COLLECTORS' INFORMATION BUREAU®

COLLECTIBLES

MARKET GUIDE & PRICE INDEX

Limited Edition

**Figurines ✦ Architecture ✦ Plates/Plaques ✦ Dolls/Plush ✦ Boxes ✦ Ornaments
Nutcrackers ✦ Graphics ✦ Steins ✦ Bells**

Eighteenth Edition

Your Complete Source for Information on Limited Edition Collectibles

Collectors' Information Bureau
Barrington, Illinois

Copyright© 2000 by Collectors' Information Bureau

All Right Reserved

Distributed by Krause Publications

No part of this book may be reproduced, transmitted
or stored in any form or by any means, electronic,
or mechanical, without prior written permission
from the publisher.

Manufactured in the United States of America

Library of Congress Catalog Card Number: 95-71406

ISBN 0-930785-30-4 Collectors' Information Bureau

ISBN 0-87341-943-X Krause Publications

ISSN 1068-4808

──────── CREDITS ────────

Printing:
Quebecor - World, Book Services

Book Design and Graphics:
Stone Design, Grand Rapids, Michigan

Cover Photography:
Camacho & Assoc., Dundee, Illinois

Design of Cover Artwork:
Pierce Design, Chicago, Illinois

Contributing Writers:
Lisa Gordey Encarnación
Susan K. Jones
Jack McCarthy
Kelly Womer

Inquiries to Collectors' Information Bureau should be mailed to:
77 W. Washington St., Suite 1815, Chicago, Illinois 60602
Phone: 847-842-2200   Fax: 847-842-2205   E-mail: askcib@collectorsinfo.com

Visit CIB on the Web at www.collectorsinfo.com

Welcome from CIB's Executive Director

Dear Reader,

Earlier this year, when I was offered the directorship of the Collectors' Information Bureau, I was thrilled to join this not-for-profit organization that has been acknowledged as the most reliable source for tracking developments in limited edition collectibles. To my way of thinking, there could be no better way to help collectors get the most fun from the hobby of collecting .

I think you'll see what I mean as you flip through the pages of this, our biggest, most comprehensive **Collectibles Market Guide & Price Index** *ever. With its behind-the-scenes stories, you'll have a unique "insider's" view of the many fine artists and companies producing limited edition artwork and collectibles today.*

As you're checking the current prices of the pieces in your own collections, remember that the book you're holding is the source to which insurance companies, appraisers, and secondary market dealers alike turn to get the most accurate, up-to-date prices on over 68,000 individual collectibles. As an independent, "third-party" authority, our price listings continue to set a standard for objective reporting that no other reporting organization can match.

Whether you're updating your insurance, adding to your collection, or just interested in learning more about the limited-edition market, you've made the right choice with the 18th Edition of the **Collectibles Market Guide & Price Index.**

Speaking on behalf of the CIB staff and our nationwide panel of retailers who participate in the annual market surveys, we hope that you enjoy this latest edition of the **Market Guide.** *If we can help you to locate one of the many retailers who specialize in the limited-edition marketplace, please don't hesitate to call or e-mail us.*

Sincerely,

Karen Feil

Karen Feil
Executive Director

A WORD OF THANKS...

A Special "Thank You" to the Staff of Collectors' Information Bureau... Amy Alexander, Joan Barcal, Gene Niemann, Carol Van Elderen, Peggy Veltri, Robin Wilkinson, and Cindy Zagumny.

TO THE CIB PANEL OF DEALERS... Finally, we wish to thank the panel of nearly 300 limited edition retailers and secondary market experts whose knowledge and dedication have helped make our Price Index possible. We wish we could recognize each of them by name, but they have agreed that to be singled out in this manner might hinder their ability to maintain an unbiased view of the marketplace.

FRONT COVER PHOTO:

1
"Swedish Father Christmas" by Prizm, Inc./Pipka Collectibles

2
Polonaise Collection's "Charlie Brown as Santa" from Kurt S. Adler, Inc.

3
Harmony Kingdom's "Cookie's Jar"

4
"Labrador Stein" by Anheuser-Busch, Inc.

5
"Eleanore Bearsevelt" from The Boyds Collection Ltd.

6
"A Little Hope..." from Little Angel Publishing

7
"Disney's Pooh Hutch" by Cardew Design of North America

8
Charming Tails' "Ready to Take a Swing" from Fitz and Floyd Collectibles

9
"Silver Heron" from Swarovski Consumer Goods, Ltd.

10
"Welcome Precious Little One" from The Bradford Group

11
"Park Ranger" from Christian Ulbricht, USA

12
"Aldenburgh Music Box Shop" from *The Heritage Village® Collection*
by Department 56®, Inc.

PHOTO A:

1 "Eyes of Wisdom" from The Hamilton Collection's *Soul of Nature Collection*
2 Willitts Designs' "Men of the Bench" from the *Our Song Collection*
3 "Labrador with Wellies" from North Light's *Premier Collection*
4 "Monarchs of the Sky" from Islandia International's *Birds of Prey Collection*
5 "Liberty Enlightening the World" from Harbour Lights' *Commerative Series*
6 "Santa's Workshop" from the *Liberty Falls Collection* by International Resources, LLC
7 "Treasures of Egypt" from David Winter Cottages
8 "Sweets and Treats" from Lilliput Lane's *Anniversary Collection*

PHOTO B:

1 "Jeweled Dragon" from *The Oliver Weber Jeweled Collection*, distributed by Swan Seekers Network
2 "Happy Birthday Musical" from Fitz and Floyd's *Honeybourne Hollow Collection*
3 "Kewpie on Goat" from The German Doll Company
4 "The Marble Champs" from Dave Grossman Creations' *Norman Rockwell Collection*
5 "Life is Worth Fighting For" from Enesco's *Precious Moments Collection*
6 "Sunday Evening Radio" from Sandy USA
7 "Collecting Friends Along the Way" from Enesco's *Cherished Teddies Collection*
8 "Wishes Come True" from Goebel's *M.I. Hummel Collection*
9 "Millennium Travel" from Halcyon Days Enamels *Millennium Collection*

PHOTO C:

1 "Janine Angel" from Seymour Mann, Inc.'s *Sheena Easton Collection*
2 "Angel of Wishes" from Imperial Graphics, Ltd.

PHOTO D:

1 "The Journey Continues" from *Santa's Journey Series/Masterpiece Collection* by G. DeBrekht Artistic Studios
2 "Cheetah" from Slavic Treasures
3 Bing & Grondahl's "Christmas at the Bell Tower"
4 Christopher Radko's "Chillin'"
5 "Everest" from The Encore Group's *Snow Buddies Collection*
6 United Design's "Polar Express" from the *Reasons to Believe™ Series*

PHOTO E:

1 Folkwood Studio's "Harvest Festival Santa" from Coyne's & Company
2 D. Morgan Santas' "Christmas Future" from Arts Uniq'
3 "Welcome 2000" from Possible Dreams' *Clothique Santa Collection*
4 *The Village Chronicle*, The Largest Independent Publication for Department 56® Collectors™
5 "2000 Santa" from Desert Specialties
6 "Santa with Sack of Gifts" from Annalee Mobilitee Dolls

PHOTO F:

1 "Madhatter" from *The Alice Collection* by Deb Canham Artist Designs, Inc.
2 "Koala" from the Artesania Rinconada *Silver Anniversary Series*, distributed by John J. Madison Company, Inc.
3 "please bee mine..." from the Will Bullas Fun Art by The Greenwich Workshop Collection
4 "Together, We're Going Places" from Islandia International's *Sonshine Promises Collection*
5 "Max" from Hallmark's *The Snowmen of Mitford Collection*
6 "I'm So Pretty" from Collectible World Studios' *Pocket Dragons*, distributed by Goebel of North America
7 "Sidewalk Sailors" from Maruri's *In a Nutshell Series*
8 "Roy L. Mole" from the *Molenniums* by Doverdale Design

PHOTO G:

1 "Fabulous Las Vegas" from *The Original Ron Lee Collection*
2 San Francisco Music Box Company's "Wicked Witch Crystal Ball Waterglobe" from *The Wizard of Oz" Collection*
(The Wizard of Oz and all related characters are trademarks of Turner Entertainment Co. ©2000. Judy Garland as Dorothy from The Wizard of Oz)
3 "Yellow Submarine" from Gartlan USA, Inc.
4 Krystonia's "Jolly Rolly" from Precious Art, Inc.
5 "Lady Bug Johnson" by Larry Fraga Designs
6 Coca Cola Collection 2000 "Polar Bears at Juke Box" Cookie Jar from Cavanagh Group International

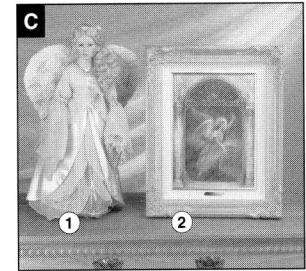
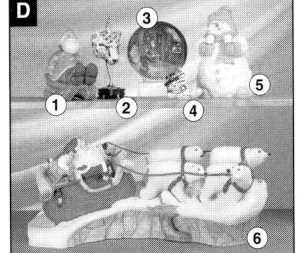

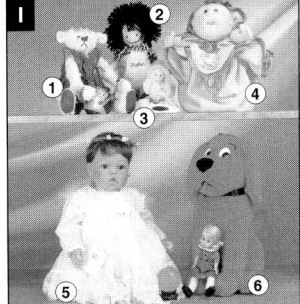

PHOTO H:

1 "Violet Overlay Basket with Hand-Painted Floral" from The Fenton Art Glass Company's *Family Signature Series*
2 "One for You, One for Me" from Lladró
3 "Summer's Light" from Reco International
4 "Gene-Twilight Rumba" from The Ashton-Drake Galleries
5 "Ivy and Roses I & II" from The Art of Glynda Turley
6 "Rachel" from Royal Doulton
7 "Dawn" by Armani, distributed by Miller Import
8 "Starry, Starry Night" from Flambro's *Center Stage Collection*

PHOTO I:

1 "Jeremy" from Mill Mountain, Inc.
2 "Mother" from Papel's *Children of the Inner Light® Series*
3 Dreamsicles® "Dressed Like Mommy" from Cast Art Industries
4 "2000 Daddy's Lil' Darlin' Edition™" from Original Appalachian Artworks, Inc.
5 Lee Middleton Original Dolls' "Bright New World" from the *Collector Series-Vinyl*
6 "Clifford and Emily Elizabeth" from The Alexander Doll Company

PHOTO J:

1 "Guardian Song" from Lenox Collections' *Annual Angels*
2 "Spring" from Margaret Furlong Designs
3 "Musical Angel" from Seymour Mann, Inc.
4 "The Valencia Nativity" from *The Valencia Collection* by Roman, Inc.
5 "Kneeling Angel" from Roman, Inc.'s *Fontanini Heirloom Nativities*
6 "Holy Family" from ANRI
7 "Millennium Angel" from GoCollect.com
8 "Hosanna" from Miss Martha Originals, Inc.'s *All God's Children Collection*
9 "Love" from United Treasures' *Angels of Inspiration™* Collection
10 Jillian "Cherish the Day" from Roman Inc.'s *Seraphim Classics Collection*

"Who's Who" in Limited Edition Collectibles

This directory provides information about many companies actively involved in the field of limited edition collectibles, and can be a helpful listing when inquiring about a company's products and services.

The Alexander Doll
Company, Inc.
615 West 131st St.
New York, NY 10027
212-283-5900
Fax: 212-283-4901
www.madamealexander.com
Specialty: See article on page 18.

American Artists
66 Poppasquash Road
Bristol, RI 02809
401-254-1191
Fax: 401-254-8881
E-mail: american_art@ids.net
Specialty: Lithos and plates.

American Mint, LLC
20 Erford Rd. Suite 100A
Lemoyne, PA 17043
717-975-8161
Fax: 717-975-8162
E-mail: tmiglino@paonline.com
www.americanmint.com
www.collorum.de
Specialty: See article on page 102.

Anheuser-Busch, Inc.
2700 South Broadway
St. Louis, MO 63118
800-305-2582
Fax: 314-577-9656
www.budweiser.com
Specialty: See article on page 20.

Annalee Mobilitee Dolls, Inc.
P.O. Box 708
Meredith, NH 03253-1137
603-279-3333
Fax: 603-279-6659
E-mail:
customerservice@annalee.com
www.annalee.com
Specialty: See article on page 22.

Anna-Perenna Inc.
35 River Street
New Rochelle, NY 10801
914-633-3777
Fax: 914-633-8727
Specialty: Figurines, ornaments
and plates.

ANRI Art
Str. Plan da Tieja, 67
1-39048 Wolkenstein
Groeden, Italy
011-39-0471-79-2233
Fax: 011-39-0471-793113
E-mail: info@anri.com
www.anri.com
Specialty: See article on page 24.

Armani
Miller Import Corp.
300 Mac Lane
Keasbey, NJ 08832-1200
800-547-2006
Fax: 732-417-0031
E-mail: society202@aol.com
www.the-society.com
Specialty: See article on page 26.

Artesania Rinconada
c/o John J. Madison Co., Inc.
29726 Ave. Banderas
Rancho Santa Margarita,
CA 92688
800-854-9338
Fax: 949-888-8416
E-mail: madison@jmadisonco.com
www.rinconada.com
Specialty: See article on page 28.

Artists of the World
2915 N. 67th Place
Scottsdale, AZ 85251
602-946-6361
Fax: 602-941-8918
Specialty: DeGrazia plates
and figurines.

Arts Uniq', Inc.
1710 S. Jefferson Avenue
P.O. Box 3085
Cookeville, TN 38502
931-526-3491
Fax: 931-528-8904
E-mail: sales@artsuniq.com
www.artsuniq.com
Specialty: See article on page 30.

The Ashton-Drake Galleries
9200 N. Maryland Avenue
Niles, IL 60714
800-634-5164
Fax: 847-966-3026
www.ashtondrake.com
www.collectiblestoday.com
Specialty: See article on page 32.

The B & J Company
P.O. Box 67
Georgetown, TX 78626
512-863-8318
Fax: 512-869-2093
Specialty: Dolls, figurines,
miniatures, plates and prints.

Belleek Collectors'
International Society
9893 Georgetown Pike
Great Falls, VA 22066
800-BELLEEK
Fax: 703-847-6201
Specialty: Belleek china and plates.

Bill Vernon Studios
4248 Burning Town Road
Franklin, NC 28734
800-327-6923
Fax: 704-349-3253
Specialty: Figurines.

Boehm Porcelain Studio
25 Princess Diana Main
Trenton, NJ 08638
800-257-9410
Fax: 609-392-1437
Specialty: Dolls, figurines
and plates.

The Boyds Collection Ltd.
350 South St.
McSherrystown, PA 17344
717-633-9898
Fax: 717-633-5137
www.boydsstuff.com
Specialty: See article on page 34.

The Bradford Exchange
9333 Milwaukee Avenue
Niles, IL 60714
800-323-5577
E-mail: custsrv@bradex.com
www.collectiblestoday.com
www.bradex.com
Specialty: See article on page 36.

Bradley Doll
1400 N. Spring Street
Los Angeles, CA 90012
323-221-4162
Fax: 323-221-8272
Specialty: Dolls.

Brandywine Collectibles
104 Greene Dr.
Yorktown, VA 23692-4800
757-898-5031
Fax: (757) 898-6895
E-mail: heartbwine@aol.com
www.brandywinecollectibles.com
Specialty: Miniature buildings.

Buccellati Silver Ltd.
460 Meadow Lane
Carlstadt, NJ 07072
201-635-1400
Fax: 201-635-1407
Specialty: Ornaments.

Byers' Choice Ltd.
4355 County Line Road
P.O. Box 158
Chalfont, PA 18914
215-822-0150
Fax: 215-822-3847
E-mail:
support@byerschoice.com
www.byerschoice.com
Specialty: Figurines.

Cairn Studio
P.O. Box 400
Davidson, NC 28036
704-892-3581
Specialty: Figurines.

Caithness Glass Inc.
141 Lanza Avenue, Bldg. 12
Garfield, NJ 07026
800-452-7987
Fax: 973-340-9415
E-mail: caithglas@aol.com
www.caithnessglass.co.uk
Specialty: Glass paperweights.

Cardew Design
North America, Inc.
17 Turntable Junction
Flemington, NJ 08822
877-9-TEAPOT
Fax: 908-806-7844
E-mail: cardewdesign@aol.com
www.cardewdesign.com
Specialty: See article on page 38.

Carlton Cards/American Greetings
One American Road
Cleveland, OH 44114
888-222-7898
Fax: 216-252-6751
Specialty: Ornaments.

Castagna by Block House
5020 W. 73rd St.
P.O. Box 2131
Beford Park, IL 60499
708-728-8400
Fax: 708-728-0022
Specialty: Figurines

Cast Art Industries, Inc.
1120 California Avenue
Corona, CA 91719
909-371-3025
Fax: 909-270-2852
E-mail: info@castart.com
www.castart.com
Specialty: See article on page 40.

Cavanagh Group International
1665 Bluegrass Lakes Pkwy.,
Ste. 100
Alpharetta, GA 30004
800-895-8100
Fax: 678-366-2801
www.cavanaghgrp.com
Specialty: See article on page 42.

Cazenovia Abroad
67 Albany Street
Cazenovia, NY 13035
315-655-3433
Fax: 315-655-4249
E-mail: dtrush@dreamscape.com
www.cazenoviaabroad.com
Specialty: Sterling silver figurines
and ornaments, silver plates.

Character Collectibles
10861 Business Drive
Fontana, CA 92337
909-822-9999
Fax: 909-823-6666
Specialty: Figurines.

Charming Tails
Fitz and Floyd Collectibles
501 Corporate Dr.
Lewisville, TX 75057
800-527-9550
Fax: 972-353-7718
Specialty: See article on page 44.

Cherished Teddies
c/o Enesco Group, Inc.
225 Windsor Drive
Itasca, IL 60143
800-632-7968
Fax: 630-875-5350
www.enesco.com
www.enescoclubs.com
Specialty: See article on page 46.

Christian Ulbricht USA
P.O. Box 99
Angwin, CA 94508
888-707-5591
Fax: 707-968-9669
E-mail: nutcracker@ulbricht.com
www.ulbricht.com
Specialty: See article on page 48.

Christina's World
27 Woodcreek Court
Deer Park, NY 11729
516-242-9664
Fax: 516-586-1918
E-mail: buytrim@aol.com
Specialty: Ornaments.

Christopher Radko Starlight Family of Collectors
P.O. Box 775249
St. Louis, MO 63177-5249
800-71-RADKO (717-2356)
www.christopherradko.com
Specialty: See article on page 50.

collectibles.com
5388 Hickory Hollow Pkwy.
Antioch, TN 37013-3128
877-365-7467
Fax: 615-263-8084
www.collectibles.com
Specialty: See article on page 52

Collectibles Insurance Agency
P.O. Box 1200
Westminster, MD 21158
888-837-9537
Fax: 410-876-9233
E-mail:
info@insurecollectibles.com
www.collectinsure.com
Specialty: See article on page 54.

CollectibleTown.com
4600 Innovation Drive
Fort Collins, CO 80525
877-600-8881
Fax: 970-226-5991
E-mail:
AuntPhoebe@collectibletown.com
www.CollectibleTown.com
Specialty: See article on page 56.

Columbus International
209 W. 12th St.
Hays, KS 67601
800-814-6287
Fax: 785-625-4094
E-mail: info@columbusintl.com
www.columbusintl.com
Specialty: See article on page 58.

The Constance Collection
11700 Rogues Rd.
Midland, VA 22728
540-788-4500
Fax: 540-788-3150
Specialty: Figurines.

Cottage Collectibles by Ganz, Inc.
908 Niagara Falls Blvd.
North Tonawanda, NY
14120-2060
800-724-5902
Fax: 905-851-6669
www.ganz.org
E-mail: headoffice@ganz.org
Specialty: Plush.

Country Artists
9305 Gerwig Lane, Ste. P
Columbia, MD 21046
410-290-8990
Fax: 410-290-5480
E-mail:
sx.rittermann@countryartists.com
www.countryartists.com
Specialty: Figurines.

Coyne's & Company
7400 Boone Avenue North
Minneapolis, MN 55428
800-336-8666
Fax: 612-425-1653
www.coynes.com
Specialty: See article on page 60.

Cross Gallery, Inc.
P.O. Box 4181
Jackson Hole, WY 83001
307-733-2200
Fax: 307-733-1414
Specialty: Graphics, ornaments
and plates.

Crystal World
120 Industrial Ave
Little Ferry, NJ 07643
800-445-4251
Fax: 201-931-0220
E-mail: collector@crystalworld.com
www.crystalworld.com
Specialty: See article on page 62.

Cybis
65 Norman Avenue
Trenton, NJ 08618
609-392-6074
Specialty: Porcelain figurines.

Dave Grossman Creations
1608 N. Warson Road
St. Louis, MO 63132
800-325-1655
Fax: 314-423-7620
E-mail: dgcrea@aol.com
Specialty: See article on page 64.

David Winter Cottages
P.O. Box 8
Libertytown, MD 21762
888-995-7005
Fax: 301-829-8554
E-mail: info@davidwinterusa.com
Specialty: See article on page 66.

Debbie Thibault's American
Collectibles
446 Anaheim Hills Rd., Ste. 188
Anaheim Hills, CA 92807
562-402-6171
Fax: 562-402-9061
Specialty: Limited edition
American-made folk art.

Deb Canham Artist Designs, Inc.
820 Albee Rd., Suite 1
Nokomis, FL 34275
941-480-1200
Fax: 941-480-1202
E-mail:
deb@deb-canham.acun.com
www.deb-canham.acun.com
Specialty: See article on page 68.

Decorative Display Products
5250 SW Tomahawk
Redmond, OR 97756
541-923-1473
Fax: 541-923-7403
www.decorativedisplays.com
Specialty: Plate hangers,
accessories and ornament stands.

Department 56®, Inc.
6436 City West Parkway
P.O. Box 44456
Eden Prairie, MN 55344-1456
800-548-8696
E-mail: Mslittown@dept56.com
www.dept56.com
Specialty: See article on page 70.

Desert Specialties, Ltd.
6280 S. Valley View Blvd.,
Suite 404
Las Vegas, NV 89118
702-253-0450
Fax: 702-253-1871
E-mail: desert3900@aol.com
www.melodyinmotion.com
Specialty: See article on page 72.

Doverdale Design
Unit 9 - Hodfar Rd.
Sandy Lane Ind. Est.
Stourport-on-Severn,
Worchestershire
DY13 9QB England
011-441-299-878867
E-mail:
graeme@doverdaledesign.com
www.doverdaledesign.com
Specialty: See article on page 74

Dram Tree/C.U.I.
1502 N. 23rd Street
Wilmington, NC 28405
910-251-1110
Specialty: Steins and promotional
products.

Duncan Royale
1141 S. Acacia St.
Fullerton, CA 92831
714-879-1360
Fax: 714-879-4611
E-mail: duncan@duncanroyale.com
www.duncanroyale.com
Specialty: Figurines.

Ebeling & Reuss Co.
6500 Chapmans Rd.
Allentown, PA 18106-1289
610-366-8304
Fax: 610-366-8307
Specialty: Figurines and teacups.

Edna Hibel Studio
P.O. Box 9967
Riviera Beach, FL 33419
561-848-9633
Fax: 561-848-9640
E-mail: ednahibel@aol.com
www.hibel.com
Specialty: Bells, crystal, dolls,
figurines, graphics (original
lithographs and serigraphs,
limited edition reproductions),
ornaments and plates.

Egg Fantasy
4040 Schiff Drive
Las Vegas, NV 89103
702-368-7747
Specialty: Egg creations.

eggspressions! inc.
1635 Deadwood Avenue
Rapid City, SD 57702-0353
800-551-9138
Fax: 605-342-8699
E-mail: shelly@hillsnet.net
Specialty: Egg art.

Eklund's Ltd.
1701 W. St. Germain
St. Cloud, MN 56301
320-252-1318
Fax: 320-252-9397
Specialty: Plates and mugs.

The Encore Group, Inc.
P.O. Box 500780
San Diego, CA 92150
800-621-3647
Fax: 800-929-9653
E-mail: sales@the-encore-group.com
www.the-encore-group.com
Specialty: See article on page 76.

Enesco Group, Inc.
225 Windsor Drive
Itasca, IL 60143
800-632-7968
Fax: 630-875-5350
www.enesco.com
www.enescoclubs.com
Specialty: See article on page 78.

Exclusively Yours
5434 Hidden Springs Rd
Fort Collins, CO 80526
970-226-5995
Fax: 970-226-5991
E-mail: cobabe@verinet.com
www.cobabe.com
Specialty: Dolls, figurines.

FJ Designs, Inc.
Makers of Cat's Meow Village
2163 Great Trails Drive
Wooster, OH 44691-3738
330-264-1377
Fax: 330-263-0219
E-mail: cmu@fjdesign.com
www.catsmeow.com
Specialty: Miniature buildings.

Federica Doll Company
4501 W. Highland Road
Milford, MI 48380
248-887-9575
Specialty: Dolls.

Fenton Art Glass
700 Elizabeth Street
Williamstown, WV 26187
304-375-6122
Fax: 304-375-7833
E-mail:
askfenton@fentonartglass.com
www.fentonartglass.com
Specialty: See article on page 80.

Figaro Import Corporation
325 South Flores Street
San Antonio, TX 78204-1178
210-225-1167
Specialty: Figurines.

Figi Graphics
3636 Gateway Center
San Diego, CA 92102
619-262-8811
Fax: 619-264-7781
Specialty: Figurines.

Flambro Imports, Inc.
1530 Ellsworth Industrial, S.W.
Atlanta, GA 30318
800-352-6276
Fax: 404-352-2150
E-mail: flambro@flambro.com
www.flambro.com
Specialty: See article on page 82.

Fontanini Heirloom Nativities
c/o Roman, Inc.
555 Lawrence Ave.
Roselle, IL 60172-1599
630-529-3000
Fax: 630-529-1121
www.roman.com
Specialty: See article on page 84.

Forest Lamps & Gifts, Inc.
728 61st Street
Brooklyn, NY 11220-4298
718-492-0200
Fax: 718-439-7719
Specialty: Figurines.

Fort USA, Inc.
54 Taylor Drive
E. Providence, RI 02916
800-678-3678
Fax: 401-434-6956
E-mail: castlebury@aol.com
www.fortusa.com
Specialty: Pewter figurines.

The Franklin Mint
U.S. Route 1
Franklin Center, PA 19091
800-THE-MINT (843-6468)
Fax: 610-459-6040
www.Franklinmint.com
Specialty: See article on page 86.

Fraser International
7811 N. Shepherd Dr., Ste. 112
Houston, TX 77088
281-260-0090
Fax: 281-260-8131
www.fraserinternational.com
Specialty: Miniature historical
buildings.

Gartlan USA, Inc.
575 Rt. 73 North, Suite A-6
West Berlin, NJ 08091-2440
856-753-9229
Fax: 856-753-9280
E-mail: info@gartlanusa.com
www.gartlanusa.com
Specialty: See article on page 88.

G. DeBrekht Artistic Studios/
Russian Gift and Jewelry
Center
18025 Sky Park Circle, Suite G.
Irvine, CA 92614
800-727-7442
Fax: 800-RUSSIA-7
E-mail: info@russiangift.com
www.russiangift.com
Specialty: See article on page 90.

Geo. Z. Lefton Co.
P.O. Box 09178
Chicago, IL 60609-0178
800-628-8492
www.gzlefton.com
Specialty: See article on page 92.

The German Doll Company
P.O. Box 483
Tipp City, OH 45371
937-335-4808
Fax: 937-440-9756
E-mail: germandoll@erinet.com
www.german-doll.com
Specialty: See article on page 94.

Glynda Turley Prints, Inc.
P.O. Box 112
74 Cliburne Park Rd.
Heber Springs, AR 72543
800-633-7931
Fax: 501-362-5020
www.glynda.com
Specialty: See article on page 96.

GoCollect.com
1000 East Woodfield Rd.,
Ste. 102
Schaumberg, IL 60173-5921
847-706-6765
Fax: 847-706-6766
E-mail: info@Gocollect.com
www.GoCollect.com
Specialty: See article on page 98.

Goebel of North America
Rt. 31 North
Goebel Plaza
Pennington, NJ 08534
609-737-8700
Fax: 609-737-1545
www.mihummel.com
Specialty: See article on page 100.

Good-Krüger Dolls
5015 E. Lincoln Hwy.
Kinzers, PA 17535
717-442-3934
Specialty: Dolls.

Great American Doll Co.
P.O. Box 576
Covina, CA 91722
800-VIP-DOLL
Specialty: Dolls.

Great American Taylor
Collectibles Corp.
110 Sandhills Blvd.
P.O. Box 428
Aberdeen, NC 28315
910-944-7447
Fax: 910-944-7449
E-mail:
jacktaylor@greatamerican.net
Specialty: Figurines.

The Greenwich Workshop
One Greenwich Place
P.O. Box 875
Shelton, CT 06484-0875
800-243-4246
Fax: 203-925-0262
www.greenwichworkshop.com
Specialty: See article on page 104.

Gund Inc.
1 Runyons Lane
P.O. Box 852
Edison, NJ 08818
732-248-1500
Specialty: Bears, stuffed toys.

H & G Studios Inc.
1490 S. Military Trail, Ste. 3
West Palm Beach, FL 33415
561-615-9900
Fax: 561-615-8400
Specialty: Music boxes.

The Hadley Companies
11300 Hampshire Avenue S.
Bloomington, MN 55438
952-943-8474
Fax: 952-943-8098
Specialty: Cottages, graphics,
ornaments, plates, steins.

Halcyon Days Enamels
P.O. Box 66599
Chicago AMF, IL 60666
877-798-1488
Fax: 630-766-5189
E-mail:
halcyondays.enamels@btinternet.com
Specialty: See article on page 106.

Hallmark Cards, Inc.
2525 Gillham Road,
Maildrop 166
Kansas City, MO 64108-2734
800-523-5839
Fax: 816-274-8092
www.hallmark.com
Specialty: See article on page 108.

The Hamilton Collection
9204 Center For The Arts Drive
Niles, IL 60714-1300
800-228-2945
Fax: 904-279-1339
www.collectiblestoday.com
Specialty: See article on page 110.

Hand & Hammer Silversmiths
2610 Morse Lane
Woodbridge, VA 22192
800-SILVERY
Fax: 703-491-2031
E-mail:
dechip@hand-hammer.com
www.hand-hammer.com
Specialty: Ornaments, sterling
silver jewelry.

Harbour Lights
1000 N. Johnson Ave.
El Cajon, CA 92020
800-365-1219
Fax: 888-579-1911
E-mail:
harbourlights@harbourlights.com
www.harbourlights.com
Specialty: See article on page 112.

Harmony Kingdom
232 Neilston St.
Columbus, OH 43215
614-469-0600
Fax: 614-469-0140
www.harmonykingdom.com
Specialty: See article on page 114.

Harold Rigsby Graphics
4108 Scottsville Rd.
Glasgow, KY 42141
800-892-4984
Specialty: Graphics.

Hawthorne Village
9210 N. Maryland Street
Niles, IL 60714-1322
800-772-4277
E-mail: custsrv@hawthorne.com
Specialty: Miniature buildings.

Hazle Ceramics
Stallion's Yard, Codham Hall
Great Warley
Brentwood, Essex,
United Kingdom CM13 3JT
011441-277-220892
Fax: 011441-277-233768
E-mail: hazle@hazle.com
www.hazle.com
Specialty: Miniatures.

Heirloom Editions, Ltd.
25100-B So. Normandie Ave.
Harbor City, CA 90710
800-433-4785
Fax: 310-539-8891
Specialty: Bells, Staffordshire dogs
and teapots, thimbles and figurines.

Helen Sabatte Designs, Inc.
6041 Acacia Avenue
Oakland, CA 94618
510-563-4616
E-mail: sabatte@autobahn.org
Specialty: Figurines.

Heritage Artists
560 Sauve West
Montreal, Quebec
Canada H3L 2A3
514-385-7000
Fax: 514-385-0026
E-mail:
customerservice@heritageartists.com
www.heritageartists.com
Specialty: Wildlife figurines,
garden accessories.

The Heritage Collections, Ltd.
6647 Kerns Road
Falls Church, VA 22042-4231
703-533-7800
Fax: 703-533-7801
Specialty: Music boxes,
ornaments, paperweights and
wall plaques.

Honeybourne Hollow
Fitz and Floyd Collectibles
501 Corporate Dr.
Lewisville, TX 75057
800-527-9550
Fax: 972-353-7718
Specialty: See article on page 116.

Hot Wheels/Mattel, Inc.
333 Continental Blvd.
El Segundo, CA 90245
800-524-8697
www.hotwheels.com
Specialty: See article on page 118.

House of Hatten, Inc.
301 Inner Loop Road
Georgetown, TX 78626
800-5HATTEN
512-819-9600
Fax: 512-819-9033
E-mail:
custserv@houseofhatten.com
Specialty: See article on page 120.

Hutschenreuther/
Eschenbach U.S.A.
14101 Sullyfield Circle, Ste. 300
Chantilly, VA 20151
800-296-7508
Fax: 703-263-2216
Specialty: Fine porcelain
sculptures.

Imperial Graphics, Ltd.
11516 Lake Potomac Dr.
Potomac, MD 20854
301-299-5711
Fax: 301-299-4837
E-mail: lliu@lenaliu.com
www.lenaliu.com
Specialty: See article on page 122.

Incolay Studios Inc.
520 Library Street
San Fernando, CA 91340-2599
818-365-2521
Fax: 818-365-9599
Specialty: Plates.

International Resources, LLC
60 Revere Dr. #725
Northbrook, IL 60062
847-291-4334
Fax: 847-291-4358
E-mail: libertyfalls@ameritech.net
www.internationalresources.com
www.libertyfalls.com
Specialty: See article on page 124.

Iris Arc Crystal
114 East Haley Street
Santa Barbara, CA 93101
888-IRIS-ARC (474-7273)
Fax: 805-965-2458
Specialty: Crystal and figurines.

Islandia International
78 Bridge Rd.
Islandia, NY 11722
516-234-9817
Fax: 516-234-9183
E-mail: islandia78@aol.com
www.sonshine-promises.com
www.islandia.com
Specialty: See article on page 126.

Jack Terry Fine Art Publishing
25251 Freedom Trail
Kerrville, TX 78028
830-367-4242
Fax: 830-367-4243
Specialty: Limited edition prints
and sculptures.

Jan Hagara Collectables, Inc.
40114 Industrial Park
Georgetown, TX 78626
512-869-1365
Fax: 512-869-2093
E-mail: info@hagaradolls.com
www.hagaradolls.com
Specialty: Dolls and figurines.

Jody Bergsma Galleries
1344 King Street
Bellingham, WA 98226
800-BERGSMA (237-4762)
Fax: 630-647-2758
E-mail: bergsma@bergsma.com
www.bergsma.com
Specialty: Graphics.

Johannes Zook Originals
P.O. Box 256
Midland, MI 48640
517-835-9388
Fax: 517-835-6689
Specialty: Dolls.

June McKenna Collectibles, Inc.
P.O. Box 846
Ashland, VA 23005
804-798-2024
Fax: 804-798-2618
Specialty: Figurines.

KVK Inc./Daddy's Long Legs
300 Bank Street
Southlake, TX 76092
817-481-4800
Fax: 817-488-8876
www.daddystrunk.com
Specialty: Dolls.

Kurt S. Adler, Inc.
1107 Broadway
New York, NY 10010
800-243-9627
Fax: 212-807-0575
www.kurtadler.com
Specialty: See article on page 128.

Ladie and Friends, Inc.
220 North Main Street
Sellersville, PA 18960
800-76-DOLLS (763-6557)
Fax: 215-453-8155
www.lizziehigh.com
Specialty: Dolls and figurines.

Lalique
400 Veterans Blvd.
Carlstadt, NJ 07072
800-CRISTAL (274-7825)
www.lalique.com
Specialty: Crystal.

Lang & Wise Ltd.
514 Wells Street
Delafield, WI 53018
414-646-5499
Fax: 414-646-4427
www.lang.com
Specialty: Ornaments
and figurines.

Larry Fraga Designs
4720 Sequoyah Rd.
Oakland, CA 94605
510-638-3900
Fax: 510-638-3900
E-mail: larryfraga@aol.com
www.larryfragadesigns.com
Specialty: See article on page 130.

The Lawton Doll Company
548 North First Street
Turlock, CA 95380
209-632-3655
Fax: 209-632-6788
Specialty: Dolls.

**Lee Middleton Original
Dolls, Inc.**
1301 Washington Blvd.
Belpre, OH 45714
740-423-1717
Fax: 740-423-5983
E-mail: lisa@leemiddleton.com
www.leemiddleton.com
Specialty: See article on page 132.

Lenox Classics
900 Wheeler Way
Langhorne, PA 19047
888-561-8808
Fax: 888-561-2155
www.lenoxclassics.com
Specialty: See article on page 134.

**Lightpost Publishing/
Media Arts Group, Inc.**
521 Charcot Avenue
San Jose, CA 95131
800-366-3733
Fax: 800-243-8533
www.thomaskinkade.com
Specialty: See article on page 136.

Lilliput Lane
P.O. Box 7
Libertytown, MD 21762
800-545-5478
Fax: 310-829-8554
E-mail: info@lilliputlaneusa.com
Specialty: See article on page 138.

**Little Angel Publishing/
Dona Gelsinger**
11232 Hwy. 62, Ste. C
Eagle Point, OR 97524
800-830-1690
Fax: 541-830-1811
E-mail: mail@donagelsinger.com
www.donagelsinger.com
Specialty: See article on page 140.

Little Gem Teddy Bears
Akira Trading Co., Inc.
6040 N.W. 84th Ave.
Miami, FL 33166
305-639-9801
Fax: 305-639-9802
E-mail: littlegem@usa.net
Specialty: See article on page 142.

Living Stone
P.O. Box 500780
San Diego, CA 92150
800-621-3647
Specialty: Figurines.

Lladró USA, Inc.
1 Lladró Drive
Moonachie, NJ 07074
800-634-9088
Fax: 201-807-1293
E-mail: lladrosociety@lladro.com
www.lladro.com
Specialty: See article on page 144.

Lynette Decor Products
4225 Prado Road, Unit 106
Corona, CA 91720
800-223-8623
Fax: (909) 279-1337
E-mail: lynette@home.com
www.lynettedecor.com
Specialty: Collectible displays and
accessories.

M C K Gifts, Inc.
P.O. Box 621848
Littleton, CO 80162-1814
303-948-1382
Fax: 303-979-6838
www.mckgifts.com
Specialty: Figurines.

M. Cornell Importers, Inc.
1462-18th St. N.W.
St. Paul, MN 55112
800-595-6898
Fax: 651-636-3568
E-mail: cornellinc@aol.com
Specialty: Steins and teapots.

Margaret Furlong Designs
210 State Street
Salem, OR 97301
503-363-6004
Fax: 503-371-0676
www.margaretfurlong.com
Specialty: See article on page 146.

Mark Hopkins Sculptures
21 Shorter Industrial Blvd.
Rome, GA 30165-1838
800-678-6564
Fax: 706-235-2814
Specialty: Sculptures.

Marty Bell Fine Art
9550 Owens Mouth Ave.
Chatsworth, CA 91311
800-637-4537
Fax: 818-709-7668
www.martybell.com
Specialty: Graphics.

Marty Sculpture, Inc.
P.O. Box 15067
Wilmington, NC 28408
800-654-0478
Fax: 910-392-3565
www.martysculpture.com
Specialty: Figurines.

Maruri, U.S.A.
21510 Gledhill St.
Chatsworth, CA 91311
818-717-9900
Fax: 818-717-9901
E-mail: marurius@pacbell.net
Specialty: See article on page 148.

Matchbox® Collectibles
P.O. Box 10490
Glendale, AZ 85318-0490
800-858-0102
Fax: 888-634-9207
www.matchbox.com
www.mattel.com
Specialty: See article on page 150.

Mattel, Inc./Barbie Collectibles®
P.O. Box 10495
Glendale, AZ 85318-0495
800-491-7514
www.barbiecollectibles.com
Specialty: See article on page 152.

Michael Boyett Studio
Hwy 225
Nacogdoches, TX 75964
409-560-4477
E-mail: mbstudio@lcc.net
www.boyettstudio.com
Specialty: Pewter and bronze
sculpture.

Michael Garman
Productions, Inc.
2418 W. Colorado Avenue
Colorado Springs, CO 80904
800-874-7144
Fax: 719-471-3659
www.michaelgarman.com
Specialty: Figurines.

Midwest of Cannon Falls
32057 64th Avenue
Cannon Falls, MN 55009
800-377-3335
507-263-4261
Fax: 507-263-7752
www.midwestofcannonfalls.com
Specialty: See article on page 154.

**M.I. Hummel
Goebel of North America**
Rt. 31 North
Goebel Plaza
Pennington, NJ 08534
800-666-CLUB
Fax: 609-737-1545
www.mihummel.com
Specialty: See article on page 156.

Mill Mountain
187 Mill Lane
Mountainside, NJ 07092
800-257-4064
Fax: 908-654-7506
E-mail: millmtn@earthlink.net
www.fromgrandmasheart.com
Specialty: See article on page 158.

Miss Martha Originals, Inc.
1119 Chastain Blvd. (Hwy. 431)
Gadsden, AL 35904
256-492-0221
Fax: 256-492-0261
Specialty: See article on page 160.

The Moss Portfolio
1 Poplar Grove Lane
Mathews, VA 23109
804-725-7378
Fax: 804-725-3040
www.p-buckley-moss.com
Specialty: Graphics.

Munro Collectibles, Inc.
1220 Waterville-Monclova Road
Waterville, OH 43566
419-878-0034
Fax: 419-878-2535
Specialty: Figurines.

Napoleon/Dear Artistic Sculpture
P.O. Box 860
Oakes, PA 19456
610-666-1650
Fax: 610-666-1379
E-mail: napusa@aol.com
Specialty: Capidimonte figurines.

New Masters Publishing Co., Inc.
2301 14th Street, Ste. 105
Gulfport, MS 39501
800-647-9578
Fax: 228-863-5145
Specialty: Bronzes and graphics.

North American Bear Co.
401 North Wabash, Suite 500
Chicago, IL 60611
312-329-0020
Fax: 312-329-1417
Specialty: Teddy bears.

North Light
41 Madison Avenue, Ste. 1601
New York, NY 10010
212-696-9667
Fax: 212-696-9683
Specialty: See article on page 162.

Oldenburg Originals
N2646 Pheasant Valley Court
Waldo, WI 53093
920-528-7127
Fax: 920-528-7127
E-mail: oldenbrg@execpc.com
Specialty: Limited edition resin
and one-of-a-kind polyclay.

Old World Christmas
P.O. Box 8000
Spokane, WA 99203
509-534-9000
Fax: 509-534-9098
E-mail:
thesource@oldworldchristmas.com
Specialty: Figurines and
ornaments.

Olszewski Studios
PNB 500 355 N. Lantana
Camarillo, CA 93010
805-484-6632
Fax: 805-484-4993
E-mail: studiosrwo@aol.com
Specialty: Miniature figurines,
jewelry and jewelry boxes.

Original Appalachian
Artworks, Inc.
1721 U.S. Hwy 75 S.
Cleveland, GA 30528
706-865-2171
Fax: 706-865-5862
www.cabbagepatchkids.com
Specialty: See article on page 164.

Pacific Rim Import Corp.
5930 4th Avenue South
Seattle, WA 98108
206-767-5000
Fax: 206-767-9179
Specialty: Figurines.

Papel Giftware
30 Engelhard Drive
Cranbury, NJ 08512
800-634-8384
Fax: 609-395-6879
www.papelgiftware.com
Specialty: See article on page 166.

Past Impressions
P.O. Box 188
Belvedere, CA 94920
800-732-7332
Specialty: Graphics.

PenDelfin Studios
c/o Miller Import Corp.
300 Mac Lane
Keasbey, NJ 08832
800-547-2006
Fax: (732) 417-0031
E-mail: society202@aol.com
www.the-society.com
Specialty: Figurines.

Penni Bears & Stuff
121 S.E. 27th
Moore, OK 73160
405-799-2165
www.pennibears.com
Specialty: Bears.

Pickard, Inc.
782 Pickard Ave.
Antioch, IL 60002
847-395-3800
www.pickardchina.com
Specialty: China.

Pipkin & Bonnet, Inc.
224 West 35th St., Ste. 1401
New York, NY 10001
212-465-1562
Fax: 212-465-1963
E-mail: pipkin@wwonline-ny.com
www.pipkinandbonnet.com
Specialty: Miniatures.

Polland Studios
P.O. Box 2468
Prescott, AZ 86302-1146
520-778-1900
Fax: 520-778-4034
Specialty: Pewter and porcelain
figurines.

Porterfield's, Fine Art in
Limited Editions
5 Mountain Road
Concord, NH 03301-5479
800-660-8345
Fax: 603-228-1888
E-mail:
porterfields@mediaone.net
www.porterfields.com
Specialty: Miniature plates.

Possible Dreams
6 Perry Drive
Foxboro, MA 02035
508-543-6667
Fax: 508-543-4255
Specialty: See article on page 168.

Precious Art, Inc.
125 W. Ellsworth
Ann Arbor, MI 48108
734-663-1885
Fax: 734-663-2343
E-mail: krystoniaclub@msn.com
www.krystoniaclub.com
www.preciousart.com
Specialty: See article on page 170.

Precious Moments
c/o Enesco Group, Inc.
225 Windsor Drive
Itasca, IL 60143
800-632-7968
Fax: 630-875-5350
www.enesco.com
www.enescoclubs.com
Specialty: See article on page 172.

Prizm, Inc./Pipka Collectibles
P.O. Box 1106
Manhattan, KS 66505
785-776-1613
Fax: 785-776-6550
E-mail: prizminc@pipka.com
www.pipka.com
Specialty: See article on page 174.

Pulaski Furniture Corporation
One Pulaski Square
Pulaski, VA 24301
800-287-4625
Specialty: See article on page 176.

R. John Wright Dolls, Inc.
15 West Main Street
Cambridge, NY 12816
518-677-8566
Fax: 518-677-5202
E-mail: rjwclub@aol.com
www.rjohnwright.com
Specialty: Plush.

Raikes Collectables
P.O. Box 8428
Tucson, AZ 85738
520-825-5788
Fax: 520-825-5789
E-mail: raikes4u@azstarnet.com
www.raikes.com
Specialty: Traditional wood
sculptures and teddy bears.

Rawcliffe Corporation
155 Public Street
Providence, RI 02903
800-343-1811
Fax: 401-751-8545
www.rawcliffe.com
Specialty: Figurines.

Reco International Corp.
138 Haven Avenue
Port Washington, NY 11050
516-767-2400
Fax: 516-767-2409
E-mail: RecoInt@aol.com
www.reco.com
Specialty: See article on page 178.

Red Mill Mfg., Inc.
1023 Arbuckle Road
Summersville, WV 26651
304-872-5231
Fax: 304-872-5234
E-mail: cwhite@mtec.net
www.red-mill.com
Specialty: Character and
wildlife figurines.

Rhyn-Rivet
395 Hwy. MM
Brooklyn, WI 53521
608-835-7886
E-mail: info@rhyn-rivet.com
www.rhyn-rivet.com
Specialty: Ornaments.

Rick Cain Studios
3500 N.E. Waldo Road
Gainesville, FL 32609
800-535-3949
Fax: 352-377-7038
Specialty: Wildlife sculptures.

Roman, Inc.
555 Lawrence Avenue
Roselle, IL 60172-1599
630-529-3000
Fax: 630-529-1121
www.roman.com
Specialty: See article on page 180.

Ron Lee's
World of Clowns, Inc.
330 Carousel Pkwy.
Henderson, NV 89014
800-829-3928
Fax: 702-434-4310
www.ronlee.com
Specialty: See article on page 182.

Royal Copenhagen/
Bing & Grondahl
41 Madison Avenue
New York, NY 10010
800-431-1992
Fax: 856-768-9726
Specialty: See article on page 184.

Royal Doulton USA
701 Cottontail Lane
Somerset, NJ 08873
800-68-CHINA (682-4462)
Fax: 732-764-4974
E-mail:
inquiries@royal-doultonusa.com
www.royal-doulton.com
Specialty: See article on page 186.

Royal Scandinavia
140 Bradford Drive
Berlin, NJ 08009
856-768-5400
Fax: 856-768-9726
Specialty: Figurines and
ornaments.

Royal Worcester
Severn Street
Worcester, England
01905-23221
Fax: 01905-23601
Specialty: Figurines, ornaments
and plates.

Salvino, Inc.
1379 Pico Street, Ste. 103
Corona, CA 91719
877-725-8466
Fax: 909-279-3409
Specialty: Sports figurines.

Sandicast, Inc.
8480 Miralani Drive
San Diego, CA 92126
800-722-3316
Fax: 858-695-0615
Specialty: Cast stone animal
figurines.

Sandy Clough Studio
25 Trail Road
Marietta, GA 30064-1535
770-428-9406
E-mail: sclough@bellsouth.net
Specialty: Limited edition prints,
open prints, framed units.

Sandy USA
3031 E. Cherry St.
Springfield, MO 65802
800-607-2639
Fax: 417-831-4477
Specialty: See article on page 188.

The San Francisco Music Box Company
390 North Wiget Lane, Ste. 200
Walnut Creek, CA 94598
925-939-4800
Mail Order: 800-227-2190
Fax: 925-927-2999
www.sfmusicbox.com
Specialty: See article on page 190.

Sarah's Attic, Inc.
126-1/2 West Broad St.
P.O. Box 448
Chesaning, MI 48616
800-437-4363
Fax: 517-845-3477
E-mail: SAATTIC@aol.com
www.sarahsattic.com
Specialty: Figurines.

Selkirk Glass
116 E. 16th Street
New York, NY 10003
212-979-6990
Fax: 212-979-8283
E-mail: giftwarelb@aol.com
Specialty: Glass

Seraphim Classics
c/o Roman, Inc.
555 Lawrence Ave.
Roselle, IL 60172-1599
630-529-3000
Fax: 630-529-1121
www.roman.com
Specialty: See article on page 192.

Seymour Mann, Inc.
225 Fifth Avenue
New York, NY 10010
212-683-7262
Fax: 212-213-4920
E-mail:
seymourmann@worldnet.att.net
www.seymourmann.com
Specialty: See article on page 194.

Shelia's, Inc.
1856 Belgrade Ave
Charleston, SC 29407
800-227-6564
Fax: 843-556-0040
E-mail: shelias@shelias.com
www.shelias.com
Specialty: Miniature buildings.

Shenandoah Designs
International, Inc.
204 W. Railroad Ave
P.O. Box 911
Rural Retreat, VA 24368-0911
800-338-7644
Fax: 540-686-4921
E-mail:
shenandoahdesigns@worldnet.att.net
www.shenandoahdesigns.com
Specialty: Figurines

Silver Deer Ltd.
963 Transport Way
Petaluma, CA 94954
800-729-3337
Fax: 707-765-0770
Specialty: Figurines.

Slavic Treasures
P.O. Box 99591
Raleigh, NC 27624-9591
877-SLAVICT (752-8428)
Fax: 919-844-4429
www.slavictreasures.com.pl
Specialty: See article on page 196.

Spencer Collin Lighthouses
24 River Road
Elliott, ME 03903
207-439-6016
E-Mail: csstudio99@aol.com
Specialty: Lighthouses.

Steiff USA
31 E. 28th Street, 9th Floor
New York, NY 10016
212-779-2582
Fax: 212-779-2594
www.steiff.com
Specialty: Plush bears.

Studio Collection
32 Jonathan-Bourne Drive
Pocasset, MA 02559
800-314-7748
Fax: 508-563-3663
Specialty: Figurines
and ornaments.

Susan Rios Co.
550 Riverdale Drive
Glendale, CA 91204
818-500-1705
Fax: 818-502-0665
E-mail: susanrios@earthlink.net
www.susanriosart.com
Specialty: Graphics.

The Susan Wakeen Doll
Company
425 Bantam Road
Litchfield, CT 06759
860-567-0007
Fax: 860-567-4636
www.susanwakeendolls.com
Specialty: Dolls.

Swan Seekers Network
9740 Campo Rd. #134
Spring Valley, CA 91977
619-462-2333
Fax: 619-462-5517
E-mail: jimer@swanseekers.com
www.swanseekers.com
www.oliverweber.com
www.jeweledcollection.com
Specialty: See article on page 198.

Swarovski Consumer
Goods Ltd.
One Kenney Drive
Cranston, RI 02920
800-426-3088
Fax: 800-870-5660
www.swarovski.com
Specialty: See article on page 200.

Towle Silversmiths
175 McClellan Highway
East Boston, MA 02128
617-568-1300
Fax: 617-568-9185
Specialty: Bells and ornaments.

The Tudor Mint
2601 South Park Road
Pembroke Park, FL 33009
800-455-8715
www.tudormint.com
Specialty: Figurines.

United Design Corporation
1600 N. Main Street
P.O. Box 1200
Noble, OK 73068
800-727-4883
Fax: 800-832-0866
E-mail: udc@ionet.net
www.united-design.com
Specialty: See article on page 202.

United Treasures
Positive Image® Division
18418 72nd Ave. South
Kent, WA 98032
800-678-2545
Fax: 425-656-0299
E-mail:
matt@unitedtreasures.com
www.unitedtreasures.com
Specialty: See article on page 204.

VF Fine Arts
1737 Stebbins #240
Houston, TX 77043
713-461-1944
Specialty: Graphics.

Vaillancourt Folk Art
145 Armsby Road
Sutton, MA 01590
508-865-9183
Fax: 508-865-4140
E-mail: valfa@valfa.com
www.valfa.com
Specialty: Figurines.

The Village Chronicle
757 Park Avenue
Cranston, RI 02910
401-467-9343
Fax: 401-467-9359
E-mail:
Peter@VillageChronicle.com
Jeanne@VillageChronicle.com
www.villagechronicle.com
Specialty: See article on page 206.

W.T. Wilson Limited Editions
185 York Avenue
Pawtucket, RI 02860
800-722-0485
E-mail: wtwgifts@aol.com
www.wtwilson.com
Specialty: Licensed and custom
collectibles.

Wade Ceramics Ltd.
PMB 333
3330 Cobb Parkway, Suite 17
Acworth, GA 30101
770-529-9908
E-mail: wade9908@aol.com
Specialty: Figurines.

Wallace Silversmiths
175 McClellan Highway
E. Boston, MA 02128-9114
617-561-2200
Fax: 617-568-9185
Specialty: Bells and ornaments.

Walnut Ridge Collectibles
39048 Webb Dr.
Westland, MI 48185
800-275-1765
Fax: 734-728-5950
Specialty: See article on page 208.

Walt Disney Art Classics
500 South Buena Vista Street
Burbank, CA 91521
800-932-5749
www.disneyartclassics.com
Specialty: Figurines.

Waterford Crystal
1330 Campus Parkway
Wall, NJ 07719
800-955-1550
Specialty: Crystal.

Wedgwood
1330 Campus Parkway
Wall, NJ 07719
800-955-1550
Specialty: Ornaments and plates.

Wild Wings
2101 South Highway 61
Lake City, MN 55041-0451
651-345-5355
Fax: 651-345-2981
Specialty: Nature art: originals,
prints and gift items.

Willitts Designs
International, Inc.
1129 Industrial Avenue
Petaluma, CA 94952
707-778-7211
Fax: 707-769-0304
E-mail: info@willitts.com
www.willitts.com
Specialty: See article on page 210.

The Wimbledon Collection
P.O. Box 21948
Lexington, KY 40522
606-277-8531
Fax: 606-277-9231
Specialty: Dolls.

Windstone Editions
13012 Saticoy Street #3
North Hollywood, CA 91605
800-982-4464
Fax: 818-982-4674
E-mail:
service@windstoneeditions.com
Specialty: Figurines.

Winston Roland Ltd.
1915 Crumline Side Road
London, Ont. Canada N5V 3B8
519-659-6601
Fax: 519-659-2923
Specialty: Graphics and plates.

Zolan Fine Arts, LLC
29 Cambridge Drive
Hershey, PA 17033-2173
717-534-2446
Fax: 717-534-1095
E-mail: DonaldZ798@aol.com
www.zolan.com
Specialty: Miniature plates.

Logging On to a New Era in Collecting

Remember the good old days of collecting? Like so many things in our lives that the computer has forever changed, the hobby of collecting has been revolutionized in just the last five years.

Still, the reports of collectible retailers closing up shop en masse, while direct marketers lick their wounds instead of postage stamps are a bit premature. In fact, if we cut through the current hype and the hysteria about the Internet and look at the reality of buying collectibles via e-commerce, one reassuring fact becomes very clear: "the more things change, the more they stay the same."

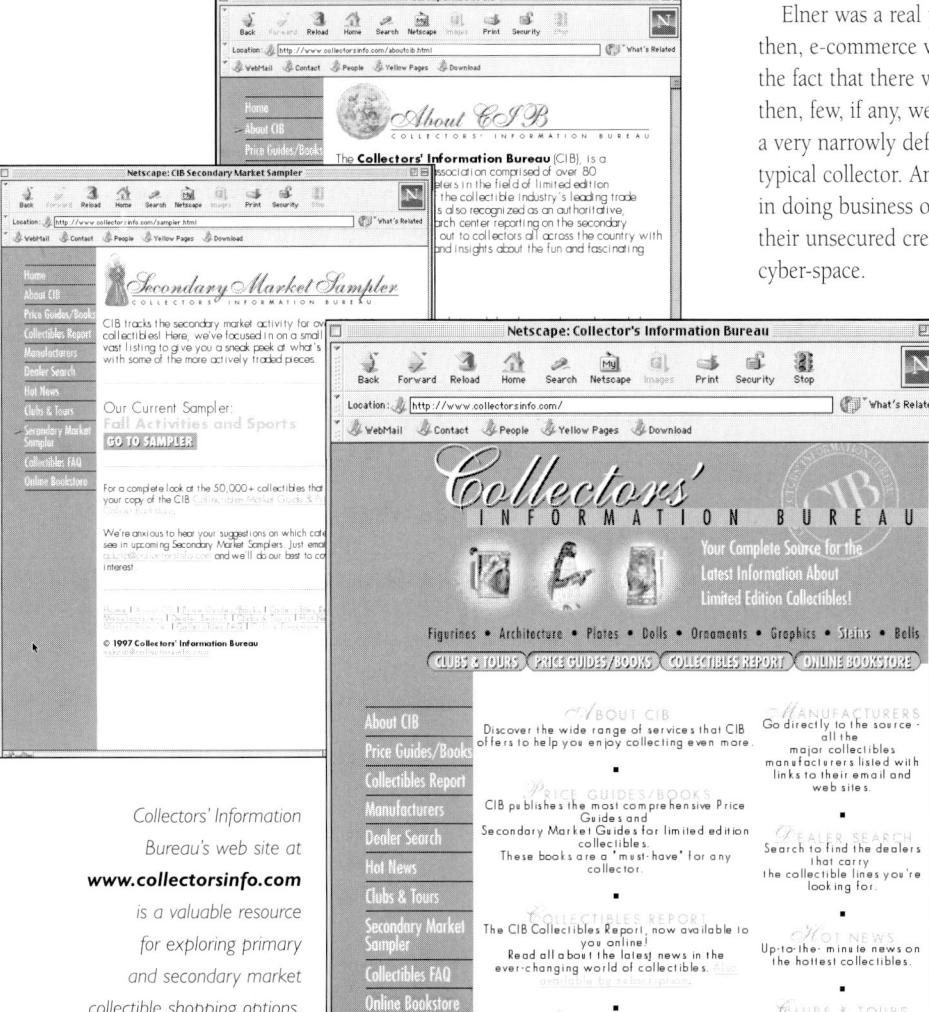

Collectors' Information Bureau's web site at **www.collectorsinfo.com** *is a valuable resource for exploring primary and secondary market collectible shopping options.*

"THE MOST EXCITING TIME IN RETAIL...EVER!"

Shopping for collectibles should be fun...otherwise, what's the point? However, buyers are finding that too many collectible sites on the Internet are far from being "user friendly." It's not the products' fault, it's just that the sites are constructed by computer wizzes who are used to serving the technology...not merchants who are used to serving customers, according to several industry watchers.

"The net just isn't set up to give customers any flexibility...most 'e-tailers' couldn't be bothered," says Ken Elner of Someone Special in Pennsylvania.

Elner was a real pioneer when he started his web site in 1996. Back then, e-commerce was a glimmer in practically nobody's eye. Despite the fact that there were a few Internet retailing success stories back then, few, if any, were actually making a profit. Plus, "web surfers" fit a very narrowly defined demographic that certainly did not reflect the typical collector. And to top things off, those who might be interested in doing business over the Internet were concerned about releasing their unsecured credit card information into the great unknown of cyber-space.

When they started their Internet site, the Elner family had three retail locations in the Philadelphia area. Now there's only one "brick and mortar site," and business has never been better. Elner estimates that 65% of their business is now generated by the store's Internet site, www.someonespecial.com.

What's the secret of their success? Elner believes that it was his refusal to subject his customers to the retailing business model that the Internet techno-designers established, and instead he applied three generations of Elner family retailing experience to the creation of his own model.

"We really broke the rules for Internet sales." If customers want their purchases gift-wrapped, shipped to another location, or need help in finding something special that they want, they get it. "It's all part of business as usual," says Elner..

In addition, collectors seeking out unusual items you don't see everywhere else have found that, with over 10,000 items listed for sale, Someone Special is an excellent resource. "We don't just carry the 'best-sellers' like other stores...we have the pieces that people have never seen before." For example, visitors to the Someone Special site can browse among the more than 800 pictures of Lladró figurines.

And if you are in the market for high-priced, high-quality items like a $1,500 Boehm sculpture, here's the place you'll find it.

The Someone Special web site is designed to create a "store experience" with products displayed and merchandised to heighten the enjoyment of browsing in this virtual shop. "With a lot of web sites, the customer has to know exactly what they're looking for before they enter the site or they're never going to find it. We give visitors the chance to look around and really 'shop.'"

Elner cautions cyber-collectors to make sure that the service they get online, matches or exceeds that which they would find in their favorite store or gallery. A small but important example of such attention to service is the fact that every single order Someone Special receives is entered individually. If two identical orders are received, the buyer will get a phone call to verify the quantity. "Ninety percent of the time the duplicate order will be an error; customers have a right to expect that kind of service."

One of the most popular secondary market sites on the web is that of Quiet Horizons in Shaftsbury, Vermont (www.quiethorizons.com). At Quiet Horizons, owner K.C. Johnson actually scours the country looking for collections to buy and then resell to eager collectors. "When we were looking to add new lines to our offerings, we first checked the values in *CIB's Collectibles Price Guide* to see which ones seemed most promising," Johnson explains. "Then we went to where most of those collectors are, and advertised heavily in those areas to buy collections." He estimates that by the time he buys 100 pieces in a particular collection, he will already have 90 of them sold. It's not hard to believe, considering that he has a hit list of 4,000 customers waiting to buy specific pieces. He also pointed out operating in this new "webbed" environment has given him the chance to test new lines quickly and inexpensively.

GOING, GOING...WENT

The past year has seen the Internet's favorite "novelty act" — online auctions — turn into big business. What many had hoped was merely a "passing fancy" has engendered a whole new kind of buying and selling. Will this affect retailing in the future? Even the experts claim that it is too early to tell.

Despite the fact that the most popular auction sites like eBay, Auction Universe, and Amazon.com are attracting an enormous number of curious collectors looking to score that one unbelievable bargain, many industry experts have observed that it is often the seller who is "making a killing."

Blaine Garfolo from Crystal Reef in Antioch, California, recounts his favorite online auction anecdote: One of his customers purchased a Real Musgrave print from his store for $35.00 and within days, that same purchaser had listed the print on eBay and sold it for $177! "People think that they're always getting a 'deal' when they buy through these auctions, but as often as not, they're going to be the loser unless they've done their homework first and tracked the primary or secondary market price of the item they're bidding on."

Auction buyers also need to be wary about the condition of the items they're bidding on. More than one unsuspecting collector has

paid the price for damaged or incomplete collectibles that were being offered as mint quality. Often the buyer has little recourse in returning goods bought through an auction or getting a refund if the quality of the merchandise is unsatisfactory.

Some of the major Internet auction sites have established safeguards to protect both buyers and sellers. Such sites as eBay and Amazon.com offer buyers insurance that provides for limited reimbursement if they feel they have been defrauded and their transaction meets each company's specific claim criteria.

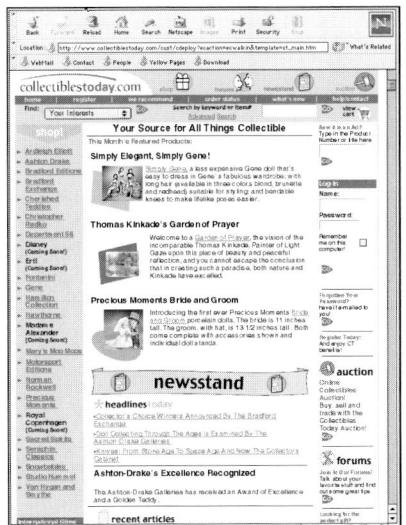

Collectors can shop online at The Bradford Group's web site at **www.collectibles-today.com** for a large variety of collectibles.

Many sites also give buyers and sellers the option of utilizing escrow services. In these transactions, an independent third party holds the buyer's payment in trust until the piece is received from the seller and accepted. Many escrow services also make it possible to buy and sell using credit cards without the seller having to go to the trouble of setting up a merchant account.

If a collector's sense of adventure should lead them to an auction site, one expert advises that they should know the value of the item they're bidding on before committing themselves to a price that may be out of line.

GETTING STARTED

Any collector interested in exploring their primary market collectibles shopping options on the Internet should first check out Collectors' Information Bureau's (CIB's) web site at www.collectorsinfo.com. There they will find a Directory of Manufacturers. With one click, they can connect to a manufacturer's web site where they will often find a Directory of Retailers.

Some member web sites, like the mega-site of The Bradford Group (www.collectibles-today.com), give you the option of purchasing a huge variety of collectibles directly through their site. Others, like the Annalee Mobilitee site (www.annalee.com) will give you the location of authorized retailers in your specific area that carry the particular lines for which you are looking.

There are a number of highly-regarded secondary market sites that collectors may want to check out as well. Collectors can locate these online dealers through any number of "search engines" like Yahoo, Alta Vista, Excite, Lycos, or AOL. Under "keyword," type in the particular line you're seeking, like "Department 56® Snow Village," or "Anheuser-Busch beer steins."

Collectors are also invited to go to CIB's web site where they can find secondary market dealers through the "Dealer Search" function.

Another way to track down online secondary market dealers is through the classified ads many run "looking to buy" pieces in various lines. If a line you're looking to buy is listed, and the dealer gives his web site address, go ahead and check it out.

Again, an educated collector is most likely to get the best deals in these marketplaces, so it's a good idea to check any prices you are quoted with those in the most current *CIB Collectibles Market Guide & Price Index* before you commit to any sale.

No matter what changes the Internet brings to the exciting world of collectibles retailing, remember this: when shopping for collectibles, buyers always have the right to excellent service, fair prices, and a fun experience. If you receive anything less...log off!

Guard Your Investment in Fine Works of Art

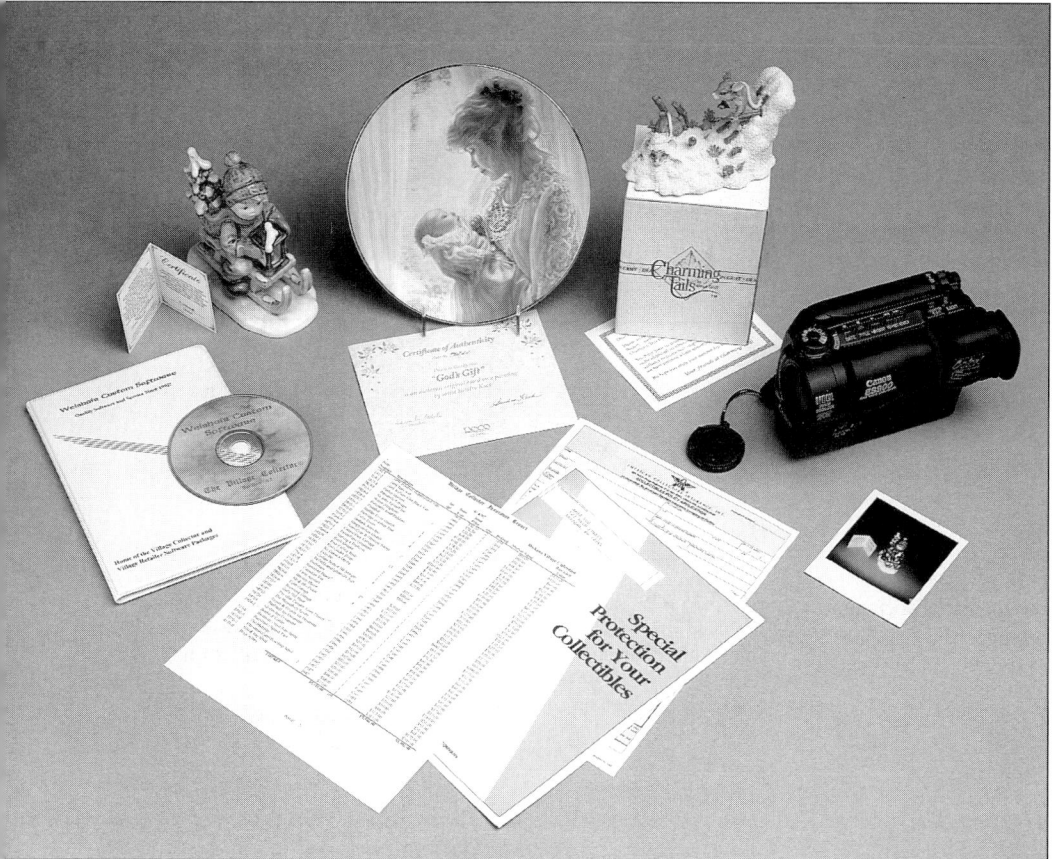

To help protect your collectibles investment, keep a visual and written record and have your collectibles properly insured.

It happens more often than we care to imagine. A burglar breaks into your house and absconds with your favorite figurine. A crystal collector's most treasured piece is shattered during a family move. Or — heaven forbid — a fire engulfs your home or an earthquake rocks it briefly on its foundation, destroying your favorite art pieces. Disaster could even strike when a pet's tail grazes a cherished item, sending it crashing to the floor — or when a well-meaning friend accidentally drops your heirloom porcelain bell while admiring it.

It's painful even to think about such events taking place, especially considering all the time, love and care you've invested in building your collection. Indeed, many collectors consider their holdings beyond price! Yet while a stolen or damaged collection may never be truly replaceable, there are important steps collectors can take to minimize their financial losses.

Experts are pleased to note that more and more collectors are making the effort to properly protect and insure their collectibles. As Jill Bookman, director of marketing for American Collectors Insurance, Inc. asks, "If collectors put an emotional and financial investment into acquiring their collection, why leave its security to chance?"

As Norman Carl, senior vice president of Horton Insurance Agency adds, "People are beginning to become more aware about insuring their collectibles. They value their collections and want to take care of their investment." Carl's firm provides collectibles coverage through a program with Atlantic Mutual Insurance Company.

Dan Walker, president of Collectibles Insurance Agency, Inc., points out the importance of specialization and taking into account the distinct needs of those who collect. "Hobby insurance is our only business," he says. "You receive coverage at your home, in a bank and worldwide coverage for travel and exhibiting. You are insured when your collectibles are sent anywhere in the world by secure mail or a secure shipping method."

A HOMEOWNER'S POLICY IS SELDOM SUFFICIENT

Experts like Carl, Bookman and Walker warn that collectors often have a false sense of security in thinking their collections are adequately covered under their homeowners' insurance policy. They suggest that collectors talk to their agents and find out if their collection is properly covered. There are basically two types of coverage: blanket and scheduled. Blanket coverage is considered much easier because the insurance covers every piece and the overall value of the collection. Scheduled coverage is for collectibles of exceptional value that need special protection. With scheduled coverage, collectors must provide a list of the pieces in a collection and tell the insurer the value. Collectors may also choose a combination of blanket and scheduled coverages.

The cost of collectibles insurance depends on the carrier and type of coverage. As an example, Atlantic Mutual Insurance Company has a minimum annual premium of $75.00 for a $10,000 collection, on a policy with no deductible. Their rates may vary 10% to 20% or so, depending on the state you live in and the value of the collection. American Collectors Insurance rates are similar, but with a $100 deductible per occurrence. Replacement value premiums from Collectibles Insurance Agency begin at $32.00 per $10,000 coverage with no deductible and no payment for losses of less than $50.00.

A recent innovation from American Collectors Insurance is the firm's comprehensive web site, which allows collectors to apply for insurance online and also find out more about insuring collectibles. Visit the site at www.americancollectorsins.com/collectibles.

Advice from Insurance Experts on
Insuring and Protecting Your Collectibles

1. Keep all receipts. Make sure you get a receipt for each piece you acquire, whether from a store, a friend or on the secondary market. Check that the receipt accurately identifies the item purchased and the price paid.

2. Record vital information. Some collectors use computer programs, while others use traditional paper logs. Whichever system you prefer, it is crucial that you record basic information about each piece you own. Keep a copy of this material in your safety deposit box or other secure, off-site location. Include:
- Item name, number and description
- Name of manufacturer
- Year of issue
- Artist's name
- Limited edition number
- Series name or number
- Special markings
- Purchase price
- Place of purchase
- Date of purchase
- Any other relevant information

3. Videotape your collection. Norman Carl says, "The single best record is to videotape the collection because you cannot only see the collectibles, but you can record a narrative, too." He recommends updating the videotape about twice a year, or as needed, when more pieces are added to a collection. Jill Bookman suggests taking photos as a supplement. If a piece is signed, a photo should also be taken of the autograph, or of other significant markings.

4. Keep records away from home. In case of fire, flood or other damage, having your receipts, item information, photos and videos and Certificates of Authenticity off site will be vital. Experts recommend placing these records in a safety deposit box.

5. Know your insurance policy. Read your policy carefully to make sure all your collectibles are insured — and insured at the proper level. Review your homeowners' policy, including all fine print, to make sure your collectibles would be adequately covered in case of an emergency. Check if the insured items are covered for their value at the time of purchase, or covered for the amount that it would take to replace them at the time you make a claim. In light of the fact that some collectibles increase in value over time, you may want a "replacement value" policy.

6. Know your insurance company. Carl says, "It's very important to deal with a company that is reputable and pays its claims promptly and fairly." At a time of personal loss, he continues, "the last thing you want is any hassles." Be sure to discuss all your special concerns with your insurance agent to make sure you have the coverage and sense of comfort you need. Ask important questions such as:
- Is it an "all risk" policy — meaning earthquakes, floods and other natural disasters are covered
- Is there a deductible? If so, how much?
- Does the policy cover breakage? If so, what constitutes breakage?
- Are the items covered if taken off the premises?

7. Update policy information regularly. If your collection appreciates to a higher value, or you acquire new pieces, it is important to update your policy. Bookman says American Collectors Insurance provides automatic 30-day coverage under an existing policy for your additional collectible purchases. "But," she notes, "collectors still need to notify us to amend their policy." Walker notes that Collectibles Insurance Agency does not require a written inventory of a collection to begin or renew coverage.

8. Establish a realistic, verifiable value for your collection. Whether you're determining the value of your collection for an insurance policy, assessing a loss or updating your coverage, turn to one of the respected reference guides published by Collectors' Information Bureau. They are recognized by insurers as one of the most reliable and credible sources.

Carl also recommends updating your personal list of collectibles each year with new secondary market prices. "Utilize the *Collectibles Market Guide & Price Index* and use the upper range of prices to insure your collection," he advises.

9. Take care of your collection. The easiest way to keep your collection safe and sound is to take proper care of each piece. Display your treasured figurines, prints or other pieces in curio cabinets, firmly secured frames and hangers, enclosed cases or away from the edges of tables or shelves. Such "tender loving care" may be your best insurance.

TO LEARN MORE, CONTACT YOUR INSURANCE AGENT OR THESE EXPERTS WHO CONTRIBUTED TO THIS ARTICLE:

American Collectors Insurance, Inc.
Jill Bookman
P.O. Box 8343
498 Kings Highway North
Cherry Hill, NJ 08002
Phone: 800-360-2277
Fax: 856-779-7289
Web Site: www.americancollectorsins.com/collectibles

Collectibles Insurance Agency, Inc.
Dan Walker
P.O. Box 1200
Westminster, MD 21158
Phone: 888-837-9537
Fax: 410-876-9233
E-mail: info@insurecollectibles.com
Web Site: www.collectinsure.com

Collectors' Information Bureau Membership Roster

Collectors' Information Bureau (CIB) is a not-for-profit trade association whose mission is to serve and educate collectors, members and dealers, and to provide them with credible, comprehensive and authoritative information on limited edition collectibles and their current values.

The Alexander Doll Company, Inc.

American Mint, LLC

Anheuser-Busch, Inc.

Annalee Mobilitee Dolls, Inc.

ANRI

Armani

Artesania Rinconada/
John J. Madison Co.

The Art of Glynda Turley

Arts Uniq'

The Ashton-Drake Galleries

The Boyds Collection Ltd.

The Bradford Exchange

Cardew Design

Cast Art Industries, Inc.

Cavanagh Group International

Charming Tails/
Fitz and Floyd Collectibles

Cherished Teddies/Enesco Group, Inc.

Christian Ulbricht USA

Christopher Radko

collectibles.com

Collectibles Insurance Agency, Inc.

CollectibleTown.com

Columbus International

Coyne's & Company

Crystal World

Dave Grossman Creations, Inc.

David Winter Cottages

Deb Canham Artist Designs, Inc.

Department 56®, Inc.

Desert Specialties, Ltd.

Doverdale Design

The Encore Group, Inc.

Enesco Group, Inc.

Fenton Art Glass

Flambro Imports, Inc.

The Franklin Mint

Gartlan USA, Inc.

Geo. Z. Lefton Co.

The German Doll Company

GoCollect.com

Goebel of North America

The Greenwich Workshop

Halcyon Days Enamels

Hallmark Cards, Inc.

The Hamilton Collection*

Harbour Lights

Harmony Kingdom

Honeybourne Hollow/
Fitz and Floyd Collectibles

Hot Wheels/Mattel, Inc.

The House of Fontanini

House of Hatten, Inc.

Imperial Graphics, Ltd.

Islandia International

Kurt S. Adler, Inc.

Larry Fraga Designs

Lee Middleton Original Dolls, Inc.

Lenox Collections

Liberty Falls Collectors Club

Lightpost Publishing

Lilliput Lane

Little Angel Publishing

Little Gem Teddy Bears

Lladró

Margaret Furlong Designs

Maruri U.S.A.

Matchbox Collectibles

Mattel, Inc./Barbie Collectibles

Midwest of Cannon Falls

M.I. Hummel *

Mill Mountain

Miss Martha Originals, Inc.

North Light

The Oliver Weber
Jeweled Collection

Original Appalachian
Artworks, Inc.

Papel Giftware

Possible Dreams

Precious Art, Inc.

Precious Moments/Enesco Group, Inc.

Prizm, Inc./Pipka Collectibles

Pulaski Furniture Corporation

Reco International Corp.*

Roman, Inc.*

Ron Lee's World of Clowns

Royal Copenhagen/
Bing & Grondahl

Royal Doulton

Russian Gift & Jewelry/
G. DeBrekht Artistic Studios

Sandy USA, Inc.

The San Francisco Music Box Co.

Seraphim Classics by Roman

Seymour Mann, Inc.

Slavic Treasures

Swarovski Consumer Goods, Ltd.

United Design Corporation

United Treasures, Inc.

The Village Chronicle

Walnut Ridge Collectibles

Willitts Designs International, Inc.

*Charter Member

Turn the page to learn more about
the past, present and future
of your favorite collectibles
as CIB presents
"Profiles of Leading
Collectibles Manufacturers."

Then, read on as CIB helps you discover…

Advice on Caring for Your
Collectible Treasures

Trends in Ornament Collecting

Taking to the Road in Search
of Collectibles

The Nations' Most Popular
Collectors' Clubs

Madame Alexander® Launches New Programs

Madame Alexander® celebrates the talent of international superstar Celine Dion with the 10" "Celine Dion™" doll.

As a child, Madame Beatrice Alexander Behrman lived in an apartment over the New York City doll hospital founded by her Russian immigrant father in 1895. This was the first facility in America where beloved dolls could be lovingly mended for their proud owners. Young Beatrice and her three sisters often played with the doll patients, fueling her desire to create her own line of dolls.

When World War I prevented importation of dolls from Germany, Madame Alexander filled the gap by producing unbreakable cloth dolls and selling them in her father's shop. These dolls were based on characters from literary classics and poems. With the assistance of her sisters, Madame Alexander added three-dimensional features and realistic clothing.

With a $5,000 loan in 1923, Madame Alexander moved her base of operation from the family kitchen table to a small shop nearby. At this time, her husband of 11 years, Philip Behrman, joined her in her efforts. Thus began The Alexander Doll Company and its long-standing tradition of handcrafted, high quality dolls.

MADAME ALEXANDER CREATES DOLL-MAKING HISTORY

Madame Alexander dolls have always been associated with "firsts" in the toy industry. Madame Alexander created the first doll based on a licensed character (Scarlett from the movie *Gone With the Wind™*). She also created dolls in honor of public figures such as the Dionne Quintuplets and Queen Elizabeth, and was the first to bring a full-figured fashion doll (Cissy™) with haute couture outfits to the marketplace.

Today, The Alexander Doll Company is located in Harlem, New York. It is one of the only major manufacturers to still produce dolls in this country. Although Madame Alexander died in 1990, the legacy of the "first lady of dolls" lives on today.

MORE AWARDS AND MORE NEW PRODUCTS

With seven DOTY "Industry Choice Awards" and one Dolls "Award of Excellence" nomination, Madame Alexander's spectacular 1999 line received acclaim throughout the doll and collectibles world.

Dolls selected for these honors include: "Madame Alexander Celebrates American Design Cissy," "Anna Sui Cissy," "Winter Wonderland," *The Little Women Journals™* "Marmee," "Porcelain Evening Star," "Limited Edition Scarlett Black Mourning," "Classic Ballerina" and the "Bent-Knee Cherry Twins."

MADAME ALEXANDER LAUNCHES *CLASSIC COLLECTIBLES*

The Alexander Doll Company provides another wonderful way to collect Madame Alexander with its launch of *Classic Collectibles*. The collection includes a new line of finely detailed, handcrafted figurines, waterglobes, music boxes, decorative porcelain boxes and collector pins based on the company's most popular dolls.

The hand-cast resin figurines are 6" tall, meticulously detailed and are based on *The Wizard of Oz™* and Betty Boop™, as well as American favorites like the "Coca-Cola® Carhop" and "Wendy Ballerina." Beloved *Storyland* characters are also vividly brought to life with "Little Red Riding Hood," "Mother Goose," "Cinderella," "Rapunzel," "Tinker Bell," "Snow White," "Row, Row, Row Your Boat," "Alice in Wonderland" and "Heidi" figurines. And to commemorate a meaningful event, *Special Occasions* figurines fit the bill beautifully with statuettes of a "Bride and Groom," a "Roaring 20s Bride," "Flower Girl," "Happy Birthday," "Spring Morning," "The Luck of the Irish," "First Communion" and "Thinking of You." And there's a holiday offering with "Santa's Little Helper" and "Guardian Angel."

Nothing evokes the pleasures and wonder of childhood like a magical waterglobe. Each of Madame Alexander's new musical waterglobes plays a special tune, and is sure to delight with themes like "Cinderella" (which

Madame Alexander® takes collecting in a new direction with the Classic Collectibles figurines based on its most popular dolls.

Madame Alexander® introduced a line of 18" Play Dolls inspired by Scholastic Entertainment's award-winning Dear America® book series.

plays "Cinderella's Dream of the Ball"), "Happy Birthday" ("Happy Birthday"), "Santa's Little Helper" ("We Wish You A Merry Christmas"), "Betty Boop" ("I Want To Be Loved By You"), and "Guardian Angel" ("Stairway To Heaven"). The "snowflakes" and sparkles within each 6" globe will add glittering excitement to any collection.

Music boxes never fail to fascinate and Madame Alexander's new collectible rotating music boxes, each 6-1/2" high, are enchanting in every way. The charming offerings include "Cinderella" (which plays "Cinderella's Dream of the Ball"), "Ring Around the Rosy" ("Ring Around the Rosy"), "Dorothy of The Wizard of Oz™" ("We're Off To See the Wizard"), "Row, Row, Row Your Boat" ("Row, Row, Row Your Boat") and "Wendy™ Makes It Special" ("Thank Heaven For Little Girls").

Lovingly made and beautifully rendered, Madame Alexander's new porcelain decorative boxes come in various sizes and make ideal gifts for numerous occasions. Exquisite detailing and rich colors enhance the beauty of this debut collection which includes scenes of "Pink Shoe Box," Madame Alexander's "Book Box" and "Pretty Bow Box." These wonderful keepsakes will be enjoyed for many years to come.

Each 2-1/2" resin collector pin is a unique hand-painted replica of a favorite Madame Alexander doll. The pins are charming, wearable renditions of some of the same whimsical figures found in the figurines, but on a more diminutive scale. "Tinker Bell," "Mother Goose," "Happy Birthday," "Alice in Wonderland," "Little Red Riding Hood," "Rapunzel," "Wendy Ballerina" and "Santa's Little Helper" are all packaged in a window box perfect for viewing these innovative collectibles.

A CELEBRATION OF DESIGN

Madame Alexander celebrates American Design in collaboration with the Council of Fashion Designers of America. Twenty famous designers, including Donna

Madame Alexander® introduced dolls based on illustrations by the popular contemporary artist Mary Engelbreit®. Featured is "Ann Estelle" wearing a white pique sailor blouse with a blue collar and blue pleated skirt, black tights and red maryjanes.

Karan, Arnold Scaasi, Linda Allard for Ellen Tracy, Jessica McClintock, Dana Buchman, Fernando Sanchez, Josie Natori, Anna Sui, Badgley Mischka, James Purcell, and more, joined forces with Madame Alexander and its Cissy™ haute couture doll to raise funds for Fashion Targets Breast Cancer. All 21 prototypes will be auctioned off in late 1999 with 100% of the proceeds going to this very important cause. Of the 21 prototypes, ten Cissy™ styles (as limited editions) will be produced with 10% of the wholesale price of the exquisite Cissys earmarked for donation to Fashion Targets Breast Cancer. Madame Alexander is honored to work with the Council of Fashion Designers of America in raising funds to help fight breast cancer.

Keeping with the tradition of Madame Alexander, licensed properties continue to play an important role. The 1999 selection includes wonderful new additions: "Celine Dion™," "Betty Boop™," "Little Orphan Annie™," "Dudley Do-Right™ and Nell," "Howdy Doody™," "Casper's friend Wendy™," "Lucy's Italian Movie," "Nostalgia Coca-Cola®," "Gone with the Wind™" and "The Wizard of Oz™."

1999 also saw the debut of adorable dolls based on Mary Engelbreit's card-illustrations – "Miss Smarty," "Ann Estelle" and "Cherry Girl."

Other additions were found in the *Baby Alexander™ Collection* including the new Meagan™ dolls – "Playtime Meagan™" and "ABC Meagan™," and the new "Baby Madison™," who drinks and wets and comes with her own layette set. Also new are the "Friends" doll featuring wonderful line drawings from the legendary singer, John Lennon™, and the fabulous Carter's® dolls: "Soft White Huggums™" and "Bunny Huggums™."

The selection of Baby Dolls, which continues to expand, includes: "Huggable Huggums™," "Classic Huggums™," "Pussycat™," 18" and 15" "Kelly," the new 12" "Katie™," and the 18" and 14" "Life-like Victoria." Each precious doll is designed to make that special someone smile.

The Alexander Doll Company has recently taken the Scholastic Books' award-winning *Dear America®* series – with over 7 million books in print – to a new medium. New introductions in this series include four 18" Play Dolls, each packaged with a Dear America® Diary. This is a wonderful addition to the company's educational/play series which includes the popular *Little Women Journals™* Play Dolls and accessories program.

Madame Alexander has dolls to suit every taste from Play Dolls to Baby Dolls, 8" dolls to 21" dolls, Storyland to Couture dolls, Bent-knee Dolls to Porcelain Dolls, and an impressive line of enchanting figurines and pins. At Madame Alexander, there truly is something for everyone.

The Alexander Doll Company, Inc.
615 West 131st Street
New York, NY 10027

Phone:
212-283-5900

Fax:
212-283-4901

Web Site:
www.madamealexander.com

A Proud American Heritage of Stein Making

Mention the name "Anheuser-Busch" today, and both beer lovers and stein collectors think of the leader – number one in the field. Yet when Eberhard Anheuser purchased his brewery in 1860, it was floundering badly. What's more, the company's first steins were little more than promotional give-aways. Yet the past 140 years tell a story of ingenuity and excellence that has taken Anheuser-Busch to the pinnacle of stein making, as well as world leadership in beer.

When Anheuser took over in 1860, his brewery was ranked only 29th of the 40 beer makers in St. Louis. But his daughter married a young brewery supplier named Adolphus Busch in 1861, and Anheuser found himself a willing ally. Busch started as a salesperson, but soon became a partner, and later president of the company. He was the driving force that transformed the small, struggling brewery into an industry giant – and thus Adolphus Busch is considered the true founder of Anheuser-Busch.

In the late 1800s, all breweries were strictly local or regional in focus, yet Busch dreamed of marketing the first national beer brand. He knew he would need to find ways to keep the beer fresh and pure during shipment. Adopting Louis Pasteur's new pasteurization process, Busch also set up the first network of rail-side ice-houses and introduced the nation's first fleet of refrigerated rail cars.

He then perfected his new beer, which he named Budweiser. It combined the finest ingredients with time-consuming, traditional brewing methods. What we now know as the "King of Beers" debuted in 1876 to great success. Today, it continues to outsell all other brands in the world. Over the years, Anheuser-Busch has added popular beers like Michelob, Busch, Bud Light, Bud Ice and many others to its product offerings. The company produced more than 92 million barrels of beer in 1998 and currently serves more than 46% of the American beer market.

The "1940-1959" stein represents the third of five issues in the 20th Century in Review series. It features highlights of the 1940s and 1950s, and has an edition limit of 5,000.

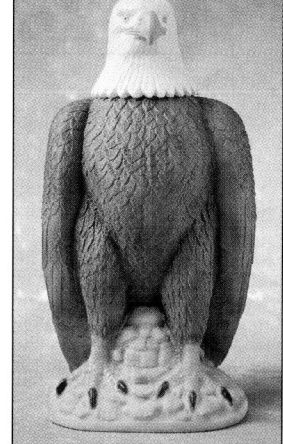

The "Bald Eagle" character stein, a limited edition of 50,000, features this most beloved American symbol in all his glory.

In 1998, Anheuser-Busch marked its 41st consecutive year as the world's largest brewer.

THE STORY OF STEINS

The German word *Steinzugkrug* translates roughly into "stoneware jug or tankard," and has been shortened in common use to "stein." Original steins had hinged covers with thumb lifts to protect the beverage from flies and debris, although today many collectible steins do not have lids. The covers were considered necessary during the 14th century, when scientists believed that the bubonic plague was spread by flies. Many towns in what is now Germany passed laws requiring that all food and beverage containers be covered.

Before long, utilitarian steins were enhanced by the designs of talented artists, transforming the drinking vessels into works of art. Even the lids provided inspiration, with colored glazes and raised decorations making the stein a status symbol for nearly all Germans. From the wealthy land owners to the lowliest laborers, most everyone proudly displayed his personal beer stein. Through force of habit, the laws about lidded steins remained in place until the 1900s. After all that time, the lidded beer stein had become an important part of German culture.

While there has long been a small "cult audience" of stein collectors in the United States and elsewhere, the hobby has enjoyed a modern renaissance since the mid-1970s. Today, steins are appreciated by people from all walks of life, both for their artistic and investment value.

While Anheuser-Busch commissioned a few steins in the 1950s and 1960s, the firm became the first U.S. brewer to seriously enter the consumer stein market in the 1970s. Many of these early steins were produced as promotional items to support the beer business, and were never intended to be "collectibles." Thus, there was little concern about edition limits or official documentation. The resulting mystery surrounding many of these steins, along with the small quantities which seem to be available, has caused some of them to soar in secondary market price over the past 20-plus years. In fact, many of the Anheuser-Busch steins from the 1970s routinely command 10 to 20 times their original retail price on the secondary market!

Second in the Budweiser Classic Car series is this "'57 Chevy Corvette" stein in a limited edition of 50,000.

A COMMITMENT TO COLLECTIBLES

In the early 1980s, Anheuser-Busch made a serious investment in the collectible stein market, providing documented item numbers, issue years and edition limits for each of its introductions. The company also began to introduce formal stein series, which added to the "collectibility" of steins. In addition to steins, the company also offers limited edition collectible figurines, plates and lithographs.

Today, Anheuser-Busch keeps between 50 and 60 stein items available at any given time. These works are designed and illustrated by a variety of artists throughout the United States and Europe. Artists are selected based on the particular style desired for each stein. Final artwork for each stein is then turned over to the stein manufacturer, most often either Ceramarte of Brazil or German manufacturers.

All of these manufacturers enjoy long-standing reputations for quality and craftsmanship, and relationships with Anheuser-Busch that date back to the 1970s. The majority of Anheuser-Busch steins are ceramic, with some being made of fine porcelain. Lids are pewter, and sometimes include a ceramic inlay, or a figurine made of ceramic, resin or pewter.

SPORTING AND WHIMSICAL THEMES

Over the years, Anheuser-Busch has developed a variety of stein themes, including brewery-related subjects, Clydesdales, sports, animals, and, of course, the famous 1975 "Bud Man" character stein. Other favorite character steins include the 1997 "Budweiser Frog" and "Bud Ice

First in a series of four steins in the Animal Family collection is "Fox Family Den," which has an edition size of 25,000.

Penguin." Notable Anheuser-Busch stein series include the *Holiday Series* and *Endangered Species* steins.

For two decades, the annual Anheuser-Busch *Holiday Stein* has played an important role in the growing popularity of stein collecting and stein gift-giving. Starting in 1990, two versions of each yearly stein were produced: the open edition, unlidded stein and the new lidded limited edition version, which is personally signed by the artist.

The *Endangered Species* steins feature eight of the world's animal species at risk, and they are among the most popular issues in Anheuser-Busch history. The first edition, "Bald Eagle," has been sought-after in the secondary market for years. The eighth and final edition, "Mountain Gorilla," was introduced in 1996. The original artwork for a number of the steins has also been reproduced in limited edition lithographs.

A THRIVING CLUB FOR STEIN COLLECTORS

A popular way to share stein collecting with friends is the Anheuser-Busch Collectors Club. Each club member receives the annual membership stein (valued at about $60.00), as well as the opportunity to purchase exclusive members-only steins. Membership also includes a one-year subscription to *First Draft*, the full-color quarterly club magazine; a collectors club binder, filled with interesting details on the early history of Anheuser-Busch, the development of beer steins, stein production and more; and admission discounts at Anheuser-Busch theme parks (Sea World, Busch Gardens, Adventure Island, Water Country USA, and Sesame Place).

Other benefits include discounts on Collectors' Information Bureau (CIB) publications, a personalized membership card, advance notice of new stein introductions and limited edition stein retirements, exclusive club member events and contests, a toll-free member's hotline and more. The annual club membership fee is $35.00.

When Anheuser-Busch introduced the club in 1995, the company set its first-year membership goal at 20,000. By early 1996, membership had reached 40,000, and it continues to grow – currently to a level of about 46,000 individuals. What's more, there is a strong base of enthusiastic Anheuser-Busch stein collectors all across America, as well as in Canada. Many collectors boast more than 300 steins in their collections, and eagerly await the 20 to 30 new issues Anheuser-Busch introduces each year.

Anheuser-Busch, Inc.
2700 South Broadway
St. Louis, MO 63118

Phone:
800-305-2582

Fax:
314-577-9656

Web Site:
www.budweiser.com

ANHEUSER-BUSCH, INC.

The Whimsy and Joy of Annalee Dolls

"Mending Teddy" is the 1999-2000 Logo Kid, free with membership in the Annalee Doll Society. The Logo Kid, which is 7" tall, changes with each membership year.

The 7" classic Annalee Santa comes complete with green burlap toy bag.

Annalee Mobilitee Dolls began on a kitchen table in the small town of Meredith, New Hampshire. It was here that creator Annalee Davis Thorndike pursued her doll-making hobby. In time, her hobby would become the family business, replacing the poultry egg farm she and her husband, Charles "Chip" Thorndike, had run.

TURNING A HOBBY INTO A BUSINESS

As a child, Annalee loved to watch her mother sew, and together, they made doll clothes. Annalee once said, "I never played 'house' with dolls, I just made clothes!"

Along with all those clothes, Annalee made dolls. These early characters were made of felt, which is still used today. What the earlier dolls lacked, however, was the internal wire frame that creates the "mobilitee" or the ability to position and pose the dolls. That addition came later from Annalee's husband, Chip.

After completing high school Annalee began offering her hand-made dolls and doll clothes for sale through outlets such as the League of New Hampshire Craftsmen. It was the dolls that caught people's fancy. "My friends wouldn't leave me alone!" says Annalee. "They kept knocking on my door and saying, 'I have an idea for a doll,' or 'I know where I can get skis for your dolls!'"

Interest in Annalee Dolls continued to grow. Stores were requesting special order pieces to use as window and product displays. The business that began on a kitchen table in the 1950s moved into a building of its own late in the 1960s. This one building soon became many as the company grew on the grounds of the former farm.

THE MAGIC OF ANNALEE DOLLS

What really set Annalee's dolls apart then, and now, is the whimsical face that shines from every doll. The expressions were taken from Annalee herself, as she studied her face, as well as others, to capture the crinkles and twinkles that animate an individual's expressions and emotions.

The clever animation that Annalee brought to her dolls was passed along to her oldest son, Chuck. Collectors are delighted when they meet Chuck and recognize those same fun-loving impish qualities in him that they love so much in their Annalee Dolls. Chuck continues to design new dolls that capture the magic of Annalee.

SECOND GENERATION ARTIST

Chuck, who is also president of the company, divides his time between running the business, designing new dolls, and meeting collectors at Artist Signings and Society Socials held around the country.

Accompanying Chuck to collector events is his wife, Karen. Over their many years together, Karen has contributed to the growth of Annalee Dolls on many fronts, from crafting the dolls to opening the Annalee Doll Gift Shop in Meredith.

A COLLECTIBLE LEGACY

The "collectibility" of Annalee Dolls was entirely consumer driven by the very passionate people who

Annalee Dolls has made bunnies for almost as long as they have made Santas. This 18" "Patchwork Bunny" is a pretty doll to display for the entire spring.

sought out the dolls for their collections. Many have celebrated the holidays with their Annalee Dolls for over three decades.

In 1983, the Annalee Doll Society was formed as a catalyst for bringing together all who love and cherish Annalee Dolls. A membership in the Society includes the annual Logo Kid, a special edition 7" doll that changes with each new Doll Society year. (The Society year begins on July 1 and ends on June 30.) Members also enjoy a subscription to the Society's magazine, *The Collector*. Four times a year, this 16-page color magazine arrives with news of special events, exclusive dolls, fun contests and members' photos and letters. Members also receive a special edition felt sun pin, an enameled lapel pin with date of membership, and a personalized membership card. For more information on the Annalee Doll Society, please visit an official Annalee Doll Society Sponsor Store, or call 1-800-433-6557. A listing of Sponsor Stores is also available on the Annalee Doll Internet site at www.annalee.com.

Membership in the Society means access to members-only exclusive dolls. The offerings are continually updated to reflect the desires of the membership. Each exclusive doll is introduced to the membership through the Society's magazine, *The Collector*.

Perhaps one of the greatest benefits of membership in the Annalee Doll Society is the invitation to the annual Summer Social at the home of Annalee Dolls in Meredith, New Hampshire. Occurring in the month of June, the Social is the largest gathering of Annalee Doll collectors to be held in the country. Over the years, members have enjoyed a myriad of activities including factory tours, clam bakes, swap and sells,

An entire menagerie of Annalee animals awaits the collector. Reindeer, in 10" and 12" sizes, complete a holiday scene.

auctions, barbecues and treasure hunts. Each attendee receives a special Annalee head pin, made exclusively for the Social. Raffles and games provide numerous opportunities to win Annalee Dolls.

For those who can't make it to Meredith for the Summer Social, the Annalee Doll Society comes to them. The Society has hosted one-day Socials filled with fun and good food in Virginia, Ohio, Tennessee, California, South Carolina and Pennsylvania, with new destinations always in the planning stages. Like the summer get-together, attendees receive an exclusive pin and the opportunity to purchase special items designed expressly for the Social.

SOMETHING FOR EVERYONE

Annalee Dolls has come a long way from the days when the Christmas line consisted of a Santa, an Elf and maybe an Angel. Today, the *Christmas Collection* is a large segment of the product line. Many of the holiday's traditional characters, like Snowmen and Gingerbread Men, are recreated as uniquely Annalee-styled characters. Santa is portrayed in four sizes, from 7" to 30" in a variety of activities. His friends, the Snowmen and Elves, are also available in a range of sizes and a multitude of accessories. There are plenty of traditional dolls too, like Carolers, Angels and Drummers. With Annalee Dolls, collectors may fill their home with the holiday theme of their choice, from humorous to traditional.

In addition to Christmas, Annalee Dolls offers collectors a complete line of seasonally appropriate dolls for every holiday, beginning with Valentine's Day. Homes filled with Annalee Dolls are colorful and cheerful the year-round.

VISIT ANNALEE DOLLS

Annalee Dolls extends an invitation to all to visit them at the Annalee Gift Shop in Meredith, New Hampshire. The shop is located on the grounds of the Annalee Doll company. Another reason to visit is the Annalee Doll Museum. The extensive collection features some of Annalee Thorndike's earliest dolls from the 1940s.

Twice a year Annalee Dolls participates in the International Collectible Expositions® held each June in Rosemont, Illinois, and each spring in alternating locations.

The Annalee Doll Society hosts an annual gathering each June in Meredith as well as "on the road" Socials across the country. Become a member of the Society to receive an invitation to these exciting events.

And, for a quick visit from the comfort of your home, visit Annalee Dolls on the Internet at www.annalee.com

Annalee Mobilitee
Dolls, Inc.
P.O. Box 708
Meredith, NH 03253-1137

Phone:
603-279-3333

Fax:
603-279-6659

Web Site:
www.annalee.com

E-Mail:
customerservice@annalee.com

ANRI Art – Creativity in Wood

From the incomparable artistry of Juan Ferrandiz comes "Wondrous Sight," a heartwarming addition to his Nativity.

Family ownership brings a special quality to any company, especially when the ownership is handed down from generation to generation. The hands-on, loving and proprietary aspect that develops over the years adds a pride of involvement that conveys something extra special to collectors, who cherish their very personal hobby. So it is with ANRI, a family-owned enterprise renowned for high quality, hand-carved and hand-painted artistry in wood sought after by connoisseurs around the world.

For over 300 years, the traditions of woodcarving have thrived in the Val Gardena (Groeden Valley) of the South Tyrol. By the turn of the 19th century, woodcarving had replaced other Valley enterprises, such as cheese-making, lace and Loden cloth, as the region's chief business activity. A unique method of distribution for the carvings was developed through itinerant sales representatives. Groedners traveling through Europe carried their wares, which ultimately led to the establishment of a major international trade. In 1866, 13-year-old Luis Riffeser was just one such representative sent abroad by his father. It was through this early start that Luis' profound devotion to the woodcarving tradition, and to his family's integrity, was nurtured.

His son, Anton, born in 1887, brought a great dream to reality. While in a Russian prisoner-of-war camp in Siberia during World War I, Anton made his plans to formalize the family's business. Using the first two letters of both his names, he christened his planned company ANRI – and a new woodcarving tradition was born.

During the war years, Anton's wife, Carolina, kept the work progressing, creating a base of operations that awaited his return. After six years as a prisoner, he was finally released. Upon returning home, startled to learn that the Austrian South Tyrol had been ceded to Italy as part of war reparations, he went to work putting his plan into effect. In 1926, the new building, complete with workshops, warehouses, offices and living space for the family, was ready. By now, the teenaged Anton Jr. was working side-by-side with his parents, ultimately playing an important role in the development of new techniques and products.

Family involvement continues to be strong today. Ernst Riffeser succeeded his father, Anton Jr., and today, Thomas, Ernst's son, is at the helm. A well-directed family enterprise with focused leadership, ANRI is moving into the new century with vitality and creativity, continuing to draw on the experiences of the past that will take the finest traditions of handcraftsmanship into the next millennium.

Sarah Kay's charming look at childhood is unmistakable. This dainty lass seems reluctant to relinquish these beautifully carved flowers in "Pretty as a Posy."

NATIVITIES DEVELOPED NATURALLY

Religious motifs have always carried weight in the Groeden Valley, with many highly detailed carvings from the 17th century still surviving today in museums and churches of the region. Among the earliest religious art forms carved by the Groedners was the Nativity, the celebration of the birth of Christ. In fact, it was the Groedners who established the tradition of adding snow to the scene. Today, Nativities in a variety of styles are an important aspect of ANRI artistry.

Among the most recognizable for many ANRI collectors is the gentle, tender spirit of Juan Ferrandiz, renowned for his poetry, as well as his painting. His love of children and his belief in them as the future of the world shines through in the cherubic quality of his Nativity. Although Ferrandiz died in 1997, ANRI is pledged to keep his spirit alive through the continuation of the production of his designs.

Highly sought after are the works of Ulrich Bernardi, whose personal appearances in the United States over the years have made him a familiar face to American collectors. Now semi-retired, Bernardi continues to carve for ANRI. Collectors can still look forward to additions to his Nativities, including the magnificent "Florentiner" which was presented to His Holiness Pope John Paul II in 1986. ANRI artisans were honored to be invited to study the

collection of religious art in the Biblioteca Apostolica Vaticana (Vatican Library). From this endeavor came the "Holy Land Nativity," now part of the official *Vatican Library Collection.*

The magnificent work of Karl Kuolt is highly recognizable by connoisseurs. The death of this renowned artist in 1937 did not diminish the attention to his work by ANRI. His stylized classicism results in the beautiful serenity of his Nativity. Much of Professor Kuolt's work can be seen in museums and private collections, while monuments and statues carved by him can be found throughout southern Germany.

Perhaps the newest star in the ANRI Nativity firmament is an artist born in 1916. Fini Martiner Moroder has been creating beauty in wood for more than 50 years. Her unique Romanesque-style Nativity has another element that differentiates it from other ANRI offerings. Produced in chestnut, rather than in the traditional alpine maple, with only a hint of color, it has a highly distinctive look.

ANRI'S ROSTER OF ARTISTS BROADENS

Sarah Kay, a beloved artist from Australia, never ceases to charm with her drawings of children, based on her own offspring. Since the early 1980s, ANRI's carvings from her art have brought three-dimensional life to her irrepressible renderings.

The world-renowned wildlife artist Gunther Granget is represented with distinctive carvings of his horses, birds and sea-dwellers. The perfect blend of his astonishing artistry with that of the ANRI masters brings magnificent works to collectors' homes.

◆ *New to ANRI is* The Ivano Collection, *debuting with the series called* Four Seasons.

Rudolph Kostner has worked with ANRI for several years and is becoming known to collectors across America. As a master carver, he is pleased to demonstrate his amazing craft in various stores across the country. Much of ANRI's translations from original two-dimensional art into the three-dimensional woodcarvings emanate from Rudi's workshop.

BRINGING THE WOOD TO LIFE

First the schooling, then the apprenticeship, followed by an arduous test. Only through this procedure may a carver be accepted by ANRI.

Four to six weeks are required before a carver is satisfied with his model. Alpine pine is generally used for a carving that will exceed 10", but if the figure will be smaller, the wood will be the harder alpine maple. The woods grow slowly at a high altitude on the shady mountainside. None is cut down before it reaches 80 to 100 years.

Once the wood is seasoned outdoors to reduce the moisture content, it rests in a kiln for about four hours before being cut into blocks. Only about 20 percent of the wood is ultimately used for carving, thus guaranteeing against imperfections which would not meet ANRI's quality standards.

Now the carver is ready to begin. The intricacies of fine carving, including facial expressions, graceful arms and fabric folds, require great skill.

A coat of lacquer provides a base for the oil paints. Colors, which are blended as needed, are applied to the figurine, then gently rubbed with a cloth. This allows the grain of the wood to shine through, giving the finished piece its utterly unique look. After a drying time of two to three days, a finishing coat of lacquer is applied to seal the wood and protect the paint.

Additions to the Karl Kuolt Nativity are always sought-after. This "Elephant and Rider" was introduced in 1999.

Ivano, a creative Renaissance man equally at home as a sculptor, painter or musician, joined ANRI's cadre of artists in 1999. The sense of rhythm he brings to his series of the *Four Seasons* – his introductory effort for ANRI – resulted in a charming new look.

With quality control at ANRI demanding the highest standards, the enduring family traditions remain very much in evidence.

ANRI Art
Str. Plan da Tieja, 67
1-39048 Wolkenstein
Groeden, Italy

Phone:
011-39-0471-79-2233

Fax:
011-39-0471-79-3113

Web Site:
www.anri.com

E-mail:
info@anri.com

Giuseppe Armani – Working to the Rhythms of Renaissance Art

Ever since Lorenzo the Magnificent, scion of the powerful Medici family, established Florence as the center of the Italian Renaissance over 500 years ago, Florentine art history has read like a "who's who" of the greatest artists who have ever lived.

For centuries, aspiring artists have traveled to Florence to worship at the shrine of such masters as Donatello, Cellini, the Della Robbias, Botticelli, Leonardo da Vinci and scores of others...both to drink in the beauty of their works and to attempt to decipher the secrets of their brilliant techniques.

Giuseppe Armani honors mothers with this delightful figurine entitled "Play Mates."

Today, the city remains the favorite locale for painters and sculptors. Among the most prominent Italian sculptors is Giuseppe Armani — a sculptor "creating art for today" in the glorious spirit of the Florentine Renaissance.

As a young child he, like many other children, loved to draw. Uniquely colorful and fresh, his drawings impressed everyone who saw them. Although his talent was obvious, it was Armani's father, Dario, who realized that his son's artistic abilities were gifts to be nurtured and developed.

Despite financial hardship, the senior Armani determined that Giuseppe would attend the prestigious Academy of Fine Arts in Florence. Because Dario became ill and died before their plans materialized, young Giuseppe was forced to abandon his studies to help his family.

The inspired young Giuseppe still continued to learn on his own. His hard work and talent were finally recognized during Pisa's local exhibition of young artists. His entry, a classically inspired male torso,

◆ *The special bond between mother and child is beautifully expressed in "Magic Touch," created by Giuseppe Armani.*

was hailed for its extraordinary precision and detail. When the sculpture was put on display at "The Gallery" in Pisa, it won Armani a permanent job offer.

While working at "The Gallery," Armani became proficient in various materials: marble, alabaster, wood and clay. He created art of such exquisite and breathtaking beauty and power that it earned him fame and admiration from visitors who flocked from around the world to Pisa.

THE ALLIANCE OF GIUSEPPE ARMANI AND FLORENCE SCULTURE D'ARTE

The people of Florence Sculture d'Arte are dedicated to continuing Tuscany's glorious artistic heritage. In their factory just outside Florence, its founders created an environment where the best Italian sculptors and painters could flourish. This same environment has encouraged Giuseppe Armani, working exclusively with the company since the 1970s, to give free reign to his artistic muse.

Today, Giuseppe Armani creates in a spartan studio attached to his house. Building on the classical traditions of Michelangelo and Leonardo da Vinci, his constant evolution, experimentation, and exploration in the ways of artistic expression have brought this living master far beyond the glorious roots of his artistic heritage. The genius of the Renaissance continues to inspire Armani to sculpt his masterpieces.

BRINGING THE ART OF GIUSEPPE ARMANI TO THE WORLD

Giuseppe Armani is the renowned and acclaimed sculptor of the Florence Sculture d'Arte Studio. Giuseppe is always quick to acknowledge the valuable contributions of his colleagues at the studio, as well as his American associates at Miller Import Corporation.

Pietro Ravenni, President of Florence Sculture d'Arte, is the son of one of the founders. He has worked at the Florence factory since the age of 20. "What symbolizes

Florence Sculture d'Arte," Pietro has stated, "is the art of Giuseppe Armani. In his 20-plus years with us, Giuseppe has strongly influenced every aspect of our studio. The Armani 'style,' which we all follow, is what gives our work its quality and distinction. Armani's style will continue to be our grounding force for the future."

Herb Miller and his wife, Pat, accompanied by their Italian agent, Attilio Vezzosi, were at an exhibition in Milan when they first discovered the work of Giuseppe Armani, who had just begun sculpting for Florence Sculture d'Arte. They realized that Armani's art would be enthusiastically received in America. Their vision led to the long and happy collaboration of Miller Import Corporation and Florence Sculture d'Arte, and brought Giuseppe Armani's figurines to one of the most receptive and appreciative audiences in the world.

RECENT RECOGNITION FOR ARMANI AND HIS WORK

This decade has been an extraordinary one for Giuseppe Armani. He has been honored by being voted "Artist of the Year" by the National Association of Limited Edition Dealers (NALED). His popularity and reputation continue to grow, as does the number of collectors who avidly acquire his work. His art has been sought by high-profile collectors. World leaders including Pope John Paul II and President Bill Clinton, along with celebrities Dionne Warwick, Tony Orlando and Herschel Walker own Giuseppe Armani sculptures.

As the millennium approaches, Giuseppe Armani and Florence Sculture d'Arte continue to strike out in exciting new directions. The *Giuseppe Armani Wall Art Collection* presents the artist's subjects with a beauty and realism that art lovers are finding irresistible.

On the home décor front, *The Giuseppe Armani Lamp Collection* has reinvented the concept of the table lamp, making lamps a true work of art. The maestro has even turned his talents to the creation

"Marjorie" exemplifies Giuseppe Armani's unique talent for inspired design, meticulous attention to detail and passion for excellence.

of Christmas ornaments, thereby applying his familiar magic in creating unique designs with unsurpassed attention to detail to the magical world of Christmas.

THE SOCIETY OF GIUSEPPE ARMANI'S STUDIO ART

Since 1990, The Society (of Giuseppe Armani's Studio Art) has helped thousands of American collectors get more enjoyment from Giuseppe Armani sculptures by sharing insider information about the artist, previewing new introductions, and helping collectors locate specific works. The Society's collectors also participate in exclusive members-only activities and events.

"Cleo" from the My Fair Ladies *collection is a limited edition of 5,000 pieces.*

The Society has its own web site (www.the-society.com) with on-line enrollment, questions and answers about the artist, news of in-store events and color pictures of new products. The Society can also be contacted via e-mail at: miller_society@prodigy.com or by phone at (800) 3-ARMANI.

The mission of Giuseppe Armani and Florence Sculture d'Arte is to bring beauty into the lives of collectors everywhere. Armani's mythic, almost mystical ability to capture the essence of his subjects — their character and their soul — amazes and intrigues people the world over. His collectors and critics agree that Giuseppe Armani Creates Art for Today!

Armani
c/o Miller Import
Corporation
300 Mac Lane
Keasbey, NJ 08832-1200

Phone:
800-547-2006

Fax:
732-417-0031

Web Site:
www.the-society.com

E-mail:
society202@aol.com

Welcome to a World of Handcrafted, Contemporary Ceramic Design

Known internationally for its unique personality, character and originality, the *Artesania Rinconada Collection* is truly one of the finest examples of contemporary ceramic design. Artesania Rinconada figurines are carefully hand-carved and detailed in fine grain, earthenware ceramic material. After initial kiln firing, decoration continues with the hand-application of colored slips and enamel glazes used to accent and highlight individual design characteristics. Each enamel glaze must be re-fired in order to preserve its distinctive coloration.

HUMBLE BEGINNINGS

Twin brothers, Jesus and Javier Carbajales, created this exquisite collection of handcrafted ceramic designs during the fall of 1972 in Montevideo, Uruguay. The Carbajales were born in Spain in 1930 and moved to Uruguay when the Spanish Civil War erupted in 1936. The brothers, however, did not forget their artistic roots. They were

Jorge De Rosa collaborates with Jesus and Javier Carbajales on Silver Anniversary designs.

strongly influenced by Pablo Picasso, Salvador Dali and Joan Miro – three Spanish artists whose work dominated the first half of the 20th century.

The Carbajales chose nature as their subject, and in their sculptures, they blend a traditional South American style with a surrealist flair.

The name Artesania Rinconada is a Spanish phrase meaning "Art of the Corner" or "Corner Art." It was chosen because the brothers worked out of a small corner of their living room for many years. Although Jesus and Javier can no longer confine themselves to a small corner studio, they continually refer to their work as Artesania Rinconada and carve the initials "AR" into each of their original designs.

THE BIRTH OF THE *SILVER ANNIVERSARY COLLECTION*

In recent years, Artesania Rinconada has evolved under the leadership of a new factory director who possesses exciting creativity and artistic vision. Jorge De Rosa apprenticed in the field of handcrafted ceramics as a young man in Montevideo, Uruguay. He studied all aspects of ceramic design and artistic development under the guidance of his father, Jorge De Rosa Thompson, who co-founded Artesania Rinconada S.R.L. along with the Carbajales brothers in the early 1970s.

Jorge became the director of the Artesania Rinconada factory in 1996 and has collaborated with Jesus and Javier in implementing creative new techniques for the company's designs. Under his leadership, Artesania Rinconada has developed a series of gold and platinum accented animal figurines to commemorate the 25th

Gold and platinum glazes highlight the ceramic craftsmanship and hand-painted accents of the "Koala" – a Silver Anniversary design for 2000 from Artesania Rinconada.

anniversary of the original *Classic Collection*. These new designs formed the beginning of the *Silver Anniversary Collection*, which is successfully leading Artesania Rinconada into the 21st century.

THE MANUFACTURING PROCESS

Because each individual artist possesses his own unique carving style and selection of paints; no two figurines in the *Artesania Rinconada Collection* are exactly the same. This gives each piece a unique style and artistic personality rarely found in the world of collectible figurines.

Creating an Artesania Rinconada design is a complicated and time-intensive undertaking. Following are the stages of development in the manufacturing process of Artesania Rinconada figurines. First, each piece is hand-carved from a flat clay mold, and then fired in kilns exceeding 1000 degrees Fahrenheit. Next, each design is hand-painted using slips and enamel glazes. Finally, each piece must re-enter the kilns to preserve the enamel glazes and distinct coloration. *Silver Anniversary* designs must undergo additional firings to preserve the gold and platinum enamel glazes.

THE BENEFITS OF MEMBERSHIP

Admirers and collectors of the Artesania Rinconada collection are invited to enroll in the Artesania Rinconada Collector's Society. The club was formed to bring together individuals who enjoy the handcrafted ceramic sculptures of Jesus and Javier Carbajales and want to be kept informed about pertinent developments within the Artesania Rinconada collection.

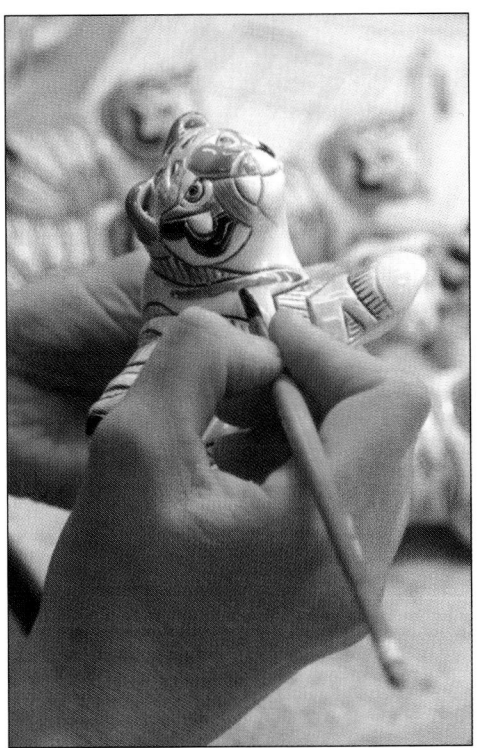

The Silver Anniversary *"Tiger" is individually hand-carved and hand-painted, then accented in gold and platinum enamel glazes, giving each piece its own unique quality, character and personality.*

Each Artesania Rinconada design is fired in kilns of temperatures exceeding 1,000 degrees Fahrenheit to preserve the distinct coloration of the enamel glazes.

The club year runs from May 1 to April 30, and the annual dues are $35.00. Upon joining, Society members receive a beautiful figurine that is limited to Artesania Rinconada Collector's Society members only. This special figurine is not available to the general public and quickly becomes among the most sought after of all Artesania Rinconada pieces.

New club members receive a complimentary copy of the *Artesania Rinconada Silver Anniversary Album* ($16.95 retail), or if they prefer, a retail guide to the value of Artesania Rinconada retired designs on the secondary market ($19.95 retail). Membership benefits entitle club members to be among the very first to learn about new introductions or when a particular group of designs is marked for retirement. Members will also have the opportunity to purchase members-only figurines, which are redeemable through their local retailer.

THE COLLECTION TODAY

Since their introduction in 1972, the artists have introduced over 480 original designs, of which 292 are currently available. Many designs have been retired over the years and can only be acquired through the secondary market.

Currently, the *Silver Anniversary Collection* features 42 intricately detailed designs. The *Large Wildlife Collection* contains 26 large animal designs and includes limited edition figurines. And rounding out the exquisite Artesania Rinconada collection is the *Classic Series*, which showcases 224 beautiful, hand-carved and hand-painted designs.

Artesania Rinconada
John J. Madison Co., Inc.
Exclusive U.S. Distributors
29726 Avenue Banderas
Rancho Santa Margarita, CA
92688

Phone:
800-854-9338

Fax:
949-888-8416

Web Site:
www.rinconada.com

E-mail:
madison@jmadisonco.com

ARTESANIA RINCONADA

Capturing the Wonder of God's Creation

"One Hundred Years Together II" by D. Morgan has a print size of 30" x 20" and a retail price of $45.00.

When Arts Uniq' President and CEO Barbara Crouch entered the world of prints and publishing nearly 20 years ago, most galleries and shops she visited devoted their space to male-oriented wildlife art. At that time, both artists and galleries focused their attention on the art itself, with very little emphasis on loving sentiments or suitability for home decor. Barbara could see a definite need for prints that would appeal to women and offer a more decorative approach in their colors, matting and framing.

Barbara and her husband, Lonnie, founded Arts Uniq' in 1985 with a distinctly different concept from that of most print publishers at the time. Barbara had soaked up considerable knowledge in sales, marketing and selection of artists. Lonnie contributed his strong background in fine art framing, gallery management and finance. The pair agreed that their firm would foster an appreciation of art and the efforts of all artists. They would focus on the wonder of God's creation, and expressions of that wonder with a deep Christian perspective. And they would strive to enhance family harmony by bringing the beauty of God's world into homes and offices everywhere.

The small version of "Mom Won't Mind" by Kathy Fincher is 20" x 16" and sells for $24.00.

Starting their business from home, Barbara and Lonnie initially sold only the prints of about a dozen carefully selected artists. Barbara found that she had a "sixth sense" about which artists' work would sell. Soon the fledgling company branched into publishing and framing, and in 1987 they signed their first "marquee" artist: D. (Doris) Morgan. Living up to its "Uniq'" name, the firm found in Morgan a painter who also created poetry to enhance each of her designs. What's more, Arts Uniq' innovated by using special mat cuts, lace insets, and other framing concepts that were fresh in the marketplace.

Many of the "serious" galleries, however, remained skeptical about Arts Uniq's focus on sentiment and décor. After all, they had based their businesses on male-oriented wildlife for many years and were inexperienced with Arts Uniq's soft florals and feminine color schemes. That meant that the early successes for Arts Uniq' centered on the gift market, offering gift shops a new opportunity to sell wonderful art with customized framing and mats, and to promote artists through their shops and shows.

A CONCEPT WHOSE TIME HAD COME

Although both Barbara and Lonnie are quick to assert that they were blessed in both the success of their business and the choice of gifted and loyal employees, the quick growth of Arts Uniq' was quite remarkable. By the end of their first year in business, the firm turned a profit — quite a coup for a brand-new firm. The second year, Arts Uniq' grew 800% — and when the partners added framing to their product mix, their sales took off once again. The home-based business then moved to a 2,000-square-foot building which soon was doubled and doubled again in size. Today, Arts Uniq' covers a total of about 48,000 square feet in three buildings.

Fueling Arts Uniq's growth has been the firm's strong relationships with artists — now a total of about 40 individuals covering landscapes, gift and sentiment lines.

Collectors always find something new with Arts Uniq', as well. For instance, the firm now is developing the framing methodology to add "fillets," which are inserts between a mat and print to add dimension and perceived value. Barbara and Lonnie find that their customer base today consists largely of "baby boomers" who appreciate extra quality touches such as the fillets, distressed looks, texturing and elegant matting.

"Waiting in the Attic," created by Gay Talbott-Boassy, measures 16" x 12" and has a retail price of $15.00.

To make sure she and her employees stay abreast of current trends, Barbara holds a coveted chair with the Colormarketing Group. This alliance of professionals meets regularly to review changes in the marketplace, the world economy, and other factors that affect consumers' color preferences. Members cover a wide range of industries including clothing, home décor and automotive — all decision-makers whose instincts help determine what consumers see in stores and showrooms and what they choose to buy.

Barbara and Lonnie both are proud to have been ranked "Number One in the Gift Market" by *Giftbeat,* a consumer report of the gift industry. This organization polls dealers nationwide to find out which firms are tops in the print and framing markets, and Arts Uniq' has consistently ranked in the top three of both home décor and wall décor categories each year since 1994. As a result, *Gift Beat* has named Arts Uniq' "The gift industry's most requested source for framed art."

MEETING THE NEEDS OF THE MARKETPLACE

One of the main reasons for this success has been Arts Uniq's willingness to adapt quickly when market conditions and needs change. They have reacted to consumers' interest in what they call "the collectible side of art" by providing more information about artists and the authenticity of their works. In addition, Arts Uniq' has opened a division called Art Express, which allows dealers to offer their customers a lower price point and quicker delivery on pieces which still represent high quality. The key to the Art Express line is that its pieces are available only with a pre-chosen set of mats and moldings in colors that are known to appeal to quality-conscious consumers.

In addition, Arts Uniq' is always on the lookout for intriguing new artists. Among recently signed artists is Jack Terry, who specializes in Western, rodeo-style creations.

For the past five years, Jane Randolph has served as Director of Licensing for Arts Uniq', expanding the firm's strategic alliances for the creation of everything from stationery and T-shirts, to canvas tote bags, and much

more. For example, artist D. Morgan's lighthouses, beach scenes, houses by the sea and shells are the focus of a book called *The Song of the Sea*, published by Harvest House Publishers, incorporating Doris' seaside imagery and poetry.

Other Arts Uniq' artists have seen their work licensed to a variety of manufacturers which meet the firm's demanding standards for family-oriented, high-quality products. These include: Dwayne Warwick's beautiful English cottages and gardens; Joyce Birkenstock's gardens, fountains, architectural motifs and portraits of children and adults; and Susan Colclough's impressionistic greenhouse interiors, gardens and fountains, and outdoor scenes focused on trout fishing and golfing. Also popular among licensees are Carolyn Shores Wright, Kathy Fincher, Laurie Hein and Gay Talbott-Boassy.

A BRIGHT LOOK AHEAD

Future plans for the company include continued growth with the assistance of a strong sales network, introductions of more innovative framing techniques, increased licensing of the images created by the talented stable of Arts Uniq' artists, stronger participation and visibility within the limited edition collectibles market, expanded dealer and artist signing events, and participation in consumer shows, including the International Collectible Expositions®.

As their business has grown, Barbara and Lonnie Crouch have remained true to their original focus. As Barbara explains, "Most of our artists have been Christian-oriented artists — and naturally they have a faith that shines through in their work. We love the idea that we

This handsome Western image, titled "When Denver Rode the Rails," is the creation of Jack Terry. At 25-1/2" x 19-1/2", it sells for $28.00.

can help enhance homes with these uplifting messages. We feel that we have been very blessed in our business. Our mission is to do more than just sell art for walls. We strive to help home life improve and relationships improve — to help people express themselves and grow closer to God and to each other."

Arts Uniq' Inc.
1710 S. Jefferson Avenue
P.O. Box 3085
Cookeville, TN 38502

Phone:
931-526-3491

Fax:
931-528-8904

Web Site:
www.artsuniq.com

E-mail:
sales@artsuniq.com

High Fashion Doll Transforms Industry

The *New York Times* has proclaimed, "A Star Is Born, and She's A Doll." The *Chicago Sun-Times* has lauded her, along with the international press. Little did designer Mel Odom know that his passion for dolls, high fashion and actresses from the '40s and '50s would lead to such a phenomenon – one named Gene Marshall.

In the late 1970s and early '80s, Odom was a hot commercial artist in New York City. His drawings of high fashion, captivating beauties graced the covers of *TIME* and *OMNI*, and also appeared in the *New York Times Magazine* and in illustrated stories by Joyce Carol Oates and Tom Robbins.

However, a drawing of a face – that of a mysterious, raven haired actress-type – came to life in Odom's mind, more so than anything else he had ever drawn. Odom attended an inspirational costume show at the Metropolitan Museum of Art, and knew he must create a high fashion doll based on that face which captured the glamour of old-time movies.

"Song of Spain" is the 1999 Annual Edition Gene doll.

INTRODUCING *GENE*

Gene Marshall, a 15-1/2" fashion doll, inspired by the legendary screen goddesses of Hollywood's Golden Age, the '40s and '50s, was born in 1995. In both quality and detail, *Gene* rivals the finest vintage fashion dolls, from the porcelain-like finish of her skin to the authentic period coutre of her wardrobe, coiffures and accessories. Intricate details, such as working garter belts, lavish hand-beading, fully lined dresses and even the racy seam on the back of her sheer stockings, all add to *Gene's* amazing appeal.

It was important to Odom, who approached the Ashton-Drake Galleries in Niles, Illinois, with six prototypes of his doll, that *Gene* be more than a glamorous figure that collectors could put on a shelf. He wanted his creation to have life – a real story behind the face, a real meaning behind the story. So he created a biography of the inimitable Ms. Marshall,

"Hello Hollywood, Hello" shows Gene receiving a star's welcome in a crisply tailored, California blue suit trimmed with matching "fur."

complete with a birth date, family background and a chronicle of her rise to fame and fortune.

HIGH FASHION DETAIL CAPTIVATES COLLECTORS

In fact, each of the dolls in the collection has her own unique story to tell, as a chapter in the movie career of *Gene*. Each doll is outfitted in a unique, high fashion costume that comes with a story line, increasing the collector's knowledge of the fictional biography of *Gene*.

The quality and fine detail of the clothing worn by *Gene* are what fascinates collectors the most about the doll. Odom, the designers and Ashton-Drake set out to create miniature versions of real, high fashion clothes – clothes that can be removed, handled, and come with snaps and buttons that work. The "realness" of the outfits is what encourages adult collectors to "play" with *Gene* – taking her out of the box and creating new and different scenarios for the doll.

Gene's unique look and high fashion wardrobe were highlighted in the first *Gene* catalog in 1995, which featured three dolls and nine outfits, and announced, "Close your eyes. A dream is about to come true." The catalog stated, "As carefully chosen as her dramatic roles, her wardrobe was the envy of all. From the Hamptons to Hollywood, she looked stunning wherever she appeared." Of those introductions, the only one still available today is "Red Venus," which depicted *Gene* in her first "bad girl" role and marked her first screen appearance as a redhead.

MORE DOLLS, MORE FASHIONS RESULT IN POPULARITY

The next year, 1996, brought two more dolls and four more outfits; in 1997, there were eight more dolls

Designed by Stephanie Bruner, winner of the Ashton-Drake Young Designers of America competition, "Breathless" is a Retailers Exclusive 1999 doll.

(including the first limited edition and several "exclusives") and six costumes. It was evident that *Gene* had catapulted to the top of the high fashion doll world with the introduction in 1998 of six dolls, five exclusives and 11 outfits.

In 1999, the collection debuted five dolls and 13 costumes. One doll, several costumes and an accessory package were designed with the theme of *Gene's* USO tour of England and France during World War II.

The welcome introduction of *Simply Gene* met collectors' demand for a less expensive *Gene* doll that's easy to dress in her fabulous wardrobe, with long hair suitable for styling and bendable knees for more life-like poses. The three *Simply Gene* dolls (a blond, brunette and redhead) were designed to encourage collectors to have fun with the collection: change the doll's hairstyle and poses and switch her outfits – even mix and match the costumes!

Gene's world also expanded with the addition of a line of accessories, a CD and a music video. Among the accessories designed to make *Gene's* life a bit easier are a dresser, the first piece in *Gene's* wardrobe suite; a director's chair and a USO accessory package. Also available are a 1950s white Christmas tree; a wardrobe trunk; a dress form; her two terriers, "Dottie" and "Dashiell," a patio set and a poolside fan set.

The CD features some of *Gene's* favorite songs from the '40s and '50s, with two new songs, "Share The Dream" (*Gene's* Theme) and "She'd Rather Dance," written and performed by *Gene's* creator Mel Odom. The music video

features "She'd Rather Dance" starring Odom and "Share The Dream" starring the 1999 *Gene* collection.

YOUNG DESIGNERS OF AMERICA COMBINE WITH *GENE*

Founded in 1995 by Ashton-Drake's Joan Greene, The Young Designers of America Program is dedicated to inspiring, recognizing and rewarding the creativity and talent of today's high school students. The competition focuses on the *Gene* collection – each student is given a basic *Gene* doll, then challenged to create a scenario and an outfit to go with it. The student competition is judged in the individual schools across the country, with judges that include art community leaders, Odom or a member of the design team.

Each and every Young Designers of America Program participant receives a special certificate of achievement and a sterling commemorative pin. Winners earn a cash prize – and possibly the satisfaction of seeing their design produced and collecting professional royalties.

"The Young Designers of America Program, in many ways, mirror's *Gene's* success," commented Greene. "You dream, you work and you're discovered. All of us at Ashton-Drake are truly proud to sponsor this program." Added Odom, "The students' talent never ceases to amaze and delight me. I am so proud that *Gene* can inspire such creativity."

GENE BECOMES HIT ON INTERNATIONAL CIRCUIT

While *Gene* took both the worlds of doll collecting and high fashion by storm in the United States, it wasn't long before the international media began to tout the success of the doll. Publications in Scotland and Japan featured *Gene* on the covers, while an edition of *Doll*, a United Kingdom magazine, headlined *Gene* as a "Hollywood star makes a sparkling appearance."

With collectors still talking about Gene's triumphant debut in Paris in the spring of 2000, what's next for Gene Marshall? Proving that Gene is the toast of both coasts, the annual Gene Convention with the theme "Broadway Medley," sold out quickly, and a West Coast convention organized by the Hollywood Gene Club and held at the Roosevelt Hotel, site of the first Academy Awards, was hailed as one of collecting's finest nights. The possibilities for Gene and her fans are limitless.

"Love Paris" shows Gene in a stunning suit given to her by a secret Parisian admirer.

"Bears and Hares... You Can Trust"™

Envision a thriving public company that's actively traded on the New York Stock Exchange, and you may picture stuffy, high-rise offices and folks in formal, navy blue pinstripe suits. But a glimpse into the world of The Boyds Collection Ltd.® breaks that corporate mold in minutes! Founded by an eccentric, fun-loving guy referred to as "The Head Bean Hisself," Boyds prides itself on being "Folksy With Attitude" in product design, craftsmanship, and culture!

Boyds began as a small antique business owned by "The Head Bean," Gary Lowenthal, and his wife, Justina (Tina). After a seven-year career in purchasing, design and merchandising at New York's famed Bloomindales Department Store, Gary left "Bloomies," eager to apply his retailing skills to the antique trade. He and Tina named their company after the small town where it was founded in 1979: Boyds, Maryland.

BEARS BRING SUCCESS TO BOYDS

Finding many of the antiques they loved to be way too costly for both themselves and their customers, Gary and Tina began selling "antique reproductions" including duck decoys and — most importantly — nostalgic teddy bears. In 1984, Gary designed a 12" fully jointed wool bear and named it after his latest "joint venture" with Tina — their newborn son, Matthew.

The plush line expanded to include poseable characteristics, as well as bears dressed for every season and occasion. Through these designs, the Boyds Bear family continued to grow. Today, the "Boyds domain" has

Meet "Rebecca and Wesley Bearimore," recent additions to the charming Boyds line of "bears and hares."

"Webber Vanguard," an appealing undressed, bean-filled bear, made his debut through Boyds in the year 2000.

expanded to serve over 19,500 dealers across the nation with bears, hares, and other assorted friends in plush and resin.

LOVINGLY MADE WITH OLD-WORLD CARE

Today, most of the plush bears, hares and friends begin as concepts developed by "The Head Bean Hisself" and the Boyds Product Development Team, through sketches or by "hands on" work with the Master Seamstress in the factory. After a prototype is developed, many modifications are made to the pattern, color, fabric, and so on until the exact "Look, Feel, and Personality" are achieved. All cutting and sewing are completed by the Master Seamstress and her associates in a manner similar to turn-of-the-century teddy bear production methods. Professional stuffers and embroiderers complete the process, with many quality control checks at each stage.

In recent years, Boyds has added fine, hand-painted resin works of art to the product mix, with rousing success. Many of the company's most beloved plush characters now can be enjoyed in figurine form as well. And of course, the same stringent quality standards apply.

BEARSTONES LEAD A VAST PRODUCT LINE

Today, the most popular of all "The Head Bean's" many lines are the *Bearstones* resin figurines — each with its own sparkling personality, vintage outfits and inspirational quote. Not one to play favorites, he also showcases his many plush products, the *Folkstones* and *Dollstones*, as well as *Wee Folkstones*, *Purrstones* and a whole realm of other figurines, resin jewelry, ornaments, waterballs, votive holders, ceramics, picture frames, wooden clocks, ceramic cookie jars and mugs.

Pieces in the resin figurine category are popularly

priced in the $9.00 to $60.00 retail range, and each comes with a number of special quality touches. These include Boyds' distinctive symbol of authenticity — the hidden bear paw — and a bottom stamp indicating the name, edition and piece name. What's more, each item is packaged with its own Certificate of Authenticity bearing the signature of "The Head Bean Hisself," Gary Lowenthal.

A perennial award nominee and winner for many of its diverse product lines, Boyds earned "Plush Collectible of the Year" and "Doll Award of 1999" from the National Association of Limited Edition Dealers (NALED). The company also received two recent nominations each for "Teddy Bear of the Year" and "Doll of the Year."

INTRODUCING *THE BEARLY-BUILT VILLAGES*™

Imagine the sort of whimsical town where the bears from Boyds would feel right at home. It's all there in *The Bearly-Built Villages* — a series of miniature houses and cottages that are perfect abodes for many of Boyds' Bears and Friends. The first Village, *Boyds Town*, was introduced in the spring of 2000 with six buildings: "Ted. E. Bear Shop," "Bailey's Cozy Cottage," "The Chapel in the Woods," "The Boyds Bearly a School," "Edmund's Hideaway" and "Public Libeary."

Boyds will limit the number of buildings in *Boyds Town* to 25, in order to give collectors an opportunity to collect the full line. Seven more buildings in *Boyds Town* made their debut in Fall of 2000: numbers seven through 15. (Boyds always skips number 13 because "The Head Bean Hisself" is quite superstitious.) Already extremely popular with collectors, *Boyds Town* saw two of the first pieces — "Bailey's Cozy Cottage" and "Public Libeary" — reach retirement in a matter of months after they were issued. In honor of "The Head Bean's" 51st birthday, each building is hand-numbered in an open edition of 5,100 pieces. They range in price from $23.00 to $25.00.

BOYDS DONATES 100% OF PROFITS FROM *BEARSTONE* AND PIN TO STARLIGHT CHILDREN'S FOUNDATION

Boyds recently announced a major, concerted commitment to donate 100% of its profits from the sale of an exclusive *Bearstone* and Pin to the Starlight Children's Foundation. Founded in 1983 by actress Emma Samms and motion picture producer Peter Samuelson, the Foundation has enhanced the lives of more than 74,000 seriously ill children each month by providing state-of-the-art audiovisual equipment for children in hospitals and by granting wishes.

Boyds has introduced a special 4 inch-tall exclusive *Bearstone* entitled "Charity Angelhug/And Every Child… Cherish the Children" to help support the Foundation's worthy efforts in "distractive entertainment therapy." The figurine features a touching comment from a child under-

100% of profits from the Starlight Bearstone "Charity Angelhug/ And Every Child…Cherish the Children" helps support the worthy efforts of the Starlight Children's Foundation.

going chemotherapy: "If I met an angel, I would ask the angel to make me healthy again."

There will be another resin Starlight piece in the fall of 2001, and the first plush piece from Boyds is slated to debut in spring of 2001. In addition, Boyds will donate a total of 50 Starlight Fun Centers – mobile units consisting of a TV, VCR and Nintendo 64 game system – to hospitals in the towns of qualifying Boyds dealers. These additional Starlight Fun Centers will help advance the organization's work to improve the quality of life of very sick children.

A BEAR-FILLED FUTURE

Today, the Folks at Boyds strive to retain the same values Gary and Tina brought to the original antiques business over 20 years ago. The "mom and pop shop…on steroids," as Gary calls Boyds, recently acquired a new CEO who takes a slightly more serious tone. "I am extremely optimistic about our future," Jean-André Rougeot asserts. "Boyds has all the keys to success…I thank you for your support, and look forward to updating you on our progress as we continue this exciting journey."

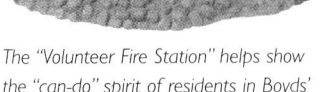

The "Volunteer Fire Station" helps show the "can-do" spirit of residents in Boyds' Bearly-Built Village.

The Boyds Collection Ltd.®
350 South Street
McSherrystown, PA 17344

Phone:
717-633-9898

Fax:
717-633-5137

Web Site:
www.boydsstuff.com

THE BOYDS COLLECTION LTD.®

The Heart of Plate Collecting

For over a quarter of a century, The Bradford Exchange has been a leader in limited edition collector plates. When legendary founder J. Roderick MacArthur helped to introduce the fascinating hobby of plate collecting to the United States, he focused the world's attention on an extraordinary art form that was born one cold December morning over one hundred years ago. On that day, Harald Bing, director of the Danish porcelain house of Bing & Grondahl, ordered his factory workers to destroy the mold for "Behind the Frozen Window,"

a small blue and white plate that would go down in history as the world's first limited edition collector plate.

Collectors of The Thomas Kinkade Simpler Times Perpetual Calendar keep current with the months by displaying different plates like "January – Lamplight Bridge."

MacArthur proceeded to establish the first organized international exchange for the buying and selling of collector plates...thus providing a legitimate foundation for this collectible form and facilitating the growth of an absorbing avocation that is now enjoyed by millions across the country, throughout North America and around the world.

Along the way, The Bradford Exchange has been proud to bring the work of some of the most talented and widely recognized artists to collectors, including Norman Rockwell, Edna Hibel, Sandra Kuck, Charles Fracé, Thomas Kinkade, Lena Liu, Charles Wysocki and many more.

The Bradford Exchange has also opened up a window to a world of exciting places, events and subjects for collectors. Plates and art from exotic locales have included the first collector plates from China and from Russia, events such as the 25th anniversary of Disney World, and diverse subjects from Elvis and Michael Jordan to spirited and endangered animals of the wild and angelic spirits guiding us from above.

Bradford has been instrumental in introducing collectors to new and exciting innovations, too, with 3-dimensional sculptural plates, musical plates, plates in the shape of angels and a Winnie-the-Pooh "honey pot." But the company has never rested on its laurels, and today, The Bradford Exchange continues to search the world and talk to collectors to find the next distinctive collectible.

CREATING DRAMATIC PANORAMAS WITH COLLECTOR PLATES

Sometimes the majesty of nature or the beauty of a rural landscape just can't be contained in a single image. You need to view the whole spectacular panorama! And that's exactly the idea behind some of Bradford's newest and most innovative collections – a series of plates that when displayed together – create one complete image.

In the past year, collectors have been held spellbound by the incredible beauty of *The Invitation* by artist Tom duBois. This epic work of art retells a favorite Bible story...that of Noah and his ark.

Each of the three rectangular ceramic plates in the series gives the collector an extraordinary view of the world's wildlife parading peacefully and majestically toward the great wooden ship that will carry them to safety and preserve life on earth to flourish anew after the floods recede.

Collectors of this panorama receive, absolutely free with their panorama collection, a solid wood plate rail on which to display their monumentally inspirational limited edition series.

The Invitation by artist Tom duBois is one of The Bradford Exchange's popular Plate Panoramas, recounting through art, the story of Noah's ark.

The Thomas Kinkade Simpler Times series Perpetual Calendar features art by the most collected living artist, known throughout the world as "The Painter of Light™."

COUNTING THE DAYS WITH COLLECTOR PLATE CALENDARS

Collectors are always on the lookout for new ways to display their prized plates, and The Bradford Exchange has introduced a new collector plate format that provides a wonderful way to give their favorite art and favorite artists special attention.

With perpetual calendars, collectors not only get a beautiful collection of 12 plates, but a unique and attractive way to display them. With each passing month, the collector can feature a different plate on the calendar display and can personalize the month with individual date and event tiles.

The Thomas Kinkade Simpler Times series Perpetual Calendar has been helping collectors count the days since it was released to an overwhelmingly enthusiastic collector response.

Thomas Kinkade is one of the best known and most beloved artists in America today...some say he is the most-collected living artist in the world. The Perpetual Calendar that bears the master's inimitable artwork, from January's lamp-lit hometown scene, to a recreation of an idyllic holiday celebration in December, takes its collectors on a year-long "celebration" of the cozy, friendly, and romantic places that we would all love to "escape" to every once in a while.

In addition to the exquisite art, *The Thomas Kinkade Simpler Times* Perpetual Calendar includes a handsome hardwood display rack with 33 moveable hardwood date tiles, and a variety of extra tiles that collectors can use to mark special holidays, birthdays and family occasions.

PORCELAINE PRINTS™ ALL READY FOR DISPLAY

Now you can get the look of custom-framed art in a collector plate that is ready to hang in a place of distinction. The Bradford Exchange has recently introduced Porcelaine Prints™, and collectors have responded enthusiastically. These 7" x 9" print-shaped plates are crafted from high-quality ceramic with properties that give it a high-luster appearance that rivals the finest porcelain. Porcelaine Prints™ feature unique raised borders that are designed to create the look of custom-framed and matted artwork, and they also come with a built-in hanging ring that allows for immediate display.

Since Bradford's Porcelaine Prints™ have hit a "home run" with collectors, it is only natural that one of the most popular images of the year would feature "the home-run king" himself – Mark McGwire. "70!," Plate One in the *Mark McGwire: King of Swing* collection of limited edition collector plates, celebrates the now-legendary major leaguer who broke Roger Maris' long-standing record of 61 home runs in a single season.

GEARING UP FOR MORE "FIRSTS" IN THE NEW CENTURY

Building on Rod MacArthur's long-standing tradition of innovation, quality and artistic excellence, The Bradford Exchange has earned an unmatched record, bringing the collecting public more exciting, historical "firsts" than any other collectibles company in the entire world.

It was The Bradford Exchange that brought the world the first three dimensional collector plate, "She Walks in Beauty," in 1976; the first genuine collector plate based on a movie, "Over the Rainbow," in 1977; the first plate ever sponsored by The Rockwell Society of America, "Scotty Gets His Tree," in 1974; and the first plate from the birthplace of porcelain, The People's Republic of China, with "Pao-Chai," in 1985.

Bradford is also responsible for introducing the first musical movie-theme collector plate with "Somewhere Over the Rainbow;" the first-ever "talking plate," "Carlton Fisk: 1975 Home Run;" and the first collector plate with movement, the carousel-themed "Swept Away."

When you see all the unique shapes of current Bradford offerings, their variety of products featuring popular themes in sports, entertainment, and world events, and their line-up of the world's most sought-after artists, you might wonder, "What will they think of next?"

Who knows what surprises the next Bradford release will hold. If the past is any indication of the future, one thing we can be sure of...it will be an exciting work of art that will make the collecting world sit up and say "Bravo!"

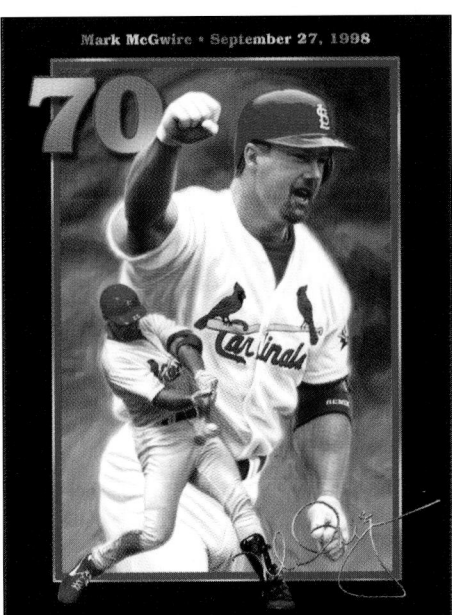

Mark McGwire · September 27, 1998

"70!," Plate One in The Bradford Exchange's Mark McGwire: King of Swing collection of limited edition collector plates, celebrates the now-legendary major leaguer's record-breaking season.

The Bradford Exchange
9333 Milwaukee Avenue
Niles, IL 60714

Phone:
800-323-5577

Web Sites:
www.bradex.com
www.collectiblestoday.com

E-mail:
custsrv@bradex.com

THE BRADFORD EXCHANGE

Where High Art Meets High Tea

Make a teapot to suit every taste and show that imagination knows no bounds. That's the goal that guides the work of the master artisans and designers of Cardew Design, including the company's illustrious and colorful founder and president, Paul Cardew.

To decide which concepts will take shape as the company's delightfully original teapots, Cardew and his design team look to see how their ideas measure up against a list of strict criteria: Is this a design that will bring a smile to everyone who sees it? Can it be produced with Cardew's high quality standards? Does the idea have the whimsy, wit and style that it takes to qualify as a truly sought-after collectible?

For nearly as long as tea has been cultivated – about 4,000 years – there have been teapots in which to make it and serve it. Cardew Design has given this once humble item of kitchenware a new lease on life, transforming it into charming and cozy vignettes featuring such familiar

"Morning Coffee" combines Cardew's trademark miniature details with antique-inspired "Old Country Rose" china in this charming teapot.

THE PURSUIT OF LOVE LEADS CARDEW TO HIS LIFE'S WORK

The success of Cardew Design is surely no surprise to the family, friends and teachers who recognized the exceptional artistic talent of Paul Cardew as he was growing up in England. Paul had always intended to be an architect, but after enrolling in architectural school, he found the work uninspiring. His grandmother, sensing his frustration, encouraged him to enroll in the prestigious Loughborough College. Here, he would find the two defining loves of his life – his wife Karen, a fellow student, and the art of ceramics.

Within ten minutes of taking his first ceramics class, Cardew knew he found his life's work. "I think it's the fact that you're working in three-dimensions, just like architecture, only all the control and decision-making is right there in your own hands," Cardew explains. "Ceramics was clearly the medium for me!"

After graduating and completing a teaching degree, Cardew accepted a position as a teacher at Exeter College, while Karen, also a ceramics designer, decided to try her hand at making brooches and earrings.

The young couple traveled to London with several samples of Karen's brooches. They were an instant success at Harrods Department Store and several big shops on fashionable Oxford Street. The Cardews returned home with an order for 5,000 brooches. From that day forward, they never looked back – it was business full speed ahead. Karen's brooches would prove to be the launching pad for what today has become a thriving ceramic business, whose classic, licensed and funky creations have been responsible for infusing the familiar old teapot with a popular new life.

CARDEW TEAPOTS DEFINE A NEW COLLECTIBLE CATEGORY

In 1991, Paul and Karen Cardew joined forces with long time friend, advertising guru, Peter Kirvan, to start Cardew Design PLC. And in 1992, the company premiered its designs in New York City. Today, Cardew Design sells its products in more than 40 countries and has developed several new product categories including: *Cardew Collectibles*, which produces novelty teapots, as well as licensed products designed and manufactured for

"Captain Pooh" from the Cardew Collectibles line translates the magic of such well-loved characters as Disney's Winnie the Pooh to fine china teapots.

and homey items as a kitchen range, a cluttered desk, an overflowing toy box and an old-fashioned sewing machine.

The metamorphosis is complete when each teapot is embellished with perfectly wrought miniature details. The result is a work of art so beguiling that it's plain to see why Cardew's marvelous limited edition creations have earned their reputation among the hottest collectibles on today's market.

Walt Disney, Royal Doulton and Portmeirion; *Cardew Studio* featuring highly decorated and elaborate works of art, products from Paul's English studio, and all limited editions; *Cardew Classic* which features tea and coffee ware; *Colour It Cardew,* a line of children's pottery paint kits; *Cardew Blue,* holiday and home accessory items, decorated in the famous Blue Willow design; and *Cardew Signature,* a line of non tea-related collectibles.

The company's pottery factory and main design studio are located in a farmhouse and buildings surrounded by a lovely setting of rolling green hills and meadows in Devon, England.

Working from the old farmhouse kitchen, which has been converted into his personal studio, Paul Cardew produces the highly decorated and elaborate works of ceramic art on which his international reputation has been built.

The origins of a Cardew teapot rests with the creativity of Cardew and his designers who develop all new concepts and then go on to handcraft the prototypes. From sketches and ideas, the sculptors work with the finest clay to bring the teapots to life. A master mold is created from plaster of paris and then meticulously cleaned of any excess clay before proceeding with the firing processes. Each teapot receives three firings. The first is a firing of the still damp clay pot at 1010° C to remove moisture and create a hard bisque pot. The teapot is then dipped into a liquid glaze and fired for a second time at 950° C turning the semi-vitrified bisque pot into a glazed pot. The precious metal lusters and picture transfers are then applied, and the pot is fired for the third and final time at 850° C.

AN INTERNATIONAL TEA PARTY

In 1995, Cardew Design premiered a collector's club dedicated to the magnetic attraction that teapots – especially the Cardew variety – hold for collectors. Members of the Cardew Collector's Club receive a unique, hand-crafted collector's club teapot; a full color Cardew Collector's Catalogue; the club newsletter, "Teapot Times," published three times annually; an invitation to purchase members-only limited edition teapots; and other special

Cardew Signature *features such non-tea items as this magnificent set of beautifully sculpted figurines from the "Matt Painted Nativity."*

offers. The club's annual subscription fee is $50.00 (U.S.); $75.00 (Canada).

From around the world, collectors make the pilgrimage to Cardew Design's Visitor Center located at Bovey Tracey in Devon, England. Here, teapot fanciers are welcome to spend the day and tour the factory for a behind-the-scenes view of teapot production. Visitors are also welcome to create, decorate and sign their own teapot designs at the Activity Center, before stopping for a spot of delicious cream tea in the Mad Hatter's Tea Room.

Their size tells the story of this mini-collection of "Cardew Tinies" from the company's line of enchanting Cardew Collectibles.

In 1998 following the highly successful launch of the company's collection of Disney licensed teapots, Cardew Design was honored with the "Gift of the Year" award by the British Retailer Association. At the *Fantasia 2000* licensing dinner held during the June, 2000 International Collectible Expo and hosted by Walt Disney Art Classics and The Disney Showcase Collection, Cardew Design received the award for "Outstanding Achievement in the Category of Storytelling" in recognition of the extraordinary teapot, "Disney Ark – Fantasia 2000." This teapot was commissioned by Roy Disney to commemorate a selected scene from the movie and was created in a limited edition of 2,000.

The year 2000 has seen Cardew Design expand its operations with the launch of Cardew Design North America. Focusing its efforts on expanding the company's sales and marketing in the U.S., Canada and the Caribbean, this new division will continue to build the Paul Cardew brand as the most sought-after name in collectibles today.

Plans are also in the works to expand the company's current retail opportunities at the Cardew Teapottery, both in the U.K. and in the U.S. In addition, the company is making plans to build a teapot museum that will house the largest teapot collection in the world.

"The pieces in our museum would be quite special," Paul Cardew says. "We would only acquire teapots that have a special meaning to us and are significant in some respect. They may be antiques, the latest designs from up-and-coming designers fresh out of school, or items found in the African bush. It makes no difference to me as long as each teapot reflects the unique taste here at Cardew Design."

Looking to the future, Cardew Design will continue to bring high quality design to the marketplace to fulfill the promise that's stated in the company's tagline, "Design, Design, Design." This commitment assures collectors that Cardew Design always has and always will be the number one source for creativity, originality and charm in the world of teapots.

Cardew Design
North America, Inc.
17 Turntable Junction
Flemington, NJ 08822

Phone:
877-9-TEAPOT

Fax:
908-806-7844

Web Site:
www.cardewdesign.com

E-mail:
Cardewdesign@aol.com

CARDEW DESIGN

Celebrating a Decade of Quality Collectibles

It seems fitting that Cast Art Industries' 10th Anniversary coincides with the millennium year 2000. In a year when everyone will be rejoicing in a new century, Cast Art will be joining in – celebrating monumental achievements accomplished in a mere decade.

In December of 1990, three gentlemen with more than 50 years of combined experience in the giftware industry came together to form Cast Art Industries. A former Florida corporate president with substantial experience in administration and marketing, Scott Sherman joined with Frank Colapinto, a gift industry sales executive, and Gary Barsellotti, an Italian-born expert in the crafting process of quality figures.

Several months later, the fledgling company teamed up with Kristin Haynes, a talented artist who would go on to create the now legendary *Dreamsicles* collection. The adorable collection of cherubs would take the collectibles world by storm, and soon Cast Art Industries would make its mark on the collectibles industry as a company with a reputation for producing fine collectibles at prices collectors could afford.

The Dreamsicles *holiday collection includes these cuddly* Angel Hugs *plush figures.*

HAYNES INSPIRED BY MOTHER'S ART

Kristin Haynes, the talented artist behind the *Dreamsicles* collection, found early inspiration in the works of her mother, noted watercolorist Abbie Whitney. She introduced Kristin and her siblings to drawing and painting when the children were quite young.

Kristin went on to major in sculpting at the University of Utah, and later went on to design small cherubs and animals, which she sold at local craft fairs. She named her company "Dicky Ducksprings," after a sentimental location from her childhood.

During this time, she and her husband, Scott Haynes, had a daughter and two sons, and Kristin fully intended to ease up on her sculpting. However, her figures continued to prove very popular, and requests continued to stream in.

Cast Art Industries offered to help ease the production

New from the Dreamsicles *collection,* Northern Lights, *are "Bunny Slope" and "Little Snowflake."*

load while maintaining Kristin's personal style and handmade look. In March of 1991, the first 29 figures were released in the *Dreamsicles* collection.

DREAMSICLES QUICKLY RECOGNIZED AS TOP GIFT LINE

Within a year of its introduction, *Dreamsicles* catapulted to the top of the collectibles industry – not a small task for a collection that was the flagship for its parent company, Cast Art. The collection was recognized as the "Best Selling New Category" by the Gift Creations Concepts group of retailers, while *Giftbeat,* an industry newsletter, named *Dreamsicles* as the Number One General Gift Line based on dollar sales volume.

Now in its eighth year of success, *Dreamsicles* has become firmly established as one of America's favorite collectibles. Each year, the collection continues to be ranked as one of the tops in the industry.

FIGURES BENEFIT CANCER RESEARCH

Since 1996, Kristin Haynes has designed special figures to benefit the American Cancer Society. The 1999 "Relay for Life" is the most recent figure, joining "We Are Winning" (1998) and "Daffodil Days" (1996-97). Cast Art Industries donates a portion of the proceeds from the sale of each figure to the fight against cancer.

COLLECTION EXPANDS TO INCLUDE CHRISTMAS, MORE ANGELS

The popularity of the *Dreamsicles* collection created several offshoots, including *Love Notes, Expressions from the Heart, Our Daily Blessings,* three dimensional greeting cards, a line of boxes, the *Golden Halo Collection* and the *Dreamsicles Garden Collection.*

Cast Art added a holiday theme to *Dreamsicles* with the addition of a series of wintertime figures called *Northern Lights.* Dressed in cuddly white snowsuits, the chubby-cheeked cherubs appear as playful snow angels,

accompanied by an array of whimsical polar animals, Santas, snowmen and crystal clear ice and snowflakes.

Angel Hugs, a collection of *Dreamsicles* beanbags, continues to be a popular addition to the line. The original group, introduced in December, 1998, consisted of three cherubs, an elephant, a cow and a blue teddy bear. The next introduction featured another trio of cherubs and three animals, along with a Christmas group including three "Santa" capped cherubs, a snowman, a moose and a green teddy bear.

Unique to 1999 is the "Millennium" cherub with a metallic gold sash and gold flowered halo.

LOVE, KRISTIN DEMONSTRATES AFFECTION FOR AMERICA

Haynes developed her distinctive style of chubby cheeked children and whimsical animals into a series of lovable characters fresh from America's heartland.

She conceived the homespun idea as a means of expressing her love for Americana. From the unique palette of yellows, reds and blues to the touching poses of each country child, the collection is distinctively her own – and aptly called *Love, Kristin*.

The country kids are dressed in polka dots, checks and stripes, in perfect harmony with the simple chiseled wood style of sculpting. In this fresh mixed media approach, Haynes adds genuine ribbon, hair, silk flowers and feathers, all a part of the folk art feel of the collection. A big, friendly cow, chickens, cats and dogs are but a few of the many animals which appear humorously on their own or as faithful pets to the kids.

CAST ART BUILDS ON SUCCESS WITH MORE ARTISTS AND COLLECTIONS

In the spring of 1997, Cast Art invited collectors to step back in time with *Ivy and Innocence*. This charming series of turn-of-the-century cottages, figurines and accessories, all based in a special place called Ivy, is characterized by its highly detailed designs and subtle use of Victorian colors. Nominated for a prestigious award upon the collection's introduction, *Ivy and Innocence* recently added boxes with themes inspired by Ivy characters. The town of Ivy continues to expand with the addition of a neighboring seaside village called "Ivy Cove."

One of the newest additions to the Ivy and Innocence *collection, this limited edition "Lighthouse at Ivy Cove" is a cherished landmark for all in the little town of Ivy.*

Humor is a central theme behind *Slapstix*, a hilarious collection of figures that pokes fun at folks in general, either at work or at play. Created by Cast Art's in-house studio team, the figures present the laughable side of life, capturing those exasperating, exciting and frustrating highs and lows that make each and every day an adventure.

The father and son team of Matt and Matthew Danko created *Gentle Expressions*, which actually consists of two collections. *Teddy Hugs'* cuddly bears and *Heart Tugs'* sweet rag dolls express heartfelt sentiments in pose and props, with a cleverly written message worked into each design.

Themes of appreciation and caring, along with special sentiments for loved ones and memorable occasions are the focus of *Gentle Expressions*. Fun sports and holiday vignettes are unique to the collections, which include figurines, water balls, magnets and covered boxes. Each piece is hand-numbered and bottom-stamped.

The pain of hammering your thumb is whimsically recaptured in "All Thumbs," a figurine from the Slapstix *collection.*

CLUB MEMBERSHIP OFFERS SPECIAL OPPORTUNITIES

Collectors can gain access to a wealth of information, along with an array of special services, by joining Cast Arts' Dreamsicles Club and Friends of Ivy. Each club provides members special benefits not available to the general public.

For just $27.50 a year, members of the Dreamsicles Club enjoy an annual symbol of membership, a plush *Angel Hugs* cherub; the special club edition of the *Collector's Value Guide*; four issues of the *Clubhouse* full-color magazine; a membership card; and exclusive offers available only to members.

Kristin Haynes has recently introduced a brand new cherub in the *Golden Halo* style, exclusively for club members. This is the first ever members-only offering to be presented in this spectacular style. Appropriately named "Golden Memories," this club exclusive is very affordable and includes a bonus gift of two "Dreamsicles Dollars," which can be spent just like cash on the purchase of any *Dreamsicles* figure. A portion of the proceeds from this figurine will be donated to the American Cancer Society.

Members of the Friends of Ivy receive an annual Symbol of Membership figure; a *Storybook of Ivy;* four issues of the "Ivy Vine" newsletter; and members-only offerings. A year's membership is just $19.95, plus shipping and handling.

In just a decade of doing business in the collectibles industry, Cast Art Industries, Inc. has achieved a level of success that has taken other companies twice as long to attain. Still, Cast Art holds true to sharing with its collectors fine quality figurines and collectibles at affordable prices.

Cast Art Industries, Inc.
1120 California Ave.
Corona, CA 91719

Phone:
909-371-3025

Fax:
909-270-2852

Web Site:
www.castart.com

E-mail:
info@castart.com

America's Leading Licensed Brand Collectibles

In 1990, Cavanagh began offering highly sought-after collectibles featuring the incomparable Coca-Cola Santa Claus and other timeless images that helped make Coca-Cola the most recognized trademark in the world. Since its inception, Cavanagh has remained The Coca-Cola Company's preeminent licensee and has broadened that line extensively to include a wide variety of both Christmas and non-seasonal categories. New launches have included collections of bean bags and large plush, figurines, buildings and accessories, animations, musicals, snow globes, cookie jars and mugs.

Building upon the popularity of its Coca-Cola brand offerings, Cavanagh has added other prime quality trademarks with such success that the company has become the established source where collectors can discover – and re-discover – the most recognized and popular licensed brands in the world. Cavanagh's exciting licensed lines include Harley-Davidson, *Monopoly*, Jerry Berta's *Neon America Collection* and, through its 1998 acquisition, the fabulous Forma Vitrum collections.

This 1999 "Coca-Cola Polar Bear Cookie Jar" is the fifth issue in the popular Coca-Cola® Heritage Collection.

INTERNATIONAL BEAN BAGS

The Coca-Cola® brand *International Bean Bag Collection* is a truly unique offering. Each animal represents an individual country in The Coca-Cola Company's vast family of nations and is detailed with the flag of its country. Each carries a miniature Coke bottle, and to ensure authenticity, features a high security holographic hang tag enclosed in a bottle-cap-shaped clear plastic protector.

The collection consists of five separate sets of ten different animals. The sets are released sequentially every two months and are simultaneously introduced and retired on a designated day. The 51st critter in the collection, "Totonca the Buffalo," is an exclusive piece available for purchase only by members of Cavanagh's Coca-Cola Christmas Collectors Society.

Bearnice Bearringer, Bearry Bearresford and Lillian Berica are three of the original designs in Cavanagh's fanciful Coca-Cola Soda Fountain Bears Collection.

COCA-COLA CHRISTMAS COLLECTION

Continuing the marvelous tradition that began in 1931 with Haddon Sundblom's first painting of the burly, happy figure that soon became the world's most famous Santa, the timeless Coca-Cola Santa again appears for this year's Cavanagh's *Coca-Cola Christmas Collection*. New Santa pieces include an ornament, a mercury glass figure, and a charming animation.

Coca-Cola Polar Bears are still the rage, and new Polar Bears have joined Santa in the 1999 collection, including a mercury glass figure and two ornaments, five new Cub and Seal ornaments, a new series of six Bottle Cap Ornaments featuring the happy critters in all kinds of festive poses, and three new miniature ornaments. Added to Cavanagh's five collectible cookie jars produced since 1994 is the "Polar Bear Soda Jerk" with a Coca-Cola fountain dispenser.

Plush ornaments are as popular as they are lovable, and Cavanagh has six new ones – two Polar Bears and one each of the Coca-Cola Reindeer, Penguin, Walrus and Seal.

Cavanagh's six brand new animations feature Polar Bears skating, dancing, rocking on a seesaw, drinking Coke, and even one riding a tricycle.

Cavanagh's two new bean bag collections, *Everyday Bean Bags* and *Winter Bean Bags,* each include three Polar Bears, two Seals and a Penguin. *The Large Plush Collection* includes eight soft and cuddly characters to warm up the holiday season: two Reindeer, four Polar Bears, and two Penguins

The *Town Square Collection* remains one of the most popular and collectible of all Cavanagh Coca-Cola Christmas offerings. Six new buildings this season include "Polar Palace Ice Cream," "Jordan Drugs," "Sleepytime Motel," "Bus Station," "Jack's Boats 'n Bait" and "Round

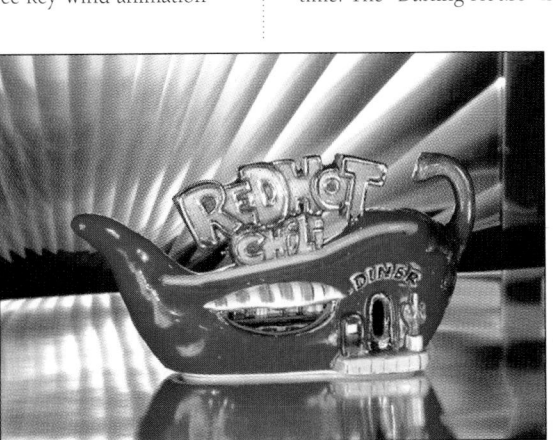

All of the Harley-Davidson magic is captured in Cavanagh's newest limited edition figurine, "Riding the Highway."

the Square Sleigh Rides." A seventh new building, a replica of "Atlanta's First Coca-Cola Bottling Plant" in 1901, is reserved for purchase only by members of Cavanagh's Coca-Cola Christmas Collectors Society. A number of new accessories has also been added.

COCA-COLA HERITAGE COLLECTION

In 1994, Cavanagh introduced the *Coca-Cola® Heritage Collection*. In 1999, the collection grew to include "Santa with a Train" in three formats – a snowglobe, a musical and a figurine – plus a key-wind animation musical.

The collection's *Coca-Cola Soda Fountain Bears* plush assemblage adds four bears, bringing the whimsical cast of characters to ten. Also new are two metal and wood accessories, a soda fountain table and chair.

New Polar Bear additions include two figurines, two snowglobe musicals, and three key-wind animation musicals, plus a very special limited edition cookie jar. All four previous cookie jars in the *Heritage Collection* have been retired. Seven new Polar Bear Cub figurines have also been added.

Additions to the collection's bean bag assortment include six *Sport Bean Bags*. Each cute Coca-Cola critter is dressed for its favorite sport. New accessories feature five finely-crafted metal and wood pieces, a bench, swing chair, bicycle, and soda fountain table and chair, plus a colorful vinyl holder.

Capturing the nostalgia of the 1950s is "Red Hot Diner" from Jerry Berta's Neon America Collection.

A notable result of Cavanagh's acquisition of Forma Vitrum is the inclusion into the *Heritage Collection* of a limited edition series of beautiful, nostalgic stained glass buildings designed by renowned artist Bill Job. Included in the *Coca-Cola Through-The-Decades* series are the "Sandy Shoal Lighthouse," "Murray's Mercantile Shop," "Corner Drug," "Town Cinema," "Grady's Barber Shop," "Sam's Grocery" and "Gus' Gas Station." Each piece has a hand-numbered signature plate to ensure its authenticity.

HARLEY-DAVIDSON

Since 1904, the Harley-Davidson brand has meant freedom and fun, and that's exactly what Cavanagh's *Harley Davidson Collection* is all about – that and collectibility. Included are finely-detailed motorcycle ornaments, limited edition figurines, snowglobes, bean bags and accessories, collectible steins, Christmas stocking holders, and new this year, black leather holiday stockings!

In addition to two new motorcycle ornaments, a limited edition figurine and three new snowglobes, Cavanagh adds seven new pieces to the *Harley Li'l Cruisers Collection*. Also new are six bean bags and accessories and two new large plush teddy bears, "Babe" and "Bosco."

GOOD FUN AND GOOD WORKS

Collectors are certain to find a special place in their hearts for Cavanagh's line of licensed *Monopoly* collectibles. John Cavanagh, Cavanagh Group International's President, explains, "We created *Monopoly Porcelain Hinged Boxes* as a way to bring to life one of America's all-time treasured games." This year, ten properties were introduced. About 3" tall, each beautifully detailed, hand-painted piece is made to represent a location on the board.

The "Woodcutter's Cottage" from *Sleeping Beauty* and the "Darling House" from *Peter Pan* are the fourth and fifth releases in the Forma Vitrum by Cavanagh *Disney Lighted Village Collection*.

The "Woodcutter's Cottage" is created from hand-painted resin, hand-cut stained glass and cast pewter – a combination of materials that is being used for the first time. The "Darling House" is constructed purely out of stained glass. These magical and exciting buildings contain original art in the windows, depicting a realistic scene from the movie. The size of the edition limit corresponds with the release date of the movie: the "Woodcutter's Cottage" is limited to 1,959 pieces, and the "Darling House" is limited to 1,953 pieces.

Jerry Berta's *Neon America Collection* by Cavanagh captures all the nostalgia of the '50s and '60s in a unique series of mini diners, each carefully crafted in ceramic, fired with shiny iridescent glazes and lighted with its own miniature "neon" signs.

Collectors looking for collectibles that will become the heirlooms of tomorrow know they can depend on Cavanagh for distinctive products licensed by the world's most respected brands and the very finest in creativity, quality and affordability.

Cavanagh Group
International
1665 Bluegrass Lakes Pkwy.
Suite100
Alpharetta, GA 30004

Phone:
800-895-8100

Fax:
678-366-2801

Web Site:
www.cavanaghgrp.com

CAVANAGH GROUP INTERNATIONAL

Dean Griff's *Charming Tails*® Come to Life

"Party Animals" perfectly captures the sense of jubilant fun that Dean Griff puts into all his Charming Tails® creations.

awards. He also started his own small business, crafting and selling hand-painted hanging ornaments like those he had made as gifts for his close friends.

In 1989, Dean moved south to work as a designer in Florida's growing television industry. In this exciting new environment, his art took on a new dimension, and soon he began creating the characters that would someday become the *Charming Tails* family.

Dean's talents were soon discovered. From his original art in 1990, came 12 delightful ornament designs that were an immediate and overwhelming success with retailers and collectors alike. *Charming Tails* was born!

"DEEP IN THE HEART OF A GREAT OLD FOREST..."

It all started with a mischievous little mouse named Mackenzie. Before too long, Dean Griff had created enough winsome wildlife characters to populate his magically imaginative village of Squashville.

From the moment Mackenzie Mouse made his debut, he and his Squashville pals ignited a whole new brand of excitement among collectors. With each character having its own distinct personality, collecting *Charming Tails* is a uniquely personal pastime. Whether their favorite "Tail" belongs to Mackenzie Mouse, Binkey Bunny, Chauncy Chipmunk, Reginald Raccoon, Sebastian Squirrel, Bunnie Bunny, Stewart Skunk, Lydia Ladybug, Sydney Snail, Sabrina Squirrel, or Mackenzie's beloved Maxine Mouse, collectors have found all of Dean's Squashville buddies uniquely appealing.

Each piece in the collection explores and enhances the irresistible charm of life in Dean's woodland paradise.

Looking at the carefree antics of Fitz and Floyd's playful *Charming Tails*® characters, it's clear that their creator, Dean Griff, has led something of an enchanted life himself. In fact, Dean was the fourth child of six brothers and sisters, raised on a farm of storybook beauty in upstate New York.

This was the perfect setting for Dean's love of animals to take root and flourish. When he wasn't at school or busy tending to his chores, he was off in the woods nearby, watching and sketching the wildlife who made their homes there.

With Dean's emerging talent and his growing interest in drawing, he vigorously pursued his art studies. In 1983, when he left the farm to become the Assistant to the Curator of the Syracuse University Art Collection, a whole new world of creative exploration opened for the gifted young man.

Soon, he was entering his wildlife paintings in University art shows, where his work brought the young artist notoriety, acclaim, and prestigious art

Artist Dean Griff.

Whether it's Mackenzie Mouse relaxing in a sugar bowl or enjoying the shelter of a mushroom during a rainstorm, or Binkey Bunny out for a drive in his delightful carrot-mobile, the *Charming Tails* gang is certain to bring a smile to all who encounter them. Summer, winter, spring, and fall, Dean Griff celebrates each day in Squashville with a heartwarming picture of love and true friendship.

COLLECTIBLES TO MAKE THE WORLD A LITTLE HAPPIER

"To this day, I still go home to my parents' farm to walk and hike through the woods," says Griff. "Through my designs of mice and other woodland animals, I reach back to that world where I grew up, where I first paid attention to wildlife and began to draw the things I saw."

Dean feels the true essence of "collectibility" has less to do with edition limits, secondary market prices and issue

Mackenzie Mouse, a Charming Tails® *"superstar," is delightfully celebrated in Dean Griff's enchanting "Reach For The Stars" figurine.*

retirements, and more about the feelings the items evoke among collectors. To be sure, *Charming Tails* collectibles have the special ability to remind us all of memories long forgotten, and making us appreciate the simple joys that life has to offer. Only when a piece has the power to touch someone's heart with meaningful sentiment, does Dean Griff deem his work a success.

Especially close to his heart is the "Wishing You Well" figurine, dedicated to the Candlelighters Childhood Cancer Foundation, with Dean and Fitz and Floyd pledging to contribute a portion of all proceeds from its sale to help that organization's commitment to finding a cure for cancer.

The variety and diversity of Dean Griff's convivial creations has led to separate classifications within the collection. The *Charming Tails* group includes non-seasonal pieces and incorporates the "dimensional greetings" figurines, which have become an enormously popular way for collectors to express and share their feelings on special occasions. *Easter Basket* celebrates springtime's rebirth. *Autumn Harvest* captures the best of fall with Halloween, harvest and Thanksgiving themes. *Squashville* continues with winter and holiday figurines, and *Deck The Halls* rounds out the collection with unforgettable holiday ornaments.

THE JOY OF BEING A *CHARMING TAILS* COLLECTOR

Since 1997, *Charming Tails* collectors have enhanced the enjoyment that their collections bring them with membership in The Leaf & Acorn® Club.

Among the members-only benefits available to club members are the exclusive club membership pieces. Leaf & Acorn members receive the opportunity to acquire charming editions created just for them.

In addition, Leaf & Acorn members will also have the exclusive opportunity (with no obligation) to purchase additional figurines and will also receive the club news in the *Squashville Gazette*. Membership kits also include the complete *Charming Tails* catalog – 44 full-color pages with all currently available *Charming Tails* figurines and ornaments, as well as a special section featuring retired *Charming Tails* collectibles.

Each member receives their own personalized membership card, and special invitations to attend important collector events, including personal appearances by Dean Griff.

Since its inception, Fitz and Floyd has taken special care to make sure that each new piece in the *Charming Tails* collection is fresh, exciting and adds to the collectibility of the entire line. Many creative and meaningful innovations are planned for *Charming Tails* in the months and years ahead.

A new collection of hand-painted resin accessories for every room of the house was recently introduced. Now collectors will be able to frame their favorite photos in the first *Charming Tails* picture frames, and hide their favorite little treasures away in beguiling lidded keepsake boxes featuring their favorite *Charming Tails* characters.

Shedding a new light on collecting are the new votive candle holders, glowing with all the magic that *Charming Tails* has to offer. And if "music be the food of love" collectors will have a feast with the new revolving music boxes that are sure to bring a touch of melodic romance to any setting.

Fitz and Floyd Collectibles is also "beary, beary" proud to invite collectors to visit their local *Charming Tails* dealer to see what all the new excitement is about down at *Honeybourne Hollow*™, the newest neighborhood for collecting fun, which made its critically-acclaimed debut this year.

A portion of the proceeds of the "Wishing You Well" figurine will be contributed to the Candlelighters Childhood Cancer Foundation, reflecting the commitment of Fitz and Floyd and Dean Griff to creating a happier and healthier world.

Fitz and Floyd Collectibles
501 Corporate Drive
Lewisville, TX 75057

Phone:
800-527-9550

Fax:
972-353-7718

Enesco Presents the Art of Priscilla Hillman

From early childhood, New England-born Priscilla Hillman sketched and painted at the family kitchen table with her twin sister Greta – but back then it was always "just for fun." A self-taught artist, she studied botany at the University of Rhode Island and after graduation went to work at the Oceanographic Office. As a young wife and mother, she resumed her interest in art, and began illustrating and writing books including nine *Merry Mouse* books for Doubleday.

Then in the late 1980s, serious back problems kept Hillman inactive for several months. During that time, she kept herself busy by looking at nostalgic photos, watching old movies and "drawing in her mind" sketches of teddy bears. When she recovered, Hillman immediately went to work to put her teddy bears on paper.

In 1990, Hillman sent 36 original oil paintings of her teddy bears to Enesco Group, Inc. Enesco decided her drawings should be transformed into three-dimensional figurines in 1992. Today, the *Cherished Teddies* collection is one of the world's leading teddy bear collectibles. The collection is sold in countries across the globe, including the United States, England, Japan, Italy and Mexico. There are now more than 600 *Cherished Teddies* figurines and accessories, including photo frames, jewelry, collector plates and clocks.

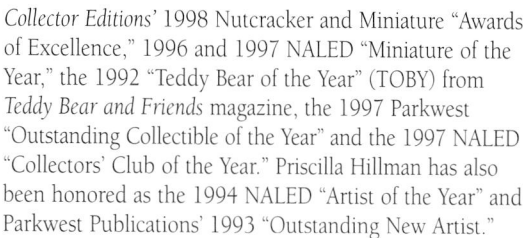

The Cherished Teddies Rare Bear, "Crystal," has real embedded crystals in her crown and rides a golden-horned unicorn atop a marble platform.

Sculpted in cold-cast resin, each *Cherished Teddies* figurine has an individual name and message of friendship and love. The names of the figurines are chosen by Priscilla Hillman herself. Often times, Hillman will use the first names of collectors she meets at trade shows and *Cherished Teddies* events. Each figurine comes with a Certificate of Adoption so collectors can officially "adopt" the teddy bears. Hundreds of thousands of figurines have been registered to date.

Cherished Teddies has been honored with numerous awards in the gift and collectible industry. In 1993, its first year of eligibility, the collection was named "Collectible of the Year" by the National Association of Limited Edition Dealers (NALED). Other awards include *Collector Editions'* 1998 Nutcracker and Miniature "Awards of Excellence," 1996 and 1997 NALED "Miniature of the Year," the 1992 "Teddy Bear of the Year" (TOBY) from *Teddy Bear and Friends* magazine, the 1997 Parkwest "Outstanding Collectible of the Year" and the 1997 NALED "Collectors' Club of the Year." Priscilla Hillman has also been honored as the 1994 NALED "Artist of the Year" and Parkwest Publications' 1993 "Outstanding New Artist."

Since the collection's first retirement of *Cherished Teddies* figurines in 1995, Enesco has retired a selection of figurines each year, enhancing their value and collectibility. Once a figurine is retired, the mold is broken, and it will never be produced again.

THEY'RE *RARE BEARS*

In an effort to create excitement and enhance the collectibility of the *Cherished Teddies* collection, Enesco recently launched the *Cherished Teddies Rare Bears* program, providing collectors with the opportunity to win limited edition *Cherished Teddies Rare Bears*.

Enesco will introduce *Rare Bears* as many as three to four times a year. Each introduction will feature *Cherished Teddies* with something unique, such as different color fur or embedded jewels. Collectors will be able to identify an authentic *Rare Bear* by its metallic gold understamp and the special *Rare Bear* symbol, a diamond with the letter "R" inside.

The first *Rare Bears* introduction took place in August, 1998. In April of 1999, Enesco unveiled the second *Rare Bear*, "Crystal. Hang On! We're in for a Wonderful Ride." "Crystal" is part of the six-piece *Cherished Teddies* carousel series, which depicts teddy bears riding animal carousels. The *Rare Bear* version of "Crystal" has real embedded crystals in its crown and rides a golden-horned unicorn that sits upon a marble platform. Each resin carousel in the series retails for $20.00. Collectors who purchase the "Crystal" *Cherished Teddies* product will learn if they have a limited edition upon opening the package.

CHERISHED TEDDIES TOURS AND EVENTS

Priscilla Hillman, creator of the Cherished Teddies collection for Enesco.

A 110-city artisan tour introduced collectors all over the United States and Canada to the art of *Cherished Teddies* in 1999. Making visits to retailers and schools, a *Cherished Teddies* sculptor or painter travels full-time throughout the tour, with Priscilla Hillman making special appearances.

"Lanny" is the 1999 Cherished Teddies Collectors Club "membearship" figurine.

To commemorate the tour, an exclusive *Cherished Teddies* figurine has been available at each of the 100 tour stops.

Another recent special event sponsored by *Cherished Teddies* was the "Reunion," which offered collectors a chance to purchase a special figurine for one day only. Titled "Old Friends Always Come Back," the event allowed collectors to acquire the "Daisy and Chelsea" figurine and to have a chance to win one of 25 retired 1993 *Cherished Teddies* pieces signed by Priscilla Hillman.

Enesco also has partnered with St. Jude Children's Research Hospital, the largest childhood cancer research center in the United States, to sponsor the "Cherished Book Drive." Collectors can donate a new book with a written message inside that will be given to children at St. Jude. Over the years, *Cherished Teddies* has donated more than $250,000 to St. Jude Children's Research Hospital.

"*Cherished Teddies* and St. Jude have teamed up for two years now, and it's a perfect fit because of the dedication of both organizations to giving back to those in need," said Marguerite Willman, product manager for Priscilla Hillman properties.

THE CHERISHED TEDDIES CLUB

Responding to overwhelming collector enthusiasm, Enesco formed the Cherished Teddies Club in 1995. Now Enesco's fastest growing club, the Cherished Teddies Club informs and entertains more than 150,000 worldwide "membears" through special events, a club newsletter, and "membears" only benefits.

Those who have joined the Club in the past have enjoyed such exclusive editions as "Lanny," the 1999 "membearship" figurine, a special mini-figurine created to commemorate the 5th anniversary of the Club, a sculpted "membership" pin, enrollment in the Customer Appreciation Program, a subscription to the "Town Tattler" newsletter, and invitations to "membears"-only

events. There is also an exclusive club web site at www.enescoclubs.com.

THE PARENT COMPANY: ENESCO

The producer of *Cherished Teddies*, Enesco, is a respected maker of fine gifts, collectibles and home décor accessories based in Itasca, Illinois. A leader in the $10 billion gift and collectibles industry, the company operates within Enesco Worldwide Giftware Group of Enesco Group, Inc., which has wholly-owned subsidiaries in Canada, Mexico, Great Britain, Germany, France and Hong Kong, as well as a network of licensed distributors located throughout the world.

Enesco's product lines include more than 10,000 gift, collectible and home accent items, including the award-winning *Precious Moments* collection by Enesco and artist Sam Butcher, which was introduced in 1978. In addition to Priscilla Hillman's *Cherished Teddies* collection, Enesco presents other Hillman creations including *Mouse Tales, Calico Kittens, My Blushing Bunnies* and *Down Petticoat Lane.* The firm also presents a host of other fine collectibles and giftware lines.

In an effort to give back to the community, Enesco became a corporate sponsor of the National Easter Seal Society in 1987. By 1996, the company had become Easter Seals' No. 1 corporate sponsor. Enesco also supports Boys and Girls Clubs of America, C.A.U.S.E.S., a social service agency preventing child abuse, Enlight Children's Charities, and through *Cherished Teddies*, St. Jude Children's Research Hospital.

Enesco Group, Inc. stands ready to provide *Cherished Teddies* collectors and others with all the information and help they may need to maximize enjoyment of their treasures. To get in touch with Enesco, call (800) NEAR-YOU (632-7968), or visit Enesco's web site at www.enesco.com.

The new Cherished Teddies – Teddies in Motion *series premieres with "Dustin and Austin" in their limited edition fire truck.*

Cherished Teddies
Enesco Group, Inc.
225 Windsor Drive
Itasca, IL 60143

Phone:
800-NEAR-YOU
800-632-7968

Fax:
630-875-5350

Web Sites:
www.enesco.com
www.enescoclubs.com

Nutcrackers and More with Heart

Nestled in the Erzgebirge Mountains in Germany, not far from to the Czech Republic border, is a region that is close to the heart of any collector of fanciful nutcrackers, incense burners and other handcrafted treasures. Prominent within the region is Holzkunst Christian Ulbricht, a family-owned company that traces its beginnings back nearly 300 years.

The personality that shines through in all the company's output reflects the attitude of a man whose mind and heart are constantly open to new ideas and influences. While production techniques haven't changed markedly over the years, Christian Ulbricht keeps his mind open to the contemporary world for inspiration for new designs, and specifically to those interests expressed by collectors in the United States.

In addition to the more traditional motifs such as kings, soldiers, hunters and folk characters, today the company features clever designs from many sources. Some are inspired by the classic animated films of Walt Disney; others come from a wide range of players out of the pages of William Shakespeare, Charles Dickens and L. Frank Baum's "Wizard of Oz." There are leading American inventors, colorful Native Americans, and so much more.

Whether open or limited editions, creations from Holzkunst Christian Ulbricht bring smiles to the faces of devotees everywhere, and add whimsical charm to collections in many homes worldwide.

THE EARLY YEARS

When Christian Ulbricht was born in 1933 in the Erzgebirge town of Seiffen, it was around the time his father, Otto, built a new factory to house his burgeoning woodturning facility. Woodturning is an industry that began to develop as far back as the 17th century, to which period the Ulbricht family can be traced. Then the region was rich in deposits of gold, silver and other minerals. But in the 18th century, the unthinkable happened. The mines dried up, and the miners turned to their long-time hobby of woodturning for their livelihood.

In the mid-1950s, Otto was forced to make a life-changing decision. Seiffen was part of the Eastern Bloc, lying on the easternmost edge of Germany. Since communism held that everything belonged to the state, not to the individual, Otto no longer controlled the family business; therefore, he decided to reestablish that business elsewhere. Late one night under cover of darkness, Otto, his wife and their four children left their beloved home and, after an arduous journey, arrived in their new surroundings in the town of Lauingen on the Danube, in Bavaria.

The second piece in the series inspired by the Walt Disney animated classic film Peter Pan is "Tinker Bell." Standing within her own bell, she looks ready to fly!
©Disney

The brooding Danish prince is the latest addition to the Plays of Shakespeare series from Holzkunst Christian Ulbricht. As he holds the skull of Yorick, we can almost hear him say "Alas."

It took time, but the traditions of the Erzgebirge were now transported to Lauingen, as Otto started his company anew. But family traditions and the need for roots are profound, and in the early 1990s, the Ulbrichts experienced still another major change. With the fall of the Berlin Wall, Christian, now the head of the family since his father's death, was able to regain the Ulbrichts' heritage by purchasing the family's holdings in Seiffen. It was time to rebuild again.

MOVING AHEAD

Today, Holzkunst Christian Ulbricht employs 80, with family members deeply involved in every aspect of the business, from the creation of new designs to quality

control. Christian's wife, Inge, is a major designer of ornaments and some nutcrackers; she also heads quality control.

Ines, their daughter, is kept very busy as a major designer and also as co-director, along with her brother Gunther, of the Christian Ulbricht Collectors' Club, which made its debut in 1998. Gunther, also a leading designer of nutcrackers, lists as a major hobby the painting of portraits and landscapes.

Christian's is the leading creative voice. His designs, which start on the wood lathe, become the models used by the master craftsmen who replicate them for the collection. The wood that is used depends in part on the designs themselves: some require a harder wood than others, and a variety may be employed in one motif. For example, the body of a nutcracker may be of linden, but the legs and arms might be beech, maple or birch. Once the wood to be used is thoroughly dried, and any not deemed satisfactory is discarded, it is cut into various sizes to fit the intricate work patterns.

Woodturning on the lathe is a painstaking process, one that requires significant training and experience. At Holzkunst Christian Ulbricht, there are only ten wood turners. Once the parts are cut, turned and stained, all the separate pieces are assembled. The figure then moves on to hand-painting and decorating, followed by costuming and the application of hair and fur, if appropriate.

Each step requires its own specialists. There are only ten women who paint, but four times that number are decorators. There are also a handful of apprentices, who learn from the experienced artisans.

CHRISTIAN ULBRICHT COLLECTORS' CLUB

Because to learn more about one's hobby is to enjoy it more, hundreds of collectors have joined the club since its inception in the spring of 1998. As a welcome gift, all new members (and in the second year, all renewing members as well) will receive "Arabian Knight," an incense burner that has special significance for Christian. It is a new look at what had been the first company logo used by his father. Otto chose it as his logo because it was also the first motif that he ever created for his own company. Christian is pleased to honor his father in this way.

The unique nutcracker that is the exclusive offering available only to members is the "Teddy Bear King," continuing the regal – and utterly charming – theme established in the club's first year with "Snow King."

Crowning the first year, club members received invitations to travel with other members of the club on the first company-sponsored trip to Germany, including three exciting days in Seiffen enjoying the warm Ulbricht

Collecting all pieces in a series brings a special enjoyment to the hobby. "Marley's Ghost" is a new addition in 1999 to Dickens' A Christmas Carol.

hospitality. Plans call for continuing this program in subsequent years, giving members the opportunity to go behind the scenes at Holzkunst Christian Ulbricht to see first-hand how their favorite collectibles come to be.

Through the pages of The *Treasure Chest,* the club's biannual colorful newsletter, members learn about new products, production techniques, company history and important happenings. To keep them apprised between publications, *Update,* aimed at conveying up-to-the-minute news, is published periodically.

This charming incense burner titled "Arabian Knight" is the unique gift for members in the second year of the Christian Ulbricht Collectors' Club.

A NEW MILLENNIUM IS DAWNING

With the start of the 21st century just a breath away, it is comforting to know that traditions begun in the 17th century are still alive and well. Fine quality and creative designs are still in the forefront of the handcraftsmanship at Holzkunst Christian Ulbricht. Because the company is also forward-looking and innovative, its timely and informative web site, e-mail and a dedicated phone line to the Christian Ulbricht Collectors' Club all provide ways for collectors to stay in touch and to learn.

As energetic ambassadors of their work, Christian, Ines and Gunther enjoy visiting the United States a few times a year, to appear at major events such as the International Collectible Exposition® and in many retail stores across the country. Bringing the traditions of the past into contemporary life is not always easy; this family does it with charm, grace and an abundance of talent. Their expertise shines through in the nutcrackers, incense burners, music boxes, ornaments, pyramids and miniature figures that bring joy to collectors of all ages.

Christian Ulbricht
Collectors' Club
P. O. Box 99
Angwin CA 94508

Phone:
888-707-5591

Fax:
707-968-9669

Web Site:
www.ulbricht.com

E-mail:
nutcracker@ulbricht.com

"Works of Heart" in Handcrafted Glass

Christopher Radko has been in the business of designing and producing dazzling holiday ornaments for over a dozen years. His luminescent holiday designs have become true collector's items. His handmade, brilliantly colored ornaments and holiday decorations have adorned the homes of millions, and *The New York Times* has proclaimed him "the Czar of Christmas Present." Christopher built a Christmas empire — and it all started by accident.

REPLACING HEIRLOOMS, REVIVING TRADITIONS

In 1983, Christopher decided that his family's old Christmas tree stand had served long enough. The family agreed to replace the stand and put their 14-foot tree in the gleaming new model. They decorated the tree in their usual tradition, with their treasures of 2,000 mouth-blown, European glass ornaments. One week before Christmas, the new stand gave way, shattering over half the collection.

When Christopher tried to restore his family's heirlooms, he ran into many difficulties. Ornaments sold in the United States were made of plastic and Styrofoam. Nothing approached the hand-made treasures his family had collected for generations. The next spring, while visiting cousins in Poland, Christopher began to look for glass ornaments and found the situation equally distressing. The workshops that produced the beautifully crafted ornaments had been closed for decades. Finally, he decided to hire a glassblower who could make the ornaments he wanted.

Christopher sketched some traditional ornament shapes, designs that had not been used since before World War II, and had several dozen ornaments produced for his family. The ornaments never made it to the tree. Instead, friends purchased all of them. On his next trip abroad, he brought back more ornaments that sold out as well. Christopher realized he had discovered something wonderful.

♦ During his lunch hour at his job with a talent agency, he began showing his ornaments to stores in New York City. By his second year, he had $75,000 in sales and was able to quit his day job. The rest, as they say, is history: a sparkling history reflected by the 5,000 designs Christopher has created since that first collection of 50 Christmas ornaments in 1986.

DYNAMIC GROWTH, DEFINING STYLE

The Christopher Radko company has grown from employing the lone glassblower who made Christopher's first ornaments, to more than 3,000 people in cottage workshops in Poland, Germany, Italy and the Czech Republic. Instead of going door-to-door to sell his products, Christopher's ornaments are now sold in over 3,000 stores, including Dayton's, Bloomingdale's, Neiman Marcus, Marshall Field's, Macy's and Saks Fifth Avenue.

Even as sales have blossomed, Christopher's attention to quality and detail has never wavered. The skills of glass blowing have been rekindled by the workers, many of whom are great-grandchildren of the original craftsmen. Each ornament still takes seven days to produce. The ornaments are mouth-blown in tempered glass for durability, lined with silver for luminescence, and painted with loving care in every intricate detail. The delicate lashes on each face, for example, are hand-painted by Christopher's famous "eyelash lady." These personalized touches create the charming variations in each ornament that make it a one-of-a-kind heirloom.

Christopher's glass ornament collection now includes designs to lend joy to every holiday, including Valentine's Day, St. Patrick's Day, Easter, the Fourth of July, Halloween, Thanksgiving, Hanukkah and Kwanzaa. And they are ideal gift selections for bridal showers, baby showers and anniversaries.

The popularity of the Christopher Radko ornaments has stimulated the development of other holiday home and décor gift accessories. The *Home for the Holidays* collection brings the spirit of the season throughout the home with candles, cookie jars, nutcrackers, paintings and snowglobes.

Christopher has also captured some of the most identifiable trademarks of business and entertainment giants in

Represented elegantly or whimsically, Santa Claus is a popular figure in Radko ornaments year after year. In "Happy Handful," Radko depicts a playful Santa in the American tradition.

"Times Square" is one of Christopher Radko's popular ornament designs that celebrates the new millennium.

This musical glitter globe from the Home for the Holidays *collection plays "Ghost Busters" as black bats swirl around the witch and her haunted mansion.*

a collection of licensed and commissioned glass ornaments known as the *Studio Collection*. New licensed ornaments from Walt Disney's *Mickey & Co.*, Universal Studios, *I Love Lucy*, Dr. Seuss, Harley-Davidson, Lucasfilm (*Star Wars*), Mattel and North American Bear are available at fine retailers from coast to coast. Kermit the Frog, Lucy Ricardo and Mickey Mouse are just a few of the characters immortalized in glass by Christopher Radko.

Christopher Radko's newest collection, *Woodland Winds*, features endearing and lively woodland characters that live in the Northern Forest. The figurines are meticulously sculpted in cold cast porcelain by skilled artisans. The collection consists of figurines, snowglobes, decorative accessories and, of course, mouth-blown glass ornaments.

RAISING FUNDS FOR CHARITY

In addition to his regular line of ornaments, Christopher makes special designs each year for charity. "It makes me feel really good to do these things. Christmas is about remembering other people, coming together, sharing feelings and helping others who are less fortunate. It is gratifying that my ornaments have been

Receiving Christopher Radko's charming totem-pole treatment, for a three-ornaments-in-one effect is "Three Blind Mice."

able to contribute in a meaningful way," Christopher explains.

"As my company grew more successful, I felt it would be good to contribute something back." Since the inception of this philosophy, Christopher has raised or donated over $3,000,000 to causes including AIDS research, pediatric cancer organizations, and the Matthew Berry Memorial Soccer Fund in Dallas, which provides uniforms, equipment and coaching for inner-city youth.

With this philosophy in mind, Christopher continues to grow his business. He received the ultimate compliment when President Clinton and Al Gore requested that Christopher decorate the mantel of the White House and the entire Vice Presidential Residence. Whether he is decorating the home of the President of the United States or an orphanage, Christopher pours his heart into his work.

"I believe the Christmas spirit transcends religious rituals," Christopher says. "It is about opening your heart and remembering others."

THE STARLIGHT FAMILY OF COLLECTORS

Christmas ornaments are the most popular collectible item in the United States, with the number of collectors growing dramatically each year. The popularity of Christopher Radko ornaments is so significant that Christopher established the Starlight Family of Collectors in 1993. Membership in 1999 swelled to 30,000.

The Starlight Family of Collectors encourages holiday traditions through the giving and sharing of fine glass ornaments and decorations — traditions like those that led Christopher Radko to his calling. With their membership, new and renewing members receive a free limited edition ornament designed by Christopher exclusively for members of the Starlight Family. They also receive a personalized membership card, one year's subscription to *Starlight* magazine and a complete set of Christopher's latest catalogs, so they can see all the ornaments for every holiday and special occasion.

"I am fortunate to be supported by many thousands of loyal collectors and enthusiasts who recognize the care and quality invested in each ornament and holiday home product with the Radko name," Christopher says. "Their devotion is an inspiration to me. I create most of my designs with them in mind, because I really treasure the traditions we're building together."

The artistry of Christopher Radko was born of a desire to bridge warm memories of holidays past with new traditions for today. Christopher takes pride in the way his creations connect families and friends, young and old, one ornament at a time. His designs are not just decorations — they are works of heart!

Christopher Radko
Starlight Family
of Collectors

P.O. Box 775249
St. Louis, MO
63177-5249

Phone:
800-71-RADKO
800-717-2356

Web Site:
www.christopherradko.com

Offering "One-Stop" Shopping

As one of the top shopping networks in the television medium, the Shop at Home Network has been offering quality products since 1986. Reaching a viewing audience of approximately 60 million households through cable affiliates, satellite and six owned and operated television stations in San Francisco, Raleigh, Cleveland, Houston, Boston and Connecticut, the Shop at Home Network holds an ideal place in the television shopping network industry. However, since the recent boom in the online retail business, the Shop at Home Network rose to the challenge of creating an online shopping source as an extension of their already existing broadcast shopping network.

In November of 1999, the Shop at Home Network introduced collectibles.com to the world. In the online retail industry, collectibles.com has staked quite a claim on the collectibles market. Combining its state-of-the-art technology with a solid collectible product base, collectibles.com has positioned itself to be one of the industry's top collectible merchandisers. With sales repeatedly exceeding the projected goals, collectibles.com has surpassed the start-up Internet industry standards by leaps and bounds, and continues to grow at an amazing rate.

AS SEEN ON TV

From the beginning, the goal of collectibles.com has been to create a one-stop shop for all things collectible. Along with an enormous product list, collectibles.com

The Shop at Home Network and collectibles.com are known for their exquisite jewelry pieces, which are made from only the finest gemstones.

The Shop at Home Network and collectibles.com feature a wide variety of products, ranging from dolls and figurines to sports memorabilia.

offers the most recent news about the collectibles industry, as well as chats with show hosts from the network and special celebrity guests. Using the latest technology, viewers are even able to watch the Shop at Home Network through the use of streaming video via collectibles.com. Both the Shop at Home Network and collectibles.com have taken advantage of their fully digital, state-of-the-art facility to be a leader in the industry in converging the Internet with interactive television.

Since collectibles.com wanted to remain a part of the Shop at Home Network, they have merged product lines to create an extensive list of merchandise that can be found on both collectibles.com and the Shop at Home Network. Over 80 percent of the products that can be found on the Shop at Home Network can also be found on collectibles.com. Though collectibles.com carries traditional collectible merchandise such as figurines, dolls and limoge, they also offer a wide variety of products including limited edition jewelry, sports and entertainment memorabilia, plush toys, knives, coins and electronics. Creating an Internet site inclusive of collectible merchandise and non-collectible merchandise has proven to be an extremely successful strategy for collectibles.com. The combination of numerous product lines with an easy way to access this merchandise has afforded customers the luxury of receiving quality products in an expeditious manner.

WHO THEY ARE

Since collectibles.com and the Shop at Home Network operate 24 hours a day 7 days a week, an integral part of their success comes from having a fully staffed customer service center, as well as a 24-hour sales center. These two facilities are conveniently located in the headquarters, allowing any customer service issues to be easily resolved. Since the customer service and sales centers are in a central location, the customer is assured that their questions and concerns will be taken care of in a timely

manner. This unique feature of collectibles.com and the Shop at Home Network allows them to maintain their strong reputation as a leader in the customer experience.

SPOTLIGHTING TOP-NAME COLLECTIBLES

In addition to offering customers fast and effective service, collectibles.com features some of the best product lines available in the collectible world. Since their launch in 1999, collectibles.com has been forming strategic alliances with the top brands in the traditional marketplace. Carrying products from such highly respected manufacturers as Harmony Kingdom, Warner Bros., *Willow Hall, M. I. Hummel, Sonshine Promises,* Collector's Edge and many more, collectibles.com stands at the forefront of the online retail industry. Along with carrying the hottest products, collectibles.com features their selection complete with enlarged photographs and detailed descriptions to give their customers the most personal and lifelike perspective of their products.

The Shop at Home Network and collectibles.com continue to offer quality products at reasonable prices.

CREATING A REALISTIC SHOPPING EXPERIENCE

In keeping with the goal of providing a more realistic and lifelike approach to viewing their products, collectibles.com is using the latest technology to offer customers 3-dimensional and rotational views of many of their items. Both of these features allow the customer to see the items they are interested in from every angle. With the Shop at Home Network having the ability to showcase their items in a way that allows the customer to almost "feel" the product because of television's visual impact, collectibles.com wanted to maintain that level of quality by offering customers the same luxury when shopping on the web site. Along with rotational views presented through streaming video, many of the product pictures and videos are accompanied

TV lunchboxes, which were made by the Lyon Company/ Vandor, feature a real-life look into the Shop at Home Network and collectibles.com.

by audio clips from the show hosts who actually sell that particular product on the Shop at Home Network. Together, the use of 3-dimensional video and narrated audio clips creates quite an impressive combination that allows the customer to really experience the product he or she is interested in, while learning about that particular piece from an experienced show host.

CONVERGENCE CREATES "ONE-STOP" SHOPPING

The Shop at Home Network has been establishing itself in the television-shopping world for almost 15 years, and continues to prove its worth in the marketplace by producing quality shows with quality merchandise. Since the inception of its web site, collectibles.com, the Shop at Home Network has become an even stronger force in the television and Internet shopping world. Now, as the two entities converge to form one center for easy, one-stop shopping, the possibilities are limitless. collectibles.com is upholding the long-standing philosophy of the Shop at Home Network by committing itself to helping the growth of the collectibles industry by introducing new products to their core customer base, as well as introducing new collectors to the industry through widespread marketing campaigns, in both traditional and online advertising campaigns. Together, collectibles.com and the Shop at Home Network are quickly rising to the top of the at-home shopping marketplace, only to continue its pattern of growth into the future of interactive shopping.

collectibles.com
5388 Hickory Hollow Pkwy.
Antioch, TN 37013-3128

Phone:
877-365-7467

Fax:
615-263-8084

Web Site:
www.collectibles.com

Protecting Your Treasures for 35 Years

Decades ago, collectors who wanted to insure their cherished possessions were often met with blank stares by insurance agents. "Why should we spend any time on postage stamps, dishes and knick-knacks?" asked the uninitiated sales reps. "They couldn't be worth much!" Then about 35 years ago, members of the American Philatelic Society finally found a "kindred spirit" in the insurance business. Collectibles Insurance Agency was founded to provide insurance coverage to stamp and postal history collectors who were members of the Society.

A life-long stamp collector and a professional insurance agent, company founder Horace W. Harrison combined his avocation with his vocation to make protecting valuable stamps easier and more affordable for his fellow philatelists. By the early 1980s, Harrison's sole business was insuring collectibles. When he decided to retire from the day-to-day running of the business, he first sought an insurance agent to purchase his firm. But eventually he realized that the major skills required to successfully run the business were knowledge of collectibles and the people involved in that field.

Company President Dan Walker attends many collectibles shows each year to meet and greet current and future policyholders in person.

Insurance For Your Collectibles

Your cherished collection

is not easily covered by your normal homeowners insurance policy. To assure that you will financially recover from the loss of your wonderful collection—from theft, fire or unfortunate occurrence—you need the easy-to-obtain specialized insurance coverage provided by Collectibles Insurance Agency. Our 30-year record of integrity in the collectibles field offers you a new kind of peace of mind. And most important: you'll know the kind of company we are if you ever experience a loss. We understand your hobby.

Insuring your collection with CIA is easy...

because we do not require a written inventory of your collection to begin or renew coverage. Enrolling for CIA insurance coverage is so simple that it only takes a few minutes to fill out our brief application. Approval of coverage is handled expediently...and we'll answer any question you may have. CIA is a full-service agency. You may enroll or renew your insurance coverage by mail, e-mail or instantly on our website on the Internet's World Wide Web. Best of all, our rates are attractive and especially competitive!

Inexpensive Protection For Your Collection

Collectibles Insurance Agency

P.O. Box 1200 · Westminster MD 21158
Phone: (888) 837-9537 · Fax (410) 876-9233
E-Mail: info@insurecollectibles.com
Website: www.collectinsure.com

Collectibles Insurance Agency insures scores of different types of collectibles and provides peace of mind to collectors nationwide.

DAN WALKER BUYS AND EXPANDS THE FIRM

In 1983, Harrison sold the stamp collecting insurance business to W. Danforth Walker. Since then, Dan Walker has devoted himself full-time to running his 100%-collectibles insurance business. Like Harrison, Walker is a life-long stamp collector, and he also is a collector of picture postcards and paper collectibles. Walker personally collects stamps and postal history from Grenada, Indian Native States and Romania; postal history from India, North Borneo and Sarawak; picture postcards from China (two visits), Valhalla, New York (hometown) and

While Plains, New York (high school town), as well as U.S. fire insurance paper and non-paper memorabilia.

By the early 1990s, Walker expanded the types of collectibles being insured to include most types of paper collectibles. Starting in late 1996-early 1997, coverage was expanded to include most types of collectibles, including limited editions. At the same time, an exclusive agreement with the American Philatelic Society to only insure members of this organization was ended.

A REPUTATION BUILT ON SERVICE

The expansion of coverage to virtually all types of collectibles has resulted in a number of advances for Collectibles Insurance Agency. In late 1999 and early 2000, the number of agents was increased 40%, and the physical space was more than doubled. Phone lines, computer servers and Internet connections were upgraded, as well. Today, the firm insures the collectibles of over 13,000 collectors and over 1,500 dealers.

Collectibles Insurance Agency has been successful because of the service it provides to both prospective and existing customers. Representatives attend collectibles shows throughout the country to answer collectors' questions, and there is an active web site at www.collectinsure.com with information about coverage and costs. The web site even provides a downloadable claim form. The firm prides itself on the expertise and longevity of its personnel. For example, the current collector claims representative has been settling collectors' claims for over 18 years!

Serving both collectors and dealers, Collectibles Insurance Agency insures collectibles against both loss and damage. Collectibles insured include:

COLLECTIBLES INSURANCE AGENCY, INC.

Limited Edition Collectibles	Figurines	Pins
	Glass	Plates
Animation Art	Jukeboxes	Postcards
Autographs	Maps	Posters
Badges	Medals	Pottery
Beanie Babies	Military/Movie/ Political/TV/Sports Memorabilia	Prints
Books		Records
Bottles		Stamps/ Postal History
Ceramics	Model Cars/ Trains	
China	Musical Instruments	Sports Cards
Clothing		Slot Machines
Coins	Ornaments	Stocks/Bonds
Comics	Paper Collectibles	Teddy Bears
Crystal	Patches	Textiles
Currency	Pens	Toys
Dolls	Photos	Trade Cards

The only exceptions are bullion, jewelry or watches containing precious metals, motor vehicles, live animals and plants. Even guns, knives and edged weapons can be insured with specialized policies.

ELIMINATING THE DREADED INVENTORY

Before Collectibles Insurance Agency, many collectors considered the meticulous inventory methods necessary for insurance coverage to be a major drain on their enjoyment of the hobby. This was especially true in the stamp-collecting realm, where collections often include thousands of individual specimens.

As Dan Walker explains, Collectibles Insurance Agency has eliminated this drudgery. "We have over 35 years' experience handling collectible claims and know that the detailed listing of lost property, and verification that this property actually existed, can be pieced together after a loss, if necessary. A brief summary description of each type of collection is all we need for an inventory prior to issuing insurance. You only need to specifically list individual items worth over $5,000.

"Also, we do not require a professional appraisal. You, the collector, estimate the replacement value for each type of collectible. Ballpark estimates are acceptable. We handle new acquisitions and inflation by automatically increasing coverage by 1% each month (not compounded) unless this option is voided by the insured. Coverage can be changed at any time by contacting our office."

WIDE-RANGING COVERAGE

Collectibles Insurance Agency prides itself on the comprehensive nature of its coverage. All policyholders have the opportunity to be insured against:

Burglary and Theft — Limited to $60,000 for a savings in premium, or full coverage for a slightly higher premium for collectors.

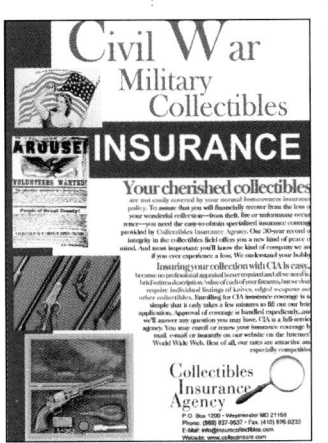

Most all information a potential customer needs is available online at www.collectinsure.com including quotes, brochures and resources.

Collectibles Insurance Agency prides itself on its friendly, knowledgeable and experienced staff members.

As an example, $100,000 coverage with full coverage for fire, flood, earthquake, hurricane and all other covered risks except burglary and theft, which is limited to $60,000, costs $238 annually. For $100,000 with full burglary and theft coverage, the annual cost is $274. If a central station alarm is protecting the property, there are additional cost savings. A $60,000 burglary and theft limit can be cost-effective when a collection is difficult to steal or to re-sell. Many limited edition collections fall into this category.

Robbery — Full policy coverage for robbery without requiring an alarm or safe. Robbery is the taking of your insured property by threat or force, such as an armed robbery.

Fire/Natural Catastrophes — Fire, earthquake, flood, hurricane, lightning, mudslide, hail, wind, tornado, cyclone and other natural catastrophes are covered up to the policy limit.

Breakage and Mysterious Disappearance — Accidental breakage and mysterious disappearance are covered.

Coverage for mail and shipping, Internet transactions and travel and exhibits also are available, including moving coverage and unattended auto coverage.

APPLYING AND MAKING CLAIMS

It is easy to apply for insurance through Collectibles Insurance Agency. There is an application available on the company's web site, or by calling the company directly. Claims ordinarily are acted upon within ten working days of receipt, and the firm works with knowledgeable dealers and experts to aid in determining replacement value. While most claims can be paid within ten working days of receipt of proof of value, some larger claims may take longer — but never more than 60 days.

There are specific, named exclusions on coverage listed in the Certificate of Insurance, and the firm will be happy to send a specimen copy on request. Exclusions include: inherent defect, gradual deterioration, insects/vermin, dampness, dishonest acts, losses of $50 or less, unsecured common carrier transits, checked baggage, government confiscation, conversion/infidelity, war and nuclear losses.

As Dan Walker asserts, "The cherished treasures that you own or sell are often not easily covered by your personal or business insurance. At Collectibles Insurance Agency, we make it our business to provide collectors, dealers and dealer/collectors with the peace of mind and protection they deserve!"

Collectibles Insurance Agency, Inc.
P.O. Box 1200
Westminster, MD
21158-0299

Phone:
888-837-9537

Fax:
410-876-9233

Web Site:
www.collectinsure.com

E-mail:
info@insurecollectibles.com

A Leading Seller of Collectibles Online

The average collector today maintains five separate collections and spends $800 a year adding to his or her holdings! Finding those special new acquisitions can take a great deal of time and effort if traditional shopping is involved, considering the commuting, parking, and searching. That's why many collectors are so excited about the opportunity to seek and purchase collectibles online.

While a growing number of collectible manufacturers and artists have their own web sites that include retail options, seeking and "surfing" all those sites can be time-consuming, as well. *But that's where CollectibleTown.com comes in.* This impressive and comprehensive web site offers more than 10,000 products from over 30 different collectibles companies — much more than most brick-and-mortar retailers can provide!

The official logo of the web-based retail company reflects the concept that CollectibleTown.com is a friendly on-line community for collectors.

LAURA COBABE'S BIG IDEA

CollectibleTown.com founder Laura Cobabe is the visionary who identified the need for a web-based retailer that could offer a variety of high-quality, new collectibles through one virtual storefront. Her initial research led her to discover that there are more than 36,000,000 Americans collecting today, whether their focus is coins, baseball cards, figurines, die-cast toy cars or limited editions. Of these collectors, about 10,000,000 already use the Internet for some aspect of their hobby.

Aunt Phoebe is CollectibleTown.com's official spokeswoman. She is a composite of the average collector — and she introduces new products, offers gift-buying suggestions and more!

In 1998, the domestic market for collectibles grew to $10.6 billion — a 10% annual growth rate since 1993. With the aging of the baby boomer generation, that number will continue to grow. Industry analysts predict that by the year 2004, the collectibles market will rise to $16 billion a year, $2 billion of which will come through e-commerce.

A "VIRTUAL STOREFRONT" ONLINE

CollectibleTown.com was established in 1999 with headquarters in Fort Collins, Colorado. Its goal is to lead the online collectibles market with extensive merchandise in a convenient, customer-friendly format.

The firm offers a "virtual storefront" that sells only top-of-the-line, new collectibles from the finest artists and manufacturers. With thousands of products to choose from, a collector or occasional buyer is assured of one-stop shopping. But there's more to CollectibleTown.com than merchandise. The web site is also chock-full of information that educates and entertains collectors of all ages and interests. There are chat rooms with artists and fellow collectors, experts on hand to answer questions, news and feature articles about artists and the collectibles industry, how-tos for maximizing a collection and much more.

Exceptional customer service is the number-one goal at CollectibleTown.com. Ensuring that customers have an enjoyable experience is the firm's constant priority. There are a number of purchasing options available to customers, as well as customer service representatives on hand to answer questions and solve problems. The call center at CollectibleTown.com is top-notch, both in its technology and its staff.

AUNT PHOEBE HELPS BUILD A COMMUNITY OF COLLECTORS

As the collectibles field grows, CollectibleTown.com intends to become a friendly "touchpoint" and a true community that welcomes everyone from avid collectors to occasional shoppers. The web site aims to become a "hometown away from home" for its visitors, with special features such as the chat room, which functions like a "Local Coffee Shop."

The "heart and soul" of the site is Aunt Phoebe, CollectibleTown.com's number-one collector, tour guide and hostess. Aunt Phoebe is an expert on the products CollectibleTown.com sells, and often has a few suggestions for those who aren't sure just which item would make the perfect gift.

Aunt Phoebe also is in charge of CollectibleTown.com's incentive program, which allows visitors to earn "Brownie Points" that count toward their next purchase. Earning Brownie Points can be as easy as registering and logging onto CollectibleTown.com.

SHOP AROUND THE CLOCK

Unlike "brick and mortar" stores that close at 5:30 p.m. or 9:00 p.m., CollectibleTown.com offers its visitors 24-hour-a-day, 365-days-a-year convenience. Its stores are always open and ready for business. Collectors can shop

This "Little Rascals" figurine from Mill Creek Studios is an example of the high-quality collectibles available at CollectibleTown.com.

evenings, weekends, holidays, or even late at night when they can't sleep – no need to make time in the busy workday for a visit to a land-based store!

Any questions or problems can be addressed directly to customer service representatives during business hours. Items purchased will be delivered to the customer's door in as little as three business days. What's more, CollectibleTown.com guarantees the privacy and confidentiality of its customers. The firm does not collect, track, sell or otherwise transfer to any third party any identifiable information about visitors to and users of its web site.

One-stop shopping for collectors is a goal of CollectibleTown.com. The selection of items available from a variety of high-quality manufacturers offers customers the luxury of shopping for a wide range of items in one place. Need a Glass Eye paperweight for Uncle George and a die-cast *American Muscle Car* for Cousin Billy? No problem. How about a *Dreamsicles* figurine for Niece Brittany and a Betty Boop snowglobe for Aunt Glory? You bet. CollectibleTown.com has it all!

A PANORAMA OF COLLECTIBLE STARS

With products from more than 30 companies already online at CollectibleTown.com, the variety available is nothing short of astounding. Firms whose works can be previewed and purchased at the site include, in alphabetical order: Cast Art Industries, Cavanagh, Classic Couture Artisan Flair, Country Artists USA, Crystal World, Ertl Collectibles, Fenton Art Glass, Glass Eye Studio, Goebel of North America, The Greenwich Workshop, Hand & Hammer Silversmiths, Harmony Kingdom, Lenox, Little Gem Teddy Bears, Mattel, Midwest of Cannon Falls, Mill Creek Studios, Miller Import Corp., Popular Imports, Possible Dreams, Robert Raikes, Roman, Russ Berrie, Schylling, Sigikids/Absolute

Collectibles Inc., Steiff, United Design Corp., Vandor and Westland Giftware.

The artists and collectible lines CollectibleTown.com features include: Kristin Haynes' *Dreamsicles* line, Cavanagh's licensed Coca-Cola collectibles, Crystal World's *Castles and Legends Series* and *Disney Showcase Collection,* Real Musgrave's *Pocket Dragons,* Will Bullas and James C. Christensen from The Greenwich Workshop, Chip de Matteo and P.D. Crowe from Hand & Hammer Silversmiths, Deb Canham and Jamie Wu of Little Gem Teddy Bears and Midwest of Cannon Falls' *Disney Classics,* Harley Davidson, Elvis Presley Enterprises, Beatrix Potter, Coca-Cola and "I Love Lucy" collectibles.

COBABE AND COMPANY LOOK TO THE FUTURE

With more than 15 years' experience in the collectibles industry as an artist, agent and producer, Laura Cobabe understands what collectors seek in the realm of high-quality new collectibles – convenience and customer service. She sees an unlimited potential for CollectibleTown.com — not only because baby boomers are joining collector ranks in large numbers – but also because of the growing number of men and boys entering the field.

With about 150 collectible manufacturers in the United States, CollectibleTown.com has a fertile field for expansion, and indeed, the firm anticipates working with most of these companies. Considering the creative talents of Ms. Cobabe and others on her team, she expects that CollectibleTown.com will produce its own collectible products as well. What's more, since home decorative accessories are such a natural partner to collectibles, CollectibleTown.com soon will add this category to its product mix.

As Ms. Cobabe concludes, "Collectors have unique sensibilities whether they are making purchases, getting new product information or keeping up-to-date on industry trends and issues. We have the experience and capability to provide a convergence point for collectors — and build strong relationships with existing online consumers!"

The popular Dreamsicles *line of precious figurines, designed by Kristin Haynes, is offered through CollectibleTown.com.*

CollectibleTown.com
4600 Innovation Drive
Fort Collins, CO 80525

Phone:
877-600-8881

Fax:
970-226-5991

Web Site:
www.CollectibleTown.com

E-mail:
AuntPhoebe@CollectibleTown.com

COLLECTIBLETOWN.COM

Importers of Unique European Collectibles

Almost a decade ago, Patrick Hobus flew from his native Germany to the United States in search of a relaxing vacation. Instead he found something much more precious and long-lasting: the love of his life and now his wife, Cathy Hobus. Proud of his German heritage, Patrick founded Columbus International to bring the fine arts and craftsmanship of Europe to the United States, where he and his wife happily reside.

Columbus International has grown rapidly since its beginning and now has a buying office in Germany. This allows Patrick and Cathy to search year-round for new and unique products in Europe. Their goal is to bring the collector limited edition collectibles with low edition sizes, made by renowned artists whose work is of the highest quality. Besides the firm's three major lines — HERMANN-Spielwaren, Füchtner nutcrackers and Zuber nutcrackers — Columbus International carries several other collectible gift items including hand-blown glass ornaments and Limoges boxes.

Columbus International is very proud of the relationship it has developed between its artists and the collectors. By bringing these talented artists to the

In a case of "turnabout is fair play," a teddy bear holds a Teddy Roosevelt doll in "My Favorite Teddy," a 15-3/4" limited edition of 500 pieces from HERMANN-Spielwaren.

International Collectible Expositions® in Rosemont, Illinois, and Long Beach, California, and to the Teddy Bear Expos, Columbus International has been able to create a unique connection between artist and collector.

As one of the first collectible gift importers in the United States to launch a web site for collectors and retailers, Columbus International features on-line catalogs, retailer listings, important news for collectors (such as artist appearances) and special introductions of new collectible pieces.

HERMANN-SPIELWAREN TEDDY BEARS

Columbus International is proud to be the sole agent of one of the oldest German teddy bear companies in the world, founded by Max Hermann in 1920. The world-renowned HERMANN-Coburg Company specializes in limited edition teddy bears that are designed for the adult collector. Dr. Ursula (Ulla) Hermann, CEO and designer of the HERMANN bears, has a unique talent for projecting music, literature and art into her teddy bears.

Since 1992, Ulla Hermann has been responsible for the design of teddy bears for HERMANN-Spielwaren in Corburg-Cortendorf, Germany. Every year Ulla, the founder's granddaughter, introduces between 60 and 80 new pieces.

Ulla's passion for designing teddy bears began as a young child. She learned her bear-making skills at her father's business and was trained by her mother, Dorle Hermann, to develop new models. After completing her doctoral degree in business, Ulla returned to her father's company and now is responsible for the management and design of the HERMANN bears. The principle of her creative work consists of conserving traditional techniques in combination with the search for new, unconventional designs.

Ulla's talents have become internationally acclaimed. For the past several years, HERMANN-Coburg bears have been nominated and have won several design awards, including the world-renowned "TOBY Award" and "Golden Teddy Award." In 1997, she won the "Golden Teddy Award" with HERMANN's first "Internet Bear," and in 1998 she claimed the "TOBY Award" with "Professor

The "Y2K Bug Bear" represents HERMANN's second Internet bear. The "Y2K" bug can be attached magnetically to different spots on the bear!

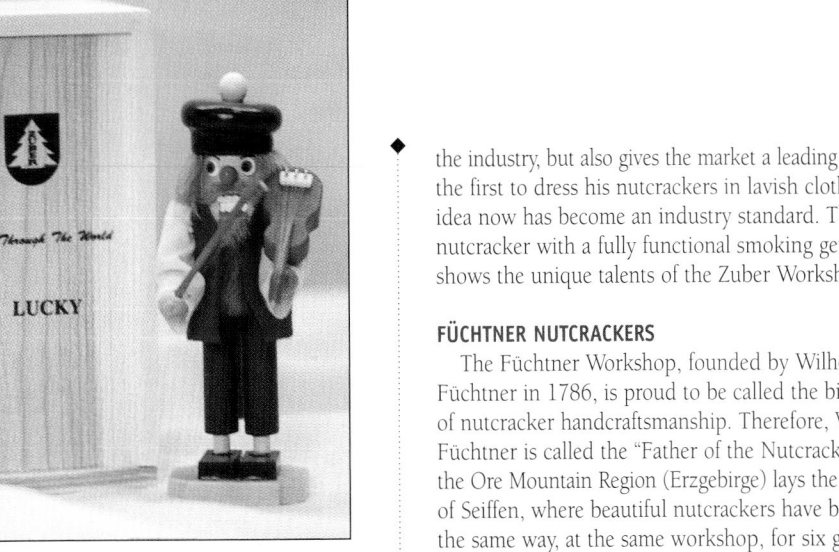

One of the miniature nutcrackers from Zuber's Travel Through the World *collection is "Lucky — from Ireland."*

Higgins" and the "Golden Teddy Award" with "Small Jacob." The year 1999 also has proven to be successful. The HERMANN bears have been nominated for five "Golden Teddy Awards" and one "TOBY Award." Since 1992, Ulla's teddy bear creations have been awarded 12 "TOBY" and 11 "Golden Teddy" nominations in all.

Today, most of the HERMANN bears are made in the same way as the original Max Hermann bears were crafted long ago in Sonneberg. They are made of rich mohair fabric, stuffed mainly with excelsior, and most of them have a deep, "growler" voice. Each teddy bear requires about three hours of hand-labor by the skilled men and women of the HERMANN bears' staff, many of whom have been with the firm for 20 or 30 years.

ZUBER NUTCRACKERS

Zuber nutcrackers became well known in the United States at the end of the 1980s. Columbus International is very proud to be the exclusive importer and distributor for the Zuber nutcrackers. Established in 1983, in Bavaria, Germany, by Norbert Zuber, this collection of nutcrackers and smokers is a true tradition of Germany. Zuber nutcrackers feature many sizes and characters that range from the traditional soldier to the "Y2K" nutcracker. The miniature nutcrackers have lately become very popular and are made in the same detail as their "big brothers." A new series of miniature nutcrackers has been launched for the holiday season. This series, called *Travel Through the World*, features miniature nutcrackers representing many countries of the world.

Norbert Zuber and his wife, Marlies, have developed high-quality wooden figurines for almost two decades. The Zuber company focuses its attention on nutcrackers, smokers, Christmas ornaments and music boxes. The Zuber Workshop artists have a talent for bringing unique wooden figurines to life, many in limited editions.

The special gift of Norbert Zuber not only challenges

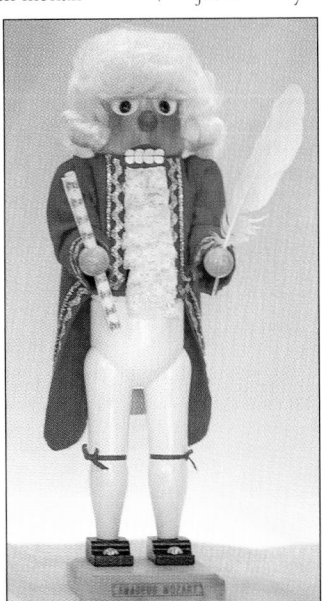

"Wolfgang Amadeus Mozart" is presented at 15-1/2" in height in a limited edition of 500 and with a $179 retail price.

the industry, but also gives the market a leading edge. Being the first to dress his nutcrackers in lavish clothing, Zuber's idea now has become an industry standard. The "Aladdin" nutcracker with a fully functional smoking genie bottle shows the unique talents of the Zuber Workshop.

FÜCHTNER NUTCRACKERS

The Füchtner Workshop, founded by Wilhelm Füchtner in 1786, is proud to be called the birthplace of nutcracker handcraftsmanship. Therefore, Wilhelm Füchtner is called the "Father of the Nutcracker." Deep in the Ore Mountain Region (Erzgebirge) lays the small village of Seiffen, where beautiful nutcrackers have been made in the same way, at the same workshop, for six generations.

The process of producing each Füchtner nutcracker involves 130 steps. The Füchtner Workshop emphasizes the classical nutcracker line that still holds, and really cracks, nuts. This is possible since the head and body are one piece. This crafting process involves much more time and effort than most contemporary nutcrackers require. Also, all of Füchtner's nutcrackers have real rabbit hair and are brand marked with the Füchtner logo. A Certificate of Authenticity is attached to each nutcracker along with a family chronicle.

The "King" nutcracker is the most famous, with a red jacket and yellow pants, copied over and over by many other manufacturers. In honor of the founder, Wilhelm Füchtner, Columbus International introduced this first limited edition nutcracker in 1998. In 1999, the second limited edition followed with the "Night Watchman." Both are shipped in beautiful wooden crates.

The Füchtner Workshop is a family-owned business, now operating in the sixth generation. With the first nutcracker developed in Seiffen by Wilhelm Füchtner in 1786, the company has carried on the family's name and expertise in producing high quality, traditional nutcrackers from Germany. Now, Volker Füchtner is proud to carry on his ancestors' creative and artistic talents.

COLUMBUS COLLECTION™

Columbus International introduces several exclusive pieces throughout the year for the United States market, and for many different events such as the International Collectible Exposition®.

Coming soon from Columbus International are new pieces to its unique line of charming, finely-crafted folk art, and a newsletter for collectors. After receiving an abundance of requests for a HERMANN Collector Club, Columbus International will be sponsoring one. And, after many inquiries from retailers and collectors, Columbus International will host a trip through Germany in the year 2001.

Columbus International
209 W. 12th St.
Hays, KS 67601

Phone:
800-814-6287

Fax:
785-625-4094

Web Site:
www.columbusintl.com

E-mail:
info@columbusintl.com

COLUMBUS INTERNATIONAL

Showcasing Artists Through the Next Millennium

Coyne's & Company is a multi-divisional company that has served the giftware industry for over four decades. As one of the few family-run companies that has survived for three generations, it is poised to take on the new millennium.

in the Studio G! division of Coyne's & Company have become very successful, and their lines are carried by over 4,000 retailers nationwide.

THE DAVID FRYKMAN PORTFOLIO COLLECTION FROM COYNE'S & COMPANY

David Frykman was the first sculptor to begin working directly with Coyne's & Company. Although the relationship began by creating *The David Frykman Portfolio Collection* in 1994, David began sculpting early in his life and had sculpted in nearly every material possible – from clay and bronze, to sand and snow. His first true carving experience was in the winter of 1992-93 when he was invited to participate as an ice-carver in local ice-carving competitions. This experience provided David with the opportunity to explore a whole new direction as a sculptor.

Today, David's medium of choice is white cedar, though he will still sneak off to the occasional ice competition. Cedar, which grows in abundance in Door County, Wisconsin, is a knotty and brittle wood which frustrates many traditional carvers, but which David carves particularly well with wood-adapted ice-carving tools.

Since 1994, *The David Frykman Portfolio Collection* has produced 16 series that have included over 300 individual designs. Three of these series are new for 1999: *The Hunter, The Firefighter* and *The Patrolman*. The designs for two of these new series capture many of the daily activities that are performed

The Golfer series from The David Frykman Portfolio Collection is definitely a hit in the right direction with creative designs depicting golfers in a variety of poses.

In 1955, Ed Coyne developed the business around the opportunity to represent the Fenton Art Glass Company. To this day, the Fenton and Coyne families enjoy a long-standing relationship. In 1959, Ed's son, John, joined the family business after graduating from the University of St. Thomas in St. Paul, Minnesota.

Coyne's & Company continued to increase the number of giftware lines they represented. Eventually, Coyne's & Company expanded into importing and warehousing giftware items from Europe that were sold to specialty stores in the upper Midwest. From these humble beginnings, Coyne's & Company has grown into a key player in the giftware industry.

In 1981, Coyne's & Company developed Parade of Gifts, a marketing and advertising tool for independent gift stores, which offers a coordinated giftware catalog featuring select giftware products produced by leading manufacturers from all over the world. This division has become a key resource for aggressive retailers and allows them to compete with national chains by advertising and promoting their own catalog and exclusive product.

In 1991, Coyne's & Company made a major move to bring new and exciting artist-driven lines to the marketplace. This gallery of artists is called Studio G!. The artists

"Winter Friends" portrays a favorite pastime of many youngsters. These three best friends from the Williraye Studio collection are fast becoming artists themselves by building snowmen and friendships.

"Flight in the Starry Night" from the American Chestnut Folk Art *collection shows that even when the sleigh has a broken runner, Santa's friends know how to improvise!*

by our public servants. There are five designs within *The Firefighter* series and seven designs within *The Patrolman* series. In total, there are 87 new designs for the nine current series within *The David Frykman Portfolio Collection*.

THE EXCITEMENT CONTINUES WITH *WILLIRAYE STUDIO*

In 1996, Coyne's & Company discovered Jeff Schuknecht and Bobbe Punzel-Schuknecht of *Williraye Studio* and a strong relationship developed.

Twenty-two years ago, Jeff and Bobbe met at the University of Wisconsin, married and formed an artistic partnership. Having both grown up in large urban settings, the couple decided to seek out a more relaxed life-style in a small town in Wisconsin. They purchased the property that is now their home and studio.

The couple had been creating original designs for their own art and antique store until the early 1990s, when they received national exposure from a featured article in *Folk Art Magazine*. The increased demand for their creations allowed Jeff and Bobbe to concentrate all their efforts on new designs which encompass a blend of American and French folk art.

Jeff and Bobbe draw on their day-to-day experiences for their whimsical themes, with family, friends, and the farm serving as both inspiration and motivation. The formation of their designs is attributed to their shared vision. This shared vision has given them the ability to think as one…from conceptualization to the finished design.

Each year, Coyne's & Company introduces new designs, including new additions to the very popular "Americana" collection. This collection, which encompasses seven designs, depicts youngsters dressed in our country's traditional colors. The highlight of the collection is "Uncle Sam," a limited edition featuring Uncle Sam and his best friend, Bald Eagle.

AMERICAN CHESTNUT FOLK ART AND *THE BAVARIAN HERITAGE COLLECTION* DEBUT

Coyne's & Company introduced two new exciting collections to the gift and collectibles industry. The first

introduction was the *American Chestnut Folk Art* collection. Award-winning artists Pete and Diane Bretz have given new life to the wood of the American chestnut tree. In their native Pennsylvania, Pete and Diane recycle antiquated American chestnut wood originally used in the construction of homes and barns. Their efforts of gathering the wood for sculpting are necessary, due to the fact that the American chestnut tree which once covered one half of the United States, was decimated nearly one hundred years ago by a chestnut blight from Asia.

Inspired by the style of traditional American folk art from the past, Pete and Diane have created wonderful characters that are sure to excite any collector. *The American Chestnut Folk Art* collection consists of spring and Christmas designs. The spring collection is comprised of five groups that include bears, rabbits, farm animals and pull toys. The *Christmas* collection was initially comprised solely of numbered limited editions that depict Santa and his friends at work and play. The recent midyear introductions include smaller Santa figurines and ornaments that are not limited editions.

The latest introduction by Coyne's & Company, created by in-house artists, is *The Bavarian Heritage Collection*. Based upon the story *The Toymaker and Bastien Bear,* this series consists of hand-painted porcelain designs and a specially designed plush bear. Each design contains *The Bavarian Heritage Collection* bottomstamp, and the porcelain Santa designs are accented with gold highlights. With porcelain, plush, ornaments, musicals and limited editions, this series has something for every collector.

Coyne's & Company is committed to developing quality collectibles from their talented artists. There are many exciting new designs in product development, and the anticipation increases as the new millennium begins.

"Santa's Sleigh of Wonder" from The Bavarian Heritage Collection *illustrates the detail and quality of this collection and plays "O'Tannenbaum."*

Coyne's & Company
7400 Boone Avenue North
Minneapolis, MN 55428

Phone:
800-336-8666

Fax:
612-425-1653

Web Site:
www.coynes.com

COYNE'S & COMPANY

Crafting the Drama of Life in Crystal

I t's 6 a.m. – the start of a new day. Already, the artists of Crystal World – Rudy Nakai, Tom Suzuki, Nicholas Mulargia and Roy Takii – are full of new ideas they can't wait to create in crystal. Where do they get these ideas? An hour or two spent in their company will tell the tale.

As Rudy and his family eat breakfast, outside in the yard, they can see a plump little bird in the nearby tree. Is that the first robin of spring, Rudy wonders? The germ of an idea is already taking shape. Watching, as the little bird turns its head from side to side, Rudy can feel a stirring in his own hands, as he imagines assembling the

"Cinderella's Castle," winner of Collector Editions "Award of Excellence," stands 7-1/2" high, and is composed of 350 individual prisms. Four sterling silver clocks, frozen in time at the magical hour of midnight, complete the castle!

◆ *An open edition figurine, "Legendary Unicorn" stands 3-1/2" tall and is part of Crystal World's popular Castles and Legends series.*

tiny pieces of crystal that may one day become the image of this very bird!

As Tom Suzuki leaves his house in the morning, he spies a small cat playing in the front yard. Tom smiles in delight as he watches the cat so intently engaged in its play. Suzuki has already received one *Collector Editions* "Award of Excellence" for his figurine "Curious Cat." Perhaps another little charmer will come from the activity of this particular morning.

Sipping coffee as he watches a television documentary, Crystal World's newest artist, Roy Takii, is impressed with the antics of the Arctic penguins profiled on the show. Penguins have always been a favorite of this artist, and what he has seen this morning will surely become part of a new penguin family sculpture, to be introduced in the near future by Crystal World.

INSPIRATION COMES FROM EVERYWHERE

On a rainy Sunday afternoon, Nicholas Mulargia takes his four children to the local mall. There, in the center of the mall is an old-fashioned carousel, reminiscent of Nicholas' youth in his native Italy. Before his little ones have a chance to hop on their favorite horse, the seed for a new crystal creation, the limited edition "Merry-Go-Round," takes root.

"Our ideas begin with the world we see around us," explains Rudy Nakai, founder and leading artist of Crystal World. "We'll be walking down a street or sitting in our homes, when we'll notice a dog playing in the yard and, before you know it, we've got an idea for a new figurine. The world is full of so many wonderful things – how can we not be inspired by it all?" Every animal in Crystal World's popular menagerie was motivated by its real counterpart, as envisioned by the artist.

Something else makes Crystal World collectibles special, and that is the sense of drama – of something actually happening before your eyes – that so many of these pieces offer. Examples include everything from "Mozart," featuring a little dog listening to an old-time Victrola, to "CompuBear," Crystal World's new cyber-age teddy. "Tee-Shot Teddy," on the other hand, is concentrating on the final putt of the day. With any luck, he'll make par. Now, there's drama!

In one Crystal World sculpture, charming "Wilbur the Pig" is sticking his head through the rails of a fence,

"Dumbo & Timothy," from the Walt Disney classic motion picture Dumbo, features everyone's favorite flying elephant in full-cut, faceted crystal with his best friend Timothy the mouse (interpreted in sterling silver) perched atop him.

gazing longingly into the distance. It's difficult to look at this figurine without becoming emotionally attached to little Wilbur.

New additions to the company's menagerie that continue this dramatic tradition include "Legendary Unicorn," rearing up in all its majesty, and one of Crystal World's most irresistible angels – "Angel of Joy" – who's engaged in blowing her little trumpet in the most joyous manner imaginable.

CRYSTAL CREATIONS FROM WILDLIFE TO CITY LIFE

In 1997, artist Nicholas Mulargia created his limited edition "Majestic Bald Eagle." Enthusiastically received by crystal collectors and wildlife lovers, a new limited edition collection was born: *The North American Wildlife Series.* The following year, Crystal World's "Timber Wolf," designed by Rudy Nakai, made its debut. And in 1999, the company's spectacular "White-Tailed Deer" and "Mountain Lion," created by Crystal World's newest artist Roy Takii, were introduced.

Crystal World is known worldwide for its exquisite array of architectural sculptures of some of the world's most famous buildings. These pieces have proven popular not only with collectors, but also with visitors to New York, Washington DC, and Paris. From the signed and numbered limited edition "Capitol Hill" to the "Eiffel Tower," along with eight different versions of New York's Empire State Building, Crystal World's *Wonders of the World* are both plentiful and dynamic.

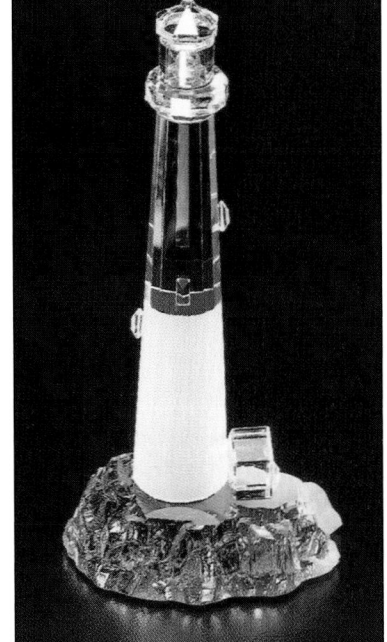

"Barnegat Lighthouse, NJ," designed by Crystal World's founding artist and award-winning designer Rudy Nakai, stands 3-1/2" high and is part of the Seaside Memories *collection.*

◆ AH, ROMANCE!

The key to much of Crystal World's success with collectors can be summed up in a single word: *romance.* This embodies the heart of collectibles, and Crystal World captures it as few others can. Crystal, after all, is the very essence of romance. Crystal gifts, from fine vases and stemware to pendants and jewelry, have been exchanged and treasured throughout the ages. Historically, truly fine crystal has always contained at least 24% lead; Crystal World's figurines contain 30% or more. It's this lead content that maximizes the refraction of the light, and gives the crystal its sharpness and brilliance.

Crystal World's extraordinary sculptures are created from the world's finest full-lead crystal, and are as shimmering and as beautiful as anything encountered in today's collectible world. The romance, in fact, is found not only in the crystal itself, but also in many of the themes Crystal World selects. In the popular *Teddyland* series, collectors are taken on a romantic journey from a chance encounter by two teddy bears on a park bench, "Loving Teddies," to their eventual honeymoon on a distant tropical paradise, "Beach Teddies."

For gifts of the heart, little charmers such as "I Love You Teddy" (featuring a teddy with a red heart) and "I Love You Bouquet Teddy" (with, yes, a bouquet of flowers) are hard to beat. One of Crystal World's recent introductions, "Broadway Ted," features a teddy dancing up a storm!

DISNEY IN CRYSTAL!

What's new from America's premier producer of faceted crystal collectibles? In July 1998, Crystal World introduced *The Disney Showcase Collection* of hand-numbered, limited edition crystal figurines, inspired by beloved Disney characters. "Just for You" (Mickey Mouse) and "Gee, You're the Sweetest" (Minnie), "Dumbo & Timothy," and "Pinocchio & Jiminy Cricket" were fast favorites among crystal collectors and Disney fans alike. This exciting series also features exquisite replicas of "Cinderella's Castle" and "Cinderella's Slipper," inspired by Walt Disney's classic animated motion picture. Certain pieces, such as "Pinocchio & Jiminy Cricket" include fine, sterling silver accents.

In 1999, "Cinderella's Castle," designed by Tom Suzuki, received the prestigious *Collector Editions* "Award of Excellence," for "Cottage or Building over $100." Look for the unveiling of several new surprises in the months ahead, including replicas of "Tinkerbell," "Steamboat Willie" and "Cinderella's Coach," interpreted in the finest full-cut faceted crystal. It's "crystal clear" that Crystal World has something for everyone!

◆

Crystal World
120 Industrial Avenue
Little Ferry, NJ 07643

Phone:
800-445-4251

Fax:
201-931-0220

Web Site:
www.crystalworld.com

E-mail:
collector@crystalworld.com

Celebrating 26 Years as an Industry Leader

In 1973, Dave Grossman Creations became the first company to produce a collectible line of figurines inspired by the works of Norman Rockwell, the world-famous artist who forever endears us with his slice of "Americana" through his illustrations in *The Saturday Evening Post.*

Since then, the company has expanded its lines to welcome products from *I Love Lucy™, Batman, Superman, The Wizard of Oz™, Gone With the Wind™, Laurel & Hardy™, The Three Stooges™, Emmett Kelly, Sr., Spencer Collin Lighthouses, Embrace, Legacy, Hal Payne's Button Box Kids* and many more!

A COMPANY THAT KEEPS THE COLLECTOR IN MIND

The company's longevity and creativity is a credit to artist and founder Dave Grossman. The pride that Dave takes in his work, his energetic spirit and his devotion to the collector are the backbone of his success. Grossman's future plans include expanding on existing licensed and limited edition collectibles while marketing new and innovative products — all with the collector in mind.

A native of St. Louis, Grossman graduated from the University of Missouri, where he was a standout on the football, baseball and track teams. Upon graduation, Grossman was commissioned to produce architectural sculptures for banks, hospitals, hotels and other private and public buildings. One of his works is on display in New York city's Lincoln Center. He was also commissioned to create sculptures for Presidents Lyndon B. Johnson and Richard M. Nixon.

A licensing agreement that was made in 1973 between Dave Grossman Creations and The Curtis Publishing Company to produce *Norman Rockwell* figurines proved to be the birth of a new company in the collectibles industry. However, the company was actually founded in 1968, when Grossman originally began designing and marketing his own unique style of welded metal sculptures.

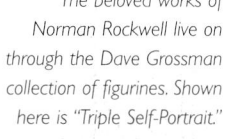

The beloved works of Norman Rockwell live on through the Dave Grossman collection of figurines. Shown here is "Triple Self-Portrait."

LICENSED PRODUCTS EQUAL SUCCESS

The *Norman Rockwell* figurines changed the company's direction. Each figurine beautifully captures Rockwell's homespun and hometown portraits that graced the covers of *The Saturday Evening Post,* among other publications. The collection has evolved since its inception, and the enthusiasm and pride among Rockwell collectors is stronger today than ever before! The collection now includes retired porcelain figurines, resin figurines and yearly limited edition porcelain and ball ornaments.

"Vitameatavegamin" is one of the most exciting licensed figurines from the I Love Lucy™ brand of collectibles.

Dave Grossman Creations continues its quest to be a leader in the field of licensed collectibles. Under a licensing agreement with Warner Bros., the company has gained a loyal following for products produced for two of the silver screen's most popular films: *The Wizard of Oz™* and *Gone With the Wind™.* 1999 marks the 60th anniversary for both films, and the company will again lead the way for these two properties with their innovative figurines, waterglobes, musicals, plaques, framed lithographs and Christmas ornaments.

Dave Grossman Creations has also signed deals with Unforgettable Licensing, Larry Harmon Pictures and Comedy III Entertainment to produce other well-known television-themed products. One of the company's most exciting new product categories is their *I Love Lucy™* brand of collectibles. The product lines include figurines, musical figurines and snowglobes. The *I Love Lucy™* show is the most watched TV show in history, and the initial collection features products from two of the most popular episodes, "The Chocolate Factory" and "Job Switching."

The lovable characters from two other classic series — *Laurel & Hardy™* and *The Three Stooges™* — are represented in figurines, musical figurines and waterglobes. These two shows were at the forefront of slapstick comedy and what we refer to today as "physical" comedy.

The beloved Emmett Kelly, the most famous circus clown of all time, continues to make people smile

Dave Grossman Creations introduces the "Ol' Fishin' Hole" from The Button Box Kids collection by artist Hal Payne.

through the works of Grossman's *Emmett Kelly, Sr.* collection of fine porcelain figurines and ornaments. Kelly's fame was based on his clown character "Weary Willie." With his big red nose, black grease face paint and a woefully sad expression, "Willie" was a down-and-out vagabond for whom nothing ever came out right. He was called "the saddest and funniest man in the world." Mr. Kelly's antics and shenanigans were enjoyed by Ringling Brothers Barnum and Bailey Circus audiences for years!

Licensed through his estate, the limited edition collection of bisque porcelain figurines features the hobo clown performing his familiar antics, including trying to sweep away the spotlight, playing an organ and trying to catch a baseball. Included in the collection are themes from the *Circus Collection*, the *Casino Series* and the *Gallery Collection*.

Dave Grossman Creations is pleased to announce a new collection of whimsical dolls called *The Button Box Kids* from renowned doll artist Hal Payne. The assortment of 12 dolls/figurines is based upon a group of children who find magic and mischief within their grandmother's button box. Each figurine has a resin base and features a fully-dressed doll. A few are encased in a decorative tin! From "Jacob" with his saxophone to "Ol' Fishin' Hole" and "Garland Makers," there is sure to be a *Button Box Kid* for any gift-giving occasion.

SPENCER COLLIN LIGHTHOUSES AND DAVE GROSSMAN CREATIONS ARE A WINNING COMBINATION

Dave Grossman Creations is proud to announce the 15th anniversary of Cheryl Spencer Collin producing her award-winning lighthouse designs. After receiving a bachelor of fine arts in 1975 and a master's degree of fine arts in 1977, Spencer Collins began sculpting her one-of-a-kind porcelain animal sculptures to sell to galleries. Later, she added a line of cottages and lighthouses. Today, her Maine barn studio is known for producing some of the finest limited edition lighthouse sculptures available. *Spencer Collin*

Lighthouses is a one-artist collection that has a well-deserved reputation for quality and attention to detail. Cheryl has won many accolades and awards, and is in fact, the Coast Guard-approved lighthouse artist, due to her many years of sculpting lighthouses and lightships.

Spencer Collin believes that the true beauty of a lighthouse is found in its setting. It is this "sense of place" that sets her intricate lighthouses apart from all others in the marketplace. Spencer Collin meticulously researches each site and lighthouse before she painstakingly sculpts them. Cheryl's joy in her work is apparent in all of her sculptures — they are the next best thing to being there!

Cheryl does all of the sculpting herself, giving the collection unique qualities of consistent style, relative scale and detail based on actual regional surroundings, flora and fauna. The observer may find sea roses, sunflowers, birch or palm trees, harbor seals or humpback whales on any given piece. Look for whimsical touches such as the keeper's dog burying a bone, a fishing pole and bait bucket, or even a New England clambake complete with lobsters, corn on the cob and fresh blueberry pie. Cheryl's personal touches include her pet bunny, Willy, and her dog, Svea, on every piece.

All *Spencer Collin Lighthouses* are limited to 2,400 pieces, with the first 500 as "Gold Label Editions" personally signed and numbered by Spencer Collin.

In recent years new introductions have included a line of 12 miniature lighthouses from the *Compass Rose Collection*. The retail prices range between $20.00 and $35.00 per item and each lighthouse is limited to 9,500 pieces.

Other lighthouses include "White Fish Point (MI)," "Old Scituate Light (MA)", "Point Cabillo (CA)," "Hilton Head (SC)," and "Chatham Light (MA)." New additions to Cheryl's lightships are the "Huron Lightship (Great Lakes)" and a wonderful trio of miniature lightships that come in a block set.

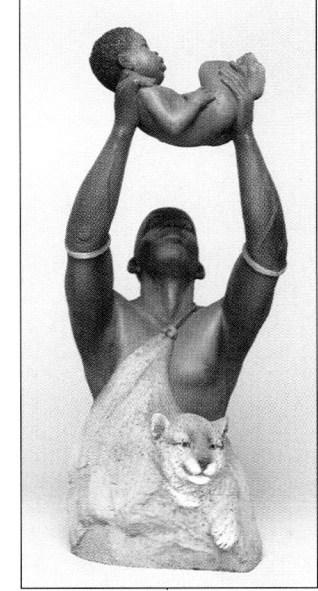

Tom Snyder's moving "Legacy" figurine from the Legacy Collection is presented by Dave Grossman Creations.

At the request of *Spencer Collin Lighthouse* enthusiasts, Dave Grossman Creations has launched a collector's club. The Spencer Collin Lighthouses Collectors Club, now in its third year, lets more people explore the magic and charm of Cheryl's sculptures.

The $30 annual membership fee entitles members to an exclusive and complimentary lighthouse figurine, sculpted lighthouse pin, personalized membership card, free subscription to the quarterly newsletter, "Studio Update," current brochures and an attractive folio with a hand-signed photo of the artist. Members also have the opportunity to purchase members-only lighthouses and learn about special events and open houses where Spencer Collin's works are featured.

Dave Grossman Creations
1608 North Warson Road
St. Louis, MO 63132

Phone:
800-325-1655

Fax:
314-423-7620

E-mail:
dgcrea@aol.com

Opening the Doors to the Past

For the past two decades, David Winter's meticulously sculpted cottages have been admired and collected all over the world. A great deal of their appeal – apart from their fine craftsmanship – stems from their ability to conjure up an earlier, less hectic way of life. They evoke an era when people had time to "stand and stare" and when people knew their neighbors.

There's even something unhurried about their creator, David Winter, who gives the impression of having all the time in the world to meet and listen to people. He sees his sculptures as "evoking and recapturing something of the past – when communities were communities, when everyone looked out for each other, and when the pace of life was slower."

HOME AND FAMILY INSPIRE WINTER'S CREATIONS

Born in Caterick, Yorkshire, Winter is the son of an army colonel and the famed British sculptor Faith Winter. While his father's army postings took the family to exotic locales like Singapore and Malaysia, Winter still loved nothing better than to live and work in a part of rural England that remains much as it was 300 years ago.

Inspired by his mother, David wanted to pursue sculpting as a career. Before heading to art college, he spent a year working as his mother's assistant. He created his first miniature cottage in 1979 titled "Mill House." It sold at a local shop on the first day it was displayed. Within a week of that first sale, there were David Winter Cottages available in several shops in Winter's home territory of Surrey. Since then, Winter has hundreds of titles to his credit. His models are rarely reproductions of "real" places, but his work is imaginative rather than totally imaginary. "Architecturally," David explains, "they all have a basis in fact."

In early 1997, David Winter signed an agreement with Enesco Corporation, a leading gifts and collectibles firm. Enesco is now manufacturing the cottages and operating the David Winter Cottages Collectors' Guild. As always, however, the cottages are completely a result of the artist's vision. "I stand alone in the concept of a subject," Winter says. "I decide how a cottage will look and I, alone, sculpt that master. As a model is manufactured, I am there, too, seeing it progress through the various stages of production."

THE MAKING OF A DAVID WINTER COTTAGE

When Winter has completed an original sculpture in wax, it is taken to the studios and workshops of Enesco Europe, where liquid silicon rubber is poured over it to

To celebrate the 20th Anniversary of the collection, David Winter has created "Bridgewater." The sculpture features a bridge symbolizing the two decades of his work, while the water represents time passing by.

The residents of Horseshoe Bay have been planning for months for the biggest celebration ever in this limited edition piece titled "The Millennium At Horseshoe Bay."

make a master mold. This is a delicate operation, and the mold must be perfect because the original is destroyed during the process. From this mold, an exact copy of the original sculpture can be cast in tough resin. This process now can be safely repeated using the "resin master" to make further molds from which the final cottages will be cast. Next, liquid gypsum is poured into the mold. At this stage, it's important to remove any pockets of air. Then, the cast is ready to be de-molded with great care. The cottage is then "fettled," which means that tiny flashes of excess gypsum are scraped away. The base of the cottage also is rubbed down until it's smooth. The cast is left for 24 hours to completely dry.

Before painting, the white cast is dipped in a special sealing solution of shellac and white polish. The coloration is applied by highly trained artists using strict guidelines, although some artistic license is permitted, provided it adheres to high levels of quality control. Metal components and other additional items are attached at this stage. After a final, careful inspection, the painted cottage has its base covered in green felt and its identification label attached. The pieces are then boxed, each with a Certificate of Authenticity, before being sent to stores around the world.

NEW INTRODUCTIONS ADD EXCITEMENT

"Merlin's Castle" from
The King Arthur Collection
*celebrates the medieval
people and places in the
legend of King Arthur.*

David Winter Cottages exist in homes worldwide because of two essential ingredients: David's enormous talent for sculpting in the finest and most exquisite detail, and the ability of the company's craftspeople in Great Britain to make exact models from David's originals. Inspiration for his sculptures comes from a variety of sources — old books, manuscripts, etchings and real buildings all play a part in the evolution of an idea. But the final shape and form of the sculpture comes firmly from David's imagination.

Several new series were added in 1999, including *The Anniversary Collection* in recognition of the 20th Anniversary of David Winter Cottages. The special 20th Anniversary piece is "Bridgewater," representing a bridge spanning those years, while the stream depicts the movement of time. "Although it spans the past 20 years, I hope it also spans the next 20," Winter says.

To ring in the new century, there's *The Millennium Collection* with "The Millennium at Horseshoe Bay" featuring residents of the town planning the biggest celebration ever. The piece is limited in edition to 2,000 pieces.

The *Traditional Crafts Collection* plays up the owners' names of the cottages: "Mr. Clinker's Cottage," "Mr. Delver's Cottage," "Mr. Kelman's Cottage" and "Mr. Cocker's Cottage." *The King Arthur Collection* takes collectors to medieval times with five introductions from the legends. The pieces are: "Merlin's Castle," "Morgan Le Fay's," "Sir Tristan's," "Dagonet the Fool's," and "Sir Perceval's."

Each year, more cottages are added to continuing series within the collection, including *The Pubs & Taverns of England* and *Pilgrims' Way*. Winter discovers out-of-the-way taverns on his travels, including "The Potted Shrimp." Winter's own home village inspired *The Pilgrims' Way* collection, featuring cottages that may have appeared in Chaucer's time. One of the recent additions to the series is "Robber's Retreat."

In other continuing series, the spooky "Casterton Railway Station" was added to the annual *Haunted House Collection.* "Bill & Nancy's House" was added as the third issue in the *The Oliver Twist Christmas Collection.*

ARTISTRY RECOGNIZED

While collectors have been captivated by David Winter Cottages, he has also received acclaim from the collectibles industry. In 1987 and 1988, the collection received the "Collectible of the Year" honors from the National Association of Limited Edition Dealers (NALED). In 1989 and 1990, the collection was first runner-up in that category. In several collectible shows — both in the U.S. and abroad — David Winter Cottages has been named the "Collectible of the Show." In 1991, David himself won "Artist of the Year" from NALED.

COLLECTORS CAN JOIN GUILD

Since 1987, David Winter collectors have had the opportunity to enjoy the privileges of membership in the David Winter Cottages Collectors' Guild. Among the many benefits available for a $42.00 yearly membership fee are opportunities to acquire the annual Guild Symbol of Membership and two members-only cottages. "I derive a great deal of satisfaction from sculpting these special cottages as they are destined for people who have shown a particular interest in and appreciation for my work," Winter says. "This in itself is a source of inspiration for me." Members also receive a membership card, a subscription to *Cottage Country* magazine and the full-color David Winter catalog.

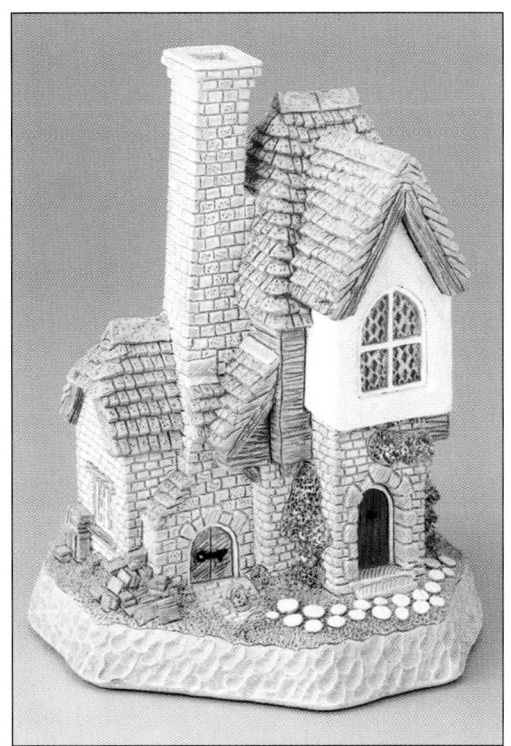

Members of the David Winter Cottages Collectors' Guild received "The Tile Maker's Cottage," the 1999 Guild Symbol of Membership.

David Winter Cottages
P.O. Box 8
Libertytown, MD 21762

Phone:
888-995-7005

Fax:
301-829-8554

E-mail:
www.info@davidwinterusa.com

DAVID WINTER COTTAGES

Old World Quality for New World Bears

Deb Canham, the chief creative force behind Deb Canham Artist Designs, Inc., joyfully relates how the "seeds" of her successful company were planted generations ago, by – of all people – England's fabled Queen Victoria!

Canham's great-grandmother was a ward of the Queen, and as such, she became one of the first pupils of the Royal School of Needlework in London. As Canham explains, "My grandmother was a fine seamstress who made beautiful crocheted tablecloths. My mother inherited her excellence as a seamstress, and she passed on to me her love for sewing...and storytelling."

"While sharing with me her passion for sewing with needle, thread and fabric, she also encouraged me to believe that each of my soft toys had its own character and personality. In fact, I never called them toys...they were my animals!"

"When I look back to see how I ended up with a collectible bear company, it is almost frightening how inevitable it was," Canham explains. "What else could I have done that would have so opened up the world to me, and given me such a universal language, as bears?"

Inspired by vintage bears of German origin, the "Good Old Days" collection features some of the most lovable, worn-out looking characters you will ever find.

"Blustery Day" was created by Deb Canham and her sister Jane Davies for the 1999 Walt Disney World Teddy Bear Convention in Orlando, Florida.

A LOVE OF OLD THINGS INSPIRES CANHAM

Ever since she was a child, Canham has appreciated time-worn objects and fabrics, and this love shines through in her contemporary works of art. Canham's father and brother are what she calls "great artists," but she herself never took to painting or sketching. Canham focused on the area where her unique talents and skills lay: creating miniatures.

"When I see items of antique clothing, I am always fascinated by the quality and feel of the actual fabric. But the greatest thrill comes in looking at the hand-stitching," Canham enthusiastically explains. "To me there is a story behind every handcrafted item."

From 1987 to 1996, Canham worked as a "bear artist," designing and making each of her bears completely by hand and selling them as one-of-a-kind collector's pieces.

Over the years, Deb won many awards for her bear originals, wrote an in-depth *Manual on Miniature Bearmaking*, and taught advanced workshops in England, America, Holland, Germany and Japan.

Eventually, she felt constrained by the small number of bears she could personally complete, and decided she could make more impact by embracing the concept of the limited edition "artist designed bear." With that change, she also made a major geographical switch, leaving her native England for new headquarters, new opportunities and new challenges in the United States.

NEW SERIES MARKS CANHAM'S U.S. DEBUT

Canham moved from the United Kingdom to the United States in April of 1996 to start Deb Canham Artist Designs, Incorporated. Their first release was a group of seven animals who made up the *Mohair Collection*. What immediately caught collectors' attention was the delicate proportions of the bears in the series. Measuring only 3" tall, they had the precise proportions, detail and cuddly look of large teddy bears that had somehow been magically miniaturized!

The Camelot Collection *numbers seven pieces, from "King Arthur" and "Merlin," to a pair of sprightly dragons.*

"My very favorite was 'Sorry' who had holes in his foot-pads and paw pads, and that 'slouched-shoulder' worn-out look," Canham reveals. "He was meant to represent all those beloved old bears who had been put away in the attic and forgotten." A few shops actually returned "Sorry" because of the holes in his pads – but once they heard he was supposed to be like that, they found him all the more endearing!

At the same time, Canham released a group of four bears called the *Country Collection,* inspired by American pioneer ingenuity and attention to thrift. As she describes, "We had 3" bears wearing dungarees and dresses, carrying little dolls wearing the same calico fabric."

To celebrate her first ten years making miniature bears in 1997, Canham released a special new collection, inspired by days spent by a roaring fire while the rain beat against the windows. Here, Canham would spend hours sewing tiny felt clothes for her soft toy "animals." "That's how I decided to design the *Rainy Day Collection* in which all the characters have felt accessories," she explains.

Canham feels a deep affinity for the little personalities she creates. As she notes, "When you spend time designing a collection of bears, it's impossible not to have the pieces develop into real characters that you get to know and care about." In the *Rainy Day Collection,* "Hattie" is a little girl in a gingham dress with a felt hat and cotton drawers. The dress has a patch on it, but what she is most proud of is her new hat decorated with flowers.

NEW ARTISTS COMPLEMENT CANHAM'S DESIGNS

The first time the company sought out the talents of other designers was for the creation of Canham's *Nutcracker Collection.* Laurie Sasaki, one of the very best miniature bear artists whose work is rarely seen except on the secondary market, designed the "Nutcracker Prince." Bonnie Windell, another bear artist who is famous for her wonderfully charming rats, was chosen to create the "Rat King." This was also the first collection the firm ever made with matching limited edition numbers.

Canadian bear artist Brenda Power contributed her first animals to the firm in 1998, designing two rabbits, a raccoon and a penguin.

WHAT'S NEW...

Inspired by her work on 1998's *Camelot* series, Deb has created the *Dappled Dragons,* a line of irresistibly cute and cuddly "fire breathers" from the middle ages. With names like "Custard," "Stan," and "The Professor," you can imagine that these limited editions will carry on the tradition of beguiling charm for which Deb Canham Artist Designs has already become famous.

The year 2000 will bring the long-awaited arrival of the 5" cloth doll range designed by Jane Davies, Deb's sister. Also brand new is the launch of *The Bigger Bear Collection,* Deb's designs produced in 6" to 12" sizes in numbered limited editions.

Part of Deb's original plan for her company is the formation of the Deb Canham Artist Designs Collectors Club to help make the art and hobby of collecting miniature bears more fun and rewarding.

The club mascot is a Deb-designed bear named "Binker." "He travels all over the place, with his owner, Monty," says Deb, clearly enjoying her storytelling prowess. "He gets himself in trouble and meets new friends all the time. We're looking for him to travel throughout the United States and to occasionally go overseas. Wherever he goes, you can be sure there will be other bears to welcome him and make him feel right at home." Members can follow "Binker's" adventures and meet his new pals through the stories in the club's newsletter.

Undoubtedly, part of the reason Deb has been so successful in such a short period of time, is that she knows what she wants and what collectors want, and she

"Binker," designed by Deb Canham as the mascot of the Deb Canham Artist Designs Collectors Club, is an adventurous teddy.

has devoted herself to making it happen.

Call it synergy, serendipity, or just plain luck, but somehow in creating the perfect company and product for herself, Deb has also delighted the thousands of collectors who have discovered her tiny teddies.

Deb Canham
Artist Designs, Inc.
820 Albee Rd., Suite #1
Nokomis, FL 34275

Phone:
941-480-1200

Fax:
941-480-1202

Web Site:
www.deb-canham.acun.com

E-mail:
deb@deb-canham.acun.com

DEB CANHAM ARTIST DESIGNS, INC.

Department 56® — The Tradition Continues

Before Department 56®, Inc. became an independent corporation, it was part of a large parent company that used a numbering system to identify each of its departments. Department 21 was administration, and the name assigned to wholesale gift imports was Department 56.

Although Department 56 began by importing fine Italian basketry, a new product line introduced in 1977 set the groundwork for the collectible products of today. Each design of *The Original Snow Village®* was handcrafted of ceramic, and hand-painted to create all the charming details of an "olden day" village. To create the glow of the windows, a switch cord and bulb assembly was included with each individually boxed piece.

Glowing lights gave the impression of cozy homes and neighborhood buildings with happy, bustling townsfolk in a wintry setting. Sales were encouraging, so Department 56 decided to develop more Village pieces.

By 1979, the company realized that in order to keep the Village at a reasonable size, buildings would have to be retired each year to make room for new designs. Being new to the world of collectibles, they did not realize the full impact of this decision. Collectors who had not yet obtained a retired model would attempt to seek out that piece on the secondary market, leading, in some cases, to significant increases in values.

1990 brought about a new extension to *The Original Snow Village: The American Architectural Series*. These pieces have been modeled after famous examples of American architecture; however, they do not portray existing structures. The 11 pieces in this sub-series are some of the most popular homes in *Snow Village*.

In 1994, the creative department started to design a new series of licensed pieces. "Coca-Cola® Brand Bottling Plant" was the first piece in this series. Through this piece, many Coca-Cola® collectors learned about Department 56 and *The Original Snow Village*. Because of their popularity, other licensed pieces have been added to the *Snow Village*.

"St. Martin-in-the-Fields Church" from The Heritage Village Collection, Dickens' Village Series *is a replica of the famous chapel located in London.*

THE TRADITION CONTINUES ...

In 1984, Department 56 became an independent company. It was also the year the first *Heritage Village® Collection, The Dickens' Village Series®*, was introduced. Extensive research, charming details and the fine hand-painting of the seven original porcelain shops and "Village Church" established them as favorites among collectors.

Other series followed with the introductions of the *New England Village® Series, Alpine Village Series®, Christmas in the City®, Little Town of Bethlehem™ Series, North Pole Series™*, and in 1994, *Disney Park Village Series™*.

Each series within *The Heritage Village Collection* captures the holiday spirit of a bygone era. *The Dickens' Village Series*, for instance, portrays the bustling, hearty and joyous atmosphere of the holidays in Victorian England. *New England Village* brings back memories of "over the river and through the woods," with a journey through the northeastern countryside.

Alpine Village recreates the charm of a quaint mountain town, while *Christmas In The City* evokes memories of busy sidewalks, street corner Santas, friendly traffic cops and bustling crowds amid cheery shops, elegant townhouses and theaters.

In 1987, Department 56 introduced the *Little Town of Bethlehem*. The unique 12-piece set inspired those who celebrate Christmas everywhere. In the year 2000, *Little Town of Bethlehem* was expanded to include three new lighted pieces, accessory figures and a variety of landscaping materials that will add character to the display.

In 1991, Department 56 presented the *North Pole Series*, which depicts the wonderful Santa Claus legend with charm and details that bring childhood dreams to life. 1998 brought a new development called *Elf Land™*, to the *North Pole*. This series is comprised of slightly smaller buildings, and the first introductions are businesses that

Filled with Christmas treasures, "Silver Bells Christmas Shop" from The Original Snow Village® *celebrates the 25th anniversary of Department 56®, Inc.*

Several North Pole Woods *mail carriers put their stamp of approval on the "Oakwood Post Office Branch."*

provide services specifically suited to elves. New for 2000 and nestled in the forest at the edge of the *North Pole* is a treetop community called *North Pole Woods*. High above the everyday world, this woodsy town is home to suppliers and cottage industries, all with the goal of providing the raw materials and services to keep the North Pole running smoothly. Made of resin, these pieces are highly detailed, and each has just a touch of whimsy.

Disney Parks Village Series was welcomed in 1994 to *The Heritage Village Collection*. Replicas of Disney theme park buildings are accompanied by Mickey and Minnie Mouse, along with other coordinated accessories. The *Disney Parks Village Series* retired in May, 1996. It was the first complete series to be retired by Department 56.

Alpine Village was the first Village in *The Heritage Village Collection* to introduce licensed pieces. In 1999, the Village echoed with the *Sound of Music®* when buildings based on the popular musical of the same name were added to the Village.

As the Villages began to grow, limited edition pieces were added along with trees, street lamps, and accessory groupings to complete the nostalgic charm of each collection. Every lighted piece is stamped on the bottom with its designated series name, title, year of introduction, and Department 56, Inc. logo to assure authenticity.

The *Historical Landmark Series*™ debuted in 1997 with reproductions of well-known architectural structures that can be displayed alone, as a vignette or incorporated into an existing Village.

In 1998, *Literary Classics*™ was created to honor the important role classic literature plays in our lives.

Seasons Bay™, the newest Village from Department 56, was introduced in 1998. This series began with six

◆ lighted pieces inspired by a nostalgic turn-of-the-century resort. It is the first Village designed without snow, so it can be displayed throughout the year. Carefully hand-painted pewter accessories complement the turn-of-the-century shingle style buildings.

SNOWBABIES™ ENCHANT COLLECTORS

Since their introduction, *Snowbabies*™ have enchanted collectors around the world and have brightened the imagination of all of us who celebrate the gentle play of youthful innocence. These adorable, whimsical figurines have bright blue eyes and creamy white snowsuits covered by flakes of new fallen snow. A bit of color has been added to special pieces in the *Snowbabies Guest Collection*™, which debuted in the fall of 1998. The first guest was Dorothy with her dog Toto from *The Wizard of Oz*, celebrating the 60th anniversary of this film. This series has been enthusiastically received by collectors, and with the addition of more guests, the series now totals six.

In 1989, a line of pewter miniature *Snowbabies* was introduced. These tiny treasures are made to reflect many of the same designs as their bisque counterparts, and come packaged in little gift boxes sprinkled with gold stars.

The newest *Snowbabies,* introduced in 2000, are made of soft plush material. Four styles include a penguin, sled dog and polar bears in two sizes.

Collectors can enhance their enjoyment of collecting *Snowbabies* by joining the Snowbabies Friendship Club™. Membership benefits include a welcome gift, four issues of the "Friendship News" newsletter, the opportunity to purchase club exclusive *Snowbabies* figurines and merchandise, as well as invitations to special events.

OTHER FAVORITES FROM DEPARTMENT 56

Another Department 56 collection, *Silhouette Treasures*™, consists of highly detailed white porcelain figurines, many with pewter, silver or gold accents.

The springtime favorites — *Snowbunnies®* — appear in creamy bisque porcelain with delicate touches of pink on their ears and on bows tied around their necks. Their little bunny suits are covered with tiny bisque crystals, and their cheerful faces are carefully hand-painted.

Alice in Wonderland pours a spot of tea for a Snowbabies *friend in "Tea For Two," part of* The Guest Collection.

The *Candle Crown*™ *Collections* are the newest collections from Department 56. Functional as well as beautiful, these exquisitely designed candle extinguishers are designed in keeping with those of 150 years ago. The first series includes "Alice in Wonderland" modeled after the original illustrations by Sir John Tenniel. Others series include "The Nutcracker Suite," "The Wizard of Oz" and "Christmas Carol."

In addition to collectibles, Department 56, Inc. continues to develop colorful and innovative giftware, as well as ongoing lines to celebrate spring, Easter, Halloween and Christmas, including many beautiful ◆ Christmas ornaments.

Department 56®, Inc.
P.O. Box 44456
Eden Prairie, MN
55344-1456

Phone:
800-LIT-TOWN
800-548-8696

Web Site:
www.dept56.com

E-mail:
Mslittown@dept56.com

DEPARTMENT 56®, INC.

Melody In Motion Figurines Engage the Emotions

*M*elody In Motion is more than just another collection of figurines; their universal appeal goes much deeper. Since the first piece was created in 1985, collectors have regularly shared stories of the tremendous satisfaction they get from the viewing, listening and displaying of their *Melody In Motion* figurines. According to Ru Kato, creative director, "When the owners talk to us, they never speak in commercial terms. They talk about how the figurines add a pleasurable aspect to their life. For this reason alone," says Kato, "every piece we produce must be capable of bringing a smile to each viewer's face when the figurine moves and the music plays."

All *Melody In Motion* pieces are a combination of exquisite craftsmanship and precision technology. Handcrafted and hand-painted, all figurines begin with Kato who, thanks to a family heritage that includes writers, movie directors and painters, has artistry in his blood. A multi-faceted individual, Kato often wears many hats as he directs the artistic development and production of the *Melody In Motion* figurines. Preferring a hands-on approach, he creates the original concept and selects the music and movements appropriate to the storyline. The design passes on to a designer who creates a drawing; a musical director who writes an arrangement; and a sculptor who makes the clay models for the basic figurine and its separate moving parts; and, finally onto an engineer who designs the internal mechanism.

Each figurine is carefully hand-assembled, adjusted and fitted with a state-of-the-art electronic motor. That single motor drives a tape player that plays the music and sets in motion a series of cams and levers that produce the figurine's movements. All parts are custom-made for that particular style of figurine, with each mechanism designed and engineered to achieve the specific

"Nocturne," the 1999 gift for Collectors Society Members, is a non-animated and non-musical figurine that is a prized collectible for club members.

movement. Each part is hand-painted and fitted with precision mechanical and electronic devices. All tolled, there are over 150 individual pieces that combine to bring the creative tableau to life.

WILLIE, THE "STAR" OF *MELODY IN MOTION*

Fifteen years ago, Willie, the "star" of *Melody In Motion* was born. Originally designed by master sculptor Seiji Nakane (now retired), Willie was crafted as a free-spirited, lovable whistling hobo that could go anywhere, be anything. With the help of concept artists, every *Melody In Motion* figurine presents a tableau that tells a story and provides a little something special for every viewer. In fact, when it comes to entertainment, it's hard to find a more delightful cast of characters than the 145-plus members of the *Melody In Motion* family.

Over the years, *Melody In Motion* has introduced new Willies as well as other characters with broad appeal. Of particular interest to collectors are the showpiece carousels, complete with moving horses, popular carousel music, masterful scroll work and exquisite detail. "The Grand Carousel" recently retired with a market value exceeding $3,000! Another popular collection features handcrafted pieces with built-in clocks. Depending on the piece, the clock can be switched on manually or set to play every hour on the hour. Or, the clock can be set as an alarm.

"Cheers!," the 1999 Melody In Motion members-only piece, celebrates Oktoberfest! As Willie raises his mug of beer in an appropriate toast to both the event and the revelers, a whistled version of "Beer Barrel Polka" sets the mood.

A TRULY PERSONALIZED COLLECTION

Every year, *Melody In Motion* presents Willie and friends in a variety of tableaus – often in response to collectors' requests. In fact, many recent pieces are a result of collectors sharing their thoughts about what they love about their collections.

In response to the popularity of the clock collection, *Melody In Motion* recently introduced a special clock base that connects to an assortment of *Melody In Motion* figurines. By using this clock base with any figurine whose base does not exceed 6" wide by 5" deep, collectors can create their own "custom" clock. Once the figurine is in place, its tune will play every hour

on the hour. As with all clocks, there is a switch to turn the mechanism off.

And because collectors have expressed a particular delight with whistled tunes, the *Melody In Motion* collection has expanded to include more figurines that feature whistled versions of familiar music. Recent whistling releases include "Clockpost Clown," "Balloon Clown," "Just for You" and "Willie the Hunter."

Another figurine that successfully incorporated collector feedback is "The Wedding Couple." Originally issued in the U.S. and then reissued for collectors in Japan and Europe, each plays the same wonderful rendition of "We've Only Just Begun" – a tune selected as the result of a collectors' poll!

THE *MELODY IN MOTION* LICENSED LINE

The *Melody In Motion* collection also includes a host of licensed products. To date, four Coke-brand musical figurines have been created: two 6,000 piece limited edition Santas inspired by the illustrator Haddon Sundblom; "Gone Fishin," a piece based on a Coca-Cola commissioned original Norman Rockwell painting; and a 6,000 piece limited edition based on the popular advertising character, the Coca-Cola Polar Bear.

A second licensed line is based on classic episodes from the TV comedy series, "I Love Lucy." The first Lucy figurine, "The Candy Factory – I Love Lucy," captures the hilarity of the famous job-switching episode in which Lucy tries frantically to

Crafted in glazed porcelain, and standing 12" tall, "Wedding Couple" rotates as the tune, "We've Only Just Begun," plays.

This "1999 Limited Edition Santa" captures the fun and happy-go-lucky days of fast sledding down a favorite hill. A "real-life" dialogue between Santa and his young companion adds a touch of realism.

keep up with a conveyor belt of freshly made chocolates. "Vitameatavegamin," released in 1997, portrays Lucy's intoxicating encounter with an alcohol-laced pep tonic as she "spoons her way to health." Both licensed "I Love Lucy" figurines showcase the theme music from the original television show, while "Vitameatavegamin" includes actual dialogue from the original television episode.

According to Kato, "Our licensed products have helped us reach new and different types of consumers, and different age groups." He adds, "Believe it or not, a lot of our new customers have come from the younger generation who know 'I Love Lucy' from watching reruns on Nick at Night."

EVERYONE LOVES SANTA — HE'S ALWAYS A SELL OUT

Almost every year since 1986, *Melody In Motion* has introduced a "Limited Edition Santa Claus." And each year that figurine has sold out and been retired. Continuing the heritage of *Melody In Motion*, these Santas add another dimension to the *Melody In Motion* slogan "see me move, hear my melody." Aside from life-like movements and wonderful studio-quality music, recent Santas have the added feature of a voice-over soundtrack that captures true-to-life dialogue between Santa and his young companions. The music is punctuated by "oohs and ahhs," squeals of delight, jingle bells, and of course, a few "Ho Ho Hos," helping listeners uniquely celebrate the Yuletide season.

SHARE IN THE *MELODY IN MOTION* MAGIC

To support the collection of the fine musicals, collectors are invited to join the Melody In Motion Collectors Society. Annual dues are $27.50, and members have the opportunity to purchase exclusive figurines, as well as receive a complimentary subscription to the "Melody Notes" newsletter, the latest Melody In Motion Yearbook, and a special savings coupon, among other items. As an enrollment bonus, members receive a distinctive hand-painted figurine that is not available for purchase anywhere else.

Whether a collection is being started or added to, membership in the Melody In Motion Collectors Society is an informative and rewarding investment.

DESERT SPECIALTIES, LTD.

Desert Specialties, Ltd.
6280 S. Valley View Blvd.
Suite 404
Las Vegas, NV 89118

Phone:
702-253-0450

Fax:
702-253-1871

Web Site:
www.melodyinmotion.com

E-mail:
desert3900@aol.com

McMillans Build Mountains With *Molenniums*

When Graeme McMillan wrote at the tender age of seven that he would like to be a salesman "just like my Dad," it was inevitable that father and son would team up in business one day. Graeme's father, Robin McMillan, has been in the gift trade for 35 years. He has sold famous names, such as Caithness Glass, and built up a business specializing in collectible pewter thimbles.

As a young adult, Graeme tried to "resist his destiny" for a time, and pursued a career as an Environmental Planner. Although he was an honors graduate in this field, he found that his post as a city architect didn't challenge his creative side. Before long, Graeme decided to join his father as an independent sales agent working for several manufacturers at one time.

Adorable moles star in The Molenniums collection from Doverdale Design.

This was a good starting point for the pair, but what they really desired was to set up their own company as Robin had done so many years before. First, however, they needed a product, and it had to be a good one if they were to survive in a fiercely competitive market.

MOLES SURFACE AS THE IDEAL SUBJECT

During one of the pair's many meetings in search of a product idea, Graeme was glancing out of Robin's window. The younger McMillan found himself admiring

The whimsical wits behind The Molenniums: Doverdale Design founders Robin (left) and Graeme McMillan.

the neatly manicured lawn in the sleepy English village where his father lives. In the middle of the grass, like a mountain in a sea of green, was a molehill!

Graeme felt instant inspiration. Moles had not yet been used as the stars of a collectible series. And while these creatures were obviously cute, they also seemed to be somewhat mystical creatures because they are rarely seen. There was no limit to the underground world that could be created for them!

Having decided on the subject matter, it was important to come up with a memorable name for the series, and here Robin's word-play skills came into their own. Thus on a spring day in 1996, *The Molenniums* were born!

THE MAKING OF THE *MOLENNIUMS*

Several talented sculptors replied to the McMillans' ad to create a series of 25 three-inch figurines, but on meeting them it was obvious that there was only one choice. Joe Bailey had sculpted for several famous companies but was now looking for a new challenge. His sense of humor was so similar to Robin and Graeme's that it was as if they had known each other for years!

Nothing official had been decided, yet Joe was so inspired by the idea of *The Molenniums* that when father and son next turned up at his studio, he had already created the first-ever *Molennium* – "Geronemole."

The figure sitting before them in soft wax was so obviously "right" that Joe was officially chosen as sculptor for *The Molenniums* – then and there.

Thus began a process of sculpting the initial series of 25 *Molennium* characters, each inspired by a mole name — for example, "Double Mole Seven," the secret agent, and "Moler," the dentist. "Molein," the wizard, is a play on Merlin of King Arthur's Camelot (or is that Camolelot!), and the commonly available English painkiller, "paracetamol," inspires "Paracetemole," the doctor.

Joe worked long and hard to produce the first 25 *Molennium* characters in time for the launch of the new company, Doverdale Design, in January 1997. Doverdale is the name of the village parish in which Robin lived at

the time. While Joe created the figurines, Robin and Graeme worked hard raising the financing for the launch, obtaining premises to work from and securing everything necessary to manufacture the product.

THE *MOLENNIUMS* MAKE THE CLUB SCENE

Doverdale began 1997 with an untested product and no customers. It ended that year with 350 retail accounts and the first members of the newly formed Molennium Collectors Club.

The Club is a great barometer of the success of the series, and after just three years, its membership numbers almost 3,000 – and is currently growing at the rate of 30 to 40 new members a week. The Club represents a large cross-section of the community with young and old and all manners of professions enjoying the innocent fun that the figurines represent.

Members of the Club don't just enjoy the figurines, however. Another important factor is the ongoing story of "The Molevern Molenniums." The collectors follow the story (written by brother and sister Steve and Julie Middleton) of a motley bunch of *Molenniums* under the leadership of "Old King Mole'" in their efforts to protect "The Moley Grail" from the clutches of the evil "Molevolent."

Twice each year, the company has added new *Molennium*s to the range, and in 1998, they launched their first-ever limited edition entitled "Formoler One." Displaying the inept "Moleboro Formoler One" team, it was limited to just 600 pieces and quickly sold out. Along with the limited editions, the first-ever retirements were announced at the end of 1999.

CROSSING THE ATLANTIC WITH *MOLENNIUMS*

Having established themselves as a force in the British market, Graeme and Robin set their sights on the American market. They frequently had calls from

The charming Panda to Your Heart *collection will surely find their way into the hearts of collectors everywhere.*

American collectors who had visited the United Kingdom and had bought a *Molennium* while there, but when they launched their web site in 1999, they soon found them-selves shipping orders out to the U.S.A.

The die was cast, and in January 2000 with the "New

◆ The Spotniks, *a wacky group of three-eyed green aliens, have been "spotted" on earth.*

Molennium" barely started, Graeme set off for the Atlanta Gift Mart where he began to establish the growing network of American dealers. It has been a steady process, but Doverdale plans to have good U.S. coverage within three years. And with the web site, collectors are always able to increase their collection wherever they live.

THE *MOLENNIUM* FUTURE

Not content to rest on their laurels, Graeme and Robin have embarked on an ambitious program to bring some of their many other ideas to the marketplace. The spark for the idea always starts with father and son who convey their thoughts to Joe. These meetings are a frenzy of laughter and sketching as the humor shines through in the first visuals. Joe then sets about sculpting the new figures, which are then cast and brought vividly to life with the expert touch of Heather Larose, the color designer.

As well as adding to *The Molenniums,* the team has created two entirely new ranges for the year 2000. *Panda to Your Heart* is a charming collection of panda characters, mostly inspired by Robin's four grandchildren, two of whom are Graeme's. The pastel colors chosen by Heather make the figurines look good enough to eat.

With the second new series, the "wild kid" in the whole team has come out. *The Spotniks* are a vagabond group of three-eyed green aliens who are searching the galaxy for their planet's dwindling life-fuel, GLUBE. The crew of five is then "spotted" trying out various activities on earth, such as "Spotted Surfing" or "Spotted in the Sixties." There is only one way to describe this series: wacky.

It doesn't stop there either. This year, the company announced the birth of "Molly - The Molennium Baby." Each year Doverdale will produce a limited edition figurine charting Molly's life until at least her 21st birthday! This will be a unique series for collectors to own if they can secure one of the first editions, which will guarantee their being able to purchase the subsequent releases.

As Graeme McMillan says in conclusion, "Over this period, the existing series will grow, and new and exciting collections will be created. You won't just become a *Molennium* collector, you will be a Doverdale collector!"

DOVERDALE DESIGN

Doverdale Design
Lowland House,
Green Street
Kidderminster,
Worchestershire
DY10 1HN
England

Tel/Fax:
011-441-562-827113

Web Site:
www.doverdaledesign.com

E-mail:
graeme@doverdaledesign.com

Snow Buddies™, *Living Stone*® and XPRES® Combine Creativity and Nostalgia

A relatively new name in the gift and collectibles industry, The Encore Group, Inc. has made a significant impact at the beginning of a new century and millennium. Its introduction of *Snow Buddies*™ has been called a phenomenon, as the enchanting little lumpy snowpeople in their silver-blue caps, scarves and mittens charm and captivate with their antics and activities in this unique collection that has captured the imagination of collectors throughout North America. It is easy to identify an authentic *Snow Buddies* figure: each genuine *Snow Buddies* piece is imprinted with a unique Snowflake on the toe of its boot!

When *Snow Buddies* made their debut in stores just before Christmas 1998, the response exceeded all expectations. Dealers found the momentum did not slow down after the holidays, and throughout 1999, collectors returned again and again to add to their collections. It soon became apparent that the whimsical figurines were

Like many of the new lighted buildings in the Snow Buddies Snowville series, "The Snowville Church" has a blue "knitted" rooftop.

in demand for year-round collecting enjoyment. The dilemma for The Encore Group was how to preserve the character of the collection as jovial, playful snowpeople and create more non-seasonal pieces. It was then that a miracle was born!

DR. VON SNOW'S FORTUNATE DISCOVERY

The mythical – and renowned – scientist Dr. Von Snow was lost during an expedition and then rescued by *Snow Buddies*, who brought him to their little village of *Snowville*™ – a very well-hidden community nestled in the protection of a cool valley that rests between the Great Woods and the High Mountains. Using their own home-made remedies and the warmth of their hearts, the *Snow Buddies* restore Dr. Von Snow to good health. Whereupon, he dedicated his research to finding a way to prevent the unfortunate meltdown of *Snow Buddies* when they leave the protection of *Snowville* and wander into the warmth of sunlight. After trial and error, Dr. Von Snow perfected the "No Melt Formula Solution" that the snowpeople can brush on themselves before entering the outside world!

SNOWVILLE AGLOW WITH LIGHTED BUILDINGS

As a result of this miracle, *Snow Buddies* made their 2000 debut in a series called *Valentine Buddies*™ — *Melt Your Heart,* a heartwarming collection for expressing love and affection; in *Springtime Buddies*™ — a delightful tribute to the season of awakening in the forest; and *Boo Buddies*™ — a collection of fearless, frolicking fall and

A toboggan ride with friends can lead to a "Crash Landing" in this Snow Buddies *vignette.*

Halloween scenes. With the advent of the "No Melt Solution," The Encore Group has promised still more year-round excursions for the *Snow Buddies* characters.

Also, in 2000, The Encore Group introduced the first lighted buildings in the village of *Snowville* – official residence of all true *Snow Buddies*. At the same time, the individual identities of the characters were born. Each of the buildings has a little story about its history and community role, and each of the characters also has his or her story that accompanies the figure. The buildings are whimsical and imaginative, reflecting their function in the village. Each one has a knitted blue roof, no doubt created in the "Snowville School of Knitting," under the able supervision of headmistress "Blizzy." Outsiders often ask her where all the blue wool comes from, and the answer is quite simple. Sometime ago, several little lambs were rescued in the deep snow of the Great Woods and brought to *Snowville*. It was so cold that their coats turned blue, and ever since, each new litter of lambs has the same soft blue color, thus giving the School all the blue wool it needs to keep knitting!

A favorite is the "Sno-Cone Shop," which specializes in Snowberry Swirl – a particular choice of "Everest," a somewhat over-endowed *Snow Buddies* family member, often spotted with a cone in each hand or an overfilled platter from the "all you can eat" buffet. Then there's "Avalanche," a family member whose feet have grown faster than he has – causing him to tumble into any number of embarrassing and unpredictable situations. The "Snowville Sports Shop" is run by "Blizzy's" husband "Flurry," the son of "Grandpa Frostbite," patriarch of the village and one of its founders. "Flurry" and "Blizzy" live in the charming "Home Sweet Home" lighted house. As you can see, the village is very intertwined with the residents! In all, the initial 2000 introduction of *Snowville* includes eight buildings, plus snow-capped accessories to complement the setting.

"BLIZZY" AND "COUSIN SLICK" MAKE THEIR DEBUT

Snow Buddies made its debut at the International Collectible Expositions® in 2000, where the first full-size costume characters brought the images to life. "Blizzy" and "Cousin Slick" – the "coolest dude in *Snowville*," are also making appearances at a select number of retail stores.

Alas, not all *Snow Buddies* are judicious about applying the "No-Melt Solution." As a result, several of the original pieces have "melted away" – retired forever from the collection. From time to time, other "melt-downs" will be announced to retailers and collectors. The *Snow Buddies* collection is sold through a network of authorized dealers throughout the United States and Canada

MORE POPULAR LINES FROM THE ENCORE GROUP

The lifelike *Living Stone*® collection of animals and wildlife is the oldest division of The Encore Group. Many of the pieces have been created by contributing artist Cliff

"Cousin Slick" is featured on this Snow Buddies character mug from XPRES Division of The Encore Group, Inc.

This family scene by Living Stone®, titled "Shell Game," depicts wolf cubs exploring the mystery of a turtle.

Sanders, a gifted Native American sculptor. The collection includes a wide range of both domestic and untamed animals, in sizes ranging from miniatures to full-size sculptures. Since 1992, the talents of Cliff Sanders have enchanted collectors of birds and animals for his true-life portrayals.

The majestic *Fireside* series features animals up to 30-inches high – dogs, bears, tigers and puma family – in realistic poses. Each one is hand-cast from the original sculpture, then meticulously hand-painted to the exact specifications of the artist. The result is an amazing realism that earns the *Living Stone* trademark of lifelike authenticity. Also new in 2000 is a series of wild animal mothers with their offspring called *Generations*. From a doe with her fawn to the white tiger with cub, the series presents the gift of motherhood in a new light.

The newest addition to The Encore Group is XPRES® Corporation, a North Carolina-based company that became a part of The Encore Group in early 2000. XPRES is a well-established maker of dimensional mugs – using an exclusive technique that has made the company the largest producer in the United States – as well as other specialty items. Its collection of familiar licensed characters which include Warner Bros. Pictures' *Looney Tunes*®, *Wizard of Oz*™ and *Scooby-Doo*™, as well as a wide range of sports-related licensed gift items, has made XPRES a leader in the giftware marketplace.

As a result of its strong position in successful licensed lines, Warner Bros. Consumer Products chose XPRES as a licensee for the new Harry Potter movie, *Harry Potter and the Sorcerer's Stone*, scheduled for release by Warner Bros. Pictures in November 2001. The series of best-selling children's books by British author J.K. Rowling has swept the world, and Warner Bros. Pictures will produce two films based on the first two books. XPRES' first product release will be in late 2000.

The Encore Group, Inc.
P.O. Box 500780
San Diego, CA 92150-0780

Phone:
800-621-3647

Fax:
800-929-9653

Web Site:
www.the-encore-group.com

E-mail:
sales@the-encore-group.com

THE ENCORE GROUP, INC.

Collectible Success 40 Years in the Making

Based in Itasca, Illinois, Enesco Group, Inc. boasts more than 40 years as a leader in the $10 billion gift and collectibles industry, producing fine gifts, collectibles and home décor accessories.

The company's success, catapulted 22 years ago by the famous *Precious Moments* collection, continues to grow with more collectibles that are known and loved around the world.

FOUNDING CHAIRMAN EUGENE FREEDMAN

Instrumental in the growth and success of Enesco Group, Inc. is Eugene Freedman, founding chairman. He joined Enesco in 1958, with the responsibilities for both sales and overseas product development. Freedman was elevated to a number of management positions before being named president and CEO of the company in the late 1960s. He was named to his current position in 1998.

Credited with the development of the *Precious Moments* collection by Enesco, Freedman discovered the artwork of artist Sam Butcher and transformed his two-dimensional art into today's popular three-dimensional figurine collection.

Freedman has been presented with a multitude of honors, including most recently the National Association of Limited Edition Dealers (NALED) "Special Recognition Award" in 1998. He was also awarded the Congressional Ellis Island Medal of Honor, the "International Collectible Achievement Award," and Epsilon Sigma Alpha's "International Vision Award," all in 1992. He also received the collectible industry's most prestigious award, the "Lee Benson Award," in 1988.

A beautiful addition to the Precious Moments collection is "Blessed Art Thou Amongst Women," featuring Madonna with Child.

Active in the community, both locally and nationally, Freedman is chairman of the National Easter Seal Society Partnership Board, national governor of the Boys & Girls Clubs of America, and vice-chairman of the Very Special Arts International Fund (VSAIF). He also serves on the Board of Directors of Opportunity, Inc. and C.A.U.S.E.S. (Child Abuse Unit for Studies and Educational Services).

PRECIOUS MOMENTS CONTINUES IMMENSE POPULARITY

One of the world's most popular collectibles, the *Precious Moments* collection was unveiled by Enesco in 1978, featuring 21 teardrop-eyed porcelain bisque figurines bearing inspirational messages.

Created by artist Sam Butcher, who had drawn the teardrop-eyed children for inspirational greeting cards,

Eternal optimism is displayed in this figure from the Cherished Teddies collection, Winfield – "Anything Is Possible When You Wish on a Star."

Precious Moments was the brainchild of Eugene Freedman. He convinced Butcher to allow Enesco to develop figures from the artwork. Freedman then turned Butcher's drawings over to Japanese Master Sculptor Yashuei Fujioka, who sculpted the first *Precious Moments* figurine, "Love One Another." The original 21 figurines were unveiled to retailers in the fall of 1978, followed by four more in 1979.

To help collectors learn more and share experiences about *Precious Moments*, Enesco launched the Precious Moments Collectors' Club® in 1981. Today, it boasts more than 200,000 members and 380 local club chapters nationwide. In 1985, the Precious Moments Birthday Club was introduced to teach children about the art of collecting. In 1998, Enesco launched the Precious Moments Fun Club, replacing the Birthday Club, providing collectors with additional benefits and opportunities for kids of all ages to enjoy all facets of *Precious Moments*.

PRECIOUS MOMENTS CELEBRATES WITH THE CARE-A-VAN

To celebrate the 20th anniversary of the collection, Enesco created the *Precious Moments* Care-A-Van, a 53' long traveling museum. In 1998, the Care-A-Van went on an eight-month tour across the United States, stopping in more than 200 cities to communicate the *Precious Moments'* message of loving, caring and sharing.

For the tour, Enesco partnered with Second Harvest, the nation's largest hunger relief organization, to sponsor food drives across the country. It donated 56,618 pounds of food, which Second Harvest distributed to local food banks across the country.

The Care-A-Van, featuring one-of-a-kind artwork, videos and items from Butcher's personal collection, continues to travel across the country.

HIGH HONORS FOR PRECIOUS MOMENTS

Precious Moments figurines have been recognized extensively by the collectibles and giftware industry. The collection has been honored with numerous awards, including a "Special Recognition Award" from NALED in 1998; "Ornament of the Year" in 1994, 1995 and 1996; "Figurine of the Year" in 1994 and "Collectible of the Year" in 1992. In 1992, NALED also named Sam Butcher "Artist of the Year." The Collectors' Club was honored by NALED for several years in a row as the "Collectors' Club of the Year."

In the 22 years since its debut, the *Precious Moments* collection has grown to include more figurines, as well as plates, bells, ornaments, photo frames, musicals and

home décor accessories. Within the collection, Enesco launched several lines, including *Sugar Town*, a porcelain village based on Sam Butcher's hometown; *Sammy's Circus*; the *Precious Moments "Forever True"* wedding line; *Little Moments*; the *Precious Moments Jewelry Collection* and the *Tender Tails®* plush.

Introduced in 1997, *Tender Tails* marked a new direction for Butcher and Enesco. The soft, poseable animals are available for "adoption," allowing "parents" to actually choose the name of their *Tender Tails* friend. The "parents" receive the "official" adoption papers, registered in the Enesco Tender Tails Nursery and a *Love and Care Guide*.

CHERISHED TEDDIES ARE TOP BEARS

Introduced by Enesco in 1992, the *Cherished Teddies* collection is one of the world's leading teddy bear collectibles. The collection debuted with 16 teddy bear figurines. Today, there are more than 600 figurines and accessories, including photo frames, jewelry, collector plates and clocks.

Each *Cherished Teddies* figurine has a unique name and a message of friendship and love. The names are chosen by the collection's creator, Priscilla Hillman, who often incorporates the names of collectors she meets at shows into her new creations.

Responding to the incredible success of the collection, Enesco formed the Cherished Teddies Club in 1995. Now Enesco's fastest growing collectors' club, the Cherished Teddies Club informs and entertains approximately 84,000 "membears" worldwide through special events, a club newsletter and "membears" only benefits.

In the Enesco tradition, *Cherished Teddies* has been honored with numerous awards by the collectibles industry. In its first year of eligibility, 1993, *Cherished Teddies* was named "Collectible of the Year" by NALED. Other honors have come from *Collector Editions* magazine; *Teddy Bear and Friends* magazine; and Parkwest Publications. Hillman herself has been honored as NALED's "Artist of the Year" in 1994 and Parkwest Publication's "Outstanding New Artist" in 1993.

New from Mary's Moo Moos collection is "Famoolies Grow With Loving Hearts," showing a close-knit dad, mom and baby cow cuddled up for the night.

POPULAR ARTISTS ARE PART OF ENESCO'S SUCCESS

While Enesco has made a name with its world-famous *Precious Moments* and *Cherished Teddies* collections, it also offers many more collections created by talented artists that appeal to a variety of collectors.

Whether it's a heartwarming reindeer, a whimsical cow or a chocolate bunny, artist Mary Rhyner-Nadig brings to life colorful animal figurines. She made her mark on the industry with *Mary's Moo Moos*, a humorous collection of cows with "pun-filled" titles. Now in its sixth year, *Mary's Moo Moos* has consistently been honored as the leading cow-themed collectible.

David Winter is the creator and sculptor of the *David Winter Cottages* collection, enjoyed by collectors for nearly 21 years. Winter draws inspiration from a variety of sources and takes his camera with him wherever he goes, always keeping an eye out for interesting or unusual architecture.

Linda Lindquist Baldwin is the creator of *Belsnickle*, a collection of vintage Santa Claus figures. She is also behind the *Snowsnickle, Broomsnickle* and *Haresnickle* collections. Baldwin's artistic career began in 1986 when she attended a garage sale and picked up a book, *Old Antique Santa Collections,* for a nickel. She was so intrigued by the 18th and 19th century European Santas pictured in the book that she wanted to purchase one for herself. However, it was more economically feasible for her to make her own out of a home-made papier mâché formula. She began selling the figures at craft fairs. Soon demand for her creations increased, resulting in the birth of the *Belsnickle* collection.

Since 1989, artist Ray Day has created miniature sculptures based on American architecture for Lilliput Lane's *American Landmarks* collection. Day researches each new sculpture by traveling throughout the United States in search of structures and landmarks representative of each state.

In 1998, Enesco expanded its licensing agreement with Mary Engelbreit, a renowned artist who has been dubbed the "Norman Rockwell of the Nineties," to include home décor and figurine collections featuring her popular characters.

ENESCO ENTERS CYBERSPACE THROUGH WEB SITE

In 1997, Enesco was one of the first collectible companies to launch a site on the World Wide Web with the debut of www.enesco.com.

The site features a variety of informational tools for collectors, including a Daily News section, a "Product Spotlight" section previewing products not yet available in stores, and a special section devoted exclusively to club members.

Based on Enesco's history and prominence, more growth and success will surely follow as the company continues giving back to the community and giving collectors new and appealing collectibles.

Enesco Group, Inc.
225 Windsor Drive
Itasca, IL 60143

Phone:
1-800-NEAR-YOU
1-800-632-7968

Fax:
630-875-5350

Web Sites:
www.enesco.com
www.enescoclubs.com

ENESCO GROUP, INC.

A Continuing Celebration in Fine Glass

The year: 2005. The event: an extravaganza to mark the 100th anniversary of Fenton Art Glass. Today – with only 5 years to go before this remarkable milestone, Fenton family members and artists are working together in a concerted effort to continue their company's rise as one of America's leading creators of collector's items.

Each year, Fenton introduces new collectibles in the spirit of the company's long-standing philosophy: to produce unique glass treatments, employing the age-old techniques of hand craftsmanship that have been passed down from generation to generation.

Figurines are an important part of the Fenton offering including these delightful Santas.

One of the first colors produced by the new company was called Chocolate Glass, and in late 1907, Fenton introduced iridescent pressed glass – 50 years later this glass has become known as Carnival Glass. High quality Carnival Glass now sells for as much as $600 to $4,500 a piece. Recently, a rare piece sold for $22,500. Iridescent glass was still selling in the 1920s, but it was made in delicate pastel colors with very little pattern in a treatment called "stretch glass."

Today, there are 12 family members working in the management of The Fenton Art Glass Company. With over 600 employees, the company is now the largest producer of hand-made colored glass giftware in the United States.

AN ARRAY OF JEWEL-LIKE FENTON GLASS CREATIONS

Fenton Art Glass is renowned for creating beautiful and unique colors in glass, including exotic varieties in rich shades such as Cranberry, Mulberry and Burmese. Its fiery Opalescent glass gleams in transparent colored glass that shades to opaque white.

With an appreciation of the past and an eye to the future, Fenton brings back the rare collectible treatments of bygone eras, while continually developing new and exciting colors to coordinate with current decorating trends.

At Fenton, each piece of glassware is an individual creation from the skilled hands of glassworking artisans. As seasoned collectors know, only an unfeeling machine can produce "glass armies" of unvarying detail. Much of the charm of true Fenton Art Glass comes from its stretched and fluted shapes that can only be created by hand.

Like most experts, the master glassworkers of Fenton make their craft appear simple. Even so, if you watch the experts making Fenton glass, you will observe the hundreds of appraising glances that carefully assay each piece as it passes from hand to hand. Many of those looks are clearly punctuated with an unmistakable expression of pride that declares, "That's mine. I created it."

Fenton has its own mould shop, which enhances the company's ability to develop and introduce new designs. Patterns and designs are chipped into the cast iron moulds by hand. Many Fenton creations are painted by hand by individual artists who proudly sign each piece.

SPECIAL FENTON OFFERINGS INTRIGUE COLLECTORS

Each year, Fenton Art Glass produces new editions for several popular series in strictly limited editions. These include the *Family Signature Series, Historical Collection,*

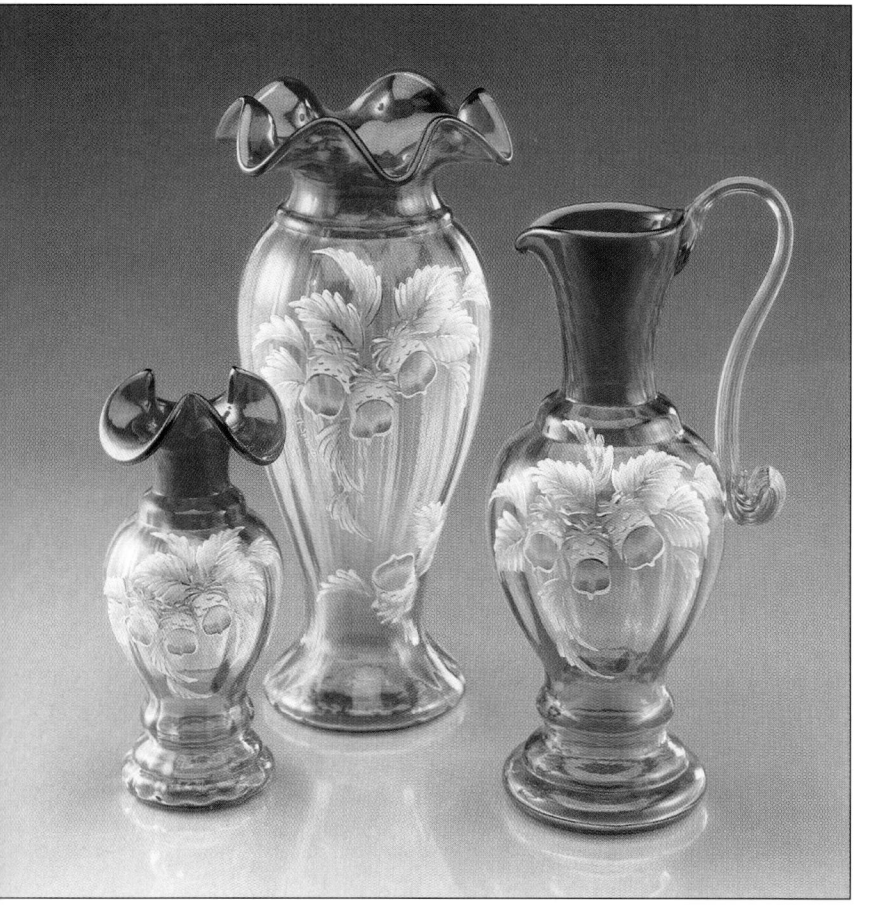

For 1999, The Historic Collection featured the historically significant color, Gold Amberina, hand-painted with open seedpods tucked among ferns.

A FAMILY OF INNOVATIVE GLASS ARTISTS

The Fenton Art Glass Company was founded in 1905 by Frank L. Fenton and his brother, John, in an old glass factory building in Martins Ferry, Ohio. Here, they painted decorations on glass blanks made by other firms. Before long, the Fentons found that they were having trouble getting the glass they wanted when they wanted it, so they decided to produce their own. The first glass from the Fenton factory in Williamstown, West Virginia, was made on January 2, 1907.

Each year a small grouping of very special pieces are created by Fenton's designers for the Connoisseur Collection.

Connoisseur Collection, Collectible Eggs, and *Christmas, Valentine's Day* and *Easter* limited editions.

The *Family Signature Series* includes a few select pieces which represent the glassworker's and decorator's finest creations. Classic moulds from the past inspire the *Historical Collection* pieces, all made in unique colors and treatments. The *Connoisseur Collection* features a small grouping of art objects made in exotic glass treatments.

For *Christmas,* Fenton produces an annual limited edition collection including a plate, bell, fairy light and lamp — all entirely hand-painted. For *Valentine's Day,* Fenton introduces new items each year in the Mary Gregory style of painting. Mouth-blown eggs and hand-pressed collectible eggs are showcased in Fenton's *Easter* offerings.

What's more, Fenton Showcase Dealers now may offer two exclusive Fenton items each year.

FENTON COLLECTORS BENEFIT BY KNOWLEDGE OF GLASS MARKINGS

The Handler's Mark, Decorator's Signature and Fenton Logo represent three markings that "savvy" Fenton collectors should know. A "Handler's Mark" – different for each craftsman – is applied to each Fenton basket by the highly skilled person who attaches the handle. The "Decorator's Signature" appears on each hand-painted piece, and the "Fenton Logo" is placed on each piece of the company's glass to forever mark it as authentically Fenton.

Fenton logos vary slightly, depending upon the era when the piece was made and what type of glass it represents. These markings typically help collectors to authenticate their holdings and provide unequivocal proof of the piece's value when collectors are evaluating potential purchases on the secondary market.

THE GLASS MESSENGER ENHANCES FENTON COLLECTING

Fenton invites collectors to subscribe to its collector publication, *The Glass Messenger.* For a subscription price of just $12.00, collectors receive four colorful issues of *The Glass Messenger,* along with a decorative storage binder, and the opportunity to purchase an exclusive piece of Fenton glass which has been designed for and is available only to subscribers. *The Glass Messenger* gives collectors an insider's look at the intricate, specialized processes involved in creating hand-made art glass, provides a priority opportunity to view new products, and fascinates with the rich history of Fenton Glass and stories about the Fenton family and the company's colorful employees.

Collectors may also join one of the two national organizations: The Fenton Art Glass Collectors of America (FAGCA) and the National Fenton Glass Society (NFGS).

Collectors visiting the Williamstown, West Virginia, facility can take regularly scheduled tours of the glass-making process and visit the Fenton Museum. Collectors are invited to call the Fenton Gift Shop at (304) 375-7772 for specifics on the free tours.

THE FENTON TRADITION: BORN OF A PROUD GLASSMAKING HISTORY

For three millennia, glass has delighted and served people in their homes, their industries and their places of worship. The first industry in the American colonies was a hand glass shop started at Jamestown, Virginia, in 1608. In America, glassware reached a new zenith during the last half of the 1800s, as a newly united nation started to realize its proud and powerful destiny.

Subscribers to Fenton's Glass Messenger quarterly publication, are eligible to purchase the annual "Subscriber Exclusive," hand-painted, numbered, and signed by a member of the Fenton family.

It is this venerable tradition of the glassmaker's art which is painstakingly recreated and preserved in Fenton Art Glass. Now, as the company approaches their Centennial as a family-owned company, the Fenton family takes pride in the fact that Fenton glass has itself become a modern American tradition. To even the casual admirer, each piece of Fenton hand-made glass reflects the affection and care that has gone into its making. No other gift seems quite as intimate as a work of Fenton glass in its ability to convey its maker's commitment to excellence, and its giver's regard. To those who collect, display and use Fenton Art Glass pieces, this may be the most important quality of all.

Fenton Art Glass
700 Elizabeth Street
Williamstown, WV 26187

Phone:
304-375-6122

Fax:
304-375-7833

Web Site:
www.fentonartglass.com

E-mail:
askfenton@fentonartglass.com

Emmett Kelly, Jr. Leads a Dynamic Line-up

Setting high standards, exceeding expectations and offering collectibles with enduring qualities and reasonable prices are considered business "musts" at Flambro Imports, where keeping collectors happy is "Job One." This philosophy has helped build long-term success for the company, founded in 1965 by Louis and Stanley Flamm. Back then, the brothers began with a simple plan: to buy gifts from importers that they could, in turn, sell to American businesses as promotional items and give-aways.

So fruitful was this venture that the Flamms soon entered the importing business for themselves. Flambro continued to import inexpensive promotional items until the 1970s, when it began purchasing higher quality giftware from Taiwan. During this time, most of the less expensive ceramic factories turned to Taiwan rather than Japan, since the labor market could still support a low-cost, yet high-quality product. Flambro soon became a stabilizing force in the Taiwanese gift market, serving as U.S. representative to the Taiwan Tao Tsu Ceramics Manufacturers Association. Malaysia, Indonesia and China were added to the Flambro Imports' roster in the 1980s, and these countries still supply most of the company's products today.

"Birthday Parade" shows the wonderful Emmett Kelly, Jr. onboard his circus wagon with a monkey friend, while a baby elephant pulls the wagon and sports a blanket that proclaims, "Happy 75th Birthday."

The 2000 Emmett Kelly, Jr. Block Set contains "The Grand Parade" and "Kodak's Clown." This 2000 release is offered in a limited edition of 1,500 at a suggested retail price of $550.

THE ART OF "AMERICA'S FAVORITE CLOWN"

The ever-popular *Emmett Kelly, Jr. Collection*, featuring "America's Favorite Clown," has remained Flambro's top-selling collectible. "Emmett Kelly is a piece of Americana – a real American classic," says Allan Flamm, President of Flambro since the 1982 retirement of his father, Louis. "We had been producing porcelain clown figures before 1980, so when we had the opportunity to do Emmett Kelly, Jr., it gave us something we could base our designs on and add a little pizzazz. The products were successful from the get-go."

Many of the early limited edition pieces in the collection have soared on the secondary market. The line now includes porcelain figurines, ornaments, waterglobes and other gift accessories. To date, Flambro has introduced about 1,500 different designs, including nearly 75 limited edition figurines.

A MILLENNIAL LANDMARK

The year 2000 marks the transition into a new century for all of us. The year 2000 also heralds several landmarks for Emmett Kelly, Jr.'s long clowning career. Among the major events to celebrate is the 40th year anniversary of Emmett Kelly, Jr.'s career as a clown. It is also the 20th anniversary of the introduction of the EKJ product line of collectible figurines.

Flambro is introducing Emmett Kelly, Jr. products to celebrate all of these — the millennium, 40 years as a clown and 20 years as a collectible. It should be a time to remember for collectors and fans alike.

FLAMBRO SHOWCASES *PEANUTS*™ COLLECTION

In 1996, Flambro welcomed the *Peanuts*™ collection, introduced to coincide with the 45th anniversary of the comic strip and the 75th birthday of its creator, Charles Schulz. The premier collection included 12 colorful resin birthday figurines featuring Snoopy, Woodstock, Charlie Brown, Lucy and the whole gang of familiar characters.

After this first introduction, several new *Peanuts*™ products have been added to the line. These introductions include limited editions, *Snoopy Sports* figurines, Snoopy "personas" such as "Joe Cool," the "Scoutmaster" and other famous Snoopy impersonations. Flambro also introduced the *Life with Peanuts* figurine collection which showcases the entire *Peanuts* gang of characters. The latest introductions include the *Peanuts* "situational" figurines – each of which features two or more *Peanuts* characters in an interactive "scene" – all humorous and endearing.

MORE POPULAR LINES FROM FLAMBRO

In 1997, Flambro became the exclusive U.S. distributor for the *Willow Hall* collection of England. *Willow Hall* is inspired by Victorian ladies' hats, shoes, handbags and purses. Each piece is sculpted with attention to the smallest detail and meticulously hand-painted. These highly decorative and collectible designs are incorporated into covered trinket boxes, decorative boxes and brooches.

Later introductions have broadened the product category to include various boxes, a miniature cottage collection called *Willow Hall Way*, miniature shoes, hats and purses of the *Age of Elegance* and *Center Stage* lines, and *Willow Hall* dolls. The latest introduction is *A Secret Place Collection* – covered trinket boxes which appear as a "solid" product, but in reality are boxes with "secret" compartments.

In 1999, Flambro entered an agreement with Vanguard Furniture, Kathy Ireland™ and Stetson™ to produce and supply home accents and decorative accessories to complement both furniture collections.

The *Kathy Ireland Home Collection* skillfully merges sophistication with practicality. The collection is inspired by Ireland's worldwide travels, with many of the items evoking visions of the English countryside and gardens. The line is an eclectic group of vases, large pottery, cachepots, boxes, frames, ornaments, and more that capture the warmth and wonder that embodies the richness of England's history, while adding a twist of American allure.

Maintaining the tradition of the classic and beloved American West, while adding a 21st century tweak, is the *Stetson Home Collection*. Flambro's *Stetson* line of home décor products reflects the evolution of an American icon,

Reflecting the Age of Elegance, the "Sweet Sparkle" hat, shoe and purse, from The Willow Hall Collection, is bejeweled with a myriad of gemstones.

from its early Western roots to the enduring face of Americana. Old-world charm meets the new millennium in a variety of products that are the perfect accents to any room. Mirrors, boxes, candelabras, ice buckets, magazine racks, large pottery, and more will decorate the bar, bath, bed and living areas of a *Stetson* home.

To round out the lines of home décor products, Flambro has created its own signature line – *The Flambro Home Collection*. The collection includes an array of candleholders, vases, bowls, frames, decorative turkeys and chickens. As the popularity for home accent pieces continues to grow, so do the ideas and products for the Flambro home. 2001 will usher in *Fashion Solids* that will help keep Flambro in step with home décor trends.

A CLUB FOR FLAMBRO AFICIONADOS

Flambro also offers collectors a way to further enjoy their favorite collectibles through the Emmett Kelly, Jr. Collectors' Society. The EKJ Club provides members with a collectors' plaque, quarterly newsletter, binder, EKJ lapel pin, membership card, free registration of figurines, a full-color catalog, annual collector registry listing, and a toll-free collectors' service hotline 800-EKJ-CLUB (355-2582). Members also have the opportunity to purchase exclusive members-only figurines and attend special club-sponsored events.

Allan Flamm, sums up the company philosophy this way: "Over the years, we've tried to maintain a good balance of quality, design and value. We try to continually offer new products and, most importantly, keep our customers happy."

Flambro Imports offers a variety of collectible figurines featuring the unforgettable Peanuts™ *characters.*

Flambro Imports, Inc.
1530 Ellsworth
Industrial, SW
Atlanta, GA 30318

Phone:
800-352-6276

Fax:
404-352-2150

Web Site:
www.flambro.com

E-mail:
flambro@flambro.com

FLAMBRO IMPORTS, INC.

Fourth Generation Continues Family Tradition

"Millennium Edition Nativity" by the House of Fontanini honors the 2000th anniversary of the birth of Christ.

For over 90 years, Italy's world-famous House of Fontanini has been creating Nativity sets and angels. In the beginning, the figures were made from *papier mâché* and attired in fabric garments. Over the years, the Fontanini family sought to create its highly detailed figures from a material so durable that it would allow even the youngest children the opportunity to safely experience first-hand the beloved tradition of the Nativity scene. In the 1940s, the Fontaninis found polymer to be the ideal new medium and began using it to create the Fontanini figures. Today, the much sought-after collection is prized for its life-like sculpting and meticulous hand-painting. The partnership with Roman, established in 1973, has made *Fontanini Heirloom Nativities* the most popular in America for more than 25 years.

The family patriarch, Emanuele Fontanini, embarked on his career of figurine crafting in 1893 as a talented 13-year-old apprentice to an artist in Bagni di Lucca, Italy. Fontanini expanded his knowledge and skill in art through travels to European cities, and returned to Bagni di Lucca to launch his company in 1908. In time, the House of Fontanini gained recognition for its work and Fontanini's sons, Ugo,

Fontanini Village buildings and accessories create extraordinarily detailed depictions of Biblical Bethlehem.

Mario and Aldo, joined him in the business. Later, Mario's sons, Ugo, Mariano and Piero, became the third generation to head up the rapidly growing enterprise.

Now the family's fourth generation is poised to take the House of Fontanini into the 21st century. As the namesake and great-grandson of the founder, Emanuele Fontanini acts as the liaison between the Master Sculptor and the artists who translate his work into finished pieces. Emanuele's cousins, Marco, Luca and Alessandro, oversee production and quality control at the House of Fontanini. Emanuele's brother, Stefano, assumes responsibility on the business side of the operation.

THE CRAFTING PROCESS

Every stage of the labor-intensive process of crafting Fontanini figures is conducted under the close supervision of the Fontanini family. The following steps detail the process of bringing the figures of *Fontanini Heirloom Nativities* to life.

First, original ideas for new pieces are conceived by the Fontanini family and members of the Roman, Inc. creative team. As the process evolves, a sketch is developed to portray the figure. Emanuele Fontanini then meets with Master Sculptor Elio Simonetti to discuss the creation of the sculpture.

Slowly and meticulously Simonetti shapes and carves the image, bringing the clay to life. Figures are developed in the size in which they will eventually be produced.

Upon completion of the clay sculpture and final approval from the Fontanini family, Simonetti prepares a highly detailed model in beeswax. Then Simonetti's youngest son, Raffaello, begins the mold-making process. He positions his father's wax model against a piece of clay which will form the base of the mold, then encases half the figure in clay, applied layer by layer. He removes the model and repeats the process to create the second half of the mold. Upon completion of the clay mold, Raffaello creates a model plaster figure from his clay mold. The final molds that will produce the figures are made from either metal or rubber.

From the plaster figure, the foundry will create a final master mold. The master mold is then used in the test production of several figures. Simonetti's son, Giuliano, perfects the mold, utilizing tiny precision instruments to correct all defects. Next, the 2-1/2", 5", 7-1/2" and 12" figures are cast in

The Exclusive Club Symbol of Membership Angel heralds the many benefits of the Fontanini Collectors' Club.

durable polymer, a compound which captures every detail of the original. Injection molding allows the polymer to be shaped into figures of extraordinary beauty with fine undercuts and delicately sculpted elements. Liquid polymer is forced into the carefully crafted mold at high temperatures and pressure. After an initial cooling period, the still-warm figure emerges from the mold. It is then submerged in continuously running cold water for about two hours.

The first Fontanini always made his mark — a spider — under each figure to identify it as a House of Fontanini exclusive. The spider represented his unique design for a popular toy, a *papier mâché* spider. Early Fontanini figures can still be identified by this special base mark of authenticity. Today, newer creations are identified by a "fountain" mark, the modern-day Fontanini authenticator.

Artisans living in Bagni di Lucca painstakingly hand-paint Nativity figures using skills that have been passed down from generation to generation. Generally, several pieces are painted at the same time. Only the best painters paint the figures' faces so that the desired expression, often one of awe and reverence, is captured.

After painting, the figures are again sent from the House of Fontanini for the last phase of production — the patina application. A compound of burnt oils, oil, burnt earth, lime and other ingredients, called patina, is applied to each piece with a brush, making the figures almost entirely brown. The figures are wiped with a cloth and placed in tubs containing special soaps. Finally, they are removed from the tubs and carefully wiped dry. As the patina is applied to the figures, it bonds with the material and cannot be removed.

INNOVATIONS FROM A MASTER STUDIO

A new dimension in the history of Fontanini premiered in 1996 with the introduction of the Lighted Nativity Village buildings. These introductions enabled collectors to recreate extraordinarily detailed depictions of Biblical Bethlehem with realistic buildings, structures, tents, walls and accessories. In addition, Roman has introduced self-contained scenes that combine such elements as a working waterfall, back lighting and mixed media.

COLLECTION HIGHLIGHTED BY SPECIAL EVENTS PROGRAM

Launched in 1990, the collection's extensive special events program began with the introduction of exclusive Limited Edition Fontanini Tour Figures and expanded significantly in 1994 with the introduction of annual Limited Edition Event Figures. The exclusive Limited Edition Fontanini Tour Figures are available exclusively at authorized Fontanini Guild Dealers in conjunction with a personal appearance by a member of the Fontanini family.

All five fourth-generation Fontanini family members periodically tour the United States to meet collectors and sign their treasured personal pieces. These personal appearances provide collectors with the extremely limited opportunity to purchase the sought-after Personal Tour Figure. The annual Limited Edition Event Figure is available exclusively at Retailers' Open House Events and can only be purchased on event days.

THE FONTANINI COLLECTORS' CLUB

With the beginning of a new millennium, the Fontanini Collectors' Club will enjoy a glorious 10-year anniversary celebration with special member benefits and promotions. As a member of the club, collectors have the opportunity to acquire two exclusive figures. An exclusive addition to the 5" *Nativity Collection*, the Symbol of Membership figure is created solely for the enjoyment of club members and can only be acquired through membership in the club.

Members also have the opportunity to purchase an annual members-only Nativity Preview Figure. The members-only Nativity Preview Figure has a special understamp authenticating it as an annual club exclusive. The Nativity Preview figure will eventually be re-introduced as an open stock figure in a new color palette to distinguish it from its club exclusive predecessor.

Club members also receive a subscription to the quarterly "Fontanini Collector" newsletter filled with new product information, retirement news, display ideas and features on fellow club members. Other membership benefits include a club pin, a personalized membership card, and a registry to assist members with tracking their often extensive personal collections. Membership dues are less than $25.00 per year, and members who choose to join for a two-year period enjoy special savings.

The Fontanini Design Edition Nativity reproduces in resin the magnificent detail of Pennsylvania artist Michael Stumpf's original handcrafted stable for Fontanini collectors to enjoy.

Fontanini Heirloom Nativities
c/o Roman, Inc.
555 Lawrence Avenue
Roselle, IL 60172-1599

Phone:
630-529-3000

Fax:
630-529-1121

Web Site:
www.roman.com

Honoring the Most Beloved Twentieth-Century Icons

I f you ever have the opportunity to visit The Franklin Mint Museum at its corporate headquarters in suburban Philadelphia, Pennsylvania — take the trip. It's a showcase for many of the fine art collectibles that this leading direct marketer creates. But even more, it's an up-close and personal look at The Franklin Mint's commitment to honoring some of the most beloved 20th century icons. Displayed there are Princess Diana's famous beaded gown and Jackie Kennedy's remarkable faux pearls — each purchased for small fortunes at newsworthy auctions where proceeds went to charities. You'll also find collectibles and memorabilia honoring legends ranging from Frank Sinatra to Mother Teresa — plus a spectacular STAR TREK® exhibit and a year-round schedule of events showcasing artists, or specialized art or collectible genres.

It's just one example of The Franklin Mint's dedication to creating collectible works of art that "touch the heart" of the collector by commemorating the people, events and memories that changed the world forever. Its broad range of artwork is recognized internationally for artistic excellence and quality of craftsmanship — and savored by an enthusiastic legion of eight million collectors.

Cutting-edge aerospace technology created "The U.S.S. ENTERPRISE NCC-1701 Illuminated Crystal Ball."

House of Faberge, Erté and the Vatican Museums; entertainment leaders like Viacom and Universal Pictures; and designers such as Bill Blass and Oleg Cassini, The Franklin Mint offers a full spectrum of themed products. Some of the most popular works pay tribute to cultural icons like Marilyn Monroe, John Wayne, Harley-Davidson motorcycles, the John Deere tractor — even Dracula and Betty Boop.

FORGING WORLDWIDE PARTNERSHIPS

At the foundation of all The Franklin Mint's offerings is an unerring commitment to quality, craftsmanship and authenticity that is evidenced in the work of resident artisans, designers and craftsmen, as well as in collaborations with world-class artists, sponsors and institutions. The result is a unique line of heirloom-quality offerings that can't be found anywhere else in the world.

Working with prestigious institutions such as The

The Franklin Mint captures the romance of a beloved epic with "The Official TITANIC™ Vinyl Portrait Doll."

DIRECT TO COLLECTORS — AN INCOMPARABLE CHOICE

Major product lines include porcelain and vinyl heirloom collector dolls, Franklin Mint Precision Models (scale die-cast replicas of cars, trucks, motorcycles and other vehicles), collector plates, sculpture, collector games, fashion and traditional jewelry, home décor accessories, coins and medals, pocket knives, pocket watches, and historic weapon and scientific instrument reproductions.

Created exclusively by The Franklin Mint and distributed through direct response mailings and catalogs, and its own retail stores, some products are also available through a new Independent Retail Program. This program features stand-alone displays stocked with die-cast model cars — a convenient way for independent retailers to add these very popular collectibles to their merchandise mix. The June 1999 Rosemont International Collectible Exposition® was the scene of the unveiling of an exciting new phase of the program: several exclusive new collections including *Muscle Cars, Cars of the '50s,* and *Fire Engines* were introduced, designed to let retailers personalize their selections to the customers they serve.

Coming very soon is The Collector's Choice Online — a unique and very personalized Internet web site and a shopping experience geared exclusively to the collector.

OH YOU BEAUTIFUL DOLL!

The Franklin Mint's growing collection of vinyl portrait dolls includes Jackie Kennedy, Princess Diana and Marilyn Monroe. Reflecting the beauty and universal allure of these inspiring women, the resemblances are remarkable, and each doll is available with her own collection of historically authentic, fully-accessorized costumes. There's even a custom-designed wardrobe trunk to store and

The "We're Off to See the Wizard" musical carousel sculpture celebrates a fantasy film classic.

protect the ensembles. Equally as authentic in capturing the faces that thrilled the 20th Century are the fine porcelain portrait dolls portraying Jackie Kennedy, Princess Diana, Marilyn Monroe, Frank Sinatra and John Wayne.

WHAT'S YOUR FANTASY?

Bored with life? Need to escape? You'll find romance, adventure, spectacle and enchanting kingdoms of the heart to explore as The Franklin Mint celebrates the wonderful world of fantasy. From *Gone With the Wind* to *The Wizard of Oz*, there are art forms like the very popular "Scarlett of Tara Collector Egg" immortalizing the legendary movie heroine and the entire cast from this epic film. Recent additions include exquisite porcelain and vinyl portrait dolls that bring to life "Rose" from the blockbuster movie *TITANIC*.

The fearsome yet fascinating world of knights and dragons is commemorated with "fiery" dragon sculptures by acclaimed fantasy artist Michael Whelan, plus gentle *Mood Dragons* — lovable creatures with "attitude," as well as new age crystals. Gargoyles lurk with glowing eyes, while the beautiful sorceress "Morgan le Fay" prepares to bewitch you.

The Franklin Mint's exclusive *STAR TREK* universe has recently expanded to include much-requested collector plates. Breakthroughs in technology are also making possible exciting new art forms, such as the unique, high-tech "U.S.S. ENTERPRISE NCC-1701 Illuminated Crystal Ball."

PAVING THE ROAD OF SUCCESS

Franklin Mint Precision Models travel through the decades with intricately crafted die-cast models, accurate down to the tiniest detail. And every vehicle has a story!

Ready to forge through the Badlands, the 11" long "Wells Fargo & Company Overland Stagecoach" captures the enduring spirit of the American frontier, complete

"The Wells Fargo Overland Stagecoach" symbolizes America's enduring frontier spirit.

with a recreation of a Wells Fargo strongbox, shotguns and luggage.

The bold and sassy "1955 Packard Caribbean" was one of the most luxurious cars of its day, and one of the rarest. Franklin Mint Precision Models captures the spirit of this legend in a detailed 1:24 scale model with all of the "bells and whistles" of the original, including a fully-functional suspension.

For the first time ever, The Franklin Mint has been able to get real with "The 1963 Corvette Sting Ray In Fiberglass," a 1:24 scale model with a fiberglass body like the original full-sized car.

The exciting lineup also includes Harley-Davidson motorcycles; Freightliner and Mack Trucks; and police and emergency vehicles; as well as vintage Rolls-Royce, Mercedes, Duesenberg, and Ford cars; classic American cars of the '50s and muscle cars; and continental dream machines like Ferrari, Porsche, Lamborghini and Bugatti. There are even legendary John Deere and Farmall tractors. Each vehicle is a perfect hand-assembled replica of the original with doors, hood and trunk that open and close, steering and road wheels that turn, fully-detailed engine recreations, and more.

LEADING THE CORPORATE COMMITMENT

At the heart of The Franklin Mint's commitment to quality in product, and in customer service, are co-owners Stewart and Lynda Resnick, who serve as The Franklin Mint's Chairman and Vice-Chairman, respectively. The Franklin Mint is a subsidiary of Roll International Corporation, a privately-held diversified network of products and services based in Los Angeles and owned by the Resnicks. Roll International is consistently listed in the Forbes 200 largest privately-held firms.

The Resnicks are also community and civic leaders, lending their talents, support and expertise to institutions including the National Gallery, The Metropolitan Museum of Art, the Philadelphia Museum of Art, Conservation International, The Aspen Institute and The Los Angeles County Museum of Art.

WELCOMING ALL TO THE MUSEUM

If you're ready to visit, The Franklin Mint Museum is located on Route 1 in historic Brandywine River Valley in Southeastern Pennsylvania. It is open Monday through Saturday from 9:30 a.m. to 4:30 p.m., and Sunday from 1:00 to 4:30 p.m.. It is closed on major holidays. Admission and parking are free. For museum information, please call 610-459-6168.

THE FRANKLIN MINT

The Franklin Mint
U.S. Route 1
Franklin Center, PA 91091

Phone:
800-THE-MINT
800-843-6468

Fax:
610-459-6040

Web Site:
www.franklinmint.com

Making Collecting More Entertaining

When Bob Gartlan founded his company, Gartlan USA in 1985, he forever redefined the concept of "the art of entertainment," by creating and sharing extraordinary, history-making collectibles with enthusiastic collectors and fans.

From the beginning, Gartlan USA has forged strong partnerships with the biggest names in sports and entertainment. The personal involvement of these superstars in the creation of the company's collector's plates, figurines, lithographs, canvas transfers, baseballs, ornaments and ceramic trading cards makes the Gartlan USA brand unique and special in the collectibles world. Just like the company's founder and president, Bob Gartlan.

ONE MAN'S ENTHUSIASM CREATES SUCCESS

Growing up in New Jersey, Gartlan was an outstanding high-school baseball player, earning All-State honors. In his junior year, he was even drafted by the Atlanta Braves, but chose instead to continue his education. By the time he graduated from college, his interest had shifted from ball playing to business, and he went to work for Royal Doulton, Great Britain's prestigious china and giftware manufacturer.

During the next 14 years, Gartlan worked his way up through a number of well-known companies, getting to know collectors and learning what they wanted. Along the way, he was responsible for initiating a variety of highly successful collectible "firsts."

In 1985, Gartlan finally fulfilled his dream – opening his own business, and the timing couldn't have been better. In anticipation of Pete Rose breaking Ty Cobb's career mark of 4,192 hits and becoming baseball's all-time hit king, Gartlan produced a series of limited editions including personally autographed figurines, collector's plates, ceramic plaques, and the first ceramic cards ever produced. Today, many of those first Pete Rose pieces trade for more than 1,600 percent above their issue price — a trend that many Gartlan USA editions would follow.

A pewter Ringo Starr flashes a "peace" sign in a sculptural portrait from Gartlan USA.

Bob Gartlan and Ringo Starr check out the figurine interpretation of Ringo's famous pose from the cover of The Beatles' "Abbey Road" album.

GARTLAN USA CREATES COLLECTING HISTORY

While Gartlan USA became the premiere source for limited edition sports collectibles — having commemorated more than 40 of the world's greatest athletes — it was destined for even bigger success in the entertainment arena.

Bob Gartlan has made collectible history by creating a line of unique collectibles celebrating the most beloved entertainment icons. Among them: Jerry Mathers from the 1950s TV show, "Leave It To Beaver," The Beatles' Ringo Starr and John Lennon, Neil Diamond, Jerry Garcia, and the rock group KISS.

The superior quality of Gartlan USA products comes from the close and intimate involvement of the family, friends, and associates of their subjects...and often from the personalities themselves.

On the Garcia project, Jerry's widow was instrumental in providing art direction and backstamp copy for the collector's plates. During a plate signing for Ringo's collector's plates, the ex-Beatle sketched the concept for the second edition, himself. KISS guitarist, Paul Stanley, took time from the band's record-setting 1996-1997 world tour to work with members of the Gartlan USA development team on the *KISS Kollection.*

Over the years, collectors have come to rely on the integrity of every Gartlan USA product:

- When the company says that a piece has been autographed, it means that the named personality actually sat down and signed the collectible by hand.
- Edition limits are established by the number of pieces released, not by the number of firing days, assuring truly limited editions.
- Gartlan USA certifies absolute authenticity, assuring collectors of the company's painstaking attention to quality, accuracy and detail.

Proceeds from the sale of this exquisite John Lennon sculpture are slated for John's and Yoko Ono's Spirit Foundation.

THE TRADITION OF INNOVATION CONTINUES

One of the company's most popular new items is the KISS Kommemorative Baseball, which combines elements of the company's sports past and its entertainment future in a delightful new collectible medium.

Yet one of the company's most exciting new product lines is its Christmas ornaments. The first, a 1996 annual featuring Ringo Starr in his famous "Abbey Road" pose, exceeded its most optimistic expectations, selling out before factory orders were even shipped.

And the company has recently released a new collection of limited edition pewter figurines featuring Ringo and designed to coordinate with the "John Lennon Pewter Figurine," released in 1998. Each of the edition of 500 has been personally autographed by Ringo Starr. Like the pewter Lennon figurine, the pewter Ringo sculptures will contain metal from melted-down firearms collected by law enforcement and civic organizations dedicated to combating violence.

In a very different tribute to another former Beatle, Gartlan USA has released a ten-piece series of John Lennon's artwork on fine porcelain collector's plates. Leading off with Lennon's "Happy Xmas," a light-hearted tribute to Christmas, the plates represent a first for the estate of John Lennon. Additional titles in the collection are "Borrowed Time," "Peace Brother," "Imagine (All the People)," and "Family Tree." A new series adapted from Lennon's art is scheduled for the coming year.

A portion of the proceeds from the sale of the Lennon art will go to John's and Yoko Ono's Spirit Foundation, providing funds for many worthy causes including abused and needy children, and caring for the aged.

Jerry Garcia continues to be a popular subject for Gartlan USA collectibles, introducing a new — and

somewhat surprising — audience to the hobby of collecting. The collector's plates and figurines in the collection make the glory days of the leader of the Grateful Dead come to life once again.

Neil Diamond, one of the century's most successful pop singers/songwriters, also takes center stage in a Gartlan USA tribute. The personally autographed collection includes collector's plates featuring an artistic montage of highlights from his career, and a choice of beautifully sculpted figurines.

Besides the KISS Baseball, the rock band has been immortalized by a traditional collector's plate, a porcelain figurine, a three-dimensional collector's plate, a masterful pewter sculpture, and a choice of unique Christmas ornaments.

TAKING COLLECTING INTO THE 21ST CENTURY

As more and more collectors look for ways to own works of art with true historical significance, Gartlan USA will continue to hold its pre-eminent place among the most creative, respected, and popular collectibles manufacturers.

Plans are already underway for new lines dedicated to the Beatles' seminal record album "Yellow Submarine," and to pop star, Ozzy Osbourne.

As Gartlan USA collectibles grow in popularity, collectors are also discovering the fun of membership in the Gartlan USA Collectors' League.

Bound by a common interest in owning a piece of sports or entertainment history, the League boasts a worldwide membership. Members are offered editions not available to the general public, and receive members-only gifts for joining and renewing their memberships. Other benefits include a quarterly newsletter, advance notice of new releases, and a personalized membership card. Annual membership dues are $35.00 for new members, and $25.00 for renewing members.

Redefining the "art of entertainment" takes vision, hard work, painstaking care, and a genuine appreciation of talent, trends and fun. Bob Gartlan and his team at Gartlan USA have most definitely brought a new meaning and a new purpose to the world of collecting.

Gartlan USA's "KISSmas" collector's plate is sure to be a hit this holiday season.

Gartlan USA, Inc.
575 Rt. 73 N., Suite A-6
West Berlin, NJ
08091-2440

Phone:
856-753-9229

Fax:
856-753-9280

Web Site:
www.gartlanusa.com

E-mail:
info@gartlanusa.com

Bringing Fine Russian Folk Art to America

Russian art – like Russian music and literature – has been admired and respected for hundreds of years. Until recently, however, few collectors had the enjoyment of owning a true work of art from Russia. Thanks to the efforts of Andrew and Vicky Gabricht, original – even one-of-a-kind – collectibles from Russia are now available to American collectors.

Andrew was the son of a successful businessman whose personal hobby of collecting folk art in the 1960s brought together the finest woodcarvers and painters from the remote art villages and led to the eventual formation of G. DeBrekht Artistic Studios, the company that bears his name. Both Andrew and Vicky were surrounded by this artistic beauty in their homeland, and it was their dream to share it with the rest of the world – particularly in America. The opportunity to live their dream came in 1990 when the young couple and their daughters immigrated to the United States, and G. DeBrekht Artistic Studios became a reality.

They formed Russian Gift & Jewelry Center to market the hand-made ornaments and figures from the Russian art villages, and to be the exclusive U.S. distributor for the fine Faberge-style jewelry from St. Petersburg jewelers

The majesty and beauty of authentic Russian art is featured in "Russian Santa with Bear," "Honey Lover Bear" and "Snowmaiden with Squirrel" from G. DeBrekht Artistic Studios.

Russkiye Samotsvety, and the famous Gzhel blue and white porcelain collectibles made near Moscow. From the beginning, Andrew and Vicky wanted to bring collectors the true art that is the heart of Russian

culture – the fine folk art that uses skills and techniques spanning centuries.

"For many people, Russian art is a shiny, brightly painted matryoshka that a friend may have bought on a street corner in Moscow, or a decal box that is being passed off as fine lacquer work. These are poor imitations of the truly magnificent art that is found in our villages," explains Andrew. "We wanted to bring this beauty and this creative originality to American collectors, and this is what we have done."

"Forest Bear" is an exclusive design from G. DeBrekht Artistic Studios, limited to only 750 pieces worldwide.

LIMITED EDITION MASTERPIECES EMANATE FROM TINY "ARTIST VILLAGES"

Russian Gift & Jewelry Center expanded over the years, and with it came the introduction of G. DeBrekht Artistic Studios – the limited editions, masterpiece originals division of Russian Gift and Jewelry. Drawing on his own artistic skills, and a deep love of folk art throughout his life, Andrew set about to develop and bring a new level of Russian art to collectors: collectibles of unique design and originality.

G. DeBrekht Artistic Studios now has locations in major art villages – tiny, sometimes remote villages – where artistic crafts have been a way of life for hundreds of years. Andrew's father had discovered that in one village lived the best woodcarvers; in another, lived the best decorative painters; and in others there were artists who painted miniature scenes that could not be duplicated. Pieces move from village to village to ensure the finest workmanship and artistic integrity.

As demand for the individually carved and hand-painted pieces grew, so did the capacity of the Russian studios. Today, there are 16 studios with more than 600 full-time artisans. Even so, production is limited by the length of time it takes artisans to finish their creative input. A lacquer-art miniaturist takes months or years to complete a single papier mâché box; a woodcarver can take days or weeks to carve an intricate figure; and painters may require weeks to paint a complex scene.

But when the work is complete, it is an original masterpiece. Although most G. DeBrekht creations are very small limited editions, each individual piece is a true original, since each artist adds his or her individual touch to every piece they work on. It's no wonder that American

Wood painted in oils and clear lacquer, this new addition to the G. DeBrekht ornament collection portrays the beautiful "Snowmaiden."

collectibles retailers and their customers are so excited about the G. DeBrekht collections.

RUSSIAN SANTAS AND FOLK ART WIN COLLECTORS' FAVOR

G. DeBrekht Studios' collection of wood-carved, old-world Santas is a collector favorite. The most popular is a series called *The Storybook Santa,* with its beautifully detailed watercolor paintings. In sizes ranging from 7" up to 20", the series has sold out production through late 2000.

Because each carver has his or her own approach to the Santa figures, the range of G. DeBrekht Santas is diverse. From the 5-1/2" "Playful Santa" to the unique "Romantic Santa" or the wily "Wilderness Santa," there's one that's sure to please the most discerning collector or anyone who enjoys the beauty of true folk art.

Another collection that has won collector favor is a unique range of bears. Unlike the traditional teddy bear, these are bears of both whimsy and strength, intricately hand-carved and meticulously hand-painted. A favorite is the limited edition "Honey Lover Bear," a jovial — fully dressed — bear carrying a honey pot. In Russian lore, animals take on the role of humans, even to wearing the peasant clothing of the day, so all G. DeBrekht bears are "dressed" by their creators.

Other collections include a wide range of matryoshka — nested dolls — regarded as synonymous with Russian artistic culture; roly-poly musical dolls; fairytale figurine sets; ornaments; hand-painted trays and brooches; wooden toys; and lacquer miniatures. Each of these pieces is created by skilled artists living in villages that have fostered these crafts for generations.

The finest of all Russian folk art is the lacquer miniature, whose artists possess a unique gift. G. DeBrekht Studios is home to the best of these artists and offers a wide selection of one-of-a-kind lacquer miniatures, as well as a range of limited editions. For hundreds of years, Russian lacquer art has been honored as the world standard, and while some villages were creating lacquer miniatures of the highest quality, other art villages excelled in painting the richly elaborate Orthodox icons. Following the Russian Revolution in 1917, icon painting was banned, and artists turned to other expressions of their talent.

Using the artistic techniques handed down by the famed icon painters dating back to the Byzantine period, today's Russian artists are now free to paint subjects of their choice — including religious scenes. G. DeBrekht artists capture these timeless subjects on magnificent pedestal eggs and nested dolls, as well as on lacquer boxes.

FAIRYTALES INSPIRE BEAUTIFUL COLLECTIBLES

Russian fairytales inspire many of the G. DeBrekht artists, just as they have inspired great music, ballet, art and theatre for centuries. Many of the most remarkable miniatures are based on such classic tales as Pushkin's *Ruslan and Ludmilla, Firebird, Snowmaiden* and *The Nutcracker,* among others.

To meet demand for more and more examples of this unique cultural art, the company introduced the *Derévo Collection™* in 2000. The collection features exquisitely hand-carved and hand-painted pieces that are then hand-cast in a special wood-based resin and meticulously hand-painted to the exact likeness of the original. These Russian designed pieces are limited editions and offer collectors the opportunity to acquire examples of fine Russian designs at a modest price. At the heart of the *Derévo Collection* is the *Russian Fairytale Village,* a series of authentic lighted buildings and figures that represent the most familiar Russian folk stories. With each fairytale set comes a little book of authentic stories translated from Russian, as well as a Certificate of Authenticity. These limited edition pieces represent a new dimension in fine Russian collectibles from G. DeBrekht Artistic Studios.

Collectors are invited to see the full range of gifts and collectibles available from G. DeBrekht Studios, as well as read the history of the company and several well-known fairytales, by visiting www.russiangift.com on the Web.

This exquisite hand-painted matryoshka, or nested doll set, is titled "Guardian Angel."

G. DeBrekht Artistic Studios
Division of Russian Gift & Jewelry Center
18025 Sky Park Circle, Suite G
Irvine, CA 92614

Phone:
800-727-7442

Fax:
800-RUSSIA-7

Web Site:
www.russiangift.com

E-mail:
info@russiangift.com

G. DeBREKHT ARTISTIC STUDIOS

Generations Enjoy Treasures from a Collectibles Pioneer

An industry pioneer with over half a century in the collectibles and decorative accessories field, Geo. Z. Lefton Company has established sterling credentials in both antique and contemporary collectibles. In a report by Warman's *Today's Collector Magazine*, April 1998, Lefton ranked in the top 15 hot collectibles on the Internet, attracting the most inquiries, according to The Internet Antique Shop. At the same time, Lefton was nominated by Unity Marketing for the "Collectibles Business Trendsetter Of The Year-1998" for its company-wide evolution branching into new sports, humor and musicals in contemporary collectibles.

Popular Lefton contemporary collectibles celebrate America's rich heritage, tradition, pastimes, humor and natural beauty with collections garnering legions of devoted followers. Foremost among these are the top-ranking illuminated porcelain *Historic American Lighthouses* and *Colonial Village Collection*.

The artist behind *The Gary Patterson Collections* by Lefton was awarded Collectors' Information Bureau's "Best of Show" Sports Artist honor at the 1998 Rosemont International Collectible Exposition®. Meanwhile, *The Child Within* talent, Maggie Garvin, walked away with CIB's "Best of Show" award for Best New Figurine.

How has this long-time producer managed to maintain superior standings in vintage and modern collectibles in a world fraught with change? Primarily because of acute sensitivity to the needs of the American public and the integrity to fill those needs with vigilant commitment to quality and creativity.

"My grandfather and founder of the company, George Zoltan Lefton, had amazing artistic flair and marvelous business instincts," informs Steven Lefton Sharp, Lefton President and Chief Executive Officer. "Following his 1939 arrival in Chicago, his passion for collecting fine porcelain led to his starting our company in 1941. He opened up shop in a small Chicago warehouse. With several family members and 50 SKUs of product, he set out to make history in the ceramics business. Following WWII, he was one of the first entrepreneurs to help revive Japan's handcrafted porcelains for American consumers. He sealed his first agreement on his initial trip to Japan in 1945. Collectors trace these earliest porcelains by the historically significant 'Made In Occupied Japan, 1946' understamp."

With creative designs and superlative crafting, Lefton earned the well-deserved title of "The China King" by 1948. Today, a strong nationwide following of fans of Lefton

"Old Baldy" from Lefton's illuminated Historic American Lighthouse Collection *represents North Carolina's first established light station.*

Lefton's innovative "Cotswold Cottage" from the Colonial Village Collection *is making big news with versatile "dormant" and "bloom" facades.*

antique china collect and hunt for this early Lefton china tableware, accessories and gifts.

COLLECTOR AUTHORS LEFTON ANTIQUE CHINA ENCYCLOPEDIAS

For more information about Lefton antique china, just ask avid Lefton china collector and chronicler of the Lefton family business history and wares, Loretta DeLozier. As President and founder of the National Society of Lefton Collectors, Delozier organized the first Annual Convention of the National Society of Lefton Collectors in 1997. She has researched and published Books 1 and 11 of the *Collector's Encyclopedia of Lefton China* devoted to identifying and evaluating representative selections of the over half a billion pieces of Lefton china produced since 1941.

Collectors of Lefton antique china, figures and accessories may contact DeLozier via the National Society of Lefton Collectors, 1101 Polk St., Bedford, IA 50833, or E-Mail: LeftonLady@aol.com.

Lefton's ties with Japan's remarkable ceramic skills are still maintained with collections like *Remembrances* musicals and figurines by gifted artist Tsunekazu Yamada of Japan who was greatly influenced by the art of the European Masters. Each piece is crafted of the finest glazed porcelain in Seto City, Japan's oldest ceramics center.

Not resting on his laurels, Lefton proceeded to establish a reputation as a major contemporary collectibles player with collections celebrating the attributes of his new homeland. He introduced *American Beauty Flowers of Porcelain* in 1977. The popular *Colonial Village Collection*, "the place everyone loves to come home to," followed in 1987. Then, Lefton was inspired to pay tribute to land-

The limited edition "Blue Millennium Rose" is Lefton's tribute to the upcoming historic milestone.

mark beacons, past and present, of the United States with the *Historic American Lighthouse Collection* in 1991.

GIFTBEAT RANKS LEFTON PORCELAIN ILLUMINATED LIGHTHOUSES NO. 1

In early 1998, *GiftBeat,* a surveyor of nationwide collectibles dealers, placed Lefton illuminated porcelain lighthouses in the top slot on national collectibles charts. Since its 1991 debut, Lefton's popular *Historic American Lighthouse Collection* has been paying tribute to well-known beacons. Each authentic replica with historical background is the result of Lefton's close working relationship with the U.S. Lighthouse Society. A portion of all lighthouse sales proceeds is donated to this group's mission of preserving and restoring U.S. national lighthouses.

"We admire the invaluable work the U.S. Lighthouse Society and others like them perform to preserve these national treasures for fellow Americans, tourists from abroad and future generations. Lefton will work very closely with these associations to insure the continued protection and preservation of lighthouses through donations and by continuing to represent them through the *Historic American Lighthouse* collection," Sharp states.

With the widest offerings of porcelain lighthouses in the industry in a variety of mediums ranging from full-sized lighted replicas, musical waterballs, decorator clocks and lamps, hanging and clip-on ornaments, wind chimes and functional tea pots, Lefton provides for all light-house lovers' desires for collecting, decorating and gift giving.

"Lefton's introduction of a series of smaller resin light-houses has met with such positive response, that collectors can look forward to more offerings in this popular medium," comments Margo Lefton, co-owner and executive vice president of research and design.

COLONIAL VILLAGE SPANS THE SEASONS

Colonial Village — a community of buildings and citizens with a continuing old-fashioned, homespun story — has carved a name as "the place everyone loves to come home to." An early *Colonial Village* building, "Hillside Church," was so much in demand on the secondary market that Collectors' Information Bureau named *Colonial Village* a Top 10 Architectural Collectible in 1994.

Thanks to creative innovations inspired by suggestions from devoted *Colonial Village* fans, Lefton designers have added a new dimension to the collection. Now, through the magic of imaginative design, action, music, lights and sound, *Colonial Village* is truly a place collectors and village builders love to live with every season of the year.

Through the heartwarming and action-filled vignettes, enthusiasts can truly have a community that lives, works and plays all year with delightful surprises at every turn!

Springtime "magic" comes via a little jewel of an English style dwelling, "Cotswold Cottage." This first seasonally convertible building is making big news with versatile "dormant" and "bloom" facades. Turn, and it's spring and summer! Turn again for an instant fall and winter setting!

Summer pleasures arrive on the *Colonial Village* landscape with the picture-perfect "Blarney Farmstead" scene conjuring the honest labors and wholesome joys of farm life many remember or hope to share with their youngsters. Also, they can circle 'round with ceramic couples and uniquely illuminated silhouettes in the musical "Blarney Barn" to the familiar strains of "Oh! Susanna." Together with the "Silo," this collector's set is full of rustic charm.

Full-blown vignettes portray a *Winter Carnival* full of snow frolics and ice skating fun; *Fall Harvest* celebrates nature's bounty; and *Halloween* high-jinks highlights include a haunted house, "Mooncrest Mansion," featuring flashing lights and eerie sounds, plus "Trick-or-Treat" and "Peek-a-Boo" figures.

Collectors are invited to explore the full world of fascinating Lefton collectibles via the "Lefton Collectors' Newsletter." An annual subscription is the collectors' key to fabulous benefits, including prior announcements of limited editions and advance notification of *Historic American Lighthouse* and *Colonial Village* retirements and introductions. There's also news about personal appearances by Lefton family members; fun-filled contests with prizes; collecting and display tips; artist features; Lefton antique china news; and the opportunity to acquire catalogs. For subscription information, please contact Lefton Collectors' Service Bureau at (800)-628-8492.

The inspirational figure of "Praying Madonna" from the Remembrances *by* Yamada *collection continues the remarkable artistic tradition begun by gifted sculptor Tsunekazu Yamada of Japan.*

A Century-Old Tradition Continues

After the death of her husband, free-lance court reporter Susan Bickert decided to travel with her two children to old East Germany. The family was on a quest to discover more of the German antique toys and holiday items they had been collecting for years.

Susan was raised in the Amana Colonies, a close-knit, German-speaking community that is now a tourist attraction in Eastern Iowa. She always wanted to see what was still available in the way of antiques in East Germany. After the Berlin Wall came down, her quest became possible.

Unfortunately, Susan and her children were a few years too late. She wasn't the first person to travel to old East Germany in search of treasured antique dolls and toys. But that first trip in March of 1996 was only the beginning of a much longer and still-continuing journey. On the family's second trip in October of 1996, they stopped in Saalfeld, Germany, to tour a famous cave. They never did get to see the cave, but instead stepped into the antique shop of Roland Schlegel.

After several more trips, a friendship developed, and Roland began telling Susan about the old porcelain factories in the region. He took her to the dumping grounds that he had been visiting for years. These expeditions were more like archeological digs — uncovering treasures from the past. It didn't matter that most were broken. Digging in streams behind the factories or pulling up the floorboards in the old factories to expose century-old doll parts gave Susan and Roland quite a rush! The original old molds also were available — either mortared into the interior and exterior walls of the factories as building materials, or to be bought from other antique dealers or locals who had acquired them over the years.

A selection of original Kewpie dolls and figurines is being reissued from Rose O'Neill's original molds found in Germany.

Susan Bickert, The German Doll Company co-founder and president, is shown at a dumping ground in the Thuringian Forest, Germany, amidst pieces of turn-of-the-century doll parts.

A NEW DOLL COMPANY IS BORN

It was only in June of 1998 when Susan was in Europe for another visit that the idea of The German Doll Company was first conceived. Upon seeing some bisque Kewpie dolls produced from original molds found in the region, she immediately saw the possibilities of reissuing Rose O'Neill's beloved Kewpies from the original molds for today's collector. That was all Roland needed to hear. Upon her arrival back in the United States, Susan received a phone call from Roland that changed everything: "I've just sold my antique shop," he said. "We are now in business."

What they have undertaken to accomplish couldn't have been foreseen. One Kewpie mold led to another, and another. Then came the discovery of the extremely rare *Kewpie Riding Series* molds from the Hermann Voigt factory in Schaala, Germany. With Roland searching in Germany and overseeing the production, and Susan in the United States, she always looked forward to their daily 5:00 p.m. telephone calls. Roland would tell Susan what molds he had discovered that day and his plans for the coming day.

Before long, Roland was developing reproduction automatons, pull toys and an endless list of *papier mâché* items all poured from old molds. The possibilities are endless, and Susan still waits for her 5:00 p.m. calls to find out just what the day was like in Germany.

THE GOLDEN AGE OF GERMAN PORCELAIN

During the heyday of the German porcelain-making industry at the turn of the 20th century, the area of the Thuringian Wald (in what was formerly East Germany) had as many as 200 factories producing dolls for the American market. The Hertwig factory in Katzhütte alone turned out 2,000 dozen dolls per day during the winter months! Seconds were usually disposed of by merely dumping them behind the factory or using them as filler beneath factory floorboards — an inexpensive substitute for insulation materials.

Along with the huge number of dolls being turned out every day also came an equally large number of plaster

Original, old molds were used as building material for this interior wall of a porcelain factory.

molds in which each porcelain doll's head, arms, legs, and body had to be poured. At the very most, one mold can be used to pour 15 doll heads, as the features of each piece become less crisp with each pouring. Instead of disposing of thousands of molds per week, molds often were mortared into the interior and exterior walls of the porcelain factories, or given to the poor factory workers who gladly used them to build chicken houses, barns or homes — again an inexpensive substitute for expensive building materials.

Uncovering these turn-of-the-century porcelains, according to Susan Bickert, is the most wonderful treasure hunt one can imagine! As these factories are now being razed or found sitting idle after years of neglect, floorboards are ripped up to expose bucketfuls of century-old porcelain. Digging in old dumping grounds yields handfuls of broken parts or an occasional complete doll or figurine.

Today, only a few of these porcelain factories remain standing, lost through ravages of war or fire, a common occurrence in factories with their massive coal-burning ovens. Most of those that did survive have been torn down since the reunification of Germany to make way for auto dealerships, gas stations and the countless other businesses springing up virtually overnight as East Germany begins its westernization.

RARE KEWPIE MOLDS ARE UNCOVERED

Through knowledge of the region's history and countless searches, Susan Bickert and Roland Schlegel have uncovered many of these turn-of-the-century molds. Among the most exciting of their discoveries has been many of the now-rare molds used for Rose O'Neill's first production of Kewpies. Miss O'Neill, an American artist,

traveled to Germany in 1910 in search of a porcelain manufacturer for her beloved Kewpies.

The German Doll Company's *Riding Series* gives today's collector an opportunity to acquire a seldom-seen Kewpie line prized today. What's more, the firm not only has the rare *Naked Kewpie Riding Series* but also the *Kewpie Soldier Riding Series,* which has never before been pictured. The *Madeleine Riding Series* is the rarest of them all. It is speculated that Rose O'Neill may have designed Madeleine, and for one reason or another, decided not to proceed with production. World War I certainly may have played a part. But for whatever reason, genuine Kewpie production came to a halt and never resumed again, until now.

Also available are an assortment of action Kewpies, along with an irresistible Christmas ornament selection issued in an edition limited to 200 pieces, and an amazing 16" Kewpie with jointed arms, limited to 500 pieces. With this extensive line of quality bisque Kewpies limited in production by color palette, a new era of Kewpie collecting begins.

The German Doll Company is once again following the time-honored method of producing quality porcelain in its factory in the Thuringian Wald. Susan Bickert and Roland Schlegel are proud to offer collectors a unique line poured in original molds, which have been carefully reworked by trained artisans. Once again, the beauty and quality of German porcelain is available for collectors to enjoy in what is sure to be the antique of tomorrow. And thus, the century-old tradition continues.

Here are two of the many automatons offered by The German Doll Company, completely hand-built in Germany and incorporating bisque doll heads poured from original old molds.

The German Doll Company
P.O. Box 483
Tipp City, OH 45371

Phone:
937-335-4808

Fax:
937-440-9756

Web Site:
www.german-doll.com

E-mail:
germandoll@erinet.com

Romancing Your Heart and Your Home

Glynda Turley, artist and president of Glynda Turley Prints, Inc.

At her home nestled in the beautiful Ozark Mountains of Arkansas, Glynda Turley finds the quiet inspiration for her exquisite oil paintings that have won her international acclaim. As president and artist of her company, *Glynda Turley Prints, Inc.,* she has turned her creative talents into a thriving family business that invites collectors to enjoy the simpler pleasures of life. Her artwork reflects the vibrant colors of a springtime garden, the country charm of beloved antiques or the playful afternoon pastimes of children.

"I strive to take the viewer into a time and place of beauty, peace and harmony – where time seems to stand still," Glynda says. "I suppose my style of work could be described as romantic." It is the captivating combination of romance and nostalgia that has blossomed Glynda Turley Prints, Inc. into a successful print and collectibles company. Collectors can now find Glynda's artwork adorning everything from limited edition prints to tapestry throws and pillows.

"I love my work," Glynda says. "My paintings are the way I share that magical place or old-fashioned bouquet that represents the way I see things and the way I feel inside. It is a very rewarding thing to know you have helped someone to smile."

INSPIRED BEGINNINGS FOR A SELF-TAUGHT ARTIST

Glynda's artistic style has evolved since her childhood. She had no formal art training, but can't recall a time when she wasn't filling blank pieces of paper or canvases with the images in her mind and heart.

"My grandmother was probably my very first influence," she recalls. "She inspired me to be creative by her constant creativity. She was always making beautiful gifts. She never had the opportunity to paint, but I have no doubt that she could have been a great artist."

Even though this self-taught artist loved to sketch, Glynda didn't begin to paint until the mid-1970s, when as a young mother and housewife, she was introduced to oil paints. Ozark Mountain scenes and barnyard animals were among her first subjects. She sold some of her paintings at arts and crafts fairs throughout the state. During this time, she also started teaching art to neighborhood children and adults in her kitchen, as well as at a local beauty shop and school gymnasium. In 1977, she opened an art supplies store in Heber Springs, Arkansas. A few years later, Glynda's first two prints were published. Soon, she was winning awards and receiving many requests for her work from galleries, gift shops and collectors.

In 1985, she founded Glynda Turley Prints, Inc. to market her prints. Since then, the number of outlets and mediums for her work has grown by leaps and bounds. Glynda's work is sold in more than 7,000 stores nationwide.

The first company-owned retail store opened in April of 1996 in Branson, Missouri, to carry the extensive line of every Glynda Turley product, including licensed products. Glynda Turley's complete *Romancing the Home® Collection* can be found in the Glynda Turley store, including products that her company produces, such as framed prints, as well as licensed products such as tapestries from Simply Country, lamp shades from A Homestead Shoppe, calendars from Amcal, and much more. A second company store recently opened in Glynda's hometown of Heber Springs, Arkansas.

Glynda Turley incorporates the themes of florals and family in her print titled "Hand In Hand."

"Treasured Times," painted in memory of Glynda Turley's friend Sherry Smith, is featured on the cover of the book Friends Are the Flowers in the Garden of the Heart.

A STRONGER COMPANY RISES FROM TRAGIC FIRE

To keep up with the demand, Glynda now employs about 45 people, including 12 family members. But the company and collectors are truly her extended family. In 1992, when a fire destroyed her manufacturing plant and 83 of her original oil paintings, her employees, suppliers, retailers and collectors came to the rescue. They gave the helping hands and encouraging words needed to rebuild the business and plant, which are located in Heber Springs, Arkansas, a picturesque resort area 80 miles north of Little Rock.

"We have a wonderful team that pulled together," Glynda says. "There's a real family bond." In recent years, Glynda has expanded the scope of her products through licensing agreements. Her designs appear on many different kinds of home décor items and gifts, including cedar chests, throws, pillows, lamp shades, keepsake boxes, coasters, night lights, and more. Other items are always in the works. "Nothing is more exciting than to see one's artwork adapted to other products." she says.

PRINTS CAPTURE FLORALS, FAMILY AND FRIENDS

Although her artwork is being translated into a variety of products, Glynda is still most renowned for her prints – especially those featuring beautiful florals. "Florals are my true love," Glynda reveals. "Flowers are so short-lived that if I can capture them on canvas, they can be enjoyed forever."

At her cottage-style home, Glynda enjoys working in her gardens, which grow among a backdrop of picket fences and are filled with multi-colored roses, delphiniums and foxgloves, among others. "I only have to look out my window for my inspiration," she says.

The Victorian house in "Ring Around the Rosy" captures the childhood home of one of Glynda Turley's friends.

But some of her ideas don't just come from her backyard. Her family also appears in many of her works. "Hand In Hand," a 1998 print release features Glynda's daughter-in-law Toni and granddaughter Crystal. This print has been very well received with numerous licensed products being produced. "Hand In Hand" was featured on the cover of the 1998 book, *Seasons of the Heart,* which told of relationships between mothers and daughters.

Glynda premiered another very special print release in January of 1999 titled "Treasured Times." This print was painted in memory of Glynda's friend, Sherry Smith. This design is featured on the cover of a book about friends from Honor Books entitled, *Friends are the Flowers in the Garden of the Heart,* which was released in March, 1999.

"Ring Around the Rosy" was a 1998 release that features a Victorian home from Nevada, Missouri. This was the childhood home of Glynda's friend, May Ann Miller. Glynda fell in love with the house and felt the print would be a very special surprise to Mary Ann. Glynda chose to paint Mary Ann in the picture as a child and included two more friends to complete the ring around the rosy circle. This painting also shows Mary Ann's grandfather, a prominent doctor, in the horse drawn buggy. Her mother watches from the doorway of the home.

"My inspiration today comes from my environment," she says. "I live in one of the most beautiful places in the world, so I only have to look around me for the inspiration to create. My head is full of ideas for paintings, many of which come from the extensive amount of travelling that I do throughout the year."

Glynda's limited edition prints include more than 150 titles, with many selling out within a matter of months. Some sold-out limited edition prints are available in smaller sizes in an open edition. Custom framing is also offered by the company.

CREATING THE HEIRLOOMS OF TOMORROW

"My personal goals as an artist are to recreate the wonderful things that I have had the privilege or opportunity to see, whether they are found in my travels, at home or in my imagination. I wish to record with my paintings some of the beauty of the past," states Glynda.

Today's lovely Glynda Turley prints, decorative accessories, and collectibles will surely be the heirlooms of tomorrow. Whether in the Ozark Mountains or traveling around the world, Glynda is always working on new ideas and expanding her collection for more collectors to enjoy.

Glynda Turley Prints, Inc.
P.O. Box 112
74 Cleburne Park Rd.
Heber Springs, AR 72543

Phone:
800-633-7931

Fax:
501-362-5020

Web Site:
www.glynda.com

The Web's Widest Selection of Contemporary Collectibles and Gifts

In less than one year's time, GoCollect.com has grown from a web site start-up to the premier online source of community, content and e-commerce for American collectors, manufacturers and retailers. More than 150,000 collectors registered on the site in its first nine months of operation alone. What's more, in May 2000, PC Data Online listed GoCollect.com as one of the world's top ten growing web sites. And by the end of the year 2000, GoCollect was on track to represent a total of 20,000 distinct products: the Web's widest selection of contemporary collectibles!

Created by collectors for collectors, GoCollect.com offers information about collections, interaction and community-building, and a convenient and fun environment in which to purchase favorite collectibles and gifts. Traditional brick-and-mortar collectibles dealers are joining GoCollect.com by the hundreds, excited by this chance to reach a wider market and share more information with current and new customers.

GoCollect.com has fresh content that is updated each day, including news, special features, games, exclusive products and free gift opportunities. The site is designed to give collectors many reasons to log on, every single day.

◆ *The GoCollect.com web site provides the widest selection of contemporary collectibles available on-line, plus a constantly updated treasure trove of information and fun for the collector community.*

LOYALTY IS AT THE HEART OF GOCOLLECT.COM

The home of the Web's widest collectibles selection seeks to delight members with a rewarding, fun and interactive Loyalty Program. Collectors truly enjoy their relationship with GoCollect.com, where fun and rewards are the name of the game!

Throughout the year, GoCollect.com offers members special ways to participate in the Loyalty Program, earning valuable loyalty points to be used towards a future purchase. Around St. Patrick's Day, members searched the site for a leprechaun's pot of gold for prizes. Shamrocks hidden throughout the site either led to the much desired "pot o' gold" or to a "bit of blarney" from the mischievous leprechaun. For Easter, an online Egg Hunt rewarded members for finding all three eggs hidden on the site. The hunt required patience, as eggs that had previously been discovered continued to reappear. In each contest, the shamrocks and eggs were hidden in new places, height-

This lovely Swarovski Crystal piece by Michael Stamey, titled "The Rose," is featured at GoCollect.com.

ening the excitement of the hunt. On the Fourth of July, the "Firecracker Frenzy" kept things popping all during the holiday weekend, too.

"At GoCollect.com, we want to offer our members exciting and entertaining features to enhance the time they spend on the site," explains CEO Shonnie Bilin. "We are glad our members have enjoyed the Loyalty Program thus far. We will continue to bring interesting and fun features to the site as a 'thank you' to our members for choosing GoCollect.com."

Members truly appreciate the Program, as one participant commented: "I thought the hunting for shamrocks was great, and the hunting for eggs was even more fun. Thanks GoCollect.com for adding fun and points to my day."

Loyalty points are awarded to members for each visit and purchase to GoCollect.com, as well as for participation in the various polls and contests.

NBA fans will love owning and giving these exclusive NBA key rings, tie tacks and money clips from GoCollect.com.

The more points members earn, the more they are awarded on future purchases.

There are lots of other ways to benefit and have fun on Go.Collect.com. A Mother's Day Contest called "Spell Your Love for M-O-M" drew nearly 1,000 entries, and the grand prizewinner enjoyed a Spa Vacation for two in Scottsdale, Arizona. Biweekly polls and frequent trivia contests keep collectors engaged and returning to the site time and again. Message Boards let collectors exchange thoughts and ideas with those of similar interests. And a "Collector of the Week" and his or her collection are featured on the site weekly.

GOCOLLECT.COM MAKES GIFT-GIVING A BREEZE

Whether it's a birthday present for your "significant other" or a Christmas gift for that friend who "has everything," GoCollect.com offers an incredible selection — and makes the process of selecting and shopping an enjoyable experience! The site's advanced "Gift Finder" helps visitors locate the items they seek, or gift-buyers can "surf around" looking for interesting possibilities.

Whenever a special day is coming up, GoCollect.com gathers a wide range of gift ideas at every possible price point. Special features tell collectors more about the holiday or event in question, and help them "gear up" to make the right selection. The entire gift-giving transaction can be handled online in a matter of minutes, complete with gift-wrapping, greetings to the recipient, and shipping.

The GoCollect.com Wish List/Gift Registry lets members create and maintain a personalized wish list or gift registry that can be e-mailed to friends and family so they can see the member's most desired products. What's more, Gift Certificates purchased at GoCollect.com can be used to purchase any product on the web site.

The diversity of products available through GoCollect.com — as well as the company's many "exclusives" and hand-signed pieces from top firms like Disney, Fenton Art Glass and Cast Art — ensures that you can always find a unique gift. For example,

Collectors and holiday gift-givers can shop a lavish Christmas selection from the comfort of home by visiting GoCollect.com.

GoCollect.com offers a wide array of exclusive NBA products and original movie posters, as well as the more traditional figurines, dolls, cottages and other collectibles.

AN INCREDIBLE ARRAY OF BRANDS AND CLUBS

Browsing through the GoCollect.com web site is like a stroll through "Who's Who" of the collectibles world. Favorite brands represented include *Precious Moments, Cherished Teddies,* Boyds plush and resin pieces, Yankee Candles, Swarovski Crystal, *Just The Right Shoe,* Walt Disney Art Classics, *Charming Tails,* Department 56, *Tender Tails, Seraphim Classics, Pooh & Friends,* Pokemon, *Mary's Moo Moos,* Harmony Kingdom, Anne Geddes, Harbour Lights, Lilliput Lane, *M.I. Hummel, Berta Hummel, Wee Forest Folk,* Annalee, Van Mark Character Collectibles, *All God's Children, Pocket Dragons,* David Winter Cottages, Lang and Wise, *Calico Kittens* and many more.

Themes covered are equally inclusive, ranging from all the major holidays and events to teddy bears, angels, lighthouses, villages, animals and people. Site visitors have the opportunity to build a community with like-minded people by joining a host of collecting clubs online, as well.

One prominent example is the *Precious Moments* Community at GoCollect.com: the place to go for those who want to know more about the award-winning artist Sam Butcher, as well as the inspiration behind his designs, latest product retirements and exclusive items. Along with the up-to-date information about *Precious Moments,* the community acts as a meeting place for collectors worldwide to participate in activities, swap stories and form friendships.

As part of GoCollect.com's expansion of offerings to *Precious Moments* collectors, the site now includes PreciousMom (www.preciousmom.com), the leading expert of *Precious Moments,* created by Kristi Schult. Schult launched PreciousMom five years ago as a place for *Precious Moments* collectors to meet and share information and stories about their collections.

GoCollect.com also is launching a new program for local collectors clubs. Local club chapters will have their own home pages to feature news and events specifically for their members. This program will also feature ways for the club to earn money.

With the advice and participation of its members, GoCollect.com will continue to add product lines, benefits of membership, and lots more ways to have fun, affiliate with fellow collectors, and earn points toward coveted purchases. As Bilin, herself an avid collector of paperweights, notes in closing, "At GoCollect.com, we think it is important to share the joys of collecting with others!"

GoCollect.com
1000 East Woodfield Road,
Suite 102
Schaumburg, IL
60173-5921

Phone:
847-706-6765

Fax:
847-706-6766

Web Site:
www.GoCollect.com

E-mail:
info@GoCollect.com

Looney Tunes Spotlight Collection Based on Classic Cartoons

Throughout its history, Goebel has distinguished itself as a leader in ceramic technology and a manufacturer with the uncanny ability to respond to popular culture and the tastes of the times.

Over the years, Goebel has worked with artists, illustrators and animators as diverse as Sister Maria Innocentia Hummel, Norman Rockwell and Walt Disney to create treasured objects and decorative accessories.

Today, as in every generation, Goebel continues to seek out, work with, license or develop fine artists to produce products that bring joy and sustained value to millions of people around the world.

The *Looney Tunes Spotlight Collection* is the result of Goebel's most recent artistic alliance. Teaming up with Warner Bros., the entertainment powerhouse, Goebel has produced a collection of superbly sculpted figurines that clearly reflects the spirit of the world's most celebrated cartoon characters. The figurines are based on actual scenes from Warner Bros. Classic Cartoons and spotlight some of the most memorable moments in the history of animation.

Warner Bros. artists and Goebel sculptors collaborated to make the lovable *Looney Tunes Spotlight Collection* characters literally jump off the screen in three dimension. Crafted of fine porcelain, all of the figurines perfectly capture the offbeat attitudes and winning personalities of the popular cartoon characters. Painstaking attention to detail — from color choices to the size and stance of the characters, to the addition of fine crystal and metals — is apparent in each piece.

TWO'S COMPANY, THREE'S A CROWD, BUT TWENTY-THREE IS A PARTY!

In 1999, the ranks of the Looney Tunes gang multiplied faster than Marvin The Martian's instant Martians as Goebel added five new figurines to its *Looney Tunes Spotlight Collection.* The new additions include many stand-outs, firsts and limited editions. The collection now offers collectors and gift givers 23 pieces to choose from.

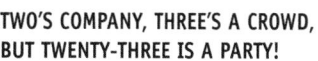

New from the Looney Tunes Spotlight Collection is "Laughing All the Way," a limited edition of 1,200 pieces which comes with a handsome hardwood base.

"Laughing All the Way," created especially for the "Mil-LOONEY-um," is an intricately crafted, sculptural masterpiece, drawn from the cartoon short called "Bugs Bunny's Looney Christmas Tales." In the cartoon — a parody of Charles Dickens' holiday classic, *A Christmas Carol* — Yosemite Sam is the acerbic Scrooge, Porky Pig is Bob Cratchet, and Bugs Bunny is the slick good samaritan who tries to teach Scrooge the meaning of Christmas.

The complex work of art features eight members of the Looney Tunes gang — Bugs Bunny, Tweety, Yosemite Sam, Pepe Le Pew, Porky Pig, Elmer Fudd and Foghorn Leghorn — riding in a sleigh with the Tasmanian Devil at the helm. It is available in a limited edition of 1,200 pieces and has a suggested retail price of $995.

"Paw De Deux," the first figurine in a special *Chuck Jones Signature Edition*, was produced to honor the legendary Warner Bros. animation director. Released in a limited edition of 2,500 pieces, each "Paw De Deux" figurine is hand-signed by Chuck Jones, one of the

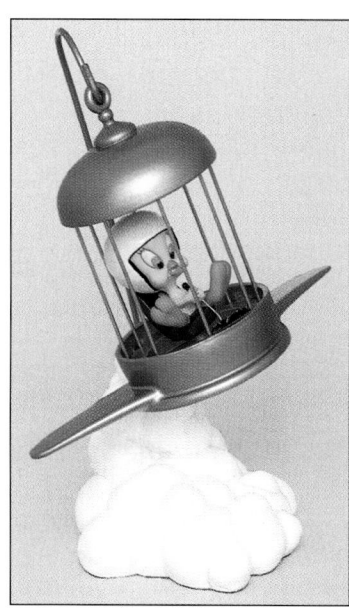

"The Only Way to Fly" hangs from a display stand of handcrafted resin and metal. Tweety may be removed and used as a Christmas ornament.

greatest animation directors of all time, winner of three Academy Awards, and recognized for Lifetime Achievement by national and international film festivals.

Based on the most popular cartoon of all time, "What's Opera, Doc?," "Paw De Deux" features Elmer Fudd, dressed as the demigod, Siegfried, and Bugs Bunny as a provocative Brunhilde. The figurine captures the moment in the cartoon when Elmer Fudd lifts Bugs Bunny above his head in a delicate flourish of operatic courtship. Bugs Bunny looks purely balletic, if not comedic, in his costume of armored bustier and pink tutu, his blonde braids sweeping out from beneath his winged helmet. Elmer Fudd wears his Valkyrie armor: a shiny breastplate and a horned helmet. The figurine retails for $245.

Based on the hilarious Warner Bros. cartoon "Rabbit Hood," "His Royal Hareness" depicts Bugs Bunny in regal attire as he outwits the slow-thinking Sheriff of Nottingham in this hilarious spoof of the literary classic, *Robin Hood*. The figurine is released in a limited edition of 5,000 pieces and retails for $70.00.

In the wacky cartoon, "The Jet Cage," birdcage-bound Tweety wants to fly like all the other birdies. So Granny sends away for a jet-powered flying bird cage, complete with crash helmet, that puts Tweety far above the reach of Sylvester's paws. But that "bad 'ol puddy tat" doesn't give up easily! Sylvester's antics land him in bandages and Tweety is free to fly like a jet.

The figural ornament, "The Only Way to Fly," features Tweety, crash helmet securely in place, soaring through the sky in his airborn aviary. The cage can be used as an ornament or hung from a stand that features a billowing cloud as the base. Released in a limited edition of 5,000 pieces, the figurine has a suggested retail price of $80.00; the hanger is $20.00.

Every figurine in the *Spotlight Collection* is a hand-numbered limited edition and comes with a Certificate of Authenticity and a Celcard that spotlights the scene that inspired the figurine. Many people consider the Celcards collector's items in their own right.

LOONEY TUNES CLASSIC COLLECTION OFFERS GIFTWARE

To complement the *Spotlight Collection* and extend the hilarity of the characters into giftware, Goebel has produced the *Looney Tunes Classic Collection*. Comprised of 19 wacky and wonderful motifs, this exciting new giftware collection features figurines, waterglobes, and ornaments. The characters are depicted in a wide array of antic situations themed to suit a variety of special occasions.

Looney Tunes Giftware has been designed to coincide with events and holidays throughout the year. Figurines like "24 Carrot X-mas" and "Snow Angel" mix the spirit of Christmas with the hijinks of the world's best-loved cartoon characters. Holiday ornaments such as "Silent Bite" and "Snow Bunny" are sure to make even the sourest Scrooge grin.

The Looney Tunes Classic Collection *figurines, "Tee'd Off" and "Oh, Father" celebrate the game of golf...with a twist!*

Birthdays, weddings, and holidays are celebrated with humor and light-hearted charm in the collection, as well. "I Do, 'Doc'" features Bugs Bunny and bride walking down the aisle, while "Nest Egg" is a figurine depicting a hatchling Tweety that doubles as a small box for keepsakes. "Birthday Tweat" and "Party Animal" cagily commemorate birthdays with Tweety and The Tasmanian Devil.

Who says love is always serious? To express affection on Valentine's Day, anniversaries, or whenever romance strikes, there are waterglobes and figurines in the collection that convey tender sentiments with a wacky twist. "Whirlwind Romance" is a musical waterglobe that features The Tasmanian Devil and his She-Devil. It plays the tune "Rock Around the Clock." The figurine "Tweet Heart" depicts Tweety as Cupid, complete with bow and arrow.

There's a *Looney Tunes Giftware* piece that's right for everyone and every occasion. Each piece is crafted of fine porcelain, affordably priced from $12.50 to $45.00, and beautifully boxed for gift-giving.

Pepe Le Pew and Penelope, Bugs Bunny and Lola Bunny, Taz and She Devil, and Tweety are poised for love and romance in a range of charming keepsakes from the Looney Tunes Classic Collection.

Goebel of North America
Rt. 31 North
Goebel Plaza
Pennington, NJ 08534

Phone:
609-737-8700

Fax:
609-737-1545

Web Site:
www.mihummel.com

Creating Rare Items for Special People

The King and Queen of Norway own their *Olympic Gold* medallions, as does multiple Olympic medal winner Peter Angerer. And Queen Elizabeth II is the owner of their solid silver *Chancellors of the Federal Republic of Germany* series. Yet even with all these celebrated admirers, The Goede Group considers each and every collector special — be they a member of royalty or an everyday hobbyist.

From a state-of-the-art facility in Waldaschaff, Northern Bavaria, Dr. Michael Goede presides over The Goede Group. He considers it a wonderful gift to be able to "make his passion his profession." As Dr. Goede explains, "Because of my personal love of collecting beautiful and rare objects, I am able to connect with my customers in a special way. Love, creativity and dedication are key ingredients in creating all of our exquisite collectors' items."

Goede considers all collectors to be special people who enjoy feeling "history in their hands." The interests of Goede Group collectors are highly diverse. Indeed, from new collecting ideas such as reproduction police badges and historical locomotives, to offerings inspired by the thousand-year history of coins and medallions, Goede has something wonderful for every collector.

Among the amazing and unique collectibles offered by The Goede Group is this telephone card that actually traveled into outer space!

FROM STUDENT TO ENTREPRENEUR

In 1978, while still a student, Dr. Michael Goede began to sell high quality collectors' items. The small firm he founded in Wuersburg, Germany, grew quickly and, in the early 1980s, it moved to larger headquarters in Aschaffenburg. Step by step, the Goede company's product lines expanded. Coins and medallions were added to stamps, and collectible offerings were broadened to include items such as decorations from famous orders, telephone cards, model cars, miniatures, reproduction badges and much more.

In 1993 the company moved to its present location in Waldaschaff. The firm's increasing success in Germany was coupled with growth in the international sector. Foreign subsidiaries now exist in the United States, Austria, France, Sweden, Finland, Norway, Denmark, the Benelux countries and Switzerland. Plans are now being made to begin operations in Canada, China and Japan. Today, Goede has more than 300 employees and serves 4.3 million customers worldwide.

Dr. Michael Goede is founder, managing director and C.E.O of The Goede Group.

CUSTOMER CONTACT YIELDS IDEAS

From the very beginning, dialogue with customers and a dedication to providing precise and accurate information have been two of the most important sales instruments of The Goede Group. The firm reaches and dialogues with customers through many media including direct marketing, TV advertising, personalized letters and the Internet.

Collectors appreciate the fact that each and every item offered by Goede is backed by an unconditional guarantee. What's more, customer service and satisfaction are top priorities. To make collecting easy and enjoyable, the firm provides customers with a subscription service for limited editions and collections. This ensures the stability of price and provides each subscriber with a "completion guarantee."

THE GERMAN MEDALLION MUSEUM

By creating the German Medallion Museum in Waldaschaff, Goede has undertaken an exciting project that preserves and celebrates a valuable aspect of art history. All friends of collecting are welcome to visit and enjoy the unique displays that feature wonderful examples from the long history of medallion minting.

For a coin, its most important attributes are rarity, condition and origin. But for a medallion, artistic appeal and craftsmanship are prime factors in determining its value. A medallion is a canvas for its creator — a mirror of the epoch in which he or she lives. The collections housed in the German Medallion Museum have been gathered and displayed to show the long history that this expressionistic art form has in virtually all cultures.

Along with displaying scores of medallions created by

well-known artists from medallion making's earliest beginning to the present, the exhibits at the German Medallion Museum also provide an interesting look at the history of engraving and minting techniques.

AMERICAN MINT BRINGS THE GOEDE GROUP TO THE U.S.A.

The Goede Group founded its U.S. subsidiary, American Mint, in 1997. Since its inception, American Mint has grown to become a major marketer of "themed" collectibles and a prime source for high quality, unique commemorative items.

Dedicated to quality, authenticity and craftsmanship, American Mint offers a stunning array of unique collectibles gathered by experts from across Europe and North America. Each item offered is a unique treasure that celebrates the history of our country, and the world, through a variety of mediums including silver, brass, pewter and porcelain. Available only by direct purchase from American Mint, all items are fully and unconditionally guaranteed.

Among American Mint's offerings you will find:

- **Commemorative Medallions**
  Meticulously crafted, polished-plate quality and struck from .999 pure silver — which is purer and brighter than sterling — these stunning medallions honor the people, events and objects that have been instrumental in building our civilization.
- **Collectible Coins**
  Select from a choice offering of rare and highly desirable uncirculated coins such as the "1999 American Eagle Silver Dollar."
- **Reproduction Badges and Medals**
  A striking selection of exacting reproductions of historic badges and medals is offered. Choose from medals representing Europe's most famous orders or badges from the Old West. All are meticulously detailed to replicate the antiques they mirror.
- **Desirable Stamps**
  A select offering of rare and wonderful stamps has been gathered from around the world, with many decorated in gold.
- **Miniature Locomotives**
  Exacting miniatures of the famous "iron horses" are featured from around the world. Each is small enough to hold in your hand, yet precise in every detail.
- **Commemorative Phone Cards**
  A new trend in collecting, these handsome phone cards pay tribute to a variety of people, places and events.
- **Porcelain Coffee and Tea Services**
  A beautiful tribute to the elegance and lavish lifestyles of the European nobility, American Mint's porcelain coffee and tea services are crafted using centuries-old techniques that speak of quality, beauty and romance.

In short, American Mint brings the joy of collecting to life. All American Mint exclusives are developed as

The headquarters of The Goede Group, located in Waldaschaff, Germany, is set in a natural environment that is conducive to creative thinking.

American Mint, the U.S. branch of The Goede Group, offers a wide variety of historically inspired collectibles, including reproduction badges.

collections making acquisition fun and simple. Their unwavering devotion to quality, integrity and customer service provides collecting confidence. And, because exceptional craftsmanship, fine materials and historical significance hallmark all American Mint collectibles, each is sure to bring years of enjoyment now and for future generations.

A ONE-STOP "COLLECTOR'S FORUM"

According to independent analysts, there are nearly 100 million collectors worldwide. To serve these enthusiasts, The Goede Group has founded "Collorum" as a universal web site. Located at Collorum.de, the European site is currently open for visitors, along with the American site at www.americanmint.com.

Collorum covers everything from autographs, coins, medallions, postage stamps and miniatures to the hottest current collectibles. The site features auction search engines, a facility to exchange collectors' items, and a game of chance. The site incorporates input from over 2,000 cooperative organizations.

As Collorum illustrates, The Goede Group faces the future with a strong emphasis on internationalization. Ultimately, it is the goal of The Goede Group to become the global partner of choice for collectors everywhere. To reach this goal, Goede will continue to listen to requests from its customers and the demands of the market. The customer alone determines what the firm will offer in the coming years.

For Goede, each business decision is made with one thing in mind: the fascination with collecting. It is this passion that transcends national borders and connects people around the world!

American Mint, LLC
20 Erford Road, Ste. 100A
Lemoyne, PA 17043

Phone:
717-975-8161

Fax:
717-975-8162

Web Sites:
www.Collorum.de
www.americanmint.com

E-mail:
tmiglino@paonline.com

Proudly Presenting "Art as Entertainment"

In 1972, David P. Usher had an idea to create a company which would improve the enjoyment of people's lives by offering high quality, affordable art. He founded The Greenwich Workshop in the suburb of Greenwich, Connecticut — hence the company's name — in a small storefront office, and with just $7,000 (charged to a credit card!).

A pioneer of the concept of hand-signed and numbered "limited edition" fine art prints, Usher chose an owl by Canadian artist Fenwick Lansdowne to be published as his new company's first print. The print sold out quickly, and success was marked by adopting the owl as part of the company's logo.

Through Usher's creative vision, leadership and integrity, The Greenwich Workshop — and the lucky owl! — quickly came to symbolize the leading fine art publisher in North America, attracting the most sought-after artists, the leading retailers of fine art and legions of loyal customers. More than 25 years later, The Greenwich Workshop remains a family-owned company trusted for quality, innovation and inspiration. Now under the care of the late David Usher's son, Scott Usher, the company continues to demonstrate its unique vision of "Art as Entertainment."

The "creative alchemists" behind the magic of The Greenwich Workshop are its artists. From the first limited edition prints and books, to the most recent introduction of three-dimensional fine art porcelain, every detail of every Greenwich Workshop product is created from a fine artist's inspiration. This is what truly sets apart The Greenwich Workshop Collection.

In "Offerings to the Little People," Howard Terpning portrays an age-old Native American tradition of sending special gifts to the tiny people in the ground that supposedly help tobacco seeds grow.

Scott Gustafson captures the magical moment when Dorothy and her friends first spy the glorious land of Oz in "Wizard of Oz."

HOWARD TERPNING HONORS A CROW CUSTOM

Among the 40-plus artists The Greenwich Workshop has proudly represented is Howard Terpning, creator of the award-winning "Offerings to the Little People." The original painting earned the "Gold Medal" (oils), "Best of Show" and "CA Award" at the prestigious 1998 Cowboy Artists of America Exhibition. It portrays a little-known Crow Indian custom in vivid and dramatic detail.

As Terpning explains, "Planting tobacco seeds was a religious event performed by the tobacco society. After the ground was prepared, members placed branches around the garden to protect the plants. Small offerings, such as bits of ribbon and feathers, were tied to the branches. Once the seeds were planted, sticks about 18" long were inserted into the ground with small medicine bunches attached. The Crow believed that little people lived in the ground and helped make the tobacco plants grow, so the bundles, containing berries, herbs, etc., along with tiny moccasins and other miniature articles of clothing, were given as offerings."

Scott Usher considers this work particularly compelling, as he notes in this word from the publisher: "I can't think of a better opportunity than the release of 'Offerings to the Little People' to reconfirm our mission as a fine art publisher: we make it possible for you to own limited edition replicas of original works of art which are otherwise accessible to a rare few and which have been approved and personalized by the artist. This award-winning painting by Howard Terpning is valued at hundreds of thousands of dollars and there is only one original. However, through a close collaboration between the artist, publisher and your authorized dealer, a wider audience — albeit one which is limited to the size of the edition — can enjoy this work of art in their own homes at an exceptionally fair price." That price is $875 for the 22-1/4" x 35" textured canvas, offered in an edition of 975 consecutive, artist-signed prints, each accompanied by a brass plate.

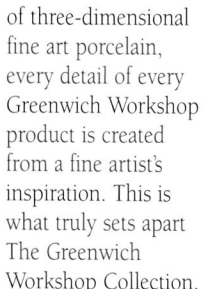

A 100TH ANNIVERSARY TRIBUTE FROM SCOTT GUSTAFSON

Another of The Greenwich Workshop's featured artists is Scott Gustafson, who has created an enchanting panorama to celebrate the 100th anniversary of the publication of the book, *The Wonderful Wizard of Oz*. From the blue Munchkin land in the West to the yellow Winkie kingdom in the East, Gustafson dots the landscape with more than a dozen memorable Oz characters.

The mustachioed Munchkin on the lower left of the print is modeled on author L. Frank Baum himself. Baum liked to be called the Royal Historian of Oz, and accordingly, Gustafson titles the hefty tome he's holding the "Royal History of Oz." Dorothy, Tin Man, Scarecrow, Cowardly Lion and other "Ozites" are pictured as well. Each of the 2,000 signed and consecutively numbered prints is available at $185.

ADDITIONAL MASTERS OF THE WORKSHOP

Two more favorite artists from The Greenwich Workshop — each of whom has an important new work now available — are Braldt Bralds and Nelson Boren. Bralds' creation is called "Diane's Broken Heart," and Boren's is named "Sittin' Pretty."

"Diane's Broken Heart" offers an artistic expression of the following poem: "The sea cast forth a heart of stone, divided but unbroken. Hold on to love, it cries to us in words unwrit, unspoken..." It was created by Bralds after a friend found the heart-shaped rock it depicts on a beach in Maine. At the time, the friend — Diane — was suffering hurt due to a misunderstanding with her "significant other." Finding the "heart rock" meant a great deal to her, and she lent it to Bralds for him to paint. At an image size of 11" x 11", the edition of 1,500 signed and consecutively numbered prints sells for $125 each.

"Sittin' Pretty" shows a group of boot-clad folks all lined up together on a set of wooden risers — but only from the knees down! The punch line comes from the fact that there are five sets of boots in all: two women on either side of one chaps-clad cowboy. Scott Usher explains that the viewer's perception of this situation depends on his or her gender.

"When we offered to help Nelson title this piece, an interesting trend revealed itself," Usher recalls. "Suggestions from guys at the Workshop ran to 'Good Odds' and 'All the Luck,' while the gals tended to come up with phrases like 'Slim Pickin's.' But the artist is used to hearing a host of responses from viewers. His gestalt-inspired technique, giving only an enticing piece of a larger, intriguing picture, invites viewers to indulge their imagination and complete each story for themselves."

Boren adds, "Maybe he's a real popular cowboy, or maybe he's babysitting his sisters. It's up to you!" This reproduction of the original "Sittin' Pretty" painting meas-

"Duck Tape" by Will Bullas whimsically captures what dastardly developments can take place when a duck or two tangle with everyone's favorite silver-gray tape.

ures 45" x 16" and has been published on deckled paper in an edition of 450 prints, signed by the artist and consecutively numbered. The price is $345.

Among the many other celebrated artists presenting their work through The Greenwich Workshop today are: Bev Doolittle, James C. Christensen, William S. Phillips, John Buxton, Simon Combes, Bonnie Marris, Paul Landry, John Weiss, Will Bullas and Stephan Lyman.

THE FUTURE INCLUDES AN IMPRESSIVE WEB PRESENCE

Scott Usher is proud to invite collectors to visit The Greenwich Workshop's newly upgraded, re-designed and re-tooled web site at www.greenwichworkshop.com. As he comments, "The old site let you get a look at what was new, but the time has come for us to take advantage of the dynamic, in-depth and responsive qualities of the Internet."

At the new web site, collectors can follow the creation of selected, new originals, as well as reserve and register the subsequent print on-line. They can browse through an artist's portfolio in-depth or check up on that artist's schedule of appearances and shows. In the future, certain editions will be exclusively released on-line, and there will be "chat" sessions with the artists.

Yet Usher wants to assure collectors that the firm has not gone "high tech" at the expense of "high touch." As he concludes, "Remember, for all this electronic wizardry, we still feel that the person-to-person relationship between you and your local authorized dealer is the most important aspect in a successful art purchase. Let us make it easier to see what we're up to; count on your local dealer to make it happen right."

The Greenwich Workshop produces handsome fine art books, as well as prints and porcelains. One outstanding, recent example is Bev Doolittle's The Forest Has Eyes.

The Greenwich Workshop
One Greenwich Place
P.O. Box 875
Shelton, CT 06484-0875

Phone:
800-243-4246

Fax:
203-925-0262

Web Site:
www.greenwichworkshop.com

THE GREENWICH WORKSHOP

One Woman's Vision Revives an 18th Century Art

Elegant 18th century English enamels had always captured Susan Benjamin's imagination. As a young girl, she spent many afternoons examining the delicate hand-painted brushstrokes on the dozens of enamel boxes that filled her family's London home.

In 1950, she opened a small antique shop in London called Halcyon Days to offer collectors a variety of 18th century English objets d'art, including the rare enameled boxes she so loved.

Word about the tiny shop, overflowing with splendid examples of the lost craft, spread throughout the United Kingdom, to the Continent, and then across the Atlantic to America. Patrons from all over the world came to call, and business was brisk.

During the 1960s, when demand for the enamels eventually exceeded their supply, Mrs. Benjamin had an inspiration, and in 1970, Halcyon Days, in partnership with a manufacturer now called Bilston & Battersea Enamels, began a new chapter in the history of English enamels. Susan Benjamin's design artistry, combined with the manufacturer's expertise, revived the 18th century craft and produced the first Halcyon Days Enamels collection.

Their imaginative designs and impeccable quality won the unique pieces instant admiration in collectors' circles. The hand-painted boxes had captured the qualities of the beautiful copper enamels of the 18th century.

The Hermitage Collection: "Lady in a Garden," limited to editions of 500 boxes, is a design from a continuing series launched in 2000 in honor of Halcyon Days Enamels' 30th anniversary.

The millennium signaled the beginning of Halcyon Days Enamels 30th anniversary celebration of the craft's revival. Three decades later, the collection of over 400 exquisite enameled and sculpted pieces still sets the standard for excellence in design and production. Sales have doubled in the United States in five years, accounting for over half of the company's business. Halcyon Days Enamels are available in the United States through fine retailers including Neiman Marcus, Nordstrom, Scully and Scully, Gump's, Jacobson's and Marshall Field's.

Royalty, Heads-of-State, and collectors worldwide share an unbounded enthusiasm for Halcyon Days

"Happy Birthday," a two-year edition, makes a thoughtful gift for a special occasion.

Enamels. In recognition of their special status, Baroness Margaret Thatcher, the first woman Prime Minister of England, officially opened the United States' first gallery at Randall Morgan Stationery, which is dedicated to the sale and display of the entire Halcyon Days Enamels collection.

HISTORY OF ENGLISH ENAMELS

Small boxes enameled on copper were first made in England in the 1740s. Examples from the period are not only rich in design, they also embrace a fascinating history of fashion, utility and craftsmanship.

Enamel boxes were used by the aristocracy of 18th century England for a variety of practical purposes: to "contain snuff," "beauty spots" made of black paper or taffeta, or cachous to sweeten the breath. Other boxes intended for breath mints, called *bonbonnières*, were made in sculptural form with a porcelain lid and enamel base.

Toward the turn of the 19th century, the little boxes simply went out of fashion and by 1840, production of English copper enamels ceased. The craft lay virtually dormant for 130 years until revived in the 20th century.

REBIRTH OF A TRADITION

Susan Benjamin, assisted by a team of artists, creates each Halcyon Days Enamels design in her Brook Street, London, studio. Mrs. Benjamin is personally involved in the design process from initial inspiration to final approval.

The exceptional variety of the designs is inspired in part by historic artifacts...an ancient tapestry, a famous painting, a motto or quotation, or an original 18th century enamel from Halcyon Days' private collection.

One-third of the collection is retired each season to make room for over 120 new designs introduced annually. Including special commissions, Susan Benjamin has created nearly 6,300 unique pieces since 1970.

In recognition of excellence for service and quality, Halcyon Days has been granted the maximum number of royal warrants a business may display – four. Only eight

"Original Teddy," issued at $125, is named for President "Teddy" Roosevelt.

English companies in the world have achieved this honor.

Following Mrs. Benjamin's specifications and the traditional enameling process, Bilston & Battersea Enamels produces the collection. The process is extremely labor intensive. The factory employs over 150 artisans who craft and paint each design by hand. To achieve the mellow, creamy finish of the pieces, each must receive numerous firings. Over a four-week period, every one will pass through at least 30 separate skilled hand-processes before it is ready to leave the factory.

Endorsed by the Royal Family, Halcyon Days Enamels is the only collection in the industry granted the privilege to display the Queen's Warrant, Elizabeth II, on the base of each design.

THE COLLECTION

From images of delicate florals to majestic creatures of the wild, the collection offers designs in a variety of objets d'art including boxes in 38 shapes and sculptural pieces. Extremely popular is the tradition of dated editions created specifically for Christmas, Valentine's Day, Easter and Mother's Day. Introduced 27 years ago, the enamel "Easter Egg" is the most established of all dated editions.

In honor of the company's 30th anniversary, two exceptional collections of limited edition, continuing series were launched in 2000. Released over the next several years, designs in *The State Box Collection* highlight the heritage of each state in America. Each design is a limited edition of 1,000 pieces per state. *The Hermitage Collection,* produced in collaboration with The State Hermitage Museum in St. Petersburg, Russia, features limited edition designs that replicate fine European paintings found in the museum's collection.

Other limited editions include "An Impressionist

This porcelain and enamel box of "Peter Rabbit™" from Frederick Warne's The World of Peter Rabbit *is a sculptural design known as a bonbonnière.*

Garden," limited to 500 boxes, and "The Calendar Box," limited to 1,000 boxes. "Flowers in a Vase," limited to 500 boxes, features the elaborate design of a late 1800's greeting card from the Smithsonian Institute. Accented with a butterfly, a spray of bold red and yellow blooms overflows a blue patterned vase. Each limited edition is numbered and includes a corresponding numbered Certificate of Authenticity.

Several splendid designs in this year's *Millennium Collection* deliver contemporary messages. Limited in production, "Children of the World" portrays youths of many nations celebrating their individual cultures, linking hands to symbolize peace and friendship.

With the success of Halcyon Days Enamels, Susan Benjamin spearheaded the revival of yet another rare 18th century art form: the *bonbonnière*. First introduced in 1997, this popular collection offers over 40 handcrafted designs including "Peter Rabbit™." "The Old Woman" is the third dated box created for the award-winning *Childhood* series. Each sculptural piece is underglazed with the Halcyon Days emblem – "HD London," together with the artist's initials.

In addition, the number of enamels handcrafted to enhance the holidays continues to grow. Limited to 750 pieces, this year's "Wrapping the Presents" is the final sphere in a series of three ornaments featuring a Victorian Christmas.

SPECIAL DESIGNS

Beginning in 1995, Halcyon Days Enamels has offered exclusive designs which depict beloved characters found in a variety of children's literature and films. From Walt Disney's classic *Winnie the Pooh,* the collection offers a piece entitled "Christopher Robin Knew…" The design is limited to 500 detailed boxes and features the E.H. Shepard illustration of Christopher gathered in discussion with friends from the Hundred Acre Wood.

A number of commissioned pieces are produced by Halcyon Days Enamels to benefit charities, honor commemorative events, or to be given as corporate gifts. Unveiled in 2000, "The Summer Tanager" benefits the Susan G. Komen Breast Cancer Foundation, the nation's leading catalyst in the fight against breast cancer. Halcyon Days Enamels may also be individualized with special messages and "Works of Art" – the reproduction of a personal photograph onto an enamel box.

The beauty of the enameling technique has been applied to other products in the collection, including desk accessories, cufflinks, clocks, watches, plaques, handbag accessories, and photograph frames…all produced with meticulous care and to the same exacting standards, and all destined to be cherished antiques.

Halcyon Days Enamels
P.O. Box 66599
Chicago AMF, IL 60666

Phone:
877-798-1488

Fax:
630-766-5189

E-mail:
halcyondays.enamels@
btinternet.com

Hallmark Keepsake Ornaments Bring Special Holiday Magic

"Jazzy Jalopy," a Keepsake Magic Ornament, plays a jaunty ragtime tune, while Santa and his reindeer go for a little joy ride.

Imagine holiday celebrations before the introduction of *Hallmark Keepsake Ornaments*. Americans decorated their Christmas trees with the same old mass-produced glass balls that everyone else used...the same old tinsel, the same old garland.

From their introduction more than 25 years ago, *Hallmark Keepsake Ornaments* have brought a special magic to holiday decorating, making each year's celebration more personal and more fun than the last. Today, thanks to new technological wonders and the special touch of each *Keepsake Ornament* studio artist, designs employ light, motion, and sound to inspire a thrilling sense of holiday cheer in grown-up collectors and children (both naughty and nice), alike.

THE MAGIC BEGINS

According to Clara Johnson Scroggins, a renowned authority on ornament collecting, "Hallmark was the very first company to date glass ornaments and to apply artistic designs on a printed band." Scroggins recalls that, "Hallmark was also the first to put a glass ornament in its own box, making it collectible as well as giftable. No one had ever done that before."

Other *Keepsake Ornament* "Firsts:"

1973 – Hallmark introduces *Keepsake Ornaments* with a collection of six decorated ball ornaments and 12 yarn figures.

1975 – First handcrafted *Keepsake Ornaments* debut.

1976 – "Baby's First Christmas" is the industry's first commemorative ornament.

1979 – First edition of the *Here Comes Santa* series, the longest-running *Keepsake Ornament* series, is introduced.

1980 – The first two Special Edition ornaments debut: "Heavenly Minstrel" and "Checking It Twice."

1983 – Clara Johnson Scroggins publishes the first complete guide to *Hallmark Keepsake Ornaments*.

1984 – First lighted *Keepsake Ornaments* appear, paving the way for the addition of music, motion and even talking *Keepsake Magic Ornaments*.

1987 – Hallmark organizes the Keepsake Ornament Collector's Club. Today, the club is more than 200,000 members strong, making it the largest organization of its kind.

1988 – Hallmark offers *Keepsake Miniature Ornaments*, the industry's first complete line of miniature ornaments.

1991 – The first national Hallmark Keepsake Ornament Collector's Club Convention is held in Kansas City.

1991 – First *Hallmark Keepsake Ornaments* for Easter are introduced.

1993 – Hallmark introduces Anniversary Editions, commemorating 20 years of *Keepsake Ornaments*.

1993 – Hallmark introduces the *Keepsake Ornament Showcase* line, a premiere offering featuring 19 ornaments in four distinctive theme groups: *Folk Art Americana, Old World Silver, Portraits in Bisque* and *Holiday Enchantment*.

1993 – First *Personalized Keepsake Ornaments* appear with 12 designs that may be personalized with name, date or even a phrase. "Messages of Christmas" becomes the first ornament that consumers can record with their own message to be replayed season after season.

1995 – Lighted *Keepsake Miniature Ornaments* light up the tree. Silent motors for *Keepsake Magic Ornaments* also debut.

1995 – *Keepsake Ornaments* celebrate the 15th Anniversary of the *Rocking Horse* series with a special "Anniversary Edition Pewter Rocking Horse."

1995 – For the first time, members of the Keepsake Ornament Collector's Club appear in photo holder ornaments.

"The Cat in the Hat" two ornament set, first in the Dr. Seuss® Book series featuring delightful characters from the classic children's books, is sculpted by Keepsake Ornament artist Nello Williams.

"Best Pals" from the Holiday Traditions group shows Santa being serenaded by a talented little cockatiel. Artist Nina Aubé sculpted this ornament for 1999.

1996 – The first *Collector's Choice* ornament, "Come All Ye Faithful" is picked by Clara Johnson Scroggins as epitomizing the spirit of the holiday and the essence of *Keepsake Ornaments*.

1997 – Favorite Disney characters, including Mickey Mouse, return to the *Keepsake Ornament* line after a 20-year absence.

1998 – The 25th Anniversary of *Keepsake Ornaments*. Thousands of club members gather in Kansas City for the gala celebration.

1999 – *Laser Gallery* ornaments debut. Each is an exciting play of light and shadow, precisely cut by an invisible beam of pure laser light and hand-assembled.

2000 – Hallmark introduces *Hallmark Keepsake Collections*. Building on the success of popular Hallmark collectible lines such as *Kiddie Car Classics* and *Merry Miniatures®* figurines, collectors can pursue their special passion, brighten someone's day, or commemorate a special moment. Each piece is a personal treasure to be cherished by future generations. Among the product lines in the collection are *Great American Railways*, *Legends in Flight*, *Merry Miniatures* and *Kiddie Car Classics*.

POPULAR CHARACTERS AND CULTURAL CHANGE

Hallmark Keepsake Ornaments pioneered many changes through the years, and they continue to change with the times. While family and friends will always select ornaments to commemorate special memories and milestones, choices now include ornaments that salute popular characters, personalities and cultural change.

Who would have predicted that BARBIE® would find her place on a Christmas tree? Or Superman? *Keepsake Ornaments* also celebrate the movies like the popular Disney film *The Lion King*. Even *Keepsake Miniature Ornaments* feature the stars of "Tiny Toon Adventures," among others.

Keepsake Ornaments traditionally commemorate historic events in innovative ways. "The Eagle Has Landed"

captures the drama of the first moon landing, complete with the actual recorded transmission, "One small step for man, one giant leap for mankind."

Changing lifestyles are reflected in *Keepsake Ornaments* such as "Santa's Answering Machine," computers in "People Friendly," and "Messages of Christmas," which gives revelers the chance to record their own messages to be enjoyed season after season.

And STAR TREK® continues to take Christmas where no holiday has gone before, with a variety of favorite starships and characters from the various STAR TREK® television series and movies.

COLLECTOR FRIENDLY GUIDES

Keepsake Ornaments: A Collector's Guide, written by Clara Johnson Scroggins and published in collaboration with Hallmark, assists collectors in keeping track of their collections.

Another helpful resource for collectors is the *Dream Book* published by Hallmark each year. It features an array of more than 200 brand-new *Keepsake Ornaments*, decorating ideas, and the artists who sculpted or designed each ornament, along with those artists' thoughts about some of their designs. *The Dream Book* is available from Hallmark Gold Crown stores at no charge.

"Frosty Friends," one of the most popular Keepsake Ornaments of all time, was first introduced 20 years ago.

KEEPSAKE ORNAMENT COLLECTOR'S CLUB

Exclusive *Keepsake Ornaments* for members only top the list of great benefits offered to members of the Hallmark Keepsake Ornament Collector's Club.

Other significant membership benefits include:

• The opportunity to purchase one each of an assortment of exclusive Club Edition Ornaments.

• Invitations to attend collector's events. Some years, the Keepsake Ornament Collector's Club hosts events for members only. In other years, the club makes special appearances at collector's shows and events that are sponsored by other groups.

• A subscription to "Collector's Courier," the official newsletter of the club, which is full of insider tips about the artists, decorating, local clubs, and more.

• The annual *Dream Book*, mailed directly to club members' homes.

• A personalized membership card that, from time to time, is good for special gifts in Hallmark stores.

Plus the joy of meeting other club members – the nicest folks around – who share the same interests.

Keepsake Ornament Collector's Club P.O. Box 419034 Kansas City, MO 64141-6034

Phone: 800-HALLMARK

Web Site: www.hallmark.com

HALLMARK CARDS, INC.

A Leader in Collecting for Over 30 Years

One of the world's leading direct response marketers of limited edition collectibles, The Hamilton Collection has delighted collectors around the world with its unique product assortment for over three decades. From fine porcelain collector plates and figurines, to die cast cars and a wide variety of sculptures, Hamilton's wide product base is just one of the reasons for its success. Today, the company continues its mission to satisfy the increasing demand from astute collectors by bringing to market exciting and innovative product lines.

In addition to enjoying prestigious joint ventures that enable the company to present a number of licensed products including Enesco's *Precious Moments®* and *Cherished Teddies®* collections, Cast Art's *Dreamsicles™*, *I Love Lucy®*, NASCAR, *Easyriders®*, and others, The Hamilton Collection has been busy over the last year developing a number of new product lines that have already met with great enthusiasm from collectors. The most exciting new brand names include *Motorsport*

Officially authorized by Dale Earnhardt, Inc., the Good Ole™ Bears collection of limited edition figurines is inspired by Earnhardt's loyal pit crew.

Motorsport Editions™, a new division solely devoted to providing race fans with the most innovative racing collectibles today. Importantly, the firm has established exciting partnerships with agents of the most popular drivers, as well as today's most talented motorsports artists like Sam Bass

"Gina" debuts the new Cherished Teddies Carousel Collection from The Hamilton Collection.

and Robert Tanenbaum. This allows collectors the opportunity to acquire officially authorized collectibles whose authenticity and quality are guaranteed. Already a driving force in the world of racing collectibles, *Motorsport Editions™* offers collectors tributes that are personally autographed by the drivers, limited edition die cast cars, sculptures, medallions, special edition prints, and more.

Fans of Dale Earnhardt will want to make an important pit stop at *Motorsport Editions™* for the introduction of the brand new *Dale Earnhardt Good Ole™ Bears Figurine Collection*. This new line of limited edition figurines is officially authorized by Dale Earnhardt, Inc. and is inspired by "The Intimidator's" loyal pit crew. The collection features "Need a Lift?," who hoists the car; "Rear Tire Changer," who quickly changes tires; "Gassin' Around," who fills the tank, and more. There's even a *Good Ole Bear™* that resembles the seven-time Winston Cup champion himself! Each adorable bear is costumed in Earnhardt's trademark team colors, hand-numbered, accompanied by a Certificate of Authenticity, and decorated by hand.

Editions™, offering collectors today's hottest racing collectibles; *Sacred Spirits™*, a new line devoted to collectibles inspired by the spirit of Native America; and *Rainbow Reef™*, a family of unique figurines and sculptures capturing the wonder of the sea.

MOTORSPORT EDITIONS™ MAKES ITS DEBUT

In response to the unprecedented growth of professional stock car racing, The Hamilton Collection launched

HAMILTON PRESENTS THE FIRST-EVER CHERISHED TEDDIES® CAROUSEL BY PRISCILLA HILLMAN

In honor of the 100th Anniversary of the American carousel, The Hamilton Collection, in association with Enesco Corporation, recently introduced the first-ever *Cherished Teddies®* Carousel by acclaimed artist Priscilla Hillman, winner of the prestigious 1996 "Miniature of the Year" Award from the National Association of Limited Edition Dealers (NALED). Thanks to their sentimental messages of love and friendship, the *Cherished Teddies*

collection reigns among today's most popular giftware lines, and is now presented to collectors in an enchanting new carousel figurine.

Collectors can relive fond childhood memories of a day at the county fair with "Gina," an adorable teddie bear dressed in red, white and blue, perched high upon a delightful carousel pony. The figurine features all the heartwarming, homespun charm that is the trademark of *Cherished Teddies* collectibles. Meticulously detailed and painted entirely by hand, the figurine also features a golden pole and finial enhanced with a real red ribbon. "Gina" debuts the new *Cherished Teddies Carousel Collection* and is available exclusively from The Hamilton Collection.

EXPLORE THE SPIRIT OF NATIVE AMERICA WITH THE *SACRED SPIRITS*™ COLLECTION

One of the most unique trends in today's collecting world is the popularity of sculptures and figurines inspired by Native American legend and lore. The Hamilton Collection has been a strong leader in presenting collectors with a wide variety of products based on American Indian subjects. And most recently, the firm underscored their commitment to collectors of this genre by introducing their new *Sacred Spirits*™ line, a family of collectibles inspired by the proud cultures and rich traditions of our country's native people. The line offers unique figurines, sculptures, ornaments, plates, and more, and will showcase some of the most talented artists in the field of Native American art, with works by such recognizable names as Ray Swanson, Steve Kehrli and Al Agnew.

The Hamilton Collection recently collaborated with artist Steve Kehrli to create *Nature's Spiritual Realm Collection*, a tribute to the harmony between Native American culture and nature's untamed elements of earth, wind, water and fire. The premier issue, "Spirit of the Wind," celebrates the spirit guides who bring the power of those elements to life. This striking tribute is of unparalleled drama as artist Steve Kehrli captures the fulfillment of a spiritual quest. Here, the magnificent spirit eagle is portrayed in fluid motion as it encircles a handsome youth with the power of the wind. The warrior's acceptance of his destiny is vividly captured as he opens his arms to the light of wisdom, like a flower opening its petals to the rays of the sun. Available exclusively from Hamilton's *Sacred Spirits* line, "Spirit of the Wind" measures an impressive 10-1/4" tall and is accompanied by a Certificate of Authenticity.

Artist Steve Kehrli brings the art of ancient cultures to life in "Spirit of the Wind" from Nature's Spiritual Realm Collection.

"I Want To Be Your Snuggle Bear" premiers Hamilton's Snuggle Figurine Collection, *featuring the fabric softener-loving character.*

◆ WHIMSICAL FIGURINES WARM THE HEARTS OF COLLECTORS

The Hamilton Collection is also enchanting collectors with a unique selection of figurines that have a special heartwarming and whimsical quality. And it seems that collectors just can't get enough of adorable figurines, whether they feature playful elephants as in the *Protect Nature's Innocents*™ line, or one of their newest offerings, the adorable Snuggle® bear figurine based on the huggable television bear icon.

Among Hamilton's newest presentations from their popular *Protect Nature's Innocents* line comes "Showered With Love," the very first glitter globe figurine from this exclusive Hamilton family of collectibles. Collectors will be captivated as they watch a tender moment unfold as a devoted mother elephant showers her baby with love. Everyone loves glitter globes, and with a gentle shake, glitter gently cascades about the baby elephant like shimmering droplets of water. Expertly crafted and lovingly painted by hand, this delightful collectible premiers the *Wonders in Water Collection*, portraying mother and child elephants in playful water scenes.

For decades, popular television icons have captured the hearts of collectors everywhere. From the nostalgic Campbell's Soup Kids to the fun-loving Coca-Cola®. Polar Bears, these charming characters and their whimsical antics have had a strong impact on the world of collectibles.

Most recently, the adorable fabric softener-loving character known simply as "Snuggle®" made its debut as the first-ever figurine inspired by the character touting a popular fabric softener. The Hamilton Collection recently introduced "I Want To Be Your Snuggle Bear," featuring a heartwarming figurine cozying up to a soft, cuddly blanket. Available exclusively from Hamilton's *Snuggle Figurine Collection,* this enchanting premier figurine measures 4-1/2" high. New issues in the series feature the adorable bear turning wash day into play in "A Basket Full of Sweet Snuggle" and "Snuggle's Story Time," portraying this lovable little bear reading a favorite book. Each is intricately handcrafted, hand-painted, and accompanied by a Certificate of Authenticity.

Contact the company to learn more about unique collectibles available from The Hamilton Collection.

The Hamilton Collection
9204 Center
For The Arts Drive
Niles, IL, 60714-1300

Phone:
800-228-2945

Fax:
904-279-1339

Web Site:
www.collectiblestoday.com

Collectibles Dedicated to Keeping the Flame

For nearly a decade, the words "Harbour Lights" have come to signify much more than simply a collectible line. Collectors will tell you, quite emphatically, that these beautiful lighthouse sculptures represent more profound things, such as history, culture and tradition.

For Bill Younger, the founder of Harbour Lights, lighthouses represent America's proud nautical heritage. He still remembers the first time that he saw a light station up close, as a child, while on a fishing trip on the Chesapeake Bay. "We sailed near Thomas Point Light, and I was awestruck. I remember thinking about the keepers and families who stayed there, what it must have been like to live and work in a lighthouse."

A DREAM IS BORN

Bill Younger, the first sales representative in the United States for David Winter Cottages, felt right at home speaking about historic architecture. While Bill loved the traditional English structural design, he yearned to offer a collectible that would represent American history. In 1989, when the Postal Service issued a stamp collection in honor of the bi-centennial of our nation's lighthouses, Bill was inspired to create a line of sculptures that would accurately depict our majestic American architecture.

The spectacular symbol of freedom, "Liberty Enlightening the World," measures 9" x 7" and retires on December 31, 2000.

Since the first introductions, lighthouse lovers and people who simply appreciate the meticulous craftsmanship of the Harbour Lights' sculptures have responded overwhelmingly to the line. When asked why they love Harbour Lights, collectors will invariably respond, "There is so much detail," or "They're so realistic!" or "It's like you're standing right there." This is exactly what Bill had hoped to achieve.

ALL IN THE FAMILY

Harbour Lights has been a family affair since its inception. Much of the original research was carried out by daughter Kim Andrews, who manages the company. Now that Bill is able to devote himself full time to Harbour Lights, he does a great deal of his own research, personally photographing many of the light stations chosen for production.

Nancy Younger, Bill's wife, serves as "Head Keeper" of the popular Harbour Lights Collectors Society, which caters to the needs of over 25,000 collectors. Although busy with two little ones at home, Bill's daughter, Tori Dawn, contributes time as an origination painting artist. Her husband, Harry Hine, heads the art and quality control department.

FROM A TWINKLE IN BILL'S EYE TO A FINISHED SCULPTURE

Every Harbour Lights replica begins on location, usually with Bill and his camera. Extensive research is required to achieve an accurate finished product. From photographs, architectural plans and drawings, sculptors begin to work their magic, painstakingly creating an authentic model, and finally a mold. Depending upon the item, high-grade gypsum or cold-cast porcelain is carefully poured into the mold.

Accuracy, while difficult to achieve, is paramount. Origination painters often use shards of stone or brick from the original lighthouse to guide their work. Each paint is carefully mixed to create the proper hue, and then, with expert dexterity, the paint is applied with fine brush strokes. From its humble beginnings as a simple cast, the sculpture is transformed into a thing of beauty, a faithful replica of the actual sentinel.

The beautiful New York lighthouse, "Sister(s) Island" measures 4" x 7-1/2" and is limited to production through March 31, 2001.

Working closely with his wife and daughters, Bill's dream became a reality in the spring of 1991, when Harbour Lights was introduced to the world. The original 17 limited editions were chosen by Bill and his family from America's most famous and beloved sentinels.

Harbour Lights' 2000-2001 Members Exclusive "Boca Grande, Florida" is only available through April 2001 to members of the Harbour Lights Collectors Society.

LIMITED AND OPEN EDITIONS

Much of Harbour Lights award-winning collection is devoted to limited editions, ranging from 5,500 to 10,000 hand-numbered pieces. Each piece is beautifully gift-boxed, and comes complete with its own history and Certificate of Authenticity. After the edition limit is reached, molds are destroyed, and the piece is officially retired.

In 1995, Harbour Lights created a wonderful new series of hand-numbered, open edition sculptures entitled *Great Lighthouses of the World*. Commemorating the world's most celebrated light stations, this remarkable series includes such favorites as "Portland Head, Maine" and "Key West, Florida." When a *Great Lighthouse* is purchased, a portion of the proceeds is donated to the organization responsible for the preservation, restoration or maintenance of that particular lighthouse.

RECENT DEVELOPMENTS

2000 marked the introduction of Harbour Lights' magnificent replica, "American Shoal, Florida." "American Shoal" lighthouse is a unique and complex metalwork screwpile, created using the latest technology and skilled craftsmanship. This distinctive sentinel also completes the original "stamp series" from Harbour Lights. In 1989, the U.S. Postal Service issued a set of five commemorative postage stamps to honor the bi-centennial of the Lighthouse Establishment. Harbour Lights created four of those five lighthouses as their first introductions and included the matching stamp with the sculptures. But the "American Shoal" beacon was too difficult to reproduce at that time, so Harbour Lights purchased the remaining stamps from the U.S. Postal Service and saved them until their artists could do the lighthouse justice. The result is a master-piece of precision and craftsmanship

In 1996, Harbour Lights introduced its first international edition, "Peggy's Cove, Nova Scotia." In the summer of 1999, a wonderful sculpture commemorating the world's oldest, active light station, "La Coruña, Spain," was released. This magnificent sentinel has been lighting the way for mariners since the second century A.D.!

Harbour Lights now offers several other products for the lighthouse aficionado. These include a wonderful

The vibrant 5th order Frensel lens, the perfect complement to a maritime collection, measures 8" x 4-1/2" and was issued as a special edition of just 4,000 hand-numbered pieces.

assortment of Christmas ornaments and *This Little Light of Mine*, a brand new collection of miniature lighthouses for the casual buyer or gift-giver looking for a memento of their visit to one of our nation's beacons.

COLLECTORS SOCIETY CELEBRATES 6TH EXCITING YEAR!

Collectors are the driving force behind Harbour Lights. In 1995, the Harbour Lights Collectors Society was founded to support the growing number of collectors. The response has been tremendous. Each member receives a number of exciting benefits, including the opportunity to purchase members-only, exclusive editions.

Harbour Lights is celebrating the Society's 6th anniversary year with the magnificent "Boca Grande, Florida" lighthouse. Legend has it that Gasparilla Island, where Boca Grande is located, was named for the infamous pirate José Gaspar. All members will receive a redemption certificate for the Christmas Ornament Exclusive "Seven Foot Knoll, Maryland." In addition, each new and renewing member will receive a handsome limited edition sculpture, "Southwest Reef, Louisiana." This $60.00 value is a special gift to members.

ANCHOR BAY SETS SAIL

In early 1997, Bill Younger announced the creation of a brand new line of collectible boats and ships, *Anchor Bay*. Because of his love for maritime history and the sea, Bill felt that *Anchor Bay* was a "natural progression" for his growing company. Each hand-painted sculpture includes numerous components and comes complete with a wooden base and mirrored glass case. *Anchor Bay* is a numbered, special edition collection, featuring tugboats, steamships, trawlers, skipjacks, and of course, the all-important lightship.

PRESERVING OUR LEGACY

Each year Bill Younger travels throughout the United States, visiting with collectors and sharing the story of Harbour Lights. When he meets collectors, Bill often conveys the importance of preserving lighthouses and the memory of those who risked their lives to keep the flames burning. Harbour Lights has been an active participant in the lighthouse preservation movement, donating substantial funds to this important cause.

In April 1999, Bill Younger received the prestigious "Achievement Award" from the International Collectible Exposition® for his years of dedication to the gift and collectibles industry. As is his way, Bill gave all of the credit to the devoted collectors and dealers, who together with Harbour Lights, are helping to ensure that lighthouses are never forgotten.

Harbour Lights
1000 North Johnson Ave.
El Cajon, CA 92020

Phone:
800-365-1219

Fax:
888-579-1911

Web Site:
www.harbourlights.com

E-mail:
harbourlights@harbourlights.com

Chance Encounters Create Collectors' Kingdom

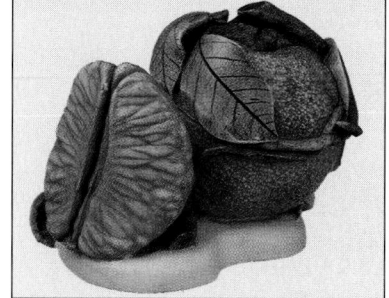

The tale of Lord Byron continues in the "Orange," where he courageously challenges and defeats Mighty Toro, the beetle.

Harmony Kingdom does not consider itself a "typical" collectibles company, which may seem understandable since the founding of the company was seemingly by happenstance. According to company lore, the story began with a shepherd, a vagabond artist and a collection of dreams. All came together at one time or another to make Harmony Kingdom what it is today.

A CHANCE MEETING

A shepherd turned designer and mold-maker, Englishman Martin Perry met an artist and entrepreneur, Noel Wiggins. Noel had built a successful importing and manufacturing business, the Harmony Ball Company, and was traveling through Europe seeking the perfect box for his chiming silver balls.

A businessman himself, Martin was the owner of Antiquark, Ltd., where he sculpted and sold original pieces. He shared with Noel his unique carvings of animals that contained hidden compartments for small keepsakes. Noel quickly recognized that the designer's sculptures blended perfectly with the ideas he had for a business venture – the items would tell a story, with a "built-in narrative, which is universally understood."

This chance meeting in 1995 led to the creation of Harmony Kingdom, which has become one of the fastest growing lines in the collectibles industry with its intriguing Box Figurines™. These handcrafted figures are actually treasure boxes – each with its own story to tell and secrets to reveal.

To celebrate the millennium, Harmony Kingdom introduced "Y2HK," a crowded boat that represents the Planet Earth.

THE BEGINNINGS

Just ten months after the initial meeting, another chance encounter took place that would directly impact the future of Harmony Kingdom.

While Noel Wiggins was attending the Chicago Gift Show in 1995, he met Paul Osnain, a collectibles expert. Noel shared with Paul the difficulty they were having copyrighting jewelry products and retaining customer loyalty due to competition from copycat companies. He also showed Paul the new line of small boxes, the *Treasure Jests*. Paul offered valuable advice to Noel on how a successful collectible company operates: a brand name is essential,

all the pieces should have colorful, creative names and be divided into distinct subsets; some pieces should be limited editions and others should be retired; and a collector's club should be formed.

When he returned, Noel shared the ideas with his partner, Lisa Yashon, and the two decided on the name "Harmony Kingdom" for the company. Then they named the 60 Box Figures currently in the line, retired four of them and introduced a limited edition piece. They also created the first Harmony Kingdom catalog and retained a booth at the 1995 Long Beach International Collectible Exposition®. At the show, collectors were enamored by the unique and humorous Box Figurines, and their popularity has continued every since.

VARIATIONS ON THE THEMES

While at the Long Beach show, Martin, Noel and Lisa discussed new themes to add to Harmony Kingdom. *Treasure Jests* had unlimited possibilities, but they didn't want to overtax the artist, Peter Calvesbert. In addition, Martin had recently met a bright new artist, David Lawrence, who was working on Harmony Kingdom's first holiday angel, "Chatelaine." From the discussions, two themes came to light: flowers and the circus. *Harmony Garden* was launched a year and a half later, with *Harmony Circus* being created eight months later. *Harmony Garden* depicts traditional British flowers in softly colored sculptures, with each opening to expose the intriguing world of an adventurous ladybug named Lord Byron. The ladybug's story unfolds with each series' introduction, creating an on-going story with each addition eagerly awaited by collectors. *Harmony Circus* is a curious collection of circus characters, each with its own story to tell.

HANDCRAFTED IN THE ENGLISH SOUTH COTSWOLDS

Harmony Kingdom's U.K. headquarters, Wimberly Mills, is located in a beautiful rural area of England, the South Cotswolds. It is here that all Harmony Kingdom items are conceived.

The creation of each Harmony Kingdom box begins when the original work from sculptors like Martin Perry, David Lawrence and Peter Calvesbert is molded using silicone rubber. This original is then used to create production molds for the casting department. Castings are created in the model using crushed marble. The casting is then fettled (cleaned up) and made ready for staining.

The stain has been exclusively formulated by Martin and is considered a "trade secret." The piece is then polished back to remove most of the stain before being sent out into the countryside for painting.

The subtle tinting and hand-painting of all the Harmony Kingdom boxes is under the direction of Martin's wife, Corinna. "The early boxes were entirely Martin's painting plan and execution," she explains.

But when it became clear that Martin could no longer make and finish each and every box by himself, Corinna left her teaching career to help him. However, the task proved too big even for the both of them, and they enlisted the assistance of some women friends. "We would sit around my kitchen table, children playing on the floor, as I initiated them into the secrets of tinting," recalls Corinna. Seemingly, they carried on the cottage industry tradition that thrived in the region during the 19th century.

Corinna's kitchen soon became home to the painters. More artists joined the close knit group, and some of Corinna's friends even offered to train new painters in their homes. The small group continued to grow and grow. "Although we have had to centralize some aspects of the business, it is still a cottage industry in the true sense of the word," explains Corinna.

The artists continue to follow a painting and quality regime, but multiple factors can alter the finished look of each piece: room temperature, base color, dilution of the tints or just simply the mood of the day. So if one animal figure appears to be particularly pleased with itself, remember each is unique and individually handcrafted!

THE ROYAL WATCH COLLECTOR'S CLUB

By the end of 1995, it became apparent that the collector base of Harmony Kingdom was growing rapidly, so Martin, Corinna, Noel and Lisa heeded the advice of Paul Osnain and formed the Royal Watch Collector's Club. It debuted in 1996 at the International Collectible Exposition® in Secaucus, New Jersey. As an incentive to join, Harmony Kingdom offered collectors a special version of the Garden Prince pendant. At the Rosemont Show in June of that same year, another variation of the pendant was offered to those who joined the club. The tradition continues, as both current members and new members who join the club receive the special event pendant while at the shows.

The club continues to grow rapidly. Member benefits include exclusive gifts, four issues of the quarterly club newsletter, "The Queen's Courier," the opportunity to purchase two annual redemption pieces, and other members-only opportunities.

THE REINCARNATION OF LORD BYRON

The inaugural issue of "The Queen's Courier" in the spring of 1996 featured an article titled "Secrets of the Kingdom." Collectors had begun to greatly enjoy the

The second box figure in the Black Box *series is "Road Kill." A group of animals sits on a cloud in heaven, bearing the tire marks of their demise.*

"secrets" carved into and found within the figurines. Noel encouraged Martin to emphasize the importance of these "secrets" to his master carvers. This unique concept has become a source of delight for both collectors and the artists themselves, who seem to enjoy encrypting their pieces.

The flowers were to be a variation on the secrets theme. Instead of having hidden secrets, they were to have elaborate interior themes. Butterflies hid inside the original flower prototypes, but it was decided that a distinct and clever character should be introduced. Noel did the original sketches for the first ten open edition *Harmony Garden* Box Figurines and created the framework for the storyline, and Lisa came up with the name Lord Byron as a play on "Ladybug" and "Ladybird." The story of Lord Byron would incorporate romance and adventure, so naming the character after a famous romantic poet seemed to fit.

The first ten open edition Box Figurines were introduced in January, 1997. In addition, six limited edition single roses were released throughout the year. "The Sunflower" was the club exclusive redemption piece in 1997, and the 1997 limited edition "Rose Basket" featured Lord Byron golfing on the moon.

HARMONY KINGDOM ON THE INTERNET

While Harmony Kingdom may be a company built on time-honored tradition and craftsmanship, the advent of cyberspace and the World Wide Web brought new opportunities to share information with collectors around the globe. Utilizing Noel's vast knowledge of computers and the Internet, Harmony Kingdom launched its web site in September, 1996. Towards the end of the year, a chat room was established, the first of its kind in the collectibles industry. In addition, top retailers were listed on the site, offering collectors the opportunity to shop for Harmony Kingdom wherever they may travel, as well as locate hard-to-find pieces.

While the founding of Harmony Kingdom may have been due to a series of chance encounters, the success of the company certainly isn't by chance. Collectors have become quite enthralled with the warmth and tongue-in-cheek humor of Harmony Kingdom's Box Figurines.

Picturesque is the first collection created by Harmony Kingdom that does not follow the Box Figurine format. "Mark of the Beast" is one of 20 tiles that portrays Noah and his companions after the flood.

Harmony Kingdom
232 Neilston Street
Columbus, OH 43215

Phone:
614-469-0600

Fax:
614-469-0140

Web Site:
www.harmonykingdom.com

It's a Wonderful Place for Bears!

Once upon a time, (as *Honeybourne Hollow* artist and writer Pat Sebern tells us) in the middle of a quiet country town, there stood a grand library. At the base of its stairs was a pair of large marble pedestals supporting two wonderfully sculpted white marble bears. While most libraries have a pair of stoic lions guarding the way, the sculptor who had carved out these pedestals was especially fond of bears. His work became the pride of the town.

On their watch over the years, these two bears saw many families come and go. On fine spring days, the children of the town would sit on the bottom steps and read aloud from the thousands of books in the library. Over the years, the two bears enjoyed hearing many tales of many things.

Preparing for a festive birthday party, a little boy bear and a little girl bear proclaim, "You Take the Cake" as they present their rose-laden confection.

"Follow Your Dreams" shows the ambitious young Byron bear setting off to seek his ideal village for bears, carrying his own "bear map."

One little girl named Patty loved the Library Bears so very much that as she walked to school each morning, she would pass the library just to say hello to the bears. She named the bear on the left Byron and the one on the right Briggs. Byron and Briggs became her special friends. She often wished the bears could come to life, so that she could really talk to them and they could talk to her.

One night when Patty was tucked into bed, she noticed an especially bright star twinkling through her window. She remembered the two wonderful bears in front of the library, and imagined them in cool green forests and flower-strewn meadows. Then, just as she drifted off to sleep…she made a fateful wish.

BYRON COMES TO LIFE IN THE WOODS

When Byron awoke the next morning…he was surprised to find himself in the woods. He couldn't quite remember how he had gotten there. He remembered the library, the wonderful books from all over the world, and of course the children…But how did he get here…and where would he go…and where was his old friend Briggs?

As he looked around, he saw the forest was a very good place for bears, with large oak trees and a small stream. But Byron wanted something special, like a place he had heard described in a story as he listened by the library steps. He would look for a place with big old trees with huge leafy branches and lots of places to hide. It had to have a meadow that was just right…with tall wispy grass that shimmered when a breeze drifted through, and lots of warm sun…a place to have wonderful picnics, and bear naps in the afternoons. Of course, it had to have a brook that wandered through, with a pond that was just wide enough, and deep enough for a perfect fishing hole.

Byron set off and traveled for days, searching for just the right spot. He stopped at several likely places along the way, each one nicer than the last…but none quite right. Finally, when he arrived in the beautiful wooded area known as *Honeybourne Hollow,* he knew he had found his new home.

After a short nap and a snack of ripe berries and wild honey, Byron began to plan. He decided where his den would be. He found a place for a bakery, a church and a

A sweet mother bear named Emma and her adorable offspring are featured in this work of art from Honeybourne Hollow titled "Moms Are Pretty Wonderful!"

A HOME FULL OF FUN AND WARMTH

The 26-page illustrated, hard cover book, *The Bears of Honeybourne Hollow,* comes with each limited edition "Follow Your Dreams" figurine, one of 15 new hand-painted resin figurines created by Pat Sebern to capture the "fun and warmth" of the bears' cozy lifestyle.

After establishing herself as a giftware artist, Pat moved to Dallas in 1995 to work for Fitz and Floyd. In 1997, she became Director of Concept Development for Fitz and Floyd Collectibles and began working on a new group of collectibles that evolved into *Honeybourne Hollow.* Delightful graphics and heartwarming, humorous family situations characterize the collection's packaging and presentation. A special limited edition piece, with a working clock, titled "Time is Precious," will also be available to celebrate the new millennium.

Speaking of *Honeybourne Hollow,* Pat Sebern says, "I wanted to create a community expressing the values of hard work, collective effort and the importance of family fun. Honeybourne was the name of the farm where my grandmother grew up in the Cotswolds in England. Memories of her and the stories she told me were an important inspiration not only for *Honeybourne Hollow* but also for myself as an artist and mother.

"Teddy bears are one of the most meaningful and identifiable American icons. They evoke a nostalgia for the warmest traditions and emotions associated with childhood. To me, expressions of family and enduring friendship are an important foundation and inspiration for the entire collection."

FITZ AND FLOYD SHOWCASES *HONEYBOURNE HOLLOW*

Honeybourne Hollow represents the latest marvelous creation of Fitz and Floyd, a renowned giftware and collectibles firm founded in 1960. Since then, Fitz and Floyd has evolved into the undisputed leader in the design and manufacture of hand-painted ceramic giftware, tableware, decorative accessories and collectibles.

From its renowned studios in Dallas, the Fitz and Floyd design team creates the company's exclusive designs – over 500 new and unique designs every year. Whether it's a tea service for Her Majesty Queen Elizabeth II, Presidential dinnerware for the White House, or a holiday centerpiece for your table, each and every Fitz and Floyd product receives the same discerning attention to meticulous craftsmanship and exquisite detail. Fitz and Floyd – often elegant, sometimes whimsical, always a prized and treasured gift. As they say in Dallas, "Fitz and Floyd...one look and you know."

carpenter's shop...and even a place for a little theater. He was very handy, and had learned a lot of useful things on the library steps. Shortly after noon, he set to work.

A few days after he had started building...a mother bear with two cubs appeared in the meadow. She watched him working from a distance; curious about the project, but wanting to keep her cubs safe. When Byron approached, he called out, "Don't be afraid! My name is Byron, and I am building a village that will be a wonderful place for bears."

"My name is Emma and these are my cubs Burke and Blossom. What kind of village are you building?" "I'm working on my carpenter's shop right now, and I plan to build the bakery next," Byron answered. "Oh!" Emma exclaimed, "I bake wonderful berry pies and tarts. Will you be needing someone to run the bakery?"

"Why, yes," Byron said. "That's perfect! And we'll have a tailor, a quilt shop, and much more! If you'll stay, I'll build a fine bakery." "I have some friends that have been searching for a new home," she said. "I'll see if they would like to join us in this wonderful new village." Soon the word spread of *Honeybourne Hollow,* a wonderful place for bears. By summer's end, the group had grown to 11 grown bears and seven cubs. All the bears agreed that Byron had done such a good job of setting up this bear village that he should be the mayor.

They also decided that they would all take care of each other, and the many other small animals living nearby. And perhaps they could even help Byron find Briggs, his old friend. Together they signed a charter...and *Honeybourne Hollow* became official. Byron had chosen the perfect spot, and he was very proud indeed!

What better way of "Sharing the Season" at Christmas than to decorate a fir tree in Honeybourne Hollow with strings of bright red cranberries?

Fitz and Floyd Collectibles
501 Corporate Drive
Lewisville, TX 75057

Phone:
800-527-9550

Fax:
972-353-7718

Fabulous Die-Cast Models of Fantastic Vehicles

The sleek "Ferrari Millennium Edition" starts a new century of Hot Wheels® collecting in high style.

Imagine this: If all the Hot Wheels® vehicles produced in the last 30 years were placed front-to-rear, they would circle the earth almost four times! Indeed, the two billion-plus Hot Wheels cars made since 1968 represent more "vehicles" than all of Detroit's "Big Three" have manufactured in that time period combined!

These facts come into clear focus, considering that 41,000,000 of today's American adults grew up "driving" Hot Wheels cars — and many of them still boast substantial collections. The younger generation continues to get onboard as well, with more than 15,000,000 boys ages three to ten currently owning an average of more than 30 Hot Wheels vehicles each. The volume is so substantial that Mattel, Inc., the number-one toy manufacturer in the world, sells an average of two Hot Wheels cars every second, three track sets every minute, and 230 play sets per hour!

Since Hot Wheels began as a line of 1:64th scale die-cast replica vehicles, more than 10,000 variations have been created, with the Corvette® reigning as the most popular vehicle in the brand's history. Many collectors strive to own at least a representative sample of this diverse line, with the average Hot Wheels aficionado boasting over 1,500 vehicles. The largest known Hot Wheels collection is valued at approximately $500,000. And the cars aren't "just for looking," either — in fact, the X-V Racers®, the Hot Wheels cars with a motor inside, have been clocked at scale speeds up to 500 mph!

Today, the Hot Wheels brand encompasses anything that rolls, flies or floats. It has evolved into a true "lifestyle brand" with segments that range from aftermarket parts to licensed apparel and merchandise. What's more, Hot

Wheels is the only product line in the die-cast business that stands behind the quality of its products with a "Guaranteed for Life" promise.

HOW HOT WHEELS VEHICLES COME TO LIFE

Each new Hot Wheels vehicle begins life in the imagination of Mattel's gifted designers. To keep up with the latest trends in the auto industry, the designers visit major auto shows, attend car-racing events and study auto magazines for the latest on the cars of tomorrow.

These creative ideas are then transferred onto an artist's drawing board. The designer may sketch hundreds of drawings as he conceives different ideas for a new vehicle. The best drawings of proposed models are then test-marketed with focus groups of children and adults. After evaluating all the research, one design is finally selected to become a Hot Wheels vehicle.

If the vehicle exists in reality, photographing the original becomes the first step. Details, both interior and exterior, from close-ups of the grill, to overhead and full-length views, are captured on film. If the vehicle is a classic or an older model, manufacturers and owners are often consulted.

Precise measurements of the full-size original come next. Detailed dimensions, such as height, wheelbase and engine compartment overhang are carefully noted.

The photographs and "specs" are then sent to the engineering department where they are translated into mechanical drawings. No dimension can be overlooked and every part and styling element must be in scale.

Next, the engineering drawings are sent to a pattern maker where a wooden model is made. The wooden model, which is four times larger than an actual Hot Wheels vehicle, is essential to make certain that all parts possess the fine, authentic detailing that has made the Hot Wheels line famous.

This Hot Wheels® grouping in 1:43rd scale is loaded with detail and authenticity.

118

The prestigious history of the premier Ferrari brand is beautifully represented in these 1:18th scale Hot Wheels® die-cast replicas.

EVERY TINY DETAIL SHINES THROUGH

Details are faithfully reproduced including door handles, emblems, logos, and the shape of a headlight or instrument panel. This realism is what gives the vehicles their unique look and personality.

The final destination is the mold shop where the molds are made. The die-cast is injected into the molds and the body of the vehicle emerges. Next, it is polished and washed, and then spray-painted. Letters, logos and such detailing as pin striping are then printed. Finally, all parts, such as the wheels, chassis and engine are assembled — and a Hot Wheels vehicle is born.

The finished product is now a 1:64th, 1:43rd, 1:24th or 1:18th scale die-cast replica of the original vehicle. All that remains is road testing to Hot Wheels' standards for quality and safety, and creating a new name for the vehicle, if it is not a standard production model.

"We have a lot of fun dreaming up names for our offbeat, California-style vehicles," says Larry Wood, the chief Hot Wheels designer since 1970. "With such past model monikers as Funny Money, Buzz Off, Rodzilla, Noodlehead, Rocket-Bye Baby and Nitty-Gritty Kitty, you can imagine what some of our brainstorming sessions are like!"

After the name and packaging are in place, the vehicles are ready to hit store shelves. Total time from concept to shipping is usually about ten to 12 months.

America's love for road cars is featured in the Hot Wheels® 1:18th scale "Mercury Woody," VW Drag Bus" and "1965 Chevy Impala Convertible."

MATTEL PROUDLY PRESENTS HOT WHEELS

The parent company of the thriving Hot Wheels brand is Mattel, Inc., a worldwide leader in the design, manufacture and marketing of family products. Mattel has offices and facilities in 36 countries and markets its products in more than 150 nations worldwide.

The company traces its beginnings to 1945, when

Harold Matson and Elliot Handler opened their garage workshop. Before long, Matson sold out to Elliot and Ruth Handler, who focused the business on toys. Advertising their products on the "Mickey Mouse Club" during the 1950s, Mattel became a household name. Then in 1959, Ruth Handler unveiled a doll named Barbie®, and it soon became the best-selling fashion doll in the world.

The year 1968 saw the entry of Hot Wheels miniature vehicles, a Mattel landmark because it captured boys' imaginations just as Barbie had captivated the girls. Hot Wheels' volume helped Mattel grow to $300 million annual revenue by the early 1970s. Since then the toy manufacturer has launched many intriguing electronics products, and merged with Fisher-Price and Tyco Toys. Yet even today, along with the beloved Barbie, Hot Wheels reigns among Mattel's most robust and best-known brands. And for the past few years, Hot Wheels has been ranked as the #1 best-selling toy according to TRST.

100% HOT WHEELS COLLECTIBLES®

For the new millennium, Hot Wheels is turning things up a notch, with an expanded portfolio of some of the world's best-known and popular cars. The new 2000 line of die-cast models includes exclusive Ferrari replicas, and is loaded with the detail and authenticity car lovers have come to expect from Hot Wheels Collectibles. The Hot Wheels Collectibles line-up includes a variety of themes: Hot Rods, Muscle Cars, Custom Cars and Performance Cars in 1:18th, 1:43rd and 1:64th scale. As the folks at Hot Wheels say, "Gentlemen, start your collections!"

Among the most notable new Hot Wheels Collectibles are the Ferrari street and race cars, and Ferrari Millennium Cars at 1:18th scale. Included are such coveted models as the 250 GT "California," the 1984 Testa Rossa, the 250 GT Testa Rossa, F512M, F 50 and 550 Maranello. Some of these replicas introduce Ferrari colors never produced before in die-cast models. All of them beautifully represent the prestigious history of the premier Ferrari brand.

With more than 30 years of Hot Wheels creation under their belts, Mattel designers continue to craft the finest and flashiest vehicles of every description. Whether it ends up in the hands of a serious collector, or a child enjoying an afternoon of play-racing, each car beautifully exemplifies the speed, power and performance that has made Hot Wheels popular with more than three generations of kids.

HOT WHEELS®/MATTEL, INC.

Hot Wheels®
Mattel, Inc.
333 Continental Boulevard
El Segundo, CA 90245

Phone:
800-524-TOYS

Fax:
310-252-3298

Web Site:
www.hotwheels.com

Gifted Artists Share Holiday Traditions

The artists of House of Hatten celebrate Christmas all year long, and pay tribute to other popular holidays as well, with their heirloom-quality home décor designs. With everything from Santa centerpieces to Halloween displays, House of Hatten's artists strive not for mass production but for creating one-of-a-kind keepsakes, while focusing on a simple commitment to innovative designs and excellence. This same drive for excellence is also found in the production of these keepsakes.

Founded more than two decades ago, House of Hatten established its place in the Christmas industry with the introduction of unique appliquéd stockings and tree skirts, and by being one of the first companies to manufacture soft-sculptured Christmas decorations. House of Hatten again made an impact on the industry in 1988 with the debut of poly-resin reproductions of original wood carvings created by Denise Calla.

Today, House of Hatten's products are found in fine department stores, boutiques and specialty stores across the country. Headquartered near Austin, Texas, the company has expanded by adding new designs and exploring different mediums to reflect each artist's talents. House of Hatten offers the largest line of exclusively designed Christmas products in today's high-end industry. Consistently retaining the highest standards of quality, House of Hatten continues to provide the finest in heirloom products for collectors to delight in today and tomorrow.

"Tea and St. Nicholas" by Denise Calla offers collectors the opportunity to acquire a stunning 14-piece ceramic tea set that is as practical as it is beautiful. Search for the twirling bell that highlights each piece of the set!

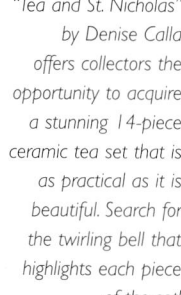

The "Santa and Fawn Centerpiece" from Susan M. Smith is part of the Santa's Kingdom *collection, available exclusively through House of Hatten, for the nature lover in all of us.*

PREMIER ARTIST DENISE CALLA

The self-taught authenticity that Denise Calla brings to her artwork has been described as pure magic and has made her one of America's most highly collected artists. As a result of her dedication to over 25 years of working professionally as an artist in many different media, her collectors can delight in her originality, knowledge of her subject matter, and the gentle life-like qualities of her pieces.

From the beginning, her artwork has always touched people in a special and personal way. Her *Twelve Days of Christmas* collection is so loved and cherished by families that it has been passed along from one generation to the next, and has long been a favorite wedding gift. Denise communicates something to the heart and soul that transcends nationality, language or background. Denise sends each piece of artwork into the world with the words "go and make someone happy."

When asked, Denise tells us she starts each day walking through the woods seeking inspiration and instruction from nature and the changing seasons. When not in her studio, she tends to her family of animals, both tame and wild, and her garden. She only uses the wood from evergreen trees to carve her Santas, so she has planted acres of pine trees to give back to the earth the wood she has used.

MORE FEATURED ARTISTS FROM HOUSE OF HATTEN

In a small Alaska town, nestled between breathtaking snow-tipped mountains and thick wilderness, one finds a tiny, cozy workshop where artist Susan M. Smith – much like a Santa's elf – toils away to carve her next creation. Inspired by the natural wildlife that surrounds her home, Susan couples Santa with some of the same animals she watches from her home on a day-to-day basis. No two pieces are alike. Each one is carefully hand-painted to bring out its own special character and detail. House of Hatten began reproducing her designs in 1995 with the *Santa's Kingdom* collection.

Rodney Leeseberg's "Scarecrow with Pumpkin" original woodcarving (reproduced in poly-resin) makes a wonderful Halloween and harvest centerpiece.

Together, Vaughn and Stephanie Rawson have become one of the most successful design teams around. Indeed, today they are so well known by House of Hatten collectors and others that Vaughn is revered by many as the "Whimsical Whittler." It all started when the Rawsons built a country home in Michigan, and Vaughn began to make its furniture himself. In doing so, the couple found that Vaughn was a gifted wood carver. Their newest series for House of Hatten is *Nursery Rhyming*, and their collections called *A Christmas Alphabet* and *Christmas Messengers* continue to grow and develop.

Rodney Leeseberg confesses that "It's really a passion for me to create." He lives in a small house filled with a variety of wonderful wood carvings. The windows of his home look out onto a beautiful lake surrounded by hundreds of pine trees. Growing up in the area, Rodney enjoyed playing outdoors among the picturesque scenery. Now, this is where one of the top Santa craftsmen draws his inspiration. Rodney's newest additions continue his *From Out of the North* series for House of Hatten. He has also diversified into other holidays, creating a handsome "Scarecrow with Pumpkin" for autumn and Halloween.

New artists who joined House of Hatten in 1999 are Paul F. Bolinger, Pamela Silin-Palmer and Kelly S. Stadelman. Paul is recognized as one of the nation's top wood carvers. His premier line for House of Hatten, *The Paul Bolinger Collection,* showcases Paul's never-ending creativity by depicting Santa with the familiar cookies and milk, to a 21st century Santa tackling the Y2K bug. Pamela lives in the redwood forest on the beautiful Northern California Coast. Her sense of style has been captured in the exquisitely detailed needlepoint pillow collection entitled *Don't Count Your Chickens.* Kelly has created a grouping of Santas from her *Heritage Arts Studio* collection reflecting her unique carving style and attention to painting detail.

COVETED LIMITED EDITIONS AND GIFTS

Collectors particularly prize limited edition pieces, and House of Hatten offers a number of these special treasures, especially Denise Calla's *Four Seasons* collection, as well as her *Heartbeats* centerpieces. Additional limited edition pieces sought by Denise Calla fans are three beautiful centerpieces from her collection entitled *Angels Triumphant.* Also desired by collectors are six pieces from Susan M. Smith's *Santa's Kingdom* collection and Ann Schreck Moore's soft-sculpted Santas from her *Santa's Legend* collection.

Although House of Hatten's artists focus primarily on Christmas products, over the years, the company has expanded to include Easter, Independence Day, Halloween, Thanksgiving and Hanukkah, as well as various giftware items. Numerous House of Hatten artists have made contributions to the expanded year-round decor and gift areas. Peggy Fairfax Herrick's *Grand Finale* collection has brought together a whimsical collection of candlesticks with or without animal motifs, as well as boxes, chests and many other items.

For spring and summer, *Honey Bees,* Denise Calla's latest tabletop and giftware design collection, offers a full tablesetting, serving compote and platter, cup, saucer and mug sets. There is also a teapot complete with honey pot, bee hive inspired cheese dome, sugar and creamer, berry bowls, a lemonade pitcher and cake stand. Sassy garden sprites, reproductions of Denise's wood carvings, round out the tabletop collection.

HOLIDAY COLLECTIONS AND SOFT SCULPTURE

Numerous collectors of House of Hatten delight in the extreme diversity of Santas that have been offered throughout the years. As a result, Santa collections can

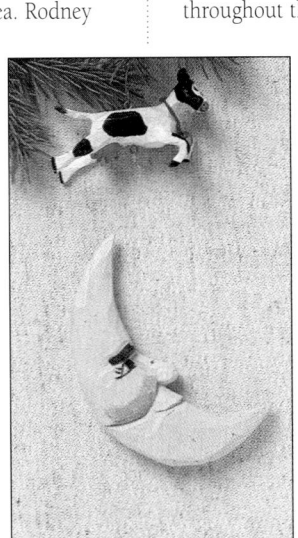

Vaughn and Stephanie Rawson collaborated to create this "Cow Over the Moon" ornament, part of a series of nine Christmas ornaments depicting nursery rhymes.

be found in many homes across the country and beyond. Along with a host of past collections, new series demonstrating success include *Fire and Ice, Tea and St. Nicholas, Glad Tidings, From Out of the North, Christmas Messengers, Grand Finale, Santa's Kingdom* and the *Twelve Days of Christmas Anniversary Collection.*

House of Hatten also is one of the leading manufacturers of soft-sculptured items. Using the finest quality fabrics and materials, the firm offers a variety of tree skirts, stockings and soft-sculpture ornaments exhibiting hand-guided machine embroidery and elaborate appliqué. Some recent favorite soft-sculpture collections include *Grandmother's Crazy Quilt, Renaissance Christmas, Rose Star Brocade* and *Peace on Earth.*

House of Hatten, Inc.
301 Inner Loop Road
Georgetown, TX 78626

Phone:
800-5-HATTEN
512-819-9600

Fax:
512-819-9033

E-mail:
custserv@houseofhatten.com

HOUSE OF HATTEN, INC.

Artist Lena Liu Shares Beauty from the Heart

"Music Room VII - Afternoon Repose" is the most recent addition to the popular Music Room series. The composition is a romantic painting that depicts a casual yet elegant room following a lively rehearsal.

Lena Liu paints the life around her – the spring bulbs that peek out of her garden to welcome the new season, the music room filled with instruments waiting to be played, the bouquet of flowers displayed in an ornate Oriental vase.

Her inspiration comes from within and from the comforts of her own home and studio in Maryland. "I surround myself with what I love," says Lena. "It's inspiring to me." It has also inspired collectors around the world, who have grown to love the simple pleasures of life and nature in Lena's award-winning artwork.

LENA SHARES ORIENTAL TRADITIONS THROUGH ARTWORK

From its studios in Potomac, Maryland, Imperial Graphics, Ltd. introduces and distributes work by Lena Liu, an artist of unparalleled popularity in today's collectibles market. Since Lena and her husband, Bill, founded their firm in 1984, Imperial Graphics has become renowned for its versatility of subjects, highly detailed compositions and Lena's delicate and tranquil style of painting.

"I strive to create a sense of poetry and music in my paintings," Lena says. "Emotion, love and nature will never change. I try to capture that in my art – in painting the human interpretation of nature, I let what touches my heart pass through my fingers."

Lena was born in Tokyo to a military Chinese family

and raised and educated in Taiwan. Her parents discovered her painting talent at a very young age and sent her to private tutors, with whom she began to learn and apply traditional Chinese brushwork. She also combined traditional Oriental brushwork with Western painting techniques, which can be seen in many of her works today.

As a young woman, Lena moved to the United States in her sophomore year in 1972 to study architecture at the State University of Buffalo. She then pursued a graduate degree at UCLA, but true love won out after her first year, as she returned to the East Coast to marry Bill. Having worked for an architectural firm for two years, Lena made the decision in 1977 to devote herself full time to art. She began selling her artwork locally, developing her own style along the way. Her popularity soared, so Lena and Bill launched Imperial Graphics, Ltd., with the express purpose of marketing her limited edition artwork.

AN ARTISTIC TRIBUTE TO MUSIC AND THE MASTERS

While Lena is renowned for her floral artistry, she has also shared her love of music with collectors. Each year, Imperial Graphics introduces annual additions to the *Music Room* series, which debuted in 1991 and has proven to be a favorite among collectors. This annual series has also been one of Lena's favorites to paint because it allows her to combine her love for music with her love for art. She enjoys going to the symphony, and it is this passion that inspires these romantic paintings.

"Music Room VII - Afternoon Repose" invites collectors to immerse themselves in a warm, intimate and romantic room while the musicians take a well-deserved break.

Lena Liu's artwork has been recreated on limited edition Art Tiles, including "Anna's Hummingbird with Fuchsia."

The cello rests against a chair in the foreground. The gold-leafed Oriental screen painted with plum blossoms stands next to a life-size reproduction of a bronze ballerina sculpture by Degas. A violin nestles in the sofa and is surrounded by beautifully embroidered pillows. Sheet music scattered on the Oriental rug signals the intensity of the rehearsal. On an ottoman, a tray holds a teacup waiting for the musicians' return. Next to a sunny window, a candelabra sits on top of the grand piano. The sweet fragrance from freshly cut peonies fills

"Homage to Mozart - Marriage of Figaro" pays tribute to the great composer and his opera. The print is limited to 2,950 signed and numbered pieces.

the room, while ivy, fern and palm all thrive in the sunlit parlor. Each of the music-themed prints is limited to 5,500 signed and numbered pieces.

In addition to the *Music Room* series, Lena has paid tribute to two of the most famous romantic composers – Mozart and Beethoven. A trip to Prague, Budapest and Vienna in 1998 inspired these paintings in the *Tribute to the Masters* series. "Homage to Mozart – Marriage of Figaro" features images of Mozart, piano, french horn, cello and red roses on a copy of Mozart's manuscript. This particular page is the aria written for the title role of Susanna from "The Marriage of Figaro." The border depicts the title of the opera and the two main characters of the play, Susanna and Figaro.

"Homage to Beethoven - Symphony No. 9 D Minor, op. 125" highlights the manuscript affectionately known as "Ode to Joy." Images of Beethoven, piano, violin, trumpet and white lilies are surrounded by a border which depicts the title of the symphony, a conductor, the chorus and musicians playing violin and cello. Both are limited in edition to 2,950 signed and numbered pieces.

ART TILES RECREATE LENA LIU'S PAINTINGS

For collectors to further enjoy Lena's artwork, some of her original paintings have been reproduced on premium quality porcelain tiles. The Art Tiles are limited in edition to 5,500 signed and numbered pieces and come with a Certificate of Limitation and Authenticity. Imperial Graphics is also offering the tiles set on a silky mat with a gold fillet atop a luxurious suede matting and framed in a lovely shadow box style frame to give them a three-dimensional look.

In the Tribute to the Masters series, "Homage to Beethoven - Symphony No. 9 D Minor, op. 125" honors the composer and the manuscript affectionately known as "Ode to Joy."

Among the Art Tiles are "Iris Bouquet" with Lena's signature bearded irises in shades of purple, blue and white. "Hydrangea Bouquet" is the perfect mate to "Iris Bouquet" with its matching green border with gold and purple accents. "Guardian Angel" stands in the entrance of an ancient gothic archway, her arms reaching out in a dramatic gesture to welcome her passenger doves. "Motif Orientale," previously released as a print, proved to be very popular among collectors and sold out quickly. After numerous requests, Lena decided to bring back this still life image on the Art Tile. Two other Art Tiles feature the beloved combination of hummingbirds and flowers: "Hummingbird with Trumpet Vine" and "Anna's Hummingbird with Fuschia."

ARTWORK APPEARS ON OTHER COLLECTIBLES

Since 1988, Lena's artwork has been produced on plates by The Bradford Exchange, one of the world's most successful marketers of collector's plates. Today, The Bradford Exchange continues marketing Lena's plates, along with other innovative products designed by this talented artist, including ornaments, music boxes and an elegant tea service collection. The Bradford Exchange honored Lena as one of the first inductees to its "Plate Hall of Fame" at the company's headquarters in Niles, Illinois. The Danbury Mint, a leading marketer of collectibles, recently introduced figurines featuring Lena's exquisite Oriental maiden sculptures. A *Butterfly Maiden Collectible Doll* Series was introduced in the year 2000 to celebrate the millennium.

No matter what the medium, Lena has been recognized for her artistry and contributions to the collectibles industry. She has been named "Artist of the Year" in both the United States and Canada, and has also received "Plate of the Year" honors from the National Association of Limited Edition Dealers (NALED).

When she's not painting, Lena also enjoys meeting her collectors by traveling to collectible conventions and galleries. Her collectors anticipate the newest releases that share Lena's love of nature and music and are of the finest quality – both in terms of composition and material. Lena's limited editions are printed on high-quality archival, acid-free paper to ensure their long-lasting beauty. Her canvases are stamped as "Archival, Museum Quality" artwork. Collectors know they are making a sound investment as they experience the beauty and tranquility of Lena Liu's artwork.

IMPERIAL GRAPHICS, LTD.

Imperial Graphics, Ltd.
11516 Lake Potomac Dr.
Potomac, MD 20854

Phone:
301-299-5711

Fax:
301-299-4837

Web Site:
www.lenaliu.com

E-mail:
lliu@lenaliu.com

Collectibles with History and Heritage

When his children were growing up during the 1970s and 1980s, Ralph Gadiel loved to take them on trips to Old Colorado. The Gadiel clan reveled in the beauty of the mountains and the rich history of the Gold Rush days. So when Ralph — a veteran of the collectibles industry — set out to develop a new series of miniature buildings for the department store market, his subject matter seemed like second nature. He'd create a series of buildings inspired by that glorious Colorado history in wonderful towns like Georgetown, Leadville, Blackhawk, Central City and Golden!

Sadly, Ralph Gadiel died in 1998 — but not before experiencing the incredible popularity of his *Liberty Falls* Colorado collectibles. Now under the leadership of new owner Larry Stern and Gadiel's own second-in-command, Debbie Gimza, International Resources, LLC still weaves fascinating tales of Colorado "days of old," while also creating wonderful Christmas collectibles like the *International Santas* and *International Christmas Trees.*

THE STORY OF *LIBERTY FALLS*

Liberty Falls is a fictitious, late-1800's Colorado mining town that is made up of miniature buildings now collected by people all over the country. These buildings are available from October until the end of December in department stores — with one store chain holding the "exclusive" in each area of the country *Liberty Falls* serves. What's more, during the decade in which the *Liberty Falls* pieces have been on sale, many of its more coveted issues have seen strong secondary market action.

Each finely detailed, hand-painted building measures 3" in height and represents a home, retail store, community outpost or other structure that might well have appeared in a thriving Colorado mining town 100 years ago. Carefully researched for architectural authenticity and historical accuracy, each

"The Liberty Falls Roller Coaster" is a special premium available to those collectors who acquire all the Liberty Falls buildings for Fall 2000. Information on how to acquire it appears in each package of Fall 2000 buildings.

building comes complete with a story that places it in the context of the overall town and introduces the people who live or work there. Hand-painted "pewter people" and accessory pieces also are available for collectors who enjoy creating authentic Colorado scenes.

CELEBRATING THE COLORADO GOLD RUSH

When John Gregory first discovered Colorado gold in 1859, word of the rich ore deposits spread like wild fire all over the world. Experienced miners from California came to Colorado in droves, as did "get rich quick" schemers with no mining background – but a whole lot of dreams.

According to the "historical fiction" that underpins this International Resources collection, one of the first outposts for miners was a little gathering of tents and lean-tos that was later named "Liberty Falls" because of the beautiful, natural falls nearby. The miners pitched their tents there to be in close proximity to the spots most likely to "hit big." And soon, tradespeople joined the miners – lured by the possibility of swapping their wares for some of that free-flowing miner cash and gold.

Mr. and Mrs. Frank Clark, Mr. and Mrs. Jason DuBois, the Tullys and the Applegates were among the earliest families to travel West in support of the mining effort. The first two gents started the Clark and DuBois Bank and Mint in what would soon become "downtown *Liberty Falls.*" They and their wives made do with "soddies" – sod-covered houses – until their mansions were built in that part of Colorado.

The Tullys started the local General Store — and in the early days, if you needed to buy something in *Liberty Falls,* the Tullys were the only source in town. But when mining became an institution in the area and the wealth kept flowing freely, the new Main Street eventually played host to a whole row of "high-class establishments" selling

"Jeremiah Sobel's Home" is one of the many stately buildings that grace the fictional Colorado mining town of Liberty Falls.

clothing, timepieces and jewelry, eyeglasses, hats, quilts, and many other specialized products.

Liberty Falls had its own stunning Opera House to rival those of the European capitals. In time, it boasted an array of churches from every denomination and religion – and unlike most Western towns of the era, it actually had more churches than saloons! Perhaps one reason for that was the strong Temperance movement in town. A whole team of ladies could be rousted for demonstrations at the drop of a hat shouting "The Saloon must go!"

Susan Applegate also was one of the first settlers in *Liberty Falls,* but her husband died young. The resourceful Mrs. A. started her own boarding house in downtown *Liberty Falls.* She hosted miners, construction workers – anyone needing a clean bed and three square meals a day. She took young Clara Goodfriend and her son Scott under her wing when Clara became a Civil War widow, encouraging Clara to start her own bakery shop in town, too.

By the 1880s and 1890s, *Liberty Falls* – though considerably smaller than Denver – rivaled the state capital for architecture, culture and civilized living. The area boasted fairgrounds, parks, a swimming hole, skating pond, civic clubs, and many annual activities to draw enthusiastic crowds. With the Union Pacific Railroad running through town, an exemplary school system, a smooth-running city government, and beautiful scenery to draw tourists, *Liberty Falls* faced the new century (1900) with optimism, energy and high spirits!

BOOKS, CLUB AND SUMMER PIECES EXTEND ENJOYMENT

Collectors have been so hungry to learn more about *Liberty Falls* that there have been two very successful books about this fictional town, as well as a club with tens of thousands of enthusiastic members. *The Life and Times of Liberty Falls* – parts one and two – tell the stories of local settlers in their own words. Everyone from the

This set of hand-painted pewter accessories is among those created to enhance the display of Liberty Falls *buildings.*

high and mighty to the everyday folks have their say in these popular "page-turners."

At just $9.95 annual dues, The Liberty Falls Collectors Club is an incredible bargain. That nominal fee brings each member a quarterly *Liberty Falls Gazette* newsletter, membership card, special advance notice about events and products, and a free gift building, "The Ski Lodge."

Each spring and summer, International Resources also introduces a series of several *Summer in Liberty Falls* pieces, which create intricate miniature scenes including people and outdoor places such as a lovely gazebo, swimming hole or park.

THE *INTERNATIONAL SANTAS* AND *CHRISTMAS TREES*

Building on the success of the *Liberty Falls* series, International Resources also sells finely crafted *International Santas* and *International Christmas Trees.* In the Santas comprehensive series of finely crafted, hand-painted figurines, all the images of St. Nick from countries that span the globe come alive in delightful, displayable form. The *Christmas Trees* also offer a worldwide perspective of festive home decorations and yuletide customs.

Each *International Santas* and *International Christmas Trees* figurine is protectively packaged, then nestled into its own gift box. On the box, you'll find a story about the Santa or Tree, its place in the country's legend and lore, and other fun facts. What could be more enjoyable than sharing these stories with friends, relatives and special youngsters as you set up your holiday display?

MORE HERITAGE COLLECTIBLES TO COME

With strong ties to numerous gifted artists and top manufacturing facilities around the world, International Resources has plans to build upon its success with "Colorado and Christmas." As President Larry Stern concludes, "Our strength is in developing affordable and high quality works of art with stories that bring them to life in the hearts and minds of our collectors. We're just getting started — so watch for our upcoming creations!"

"Joulupukki", the Santa Claus figure from Lapland, makes a colorful addition to the International Santas Collection.

International Resources, LLC
60 Revere Drive, Suite 725
Northbrook, IL 60062

Phone:
847-291-4334

Fax:
847-291-4358

Web Site:
www.LibertyFalls.com

E-mail:
LibertyFalls@ameritech.net

INTERNATIONAL RESOURCES, LLC

Bringing Inspiration and Beauty to Collectors

The Sonshine Promises® figurine, "Faith For The Future," is the cornerstone of Islandia's Millennium Collection.

Islandia President Joseph Timmerman has devoted more than 20 years to bringing unique gifts and collectibles to market. His newest venture is touching the lives of collectors through a diverse array of artist-driven lines, ranging from the popular *Sonshine Promises®* collection of whimsical blue birds with uplifting messages by Gretchen Clasby to the majestic wildlife art of painter Trevor Swanson.

Joe Timmerman has a special affection for collector plates and a reputation for creating high quality plates of exceptional beauty. So it was inevitable that plates would comprise an important part of Islandia International. "I personally love collector plates, because they enable collectors to own a beautiful piece of art at a fraction of the cost of a quality lithograph," he explains. "There is so much wonderful art that translates into plates but could lose the magic in three-dimensional format. On the other hand, there is art that begs to be expanded into figurines, and we are blessed to have both kinds of artwork in our Islandia lines."

COLLECTORS FALL IN LOVE WITH SONSHINE PROMISES

Joe Timmerman discovered artwork in early 1998 that would change the character of his new business overnight. He saw the endearing watercolor art of Gretchen Clasby: chubby birds with big expressive eyes, webbed feet, wings that worked like arms, a cherubic yellow beak and painted a soft blue – "because blue is my favorite color," the artist tells collectors.

What Joe Timmerman didn't know was that six other companies had tried their skills at interpreting the little birds that the artist lovingly called *Sonshine Promises*. But he was undeterred when Gretchen was skeptical that this

unknown little company could do what the industry's leaders could not. In a few short weeks, Joe had created a sample of "God Blesses This House But He Doesn't Clean It" and earned the approval of the artist.

"After so many sharp beaks, flat faces and unexpressive eyes, I was overwhelmed that Joe had actually brought my art to life," says Gretchen Clasby. "Everything I felt when I painted my blue birds was right there in a figurine! It was wonderful."

The next step was to put together a collection that could be presented at the 1998 International Collectible Exposition® at Rosemont, Illinois. Not only did he accomplish this seemingly undoable feat, but also he engaged the artist for a collectors' seminar — a bold move when introducing a new collection by a new artist.

"I like a challenge," admits Joe. "I knew that if we were going to introduce the collection, we had to go all out. What I didn't know, at the time, was what a remarkable person Gretchen Clasby is. She absolutely captivated collectors with her wit and candor, and they loved her."

In the months that followed its launch, the *Sonshine Promises* collection won the hearts of collectors throughout America. When Gretchen Clasby returned to Rosemont for the 1999 Expo, she had a following of enthusiastic collectors — including many who had met her the previous year — who once again filled the Islandia booth and her seminars.

MILLENNIUM COLLECTION HERALDS NEW CENTURY

On the brink of the 21st century, Gretchen Clasby created special artwork for the event, which Islandia unveiled at the Rosemont Expo. The *Millennium Collection* is comprised of three different subjects to commemorate the occasion.

"Faith For The Future" is a limited edition figurine and dated ornament portraying four different birds with a bucket of stars. The figurine is limited to 2,000 pieces, with a special Artist Proof Edition of 200, hand-signed and numbered by the artist.

"The Sky's The Limit" is a dated figurine and pin that portrays a little bird nestled in the

Gretchen Clasby's Sonshine Promises® figurine touches a familiar theme with her endearing portrayal of temptation – "After This Sundae, The Diet Starts on Monday!"

crescent of a moon, with the title and date on its side.

"Celebrate – It's A Boy!" and "Celebrate – It's A Girl!" are two figurines that depict a blue bird carrying two heart-shaped balloons with the good news on the balloons, especially created for the fortunate families who welcome a new addition in the first year of the millennium.

To celebrate the first year of the collection, Islandia introduced a grouping of six popular subjects from the premier year in a larger size and each limited to 5,000 pieces worldwide. Included is an oversized tribute to that very first figurine of the bird carrying a mop, which has proved to be a collector favorite; and two of Gretchen Clasby's *Blessed Are...*™ cardinals, a limited series of whimsical red birds with such charming titles as "Blessed Are The Playful...For Theirs Is A World Of Fun."

TREVOR SWANSON'S ART CAPTURES WILDLIFE IN THEIR NATURAL HABITAT

The most popular of Islandia's plate artists is gifted wildlife painter Trevor Swanson. The young Arizona artist, whose father is acclaimed wildlife artist Gary Swanson, has carved his own niche in the art world with his realistic paintings of nature's most ferocious and beautiful animals. Trevor Swanson travels worldwide to capture his subjects in their natural habitat, and the results are paintings of great realism and detail.

Among his most popular series for Islandia are his *Rocky Mountain Wildlife and Wolves — Dusk to Dawn*. But a small grouping of familiar barnyard animals in a series called *Trevor's Farm Friends* is proving to be an award-winning collection for the artist. This simple series includes a rooster, cow, pig and goat — each named.

"When Joe asked me to paint farm animals, I didn't know where to start," recalls the artist. "So I visited my uncle's farm in Colorado. Each of the four animals I painted are real, and it was a brand-new experience for me."

Far and away the biggest seller is "Rollie the Rooster," who sits in regal splendor on a split rail fence, overseeing the farm. Islandia has also interpreted the art in figurines that are equally successful. Trevor's latest plates for Islandia include *Large Cats of North America* and a group of six diverse limited edition plates titled *The Wildlife Art of Trevor Swanson.*

Islandia added a second member of the talented Swanson family in 1999. Kimberly Swanson, Trevor's

This poignant portrayal of beauty is titled "Seneca" and is the first issue in the Seasonal Winds *series by artist Jonnié K.C. Chardonn.*

Trevor Swanson's "Rollie The Rooster," was chosen "Best New Plate" by collectors at the 1999 Long Beach International Collectible Exposition®.

sister, is an accomplished painter of horses, dogs and birds. Kimberly's first plates are two of her commissioned paintings of dogs. *The Sporting Hound* series includes "Badger," a Golden Retriever, and "Gopher," a Labrador Retriever.

The newest artist to join the company is acclaimed ethnic artist Jonnié K. C. Chardonn. A college art instructor in Illinois for more than 17 years, Jonnié has had her artwork reproduced in many forms, including more than 6 million lithographs of her works.

Islandia has selected her remarkable paintings of Native American images for its 1999 premier series. Jonnié demonstrates unique insight into the strength and beauty of her subjects, each of which she has researched with exacting detail. The result is a collection as distinctive as the artist herself.

To better portray the artwork, Joe Timmerman chose a larger, more translucent plate for the collection. Every border is an extension of the art, especially designed for each plate in the series. From the raw beauty of "Seneca" and "Bmola," to the strength of "Chief Titichakyo" and "Chief Pautiwa," the art of Jonnié Chardonn is a classic addition to the Islandia range.

AWARD-WINNING ARTISTS TOP ISLANDIA'S ROSTER

Islandia received validation of their choice of artists in the form of several "Best of Show" awards from Collectors' Information Bureau (CIB). Collectors voting in the 1998 "Best of Show" balloting held in conjunction with the International Collectible Exposition® (I.C.E.) in Rosemont, Illinois, chose Islandia's Sue Etém as "Best Plate Artist." The first and second place awards for "Best New Plate" were presented to Islandia for Sue Etém's "Bluebird of Happiness" and Trevor Swanson's "Grizzly Bear," respectively. At the 1999 I.C.E. in Long Beach, California, Swanson was singled out as "Best Plate Artist" and his best-selling plate, "Rollie the Rooster," was chosen as "Best New Plate."

Other prominent artists in the Islandia International lineup are Robert Tanenbaum, Gale Pitt, Wayne Anthony Still and Cliff Hayes. Islandia International gifts and collectibles are available through leading retailers and specialty shops.

Islandia International
78 Bridge Road
Islandia, NY 11722

Phone:
516-234-9817

Fax;
516-234-9183

E-mail:
islandia78@aol.com

Web Sites:
www.sonshine-promises.com
www.islandia.com

World's Leading Resource for Christmas Collectibles

Christmas may only come once a year, but at Kurt S. Adler, Inc., every day feels like Christmas. During the past 50-plus years, Kurt S. Adler has evolved into a leading supplier and designer of holiday decorative accessories and collectibles, making the firm's name synonymous with this great holiday. Kurt S. Adler has created and designed products that have made holiday memories for millions of collectors.

A soft-spoken, charming businessman and a true gentleman in every sense of the word, Adler was gifted with an uncanny design savvy and a keen eye for style. Capturing the imagination of well-heeled, post-war consumers, he combined a European flavor and sense of fashion with American tastes at affordable prices, bringing a whole new look to Christmas in the United States. Before long, Kurt S. Adler would become a name that consumers would come to know and trust.

When he wasn't buying and designing new products, Adler traveled all over the U.S., learning what collectors wanted. Gifted with the talent for knowing his market and a great eye for appealing designs and colors, he carried prototypes of his ideas overseas. He learned quickly that the American consumer was quality-conscious, and that his products would have to meet stringent standards to succeed in the marketplace.

Kurt S. Adler presents the "Carousel Horse," an exclusive mouth-blown European glass ornament for members of the Polonaise® Collector's Guild.

CHANGING THE WAY AMERICAN DECORATES FOR CHRISTMAS

During its history, Kurt S. Adler has been recognized for many breakthroughs and significant achievements. Ornaments have always been one of the mainstays of the line. Kurt S. Adler was the first to design, develop, import and distribute ornaments crafted of high-quality materials including woods, ceramics, stained glass, resin, fabric mâché and mouth-blown glass.

Supported by one of the largest teams of exclusive designers, Kurt S. Adler was one of the first companies to contact factories in the Far East and commercially manufacture ornaments and holiday accessories. The company has maintained stringent quality control standards to meet the buying preferences of American consumers and has helped transform a cottage industry

into the modern Christmas industry of today.

The firm introduced the age-old tradition of wood-turned ornaments to the Orient. In the mid-1950s and well in to the '60s, Kurt S. Adler imported the first quality-made snowglobes from West Germany. These snowglobes, also called snowdomes, featured Christmas scenes with Santa and other holiday characters.

When country styles and colors became popular in home furnishings in the 1970s, Kurt S. Adler, Inc. unveiled the first ornaments with "country" motifs and colorations. From that point on, the company continued to create decorations with innovative designs, such as Victorian, contemporary, folkart, and many others.

Since the early '70s, the firm utilized the unique talents of its art director and veteran designer, Marjorie Grace Rothenberg, to introduce a variety of Christmas themes – which have included ornaments and accessories that have been saved by collectors and passed down from generation to generation. Today, the firm introduces 12 to 15 new themes and adds thousands of collectibles annually.

Kurt S. Adler retains the largest team of exclusive designers "under one roof" for collectible holiday ornaments and accessories. The firm is credited with creating the first ornaments and figurines featuring African-American Santas and angels. The company also introduced the first line of Santas designed in unique, whimsical settings, from postal carrier, policeman and fireman, to fisherman, golfer and baseball player.

Kurt S. Adler was one of the foremost companies to introduce licensed products in the Christmas industry. Some current licenses include: Peanuts™, Coca-Cola®, The Vatican Library, Smithsonian Institution®, Sesame Street®, Mary Engelbreit®, Campbell's Soup®, Pink Panther™, United States Post Office Stamps, Popeye®, Garfield®, Madeline™, Babe Ruth™, Paddington Bear™, Pillsbury Doughboy™, James Dean™, Ford Motor

The Steinbach Collector's Club members-only piece features "Otto, The Royal Drummer," which stands 17" tall and has a retail price of $250.

"Sunday Drive," from the Fabriche Collection, features Mr. and Mrs. Claus driving an old-fashioned automobile.

Company®, Mr. Peanut™, Gone With The Wind™, Wizard of Oz™, Betty Boop™, Raggedy Ann & Andy™, Casablanca™, King Kong™, It's A Wonderful Life™, Marilyn Monroe™, and more.

LIMITED EDITION STEINBACH NUTCRACKERS ARE COLLECTOR FAVORITES

In 1991, Kurt S. Adler introduced one of the first limited edition nutcrackers, "Merlin The Magician," from the world-famous Steinbach factory. Since then, Merlin's value has soared dramatically on the secondary market. In recent years, the firm introduced popular collections depicting characters of Camelot, Robin Hood, American Presidents, Native American Chiefs, and others. The Steinbach Factory, the leading producer of collectible nutcrackers and smoking figures in the world, was founded in 1832 and continues to manufacture nutcrackers, smoking figures, ornaments and music boxes in the age-old tradition. Handcrafted and hand-painted from the finest northern European woods, these handicrafts are among the best examples of the medieval art of wood-turning. The Steinbach Collector's Club offers members-only pieces, gifts and other items, and is gaining members every day.

ORNAMENTS THAT CAPTURE COLLECTORS' HEARTS AND IMAGINATIONS

The Polonaise® Collection, which won the "Collector's Choice Award" for several consecutive years, has captivated collectors from around the world with its spectacular array of glass ornaments handcrafted in Poland in the age-old tradition of European master glassblowers. The hand-workmanship is very involved – from creating forms and fashioning hand-blown glass shapes, to silvercoating, lacquering and decorating the ornaments. All the work is done by Europe's most highly skilled and well-trained artisans. Collectors can join the Polonaise™ Collector's Guild to receive members-only ornaments, exciting videos, and more.

In 1999, Kurt S. Adler reintroduced the world-renowned *Louis Nichole Heirloom Collection*, which originally debuted in the early 1980s as one of the most elegant ornament lines ever produced. Designed by famed

These three ornaments, depicting Old World styled doll ornaments, are featured in the The House of Louis Nichole Collection.

designer Louis Nichole, the new collection features elegant home décor and Victorian-styled doll ornaments dressed in elaborate fabric and lace costumes with stunning colors. Some of the originals are included in the prestigious *White House Collection*.

UNCLE NICK AND FABRICHE SANTAS

Created exclusively for Kurt S. Adler by Mary Beth Designs, *Uncle Nick Santas* are designed with distinctive personalities. They are individually handcrafted with faces of resin, and bodies and costumes of fine fabrics such as velvets, tapestries and wools, along with unique trims and accessories. Standing from 12" to 24" tall, *Uncle Nick Santas* take on the role of fisherman, gardener, cook, and more. There are *Uncle Nick Santas* for nearly every occasion and taste.

The popular *Fabriche Collection* features a broad range of Santas in whimsical poses and charming designs. The engaging collection shows Santa as he is seldom seen – driving an old fashioned car and golf cart, teeing-up on the golf course with Mrs. Santa, and in the uncharacteristic garb of a fisherman or a lawyer.

Each Santa is noted for unparalleled design, superior quality and skillful workmanship. Fabriche is a mixed media technique that combines the Old World art of papier mâché with modern methods and materials. This merging of different media gives the effect of movement and life-like expressions.

ANGEL HEIGHTS AND OTHER DELIGHTS

Angel Heights, a unique celestial village that appeals to collectors all year 'round, includes whimsical angels and houses with a hand-carved look. The wood resin village has been designed as a place high in the heavens that will "Make All of Your Dreams Come True." Inside each building, you can watch the angels working to grant wishes to all good people on earth. The group, which is highlighted with pastel colorations, offers matching ornaments, stockings, a treetopper, door décor and tabletop accessories.

The Mystique Collection is another unique line of ornaments crafted of vintage hand-blown glass in Italy. Created in Art Deco style, these holiday ornaments are elaborately attired with striking head dresses, feather boas and spangles galore.

The Coca-Cola Christmas Village, one of the first licensed villages available today, has been designed by award-winning artist Michael Stoebner. This illuminated, wood resin holiday village features magical buildings. Inside each building is a special, secret story of holiday love and friendship.

With such a rich tradition of creating holiday treasures, collectors of Kurt S. Adler's products can be assured of many more years of collecting pleasures.

KURT S. ADLER, INC.

Kurt S. Adler, Inc.
1107 Broadway
New York, NY 10010

Phone:
800-243-9627

Fax:
212-807-0575

Web Site:
www.kurtadler.com

The Ultimate in Elegant Christmas Ornaments

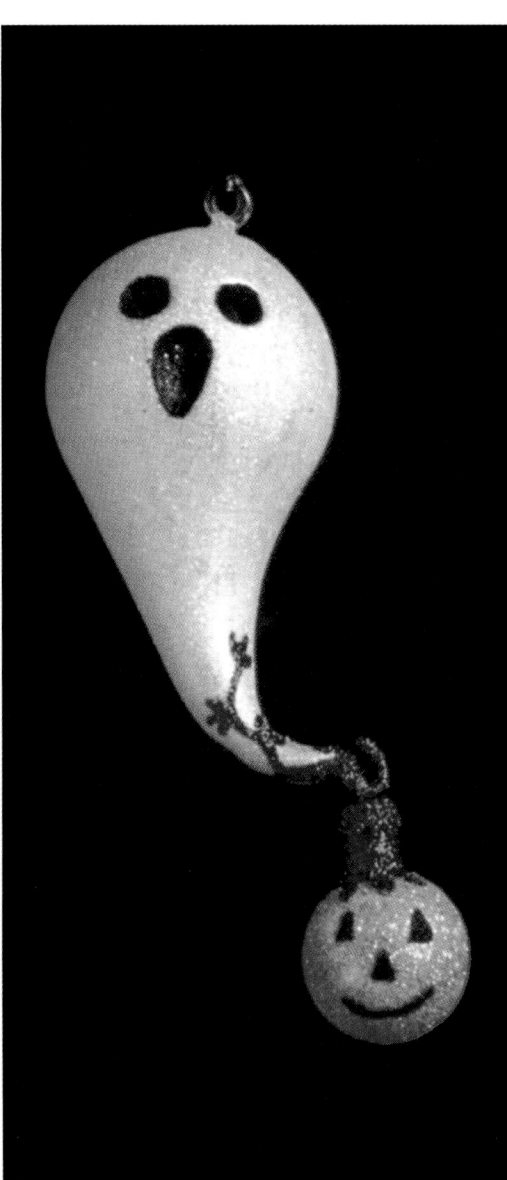

"The Ghost that Stole the Pumpkin" is one of the free-form ghost designs individually mouth-blown by designer Larry Fraga.

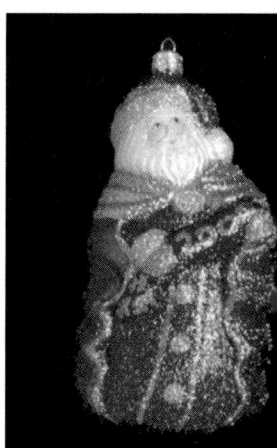

"Christmas 2000" is Larry Fraga Designs tribute to the millennium.

While Larry Fraga's childhood friends were collecting baseball cards in Oakland, California, Larry already was assembling his prized collection of antique mouth-blown Christmas ornaments. Whether those ornaments came from the local Goodwill store or as a gift from a neighbor, Larry treasured each and every one. For him, every day was Christmas, as he kept ornaments on display year-round. Today his personal collection exceeds 18,000 ornaments!

Larry grew up decorating his neighbors' Christmas trees as well as those of local churches, convalescent homes and convents. By 1977, he had become President of the Dunsmuir Estate, an Oakland landmark. One of the most pleasant parts of his duties was decorating the estate during the holidays, and sharing the results with thousands of visitors.

FRAGA'S CREATIVE FORCE

Today, Larry is the owner and designer of Larry Fraga Designs, a rapidly expanding company creating highly collectible Christmas ornaments. Without formal training in design or art, Larry has developed a natural, instinctive talent. His line now is composed of more than 700 designs. Many of those are from his original artwork, while others are antique molds that Larry discovered and then re-colored to fit his artistic vision.

The process of creating a new mouth-blown ornament spans many months. Larry starts with an idea, which he then sketches and hand-colors. Next, Larry's original artwork is sent to a glassblowing factory in Germany or Poland. From that drawing, a plaster mold is created and returned to Larry for refinement. Next, a hard mold is created, and then the prototypes are mouth-blown in glass. Larry hand-paints the prototypes and returns those to the factory for the painters to follow his exact colorations. Within a very short time after Larry started in the industry, he was acclaimed for his innovative colorations and unique designs, as well as the incredibly life-like skin tones he achieves in porcelain.

THE *GLITTER SERIES* DEBUTS

Recently, Larry introduced a new line called the *Glitter Series,* a collection of ornaments which are hand-painted and glittered by Larry himself, in his studio in Oakland. Because of the labor-intensive work involved, each design is limited to a production of 300 pieces. This line is truly the jewel of Larry Fraga Designs! When placed on ornamotors, the ornaments reveal both their sparkle and the spectrum of the rainbow. The *Glitter Series* has taken the ornament market by storm, with its early issues selling out at a record pace. The introduction of the line was combined with the opening of the Larry Fraga Designs' web site, where collectors and retailers alike got their first glimpse of these incredible, glittery designs in April, 1999.

"Settling In" from the *Glitter Series* depicts Santa in a large overstuffed, tufted chair, as he relaxes with a good book and his favorite kitty for company. The very striking fuschia chair, with button and quilting accents of gold, is the perfect complement to Santa's rich, teal-glittered robe.

"Playing the Blues" portrays Santa on one knee with his saxophone and his eyes closed. The expression on his face is one of pure joy, as he is lost in his music. Santa is attired in a fully glittered silver suit, trimmed in green and gold.

"Santa Baby" is a whimsical design with Santa leaning against an old-fashioned jukebox listening to his favorite tunes. You can almost feel that Santa is ready to break out in a holiday song. Santa's red suit against the gold jukebox is a striking combination.

"Christmas 2000" is Larry Fraga Designs' tribute to the millennium. Larry wanted a design that went beyond the ordinary champagne bottle or another

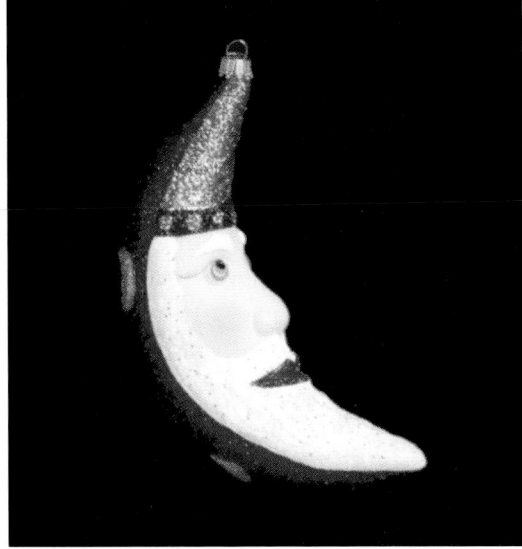

"Moon & Stars" is a striking quarter moon face, with Larry Fraga's signature porcelain skin tone. The back is fully glittered in stunning emerald green, with molded stars and moons.

rendition of Times Square. He has presented us with a Santa dressed in a flowing robe of teal and magenta glitter, trimmed in green and silver. Santa holds a banner announcing 2000.

"Renaissance Santa" and "Chartreuse Sparkler" are new additions in the 1999 *Glitter Series.* "Renaissance Santa" is a showstopper in his copper coat, and "Chartreuse Sparkler" shimmers with hints of gold shot through his very distinctive coat.

FAVORITES AND EXCLUSIVES ABOUND

Two of the most popular Larry Fraga Designs are the series of *Father Christmas* and *Mr. Fabulous.*

"Father Christmas" is a 7" tall, tradi-tional Santa that was released in brown, purple, pink, blue, yellow and green. At the request of both collectors and retailers, 1999 has seen the addition of "Winter Mint," "Snowflake Santa," "Halloween Santa," "Fireball" and "Shades of Royal," all fully glittered versions of "Father Christmas." "Sterling Silver" was previewed in March at Christmas in Seattle in Seattle, Washington, as their store exclusive. "Father Christmas" will retire at the end of 1999.

"Mr. Fabulous" is 5-1/2" in height and was originally released in fuschia. During 1999, the "Mr. Fabulous" mold was the most requested mold by retailers to be created as an exclusive for their stores in "full glitter." Other stores also have selected Larry Fraga Designs' exclusives for 1999: for instance, East Bay Nursery in Berkeley, California, has chosen "Gift of Giving" in a magnificent ruby red. Holiday Treasures in Birmingham, Alabama, has selected "Sapphire Santa," with his rich, deep blue coat accented with a gold rope, and red ornaments highlighting his tree.

Lil' Treasures in Fullerton, California, chose

"Black Tie Santa," a courtly gentleman ready for a night on the town in his robe of black glitter with accents of gold, silver and purple. "Black Tie Santa's" mold will be retired at the end of 1999. Lyal Nickals in San Leandro, California, is featuring "St. Nickals," an exquisite Santa in billowing robes of brilliant red and gold. Tickled Pink in Portland, Oregon, has a two-sided ornament designed specifi-cally for that store. "Mr. and Mrs. Claus" wear diamond-patterned robes in deep burgundy red. The package at Mrs. Claus' feet is wrapped in the signature pink of Tickled Pink, including the feather plume in the ribbon. Each of these Larry Fraga Designs exclusives is limited to 54 pieces.

THE LARRY FRAGA DESIGNS COLLECTORS' CLUB

The year 2000 saw the introduction of many new and original designs by Larry, reflecting the new twist that artist is giving his work now that the new millennium has begun. The Larry Fraga Designs Collectors' Club also premiered in 2000, with membership initially limited to 1,000 collectors and an annual fee of $45.00. A wonderfully elegant, timeless and traditional Santa was created as the exclusive-members-only piece. This Santa is titled "Christmas I Bring," and is 6" tall. He is robed in royal purple and brilliant red.

Club members will have the opportu-nity to purchase a second exclusive, available only with collectors' club membership, through a Golden Wing Retailer in August. 2000. Members also will receive advance notification of new releases, the Larry Fraga Designs Catalog for 2000 and the official member-ship card.

During the year, Larry will be doing signing events and personal appearances across the United States. As he comments, "I truly enjoy my signing events because it gives me the opportu-nity to meet the collectors and share stories about their Christmas traditions. I love to laugh, and I want this company to be built on the belief that people can have a great time collecting Christmas ornaments, with joy and laughter and high energy all year long."

"Christmas I Bring" is the members-only gift exclusive for the premier year of the Larry Fraga Designs Collectors' Club in 2000.

Larry Fraga Designs
4720 Sequoyah Road
Oakland, CA 94605

Phone:
510-638-3900

Fax:
510-638-3900

Web Site:
www.larryfragadesigns.com

E-mail:
larryfraga@aol.com

LARRY FRAGA DESIGNS

"The Babies That Love You Back"

Imagine collectible dolls so real that grown men send for rescue squads to "save the baby" from a locked car! That kind of "mistaken identity" happens all the time with designer Reva Schick's creations for Lee Middleton Original Dolls, Inc. In fact, Reva's husband, Wayne, says he and his wife either have to stop taking her doll creations with them on trips, or he's going to create a sign to hang in his car window, "Doll On Board!"

The "Babies That Love You Back" also are being used today in Red Cross certified babysitting and parenting classes to teach proper infant handling. What's more, in November of 1998, Middleton dolls made their debut on NBC's top-rated show, "ER," playing the parts of infants in "long shots" in the emergency room setting.

The "My Own Baby" dolls are so realistic that they have played infants on the NBC television show, "ER."

Reva Schick's "Little Sweetheart" vinyl doll is presented in a limited edition of 5,000.

Also fueling the firm's continued success has been a heightened profile on the national media scene, with Middleton dolls appearing on "The Oprah Winfrey Show" and the "Weekend Today Show," and serving as prizes on "The Price is Right." On "Oprah," the dolls actually appeared twice: once to demonstrate the proper way to hold babies, and again in a Christmas show on favorite gifts. In addition, the company's "My Own Baby" designs are the only dolls ever awarded a "UL Classification" for safety from Underwriter's Laboratory, underscoring their use for children ages three and older. Middleton dolls are perfect as a child's first collectible play doll, bridging the gap between toys and collectibles.

Recognizing Lee Middleton Original Dolls' growing status on the world stage, Mayor Richard Thomas of Belpre, Ohio, honored the firm as the top tourist attraction in the region in 1998. He dubbed the town "The Baby Doll Capital of the World," noting that thousands visit the doll studio each year from all over the globe. One of the highlights of the tour is a visit to the "hospital" where each doll's new "parents" are invited to don hospital gowns and rock their "babies" for the first time in cozy rocking chairs!

AN INVENTIVE ARTISTS' LEGACY LIVES ON

Setting the stage for this outstanding success was Lee Middleton herself – the company's founder and original artist. For nearly two decades, before her unexpected death on January 30, 1997, her superb artistry captivated doll collectors nationwide.

The granddaughter of an inventor, Lee Middleton was always resourceful in developing her own techniques for sculpture and doll production. Lee became something of an inventor herself, introducing the "porcelain look" in vinyl collectibles, and creating the first vinyl dolls to be considered truly collectible. Her "BABY SKIN"™ vinyl dolls are so life-like that it seems they almost breathe!

When Lee founded her company in 1980, her plan was to work from home and create only as many dolls as she could produce herself. But gift and doll shop owners had other ideas. They soon placed so many orders for Middleton dolls, that Lee had to create a "cottage industry," with family members and other helpers working from their homes. Eventually, Lee spearheaded the construction of a state-of-the-art manufacturing facility, that combines a one-of-a-kind production plant, with a beautiful pastel "gingerbread" facade that looks like a larger-than-life doll house.

AWARD-WINNING SCULPTOR REVA SCHICK

In honor of Lee and her indomitable spirit, Lee Middleton Original Dolls lives on and prospers. Many of Lee's own designs are still in production, and the firm's fruitful alliance with the gifted Canadian artist Reva Schick keeps more dolls coming with that "Middleton touch."

Just days after Lee Middleton's death, officials from her firm discovered Reva Schick's work at the 1997 International Toy Fair in New York. Reva had been making her own one-of-a-kind dolls for collectors, but before long, her originals inspired a new line of Middleton dolls with the same true-to-life magic as those of Lee herself.

Like Lee Middleton, Reva is a devout Christian who believes her talent is God-given. As Reva comments, "I can't explain to anybody what the characteristics of the face are, or about the dimensions. Once I start sculpting, it's whatever expression comes out, comes out. It's like having a real baby – you don't know what it is, who it is, or what it looks like until it's done! I believe that my strong religious background fits in well with the direction of the Lee Middleton Doll Studio. The Bible that Middleton places in each doll box was a factor in my deciding to go with the company."

THE MIDDLETON "BABY BOOM"

Already renowned for its incredibly realistic porcelain and vinyl babies, Middleton introduced ten new porcelain newborns, infants and toddlers during 1999, as well as 31 new vinyl dolls. In addition, the firm unveiled a brand-new line of mohair *Nursery Bear Babies*™ – three years in the making – from the gifted artist Linda Henry.

"Just think, I get to play with bears and dolls all day and get paid for it!" Linda exclaimed upon signing an exclusive, five-year contract with Lee Middleton Original Dolls. Linda studied with Lee Middleton before starting to design teddy bears more than a decade ago. She has won several national awards, and has shown her teddy bears and dolls in Europe and in Japan, including Japanese television.

Each of the six newborn teddy bears is crafted with the same degree of expertise as Middleton's collectible line of dolls. Each of them has a floppy, weighted head, squeezable body, and fully jointed arms and legs. Beautifully dressed, each with his or her own lively personality, the *Nursery Bear Babies* can't wait to "bond" with their new families.

OUR DOLL FAMILY

Seasoned and new Lee Middleton doll collectors alike enjoy membership in Our Doll Family, the club that debuted only four years ago, yet already boasts several thousand members. The first two years'

"Sleepy Bear Baby" by Linda Henry is one of Middleton's first six Nursery Bear Babies™ teddy bears.

members-only designs were Lee Middleton creations, while the third and fourth years featured a Reva Schick doll.

The 2000 premium for joining the club is a delicate pair of handwoven booties and cap made especially to accent our club doll, "Dressed for the Holidays," or any of our babies. Club members also receive first news about upcoming products and events through an exclusive newsletter.

MIDDLETON EARNS TOP AWARDS

Lee Middleton Original Dolls won two coveted "Doll of the Year" awards for "Growing Up" in Category Four: Plastic/Vinyl Retail $150-$350; and for "Cuddle Me" in Category One: Children's Play Dolls in 1999.

The firm also received two "Awards of Excellence" nominations from *Dolls* magazine: for "Growing Up" in the Vinyl/Resin/Plastic category $100-$200; and for "Little Princess' Hispanic" in the Vinyl/Resin/Plastic category $201-$400. The nomination for "Little Princess' Hispanic" is especially notable in that it represents the firm's first-ever Hispanic doll design.

What's more, Middleton was tapped as a Top 10 Finalist for the NALED Achievement Award, for Producer/ Manufacturer of the Year from the National Association of Limited Edition Dealers.

No matter how many awards the firm wins, how many artists it brings under contract and how much its product lines and manufacturing capabilities grow, Lee Middleton Original Dolls is dedicated to keeping its founder's values alive. As Jim Armour, Chief Operating Officer of the company, asserts, "Lee left us a legacy of beauty and quality which is unparalleled in the doll business. We will use this legacy as the foundation upon which to build a living memorial to the talent, creativity and spirit of its founder, Lee Middleton."

"Love and Prayers" by Reva Schick is the official 1999 exclusive for Our Doll Family club members.

Lee Middleton
Original Dolls, Inc.
1301 Washington Blvd.
Belpre, OH 45714

Phone:
740-423-1717

Fax:
740-423-5983

Web Site:
www.leemiddleton.com

E-mail:
lisa@leemiddleton.com

A Tradition of Quality, Artistry and Beauty

Dressed "to the nines" in late 19th-century style, this elegant lady in hand-painted porcelain is seen "Shopping on Fifth Avenue."

For a century, the name Lenox has been synonymous with a relentless pursuit of excellence in quality, artistry and beauty. And now the emergence of Lenox Classics represents a natural and clear extension of the Lenox legacy. Lenox Classics exhibit the firm's high standards through two exquisite modes of execution: gold-accented ivory china and brilliant crystal.

HISTORY OF LENOX

It all began with a dream... when Walter Scott Lenox, who was born in Trenton, New Jersey, in 1859, was but a schoolboy. The sight of the potter's wheel awoke in him longings which later led him along the path of greatness. This youth became a potter, learning the rudiments of a trade before assaying the possibilities of an art.

Lenox, dreaming of better things, yearning for an opportunity to give vent to his own aspirations and individuality, perceived the fact that only by establishing his own factory could he attain his own ideals of producing a grade of china equal to the finest created abroad. There were years of struggle, but Lenox was adamant in his determination to make no compromise with his conscience. Nothing could stir him from his resolution to make the best china of which he was capable – or none at all.

Blindness and paralysis struck Walter Scott Lenox as he was about to reap the reward of artistic success. Until the day of his death, January 11, 1920, Walter Scott Lenox continued to visit his factory regularly, lovingly caressing the new products to supplement the loss of sight through the delicate nerves of his fingers. His boyhood dream had been realized!

And then one day he came no more. But the idealism, the personality, the spirit of Walter Scott Lenox lived on. The first complete Lenox table service was displayed by Tiffany & Co. Today, Lenox china services are found in the White House and in homes of culture and refinement throughout the land. What's more, Lenox Classics has recently introduced china and crystal figurines. Continuously measuring up to the long-established expectations of this fabled firm, these additions are as superb in the quality of high standard craftsmanship, as they are in the splendid skillful artistry.

THE BEAUTY OF LENOX CHINA

Offering a wide variety of collectibles for any occasion, the latest china collections to join the Lenox Classics family include *Gala Fashion Figurines, Mother and Child Sculpture Collection* and the *Ivory Snowman Collection.*

The *Gala Fashion Figurines* collection features two graceful figurines – "Belle of the Ball™" and "Evening at the Opera™" – ready for a special evening attired in elegant dresses with pastel accents. Lenox Classics has introduced a fourth and fifth addition to the *Victorian Ladies of Fashion Collection*, titled "Shopping on Fifth Avenue" and "Picnic in the Park." These works of art exhibit both grace and elegance – like a true lady from the Victorian era.

Marking the beginning of the heartwarming *Mother and Child Sculpture* collection, "A Time to Cherish™" is a spectacular portrayal of the timeless bond between mother and baby.

The *Ivory Snowman Collection* features everyone's favorite symbol of winter fun in an adorable ivory china figurine called "Special Delivery." Representing another symbol of winter is "North Pole Express," the third Santa in a series of annuals. Making the tree come to life, this lovable sculpture showcases a playful string of trains wrapped around jolly St. Nick.

The third in a series of annual angels is "Guardian of the Millennium." Standing approximately 10" high, this beautiful 24K gold-accented ivory china piece commemorates the end of the century and the beginning of a new

From Lenox Classics' Crystal Elephant Collection comes this intimate family scene called "Tender Embrace."

"The Ascension" is a heavenly collectible, combining clear and frosted crystal to add depth and dimension.

era. In celebration of the year 2000, "Guardian of the Millennium" is limited to only 2,000, and production will end on December 31, 1999.

For 1999, Lenox Classics also introduced its first African American Santa, "Santa's List."™ This limited edition figurine features a detachable elf ornament to be displayed with Santa or hung separately on the tree.

"The Children's Blessing" continues the *Inspirational Collection* with a divine scene of love and blessing of the children. This is the second work of art in the collection.

Little Graces, the truly angelic collection of limited edition, hand-numbered cherubs, marks the third season of special ornaments with "Peaceful Messenger™," a beautiful angel carrying the 1999 insignia. Also limited to 5,000 is "Enlightenment" – the first African-American angel in this collection.

Lenox is introducing several new figurines to its *Barefoot Blessings* collection, which features adorable little barefoot children, each captured in a special moment of life. "Little MVP" captures a joyous moment in the game of soccer. "A Boy's Best Friend" shows an intimate moment of friendship between a boy and his pup. "The Graduate" celebrates a glorious time of achievement; "Chatterbox" shows how a bond is created through conversations on the phone. "First Recital" recalls wonderful memories of a little girl's premier ballet performance.

Disney Showcase Collection features "Doc," "Happy" and "Bashful," three long-awaited additions to the popular Lenox Classics collection. An authentic portrayal of the beloved Disney characters, each is artistically designed and skillfully crafted, providing for an unmistakable recognition of these delightful dwarfs. Truly lovable and charming, they are an irresistible attraction for all ages.

THE BRILLIANCE OF LENOX CRYSTAL

Lenox's Crystal Collection shimmers with elegance and beauty! Two new items mark the introduction of the *Crystal Inspirational* collection, which translates religious

passages into heavenly collectibles. "Crystal Footprints™" depicts a divine scene reflecting a Bible passage, and "The Ascension" portrays Jesus ascending on a cloud in brilliant crystal. *Seasonal Christmas,* the newest crystal holiday collection in the Lenox Classics family, features a crystal "Jolly Santa Claus™" and "Winter Magic," a crystal snowman.

The "Regal Lion" from the *Crystal Cat Collection* shows the lord of the wilderness gazing into the distance. "Dolphin's Love" and "Sea Surrender" portray magnificent dolphins. "Cute and Cuddly" from the *Crystal Collection* portrays two lovable teddy bears, one clear and one frosted, while that series' "Woodland Spirit" suspends a wolf in mid-air. "Racing the Wind," another *Crystal Collection* entry, shows a galloping horse.

Also from the *Crystal Elephant Collection* are "Tender Embrace" and "Bashful and Bold." Each combines clear and frosted crystal, with the first piece showcasing a mother and baby and the second showing playful friends.

THE LENOX TRADITION LIVES ON

Today in the new millennium, the dream of Walter Scott Lenox continues. Lenox designers still strive to enrich people's lives through beautifully crafted products. What's more, Lenox Classics looks forward to years of continuing growth, providing collectors with works of art that combine classic techniques and designs with quality, artistry and beauty.

Created to mark the year 2000 is this stunning "Guardian of the Millennium" figurine from Lenox Classics. Note the rich touches of 24K gold on the globe.

Lenox Classics
900 Wheeler Way
Langhorne, PA 19047

Phone:
888-561-8808

Fax:
888-561-2155

Web Site:
www.lenoxclassics.com

Thomas Kinkade, "Painter of Light™"

Thomas Kinkade is America's most collected living artist, a painter-communicator whose tranquil, light infused paintings bring hope and joy to millions each year. Each painting Thomas Kinkade creates is a quiet messenger in the home, affirming the basic values of family and home, faith in God and the luminous beauty of nature.

It was while growing up in the small town of Placerville, California, that these simple, life-affirming values were instilled in Thomas. It was also during this time that he began to explore the world around him. He once spent a summer on a sketching tour with a college friend, producing the best-selling instructional book, *The Artist's Guide to Sketching*. The success of the book landed the two young artists at Ralph Bakshi Studios to create background art for the animation feature, "Fire and Ice," where Kinkade was able to explore light and imaginative worlds with abandon.

After the film, Kinkade earned his living as a painter, selling his originals in galleries throughout California. In 1982, he married his childhood sweetheart, Nanette, and two years later, they began to publish his art.

"Paris, City of Lights" reflects the love affair between this immortal city and the "Painter of Light™," Thomas Kinkade.

"Bridge of Faith" offers a symbolic and inspirational message from Thomas Kinkade.

FAMILY AND FAITH

Kinkade is a devout Christian and credits the Lord for both the ability and the inspiration to create his paintings. His goal as an artist is to touch people of all faiths, to bring peace and joy to their lives through the images he creates. The letters he receives every day testify to the fact that he is achieving this goal. Though a committed Christian, Kinkade believes that art is a universal language and has the power to touch people of all faiths.

A devoted husband and doting father to their four little girls, Kinkade hides the letter "N" in his paintings to pay tribute to his wife, Nanette, and the girls find their names and images in many of his paintings.

AWARDS AND ACCOLADES

Kinkade has received numerous awards for his works. He has been named by the National Association of Limited Edition Dealers (NALED) as "Graphic Artist of the Year" for the fourth year in a row. He has also been named NALED's "Artist of the Year," and his works have been named "Graphic Art Print of the Year" for seven years in a row.

Kinkade has also won *Collector Editions'* "Award of Excellence" and was a charter inductee, along with his idol, Norman Rockwell, to the Bradford International Hall of Fame for plate artists. In 1989, he was the "Official Artist" for the National Parks Collectors' Print and has donated his art for the Veterans of Foreign Wars (VFW) Christmas program, as well as granting the VFW the right to use his images on their Christmas cards. Kinkade also has recently been inducted into *U.S. Art* magazine's "Hall of Fame."

ABOUT MEDIA ARTS GROUP, INC.

Thomas Kinkade's diverse creations are presented by Media Arts Group, Inc., a leading designer, manufacturer, marketer and branded retailer. The firm produces canvas and paper lithographs, art-based home decorative accessories, collectibles and gift products based on Kinkade's works. All of this fine art features Thom's unique use of light and his peaceful and inspiring themes.

Media Arts Group's products are sold nationwide through a network of individually owned Signature Galleries. During the firm's fiscal year 1999, 112 new Signature Galleries were opened, and plans for fiscal year 2000 call for 115 more new galleries. Bud Peterson, President and CEO of Media Arts Group, notes that, "With the rapid expansion of our Signature Gallery

Thomas Kinkade's "Cobblestone Brooke" portrays a charming English town with inviting lights in the windows of each home.

program, we are committed to providing our dealers with more retail services and support to help them manage and grow their businesses."

In addition to enhancing support for these retail concerns, Media Arts Group has allocated significant resources to the development of its Internet and e-commerce strategy, and diversification through a broader offering of artist-based products on the Internet. According to Peterson, "We believe that the e-commerce opportunities for the Thomas Kinkade lifestyle brand are enormous. Our vision is to create the web's largest art-based on-line community and to provide Internet visitors with an experience that is creative, interactive and enjoyable."

Signature Gallery Advisory Committee member Mike Johnson, who owns four galleries in the Omaha, Nebraska area, adds, "As a Signature Gallery owner, I am extremely excited about the introduction of this Internet strategy and the positive impact it will have on my business. By taking the lead in establishing a strong, centralized e-commerce presence, Media Arts is giving all of its Signature Gallery owners an equal opportunity to take advantage of the Internet's powerful capabilities."

In addition to expanded retail and Internet ventures for Thomas Kinkade and Media Arts Group, in April 1999, Warner Books published Kinkade's *Lightposts for Living,* a hugely popular new book that already has landed on a number of prominent best seller lists. This effort has played a significant role in raising consumer awareness of and demand for the Kinkade lifestyle brand.

THOMAS KINKADE HOME STYLE

Media Arts group has launched a strategic alliance with La-Z-Boy Incorporated and Kincaid Furniture Company, Inc., a subsidiary of La-Z-Boy, to present a furniture collection created by Thomas Kinkade. "We are very excited to associate the Thomas Kinkade brand name with a company as highly recognized and respected as La-Z-Boy," said Ken Raasch, Media Arts Group, Inc.'s Chairman.

Kincaid Furniture Company (no relation to Thomas Kinkade) is the largest solid wood manufacturer in the

industry, and has introduced a line of "Thomas Kinkade, Painter of Light" solid wood furniture. The line premiered in October, 1998 at the furniture show in High Point, North Carolina, featuring sofas, chairs, bedroom, dining room and occasional furniture.

THE ARTIST'S PHILOSOPHY OF LIFE

While Media Arts Group takes care of Thomas Kinkade's business concerns, the artist himself works hard to provide his family with a calm and gentle lifestyle. Kinkade has recently published *Simpler Times,* a best-selling book which shares some of his philosophy about faith and family and is illustrated with his work. In it, he encourages everyone to simplify their lives, to spend time with family and friends. The book, like his paintings, offers "an off ramp from the fast lane..."

In an interview which appeared in the Christian publication *Release Ink* magazine, Kinkade told journalist Cara Denny about his efforts to reestablish a simpler way of life as we greet the millennium. The Kinkade family spends much time together, and they live a life that is nearly devoid of "consumerism" and media influence. As Kinkade related to Denny, "Remember the old fashioned thing, when people used to take a walk in the evenings? We do that almost every night. Sounds simple enough, but what a meaningful thing."

Kinkade has eliminated television and newspapers from his home. "Media is a peer group that will overwhelm just about anything if you allow it. It will be the thing that shapes the ideas of the next generation. I don't want to be reading a newspaper when I should be talking to my children in the morning," asserts the "Painter of Light."

"We'll be okay," Kinkade told Denny, "when we return to the basic dignity of life – to moments spent in the sunshine, moments spent with each other, spending life with people one on one. What really matters is making those little choices day by day to simplify your life and to enjoy the moments that God has given us."

A stunning autumn panorama is captured in "The Valley of Peace" by Thomas Kinkade.

Lightpost Publishing/
Media Arts Group, Inc.
521 Charcot Avenue
San Jose, CA 95131

Phone:
800-366-3733

Fax:
800-243-8533

Web Site:
www.thomaskinkade.com

Five Fine Hallmarks Set These Cottages Apart

"The Planetarium" features the Old Royal Observatory at Greenwich, building on a tradition begun in 1675 by King Charles II of England.

Back in 1982, a quaint old barn in Cumbria, England, became the first "corporate home" for Lilliput Lane. Born of the imagination of artist David J. Tate, the fledgling firm and its original seven team members were dedicated to five outstanding hallmarks: Authenticity, Detail, Quality, Color and Collectibility.

Since then, Lilliput Lane's friendly staff has grown to more than 500 members working in studios in Penrith, Workington and Carlisle. As the creative force behind Lilliput Lane's *American Landmarks* collection, Ray Day reigns as lead American artist for the firm today. David Tate — though currently retired — still shares his inspiration as Special Projects Consultant. Now as in the past, the genius of Lilliput Lane springs from Tate's life-long love of British vernacular architecture.

PROMPT PRAISE FOR A GROWING STUDIO

Within five years of its establishment, Lilliput Lane had received the "Cumbria County Export Award," and had been a finalist twice in the Confederation of British Industry (CBI) "Company of the Year" Award. In the New Year's Honors of 1988, David Tate was awarded the M.B.E., Member of the Order of the British Empire in recognition of his achievements. He received this honor from Queen Elizabeth during a ceremony at Buckingham Palace. By mid-1988, Lilliput Lane cottages could be bought throughout the world — in Australia, New Zealand, Canada, the United States, and many European countries. Such success brought Lilliput Lane another honor in

♦ 1988: the "Queen's Award" for Export and Achievement.

To ensure that Lilliput Lane consistently produces the world's most definitive cottage sculptures, every piece bears five outstanding hallmarks: authenticity, detail, quality, color and collectibility. *Authenticity* is reflected in the way each Lilliput Lane cottage accurately captures the essence of picturesque and vernacular architecture. The attention to *detail* eminates from the craftspeople of Lilliput Lane who are famous for producing sculptures of remarkably fine detail. Research is thorough, involving months of dedicated study. *Quality* is never uncompromised at Lilliput Lane. Exhaustive research and development constantly improve techniques and materials. Rich, brilliant, permanent *colors* are hand-painted by highly skilled, trained artisans. Lilliput Lane offers a wealth of choice to the collector, fostering the *collectibility* of the line.

THE LATEST FROM LILLIPUT LANE

Three lovely new cottages and Ray Day's 10th Anniversary introduction star among Lilliput Lane's current product lineup. "Say It With Flowers" captures a colorful scene in Aldbourne, Wiltshire, just as it might have appeared circa 1900. Freshly cut flowers were not such a luxury

This idyllic setting for a country wedding is titled "To Have and To Hold." It captures the charm of lovely St. James Church in Defford, Worcestershire.

then, and a flower seller like this could provide delightful decorations for the village church, centerpieces for the local gentry's dining tables, and pretty posies for the sweethearts of soldiers. Rather than have a market stall, the florist found this ideal permanent site: a compact, 17th-century timber structure raised off the ground on straddle stones.

"Pen Pals" takes us to a pretty cottage in Eastnor, Herefordshire, where a little girl named Polly is just in time to give her latest letter to the postman. Polly's letters always describe her lovely village, which is full of wonderful old timber box-frame and thatch cottages. Then there is "Stargazer's Cottage" from Wickhamford, Worcestershire, where the owner celebrates the millennium by charting the starry skies throughout the year.

RAY DAY'S ANNIVERSARY SPECIAL

Over the past decade, Ray Day has earned international renown for his *American Landmarks* collection. In addition, he creates popular pieces for Lilliput Lane in series

For his 10th Anniversary as a Lilliput Lane artist, Ray Day unveils "Nature's Bounty," inspired by the Wayside Inn Gristmill near Sudbury, Massachusetts.

known as *America's Favorites, An American Journey, The Allegiance Collection,* and *Coca-Cola Country Collection.*

Day's sculpting talent encompasses a wide range of architectural designs — from rural structures to elegant Victorian homes. Now, to mark his 10th Anniversary creating *American Landmarks* for Lilliput Lane, he has created "Nature's Bounty," portraying the Wayside Inn Gristmill near Sudbury, Massachusetts.

As Day explains, "It was in the summer of 1990 while on a Lilliput Lane promotional tour of New England, that I first visited the Wayside Inn Gristmill. My love of rural architecture drew me there, and the beauty of the place made it difficult to leave. The structure's native stones create a textural delight for the eyes, while the rushing waterfall is a constant reminder that the power of nature, when harnessed, is more than enough to turn the massive 'buhr' stones to grind the grain." Henry Ford's interest in recreating and preserving architecture for educational purposes led to the original construction of this structure in 1929. Now a National Historic Site, the mill was restored following a fire in 1955.

In addition to Day's several series for Lilliput Lane, the firm keeps up a thriving *British Collection* which includes: *The Bed and Breakfast Collection, The Victorian Shops Collection, The English Tea Room Collection, The Village Shops Collection, Britain's Heritage, Anniversary Special, Christmas Special, Christmas Ornament, Moments in Time* and *Secret Gardens.*

HOW LILLIPUT LANE COTTAGES ARE MADE

The most important decision in the entire creative process of developing a Lilliput Lane cottage comes as part of the research phase. A suitable region and price point are selected, and then an appropriate cottage is photographed and researched. From two-dimensional drawings, the cottage first takes its three-dimensional shape in wax. Nearly 200 sculpting tools have been devised for the intricate tasks of sculpting!

Every roof tile is cut out of thin sheets of wax and placed onto the roof, one by one — with thousands of tiles needed for some pieces.

Tooling and molding come next — a process that requires up to three months and involves over 40 different processes. Next, each piece is hand-cast in amorphite, a type of gypsum rock mined in the United Kingdom. While still "green" (not completely hardened), the casts are "fettled," or made good through hand-detailing, then dipped in one or more of eight different substances, representing the different stone colors throughout the United Kingdom.

After the pieces are dry, they move to the painting studio, where each cottage is painted from start to finish by one of 300 Lilliput Lane painters. Over 72 permanent, waterproof paints are used. On completion, the cottages are carefully packed to ensure that collectors worldwide receive their pieces in perfect condition.

THE LILLIPUT LANE COLLECTORS' CLUB

In response to many requests, The Lilliput Lane Collectors' Club was formed in 1986, with branches worldwide. Benefits include an exclusive collectors' cottage, a complimentary cottage on joining, regular issues of the club's quarterly magazine, *Gulliver's World,* and many more advantages such as special events and exclusive studio tours. U.S. club fees are $40.00 per year.

In the past, club members have enjoyed such members-only exclusives as "The Good Life." It captures a charming, rustic scene inspired by a 17th century farmhouse near Aldbourne — an upland village in Wiltshire, England. By Victorian times the farm is doing so well that one of the nearby cottages has been converted to a little shop, which club members will recognize as the 1999/2000 club Symbol of Membership piece. It's called "Fresh Today," and it shows off the wonderful eggs, butter and milk from the thriving farm.

With products now widely available in over 40 countries, Lilliput Lane attributes its phenomenal growth and success to the care and attention it gives to everything it does. From the tiniest tile or leaf in a sculpture, to the meticulous business plans for growth, attention to detail is the creed of Lilliput Lane. Lilliput Lane's mission is to continually improve its products and services to meet collector aspirations and customer needs. Lilliput Lane cares about its image in the giftware and collectibles market, that it meets the expectations of collectors and retailers alike, and that it shares a sense of pride in its work and achievement.

The 1999/2000 Symbol of Membership piece in the Lilliput Lane Collectors' Club is "Fresh Today," portraying a little shop packed full with newly laid eggs, just-churned butter, and this morning's milk, all from the family farm.

Lilliput Lane
P.O. Box 7
Libertytown, MD 21762

Phone:
800-545-5478

Fax:
301-829-8554

E-mail:
www.info@lilliputlaneusa.com

An Angel Made the Difference

A love of nostalgia, a close-knit family and more than just a little divine inspiration went into the formation of one of the country's hottest, up-and-coming print and collectibles companies, Little Angel Publishing.

By the time Dona and Brian Gelsinger founded the company (which they lovingly refer to as LAP for the initials of Little Angel Publishing) in 1994 as the principal showcase for Dona's ever-growing portfolio of transcendent art, the young couple had already triumphed over tragedy, with their faith helping them to cope with the devastating loss of their infant son.

A LIFE DEVOTED TO ART

Artist Dona Gelsinger grew up in the 1960s near Los Angeles, California. Her father was a school teacher,

In "Tender Love" Dona Gelsinger depicts a mother's love for her son as she quiets his fears before bedtime.

principal and school administrator. Her mother was a nurse. From both her parents, Dona inherited her deep appreciation for the strong, loving family values that were the foundation for both her happy childhood and the art she started to create at a very early age.

In fact, from the time she could walk, Dona had been fascinated by art. For hours on end, she would sit and watch her grandfather as he painted. As she studied every stroke of his brush, the talented youngster was learning her craft – so much so that young Dona received several awards as an art student in high school. In recognition of her skills, she was rewarded with an art scholarship to Cal State Long Beach.

Once she graduated, Dona accepted a position as a staff artist for a large corporation in southern California. There she spent her days designing and drawing advertising layouts. Although she was very thankful to have a steady job, in time she started to feel out of touch in the impersonal corporate culture, and longed to set her creative spirit soaring.

With the support and encouragement of her devoted family, Dona left the safety of her corporate job and struck out on her own to pursue her heart's desire. She set up a studio in her home and started painting portraits and illustrations.

A MESSAGE THAT CHANGED HER FAMILY'S LIVES

One Sunday in 1987, while Dona and her family were attending services at their small church, something that would change the lives of the whole family happened. From out of nowhere a powerful thought suddenly overtook her...why not use her gifts to create a life size painting of Jesus Christ for the new church her congregation was building?

After thinking and praying for the right decision, she talked to the parish priest and learned that the church was considering hiring an artist from overseas to paint the Stations of the Cross. At that moment, she was sure what the Lord had meant for her to do.

She applied for the commission herself, offering to contribute additional work beyond the massive project at hand, and after demonstrating her abilities, she landed the job.

In her Angel's Light *series, Dona Gelsinger reminds us that angels can guide us to safety, if only we let them.*

Like a modern day Michelangelo, Dona spent the better part of the next two years high up in the new church, creating the inspiring scenes of the Passion of Jesus Christ.

Her paintings have helped to make the new St. Denis Church in Diamond Bar, California, a destination for devout pilgrims throughout America, and forever changed the fate of the little-known artist who was selected to paint them.

In no time, Dona found herself traveling in the art world's most exalted circles. But even working with a prestigious art publisher failed to provide the creative stimulus she had been seeking since her work on the church. So in 1994, Dona and Brian once again put their faith and future in God's hands. They started their own company, Little Angel Publishing, a name they chose as a tribute to their baby, Jacob, who died from a heart defect.

LAP – THE REALIZATION OF A HEART'S DESIRE

From its inception, Little Angel Publishing has been bringing Dona Gelsinger's sublime vision of the world to collectors on paper and on canvas. As meticulous with her prints as she is with her original works, Dona insists on maintaining the highest standards. In fact, one of Dona's inviolable policies is that no art leaves the company until it has been fully inspected and approved by herself, Brian, or a member of their quality control team.

"Quality" has always been the cornerstone of the company. This has been acknowledged by the dealers who carry Dona's artwork, and her growing number of collectors. Although the company is widely known in the western U.S., LAP has recently started to make a name for itself all over the country, emerging to the forefront in fine art collectibles.

AT HOME WITH THE LOVE OF ART

LAP is headquartered in a rural community called Eagle Point, outside of Medford, Oregon, near Dona's studio. Living and painting in southern Oregon, with its incredible natural beauty, provides Dona with an endless source of inspiration.

In this paradise of clear lakes, blue skies and green trees, Dona has merely to step outside to find fascinating subjects, while the quiet grandeur of the area provides the spiritual tranquillity with which all of the artist's work is suffused.

Her proximity to LAP's headquarters also allows Dona to stop by the offices to check on the progress of new prints, and share in the excitement when a new edition is ready for release.

A BRIGHT FUTURE WITH GOD'S HELP

LAP recently teamed up with Bentley House, a highly-respected distributor, to help distribute Dona's artwork in several countries, enabling more collectors than ever to own Dona's art.

Soon, several paintings new to the print market are destined to go to press. These include Dona's popular plate art such as "Garden Blessing," and the new series which combines angels and lighthouses, *An Angel's Light.*

The scene in the "Heceta Head Lighthouse" is magically reminiscent of Norman Rockwell's masterworks, depicting a happy relationship between the young and old.

Collectors are also looking forward to seeing Dona's art on plates and ornaments from The Bradford Exchange, needlework kits from Candamar, puzzles by SunsOut, holiday candles from Lava Enterprises, and Christmas cards from Crown Point Graphics. Even more products are planned for introduction in the near future.

Dona recently completed a life-size painting of actress Ginger Rogers for display in the Craterian Ginger Rogers Theater in Medford, Oregon. Miss Rogers once performed there and was so taken with the beauty of the countryside, she purchased property and lived there for most of her career.

One of Dona Gelsinger's trademarks is her inclusion of an angelic figure hidden within her paintings. Collectors enjoy searching for the image, and those who have suffered a tragic loss as Dona and Brian have, often say that they take comfort in the celestial presence they find in Dona's work.

Dona's original paintings can be found on display at the Galleria di Sorrento at Caesar's Palace, Las Vegas, Nevada. The friendly people who work there are always willing to provide collectors with any information they may want, and answer any questions they have about Dona's art.

"An Angel's Touch," has been interpreted by The Bradford Exchange as a hand-numbered, fine porcelain collector's plate.

Little Angel Publishing
11232 Hwy. 62, Ste. C
Eagle Point, OR 97524

Phone:
800-830-1690

Fax:
541-830-1811

Web Site:
www.donagelsinger.com

E-mail:
mail@donagelsinger.com

Look for "Little Gem" on the Paw Pad!

Little Gem's 1999 collection features designs by talented artists Carol Stewart, Lisa Lloyd and Linda Spiegel.

"**I**f the bear does not have 'Little Gem' written on its paw pad, then it's not a Little Gem!" asserts Chu-Ming (Jamie) Wu with a smile. The Taiwanese native has made teddy bears his life – with award-winning results – since he left his homeland in 1983 to settle in Southeast Florida. Today, Wu counts teddy bear luminaries Deb Canham, Lisa Lloyd, Carol Stewart, Bev White, Linda Spiegel and Linda Mullins among his "house designers," and he creates many a Little Gem teddy himself. Indeed, Wu now reigns over his own "teddy bear empire," selling more than 57,000 bears per year!

Sixteen years ago, Wu fled Taiwan to try to escape the deep grief he felt after his wife's death from leukemia. Searching for solace, he thought about the kind of atmosphere he and his children would enjoy most. Sunshine and fishing were high on the list, and thus Florida became the Wu's new home.

At first, the transition was difficult. Wu spoke only a few words of English, and although he had been a Ford Motor Company sales manager in Taiwan, he considered himself lucky to acquire an American job as a landscaper at $5.00 an hour. For fun and to help feed his family, Wu pursued his favorite hobby of fishing. As luck would have it, he discovered a bait and tackle store owned by Tom and

The delightful Golfer Collection and 1" Pin Bears were designed by Chu-Ming (Jamie) Wu.

Carol Stewart. One day when Wu entered the store, he found Carol working on one of her charming miniature teddy bears.

A NATURAL TALENT FOR TEDDIES

As Patrick Lee reported in an issue of *Teddy Bear Review,* Stewart vividly recalls the encounter. "He seemed fascinated, insisting I teach him how," says Stewart. "My thought was, 'Yeah, right!'" She couldn't imagine that this strapping fisherman would really want to spend his time creating and clothing tiny teddy bears. "But I taught him, and he took to it like a duck to water!"

While Wu loved making teddy bears right from the start, it didn't necessarily come easily to him. It took him 27 evenings to make his first teddy bear, but when it was complete, Wu was hooked! It's hard for him to determine exactly why making bears appeals to him so much. Wu recalls many happy hours spent with his grandfather back in Taiwan, where he learned to carve miniature animals from wood as a child. His grandfather also instilled determination and drive in young Chu-Ming Wu, telling the youngster, "If you are interested in something, stay with it!"

When Wu had a small grouping of adorable bears made from upholstery cloth, Stewart christened them the "Little Gems," and the name stuck. While Wu's firm is formally known as Akira Trading Company, his creations are called Little Gem Teddy Bears.

FROM AVOCATION TO CAREER

During the 1980s, Wu perfected his talents through experimentation and hard work. At the time, he made individual miniature teddies by hand and sold them for $200 or more. Because he could make such a limited number, it was not possible for him to support his family on the teddy bear business alone. While the teddies were his true love, he sold and installed satellite dishes for extra money.

Wu realized that if he could have his original designs crafted in quantity, he could make bears that more collectors could afford – and have sufficient volume to make a living in the bargain. In 1989, he traveled to China to personally train workers in a "cottage industry" setting so that they could craft his bears according to his particular standards.

Wu's first major success occurred in 1993 when he exhibited his Little Gems at a show in England. When show attendees saw the paw pads reading, "Made with 617 loving stitches," they purchased the wonderfully detailed bears in droves. Wu was amazed when he

Artist Deb Canham created this fun-loving troupe of animals for *Little Gem's* The Circus Collection.

counted the proceeds: "In two days, we sold enough bears to make £4,000!"

TWO TEDDY BEAR MASTERS MEET

That English show had even more significance for Wu in that the renowned teddy bear maker Deb Canham occupied the booth next to his. Deb recalls the moment very clearly. She had been in a car accident and was "In plaster from my fingers to shoulder, and on strong pain killers. Jamie spoke hardly a word of English. We communicated in sign language. He asked me to design for him, and I sent him some of my bears but doubted he could maintain the quality. When I opened the box he sent back, I thought he had returned my own samples, instead of his copies! The quality was that high."

Another happy meeting for Wu was his introduction to a manufacturer's representative named Tommy Thompson. Thompson remembers, "He told me he made bears, but I dismissed it. I assumed he produced big cheap bears. Some time later, I saw some wonderful miniature bears and found out they were Jamie's! I started representing him in August of 1993. I took his bears to Toy Fair in 1994, and that's when he went national."

A FAMILY-ORIENTED BUSINESS FLOURISHES IN MIAMI AND CHINA

Today, Wu's daughter, Jenny, manages the Akira Trading office in Miami, Florida. Originals done by Wu and his designer friends are produced in China, then distributed through a team of sales representatives to more than 1,500 stores nationwide. Wu is delighted to provide an excellent way of making a living for his "cottage industry" artists in China. As he notes, "Over 350 families in seven villages make my bears. The average age of our workers is 32, mostly mothers who want to stay home with their children. Workers in one village will make only arms and legs, in another, only heads. Another will do only assembly. I have one supervisor for every ten workers. I interview every worker myself for quality!"

Little Gem favorites are The Garden Harvest Pincushion Collection *by Linda Mullins and "Lucky Locket" and "Ginger and Snaps" by Durae Allen.*

When Wu makes personal appearances, he often brings a few special bears that he sells only on such occasions. They cost about $100 each, while the regular run of 1-1/2" to 3" bears range in price from about $15.00 to $70.00. All dressed bears and special edition bears are numbered and signed. Wu does not plan to introduce any large editions, preferring to add new designs to his line in January and July and sell them in smaller numbers per design. Little Gem does make some exclusive editions for dealers as well, with minimum editions of 500.

Testimonials from dealers and collectors alike show how beloved the Little Gems have become in recent years. They compliment Wu on his designs, execution, variety of styles, affordability of products, creativity, customer service and much more. What's more, as collectors "downsize" to smaller homes, they find themselves drawn to miniature works like Wu's. They can still own and exhibit a variety of pieces, even in limited space.

As Debbye Jackson of Decatur, Illinois, describes, "I have over 20 Little Gems, and I display them in old cups and saucers or with a tool box. I have a smaller home, and this size suits me well. Jamie's dedication shows in the quality of his work."

WU'S PERSONALITY SHINES THROUGH

Collectors and dealers will recognize Jamie Wu at shows because of his trademark attire – a blue vest adorned with about a dozen of his tiny bears. His enthusiasm for all aspects of life is apparent to his friends and collaborators. As artist Carol Stewart says, "Jamie is very energetic and rambunctious, very personable, and motivated by a genuine love for what he's doing. He's very reputable." Deb Canham agrees, noting, "He is such an honorable person, one of the world's nice guys!" Tommy Thompson chimes in admiringly, "If you could bottle Jamie's personality, you could sell it!"

A natural competitor who earned archery championships in international competition as a youth in Taiwan, Wu is thrilled by the awards and nominations his Little Gem bears have received in recent years. These include Golden Teddy Awards in 1996, 1997 and 1998, and a TOBY nomination in 1998. He is gratified to report that a one-of-a-kind piece he made for the Disney Doll and Bear Convention in 1997 sold at auction for $17,000.

Because Wu is an archer, it may come as no surprise that his company name "Akira" means "rising star" in Chinese. As he explains, "When I was an archery sportsman, I aimed for the target. Now the Teddy Bear is my target. Before, I used an arrow. Now I use a needle!"

Collectors' Information Bureau thanks Teddy Bear Review and Patrick Lee, author of "Shrunken Treasures" from that publication's July/August 1997 issue, for substantial contributions to this article.

Akira Trading Co.
Little Gem Teddy Bears
6040 NW 84th Avenue
Miami, FL 33166

Phone:
305-639-9801

Fax:
305-639-9802

E-mail:
littlegem@usa.net

LITTLE GEM TEDDY BEARS

Lladró – Art in Fine Porcelain

The name Lladró brings to mind an internationally renowned collection of porcelain figurines hand-crafted in Spain. Few today could imagine that a porcelain company of such prestige would have such humble beginnings. However, Lladró porcelain was born from the perseverance, imagination and determination of three ambitious brothers – Juan, Jose and Vicente Lladró.

In 1951, drawing on meager resources, the Lladró brothers built their first kiln. A moruno (Moorish-style) brick structure shaped like a beehive and measuring one meter high, the kiln was built in their parents' back yard. They began experimenting with different glazing and firing techniques, and used the kiln to create their first diminutive flowers for which Lladró is still known today.

The Lladró brothers soon built a larger furnace which was able to attain high temperatures and vitrify porcelain. They quickly found that the demand for their artwork exceeded what they alone could produce. While continuing to experiment in other areas, Juan, Jose and Vicente hired and trained friends from the neighborhood to be their first workers.

The Lladró Gres Collection figurine, "Spring Inspiration," illustrates the celebration of multicultural beauty that is typical of Lladró.

As their business grew, the Lladró brothers heard of a kiln in Almacera left unfinished because of defects in construction. The enterprising young men rented the premises, renovated the kiln, and formed the foundation for what would one day come to be called Porcelain City.

Today, Lladró has become one of the leading producers of fine porcelain in the world. Together with their children, the brothers have named a Lladró Family Council. The board currently consists of Rosa Maria Lladró, daughter of Jose; Rosa Lladró, daughter of Juan; and Juan Vicente Lladró, son of Vicente. Working closely with their fathers, each of the children has contributed greatly to the recent growth of the company and is certain to carry on Lladró's tradition of excellence with capable hands.

After nearly 50 years, Lladró's studies in color, form and posture continue to represent a never-ending foundation of invention, a constant merging of technical expertise and supreme artistry. Lladró truly is "Art in Fine Porcelain."

The Lladró trademark color palette is one of the most instantly recognizable in the world. Soft pastel shades of blue, cream, gray and brown form a palette of well over 5,000 colors! These delicate hues decorate the figurines that form the *Lladró Core Collection*.

◆   *"A Wish for Love" portrays an elegant maiden by a traditional wishing well.*

The *Lladró Core Collection* is the collection for which Lladró is best known. These elegant and charming figurines are displayed and collected the world over. Many figurines in the *Core Collection* are available in a choice of finishes: glazed, or matte, which is also often called bisque. The glazed finish is the high-gloss finish found on most *Core Collection* figurines. Matte is often found as an alternative to the glazed finish and provides a softer, warmer feel to the figurine.

LLADRÓ CORE COLLECTION ATTRACTS WORLD-WIDE ATTENTION

All Lladró figurines begin life in the same place – the drawing board. Sketches are used to study the position, movement and size of the porcelain. Once the sketch is approved, a figurine is molded in clay and carefully divided into numerous parts to produce special molds.

These molds are filled with porcelain paste to create the individual pieces from which the figurine is carefully assembled. The figurines are then painstakingly hand-painted by skilled artisans. Great care must be taken to ensure that all figurines achieve the same consistency of

Among the many bridal figurines available from Lladró, "A Kiss to Remember" is a special favorite.

color. However, as with any hand-made product, slight variations serve to make each figurine unique.

Before firing, the painted figurine is virtually unrecognizable as compared to the finished product. Unfired figurines are up to 20% larger than their final size, due to shrinkage during the firing process. They are also covered in a white glaze, which crystallizes and becomes clear during firing.

Figurines are fired for hours at extremely high temperatures in scientifically-controlled kilns. After firing, the figurines are allowed to cool and are meticulously inspected for any defects. After passing these rigorous tests, the finished figurine is on its way to becoming an elegant part of a porcelain connoisseur's collection.

LLADRÓ GRES COLLECTION CELEBRATES THE VIBRANT SPIRIT OF SPAIN

In 1971, Lladró introduced a new line of porcelain to the world known as Gres. The *Gres Collection* from Lladró combines warm, expressive colors with a distinctive finish that complements any home decor. *Gres* possesses all the earth tones of the Spanish countryside – mellow colors from the plains of Castile and the sandstone cliffs of Aragon. Sun-drenched shades reflective of Costa del Sol and vivid contrasts of Andalucia are evident. The vibrant spirit of Spain comes to life in this rich, colorful porcelain.

Like all Lladró figurines, each *Gres* figurine is exquisitely crafted by hand. Unlike the white-based, hard paste porcelain of the *Core Collection, Gres* has a distinctive texture with the slightly porous quality of skin and a palette of lively colors.

◆ The unique texture and coloration result from a secret blend of porcelain paste and enamel pigments. This special blend evolved after years of experiments directed by the Lladró brothers with the artisans and technicians in their state-of-the-art facilities at Porcelain City.

Gres gives Lladró artisans another avenue to explore in their expressive sculpting and painting. The warmth of the *Gres* palette harmonizes with Lladró's sensitive portraits of subjects renowned for their universal appeal. *Gres* also provides admirers with the popular traditional themes of Lladró in a color scheme that coordinates well with many home décors.

In fact, what is extraordinary about the *Gres Collection* is how comfortably, and graciously, it fits into any decorating style. Its warm palette enlivens the most traditional homes. Similarly, a more contemporary décor can be enriched by the classical qualities of *Gres* sculpture. Even a country casual interior can achieve a level of relaxed sophistication with the addition of Lladró *Gres*. The beauty of the *Gres Collection* is that it is at home wherever it goes.

EXQUISITE WEDDING KEEPSAKES

To celebrate the beauty of brides and the glories of marriage, Lladró offers a large variety of lovely bridal figurines in a wide range of price points. They're perfect as a gift for the couple-to-be, for a bridal registry, as a cake topper, or as a gift for the members of the bridal party.

Many bridal figurines can also be personalized to commemorate the date. They are engraved on the bottom of the figurine with the desired information. Personalization for bridal figurines is $15.00 and is free to members of the Lladró Society.

Two wistful pups beckon to their master, "Please Come Home!," in this finely hand-painted figurine.

THE BENEFITS OF MEMBERSHIP

In addition to free personalization of bridal figurines, members of the Lladró Society enjoy many valuable benefits for annual dues of $45.00 for new members and $35.00 for renewing members. In addition to a membership gift and yearly renewal gifts, Society members receive: the opportunity to purchase members-only figurines; the quarterly magazine, *Expressions;* a membership card; a binder for newsletters; a Lladró video; associate membership to the Lladró Museum in New York City; figurine research service, opportunity to participate in society-sponsored trips to Spain, and members-only signing events.

The Lladró family has built one of the most creative and exquisite houses of fine porcelain in the world. Each handcrafted figurine is a unique work of art worthy of a place of prominence in any collection.

◆

Lladró
1 Lladró Drive
Moonachie, NJ 07074

Phone:
800-634-9088

Fax:
201-807-1293

Web Site:
www.lladro.com

E-Mail:
lladrosociety@lladro.com

LLADRÓ

Finding Inspiration in Heaven and Nature's Beauty

Nearly two decades ago, Margaret Furlong Designs began in a small Midwestern studio – born out of the artist's love of nature and a heart of faith. After earning her master of fine arts degree from the University of Nebraska, Margaret opened a modest art studio in Lincoln, Nebraska.

The Madonna and Child series features "Madonna of the Cross" (1996), "Madonna of the Heavens" (1998) and "Madonna of the Flowers" (1997).

Drawing on her background in painting, pottery and sculpture, she sought to use her creative talents to celebrate God and nature's amazing beauty. For one project, she was asked to create a set of dishes adorned with a shell motif. So she studied her drawings and an array of seashells that were scattered about her studio. Moved by the incredible simplicity and beauty of this elegant and natural design, she began combining several shell forms, adding a molded face, a textured coil and a tapered trumpet. The result was her very first shell ornament, the "Trumpeter Angel," which was introduced in 1980.

Margaret then launched a series of white-on-white angel ornaments based on the shell form. She chose white bisque porcelain as the medium, which allowed her to highlight the subtleties of the shell's delicate pattern and rich texture. It's a combination that has become the hallmark of her designs – each creation hand-cast from shells she has often found along the beach.

Today, her angels wear robes of rippled scallop shells and have formed a full choir of about 80 different designs. The angels are also joined by a collection of other creations that blend the symbols of heaven and earth and celebrate the things Margaret values the most: God, nature, family and friendship. "Shells are such a beautiful

The "Celebration Cherubs" are perfect for birthdays, anniversaries, showers or other festive occasions.

motif used in just about every culture," she explains. "I combine them with images that represent the blessings of the world."

ANGELS RESIDE IN HEARTS AND HOMES OF COLLECTORS

It was a humbling beginning to Margaret's career. With borrowed money, she set up shop in an old stone carriage house in Nebraska and moved into the apartment above it. She began by sending letters to museum shops, earning sales of $50,000 in 1979. The following year, she got married to Jerry Alexander and moved to Seattle. In 1981, she moved to Salem, Oregon, and set up the Carriage House Studio – named after her first studio in Nebraska. Her husband gave up his job to become a full-time partner, and together they were determined to go national.

The National Trust for Historic Preservation put her angels in its catalog – and on the White House Christmas tree in 1981. A selection of Margaret's angels adorned Ronald Reagan's personal tree. Given this remarkable exposure, it wasn't long before the media took notice. America's top publications featured Margaret's work in their holiday issues. *Victoria, Good Housekeeping, Redbook* and *Ladies Home Journal* were among the magazines spreading the joy of Margaret's angels to millions of readers. In 1983, Margaret produced her most distinguished work of art, daughter Caitlin Alexander. The birth of her child took Margaret's artistic spirits to new heights.

COLLECTORS DISCOVER LIMITED EDITION SERIES

Beginning in 1980, Margaret launched her first limited edition series and also introduced angels in 3", 4" and 5" sizes. For five consecutive years, Margaret's definition of the true meaning of Christmas was shared with collectors in the *Musical* series with each 5" design limited to 3,000 pieces. In 1985, Margaret debuted her next 5" collectible series: *Gifts from God,* also limited to 3,000 of each design.

In 1990, Margaret introduced *Joyeux Noel,* a five-year series of 5" angels limited to 10,000 of each design. With the completion of *Joyeux Noel,* the *Flora Angelica* series was launched in 1995. The series combines the radiance of angels with the symbolism of flowers. The series is limited to just 10,000 pieces of each annual 5" angel. The fifth and final issue in the series, "The Angel of Love," holds a heart of lilies, roses and forget-me-nots – all of the flowers held by the first four angels in the series. A new series starts in 2000.

Charter members of the Margaret Furlong Collectors Club receive this 4-1/2" angel named "Coral Bells and Cockle Shells," inspired by the childhood rhyme, "Mary, Mary Quite Contrary."

DEVOTION AND LOVE CAPTURED IN *MADONNA* AND *CHILD SERIES*

In 1996, Margaret proudly introduced a three-part limited edition *Madonna and Child* series, inspired by Russian icons and Italian Renaissance paintings that she discovered during a trip to Europe. Her personal attraction and devotion to the theme of mother and child is influenced by her desire to protect, cherish and celebrate the precious gift of children.

The first design, "Madonna of the Cross," features a Madonna with her face accented with a beautifully detailed veil and elegant crown. "Madonna of the Flowers" continues the series with clusters of forget-me-nots adorning the Madonna's gown, and the baby Jesus also holding a bouquet of these dainty flowers. In the third and final issue, "Madonna of the Heavens," Mary cradles the Christ Child, who holds the sun or the morning star – as He is often referred to in Scripture. Each design in the series is a limited edition of 20,000 and measures approximately 6-1/2".

TAKING A STROLL THROUGH THE GARDEN

Margaret Furlong's 1999 collection continues her love of flowers, nature and feathered friends. The 4" Special Edition "Hummingbird" angel holds a trumpet flower, attracting this precious little bird to its sweet nectar. Margaret's inspiration for this angel comes from her love and appreciation of the hummingbirds that make their home in her garden.

Margaret's 3" angel "Coneflower and Goldfinch" and 2" "Flower Basket" angel are inspired by Margaret's fond childhood memories of birdwatching with her mother and making May Day baskets filled with flowers from the garden. Her 2-1/2" "Love Song" heart sings the theme of love through nature by featuring flowers, a hummingbird and vines that gently climb the heart's edge.

Margaret continues to celebrate her Irish heritage with a second cross, "Everlasting Hope." This 3" Celtic-inspired cross is adorned with ivy, the symbol of everlasting hope through Christ. Collectors have also fallen in love with Margaret's angel sets. In "Celebration Cherubs," one angel holds a two-tiered polka dot cake and the other carries a polka dot wrapped gift. This tiny 1-1/2" duo was inspired by Margaret's love of decorating cakes for family and friends.

Each year, Margaret also retires one 3" and one 4" angel. Those retired in 1999 were the 3" and 4" "Sun" angels. Created in 1994, these angels are sure to become sought-after collectibles. Collectors can go online to find all of their favorite collectibles on the Margaret Furlong web site at www.margaretfurlong.com. The site features the company's entire line of ornaments, as well as decorating ideas, history about Margaret Furlong, collectors club information and local retailers.

COLLECTORS CLUB WELCOMES NEW MEMBERS

Launched in 1999, Margaret Furlong Collectors Club provides another opportunity for Margaret to share the joy of her work, and for collectors to enjoy the artist's designs and special rewards. The 1999 collectors-only piece is the 4-1/2" angel "Coral Bells and Cockle Shells," inspired by the childhood rhyme "Mary, Mary Quite Contrary." Other benefits include a porcelain display easel, video from Margaret, "Wild Rose" cameo lapel pin, charter member certificate, membership card and history of Margaret and her company. A special collector's edition "Hummingbird" keepsake box is also available for members to purchase. The box comes inscribed with the message: "Friends are the flowers in the garden of life."

CREATING A WORK OF ART

Today, Margaret Furlong's dreams and creations have come full circle. Each is a reflection of her personal commitment to quality, value and good design. Toward that end, Margaret uses a meticulous production process that moves her creations from prototype to first modeling, and from carving to a master mold, all with methodical care. Each step of the crafting and finishing process is overseen by Margaret and her growing staff of artisans and crafters, now numbering more than 85. Her designs are also proudly made in the United States, using the exacting techniques and standards that she pioneered back in her Nebraska studio.

With all this growth and excitement, Margaret still finds time to make herself available to collectors with tours of her studios and facility in Salem, as well as personal appearances across the country. "I think I've been successful because I've used imagery that God designed," she explains. "We can never come close to making a design as beautiful as His. I love casting shells, leaves and flowers. My work celebrates God's handiwork."

The popular Flora Angelica series ended in 1999 with the fifth and final issue, "The Angel of Love." The 5" angel holds a heart of lilies, roses and forget-me-nots – all of the flowers held by the first four angels in the series.

Margaret Furlong Designs
210 State Street
Salem, OR 97301

Phone:
503-363-6004

Fax:
503-371-0676

Web Site:
www.margaretfurlong.com

A Modern Interpretation of Classic Japanese Art

The graceful beauty of the "Northern Parula" is displayed in this edition from Maruri's Premier Bird collection.

Centuries ago, sculptors in the fabled ceramic capital of Seto, Japan, mastered the art of ceramics. There, near the exotic, old-world city of Nagoya, some of the world's finest porcelain workshops have reigned for generations. One particularly successful enterprise in Seto is that of the Mizuno brothers, who carefully selected the name "Maruri" for their design studio. The "ri" means "benefits." "Maru" is a time-honored symbol for a circle meaning the never-ending nature of classic fine art.

Together, the brothers lived up to their name. Their studio quickly earned a distinguished reputation for excellent bone china, delicate figurines and true-to-nature bird and animal sculptures. Just as artists did centuries ago, today's skilled Maruri craftspeople produce the world's most treasured porcelain giftware and collectibles. And now for well over a decade, Maruri has shared this artistic treasury with connoisseurs in the New World. Indeed, today's American collectors consider Maruri a benchmark for all other wildlife sculptures on the market.

OLD-WORLD ARTISTRY CONTINUES TODAY

To create exquisite porcelain sculptures requires two things above all else: talented art masters and a total commitment to quality. Maruri prides itself on upholding such a "studied approach" in creating its limited edition sculptures. Each flower, bird and animal takes many days to complete using a multi-step process that has been faithfully followed over the years.

Artisans begin by crafting multiple molds for each piece to capture every detail to perfection. Once the molds are approved, a creamy feldspar mixture in the form of liquid slip is carefully poured. This so-called Grand Feu formula is the same one used in ancient times and continues to be the preferred ceramic material, prized for its excellent finished look and feel. When the molds are filled to a specific thickness, they are allowed to dry very slowly to meet Maruri's stringent specifications.

Next, pieces are carefully removed from the molds and placed together. Seam lines and points of juncture are smoothed and refined. Sculptures are next placed in a temperature-controlled drying room for several days, then fired in a kiln for 16 hours. A careful inspection by Maruri artists after the kiln firing leads to the rejection of as many as 40% of the sculptures that are deemed "less than perfect." Those that pass inspection are sandblasted to a brilliant, strong finish before painting by highly trained artists. The resulting sculptures are finally ready to be wrapped and shipped to fine stores around the world.

WILLY WHITTEN CAPTURES EXOTIC LOCALES

To ensure a constant flow of new ideas and artistic concepts, Maruri works with a host of gifted sculptors — including both studio artists and gifted individuals from other walks of artistic life. One of Maruri's featured master sculptors today is Willy Whitten, who admits he always wanted to live on an island somewhere in the South Pacific. Now he has given collectors a way to escape to paradise in his new collection of hut sculptures, *The Tropics*. The line is one of Willy's pet projects. He has created places we can dream about by imagining ourselves actually being there. According to Willy, "You can put these in your home or office and when you get stressed out, just sit back and dream a little."

Before taking on this labor of love for Maruri, Whitten spent years as a sculptor for several movie studios, working on movies including "Ghostbusters," "The Terminator" and others. He has also done work for the Los Angeles County Museum, Marvel Comics, Disney, and many more. His six

"Shaman Hut" from Maruri's The Tropics collection represents the exotic artistry of famed movie studio sculptor Willy Whitten.

This charming "Bluebird Family" is part of Maruri's popular Songbird Serenade collection.

Maruri cold-cast porcelain huts range in price from $40.00 to $85.00 retail. "Shaman Hut" features ceremonial shields and carved masks, "Tiki Hut" is the tiki carver's house, and there is "Happy Hut" from Fiji, "Tahiti Dream" and "Baja Surfer," which features an old trailer, scuba gear, surfboard and hammock.

FOUR EXQUISITE BIRD COLLECTIONS DEBUT

Collectors may do a double-take when they see that the retail price of each new Maruri *Premier Bird Collection* piece is just $24.95. Indeed, this line represents superior value. The sculpting detail and painstaking hand-painting make these pieces outstanding at that price.

The line consists of small North American birds: "Black-capped Chickadee," "House Wren," "Golden-crowned Kinglet," "American Goldfinch," "Tufted Titmouse," "Yellow Warbler," "Pine Warbler," "Savannah Sparrow," "Red-breasted Nuthatch," "Barn Swallow," "Northern Parula" and "Yellow-throated Warbler." All birds come with wood bases attached, and range from 4-1/4" to 5" in overall height.

Songbird Serenade represents a collection of fine Maruri porcelain songbird sculptures featuring some of the most beloved and familiar North American species. These elegant sculptures will transport their viewers to the tranquil forests and breezy meadows where these colorful little creatures sing to their hearts' content.

The songbirds portrayed include the "Goldfinch," "Robin," "Blue Jay," "Chickadee," "Cardinal" and others. Each bird species is depicted in its natural environment — perched on a branch and surrounded by colorful

Maruri's Treasures of the Sky plates each portray a pair of hummingbirds sharing the sweet nectar of a garden's floral bounty.

flowers and other foliage. Every detail of these delicately crafted sculptures is hand-painted for realistic effect. A Certificate of Authenticity and wooden base is included with each piece. Prices range from $65.00 to $95.00 at retail, and sizes are between 5-1/4" and 7-1/2" in height.

Another recent addition to the magnificent *Maruri Collection* is a series of *Four Seasons* plates, each reflecting all the natural beauty unique to the season it represents. Each three-dimensional, sculptured plate is hand-painted and handcrafted of fine Maruri cold-cast porcelain and comes complete with a hook on the back for wall hanging and a Certificate of Authenticity. The plates measure 8-1/4" in diameter and feature cardinals and pine trees for winter; bluebirds and iris for spring; goldfinch and sunflowers for summer; and cedar waxwing and autumn foliage for fall. The retail price is $45.00 per plate.

Portraying graceful hummingbirds is Maruri's *Treasures of the Sky* plate collection, presented in sculptural bas-relief and hand-painted in cold cast porcelain. Each plate captures two tiny hummingbirds sharing the nectar of a favorite flower variety. At 8-1/2" in diameter, plates presented so far are "Anna's with Lily," "Allen's with Hibiscus" and "Ruby-throated with Trumpet Creeper."

A FANTASY RIDE WITH SANTA

Maruri has added five whimsical figurines to its *Santa's World Travels* collection of limited edition sculptures. With these latest additions to the popular series, Santa's journeys continue through far-flung corners of the globe.

"Winter's Bear Necessities" shows Santa as a Canadian Mountie, while a baby hippo receives a mouthful of candy in "Fill'er Up!" "Tall Order for Christmas" has Santa being assisted by a giraffe family. The largest of the five new pieces is "Clydesdale Christmas," at 8" high and 17" long. Clydesdales pull Santa and his sleigh across the Scottish countryside. These four pieces range in retail price from $60.00 to $195. They are limited to 5,000 pieces each, except "Clydesdale Christmas," which is limited to 3,500 pieces.

"Bringing Joy to the World" is the series' first open edition piece, and it portrays a traditionally dressed Santa sitting on top of the world. It can be purchased for just $25.00, and can be used as a sign for the collection, since the front of the piece says *Santa's World Travels.* All of these cold cast porcelain sculptures are hand-painted to capture every delightful detail.

With age-old methods and award-winning sculptures, Maruri will continue spreading its wings with new introductions to delight generations of collectors. The company's time-honored traditions offer an enduring tribute to some of the world's most enchanting creatures.

Maruri U.S.A.
21510 Gledhill Street
Chatsworth, CA 91311

Phone:
818-717-9900

Fax:
818-717-9901

E-mail:
marurius@pacbell.net

MARURI U.S.A.

The Greatest Name in Die-Cast

Today's Matchbox is a very different organization than the company that inspired generations of children in Europe and America to first experience the joy of building their own first collections.

Yet, the spirit and popularity of Matchbox today, as in years gone by, continue to spring from our fascination with miniature precision, authenticity and nostalgia. The detail, accuracy and construction of each Matchbox® Collectibles vehicle are testaments to the fact that each meticulously crafted limited edition bears the greatest name in die-cast.

A YOUNG QUEEN AND A CLASSROOM RULE HELP MAKE A NEW COMPANY SUCCESSFUL

In June of 1947, Rodney Smith, who was working in the engineering firm of Die-Cast and Machine Tools in London, teamed up with former schoolmate Leslie Smith, and along with ex-soldier Jack Odell, formed a toy company which they named Lesney Products.

At first, the company made many different types of toys. Then, in 1953, to commemorate the crowning of England's young new queen, the company released a die-cast replica of the golden eight-horse ceremonial carriage that carried Queen Elizabeth to Westminster Abbey. Their miniature model, "Coronation Coach," was such a great success that ultimately over one million were produced. It seemed inevitable that more die-cast miniatures would soon be on their way.

Which leads to the story of how Matchbox eventually got its well-known name. Jack Odell had a daughter in school at the time, and word is that she and her playmates were only allowed to bring toys to school if they

The "1937 Cord 812 Supercharged Viton" from the Cars of the Rich and Infamous collection perfectly replicates the streamlined Art Deco lines of this legendary motorcar.

could fit in a matchbox. This rule inspired the size specifications for Lesney's first "Matchbox" model, a diesel "Road Roller."

Soon, the "Road Roller" was followed by a "Cement Mixer" and a "Crawler Tractor." And thus Matchbox,

◆ *Among the most beautiful Fords ever, the "1940 Ford Pickup" from the '30s and '40s Classic American Pickup collection captures all the detail that made it a classic — the distinctive grille and one-piece stamped steel front panel.*

along with its I-75 Series, which can still be found in popular chain store locations today, got its start!

In 1956, Matchbox released the first of its *Models of Yesteryear* series. With the introduction, the company's goal of creating a line of models that were more intricately and authentically detailed than any other die-cast model ever before produced, was finally realized. The series has since become a classic favorite and is still sought after by collectors today.

TODAY'S MATCHBOX SPRINGS FROM A LONG AND DISTINGUISHED PEDIGREE

In the world of die-cast models, it seems that the greatest names – those that have most influenced the history of this unique art form – have gravitated towards each other. To fully understand the Matchbox magic, it helps to know how the company grew from its origins as a British toy company to the highly respected, international maker of serious collectibles that it has become, today.

Until 1971, the Matchbox® brand was little known in the United States, available from only a few specialty retailers who carried English imports. In that year, Matchbox made a major investment in their United States market, building a state-of-the-art manufacturing facility in New Jersey.

Finally in 1973, *Models of Yesteryear* vehicles officially made their first appearance on store shelves in America. Over the next few years, as the original owners of Lesney looked to divest themselves of their investment, new corporate suitors came courting in hopes of acquiring the Matchbox brand. One in particular was Hong Kong Universal.

In 1980, two models were produced under the auspices of Hong Kong Universal. Then in 1983, Hong Kong Universal purchased Matchbox, and Matchbox International was formed. By 1986, Matchbox was declared the best-selling line in Europe. Matchbox toys were being sold in 120 countries, and Universal had also acquired Dinky.

Dinky itself had a long, successful and colorful history, established even before Lesney had emerged on the scene. The English Company Meccano, Ltd. had become known for its model train sets and accessories. In April 1934, it had renamed its brand and expanded its die-cast line

under the name, "Dinky Toys." Within a few years, the Dinky Toys line was firmly established with nearly 200 model cars and trucks. Ironically, they were intended to be model train accessories — mere props — to add realism to the miniature towns through which electric trains coursed.

Matchbox remained under the roof of Universal until Tyco Toys acquired both Matchbox and Dinky in 1992. Wasting no time, Tyco launched Matchbox Collectibles in 1993, with a reincarnation of their historic *Models of Yesteryear* line entitled, "A Taste of France." By June 1997, more transition was in store for Matchbox Collectibles.

Mattel purchased its parent company, Tyco Toys, and the company moved its facilities to Phoenix, Arizona. In addition, the decision was made to reintroduce Matchbox Collectibles in specialty retail stores.

Today, Matchbox Collectibles boasts over 1,500 retail outlets in the U.S.,

"Austin Powers Shaguar"
takes '60s "mod" styling to new
heights. The secret agent's "shagadelic"
E-Type Jaguar sports a pop-art Union Jack paint job, plus
intricately wrought wire wheels and full dashboard instrumentation.
Authorized by New Line Cinema.

with ambitious plans in the works to expand its retail presence in Canada. And so it goes in the history of die-cast…Dinky became part of Matchbox; Matchbox became part of Tyco; Tyco became part of Mattel.

And as collectors all over the world can attest, the models just keep getting better and better.

AMERICA'S LOVE AFFAIR WITH DIE-CAST INSPIRES UNIQUE DESIGNS

When someone mentions "Matchbox," most people tend to think of the Matchbox toys with which they played as children. Still, there are many things that distinguish Matchbox Collectibles from the Matchbox Toy Brand.

While Matchbox Toys continues to focus on the inexpensive 1:64th scale cars that are available at most popular toy retailers, Matchbox Collectibles' focus has been on the larger scale cars, primarily 1:43rd scale, but also including 1:100th, 1:64th and 1:58th scales.

A higher level of detail goes into creating each authentic Matchbox Collectible replica, with each extensively researched to ensure a level of satisfaction that surpasses the expectations of even the most discerning collector.

Keeping tradition alive, Matchbox Collectibles continues to identify each model with a specific collector number that is unique to the *Models of Yesteryear* and Dinky lines. This tradition was started with the first

The all-time favorite '50s car, the 1957 Bel Air is a classic in every sense of the word. It was acclaimed for its meticulous workmanship, long, elegant body and the first fuel injection system offered by an American automaker.

Models of Yesteryear vehicle, and collectors today still look for that identification on every model.

Another factor that distinguishes the toy and collectible lines is the packaging. Each collectible model is packaged in a unique collector box. Most models are packaged in a standard yellow collector's box, while limited editions come in a maroon limited edition collector's box. Still, other collections, such as *Fire Engines* and *Great Beers of the World,* are packaged in boxes specially designed to capture the theme of the collection and preserve each model's history and heritage.

For many Matchbox enthusiasts, their collecting represents more than just a passion for acquiring highly authentic, precision-engineered models of some of history's favorite cars, trucks, rigs and other modes of transportation. For many of us, it also means a nostalgic trip down Memory Lane, whisking us back in time to revisit the happiest experiences of our lives.

Of course, many Matchbox owners also relish a different kind of reward when a model from their collection appreciates in value, as many have over the years. Yet for most collectors, potential price appreciation is seldom the driving motivation for selecting a particular Matchbox replica. Their hearts and their own taste are the best guide for acquiring a treasure that will keep its special meaning for its owner over time.

Each year, Matchbox releases nearly 15 new collections, in addition to a host of special limited edition models. The year 2000 marks another milestone in the company's history, with the release of the first collection of die-cast planes ever produced by Matchbox Collectibles. Featuring six models, including the "P-51 Mustang" and the legendary "Grumman Hellcat," these famous *W.W.II Fighter Planes* are proving to be a hit with collectors.

With the company's great success with the *International Fire Engine Collection,* Matchbox will be expanding its line of emergency vehicles to include *Vintage City Police Cars* and a collection of *International Ambulances.* And of course, collectors have continued to be delighted with the company's precision-engineered replicas of the *Classic Cars* we all remember from the '50s, '60s and '70s.

For many of us, Matchbox models were the first things we collected. And for today's Matchbox collector, "The Greatest Name in Die-Cast" continues to ignite collecting excitement with new model releases and strategic collection retirements to maintain the line's superb collectibility.

Matchbox® Collectibles
P.O. Box 10490
Glendale, AZ 85318-0490

Phone:
800-858-0102

Fax:
800-634-9207

Web Sites:
www.mattel.com
www.matchbox.com

Presenting the Most Collectible Doll in the World™

"Delphine™ Barbie," as the ultimate fashion model, wears a strapless evening gown of pale delphinium blue satin and taffeta with dramatic bow and draped train.

Handler had an inspiration while watching her daughter, Barbara, have fun with her paper dolls. Barbara and her friends loved to play make-believe with the cardboard characters, imagining them as teenagers or grown-ups with glamorous lives. While Ruth's all-male design staff expressed doubts about creating a three-dimensional fashion doll, she eventually prevailed. Barbie was unveiled to buyers at the annual New York Toy Fair in 1959!

BARBIE CELEBRATES CHANGING TIMES

Since her debut, Barbie has evolved with the times and even set some trends of her own. Starting as a teen-age fashion model, she reflected the Jacqueline Kennedy and "Mod" looks in the early 1960s, wore granny dresses and disco outfits in the 1970s, and became a powerful executive (and part-time aerobics instructor) in the 1980s. By the 1990s, Barbie was active in sports — basketball, car racing and soccer, to name a few. She's also been an astronaut, diplomat, dentist and surgeon. "Girls Can Do Anything™" certainly applies to Barbie!

Over the years, Barbie has enjoyed the company of her boyfriend Ken®, best friend Midge®, sisters Skipper®, Stacie® and Kelly®, and pals of diverse backgrounds including African-American Christie®, Hispanic Teresa®, Asian Kira®, and Becky® who uses a wheelchair.

Keeping up with the times as always, Barbie has become fully techno-savvy, offering a full range of software titles and digital and interactive products for her friends and collectors. These include tools for fashion design, hairstyling, and a Barbie digital camera and CD-ROM. Most recently, Barbie has gone on-line with My Design™, a product that allows consumers to customize and order special friends of Barbie doll.

Dress Barbie for a nostalgic outdoor gathering in this "Garden Party™ Fashion" including a rose print organza dress with lovely accessories. (Doll not included.)

When the beautiful Barbie® doll debuted two generations ago, even her creators at Mattel could not have predicted her lasting, worldwide impact. Today, after marking her 40th anniversary, Barbie reigns as a successful businesswoman, member of a rock band, Women's World Cup Soccer player…and world-class collectible! Still a role model for girls who dream of dynamic achievements, Barbie greets the new millennium in high style!

Barbie first came of age when Americans were buoyed by the benefits of the strong, post-World War II economy. "Rosie the Riveter" was replaced by "June Cleaver" as the ideal woman. Cars sported huge tailfins, "Ike" ruled the White House, and *Ben-Hur* dominated the box office. Teenagers thrilled to the music of Elvis, Fabian and Frankie Avalon. Little girls dressed paper dolls and played mommy with their vinyl "babies."

During this time period, Mattel co-founder Ruth

GROWN-UPS LOVE BARBIE, TOO

While little girls were the first Barbie enthusiasts, today there are many female and male adult collectors who flock to own each new Barbie introduction. They enjoy affiliating through clubs, conventions, magazines, newsletters and the Internet.

Adult collectors appreciate the haute couture created for Barbie by famed designer Nolan Miller, as well as nostalgic Barbie recreations from the early years, and the X-Files™ Barbie and Ken. Many of these stunning dolls

Barbie joins the "ladies who lunch" in dramatic style with her "Lunch at the Club™ Fashion," including slim navy suit, faux fur stole and gorgeous accessories. (Doll not included.)

have risen sharply in price on the secondary market as more and more collectors compete to own them.

THE OFFICIAL BARBIE COLLECTOR'S CLUB℠

One of the most enjoyable ways to become immersed in "all things Barbie" is to join The Official Barbie Collector's Club for just $39.99 (plus shipping and handling and applicable tax) per year. Members receive a colorful kit chock-full of benefits and opportunities.

The 2001 kit includes: an official Membership Card; a pink padfolio with lovely club stationery; and the first-ever Club diorama setting so members can place their Barbie dolls in a setting as glorious as they are. Membership also brings a year's subscription (four issues) to the very popular newsletter, *The Barbie Insider*™. This exciting publication provides readers with an exclusive, behind-the-scenes look at the world of the Barbie doll, lets them meet the designers, get sneak peeks at upcoming dolls and find out the latest Barbie news. Additionally, members receive an elegant ink pen with a Barbie logo and a stunning silver-toned pin.

Members also have an opportunity to purchase Exclusive Club Dolls. Recent Club-Exclusive Dolls include the "Club Couture™ Barbie," "Café Society® Barbie" (sold out), "Embassy Waltz™ Barbie," "Gala Barbie," "Holiday Treasures Barbie 1999" (sold out) and "Holiday Treasures Barbie 2000." Each membership entitles individuals to purchase up to two of these dolls.

"Midnight Tuxedo™ Barbie," the official Club Doll for the year 2001, is the fifth doll from the *Members' Choice*™ series. This glamorous Barbie is the very picture of evening elegance. From her lustrous, platinum-blonde hair to her midnight-black, slim-fitting, tuxedo-style gown with dazzling rhinestone buttons, she is truly a vision of contemporary sophistication. Accompanied by a luxuriously long, chiffon stole with faux fur trim, "Midnight Tuxedo™ Barbie" doll is exclusively available to members of The Official Barbie Collector's Club for only $59.00 (plus shipping and handling and applicable tax).

♦ *BARBIE® FASHION MODEL COLLECTION* DEBUTS

To indulge the wishes of Barbie doll's most ardent collectors, Mattel has introduced a new body material for Barbie called Silkstone™. Silkstone offers the silky smooth touch and heavy feel of porcelain, and adds a dimension of durability. Lifelike sculpting adds both expression and versatility of pose to each new Barbie.

The Silkstone Barbie dolls will make their first entrance as part of the *Barbie® Fashion Model Collection*. "The Lingerie Barbie®" comes in both brunette and blonde versions, each wearing lovely white satin bra-and-panty ensembles with white lace and pale pink bows. White stockings, garters and a wrist tag complete each doll presentation.

The "Delphine™ Barbie" embodies glamour with a strapless evening gown of pale delphinium blue satin and taffeta that combines a dramatic bow, draped train and delicate pink flower accents. Her white faux fur stole is lined in pale pink charmeuse.

Barbie also has two exceptional new fashions entitled "Lunch at the Club™" and "Garden Party™." Barbie doll's lunch ensemble begins with a chic navy suit to wear over a pink halter bodysuit. A gray faux fur stole with pink satin lining, pillbox hat, black "patent" handbag, bouquet of pink roses and white gloves complete the look. For the "Garden Party," Barbie will slip into a pretty daytime ensemble, featuring a rose print organza dress, pink chiffon cardigan, straw cloth hat and straw handbag.

THE WORLD'S MOST BELOVED FASHION DOLL

Over the years, Barbie earned the title of most popular fashion doll ever created. She has held that honor for over four decades, throughout changing times and clothing styles. Barbie has the unique ability to inspire self-esteem, glamour, and a sense of adventure in all who love her. The Barbie line has also developed into a broad array of exciting licensed products for girls, including publishing, apparel, food, home furnishings and home electronics.

Today, Barbie still reflects the dreams, hopes and future realities of an entire generation of little girls, who still see her as representing the same American aspirations as when she was introduced. What's more, fans of all ages enjoy collecting and displaying the line of collector edition and limited edition Barbie dolls. With more than 75 careers to her credit already, Barbie faces the 21st century with anticipation of more adventures, fashion and fun with all her admirers and collectors.

Our lovely model shows off her favorite "underpinnings" in "The Lingerie Barbie®," with white satin bra and panties, white stockings and garters.

Each sold separately, subject to availability. Fashions designed especially for the Silkstone™ Barbie® doll. Not for use with other Barbie dolls.

Barbie is a trademark owned by and used with permission of Mattel, Inc. ©2000 Mattel, Inc. All Rights Reserved.

Mattel, Inc./
Barbie Collectibles®
P.O. Box 10495
Glendale, AZ 85318-0495

Phone:
800-491-7514

Web Site:
www.barbiecollectibles.com

Exclusive Designs... Crafted Worldwide

Eddie Walker's four-piece "Twas the Night Before Christmas" limited edition set features a holiday fireplace with a plate of cookies and a family cat waiting for Santa to deliver gifts under the Christmas tree.

Midwest of Cannon Falls® ranks as one of the United States' top designers and distributors of seasonal and year-round giftware, exclusive collectibles and distinctive home decor. The current Midwest of Cannon Falls line features more than 5,000 highly creative and innovative products that spring from nostalgic and traditional themes.

A COMPANY BORN OF UNSINKABLE DETERMINATION

Lutheran pastor Kenneth Althoff originally opened a small family-owned business in 1955 specializing in importing European products. His first European shipment was lost at sea in the1956 sinking of the Italian liner Andrea Doria. But that didn't dampen Althoff's spirits. After noting that other retailers were turning to him as a source of fine imports, he focused his attention on importing and wholesaling full time. To ensure high quality at an affordable cost, Midwest of Cannon Falls began working with international manufacturers long before many companies even began to consider global business relationships.

Creepy Hollow's "Creepy Commons Apartments and Shops" porcelain lighted haunted house has a removable interior room with two charming witches enjoying a frightful hour of television.

Kathleen Brekken, daughter of Kenneth Althoff, has served as President and Chief Executive Officer of the company since 1985. She joined the firm in 1972, after graduating from the University of Minnesota. She also attended the Owner/President Management program at Harvard University School of Business Administration.

Midwest of Cannon Falls is headquartered in Cannon Falls, Minnesota, less than an hour's drive from Minneapolis/St. Paul. Branch offices in Asia give the company a competitive edge based on long-standing relationships with manufacturers. Working closely with these manufacturers offers a degree of quality, integrity, trust and high performance.

A WORLD OF EXCLUSIVE PRODUCTS

Collectibles from the Erzgebirge region of Germany were among the first items imported by Althoff, and the company's relationship with these fine artists continues. However, today the majority of the company's products are designed exclusively by Midwest of Cannon Falls artists and crafted around the world. About 90 percent of Midwest of Cannon Falls items are original designs, created by in-house designers or are the work of exceptional artists under contract.

Christmas ornaments, collectible porcelain hinged boxes and decorative accessories represent a large portion of the company's business. Product lines range from elegant European blown glass ornaments and limited edition folk art figurines, to charmingly rustic home accessories and licensed reproductions of much-loved characters of the classics. Each year, the company creates over 2,000 new products using a wide range of handcrafted materials, including resin, fabric, wood, metal, glass and ceramics, and incorporates techniques such as hand-painting to achieve a very distinctive look.

Being a trend-setter in the industry, Midwest of Cannon Falls has helped change how Americans decorate Christmas trees. In contrast to the 1960s, when every tree had the requisite tinsel and predictable glass-ball ornaments, consumers today are opting for items that symbolize their lifestyles and special interests. From sports and hobby related items, to ornaments that commemorate special events, consumers increasingly are making a personal statement with the family Christmas tree.

The firm's reputation for quality has led to a number of breakthrough licensing agreements for well-known figures. Its expanding line of licensed properties include characters from Disney Classics™, Harley Davidson™, Elvis Presley Enterprises™, Beatrix Potter™, Coca Cola®, Hasbro™, Heinz©, Hershey Foods™, I Love Lucy™, Jim Henson's Kermit Collection™, Kellogg's®, Madeline™, Nabisco™, Tabasco®, Tootsie Roll® and Universal Studios characters, Curious George™ and Woody Woodpecker®.

Midwest of Cannon Falls recently received an award for "Best Three-Dimensional Design" from The Walt Disney Company©, one of the highest awards given to licensees by Disney© each year.

PHB™ COLLECTION UPDATES 18TH CENTURY TRADITION

Midwest of Cannon Falls' *PHB Collection* has rapidly become popular for collectors of fine porcelain hinged boxes. Originally developed in 18th century France to hold perfume or small jewels, porcelain hinged boxes

have proven to be treasured collectibles for centuries. Boasting over 400 designs, these *PHBs* have been designed exclusively by Midwest of Cannon Falls artists and carefully sculpted and hand-painted in intricate detail. Many boxes contain an interior decal message or a coordinating porcelain piece tucked inside.

CREEPY HOLLOW™ COLLECTION BREAKS NEW GROUND

Midwest of Cannon Falls introduced *Creepy Hollow* in 1992 to fill collectors' desire for holiday villages other than those offered for the Christmas season. *Creepy Hollow* began with five porcelain lighted houses, resin figurines and accessories. By 1999, with many lighted houses added to the line, 16 had already been retired. The *Creepy Hollow* line consists of lighted porcelain pieces with spooky houses, mansions and cottages, as well as a haunted "Gasp N' Go Gas Station," a "Cozy Coffin Motel" and a "Fright Club and Disco." Goulish accessories support the story line of each spooky village scene. For example, frightening characters, a "Halloween Bone Fence," a "Creepy Mail Box" and an "Ice Scream Truck" can be combined to create a truly bewitching village scene. Visual humor appeals to the serious collector along with high quality sculpting and detailed handpainting. Increased interest in animation and novelty sound chips for hauntingly fun effects add to the special-effect features of *Creepy Hollow.*

"Darn Lights," "All Decked Out" and "Snowed Under" are from Sandi Gore Evans' Jolly Follies™ collection for Midwest of Cannon Falls.

NUTCRACKERS AND OTHER GERMAN COLLECTIBLES

As the largest U.S. importer of Erzgebirge nutcrackers, Midwest of Cannon Falls offers handcrafted wooden treasures that come direct from the nutcracker's 17th century birthplace in Germany. New designs are introduced each year, ranging from the classic "Guard Nutcracker," "Drummer Nutcracker" and "Prince With Red Coat Nutcracker," to the unique "Hippie Nutcracker" and "Biker Nutcracker." *Ken Althoff's European Collection* offers a unique selection of wooden angels, animals and other characters that bring some of the best of German craftsmanship to collectors.

Seeds of friendship, happiness and hope are gathered together in Sue Dreamer's Simple Delights™ *collection of sweet garden characters, pot sitters, photo frames and stoneware.*

TALENTED ARTISTS LEAD THE WAY

Midwest of Cannon Falls partners with talented artists to create a collection of reproductions of original work. Among these artists are Eddie Walker, Sandi Gore Evans, Greg Guedel, Iona Steelhammer, Fran Welch, Teena Flanner and Sue Dreamer.

An artist from Walla Walla, Washington, Eddie Walker has turned her love of carving into a collection of hundreds of smiling characters. Since 1993, Midwest of Cannon Falls has exclusively created precise reproductions of Eddie Walker's original carvings. Eddie Walker started carving in 1989. Her enchanting characters, ranging from chummy bunnies to adorable Santas, celebrate the seasons, while generating smiles and praise across the country. Eddie Walker's limited editions and limited-to-year-of-issue designs are in high demand. Many pieces have been retired. More information about Eddie Walker and pictures of her work can be found on her web site at www.eddiewalker.com.

Sandi Gore Evans, another Midwest of Cannon Falls artist, works out of her home studio in Augusta, Kansas, bringing watercolors to life with the stroke of a brush. Inspiration for many of her designs comes from the delights of the beauty and simplicity of everyday life. One of her limited edition pieces, "Wee Miracles Everywhere," was inspired by her granddaughter's discovery that each snowflake is different. Sandi's collection of figurines, ornaments and functional dishes have become increasingly popular as collectibles. The distinctive style of Sandi is clear in the characters of her *Jolly Follies*® collection of robust snowmen and Santas, her *Tattertales*® collection of angels, and the delightful designs of *Rabbit Rascals*® and *Bunny Frolics*®.

Midwest of Cannon Falls artist Sue Dreamer majored in painting at the Massachusetts College of Art. While there, Sue enjoyed drawing, furniture painting, soft sculpture and quilting her own hand-painted fabric. Now, Sue lives in the Boston area where she works in her home studio, creating images that continue to grow in popularity. For Sue, drawing is a magical process that comes from the love and happiness in her heart. Along with the *Simple Delights*™ collection designed exclusively for Midwest of Cannon Falls, Sue also has a complete line of greeting cards, calendars and home decor textiles, as well as a series of books she has illustrated. Sue Dreamer's colorful collection of whimsical, smiling figurines, ornaments and porcelain hinged boxes are destined to become collectors' favorites.

Through this combination of talented artists, high quality production and innovative marketing programs, Midwest of Cannon Falls holds a unique niche in the giftware market. They provide products that evoke a sense of nostalgia and tradition, yet are innovative, fresh and relevant to today's tastes.

Midwest of Cannon Falls®
32057 64th Avenue
Cannon Falls, MN 55009

Phone:
800-377-3335

Fax:
507-263-7752

Web Site:
www.midwestofcannonfalls.com

A Tradition of Excellence: A Passion for Porcelain

Rich detail and exquisite artistry are evident in the M.I. Hummel limited edition figurine, "Worldwide Wanderers." Part of the Millennium Collection, it measures 9-3/4" high x 17-1/4" long x 8-1/2" wide and retails for $4,500.

The year was 1871 when Franz Detleff Goebel and his son, William, realized their life-long dream of creating their own company. Their original aim was to produce the fresh, simple and popular porcelain of Germany's Thuringia region: a goal that continues today under the guidance of the Goebel family. Over the past 125-plus years, this dream has inspired consistent innovation in the ceramics industry, and it has touched the hearts of millions around the world.

In the last 20 years, Goebel has been a leader in maintaining the highest quality of craftsmanship and artistic integrity in highly competitive markets. With a keen sensibility for popular trends and the interests of the collecting public, Goebel's innovations and artistic excellence have defined an international standard. Today, the company concentrates on manufacturing and distributing products to over 100 markets, while its close to 2,000 employees are dedicated to continuing Franz Detleff Goebel's dream on a global scale.

M.I. HUMMEL CAPTURES THE MAGIC OF CHILDHOOD

Goebel is perhaps known best for its *M.I. Hummel* line of figurines. Renowned throughout the world for their gentle reflection of childhood joys, these charming

figurines began as drawings by the gifted artist, Sister Maria Innocentia Hummel, who lived in Southern Germany during the first half of this century. With meticulous craftsmanship, her drawings were transformed by Goebel master artisans into hand-sculpted, hand-painted earthenware treasures. The figurines made their debut at the Leipzig Spring Fair in March of 1935 and were an instant hit with foreign buyers. Introduced into the United States market by Marshall Fields in the summer of 1935, *M.I. Hummel* figurines were warmly received in America, where their popularity continues to this day.

M.I. HUMMEL PRESENTS YEAR 2000 BACKSTAMP

Since 1935, each *M.I. Hummel* collectible has carried two definitive marks of identification which attest to the product's authenticity. One is the incised signature of Sister Maria Innocentia Hummel; the other is the official Goebel Backstamp. Over the years, Goebel has occasionally changed its backstamp, sometimes for sentimental reasons and other times to denote historical events. The last time the Goebel backstamp changed was in 1991 to mark the reunification of East and West Germany.

This year, to honor the new millennium, Goebel has made a dramatic change to the entire *M.I. Hummel* product line. Each *M.I. Hummel* figurine will bear the new Year 2000 Backstamp.

The Year 2000 Backstamp incorporates the Goebel name with the full bee symbol, which was part of the backstamp used in the 1950s. The bee is a tribute to Sister Maria Innocentia Hummel, since Hummel is the German word for bumblebee.

"American Wanderer" is one of five individual Wanderer figurines from the M.I. Hummel Millennium Collection. It measures 4-3/4" x 6" x 3-1/2" and retails for $250.

Back in 1934, Franz Goebel, fourth generation owner and head of W. Goebel Porzellanfabrik, knew instinctively that Sister Maria Innocentia's enchanting portraits would give rise to a new product line perfect for a public anxious to escape from the hardships of the day. Today as we move toward the millennium, Goebel continues to count on the appeal of the innocence of youth to spread a message of hope and inspiration.

M.I. HUMMEL CELEBRATES A NEW CENTURY WITH THE MILLENNIUM COLLECTION

As a new century approaches, Goebel introduces an important new collection of *M.I. Hummel* figurines, created especially for the millennium. Named the *Millennium Collection*, these figurines explore the amazing gift that allows children to imagine a world where cultural diversity is celebrated and dreams of peace and friend-

ship are shared by people everywhere.

The centerpiece of the collection is an exquisite figurine called the "Worldwide Wanderers." The intricately detailed *M.I. Hummel* work of art depicts a band of neighborhood kids playing dress-up. It is based on classic motifs led by the renowned "Merry Wanderer," but the children have donned their own versions of costumes worn by children in lands far away. A worn blanket, mom's bathrobe, and a favorite stuffed toy are all that's needed to transport these "Worldwide Wanderers" to exotic locales.

"Worldwide Wanderers" has been created in a sequentially numbered edition, limited to 2,000 pieces. It sits atop a hardwood, velvet-covered base and comes with a ceramic plaque honoring its special status. The figurine is hand-sculpted and hand-painted in the Goebel tradition of excellence.

All five of the costumed children depicted in the "Worldwide Wanderers" figurine are available as individual figurines. "Asian Wanderer," "Australian Wanderer," "European Wanderer," "American Wanderer" and "African Wanderer" all come with a ceramic globe that actually spins. Both the figurine and the globe sit atop a black wooden base.

Bid a fond good-bye to the century and to a M.I. Hummel *classic, when "Auf Wiedersehen" retires on December 31, 2000.*

"AUF WIEDERSEHEN" RETIRES

It's been a century of incredible change, and as it draws to an end, there is one more change taking place in the world of *M.I. Hummel*. "Auf Wiedersehen," a pair of beloved friends, will officially retire on the last day of the 20th century.

This Bavarian boy and girl have captured the hearts of *M.I.Hummel* enthusiasts since 1943, when the figurine was modeled by Master Sculptor Arthur Möller and introduced to the world.

They've stood vigil, hankies in hand, over many a bittersweet separation – children going off to college, friends moving away, colleagues changing jobs. "Auf Wiedersehen" has served as a perfect tribute to friendship and the emotions that accompany saying good-bye.

"Auf Wiedersehen" will be available, bearing a final issue medallion and backstamp, until December 31, 2000. At that time, the molds will be broken and the figurine will wave a final goodbye.

"Private Conversation," a new M.I. Hummel *Club Exclusive, depicts a boy and a bunny. It is available to club members only during Club Year 23.*

M.I. HUMMEL CLUB CELEBRATES YEAR 24

Membership has its advantages and members of the M.I. Hummel Club would be quick to agree. Now in its 24th year, the Club boasts over 250,000 members in 50 countries! Its quarterly newsletter, "INSIGHTS," has expanded into a handsome and entertaining magazine, full of information about *M.I. Hummel* history, handcraftsmanship and

future product offerings. The club also provides research services, drawing on its vast reference files and factory records from Germany. Perhaps its most exciting service — and its newest — is the special area on the *M.I. Hummel* web site, www.mihummel.com, created exclusively for Club members. By entering their individual membership numbers, club members can gain access to the "M.I. Hummel Club House" and receive information and special services not available to the general public. Members can purchase club products, check itineraries of upcoming club trips and events, and correspond directly with Goebel and with other club members.

The M.I. Hummel Club (formerly the Goebel Collector's Club) was founded in the spring of 1977 to provide information that would be valuable to collectors of *M.I. Hummel* and other Goebel products. Since 1978, an extensive travel program has been a prime benefit to M.I. Hummel Club members. Beginning in 1985, there have been as many as ten deluxe, privately escorted trips a year to countries such as Germany, Switzerland, Italy, Austria and Holland.

Club Year 24 – June 1, 2000 through May 31, 2001 – presents a wonderful selection of M.I. Hummel products that are only available for members to enjoy. For starters there is the free club Welcome Figurine, "Honor Student," portraying a serious little scholar whose attention has been captivated by the wonders of knowledge he finds as he reads his big book. New and renewing M. I. Hummel Club members will receive "Honor Student" as a gift. Valued at $90.00, this 3-3/4" figurine will never again be available to non-members from Goebel.

There are three new Club Members' Exclusive editions for 1999-2000. The first is "Sharpest Student," the companion piece to "Honor Student." This diligent little lass looks like she can't wait to study with her book-loving counterpart. "Sharpest Student" is only available to club members for one year and will never be available to the general public from Goebel at any price.

"Will it Sting" is another new Club Members' Exclusive available throughout the club year. Measuring 5", the figurine recreates the sweet joy of springtime when the world is filled with happy pastimes and buzzing with newfound friends. And finally members can acquire the first piece in a remarkable new figurine collection - *The Wonder of Childhood*. Celebrating the moment when children's dreams become happy realities, this adorable work of art, "Wishes Come True" will make you believe in the magic of youth as seen through the innocent eyes of one

Goebel of North America
Rt. 31 North
Goebel Plaza
Pennington, NJ 08534

Phone:
800-666-CLUB

Fax:
609-737-1545

Web Site:
www.mihummel.com

Capturing Nostalgia and Memories in Chenille

Mill Mountain™ was created to fulfill a dream. Ivan Cohen, president of Westwater Enterprises® in Mountainside, New Jersey, remembered the warmth and security he always felt when he visited his Grandmother – especially when taking naps or spending the night with her wonderful old chenille spread on the bed. But chenille was no longer in vogue, and certainly not being used beyond the occasional robe or bedspread.

As president of Westwater Enterprises, one of the foremost makers and suppliers of products for the hobby and craft industry, Ivan was familiar with trends and fabrics – particularly in the plush market. No one was using chenille, and he wasn't even certain that his idea

Wearing an old-fashioned batiste baby dress, "Victoria" is 16" tall and fully poseable.

The chenille was being made on ancient looms more than 75 years old. The work was slow and required multiple steps to create the varied designs so familiar in old chenille. Ivan was not deterred. He contracted to purchase all the fabric the little factory could make. Then he went to a manufacturer with his idea. This was more difficult, because plush product was at an all-time high demand, and factories were not inclined to try speculative new lines.

Ivan prevailed, and a quality plush maker agreed to test his idea. What he found was that working with chenille is much different than with plush. The patterns and the varied thickness made work more complex for both machine sewing and the extensive handwork required. But the samples fulfilled Ivan's dream, and he knew right away that he must continue his mission.

THE FULFILLMENT OF A DREAM

Ivan called on designer Karen Drayne, well-known for her handmade collection of limited edition animals called *Dirty Bunnies*. Karen immediately saw the possibilities in Ivan's dream and set about designing and handcrafting samples, using scraps of chenille in whatever colors she could find. Because of the unique patterns in chenille, each little animal took on a personality of its own. Karen added clothes and accessories to some; ribbons and little mementos to others. The samples were endearing and evoked fond memories for everyone who saw them.

Ivan appealed to his Board of Directors to take a bold new step: create a company to market this new line to the gift and collectibles industry. Thus, in early 1999, Mill Mountain was formed, and shortly thereafter, *From Grandma's Heart*™ – a warm and nostalgic collection of animals made of chenille and other aged fabrics – was born.

"Jeremy" has become the signature bear for From Grandma's Heart collection with his chenille gardening vest, shovel, watering can and packets of "Bear Seeds."

was feasible. His "idea" was to create a line of soft-bodied animals made of chenille and other nostalgic, seldom-used materials from another era. But first he had to find a source for chenille and then he had to convince a major plush manufacturer to use it.

What Ivan found was a very limited supply of authentic, all-cotton chenille – the kind on his Grandmother's bed.

The little animals – including teddy bears, bunnies, kittens, puppies and lambs – are each named and come with a "letter" from "Grandma" to the child for whom she made it. The premise is that "Grandma" used the scraps in her sewing basket and old chest to make the little soft-bodied animals for special children. An original poem is printed on each gift card that comes with the animal:

Her sewing basket by her chair,
Her scraps so soft and worn,
With loving care, she sews each seam,
From Grandma's Heart™ they're born!

The logo is a silhouette of "Grandma" in her rocker with a sewing basket in her lap, set against a large pink heart.

COLLECTION RECEIVES OVERWHELMING RESPONSE

Retailers were introduced to "Grandma" and the endearing line during the summer of 1999, with the first pieces arriving at shops in late fall. The initial response from consumers was overwhelming! Dealers told stories of pieces being bought as they were unpacked – before they could even be placed on shelves. Store associates wanted to buy the little animals before customers saw them, and consumers bought one as a gift and returned to buy more for themselves, only to find them sold out! The first shipments were hardly out the door, when Ivan found that Mill Mountain's entire production capacity was oversold!

Meanwhile, designer Karen Drayne was busily working on the first introductions of the new millennium. As she worked more with the old fabrics, her creativity increased. She began combining different chenille patterns; adding touches of gingham and chambray; experimenting with wool and ticking; even sculpting add-ons like pins and toys. The result was a second round of introductions in January, 2000 that complemented and eclipsed the premiere line. When these new introductions arrived at stores, they were met with equal enthusiasm, as the new *From Grandma's Heart* collection added to the line's momentum.

NEW INTRODUCTIONS ADD TO EXCITEMENT

Also in 2000, Mill Mountain added *Grandpa's Workbench™*, a collection of wooden animal "toys" that are also designed by Karen Drayne. The old-fashioned, primitive-style pieces are "made by 'Grandpa' in his little workshop, while 'Grandma' is busily making her chenille animals." The opening line includes pull toys, jack-in-the-boxes and other examples of homemade toys that might have been made by "Grandpa" over the years. Each one is titled and comes with a silly verse "that 'Grandpa' makes up as he whittles and paints each toy."

The other extension to *From Grandma's Heart* is *From Grandma's Heart Baby™*, a charming collection of nursery accessories in chenille designed by Trena Hegdahl.

"Danielle," from the American Classics Series *of* From Grandma's Heart *is hand-sewn in old-fashioned check gingham and wears a matching chenille dress and hat appliqued with big hearts.*

The new line includes three design groups and complements the chenille animals in the *From Grandma's Heart* collection.

Mill Mountain made its first appearance at the 2000 International Collectible Exposition® in Atlanta. Retailers and collectors greeted the new company warmly, and its reward came with the announcement that the limited edition bear, "Victoria," was voted "Best New Plush" by collectors in the annual Collectors' Information Bureau's "Best of Show" balloting.

FROM GRANDMA'S HEART NOW ONLINE

From Grandma's Heart now has it's own website – www.fromgrandmasheart.com – where visitors are taken on a personal tour of the collection by "Grandma." Collectors can see the complete collection and read each of "Grandma's" letters that accompany the handmade animals. One of the favorites is the letter that comes with "Jeremy," known as the "garden bear," and one of the premiere introduction pieces. "Jeremy" is a white chenille bear dressed in a rust chenille vest and comes complete with a watering can, shovel and packets of "Bear Seeds." Noteworthy are the soles of his feet, which are made of green chenille. The letter reads:

Dear Jeremy,
You were always the best garden helper I ever had, so this little bear is to remind you how much I miss you. The green feet are like yours the day you took the shortcut through the freshly painted gazebo! Come back soon.
Love, Grandma

One of the "toys" from Grandpa's Workbench *is "Crissy the Cow," a wood and metal reproduction of an old children's plaything.*

Mill Mountain™
187 Mill Lane
Mountainside, NJ 07092

Phone:
800-257-4064

Fax:
908-654-7506

Web Site:
www.fromgrandmasheart.com

E-mail:
millmtn@earthlink.net

All God's Children – Love from Above

It all began almost two decades ago when a pastor at Martha Holcombe Root's church in Gadsden, Alabama, made an appeal to his congregation for money to replace a leaky church roof. At the time, Martha was a stay-at-home mother, raising three children, and the family finances were tight. She looked deep within her heart and the following Sunday pledged $800 – an enormous amount of money for her.

Without start-up funds or a formal art education, Martha began searching for a way to meet her pledge. While she had never worked outside the home, Martha knew she could sew. She created a single doll, which she used as a basis for making doll patterns. She sold the patterns by mail order through a craft magazine, calling her fledgling business "Miss Martha Originals."

Her initial ad elicited 20 responses, each with a $5.00 check for a pattern. Orders continued to come in, and Martha was able to pay her pledge to her church, and also contributed money towards other repairs.

At this time, her business continued to grow. She moved her operation from the living room to her garage, and then to a vacant store building. In 1985, she finally moved, along with 33 employees, to an industrial park in East Gadsden.

"Nate" is one of the new figures in the Inspirational Series, *reminding us that "God's Promises Are True."*

"Serenity" is the first release from the new Angel Series.

However, about this time, the demand for doll patterns dwindled, and Martha was forced to downsize her business. With only four employees, she started sculpting *All God's Children* (AGC), focusing on African Americans. She felt there was a void in the marketplace for this type of art that was done in a loving and dignified manner. The name, *All God's Children*, was chosen from the Bible verse 1 John 3:1: "See how much the Father has loved us! His love is so great that we are called God's children."

Each figure carries the message, "God is Love." Martha prays that through the collecting of her figures, hurting hearts will be healed, bitterness will be turned into forgiveness and each person will realize that we are "All God's Children."

Today, Martha employs more than 200 employees and *All God's Children* are a top-selling ethnic collectible. Quite a change from the days when the former housewife turned entrepreneur operated her doll business out of her living room, trying to make good on her pledge to her church!

WITH HONOR AND PRAISE TO THOSE WHO MADE HISTORY

In 1989, Martha introduced a *Historical Series* of black figurines to heighten awareness of the unsung heroes and heroines of American history. Their courage, beliefs and determination positively influenced the history of our country.

Figures in the series include such notable African Americans as George Washington Carver, Frederick Douglass and Bessie Smith. Also honored in this group is Richard Allen, founder of The Bethel (House of God) Church; Mary Bethune, the foremost black educator of her time; Bessie Coleman, the first African-American woman pilot; Frances E. Harper, an American author and lecturer; and Mary Mahoney, the first African-American graduate nurse in the United States. The series gains additional popularity during Black History Month in February.

Other series in the *All God's Children* collection include *Count Your Blessings*, seven birthday-themed children, ranging in age from birth to six years old; *Nativity Series*, ten figures that tell the story of Christ's birth; and *Ragbabies*, adorable ragdoll figures that portray the virtues of friendship.

SCULPTING PROCESS BASED IN CLAY

To this day, Martha continues to use soft clay to sculpt the original figures, just as she did when she began AGC in 1985. Prototypes are then made from

the original sculptures, and molds are made using silicone rubber. A special blend of resin and pecan shell flour is carefully mixed, and each mold is cast by hand. Each figure is then washed in a special solution and checked for quality. Martha then chooses paint colors, and the figures are sent to artists, who carefully hand paint each figure. The next step is the application of the antiquing glaze using a special formula. After a final quality control inspection, the figures are boxed and ready to be shipped.

ANNUAL COLLECTORS REUNION PART OF AGC TRADITION

Just as Martha refers to all her figures as her "children," the annual gathering in Gadsden, Alabama, of collectors from all over the world is a "family reunion."

For long-time and just beginning collectors of *All God's Children,* the reunion offers opportunities to meet other collectors, to see firsthand the Miss Martha Originals production facilities and to actually meet Martha Root. More than 3,000 enthusiastic collectors and their families attend the reunion annually. Every state is represented, along with many foreign countries.

Held in late June over a three-day weekend, the ninth annual Reunion featured a luau theme. Collectors were treated to food and entertainment, gifts and prizes, swap and sells, and rides for the children.

NEW FIGURE INTRODUCED AT REUNION

A popular "Ann" collection was introduced in 1999 at the ninth annual *All God's Children Reunion.* The first doll, "Hawaiian Ann", could only be purchased by those attending the event. "Ann, Schoolgirl" was the next in the collection. "Holiday Ann" is the latest release. Dressed in her new Christmas outfit, including a bright red coat with white fur collar and muff, Ann waits with excitement to join the carol-singing in the big Christmas parade.

COLLECTOR'S CLUB OFFERS INSIGHTS INTO COLLECTION

The All God's Children Collector's Club features "Daniel," the 2000-2001 membership piece, available for puchase by members only. "Hubcap," the dog who loves to ride, is the free gift. New and renewing members receive "Hubcap" free.

Also included among the many club amenities are a subscription to the *All God's Children Collectors' Edition Magazine,* a quarterly publication which keeps members up-to-date on

"Fannie Lou Hamer" is the 1999 introduction in the Historical Series.

"Ann, Schoolgirl" is the second doll in the new Ann series, which was introduced at the ninth annual All God's Children Family Reunion.

the latest happenings; a listing of Miss Martha's personal appearances; a checklist to keep track of purchases; and an official club membership card.

Club members also receive a club checklist and a personal invitation to the very popular annual All God's Children Family Reunion in Gadsden, Alabama.

The annual fee for membership is $20.00. Membership is valid for one year from the time the membership fee is received.

Collectors wanting to gain further insight into their favorite collection are encouraged to visit the Miss Martha Originals, Inc. showroom in Glencoe, Alabama, which features displays of all the figures from the collection. Martha also has on display the legendary soft-sculpture dolls that began Miss Martha Originals. The showroom is open to the public daily, Monday through Thursday.

Martha Root continues to sculpt today with the same enthusiasm and dedication that motivated her almost 20 years ago to create Miss Martha Originals. It is her delight in children and her strong belief that each is a reflection of God's love that continue to inspire her daily.

Martha's collectors often tell her that they feel God is using the *All God's Children* collection to build a bridge between all races. She and her staff are thankful that God has chosen to use the collection in this way.

Miss Martha Originals, Inc.
1119 Chastain Blvd.
(Hwy. 431)
Gadsden, AL 35904

Phone:
256-492-0221

Fax:
256-492-0261

Animal Figurines with British Elegance

The noble "Valoroso" in medium grey is a limited edition sculpture of an Andalucian horse. Only 1,000 pieces will be produced for worldwide distribution.

Stoke-on-Trent, England, is renowned throughout the world as an area steeped in the history and tradition of handcraftsmanship. There, at the North Light studios, both ceramic and resin figurines are made by artists whose skills and techniques have been handed down through generations. Recognized as one of the leading makers of resin figurines in Europe, North Light's collections are now widely available in the United States. The firm's recent association with Q. A. Products has facilitated this expanded distribution, much to the delight of collectors.

"This is really an exciting time for North Light," says Clare Beswick, the firm's U.S.A. sales manager. "We knew our sculptures were in demand in the United States, but as a boutique studio we have not previously had the resources to set up a distribution system in the States. Our cooperation with Q. A. Products is a perfect marriage. Their established offices and showroom at 41 Madison Avenue, New York City, and their distribution facility in Brooklyn allow us to concentrate on determining which of our figurines are right for the American collector. Our current range is extensive, and the logistics of stocking each line was challenging. Thus, we have decided to put together an initial collection of our best-loved dogs and horses for the American market."

◆ CANINE AND EQUINE SUBJECTS

Premier Dogs and Horses was launched in the United States in January of 1999. *Premier Dogs* is a collection of over 50 of North Light's best-selling dog figurines, all of which are hand-painted in the most popular breed colors. The *Premier Horse* collection features over 30 horses of various breeds in traditional stances, each handsomely hand-painted. Each collection has its own catalog which is unique in design, giving information about the artist, including praise from respected experts in the dog and horse worlds. These catalogs are a great source of information, providing a short history of the breed and individual photographs of each model.

Clare Beswick points out that although North Light figurines are primarily collectibles — and are easily recognized as such by discerning collectors and horse and dog specialists — "our aim is to open our collections to a much wider audience of all generations. My hope is," she adds, "that people who would not normally buy an animal figurine will be attracted to North Light because of its life-like quality and color, perhaps reminding them of a beloved pet, and thereby encouraging them to go on and become collectors themselves. Our retail prices, from $20.00 up to $60.00, have been structured with this in mind."

LIMITED EDITIONS ARE SPECIAL

In addition to its open edition pieces, North Light also offers limited editions which are larger in size and richer in detail than those in the *Premier Collections*. A signed

The limited edition pug, "Joe," is painted in a delicate fawn hue. There will be only 350 in the world.

Certificate of Authenticity is issued with each sculpture guaranteeing the total number in the edition and the name and number on each piece.

This line has especially attracted the attention of international judges and breeders from whom North Light has many testimonials of excellence. The firm's limited editions are made to order, and waiting lists are normally supplied with a delivery within six to ten weeks.

GUY POCOCK'S VISION FOR NORTH LIGHT

Two decades ago, working from his studio in Cornwall, England, Guy Pocock conceived the beginnings of North Light figurines. His concept was to combine the artistic flair of the 19th century French Animalia bronzes with the realism admired today.

Pocock was born and spent his formative years in the India of the British Raj. In England, he obtained Honors

in Literature at Exeter University and studied painting and sculpture at Sir John Cass College of Art and Design at White Chapel, London. He learned stone carving from a pupil of Barbara Hepworth at Redruth and St. Ives, and later sought the illusive realism of art by apprenticing himself to Walter Crang of Somerset, a restoration wood and stone carver famed for his work on medieval carvings.

In the late 1970s, during a meeting with a prominent member of the British Kennel Club, Pocock learned that there were no models available of dogs true to Kennel Club breed standards. This led him to create the first models of dogs true to modern pedigree. In the following years, he painstakingly built up the comprehensive collection of over 150 models of dogs that North Light is proud to show today.

In the late1980s, Pocock decided it was time to extend the range of North Light's figurines to include studies of the horse with the same exacting artistic approach found so rewarding in sculpting dogs. The idea for the range came from Clare Beswick, who with a practical under-standing of horses and an extensive knowledge of figurines, had joined the team as sales manager.

Collectors of figurines will no doubt connect Clare's surname with Beswick Horses, which are highly collectible today. When her family sold Beswick's, she dedicated her life to bringing up her two children. In the early 1980s, she joined North Light. She added her extensive knowledge and inimitable personality to strengthen and promote the North Light range of figurines in the continued growth of which she has become an integral and essential part.

THE NORTH LIGHT DIFFERENCE

North Light's line of high-quality, ceramic and resin figurines is unique in many ways. The firm emphasizes a true anatomy in each of its animal figurines, focusing on good bone and muscle structure and a fine, life-like expression of face. For this purpose with every model, North Light seeks out animals of exceptional phys-ical conformation and color.

The particular attention paid to the authentic breed colors gives a vividness of life which further demonstrates North Light's uniqueness. What's more, for each year during the past 14 years, North Light has met, measured and made portrait models of the Supreme Champion at Crufts. Guy Pocock also believes that another key to North Light's unusual excellence is vision and steadfast

◆ The "Annes Dog Jack" set from North Light can be purchased as a set, or individually at just $20.00 each.

continuity, a continuity that has been unbroken since the mid-1970s in keeping together the very talented and dedicated craftsmen who have built up North Light's reputation for excellence.

THE MILLENNIUM AND BEYOND

Today, North Light is increasing its resources to reach an ever-growing number of collectors, which continues to include members of the Royal Family, famous actors, owners of Crufts Champions, respected breeders and international judges. Thus, the pursuit of excellence will go on.

Plans are underway to widen the scope of North Light's figurine range to include the human figure. That cele-brated tradition of models, the lady figurine, will emerge in a line of beauty, fashion and finery not easily equaled.

There will also be a magnificent collection of limited editions depicting the bond between animals and mankind. In this line, Pocock seeks to portray aspects of the millennium while reminding us of the preceding birth of the 20th century. As Clare Beswick concludes, "We know you will see in these new lines that the North Light style will continue to prevail into the 21st century."

This handsome grey "Rolling Horse" from North Light is part of an edition limited to 2,000 pieces worldwide, issued at a retail price of $395.

North Light
41 Madison Avenue
Suite 1601
New York, NY 10010

Phone:
212-696-9667

Fax:
212-696-9683

Sharing the Charms of *Cabbage Patch Kids*®

The "Nifty 50's Special Edition™" doll captures the nostalgic charm of a bobbysoxer in her varsity sweater, rolled jeans and saddle oxfords.

I t's been less than 25 years since a 21-year-old art student named Xavier Roberts unleashed the *Cabbage Patch Kids*® upon the world, but already they're an American institution! So much so that these life-size cloth "babies" will appear on their very own U.S. Postage Stamp for the year 2000 as part of the "Celebrate the Century" series, featuring the decade of the 1980s.

Born in the Appalachian Mountains, Roberts' 'Kids™ combined their creator's interest in sculpture with the quilting skills passed down for generations in mountain families. Roberts dressed his original babies, which were first called Little People®, in yard sale clothing and gave them each a name from a 1937 baby book.

By 1978, demand to adopt these *Little People* was so great that Roberts and five college friends renovated an old doctor's clinic in Cleveland, Georgia, to house them. In that office just 70 miles north of Atlanta, BabyLand General® Hospital was officially opened to the public in July 1978, and is now one of northeast Georgia's most popular tourist attractions.

Roberts' creative company was incorporated as Original Appalachian Artworks, Inc. — the business that started a worldwide phenomenon with national publications filling their pages with feature stories on Roberts' adoptable and adorable babies. Then in 1982, the babies became known as *Cabbage Patch Kids* – a name as recognizable as the babies' smiles, personality and charm. Today, millions of people all over the world enjoy the fun and fantasy of the *Cabbage Patch Kids*, brought to life by a young artist and made possible by his dreams.

A LEGENDARY COLLECTIBLE

Those early days were hectic in Cleveland, Georgia, as prospective "parents" and reporters from around the globe descended on the town. Before long, "Adoption Centers" were set up in many other cities as well – such that 650,000 of these hand-stitched original babies soon found happy homes. To ensure authenticity, each baby came with a Birth Certificate and Adoption Papers, which are still recorded at BabyLand in Cleveland. Through the Oath of Adoption, the babies are assured of a caring "parent."

The growing popularity of the hand-stitched *Little People* was only a hint of the fame the babies would find. In August 1982, Roberts signed his first licensing agreement to produce a smaller, mass-market version of his babies. These babies featured vinyl heads and soft, pillow-like bodies. During this period, Roberts changed the name *Little People* to *Cabbage Patch Kids*, a name that could be registered and protected as a trademark in all product categories.

Cabbage Patch Kids encourage a nurturing behavior in children and adults alike. Their smiling faces and outstretched arms place them among the classic favorites in the toy line. Three million 'Kids were delivered in 1983 and set a record as the most successful new doll in the history of the toy industry. Christmas shoppers literally could not get enough of the huggable 'Kids. A decade later, the licensed version of *Cabbage Patch Kids* still held its position as one of the four best-selling toys of all time. Since 1983, more than 90 million licensed *Cabbage Patch Kids* have been adopted worldwide.

Beginning in 1995, Mattel, the world's largest toy manufacturer, began producing and marketing licensed *Cabbage Patch Kids* through an exclusive worldwide agreement with Original Appalachian Artworks. Mattel was

All ready for a loving home, this "newborn" Cabbage Patch Kid is the latest "special delivery!"

The 1999 Cabbage Patch Kids Collectors Club special edition is the adorable "Harley."

chosen because of its expertise in the design, manufacture and marketing of children's toys. In addition to the Mattel license, current licensing agreements for the *Cabbage Patch Kids* property in the U.S. include products in the categories of toys, gifts and collectibles.

Adoption fees for the original soft sculpture 'Kids range from $170 for limited editions, to $650 for extremely limited, special collectors' editions, hand-signed by Xavier Roberts. Some early editions of the babies, with original adoption fees of $30.00, are now valued at $8,000 or more, according to Collectors' Information Bureau. New special editions of Xavier's soft-sculpture 'Kids continue to be "stitched-to-birth" at the Cabbage Patch each year.

The *'Kids* from Mattel are molded in vinyl and are usually priced under $40.00. Like the original hand-made versions, the Mattel *'Kids* have soft bodies, cute little fingers, "outie" belly buttons and adorable toes.

THE LATEST FROM THE CABBAGE PATCH

In addition to the new *Cabbage Patch Kids* Postage Stamp, some of the biggest news from Cleveland, Georgia, includes the *Favorite Memories Series™* Special Editions, "One-of-a-Kind Wonderful" *'Kids*, Limited Edition *Blue Creek 'Kids Editions* and a special Christmas edition.

If you've ever enjoyed looking back through old family photos, you'll appreciate the fun of *Favorite Memories*. These special editions capture special times from childhood that most everyone can recall. Among collector favorites have been the 1999 Collectors Club Special Edition™, "Harley," reminiscent of the early 1920s. With denim knickers and his own teddy bear. Then there's the "Terrific 30's" Special Edition, swinging into the era of glamour and style with her velvet-and-satin outfit and white poodle.

For "Fabulous 40's," there's a jump-roping charmer in cotton print with rick-rack trim, and the "Nifty 50's" remembers the early days of rock 'n roll and slinkys. For the "Super 70's," love and peace are recalled with a "cool chick" dressed in daisies and crop top. Each *Favorite*

Memories doll has an adoption fee of $345, and each (except "Harley," available only to club members) is limited to an edition of 200.

The "One-of-a-Kind Wonderful" 'Kids are exclusive, soft-sculpture dolls in the original tradition of *Little People*. There are also limited editions available for the 1999 "Blue Creek Preemie" and "Blue Creek Newborn." The "Mobile 'Patch Newborn" is available exclusively through "Adoption Centers" hosting an appearance of the Mobile 'Patch delivery team. Adoption fees range from $190 to $235.

The *Blue Creek 'Kid Edition* offers an amazing variety of features for prospective parents including four skin tones, seven hair colors and a host of hairstyles. The 'Kid's name and birth date can also be selected. Adoption fee for each of the customized dolls is $235.

A special edition for Christmas 2000 is "Merry," a Christmas cutie, just old enough to really enjoy Christmas morning. At 17" in height, "Merry" wears a cascade of blonde ringlets and a designer ensemble of smart red and green plaid trimmed with shimmering golden bows. Limited to only 300 babies, her adoption fee is $295.

SEND YOUR 'KID TO BATH CAMP

BabyLand General Hospital provides a bathing service for soft-sculpture *Cabbage Patch Kids* with fabric faces. During the procedure, the baby is bathed from head to toe including a hair washing. The fee is $30.00 per baby, and full details are available from headquarters in Cleveland.

BabyLand General also assists "parents" with secondary market values (through CIB), research and replacement papers for their *'Kids,* and other customer services.

Capturing the glamour and style of the 1930s in her smart-looking velvet and satin outfit, it's the "Terrific 30's Special Edition™."

A CLUB FOR 'KIDS COLLECTORS

Since 1987, *Cabbage Patch Kids* collectors all over the world have enjoyed membership in their own collectors club. Membership includes a year's subscription to the "Limited Edition," the club's quarterly newsletter packed with the latest information on *Cabbage Patch Kids*; special club offerings created exclusively for club members; a membership card and pin entitling collectors to special privileges exclusive to members; and a customized binder filled with information about the club and 'Kids. Annual dues are $30.00.

Now with their postage stamp on the horizon and *Cabbage Patch Kids* thriving as popular collectibles, things are as exciting as ever at BabyLand General Hospital. As long as the sun shines, the adventures of the *Cabbage Patch Kids* will grow.

Original Appalachian Artworks, Inc.
1721 U.S. Hwy. 75 South
Cleveland, GA 30528

Phone:
706-865-2171

Fax:
706-865-5862

Web Site:
www.cabbagepatchkids.com

The Windsor Bears of Cranbury Commons Share Family Values

Love grows in a very special town, nestled deep in the woods. It's a town where folks always leave their doors open for family and friends… a town where everyone knows each other and neighbors are considered family… a town called Cranbury Commons.

It's a town that collectors have grown to love, filled with bears that make them feel right at home. It's *The Windsor Bears of Cranbury Commons* by Papel Giftware. On Main Street there's a big white house with green shutters and a white picket fence where the *Windsor Bears* live. The bears believe in old-fashioned ideals like love, trust and sharing. They work hard and take pride in everything they do. But there's always time for family and friends… and family and friends are what the *Windsor Bears* are all about. They love spending time together and celebrating life's cherished moments, like their baby's first step. Or that special Christmas when dad lifts the little one way up high to put the star on the family tree. *The Windsor Bears of Cranbury Commons* treasure all those delightful memories of special moments spent together.

At the heart of this happy community is a secret… a secret that makes Cranbury Commons such a wonderful place to live. And the *Windsor Bears* want to pass along

"The Windsor Family — A Time To Remember" is the first limited edition from The Windsor Bears of Cranbury Commons. *It is limited to 2,750 pieces.*

Everyone wants to reach for their dreams. "Andy — Reach for the Stars" shares the sentiment with family and friends.

this secret: happiness is sharing love and memories with a special friend – you!

WINDSOR BEARS INSPIRED BY FEELINGS OF FRIENDSHIP

The folks at Papel Giftware, located in Cranbury, New Jersey, found their inspiration for the *Windsor Bears* while having lunch in the gazebo by the lake in Cranbury Park. There's always lots going on in the park – family picnics, couples walking hand-in-hand, and kids playing all kinds of sports and games. The park and the gazebo inspired a feeling of friendship, and this led to the creation of *The Windsor Bears of Cranbury Commons*.

The bears made their first appearance in the summer of 1996. The first seven figurines – all Christmas and winter-themed – were developed as "gifts for the holiday season," and they were very well received by consumers. So much so that Papel began receiving letters and cards from the customers who bought or were given the figurines. The love and emotion expressed in each piece appeared to touch a chord in people and capture a special memory for them. In response, Papel added a few more figurines to the line, and then a few more. Today, there are more than 100 figurines in the collection.

BEARS CELEBRATE EVERY MOMENT IN LIFE

Since family and friends are so important in Cranbury Commons, it's no surprise that each bear comes with its own name – and seems to know all its neighbors who join in the special times! Among the most recent introductions is "Sammy – Take Me Out To The Ball Game." This adorable new player is sure to become Rookie of the Year!

The first limited edition of the *Windsor Bears* is entitled "A Time To Remember" and is limited to 2,750 pieces. It features Papa Windsor in his chair reading to little Windsor bear, while Mama Windsor is rocking baby in her chair and listening to Papa's story. The figurine also comes with a working (miniature) grandfather clock.

Another first for the collection was "The New Mr. and

"The New Mr. and Mrs. Windsor – Dearly Beloved…" is the happy couple in this first wedding piece introduced in 1997.

Mrs. Windsor – Dearly Beloved…" It was the first wedding piece introduced in 1997. The couple has since been joined by other members of the wedding party and other special wedding moments such as cutting the cake and crossing the threshold.

Throughout the line, collectors will also find figurines for each of the seasons and family milestones. From time to time, figurines are also honored with retirement. Collectors can often catch up with their favorite bears and news during collectible shows. In 1998, Papel Giftware received the "Outstanding Booth Award" during the International Collectible Exposition®, where all the latest *Windsor Bear* introductions greeted collectors.

THE MAKING OF A WINDSOR BEAR

All the *Windsor Bears* are designed in-house by the folks in Cranbury, New Jersey. They work together as a team, or maybe even a family. Some of them write the stories that go along with the figurines. Some draw and some paint. But each *Windsor Bear* is designed to be part of the town called Cranbury Commons.

Every piece from *The Windsor Bears of Cranbury Commons* starts with a moment in time. From this initial concept, the talented artists in Cranbury Commons sketch each figurine to capture that special memory. In great detail, the drawings illustrate all sides of the piece, showing all the little touches that make the *Windsor Bears* so special.

Next, the experienced sculptors translate these renderings into three-dimensional pieces. Skilled hands carefully sculpt in special clays. The creative team reviews and revises each clay sculpture many times to get it just right. Once approved, the sculptors create what is called a production sample. From this production sample, special molds are made. And from these, actual figurines are created. This process results in the exquisite detail that makes each *Windsor Bear* unique.

Each figurine comes out of the mold completely white. Only the most skilled artisans paint the figurines to achieve the authentic *Windsor Bear* look. Artisans carefully inspect each *Windsor Bear.* Only those that meet their highest standards become true *Windsor Bears of Cranbury*

Commons. Through the entire process, the artists keep in mind that every *Windsor Bear* is special and is headed to someone's home. They guarantee that lots of love and care go into each figurine: from concept to creation, from their home to your home.

On the bottom of each figurine there is *The Windsor Bears of Cranbury Commons* backstamp. This is the official "seal of approval" that promises each piece is made in strict accordance to the company's standards. The bottom of the piece also has the year the piece was introduced, its name and title, and its registration number. All *Windsor Bears* come with a Certificate of Friendship, a tent card, and a registration card. Collectors are encouraged to return the card with their comments.

PAPAL GIFTWARE FOCUSES ON SPECIAL MOMENTS

In addition to the *Windsor Bears*, Papel offers a wide range of social expression products, seasonal accents and home fragrances. Papel has a long history in the gift industry, beginning in 1955 as a mug and ceramic giftware company and evolving over the years. In 1996, Gift Holdings LLC, a private investment group, and the Papel management team bought the company from its then owner, Russ Berrie.

"We are a design-oriented, social expression gift company," says Jim Godsill, president of Papel. "We never forget this fundamental philosophy. It permeates all of our creative thinking and goes into all of the products we produce."

In the *Windsor Bears of Cranbury Commons* and all its products, Papel continues its focus on family values and special moments.

It's a big step in every child's – and parent's – life! "Mommy, Daddy and Me – Baby's First Step" captures the moment that will be remembered forever.

Papel Giftware
30 Engelhard Drive
Cranbury, NJ 08512

Phone:
800-634-8384

Fax:
609-395-6879

Web Site:
www.papelgiftware.com

Where Every Day Is Christmas

Fifteen years ago, Warren Stanley had a dream. He wanted to make the best Santa figurines that collectors could find anywhere. So he founded Possible Dreams in order to make his own dream a reality. His company started with a few Santa designs and today has more than 250 in its line, as well as other unique Christmas collectibles and gifts. And while the company and its artists are still focused on the holiday season, Possible Dreams also offers non-Christmas-themed gifts that are just as popular. It seems the company is making dreams come true for collectors, too!

CLOTHTIQUE SANTAS BRING HOME THE HOLIDAYS

In wanting to create the best Santas, Possible Dreams President Warren Stanley designed a special line in which the Santas wear real cloth clothing that has been treated with a stiffening agent. Although techniques for stiffening cloth have existed since the 1800s in countries such as Spain, Italy and France, Stanley and his factory were the first to come up with the idea of using the process to make reproductions of Santa Claus. *The Clothtique Santa Collection* features many Santas created by Stanley himself,

Artist Wayne Still captures the people and customs of Africa with "Hausa Man" and other figurines in the African Spirit collection.

Possible Dreams now often licenses designs from independent artists. *The Clothtique American Artist Collection* features well-known artists such as Tom Browning, Lyn Fletcher, Judi Vaillancourt, Mark Alvin, Judith Ann Griffith and David Wenzel. They all create collectible Santas dressed and accessorized in very original ways.

There are also licensed *Clothtique Santas* featuring the world's most popular brands. Additions to *The Coca-Cola Brand Clothtique Santas* and *McDonald's Clothtique Santas* are always very popular with collectors of all ages. *Saturday Evening Post Cover Clothtique Santas,* inspired by the art of Norman Rockwell and J.C. Leyendecker, continue to please, especially with Possible Dreams' reintroduction of smaller, less expensive versions.

To welcome the 21st century, "Greeting the Millennium" is a very special offering from the *Clothtique* line. A breakthrough piece also made from *Clothtique* is a rock and roll Santa called "Santa Be Good." Santa comes complete with an electric guitar, amp and red glitter smoking jacket.

FROM THE HOLIDAYS AND BEYOND

In addition to celebrating the holidays, Possible Dreams extends its collections to capture other themes, times and adventures. *Thickets At Sweetbriar* is the fanciful world of artist Bronwen Ross, who has a talent for capturing the whimsy of yesteryear. Her backyard wildlife is dressed in sophisticated wardrobes borrowed from the Victorian era. Year after year, Ross adds characters to the *Thickets At Sweetbriar* collection that are entertaining, charming and a delight to collectors.

Spangler's Realm has artist Randal Spangler's house dragons involved in mischievous deeds. *African Spirit* by Wayne Still is a sculpted tribute to members of tribes in sub-Saharan Africa. The figurine collection shares Still's discoveries about the people and customs of Africa. "It is

Rock and roll is here to stay in "Santa Be Good" by artist Lyn Fletcher from the Clothtique American Artist Collection.

who tries to sit down at the drawing board as often as possible. The figurines, which are crafted in stiffened cloth, porcelain and cold cast, highlight a range of whimsical themes and traditional motifs.

While Stanley designed many of the original Santas,

Santa is checking out his Christmas Eve route in this Clothtique *Saturday Evening Post Cover figurine. "Santa With Globe" is based on the artwork of Norman Rockwell.*

my hope that this project will enlighten many to the intriguing and mysterious culture that is the people of Africa — to help preserve a way of life that is being lost to the industrialization of a continent," Still says.

Baby's Roots are charming African-American children as envisioned by author and artist Debbie Bell Jarratt. *Tender Treasures* is full of Old World European charm as artist Lynn Norton Parker creates lovely little girls with lots of color and details.

RECENT ADDITIONS FOR COLLECTORS TO ENJOY

Possible Dreams also offers new collections that can be enjoyed year 'round. Bob Stebleton's *Cagey Critters* feature cats and sometimes mice, which are sculpted in resin from this Maine artist's hand-carved menagerie. Stebleton's kooky themes are whimsically executed with skilled artistry. There is also a small line of Christmas-themed designs of a whale and Santa, as well as a dinosaur and Santa.

Veteran artist Judi Vaillancourt has conformed her famous antique chocolate molds into old Christmas chess pieces in a stained wood box that's also the chess board. Artist Jeanne Beury is a new *Clothtique* artist who has created a line of cast figurines called *Jingle Journey* that depicts Santa riding various animals. "I remember painting Santas when I was just nine years old," Beury recalls. "He's always represented every-thing good in this world."

Flights of Fancy soars with a variety of Santas and aviators that balance overhead in motion, thanks to propellers that are battery powered.

COLLECTORS CAN JOIN THE CLUBS

To keep the magic of Christmas alive throughout the year, Possible Dreams introduced the Santa Claus Network. The collector's club is dedicated to those who experience the magic of Christmas every day of their lives. Members receive an exclusive *Clothtique* figurine, along with a quarterly newsletter, membership card, and *Collector Guide Book,* featuring color photos of the *Clothtique* collection and fascinating folklore.

Collectors can also purchase exclusive members-only offerings during the year.

Possible Dreams also invites collectors to join the Crinkle Claus Collectors Club. It's for everyone who is crazy about *Crinkle Claus,* a colorful line of Santas that come in unique shapes and sizes. Members receive a complimentary *Crinkle Claus* Santa figurine, along with a 14-K gold membership pin, newsletter and guidebook that features all the *Crinkles*. In addition, members have the opportunity to purchase members-only *Crinkles* that they can't find anywhere else.

MAKING THE BEST COLLECTIBLES POSSIBLE

No matter what the collection, design or collector's club, Possible Dreams is dedicated to creating the highest quality collectibles and meeting the needs of its collectors. This commitment and creativity was first seen in the *Clothtique* collection and now extends throughout the company's line. "Discovering new ways to bring *Clothtique Santas* into the hearts of a wider audience is my first joy," says Stanley. "But I also know that if I don't follow each piece through from sketchpad to brushstroke, then our strict standard of high quality and dauntless service will be compromised."

That kind of dedication at Possible Dreams is why collectors around the world look forward year after year to new *Clothtique Santas,* along with a broad spectrum of innovative holiday and non-seasonal treasures.

With a touch of whimsy, artist Bob Stebleton lets Santa trade in his reindeer for a dinosaur. The 7-1/2" figurine, "Jolly Jurassic," is from the popular Stebleton Folkart Collection.

Possible Dreams
6 Perry Drive
Foxboro, MA 02035

Phone:
508-543-6667

Fax:
508-543-4255

A World of Whimsical Fantasy and Animals

"When we opened Precious Art, we wanted to create quality giftware that was innovative in nature," says David Woodard of himself and his two partners, Pat and Sam Chandok. "We wanted to incorporate new ideas into existing items, as well as create new designs." It was back in 1980 when the trio of veteran gift shop owners pooled their experience in the gift industry and their knowledge of collectors to open their own thriving firm. Since then, their creations, based on fantasy and fun, have delighted fans all over the world.

"The first items we introduced were imported from Asia," Woodard recalls. "We took an ancient Japanese art called Chokin and created pictures and music boxes, and later expanded into vases, accessories and other items. We found that collectors liked to have a variety of choices in a product they enjoyed." Musicals became very important in Precious Art's early designs. Woodard explains, "We worked with woods, etched glass and metals. Limited edition carousels were an important part of the line, especially with the creation of a vertical movement to resemble a real carousel. To complement the carousel pieces, we added brass designs, ornaments and larger pieces."

Here, "Kephren the Recorder" tends to his work while all the fantasy activity of the Krystonia baby dragons continues around him.

Funny Galore's *innovative designs include these googly-eyed* Funny Frogz® *from Precious Art, Inc.*

PRECIOUS ART UNVEILS *KRYSTONIA*®

In 1987, Precious Art introduced what has become its "signature line" – the whimsically fantastic *World of Krystonia*. Four *Krystonia* books tell the stories of a magical kingdom where good and evil battle for control – with the virtuous always winning, of course. The good wizards are helped in this effort by the dragons, and many other characters, in their search for krystals.

The World of Krystonia started in a tiny factory in England, but is now produced in the Far East. Using cold-cast porcelain, the hand-painted figurines are carefully monitored throughout the production process. Of course, each character must have its own sparkling krystal adornment for the finishing touch.

While *Krystonia* is manufactured in China, the collection was born from the hearts and minds of David Woodard and Pat Chandok. They spend countless hours making sure that no two characters are the same, and they lead a creative team of artists who breathe life into every *Krystonia* resident. Without just the right design and color, each figurine may never make it to the stage of production and naming.

Storylines for the books come from Dave, Pat and Mark Scott. They collaborate to bring to life all the different characters and adventures. After one book is completed, they start planning the next – which always is sure to be filled with pages of fantasy and fun!

The four fascinating *Krystonia* books, as narrated by "Kephren the Recorder," give collectors a way to further enjoy their figurines – and to follow the storylines of their beloved characters. It's an up-close and personal approach that sparks the imagination and has led to great success for Precious Art. What's more, the books reveal the magic found throughout the wonderful land, where the search is always on for magic krystals. Whoever controls the krystals rules all of *Krystonia!*

Among the most intriguing book characters of all time is the evil "N'Borg," who dreams of the day when he will make *Krystonia* a bleak and barren wasteland. With his

Welcome to Happy Acres *– a place where cows "m-o-o-ve" about and every animal is a little "quakkers!"*

henchdragon "N'Grall," "N'Borg" plots to crush the Council of Wizards from his menacing castle, "Krak N'Borg." He also has a score to settle with "Klip," who took away his beautiful "N'Leila."

The Council of Wizards looks out for the best interests of *Krystonia* by thwarting "N'Borg's" plans. A host of wizards, each with his own spell-casting specialty, rules the day. Most agree that "Graffyn" has the toughest job of all the wizards: he negotiates the transportation contracts with the dragons' leader, "Grumblypeg Grunch." All of this and much more is ours to enjoy – thanks to the writings of "Kephren," who has delivered more scrolls to translate each day by dragon transport!

PRECIOUS ART'S AMAZING ANIMALS

In addition to *The World of Krystonia*, Precious Art is proud to offer collectors three other lovable lines, each inspired by an outlandish vision of creatures in their own make-believe worlds.

Funny Galore combines brightly colored frogs, cats, elephants and penguins in comical poses. Most of the pieces have been created in smaller sizes, but Precious Art plans to add more large designs of crabs, lobsters, armadillos and various other animals. These designs can be used for home décor but are also ideal for those who collect certain animals.

Petal Pets® offers a marvelous mix of musical candleholders and figurines. Each piece is very attractively gift boxed and has the story of *Petal Pets* on the back. It's a tale of how tiny seeds were carried high above the earth across the skies, then gently sprinkled over a fertile valley filled with rich, dark soil. According to legend, from the warmth of this Mother Earth come the *Petal Pets*: "Samantha Straw Beary," "Darius Dandee Lion," "Polly Poin Setter" and "Sylvester Snap Dragon."

"Samantha Straw Beary" is one of the first works of art introduced in Precious Art, Inc.'s Petal Pets collection.

◆ *Happy Acres* depicts barnyard animals in whimsical poses, including sheep, cows, ducks, pigs, dogs, chickens and even a sly fox or two. Horses are the most recent addition to the collection.

KRYSTONIA COLLECTORS' CLUB HAS BEEN CHARMING COLLECTORS FOR OVER A DECADE

The Krystonia Collector's Club offers a fine array of benefits to its enthusiastic members. For a $30.00 annual fee, members receive the "Phargol Horn" club newsletter, featuring an exclusive *Krystonia* story in each issue. Members also receive a membership card and a redemption certificate that allows them to purchase a members-only figurine. Club members also are sent invitations to special events.

Each member receives a special club figurine every year, as well as a coupon to purchase a members-only redemption piece. As David Woodard comments, "We have always enjoyed designing the club figurine and the special member redemption figurine together so they form a scene." The special club figurine was a small dragon called "Which Way." The redemption figurine was entitled "Krystonia This Way." "Krystonia This Way" showed Groza the Troll putting a sign up showing the way to *Krystonia*. Collectors of the "Which Way" figurine can place it on "Krystonia This Way" to create a scene of the small dragon asking for directions.

MORE CREATIVE IDEAS TO COME

Woodard characterizes the works he and Pat Chandok create as "feel-good" designs. "Our designs lean toward the whimsical," he notes, "but we have been known to create realistic designs as well. The process begins with brainstorming. We talk about our initial concept and continue by looking for unique ways to develop our ideas. We always look for a special niche that has not been addressed before. Once the concept is developed, we work with sculptors all over the world, carefully supervising each design and color choice.

"We feel some products are better suited to be limited editions while others should be open stock. In all that we do, we think the reason people should collect a line is for enjoyment." Woodard concludes, "The reward of creating a collectible line is to see the joy in the faces of our collectors!"

Precious Art, Inc.
125 W. Ellsworth
Ann Arbor, MI 48108

Phone:
734-663-1885

Fax:
734-663-2343

Web Sites:
www.preciousart.com
www.krystoniaclub.com

E-mail:
krystoniaclub@msn.com

The Art of Joy and Innocence

The history of art has taught us that every once in a great while, an artist will come along, whose work is so truthful and so touching that it speaks to the very core of who we are, and helps us define our beliefs, our values, and ourselves. Such artistic talent is extraordinary and rare. So it's not surprising that those who possess it also have the power to attract collectors who, themselves, are a very special group – like those who collect *Precious Moments*.

Precious Moments was created by artist Sam Butcher, whose drawings of the adorable, teardrop-eyed children appeared on his popular, inspirational greeting cards in the 1970s. When Eugene Freedman, Founding Chairman of Enesco, one of the most successful giftware companies in the world, discovered the cards, he was instantly captivated by the charm and innocence of the drawings.

Mr. Freedman convinced Butcher to allow Enesco to develop porcelain bisque figurines based on his artwork. With Butcher's blessing, Freedman turned the artist's drawings over to renowned Japanese master sculptor Yasuhei Fujioka and charged him with translating the two-dimensional images into three dimensions, while preserving all the tenderness and charm of the originals.

Fujioka's first *Precious Moments* figurine, completed in 1978, was appropriately titled, "Love One Another." An additional 20 figurines were unveiled that first year, followed by an additional four more figurines in 1979. To date, more than 1,000 *Precious Moments* figurines have been created.

In the 22 years since its debut, the collection has expanded to include many more figurines, as well as plates, bells, ornaments, photo frames, musicals, and home decor giftware. Within the collection, Enesco has launched several lines, including *Sugar Town*, a porcelain village based on artist Sam Butcher's hometown (1992); the *Precious Moments Forever True* wedding line (1994); *Little Moments* (1996); the *Precious Moments Jewelry Collection* (1997); the *Tender Tails* plush collection (1998); and *Hugs for the Soul* collectible plush collection (1999).

THE ARTIST WHO BRINGS *PRECIOUS MOMENTS* TO LIFE

More than two decades after the introduction of the *Precious Moments* collection, Sam Butcher is still responsible for creating all artwork. He works closely with the folks at Enesco and the *Precious Moments* Design Studio to create dozens of new subjects each year, all inspired by his own personal experience, his faith and stories from *Precious Moments*' collectors.

Sam Butcher, the creator and artist of the Precious Moments *collection by Enesco.*

◆ *The first* Precious Moments *wedding figurine to feature a bride dancing with her father, "You Will Always Be Daddy's Little Girl," was introduced in 2000.*

From the beginning of his artistic career, Butcher has been creating the teardrop-eyed children, now so dear and familiar to every *Precious Moments* fan, for greeting cards and posters. Originally, the cards and posters were created under the auspices of his first business, a company called Jonathon and David, which he and his friend, Bill Biel, founded in order to create and sell merchandise that expressed their social beliefs.

Then, as now, Butcher's talents were not limited to creating *Precious Moments* artwork. He is also a master of contemporary art that depicts men, women and children.

Sam Butcher's devotion to both his faith and his art has led to the construction of the Precious Moments Chapel in Carthage, Missouri. The Chapel, which opened in 1989, sits on more than 2,000 acres, and houses a myriad of hand-painted murals, sculpted bronze statues, stained glass windows and a painted ceiling, all featuring *Precious Moments* children.

Each year, nearly a million collectors make the journey deep into the heart of the nation's midwestern countryside to visit the Chapel. Recent guests have found such beautiful new additions to the grounds as the lovely Fountain of the Angels, a quaint Victorian wedding chapel, and the charmingly romantic Honeymoon Island.

Sam Butcher has also been honored with a multitude of awards for his work in the collectible and art world, including the "International Collectible Artist Award" (1995); the "Special Recognition Award" by the National Association of Limited Edition Dealers (NALED, 1988); and the NALED "Artist of the Year" designation (1992 and 1995). His artwork has also been recognized with such prestigious awards as the NALED "Figurine of the Year" (1994); NALED "Ornament of the Year" (1994, 1995, 1996); and NALED "Collectible of the Year" (1992).

Also in 1992, at the Midwest Gathering of the Artists, an annual event held in Carthage, Missouri, the town's mayor proclaimed September 18-20 as "Sam Butcher Days" in recognition of his outstanding artistic talent, achievements and community service.

A native of Jackson, Michigan, Butcher attended the College of Arts and Crafts in Berkeley, California. He is the father of seven children and grandfather of 23.

Butcher divides his time among his home on the Chapel grounds, his residence near Chicago, and an art studio overseas. But wherever in the world he might be at any given time, you can be sure that his life's work – touching the hearts of collectors with his winsome creations – is always close at hand.

A portion of proceeds from of "Life is Worth Fighting For" benefit the National Alliance of Breast Cancer Organizations. The "pink ribbon" symbol of breast cancer awareness is sculpted on the figurine.

COLLECTORS MAKE *PRECIOUS MOMENTS* SO SPECIAL

The Enesco *Precious Moments* collection is ranked as the nation's Number One collectible, a distinction it has held for nearly 20 years, according to retailers. To help collectors get the most enjoyment from their collections, Enesco launched the national Precious Moments Collectors' Club in 1981. The Club is one of the world's largest collectors' club with more than 160,000 members and 4,000 local club chapter members nationwide. It offers *Precious Moments* enthusiasts the opportunity to learn more about the artwork and its creator, as well as meet and make friends with other *Precious Moments* collectors from around the country.

For the Collectors' Club's 20th anniversary, more than a 1,000 collectors sailed on a seven-day *Precious Moments*-sponsored cruise to Alaska. In 1985, the Enesco Precious Moments Birthday Club was formed to introduce children to the fun of collecting. In 1998, the Birthday Club was replaced by the Precious Moments Fun Club, which emphasizes and encourages collecting as a joyfully shared family activity for children ages eight to 12.

With the collection's underlying themes of reaching

The master sculptor behind the Precious Moments *collection, Yasuhei Fujioka, is portrayed in the figurine, "Mr. Fujioka."*

out, acceptance and inclusion, there could hardly be a more fitting way to celebrate the 20th anniversary of the collection than with the Precious Moments Care-A-Van. Launched in 1998, this 53-foot long traveling museum embarked on an eight-month tour across the United States and Canada, stopping at more than 200 cities to spread the *Precious Moments* message of loving, caring, and sharing.

The Care-A-Van features one-of-a-kind artwork, videos and giftware items. Today, the Care-A-Van continues to travel across the country making more than 80 stops nationally, with the Year 2000 Tour including stops at military bases and key Special Olympics events nationwide.

PRECIOUS MOMENTS — AN INTERNATIONAL SYMBOL OF CARING AND SHARING

Each year, Enesco introduces new figurines to the *Precious Moments* collection and retires or suspends existing figurines. Once a figurine is retired, the mold is broken, and it will never again be produced. Figurines that have been "suspended" are indefinitely withdrawn from production. "Retirement" is the highest honor bestowed upon a figurine, as it enhances the figurine's secondary market value and its collectibility.

With all the *Precious Moments* figurines that have been released over the years, collectors always want to know which one has sold the most. The big answer is "The Lord Bless You and Keep You," a bride-and-groom double figurine, which has topped well over a million wedding cakes since it was first introduced in 1979.

More than 60 percent of *Precious Moments* collectors get their start in collecting when they receive a figurine as a gift. In fact, *Precious Moments* figurines have such extensive recognition within the collectible and giftware industry, that they have been chosen for presentation to three United States presidents – Bill Clinton, George Bush, and Ronald Reagan.

For more than 40 years, Enesco Group, Inc. has been a global leader in the gift, collectibles, and home décor industries. In addition to *Precious Moments*, one of the world's most popular collectible lines, the company offers products from such notable licenses as *Cherished Teddies*, Mary Engelbreit, Kim Anderson's *Pretty As A Picture*, and Harry Potter among others.

Precious Moments
c/o Enesco Group, Inc.
225 Windsor Drive
Itasca, IL 60143

Phone:
800-632-7968

Fax:
638-875-5350

Web Sites:
www.enesco.com
www.enescoclubs.com

Celebrating Christmas Traditions All Year 'Round

Pipka Ulvilden's story begins at the end of World War II when her family emigrated from Germany to America. Her father was a doctor, but his first love was art – a talent that he shared with his children. Pipka remembers drawing since the age of five in her new home in a small North Dakota town, where she admired and studied the paintings of Old Masters found in her parents' books.

Each year, her family would return to Germany to visit relatives and maintain the customs and values of their heritage. "It was in Germany that my appreciation for primitive art blossomed," she says. While Pipka loved art, her own creative talents remained dormant until she received an unexpected gift from her mother in 1972.

While visiting Germany, her mother packed up a box filled with unpainted wood, paint brushes and books on a Bavarian folk art known as "Bauernmalerei," or peasant painting. At this point, Pipka was a divorced mother with two small children. "I used the supplies to relax and get in touch with my feelings," she says. "I loved art so much that I decided this was how I would make a living and support my family."

Since then, Pipka has been sharing her beautiful artwork of Santas, angels and florals which also weave wonderful stories of folklore, customs and traditions. Today, her work has been transformed into a line of limited edition collectibles exclusively distributed by Prizm, Inc.

Charter members of Pipka's Memories of Christmas Collector's Club have the opportunity to purchase two members-only figurines: "Knock, Knock Santa" and the "Knock, Knock Santa Door."

PRIZM FEATURES PIPKA'S FOLK ART TRADITIONS

In 1992, a friend of Pipka sent her drawings to Gary Meidinger and Michele Johnson, then in-house artists for TLC, a card company owned by McCall's Pattern Company. The company's artists envisioned translating Pipka's artwork into a line of Santas featuring figurines, mugs and other giftware items. Unfortunately, TLC closed. But Gary and Michele still wanted to pursue their dream. So in 1994, they founded Prizm, Inc. to produce collectibles and gifts featuring Pipka's talents. With Gary and Michele's experience in the gift industry and Pipka's work, they knew a unique line of limited edition Santas could be introduced to collectors. Prizm sent Pipka's artwork to China, where a talented sculptor interpreted them as three-dimensional figurines.

As the first issue in the Artist Choice series, "Laplander Santa" celebrates the traditions of the Samis people near the Arctic Circle.

"Pipka, Gary and I aren't related, but we're family," says Michele. "We are dedicated to one another as life partners. We started this company with a deep devotion to each other and to Pipka's wonderful artwork. Every item we bring to the gift and collectible industry is with a tremendous amount of love and support."

The founders also built the company with the collector in mind, ensuring that each product and program that bears Pipka's name will be of the highest standards and quality. Their vision is to build a collectible line that excites and warms the hearts of all. For now, Pipka is Prizm's only artist. "We see ourselves as a company devoted to one line," Gary says.

PIPKA'S MEMORIES OF CHRISTMAS COLLECTOR'S CLUB

Pipka's Memories of Christmas Collector's Club was founded in 1998 to further share the artist's folk art Santa traditions and inspirations. Charter members can unlock the door to Santa's world by receiving exclusive benefits. Members receive a decorative tin filled with the "Knock, Knock Santa" ornament, an autographed picture of Pipka and the Club Key Pin (a pewter lapel pin). Members also receive a subscription to the club newsletter, "Pipka's Scrapbook Pages," which is packed with information about Pipka and her Old World Santas. Members also have the opportunity to purchase two members-only figurines: "Knock, Knock Santa" and the "Knock, Knock Santa Door."

SERIES CELEBRATE CHRISTMAS TRADITIONS

In researching every Santa that she creates, Pipka has discovered that people share many of the same Christmas traditions that have been passed down through the ages.

Santa Claus, or Father Christmas, is a mythical figure that transcends all race, nationalities and countries. In that respect, Pipka sees him as being holy and spiritual – a character that brings us together in the spirit of hope.

Pipka's *Christmas Memories* series, originally launched in 1995, features large, limited edition Santas that bring back warm thoughts of the holiday season. There are now a total of 26 Santas, and the edition size was increased from 3,600 to 4,500 pieces in 1999.

The *Artist Choice Santa* series was introduced in 1999 with "Laplander Santa." The 11" Santa – representing the Samis people from Lapland near the Arctic Circle – is dressed in traditional clothing of wool and deerskin, trimmed with decorative hand-woven braids. In his basket, he carries the toys that Samis children love: a reindeer, hand-made doll, sled and knitted mittens. The *Artist Choice* pieces are limited to one year of production.

Another inspiring part of the Christmas story is the Madonna, which is featured in the *Pipka – The Madonna Collection*. The first Madonna is "Queen of Roses" and is limited in edition to 5,400 pieces. "One of my earliest memories as a little girl is of drawing pictures of religious figures, saints, angels and the Virgin Mary," Pipka says. "I wanted to design my Mary, Queen of Roses, to depict sweetness, humility and strength."

In 1997, Prizm launched another series of Old World Santa figurines, which are smaller versions of sold-out *Christmas Memories* figurines. Some of the pieces in *Pipka's Reflections of Christmas* series will never be issued as larger *Memories* figurines. The series debuted with six cold cast figurines, each limited in edition to 9,700 pieces and standing 6" tall. There are now a total of 24 Santas.

For trimming the tree, collectible ornaments known as the *Stories of Christmas* also debuted in 1997 with six designs. The line now has 24 Santa ornaments.

PIPKA'S THREE YEAR NATIVITY COLLECTION

Pipka Collectibles brings the story of the first Christmas to collectors with the recent introduction of the "First Christmas by Pipka Nativity." Over three years, collectors will have the opportunity to acquire this stunningly moving portrayal of the Nativity, with a bonus gift of "First Christmas Angel" (a $50 value) going to those who complete the collection, at the end of 2002.

EARTH ANGELS WATCH OVER ALL

Pipka believes that angels are spiritual beings that bring us messages and guidance. They are the thoughts of God. With this in mind, Pipka designed her *Earth Angels* series to represent the heavenly messengers that live among us. An angel can be found in a stranger, friend

Pipka's Earth Angels *include "Sissy – The Little Helper Angel" (left) and "Michele – The Snow Angel" – both of which represent the heavenly angels that live among us. Each hand-painted figurine is limited to 5,400 pieces.*

or loved one.

Each of the figurines – portraying either an adult or child angel – is limited to 5,400 pieces and stands 9-1/2" tall. There are a total of 17 designs. Among the two most recent introductions are "Michele – The Snow Angel" and "Sissy – The Little Helper Angel." "The Snow Angel" teaches that the most fun activities are those that can be enjoyed by all. "The Little Helper Angel" loves to play in the snow and make snowmen – or "snow friends" as she calls them. She decided that even a snow friend must keep warm, and she offers him her own little coat as a gesture of kindness.

PIPKA SHARES HER TALENTS WITH OTHERS

For more than 25 years, Pipka has taught classes from America to Australia, and she has also authored dozens of art instruction books. Her classes and seminars are held from May through December at the Folk Art Studio in beautiful Door County, Wisconsin. Despite her demanding schedule and the growing popularity of her designs, she still puts teaching high on her list of priorities. "I love the students," she says. "Their enthusiasm and intention to learn is so contagious. What they might not guess is that I learn as much from them as they learn from me." Pipka also takes time to meet her collectors by doing in-store signings and attending the two major collectible shows annually.

Pipka created the "Queen of Roses" as the first introduction in the Pipka – The Madonna Collection.

Prizm, Inc./
Pipka Collectibles
P.O. Box 1106
Manhattan, KS 66505

Phone:
785-776-1613

Fax:
785-776-6550

Web Site:
www.pipka.com

E-mail:
prizminc@pipka.com

PRIZM, INC./
PIPKA COLLECTIBLES

A Name Synonymous with Collectors Curios

As the new millennium dawns, Pulaski Furniture Corporation sees a bright future. The nation's largest curio manufacturer, Pulaski has built a strong following of collectors whose aim is to display and protect their collectible treasures. Pulaski Vice President of Sales, Randy Chrisley, attributes the success of the curio business, in large part, to the Internet. "Auction sites such as eBay and Amazon.com are attracting millions of people everyday," said Chrisley. "Collectibles and memorabilia are being bought and sold in record numbers, and what that means is more demand for displaying and protecting these collectibles."

Pulaski sees an increased interest in collectible curios as more and more collectors nationwide are educating themselves on caring for and displaying their cherished collectibles. In doing so, they are turning to Pulaski for the answers. In response to collector demand, the company repositioned its curio line over three years ago, and began marketing them as PFC Collectors Curios. With broad national advertising and point-of-purchase displays at the company's 2,000-plus authorized dealers, Pulaski has become a name synonymous with "collectibles."

There is a PFC Collectors Curio to complement every décor.

Thousands of consumers have responded to the company's ads and called its toll free number (800-Curio 25) for the name of their nearest dealer. Most are referred to Pulaski's large core retailers and department stores such as Heilig-Meyers, JC Penney, Levitz and Federated Department Stores. But, according to Chrisley, Pulaski also sells to many smaller, independent retailers, too. Consumers have responded well to Pulaski's PFC Collectors Club. The $29.95 annual membership includes a very informative newsletter and a gift. Most recently, the

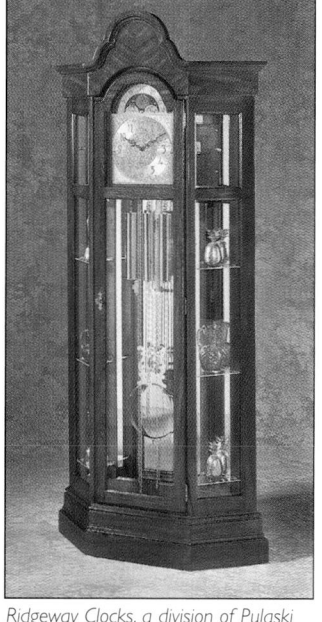

Ridgeway Clocks, a division of Pulaski Furniture, offers a line of curio clocks that make timeless keepsakes.

gift was a limited edition print of "Rembrandt Russell," a Jack Russell Terrier "self pawtrait."

EXTRA GLASS SHELVES A BIG HIT

Responding to collectors needs, Pulaski now offers a program through which consumers can literally double the shelf space in their PFC Collectors Curios. Each curio comes with an order form for acquiring extra glass shelves and a bracket kit directly from Pulaski. So, three-shelf curios can expand to six shelves. Four-shelf curios can expand to eight shelves. "This program has been great for our customers," said Chrisley. "They can literally customize their curio to fit their collection, with large and small items on different shelf configurations."

There is a PFC Collectors Curio complementing every décor. Light, dark and medium finishes abound in a wide variety of styles. All PFC Collectors Curios feature interior lighting and mirrored backs. And there is a price point for everyone, too. PFC Collectors Curios have been seen on sale for as little as $199. According to Chrisley, the average curio purchased is in the $599 to $699 range.

AN INVESTMENT IN TIME

On the eve of the 21st century, Pulaski challenged the designers at its Ridgeway Clocks division to put their names on an historic timepiece: a clock that would pay homage to the history of timekeeping. The result is the "Millennia," a limited edition Grandfather clock. The "Millennia" will be available at select Ridgeway dealers. It is being crafted in a limited edition of only 1,000 clocks. Each numbered clock comes with its own Certificate of Authenticity and consumer registration number.

While keeping accurate time, this curio clock from Pulaski Furniture's Ridgeway Clocks division beautifully displays a collector's favorite treasures.

The "Millennia" is traditional in style but high-tech in performance. Its West German movements are among the most precise in the world. And its time-honored chimes are the ones most familiar and cherished — Westminster, St. Michael's and Whittington, plus the Big Ben hour count. The deep wooden echo box featured in the "Millennia" greatly enhances all of these historic sounds. This timeless timepiece is expected to retail for approximately $2,000.

PULASKI QUALITY AND DESIGN MOVE ALL THROUGH THE HOUSE

Pulaski Furniture was founded in Pulaski, Virginia, in 1955, and is one of the nation's largest furniture producers. The company's domestic and export sales exceed $175 million.

Besides making PFC Collectors Curios, the company also produces casual dining and bedroom furniture. And its stylish Accentrics division is an innovative source for home accents.

"We're a complete source for furniture," said Chrisley. "Our curio business and the advertising we've put behind it has no doubt helped drive our other categories. Pulaski is becoming a top-of-mind furniture name with consumers." Chrisley believes PFC Collectors Curio customers are discovering other Pulaski items such as bedroom and casual dining pieces right along side the curios. They're delighted to know that the same sense of style and dedication to quality can be found in products for the entire home.

Pulaski Furniture exhibits at the International Home Furnishings Center (IHFC) in High Point, North Carolina.

IHFC is the largest showroom under one roof in the world. Pulaski also exhibits at regional markets including the Dallas and San Francisco markets.

MORE COLLECTIBLES?

With the advent of its PFC Collectors Curio program in 1996, Pulaski launched its first figurine: a hand-painted resin piece named "Curios Henry." It was in the likeness of a Jack Russell Terrier. The breed selected was not a random choice. Randy Chrisley and Pulaski's VP of Manufacturing, Jim Kelly, both own this breed of dog.

Chrisley says that future figurines are possible, but only for promotions such as "A Gift with Purchase" promotion. "We're not in the the business of making figurines," notes Chrisley. "We're in the business of protecting and displaying them."

Pulaski does plan to pursue licensing ventures with collectibles manufacturers, however. One successful venture so far has been with Enesco's *Precious Moments* brand. In a joint venture between Pulaski and the Levitz furniture chain, members of the Precious Moments Collector's Club were introduced to an exclusive curio designed just for their figurines.

"This is the kind of business we're looking for," said Chrisley. "We believe there are a lot of opportunities out there for Pulaski to enhance the collecting experience through the development of exclusive curios."

These dolls are attractively and safely displayed in this PFC Collectors Curio.

Pulaski Furniture
Corporation
One Pulaski Square
Pulaski, VA 24301

Phone:
800-CURIO-25
800-287-4625

PULASKI FURNITURE CORPORATION

Celebrating 20 Happy Years with Sandra Kuck

◆

Lovely "Little Valentina," the christening doll, represents the touching and timeless art of Sandra Kuck.

Two decades ago, Heio Reich was enjoying the results of more than 12 years of hard work establishing Reco International as a purveyor of world-class collectibles. A native of Berlin, Reich had earned awards and kudos for importing elegant works from some of Europe's leading art studios, including Fuerstenberg, Royale, Dresden, Royal Germania Crystal, King and Moser. Then in the mid-1970s, Reich formed a warm and fruitful association with the gifted John McClelland, creator of beautiful and artistic child-subject works.

It came almost as a gift when Reich discovered another painter of children who was destined to become one of the brightest shining stars in the history of collectibles. Sandra Kuck was a gifted young mother, displaying her paintings in a Long Island art gallery when Reco signed her to create collector plates. Her first plates debuted in 1979. But it was not until "Sunday Best" was unveiled in

also has graced the collectibles world with many other wonderful creations. Indeed, while some studios specialize in only one content area such as children or wildlife, Reco seeks out artists who paint in many styles and capture a variety of subjects. In addition to the child-subject works of McClelland and Kuck, Dot and Sy Barlowe have crafted vivid portraits of wildlife and nature for Reco. And Clemente Micarelli has painted homages to the ballet, religious events and weddings. Subjects as diverse as French café scenes, lighthouses and hot air balloons also may be found in the Reco archives.

Striving to be the best also brings well-deserved recognition. Reich and his artists have never sought personal glory or awards. Indeed, they consider their finest accolade the gleam in a happy collector's eyes. Nonetheless, Reich has received nearly every prestigious honor available to a collectibles marketer or producer. These awards include: "Vendor of the Year," "Producer of the Year," the "Lee Benson Memorial Award," the "International Collectible Achievement Award" and the "Silver Chalice Award" for selected plates.

Reich also has long been an active member and leader in the National Association of Limited Edition Dealers (NALED) and the Collectibles and Plate Makers Guild. He also was a charter member of the Board of Directors of Collectors' Information Bureau (CIB).

In addition to the company's leader receiving recognition, Reco's artists have also been singled out for their work. McClelland and Kuck have been lauded at scores of conventions and collectors' gatherings with "Plate of the Year," "Artist of the Year" and many other honors. Kuck is readily acknowledged as the most honored collectibles artist of all time – including an unprecedented six consecutive "Artist of the Year" awards from NALED.

The company and its artists also enjoy a visible presence before collectors. Reco has exhibited at every International Collectible Exposition® since that famous show began 25 years ago in South Bend, Indiana.

SANDRA KUCK: ROMANTIC REALIST

After many successful years as a plate artist, Sandra Kuck has widened her horizons to develop marvelous new pieces in three dimensions. For several years now, her *Sandra Kuck's Treasures*™ figurines have earned interna-

"Friendship and Sharing" continues the heartwarming and nostalgic theme of Sandra Kuck's Treasures series of figurines from Reco International Corp.

1982 that she took the collecting world by storm. Kuck's combination of gorgeous, sweet-faced youngsters with gentle Victorian scenes and incredible detail work won her and Reco "Plate of the Year" honors for "Sunday Best" – just the first of a string of awards and kudos that continues to this day.

A DIVERSE ARRAY OF AWARD-WINNING ART

While the names "Sandra Kuck" and "Reco" remain synonymous with quality in child-subject art, Heio Reich

◆

Now the beloved Sandra Kuck Treasures *collection figurines have garden accessories to complement their Victorian charms.*

tional acclaim. Now totaling nearly 30 individual issues, the figurines express the same youthful joy and nostalgic charm that endears collectors to her plate art. One of the newest *Treasures* in the series is titled "Friendship and Sharing." In the most intricate detail of sculpting and hand-painting, it shows two lively little girls, dressed in Victorian finery, sharing a cup of tea while their tabby cat rests at their feet. It measures 3-1/2" in height and retails for $50.00. The majority of the figurines retail from $20.00 to $30.00.

To complement her *Treasures*, Kuck and Reco have unveiled a new set of garden accessories that enhance the line. Among the first introductions are a lovely "Rose Gazebo" and a graceful "Cherub Fountain."

Now a very youthful grandmother, Sandra Kuck was inspired to create "Little Valentina" as a christening doll for her *Sandra Kuck Doll* collection. This pretty baby boasts a radiant blush of color and a joyful sparkle in her blue eyes. Her gown is painstakingly tailored by hand and features delicate lace, satin ribbons and layers of eyelet detailing. Her head, arms and legs are crafted of fine, hand-painted porcelain. Each doll is hand-numbered and accompanied by a same-numbered Certificate of Authenticity. At 16-1/2" in length, "Little Valentina" has a retail price of $99.00.

The stunning bride doll "Jennifer Rose" is accompanied by her junior bridesmaid, "Lindsay" and her flower girl, "Aubrey" in another exceptional creation by Sandra Kuck. "Jennifer Rose" wears an heirloom gown combining tiers of satin, lace and tulle. Lavish details abound, from

Reco's Purr-fect Views *plaques, including this whimsical "Town House Cats" piece, are part of the ever-expanding* Art With Dimension *series.*

her embroidered lace "necklace," hem and train, to her elegant bodice, puffed sleeves, headpiece and veil. On the back of her dress, rows of tiny faux pearl buttons lead to a band of elaborate white lace and a richly tailored satin bow at the waistline. The little girls' ruffled outfits and flowing lace hairbows provide the perfect accompaniment. All three dolls are meticulously crafted of fine, bisque porcelain, and painted lovingly by hand.

Also new from Sandra Kuck and Reco is their *Victorian Home* collection, uniting the artist's favorite designs with useful and decorative objects. There are frames, candlesticks, bowls, vases, wreaths, mugs and figurines in this charming new series. Kuck's *Enchanted Gardens* plates feature a unique, decorative gold border and depict children's quiet play in garden settings.

NEW ADDITIONS TO FAVORITE SERIES

Reco is expanding its *Art With Dimension* series from the original *Rooms With a View* to include *Shops With a View, Views of Faith* and *Purr-fect Views.* These bas-relief plaques add a perspective beyond traditional art, and can be hung on a wall or displayed on a small easel. There are a variety of contemporary artists whose works are represented in this unique series, including Fanch Ledan, John O'Brien, Erin Dertner, Guy Buffet, Jimi Claybrooks and Jean Everett.

Reco has recently contracted with Graceland/Elvis Presley Enterprises, Inc., the home of Elvis Presley, to portray rooms from his famous Graceland home in Memphis, Tennessee. These rooms will be portrayed in *Art With Dimension* style.

A new collection in this series will be Gregory Perillo's *Native American Views,* highlighting portraits and scenery of the American Indian. What's more, Reco has new plate series underway with renowned artists, including Gamini Ratnavira, Alan Grant, Sheila Sommerville, Clemente Micarelli, Norbert McNulty, Bradford Brown, Jimi Claybrooks, Sy Barlowe, Vincent DiFate and the late Alan Maley. For more on this diverse array of upcoming introductions, check the Reco web site at www.reco.com.

While Reco's products represent a panorama of artistic styles, media and subjects, Heio Reich's company philosophy unites all creations with a shared vision of excellence. Reich's goal is for the company to create beautiful products to bring enjoyment and a life-long interest and hobby to collectors. Reco's commitment to produce only the very best art on plates and in other media will continue will into the 21st century – just as it has since 1967.

Reco International Corp.
138 Haven Avenue
Port Washington, NY 11050

Phone:
516-767-2400

Fax:
516-767-2409

Web Site:
www.reco.com

E-mail:
RecoInt@aol.com

Collectibles for Every Day and Every Occasion

Among the largest privately owned and operated firms in the industry, Roman, Inc. — an extraordinary blend of creativity, marketing and experience — was founded in 1963 by its President and Owner Ronald T. Jedlinski. A leading producer and exclusive distributor of more than 15,000 giftware items, Roman, Inc. has well established itself in the collectibles arena with its world-renowned *Fontanini® Heirloom Nativities* and award-winning *Seraphim Classics® Collection*. The story of Roman, Inc. is the story of Ron Jedlinski. He started his company with $500 and a car trunk full of inspirational products for the religious market, and now leads one of the foremost gift companies in the U.S.

With a sprinkling of magic dust, the "Magic of Christmas" by D. Morgan, exclusively for Roman, Inc., captures the warmth and tranquillity of the season.

FONTANINI HEIRLOOM NATIVITIES AND SERAPHIM CLASSICS COLLECTION

In 1973, Roman, Inc. became the exclusive North American distributor for *Fontanini Heirloom Nativities*. With this splendid line, Jedlinski partnered Roman with a world-famous name in Italian craftsmanship and positioned his company as the singular North American source for the sought-after collection, prized for its life-like sculpting, meticulous hand-painting and extraordinary attention to detail. For more about *Fontanini Heirloom Nativities*, see pages 76-77.

Renowned for its range of angels, Roman introduced the *Seraphim Classics Collection* in 1994. One of the world's greatest artisans, *Seraphim Classics* Master Sculptor Gaylord Ho has been an integral member of the creative team since the collection's debut. In addition to possessing an exceptional artistic gift, Ho shares with Roman the unwavering commitment to the creation of angels whose ethereal beauty touches the furthest reaches of the imagination. For more about *Seraphim Classics,* see pages 186-187.

HOLIDAY TRADITIONS

Working with the wealth of legends, customs and symbols associated with the holiday season, Roman brilliantly recreates all the traditions of Christmas and more through an impressive array of high quality, attractively priced and imaginative collectibles. Focused on connecting family members in joyful celebration, Roman seeks to foster the sharing of beloved traditions with future generations and to enthusiastically support the creation of lasting happy memories. Each piece in the *Holiday Traditions Collection* honors a specific Christmas legend or custom, and includes the story that inspired it. Introduced in 1997, the collection features the artistry of a number of the company's in-house artists and consistently ranks among the top sellers.

THE MAGIC OF CHRISTMAS COLLECTION

In 1999, Roman enlisted the talents of another extraordinary artist in the celebration of Christmas. One of the most widely published artists in America, D. Morgan honors the truly important things in life with paintings and gentle verses celebrating love and joy. In *The Magic of Christmas Collection*, Morgan's captivating portrayals of tranquillity, embrace the spirit of this enchanting season in three-dimensional form. Based on Morgan's extremely popular Christmas card artwork, each of the four titles in the collection includes a Santa figure and collection of mini-ornaments with a card featuring the art that inspired the designs. The set also includes a verse by the artist and a clear glass star ornament filled with glitter to represent the twinkle always found in Morgan's memorable images.

THE VALENCIA COLLECTION

In 1980, Roman debuted *The Valencia Collection* and captured the aura of the blue Mediterranean in affordably priced glazed porcelain depictions of the Holy Family. Enthusiastically received by retailers and collectors nationwide, the collection remains a cornerstone of the Roman product mix and has expanded to include St. Francis and highly detailed images of the life of Christ. *The Valencia Collection* was produced in Japan exclusively for Roman. Due to significant changes in the Japanese economy, Roman could no longer offer the serenely beautiful, high quality figures at the affordable price. After serious consideration, Roman ceased production of the well-loved *Valencia Collection* in 1995.

In 1997, the prayers of many were answered with the

"The Valencia Nativity" powerfully depicts the arrival of Jesus as an infant in a lowly stable."

re-introduction of *The Valencia Collection*. Jedlinski enlisted Gaylord Ho, the master sculptor responsible for the award-winning *Seraphim Classics* angels, in the recreation of *The Valencia Collection*. The cover of the 1997-98 Inspirational Giftware catalog from Roman featured the "Last Supper" from the new *Valencia Collection* and introduced 11 figurines. Almost unimaginable, the re-introduction of *The Valencia Collection* was more beautiful than ever before and as affordable. In fact, the compelling depiction of the "Last Supper" that debuted in 1997 was priced less than the "Last Supper" from *The Valencia Collection* that debuted in 1983. Crafted with extraordinary grace by Gaylord Ho, *The Valencia Collection's* three dimensional portraits of beloved sacred subjects are painted in the palest of blue-tinted hues, using carefully applied layers of underglazing to further underscore the celestial beauty and flowing artistry that are the signatures of the collection. Seven new figurines were added to the collection in 1998 including "Flight into Egypt," a compelling presentation of Mary and the Baby Jesus riding a weary donkey as Joseph leads the young family to Egypt. This figure would mark another milestone in the collection's history with the first award in 1999 — a much coveted *Collector Editions* "Award of Excellence" in the highly competitive Figurines $50 - $100 category.

"Joyful Promise" is the ninth edition in The Millenium™ Collection, *which will close forever in the year 2000.*

THE MILLENIUM™ COLLECTION

In 1992, long before many of its competitors acknowledged the coming millennium, Roman debuted *The Millenium™ Collection* — the translation of Sister Mary Jean Dorcy's extraordinary scissor-cuttings from the page into new dimensions. Sister Mary Jean's artistic gift was revealed in response to a stern request made by her superior while Sister Mary Jean was only a novice. She had tried all the practical details of convent life, such as cooking, teaching, nursing and bookkeeping, and had repeatedly failed. As a result, she doubted her chances of ever becoming a full-fledged member of the Dominican Order. Well aware of Sister Mary Jean's failures, the Mistress of Novices sent for her, handed her a framed silhouette, and said "here is a perfect paper-cutting; and here is some paper. I presume you have your own scissors. Now go make one just like it." Looking at the elaborately detailed cutting, Sister Mary Jean was nearly certain this seemingly impossible task would lead to her dismissal. Refusing to abandon her dream, she took her scissors, made "one just like it" and stunned the Mistress of Novices with the incredible result. Subsequently, Sister Mary Jean achieved world-wide fame, and her designs appeared

in newspapers, magazines, books and greeting cards for over 50 years. As a devoted member of the Dominican Order, her artistic achievements are paled only by her humanitarian contributions to the world.

From the acclaimed Faro Studios in Italy, Sister Mary Jean's serene depiction of Mary and the infant Jesus quickly sold out as a 2,000-piece limited edition plate. In 1994, limited edition ornaments were introduced to accompany the sought-after collectible plates. Fully dimensional open edition figurines made their *Millenium Collection* debut in 1996. In response to collector enthusiasm, *The Millenium Collection* added beautifully detailed crib medals, wall crosses, photo frames and musicals. In 1998, inspired by Sister Mary Jean Dorcy's flowing style, the collection heralded the addition of new subjects: beautiful depictions of children kneeling in prayer and an enchanting bridal couple.

THE REMEMBER WHEN™ COLLECTION

Slated to feature annually the talent of different artists, the *Remember When™ Collection*, which debuted in 1999, honors and celebrates the wondrous experience of childhood. The 1999 *Remember When Collection* is a brilliant revival of the timeless renderings of children fashioned by Frances Hook. *Remember When* readily captures Hook's enchanting images of children that are both universal in appeal and unlike any other depictions before or since. Understamped with an inspirational verse and featuring a rich blend of bisque and gloss finishes, each highly detailed figure is crafted in Porcelique™ — an innovative ceramic process requiring hand-painting and multiple firings.

For over 40 years, Roman has enchanted collectors with a wide variety of award-winning collectibles. *Fontanini Heirloom Nativities* have become a part of Christmas celebrations for generations. *The Seraphim Classics Collection* inspires many to envision themselves closer to these celestial beings. *Holiday Traditions* seeks to foster joyful celebration and the sharing of beloved customs. In a glitter-filled twinkle, *The Magic of Christmas Collection* memorably captures the spirit of this heartwarming season. *The Valencia Collection* brilliantly presents beloved sacred subjects of the highest quality at extremely affordable prices. *The Millenium Collection* translates Sister Mary Jean Dorcy's extraordinary scissor-cuttings depicting Mary and the infant Jesus into dimensional collectibles, while the *Remember When Collection* honors and celebrates the wondrous experience of childhood. What these diverse lines have in common is Roman, Inc. and a long history of innovative, high quality collectibles.

"Sounds of the Sea" is one of eight introductions from the 1999 Remember When™ Collection *by Roman, Inc.*

Roman, Inc.
555 Lawrence Ave.
Roselle, IL 60172-1599

Phone:
630-529-3000

Fax:
630-529-1121

Web Site:
www.roman.com

It's Like The Circus Coming To Town Every Day!

Growing up in southern California, Ron Lee had two passions: to entertain and to create. Today, he is proud to be accomplishing both, to the delight of collectors everywhere, through his *World of Clowns* collection of figures.

Each character is magnificently sculpted by Ron and hand-painted with a broad spectrum of primary or pastel colors to catch the eyes and hearts of collectors. Ron Lee's *World of Clowns* continues to expand, both in size and success, whether it's with a new license to sculpt more figurines or another attraction at the 30,000 square-foot factory and museum of circus and clown memorabilia, located in Henderson, Nevada. Ron still clings to his original passions and continues to masterfully create collectibles, entertaining all who walk through his company's doors or experience his fabulous sculptures.

RON LEE DEVELOPS SCULPTING TALENTS

Born into a talented family in Burbank, California, Ron literally grew up in the back room of his father's

later, he met and married his wife, Jill, who now manages Ron Lee's World of Clowns. It was also at that time that Ron began sculpting little animal figures in his garage by making wax molds and pouring metal into them. He began by renting space in his father's shop, and as he started making more figurines, he found he required more room. Eventually, Ron pushed his father out of his own store!

However, Ron, who had always loved characters, grew tired of doing bronze figures of animals and wildlife and using dull colors. He created a single small clown – "Hobo Joe" – which has since become his beloved mascot. Ron's

"Ching Ching" is one of 16 figures to debut in Ron Lee's new The Millennium Collection.

father introduced "Hobo Joe" to area gift shops, and a few owners expressed their interest by placing orders, saying, "We think you have something there." As Ron sold more figures, he was encouraged to continue designing and creating new pieces. His collection grew tremendously. It became necessary for him to hire sales representatives to expand the distribution of the collection to gift shops, galleries and collectible stores.

Eventually, Ron rented a building next door to his father's shop and bought that building, as well. In 1990, he sold the buildings and moved his operation to a larger facility in Simi Valley, California, starting his own casting business. He now was completely free to make his popular figurines and share his favorite art form of sculpting.

"I needed to be able to touch, to feel, to turn, to lift, to know it has dimension, a sense of reality," commented Ron. "Even though the figurines I create are, what would you say, fanciful, if I could hold them in my hands, to me they suddenly become alive. They take on life and seem real, almost like children to be cherished and cared for."

FACTORY TOUR GIVES INSIDE LOOK AT RON LEE'S WORLD OF CLOWNS

When Ron Lee decided to expand his business, he also fulfilled a life-long ambition of creating a family-oriented

Ron Lee invites collectors of all ages to visit the Ron Lee World of Clowns Factory and Tour in Henderson, Nevada. The crown jewel of the museum is an authentic, 30' carousel.

floral shop where his love for crafting and natural artistic ability blossomed. It was there that he also learned to work with his hands, using clay, wood and metal. When Ron was ready, his father helped him get started in the business.

A 21-year-old Ron opened a foundry, making bronze sculptures of wildlife and western scenes. Seven years

tour and amusement center. His dreams eventually brought him to the Las Vegas suburb of Henderson, Nevada, where he established the city's premier attraction – Ron Lee's World of Clowns Factory and Tour.

The $3 million project, which took two and a half years to complete, houses the magnificent sculptures that have sold worldwide and now grace the homes of discerning collectors of quality craftsmanship.

The Ron Lee World of Clowns Factory and Tour is an experience unlike any other. Ron didn't just create a factory tour – he provided a wonderland for all ages, a place where you can bring a family and spend the day touring the factory, seeing how clown and animation characters are made from start to finish, visiting the museum, having lunch or a snack in the famed "Carousel Café," browsing in the Ron Lee Gallery and riding the Chance Carousel.

And what a carousel! It's a magnificent and authentic 30', $250,000 carousel, with lights, music and a glorious menagerie of animals and carousel horses that go round and round. Enclosed in a glass pavilion, the breathtaking carousel is a sight to behold at the factory, which sits on 3-1/2 acres in the middle of an 80-acre master plan. Exquisitely designed, the factory boasts beautiful hallways and a charming décor. The museum also houses costumes and props belonging to famous clowns from the past and present.

This enjoyable experience was envisioned by Ron as an "educational and exciting place to be." Visitors can take the self-guided visual and audio tour and actually see each and every step that leads up to a completed Ron Lee sculpture.

RON LEE PRODUCES LIMITED EDITION COLLECTIBLES, FINE ART PRINTS

Ron Lee has carved out another niche in the collectibles market with limited edition sculptures based on familiar circus scenes, classic cartoons, and live action characters from the golden age of television and movies.

"Side Kicks," new from The Millennium Collection, *depicts two merry clown buddies taking a ride on the town.*

As reflected in his company's name, the most recognized collectibles often feature clowns.

Ron has also added a collection of limited edition Giclee fine art canvas prints, each framed and limited to 750 signed and numbered pieces. Four of the prints focus on clowns taking to the

Focused and determined is this clown in "A Swinging Par-Tee" – let's hope he hits the ball!

greens, playing golf; three others feature clowns on trains, planes and a carousel. He is also currently in production on several new series.

COLLECTORS CLUB CAPTURES ENTHUSIASM

Collectors are invited to join Ron Lee's World of Clowns Collectors Club, which continues to grow rapidly due to the increased benefits for members. Currently, over 30,000 avid collectors worldwide proudly call themselves members of the club.

Annual dues are just $30.00 a year, which includes the membership gift of a new clown sculpture annually, newsletters, brochures on new figures and the opportunity to purchase members-only pieces.

Members receive special invitations to grand openings, special events and collectible conventions, where they can meet fellow club members and catch up on all the updates.

CD'S, GALLERY OPENINGS AND MORE

Enormous talent runs through the family. This is evident with the exclusive recording of Ron's daughter's music. Robyn Lee's CD, "A Man With A Dream...," tells the story of Ron's beloved Hobo Joe. Robyn is working on more CD's which will soon be available.

This spring, the second Ron Lee Gallery opened at Masquerade Village, in the Rio Suites Hotel and Casino in Las Vegas.

Collectors can "surf the net" and check out Ron's web site, www.ronlee.com, for up-to-the-minute information on the Ron Lee's World of Clowns, as well as the Factory and Tour.

Ron Lee's enthusiasm is contagious – he loves to share his artistry and his *World of Clowns* with everyone he meets, whether it be through attending collectible conventions, creating new sculptures, or adding memorabilia and fun rides to his museum. He holds all his collectors in the highest regard. He shares that his work – his passion – is like the circus coming to town every day!

Ron Lee's World of Clowns, Inc.
330 Carousel Parkway
Henderson, NV 89014

Phone:
800-829-3928

Fax:
702-434-4310

Web Site:
www.ronlee.com

Purveyors of Exquisite Danish Porcelain

"The goal of my grandfather, the late Harald Bing, was to bring the history and customs of Denmark, 'the world's oldest kingdom,' to collectors everywhere," recalls Ebbe Simonsen, former president of Bing & Grondahl of Denmark. "In 1895, he conceived the idea of the world's first Christmas plate. He wanted not only to create a Christmas greeting or gift of particular quality and beauty, but also a series of Danish sceneries, historic buildings, etc., that would appeal to collectors all over the world, and at the same time make them interested in his beloved mother country."

In centuries past, the European elite would gift their servants at Christmastime with plates of holiday delicacies – cookies, fruits, candies and other treats. Over the years, the plates themselves began to take on more significance for servants and nobles alike. It was here that Harald Bing entered the picture. The entrepreneur wondered if the holiday plate tradition could be extended throughout Danish society. Determined to test his idea during the 1895 Christmas season, Bing commissioned artist F.A. Hallin to create an original work entitled "Behind the Frozen Window." The hand-painted, limited edition plate showcased the Copenhagen skyline as seen through a frosty window pane. The year 1895 and the message "Jule Aften" (Christmas Eve) were scrolled in blue and white around the bottom of the plate.

Bing's idea was embraced by the Danish public with enthusiasm, and "Behind the Frozen Window" became a legendary work of art throughout Europe, and later the world. Made in an edition size of just 400, all plates sold out in quick order, despite what

Royal Copenhagen presents "The Millennium Plate" to celebrate the year 2000.

was then considered a "hefty" price tag of 50¢ per plate. Today, most of the remaining plates from this small edition reside in museums and substantial private collections. On the rare chance that a "Behind the Frozen Window" becomes available at auction, it could command $4,500 to $6,700 or more, according to collectibles experts.

THE HISTORY OF DANISH PORCELAIN

While Bing & Grondahl was the first to present an annual blue-and-white Christmas plate, Royal Copenhagen is the older of the two prestigious Danish porcelain firms. Denmark's Queen Dowager, Juliane Marie, christened what is now Royal Copenhagen as the "Danish Porcelain Factory" in 1775. The Queen had become intrigued by the discovery of Franz Heinrich Muller, a Danish pharmacist and chemist, who happened upon the secret of true hardpaste porcelain in 1772. She was delighted that – like other royal families of Europe – she would now have her own source for treasured hardpaste porcelain.

Because of Denmark's international renown as a seafaring nation, the factory's trademark was developed as three wavy lines, symbolizing the ancient Danish waterways from the Kattegat to the Baltic: the Sound, the Great Belt and the Little Belt. Before long, the trademark and the creations of the Danish Porcelain Factory brought an emotional resurgence of national pride to the people of Denmark.

Arnold Krog, an architect, became art director of Royal Copenhagen in January 1885, and proceeded to develop a fine technique for Danish underglaze painting. This method became the basis for the Royal Copenhagen blue-and-white Christmas plate series.

Bing & Grondahl presents the 1999 "Dancing on Christmas Eve" as its 105th annual Christmas plate.

The Bing & Grondahl studio was founded in 1853 by artist Frederick Grondahl and the brothers Meyer and Jacob Bing. Initially, Bing & Grondahl manufactured and sold figurines, but the popularity of these sculptures was so significant that Danish consumers clamored for more variety. In response, Bing & Grondahl produced elegant dinnerware and coffee services. This remarkable collection rapidly became a benchmark of tabletop fashion across Denmark.

THE CREATION OF "DANISH BLUES"

Both Bing & Grondahl and Royal Copenhagen use a similar process to create their fine collector plates – a method that has remained virtually unchanged for more

"Christmas Eve at Mount Rushmore" is part of The American Heritage Collection.

than 100 years! First, years of drawing, planning and subject evaluation are undertaken by the staff to pick the ideal art. Today at Royal Copenhagen, every employee in the factory is eligible to submit ideas and artwork. When everyone has agreed on the design, a master sculptor crafts a bas-relief model.

Painstakingly, a plaster of Paris copy is sculpted. This will determine the all-important master mold, so it must be perfect. Finally, a cast bronze image becomes central to the production process, acting as the permanent master. From it, plaster molds are recreated, and only 20 plates are made from each before the plaster is destroyed. This is a demanding production method, but one that must be followed to meet stringent quality control standards.

Plates are now ready for firing and decorating in the world-famous "underglaze technique." Colors are applied carefully by artisans receiving special training. Because exact shades of blue don't emerge until the final firing has taken place, craftsmen must know how to adjust the intensity of their colors to attain a perfect finished product.

Before the final firing, the authentication process must be completed. The date and artist's initials are placed on the backstamp, and the studio's logo is applied. Each plate is carefully dipped into glaze, then fired. In the kiln, kaolin, quartz and feldspar meld into a hard paste over a 24-hour period. The precise 2700°F temperature melts the glaze and creates an everlasting, glass-like surface of shimmering "Copenhagen Cobalt Blue."

If an issue is examined and found undesirable for a reason determined by the quality control team, the plate is destroyed. Since production of all Bing & Grondahl and Royal Copenhagen plates is strictly limited by year, this examination process is particularly critical. Of course, all molds are destroyed at the end of a year's production.

TWO STUDIOS RETAIN DISTINCTIVE STYLES

While Christmas plates were the initial claims to international collectible fame for both Bing & Grondahl and Royal Copenhagen, each firm has enjoyed many other successes as well. Bing & Grondahl, for example, initiated the world's first *Mother's Day* plate series in 1969 with "Dog and Puppies." The collection continues with sought-after annual issues to this day. Royal Copenhagen also produced a very popular *Motherhood* plate series from 1982 to 1987.

For 1999, Royal Copenhagen looks forward to the next 1,000 years with *The Millennium Collection*, featuring "The Millennium Plate," "The Millennium Plaquette" and "The Millennium Figurines." The motif for these pieces, designed by artist Sven Vestergaard, contains a wealth of symbolic details, illustrating our hopes for the new generations. The 7" plate comes with a Certificate of Authenticity and has a retail price of $72.50.

The 1999 Royal Copenhagen Christmas plate is "The Sleigh Ride."

The plaquette, a 3" miniature plate, retails for $19.50. The figurines portray the two children from the plate artwork. Each measures 3-1/2" in height, sells for $49.50, and is handsomely gift-boxed.

Royal Copenhagen's 2000 annual Christmas plate is "Trimming the Tree," by Sven Vestergaard. The plate's delicate motif is reproduced in miniature on the Christmas Bell and Christmas Drop Ornament. The Christmas Cup and Saucer and the small Figurine Ornament entitled "Hans" also belong to this grouping. The Christmas Plate, "Trimming the Tree," measures 7-1/8 in diameter. Its suggested retail price is $72.50. "Hans," the Figurine Ornament, is 3" tall and has a suggested retail price of $25.00. To learn more about these new releases, and the new Bing and Grondahl Christmas Plate, call Royal Copenhagen at (800) 431-1992.

Although Bing & Grondahl and Royal Copenhagen have exchanged technicians and artists over the years, their Christmas plates and other elegant issues have maintained their distinctive styles, which are obvious to the discerning collector. No other Christmas plates in the world have ever come close to the popularity of the "Danish Blues." Part of their strength is due to tradition, part to artistic brilliance. But perhaps most important of all is the fact that these are the only truly hand-decorated plates in the world of collectibles.

Royal Copenhagen/
Bing & Grondahl
41 Madison Avenue
New York, NY 10010

Phone:
800-431-1992

Fax:
856-768-9726

A World-Renowned Leader in Collectibles

In 1815, John Doulton invested his life savings in a small London pottery, which produced practical and decorative stoneware with a single kiln. By the turn of the century, the business was at the forefront of the ceramics and china industry, and was authorized by His Majesty King Edward VII to use the word "Royal" to describe its products.

Today, Royal Doulton is a world-renowned leader in bone china giftware and collectibles. Five generations have treasured the fine collectibles from the famed British firm. From the familiar and beloved characters of Beatrix Potter™ and Winnie-the-Pooh™ to the timeless *Bunnykins*™, Royal Doulton achieves excellence in quality and design.

Regarded as the world's largest manufacturer and distributor in the premium ceramic tableware and giftware market, Royal Doulton also includes the Royal Crown Derby, Minton and Royal Albert brands — each of which is internationally recognized for its innovative designs and modern production techniques. Together, these divisions total more than 1,000 years of history and tradition.

Royal Doulton continues this history. Many of the company's collectibles have or will soon become heirlooms, passed down for children and future generations to enjoy.

PRETTY LADIES ENCHANT COLLECTORS

To collect in harmonious themes, to celebrate special occasions, to mark memorable family moments... what could be more appropriate than a beautiful figure from this superb range of lady figurines? From the charming elegance of society ladies to the graceful movement implied by the ballroom dancers, they offer romantic inspiration for collectors and gift buyers alike. Every new figure launched in this collection has been carefully researched, sensitively modeled and decorated to complement the tastes of today. This collection includes modern colorful interpretations of traditional ideals, elegant poses honoring charitable causes, and graceful models based on famous people. Some are simply exquisite new ideas for the ever-popular *Crinoline Ladies Collection*.

The fourth figure in the Seaside Holiday collection, *"Mother Bunnykins," is the 1999 "Bunnykins of the Year."*

CHARACTER JUGS ARE "HANDLED" CREATIVELY

Royal Doulton Character Jugs can trace their ancestry to the beginning of the pottery industry. All Character Jugs are supremely detailed and decorated to reflect with expressive clarity the features of the subject. The handles of Character Jugs, which have been an integral part of the overall design since the mid-1950s, have become even more elaborate on limited edition jugs produced in the

"Faith" is the second in a series of Royal Doulton figurines to benefit breast cancer charities worldwide.

1990s. Intricate handles have included modeled faces or figures, while the first three-handled model was issued in 1992. The almost limitless scope of Royal Doulton Character Jugs promises subjects to suit collectors of all interests!

BUNNYKINS™ CELEBRATE FAMILY AND CHILDHOOD DELIGHTS

For more than 60 years, Royal Doulton's *Bunnykins* characters have been found in nurseries and homes around the world. The whimsical *Bunnykins* family has delighted collectors for generations.

The world of *Bunnykins* was created in 1934 by Barbara Vernon, a young nun who taught history at an English convent school. In her spare time, she illustrated the simple antics of a family of bunnies. Her sketches caught the attention of her father, the general manager of Royal Doulton's Burslem Pottery Studio, who had them turned into a range of products. By 1937, there was a new world of *Bunnykins* in earthenware and bone china. *Bunnykins* has stood the test of time, proving itself with an enduring appeal of childhood imagination and innocent pleasures.

BEATRIX POTTER'S FAMOUS CHARACTERS COME TO LIFE

A little over 100 years ago, the fairy tale world of Beatrix Potter began with the charming stories of Peter Rabbit, Jemima Puddleduck and Benjamin Bunny. For half of those years, Beatrix Potter's animal creations have delighted collectors and children all over the world as ceramic sculptures and nurseryware by Royal Doulton.

Royal Doulton's development of the Beatrix Potter

figurines is credited to Lucy Beswick, wife of the studio's chairman. In the 1940s, she was fascinated with Potter's stories and illustrations and thought the character Jemima Puddleduck would make a charming clay figurine. The sculpture was so well received that Beswick Studios received permission to reproduce other familiar characters. By the middle of 1947, Jemima was joined by friends Peter Rabbit, Tom Kitten, Timmy Tiptoes, Squirrel Nutkin and Mrs. Tittlemouse, among several others.

Many of Potter's stories are told through the figurines, which are portrayed in characteristic settings. Today, millions of collectors eagerly await the newest introductions.

CLASSIC POOH® CHARMS COLLECTORS OF ALL AGES

A much loved range of items by Royal Doulton is inspired by classic Ernest H. Shepard illustrations from *Winnie the Pooh* and *The House at Pooh Corner*. Pooh and his friends Christopher Robin, Eeyore, Tigger, Piglet, Owl, Rabbit, Kanga and Roo are featured in some of the best-loved scenes from the books. Children and their parents continue to be captivated by these stories.

The *Classic Pooh* range by Royal Doulton is composed of nursery, gift and teaware items of heirloom quality to be used and enjoyed now, and then passed down from one generation to the next. They make mealtime more enjoyable, and can provide the finishing touch to a nursery or bedroom with images of childhood, playtime and friends.

Dressed in early 1930s evening wear, "Eve" from the Classique Collection has stolen away from the ball for a moment of reverie.

ROYAL CROWN DERBY PAPERWEIGHTS ADD TO COMPANY'S SUCCESS

The birth of the Royal Crown Derby series of paperweights can be traced to a special event held at Chatsworth House in 1981, when, together with a number of new designs for tableware, the firm introduced six paperweights in animal form. The initial offering included an Owl, Duck, Quail, Penguin, Wren and Rabbit. These new designs signified Royal Crown Derby's commitment to the processes of renewal and innovation. These processes are vital in developing new products suited to contemporary fashions and tastes. As its subsequent history proves, the paperweight range was an imaginative and well-conceived response to new challenges, and the first six weights provided the foundations for a remarkable success story for Royal Crown Derby.

Since the product line launch, nearly one hundred models of *Royal Crown Derby Paperweights* have been created, achieving enduring popularity and quickly becoming collectors' items. Originally, they were filled with sand at the factory, and a small simulated-gold stopper was inserted in the basal holes after filling. Due

Royal Crown Derby's "Sleeping Piglet" and "Sitting Piglet" paperweights reveal the designer's distinctive approach to integrating his sculptural work and graphic decoration.

to increased transport costs, the addition of sand was discontinued, and the weight of the clay was increased to be more robust. The practice of adding the simulated-gold stoppers has continued. These paperweights are a series of useful and aesthetically attractive objects that have broad appeal.

CLASSIQUE COLLECTION RECREATES THE AGE OF ELEGANCE

The *Classique Collection* is a new style of figures which has proven appeal among new customers and which promises to widen the Royal Doulton customer base beyond traditional collectors.

The *Classique Collection* uses the properties of cold cast resin to introduce slim, elegant figures, all with a wealth of sculpted and hand-painted detail. These exquisite figurines faithfully recreate the designs of the early 1900s, which defined great epochs in style. One can easily note that the folds and textures of the dresses and jewelry are all reproduced to perfection. Poised in a moment from the past, these sophisticated ladies speak proudly of the elegance of their era!

INTERNATIONAL COLLECTORS CLUBS

The tremendous enthusiasm for The Royal Doulton Company's gifts and collectibles prompted them to form the Royal Doulton International Collectors Club and the Royal Crown Derby Collectors Guild. Thousands of members worldwide receive information to further their awareness and understanding of Royal Doulton and Royal Crown Derby. Members also have the opportunity to add to their collections as the Club and Guild offer exclusive pieces each year. Among the other benefits are a quarterly magazine, free tours of the factories in England, and a historical inquiry service helping members identify and date unusual items.

Club headquarters is established in England with branches in Australia, Canada, Europe, New Zealand and America, ensuring that all members are kept up-to-date with what is happening in their part of the Royal Doulton and Royal Crown Derby worlds. For more information on the Royal Doulton International Collectors Club and Royal Crown Derby Collectors Guild, see page 223.

Royal Doulton USA
701 Cottontail Lane
Somerset, NJ 08873

Phone:
800-68-CHINA
800-682-4462

Fax:
732-764-4974

Web Site:
www.royal-doulton.com

E-mail:
inquiries@royaldoultonusa.com

Capturing the Proud Spirit of Ethnic Collectibles

When Sandy Dolls' made their debut with the *Native American* series and *The Warrior & Princess* series in April, 1994, it was a dream-come-true for Robert N. Nocera. For years, he had dreamed of presenting historically researched and authentically attired Native American dolls to the collectibles market. And when the Sandy Corporation of Manila, the Philippines, approached him to do just that only a few months earlier, he moved quickly.

Since then, Sandy Dolls has become Sandy USA and has grown and flourished, expanding its lines to bring to market high quality, ethnic products designed with respect and dignity according to the needs and wishes of the collector.

DEDICATED TO HEAVENLY DIVERSITY

Near the end of its first year of operation, Sandy Dolls introduced its first collection of angels featuring the same exquisite sculpting as its dolls, and each lavishly robed in sumptuous gowns of satin and velvet. *The Angelic Collection* met with instant success and, over the years, has developed into a full line of holiday designs that include coordinating ornaments.

Realizing that interest in ethnic art extended far beyond Native American designs, the company debuted *The African American Angelic Collection* in 1995. The very first angel in the series, "Asha," was such a success that even on Christmas Eve, retailers were still trying to order her! Since then, each design in the collection has been created based on the advice and comments of both consumers and retailers, assuring tremendous success for each new introduction.

The Santa Collection features both Caucasian and African-American characters and brings new meaning to the Yuletide holiday, while renewing the belief of young and old in the jovial goodness of Father Christmas.

"Gentle Moon - Nez Perce Girl" from the Gentle Dreams Baby *series by doll artist Ruben Tejada is authentically costumed and sits on a blanket based on Native American designs.*

The success of the Native American doll lines and the African-American holiday line quickly led to the development of new products in those market segments. *The Sweet Spirit Baby* series of toddler dolls debuted in 1995. These delightful dolls are the work of acclaimed artist Ruben M. Tejada, whose 20 years' experience as an ethnic doll designer shines through in every one of these marvelous, vinyl and cloth creations.

"Tahirah" from the African American Angelic Collection by Gigi Dy-Sy is robed in heavenly elegance...a white satin gown with gold satin inlays.

Each doll in the series carries a handcrafted and authentic accessory which can be detached. For example, the first in the series, "Little Blossom," carries a dream-catcher made by Native American craftsmen. It can be removed from her hand and used over the bed, cradle, or crib of a baby or small child.

SARAH'S GANG...LESSONS IN VALUES

Since 1995, the company has been introducing new dolls based on the popular *Sarah's Gang* figurines from Sarah's Attic. Designed by Sarah Schultz, this multicultural line has been well received, especially in the educational market where they are used to teach children understanding and encourage the development of values. There are currently eight dolls in the collection: "Willie," who focuses on respect; "Tillie" and "Buddy," who teach about manners; "Katie," who stresses responsibility; "Maria," who celebrates gratitude; "Miguel," who espouses patience; "Shina," who offers forgiveness; and "Sammy," who recommends honesty.

Each 11" *Sarah's Gang* doll comes with an eight-page booklet proclaiming a specific value and written as if that character were speaking to other children. As their creator Sarah Schultz says, "Our world needs this 'Good Gang.'"

ANNIE LEE'S PAINTINGS COME TO LIFE

Sandy USA is also the exclusive licensee of *Sass 'N Class by Annie Lee*. Lee's paintings of African-American family life are sold throughout the United States and Europe, and her work has been shown on episodes of such television shows as "ER," "Hanging with Mr. Cooper," "A Different World," "227," and "Amen," and in Eddie Murphy's movies *Coming to America* and *Boomerang*. Indeed Lee's art

"Love Song" from the Sass 'N Class by Annie Lee *collection captures a warm, romantic moment with the artist's special brand of humor and nostalgia.*

has been internationally acclaimed and warmly received not only by the African-American culture, but also by art lovers everywhere.

The *Sass 'N Class by Annie Lee* series is currently composed of resin figurines recreated from the artist's original canvas artwork. The collection, which has captured the satire, humor, and real life emotions of Annie Lee's paintings, has been a huge success since the very first pieces were unveiled in October of 1997.

ANGELIC MESSENGERS OF GOOD WILL

During the same period, *SoulMates* by Sandra Bedard was introduced. Each adorable, little 4" African-American angel, with its delightfully heart-melting expression, is costumed in a special occasion outfit. Each of these brightly costumed little angel children is the bearer of happy tidings: "Happy Birthday," "Get Well," "Missing You," and "To a Special Friend." In addition, the second release of the popular *Birthstone Babies* collection of little resin figurines, also by Sandra Bedard, was announced in January, 1999.

In the summer of 1998, the company introduced *The Angelic Maille' Collection* comprised of angels exquisitely crafted of wire mesh. Each angel appears to be floating – as only an angel can – and is simultaneously delicate, elegant and strong. A truly unique type of angel that captures the essence of beauty and grace, these works of art are available in Caucasian and African-American designs, and in a choice of gold or silver gowns.

Also released at that time was the *Gentle Dreams Baby* series of Native American dolls, posed in seated positions, and only 7" in height. Each little doll comes clutching a woven blanket based on authentic Native American designs. This series was developed in response to collectors' many requests for a smaller version of the *Sweet Spirit Baby* series which sits at 11" tall. The *Gentle Dreams Baby* dolls are not only adorable, but their authentic attire is completely accurate in every detail, so that each is a lovable tribute to the very first Americans.

SANDY DECKS THE HALLS WITH HOLIDAY ELEGANCE

To enhance Sandy USA's angels in holiday displays, the firm also has introduced a series of handcrafted and very elegant ball ornaments made of high quality velvets, velours and satins. Their exquisite trims include faux pearls and gems, gold decorative braid, colored bead and ribbon. All have been specifically designed to coordinate with and enhance the firm's richly gowned angels and elaborately garbed Santas, but of course, each ball may also be purchased independent of their angel or Santa counterpart.

Because of Sandy USA's exclusive relationship to its parent company, Sandy Corporation, the firm has been able to respond immediately to the needs and wants of customers – bringing new designs to the marketplace within four to six months of origination.

Since extensive research is required for all of the authentic, ethnic-themed products, there is a constant and ongoing education process which has been both fascinating and inspirational. Sandy USA never releases a product until its management team is completely satisfied with it, and certain of its quality, accuracy and authenticity.

A CONTINUING COMMITMENT TO COLLECTORS

With all the firm's products, including its seasonal designs, Sandy Corporation helps ensure that all fabrics and adornments are of the highest quality available. The dolls and seasonal collections are crafted in Manila, while the resin figurines are made both in Manila and in Guangzhou, China.

Sandy USA pledges always to grow and diversify according to the demands of its collectors and its dealers. Returning the loyalty of its collectors by providing them with the products that will bring them joy is the goal of Sandy USA. Six years after Sandy USA's founding, Robert Nocera and his staff confirm that they are thrilled and proud to be part of the collectibles industry!

"February" from Birthstone Babies by Sandra Bedard *portrays a precious little angel holding a faux amethyst, while she gets comfortable on a cloud.*

Sandy USA
3031 E. Cherry St.
Springfield, MO 65802

Phone:
800-607-2639

Fax:
417-831-4477

The Premier Resource for Rare and Exceptional Gifts

Designed by Ellen Kamysz, the "Scheherazade Carousel" is crafted in cloisonné and part of an edition limited to 500.

When San Francisco's bustling Pier 39 opened in 1978, The San Francisco Music Box & Gift Company was one of the original stores at the internationally famous shopping site. Just a stone's throw from the famed Fisherman's Wharf, that first store opened its door on October 4, 1978 with only 500 square feet of space. Within weeks, it was clear that this would become one of the most popular establishments on the Pier.

Buoyed by their success, store founders Marcia and John Lenser exercised their entrepreneurial flair with great optimism, and soon opened a second location in a traditional suburban mall. The mall store also proved successful, so the Lensers expanded their scope again and again. By 1991, when the Venator Group bought the thriving chain, there were already 100 locations nationwide. Now, the company boasts 165 stores in 35 states (plus approximately 175 more stores for the holiday season) — as well as a nationally-distributed catalog reaching over 10,000,000 households annually.

In January 1999, the company introduced its wholesale channel of distribution, making available to select giftware dealers the first fully assorted collection of musical giftware. Currently, over 350 retailers have signed agreements to become authorized dealers. The company is one of the first gift and collectibles retailers to ever expand into the wholesale market, presenting the unique ability to provide dealers with authoritative knowledge on the existing or potential success of their product lines.

ADAPTING TO CHANGING TRENDS

The San Francisco Music Box & Gift Company carries over 2,000 musical gifts and collectibles. These truly unique gifts, designed with a touching, personal quality, and combined with the sweet, nostalgic sound of a music box, entice customers back time and time again. It's the old-fashioned gentle chiming of a music box that makes these gifts so distinctive, bringing back memories and touching the heart every time the music plays. The

company's wide variety of products is sure to satisfy anyone searching for all-occasion gifts — from the thoughtful, "just-because" gifts, to exquisite heirloom-quality collections for milestone events.

Exclusive licensed products developed by the company include *Phantom of the Opera, Betty Boop, National Geographic* and *Raggedy Ann and Andy.* In 1999, the company premiered their eight-piece *Gone With the Wind* and eleven-piece *Wizard of Oz* collections. Time has not diminished the appeal of these two classic films, nor the quest for collectibles from these icons of the entertainment industry. Therefore, the company is confident these new lines of licensed collectibles will become very popular.

The San Francisco Music Box & Gift Company is the largest purveyor of handcrafted wood-inlay music boxes from Sorrento, Italy, offered with 18-note and 36-note musical movements. These treasured boxes are created from the Renaissance art of intarsio, a traditional craft of wood inlay practiced only in a few tiny workshops in the region. When you add the personalization of selecting a tune close to one's heart, these wonderful masterpieces are truly a treasured keepsake.

The San Francisco Music Box & Gift Company's product development group creates over 70% of the company's proprietary lines of musical gifts and collectibles. Led by Diane Burlando, vice president of product development, their offerings include a line of collectible dolls, an extensive selection of figurines and their signature product — beautiful carousels of heirloom quality.

AN UNPARALLED COLLECTION OF MUSICAL CAROUSELS

The company's line of carousels is designed exclusively for its stores, catalogs and wholesale division. The company considers itself without peer when it comes to creating the four-horse, six-horse, and 12-animal merry-go-round. During its 21-year history, the company has developed over 200 exclusive carousel subjects. In fall 1999, the company introduced The *Chinoiserie Collection* by Maureen Drdak which carries oriental embellishments. This collection includes a limited edition

The new musical "Wizard of Oz" figurine is sure to be welcomed by a whole new generation of fans of this American classic.

The "Victorian Father Christmas" and "Victorian Snow Angel" are part of the Sentimental Rose Christmas Collection *designed by Ellen Kamysz.*

6-horse merry-go-round, a double-horse with canopy, and an 8" horse, as well as two waterglobes.

In 1999, the San Francisco Music Box & Gift Company introduced a 500-piece limited edition cloisonné carousel titled "Scheherazade." Each of these stunning limited edition showpieces is signed and hand-numbered by the artist, Ellen Kamysz. Collectors will be mesmerized by these exotic animals that glide up and down on 24K gold-plated brass poles, as they revolve beneath the turning canopy. A press of the gold coin, minted with the edition number and mounted on the base, sets the horses in motion to the tune of "Scheherazade" by composer/writer Kimsky Korsakov. Developed during the Byzantine Empire over a millennium ago, the art of cloisonné enamel is still practiced with the same meticulous handcraftsmanship by master artisans. The fine craft is exacted in this solid work made of brass and enamels in graduating shades of rich color. The intricate cloisonné carousel, standing 15" tall, is truly a work of art to be appreciated by the most discriminating collector.

OFFERING AN EVER-GROWING MAGICAL HOLIDAY COLLECTION

The San Francisco Music Box & Gift Company's collection of magical holiday products has steadily grown over the years. Recent introductions include the *Sentimental Rose Collection* featuring Victorian figurines and the *Winter Wonderland Collection* of dynamically sculpted, pearlescent figurines accented with brilliant red, green and gold. Additionally, the company is introducing a very special collectible line appropriately named *Peaceful Kingdom*. Designed by John Kissling, this series of figurines is inspired by nature's wonders and serenity, and centers around a nostalgic Father Christmas and a gathering of his forest friends. The hallmark of each

Artist Marjorie Sarnat creates mystical magic as Merlin meets the Dragon in a challenging game of chess, which is part of the Crystal Visions® Collection.

piece is his ever-vigilant feathered friend, a cardinal who can always be found somewhere on the sculptured piece.

Over 60 musical ornaments were introduced in 1999 which have been developed exclusively for the company. From the elegant *Le Blanc* and *Designer Collections*, to dozens of other heirloom-qulaity, hand-painted musical ornaments, each ornament is crafted to the company's high standards and designed to be cherished for many happy years.

Each graceful ornament in the *Le Blanc Collection* is made from the finest jade porcelain, known for its rich, glossy cream color. Exquisitely cast details, hand-painted gold highlights and the translucent porcelain make the ornaments an heirloom for the collector, touching the heart with the joy of music. The *Designer Series* features creations from artists Matthew Danko, Maureen Drkak and Marjorie Sarnat. This collection includes ornaments inscribed with endearing sentiments, storybook characters and plenty of rich, striking colors, as well as original themes.

These ornaments, along with many other holiday collectibles and gifts for the home, can be found in The San Francisco Music Box & Gift Company stores located across the country, as well as in the pages of their most recent catalog, and online at www.sfmusicbox.com.

INCREASING CONSUMER RECOGNITION AND COLLECTIBILITY

The company is constantly evolving their product assortment to adapt to the changing trends within the gift and home decorating industries. This fact, along with the positive response from gift retailers to The San Francisco Music Box & Gift Company's recent entrance into the wholesale gift market, has led to the company's high expectations for increasing consumer recognition and collectibility of their exclusive product lines.

Janet Thompson, vice president of marketing communications for the company, says, "It would be hard to find another resource for the rare and exceptional treasures we offer. Like the city we call home, we are an original." Thompson invites collectors to discover this for themselves by visiting the company on the World Wide Web at www.sfmusicbox.com. The site's unique attribute is a "Play Me" feature where customers can listen to tune selections. By listening to the tune and having the product pictured, the true musical charm of The San Francisco Music Box & Gift Company products is captured.

The company prides itself on its very generous Lifetime Guarantee which states: "We guarantee your satisfaction with every wind-up music box you purchase from us for life. If you are ever dissatisfied with your purchase for whatever reason — at any time — we'll replace it at no cost to you or reimburse you 100%."

THE SAN FRANCISCO MUSIC BOX & GIFT COMPANY

The San Francisco
Music Box & Gift Company
390 North Wiget Lane,
Suite 200
Walnut Creek, CA 94598

Phone:
925- 939-4800

Mail Order:
800-227-2190

Fax:
925-927-2999

Web Site:
www.sfmusicbox.com

The Most Angels This Side of Heaven

"Serenity — Trusting Soul" represents a recent addition to the Seraphim Classics® Collection.

For more than three decades, Roman, Inc., has been a recognized leader in inspirational gifts and collectibles. Founder and CEO Ron Jedlinski made his company renowned for its range of angels — the most angels this side of heaven. So when the national trend turned once again toward angels in a wide scope of roles and interpretations, Roman was already positioned as the industry source for the most majestic of winged heralds.

It was in the early 1990s that Jedlinski moved to form Seraphim Studios, a creative umbrella of world-famous artists and sculptors. Their singular assignment was to research and develop a collection that would be modern interpretations of the world's most beautiful angels. Seraphim Studios took advantage of more than 2,000 years of writings and works of art to achieve their objective. The result was introduced to the world in 1994: the *Seraphim Classics® Collection.*

Based on the greatest artistic achievements of the Renaissance Masters, the collection immediately won the enthusiastic acceptance of both retailers and consumers. Within a single year, it was apparent that the collection was destined to be a collectible. Numerous awards

These five Heavenly Reflections *figurines and their resin pond base have been created to mark the fifth anniversary of the* Seraphim Classics® Collection.

followed, including extensive honors from *Collector Editions* magazine and NALED. These prestigious awards confirmed collector enthusiasm, as authorized dealers found it difficult to keep up with demand for the highly detailed, flowing sculptures with their pale, pastel wings.

CREATING *SERAPHIM CLASSICS*

Creating the world's most beautiful angels is a complicated and time-intensive undertaking. Following are the details of the process used in creating "America's Number One Angel Collection."

Angel design begins with sketches and may spring from a variety of sources including artists, collectors and store owners. Gaylord Ho, Master Sculptor for Seraphim Studios, transforms the sketch into a three-dimensional clay model. Seraphim Studios creates a "mother mold" using thin layers of silicone painted over the clay model. Additional layers of silicone are added to thicken the mold. The silicone mother mold is peeled from the clay. Upon completion, a perfect negative of the sculpt is created.

After the mother mold is cleaned and all remnants of clay are removed, a sample figurine is cast. Only 4 or 5 of these samples can be cast in the mother mold before the intricate details begin to deteriorate. Once the sample is approved, a "master mold" is cast in the mother mold. One master mold is used to make production molds from which the *Seraphim Classics* angels are cast.

The *Seraphim Classics* figurines are formulated of resin, porcelain powder and marble dust which yields a mixture with the consistency of pancake batter. It is poured into the production molds and left to harden for approximately five minutes. The hardened figure — with all of the details on the original sculpt — is removed from the mold.

After washing, the figure is trimmed to eliminate any mold lines. Polishing is a step that is unique to the *Seraphim Classics Collection*, and involves hours of painstaking hand labor. It is this step that creates the translucence that gives the figures their life-like glow.

Each figurine then is meticulously hand-painted using a special pastel palette. Talented and well-trained artists paint the features of each *Seraphim Classics* angel.

A gold understamp on the base of each *Seraphim Classics* angel provides an assurance of authenticity. Since 1996, the understamp has also included a year of production mark: a harp for 1996, a dove for 1997, a heart for 1998 and a long-stemmed rose adorning the number five for 1999, the fifth anniversary of the line.

At each step of the production process, quality inspections are done before a figure moves to the next phase. At the packing table, a final inspection assures that every *Seraphim Classics* angel shipped is as perfect as humanly possible. Each angel is then wrapped, packed and shipped to Roman for distribution to *Seraphim Classics* dealers, and ultimately to *Seraphim Classics* collectors.

The 1999 Symbol of Membership Angel for the Seraphim Classics Collectors Club is "Eve — Tender Heart."

COLLECTION HIGHLIGHTED BY SPECIAL EVENTS PROGRAM

Although the collection is relatively small — necessitated both by the intricacy of production and the limited time the collection has been offered — it is nonetheless well established in the collectibles industry. In 1996, the first figures were retired; in 1997, three more attained this status; in 1998, an additional four were heralded with this honor; and, in 1999, five joined the celebrated ranks of retired figurines. Annual limited editions and special editions are offered, already gaining in value on the secondary market as they are withdrawn from production.

The collection is supported by an extensive special events program, launched in 1996. The program consists of annual Limited Edition Event Angels featured at authorized *Seraphim Classics* dealers' open houses and personal appearances. The annual Limited Edition Event Angel is available exclusively at special events and can only be purchased on event days.

In 1997, personal appearances by The Seraphim Classics Angel and Rosemary, the Seraphim Classics Messenger, were added to the special events program. The majestically winged *Seraphim Classics* Angel is available for free keepsake photographs with collectors and is authorized to mark angels purchased during events with an "Angel's Touch." Rosemary is the official spokesperson for the *Seraphim Classics Collection* and is authorized to sign angels purchased during events.

The angelic emissaries of America's number-one angel collectible were warmly received by collectors as they participated in a variety of activities, including presentation of "Angel on Earth Awards"

"Hope —Light in the Distance" was an event-exclusive musical figurine from which part of the proceeds went to support the Susan G. Komen Breast Cancer Foundation.

to local citizens. These awards, presented by the dealer and Roman, recognize individuals and their selfless acts and deeds that exemplify the qualities associated with angels.

For three years, the *Seraphim Classics* special events program has been dedicated to the good works and caring spirit of The Sunshine Foundation®, a not-for-profit organization that grants wishes to critically and terminally ill children. Recognized as "The Original Dream Makers®," The Sunshine Foundation was founded more than 30 years ago by Bill Sample, who remains at the helm of the organization. As a result of the *Seraphim Classics* events program, Roman has donated more than $200,000 to the Foundation.

Since 1998, Roman has sponsored "Be An Angel Month" and marshaled the efforts of its nationwide network of authorized *Seraphim Classics* dealers to support the Susan G. Komen Breast Cancer Foundation. An aggressive awareness and fundraising campaign, "Be An Angel Month" teams *Seraphim Classics* dealers with the Komen Foundation in its efforts to eradicate breast cancer as a life-threatening disease. Roman further supports the cause with a $500,000 pledge generated through sales of special limited edition angels dedicated to the Komen Foundation. The event-exclusive musical version of "Hope —Light in the Distance," was the primary focus of the October 1999 "Be An Angel Month." "Hope" graces the top of a heart-shaped music box brilliantly accented with intricately sculpted roses and ribbons. This musical followed two successful predecessors from the *Seraphim Classics Collection* featuring the image of "Hope" — the limited edition figurine and ornament.

THE SERAPHIM CLASSICS COLLECTORS CLUB℠

The popularity and collectibility of the collection was validated when, in 1997, Roman, Inc. announced the formation of The Seraphim Classics Collectors Club℠...A Club For People Who Care. Beginning in its 1998 charter year, the club has focused on the premise that helping others is the highest calling for its members. Members receive an exclusive Symbol of Membership angel figure; a specially designed club pin; a personalized membership card; a 12-month subscription to the official club newsletter, "The Seraphim Classics Herald," mailed quarterly; an annual *Seraphim Classics* catalog; and the opportunity to purchase the exclusive members-only Angel. Dues for 1999 are $55.00, plus $4.50 shipping and handling, with $5.00 of each charter membership donated to The Sunshine Foundation.

Roman, Inc.
555 Lawrence Avenue
Roselle, IL 60172-1599

Phone:
630-529-3000

Fax:
630-529-1121

Web Site;
www.roman.com

Creating a Legacy of Fine Doll Making

From its beginning over 30 years ago, Seymour Mann, Inc. has become internationally recognized as one of the great collectible doll companies in the world. "Dolls are our passion," states Gideon Oberweger, CEO of Seymour Mann. "Any company can make a doll, but only an artist can breathe life into it."

When Seymour Mann started making its own dolls, the firm mainly created versions of antiques. They were highly successful, as were Seymour Mann's stunning art deco dolls created in the 1970s. Seymour Mann himself enjoys a great love of porcelain. As Oberweger notes, "He always treats it as a precious medium. He knew from the beginning that great makers could translate the artist's originals into more affordable versions." Indeed, Seymour Mann's marketing and design staff wanted to grow and improve, and they knew that the industry was capable of producing dolls that had never really existed before, except as one-of-a-kinds.

Valerie Pike created "Turandot," and she and Seymour Mann have been tapped for a "Doll of Excellence" nomination for this work of art.

FRUITFUL ARTISTIC COLLABORATIONS

The studio's first doll artist was a lady who Oberweger describes as "The Incredible Pat Kolesar." He credits her with teaching everyone at Seymour Mann how to respect a doll artist's vision. Kolesar remains one of the firm's best friends, even as Seymour Mann continues licensing new artists. The goal of Seymour Mann is to work hard to reproduce a new version of an expensive doll at an accessible price, rather than to cheapen it into something more prosaic.

As Oberweger states, "We have many artists who are stunned at how much our dolls replicate their originals. This is great for the collector because they get the advantage of buying superior dolls at very reasonable prices. On the other hand, it also forces the artists to be more creative in their own editions, which is also great for collectors." As an example, Oberweger points out that artist Hanna Hyland ordinarily sculpts in wood, but

creates in porcelain for Seymour Mann. Thus, she maintains two completely different collector bases.

After more than 30 years in the business, Seymour Mann's staff often is asked which are their favorite dolls. They usually reply that picking just a few from the many beautiful dolls is truly impossible. What's more, because the doll industry advances quickly, dolls improve dramatically from year to year. A Seymour Mann doll produced in 1995 is still beautiful, but it is not as complicated or as great a value as a doll produced in 1999, according to Oberweger. He adds, "Of course, some dolls stick in our minds, such as Pamela Phillips' 'Nizhoni' or Sandra Billato's 'Precious.' These were very special at the time of their creation and have remained special."

AWARDS AND ACHIEVEMENTS

During its three decades in business, Seymour Mann has been the recipient of more nominations and awards than any other doll maker in history. Especially dear to Seymour Mann and his wife Eda, is the "Lifetime Achievement Award" presented by *Doll Reader* magazine. This award recognized their pioneering efforts at introducing artists' dolls at affordable prices. Seymour and Eda have always stressed that they wanted to keep their dolls very reasonable. As a painter and the daughter of a painter, Eda Mann knows first hand that only one person

Hanna Hyland's "Sarah" was nominated for a "Doll of Excellence" award in 1999.

"Masquerade" by Cindy Koch is a 1999 "Doll of Excellence" Nominee.

could own an original. "Licensed artist dolls are what lithographs are to original oils, simply a more affordable version," she explains.

Seymour Mann recalls that many people in the doll business told him he was crazy and that artist techniques could not be replicated in large quantities. He laughs when he remembers that the dolls of the 1970s did not even come with eyelashes! "Our first efforts," he says, "were less than successful. All our dolls looked like Mae West! Today, of course, everyone takes eyelashes and feathered brows for granted!" Many techniques in porcelain doll making originated at Seymour Mann.

In addition, Seymour Mann's costume design department is considered by many to be the best in the world. Many of the firm's artists no longer bother to costume their originals — instead they turn them over to Seymour Mann for dressing. Doll artist Cindy Koch, for example, says, "Seymour Mann costumes my dolls better than I do!"

For years, the company has been proud of its involvement with charities and hospitals. Many Seymour Mann dolls have been donated to causes aiding children less fortunate than others. Some of the recipients have been Cancer Care, Cystic Fibrosis Foundation, Heart Share and Mount Sinai Medical Center, as well as many schools. These philanthropic commitments are dedicated to all in need, and especially children.

A CLUB FOR CONNOISSEURS

In 1987, Seymour Mann assembled a small group of collectors to form the Connoisseur Collectors Club. Since then it has grown to over 100,000 members. These members are offered special promotions, newsletters and collectible items not available to the general public. The club has been a huge success and illustrates the involvement of Seymour Mann collectors.

In addition to the doll business, the Studios of Seymour Mann, Inc., have created collectible musicals, plates, bells, figurines and clocks as part of the *Bernini Series*. The nature themes of beautiful flowers and birds have highlighted many of the new designs, which include magnolias, lilies, hummingbirds, monarch butterflies, cardinals and turtle doves. The limited edition pieces have

been retired when their original run has sold out. Many of these collectibles have been award winners, as well.

Also crafted by Seymour Mann are fashion hats from Italy. Known as "Milano," these porcelain hats are all original designs and are available in many color groups, all with coordinating baskets. In tabletop and gifts, the firm offers *China Blue* porcelains combining traditional English and Chinese accessories featuring floral and natural motifs. Included in the collection are vases, umbrella jars, pitchers and mugs, as well as oversized urns.

LOOKING TO THE FUTURE

Gideon Oberweger speaks for everyone at Seymour Mann when he says, "It is the golden age of dolls. The collector is being offered absolutely incredible creations at remarkably low prices." Even so, he pledges that Seymour Mann will "compete with itself" to offer its collectors a more beautiful collection each year, always with a distinct and apparent value price. One way to do this is to encourage artists to try new techniques rather than creating dolls that resemble each other. Since doll lovers enjoy things that are new, this can easily become a never-ending quest.

As Oberweger concludes, "When I joined Seymour Mann over three decades ago, our cable address was 'What's new New York.' This philosophy has always driven us at Seymour Mann, and it always will. Creating collectible dolls is a wonderful, rewarding business. I don't think a week goes by that we don't get letters and pictures from collectors who want to share the joy our dolls have brought into their lives. Really, who could ask for anything more?"

Also nominated for a "Doll of Excellence" award is J.C. Lee's "The Murphy Kids."

Seymour Mann, Inc.
225 Fifth Avenue
New York, NY 10010

Phone:
212-683-7262

Fax:
212-213-4920

Web Site:
www.seymourmann.com

E-mail:
seymourmann@
worldnet.att.net

SEYMOUR MANN, INC.

Creating Contemporary Heirlooms Using Centuries-Old Traditions

Starting an ornament company was the last thing on his mind when Glenn Lewis, co-President of Slavic Treasures, moved to Krakow, Poland, in January 1993. He had just formed a Polish-American architectural firm with the head of the College of Architecture from the Technical University in Krakow, Poland. Since its inception in 1993, their firm Wizja (which means "vision" in Polish), has been participating in the restoration and modernization of structures throughout Poland following the fall of communism.

On his second day in Krakow, as Glenn was looking up admiring the extraordinary architecture of the city, he quite literally almost knocked down a young Polish lady. Ever the Southern gentleman, Glenn tried to apologize, but stopped mid-sentence when he realized she would not understand a word he was saying. Imagine his surprise when Basia responded using fluent English! Fifteen months later, they were married in Krakow. Basia Lewis is now vice-president of Slavic Treasures and brings to the partnership her skills in multiple languages, plus the ability to bridge the complex cultural differences between people from both countries.

Dave Wegerek, Glenn's life-long friend, is the third partner in this collaboration and shares the title and duties of president. His financial and business acumen provides the cement that forms the foundation of this partnership.

The inspiration to design Christmas ornaments came to Glenn and Basia as an additional outlet for Glenn's artistic talents, as well as a means to fully utilize Basia's artistic and language skills. Little did they know their venture would alter their life's journey. In just two years, Slavic Treasures has

The Slavic Treasures "African Elephant," which debuted in 1998, stands out in the ornament industry as the first to feature blown-glass tusks.

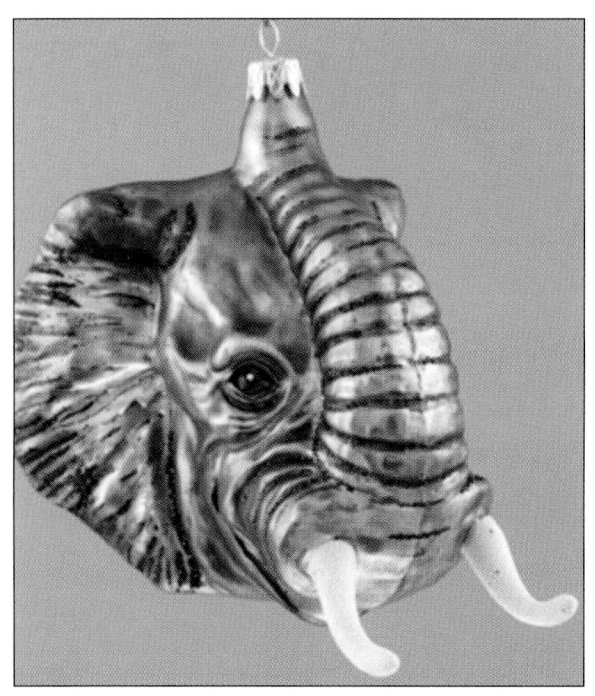

"Rainbow Kootie-99," limited to only 600 pieces, is the second coloration of the very popular Kootie bug.

gone from one young couple's hobby to a full-time enterprise that currently employs over 200 artisans!

ORIGINAL DESIGNS FOR TODAY'S COLLECTOR

All ornaments in the Slavic Treasures line are made from original molds. Many of the pieces are a cooperative effort between several artists, but Glenn is the primary creative force and designer. All the ornaments are mouth blown and silvered in the centuries-old tradition. They are then hand-painted and glittered using only the finest lacquers and premium diamond-dust glitters available.

Glenn studied art quite extensively and has even had several one-man exhibitions of his painted and sculpted works. Though he leans towards abstract impressionism, Glenn's astonishingly realistic animal designs are unequalled in the marketplace. Collectors were awestruck when, for the first time, elephants and rhinos had extended glass tusks. Glenn designed a limited edition "White-Tailed Deer" for the 1999 collection with a majestic rack of glass antlers. Collectors were spellbound during one of Glenn's 1998 signing events, as they watched a customer's pet chimp lean out of her owner's arms to kiss the life-like "Chimpanzee" head ornament! The piercing eyes on the big cats like the "Cheetah," "Lion," and "Bengal Tiger" are mesmerizing. Gentle giants like the "Giraffe," "Panda," "Polar Bear" and "Mountain Gorilla" ornaments will capture the hearts of all animal lovers.

In addition to the wild animal heads, Slavic Treasures offers collectors the chance to own glass replicas of companion animals including dogs, cats and tropical fish. The 1999 line has both yellow and black "Labradors," a "Dalmatian," an "English Bulldog" and a "Yorkshire Terrier." Cat lovers can choose from the sophisticated "Flame Point Himalayan" or the suave "Alley Cat." Each year, Slavic Treasures adds several new breeds of dogs and cats.

BASIA LEWIS ADDS HER ARTISTIC GIFTS TO THE LINE

In 1999, Basia Lewis joined her husband, Glenn, in designing some highly detailed ornaments. The result was several exquisite limited edition ball ornaments that were an instant sell-out. These pieces are part of a grouping

In 1999, the three-piece set including "Dasher," "Dancer" and "Santa Driver" launched the Night Before Christmas *series, limited to only 2,800 sets per year.*

called *Allyson's Corner* to honor Basia and Glenn's darling two-year old daughter who inspires them both. Basia's designs feature a variety of motifs, ranging from a traditional Christmas scene in the "Winter Cardinal Ball," to a serene Japanese koi pond ornament called "Fish and Coral Ball."

FREE-BLOWN DESIGNS ARE UNIQUE IN BLOWN GLASS

The hallmark of the Slavic Treasures line is the free-blown designs that are unparalleled in the ornament world. Slavic Treasures exploded onto the market in their debut year with ornaments with incredibly delicate arms, legs, noses and antennae. The reception to these extraordinary designs was outstanding! Only the most skilled master blowers are capable of creating these intricate designs. Many of the free-blown pieces require several hours to blow a single ornament. Thus, all of the free-blown styles are limited editions ranging from 150 to 1,000 pieces.

Free-blown toads and frogs frolic throughout the Slavic Treasures line. There are graceful dancing frogs such as "Frog Astaire," relay racing frogs and lavish royal frogs. There is even an amphibious band where the "Maestro" leads the way.

When most people see a bug they grab the nearest shoe with thoughts of eradication in mind. But when collectors see a Slavic Treasures free-blown bug, they just want to hold it, admire it from every angle, and take it home for their own collection. There is a family of mosquitoes, a ladybug, a grasshopper, a fly, and an extraordinary yellow jacket called "Goldstinger." Of course, no bug collection would be complete without the very popular "Kootie" bug.

THE *NIGHT BEFORE CHRISTMAS* SERIES BEGINS

1999 marked the beginning of a brand new limited edition series based on the cherished Christmas poem by Clement C. Moore: "The Night Before Christmas." For

The licensed "Georgia Tech Yellow Jackets" ornament is one of the more than 100 college and university mascots represented in Slavic Treasures Glasscots line.

these designs, Slavic Treasures combines both free-blown and molded glass to create the most artistic and technically challenging ornaments on the market. The first set in this series includes "Dasher," "Dancer" and "Santa Driver." Each reindeer is made from at least ten individual pieces of glass! They have delicate legs and antlers, as well as harness hooks to attach reins from each reindeer to Santa's hand. Santa's sleigh even has glass runners. The series is strictly limited to 2,800 sets each year explains Glenn Lewis, "to maintain its credibility as a true collectible." Look for a new pair of reindeer to join Santa's team in 2000, 2001 and 2002. "After that," Glenn adds, "the series will continue as each stanza of the poem inspires me to design another pair or perhaps another trio of ornaments."

COLLEGE AND UNIVERSITY MASCOTS

There is yet another facet to the Slavic Treasures line known as *Glasscots*. In 1998, Slavic Treasures debuted a line of fantastic licensed glass figurals representing the major university mascots from across the country. Currently over 100 colleges and universities have given their approval to Slavic's wonderful blown glass creations. Slavic Treasures will constantly be adding additional designs, largely based on input they receive from retailers and the universities themselves. The ornaments make excellent graduation or corporate executive gifts. When displayed on one of Slavic Treasures solid brass stands, these designs are transformed from a blown-glass Christmas ornament into a year-round glass figurine!

COLLECTOR'S CLUB KICKS OFF THE NEW MILLENNIUM

Slavic Treasures will usher in the millennium with the launch of their new collectors' club. Plans for this new club are still in the works. From what has been seen from this innovative new line thus far, collectors can be assured that the benefits offered to members of the club will be creative and unrivaled in the ornament industry.

In just two years, the Slavic Treasures line has become one of the leading sources for handcrafted blown-glass ornaments. In 1998, Glenn retired two thirds of the line saying, "I wanted to do something for the collectors who got behind us in our inaugural year." Glenn adds, "I'm committed to continually bringing fresh ideas to the marketplace, while maintaining the true collectibility of cherished heirloom ornaments." By blending modern techniques with the centuries-old glass-making traditions, Slavic Treasures creates timeless ornaments which kindle the magic spirit of Christmas past, present and future.

Slavic Treasures
P.O. Box 99591
Raleigh, NC 27624-9591

Phone:
877-SLAVICT
877-752-8428

Fax:
919-844-4429

Web Site:
www.slavictreasures.com.pl

Presenting the Shimmering Art of Oliver Weber

When Oliver Weber unveiled his elegant, crystal-encrusted originals to the collectibles world in the spring of 2000, his unique and sparkling art took the market by storm. The lavish *Oliver Weber Jeweled Collection* features intricately detailed pieces, each of which is adorned with hundreds of sparkling Swarovski crystal stones.

Born in Leoben, Austria, on January 19, 1964, Weber attended a special high school for snow ski racers. After graduation in 1983, he became a professional ski racer in the United States and Japan from 1984 to 1989. Weber then studied business and marketing at the University of Innsbruck, Austria, and later took a position as marketing and sales manager for Swarovski's Jewelry Division.

A PAINSTAKING CREATIVE PROCESS

In 1995, Oliver teamed up with 15-year Swarovski veteran Alexander Stabinger to form the WeSta Company. Stabinger's experience as Swarovski's financial director harmonized well with Weber's artistic and marketing flair.

Breathing fire and looking fierce, the "Dragon" is nonetheless an elegant presence with his body of Swarovski crystals and his many touches of rich gold.

This first-ever piece from the Oliver Weber Jeweled Collection features a quartet of dolphins, which took over four years to create.

The pair inaugurated their firm with the creation of a dolphin figurine using 22K gold-plated metal highlighted with pave stones. That premier piece, a family of four dolphins, took over four years to create. It is displayed on an elaborate, blue aluminum base with a thick, beveled-edge glass background of Swarovski stones forming a transparent wave.

In the past two years, the *Oliver Weber Jeweled Collection* has grown to include several intricately detailed musical instruments and animal figurines designed in brushed rhodium or polished gold, combined with pave stones and rich accents of enameling. The company plans to introduce three or four new pieces per year until the collection totals approximately 30 current designs.

The first piece in the collection to be "closed" was the "Harp." The precision and intricacy involved with the strings on the "Harp" made this piece far too difficult to manufacture. Each string was strung by hand and had to be 1/8th of an inch apart. The newest addition to the collection is a beautiful "Eagle" with its wings spread. This piece stands approximately 2-1/2" tall.

At this point, there is no collectors club for this line of collectibles, however within the next two years, announcements and subscriptions will be available, along with an introduction of an annual piece.

A NEW ASSOCIATION WITH SWAN SEEKERS

Before Oliver Weber forged his agreement with Swan Seekers Network, WeSta's Oliver Weber creations were sold exclusively at Swarovksi's Gift Shop in Wattens, Austria, and at the Arribas Brothers shops located in Disneyland and Disney World. Now Swan Seekers has earned authorization to offer the *Oliver Weber Jeweled Collection,* with Weber's personal blessing. Being familiar with Swan Seeker's excellent reputation in the Swarovski secondary market, Weber successfully made his first foray into the collectibles arena.

To inaugurate this new arrangement, Weber attended the International Collectible Exposition® in Atlanta in May of 2000 and the Rosemont, Illinois, collectibles show in June of 2000, signing autographs and greeting collectors at the Swan Seekers Network booth. Special pieces were on display, including the sold-out "Millennium Mickey," which was limited to 2,000 pieces, and the "Signature Series Mickey 2000," now being offered exclusively at Arribas Brothers in Disney theme parks. Weber designed

A crystal-and-gold tribute to fine music includes, from left to right, the "Saxophone," retired "Harp," "Violin" with stand and "Guitar" with stand.

these two pieces specifically for *The Arribas Collection.*

Jimer F. DeVries of Swan Seekers Network was delighted with the response to the firm's new artist, and also found some collectors' reactions quite amusing. "Oliver Weber could be (actor) Kurt Russell's brother," DeVries asserts. "We actually had two people come up to our booth in Atlanta to ask if he was Kurt Russell!"

WORKS INSPIRED BY ANIMALS AND MUSIC

The current *Oliver Weber Jeweled Collection* includes fanciful and graceful animals as well as shimmering musical instruments. "The Jeweled Dragon" combines crystals, gold and silver with red accents for a fearsome yet beautiful presence. The "Dolphin Set" pays homage to these intelligent and charming animals, and a separate "Dolphin Father" and "Dolphin Mother" are showcased as the leaders of the family in all their natural glory.

A whimsical "Polar Bear" seems to smile as he lounges contentedly, and small and large "Elephants" look as if they're all ready for a formal parade. A funny little "Snowman" makes a fine addition to this collection, as well.

With its golden body and crystal inner workings, the "Piano" pays homage to any musical collector's passion. Don't forget the "Saxophone," "Violin" and "Guitar" — as well as that now-retired "Harp," which may be available to avid collectors on the secondary market. With prices in the $58.00 to $495 range, connoisseurs will find these works of art remarkably affordable, especially considering the opulent impression they make.

THE SWAROVKSI CONNECTION

Oliver Weber's artistry is beautifully enhanced by the wonderful crystals he uses to adorn each of his original creations. He insists on using only Swarovski crystals — as befits his Austrian heritage and appreciation of quality. Known for their "fiery brilliance, magical interplay of spectral colors, intensity and harmony of color, and perfect cut," Swarovski crystals rival fine jewels for their stunning beauty and elegance.

The company Weber once worked for began over 100 years ago when Bohemian entrepreneur Daniel Swarovski invented and patented a crystal stone cutting machine. The resulting crystals were crafted with such precision and consistency that the small glass-cutting works in the Tyrol grew rapidly into an international success.

Having provided crystal "trimmings" for the fashion world since the 1930s, Swarovski Crystal gained even more fame in the mid-1950s working with Parisian designer Christian Dior. The "Aurora Borealis," a coated crystal stone that flashed with rainbow-colored lights, became a fashion sensation.

Already established making fashion accoutrements as well as glass reflectors, binoculars and crystal chandelier parts, Swarovski began making jewelry in the late 1960s. Indeed, the firm was the first to cut cubic zirconia by mechanical methods. Then in 1976, the introduction of a crystal mouse heralded the firm's entry into the collectibles market.

With the international success of the Swarovski Collectors Society and its many splendid introductions, Swarovski reigns today among the world's most elite collectibles makers, with more than 9,000 employees worldwide. The company changed its logo in 1988 from the Tyrolean Edelweiss to the Swan — embodiment of metamorphosis and all that is pure and elegant. Still family owned and run, Swarovski is one of the largest and most successful of all Austrian companies.

Yet, the firm also retains the vision to work with fledgling entrepreneurs like Oliver Weber, exemplifying the spirit that ensured the success of its founder, Daniel Swarovski. Weber's goal for his firm is to become as renowned and respected as Swarovski itself, and he spares no effort in achieving this mission.

This whimsical "Snowman" adds a touch of fun to the Oliver Weber Jeweled Collection, presented by Swan Seekers Network.

Of course, he knows the saying about "all work and no play," as well. Indeed, when Weber is not traveling around the world promoting his *Jeweled Collection*, or in his studio creating new images, he is "hard at work" on the golf course. He believes that, "If you work hard, you need to play hard and enjoy life — or it's all for nothing." Golf is just another challenge, which Weber takes on with gusto!

Swan Seekers Network
9740 Campo Road, #134
Spring Valley, CA 91977

Phone:
619-462-2333

Fax:
619-462-5517

Web Sites:
www.swanseekers.com
www.oliverweber.com
www.jeweledcollection.com

E-mail:
Jimer@swanseekers.com

Shimmering Crystal to Fire the Imagination

His dream: to establish a factory producing cut crystal jewelry stones. His destination: Wattens, in the Austrian Tyrol. The year was 1895 when Daniel Swarovski I, along with his wife and three sons, said farewell to their Bohemian homeland. At that time, Swarovski could hardly have foreseen that he was laying the foundation of a corporation which, less than a century later, would be the world's leading manufacturer of cut crystal jewelry stones. Today, Swarovski produces billions of crystal stones annually, as well as decorative objects, jewelry, accessories, chandelier parts, grinding and abrasive instruments, and glass reflecting elements for road and rail safety.

Swarovski's renowned manufacturing facility is nestled in the glorious Alps in Wattens, Austria.

THE SWAROVSKI STORY

Daniel Swarovski was born in Georgenthal, a small village located in the Iser mountains of northern Bohemia. He was the first of four children of a glasscutter who – like countless other skilled artisans in Bohemia – had a workshop at home. As a young man, Daniel Swarovski completed a two-year apprenticeship in gem engraving with his father. They produced small hand-cut stones which were fitted with copper studs and used to decorate pins, combs, hat pins, and other accessories. Even then, he realized that the days of manual cutting were numbered, and he had already started experimenting with ways of automating the process.

In 1883, Daniel visited the International Electric Exhibition in Vienna and saw machines invented by the early giants of technology such as Edison, Schuckert and Siemens. He realized the world stood on the threshold of a major technological revolution.

Nine years later in 1892, Daniel applied for a patent on his first invention, a machine which cut crystal jewelry stones with unmatched speed and precision. It also gave him a significant edge over the local competition, an advantage which he was reluctant to lose.

He began to scout around for a site that would enable him to develop his idea. Eventually, he found an old factory in Wattens, a small village outside of Innsbruck in the Tyrolean Inn valley. The Alpine setting was idyllic – the mountain stream running through the village supplied water power in abundance, while local trains provided a direct link to the West and Paris, which was to be a major market for Swarovski crystal. By the end of the century, his Tyrolean cut stones had established a reputation for such quality and precision that they were in demand not only in jewelry making centers in England, France and Germany, but also on the other side of the Atlantic in America.

By 1908, he and his three sons, Wilhelm, Friedrich and Alfred, were carrying out experiments in the manufacture of glass. Within three years, they had designed furnaces and perfected a method of producing and refining crystal to a state of flawless brilliance.

THE ORIGINS OF THE "SWAROVSKI SPARKLE"

The basic material used in the production of Swarovski crystal is a unique man-made substance produced from a combination of natural minerals, including quartz sand, potash and sodium carbonate. When these materials are fused together at a very high temperature (2,732°F), they attain a clarity and brilliance far surpassing natural rock or quartz crystal. Each solid crystal mass is then precisely cut, polished and faceted. A facet is a small angular cut plane or slanted edge, designed to give optimum color refraction to a stone. The precise edges on each facet are the hallmark of Swarovski crystal stones and give the product the famous "Swarovski sparkle."

People often wonder how Swarovski achieves the frosted effect featured in pieces like the "Baby Lovebirds," "Dragonfly" and "Butterfly on Leaf." A crystal piece is finished according to design specifications and dipped in a specially formulated liquid acid solution. The acid wears away the surface area, creating the smooth, fine frosted surface. These frosted pieces are made with the same careful attention to detail as any other Swarovski stone. Swarovski uses the frosted effect on certain design elements in a piece to create a wonderful contrast between it and the sharp, crystal clear focal stones.

Each Swarovski object is designed by an artist, and each component stone is cut specifically for that design. These component pieces are not available to any other

This graceful Swarovski Silver Crystal "Silver Heron" is from the Feathered Friends series.

Favorite activities and interests are lovingly portrayed in crystal with gold-plated details in the Swarovski Crystal Memories collection.

company. However, other manufacturers do purchase standard Swarovski chandelier stones and assemble them into decorative objects. Swarovski's continuing technological advances in stone cutting are resulting in more complex and realistic designs to delight collectors.

SWAROVSKI CRYSTAL TODAY

Swarovski reigns as the world's leading manufacturer of full cut crystal for the giftware, fashion, jewelry and lighting industries. Swarovski's own consumer goods labels include *Swarovski Silver Crystal, Swarovski Collectors Society, Swarovski Crystal Memories, Swarovski Selection* and *Swarovski Jewelry.*

Swarovski Silver Crystal was not named so because the crystal contains traces of silver, but because if you hold up a piece of crystal to the light, its spectral brilliance creates a "silvery" glow. The *Silver Crystal* line consists of more than 140 figurines and decorative items inspired by themes such as *African Wildlife, Woodland Friends, When We Were Young* and *South Sea.*

Swarovski Crystal Memories is a collection of more than 130 adorable miniature objects, key rings, pendants and brooches, created to symbolize life's special moments. They're perfect as small gifts to celebrate joyous occasions, table setting enhancements or spontaneous treats. Each miniature unites brilliantly faceted crystal with meticulously designed 18K gold-plated details.

Since 1992, Swarovski has commissioned acclaimed artists and architects such as Andrée Putman, Joël Desgrippes and Borek Sipek for the creation of its *Swarovski Selection* tabletop objects. They unite state-of-the-art Swarovski crystal cutting technology with natural and man-made materials in works of art for the home. Each piece carries its designer's signature.

A stunning line of opulent crystal *Swarovski Jewelry* uses pavé settings and colored stones for day-into-night dressing. The collection includes earrings, necklaces, bracelets, pins and rings. Exceptional design and quality are trademarks of this contemporary collection. Four collections are created each year.

A THRIVING SOCIETY FOR SWAROVSKI COLLECTORS

The popularity of the *Swarovski Silver Crystal* collection led to the creation of the Swarovski Collectors Society (SCS) in 1987. The Society now boasts more than 400,000 members worldwide, with over 120,000 in the United States. Indeed, for many owners of *Swarovski Silver Crystal,* their figurines are more than just decorative objects – they are a passion.

Through publications, events and trips, members meet other collectors and obtain information about their pieces, Swarovski products, and the company. Membership also provides collectors with the exclusive opportunity to purchase the SCS Annual Edition.

Annual Editions are presented as part of a themed three-piece series. The first Annual Edition series was named "Togetherness," and included the Lovebirds, Woodpeckers and Turtledoves. Next came "Mother and Child," which featured the Dolphins, Seals and Whales. The year 1993 introduced the "Inspiration Africa" series which was comprised of the Elephant, Kudu and Lion. The "Fabulous Creatures" trilogy was introduced in 1996 with the Unicorn, Dragon and Pegasus. Now for 1999 to 2001, the new trilogy is titled "Masquerade." The first piece portrays a "Pierrot," one of the most popular figures of the Italian *Commedia dell 'arte.*

Given the spirited excitement and enthusiasm of its members around the world, the Swarovski Collectors Society can look forward to years of continued growth and success.

Sparkling crystals and striking designs make Swarovski jewelry sought after by women around the world.

Swarovski Consumer
Goods, Ltd.
One Kenney Drive
Cranston, RI 02920

Phone:
800-426-3088

Fax:
800-870-5660

Web Site:
www.swarovski.com

SWAROVSKI CONSUMER GOODS, LTD.

Bringing Delightful Designs to Life

It was once just a backyard hobby for its founders, but today United Design™ offers a wealth of creations — and has the distinction of being the largest manufacturer of animal figurines in the country. What's more, today this thriving company sells its products all over the world.

Anyone visiting the stunning 200,000 square foot plant and office complex of United Design Corporation will find it difficult to believe that this business was started in a chicken coop! The firm's devotion to creativity, quality and "hands on" craftsmanship has ultimately set it and its multitude of appealing products apart from the competition.

United Design currently manufactures 5,400 designs that are sold in 13 different wholesale product catalogs. Present designs include everything from miniature animal and angel figurines, to imaginative and intricate limited edition Santa and Angel designs, to near life-size animal sculptures. Also offered by this versatile company is a broad selection of home and garden decor accessories.

The menagerie of animals produced for *Classic Critters™*, *Stone Critters®*, *Animal Magnetism®* and *Itty Bitty World®* collections bring the wonder of nature indoors. Animal statuary, birdfeeders, fountains, chimes and garden furniture created for the *Stone Garden®* collection are designed for outdoor use. Nature's endless charm is also the focus in many of United Design's home decor and accessory lines — *Candlelights™* candle holders, *frame•ology®* photo frames, and *StoneGlow®* oil lamps. The new *Hayes Parker®* *Collection* of cache pots, wall plaques, birdbaths and feeders, candle-holders, orbs and lamps are equally suitable for both indoor and outdoor use.

Oklahoma-based United Design is joined by European and Canadian sales and distribution companies headquartered in Nottingham, England, and Norwich, Ontario. The efforts of all involved account for the fact that United Design's fine collectible, gift and decorative accessory lines are enjoyed by millions of satisfied customers around the world.

"Angel in Flight" by artist G. G. Santiago lifts the sculptural interpretation of angels to new heights.

It's a "Warm & Fuzzy Christmas" for Santa and his pets as they check the list of good boys and girls from the comfort of Santa's North Pole hideaway.

SANTA AND ANGEL DESIGNS ABOUND

The artists of United Design pride themselves on honoring the legendary figure of Santa Claus — and providing cherished memories for collectors. They have created a series of richly detailed, limited edition figurines called *The Legend of Santa Claus™*. Hand-made and hand-painted, some *Legend of Santa* figurines depict St. Nick as he appears in various cultures and situations. Others provide a unique glimpse of Santa going about his typical yearly routine.

The original artist for this collection was Larry Miller, who died in 1997. Picking up on Miller's brilliant legacy are Jeff Littlejohn and Denise Vaughan, who add their many talents to *The Legend of Santa Claus* collection today. Every limited edition Santa is accompanied by a Certificate of Authenticity and a collectors' booklet.

Among the newer *Legend of Santa Claus* pieces is "Warm & Fuzzy Christmas," showing St. Nick and his favorite pets checking the list of good boys and girls. Then there's "Up on the Rooftop" by Jeff Littlejohn, depicting Santa and a pair of reindeer busy bringing gifts to youngsters. Denise Vaughan's first contribution to this limited edition collection is "Woodland Santa."

From 1991 to 1999, the *Angels Collection* has been pleasing collectors around the world. The mainstay of the collection is the annual "The Gift" design, representing an Angel giving a star to a young child. The star is a symbol

"The Gift" for 1999 was sculpted as a special benefit for the Starlight Foundation.

of wishes granted, and serves as a benefit for the Starlight Foundation, renowned for granting the wishes of seriously and terminally ill children. Another lovely Angel is the work of G. G. Santiago, titled "Angel in Flight." Penni Jo Couch's "Musical Motion" also is a new Angel presentation.

CHARMING "CRITTERS" COLLECTIONS

In recent years, United Design has introduced hundreds of new designs in its animal collection. *Classic Critters*™ and *Stone Critters*® figurines, *Animal Magnetism*® magnets and *Itty Bitty Critters*® miniatures, as well as several other animal collections, are featured in the company's catalog that showcases over 1,500 charming animal "critters."

Two new collections, *Flora and Fauna* and *Critter Keepers,* have captured collectors' hearts. *Flora and Fauna's* innovative box design opens to reveal an animal figure surrounded by the petals of a flower bouquet. *Critter Keepers* resemble chubby animal-shaped figurines, but do double duty as trinket boxes. The political *Party Animals* collection returns with the "Democratic Donkey" and "Republican Elephant" made an appearance just in time for the 2000 presidential election. All of these wonderful animals are hand-made in bonded porcelain or hydrostone, and are hand-painted.

TYBER KATZ™ FEATURES DELIGHTFUL FELINES

Renowned artists Peter and Patricia Tyber have teamed up with United Design to present a new and whimsical limited edition feline figurine line called *Tyber Katz*™. This creative collaboration begins with 12 inaugural designs including *Talltailz*™, *Teapot Catz*™ and *Grinski Boxes*™. *Talltailz* cats keep their cool even though their long, tall tails make a perfect place for mice to swing, or birds and butterflies to hitch a ride. The *Teapot Catz* climb headfirst into decorative teapots searching for unseen delights, while *Grinski Boxes* offer the proverbial grinning Cheshire cat to watch over caches of trinkets and treasures.

IN THE GARDEN WITH MARY ENGLEBREIT®

United Design and renowned artist Mary Engelbreit have teamed up as well, to tend the home and garden. Together, they give her unique and popular colors and designs a

new place to grow in lawn. patio and garden accessories.

The first products to bloom within the *In the Garden With ME*® collection are wall plaques, garden markers, pots, stepping stones, candleholders and the precious "Beehive" and "Chair of Bowlies" fountains. Each of Engelbreit's original graphic designs is sculpted in exacting detail and has been carefully hand-painted based on her trademark color schemes. A "Cherry Girl" garden sculpture features one of Mary's most endearing characters.

WARM COMMUNICATION WITH COLLECTORS

Collectors of United Designs' limited edition Santas and Angels can access the annual *The Legend of Santa Claus* and *Angels Collection* newsletters on United Design's web site at www.united-design.com. The newsletters keep collectors informed about new releases and retirements, and provide a checklist of all pieces offered in the collection. Sometimes they even provide collectors with a peek at designs the sculptors are working on for the next collection. Photocopies of the online newsletter are provided for those collectors needing printed copies.

Collectors are invited to visit and experience the fascinating processes involved in creating a United Design collectible. A tour guide at the Noble, Oklahoma facility explains the procedure and points out interesting details as visitors watch the mold making, pouring and pulling, painting and finishing techniques first-hand. On completing the tour, collectors are also invited to visit the on-site Showroom where thousands of the company's figurines are displayed.

United Design's goal — "put a twinkle in the eye of every beholder" — remains unchanged. It is faithfully supported by an award-winning design staff that includes several talented sculptors, numerous skilled artisans and craftspeople, and an enterprising support staff. Working together as a team, they are dedicated to giving the consumer an uncharacteristic selection of quality products.

The Cowboy Santa, "Runnin' Late," is part of The Legend of Santa Claus Edition Unlimited *from United Design.*

United Design Corp.
1600 North Main
P.O. Box 1200
Noble, OK 73068

Phone:
800-727-4883

Fax:
800-832-0866

Web Site:
www.united-design.com

E-mail:
udc@ionet.net

United Treasures – A Positive Image®

While the world may be getting smaller, the world of collecting is growing through the contributions of new companies like United Treasures. Founded in 1995, this dynamic producer and designer of figurines entered the collectible field in late 1998 with its Positive Image® Division. Featuring the works of leading artists, designers and sculptors, the Positive Image® Division of United Treasures is more than just a name.

From its beginning, the company sought to bring the finest gifts and figurines to the collector at the most affordable cost. In order to guarantee the highest possible quality for the collector, United Treasures opened its first production studio in 1997. Within one year, the demand for United Treasures products was so high that in 1998, United Treasures opened a new state-of-the-art 98,000 square foot art studio and production facility. Setting a new standard for high quality cold cast figurines, United Treasures now produces some of the finest resin collectible figurines in the world.

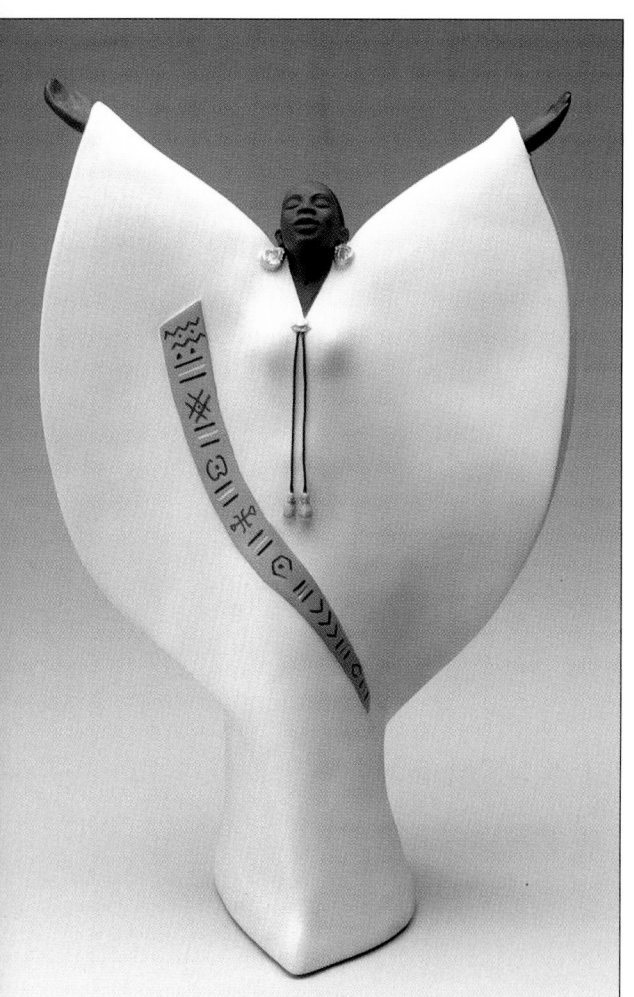

Nyame Dua "Joy" from the Sankofa collection is limited to 5,000 pieces.

In late 1997, a meeting between United Treasures' founder and President Gary Harrison and Master Sculptor Norman A. Hughes led to the development of the Positive Image® Division. Originally founded by Hughes as a vehicle for his most personal and artistic creations, the Positive Image® collection became a highly sought-after collection of figurines. Hughes soon found himself increasingly absorbed in the daily business and farther from his true avocation of sculpting and designing. United Treasures provided Hughes with the ideal solution. Positive Image® became a division of United Treasures, which handles the production, marketing and

From Emma Jane's Children Remember When series comes "Papa took Nate to his First Day of School," "Bertie Mae Watched over little Hattie," and "Babie Lexie wore her first Sunday Go to Meeting Dress."

distribution, allowing Hughes to return to his studio and his first love: Art.

THE SPIRIT OF A MASTER SCULPTOR

A truly visionary artist involved with every step in the creation, design, sculpting and detailing of his work, Norman A. Hughes had long sought to develop a collection that reflected the feelings, the look and the spirituality he felt as an African-American artist. His first collection for the new Positive Image® Division, *The Sankofa Collection*, would achieve that goal. Sankofa is the name given to one of the many Adrinka symbols that the Ashanti people of West Africa use to decorate their cloth. The *Sankofa* symbol means "look to your past for the knowledge to prepare for your future." Each of the nine designs in the *Sankofa* collection is based on an Adrinka symbol that inspires both the design and spiritual meaning of the figurine.

Sankofa's stylistically simple designs were anything but simple to make. Involving dozens of skilled artisans and proprietary formulas, each *Sankofa* figurine is a hand-crafted work of art. Available in editions limited to 5,000 pieces, each cold cast resin figurine is hand-painted and is carefully packaged in a collector's box with an original verse about the design, an information card about the artist, and a folding tent card about the design. The base of every *Sankofa* statuette is carefully stamped in gold with the edition size, the name of the piece, the artist's signature and is hand-numbered with a corresponding Certificate of Authenticity.

REMEMBER WHEN...

United Treasures and Positive Image's® reputation for bringing the best collectible figurines to market caught the attention of artist Emily Watkins. Watkins, already very well known through her work with leading collectible companies, sought a company that could

provide her *Emma Jane's Children* collection the commitment it deserved. Meanwhile, United Treasures had long admired Watkins' work, and so another perfect match was made. Positive Image® is now proud to announce the release of *Emma Jane's Children* from artist Emily Watkins.

Each piece in the *Emma Jane's Children* collection is a snapshot of a time gone by, evoking the memories of yesteryear through the eyes of a child. Each figurine is limited to just 5,000 pieces and includes a Certificate of Authenticity, artist biography, and comes with a story card about the design. With the overwhelming response the collection has generated, Emily Watkins created a special collection: *Emma Jane's Babies*. Each *Emma Jane's Baby* is an adorable miniature version of an *Emma Jane's Children* design. All of the charm of the original is packed into this open edition series that is designed to be affordable for every collector.

◆ *"From the Garden," "Wake Up," and "First School Day" are from United Treasures Sarah Kay Collection.*

A NEW ROMANCE COLLECTION FROM ARTIST/ACTOR BILLY DEE WILLIAMS

Another first for Positive Image® is the debut collection from one of America's most talented artists and actors, Billy Dee Williams. While audiences know Williams from his starring roles in movies like *The Lady Sings the Blues* and *Star Wars*, collectors have avidly sought his passionate canvases. Williams' works hang in galleries and homes around the world, and can be seen in the Smithsonian Portrait Gallery and the Schomberg Museum in New York. Billy Dee Williams' *Romance Collection* is sure to set hearts afire with romantic figurines drawn from a lifetime of painting. Williams will bring a new audience to the world of collecting through the release of his first 5,000-piece limited edition collectible from Positive Image®.

NEW PARTNERSHIPS MAKE ESTABLISHED ARTWORK AFFORDABLE

United Treasures is also proud to announce the first license ever granted to any company from ANRI GmbH of Italy. United Treasures is releasing an exclusive open edition, cold cast collection based on the designs of the beloved Australian artist Sarah Kay. This series consists of new sculptures that reflect the stunning artistry of the hand-carved wood originals from ANRI, setting a new standard in high quality cold cast figurines. This new affordable series is bringing more collectors than ever before to these cherished children created by Sarah Kay, and introducing new collectors to the museum quality ANRI originals.

United Treasures is also proud to be working with Oldham & Company. Founded by Charles & Victoria Oldham, the Oldham & Company collection currently has two wonderful series available in open edition collec-

Billy Dee Williams Romance Collection features "Billy Dee Williams' Self-Portrait." It has a retail price of $125 and is limited to 5,000.

tions. The *Guardian Angel* series is a special tribute to the Guardian Angels who watch over those who watch over us – our pets. Exquisite details that are characteristic of Charles' and Victoria's work are highlighted in the charming "Guardian Angel of Cats" and the "Guardian Angel of Puppies." Each of these delightful angels comes with an information card about the artists and a wonderful original poem by Victoria Oldham.

With a yowling "Let's play ball!" it's a whole new game in Oldham & Company's newest collection for United Treasures, the *Cats of Baseball*. A more colorful collection of kitties can't be found as the Barncats take on the crosstown rival, the Alleycats, in an open edition series. Each cat comes with its very own tradeable collector's card featuring all the statistics of each cat's career. These cool and colorful kitties are sure to be a favorite with baseball and animal fans alike. The exquisite sculpting and painstaking details mark this collection as another masterpiece from Oldham & Company.

POSITIVE IMAGE INVITES COLLECTORS' IDEAS

With a growing cadre of the finest designers and artists in the collectible industry, United Treasures and its Positive Image® division are set to open a new chapter in the collectible world. Maintaining their commitment to present works that truly reflect the best in design, quality, and more importantly – the best in all of us, United Treasures and Positive Image® are truly setting the foundations for the next greatest collectible company.

United Treasures is also soliciting suggestions and ideas for a forthcoming collector's club. In order to create a club that truly reflects the Positive Image® philosophy, help from collectors is paramount. Artist events, specialty pieces, promotional items, tours and events are all being actively planned. Please feel free to submit your idea and become a part of the beginning of the next great club.

**United Treasures
Positive Image® Division
18418 72nd Ave, South
Kent, WA 98032**

**Phone:
800-678-2545**

**Fax:
425-656-0299**

**Web Site:
www.unitedtreasures.com**

**E-mail:
matt@unitedtreasures.com**

The Magazine for Fans of Department 56®, Inc.

Vol. IX No. 5 — September - October '99 — $4.50

the Village Chronicle

The Largest Independent Publication for Department 56 Collectors®

All The News That's Lit To Print

Covers of The Village Chronicle *are lively and engaging, as this example demonstrates.*

Before husband-and-wife-to-be Peter and Jeanne George tied the knot in 1990, they received two engagement gifts that would chart the course for their personal and professional lives. The gifts? Two pieces from the Department 56®, Inc. collectibles line called *Dickens' Village.*

Peter was quickly hooked, becoming an avid collector of items from the *Dickens' Village* collection. Now the publisher of *The Village Chronicle,* he recalls, "Between the two of us, I was the primary collector of that line. I've always been a fan for Dickens' works. Today, Jeanne and I own over 150 Department 56 village buildings and *Snowbabies* — and that doesn't include our accessories!"

Initially, Peter says, he and Jeanne really weren't acquainted with the company. "We were just like most collectors, who look at a piece, find it appealing and then begin to collect and learn more about the item they cherish and the company who makes it," adds Peter.

"Somehow, though, the warmth and glow of these wonderful little houses from Department 56 have not been restricted to the inside of our home's walls. They also found their way into our hearts. What began with two pieces, erupted into a collection that transcends the Department 56 villages and enters the vast territory of the firm's collectibles and giftware."

A COLLECTOR BECOMES AN ENTREPRENEUR

As the couple's interest in Department 56 spiraled, they attempted to become better informed about the lines they collected. While attending the International Collectible Exposition® in South Bend, Indiana, in 1991, Peter says, "I realized that many collectors like Jeanne and myself

were looking for information on Department 56, and that there was very little information in print at that time. I recognized that here was a niche that needed to be filled. I decided to go after it." Peter published the first issue of *The Village Chronicle* later that year.

The first issues of *The Village Chronicle* were eight-page newsletters. Today, it is a 64 to 72-page, full-color magazine with a circulation of approximately 16,000. In each bi-monthly issue, *The Village Chronicle's* eight feature writers deliver the world of Department 56 to the collector's door with page after page of authoritative, well-researched articles. Readers also enjoy display-making advice and tips; product highlights; the "New Stand," a special section for new Department 56 collectors; secondary market reports; a calendar of Department 56 events; and the latest news about each of the Department 56 villages, as well as the company itself.

One of the magazine's most popular feature articles, Peter notes, is one the staff calls a "historical article." If Department 56 has released a piece that replicates a famous location or building, such as London's Big Ben, *The Village Chronicle* will set to work "chronicling" the history of the structure, even showcasing a photograph of the actual property.

Today, Peter and Jeanne serve as publisher and editor of *The Village Chronicle,* respectively. The couple attends approximately 30 events related to Department 56 each year, including the renowned Bachman's Gathering, industry trade shows, open houses and group events, where they are often the featured speakers or guests.

The Georges have also positioned *The Village Chronicle* on the Internet via a user-friendly collectors' web site at www.villagechronicle.com. This lively site includes a feature article from the magazine's current issue, a monthly puzzle, a marketplace where collectors can purchase items that enhance collecting and display-making, and classified ad pages where collectors can buy, sell and trade their Department 56 collectibles. There is also an on-line subscription to *The Village Chronicle* at $12.95 for six issues.

Publisher Peter George and Editor Jeanne George of The Village Chronicle *are noted experts on Department 56 and its many product lines.*

LIVING UP TO HIGH GOALS

Over the years, Peter says, the goal of *The Village Chronicle* has remained consistent: to provide information, whether it be historical, current or breaking news, to Department 56 collectors and to enhance the enjoyment

they receive from their personal collections.

To ensure that material printed in *The Village Chronicle* is accurate, the magazine's writers regularly survey a variety of industry sources. These sources have been cultivated over the past nine years and include a cadre of knowledgeable dealers, manufacturers' representatives and collectors.

The news scoops that frequently result from this careful checking of sources prove quite exciting for Department 56 devotees. Readers, Peter says, are also delighted to learn where unannounced Department 56 pieces are available and how long they will likely remain in stock.

To stay abreast of the field and gain new subscribers, the Georges travel widely and frequently write or contribute to articles in other publications. They also have published *Collecting Department 56: The Fun - The Facts - The Tradition,* which is now in its fourth printing. And they serve as Department 56 historians for the *Greenbook* secondary market guides and as featured Department 56 experts at GoCollect.com.

Trips to England with as many as 40 collectors took place in 1996 and 1998 with the Georges as hosts, and the couple plans more such "historic discovery" tours in the years to come.

THE BOTTOM LINE: F-U-N

"I believe that collecting Department 56 is ultimately about fun, not about trying to accumulate wealth with a collection," Peter says. "The value is what they mean to you as a collector, not what they're worth on the secondary market," he adds.

"The display-making aspect of collecting Department 56 collectibles is a big part of the appeal of the villages," Peter notes. "These are pieces that collectors take home and play with. People who collect Department 56 are really just big kids!"

As Peter and Jeanne travel across the country presenting lectures on Department 56 collectibles, they regularly stress the importance of having fun and being creative with the captivating pieces in the company's lines.

Indeed, Peter will stop at almost nothing to share a good time with collector friends. At the Department 56 10th Annual Village Gathering in Minneapolis, for example, he announced that if he sold 200 subscriptions to *The Village Chronicle,* he'd shave off his hair! After the final tally reached 208 subscriptions sold, Peter smiled in his chair while Shannon Jenson, a Minnesota barber, buzzed and clipped away his "crowning glory"!

To involve their readers "to the ultimate," Peter and Jeanne also led a tour last April to Quebecor World Pendell in Midland, Michigan, for the first-ever "I saw *The Village Chronicle* being printed" gathering. Some 45 enthusiastic readers showed up for the two-day happening, which included a Quebecor tour, great food, games, prizes and camaraderie. A side trip to historic Frankenmuth, Michigan, and Bronner's world-famous Christmas store capped off the event.

Department 56 enthusiasts and The Village Chronicle *subscribers from all over the nation gathered in Midland, Michigan, to tour the Quebecor printing plant and see their favorite publication being printed.*

Just as Peter and Jeanne like to bring a feeling of fun to their Department 56 collection, they encourage others to do likewise. As Jeanne explains, "I think our magazine is so popular because it is written from a collector's point of view. We love our Department 56 collection. And we love learning more about each building and accessory, as well as new ways to display them. It is this love and fun that we put into each issue. There is no better way to make a living than to do what you love every single day of the week!"

Members of the Treasure Coast 56ers of Stuart, Florida, stopped by The Village Chronicle's *booth at a Department 56 event to have their picture taken with the Georges.*

The Village Chronicle
757 Park Avenue
Cranston, RI 02910

Phone:
401-467-9343

Fax:
401-467-9359

Web Site:
www.villagechronicle.com

E-mail:
Peter@VillageChronicle.com
Jeanne@VillageChronicle.com

Classic Molds Inspire Kathi Lorance Bejma

Artist Kathi Lorance Bejma, surrounded by her charming creations for Walnut Ridge Collectibles.

Kathi Lorance Bejma loves Father Christmas. So much so that for years, she collected "everything Santa" — that is, until she bought her first antique Santa Claus chocolate mold! Today, Bejma still favors St. Nick, but her Santa Claus collection has been overshadowed by her devotion to chocolate molds of every description — a total of more than 4,000 in all!

While many people enjoy a collecting hobby, Bejma found that her creativity was fueled by that first Santa mold and the many other molds she soon added to her trove. "I decided to experiment with my Father Christmas

The most popular of Walnut Ridge's angel designs, "Alexandra" now has her own elegant lithograph. At 16"x20", this framed graphic sells for $300.

Kathi Bejma's collectors often marvel at the fact that she is completely self-taught. Although she liked to draw and paint from the time she was in kindergarten, her youthful artistic energies were invested in dancing. Married at 19 after a brief career in modeling and cosmetology, Bejma was a full-time homemaker until she and a pair of friends decided to sign up for a craft show in 1980. While her partners considered this a one-time lark, Bejma was intrigued. She started doing a few more shows, selling a variety of soft sculpture dolls and animals, as well as reproduction furniture.

HER OWN CHALKWARE FORMULA

By 1985, Bejma was "real heavy into Santa collecting," as she recalls. "I bought every Santa imaginable, including my first antique Santa mold, and the rest is history! Once the first chalkware piece was created, all of my friends admired it and wanted one. So I made 10 or 15 more, and they were gone in a flash! I knew I was on to something, so I started actively pursuing my quest for chocolate molds and found a few more. Even though I now have thousands, I've been very particular in what I choose. I don't like 'cutesy' molds," states Kathi.

"I started doing chalkware out of my basement on a small scale, but then in the fall of 1986, I was invited to show my work at the first country wholesale show in Valley Forge, Pennsylvania." Bejma was apprehensive, but much to her surprise, she returned home with $50,000 in orders! Since then, her company's growth has been phenomenal. She has moved twice to larger quarters to ensure that she can personally supervise the hand-crafting of every Walnut Ridge product under one roof. She has also upgraded and expanded her showroom space at the Atlanta Gift Mart.

In addition to her talents as an artist, Bejma enjoys the design aspect of displaying her creations, especially in her Atlanta space. As she relates, "Customers told me the Atlanta showroom was like walking into a fairyland! I wanted to make it a real warm and inviting setting to show customers that you can display our products all year — not just at Christmas. We have a whole line of fruit and vegetable ornaments that make a nice addition to a kitchen or dining room. We created a library setting

mold to see if I could create a piece of chalkware in his image," she recalls. Already a successful maker and marketer of crafts and furniture, Bejma introduced her chalkware Santa to her customers with immediate success. Since that day in 1985, Bejma's Walnut Ridge Collectibles has grown and flourished, thanks to the ingenuity of its founder.

Kathi Bejma has extended her line to include both potpourri and candles with a wonderful pine-and-spice scent.

with a sofa and chairs that the buyers find relaxing. They can sit on the sofa and look at our large library bookcase filled with product."

While most of the original Walnut Ridge products were chalkware Santa figurines, Bejma has always made Santa lamps, too. She expanded into a rabbit line — again made from antique molds — her second year in the chalkware business. With hundreds of items in the present line, Walnut Ridge continues to diversify. Holiday pieces represent all major holidays except the Fourth of July, which is on Bejma's list to commemorate. "We have a garden line," she adds, "birdhouses and bird feeders in a grouping called Walnut Ridge Outdoors, as well as snowmen, angels, rabbits, roosters and topiaries. We have porcelain ornaments, too, because chalkware is too heavy to hang on trees."

NEW PRODUCTS FOR WALNUT RIDGE

Bejma also has introduced a new line of Walnut Ridge potpourri and candles. The potpourri and candles are scented with the wonderful fragrance of pine and spice and are ideal for the holidays, yet versatile enough to use all year. The potpourri features many small pinecones adorned with Bejma's signature glitter, which she calls "diamond dusting." The candles are in a clear glass container, which makes them appropriate for both casual and formal settings. The potpourri has a retail price of $18.00, and the candles sell for $15.00 each.

What's more, Kathi Bejma has introduced a series of six lithographs on canvas, portraying some of Walnut Ridge's most popular items. The "Alexandra" features the company's most beloved angel figurine. The "Herr" *Belsnickle* collection is also represented, as well as favorite snowmen, cats and limited

"Snowy Christmas" represents the 1999 limited edition Santa Claus creation of Walnut Ridge Collectibles.

edition Santa figures. The lithographs are 16" x 20" and are framed in a gilded gold frame. Their retail price is $300 each.

Recent additions to her series of *Annual Limited Edition Santas* have been notable works like "Snowy Christmas," representing 1999. He is 8" tall and has an issue price of $60.00 retail. "Snowy Christmas" is a bright holiday red Santa with snowflakes decorating his coat, and a jolly hand-painted snowman in front of him. While some of her designs are more serious, this Santa represents Bejma's sense of whimsy. As she says, "I wanted to do something fun with this Santa. He has a very happy snowman hand-painted on his coat and the colors are very rich and festive."

A WAY TO GIVE BACK

To show how grateful she is for the success of Walnut Ridge Collectibles, Bejma has established an annual charity ornament issue to provide a "Glimmer of Hope" to the children helped by Communities In Schools (CIS). CIS "helps kids to help themselves" by championing the connection of community resources with schools. The program serves over 500,000 students annually in 1,100 school sites, representing the largest stay-in-school network in America today.

There have been three previous "Glimmer of Hope" ornaments, netting about $10,000 for CIS. For 1999, "Glimmer of Hope IV" depicts a sweet little angel crafted from one of Bejma's own molds. The artist notes, "These ornaments are a versatile size. They can sit on a table or counter, as well as hang from a tree or other display device. For something different this time around, we have an angel on skis!" The little blonde angel wears a pale pink gown with brighter pink patches. She holds a tiny, decorated fir tree as she glides across the snow on golden skis. At 4" tall by 2-3/4" wide, the ornament has a suggested retail price of $36.00, with a portion of the proceeds for each going to CIS.

Looking toward the future, Kathi Lorance Bejma says her main aspiration is "just to keep producing a quality product that makes collectors happy." She adds, "I feel very fortunate with my life, and where I'm at, and wish to give something back." With innovative introductions each year, a continued commitment to hand-made products crafted in the U.S.A., and her thriving "Glimmer of Hope" charity ornament campaign, Bejma is doing just that!

Walnut Ridge Collectibles
39048 Webb Drive
Westland, MI 48185

Phone:
800-275-1765

Fax:
734-728-5950

Bringing Artistry and Entertainment to Collectors

From its beginnings in 1961 as a small gift company, Willitts Designs International, Inc. has become one of the leading manufacturers of collectibles. Today, Willitts Designs creates, manufactures and markets high quality, innovative, limited edition collectibles within two divisions. The Classic Collectibles Division utilizes a cadre of uniquely talented artists to develop — under exclusive contract — proprietary limited edition collectibles based on distinct cultural and artistic themes. Through its Entertainment Division, Willitts Designs features a popular category of limited edition collectibles based upon one-of-a-kind film cels and lenticular motion cels. Together, these divisions have helped Willitts Designs provide the variety and quality that collectors both seek and demand.

THOMAS BLACKSHEAR'S *EBONY VISIONS* SHARE THE HUMAN EXPERIENCE

Among the leading artists for Willitts Designs is Thomas Blackshear, a world-class illustrator best known for his limited edition prints and collector plates. For Willitts Designs, Blackshear's extraordinary versatility as a fine artist is displayed in limited edition sculptures from the *Ebony Visions* collection. The collection emphasizes the beauty of the human form and symbolizes the universal aspirations and ideals of humankind depicted through images that reflect the unique characteristics of African-American culture. Blackshear deliberately portrays the figures in a timeless setting in order to transcend a specific time, place or culture.

Response to *Ebony Visions* in its first year of introduction in 1995 was so overwhelming that the National Association of Limited Edition Dealers (NALED) awarded Blackshear its 1996 "Rising Star Award." Today, the collection features more than 35 figurines. "The designs reflect visions we all share, regardless of the color of our skin," says Blackshear. "Emotions like hope, love, tenderness, faith and serenity know no boundaries. My work is meant to transcend all racial and cultural lines, because in essence, the physical and spiritual expression in my sculptures are all part of the human experience."

In "The Comforter" from Ebony Visions, Thomas Blackshear pays homage to women who nurture others throughout their lifetime.

Based on the popularity of his artwork, Willitts Designs is introducing the *TBII Jewelry Collection* in 2000. It's a full line of earrings, necklaces and accessories inspired by the most popular *Ebony Visions* designs. *TBII Jewelry* is the first of a series of new product categories to be released under the Blackshear Style umbrella — a lifestyles brand of fashion accessories and home decor.

Willitts also invites collectors to join The Blackshear Circle, which was launched in 1997. Members have the opportunity to purchase the club's members-only sculpture. Membership benefits also include a framed bas relief plaque, a personalized membership card, quarterly newsletters, catalogs and invitations to special events. Collectors wanting to find more information about *Ebony Visions* can go on-line at www.ebony-visions.com.

MAKING A COLLECTIBLES FASHION STATEMENT

Putting her best foot forward, artist Raine offers a delightful commentary on art, culture and taste with her collection called *Just the Right Shoe*. A successful illustrator and sculptor with strong formal training in composition and form, Raine has received broad recognition in the art world. Raine entered the art world with an apprenticeship at the age of 15, followed by a full scholarship for a bachelor of fine arts degree. Her impressive career includes numerous publications, gallery exhibits, public and private commissions and collections, television appearances and awards.

Her forte is a rich combination of realism, symbolism and fantasy — all of which are found in *Just the Right Shoe*. Through miniature figurines, boxes and jewelry, the collection provides an historical perspective of women's shoes, purses, hats and other fashion accessories. The addition of women's hats and purses expands the existing line of *Just the Right Shoe* with the introduction of *Just the Right Shoe* accessories. Collector boxes, musicals and sterling silver jewelry are the newest additions to the collection. For more details, collectors can log onto www.just-the-right-shoe.com.

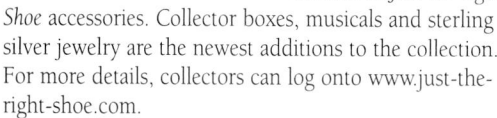

"Frosted Fantasy," a miniature figurine from the Just the Right Shoe collection, steps out in style with a shoe circa 1990 that's adorned with shimmering pearls and frosted beads.

EVERYDAY LIFE CAPTURED IN *OUR SONG* COLLECTION

Willitts Designs also proudly presents *Our Song*, a limited edition collection based on the pastel paintings of

award-winning artist Brenda Joysmith. Joysmith is renowned for her paintings depicting African Americans in everyday living situations from reading bedtime stories to telling secrets. "Rather than convey something grand or extraordinary, I'm interested in reminding people of something they already know," she says. "I want people to relate to the positive aspects of our lives, those aspects that reflect everyday life that is as common as sunshine."

Working with Willitts Designs, her artwork has been brought to life in three-dimensional sculptures that are hand-painted and sculpted in cold cast porcelain. Recent introductions included five figurines, one premiere sculpture and a sculpted plate. For more information on the latest releases based on Brenda Joysmith's art, please visit the Willits Designs Web Site at www.willitts.com.

BRINGING BACK THE MAGIC OF CHRISTMAS

Collectors can start new holiday traditions with *The Life and Adventures of Santa Claus*, a collection of books and figurines based on the literary work of the same name by L. Frank Baum. As the world renowned author of *The Wizard of Oz*, Baum shares the origins and secrets of Santa Claus' life in this three-volume set of newly illustrated and published books adapted from his original work. Exquisitely hand-painted cold cast porcelain figurines accompany each 36-page volume, enriching the story and bringing life to Baum's characters.

The figurines that complement the stories are designed by Ann Dezendorf, an award-winning artist and designer. Baum and the collection chronicle Santa's journey through life and reveal answers to the age-old questions posed by children: How did Santa grow up?; Why does he go down chimneys?; How did he come to choose the reindeer?;

Based on Brenda Joysmith's original pastel painting, "Barefoot Dreams" captures the everyday life events that the artist says "are as common as sunshine." The figurine is from the Our Song collection.

What is the role he has assigned parents?; and Why is he rarely seen?

"By retelling L. Frank Baum's classic, we hope to bring back the magic of Christmas for many adults, as well as helping to create wonderful memories of Santa Claus for all children," says Paul Watson, vice president of Willitts.

OTHER COLLECTIONS KEEP WILLITTS DESIGNS ON THE MOVE

Willitts also features several other collections that celebrate the classics and fine art. *Carousel Memories* by Ann Dezendorf showcases the artistry and imagination of the great international carvers of the golden era of carousels. Each figurine is carefully researched and designed to continue the tradition.

Ami Blackshear's *Rainbow Babies* were inspired by the artist's beautiful watercolor illustrations. The figurines reflect Ami's faith in God and love for babies and nature. The idea of rainbow-colored, butterfly-winged babies in a beautiful garden came to her while visiting the Garden of the Gods in Manitou Springs, Colorado. She feels the babies represent a unity and purity of spirit alive in the souls of all children.

The *Masterpeace Collection* recreates Thomas Blackshear's "Watchers in the Night" as a figurine and framed print. The design depicts the powerful image of an angel providing covering and protection.

Willitts Designs helped create a whole new collecting category in 1995, when it introduced a series of limited edition collectible cels. Following the initial series featuring characters from *Star Wars*, the collection now includes film cels taken from classic Disney animated films including *Cinderella* and *Snow White and the Seven Dwarfs*. An introduction from 1998 was the limited edition collectible film cels taken from James Cameron's epic *Titanic*. In 1999, Willitts added the *Signature Series* in which the voice actors for Cinderella, Beauty and the Beast, and Mickey Mouse have signed a limited number of lithographs.

As a company "on the move," Willitts Designs keeps abreast of the evolving collectibles market and stands ready to serve the changing needs and wants of collectors. One of the company's slogans says it all: "The customer is the boss at Willitts Designs."

The Life and Adventures of Santa Claus collection based on the original work by L. Frank Baum is recreated in newly illustrated and published books. These "Christmas Eve" figurines designed by Ann Dezendorf beautifully complement the stories.

Willitts Designs International, Inc.
1129 Industrial Avenue
Petaluma, CA 94952

Phone:
707-778-7211

Fax:
707-769-0304

Web Site:
www.willitts.com

E-mail:
info@willitts.com

How to Keep Your Treasures Safe and Sound

You select them with love...as an expression of your interests and passions. And you want to show off your collectibles for family and friends to enjoy as much as you do. But you also want your favorite works of art to endure so that they can become heirlooms for the next generation! So how do you make sure they retain their original condition and beauty?

We've asked the manufacturers of a broad range of artworks for their advice. And if you follow their directions, you can help ensure that your favorite treasures will be as beautiful in your great-grandchildren's homes as they are in yours today.

MANUFACTURERS KNOW BEST

Stephen Richardson, general manager of Hazle Ceramics, advises, "Follow the manufacturer's instructions for the care of your collection. Your fragile pieces will probably require specific care and attention." When you buy a new piece, look for hangtags or enclosures that include such information. Also check a company's club newsletter or Internet site for tips.

STORE AND SHIP IN ORIGINAL BOXES

Collectibles are packed in boxes specially designed and tested to ensure they can keep their contents safe in shipping – even when handled somewhat roughly. So keep the boxes your pieces come in, along with all wrapping materials. They'll prove handy for storage or when moving. They'll also help fetch the best possible price if you ever care to sell items on the secondary market.

AVOID SUNLIGHT

This is especially true if you live in a climate with strong sun, since harsh rays can be harmful to the coloring or detail of a collectible.

SELECT WELL-CONSTRUCTED DISPLAYS

Place your collectibles in sturdy displays that are away from busy traffic areas in your home. Whether you're choosing a curio cabinet, adjustable shelves, plate hangers or a Christmas tree, make sure it's strong and stable enough to support your pieces. Select glassed-in cabinets over open table displays for especially fragile pieces. And if you live in an area where earthquakes may occur, consider using a product like Quake Hold! putty or wax, which fastens collectibles in place.

ADVICE AND CARE FOR SPECIFIC COLLECTIBLES

Each collectible – from plates to prints, figurines to ornaments, steins to dolls – has its own unique requirements for safety and

Before

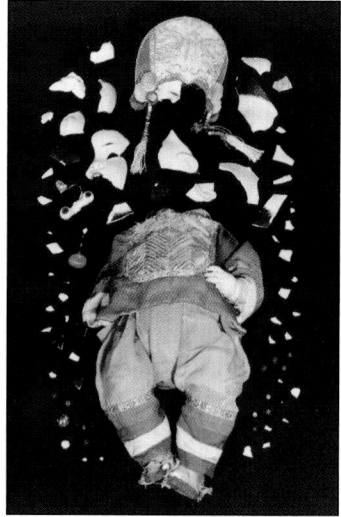

After

This Chinese doll was restored to its original beauty by the experts at Venerable Classics.

security. Here we present general guidelines, but we also suggest checking with the manufacturer of your collectibles if you have a special concern.

Figurines, Cottages, Steins and Bells

Because of their delicate detail work and crevices, three-dimensional pieces such as figurines, cottages, steins and bells, often require more cleaning than flat works of art. Dust gently with a feather duster or small shaving brush for regular care. When deeper cleaning is needed, the manufacturer's advice is crucial. For example, Enesco Corporation recommends that its porcelain bisque figurines from the *Precious Moments* collection be wiped with a damp cloth – never immersed in water. Roman, Inc. suggests that its *Fontanini* figurines be cleaned with a damp cloth dipped in clear water. These pieces are made of a high-density polymer, which means they are impossible to chip, break or nick. However, if subjected to heat or chemicals, they may be damaged beyond repair. "Just be sure not to store or display the figures near a heat source, such as the top of a hot radiator or register," says Jennifer Wigman, Fontanini Collectors' Club coordinator. "Distortion or damage could result," she warns.

Crystal figurines can be washed with warm water. Experts recommend lining your sink with towels before gently immersing crystal pieces. Rinse in a towel-lined tub of cool, clean water. Then, let your crystal air-dry or use a polishing cloth or chamois to bring out its sparkle.

Plates

Although they are breakable, most collectible plates are remarkably durable because of the way their decorations are fired on. In most cases, they can be wiped clean with a damp cloth or even washed gently by hand in a sink with lukewarm water and mild soap. On the other hand, unglazed plate surfaces or hand-painted, unfired plates should never be immersed in water. In these cases, dusting is your best option. If your plate has been hand-signed by the artist, you should completely avoid using water. Plates on secure hangers, displayed on well-sunk nails, are usually safe from most harm. However, if your plates are to be shown in a high-traffic area, you might choose plate frames for more protection against bumps and bangs.

Collectible Dolls

Because of their fabric clothing, synthetic wigs and delicate features and fingers, it is best to keep collectible dolls in glass cases or wooden displays with glass fronts. Dolls should be kept away from sunlight to

avoid damage to fabrics, hair and painting. If a doll's clothing becomes soiled, the best option is to remove it and have it dry-cleaned, unless the manufacturer says the fabric can be washed without damage or shrinking. Annalee Mobilitee Dolls offers this caveat: If there is any concern that the cleaning may do more harm than good, leave it as is.

If your doll's coiffeur needs attention, it's not advisable to attempt a complete re-style. This often ends in disaster. Instead, use your fingers to gently smooth down any out-of-place hairs.

Ornaments

At one time, ornaments only saw the light of day at Christmas. However, many of today's collectors choose to show these elegant works of art all year. If you still choose to put your collectible ornaments away each January, the best option is to store them in their original boxes.

Christopher Radko adds that it is wise to wrap ornaments in acid-free paper for extra protection. They can then be stored in boxes with divided compartments or stackable rubber tray containers lined with bubble wrap. Ornaments should never be stored in an attic or basement where water, humidity or extreme temperatures exist.

Graphics

A museum-mounted, framed print is well protected, but it should still be hung out of direct sunlight to avoid fading. Other important rules in preserving your print are to minimize handling and maintain consistent temperatures in your home to prevent the build-up of moisture between the print and glass. Also, be sure never to spray liquid glass cleaner directly onto the glass: it may drip down between the frame and the mat, causing damage. Instead, spray a dry, lint-free cloth with cleaner and then gently wipe the glass. If a canvas reproduction or oil painting cannot be dusted clean with a lint-free silk cloth or brush, take it to a professional framer for cleaning. Unframed prints should be stored within protective acetate sleeves.

A COLLECTIBLES RESTORATION GUIDE

If one of your prized collectibles is broken or damaged, don't despair: often it can be restored to its original beauty, if not its original value. Indeed, many collectors love their artwork so much that they prefer to have it restored rather than accept an insurance settlement. A qualified restorer can assist with a variety of collectibles and recover 50% to 100% of the item's original issue price.

The following list of restorers has been recommended through various sources. Since we have not had the occasion to use the services of the businesses listed, CIB cannot guarantee their workmanship. You can also call a restoration expert in your area.

T.S. Restoration
2015 N. Dobson Rd., Suite 4
PMB 59B
Chandler, AZ 85224
480-963-3148
Specialty: Porcelain.

China & Crystal Clinic
1808 N. Scottsdale Rd.
Tempe, AZ 85281
800-658-9197
Specialty: Porcelain and crystal.

Crystal World
2743 N. Campbell Ave.
Tuscon, AZ 85719
520-326-5990
Specialty: Crystal.

Pick Up The Pieces
711 W. 17th St. #C12
Costa Mesa, CA 92627
949-720-8183
Specialty: Porcelain, oil paintings and frames, crystal, glass, wood, jade, ivory, bronze, brass, gold, silver, pewter, resin, papier mâché, iron, white metal, soapstone and china.

Brookes Restorations
930 S. Robertson Blvd.
Los Angeles, CA 90035
310-659-8253
Fax: 310-659-8262
Specialty: Porcelain, ceramic, jade, marble, ivory, alabaster, wood, crystal, glass, paintings, soapstone, resin and china.

Venerable Classics
645 Fourth St., Suite 208
Santa Rosa, CA 95404
707-575-3626
800-531-2891
Specialty: Porcelain, ceramic, resin, pottery, glass, crystal, jade, ivory, marble, wood, frames, brass, bronze and pewter.

Geppetto's Restoration
31121 Via Colinas, Suite 1003
Westlake Village, CA 91362
818-889-0901
Fax: 818-889-8922
Specialty: Porcelain, glass, crystal, ivory, jade, marble, ceramics, resin, pottery and wood.

Herbert F. Klug Conservation and Restoration
Box 28002 #16
Denver, CO 80228
303-985-9261
Specialty: Porcelain, marble and ivory.

Dean Schulefand & Associates Porcelain & Crystal Restoration
324 Guinevere Ridge
Cheshire, CT 06410
203-271-3659
800-669-1327
Specialty: Pottery, jade, ivory, glass, crystal, ceramic, cold cast, resin, porcelain, marble, plaster, china, bronze, silver, pewter and brass.

The Crystal Doctor
3633 Bramble Rd.
Jacksonville, FL 32210
904-781-9702
Specialty: Swarovski crystal.

A Fine Touch
5740 Lakefield Court
Orlando, FL 32810
407-298-7129
Specialty: Porcelain, ceramic, pottery, clay, china, jade, marble, resin and plaster.

Beckus Studios
4511 32nd Avenue North
St. Petersburg, FL 33713
727-522-4288
Specialty: Wood, porcelain, metal, ceramic, pottery, ivory, jade, marble, plaster, resin, china and cold cast.

Doe Lasky Repair and Restoration
Oak Park, IL 60302
708-386-1772
Specialty: Porcelain, crystal, bronze, ivory, jade, oriental screens, oil paintings, frames and wood carvings.

Rosine Green Associates , Inc.
89 School St.
Brookline, MA 02446
617-277-8368
Specialty: Porcelain, paintings, wood, ceramic, pottery, resin, jade, marble, lacquer, granite, alabaster, glass, soapstone, cold cast, brass, pewter and bronze.

Trefler and Sons Antique Restoring Studio, Inc.
99 Cabot St.
Needham, MA 02494
781-444-2685
Specialty: Crystal, paintings, furniture, silver, resin, glass, pottery, ceramic, wood, ivory, jade and soapstone.

Imperial China
27 North Park Avenue
Rockville Center, NY 11570
516-764-7311
Specialty: Porcelain, ceramic and resin.

Collector's Clinic
3009 W. Genesee St.
Syracuse, NY 13219
315-488-7123
Specialty: Porcelain, cold cast, resin, antique dolls, frames, pottery, china, ivory, papier mâché, jade and soapstone.

Old World Restorations, Inc.
5729 Dragon Way
Cincinnati, OH 45227
513-271-5459
Specialty: Porcelain, paintings, glass, frames, works on paper, photographs, furniture, metals and on-site architectural restoration such as murals, frescos and gold leaf.

Antique & Hummel Restoration by Wiebold
413 Terrace Place
Terrace Park, OH 45174
800-321-2541
Specialty: Porcelain, ceramic, pottery, metal art, glass, oil paintings, frames, crystal, jade, marble, soapstone, alabaster and plaster chalk.

A. Ludwig Klein & Son, Inc.
P.O. Box 145
683 Sumneytown Pike
Harleysville, PA 19438
215-256-9004
Specialty: Glass, ivory, jade, metal art, crystal, pottery, leather, statuary and porcelain.

Harry A. Eberhardt & Sons, Inc.
2010 Walnut St.
Philadelphia, PA 19103
215-568-4144
Specialty: Porcelain, glass, metal, crystal and orientalia.

Sharon Lewis Restoration & Repairs
8902 Deer Haven Rd.
Austin, TX 78737
512-301-2294
Specialty: Porcelain, ceramic, plaster, stoneware, china and pottery.

McHugh's
3461 West Cary St.
Richmod, VA 23221
804-353-9596
Specialty: Crystal, glass, ivory, marble, jade, pottery, soapstone and porcelain.

Kingsmen Antique Restoration Inc.
19 Passmore Avenue, Unit 28
Scarborough, ONT M1V 4T5
Canada
416-291-8939
Specialty: Porcelain, bronze, pewter, ivory, pottery, glass, crystal, jade, marble, soapstone, wood, lacquer, papier mâché, brass, iron, white metal and oil paintings.

Artwork Restoration
30 Hillhouse Road
Winnipeg, MB R2V 2V9, Canada
204-334-7090
Specialty: Crystal, china, glass, marble, pottery, soapstone, ivory, dolls, paintings, wood frames and porcelain.

A New Collecting Tradition Begins

The tradition of decorating Christmas trees was largely unknown in America until the mid to late 1800s. German immigrants arrived on our shores carefully cradling the precious glass "kugel" decorations that they'd carried across rough seas to the New World. In 1856, President Franklin Pierce set up the first decorated Christmas tree in the White House, establishing a new American tradition.

In a few short years, nearly every family would have their own splendid display of fragrant greenery, flickering candlelight and lovingly crafted ornaments. Christmas trees provided an ideal showcase for 19th century Americans' love of opulence - it wasn't long before the Christmas tree would become as American as apple pie.

The Victorian era of extravagance demanded ever-new Christmas tree decorations and while German artisans complied with a myriad of fanciful designs, the American retailing legend, F.W. Woolworth,

Swarovski Crystal sparkles brightly in the "2000 Annual Edition Ornament."

was largely responsible for the popularization of glass Christmas tree ornaments. He started bringing them from Europe and making them available to virtually everybody, from the wealthy to the working class, in his famous five-and-dime stores.

No longer were tree decorations confined to perishable paper flowers, consumable candy and cookies, or fragile scraps of printed paper. Woolworth's imported glass ornaments were affordable, retained their beauty year after year, and attained the status of family treasures.

Fads and fashions in ornament design over the years have generally reflected the changing lifestyles and tastes of America through the twentieth century. But in recent years, a number of innovative makers of fine art limited editions – their names read like a "Who's Who" in collectibles – have started producing their own remarkable brands of ornaments…original works of Christmas art that are revolutionizing the decorating and collecting world.

MORE THAN JUST ONE SEASON TO BE JOLLY!

Ornaments have burst on the scene as one of the newest and hottest categories in collecting, yet virtually everyone who celebrates the holiday has been quietly and lovingly amassing their own collections for generations.

And like collectors of every other category, it becomes clear that the value of the ornaments truly lies in the memories and sentimental associations each conjures up for its owners — "We got this ornament the year our baby was born." "Remember the little shop where we bought this, that first time we all went on vacation together?" "This was always my mother's favorite ornament, and she handed it down to me."

Sentiment aside, the works of the leading ornament makers are generating enough demand to create a secondary market for ornaments that is as healthy and vigorous as that of other collectible categories.

A WHOLE NEW WORLD OF COLLECTING EXCITEMENT

From reverent solemnity to irreverent humor, from ancient themes to rock 'n roll, from homespun charm to glamorous sparkle, today's ornaments run the gamut of styles, subjects, materials, looks and price ranges. Collectors have developed a remarkable level of discernment, and exhibit extraordinary brand and style loyalty when they are making a decision about a new acquisition. A perfect example is the selection of nostalgic looking molded, blown glass ornaments from Eastern Europe.

Christopher Radko's handcrafted glass ornaments have helped to revive the public's taste for the brightly painted, whimsical mouth-blown glass ornaments that were so common back in the first half

Christopher Radko's ornaments reflect the magic of Christmas.

Artist Will Bullas' good humor comes through in his "bearing gifts…" ornament.

of the twentieth century. Santas, nutcracker characters, the Nativity, and storybook, cartoon and television personalities have all been given the "Radko treatment," which can be characterized by a rich, jewel-like opulence that is timeless.

No wonder Radko's distinctive ornament designs are featured by some of the most prestigious retailers in the world like Neiman Marcus, Saks Fifth Avenue, Bloomingdale's and Marshall Field & Co., and are found in the homes of such luminaries as the President and Vice-President of the United States.

The age-old European tradition of glass blowing and hand-painting also shines through the ornaments of Kurt S. Adler's *Polonaise Collection*. But the innovative supplier of high-end holiday decorations also offers unique ornaments of extraordinary elegance like the Victorian-styled *Louis Nichole Heirloom Collection*, many pieces of which have helped to make the White House Christmas more festive.

Larry Fraga, of Larry Fraga Designs, is another well-known designer of Old World style glass ornaments. Created from both his own original designs and from forgotten antique glass blowing molds he has discovered, Larry has developed his own trademark ornament colorations that savvy collectors immediately recognize as the artist's signature. The porcelain like quality of the ornaments' skin tones, and the inspired use of a palette of colorful glitters give Larry Fraga's designs a distinctive caché that has attracted collectors for over a decade.

In creating contemporary ornaments that will be tomorrow's family heirlooms, the artisans of Slavic Treasures collaborate with nature on the company's magnificent hand-blown and hand-painted wildlife designs that are astonishingly realistic. Their interpretations of college mascots have also proven to be overwhelmingly popular in bringing good-natured academic rivalry to holiday celebrating.

MORE POPULAR DESIGNS JUST RIGHT FOR HANGING

Margaret Furlong Designs has also taken a page from nature's design portfolio by incorporating the perfect elegance of the seashell into the company's signature angels. Margaret's series of white-on-white angel ornaments are crafted of white bisque porcelain, which allows her to highlight the subtleties of the shell's delicate pattern and rich texture.

For the last 25 years, *Hallmark Keepsake Ornaments* have been enchanting collectors with new, original and irresistible decorating possibilities based on our most cherished Christmas traditions and the most beloved cultural icons. In fact, the company was a real pioneer in helping this category make the transition from generic commodity to gift-quality collectible.

Hallmark Keepsake Ornaments can boast so many "firsts" among their limited edition releases over the years, that it's little wonder they're acknowledged as the industry's leading innovator. The first "Special Edition" ornaments, the first lighted ornaments, and the first ornaments with audio messages that can be customized have all come from Hallmark's team of top ornament artists.

Favorite pop culture icons like Barbie®, sports figures like Mark McGwire, cartoon characters like "Snoopy" and science fiction fantasy like *Star Wars*™ have all been translated into *Hallmark Keepsake Ornaments* over the years. Each year's unveiling of the new additions to the *Keepsake Ornament* line is an event for collectors across the nation, as Hallmark continues to delight young and old with the wit and whimsy of their miniature holiday creations.

The Old World charm of mouth-blown glass ornaments is captured in Kurt S. Adler's "Coming Down the Chimney" from the Polonaise Collection.

Well known artists have also found Christmas ornaments to be an irresistible medium. The humor of Will Bullas, which has been captivating patrons of the prestigious Greenwich Workshop for many years, has found its way onto Christmas trees. The artist's new line of whimsical and witty ornaments are executed in the company's exquisite Pearl Bisque™, a proprietary blend of cold cast porcelain and finely ground pearl.

Nothing gleams and sparkles like the flawless, fiery brilliance of Swarovski Crystal — which is why the faceted twinkle of the famous crystals has been the choice for fine jewelry makers for over a century.

And as collectors have demanded ever-higher quality for the ornaments they treasure, Swarovski crystal has been an obvious and precious choice. The company's magnificent *Annual Edition Christmas Ornaments, Annual Edition Angel Ornaments,* and exquisite *Crystal Memories Ornaments* are masterpieces of intricate, original and beautiful design.

In just a few decades, Christmas ornaments have come a long, long way. Today's limited edition ornaments are crafted from more precious materials than ever used in days gone by, and they have become a uniquely appropriate medium for the finest artists in the world to work. Ornaments have come of age as treasured gifts, delightfully festive statements of self-expression, and collectibles to be cherished for a lifetime.

Hallmark's Barbie® ornament series continues in 2000 with "Commuter Set."

Tours and Museums in the U.S.A. and Around the World

There's nothing more fascinating to a serious collector than visiting the place where his treasures are made, or strolling through a museum boasting the work of her favorite artist. Many of your favorite collectibles studios have organized wonderful travel tours to sites around the corner — or even on the other side of the world. And many more recommend special museums and showcases of special interest to their collectors. Here, we present a guide to some of the most popular collector travel sites both in the United States and in other parts of the world. Next time you have a trip planned, make sure you add on a visit to a special museum or take in a collectibles tour. And perhaps your next vacation could focus on a travel tour sponsored by your favorite collectibles manufacturer!

Lee Middleton Original Dolls welcomes thousands of visitors each year to its facility in Belpre, Ohio.

MUSEUMS AND FACTORY TOURS IN THE U.S.A.

THE ANNALEE DOLL MUSEUM
44 Reservoir Road
Meredith, NH 03253
603-279-3333
HOURS: Memorial Day to Columbus Day; call ahead for hours.
ADMISSION: Free
Museum houses thousands of Annalee Thorndike's creations from the 1930s to the present.

BABYLAND GENERAL® HOSPITAL
73 W. Underwood Street
Cleveland, GA 30528
706-865-2171
HOURS: Mon.-Sat. 9 a.m. to 5 p.m.; Sun. 10 a.m. to 5 p.m.
ADMISSION: Free
Witness the "birth" of a soft-sculpture Cabbage Patch Kid® in a turn-of-the-century medical clinic, which formerly served the small Appalachian community.

THE BRADFORD MUSEUM OF COLLECTOR'S PLATES
9333 Milwaukee Avenue
Niles, IL 60714
800-323-5577
HOURS: Mon.-Fri. 9 a.m. to 5:30 p.m.; closed weekends.
ADMISSION: Free
The Bradford Museum of Collector's Plates houses almost 800 plates, spanning the 100-plus year history of collector's plates.

BRANDYWINE COLLECTIBLES FACTORY TOUR
104 Greene Drive
Yorktown, VA 23692
757-898-5031
HOURS: Mon.-Fri. 9 a.m. to 5 p.m.
ADMISSION: Free to Club Members.
Club members are invited to tour Brandywine's 9,400 square foot manufacturing and distribution center and

observe the fine craftsmanship that goes into the making of every Brandywine building.

BYERS' CHOICE LTD.
GALLERY & EMPORIUM
4355 County Line Road
Chalfont, PA 18914
215-822-0150
HOURS: Mon.-Sat. 10 a.m. to 4 p.m.; Closed Sun. and major holidays.
ADMISSION: Free
Visit the factory and see how Byers' Choice Carolers® are made. Over 400 figurines are on display in various winter settings. Selected gifts and Carolers are sold at the Emporium.

DEPARTMENT 56® SHOWROOM TOUR
One Village Place
6436 City West Parkway
Eden Prairie, MN 55344
800-LIT-TOWN (548-8696)
HOURS: Every Friday during the summer; one-hour tours from 9 a.m. to 4 p.m. Advance reservations required.
ADMISSION: Free
Enjoy a walk through Department 56 headquarters' showroom and see the over 3,000 products the company makes, as well as imaginative displays.

FENTON ART GLASS COMPANY MUSEUM & TOUR
420 Caroline Avenue
Williamstown, WV 26187
304-375-7772
HOURS: April-Dec. Mon.-Fri. 8 a.m. to 8 p.m.; Sat. 8 a.m. to 5 p.m.; Sun. 12:15 p.m to 5 p.m.
Jan.-Mar. Mon.-Sat. 8 a.m. to 5 p.m.; Sun. 12:15 p.m. to 5 p.m.
ADMISSION: Free
The Fenton Art Glass Museum offers examples of Ohio Valley glass, with major emphasis on Fenton glass made from 1905 to 1955. A 30-minute movie on the making

of Fenton glass is shown throughout the day.
TOURS: Mon.-Fri. only, 8 a.m. to 4 p.m. The 40-minute factory tour allows visitors to watch highly-skilled craftsmen create hand-made glass from its molten state to the finished product. A gift shop is also located on the premises.

THE FRANKLIN MINT MUSEUM
Franklin Center, PA 19091
610-459-6582
HOURS: Mon.-Sat. 9:30 a.m. to 4:30 p.m.; Sun. 1 p.m. to 4 p.m.
ADMISSION: Free
The museum houses many icons of the 20th century, including a famous Princess Diana gown and the original Jacqueline Kennedy Onassis faux pearl triple strand necklace.

HALLMARK VISITORS CENTER
Located in Hallmark Square in Crown Center
P.O. Box 419580, Mail Drop 132
Kansas City, MO 64141-6580
816-274-5672
HOURS: Mon.-Fri. 9 a.m. to 5 p.m.; Sat. 9:30 a.m. to 4:30 p.m.; closed Sun. Open most holidays. Reservations required for groups of ten or more.
ADMISSION: Free; also free parking with three-hour validation.
Learn about the history of the Hallmark company, its products and promotions.

THE HUMMEL MUSEUM
199 Main Plaza
New Braunfels, TX 78130
210-625-5636
HOURS: Mon.-Sat. 10 a.m. to 5 p.m.; Sun. Noon to 5 p.m.
ADMISSION: $5.00 adults; $4.50 seniors; $3.00 students.
The Hummel Museum displays the world's largest collection of Sister Maria Innocentia Hummel's original art. This one-of-a-kind

museum offers guided tours, video presentations, historical vignette rooms of Sister Hummel's personal items, and an extensive display of rare M.I. Hummel figurines (over 1,100 on exhibit). The Museum Gift Shop offers a great variety of Hummel collectibles.

LEE MIDDLETON ORIGINAL DOLLS FACTORY TOUR
1301 Washington Blvd.
Belpre, OH 45714
740-423-3125
HOURS: Mon.-Fri. 9 a.m. to 2:15 p.m.
ADMISSION: Free
Travel to Belpre, Ohio, dubbed by its mayor as "The Baby Doll Capital of the World," to see how Lee Middleton Original Dolls are made. Tour includes a visit to the "hospital" where each doll's new "parents" are invited to don hospital gowns and rock their "babies" for the first time.

LIZZIE HIGH MUSEUM
A Country Gift Shoppe
Rt. 313, Dublin Pike
Dublin, PA 18917
215-249-9877
HOURS: Mon., Wed., Thurs. and Fri. 10 a.m. to 7 p.m.; Tues. and Sat. 10 a.m. to 5 p.m.; Sun. 11 a.m. to 4 p.m.
ADMISSION: Free
All retired and limited special edition Lizzie High dolls are on display in the museum, as well as historical information about the company's development. Current dolls are available in the gift shop.

LLADRÓ MUSEUM
43 West 57th Street
New York, NY 10019
212-838-9356
HOURS: Tues.-Sat. 10 a.m. to 5:30 p.m.; closed Sun. and Mon.
ADMISSION: Free
The world's largest collection of retired

Lladró figurines – over 1,000 pieces – occupy five floors of the building.

MARGARET FURLONG DESIGNS STUDIO TOUR
210 State Street
Salem, OR 97301
503-363-6004
HOURS: Mon.-Fri.; closed weekends.
Please call for an appointment.
ADMISSION: Free
Visitors can tour the production area at Margaret Furlong Designs Studio, where skilled craftspeople make each porcelain design by hand.

MISS MARTHA ORIGINALS, INC. SHOWROOM
1119 Chastain Blvd. (Hwy. 431)
Gadsden, AL 35904
256-492-0221
HOURS: Mon.-Thurs. 8 a.m. to 5 p.m.; closed Fri. and weekends.
ADMISSION: Free
The showroom features displays of figurines in the All God's Children collection.

PIPKA'S GALLERY
334 Mill Road
Sister Bay, WI 54234
800-829-9235
HOURS: By appointment or during regular business hours.
ADMISSION: Free
Browse through Pipka's Gallery, filled with original sculpts, and learn the history of her artwork and collectible line.

RON LEE'S WORLD OF CLOWNS FACTORY AND TOUR
330 Carousel Pkwy.
Henderson, NV 89014
702-434-1700
HOURS: Mon.-Fri. 8 a.m. to 5 p.m.; Sat. 9 a.m. to 5 p.m.; closed Sun.
ADMISSION: Free
Take a self-guided audio and video tour to view the making of clown figurines from start to finish. There is also a museum of

circus and clown costumes, props and memorabilia, a miniature carnival, a café, a Gallery featuring Ron Lee's clown and animation sculptures, the 30-foot Chance Carousel, and more.

SARAH'S ATTIC
126-1/2 W. Broad Street
Chesaning, MI 48616
800-437-4363
HOURS: Mon.-Fri. 8 a.m. to 4:30 p.m.; closed weekends.
ADMISSION: Free
Tour the production factory and home of Sarah's Attic.

SHELIA'S, INC.
1856 Belgrade Avenue
Charleston, SC 29407
800-227-6564
HOURS: By appointment.
ADMISSION: Free to members of Shelia's Collectors Society; $3.00 for non-members.
See Shelia's, Inc. historic architectural replicas made from start to finish.

UNITED DESIGN GIFT SHOP
1600 N. Main
Noble, OK 73068
800-527-4883
HOURS: Mon.-Fri. 9 a.m. to 5 p.m.; 10 a.m. to 4 p.m. on the first Saturday of every month only. Call for tour times.
ADMISSION: Free
Over 4,000 handcrafted products are on display. The tour showcases hundreds of figurine designs being made by artists and craftsmen.

OUTSIDE THE U.S.A.

ANRI WORKSHOPS TOURS
ANRI ART
Str. Plan da Tieja, 67
1-39048 Wolkenstein
Groeden, Italy
011-39-0471-79-2233
HOURS: Contact company.
ADMISSION: Free

Advance reservations are requested to ensure that an English-speaking guide is available to escort collectors through the carving and painting studios.

CAPODIMONTE MUSEUM THE PRINCIPE SOCIETY
Napoli, Italy
410-823-6080
HOURS: Private tours with special guides are provided for members of the Principe Society. Call ahead for reservations.
ADMISSION: Free to Society members.
Capodimonte Museum of Porcelain displays a breathtaking area of rare Capodimonte art from 1746 to 1902.

HAZLE CERAMICS VISITORS CENTRE
Stallions Yard, Codham Hall,
Great Warley
Brentwood, Essex CM13 3JT
United Kingdom
011-44-1277-220892
HOURS: Fri.-Sun. (and bank holidays) 11 a.m. to 5 p.m.
ADMISSION: Free
See the whole ceramic-making process of this award-winning range of miniature wall sculptures, from artist's drawings to signed and boxed limited edition pieces.

LILLIPUT LANE VISITORS CENTER/TOURS
Skirsgill, Penrith
Cumbria, England CA11 0DP
011-44-1768-212700
HOURS: Mon.-Thurs. 9:30 a.m. to 2:30 p.m.; Fri. 9:30 a.m. to 12:30 p.m.; closed weekends.
ADMISSION: Free to Club members.
This one-hour tour takes visitors through the research, development, casting and painting departments.

PIPKIN AND BONNET
Park House, Victoria Place, Henry St.
New Ross, Wexford
Ireland
011-353-51-425695
HOURS: Contact company.

ADMISSION: Free
View Pipkin and Bonnet designers at the millinery headquarters in New Ross, County Wexford, Ireland.

ROYAL CROWN DERBY MUSEUM
184 Osmaston Road, Derby
England
011-44-1782-292292
HOURS: Mon.-Fri. 9 a.m. to 4 p.m.; closed weekends.
ADMISSION: Free
A wide variety of pieces from the archives of Royal Crown Derby and Minton dinnerware and giftware lines are on display for collectors to admire and study.

ROYAL DOULTON MUSEUM AND FACTORY TOURS
Nile Street
Burslem Stoke-on-Trent Staffs
ST6 2AJ England
011-44-1782-292292
MUSEUM HOURS: Daily 9 a.m. to 4 p.m.
TOUR HOURS: Mon.-Fri. 10:30 a.m. to 2 p.m.; no tours on weekends.
ADMISSION: Nominal charge. For safety reasons, the tour is not available for children under 10 years of age.
The Royal Doulton Factory Tour takes you behind the scenes at one of the world's leading fine china companies. The tour also includes the Sir Henry Doulton Gallery, displaying examples of Royal Doulton products spanning over 170 years, and a factory gift shop.

THE SOCIETY — GIUSEPPE ARMANI ART FACTORY TOUR IN ITALY
c/o Miller Import
300 Mac Lane
Keasbey, NJ 08832
800-3-ARMANI
HOURS: Society members should call ten days prior to their visit of the Florence Sculture d'Arte Studio.
ADMISSION: Free to Society members.
Members of the Society — Giuseppe Armani Art and their guests can tour the Florence Sculture d'Arte Studio located in Florence, Italy.

TRAVEL TOURS FOR COLLECTORS

CHRISTIAN ULBRICHT COLLECTORS' CLUB TOUR
P.O. Box 99
Angwin, CA 94508
888-707-5591
The company sponsors a two-week annual trip to Germany that includes a visit to the factory and other sites.

LLADRÓ SOCIETY
1 Lladró Drive
Moonachie, NJ 07074
800-634-9088
Members-only Society-sponsored trips to Spain include a tour of Porcelain City in Valencia, Spain — where all Lladró figurines are created.

M.I. HUMMEL CLUB TOURS
c/o M.I. Hummel Club
Goebel Plaza
P.O. Box 11
Pennington, NJ 08534-0011
800-666-CLUB
Eleven superb millennium tours are planned in 2000 for M.I. Hummel Club members. Eight 15-day tours are offered to Oberammergau, Germany, for the Passion Play, and two 15-day tours to Rome. An 11-day "Fairy Tale Christmas Tour" to Germany is also planned for Dec., 2000.

THE PRINCIPE SOCIETY
Napoli, Italy
410-823-6080

Principe Society members are offered a trip to the foundry in Italy three times a year.

SWAROVSKI EUROPEAN TOURS
c/o Swarovski Collectors Society
One Kenney Drive
Cranston, RI 02920
800-426-3088
Each year, a variety of tours is offered to SCS members and a guest. Participants are escorted through the picturesque countryside of Europe, stopping at local points of interest. Tours are offered in spring, fall and at the holidays, with an average tour length of between ten and 13 days.

The Hummel Museum in New Braunfels, Texas, displays the world's largest collection of original art by Sister M.I. Hummel.

National Collectors' Clubs

	Annual Dues/Renewals	Club Year	Membership Gift	Members-Only Piece	Club Publication	Binder	Membership Card	Buy-Sell Matching Service	Local Chapters	Tours/Special Events	Other Benefits
All God's Children Collector's Club* **Miss Martha Originals** P.O. Box 5038 Glencoe, AL 35905 (256) 492-0221	$20	Anniv. of Sign-Up Date	●	●	4/yr.		●		●	●	• Invitation to Collector's Family Reunion • Personal Checklist
The Anheuser-Busch Collectors Club* 2700 South Broadway St. Louis, MO 63118 (800) 305-2582 www.budweiser.com	$40	Jan.-Dec.	●	●	4/yr.	●	●			●	• Discounts to Anheuser-Busch Theme Parks • Monthly Contests • Notification of Artist Events
Annalee Doll Society* P.O. Box 1137 Meredith, NH 03253-1137 (800) 433-6557 www.annalee.com	$37.95	July 1-June 30	●	●	4/yr.	●	●			●	• Discounts on CIB Books • Membership Pin • Advance Notice of Retirements • Contests and Prizes
Artesania Rinconada Collector's Society* **John J. Madison Co., Inc.** P.O. Box 2190 Laguna Hills, CA 92654 949) 888-8415 www.rinconada.com	$35.00	May 1-April 30	●	●	4/yr.						• Silver Anniversary Album or • Collector's Pricing Guide • Membership Certificate
The Belleek Collectors International Society 9893 Georgetown Pike, Suite 525 Great Falls, VA 22066 (800)-BELLEEK (235-5335)	$38.50/ $31	Anniv. of Sign-Up Date	●	●	3/yr.	●	●	●	●	●	• Membership Certificate • Full Color Catalog • Annual Renewal Gift
Boehm Porcelain Society 25 Fairfacts Street Trenton, NJ 08638 (800) 257-9410	$15	Jan.-Dec.		●	1/yr.		●			●	• Invitations to Special Events • Catalogs
Brandywine Neighborhood Association 4303 Manchester Rd. Portsmouth, VA 23703 (757) 898-5031 www.brandywinecollectibles.com	$30/$25	Anniv. of Sign-Up Date	●	●	4/yr.	●				●	
Cabbage Patch Kids® Collectors Club* **Original Appalachian Artworks** P.O. Box 714 Cleveland, GA 30528 (706) 865-2171 www.cabbagepatchkids.com	$30	Anniv. of Sign-Up Date	●	●	4/yr.	●	●			●	• Pin • Members-Only Merchandise Available
Caithness Glass Paperweight Collectors' Club 141 Lanza Ave., Bldg. 12 Garfield, NJ 07026 (973) 340-3330	$40-1yr. $70-2yrs.	Anniv. of Sign-Up Date	●	●	2/yr.	●	●	●		●	• Catalogs
The Cardew Collectors' Club* 200 South 31st Street Paducah, KY 42001 (877) 9-TEAPOT www.cardewdesign.com	$50-1yr. $90-2yrs.	Anniv. of Sign-Up Date	●	●	3/yr.		●			●	• Catalog
Cat's Meow Collectors Club FJ Designs 2163 Great Trails Dr. Wooster, OH 44691-3738 (330) 264-1377 Ext. 225	$33/$22	Anniv. of Sign-Up Date	●	●	3/yr.	●	●	●		●	• Deed Holder
Cavanagh's Coca-Cola Collectors Society* P.O. Box 768090 Roswell, GA 30076 (800) 653-1221 www.cavanaghgrp.com	$25	Jan.-Dec.	●	●	4/yr.		●				• Membership Certificate
The Cherished Teddies Club* **Enesco Group, Inc.** P.O. Box 689 Itasca, IL 60143-0689 (800) NEAR-YOU (632-7968) www.enescoclubs.com	$20-1yr. $38-2yrs.	Jan. 1-Dec. 31	●	●	●		●			●	• Catalog
Cheryl Spencer Collin Lighthouse Collectors Club* **Dave Grossman Creations** 1608 N. Warson Rd. St. Louis, MO 63132 (800) 325-1655	$30/ $25	Jan.-Dec.	●	●	4/yr.	●	●			●	

National Collectors' Clubs

	Annual Dues/Renewals	Club Year	Membership Gift	Members-Only Piece	Club Publication	Binder	Membership Card	Buy-Sell Matching Service	Local Chapters	Tours/Special Events	Other Benefits
Christian Ulbricht Collectors' Club* P.O. Box 99 Angwin, CA 94508 (888) 707-5591 www.ulbricht.com	$45/ $35	Anniv. of Sign-Up Date	●	●	2/yr.	●	●			●	• Button • Product Catalogs
Crinkle Claus Collectors Club* Possible Dreams 6 Perry Dr. Foxboro, MA 02035 (508) 543-6667	$25	Anniv. of Sign-Up Date	●	●	2/yr.		●				• Contests
D.C.A.D. Collectors Club* Deb Canham Artist Designs, Inc. 820 Albee Rd., Ste. 1 Nokomis, FL 34275 (800) 789-8767 www.deb-canham.acun.com	$35	June - May	●	●	4/yr.	●	●	●			• Contests
Daddy's Long Legs Collectors Club 300 Bank St. Southlake, TX 76092 (888) 2-DADDYS (232-3397)	$30-1yr. $50-2yrs.	Anniv. of Sign-Up Date	●	●	4/yr.		●	●		●	• Advance Notice of Retirements • New Releases
David Winter Cottages Collectors' Guild* Enesco Group, Inc. P.O. Box 8 Libertytown, MD 21762 (888) 995-7005	$42-1yr. $80-2yrs.	Anniv. of Sign-Up Date	●	●	4/yr.		●		●	●	• Notification of Retirements • New Releases • Catalog
The Donald Zolan Society 29 Cambridge Dr. Hershey, PA 17033-2173 (717) 534-2446 www.zolan.com	$29.95/ $25	Anniv. of Sign-Up Date	●	●	4/yr.		●			●	• 24K Gold Membership Pin • Contests
Dreamsicles Collectors' Club* Cast Art Industries 1120 California Avenue Corona, CA 91719 (800) 437-5818 www.dreamsiclesclub.com	$27.50/ $23.50	Anniv. of Sign-Up Date	●	●	4/yr.		●	●		●	• *Dreamsicles Value Guide* • Members-only Offerings
Duncan Royale Collectors Club 1141 S. Acacia Ave. Fullerton, CA 92631 (714) 879-1360	$30	Anniv. of Sign-Up Date	●	●	●	●	●	●			• Certificate • Catalog • Free Figurine Registration
EKJ Collectors' Society* Flambro Imports P.O. Box 93507 Atlanta, GA 30377 (800) 355-2582 www.flambro.com	$30	Jan.-Dec.	●	●	4/yr.	●	●			●	• Toll Free Hotline • EKJ Pin • Catalog • Figurine Registration • Collector Registry Listing
The Ebony Visions Circle* Willitts Designs International P.O. Box 750009 Petaluma, CA 94975 (888) 701-2373 www.willitts.com	$40	Jan.-Dec.	●	●	4/yr.	●	●		●	●	
Edna Hibel Society P.O. Box 9721 Coral Springs, FL 33075 (561) 848-9633	$20-1yr. $35-2yrs.	Anniv. of Sign-Up Date	●	●	4/yr.		●			●	• Previews of Hibel Artworks • 5 Types of Membership Available
Enchantica Collectors Club Munro Collectibles, Inc. 1220 Waterville-Monclova Rd. Waterville, OH 43566 (419) 878-0034 www.enchantica.com	$35-1yr. $60-2yrs.	Jan.-Dec.	●	●	3/yr.		●			●	• Catalog
Fenton Art Glass Collectors of America (FAGCA)* P.O. Box 384 Williamstown, WV 26187 (304) 375-6196	$20	Anniv. of Sign-Up Date		●	6/yr.			●	●	●	
Fontanini Collectors' Club* Roman, Inc. 555 Lawrence Avenue Roselle, IL 60172 (630) 529-3000 www.roman.com	$22	Anniv. of Sign-Up Date	●	●	4/yr.	●	●			●	• Pin • Registry

*For more information, see company feature articles (pages 18-211).

National Collectors' Clubs

	Annual Dues/Renewals	Club Year	Membership Gift	Members-Only Piece	Club Publication	Binder	Membership Card	Buy-Sell Matching Service	Local Chapters	Tours/Special Events	Other Benefits
Forever Friends Collectors' Club Sarah's Attic P.O. Box 448 Chesaning, MI 48616 (800) 437-4363 www.sarahsattic.com	$30	Annual	●	●	●		●		●	●	• *Schnookums* Postcards
Friends of Ivy* **Cast Art Industries** 1120 California Ave. Corona, CA 91719 (800) 437-5818 www.ivy-innocence.com	$19.95	Anniv. of Sign-Up Date	●	●	4/yr.						• Members-only Offerings
Gartlan USA Collectors' League* 575 Rt. 73 N., Ste. A-6 West Berlin, NJ 08091-2440 (856) 753-9229 www.gartlanusa.com	$35/ $25	Anniv. of Sign-Up Date	●	●	2/yr.	●				●	
The Glass Messenger* **Fenton Art Glass** 700 Elizabeth St. Williamstown, WV 26187 (304) 375-6122 www.fentonartglass.com	$12	Anniv. of Sign-Up Date		●	4/yr.	●				●	
The Great American Collectors' Club P.O. Box 428 Aberdeen, NC 28315 (910) 944-7447	None	Jan.-Dec.		●	3/yr.			●		●	• Membership Free with Purchase of Club Piece • Early Preview of New Releases
Hallmark Keepsake Ornament Collector's Club* P.O. Box 419034 Kansas City, MO 64141-6034 (800) 523-5839 www.hallmark.com	$22.50- 1yr. $43.-2yrs.	Jan.-Dec.	●	●	4/yr.		●	●	●	●	• Early Mailing of *Dreambook* and Events
Harbour Lights Collectors Society* 1000 N. Johnson Ave. El Cajon, CA 92020 (800) 365-1219 www.harbourlights.com	$30	May 1- Apr. 30	●	●	4/yr.	●	●		●		• Membership Certificate • Print of Redemption Piece Free to Renewing Members
Heirloom Collection Collector's Club Carlton Cards One American Rd. Cleveland, OH 44144 (888) 222-7898	$22.50	July 1- June 30	●	●	4/yr.		●			●	• Carlton Cards History Brochure
Jan Hagara Collectors' Club 40114 Industrial Park Georgetown, TX 78626 (512) 863-9499	$44/$39	July 1- June 30	●	●	2/yr.	●	●	●	●	●	• Cloisonné Pin • Contests • National Convention • Savings on Products
Hutschenreuther Collector's Circle 3412 Milwaukee Ave. Northbrook, IL 60062 (800) 296-7508 www.eschenbachusa.com	Free for 2000	Jan.-Dec.		●			●				• Catalog
Just the Right Club™* **Willitts Designs** P.O. Box 775636 St. Louis, MO 63177 (877) 587-5877 www.justtherightshoe.com	$40	Jan.-Dec.	●	●	4/yr.		●				
Keeper's™ Klub Shenandoah Designs International, Inc. P.O. Box 911 Rural Retreat, VA 24368 (800) 338-7644 www.shenandoahdesigns.com	$37.50	Anniv. of Sign-Up Date	●	●	4/yr.		●				• Travel Kit
Krystonia Collectors Club* **Precious Art** 125 W. Ellsworth Rd. Ann Arbor, MI 48108 (734) 663-1885 www.krystoniaclub.com	$30	Anniv. of Sign-Up Date	●	●	4/yr.		●			●	• Signings • Give-aways • Drawings

National Collectors' Clubs

	Annual Dues/Renewals	Club Year	Membership Gift	Members-Only Piece	Club Publication	Binder	Membership Card	Buy-Sell Matching Service	Local Chapters	Tours/Special Events	Other Benefits
Larry Fraga Designs Collectors' Club* 4720 Sequoyah Rd. Oakland, CA 94605 (510) 638-3900 www.larryfragadesigns.com	$45	Jan.-Dec.	●	●			●			●	
The Leaf & Acorn Club* **Charming Tails/Fitz and Floyd Collectibles** P.O. Box 78218 St. Louis, MO 63178-8218 (800) 486-1065	$27.50	Jan.-Dec.	●	●			●			●	• Members-Only Offers
Liberty Falls Collector's Club* **International Resources, LLC** 60 Revere Drive #725 Northbrook, IL 60062 (847) 291-0282 www.libertyfalls.com	$9.95	Jan.-Dec.	●	●	4/yr.		●	●	●		• Advance Notice of Events and Products
Lilliput Lane Collectors' Club* P.O. Box 7 Libertytown, MD 21762 (800) 545-5478	$40- 1yr $65-2yrs.	Anniv. of Sign-Up Date	●	●	4/yr.		●			●	• Catalog
The Lizzie High Society Ladie and Friends 220 North Main Street Sellersville, PA 18960 (800) 76-DOLLS (763-6557) www.lizziehigh.com	$29/$19	Jan.-Dec.	●	●	2/yr.		●	●		●	• Catalog • Pewter Pin
Lladró Society* 1 Lladró Drive Moonachie, NJ 07074 (888) 634-9088 www.lladro.com	$50-1yr. $75-2yrs.	Anniv. of Sign-Up Date	●	●	4/yr.	●	●			●	• Video • Research Service • Associate Membership to Lladró Museum
The Loyal Order of Friends of Boyds* **Boyds Collection Ltd.** P.O. Box 4386 F.O.B. Dept. Gettysburg, PA 17325-4386 (717) 633-7080 www.boydsstuff.com	$32.50-1yr. $63-2yrs.	Jan.-Dec.	●	●	4/yr.		●			●	
M.I. Hummel Club* Goebel Plaza, P.O. Box 11 Pennington, NJ 08534-0011 (800) 666-CLUB (2582) www.mihummel.com	$50	June 1-May 31	●	●	4/yr.		●	●	●	●	• Research Service • Annual Contests
Madame Alexander Doll Club* P.O. Box 330 Mundelein, IL 60060 (847) 949-9200 www.madc.org	$25	Anniv. of Sign-Up Date		●	6/yr.		●	●		●	• Club Pin
Margaret Furlong Collectors Club* 210 State St. Salem, OR 97301 (503) 363-6004 www.margaretfurlong.com	$49.50	Jan.-Dec.	●	●	4/yr.	●	●	●			• Video • Lapel Pin • Membership Certificate
Matchbox Collectors Guild* P.O. Box 10490-9955 Glendale, AZ 85318-0490 (800) 858-0102 www.matchbox.com	$29.95	Anniv. of Sign-Up Date	●		4/yr.		●			●	• Gift Certificate • Bumper Sticker • Model Blueprint Suitable for Framing
Melody In Motion Collectors Club* **Desert Specialties** 6280 S. Valley View Blvd. #404 Las Vegas, NV 89118 (702) 253-0450 www.melodyinmotion.com	$27.50-1yr. $50-2yrs.	Anniv. of Sign-Up Date	●	●	2/yr.		●				• Catalog • Savings Coupon • Retired Edition Summary • List of Collectors' Centers
Muffy VanderBear Club North American Bear Co. 401 N. Wabash, Ste. 500 Chicago, IL 60611 (800) 682-3427 www.nabear.com	$25/$22	Anniv. of Sign-Up Date	●	●	3/yr.	●	●	●		●	• Exclusive Club Merchandise

For more information, see company feature articles (pages 18-211).

National Collectors' Clubs

	Annual Dues/Renewals	Club Year	Membership Gift	Members-Only Piece	Club Publication	Binder	Membership Card	Buy-Sell Matching Service	Local Chapters	Tours/Special Events	Other Benefits
Myth and Magic Collectors' Club The Tudor Mint 2601 South Park Rd. Pembroke Park, FL 33009 (800) 455-8715	$37.50	July 1-June 30	●	●	2/yr.	●				●	• Catalog • Updates
National Fenton Glass Society (NFGS)* P.O. Box 4008 Marietta, OH 45750 (740) 374-3345	$20	Anniv. of Sign-Up Date		●	6/yr.		●	●	●		
Neiman Marcus Collectors Society* **Halcyon Days Enamels** 14-16 Barton Park Bilston, West Midlands England WV14 7LH 011-441-902-408440	$50	Anniv. of Sign-Up Date	●	●		●					• Membership Certificate • Historical Booklet
North American Tusker's Club Country Artists 9305 Gerwig Lane, Ste. P Columbia, MD 21046 (800) 456-4660	Free with Purchase		●	●	2/yr.	●					
The Official Barbie® Collectors Club™* P.O. Box 903 El Segundo, CA 90245-9792 (800) 491-7503 www.Barbiecollectibles.com	$39.99	Jan.-Dec.	●	●	4/yr.	●	●				• Membership Pin • Contests • Exclusive Club Doll Offers
Old World Christmas Collectors' Club P.O. Box 8000 Department C Spokane, WA 99203 (800) 962-7669	$30-1yr. $57-2yrs. $83-3yrs.	Anniv. of Sign-Up Date	●	●	●	●					• Collectors' Guide • Local Retailer Listings • Video
Our Doll Family* **Lee Middleton Original Dolls** 1301 Washington Blvd. Belpre, OH 45714 (740) 423-3125 www.leemiddleton.com	$35	Anniv. of Sign-Up Date	●	●	4/yr.	●	●			●	• Pin • Contests • Catalogs
P. Buckley Moss Society 801 Shenandoah Village Dr. Box 1C Waynesboro, VA 22980 (540) 943-5678 www.mosssociety.org	$30	Anniv. of Sign-Up Date	●	●	4/yr.	●	●		●	●	
PFC Collectors Club* **Pulaski Furniture Corporation** P.O. Box 1371 Pulaski, VA 24301 (540) 980-7330	$29.95/ $24.95	Anniv. of Sign-Up Date	●		4/yr.		●				• Sneak Previews • Members Incentives for Purchase of Pulaski Furniture
PenDelfin Family Circle Miller Import Corp. 230 Spring Street N.W. Atlanta Gift Mart, Suite 1238 Atlanta, GA 30303 (404) 523-3380 or (800) 872-4876	$30	Jan.-Dec.	●	●	4/yr.		●	●		●	
PipClub® Pippsywoggins® Club 521 Eighth St. S.W., Suite D Auburn, WA 98001 (800) 747-7257 www.pippsywoggins.com	$35 for 10yrs.	Anniv. of Sign-Up Date	●	●	2/yr.		●				
Pipka's Memories of Christmas Collectors' Club* **Prizm, Inc.** P.O. Box 1106 Manhattan, KS 66506 (888) 427-4752 www.pipka.com	$40	Anniv. of Sign-Up Date	●	●	4/yr.	●	●			●	• Christmas Gift • Membership Certificate Suitable for Framing • Autographed Photo of Pipka • Pin
Pocket Dragons and Friends Collectors Club* **Goebel of North America** P.O. Box 7 – Goebel Plaza Pennington, NJ 08534-0007 (800) 563-6559 www.pocketdragonsclub.com	$29.50- 1 yr. $54-2yrs.	June 1-May 31	●	●	4/yr.		●			●	• Catalog

For more information, see company feature articles (pages 18-211). ◆ 222 ◆

National Collectors' Clubs

Club	Annual Dues/Renewals	Club Year	Membership Gift	Members-Only Piece	Club Publication	Binder	Membership Card	Buy-Sell Matching Service	Local Chapters	Tours/Special Events	Other Benefits
Polonaise Collector's Guild* Kurt S. Adler, Inc. 1107 Broadway New York, NY 10010 (212) 924-0900 www.kurtadler.com	$50/$40	Anniv. of Sign-Up Date	●	●	4/yr.	●	●			●	• Membership Certificate • Pin • Artist Tour Updates • Collector's Hotline
Precious Moments Collectors' Club* Enesco Group, Inc. P.O. Box 689 Itasca, IL 60143-0689 (877) 4-YOUR CLUB www.enescoclubs.com	$28-1yr. $54-2yrs.	Jan. 1- Dec. 31	●	●	4/yr.		●			●	• Journal • Memory Box
Precious Moments Fun Club* Enesco Group, Inc. P.O. Box 689 Itasca, IL 60143-0689 (877) 4-YOUR CLUB www.enescoclubs.com	$22.50	Jan. 1- Dec. 31	●	●	4/yr.		●				
R. John Wright Collector Club 15 West Main St. Cambridge, NY 12816 (518) 677-8566 www.rjohnwright.com	$45	May 1- April 30	●	●	4/yr.	●	●	●		●	• Members-Only Hotline • Dealer Directory
Red Mill Collectors Society One Hunters Ridge Summersville, WV 26651 (304) 872-5237	$15	Mar. 31 and Sept. 30		●	2/yr.	●	●				
Rob Anders Collectors Society Porterfield's 5 Mountain Rd. Concord, NH 03301-5479 (800) 660-8345 www.porterfields.com	$19	Jan.-Dec.	●		4/yr.		●				• Publication Subscription Discounts • Sneak Previews • Special Contests • Secondary Market Updates
Ron Lee's Collectors Club* 330 Carousel Parkway Henderson, NV 89014 (800) 829-3928 www.ronlee.com	$30	Anniv. of Sign-Up Date	●	●	4/yr.					●	• New Product Brochures
Royal Crown Derby Collectors Guild* Royal Doulton 701 Cottontail Lane Somerset, NJ 08873 (800) 747-3045 www.royal-doulton.com	$50/$45	Anniv. of Sign-Up Date	●	●	4/yr.		●	●		●	• Free Admission to Royal Crown Derby Museum and Factory Tours • Historical Enquiry Services
Royal Doulton International Collectors Club* 701 Cottontail Lane Somerset, NJ 08873 (800) 747-3045 www.royal-doulton.com	$55	Anniv. of Sign-Up Date	●	●	4/yr.	●	●	●		●	• Free Admission to Royal Doulton Museum and Factory Tours • Historical Enquiry Services • Advance Mailings
Royal Watch™ Collectors Club* Harmony Kingdom 232 Neilston St. Columbus, OH 43215 (614) 469-0600 www.RoyalWatch@HarmonyBall.com	$40	Jan. 1- Dec. 31	●	●	4/yr.		●		●	●	• Members-Only Merchandise Available • Contests
Sandicast Collectors Guild P.O. Box 910079 San Diego, CA 92191 (800) 722-3316	Free with Purchase	Jan.-Dec.		●	●		●				• Free Membership with Purchase of a Sandicast Sculpture
San Francisco Music Box Company Collector's Club* P.O. Box 7465 San Fransisco, CA 94120 (800) 635-9064 www.sfmusicbox.com	Free with Purchase	Anniv. of Sign-Up Date			●		●				• $10 Collector's Certificate Awarded Every Time Customer Accumulates $100 in Purchases • Advance Notice of Sales • Members-Only Collectible Items Available
Santa Claus Network* Possible Dreams 6 Perry Drive Foxboro, MA 02035-1051 (508) 543-6667	$25	Anniv. of Sign-Up Date	●	●	4/yr.		●	●		●	

For more information, see company feature articles (pages 18-211).

National Collectors' Clubs

Club	Annual Dues/Renewals	Club Year	Membership Gift	Members-Only Piece	Club Publication	Binder	Membership Card	Buy/Sell Matching Service	Local Chapters	Tours/Special Events	Other Benefits
Seraphim Classics Collectors Club* Roman, Inc. P.O. Box 78575 St. Louis, MO 63178-8575 (800) 540-4754 www.roman.com	$59.50	Anniv. of Sign-Up Date	●	●	4/yr.	●					• Catalog • Pin
Seymour Mann Doll Club* 225 Fifth Avenue Dept. MDC New York, NY 10010 (212) 683-5229 Ext. 202 www.seymourmann.com	$35	Anniv. of Sign-Up Date	●	●	4/yr.	●				●	• Catalog • Updates
Shelia's Collectors Society 1856 Belgrade Avenue Charleston, SC 29407 (800) 227-6564 www.shelias.com	$35	Anniv. of Sign-Up Date	●	●	4/yr.	●	●	●	●		
Snowbabies Friendship Club™* Department 56, Inc. P.O. Box 120 S. St. Paul, MN 55075-0120 (888) SNOWBABY (766-9222) www.dept56.com	$37.50	Jan.-Dec.	●	●	4/yr.					●	• Membership Certificate • Renewal Gifts
The Society – Giuseppe Armani Art* 300 Mac Lane Keasbey, NJ 08832 (800) 3-ARMANI (327-6264) www.the-society.com	$50/ $37.50	Jan.-Dec.	●	●	3/yr.	●	●		●	●	• Advance Notice of Special Introductions
Starlight Family of Collectors* Christopher Radko P.O. Box 775249 St. Louis, MO 63177-5249 (800) 71-RADKO (717-2356) www.christopherradko.com	$49.50	Jan.-Dec.	●	●	●		●			●	• Catalogs • Binder Available for Purchase
The Steinbach Collectors' Club* Kurt S. Adler, Inc. 1107 Broadway New York, NY 10010 (212) 924-0900 www.kurtadler.com	$45/$35	Anniv. of Sign-Up Date	●	●	4/yr.	●	●	●		●	• Artist Tour Updates • Collector's Hotline
Swarovski Collectors Society* One Kenney Dr. Cranston, RI 02920 (800) 426-3088 www.swarovski.com	$45/$35	Anniv. of Sign-Up Date	●	●	4/yr.	●				●	
Thomas Kinkade Collectors' Society* Media Arts Group, Inc. P.O. Box 90267 San Jose, CA 95109 (800) 544-4890 www.thomaskinkade.com	$50	Anniv. of Sign-Up Date	●	●	4/yr.	●	●			●	
Treasure Hunters Club* Slavic Treasures P.O. Box 99591 Raleigh, NC 27624-9591 (877) SLAVICT www.slavictreasures.com.pl	$49.50	Jan.-Dec.	●		●					●	• Catalog
Walt Disney Collectors Society 500 S. Buena Vista St. Burbank, CA 91521-8028 (800) 932-5749 www.disneyartclassics.com	$50-1yr. $95-2yrs.	Anniv. of Sign-Up Date	●	●	4/yr.	●				●	• Binder Available for Purchase • Cloissoné Pin

The following publications and show listings are designed to keep you current on the latest news about limited edition collectibles. In addition, many manufacturers and collectors' clubs publish newsletters that will help you enjoy your hobby to the fullest. See the club listing beginning on page 218 for more information.

BOOKS

AMERICAN TEDDY BEAR ENCYCLOPEDIA
by Linda Mullins.
Hobby House Press.

THE CHARLESTON STANDARD CATALOG OF ROYAL DOULTON BESWICK FIGURINES (6TH EDITION)
by Jean Dale.

CHRISTMAS THROUGH THE DECADES
by Robert Brenner.
Schiffer Publishing.

CHRISTOPHER RADKO – THE FIRST DECADE (1986-1995)
by Christopher Radko
for Starad, Inc.

DECK THE HALLS: TREASURES OF CHRISTMAS PAST
by Robert Merck.
Abbeville Press.

DECORATING WITH COLLECTIBLES
by Annette R. Lough.
Krause Publications.

FENTON GLASS, THE FIRST TWENTY-FIVE YEARS (1905-1930)
by William Heacock.
Richardson Printing.

FENTON GLASS, THE SECOND TWENTY-FIVE YEARS (1931-1955)
by William Heacock.
Richardson Printing.

FENTON GLASS, THE THIRD TWENTY-FIVE YEARS (1956-1980)
by William Heacock.
Richardson Printing.

HALLMARK KEEPSAKE ORNAMENTS: A COLLECTOR'S GUIDE 1994-1998
by Clara Johnson Scroggins, Hallmark (Editor).
Meredith Books.

LLADRÓ – THE MAGIC WORLD OF PORCELAIN
by Several.
Salvat.

LUCKEY'S HUMMEL FIGURINES & PLATES: IDENTIFICATION AND VALUE GUIDE (11TH EDITION)
by Carl F. Luckey.

NUMBER ONE PRICE GUIDE TO M.I. HUMMEL FIGURINES, PLATES, MINIATURES AND MORE
by Robert Miller.
Portfolio Press.

THE OFFICIAL LLADRÓ COLLECTION IDENTIFICATION CATALOG AND PRICE GUIDE
by Glenn S. Johnson.
Lladró Collectors Society.

ROYAL COPENHAGEN PORCELAIN: ANIMALS AND FIGURINES
by Robert J. Heritage.
Schiffer Book for Collectors.

THE STRACYL OF UNITY
by Allan Frost.
AJF Desk Top Publishing.

SWAROVSKI: THE MAGIC OF CRYSTAL
by Vivienne Becker.
Abrams, New York.

MAGAZINES/NEWSLETTERS

AMERICAN ARTIST
1515 Broadway
New York, NY 10036
212-536-5178

ANTIQUES & COLLECTING
1006 S. Michigan Avenue
Chicago, IL 60605
312-939-4767

THE ANTIQUE TRADER
P.O. Box 1050
Dubuque, IA 52004
800-334-7165

CIB COLLECTIBLES REPORT
77 West Washington Street, Suite 1815
Chicago, IL 60602
847-842-2200

COLLECTOR EDITIONS
1107 Broadway #1210–North
New York, NY 10010
800-588-1692

COLLECTOR'S MART
700 E. State Street
Iola, WI 54990
715-445-2214

COLLECTORS NEWS
P.O. Box 156
Grundy Center, IA 50638
319-824-6981

CONTEMPORARY DOLL COLLECTOR
30595 Eight Mile Rd.
Livonia, MI 48152-1798
248-477-6650

DOLLS MAGAZINE
1107 Broadway #1210–North
New York, NY 10010
800-588-1691

THE DOLL READER
6405 Flank Drive
Harrisburg, PA 17112
717-657-9555

KOVELS ON ANTIQUES & COLLECTIBLES
P.O. Box 420347
Palm Coast, FL 32142-0347
800-829-9158

MINIATURE COLLECTOR
30595 Eight Mile Rd.
Livonia, MI 48152-1798
248-477-6650

SOUTHWEST ART
5444 Westheimer, Suite 1440
Houston, TX 77056
713-296-7900

TEDDY BEAR AND FRIENDS
6405 Flank Drive
Harrisburg, PA 17112
717-657-9555

TEDDY BEAR REVIEW
1107 Broadway #1210–North
New York, NY 10010
800-728-2729

U.S. ART
220 S. 6th Street, Suite 500
Minneapolis, MN 55402
612-339-7571

VILLAGE CHRONICLE
757 Park Ave.
Cranston, RI 02910
401-467-9343

SHOWS

COLLECTORS' FESTIVAL
One Penn Plaza, 10th Floor
New York, NY 10119
212-615-2262
www.collectorfest.com

INTERNATIONAL COLLECTIBLE EXPOSITION
c/o Krause Publications
700 E. State Street
Iola, WI 54990
715-445-2214

Biographies of Today's Most Popular and Talented Artists in the Field of Limited Edition Collectibles

MICHAEL ADAMS

Michael Adams is an award-winning artist of many talents. Michael began his freelance career as an editorial cartoonist after completing his studies in illustration at the Philadelphia College of Art. After he illustrated numerous text, trade, medical and children's books, Michael became a senior giftware designer for a major collectible company. Over the past 15 years, he has designed many giftware lines which have included wildlife and garden birds. For The San Francisco Music Box Company, he has designed the *Angel's Flight Carousel Collection,* the *Divinity Collection,* as well as several inspirational pieces. Michael has also designed two special millennium pieces for The San Francisco Music Box Company which exemplify *Peace on Earth.*

Michael works as a consultant and designer in collectibles and in retail giftware. He is an avid wildlife artist with an established reputation for richness of detail and faithfulness to nature. He is a participant in many national and state competitions, and enjoys nature and fishing.

HOLLY ADLER

Transforming animal characters into delightful holiday accessories from figurines and ornaments, to candle-holders and tree toppers, Holly Adler views Christmas with a creative eye unlike any other artist today.

A highly skilled sculptor, painter and illustrator, Holly has created many award-winning designs for Kurt S. Adler, Inc., a leading manufacturer of holiday accessories and collectibles.

Using her friends and family for inspiration, Holly has designed new plush bears like "Stefan" and "Brittany," and ornaments like the all-new "Star Catcher" (with a portion of its sales going to the Starlight Children's Foundation) for her *Holly Bearies* collection.

She has added adorable Black Bears and Moose to her *Holly Dearies & Friends* collection, as both ornaments and figurines. And she has expanded the *Snow Bearies* collection to include several new Polar Bears.

Last year, *Holly Bearies* was named one of the top ornament lines at the International Collectible Exposition®, yet Holly Adler knows it is the continuing excitement she sees in her collectors that is her greatest honor.

MARTYN ALCOCK

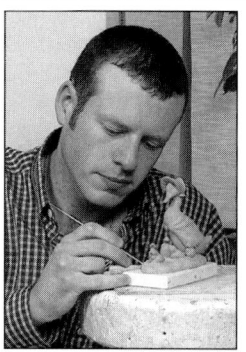

Martyn Alcock became a modeller for Royal Doulton at the John Beswick Studio in 1986. Through the years, he has worked on several figurines for the *Bunnykins* collection. Martyn has contributed several studies of *Beatrix Potter* characters to the Royal Albert figure collection, including "Peter and the Red Handkerchief" and "Christmas Stocking." He also recreated several of the most popular *Beatrix Potter* subjects in a large size.

Like all the modellers in the Beswick Studio, Martyn has been encouraged to show his versatility, and more recently has turned his hand to Character Jugs. His first Character Jug, "Captain Hook," was selected to be Royal Doulton's "Character Jug of the Year" for 1994. He also modelled the charming miniature "Snowman" Character Jug.

Away from the studio, Martyn spends time with his family and still finds time to be the goalkeeper for Royal Doulton's Nile Street soccer team. As Martyn says, "To know that people enjoy and appreciate my work is the most rewarding part of my job."

PATRICIA ANDREWS

Patricia Andrews subscribes to the adage, "Time flies when you're having fun." She's worked at Hallmark since 1976 and can hardly believe that *Keepsake Ornaments* have passed the 25-year milestone!

Patricia first worked as an engraver, then joined the *Keepsake Ornament* studio in 1987. She enjoys creating ornaments based on real people and has crafted images of several movie stars, including Marilyn Monroe, Humphrey Bogart, and Vivien Leigh as Scarlett O' Hara. Many collectors call Patricia "the BARBIE™ lady;" she has sculpted most of the *Keepsake Ornaments* based on Mattel's doll.

Patricia is in awe of collectors' reaction to *Keepsake Ornaments.* She met one woman at a 1993 Hallmark Keepsake Ornament Collector's Club convention who was dressed as an ornament that Patricia had sculpted. Since then, they've built a valued friendship. Patricia is married to Dill Rhodus, another *Keepsake Ornament* artist.

GIUSEPPE ARMANI

Giuseppe Armani has had an extraordinary life. Born in Calci, Italy, in 1935, his talent and his passion for art were recognized very early on. Yet a family tragedy – the death of his father – forced the youngster to abandon his art studies for more practical family needs.

Still, young Giuseppe persevered. When his entry in a local art exhibition led to a job offer at Pisa's prestigious Art Gallery, he immersed himself in the process of learning the secrets of the great Master Artists of the Renaissance.

In the mid 1970s, Giuseppe Armani teamed up with Florence Sculture d'Arte, which is dedicated to continuing Tuscany's glorious artistic heritage. Thus began an inspired, exclusive and extraordinarily successful relationship.

The artist's sculptural works include diverse subjects such as elegant ladies, weddings and maternities, children, social events, gardens, religious figurines, Capodimonte, wildlife, home-décor items, and a special *Disney Showcase Collection*. Always, Giuseppe infuses his figurines with breathtaking realism — the spark of life. This ability continues to amaze his many admirers the world over.

LINDA LINDQUIST BALDWIN

Today, Linda Lindquist Baldwin, creator of the *Belsnickle, Snowsnickle, Broomsnickle,* and *Haresnickle* collections of figurines and accessories produced by Enesco Group, Inc., lives in Joplin, Missouri, with her husband and son.

She credits her childhood – spent on an out-of-the-way farm in the Ozarks that had no electricity – for giving her the determination and character to turn a garage sale purchase into a successful career.

It was at a garage sale in 1986 that Baldwin paid a nickel for a book, *Old Antique Santa Collections*. As a single parent working two jobs teaching the developmentally disabled, Baldwin knew she couldn't afford the 18th and 19th century European Santas pictured in the book. Instead, she decided to make her own out of homemade *papier mâché*.

Baldwin began selling her creations at local craft fairs, and interest and demand quickly spread. Today, the *Belsnickle* collection includes more than 50 figurines and accessories, with each piece containing a nickel in the base to commemorate Baldwin's very special nickel purchase at that garage sale.

KATHY BARRY-HIPPENSTEEL

Kathy Barry-Hippensteel has received widespread acclaim for the lifelike quality of her child and baby dolls and has had many awards bestowed upon her.

"Chen" was nominated for *Dolls* magazine's 1989 "Award of Excellence" and received the National Association of Limited Edition Dealers' (NALED) 1990 "Achievement Award." "Patricia, My First Tooth" was also nominated for an "Award of Excellence," plus *Doll Reader's* DOTY award. In 1993, "Tickles," one of her most sought-after dolls, was nominated for the same two awards.

In 1994, the International Doll Exposition (IDEX) recognized Kathy for her exceptional work, giving her international acclaim. She displays her dolls in Canada and the United States, and both "Tickles" and "Elizabeth's Homecoming" have received the prestigious "Canadian Collectibles of the Year Award" given by *Collectibles Canada*.

SANDRA BEDARD

Ever since she can remember, Sandra Bedard has loved to draw and create. Growing up in the Northeast, art was Sandra's favorite subject all through school. School officials took notice of her artistic talent and commissioned her to paint a mural for them. Sandra proudly recalls that she paid one year of her school tuition with the money she received from that commission.

Before she could begin a career in commercial art, Sandra fell in love, married, and became a mother. Every night after the children were settled in their beds and the household was quiet, Sandra would enter her own little world and draw angels which came into her imagination. She thought of them as her *SoulMates*.

Until recently, all of Sandra's angels were just drawings. Then, explains Sandra, "I found sculpting, or it found me!" Sculpting is where her heart is because it allows her to create adorable little *SoulMates* from Sandy USA to share with everyone.

Now that her family is grown, Sandra's dream is to make everyone happy through these adorable little angel babies – her *SoulMates*.

KATHI LORANCE BEJMA

From the time she was a young girl, Kathi Lorance Bejma was fascinated by both antiques and history. As an adult, she began collecting Father Christmases and exhibiting at craft shows, where she sold items made of clay, wood and soft sculpture.

At about the time her *Father Christmas* collection numbered 400, Bejma discovered an antique chocolate mold to add to her collection. She experimented with the mold, creating a piece of chalkware. This design was so popular with her customers that she began collecting these fascinating antique molds, which now number nearly 4,000, and founded a thriving business. Through her company, Walnut Ridge Collectibles, Bejma creates numerous chalkware and porcelain designs for both the giftware and limited edition collectibles industries. Subjects include Santas, angels, snowmen, rabbits, cats, trees, and many others.

Bejma oversees the entire operation at Walnut Ridge Collectibles, where all products are tagged "Made in the USA."

YOLANDA BELLO

As a child in Venezuela, Yolanda Bello "restyled" her dolls into new and exciting characters. At age 14, Bello moved to Chicago, where she worked as a figurine sculptor and pursued doll design and sculpture. In 1981, Bello created a pair of porcelain Spanish dolls, which turned her doll making into a full-time profession.

Bello has earned more than 60 awards, including a "Doll of the Year" (DOTY) award in 1985 for one of her studio dolls, and in 1993 for her Ashton-Drake doll, "Meagan Rose."

Bello's designs range from one-of-a-kind dolls portraying characters of the opera *Carmen*, to her most sought-after limited edition dolls. Collectors the world over are familiar with *Yolanda's Picture-Perfect Babies®* collection, her first dolls for Ashton-Drake, which sold out years ago.

Bello is still best known for her lifelike, lovable baby dolls for Ashton-Drake, among which are the popular *Yolanda's Lullaby Babies®*, *Yolanda's Heaven-Scent* collection, and the *Yolanda's Rainbow of Love* collection. Her newest collection for Ashton-Drake is the *Disney Babies in Dreamland* collection.

ULRICH BERNARDI

A native of the Groeden Valley of the South Tyrol in Northern Italy's Dolomite Mountains, Ulrich Bernardi dreamed of becoming a woodcarver, continuing a tradition that has been passed from generation to generation for more than 300 years.

His grandfather, an altar builder, and his grandmother, who carved ornamental designs, shared their knowledge and skills with him. He achieved the rank of master carver at the age of 30, with a wood sculpture of a Madonna. He had already earned a master of art degree at the Academy of Art in St. Ulrich (in Groeden) and had served a four-year apprenticeship.

With ANRI for nearly 40 years, Bernardi's religious woodcarvings, including the *Florentine Nativity*, as well as his carvings of the works of Sarah Kay and others, have earned him a worldwide reputation for finely detailed art. Now semi-retired, he is still carving for ANRI.

JERRY BERTA

Jerry Berta has loved working with clay since his first seventh grade art class. At Wayne State University, he received a bachelor of fine arts degree in sculpture with a major in ceramics.

About 1977, Jerry's fascination for streamline shapes led him to create diners. His attention to detail required that the interiors be lit. He figured out that neon would be the most unique and appropriate way to enhance the metallic surfaces and complete the diner theme.

This fascination with diners led the artist to research diners far and wide. Jerry couldn't believe the rate at which diners were being demolished. He eventually saved one, and it became his gallery and studio. Before he knew it, he had another diner serving food right next door. It wasn't just any diner, but America's most famous "Rosie's Diner" of the "quicker picker upper" Bounty paper towel TV commercial fame.

Jerry Berta's *Neon America Collection* by Cavanagh introduces a brand new collection in ceramic and neon with eight beautifully sculpted reproductions, each based on a Jerry Berta original.

MARY BETH

With the 1999 premiere of the *Uncle Nick Collection*, artist Mary Beth made her design debut for Kurt S. Adler, Inc., a leading supplier of holiday ornaments and collectibles.

Mary Beth's extensive experience in tailoring and original dress design has served her well in the creation of this group of 12 captivating Santa figures. She has given each Santa a distinctive personality using unique trims, accessories and a variety of rich fabrics such as velvets, tapestries and wools.

The new collection features a dozen Santas designed in a broad range of styles. There's Santa posing as a fisherman in "Big Catch," a gardener in "Welcome to My Garden," a Santa stockbroker in "Market Trends" and a cook in "What's Cookin'?." One whimsical Santa, titled "A Moment to Relax," is even shown relaxing in a pair of moose slippers.

In addition to their unique styles, Mary Beth's Santas all stand 12" to 24" tall. Their size, along with the artist's elaborate costumes and attention to detail, makes them the holiday's most enchanting attention-getters.

THOMAS BLACKSHEAR

In 1999, Thomas Blackshear was named "Artist of the Year" by the National Association of Limited Edition Dealers (NALED). His most recent creation, Thomas Blackshear's *Ebony Visions,* is a collection of three-dimensional figurines that capture the beauty, elegance and emotions of the African-American culture. In his own words, "*Ebony Visions,* does not reflect only my own visions as a black man, but also unique visions of black people. The designs reflect visions we all share, regardless of the color of our skin."

As an artist, it has always been his dream to create paintings and sculptures that have lasting quality to them. When asked where his inspiration comes from, Thomas' response was "through prayer and intervention from the Creator."

Blackshear entered the Art Institute of Chicago on a scholarship and later attended and graduated from the American Academy of Art in Chicago. In 1982, after working for Hallmark Cards and an advertising agency, he became a free-lance illustrator.

Thomas Blackshear's fascination with the movie industry led him to Marin County in California, where he earned the assignment for George Lucas' "Tucker" video cover. His entry into the collectible

arena came when the art director at Lucas Studios invited him to paint a series of eight limited edition *STAR WARS* collectible plates.

Blackshear's illustrations from the book, *I Have a Dream*, were on exhibit at the Smithsonian Institution, and his art has also graced a collection of Black Heritage Stamps created for the U.S. Postal Service.

COLLIN BOGLE

Collin Bogle, who has been published in the limited edition art market for over four years, is a bright, emerging star in plate collecting as well. Widely admired for his floral, wildlife and figurative art, Collin has graced the plate market with three outstanding collections in the past three years that have met with enthusiastic response.

His first series, a collection of musical plates entitled *Remembering England's Rose*, debuted in 1997. It was a floral-art tribute to Princess Diana. Just one year later, his *Sisters Forever* collection followed, portraying exquisite flowers and inscribed with inspirational sayings celebrating sisterhood.

In recognition of these plate-market triumphs, Collin Bogle was selected by The Bradford Exchange as the 1998 Collector's Choice "New Artist of the Year."

A native of Washington, Collin grew up near beautiful Puget Sound, a natural source of inspiration. At an early age, he became interested in art, and began to apprentice for his father, Lee Bogle, a renowned artist who has become a plate-market favorite with his romantic Native American themed editions offered by The Bradford Exchange.

Inspired by nature's beauty, Collin also enjoys photography. His special interest is interpreting light upon his subjects – a passion also demonstrated in his highly sought artwork.

PAUL F. BOLINGER

Paul Bolinger was educated in engineering, spent six years in the Navy, and 11 years as vice president of a Silicon Valley chip maker – an unlikely background for one of the nation's top wood carvers and collectible artists.

Paul Bolinger began carving in 1980 when a friend gave him a block of wood and a chisel for Christmas. Starting simply, Paul practiced until he achieved self-taught success with his *Father Christmas* wood carvings.

He completed his move from silicon chips to wood chips in 1993, moving to Spokane, Washington, and a full time art career. Paul's figures range from serious one-of-a-kind sculptures, to his popular, humorous line of resin-cast collectibles.

He has been a featured artist at Disney World, MGM Grand and Knott's Berry Farm. The book, *The Forever Wreath*, authorized by Camille Bolinger and illustrated with Paul's wood carvings, is recognized as a collector's treasure.

Paul and his wife have also authored six wood-carving "how to" books...just one way they hope to pass on the love of their art to aspiring wood carvers.

BRALDT BRALDS

Braldt Bralds combines "domestic whimsy" with a bright, unique art style, developed through years of commercial artwork in his homeland of the Netherlands. His first job in the U.S. was illustrating a cover for *Time* magazine. This led to illustrations in *Newsweek, Omni, TV Guide, Rolling Stone* and *National Geographic,* among many others. His awards include three gold medals, three silver medals, and the "Hamilton King Award" from the Society of Illustrators.

Bralds is proud of his contribution to education. He has taught at New York's School of Visual Arts and was an independent student counselor for their masters program. He now serves on the International Advisory Board of Art Institutes International, which established a Braldt Bralds Illustration Scholarship in 1993. He joined The Greenwich Workshop in 1995 and embarked on a string of sold-out limited editions.

PETE & DIANE BRETZ

In the rolling hill country of Pennsylvania, award-winning artists Pete and Diane Bretz have given new life to the wood of the American chestnut tree. In their native Pennsylvania, Pete and Diane recycle antiquated American chestnut wood originally used in the construction of homes and barns. Their efforts of gathering the wood for sculpting are necessary, due to the fact that the American chestnut tree, which once covered one half of the United States, was decimated nearly 100 years ago by a chestnut blight from Asia.

Inspired by the style of traditional American folk art from the past, Pete and Diane have created wonderful characters that are sure to excite any collector. The *American Chestnut Folk Art* collection, introduced by Coyne's & Company in 1999, consists of spring and Christmas designs. The spring collection is comprised of five groups that includes bears, rabbits, farm animals and pull toys. The Christmas collection, many of which are numbered limited editions, depicts Santa and his friends at work and at play.

DENNIS BROSE

Dennis Brose is the creator of *Seasons Bay*™, the latest Village collection from Department 56®. Dennis has been actively involved in the design, restoration and adaptive reuse of traditional "period" and historic architecture for more than two decades.

His interest in 19th century resort architecture began in 1985 with a visit to Newport, Rhode Island. Since then, numerous architectural "expeditions" to document the buildings of resort towns and villages throughout the country have resulted in an extensive collection of photographs, drawings and printed material related to

Shingle Style architecture. From this vast store came the inspiration for the designs of *Seasons Bay.*

Dennis particularly enjoys Shingle Style architecture because of its picturesque irregularity. His favorite pieces in the *Seasons Bay* collection are the "Grandview Shores Hotel" and the "Bay Street Shops."

In creating the pieces for *Seasons Bay,* Dennis has attempted to capture the spirit and mood of the architecture and the era. The profusion of porches, gables, loggias, towers, chimneys and dormers is designed to evoke romantic images of the past – sentiments collectors have come to expect from the lighted Village collections of Department 56.

ADRIENNE BROWN

Adrienne Brown descended from two generations of accomplished artists, and was raised in a home where the love of dolls was encouraged. After earning a degree in fine art from the Philadelphia College of Art, Brown designed and sculpted porcelain dolls professionally, earning several prestigious awards for her work. She lived and worked in London, designing baby dolls that earned wide recognition in the European market. Today, she lives and works in the U.S., creating her own doll designs for discriminating customers.

Working with Ashton-Drake for the past five years, Adrienne Brown has created two very popular collections that were inspired by her three sons. *Just Caught Napping* portrays four toddlers who have fallen asleep while playing, and the *Boys and Bears* collection features little boys with their cuddly teddy bear companions.

MICHELE BROWN

Columbus International is delighted to add the artistic talents of teddy bear designer Michele Brown to the HERMANN-Spielwaren collection. In 1988, she left New York City and her clothing design studio to return to her quiet hometown of Stephenville, Texas, where she began her bear-making business.

Michele's strong fashion background is evident in her creations. She uses her extensive knowledge of design and pattern-making to develop wonderfully costumed bears. Inspired by the colors and textures of nature and her surroundings, her themes range from the very elegant to the rustic woodland. Her repertoire is not limited to the mighty bruin, but also includes horses, rabbits, cats, moles and badgers, to name a few. Michele became known early in her career for her highly sought after bearded bears. She has created a woodsy bearded bruin, along with several other wonderful bears for the Hermann-Coburg line.

Among Michele's numerous awards are a 1996 "Golden Teddy Award" winner for "Jack Frost and Sno," 1997 "Golden Teddy" nomination for "Snow White," 1997 "TOBY" nomination for "Chen Lu & Zhen Zhen," and a 1998 "Golden Teddy" nomination for "Little Red Riding Hood."

TOM BROWNING

"I always knew what I wanted to do," says Tom Browning. "On Saturday mornings, I'd tune into a learn-to-draw program on television and follow the instructions." By the time he was 10, there was no doubt in Browning's mind — he was going to be an artist.

Browning says the list of established artists who have influenced him is a long one. "There's Sargent, William Merritt Chase, Elizabeth Nourse and Frank Benson, to name a few." As he talks about his work, Browning becomes introspective. "Painting is a pretty involved process. I like to say it's like a golf swing; a lot of things have to happen at once to make it a good shot."

Tom Browning's subject matter has changed over the years from wildlife to landscapes, still life to figure work. "I'm a little more romantic now," he admits. And that romance is evident in every Santa Claus he creates for his *Clothtique Santas* from Possible Dreams. Each has the power to create nostalgic yearnings for the joys of a bygone era.

WILL BULLAS

The enormous appeal of Will Bullas' work is very simple: he makes fine art fun! An award-winning watercolorist, Will's popularity has grown from his quirky sense of humor and positive outlook. The image or sculpture is the set up for his humor, and the caption is the payoff. His *Indian Runner* ducks have provided endless ideas – along with other "critters" he adores.

Bullas was born in Ohio and raised in the Southwest. While studying at Arizona State University, he was drafted and fought in Vietnam. His first professional pieces were pencil portraits of fellow soldiers, which were sent to loved ones back home. After returning from military duty, Bullas enrolled in the Brooks Institute of Fine Art in Santa Barbara, California, where he was classically trained in painting and majored in landscape and figure drawing.

He has been honored with many awards including the "President's Award" at the 1986 American Watercolor Society Exhibition and the "First Place Award" for the 1990 Signature Membership Exhibition of the National Watercolor Society.

Bullas joined The Greenwich Workshop in 1992, and his art appears on limited edition prints, fine art porcelains from The Greenwich Workshop Collection®, and popular books, including *fool moon...more art of Will Bullas* and *a fool and his bunny...,* both published by The Greenwich Workshop Press. In addition, his art appears on his own line of greeting cards, mugs and clothing.

Recently, Bullas' delightful works of art have been brought to life with Pearl Bisque™, a proprietary blend of cold-cast porcelain and finely ground pearl developed by The Greenwich Workshop. This unique medium, combined with innovative sculpting and molding techniques and meticulous hand-painting, results in exceptionally refined and detailed works of art, at a very affordable price.

FRANCES BURTON

Frances Burton loved art long before beginning training as a decorator for Fenton Art Glass in 1973. Initially balancing her job with raising a family, Frances later worked full-time at Fenton Art Glass and quickly progressed from decorator to trainer, designer, head designer and, finally, department supervisor, the position she holds today.

Frances was honored in 1998 with a "Discovery Award" from the Society of Glass and Ceramic Decorators. Her decoration designs have graced many items in the Fenton *Connoisseur Collection*, and she was responsible for the elegant Colonial Scroll on Fenton's *Historic Collection* Royal Purple glass in 1998.

Frances enjoys growing the beautiful flowers she later brings to life on glass. Romance novels and old movies also capture her interest. Frances and Lanny, her husband of 30 years, love to escape to Vermillion on Lake Erie where they fish and share the area's quiet beauty, while dreaming of residing there someday.

SAM BUTCHER

Sam Butcher is the artist and creator behind the Enesco *Precious Moments* collection, one of the most popular collectibles in the world. The collection depicts Butcher's teardrop-eyed children through porcelain bisque figurines with inspirational messages.

Butcher creates all art work for the collection and coordinates with Enesco and the Precious Moments Design Studio in Japan to create dozens of new subjects each year, all inspired by personal events and collector requests.

Butcher has been honored with a multitude of awards within the collectibles industry including NALED's 1988 "Special Recognition Award" and "Artist of the Year" in 1992 and 1996. His artwork has won the 1992 "Collectible of the Year," 1994 "Figurine of the Year," and 1994, 1995, and 1996 "Ornament of the Year," also from NALED.

Butcher's devotion to his faith and art has led to the construction of the Precious Moments Chapel located in Carthage, Missouri. It houses a myriad of hand-painted murals, statues, stained glass windows and a painted ceiling, all featuring *Precious Moments* children.

Sam Butcher has seven children and 23 grandchildren.

DENISE CALLA

The self-taught authenticity that Denise Calla brings to her artwork has been described as pure magic and has made her one of America's most highly collected artists. Denise's inspiration stems from taking daily walks within majestic woods. She says that she lives her life being led through the course of a year by the instructions coming from nature and the changing seasons.

Denise only uses the wood of evergreen trees to carve her Santas, so she has planted acres of pine trees to give back to the earth the wood she has used for her artwork. Not only is she a superb wood-carver and accomplished painter, but she also designs and makes

furniture with her husband.

In order to meet the overwhelming demand for her creations, while continuing to meet high-quality standards, Denise joined House of Hatten, Inc. Her first designs, *Enchanted Forest*, were introduced in 1988. Now 25 of her collections make up a significant portion of House of Hatten's popular Christmas and gift lines.

PETER CALVESBERT

Peter Calvesbert is one of the most beloved artists in the collectibles industry. His animal Box Figurines for Harmony Kingdom have gained an astonishing reputation, and he has built a fanatic following on both sides of the Atlantic.

Peter lives in England's West Country with his wife and a menagerie of treasured pets. Here, he sculpts animals that live in his backyard and in his imagination, depicting their humorous behavior and unusual proportions. Despite having no formal artistic training, Peter is Harmony Kingdom's most recognized carver.

His series of *Cake Toppers* is an ongoing celebration of Peter's marriage. "The Big Day" was carved in 1995 for his wedding cake and became Harmony Kingdom's inaugural club piece. Each year, he carves a new "Cake Topper" to commemorate his wedding anniversary and the anniversary of The Royal Watch Collector's Club.

DEB CANHAM

English artist Deb Canham spent many years working as a police officer on the streets of London. As a hobby, she designed animal characters that sprang from her creative imagination.

In 1991, Deb started working with Jamie Wu, founder of Little Gem Teddy Bear Company, designing and fine tuning the production of collectible, miniature teddy bears. To date, she has created 95 designs for the company and is their top-selling designer. In 1996, Deb started her own company, Deb Canham Artist Designs, Inc., producing her signature mohair designs in collections which have become well known worldwide. The *Rainy Days*, *Have a Heart* and *Camelot* collections have inspired a new range of miniature fabric "dappled dragons."

Deb's miniature designs, which only measure around 3" in height, are easily identified because of their intricate detail and well balanced proportions. Her collections include bears, cats, dragons, and even mice and rats.

Through the years, Deb Canham's miniature bears and animals have received numerous awards and nominations.

In 1999, the Deb Canham Artist Design (DCAD) Collectors Club was launched in response to collectors' wishes for more information about Deb's popular creations.

PAUL CARDEW

Paul Cardew, owner of Cardew Design, is an intensely creative, life-is-an-adventure sort of entrepreneur.

Cardew's artistic talents surfaced during his school years, and later he enrolled in Loughborough University, a local art school, where he immersed himself in the field of ceramics. After completing his bachelor of honors degree and a year-long teaching degree course, Cardew accepted a position as a part-time teacher at Exeter University. During that time, he exhibited his work around the world, and also met his wife, Karen, who designed brooches. After the couple received an order for 5,000 of Karen's designs, Cardew quit his university position, and they bought a small workshop and a kiln and began producing brooches. Eventually, their company became known as Cardew Design.

Cardew premiered his teapots in 1975, tapping into the up-and-coming consumer frenzy for 'all things teapots.' "Over the years, we've prided ourselves on being a very cutting-edge business in the area of design," says Cardew. "For example, we were one of the first companies to make what we call 'funky' teapots, decorated with animal patterns such as zebra and leopard motifs."

Cardew's design talents are being turned to a variety of new directions, such as the *Cardew Blue* home decorative accessories. Cardew says, "I am always striving to create new designs, techniques and products. I like the accolades I've received in my career. But I like to look forward and search for that next idea that says, 'Eureka!'"

ROBERT CHAD

"I love the idea that after I'm gone my ornaments will remain, and may be passed down through families for generations," says Robert Chad, a sculptor since 1987 in the *Keepsake Ornament* studio.

After studying at the Kansas City Art Institute, and with previous animation experience, Chad worked for Hallmark on a freelance basis. He began sculpting pewter pieces, designing stuffed animals and creating other licensed properties that were developed by Hallmark.

He may best be known for his *Mary's Angels Keepsake Ornaments*, which he sculpts from sketches by Hallmark Master Artist Mary Hamilton. Chad also creates many *Keepsake Ornaments* based on licensed designs from Warner Bros. and others.

PAT CHANDOK

Pat Chandok was always surrounded by innovation in her native Bombay, India. Coming from a large family of business people, she grew up hearing a great deal of discussion about the newest and most exciting happenings. Her family was always involved in a variety of ventures, and she followed this pattern when she and her husband moved to the United States. Pat's enjoyment of fine art inspired her to concentrate on the gift industry.

One of her first ventures was to develop gift shops in Michigan. Before long, she was importing products from Asia and opening a

factory in Europe to manufacture her own designs.

Her first creations were mostly musicals crafted in wood, glass, antimony, and other materials. She worked with ancient Japanese art, as well as modern glass etchings. Soon prints were created, and many other lines were added.

Pat especially loves to work with figurines. She is particularly proud of her creation of the *World of Krystonia* from Precious Art, Inc. She truly enjoys making people smile, which is why she is attracted to whimsical products. Recently, Pat has also returned to her musical roots through her work on the new *Petal Pets* line.

JONNIÉ K.C. CHARDONN

Jonnié Chardonn's popularity as an artist soared right from the beginning. During her first four years as a working artist, she sold more that six million prints on paper. From her Illinois studio, "The Finest Touch of Art," Jonnié Chardonn now paints more than 30 images per year. Using a variety of subjects as her inspiration, Chardonn employs a wide range of media to create her vibrantly colored works of art.

During her extensive career, her work has appeared in many national galleries, shows and businesses. In addition to her signature canvases, she has also designed a postal stamp commemorating the U.S. Postal Service's 150th year. While a working artist, Chardonn helped others hone their artistic talents by teaching art at an Illinois college for 17 years.

In 1999, Chardonn's creations premiered in a line of collectible plates from Islandia International. The collection, *The Art of Jonnié Chardonn*, showcases the artist's renowned Native American art and is a celebration of Chardonn's own Native American heritage.

Trained in commercial art at the American Academy of Art in Chicago, and fine art at the Layton School of Art in Milwaukee, Chardonn shares her talents by presenting art lectures across the country.

JAMES C. CHRISTENSEN

Inspired by the world's myths, fables and tales of imagination, James C. Christensen's hope is that through whatever he creates – be it a porcelain, fine art print or book – he can convey a message, inspiration or a simple laugh.

Born and raised in Culver City, California, Christensen studied painting at Brigham Young University and the University of California at Los Angeles. Christensen finished his formal education at BYU, where he was a professor of art for over 20 years.

Since that time, he has had one man shows in the West and Northeast, and his work is prized in collections throughout the United States and Europe. In addition, he has been commissioned by both Time/Life Books and *Omni* magazine to create illustrations

for their publications.

Awards include a 1992 World Science Fiction "Judges' Award" for "The Royal Processional," the Association of Science Fiction and Fantasy Artists' 1990 "Chesley Award" for "The Fish Walker," and the 1991 World Science Fiction Convention's "Best in Show" award for "Once Upon a Time." He was also a finalist for the National Association of Limited Edition Dealers' (NALED) 1998 "Artist of the Year" Award.

Christensen's creations appear as fine art prints, porcelains and books published by The Greenwich Workshop Press, including *A Journey of the Imagination, Voyage of the Bassett* and *Rhymes and Reasons.*

GRETCHEN CLASBY

More than a decade ago, Gretchen Clasby began drawing and selling blue birds for $5.00 at sidewalk art shows. The artist's faith and determination transformed these drawings into popular stationery products and, most recently, a new line of enchanting figurines produced by Islandia International.

The collection, which she lovingly named *Sonshine Promises* to commemorate her faith, premiered to collector acclaim at the 1998 International Collectible Exposition® at Rosemont, Illinois. In just two years, this new line has captured the hearts of collectors around the country, who relate to the little birds and their uplifting messages and scriptural passages.

People wanted to know everything about her birds, and Gretchen's answers were simple and direct. "They're just funny little birds with webbed feet – not like any real bird – and I painted them blue because that's my favorite color." The collection now includes a series of light-hearted Cardinals with endearing titles such as "Blessed Are the Trusting...for Theirs Is a World of Belief."

During her 25 years as an artist, Gretchen Clasby has specialized in portraits of children and scenes of natural beauty that cause the viewer to become involved in the "wonder of life."

JIMI CLAYBROOKS

From the time Jimi Claybrooks was a small boy, he knew he was destined to draw and paint. His professional career began in Chicago when he won "Best of Show" at the DuSable Black History Museums' First Annual Art Show. That same year, he won the Lake Meadows 25th Annual Art Exhibit. Recognition from the latter lead him into a position as art director with a record company. From that moment on, Jimi became a full-time artist.

Claybrooks' works have been collected by enthusiasts as far away as Australia and England, as well as by prominent Hollywood celebrities, professional athletes, politicians and wealthy industrialists. His art holds a commitment to both children and his African heritage, and each image reflects a special significance to his life.

With Reco International, Jimi introduced the *Pure Potential* figurine series, created from Jimi's original art, and "Gettin' Ready" an inspirational relief plaque.

CHERYL SPENCER COLLIN

Celebrating her 16th year of designing and sculpting intricate lighthouse designs, Cheryl Spencer Collin recently received the distinct honor of being selected as an Official Coast Guard Artist for her achievements and her years of dedicated work in the industry.

After receiving a bachelor of fine arts in 1975 and master of fine arts in 1977, Cheryl began sculpting one-of-a-kind porcelain animal miniatures. In 1984, she added a line of cottages and lighthouses. Today, her studio that is housed in her Maine barn is known for producing some of the finest lighthouse sculptures available. Attention to detail has earned *Spencer Collin Lighthouses* a well-deserved reputation for quality and detail.

Cheryl researches and painstakingly sculpts each site, as well as the lighthouse itself. This gives the collection unique qualities of consistent style, relative scale, and detail based on *actual* regional surroundings.

A new collection for Cheryl is the *Compass Rose Collection.* The initial offering features 12 popular lighthouses from around the United States produced in miniature form. Also look for new lighthouse designs, new lightships and a collection of mini ightships.

PENNI JO COUCH

Penni Jo Couch is known as a "master miniaturist." Along with sculpting many small and miniature figurines for United Design™, she is spreading her talents to the large and limited edition *Angels Collection.* Penni Jo created "The Gift" angels in 1997 and 1998.

Penni Jo began her career sculpting tiny figurines in her kitchen, which she sold at craft shows. Using colored clays, a food processor and a toaster oven, Penny Jo created miniature teddy bears that propelled her into the national spotlight among collectible figurine artists.

Today, Penni Jo still uses the toaster oven, along with many other innovative tools, to create designs for several figurine collections. Many of the lively animals featured in the *Stone Critters*® and *Itty Bitty Critters*® series are a reflection of Penni Jo's creativity. Penni Jo says, "We can learn noble qualities from animals – like self-reliance and loyalty." This point is echoed in her charming collection of teddy bear angels called *Teddy Angels*™.

KEN CROW

"I have a mind for putting things together," Ken Crow explains. He classifies his work as "little boy, juvenile," although people of all ages are attracted to his moving creations. Pull the string on the "Mistletoad" *Keepsake Ornament,* for instance, and the festive amphibian grins and "ribbits." Ken engineered the works himself.

Before coming to Hallmark in 1979, Ken wanted to be an editorial cartoonist or a Disney animator. He says that his work at Hallmark is much more satisfying. "I can use my own ideas and style, and animate my own characters," he says. That's been

especially true since he joined the *Keepsake Ornament* studio in 1983. Ken's favorite *Keepsake Ornament* is the 1995 "Our Little Blessings" because he modeled it after his own son and daughter, Paul (then four years old) and Michelle (then two).

Ken says he has a special memory of a blind collector who smiled from the heart when she "saw" his Santa ornament through the touch of her fingertips.

MATT & MATTHEW DANKO

Matt Danko and his son, Matthew, first created *Heart Tugs™* and *Teddy Hugs™* out of their love of collecting antique teddy bears, dolls and nostalgic keepsakes. Each piece is designed to include a message that is appropriate to a specific gift occasion. A touching sentiment and keepsake heart clearly appears as a part of a charmingly complete vignette.

The Dankos have enjoyed great success in giftware design. Matt began his career as a greeting card designer for American Greetings. More recently, he and his son successfully created *Heart Tugs* and *Teddy Hugs* as musical giftware designed for The San Francisco Music Box Company. "Love is sharing," a *Teddy Hugs* musical figurine, received a nomination for *Collector Editions'* 1999 "Awards of Excellence."

In 1999, a non-musical message figurine line featuring the same precious vignettes was introduced by Cast Art Industries under the "Gentle Expressions" trade name.

JANE DAVIES

At an early age, Jane Davies was fascinated by all types of arts and crafts and wanted to be a potter. However, she followed another career path which included fashioning gold and silver jewelry, china restoration and doll repair. From there, it was just a short step to making her own all-porcelain miniature dolls.

Jane specializes in creating small dolls. Her current work in porcelain includes one-of-a-kind artist figures that are 12" tall, limited editions of 6" and smaller sized dolls, and one-twelfth scale dollhouse dolls. Recently, Jane began creating cloth dolls. Her designs for Deb Canham Artist Designs, Inc. include a 5" fully jointed cloth doll available in a numbered limited edition.

Jane has been involved in the doll industry for more than 20 years and has been active in the Global Doll Society as an exhibitor, judge and lecturer. In 1991, she was selected as an artist member of the National Institute of American Doll Artists and has served as its first vice-president since 1995.

RAY DAY

1999 marked the 10th anniversary of Ray Day's first Lilliput Lane collection, *American Landmarks,* which beautifully captures the essence of regional American architecture.

Ray, believing that we are stewards, preserving the past for the next generation, creates nostalgic, historic, artistic sculptures based on real places located throughout America.

The architecture, built by everyday people for everyday purposes, is selected for its ability to touch heartstrings and rekindle fond memories. Among his collections are *The Allegiance Collection,* inspired by our national flag; *An American Journey,* endorsed by The National Trust for Historic Preservation and the *Coca-Cola® Country Collection.*

Each year, Ray has created a special piece for the annual Disneyana Convention. His 1999 selection, "Main Street Cinema," depicts the world-famous Walt Disney World's nineteenth century-style Main Street in Orlando.

Since 1973, Ray and his wife Eileen have published limited editions of his watercolor subjects, such as the picturesque covered bridge at Fuzzy Zoeller's "Covered Bridge Golf Club" in southern Indiana.

JORGE DE ROSA

As a young man in Montevideo, Uruguay, Jorge De Rosa apprenticed in the field of handcrafted ceramics. He studied all aspects of ceramic design and artistic development under the guidance of his father, Jorge De Rosa Thompson, who co-founded Artesania Rinconada S.R.L. in the early 1970s with twin brothers, Jesus and Javier Carbajales.

Jorge devoted his professional career to the craft of ceramic design and became the Director of the Rinconada factory in 1996. Under his leadership, Artesania Rinconada developed a series of gold and platinum accented animal figurines to commemorate the 25th anniversary of the original *Classic Collection.* These new designs formed the beginning of the *Silver Anniversary Collection,* which is successfully leading the Artesania Rinconada collection into the 21st century.

BRIGITTE DEVAL

Brigitte Deval has been creating dolls since her childhood days in Munich, Germany. Her first dolls were *stoche puppe* — dolls modeled over sticks and bottles — that she made as family gifts. In 1968, she began creating one-of-a-kind dolls in wax over ceramic, which won her international acclaim.

Her latest offering under the Ashton-Drake name is the *Fairy Tale Princess* collection. The first issue in the series, "Cinderella," was nominated for the 1997 "Doll of the Year" (DOTY) Award. Dressed in pale blue from head to toe, she's been a sensation with collectors and critics. This

is a new direction for Brigitte, who is probably best known for her breathtaking Madonnas for *Visions of Our Lady* and her angels for *Blessed Are the Children*.

ANN DEZENDORF

Her love of children and strong traditional values have always led Ann Dezendorf to create lines that touch the hearts of people – at any age. Her *Carousel Memories* and *The Life and Adventures of Santa Claus* collections are no exceptions.

Ann has taken the majestic carousel horse/menagerie animal designs from the master carvers of the late 1800s to a new level. Each carousel base is inspired from the rounding boards of the great carousels and decorated with a cabochon stone. On the top of each brass pole, Ann has created a finial (Willitts Designs exclusive) that is unique in design to match each horse.

Ann's children have brought back the excitement of Christmas she thought she had lost. Her new line of figurines and book collection bring to life the charming characters from L. Frank Baum's classic children's book, *The Life and Adventures of Santa Claus*. Ann combines the traditional Christmas theme of loving one another with a new understanding of the magic of Santa.

Ann graduated from the Paier College of Art in Connecticut in 1974. Since then, she has won numerous awards for product and package designs at several top gift and collectibles companies, including Willitts Designs, Inc., where she currently creates award-winning figurines.

BEV DOOLITTLE

One of the most popular and innovative concept artists in print, Bev Doolittle creates artwork that has been called visual poetry, and even magical. After studying at the Art Center College of Design in Los Angeles, Doolittle embarked on a fine arts career, anxious to share her message of conservation and to give something back to nature.

After developing her own water-color technique and joining The Greenwich Workshop in 1979, Doolittle's artwork was so unique that a category was named for it — Camouflage Art. It gave her collectors a new way of appreciating art, which was beyond the obvious. Doolittle continues to explore the wonders of nature and the unlimited opportunities of art. Her newest work is the book titled *The Earth is My Mother*.

KAREN DRAYNE

Artist Karen Drayne is the artist behind *From Grandma's Heart*™, the successful new collection of nostalgic chenille animals by Mill Mountain™. Each animal in the collection has been handmade by "Grandma" and is named for the child to whom it will be given. Along with the little animal is a "letter from Grandma" with the story behind the gift.

Growing up in Florida, Karen designed clothes for her dolls and learned sewing from her mother. She never outgrew her love of sewing and creating craft projects, and her hobby became a

business in 1982. Her charming muslin bunnies were an overnight success at local shows, and she named her thriving business, Dirty Bunnie Originals. By 1987, she had added a full range of animals to her repertoire, and collectors and shop owners were happy to wait up to two years for one of her originals.

Karen's reputation as a craft artist and designer grew to a national level. She was featured in *Country Folk Art* magazine and also developed ties to Westwater Enterprises® and their craft supplies business, also part of the Mill Mountain organization. Karen initially designed and made original creations for Westwater's *Bear Paws*™ bears and accessories line. Now she designs and sews her endearing little characters for *From Grandma's Heart* collection.

MAUREEN DRDAK

As a young girl, Maureen Drdak was so crazy about horses that she would tie a rope around the handle bars of her bike, pretending they were reins. She would then simulate jumping, as if her bike was the horse she always dreamed of owning. So, it seemed a natural progression for Maureen to later design beautiful horses.

After completing her studies and receiving a bachelor of fine arts degree, Drdak served as the head of the design studio for The Franklin Mint and also specialized as a designer for Fabergé. Most recently, The San Francisco Music Box Company licensed her to design a line of carousel horses.

Drdak works out of her home studio in Ardmore, Pennsylvania, which she shares with her husband and daughter, and a menagerie of pets. Inspiration for her designs comes from reading a variety of magazines, visiting antique shops and even channel surfing on the TV to keep up on the latest trends. She enjoys gardening and loves to read and travel.

SUE DREAMER

Sue Dreamer has loved to draw for as long as she can remember, and always knew she would become a professional artist. While majoring in painting at the Massachusetts College of Art, Sue enjoyed pursuing crafts like furniture painting, soft sculpture and quilting her own hand-painted fabrics.

Today, Sue and her family live in the Boston area where she works in her home studio, creating images that continue to grow in popularity. Drawing for Sue is a magical process that comes from the love and happiness in her heart. Her current medium of choice is Tria markers, a medium that perfectly complements her unique sense of color and imagery. Along with the *Simple Delights*™ collection designed exclusively for Midwest of Cannon Falls®, Sue also has a complete line of greeting cards, calendars and home décor textiles, as well as a series of books she has illustrated.

SCOTT ENTER

Scott Enter was born in Minneapolis, Minnesota. Early in his life, he developed an interest in drawing and photography. In 1990, he graduated from St. Paul School of Associated Arts, where he earned a degree in illustration and design.

That same year, he began working for Department 56®. He started by designing Village accessories, building paper models of the houses, and painting samples of Village pieces. His first lighted building was the "Village Greenhouse." Now Scott designs all *The Original Snow Village*® pieces.

Introduced in 1976, *The Original Snow Village* was inspired by the warm, nostalgic image of a snow covered old-fashioned American town. Scott's extensive research contributes to the charm and detail of each lighted ceramic building.

One of the things that Scott enjoys most about designing *Snow Village* pieces is that it allows him to draw upon his own childhood memories and family traditions. His appreciation of small towns and days gone by helps collectors identify with the gentler time *The Original Snow Village*® has come to represent.

SUE ETÉM

From the age of three, Sue Etém has been perfecting her art. In high school, she won many awards while studying various art techniques. Traveling throughout Europe in the '60s and '70s, Etém studied the works of master painters, and she explored multiple painting styles.

By the late 1970s, Etém had developed a personal style, painting boats, portraits and children at play. She would later become well-known for her very successful artistic creations of toddlers and children. In 1980, she entered the collectibles market with her first plate, "Renee," which was awarded the prestigious title of "Plate of the Year 1981." Etém was an "instant" success, and every plate and lithograph produced was a sell-out through 1983. In 1982 and 1983, she was voted "Artist of the Year" by the plate collectors of the U.S. and Canada.

More recently, private commissions for her artwork and sculpting have kept Etém busy. In 1997, a past friendship with the President of Islandia International, Joe Timmerman, was rekindled, and Etém has proudly joined forces with this fast-growing collectibles company. She has already developed many new masterpieces for her exclusive fine art collection from Islandia International.

SANDI GORE EVANS

Working out of her home studio in Augusta, Kansas, self-taught artist Sandi Gore Evans brings watercolors to life with the stroke of a brush. Artistic since childhood, Sandi credits her early interest in art to her father, who allowed her to "mess with his paints and brushes." Sandi combines her passion for all things old with her love for the adventure of today. She owns a retail gift store and gallery, and enjoys puttering around her flowerbeds and collecting antique toys.

Inspiration for many of her designs comes from the beauty and simplicity of everyday life. One of her limited edition pieces, "Wee Miracles Everywhere," was inspired by her granddaughter's discovery that each snowflake is different.

The distinctive style of Sandi is clear in the characters of her *Jolly Follies*® collection of robust snowmen and Santas, her *Tattertales*® collection of angels, and the playful designs of *Rabbit Rascals*® and *Bunny Frolics*®.

Sandi's watercolors come to life in the delightful collection of figurines, ornaments and functional dishes designed by Midwest of Cannon Falls®.

JEAN EVERETT

Jean Everett was born in England, but moved to South Africa as a young child. Much of her childhood was spent traveling around Africa, where she developed a deep and lasting love of the continent.

Everett studied art at the St. Martin's School of Art and the Central School of Advanced Art in London. After completing her studies, she found much enjoyment in exhibiting her paintings, along with illustrating and designing. She married and eventually moved to the United States with her husband and two sons. Her creativity is now enhanced by her Connecticut studio, which is surrounded by magnificent stone walls and abundant nature.

With Reco International, Everett has introduced two series of relief plaques. *Purr-Fect Views* interprets her personal creative style, bringing playful cats into three dimensional art. *Fancy Footwork* features a lovely and unique series of shoes with her favorite animals.

JUAN FERRANDIZ

Claimed by Barcelona as a native son, Juan Ferrandiz was beloved by the world. A poet, painter, author and illustrator of children's books, his wide acclaim in the United States came from his distinctive ANRI carved figurines.

Ferrandiz studied at the Bellas Artes School in Barcelona, as well as in private art schools. He also worked on his own to perfect his inimitable style. It was his belief that children are the hope for the salvation of mankind, and he envisioned a unique harmony between children and nature. This is evident in much of his work by his use of small animals, such as cats, dogs, forest animals and even birds, in tender combination with children.

Although Ferrandiz died in 1997, ANRI continues to bring his art to countless admirers around the world.

KATHRYN ANDREWS FINCHER

Kathryn (Kathy) Andrews Fincher had been a successful artist of wildlife and landscapes for many years when she redirected her focus to the innocent faces of children.

"When I discovered that one little shadow or slight change of the angle of a child's mouth could change an entire expression...I was hooked!" exclaims Kathy. In her popular *Spirit of Innocence*™ collection for Arts Uniq', it's the wonderful look on a child's face when they are on the brink of a new discovery that she tries to capture.

Because the artist's favorite models are real kids, like her own two daughters, Maggie and Kelley, and children of family and friends, the *Spirit of Innocence* collection has touched many hearts all over the country.

The *Spirit of Innocence* collection and Kathy's other works are available in books, calendars, cards, stationery, gifts and needlework kits.

Although she has traveled all over the world, Kathy delights in the home town atmosphere of Duluth, Georgia, where she was raised, and where she, her husband and their two daughters live today.

LYN FLETCHER

Artist Lyn Fletcher was born on Long Island, New York, and grew up in Riverside, Rhode Island. She earned a bachelor of fine arts degree from Rhode Island School of Design and later worked as a fashion illustrator, graphic designer, illustrator and product conceptualist. Lyn has designed dolls, giftware and toys for a number of leading manufacturers, and for the past 12 years, has enjoyed a successful freelance art career. Lyn has designed several Santas for the *American Artist Collection* from Possible Dreams.

"Although I love drawing flowers, birds and wildlife, there's nothing I like better than drawing people," explains Lyn. "I especially like illustrating people in warm, funny situations, the way Norman Rockwell did. Like Rockwell, I take snap shots of my friends and family as reference to draw from. Just about everyone in the neighborhood has posed for me, and they're always amused to find out what 'part' they get to play. My next door neighbor, Deb, is my Mrs. Claus, and my husband, Jon, has always been my model for Santa. I like to think that drawing from models I know gives the artwork a 'real personality' that will touch its viewer."

EMANUELE FONTANINI

Emanuele Fontanini is one of five fourth-generation family members now managing the celebrated House of Fontanini® in the village of Bagni di Lucca, Italy, where it was founded more than nine decades ago. Famous for magnificent old-world crafting, *Fontanini Nativities* are treasured for their exquisite, lifelike sculpting, meticulous hand-painting and painstaking attention to detail. Roman, Inc. became the exclusive U.S. distributor for *Fontanini Heirloom Nativities* more than two decades ago.

As the namesake and great-grandson of the founder of the House

of Fontanini, Emanuele has a rich and colorful legacy to preserve. He began his apprenticeship in the Nativity crafting process as a young boy and studied all facets of Fontanini operations at his father's side. He took on an increasingly active role as he learned about production schedules, sculpting techniques, and shipping dilemmas. In his current role, Emanuele acts as the liaison between Master Sculptor Elio Simonetti and the artisans who translate Simonetti's models into finished pieces. In addition to his responsibilities with the family business, Emanuele makes time for a second professional passion, auto racing.

BART FORBES

Bart Forbes' unique approach to painting is a result of many years spent both as a fine artist and illustrator. His interest in sports has led to a wide variety of major commissions.

Forbes has done theme paintings for a variety of PGA and Seniors tournaments, and is known for his many posters and prints. He has also designed over 20 commemorative postage stamps for the U.S. Postal Service including the 1988 Olympic Stamps, Lou Gehrig and Jesse Owens stamps and the *America the Beautiful* series. His work has appeared in countless magazines, including *Sports Illustrated* and *TIME*. Corporate clients include Exxon, Pepsi-Cola, ABC-TV, Eastman Kodak, General Electric, Lockheed, American Airlines and the National Football League.

In 1988, Forbes was selected by the Korean Olympic Committee to be the Official Artist for the Seoul Olympics. In addition, he has painted official posters for the Boston Marathon, The America's Cup, Indianapolis 500, as well as the 1992 and 1996 Olympic Games.

For Gartlan USA, Forbes created the original artwork of Ringo Starr featured on the Drumstick and Lithograph which are personally autographed by Ringo.

Bart and his wife, Mary Jo, live and work in Dallas, Texas.

LARRY FRAGA

Artist Larry Fraga's love for Christmas began when he was a small child growing up in Oakland, California, and has continued to this day. For the past 29 years, Larry has worked within the Christmas industry. In 1994, he started designing glass ornaments and introduced his line, Larry Fraga Designs, in 1995. They were an immediate national success and were featured in magazine and newspaper articles, on television, and at local and national artist signing events.

The creation of a Larry Fraga Christmas ornament begins when he sketches the design at his studio. After a few months of work, a mold is cast, and the prototypes are mouth blown by skilled artisans in Germany. Larry then hand paints each design, creating the magic that brings these Christmas wonders to life!

Noted in the industry for having an exceptional eye for coloration and design, Larry Fraga's creations have introduced a new element of excitement in the glass ornament industry. The introduction of the *Glittered Series* again took the industry by storm! Each piece in the series is limited to 300 and is hand-painted by the artist. Larry creates an extraordinary collection of sparkling and spectacular ornaments of unmatched craftsmanship.

DAVID FRYKMAN

David Frykman was born in Door County, Wisconsin. When he was just a small boy, his mother introduced him to the craft of sculpture. Her talents and magical displays captivated children of all ages, including David! He began sculpting early in his life and has sculpted in nearly every material possible from clay and bronze, to sand and snow. His first true carving experience was in the winter of 1992-93 when he was invited to participate as an ice carver in local ice carving competitions. This experience provided David with the opportunity to explore a whole new direction as a sculptor.

Today, David's medium of choice is white cedar, though he will still sneak off to the occasional ice competition! Cedar, which grows in abundance in Door County, is a knotty and brittle wood which frustrates many traditional carvers. However, David finds that it carves particularly well with wood-adapted ice carving tools.

For Coyne's & Company, David has created 15 series within *The David Frykman Portfolio Collection,* now in its 6th year.

MARGARET FURLONG

Twenty-one years ago, artist Margaret Furlong thought about starting a small business that would let her merge her love of nature and her artistic impulses. Drawing on her pottery and painting background, Margaret Furlong established a modest art studio in 1979 and began experimenting with the design of things found in nature. Working on a shell motif, the talented artist began combining several shell forms; she added a molded face, a textured coil and a tapered trumpet, forming her first "shell angel" ornament.

Margaret then launched a heavenly series of all-white angel ornaments fashioned after sea shells. She wanted the ornaments to exemplify the real meaning of Christmas — "a celebration of God and nature."

Furlong is the sole designer for her company. She gets her inspiration from God, nature, family and friends. Each of her limited edition angels carries a theme and comes with a scriptural quote.

Margaret's deep-seated Christian beliefs are at the heart of her artwork. She hopes that when people look at her designs, they will sense her love and celebration of God and His beautiful creations.

ANDRÉ GABRICHT

Son of the founder of G. DeBrekht Artistic Studios, André Gabricht was trained as an engineer but is also a gifted artisan in his own right. Born in the Ukraine, André grew up in an artistic environment. His father had a passion for the unique folk art found in small Russian villages, and it was his hobby of collecting this art that led to the creation of G. DeBrekht Studios when André was quite young.

Over the years, his close friendships and associations with many of Russia's most gifted artists have been an on-going learning experience for André. He is gifted as a wood carver and as a painter, but it is his designing skills in product development that has cast G. DeBrekht Artistic Studios into the international collectibles spotlight.

In 1990, André, his wife Vicky, and their two daughters came to America. They established Russian Gift & Jewelry Center, which includes the G. DeBrekht Division. As André and Vicky learned more about the U.S. market, they introduced the unique G. DeBrekht collection of hand-made, hand-painted Russian art. André travels several times a year to work in the Russian studios with artists to develop new pieces and to perfect his own designs, as G. DeBrekht creations become more sought after by American collectors.

DONA GELSINGER

As Dona Gelsinger was growing up in the 1960s, her parents gave her a loving gift that would later have a profound influence on her art — a deep appreciation for strong, loving family values.

After graduating from Long Beach State, Dona worked as a staff artist for a large corporation before striking out on her own to paint portraits and illustrations.

Dona's first major commission — painting the Stations of the Cross for a church in Diamond Bar, California — won her widespread acclaim, and helped fuel the growing demand for her work. Dona and her husband, Brian, later established Little Angel Publishing (LAP), to create prints of her inspirational paintings on paper and canvas.

LAP is headquartered in rural Eagle Point, Oregon, near Dona's studio. Living and painting in southern Oregon, with its incredible natural beauty, provides Dona with the spiritual tranquillity which is found in all her work.

Dona's art can be found on plates and ornaments from The Bradford Exchange, needlework kits from Candamar, puzzles by SunsOut, and Christmas cards from Crown Point Graphics.

In 1998, The Bradford Exchange awarded Dona its "Collector's Choice Artist of the Year" award. The annual award recognizes the achievements of outstanding artists in the field of limited edition collectors' plates and an artist's ability to win the widespread admiration of collectors.

JULIE GOOD-KRÜGER

Julie Good-Krüger has been designing dolls for 22 years. Her lovable, lifelike dolls tell a story, capture a feeling and often represent contemporary or old-fashioned children at play. She gathers inspiration for her creations from her two children and from her own childhood memories.

On the road to becoming a doll designer, Julie entered St. Olaf College in Minnesota and then studied abroad at Manchester College in Oxford, England for two years. She received a bachelor of arts degree in classics and was accepted into a doctorate program. Her parents wanted her to return to the United States and sent her a one-way plane ticket home. On the night she received the ticket, Julie had a dream. She saw herself sculpting dolls, and when she awoke, she knew that this was her life's calling.

Julie started her own company, Good-Krüger Dolls, and through the years, her creations have won numerous awards. Recently, she joined The Boyds Collection Ltd.® to introduce a new series of dolls.

FRANK GRAU

A talented illustrator and designer, Frank Grau has been a member of Cast Art's in-house art staff since 1995. He plays an important role in the company's new product development.

In collaboration with in-house sculptor LeoLeo, Frank originated and developed the hilarious *Slapstix*™ line. The collection was an immediate success and is presently offered by more than 4,000 retail outlets from coast to coast. The *Slapstix*™ collection has been expanded to more than 75 delightful figurines, miniatures and water globes that poke fun at folks from all walks of life, at work and play. Frank has many more designs on the drawing board.

Frank also illustrates many of the *Dreamsicles*® cherubs adorning licensed products by a variety of other manufacturers, and his creative ideas have been an inspiration for some of Kristin Haynes' most popular sculptures.

DEAN GRIFF

The fourth of six children, Dean Griff grew up on a 500-acre farm in rural Oneida, New York. As early as elementary school, Dean began to develop a talent in drawing and art. Eventually, this interest led him to pursue an artistic career rather than follow in the footsteps of his siblings who went on to study agriculture. In 1989, at the age of 23, Dean left the family farm to take a job as Assistant to the Curator of the Syracuse University Art Collection. Awards for his wildlife paintings in university art shows followed, as did a small business in hand-painted, hanging ornaments.

Since 1990, Dean Griff has produced hundreds of delightful *Charming Tails*® figurines, ornaments, water globes and lighted houses. The most recent additions to *Charming Tails* is a collection of functional giftware featuring picture frames, votive candleholders and music boxes.

In 1998, Dean was honored with the prestigious "Artist of the Year" award and the "Rising Star" award for *Charming Tails*, presented by the National Association of Limited Edition Dealers (NALED).

From his home in Florida, Dean Griff expresses the love of nature he learned on the farm through his artistry and the ever expanding world of *Charming Tails*.

DAVE GROSSMAN

An artist for more than 27 years, Dave Grossman relishes his current role as the creative and artistic force behind Dave Grossman Creations. A native of St. Louis, Dave graduated from the University of Missouri, where he was also a stand-out running back for the Tigers football team. After graduation, he was commissioned to design architectural sculptures for banks, hospitals, hotels and other public and private buildings. One of Dave's more intricate works is on display in New York's Lincoln Center. He was also commissioned to create sculptures for Presidents Lyndon B. Johnson and Richard Nixon.

Dave Grossman Creations began producing limited edition collectibles in 1973, most notably figurines inspired by the works of Norman Rockwell. From that successful beginning, the company has expanded to include many other licensed collectibles such as *The Wizard of Oz, The Original Emmett Kelly Circus Collection, I Love Lucy, Gone With the Wind, The Three Stooges, Laurel & Hardy,* and many others.

Dave's plans include expanding on existing licensed and limited edition collectibles and marketing new and exciting proprietary collectibles.

SCOTT GUSTAFSON

Scott Gustafson creates fairy tale treasures for the child in each of us. His paintings and porcelains are rich in imagination and possess a visual richness. His creations breathe life back into stories from long ago, reinventing and interpreting fairy tales in ways which appeal to all ages.

Born and raised in Illinois, Gustafson pursued animation art throughout his years at the Chicago Academy of Fine Arts and Columbia College. Among his first inspirations were Walt Disney cartoons – now one of Scott's works hangs in the work area of an animator at Disney Studios.

Publications as diverse as *The Saturday Evening Post* and *Playboy* have used his work. Gustafson has illustrated anew such children's classics as *The Night Before Christmas, The Nutcracker* and *Peter Pan* – and received rave reviews. His own books, including *Animal Soup* and *Animal Orchestra*, published by The Greenwich Workshop Press, have been lauded as classics in the making.

Since 1993, Gustafson's limited edition fine art prints from The Greenwich Workshop have delighted collectors. Now his

work also appears in fine art porcelain from The Greenwich Workshop Collection®.

HANS HENRIK HANSEN

Born in 1952, Hans Henrik Hansen graduated from the Academy of Applied Art in Copenhagen with an emphasis on graphic design.

For 12 years, he was the principal decorator at the retail store for the Royal Copenhagen Porcelain Manufactory, where his window decorations were the rage of fashionable Copenhagen. Since 1987, Hansen has been devoted almost exclusively to creating designs and illustrations for the porcelain manufactory. His first Christmas series, *Jingle Bells,* was very successful.

With the introduction of the *Santa Claus* collection in 1989, Hansen became the first artist since 1895 to create a colorful Christmas plate for Bing & Grondahl.

For the first time since 1908, Royal Copenhagen issued a series of six colorful annual Christmas plates and coordinating ornaments titled *Christmas in Denmark.* The original art for this epoch-making series was created by Hans Henrik Hansen.

KRISTIN HAYNES

Kristin Haynes and her *Dreamsicles®* continue to gain in popularity. It was less than a decade ago that Cast Art Industries introduced 29 adorable cherubs and animals that made up the original *Dreamsicles®* collection. Now this collection is one of America's best-selling collectibles, propelling Kristin into the spotlight alongside the most collected figurine artists.

Today, Kristin's talent touches more hearts than ever, both within the *Dreamsicles* line and beyond. *Dreamsicles Angel Hugs* is a collection of plush bean bag characters based on popular cherubs and animal characters; *Dreamsicles Northern Lights™* depicts lovable snow angels and their frosty friends in a winter wonderland; and the *Dreamsicles Garden Collection* offers a whimsical accent to any patio, porch or garden setting. As an entirely new line of figurines, *"Love, Kristin"* features home-spun kids and their animal friends in a heartland collection that celebrates the American folk art style.

Kristin continues to create her sweet-faced characters from her farmhouse studio. Collectors can be assured that much love and pride are put into creating each and every one of these precious collectible treasures.

LINDA HENRY

Internationally renowned doll and bear artist Linda Henry began her doll sculpting career over 15 years ago. In 1987, she began designing her own original teddy bears which have won numerous awards. She has also designed dolls and teddy bears for several leading manufacturers.

In 1997, Henry made her first appearance on Japan's premier home shopping network with her "Tobey" bear, which quickly sold out. Since then, her bears have been featured on several other

home shopping channels in Japan and in several prestigious Japanese catalogs.

In her current association with Lee Middleton Original Dolls, Linda designed the popular new *Nursery Bear Babies™* line of quality teddy bears. The collection's six designs are crafted of fine, soft German mohair and have jointed bodies, floppy heads and "human personalities" all their own.

DR. URSULA HERMANN

Since 1992, Dr. Ursula (Ulla) Hermann has been responsible for the design of teddy bears and cuddly toys for HERMANN-Spielwaren GmbH in Coburg-Cortendorf, Germany. Every year, the founder's granddaughter introduces 60 to 80 new models.

Ulla's passion for designing teddy bears began as a young child. She learned her bear-making skills at her father's business and was trained by her mother, Dorle Hermann, to develop new models. In spite of her love for designing cuddly toys, she decided to study business management at the Friedrich-Alexander University, Erlangen-Nuremberg. She then went on to achieve her doctorate degree.

In addition to managing the HERMANN Company, she is responsible for the production and design of the HERMANN Bears. The principle of her creative work consists of conserving traditional techniques in combination with the search for new, unconventional designs.

Ulla's talents have become internationally acclaimed. In 1997, she won the "Golden Teddy Award" with "HERMANN's 1st Internet Bear," and in 1998, she claimed the "TOBY Award" with "Professor Higgins" and the "Golden Teddy Award" with "Small Jacob." Since 1992, her teddy bear creations have been awarded 12 "TOBY" and 11 "Golden Teddy" nominations.

PEGGY FAIRFAX HERRICK

Since childhood, Peggy Fairfax Herrick knew she had uncommon artistic abilities. However, it was only 17 years ago that she realized her unique carving talent, for which she would become famous.

In order to be closer to her husband, an avid woodworker, Peggy began spending time with him in his workshop. She even amazed herself with her own carving ability. Peggy remembers that "in no time, my hobby became my profession, and my poor husband was doomed to share his shop forever."

Her charming, self-created style is perfect for conveying her love for both animals and antique toys. In fact, her *Old Fashioned Toys* collection was so delightful, it was the first to be reproduced in resin by House of Hatten, Inc. This was closely followed in 1998 with the extensive *Grand Finale* collection of home décor items and an array of Christmas decorations.

Peggy finds that the most rewarding aspect of her work is her ability to bring a smile to collectors' faces when they see her carved creations.

PRISCILLA HILLMAN

Priscilla Hillman is the creator of Enesco's award winning *Cherished Teddies®* collection, featuring some of the world's most popular teddy bear collectibles.

A self-taught artist, Hillman sketched and painted as a child. She didn't seriously pursue art until the late 1960s, when she began illustrating and writing children's books, including nine "Merry Mouse" books for Doubleday.

Twenty years later, a back problem kept Hillman inactive for several months. During that time, she kept herself busy by "drawing in her mind" sketches of teddy bears. When she recovered and put those same teddy bears on paper, *Cherished Teddies* came to life.

From the original 16 figurines introduced in 1992, *Cherished Teddies* has expanded to include more than 600 figurines and accessories which are distributed in more than 25 countries.

In addition to *Cherished Teddies*, Hillman has created four other figurine lines for Enesco, including the award-winning *Calico Kittens, Priscilla's Mouse Tales, Down Petticoat Lane,* and *My Blushing Bunnies.*

Hillman's list of honors includes the 1992 "Teddy Bear of the Year" (TOBY) award from *Teddy Bear and Friends* magazine; Parkwest Publication's 1993 "Outstanding New Product Line;" the National Association of Limited Edition Dealers (NALED) "Collectible of the Year" and the 1996 "Miniature of the Year" awards. Hillman was also named NALED's 1994 "Artist of the Year," and in 1999, she received the "International Collectible Artist Award" from the International Collectible Exposition®.

Hillman and her husband, Norman, live in a small town in New England.

ANTON HIRZINGER

Anton Hirzinger was born in 1955 in Kramsach, Tyrol, home of the famous technical school for glass craft and design. "Even as a child, I was fascinated by glass production, and knew at a very early age that when I grew up, I wanted to make it my career," says Anton, who studied at his "hometown school." He initially worked as a hollow glass craftsman.

Now, Anton has been working for Swarovski for more than ten years. He initially started work in the Swarovski Crystal Shop in Wattens, providing countless visitors from all over the world a closer insight to glass and crystal craftsmanship. Transferring to the Design Center in 1991, Anton created the Swarovski Silver Crystal "Pelican" and "Owlet." His latest designs include "The Four-Leaf Clover" and "The Reindeer." His greatest achievements so far are the "Centenary Swan" design, a commemorative edition for the company's 100th anniversary in 1995, and the Swarovski Collectors Society 10th Anniversary Edition, "The Squirrel."

GAYLORD HO

Renowned for its range of angels, Roman, Inc. introduced the *Seraphim Classics* collection in 1994. One of the world's greatest artisans, Master Sculptor Gaylord Ho has been an integral member of the creative team since the collection's debut. In addition to possessing an extraordinary artistic gift, Ho shares with Roman the unwavering commitment to the creation of angels, whose ethereal beauty touches the furthest reaches of the imagination.

The first angels created by Ho in 1994 possessed a celestial beauty never seen before, and each year the collection reaches new heights in craftsmanship and design. Rendering elaborately detailed wings, flowing gowns and exquisite angelic features, Ho has created ethereal beauties with unequaled grace and elegance. He instills a sense of motion into every angel, creating a depiction where one can almost feel the heavenly breeze that gently sweeps the angel's luxurious hair and robes.

RUTH HOLLIS

Ruth Hollis, creator of the haunting portraits that appear on the exciting "Psycho Circus" and "KISSmas" collector plates by Gartlan, USA, received her masters of fine arts degree from California State University at Fullerton. She later continued her portraiture study in France.

Her avid pursuit of excellence in the very specialized area of portrait painting was sparked by her personal fascination with the human face – a fascination that comes through in all of Ruth Hollis' work.

Critics have noted her skill in observing the specific characteristics that make each person unique. Hollis then translated that in her portraits, making them particularly emotional and moving. She is particularly effective in conveying the "life spark" of her youngest subjects and capturing the wisdom of her more mature subjects.

Hollis is also well known for recreating art from the past. Her museum replications are painted using the methods, materials and the techniques of the original artist – even the original brushstrokes are duplicated.

FRANCES HOOK

In the 1950s, illustrator Frances Hook secured the assignment that would become her benchmark: the Northern Tissue campaign. The images of children that appeared on the packaging were rendered so brilliantly that millions of requests for Hook's artwork were received. Subsequently, Hook brought her talent to book illustration, lavishing her imagination across the pages of inspirational books for children.

A new audience of devoted fans discovered her artistry in the late 1970s when Roman, Inc.

commissioned her to design her very first limited edition figurine.

Within two years of its introduction, Hook's work helped the company double its sales. "The work of Frances Hook has lost none of its appeal," said Ron Jedlinski, president and founder of Roman. "Her heartwarming portrayals of children have withstood the test of time and remain as compelling as ever. These enduring and endearing qualities are the signature of the *Remember When* collection."

Readily capturing Hook's enchanting images of children, the *Remember When* collection is a brilliant revival of the timeless renderings of children fashioned by Hook.

NORMAN A. HUGHES

Master sculptor and visionary artist Norman A. Hughes has led the collectibles industry with his designs of African-American and ethnic figurines for more than 20 years. Hughes began his career as a child sculpting the red clay of his native Georgia.

Throughout his career as one of America's leading sculptors, Hughes has released some of the most treasured designs in the collectible world. Hughes' creations are instantly recognizable through his unique talent in representing the deep values of love, faith, family, and history that he feels as an African-American artist. Committed to creating works that reflect the best in the subjects he portrays, Hughes' works continue to garner critical success and win the hearts of collectors everywhere.

The *Sankofa Collection,* featuring some of his most sought after designs and new collections, are offered by the Positive Image® Division of United Treasures. The *Sankofa* symbol means "look to your past for the knowledge to prepare for your future."

AMANDA HUGHES-LUBECK

Amanda Hughes-Lubeck was one of the first students at the Sir Henry Doulton School of Sculpture. Over the two-year course, she developed her skills in drawing and sculpture through human and animal studies. Upon completion of the course, she began her career as a modeller in the Beswick Studio at Royal Doulton.

After five years as a sculptor, Amanda was promoted to "Head of Studio," where her role was broadened to encompass administrative and project management duties.

Her favorite subject matter is horses, and she has modelled a number of breeds, including Red Rum. Amanda has exhibited her work alongside Dame Elizabeth Frink at Keele University, and at Shugborough Hall. She continues her creativity at home, sketching and modelling both figure and animal studies.

In her spare time, Amanda enjoys golfing and keeping fit.

VALENTINA IVANOVA

Valentina Ivanova is ranked as one of the most talented wood carvers in Russia and has worked at her craft since she was a child. Born in 1948, Valentina was a young student when a teacher asked her to draw a cat. She became so absorbed in the project that she lost track of time, and Valentina knew she would be an artist.

She was trained at the School of Art Carving in the ancient art village of Bogorovska, famous for its folk art wood carvers and wooden toys that have been hand-made in the village for more than 350 years. Valentina worked with the toy makers and began to create her own designs, developing her techniques as a painter and wood carver.

In 1990, she joined G. DeBrekht Artistic Studios, where her wood sculptures and fine painting include *Snow Maidens* and the touching double figure of two sisters. Her newest achievement is a collection of 12 wooden bears.

Valentina is the mother of four children and resides in the village of Bogorovska.

BILL JOB

A native of Tennessee, artist Bill Job grew up among the local mountain craftspeople of the region. Later, his Navy experience in Asia drew him to China, and in 1987, Bill moved his wife and two daughters there permanently.

In China, he learned the stained glass technique made famous by Louis Comfort Tiffany. The Tiffany technique Bill uses includes hand cutting the stained glass, wrapping it in copper foil, cleaning with flux, soldering with tin and applying patina, which darkens the shiny tin. He has experimented with fusing glass, mixing glass with pewter, adding blown glass, and drilling the glass to create works of art that are uniquely his own.

In 1999, Forma Vitrum by Cavanagh created the *Bill Job Signature Series,* identifying new introductions designed by the artist and produced in his studio. Earlier pieces, with Bill's signature on the plate, were made this way, but some new pieces from current production will be crafted outside of Bill's studio. They will not bear the special "chop" – Bill's name in Chinese.

BRENDA JOYSMITH

Brenda Joysmith, the artist behind the enchanting *Our Song* collection from Willitts Design, is best known for presenting everyday African-American life in a way that highlights the positive aspects of ordinary lives that are sometimes overlooked or often simply taken for granted.

A native of Memphis, Tennessee, Brenda began her formal training in 1968 at the School of the Art Institute in Chicago. She then studied at the University of Chicago where, in 1974, she received her bachelor of fine arts degree.

Moving to Northern California, Joysmith opened her first studio in 1980, and in 1984, self-published her first limited edition print

portfolio of six paintings titled *Tapestry,* which included her signature painting of "Madonna with Child."

Over the years, her artwork has received valued exposure on the sets of network television series, including *The Cosby Show, A Different World, Amen, Family Matters, In the Heat of the Night* and *The Hughleys,* and in the feature films *Philadelphia, Lethal Weapon II, and The Preacher's Wife.*

LYNN R. KAATZ

Lynn Kaatz has established an international reputation as a result of his artistic talent and versatile skills. He paints from knowledge and experience. His formal art training, combined with extensive field research, gives Kaatz' paintings a realistic, true-to-life feel.

Kaatz, a native of the Great Lakes region of northern Ohio, is a demanding and dedicated artist who excels in painting scenes of nature – from landscapes and wildlife to seascapes. He spends hours observing his subjects, so his paintings feature accurate details, quality and realism.

When one of his paintings conveys not only a scene, but his emotions as well, then Kaatz feels that he and the viewer have a special relationship. And that relationship is the greatest tribute any artist can achieve.

Kaatz' work is marketed under the title *Sportsman Collection by Lynn Kaatz.* The collection of figurines Kaatz has designed exclusively for Flambro Imports of Atlanta, Georgia, is focused on puppies of popular sporting dog breeds. These puppies are shown in various sporting situations including hunting, fishing and golf, as well as in Christmas scenes.

ELLEN KAMYSZ

Ellen Kamysz was just nine years old when she was first asked to show her artwork on the local TV station in her hometown of South Bend, Indiana. This early recognition, paired with her love of and aptitude for drawing, were the catalysts for her artistic career. Ellen completed her education at the American Academy of Art in Chicago with an apprenticeship in illustration and layout design, laying the groundwork for her successful freelance career.

In 1995 when Ellen was introduced to the world of giftware design, she was immediately drawn to the freedom to go anywhere her imagination took her. Practically overnight, Ellen's focus changed from print advertising to designing giftware. Ellen has designed the *Arabesque Carousel Collection,* the *Four Seasons Carousel Collection,* juvenile inspirational figurines and Christmas ornaments for The San Francisco Music Box Company. Ellen's newest creations are the *Sentimental Rose Christmas Collection* and the *Scheherazade Cloisonné Carousel.*

RU KATO

All *Melody In Motion* (MIM) figurines begin with Ru Kato, the *MIM* Creative Director. He writes a story line describing the concept and the movement, and selects the music, thus beginning a process that unites the 150 pieces found in a typical figurine. Recently asked where he finds his creative motivation for the unique line, he responded "just about everywhere!"

Born in Kamakura, an ancient, historical city in eastern Japan, Ru grew up in an artistic environment. His father, a scenario writer for a Japanese movie company, and his late uncle, the Academy award-winning director, Akira Kurosawa, provided real-life confirmation of the importance of imagination and its ability to transport us away from the mundane and commonplace.

For Kato, entertainment is every bit as important as the complex manufacturing process that brings the *Melody In Motion* figurines to life. As *MIM* celebrates its 15th anniversary, Ru is pleased that so many collectors enjoy what took so many years to create.

SARAH KAY

Since the early 1980s, Sarah Kay's name has been linked with ANRI in a mutually successful enterprise.

Her figures of children – happy, thoughtful, enterprising, studious – are based on drawings of her own offspring. The carvings of these figures are three-dimensional translations that capture the wonder, simplicity and joy of childhood. The sunny aspect of life has continued in Sarah Kay's recent *Santa* series, with the fifth and final edition issued in 1999.

Cold cast porcelain figures were introduced in 1999, with the launch of the *Sarah Kay Collection* by United Treasures, Inc., under a unique licensing agreement with ANRI. The winsome children are superbly captured in this new medium, with the sculpted figurines as masterfully done as those originally handcrafted in wood.

Sarah Kay's art continues to warm the hearts of collectors, as ANRI and United Treasures continue to produce her nostalgic and loving appreciation of children for her devoted audience.

DONNA KENNICUTT

Primarily self-taught, Donna Kennicutt says she loved art during her high school years but never pursued it as a career until her children were grown. Even then, her painting and sculpting began as a hobby. Her talents, however, have won her wide recognition as one of Oklahoma's outstanding women artists.

Early on, Donna's subjects for her cast bronze pieces were primarily animals. This gave her an ideal background for creating the originals for the animal figurines produced by United Design™. Donna says she never tires

243

of working with animals because they are so fascinating. "Doing my hobby and getting paid for it is the best part of working for United Design," comments Donna.

One of the most popular collectible editions Donna has created and sculpted since working with United Design is the *Easter Bunny Family*™ collection. She is also responsible for *Children's Garden of Critters*™ and many of the *Stone Critters*® and *Animal Magnetism*® designs.

THOMAS KINKADE

Thomas Kinkade is America's most collected living artist, a painter-communicator whose tranquil, light infused paintings bring hope and joy to millions each year. Each painting Thomas Kinkade creates is a quiet messenger in the home, affirming the basic values of family, faith in God, and the luminous beauty of nature.

Kinkade is a devout Christian and credits the Lord for both the ability and the inspiration to create his paintings. His goal as an artist is to touch people of all faiths, bringing peace and joy into their lives through the images he creates. The letters he receives every day testify to the fact that he is achieving this goal.

A devoted husband and doting father to their four little girls, Kinkade hides the letter "N" in his paintings to pay tribute to his wife, Nanette, and the girls also find their names in many of his paintings.

Kinkade has received numerous awards for his works. Most recently, he was inducted into the *U.S. Arts'* Hall of Fame. The National Association of Limited Edition Dealers (NALED) has named him "Graphic Artist of the Year" for the fourth year in a row. Kinkade has also won *Collector Editions'* "Award of Excellence," was a charter inductee to The Bradford International Hall of Fame for plate artists, and won The Bradford Exchange's 1999 "Collector's Choice Artist of the Year" award.

RUDOLPH KOSTNER

Born in Bolzano (Bozen), the capital of the South Tyrol, in 1958, Master Carver Rudi Kostner now lives in Ortisei (St. Ulrich) in the heart of the Groeden Valley. He is descended from a long tradition of carvers, following in the footsteps of his father, grandfather and great-grandfather.

Following school, where he received his basic training, he worked in his father's woodworking shop, specializing in sacred motifs for seven years before apprenticing at age 22 with a master. In three short years, Rudi himself became a master wood sculptor.

With ANRI for several years, one of Rudi's great pleasures is coming to the United States to make personal appearances in stores to demonstrate his exacting artistry. To watch this captivating experience is to be enthralled.

SANDRA KUCK

In 1979, Heio Reich, President of Reco International Corp., discovered Sandra Kuck's paintings of children in a Long Island gallery. Sandra's career skyrocketed with the creation of the plate "Sunday Best" in 1983. Since then, NALED honored her with many awards, including an unprecedented six-time honor as "Artist of the Year."

Sandra's list of awards and accomplishments in the collectibles field are far too lengthy to list. Her most recent works include the *Everlasting Friends* and *Gardens of Innocence* plate series. "Mother's Love" is the first issue in a new Mother's Day series titled *Reflections of Love*. Her newest dolls include two bridesmaids, "Aubrey" and "Lindsay," and a christening doll, "Little Valentina."

Adding another successful category, Reco International released *Sandra Kuck's Treasures*™ in 1997. This exquisite line of figurines continues to grow in popularity, and numbers over 30 pieces. There are new *Garden Accessories* to complement the line, all with the incredible detail of Sandra's artistry.

KARL KUOLT

In the annals of European wood carving, no artist is held in higher esteem than Professor Karl Kuolt. Born in Spalchingen, Germany, in 1878, he studied at the Munich School of Art. He also attended the Munich Academy of Applied Art and was later on the faculty of this prestigious school. In addition to many monuments and memorial chapels throughout Southern Germany, countless of his smaller works are owned by private collectors and museums.

ANRI's master craftsmen have kept his art alive by faithfully reproducing Professor Kuolt's works, including his world-famous Nativity, which has endured for decades. Although he died in 1937, each piece produced by ANRI is created with the same love and care as the original.

DAVID LAWRENCE

After working for many years in London's hectic and competitive advertising industry, David Lawrence fled the city and settled in rural Somerset. Here, he met Martin Perry and turned his two-dimensional artistic expertise into three-dimensional sculptures for Harmony Kingdom.

Gathering inspiration from his young daughter, Rose, and his charming village, he carved his first series for Harmony Kingdom entitled *Angelique*. These angel Box Figurines are a unique combination of classical elegance and childlike innocence. His humorous and irreverent *Harmony Circus* has secured David a cult following, and collectors have eagerly anticipated David's annual holiday angels, a tradition since 1995.

ANNIE LEE

Annie Lee began painting at the ripe old age of ten, winning her first competition during that year. Her accomplishments continued throughout her teens, culminating in an offer of a four-year scholarship to the prestigious Northwestern University. Though declining that scholarship, Annie Lee later returned to northern Illinois to study art at Mundelein College and the American Academy of Art. She also earned a master of education degree from Loyola University.

Annie Lee's art reflects her remarkable ability to observe and draw life as she sees it, combining the elements of humor, satire and realism to relay those observations to the viewer. As a result, her work has been internationally acclaimed and warmly received by not only African Americans, but by art lovers everywhere.

The *Sass 'N Class* by Annie Lee exclusive license from Sandy USA recreates the artwork of Annie Lee from the canvas into resin figurines, each full of life, satire and humor. The *Sass 'N Class by Annie Lee* series contains both open and limited edition pieces.

RON LEE

Ron Lee started his world-renowned clown and animation figurine collection when he decided to create a little clown, "Hobo Joe," which has become his mascot. Ron has worked feverishly to create an unprecedented array of exciting sculptures that have found their way to the homes of the most discerning collectors.

His imaginative and whimsical sculptures are forever preserved in fine white metal, 24K gold-plated, hand-painted and mounted on imported onyx. His work is manufactured at Ron Lee's World of Clowns Factory and Tour in Henderson, Nevada, which fulfilled Ron's life-long ambition of creating a family-oriented tour where people could view the different stages of production of his figurines. Visitors can also see beautiful displays, relax in the Carousel Café, shop in the Ron Lee Gallery and take a ride on the Chance Carousel.

Ron is married and the father of four children. He is an inspiring example of a self-made man who, due to his natural and unique talent, coupled with untiring hard work, has achieved much recognition within the art world. Ron and his wife, Jill, recently opened a new Ron Lee Gallery at the Rio Hotel in Las Vegas, fulfilling yet another dream of expanding their own retail distribution. In addition, Ron has one of the largest collectors clubs in the world, where his members feel that they are part of the Ron Lee family.

RODNEY LEESEBERG

Rodney Leeseberg lives in a small house on a beautiful lake surrounded by hundreds of pines trees. Growing up in the area, Rodney enjoyed playing outdoors among the picturesque scenery. Now it's where one of the country's top Santa craftsmen draws his inspiration.

For this fourth grade teacher from northern Minnesota, Christmas is a very special time of year. Rodney carved his first Santa in 1988.

Even his young students saw something special in those first Santa carvings. "Hey," they told him, "they look just like you!"

He has experimented with painting, stained glass and hand pottery but enjoys whittling most, because it allows him to work in three dimensions. Rodney carves or paints every day, saying, "It's really a passion for me to create. You can't think of anything else except what you are working on. The rest of the world is blocked out of your mind."

Rodney's newest additions to his *From Out of the North* series are presented by House of Hatten.

MARGO LEFTON

As the only daughter of the founder of the 59-year collectibles pioneer Geo. Zoltan Lefton Co., Margo Lefton brings an impressive artistic and business background to the challenges of preserving the family legacy. She serves as co-owner and Executive Vice President of Research and Design for the Chicago-based giftware and collectibles company.

Since 1971, Margo has worked in every Lefton department. Her formal art studies began at Illinois' Bradley University and Roosevelt University. Margo's quest for artistic development has taken her to the School of Representational Art at the Atelier Neo Medici in Monflaquin, France, and an apprenticeship with famous Chicago glassblower, Jim Wilbat. Margo has also explored bead art, sculpture and working in various fiber media.

The Chicago-born artist fondly remembers the day her father, George Zoltan Lefton, was inspired to introduce the popular *Historic American Lighthouse Collection*. "He was so taken by the majesty of a lighthouse, he decided to create replicas of beacons as tributes to these guardians of the seas." This inspired Margo to paint lighthouses in tribute to her father's memory after his death in 1996.

Margo is thrilled to be sharing the family business leadership responsibilities with her son, President and CEO Steve Lefton Sharp. "Dad would have loved the idea of us working together to carry on the company he started in 1941," says Margo.

LEOLEO

LeoLeo is a talented sculptor who has been a member of Cast Art's studio art team since 1996. After years of producing, packaging and marketing his own gift products, this entrepreneur turned to Cast Art for help. Now he can devote 100% of his energy to his first love – art. Today, he plays an important role in developing characters from cherubs to chimpanzees.

Along with illustrator and designer Frank Grau, LeoLeo developed the *Slapstix*™ line. Grau first illustrates his offbeat clown characters, and LeoLeo then sculpts them in clay using fabrics and other materials to achieve a uniquely textured finish. The collection became an instant success and is now offered in more than 4,000 retail outlets

across the nation. *Slapstix™* has been expanded to include more than 75 cleverly designed figurines, miniatures and water globes that poke fun at folks at work and at play.

GLENN H. LEWIS

Glenn Lewis was born and raised in North Carolina. He earned a degree in design from Clemson University and a graduate degree in architecture from the University of Tennessee, Knoxville. In late 1992, he moved to Krakow, Poland, to become the co-founder of the Polish-American architectural firm, Wizja, where today he maintains a permanent seat on the company's Board of Directors.

Because of their interest in blown-glass ornaments, Glenn and his Polish wife, Basia, began creating ornaments as a hobby in 1995. A short time later, they formed Slavic Treasures with Glenn's life-long friend, Dave Wegerek. At first, they provided products for other companies, but in 1998 they decided to launch their own designs using their privately-organized manufacturing facilities.

Glenn does all the conceptualization and design work for both the *Slavic Treasures Collection* and the Licensed Products Division. An extremely talented team of craftspeople, including the firm's accomplished sculptor, glass blowers and painters, bring to life the distinguishing style of Slavic Treasures products, as directed and visualized by Glenn.

Glenn resides in Krakow with his wife and family, and looks forward to his visits and signing tours back home in the USA.

JEFF LITTLEJOHN

Jeff Littlejohn's eye for detail and expression is most often recognized in his sculptures of nature's wildlife. It was his talent in portraying some of earth's most captivating creatures that brought him to the attention of United Design.

Jeff received his degree to teach art from Central Missouri State. After graduation, he taught high school art in Missouri. Not totally satisfied with teaching, he began exploring his talent in three-dimensional sculpture. Jeff sculpted on a freelance basis for various gift and collectible companies.

Jeff's work has been exhibited at wildlife art shows, and he's won numerous awards for his wildlife sculptures. Several commissioned sculptures and bronzes are on permanent display.

Jeff joined the United Design staff of artists in 1997. He is responsible for many new wildlife designs in United Design's *Stone Critters®* and *Classic Critters™* collections. He contributes his talent to the popular *The Legend of Santa Claus™* collection and is responsible for creating the new *Snow Zone™* snowmen characters.

LENA LIU

Lena Liu is an artist of unparalleled popularity in today's collectible market. Art lovers the world over enjoy the universal yet personal character of her paintings of beautiful birds, tranquil landscapes and breathtaking floral and musical still lifes.

Lena had her first painting lessons as a child in Taiwan under the guidance of renowned painters. She came to the United States in 1972 to study architecture at the State University of Buffalo, and later did graduate work at the School of Architecture at U.C.L.A.

However, her true passion for painting never left her, and in 1977, she began to paint full time.

Today, her work is enjoyed as limited edition prints, porcelain collector plates, ornaments, figurines, music boxes, sculptures, cards, tapestries, bookmarks and calendars. Lena has achieved recognition at national shows and exhibits. She was honored by Collectors' Information Bureau as "Best Plate Artist of the Year," as Bradford's "Collector's Choice Artist of the Year," and by the National Association of Limited Edition Dealers as "Artist of the Year." She was named the Canadian "Artist of the Year" at the Canadian Collectible of the Year Awards. She was also an inaugural inductee into the prestigious Bradford Exchange Plate Artist Hall of Fame.

Lena and her husband, Bill, live in Maryland, in the home she designed to accommodate their joint love of art, music and nature.

JOSE LLADRÓ

Nearly 50 years ago, Jose Lladró joined his brothers in founding what would become one of the most famous houses of porcelain in the world.

As Jose was decorating ceramics with his brothers at their Valencia home, the increasing demands of their business turned the young artists into businessmen and entrepreneurs. A born organizer, Jose has been credited with possessing the imagination and foresight necessary to bring to fruition the dreams of a family porcelain dynasty.

On a private note, he enjoys playing squash and has been instrumental in developing the Lladró sports facilities and fostering a basketball team for the handicapped. Jose, along with his brothers, has also been granted the "Medal of Civic Merit" by the Spanish Ministry of Foreign Affairs for their activities abroad and their contribution to the export of Spanish products.

In 1998, the Lladró brothers were presented the "International Collectible Artist Award" for devoting their talents to furthering the limited edition collectible industry.

JUAN LLADRÓ

Juan Lladró is the eldest of the three brothers who founded Lladró, one of the world's most respected houses of porcelain. A connoisseur and collector of fine art, Juan possesses an intense curiosity about nature, people and landscapes that constantly fuels his imagination.

With a small kiln in their backyard in Valencia, Spain, Juan and his brothers began their experiments in porcelain in 1951. Using the skills they obtained at Valencia's San Carlos School of Arts and Crafts, he began decorating lamps with delicate porcelain flowers that have become the Lladró signature.

Juan Lladró has been described as possessing an "ever-critical spirit that demands accuracy and elaborate delicacy." And these

standards are applied to all of the products made by Lladró. As an artist, he is constantly looking for new discoveries in line, color and shadow. As an art expert, Juan is always searching for new interpretations of subjects and themes.

VICENTE LLADRÓ

The youngest of the three Lladró brothers, Vicente Lladró pooled his sculpting talents with his older brothers' and established what would become the internationally renowned porcelain house that bears their name.

As the brothers worked at their backyard kiln in Valencia, each brother continued to develop his talents. Vicente began specializing in sculpting and supervising the firing process, while his brothers decorated the ceramics.

Today, when not in his office, Vicente is often found in various departments of the factory, sharing with fervor his ideas and enthusiasm. When he is not contributing his time and expertise to the Lladró enterprise in Valencia, he travels extensively, attending trade shows and other related events around the world.

BARBARA LUND

Barbara Lund is the talented daughter of Neilan Lund, master architect of Department 56®'s *Heritage Village Collection®*. She was working for an advertising and publishing company when she was "drafted" to help her father with the growing design responsibilities that came with the explosive popularity of the *Heritage Village Collection*.

She found that having no previous experience in design was a real advantage, as it allowed her to completely absorb her father's concepts, his method of solving problems and his brilliant technique.

Barbara works on designing *Dickens' Village®*, *Alpine Village*™, and the *North Pole Series*™. She finds that each series has advantages and challenges that are unique. With the exception of the *North Pole Series*, the Villages all have quite specific architectural styles that she must replicate. She does extensive research to execute a classic look, while keeping her designs fresh.

Barbara's goal has been to create collectibles with the same warmth, charm, and feeling that *Heritage Village* collectors have come to expect and appreciate from the Lund family's continuing tradition of design excellence.

NEILAN LUND

Neilan Lund is the master architect for *The Heritage Village Collection®*. He designs the buildings for the *Dickens' Village®*, *New England Village®*, *Alpine Village*™ and the *North Pole Series*™.

Neilan made his substantial reputation in both the commercial and fine art worlds. Before his retirement as Advertising and Art Services Manager for General Mills, he did house drawings for local real estate companies.

Over the years, his travels in England stimulated his interest in villages. Neilan takes many photographs on these extensive

research expeditions, and keeps a file of house information as the basis for his designs.

When he first began designing for Department 56®, Neilan kept the details of his buildings fairly simple. But as production techniques developed and improved, he has become more creative, adding additional elements much like an architect of full-size buildings would do.

Although a few of the pieces are designed after actual buildings, including "Victoria Station," "The Old Curiosity Shop" and the "Old North Church," most are completely original designs.

ALAN MASLANKOWSKI

Alan Maslankowski was born in 1952 in Stoke-on-Trent, England. His mother was a semi-skilled pottery worker, and his father a coal miner from Gdansk in Northern Poland. He had an interest in modelling from an early age, and after leaving school, was offered an apprenticeship at Royal Doulton.

Among his early successful works were a "Cat and Owl" made in Flambe and "The Wizard." More recent works include: *The Sentiment Collection, The Elegance Collection, The Charleston Collection*, and two very prestigious pieces, "The Charge of the Light Brigade" and "Henry V at Agincourt." He has also modelled various animal studies for John Beswick which reflect his love for animals.

JOHN McCLELLAND

Some years back, John McClelland created a life-sized portrait of his daughter Susan. The portrait was used for an ad in a trade magazine, and Miles Kimball, the mail order company, spotted it and asked McClelland to do a Christmas cover for their catalog. That was the beginning of an association which continues today.

In the mid-1970s, Reco International arranged for McClelland to create limited edition plates. Today, he is one of the field's most celebrated artists with numerous "Plate of the Year" and "Artist of the Year" awards. He also has designed several figurine series and a number of limited edition lithographs.

McClelland is a portraitist and has taught both intermediate and advanced classes in portrait painting. Scores of his illustrations have appeared in magazines, and he has written two "how to" books for artists.

Among his works for Reco are *The Treasured Songs of Childhood, The Wonder of Christmas* and *A Children's Garden* plate series, as well as *The Children's Circus Doll Collection*, based upon the popular Reco plate series.

CINDY MCCLURE

Ashton-Drake is proud of its long-standing association with acclaimed doll artist Cindy McClure. Both talented and highly versatile, she has won the hearts of collectors with her pretty little girls, adorable babies and toddlers, and elegant bride dolls. Her most notable collections for the Galleries include *Heavenly Inspirations,* featuring beautiful winged messengers from on high; *Forever Starts Today,* her first-ever bride collection; and *A Joy Forever,* her collection of gorgeous infants dressed in Victorian christening gowns. Many new fans were introduced to Cindy's work with the 1998 release of "You Need a Hug, Pooh," a tremendously popular and critical success for the artist.

Cindy is one of only a few artists in the world to win the prestigious "Doll Of The Year" (DOTY) Award from the International Doll Academy in back-to-back years. Other recent triumphs include "Victorian Lullaby," nominated for the 1995 *Dolls* "Award of Excellence" and "Melody," nominated for a 1997 DOTY, as well as for a *Dolls* "Award of Excellence." In all, Cindy has been recognized with more than 20 important awards for her creations.

Her newest collection, *Tied Up in Dreams,* has been released by The Ashton-Drake Galleries.

KEN MEMOLI

Ken Memoli grew up surrounded by art. His grandfather was one of the sculptors of Mount Rushmore and the General Lee monument in Stone Mountain, Georgia. "That influence," Ken says, "and a lot of good art in the house inspired my interest in nature and the arts."

Ken studied sculpture at the University of Hartford Art School. Since then, he has been known for his intricately detailed wildlife and domestic animal sculptures. His sculpting talents also include figures of Santa Claus and angels.

For United Treasures, Inc., Ken has created the *Troubadour* series, sculptures that echo the magic, mystery and muse of our human journeys. In each piece, the storytelling *Troubadour* leans forward and quietly relates to the viewer suggestions of the tales of the millennia.

"My goal is not to be an artist, but to live a creative life," states Ken. "That means leaving more than what was here when you came." Ken works in his studio daily and enjoys photography and playing the guitar.

CLEMENTE MICARELLI

Clemente Micarelli studied art at both the Pratt Institute and The Art Students League in New York and the Rhode Island School of Design.

His paintings have been exhibited in numerous shows and have won many awards. Represented nationally by Portraits, Inc. and C.C. Price Gallery in New York, Micarelli has painted the portraits of prominent personalities throughout the United States and Europe.

Micarelli has done fashion illustrations for many leading department stores and has taught at the Rhode Island School of Design, the Art Institute of Boston and the Scituate Arts Association and South Shore Art Center.

For Reco International, Micarelli has created *The Nutcracker Ballet* plate series, a *Wedding Series* of plates and bells, and *The Glory of Christ Collection,* a plate series depicting revered events in the life of Jesus Christ.

LARRY MILLER

Larry Miller described sculpture as "more than just capturing an animal portrait in clay — it's revealing the creature's essence, giving it personality, and telling a story."

When he sculpted for the United Design™ collection of large and exceptionally lifelike *Classic Critters*™, Larry said, "I do research, go to the zoo, watch how the animal moves and reacts – that's where my inspiration comes from."

After working in graphic arts, Larry went to United Design in 1981, seeking the opportunity to work in three dimensional art. He had always loved the feel and texture of sculpture, so working independently, he developed his technique by sculpting western bronzes. Larry's love for the work he did is evident in the charming humor and rich detail he sculpted into all his designs.

Larry Miller is also credited with creating many of *The Legend of Santa Claus*™ limited edition figurines and many designs in the *Stone Garden*® line of outdoor animals and statuary.

Larry Miller died on March 14, 1997. His life and his talent are truly missed.

D. MORGAN

A native of Atlanta, Georgia, Doris Whitten Morgan began showing her work at sidewalk art shows in 1972. Today, she is one of the most published and widely distributed artists in America.

Doris studied art formally at The High Museum School of Art in her hometown, but she continues to credit her father, the late John Lovic Whitten, as her most influential teacher. With paint and pen, Doris has fashioned her God-given talent into a unique style which is unequaled.

Collectors of Doris' art can immediately recognize her work by her trademark blending of lovely sentimental verses, beautiful watercolor artistry and her proclivity to extend her painting's boundaries with creative matting.

Aside from the sale of her prints, D. Morgan's art can be found on everything from three-dimensional sculptured figurines to afghans, pillows, needlecraft and greeting cards.

The Magic of Christmas Collection, exclusively for Roman, Inc., is based on Doris' extremely popular Christmas card artwork. Each of the four titles includes a Santa figure, a collection of mini-

ornaments, the card featuring the art that inspired the designs, a verse by the artist, and a clear glass star ornament filled with glitter, representing the twinkle found in Morgan's memorable images.

Many of her most avid collectors are introduced to her art through the host of prestigious mail order catalogs that feature her work, like *Potpourri, Casual Living, Faith Mountain, Linda Anderson* and *Cats, Cats & More Cats*.

JANICE MORGAN

Halcyon Days Enamel's collection of over 400 enameled boxes, accessories and sculptural designs is filled with delicate florals, exotic wildlife and treasured works of art. "Contributing to the revival of an art form is rewarding, both professionally and personally," says Janice Morgan, premier artist for Halcyon Days Enamels.

Born in Bilston, the original center of the 18th century English craft, Janice has a unique gift for hand-painting on copper enamel. Always eager for a challenge, she prefers to paint the more complex designs, which require the highest level of skill. Notable pieces include the enamel plaques of the "Cheetahs," two representative works from the artist Graham Rust. Each took 44 hours to paint.

Janice's initial interest in art began in school, and at age 16, she joined Halcyon Days Enamels as an apprentice to fully develop her artistic ability. Eighteen years later, with her personable manner, excellent communication skills and expertise, Janice often travels to the U.S. to share her knowledge and demonstrate the centuries-old techniques used to create this fascinating and demanding art form.

FINI MARTINER MORODER

Born in Ortisei (St. Ulrich) in 1916, Fini Martiner Moroder is truly a daughter of the Groeden Valley. She apprenticed at the Ortisei Academy of Arts for three years and, since then has created many models for ANRI.

Deeply religious, Moroder was inspired to create her unusual Nativity by a vision which showed her exactly how the figures should look. Their dark eyes, expressionless faces and simple robes carried out the vision, evoking dramatic, uplifting emotions.

One of the most famous artists in the South Tyrol, Moroder's personal style makes the beauty of her distinctively Romanesque Nativity an outstanding example of sublime creativity.

ALEXEI MOROZOV

Alexei Morozov was destined to be an artist. He was born in 1964 in the famous Sergei Posad region near Moscow, which is renowned for its watercolor artists. Both his parents were artists, and Alexei demonstrated his own artistic abilities at a very early age.

In 1980, he began his studies at Abramtzevo Artistic College, where he developed his talents in painting, sculpting, wood carving and stone sculpture. He joined G. DeBrekht

Artistic Studios in 1992, where he not only creates his own art, but also instructs new artists. He heads the design team at G. DeBrekht and teaches techniques to other artists.

Alexei works with his artist wife, Tatiana, also born into an artistic family. The couple met in college and work together at G. DeBrekht, where they have been responsible for such impressive designs as the nutcracker illustrations on carved Santas, dolls and roly-poly limited editions; the majestic "Night Before Christmas Storybook Santa;" and the new bear figures. They are the parents of three sons.

NICHOLAS MULARGIA

Full of warmth, humor and the charm of his native Italy, Nicholas Mulargia brings his own special passion and vitality to everything around him. Raised on the beautiful Mediterranean island of Sardinia, his love of life and family is reflected in each piece he creates.

Two years ago, Nicholas designed the amazing wildlife sculpture titled "Majestic Bald Eagle" for Crystal World. So popular did this single piece become that it spawned an entirely new series, *The North American Wildlife Series*.

Nominated for numerous awards, Nicholas was one of the first crystal designers in the world to translate emotion and character into the enormously challenging medium of crystal. His delightful crystal teddy bears in the *Teddyland* series are now legendary – evidence of the artist's tremendous ability.

REAL MUSGRAVE

Real Musgrave carefully sculpts every piece in *The Whimsical World of Pocket Dragons*, infusing the characters with their wonderful personality and charm. Using the events in his own household, he brings each *Pocket Dragon* to life with a clever sense of humor. Real's whimsical style and obvious talent attracted the attention of Bill Dodd, President of Collectible World Studios in Staffordshire, England. *The Whimsical World of Pocket Dragons* is distributed in the United States by Goebel of North America.

In the fall of 1997, *Pocket Dragons* debuted in a televised animated series, "Pocket Dragon Adventures," produced by Bohbot Enterprises. Also on Real's drawing board are illustrations for a wonderful new line of Golden Books featuring his whimsical *Pocket Dragons*. Who knows where these little characters may take him next!

RUDY NAKAI

Founding artist and leading Crystal World designer, Rudy Nakai seems to live and breathe exciting new concepts in crystal each and every year. Winner of the prestigious *Collector Editions*' "Award of Excellence," this enormously talented artist has delighted collectors with his replicas of castles, buildings and wildlife for more than 16 years.

In 1998, he brought his creativity to new heights with the

introduction of the *Disney Showcase Collection*. He also delighted wildlife collectors with his haunting and beautiful "Timber Wolf," while providing lighthouse lovers with his exquisite "Barnegat Lighthouse - New Jersey" and "Nubble Lighthouse - Maine". Newest from this prolific and talented artist are "Tinkerbell" and "Cinderella's Coach," both part of the exciting *Disney Showcase Collection*.

DIANNA NEWBURN

"I married early, had my children young, and now this is my time," declares Dianna Newburn. These days, her time and energies are directed toward her life-long interest in art.

When Dianna's children were small, she taught decorative painting, but her true talent and love of sculpture was discovered when she began experimenting with making miniature clay dolls. In 1990, Dianna's work had become so popular that she was exhausted from trying to keep up with demand. It was then that she agreed to join the staff of artists at United Design™, where she continues to create figurines for the company's various figurine lines.

Currently, Dianna is sculpting figurines for several collections. In the *Angels Collection,* she has created several designs of limited edition and small angels. Dianna is also kept busy working on *Itty Bitty Critters®* and *Stone Critters® Littles™*.

LOUIS NICHOLE

Designer, craftsman, author, musician, inventor, *raconteur extraordinaire —* for over 20 years, Louis Nichole has been charming American consumers and collectors with the Old World romance of his unique Christmas ornaments, heirloom dolls, bed and bath linens, fabrics, laces, wallpaper, decorative accessories, and other home furnishings.

In 2000, Louis has once again created a line of Christmas and home decorative products exclusively for Kurt S. Adler, Inc. Headlining the collection is a stunningly intricate grouping of ornaments based on original designs created for the White House during President Carter's administration.

Also featured in this new line are dolls and doll accessories with coordinating fabric trim, and tabletop items that create a complete decorative home statement.

Nichole has made fantasy attainable with his fresh approach to Old World elegance which he combines with classic designs. His ability to bring together the best of both worlds, where the "past is present" and "once upon a time" remains tasteful, brought him to the attention of the White House, where he was commissioned as Decorative Arts Designer.

MEL ODOM

Mel Odom's story is not unlike that of his creation, *Gene*. Mel was raised in tiny Ahoskie, North Carolina, far from the complexity of life in New York City that he would ultimately embrace. Like *Gene*, Mel knew early in life what dream he wanted to fulfill.

Mel majored in fashion illustration at Virginia Commonwealth University, followed by graduate work at the Leeds Polytechnic Institute of Art and Design in England. Mel's work has been widely exhibited, most notably at the Cooper-Hewitt Museum, the Chrysler Museum, and the Santa Barbara Museum of Art. He is a multiple recipient of the "Award of Excellence" from the Society of Illustrators. Mel's distinctive, captivating artwork has appeared in the *New York Times Magazine,* in illustrated stories by Joyce Carol Oates and Tom Robbins, and on the covers of *Time* and *OMNI*.

Mel made his mark in collectibles with his creation of "Gene Marshall", a 15-1/2" vinyl fashion doll inspired by all the legendary screen goddesses of Hollywood's Golden Age, the '40s and '50s. She rivals the finest vintage fashion dolls, from the porcelain-like finish of her skin to the authentic period *couture* of her wardrobe, coiffures and accessories. *The Gene Marshall Collection* is produced by the Ashton-Drake Galleries.

CHARLES & VICTORIA OLDHAM

A serious collector would recognize the works of talented artists Charles and Vicky Oldham, but may not know who they are. Charles and Vicky are the "ghost" designers behind many of the most successful collectible figurines ever sold by some of the world's best-known collectible companies. For more than 20 years, their designs have appeared in porcelain, crystal and resin. Sculptures such as "The Great Horned Owl," "The American Bald Eagle," and the "Gyre Falcon" are the works of Charles Oldham and were presented to foreign Heads of State as Presidential gifts. One of the most successful collectibles ever released from The Franklin Mint was Vicky Oldham's "Moonlight and Platinum."

Now Charles and Vicky have devoted their considerable talents to creating wonderful new collections for United Treasures, including the *Guardian Angels* series and the all-new *Cats of Baseball.*

MICHAEL V. PASCUCCI

More than just a talented sculptor, Michael Pascucci's range of knowledge and experiences in figural production span the scope of figurine development. Sculpting, molding, casting and final production in porcelain, bronze, plastic and a multitude of other media have made Pascucci a valued member of the Gartlan USA team. He created original art for the company's popular *KISS* figurine collection.

With more than 20 years of related experience, Pascucci earned a master's degree in sculpture and foundry from Southern Illinois University – Carbondale, in 1983. His bachelor's in fine arts was earned at Pennsylvania State University in 1976. Since then,

Pascucci has been featured in national media campaigns, has managed world-renowned foundries, and built his own flourishing sculpting business.

For Gartlan USA, Michael created the 11-piece figurine collection from the *Yellow Submarine Series,* which includes figurines of four of the Beatles and animated characters from the movie.

When he is not crafting figural designs or building businesses, Pascucci, an Army veteran, spends his time actively involved in his children's interests, including coaching basketball and soccer teams, and volunteering with the Boy Scouts. He resides in Yardley, Pennsylvania, with his wife, Beth, and their three children.

HAL PAYNE

As a doll artist, Hal Payne has been described as a "true Renaissance man." Hal is not limited or confined to one range of subject matter or in his exceptional range of techniques. His works have been described as "masterpieces" and have gained acclaim and admiration whenever they are shown. Indeed, Hal Payne is a serious and dedicated artist, who happens to have chosen doll making as an exciting medium for his art.

In high school, Hal won honors in art and continued his studies at the University of Texas - El Paso. After four years in the Navy, he began working for a local department store, creating in-store and window displays. Later, Hal's love of art catapulted his efforts into the genre of dolls.

Hal Payne's collection of *Button Box Kids* for Dave Grossman Creations is based upon the fun and mischief that a group of young children display when they search through their grandmother's button box. Each figurine combines the uniqueness of a resin base with a fully-dressed doll attached.

SIOBHAN PENDERGAST

As the Manager of Product Development for *Lenox Classics,* Siobhan Pendergast is responsible for initiating and creating new items for the *Lenox Classics* line of collectible figurines, taking them from the concept stage through final production.

Siobhan believes that "the selection of the artist is critically important, as they must capture the elegance, sweetness and refinement that is expected from all new *Lenox Classics* products." To this end, Siobhan is responsible for reviewing the portfolios of numerous artists and sculptors to identify their style for upcoming projects.

"I have a great love of art, sculptures and antiques, and enjoy attending art auctions with family and friends," Siobhan relates. This love of art is evident in the work that she helps create for the *Lenox Classics* collection.

A current resident of Haverford, Pennsylvania, Siobhan studied drawing, painting, and sculpture at the Pennsylvania Academy of Fine Arts. An avid traveler, Siobhan likes to spend her free time touring other countries to learn about their history, art and culture.

GREGORY PERILLO

Though he was born in New York, Gregory Perillo was drawn to the American West at an early age. After a tour with the U.S. Navy, Perillo studied at New York's Pratt Institute, the Art Student's League and the School of Visual Arts. His interest in Native Americans had not diminished, and Perillo traveled extensively to learn the customs and lifestyles of the Sioux, Cheyenne, Apache and Blackfoot.

Now a major artist of the dominant Indian Nations, this American Master's oil paintings and bronzes adorn many major museums, corporate headquarters and galleries throughout the United States, including the Kennedy Gallery in New York City. His works hold a place of honor as part of the permanent collection housed by the Pettigrew Museum in Sioux Falls, South Dakota. Perillo holds the proud distinction to be the only Western artist exhibited in the prestigious Denver Museum of Natural History. Additionally, Perillo's collector plates can be found in thousands of private collections.

For Reco International, Perillo has recently created the *Majestic Spirits* plates series, depicting proud horses of the American Indian; and *Native American Views,* a series of unique relief plaques representing American Indian dwellings.

MARTIN PERRY

Martin Perry is the founder and artistic director of Harmony Kingdom, an award-winning collectible company specializing in Box Figurines. After pairing up nearly five years ago with Noel Wiggins and Lisa Yashon, Martin's modest cottage industry has steadily grown into the worldwide sensation that it is today.

In 1995, Martin, Noel and Lisa introduced their new collectible concept in the United States. At that time, no other company in the collectible industry had crafted a figurine that was actually a seamless box. Today, Martin's "Westerner's idea of a Japanese netsuke" has received numerous awards in both the United States and Europe, and Harmony Kingdom's collector's club, The Royal Watch, has thousands of avid members.

Recently, this shepherd-turned-artist introduced another innovation, *Picturesque* tile figurines. Each tile is a stand-alone object of art, but when viewed together as a complete picture of 20 tiles, an endlessly engaging story unfolds.

Martin lives in England's Cotswolds region with his wife and two children. Though his days as a shepherd are well behind him, he still enjoys a special relationship with nature, which is evident in all of Harmony Kingdom's creations.

CHRIS PETERSON

As a child, Chris Peterson enjoyed "years of watching Looney Tunes cartoons," now evident in the extraordinary collection of porcelain figurines he sculpted for Goebel's *Looney Tunes Spotlight Collection*.

Born in Manchester, Connecticut, Chris moved to southern California and earned his first job at a major animation studio at the tender age of 16. As an assistant animator and designer for projects ranging from "Fat Albert" and "He Man" to "BraveStar," he exhibited an enviable talent which landed him his first sculpting assignment at Filmation Studio at age 19.

After successfully designing and sculpting products for various toy and gift manufacturers, Chris began a free-lance operation in 1990. Since then, he has established a distinguished roster of sculpting and design credits, including those for his contributions to "Ferngully," "The Secret of N.I.M.H.," "Rover Dangerfield," as well as numerous Warner Bros. and Disney projects. He currently maintains a working residence in Ventura, California.

Each of Chris' sculpts is marked by his meticulous attention to detail and a unique style, which those in the know can identify as having "the Peterson look." Goebel and Warner Bros. are honored to have Chris Peterson as a sculptor of the *Looney Tunes Spotlight Collection*.

KRISTI JENSEN PIERRO

Kristi Jensen Pierro was born in Minneapolis, Minnesota. She always loved to draw and started her career designing porcelain decanters while still a student at Saint Cloud State University.

After graduation, Kristi worked for various companies and freelanced for Department 56® until 1987, when she was hired as a full-time illustrator/designer. One of her first projects was the development of the newly created *Snowbabies*™ series.

Kristi's ideas for *Snowbabies* are inspired by watching children and by thinking about her own childhood experiences. She begins with rough sketches of her ideas which she then refines into illustrations that are used by sculptors in creating the three-dimensional figurines.

Department 56 *Snowbabies* have bright blue eyes and creamy white snowsuits covered by hand-applied crystal flakes of new fallen snow. They play together and frolic with their animal friends, while brightening the imagination of all of us who celebrate the gentle play of youthful innocence.

Kristi uses her creative talents in the development of fine porcelain figurines, ornaments, water globes and music boxes for other Department 56 lines, including *Silhouette Treasures*™, and *Snowbunnies*®.

PIPKA

Born in Germany, folk artist Pipka came to America with her parents and brother after World War II, settling in North Dakota.

Pipka's interest in folk art began when her mother sent her a

package filled with art supplies, wooden boxes, and instruction books on Bauermalerei, Bavarian peasant painting. When she picked up the brush, she never put it down again.

Pipka designed her first "Father Christmas" image, a Russian Santa for her mother. Since that time, she has studied, researched and become enamored with the stories, myths, and traditions surrounding Father Christmas, or Santa Claus.

While painting her Santas, Pipka was also inspired to research and design Angels. Her Angels have become a part of her spiritual journey, and they reflect the warm, giving spirit that is found in Pipka.

Through her Santas and Angels, Pipka celebrates Christmas and life. She shares her passion for folk art by teaching her painting techniques and sharing the stories and traditions of Santa Claus with students and Christmas enthusiasts around the world.

GALE PITT

Combining her personal interests in travel, gourmet food and felines has enabled Gale Pitt to parlay her gift for art into a successful career. The London resident has traveled around the world, including the U.S., Russia, Egypt, Tunisia and Pakistan, to obtain inspiration for her unique artistic creations.

Her mastery of varied artforms such as pastel, oil and watercolor, have earned her commissions to paint directory book covers for British Telecom and to illustrate four children's books.

Three years ago, Pitt partnered with Islandia International, which added her adorable *International Fat Cat* art to its exclusive fine art collections. The series features cats dressed in the native costume of various countries around the world. Each cat is surrounded by the famous sights and gourmet food delicacies best known from each respective country.

An honors graduate in English language and literature from the University of London, Pitt has had solo exhibitions of her paintings in Oxford, Stamford, Birmingham and Ilford, England.

WARREN PLATT

Warren Platt joined the John Beswick modelling team in 1985 on a Youth Training Program. In 1986, he became a full-time modeller and continued his art education by attending Stafford Art College. All modellers at Beswick must be adaptable and versatile, and Warren has demonstrated this through his excellent work.

His works are featured in the *Beatrix Potter, Snowman* and *Bunnykins* collections, including "Ice Cream and Brownie" *Bunnykins*. He also designed "Bulldog" and "Jack Russell," horse models for the *Spirit Horse* collection, and the small size "Desert Orchid" and "Mr. Frisk." Warren feels that horses are his favorite subject to model and enjoys visiting them and getting to

know their character. He likes the challenge of developing an idea into a three dimensional model.

Warren's leisure activities include cycling and sketching.

KIM PLAUCHÉ

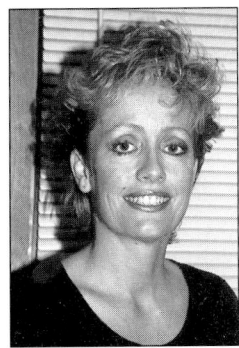

Sometimes one identifies so completely with an occupation that it's difficult to separate who they are from what they do! That's the case with Fenton Art Glass decorating designer Kim Plauché.

Kim sees herself as an artist and a Pisces, and she is particularly interested in scenes which include water. Her design concepts have contributed to the Fenton *Connoisseur Collection,* and she designed the floral motif which graces Fenton's Violet Satin glass, a 1999 *Historic Collection* color.

Kim is also drawn to people. She began working at Fenton Art Glass in 1979 and moved up through many different departments, getting to know the nature of handmade glass and her fellow employees. "Most of my art education has been on-the-job experience at Fenton," she says. "I believe in staying busy with my job, and I enjoy spending time with my family." Kim collects Elvis, Marilyn Monroe and Princess Diana memorabilia.

GUY POCOCK

Guy Pocock was born and raised in the India of the British Raj. Returning to England, he obtained Honors in Literature at Exeter University, and studied painting and sculpture at Sir John Cass College of Art and Design at White Chapel, London.

Two decades ago, working in his studio in Cornwall, England, Guy Pocock conceived the beginnings of North Light figurines. His concept was to combine the artistic flair of the 19th century French *animalia* bronzes with the realism collectors value so highly today.

In the late 1970s, during a meeting with a member of the British Kennel Club, Pocock learned that there were no models available of dogs true to Kennel Club breed standards. This led him to create the first models of dogs true to pedigree.

In following years, he painstakingly built up the comprehensive collection of over 150 models of dogs that North Light is proud to show today. In the late 1980s, he began the present collection of 35 horse models, which complete North Lights' current offerings.

CHANTAL POULIN

Chantal Poulin's art career began to take shape in early childhood. At the age of five, she drew praise for her kindergarten drawings, and has been painting ever since. Poulin studied fine arts in Montreal, where she graduated from the College of Old Montreal and the Mission Renaissance School of Fine Arts.

Although she is best known today for the freshness and spontaneity she brings to her paintings that feature children, it was actually her landscapes that launched Poulin's career in a successful 1978 solo exhibition.

Today, Chantal Poulin creates her highly-sought works of art

in a century-old house turned studio, built near a waterfall in the Canadian village of Ste. Beatrix. Certainly, her beautiful surroundings influence the look and feel of her uniquely romantic and sensitive works.

Chantal Poulin has had several successful series for The Bradford Exchange, beginning with the memorable *Kindred Memories* collection. She was named "Collector's Choice New Artist of the Year" in 1996 by The Bradford Exchange.

BRENDA POWER

Brenda Power has had a life-long involvement in art. She started making full-size dolls and soft toys over 20 years ago which she sold at local craft shows. She then began to paint scenes on Christmas ornaments made of eggshells and did portrait paintings of children. However, when she discovered the joys of designing miniature bears, she states, "I came full circle."

Drawing on her considerable talents as an artist and her previous experience with soft toys, Brenda has been able to design and create tiny realistic, three-dimensional animals using mohair. In 1997, she was invited to design some pieces for Deb Canham Artist Designs, Inc. The *Brenda Power Collection* features a push-a-long penguin, a raccoon, a standing rabbit and a rabbit on wheels. More designs are planned including a duck, goose and two realistic cats.

HEIDE PRESSE

Born in Heidelberg, Germany, and raised in Monroe Louisiana, Heide Presse graduated from Stephen F. Austin University in Texas with a bachelor of fine arts degree.

She worked in commercial art for six years, but when her husband was transferred to Michigan, she saw an opportunity to try something else. That "something else" included restoring old houses, making stained glass windows and hand-painting furniture.

"I'm attracted to images with nostalgic objects reflecting a different era...whether it's sun-splashed porches, window boxes, hand-made quilts, antique bowls or sparkling crystal...I paint to preserve the feeling these subjects evoke in me," she says.

After starting a family, she returned to painting with a renewed conviction. Since then, she has been awarded signature membership in the National Watercolor Society, Watercolor U.S.A. and the Adirondacks Exhibition of American Watercolors, among others. She has also been an award winner at the Arts for the Parks national competition.

In her work for The Greenwich Workshop, using shadows, light and her superlative sense of design, Presse transforms the most simple objects into magnificent images capturing fleeting moments of drama and emotion.

CHRISTOPHER RADKO

Since 1986, Christopher Radko has devoted himself to restoring magic, heart and fine craftsmanship to holiday celebrations – and it all began with a family calamity. His family's Christmases centered around a 14-foot tree filled with glass ornaments collected by three generations. In 1984, the tree crashed to the floor one week before the holiday, shattering almost every ornament. Determined to restore them, Christopher found a glassblower in Europe eager to revive an art dormant since the turn-of-the-century.

Each of Christopher's glass ornaments is made entirely by hand, using techniques dating back to the 1800s – a process that requires seven days to produce a single ornament! The ornaments are blown by European craftsmen in tempered glass for durability, lined with sterling silver for luminescence, and painted with loving care in very intricate detail.

Christopher has created more than 5,000 designs since his first collection in 1986. His collection now includes the *Studio* line, depicting beloved characters from the entertainment world, as well as *Woodland Winds*, a world of figurines, snowglobes and ornaments in glass and cold cast porcelain.

RAINE

Raine always knew she was meant to be an artist, and from an early age, she was completely focused on pursuing her passion for art. Her talent was recognized when she was awarded a full scholarship to attend the University of the Arts in Philadelphia, where she received classical training in illustration. Yet, feeling the constraints of working in only two dimensions, she turned to sculpture where she ultimately found her life's work.

Today, Raine is a skillful and versatile artist who can move from large bronze sculptures to collectible miniatures without sacrificing artistic excellence.

Her latest works represent life in miniature (tiny shoes that bear a subtle crease suggesting a human presence). All of her work seems to be bursting with a story, whether mythical, humorous, historical or other-worldly.

Teaming up with Willitts Designs, Raine's whimsy, historical insight, and sculpturally realistic style are combined in the creation of *Just the Right Shoe*, a series of miniature collectibles that honor and memorialize the great creations in women's fashion accessories throughout history.

VAUGHN & STEPHANIE RAWSON

Together Vaughn and Stephanie Rawson have become one of the most successful design teams around. However, they didn't start out that way...it took the building of their dream house to realize the talents that would one day earn Vaughn the nickname "Whimsical Whittler."

Vaughn and Stephanie wanted their new home to be furnished in their very personal American taste. So, instead of buying furniture, Vaughn began to make it himself. In doing so, the couple

found that Vaughn was indeed a gifted wood carver.

Eventually he carved his first Santa, and continued to carve others, while Stephanie designed and painted them. Soon, they began to sell their creations, and before long, what had once been a hobby became a career.

Fascinated by old books and postcards found while doing research, Vaughn and Stephanie designed the popular *Christmas Messengers*, their first series for House of Hatten, Inc. Other designs include *A Christmas Alphabet* and their new *Nursery Rhyming* series.

MARTHA REYNOLDS

The word "vibrant" is the perfect term to describe both Martha Reynolds and her work. A decoration designer at Fenton Art Glass since 1990, Martha is always experimenting with new materials and styles. Her designs range from the simple and contemporary, to the ornate and richly-embellished look of Victorian glass.

Many of Martha's decoration designs have appeared in the Fenton *Connoisseur Collection,* and she created the Floral Interlude motif for Fenton's *Sea Green* Satin glass in 1998.

Martha has often been honored with design awards since graduating cum laude from Shepherd College. In 1993, the Society of Glass and Ceramic Decorators presented her with their prestigious "Vandenoever Award," and she has recently been recognized by *Collector Editions* magazine.

On weekends, Martha and her husband, Gary, search for old jewelry, antiques and figurines to add to their growing collection. Their daughter, Johanna, is also a decorator at Fenton.

MARY RHYNER-NADIG

Whether a heartwarming reindeer, whimsical cow or chocolate bunny, Enesco's Senior Stylist Mary Rhyner-Nadig brings to life colorful animal figurines through her creative artwork.

Nadig made her mark in the giftware and collectibles industry with *Mary's Moo Moos,* a whimsical collection of cows with "punny" titles. Now entering its sixth year, the collection is ranked as the leading collectible in the cow-theme category, according to *Giftbeat,* an industry research organization. Some of Nadig's other popular collections include *This Little Piggy*™ and *Santa's Deerlivery,* which join her other endearing animal lines.

Since joining Enesco in 1990, Nadig has received many awards including "Division Designer of the Year" and "Enesco Associate of the Month." She was also recognized by Stanhome, previously Enesco's parent company, when she received the Stanhome Achievement Award.

Nadig received her degree from the American Academy of Art, located in Chicago, and resides in the area with her family.

SHANE RIDGE

Shane Ridge entered the pottery industry in 1978 as a moldmaker. Four years later, he began a new career as a tableware and low-relief modeller. In 1987, Shane joined Royal Doulton as their tableware modeller.

Since then, he has worked on various projects, ranging from standard tableware items to more elaborate semi-sculptural pieces. He modelled the "Monkey/ Cockerel Teapot" and "Flat Iron Teapot" for *The Minton Archive Teapot Collection*.

In 1994, Shane was invited to spend six months in the John Beswick Studio, where he was able to develop his skills on wholly sculptural projects including *Bunnykins* and a large size horse, "The Lipizzaner." Having shown great potential as a sculptural modeller, Shane was offered a permanent position in the John Beswick Studio, and to date, Shane's modelling projects have covered the entire Beswick product range.

In his spare time, Shane likes spending time with his family. He also enjoys playing football and video games.

XAVIER ROBERTS

Xavier Roberts drew upon Georgia Mountain folklore, the art of needle molding, and his own creativity to build the foundation for the internationally famous *Cabbage Patch Kids*®.

After dressing his soft-sculpture creations in clothes found at yard sales, the college art student put the "babies" up for adoption. By 1977, the "Little People®," now called *Cabbage Patch Kids*, gained recognition as award-winning works of art.

In 1978, the artist formed Original Appalachian Artworks Inc., and transformed a country doctor's clinic in Cleveland, Georgia, into BabyLand General® Hospital, staffed with "doctors" and "nurses" to deliver the 'Kids. The tradition, which started more than 21 years ago, continues with the highly collectible, soft-sculpture 'Kids™ still hand-stitched to birth.

Based on his belief that no dream is ever too big, Xavier continues to throw himself into his creations with an enthusiasm that matches the excitement of those who enjoy them.

ANITA MARRA ROGERS

When Hallmark rejected Anita Marra Rogers' portfolio of two-dimensional art, she didn't take no for an answer. She met another artist who encouraged her to try three-dimensional work, and that began her career in sculpting. After freelancing for two years, Anita joined the *Keepsake Ornament* studio full time in 1987. She may be best known for her *Puppy Love* series, as well as for ornaments based on the Beatles, STAR TREK® characters and other licensed figures.

Anita's favorite ornament is "Holiday Teatime," which she designed to honor a teatime tradition she shared with her best friend. When Anita gave the ornament to her friend, the tears and hugs made it all the more meaningful.

Anita says every meeting with collectors is special. "They're all great people," she adds.

MARTHA ROOT

Martha Root has affectionately been called Miss Martha since the name was first bestowed upon her by her Sunday school class many years ago. To friends and collectors alike, the name seems to fit perfectly, as it reflects her gentle nature and warm, ready smile.

Her own childhood is sculpted into each piece of art she creates. She draws upon the multitude of memories that rest gently in her heart, memories that are part and parcel of the summers spent on her grandmother's farm. It was there that childhood came alive in the cotton fields, the watermelon patch and the ol' swimming hole.

Martha's deep personal faith and precious childhood memories give birth to her sculptures, whose expressions and situations reflect the tenderness, innocence and love of childhood. The name of the line, *All God's Children*, fittingly carries the message of her life and her work.

Each piece sculpted by Martha is handcrafted in the USA at the Miss Martha Originals factory located in Gadsden, Alabama.

BRONWEN ROSS

Bronwen Ross is an internationally known wildlife artist with a talent for capturing the whimsy of yesteryear. Since early childhood, this beloved Southern belle has been creating a delicate world of make-believe – a garden grandeur populated by lavishly attired animals among arabesque shrubs and flowers. Her eye for intricate detailing and compositional color is uncanny! Many of her pieces have been produced in a number of mediums, including greeting and note cards, stationery and limited edition prints.

Her knack for lighthearted themes was what first attracted Bronwen to Possible Dreams. Year after year, she adds characters to *The Thickets at Sweetbriar* collection that are entertaining, charming and a delight to loyal collectors. That illusion of nature, so intrinsic in all Bronwen's work, transcends the passage of time and makes us believe, for a little while, that all our childhoods are as perpetual as hers.

JON SAFFELL

Many figurines produced by the Fenton Art Glass Company are the result of Jon Saffell's expertise in designing objects to be made in glass. Several Fenton limited edition Christmas items, such as the Nativity Set and the popular Santa figurines, are the most recent testaments to Jon's talent. He has also designed a wide variety of giftware and lighting ware items.

Glass demands a knowledge of the working characteristics of a unique molten material, as well as the mechanics of glass molds.

Working in clay or plaster, Jon sculpts beautiful shapes which both take advantage of the properties of colored glass and anticipate production challenges.

Jon particularly enjoys children, and Fenton's new "Praying Children" figurines were modelled after his grandchildren, Ashley and Dax. A designer at Fenton since 1994, Jon has been involved with glass design since 1957, when he was first employed at the Fostoria Glass Company.

G.G. SANTIAGO

G.G. Santiago has a natural and instinctive talent when it comes to creating art. She had just graduated from high school when she joined American Greetings, quickly becoming one of their top illustrators. From there, she continued her self-guided art education, working in Hallmark's creative licensing department where she is credited with developing several new character lines.

G.G. spent the next few years at Enesco, as creative director and designer. As the expression and detail in her art continued to grow, she soon began doing her own sculpting to interpret her drawings into three-dimensional art. During the next nine years, she was the recipient of several prestigious creative awards.

In 1997, United Design™ commissioned G.G. to design and sculpt an angel series to add to its *Angels Collection*. The result was a succession of four limited edition angels, each with a seasonal theme. Since then, G.G. has created two other angel lines for United Design, *Studies in Grace*™ and *Cupid, the Gift of Love*™.

MARJORIE SARNAT

For the past ten years, Marjorie Sarnat's designs for The San Francisco Music Box Company have captured consumers' hearts. Her *Folk Art Figurines, Nine Lives Cat Collection,* mythological *Crystal Visions*™ and *Rainbow Visions*® lines, *Sweet Inspirations*™ and *Angel Teddy Bears* are perennial favorites.

Sarnat attended the Chicago Art Institute and the Boston Museum of Fine Arts, earning a bachelor's degree in fine arts. She now lives with her husband and young son in Granada Hills, California, where her home studio is located.

Sarnat's greatest satisfaction comes from "seeing her art come to life." Inspired by her desire to communicate emotions through her work, her designs frequently take their cues from art history or pop culture. "In my work, I like to create the comfort of tradition with the surprise of originality," says the artist.

Sarnat believes that each item she creates must have special meaning. "I view each piece that I design as a tribute to the human spirit. My hope is that people will look at that piece and be reminded that someone loves and believes in them."

REVA SCHICK

Award-winning artist Reva Schick discovered her God-given talent for sculpture when she created several full-size Halloween monsters to delight her children. Later, when she created an infant mannequin for a retail shop, doll collectors started clamoring for her custom-made, one-of-a-kind baby dolls.

Soon, her *Butterfly Babies* caught the attention of Lee Middleton Original Dolls who recognized the lifelike quality of her dolls. Of her self-taught approach to dollmaking, Schick says, "Once I start sculpting...whatever expression comes out, comes out. It's like having a real baby — you don't know what it is, who it is, or what it looks like until it's done!"

Reva Schick has sculpted several new faces for the line, including some being used for the first time in the *My Own Baby* collection. Once again, her designs have taken the doll market by storm, receiving several awards and two nominations at the New York International Toy Fair. "Growing Up" won a "Doll of the Year" (DOTY) Award, "Public Choice" DOTY award and the *Dolls* "Award of Excellence." "Cuddle Me" (Girl) from the *My Own Baby* series also won a "Public Choice" DOTY award.

JEFF SCHUKNECHT & BOBBE PUNZEL-SCHUKNECHT

From their Princeton, Wisconsin farmstead, Jeff Schuknecht and Bobbe Punzel-Schuknecht create the art that reflects the rural life they live. Bobbe creates the designs and finishing work, while Jeff translates her designs into three-dimensional reality.

Twenty-three years ago, Jeff and Bobbe met at the University of Wisconsin, married and formed an artistic partnership. They had been creating original designs for their own art and antique store until the early 1990s, when they received national exposure from a feature article in *Folk Art Magazine*. The increased demand for their work allowed Jeff and Bobbe to concentrate all their efforts on creating new designs.

In 1996, these talented artists joined Coyne's & Company to introduce *Williraye Studio*. The creations are unique designs which encompass a blend of American and French folk art. The formation of their designs is attributed to their shared vision. They draw on their day-to-day experiences for their whimsical themes, with family, friends and the farm serving as both inspiration and motivation. This shared vision has given them the ability to think as one...from conceptualization to the finished design.

PAT SEBERN

Pat Sebern began her art career in fashion illustration and moved into the fine arts field in the early 1970s, painting in oils and pastels. Living in Colorado, she found her greatest interest was Western art. She was frequently invited to exhibit her work, which garnered many awards.

In 1988, Pat moved to Seattle and began her career in the giftware industry, designing collectibles. Two of her collections, a waterfront style porcelain village and a resin figurine collection of

rabbits, came to have quite an extensive collector following.

Pat relocated to Dallas in 1995 to work for Fitz and Floyd, briefly designing tabletop products. In 1997, she became Director of Concept Development for Fitz and Floyd Collectibles, working on a new group of collectibles that evolved into *Honeybourne Hollow,* named for her grandmother's farm in England.

This delightful collection consists of hand-painted resin figurines and musicals. Included in the line is the limited edition piece, "Follow Your Dreams," which comes with a 26-page illustrated storybook of *Honeybourne Hollow.* Charming graphics and heartwarming, humorous family situations characterize the collection's packaging and presentation. A special limited edition piece, "Time Is Precious," celebrates the new millennium.

ELIO SIMONETTI

Creating the life-sized *Fontanini® Heirloom Nativities* by Roman, Inc. is the crowning achievement of Elio Simonetti's distinguished artistic career. Receiving the Fontanini family gift of a 50" nativity, Pope John Paul II expressed his admiration of Simonetti's work with the statement, "I hope God grants him a long life to continue his fantastic sculpting." The Pontiff's prayer has been answered, and Simonetti's talent spans more than five decades of sculpting with the House of Fontanini.

Born in Lucca in 1924, Simonetti studied at the Liceo of Arts in Lucca before leaving school to help support his large family. From the very beginning, Simonetti was lauded for his magical ability to infuse sculptures with lifelike qualities. This mastery has led to a collection of hundreds of *Fontanini Nativity* pieces in seven different sizes — from 2-1/2" miniatures to near life-size scenes.

GERHARD SKROBEK

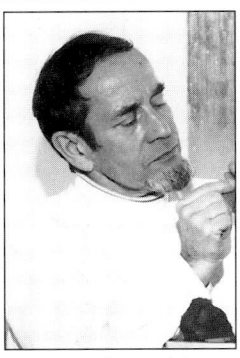

Gerhard Skrobek, a master sculptor of the Goebel company, was born in Silesia, the northernmost part of Germany. He subsequently moved with his family to Berlin. There, surrounded by museum art treasures and encouraged by his artist mother, young Skrobek became immersed in the heady climate of artistic tradition. From early childhood, he was fascinated with sculpture and its many artistic forms. He studied at the Reimannschule in Berlin, a renowned private academy of the arts. Later, he continued his studies in Coburg. Through one of his professors, he was introduced to porcelain sculpture at the world renowned W. Goebel Porzellanfabrik.

Skrobek joined Goebel in 1951, and soon became one of its leading sculptors. Eventually he emerged as the predominant interpreter of Sister Maria Innocentia Hummel's drawings into three-dimensional form.

According to his interpretation, Skrobek is able to capture the life and vitality of the two-dimensional art through the use of a textured surface in the sculpting process. Gerhard Skrobek is articulate and personable, and a delight to meet and to talk with about *M.I. Hummel* figurines.

SUSAN M. SMITH

In a small, cozy workshop in Alaska, Susan M. Smith toils away like one of Santa's elves, carving her next creation.

When she first began to carve, she concentrated on depicting real life with all its details and intricacies. She soon realized she was only expressing what she saw, instead of what she felt.

Susan relaxed her style and began to have more fun with her designs. Changing her style resulted in designs that were whimsical and fun. "I'm always making something," Susan says, "Sometimes serious, sometimes silly." Inspired by the natural wildlife that surrounds her home, Susan often features Santa with some of the same animals she watches from her home.

She was elated when House of Hatten began to reproduce her designs in 1995 and introduced her *Santa's Kingdom* collection. As *Santa's Kingdom* has gained momentum, Susan and the House of Hatten have continued to expand the collection each year. She is rewarded by the smiles her designs bring, and is even more delighted when they evoke genuine laughter as they often do.

RANDAL SPANGLER

Fantastically delightful describes the fantasy art that Randal Spangler creates. The seeds of his wonderfully fertile imagination were planted early at his grandparent's farm. There, in the wooded hills of Missouri, he would while away the days engaged in pretend games with gentle dragons, mischievous elves, flying fish, caroling kitties – anything that suited his fancy. Says Randal, "My fantasy world is based on my childhood memories of playing at the farm and the hours I sat entranced listening to the marvelous stories my grandfather would spin. And every story grandpa would tell was done with a twinkle and a smile."

At the Art Institute of Kansas City, Randal learned to translate his loving memories into works of art using ink, watercolor, colored pencil and gouache. Today, his work is shown nationwide at over 40 major art festivals and over 50 science fiction conventions a year. Randal's work has earned him numerous awards and a loyal following. For Possible Dreams, Randal has created *Spangler's Realm,* a collection of delightful "Draglings."

ROBIN SPINDLER

When you find a Fenton Art Glass collectible signed "J.K. Spindler" (Judith Kay), then you've found Robin!

Born and reared in Morgantown, West Virginia, Robin loves the outdoors, and animals are among her favorite subjects. "I like to capture the spirit in their eyes," she says. Some of Robin's most recent work has won awards from *Collector Editions* magazine and

from the prestigious Society of Glass and Ceramic Decorators.

Employed at Fenton Art Glass since 1979, Robin became a Fenton designer in 1994. She has created decoration designs for many of the pieces in Fenton's elite *Connoisseur Collection*.

While visiting the Fenton Gift Shop years ago, Spindler and her mother admired the hand-painted glass. "You can paint like that," exclaimed Robin's mother. That thought stayed with Robin as she developed the personal style which is reflected in her work.

GABRIELE STAMEY

Born in the small Tyrolean town of Worgl, Gabriele Stamey began her professional career designing hand-blown stemware after studying at the world-famous technical school of glass-making and design in Kramsach, Tyrol.

In 1986, Gabriele accepted a full-time design position with Swarovski Silver Crystal. Her professional skills and lively imagination were immediately evident in her first designs comprising a whimsical "Miniature-Rooster," a "Miniature-Hen" and three "Miniature-Chicks" in fine cut crystal.

She created the first designs in the theme group, "When We Were Young," which brings back childhood memories. Her designs in this series include a cut crystal train complete with "Locomotive," "Tender" and three "Wagons," as well as the "Rocking Horse" and "Puppet."

Gabriele is the designer of the Swarovski Collectors Society 1997 Annual Edition, "Fabulous Creatures" - The Dragon. This was her first design for the Collectors Society.

MICHAEL STAMEY

Michael Stamey was born in Munich, West Germany, in 1951. He developed his handcrafting skills through a thorough four-year education at the world- famous technical school of glass craft and design at Kramsach in the Austrian Tyrol.

In 1977, Michael started work for Swarovski Silver Crystal. Among his designs are such popular items as "The Rose," "Cheetah," "Baby Giraffe," "Tiger," and "Miniature Alligator." Many years of snorkeling gave him the inspiration for his designs in the *South Seas* series, including the "Dolphin," "Maxi Dolphin," "Miniature-Crab," "Shell with Pearl" and "Maritime Trio."

Stamey also created the Swarovski Collectors Society Annual Editions, "Lead Me" - The Dolphins, "Save Me" - The Seals, and "Care For Me" - The Whales for the *Mother and Child* trilogy, and the "Kudu" in the *Inspiration Africa* trilogy.

The most important influence in his artistic work is nature. "If you just look at something beautiful or complex long enough, parallels to nature become obvious," says Stamey. Through the brilliant crystal objects he creates for Swarovski, this philosophy becomes clearly visible.

BOB STEBLETON

At a remote studio in Woolwich, Maine, folk artist Bob Stebleton brings figments of his colorful imagination to life. Drawing from his earliest commercial art training at Ferris State University in Big Rapids, Michigan, and at painting seminars in Maine, Bob never fails to amaze and entertain viewers of all ages.

His unique designs have appeared at one-man exhibits and group art shows across the country. His art has been displayed at the Museum of American Folk Art in New York City, and his creations have adorned the Christmas tree in the Blue Room of the White House.

In 1997, Bob joined Possible Dreams' family of remarkable artists. His inventive artistry affects everything around him, especially his unique perspective on old St. Nick. Bob's visions have materialized into the *Stebleton Folk Art* and *Cagey Critters* collections of thoroughly original designs, executed with an architect's grasp of form and space. If any holiday images point in style and grace to the new millennium, it is Bob Stebleton's poignant sculptures.

KEITH STEFAN

Keith Stefan is a multi-talented designer who combines original concepts and design skills to create unique, quality Christmas products exclusively for Kurt S. Adler, Inc.

His artistic prowess began to develop while he was still a small child. At seven, he won his first scholarship to attend Saturday morning art classes. Later, his work earned him a scholarship at the Columbus College of Art and Design, and he continued his education at the Kansas City Art Institute and at The London Polytech Institute.

In 1988, after establishing himself at Hallmark Cards, Inc., he joined the staff at Kurt S. Adler, Inc. as a product designer, and has remained one of the key members of the KSA design team. His work for the *Polonaise*® collection includes the "Coca-Cola® Snowman," "Couch Cat," "North Star Santa," "Santa with Bells" and "Six Geese-A-Laying" from the *Twelve Days of Christmas* series.

"The most significant influence in my life was growing up in an artistic family," Keith says. "My father is a professional musician currently playing piano for the American Orient Express. My mother is a successful fine art painter in landscapes. We always had a variety of musical instruments, artist supplies, and a library I am still exploring."

HERR CHRISTIAN STEINBACH & KARLA STEINBACH

Herr Christian Steinbach and Karla Steinbach are the current President and Vice President of the Steinbach factory in Germany, the leading producer of collectible nutcrackers and smoking figures in the world. Together they oversee product development and manufacturing of limited edition nutcrackers and smoking figures for Kurt S. Adler, Inc.

Founded in 1832, the Steinbach company continues to manufacture nutcrackers, smoking figures, ornaments and music boxes in

the age-old tradition. Kurt S. Adler, Inc. introduced the first limited edition design from the Steinbach factory in 1991. Each year, new designs appear in such sought-after groups as the *Biblical Series, Christmas Legends, A Christmas Carol, Tales of Sherwood Forest* and *Camelot Series.* Not just limited to larger nutcrackers ranging from 16" to 19" tall, Kurt S. Adler also offers 6" and 7" mini nutcrackers.

The popular Steinbach Collector's Club, which began in 1996, is growing by leaps and bounds.

ADI STOCKER

Born in St. Johann in Tyrol, Austria, Adi Stocker studied at the world-famous technical school for glass craft and design in Kramsach, Tyrol. After graduating in 1977, he worked in a glass studio in New Hampshire for four years. Then he traveled around the world for a year, visiting Japan, China, Thailand, Nepal and India. Upon his return, he began working for Swarovski.

From his home in St. Ulrich, Stocker creates his newest figures, but maintains contact with his colleagues in Wattens, Austria.

His Swarovski Silver Crystal designs include the limited editions "Eagle" and "Peacock." His Collectors Society designs include "The Woodpeckers," "The Turtledoves," "The Lion," "The Pegasus" and "Pierrot." Designer objects, such as jewelry boxes and pen holders designed for Swarovski Selection, testify to Adi's highly diversified talent.

NADEZHDA STRELKINA

The creation of her first limited edition plate collection for The Bradford Exchange, *A Symphony of Angels,* has helped fulfill a life-long dream for Nadezhda Strelkina. A native of the village of Fedoskino, Russia's oldest center of lacquer painting, Nadezhda has been commissioned time and again to create original designs for world renowned Russian Lacquer Boxes. A direct descendent of the founder of the famed Burbyshev's Lacquer Box Workshop, Nadezhda is also one of the most gifted graduates of Fedoskino's Lacquer Art College. Nadezhda's original works often take months to complete and are much in demand throughout Europe and the world.

But it is only now, with her work in limited edition collectibles, that Nadezhda feels she can truly communicate her true artist's spirit to a broader audience of art lovers. Nadezhda Strelkina's wondrous collection of angel musician collector plates earned her the 1997 "Collector's Choice New Artist of the Year" award from The Bradford Exchange. This collection was a dream come true for Nadezhda, as well as for collectors.

TOM SUZUKI

By nature a shy but charming fellow, Tom Suzuki prefers his home and family to the limelight of fame. But every year, this award-winning artist keeps collectors enraptured with his latest creations.

His extraordinary "Cinderella's Castle" for the *Disney Showcase Collection* recently won the prestigious *Collector Editions* "Award of Excellence," as did his "Curious Cat" of some years back. Tom's whimsical "Glamour Puss" also received an award nomination for 1998.

Possessing an amazing range of talent, Tom is able to design incredibly detailed miniatures such as the 3 inch-high "Carousel Horse," the delightful tap-dancing Teddy Bear known as "Broadway Ted," and impressive architectural masterpieces like the "Eiffel Tower." Some of Tom's newest pieces for Crystal World include "Rocking Horse" and the *Disney Showcase Collection's* new "Steamboat Willie."

TREVOR SWANSON

Trevor Swanson grew up surrounded by art. Members of his immediate family, including his father, world-renowned wildlife artist Gary R. Swanson, have made art their livelihood. Like other family members, Swanson draws inspiration for his paintings by studying and photographing wildlife in their natural environment. With patience and appreciation for his subjects, he painstakingly paints the scenes of wildlife with accuracy and skill, giving each a vitality and realism that have placed his works of art in great demand.

Swanson's paintings have captured the interest of thousands of wildlife art enthusiasts, and now can be found in plate and figurine form from Islandia International. Each plate and figurine is an exact full-color reproduction of Swanson's original artwork, including the popular renderings from his *African Wildlife* and *Great Bears of the World* collections.

The artist's mastery has not only won over wildlife art fans, but also recognition from prestigious organizations such as the Foundation for North American Wild Sheep, which honored Swanson with its "Artist of the Year" award. He was also voted "Best Plate Artist" by collectors at the 1999 International Collectible Exposition®.

ROBERT TABBENOR

Robert Tabbenor joined the Royal Doulton sculpture studio in 1973. Although he had always enjoyed drawing and painting, he had no experience in clay modelling before joining Royal Doulton. He quickly realized what a rewarding challenge it was to be able to form a lump of clay into any shape he desired.

Robert's first few production models were character figures. Now his work is represented in most of Royal Doulton's lines, including the *Pretty Ladies, Vanity Fair, Images* and *Reflections* series, as well as International Collector Club commissions, Character Jugs and Royal Crown Derby paperweights.

Recently, he has modelled limited edition pieces including "Robert E. Lee," "General Ulysses S. Grant" and "Field Marshall Montgomery."

He combines his sculptural duties at Royal Doulton with that of Studio Head. Acting in this capacity as the liaison for the company's production staff helps alleviate any problems that may arise during the manufacturing process.

SUE TAGUE

"It's rewarding to create products that help people celebrate important relationships and events," says Sue Tague about her Hallmark career, which began in 1964. She has designed greeting cards, stuffed animals, figurines and other products.

While her children were growing up, she worked for Hallmark from home. For seven years, she was among the artists who drew the "Charmers by Hallmark" cartoon that was syndicated in newspapers, and she has created many delightful *Merry Miniatures*® figurines.

Although Sue did not join the *Keepsake Ornament* studio full time until 1994, she designed the artwork that appeared on one of the first Hallmark ball ornaments. The artwork captured tiny Christmas elves as they sledded and skated in a whimsical winter wonderland.

Sue also created the *Thimble* and *Bell Ringer* series, but is most proud of "Pansy" in the *Language of Flowers* series.

GAY TALBOTT-BOASSY

An antique collector and mother of eight children, Gay Talbott-Boassy loves to paint while "listening" to old movies late at night. However, with her demanding duties as a mom, most of her work is done during the day, when the children aren't home.

In the late 1980s, Gay's work was discovered by Arts Uniq', for whom she has created a wide variety of pieces inspired by music, romance, elegant jewels, Victorian postcards, garden and floral themes, children, and pets and teddy bears.

Her favorite subject matter is anything old, and her detailed pieces have the power to propel collectors back through time to a simpler way of life. They are enchanted by the sharp detail, delicate colorations, grace and gentility of Gay's work. Many pieces feature their own touching verses, as well.

Alongside her love for art is a passion for travel. She has a long list of places she wishes to visit, but most days you'll find her happily juggling the needs of her family with her artistic pursuits in painting, dollmaking and writing.

ROBERT TANENBAUM

During his extensive art career, Robert Tanenbaum has worked on more than 200 movie posters and crafted the book cover for James Michener's *Centennial*. He was also commissioned to paint portraits of famous celebrities and business figures. His full-length rendering of the reclusive Howard Hughes at the age of 33 earned him wide acclaim. Word of the artist's abilities spread quickly, and he was soon commissioned for several Hollywood and corporate portrait designs.

Tanenbaum is now teaming up with Islandia International on a line of love and marriage-inspired plates, titled *To Have and to Hold*. Among the images are "The Engagement," "The Bridal Shower," and "The First Dance." One of the artist's most striking portraits of the late Mother Teresa has been reproduced on a special edition plate by the company.

A self-taught artist, Tanenbaum has received numerous awards for his work. In the 1980s, he was one of only 22 artists to receive certification from the American Portrait Society. He has also been inducted into the prestigious National Watercolor Society.

FABRIZIO TANI

Fabrizio Tani was born in 1965 in Vico d'Elsa, a charming small town near Florence, Italy. He was trained in painting at the Institute of Arts in Siena and attended the Academy of Fine Arts in Florence for four years, graduating in 1987 with a painting degree.

Fabrizio is a fervent follower of the Renaissance style. He trained as a sculptor under Giuseppe Armani's tutelage and, like Armani, is attracted to sculpting figurines "in motion" because it allows him to express fluidity of form and dimension.

Fabrizio joined the Florence Sculture d'Arte team in 1989. Since then he has become a key member of the sculpting team, representing Giuseppe Armani/Florence Sculture d'Arte at sculpting events throughout the world.

Fabrizio was the featured sculptor at an event in London sponsored by Harrods Department Store. At that event, he demonstrated his talents by sculpting an original work of art in the "Armani style." As can be expected of a member of the Florence Art Studio, Fabrizio's talents were lauded by all who attended the event.

MICHAEL J. TAYLOR

Influenced by an artistic correspondence course during his collegiate days, Gartlan USA artist Michael J. Taylor has spent more than a dozen years doing commercial and advertising illustrations.

In his spare time, Taylor created drawings and paintings for local art shows in his native state of Michigan. With a passion for sports, his moonlighting efforts featured many local heroes, and he was often asked by parents to draw a portrait of their son or daughter athletes.

In 1984, Taylor began creating original portraits of renowned athletes and worked to get them autographed. Taylor's enthusiasm

for sports and artistic talent attracted the critical eye of Gartlan USA, a leading producer of limited edition sports and entertainment collectibles.

Subsequently, Taylor has created original art for Gartlan USA featuring Kareem Abdul-Jabar, Joe Montana, John Wooden, Yogi Berra, Whitey Ford, Kristi Yamaguchi, Sam Snead, Bob Cousy, Rod Carew, and Brett and Bobby Hull.

Taylor also produced the original artwork featured on the *KISS Kollection, Leave It To Beaver, Ringo Starr* and *Ozzy Osbourne* series of collector plates for Gartlan USA.

His pencil study featured on the *Jerry Garcia* collector plate series was a collaborative effort, directed by Garcia's widow, Deborah Koons Garcia.

RUBEN M. TEJADA

Artist Ruben M. Tejada, a fine arts graduate, brings over 20 years of designing experience to his doll creations. Specializing in Native American designs which he carefully researches for authenticity in costume design and sculpting, Tejada's efforts have indeed resulted in awards and recognition.

The *Sweet Spirit Baby* series and the new *Gentle Dreams Baby* series of infant dolls from Sandy USA proudly carry on that great tradition. Each doll is created to be hugged, with outstretched hands and adorable expressions.

Sandy USA is proud to exclusively represent the great doll artistry of Ruben M. Tejada.

JACK TERRY

Jack Terry has become the foremost painter of classic Western American art.

A fourth-generation Texan, he credits much of his inspiration to his grandfather, a rancher who cowboyed on some of the last great cattle drives of the West, and his grandmother, who painted the landscapes and people of West Texas. His roots are deeply planted in the ways of the West, and he continually seeks inspiration from the people and places that carry on the tradition.

A graduate of the University of Texas, Jack studied anatomy and design, while seeking every opportunity to do day work on various ranches in search of inspiration. Jack and his wife, Mary, travel extensively throughout the year, appearing at gallery shows and print signings. They currently reside on their ranch near San Antonio, Texas, where they raise cattle and exotic deer.

Now Jack Terry has joined forces with Arts Uniq' for distribution of his existing paintings, as well as the publication of exclusive art.

ALLAN THERKELSEN

Artist Allan Jochum Therkelsen has created all six motifs in Bing & Grondahl's popular *Annual Figurine Collection*. He is also credited with the creation of three new and very successful underglaze figurine collections — *Swans, Cats* and *Pandas* — for Royal Copenhagen, one of Europe's oldest porcelain manufacturers.

Recognized as a sculptor, Therkelsen's work is a part of many permanent museum collections, including the McHenry Library at the University of California in Santa Cruz. In addition to a successful career in sculpting, Therkelsen has taught art at the University of California in Santa Cruz, the Skolen for Bildedkunst in Copenhagen and Grundtvig Hojskolen in Denmark.

Allan Therkelsen, representing the next generation of Royal Copenhagen sculptors, currently resides in Copenhagen.

CHUCK THORNDIKE

You could say Chuck Thorndike was literally born into the doll world. As the son of Annalee Dolls founder and creator, Annalee Thorndike, and her husband, Charles "Chip" Thorndike, Chuck found himself eye-to-eye with dozens of Annalee Dolls as he grew up in the family home in Meredith, New Hampshire. It was in this home that Chuck first helped his mom make dolls. Chuck was more than an apprentice though – his animated expressions and many hobbies became part of the dolls.

Today, Chuck oversees Annalee Dolls as the company president. But the role that Chuck most enjoys at Annalee Dolls is that of head of design, creating whimsy and wonder from the materials of felt and paint. Collectors delight in seeing the same twinkle in Chuck's eye that they see in the eyes of an Annalee Doll.

Chuck and his wife, Karen, still reside in Meredith. He maintains an active role in the community, serving as a Rotary member, a Land Conservation Trust volunteer, and an active participant in numerous charities. And, like his mom's earliest dolls, Chuck is a skier, competing throughout the winter in Masters Ski Races.

TITUS TOMESCU

Titus Tomescu is one of the leading names in the doll collecting world. His dolls have been praised for their realism and intricate detailing. The breadth of his images range from the gentle innocence of babies, to the towering spiritual strength of Jesus.

Among his most recent achievements is *Flurry of Activity,* a follow-up collection to his first Ashton-Drake *SnowBabies* series. Also new from Tomescu is a collection of babies, each one offering a clever answer to the question, *Where Do Babies Come From?*

A collection that introduces collectors to favorite storybook

characters as babies is called *Tales From the Nursery.* And *Twinkle Toes' Recital,* an all-porcelain collection, features toddler ballerinas in interactive dancing poses.

Tomescu's work has received many nominations for prestigious awards, and "Cute As a Button" was the 1994 dual winner of a DOTY® Award from *Doll Reader* magazine and the "Award of Excellence" from *Dolls* magazine.

JILL TRENHOLM

Artist Jill Trenholm has gone absolutely "nuts" about her new collection for Maruri USA. After showing her little animal sculptures to Maruri, they suggested putting them in nutshells. "The result was incredibly heart-warming," says Jill. "Now my little critters have their own secret environment, and I feel like there's a constant sparkler of ideas on fire inside me!"

Jill was born in Wyoming and attended Utah State University, where she studied art, music and poetry. For the last ten years, between raising her children and playing music with her husband, Jill has freelanced in concept design, sculpture, painting, stained glass, computer graphics and wood carving.

Each *In A Nutshell* piece is full of intricate details. "When I'm holding a finished piece in my hand," explains Jill, "I'm amazed that Maruri has been able to recreate every teeny, tiny detail I sculpted or painted." Jill has even hidden little bugs and her children's initials, S & J for Shane and Jamie, on each figurine.

Jill lives in sunny La Crescenta, California, with her husband, two children and their dog.

GLYNDA TURLEY

At her home nestled in the beautiful Ozark Mountains of Arkansas, Glynda Turley, one of the country's most collected artists, finds the quiet inspiration for her exquisite oil paintings that have won her international acclaim. Her romantic, nostalgic style opens windows to the Victorian era and days gone by.

Glynda is the president and sole artist of her company, Glynda Turley Prints, Inc., which was established in 1985. Glynda has turned her creative talents into a thriving family business that invites collectors to enjoy the simpler pleasures of life. "I strive to take the viewer into a time and place of beauty, peace, and harmony – where time seems to stand still," Glynda says. "I suppose my style of work could be described as romantic."

Glynda is always working on new ideas, including new collectible and decorative products for the home, as well as her paintings that collectors love so much. Glynda Turley's prints, decorative accessories and collectibles are sure to romance your home and your heart.

CHRISTIAN ULBRICHT

Taking centuries-old traditions and bringing them into the modern world is something Christian Ulbricht loves to do. As founder of Holzkunst Christian Ulbricht, he has truly earned the title of master wood carver, a family tradition begun by his father more than 65 years ago. Ulbricht carries on the centuries-old tradition of wood turning on the lathe, letting his natural warmth and humor shine through. These are the attributes that distinguish his intriguingly hand-carved wooden creations and bring delight to those who collect his nutcrackers, ornaments, music boxes, incense burners, and more.

Christian and his family take great pride in continuing the legendary handcraftsmanship that has existed for generations. It is easy to see why the nutcrackers that carry the Ulbricht family name are so popular. Not only do they bring to life the folklore of the beautiful German region that is their home, they also depict up-to-date life everywhere in the world today. Included among the more traditional motifs one expects to see, such as kings, soldiers and hunters, are bikers, Santa Claus, literary figures, American heroes, and even a computer hacker!

Holzkunst Christian Ulbricht is truly a family affair. Working along with Christian, and the trained artisans who carry out the master designs, are his wife, Inge, and their son and daughter, Gunther and Ines. Together, they have developed their studio into a creative, well-knit, productive organization dedicated to bringing high-quality craftsmanship to collectors.

DUANE UNRUH

Duane Unruh could retire, but he says he continues to work because he enjoys it so much. A *Keepsake Ornament* artist since 1984 and part of Hallmark since 1979, Duane still dreams up new designs. "I like to use colors that are particularly beautiful against a tree," he says. That's why he draped "Magical Unicorn," a limited edition ornament that he sculpted for the 1986 line, in pink and mint-green ribbons.

Before joining Hallmark, Duane was a football coach and biology teacher – and a sculptor. He created a series of limited edition bronze sculptures (of which several were inspired by his five children) that were sold through Kansas City's Halls Crown Center department store. Hallmark design managers noticed his artistry and offered him freelance assignments, which led to full-time work in the *Keepsake Ornament* studio. Today, he has 19 grandchildren and scores of *Keepsake Ornament* designs to his credit.

SVEN VESTERGAARD

Sven Vestergaard became an apprentice at the Royal Copenhagen Porcelain Manufactory at the age of 16. Four years later, he was given the highest award — the Silver Medal — and remained at the factory as an overglaze painter until 1959.

He then worked as a designer at Denmark's oldest newspaper, Berlinske Tidenede, as well as at various advertising agencies. In 1965, he returned to the factory as a draftsman and became the head of Royal Copenhagen's drawing office in 1976.

Vestergaard has become well known and respected throughout the world for his designs for Royal Copenhagen's *Christmas, Olympic, Hans Christian Andersen, National Parks of America* and *Mother's Day* plates and *Children's Day* series.

Vestergaard lives 30 miles south of Copenhagen on an estate originally owned by nobility, where he creates the many themes for Royal Copenhagen plates, and his oil paintings of peaceful Danish landscapes, animals and nature.

EDDIE WALKER

As a child, Eddie Walker noticed how much love went into the things her family made, like cookies, quilts and crafts. It was natural for her to express her feelings of love in her own work.

Eddie began woodcarving in 1989 when a neighbor convinced her to take a carving class in her hometown of Walla Walla, Washington. After spending nine hours carving her first Santa, Eddie realized the possibilities were endless. Eddie admits that she does very little planning when she carves. Using a bench knife and the process of "peeling potatoes," as she puts it, she simply draws a rough sketch on the wood and begins to carve. Sometimes she cuts wood into random shapes and finds the character inside waiting to take form. What evolves are chubby, endearing figures that come alive with warm and inviting expressions.

Eddie's art offers a glimpse of the people in her life. Whether it's a child's story, a part of her own childhood or something her grown children have experienced, Eddie tries to see through the eyes of a child, where everything is filled with magic and wonder.

In 1994, Midwest of Cannon Falls® began producing high-quality, affordable reproductions of Eddie's work.

EMMA JANE WATKINS

"Look deep into a child's eyes, and you'll find everything you'll ever need in life; pure love, simple joy, honest sadness, and most importantly, an irrepressible hope for and belief in the future," says artist Emma Jane Watkins.

Emma Jane started sculpting as a child and even opened an Art School in the basement of her parents home. While her friends often played hopscotch, Emma Jane baked delicately formed clay animals and people in the family oven. By high school, Watkins was already receiving portrait commissions, and her career as one of America's premier sculptors was well under way.

Emma Jane Watkins' work continues to touch on themes shared in the hearts of children of every age. Her newest collection for United Treasures, the *Remember When...* series, captures the heart and soul of the child in all of us in a portrait of simpler times gone by. Each piece in the collection is a snapshot of a time gone by, evoking the memories of yesteryear through the eyes of a child.

OLIVER WEBER

Oliver Weber is taking the collectibles market by storm with the *Oliver Weber Jeweled Collection!* The lavish collection, distributed in the United States exclusively by Swan Seekers Network, features intricately detailed pieces that are encrusted with hundreds of sparkling Swarovski stones.

Born in Leoben, Austria, Oliver Weber attended a special high school for snow ski racers. After graduation, he became a professional ski racer in the United States and Japan. He then studied business and marketing at the University of Innsbruck, Austria, and later took a position as marketing and sales manager for Swarovski's Jewelry Division.

In 1995, Oliver and his partner, Alexander Stabinger, formed the WeSta Company with the idea of developing a dolphin figurine using 22K gold plated metal highlighted with pave stones. The premier piece, a family of four dolphins, took over four years to create. It is displayed on an elaborate aluminum blue base with a thick, beveled-edged glass background of Swarovski stones that form a transparent wave. The collection has grown to include several intricately detailed musical instruments and animal figures designed in brushed rhodium or polished gold, combined with pave stones and rich accents of enameling. The company plans to introduce three or four new pieces per year until the collection totals 30 current designs.

When Oliver is not traveling around the world on business, he is hard at work on the golf course. He believes that "If you work hard, you need to play hard and enjoy life – or it's all for nothing." Golf is just another challenge, which Oliver takes on with "gusto."

WILLY WHITTEN

Artist and sculptor Willy Whitten first realized his talent when he was five years old, making animated drawings with the help of his grandfather.

During his career, Willy has sculpted for several movie studios and worked on movies including *Ghostbusters, Terminator* and others. He has also created works for The L.A. County Museum, Landmark Entertainment, Disney, Marvel Comics, and many more.

For Maruri, Willy has created *The Tropics*, a collection of intricately detailed figurines that draw their inspiration from a tropical paradise. "Maruri's *Tropics* line has been

a passionate dream for a long time," explains the artist. "I guess it's because I'd love to be working in some tropical paradise." Now when collectors feel the need to relax and dream about the less stressful things in life, they can place a piece of *The Tropics* in their home or office and escape any time they would like.

BILLY DEE WILLIAMS

Billy Dee Williams grew up in Harlem with a family that actively encouraged the artistic abilities of their children. Billy Dee began drawing at an early age, and developed his fundamental skills in painting while attending New York's High School of Music and Art. In 1955, he won the coveted Hallgarten Award Scholarship to the National Academy of Fine Art and Design.

While studying under artists like Robert Phillip and Boris Wolensky, Billy Dee also pursued his acting career that would ultimately lead to worldwide fame. Starring in movies such as *Lady Sings the Blues* and *Star Wars* brought Williams instant recognition for his acting talents, while his paintings found an audience with art collectors around the world. Williams' paintings hang in the Smithsonian Portrait Gallery, The Schomberg Museum in New York, and in homes and galleries around the world.

Presented by United Treasures, *The Romance Collection* by Billy Dee Williams is sure to set hearts afire with these passionate interpretations of his works.

DAVID WINTER

Gifted English sculptor David Winter has gained international acclaim as one of the world's foremost creators of unique miniature architectural cottages.

Born in Catterick, in Yorkshire, England, David is the son of an army colonel and the famed British sculptor, Faith Winter. Inspired by his mother, David created his first miniature cottage in 1979. Since then, David has received worldwide acclaim, winning such coveted honors as the National Association of Limited Edition Dealers (NALED) "Collectible of the Year Award" in 1987 and 1988, NALED's "Artist of the Year" in 1991, and Collectors' Information Bureau's "Best Cottage Artist" in 1998 and 1999.

Every David Winter cottage has a unique story to tell. Each model comes with a Certificate of Authenticity and a card that tells the story of the cottage's occupants or relays historical facts connected with the subject matter.

1999 marked an important milestone in David Winter's career – the 20th Anniversary of the *David Winter Cottages*® collection.

IWONA WISZNIEWSKA

Iwona Wiszniewska (pronounced Eev-oh-na Vish-nee-ef-ska) was born in Poland and came to the United States in 1992. She is an accomplished artist, educated in home décor, fashion accessories, interior design and crafts. Iwona especially loves to design Christmas decorations including fabric and paper ornaments,

and "stroik," table pieces made up of fragrant evergreens, candles, and glass ornaments.

When she joined the staff at Kurt S. Adler, Inc., she was trained in the Komozja factory, where the *Polonaise*® collection of hand-blown glass ornaments is created.

"I was taught how to paint on glass, which is totally different than painting on any other surface, because it is slippery and rounded. You must know the right techniques, or your ornaments will be lopsided!"

Among her most beloved ornaments in the *Polonaise* collection are "The Lamb of God," which shows a baby Jesus cuddling a mother lamb, and on the other side, a baby lamb nuzzling Jesus' hand; and the "The Adoring Santa" ornament which features Santa Claus and the child Jesus in a loving embrace.

DAVID LEE WOODARD

Everyone has an imagination, but the true challenge to imagination is to take something ordinary and change it into something that brings pleasure. Since his early years, David Lee Woodard has been striving to meet that challenge. Looking at things from a different perspective has allowed him to create new ideas.

David likes to have fun and have others enjoy his creative endeavors. He especially likes making up stories and swapping tales with others. He has great fun sitting with a group of friends, each trying to top the other by making up a better story. David has always enjoyed writing stories and poetry. When he was 19 years old, he had the opportunity to publish some of his compositions. Not until he helped develop the *World of Krystonia* books did he pursue his creative skills again.

Over the past 20 years, David has developed figurine lines for Precious Art, Inc., ranging from music boxes and animals to fantasy figurines. As in the past, he continues to look for ways to stretch the imagination through his designs.

ANDREA WORKMAN

There are few New Jersey artists working today that enjoy the exposure and popularity that Andrea Workman has attained in her career. Painter, designer, sculptor, illustrator of dolls, figurines and collectibles, and teacher... her talent runs the gamut of the most-collected artistic forms. It's no wonder that her work has been featured by many of the most prestigious collectible manufacturers, including The Franklin Mint, Lenox, Paradise Galleries, Royal Doulton and Gartlan USA, to name but a few.

"I love to sculpt and paint all people, from celebrities to 'everyday' women, women with children, men, flowers and animals," she enthusiastically states.

She has just completed her newest work for Gartlan USA, based

on a classic Beatles' album, "Yellow Submarine." Of her "Yellow Submarine" figurine for Gartlan USA, she says, "I try for the inner joy and beauty. All life is interwoven and magic. I love to work with companies on the cutting edge, dedicated to quality and services — and Gartlan USA is such a company."

CHU-MING "JAMIE" WU

A chance meeting in 1983 with an artist who made miniature bears led Chu-Ming "Jamie" Wu to become a top teddy bear designer and successful entrepreneur. Jamie had just immigrated to the United States, spoke little English, and was a day laborer when he met Carol Stewart. Under her guidance, Jamie made his first bear, working diligently for 27 nights! Fifteen years later, his company, Akira Trading Company, sells thousands of *Little Gem Teddy Bears* that are made by cottage workers in China.

Chu-Ming Wu, known to his English speaking friends as "Jamie," was born in 1947 in Taiwan. At an early age, his grandfather taught him to carve small animals and encouraged him to follow his interests. A delightful, down-to-earth and honorable man, Jamie is motivated by a genuine love for what he is doing. Renowned for his work, he has been invited as a guest artist to the Walt Disney World Teddy Bear & Doll Convention in 1997, 1998 and 1999. His unique designs, combined with fine craftsmanship and an affordable price, make his teddy bears truly "Little Gems."

BILL YOUNGER

Bill Younger has loved lighthouses as long as he can remember. In the spring of 1991, working closely with his family, he developed the first 17 pieces of Harbour Lights, hand-painted sculptures that honor the history of our nation's extraordinary sentinels.

Since those humble beginnings, Harbour Lights has captured the imaginations of people the world over. During the past eight years, Bill has won numerous awards, including two "Awards of Excellence" from *Collector Editions* magazine, as well as the "Award of Devotion" from the National Association of Limited Edition Dealers (NALED). In 1999, he received the prestigious "International Collectible Achievement Award."

Three years ago, Bill set his sights beyond our shores with the release of Anchor Bay. A stunning collection of hand-painted boat and ship sculptures, Anchor Bay commemorates watercraft from recent and past history.

Bill Younger hopes that through Harbour Lights and Anchor Bay, future generations will remember our proud nautical heritage and the courageous men and women who kept the flame.

MARTIN ZENDRON

Born in the medieval town of Hall in Tyrol, Austria, Martin Zendron now lives and works only a few miles away in Wattens, the home of Swarovski.

In his late teens, Martin attended the world-famous technical school for glass craft and design in Kramsach in Tyrol, where he studied glass design with a special course in cutting and engraving. After graduation, he worked for a well-known Tyrolean retailer specializing in glass objects. His work came to Swarovski's attention, and he became a designer in 1988.

His first creations for Swarovski Silver Crystal were the "Harp" and the "Lute," followed by the "Grand Piano." Zendron also designed the "Fawn," "Santa Claus," "Sleigh," and all of the "Kris Bear" offerings. He also created the first piece in the *Inspiration Africa* series, the "Elephant," and the "Unicorn" in the *Fabulous Creatures* series for the Swarovski Collectors Society.

Although Martin spends much of his spare time in the mountains, his real passion is deep-sea diving. For him, it is a wonderful way of relaxing from the precision and concentration required for his work with Swarovski.

NORBERT ZUBER

Columbus International is proud to represent the artistic craftsmanship of Norbert Zuber, creator of the Zuber nutcrackers, smokers, Christmas ornaments and music boxes. Since 1983, Norbert and his wife, Marlies, have developed high-quality wooden figurines, many in limited editions, for the collectible market. Being the first to dress his nutcrackers in lavish clothing, Zuber's idea has now become an industry standard.

Zuber has a talent for bringing unique wooden figurines to life. In 1999, two special millennium pieces were introduced to bring in the New Year. The "Y2K" nutcracker was also introduced. A special "Around the World" miniature nutcracker series highlights Zuber's collection. This series contains a selection of unique miniature nutcrackers representing many countries of the world.

10 Most Frequently Asked Questions
About Buying and Selling Limited Edition Collectibles

Q. How are prices for limited edition collectibles established on the secondary market?

A. As with most items in an open marketplace, prices are established in response to the supply of and demand for each individual item. Since limited edition pieces are, by definition, limited in the number of pieces available, demand for each piece will impact the market value of the item.

Over time, the "supply" of a particular piece may decrease, as natural disasters and home accidents result in damage or breakage. As the supply shrinks, the price may increase again.

Similarly, items that are in relatively large supply and experience small to moderate demand may see modest or low appreciation on the secondary market. Some items with broad distribution and low demand do not appreciate at all on the secondary market.

These fluctuations in the secondary market value of items are tracked by organizations like the COLLECTORS' INFORMATION BUREAU. Twice a year, the CIB surveys over 300 secondary market dealers and asks them to report back on the actual prices collectors have paid for individual pieces. This input is compiled and reported in the COLLECTIBLES PRICE GUIDE (published each May) and the COLLECTIBLES MARKET GUIDE & PRICE INDEX (published each November).

Q. What does a collector need to know if they are planning to buy or sell on the secondary market?

A. There are 4 things to consider when you begin thinking about buying or selling on the secondary market.

1.) *Know the value of the piece you want to buy or sell.* This information can be found by checking reputable price guides like the CIB's COLLECTIBLES PRICE GUIDE. Since these books list actual prices paid by collectors in recent transactions, they represent an excellent starting point for determining the market value of an item.

2.) *Understand the "terms of sale" used by the secondary market dealer that you're considering.* Individual dealers vary greatly in the services they offer the collectors and the fees they charge for these services. Some dealers buy pieces outright, while others provide a listing service or take goods on consignment. Some dealers charge as little as 10% commission, while others charge upwards of 30% to 50%. In most cases, the buyer pays the fee, however some dealers will ask the seller to pay all or part of the fee.

3.) *Be realistic about the condition of your piece.* Note any markings, mold numbers, etc. Carefully check your piece for any scratches, blemishes or cracks. If you are upfront with the dealer, you'll save yourself time and aggravation. Gather the original paperwork and box. If you don't have these materials, ask the dealer how this will affect the price of the piece you're selling. If you're looking to buy and have no intention of reselling, let the dealer know that you would accept a piece without the original paperwork. But be sure that you will not want to resell the piece later, since this will have an impact on the price you can demand.

4.) *Ask if the piece will be inspected by the dealer.* Many dealers will suggest that you write your initials or some other "code" on the bottom of the piece in pencil. By doing so, you can be sure that the piece you send in is the piece you get back should the sale fall through. Check with the dealer before putting any markings on the piece to ensure that it will not effect the value of the piece.

Q. Does a factory flaw or variation effect the selling price of a piece?

A. Usually, factory flaws are not a problem unless they are very pronounced. That's why it is extremely important to inspect each piece you buy...whether it's on the primary market (through a retailer or direct mail) or on the secondary market (at a "swap and sell" or through a dealer/exchange). And remember, everyone's definition of "perfection" is different. What one collector may find acceptable, another would reject. Variations usually do not effect the value of a piece. The exception to this rule is variations that qualify as "mistakes." Misspelling and other obvious mistakes will usually make a piece more valuable.

Q. Does the presence of an artist's signature on a piece increase its value?

A. Though the presence of a signature is not as important as it used to be, in some cases the value of a signed piece may be 15% to 25% higher than a comparable unsigned piece. Factors that impact the value of a signature include:

1.) *Age of the artist* — Artists who are reaching the end of their career may be doing fewer signings, making a signed piece more valuable to many collectors.

2.) *Accessibility of an artist* — Signatures from artists that rarely make themselves available for signings are often more coveted and therefore add to the value of a signed piece.

3.) *Buyer's preference* — More and more artists are taking to the road for personal appearances. These events give the collector the chance to share a personal experience with the artist. Some collectors prefer to buy unsigned pieces because they plan to have the artist sign the piece for them personally at an upcoming event.

Q. How important is it to save the original box?

A. Boxes are very important and the absence of an original box will often result in a lower selling price.

If you have a collectible that breaks, and you have your original box, you can buy a replacement piece without the box (since you don't need it) and usually save some money.

On a more practical note, the manufacturer designs the box to afford the best possible protection for the piece during shipment. If you and your collectible move, the original box will be your best shot at getting your collection safely to its new home.

Q. What steps should I expect to go through in buying or selling collectibles through a secondary market dealer or exchange?

A. The average secondary market transaction takes about 3 weeks to complete and will usually include the following steps:

1.) *Call the secondary market dealer/exchange and tell them about the piece you want to buy or sell.* Be specific and include the product number if possible.

2.) *If you are looking to buy a piece, the dealer will tell you if they currently have it listed (available from a seller) or in stock, and what the selling price is.* The selling price will usually include a commission or service fee for the dealer/exchange. If you are looking to sell a piece, you should be prepared to tell them your "asking price." This price is the amount of money you expect to clear after the transaction is completed, and should not include the commission. In most cases, the dealer will add the commission on top of your asking price. Keep in mind that you must pay the shipping and insurance charges necessary to get your piece to the dealer/exchange. The buyer will usually pay to have the item shipped to them from the dealer/exchange.

3.) *Once a buyer agrees to pay the price asked, the dealer contacts the seller and has the piece shipped to the dealer for inspection.* At the same time, the buyer sends his/her payment to the dealer.

4.) *After the piece is inspected by the dealer and found to be in acceptable condition, the piece is shipped to the buyer for their inspection.* Before it is shipped, most dealers will put a marking (often invisible) on the bottom of the piece. This is a safeguard to ensure that if the piece is not accepted, the same piece is returned.

5.) *The buyer usually will have a set time-period (3 to 5 days) to either accept or reject the piece.* If the piece is accepted by the buyer, the dealer pays the seller the agreed-upon asking price. If the piece is not acceptable, it is returned to the dealer who can either return it to the seller, or sell it to another buyer for the original asking price.

Q. How has the emergence of the Internet effected the secondary market?

A. There is no denying that the Internet has broadened the scope of the secondary market for collectibles and changed the way some people buy and sell retired pieces. From popular auction sites like eBay and Auction Universe, to established secondary market dealers who have expanded their businesses to include an e-commerce component, the Internet provides another avenue for the anxious buyer or seller to meet.

We advise collectors, however, that auction sites have been referred to as electronic classifieds, and as a result should be approached with caution. As with a traditional classified ad, buyer and seller do not meet before the sale and may be hard to track down after it. So "caveat emptor" or" buyer beware" when it comes to dealing through an unknown party. Safeguards, such as buyer and seller feedback reports and escrow provisions, have been put in place by the auction sites and should be employed by collectors eager to use this avenue.

With that being said, some of the best bargains in the secondary market are often found on the Internet, where overhead is low, middlemen are often eliminated and hard-to-find pieces are exposed to willing buyers. When used judiciously, the Internet can be the answer to the avid collectors' prayers!

Q. Is trading or bartering an option for acquiring limited edition collectibles?

A. Trading and/or bartering is an alternative to buying and selling on the secondary market. Collectors clubs and "swap and sell" events offer the best avenue for trading or bartering, since you have the opportunity to inspect the piece and negotiate right on the spot.

Q. If you have a large collection, is it better to sell it as a "collection" or as single pieces?

A. It is very difficult to sell an entire collection unless it is comprised of all older pieces, since collectors usually have some of the pieces from the collection that they're building. Often, they are looking to supplement their own collection of later issues with some of the earlier pieces that they missed.

It's also typically quite expensive to purchase an entire collection at once, so collectors will add to a collection piece-by-piece as they can afford the investment.

You will usually receive greater value for your collection if you sell it one piece at a time, rather than trying to sell the whole collection at once to one buyer. By listing your collection as individual pieces with a secondary market dealer, you have a better chance of moving all the pieces, though it may take some time.

Q. Do club pieces increase in value faster than other collectibles?

A. Club issues tend to appreciate quickly because they are only available for one year. The first club issue may be harder to find because club membership is smaller in the beginning, making fewer pieces available and thus driving up demand.

Generally, though, club pieces are not more in demand than some very specific pieces in a line.

Terms Often Used by Collectors, Dealers and Manufacturers to Describe Limited Edition Collectibles

Acid-free. A description of paper and materials treated to remove the acids that cause deterioration.

Alabaster. A fine-textured gypsum which is usually white and translucent. Some collectors' plates are made of a material called ivory alabaster which is not translucent, but has the look and patina of old ivory.

Allotment. The number within a limited edition which a manufacturer allows to a given dealer, direct marketer or collector.

Annual. The term is used to describe a plate or other limited edition which is issued yearly. Many annual plates commemorate holidays or anniversaries, and they are commonly named by that special date, i.e. the Annual Bing & Grondahl Christmas plate.

Art deco. A popular art style, recognized by its clean, dramatic lines, bold colors and distinct patterning, that originated in the 1920s and 1930s.

Artist/gallery/publishers' proofs. Originally, the first few prints in an edition of lithographs were used to test colors and then given to the artist. They were not numbered but were signed. Artist's proofs are not considered part of the edition. Gallery and publishers' proofs are used as a means of increasing the number of prints in an edition.

Baby doll. A doll with the proportions of a baby; with a short-limbed body and lips parted to take a nipple.

Back issue. An issue in a series other than the issue that is currently being produced. It can be either open or closed and may or may not be available.

Backstamp. The information on the back of a plate or other limited edition which documents it as part of a limited edition. This information may be hand-painted onto the plate, or it may be incised, or applied as a transfer (decal). Information which typically appears on the backstamp includes the name of the series, name of the item, year of issue, some information about the subject, the artist's name and/or signature, the edition limit, the item's number within that edition, initials of the firing master or production supervisor, etc.

Band. Also known as a rim, as in "24K gold banded, or rimmed." A popular finishing technique is to band plates and bells with gold, platinum or silver which is then adhered to the plate through the firing process. Details from the primary artwork may also be adapted to form a decorative rim.

Bas-relief. A technique in which the collectible has a raised design. This design may be achieved by pouring liquid material into a mold before firing, or by applying a three-dimensional design element to the flat surface of a plate, figurine or other "blank" piece.

Bavaria. A section of Germany that is one of the world's richest sources of kaolin clay, an essential component of fine porcelain. The region is home to a number of renowned porcelain factories.

Bent glass. Flat piece of glass which is reheated and allowed to sag into a decorative curved shape.

Bisque or biscuit. A fired ware which has neither a glaze nor enamel applied to it. Bisque may be white or colored. The name comes from its biscuit-like, matte texture.

Blank. An undecorated piece, which usually will have further processing.

Blown glass. Technique of shaping glass by air pressure with or without a mold.

Body. The basic form of a plate, figurine, bell or other collectible, or its component materials.

Bone ash. Fire is used to reduce animal bones to calcium phosphate, a powder which is an ingredient of bone china or porcelain.

Bone china/bone porcelain. Bone porcelain is similar to hard porcelain in its ingredients, except that bone ash is the main component of the mix and is the primary contributor to the vitrification and translucency. Bone clay allows for extreme thinness and translucency without sacrificing strength or durability.

Bottomstamp. The same as a backstamp, but usually refers to documentation material found on the bottom of a figurine or the inside of a bell. Also known as an understamp.

Bye-lo-baby. Grace Storey Putman copyrighted this life-sized baby doll (three days old) in 1922. This style of baby doll is a favorite among limited edition collectors.

Cameo. Relief decoration with a flat surface around it, similar to the look of a jeweler's cameo. A technique used by Wedgwood, Incolay, Avondale and others.

Canceled plate. A plate that was planned as part of a series, but never produced because of technical problems or lack of interest in early issues.

Canvas transfer process. A lithograph is treated with a latex emulsion. The paper is removed and the image on the latex emulsion is placed on a cotton duck canvas. It is then topcoated, retouched and highlighted by hand before being hand-numbered.

Capodimonte. Originally a fine porcelain produced at a "castle on the mountain" overlooking Naples. The term currently describes a highly ornate style rather than an actual product. Frequently features flowers, fruits and courtly or native figures.

Cased glass. The process whereby one layer of glass is applied over another.

Cast. The process of creating a copy of an original model by pouring liquid clay or slip into a mold.

Ceramic. The generic term for a piece which is made of some form of clay and finished by firing at high temperatures.

Certificate/Certificate of Authenticity. A document which accompanies a limited edition item to establish its place within the edition. Certificates may include information such as the series name, item title, artist's name and/or signature, brief description of the item and its subject, signatures of sponsoring and marketing organizations' representatives, and other documentation material, along with the item's individual number or a statement of the edition limit.

Character dolls. These dolls are often created to resemble actors or celebrities. Character dolls also include fairytale images, folk heroes and cartoon characters.

Chasing. A sculpting process in which tiny hammers and punches are used to create decorative details on ornaments.

China. Originally "china" referred to all wares which came from China. Now the term means products which are fired at a high temperature. China usually consists of varying percentages of kaolin clay, feldspar and quartz. Also see "porcelain."

Cinnabar. A red mineral found in volcanic regions, and an ingredient in mercury. It is used to create collectors' items.

Cire perdue. See lost wax.

Clay. A general term for materials used to make ceramic items. Pliable when moist, clay becomes hard and strong when fired. It may be composed of any number of earthen materials.

Cloisonné. An enameling process in which thin metal strips are soldered on the base of a piece to create a pattern. Then, various enamels are poured in to provide the color.

Closed edition. A limited edition that is no longer being issued because it has reached the designated limit, or no longer has market appeal.

Closed end edition. A series with a pre-determined, and usually pre-announced, number of issues.

Cobalt blue. Also known as Copenhagen blue, this rich color was an early favorite because it was the only color that could withstand high firing temperatures needed for glazing. Cobalt oxide is a black powder when applied, but fires to a deep blue.

Cold cast. A relatively new process which combines polyester resins and a variety of materials (metal powders, ground porcelain, wood shavings and other natural materials). The combination is forced into a mold or die under high pressure and a forging process occurs. Allows for exceptional detailing which can be easily hand-painted.

Cold painting. Decorative glass technique using lacquer oil-based pigments with no subsequent firing.

Collector plate. A limited edition plate which is created to be collected for its decorative appearance.

Commemorative. An item created to mark a special date, holiday or event.

Crazing. A defect in the glaze caused by the difference in the rate of contraction between the body of the item and the glaze.

Crystal. Clear, colorless glass.

Cut glass. Glass whose surface is decorated with cuttings applied by an abrasive wheel.

Dealer. An individual or store where collectors can purchase collectibles at retail prices.

Decal. Also known as a transfer, this is a lithographic or silk-screen rendering of a piece of artwork, which is applied to ceramic or other materials and then fired on to fuse it to the surface.

Delftware. Heavy earthenware coated with an opaque white glaze that contains tin oxide. First developed in Delft, Holland, in the 16th century.

Diptych. Two pieces of complementary art, intended to be displayed side-by-side.

Drafting. Process for shaping metal into hollowware.

Dresden. White china, usually heavily decorated.

Earthenware. A non-vitrified ceramic made of ball clay, kaolin and pegmatite. Remains porous until glazed and fired at a low temperature.

Edition. A term referring to the number of items created with the same name and decorations.

Embossing. A process of producing an image in relief by using dies or punches on a surface.

Enameling. Metallic oxides ground to a fine powder and fired at low temperatures used to decorate already glazed pottery.

Encrustation. Decoration of precious metal applied in liquid form and then fired.

Engraving. An intaglio process in which an image is cut into the surface. Term also used to describe a print made by an engraving process.

Etched design. Decoration produced by cutting into a surface with acid. An acid-resistant paint or wax is applied and the design is inscribed through this coating. When immersed in acid, the acid etches the surface to form the design.

Faceting. Decorative technique of cutting diamond-shaped or other patterns into the surface of glass.

Faience. Named after an Italian town, Faenza, faience is similar to Delftware and Majolica because it is earthenware coated with a glaze that contains tin oxide.

Feldspar. When decomposed, this mineral becomes kaolin, which is the essential ingredient in china and porcelain. Left in its undecomposed form, feldspar adds hardness to a ware.

Filling-in. Decorating process where transfer print outlines are filled in by hand to produce multi-color effects.

Firing. Baking process in a kiln where all ceramics are subject to hardening, strengthening or fusing.

Firing period. A time period — usually 10 to 75 days, which serves to limit an edition, usually of plates. The number of items is limited to the capacity of the manufacturer during that time period.

First issue. The premiere item in a series, whether closed-ended or open-ended.

Flashed glass. Clear glass covered with a thin second layer of colored glass which can be cut to produce various effects similar to cased glass.

Folk art. An art style known for simple but rich colors, originating from the common people, both past and present. Sometimes called "primitive art."

French bronze. Also known as "spelter," this is zinc refined to 99.97% purity. It has been used as an alternative to bronze for casting for more than a century.

Frosted glass. Semi-opaque glass with a gray-textured surface.

Full lead. Glass with a high lead content, usually 24% or 30%.

Gilding. The process of using gold or platinum to decorate a piece.

Glaze. The liquid material which is applied to a ware for various purposes. Cosmetically, it provides shine and decorative value. It also makes the item more durable. Decorations may be applied before or after glaze is applied.

Graphic. A print produced by one of the "original" print processes such as etching, engraving, woodblocks, lithographs and serigraphs. This term is frequently used interchangeably with "print."

Greenware. Undecorated ceramic before it is fired.

Hallmark. The mark or logo of the manufacturer of an item.

Glossary

Hard paste porcelain. The hardest porcelain made, this material uses feldspar to enhance vitrification and translucency, and is fired at about 2642 degrees Fahrenheit.

Hydrostone. The hardest form of gypsum cement from which many limited edition collectibles are produced. A registered trademark of the United States Gypsum Co.

Incised. Writing or design which is etched or inscribed into a piece to provide a backstamp or decorative design.

Incolay stone. A man-made material combining minerals including carnelian and crystal quartz. Used by Incolay Studios to make cameo-style collectibles.

Inlay. To fill an etched or incised design with another material such as enamel, metal or jewels.

In stock. A term used to refer to an item of a given edition still available from the producers' inventory.

Iridescent glass. Glass with a special coating, that when struck by light, reflects a rainbow.

Issue. As a verb, to introduce. As a noun, the term means an item within a series.

Issue Price. The price established by the manufacturer or principal marketer when a collectible is introduced.

Jasper ware. Josiah Wedgwood's unglazed stoneware material, first introduced in the 1770s. Although jasper is white in its original form, it can be stained a medium blue called "Wedgwood Blue," or a darker blue, black, green, lilac, yellow, brown and gray. Colored Wedgwood "bodies" are often decorated with white bas-relief, or vice/versa.

Jiggering. Jigger machine used to shape plates.

Kaolin. The essential ingredient in china and porcelain, this special clay is found in several spots throughout the world. Many famous porcelain factories are located near these deposits.

Kiln. Oven in which ceramics are fired or baked.

Lace glass. Glass decorated with a maze of thread-like lines resembling lace fabric.

Lead crystal. Lead oxide is added to glass to give it weight, brilliance and a clear ring. Lead crystal has a lead oxide content of 24%, while "full" lead crystal contains more than 30%.

Limited edition. An item produced only in a certain quantity or only during a certain time period. Collectible editions are limited by: specific numbers, years, specific time periods or firing periods.

Limoges. A town in France with rich deposits of kaolin clay and other essential ingredients for making china and porcelain. Home of a number of famed porcelain manufacturers.

Lithograph. Limited reproductions of original paintings or drawings. Also known as a graphic or print.

Lost wax. An ancient method used by sculptors to create a detailed wax "positive" which is then used to form a ceramic "negative" shell. This shell becomes the original mold used in the creation of finely carved three-dimensional pieces.

Luster. Ceramic glaze coating which gives the finished piece an iridescent effect.

Majolica. Similar to Delftware and Faience, this glazed earthenware was first produced on the Spanish island, Majorca.

Market. The organized buy-sell medium for collectibles.

Marks or markings. The logo or insignia which certifies that an item was made by a particular firm.

Matte Finish. Flat glaze without gloss.

Meissen. Europe's first factory to produce hard-paste porcelain.

Milk glass. White opaque glass used mostly in the reproduction of early decorative pieces.

Miniatures. Collectibles, including figurines, plates, graphics, dolls, ornaments and bells, which are very small originals or smaller versions of larger pieces. Usually finely detailed, many figurine miniatures are created using the lost wax process.

Mint condition. The term originated in coin collecting. In limited edition collectibles, it means that an item is still in its original, like-new condition, with all accompanying documents.

Mold. The form that supplies the shape of a plate, bell, figurine or other items.

Mold-blown. Glass manufactured by blowing molten glass into a mold.

Mold-pressed. A mechanized process in which a gob of glass is forced into a mold and plunged into the center to form a hollow section.

Open edition. A reproduction of an original with no limit on time of production or the number of pieces produced, and no announcement of edition size.

Open-ended series. A collection of plates or other limited editions which appear at intervals, usually annually, with no limit as to the number of years it will be produced.

Optic. Decoration that yields swirls or ripples which are made by forming glass in a mold.

Original. One-of-a-kind piece created by an artist.

Overglaze. A decoration which is applied to an item after its original glazing and firing.

Palette. A specific range of colors used by an artist. Also the surface used by the artist to mix colors.

Paste. The raw material of porcelain before shaping and firing. See "slip."

Patina. The special soft sheen, color and feel that develops years after using silver.

Pattern glass. Pressed glassware originally produced in America between 1890 and 1940.

Pewter. An alloy containing at least 85% tin.

Pontil mark. The rough mark made on the base of glass when the pontil (the iron rod used to handle hand-made glass) is removed. A true sign of hand-made, mouth-blown glass.

Porcelain. Made of kaolin, quartz and feldspar, porcelain is fired at up to 1450 degrees centigrade. Porcelain is noted for its translucency and its true ring. Also called "china."

Pottery. Ceramic ware, more specifically that which is earthenware or non-vitrified. Also a term for manufacturing plants where such objects are made and fired.

Pressed glass. Glassware formed in a mold.

Primary market. The first buy-sell market used by manufacturers to reach collectors. Sold at issue price, collectibles are offered to the public through retailers, direct mail and home shopping networks.

Print. A photomechanical reproduction process such as offset, lithography, collotypes and letterpress.

Printed remarque. A hand drawn image by the artist that is photomechanically reproduced in the margin of a print.

Queen's ware. Cream-colored earthenware developed by Josiah Wedgwood; now used as a generic term for similar materials.

Quote. The average selling price of a collectible at any given time. It may be the issue price, or above or below.

Refractories. Materials which can withstand high temperatures.

Release price. The price for which each print in the edition is sold until the edition is sold out and a secondary market price is established.

Relief. A raised design in various levels above a background.

Remarque. A hand-drawn original image by the artist, either in pencil, pen and ink, watercolor or oil, that is sketched in the margin of a limited edition print.

Resin. A bonding compound mixed with powdered, ground or chipped materials (pulverized porcelain, wood, shells and other materials) to form cold-cast products. Cold-cast porcelain is made by mixing resin with porcelain dust; cold-cast bronze is made by blending resin with ground bronze.

Retired. No longer available from the producer, and none of the pieces will ever be produced again.

Sandwich glass. Early pressed glass from Sandwich, Massachusetts.

Screen printing. Decoration in which stencil-like screens are used to apply colors.

Sculpted crystal. A general term for products made by assembling faceted Austrian crystal prisms with a 32% lead content

Second. An item which is not first quality and should not be included in the limited edition. Normally, such items are destroyed or at least marked on the backstamp or bottomstamp to indicate they are not first quality.

Secondary market. Once the original edition has been sold out, the buying and selling among collectors, through dealers or exchanges, takes place on the "secondary" market.

Secondary market price. The price a customer is willing to sell or buy an item for once it is no longer available on the primary market. These prices will vary from one part of the country to another, depending on the supply and demand for the collectible.

Serigraphy. A direct printing process used by artists to design, make and print their own stencils. A serigraph differs from other prints in that its images are created with paint films instead of printing inks.

Signed and numbered. Each print is signed and consecutively numbered by the artist, in pencil, either in the image area or in the margin. Edition size is limited.

Signed in the plate. The only signature on the artwork is reproduced from the artist's original signature. Not necessarily limited in edition size.

Signed only. Usually refers to a print that is signed without consecutive numbers. May not be limited in edition size.

Silver crystal. Faceted Austrian crystal prisms with a 32% lead content used to produce sculpted crystal. The name is registered by Swarovski.

Silverplate. A process of manufacturing ornaments in which pure silver is electroplated onto a base metal, usually brass or pewter.

Slip. A creamy material used to fill the molds in making greenware. Formulas for slip are closely guarded secrets.

Soft paste. A mixture of clay and ground glass first used in Europe to produce china. The vitrification point of soft paste is too low to produce the hardness required for true porcelain.

Soldering. Attaching bases, handles, fittings, or bodies by fusing the metallic surfaces together with a soldering iron.

Sold out. The classification given to an edition which has been 100% sold out by the producer.

Spin casting. A process of casting multiple ornaments from rubber molds; commonly used for low-temperature metals such as pewter.

Stained glass. Glass that is colored in various ways, by fusing metallic oxides into it, by enameling, or by burning pigments into its surface.

Sterling silver. An alloy of 92-1/2% pure silver and 7-1/2% copper.

Stoneware. A vitrified ceramic material, usually a silicate clay that is very hard, heavy and impervious to liquids and most stains.

Suspended. Not currently available from the producer — production has ceased but may be resumed at a later date.

Temper. Process used to increase the strength of glass by reheating it after it is formed and then rapidly cooling it.

Terra cotta. A reddish earthenware or a general term for any fired clay.

Throwing. Forming clay manually by shaping it as it's rotated on a potter's wheel.

Tin glaze. The glaze on Delftware, Faience or Majolica. This material results in a heavy white and opaque surface after firing.

Transfer. See decal.

Translucency. Allowing light to shine through a non-transparent object. A positive quality of fine china or porcelain.

Triptych. A three-panel art piece, often of religious significance.

Underglaze. A decoration which is applied before the final glazing and firing of an item. Most often, such decorations are painted by hand.

Understamp. See bottomstamp.

Vinyl. A synthetic material developed with the special properties of color, durability and skin-like texture which is molded into collectible dolls.

Vitrification. The process by which ceramic artwork becomes vitrified or totally nonporous at high temperatures.

Collectible Inventory Record

Item Name: _____

Manufacturer's Name: _____ Artist's Name: _____

Series Name/Number: _____

Special Markings: _____

Year of Issue: _____ Edition Limit: _____

Purchase Price: _____ Date of Purchase: _____

Purchased From: _____

Address: _____ Phone: _____

Secondary Market Price: _____

Additional Information: _____

Item Name: _____

Manufacturer's Name: _____ Artist's Name: _____

Series Name/Number: _____

Special Markings: _____

Year of Issue: _____ Edition Limit: _____

Purchase Price: _____ Date of Purchase: _____

Purchased From: _____

Address: _____ Phone: _____

Secondary Market Price: _____

Additional Information: _____

Item Name: _____

Manufacturer's Name: _____ Artist's Name: _____

Series Name/Number: _____

Special Markings: _____

Year of Issue: _____ Edition Limit: _____

Purchase Price: _____ Date of Purchase: _____

Purchased From: _____

Address: _____ Phone: _____

Secondary Market Price: _____

Additional Information: _____

PRICE INDEX

Limited Edition

Figurines ✦ Architecture ✦ Plates/Plaques ✦ Dolls/Plush ✦ Boxes ✦ Ornaments
Nutcrackers ✦ Graphics ✦ Steins ✦ Bells

This index includes over 67,000 of the most widely traded limited editions in today's collectibles market. It is based on surveys and interviews with several hundred of the most experienced and informed limited edition dealers in the United States, as well as many independent market advisors. In some cases, dealers outside the U.S. are also consulted.

HOW TO USE THIS INDEX

Listings are set up using the following format:

Harbour Lights ❶

❷   ❸
Western Region — Harbour Lights

❹   ❺   ❻   ❼   ❽   ❾
1991   Coquille River OR-111   1138   1993   60.00 2270-2700

❶ Harbour Lights = Company Name

❷ Western Region = Series Name

❸ Harbour Lights = Artist's Name. In this case, the presence of the company name indicates that Harbour Lights staff artists created the piece. In some cases, a single artist's name may appear here. The word "Various" may also appear, meaning that several artists have created pieces within the series. The artist's name then appears after the title of the collectible. In some cases, the artist's name will be indicated after the series name "with exceptions noted." If no artist name is listed, company staff artists have created the piece.

❹ 1991 = Year of Issue

❺ Coquille River OR-111 = Title of the collectible. Many titles also include the model number for further identification purposes.

❻ 1138 = Edition Limit. This indicates that this collectible was produced in an edition limited to 1,138 pieces. The edition limit category generally refers to the number of items created with the same name and decoration. Edition limits may indicate a specific number (i.e. 10,000) or the number of firing days for plates (i.e. 100-day, the capacity of the manufacturer to produce collectibles during a given firing period). You may also see a term like "Retrd.," "Open," "Suspd.," "Annual," and "Yr. Iss." Refer to "Terms and Abbreviations" below for their meanings.

❼ 1993 = Year of Retirement. May also indicate the year the manufacturer ceased production of the collectible. If N/A appears in this column, it indicates the information is not available at this time, but research is continuing.
Note: In the plate section, the year of retirement may not be indicated because many plates are limited to firing days and not years.

❽ 60.00 = Original Issue Price in U.S. Dollars

❾ 2270-2700 = Current Quote Price listed may show a price or price range. Quotes are based on interviews with retailers across the country, who provide their actual sales transactions. Quotes have been rounded up to the nearest dollar. Quote may also reflect a price increase for pieces that are not retired or closed.

> A Special Note to Beanie Babies, Beatrix Potter, Boyds Bears, Cherished Teddies, Disney Classics, Goebel Miniatures, M.I. Hummel and Precious Moments Collectors: *These collectibles carry special marks which change according to production and/or year. The secondary market value for each piece may vary because of these distinctive markings. Our pricing reflects a range for all marks.*
> A Special Note to Hallmark Keepsake Ornament Collectors: *All quotes in this section are for ornaments in mint condition in their original box.*
> A Special Note to Department 56 Collectors: *Year of Introduction indicates the year in which the piece was designed, sculpted and copyrighted. It is possible these pieces may not be available to collectors until the following calendar year.*
> A Special Note to Annalee Doll Collectors: *Previous editions of this book have only reflected prices paid at Annalee auctions. In this edition, secondary market dealer prices are also reported. As a rule, auction prices are higher than secondary market dealer prices.*

TERMS AND ABBREVIATIONS

Annual = Issued once a year.
A/P = Artist Proof.
Closed = An item or series no longer in production.
G/P = Gallery Proof.
N/A = Not available at this time.
Numbrd. = Numbered series.
P/P = Publisher's Proof.

Open = Not limited by number or time, available until manufacturer stops production, "retires" or "closes" the item or series.
Retrd. = Retired.
R/E = Renaissance Proof.
S/N = Signed and Numbered.
S/O = Sold Out.
S/P = Studio Proof.

Set = Refers to two or more items issued together for a single price.
Suspd. = Suspended (not currently being produced: may be produced in the future).
Unkn. = Unknown.
Yr. Iss. = Year of issue (limited to a calendar year).
28-day, 10-day, etc. = Limited to this number of production (or firing) days, usually not consecutive.

Finding Your Way Through CIB's Price Index Is As Easy As 1, 2, 3!

1. Determine the category that your collectible falls into. CIB's Price Index is divided into 10 general categories that are organized alphabetically. They include: Architecture, Bells, Boxes, Dolls/Plush, Figurines, Graphics, Nutcrackers, Ornaments, Plates/Plaques and Steins. Hint: Figurines is by far our most extensive category. If the product you're looking for doesn't fit neatly into one of the other categories, chances are you'll find it in the Figurines section.

2. Locate your manufacturer. Manufacturers are listed alphabetically within each category.

3. Once you turn to the pages that contain information about the manufacturer you're looking for, you'll find that products are listed by line, and by series within each line, if applicable.

ARCHITECTURE

Boyds Collection Ltd.

The Bearly-Built Villages™ - The Boyds Collection

YEAR ISSUE	EDITION LIMIT	YEAR RETD.	ISSUE PRICE	*QUOTE U.S.$
2000 Bailey's Cozy Cottage - Boyds Town Village #2 19002	Retrd.	2000	24.00	24
2000 Boyds Bearly a School - Boyds Town Village #4 19004	Open		23.00	23
2000 The Chapel in the Woods - Boyds Town Village #3 19003	Open		24.00	24
2000 Edmund's Hideaway - Boyds Town Village #5 19005	Open		25.00	25
2000 Public Libeary - Boyds Town Village #6 19006	Retrd.	2000	24.00	24
2000 Ted E. Bear Shop - Boyds Town Village #1 19001	Open		24.00	24

Brandywine Collectibles

The Brandywine Neighborhood Association - M. Whiting

YEAR ISSUE	EDITION LIMIT	YEAR RETD.	ISSUE PRICE	*QUOTE U.S.$
1997 Moore House	Yr.Iss.	1997	Gift	N/A
1997 Manhassett House-Hometown	Yr.Iss.	1997	32.00	32
1997 Manhassett House-Country Lane	Yr.Iss.	1997	32.00	32
1998 Moore House	Yr.Iss.	1998	Gift	N/A
1998 Brandywine Shop-Hometown	Yr.Iss.	1998	32.00	32
1998 Brandywine Shop-Country Lane	Yr.Iss.	1998	32.00	32
1999 Country Interiors	Yr.Iss.	1999	Gift	N/A
1999 Marquette	Yr.Iss.	1999	25.00	25

Hometown I - M. Whiting

YEAR ISSUE	EDITION LIMIT	YEAR RETD.	ISSUE PRICE	*QUOTE U.S.$
1990 Barber Shop	Closed	1992	14.00	14
1990 General Store	Closed	1992	14.00	14
1990 School	Closed	1992	14.00	14
1990 Toy Store	Closed	1992	14.00	14

Hometown II - M. Whiting

YEAR ISSUE	EDITION LIMIT	YEAR RETD.	ISSUE PRICE	*QUOTE U.S.$
1991 Church	Closed	1993	14.00	14
1991 Dentist	Closed	1993	14.00	14
1991 Ice Cream Shop	Closed	1993	14.00	14
1991 Stitch-N-Sew	Closed	1993	14.00	14

Hometown III - M. Whiting

YEAR ISSUE	EDITION LIMIT	YEAR RETD.	ISSUE PRICE	*QUOTE U.S.$
1991 Basket Shop	Closed	1993	15.50	16
1991 Dairy	Closed	1993	15.50	16
1991 Firehouse	Closed	1993	15.50	16
1991 Library	Closed	1993	15.50	16

Hometown IV - M. Whiting

YEAR ISSUE	EDITION LIMIT	YEAR RETD.	ISSUE PRICE	*QUOTE U.S.$
1992 Bakery	Closed	1994	21.00	21
1992 Country Inn	Closed	1994	21.50	22
1992 Courthouse	Closed	1994	21.50	45
1992 Gas Station	Closed	1994	21.00	21

Hometown V - M. Whiting

YEAR ISSUE	EDITION LIMIT	YEAR RETD.	ISSUE PRICE	*QUOTE U.S.$
1992 Antiques Shop	Closed	1995	22.00	45
1992 Gift Shop	Closed	1995	22.00	45
1992 Pharmacy	Closed	1995	22.00	45
1992 Sporting Goods	Closed	1995	22.00	45
1992 Tea Room	Closed	1995	22.00	45

Hometown VI - M. Whiting

YEAR ISSUE	EDITION LIMIT	YEAR RETD.	ISSUE PRICE	*QUOTE U.S.$
1993 Church	Closed	1995	24.00	45
1993 Diner	Closed	1995	24.00	45
1993 General Store	Closed	1995	24.00	45
1993 School	Closed	1995	24.00	45
1993 Train Station	Closed	1995	24.00	45

Hometown VII - M. Whiting

YEAR ISSUE	EDITION LIMIT	YEAR RETD.	ISSUE PRICE	*QUOTE U.S.$
1993 Candy Shop	Closed	1996	24.00	24
1993 Dress Shop	Closed	1996	24.00	24
1993 Flower Shop	Closed	1996	24.00	24
1993 Pet Shop	Closed	1996	24.00	45
1993 Post Office	Closed	1996	24.00	45
1993 Quilt Shop	Closed	1996	24.00	24

Hometown VIII - M. Whiting

YEAR ISSUE	EDITION LIMIT	YEAR RETD.	ISSUE PRICE	*QUOTE U.S.$
1994 Barber Shop	Closed	1996	28.00	28
1994 Country Store	Closed	1996	28.00	45
1994 Fire Company	Closed	1996	28.00	45
1994 Professional Building	Closed	1996	28.00	45
1994 Sewing Shop	Closed	1996	26.00	26

Hometown IX - M. Whiting

YEAR ISSUE	EDITION LIMIT	YEAR RETD.	ISSUE PRICE	*QUOTE U.S.$
1994 Bed & Breakfast	Closed	1997	29.00	45
1994 Cafe/Deli	Closed	1997	29.00	30
1994 Hometown Bank	Closed	1997	29.00	30-45
1994 Hometown Gazette	Closed	1997	29.00	45
1994 Teddys & Toys	Closed	1997	29.00	45

Hometown X - M. Whiting

YEAR ISSUE	EDITION LIMIT	YEAR RETD.	ISSUE PRICE	*QUOTE U.S.$
1995 Brick Church	Closed	1997	29.00	30
1995 The Doll Shoppe	Closed	1997	29.00	30
1995 General Hospital	Closed	1997	29.00	45
1995 The Gift Box	Closed	1997	29.00	30-45
1995 Police Station	Closed	1997	29.00	45

Hometown XI - M. Whiting

YEAR ISSUE	EDITION LIMIT	YEAR RETD.	ISSUE PRICE	*QUOTE U.S.$
1995 Antiques	Closed	1998	29.00	36
1995 Church II	Closed	1998	29.00	36
1995 Grocer	Closed	1998	29.00	36
1995 Pharmacy	Closed	1998	29.00	36
1995 School II	Closed	1998	29.00	36

Hometown XII - M. Whiting

YEAR ISSUE	EDITION LIMIT	YEAR RETD.	ISSUE PRICE	*QUOTE U.S.$
1996 Bridal & Dress Shoppe	Closed	1998	29.00	36
1996 Five & Dime	Closed	1998	29.00	36
1996 Hometown Theater	Closed	1998	29.00	36
1996 Post Office	Closed	1998	29.00	36
1996 Travel Agency	Closed	1998	29.00	36

Hometown XIII - M. Whiting

YEAR ISSUE	EDITION LIMIT	YEAR RETD.	ISSUE PRICE	*QUOTE U.S.$
1996 Baby Shoppe	Closed	1998	29.00	36
1996 Beauty Shoppe	Closed	1998	29.00	36
1996 Gem Shoppe	Closed	1998	29.00	36
1996 House of Flowers	Closed	1998	29.00	36
1996 Robins & Roses	Closed	1998	29.00	36

Cast Art Industries

Dreamsicles Northern Lights Village - K. Haynes

YEAR ISSUE	EDITION LIMIT	YEAR RETD.	ISSUE PRICE	*QUOTE U.S.$
2000 Ice Castle-60135	Open		59.00	59
2000 The Ice Works-60134	Open		59.00	59
2000 Santa's Place-60131	Open		59.00	59
2000 Ski Lodge-60133	Open		55.00	55
2000 Snowed Inn-60132	Open		49.00	49

The Cat's Meow

Collector Club Gift - Houses - F. Jones

YEAR ISSUE	EDITION LIMIT	YEAR RETD.	ISSUE PRICE	*QUOTE U.S.$
1989 Betsy Ross House	Retrd.	1989	Gift	200
1990 Amelia Earhart	Retrd.	1990	Gift	100
1991 Limberlost Cabin	Retrd.	1991	Gift	50
1992 Abigail Adams Birthplace	Retrd.	1992	Gift	50
1993 Pearl S. Buck House	Retrd.	1993	Gift	10-50
1994 Lillian Gish	Retrd.	1994	Gift	7-30
1995 Eleanor Roosevelt	Retrd.	1995	Gift	11-25
1996 Mother's Day Church	Retrd.	1996	Gift	25
1997 Barbara Fritchie House	Retrd.	1997	Gift	12
1997 Playhouse	Retrd.	1997	Gift	12
1998 The Elizabeth Cady Stanton House	Retrd.	1998	Gift	12
1999 Mary McCloud Bethune	Retrd.	1999	Gift	12
2000 Whitehead Lighthouse	Yr.Iss.		Gift	N/A

Collector Club - Famous Authors - F. Jones

YEAR ISSUE	EDITION LIMIT	YEAR RETD.	ISSUE PRICE	*QUOTE U.S.$
1989 Harriet Beecher Stowe	Retrd.	1989	8.75	N/A
1989 Orchard House	Retrd.	1989	8.75	N/A
1989 Longfellow House	Retrd.	1989	8.75	N/A
1989 Herman Melville's Arrowhead	Retrd.	1989	8.75	N/A
1989 Set	Retrd.	1989	35.00	225-800

Collector Club - Great Inventors - F. Jones

YEAR ISSUE	EDITION LIMIT	YEAR RETD.	ISSUE PRICE	*QUOTE U.S.$
1990 Thomas Edison	Retrd.	1990	9.25	N/A
1990 Ford Motor Co.	Retrd.	1990	9.25	N/A
1990 Seth Thomas Clock Co.	Retrd.	1990	9.25	75
1990 Wright Cycle Co.	Retrd.	1990	9.25	50
1990 Set	Retrd.	1990	37.00	343-400

Collector Club - American Songwriters - F. Jones

YEAR ISSUE	EDITION LIMIT	YEAR RETD.	ISSUE PRICE	*QUOTE U.S.$
1991 Benjamin R. Hanby House	Retrd.	1991	9.25	N/A
1991 Anna Warner House	Retrd.	1991	9.25	N/A
1991 Stephen Foster Home	Retrd.	1991	9.25	22
1991 Oscar Hammerstein House	Retrd.	1991	9.25	22
1991 Set	Retrd.	1991	37.00	200-350

Collector Club - Signers of the Declaration - F. Jones

YEAR ISSUE	EDITION LIMIT	YEAR RETD.	ISSUE PRICE	*QUOTE U.S.$
1992 Josiah Bartlett Home	Retrd.	1992	9.75	N/A
1992 George Clymer Home	Retrd.	1992	9.75	N/A
1992 Stephen Hopkins Home	Retrd.	1992	9.75	N/A
1992 John Witherspoon Home	Retrd.	1992	9.75	N/A
1992 Set	Retrd.	1992	39.00	165

Collector Club -19th Century Master Builders - F. Jones

YEAR ISSUE	EDITION LIMIT	YEAR RETD.	ISSUE PRICE	*QUOTE U.S.$
1993 Henry Hobson Richardson	Retrd.	1993	10.25	25
1993 Samuel Sloan	Retrd.	1993	10.25	25
1993 Alexander Jackson Davis	Retrd.	1993	10.25	25
1993 Andrew Jackson Downing	Retrd.	1993	10.25	25
1993 Set	Retrd.	1993	41.00	60-100

Collector Club - Williamsburg Merchants - F. Jones

YEAR ISSUE	EDITION LIMIT	YEAR RETD.	ISSUE PRICE	*QUOTE U.S.$
1994 East Carlton Wigmaker	Retrd.	1994	11.15	12
1994 J. Geddy Silversmith	Retrd.	1994	11.15	12
1994 Craig Jeweler	Retrd.	1994	11.15	12
1994 M. Hunter Millinery	Retrd.	1994	11.15	12
1994 Set	Retrd.	1994	44.60	60-100

Collector Club - Mt. Rushmore Presidential Series - F. Jones

YEAR ISSUE	EDITION LIMIT	YEAR RETD.	ISSUE PRICE	*QUOTE U.S.$
1995 George Washington Birthplace	Retrd.	1995	12.00	12
1995 Metamora Courthouse	Retrd.	1995	12.00	12
1995 Theodore Roosevelt Birthplace	Retrd.	1995	12.00	12
1995 Tuckahoe Plantation	Retrd.	1995	12.00	12
1995 Set	Retrd.	1995	48.00	60-75

Collector Club - American Holiday Series - F. Jones

YEAR ISSUE	EDITION LIMIT	YEAR RETD.	ISSUE PRICE	*QUOTE U.S.$
1996 And to all a Goodnight	Retrd.	1996	11.00	12
1996 Boo to You	Retrd.	1996	11.00	12
1996 Easter's On Its Way	Retrd.	1996	11.00	12
1996 Let Freedom Ring	Retrd.	1996	11.00	45-85
1996 Set	Retrd.	1996	44.00	50-70

Collector Club - The Civil War Generals - F. Jones

YEAR ISSUE	EDITION LIMIT	YEAR RETD.	ISSUE PRICE	*QUOTE U.S.$
1997 Sherman Home	Retrd.	1997	12.00	12
1997 Jackson Home	Retrd.	1997	12.00	12
1997 Lee Memorial Chapel	Retrd.	1997	12.00	12
1997 Grant House	Retrd.	1997	12.00	12

Collector Club - F. Jones

YEAR ISSUE	EDITION LIMIT	YEAR RETD.	ISSUE PRICE	*QUOTE U.S.$
1998 Boots Motel (available 3/98)	Retrd.	1998	14.00	14
1998 3 Ghosts of Christmas (set/3) (available 7/98)	Retrd.	1998	20.00	20
1998 The Ingalls Family (available 11/98)	Retrd.	1998	7.00	7
1998 Club House Diner	Retrd.	1998	11.50	12-15

Collector Club - F. Jones

YEAR ISSUE	EDITION LIMIT	YEAR RETD.	ISSUE PRICE	*QUOTE U.S.$
1999 Molly Pitcher	Retrd.	1999	10.00	10-12
1999 Eagle Harbor Light	Retrd.	1999	15.00	15
1999 Currier & Ives Sled Ride	Retrd.	1999	12.00	12-15
1999 Village Jewelers	Retrd.	1999	12.00	12-15

Collector Club - F. Jones

YEAR ISSUE	EDITION LIMIT	YEAR RETD.	ISSUE PRICE	*QUOTE U.S.$
2000 Port Grace Lighthouse	Yr.Iss.		13.00	13
2000 A Sign - Port Grace	Yr.Iss.		11.00	11
2000 Port Grace Pilot	Yr.Iss.		15.00	15

Open House - F. Jones

YEAR ISSUE	EDITION LIMIT	YEAR RETD.	ISSUE PRICE	*QUOTE U.S.$
1998 Cat's Meow Diner	Retrd.	1998	12.00	12-17
1999 Hospice Tree	Retrd.	1999	14.00	14
2000 Humane Society Tree	Yr.Iss.		14.00	14

Black Heritage Series - F. Jones

YEAR ISSUE	EDITION LIMIT	YEAR RETD.	ISSUE PRICE	*QUOTE U.S.$
1994 Martin Luther King Birthplace	Retrd.	1994	8.00	15-50

Christmas 1983-Williamsburg - F. Jones

YEAR ISSUE	EDITION LIMIT	YEAR RETD.	ISSUE PRICE	*QUOTE U.S.$
1983 Christmas Church	Retrd.	1983	6.00	N/A
1983 Federal House	Retrd.	1983	6.00	N/A
1983 Garrison House	Retrd.	1983	6.00	N/A
1983 Georgian House	Retrd.	1983	6.00	450
1983 Set	Retrd.	1983	24.00	3500-4000

Christmas 1984-Nantucket - F. Jones

YEAR ISSUE	EDITION LIMIT	YEAR RETD.	ISSUE PRICE	*QUOTE U.S.$
1984 Christmas Shop	Retrd.	1984	6.50	N/A
1984 Powell House	Retrd.	1984	6.50	350
1984 Shaw House	Retrd.	1984	6.50	350
1984 Wintrop House	Retrd.	1984	6.50	250
1984 Set	Retrd.	1984	26.00	1600-1800

Christmas 1985-Ohio Western Reserve - F. Jones

YEAR ISSUE	EDITION LIMIT	YEAR RETD.	ISSUE PRICE	*QUOTE U.S.$
1985 Bellevue House	Retrd.	1985	7.00	175
1985 Gates Mills Church	Retrd.	1985	7.00	200
1985 Olmstead House	Retrd.	1985	7.00	137-175
1985 Western Reserve Academy	Retrd.	1985	7.00	137-175
1985 Set	Retrd.	1985	27.00	600-1500

Christmas 1986-Savannah - F. Jones

YEAR ISSUE	EDITION LIMIT	YEAR RETD.	ISSUE PRICE	*QUOTE U.S.$
1986 J.J. Dale Row House	Retrd.	1986	7.25	117-150
1986 Lafayette Square House	Retrd.	1986	7.25	140-150
1986 Liberty Inn	Retrd.	1986	7.25	88-200
1986 Simon Mirault Cottage	Retrd.	1986	7.25	117-200
1986 Set	Retrd.	1986	29.00	500-925

Christmas 1987-Maine - F. Jones

YEAR ISSUE	EDITION LIMIT	YEAR RETD.	ISSUE PRICE	*QUOTE U.S.$
1987 Cappy's Chowder House	Retrd.	1987	7.75	250
1987 Captain's House	Retrd.	1987	7.75	250
1987 Damariscotta Church	Retrd.	1987	7.75	85-250
1987 Portland Head Lighthouse	Retrd.	1987	7.75	150-450
1987 Set	Retrd.	1987	31.00	800-1050

Christmas 1988-Philadelphia - F. Jones

YEAR ISSUE	EDITION LIMIT	YEAR RETD.	ISSUE PRICE	*QUOTE U.S.$
1988 Elfreth's Alley	Retrd.	1988	7.75	150-200
1988 Graff House	Retrd.	1988	7.75	150-200
1988 The Head House	Retrd.	1988	7.75	150-200
1988 Hill-Physick-Keith House	Retrd.	1988	7.75	150-200
1988 Set	Retrd.	1988	31.00	125-520

Christmas 1989-In New England - F. Jones

YEAR ISSUE	EDITION LIMIT	YEAR RETD.	ISSUE PRICE	*QUOTE U.S.$
1989 Hunter House	Retrd.	1989	8.00	50-70
1989 The Old South Meeting House	Retrd.	1989	8.00	80-125
1989 Sheldon's Tavern	Retrd.	1989	8.00	125
1989 The Vermont Country Store	Retrd.	1989	8.00	80-125
1989 Set	Retrd.	1989	32.00	125-475

Christmas 1990-Colonial Virginia - F. Jones

YEAR ISSUE	EDITION LIMIT	YEAR RETD.	ISSUE PRICE	*QUOTE U.S.$
1990 Dulany House	Retrd.	1990	8.00	35-100
1990 Rising Sun Tavern	Retrd.	1990	8.00	70-100
1990 Shirley Plantation	Retrd.	1990	8.00	50-75
1990 St. John's Church	Retrd.	1990	8.00	100-150
1990 St. John's Church (blue)	Retrd.	1990	8.00	100-500
1990 Set	Retrd.	1990	32.00	175-775

Christmas 1991-Rocky Mountain - F. Jones

YEAR ISSUE	EDITION LIMIT	YEAR RETD.	ISSUE PRICE	*QUOTE U.S.$
1991 First Presbyterian Church	Retrd.	1991	8.20	9-30
1991 Tabor House	Retrd.	1991	8.20	55-75
1991 Western Hotel	Retrd.	1991	8.20	25-55
1991 Wheller-Stallard House	Retrd.	1991	8.20	25-55
1991 Set	Retrd.	1991	32.80	95-260

Christmas 1992-Hometown - F. Jones

YEAR ISSUE	EDITION LIMIT	YEAR RETD.	ISSUE PRICE	*QUOTE U.S.$
1992 August Imgard House	Retrd.	1992	8.50	9-50
1992 Howey House	Retrd.	1992	8.50	9-50
1992 Overholt House	Retrd.	1992	8.50	9-50
1992 Wayne Co. Courthouse	Retrd.	1992	8.50	9-40
1992 Set	Retrd.	1992	34.00	50-120

Christmas 1993-St. Charles - F. Jones

YEAR ISSUE	EDITION LIMIT	YEAR RETD.	ISSUE PRICE	*QUOTE U.S.$
1993 Lewis & Clark Center	Retrd.	1993	9.00	15-20
1993 Newbill-McElhiney House	Retrd.	1993	9.00	15-20
1993 St. Peter's Catholic Church	Retrd.	1993	9.00	15-20
1993 Stone Row	Retrd.	1993	9.00	15-20
1993 Set	Retrd.	1993	36.00	60-85

Christmas 1994-New Orleans Series - F. Jones

YEAR ISSUE	EDITION LIMIT	YEAR RETD.	ISSUE PRICE	*QUOTE U.S.$
1994 Beauregard-Keyes House	Retrd.	1994	10.00	14-20
1994 Gallier House	Retrd.	1994	10.00	10-15
1994 Hermann-Grima House	Retrd.	1994	10.00	14-20

*Quotes have been rounded up to nearest dollar

YEAR ISSUE	EDITION LIMIT	YEAR RETD.	ISSUE PRICE	*QUOTE U.S.$
1994 St. Patrick's Church	Retrd.	1994	10.00	10-50
1994 Set	Retrd.	1994	40.00	50-65

Christmas 1995-New York Series - F. Jones

YEAR ISSUE	EDITION LIMIT	YEAR RETD.	ISSUE PRICE	*QUOTE U.S.$
1995 Clement C. Moore House	Retrd.	1995	10.00	15
1995 Fraunces Taver	Retrd.	1995	10.00	15
1995 Fulton Market	Retrd.	1995	10.00	10-15
1995 St. Marks-In-the-Bowery	Retrd.	1995	10.00	15
1995 Set	Retrd.	1995	40.00	52-55

Christmas 1996-Atlanta Series - F. Jones

YEAR ISSUE	EDITION LIMIT	YEAR RETD.	ISSUE PRICE	*QUOTE U.S.$
1996 Callanwolde	Retrd.	1996	11.00	15
1996 First Baptist Church	Retrd.	1996	11.00	15
1996 Fox Theatre	Retrd.	1996	11.00	15
1996 Swan House	Retrd.	1996	11.00	15
1996 Set	Retrd.	1996	44.00	44-60

Christmas 1997-Stockbridge - F. Jones

YEAR ISSUE	EDITION LIMIT	YEAR RETD.	ISSUE PRICE	*QUOTE U.S.$
1997 Housatonic National Bank	Retrd.	1997	12.00	15
1997 Nejaimie's Stockbridge Shop	Retrd.	1997	12.00	15
1997 Town Offices	Retrd.	1997	12.00	15
1997 William's & Sons	Retrd.	1997	12.00	12-15

Christmas 1998-Dickens Christmas Carol Series - F. Jones

YEAR ISSUE	EDITION LIMIT	YEAR RETD.	ISSUE PRICE	*QUOTE U.S.$
1998 The Crachit's House	Retrd.	1998	12.00	12
1998 Fezziwig's Warehouse	Retrd.	1998	12.00	12
1998 Scrooge & Marley	Retrd.	1998	12.00	12
1998 Scrooge's Flat	Retrd.	1998	12.00	12

Christmas 1999-Annapolis Series - F. Jones

YEAR ISSUE	EDITION LIMIT	YEAR RETD.	ISSUE PRICE	*QUOTE U.S.$
1999 Chase-Lloyd House	Retrd.	1999	12.00	12
1999 Maryland Inn	Retrd.	1999	12.00	12
1999 St. Anne's Church	Retrd.	1999	12.00	12
1999 Thomas Point Light	Retrd.	1999	12.00	12

Christmas 2000-San Francisco Series - F. Jones

YEAR ISSUE	EDITION LIMIT	YEAR RETD.	ISSUE PRICE	*QUOTE U.S.$
2000 Saint Mary's Cathedral	Yr.Iss.		12.00	12
2000 Sea Lions with Christmas Bows	Yr.Iss.		7.50	8
2000 Spencer House Bed & Breakfast	Yr.Iss.		12.00	12
2000 Spreckels Mansion	Yr.Iss.		12.00	12
2000 Union Street Boutique	Yr.Iss.		12.00	12

Limited Edition Promotional Items - F. Jones

YEAR ISSUE	EDITION LIMIT	YEAR RETD.	ISSUE PRICE	*QUOTE U.S.$
1998 Black Cat Alley	Retrd.	1998	12.00	12
1993 Convention Museum	Retrd.	1993	12.95	13
1993 FJ Factory	Open		12.95	13
1994 FJ Factory/5 Yr. Banner	Retrd.	1994	10.00	16-18
1993 FJ Factory/Gold Cat Edition	Retrd.	1993	12.95	490
1994 FJ Factory/Home Banner	Retrd.	1994	10.00	10
1990 Frycrest Farm Homestead	Retrd.	1991	10.00	125
1992 Glen Pine	Retrd.	1993	10.00	16
1998 Goblins & Giggles	Retrd.	1998	12.00	15
1993 Nativity Cat on the Fence	Retrd.	1993	19.95	30
1998 Two Brothers Statue	Retrd.	1998	9.00	9

Cavanagh Group Intl.

Coca-Cola Brand North Pole Bottling Works - CGI

YEAR ISSUE	EDITION LIMIT	YEAR RETD.	ISSUE PRICE	*QUOTE U.S.$
1995 All in a Day's Work	Closed	1997	25.00	25-30
1996 Art Department	Closed	1997	50.00	50-55
1996 An Artist's Touch	Closed	1997	25.00	25-30
1996 Big Ambitions	Closed	1997	25.00	25-30
1995 Checking His List	Closed	1997	30.00	30
1996 Delivery for Mrs. Claus	Closed	1997	25.00	25-30
1996 Elf in Training	Closed	1997	25.00	25-35
1995 An Elf's Favorite Chore	Closed	1997	30.00	30-50
1995 Filling Operations	Closed	1997	45.00	50-55
1995 Front Office	Closed	1997	50.00	50-60
1995 The Kitchen Corner	Closed	1997	55.00	35-55
1995 Maintenance Mischief	Closed	1997	25.00	25-35
1995 Making the Secret Syrup	Closed	1997	30.00	30-35
1996 Oops!	Closed	1997	25.00	25-30
1996 Order Department	Closed	1997	55.00	50-60
1996 Precious Cargo	Closed	1997	25.00	25-30
1995 Quality Control	Closed	1997	25.00	30-35
1996 Shipping Department	Closed	1997	55.00	50-60
1996 Special Delivery	Closed	1997	25.00	25-30
1996 A Stroke of Genius	Closed	1997	25.00	25-30
1995 Top Secret	Closed	1997	30.00	30-35

Coca-Cola Brand Town Square Collection - CGI

YEAR ISSUE	EDITION LIMIT	YEAR RETD.	ISSUE PRICE	*QUOTE U.S.$
1995 Barber Shop (House of Lloyd Exclusive)	10,000	1995	25.00	55-120
2000 Broad Street Café	Yr.Iss.		35.00	35
1999 Bus Station	Closed	1999	40.00	40
1994 Café (House of Lloyd Exclusive)	5,000	1994	25.00	80-120
1992 Candler's Drugs	Closed	1993	40.00	110-120
1996 Carlson's General Store	Closed	1997	40.00	90
1997 Central High	Closed	1997	40.00	75-80
1996 Chandler's Ski Resort	Closed	1997	40.00	50-70
2000 Chinese Restaurant	Yr.Iss.		35.00	35
1993 City Hall	Closed	1994	40.00	150-180
1996 Clara's Christmas Shop	Closed	1996	40.00	95-150
1995 Coca-Cola Bottling Works	Closed	1995	40.00	80-95
1993 Coca-Cola Pharmacy (House of Lloyd Exclusive)	25,000	1993	25.00	90-120
1996 Cooper's Tree Farm	Closed	1997	20.00	35-80
1992 Dee's Boarding House	Closed	1993	40.00	600-700
1997 Dew Drop Inn	Closed	1998	40.00	50
1996 Diamond Service Station	Closed	1996	40.00	175-200
1992 Dick's Luncheonette	Closed	1993	40.00	100-120
2000 Eckerd Drugs, 2nd Ed. (Exclusive)	Yr.Iss.		25.00	25
1999 Eckerd Drugstore (Eckerd's Exclusive)	Closed	1999	40.00	40
1994 Flying "A" Service Station	Closed	1996	40.00	90-100
1992 Gilbert's Grocery	Closed	1993	40.00	160-165
1995 Grist Mill	Closed	1995	40.00	65-90
1992 Howard Oil	Closed	1993	40.00	150-175
1999 Jack's Boats 'N Bait	Closed	1999	40.00	36-40
1993 Jacob's Pharmacy	5,000	1993	25.00	750-850
1995 Jenny's Sweet Shoppe	Closed	1995	40.00	65-80
1998 Joe's Diner	Closed	1999	40.00	40-60
1999 Jordan Drugs	Closed	1999	40.00	36-40
2000 Lighthouse Gift Shop	Yr.Iss.		35.00	35
1995 Lighthouse Point Snack Bar	Closed	1996	40.00	60-70
2000 Mary's Music/Laundry	Yr.Iss.		35.00	35
1994 McMahon's General Store	Closed	1995	40.00	60
1998 Moe's Café & Grill	Closed	1998	40.00	50
1993 Mooney's Antique Barn	Closed	1994	40.00	125-150
1997 Mrs. Murphy's Chowder House	Closed	1998	40.00	42-50
2000 Newstand	Yr.Iss.		30.00	30
2000 Original Publix Grocery (Exclusive)	Yr.Iss.		25.00	25
2000 Pet Store	Yr.Iss.		35.00	35
1994 Plaza Drugs	Closed	1995	20.00	75
1999 Polar Palace	Closed	1999	40.00	36-40
1993 Route 93 Covered Bridge	Closed	1995	20.00	55-75
1996 Scooter's Drive In	Closed	1997	40.00	40-60
1999 Sleepytime Motel	Closed	1999	40.00	40-60
1999 Sleigh Rides	Closed	1999	29.00	29-34
1997 South Station	Closed	1998	40.00	42-60
1998 Speedy Burger	Closed	1998	40.00	40-55
1998 Star Drive-In	Closed	1998	40.00	40-55
1998 State Theater	Closed	1998	40.00	40-55
1994 Station #14 Firehouse	Closed	1996	40.00	75
1994 Strand Theatre	Closed	1996	40.00	65-70
1993 T. Taylor's Emporium	Closed	1994	40.00	75
1993 The Tick Tock Diner	Closed	1995	40.00	65-70
1998 Tommy's Service Station	Closed	1999	40.00	40-42
1997 Tony's Pizza (Target Exclusive)	Closed	1998	40.00	60
1996 Town Barber Shop	Closed	1997	40.00	45-60
1994 Town Gazebo	Closed	1995	20.00	65-100
1992 Train Depot	Closed	1993	40.00	300
1993 Trolley (House of Lloyd Exclusive)	Closed	1993	N/A	30-100
1997 Variety Store	Closed	1997	40.00	45-70
1996 Walton's 5 & 10	Closed	1997	40.00	80
1997 Wiley's Hardware	Closed	1997	40.00	70

Coca-Cola Brand Town Square Collection Accessories - CGI

YEAR ISSUE	EDITION LIMIT	YEAR RETD.	ISSUE PRICE	*QUOTE U.S.$
1992 Ad Car "Coca-Cola"	Closed	1993	9.00	30
1992 After Skating	Closed	1993	8.00	16-25
1998 Airplane Ads (motion)	Closed	1999	36.50	37-65
1997 Angela	Closed	1997	8.00	16-20
1998 Bandstand	Closed	1998	30.00	35-60
1996 Billboard (large)	Closed	1997	15.00	15-40
1999 Boy Fishing	Closed	1999	12.00	12-30
1995 Boys with Snowballs	Closed	1996	11.00	20-28
1992 Bringing It Home	Closed	1993	8.00	18-25
1999 Bus	Closed	1999	11.00	11-15
1999 Bus Driver at Vending Machine	Closed	1999	11.00	11-15
2000 Cable Car on Track (Electronic)	Yr.Iss.		75.00	75
1994 Carolers	Closed	1996	9.00	13-20
1997 Charity Santa	Closed	1998	9.00	9-25
1994 Checker Players	Closed	1995	15.00	15-30
1993 Coca-Cola Park Bench	Open		7.00	7
1997 Conductor	Closed	1998	8.00	15
1995 Couple on Bench	Closed	1997	11.00	11-20
2000 Couple w/Take-Out Chinese	Yr.Iss.		12.00	12
1999 Couple Waiting	Closed	1999	11.00	11-15
1998 Couple with Vending Machine	Closed	1998	14.00	16-30
1996 Covertible	Closed	1996	9.00	15-40
1994 Crowley Cab Co.	Closed	1995	11.00	40
1992 Delivery Man	Closed	1993	8.00	23-25
2000 Delivery Truck	Yr.Iss.		14.00	14
1992 Delivery Truck "Coca-Cola"	Closed	1993	15.00	40
1996 Drive-In Girl	Closed	1997	7.00	10-30
1997 Elderly Couple on Bench	Closed	1997	15.00	15-30
1993 Extra! Extra!	Closed	1994	7.00	25
1997 Father/Son Cutting Tree	Closed	1998	15.00	15-30
1998 Fence Strips with Banner	Closed	1999	16.00	16-25
1998 Fence with Banner	Closed	1998	16.00	16-25
1998 Gas Station Attendent	Closed	1998	12.00	15-25
1992 Gil the Grocer	Closed	1993	8.00	20
2000 Girl w/Cat and Sled	Yr.Iss.		14.00	14
1993 Gone Fishing	Closed	1994	11.00	15-25
1994 Homeward Bound	Closed	1995	8.00	16-25
1999 Horse Pulling Sled	Closed	1999	14.00	15
1992 Horse-Drawn Wagon	Closed	1993	12.00	50
1997 Kids on Cooler	Closed	1998	15.00	17-25
1998 Kids Toasting Marshmellows	Closed	1998	12.00	15-30
1997 Last Minute Shoppers	Closed	1997	11.00	15-25
2000 Laundry Ladies	Yr.Iss.		12.00	12
1998 Lighted Café Sign	Closed	1998	14.00	15-25
1998 Lighted Diner Sign	Closed	1999	14.00	14-25
1995 Lunch Wagon	Closed	1995	15.00	20-30
1996 Mailbox	Closed	1996	7.00	9-30
1996 Mailman	Closed	1996	7.00	15-25
1998 Man with Shovel	Closed	1998	11.50	15-25
1993 Model "T" Truck w/ Barrels	Closed	1995	12.00	20
2000 Mom, Boy & Dog	Yr.Iss.		14.00	14
2000 Natural Wood Bench	Open		10.00	10
1993 Newsstand	Closed	1994	15.00	25
1993 Officer Pat	Closed	1995	7.00	25
1993 Old Number Seven	Closed	1995	15.00	25-30
1997 Pizza Delivery Man	Closed	1997	16.00	16-25
1997 Pizza Delivery Truck	Closed	1997	16.00	20-30
1998 Popcorn Vendor	Closed	1998	7.00	20-30
1996 Proprietor	Closed	1997	7.00	11-25
2000 Red Coca-Cola Cases	Open		12.00	12
1997 Red Delivery Truck	Closed	1998	16.00	15-25
1999 Sea Captain and Boy	Closed	1999	14.00	15
2000 Shoppers at Vending Machine	Yr.Iss.		14.00	14
1995 Skiers From Ad	Closed	1995	8.00	13-25
1994 Sledders	Closed	1995	11.00	14-25
1994 Sleigh Ride	Closed	1995	15.00	25
1997 Snow Day Fun	Closed	1997	8.00	9-25
1994 Snowbear	Closed	1995	8.00	12-25
1993 Soda Jerk	Closed	1995	7.00	20-25
1994 Sparky and the Fireman	Closed	1996	10.00	17-25
1994 Special Delivery	Closed	1995	9.00	16-25
1999 Station Wagon	Closed	1999	11.00	11-15
1993 Street Vendor	Closed	1994	11.00	25
1996 Telephone Booth	Closed	1996	15.00	35-40
1996 Thermometer	Closed	1998	12.00	15-25
1992 Thirsty the Snowman	Closed	1993	9.00	25-30
1998 Toboggan Sledders	Closed	1998	12.00	12-17
1998 Town Clock Tower with Clock	Closed	1999	29.00	29
2000 Tuba Player	Yr.Iss.		12.00	12
1994 W.J. Davis Delivery Truck	Closed	1996	12.00	20-25
1998 Waitress on Roller Skates	Closed	1999	7.00	7
1997 Yellow Delivery Truck	Closed	1997	16.00	20-28

Jerry Berta's Neon America Collection - J. Berta

YEAR ISSUE	EDITION LIMIT	YEAR RETD.	ISSUE PRICE	*QUOTE U.S.$
1999 Big Fish Diner	5,000		225.00	225
1998 Blue Diner	5,000		175.00	175
1998 The Diner	5,000	1999	200.00	200
1999 Diner Cookie Jar	5,000		40.00	40
1999 Red Hot Chili Diner	5,000		225.00	225
1998 Rosie's Diner	3,000		250.00	250
1999 Rosie's Salt & Pepper	Open		20.00	20
1999 Salt & Pepper	Open		20.00	20
1998 Star Theater	5,000		175.00	175
1999 Teapot	Open		40.00	40
1998 Teapot Diner	5,000		200.00	200

Charming Tails/Fitz and Floyd Collectibles

Charming Tails Squashville Lighted Village - D. Griff

YEAR ISSUE	EDITION LIMIT	YEAR RETD.	ISSUE PRICE	*QUOTE U.S.$
1994 Acorn Street Lamp 87/948	Closed	1997	5.00	6-20
1995 Butternut Squash Dairy 87/562	7,500	1995	45.00	45-144
1996 Candy Apple Candy Store 87/611	9,000	1997	45.00	48-113
1996 Cantaloupe Cathedral 87/597	Closed	1997	45.00	48-125
1995 Carrot Post Office 87/583	Closed	1996	45.00	45-125
1994 Chestnut Chapel 87/521	Closed	1996	45.00	45-125
1995 Great Oak Town Hall 87/584	Closed	1997	45.00	48-100
1994 Leaf Fence 87/947	Closed	1997	6.00	6-25
1995 Mail Box, Bench 87/560	Closed	1995	11.00	12-35
1995 Mushroom Depot 87/563	Closed	1997	45.00	48-107
1994 Old Cob Mill 87/524	7,500	1997	45.00	63-157
1994 Pumpkin Inn 87/522	Closed	1997	45.00	48-119
1995 Street Light/Sign 87/561	Closed	1997	11.00	12-30
1994 Village Sign 87/533	Closed	2000	30.00	25-42

Cherished Teddies/Enesco Group, Inc.

Our Cherished Neighbearhood - P. Hillman

YEAR ISSUE	EDITION LIMIT	YEAR RETD.	ISSUE PRICE	*QUOTE U.S.$
1998 Christmas Decorated House 352667	Closed	1999	20.00	20
1998 Winter Church 352659	Closed	1999	20.00	20
1998 Winter Post Office 352675	Closed	1999	20.00	20
1998 Winter Train Depot 352683	Closed	1999	20.00	20

Dave Grossman Creations

Spencer Collin Lighthouses Collector Club - C. Spencer Collin

YEAR ISSUE	EDITION LIMIT	YEAR RETD.	ISSUE PRICE	*QUOTE U.S.$
1997 Portsmouth Harbor, NH	Yr.Iss.	1997	40.00	40
1997 Membership Lighthouse	Yr.Iss.	1997	Gift	N/A
1998 Willy & Svea Charting a New Course CSC-CP2	Yr.Iss.	1998	Gift	N/A
1998 Old Alcatraz Lighthouse	Yr.Iss.	1998	40.00	40
1999 Old Presque Isle Light	Yr.Iss.	1999	Gift	N/A
1999 San Francisco Lightship	Yr.Iss.	1999	30.00	40
2000 Millennium's Dawn	Yr.Iss.		25.00	25

Spencer Collin Special Event - C. Spencer Collin

YEAR ISSUE	EDITION LIMIT	YEAR RETD.	ISSUE PRICE	*QUOTE U.S.$
1999 Rose Cottage	Yr.Iss.	1999	30.00	50

Spencer Collin-Admiral's Flag Quarters Series - C. Spencer Collin

YEAR ISSUE	EDITION LIMIT	YEAR RETD.	ISSUE PRICE	*QUOTE U.S.$
1996 Alki Point Light, VA 748G	5,000	2000	74.00	74
1994 Alki Point Light, VA 748M	3,000	1996	74.00	70-74
1996 Diamond Head Light, CT 749G	5,000	2000	130.00	130
1994 Diamond Head Light, CT 749M	3,000	1996	130.00	124-130
1996 Hospital Point Light, MA 750G	5,000	2000	71.00	71
1994 Hospital Point Light, MA 750M	3,000	1996	71.00	68-71
1996 Yerba Buena Light, CA 747G	5,000	2000	101.00	101
1994 Yerba Buena Light, CA 747M	3,000	1996	101.00	96-101

Spencer Collin-Commemorative Series - C. Spencer Collin

YEAR ISSUE	EDITION LIMIT	YEAR RETD.	ISSUE PRICE	*QUOTE U.S.$
1996 Admirality Head, WA 720G	2,400	1997	118.00	118
1990 Admirality Head, WA 720M	1,500	1996	98.00	110
1996 American Shoals, FL 722G	2,400	1997	97.00	97
1990 American Shoals, FL 722M	1,500	1996	90.00	93-97
1990 Cape Hatteras, NC 718M	1,500	1994	70.00	70-112
1996 Sandy Hook Light, NJ 721G	2,400	2000	95.00	95
1990 Sandy Hook Light, NJ 721M	1,500	1996	84.00	90-120
1996 West Quoddy Light, ME 719G	2,400	2000	107.00	107
1990 West Quoddy Light, ME 719M	1,500	1996	95.00	102-107

*Quotes have been rounded up to nearest dollar

Spencer Collin-Gold Label Signature Series - C. Spencer Collin

YEAR ISSUE	EDITION LIMIT	YEAR RETD.	ISSUE PRICE	*QUOTE U.S.$
1998 Absecon, NJ (signed/gold label) 776	500		90.00	90
1998 Absecon, NJ 776	1,900		90.00	90
1998 Boon Island, ME (signed/gold label) 775	500	2000	85.00	85
1998 Boon Island, ME 775	1,900	2000	85.00	85
1998 Hillsboro Inlet, FL (signed/gold label) 774	500	2000	80.00	80
1998 Hillsboro Inlet, FL 774	1,900	2000	80.00	80
1997 Holland Light, MI (signed/gold label) 766	500	1998	70.00	70
1997 Holland Light, MI 766	1,900		70.00	70
1997 Lightship Nantucket (signed/gold label) 767	500	1997	120.00	120
1997 Lightship Nantucket 767	1,900		120.00	120
1997 Mukiteo, WA 772	1,900		55.00	55
1997 Mukiteo, WA (signed/gold label) 772	500		55.00	55
1997 New Dungeness, WA (signed/gold label) 765	500	1998	70.00	70
1997 New Dungeness, WA 765	1,900		70.00	70
1997 Piedras Blancas, CA (signed/gold label) 770	500	2000	75.00	75
1997 Piedras Blancas, CA 770	1,900	2000	75.00	75
1998 S.F. Lightship (signed/gold label) 773	500	2000	120.00	120
1998 S.F. Lightship 773	1,900	2000	120.00	120
1997 San Luis Obispo, CA (signed/gold label) 771	500		90.00	90
1997 San Luis Obispo, CA 771	1,900		90.00	90
1997 Twin Lights, NJ (signed/gold label) 769	500		120.00	120
1997 Twin Lights, NJ 769	1,900		120.00	120

Spencer Collin-The Guardian Lights - C. Spencer Collin

YEAR ISSUE	EDITION LIMIT	YEAR RETD.	ISSUE PRICE	*QUOTE U.S.$
2000 Alcatraz LUC-2	Open		30.00	30
2000 Barnegat LUC-7	Open		30.00	30
2000 Block Island LUC-3	Open		30.00	30
2000 Cape Hatteras LUC-1	Open		30.00	30
2000 Cape Neddick LUC-12	Open		30.00	30
2000 Marblehead LUC-11	Open		30.00	30
2000 Montauk Point LUC-5	Open		30.00	30
2000 Portland Head LUC-4	Open		30.00	30
2000 Split Rock LUC-8	Open		30.00	30
2000 St. Augustine's LUC-9	Open		30.00	30
2000 Thomas Point LUC-10	Open		30.00	30
2000 White Shoals LUC-6	Open		30.00	30

Spencer Collin-Lighthouses - C. Spencer Collin

YEAR ISSUE	EDITION LIMIT	YEAR RETD.	ISSUE PRICE	*QUOTE U.S.$
1996 10th Year Anniversary 751G	2,400		100.00	100
1994 10th Year Anniversary 751M	Retrd.	1994	100.00	100
1996 Annisquam Harbor Light, MA 742G	2,400		50.00	50
1993 Annisquam Harbor Light, MA 742M	2,000	1996	45.00	48-50
1996 Assateague Light, VA 727G	2,400		76.00	76
1991 Assateague Light, VA 727M	Retrd.	1996	69.00	72-76
1996 Barnegat Light, NJ 723G	2,400	1998	71.00	71
1990 Barnegat Light, NJ 723M	Retrd.	1996	71.00	68-71
1996 Bass Harbor Light, ME 715G	2,400		103.00	103
1989 Bass Harbor Light, ME 715M	Retrd.	1996	95.00	98-103
1998 Boston Harbor Light, MA 710G	2,400		61.00	61
1996 Boston Harbor Light, MA 710G	2,400		61.00	61
1987 Boston Harbor Light, MA 710M	Retrd.	1996	45.00	58-61
1985 Brant Point Lighthouse, MA 703M	Retrd.	1996	75.00	75
1996 Cape Hatteras Lighthouse, NC 802G	2,400	1998	118.00	112-118
1995 Cape Hatteras Lighthouse, NC 802M	Retrd.	1996	118.00	101-175
1996 Cape May Light, NJ 738G	2,400	2000	88.00	88
1992 Cape May Light, NJ 738M	Retrd.	1996	79.00	84
1996 Cape Neddick "Nubble" Light, ME 709G	2,400	1998	95.00	95
1987 Cape Neddick "Nubble" Light, ME 709M	Retrd.	1996	80.00	90-95
1996 Castle Hill Light, RI 716	2,400	1999	30.00	30
1996 Castle Hill Light, RI 716G	2,400	2000	32.00	32
1990 Castle Hill Light, RI 716M	Retrd.	1996	22.00	30-32
1985 Chatham Light, MA 706M	Retrd.	1996	68.00	80
1998 Chatham Light, MA 781	2,400	2000	80.00	80
1996 Christmas Eve Light 760G	2,400	1997	86.00	86
1995 Christmas Eve Light 760M	Retrd.	1996	86.00	82-86
1996 Concord Point Light, MD 761G	2,400	2000	60.00	60
1995 Concord Point Light, MD 761M	2,000	1996	60.00	54-60
1996 Curtis Island Light, ME 734G	2,400		44.00	44
1992 Curtis Island Light, ME 734M	Retrd.	1996	40.00	44
1996 Edgartown Light, MA 801G	2,400	2000	48.00	48
1994 Edgartown Light, MA 801M	Retrd.	1996	48.00	48
1985 Edgartown, MA (1st ed.) 705M	Retrd.	1996	24.00	24
1996 Eggrock Light, ME 731G	2,400	1997	99.00	99
1992 Eggrock Light, ME 731M	Retrd.	1996	91.00	94-99
1996 Fire Island Light, NY 732G	2,400		122.00	122
1992 Fire Island Light, NY 732M	Retrd.	1996	114.00	116-122
1996 Fort Gratiot Light, MI 746G	2,400		57.00	57
1994 Fort Gratiot Light, MI 746M	2,000	1996	54.00	54-57
1996 Goat Island Light, ME 763G	2,400		50.00	50
1995 Goat Island Light, ME 763M	2,000	1996	50.00	50
1996 Great Point Light, MA 717	2,400	2000	38.00	38
1990 Great Point Light, MA 717M	Retrd.	1996	36.00	38-40
1996 Heceta Head Light, OR 753G	2,400	2000	155.00	155
1994 Heceta Head Light, OR 753M	2,000	1996	155.00	148-155
1996 Highland "Cape Cod" Light, MA 733G	2,400	1997	101.00	101
1992 Highland "Cape Cod" Light, MA 733M	Retrd.	1996	94.00	86-101
1996 Jeffrey's Hook Light, NY 735G	2,400	2000	50.00	50
1992 Jeffrey's Hook Light, NY 735M	Retrd.	1996	45.00	48-50
1996 Jupiter Inlet Light, FL 743G	2,400		88.00	88
1993 Jupiter Inlet Light, FL 743M	2,000	1996	82.00	84-88
1986 Kennebec River Light, ME 707M	Retrd.	1995	23.00	27
1995 Logo Light w/Flashing Beacon 755M	Retrd.	1995	116.00	116
1996 Logo Mini-Plaque 757G	Retrd.	2000	53.00	53
1995 Logo Mini-Plaque 757M	Retrd.	1996	53.00	53
1996 Marblehead Light, OH 724G	2,400	2000	46.00	46
1990 Marblehead Light, OH 724M	Retrd.	1996	36.00	44-46
1996 Marshall Point Light, ME 741G	2,400		50.00	50
1993 Marshall Point Light, ME 741M	2,000	1996	45.00	48-50
1996 Minots Ledge Light, MA 714G	2,400	2000	59.00	59
1989 Minots Ledge Light, MA 714M	Retrd.	1996	50.50	56-59
1996 Monhegan Island Light, ME 730G	2,400		50.00	50
1991 Monhegan Island Light, ME 730M	Retrd.	1996	44.00	48-50
1996 Montauk Point 711	2,400	1999	84.00	84
1996 Montauk Point Light, NY 711G	2,400	1999	88.00	88
1988 Montauk Point Light, NY 711M	Retrd.	1996	80.00	94
1996 Mystic Seaport Light, CT 728	2,400	1999	30.00	30
1996 Mystic Seaport Light, CT 728G	2,400	1999	32.00	30-32
1991 Mystic Seaport Light, CT 728M	Retrd.	1996	29.00	32-37
1986 Nauset Beach Light, MA 708M	Retrd.	1995	32.00	36-40
1996 New London Ledge Light, CT 745G	2,400	1998	126.00	126
1993 New London Ledge Light, CT 745M	2,000	1996	124.00	120-126
1996 Nobska Light, MA 729G	5,000	2000	40.00	40
1991 Nobska Light, MA 729M	Retrd.	1996	35.00	38-40
1996 Old Point Loma Light, CA 726G	2,400	2000	86.00	86
1991 Old Point Loma Light, CA 726M	Retrd.	1996	80.00	82-86
1999 Old Scituate Light 779	2,400		70.00	70
1996 Peggy's Point Light, Nova Scotia 739G	2,400	1999	44.00	44
1993 Peggy's Point Light, Nova Scotia 739M	Retrd.	1996	38.00	42-44
1996 Pemaquid Bell House, ME 704G	2,400		29.00	29
1984 Pemaquid Bell House, ME 704M	Retrd.	1996	16.00	29
1996 Pemaquid Bell Light 704	2,400	N/A	28.00	28
1996 Personalized Lighthouse 712G	2,400		34.00	34
1988 Personalized Lighthouse 712M	Retrd.	1996	24.00	32-34
1999 Point Cabrillo Light 777	2,400		80.00	80
1996 Point Isabel, TX 752G	2,400		55.00	55
1994 Point Isabel, TX 752M	2,000	1996	55.00	52-55
1997 Polar Light	2,400		60.00	60
1996 Ponce Inlet Light, FL 744G	2,400	2000	90.00	90
1993 Ponce Inlet Light, FL 744M	2,000	1996	83.00	86-90
1996 Portland Head Light, ME 701G	2,400	1997	82.00	82
1984 Portland Head Light, ME 701M	Retrd.	1996	75.00	75
1984 Portsmouth Light, NH 702M	Retrd.	1994	16.00	16
1996 Rock of Ages Light, OH 725G	2,400	1997	63.00	63
1991 Rock of Ages Light, OH 725M	Retrd.	1996	58.00	54-63
1996 Round Island Light, MI 758G	2,400	2000	120.00	120
1995 Round Island Light, MI 758M	2,000	1996	120.00	114-120
1996 Rudolph's Light 759G	2,400	1997	68.00	68
1995 Rudolph's Light 759M	Retrd.	1996	68.00	64-68
1996 Sand Island Light, AL 740G	2,400	2000	71.00	71
1993 Sand Island Light, AL 740M	Retrd.	1996	65.00	68-71
1996 Split Rock Lighthouse, MI 737G	2,400		118.00	118
1992 Split Rock Lighthouse, MI 737M	Retrd.	1996	99.00	112-118
1996 St. Joseph's Pier Lights, MI 762G	2,400		114.00	114
1995 St. Joseph's Pier Lights, MI 762M	2,000	1996	114.00	108-114
1996 St. Simons Island Light, GA 736G	2,400		124.00	124
1992 St. Simons Island Light, GA 736M	Retrd.	1996	116.00	118-124
1996 Thomas Point Light, MD 754G	2,400		109.00	109
1995 Thomas Point Light, MD 754M	2,000	1996	109.00	104-109
1996 West Quoddy 719	2,400	1999	102.00	102
1996 Whaleback Light, NH 713	2,400	2000	36.00	36
1996 Whaleback Light, NH 713G	2,400	1999	38.00	38
1989 Whaleback Light, NH 713M	Retrd.	1996	30.00	36-38
1999 Whitefish Point Light 778	2,400		85.00	85
1995 Willie & Svea's Light 756M	Retrd.	1995	N/A	N/A

Spencer Collin-Lightships - C. Spencer Collin

YEAR ISSUE	EDITION LIMIT	YEAR RETD.	ISSUE PRICE	*QUOTE U.S.$
2000 Edmund Fitzgerald	500		75.00	75
1999 Huron Lightship CSC-780	2,400		120.00	120
1999 Mini Lightships, set/3 CSC-BSM	2,400		72.00	72
1998 Nantucket CSC-767	2,400	2000	120.00	120
1998 San Francisco CSC-773	2,400	2000	120.00	120

Spencer Collin-Lighted Lighthouses - C. Spencer Collin

YEAR ISSUE	EDITION LIMIT	YEAR RETD.	ISSUE PRICE	*QUOTE U.S.$
1997 Cape Neddick "Nubble", ME	Closed	1999	50.00	50
1997 Old Point Loma, CA	Closed	1999	50.00	50
1997 Split Rock Lighthouse, MN	Closed	1999	50.00	112

Spencer Collin-Mini Lighthouses - C. Spencer Collin

YEAR ISSUE	EDITION LIMIT	YEAR RETD.	ISSUE PRICE	*QUOTE U.S.$
1999 Barnegat	Open		25.00	25
1999 Boston Harbor	Open		25.00	25
1999 Chicago Harbor	Open		25.00	25
2000 Compass Rose - Point Arena	7,500		25.00	25
2000 Compass Rose - Portland Head	7,500		30.00	30
2000 Compass Rose - Race Point	7,500		30.00	30
1999 Hatteras	Open		30.00	30
1999 Heceta Head	Open		30.00	30
1999 Holland Harbor	Open		25.00	25
1999 Jupiter Inlet	Open		25.00	25
1999 Navesink Twin	Open		35.00	35
1999 Nubble	Open		25.00	25
1999 Old Pt. Loma	Open		25.00	25
1999 Portsmouth Harbor	Open		20.00	20
1999 Split Rock	Open		30.00	30

Spencer Collin-Musical Waterglobes - C. Spencer Collin

YEAR ISSUE	EDITION LIMIT	YEAR RETD.	ISSUE PRICE	*QUOTE U.S.$
1997 Cape Hatteras, NC CSCW-3	Closed	1999	50.00	50
1997 Cape May, NJ CSCW-6	Closed	1999	50.00	50
1997 Cape Neddick-"Nubble", ME CSCW-5	Closed	1999	50.00	50
1997 Hecata Head, OR CSCW-2	Closed	1999	50.00	50
1997 Split Rock, MN CSCW-1	Closed	1999	50.00	50
1997 Thomas Point Shoals, MD CSCW-4	Closed	1999	50.00	50

Spencer Collin-New England Collection - C. Spencer Collin

YEAR ISSUE	EDITION LIMIT	YEAR RETD.	ISSUE PRICE	*QUOTE U.S.$
1984 Historical Homes, set/10	Retrd.	1990	N/A	N/A
1984 Home Town, set/10	Retrd.	1990	200.00	200
1984 New England Cottages, set/10 w/base	Retrd.	1990	195.00	195
1984 New England Village, set/12 w/base	Retrd.	1990	227.00	227

Norman Rockwell Village - Rockwell-Inspired

YEAR ISSUE	EDITION LIMIT	YEAR RETD.	ISSUE PRICE	*QUOTE U.S.$
2000 Bake Shop NRV-3	7,500		20.00	20
2000 Barber Shop NRV-2	7,500		20.00	20
2000 Train Station NRV-1	7,500		20.00	20

David Winter Cottages/Enesco European Giftware Group

David Winter Collectors Guild Exclusives - D. Winter

YEAR ISSUE	EDITION LIMIT	YEAR RETD.	ISSUE PRICE	*QUOTE U.S.$
1987 Robin Hood's Hideaway	Closed	1987	54.00	275
1987 Queen Elizabeth Slept Here	Closed	1987	183.00	225
1988 Black Bess Inn	Closed	1988	60.00	85
1988 The Pavillion	Closed	1988	52.00	100
1988 Street Scene	Closed	1988	Gift	85
1989 Home Guard	Closed	1989	105.00	90
1989 Coal Shed	Closed	1989	112.00	100
1990 The Plucked Ducks	Closed	1990	Gift	50
1990 The Cobblers Cottage	Closed	1990	40.00	75
1990 The Pottery	Closed	1990	40.00	50
1991 Pershore Mill	Closed	1991	Gift	50
1991 Tomfool's Cottage	Closed	1991	100.00	50-100
1991 Will-O' The Wisp	Closed	1991	120.00	100-120
1992 Irish Water Mill	Closed	1992	Gift	45
1992 Patrick's Water Mill	Closed	1992	Gift	75
1992 Candlemaker's	Closed	1992	65.00	60
1992 Beekeeper's	Closed	1992	65.00	65
1993 On The River Bank	Closed	1993	Gift	45
1993 Thameside	Closed	1993	79.00	60-110
1993 Swan Upping Cottage	Closed	1993	69.00	60
1993 Plum Cottage (U.K. only/Guild Membership incentive piece)	Closed	1993	N/A	110-150
1994 15 Lawnside Road	Closed	1994	Gift	40-135
1994 While Away Cottage	Closed	1994	70.00	75-100
1994 Ashe Cottage	Closed	1994	62.00	90-120
1995 Buttercup Cottage	Closed	1995	60.00	70-140
1995 The Flowershop	Closed	1995	150.00	175-250
1995 Gardener's Cottage	Closed	1995	Gift	57-125
1996 Punch Stables	Closed	1996	150.00	150
1996 Plough Farmstead	Closed	1996	125.00	125
1996 Model Dairy	Closed	1996	Gift	30-35
1997 Abbots	Closed	1997	75.00	75
1997 Gameskeeper	Closed	1997	85.00	85
1997 Sextons	Closed	1997	Gift	65
1998 The Charcoal Burner's	Closed	1998	85.00	85
1998 The Coppicer's Cottage	Closed	1998	90.00	90
1998 Mistletoe Cottage	Closed	1998	Gift	40-76
1999 The Joinery	Closed	1999	95.00	95
1999 The Architect's	Closed	1999	95.00	95
1999 Tile Maker's Cottage	Closed	1999	Gift	45
2000 The Porter's Lodge	Yr.Iss.		90.00	90
2000 The Station Master's House	Yr.Iss.		90.00	90
2000 The Signal Box	Yr.Iss.		Gift	N/A

Painting Event Pieces - D. Winter

YEAR ISSUE	EDITION LIMIT	YEAR RETD.	ISSUE PRICE	*QUOTE U.S.$
1992 Birthstone Wishing Well	Closed	1992	40.00	65
1993 Birthday Cottage (Arches Thwonce)	Closed	1994	55.00	60
1994 Wishing Falls Cottage	Closed	1995	65.00	65
1995 Whisper Cottage	Closed	1995	65.00	100
1996 Primrose Cottage	Closed	1996	65.00	56

Appearance Piece - D. Winter

YEAR ISSUE	EDITION LIMIT	YEAR RETD.	ISSUE PRICE	*QUOTE U.S.$
1993 Arches Thrice	Closed	1993	150.00	90-150
1994 Winter Arch	Closed	1995	N/A	42-50
1995 Grumbleweed's Potting Shed	Closed	1995	99.00	140
1995 Grumbleweed's Potting Shed Colorway	Closed	1995	99.00	100
1996 The Derby Arms	Closed	1996	65.00	85
1997 Suffolk Gardens	Yr.Iss.	1997	60.00	60
1998 The Truffleman's	Yr.Iss.	1998	75.00	75
1999 The Stained Glass Studio	Yr.Iss.	1999	60.00	60
2000 The Guard's Van	Yr.Iss.		70.00	70

20th Anniversary - D. Winter

YEAR ISSUE	EDITION LIMIT	YEAR RETD.	ISSUE PRICE	*QUOTE U.S.$
1999 Bridgewater	Yr.Iss.	1999	190.00	190

At The Centre of the Village Collection - D. Winter

YEAR ISSUE	EDITION LIMIT	YEAR RETD.	ISSUE PRICE	*QUOTE U.S.$
1983 The Bakehouse	Closed	1996	31.40	40-125
1984 The Chapel	Closed	1992	48.80	50-100
1985 The Cooper Cottage	Closed	1993	57.90	75-80
1983 The Green Dragon Pub/ Inn	Closed	1996	31.40	39-78
1982 Ivy Cottage	Closed	1992	22.00	35
1980 Little Market	Closed	1993	28.90	40-60
1980 Market Street	Closed	1996	48.80	90
1984 Parsonage	Closed	1996	390.00	530-560
1980 Rose Cottage	Closed	1996	28.90	45-53
1984 Spinner's Cottage	Closed	1991	28.90	40-100
1982 The Village Shop	Closed	1996	22.00	30-50
1980 The Wine Merchant	Closed	1993	28.90	39-80

British Traditions - D. Winter

YEAR ISSUE	EDITION LIMIT	YEAR RETD.	ISSUE PRICE	*QUOTE U.S.$
1990 Blossom Cottage	Closed	1995	59.00	52-65
1990 The Boat House	Closed	1995	37.50	60-104
1990 Bull & Bush	Closed	1995	37.50	30-50
1990 Burns' Reading Room	Closed	1995	31.00	45-50
1990 Grouse Moor Lodge	Closed	1995	48.00	35-52
1990 Guy Fawkes	Closed	1995	31.00	30-50

*Quotes have been rounded up to nearest dollar

YEAR ISSUE	EDITION LIMIT	YEAR RETD.	ISSUE PRICE	*QUOTE U.S.$
1990 Harvest Barn	Closed	1995	31.00	40-60
1990 Knight's Castle	Closed	1995	59.00	85
1991 The Printers and The Bookbinders	Closed	1994	120.00	150-171
1990 Pudding Cottage	Closed	1995	78.00	50-110
1990 St. Anne's Well	Closed	1995	48.00	59-70
1990 Staffordshire Vicarage	Closed	1995	48.00	50-75
1990 Stonecutters Cottage	Closed	1995	48.00	46-72

Cameos - D. Winter

YEAR ISSUE	EDITION LIMIT	YEAR RETD.	ISSUE PRICE	*QUOTE U.S.$
1992 Barley Malt Kilns	Closed	1996	12.50	20
1992 Brooklet Bridge	Closed	1996	12.50	20
1992 Diorama-Bright	Closed	1996	50.00	50
1992 Diorama-Light	Closed	1992	30.00	30-50
1992 Greenwood Wagon	Closed	1996	12.50	20
1992 Lych Gate	Closed	1996	12.50	25-40
1992 Market Day	Closed	1996	12.50	20-25
1992 One Man Jail	Closed	1996	12.50	20
1992 Penny Wishing Well	Closed	1996	12.50	20
1992 The Potting Shed	Closed	1996	12.50	20-25
1992 Poultry Ark	Closed	1996	12.50	20
1992 The Privy	Closed	1996	12.50	20-30
1992 Saddle Steps	Closed	1996	12.50	20-30
1992 Welsh Pig Pen	Closed	1996	12.50	20

Carnival Premier Castles-England - D. Winter

YEAR ISSUE	EDITION LIMIT	YEAR RETD.	ISSUE PRICE	*QUOTE U.S.$
1993 Castle Cottage of Warwick	Closed	1993	160.00	525-575
1994 Kingmaker's Castle	Closed	1994	240.00	312-360
1995 Castle Tower of Windsor	Closed	1995	280.00	435
1996 Rochester Castle	Closed	1996	312.00	375-425
1997 Richard III Castle	Closed	1997	184.00	351-450
1999 Solent Fortress	Yr.Iss.	1999	200.00	475

Castle Collection - D. Winter

YEAR ISSUE	EDITION LIMIT	YEAR RETD.	ISSUE PRICE	*QUOTE U.S.$
1995 Bishopsgate	Closed	1996	175.00	149-175
1995 Bishopsgate Premier	Closed	1996	225.00	201-225
1994 Castle Wall	Closed	1996	65.00	75-90
1996 Christmas Castle	Closed	1996	160.00	160
1996 Guinevere's Castle	Closed	1996	299.00	248-400
1996 Guinevere's Castle Premier	Closed	1996	350.00	550-775
1994 Kingmaker's Castle (w/Ivy)	Closed	N/A	N/A	390-460
1996 Rochester Castle (without snow)	Closed	1996	312.00	160-325

Celebration Cottages - D. Winter

YEAR ISSUE	EDITION LIMIT	YEAR RETD.	ISSUE PRICE	*QUOTE U.S.$
1994 Celebration Chapel	Closed	1996	75.00	68-75
1994 Celebration Chapel Premier	Closed	1996	150.00	147-175
1995 Mother's Cottage	Closed	1996	65.00	65
1995 Mother's Cottage Premier	Closed	1996	89.50	82-90
1994 Spring Hollow	Closed	1996	65.00	59-65
1994 Spring Hollow Premier	Closed	1996	125.00	125-150
1995 Stork Cottage Boy	Closed	1996	65.00	52-65
1995 Stork Cottage Girl	Closed	1996	65.00	63
1994 Sweetheart Haven	Closed	1996	60.00	54-60
1994 Sweetheart Haven Premier	Closed	1996	115.00	115-120

Charitable Models - D. Winter

YEAR ISSUE	EDITION LIMIT	YEAR RETD.	ISSUE PRICE	*QUOTE U.S.$
1988 Jim'll Fixit-Wintershill	Closed	1988	350.00	2500-3000
1990 Cartwright's Cottage	Closed	1990	45.00	40-70

The Churches & Chapels of Britain Collection - D. Winter

YEAR ISSUE	EDITION LIMIT	YEAR RETD.	ISSUE PRICE	*QUOTE U.S.$
1999 The Church of the Good Shepherd	Open		110.00	110
1999 The Copse Chapel	Open		110.00	110
2000 St. Barbara's	Open		160.00	160
1998 St. Christopher's Church	Open		110.00	110
1998 Thornhill Chapel	Open		90.00	90

Crack The Code - D. Winter

YEAR ISSUE	EDITION LIMIT	YEAR RETD.	ISSUE PRICE	*QUOTE U.S.$
2000 The Assayer's Tower	Closed	2000	220.00	220

Dicken's Christmas - D. Winter

YEAR ISSUE	EDITION LIMIT	YEAR RETD.	ISSUE PRICE	*QUOTE U.S.$
1987 Ebenezer Scrooge's Counting House	Closed	1988	96.90	195-208
1988 Christmas in Scotland & Hogmanay	Closed	1988	100.00	75-100
1989 A Christmas Carol	Closed	1989	135.00	100-195
1990 Mr. Fezziwig's Emporium	Closed	1990	135.00	75-120
1991 Fred's Home: "A Merry Christmas, Uncle Ebenezer saids Scrooge's Nephew Fred, and a Happy New Year.	Closed	1991	145.00	85-150
1992 Scrooge's School	Closed	1992	160.00	113-190
1993 Old Joe's Beetling Shop, A Veritable Den of Iniquity!	Closed	1993	175.00	250-275
1994 Scrooge's Family Home	Closed	1994	175.00	149-175
1994 Scrooge's Family Home Premier	Closed	1994	230.00	230-280
1994 Scrooge's Family Home, Plaque	3,500	1994	125.00	33-80
1995 Miss Belle's Cottage	Closed	1995	185.00	99-130
1995 Miss Belle's Cottage Premier	2,200	1995	235.00	235-298
1995 Miss Belle's Christmas Plaque	4,000	1995	120.00	33-112
1996 Tiny Tim	Closed	1996	150.00	150-250
1996 Tiny Tim Premier	2,200	1996	180.00	180-298
1996 Tiny Tim Christmas Plaque	4,000	1996	110.00	104-150

The Eccentrics Collection - D. Winter

YEAR ISSUE	EDITION LIMIT	YEAR RETD.	ISSUE PRICE	*QUOTE U.S.$
2000 The Beachcombers	Open		110.00	110
2000 Guano Heights	Open		170.00	170
2000 Hornblowers	Open		100.00	100
2000 Knights Folly	Open		150.00	150
2000 The Recluses	Open		125.00	125
2000 The Treehouse	Open		110.00	110

English Village - D. Winter

YEAR ISSUE	EDITION LIMIT	YEAR RETD.	ISSUE PRICE	*QUOTE U.S.$
1994 Cat & Pipe Inn	Closed	1997	53.00	55-95
1994 Chandlery	Closed	1997	53.00	55
1994 Church & Vestry	Closed	1997	57.00	55
1994 Constabulary	Closed	1997	60.00	55-65
1994 Crystal Cottage	Closed	1997	53.00	55
1995 Engine House (brown door)	Closed	1997	55.00	55
1994 Engine House (Disney/red door)	Closed	1997	55.00	55
1994 Glebe Cottage	Closed	1997	53.00	55-65
1994 Guardian Castle	8,490	1994	275.00	275-400
1994 Guardian Castle Premier	1,500	1994	350.00	495-625
1994 The Hall	Closed	1997	55.00	55-63
1994 One Acre Cottage	Closed	1997	55.00	55-88
1994 The Post Office	Closed	1997	53.00	55-93
1994 The Quack's Cottage	Closed	1997	57.00	55-65
1994 The Rectory	Closed	1997	55.00	55
1994 The Seminary	Closed	1997	57.00	55-132
1994 The Smithy	Closed	1997	50.00	55
1994 The Tannery	Closed	1997	50.00	55

Forest of Dean Collection - D. Winter

YEAR ISSUE	EDITION LIMIT	YEAR RETD.	ISSUE PRICE	*QUOTE U.S.$
1996 Abbey Ruins	Closed	2000	55.00	55
1997 The Artist's Studio	Closed	2000	55.00	55
1996 The Citadel	Closed	2000	55.00	55
1999 The Firewatchers Tower	Closed	2000	55.00	55
1996 Forest of DEAN MINE	Closed	2000	55.00	55
1997 The Observatory	Closed	2000	55.00	55
1997 The Sawmill	Closed	2000	55.00	55

Garden Cottages of England - D. Winter

YEAR ISSUE	EDITION LIMIT	YEAR RETD.	ISSUE PRICE	*QUOTE U.S.$
1996 The Park	Closed	1996	275.00	275
1996 The Park, Premier	Closed	1996	299.50	300-475
1995 Spencer Hall Gardens	Closed	1996	395.00	395
1995 Spencer Hall Gardens, Premier	Closed	1996	495.00	484-495
1995 Willow Gardens	Closed	1995	225.00	288
1995 Willow Gardens, Premier	Closed	1995	299.00	299-340

The Haunted House Collection - D. Winter

YEAR ISSUE	EDITION LIMIT	YEAR RETD.	ISSUE PRICE	*QUOTE U.S.$
1999 Casterton Railway Station	Yr.Iss.	1999	190.00	190
1998 The House of Usher	Yr.Iss.	1998	175.00	175
2000 Phantom's Ruin	Closed	2000	200.00	200

Heart of England Series - D. Winter

YEAR ISSUE	EDITION LIMIT	YEAR RETD.	ISSUE PRICE	*QUOTE U.S.$
1985 The Apothecary Shop	Closed	1995	24.10	34-55
1985 Blackfriars Grange	Closed	1994	24.10	50
1985 Craftsmen's Cottage	Closed	1995	24.10	45
1985 The Hogs Head Tavern/Beer House	Closed	1995	24.10	35
1985 Meadowbank Cottages	Closed	1995	24.10	30
1985 The Schoolhouse	Closed	1995	24.10	25-30
1985 Shirehall	Closed	1995	24.10	35
1985 St. George's Church	Closed	1995	24.10	35-51
1985 The Vicarage	Closed	1995	24.10	51-117
1985 The Windmill	Closed	1995	37.50	38
1985 Yeoman's Farmhouse	Closed	1995	24.10	28-39

In The Country Collection - D. Winter

YEAR ISSUE	EDITION LIMIT	YEAR RETD.	ISSUE PRICE	*QUOTE U.S.$
1983 The Bothy	Closed	1996	31.40	45-94
1982 Brookside Hamlet	Closed	1991	74.80	32-45
1981 Drover's Cottage	Closed	1996	22.00	45-85
1983 Fisherman's Wharf	Closed	1996	31.40	30-97
1994 Guardian Gate	Closed	1996	150.00	98-129
1994 Guardian Gate Premier	Closed	1996	199.00	248-429
1987 John Benbow's Farmhouse	Closed	1993	78.00	80-115
1996 Lover's Tryst	Closed	1996	125.00	125-238
1983 Pilgrim's Rest	Closed	1993	48.80	59-94
1984 Snow Cottage	Closed	1992	24.80	65-100
1986 There was a Crooked House	Closed	1996	96.90	186-200
1996 There was a Narrow House	Closed	1996	115.00	115
1984 Tollkeeper's Cottage	Closed	1992	87.00	75-85

Irish Collection - D. Winter

YEAR ISSUE	EDITION LIMIT	YEAR RETD.	ISSUE PRICE	*QUOTE U.S.$
1992 Fogartys	Closed	1994	75.00	72-110
1992 Irish Round Tower	Closed	1996	65.00	56-65
1992 Murphys	Closed	1996	100.00	91
1992 O'Donovan's Castle	Closed	1996	145.00	170
1991 Only A Span Apart	Closed	1993	80.00	88-150
1991 Secret Shebeen	Closed	1993	70.00	60-100

The King Arthur Collection - D. Winter

YEAR ISSUE	EDITION LIMIT	YEAR RETD.	ISSUE PRICE	*QUOTE U.S.$
1999 Dagonet the Fool's	Open		50.00	50
2000 Mabon's House	Open		80.00	80
1999 Merlin's Castle	4,250		160.00	160
2000 Mordred's Cottage	Open		80.00	80
1999 Morgan Le Fay	Open		50.00	50
2000 Nimue's Tower	Open		50.00	50
2000 Sir Griflet's Hovel	Open		35.00	35
1999 Sir Perceval's	Open		50.00	50
1999 Sir Tristan's	Open		50.00	50

Landowners - D. Winter

YEAR ISSUE	EDITION LIMIT	YEAR RETD.	ISSUE PRICE	*QUOTE U.S.$
1984 Castle Gate	Closed	1992	155.00	176-270
1982 The Dower House	Closed	1993	22.00	25-35
1988 The Grange	Closed	1989	120.00	800-1100
1985 Squire Hall	Closed	1990	92.30	65-80
1981 Tudor Manor House	Closed	1992	48.80	60-120

Main Collection - D. Winter

YEAR ISSUE	EDITION LIMIT	YEAR RETD.	ISSUE PRICE	*QUOTE U.S.$
1983 The Alms Houses	Closed	1987	59.90	250-400
1992 Audrey's Tea Room	Closed	1992	90.00	60-99
1992 Audrey's Tea Shop	Closed	1992	90.00	165-510
1982 Blacksmith's Cottage	Closed	1986	22.00	200-473
1991 Castle in the Air	Closed	1996	675.00	450-750
1981 Castle Keep	Closed	1982	30.00	1400
1981 Chichester Cross	Closed	1981	50.00	3000-3200
1980 The Coaching Inn	Closed	1983	165.00	3600
1981 Cornish Cottage	Closed	1986	30.00	700
1983 Cornish Tin Mine	Closed	1989	22.00	40-50
1983 Cotton Mill	Closed	1989	41.30	250-360
1981 Double Oast	Closed	1982	60.00	3300
1980 Dove Cottage	Closed	1983	60.00	825-900
1982 Fairytale Castle	Closed	1989	115.00	175-240
1986 Falstaff's Manor	10,000	1990	242.00	223-360
1980 The Forge	Closed	1983	60.00	825-900
1999 Gallow's Gate	Closed	1999	55.00	55
1996 Golf Clubhouse	Closed	1996	160.00	160-275
1996 Haunted House	4,900	1996	325.00	600
1983 The Haybarn	Closed	1987	22.00	182-341
1997 Hereward the Wake's Castle	3,500	1997	175.00	175
1985 Hermit's Humble Home	Closed	1988	87.00	248-300
1993 Horatio Persnickety's Amorous Intent	9,900	1993	375.00	150-200
1984 House of the Master Mason	Closed	1988	74.80	165-200
1982 House on Top	Closed	1988	92.30	157-250
1991 Inglenook Cottage	Closed	1996	60.00	75-80
1980 Little Forge	Closed	1983	40.00	935-1680
1980 Little Mill	Closed	1980	40.00	750-950
1980 Little Mill-remodeled	Closed	1983	Unkn.	825-999
1992 Mad Baron Fourthrite's Folly	Closed	1992	275.00	125-175
1997 Milestone Cottage	Closed	1999	130.00	130
1980 Mill House	Closed	1980	50.00	2500
1980 Mill House-remodeled	Closed	1983	50.00	999-1250
1999 The Millennium at Horseshoe Bay	2,000	1999	850.00	850
1982 Miner's Cottage	Closed	1987	22.00	150-195
1991 Moonlight Haven	Closed	1996	120.00	104-155
1982 Moorland Cottage	Closed	1987	22.00	185-300
1995 Newtown Millhouse	Closed	1996	195.00	195
1981 The Old Curiosity Shop	Closed	1983	40.00	799-1300
1980 Provencal One (French Market Only)	Closed	N/A	N/A	N/A
1980 Provencal Two (French Market Only)	Closed	N/A	N/A	N/A
1980 Quayside	Closed	1985	60.00	799-1100
1994 Quindene Manor	3,000	1994	695.00	605-650
1994 Quindene Manor Premier	1,500	1994	850.00	782-1050
1982 Sabrina's Cottage	Closed	1982	30.00	1250-2000
1996 St. George & The Dragon	Closed	1996	150.00	127-150
1997 St. George & The Dragon (modified)	Open		150.00	150
1981 St. Paul's Cathedral	Closed	1982	40.00	825-999
1985 Suffolk House	Closed	1989	48.80	40-100
1980 Three Duck Inn	Closed	1983	60.00	699-1500
1998 Tom's Yard	5,000	2000	130.00	130
2000 Trainspotters	1,999	2000	55.00	55
2000 Treasures of Egypt	2,500		300.00	300
1981 Tythe Barn	Closed	1986	39.30	900-1452
1981 The Village	Closed	1996	362.00	495-585
1986 The Village-remodeled	Closed	N/A	580.00	580
1999 Watt's Cottage	Open		180.00	180
1991 The Weaver's Lodgings	Closed	1996	65.00	54-75
1995 Welcome Home Cottage	Closed	1995	99.00	135-145
1995 Welcome Home Cottage Military	Closed	1995	99.00	135
1999 Wellstead Cottage	Closed	1999	50.00	50
1982 William Shakespeare's Birthplace (lg)	Closed	1984	60.00	900-1573
1983 Woodcutter's Cottage	Closed	1988	87.00	175-250

Midlands Collection - D. Winter

YEAR ISSUE	EDITION LIMIT	YEAR RETD.	ISSUE PRICE	*QUOTE U.S.$
1988 Bottle Kilns	Closed	1991	78.00	72
1988 Coal Miner's Row	Closed	1996	90.00	90-120
1988 Derbyshire Cotton Mill	Closed	1994	65.00	55-70
1988 The Gunsmiths	Closed	1996	78.00	65-104
1988 Lacemaker's Cottage	Closed	1996	120.00	165
1988 Lock-keepers Cottage	Closed	1996	65.00	85

Millennium Special - D. Winter

YEAR ISSUE	EDITION LIMIT	YEAR RETD.	ISSUE PRICE	*QUOTE U.S.$
1999 The Millennium at Horseshoe Bay	Closed	1999	850.00	850

The Mystical Castles of Britain - D. Winter

YEAR ISSUE	EDITION LIMIT	YEAR RETD.	ISSUE PRICE	*QUOTE U.S.$
1999 The Astrologer's Castle	3,500		200.00	200
2000 Daresbury Castle	2,750		140.00	140
1998 Halidon Hill	Closed	2000	130.00	130
1998 Hotspur's Keep	Closed	2000	110.00	110
2000 Looking for George	Open		165.00	165
1998 Myton Tower	Closed	2000	130.00	130
1998 Witch's Castle	4,250		175.00	175

The Oliver Twist Christmas Collection - D. Winter

YEAR ISSUE	EDITION LIMIT	YEAR RETD.	ISSUE PRICE	*QUOTE U.S.$
1997 Mr. Bumble's	Closed	1997	110.00	110-249
1998 Mr. Fang The Magistrate's House	Closed	1998	110.00	110
1999 Bill & Nancy's House	Yr.Iss.	1999	130.00	130
2000 The Bottle'n Glass	Yr.Iss.		140.00	140

The Pilgrim's Way Collection - D. Winter

YEAR ISSUE	EDITION LIMIT	YEAR RETD.	ISSUE PRICE	*QUOTE U.S.$
1997 The Alchemist's Cottage	Closed	1999	50.00	50
1997 The Brickies	Closed	1999	50.00	50
1997 The Dingle	Closed	1999	50.00	50
1997 The Falconry	Closed	1999	50.00	50
1998 Griselda's Cottage	Closed	1999	90.00	90
1998 Marquis Walter's Manor	5,000	1999	150.00	150
1999 Robbers Retreat	Closed	1999	110.00	110
1997 The Serf's Cottage	Closed	1999	50.00	50
1997 St. Joseph's Cottage	Closed	1999	50.00	50

Porridge Pot Alley - D. Winter

YEAR ISSUE	EDITION LIMIT	YEAR RETD.	ISSUE PRICE	*QUOTE U.S.$
1995 Cob's Bakery	Closed	1996	125.00	125
1995 Cob's Bakery Premier	Closed	1996	165.00	165
1995 Porridge Pot Arch	Closed	1996	50.00	50-63
1995 Sweet Dreams	Closed	1996	79.00	80
1995 Sweet Dreams Premier	Closed	1996	99.00	99
1995 Tartan Teahouse	Closed	1996	99.00	99
1995 Tartan Teahouse Premier	Closed	1996	129.00	129

The Pubs & Taverns of England - D. Winter

YEAR ISSUE	EDITION LIMIT	YEAR RETD.	ISSUE PRICE	*QUOTE U.S.$
1998 The Bird Cage	Closed	2000	100.00	100
1998 The Good Intent	Closed	2000	100.00	100
1998 The Hop Pickers	Open		130.00	130
1999 The Potted Shrimp	Open		160.00	160
2000 Rapunzel's Tower	Open		170.00	170
1998 The Tickled Trout	4,500	2000	150.00	150

*Quotes have been rounded up to nearest dollar

Regions Collection - D. Winter

YEAR ISSUE	EDITION LIMIT	YEAR RETD.	ISSUE PRICE	*QUOTE U.S.$
1981 Cotswold Cottage	Closed	1996	22.00	30-45
1982 Cotswold Village	Closed	1990	59.90	50-99
1983 Hertford Court	Closed	1992	87.00	65-100
1985 Kent Cottage	Closed	1996	48.80	80
1981 Single Oast	Closed	1993	22.00	35-45
1981 Stratford House	Closed	1996	47.80	75-138
1981 Sussex Cottage	Closed	1996	22.00	34-50
1981 Triple Oast (old version)	Closed	1994	59.90	135-163

Scottish Collection - D. Winter

YEAR ISSUE	EDITION LIMIT	YEAR RETD.	ISSUE PRICE	*QUOTE U.S.$
1986 Crofter's Cottage	Closed	1989	51.00	45
1989 Gatekeeper's Cottage	Closed	1996	65.00	55-100
1990 Gillie's Cottage	Closed	1996	65.00	55-100
1989 The House on the Loch	Closed	1994	65.00	90-100
1989 MacBeth's Castle	Closed	1996	200.00	201-260
1982 Old Distillery	Closed	1993	312.00	462-550
1992 Scottish Crofter's	Closed	1996	42.00	65

Seaside Boardwalk - D. Winter

YEAR ISSUE	EDITION LIMIT	YEAR RETD.	ISSUE PRICE	*QUOTE U.S.$
1995 The Barnacle Theatre	4,500	1996	175.00	175-240
1995 Dock Accessory	Closed	1998	N/A	N/A
1995 The Fisherman's Shanty	Closed	1998	110.00	110-120
1995 Harbour Master's Watch-House	Closed	1998	125.00	125
1995 Jolly Roger Tavern	Closed	1998	199.00	199-220
1995 Lodgings and Sea Bathing	Closed	1998	165.00	165-180
1995 Trinity Lighthouse	Closed	1998	135.00	135-150
1995 Waterfront Market	Closed	1998	125.00	125

Sherwood Forest Collection - D. Winter

YEAR ISSUE	EDITION LIMIT	YEAR RETD.	ISSUE PRICE	*QUOTE U.S.$
1998 Alan-a-Dale	Retrd.	1998	55.00	55-65
1995 Friar Tuck's Sanctum	Retrd.	1998	45.00	45-50
1995 King Richard's Bower	Retrd.	1998	45.00	45-50
1995 Little John's Riverloft	Closed	1999	45.00	45-50
1995 Loxley Castle	Closed	1999	150.00	150
1995 Maid Marian's Retreat	Closed	1999	49.50	50-80
1995 Much's Mill	Closed	1998	45.00	50-80
1995 Sherwood Forest Diorama	Closed	1998	100.00	100-130
1995 Will Scarlett's Den	Closed	1998	49.50	50

Shires Collection - D. Winter

YEAR ISSUE	EDITION LIMIT	YEAR RETD.	ISSUE PRICE	*QUOTE U.S.$
1993 Berkshire Milking Byre	Closed	1995	38.00	30-40
1993 Buckinghamshire Bull Pen	Closed	1994	38.00	24
1993 Cheshire Kennels	Closed	1995	36.00	25-30
1993 Derbyshire Dovecote	Closed	1995	36.00	25-30
1993 Gloucestershire Greenhouse	Closed	1995	40.00	25-30
1993 Hampshire Hutches	Closed	1995	34.00	25-30
1993 Lancashire Donkey Shed	Closed	1995	38.00	30-40
1993 Oxfordshire Goat Yard	Closed	1994	32.00	25-30
1993 Shropshire Pig Shelter	Closed	1995	32.00	30-40
1993 Staffordshire Stable	Closed	1995	36.00	30-40
1993 Wiltshire Waterwheel	Closed	1995	34.00	30-40
1993 Yorkshire Sheep Fold	Closed	1995	38.00	25-30

South Downs - D. Winter

YEAR ISSUE	EDITION LIMIT	YEAR RETD.	ISSUE PRICE	*QUOTE U.S.$
1996 Elfin Cottage (10th Anniversary of the Collectors' Guild)	Closed	1996	65.00	65-100
1996 The Parish School House	Closed	1997	55.00	55
1997 Sunday School	Closed	1997	55.00	55

Special Pieces - D. Winter

YEAR ISSUE	EDITION LIMIT	YEAR RETD.	ISSUE PRICE	*QUOTE U.S.$
1987 The Village Scene, 1988 Street Scene - Bas Relief Plaque	Closed	1987	Gift	70-134
1997 Thank You	Yr.Iss.	1997	Gift	50

Tiny Series - D. Winter

YEAR ISSUE	EDITION LIMIT	YEAR RETD.	ISSUE PRICE	*QUOTE U.S.$
1980 Anne Hathaway's Cottage	Closed	1982	Unkn.	325-500
1980 Cotswold Farmhouse	Closed	1982	Unkn.	450-525
1980 Crown Inn	Closed	1982	Unkn.	525
1981 Provencal A (French Market Only)	Closed	N/A	N/A	N/A
1981 Provencal B (French Market Only)	Closed	N/A	N/A	N/A
1980 St. Nicholas' Church	Closed	1982	Unkn.	525
1980 Sulgrave Manor	Closed	1982	Unkn.	325-1050
1980 William Shakespeare's Birthplace	Closed	1982	Unkn.	325-550

The Traditional Crafts Collection...What's In A Name? - D. Winter

YEAR ISSUE	EDITION LIMIT	YEAR RETD.	ISSUE PRICE	*QUOTE U.S.$
1999 Mr. Clinkers Cottage	Open		45.00	45
1999 Mr. Cockers Cottage	Open		45.00	45
1999 Mr. Delvers Cottage	Open		40.00	40
2000 Mr. Fletcher's Cottage	Open		35.00	35
1999 Mr. Kelmen's Cottage	Open		40.00	40
2000 Mr. Turner's Cottage	Open		35.00	35

Welsh Collection - D. Winter

YEAR ISSUE	EDITION LIMIT	YEAR RETD.	ISSUE PRICE	*QUOTE U.S.$
1993 A Bit of Nonsense	Closed	1996	50.00	50-97
1993 Pen-y-Craig	Closed	1996	88.00	90-97
1993 Tyddyn Siriol	Closed	1994	88.00	104
1993 Y' Ddraig Goch	Closed	1994	88.00	90-112

West Country Collection - D. Winter

YEAR ISSUE	EDITION LIMIT	YEAR RETD.	ISSUE PRICE	*QUOTE U.S.$
1988 Cornish Engine House	Closed	1996	120.00	90-150
1988 Cornish Harbour	Closed	1996	120.00	124
1986 Devon Combe	Closed	1994	73.00	60-113
1987 Devon Creamery	Closed	1996	62.90	55-150
1986 Orchard Cottage	Closed	1991	91.30	60-80
1987 Smuggler's Creek	Closed	1996	390.00	282-475
1987 Tamar Cottage	Closed	1996	45.30	75-80
1996 Wreckers Cottages	Closed	1996	225.00	179-225
1996 Wreckers Cottages Premier	Closed	1996	275.00	325

Winterville Collection - D. Winter

YEAR ISSUE	EDITION LIMIT	YEAR RETD.	ISSUE PRICE	*QUOTE U.S.$
1996 At Home with Comfort & Joy	Closed	1996	110.00	110-120
1996 At Home with Comfort & Joy Premier	Closed	1996	145.00	145
1994 The Christmastime Clockhouse	Closed	1996	165.00	126
1994 The Christmastime Clockhouse Premier	3,500	1994	215.00	215-225
1995 St. Stephen's	Closed	1996	150.00	83-99
1995 St. Stephen's Premier	1,750	1995	195.00	171-195
1994 Toymaker	Closed	1996	135.00	112-135
1994 Toymaker Premier	3,500	1994	175.00	168-250
1995 Winterville Square	Closed	1996	75.00	75
1995 Ye Merry Gentlemen's Lodgings	Closed	1996	125.00	105-125
1995 Ye Merry Gentlemen's Lodgings Premier	1,750	1995	170.00	156-170

Disneyana Convention - John Hine Studio

YEAR ISSUE	EDITION LIMIT	YEAR RETD.	ISSUE PRICE	*QUOTE U.S.$
1992 Cinderella Castle	500	1992	250.00	1100-1528
1993 Sleeping Beauty Castle	500	1993	250.00	650-850
1994 Euro Disney Castle	500	1994	250.00	350-845

David Winter Scenes - Cameo Guild, unless otherwise noted

YEAR ISSUE	EDITION LIMIT	YEAR RETD.	ISSUE PRICE	*QUOTE U.S.$
1992 At Rose Cottage Vignette - D. Winter	Closed	1996	39.00	39
1992 Daughter - D. Winter	Closed	1996	30.00	30
1992 Father	Closed	1996	45.00	45
1992 Mother	Closed	1996	50.00	50
1992 Son	Closed	1996	30.00	30
1992 At The Bake House Vignette - D. Winter	Closed	1996	35.00	35
1992 Girl Selling Eggs	Closed	1996	30.00	30
1992 Hot Cross Bun Seller	Closed	1996	60.00	60
1992 Lady Customer	Closed	1996	45.00	45
1992 Small Boy And Dog	Closed	1996	45.00	45
1992 Woman At Pump	Closed	1996	45.00	45
1992 At The Bothy Vignette Base - D. Winter	Closed	1996	39.00	39
1992 Farm Hand And Spade	Closed	1996	40.00	40
1992 Farmer And Plough	Closed	1996	60.00	60
1992 Farmer's Wife	Closed	1996	45.00	45
1992 Goose Girl	Closed	1996	45.00	45
1993 Christmas Snow Vignette - D. Winter	Closed	1996	50.00	50
1993 Bob Cratchit And Tiny Tim	Closed	1996	50.00	50
1993 Ebenezer Scrooge	Closed	1996	45.00	45
1993 Fred	Closed	1996	35.00	35
1993 Miss Belle	Closed	1996	35.00	35
1993 Mrs. Fezziwig	Closed	1996	35.00	35
1993 Tom The Street Shoveler	Closed	1996	60.00	60

Department 56

Alpine Village Series - Department 56

YEAR ISSUE	EDITION LIMIT	YEAR RETD.	ISSUE PRICE	*QUOTE U.S.$
1987 Alpine Church 6541-2	Closed	1991	32.00	195
1987 Alpine Church (white) 6541-2	Closed	N/A	32.00	395
1992 Alpine Shops 5618-9, set/2	Open		75.00	75
1992 • Kukuck Uhren 56191	Open		37.50	38
1992 • Metterniche Wurst 56190	Closed	1997	37.50	28-45
1986 Alpine Village 6540-4, set/5	Closed	1997	150.00	120-148
1986 • Apotheke 65407	Closed	1997	39.00	25-39
1986 • Besson Bierkeller 65405	Closed	1996	30.00	25-58
1986 • Gasthof Eisl 65406	Closed	1996	30.00	25-45
1986 • Milch-Kase 65409	Closed	1996	30.00	25-40
1986 • E. Staubr Backer 65408	Closed	1997	39.00	21-40
1990 Bahnhof 5615-4	Closed	1993	42.00	35-90
1997 Bernhardiner Hundchen 56174	Open		50.00	50
1998 Federbetten Und Steppdecken 56176	Open		48.00	48
1999 Glockenspiel 56210	Open		80.00	80
1988 Grist Mill 5953-6	Closed	1997	42.00	30-100
1998 Heidi's Grandfather's House 56177	Open		64.00	64
2000 Hofburg Castle 56216	Open		68.00	68
1987 Josef Engel Farmhouse 5952-8	Closed	1989	33.00	975-1080
1995 Kamm Haus 5617-1	Closed	1999	42.00	42-63
1994 Konditorei Schokolade (Bakery & Chocolate Shop) 5614-6	Closed	1998	37.50	30-40
1998 The Sound of Music® von Trapp Villa 56178, set/5	Open		130.00	130
1999 The Sound of Music® Wedding Church 56211	Open		60.00	60
1997 Spielzeug Laden 56192	Open		65.00	65
1993 Sport Laden 5612-0	Closed	1998	50.00	38-75
1991 St. Nikolaus Kirche 5617-0	Closed	1999	37.50	37-45

Christmas In the City Series - Department 56

YEAR ISSUE	EDITION LIMIT	YEAR RETD.	ISSUE PRICE	*QUOTE U.S.$
1989 5607 Park Avenue Townhouse 5977-3	Closed	1992	48.00	75-88
1989 5609 Park Avenue Townhouse 5978-1	Closed	1992	48.00	75-88
1999 5th Avenue Salon 58950	Open		68.00	68
1991 All Saints Corner Church 5542-5	Closed	1998	96.00	58-110
1991 Arts Academy 5543-3	Closed	1993	45.00	60-85
1995 Brighton School 5887-6	Closed	1998	52.00	46-72
1994 Brokerage House 5881-5	Closed	1997	48.00	45-69
1995 Brownstones on the Square 5887-7, set/2 (Beekman House)	Open		90.00	90
1995 • Pickford Place 58879	Closed	1998	45.00	45-63
1997 The Capitol 58887	Closed	1998	110.00	90-125
1987 The Cathedral 5962-5	Closed	1990	60.00	275-425
1991 Cathedral Church of St. Mark 5549-2	3,024	1993	120.00	1400-1895
1988 Chocolate Shoppe 5968-4	Closed	1991	40.00	110-245
1987 Christmas In The City 6512-9, set/3	Closed	1990	112.00	534-650
1987 • Bakery 6512-9	Closed	1990	37.50	110-140
1987 • Tower Restaurant 6512-9	Closed	1990	37.50	235-244
1987 • Toy Shop and Pet Store 6512-9	Closed	1990	37.50	185-235
1997 The City Globe 58883	Open		65.00	65
1988 City Hall (small) 5969-2	Closed	1991	65.00	110-188
1988 City Hall (standard) 5969-2	Closed	1991	65.00	110
1999 Clark Street Automat 58954	Open		68.00	68
1999 The Consulate 58951, set/2	12/00		95.00	95
1991 The Doctor's Office 5544-1	Closed	1994	60.00	55-120
1989 Dorothy's Dress Shop 5974-9	12,500	1991	70.00	235-425
1994 First Metropolitan Bank 5882-3	Closed	1997	60.00	50-82
1996 Grand Central Railway Station 58881	Closed	1999	90.00	79-125
1998 The Grand Movie Theater 58870	Closed	1999	50.00	50-80
1988 Hank's Market 5970-6	Closed	1992	40.00	80-175
1994 Heritage Museum of Art 5883-1	Closed	1998	96.00	64-127
1997 Hi-De-Ho Nightclub 58884	Closed	1999	52.00	55
1991 Hollydale's Department Store 5534-4	Closed	1997	75.00	70-100
1995 Holy Name Church 5887-5	Open		96.00	96
1995 Ivy Terrace Apartments 5887-4	Closed	1997	60.00	55-85
2000 Jenny's Corner Book Shop 58912	Open		65.00	65
1997 Johnson's Grocery & Deli 58886	Open		60.00	60
1999 Lafayette's Bakery 58953	Open		62.00	62
1991 Little Italy Ristorante 5538-7	Closed	1995	50.00	75-95
1999 Molly O'Brien's Irish Pub 58952	Open		62.00	62
1998 Old Trinity Church 58940	Open		96.00	96
1987 Palace Theatre 5963-3	Closed	1989	45.00	855
2000 Paramount Hotel 58911	Open		85.00	85
1999 Parkview Hospital 58947	Open		65.00	65
1998 Precinct 25 Police Station 58941	Open		56.00	56
1990 Red Brick Fire Station 5536-0	Closed	1995	55.00	63-85
1989 Ritz Hotel 5973-0	Closed	1994	55.00	65
1997 Riverside Row Shops 58888	Closed	1999	52.00	52-60
1997 Scottie's Toy Shop Gift Set (Home For the Holidays) 58871, set/10	Yr.Iss.	1998	65.00	88-115
1987 Sutton Place Brownstones 5961-7	Closed	1989	80.00	650-795
1998 The University Club 58945	Open		60.00	60
1992 Uptown Shoppes 5531-0, set/3	Closed	1996	150.00	125-145
1992 • Haberdashery 55311	Closed	1996	30.00	22-40
1992 • City Clockworks 55313	Closed	1996	30.00	50-60
1992 • Music Emporium 55312	Closed	1996	30.00	41-57
1988 Variety Store 5972-2	Closed	1990	45.00	175-185
1996 Washington Street Post Office 58880	Closed	1998	52.00	52-80
1998 The Wedding Gallery 58943	Open		60.00	60
1993 West Village Shops 5880-7, set/2	Closed	1996	90.00	95-128
1993 • Potters' Tea Seller 58808	Closed	1996	45.00	41-69
1993 • Spring St. Coffee House 58809	Closed	1996	45.00	60-70
1999 Wintergarten Café 58948	Closed	1999	60.00	85
1990 Wong's In Chinatown 5537-9	Closed	1994	55.00	75-125

Dickens' Village Series - Department 56

YEAR ISSUE	EDITION LIMIT	YEAR RETD.	ISSUE PRICE	*QUOTE U.S.$
1999 Aldeburgh Music Box Shop 58441	Open		60.00	60
1999 Aldeburgh Music Box Shop (Discover Department 56® Spring Promotion) 58442, gift set/3	35,000		85.00	85
1991 Ashbury Inn 5555-7	Closed	1995	55.00	46-85
1997 Ashwick Lane Hose & Ladder 58305	Open		54.00	54
1987 Barley Bree 5900-5, set/2 (Farmhouse, Barn)	Closed	1989	60.00	250-275
1997 Barmby Moor Cottage 58324	Open		48.00	48
1990 Bishops Oast House 5567-0	Closed	1992	45.00	50-85
1995 Blenham Street Bank 5833-0	Closed	1998	60.00	44-85
1986 Blythe Pond Mill House 6508-0	Closed	1990	37.00	169-300
1986 By The Pond Mill House 6508-0	Closed	1990	37.00	60-80
1994 Boarding & Lodging School 5810-6	Closed	1998	48.00	48-78
1993 Boarding and Lodging School 5809-2 (Christmas Carol Commemorative Piece)	Yr.Iss.	1993	48.00	55-75
1987 Brick Abbey 6549-8	Closed	1989	33.00	264-385
1996 Butter Tub Barn 58338	Closed	1999	48.00	48-89
1996 Butter Tub Farmhouse 58337	Closed	1999	40.00	38-50
1988 C. Fletcher Public House 5904-8	12,500	1989	35.00	360-550
1997 Canadian Trading Co. (Canadian Version) 58306	Closed	1998	65.00	150
1986 Chadbury Station and Train 6528-5	Closed	1989	65.00	190-360
1999 Chancery Corner (Discover Department 56® Holiday Program) 58352, set/8	Yr.Iss.	1999	65.00	78-105
1987 Chesterton Manor House 6568-4	7,500	1988	45.00	1200-1395
1999 The China Trader 58447	Open		72.00	72
1986 Christmas Carol Cottages 6500-5, set/3	Closed	1995	75.00	99-150
1986 • The Cottage of Bob Cratchit & Tiny Tim 6500-5	Closed	1995	25.00	60-75
1986 • Fezziwig's Warehouse 6500-5	Closed	1995	25.00	22-40
1986 • Scrooge and Marley Counting House 6500-5	Closed	1995	25.00	42-65
1996 The Christmas Carol Cottages (revisited) 58339	Open		60.00	60
1988 Cobblestone Shops 5924-2, set/3	Closed	1990	95.00	300-460
1988 • Booter and Cobbler 5924-2	Closed	1990	32.00	88-119
1988 • T. Wells Fruit & Spice Shop 5924-2	Closed	1990	32.00	50-69
1988 • The Wool Shop 5924-2	Closed	1990	32.00	119-138
1989 Cobles Police Station 5583-2	Closed	1991	37.50	113-128
1988 Counting House & Silas Thimbleton Barrister 5902-1	Closed	1990	32.00	75-80
1997 Crooked Fence Cottage 58304	Open		60.00	60
1992 Crown & Cricket Inn (Charles Dickens' Signature Series), 5750-9	Yr.Iss.	1992	100.00	98-185
1989 David Copperfield 5550-6, set/3	Closed	1992	125.00	115-157
1989 • Betsy Trotwood's Cottage 5550-6	Closed	1992	42.50	40-80
1989 • Peggotty's Seaside Cottage 5550-6 (green boat)	Closed	1992	42.50	48-80
1989 • Peggotty's Seaside Cottage 5550-6 (tan boat)	Closed	1992	42.50	104-157
1989 • Mr. Wickfield Solicitor 5550-6	Closed	1992	42.50	48-110
1989 David Copperfield 5550-6, set/3 with tan boat	Closed	1992	125.00	130-195
1994 Dedlock Arms 5752-5 (Charles Dickens' Signature Series)	Yr.Iss.	1994	100.00	75-150
1985 Dickens' Cottages 6518-8 set/3	Closed	1988	75.00	850-920
1985 • Stone Cottage 6518-8	Closed	1988	25.00	298-399
1985 • Thatched Cottage 6518-8	Closed	1988	25.00	100-225

*Quotes have been rounded up to nearest dollar

YEAR ISSUE	EDITION LIMIT	YEAR RETD.	ISSUE PRICE	*QUOTE U.S.$
1985 • Tudor Cottage 6518-8	Closed	1988	25.00	215-325
1986 Dickens' Lane Shops 6507-2, set/3	Closed	1989	80.00	399-550
1986 • Cottage Toy Shop 6507-2	Closed	1989	27.00	115-200
1986 • Thomas Kersey Coffee House 6507-2	Closed	1989	27.00	98-130
1986 • Tuttle's Pub 6507-2	Closed	1989	27.00	125-168
1985 Dickens' Village Church (lt. cream) 6516-1	Closed	1989	35.00	190-265
1985 Dickens' Village Church (cream-yellow) 6516-1	Closed	1989	35.00	175-200
1985 Dickens' Village Church (dark) 6516-1	Closed	1989	35.00	89-150
1985 Dickens' Village Church (green) 6516-1	Closed	1989	35.00	350-515
1985 Dickens' Village Church (tan) 6516-1	Closed	1989	35.00	150-200
1985 Dickens' Village Mill 6519-6	2,500	1986	35.00	4480-4850
1995 Dudden Cross Church 5834-3	Closed	1997	45.00	38-55
1999 Dudley Docker 58353	Open		70.00	70
1995 Dursley Manor, 5832-9	Closed	1999	50.00	52-69
1997 East Indies Trading Co. 58302	Closed	1999	65.00	52-82
1991 Fagin's Hide-A-Way 5552-2	Closed	1995	68.00	47-95
2000 Fezziwig's Ballroom (Discover Department 56® Holiday Program) 58470, set/6	12/00		75.00	75
1989 The Flat of Ebenezer Scrooge 5587-5	Open		37.50	38
1997 Gad's Hill Place (Charles Dickens' Signature Series), 57535	Yr.Iss.	1997	98.00	58-133
1994 Giggelswick Mutton & Ham, 5822-0	Closed	1997	48.00	32-94
1996 The Grapes Inn, 57534 (Charles Dickens' Signature Series)	Yr.Iss.	1996	120.00	64-135
1993 Great Denton Mill 5812-2	Closed	1997	50.00	35-63
1989 Green Gate Cottage 5586-7	22,500	1990	65.00	168-450
1994 Hather Harness 5823-8	Closed	1997	48.00	32-70
1998 Heathmoor Castle 58313	Closed	1999	90.00	72-90
1992 Hembleton Pewterer, 5800-9	Closed	1995	72.00	37-90
1998 The Horse And Hounds Pub 58340	Open		70.00	70
1988 Ivy Glen Church 5927-7	Closed	1991	35.00	55-95
1995 J.D. Nichols Toy Shop 5832-8	Closed	1998	48.00	46-60
1997 J. Lytes Coal Merchant 58323	Closed	1999	50.00	40-64
1987 Kenilworth Castle 5916-1	Closed	1988	70.00	350-545
1998 Kensington Palace (Home For the Holidays) 58309	Yr.Iss.	1998	195.00	125-165
1989 Knottinghill Church 5582-4	Closed	1995	50.00	45-75
1992 King's Road Post Office 5801-7	Closed	1998	45.00	30-50
1993 Kingford's Brewhouse 5811-4	Closed	1996	45.00	40-57
1990 Kings Road 5568-9, set/2	Closed	1996	72.00	50-100
1990 • Tutbury Printer 55690	Closed	1996	36.00	19-45
1990 • C.H. Watt Physician 55691	Closed	1996	36.00	48-63
1997 Leacock Poulterer (Revisited) 58303	Closed	1999	48.00	39-65
1999 Leed's Oyster House 58446	Open		68.00	68
1998 Lynton Point Tower 58315	Open		80.00	80
1995 The Maltings 5833-5	Closed	1998	50.00	36-63
1997 Manchester Square 58301, set/25 (G. Choir's Weights & Scales, Frogmore Chemist, Custom House, Lydby Trunk & Satchel Shop, Manchester Square Accessories, set/7, 12 trees, road, snow)	Open		250.00	250
1999 Margrove Orangery 58440	Open		98.00	98
1999 McShane Cottage 58444, set/2	Open		55.00	55
1996 The Melancholy Tavern (Revisited) 58347	Closed	1999	45.00	36-57
1988 Merchant Shops 5926-9, set/5	Closed	1993	150.00	188-450
1988 • Geo. Weeton Watchmaker 5926-9	Closed	1993	30.00	30-44
1988 • The Mermaid Fish Shoppe 5926-9	Closed	1993	30.00	40-57
1988 • Poulterer 5926-9	Closed	1993	30.00	30-53
1988 • Walpole Tailors 5926-9	Closed	1993	30.00	20-48
1988 • White Horse Bakery 5926-9	Closed	1993	30.00	30-57
1996 Mulberrie Court 58345	Closed	1999	90.00	73-113
1991 Nephew Fred's Flat 5557-3	Closed	1994	35.00	60-85
1996 Nettie Quinn Puppets & Marionettes 58344	Open		50.00	50
1988 Nicholas Nickleby 5925-0, set/2	Closed	1991	72.00	135-150
1988 • Nicholas Nickleby Cottage 5925-0	Closed	1991	36.00	48-88
1988 • Wackford Squeers Boarding School 5925-0	Closed	1991	36.00	48-75
1988 Nickolas Nickleby Cottage 5925-0-misspelled	Closed	1991	36.00	48-90
1988 Nickolas Nickleby set/2, 5925-0-misspelled	Closed	1991	36.00	175-200
1986 Norman Church 6502-1	3,500	1987	40.00	2250-3200
1998 North Eastern Sea Fisheries Ltd. 58316	Closed	1999	70.00	56-88
1987 The Old Curiosity Shop 5905-6	Closed	1999	32.00	24-50
1992 Old Michaelchurch, 5562-0	Closed	1996	42.00	34-52
1999 Old Queensbridge Station 58443, set/2	Open		100.00	100
1996 The Olde Camden Town Church (Revisited) 58346	Closed	1999	55.00	44-69
1991 Oliver Twist 5553-0, set/2	Closed	1993	75.00	70-90
1991 • Brownlow House 5553-0	Closed	1993	38.00	46-85
1991 • Maylie Cottage 5553-0	Closed	1993	38.00	34-70
1984 The Original Shops of Dickens' Village 6515-3, set of 7	Closed	1988	175.00	990-1250
1984 • Abel Beesley Butcher 6515-3	Closed	1988	25.00	98-110
1984 • Bean And Son Smithy Shop 6515-3	Closed	1988	25.00	140-175
1984 • Candle Shop 6515-3	Closed	1988	25.00	115-150
1984 • Crowntree Inn 6515-3	Closed	1988	25.00	150-240
1984 • Golden Swan Baker 6515-3	Closed	1988	25.00	122-161
1984 • Green Grocer 6515-3	Closed	1988	25.00	138-175
1984 • Jones & Co. Brush & Basket Shop 6515-3	Closed	1988	25.00	200-248
1993 The Pied Bull Inn (Charles Dickens' Signature Series), 5751-7	Closed	1993	100.00	98-165
1994 Portobello Road Thatched Cottages 5824-6, set/3	Closed	1997	120.00	120-150
1994 • Browning Cottage 58249	Closed	1997	40.00	24-45
1994 • Cobb Cottage 58248	Closed	1997	40.00	24-50
1994 • Mr. & Mrs. Pickle 58247	Closed	1997	40.00	24-60
1993 Pump Lane Shoppes 5808-4, set/3	Closed	1996	112.00	75-140
1993 • Bumpstead Nye Cloaks & Canes 58085	Closed	1996	37.35	22-40
1993 • Lomas Ltd. Molasses 58086	Closed	1996	37.35	27-45
1993 • W.M. Wheat Cakes & Puddings 58087	Closed	1996	37.35	35-55
1996 Quilly's Antiques 58348	Closed	1999	46.00	38-68
1996 Ramsford Palace 58336, set/17 (Ramsford Palace, Palace Guards, set/2 Accessory, Palace Gate Accessory, Palace Fountain Accessory, Wall Hedge, set/8 Accessory, Corner Wall Topiaries, set/4 Accessory)	27,500	1996	175.00	295-465
1998 Royal Coach (hinged box) 57501	Open		25.00	25
1989 Ruth Marion Scotch Woolens 5585-9	17,500	1990	65.00	225-330
1998 Seton Morris, Spice Merchant Gift Set (Home For the Holidays) 58308, set/10	Yr.Iss.	1998	65.00	40-75
1995 Sir John Falstaff Inn 5753-3 (Charles Dickens' Signature Series)	Closed	1995	100.00	63-135
1999 The Spider Box Locks 58448	Open		60.00	60
2000 St. Martin-in-the-Fields Church 58471	Open		96.00	96
1999 Staghorn Lodge 58445	Open		72.00	72
1995 Start A Tradition Set 5832-7, set/13 (The Town Square Carolers Accessory, set/3, 6 Sisal Trees, Bag of Real Plastic Snow, Cobblestone Road)	Closed	1996	85.00	70-110
1995 • Faversham Lamps & Oil	Closed	1996	N/A	63
1995 • Morston Steak and Kidney Pie	Closed	1996	N/A	43
1997 Start A Tradition Set 58322, set/13 (Sudbury Church, Old East Rectory, The Spirit of Giving Accessory, set/3, 6 Sisal Trees, Bag of Real Plastic Snow, Cobblestone Road)	Closed	1998	75.00	60-80
1998 Tattyeave Knoll 58311	Closed	1999	55.00	44-69
1998 Teaman & Crupp China Shop 58314	Open		64.00	64
1989 Theatre Royal 5584-0	Closed	1992	45.00	60-95
1998 Thomas Mudge Timepieces 58307	Open		60.00	60
1989 Victoria Station 5574-3	Closed	1998	100.00	86-125
1994 Whittlesbourne Church, 5821-1	Closed	1998	85.00	60-100
1999 Wingham Lane Parrot Seller 58449	Open		68.00	68
1995 Wrenbury Shops 5833-1, set/3	Closed	1997	100.00	138
1995 • The Chop Shop 58333	Closed	1997	35.00	30-88
1995 • Wrenbury Baker 58332	Closed	1997	35.00	35-75
1995 • T. Puddlewick Spectacle Shop 58334	Closed	1998	35.00	36-45

Disney Parks Village Series - Department 56

YEAR ISSUE	EDITION LIMIT	YEAR RETD.	ISSUE PRICE	*QUOTE U.S.$
1994 Fire Station No. 105 5352-0 Disneyland, CA	Closed	1996	45.00	38-50
1994 Fire Station No. 105 744-7 (theme park backstamp) Disneyland, CA	Closed	1996	45.00	63-75
1994 Mickey's Christmas Shop 5350-3, set/2 Disney World, FL	Closed	1996	144.00	72-165
1994 Mickey's Christmas Shop 742-0 (theme park backstamp), set/2 Disney World, FL	Closed	1996	144.00	350-435
1994 Olde World Antiques 5351-1, set/2 Disney World, FL	Closed	1996	90.00	44-100
1994 Olde World Antiques 743-9 (theme park backstamp), set/2 Disney World, FL	Closed	1996	90.00	56-100
1995 Silversmith 5352-1 Disney World, FL	Closed	1996	50.00	198-225
1995 Silversmith 744-8 (theme park backstamp) Disney World, FL	Closed	1996	50.00	225-288
1995 Tinker Bell's Treasures 5352-2 Disney World, FL	Closed	1996	60.00	198-238
1995 Tinker Bell's Treasures 744-9 (theme park backstamp) Disney World, FL	Closed	1996	60.00	225-238

Disney Parks Village Series Accessories - Department 56

YEAR ISSUE	EDITION LIMIT	YEAR RETD.	ISSUE PRICE	*QUOTE U.S.$
1995 The Balloon Seller 5353-9, set/2	Closed	1996	25.00	30-50
1994 Disney Parks Family 5354-6, set/3	Closed	1996	32.50	18-30
1994 Mickey and Minnie 5353-8, set/2	Closed	1996	22.50	18-30
1994 Olde World Antiques Gate 5355-4	Closed	1996	15.00	12-30

Event Piece - Heritage Village Collection Accessory - Department 56

YEAR ISSUE	EDITION LIMIT	YEAR RETD.	ISSUE PRICE	*QUOTE U.S.$
1992 Gate House 5530-1	Closed	1992	22.50	25-30
1996 Christmas Bells 98711	Closed	1996	35.00	26-57
1997 The Holly & The Ivy, set/2 56100	Yr.Iss.	1997	17.50	10-15
1998 Stars And Stripes Forever 55502	Yr.Iss.	1998	50.00	48-50

Heritage Village Special Edition - Department 56

YEAR ISSUE	EDITION LIMIT	YEAR RETD.	ISSUE PRICE	*QUOTE U.S.$
1999 The Times Tower 55510, set/3	Closed	1999	185.00	185-312

The Historical Landmark Series™ - Department 56

YEAR ISSUE	EDITION LIMIT	YEAR RETD.	ISSUE PRICE	*QUOTE U.S.$
1997 The Old Globe Theatre 58501, set/4	Yr.Iss.	1998	175.00	98-225
1997 Tower of London 58500, set/5	Closed	1997	165.00	195-265
1998 Big Ben 58341, set/2	Closed	2000	95.00	95
1998 Independence Hall 55500	Open		110.00	110
1999 The Old Royal Observatory 58453, set/2	35,000		95.00	95

Homes For The Holidays - Department 56

YEAR ISSUE	EDITION LIMIT	YEAR RETD.	ISSUE PRICE	*QUOTE U.S.$
1997 Ronald McDonald House ® (Fund Raiser Piece) 8960	Yr.Iss.	1997	N/A	130-300

Hot Properties - Department 56

YEAR ISSUE	EDITION LIMIT	YEAR RETD.	ISSUE PRICE	*QUOTE U.S.$
2000 How The Grinch Stole Christmas! "Cindy Lou Who's House", set 59004	Open		75.00	75

Literary Classics™ Collections - Department 56

YEAR ISSUE	EDITION LIMIT	YEAR RETD.	ISSUE PRICE	*QUOTE U.S.$
1998 Great Expectations - Satis Manor 58310, set/4	Open		110.00	110
1999 Little Women - The March Residence 56606, set/4	Open		90.00	90
1999 The Great Gatsby - West Egg Mansion 58939, set/4	Open		135.00	135
2000 The Adventures of Tom Sawyer - Aunt Polly's House 58600, set/5	Open		90.00	90

Little Town of Bethlehem Series - Department 56

YEAR ISSUE	EDITION LIMIT	YEAR RETD.	ISSUE PRICE	*QUOTE U.S.$
1999 Gatekeeper's Dwelling 59797	Open		55.00	55
1999 Innkeeper's Caravansary 59795	Open		70.00	70
1987 Little Town of Bethlehem 5975-7, set/12	Closed	1999	150.00	150-156
1999 Nativity 59796, set/2	Open		55.00	55

New England Village Series - Department 56

YEAR ISSUE	EDITION LIMIT	YEAR RETD.	ISSUE PRICE	*QUOTE U.S.$
1993 A. Bieler Farm 5648-0, set/2	Closed	1996	92.00	90-92
1993 • Pennsylvania Dutch Farmhouse 56481	Closed	1996	46.00	38-88
1993 • Pennsylvania Dutch Barn 56482	Closed	1996	46.00	40-78
1988 Ada's Bed and Boarding House (lemon yellow) 5940-4	Closed	1991	36.00	195-240
1988 Ada's Bed and Boarding House (pale yellow) 5940-4	Closed	1991	36.00	98-112
1996 Apple Valley School 56172	Open		35.00	35
1994 Arlington Falls Church 5651-0	Closed	1997	40.00	26-45
1989 Berkshire House (medium blue) 5942-0	Closed	1991	40.00	128-163
1989 Berkshire House (teal) 5942-0	Closed	1991	40.00	80-88
1993 Blue Star Ice Co. 5647-2	Closed	1997	45.00	40-70
1992 Bluebird Seed and Bulb 5642-1	Closed	1996	48.00	24-38
1996 Bobwhite Cottage 56576	Open		50.00	50
1995 Brewster Bay Cottage 5657-0, set/2	Closed	1997	90.00	75-95
1995 • Jeremiah Brewster House 56568	Closed	1997	45.00	32-50
1995 • Thomas T. Julian House 56569	Closed	1997	45.00	38-60
1994 Cape Keag Cannery 5652-9	Closed	1998	48.00	24-55
1990 Captain's Cottage 5947-1	Closed	1996	40.00	38-45
1988 Cherry Lane Shops 5939-0, set/3	Closed	1990	80.00	210-253
1988 • Anne Shaw Toys 5939-0	Closed	1990	27.00	112-175
1988 • Ben's Barbershop 5939-0	Closed	1990	27.00	75-135
1988 • Otis Hayes Butcher Shop 5939-0	Closed	1990	27.00	75-119
1987 Craggy Cove Lighthouse 5930-7	Closed	1994	35.00	35-68
1995 Chowder House 5657-1	Closed	1998	40.00	34-57
1998 Deacon's Way Chapel 56604	Open		68.00	68
1997 East Willet Pottery 56578	Closed	1999	45.00	36-46
1998 The Emily Louise 56581, set/2	Open		70.00	70
1998 Franklin Hook & Ladder Co, 56601	Open		55.00	55
1999 Hale & Hardy House 56610	Open		60.00	60
1998 Harper's Farm 56605	Open		65.00	65
1999 Harper's Farmhouse 56612	Open		57.00	57
1996 J. Hudson Stoveworks 56574	Closed	1998	60.00	42-75
1986 Jacob Adams Farmhouse and Barn 6538-2	Closed	1989	65.00	350-465
1989 Jannes Mullet Amish Barn 5944-7	Closed	1992	48.00	70-115
1989 Jannes Mullet Amish Farm House 5943-9	Closed	1992	32.00	86-125
1991 McGrebe-Cutters & Sleighs 5640-5	Closed	1995	45.00	28-70
1998 Moggin Falls General Store 56602	Open		60.00	60
1996 Navigational Charts & Maps 56575	Closed	1999	48.00	48-62
1986 New England Village 6530-7, set/7	Closed	1989	170.00	1000-1300
1986 • Apothecary Shop 6530-7	Closed	1989	25.00	75-135
1986 • Brick Town Hall 6530-7	Closed	1989	25.00	124-239
1986 • General Store 6530-7	Closed	1989	25.00	295
1986 • Livery Stable & Boot Shop 6530-7	Closed	1989	25.00	128-138
1986 • Nathaniel Bingham Fabrics 6530-7	Closed	1989	25.00	138-148
1986 • Red Schoolhouse 6530-7	Closed	1989	25.00	238-290
1986 • Steeple Church (Original) 6530-7	Closed	1989	25.00	139-300
1988 Old North Church 5932-3	Closed	1998	40.00	28-48
1995 Pierce Boat Works 5657-3	Open		55.00	55
1994 Pigeonhead Lighthouse 5653-7	Closed	1998	50.00	35-55
1999 P.L. Wheeler's Bicycle Shop 56613	Open		57.00	57
1999 Platt's Candles & Wax 56614	Open		60.00	60
1997 Semple's Smokehouse 56580	Closed	1999	45.00	38-56
1990 Shingle Creek House 5946-3	Closed	1994	37.50	32-40
1990 Sleepy Hollow 5954-4, set/3	Closed	1993	96.00	125-264
1990 • Ichabod Crane's Cottage 5954-4	Closed	1993	32.00	30-50
1990 • Sleepy Hollow School 5954-4	Closed	1993	32.00	60-100
1990 • Van Tassel Manor 5954-4	Closed	1993	32.00	48-69
1990 Sleepy Hollow Church 5955-2	Closed	1993	36.00	44-58
1987 Smythe Woolen Mill 6543-9	7,500	1988	42.00	1050-1125
1997 Steen's Maple House (Smoking House) 56579	Open		60.00	60
1986 Steeple Church (Second Version) 6539-0	Closed	1989	30.00	88-135
1986 Steeple Church (Third Version) 6539-0	Closed	1990	30.00	75
1992 Stoney Brook Town Hall 5644-8	Closed	1995	42.00	30-57
2000 Susquehanna Station 56624, set/2	Open		60.00	60
1987 Timber Knoll Log Cabin 6544-7	Closed	1990	28.00	150-157
1999 Trinity Ledge 56611	Open		85.00	85
1997 Van Guilder's Ornamental Ironworks 56577	Closed	1999	50.00	50-58
1987 Weston Train Station 5931-5	Closed	1989	42.00	230-275
1995 Woodbridge Post Office 5657-2	Closed	1998	40.00	36-45
1992 Yankee Jud Bell Casting 5643-0	Closed	1995	44.00	26-30

North Pole Series - Department 56

YEAR ISSUE	EDITION LIMIT	YEAR RETD.	ISSUE PRICE	*QUOTE U.S.$
1994 Beard Barber Shop 5634-0	Closed	1997	27.50	16-41
1999 Cold Care Clinic, Elf Land™ 56703	Open		42.00	42
2000 Crayola® Polar Palette Art Center 56726	Open		65.00	65
1998 Custom Stitchers, Elf Land™ 56400	Open		37.50	38
1999 Elf Mountain Ski Resort 56700	Open		70.00	70
1998 The Elf Spa, Elf Land™ 56402	Open		40.00	40
1992 Elfie's Sleds & Skates 5625-1	Closed	1996	48.00	48-60

*Quotes have been rounded up to nearest dollar

Year Issue	Edition Limit	Year Retd.	Issue Price	*Quote U.S.$
1995 Elfin Forge & Assembly Shop 5638-4	Closed	1998	65.00	44-75
1994 Elfin Snow Cone Works 5633-2	Closed	1997	40.00	38-52
1997 Elsie's Gingerbread (Smoking House) 56398	Yr.Iss.	1998	65.00	82-144
1995 Elves' Trade School 5638-7	Closed	1998	50.00	34-80
1993 Express Depot 5627-8	Closed	1998	48.00	38-50
1997 The Glacier Gazette 56394	Closed	1999	48.00	39-100
1997 Glass Ornament Works 56396	Open		60.00	60
1996 Hall of Records 56392	Closed	1999	50.00	40-63
1999 Jack In The Box Plant No. 2 56705	12/00		65.00	65
1999 Marie's Doll Museum 56408	Closed	1999	55.00	55-85
1999 Mini-Donut Shop, Elf Land™ 56702	Open		42.00	42
1997 Mrs. Claus' Greenhouse 56395	Open		68.00	68
1991 Neenee's Dolls & Toys 5620-0	Closed	1995	37.50	33-60
1990 North Pole 5601-4, set/2	Closed	1996	70.00	64-119
1990 • Elf Bunkhouse 56016	Closed	1996	35.00	22-45
1990 • Reindeer Barn 56015	Closed	1996	35.00	38-40
1993 North Pole Chapel 5626-0	Open		45.00	45
1994 North Pole Dolls & Santa's Bear Works 5635-9, set/3 (North Pole Dolls, Santa's Bear Works, Entrance)	Closed	1997	96.00	88-125
1992 North Pole Post Office 5623-5	Closed	1999	45.00	40-50
1991 North Pole Shops 5621-9, set/2	Closed	1995	75.00	85-119
1991 • Orly's Bell & Harness Supply	Closed	1995	37.50	42-55
1991 • Rimpy's Bakery	Closed	1995	37.50	50-85
1999 Northern Lights Stinsel Mill 56704	Open		55.00	55
1992 Obbie's Books & Letrinka's Candy 5624-3	Closed	1996	70.00	68-90
1999 The Peanut Brittle Factory 56701	Open		80.00	80
1996 Popcorn & Cranberry House 56388	Closed	1997	45.00	65-107
1998 Real Plastic Snow Factory 56403	Open		80.00	80
1998 Reindeer Flight School 56404	Open		55.00	55
1996 Route 1, North Pole, Home of Mr. & Mrs. Claus 56391	Open		110.00	110
1996 Santa's Bell Repair 56389	Closed	1998	45.00	36-63
1997 Santa's Light Shop 56397	Open		52.00	52
1993 Santa's Lookout Tower 5629-4	Open		45.00	48
1995 Santa's Rooming House 5638-6	Closed	1999	50.00	42-54
1999 Santa's Visiting Center (Discover Department 56® Holiday Program) 56407, set/6	Yr.Iss.	1999	65.00	72-157
1993 Santa's Woodworks 5628-6	Closed	1996	42.00	48-75
1990 Santa's Workshop 5600-6	Closed	1993	72.00	256-348
1996 Start a Tradition Set 56390, set/12 (Candy Cane Elves, set/2 Accessory)	Closed	1996	85.00	64-124
1996 • Candy Cane & Peppermint Shop	Closed	1996	N/A	63-120
1996 • Gift Wrap & Ribbons	Closed	1996	N/A	60
2000 Sweet Rock Candy Co. (Discover Department 56® Holiday Program) 56725, set/9	12/00		75.00	75
1991 Tassy's Mittens & Hassel's Woolies 5622-7	Closed	1995	50.00	64-75
1998 Tillie's Tiny Cup Café Elf Land™ 56401	Open		37.50	38
1995 Tin Soldier Shop 5638-3	Closed	1997	42.00	47-91
1995 Weather & Time Observatory 5638-5	Closed	1999	50.00	40-54

North Pole Woods - Department 56

Year Issue	Edition Limit	Year Retd.	Issue Price	*Quote U.S.$
2000 Oakwood Post Office Branch 56881, set/2	Open		65.00	65
2000 Reindeer Care & Repair 56882	Open		60.00	60
2000 Town Meeting Hall 56880	Open		68.00	68
2000 Trim-A-Tree Factory 56884, set/2	Open		50.00	50

The Original Snow Village Collection - Department 56

Year Issue	Edition Limit	Year Retd.	Issue Price	*Quote U.S.$
1999 2000 Holly Lane (Discover Department 56® Holiday Program) 54977, set/11	Yr.Iss.	1999	65.00	82-98
1986 2101 Maple 5043-1	Closed	1986	32.00	285-360
1990 56 Flavors Ice Cream Parlor 5151-9	Closed	1992	42.00	143-195
1979 Adobe House 5066-6	Closed	1980	18.00	2424-2650
1992 Airport 5439-9	Closed	1996	60.00	75-95
1992 Al's TV Shop 5423-2	Closed	1995	40.00	31-60
1986 All Saints Church 5070-9	Closed	1997	38.00	34-50
1998 ...Another Man's Treasure Garage 54945, set/22	Open		60.00	60
1986 Apothecary 5076-8	Closed	1990	34.00	75-100
1987 Bachman's Hometown Boarding House 6700-0	Closed	1988	34.00	156
1987 Bachman's Hometown Church 6718-0	Closed	1988	39.00	160
1988 Bachman's Hometown Drugstore 6726-0	Closed	1988	29.00	200
1997 Bachman's Flower Shop 8802-0	Closed	1997	50.00	98-100
1998 Bachman's Greenhouse 2203-0	Closed	1998	60.00	75-92
1999 Bachman's Original Homestead 1885	7,500	1999	75.00	113-122
1981 Bakery 5077-6	Closed	1983	30.00	215-225
1986 Bakery 5077-6	Closed	1991	35.00	59-107
1982 Bank 5024-5	Closed	1983	32.00	490-545
1981 Barn 5074-1	Closed	1984	32.00	295-486
1984 Bayport 5015-6	Closed	1986	30.00	215-250
1986 Beacon Hill House 5065-2	Closed	1988	31.00	121-213
1995 Beacon Hill Victorian 5485-7	Closed	1998	60.00	45-82
1996 Birch Run Ski Chalet 54882	Closed	1999	60.00	49-78
1979 Brownstone 5056-7	Closed	1981	36.00	495-625
1996 Boulder Springs House 54873	Closed	1997	60.00	48-69
1995 Bowling Alley 5485-8	Closed	1998	42.00	34-59
1997 The Brandon Bungalow 54918	Closed	1999	55.00	48-58
1978 Cape Cod 5013-8	Closed	1980	20.00	400-426
1994 Carmel Cottage 5466-6	Closed	1997	48.00	33-67
1998 The Carnival Carousel (musical) 54933	Open		150.00	150
2000 Carpenter Gothic Bed & Breakfast (American Architecture Series), 55043	Open		75.00	75
1982 Carriage House 5021-0	Closed	1984	28.00	240-348

Year Issue	Edition Limit	Year Retd.	Issue Price	*Quote U.S.$
1986 Carriage House 5071-7	Closed	1988	29.00	94-130
1987 Cathedral Church 5019-9	Closed	1990	50.00	70-100
1980 Cathedral Church 5067-4	Closed	1981	36.00	2740-3500
1999 Cedar Point Cabin 55009	Open		66.00	66
1982 Centennial House 5020-2	Closed	1984	32.00	260-295
1998 Center For The Arts 54940	Open		64.00	64
1999 Champsfield Stadium 55001, set/24	Open		195.00	195
1983 Chateau 5084-9	Closed	1984	35.00	415-507
1997 Christmas Barn Dance 54910	Closed	1999	65.00	55-82
1995 Christmas Cove Lighthouse 5483-6	Open		60.00	60
1996 Christmas Lake High School 54881	Closed	1999	52.00	48-87
1991 The Christmas Shop 5097-0	Closed	1996	37.50	40-75
1985 Church of the Open Door 5048-2	Closed	1988	34.00	85-169
1999 Cinema 56 54978	Open		85.00	85
1988 Cobblestone Antique Shop 5123-3	Closed	1992	36.00	49-82
1994 Coca-Cola® Brand Bottling Plant 5469-0	Closed	1997	65.00	68-95
1995 Coca-Cola® Brand Corner Drugstore 5484-4	Closed	1998	55.00	55-85
1989 Colonial Church 5119-5	Closed	1992	60.00	40-92
1980 Colonial Farm House 5070-9	Closed	1982	30.00	250-300
1984 Congregational Church 5034-2	Closed	1985	28.00	520-590
1988 Corner Cafe 5124-1	Closed	1991	37.00	62-98
1981 Corner Store 5076-8	Closed	1983	30.00	170-225
1976 Country Church 5004-7	Closed	1979	18.00	375
1979 Countryside Church 5051-8 Meadowland Series	Closed	1980	25.00	360-650
1979 Countryside Church 5058-3	Closed	1984	27.50	200-250
1989 Courthouse 5144-6	Closed	1993	65.00	159-207
1992 Craftsman Cottage (American Architecture Series), 5437-2	Closed	1995	55.00	53-80
1987 Cumberland House 5024-5	Closed	1995	42.00	35-88
1993 Dairy Barn 5446-1	Closed	1997	55.00	45-75
1984 Delta House 5012-1	Closed	1986	32.00	250-270
1985 Depot and Train w/2 Train Cars 5051-2	Closed	1988	65.00	135-175
1993 Dinah's Drive-In 5447-0	Closed	1996	45.00	113-148
1989 Doctor's House 5143-8	Closed	1992	56.00	89-135
1991 Double Bungalow 5407-0	Closed	1994	45.00	31-70
1985 Duplex 5050-4	Closed	1987	35.00	106-158
1995 Dutch Colonial (American Architecture Series) 5485-6	Closed	1996	45.00	36-82
2000 Elvis Presley's Graceland® (Discover Department 56® Holiday Program) 55041, set/6	12/00		165.00	165
1981 English Church 5078-4	Closed	1982	30.00	400-474
1981 English Cottage 5073-3	Closed	1982	25.00	280-325
1983 English Tudor 5033-4	Closed	1985	30.00	184-252
1987 Farm House 5089-0	Closed	1992	40.00	46-75
1997 Farm House 54912	Open		50.00	50
1998 The Farmer's Co-op Granary 54946	Open		64.00	64
1994 Federal House (American Architecture Series) 5465-8	Closed	1997	50.00	56-65
1991 Finklea's Finery: Costume Shop 5405-4	Closed	1993	45.00	45-82
1983 Fire Station 5032-6	Closed	1984	32.00	480-550
1987 Fire Station No. 2 5091-1	Closed	1989	40.00	145-195
1998 Fire Station No. 3 54942	Open		70.00	70
1994 Fisherman's Nook Cabins 5461-5, set/2, (Fisherman's Nook Bass Cabin, Fisherman's Nook Trout Cabin)	Closed	1999	50.00	40-85
1994 Fisherman's Nook Resort 5460-7	Closed	1999	75.00	45-110
1982 Flower Shop 5082-2	Closed	1983	25.00	410-462
1976 Gabled Cottage 5002-1	Closed	1979	20.00	320-390
1982 Gabled House 5081-4	Closed	1983	30.00	360-370
1984 Galena House 5009-1	Closed	1985	32.00	350-402
1978 General Store (gold) 5012-0	Closed	1980	25.00	550
1978 General Store (tan) 5012-0	Closed	1980	25.00	700-770
1978 General Store (white) 5012-0	Closed	1980	25.00	400-522
1979 Giant Trees 5065-8	Closed	1982	20.00	252-295
1983 Gingerbread House Bank (Non-lighted) 5025-3	Closed	1984	24.00	460-650
1983 Gingerbread House Bank (lighted) 5025-3	Closed	1984	24.00	425
1994 Glenhaven House 5468-2	Closed	1997	45.00	40-63
1992 Good Shepherd Chapel & Church School 5424-0, set/2	Closed	1996	72.00	35-68
1983 Gothic Church 5028-8	Closed	1986	36.00	211
1991 Gothic Farmhouse (American Architecture Series), 5404-6	Closed	1997	48.00	44-75
1983 Governor's Mansion 5003-2	Closed	1985	32.00	275-360
1997 Gracie's Dry Goods & General Store 54915, set/2	Open		70.00	70
1992 Grandma's Cottage 5420-8	Closed	1996	42.00	59-88
1999 Grimsley Manor 55004	Open		120.00	120
1983 Grocery 5001-6	Closed	1985	35.00	290-348
1998 Harley-Davidson® Manufacturing 54948, set/3	Open		80.00	80
1996 Harley-Davidson® Motorcycle Shop 54886	Open		65.00	65
1992 Hartford House 5426-7	Closed	1995	55.00	55-100
1998 Haunted Mansion (green roof) 54935	Closed	2000	110.00	110-245
1984 Haversham House 5008-3	Closed	1987	37.00	182-247
1997 Hershey's® Chocolate Shop 54913	Open		55.00	55
1998 Hidden Ponds House 54944	Open		50.00	50
1986 Highland Park House 5063-6	Closed	1988	35.00	105-200
1995 Holly Brothers Garage 5485-4	Closed	1998	48.00	47-67
1999 Holy Spirit Church 55003, set/2	Open		70.00	70
1999 A Home In The Making 54979, set/5	Open		95.00	95
1988 Home Sweet Home/House & Windmill 5126-8	Closed	1991	60.00	65-119
1978 Homestead 5011-2	Closed	1984	30.00	195-294
1991 Honeymooner Motel 5401-1	Closed	1993	42.00	72-118

Year Issue	Edition Limit	Year Retd.	Issue Price	*Quote U.S.$
1998 The House That Love Built™ 1998 (Home For the Holidays) 2210	Yr.Iss.	1998	N/A	130
2000 How The Grinch Stole Christmas! - Movie Premiere, set/2 55103	Open		17.50	18
1993 Hunting Lodge 5445-3	Closed	1996	50.00	137-175
1976 The Inn 5003-9	Closed	1979	20.00	365
1997 Italianate Villa (American Architecture Series), 54911	Open		55.00	55
1989 J. Young's Granary 5149-7	Closed	1992	45.00	66-98
1991 Jack's Corner Barber Shop 5406-2	Closed	1994	42.00	59-88
1987 Jefferson School 5082-2	Closed	1991	36.00	129-188
1989 Jingle Belle Houseboat 5114-4	Closed	1991	42.00	150-235
1988 Kenwood House 5054-7	Closed	1990	50.00	100-150
1979 Knob Hill (gold) 5055-9	Closed	1981	30.00	320-370
1979 Knob Hill 5055-9	Closed	1981	30.00	295-358
1981 Large Single Tree 5080-6	Closed	1989	17.00	20-45
1999 Last Stop Gas Station 55012, set/2	Open		72.00	72
1987 Lighthouse 5030-0	Closed	1988	36.00	320-660
1986 Lincoln Park Duplex 5060-1	Closed	1988	33.00	125-140
1997 Linden Hills Country Club 54917, set/2	Open		60.00	60
1998 Lionel® Electric Train Shop 54947	Open		55.00	55
1979 Log Cabin 5057-5	Closed	1981	22.00	525-600
1999 Lucky Dragon Restaurant 55011	Open		75.00	75
1997 Main Street Gift Shop 5488-7	Closed	1998	50.00	28-50
1984 Main Street House 5005-9	Closed	1986	27.00	190-250
1990 Mainstreet Hardware Store 5153-5	Closed	1993	42.00	64-119
1977 Mansion (blue-green) 5008-8	Closed	1979	30.00	500-540
1977 Mansion (dark green) 5008-8	Closed	1979	30.00	800-850
1988 Maple Ridge Inn 5121-7	Closed	1990	55.00	40-88
1994 Marvel's Beauty Salon 5470-4	Closed	1997	37.50	34-54
1997 McDonald's® 54914	Closed	1999	65.00	50-65
1986 Mickey's Diner 5078-4	Closed	1987	22.00	550-690
1979 Mission Church 5062-5	Closed	1980	30.00	1174-1300
1979 Mobile Home 5063-3	Closed	1980	18.00	2200-2800
1990 Morningside House 5152-7	Closed	1992	45.00	48-82
1993 Mount Olivet Church 5442-9	Closed	1996	65.00	56-95
1976 Mountain Lodge 5001-3	Closed	1979	20.00	377-395
1978 Nantucket 5014-6	Closed	1986	25.00	165-270
1993 Nantucket Renovation 5441-0	Closed	1993	55.00	31-88
1997 New Hope Church 54904	Closed	1998	60.00	48-82
1984 New School House 5037-7	Closed	1986	35.00	199-225
1982 New Stone Church 5083-0	Closed	1984	32.00	350-432
1996 Nick's Tree Farm 54871, set/10 (Nick's Tree Farm, Nick The Tree Farmer Accessory)	Closed	1999	40.00	34-45
1989 North Creek Cottage 5120-9	Closed	1992	45.00	37-79
1991 Oak Grove Tudor 5400-3	Closed	1994	42.00	30-75
1997 Old Chelsea Mansion 54903	Closed	1998	85.00	50-85
1994 The Original Snow Village Starter Set 5462-3 (Sunday School Serenade Accessory, 3 asst. Sisal Trees, 1.5 oz. bag of real plastic snow)	Closed	1996	50.00	40-45
1994 • Shady Oak Church	Closed	1996	N/A	N/A
1986 Pacific Heights House 5066-0	Closed	1988	33.00	75-125
1988 Palos Verdes 5141-1	Closed	1990	37.50	48-82
1989 Paramount Theater 5142-0	Closed	1993	42.00	130-195
1984 Parish Church 5039-3	Closed	1986	32.00	290-354
1983 Parsonage 5029-6	Closed	1985	35.00	365-396
1995 Peppermint Porch Day Care 5485-2	Closed	1997	45.00	45-68
1989 Pinewood Log Cabin 5150-0	Closed	1995	37.50	37-70
1982 Pioneer Church 5022-9	Closed	1984	30.00	372-385
1995 Pisa Pizza 5485-1	Closed	1998	35.00	32-50
1985 Plantation House 5047-4	Closed	1987	37.00	88-138
1992 Post Office 5422-4	Closed	1995	35.00	62-82
1990 Prairie House (American Architecture Series), 5156-0	Closed	1993	42.00	60-80
1992 Print Shop & Village News 5425-9	Closed	1994	37.50	60-90
1990 Queen Anne Victorian (American Architecture Series), 5157-8	Closed	1996	48.00	43-94
1986 Ramsey Hill House 5067-9	Closed	1989	36.00	70-119
1987 Red Barn 5081-4	Closed	1992	38.00	65-107
1988 Redeemer Church 5127-6	Closed	1992	42.00	37-77
1996 Reindeer Bus Depot 54874	Closed	1997	42.00	33-59
1985 Ridgewood 5052-0	Closed	1987	35.00	115-160
1984 River Road House 5010-5	Closed	1987	36.00	138-250
1984 River Road House (open transom) 5010-5	Closed	1987	36.00	330-350
1996 Rockabilly Records 54880	Closed	1998	45.00	34-63
1998 Rock Creek Mill 54932	Closed	1998	64.00	59-78
1997 Rollerama Roller Rink 54916	Closed	1999	56.00	45-56
1996 Rosita's Cantina 54883	Closed	1999	50.00	40-75
1995 Ryman Auditorium 5485-5	Closed	1997	75.00	68-107
1986 Saint James Church 5068-7	Closed	1988	37.00	100-194
1979 School House 5060-9	Closed	1982	30.00	370-396
1996 The Secret Garden Florist 54885	Open		50.00	50
1998 The Secret Garden Greenhouse 54949	Open		60.00	60
1988 Service Station 5128-4	Closed	1991	37.50	158-285
1999 Shelly's Diner 55008, set/12	Open		110.00	110
1996 Shingle Victorian (American Architecture Series), 54884	Closed	1999	55.00	45-68
2000 Silver Bells Christmas Shop (Discover Department 56® Holiday Program) 55040, set/4	12/00		75.00	75
1988 Single Car Garage 5125-0	Closed	1990	22.00	35-55
2000 Sitting in the Park, set/4 55100	Open		28.00	28
1994 Skate & Ski Shop 5467-4	Closed	1998	50.00	30-69
1982 Skating Pond 5017-2	Closed	1984	25.00	320-396
1978 Skating Rink, Duck Pond (set) 5015-3	Closed	1979	16.00	898-975
1976 Small Chalet 5006-2	Closed	1979	15.00	456-550
1978 Small Double Trees w/ blue birds 5016-1	Closed	1989	13.50	157-175

*Quotes have been rounded up to nearest dollar

YEAR ISSUE	EDITION LIMIT	YEAR RETD.	ISSUE PRICE	*QUOTE U.S.$
1978 Small Double Trees w/ red birds 5016-1	Closed	1989	13.50	45
1996 Smokey Mountain Retreat 54872	Open		65.00	65
1995 Snow Carnival Ice Palace 5485-0	Closed	1998	95.00	70-135
1987 Snow Village Factory 5013-0	Closed	1989	45.00	96-144
1987 Snow Village Resort Lodge 5092-0	Closed	1989	55.00	85-165
1993 Snowy Hills Hospital 5448-8	Closed	1996	48.00	94-125
1998 Snowy Pines Inn Gift Set (Home For the Holidays) 54934, set/9	Yr.Iss.	1998	65.00	75-95
1986 Sonoma House 5062-8	Closed	1988	33.00	115-150
1991 Southern Colonial (American Architecture Series), 5403-8	Closed	1994	48.00	62-90
1990 Spanish Mission Church 5155-1	Closed	1992	42.00	68-125
1987 Springfield House 5027-0	Closed	1990	40.00	39-95
1985 Spruce Place 5049-0	Closed	1987	33.00	180-311
1987 St. Anthony Hotel & Post Office 5006-7	Closed	1989	40.00	75-132
1992 St. Luke's Church 5421-6	Closed	1994	45.00	34-82
1995 Starbucks Coffee 5485-9	Open		48.00	48
1997 Start A Tradition Set 54902, set/8 (Kringle's Toy Shop, Hot Chocolate Stand, Saturday Morning Downtown accessory, set/4, Bag of Real Plastic Snow, Cobblestone Road)	Closed	1998	75.00	45-100
1976 Steepled Church 5005-4	Closed	1979	25.00	480-600
1998 Stick Style House (American Architecture Series) 54943	Open		60.00	60
1977 Stone Church (10") 5009-6	Closed	1979	35.00	690-800
1979 Stone Church (8") 5059-1	Closed	1980	32.00	780-900
1980 Stone Mill House 5068-2	Closed	1982	30.00	400-546
1988 Stonehurst House 5140-3	Closed	1994	37.50	44-72
1984 Stratford House 5007-5	Closed	1986	28.00	135-232
1982 Street Car 5019-9	Closed	1984	16.00	330-403
1985 Stucco Bungalow 5045-8	Closed	1986	30.00	325-378
1984 Summit House 5036-9	Closed	1985	28.00	300-390
1999 Super Suds Laundromat 55006	Open		60.00	60
1982 Swiss Chalet 5023-7	Closed	1984	28.00	330-438
1979 Thatched Cottage 5050-0 Meadowland Series	Closed	1980	30.00	680-700
1980 Town Church 5071-7	Closed	1982	33.00	276-300
1983 Town Hall 5000-8	Closed	1984	32.00	300-360
1986 Toy Shop 5073-3	Closed	1990	36.00	64-110
1980 Train Station (8 window panes) w/ 3 Train Cars 5085-6	Closed	1985	100.00	325-345
1980 Train Station (6 window panes) w/ 3 Train Cars 5085-6	Closed	1985	100.00	395-425
1996 Treetop Tree House 54890	Open		35.00	37
1984 Trinity Church 5035-0	Closed	1986	32.00	200-360
1979 Tudor House 5061-7	Closed	1981	25.00	250-348
1983 Turn of the Century 5004-0	Closed	1986	36.00	195-288
1986 Twin Peaks 5042-3	Closed	1986	32.00	325-462
1998 Uncle Sam's Fireworks Stand 54974, set/2	Open		45.00	45
1998 Uptown Motors Ford® 54941, set/3	Open		95.00	95
1979 Victorian 5054-2	Closed	1982	30.00	235-360
1983 Victorian Cottage 5002-4	Closed	1984	35.00	300-375
1977 Victorian House 5007-0	Closed	1979	30.00	460-492
1999 Village Bank & Trust 55002	Open		75.00	75
1983 Village Church 5026-1	Closed	1984	30.00	400-450
1991 Village Greenhouse 5402-0	Closed	1995	35.00	30-75
1988 Village Market 5044-0	Closed	1991	39.00	59-95
1995 Village Police Station 5485-3	Closed	1998	48.00	44-67
1993 Village Public Library 5443-7	Closed	1997	55.00	53-82
1990 Village Realty 5154-3	Closed	1993	42.00	54-82
1992 Village Station 5438-0	Closed	1997	65.00	50-70
1988 Village Station and Train 5122-5	Closed	1992	65.00	57-120
1992 Village Vet and Pet Shop 5427-5	Closed	1995	32.00	70-100
1989 Village Warming House 5145-4	Closed	1992	42.00	45-85
1986 Waverly Place 5041-5	Closed	1986	35.00	248-305
1994 Wedding Chapel 5464-0	Open		55.00	55
1985 Williamsburg House 5046-6	Closed	1988	37.00	95-130
1993 Woodbury House 5444-5	Closed	1996	45.00	39-82
1983 Wooden Church 5031-8	Closed	1985	30.00	275-384
1981 Wooden Clapboard 5072-5	Closed	1984	32.00	180-300
1999 WSNO Radio 55010	Open		75.00	75

The Original Snow Village Collection Accessories Retired - Department 56

YEAR ISSUE	EDITION LIMIT	YEAR RETD.	ISSUE PRICE	*QUOTE U.S.$
1987 3 Nuns With Songbooks 5102-0	Closed	1988	6.00	120-154
1988 Apple Girl/Newspaper Boy 5129-2, set/2	Closed	1990	11.00	10-30
1979 Aspen Trees 5052-6, Meadowland Series	Closed	1980	16.00	450-515
1997 At The Barn Dance, It's Allemande Left 54927, set/2	Closed	1999	30.00	30-49
1989 Bringing Home The Tree 5169-1	Closed	1992	15.00	16-32
1989 Calling All Cars 5174-8, set/2	Closed	1991	15.00	58-75
1979 Carolers 5064-1	Closed	1986	12.00	95-126
1987 Caroling Family 5105-5, set/3	Closed	1990	20.00	14-38
1996 Caroling Through The Snow 54896	Closed	1999	15.00	15
1980 Ceramic Car 5069-0	Closed	1986	5.00	45-54
1981 Ceramic Sleigh 5079-2	Closed	1986	5.00	45-54
1993 Check It Out Bookmobile 5451-8, set/3	Closed	1995	25.00	17-38
1987 Children In Band 5104-7	Closed	1989	15.00	13-31
1989 Choir Kids 5147-0	Closed	1992	15.00	13-32
1993 Christmas at the Farm 5450-0, set/2	Closed	1996	16.00	12-16
1991 Christmas Cadillac 5413-5	Closed	1994	9.00	10-21
1987 Christmas Children 5107-1, set/4	Closed	1990	20.00	19-44
1997 Christmas Kids 54922, set/5	Closed	1999	27.50	28
1992 Christmas Puppies 5432-1, set/2	Closed	1996	27.50	18-41
1993 Classic Cars 54577, set/3	Closed	1998	22.50	15-35
1994 Coca-Cola® Brand Billboard 5481-0	Closed	1997	18.00	12-30
1994 Coca-Cola® Brand Delivery Men 54801, set/2	Closed	1998	25.00	19-38
1994 Coca-Cola® Brand Delivery Truck 54798	Closed	1998	15.00	20-27
1991 Cold Weather Sports 5410-0, set/4	Closed	1994	27.50	23-50
1991 Come Join The Parade 5411-9	Closed	1992	13.00	7-27
1991 Country Harvest 5415-1	Closed	1993	13.00	14-30
1989 Crack the Whip 5171-3, set/3	Closed	1996	25.00	13-38
1988 Doghouse/Cat In Garbage Can 5131-4, set/2	Closed	1992	15.00	20-57
1990 Down the Chimney He Goes 5158-6	Closed	1993	6.50	4-22
1992 Early Morning Delivery 5431-3, set/3	Closed	1995	27.50	12-40
1997 Everybody Goes Skating At Rollerama 54928, set/2	Closed	1999	25.00	15-25
1985 Family Mom/Kids, Goose/Girl 5057-1	Closed	1988	11.00	21-60
1994 Feeding The Birds 5473-9, set/3	Closed	1997	25.00	15-38
1995 Firewood Delivery Truck 54864	Closed	1999	15.00	12-15
1989 Flag Pole 51772	Closed	1999	8.50	6-19
1987 For Sale Sign 5108-0	Closed	1989	3.50	4-20
1990 Fresh Frozen Fish 5163-2, set/2	Closed	1993	20.00	30-55
1995 Frosty Playtime 54860, set/3	Closed	1997	30.00	28-30
1986 Girl/Snowman, Boy 5095-4	Closed	1987	11.00	60-75
1995 Grand Ole Opry Carolers 54867	Closed	1997	25.00	15-35
1996 A Harley-Davidson® Holiday 54898, set/2	Closed	1999	25.00	18-25
1988 Hayride 5117-9	Closed	1990	30.00	34-69
1997 He Led Them Down The Streets Of Town 54927, set/3	Closed	1999	30.00	30
1993 A Herd Of Holiday Heifers 5455-0, set/3	Closed	1997	18.00	18-30
1990 Here We Come A Caroling 5161-6, set/3	Closed	1992	18.00	11-35
1997 Hitch-up The Buckboard 54930	Closed	1999	40.00	17-38
1996 Holiday Hoops 54893, set/3	Closed	1999	20.00	20
1990 Home Delivery 5162-4, set/2	Closed	1992	16.00	22-45
1990 A Home For the Holidays 5165-9	Closed	1996	7.00	6-7
1986 Kids Around The Tree (large) 5094-6	Closed	1990	15.00	50-69
1986 Kids Around The Tree (small) 5094-6	Closed	1990	15.00	19-40
1997 Kids, Candy Canes....& Ronald Mc Donald® 54926, set/3	Closed	1999	30.00	24-30
1990 Kids Decorating the Village Sign 5134-9	Closed	1993	13.00	11-48
1989 Kids Tree House 5168-3	Closed	1991	25.00	33-50
1988 Man On Ladder Hanging Garland 5116-0	Closed	1992	7.50	10-24
1997 McDonald's®...Lights Up The Night 54925	Closed	1999	30.00	28-30
1996 Men At Work 54894, set/5	Closed	1998	27.50	12-22
1982 Monks-A-Caroling 6460-2	Closed	1983	6.00	135-180
1984 Monks-A-Caroling (brown) 5040-7	Closed	1988	6.00	26-35
1983 Monks-A-Caroling (butterscotch) 6459-9	Closed	1984	6.00	45-60
1996 Moving Day 54892, set/3	Closed	1998	32.50	22-47
1994 Mush! 5474-7, set/2	Closed	1997	20.00	13-32
1992 Nanny and the Preschoolers 5430-5, set/2	Closed	1994	27.50	13-41
1987 Park Bench (green) 5109-8	Closed	1993	3.00	5-10
1994 Pets on Parade 54720, set/2	Closed	1998	16.50	14-29
1996 Pick-Up & Delivery (St. Nick's) 5454-2	Closed	1996	10.00	30
1993 Pint-Size Pony Rides 5453-4, set/3	Closed	1996	37.50	24-54
1995 Pizza Delivery 54866, set/2	Closed	1998	20.00	16-32
1995 Poinsettias For Sale 54861, set/3	Closed	1998	30.00	21-44
1987 Praying Monks 5103-9	Closed	1988	6.00	35-40
1996 A Ride On The Reindeer Lines 54875, set/3	Closed	1997	35.00	25-38
1992 Round & Round We Go! 5433-0, set/2	Closed	1995	18.00	16-34
1993 Safety Patrol 5449-6, set/4	Closed	1997	27.50	10-41
1985 Santa/Mailbox 5059-8	Closed	1988	11.00	30-49
1994 Santa Comes To Town, 1995 5477-1	Closed	1995	30.00	36-57
1995 Santa Comes To Town, 1996 54862	Closed	1996	32.50	22-47
1996 Santa Comes To Town, 1997 54899	Closed	1997	35.00	22-50
1997 Santa Comes To Town, 1998 54920	Closed	1998	30.00	30-44
1998 Santa Comes To Town, 1999 54958	Closed	1999	30.00	30
1988 School Bus, Snow Plow 5137-3, set/2	Closed	1991	16.00	42-59
1988 School Children 5118-7, set/3	Closed	1990	15.00	10-30
1984 Scottie With Tree 5038-5	Closed	1985	3.00	176-220
1995 Service With a Smile 54865, set/2	Closed	1998	25.00	17-38
1979 Sheep, 9 White, 3 Black 5053-4 Meadowland Series	Closed	1980	12.00	400
1986 Shopping Girls w/Packages (large) 5096-2	Closed	1988	11.00	45-60
1986 Shopping Girls w/Packages (small) 5096-2	Closed	1988	11.00	24-35
1985 Singing Nuns 5053-9	Closed	1987	6.00	120-136
1988 Sisal Tree Lot 8183-3	Closed	1991	45.00	50-104
1989 Skate Faster Mom 5170-5	Closed	1991	13.00	11-35
1990 Sleighride 5160-8	Closed	1992	30.00	23-65
1990 Sno-Jet Snowmobile 5159-4	Closed	1993	15.00	19-35
1995 Snow Carnival Ice Sculpture 54868, set/2	Closed	1998	27.50	18-41
1995 Snow Carnival King & Queen 54869	Closed	1998	35.00	27-50
1987 Snow Kids 5113-6, set/4	Closed	1990	20.00	35-60
1985 Snow Kids Sled, Skis 5056-3	Closed	1987	11.00	39-50
1991 Snowball Fort 5414-3, set/3	Closed	1993	27.50	29-48
1982 Snowman With Broom 5018-0	Closed	1990	3.00	10-22
1992 Spirit of Snow Village Airplane 5440-2	Closed	1996	32.50	25-42
1993 Spirit of Snow Village Airplane 5458-5, 2 asst.	Closed	1996	12.50	42-58
1989 Statue of Mark Twain 5173-0	Closed	1991	15.00	16-57
1994 Stuck In The Snow 54712, set/3	Closed	1998	30.00	21-44
1989 Street Sign, set/6 5167-5	Closed	1992	7.50	19-50
1990 SV Special Delivery 5197-7, set/2	Closed	1992	16.00	38-43
1997 Television Antenna 52658, set/4	Closed	1999	5.00	5
1996 Terry's Towing 54895, set/2	Closed	1999	20.00	16-24
1993 Tour The Village 5452-6	Closed	1997	12.50	8-16
1989 Through the Woods 5172-1, set/2	Closed	1991	18.00	12-45
1990 A Tree For Me 5164-0, set/2	Closed	1995	8.00	7-24
1988 Tree Lot 51381	Closed	1999	37.50	21-35
1989 US Mailbox 5179-9	Closed	1990	3.50	8-12
1989 US Special Delivery 51489, (red, white, blue) set/2	Closed	1990	16.00	32-56
1990 US Special Delivery 51977, (red, green) set/2	Closed	1992	16.00	17-34
1989 Village Birds 5180-2, set/6	Closed	1994	3.50	7-16
1989 Village Gazebo 5146-2	Closed	1995	30.00	25-45
1991 Village Greetings 5418-6, set/3	Closed	1994	5.00	6-10
1993 Village News Delivery 5459-3, set/2	Closed	1996	15.00	11-21
1991 Village Marching Band 5412-7, set/3	Closed	1992	30.00	40-75
1992 Village Used Car Lot 5428-3, set/5	Closed	1997	45.00	25-44
1988 Water Tower 5133-0	Closed	1991	20.00	69-95
1989 Water Tower-John Deer 568-0	Closed	1991	20.00	650-985
1992 We're Going to a Christmas Pageant 5435-6	Closed	1994	15.00	12-27
1997 The Whole Family Goes Shopping 54905, set/3	Closed	1999	25.00	25
1991 Winter Fountain 5409-7	Closed	1993	25.00	37-85
1992 Winter Playground 5436-4	Closed	1995	20.00	23-44
1988 Woodsman and Boy 5130-6, set/2	Closed	1991	13.00	15-19
1988 Woody Station Wagon 5136-5	Closed	1990	6.50	17-40
1991 Wreaths For Sale 5408-9,set/4	Closed	1994	27.50	17-50

Profile Series - Department 56

YEAR ISSUE	EDITION LIMIT	YEAR RETD.	ISSUE PRICE	*QUOTE U.S.$
1996 Heinz House	Closed	1996	28.00	49-95
1997 State Farm Insurance 75th Anniversary 56000	Closed	1997	35.50	68-94

Retired Heritage Village Collection Accessories - Department 56

YEAR ISSUE	EDITION LIMIT	YEAR RETD.	ISSUE PRICE	*QUOTE U.S.$
1995 The 12 Days of Dickens' Village, A Partridge In A Pear Tree 58351	Closed	1999	35.00	35-44
1995 The 12 Days of Dickens' Village, Two Turtle Doves 58360, set/4	Closed	1999	32.50	32-41
1995 The 12 Days of Dickens' Village, Three French Hens 58378, set/3	Closed	1999	32.50	33-50
1995 The 12 Days of Dickens' Village, Four Calling Birds 58379, set/2	Closed	1999	32.50	33-55
1995 The 12 Days of Dickens' Village, Five Golden Rings 58381, set/2	Closed	1999	27.50	28-50
1995 The 12 Days of Dickens' Village, Six Geese A-Laying 58382, set/2	Closed	1999	30.00	30-50
1991 All Around the Town 5545-0, set/2	Closed	1993	18.00	20-30
1987 Alpine Village Sign 6571-4	Closed	1993	6.00	5-24
1986 Alpine Villagers 6542-0, set/3	Closed	1992	13.00	22-36
1990 Amish Buggy 5949-8	Closed	1992	22.00	65
1990 Amish Family 5948-0, set/3	Closed	1992	20.00	22-65
1990 Amish Family, w/Moustache 5948-0, set/3	Closed	1992	20.00	22-75
1997 Animated Ski Mountain With 3 Skiers 52641	Closed	1998	85.00	65-85
1997 Ashley Pond Skating Party 58405, set/6	Closed	1999	70.00	65-88
1987 Automobiles 5964-1, set/3	Closed	1996	22.00	12-20
1995 Bachman's Squash Cart 753-6	Closed	1996	50.00	75-98
1997 Bachman's Wilcox Truck 880-8	Closed	1997	29.95	42
1991 Baker Elves 5603-0, set/3	Closed	1995	27.50	14-47
1997 Big Smile For The Camera 58900, set/2	Closed	1999	27.50	24-28
1992 The Bird Seller 5803-3, set/3	Closed	1995	25.00	15-35
1987 Blacksmith 5934-0, set/3	Closed	1990	20.00	44-85
1993 Blue Star Ice Harvesters 5650-2, set/2	Closed	1997	27.50	23-28
1989 Boulevard 5916-6, set/14	Closed	1993	25.00	36-44
1993 Bringing Fleeces To The Mill 58190, set/2	Closed	1998	35.00	26-40
1991 Bringing Home The Yule Log 55581, set/3	Closed	1998	28.00	15-32
1995 Brixton Road Watchman 58390, set/2	Closed	1999	25.00	24-32
1995 A Busy Elf North Pole Sign 56366	Closed	1999	20.00	16-20
1990 Busy Sidewalks 5535-2, set/4	Closed	1992	28.00	35-50
1992 Buying Bakers Bread 5619-7, set/2	Closed	1995	20.00	14-38
1993 C. Bradford, Wheelwright & Son 5818-1, set/2	Closed	1996	24.00	18-31
1990 Carolers on the Doorstep 5570-0, set/4	Closed	1993	25.00	19-45
1984 Carolers, w/ Lamppost (bl) 6526-9, set/3	Closed	1990	10.00	23-29
1984 Carolers, w/ Lamppost (wh) 6526-9, set/3	Closed	1990	10.00	65-90
1991 Caroling Thru The City 55484, set/3	Closed	1998	27.50	22-28
1994 Chamber Orchestra 58840, set/4	Closed	1998	37.50	28-54
1995 Charting Santa's Course 56364, set/2	Closed	1997	25.00	24-38
1993 Chelsea Lane Shoppers 58165, set/4	Closed	1999	30.00	22-30
1994 Chelsea Market Curiosities Monger & Cart 58270, set/2	Closed	1998	27.50	28-32
1993 Chelsea Market Fish Monger & Cart 5814-9, set/2	Closed	1997	25.00	15-32
1993 Chelsea Market Fruit Monger & Cart 5813-0, set/2	Closed	1997	25.00	15-25
1994 Chelsea Market Mistletoe Monger & Cart 58262, set/2	Closed	1998	25.00	25-32
1988 Childe Pond and Skaters 5903-0, set/4	Closed	1991	30.00	45-94
1995 Choirboys All-In-A-Row 58892	Closed	1998	20.00	22-40
1997 Christmas Bazaar...Flapjacks & Hot Cider 56595, set/2	Closed	1999	27.50	26-30
1996 Christmas Bazaar...Handmade Quilts 56594, set/2	Closed	1999	25.00	25

*Quotes have been rounded up to nearest dollar

Collectors' Information Bureau

283

ARCHITECTURE

YEAR ISSUE	EDITION LIMIT	YEAR RETD.	ISSUE PRICE	*QUOTE U.S.$
1997 Christmas Bazaar...Sign 56598, set/2	Closed	1999	16.00	14-20
1997 Christmas Bazaar...Toy Vendor & Cart 56597, set/2	Closed	1999	27.50	22-30
1996 Christmas Bazaar...Woolens & Preserves 56595, set/2	Closed	1999	25.00	20-25
1986 Christmas Carol Figures 6501-3, set/3	Closed	1990	12.50	48-84
1996 A Christmas Carol Reading by Charles Dickens 58404, set/7 (Charles Dickens' Signature Series)	42,500	1997	75.00	88-165
1994 Christmas Carol Revisited Holiday Trimming Set 5831-9, set/21	Closed	1997	65.00	45-65
1987 Christmas in the City Sign 5960-9	Closed	1993	6.00	8-25
1990 Christmas Trash Cans 52094, set/2	Closed	1998	7.00	7-15
1992 Churchyard Fence Extensions 5807-6, set/4	Closed	1997	16.00	14-17
1992 Churchyard Gate & Fence 5806-8, set/3	Closed	1997	15.00	15-17
1992 Churchyard Gate and Fence 5563-8, set/3	Closed	1992	15.00	55-65
1988 City Bus & Milk Truck 5983-8, set/2	Closed	1991	15.00	27-32
1988 City Newsstand 5971-4, set/4	Closed	1991	25.00	105
1987 City People 5965-0, set/5	Closed	1990	27.50	45-65
1991 City Subway Entrance 55417	Closed	1998	15.00	15-18
1987 City Workers 5967-6, set/4	Closed	1988	15.00	29-40
1995 Cobbler & Clock Peddler 58394, set/2	Closed	1997	25.00	20-38
1994 Coca-Cola® Brand Neon Sign 54828	Closed	1998	16.50	15-17
1991 Come into the Inn, 5560-3	Closed	1994	22.00	20-40
1989 Constables 5579-4, set/3	Closed	1991	17.50	57-68
1992 Courtyard Fence With Steps 52205	Closed	1998	4.00	12
1986 Covered Wooden Bridge 6531-5	Closed	1990	10.00	20-26
1989 David Copperfield Characters 5551-4, set/5	Closed	1992	32.50	22-45
1997 Delivering Coal For The Hearth 58326, set/2	Closed	1999	32.50	33-41
1987 Dickens' Village Sign 6569-2	Closed	1993	6.00	13-20
1992 Don't Drop The Presents! 5532-8, set/2	Closed	1995	25.00	28-38
1987 Dover Coach 6590-0	Closed	1990	18.00	44-48
1987 Dover Coach w/o Mustache 6590-0	Closed	1990	18.00	75-90
1996 Early Rising Elves 56369, set/5	Closed	1999	32.50	26-44
1996 End Of The Line 56370, set/2	Closed	1999	28.00	23-57
1989 Farm Animals 5945-5, set/4	Closed	1991	15.00	29-47
1987 Farm People And Animals 5901-3, set/5	Closed	1989	24.00	77-88
1988 Fezziwig and Friends 5928-5, set/3	Closed	1990	12.50	48-65
1991 The Fire Brigade 5546-8, set/2	Closed	1995	20.00	18-35
1988 Fire Hydrant & Mailbox 51322, set/2	Closed	1998	6.00	8-19
1991 Fire Truck, "City Fire Dept." 5547-6, set/2	Closed	1995	18.00	23-35
1990 The Flying Scot Train 55735, set/4	Closed	1998	50.00	35-63
1989 For Sale Sign (Bachman's) 51667	Closed	1998	4.50	32-40
1989 For Sale Sign 51667	Closed	1998	4.50	5-10
1996 Going Home For The Holidays 58896, set/3	Closed	1999	27.50	28
1995 Harvest Pumpkin Wagon 56591	Closed	1999	45.00	45
1992 Harvest Seed Cart 5645-6, set/3	Closed	1995	27.50	24
1989 Heritage Village Sign 9953-8	Closed	1989	6.00	14-17
1991 Holiday Coach 55611	Closed	1998	70.00	44-70
1994 Holiday Field Trip 58858, set/3	Closed	1998	27.50	24-41
1990 Holiday Travelers 5571-9, set/3	Closed	1999	25.00	20-25
1994 Hot Dog Vendor 5886-6, set/3	Closed	1997	27.50	19-41
1995 I'll Need More Toys 56365, set/2	Closed	1998	25.00	20-30
1995 King's Road Cab 55816	Closed	1998	30.00	19-36
1993 Knife Grinder 5649-9, set/2	Closed	1996	22.50	18-24
1994 Last Minute Delivery 56367	Closed	1998	35.00	24-40
1997 Let's Go Shopping In The City 58899, set/3	Closed	1999	35.00	35
1992 Letters for Santa 5604-9, set/3	Closed	1994	30.00	57-75
1986 Lighted Tree With Children & Ladder 6510-2	Closed	1989	35.00	150-225
1992 Lionhead Bridge 5864-5	Closed	1997	22.00	14-22
1995 Lumberjacks 56590, set/2	Closed	1998	30.00	18-44
1991 Mail Box & Fire Hydrant 52140, set/2	Closed	1998	5.00	12-20
1987 Maple Sugaring Shed 6589-7, set/3	Closed	1989	19.00	195-200
1991 Market Day 5641-3, set/3	Closed	1993	35.00	16-50
1987 New England Village Sign 6570-6	Closed	1993	6.00	7-20
1986 New England Winter set 6532-3, set/5	Closed	1990	18.00	35-63
1996 A New Potbellied Stove For Christmas 56593, set/2	Closed	1998	35.00	28-40
1988 Nicholas Nickleby Characters 5929-3, set/4	Closed	1991	20.00	20-27
1996 North Pole Express 56368, set/3	Closed	1999	37.50	30-63
1993 North Pole Gate 56324	Closed	1998	32.50	27-35
1994 The Old Man And The Sea 56553, set/3	Closed	1998	25.00	20-38
1992 The Old Puppeteer 5802-5, set/3	Closed	1995	32.00	24-40
1991 Oliver Twist Characters 5554-9, set/3	Closed	1993	35.00	24-50
1988 One Horse Open Sleigh 5982-0	Closed	1993	20.00	24-40
1995 One-Man Band And The Dancing Dog 58891, set/2	Closed	1998	17.50	14-30
1989 Organ Grinder 5957-9, set/3	Closed	1991	21.00	28-35
1994 Over The River And Through The Woods 56545	Closed	1998	35.00	30-50
1987 Ox Sled (blue pants) 5951-0	Closed	1989	20.00	78-96
1987 Ox Sled (tan pants) 5951-0	Closed	1989	20.00	255-270
1993 Pine Cone Trees 522-13, set/2	Closed	1995	15.00	10-15
1993 Playing in the Snow 5556-5, set/3	Closed	1996	25.00	20-38
1997 Poinsettia Delivery Truck 59000	Closed	1999	32.50	14-38
1994 Polka Fest 56073, set/3	Closed	1999	30.00	30-38
1989 Popcorn Vendor 5958-7, set/3	Closed	1992	22.00	24-40
1986 Porcelain Trees 6537-4, set/2	Closed	1992	14.00	27-35
1994 Portobello Road Peddlers 58289, set/3	Closed	1998	27.50	23-41
1994 Postern 9871-0, (Dickens' Village Ten Year Accessory Anniversary Piece)	Closed	1994	17.50	12-40

YEAR ISSUE	EDITION LIMIT	YEAR RETD.	ISSUE PRICE	*QUOTE U.S.$
1991 Poultry Market 5559-0, set/3	Closed	1995	32.00	25-45
1988 Red Covered Bridge 5987-0	Closed	1994	17.00	18-30
1989 River Street Ice House Cart 5959-5	Closed	1991	20.00	38-52
1989 Royal Coach 5578-6	Closed	1992	55.00	50-85
1988 Salvation Army Band 5985-4, set/6	Closed	1991	24.00	78-100
1990 Santa's Little Helpers 5610-3, set/3	Closed	1993	28.00	48-60
1987 Shopkeepers 5966-8, set/4	Closed	1988	15.00	25-29
1987 Silo And Hay Shed 5950-1	Closed	1989	18.00	136-148
1993 Sing a Song For Santa, set/3 5631-6	Closed	1998	28.00	24-32
1991 Sisal Wreath 54194, set/6	Closed	1998	4.00	7-10
1987 Skating Pond 6545-5	Closed	1990	24.00	25-85
1990 Sleepy Hollow Characters 5956-0, set/3	Closed	1992	27.50	28-55
1986 Sleighride 6511-0	Closed	1990	19.50	32-60
1988 Snow Children 5938-2	Closed	1994	17.00	20-30
1994 Snow Cone Elves 5637-5, set/4	Closed	1997	30.00	32-34
1997 Spirit Of The Season 58898	Closed	1999	20.00	20
1997 Steppin' Out On The Town 58885, set/5	Closed	1999	35.00	35
1987 Stone Bridge 6546-3	Closed	1990	12.00	38-48
1993 Street Musicians 5564-6, set/3	Closed	1997	25.00	20-25
1995 Tallyho 58391, set/5	Closed	1998	50.00	38-69
1996 Tending New Calves with Kids 58398, set/3	Closed	1999	30.00	22-38
1998 Tending The Cold Frame 58416, set/3	Closed	1999	32.50	32-41
1992 Testing The Toys 56057, set/2	Closed	1999	16.50	14-17
1994 Thatchers 5829-7, set/3	Closed	1997	35.00	27-40
1990 Tis the Season 5539-5	Closed	1994	12.95	10-25
1989 Town Square Gazebo 5513-1	Closed	1997	19.00	21
1992 Town Tinker 5646-4, set/2	Closed	1995	24.00	19-28
1990 The Toy Peddler 56162, set/3	Closed	1998	22.00	11-34
1991 Toymaker Elves 5602-2, set/3	Closed	1995	27.50	19-45
1990 Tree-Lined Courtyard Fence 52124	Closed	1998	4.00	4
1990 Trimming the North Pole 5608-1	Closed	1993	10.00	34-45
1994 Two Rivers Bridge 5656-1	Closed	1997	35.00	23-35
1989 U.S. Mail Box and Fire Hydrant 5517-4	Closed	1990	5.00	18-20
1993 Utility Accessories 55123, set/8	Closed	1998	12.50	12-15
1990 Victoria Station Platform 5575-1	Closed	1999	22.00	21-25
1995 Village Arctic Pines 52608, set/3	Closed	1998	12.00	12
1995 Village Autumn Trees 52616, set/3	Closed	1998	13.50	14
1995 Village Cedar Pine Forest 52606, set/3	Closed	1998	15.00	15
1993 Village Chain Link Fence Extensions 52353, set/4	Closed	1998	15.00	9-15
1993 Village Chain Link Fence w/Gate 52345, set/3	Closed	1998	12.00	12
1995 Village Double Pine Trees 52619	Closed	1998	13.50	14
1987 Village Express Train (electric, black), 5997-8	Closed	1988	89.95	195-225
1988 Village Express Train 5980-3, set/22	Closed	1996	95.00	138-145
1993 Village Express Van (black), 9951-1	Closed	1993	25.00	35-125
1993 Village Express Van (gold), 9977-5 (promotional)	Closed	1993	N/A	451-500
1992 Village Express Van (green) 5865-3	Closed	1996	25.00	18-32
1994 Village Express Van-Bachman's 729-3	Closed	1994	22.50	34-65
1994 Village Express Van-Bronner's 737-4	Closed	1994	22.50	18-32
1995 Village Express Van-Canadian 2163-7	Closed	1995	N/A	36-58
1994 Village Express Van-Christmas Dove 730-7	Closed	1994	25.00	38-69
1994 Village Express Van-European Imports 739-0	Closed	1994	22.50	38-42
1994 Village Express Van-Fortunoff's 735-8	Closed	1994	22.50	60-75
1994 Village Express Van-Limited Edition 733-1	Closed	1994	25.00	63-70
1994 Village Express Van-Lock, Stock & Barrel 731-5	Closed	1994	22.50	50-110
1994 Village Express Van-North Pole City 736-6	Closed	1994	25.00	42-54
1995 Village Express Van-Park West 0755-2	Closed	1995	N/A	460
1994 Village Express Van-Robert's Christmas Wonderland 734-0	Closed	1994	22.50	25-40
1995 Village Express Van-St. Nicks 756-0	Closed	1995	25.00	47-55
1994 Village Express Van-Stat's 741-2	Closed	1994	22.50	28-38
1994 Village Express Van-The Incredible Christmas Place (Pigeon Forge) 732-3	Closed	1994	24.98	40-42
1994 Village Express Van-The Lemon Tree 721-8	Closed	1994	30.00	35-40
1994 Village Express Van-William Glen 738-2	Closed	1994	22.50	31-42
1994 Village Express Van-Windsor Shoppe 740-4	Closed	1994	25.00	32-45
1995 Village Frosted Fir Trees 52605, set/4	Closed	1998	15.00	15
1996 Village Frosted Hemlock Tree 52638, set/2	Closed	1998	32.50	33
1991 Village Frosted Norway Pines 51756, set/3	Closed	1998	12.95	13
1988 Village Harvest People 5941-2, set/4	Closed	1991	27.50	44-55
1995 Village Let It Snow Snowman Sign 52594	Closed	1998	12.50	13
1997 Village Lighted Christmas Tree 52690	Closed	1998	48.00	50
1990 Village Mail Box 51985	Closed	1998	3.50	4-10
1996 Village Mini Lights 52626	Closed	1998	10.00	10
1989 Village Parking Meter 51780, set/4	Closed	1998	6.00	6-10
1994 Village Pencil Pines 52469, set/3	Closed	1998	15.00	15-18
1996 Village Pole Pine Forest 55271, set/5	Closed	1998	48.00	38-46
1991 Village Pole Pine Tree, large 55298	Closed	1998	12.50	13-15
1991 Village Pole Pine Tree, small 55280	Closed	1998	10.00	13-15
1995 Village Ponderosa Pines 52607, set/3	Closed	1998	13.00	13
1994 Village Porcelain Pine Trees 5251-5, set/2	Closed	1997	15.00	22-25
1992 Village Porcelain Pine, large 5218-3	Closed	1997	12.50	15-20
1992 Village Porcelain Pine, small 5219-1	Closed	1997	10.00	12-15
1989 Village Sign with Snowman 5572-7	Closed	1994	10.00	12-15
1991 Village Snow Fence 52043	Closed	1998	7.00	7-20

YEAR ISSUE	EDITION LIMIT	YEAR RETD.	ISSUE PRICE	*QUOTE U.S.$
1989 Village Stop Sign 51764, set/2	Closed	1998	5.00	6-10
1992 Village Street Peddlers 5804-1, set/2	Closed	1994	16.00	14-30
1994 Village Streetcar 52400, set/10	Closed	1998	65.00	50-62
1991 Village Town Clock 51101, 2 asst.	Closed	1998	3.00	5
1985 Village Train Brighton 6527-7, set/3	Closed	1986	12.00	295-369
1988 Village Train Trestle 5981-1	Closed	1990	17.00	32-63
1995 Village Wagon Wheel Pine Grove 52617	Closed	1998	22.50	20-23
1987 Village Well And Holy Cross 6547-1, set/2	Closed	1989	13.00	88-138
1996 Village White Picket Fence Extensions 52625, set/6	Closed	1998	10.00	10
1996 Village White Picket Fence With Gate 52624, set/5	Closed	1998	10.00	10
1989 Violet Vendor/Carolers/Chestnut Vendor 5580-8, set/3	Closed	1992	23.00	22-50
1993 Vision of a Christmas Past 5817-3, set/3	Closed	1996	27.50	18-35
1992 Welcome Home 5533-6, set/3	Closed	1995	27.50	16-40
1988 Woodcutter And Son 5986-2, set/2	Closed	1990	10.00	29-55
1993 Woodsmen Elves 5630-8, set/3	Closed	1995	27.50	45-65
1991 Wrought Iron Fence 59986, 2 asst.	Closed	1998	2.50	12-17
1991 Wrought Iron Fence Extensions 55158, set/9	Closed	1998	12.50	14-15
1991 Wrought Iron Gate And Fence 55140, set/9	Closed	1998	15.00	14-21
1996 Yeomen of the Guard 58397, set/5	Closed	1997	30.00	58-63

Seasons Bay Series - Department 56

YEAR ISSUE	EDITION LIMIT	YEAR RETD.	ISSUE PRICE	*QUOTE U.S.$
1998 Bay Street Shops 53401, set/2	Open		135.00	135
1998 Bay Street Shops (1st Ed.) 53301, set/2	Closed	1999	135.00	135
1998 Chapel On The Hill 53402	Open		72.00	72
1998 Chapel On The Hill (1st Ed.) 53302	Closed	1999	72.00	72
1998 The Grand Creamery 53405	Open		60.00	60
1998 The Grand Creamery (1st Ed.) 53305	Closed	1999	60.00	60
1998 Grandview Shores Hotel 53400	Open		150.00	150
1998 Grandview Shores Hotel (1st Ed.) 53300	Closed	1999	150.00	150
1998 Inglenook Cottage #5 53404	Open		60.00	60
1998 Inglenook Cottage #5 (1st Ed.) 53304	Closed	1999	60.00	60
2000 Mystic Ledge Lighthouse 53445	5,600		96.00	96
1999 Parkside Pavilion (Discover Department 56® Spring Promotion) 53412, gift set/9	Open		75.00	75
1999 Parkside Pavilion 53411, set/2	Open		65.00	65
1998 Side Porch Café 53403	Open		50.00	50
1998 Side Porch Café (1st Ed.) 53303	Closed	1999	50.00	50
1999 Springlake Station 53413	Open		90.00	90
1999 Stillwaters Boathouse 53414	Open		70.00	70

Storybook Village - Department 56

YEAR ISSUE	EDITION LIMIT	YEAR RETD.	ISSUE PRICE	*QUOTE U.S.$
1999 The Butcher, Baker and Candlestick Maker 13186, set/2	Open		75.00	75
1996 Goldilocks Bed And Breakfast 13193, set/4	Closed	1999	75.00	75
1998 H.D. Diddle Fiddles 13183, set/4	Open		75.00	75
1996 Hickory Dickory Dock 13195, set/3	Closed	1998	95.00	95
1996 Lambsville School 13194, set/5	Closed	1999	75.00	75
1999 Lil' Boy Blue Petting Farm 13172, set/3	Open		75.00	75
2000 Little Bo-Peep's Woolery, set/3 13174	Open		75.00	75
1999 Mother Goose Book Cellar 13171, set/5	Open		75.00	75
1998 Old House In Paris That Was Covered With Vines 13185, set/9	Open		75.00	75
1996 Old Woman Cobbler 13191, set/5	Closed	1999	75.00	75
1996 Peter Piper Pickle And Peppers 13192, set/4	Closed	1998	95.00	95
1998 Peter Piper's 13184, set/3	Open		75.00	75
1999 Queen's House of Cards 13173, set/8	Open		85.00	85
1999 Storybook Village Collection Landscape Set 13179, set/6	Open		10.00	10
1999 Storybook Village Collection Sign 13169	Open		10.00	10

Village CCP Miniatures - Department 56

YEAR ISSUE	EDITION LIMIT	YEAR RETD.	ISSUE PRICE	*QUOTE U.S.$
1987 Christmas Carol Cottages 6561-7, set/3	Closed	1989	30.00	83-93
1987 • The Cottage of Bob Cratchit & Tiny Tim 6561-7	Closed	1989	10.00	38-50
1987 • Fezziwig's Warehouse 6561-7	Closed	1989	10.00	26-30
1987 • Scrooge/ Marley Countinghouse 6561-7	Closed	1989	10.00	40-42
1987 Dickens' Chadbury Station & Train 6592-7	Closed	1989	27.50	50-55
1987 Dickens' Cottages 6559-5, set/3	Closed	1989	30.00	345
1987 • Stone Cottage 6559-5	Closed	1989	10.00	98-130
1987 • Thatched Cottage 6559-5	Closed	1989	10.00	105-125
1987 • Tudor Cottage 6559-5	Closed	1989	10.00	121-140
1988 Dickens' Kenilworth Castle 6565-0	Closed	1989	30.00	120-125
1987 Dickens' Lane Shops 6591-9, set/3	Closed	1989	30.00	140-150
1987 • Cottage Toy Shop 6591-9	Closed	1989	10.00	25-30
1987 • Thomas Kersey Coffee House 6591-9	Closed	1989	10.00	40-56
1987 • Tuttle's Pub 6591-9	Closed	1989	10.00	28-50
1987 Dickens' Village Assorted 6560-9, set/3	Closed	1989	48.00	140
1987 • Blythe Pond Mill House 6560-9	Closed	1989	16.00	40-42
1987 • Dickens Village Church 6560-9	Closed	1989	16.00	38-40
1987 • Norman Church 6560-9	Closed	1989	16.00	130-138

*Quotes have been rounded up to nearest dollar

YEAR ISSUE		EDITION LIMIT	YEAR RETD.	ISSUE PRICE	*QUOTE U.S.$
1987	Dickens' Village Assorted 6562-5, set/4	Closed	1989	60.00	300
1987	• Barley Bree Farmhouse 6562-5	Closed	1989	15.00	22-55
1987	• Brick Abbey 6562-5	Closed	1989	15.00	88-105
1987	• Chesterton Manor House 6562-5	Closed	1989	15.00	120-130
1987	• The Old Curiosity Shop 6562-5	Closed	1989	15.00	72-75
1987	Dickens' Village Original 6558-7, set/7	Closed	1989	72.00	219
1987	• Abel Beesley Butcher 6558-7	Closed	1989	12.00	24-30
1987	• Bean and Son Smithy Shop 6558-7	Closed	1989	12.00	32-40
1987	• Candle Shop 6558-7	Closed	1989	12.00	35-40
1987	• Crowntree Inn 6558-7	Closed	1989	12.00	35-38
1987	• Golden Swan Baker 6558-7	Closed	1989	12.00	17-25
1987	• Green Grocer 6558-7	Closed	1989	12.00	17-45
1987	• Jones & Co Brush & Basket Shop 6558-7	Closed	1989	12.00	28-68
1987	Little Town of Bethlehem 5976-5, set/12	Closed	1989	85.00	215-285
1988	New England Village Assorted 5937-4, set/6	Closed	1989	85.00	400-500
1988	• Craggy Cove Lighthouse 5937-4	Closed	1989	14.50	89-105
1988	• Jacob Adams Barn 5937-4	Closed	1989	14.50	49-55
1988	• Jacob Adams Farmhouse 5937-4	Closed	1989	14.50	47-50
1988	• Maple Sugaring Shed 5937-4	Closed	1989	14.50	46-60
1988	• Smythe Wollen Mill 5937-4	Closed	1989	14.50	75-80
1988	• Timber Knoll Log Cabin 5937-4	Closed	1989	14.50	48-50
1988	New England Village Original 5935-8, set/7	Closed	1989	72.00	680
1988	• Apothecary Shop 5935-8	Closed	1989	10.50	38-45
1988	• Brick Town Hall 5935-8	Closed	1989	10.50	55-60
1988	• General Store 5935-8	Closed	1989	10.50	62-70
1988	• Livery Stable & Boot Shop 5935-8	Closed	1989	10.50	55-60
1988	• Nathaniel Bingham Fabrics 5935-8	Closed	1989	10.50	63-65
1988	• Red Schoolhouse 5935-8	Closed	1989	10.50	80-90
1988	• Village Steeple Church 5935-8	Closed	1989	10.50	155-200
1986	Victorian Miniatures, set/2 6564-1	Closed	1987	45.00	219-248
1986	• Church 6564-1	Closed	1987	22.50	40-93
1986	• Estate 6564-1	Closed	1987	22.50	40-88
1986	Victorian Miniatures 6563-3, set/5	Closed	1987	65.00	275
1986	Williamsburg Snowhouse Series, set/6	Closed	1987	60.00	625
1986	• Williamsburg Church, White 6566-8	Closed	1987	10.00	30-62
1986	• Williamsburg House Brown Brick 6566-8	Closed	1987	10.00	61
1986	• Williamsburg House, Blue 6566-8	Closed	1987	10.00	20-50
1986	• Williamsburg House, Brown Clapboard	Closed	1987	10.00	50-75
1986	• Williamsburg House, Red 6566-8	Closed	1987	10.00	20-50
1986	• Williamsburg House, White 6566-8	Closed	1987	10.00	30-62

The Encore Group

Snow Buddies Snowville™ - Encore

YEAR ISSUE		EDITION LIMIT	YEAR RETD.	ISSUE PRICE	*QUOTE U.S.$
2000	Boot Repair Shop	Open		25.00	25
2000	Bridge	Open		5.00	5
2000	Church	Open		25.00	25
2000	Flurry's Home Sweet Home	Open		25.00	25
2000	Hat Shop	Open		19.00	19
2000	Ice Pond	Open		15.00	15
2000	Knitting School	Open		25.00	25
2000	Lamp Post	Open		3.00	3
2000	Sno Cone Shop	Open		15.00	15
2000	Sports Shop	Open		30.00	30
2000	Sports Shop, 20"	Yr.Iss.		350.00	350
2000	Tree, lg.	Open		8.00	8
2000	Tree, med.	Open		4.00	4
2000	Tree, sm.	Open		2.50	3
2000	Welcome To Snowville Sign	Open		4.00	4

Forma Vitrum/Cavanagh Group Intl.

American Coastal Heritage - Cavanagh

YEAR ISSUE		EDITION LIMIT	YEAR RETD.	ISSUE PRICE	*QUOTE U.S.$
1999	Assetauge (VA) 6901	Open		40.00	40
1999	Bodie Island (NC) 6904	Open		40.00	40
1999	Cape May (NJ) 6906	Open		40.00	40
1999	Grosse Point (IL) 6902	Open		40.00	40
1999	Marblehead (OH) 6905	Open		40.00	40
1999	Ponce De Leon (FL) 6903	Open		40.00	40

Annual Christmas - B. Job

YEAR ISSUE		EDITION LIMIT	YEAR RETD.	ISSUE PRICE	*QUOTE U.S.$
1995	Confectioner's Cottage 41101	2,500	1995	100.00	157-250
1996	Lollipop Shoppe 41102	2,500	1996	110.00	110-175
1997	Peppermint Place 41103	2,500	1997	100.00	100-138
1998	Holly Day Chapel 41104	1,500	1998	120.00	120
1998	Holly Day Home 41105	1,500	1998	120.00	150

Bed & Breakfast - B. Job

YEAR ISSUE		EDITION LIMIT	YEAR RETD.	ISSUE PRICE	*QUOTE U.S.$
1997	Bavarian Lodge 11306	1,500	2000	225.00	225-282
1995	Brookview Bed & Breakfast 11303	1,250	1995	295.00	295-788
1996	Edgewater Inn 11305	1,500	1996	310.00	310-469
1997	Whispering Pines 11308	1,250		250.00	250
1998	White Oak Inn 11309	1,250		275.00	275

Coastal Classics - B. Job

YEAR ISSUE		EDITION LIMIT	YEAR RETD.	ISSUE PRICE	*QUOTE U.S.$
1995	Bayside Beacon Lighthouse 21013	Closed	1998	65.00	65
1996	Cape Hope Lighthouse 21014	Open		100.00	100
1993	Carolina Lighthouse 21003	Open		65.00	65
1996	Cozy Cottage 21500	Closed	1998	70.00	70-88
1994	Lookout Point Lighthouse 21012	Closed	1998	60.00	60
1993	Maine Lighthouse 21002	Open		50.00	50
1993	Michigan Lighthouse 21001	Closed	1998	50.00	50-107
1994	Patriot's Point 29010	Closed	2000	70.00	70
1994	Sailor's Knoll Lighthouse 21011	Closed	2000	65.00	65

Coastal Heritage - B. Job

YEAR ISSUE		EDITION LIMIT	YEAR RETD.	ISSUE PRICE	*QUOTE U.S.$
1996	Barnegat (NJ) 25006	2,996		85.00	85
1996	Cape Hatteras (NC) 25102	3,867		120.00	120
1997	Cape Lookout (NC) 25105	1,997		80.00	80
1995	Cape Neddick (ME) 25002	1,995	1995	140.00	175
1996	Fire Island (NY) 25005	2,996		150.00	150
1998	Harbor Towne @ Hilton Head (SC) 25106	2,998		65.00	65
1996	Holland Harbor (MI) 25203	1,996		125.00	125
1997	Jupiter (FL) 25104	1,997		80.00	80
1995	Marble Head (OH) 25201	1,995	1996	75.00	90-108
1997	Montauk Point (NY) 25008	997		145.00	145
1996	New London (CT) 25004	2,996		145.00	145
1995	North Head (WA) 25302	1,995		100.00	120
1995	Old Point Loma (CA) 25301	1,995	1999	100.00	120-125
1996	Peggy's Cove (NS) 25501	2,500		75.00	75
1996	Pigeon Point (CA) 25303	2,996		125.00	125
1995	Portland Head (ME) 25003	1,995	1997	140.00	170
1995	Sandy Hook (NJ) 25001	3,759		140.00	156
1998	SE Block Island (RI) 25009	998		160.00	160
1996	Split Rock (MN) 25202	2,996		130.00	130
1996	St. Augustine (FL) 25103	2,996		130.00	130
1995	St. Simon's (GA) 25101	1,995	1997	120.00	130-150
1997	West Quoddy (ME) 25007	1,997		140.00	140
1998	Wind Point (WI) 25204	1,997		140.00	140

Coastal Heritage Signature Series - B. Job

YEAR ISSUE		EDITION LIMIT	YEAR RETD.	ISSUE PRICE	*QUOTE U.S.$
2000	Alcatraz CA 6911	2,000		180.00	180
1999	Cape Elizabeth ME 6908	1,999		100.00	100
2000	Chicago/Lake Michigan IL 6910	2,000		140.00	140
1999	Hudson/Athens NY 6907	1,999		100.00	100
2000	Sandy Point NJ 6909	2,000		140.00	140

Disney Lighted Village - B. Job

YEAR ISSUE		EDITION LIMIT	YEAR RETD.	ISSUE PRICE	*QUOTE U.S.$
1998	Belle's Cottage 11703	1,991		225.00	225
2000	Darling House from Peter Pan 6701	1,953		150.00	150
1997	Dwarf's Cottage from Snow White 11701	1,937		215.00	215
1998	Geppetto's Toy Shop 11702	1,940		215.00	215
2000	Woodcutter's Cottage from Sleeping Beauty 6703	1,959		200.00	200

Event Piece - B. Job

YEAR ISSUE		EDITION LIMIT	YEAR RETD.	ISSUE PRICE	*QUOTE U.S.$
1997	Gifts and Collectibles ART01	Closed	1998	60.00	60

Special Production - B. Job

YEAR ISSUE		EDITION LIMIT	YEAR RETD.	ISSUE PRICE	*QUOTE U.S.$
1994	Gingerbread House 19111	1,020	1994	100.00	360

Through The Decades "Coca Cola" - B. Job

YEAR ISSUE		EDITION LIMIT	YEAR RETD.	ISSUE PRICE	*QUOTE U.S.$
1997	Corner Drug 11903	5,000		100.00	100
1998	Grady's Barber Shop 11906	5,000		65.00	65
1998	Gus' Gas Station 11905	5,000		75.00	75
1998	Murray's Mercantile Company 11904	5,000		70.00	70
1997	Sam's Grocery 11901	5,000		70.00	70
1998	Sandy Shoal Lighthouse 11907	5,000		70.00	70
1997	Town Cinema 11902	5,000		100.00	100

Vitreville™ - B. Job

YEAR ISSUE		EDITION LIMIT	YEAR RETD.	ISSUE PRICE	*QUOTE U.S.$
1993	The Bavarian Chapel 11503	2,712	1994	90.00	120
1997	Breadman's Bakery (Renovation) 11301R	200	1997	85.00	400
1993	Breadman's Bakery 11301	5,933	1996	70.00	72-85
1993	Candlemaker's Delight 11801	4,997	1996	60.00	65-125
1993	Candymaker's Cottage 11102	8,368	1996	65.00	70-100
1994	Community Chapel 19510	Closed	2000	95.00	95
1993	Country Church 11502	12,500	1995	100.00	105-123
1993	Doctor's Domain 11201	Open		70.00	74
1998	Farah's Flower Shop 11311	Open		80.00	80
1995	Fire Station 11403	Closed	1998	100.00	100
1996	First Bank & Trust 11405	Closed	2000	110.00	110
1998	Jessie's Barber Shop 11310	Open		75.00	75
1997	Klaus' Clock Shoppe 11307	Open		75.00	75
1996	Kramer Building 11404	Closed	2000	100.00	100
1994	Maplewood Elementary School 11401	Open		100.00	100
1995	Mayor's Manor 11205	Closed	1998	85.00	85
1995	Miller's Mill (Musical) 11304	Closed	1998	115.00	115
1993	Painter's Place 11202	Closed	2000	70.00	50-74
1993	Pastor's Place 11101	Open		65.00	70
1993	Pillars of Faith 11504	2,448	1994	90.00	110-165
1993	Roofer's Roost 11203	7,250	1995	70.00	50-110
1993	Tailor's Townhouse 11204	5,215	1995	70.00	70-94
1994	Thompson's Drug 11302	5,000	1996	140.00	140-200
1993	Tiny Town Church 11501	Closed	2000	95.00	100
1994	Trinity Church 11511	7,000		130.00	130
1994	Vitreville Post Office 11402	3,908	1997	90.00	90-94
1998	White Stone Chapel 11506	1,250		85.00	85
1997	Wildwood Chapel 11505	Retrd.	1998	60.00	60

Vitreville™ Main Street - Cavanagh

YEAR ISSUE		EDITION LIMIT	YEAR RETD.	ISSUE PRICE	*QUOTE U.S.$
1999	A-1 Hardware Store 6403	Open		50.00	50
1999	Firehouse 36 6404	Open		50.00	50
1999	Kelsey's 5 & 10 Store 6401	Open		60.00	60
1999	PJ's Drug Store 6408	Open		70.00	70
1999	Steakhouse Restaurant 6402	Open		75.00	75
1999	Town Hall w/Steeple & Clock 6407	Open		75.00	75

Vitreville™ Signature Series - B. Job

YEAR ISSUE		EDITION LIMIT	YEAR RETD.	ISSUE PRICE	*QUOTE U.S.$
1999	North End Train Station 6406	Open		70.00	70

Vitreville™ Signature Series Annual Bed and Breakfast - B. Job

YEAR ISSUE		EDITION LIMIT	YEAR RETD.	ISSUE PRICE	*QUOTE U.S.$
2000	Ginny's Bed & Breakfast 6414	N/A		270.00	270
1999	Patty Ann's B & B 6405	1,250		270.00	270

Vitreville™ Signature Series Annual Christmas - B. Job

YEAR ISSUE		EDITION LIMIT	YEAR RETD.	ISSUE PRICE	*QUOTE U.S.$
1999	The Gumdrop Shoppe 6413	2,500		90.00	90
2000	Tudor Rose Doll Cottage 6415	N/A		70.00	70

Woodland Village™ - B. Job

YEAR ISSUE		EDITION LIMIT	YEAR RETD.	ISSUE PRICE	*QUOTE U.S.$
1993	Badger House 31003	1,056	1996	80.00	85-125
1993	Chipmunk House 31005	1,080	1996	80.00	85-125
1993	Owl House 31004	991	1996	80.00	85-129
1993	Rabbit House 31001	926	1996	90.00	125
1993	Racoon House 31002	1,154	1996	80.00	75-125

Geo. Zoltan Lefton Company

Accessories - Lefton

YEAR ISSUE		EDITION LIMIT	YEAR RETD.	ISSUE PRICE	*QUOTE U.S.$
1990	Abe Smith 07483	Suspd.		5.00	8-24
1988	Allison Davis 06547	Suspd.		5.00	22-40
1991	Annette & Rebecca 07827	Suspd.		10.00	8-35
1999	Autumn Colors 11582	Open		13.00	13
1988	Billy O'Malley 06740	Suspd.		7.00	26-45
1990	Bonnie Charles & Spot 07824	Suspd.		10.00	12-35
1999	Brown Tree (11") 12454	Open		6.00	6
1999	Brown Tree (9") 12455	Open		4.00	4
1987	Cab 06459	Suspd.		13.00	25-57
1991	Cart 07830	Suspd.		11.00	15-28
1988	CV Express 05826	Suspd.		27.00	99-124
1991	Da Vinci Bros. 00269	Suspd.		12.00	8-32
1990	Dashing Through Snow 07322	Suspd.		16.00	10-16
1988	Dick's Delivery 06548	Suspd.		8.00	15-45
1999	Direction Sign 12130	Open		16.00	16
1987	Doc Olsens' Wagon 06457	Suspd.		14.00	28
1988	Double Tree 06467	Suspd.		5.00	10-40
1987	Eberhardt's (4pc./set) 05910	Suspd.		20.00	10-79
1987	Fire Engine Co. NO. 5 06458	Suspd.		14.00	19-50
1991	Frank Pendergast 07776	Suspd.		5.50	25-40
1999	George Blarney 11580	Open		22.00	22
1991	The Griffiths 00661	Suspd.		13.00	10-35
1999	Harvest Pickens 11579	Open		12.00	12
1987	Ivan the Lamplighter 06741	Suspd.		7.00	7-35
1991	Jeffrey Sawyer 00659	Suspd.		8.00	8-28
1988	Kalenko Family Choir 06887	Suspd.		13.00	47-67
1988	Large Tree 06465	Suspd.		6.50	10-40
1999	Lillian Blarney 11577	Open		15.00	15
1988	Lisa & Selena 06549	Suspd.		7.00	12-30
1991	Major & Mrs. 00214	Suspd.		12.00	12-30
1999	Maple Tree (10") 12453	Open		13.00	13
1999	Maple Tree (12") 11988	Open		17.00	17
1999	Maple Tree (12") 12452	Open		17.00	17
1990	Mary & Jack Cobb 07825	Suspd.		10.00	12-35
1987	Matt's Milk Wagon 06461	Suspd.		13.00	30-63
1988	Merrymaker Ed 06739	Suspd.		7.00	10-33
1988	Mr. Watts 06742	Suspd.		7.00	9-35
1999	Needle in a Haystack 11581	Open		15.00	15
1988	Nina & Fillipe 06737	Suspd.		9.00	10-35
1987	One Horse Open Sleigh 06460	Suspd.		13.00	24-42
1991	The Parkers 00218	Suspd.		13.00	6-13
1999	Peek-A-Boo 11575	Open		13.00	13
1999	Season's Greetings 11585	Open		17.00	17
1999	Sharon Blarney 11576	Open		15.00	15
1988	Small Tree 06466	Suspd.		4.00	15-30
1988	Steven & Stacey 06744	Suspd.		9.00	15-35
1988	Stone Church Carolers 06554	Suspd.		12.00	39-63
1990	Sylvester The Sweep 07778	Suspd.		5.00	15-25
1992	Tim & Lucy Morgan 00662	Suspd.		9.00	5-9
1999	Trick or Treat 11574	Open		13.00	13
1999	William Blarney 11578	Open		15.00	15

Colonial Village - Lefton

YEAR ISSUE		EDITION LIMIT	YEAR RETD.	ISSUE PRICE	*QUOTE U.S.$
1993	Antiques & Curiosities 00723	Closed	1998	50.00	50
1995	Applegate-CVRA Exclusive 01327	Closed	1995	50.00	125-188
1990	The Ardmore House 07338	Closed	1995	45.00	50-75
1997	Ashton House-CVRA Exclusive 10829	Open		50.00	50
2000	Auntie June's House 13517	Open		50.00	50
1993	Baldwin's Fine Jewelry 00722	Closed	1997	50.00	39-59
2000	Bed & Breakfast 13501	Open		50.00	50
1991	Belle-Union Saloon 07482	Closed	1994	45.00	63-94
1998	Berkely House-CVRA Exclusive 11262	Open		50.00	50
1989	Bijou Theatre 06897	Closed	1990	40.00	625-1063
1994	Black Sheep Tavern 01003	Closed	1999	50.00	50
1993	Blacksmith 00720	Suspd.		47.00	47-63
1999	Blarney Barn/Blarney Silo (Collector's Set) 12330	Closed	1999	150.00	150
1999	Blarney Farmhouse 11587	Open		50.00	50
1998	Blue Bell Flour 11263	Open		50.00	50
1999	Bradley House 11999	Open		65.00	65
1992	Brenner's Apothecary 07961	Open		45.00	50
1996	The Brookfield 11996	5,500	1996	75.00	75-188
1994	Brown's Book Shop 01001	Closed	1999	50.00	50
1993	Burnside 00717	Open		50.00	50
1989	Capper's Millinery 06904	Suspd.		40.00	50-94
1988	City Hall 06340	Suspd.		40.00	82-194
1989	Cobb's Bootery 06903	Suspd.		40.00	82-188
1990	Coffee & Tea Shoppe 07342	Suspd.		45.00	75-188
1996	Collectors Set 10740	Closed	1998	100.00	100
1989	Cole's Barn 06750	Closed	1994	40.00	63-94
1998	Colonial Queen Showboat (Collectors' Set - musical)11266	Closed	1998	100.00	100
1995	Colonial Savings and Loan 01321	Closed	1998	50.00	40-50
1995	Colonial Village News 01002	Closed	1999	50.00	50
1998	Cooper's Shop 11259	Open		50.00	50
1999	Cotswold Cottage, set/3 12218	Open		49.00	49
1990	Country Post Office 07341	Closed	1994	45.00	63-94
1992	County Courthouse 00233	Open		45.00	50
1991	Daisy's Flower Shop 07478	Closed	1996	45.00	75-138
1993	Dentist's Office 00724	Suspd.		50.00	50

*Quotes have been rounded up to nearest dollar

YEAR ISSUE	EDITION LIMIT	YEAR RETD.	ISSUE PRICE	*QUOTE U.S.$
1993 Doctor's Office 00721	Open		50.00	50
1992 Elegant Lady Dress Shop 00232	Suspd.		45.00	60-94
1988 Engine Co. No. 5 Firehouse 06342	Open		40.00	50
1996 Fairbanks House 10397	Open		50.00	50
1988 Faith Church 06333	Closed	1991	40.00	130-407
1990 Fellowship Church 07334	Suspd.		45.00	78-188
1990 The First Church 07333	Open		45.00	50
1988 First Post Office 06343	Open		40.00	50
2000 The Fountain 12897	Open		11.00	11
1996 Franklin College 10393	Closed	1999	50.00	50
1988 Friendship Chapel 06334	Closed	1994	40.00	63-188
2000 Grandma's House 12000	Open		60.00	60
2000 Gazebo 12898	Open		24.00	24
1993 Green's Grocery 00725	Open		50.00	50
1988 Greystone House 06339	Closed	1995	40.00	40-100
1989 Gull's Nest Lighthouse 06747	Open		40.00	50
1990 Hampshire House 07336	Closed	1996	45.00	57-157
1996 The Hermitage 10394	Closed	1998	55.00	98-100
1991 Hillside Church 11991	Closed	1991	60.00	469-619
1995 Historical Society Museum 01328	Closed	1999	50.00	98
1998 Holmer's Bait Shop, set/3 11534	Open		60.00	60
1988 House of Blue Gables 06337	Closed	1995	40.00	50-75
1988 Johnson's Antiques 06346	Closed	1993	40.00	69-125
1993 Joseph House 00718	Open		50.00	50
1999 Kidgloo 12132	Open		24.00	24
1993 Kirby House-CVRA Exclusive 00716	Closed	1994	50.00	75-157
1999 Kringle's Snow Castle 12129	Closed	1999	150.00	150
1992 Lakehurst House 11992	Closed	1992	55.00	313-388
1996 Lattimore House-CVRA Exclusive 10391	Closed	1997	50.00	63-125
1997 Law Office 10825	Closed	1999	50.00	40-50
1992 Main St. Church 00230	Open		45.00	50
1989 The Major's Manor 06902	Closed	1998	40.00	63-94
1989 Maple St. Church 06748	Closed	1993	40.00	63-107
1993 Mark Hall 00719	Open		50.00	50
1989 Miller Bros. Silversmiths 06905	Suspd.		40.00	100-194
1998 M.S. Miller-Painter 11261	Open		50.00	50
1997 Montrose Manor 10828	Open		50.00	50
1999 Mooncrest Mansion 11588	Closed	1999	50.00	50
1999 Mortimer & Friends 11589	Closed	1999	35.00	35
1994 Mt. Zion Church 11994	5,500	1994	70.00	75-113
1994 Mt. Zion Church (Hillside Church-error) 11994	Closed	1994	70.00	255-553
1990 Mulberry Station 07344	Open		50.00	65
1995 Mundt Manor 01008	Closed	1999	50.00	50
2000 Nativity, set/3 12220	Open		32.00	32
2000 Nativity, set/4 12221	Open		44.00	44
1988 New Hope Church (musical) 06470	Suspd.		40.00	500-750
1990 The Nob Hill 07337	Closed	1995	45.00	52-67
1992 Northpoint School 07960	Open		45.00	50
1994 Notfel Cabin 01320	Open		50.00	50
1999 O' Christmas Tree 12113	Closed	1999	33.00	33
1995 O'Doul's Ice House 01324	Open		50.00	50
1988 Old Stone Church (musical) 06471	Suspd.		25.00	300-580
1988 Old Time Station 06335	Closed	1997	40.00	69-94
1998 Opera House 11260	Open		50.00	50
1987 Original Set of 6 05818	Unkn.		210.00	N/A
1987 • Charity Chapel 05818 (05895)	Closed	1989	35.00	886-938
1987 • King's Cottage 05818 (05890)	Closed	1997	35.00	39-49
1987 • McCauley House 05818 (05892)	Closed	1988	35.00	519-938
1987 • Nelson House 05818 (05891)	Closed	1989	35.00	688-813
1987 • Old Stone Church 05818 (05825)	Open		35.00	50
1987 • The Welcome Home 05818 (05824)	Closed	1997	35.00	50
1987 Original Set of 6 05819	Unkn.		210.00	N/A
1987 • Church of the Golden Rule 05819 (05820)	Closed	1999	35.00	50
1987 • General Store 05819 (05823)	Closed	1988	35.00	750-920
1987 • Lil Red School House 05819 (05821)	Open		35.00	50
1987 • Penny House 05819 (05893)	Closed	1988	35.00	750-1000
1987 • Ritter House 05819 (05894)	Closed	1989	35.00	700-850
1987 • Train Station 05819 (05822)	Closed	1989	35.00	1065-1244
1997 Park Vista-Convention Piece 11141	Closed	1997	50.00	250-720
1995 Patriot Bridge 01325	Open		50.00	50
1997 Photography Studio 10872	Open		50.00	50
1990 Pierpont-Smithe's Curios 07343	Closed	1993	45.00	63-113
1997 Potter House 10826	Open		50.00	50
1995 Queensgate 01329	Closed	1999	50.00	50
1989 Quincy's Clock Shop 06899	Suspd.		40.00	75-188
1995 Rainy Days Barn 01323	Open		50.00	50
2000 Rathbone Retreat 13518	Open		50.00	50
1994 Real Estate Office -CVRA Exclusive 01006	Open		50.00	50
1988 The Ritz Hotel 06341	Closed	1997	40.00	188-375
1999 River Queen 12216	Open		50.00	50
1994 Rosamond 00988	Closed	1999	50.00	50
1990 Ryman Auditorium-Special Edition 08010	Suspd.		50.00	50-113
1992 San Sebastian Mission 00231	Closed	1995	45.00	60-94
1991 Sanderson's Mill 07927	Open		45.00	50
1997 Sawyer's Creek 11030	Open		55.00	55
1990 Ship's Chandler's Shop 07339	Suspd.		45.00	75-157
1997 Sir George's Manor 11997	5,500	1997	75.00	75-113
1994 Smith and Jones Drug Store 01007	Open		50.00	50
1991 Smith's Smithy 07476	Closed	1991	45.00	732-1063
1994 Springfield 00989	Open		50.00	50
1993 St. James Cathedral 11993	Closed	1993	75.00	125-213
1996 St. Paul's Church 10735	Closed	1999	50.00	55
1993 St. Peter's Church w/Speaker 00715	Suspd.		60.00	75-100
1996 Stable 10395	Open		33.00	33
1988 The State Bank 06345	Closed	1997	40.00	63-94
1992 Stearn's Stable 00228	Closed	1999	45.00	60
1988 The Stone House 06338	Closed	1998	40.00	63-100
1991 Sweet Shop 07481	Suspd.		45.00	50
1989 Sweetheart's Bridge 06751	Suspd.		40.00	50-94
2000 Town Meeting Hall 13500	Open		50.00	50
1991 The Toy Maker's Shop 07477	Open		45.00	50
1988 Trader Tom's Gen'l Store 06336	Closed	1999	40.00	69-94
1996 Trading Post 10732	Open		50.00	50
1996 Treviso House 10392	Closed	1999	50.00	50
1998 Trinity Church 11998	5,500	1998	75.00	75-219
1992 Vanderspeck's Mill 00229	Closed	1996	45.00	57-125
1997 Variety Store 10827	Open		50.00	50
1990 The Victoria House 07335	Closed	1993	45.00	63-94
1989 Victorian Apothecary 06900	Closed	1991	40.00	282-375
1991 Victorian Gazebo 07925	Suspd.		45.00	25-63
1989 The Village Bakery 06898	Open		40.00	50
1989 Village Barber Shop 06901	Suspd.		40.00	50-63
2000 The Village Church 13502	Open		50.00	50
1986 Village Express 05826	Closed	1990	27.00	94-219
1992 Village Green Gazebo 00227	Suspd.		22.00	22-32
1990 Village Hardware 07340	Closed	1996	45.00	69-125
1994 Village Hospital 01004	Open		50.00	50
1992 The Village Inn 07962	Closed	1998	45.00	117
1989 Village Library 06752	Suspd.		40.00	63-94
2000 The Village Lighthouse 13537	Open		50.00	50
1988 Village Police Station 06344	Suspd.		40.00	50-82
1989 Village School 06749	Closed	1991	40.00	200-432
1991 Watt's Candle Shop 07479	Closed	1994	45.00	63-94
1987 Welcome Home 05824	Closed	1997	50.00	63-105
1994 White's Butcher Shop 01005	Open		50.00	50
1999 Winter Carnival (set/7) 11584	Open		120.00	120
1999 Winter Carnival (set/3) 12194	Open		40.00	40
1999 Winter Carnival (set/2) 12195	Open		34.00	34
1999 Winter Carnival (set/2) 12196	Open		34.00	34
1998 Wright's Emporium 11264	Open		50.00	50
1990 Wig Shop 07480	Suspd.		45.00	50-100
1995 Wycoff Manor 11995	5,500	1995	75.00	107-150
1995 Zachary Peters Cabinet Maker 01322	Closed	1999	50.00	50

Colonial Village Special Event - Lefton

YEAR ISSUE	EDITION LIMIT	YEAR RETD.	ISSUE PRICE	*QUOTE U.S.$
1995 Bayside Inn 01326	Yr.Iss.	1995	50.00	100-194
1996 Town Hall 10390	Yr.Iss.	1996	50.00	78-132
1997 Meeting House 10830	Yr.Iss.	1997	65.00	65-125
1998 Good Neighbor's Haven 11505	Yr.Iss.	1998	55.00	55-75
1999 Christmas Wishes 12114	Yr.Iss.	1999	25.00	25

Historic American Lighthouse Collection - Lefton

YEAR ISSUE	EDITION LIMIT	YEAR RETD.	ISSUE PRICE	*QUOTE U.S.$
1995 1716 Boston Lighthouse 08607	7,500	1995	50.00	250-313
2000 Abselon, NJ 13522	Open		43.00	43
1994 Admirality Head, WA 01126	Open		40.00	43
1997 Alcatraz Island-1854 08649	9,000	1997	55.00	138-175
1998 Alcatraz, CA 11526	Open		65.00	65
2000 Amelia Isl., FL 13523	Open		43.00	43
1992 Assateaque, VA 00137	Open		40.00	43
1995 Barneget, NJ 01333	Open		40.00	43
1993 Big Sable Point, MI 00885	Open		40.00	43
1998 Biloxi Lighthouse, MS 11522	Open		40.00	43
1996 Block Island, RI 10105	Open		50.00	50
1994 Bodie Island, NC 01118	Open		40.00	43
2000 Boon Isl., ME 12717	Open		45.00	45
1993 Boston Harbor, MA 00881	Open		40.00	43
1996 Buffalo, NY 10076	Open		40.00	43
1994 Cana Island, WI 01117	Open		40.00	43
1999 Cape Canaveral, FL 11569	Open		43.00	43
1993 Cape Cod, MA 00882	Open		40.00	43
1994 Cape Florida, FL 01125	Closed	1998	40.00	50
1998 Cape Florida, FL 11537	Open		43.00	43
1992 Cape Hatteras, NC 00133	Closed	1998	40.00	40-125
1998 Cape Hatteras, NC 11533	Open		45.00	45
1997 Cape Henlopen, DE	9,000	1997	55.00	65-125
1992 Cape Henry, VA 00135	Open		40.00	43
1992 Cape Lookout, NC 00134	Open		40.00	43
1994 Cape May, NJ 01013	Closed	1995	40.00	185-272
1995 Cape May, NJ 01013R	Open		40.00	43
1996 Cape Neddick, ME 10106	Open		47.00	47
2000 Cape St. George, FL 13524	Open		43.00	43
1994 Chicago Harbor, IL 01010	Open		40.00	43
1999 Concord Point, MD 11567	Open		47.00	47
1997 Currituck Beach, NC 10834	Open		40.00	43
1996 Destruction Island, WA 10108	Open		40.00	43
2000 Diamond Head, HI 12858	Open		43.00	43
1995 Fire Island, NY 01334	Open		40.00	43
1997 Fort Niagara, NY 10965	Open		40.00	43
1994 Ft. Gratiot, MI 01123	Open		40.00	43
2000 Grand Haven, MI 13525	Open		50.00	50
1993 Gray's Harbor, WA 00880	Open		40.00	43
1998 Harbour Town, SC 11527	Open		45.00	45
1994 Heceta Head, OR 01122	Open		40.00	43
2000 Hereford Inlet, NJ 13526	Open		50.00	50
2000 Hillsboro Inlet, FL 13527	Open		50.00	50
1996 Holland Harbor, MI 10104	Open		45.00	45
1995 Jupiter Inlet, FL 01336	Open		40.00	43
1996 Key West, FL 10075	Open		40.00	43
1996 Los Angeles Harbor, CA 10109	Open		45.00	45
1993 Marblehead, OH 00879	Open		40.00	43
1999 Minots Ledge, MA 11568	Open		43.00	43
1993 Montauk, NY 00884	Open		40.00	43
1998 Morris Island, SC 08657	9,000	1998	50.00	60-155
2000 Mukilteo Light Possession Sound, WA 12257	Open		56.00	56
1998 New London Harbor, CT 11524	Open		40.00	43
1994 New London Ledge, CT 01119	Open		40.00	43
1998 New Presque Isle, MI 11523	Open		40.00	43
2000 Oak Island, NC 08683	9,000		45.00	45
1994 Ocracoke, NC 01124	Open		40.00	43
2000 Old Baldy Smith Isl., NC 12256	Open		45.00	45
1996 Old Cape Henry, VA 08619	7,500	1996	47.00	207-285
1999 Old Mackinac Pt., MI 08676	9,000	2000	79.00	79
2000 Old Point Comfort, VA 12715	Open		43.00	43
1994 Old Point Loma, CA 01011	Open		40.00	43
1998 Pemaquid Point, ME 11525	Open		42.00	42
1999 Pensacola, FL 11566	Open		43.00	43
1995 Pigeon Point, CA 01289	Open		40.00	43
1997 Point Arena, CA 10968	Open		40.00	43
1995 Point Betsie, MI 01335	Open		47.00	47
1997 Point Bolivar, TX 10967	Open		40.00	43
1995 Point Cabrillo, CA 01330	Open		47.00	47
1999 Point Pinos, CA 11571	Open		56.00	56
1993 Point Wilson, WA 00883	Open		40.00	43
1995 Ponce De Leon, FL 01332	Open		40.00	43
1994 Portland Head, ME 01121	Open		40.00	43
1996 Pt. Isabel, TX 10074	Open		40.00	43
2000 Rockland Breakwater, ME 13529	Open		47.00	47
1997 Round Island, MI 10969	Open		47.00	47
1992 Sandy Hook, NJ 00132	Open		40.00	43
1994 Split Rock, MN 01009	Open		40.00	43
1994 St. Augustine, FL 01015	Open		40.00	43
2000 St. Marks Light, FL 13530	Open		50.00	50
1994 St. Simons, GA 01012	Open		40.00	43
2000 Tawas, MI 12716	Open		43.00	43
1996 Thomas Point, MO 10107	Open		45.00	45
1995 Toledo Harbor, OH 01331	Open		47.00	47
2000 Two Harbors, MI 13531	Open		50.00	50
1994 Tybee Island, GA 01014	Closed	1999	40.00	40-43
1999 Tybee Island, GA 12217	Open		43.00	43
1992 West Quoddy Head, ME 00136	Open		40.00	43
1993 White Shoal, MI 00878	Open		40.00	43
1997 Wind Point, WI 10966	Open		40.00	43
1994 Yerba Buena, CA 01120	Open		40.00	43

Historic American Lighthouse Collection Special Event - Lefton

YEAR ISSUE	EDITION LIMIT	YEAR RETD.	ISSUE PRICE	*QUOTE U.S.$
1999 Diamond Head, HI 11570	Yr.Iss.	1999	50.00	50
2000 Gays Head, MA 13528	Yr.Iss.		45.00	45

Historic Williamsburg Collection - Lefton

YEAR ISSUE	EDITION LIMIT	YEAR RETD.	ISSUE PRICE	*QUOTE U.S.$
1997 Bruton Parish Church 11051	Open		55.00	55
1997 The Capitol 11054	Open		75.00	75
1998 Christiana Campbell's Tavern 11705	Open		55.00	55
1998 Courthouse 11704	Open		70.00	70
1997 George Wythe House 11053	Open		50.00	50
1997 The Govenor's Palace 11052	Open		75.00	75
1997 King Arms Taverns 11050	Open		50.00	50
1998 Prentis Store 11703	Open		50.00	50

GiftStar

Collectors' Corner - B. Baker

YEAR ISSUE	EDITION LIMIT	YEAR RETD.	ISSUE PRICE	*QUOTE U.S.$
1993 City Cottage-rose/grn. (Membership Sculpture)1682	Retrd.	1994	35.00	95-135
1993 Brian's First House-red (Redemption Sculpture) 1496	Retrd.	1994	71.00	150-175
1994 Gothic Cottage (Membership Sculpture) 1571	Retrd.	1995	35.00	95-100
1994 Duke of Gloucester Street (Redemption Sculpture) 1459	Retrd.	1995	108.00	150-165
1995 Marie's Cottage-grey (Membership Sculpture) 1942	Retrd.	1996	35.00	75-95
1995 Welcome Home-brick (Redemption Sculpture) 1599	Retrd.	1996	65.00	85-95
1996 Queen Ann Cottage-rose/blue (Membership Sculpture) 1676	Retrd.	1997	39.00	39
1996 Oak Street-brick/brown (Redemption Sculpture) 1685	Retrd.	1997	65.00	75
1997 Michael's House-blue (Membership Sculpture) 1719	Retrd.	1998	40.00	40
1997 Michael's Garage (Redemption Sculpture) 1720	Retrd.	1998	34.50	35
1998 Empire Tower House (Membership Sculpture) 16510	Retrd.	1998	40.00	40
1998 Main Street Café Ornament (Redemption Sculpture) 18000	Retrd.	1998	17.00	17

Signing Piece - B. Baker

YEAR ISSUE	EDITION LIMIT	YEAR RETD.	ISSUE PRICE	*QUOTE U.S.$
1995 Joe's Newstand 1348	Yr.Iss.	1995	27.00	27
1996 Yellow Rose Cottage 1444	Yr.Iss.	1996	62.00	62
1997 Umbrella Shop 1179	Yr.Iss.	1997	29.50	30
1998 The Coffee House 11780	Yr.Iss.	1998	34.00	34

Limited Editions From Brian Baker - B. Baker

YEAR ISSUE	EDITION LIMIT	YEAR RETD.	ISSUE PRICE	*QUOTE U.S.$
1993 American Classic-rose 1566	500	1993	99.00	450-550
1987 Amsterdam Canal-brown, S/N 1030	1,000	1993	79.00	225
1998 Get Hooked 14080	750		68.00	68
1998 Haight Ashbury 16320	2,500		67.50	68
1994 Hill Top Mansion 1598	1,200	1995	97.00	125-150
1993 James River Plantation-brick 1454	Retrd.	1994	108.00	300-400
1996 London 1045	1,200	1997	119.00	119-135
1994 Painted Ladies 1190	1,200	1996	125.00	125
1995 Philadelphia-brick 1441	1,500	1997	110.00	110-125
1997 Riverside Plantation 1739	1,200		60.00	60
1994 White Point 1596	700	1996	100.00	165

Goebel/M.I. Hummel

M.I. Hummel Bavarian Village Collection - M.I. Hummel

YEAR ISSUE	EDITION LIMIT	YEAR RETD.	ISSUE PRICE	*QUOTE U.S.$
1996 All Aboard	Open		60.00	60
1995 Angel's Duet	Open		50.00	60
2000 Apple Tree Cottage	Open		65.00	65

*Quotes have been rounded up to nearest dollar

YEAR ISSUE	EDITION LIMIT	YEAR RETD.	ISSUE PRICE	*QUOTE U.S.$
1995 The Bench and Tree Set (accessory)	Open		25.00	30
1995 Christmas Mail	Open		50.00	60
2000 Clock Shop	Open		65.00	65
1995 Company's Coming	Open		50.00	60
1997 Evergreen Tree Set (accessory)	Open		30.00	30
1998 Heavenly Harmony Church	Open		60.00	60
1996 Holiday Fountain (accessory)	Open		35.00	35
1997 Holiday Lights (accessory)	Open		30.00	20
1996 Horse With Sled (accessory)	Open		35.00	35
1997 The Mailbox (accessory)	Open		30.00	20
1996 Off for the Holidays	Open		60.00	60
1998 Practice Makes Perfect	Open		65.00	65
1998 Scholarly Thoughts	Open		65.00	65
1996 Shoe Maker Shop	Open		60.00	60
1995 The Sled and Pine Tree Set (accessory)	Open		25.00	30
2000 Tending the Geese	Open		65.00	65
1995 The Village Bakery	Open		50.00	60
1995 The Village Bridge (accessory)	Open		25.00	30
2000 Village Pharmacy	Open		65.00	65
1998 Warm Winter Wishes	Open		65.00	65
1995 Winter's Comfort	Open		50.00	60
1995 The Wishing Well (accessory)	Open		25.00	30

Hamilton Collection

Cherished Teddies Christmas Village - P. Hillman

YEAR ISSUE	EDITION LIMIT	YEAR RETD.	ISSUE PRICE	*QUOTE U.S.$
2000 Boat House	Open		49.95	50
2000 Christmas Cottage	Open		49.95	50
2000 Santa Bear's Sweet Shoppe	Open		49.95	50
2000 Teddies Toy Shop	Open		49.95	50

Dreamsicles Heavenly Village - K. Haynes

YEAR ISSUE	EDITION LIMIT	YEAR RETD.	ISSUE PRICE	*QUOTE U.S.$
1997 Cherub Concerto	Open		49.95	50
1996 Flight School	Open		49.95	50
1996 Star Factory	Open		49.95	50
1997 Wreath Makers	Open		49.95	50

Harbour Lights

Harbour Lights Collector's Society - Harbour Lights

YEAR ISSUE	EDITION LIMIT	YEAR RETD.	ISSUE PRICE	*QUOTE U.S.$
1995 Point Fermin CA 501 (Charter Member Piece)	Retrd.	1996	80.00	150-241
1995 Framed Point Fermin CA Print (numbrd.)	Retrd.	1996	Gift	20-45
1996 Stonington Harbor CT 502	Retrd.	1997	70.00	94-188
1996 Spyglass Collection 503	Retrd.	1997	Gift	70-90
1996 Point Fermin CA (Ornament)	Retrd.	1997	15.00	15-50
1997 Port Sanilac MI 506	Retrd.	1998	80.00	80-200
1997 Amelia Island FL	Retrd.	1998	Gift	55-144
1997 Stonington Harbor CT (Ornament)	Retrd.	1998	15.00	15-63
1998 Sea Girt NJ	Retrd.	1999	80.00	80
1998 Cockspur GA	Retrd.	1999	Gift	65-75
1998 Port Sanilac MI (Ornament)	Retrd.	1999	15.00	15-50
1999 Seven Foot Knoll MD 521	Retrd.	2000	99.00	99
1999 Baltimore MD 524	Retrd.	2000	Gift	N/A
1999 Sea Girt NJ 527 (Ornament)	Retrd.	2000	15.00	15
1999 Pt. Fermin CA (Charter Member 5 Year)	Retrd.	2000	29.00	29
1999 Pt. Fermin CA (Member 5 Year)	Retrd.	2000	29.00	29
2000 Boca Grande FL 531	4/01		90.00	90
2000 S.W. Reef LA 530	4/01		Gift	N/A
2000 Seven Foot Knoll MD (Ornament) 532	4/01		15.00	15

Event Piece - Harbour Lights

YEAR ISSUE	EDITION LIMIT	YEAR RETD.	ISSUE PRICE	*QUOTE U.S.$
1996 Sunken Rock NY 602	8,132	1996	25.00	41-63
1997 New Point Loma 604 (1997 Collector's Reunion)	950	1997	70.00	625-1035
1997 New Point Loma-mini 605 (1997 Collector's Reunion)	480	1997	Gift	188-380
1997 Edgartown MA 603	8,008	1997	35.00	60-75
1997 Thumbnail-Assateague	Closed	1997	Gift	15-25
1997 Thumbnail-Cape Hatteras	Closed	1997	Gift	15-25
1997 Thumbnail-Sandy Hook	Closed	1997	Gift	15-25
1997 Thumbnail-St. Simons	Closed	1997	Gift	15-25
1998 Roosevelt Island NY 612	7,884	1998	25.00	40-44
1998 Rose Island RI 614	700	1998	70.00	100-150
1998 Rose Island RI (mini) 615	700	1998	Gift	50
1998 Rose Island RI (Society Members Only) 616	6,100	1998	70.00	215-300
1998 Thumbnail-Beavertail	Closed	1998	Gift	15
1998 Thumbnail-Point Judith	Closed	1998	Gift	15
1998 Thumbnail-Rose Island	Closed	1998	Gift	15
1998 Thumbnail-SE Block Island	Closed	1998	Gift	15
1999 Kilauea HI 620	Closed	1999	65.00	65-110
2000 Hatteras-on-the-Move 632	12/00		65.00	65
2000 Lady Liberty 627	12/00		125.00	125

Chesapeake Series - Harbour Lights

YEAR ISSUE	EDITION LIMIT	YEAR RETD.	ISSUE PRICE	*QUOTE U.S.$
1996 Concord MD 186	8,450	1999	66.00	66-76
1997 Drum Point MD 180	9,500	1997	99.00	99-150
1996 Sandy Point MD 167	9,500	1999	70.00	70-90
1996 Sharps Island MD 185	9,500	1997	70.00	70-120
1996 Thomas Point MD 181	9,500	1996	99.00	130-300

Christmas - Harbour Lights

YEAR ISSUE	EDITION LIMIT	YEAR RETD.	ISSUE PRICE	*QUOTE U.S.$
1995 Christmas 1995 - Big Bay Point MI 700	5,000	1995	75.00	231-500
1996 Christmas 1996 - Colchester VT 701	8,200	1996	75.00	80-200
1997 Christmas 1997 - White Shoal MI 704	8,000	1997	80.00	80-150
1998 Christmas 1998 - Old Field Point NY 707	10,000	1998	80.00	80-150
1999 Christmas 1999 -East Quoddy Canada 708	10,000	1999	80.00	80-125
2000 Christmas 2000 -Hereford Inlet NJ 710	10,000		75.00	75

From Glow to Limited - Harbour Lights

YEAR ISSUE	EDITION LIMIT	YEAR RETD.	ISSUE PRICE	*QUOTE U.S.$
1996 Alcatraz CA 407 to 177	Closed	1996	77.00	122-125
1996 Cape Lookout 405 to 175	Closed	1996	64.00	64-100
1996 Fire Island NY 406 to 176	Closed	1996	70.00	70-84
1996 Mukilteo WA 417 to 178	Closed	1996	55.00	55
1996 Spectacle Reef MI 410 to 182	Closed	1996	60.00	60-88
1996 St. Joseph MI 411 to 183	Closed	1996	60.00	60-110
1996 Thirty Mile Point NY 414 to 184	Closed	1996	62.00	60-90

Gone But Not Forgotten - Harbour Lights

YEAR ISSUE	EDITION LIMIT	YEAR RETD.	ISSUE PRICE	*QUOTE U.S.$
2000 Cape Henlopen DE 243	4/01		80.00	80

Great Lakes Region - Harbour Lights

YEAR ISSUE	EDITION LIMIT	YEAR RETD.	ISSUE PRICE	*QUOTE U.S.$
1999 Big Sable MI 228	10,000		70.00	70
1992 Buffalo NY 122	5,500	1996	60.00	97-182
1992 Cana Island WI 119	5,500	1995	60.00	93-163
1996 Charlotte-Genesee NY 165	7,100	1999	77.00	77
1998 Chicago Harbor IL 208	10,000		73.00	73
2000 Eagle Bluff WI 249	6,500		65.00	65
2000 Fairport Harbor OH	6,500		68.00	68
2000 Fort Gratiot MI	7,000		65.00	65
1991 Fort Niagara NY 113	5,500	1995	60.00	99-182
1998 Grand Haven MI 212	10,000		90.00	90
1997 Grand Traverse MI 191	9,500	1999	80.00	80-90
1992 Grosse Point IL 120	5,500	1996	60.00	60-98
1994 Holland (Big Red) MI 142	5,500	1995	60.00	156-250
1998 Lorain OH 207	10,000		75.00	75
1992 Marblehead OH 121	5,500	1995	50.00	50-175
1992 Michigan City IN 123	5,500	1996	60.00	94-139
1992 Old Mackinac Point MI 118	5,500	1995	65.00	145-350
1999 Old Mission Point MI 236	10,000		70.00	70
1998 Point Betsie MI 218	10,000		75.00	75
1997 Presque Isle PA 201	9,500		75.00	75
1995 Round Island MI 153	9,500	1999	85.00	85-124
1991 Sand Island WI 112	5,500	1996	60.00	75-125
1995 Selkirk NY 157	6,500	1999	75.00	74-94
2000 Sister Island NY (Collector's Choice) 252	3/01		68.00	68
1999 South Bass Island OH 237	10,000		80.00	80
1992 Split Rock MI 124 (incorrect state)	Closed	1992	60.00	1800-2500
1992 Split Rock MN 124	5,500	1995	60.00	60-107
1998 Sturgeon Bay WI 217	10,000		90.00	90
1995 Tawas Pt. MI 152	5,500	1996	75.00	75-157
1996 Toledo OH 179	6,437	1999	85.00	84-94
1999 White River MI 226	10,000		73.00	73
2000 Whitefish Point MI 254	6,500		99.00	99
1995 Wind Point WI 154	7,783	1999	78.00	77-92

Great Lighthouses of the World - Harbour Lights

YEAR ISSUE	EDITION LIMIT	YEAR RETD.	ISSUE PRICE	*QUOTE U.S.$
1998 Alcatraz CA 417	Open		70.00	70
1999 Assateague VA 425	Open		60.00	60
1997 Barnegat NJ 414	Closed	1997	45.00	45-50
1998 Barnegat NJ 414R	Open		50.00	50
1998 Bolivar TX 422	Open		65.00	65
1996 Boston Harbor MA 402	Closed	1998	50.00	250
1999 Boston Harbor MA 402R	Open		55.00	55
1998 Cape Canaveral FL 420	Open		50.00	50
1994 Cape Hatteras NC 401	Open		50.00	50
2000 Cape May NJ 428	Open		55.00	55
1997 Cape Neddick ME 410	Open		50.00	50
1999 Grosse Point IL 426	Open		60.00	60
1998 Holland MI 407	Open		50.00	50
1999 Key West FL 424	Open		65.00	65
1997 Montauk NY 405	Open		55.00	55
1997 New London Ledge CT 406	Open		55.00	55
1998 Old Mackinac MI 419	Open		65.00	65
2000 Pensacola FL 430	Open		60.00	60
1997 Point Loma CA 409	Open		50.00	50
1997 Ponce De Leon FL 408	Open		55.00	55
1995 Portland Head ME 404	Closed	1998	50.00	50-88
1999 Portland Head ME 404R	Open		55.00	55
1996 Sandy Hook NJ 418	Open		50.00	50
2000 Sanibel FL 429	Open		90.00	90
1997 Sea Pines (Hilton Head) SC 415	Open		50.00	50
1995 Southeast Block Island RI 403	Closed	1998	50.00	50
1999 Southeast Block Island RI 403R	Open		55.00	55
1997 St. Augustine FL 411	Open		45.00	45
1997 St. Simons GA 416	Open		50.00	50
1998 Thomas Point MD 421	Open		90.00	90

Gulf Coast Region - Harbour Lights

YEAR ISSUE	EDITION LIMIT	YEAR RETD.	ISSUE PRICE	*QUOTE U.S.$
1995 Biloxi MS 149	5,500	1997	60.00	60-125
1995 Bolivar TX 146	5,500	1997	70.00	70-107
1997 Middle Bay AL 187	9,500	1997	99.00	99-182
1995 New Canal LA 148	5,500	1996	65.00	65-107
1995 Pensacola FL 150	9,000	1997	80.00	79-175
1995 Port Isabel TX 147	5,500	1997	65.00	65-182
2000 Round Island MS "Then & Now" 242	Retrd.	2000	65.00	65-75

Hudson River Series - Harbour Lights

YEAR ISSUE	EDITION LIMIT	YEAR RETD.	ISSUE PRICE	*QUOTE U.S.$
1999 Esopus Meadows NY 231	10,000		70.00	70
1999 Hudson-Athens NY 230	10,000		78.00	78
1999 Tarrytown NY 232	10,000		75.00	75

International Series - Harbour Lights

YEAR ISSUE	EDITION LIMIT	YEAR RETD.	ISSUE PRICE	*QUOTE U.S.$
1999 Cape Agulhas South Africa 227	10,000		73.00	73
1999 Cove Canada Ontario 233	8,000		68.00	68
1999 Fisgard British Columbia 234	8,000		69.00	69
1997 Hook Head Ireland 198	9,500		71.00	71
1999 La Coruna Spain 235	6,500		65.00	65
1997 La Jument France 192	9,500	1998	68.00	67-150
2000 La Marte Quebec 255	6,500		75.00	75
1997 Longship UK 193	9,500		68.00	68
1997 Macquarie Australia 197	9,500		68.00	68
1999 Panama (Miraflores & Gatun Locks) Matched Numbered Set 241	4,000	1999	65.00	65
1996 Peggy's Cove Canada 169	Closed	1999	68.00	63-100

Lady Lightkeepers - Harbour Lights

YEAR ISSUE	EDITION LIMIT	YEAR RETD.	ISSUE PRICE	*QUOTE U.S.$
1996 Chatham MA 172	8,032	1998	70.00	70-150
1996 Ida Lewis RI 174	5,886	1999	70.00	70
1996 Matinicus ME 173	6,800	1999	77.00	77
1996 Point Piños CA 170	6,700	1999	70.00	70
1996 Saugerties NY 171	8,100	1999	75.00	75-110

Northeast Region - Harbour Lights

YEAR ISSUE	EDITION LIMIT	YEAR RETD.	ISSUE PRICE	*QUOTE U.S.$
1994 Barnegat NJ (blue water)139	5,500	1995	60.00	245-391
1994 Barnegat NJ (green water) 139	5,500	1995	60.00	275-360
1998 Bass Harbor ME 214	10,000		75.00	75
1997 Beavertail RI (gray) 188	6,500	1999	80.00	80
1997 Beavertail RI (tan) 188	3,000	1999	80.00	63-110
1991 Boston Harbor MA 117	5,500	1995	60.00	133-300
1995 Brant Point MA 162	Closed	1999	66.00	60-80
1998 Cape Elizabeth ME 215	10,000		75.00	75
1997 Cape Henry VA 196	9,500	1997	82.00	82-150
1996 Cape May NJ 168	9,500	1997	75.00	75-190
1994 Cape Neddick (Nubble) ME 141	5,500	1995	66.00	185-400
1991 Castle Hill RI 116	5,500	1996	60.00	79-175
1998 Dunkirk NY 221	10,000		70.00	70
1998 Execution Rock NY 210	10,000		78.00	78
1998 Faulkner's Island CT 216	10,000		70.00	70
1998 Fenwick DE 213	10,000		82.00	82
1996 Fire Island NY 176	9,500	1998	70.00	70-150
1998 Gay Head MA 219	10,000		75.00	75
1998 Goat Island ME 222	10,000		75.00	75
1991 Gt. Captain Island CT 114	5,500	1996	60.00	82-150
1995 Highland MA (w/o "s") 161	3,500	1998	75.00	75-150
1995 Highlands MA (w/ "s") 161	6,000	1998	75.00	175
1998 Horton Point NY 205	10,000		75.00	75
1997 Jeffrey's Hook NY 195	9,500	1999	66.00	66-125
1992 Minot's Ledge MA (blue water) 131	5,500	1996	60.00	150-275
1992 Minot's Ledge MA (green water) 131	5,500	1996	60.00	200-275
1994 Montauk NY 143	5,500	1995	85.00	162-250
1992 Nauset MA 126	5,500	1995	66.00	200-375
1992 New London Ledge CT (blue water) 129	5,500	1995	66.00	145-175
1992 New London Ledge CT (green water) 129	5,500	1995	66.00	250
1997 Nobska MA 203	9,500	1998	75.00	74-80
1998 Old Saybrook CT 206	10,000		69.00	69
1996 Pemaquid ME 164	9,500	1998	90.00	90-175
1998 Point Judith RI 223	10,000		82.00	82
1992 Portland Breakwater ME 130	5,500	1996	60.00	82-115
1992 Portland Head ME 125	5,500	1994	66.00	600-875
1996 Pt. Pinos CA 170	6,700	1999	70.00	70
1991 Sandy Hook NJ 104	5,500	1994	60.00	275-550
1996 Scituate MA 166	9,500	1998	77.00	77-150
2000 Ship John Shoal DE 245	6,500		68.00	68
1992 Southeast Block Island RI 128	5,500	1994	71.00	369-500
1991 West Quoddy Head ME 103	5,500	1995	60.00	133-313
1992 Whaleback NH 127	5,500	1996	60.00	63-112

Northwest Region - Harbour Lights

YEAR ISSUE	EDITION LIMIT	YEAR RETD.	ISSUE PRICE	*QUOTE U.S.$
2000 Eldred Rock AK 257	4,000		65.00	65

Restoration Series - Harbour Lights

YEAR ISSUE	EDITION LIMIT	YEAR RETD.	ISSUE PRICE	*QUOTE U.S.$
2000 Rockland Breakwater ME 248	6,500		70.00	70
1999 Sapelo Island GA 239	8,000		60.00	60

Signature Series - Harbour Lights

YEAR ISSUE	EDITION LIMIT	YEAR RETD.	ISSUE PRICE	*QUOTE U.S.$
1999 Coquille OR 427, S/N	Open		55.00	55
1998 Thomas Point MD 421, S/N	Open		90.00	90
1998 Tybee GA 423, S/N	Open		65.00	65

Southeast Region - Harbour Lights

YEAR ISSUE	EDITION LIMIT	YEAR RETD.	ISSUE PRICE	*QUOTE U.S.$
2000 American Shoal FL 229	6,500	2000	99.00	99
1994 Assateague VA 145-mold one	988	1994	69.00	150-275
1994 Assateague VA 145-mold two	4,512	1995	69.00	150-188
1996 Bald Head NC 155	9,500	1998	75.00	75-155
1996 Cape Canaveral FL 163	9,500	1996	80.00	75-188
1998 Cape Florida FL 209	10,000	1998	78.00	78-150
1991 Cape Hatteras NC 102 (with house)	Retrd.	1991	60.00	3400-3481
1992 Cape Hatteras NC 102R	5,500	1993	60.00	615-1250
2000 Fort Jefferson FL 247	8,000		75.00	75
2000 Haig Point SC 246	8,000		75.00	75
1999 Hillsboro FL 225	6,500	1999	125.00	125-238
1993 Hilton Head SC 136	5,500	1994	60.00	420-500
1998 Hunting Island SC 211	10,000		75.00	75
1995 Jupiter FL 151	9,500	1996	77.00	125-195
1993 Key West FL 134	5,500	1995	60.00	275-379
2000 Oak Island NC 240	6,500	2000	78.00	78
1993 Ocracoke NC 135	5,500	1995	60.00	300-450
2000 Old Point Comfort VA 244	8,000		82.00	82
1993 Ponce de Leon FL 132	5,500	1994	60.00	350-469
1997 Sanibel FL 194	9,500	1997	120.00	120-250
1993 St. Augustine FL 138	5,500	1994	71.00	447-500
1999 St. Marks FL 220	10,000		75.00	75
1993 St. Simons GA 137	5,500	1995	66.00	300-375
1993 Tybee GA 133	5,500	1995	60.00	250-374

Special Editions - Harbour Lights

YEAR ISSUE	EDITION LIMIT	YEAR RETD.	ISSUE PRICE	*QUOTE U.S.$
2000 5th Order Fresnel Lens 631	4,000		80.00	80
1999 Bob Younger Memorial 623	Open		10.00	10
1997 Keepers & Friends 606	Open		55.00	55
1995 Legacy Light (blue) 601	Retrd.	1996	65.00	65-150
1995 Legacy Light (red) 600	Retrd.	1996	65.00	65-188

*Quotes have been rounded up to nearest dollar

YEAR ISSUE	EDITION LIMIT	YEAR RETD.	ISSUE PRICE	*QUOTE U.S.$
2000 Liberty Enlightening The World 627	Yr.Iss.		125.00	125
1997 Navesink NJ 200	9,500		245.00	245
1997 Spyglass Collection-New England 607	Open		83.00	83
1998 Spyglass Collection-Southern Belles, set/7 613	Open		83.00	83

Stamp Series - Harbour Lights

YEAR ISSUE	EDITION LIMIT	YEAR RETD.	ISSUE PRICE	*QUOTE U.S.$
1995 Marblehead OH 413	Open		50.00	50
1995 Spectacle Reef MI 182	9,500	1996	60.00	60
1995 Split Rock MN 412	Open		60.00	60
1995 St. Joseph MI 183	9,500	1996	60.00	60-95
1995 Thirty Mile Point NY 184	9,500	1996	62.00	62
1995 Five Piece Matched Numbered Set 400	5,300	1995	275.00	275-350

Tall Towers - Harbour Lights

YEAR ISSUE	EDITION LIMIT	YEAR RETD.	ISSUE PRICE	*QUOTE U.S.$
1996 Bodie NC 159	9,500	1998	77.00	144-188
1996 Cape Lookout NC 175	9,500	1997	64.00	64-150
1995 Currituck NC 158	9,500	1997	80.00	80-150
1997 Morris Island - Now, SC 190	9,500	1997	65.00	65-163
1997 Morris Island - Then, SC 189	9,500	1997	85.00	85-195
1997 Morris Island - Now & Then, set SC 189	9,500	1997	170.00	175-300

Western Region - Harbour Lights

YEAR ISSUE	EDITION LIMIT	YEAR RETD.	ISSUE PRICE	*QUOTE U.S.$
1991 Admirality Head WA 101(misspelled)	Closed	1994	60.00	125-188
1991 Admiralty Head WA 101	Retrd.	1994	60.00	87-250
1996 Alcatraz CA 177	9,500	1996	77.00	122-195
1991 Burrows Island OR 108 (incorrect state)	Closed	1991	60.00	1063-1250
1991 Burrows Island WA 108	2,563	1994	60.00	300-425
1991 Cape Blanco OR 109	5,500	1997	60.00	60-94
1999 Cape Disappointment WA 238	8,000		65.00	65
1996 Cape Meares OR 160	5,656	1999	68.00	68
1991 Coquille River OR 111	1,138	1993	60.00	2270-2700
1994 Diamond Head HI 140	5,500	1995	60.00	150-325
1997 Gray's Harbor WA 202	9,500		75.00	75
1994 Heceta Head OR 144	5,500	1996	65.00	72-138
1996 Mukilteo WA 178	9,500	1999	55.00	55
1991 North Head WA 106	5,500	1996	60.00	72-93
1991 Old Point Loma CA 105	5,500	1995	60.00	122-235
1997 Pigeon Point CA 199	9,500		68.00	68
1995 Pt. Arena CA 156	5,428	1996	80.00	128-295
1991 St. George's Reef CA 115	5,500	1996	60.00	63-90
1998 Tillamook OR 224	10,000		75.00	75
1991 Umpqua River OR 107	5,500	1996	60.00	68-125
1997 Yaquina Bay OR 204	9,500		77.00	77
1991 Yaquina Head WA 110	5,500	1996	60.00	75-104

Hazle Ceramics

A Nation of Shopkeepers Collectors' Club - H. Boyles

YEAR ISSUE	EDITION LIMIT	YEAR RETD.	ISSUE PRICE	*QUOTE U.S.$
1995 Anne Frank's "The Hiding Place"	Retrd.	1998	76.00	76
1996 Jewellers	200	1997	68.00	68-116
1996 County Bank	200	1998	76.00	76-145
1998 Street Scenes - The Telephone Box Queue	Yr.Iss.	1998	Gift	25
1999 Street Scenes - The Walled Garden	Yr.Iss.	1999	Gift	N/A
2000 Village Sign	Yr.Iss.		Gift	N/A

A Nation of Shopkeepers - H. Boyles

YEAR ISSUE	EDITION LIMIT	YEAR RETD.	ISSUE PRICE	*QUOTE U.S.$
1993 Bagel Bakery	Retrd.	1997	63.00	112
1995 Bakery/Coffee Shop	Retrd.	1998	72.00	72
1991 Barber	Retrd.	1997	64.00	112
1998 Batchelor's Saddlemaker	200	1999	120.00	120
1993 Bookshop	Retrd.	1998	72.00	76
1993 Bookshop & Postbox	Retrd.	1998	76.00	76
1991 Butcher Shop	Retrd.	1997	64.00	115-145
1994 Christmas Ironmonger-red	300	1996	84.00	651-913
1990 Clock Shop	Retrd.	1992	54.00	54
1998 Collect It!	300	1998	70.00	70
1996 Corner Grocer	2,000	1998	85.00	85
1991 Corner Shop	Retrd.	1998	62.00	62
1995 East End Deli (London)	Retrd.	1998	75.00	112
1996 East Side Deli (NY)	Retrd.	1998	75.00	80
1994 Fine Art Saleroom	Retrd.	1998	124.00	170
1990 Fish & Chips (no line up)	Retrd.	1993	50.00	215
1991 Fishmonger	Retrd.	1997	68.00	95-116
1995 Forever Flowers	50	1997	70.00	70
1990 Gents Hats	Retrd.	1992	54.00	54
1993 Gift Shop	Retrd.	1997	72.00	76
1995 Green Fingers	50	1997	70.00	70
1991 Greengrocer	Retrd.	1995	62.00	62
1991 Hairdresser	Retrd.	1997	64.00	110
1994 Hardware/Ironmonger-green	1,200	1996	84.00	205-362
1991 Harvard House	Retrd.	1997	58.00	58
1992 Indian Restaurant	Retrd.	1997	72.00	72
1990 Ladies Hat Shop	Retrd.	1992	54.00	54
1993 Needlewoman	300	1995	72.00	72-362
1993 Nell Gwynn's House	250	1996	90.00	90-362
1998 The Optician	Retrd.	1998	70.00	116
1991 The Pawnbroker	Retrd.	1994	72.00	165
1998 Post Office/Newsagent	Retrd.	1999	76.00	76
1994 Saddlery	Retrd.	1997	76.00	140
1995 Sewing Room	500	1996	76.00	200-254
1990 Shoe Shop	Retrd.	1992	54.00	54
1990 Small Post Office	Retrd.	1992	54.00	205-290
1993 Smiths of Bermuda	200	1996	70.00	95
1994 Tom Morris Golf Shop	Retrd.	1997	76.00	110-145
1993 Trick or Treat	Retrd.	1997	70.00	70
1995 Tudor Pub-Fox & Hounds	Retrd.	1997	72.00	145
1994 Turret Pub	Retrd.	1998	78.00	78
1996 Victorian Police Station	Retrd.	1997	75.00	145-175
1993 Victorian Post Office	Retrd.	1997	78.00	165
1997 Victorian Pub-Red Lion	Retrd.	1999	74.00	76
1997 Victorian Pub-Victoria & Albert	Retrd.	1997	74.00	74

Kiddie Car Classics/Hallmark Keepsake Collections

Kiddie Car Corner Collection - L. Sickman

YEAR ISSUE	EDITION LIMIT	YEAR RETD.	ISSUE PRICE	*QUOTE U.S.$
1999 "Cinder says..." QHG3621	Open		30.00	30
1999 "Cinder" & "Ella" Dalmatians QHG3619	Open		15.00	15
1999 Call Box & Fire Hydrant QHG3618	Open		25.00	25
1998 Corner Drive-In QHG3610	39,500		70.00	70
1999 Corner Drive-In Sidewalk Signs QHG3616	Open		15.00	15
2000 Don's Sign QHG3623	Open		16.00	16
1998 Famous Food Sign QHG3614	Open		30.00	30
1999 Fire Station No.1 QHG3617	39,500		70.00	70
1999 Flagpole QHG3620	Open		20.00	20
1997 KC's Garage QHG3601	Retrd.	1998	70.00	70-125
1998 KC's Motor Oil QHG3609	Retrd.	2000	15.00	15
1998 Mechanic's Lift & Tool Box QHG3608	Retrd.	2000	25.00	25
1998 Menu Station with Food Trays QHG3611	Open		30.00	30
1998 Newspaper Box and Trash Can Set QHG3613	Open		20.00	20
2000 Parking Sign QHG3630	Open		8.00	8
1997 Pedal Petroleum QHG3602	Retrd.	1999	25.00	25
1999 Pedal Power Premium Gas Pump QHG3603	Retrd.	1999	30.00	30-50
1997 Sidewalk Sale Signs QHG3605	Retrd.	1999	15.00	15
1997 Sidewalk Service Signs QHG3604	Retrd.	1999	15.00	15-25
2000 Stop Sign QHG3622	Open		10.00	10
2000 Street Signs QHG3629	Open		10.00	10
2000 Streetlamp QHG3624	Open		15.00	15
1999 Table & Benches QHG3615	Open		20.00	20
1997 Welcome Sign QHG3606	Retrd.	1999	30.00	30

The Liberty Falls Collection/International Resources, LLC.

The Liberty Falls Collectors Club - Liberty Falls

YEAR ISSUE	EDITION LIMIT	YEAR RETD.	ISSUE PRICE	*QUOTE U.S.$
1993 Clara's Bakery - Gift	Retrd.	1999	Gift	7-20
1994 Liberty Falls Bandstand - Gift	Open		Gift	N/A
1994 Welcome to Liberty Falls Road Sign - Gift	Open.		Gift	N/A
1995 Skating Pond - Gift	Open		Gift	N/A
1995 Community Christmas Tree - Gift	Open		Gift	N/A
1996 Liberty Falls Wishing Well - Gift	Open		Gift	N/A
1996 Liberty Falls Playground - Gift	Open		Gift	N/A
1997 Liberty Falls Windmill - Gift	Open		Gift	N/A
1997 Sledder's Paradise - Gift	Open		Gift	N/A
1998 Liberty Falls Water Tower - Gift	Open		Gift	N/A
1998 Covered Bridge & One Horse Open Sleigh - Gift	Open		Gift	N/A
1999 The Oldest Tree - Gift	Open		Gift	N/A
1999 Liberty Falls Apple Orchard - Gift	Open		Gift	N/A
1999 Ski Lodge	Open		Gift	N/A

The Liberty Falls Collection - Liberty Falls

YEAR ISSUE	EDITION LIMIT	YEAR RETD.	ISSUE PRICE	*QUOTE U.S.$
1994 Albert Buck Law Office	Retrd.	1995	5.00	8-20
1996 Alexander Mansion	Retrd.	1996	5.00	5
1997 Aunt Alice's Quilt Shop	Retrd.	1997	5.00	15-35
1994 Ausberg's Brewery	Retrd.	1995	5.00	7-15
1997 B. Cummings Signmaker	Retrd.	1997	5.00	7-12
1999 Baseball Game	Open		12.50	13
1997 Berghoff Butcher Shop	Retrd.	1997	5.00	7-12
1998 Bergman Residence	Retrd.	1998	5.00	5-20
1996 Bergman's Clock Shop	Retrd.	1996	5.00	7-13
1998 Billy Atwell's Homestead	Retrd.	1998	5.00	15-20
1991 Blue Whale Tavern	Retrd.	1991	5.00	15-60
1995 Boots & Shoes Store	Retrd.	1995	5.00	5
1997 Carriage & Wagon Works	Retrd.	1997	5.00	12
1997 Church of the Epiphany	Retrd.	1997	5.00	6-13
1998 Church of the Holy Redeemer	Retrd.	1998	5.00	6-8
1998 Circus Big Top	Open		12.50	13
1998 Circus Train	Retrd.	1998	15.00	15
1994 City Hall (original)	Retrd.	1994	5.00	10-35
1995 City Hall (revised)	Retrd.	1995	5.00	7-12
1999 Civil War Veteran's Home	Retrd.	1999	6.00	6-10
1999 Civil War Veteran's Home w/Memorial	Retrd.	1999	10.00	7-12
1994 Clark Mansion	Retrd.	1994	5.00	7-15
1992 Clark, DuBois Bank & Mint	Retrd.	1995	5.00	15-45
1992 Clemen's School	Retrd.	1995	5.00	20-55
1995 Clock Tower & Civic Center	Retrd.	1995	10.00	35-45
1996 Cluny & Cluny Real Estate	Retrd.	1996	5.00	7-12
1999 Commercial Layout	Open		10.00	10
1993 Cox's Furniture & Undertakers	Retrd.	1994	5.00	8-31
1993 Daily News	Retrd.	1994	5.00	7-15
1998 Dawson's Livery	Retrd.	1998	5.00	6-16
1998 Dearly's Grocery Store	Retrd.	1998	5.00	6-13
1999 Dr. Sandy Veterinarian	Retrd.	1999	6.00	10-20
1994 Dr. Steven's Home & Office	Retrd.	1994	5.00	5-35
1997 Dr. Wilson's Dentist Office	Retrd.	1997	5.00	5-35
1992 DuBois Mansion	Retrd.	1995	5.00	7-45
1991 Duffy's Mill (original)	Retrd.	1991	5.00	40-115
1993 Duffy's Mill (revised)	Retrd.	1993	5.00	14-35
1996 Emma's Family Restaurant	Retrd.	1996	5.00	5-25
1995 Fannie's Ice Cream Parlor	Retrd.	1995	5.00	25
1992 First Congregational Church	Retrd.	1993	5.00	7-20
2000 First Lakeview Church	Retrd.	2000	6.00	6
1991 First Prarie Church (original)	Retrd.	1991	5.00	35-46
1992 First Prarie Church (revised)	Retrd.	1995	5.00	25-40
1999 Forest Glen Church	Retrd.	1999	6.00	6-8
1996 Friends Community Church	Retrd.	1996	5.00	5-25
1996 Frontier Card Parlor	Retrd.	1996	5.00	5
1999 Gadiel Home	Retrd.	1999	6.00	6
1999 Gadiel Home w/Studio	Retrd.	1999	10.00	7-12
1998 General Miles Memorial Park	Open		12.50	13
1999 General Miles' Home	Retrd.	1999	6.00	5-6
1993 Gold King Mines	Retrd.	1993	5.00	5-35
1997 Gold Mining Stock Exchange	Retrd.	1997	5.00	12-20
1993 Gold Nugget Tavern	Retrd.	1993	5.00	7-35
1998 Goldman's Home	Retrd.	1998	5.00	5
1996 Govenor's Mansion	Retrd.	1996	5.00	6-13
1991 Greller's Pharmacy (original)	Retrd.	1991	5.00	10-34
1993 Greller's Pharmacy (revised)	Retrd.	1993	5.00	7-15
1994 Gunsmith Shop (original)	Retrd.	1994	5.00	5
1995 Gunsmith Shop (revised)	Retrd.	1995	5.00	15-20
1997 Handy Andy Malloy's House	Retrd.	1997	5.00	6-35
2000 Hayride	Open		12.50	13
1999 Henshaw House	Retrd.	1999	6.00	10
1999 Henshaw House w/Mother-In-Law Cottage	Retrd.	1999	10.00	7-12
1999 Hillside Farm	Retrd.	1999	6.00	8
1999 Hillside Farm w/Cow Barn	Retrd.	1999	10.00	7-12
1998 Home of Artist Anabelle Phillips	Retrd.	1998	5.00	15-20
1998 Home of Seamstress Ida Penney	Retrd.	1998	5.00	10-25
1999 Hook Family Home	Retrd.	1999	6.00	7-20
1996 Howard's Hardware	Retrd.	1996	5.00	7-13
2000 Jeremiah Sobel's Home	Retrd.	2000	6.00	6
1998 John T Boone's Home	Retrd.	1998	5.00	10-15
1996 Johnson Farmhouse	Retrd.	1996	5.00	5
2000 Joss's Barber Shop	Retrd.	2000	6.00	6
1997 Ladies Temperance Society	Retrd.	1997	5.00	6-18
1994 Land Surveyor & Assay Office	Retrd.	1995	5.00	7-20
1999 Lemonade Stand	Retrd.	1999	15.00	15
1999 Liberty Church	Retrd.	1999	6.00	6
1999 Liberty Church w/Social Hall	Retrd.	1999	10.00	7-12
1998 Liberty Falls Airship	Retrd.	1998	15.00	15-25
2000 Liberty Falls Art Museum	Retrd.	2000	6.00	6
1996 Liberty Falls Bell Tower	Retrd.	1996	12.00	15-35
1997 Liberty Falls Carousel	Retrd.	1997	15.00	15-50
2000 Liberty Falls Children's Hospital	Retrd.	2000	6.00	6
1993 Liberty Falls Courthouse	Retrd.	1994	5.00	7-35
1999 Liberty Falls Ferris Wheel	Retrd.	1999	15.00	15
1992 Liberty Falls Fire Station	Retrd.	1995	5.00	55-60
1996 Liberty Falls Historical Society	Retrd.	1996	5.00	5-30
1998 Liberty Falls Hot Springs & Spa	Retrd.	1998	5.00	10-15
1995 Liberty Falls Laundry	Retrd.	1995	5.00	5
1996 Liberty Falls Middle School	Retrd.	1996	5.00	5
1993 Liberty Falls Opera House	Retrd.	1993	5.00	6-35
1996 Liberty Falls Post Office	Retrd.	1996	5.00	8-20
2000 The Liberty Falls Roller Coaster	Retrd.	2000	15.00	15
1998 Liberty Falls Secondary School	Retrd.	1998	5.00	10-20
2000 Liberty Falls Theatre	Retrd.	2000	6.00	6
1991 Liberty Falls Train Station (original)	Retrd.	1991	5.00	45-120
1991 Liberty Falls Train Station (revisedl)	Retrd.	1993	5.00	20-41
1994 Library & Reading Room	Retrd.	1995	5.00	8-15
1994 Life & Times of Liberty Falls	Retrd.	1995	9.95	10-15
1998 Life & Times of Liberty Falls II	Retrd.	1998	9.95	10
2000 Livestock Judging	Open		12.50	13
1995 Lucky's Billiard Hall	Retrd.	1995	5.00	5
1992 Marshal's Office	Retrd.	1995	5.00	20-50
2000 Mayor Griffin's Home	Retrd.	2000	6.00	6
1991 Mayor Johnson's Home	Retrd.	1995	5.00	66-140
1999 McKee Photography Studio	Retrd.	1999	6.00	6-20
1998 Miller Family Shingle House	Retrd.	1998	5.00	10-20
1998 Mountainview Church	Retrd.	1998	5.00	10-15
1993 Mrs. Applegate's Boarding House	Retrd.	1993	5.00	5-35
1994 Muriel Phillips' Piano & Violin School	Retrd.	1995	5.00	6-20
2000 Murray's Grist Mill	Retrd.	2000	6.00	6
1994 Old Homestead Restaurant	Retrd.	1994	5.00	7-12
1998 Old Swimming Hole	Open		12.50	13
1999 Ornithologist's House	Retrd.	1999	6.00	6-10
1999 Ornithologist's House w/Dove Cote	Retrd.	1999	10.00	7-15
1997 Owen Conkling's Books & Stationary	Retrd.	1997	5.00	15
1995 P&M Stagecoach Station	Retrd.	1995	5.00	25
1995 Pacific & Mountain Telegraph Co.	Retrd.	1995	5.00	9-12
1996 Palace Dance Hall & Saloon	Retrd.	1996	5.00	7-18
1996 Palace Dance Hall New Year's Eve	Retrd.	1996	5.00	20-30
1999 Panning For Gold	Open		12.50	13
1997 Pastor George Kendall's Parsonage	Retrd.	1997	5.00	6-13
1998 Perfect Day For a Picnic	Open		12.50	13
2000 Pie Easting Contest	Open		12.50	13
1996 Pioneer's Church	Retrd.	1996	5.00	8-13
1994 Pipe & Tobacco Shop (original)	Retrd.	1994	5.00	5-45
1994 Pipe & Tobacco Shop (revised)	Retrd.	1995	5.00	15-20
1992 Pony Express Station	Retrd.	1995	5.00	60
1995 Port Clinton Jewelers/Optical Shop	Retrd.	1995	5.00	9-25
1997 Prospector's Cabin	Retrd.	1997	5.00	15
1999 Purdy Dairy Farm	Retrd.	1999	6.00	10-15
1996 Red Crown Barn	Retrd.	1996	5.00	5-35
1996 Red Rudder Antiques	Retrd.	1996	5.00	5-15
1999 Residential Layout	Open		10.00	10
1998 Rev. Muir's Cottage	Retrd.	1998	5.00	7-13
1994 Rev. Watkins' House	Retrd.	1994	5.00	7-15
1999 Riverside Lodge	Retrd.	1999	6.00	6-8
1999 Riverside Lodge w/Bath House	Retrd.	1999	10.00	7-12
1999 Rodeo	Open		12.50	13
1999 Rosie's Flower Shop	Retrd.	1999	6.00	10
1999 Rosie's Flower Shop w/Greenhouse	Retrd.	1999	10.00	7-12
1993 Ross Brothers Clothiers	Retrd.	1995	5.00	7-35
1997 Ross Family Home	Retrd.	1997	5.00	12-25
1999 Sally's Dancing School	Retrd.	1999	6.00	8-10
1998 Scenic Overlook	Open		12.50	13
1999 Sideshow Tent	Open		12.50	13
1998 Silver Spoon Silversmith	Retrd.	1998	5.00	15-20

*Quotes have been rounded up to nearest dollar

YEAR ISSUE	EDITION LIMIT	YEAR RETD.	ISSUE PRICE	*QUOTE U.S.$
2000 Sinclair Home	Retrd.	2000	6.00	6
1999 Sinclair Hotel	Retrd.	1999	6.00	6-8
1999 Sinclair Hotel w/Carriage House	Retrd.	1999	10.00	6-12
2000 Sports & Apothecary Shops	Retrd.	2000	6.00	6
2000 Square Dance	Open		12.50	13
1997 St. Paul's United Church	Retrd.	1997	5.00	10-15
1999 Stern House	Retrd.	1999	6.00	6-20
2000 The Stone Bridge	Retrd.	2000	Gift	N/A
1992 Stubbs Blacksmith & Saddlery	Retrd.	1995	5.00	10-55
1997 Susan's Hat Shop	Retrd.	1997	5.00	6-12
1994 Swanson's Feed and Grain	Retrd.	1994	5.00	7-12
1996 Timberline Lumber	Retrd.	1996	5.00	8-13
1997 Trapper Big Mike's Cabin	Retrd.	1997	5.00	10-30
1995 Trinity Church	Retrd.	1995	5.00	6-12
1994 Tully House	Retrd.	1995	5.00	7-20
1991 Tully's General Store (original)	Retrd.	1991	5.00	37-60
1993 Tully's General Store (revised)	Retrd.	1993	5.00	5-20
1997 Vedder Home	Retrd.	1997	5.00	15
1998 Wedding Portrait	Open		12.50	13
1998 Welbourne Estate	Retrd.	1998	5.00	15
1998 White's Wheel Company	Retrd.	1998	5.00	15
1995 Wilson Ranch House	Retrd.	1995	5.00	10-16
1999 Winthrop's Carpet Mill	Retrd.	1999	6.00	5-10
1999 Winthrop's Carpet Mill w/Warehouse	Retrd.	1999	10.00	7-12
1994 Wooden Nickel Inn	Retrd.	1994	5.00	6-15
1993 Wooden Wall Rack	Retrd.	1997	9.95	10

The Liberty Falls Collection Accessories - Liberty Falls

YEAR ISSUE	EDITION LIMIT	YEAR RETD.	ISSUE PRICE	*QUOTE U.S.$
1994 Accessory Set, AH49	Open		6.00	6
1995 Accessory Set, AH50	Open		6.00	6
1996 Accessory Set, AH51	Open		6.00	6
1997 Accessory Set, AH52	Open		6.00	6
1998 Accessory Set, AH121	Open		6.00	6
1999 Accessory Set, AH122	Open		6.00	6
2000 Accessory Set, AH221	Open		6.00	6
2000 Accessory Set, AH224	Open		6.00	6
2000 Accessory Set, AH225	Open		6.00	6

The Liberty Falls Collection Pewter Set - Liberty Falls

YEAR ISSUE	EDITION LIMIT	YEAR RETD.	ISSUE PRICE	*QUOTE U.S.$
1991 Pewter Set, AH09	Retrd.	1991	5.00	15
1992 Pewter Set, AH18	Retrd.	1995	5.00	9-20
1992 Pewter Set, AH19	Retrd.	1995	5.00	10-25
1993 Pewter Set, AH30	Retrd.	1993	5.00	75
1993 Pewter Set, AH31	Retrd.	1993	5.00	15-20
1993 Pewter Set, AH45	Retrd.	1993	5.00	5
1994 Pewter Set, AH47	Retrd.	1994	5.00	6-20
1994 Pewter Set, AH48	Retrd.	1994	5.00	6-20
1995 Pewter Set, AH71	Retrd.	1995	5.00	6-15
1995 Pewter Set, AH72	Retrd.	1995	5.00	6-20
1996 Pewter Set, AH109	Retrd.	1996	5.00	10-18
1996 Pewter Set, AH110	Retrd.	1996	5.00	8-12
1997 Pewter Set, AH135	Retrd.	1997	5.00	8-15
1997 Pewter Set, AH136	Retrd.	1997	5.00	10-18
1998 Pewter Set, AH161	Retrd.	1998	5.00	7-13
1998 Pewter Set, AH162	Retrd.	1998	5.00	7-13
1998 Pewter Set, AH19C	Retrd.	1998	5.00	5
1998 Pewter Set, AH72C	Retrd.	1998	5.00	5
1999 Pewter Set, AH195	Retrd.	1999	6.00	6
1999 Pewter Set, AH196	Retrd.	1999	6.00	6
1999 Pewter Set, AH199	Retrd.	1999	10.00	10
2000 Pewter Set, AH222P	Retrd.	2000	6.00	6
2000 Pewter Set, AH223	Retrd.	2000	6.00	6

Lilliput Lane Ltd./Enesco European Giftware Group

Collectors Club Specials - Lilliput Lane, unless otherwise noted

YEAR ISSUE	EDITION LIMIT	YEAR RETD.	ISSUE PRICE	*QUOTE U.S.$
1986 Packhorse Bridge - D. Tate	Retrd.	1987	Gift	375-650
1986 Packhorse Bridge (dealer) - D. Tate	Retrd.	1987	Gift	450-600
1986 Crendon Manor - D. Tate	Retrd.	1989	285.00	838-925
1986 Gulliver - Unknown	Retrd.	1986	65.00	250-375
1987 Little Lost Dog - D. Tate	Retrd.	1988	Gift	525-625
1987 Yew Tree Farm - D. Tate	Retrd.	1988	160.00	219-375
1988 Wishing Well - D. Tate	Retrd.	1989	Gift	75-138
1989 Dovecot - D. Tate	Retrd.	1990	Gift	57-82
1989 Wenlock Rise - D. Tate	Retrd.	1989	175.00	132-225
1990 Cosy Corner - D. Tate	Retrd.	1991	Gift	30-94
1990 Lavender Cottage - D. Tate	Retrd.	1991	50.00	49-75
1990 Bridle Way - D. Tate	Retrd.	1991	100.00	119-163
1991 Puddlebrook - D. Tate	Retrd.	1992	Gift	33-90
1991 Gardeners Cottage - D. Tate	Retrd.	1992	120.00	63-125
1991 Wren Cottage - D. Tate	Retrd.	1993	13.95	119-188
1992 Pussy Willow - D. Tate	Retrd.	1993	Gift	34-55
1992 Forget-Me-Not - D. Tate	Retrd.	1993	130.00	100-144
1993 The Spinney	Retrd.	1994	Gift	29-35
1993 Heaven Lea Cottage	Retrd.	1994	150.00	73-195
1993 Curlew Cottage	Retrd.	1995	18.95	110-219
1994 Petticoat Cottage	Retrd.	1995	Gift	25-40
1994 Woodman's Retreat	Retrd.	1995	135.00	94-120
1995 Thimble Cottage	Retrd.	1996	Gift	30-50
1995 Porlock Down	Retrd.	1996	135.00	135
1996 Wash Day	Retrd.	1997	Gift	25
1996 Meadowsweet Cottage	Retrd.	1997	110.00	110
1996 Nursery Cottage	Retrd.	1997	Gift	45-60
1996 Winnows	Retrd.	1998	22.50	50
1997 Hampton Moat	Retrd.	1998	Gift	28
1997 Hampton Manor	Retrd.	1998	100.00	100
1997 Cider Apple Cottage	Retrd.	1998	Gift	60-107
1998 The Pottery	Retrd.	1999	170.00	113-120
1998 Kiln Cottage	Retrd.	1999	Gift	30
1999 Fresh Today	Retrd.	1999	Gift	N/A
1999 The Good Life	Retrd.	1999	150.00	150

YEAR ISSUE	EDITION LIMIT	YEAR RETD.	ISSUE PRICE	*QUOTE U.S.$
2000 Little Bee	Yr.Iss.		Gift	N/A
2000 Beekeeper's Cottage	Yr.Iss.		150.00	150

Anniversary Collection - Lilliput Lane

YEAR ISSUE	EDITION LIMIT	YEAR RETD.	ISSUE PRICE	*QUOTE U.S.$
1992 Honeysuckle Cottage	Yr.Iss.	1992	195.00	107-250
1993 Cotman Cottage	Yr.Iss.	1993	220.00	119-220
1994 Watermeadows	Yr.Iss.	1994	189.00	130-189
1995 Gertrude's Garden	Yr.Iss.	1995	192.00	95-192
1996 Cruck End	Yr.Iss.	1996	130.00	104-130
1997 Summer Days	Yr.Iss.	1997	165.00	95-150
1998 Shades of Summer	Yr.Iss.	1998	170.00	105-213
1999 Pen Pals	Yr.Iss.	1999	170.00	136-170
2000 Sweets & Treats	Yr.Iss.		160.00	160

South Bend Dinner Collection - Various

YEAR ISSUE	EDITION LIMIT	YEAR RETD.	ISSUE PRICE	*QUOTE U.S.$
1989 Commemorative Medallion - D. Tate	Retrd.	1989	N/A	130-200
1990 Rowan Lodge - D. Tate	Retrd.	1990	N/A	300
1991 Gamekeepers Cottage - D. Tate	Retrd.	1991	N/A	200-360
1992 Ashberry Cottage - D. Tate	Retrd.	1992	N/A	194-250
1993 Magnifying Glass - Lilliput Lane	Retrd.	1993	N/A	N/A

Special Event Collection - Lilliput Lane

YEAR ISSUE	EDITION LIMIT	YEAR RETD.	ISSUE PRICE	*QUOTE U.S.$
1990 Rowan Lodge	Retrd.	1990	50.00	82-145
1991 Gamekeepers Cottage	Retrd.	1991	75.00	100
1992 Ploughman's Cottage	Retrd.	1992	75.00	68-128
1993 Aberford Gate	Retrd.	1993	95.00	95-157
1994 Leagrave Cottage	Retrd.	1994	75.00	39-75
1995 Vanbrugh Lodge	Retrd.	1995	60.00	60-82
1996 Amberly Rose	Retrd.	1996	45.00	45
1997 Dormouse Cottage	Retrd.	1997	60.00	48-60
1998 Comfort Cottage	Retrd.	1998	50.00	40-50
1999 Rainbow's End	Retrd.	1999	55.00	44-55
2000 Candy Cottage	Open		65.00	65

American Collection - D. Tate

YEAR ISSUE	EDITION LIMIT	YEAR RETD.	ISSUE PRICE	*QUOTE U.S.$
1984 Adobe Church	Retrd.	1985	22.50	500
1984 Adobe Village	Retrd.	1985	60.00	1000-1157
1984 Cape Cod	Retrd.	1985	22.50	325
1984 Country Church	Retrd.	1985	22.50	150-350
1984 Covered Bridge	Retrd.	1985	22.50	1500
1984 Forge Barn	Retrd.	1985	22.50	600
1984 General Store	Retrd.	1985	22.50	580-750
1984 Grist Mill	Retrd.	1985	22.50	500-750
1984 Light House	Retrd.	1985	22.50	625-938
1984 Log Cabin	Retrd.	1985	22.50	600-875
1984 Midwest Barn	Retrd.	1985	22.50	250-375
1984 San Francisco House	Retrd.	1985	22.50	550-875
1984 Wallace Station	Retrd.	1985	22.50	563-725

The Beatrix Potter Collection - Lilliput Lane, unless otherwise noted

YEAR ISSUE	EDITION LIMIT	YEAR RETD.	ISSUE PRICE	*QUOTE U.S.$
1999 Buckle Yeat	Open		95.00	95
1999 Ginger & Pickles Shop	Open		53.00	53
1999 Hill Top	Open		120.00	120
1999 The House of the Tailor of Gloucester	Open		65.00	65
1999 Tabitha Twitchit's Shop	Open		65.00	65
1999 Tower Bank Arms	Open		65.00	65

The Bed & Breakfast Collection - Lilliput Lane, unless otherwise noted

YEAR ISSUE	EDITION LIMIT	YEAR RETD.	ISSUE PRICE	*QUOTE U.S.$
1998 Seaview	Retrd.	2000	80.00	80
1998 Tarnside	Retrd.	2000	85.00	85
1998 Walker's Rest	Open		85.00	85
1998 York Gate	Retrd.	2000	85.00	85

Blaise Hamlet Classics - Lilliput Lane

YEAR ISSUE	EDITION LIMIT	YEAR RETD.	ISSUE PRICE	*QUOTE U.S.$
1993 Circular Cottage	Retrd.	1995	95.00	66-70
1993 Dial Cottage	Retrd.	1995	95.00	57
1993 Diamond Cottage	Retrd.	1995	95.00	55-100
1993 Double Cottage	Retrd.	1995	95.00	55
1993 Jasmine Cottage	Retrd.	1995	95.00	55
1993 Oak Cottage	Retrd.	1995	95.00	55-95
1993 Rose Cottage	Retrd.	1995	95.00	55
1993 Sweet Briar Cottage	Retrd.	1995	95.00	50-95
1993 Vine Cottage	Retrd.	1995	95.00	55-135

Blaise Hamlet Collection - D. Tate

YEAR ISSUE	EDITION LIMIT	YEAR RETD.	ISSUE PRICE	*QUOTE U.S.$
1989 Circular Cottage	Retrd.	1993	110.00	75-175
1990 Dial Cottage	Retrd.	1995	110.00	112-144
1989 Diamond Cottage	Retrd.	1993	110.00	113-157
1991 Double Cottage	Retrd.	1996	200.00	115
1991 Jasmine Cottage	Retrd.	1996	140.00	90-110
1989 Oak Cottage	Retrd.	1993	110.00	135-250
1991 Rose Cottage	Retrd.	1997	140.00	90-110
1990 Sweetbriar Cottage	Retrd.	1995	110.00	75-138
1990 Vine Cottage	Retrd.	1995	110.00	100-156

Britain's Heritage - Lilliput Lane

YEAR ISSUE	EDITION LIMIT	YEAR RETD.	ISSUE PRICE	*QUOTE U.S.$
2000 Balmoral	Open		110.00	110
1998 Big Ben	Open		55.00	55
1999 Big Ben in Winter	Retrd.	2000	70.00	75-80
1999 Blacksmith's Shop-Gretna Green	Retrd.	2000	100.00	100
1999 Buckingham Palace	Open		100.00	100
2000 Caernarfon Castle	Open		70.00	70
1999 Edinburgh Castle	Open		110.00	110
1999 Eros	Open		60.00	60
1999 Hampton Court Palace	Open		60.00	60
1999 Marble Arch	Open		60.00	60
1998 Mickelgate Bar-York	Retrd.	2000	37.00	37
2000 Nelson's Column	Open		55.00	55
1999 Nelson's Column in Winter	Retrd.	2000	60.00	60
1998 Round Tower-Windsor Castle	Open		50.00	50
2000 The Royal Albert Hall	Open		70.00	70
2000 The Royal Pavilion, Brighton	Open		125.00	125

YEAR ISSUE	EDITION LIMIT	YEAR RETD.	ISSUE PRICE	*QUOTE U.S.$
1998 Shakespeare's Birthplace	Retrd.	2000	50.00	50
2000 St. Paul's Cathedral	Open		90.00	90
1998 Tower Bridge	Open		55.00	55
1998 Tower of London	Open		50.00	50

Christmas Collection - Various

YEAR ISSUE	EDITION LIMIT	YEAR RETD.	ISSUE PRICE	*QUOTE U.S.$
1992 Chestnut Cottage	Retrd.	1996	46.50	45-63
1992 Cranberry Cottage	Retrd.	1996	46.50	27-35
1988 Deer Park Hall - D. Tate	Retrd.	1989	120.00	107-188
1993 The Gingerbread Shop	Retrd.	1997	50.00	28-63
1992 Hollytree House	Retrd.	1996	46.50	20-35
1991 The Old Vicarage at Christmas - D. Tate	Retrd.	1992	180.00	94-200
1993 Partridge Cottage	Retrd.	1997	50.00	30-50
1994 Ring O' Bells	Retrd.	1997	50.00	35-50
1993 St. Joseph's Church	Retrd.	1997	70.00	35-50
1994 St. Joseph's School	Retrd.	1997	50.00	35-50
1989 St. Nicholas Church - D. Tate	Retrd.	1990	130.00	100-225
1994 The Vicarage	Retrd.	1997	50.00	35-125
1990 Yuletide Inn - D. Tate	Retrd.	1991	145.00	57-188

Christmas Lodge Collection - Lilliput Lane

YEAR ISSUE	EDITION LIMIT	YEAR RETD.	ISSUE PRICE	*QUOTE U.S.$
1993 Eamont Lodge	Retrd.	1993	185.00	118-185
1992 Highland Lodge	Retrd.	1992	180.00	138-185
1995 Kerry Lodge	Retrd.	1995	160.00	85-160
1994 Snowdon Lodge	Retrd.	1994	175.00	100-175

Christmas Special - Lilliput Lane

YEAR ISSUE	EDITION LIMIT	YEAR RETD.	ISSUE PRICE	*QUOTE U.S.$
1996 St. Stephen's Church	Yr.Iss.	1996	100.00	70-100
1997 Christmas Party	Yr.Iss.	1997	150.00	90-150
1998 Frosty Morning	Yr.Iss.	1998	150.00	100-150
1999 The First Noel	Yr.Iss.	1999	150.00	120-150
2000 The Star Inn	Yr.Iss.		150.00	150

Disneyana Convention - R. Day

YEAR ISSUE	EDITION LIMIT	YEAR RETD.	ISSUE PRICE	*QUOTE U.S.$
1995 Fire Station 105	501	1995	195.00	350-595
1996 The Hall of Presidents	500	1996	225.00	330-715
1997 The Haunted Mansion	500	1997	250.00	605-655
1998 "Magic Kingdom Memories"	500	1998	275.00	400-550
1999 Main Street Cinema	500	1999	275.00	636-415
2000 It's A Small World	400		325.00	325

Dutch Collection - D. Tate

YEAR ISSUE	EDITION LIMIT	YEAR RETD.	ISSUE PRICE	*QUOTE U.S.$
1991 Aan de Amstel	Retrd.	1998	79.00	50-80
1991 Begijnhof	Retrd.	1998	55.00	30-35
1991 Bloemenmarkt	Retrd.	1998	79.00	60-80
1991 De Branderij	Retrd.	1998	72.50	40-55
1991 De Diamantair	Retrd.	1998	79.00	60-85
1991 De Pepermolen	Retrd.	1998	55.00	30-60
1991 De Wolhandelaar	Retrd.	1998	72.50	40-55
1991 De Zijdewever	Retrd.	1998	79.00	60-85
1991 Rembrant van Rijn	Retrd.	1998	120.00	70-80
1991 Rozengracht	Retrd.	1998	72.50	35-80

English Cottages - Lilliput Lane, unless otherwise noted

YEAR ISSUE	EDITION LIMIT	YEAR RETD.	ISSUE PRICE	*QUOTE U.S.$
1982 Acorn Cottage-Mold 1 - D. Tate	Retrd.	1983	30.00	250
1983 Acorn Cottage-Mold 2 - D. Tate	Retrd.	1987	30.00	44-69
2000 All Things Bright and Beautiful	Open		75.00	75
1999 Amazing Grace	Open		75.00	75
1996 The Anchor	Retrd.	2000	85.00	85
1982 Anne Hathaway's-Mold 1 - D. Tate	Retrd.	1983	40.00	1000-2148
1983 Anne Hathaway's-Mold 2 - D. Tate	Retrd.	1984	40.00	300
1984 Anne Hathaway's-Mold 3 - D. Tate	Retrd.	1988	40.00	45-75
1989 Anne Hathaway's-Mold 4 - D. Tate	Retrd.	1997	130.00	90-182
1991 Anne of Cleves - D. Tate	Retrd.	1996	360.00	269-360
2000 Anyone for Tennis	Open		85.00	85
1997 Appleby East	Retrd.	1999	70.00	50-70
1994 Applejack Cottage	Retrd.	1999	45.00	25-35
1982 April Cottage-Mold 1 - D. Tate	Retrd.	1984	Unkn.	300-350
1982 April Cottage-Mold 2 - D. Tate	Retrd.	1989	Unkn.	39-82
1991 Armada House - D. Tate	Retrd.	1997	175.00	100-125
1989 Ash Nook - D. Tate	Retrd.	1995	47.50	40-60
1986 Bay View - D. Tate	Retrd.	1988	39.50	52-88
1987 Beacon Heights	Retrd.	1992	125.00	113-175
1989 Beehive Cottage - D. Tate	Retrd.	1995	72.50	62-95
1997 Best Friends	Retrd.	1999	25.00	20-25
2000 Bill and Ben's	Open		65.00	65
1996 Birchwood Cottage	Retrd.	1998	55.00	44-55
1993 Birdlip Bottom	Retrd.	1998	80.00	45-50
2000 Birthday Cottage	Open		50.00	50
1996 Blue Boar	Retrd.	1999	85.00	65-85
1996 Bluebell Farm	Retrd.	1998	250.00	200-250
1998 The Bobbins	Open		85.00	85
1998 Bobby Blue	Open		120.00	120
1999 Bottle of Cheer	Open		25.00	25
1992 Bow Cottage - D. Tate	Retrd.	1995	128.00	60-188
1998 Bowbeams	Retrd.	1999	180.00	150-180
1996 Boxwood Cottage	Retrd.	1999	30.00	25-30
1990 Bramble Cottage - D. Tate	Retrd.	1995	55.00	45-70
1988 Bredon House - D. Tate	Retrd.	1990	145.00	75-145
1989 The Briary - D. Tate	Retrd.	1995	47.50	40-60
1982 Bridge House-Mold 1 - D. Tate	Retrd.	N/A	15.95	450-500
1982 Bridge House-Mold 2 - D. Tate	Retrd.	1990	15.95	175-250
1991 Bridge House-Mold 3 - D. Tate	Retrd.	1998	25.00	15-34
2000 Bridle & Bit Stables	Open		170.00	170
1988 Brockbank - D. Tate	Retrd.	1993	58.00	50-88
1985 Bronte Parsonage - D. Tate	Retrd.	1987	72.00	107-194
1998 Buckle My Shoe	Retrd.	2000	85.00	85
1997 Bumble Bee Cottage	Retrd.	1999	35.00	30-35
2000 Burley Street Garage	Open		170.00	170
1982 Burnside - D. Tate	Retrd.	1985	30.00	107-350
1990 Buttercup Cottage - D. Tate	Retrd.	1992	40.00	35-50
1999 Butterfly Cottage	Retrd.	1999	70.00	56-70
1997 Buttermilk Farm	Retrd.	2000	120.00	120

Lilliput Lane Ltd./Enesco European Giftware Group
to Lilliput Lane Ltd./Enesco European Giftware Group

ARCHITECTURE

YEAR ISSUE	EDITION LIMIT	YEAR RETD.	ISSUE PRICE	*QUOTE U.S.$
1989 Butterwick - D. Tate	Retrd.	1996	52.50	60-65
1995 Button Down	Retrd.	1998	37.50	25-30
1996 Calendar Cottage	Retrd.	1999	55.00	45-55
1994 Camomile Lawn	Retrd.	1997	125.00	75-90
1998 Campden Cot	Open		35.00	35
1997 Canterbury Bells	Retrd.	1999	170.00	125-170
1982 Castle Street - D. Tate	Retrd.	1986	130.00	275-375
1993 Cat's Coombe Cottage	Retrd.	1995	95.00	45-95
1999 The Cat's Whiskers	Open		85.00	85
1997 Catkin Cottage	Retrd.	2000	70.00	70
1996 Chalk Down	Retrd.	1999	35.00	25-35
1998 Chatsworth Blooms	Retrd.	2000	120.00	120
1991 Chatsworth View - D. Tate	Retrd.	1996	250.00	175-182
2000 Chatterbox Corner	Open		75.00	75
1995 Cherry Blossom Cottage	Retrd.	1997	128.00	65-76
1990 Cherry Cottage - D. Tate	Retrd.	1995	33.50	24-45
1989 Chiltern Mill - D. Tate	Retrd.	1995	87.50	70-125
1989 Chine Cot-Mold 1 - D. Tate	Retrd.	1989	36.00	70
1989 Chine Cot-Mold 2 - D. Tate	Retrd.	1996	35.00	30-35
1995 Chipping Combe	3,000	1998	525.00	525
1992 The Chocolate House	Retrd.	1998	130.00	59-70
1985 Clare Cottage - D. Tate	Retrd.	1993	30.00	30-63
1993 Cley-next-the-sea	2,500	1995	725.00	695-1000
1987 Clover Cottage - D. Tate	Retrd.	1994	27.50	25-60
1997 The Coach & Horses	Retrd.	2000	90.00	90
1982 Coach House - D. Tate	Retrd.	1985	100.00	1125
1986 Cobblers Cottage - D. Hall	Retrd.	1994	42.00	40-65
2000 Cockington Forge	Open		65.00	65
1997 Cockleshells	Retrd.	2000	25.00	25
1998 Coniston Crag	3,000		650.00	650
1990 Convent in The Woods - D. Tate	Retrd.	1996	175.00	150-175
1983 Coopers - D. Tate	Retrd.	1986	15.00	375-500
1998 Country Living	Retrd.	2000	275.00	275
1998 Cowslip Cottage	Open		120.00	120
1996 Cradle Cottage	Retrd.	1999	100.00	80-150
1994 Creel Cottage	Retrd.	1997	40.00	35-40
1996 Crispin Cottage	Retrd.	1999	50.00	35-50
1988 Crown Inn - D. Tate	Retrd.	1992	120.00	157-200
1996 The Cuddy	Retrd.	1999	30.00	25-40
1991 Daisy Cottage - D. Tate	Retrd.	1997	37.50	25
1982 Dale Farm-Mold 1 - D. Tate	Retrd.	1986	30.00	825-1225
1982 Dale Farm-Mold 2 - D. Tate	Retrd.	1986	30.00	500-875
1986 Dale Head - D. Tate	Retrd.	1988	75.00	50-135
1982 Dale House - D. Tate	Retrd.	1986	25.00	500-840
1996 The Dalesman	Retrd.	1998	95.00	76-95
2000 Davy Jones' Locker	Open		85.00	85
1992 Derwent-le-Dale	Retrd.	1998	75.00	50-55
1997 Devon Leigh	Retrd.	1999	90.00	70-90
1983 Dove Cottage-Mold 1 - D. Tate	Retrd.	1984	35.00	500-725
1984 Dove Cottage-Mold 2 - D. Tate	Retrd.	1988	35.00	65-95
1991 Dovetails - D. Tate	Retrd.	1996	90.00	50-75
1982 Drapers-Mold 1 - D. Tate	Retrd.	1983	15.95	2500
1982 Drapers-Mold 2 - D. Tate	Retrd.	1983	15.95	2000
2000 The Drayman	Open		100.00	100
1995 Duckdown Cottage	Retrd.	1997	95.00	40-70
1994 Elm Cottage	Retrd.	1997	65.00	30-50
2000 Faithful Friends	Open		25.00	25
1985 Farriers - D. Tate	Retrd.	1990	40.00	35-50
1991 Farthing Lodge - D. Tate	Retrd.	1996	37.50	30-40
1996 Fiddlers Folly	Retrd.	1999	35.00	28-35
1992 Finchingfields	Retrd.	1995	82.50	57-95
1999 Finders Keepers	Retrd.	1999	Gift	20
2000 Fireman's Watch	Open		170.00	170
1997 First Snow at Bluebell	3,500	1998	250.00	180-250
1985 Fisherman's Cottage - D. Tate	Retrd.	1989	30.00	35-75
1989 Fiveways - D. Tate	Retrd.	1995	42.50	25-55
1999 Flatford Lock	Retrd.	2000	275.00	275
1991 The Flower Sellers - D. Tate	Retrd.	1996	110.00	70-80
1996 Flowerpots	Retrd.	1999	55.00	35-55
1987 Four Seasons - M. Adkinson	Retrd.	1991	70.00	50-110
1993 Foxglove Fields	Retrd.	1997	130.00	60-85
1998 Free Range	Retrd.	2000	35.00	35
1996 Fry Days	Retrd.	2000	70.00	70
1996 Fuchsia Cottage	Retrd.	1999	30.00	25-30
2000 Full Stream Ahead	Open		225.00	225
1987 The Gables	Retrd.	1992	145.00	138-165
1997 The George Inn	Retrd.	2000	225.00	225
1998 Golden Memories	Retrd.	1999	90.00	65-90
1997 Golden Years	Open		25.00	25
1996 Gossip Gate	Retrd.	1999	170.00	125-170
2000 Grandma & Grandpa's	Open		30.00	30
1992 Granny Smiths - D. Tate	Retrd.	1996	60.00	25-45
1997 Granny's Bonnet	Open		25.00	25
1992 Grantchester Meadows	Retrd.	1996	275.00	148-150
1997 Green Gables	Retrd.	2000	225.00	225
1989 Greensted Church - D. Tate	Retrd.	1995	72.50	95
1994 Gulliver's Gate	Retrd.	1997	45.00	35-40
1998 Gulls Cry	Retrd.	2000	35.00	35
1997 Halcyon Days	Retrd.	1999	150.00	120-150
1998 Harebell Cottage	Open		35.00	35
1996 Harriet's Cottage	Retrd.	1999	85.00	68-85
1997 Harvest Home	4,950	1998	250.00	176-200
1989 Helmere Cottage - D. Tate	Retrd.	1995	65.00	60-90
1997 Hestercombe Garden	3,950	1998	350.00	235-280
1998 The Hideaway	Retrd.	2000	120.00	120
1992 High Ghyll Farm	Retrd.	1998	360.00	195-275
1999 High Spirits	Open		85.00	85
1982 Holly Cottage - D. Tate	Retrd.	1988	42.50	60-85
1987 Holme Dyke - D. Tate	Retrd.	1990	50.00	50
2000 Home Is Where The Heart Is	Open		50.00	50
1996 Honey Pot Cottage	Retrd.	1999	60.00	45-60
1982 Honeysuckle Cottage - D. Tate	Retrd.	1987	45.00	90-190
1991 Hopcroft Cottage - D. Tate	Retrd.	1995	120.00	117-130
1998 Hubble Bubble	Open		35.00	35
2000 I.N. Mongers & Sons	Open		90.00	90
1987 Inglewood - D. Tate	Retrd.	1994	27.50	24-40
1987 Izaak Waltons Cottage - D. Tate	Retrd.	1989	75.00	68-125
1991 John Barleycorn Cottage - D. Tate	Retrd.	1995	130.00	113-140
2000 Juliet's Tower	Open		25.00	25
1993 Junk and Disorderly	Retrd.	1998	150.00	100-110
1987 Keepers Lodge - D. Tate	Retrd.	1988	75.00	88-100
1999 Kentish Brew	Open		35.00	35
1985 Kentish Oast - D. Tate	Retrd.	1990	55.00	83-150
1990 The King's Arms - D. Tate	Retrd.	1995	450.00	275-338
1991 Lace Lane - D. Tate	Retrd.	1997	90.00	70-110
1982 Lakeside House-Mold 1 - D. Tate	Retrd.	1983	40.00	875-1125
1982 Lakeside House-Mold 2 - D. Tate	Retrd.	1986	40.00	600-750
1991 Lapworth Lock - D. Tate	Retrd.	1993	82.50	75-85
1995 Larkrise	Retrd.	1998	50.00	35-45
1999 Lavender Lane	Open		75.00	75
1995 Lazy Days	Retrd.	1998	60.00	50-60
1994 Lenora's Secret	2,500	1995	350.00	375-450
1997 Lilac Lodge	Open		60.00	60
2000 Lily of the Valley	Open		25.00	25
1998 The Lion House	Retrd.	2000	70.00	70
1995 Little Hay	Retrd.	1998	55.00	40-50
1996 Little Lupins	Retrd.	1999	40.00	32-40
1995 Little Smithy	Retrd.	1998	65.00	45
1999 Little Watermill	Open		55.00	55
1996 Loxdale Cottage	Retrd.	1999	35.00	25-35
1999 Lucky Charms	Open		35.00	35
1987 Magpie Cottage - D. Tate	Retrd.	1990	70.00	40-110
1997 Mangerton Mill	Retrd.	1999	185.00	140-185
1993 Marigold Meadow	Retrd.	1998	120.00	80
1998 Medway Manor	Retrd.	1999	120.00	90-120
1991 Micklegate Antiques - D. Tate	Retrd.	1997	90.00	65-80
1995 Milestone Cottage	Retrd.	1998	40.00	28-40
1983 Millers - D. Tate	Retrd.	1986	15.00	100-120
1983 Miners-Mold 1 - D. Tate	Retrd.	1985	15.00	500-590
1983 Miners-Mold 2 - D. Tate	Retrd.	1985	15.00	325-400
2000 Montacute Crown	Open		55.00	55
1991 Moonlight Cove - D. Tate	Retrd.	1996	82.50	48-65
1985 Moreton Manor - D. Tate	Retrd.	1989	55.00	68-94
1998 Mosswood	Open		85.00	85
2000 Mother's Garden	Open		30.00	30
1990 Mrs. Pinkerton's Post Office - D. Tate	Retrd.	1997	72.50	55-75
2000 Mystery Manor	Open		85.00	85
1998 Nest Egg	Retrd.	1998	25.00	17-25
1999 New Neighbours	Open		85.00	85
1998 Nightingale Cottage	Retrd.	1998	25.00	15-25
1992 The Nutshell	Retrd.	1995	75.00	40-80
1982 Oak Lodge-Mold 1 - D. Tate	Retrd.	N/A	40.00	450-1000
1982 Oak Lodge-Mold 2 - D. Tate	Retrd.	1987	40.00	50-88
1992 Oakwood Smithy - D. Tate	Retrd.	1998	450.00	230-300
1999 Old Crofty	Retrd.	2000	85.00	85
1985 Old Curiosity Shop - D. Tate	Retrd.	1989	62.50	60-94
1998 Old Forge, The	Open		55.00	55
1982 Old Mine - D. Tate	Retrd.	1983	15.95	2500-4000
1993 Old Mother Hubbard's	Retrd.	1998	185.00	90-120
1982 The Old Post Office - D. Tate	Retrd.	1986	35.00	450-625
1984 Old School House - D. Tate	Retrd.	1985	25.00	1000-1125
1991 Old Shop at Bignor - D. Tate	Retrd.	1995	215.00	188-200
1989 Olde York Toll - D. Tate	Retrd.	1991	82.50	125-150
2000 Open All Hours	Open		50.00	50
1994 Orchard Farm Cottage	Retrd.	1998	145.00	85-110
1985 Ostlers Keep - D. Tate	Retrd.	1991	55.00	40-90
1990 Otter Reach - D. Tate	Retrd.	1996	33.50	25-30
1999 Out For a Duck	Open		75.00	75
1997 Out of the Storm	3,000	1998	1250.00	1000-1250
1991 Paradise Lodge - D. Tate	Retrd.	1996	130.00	95-125
1988 Pargetters Retreat - D. Tate	Retrd.	1990	75.00	44-88
1998 Parson's Retreat	Retrd.	2000	90.00	90
1998 Pastures New	Open		350.00	350
1991 Pear Tree House - D. Tate	Retrd.	1995	82.50	40-85
1995 Penny's Post	Retrd.	1998	55.00	40
2000 Pepper Mill Cottage	Open		50.00	50
1990 Periwinkle Cottage - D. Tate	Retrd.	1996	165.00	145-175
2000 Piggy Bank	Open		85.00	85
1995 Pipit Toll	Retrd.	1998	64.00	28-35
1992 Pixie House - D. Tate	Retrd.	1995	55.00	33-60
1999 Playtime	Open		75.00	75
1997 Poppies, The	Open		50.00	50
1996 Potter's Beck	Retrd.	1998	35.00	28-35
1991 Priest's House, The - D. Tate	Retrd.	1995	180.00	125-195
1991 Primrose Hill - D. Tate	Retrd.	1996	46.50	40-45
1998 Puddle Duck	Retrd.	2000	80.00	80
1992 Puffin Row - D. Tate	Retrd.	1997	128.00	60-75
1993 Purbeck Stores	Retrd.	1997	55.00	28-35
1996 Railway Cottage	Retrd.	1999	60.00	45-60
1983 Red Lion Inn - D. Tate	Retrd.	1987	125.00	250-350
1996 Reflections of Jade	3,950	1998	350.00	280-350
1999 Right Note, The	Open		85.00	85
1988 Rising Sun - D. Tate	Retrd.	1992	58.00	50-100
1987 Riverview - D. Tate	Retrd.	1994	27.50	40-75
1990 Robin's Gate - D. Tate	Retrd.	1996	33.50	25-30
1999 Rock-A-Bye Baby	Open		35.00	35
1997 Rose Bouquet	Open		25.00	25
1996 Rosemary Cottage	Retrd.	1999	70.00	55-70
2000 Roses are Red	Open		25.00	25
1988 Royal Oak - D. Tate	Retrd.	1991	145.00	150-188
1990 Runswick House - D. Tate	Retrd.	1998	62.50	40-55
1992 Rustic Root House - D. Tate	Retrd.	1997	110.00	50-80
1995 The Rustlings	Retrd.	1998	128.00	75-95
1987 Rydal View - D. Tate	Retrd.	1989	220.00	125-220
1987 Saddlers Inn - M. Adkinson	Retrd.	1989	50.00	40-75
1994 Saffron House	Retrd.	1997	220.00	170
2000 The Sandcastle	Open		35.00	35
1985 Sawrey Gill - D. Tate	Retrd.	1992	30.00	45-90
1991 Saxham St. Edmunds - D. Tate	Retrd.	1994	1550.00	1188-1650
1988 Saxon Cottage - D. Tate	Retrd.	1989	245.00	160-300
1999 Say It With Flowers	Open		35.00	35
1997 Scotney Castle Garden	4,500	1998	300.00	200-300
1986 Scroll on the Wall - D. Tate	Retrd.	1987	55.00	125-137
1987 Secret Garden - M. Adkinson	Retrd.	1994	145.00	125-138
1988 Ship Inn	Retrd.	1992	210.00	180-230
1997 Silver Bells	Retrd.	2000	25.00	25
1988 Smallest Inn - D. Tate	Retrd.	1991	42.50	63-82
2000 Smuggler's Rest	Open		65.00	65
1996 Sore Paws	Retrd.	2000	70.00	70
1996 The Spindles	Retrd.	1998	85.00	68-85
1986 Spring Bank - D. Tate	Retrd.	1991	42.00	30-60
1994 Spring Gate Cottage	Retrd.	1997	130.00	95
1996 St. John the Baptist	Retrd.	1998	75.00	75
1989 St. Lawrence Church - D. Tate	Retrd.	1998	110.00	85
1988 St. Marks - D. Tate	Retrd.	1991	75.00	90-125
1985 St. Mary's Church - D. Tate	Retrd.	1988	40.00	97-160
1989 St. Peter's Cove - D. Tate	Retrd.	1991	1375.00	1000-1519
1993 Stocklebeck Mill	Retrd.	1998	325.00	156-175
1982 Stone Cottage-Mold 1 - D. Tate	Retrd.	1983	40.00	250-375
1982 Stone Cottage-Mold 2 - D. Tate	Retrd.	1986	40.00	185-200
1986 Stone Cottage-Mold 3 - D. Tate	Retrd.	1986	40.00	200
1998 The Stonemason	Retrd.	1999	120.00	80-120
1987 Stoneybeck - D. Tate	Retrd.	1992	45.00	40-60
1993 Stradling Priory	Retrd.	1997	130.00	80-125
1990 Strawberry Cottage - D. Tate	Retrd.	1998	36.00	30-35
1987 Street Scene No. 1 - Unknown	Retrd.	1987	40.00	125-240
1987 Street Scene No. 2 - Unknown	Retrd.	1987	45.00	188-250
1987 Street Scene No. 3 - Unknown	Retrd.	1987	45.00	125
1987 Street Scene No. 4 - Unknown	Retrd.	1987	45.00	125
1987 Street Scene No. 5 - Unknown	Retrd.	1987	40.00	75-120
1987 Street Scene No. 6 - Unknown	Retrd.	1987	40.00	75-120
1987 Street Scene No. 7 - Unknown	Retrd.	1987	40.00	75-120
1987 Street Scene No. 8 - Unknown	Retrd.	1987	40.00	98-120
1987 Street Scene No. 9 - Unknown	Retrd.	1987	45.00	125
1987 Street Scene No. 10 - Unknown	Retrd.	1987	45.00	75-120
1987 Street Scene Set - Unknown	Retrd.	1987	425.00	800-1125
1990 Sulgrave Manor - D. Tate	Retrd.	1992	120.00	115-150
1987 Summer Haze - D. Tate	Retrd.	1993	90.00	75-130
1994 Sunnyside	Retrd.	1997	40.00	24-35
1982 Sussex Mill - D. Tate	Retrd.	1986	25.00	500-575
1988 Swan Inn - D. Tate	Retrd.	1992	120.00	135-190
1994 Sweet Pea Cottage	Retrd.	1997	40.00	25-28
1997 Sweet William	Retrd.	1998	25.00	20-25
1988 Swift Hollow - D. Tate	Retrd.	1990	75.00	45-95
1989 Tanglewood Lodge - D. Tate	Retrd.	1992	97.00	103-120
1987 Tanners Cottage - D. Tate	Retrd.	1992	27.50	34-65
1994 Teacaddy Cottage	Retrd.	1998	79.00	45
1999 Temple Bar Folly	Open		55.00	55
1983 Thatcher's Rest - D. Tate	Retrd.	1988	185.00	219-239
1986 Three Feathers - D. Tate	Retrd.	1989	115.00	175
1991 Tillers Green - D. Tate	Retrd.	1995	60.00	40-65
1984 Tintagel - D. Tate	Retrd.	1988	39.50	138-265
1994 Tired Timbers	Retrd.	1997	80.00	40-60
1989 Titmouse Cottage - D. Tate	Retrd.	1995	92.50	75-120
1993 Titwillow Cottage	Retrd.	1997	70.00	30-45
1999 To Have and to Hold	Open		60.00	60
2000 The Toadstool	Open		25.00	25
1983 Toll House - D. Tate	Retrd.	1987	15.00	125-235
1995 Tranquillity - D. Tate	2,500	1995	425.00	425
1983 Troutbeck Farm - D. Tate	Retrd.	1987	125.00	238-325
1983 Tuck Shop - D. Tate	Retrd.	1986	35.00	500-760
1986 Tudor Court	Retrd.	1992	260.00	195-350
1998 Tuppeny Bun	Open		35.00	35
1994 Two Hoots	Retrd.	1997	75.00	35-55
1999 Ullswater Boat House	Open		32.00	32
1989 Victoria Cottage - D. Tate	Retrd.	1993	52.50	50-75
1991 Village School - D. Tate	Retrd.	1996	120.00	60-85
2000 Violets are Blue	Open		25.00	25
1998 Wagtails	Retrd.	2000	35.00	35
1997 Walton Lodge	Retrd.	1999	65.00	50-65
1983 Warwick Hall-Mold 1 - D. Tate	Retrd.	1983	185.00	1813-3000
1983 Warwick Hall-Mold 2 - D. Tate	Retrd.	1985	185.00	1500
1985 Watermill - D. Tate	Retrd.	1993	40.00	32-60
1998 Waters Edge	Open		170.00	170
1994 Waterside Mill	Retrd.	1999	65.00	46-50
1987 Wealden House - D. Tate	Retrd.	1990	125.00	100-155
1992 Wedding Bells	Retrd.	1999	75.00	40-50
1991 Wellington Lodge - D. Tate	Retrd.	1995	55.00	40-60
1992 Wheyside Cottage	Retrd.	1998	46.50	35
2000 The White Hart	Open		55.00	55
1989 Wight Cottage - D. Tate	Retrd.	1994	52.50	35-65
1982 William Shakespeare-Mold 1 - D. Tate	Retrd.	1983	55.00	1000-1500
1983 William Shakespeare-Mold 2 - D. Tate	Retrd.	1986	55.00	150-190
1986 William Shakespeare-Mold 3 - D. Tate	Retrd.	1989	55.00	100-225
1989 William Shakespeare-Mold 4 - D. Tate	Retrd.	1992	130.00	80-150
1999 Windmill, The	Open		70.00	70
1996 Windy Ridge	Retrd.	1998	50.00	40-50
1999 With Thanks	Open		50.00	50
1991 Witham Delph - D. Tate	Retrd.	1994	110.00	100
1983 Woodcutters - D. Tate	Retrd.	1987	15.00	94-175
1997 Yorkvale Cottage	Retrd.	1999	50.00	40-50

English Tea Room Collection - Lilliput Lane

YEAR ISSUE	EDITION LIMIT	YEAR RETD.	ISSUE PRICE	*QUOTE U.S.$
1995 Bargate Cottage Tea Room	Retrd.	1999	160.00	90-120
1995 Bo-Peep Tea Rooms	Retrd.	1997	120.00	60-85
1995 Grandma Batty's Tea Room	Retrd.	1998	120.00	72-90

*Quotes have been rounded up to nearest dollar

YEAR ISSUE	EDITION LIMIT	YEAR RETD.	ISSUE PRICE	*QUOTE U.S.$
1995 Kendal Tea House	Retrd.	2000	120.00	85-120
1995 New Forest Teas	Retrd.	1999	160.00	120-165
1998 Strawberry Teas	Retrd.	2000	100.00	100
1996 Swalesdale Teas	Retrd.	1999	85.00	65-85

Founders Collection - Lilliput Lane

YEAR ISSUE	EDITION LIMIT	YEAR RETD.	ISSUE PRICE	*QUOTE U.S.$
1996 The Almonry	Yr.Iss.	1996	275.00	225-275

French Collection - D. Tate

YEAR ISSUE	EDITION LIMIT	YEAR RETD.	ISSUE PRICE	*QUOTE U.S.$
1991 L' Auberge d'Armorique	Retrd.	1997	220.00	120-170
1991 La Bergerie du Perigord	Retrd.	1997	230.00	150-170
1991 La Cabane du Gardian	Retrd.	1997	55.00	45-50
1991 La Chaumiere du Verger	Retrd.	1997	120.00	75-95
1991 La Maselle de Nadaillac	Retrd.	1997	130.00	60-100
1991 La Porte Schoenenberg	Retrd.	1997	75.00	50-60
1991 Le Manoir de Champfleuri	Retrd.	1997	265.00	145
1991 Le Mas du Vigneron	Retrd.	1997	120.00	60-85
1991 Le Petite Montmartre	Retrd.	1997	130.00	70-135
1991 Locmaria	Retrd.	1997	65.00	35-50

German Collection - D. Tate

YEAR ISSUE	EDITION LIMIT	YEAR RETD.	ISSUE PRICE	*QUOTE U.S.$
1992 Alte Schmiede	Retrd.	1998	175.00	80-150
1987 Das Gebirgskirchlein	Retrd.	1998	120.00	90-120
1988 Das Rathaus	Retrd.	1998	140.00	125-150
1992 Der Bücherwurm	Retrd.	1998	140.00	70-100
1988 Der Familienschrein	Retrd.	1991	52.50	90-100
1988 Die Kleine Backerei	Retrd.	1994	68.00	60-80
1987 Haus Im Rheinland	Retrd.	1998	220.00	150-215
1987 Jaghutte	Retrd.	1998	82.50	70-83
1987 Meersburger Weinstube	Retrd.	1998	82.50	60-70
1987 Moselhaus	Retrd.	1998	140.00	95-140
1987 Nurnberger Burgerhaus	Retrd.	1998	140.00	140-150
1992 Rosengartenhaus	Retrd.	1998	120.00	65-90
1987 Schwarzwaldhaus	Retrd.	1998	140.00	84-120
1992 Strandvogthaus	Retrd.	1998	120.00	70-90

The Helen Allingham Collection - Lilliput Lane

YEAR ISSUE	EDITION LIMIT	YEAR RETD.	ISSUE PRICE	*QUOTE U.S.$
1999 Chalfont St. Giles	Retrd.	1999	150.00	150
1999 Great Wishford	Retrd.	1999	70.00	70
1999 Midhurst	Retrd.	1999	100.00	100
1999 Witley	Retrd.	1999	100.00	100

Historic Castles of England - Lilliput Lane

YEAR ISSUE	EDITION LIMIT	YEAR RETD.	ISSUE PRICE	*QUOTE U.S.$
1994 Bodiam Castle	Retrd.	1997	129.00	100-180
1994 Castell Coch	Retrd.	1998	149.00	100
1995 Penkill Castles	Retrd.	1998	130.00	80
1994 Stokesay Castle	Retrd.	1998	99.00	60

Irish Cottages - D. Tate

YEAR ISSUE	EDITION LIMIT	YEAR RETD.	ISSUE PRICE	*QUOTE U.S.$
1989 Ballykerne Croft	Retrd.	1996	75.00	60-80
1987 Donegal Cottage	Retrd.	1992	29.00	40-65
2000 A Drop Of The Irish	Open		65.00	65
1989 Hegarty's Home	Retrd.	1992	68.00	138-150
1989 Kennedy Homestead	Retrd.	1996	33.50	40-82
1989 Kilmore Quay	Retrd.	1992	68.00	93-113
1989 Limerick House	Retrd.	1992	110.00	95-110
1989 Magilligan's	Retrd.	1996	33.50	25-30
2000 Morning Post	Open		85.00	85
1989 O'Lacey's Store	Retrd.	1996	68.00	40-60
1989 Pat Cohan's Bar	Retrd.	1996	110.00	70-130
1989 Quiet Cottage	Retrd.	1992	72.50	75-100
1989 St. Columba's School	Retrd.	1996	47.50	35
1989 St. Kevin's Church	Retrd.	1996	55.00	45
1989 St. Patrick's Church	Retrd.	1993	185.00	180-210
1989 Thoor Ballylee	Retrd.	1992	105.00	157-189

Lakeland Christmas - Lilliput Lane

YEAR ISSUE	EDITION LIMIT	YEAR RETD.	ISSUE PRICE	*QUOTE U.S.$
1995 Langdale Cottage	Retrd.	1998	48.00	20-35
1995 Patterdale Cottage	Retrd.	1998	48.00	35-48
1995 Rydal Cottage	Retrd.	1998	44.75	35-45
1996 All Saints Watermillock	Retrd.	1999	50.00	40-50
1996 Borrowdale School	Retrd.	1999	35.00	30-35
1996 Millbeck Cottage	Retrd.	1999	35.00	28-35

Millennium Specials - Lilliput Lane

YEAR ISSUE	EDITION LIMIT	YEAR RETD.	ISSUE PRICE	*QUOTE U.S.$
1999 Great Equatorial, The	Retrd.	2000	90.00	90
1999 Millennium Gate, The	2,000	1999	500.00	400-500
1999 Planetarium, The	Retrd.	2000	210.00	210
1999 Stargazers Cottage	Retrd.	2000	90.00	90

Moments in Time - Lilliput Lane, unless otherwise noted

YEAR ISSUE	EDITION LIMIT	YEAR RETD.	ISSUE PRICE	*QUOTE U.S.$
1998 Bananas Are Back	Retrd.	1999	80.00	50-80
1998 Our First Telly	Retrd.	1999	100.00	75-100
1998 Short, Back and Sides?	Retrd.	1999	90.00	50-90
1998 Time Gentlemen, Please	Retrd.	1999	90.00	70-90

Ray Day/Allegiance Collection - R. Day

YEAR ISSUE	EDITION LIMIT	YEAR RETD.	ISSUE PRICE	*QUOTE U.S.$
1998 By Dawn's Early Light	Retrd.	2000	70.00	56-70
1998 Fourth of July	1,776	2000	70.00	56-70
1997 Home of the Brave	Retrd.	1999	75.00	64-80
1997 I Pledge Allegiance	Retrd.	1999	75.00	64-80
1998 I'll Be Home For Christmas	Open	2000	75.00	75
1997 In Remembrance	Retrd.	1999	75.00	64-80
1997 One Nation Under God	Retrd.	1999	75.00	64-80
1998 Stars & Stripes Forever	Retrd.	2000	75.00	60-75

Ray Day/America's Favorites - R. Day

YEAR ISSUE	EDITION LIMIT	YEAR RETD.	ISSUE PRICE	*QUOTE U.S.$
1998 "Nothing Runs Like a Deere"	Retrd.	2000	37.50	38
1998 "See The USA in Your Chevrolet"	Retrd.	2000	37.50	30-38
1998 "Sign of Good Taste"	Retrd.	2000	37.50	38
1998 "This Bud's For You"	Retrd.	2000	37.50	30-38
1998 "Trust Your Car to the Star"	Retrd.	2000	37.50	30-38

Ray Day/American Landmark Series - R. Day

YEAR ISSUE	EDITION LIMIT	YEAR RETD.	ISSUE PRICE	*QUOTE U.S.$
1992 16.9 Cents Per Gallon	Retrd.	1999	150.00	80-95
1995 Afternoon Tea	1,995	2000	495.00	400-520
1994 Birdsong	Retrd.	1997	120.00	60-85
1990 Country Church	Retrd.	1992	82.50	100-125
1989 Countryside Barn	Retrd.	1992	75.00	70-113
1990 Covered Memories	Retrd.	1993	110.00	88-110
1989 Falls Mill	Retrd.	1992	130.00	100-135
1991 Fire House 1	Retrd.	1997	87.50	60-72
1994 Fresh Bread	Retrd.	1999	150.00	80-95
1992 Gold Miners' Claim	Retrd.	1997	110.00	65-95
1992 Gold Miners' Claim (no snow)	Retrd.	N/A	95.00	600
1990 Great Point Light	Retrd.	1999	39.50	40-69
1994 Harvest Mill	3,500	1999	395.00	275-308
1994 Holy Night	Retrd.	1999	225.00	150
1996 Home For the Holidays	2,596	2000	495.00	495
1992 Home Sweet Home	Retrd.	1998	120.00	56-130
1990 Hometown Depot	Retrd.	1993	68.00	75-95
1997 Let Heaven & Nature Sing	Yr.Iss.	1997	158.00	110-158
1998 Lobster at the Pier	Retrd.	2000	90.00	72-90
1989 Mail Pouch Barn	Retrd.	1993	75.00	95-110
1999 Nature's Bounty (Ray Day's 10th Anniversary)	Retrd.	2000	140.00	112-140
1990 Pepsi Cola Barn	Retrd.	1991	87.00	82-128
1990 Pioneer Barn	Retrd.	1991	30.00	50-63
1991 Rambling Rose	Retrd.	1995	60.00	60-65
1990 Riverside Chapel	Retrd.	1993	82.50	107-130
1990 Roadside Coolers	Retrd.	1994	75.00	75-110
1991 School Days	Retrd.	1997	60.00	36-60
1993 See Rock City	Retrd.	1997	60.00	30-35
1998 Seek and Find	Retrd.	2000	80.00	64-80
1993 Shave and A Haircut	Retrd.	1997	160.00	64-95
1990 Sign Of The Times	Retrd.	1996	27.50	30-35
1993 Simply Amish	Retrd.	1998	160.00	75-110
1992 Small Town Library	Retrd.	1995	130.00	103-140
1994 Spring Victorian	Retrd.	1998	250.00	150-170
1997 To Grandmother's House We Go	Yr.Iss.	1997	158.00	127-158
1999 Victorian Romance	Retrd.	2000	250.00	250
1991 Victoriana	2,500	1992	295.00	175-288
1999 Watson's Collectibles	Retrd.	2000	110.00	88-110
1992 Winnie's Place	Retrd.	1993	395.00	313-450

Ray Day/An American Journey - R. Day

YEAR ISSUE	EDITION LIMIT	YEAR RETD.	ISSUE PRICE	*QUOTE U.S.$
1998 Day Dreams	Retrd.	2000	75.00	60-75
1998 Dog Days of Summer	Retrd.	2000	55.00	44-55
1998 Lace House	Retrd.	2000	85.00	68-85
1998 Morning Has Broken	Retrd.	2000	85.00	68-85
1998 Safe Harbor	1,783	2000	75.00	60-75
1998 Victorian Elegance	Retrd.	2000	130.00	104-130

Ray Day/Coca Cola Country - R. Day

YEAR ISSUE	EDITION LIMIT	YEAR RETD.	ISSUE PRICE	*QUOTE U.S.$
1996 A Cherry Coke...Just the Prescription	Retrd.	1999	95.00	80-100
1997 Country Canvas	Retrd.	1999	15.00	16
1996 Country Fresh Pickins	Retrd.	1999	150.00	100-160
1999 Dixie Bottling Company	Retrd.	2000	160.00	128-160
1996 Fill'er Up & Check the Oil	Retrd.	1999	125.00	60-130
1996 Hazards of the Road	Retrd.	1999	50.00	45-55
1996 Hook, Line & Sinker	Retrd.	1999	95.00	80-100
1997 The Lunch Line	Retrd.	2000	40.00	34-65
1998 Milk For Mom & A Coke For Me	Retrd.	2000	95.00	76-95
1997 Mmmmm...Just Like Home	Retrd.	1999	125.00	104-130
1997 Oh By Gosh, By Golly	Yr.Iss.	1997	85.00	50-90
1997 Saturday Night Jive	Retrd.	1999	95.00	80-100
1998 They Don't Make 'em Like They Used To	Retrd.	2000	70.00	56-70
1996 We've Got it or They Don't Make it	Retrd.	2000	95.00	80-100
1997 Wet Your Whistle	Retrd.	1999	40.00	34-43

Ray Day/Special Commissions - R. Day

YEAR ISSUE	EDITION LIMIT	YEAR RETD.	ISSUE PRICE	*QUOTE U.S.$
1999 The Precious Moments Chapel	Open		75.00	75
1999 Universal Studios Lighthouse of Adventure	Open		50.00	50

Scottish Collection - D. Tate, unless otherwise noted

YEAR ISSUE	EDITION LIMIT	YEAR RETD.	ISSUE PRICE	*QUOTE U.S.$
1985 7 St. Andrews Square - A. Yarrington	Retrd.	1986	15.95	125-175
1995 Amisfield Tower - Lilliput Lane	Retrd.	1998	55.00	40-50
1989 Blair Atholl	Retrd.	1992	275.00	282-350
1985 Burns Cottage	Retrd.	1988	35.00	135-225
1989 Carrick House	Retrd.	1998	47.50	40
1990 Cawdor Castle	3,000	1992	295.00	344-375
1989 Claypotts Castle	Retrd.	1997	72.50	65-70
1989 Craigievar Castle	Retrd.	1991	185.00	215-265
1997 Crathie Church, Balmoral	Retrd.	1999	60.00	48-60
1984 The Croft (renovated)	Retrd.	1991	36.00	50-100
1982 The Croft (without sheep)	Retrd.	1984	29.00	750-1000
1989 Culloden Cottage	Retrd.	1998	36.00	20-35
1992 Culross House	Retrd.	1997	90.00	50-70
1992 Duart Castle	3,000	1997	450.00	300-361
1987 East Neuk	Retrd.	1991	29.00	35-75
1993 Edzell Summer House - Lilliput Lane	Retrd.	1997	110.00	70-110
1990 Eilean Donan	Retrd.	1998	145.00	136-140
1992 Eriskay Croft	Retrd.	1999	50.00	32
1990 Fishermans Bothy	Retrd.	1999	36.00	113-130
1990 Glenlochie Lodge	Retrd.	1993	110.00	80-100
1990 Hebridean Hame	Retrd.	1992	55.00	82-107
1989 Inverlochie Hame	Retrd.	1999	47.50	32
1989 John Knox House	Retrd.	1992	68.00	79-125
1989 Kenmore Cottage	Retrd.	1993	87.00	80-110
1990 Kinlochness	Retrd.	1993	79.00	75-85
1990 Kirkbrae Cottage	Retrd.	1993	55.00	70
1998 Lady Jane's Cottage	Retrd.	2000	35.00	35
1994 Ladybank Lodge - Lilliput Lane	Retrd.	1998	80.00	60
1998 Loch Ness Lodge	Open		170.00	170
1992 Mair Haven	Retrd.	1999	46.50	30
2000 Over the Sea to Skye	Open		65.00	65
1998 Pineapple House, The	Open		60.00	60
1985 Preston Mill-Mold 1	Retrd.	1986	45.00	125-140
1986 Preston Mill-Mold 2	Retrd.	1992	62.50	69-73
1999 Salmon's Leap	Retrd.	2000	55.00	55
1998 Scotch Mist	Open		70.00	70
1989 Stockwell Tenement	Retrd.	1996	62.50	50-63
1999 Yaird O' Tartan	Open		55.00	55

Secret Gardens Collection - Lilliput Lane

YEAR ISSUE	EDITION LIMIT	YEAR RETD.	ISSUE PRICE	*QUOTE U.S.$
1998 Fragrant Haven	Retrd.	2000	90.00	90
1999 Fruits of Eden	Retrd.	2000	80.00	80
1999 Nature's Doorway	Retrd.	2000	90.00	90
1998 Peaceful Pastimes	Retrd.	2000	90.00	90
1998 Picnic Paradise	Retrd.	2000	80.00	80
1998 Tranquil Treasure	Retrd.	2000	80.00	80

Show Place Like Home - Lilliput Lane

YEAR ISSUE	EDITION LIMIT	YEAR RETD.	ISSUE PRICE	*QUOTE U.S.$
2000 Chill Out	Open		30.00	30
2000 Frost Bite	Open		30.00	30
2000 I Cycle	Open		30.00	30
2000 Santa's Little Helper	Open		25.00	25
2000 Snow Stories	Open		30.00	30

Specials - Various

YEAR ISSUE	EDITION LIMIT	YEAR RETD.	ISSUE PRICE	*QUOTE U.S.$
1997 Arbury Lodge - Lilliput Lane	Retrd.	1997	N/A	130
1985 Bermuda Cottage (3 Colors) - D. Tate	Retrd.	1991	29.00	200-350
1985 Bermuda Cottage (3 Colors)-set - D. Tate	Retrd.	1991	87.00	600-688
1983 Bridge House Dealer Sign - D. Tate	Retrd.	1984	N/A	375-525
1988 Chantry Chapel - D. Tate	Retrd.	1991	N/A	300
1983 Cliburn School - D. Tate	Retrd.	1984	Gift	4000-6000
1987 Clockmaker's Cottage - D. Tate	Retrd.	1990	40.00	225
1996 Cornflower Cottage	Retrd.	1996	N/A	110-150
1993 Counting House Corner (mounted) - Lilliput Lane	Retrd.	1993	N/A	850
1993 Counting House Corner - Lilliput Lane	3,093	1993	N/A	750
1998 Dove Cottage-Grasmere	Open		N/A	N/A
1987 Guildhall - D. Tate	Retrd.	1989	N/A	200-275
1998 Hadleigh Cottage - Lilliput Lane	5,000	1998	95.00	95-100
1997 Honeysuckle Cottage Trinket Box	Retrd.	1999	N/A	60
1997 Honeysuckle III - Lilliput Lane	Open		N/A	N/A
1989 Mayflower House - D. Tate	Retrd.	1990	79.50	150-188
1999 Queen Alexandra's Nest - Lilliput Lane	Retrd.	1999	50.00	50
1991 Rose Cottage Skirsgill-Mold 1 - Lilliput Lane	200	1991	N/A	450-700
1991 Rose Cottage Skirsgill-Mold 2 - Lilliput Lane	Retrd.	1991	N/A	175
1994 Rose Cottage Skirsgill-Mold 3 - Lilliput Lane	Open		N/A	N/A
1991 Settler's Surprise - Lilliput Lane	Retrd.	1996	135.00	200-282
1986 Seven Dwarf's Cottage - D. Tate	Retrd.	1986	146.80	594-900
2000 Syon Conservatory	Retrd.	2000	N/A	N/A
1998 Thornery - Lilliput Lane	Retrd.	1998	N/A	140-150
1998 Winter at Skirsgill	Open		N/A	N/A
1994 Wycombe Toll House - Lilliput Lane	Retrd.	1994	33.00	282-313

Studley Royal Collection - Lilliput Lane

YEAR ISSUE	EDITION LIMIT	YEAR RETD.	ISSUE PRICE	*QUOTE U.S.$
1994 Banqueting House	5,000	1998	65.00	45-65
1995 Fountains Abbey	3,500	1998	395.00	395
1994 Octagon Tower	5,000	1998	85.00	64-85
1994 St. Mary's Church	5,000	1998	115.00	99-115
1994 Temple of Piety	5,000	1998	95.00	60-95

Victorian Shops - Lilliput Lane

YEAR ISSUE	EDITION LIMIT	YEAR RETD.	ISSUE PRICE	*QUOTE U.S.$
1997 Apothecary	Retrd.	1999	90.00	90
1997 Book Shop	Retrd.	1999	75.00	75
1997 Haberdashery	Open		90.00	90
1997 Horologist	Retrd.	1999	75.00	60-75
1997 The Jeweller's	Retrd.	1999	75.00	75
1997 Pawnbroker	Retrd.	1999	75.00	55-75
1997 Tailor	Retrd.	1999	90.00	72-90

Village Shop Collection - Lilliput Lane, unless otherwise noted

YEAR ISSUE	EDITION LIMIT	YEAR RETD.	ISSUE PRICE	*QUOTE U.S.$
1995 The Baker's Shop	Retrd.	1999	120.00	65-85
1995 The Chine Shop	Open		120.00	85-120
1992 The Greengrocers - D. Tate	Retrd.	1998	120.00	60-80
1993 Jones The Butcher	Retrd.	1998	120.00	55-80
1992 Penny Sweets	Retrd.	1998	130.00	60-80
1993 Toy Shop	Retrd.	1999	120.00	60-80

Welsh Collection - Various

YEAR ISSUE	EDITION LIMIT	YEAR RETD.	ISSUE PRICE	*QUOTE U.S.$
1986 Brecon Bach - D. Tate	Retrd.	1993	42.00	40-69
1991 Bro Dawel - D. Tate	Retrd.	1998	37.50	30
1998 Bythyn Bach Gwyn	Open		35.00	35
1985 Hermitage - D. Tate	Retrd.	1986	30.00	107-188
1987 Hermitage Renovated - D. Tate	Retrd.	1990	42.50	65
1999 Labour of Love	Open		55.00	55
1995 Ladybird Cottage	Retrd.	1998	40.00	25-28
1992 St. Govan's Chapel	Retrd.	2000	75.00	50-80
1991 Tudor Merchant - D. Tate	Retrd.	1997	90.00	60-70
1991 Ugly House - D. Tate	Retrd.	1999	55.00	40-50

World Heritage - Lilliput Lane

YEAR ISSUE	EDITION LIMIT	YEAR RETD.	ISSUE PRICE	*QUOTE U.S.$
1999 Dutch Merchant's Shop/Zaane Koopmanshule	Open		50.00	50
1999 Dutch Windmill/Hollandse Poldermolen	Open		65.00	65

A Year In An English Garden - Lilliput Lane

YEAR ISSUE	EDITION LIMIT	YEAR RETD.	ISSUE PRICE	*QUOTE U.S.$
1994 Autumn Hues	Retrd.	1997	120.00	80-85
1995 Spring Glory	Retrd.	1997	120.00	44-85
1995 Summer Impressions	Retrd.	1997	120.00	55-65

*Quotes have been rounded up to nearest dollar

YEAR ISSUE	EDITION LIMIT	YEAR RETD.	ISSUE PRICE	*QUOTE U.S.$
1994 Winter's Wonder	Retrd.	1997	120.00	50-55

Midwest of Cannon Falls

Cottontail Lane Figurines and Accessories - Midwest

YEAR ISSUE	EDITION LIMIT	YEAR RETD.	ISSUE PRICE	*QUOTE U.S.$
1993 Arbor w/ Fence Set 02188-0	Retrd.	1998	14.00	14-28
1993 Birdbath, Bench & Mailbox, 02184-2	Retrd.	1993	4.00	8-12
1994 Birdhouse, Sundial & Bunny Fountain, 3 asst. 00371-8	Retrd.	1998	4.50	12
1993 Bridge & Gazebo, 2 asst. 02182-9	Retrd.	1996	11.50	24-50
1998 Bunnies Around Maypole 23657-4	Retrd.	1997	11.00	33-50
1998 Bunnies at Fence 23656-7	Retrd.	1998	7.00	21-30
1997 Bunnies on an Afternoon Stroll 18656-5	Retrd.	1998	5.00	10
1998 Bunnies on Bench 23655-0	Retrd.	1997	7.50	22-50
1996 Bunnies Sitting in Gazebo 15801-2	Retrd.	1998	10.00	10
1998 Bunnies Under Tree 23658-1	Retrd.	1997	7.50	38-50
1998 Bunnies with Wagon 23659-8	Retrd.	1998	6.50	18-35
1996 Bunny Band Quartet, set/4 15799-2	Retrd.	1997	16.00	16-33
1995 Bunny Chef, 2 asst. 12433-8	Retrd.	1998	4.50	10
1993 Bunny Child Collecting Eggs, 2 asst. 02880-3	Retrd.	1993	4.20	20
1996 Bunny Children Working in Garden, 2 asst. 15796-1	Retrd.	1998	3.50	4
1997 Bunny Clown, 2 asst. 18659-6	Retrd.	1998	4.00	4
1995 Bunny Couple at Cafe Table 12444-4	Retrd.	1998	7.00	7-12
1993 Bunny Couple on Bicycle 02978-7	Retrd.	1993	5.30	6-69
1997 Bunny Flower Girl & Ring Bearer, 2 asst. 18651-0	Retrd.	1998	3.50	17
1995 Bunny Kids at Carrot Juice Stand 12437-6	Retrd.	1998	5.30	6-19
1997 Bunny Kissing Booth 18660-2	Retrd.	1998	9.00	9
1994 Bunny Marching Band, 6 asst. 00355-8	Retrd.	1998	4.20	5-40
1995 Bunny Minister, Soloist, 2 asst. 12434-8	Retrd.	1998	5.00	5-22
1996 Bunny Picnicking, set/4 15798-5	Retrd.	1998	15.00	15
1995 Bunny Playing Piano 12439-0	Retrd.	1998	5.30	6
1995 Bunny Playing, 2 asst. 12442-0	Retrd.	1998	6.50	7-63
1995 Bunny Popcorn, Balloon Vendor, 2 asst. 12443-7	Retrd.	1998	6.70	19-22
1994 Bunny Preparing for Easter, 3 asst. 02971-8	Retrd.	1996	4.20	40-45
1994 Bunny Shopping Couple, 2 asst. 10362-3	Retrd.	1998	4.20	17-20
1997 Bunny Throwing Pie 18657-2	Retrd.	1998	3.00	3
1997 Bunny Vendor 18658-9	Retrd.	1998	4.00	10
1998 Bunny with Toys 23660-4	Retrd.	1998	3.50	30
1997 Carrot Fence 19625-0	Retrd.	1997	10.00	20
1994 Cobblestone Road 10072-1	Retrd.	1996	9.00	18
1994 Cone-Shaped Tree Set 10369-2	Retrd.	1996	7.50	16
1997 Cotton Candy Vendor Bunny 18661-9	Retrd.	1998	5.00	10-12
1994 Cottontail Lane Sign 10063-9	Retrd.	1998	5.00	10-25
1994 Easter Bunny Figure, 2 asst. 00356-5	Retrd.	1998	4.20	5
1994 Egg Stand & Flower Cart, 2 asst. 10354-8	Retrd.	1998	6.00	12
1995 Electric Street Lamppost, set/4 12461-1	Retrd.	1996	25.00	50
1996 Garden Shopkeeper, set/2 15800-5	Retrd.	1998	10.00	10-12
1996 Garden Table with Potted Plants and Flowers 15802-9	Retrd.	1998	9.00	18
1996 Garden with Waterfall and Pond 15797-8	Retrd.	1996	15.00	30
1997 Just Married Getaway Car 18650-3	Retrd.	1998	10.00	20
1993 Lamppost, Birdhouse & Mailbox, 3 asst. 02187-3	Retrd.	1993	4.50	9
1995 Mayor Bunny and Bunny with Flag Pole, 2 asst. 12441-3	Retrd.	1998	5.50	12
1995 Outdoor Bunny, 3 asst. 12435-2	Retrd.	1998	5.00	5-17
1994 Policeman, Conductor Bunny, 2 asst. 00367-1	Retrd.	1998	4.20	10
1995 Professional Bunny, 3 asst. 12438-3	Retrd.	1998	5.00	5-8
1995 Street Sign, 3 asst. 12433-8	Retrd.	1998	4.50	9-19
1993 Strolling Bunny, 2 asst. 02976-3	Retrd.	1993	4.20	5-150
1995 Strolling Bunny, 2 asst. 12440-6	Retrd.	1998	5.50	12
1994 Sweeper & Flower Peddler Bunny Couple, 2 asst. 00359-6	Retrd.	1998	4.20	5
1997 Ticket Vendor 18654-1	Retrd.	1998	10.00	12
1994 Topiary Trees, 3 asst. 00346-6	Retrd.	1994	2.50	5
1994 Train Station Couple, 2 asst. 00357-2	Retrd.	1998	4.20	12-113
1994 Tree & Shrub, 2 asst. 00382-4	Retrd.	1997	5.00	10-50
1996 Tree with Painted Flowers, set/3 15924-8	Retrd.	1998	20.00	25-27
1993 Trees, 3 asst. 02194-1	Retrd.	1994	6.20	12-50
1997 Wedding Bunny Couple 18652-7	Retrd.	1998	5.00	20
1994 Wedding Bunny Couple, 2 asst. 00347-3	Retrd.	1998	4.20	5
1993 Wishing Well, Vegetable Stand, 2 asst. 02185-5	Retrd.	1993	6.50	150
1993 • Wishing Well 02185-5	Retrd.	1993	N/A	15
1993 • Vegetable Stand 02185-5	Retrd.	1993	N/A	15

Cottontail Lane Houses - Midwest

YEAR ISSUE	EDITION LIMIT	YEAR RETD.	ISSUE PRICE	*QUOTE U.S.$
1997 Arcade Booth (lighted) 18655-8	Retrd.	1998	33.00	33
1993 Bakery (lighted) 01396-0	Retrd.	1996	43.00	21-94
1996 Bandshell (lighted) 15753-4	Retrd.	1997	50.00	24-63
1994 Bed & Breakfast House (lighted) 00337-4	Retrd.	1997	43.00	22-69
1995 Boutique and Beauty Shop (lighted) 12301-0	Retrd.	1997	45.00	24-45
1996 Bungalow (lighted) 15752-7	Retrd.	1997	45.00	24-63
1997 Bunny Chapel (lighted) 18653-4	Retrd.	1998	40.00	21-40
1995 Cafe (lighted) 12303-4	Retrd.	1997	45.00	24-45
1997 Carousel (lighted & musical) 18649-7	5,000	1998	47.00	25-69
1995 Cathedral (lighted) 12302-7	Retrd.	1997	47.00	25-94
1994 Chapel (lighted) 00331-2	3,000	1993	43.00	180-238
1993 Church (lighted) 01385-4	3,000	1993	42.00	150
1992 Confectionary Shop (lighted) 06335-5	Retrd.	1994	43.00	69-107
1998 Cottage (lighted) 23667-3	Retrd.	1998	43.00	43-94
1993 Cottontail Inn (lighted) 01394-6	Retrd.	1996	43.00	24-78
1996 Fire Station w/Figures, set/6 (lighted) 15830-2	5,000	1997	90.00	46-125
1992 Flower Shop (lighted) 06333-9	Retrd.	1994	43.00	69-100
1994 General Store (lighted) 00340-4	Retrd.	1998	43.00	22-35
1998 Library (lighted) 23671-0	Retrd.	1998	43.00	43-94
1998 Mansion (lighted) 23672-7	2,500	1998	47.00	188-200
1993 Painting Studio (lighted) 01395-5	Retrd.	1994	43.00	60-88
1993 Rose Cottage (lighted) 01386-1	Retrd.	1994	43.00	38-94
1995 Rosebud Manor (lighted) 12304-1	3,500	1994	45.00	44-157
1998 Row House (lighted) 23670-3	Retrd.	1998	45.00	45-94
1993 Schoolhouse (lighted) 01378-6	Retrd.	1997	43.00	24-94
1992 Springtime Cottage (lighted) 06329-8	Retrd.	1994	43.00	88-107
1996 Town Garden Shoppe (lighted) 15751-0	Retrd.	1997	45.00	24-63
1995 Town Hall (lighted) 12300-3	Retrd.	1997	45.00	50-63
1998 Toy Store (lighted) 23668-0	Retrd.	1998	37.00	145-157
1994 Train Station (lighted) 00330-5	Retrd.	1997	43.00	24-94
1997 Tunnel of Love w/Swan (lighted)18648-0	Retrd.	1998	40.00	21-40
1992 Victorian House (lighted) 06332-1	Retrd.	1997	43.00	24-94

Creepy Hollow Figurines and Accessories - Midwest

YEAR ISSUE	EDITION LIMIT	YEAR RETD.	ISSUE PRICE	*QUOTE U.S.$
1994 Black Picket Fence 10685-3	Retrd.	1996	3.50	35-40
1996 Bone Fence 16961-2	Retrd.	2000	9.50	11-17
1999 Boo News Newsstand 30907-0	Open		11.00	11
1993 Bride of Frankenstein 06663-8	Retrd.	1993	5.00	90-225
1995 Cemetery Gate 13366-8	Retrd.	1997	16.00	45-55
2000 Clock & Fire Hydrant, 2 asst. 35479-7	Open		5.50	6
1996 Covered Bridge 16664-2	Retrd.	1997	22.00	30-65
1994 Creepy Hollow Sign 10647-1	Open		5.50	6
1992 Dracula (standing) 06707-9	Retrd.	1994	7.30	200-250
1996 Dragon 16936-0	Retrd.	1998	8.50	9-12
1995 Flying Witch, Ghost, 2 asst. 13362-0	Retrd.	1996	11.00	25-60
1992 Frankenstein 06704-8	Retrd.	1994	6.00	75-125
2000 Frankenstein, Waitress, 2 asst. 35482-7	Open		7.00	7
2000 • Frankensteinon Motorcycle 35482-7	Open		N/A	N/A
2000 • Waitress on Rollerskates 35482-7	Open		N/A	N/A
1997 Garden Statue, 2 asst. 19827-8	Open		7.50	8
1994 Ghost, 3 asst. 10652-5	Retrd.	1997	6.00	12-25
1996 Ghostly King 16659-8	Retrd.	1997	8.00	8-24
1995 Ghoul Usher 13515-0	Open		6.50	7
2000 Ghoulish Couple Out Crusin' 35488-9	Open		7.00	7
1995 Ghoulish Organist Playing Organ 13363-7	Retrd.	1997	13.00	18-37
2000 Ghoulish Street Light 35480-3	Open		7.00	7
1999 Ghouly Characters, 4 asst. 30908-7	Open		7.00	7
1995 Grave Digger, 2 asst. 13360-6	Retrd.	1997	10.00	22-28
1996 Gypsy 16656-7	Retrd.	1997	8.00	10-18
1996 Gypsy Witch 16655-0	Open		8.00	8
1992 Halloween Sign, 2 asst. 06709-3	Retrd.	1995	6.00	25-40
1992 • Keep Out 06709-3	Retrd.	1995	N/A	23-35
1992 • Ghost Town 06709-3	Retrd.	1995	N/A	25-35
1997 Haunted Lighted Trees, 2 asst. 21458-9	Retrd.	1999	24.00	16-24
1993 Haunted Tree, 2 asst. 05892-3	Retrd.	1997	7.00	12-25
1996 Headless Horseman 16658-1	Retrd.	1997	11.00	20-27
1995 Hearse with Monsters 13364-4	Retrd.	1997	15.00	19-50
1993 Hinged Dracula's Coffin 08545-5	Retrd.	1995	11.00	38-94
1995 Hinged Tomb 13516-7	Retrd.	1995	15.00	80-125
1995 Hunchback 13359-0	Retrd.	1997	9.00	12-28
1999 Ice Scream Truck 30909-4	Open		17.00	17
1996 Inn Keeper 16660-4	Retrd.	1999	7.00	7-10
1994 Mad Scientist 10646-4	Retrd.	1997	6.00	9-24
1998 Mailbox 24374-9	Open		7.00	7
2000 Monster Band, 3 asst. 35481-0	Open		7.00	7
2000 Monster Pound Truck (sound & light) 35483-4	Open		18.00	18
1993 Mummy 06705-5	Retrd.	1994	6.00	82-94
1997 Mummy Box 19846-9	Retrd.	1998	16.00	17-32
1994 Outhouse 10648-8	Retrd.	1997	7.00	15-38
1994 Phantom of the Opera 10645-7	Retrd.	1997	6.00	15-35
1997 Potted Plant, 3 asst. 19826-1	Retrd.	1998	7.00	15-39
1993 Pumpkin Head Ghost 06661-4	Retrd.	1993	5.50	75-157
1993 Pumpkin Patch Sign, 2 asst. 05898-5	Retrd.	1995	6.50	35-50
1993 • Dead End 05898-5	Retrd.	1995	N/A	35-40
1993 • Pumpkin Patch (Cat Crossing) 05898-5	Retrd.	1995	N/A	30-38
1995 Pumpkin Street Lamp, set/4 13365-1	Retrd.	1996	25.00	60-107
1998 Railroad Conductor, Railroad Crossing Sign, Traveler, 3 asst. 24370-1	Open		7.00	7
1993 Resin Skeleton 06651-5	Retrd.	1994	5.50	85-100
1995 Road of Bones 13371-2	Retrd.	1997	9.00	12
1996 School Teacher 16657-4	Retrd.	2000	8.00	8-18
1997 Sea Captains, 2 asst. 19823-0	Open		7.50	8
1997 Servant, 2 asst. 19825-4	Open		7.50	8
1998 Sign, 3 asst. 24372-5	Open		6.00	6
1997 Siren on Rock, 3 asst. 19824-7	Open		7.50	8
1996 Skeleton Butler 16661-1	Open		7.00	7
1997 Skeleton in Dinghy 19821-6	Open		12.00	12
1995 Spooky Black Tree 13752-9	Open		4.50	5
1994 Street Sign, 2 asst. 10644-0	Retrd.	1996	5.70	16-63
1995 Street Sign, 3 asst. 13357-6	Retrd.	1996	5.50	15-46
1995 Theatre Goer, set/2 13358-3	Retrd.	1997	9.00	12-45
1995 Ticket Seller 13361-3	Retrd.	1997	10.00	10-45
1993 Tombstone 06712-3	Retrd.	1993	6.00	100-120
1994 Tombstone Sign, 3 asst. 10642-6	Retrd.	1997	3.50	11-40
1998 Train with Engineer (sound activated) 24373-2	Open		18.00	18
1993 Trick or Treater, 3 asst. 08591-2	Retrd.	1995	5.50	8-60
1998 Trick or Treaters, 3 asst. 24371-8	Retrd.	1999	6.00	6
1994 Werewolf 10643-4	Retrd.	1997	6.00	12-28
1992 Witch 06706-2	Retrd.	1996	6.00	27-33
1997 Witch with Telescope 19822-3	Open		7.50	8

Creepy Hollow Lighted Houses - Midwest

YEAR ISSUE	EDITION LIMIT	YEAR RETD.	ISSUE PRICE	*QUOTE U.S.$
1999 Beastly Bungalow 29837-4	2,500	1999	48.00	48-110
1995 Bewitching Belfry 13355-2	Retrd.	1997	50.00	75-94
1993 Blood Bank 08548-6	Retrd.	1996	40.00	95-120
1999 Butcher Shop 29835-0	Open		30.00	30
2000 Camping Store 35484-1	Retrd.	2000	35.00	35
1998 Candy, Costume and Barbershop 23274-3	Retrd.	1999	48.00	48-70
1997 Cape Odd Lighthouse 19569-7	Retrd.	1998	45.00	50-82
1996 Castle 16959-9	5,000	1997	50.00	50-113
1994 Cauldron Cafe 10649-5	Retrd.	1996	40.00	70-113
1998 Cozy Coffin Motel 23276-7	Retrd.	1999	35.00	40-57
1999 Creepy Commons Apt & Shops 29836-7	Retrd.	2000	45.00	45
1992 Dr. Frankenstein's House 01621-3	Retrd.	1995	40.00	113-188
1992 Dracula's Castle 01627-5	Retrd.	1995	40.00	188-250
1997 Drearydale Manor House (sound activated) 19568-0	5,000	1999	50.00	65-107
1997 Eerie Eatery House 19571-0	Retrd.	1998	45.00	55-75
2000 Frankie's Dis-Em-Bowling Alley 35486-5	Retrd.	2000	45.00	45
1999 Fright Club and Disco 29839-8	Retrd.	2000	35.00	35
1995 Funeral Parlor 13356-9	Retrd.	1997	50.00	63-88
1998 Gasp N Go Gas Station 23275-0	Retrd.	2000	35.00	40-50
1998 Ghost Post Office 23273-6	Retrd.	1999	30.00	30-50
2000 Ghoul's Gym 35485-8	Retrd.	2000	35.00	35
1996 Gypsy Wagon 16663-5	Open		45.00	45
1993 Haunted Hotel 08549-3	Retrd.	1996	40.00	88-125
1999 Haunted Library 29838-1	Retrd.	2000	35.00	35
1996 Jack-O' Lant-Inn 16665-9	Retrd.	1997	45.00	85-100
1994 Medical Ghoul School 10651-8	Retrd.	1997	40.00	65-107
1992 Mummy's Mortuary 01641-1	Retrd.	1995	40.00	250
1997 Norman's Bait & Tackle House 19572-7	Retrd.	1998	36.00	45-60
1994 Phantom's Opera 10650-1	Retrd.	1996	40.00	100-125
1996 School House 16662-8	Retrd.	1997	45.00	60-88
1997 Shipwreck House 19570-3	Retrd.	1998	45.00	50-75
1993 Shoppe of Horrors 08550-9	Retrd.	1995	40.00	88-169
1995 Skeleton Cinema 13354-5	5,000	1995	50.00	50-175
2000 Skully's Drive-In Diner 35487-2	2,500	2000	50.00	50
2000 Stray Pet Store 35489-6	Open		33.00	33
1998 Train Depot 23272-9	3,500	1998	45.00	57-65
1992 Witches Cove 01665-7	Retrd.	1995	40.00	188-250

Possible Dreams

Crinkle Village - Staff

YEAR ISSUE	EDITION LIMIT	YEAR RETD.	ISSUE PRICE	*QUOTE U.S.$
1997 Crinkle Barn 659654	Open		43.30	44
1998 Crinkle Candy Store (lighted) 659661	Open		62.00	62
1996 Crinkle Castle (lighted) 659652	Retrd.	1998	70.00	75
1996 Crinkle Church (lighted) 659651	Retrd.	1998	70.00	70
1997 Crinkle Claus Village Display 965006	Open		10.00	10
1996 Crinkle Cottage (lighted) 659653	Retrd.	1998	70.00	70
1997 Crinkle Farmhouse 659657	Open		43.30	44
1998 Crinkle Fire Station (lighted) 659660	Open		62.00	62
1997 Crinkle Grist Mill 659656	Open		43.30	44
1997 Crinkle Inn 659655	Open		43.30	44
1998 Crinkle Police Station (lighted) 659662	Open		62.00	62
1998 Crinkle Post Office (lighted) 659659	Open		62.00	62
1998 Crinkle Toy Shop (lighted) 659658	Open		62.00	62
1996 Crinkle Workshop (lighted) 659650	Retrd.	1998	70.00	75
1996 Santa Castle 659019	Open		15.00	15
1996 Santa Christmas House 659017	Open		15.00	15
1996 Santa Church 659020	Open		15.00	15
1996 Santa Farm House 659018	Open		15.00	15
1996 Santa Palace 659016	Open		15.00	15
1996 Santa Windmill 659021	Open		15.00	15

Reco International

Mini Views - Various

YEAR ISSUE	EDITION LIMIT	YEAR RETD.	ISSUE PRICE	*QUOTE U.S.$
1999 Afternoon in Venice - B. Pejman	Open		20.00	20
1999 Almost There - R. Lee	Retrd.	2000	20.00	20
2000 Angel Lighting the World - D. Gelsinger	Open		20.00	20
2000 Anna - H. Fisher	Open		20.00	20
2000 Ballerina - N. Mirkovich	Open		20.00	20
2000 Beach Duet - P. Brent	Open		20.00	20
1999 Birth of Hiawatha - G. Perillo	Retrd.	2000	20.00	20
2000 Cape Hatteras - P. Brent	Open		20.00	20
2000 Cape Lookout - P. Brent	Open		20.00	20
1999 Capri Terrace - B. Pejman	Open		20.00	20
1999 Champaign Wishes - S. Hatchett	Open		20.00	20
2000 Cherub with Wren - C. Shoresright	Open		20.00	20
2000 Chickadees in the Snow - D. Balke	Open		20.00	20
2000 Christmas Joy - B. Harris Tustian	Open		20.00	20
2000 Christmas Memories - B. Harris Tustian	Open		20.00	20
1999 Duck Crossing - R. Lee	Retrd.	2000	20.00	20
2000 Dune Hideaway - P. Brent	Open		20.00	20
2000 Follow Me - D. DeVary	Open		20.00	20
1999 From Santorini With Love - S. Hatchett	Open		20.00	20
2000 The Gallery - J. Haney-Neal	Open		20.00	20
2000 The Grand Finale - M. Grimball	Open		20.00	20

*Quotes have been rounded up to nearest dollar

YEAR ISSUE	EDITION LIMIT	YEAR RETD.	ISSUE PRICE	*QUOTE U.S.$
2000 Grandma's Backyard - N. Mirkovich	Open		20.00	20
1999 Green Ledge Lighthouse - H. Schaare	Open		20.00	20
2000 Hope - P. Church	Open		20.00	20
1999 The Hunt - G. Perillo	Retrd.	2000	20.00	20
2000 In Disgrace - M. Grimball	Open		20.00	20
2000 Jazz - T. Wilson	Open		20.00	20
2000 Lilies of the Mohawk - G. Perillo	Open		20.00	20
1999 Lily Pond - G. Perillo	Retrd.	2000	20.00	20
1999 Love Song - G. Ratinavera	Retrd.	2000	20.00	20
2000 Loving Care - C. Shoresright	Open		20.00	20
1999 Memories in Blue - A. Berman	Open		20.00	20
2000 Mystical Santa - D. Gelsinger	Open		20.00	20
2000 The Old Barn - N. Mirkovich	Open		20.00	20
2000 On Guard - M. Grimball	Open		20.00	20
1999 Once Upon a Time - S. Hatchett	Open		20.00	20
2000 The Optimist - J. Haney-Neal	Open		20.00	20
2000 Pansies & Lace - S. Wall	Open		20.00	20
2000 Peace - P. Church	Open		20.00	20
2000 The Rebel - J. Haney-Neal	Open		20.00	20
1999 Rhapsody in Blue - G. Ratinavera	Retrd.	2000	20.00	20
2000 Rhythm - T. Wilson	Open		20.00	20
2000 Ride the Pony - D. DeVary	Open		20.00	20
1999 Room Service - G. Buffet	Open		20.00	20
2000 The Run Away - D. DeVary	Open		20.00	20
1999 The Rustler - G. Perillo	Open		20.00	20
2000 Snowman Family - D. Gelsinger	Open		20.00	20
2000 Still Life - A. Kaercher	Open		20.00	20
2000 Three for Tea - S. Wall	Open		20.00	20
2000 Three Little... - S. Wall	Open		20.00	20
2000 Three Sisters - C. Shoresright	Open		20.00	20
1999 The Vanishing West - D. Cook	Open		20.00	20
2000 Vase of Roses - J. L. Jensen	Open		20.00	20
2000 Who's Afraid - M. Grimball	Open		20.00	20

Native American Views - G. Perillo

YEAR ISSUE	EDITION LIMIT	YEAR RETD.	ISSUE PRICE	*QUOTE U.S.$
1999 Anasazis Sanctuary	Open		45.00	45
1999 Cheyenne's Pride	Open		45.00	45
1999 Iroquois Dignity	Open		45.00	45
1999 Navaho's Refuge	Open		45.00	45
1999 Pueblo Abode	Open		45.00	45

Nautical Views - R. Reichardt

YEAR ISSUE	EDITION LIMIT	YEAR RETD.	ISSUE PRICE	*QUOTE U.S.$
1999 Cape Hatteras	2,400		45.00	50

Purr-fect Views - J. Everett

YEAR ISSUE	EDITION LIMIT	YEAR RETD.	ISSUE PRICE	*QUOTE U.S.$
1999 Country Store	Open		40.00	40
1999 The Potting Shed	Open		40.00	40
1999 Townhouse Cats	Open		40.00	40

Rooms With A View - Various

YEAR ISSUE	EDITION LIMIT	YEAR RETD.	ISSUE PRICE	*QUOTE U.S.$
2000 Afternoon Remembered - J. O'Brien	Open		40.00	40
1998 Archway - J. O'Brien	Retrd.	2000	40.00	40
2000 The Arrangement - J. O'Brien	Open		40.00	40
2000 Castle View - J. O'Brien	Open		40.00	40
2000 Country Elegance - E. Dertner	Open		40.00	40
1998 Gourmet Delight - B. Ternay	Open		40.00	40
2000 Grand Ma's Kitchen - E. Dertner	Open		40.00	40
1998 In The Garden - J. O'Brien	Retrd.	2000	40.00	40
1999 Lighthouse - R. Reichardt	Open		40.00	40
1998 Nantucket - F. Ledan	Open		40.00	40
1998 New York Nights - F. Ledan	Open		40.00	40
1998 Remembering - J. O'Brien	Retrd.	2000	40.00	40
1999 Romantic Belliago - S. Hatchett	Open		40.00	40
1998 Rustic Repose - E. Dertner	Open		40.00	40
1998 Salinger Mansion - F. Ledan	Open		40.00	40
1998 Salon Sur La Cite - F. Ledan	Open		40.00	40
2000 Summer's Light - J. O'Brien	Open		40.00	40
1998 Terrasse-Sur-Riviera - F. Ledan	Open		40.00	40
1998 Top of the Morning - E. Dertner	Open		40.00	40
1999 Tropical Hideaway - S. Hatchett	Open		40.00	40
1998 Yellow Roses, Red Poppies - F. Ledan	Open		40.00	40

Rooms With A View-Graceland - Based on Graceland Rooms

YEAR ISSUE	EDITION LIMIT	YEAR RETD.	ISSUE PRICE	*QUOTE U.S.$
1999 The Graceland Mansion	Open		45.00	50
1999 The Jungle Room	Open		45.00	50
1999 The Living Room & Music Room	Open		45.00	50
1999 The Mansion Foyer	Open		45.00	50

Shops With A View - Various

YEAR ISSUE	EDITION LIMIT	YEAR RETD.	ISSUE PRICE	*QUOTE U.S.$
1999 Bottle Brigade - G. Buffet	Open		45.00	45
1999 Clip Art - R. Souders	Open		40.00	40
1999 Diner - W. Ternay	Open		40.00	40
2000 The Flower Shop - J. O'Brien	Open		40.00	40
1999 La Cacioteca - G. Buffet	Open		45.00	45
2000 Menu of the Day - G. Buffet	Open		45.00	45
2000 The Old Antique Shop - J. O'Brien	Open		40.00	40
2000 Palace of Treasures - J. O'Brien	Open		40.00	40
1999 Panetteria - G. Buffet	Open		45.00	45
1999 Pop's - R. Souders	Open		40.00	40

Views of Faith - Various

YEAR ISSUE	EDITION LIMIT	YEAR RETD.	ISSUE PRICE	*QUOTE U.S.$
1999 The Conception - S. Tiepolo	Open		40.00	40
1999 Gett'n Ready - J. Claybrooks	2,400		45.00	45
1999 Madonna in Prayer - S. Tiepolo	Open		40.00	40
1999 Sharing Harmony - S. Kuck	2,400		45.00	45

Roman, Inc.

Fontanini Club Members Only Midyear Exclusive - E. Simonetti

YEAR ISSUE	EDITION LIMIT	YEAR RETD.	ISSUE PRICE	*QUOTE U.S.$
2000 The Harbor	Yr.Iss.		75.00	75

Fontanini Life of Christ 5" - E. Simonetti

YEAR ISSUE	EDITION LIMIT	YEAR RETD.	ISSUE PRICE	*QUOTE U.S.$
1999 Crucifixion Scene	Open		100.00	100
2000 Resurrection Scene	Open		85.00	85

Fontanini Nativity Village 2.5" - E. Simonetti

YEAR ISSUE	EDITION LIMIT	YEAR RETD.	ISSUE PRICE	*QUOTE U.S.$
1996 Blue King's Tent	Open		17.50	18
1996 Inn	Open		29.50	30
1996 Shepherd's Camp	Retrd.	1999	29.50	30
1996 Stable (original design)	Retrd.	1997	29.50	30
1996 Town Building	Retrd.	1998	25.00	25
1996 Town Store	Retrd.	1998	25.00	25
1996 6 pc. set w/ lighted base	Retrd.	1998	270.00	270
1997 Gold King's Tent	Open		22.50	23
1997 Marketplace	Open		32.50	33
1997 Pottery Shop	Open		32.50	33
1997 Purple King's Tent	Open		22.50	23
1997 Town Gate	Open		32.50	33
1998 Carpenter's Shop	Open		32.50	33
1998 Corral (For Animals)	Open		32.50	33
1998 Lighted Stable (revised design)	Open		32.50	33
1998 Poultry Shop	Retrd.	2000	32.50	33
2000 Basket Shop	Open		32.50	33
2000 Weaver's Shop	Open		32.50	33

Fontanini Nativity Village 5" - E. Simonetti

YEAR ISSUE	EDITION LIMIT	YEAR RETD.	ISSUE PRICE	*QUOTE U.S.$
1996 Bakery	Retrd.	1999	80.00	80
2000 Basket Shop	Open		80.00	80
1996 Blue King's Tent	Open		50.00	50
1998 Carpenter's Shop	Retrd.	2000	90.00	90
1999 Census Building	Open		85.00	85
1998 Corral (For Animals)	Open		90.00	90
1997 Gold King's Tent	Open		65.00	65
2000 Home	Open		125.00	125
1996 Inn	Open		85.00	85
1997 Marketplace	Retrd.	1999	90.00	90
1997 Pottery Shop	Open		90.00	90
1998 Poultry Shop	Retrd.	2000	90.00	90
1997 Purple King's Tent	Open		60.00	65
1996 Shepherd's Camp	Retrd.	1998	80.00	80
1996 Stable	Open		75.00	75
1999 Temple	Open		125.00	125
1997 Town Gate	Open		90.00	90
2000 Vineyard	Open		80.00	80
1999 Weaver's Shop	Open		75.00	75

Fontanini Nativity Village 7.5" - E. Simonetti

YEAR ISSUE	EDITION LIMIT	YEAR RETD.	ISSUE PRICE	*QUOTE U.S.$
1997 Blue King's Tent	Open		99.50	100
1998 Fish Market	Open		120.00	120
1998 Gold King's Tent	Open		110.00	110
1997 Inn	Retrd.	1998	55.00	55
1998 Lighted Stable	Open		125.00	125
1997 Lighted Stable	Retrd.	1998	75.00	85
1999 Marketplace	Open		120.00	120
1997 Marketplace	Retrd.	1998	65.00	70
1998 Purple King's Tent	Open		95.00	95
1997 Town Building	Retrd.	1998	70.00	70
1997 Town Gate	Retrd.	1998	35.00	35
2000 Weaver's Shop	Open		110.00	110

Shelia's Collectibles

Shelia's Collectors' Society - S. Thompson

YEAR ISSUE	EDITION LIMIT	YEAR RETD.	ISSUE PRICE	*QUOTE U.S.$
1993 Anne Peacock House SOC01	Retrd.	1994	16.00	132-250
1993 Susan B. Anthony CGA93	Retrd.	1994	Gift	94-125
1993 Anne Peacock House SOC01 & Susan B. Anthony CGA93, set/2	Retrd.	1994	16.00	132-300
1993 Anne Peacock House Print	Retrd.	1994	Gift	47-75
1994 Seaview Cottage SOC02	Retrd.	1995	17.00	75-125
1994 Helen Keller's Birthplace-Ivy Green CGA94	Retrd.	1995	Gift	75
1994 Seaview Cottage SOC02 & Helen Keller's Birthplace-Ivy Green CGA94, set/2	Retrd.	1995	17.00	97-113
1994 Collector's Society T-Shirt	Retrd.	1995	Gift	N/A
1995 Pink Lady SOC03	Retrd.	1996	20.00	40-57
1995 Red Cross CGA95	Retrd.	1996	Gift	47-88
1995 Pink Lady SOC03 & Red Cross CGA95, set/2	Retrd.	1996	20.00	50-200
1995 Collector's Society T-Shirt & Collector's Society Pin	Retrd.	1996	Gift	45-115
1996 Tinker Toy House SOC04	Retrd.	1997	20.00	39-47
1996 Tatman House CGA96	Retrd.	1997	Gift	30-50
1996 Tinker Toy House SOC04 & Tatman House CGA96, set/2	Retrd.	1997	20.00	200
1996 Tinker Toy House Ornament	Retrd.	1997	Gift	45
1997 25 Meeting St. SOC97	Retrd.	1998	26.00	45-47
1997 23 Meeting Street CGA97	Retrd.	1998	Gift	45
1997 23 Meeting St. SOC97 & 23 Meeting Street CGA97, set/2	Retrd.	1998	26.00	150
1997 25 Meeting Street Ornament OCS02	Retrd.	1998	Gift	40-63
1998 Old North Church II CGA98	Retrd.	1998	Gift	20-25
1998 Paul Revere's Ride CGA98	Retrd.	1998	Gift	15-20
1998 Munroe Tavern SOC98	Retrd.	1999	26.00	28
1999 Eugenia's Flower Garden SOC99	Retrd.	1999	Gift	N/A
1999 Eugenia's Cottage CGA99	Retrd.	1999	Gift	25
2000 Betsy Ross CSA00	Yr.Iss.		Gift	N/A
2000 Betsy Ross House CGA00	Yr.Iss.		Gift	N/A

Signing & Event Pieces - S. Thompson

YEAR ISSUE	EDITION LIMIT	YEAR RETD.	ISSUE PRICE	*QUOTE U.S.$
1994 Star Barn SOP01	Retrd.	1994	24.00	60-75
1995 Shelia's Real Estate Office SOP02	Retrd.	1995	20.00	20-44
1996 Thompson's Mercantile SOP03	Retrd.	1996	24.00	25-55
1997 27 Meeting St. SOP97	Retrd.	1997	26.00	44-50
1998 The Old Manse SOP98	Retrd.	1998	26.00	26
1999 Gilson Residence EVT99	Retrd.	1999	23.00	23-30
2000 Buckeye Tree SOP04	Retrd.	2000	15.00	15
2000 Golden Gate Bridge SOP05	Retrd.	2000	17.00	17
2000 A Day at the Beach SOP06	Yr.Iss.		N/A	N/A
2000 Thanksgiving Blessings SOP07	Yr.Iss.		N/A	N/A

Accessories - S. Thompson

YEAR ISSUE	EDITION LIMIT	YEAR RETD.	ISSUE PRICE	*QUOTE U.S.$
1994 Amish Quilt Line COL12	Retrd.	1994	18.00	35-48
1993 Apple Tree COL09	Retrd.	1996	12.00	20-35
1996 Autumn Tree ACC09	Open		14.00	15
1996 Barber Gazebo ACC05	Retrd.	2000	13.00	14
1999 Biltmore Conservatory ACC15	Retrd.	2000	24.00	24
1997 Crepe Myrtle ACC13	Open		15.00	15
1993 Dogwood Tree COL08	Retrd.	1996	12.00	24-55
1999 Evergreen Trees ACC16	Open		13.00	13
1992 Fence 5" COL04	Retrd.	1993	9.00	25-30
1992 Fence 7" COL05	Retrd.	1995	10.00	27-35
1995 Flower Garden ACC02	Retrd.	1998	13.00	13-18
1994 Formal Garden COL13	Retrd.	1994	18.00	30-35
1992 Gazebo With Victorian Lady COL02	Retrd.	1995	11.00	25-35
1996 Grazing Cows ACC04	Retrd.	2000	12.00	12
1992 Lake With Swan COL06	Retrd.	1993	11.00	23-35
1997 Magnolia Tree ACC11	Open		15.00	15
1992 Oak Bower COL03	Retrd.	1993	11.00	35-45
1996 Palm Tree ACC07	Open		14.00	15
1995 Real Estate Sign ACC03	Retrd.	1998	12.00	15-18
1997 Sabal Palm ACC12	Open		14.00	14
1996 Sailboat ACC06	Open		12.00	13
1996 Spring Tree ACC10	Open		14.00	15
1996 Summertime Picket Fence ACC08	Open		12.00	13
1994 Sunrise At 80 Meeting COL10	Retrd.	1994	18.00	30-65
1998 Town Square Evergreen TSN06	Retrd.	1998	10.00	18
1992 Tree With Bush COL07	Retrd.	1996	10.00	24-35
1994 Victorian Arbor COL11	Retrd.	1994	18.00	30-45
1997 White Dogwood ACC14	Open		15.00	15
1995 Wisteria Arbor ACC01	Retrd.	1998	12.00	12-14
1992 Wrought Iron Gate With Magnolias COL01	Retrd.	1993	11.00	30-50

American Barns - S. Thompson

YEAR ISSUE	EDITION LIMIT	YEAR RETD.	ISSUE PRICE	*QUOTE U.S.$
1995 Casey Barn AP BAR04	Retrd.	1997	18.00	20-35
1995 Casey Barn BAR04	Retrd.	1997	18.00	24-27
1999 Dr. Pierce's Barn BAR07	Retrd.	2000	24.00	24
1999 King Midas Barn BAR06	Retrd.	2000	22.00	22
1995 Mail Pouch Barn AP BAR03	Retrd.	1996	18.00	18
1995 Mail Pouch Barn BAR03	Retrd.	1999	18.00	22-25
1996 Mr. Peanut Barn BAR05	Retrd.	2000	19.00	21
1996 Mr. Peanut Barn, AP BAR05	97	1996	24.00	35-60
1995 Pennsylvania Dutch Barn AP BAR02	Retrd.	1995	20.00	90
1995 Pennsylvania Dutch Barn BAR02	Retrd.	1996	18.00	25-35
1994 Rock City Barn AP BAR01	Retrd.	1994	20.00	22-25
1994 Rock City Barn BAR01	Retrd.	1999	18.00	22

Amish Village - S. Thompson

YEAR ISSUE	EDITION LIMIT	YEAR RETD.	ISSUE PRICE	*QUOTE U.S.$
1993 Amish Barn AMS04	Retrd.	1997	17.00	30
1993 Amish Barn, AP AMS04	Retrd.	1993	20.00	30-35
1994 Amish Barn (renovated) AMS04II	Retrd.	1997	17.00	60
1997 Amish Barnraising AMS09	Retrd.	1999	22.00	23
1993 Amish Buggy AMS05	Retrd.	1997	12.00	26-35
1993 Amish Buggy, AP AMS05	Retrd.	1994	16.00	20-35
1994 Amish Buggy (renovated) AMS05II	Retrd.	1997	12.00	20-30
1997 Amish Corn Cribs AMS07	Retrd.	1999	18.00	19-21
1997 Amish Farmhouse AMS08	Retrd.	1999	22.00	23-27
1993 Amish Home AMS01	Retrd.	1994	17.00	31-35
1993 Amish Home, AP AMS01	Retrd.	1993	20.00	35-42
1994 Amish Home (renovated) AMS01II	Retrd.	1997	17.00	28-35
1993 Amish School AMS02	Retrd.	1994	15.00	22-34
1993 Amish School, AP AMS02	Retrd.	1993	20.00	35-60
1994 Amish School (renovated) AMS02II	Retrd.	1997	15.00	20-27
1997 Amish Schoolhouse AMS10	Retrd.	1999	18.00	19
1993 Covered Bridge AMS03	Retrd.	1994	16.00	18-40
1993 Covered Bridge, AP AMS03	Retrd.	1993	20.00	20-60
1994 Covered Bridge (renovated) AMS03II	Retrd.	1997	16.00	28-30
1995 Roadside Stand AMS06	Retrd.	1999	17.00	19-23
1995 Roadside Stand, AP AMS06	Retrd.	1995	24.00	30-35

Arkansas Ladies - S. Thompson

YEAR ISSUE	EDITION LIMIT	YEAR RETD.	ISSUE PRICE	*QUOTE U.S.$
1996 Handford Terry House ARK02	Retrd.	1999	19.00	23-25
1996 Handford Terry House, AP ARK02	50	1996	24.00	47
1996 Pillow-Thompson House ARK04	Retrd.	1999	19.00	23
1996 Pillow-Thompson House, AP ARK04	101	1996	24.00	47-65
1996 Rosalie House ARK01	Retrd.	1999	19.00	23
1996 Rosalie House, AP ARK01	102	1996	24.00	48
1996 Wings ARK03	Retrd.	1999	19.00	23-25
1996 Wings, AP ARK03	103	1996	24.00	47

Artist Choice-American Gothic - S. Thompson

YEAR ISSUE	EDITION LIMIT	YEAR RETD.	ISSUE PRICE	*QUOTE U.S.$
1993 Gothic Revival Cottage ACL01	Retrd.	1993	20.00	37-45
1993 Mele House ACL04	Retrd.	1993	20.00	38-57
1993 Perkins House ACL02	Retrd.	1993	20.00	35-57
1993 Rose Arbor ACL05	Retrd.	1993	14.00	27-65
1993 Roseland Cottage ACL03	Retrd.	1993	20.00	35-43
1993 Set of 5	Retrd.	1993	94.00	219-275

Artist Choice-Barber Houses - S. Thompson

YEAR ISSUE	EDITION LIMIT	YEAR RETD.	ISSUE PRICE	*QUOTE U.S.$
1995 Banta House ACL12	4,000	1995	24.00	45-60
1995 Greenman House ACL11	4,000	1995	24.00	40-45
1995 Riley-Cutler House ACL10	4,000	1995	24.00	32-35
1995 Weller House ACL13	4,000	1995	24.00	40
1995 Set of 4	4,000	1995	96.00	144

Artist Choice-Mail-Order Victorians (Barber Houses) - S. Thompson

YEAR ISSUE	EDITION LIMIT	YEAR RETD.	ISSUE PRICE	*QUOTE U.S.$
1994 Brehaut House ACL09	3,300	1994	24.00	40
1994 Goeller House ACL08	3,300	1994	24.00	40
1994 Henderson House ACL07	3,300	1994	24.00	55

*Quotes have been rounded up to nearest dollar

YEAR ISSUE	EDITION LIMIT	YEAR RETD.	ISSUE PRICE	*QUOTE U.S.$
1994 Titman House ACL06	3,300	1994	24.00	75-80
1994 Set of 4	3,300	1994	96.00	145-210

Artist Choice-My Favorite Places - S. Thompson

YEAR ISSUE	EDITION LIMIT	YEAR RETD.	ISSUE PRICE	*QUOTE U.S.$
1997 Garden Bench ACL18	5,000	1997	24.00	25-30
1997 Reflecting Pond ACL19	5,000	1997	24.00	25-30
1997 Sunflower Field ACL21	5,000	1997	21.00	23-25
1997 Tranquil Arbor ACL20	5,000	1997	22.00	25

Artist Choice-Noah's Ark - S. Thompson

YEAR ISSUE	EDITION LIMIT	YEAR RETD.	ISSUE PRICE	*QUOTE U.S.$
1999 Noah's Ark ACL24	5,000		45.00	45
1999 Rainbow ACL25	5,000		set	set

Artist Choice-The Night Before Christmas - S. Thompson

YEAR ISSUE	EDITION LIMIT	YEAR RETD.	ISSUE PRICE	*QUOTE U.S.$
1998 The Night Before Christmas ACL22	7,500		55.00	55
1998 Frozen Lawn ACL23	7,500		set	set

Artist Choice-Winter White Collection - S. Thompson

YEAR ISSUE	EDITION LIMIT	YEAR RETD.	ISSUE PRICE	*QUOTE U.S.$
1996 Drain House ACL16	4,500	1996	25.00	27-40
1996 Moses Bulkeley House ACL14	4,500	1996	25.00	32-43
1996 Paul House ACL17	4,500	1996	25.00	27-43
1996 Penn House ACL15	4,500	1996	25.00	35-40

Atlanta - S. Thompson

YEAR ISSUE	EDITION LIMIT	YEAR RETD.	ISSUE PRICE	*QUOTE U.S.$
1995 Fox Theatre ATL06	Retrd.	1998	19.00	22-35
1995 Fox Theatre, A/P ATL06	Retrd.	1995	24.00	24
1995 Hammond's House ATL05	Retrd.	1997	18.00	19-26
1995 Hammond's House, A/P ATL05	Retrd.	1995	24.00	24
1996 Margaret Mitchell House ATL07	Retrd.	1996	19.00	21-25
1996 Margaret Mitchell House, AP ATL07	89	1996	24.00	35
1995 Swan House ATL03	Retrd.	1998	18.00	22-37
1995 Swan House, A/P ATL03	Retrd.	1995	24.00	25
1995 Tullie Smith House ATL01	Retrd.	1997	17.00	18-35
1995 Tullie Smith House, A/P ATL01	Retrd.	1995	24.00	24
1995 Victorian Playhouse ATL02	Retrd.	1997	17.00	18-35
1995 Victorian Playhouse, A/P ATL02	Retrd.	1995	24.00	24
1995 Wren's Nest ATL04	Retrd.	1998	19.00	22-35
1995 Wren's Nest, A/P ATL04	Retrd.	1995	24.00	24

Charleston - S. Thompson

YEAR ISSUE	EDITION LIMIT	YEAR RETD.	ISSUE PRICE	*QUOTE U.S.$
1991 #2 Meeting Street CHS06	Retrd.	1994	15.00	18-25
1994 #2 Meeting Street (renovated) CHS06II	Retrd.	1997	16.00	31-50
1999 #7 Meeting Street CHS70	Open		24.00	24
1990 90 Church St. CHS17	Retrd.	1993	12.00	45-85
1993 Ashe House CHS51	Retrd.	1994	16.00	26-50
1994 Ashe House (renovated) CHS51II	Retrd.	1997	16.00	45
1991 Beth Elohim Temple CHS20	Retrd.	1993	15.00	30-35
1993 The Citadel CHS22	Retrd.	1994	16.00	31-45
1994 The Citadel (renovated) CHS22II	Retrd.	1997	16.00	40-45
1993 City Hall CHS21	Retrd.	1993	15.00	94
1993 City Hall (No banner) CHS21	Retrd.	1993	15.00	200-450
1993 City Hall (without Spoleto colors) CHS21	Retrd.	1993	15.00	275
1991 City Market (closed gates) CHS07	Retrd.	1991	15.00	100
1991 City Market (open gates) CHS07	Retrd.	1994	15.00	35-50
1994 City Market (renovated) CHS07II	Retrd.	1998	15.00	20-25
1993 College of Charleston CHS40	Retrd.	1994	16.00	30-47
1993 College of Charleston, AP CHS40	Retrd.	1993	20.00	30-69
1994 College of Charleston (renovated) CHS40II	Retrd.	1996	16.00	85
1992 Dock Street Theater (chimney) CHS08	Retrd.	1993	15.00	30-50
1991 Dock Street Theater (no chimney) CHS08	Retrd.	1992	15.00	58-60
1991 Edmonston-Alston CHS04	Retrd.	1994	15.00	31-50
1994 Edmonston-Alston (renovated) CHS04II	Retrd.	1995	16.00	50
1990 Exchange Building CHS15	Retrd.	1994	15.00	40
1990 Heyward-Washington House CHS02	Retrd.	1993	15.00	35-40
1993 John Rutledge House Inn CHS50	Retrd.	1994	16.00	30-35
1994 John Rutledge House Inn (renovated) CHS50II	Retrd.	1997	16.00	45
1991 Magnolia Plantation House (beige curtains) CHS03	Retrd.	1994	16.00	45-50
1991 Magnolia Plantation House (white curtains) CHS03	Retrd.	1994	16.00	26-35
1994 Magnolia Plantation House (renovated) CHS03II	Retrd.	1996	16.00	26-50
1990 Manigault House CHS01	Retrd.	1993	15.00	40-57
1990 Middleton Plantation CHS19	Retrd.	1991	9.00	225-260
1999 Open Air City Market CHS69	Open		24.00	24
1990 Pink House CHS18	Retrd.	1993	12.00	35-40
1990 Powder Magazine CHS16	Retrd.	1991	9.00	300-344
1993 Single Side Porch CHS30	Retrd.	1994	16.00	27-35
1993 Single Side Porch, AP CHS30	Retrd.	1993	20.00	20-45
1994 Single Side Porch (renovated) CHS30II	Retrd.	1997	16.00	30-35
1990 St. Michael's Church CHS14	Retrd.	1994	15.00	33-40
1991 St. Philip's Church CHS05	Retrd.	1994	15.00	32-37
1994 St. Philip's Church (renovated) CHS05II	Retrd.	1996	15.00	55-60
1991 St. Phillip's Church (misspelling Phillips) CHS05	Retrd.	1991	15.00	90

Charleston Battery - S. Thompson

YEAR ISSUE	EDITION LIMIT	YEAR RETD.	ISSUE PRICE	*QUOTE U.S.$
1996 22 South Battery CHB01	Open		19.00	21
1996 22 South Battery, AP CHB01	109	1996	24.00	35
1996 24 South Battery CHB02	Open		19.00	21
1996 24 South Battery, AP CHB02	99	1996	24.00	35
1996 26 South Battery CHB03	Open		19.00	21
1996 26 South Battery, AP CHB03	74	1996	24.00	35
1996 28 South Battery CHB04	Open		19.00	21
1996 28 South Battery, AP CHB04	74	1996	24.00	35
1998 30 South Battery CHB05	Open		21.00	21
1998 30 South Battery, AP CHB05	275		25.00	25

Charleston Gold Seal - S. Thompson

YEAR ISSUE	EDITION LIMIT	YEAR RETD.	ISSUE PRICE	*QUOTE U.S.$
1988 90 Church St. CHS17	Retrd.	1990	9.00	40
1988 CHS31 Rainbow Row-rust	Retrd.	1990	9.00	30-35
1988 CHS32 Rainbow Row-tan	Retrd.	1990	9.00	30-35
1988 CHS33 Rainbow Row-cream	Retrd.	1990	9.00	30-35
1988 CHS34 Rainbow Row-green	Retrd.	1990	9.00	30-35
1988 CHS35 Rainbow Row-lavender	Retrd.	1990	9.00	30-35
1988 CHS36 Rainbow Row-pink	Retrd.	1990	9.00	30-35
1988 CHS37 Rainbow Row-blue	Retrd.	1990	9.00	30-35
1988 CHS38 Rainbow Row-lt. yellow	Retrd.	1990	9.00	30-35
1988 CHS39 Rainbow Row-lt. pink	Retrd.	1990	9.00	30-35
1988 Exchange Building CHS15	Retrd.	1990	9.00	35
1988 Middleton Plantation CHS19	Retrd.	1990	9.00	222
1988 Pink House CHS18	Retrd.	1990	9.00	29-35
1988 Powder Magazine CHS16	Retrd.	1990	9.00	188
1988 St. Michael's Church CHS14	Retrd.	1990	9.00	60

Charleston II - S. Thompson

YEAR ISSUE	EDITION LIMIT	YEAR RETD.	ISSUE PRICE	*QUOTE U.S.$
1995 Boone Hall Plantation CHS56	Retrd.	1999	18.00	22-25
1995 Boone Hall Plantation, AP CHS56	Retrd.	1995	24.00	35-46
1998 Dr. Vincent LeSigneur House CHS68	Open		22.00	22
1998 Dr. Vincent LeSigneur House, AP CHS68	130	1998	43.00	45
1994 Drayton House CHS52	Retrd.	1999	18.00	22-30
1994 Drayton House, AP CHS52	Retrd.	1994	24.00	44-58
1996 Huguenot Church CHS58	Retrd.	1999	19.00	21-25
1996 Huguenot Church, AP CHS58	95	1996	24.00	20-44
1996 Magnolia Garden CHS57	Open		19.00	21
1996 Magnolia Garden, A/P CHS57	Retrd.	1996	24.00	24-35
1998 Middleton Plantation II CHS67	Retrd.	1999	24.00	24-27
1995 O'Donnell's Folly CHS55	Retrd.	1999	18.00	22-24
1995 O'Donnell's Folly, AP CHS55	Retrd.	1995	24.00	46-50
1996 Sotille CHS59	Retrd.	1999	19.00	22
1996 Sotille, AP CHS59	98	1996	24.00	20-45

Charleston III - S. Thompson

YEAR ISSUE	EDITION LIMIT	YEAR RETD.	ISSUE PRICE	*QUOTE U.S.$
1997 South of Broad, Cream CHS65	Retrd.	1999	18.00	19-21
1997 South of Broad, Cream, AP CHS65	197	1998	24.00	35-46
1997 South of Broad, Dark Pink CHS64	Retrd.	1999	18.00	19-21
1997 South of Broad, Dark Pink, AP CHS64	214	1998	24.00	35-46
1997 South of Broad, Lavender CHS63	Retrd.	1999	18.00	19-21
1997 South of Broad, Lavender, AP CHS63	205	1998	24.00	35-46
1997 South of Broad, Light Pink CHS66	Retrd.	1999	18.00	19-21
1997 South of Broad, Light Pink, AP CHS66	207	1998	24.00	35-46
1997 South of Broad, Tan CHS62	Retrd.	1999	18.00	19-21
1997 South of Broad, Tan, AP CHS62	198	1998	24.00	35-46

Charleston Rainbow Row '97 - S. Thompson

YEAR ISSUE	EDITION LIMIT	YEAR RETD.	ISSUE PRICE	*QUOTE U.S.$
1997 89 East Bay CRR05	Open		18.00	18
1997 91 East Bay CRR06	Open		18.00	18
1997 93 East Bay CRR07	Open		18.00	18
1997 95 East Bay CRR08	Open		18.00	18
1997 97 East Bay CRR09	Open		18.00	18
1997 99-101 East Bay CRR10	Open		18.00	18
1997 103 East Bay CRR11	Open		18.00	18
1997 105 East Bay CRR12	Open		18.00	18
1997 107 East Bay CRR13	Open		18.00	18

Charleston Rainbow Row - S. Thompson

YEAR ISSUE	EDITION LIMIT	YEAR RETD.	ISSUE PRICE	*QUOTE U.S.$
1990 CHS31 Rainbow Row-rust	Retrd.	1993	9.00	35-60
1990 CHS32 Rainbow Row-cream	Retrd.	1993	9.00	35-69
1990 CHS33 Rainbow Row-tan	Retrd.	1993	9.00	38-40
1990 CHS34 Rainbow Row-green	Retrd.	1993	9.00	35-40
1990 CHS35 Rainbow Row-lavender	Retrd.	1993	9.00	35-43
1990 CHS36 Rainbow Row-pink	Retrd.	1993	9.00	40-52
1990 CHS37 Rainbow Row-blue	Retrd.	1993	9.00	38-40
1990 CHS38 Rainbow Row-lt. yellow	Retrd.	1993	9.00	40
1990 CHS39 Rainbow Row-lt. pink	Retrd.	1993	9.00	33-42
1993 CHS41 Rainbow Row-aurora	Retrd.	1994	13.00	18-30
1994 CHS41II Rainbow Row-aurora (renovated)	Retrd.	1997	13.00	30
1993 CHS42 Rainbow Row-off-white	Retrd.	1994	13.00	18-30
1994 CHS42II Rainbow Row-off-white (renovated)	Retrd.	1997	13.00	30
1993 CHS43 Rainbow Row-cream	Retrd.	1994	13.00	18-30
1994 CHS43II Rainbow Row-cream (renovated)	Retrd.	1997	13.00	30
1993 CHS44 Rainbow Row-green	Retrd.	1994	13.00	18-26
1994 CHS44II Rainbow Row-green (renovated)	Retrd.	1997	13.00	30
1993 CHS45 Rainbow Row-lavender	Retrd.	1994	13.00	18-30
1994 CHS45II Rainbow Row-lavender (renovated)	Retrd.	1997	13.00	30
1993 CHS46 Rainbow Row-pink	Retrd.	1994	13.00	18-30
1994 CHS46II Rainbow Row-pink (renovated)	Retrd.	1997	13.00	30
1993 CHS47 Rainbow Row-blue	Retrd.	1994	13.00	18-30
1994 CHS47II Rainbow Row-blue (renovated)	Retrd.	1997	13.00	30
1993 CHS48 Rainbow Row-yellow	Retrd.	1994	13.00	18-30
1994 CHS48 Rainbow Row-yellow (renovated)	Retrd.	1997	13.00	30
1993 CHS49 Rainbow Row-gray	Retrd.	1994	13.00	18-21
1994 CHS49II Rainbow Row-gray (renovated)	Retrd.	1997	13.00	30
1993 Rainbow Row Sign	Retrd.	N/A	12.50	25-40

Churches of America - S. Thompson

YEAR ISSUE	EDITION LIMIT	YEAR RETD.	ISSUE PRICE	*QUOTE U.S.$
1999 Old Church on the Hill COA06	Retrd.	2000	23.00	23

Colored Metal Accessories - S. Thompson

YEAR ISSUE	EDITION LIMIT	YEAR RETD.	ISSUE PRICE	*QUOTE U.S.$
1997 Burma Shave Sign: Past...Schoolhouse, set/6 CMA01	Retrd.	1997	17.00	19
1997 Burma Shave Sign: Don't Lose Your Head, set/6 CMA02	Retrd.	1997	17.00	19

YEAR ISSUE	EDITION LIMIT	YEAR RETD.	ISSUE PRICE	*QUOTE U.S.$
1997 Daimler 1910 Car CMA03	Retrd.	1997	18.00	20

Dicken's Village - S. Thompson

YEAR ISSUE	EDITION LIMIT	YEAR RETD.	ISSUE PRICE	*QUOTE U.S.$
1991 Butcher Shop XMS03	Retrd.	1993	15.00	35-40
1991 Evergreen Tree XMS08	Retrd.	1993	11.00	40-50
1991 Gazebo & Carolers XMS06	Retrd.	1993	12.00	35-50
1991 Scrooge & Marley's Shop XMS01	Retrd.	1993	15.00	35-50
1991 Scrooge's Home XMS05	Retrd.	1993	15.00	35-40
1991 Toy Shoppe XMS04	Retrd.	1993	15.00	35-40
1991 Victorian Apartment Building XMS02	Retrd.	1993	15.00	40
1992 Victorian Church XMS09	Retrd.	1993	15.00	100-175
1991 Victorian Skaters XMS07	Retrd.	1993	12.00	30-45
1992 Set of 9	Retrd.	1993	125.00	190-282

Exclusive Designs - S. Thompson

YEAR ISSUE	EDITION LIMIT	YEAR RETD.	ISSUE PRICE	*QUOTE U.S.$
1998 Drayton Hall Privy (Drayton Hall) EXC15	400	1998	17.00	34
1998 Drayton River Front (Drayton Hall) EXC14	300	1998	29.00	44-58
1999 Alladin's Castle (Disney) EXC26	Open		42.00	42
1999 Beauty and the Beast's Castle (Disney) EXC23	Open		42.00	42
1999 Cinderella's Castle (Disney) EXC22	Open		42.00	42
1999 The Little Mermaid's Castle (Disney) EXC25	Open		42.00	42
1999 Sleeping Beauty's Castle (Disney) EXC27	Open		42.00	42
1999 Snow White's Castle (Disney) EXC24	Open		42.00	42
1999 Castles w/certificate, set/6 (Disney)	750		255.00	255
1997 Donald's House (Disney) EXC03	Retrd.	1997	30.00	50
1997 Goofy's House (Disney) EXC02	Retrd.	1997	30.00	30
1997 Mickey's House (Disney) EXC04	Closed	1997	30.00	36-52
1997 Minnie's House (Disney) EXC05	Closed	1997	30.00	30-36
1997 Set of Four Houses w/certificate (Disney)	500	1997	120.00	N/A

Famous Homes of America - S. Thompson

YEAR ISSUE	EDITION LIMIT	YEAR RETD.	ISSUE PRICE	*QUOTE U.S.$
1998 Biltmore FHA03	Open		27.00	27
1998 Biltmore, AP FHA03	130	1998	41.00	50
1998 Monticello FHA01	Open		24.00	24
1998 Monticello, AP FHA01	130	1998	45.00	45
1998 Orchard House FHA02	Retrd.	1999	20.00	21
1998 Orchard House, AP FHA02	130	1998	48.00	48

Food For Thought - S. Thompson

YEAR ISSUE	EDITION LIMIT	YEAR RETD.	ISSUE PRICE	*QUOTE U.S.$
1999 Doumar's FTO01	Retrd.	2000	23.00	23
1999 Springer's Homemade Ice Cream, NJ (no custom logo) C0053	Retrd.	1999	23.00	23

Galveston - S. Thompson

YEAR ISSUE	EDITION LIMIT	YEAR RETD.	ISSUE PRICE	*QUOTE U.S.$
1995 Beissner House GLV04	Retrd.	1998	18.00	20-35
1995 Beissner House, A/P GLV04	Retrd.	1995	24.00	24-35
1995 Dancing Pavillion GLV03	Retrd.	1998	18.00	20-35
1995 Dancing Pavillion, A/P GLV03	Retrd.	1995	24.00	24
1995 Frenkel House GLV01	Retrd.	1998	18.00	20-35
1995 Frenkel House, A/P GLV01	Retrd.	1995	24.00	24
1995 Reymershoffer House GLV02	Retrd.	1998	18.00	20-35
1995 Reymershoffer House, A/P GLV02	Retrd.	1995	24.00	35

George Barber - S. Thompson

YEAR ISSUE	EDITION LIMIT	YEAR RETD.	ISSUE PRICE	*QUOTE U.S.$
1996 Newton House GFB03	Retrd.	1999	19.00	20-25
1996 Newton House, AP GFB03	71	1996	24.00	32
1997 Nunan House GFB05	Retrd.	1999	22.00	25
1996 Phillippi House GFB02	Retrd.	1999	19.00	20-25
1996 Phillippi House, AP GFB02	46	1996	24.00	32
1996 Pine Crest GFB04	Retrd.	1999	19.00	25
1996 Pine Crest, AP GFB04	95	1996	24.00	32
1996 Renaissance GFB01	Retrd.	1999	19.00	23-25
1996 Renaissance, AP GFB01	67	1996	24.00	33

Ghost House Series - S. Thompson

YEAR ISSUE	EDITION LIMIT	YEAR RETD.	ISSUE PRICE	*QUOTE U.S.$
1996 31 Legare St. GHO06	Retrd.	1999	19.00	23-25
1997 Catfish Plantation GHO07	Retrd.	1999	22.00	23-25
1997 Catfish Plantation, A/P GHO07	Retrd.	1997	28.00	28
1995 Gaffos House GHO04	Retrd.	1998	19.00	21-45
1995 Gaffos House, A/P GHO04	Retrd.	1995	24.00	24
1997 Hampton Lillbridge Home GHO08	Retrd.	1999	22.00	23
1997 Hampton Lillbridge Home, A/P GHO08	Retrd.	1997	24.00	24
1994 Inside-Outside House GHO01	Retrd.	1996	18.00	19-40
1994 Inside-Outside House, AP GHO01	Retrd.	1994	20.00	30-40
1996 Kings Tavern GHO05	Retrd.	1999	19.00	23
1996 Kings Tavern, AP GHO05	102	1996	24.00	28-46
1994 Pirates' House GHO02	Retrd.	1996	18.00	52-57
1994 Pirates' House, AP GHO02	Retrd.	1994	20.00	75-125
1995 Red Castle GHO03	Retrd.	1998	19.00	21-45
1995 Red Castle, A/P GHO03	Retrd.	1995	24.00	24

Gone with the Wind - S. Thompson

YEAR ISSUE	EDITION LIMIT	YEAR RETD.	ISSUE PRICE	*QUOTE U.S.$
1995 Aunt Pittypat's GWW03	Retrd.	1996	24.00	43-63
1995 Aunt Pittypat's, AP GWW03	Retrd.	1995	30.00	58-75
1998 Butler's Atlanta Mansion GWW09	Retrd.	1998	27.00	28
1998 Butler's Atlanta Mansion, AP GWW09	130	1998	48.00	48
1995 General Store GWW04	Retrd.	1996	24.00	25-63
1995 General Store, AP GWW04	Retrd.	1995	30.00	50-58
1998 Home of Ashley Wilkes GWW08	Retrd.	1998	29.00	35
1998 Home of Ashley Wilkes, AP GWW08	130	1998	50.00	50
1998 Honeymoon Embrace Poster GWW10	Retrd.	1998	20.00	23
1998 Honeymoon Embrace Poster, AP GWW10	130	1998	41.00	41
1995 Loew's Grand GWW05	Retrd.	1995	24.00	75-125
1995 Loew's Grand, AP GWW05	Retrd.	1995	30.00	75-150
1999 Scarlett GWW13	Retrd.	1999	14.00	15
1998 Scarlett's Passion, Tara GWW07	Retrd.	1998	29.00	30-35
1998 Scarlett's Passion, Tara, AP GWW07	130	1998	50.00	50

*Quotes have been rounded up to nearest dollar

YEAR ISSUE	EDITION LIMIT	YEAR RETD.	ISSUE PRICE	*QUOTE U.S.$
1996 Silhouette GWW06	Retrd.	1996	16.00	35
1995 Tara GWW01	Retrd.	1996	24.00	35-50
1995 Tara, AP GWW01	Retrd.	1995	30.00	50-60
1999 Tara Revisited GWW11	Retrd.	1999	29.00	30
1999 Twelve Oaks Revisited GWW12	Retrd.	1999	29.00	30
1995 Twelve Oaks GWW02	Retrd.	1996	24.00	35-45
1995 Twelve Oaks, AP GWW02	Retrd.	1995	30.00	40-55
1995 Set of 5, AP	Retrd.	1995	150.00	288
1995 Set of 6 GWW01-GWW06	Retrd.	1995	160.00	230

Heartsville Christmas - S. Thompson

YEAR ISSUE	EDITION LIMIT	YEAR RETD.	ISSUE PRICE	*QUOTE U.S.$
1999 Heartsville Skaters TSN10	Retrd.	2000	14.00	14
1999 Heartsville Victorian TSN07	Retrd.	2000	23.00	23

Hook Houses - S. Thompson

YEAR ISSUE	EDITION LIMIT	YEAR RETD.	ISSUE PRICE	*QUOTE U.S.$
1993 #2 Meeting St. HHH14	Retrd.	N/A	25.00	18-32
XX 90 Church St. CHS26	Retrd.	N/A	21.00	85
1993 Amish House HHH19	Retrd.	N/A	25.00	43-63
1993 Anne Peacock House HHH15	Retrd.	N/A	25.00	43-63
1993 Ashe House HHH17	Retrd.	N/A	25.00	18-32
1993 Atlanta Queen Anne HHH16	Retrd.	N/A	25.00	43-63
1993 Cape May Linda Lee HHH18	Retrd.	N/A	25.00	17-33
1993 Cape May Pink House HHH11	Retrd.	N/A	25.00	17-34
1993 Edmonston-Alston HHH13	Retrd.	N/A	25.00	33
1994 Ford Motor Company HHH20	Retrd.	N/A	25.00	17-33
1994 Gingerbread House HHH22	Retrd.	N/A	25.00	43-63
1994 Thomas Point Light HHH21	Retrd.	N/A	25.00	17-38
1993 Victorian Blue Rose HHH12	Retrd.	1993	24.00	17-25

Hook Houses-History For Keeps - S. Thompson

YEAR ISSUE	EDITION LIMIT	YEAR RETD.	ISSUE PRICE	*QUOTE U.S.$
1996 Chestnut House HFK04	Retrd.	1997	28.00	46
1996 Drayton House HFK01	Retrd.	1997	28.00	46
1996 E.B. Hall House HFK03	Retrd.	1997	28.00	42
1996 Eclectic Blue HFK06	Retrd.	1997	28.00	42
1996 Southernmost House HFK05	Retrd.	1997	28.00	46
1996 Victoria HFK02	Retrd.	1997	28.00	46

Inventor Series - S. Thompson

YEAR ISSUE	EDITION LIMIT	YEAR RETD.	ISSUE PRICE	*QUOTE U.S.$
1993 Ford Motor Company (green) INV01	Retrd.	1993	17.00	18-50
1993 Ford Motor Company (grey) INV01	Retrd.	1994	17.00	35-50
1993 Ford Motor Company, AP INV01	Retrd.	1993	20.00	20-45
1993 Menlo Park Laboratory (cream) INV02	Retrd.	1993	16.00	17-50
1993 Menlo Park Laboratory (grey) INV02	Retrd.	1994	16.00	40
1993 Menlo Park Laboratory, AP INV02	Retrd.	1993	20.00	35-70
1993 Noah Webster House INV03	Retrd.	1994	15.00	16-50
1993 Noah Webster House, AP INV03	Retrd.	1993	20.00	40-70
1993 Wright Cycle Shop INV04	Retrd.	1994	17.00	18-35
1993 Wright Cycle Shop, AP INV04	Retrd.	1993	20.00	14-27

Jazzy New Orleans Series - S. Thompson

YEAR ISSUE	EDITION LIMIT	YEAR RETD.	ISSUE PRICE	*QUOTE U.S.$
1994 Beauregard-Keys House JNO04	Retrd.	1996	18.00	26-63
1994 Beauregard-Keys House, AP JNO04	Retrd.	1994	20.00	45-65
1994 Gallier House JNO02	Retrd.	1998	18.00	30-36
1994 Gallier House, AP JNO02	Retrd.	1994	20.00	17-22
1994 La Branche Building JNO01	Retrd.	1998	18.00	30-36
1994 La Branche Building, AP JNO01	Retrd.	1994	20.00	17-22
1994 LePretre House JNO03	Retrd.	1998	18.00	22-36
1994 LePretre House, AP JNO03	Retrd.	1994	20.00	50

Key West - S. Thompson

YEAR ISSUE	EDITION LIMIT	YEAR RETD.	ISSUE PRICE	*QUOTE U.S.$
1995 Artist House KEY06	Retrd.	1999	19.00	23
1995 Artist House, AP KEY06	Retrd.	1995	24.00	46
1995 Eyebrow House KEY01	Retrd.	1998	18.00	20-23
1995 Eyebrow House, AP KEY01	Retrd.	1995	24.00	36
1995 Hemingway House KEY07	Retrd.	1999	19.00	23
1995 Hemingway House, AP KEY07	Retrd.	1995	24.00	35-46
1995 Illingsworth Gingerbread House KEY05	Retrd.	1999	19.00	23
1995 Illingsworth Gingerbread House, AP KEY05	Retrd.	1995	24.00	46
1995 Shotgun House KEY03	Retrd.	1997	17.00	30-46
1995 Shotgun House, AP KEY03	Retrd.	1995	24.00	24-75
1995 Shotgun Sister KEY04	Retrd.	1997	17.00	30-45
1995 Shotgun Sister, AP KEY04	Retrd.	1995	24.00	24-75
1995 Southernmost House KEY02	Retrd.	1999	19.00	22-28
1995 Southernmost House, AP KEY02	Retrd.	1995	24.00	46
1996 Southernmost Point KEY08	Retrd.	1999	12.00	14-17

Ladies By The Sea - S. Thompson

YEAR ISSUE	EDITION LIMIT	YEAR RETD.	ISSUE PRICE	*QUOTE U.S.$
1996 Abbey II LBS01	Open		19.00	22
1996 Abbey II, AP LBS01	93	1996	24.00	35
1998 Cape S Cape LBS06	Retrd.	1999	22.00	24
1998 Cape S Cape, AP LBS06	250	1998	26.00	26
1996 Centennial Cottage LBS02	Retrd.	1999	19.00	24
1996 Centennial Cottage, AP LBS02	94	1996	24.00	35
1996 Hall Cottage LBS04	Retrd.	1999	19.00	24
1996 Hall Cottage, AP LBS04	108	1996	24.00	35
1996 Heart Blossom LBS03	Retrd.	1999	19.00	24
1996 Heart Blossom, AP LBS03	107	1996	24.00	24
1998 Ocean Pathway Princess LBS05	Retrd.	1999	22.00	22
1998 Ocean Pathway Princess, AP LBS05	275	1998	26.00	35

Lighthouse Series - S. Thompson

YEAR ISSUE	EDITION LIMIT	YEAR RETD.	ISSUE PRICE	*QUOTE U.S.$
1991 Anastasia Lighthouse (burgundy) FL103	Retrd.	1991	15.00	22-32
1991 Anastasia Lighthouse (red) FL103	Retrd.	1994	15.00	75-100
1993 Assateague Island Light LTS07	Retrd.	1997	17.00	30-37
1994 Assateague Island Light, AP LTS07	Retrd.	1994	20.00	44
1995 Cape Hatteras Light LTS09	Retrd.	1997	17.00	26-35
1995 Cape Hatteras Light, AP LTS09	Retrd.	1995	24.00	60
1991 Cape Hatteras Lighthouse NC103	Retrd.	1994	15.00	20-50
1993 Charleston Light LTS01	Retrd.	1995	15.00	32
1994 Charleston Light (renovated) LTS01	Retrd.	1995	15.00	60
1993 New London Ledge Light LTS08	Retrd.	1996	17.00	20-35
1994 New London Ledge Light, AP LTS08	Retrd.	1994	20.00	55
1993 Round Island Light LTS06	Retrd.	1997	17.00	18-32
1994 Round Island Light, AP LTS06	Retrd.	1994	20.00	65
1990 Stage Harbor Lighthouse NEW06	Retrd.	1993	15.00	250
1993 Thomas Point Light LTS05	Retrd.	1997	17.00	20-29
1994 Thomas Point Light, AP LTS05	Retrd.	1994	20.00	55-65
1990 Tybee Lighthouse SAV07	Retrd.	1994	15.00	110-150

Limited Pieces - S. Thompson

YEAR ISSUE	EDITION LIMIT	YEAR RETD.	ISSUE PRICE	*QUOTE U.S.$
1991 Bridgetown Library NJ102	Retrd.	N/A	16.00	75-85
1993 Comly-Rich House XXX01	Retrd.	N/A	12.00	77-125
1993 Comley-Rich House (misspelling) XXX01	Retrd.	N/A	12.00	25-77
1991 Delphos City Hall OH101	Retrd.	N/A	15.00	250-265
1991 Historic Burlington County Clubhouse NJ101	Retrd.	N/A	16.00	75-125
1991 Mark Twain Boyhood Home MO101	Retrd.	N/A	15.00	395
1990 Newton County Court House GA101	Retrd.	N/A	16.00	65-100

Lone Star State - S. Thompson

YEAR ISSUE	EDITION LIMIT	YEAR RETD.	ISSUE PRICE	*QUOTE U.S.$
1998 Ashton Villa LSS02	Retrd.	1999	22.00	23
1998 Ashton Villa, AP LSS02	250	1998	26.00	35
1998 Blue Bonnets LSS03	Open		13.00	13
1998 Redington House LSS01	Retrd.	1999	22.00	25
1998 Redington House, AP LSS01	250	1998	26.00	35

Louisiana - S. Thompson

YEAR ISSUE	EDITION LIMIT	YEAR RETD.	ISSUE PRICE	*QUOTE U.S.$
1998 Commander's Palace LOU02	Open		22.00	22
1998 Commander's Palace, AP LOU02	275	1998	26.00	35
1998 Jackson Square LOU01	Open		22.00	22
1998 Jackson Square, AP LOU01	275	1998	26.00	35

Mackinac - S. Thompson

YEAR ISSUE	EDITION LIMIT	YEAR RETD.	ISSUE PRICE	*QUOTE U.S.$
1996 Amberg Cottage MAK01	Open		19.00	22
1996 Amberg Cottage, AP MAK01	102	1996	24.00	26-30
1996 Anne Cottage MAK02	Retrd.	1999	19.00	25-32
1996 Anne Cottage, AP MAK02	95	1996	24.00	28-46
1996 Grand Hotel (3 pc. set) MAK05	Retrd.	1998	57.00	70-80
1996 Grand Hotel (3 pc. set), AP MAK05	95	1996	72.00	72
1996 Rearick Cottage MAK03	Open		19.00	22
1996 Rearick Cottage, AP MAK03	103	1996	24.00	28-46
1996 Windermere Hotel MAK04	Open		19.00	22
1996 Windermere Hotel, AP MAK04	105	1996	24.00	28-46

Martha's Vineyard - S. Thompson

YEAR ISSUE	EDITION LIMIT	YEAR RETD.	ISSUE PRICE	*QUOTE U.S.$
1993 Alice's Wonderland MAR08	Retrd.	1994	16.00	19-25
1993 Alice's Wonderland, AP MAR08	Retrd.	1993	20.00	20-35
1994 Alice's Wonderland (renovated) MAR08II	Retrd.	1998	16.00	20-24
1995 Blue Cottage MAR13	Retrd.	1999	17.00	22
1995 Blue Cottage, AP MAR13	Retrd.	1995	24.00	24-45
1997 Butterfly Cottage MAR14	Open		20.00	20
1993 Campground Cottage MAR07	Retrd.	1995	16.00	35-45
1993 Campground Cottage, AP MAR07	Retrd.	1993	20.00	35-45
1994 Campground Cottage (renovated) MAR07II	Retrd.	1995	16.00	18-35
1993 Gingerbread Cottage-grey MAR09	Retrd.	1996	16.00	35-40
1993 Gingerbread Cottage-grey AP MAR09	Retrd.	1993	20.00	20-40
1994 Gingerbread Cottage-grey (renovated) MAR09II	Retrd.	1996	16.00	25-35
1998 Summer Love MAR16	Open		21.00	21
1998 Summer Love, AP MAR16	275	1998	25.00	25
1995 Trails End MAR11	Retrd.	1998	17.00	21-35
1995 Trails End, AP MAR11	Retrd.	1995	24.00	24-46
1998 Tranquility MAR15	Open		21.00	21
1998 Tranquility, AP MAR15	275	1998	25.00	25
1995 White Cottage MAR12	Open		17.00	20
1995 White Cottage, AP MAR12	Retrd.	1995	24.00	35
1993 Wood Valentine MAR10	Retrd.	1994	16.00	19-25
1993 Wood Valentine, AP MAR10	Retrd.	1993	20.00	20-46
1994 Wood Valentine (renovated) MAR10II	Retrd.	1998	16.00	20-25

Nantucket - S. Thompson

YEAR ISSUE	EDITION LIMIT	YEAR RETD.	ISSUE PRICE	*QUOTE U.S.$
1998 Brant Point Lighthouse NTK01	Open		22.00	22
1998 Brant Point Lighthouse, AP NTK01	265	1998	26.00	35
1998 Pedal Shop NTK03	Open		13.00	13
1998 Swain Cottage NTK02	Open		22.00	22
1998 Swain Cottage, AP NTK02	265	1998	26.00	35

National Park Treasures - S. Thompson

YEAR ISSUE	EDITION LIMIT	YEAR RETD.	ISSUE PRICE	*QUOTE U.S.$
1998 Independence Hall NPT04	Open		21.00	21
1998 Independence Hall, AP NPT04	130	1998	42.00	45
1998 Liberty Bell NPT05	Open		15.00	15
1998 Liberty Bell, AP NPT05	130	1998	36.00	40
1998 Mount Rushmore National Memorial NPT03	Open		20.00	20
1998 Mount Rushmore National Memorial, AP NPT03	130	1998	41.00	45
1998 Statue of Liberty NPT02	Open		20.00	20
1998 Statue of Liberty, AP NPT02	130	1998	41.00	45
1999 Vietnam Veteran's Memorial NPT06	Open		23.00	23
1998 White House NPT01	Open		26.00	26
1998 White House, AP NPT01	130	1998	47.00	50

National Trust Houses - S. Thompson

YEAR ISSUE	EDITION LIMIT	YEAR RETD.	ISSUE PRICE	*QUOTE U.S.$
1997 Cliveden NHP03	Retrd.	1999	24.00	26
1997 Cliveden, AP NHP03	240	1997	30.00	35
1998 Decatur House NHP04	Retrd.	1999	24.00	26
1998 Decatur House, AP NHP04	130	1998	44.00	44
1997 Drayton Hall NHP01	Open		24.00	24
1997 Drayton Hall, AP NHP01	266	1997	30.00	35
1997 Montpelier NHP02	Retrd.	1999	24.00	26
1997 Montpelier, AP NHP02	200	1997	30.00	35-42
1998 Oatlands NHP07	Retrd.	1999	24.00	26
1998 Oatlands, AP NHP07	130	1998	44.00	45
1998 Woodlawn Plantation NHP05	Retrd.	1999	24.00	26
1998 Woodlawn Plantation, AP NHP05	130	1998	44.00	35-44
1998 Woodrow Wilson House NHP06	Retrd.	1999	24.00	26
1998 Woodrow Wilson House, AP NHP06	130	1998	44.00	44

New England - S. Thompson

YEAR ISSUE	EDITION LIMIT	YEAR RETD.	ISSUE PRICE	*QUOTE U.S.$
1991 Faneuil Hall NEW09	Retrd.	1993	15.00	38-50
1990 Longfellow's House NEW01	Retrd.	1993	15.00	28-45
1990 Malden Mass. Victorian Inn NEW05	Retrd.	1992	10.00	63-94
1990 Martha's Vineyard Cottage -blue/mauve MAR06	Retrd.	1993	15.00	60
1990 Martha's Vineyard Cottage -blue/orange MAR05	Retrd.	1993	15.00	30-45
1990 Motif #1 Boathouse NEW02	Retrd.	1993	15.00	50
1990 Old North Church NEW04	Retrd.	1993	15.00	42-45
1990 Paul Revere's Home NEW03	Retrd.	1993	15.00	40-45
1991 President Bush's Home NEW07	Retrd.	1993	15.00	63-75
1991 Wedding Cake House NEW08	Retrd.	1993	15.00	43-63
1991 Set of 10	Retrd.	1993	145.00	385

North Carolina - S. Thompson

YEAR ISSUE	EDITION LIMIT	YEAR RETD.	ISSUE PRICE	*QUOTE U.S.$
1990 Josephus Hall House NC101	Retrd.	1993	15.00	40-45
1990 Presbyterian Bell Tower NC102	Retrd.	1993	15.00	29-32
1991 The Tryon Palace NC104	Retrd.	1993	15.00	36-40

Old-Fashioned Christmas - S. Thompson

YEAR ISSUE	EDITION LIMIT	YEAR RETD.	ISSUE PRICE	*QUOTE U.S.$
1994 Conway Scenic Railroad Station OFC04	Retrd.	1997	18.00	20-30
1994 Conway Scenic Railroad Station, AP OFC04	Retrd.	1994	20.00	28-50
1994 Dwight House OFC02	Retrd.	1996	18.00	22-35
1994 Dwight House, AP OFC02	Retrd.	1994	20.00	50
1994 General Merchandise OFC03	Retrd.	1997	18.00	19-38
1994 General Merchandise, AP OFC03	Retrd.	1994	20.00	28-60
1994 Old First Church OFC01	Retrd.	1997	18.00	23-30
1994 Old First Church, AP OFC01	Retrd.	1994	20.00	29-60
1994 Set of 4 1994 AP	Retrd.	1994	80.00	240
1995 Christmas Inn OFC05	Retrd.	1997	18.00	30-32
1995 Town Square Tree OFC06	Retrd.	1997	18.00	17-21

Painted Ladies I - S. Thompson

YEAR ISSUE	EDITION LIMIT	YEAR RETD.	ISSUE PRICE	*QUOTE U.S.$
1990 The Abbey LAD08	Retrd.	1992	10.00	94-150
1990 Atlanta Queen Anne LAD07	Retrd.	1992	10.00	50-94
1990 Cincinnati Gothic LAD05	Retrd.	1992	10.00	48-113
1990 Colorado Queen Anne LAD04	Retrd.	1992	10.00	50-63
1990 Illinois Queen Anne LAD06	Retrd.	1991	10.00	550-620
1990 San Francisco Italianate-yellow LAD03	Retrd.	1992	10.00	50-94
1990 San Francisco Stick House-blue LAD02	Retrd.	1991	10.00	60-75
1990 San Francisco Stick House-yellow LAD01	Retrd.	1991	10.00	57-70
1990 Painted Ladies I Sign	Retrd.	N/A	12.50	30

Painted Ladies II - S. Thompson

YEAR ISSUE	EDITION LIMIT	YEAR RETD.	ISSUE PRICE	*QUOTE U.S.$
1992 Cape May Gothic LAD13	Retrd.	1994	15.00	30-45
1994 Cape May Gothic (renovated) LAD13II	Retrd.	1995	16.00	31-35
1992 Cape May Victorian Pink House LAD16	Retrd.	1994	15.00	28-63
1994 Cape May Victorian Pink House (renovated) LAD16II	Retrd.	1996	16.00	28-30
1992 The Gingerbread Mansion LAD09	Retrd.	1994	15.00	35-45
1994 The Gingerbread Mansion (renovated) LAD09II	Retrd.	1994	16.00	30-63
1992 Morningstar Inn LAD15	Retrd.	1994	15.00	25-63
1994 Morningstar Inn (renovated) LAD15II	Retrd.	1994	16.00	18-25
1992 Pitkin House LAD10	Retrd.	1994	15.00	25-57
1994 Pitkin House (renovated) LAD10II	Retrd.	1996	16.00	25-30
1992 Queen Anne Townhouse LAD12	Retrd.	1994	15.00	30-63
1994 Queen Anne Townhouse (renovated) LAD12II	Retrd.	1994	16.00	30-35
1992 The Victorian Blue Rose LAD14	Retrd.	1994	15.00	30-45
1994 The Victorian Blue Rose (renovated) LAD14II	Retrd.	1996	16.00	28-63
1992 The Young-Larson House LAD11	Retrd.	1994	15.00	25-45
1994 The Young-Larson House (renovated) LAD11II	Retrd.	1996	16.00	28-63

Painted Ladies III - S. Thompson

YEAR ISSUE	EDITION LIMIT	YEAR RETD.	ISSUE PRICE	*QUOTE U.S.$
1993 Cape May Green Stockton Row LAD20	Retrd.	1994	16.00	28-35
1994 Cape May Green Stockton Row (renovated) LAD20II	Retrd.	1995	16.00	25-35
1993 Cape May Linda Lee LAD17	Retrd.	1994	16.00	30-40
1994 Cape May Linda Lee (renovated) LAD17II	Retrd.	1996	16.00	20-30
1993 Cape May Pink Stockton Row LAD19	Retrd.	1994	16.00	27-39
1994 Cape May Pink Stockton Row (renovated)LAD19II	Retrd.	1998	16.00	18-23
1993 Cape May Tan Stockton Row LAD18	Retrd.	1994	16.00	25-39
1994 Cape May Tan Stockton Row (renovated)LAD18II	Retrd.	1998	16.00	20-23
1996 Cream Stockton LAD22	Retrd.	1998	19.00	25-40
1996 Cream Stockton, AP LAD22	101	1996	24.00	29-50
1995 Steiner Cottage LAD21	Retrd.	1998	17.00	20-25
1995 Steiner Cottage, AP LAD21	Retrd.	1995	24.00	28-40

Panoramic Lights - S. Thompson

YEAR ISSUE	EDITION LIMIT	YEAR RETD.	ISSUE PRICE	*QUOTE U.S.$
1996 Jeffrys Hook Light PLH02	Retrd.	1999	19.00	23
1996 Jeffrys Hook Light, AP PLH02	97	1996	24.00	35
1996 New Canal Light PLH03	Open		19.00	21

*Quotes have been rounded up to nearest dollar

YEAR ISSUE	EDITION LIMIT	YEAR RETD.	ISSUE PRICE	*QUOTE U.S.$
1996 New Canal Light, AP PLH03	104	1996	24.00	24-35
1997 Portland Head Light PLH05	Open		21.00	21
1996 Quoddy Head Light PLH04	Retrd.	1999	19.00	23
1996 Quoddy Head Light, AP PLH04	102	1996	24.00	24-35
1996 Split Rock Light PLH01	Retrd.	1999	19.00	23
1996 Split Rock Light, AP PLH01	105	1996	24.00	35

Philadelphia - S. Thompson

YEAR ISSUE	EDITION LIMIT	YEAR RETD.	ISSUE PRICE	*QUOTE U.S.$
1990 "Besty" Ross House (misspelling) PHI03	Retrd.	1990	15.00	69-94
1990 Betsy Ross House PHI03	Retrd.	1993	15.00	65-80
1990 Carpenter's Hall PHI01	Retrd.	1993	15.00	35-40
1990 Elphreth's Alley PHI05	Retrd.	1993	15.00	42-45
1990 Graff House PHI07	Retrd.	1993	15.00	45-69
1990 Independence Hall PHI04	Retrd.	1993	15.00	90-94
1990 Market St. Post Office PHI02	Retrd.	1993	15.00	38-45
1990 Old City Hall PHI08	Retrd.	1993	15.00	48-57
1990 Old Tavern PHI06	Retrd.	1993	15.00	38-50
1990 Set of 8	Retrd.	1993	120.00	275

Plantations - S. Thompson

YEAR ISSUE	EDITION LIMIT	YEAR RETD.	ISSUE PRICE	*QUOTE U.S.$
1996 Dickey House PLA05	Retrd.	1998	19.00	23-43
1995 Farley PLA04	Retrd.	1996	18.00	22-30
1995 Farley, AP PLA04	Retrd.	1995	24.00	16-28
1995 Longwood PLA02	Retrd.	1998	19.00	22-29
1995 Longwood, AP PLA02	Retrd.	1995	24.00	38-43
1995 Merry Sherwood PLA03	Retrd.	1998	18.00	22-30
1995 Merry Sherwood, AP PLA03	Retrd.	1995	24.00	33-50
1995 San Francisco PLA01	Retrd.	1999	19.00	23-30
1995 San Francisco, AP PLA01	Retrd.	1995	24.00	24-32

San Francisco - S. Thompson

YEAR ISSUE	EDITION LIMIT	YEAR RETD.	ISSUE PRICE	*QUOTE U.S.$
1995 Brandywine SF101	Retrd.	1998	18.00	21-37
1995 Brandywine, AP SF101	Retrd.	1995	24.00	50
1995 Eclectic Blue SF103	Retrd.	1998	19.00	21-38
1995 Eclectic Blue, AP SF103	Retrd.	1995	24.00	50
1995 Edwardian Green SF104	Retrd.	1998	18.00	21-37
1995 Edwardian Green, AP SF104	Retrd.	1995	24.00	50
1995 Queen Rose SF102	Retrd.	1998	19.00	21-38
1995 Queen Rose, AP SF102	Retrd.	1995	24.00	52

San Francisco II/ Postcard Row - S. Thompson

YEAR ISSUE	EDITION LIMIT	YEAR RETD.	ISSUE PRICE	*QUOTE U.S.$
1998 716 Steiner Street SF108	Retrd.	1999	21.00	23
1998 716 Steiner Street, AP SF108	275	1998	25.00	25
1998 718 Steiner Street SF107	Retrd.	1999	21.00	22
1998 718 Steiner Street, AP SF107	275	1998	25.00	25
1998 720 Steiner Street SF106	Retrd.	1999	21.00	22
1998 720 Steiner Street, AP SF106	275	1998	25.00	25
1998 722 Steiner Street SF105	Retrd.	1999	21.00	21
1998 722 Steiner Street, AP SF105	275	1998	25.00	25

Savannah - S. Thompson

YEAR ISSUE	EDITION LIMIT	YEAR RETD.	ISSUE PRICE	*QUOTE U.S.$
1990 Andrew Low Mansion SAV02	Retrd.	1994	15.00	40-57
1996 Asendorf House SAV13	Open		19.00	22
1996 Asendorf House, AP SAV13	100	1996	24.00	32-60
1992 Cathedral of St. John SAV09	Retrd.	1994	16.00	128-138
1994 Cathedral of St. John (renovated) SAV09II	Retrd.	1995	16.00	110-150
1994 Chestnutt House SAV11	Open		18.00	22
1994 Chestnutt House, AP SAV11	Retrd.	1994	24.00	55
1990 Davenport House SAV03	Retrd.	1994	15.00	37-86
1990 Herb House SAV05	Retrd.	1993	15.00	50-75
1990 Juliette Low House (w/logo) SAV04	Retrd.	1994	15.00	22-35
1990 Juliette Low House (w/o logo) SAV04	Retrd.	1990	15.00	100-130
1994 Juliette Low House (renovated) SAV04II	Retrd.	1998	15.00	23-30
1998 King Tisdale SAV14	Open		22.00	22
1995 Mercer House SAV12	Retrd.	1998	18.00	22-45
1995 Mercer House, AP SAV12	Retrd.	1995	24.00	50-225
1990 Mikve Israel Temple SAV06	Retrd.	1994	15.00	50-86
1990 Olde Pink House SAV01	Retrd.	1994	15.00	35-50
1994 Olde Pink House (renovated) SAV01II	Retrd.	1996	15.00	40-195
1993 Owens Thomas House SAV10	Retrd.	1994	16.00	29-40
1993 Owens Thomas House, AP SAV10	Retrd.	1993	20.00	27-140
1994 Owens Thomas House (renovated) SAV10II	Retrd.	1996	16.00	55-80
1990 Savannah Gingerbread House I SAV08	Retrd.	1990	15.00	210-238
1990 Savannah Gingerbread House II SAV08	Retrd.	1992	15.00	325
1998 Tybee Island Light Station II SAV15	Open		23.00	23

Show Pieces - S. Thompson

YEAR ISSUE	EDITION LIMIT	YEAR RETD.	ISSUE PRICE	*QUOTE U.S.$
1995 Baldwin House SHW01	Retrd.	1995	20.00	30-63
1996 The Winnie Watson House SHW02	Retrd.	1996	20.00	30-63

Sights to See - S. Thompson

YEAR ISSUE	EDITION LIMIT	YEAR RETD.	ISSUE PRICE	*QUOTE U.S.$
1998 Space Needle SEE06	Retrd.	2000	24.00	24

South Carolina - S. Thompson

YEAR ISSUE	EDITION LIMIT	YEAR RETD.	ISSUE PRICE	*QUOTE U.S.$
1991 All Saints' Church SC105	Retrd.	1993	15.00	28-45
1990 The Governor's Mansion SC102	Retrd.	1995	15.00	30-45
1990 The Governer's Mansion (misspelling) SC102	Retrd.	1990	15.00	37-100
1994 The Governor's Mansion (renovated) SC102II	Retrd.	1995	15.00	30
1990 The Hermitage SC101	Retrd.	1994	15.00	29-50
1994 The Hermitage (renovated) SC101II	Retrd.	1995	15.00	45-50
1990 The Lace House SC103	Retrd.	1994	15.00	29-32
1994 The Lace House (renovated) SC103II	Retrd.	1995	15.00	15-75
1991 The State Capitol SC104	Retrd.	1994	15.00	29-63
1994 The State Capitol (renovated) SC104II	Retrd.	1994	15.00	22-115

South Carolina Ladies - S. Thompson

YEAR ISSUE	EDITION LIMIT	YEAR RETD.	ISSUE PRICE	*QUOTE U.S.$
1996 Cinnamon Hill SCL04	Retrd.	1999	19.00	23
1996 Cinnamon Hill, AP SCL04	93	1996	24.00	24-35
1996 Davis-Johnsey House SCL02	Retrd.	1999	19.00	23
1996 Davis-Johnsey House, AP SCL02	104	1996	24.00	32-35
1996 Inman House SCL01	Retrd.	1999	19.00	23
1996 Inman House, AP SCL01	107	1996	24.00	28-35
1996 Montgomery House SCL03	Retrd.	1999	19.00	23
1996 Montgomery House, AP SCL03	105	1996	24.00	24-35
1996 Set of 4 Aps	Retrd.	1996	96.00	80-96

St. Augustine - S. Thompson

YEAR ISSUE	EDITION LIMIT	YEAR RETD.	ISSUE PRICE	*QUOTE U.S.$
1991 Anastasia Lighthousekeeper's House FL104	Retrd.	1993	15.00	52-88
1991 Mission Nombre deDios FL105	Retrd.	1993	15.00	51-75
1991 Old City Gates FL102	Retrd.	1993	15.00	33-35
1991 The "Oldest House" FL101	Retrd.	1993	15.00	37-42
1991 Set	Retrd.	1993	60.00	130

Texas - S. Thompson

YEAR ISSUE	EDITION LIMIT	YEAR RETD.	ISSUE PRICE	*QUOTE U.S.$
1990 The Alamo TEX01	Retrd.	1993	15.00	157-350
1990 Mission Concepcion TEX04	Retrd.	1993	15.00	45-75
1990 Mission San Francisco TEX03	Retrd.	1993	15.00	45-75
1990 Mission San Jose' TEX02	Retrd.	1993	15.00	47-94
1990 Texas Sign	Retrd.	N/A	12.50	23

Town Square Nativity Series - S. Thompson

YEAR ISSUE	EDITION LIMIT	YEAR RETD.	ISSUE PRICE	*QUOTE U.S.$
1998 Borrowed Eli TSN04	Retrd.	1998	15.00	16-22
1998 Heartsville Gazebo TSN01	Retrd.	1998	26.00	27
1998 Heartsville's Lil Angels TSN03	Retrd.	1998	19.00	20-30
1998 Michael Keeping Watch TSN02	Retrd.	1998	19.00	20-26
1998 Town Square Church TSN05	Retrd.	1998	22.00	23
1998 Town Square Church, AP TSN05	130	1998	43.00	43-45
1998 Town Square Nativity OFC07L	11,997	1998	27.00	35-40

Victorian Springtime - S. Thompson

YEAR ISSUE	EDITION LIMIT	YEAR RETD.	ISSUE PRICE	*QUOTE U.S.$
1993 Heffron House VST03	Retrd.	1996	17.00	20-50
1993 Heffron House, AP VST03	Retrd.	1993	20.00	45-50
1993 Jacobsen House VST04	Retrd.	1996	17.00	20-45
1993 Jacobsen House, AP VST04	Retrd.	1993	20.00	60
1993 Ralston House VST01	Retrd.	1996	17.00	20-40
1993 Ralston House, AP VST01	Retrd.	1993	20.00	100
1993 Sessions House VST02	Retrd.	1996	17.00	20-44
1993 Sessions House, AP VST02	Retrd.	1993	20.00	70
1993 Set of 4, AP	Retrd.	1993	100.00	169

Victorian Springtime II - S. Thompson

YEAR ISSUE	EDITION LIMIT	YEAR RETD.	ISSUE PRICE	*QUOTE U.S.$
1995 Dragon House VST07	Retrd.	1997	18.00	30-45
1995 Dragon House, AP VST07	Retrd.	1995	24.00	24-60
1995 E.B. Hall House VST08	Retrd.	1997	19.00	30-35
1995 E.B. Hall House, AP VST08	Retrd.	1995	24.00	50-60
1995 Gibney Home VST09	Retrd.	1997	18.00	19-30
1995 Gibney Home, AP VST09	Retrd.	1995	24.00	24-60
1995 Ray Home VST05	Retrd.	1997	18.00	20-30
1995 Ray Home, AP VST05	Retrd.	1995	24.00	24-60
1995 Victoria VST06	Retrd.	1997	18.00	40-46
1995 Victoria, AP VST06	Retrd.	1995	24.00	25-60

Victorian Springtime III - S. Thompson

YEAR ISSUE	EDITION LIMIT	YEAR RETD.	ISSUE PRICE	*QUOTE U.S.$
1996 Clark House VST14	Retrd.	1998	19.00	23-26
1996 Clark House, AP VST14	96	1996	24.00	28-50
1996 Goodwill House VST13	Retrd.	1998	19.00	24
1996 Goodwill House, AP VST13	88	1996	24.00	25-50
1996 Queen-Anne Mansion VST12	Retrd.	1998	19.00	24
1996 Queen-Anne Mansion, AP VST12	103	1996	24.00	28-50
1996 Sheppard House VST11	Retrd.	1998	19.00	24-30
1996 Sheppard House, AP VST11	98	1996	24.00	28-50
1996 Urfer House VST10	Retrd.	1998	19.00	24
1996 Urfer House, AP VST10	71	1996	24.00	25-50

Victorian Springtime IV - S. Thompson

YEAR ISSUE	EDITION LIMIT	YEAR RETD.	ISSUE PRICE	*QUOTE U.S.$
1997 Allyn Mansion VST19	Retrd.	1999	22.00	25
1997 Allyn Mansion, AP VST19	200	1997	28.00	28
1997 Halstead House VST16	Retrd.	1999	22.00	22
1997 Halstead House, AP VST16	217	1997	28.00	28
1997 Harvard House VST15	Retrd.	1999	22.00	25
1997 Harvard House, AP VST15	234	1997	28.00	28
1997 Rosewood VST18	Retrd.	1999	22.00	25
1997 Rosewood, AP VST18	244	1997	28.00	22-28
1997 Zabriskie House VST17	Retrd.	1999	22.00	25
1997 Zabriskie House, AP VST17	230	1997	28.00	28

Washington D.C. - S. Thompson

YEAR ISSUE	EDITION LIMIT	YEAR RETD.	ISSUE PRICE	*QUOTE U.S.$
1992 Cherry Trees DC005	Retrd.	1993	12.00	35-40
1992 Library of Congress DC002	Retrd.	1993	16.00	69-80
1991 National Archives DC001	Retrd.	1993	16.00	47-69
1991 Washington Monument DC004	Retrd.	1993	16.00	40-63
1992 White House DC003	Retrd.	1993	16.00	175-280
1992 Set of 5	Retrd.	1993	76.00	288-500

West Coast Lighthouse Series - S. Thompson

YEAR ISSUE	EDITION LIMIT	YEAR RETD.	ISSUE PRICE	*QUOTE U.S.$
1995 East Brother Light WCL01	Retrd.	1998	19.00	20-25
1995 East Brother Light, AP WCL01	Retrd.	1995	24.00	48
1995 Mukilteo Light WCL02	Retrd.	1998	18.00	20-25
1995 Mukilteo Light, AP WCL02	Retrd.	1995	24.00	48
1995 Point Fermin Light WCL04	Retrd.	1998	18.00	20-23
1995 Point Fermin Light, AP WCL04	Retrd.	1995	24.00	25-48
1995 Yaquina Bay Light WCL03	Retrd.	1998	18.00	20-23
1995 Yaquina Bay Light, AP WCL03	Retrd.	1995	24.00	48

Williamsburg - S. Thompson

YEAR ISSUE	EDITION LIMIT	YEAR RETD.	ISSUE PRICE	*QUOTE U.S.$
1990 Apothecary WIL09	Retrd.	1994	12.00	35-48
1992 Bruton Parish Church WIL13	Retrd.	1994	15.00	17-35
1994 Bruton Parish Church (renovated) WIL13II	Retrd.	1997	15.00	28-30
1995 Capitol WIL15	Retrd.	1999	18.00	19-23
1995 Capitol, AP WIL15	Retrd.	1995	24.00	24-50
1990 Courthouse WIL11	Retrd.	1994	15.00	23-35
1994 Courthouse (renovated) WIL11II	Retrd.	1995	15.00	29-63
1990 The Golden Ball Jeweler WIL07	Retrd.	1994	12.00	34-45
1997 Govenor's Palace Formal Entrance WIL17	Retrd.	1999	22.00	24-30
1997 Govenor's Palace Formal Entrance, AP WIL17	265	1997	28.00	28
1990 Governor's Palace WIL04	Retrd.	1994	15.00	17-48
1994 Governor's Palace (renovated) WIL04II	Retrd.	1997	15.00	22-30
1990 Homesite WIL12	Retrd.	1996	15.00	29-48
1994 Homesite (renovated) WIL12II	Retrd.	1996	15.00	17-35
1990 King's Arm Tavern WIL10	Retrd.	1994	15.00	33-57
1994 King's Arm Tavern (renovated) WIL10II	Retrd.	1995	15.00	32-50
1990 Milliner WIL06	Retrd.	1994	12.00	33-45
1990 Nicolson Shop WIL08	Retrd.	1994	12.00	35-48
1990 The Printing Offices WIL05	Retrd.	1993	12.00	32-35
1995 Raleigh Tavern WIL14	Retrd.	1999	18.00	19-25
1995 Raleigh Tavern, AP WIL14	Retrd.	1995	24.00	24-45
1997 Tayloe House WIL16	Retrd.	1999	21.00	21-23
1997 Tayloe House, AP WIL16	235	1997	27.00	27

BELLS

Artists of the World

DeGrazia Bells - T. DeGrazia

YEAR ISSUE	EDITION LIMIT	YEAR RETD.	ISSUE PRICE	*QUOTE U.S.$
1980 Festival of Lights	5,000	N/A	40.00	39-75
1980 Los Ninos	7,500	N/A	40.00	46-80
1980 Los Ninos (signed)	500	N/A	80.00	250

Belleek

Belleek Bells - Belleek

YEAR ISSUE	EDITION LIMIT	YEAR RETD.	ISSUE PRICE	*QUOTE U.S.$
1988 Bell, 1st Ed.	Yr.Iss.	1988	38.00	38
1989 Tower, 2nd Ed.	Yr.Iss.	1989	35.00	35
1990 Leprechaun, 3rd Ed.	Yr.Iss.	1990	30.00	30
1991 Church, 4th Ed.	Yr.Iss.	1991	32.00	32
1992 Cottage, 5th Ed.	Yr.Iss.	1992	30.00	30
1993 Pub, 6th Ed.	Yr.Iss.	1993	30.00	30
1994 Castle, 7th Ed.	Yr.Iss.	1994	30.00	30
1995 Georgian House, 8th Ed.	Yr.Iss.	1995	30.00	44
1996 Cathedral, 9th Ed.	Yr.Iss.	1996	30.00	30
1997 Hazlewood House, 10th Ed.	Yr.Iss.	1997	30.00	30-44
1998 Ballylist Mill, 11th Ed.	Yr.Iss.	1998	30.00	30-44
1999 Dunore Lighthouse, 12th Ed.	Yr.Iss.	1999	25.00	40
2000 Clegga Boat House, 13th Ed.	Yr.Iss.		30.00	30

Twelve Days of Christmas - Belleek

YEAR ISSUE	EDITION LIMIT	YEAR RETD.	ISSUE PRICE	*QUOTE U.S.$
1991 A Partridge in a Pear Tree	Yr.Iss.	1991	30.00	30
1992 Two Turtle Doves	Yr.Iss.	1992	30.00	30
1993 Three French Hens	Yr.Iss.	1993	30.00	30
1994 Four Calling Birds	Yr.Iss.	1994	30.00	30

Cherished Teddies/Enesco Group, Inc.

Cherished Teddies Bell - P. Hillman

YEAR ISSUE	EDITION LIMIT	YEAR RETD.	ISSUE PRICE	*QUOTE U.S.$
1992 Angel Bell 906530	Suspd.		20.00	63-86

Dave Grossman Creations

Norman Rockwell Collection - Rockwell-Inspired

YEAR ISSUE	EDITION LIMIT	YEAR RETD.	ISSUE PRICE	*QUOTE U.S.$
1975 Faces of Christmas NRB-75	Retrd.	N/A	12.50	35-40
1976 Drum for Tommy NRB-76	Retrd.	N/A	12.00	30
1976 Ben Franklin (Bicentennial)	Retrd.	N/A	12.50	25-35
1980 Leapfrog NRB-80	Retrd.	N/A	50.00	50-60

Fenton Art Glass Company

1996 Designer Bell - Various

YEAR ISSUE	EDITION LIMIT	YEAR RETD.	ISSUE PRICE	*QUOTE U.S.$
1996 Floral Medallion, 6" - M. Reynolds	2,500	1996	50.00	60
1996 Gardenia, 7" - R. Spindler	2,500	1996	55.00	60
1996 Gilded Berry, 6 1/2" - F. Burton	2,500	1996	60.00	75
1996 Wild Rose, 5 1/2" - K. Plauché	2,500	1996	60.00	75

1997 Designer Bell - Various

YEAR ISSUE	EDITION LIMIT	YEAR RETD.	ISSUE PRICE	*QUOTE U.S.$
1997 Butterflies, 6" - M. Reynolds	2,500	1997	59.00	59
1997 Feathers, 6 3/4" - R. Spindler	2,500	1997	59.00	59
1997 Forest Cottage, 7" - F. Burton	2,500	1997	59.00	59
1997 Roses on Ribbons, 6 1/2" - K. Plauché	2,500	1997	59.00	59

1998 Designer Bell - Various

YEAR ISSUE	EDITION LIMIT	YEAR RETD.	ISSUE PRICE	*QUOTE U.S.$
1998 Bleeding Hearts, 7" - R. Spindler	2,500	1998	59.00	59
1998 Fairy Roses, 6" - K. Plauché	2,500	1998	59.00	59
1998 Hibiscus, 6 1/2" - F. Burton	2,500	1998	59.00	59
1998 Topaz Swirl, 7" - M. Reynolds	2,500	1998	59.00	75

1999 Designer Bell - Various

YEAR ISSUE	EDITION LIMIT	YEAR RETD.	ISSUE PRICE	*QUOTE U.S.$
1999 Butterfly on Blue Burmese, 7" - F. Burton	2,500	1999	75.00	95
1999 Deco Fushia, 7" - K. Plauché	2,500	1999	65.00	65
1999 Gilded Daisy, 6" - R. Spindler	2,500	1999	65.00	65
1999 Iridescence, 7" - M. Reynolds	2,500	1999	65.00	65

296 Collectors' Information Bureau *Quotes have been rounded up to nearest dollar

2000 Designer Bell - Various

YEAR ISSUE	EDITION LIMIT	YEAR RETD.	ISSUE PRICE	*QUOTE U.S.$
2000 Dolphin Frolic, 5 1/2" - K. Plauché	2,500		65.00	65
2000 Lush Garden, 6" - F. Burton	2,500		75.00	75
2000 Victorian Stripes, 6" - M. Reynolds	2,500		65.00	65
2000 Water Lilies, 6 1/2" - R. Spindler	2,500		65.00	65

Christmas - Various

YEAR ISSUE	EDITION LIMIT	YEAR RETD.	ISSUE PRICE	*QUOTE U.S.$
1978 Christmas Morn - M. Dickinson	Yr.Iss.	1978	25.00	50
1979 Nature's Christmas - K. Cunningham	Yr.Iss.	1979	30.00	50
1980 Going Home - D. Johnson	Yr.Iss.	1980	32.50	60
1981 All Is Calm - D. Johnson	Yr.Iss.	1981	35.00	50
1982 Country Christmas - R. Spindler	Yr.Iss.	1982	35.00	50
1983 Anticipation - D. Johnson	7,500	1983	35.00	50
1984 Expectation - D. Johnson	7,500	1984	37.50	50
1985 Heart's Desire - D. Johnson	7,500	1986	37.50	50
1987 Sharing The Spirit - L. Everson	Yr.Iss.	1987	37.50	50
1987 Cardinal in the Churchyard - D. Johnson	4,500	1987	29.50	60
1988 A Chickadee Ballet - D. Johnson	4,500	1988	29.50	50
1989 Downy Pecker - Chisled Song - D. Johnson	4,500	1989	29.50	60
1990 A Blue Bird in Snowfall - D. Johnson	4,500	1990	29.50	55
1990 Sleigh Ride - F. Burton	3,500	1990	39.00	55
1991 Christmas Eve - F. Burton	3,500	1991	35.00	55
1992 Family Tradition - F. Burton	3,500	1992	39.00	55
1993 Family Holiday - F. Burton	3,500	1993	39.50	55
1994 Silent Night - F. Burton	2,500	1994	45.00	65
1995 Our Home Is Blessed - F. Burton	2,500	1995	45.00	65
1996 Star of Wonder - F. Burton	2,500	1996	48.00	65
1997 The Way Home - F. Burton	2,500	1997	65.00	65
1998 The Arrival - F. Burton	2,500	1998	55.00	55
1999 The Announcement - F. Burton	2,500	1999	59.00	59
2000 The Journey - F. Burton	2,500		59.00	59

Connoisseur Bell - Various

YEAR ISSUE	EDITION LIMIT	YEAR RETD.	ISSUE PRICE	*QUOTE U.S.$
1983 Bell, Burmese Handpainted - L. Everson	2,000	1983	50.00	125
1983 Craftsman Bell, White Satin Carnival - Fenton	3,500	1983	25.00	50
1984 Bell, Famous Women's Ruby Satin Irid. - Fenton	3,500	1984	25.00	65
1985 Bell, 6 1/2" Burmese, Hndpt. - L. Everson	2,500	1985	55.00	125
1986 Bell, Burmese-Shells, Hndpt. - D. Barbour	2,500	1986	60.00	150
1988 Bell, 7" Wisteria, Hndpt. - L. Everson	4,000	1988	45.00	150
1989 Bell, 7" Handpainted Rosalene Satin - L. Everson	3,500	1989	50.00	85
1991 Bell, 7" Roses on Rosalene, Hndpt. - M. Reynolds	2,000	1991	50.00	85

Mary Gregory - M. Reynolds

YEAR ISSUE	EDITION LIMIT	YEAR RETD.	ISSUE PRICE	*QUOTE U.S.$
1993 Bell, 6" Ruby	Closed	1993	49.00	95
1994 Bell, 6" Ruby - Loves Me, Loves Me Not	Closed	1994	49.00	95
1995 Bell, 6 1/2"	Closed	1995	49.00	95
2000 Swan Lake Bell, 6 1/2"	2,350		109.50	110

The German Doll Company

Kewpie - Staff

YEAR ISSUE	EDITION LIMIT	YEAR RETD.	ISSUE PRICE	*QUOTE U.S.$
1999 Bell (blue)	Yr.Iss.	1999	150.00	150

Goebel/M.I. Hummel

M.I. Hummel Collectibles Annual Bells - M. I. Hummel

YEAR ISSUE	EDITION LIMIT	YEAR RETD.	ISSUE PRICE	*QUOTE U.S.$
1978 Let's Sing 700	Closed	N/A	50.00	20-195
1979 Farewell 701	Closed	N/A	70.00	20-170
1980 Thoughtful 702	Closed	N/A	85.00	20-95
1981 In Tune 703	Closed	N/A	85.00	20-115
1982 She Loves Me, She Loves Me Not 704	Closed	N/A	90.00	20-140
1983 Knit One 705	Closed	N/A	90.00	30-125
1984 Mountaineer 706	Closed	N/A	90.00	20-145
1985 Sweet Song 707	Closed	N/A	90.00	20-145
1986 Sing Along 708	Closed	N/A	100.00	50-150
1987 With Loving Greetings 709	Closed	N/A	110.00	65-150
1988 Busy Student 710	Closed	N/A	120.00	35-225
1989 Latest News 711	Closed	N/A	135.00	40-240
1990 What's New? 712	Closed	N/A	140.00	50-265
1991 Favorite Pet 713	Closed	N/A	150.00	50-245
1992 Whistler's Duet 714	Closed	N/A	160.00	70-273

Gorham

Currier & Ives - Mini Bells - Currier & Ives

YEAR ISSUE	EDITION LIMIT	YEAR RETD.	ISSUE PRICE	*QUOTE U.S.$
1976 Christmas Sleigh Ride	Annual	1976	9.95	35
1977 American Homestead	Annual	1977	9.95	25
1978 Yule Logs	Annual	1978	12.95	20
1979 Sleigh Ride	Annual	1979	14.95	20
1980 Christmas in the Country	Annual	1980	14.95	20
1981 Christmas Tree	Annual	1981	14.95	18
1982 Christmas Visitation	Annual	1982	16.50	18
1983 Winter Wonderland	Annual	1983	16.50	18
1984 Hitching Up	Annual	1984	16.50	18
1985 Skaters Holiday	Annual	1985	17.50	18
1986 Central Park in Winter	Annual	1986	17.50	18
1987 Early Winter	Annual	1987	19.00	19

Mini Bells - N. Rockwell

YEAR ISSUE	EDITION LIMIT	YEAR RETD.	ISSUE PRICE	*QUOTE U.S.$
1981 Tiny Tim	Annual	1981	19.75	20
1982 Planning Christmas Visit	Annual	1982	20.00	20

Various - N. Rockwell

YEAR ISSUE	EDITION LIMIT	YEAR RETD.	ISSUE PRICE	*QUOTE U.S.$
1975 Sweet Song So Young	Annual	1975	19.50	50
1975 Santa's Helpers	Annual	1975	19.50	50
1975 Tavern Sign Painter	Annual	1975	19.50	30
1976 Flowers in Tender Bloom	Annual	1976	19.50	40-45
1976 Snow Sculpture	Annual	1976	19.50	45
1977 Fondly Do We Remember	Annual	1977	19.50	55
1977 Chilling Chore (Christmas)	Annual	1977	19.50	35
1978 Gaily Sharing Vintage Times	Annual	1978	22.50	23-45
1978 Gay Blades (Christmas)	Annual	1978	22.50	45
1979 Beguiling Buttercup	Annual	1979	24.50	45-50
1979 A Boy Meets His Dog (Christmas)	Annual	1979	24.50	50
1980 Flying High	Annual	1980	27.50	45
1980 Chilly Reception (Christmas)	Annual	1980	27.50	28
1981 Sweet Serenade	Annual	1981	27.50	45
1981 Ski Skills (Christmas)	Annual	1981	27.50	45
1982 Young Mans Fancy	Annual	1982	29.50	30
1982 Coal Season's Coming	Annual	1982	29.50	30
1983 Christmas Medley	Annual	1983	29.50	30
1983 The Milkmaid	Annual	1983	29.50	30
1984 Tiny Tim	Annual	1984	29.50	45
1984 Young Love	Annual	1984	29.50	45
1984 Marriage License	Annual	1984	32.50	45
1984 Yarn Spinner	5,000	1984	32.50	33
1985 Yuletide Reflections	5,000	1985	32.50	45-50
1986 Home For The Holidays	5,000	1986	32.50	45
1986 On Top of the World	5,000	1986	32.50	45-50
1987 Merry Christmas Grandma	5,000	1987	32.50	33
1987 The Artist	5,000	1987	32.50	33
1988 The Homecoming	15,000	1988	37.50	38

Greenwich Workshop

The Greenwich Workshop Collection - J. Christensen

YEAR ISSUE	EDITION LIMIT	YEAR RETD.	ISSUE PRICE	*QUOTE U.S.$
1997 The Sound of Christmas	4,896		59.00	59
1997 Christmas Bell	5,000		59.00	59
1998 '98 Mrs. Claus Bell	Open		59.00	59

Jan Hagara Collectables

Figural Bells - J. Hagara

YEAR ISSUE	EDITION LIMIT	YEAR RETD.	ISSUE PRICE	*QUOTE U.S.$
1986 Jenny Bell	2-Yr.	1988	25.00	25-35
1986 Jody Bell	2-Yr.	1988	25.00	25-35
1986 Lisa Bell	2-Yr.	1988	25.00	25-35
1986 Carol Bell	2-Yr.	1988	25.00	25
1986 Chris Bell	2-Yr.	1988	25.00	25
1986 Noel Bell	2-Yr.	1988	25.00	25
1986 Lydia Bell	2-Yr.	1988	25.00	25-35
1986 Betsy Bell	2-Yr.	1988	25.00	25-35
1986 Jimmy Bell	2-Yr.	1988	35.00	35-75
1986 Jill Bell	2-Yr.	1988	35.00	35-75
1987 Holly Bell	Yr.Iss.	1988	35.00	35
1988 Marie Bell	Yr.Iss.	1989	35.00	25-35

Kirk Stieff

Bell - Kirk Stieff

YEAR ISSUE	EDITION LIMIT	YEAR RETD.	ISSUE PRICE	*QUOTE U.S.$
1992 Santa's Workshop	3,000		40.00	40
1993 Santa's Reindeer	Closed	N/A	30.00	20-30

Musical Bells - Kirk Stieff

YEAR ISSUE	EDITION LIMIT	YEAR RETD.	ISSUE PRICE	*QUOTE U.S.$
1977 Annual Bell 1977	Closed	N/A	17.95	40
1978 Annual Bell 1978	Closed	N/A	17.95	40
1979 Annual Bell 1979	Closed	N/A	17.95	40
1980 Annual Bell 1980	Closed	N/A	19.95	40
1981 Annual Bell 1981	Closed	N/A	19.95	30
1982 Annual Bell 1982	Closed	N/A	19.95	30
1983 Annual Bell 1983	Closed	N/A	19.95	30
1984 Annual Bell 1984	Closed	N/A	19.95	30
1985 Annual Bell 1985	Closed	N/A	19.95	30
1986 Annual Bell 1986	Closed	N/A	19.95	30
1987 Annual Bell 1987	Closed	N/A	19.95	21-30
1988 Annual Bell 1988	Closed	N/A	22.50	21-30
1989 Annual Bell 1989	Closed	N/A	25.00	30
1990 Annual Bell 1990	Closed	N/A	27.00	30
1991 Annual Bell 1991	Closed	N/A	28.00	30
1992 Annual Bell 1992	Closed	N/A	30.00	21-30
1993 Annual Bell 1993	Closed	N/A	30.00	21-30
1994 Annual Bell 1994	Closed	N/A	30.00	30

Lenox China

Songs of Christmas - Unknown

YEAR ISSUE	EDITION LIMIT	YEAR RETD.	ISSUE PRICE	*QUOTE U.S.$
1991 We Wish You a Merry Christmas	Yr.Iss.	1992	49.00	49
1992 Deck the Halls	Yr.Iss.	1993	53.00	53
1993 Jingle Bells	Yr.Iss.	1994	57.00	57
1994 Silver Bells	Yr.Iss.	1995	62.00	62
1995 Hark The Herald Angels Sing	Yr.Iss.	1996	62.50	63

Lenox Crystal

Annual Bell Series - Lenox

YEAR ISSUE	EDITION LIMIT	YEAR RETD.	ISSUE PRICE	*QUOTE U.S.$
1987 Partridge Bell	Yr.Iss.	1990	45.00	45
1988 Angel Bell	Closed	1991	45.00	45
1989 St. Nicholas Bell	Closed	1991	45.00	45
1990 Christmas Tree Bell	Closed	1993	49.00	49
1991 Teddy Bear Bell	Yr.Iss.	1992	49.00	49
1992 Snowman Bell	Yr.Iss.	1993	49.00	49
1993 Nutcracker Bell	Yr.Iss.	1994	49.00	49
1994 Candle Bell	Yr.Iss.	1995	49.00	49
1995 Bell	Yr.Iss.	1996	49.50	50
1996 Bell	Yr.Iss.	1996	49.50	50

Lladró

Four Seasons Bell - Lladró

YEAR ISSUE	EDITION LIMIT	YEAR RETD.	ISSUE PRICE	*QUOTE U.S.$
1991 Spring 17613	Annual	1991	35.00	36-75
1992 Summer 17614	Annual	1992	35.00	30-75
1993 Autumn 17615	Annual	1993	35.00	34-75
1994 Winter 17616	Annual	1994	35.00	36-75

Lladró Bell - Lladró

YEAR ISSUE	EDITION LIMIT	YEAR RETD.	ISSUE PRICE	*QUOTE U.S.$
XX Crystal Wedding Bell L4500	Closed	1985	35.00	195

Lladró Christmas Bell - Lladró

YEAR ISSUE	EDITION LIMIT	YEAR RETD.	ISSUE PRICE	*QUOTE U.S.$
1987 Christmas Bell - L5458M	Annual	1987	29.50	90-150
1988 Christmas Bell - L5525M	Annual	1988	32.50	40-67
1989 Christmas Bell - L5616M	Annual	1989	32.50	100-125
1990 Christmas Bell - L5641M	Annual	1990	35.00	67-75
1991 Christmas Bell - L5803M	Annual	1991	37.50	45-67
1992 Christmas Bell - L5913M	Annual	1992	37.50	45-67
1993 Christmas Bell - L6010M	Annual	1993	39.50	45
1994 Christmas Bell - L6139M	Annual	1994	39.50	45-75
1995 Christmas Bell - L6206M	Annual	1995	39.50	45-60
1996 Christmas Bell - L6297M	Annual	1996	39.50	45-55
1997 Christmas Bell - L6441M	Annual	1997	40.00	45-55
1998 Christmas Bell - 16560	Annual	1998	40.00	45-55
1999 Christmas Bell - 16636	Annual	1999	40.00	45-70
2000 Christmas Bell - 16700	Annual		45.00	45

Lladró Limited Edition Bell - Lladró

YEAR ISSUE	EDITION LIMIT	YEAR RETD.	ISSUE PRICE	*QUOTE U.S.$
1994 Eternal Love 7542M	Annual	1994	95.00	95-115

Lowell Davis Farm Club

RFD Bell - L. Davis

YEAR ISSUE	EDITION LIMIT	YEAR RETD.	ISSUE PRICE	*QUOTE U.S.$
1979 Blossom	Closed	1983	65.00	400
1979 Kate	Closed	1983	65.00	375-400
1979 Willy	Closed	1983	65.00	375
1979 Caruso	Closed	1983	65.00	275
1979 Wilbur	Closed	1983	65.00	375-400
1979 Old Blue Lead	Closed	1983	65.00	275
1993 Cow Bell "Blossom"	Closed	1994	65.00	75
1993 Mule Bell "Kate"	Closed	1994	65.00	75
1993 Goat Bell "Willy"	Closed	1994	65.00	75
1993 Rooster Bell "Caruso"	Closed	1994	65.00	75
1993 Pig Bell "Wilbur"	Closed	1994	65.00	75
1993 Dog Bell "Old Blue and Lead"	Closed	1994	65.00	75

Memories of Yesterday/Enesco Group, Inc.

Annual Bells - M. Attwell

YEAR ISSUE	EDITION LIMIT	YEAR RETD.	ISSUE PRICE	*QUOTE U.S.$
1990 Here Comes the Bride-God Bless Her 523100	Retrd.	1999	25.00	25
1994 Time For Bed 525243	Retrd.	1999	25.00	25

Precious Moments/Enesco Group, Inc.

Annual Bells - S. Butcher

YEAR ISSUE	EDITION LIMIT	YEAR RETD.	ISSUE PRICE	*QUOTE U.S.$
1981 Let the Heavens Rejoice E-5622	Yr.Iss.	1981	17.00	82-173
1982 I'll Play My Drum for Him E-2358	Yr.Iss.	1982	17.00	51-60
1983 Surrounded With Joy E-0522	Yr.Iss.	1983	18.00	47
1984 Wishing You a Merry Christmas E-5393	Yr.Iss.	1984	19.00	22-47
1985 God Sent His Love 15873	Yr.Iss.	1985	19.00	17-35
1986 Wishing You a Cozy Christmas 102318	Yr.Iss.	1986	20.00	20-42
1987 Love is the Best Gift of All 109835	Yr.Iss.	1987	22.50	20-32
1988 Time To Wish You a Merry Christmas 115304	Yr.Iss.	1988	25.00	25-40
1989 Oh Holy Night 522821	Yr.Iss.	1989	25.00	25-36
1990 Once Upon A Holy Night 523828	Yr.Iss.	1990	25.00	22-38
1991 May Your Christmas Be Merry 524182	Yr.Iss.	1991	25.00	28-35
1992 But The Greatest Of These Is Love 527726	Yr.Iss.	1992	25.00	22-30
1993 Wishing You The Sweetest Christmas 530174	Yr.Iss.	1993	25.00	22-40
1994 You're As Pretty as a Christmas Tree 604216	Yr.Iss.	1994	27.50	24-28

Various Bells - S. Butcher

YEAR ISSUE	EDITION LIMIT	YEAR RETD.	ISSUE PRICE	*QUOTE U.S.$
1981 Jesus Loves Me (B) E-5208	Suspd.		15.00	27-31
1981 Jesus Loves Me (G) E-5209	Suspd.		15.00	38-47
1981 Prayer Changes Things E-5210	Suspd.		15.00	29-36
1981 God Understands E-5211	Retrd.	1984	15.00	27-38
1981 We Have Seen His Star E-5620	Suspd.		15.00	32
1981 Jesus Is Born E-5623	Suspd.		15.00	40-50
1982 The Lord Bless You and Keep You E-7175	Suspd.		17.00	19-22
1982 The Lord Bless You and Keep You E-7176	Suspd.		17.00	44
1982 The Lord Bless You and Keep You E-7179	Suspd.		22.50	30-35
1982 Mother Sew Dear E-7181	Suspd.		17.00	25-28
1982 The Purr-fect Grandma E-7183	Suspd.		17.00	25-28

Reed & Barton

Noel Musical Bells - Reed & Barton

YEAR ISSUE	EDITION LIMIT	YEAR RETD.	ISSUE PRICE	*QUOTE U.S.$
1980 Bell 1980	Closed	1980	20.00	40-60
1981 Bell 1981	Closed	1981	22.50	26-30
1982 Bell 1982	Closed	1982	22.50	25-50
1983 Bell 1983	Closed	1983	22.50	25-60
1984 Bell 1984	Closed	1984	22.50	25-60
1985 Bell 1985	Closed	1985	25.00	25-55

*Quotes have been rounded up to nearest dollar

YEAR ISSUE	EDITION LIMIT	YEAR RETD.	ISSUE PRICE	*QUOTE U.S.$
1986 Bell 1986	Closed	1986	25.00	25-60
1987 Bell 1987	Closed	1987	25.00	25-60
1988 Bell 1988	Closed	1988	25.00	25-60
1989 Bell 1989	Closed	1989	25.00	25-60
1990 Bell 1990	Closed	1990	27.50	26-30
1991 Bell 1991	Closed	1991	30.00	26-30
1992 Bell 1992	Closed	1992	30.00	26-30
1993 Bell 1993	Yr.Iss.	1993	30.00	26-30
1994 Bell 1994	Yr.Iss.	1994	30.00	26-30
1995 Bell 1995	Yr.Iss.	1995	30.00	26-30
1996 Bell 1996	Yr.Iss.	1996	35.00	25-35
1997 Bell 1997	Yr.Iss.	1997	35.00	25-35
1998 Noel Bell 1998	Yr.Iss.	1998	35.00	25-35
1999 Noel Bell-Snowman Finial	Yr.Iss.	1999	35.00	26-35
2000 Noel Music Bell	Yr.Iss.		39.50	40

Yuletide Bell - Reed & Barton

YEAR ISSUE	EDITION LIMIT	YEAR RETD.	ISSUE PRICE	*QUOTE U.S.$
1981 Yuletide Holiday	Closed	1981	14.00	15-25
1982 Little Shepherd	Closed	1982	14.00	15-25
1983 Perfect Angel	Closed	1983	15.00	15-25
1984 Drummer Boy	Closed	1984	15.00	15-25
1985 Caroler	Closed	1985	16.50	15-25
1986 Night Before Christmas	Closed	1986	16.50	15-25
1987 Jolly St. Nick	Closed	1987	16.50	15-25
1988 Christmas Morning	Closed	1988	16.50	15-25
1989 The Bell Ringer	Closed	1989	16.50	15-25
1990 The Wreath Bearer	Closed	1990	18.50	15-20
1991 A Special Gift	Closed	1991	22.50	15-25
1992 My Special Friend	Closed	1992	22.50	15-25
1993 My Christmas Present	Yr.Iss.	1993	22.50	15-25
1994 Holiday Wishes	Yr.Iss.	1994	22.50	15-25
1995 Christmas Puppy	Yr.Iss.	1995	20.00	15-20
1996 Yuletide Bell	Yr.Iss.	1996	22.50	15-23
1997 Angel Bell	Yr.Iss.	1997	20.00	15-20
1998 Angel Bell	Yr.Iss.	1998	20.00	15-20
1999 Angel Bell	Yr.Iss.	1999	20.00	15-20

River Shore

Norman Rockwell Single Issues - N. Rockwell

YEAR ISSUE	EDITION LIMIT	YEAR RETD.	ISSUE PRICE	*QUOTE U.S.$
1981 Grandpa's Guardian	7,000	N/A	45.00	45-75
1981 Looking Out to Sea	7,000	N/A	45.00	95-125
1981 Spring Flowers	347	N/A	175.00	150-175

Rockwell Children Series I - N. Rockwell

YEAR ISSUE	EDITION LIMIT	YEAR RETD.	ISSUE PRICE	*QUOTE U.S.$
1977 First Day of School	7,500	N/A	30.00	50-75
1977 Flowers for Mother	7,500	N/A	30.00	50-60
1977 Football Hero	7,500	N/A	30.00	50-75
1977 School Play	7,500	N/A	30.00	50-75

Rockwell Children Series II - N. Rockwell

YEAR ISSUE	EDITION LIMIT	YEAR RETD.	ISSUE PRICE	*QUOTE U.S.$
1978 Dressing Up	15,000	N/A	35.00	50
1978 Five Cents A Glass	15,000	N/A	35.00	40-50
1978 Future All American	15,000	N/A	35.00	50
1978 Garden Girl	15,000	N/A	35.00	40-50

Roman, Inc.

F. Hook Bells - F. Hook

YEAR ISSUE	EDITION LIMIT	YEAR RETD.	ISSUE PRICE	*QUOTE U.S.$
1985 Beach Buddies	15,000	N/A	25.00	28
1986 Sounds of the Sea	15,000	N/A	25.00	28
1987 Bear Hug	15,000	N/A	25.00	28

The Masterpiece Collection - Various

YEAR ISSUE	EDITION LIMIT	YEAR RETD.	ISSUE PRICE	*QUOTE U.S.$
1979 Adoration - F. Lippe	Closed	N/A	20.00	20
1980 Madonna with Grapes - P. Mignard	Closed	N/A	25.00	25
1981 The Holy Family - G. Notti	Closed	N/A	25.00	25
1982 Madonna of the Streets - R. Ferruzzi	Closed	N/A	25.00	25

Seymour Mann, Inc.

Connoisseur Christmas Collection™ - Bernini™

YEAR ISSUE	EDITION LIMIT	YEAR RETD.	ISSUE PRICE	*QUOTE U.S.$
1996 Cardinal CLT-312	Open		15.00	15
1996 Chickadee CLT-302	Open		15.00	15
1996 Dove CLT-307	Open		15.00	15

Connoisseur Collection™ - Bernini™

YEAR ISSUE	EDITION LIMIT	YEAR RETD.	ISSUE PRICE	*QUOTE U.S.$
1995 Bluebird CLT-15	Closed	1996	15.00	15
1995 Canary CLT-12	Closed	1997	15.00	15
1995 Cardinal CLT-9	Closed	1997	15.00	15
1995 Dove CLT-3	Closed	1997	15.00	15
1995 Hummingbird CLT-6	Closed	1997	15.00	15
1995 Pink Rose CLT-72	Open		15.00	15
1995 Robin CLT-18	Closed	1997	15.00	15
1995 Swan CLT-52	Open		15.00	15
1996 Butterfly/Lily CLT-332	Open		15.00	15
1996 Hummingbirds, Morning Glory, Blue CLT-322B	Open		15.00	15
1996 Hummingbirds, Morning Glory, pink CLT-322	Open		15.00	15
1996 Magnolia CLT-78	Open		15.00	15
1996 Roses/Forget-Me-Not CLT-342	Open		15.00	15
1997 Bluebird/Lily CLT-392	Open		15.00	15
1997 Cardinal/Dogwood CLT-407	Open		15.00	15
1997 Dove/Magnolia CLT-352	Open		15.00	15
1997 Love Doves/Roses	Open		15.00	15
1997 Star Gazer Lily	Open		15.00	15
1997 Anna's Hummingbird	Open		15.00	15
1997 Violet Crowned Hummingbird	Open		15.00	15
1997 Blue Butterfly	Open		15.00	15
1998 Ruby Hummingbird Chicks CLT-462	Open		12.00	12
1998 Costa's Hummingbird CLT-472	Open		12.00	12

BOXES

Boyds Collection Ltd.

Uncle Ben's Treasure Boxes™ - The Boyds Collection

YEAR ISSUE	EDITION LIMIT	YEAR RETD.	ISSUE PRICE	*QUOTE U.S.$
2000 Candice's Apple Crate w/"Doc" McNibble 392105	6,000		14.00	14
2000 Devon's Pile O'Leaves w/Rake McNibble 392106	6,000		14.00	14
2000 Fuzzface's Yarn Basket w/"Purl Too" McNibble 392104	6,000		14.00	14
2000 Indy's Treasure Chest w/Pirate McNibble 392103	6,000		14.00	14
2000 Laurel Bearibean w/Picasso Mouski...Hidden Surprises	6,000	2000	13.00	13
2000 Potter Bloombeary w/Nibbles	6,000	2000	13.00	13
2000 Zazu's Attic Trunk w/Snoozy McNibble 392102	6,000		14.00	14

Cast Art Industries

Dreamsicles - K. Haynes

YEAR ISSUE	EDITION LIMIT	YEAR RETD.	ISSUE PRICE	*QUOTE U.S.$
1999 Sunflower Birdhouse-10772	Suspd.		19.00	19
1997 Tiny Dancer-10036	Suspd.		19.50	20

Cavanagh Group Intl.

Prince of Egypt - Dreamworks

YEAR ISSUE	EDITION LIMIT	YEAR RETD.	ISSUE PRICE	*QUOTE U.S.$
1998 Desert Flower-Hinged Porcelain Box	5,000		25.00	25
1998 Gamalu-Hinged Porcelain Box	5,000		25.00	25
1998 Queen of the Nile-Hinged Porcelain Box	5,000		25.00	25

Charming Tails/Fitz and Floyd Collectibles

Moon & Star Nursery Gifts - D. Griff

YEAR ISSUE	EDITION LIMIT	YEAR RETD.	ISSUE PRICE	*QUOTE U.S.$
2000 Mini Lidded Box (blue) 93/608	Open		12.00	12
2000 Mini Lidded Box (pink) 93/605	Open		12.00	12

Chubby Charmers/Miss Martha Originals

Chubby Charmers - M. Root

YEAR ISSUE	EDITION LIMIT	YEAR RETD.	ISSUE PRICE	*QUOTE U.S.$
2000 Poppy - 6009	Open		18.00	18

Department 56

Alpine Village Boxes - Department 56

YEAR ISSUE	EDITION LIMIT	YEAR RETD.	ISSUE PRICE	*QUOTE U.S.$
1995 Silent Night Music Box 56180	Closed	1999	32.50	33

Dickens' Hinged Boxes - Department 56

YEAR ISSUE	EDITION LIMIT	YEAR RETD.	ISSUE PRICE	*QUOTE U.S.$
1997 Bah, Humbug! 58430	Closed	2000	15.00	15
1997 God Bless Us, Every One! 58432	Closed	2000	15.00	15
1998 Royal Coach 57501	Closed	2000	25.00	25
1998 Sleighride 57502	Closed	2000	20.00	20
1997 The Spirit of Christmas 58431	Closed	2000	15.00	15

Heritage Village Boxes - Department 56

YEAR ISSUE	EDITION LIMIT	YEAR RETD.	ISSUE PRICE	*QUOTE U.S.$
1998 Stars and Stripes Forever Gazebo Music Box 55502	Closed	1999	50.00	50

Hot Properties Harry Potter Secret Boxes - Department 56

YEAR ISSUE	EDITION LIMIT	YEAR RETD.	ISSUE PRICE	*QUOTE U.S.$
2000 Golden Snitch 59007	Open		12.50	13
2000 Harry And Hagrid At Gringotts 59012	Open		27.50	28
2000 Harry And The Sorting Hat 59010	Open		19.50	20
2000 Harry Potter 59008	Open		19.50	20
2000 Hedwig The Owl 59009	Open		19.50	20
2000 Hermione The Bookworm 59011	Open		19.50	20

North Pole Hinged Boxes - Department 56

YEAR ISSUE	EDITION LIMIT	YEAR RETD.	ISSUE PRICE	*QUOTE U.S.$
1998 Caroling Elf 57506	Closed	2000	15.00	15
1998 Elf on Sled 57505	Closed	2000	15.00	15

Silhouette Treasures (Winter Silhouette)-Music Boxes - Department 56

YEAR ISSUE	EDITION LIMIT	YEAR RETD.	ISSUE PRICE	*QUOTE U.S.$
1992 Decorating The Mantel (waterglobe, music box) 78395	Closed	1999	30.00	30
1996 Father Time: As Time Goes By Music Box 78589	Closed	1999	65.00	65
1996 Father Time: Counting The Minutes Music Box 78588	Closed	1999	75.00	75
1992 Hanging The Ornaments (waterglobe, music box) 78409	Closed	1999	30.00	30
1993 Sharing A Christmas Moment Music Box 78425	Closed	1999	36.00	36
1995 Sliding In The Snow (waterglobe, music box) 78581	Closed	1999	30.00	30

Snowbabies - Department 56

YEAR ISSUE	EDITION LIMIT	YEAR RETD.	ISSUE PRICE	*QUOTE U.S.$
1999 Fly With Me 68949	Open		15.00	15
1999 Hard Landing 68948	Open		15.00	15
1998 Hold On Tight 68884	Closed	1999	15.00	15
2000 Home Sweet Home 69060	Open		15.00	15
1998 I Love You, (Mother's Day Event Piece) 68867	Closed	1998	15.00	15-25
1998 I'll Ring For You 68928	Open		15.00	15
1998 Once Upon A Time... 68883	Open		15.00	15
1997 Polar Express 68869	Open		15.00	15
1999 Reach Out 69030	Open		17.50	18
1999 Sending Hugs To You (Discover Department 56® Spring Promotion) 69027	Open		15.00	15
1999 Super Star 69029	Open		15.00	15
1997 Sweet Dreams 68868	Open		15.00	15
1998 Sweet Heart (1999 Mother's Day Event) 68930	Closed	1999	15.00	15
1999 Take The First Step 69028	Open		15.00	15
1999 Time Out 68947	Open		15.00	15

Snowbabies-Bisque Porcelain Boxes - Department 56

YEAR ISSUE	EDITION LIMIT	YEAR RETD.	ISSUE PRICE	*QUOTE U.S.$
1997 Celebrate 68847	Closed	1999	15.00	15
1997 Polar Express 79782	Open		15.00	15
1997 Surprise 68846	Open		15.00	15
1997 Sweet Dreams 68868	Open		15.00	15

Snowbabies-Music Boxes - Department 56

YEAR ISSUE	EDITION LIMIT	YEAR RETD.	ISSUE PRICE	*QUOTE U.S.$
1993 Can I Open it Now?, mini 7648-1	Closed	1994	20.00	28-39
1994 Catch a Falling Star 6871-3	Closed	1997	37.50	40-45
1986 Catch a Falling Star 7950-2	Closed	1987	27.50	553-577
1987 Don't Fall Off 7972-3	Closed	1993	30.00	55-60
1997 Did He See You? 68870	Open		37.50	38
1991 Frosty Frolic 7634-1	Closed	1993	110.00	121-138
1993 Frosty Fun, mini 7650-3	Closed	1994	20.00	36-39
1993 I'm So Sleepy 6851-9	Open		37.50	38
1998 I Love You From The Bottom Of My Heart (1999 Mother's Day Event) 68921	Closed	1999	30.00	30
1998 Just Follow The Star 68916	Open		48.00	48
1993 Let It Snow 6857-8	Closed	1995	100.00	100-110
1996 Once Upon a Time 68832	Closed	1999	30.00	30
1991 Penguin Parade 7633-3	Closed	1994	72.00	52-77
1993 Penquin Parade, mini 7646-5	Closed	1994	20.00	36-40
1995 Play Me a Tune 68809	Closed	1998	37.50	42-45
1993 Play Me a Tune, mini 7651-1	Closed	1994	20.00	36-46
1991 Playing Games Is Fun 7632-5	Closed	1993	72.00	97-105
1993 Reading a Story, mini 7649-0	Closed	1994	20.00	32-46
1996 Sliding Through The Milky Way 6883-3	Closed	1999	37.50	38
1991 We Wish You a Merry Christmas (Advent Tree) 7635-0	Closed	1994	135.00	225-245
1992 What Will I Catch? 6826-8	Closed	1998	48.00	48-65
1993 Wishing on a Star 7647-3	Closed	1994	20.00	32-39

Snowbunnies - Department 56

YEAR ISSUE	EDITION LIMIT	YEAR RETD.	ISSUE PRICE	*QUOTE U.S.$
1997 Abracadabra 26298	Closed	1999	15.00	15
1998 Alleluia 26313	Closed	2000	20.00	20
1997 And 'B' Is For Bunny (music box) 26290	Closed	1999	30.00	30
1997 Be My Baby Bunny Bee (music box) 26294	Closed	1999	32.50	35
1999 Bunny in Bloom 26332	Open		15.00	15
1999 Eye to Eye 26331	Open		15.00	15
2000 Go Bunny, Go! 26362	Open		15.00	15
1997 Is There Room For Me? (waterglobe, music box) 26295	Closed	2000	25.00	25
1995 Let's Play In The Meadow (waterglobe, music box) 26271	Closed	1998	25.00	25
1999 Look For The Rainbow (music box) 26337	Open		32.50	33
1995 Look What I've Got! (waterglobe, music box) 26263	Closed	1997	25.00	20-25
1997 Piggyback? 26299	Closed	2000	15.00	15
2000 Rock-A-Bye Birdie 26363	Open		15.00	15
1996 Rock-A-Bye Bunny (waterglobe, music box) 26285	Closed	1999	25.00	25
1999 Sunny Side Up 26334	Open		15.00	15
1999 Sweet Violet 26333	Open		15.00	15
1999 Talk To The Animals (waterglobe, music box) 26338	Open		25.00	25
1997 Tweet, Tweet, Tweet 26297	Closed	2000	15.00	15
1996 You Make Be Laugh (music box) 26284	Closed	1999	32.50	33-35

G. DeBrekht Artistic Studios/Russian Gift & Jewelry

Heritage Fairy Tales and Fantasy - G. DeBrekht Artistic Studios

YEAR ISSUE	EDITION LIMIT	YEAR RETD.	ISSUE PRICE	*QUOTE U.S.$
1998 Alenushka	Open		39.00	39
1998 As if by Magic	Open		39.00	39
1998 Bear on Troika	Open		39.00	39
1998 Chase	Open		39.00	39
1998 Dance	Open		39.00	39
1998 Fall	Open		39.00	39
1998 Fire Bird KHB/MD#326	Open		39.00	39
1998 Fire Bird KHB/MD#342	Open		39.00	39
1998 Flowers	Open		39.00	39
1998 Gold Cockerel	Open		39.00	39
1998 Ivan Tsarevich	Open		39.00	39
1998 Lell	Open		39.00	39
1998 The Maiden with Looking-Glass	Open		39.00	39
1998 Morozko	Open		39.00	39
1998 Pokrov	Open		39.00	39
1998 Russian North	Open		39.00	39
1998 Russian Winter	Open		39.00	39
1998 Scarlet Flower	Open		39.00	39
1998 Snow-Maiden	Open		39.00	39
1998 Storm	Open		39.00	39
1998 Suzdal	Open		39.00	39
1998 Troika	Open		39.00	39

Heritage Magical Myths - G. DeBrekht Artistic Studios

YEAR ISSUE	EDITION LIMIT	YEAR RETD.	ISSUE PRICE	*QUOTE U.S.$
1998 Alenushka	500		150.00	150
1998 At the Fence	500		150.00	150
1998 Fairy-Tale	2,000		90.00	90
1998 Ivan Princess	150		790.00	790
1998 Lady on Horse	150		790.00	790

*Quotes have been rounded up to nearest dollar

Halcyon Days Enamels

Bonbonnieres - Halcyon Days Enamels

YEAR ISSUE	EDITION LIMIT	YEAR RETD.	ISSUE PRICE	*QUOTE U.S.$
1998 Owl & Pussycat	Retrd.	1998	250.00	350-375
1999 Humpty Dumpty	Retrd.	1999	285.00	285
2000 Old Woman in A Shoe	Open		285.00	285

Christmas Boxes - Halcyon Days Enamels

YEAR ISSUE	EDITION LIMIT	YEAR RETD.	ISSUE PRICE	*QUOTE U.S.$
1973 Christmas Box (UK)	Retrd.	1973	25.00	1250-1400
1973 Christmas Box (US)	Retrd.	1973	35.00	900
1974 Christmas Box (UK)	Retrd.	1974	25.00	700-1400
1974 Christmas Box (US)	Retrd.	1974	35.00	675-725
1975 Christmas Box	Retrd.	1975	30.00	625
1976 Christmas Box	Retrd.	1976	30.00	490-495
1977 Christmas Box	Retrd.	1977	30.00	195
1978 Christmas Box	Retrd.	1978	30.00	490-495
1979 Christmas Box	Retrd.	1979	35.00	425
1980 Christmas Box	Retrd.	1980	50.00	380-395
1981 Christmas Box	Retrd.	1981	75.00	335
1982 Christmas Box	Retrd.	1982	75.00	340
1983 Christmas Box	Retrd.	1983	85.00	265
1984 Christmas Box	Retrd.	1984	85.00	295
1985 Christmas Box	Retrd.	1985	95.00	260
1986 Christmas Box	Retrd.	1986	100.00	235
1987 Christmas Box	Retrd.	1987	100.00	235
1988 Christmas Box	Retrd.	1988	110.00	210
1989 Christmas Box	Retrd.	1989	110.00	210
1990 Christmas Box	Retrd.	1990	125.00	210
1991 Christmas Box	Retrd.	1991	125.00	195
1992 Christmas Box	Retrd.	1992	135.00	210
1993 Christmas Box	Retrd.	1993	145.00	210
1994 Christmas Box	Retrd.	1994	155.00	210
1995 Christmas Box	Retrd.	1995	155.00	195
1996 Christmas Box	Retrd.	1996	155.00	185
1997 Christmas Box	Retrd.	1997	165.00	185
1998 Christmas Box	Retrd.	1998	175.00	185
1999 Christmas Box	Retrd.	1999	185.00	185
2000 Christmas Box	Open		185.00	185

Christmas Oval Boxes - Halcyon Days Enamels

YEAR ISSUE	EDITION LIMIT	YEAR RETD.	ISSUE PRICE	*QUOTE U.S.$
1971 Christmas Box	365	1971	25.00	925-1100
1972 Christmas Box	366	1972	25.00	835-950
1973 Christmas Box	365	1973	35.00	510-550
1974 Christmas Box	365	1974	38.00	550-625
1975 Christmas Box	365	1975	38.00	495
1976 Christmas Box	366	1976	40.00	435-465
1977 Christmas Box	365	1977	40.00	435-465
1978 Christmas Box	365	1978	40.00	400-435
1979 Christmas Box	365	1979	54.00	400-435
1980 Christmas Box	366	1980	73.00	400-435
1981 Christmas Box	365	1981	62.00	400-435
1982 Christmas Box	365	1982	63.00	400-435

Classic Pooh Series - Halcyon Days Enamels

YEAR ISSUE	EDITION LIMIT	YEAR RETD.	ISSUE PRICE	*QUOTE U.S.$
1995 An Astute & Helpful Bear	1,000	1998	195.00	215
1998 At Mr. Saunders House	2,500	1999	325.00	325
1999 A Bear and His Honey	750	1999	195.00	195
1995 Do Nothing Bear	1,500	1997	95.00	135
1998 Heffalumps	Open		185.00	185
1999 If You're Stuck	500	1999	345.00	345
1997 Just A Smackeral Higher	2,500	1999	195.00	195
1998 Picnic Basket Egg	1,000	1999	235.00	235
1995 Pooh and Honey Pot	Retrd.	1997	80.00	105
1997 Pooh Ornament (Event Piece)	Retrd.	1998	185.00	195
1995 Silly Old Bear Pink	Retrd.	1997	80.00	100
1995 Silly Old Blue Bear	Retrd.	1997	80.00	100
1995 Three Cheers For Pooh	Retrd.	1997	165.00	210-225
1997 Tiggers Don't Like Honey	2,500	1999	250.00	250
1998 Winnie & Fircones	1,500	1999	245.00	245

Disney Boxes - Halcyon Days Enamels

YEAR ISSUE	EDITION LIMIT	YEAR RETD.	ISSUE PRICE	*QUOTE U.S.$
1995 Winnie the Pooh Christmas Box	Retrd.	1995	165.00	225
1998 Let The Good Times Roll	1,250	1998	165.00	185-195
1998 Goofy Diet	1,250	1998	145.00	150-160

Easter Egg - Halcyon Days Enamels

YEAR ISSUE	EDITION LIMIT	YEAR RETD.	ISSUE PRICE	*QUOTE U.S.$
1973 Easter Egg	Retrd.	1973	32.00	950
1974 Easter Egg	Retrd.	1974	32.00	595
1975 Easter Egg	Retrd.	1975	32.00	575-595
1976 Easter Egg	Retrd.	1976	32.00	475
1977 Easter Egg	Retrd.	1977	32.00	460
1978 Easter Egg	Retrd.	1978	32.00	325
1979 Easter Egg	Retrd.	1979	35.00	325
1980 Easter Egg	Retrd.	1980	50.00	375
1981 Easter Egg	Retrd.	1981	60.00	295-375
1982 Easter Egg	Retrd.	1982	75.00	275-375
1983 Easter Egg	Retrd.	1983	75.00	295-375
1984 Easter Egg	Retrd.	1984	85.00	265-375
1985 Easter Egg	Retrd.	1985	95.00	265-375
1986 Easter Egg	Retrd.	1986	100.00	265-375
1987 Easter Egg	Retrd.	1987	110.00	265-300
1988 Easter Egg	Retrd.	1988	110.00	265
1989 Easter Egg	Retrd.	1989	110.00	265-300
1990 Easter Egg	Retrd.	1990	145.00	250
1991 Easter Egg	Retrd.	1991	145.00	250
1992 Easter Egg	Retrd.	1992	150.00	235
1993 Easter Egg	Retrd.	1993	165.00	235
1994 Easter Egg	Retrd.	1994	180.00	210
1995 Easter Egg	Retrd.	1995	180.00	200
1996 Easter Egg	Retrd.	1996	185.00	200
1997 Easter Egg	Retrd.	1997	195.00	235
1998 Easter Egg	Retrd.	1998	210.00	210
1999 Easter Egg	Retrd.	1999	225.00	225
2000 Easter Egg	Open		235.00	235

Mickey Christmas Boxes - Halcyon Days Enamels

YEAR ISSUE	EDITION LIMIT	YEAR RETD.	ISSUE PRICE	*QUOTE U.S.$
1997 Mickey	750	1997	135.00	160
1998 Mickey	750	1998	135.00	145

Millennium - Halcyon Days Enamels

YEAR ISSUE	EDITION LIMIT	YEAR RETD.	ISSUE PRICE	*QUOTE U.S.$
1998 Architecture	1,000	1999	325.00	350
1998 The Arts	1,000	1999	325.00	350
1999 Champagne 2000	Open		90.00	90
1999 Children of the World	Open		185.00	185
1999 International Box	Open		275.00	275
1999 International Music Box	1,000	1999	495.00	550-575
1999 Millennium Bug	Open		125.00	125
1999 Millennium Globe	Open		295.00	295
2000 Millennium Teddy	Open		125.00	125
1999 Millennium Time Capsule	500	1999	295.00	350-375
1999 Nearly the Millennium	Retrd.	1999	115.00	115-125
1998 The Sciences	1,000	1999	325.00	350
1999 Time Capsule II	Open		295.00	295
2000 Travel Through the Ages	1,000		325.00	325
1999 World 2000	Open		125.00	125

Mother's Day Boxes - Halcyon Days Enamels

YEAR ISSUE	EDITION LIMIT	YEAR RETD.	ISSUE PRICE	*QUOTE U.S.$
1975 Mother's Day Box	Retrd.	1975	30.00	295-325
1976 Mother's Day Box	Retrd.	1976	30.00	310-319
1977 Mother's Day Box	Retrd.	1977	30.00	300
1978 Mother's Day Box	Retrd.	1978	30.00	265
1979 Mother's Day Box	Retrd.	1979	35.00	265
1980 Mother's Day Box	Retrd.	1980	50.00	250

Non Dated Enamel Boxes - Halcyon Days Enamels

YEAR ISSUE	EDITION LIMIT	YEAR RETD.	ISSUE PRICE	*QUOTE U.S.$
1999 Arab Tent (based on painting by E. Landseer)	250		725.00	725
1998 Aubrey Beardsley	250	1999	235.00	265
1998 Becket's Casket	250	1999	350.00	395
1996 Birds on a Wire	Retrd.	1999	165.00	200
1999 Book of Common Prayer	450		275.00	275
1998 British Humane Society	500	1999	225.00	250
1998 California Gold Rush	500	1999	295.00	295
1997 Canaletto Tercentenary	300	1997	255.00	425
1985 Cezanne's Blue Vase	250	1986	275.00	525
1992 Christopher Columbus	500	1992	275.00	395
1970 Composer, set/5	1,000	1972	500.00	2750
1999 Fantin-Latour Flowers	500		695.00	695
1996 Front Garden Buckingham Palace	500	1997	350.00	495
1999 George Washington	200	1999	245.00	245
1995 Hancock's Tea Party 25th Anniversary	Retrd.	1995	220.00	285
1999 Hassam Impressionist Garden	500		385.00	385
1997 Hong Kong Box	2,187	1997	295.00	385
1997 It Started with a Mouse (Mickey)	2,500	N/A	225.00	265
1975 Jane Austen Bicentenary	500	1975	80.00	675
1996 Jerusalem 3000th Anniversary	3,000	1996	295.00	375
1999 La Musique Music Box	200	1999	590.00	590
1998 Lady Diane Memento Box	2,965	1998	135.00	160-185
1998 Lady Diane Memorial Box	3,354	1998	225.00	225-265
1976 Liberty Bell	250	1976	45.00	255-275
1996 Monet's House At Argentuil	Retrd.	1998	375.00	395-410
1999 Monet's Lady In A Garden	500		395.00	395
1999 Monet's Sunflowers	250	1999	425.00	425
1991 Moulin Rouge	250	1992	175.00	475
1999 Napoleon Bonbonniere	250		250.00	250
1999 Nelson Bonbonniere	250		250.00	250
1994 Pennsylvania Box	350	1994	250.00	325-345
1999 Pissaro's Boulevard Montmarte	500		475.00	475
1990 Pre Raphaelite	500	1991	200.00	495
1981 Prince Charles & Lady Diana Wedding (oval)	Retrd.	1981	65.00	265-285
1998 The Quakers	200	1999	195.00	195
1990 Queen Mother's 90th Birthday	Retrd.	1990	140.00	195
1998 Renoir's Two Sisters	750	1999	375.00	375
1999 Royal Wedding	500	1999	275.00	275
1994 Rupert Bear	Retrd.	1994	175.00	225
1994 San Marco Venice	Retrd.	1995	250.00	450
1999 Shakespeare 400th Anniversary	200	1999	175.00	240-265
1991 Sherlock Homes Centenary	250	1992	280.00	550
1977 Silver Jubilee	1,000	1977	125.00	925
1972 Silver Wedding Queen Elizabeth	100	1972	95.00	945
1998 Still Life w/Flowers	100	1998	325.00	395
1993 Table of the Grand Commanders	Retrd.	1998	230.00	385
1998 Tissot's Ball on Shipboard	350	1999	425.00	425
1998 Van de Meer's Lady with Guitar Music Box	250	1999	425.00	425
1997 Watership Down	500	1999	325.00	365
1999 Wellington Bonbonniere	250		250.00	250
1998 Whistlejacket (based on painting by Stubbs)	250	1999	575.00	625
1974 Winston Churchill	500	1975	125.00	585
1976 World Wildlife, set/6	750	1976	600.00	2400

State Boxes - Halcyon Days Enamels

YEAR ISSUE	EDITION LIMIT	YEAR RETD.	ISSUE PRICE	*QUOTE U.S.$
2000 Florida	1,000		295.00	295
2000 Michigan	1,000		295.00	295

Valentines Day Boxes - Halcyon Days Enamels

YEAR ISSUE	EDITION LIMIT	YEAR RETD.	ISSUE PRICE	*QUOTE U.S.$
1974 Valentine Box	Retrd.	1974	21.00	600-650
1975 Valentine Box	Retrd.	1975	30.00	425
1976 Valentine Box	Retrd.	1976	30.00	385
1977 Valentine Box	Retrd.	1977	30.00	385
1978 Valentine Box	Retrd.	1978	30.00	310
1979 Valentine Box	Retrd.	1979	35.00	300
1980 Valentine Box	Retrd.	1980	50.00	265-285
1981 Valentine Box	Retrd.	1981	50.00	250
1982 Valentine Box	Retrd.	1982	50.00	240
1983 Valentine Box	Retrd.	1983	60.00	240
1984 Valentine Box	Retrd.	1984	65.00	235
1985 Valentine Box	Retrd.	1985	75.00	235
1986 Valentine Box	Retrd.	1986	80.00	235
1987 Valentine Box	Retrd.	1987	85.00	235
1988 Valentine Box	Retrd.	1988	85.00	235
1989 Valentine Box	Retrd.	1989	95.00	235
1990 Valentine Box	Retrd.	1990	95.00	225
1991 Valentine Box	Retrd.	1991	125.00	225

Yearly Boxes - Halcyon Days Enamels

YEAR ISSUE	EDITION LIMIT	YEAR RETD.	ISSUE PRICE	*QUOTE U.S.$
1977 Year Box	Retrd.	1977	25.00	600
1978 Year Box	Retrd.	1978	30.00	365
1979 Year Box	Retrd.	1979	30.00	300
1980 Year Box	Retrd.	1980	35.00	325
1981 Year Box	Retrd.	1981	50.00	275
1982 Year Box	Retrd.	1982	65.00	275
1983 Year Box	Retrd.	1983	65.00	250
1984 Year Box	Retrd.	1984	75.00	235
1985 Year Box	Retrd.	1985	85.00	235
1986 Year Box	Retrd.	1986	85.00	250
1987 Year Box	Retrd.	1987	95.00	235
1988 Year Box	Retrd.	1988	100.00	225
1989 Year Box	Retrd.	1989	110.00	225
1990 Year Box	Retrd.	1990	125.00	240
1999 Year Box	Retrd.	1999	185.00	185
2000 Year Box	Open		185.00	185

Hamilton Collection

Dreamsicles Special Friends Music Box - K. Haynes

YEAR ISSUE	EDITION LIMIT	YEAR RETD.	ISSUE PRICE	*QUOTE U.S.$
1997 The Best Gift of All	Open		29.95	30
1997 Bless Us All	Open		29.95	30
1997 Heaven's Little Helper	Open		29.95	30
1997 A Heavenly Hoorah!	Open		29.95	30
1997 A Hug From The Heart	Open		29.95	30
1997 A Love Like No Other	Open		29.95	30

Sacred Encounters Totem Box - S. Kerhli

YEAR ISSUE	EDITION LIMIT	YEAR RETD.	ISSUE PRICE	*QUOTE U.S.$
1999 Keeper of Courage	Open		39.95	40
1999 Keeper of Dreams	Open		39.95	40
1999 Keeper of Strength	Open		39.95	40
1999 Keeper of Wisdom	Open		39.95	40

Sacred Keepsakes Box Collection - S. Kerhli

YEAR ISSUE	EDITION LIMIT	YEAR RETD.	ISSUE PRICE	*QUOTE U.S.$
1998 Future Pack	Open		29.95	30
1998 Guardian of Tomorrow	Open		29.95	30
1998 Legend of the Wolf	Open		29.95	30
1998 Night Watch	Open		29.95	30
1998 Priceless Treasure	Open		29.95	30
1998 Pride of the Pack	Open		29.95	30
1998 Spirit of the Hunt	Open		29.95	30
1998 Wolf Guide	Open		29.95	30

Harmony Kingdom

Royal Watch™ Collector's Club - Various

YEAR ISSUE	EDITION LIMIT	YEAR RETD.	ISSUE PRICE	*QUOTE U.S.$
1996 Big Blue - P. Calvesbert	Retrd.	1997	75.00	288-350
1996 The Big Day - P. Calvesbert	Retrd.	1996	Gift	150-188
1996 Purrfect Fit - D. Lawrence	Retrd.	1996	Gift	390-450
1996 Complete Charter Member Kit	Retrd.	1996	35.00	390-600
1997 Paper Anniversary - P. Calvesbert	Retrd.	1997	20.00	140
1997 Toad Pin - P. Calvesbert	Retrd.	1997	Gift	25-95
1997 Sweet as a Summer's Kiss - D. Lawrence	Retrd.	1997	Gift	55-125
1997 Big Blue 1997 - P. Calvesbert	Retrd.	1997	75.00	200-250
1997 The Sunflower - M. Perry	Retrd.	1997	70.00	138-175
1998 Cat Pin - P. Calvesbert	Retrd.	1998	Gift	30-70
1998 Mutton Chops - P. Calvesbert	Retrd.	1998	Gift	45-125
1998 Behold The King - D. Lawrence	Retrd.	1998	100.00	135-195
1998 The Mushroom - M. Perry	Retrd.	1998	120.00	135-223
1998 April's Fool Pen - D. Lawrence	Retrd.	1998	45.00	80-120
1998 Friends of the Royal Watch - D. Lawrence	526	1998	Gift	N/A
1999 Beneath the Ever Changing Seas - D. Lawrence	Yr.Iss.	1999	Gift	45
1999 Murphy Lapel Pin - M. Perry	Yr.Iss.	1999	Gift	N/A
1999 Pell Mell - D. Lawrence	Yr.Iss.	1999	120.00	120-200
1999 Byron's Lonely Heart Club - M. Perry	Yr.Iss.	1999	65.00	65
1999 The Mouse That Roared - P. Calvesbert	Yr.Iss.	1999	45.00	45
1999 Sole Mate - D. Lawrence	Yr.Iss.	1999	35.00	35
2000 Merry-go-round - M. Perry	Yr.Iss.		Gift	N/A
2000 Lover's Leap - M. Perry	Yr.Iss.		Gift	N/A
2000 Field Day - M. Perry	Yr.Iss.		Gift	N/A
2000 Byron & Bumbles - M. Perry	Yr.Iss.		75.00	75
2000 Cow Town - D. Lawrence	Yr.Iss.		75.00	75
2000 Silk Anniversary - P. Calvesbert	Open		20.00	20

Event Pieces - Various

YEAR ISSUE	EDITION LIMIT	YEAR RETD.	ISSUE PRICE	*QUOTE U.S.$
1997 Oktobearfest - P. Calvesbert	Retrd.	1997	38.50	40-82
1997 Octobearfest (misprint on label) - P. Calvesbert	Retrd.	1997	38.50	70-95
1998 Pumpkinfest - D. Lawrence	Retrd.	1998	45.00	50-75
1999 Chucky Pig - P. Calvesbert	300	1999	Gift	375-710
1999 Gobblefest - P. Calvesbert	12,000	1999	49.00	49-58
1999 Queen of the Jungle - D. Lawrence	6,000	1999	95.00	95-125
1999 QVC Pin - M. Baldwin	7,000	1999	Gift	20-25
1999 Noah's Hideaway-Carlsbad - Martin Perry Studios	500	1999	75.00	100-150
1999 Noah's Hideaway-Portland - Martin Perry Studios	500	1999	75.00	100-150

*Quotes have been rounded up to nearest dollar

BOXES

YEAR ISSUE	EDITION LIMIT	YEAR RETD.	ISSUE PRICE	*QUOTE U.S.$
1999 Noah's Hideaway-Tampa - Martin Perry Studios	500	1999	75.00	100-150
1999 Noah's Hideaway-Chicago - Martin Perry Studios	500	1999	75.00	100-150
1999 Noah's Hideaway-Rockville - Martin Perry Studios	500	1999	75.00	100-150
1999 Cat's Meow - P. Calvesbert	12/00		20.00	20
1999 Noah's Hideaway-Merrick, NY - Martin Perry Studios	500	1999	75.00	100-150
2000 Fat Cat's Meow - M. Baldwin	Yr.Iss.		35.00	35
2000 Alley Cat's Meow - M. Baldwin	3,600		45.00	45
2000 Cat Nap's Meow - S. Rickett	3,600		35.00	35

Show Pieces - P. Calvesbert, unless otherwise noted

YEAR ISSUE	EDITION LIMIT	YEAR RETD.	ISSUE PRICE	*QUOTE U.S.$
1996 Secaucus Frog Pendant	210	1996	Gift	300-500
1996 Rosemont Frog Pendant	403	1996	Gift	200-350
1997 Long Beach Rose Pendant	552	1997	Gift	75-175
1997 Rosemont Rose Pendant	847	1997	Gift	150-188
1997 Puffin Pin	177	1997	Gift	300-500
1998 Edison Pendant	Retrd.	1998	Gift	95-130
1998 Newark Pendant	295	1998	Gift	175
1998 Rosemont Pendant	1,912	1998	Gift	95-175
1998 Stoneleigh Pendant	270	1998	Gift	150
1998 Tin Cat's Cruise	575	1998	Gift	360-650
1999 Camelot	1,455	1999	Gift	262-650
1999 Crooze Cat	739	1999	45.00	45
1999 Dragon's Breath - Martin Perry Studios	Retrd.	1999	Gift	N/A
1999 Long Beach Pendant - M. Baldwin	2,000	1999	Gift	75-100
1999 Primordial Sloop	855	1999	Gift	219-325
1999 Rosemont Pendant - M. Baldwin	1,956	1999	Gift	50-75
1999 Tubs Pin	566	1999	Gift	N/A

I.C.E. Piece - P. Calvesbert

YEAR ISSUE	EDITION LIMIT	YEAR RETD.	ISSUE PRICE	*QUOTE U.S.$
1998 Sneak Preview	5,000	1998	65.00	94-200
1999 Swap N Sell	5,000	1999	75.00	75-119
1999 Swap N Sell Groucho	200	1999	75.00	650-750
2000 Signing Line	5,000		75.00	75

GCC Exclusive - P. Calvesbert, unless otherwise noted

YEAR ISSUE	EDITION LIMIT	YEAR RETD.	ISSUE PRICE	*QUOTE U.S.$
1998 Queen's Council	Retrd.	1998	45.00	45
1998 Boarding School	Retrd.	1998	45.00	45
1999 Thin Ice - Martin Perry Studios	6,000	1999	45.00	55-64
1999 Jump Shot - Martin Perry Studios	3,600	1999	45.00	55-95

Angelique - D. Lawrence

YEAR ISSUE	EDITION LIMIT	YEAR RETD.	ISSUE PRICE	*QUOTE U.S.$
1996 Bon Chance	Open		35.00	35
1996 Fleur-de-lis	7,888	1998	35.00	35-38
1996 Fleur-de-lis (wide-wing)	Retrd.	N/A	35.00	250
1996 Gentil Homme	6,786	1998	35.00	35-45
1996 Ingenue	8,062	1998	35.00	35-38
1996 Joie De Vivre	8,170	1998	35.00	35-90

Buying Group (Fall) - A. Richmond

YEAR ISSUE	EDITION LIMIT	YEAR RETD.	ISSUE PRICE	*QUOTE U.S.$
2000 Night Light	3,600		49.00	49

Disney Gallery - Disney, unless otherwise noted

YEAR ISSUE	EDITION LIMIT	YEAR RETD.	ISSUE PRICE	*QUOTE U.S.$
1998 Fab 5	Open		95.00	95
1998 Lion King's Pride Rock - R. King	Open		95.00	95
1997 Pooh and Friends	Open		60.00	75
1999 Snow White	Open		95.00	95

Garden Party - Various

YEAR ISSUE	EDITION LIMIT	YEAR RETD.	ISSUE PRICE	*QUOTE U.S.$
1996 Baroness Trotter - P. Calvesbert	Open		17.50	18
1997 Count Belfry - D. Lawrence	6,978	1999	17.50	18-20
1996 Courtiers At Rest - P. Calvesbert	Open		17.50	18
1997 Duc de Lyon - D. Lawrence	7,220	1999	17.50	18-20
1997 Earl of Oswald - D. Lawrence	9,253	1999	17.50	18-20
1996 Garden Prince - P. Calvesbert	Open		17.50	18
1996 Ladies In Waiting - P. Calvesbert	Open		17.50	18
1997 Lord Busby - D. Lawrence	6,964	1999	17.50	18-20
1997 Major Parker - D. Lawrence	6,262	1999	17.50	18-20
1997 Marquis de Blanc - D. Lawrence	9,222	1999	17.50	18-20
1996 Royal Flotilla - P. Calvesbert	11,488	1998	17.50	18-20
1996 Yeoman Of The Guard - P. Calvesbert	Open		17.50	18

Harmony Circus - D. Lawrence

YEAR ISSUE	EDITION LIMIT	YEAR RETD.	ISSUE PRICE	*QUOTE U.S.$
1996 The Audience	1,359	1998	150.00	150-175
1996 Ball Brothers	2,608	1998	35.00	39-50
1996 Beppo And Barney The Clowns	2,881	1998	35.00	35-50
1996 Circus Ring	640	1998	100.00	80-175
1996 Clever Constantine	1,902	1998	35.00	39-50
1996 Great Escapo	1,733	1998	35.00	39-50
1996 Harmony Circus Arch	734	1998	80.00	80-90
1996 Henry The Human Cannonball	1,886	1998	35.00	35-50
1996 Il Bendi	1,468	1998	35.00	39-50
1996 Lionel Loveless	1,983	1998	35.00	35-50
1996 Mr. Sediments	1,916	1998	35.00	35-50
1996 Olde Time Carousel	3,322	1998	35.00	35-50
1996 Pavareata The Little Big Girl	3,613	1998	35.00	35-50
1996 The Ringmaster	1,649	1998	35.00	39-50
1996 Road Dogs	3,340	1998	35.00	35-50
1996 Suave St. John	1,744	1998	35.00	39-95
1996 Top Hat	3,154	1998	35.00	35-50
1996 Vlad The Impaler	2,538	1998	35.00	35-50
1996 Winston The Lion Tamer	2,716	1998	35.00	35-38
1996 Matched Number Harmony Circus Set	1,000	1998	890.00	890
1998 Bozini the Clown	10,000	1998	29.50	30-50
1998 Madeline of the High Wire	10,000	1998	29.50	40-50

Hi-Jinx - P. Calvesbert

YEAR ISSUE	EDITION LIMIT	YEAR RETD.	ISSUE PRICE	*QUOTE U.S.$
1994 Antarctic Antics	3,291	1998	100.00	100
1994 Hold That Line	4,740	1998	100.00	100-150
1994 Mad Dogs and Englishmen	4,625	1998	100.00	100
1995 Open Mike	3,032	1998	100.00	100-150

Holiday Edition - D. Lawrence, unless otherwise noted

YEAR ISSUE	EDITION LIMIT	YEAR RETD.	ISSUE PRICE	*QUOTE U.S.$
1995 Chatelaine	7,988	1995	35.00	420-500
1996 Bon Enfant	Retrd.	1996	35.00	250-300
1996 Bon Enfant (1st ed.)	Retrd.	1996	35.00	600-700
1996 Nick Of Time - P. Calvesbert	7,804	1996	35.00	175-280
1997 Celeste	Retrd.	1997	45.00	45-70
1997 Something's Gotta Give - P. Calvesbert	16,368	1997	35.00	35-65
1998 La Guardienne	16,130	1998	45.00	45-53
1998 Jingle Bell Rock - P. Calvesbert	19,019	1998	45.00	45-69
1999 Holy Roller - P. Calvesbert	9,948	1999	45.00	45-121
1999 Joyeaux	Retrd.	1999	45.00	45
1999 Noel	Retrd.	1999	45.00	45
1998 Ruffians' Feast Tile - A. Richmond	Retrd.	2000	55.00	45
1999 Snowdonia Fields - Martin Perry Studios	Retrd.	2000	55.00	55
1999 Purrfect Tidings Tile - A. Richmond	Retrd.	2000	55.00	55
2000 Bon Bon	Yr.Iss.		45.00	45
2000 Pastille	Yr.Iss.		45.00	45
2000 Easy Slider - S. Drackett	Yr.Iss.		45.00	45
2000 King of the Road - P. Calvesbert	Yr.Iss.		55.00	55

Large Treasure Jest® - P. Calvesbert, unless otherwise noted

YEAR ISSUE	EDITION LIMIT	YEAR RETD.	ISSUE PRICE	*QUOTE U.S.$
1991 Awaiting A Kiss	Open		55.00	55
1990 Drake's Fancy	4,512	1999	55.00	45-75
1995 Holding Court	Open		55.00	55
1991 Horn A' Plenty	6,910	1997	55.00	75-145
1991 Journey Home	Open		55.00	55
1990 Keeping Current	4,448	1998	55.00	55
1992 On A Roll	Retrd.	2000	55.00	55-65
1994 One Step Ahead	Retrd.	1999	55.00	55-70
1991 Pen Pals	Retrd.	2000	55.00	55
1990 Pondering	3,918	1997	55.00	125-200
1993 Pride And Joy	10,750	1998	55.00	55-70
1990 Quiet Waters	3,518	1999	55.00	55-65
1993 Standing Guard	3,646	1997	55.00	90-125
1993 Step Aside	Open		55.00	55
1991 Straight From The Hip	Retrd.	2000	55.00	55
1991 Sunnyside Up	Open		55.00	55
1999 Tally Ho! - D. Lawrence	Open		65.00	65
1991 Tea For Two	5,384	1999	55.00	55
1997 Terra Incognita - D. Lawrence	Open		75.00	75

Limited Editions - P. Calvesbert, unless otherwise noted

YEAR ISSUE	EDITION LIMIT	YEAR RETD.	ISSUE PRICE	*QUOTE U.S.$
1999 Christmas Bouquet - Martin Perry Studios	5,000	1999	75.00	75
1999 Easter Bouquet - M. Perry	5,000	1999	75.00	75-120
1998 Family Reunion - D. Lawrence	7,200	1998	120.00	120-150
1999 Halloween Bouquet - Martin Perry Studios	5,000	1999	75.00	75
1998 Have a Heart	3,600	1998	55.00	200-295
1998 Ivory Tower - D. Lawrence	7,200	1998	120.00	120-250
1997 Killing Time (black sand) - D. Lawrence	3,600	1997	100.00	225-250
1997 Killing Time (gold sand) - D. Lawrence	3,600	1997	100.00	225-300
1999 Mother's Day Bouquet - M. Perry	5,000	1999	75.00	100-119
1995 Noah's Lark (Biblical)	5,000	1998	400.00	500-805
2000 Noah's Quack - M. Ricketts	Yr.Iss.		175.00	175
2000 Nose Bleed	5,000	2000	55.00	55-179
1997 Original Kin (Biblical)	2,500	1998	250.00	300-480
1998 Pieces of Eight (orange) - D. Lawrence	5,000	1998	120.00	650-1200
1998 Pieces of Eight (pink) - D. Lawrence	5,000	1998	120.00	250-450
1998 Pieces of Eight (red) - D. Lawrence	5,000	1998	120.00	120-230
1998 Play Ball - D. Lawrence	7,200	1998	120.00	120-150
2000 Retired Racers - D. Lawrence	5,000	2000	65.00	65
1999 Road Kill	3,600	1999	55.00	135-200
1998 SinCity (Biblical)	5,000	1998	600.00	600-720
2000 Spring Bouquet - M. Perry	5,000	2000	75.00	75
2000 Summer Bouquet - M. Perry	5,000	2000	75.00	75
1995 Unbearables	2,500	1998	400.00	400-480
1999 Y2HK - Martin Perry Studios	Yr.Iss.	1999	175.00	175-240

Lord Byron's Harmony Garden™ - M. Perry, unless otherwise noted

YEAR ISSUE	EDITION LIMIT	YEAR RETD.	ISSUE PRICE	*QUOTE U.S.$
2000 Albatross - M. Baldwin	Open		45.00	45
1999 Alpine Flower	Open		45.00	45
1997 Basket of Roses	3,600	1997	65.00	180-250
1998 Begonia	Retrd.	2000	45.00	45
1998 Cactus	Open		45.00	45
2000 Cherry Blossom - M. Baldwin	Open		45.00	45
1997 Chrysanthemum	Open		38.50	39
1997 Cranberry	12,667	1999	38.50	39-75
1997 Daisy	Retrd.	1999	38.50	39-69
1998 Double Rose (red)	5,000	1998	55.00	95-145
1998 Double Rose (pink)	5,000	1998	55.00	75-125
1998 Double Rose (violet)	5,000	1998	55.00	75-125
1998 Double Rose (yellow)	5,000	1998	55.00	75-138
1999 Double Silver Rose - R. Glover	1,500	1999	500.00	500
2000 Egyptian Rose - M. Baldwin	Open		45.00	45
1997 English Chrysanthemum	Retrd.	1997	38.50	82-120
1997 English Cranberry	Retrd.	1997	38.50	82-120
1997 English Daisy	Retrd.	1997	38.50	82-120
1997 English Hyacinth	Retrd.	1997	38.50	69-120
1997 English Hydrangea	Retrd.	1997	38.50	63-120
1997 English Marsh Marigold	Retrd.	1997	38.50	69-120
1997 English Morning Glory	Retrd.	1997	38.50	69-125
1997 English Peace Lily	Retrd.	1997	38.50	75-120
1997 English Rhododendron	Retrd.	1997	38.50	69-120
1997 English Snow Drop	Retrd.	1997	38.50	69-120
1997 English Roses, set/10	Retrd.	1997	385.00	600-875
2000 Fall Bouquet - S. Drackett	5,000	2000	75.00	75
1998 Forget Me Not	Retrd.	2000	45.00	45
1998 Gardenia	11,538	1999	45.00	45-63
1999 Gill	Retrd.	1999	45.00	45
2000 Grapes - M. Baldwin	Open		45.00	45
2000 Home Sweet Home	3,600	2000	250.00	250
1999 Hops	Open		45.00	45
1999 Hot Pepper	Open		45.00	45
1997 Hyacinth	Retrd.	1999	38.50	39-75
1997 Hydrangea	Retrd.	1999	38.50	39-75
1998 Iris	Open		45.00	45
2000 Lemon - M. Baldwin	Open		45.00	45
2000 Lotus - M. Baldwin	Open		45.00	45
1999 Marigold	Open		45.00	45
1997 Marsh Marigold	Retrd.	1999	38.50	39-75
1997 Morning Glory	Retrd.	2000	38.50	39-45
1999 Orange	Open		45.00	45
1997 Orange Rose	3,600	1998	38.50	94-150
1997 Peace Lily	Open		38.50	39
1997 Peach Rose	3,600	1997	38.50	119-125
1998 Peony	Open		45.00	45
1997 Pink Rose	3,600	1997	38.50	105-135
1999 Pomegranate	Open		45.00	45
2000 Poppy - M. Baldwin	Open		45.00	45
1997 Red Rose	3,600	1997	38.50	175-450
1997 Rhododendron	Retrd.	1999	38.50	39-75
1997 Rose Basket	3,600	1997	65.00	155-188
1998 Rose Bud	Open		45.00	45
1998 Rose Party	5,000	1998	100.00	105-175
1998 Snapdragon	Retrd.	2000	45.00	45
1998 Silver Rose	1,000	1998	400.00	480-600
1997 Snow Drop	11,893	1999	38.50	39-75
1998 Sunflower	Open		45.00	45
1999 Sunflower (II)	Open		45.00	45
1999 Tulip	Open		45.00	45
1997 Violet Rose	3,600	1997	38.50	90-145
1997 White Rose	3,600	1997	38.50	105-138
2000 Winter Bouquet - S. Drackett	5,000	2000	75.00	75
1997 Yellow Rose	3,600	1997	38.50	119-150

Mini Treasure Jest® - P. Calvesbert

YEAR ISSUE	EDITION LIMIT	YEAR RETD.	ISSUE PRICE	*QUOTE U.S.$
2000 Catch As Catch Can	Open		30.00	30
2000 The Good Race	Open		30.00	30
2000 Moggy Bag	Open		30.00	30
2000 Orange Crush	Open		30.00	30
2000 Pot Sticker	Retrd.	2000	30.00	30
2000 Trunk Call	Open		30.00	30

NALED Special Editions - D. Lawrence, unless otherwise noted

YEAR ISSUE	EDITION LIMIT	YEAR RETD.	ISSUE PRICE	*QUOTE U.S.$
1997 Cat's Cradle	1,000	1997	38.50	260-300
1997 Cat's Cradle Too	1,000	1997	38.50	225-300
1998 Kitty's Kippers	5,600	1998	45.00	45-75
1998 Peace Offering	4,200	1998	45.00	69-110
1999 Beware the Hare	4,200	1999	45.00	65-108
1999 Harmony Bull - P. Calvesbert	5,600		45.00	45

NetsUKe - P. Calvesbert

YEAR ISSUE	EDITION LIMIT	YEAR RETD.	ISSUE PRICE	*QUOTE U.S.$
2000 Francis	1,345	2000	20.00	20
2000 Georgie	Open		20.00	20
2000 Harry	Open		20.00	20
2000 Nell	Open		20.00	20
2000 Ollie	Open		20.00	20
2000 Sammy	Open		20.00	20
2000 Squee	Open		20.00	20
2000 Tarka	Open		20.00	20
2000 Waddles	Open		20.00	20

Parade of Gifts - Martin Perry Studios

YEAR ISSUE	EDITION LIMIT	YEAR RETD.	ISSUE PRICE	*QUOTE U.S.$
1999 The Parade of Gifts	5,000		75.00	75
1999 Pet Parade	5,000		45.00	45

Paradoxicals - P. Calvesbert

YEAR ISSUE	EDITION LIMIT	YEAR RETD.	ISSUE PRICE	*QUOTE U.S.$
1995 Paradise Found	7,628	1997	35.00	40-100
1995 Paradise Lost	9,855	1998	35.00	55-65

Picturesque Lord Byron's Secret Garden Tiles - M. Perry/A. Richmond

YEAR ISSUE	EDITION LIMIT	YEAR RETD.	ISSUE PRICE	*QUOTE U.S.$
1999 Bell Tower	Open		25.00	25
1999 Bumble's Bridge	Open		25.00	25
1999 Byron's Bower	Open		25.00	25
1999 Cata's Pillow	Open		25.00	25
1999 Fountain Blue	Open		25.00	25
1999 A Frog's Life	Open		25.00	25
1999 Garter of Eden	Open		25.00	25
1999 Gourmet Gazebo	Open		25.00	25
1999 Honey Brew	Open		25.00	25
1999 The Long Sleep	Open		25.00	25
1999 Love's Labours	Open		25.00	25
1999 Martin's Minstrels	Open		25.00	25
1999 Mayfly Madame	Open		25.00	25
1999 Mum's Reading Room	Open		25.00	25
1999 Slow Downs	Open		25.00	25
1999 Sun Worshipper	Open		25.00	25
1999 Swing Time	Open		25.00	25
1999 Two Blind Mice	Open		25.00	25
1999 Webmaster's Woe	Open		25.00	25
1999 Zen Garden	Open		25.00	25
1999 Byron's Hideaway	Open		55.00	55

Picturesque Noah's Park Tiles - M. Perry/A. Richmond

YEAR ISSUE	EDITION LIMIT	YEAR RETD.	ISSUE PRICE	*QUOTE U.S.$
1999 Beaky's Beach	Open		25.00	25
1999 Bungees in the Mist	Open		25.00	25

*Quotes have been rounded up to nearest dollar

YEAR ISSUE	EDITION LIMIT	YEAR RETD.	ISSUE PRICE	*QUOTE U.S.$
1999 Cliff Hangers	Open		25.00	25
1999 Dolphin Downs	Open		25.00	25
1999 Flamingo East	Open		25.00	25
1999 Flume Lagoon	Open		25.00	25
1999 Glacier Falls	Open		25.00	25
1999 Heart of Darkness	Open		25.00	25
1999 Krakatoa Lounge	Open		25.00	25
1999 The Lost Ark	Open		25.00	25
1999 Mark of the Beast	Open		25.00	25
1999 Nessie's Nook	Open		25.00	25
1999 Pelican Bay	Open		25.00	25
1999 Point Siren Song	Open		25.00	25
1999 Sky Master	Open		25.00	25
1999 Sun Catcher	Open		25.00	25
1999 Thunder Dome	Open		25.00	25
1999 Tilt-A-Whirl	Open		25.00	25
1999 Whale Watch	Open		25.00	25
1999 Whirligig Rainbow	Open		25.00	25
1999 Noah's Hideaway	Open		55.00	55

Picturesque Wimberley Tales - M. Ricketts

YEAR ISSUE	EDITION LIMIT	YEAR RETD.	ISSUE PRICE	*QUOTE U.S.$
1999 Wimberley Tales Premiere Set	Retrd.	1999	650.00	650-700
2000 The Builder	Open		35.00	35
2000 The Scientist	Open		35.00	35
2000 The Chef	Open		35.00	35
2000 The Doctor	Open		35.00	35
2000 The Dentist	Open		35.00	35
2000 The Clouds	Open		25.00	25
2000 The Sun	Open		25.00	25
2000 The Sea	Open		25.00	25
2000 The Fireman	Open		25.00	25
2000 The Harlot	Open		35.00	35
2000 The Chimney	Open		25.00	25
2000 The Rooftop	Open		35.00	35
2000 The Lovers	Open		35.00	35
2000 The Teacher	Open		35.00	35
2000 The Masquerade	Open		35.00	35
2000 The Artist	Open		35.00	35
2000 The Lawyer	Open		35.00	35
2000 The Birthday	Open		35.00	35
2000 The Baker	Open		35.00	35
2000 The Butcher	Open		35.00	35
2000 Wimberley Tales Set	Open		650.00	650

Rather Large Series - P. Calvesbert

YEAR ISSUE	EDITION LIMIT	YEAR RETD.	ISSUE PRICE	*QUOTE U.S.$
1996 Rather Large Friends	9,350	1998	65.00	65
1996 Rather Large Hop	4,330	1998	65.00	65-150
1996 Rather Large Huddle	5,423	1998	65.00	65
1996 Rather Large Safari	6,692	1998	65.00	65-150

Romance Annual - D. Lawrence, unless otherwise noted

YEAR ISSUE	EDITION LIMIT	YEAR RETD.	ISSUE PRICE	*QUOTE U.S.$
1997 Pillow Talk	Retrd.	1998	120.00	92-150
1998 Love Nest	Retrd.	1998	90.00	90-98
1999 Tender is the Night - Martin Perry Studios	Retrd.	2000	75.00	75
2000 Love and Peace - S. Drackett	Open		75.00	75

Small Treasure Jest® - P. Calvesbert

YEAR ISSUE	EDITION LIMIT	YEAR RETD.	ISSUE PRICE	*QUOTE U.S.$
1998 Algenon (1st Ed.)	3,000	1998	45.00	45-95
1998 Algenon (2nd Ed.)	Open		45.00	45
1994 All Angles Covered	Retrd.	2000	35.00	35
1993 All Ears	6,668	1996	35.00	250
1993 All Tied Up	4,566	1996	35.00	250
1998 Antipasto	Retrd.	1999	45.00	45-75
1998 Aria Amorosa	9,555	1998	45.00	45-69
1993 At Arm's Length	2,029	1996	35.00	360-600
1995 At The Hop	Open		35.00	35
1998 Baby Boomer (1st Ed.)	3,000	1998	45.00	55-95
1998 Baby Boomer (2nd Ed.)	Retrd.	1999	45.00	45
1993 Baby on Board	13,217	1997	35.00	40-100
1993 Back Scratch	554	1995	35.00	2000-4500
1997 Bamboozled	Open		45.00	45
1995 Beak To Beak	12,422	1997	35.00	40-100
2000 Beau Brummel	Open		45.00	45
1996 Brean Sands	Open		35.00	35
1998 Catch A Lot	Retrd.	1999	45.00	45
1999 Caw of the Wild	Open		45.00	45
1996 Changing of the Guard	Open		35.00	35
1996 Close Shave	10,913	1998	35.00	38-50
2000 Cookie's Jar	Open		45.00	45
1998 Croc Pot (1st Ed.-w/McD)	3,000	1998	45.00	82-95
1998 Croc Pot (2nd Ed.)	Retrd.	2000	45.00	45
1995 Damnable Plot	16,257	1999	35.00	35-63
1993 Day Dreamer	4,247	1996	35.00	480-675
1999 Dead Ringer	Open		45.00	45
1995 Den Mothers	6,264	1996	35.00	175-200
1994 Dog Days	Open		35.00	35
1997 Down Under	Retrd.	1999	35.00	35-57
1997 Driver's Seat	Open		45.00	45
1995 Ed's Safari	Open		35.00	35
1999 Ed's Safari II	Open		45.00	45
2000 Ed's Safari III	Open		45.00	45
1994 Family Tree	Retrd.	2000	35.00	35-38
1997 Faux Paw	Retrd.	1999	45.00	45-50
1992 Forty Winks	5,385	1996	35.00	280-300
1999 Foul Play	Open		45.00	45
1997 Friends in High Places	Open		45.00	45
1995 Fur Ball	Open		35.00	35
2000 Fusspot	Open		45.00	45
1999 The Great Escape	Open		45.00	45
2000 The Great Escape II	Open		45.00	45
1994 Group Therapy	3,170	1996	35.00	275-300
1993 Hammin' It Up	13,217	1996	35.00	135-225
1996 Hog Heaven	Retrd.	2000	35.00	35
1995 Horse Play	1,907	1996	35.00	270-400
1997 In Fine Feather	Retrd.	2000	45.00	45
1994 Inside Joke	Retrd.	2000	35.00	35-45
1993 It's A Fine Day	4,916	1996	35.00	250-450
1995 Jersey Belles	Open		35.00	35
1993 Jonah's Hideaway	7,342	1996	35.00	360-400
1999 The Last Laugh	Open		45.00	45
2000 Leatherneck's Lounge	Open		45.00	45
1994 Let's Do Lunch	1,269	1995	35.00	480-780
1996 Liberty and Justice	Retrd.	2000	45.00	45-55
1995 Life's a Picnic	17,842	1998	35.00	35-55
1994 Love Seat	11,510	1997	35.00	35-100
1995 Major's Mousers	9,372	1997	45.00	45-138
1998 Menage A Trois	Open		45.00	45
1995 Mud Bath	3,958	1997	35.00	90-225
1997 Murphy's Last Stand	10,168	1997	35.00	35-99
1994 Neighborhood Watch	8,837	1997	35.00	120-150
1993 Of The Same Stripe	Open		35.00	35
1999 Package Tour	Open		45.00	45
1991 Panda	100	1995	35.00	2000-2500
1999 Peace Summit	Open		45.00	45
1999 Pecking Order	Open		45.00	45
1999 Petty Teddies	Open		45.00	45
1997 Photo Finish	Retrd.	2000	45.00	45
1996 Pink Paradise	Retrd.	2000	35.00	35
1996 Pink Paradise (black beaks)	Retrd.	1996	35.00	35-57
1994 Play School	19,780	1998	35.00	35-38
1992 Princely Thoughts	9,682	1996	35.00	100-280
1995 Puddle Huddle	Open		35.00	35
1994 Purrfect Friends	Open		35.00	35
1991 Ram	100	1995	35.00	1000-1250
1993 Reminiscence	15,957	1996	35.00	125-260
1998 Rocky's Raiders	Retrd.	2000	45.00	45
1997 Rooster	300	1997	35.00	486-650
1996 Rumble Seat	Open		45.00	45
1993 School's Out	33,230	1999	35.00	35-38
1997 Shaggy Dog (Sheep Dog)	300	1997	35.00	550-750
1991 Shark	100	1995	35.00	1025-2000
1993 Shell Game	Open		35.00	35
1997 Shoe Bill	300	1997	35.00	650-750
1993 Side Steppin'	6,813	1996	35.00	115-150
1997 Sleepy Hollow	Open		35.00	35
2000 Special Delivery	Open		45.00	45
1997 Splashdown	Retrd.	2000	45.00	45
1994 Sunday Swim	Open		35.00	35
1993 Swamp Song	16,540	1997	35.00	35-100
1995 Sweet Serenade	Open		35.00	35
1994 Teacher's Pet	7,182	1997	35.00	100-225
1995 Teapot Angel I (UK)	43	1996	20.00	2000-4000
1995 Teapot Angel II (UK)	43	1996	20.00	2000-4000
1996 Tin Cat	14,418	1998	35.00	35-55
1996 Tin Cat (brown boat)	990	1996	35.00	200-207
1994 Tongue And Cheek	Open		35.00	35
1997 Tony's Tabbies	Open		45.00	45
2000 Tony's Tabbies II	Open		45.00	45
1994 Too Much of A Good Thing	15,631	1999	35.00	35-45
1993 Top Banana	1,499	1996	35.00	225
1996 Trumpeter's Ball	Open		45.00	45
1996 Trumpeter's Ball w/extra trunk	Retrd.	1996	45.00	320
1993 Trunk Show	6,467	1996	35.00	250-350
1999 Turdus Felidae	Open		45.00	45
1995 Unbridled & Groomed	20,382	1998	35.00	55-120
1994 Unexpected Arrival	Retrd.	2000	35.00	35-38
1994 Untouchable	1,889	1995	35.00	360-400
1997 Whale of a Time	15,154	1998	35.00	35-52
1999 When Nature Calls	Open		45.00	45
1993 Who'd A Thought	935	1995	35.00	1500-2750
1995 Wise Guys	Retrd.	2000	35.00	35
1998 Wishful Thinking (1st Ed.)	3,000	1998	45.00	45-100
1998 Wishful Thinking (1st Ed.-Full Screw)	Retrd.	1998	45.00	95-150
1998 Wishful Thinking (2nd Ed.)	Retrd.	1999	45.00	45-60

Special Edition - P. Calvesbert

YEAR ISSUE	EDITION LIMIT	YEAR RETD.	ISSUE PRICE	*QUOTE U.S.$
1996 Angel Baroque	62	1997	45.00	2000
1995 Primordial Soup	Retrd.	1999	150.00	150-200
1997 Scratching Post (HK Pen)	10,000		45.00	45
1997 Tabby Totem (HK Pen)	10,000		45.00	45

Wee Beasties - Martin Perry Studios

YEAR ISSUE	EDITION LIMIT	YEAR RETD.	ISSUE PRICE	*QUOTE U.S.$
1998 Helen the Owl	Open		Gift	N/A
1998 Marty the Polar Bear	Open		Gift	N/A
1998 Pip the Pelican	Open		Gift	N/A
1998 Zephyr the Monkey	Open		Gift	N/A

Wild Birds Unlimited Special - D. Lawrence

YEAR ISSUE	EDITION LIMIT	YEAR RETD.	ISSUE PRICE	*QUOTE U.S.$
1999 Jewels of the Wild	5,000	1999	75.00	75

Little Angel Publishing

Heaven's Little Angel - D. Gelsinger

YEAR ISSUE	EDITION LIMIT	YEAR RETD.	ISSUE PRICE	*QUOTE U.S.$
1999 Ornament Box	Open		34.99	35
1999 Photo Box	Open		14.99	15

Heaven's Little Guardian - D. Gelsinger

YEAR ISSUE	EDITION LIMIT	YEAR RETD.	ISSUE PRICE	*QUOTE U.S.$
1999 Angel's Prayer Music Box	Open		29.95	30

Memories of Yesterday/Enesco Group, Inc.

Covered Boxes - M. Attwell

YEAR ISSUE	EDITION LIMIT	YEAR RETD.	ISSUE PRICE	*QUOTE U.S.$
1998 Can I Keep Her, Mommy? 314862	Retrd.	1999	25.00	25
1998 Here Comes The Bride-God Bless Her 314870	Retrd.	1999	25.00	25
1998 Hoping To See You Soon 279706	Retrd.	1999	25.00	25
1998 How 'bout A Little Kiss 279730	Retrd.	1999	25.00	25
1998 I Pray Thee Lord My Soul To Keep 279714	Retrd.	1999	25.00	25
1998 Let Me Be Your Guardian Angel 279722	Retrd.	1999	25.00	25
1998 May Your Birthday Be Happy And Bright 314889	Retrd.	1999	25.00	25
1998 Mommy, I Teared 314897	Retrd.	1999	25.00	25
1998 Now I Lay Me Down To Sleep 279749	Retrd.	1999	25.00	25
1998 Time For Bed 279765	Retrd.	1999	25.00	25

Midwest of Cannon Falls

Porcelain Hinged Box-Beatrix Potter Limited Edition Collection - Midwest

YEAR ISSUE	EDITION LIMIT	YEAR RETD.	ISSUE PRICE	*QUOTE U.S.$
1998 Benjamin Bunny 27676-1	5,000	2000	25.00	25
1998 Jemima Puddle-duck 28289-2	5,000	1999	25.00	25
1998 Jeremy Fischer 27674-7	5,000		25.00	25
1998 Peter Rabbit 28290-8	10,000	2000	25.00	25
1998 Tailor of Gloucester 27675-4	5,000		25.00	25
1998 Tom Kitten 27673-0	5,000	2000	25.00	25

Porcelain Hinged Box-Coca Cola - Midwest

YEAR ISSUE	EDITION LIMIT	YEAR RETD.	ISSUE PRICE	*QUOTE U.S.$
2000 Coca Cola Santa, set/2 38342-1	Yr.Iss.		45.00	45
1999 Santa with Coke PHB set/2 33812-4	Yr.Iss.	1999	35.00	35

Porcelain Hinged Box-Retrospect Series - Midwest

YEAR ISSUE	EDITION LIMIT	YEAR RETD.	ISSUE PRICE	*QUOTE U.S.$
2000 Betty Boop w/Mirror, set/2 39456-4	3,600		25.00	25
2000 Betty Boop w/Pudgy, set/2 39457-1	3,600		25.00	25
2000 Betty Boop, waving w/Credit Card, set/2 39458-8	3,600		25.00	25
2000 Budweiser Clydesdale Horses & Wagon, set/6 38480-0	Yr.Iss.		65.00	65
2000 Tonka Crane w/Hard Hat, set/2 39465-6	3,600		30.00	30
2000 Tonka Fire Truck w/Hydrant, set/2 39464-9	3,600		30.00	30
2000 Tonka Mighty Mike w/Hard Hat, set/2 39466-3	3,600		30.00	30

Porcelain Hinged Box-Songbird Series - Midwest

YEAR ISSUE	EDITION LIMIT	YEAR RETD.	ISSUE PRICE	*QUOTE U.S.$
1998 American Goldfinch 26929-9	5,000		19.00	19
1998 American Robin 26934-3	5,000		19.00	19
1998 Black Capped Chickadee 26931-2	5,000	1998	19.00	19
1998 Cardinal 26932-9	5,000	1998	19.00	19
1998 Eastern Bluebird 26933-6	5,000	2000	19.00	19
1998 Ruby Throated Hummingbird 26930-5	5,000	1999	19.00	19

Porcelain Hinged Box-That's Entertainment Series - Midwest

YEAR ISSUE	EDITION LIMIT	YEAR RETD.	ISSUE PRICE	*QUOTE U.S.$
2000 Elvis Blue Suede Shoes w/Record, set/2 39600-1	3,600		25.00	25
2000 Elvis Guitar and Gold Record w/Pick, set/2 39467-0	3,600		25.00	25
2000 Elvis Record Player w/Record, set/2 39524-0	3,600		25.00	25
2000 Graceland w/Guitar, set/2 39541-7	3,600		25.00	25

Prizm, Inc./Pipka

Pipka's Music Boxes - Pipka

YEAR ISSUE	EDITION LIMIT	YEAR RETD.	ISSUE PRICE	*QUOTE U.S.$
2000 Christmas Ark 11604	200		170.00	170
2000 Christmas Tree 11606	200		120.00	120
2000 Teddy Bear Santa 11605	200		120.00	120

Reco International

Hearts & Flowers Music Boxes - S. Kuck

YEAR ISSUE	EDITION LIMIT	YEAR RETD.	ISSUE PRICE	*QUOTE U.S.$
2000 Tea Party	95-day		30.00	30

Precious Child Music Boxes - S. Kuck

YEAR ISSUE	EDITION LIMIT	YEAR RETD.	ISSUE PRICE	*QUOTE U.S.$
2000 Monday's Child	95-day		30.00	30
2000 Tuesday's Child	95-day		30.00	30
2000 Wednesday's Child	95-day		30.00	30
2000 Thursday's Child	95-day		30.00	30
2000 Friday's Child	95-day		30.00	30
2000 Saturday's Child	95-day		30.00	30
2000 Sunday's Child	95-day		30.00	30

School Days Lunch Boxes/Hallmark Keepsake

School Days Lunch Boxes - Hallmark Keepsake Collections

YEAR ISSUE	EDITION LIMIT	YEAR RETD.	ISSUE PRICE	*QUOTE U.S.$
1999 1950s Donald Duck QHM8806	Numbrd.		10.95	11
2000 1950s Hopalong Cassidy QHM8809	Numbrd.		10.95	11
1998 1950s Howdy Doody QHM8801	Retrd.	1999	10.95	11
1998 1950s Lone Ranger QHM8802	Retrd.	1999	10.95	11
2000 1950s Mickey Mouse Circus QHM8816	Numbrd.		10.95	11
1998 1950s Superman QHM8803	Retrd.	1999	10.95	11
2000 1960s Mickey's School Days QHM8804	12/00		10.95	11
1999 1960s Star Trek™ QHM8810	Numbrd.		10.95	11
2000 1960s Yellow Submarine™ QHM8901	29,500		11.95	12
1999 1962 BARBIE™ QHM8807	12/00		10.95	11
2000 1963 The Jetsons™	29,500		11.95	12
1998 1970s Hot Wheels QHM8813	Retrd.	1999	10.95	11
1999 1970s Snow White QHM8814	Numbrd.		10.95	11
1999 1973 Super Friends™ QHM8815	Numbrd.		10.95	11
1999 1977 Star Wars™ QHM8817	12/00		10.95	11

*Quotes have been rounded up to nearest dollar

YEAR ISSUE	EDITION LIMIT	YEAR RETD.	ISSUE PRICE	*QUOTE U.S.$
1999 1980 Peanuts® QHM8812	12/00		10.95	11
2000 Batman™ and Robin™	29,500		12.95	13
2000 Bewitched QHM8824	Numbrd.		10.95	11
2000 Bozo QHM8906	24,500		11.95	12
2000 Cinderella QHM8826	19,500		13.95	14
2000 Disney School Bus QHM8907	24,500		11.95	12
2000 The Empire Strikes Back Star Wars™ QHM8820	Numbrd.		10.95	11
2000 Flintstones QHM8828	19,500		13.95	14
2000 GI Joe QHM8827	19,500		13.95	14
2000 Harry Potter	Numbrd.		10.95	11
1999 Looney Tunes™ Rodeo QHM8805	Numbrd.		10.95	11
2000 Porky's Lunch Wagon QHM8903	24,500		11.95	12
2000 Return of the Jedi QHM8825	Numbrd.		10.95	11
1999 Scooby-Doo™ QHM8818	Numbrd.		10.95	11
2000 Snoopy QHM8905	24,500		11.95	12
2000 Three Little Pigs QHM8908	24,500		11.95	12
2000 Walt Disney Character Fire Fighters QHM8904	24,500		11.95	12
2000 Winnie the Pooh QHM8821	Numbrd.		10.95	11
2000 Wizard of Oz QHM8822	19,500		13.95	14

Willitts Designs

The Blackshear Style - T. Blackshear

YEAR ISSUE	EDITION LIMIT	YEAR RETD.	ISSUE PRICE	*QUOTE U.S.$
2000 Father's Keepsake Box	Open		125.00	125
2000 Heart Treasures Keepsake Box	Open		50.00	50
2000 Lover's Keepsake Box	Open		50.00	50
2000 Mother's Keepsake Box	Open		42.50	43

DOLLS/PLUSH

Alexander Doll Company

Madame Alexander Doll Club (M.A.D.C.)-Convention Dolls - Madame Alexander Design Staff

YEAR ISSUE	EDITION LIMIT	YEAR RETD.	ISSUE PRICE	*QUOTE U.S.$
1984 Ballerina 8" - Schumburg, IL	360	1984	N/A	N/A
1985 Happy Birthday 8" - Miami, FL	450	1985	N/A	N/A
1986 Scarlett 8" - Atlanta, GA	625	1986	N/A	N/A
1987 Cowboy 8" - San Antonio, TX	720	1987	N/A	275-325
1988 Flapper 10" - Chicago, IL	720	1988	N/A	175
1989 Briar Rose 8" - Los Angeles, CA	804	1989	N/A	225
1990 Riverboat Queen (Lena) 8" - New Orleans, LA	925	1990	N/A	N/A
1991 Queen Charlotte 10" - Charlotte, NC	900	1991	N/A	N/A
1992 Prom Queen (Memories) 8" - Chicago, IL	1,100	1992	N/A	N/A
1993 Diamond Lil (Days Gone By) 10" - Kansas City, MO	876	1993	N/A	N/A
1994 Navajo Women 8" - Phoenix, AZ	835	1994	N/A	N/A
1995 Frances Folsom 10" - Washington DC	N/A	1995	N/A	200
1996 Showgirl 10" - Las Vegas, NV	N/A	1996	N/A	N/A
1997 A Little Bit of Country 8" - Nashville, TN	N/A	1997	N/A	N/A

Madame Alexander Annual Member's Only - Madame Alexander Design Staff

YEAR ISSUE	EDITION LIMIT	YEAR RETD.	ISSUE PRICE	*QUOTE U.S.$
1989 Wendy 8"	4,878	1989	49.95	100
1990 Polly Pigtails 8"	4,896	1990	49.95	50-100
1991 Miss Liberty 10"	Retrd.	1992	69.95	N/A
1992 Little Miss Godey 8"	Retrd.	1993	79.95	N/A
1994 Wendy's Best Friend Maggie 8"	Retrd.	1994	74.95	N/A
1995 Wendy Joins M.A.D.C. 8"	Retrd.	1995	49.95	125
1996 Wendy Honors Margaret Winson 8"	Retrd.	1996	69.95	N/A
1997 From The Madame's Sketchbook 8"	Retrd.	1997	69.95	N/A

Alice in Wonderland - Madame Alexander Design Staff

YEAR ISSUE	EDITION LIMIT	YEAR RETD.	ISSUE PRICE	*QUOTE U.S.$
1996 Alice in Wonderland 13001	Open		69.95	70
1996 Cheshire Cat 13070	Open		54.95	60
1998 Dormouse 13090	Open		89.95	90
1996 Humpty Dumpty 13060	Retrd.	1999	64.95	70
1996 Knave 13040	Open		69.95	75
1996 Red Queen 13010	Open		109.95	115
1997 Red Queen and White King, set 13030	Retrd.	N/A	199.95	200
1998 Tweedledee 13120	Open		79.95	80
1998 Tweedledum 13110	Open		79.95	80
1998 Tweedledum and Tweedledee 13080, set	Open		159.95	160
1996 White King 13020	Retrd.	N/A	89.95	95
1997 White Rabbit 13050	Retrd.	1997	59.95	60

Cinderella - Madame Alexander Design Staff

YEAR ISSUE	EDITION LIMIT	YEAR RETD.	ISSUE PRICE	*QUOTE U.S.$
1997 Cinderella's Prince, 8" 13420	Retrd.	1997	64.95	65
1997 Cinderella, 8" 13400	Open		64.95	70
1997 Fairy Godmother, 8" 13430	Open		69.95	75
1997 Poor Cinderella, 8" 13410	Open		69.95	75
1997 Really Ugly Stepsister, 8" 13450	Open		79.95	85
1997 Ugly Stepsister, 10" 13440	Open		79.95	85

Cissette - Madame Alexander Design Staff

YEAR ISSUE	EDITION LIMIT	YEAR RETD.	ISSUE PRICE	*QUOTE U.S.$
1997 Cissette Houndstooth (African American) 22193	Retrd.	1999	119.95	120
1997 Cissette Houndstooth 22190	Retrd.	1999	119.95	120
1997 Cissette Onyx 22170	Retrd.	1999	119.95	120
1997 Cissette Café Rose (African American) 22203	Retrd.	1999	119.95	120
1997 Cissette Café Rose 22200	Retrd.	1999	119.95	120
1997 Cissette Leopard w/ Shopping Bag (African American) 22183	Retrd.	1999	119.95	120
1997 Cissette Leopard w/ Shopping Bag 22180	Retrd.	1999	119.95	120
1997 Cissette Onyx (African American) 22173	Retrd.	1999	119.95	120

Cissy - Madame Alexander Design Staff

YEAR ISSUE	EDITION LIMIT	YEAR RETD.	ISSUE PRICE	*QUOTE U.S.$
1998 Cissy Barcelona (African American) 22333	1,500		589.95	590
1998 Cissy Barcelona 22330	1,500		589.95	590
1998 Cissy Budapest 22340	1,500		589.95	590
1998 Cissy Milan 22320	1,500		589.95	590
1998 Cissy Paris 22300	1,500		589.95	590
1998 Cissy Venice 22310	1,500		589.95	590

The Dionne Quintuplets - Madame Alexander Design Staff

YEAR ISSUE	EDITION LIMIT	YEAR RETD.	ISSUE PRICE	*QUOTE U.S.$
1998 Annette (yellow) 12250	Retrd.	1999	84.95	85
1998 Cécile (green) 12270	Retrd.	1999	84.95	85
1998 Emilie (lilac) 12280	Retrd.	1999	84.95	85
1998 Marie (blue) 12260	Retrd.	1999	84.95	85
1998 Yvonne (pink) 12240	Retrd.	1999	84.95	85

Disneyana Convention - Madame Alexander Design Staff

YEAR ISSUE	EDITION LIMIT	YEAR RETD.	ISSUE PRICE	*QUOTE U.S.$
1993 Annette	1,000	1993	395.00	605-780

Gone With The Wind™ - Madame Alexander Design Staff

YEAR ISSUE	EDITION LIMIT	YEAR RETD.	ISSUE PRICE	*QUOTE U.S.$
1997 Mammy 15010	Open		89.95	95
1998 Poor Scarlett 14970	Open		94.95	95
1997 Rhett 15050	Retrd.	1997	89.95	90
1997 Scarlett 15040	Retrd.	1997	109.95	110
1996 Scarlett Hoop-Petti 15000	Open		99.95	100
1996 Scarlett Hoop-Petti Mammy & Flower Dress 15020	Open		219.95	230
1997 Scarlett Rose Picnic Dress 15070	Retrd.	1997	349.95	350
1997 Shadow Scarlett Rose Picnic 15030	Retrd.	1999	74.95	80

Harley Davidson® - Madame Alexander Design Staff

YEAR ISSUE	EDITION LIMIT	YEAR RETD.	ISSUE PRICE	*QUOTE U.S.$
1997 Billy 17410	Retrd.	1997	99.95	100
1998 Cissette 17390	Retrd.	N/A	149.95	150
1997 Cissette 17440	Retrd.	1997	120.00	120
1997 David 17430	Retrd.	1997	120.00	120
1997 Wendy 17420	Retrd.	1997	99.95	100

Sleeping Beauty - Madame Alexander Design Staff

YEAR ISSUE	EDITION LIMIT	YEAR RETD.	ISSUE PRICE	*QUOTE U.S.$
1997 Evil Sorceress, 8" 13610	Retrd.	1997	69.95	75
1997 Fairy of Beauty (pink), 8" 13620	Open		69.95	75
1997 Fairy of Song (green), 8" 13630	Open		69.95	75
1997 Fairy of Virtue (blue), 8" 13640	Open		69.95	75
1997 Sleeping Beauty, 8" 13600	Open		69.95	70

The Sound of Music™ - Madame Alexander Design Staff

YEAR ISSUE	EDITION LIMIT	YEAR RETD.	ISSUE PRICE	*QUOTE U.S.$
1998 Brigitta Von Trapp 14040	Open		99.95	100
1998 Captain Von Trapp 14030	Open		124.95	125
1998 Friedrick Von Trapp, 9" 14020	Open		99.95	100
1998 Gretl Von Trapp 14060	Open		99.95	100
1998 Kurt Von Trapp, 10" 14090	Open		99.95	100
1998 Liesl Von Trapp, 10" 14170	Open		99.95	100
1998 Louisa Von Trapp, 10" 14160	Open		99.95	100
1997 Maria at the Abbey 13890	Open		124.95	125
1997 Maria Travel Ensemble 13880	Open		124.95	125
1998 Marta Von Trapp 14050	Open		99.95	100
1997 Mother Superior 13870	Open		114.95	115

The Wizard of Oz™ - Madame Alexander Design Staff

YEAR ISSUE	EDITION LIMIT	YEAR RETD.	ISSUE PRICE	*QUOTE U.S.$
1993 The Cowardly Lion™ 13220	Open		64.95	70
1991 Dorothy™ with Toto™ 13200	Open		46.95	60
1997 Glinda the Good Witch™ 13250	Open		109.95	115
1997 Miss Gulch™ with Bicycle and Toto™ 13240	Open		119.95	120
1993 The Scarecrow™ 13230	Open		59.95	65
1993 The Tin Man™ 13210	Open		64.95	70
1997 The Wicked Witch of the West™ 13270	Open		99.95	100
1998 The Wizard of Oz™ 13281	Open		94.95	95
1998 The Wizard™ with State Fair Balloon 13280	Open		139.95	140

All God's Children/Miss Martha Originals

Anika Series - M. Root

YEAR ISSUE	EDITION LIMIT	YEAR RETD.	ISSUE PRICE	*QUOTE U.S.$
1996 Anika - 2600	5,000	1996	175.00	250-280
1997 Skating Anika - 2601	7,500	1998	125.00	150
1998 Anika III - 2602	5,000	1998	135.00	135

Ann Series - M. Root

YEAR ISSUE	EDITION LIMIT	YEAR RETD.	ISSUE PRICE	*QUOTE U.S.$
1999 Ann (Hawaiian) - Reunion Piece	Retrd.	1999	125.00	125
1999 Ann (school girl) 2401	Open		87.00	87

Doll Series - M. Root

YEAR ISSUE	EDITION LIMIT	YEAR RETD.	ISSUE PRICE	*QUOTE U.S.$
2000 Jody - 2402	Open		87.00	87
2000 Holiday Ann - 2403	2,500		135.00	135

Annalee Mobilitee Dolls, Inc.

Doll Society-Animals - A. Thorndike

YEAR ISSUE	EDITION LIMIT	YEAR RETD.	ISSUE PRICE	*QUOTE U.S.$
1985 10" Penguin and Chick	3,000	N/A	29.95	80-85
1985 10" Penguin and Chick w/ dome	3,000	N/A	29.95	100
1986 10" Unicorn	3,000	N/A	36.95	110
1987 7" Kangaroo 9624	3,000	N/A	37.45	85-100
1988 5" Owl 9630	3,000	N/A	37.45	95-100
1989 7" Polar Bear Cub 9636	3,000	N/A	37.50	90-100
1990 7" Thorndike Chicken 9642	3,000	N/A	37.50	90

Doll Society-Folk Heroes - A. Thorndike

YEAR ISSUE	EDITION LIMIT	YEAR RETD.	ISSUE PRICE	*QUOTE U.S.$
1984 10" Johnny Appleseed w/ dome	1,500	N/A	80.00	550
1984 10" Robin Hood w/ dome	1,500	N/A	90.00	550
1985 10" Annie Oakley w/ dome	1,500	N/A	95.00	450
1986 10" Mark Twain w/ dome	2,500	N/A	117.50	350
1987 10" Ben Franklin w/ dome 9622	2,500	N/A	119.50	325
1988 10" Sherlock Holmes w/ dome 9628	2,500	N/A	119.50	300
1989 10" Abraham Lincoln w/ dome 9634	2,500	N/A	119.50	275
1990 10" Betsy Ross w/ dome 9644	2,500	N/A	119.50	275
1991 10" Christopher Columbus w/dome 9649	2,500	N/A	119.50	275
1992 14" Uncle Sam 9652	2,500	N/A	87.50	275-295
1993 10" Pony Express Rider 9654	2,500	N/A	97.50	275
1994 10" Bean Nose Santa w/dome 9657	2,500	N/A	119.50	275
1995 10" Pocahontas w/dome 9659	1,300	N/A	87.50	275

Doll Society-Great American Era - A. Thorndike

YEAR ISSUE	EDITION LIMIT	YEAR RETD.	ISSUE PRICE	*QUOTE U.S.$
1996 10" Fabulous 50's Couple w/ dome 9961	1,500	1997	150.00	275
1997 10" Roaring Twenties 9663	Yr.Iss.	1997	160.00	225-250
1998 10" Gay Nineties 9665	Retrd.	1999	175.00	175-250
1999 10" Hippie Couple 9677	Retrd.	2000	175.00	175
2000 10" Wild & Romantic 1880's 9679	6/01		195.00	195

Doll Society-Logo Kids - A. Thorndike

YEAR ISSUE	EDITION LIMIT	YEAR RETD.	ISSUE PRICE	*QUOTE U.S.$
1985 7" Kid w/Milk & Cookies w/ pin 9605	3,562	1986	10.00	375
1985 7" Kid w/Milk & Cookies w/ pin (signed) 9605	Closed	1986	10.00	595
1986 7" Sweetheart Kid w/ pin 9614	6,271	1987	18.00	175-190
1987 7" Naughty Kid w /pin 9626	11,100	1988	18.00	125-130
1987 7" Naughty Kid w /no pin 9626	Closed	1988	18.00	75
1988 7" Raincoat Kid w/ pin 96932	13,646	1989	20.00	80-110
1989 7" Christmas Morning Kid w/ pin 9638	16,641	1990	20.00	80-100
1990 7" Clown Kid w/ pin 9648	20,049	1991	20.00	80-100
1991 7" Reading Kid w/ pin 9650	26,516	1992	20.00	70-80
1992 7" Back To School Kid w/ pin 9651	17,524	1993	25.00	60-70
1993 7" Ice Cream Logo w/ pin 9653	Yr.Iss.	1994	28.00	50-60
1994 7" Dress Up Santa Logo 9656	Yr.Iss	1995	28.00	50
1995 7" Goin' Fishin' Logo 9658	Yr.Iss	1995	30.00	40
1996 7" Little Mae Flower Logo 9660	Yr.Iss.	1997	30.00	50
1997 7" Tea For Two 9662	Yr.Iss	1997	30.00	30-45
1998 7" 15th Anniversary	Retrd.	1999	37.95	38-45
1999 7" Mending My Teddy Logo 9666	Retrd.	2000	37.95	38
2000 7" Precious Cargo 9678	6/01		37.95	38

Doll Society-Around The World Couples - A. Thorndike

YEAR ISSUE	EDITION LIMIT	YEAR RETD.	ISSUE PRICE	*QUOTE U.S.$
1997 India Couple	N/A	1998	90.00	150
1998 Japan Couple	Retrd.	1999	95.00	95
1999 Spanish Couple	Open		95.00	95
2000 Dutch Couple 9853	Open		80.00	80

Doll Society-Collector Kids - A. Thorndike

YEAR ISSUE	EDITION LIMIT	YEAR RETD.	ISSUE PRICE	*QUOTE U.S.$
1999 7" Rosie 9668	Closed	2000	40.00	40
1999 7" Summer Solitude 9669	Closed	2000	40.00	40
1999 7" Teacher's Pet 9670	Closed	2000	40.00	40
1999 7" Apres Ski 9667	Closed	2000	40.00	40
2000 7" Dressing Like Mommy 9671	6/01		40.00	40
2000 7" Chores First Kid 9672	6/01		40.00	40

Event Pieces - A. Thorndike

YEAR ISSUE	EDITION LIMIT	YEAR RETD.	ISSUE PRICE	*QUOTE U.S.$
1994 10" Redcoat w/Cannon, signed by Annalee	Yr.Iss	1994	84.00	195-250
1995 10" Tennessee Fiddler, signed by Annalee	Yr.Iss	1995	80.00	195-225
1995 3" C'mas Morn Itsie Vignette, signed by Chuck	Yr.Iss	1995	68.00	195-250
1996 3" Dreams of Gold Vignette (w/ dome)	Yr.Iss	1996	85.00	175
1996 10" Candlemaker Women (Fall Auction) 9703	Yr.Iss	1996	90.00	275
1997 10" Summer School Elf (June Auction) 9706	Yr.Iss	1997	23.00	50-65
1997 7" Ringmaster Mouse, signed by Chuck 9705	Yr.Iss	1997	50.00	50
1998 10" Fabulous Floozy Frogs (trunk show) 9709	Yr.Iss	1998	50.00	65
1998 3" Hugs and Kisses (National Open House) 9887	Yr.Iss	1998	25.00	25-35
1998 Percy Pirate	Yr.Iss	1998	39.00	60
1999 8" Nautical Bear (June Social)	Closed	1999	30.00	75
1999 7" Celebrate 2000 Mouse (signed by Chuck)	Yr.Iss.	1999	30.00	55-75
1999 3" Pick-of-the-Patch Mouse (National Open House) 9881	Closed	1999	25.00	25-35
1999 3" Sweet Pea Mouse 9883	Closed	1999	25.00	25-35
2000 3" Fantasy Flight (April Open House) 9880	Closed	2000	35.00	35
2000 8" Hiking Bear (June Social) 9706	550	2000	36.00	36
2000 Factory Tour Pin 9731	Closed	2000	5.00	35

Limited Editions - A. Thorndike

YEAR ISSUE	EDITION LIMIT	YEAR RETD.	ISSUE PRICE	*QUOTE U.S.$
1997 5" Don't Open Til Christmas I (Parkwest) 9903	500	1997	27.50	75
1997 5" Don't Open Til Christmas II (Parkwest) 9889	625	1997	30.00	60
1997 5" Sleigh Ride Couple 4539	2,500	1997	100.00	150
1998 7" Barrows of Spring Wishes (Parkwest) 9890	1,000	1998	29.50	75
1997 7" Bathtime For Buddy 2336	3,500	1997	55.00	70
1997 7" Fortunoff 75th Anniversary 9919	750	1997	29.00	65
2000 7" Patriotic Boy (Sue Coffee Exclusive) 9845	1,200	2000	50.00	55
2000 7" Patriotic Girl #2 (Sue Coffee Exclusive) 9844	600	2000	55.00	75-95
2000 7" Patriotic Girl (Sue Coffee Exclusive) 9876	500	2000	45.00	50

*Quotes have been rounded up to nearest dollar

YEAR ISSUE	EDITION LIMIT	YEAR RETD.	ISSUE PRICE	*QUOTE U.S.$
2000 8" Fiona Fox (signed by Chuck) 8506	Closed	2000	50.00	N/A
2000 8" Frederick Fox (signed by Chuck) 8507	Closed	2000	50.00	N/A
2000 8" Frederick Fox (signed by Chuck) 8507 & Fiona Fox (signed by Chuck) 8506	Closed	2000	100.00	300
1999 8" Rosie Bear (Rosemont Show) 9749	149	1999	37.00	250-295
1998 10" Christmas Tree-ditions (Parkwest) 9892	1,500	1998	95.00	150
1997 10" Crystal Angel (QVC Exclusive) 9917	1,000	1997	55.00	165
1998 10" Harvest Angel 3026	5,000	1998	60.00	80
1997 10" Little Lord Taylor (green) 9904	375	1997	65.00	250-275
1997 10" Little Lord Taylor (red) 9934	1,000	1997	65.00	165
1998 10" Little Lord Taylor Katie Kat	250	1998	45.00	225
1998 10" Little Lord Taylor Katie Kat (signed by Chuck & Karen) 9928	250	1998	45.00	295
1998 10" Little Miss Taylor 9899	1,300	1998	65.00	125
1999 10" Macy's Elf 9879	2,000	1999	38.00	38
1997 10" Merry Christmas to All (Parkwest) 9901	750	1997	85.00	165
1997 10" Merry Christmas To All 9705	750	1997	85.00	150
1999 10" Patriotic Elf (Smithsonian Folklife Festival) 9720	1,736	1999	60.00	60
1998 10" Tea Tyme Toads 9709	Closed	1998	60.00	95
1998 10" Wanda the Witch 3029	5,000	1998	55.00	75
1987 18" Macy's Workshop Santa 9908	Closed	1987	40.00	150
1997 18" Tis The Night Before Christmas 5611	3,500	1997	95.00	120-125
1999 8" Poodle Gigi Lord & Taylor (signed by Chuck & Karen) 9877	350	1999	45.00	175
1998 In From The Cold 7776	2,200	1998	70.00	125

Museum Collection - A. Thorndike

YEAR ISSUE	EDITION LIMIT	YEAR RETD.	ISSUE PRICE	*QUOTE U.S.$
1997 12" 1956 Ski Doll 9752-97	3,500		95.00	95
1997 14" Rogers Clothing Store Man & Woman 9750-97	3,500		225.00	225
1997 15" Woman with Red Felt Coat 9751-97	3,500		65.00	65

Disney Pieces - A. Thorndike

YEAR ISSUE	EDITION LIMIT	YEAR RETD.	ISSUE PRICE	*QUOTE U.S.$
1991 7" Fun in the Sun w/pin, signed	300	1991	65.00	300-325
1992 7" Nick w/pin, signed	300	1992	95.00	300-325
1993 7" Eric & Shane w/pin, signed	100	1993	110.00	425
1994 10" Piper Bear w/pin, signed	200	1994	130.00	275-295
1995 10" Chip Bear in Boat w/pin, signed	200	1995	125.00	295-300
1996 10" Indian Chief Bear w/pin, signed	200	1996	130.00	275-295

Angels - A. Thorndike

YEAR ISSUE	EDITION LIMIT	YEAR RETD.	ISSUE PRICE	*QUOTE U.S.$
1995 5" Angel w/ 18" Christmas Moon (yellow) 7173	Closed	1995	55.00	45-95
1993 7" Angel (Blonde Hair) 7108	Closed	1996	25.00	40
1976 7" Angel on Cloud 7105	Closed	1976	13.00	30
1992 7" Angel on Moon (white) 7171	Yr.Iss.	1992	40.00	100
1990 7" Angel on Sled w/ Cloud 7168	Closed	1991	30.00	65
1984 7" Angel on Star 7150	Closed	1984	33.00	225
1995 7" Angel Playing Harp 7111	Closed	1996	27.00	45
1982 7" Angel w/ Instrument 7110	Closed	1996	22.00	30
1976 7" Angel w/ Mistletoe 7140	Closed	1993	19.00	30
1950 7" Baby Angel w/ Feather Hair & Wreath on Head	Closed	N/A	3.00	300
1994 7" Flying Angel 7113	Closed	1996	26.00	26-45
1968 7" Flying Star Angel	Closed	1969	3.00	225
1981 7" Naughty Angel 7115	Closed	1986	18.00	28-50
1956 10" Baby Angel (feather hair)	Closed	1957	N/A	550
1991 10" Nativity Angel w/ plaque 5430	Yr.Iss.	1991	60.00	110
1976 12" Angel on Cloud N-125	Closed	1983	11.00	85
1987 12" Flying Angel w/ Instrument 7162	Closed	1987	37.00	85
1984 12" Naughty Angel 7160	Closed	1986	37.00	85
1984 12" Tree Top Angel (holds gold star) 7165	Closed	1985	37.00	75
1991 12" Tree Top Angel (white outfit w/ red bow) 7165	Closed	1991	43.00	65
1990 18" Angel w/ Instrument 7170	Closed	1991	56.00	110
1990 30" Angel 7172	Closed	1990	76.00	150

Assorted Animals & Birds - A. Thorndike

YEAR ISSUE	EDITION LIMIT	YEAR RETD.	ISSUE PRICE	*QUOTE U.S.$
1979 4" Boy Pig (white body) N-571	Closed	1979	N/A	65
1997 4" Fifi the Poodle 2420	Closed	1997	20.00	35
1979 4" Girl Pig (white body) N-570	Closed	1979	N/A	65
1980 4" Pig (beige body) R-541	Closed	1981	N/A	65
1996 4" Puppy Present 7421	Closed	1997	21.00	35
1997 4" Spot the Dalmation 2421	Closed	1997	20.00	35
1989 5" Baby Swan 7408	Closed	1991	14.00	30
1993 5" Christmas Lamb (black) 7425	Closed	1996	18.00	30
1992 5" Christmas Lamb (white) 7424	Closed	1996	18.00	30
1998 5" Christmas Monkey 7432	Closed	1998	23.00	43
1988 5" Duck in Egg 1532	Closed	1990	21.00	45-50
1986 5" Duck on Sled 8070	Closed	1994	27.00	27-45
1986 5" Duck w/ Raincoat & Umbrella 1565	Closed	1986	20.00	60
1983 5" Duckling in Hat 7955	Closed	1984	13.00	50
1985 5" E.P. Boy & Girl Duckling 1510, 1505	Closed	1985	28.00	22-55
1994 5" E.P. Boy Duck 1510	Closed	1994	14.00	25
1985 5" E.P. Girl Duckling 1505	Closed	1985	14.00	45
1991 5" Fawn (spotted) 6426	Closed	N/A	17.00	20
1991 5" Fluffy Yellow Chick 1728	Closed	1992	18.00	25-45
1989 5" Lamb 5424	Closed	1991	17.00	35
1984 5" Pilot Duckling 1515	Closed	1985	16.00	60
1992 5" Raincoat Duck 1560	Closed	1994	28.00	28-50
1989 5" Sailor Duck 1724	Closed	1991	22.00	22-55
1995 5" Sailor Duck 1724	Closed	1996	28.00	35-40
1991 5" Spring Lamb 1726	Closed	1992	18.00	10-35
1981 7" Boy Monkey w/ Banana Trapeze R-572	Closed	1981	10.00	175
1993 7" Christmas Chicken 7428	Closed	1993	35.00	70
1993 7" Christmas Dove 7426	Closed	1995	28.00	50
1981 7" Lady & Escort Fox (Designer Series) R630	Closed	1981	26.00	350
1976 7" Rooster A-352	Closed	1977	6.00	225
1981 7" Santa Fox w/ Bag R-173	Closed	1982	13.00	165-195
1981 7" Santa Monkey R-181	Closed	1981	10.00	150-155
1992 7" Santa Skunk 7422	Closed	1993	28.00	45-50
1993 7" Spring Boy Rooster 1596	Closed	1993	35.00	70
1992 7" Spring Girl Chicken 1595	Closed	1993	35.00	60
1992 7" Spring Skunk 1590	Closed	1993	23.00	45
1981 8" Ballerina Pig w/ Umbrella G-575	Closed	1982	13.00	145-150
1980 8" Boy Barbecue Pig (frying pan or spatula) G-570	Closed	1982	22.00	115
1999 8" Dapple Grey Horse 8797	34	1999	30.00	375
1976 8" Elephant A-310	Closed	1976	N/A	225-295
1968 8" Elephant C-47	Closed	1968	4.00	275
1972 8" Elephant R-3	Closed	1972	4.00	250
1980 8" Girl Barbecue Pig R-542	Closed	1981	11.00	130
2000 8" Graduate Panda 2794	50	2000	24.00	24
2000 8" Groom Panda 2788	50	2000	30.00	30
2000 8" Summer Chaos Elephant 9725	200	2000	50.00	50
1989 10" Barbecue Pig 2410	Yr.Iss.	1989	28.00	65-70
1991 10" Black Cat 2984	Closed	1992	26.00	75-80
1987 10" Bride and Groom Cats 2904	Closed	1987	72.00	295
1987 10" Christmas Goose 7402	Closed	1989	31.00	60
1989 10" Country Boy & Girl Goose 1574	Closed	1989	64.00	135
1989 10" Country Boy & Girl Pig 1544, 1543	Yr.Iss.	1989	52.00	125
1989 10" Country Boy Pig 1544	Yr.Iss.	1989	26.00	65
1989 10" Country Girl Pig 1543	Yr.Iss.	1989	26.00	65
1988 10" E.P. Boy & Girl Pig 1542,1540	Yr.Iss.	1988	50.00	125
1988 10" E.P. Boy Pig 1542	Yr.Iss.	1988	25.00	70
1988 10" E.P. Girl Pig 1540	Yr.Iss.	1988	25.00	70
1987 10" Easter Parade Goose 1566	Closed	1988	30.00	65
1968 10" Honkey Donkey C-45	Closed	1968	4.00	275
1991 10" Huskie w/ 5" Puppy in Dog Sled 8057	Closed	1991	55.00	125
1987 10" Kitten on Sled 8062	Closed	1991	36.00	65
1987 10" Kitten w/ Knit Mittens 8064	Closed	1992	34.00	55
1993 10" Kitten w/ Ornament 7427	Closed	1995	36.00	60-65
1986 10" Kitten w/ Yarn & Basket 2900	Closed	1987	30.00	85-95
1999 10" Murray Chrismoose 8075	Closed	1999	50.00	95
1970 10" Reindeer C-144	Closed	1974	N/A	75
1965 10" Reindeer w/ 10" Elf	Closed	1965	8.00	625
1987 10" Reindeer w/ Santa Hat & Bell 6434	Closed	1995	25.00	25
1970 10" Reindeer w/ Santa Hat C-141	Closed	1974	6.00	75
1975 10" Reindeer w/ Santa Hat R-100	Closed	1982	18.00	75
1990 10" Santa Pig 7414	Closed	1991	32.00	65
1993 10" Skating Penguin 7430	Closed	1995	36.00	60
1987 10" Stork w/ 3" Baby in Basket 1958	Closed	1988	50.00	200-295
1976 10" Vote 76 Donkey A-313	Closed	1976	6.00	200
1982 12" Boy & Girl Skunk G-655, G-650	Closed	1982	56.00	300
1981 12" Boy Monkey w/ Banana Trapeze R-573	Closed	1981	24.00	275
1982 12" Boy Skunk G-655	Closed	1982	28.00	150
1996 12" Brown Horse 2885	Closed	1996	36.00	80
1997 12" Buffalo 3310	Closed	1998	49.00	75
1967 12" Cat Sneaky	Closed	1969	7.00	325
1997 12" Champagne the Carousel Horse (last in series) 2842	Closed	1997	68.00	90-100
1991 12" Christmas Swan 7403	Closed	1991	64.00	120
1985 12" Duck w/ Raincoat & Umbrella 1560	Closed	1986	40.00	90-95
1983 12" E.P. Duck w/ Basket 1555	Closed	1986	29.00	90
1990 12" Easter Duck w/ Watering Can 1552	2,891	1991	50.00	65
1995 12" Empress the Carousel Horse (1st in series) 2840	Closed	1996	62.00	100
1982 12" Girl Skunk G-650	Closed	1982	28.00	150-175
1996 12" Mother Duck 1550	Closed	1996	50.00	75
1997 12" Mr & Mrs Quack Quack 1551, 1553	Closed	1997	120.00	225
1997 12" Mr Quack Quack 1551	Closed	1997	60.00	125
1997 12" Mrs Quack Quack 1553	Closed	1997	60.00	125
1990 12" Santa Duck 7416	Closed	1991	54.00	95-150
1981 12" Santa Monkey R-181	Closed	1981	24.00	250
1982 12" Skunk w/ Snowball S-659	Closed	1982	29.00	225-235
1979 14" Mother & Father Pig N-572, N-573	Closed	1979	38.00	295-350
1979 14" Mother Pig N-572	Closed	1979	19.00	150-160
1986 15" Hobo Cat 3040	Closed	1988	36.00	85-95
1985 15" Jazz Cat w/Trumpet 7585	Closed	1985	32.00	160
1976 15" Rooster A-353	Closed	1977	14.00	375
1972 16" Elephant R-4	230	1972	13.00	425
1981 18" Cat w/ Mouse 7590	Closed	1988	47.00	160
1975 18" Horse A-354	Closed	1976	17.00	250
1981 18" Lady & Escort Fox (Designer Series) R639	Closed	1981	58.00	625-650
1994 18" Old World Reindeer w/ Bells 6650	Closed	1995	62.00	62-75
1978 18" Reindeer w/ Saddlebags (red nose) C-144	Closed	1978	N/A	125
1986 18" Reindeer w/ Saddlebags 6600	Closed	1994	60.00	70
1981 18" Santa Fox w/Bag R-173	Closed	1982	30.00	295
1981 18" Santa Fox w/Bag R-245	Closed	1982	30.00	275
1981 22" Giraffe w/ 10" Elf R-280	Closed	1982	37.00	375
1987 24" Christmas Goose w/ Basket 7404	Closed	1989	58.00	150
1989 24" Christmas Swan 7406	Closed	1990	63.00	150
1987 24" Easter Parade Goose 1568	Closed	1988	53.00	150
1983 24" Flying Stork w/ Baby 1700	Closed	1983	37.00	150
1989 24" Spring Swan 1575	Closed	1990	63.00	125
1975 36" Horse	Closed	1975	48.00	550

Bears - A. Thorndike

YEAR ISSUE	EDITION LIMIT	YEAR RETD.	ISSUE PRICE	*QUOTE U.S.$
1973 7" Christmas Panda C-310	Yr.Iss.	1973	9.00	295-350
1993 10" Angel Bear 8053	Closed	1994	36.00	65
1986 10" Baby Bear w/ Bee 2800	Closed	1986	20.00	90-100
1987 10" Bear in Nightshirt w/Candle 8056	Closed	1993	34.00	60
1987 10" Bear in Velour Santa Suit 8054	Closed	1992	33.00	60-75
1986 10" Bear w/ Sled 8060	Closed	1989	29.00	60-75
1987 10" Bear w/ Snowball, Knit Hat & Scarf 8052	Closed	1992	30.00	41-60
1991 10" Bride & Groom Bear 2324	Closed	1991	80.00	165
1985 10" Christmas Panda w/Toy Bag 7595	Closed	1986	19.00	75-85
1996 10" Country Boy & Girl Bear 0943	Closed	1996	90.00	125
1996 10" Country Boy Bear w/ Wheelbarrow (sunflower) 0943	Closed	1996	44.00	75
1996 10" Country Girl Bear 0943	Closed	1996	44.00	75
1993 10" Doctor Bear 2829	Yr.Iss.	1993	36.00	90
1988 10" Eskimo Bear 8058	Closed	1990	36.00	90
1986 10" Fishing Bear 2830	Yr.Iss.	1986	20.00	175
1986 10" Girl Bear 2835	Closed	1987	21.00	85
1996 10" Lover Boy Bear 0356	Closed	1996	40.00	75
1992 10" Mrs Nightshirt Bear 8059	Closed	1993	39.00	70-95
1993 10" Santa's Helper Bear 8051	Closed	1993	33.00	34-70
1985 18" Ballerina Bear 2820	918	1985	40.00	195-225
1984 18" Bear w/ Brush 2810	Yr.Iss.	1984	40.00	195-220
1973 18" Bear w/ Butterfly S-201	Yr.Iss.	1973	11.00	400
1985 18" Bear w/ Honey Pot & Bee 2815	2,032	1986	42.00	165-175
1984 18" Christmas Panda w/Toy Bag 7595	Closed	1986	46.00	125-150

Bunnies - A. Thorndike

YEAR ISSUE	EDITION LIMIT	YEAR RETD.	ISSUE PRICE	*QUOTE U.S.$
1984 5" E.P. Boy & Girl Bunny 0520	Yr.Iss.	1984	24.00	195
1983 5" Floppy Ear Boy & Girl Bunny w/ Egg 0510, 0505	Closed	1984	24.00	150
1978 7" Artist Bunny S9	Closed	1978	N/A	80
1991 7" Artist Bunny w/ palette 0622	Closed	1993	23.00	40
1993 7" Artist Bunny w/ palette (has mustache) 0622	Closed	1993	21.00	60
1994 7" Baby Bunny w/ Bottle 0930	Closed	1995	21.00	45-50
1985 7" Boy Bunny w/ Carrot 0640	Closed	1985	15.00	55
1992 7" Bride & Groom Bunny2915	Closed	1993	46.00	100
1976 7" Bunnies (2) w/ Basket S25	Closed	1976	11.00	80
1988 7" Bunnies (3) on Revolving Maypole Music Box 0648	Closed	1988	70.00	325
1970 7" Bunny (yellow)	Closed	1970	N/A	150
1992 7" Bunny in Slipper (green) 0920	Closed	1993	20.00	45
1992 7" Bunny in Slipper (yellow) 0925	Closed	1993	20.00	45
1986 7" Bunny w/ Sled 8065	Closed	1988	18.00	50
1981 7" Country Boy & Girl Bunny D1, D2	Closed	1981	20.00	60-95
1993 7" Country Boy & Girl Bunny w/ Vegetables 0625, 0617	Closed	1993	42.00	21-60
1988 7" Country Boy Bunny w/ Hoe 0625	Closed	1988	16.00	25-35
1991 7" Country Bunny & Girl Bunny 0625-0617	Closed	1991	42.00	60
1994 7" Country Bunny & Girl Bunny w/ Hoe & Basket 0625-0617	Closed	1994	45.00	65
1983 7" Country Girl Bunny w/ Flower Pot 0620	Closed	1983	11.00	50
1991 7" Country Girl Bunny w/ Flowers 0617	Closed	1992	25.00	35
1984 7" E.P. Boy Bunny 0615	Closed	1984	13.00	32-35
1993 7" E.P. Girl Bunny w/ 14" Wreath 0616	Closed	1994	35.00	50
1981 7" I'm Late Bunny (special order)	100	1981	N/A	295
1996 7" E.P. Boy & Girl Bunny 0615, 0610	Closed	1998	50.00	70
1994 7" E.P. Boy & Girl Bunny w/ Purse 0615, 0610	Closed	1994	50.00	85
1983 7" Floppy Ear Bunny w/ Butterfly 0625	Closed	1983	13.00	50
1995 8" E.P. Boy & Girl Bunny 0606, 0600	Yr.Iss.	1995	56.00	110
1995 8" E.P. Girl Bunny 0600	Yr.Iss.	1995	25.00	65
1988 10" Artist Bunny 0658	Closed	1989	32.00	95
1989 10" Bunnies (2) on Flexible Flyer Sled 8058	4,104	1989	53.00	115-125
1989 10" Bunnies (3) on Revolving Maypole 0646	647	1989	190.00	295
1987 10" Carrot Balloon w/ 7" Bunny 1572	Closed	1987	50.00	50-150
1993 10" Country Boy Bunny & Girl Bunny w/ Vegetables 0662, 0664	Closed	1993	70.00	150
1989 10" Country Boy Bunny w/ Basket & Girl w/ Flowers 0652, 0650	Closed	1989	90.00	85-125
1991 10" Country Boy Bunny w/ Wheelbarrow 0664	Closed	1991	43.00	75
1989 10" Country Girl Bunny w/ Flowers 0650	Closed	1989	30.00	70
1991 10" Country Girl Bunny w/ Flowers 0662	Closed	1991	35.00	75
1988 10" E.P. Boy & Girl Bunny (blue-mint) 0655, 0654	Closed	1988	60.00	140
1997 10" E.P. Boy & Girl Bunny (pink daffodils) 0656, 0654	Closed	1997	90.00	140
1990 10" E.P. Boy & Girl Bunny (purple-mint) 0655, 0654	Closed	1990	70.00	130
1989 10" E.P. Girl Bunny 0654	Closed	1989	32.00	70
1991 10" Skating Bunny 8074	Closed	1992	44.00	41-80
1990 10" Strawberry Girl Bunny 0660	Closed	1990	35.00	95
1997 10" Strolling Bunny w/ 7" Baby 0665	Closed	1997	70.00	135-145
1999 12" Benny Bunny (w/green watering can) 0672	Closed	1999	52.00	80
1988 18" Artist Bunny 0739	Closed	1989	52.00	110-120
1978 18" Boy Bunny w/ Basket S-41	Closed	1978	14.00	150
1988 18" Country Boy & Girl Bunny 0725, 0720	Closed	1988	90.00	68-135
1993 18" Country Boy Bunny w/Vegetables 0720	Closed	1993	55.00	95
1985 18" Country Boy Bunny w/Watering Can 0730	Closed	1988	55.00	150
1985 18" Country Boy Bunny w/Wheelbarrow (blue) 0725	Closed	1986	57.00	150

*Quotes have been rounded up to nearest dollar

YEAR ISSUE	EDITION LIMIT	YEAR RETD.	ISSUE PRICE	*QUOTE U.S.$
1996 18" Country Boy Bunny w/Wheelbarrow (denim) 0725	Closed	1996	68.00	135
1984 18" Country Boy Bunny w/Wheelbarrow (sunflower) 0725	Closed	1984	40.00	150
1996 18" Country Girl Bunny (sunflower) 0720	Closed	1996	68.00	125
1988 18" Country Mother Bunny w/ 10" Baby Bunny 0738	Closed	1989	69.00	125-135
1996 18" E.P. Boy & Girl Bunny 0715, 0710	Closed	1996	135.00	70-145
1977 18" E.P. Boy & Girl Bunny S-45, S-44	Closed	1977	28.00	250
1990 18" E.P. Boy Bunny 0715	Closed	1990	70.00	68-95
1999 18" Metallic Egg Bunny 9717	48	1999	75.00	250
1999 18" Nautical Bunny 9714	99	1999	75.00	275
1990 18" Strawberry Girl Bunny 0740	Closed	1990	60.00	100
1987 18" Victorian Country Boy & Girl Bunny 0734, 0732	Closed	1987	100.00	200
1982 29" Country Girl Bunny D50	Closed	1982	62.00	295
1983 29" Country Girl Bunny w/ Basket 0805	Closed	1983	70.00	295
1982 29" E.P. Boy & Girl Bunny D54, D52	Closed	1982	132.00	550
1982 29" E.P. Girl Bunny D-52	Closed	1982	66.00	225
1979 29" Pop Bunny B-56	Closed	1979	43.00	225-245
1986 30" E.P. Boy & Girl Bunny 0815, 0810	Closed	1986	190.00	450

Clowns - A. Thorndike

YEAR ISSUE	EDITION LIMIT	YEAR RETD.	ISSUE PRICE	*QUOTE U.S.$
2000 7" Trunk of Clowns 9726	200	2000	75.00	75
1987 10" Clown 1956	Closed	1987	18.00	80
1984 10" Clown 2950	Closed	1984	14.00	55-85
1985 10" Clown 2950	Closed	1986	15.00	75
1978 10" Clown A-340	Closed	1978	7.00	40-75
1976 10" Clown A-340	Closed	1976	11.00	115-125
1981 10" Clown R-620	Closed	1981	10.00	85
1980 10" Clown R-620	Closed	1980	10.00	80
1990 10" Clown w/ stand 2966	Closed	1990	28.00	50
1990 10" Hobo Clown 2974	Closed	1991	26.00	60
1994 10" Hobo Clown 2974	Closed	1994	31.00	45-55
1991 15" Hobo Clown 2975	Closed	1991	48.00	125
1981 18" Clown	Closed	1981	N/A	200-225
1978 18" Clown	Closed	1978	14.00	225
1980 18" Clown	Closed	1980	N/A	225
1976 18" Clown A-341	Closed	1976	14.00	295
1985 18" Clown w/ Balloon 2955	Closed	1986	56.00	150-165
1990 30" Clown (yellow) 2971	Closed	1990	100.00	150
1981 48" Clown	Closed	1981	N/A	620
1985 Hot Air Balloon w/ 10" Clown 2925	Closed	1986	50.00	150

Elves/Fairies/Gnomes - A. Thorndike

YEAR ISSUE	EDITION LIMIT	YEAR RETD.	ISSUE PRICE	*QUOTE U.S.$
1994 5" Frosty (Winter) Elf (white w/ tinsel) 7345	Closed	1997	16.00	25
1991 7" Christmas Gnome 7367	Closed	1993	19.00	19-45
1998 10" Baking Friends 7352	Closed	1998	20.00	45
1970 10" Casualty Ski Elf w/ Arm in Sling	Closed	1972	N/A	275
1970 10" Casualty Ski Elf w/ Crutch & Leg in Cast C-170	Closed	1972	5.00	300
1980 10" Christmas (green) 7358	Closed	1996	17.00	100
1960 10" Christmas Elf (white)	Closed	N/A	N/A	175
1980 10" Christmas Elf (white)	Closed	1995	17.00	75
1950 10" Christmas Elf w/ Instrument	Closed	N/A	N/A	250
1989 10" Christmas Faire 7564	Closed	1990	41.00	60
1978 10" Elf w/ Planter	Yr.Iss.	1978	7.00	195
1987 10" Elves (two) w/ Tree, Sled & Axe 7360	Closed	1988	44.00	125
1987 10" Fall Elf 3300	Closed	1989	15.00	45
1974 10" Fur Trimmed Elf w/ Candy Basket C-150	Closed	1974	6.00	125
1982 10" Jack Frost Elf w/ 10" Snowflake R-820	Closed	1982	14.00	135-225
1981 10" Jack Frost Elf w/ 5" Snowflake R-200	Closed	1981	12.50	125
1996 10" Jester and Friend 7473	Closed	1998	35.00	52
1998 10" Mailman Elf 7351	Closed	1998	25.00	45
1999 10" Patriotic Elf 9719	425	1999	30.00	60
1964 10" Robin Hood Elf	Closed	1965	N/A	225
1985 10" Ski Elf 8180	Closed	1986	18.00	85
1987 10" Ski Elf w/ Sweater 8180	Closed	1987	20.00	115-125
1960 10" Spring Elf (pink)	Closed	N/A	N/A	225
1987 10" Spring Elf 2962	Closed	1991	16.00	45
1993 10" Winter Elf w/ 14" Wreath 7366	Yr.Iss	1993	26.00	50
1960 10" Woodsprite w/ Broom	Closed	1960	N/A	475
1981 10" Workshop Elf 7350	Closed	1983	12.00	65
1978 12" Gnome C-151	Closed	1978	10.00	150
1969 12" Gnome w/ Candy Basket	Closed	1972	7.00	225
1991 12" Santa's Helper Painting Boat 7646	Closed	1992	39.00	75
1991 12" Santa's Postman w/ Cardholder Mailbag 7674	Closed	1993	41.00	75
1981 18" Butterfly w/ 10" Elf G-610	Closed	1982	28.00	175-200
1979 18" Gnome R-111	Closed	1980	20.00	225
1970 18" Gnome w/ Apron - Santa's Helper X-43	Closed	1970	8.00	325
1971 18" Gnome w/ Pajama Suit & Buttons	Closed	1972	9.00	300
1973 18" Santa's Helper C-151	Closed	1973	10.00	275
1976 18" Snow Gnome C-155	Closed	1976	14.00	275
1990 20" Spring Elf (pink) 1585	Yr.Iss.	1990	35.00	80-100
1990 20" Spring Elf (yellow) 1585	Yr.Iss.	1990	35.00	95
1974 22" Workshop Elf w/ Apron (red) C-152	Closed	1974	N/A	175
1997 30" Autumn Jester 3301	Yr.Iss.	1997	100.00	190-195
1991 Tinsel the "Elf" 7365	Closed	1992	21.00	45

Frogs - A. Thorndike

YEAR ISSUE	EDITION LIMIT	YEAR RETD.	ISSUE PRICE	*QUOTE U.S.$
1996 3" Froggie (no lily pad) 2401	Closed	1996	20.00	35
1991 10" Avaitor Frog 9937	Closed	1991	20.00	60
1979 10" Boy Frog R-503	Closed	1981	10.00	75
1980 10" Bride and Groom Frog R507, R508	Closed	1981	30.00	250
1999 10" Floating Flo Frog (2 pc suit) 2405	45	1999	84.00	275
1988 10" Frog 2406	Closed	1988	16.00	40-50
1992 10" Frog in Boat 2408	Closed	1993	32.00	65
1987 10" Frog in Top Hat w/ Tails and Brass Instrument 2400	Closed	1988	24.00	60
1987 10" Frog w/ Wooden Instrument 2404	Closed	1987	20.00	85
1981 10" Girl Frog R-502	Closed	1981	10.00	95
1979 10" Girl Frog R-502	Closed	1980	10.00	75
1987 10" Leap Frogs 2402	Closed	1987	32.00	95
1999 10" Lucky Leaper (vest w/ Chain) 1715	45	1999	68.00	225
1994 10" Santa Frog on Bang Hat (green-employee) 7999	Closed	1994	N/A	130
1994 10" Santa Frog on Bang Hat (June Auction-red) 7999	Closed	1994	29.50	70
1987 10" Santa Frog w/ Toy Bag & Stand 8080	Closed	1987	20.00	55-65
1980 10" Santa Frog w/ Toy Bag R-163	Closed	1980	10.00	90
1980 18" Boy & Girl Frog R-505, R-504	Closed	1980	46.00	350
XX 18" Frog (all yellow) RARE	Closed	N/A	N/A	675
1980 18" Girl Frog R-504	Closed	1980	23.00	225
1980 18" Santa Frog w/ Toy Bag R-164	2,126	1980	25.00	275-295

Halloween - A. Thorndike

YEAR ISSUE	EDITION LIMIT	YEAR RETD.	ISSUE PRICE	*QUOTE U.S.$
1995 2" Pumpkin 9028	Closed	1996	7.00	15
1987 3" Baby Witch w/Diaper 3004	Yr.Iss.	1987	14.00	125
1986 3" Ghost Mouse 2998	Closed	1998	22.00	42
1987 3" Jack O. Lantern 2997	Closed	1998	24.00	45
1995 3" Witch Kid w/ Broom 3004	Closed	1997	20.00	30
1996 3" Wizard Mouse 2999	Closed	1996	24.00	40
1992 7" Ballerina Kid 3052	Closed	1993	28.00	50-55
1996 7" Banana Kid 3065	Closed	1996	28.00	50-55
1988 7" Bunny Trick or Treat Kid 3032	Closed	1991	26.00	45-55
1994 7" Butterfly Kid (orange) 3061	Closed	1994	29.00	65
1993 7" Butterfly Kid (yellow) 3061	Closed	1994	29.00	50-55
1992 7" Devil Kid 3043	Closed	1993	24.00	50-55
1992 7" Dracula Kid 3054	Closed	1994	27.00	50
1989 7" Dragon Kid 3033	Closed	1991	32.00	55-60
1989 7" Duck Kid 1675	Closed	1989	26.00	50
1993 7" Flower Kid (yellow)	Closed	1994	29.00	50-55
1987 7" Ghost Kid w/ Pumpkin 3002	Closed	1991	26.00	55
1993 7" Ghost Mouse 3060	Closed	1995	28.00	55
1995 7" Gypsy Girl 3035	Closed	1996	32.00	50-55
1992 7" Ladybug Kid 3056	Closed	1993	30.00	50-55
1997 7" Lone Pumpkin Mouse 2903	Closed	1998	26.00	26-45
1995 7" Mouse Kid 3037	Closed	1996	26.00	50
1998 7" Mummy Kid 3057	Closed	1998	32.00	32-50
1992 7" Pirate Kid 3038	Closed	1994	25.00	50-55
1989 7" Pumpkin Kid 3031	Closed	1992	28.00	50-55
1992 7" Scarecrow Kid 3058	Closed	1993	28.00	34
1998 7" Scarecrow Kid 3058	Closed	1998	34.00	50
1988 7" Skeleton Kid 3034	Closed	1991	25.00	50
1996 7" Spider Kid 3064	Yr.Iss.	1996	28.00	55
1997 7" Tags 3053	Closed	1997	42.00	65
1997 7" Tatters & Tags 3051, 3053	Closed	1997	84.00	130
1997 7" Tatters 3051	Closed	1997	42.00	65
1977 7" Trick or Treat Mouse 3005	Closed	1989	17.00	17-45
1988 7" Witch Kid w/ Nose 3036	Closed	1992	28.00	50-55
1993 7" Witch Mouse 3009	Closed	1996	28.00	40
1980 7" Witch Mouse on Broom 3010	Closed	1986	20.00	17-55
1981 7" Witch Mouse on Broom w/ Moon 3015	Closed	1985	34.00	125-140
1997 7" Wiz Kid 3041	Closed	1997	32.00	45
1993 7" Wizard Mouse 3007	Closed	1995	30.00	40-45
1996 10" Candy Basket Elves 2992	Closed	1996	42.00	65
1987 10" Pumpkin (medium) 3027	Yr.Iss.	1987	35.00	195-125
1996 10" Trick or Treat Elf 2991	Closed	1997	22.00	22-40
1991 12" Bat 2980	Closed	1992	32.00	80
1994 12" Cat Kid 3063	Closed	1995	37.00	37-75
1994 12" Devil Kid 3062	Closed	1994	40.00	75
1991 12" Spider 2982	Closed	1992	39.00	80
1986 12" Trick or Treat Halloween Mouse 3045	Closed	1990	43.00	85
1986 12" Witch Mouse Holding Trick or Treat Bag 3045	Closed	1990	43.00	75
1980 12" Witch Mouse on Broom 3030	Closed	1984	36.00	95-125
1986 14" Pumpkin (solid) 3025	Closed	1992	49.00	125-150
1986 14" Pumpkin Balloon w/ 7" Witch Mouse 3020	Closed	1987	60.00	225-300
1993 14" Pumpkin w/ Removable Lid 3028	Closed	1995	50.00	125-150
1996 15" Haunted Tree 3024	Closed	1996	45.00	90
1990 18" Dragon Kid 3012	Closed	1990	70.00	160
1990 18" Pumpkin Kid 3014	Closed	1991	76.00	150
1997 18" Spellbinder 3021	Closed	1997	90.00	175-195
1989 18" Thorny the Ghost 3006	Closed	1991	52.00	125
1990 18" Trick or Treat Bunny Kid 3016	Closed	1991	50.00	150
1989 18" Witch (flying) 3008	Closed	1992	64.00	100
1992 18" Witch w/ Stand 3011	Closed	1995	70.00	100
1996 30" Skeleton Kid 3019	Closed	1996	85.00	225
1993 30" Witch Kid 3013	Closed	1995	150.00	275-295
1995 Bewitching Moon Mobile 3003	Closed	1996	45.00	75-85

Mice - A. Thorndike

YEAR ISSUE	EDITION LIMIT	YEAR RETD.	ISSUE PRICE	*QUOTE U.S.$
1997 3" Sweet Surprise Mouse 7928	Closed	1997	22.50	38
1996 3" Teacher Mouse 1992	Closed	1997	22.00	35
2000 7" Amber Skier Mouse 9728	100	2000	45.00	45
1990 7" Artist Mouse 2006	Closed	1990	24.00	45
1994 7" Auction Times Mouse 2019	Yr.Iss.	1994	30.00	50
1991 7" Baker Mouse 2013	Yr.Iss.	1991	26.00	45
1991 7" Ben Franklin Mouse 2011	Yr.Iss.	1991	30.00	50
1998 7" Blossom Mouse 0830	Closed	1998	28.50	48
1986 7" Boating Mouse 2320	Yr.Iss.	1986	16.00	65
1984 7" Bowling Mouse 2275	Yr.Iss.	1984	23.00	75
1980 7" Bride & Groom Mice 2055, 2065	Closed	N/A	30.00	85
1989 7" Business Man Mouse 2002	Yr.Iss.	1989	22.00	45
1995 7" California Mudslide Mouse 9961	Closed	1995	30.00	50
1992 7" Caroller Mouse w/ Hat & Tree 7754	Closed	1995	22.00	35
1992 7" Champagne Mouse in Glass (New Years) 8204	Closed	1994	28.00	55
1995 7" Cheerleader Mouse 2025	Closed	1995	12.00	75
1995 7" Chef Mouse (bread rolling pin) (blue scarf) 2125	Closed	1995	28.00	60
1982 7" Chef Mouse (frying pan) 2125	Closed	1983	14.00	60
1995 7" Chef Mouse (wisk/bowl) 2125	Closed	1995	28.00	60
1982 7" Chef Mouse-Barbeque (hamburgers) 2125	Closed	1989	18.00	60
1997 7" Cleaning Day Mouse (holds mop & bucket) 2135	Closed	1997	27.00	26-45
1975 7" Colonial Boy & Girl Mouse M-493, M-492	Closed	1976	12.00	225-250
1975 7" Colonial Boy mouse M-493	Closed	1976	18.00	75
1968 7" Country Cousin Boy Mouse	Closed	1968	N/A	225
1968 7" Country Cousin Girl Mouse	Closed	1968	N/A	225
1996 7" Country Girl Mouse 2233	Closed	1997	26.00	40
1991 7" Desert Storm Mouse 9931	Closed	1991	30.00	50
1991 7" Desert Storm Nurse Mouse 9932	Closed	1991	30.00	45
1982 7" Equestrienne Mouse 2185	Closed	1983	13.00	125
1994 7" Football Mouse 2027	Yr.Iss.	1991	30.00	40
1990 7" Friar Tuck Mouse 2010	Yr.Iss.	1990	27.00	45-50
1994 7" Graduation Mouse (white gown) 2095/2100	Closed	1994	14.00	50
1992 7" Green Thumb Mouse 2045	Yr.Iss.	1992	26.00	45
1993 7" Habitat Mouse 9954	Closed	1995	31.00	50-55
1985 7" Hiker Mouse w/Backpack 2305	Closed	1985	15.00	55
1970 7" Housewife Mouse	Closed	N/A	12.00	60-85
1992 7" Housewife Mouse (vacumn) 2135	Closed	1992	26.00	65
1993 7" Ironing Day Mouse 2024	Closed	1995	28.00	40
1985 7" Jail House Mouse 2029	Yr.Iss.	1985	26.00	45
1996 7" Laundry Day Mouse (clothes basket) 2135	2,845	1996	26.00	50-60
1970 7" Maid Marion Mouse 2009	Yr.Iss.	1989	27.00	50
1995 7" Motorcycle Mouse 2030	Yr.Iss.	1995	31.00	45
1993 7" Mouse (white) on Toboggan 7726	Closed	1995	32.00	31-50
1992 7" Mouse on Cheese 7756	Closed	1993	27.00	27-45
1991 7" Mouse w/ Mailbag and Letters 7752	Closed	1993	26.00	26-45
1993 7" Mouse w/ Present (white) 7721	Closed	1994	23.00	45
1984 7" Mouse w/Presents 7735	Closed	1992	18.00	18-45
1991 7" Mr & Mrs Tuckered Mice 7747, 7749	Closed	1993	40.00	23-65
1996 7" New Year's Eve Mouse 8205	Closed	1995	20.00	50-55
1998 7" Paddy O'Mouse 1711	Closed	1998	28.00	50
1997 7" Par Four Mouse 2295	Closed	1997	27.00	50
1986 7" Planter Mouse w/ Wheelbarrow 2050	Closed	1986	17.00	65
1994 7" Policeman Mouse 2028	Yr.Iss.	1994	28.00	45
1978 7" Policeman Mouse M409	Closed	1978	7.00	95
1979 7" Quilting Mouse (Quilt Loft)	213	1979	18.00	160
1982 7" Quilting Mouse G420	Closed	1983	12.00	80
1990 7" Robin Hood Mouse 2008	Yr.Iss.	1990	27.00	45
1990 7" Sailor Mouse (signed by Chuck) 2007	Closed	1990	24.00	70
1990 7" Sailor Mouse 2007	Closed	1990	24.00	45
1997 7" Santa Mouse Centerpiece 7746	Closed	1997	29.00	60
1989 7" Science Center of N.H. Fishing Mouse w/dome 9911	500	1989	75.00	150
1991 7" Secretary Mouse 2012	Yr.Iss.	1991	30.00	60
1991 7" Sheriff Mouse w/ plaque 9930	Closed	1991	30.00	95
1980 7" Skater (Ice) Mouse (pink outfit) R492	Closed	1981	11.00	70
1998 7" Star Spangled Mouse 2031	Closed	1998	24.50	55
1982 7" Mouse w/ Strawberry 2115	Closed	1995	13.00	50
1984 12" Devil Mouse 2895	Closed	1984	30.00	135

Miscellaneous - A. Thorndike

YEAR ISSUE	EDITION LIMIT	YEAR RETD.	ISSUE PRICE	*QUOTE U.S.$
1995 2" Tomatoes (3) , 8 " Ear Corn w/ faces, set 9024, 9025	Closed	1996	N/A	150
1995 2" Tomatoes w/ Face (3) 9024	Closed	1996	13.50	30
1990 5" Christmas Dragon 7420	15,549	1992	N/A	50
1982 5" Dragon w/ Boy G590	1,066	1982	18.00	225
1987 5" Leprechaun 1706	Closed	1992	22.00	22-45
1993 5" Leprechaun w/ Pot O' Gold 1706	Closed	1996	22.00	35-45
1995 7" Cabbage (with face) 9023	Closed	1996	19.00	45
1997 7" Lucky the Leprechaun 1707	Closed	1998	35.00	55
1991 7" Snowman "Ritz" 7507	Closed	1995	29.00	45-50
1983 7" Snowman (holding broom) 7505	Yr.Iss.	1983	13.00	85
1993 7" Snowman on Toboggan (carrot nose) 7508	Closed	1995	31.00	55
1984 7" Snowman w/ Pipe 7505	Closed	1992	24.00	35
1993 7" Snowwoman 7506	Closed	1995	27.00	40-50
1995 8" Corn (with face) 9025	Closed	1996	13.00	40
1996 8" Corn Stalk w/ Mini Pumpkin 9029	Closed	1997	12.00	25
1996 8" Flowering Lily Pad 1847	Closed	1997	22.00	22-40
1997 10" Country Snowman (birds) 7512	Closed	1997	37.50	90
1997 10" Country Snowman (birds) 7513	Closed	1997	37.50	75
1991 10" Gingerbread Boy 7295	Closed	1994	24.00	45
1984 10" Gingerbread Boy 7295	Closed	1984	16.00	24-55
1978 10" Leprechaun (lime green body) N-501	Closed	1979	7.00	75
1977 10" Leprechaun S-356	Closed	1977	6.00	100
1992 10" Leprechaun w/ Pot O' Gold 1710	Yr.Iss.	1992	21.00	60
1974 10" Leprechaun w/ Sack S-202	Closed	1974	6.00	125
1978 10" Scarecrow (blue/maroon patchwork, red vest) A-345	Closed	1978	7.00	140
1983 10" Scarecrow (blue/wh ticking, red vest) 3105	Closed	1984	16.00	100
1976 10" Scarecrow (denim patchwork) A-345	Closed	1976	6.00	125-170

*Quotes have been rounded up to nearest dollar

YEAR ISSUE	EDITION LIMIT	YEAR RETD.	ISSUE PRICE	*QUOTE U.S.$
1977 10" Scarecrow (multicolored patchwork, burlap hat) A-345	Closed	1977	6.00	175
1996 10" Scarecrow Country Bumpkin 3072	Closed	1997	38.00	60
1998 10" Scarecrow w/ Cornucopia 3106	Closed	1998	45.00	70-80
1997 10" Scarecrow w/ Cornucopia 3106	Closed	1997	50.00	80
1978 10" Snowman N-160	Closed	1979	6.95	55
1988 10" Toy Soldier 7560	762	1990	33.00	55-75
1994 12" Girl Scarecrow (blue stone washed dress) 3073	Closed	1995	50.00	75-90
1989 12" Scarecrow (blue stone washed, red shirt) 3047	Closed	1993	42.00	75-90
1992 12" Snowman 7510	Closed	1993	42.00	70
1980 14" Dragon w/ 7" Bushbeater R-555	1,634	1982	33.00	275
1990 15" Christmas Dragon 7418	3,703	1990	50.00	100
1983 18" Gingerbread Boy 7300	Closed	1984	29.00	135
1991 18" Gingerbread Boy 7300	Closed	1992	51.00	135
1978 18" Scarecrow (blue/maroon patchwork, red vest) A-346	Closed	1978	N/A	295
1983 18" Scarecrow (blue/wh ticking, red vest) (no stand) 3150	Closed	1984	33.00	200
1976 18" Scarecrow (denim patchwork) (no stand) A-346	Closed	1976	13.50	275
1996 18" Snowman "Puttin on the Ritz" 7527	Yr.Iss.	1996	65.00	100
1978 18" Snowman (holding bird) N-161	Closed	1979	16.00	165
1983 18" Snowman w/ Broom 7525	Closed	1996	55.00	60
1996 18" Sunflower 1841	Closed	1996	24.00	50-60
1988 18" Toy Soldier 7562	Closed	1990	55.00	95-110
1981 22" Sun Mobile 1850	Closed	1985	37.00	195-225
1996 24" Country Cattail 1843	Closed	1996	30.00	50-60
1996 25" Sunflower 1842	Closed	1996	26.00	60-65
1978 29" Snowman N-162	Closed	1979	43.00	250
1994 30" Snowman w/ broom 7536	Closed	1995	120.00	225
1989 30" Toy Soldier (Animated) 9922	276	1989	280.00	625
1989 30" Toy Soldier 7558	762	1989	100.00	295
1987 48" Carrot 1570	Yr.Iss.	1987	40.00	175
1976 48" Scarecrow A-348	Closed	1978	58.00	875
1995 5' & 12" Cactus Set 9027	Closed	1996	24.00	45
1994 Carrots & Pea Pods -3 (large) (no faces) 9018	Closed	1994	15.00	35
1995 Carrots & Pea Pods -3 (large) (with faces) 9018	Closed	1996	23.00	45
1994 Carrots & Pea Pods -3 (small) (no faces) 9017	Closed	1994	13.00	25
1992 Flower (large) (no face) 1592	Closed	1992	18.00	40
1993 Flower (large) (with face) 1592	Closed	1995	21.00	50
1996 Scrooge's Bed 5458	Closed	1996	44.00	85
1999 Under the Sea w/Annalee-SSE	Closed	1999	60.00	85
1995 Vegetable Set w/ Faces, Carrots, Pea Pods (3), 7" Cabbage, 2" Tomatoes (3) & 8 " Corn	Closed	1996	N/A	150

Nativity - A. Thorndike

YEAR ISSUE	EDITION LIMIT	YEAR RETD.	ISSUE PRICE	*QUOTE U.S.$
1998 3" Baby Jesus 5429	Closed	1999	18.00	35
1999 5" Angel 5427	Open		20.00	20
1993 5" Baby Jesus in Manger 7175	Closed	1995	35.00	50
1998 7" Drummer Boy 5440	Closed	1999	30.00	55
1995 7" Joseph (child) 7070	Closed	1995	29.00	60
1995 7" Mary w/Baby Jesus (child) 7071	Closed	1995	29.00	70
1995 7" Shepherd Child w/Lamb 7072	Closed	1995	40.00	70
1996 10" Joseph 5432	Closed	1999	N/A	75
1996 10" Mary Holding Baby Jesus w/plaque 5431	Closed	1996	45.00	95
1998 10" Ox 5441	Closed	1999	37.00	65
1996 10" Wiseman w/Frankincense 5433	Closed	1999	45.00	75
1996 10" Wiseman w/Gold 5434	Closed	1996	45.00	75
1998 10" Wiseman w/Myrrh 5435	Closed	1999	45.00	75
1997 12" Camel 5437	Closed	1999	42.00	95

Picks/Pins - A. Thorndike

YEAR ISSUE	EDITION LIMIT	YEAR RETD.	ISSUE PRICE	*QUOTE U.S.$
2000 3" Bear in Back Pack (June Social) 9707	1,000	2000	N/A	N/A
1982 3" Butterfly Pin 1816	Closed	1982	N/A	35-80
1996 3" Ladypick Pick 1818	Closed	1997	N/A	25-30
1994 3" Spring Pixie Pick 1840	Closed	1995	11.00	40
1982 Bunny (boy) Head Pick G-692	Closed	1982	5.50	45
1982 Bunny (girl) Head Pick G-690	Closed	1982	6.00	45
1976 Colonial Boy & Girl Heads Pin, set A-357, A-356	Closed	1976	2.00	225
1976 Colonial Boy Head Pin A-357	Closed	1976	1.00	120
1976 Colonial Girl Head Pin A-356	Closed	1976	1.00	120
1999 Cow Head Pin 9713	200	1999	15.00	95
1991 Desert Storm Mouse Head Pin 9935	Closed	1991	8.00	30
1991 Desert Storm Nurse Mouse Head Pin 9936	Closed	1991	8.00	30
1972 Donkey Head Pin	Closed	1972	N/A	90-100
1968 Elephant Head Pin	Closed	1968	N/A	125
1976 Elephant Head Pin A-361	Closed	1976	N/A	110
1995 Frog Head Pin	Closed	1995	N/A	95-100
1997 Graduate Girl Head Pin 9707	Closed	1997	N/A	95
1999 Millennium Sun Pin 8207	Open		8.00	8
1995 Nashville Santa Head Pin	Closed	1995	N/A	55-75
1999 Nautical Bear Head Pin (June Social) 9709	Closed	1999	N/A	55-75
1998 Pirate Head Pin (Percy) (June Social) 9709	Closed	1998	N/A	45-65
1996 Poodle Head Pin	Closed	1996	N/A	95
1996 Williamsburg Man Head Pin (Williamsburg Auction) 9704	Closed	1996	N/A	125
1994 Witch Head Pin (Williamsburg Auction)	Closed	1994	N/A	125

Santas - A. Thorndike

YEAR ISSUE	EDITION LIMIT	YEAR RETD.	ISSUE PRICE	*QUOTE U.S.$
1989 3" Santa in Metal Sleigh 7962, 8032	Closed	1997	24.00	35
1983 5" Mr & Mrs Tuckered 4600	Closed	1983	23.00	175
1984 5" Mrs Santa 4505	Closed	1985	12.00	50
1982 5" Mrs Santa w/ Gift Box 4525	Closed	1984	12.00	50
1994 5" Old World Santa w/ 9" Wreath 4550	Closed	1996	33.00	60-65
1982 5" Santa w/ 5" Deer & Sleigh 4540	Closed	1984	60.00	250
1981 5" Santa w/ 5" Deer 4535	Closed	1984	23.00	80
1982 5" Santa w/ Bag 4510	Closed	1985	12.00	55
1982 5" Santa w/ Stove 4530	Closed	1984	14.00	60
1982 5" Santa with Gift Box & Card 4520	Closed	1985	13.00	45
1992 7" Chef Santa 5045	Closed	1996	30.00	45
1979 7" Cross Country Santa w/ Skis & Poles R-4	Closed	1981	11.00	70
1960 7" Mr & Mrs Santa	Closed	N/A	N/A	150
1993 7" Mr & Mrs Victorian Santa 6810, 6815	Closed	1993	60.00	95
1986 7" Mr & Mrs Victorian Santa 6810, 6815	Closed	1988	N/A	90
1984 7" Mrs Santa 5010	Closed	1984	N/A	40
1977 7" Mrs Santa C-4	Closed	1977	N/A	40
1991 7" Mrs Santa Hanging Merry Christmas Sign 5236	Closed	1993	28.00	40
1992 7" Santa & Mrs Santa w/ Candle Holder 5042, 5040	Closed	1993	52.00	80-95
1976 7" Santa & Toy Sack in Sleigh C-21	Closed	1978	8.00	45
1983 7" Santa at North Pole 5030	Closed	1987	18.00	30
1991 7" Santa Bringing Home Christmas Tree 5232	Closed	1993	28.00	50
1982 7" Santa in Sleigh 5025	Closed	1986	20.00	36-40
1975 7" Santa on Bike C-14	Closed	1978	7.00	65
1970 7" Santa w/ 10" Deer C-143	Closed	N/A	35.00	125
1970 7" Santa w/ 10" Deer on Christmas Mushroom C-253	Closed	1970	11.00	275
1976 7" Santa w/ Firewood C-12	Closed	1977	6.00	55
1975 7" Santa w/ Fur Trim	Closed	1982	N/A	30
1985 7" Santa w/ Gift List & Toy Bag 5225	Closed	1992	24.00	25
1991 7" Santa w/ Mailbag & Letters 5234	Closed	1993	28.00	50
1976 7" Santa w/ Pot Belly Stove R-10	Closed	1982	N/A	50
1975 7" Santa w/ Skis & Poles C-8	Closed	1977	N/A	85
1987 7" Santa w/ Sleigh & One Reindeer 5110	Closed	1990	66.00	120
1994 7" Santa w/ Snowshoe & Tree 5243	Closed	1995	29.00	30-55
1994 7" Santa w/ Tree & Sled 5244	Closed	1994	29.00	55
1983 7" Santa w/ White Felt Moon 5200	Closed	1984	25.00	100
1993 7" Skiing Santa 5242	Closed	1996	30.00	45
2000 7" Sleigh Ride Santa & Elf 9729	180	2000	75.00	75
1977 7" Tennis Santa N-5	Closed	1979	8.00	50
1986 7" Victorian Santa w/ Sleigh & Deer 6820	Closed	1988	52.00	100
1992 10" Fishing Mr & Mrs Santa in Boat w/ plaque 5415	Closed	1992	100.00	180
1994 10" Mrs Santa Last Minute Mend w/ plaque 5399	Yr.Iss.	1994	48.00	100
1993 10" Skating Mr & Mrs Santa w/ plaque 5409, 5411	Yr.Iss.	1993	100.00	190
1988 10" St. Nicholas w/ plaque 5410	Yr.Iss.	1990	70.00	50-100
1997 10" True Blue Santa w/ Certificate 5390	Closed	1997	63.00	125
1991 12" Tuckered Couple 5487	Closed	1994	90.00	63-125
1997 18" Catch of the Day Santa 5635	Yr.Iss.	1997	85.00	130
1988 18" Chef Santa (animated) (bowl) 5632	Closed	1989	120.00	295-300
1987 18" Chef Santa (Gingerbread) 5632	Closed	1996	61.00	75-95
1990 18" Day-After-Christmas Santa 5514	Closed	1991	80.00	140
1999 18" Feeding Time Mrs Santa 5522	37	1999	150.00	335
1987 18" Mr & Mrs Santa in Rocking Chair 5610,5627	Closed	1988	125.00	275
1996 18" Mrs Santa Hanging Popcorn & Cranberry 5521	Closed	1996	59.50	125-140
1996 18" Old World Mrs Santa Hugging Lamb 5653	Closed	1996	85.00	150
1996 18" Old World Santa 5652	Closed	1996	76.00	125
1988 18" Santa	Closed	1988	36.00	50
1996 18" Santa Hanging Gingerbread Ornament 5601	Yr.Iss.	1996	77.00	125
1981 18" Santa w/ 18" Reindeer R-103	Closed	1981	52.00	100
1991 18" Santa w/ Cardholder Mail Bag 5640	Yr.Iss.	1992	60.00	125
1985 18" Velour Mr & Mrs Santa 5615, 5620	Closed	1990	122.00	110
1986 18" Victorian (Velour) Mr & Mrs Santa 6862, 6855	Closed	1987	115.00	250
1986 18" Victorian (Velour) Mr Santa 6862	Closed	1987	57.50	125
1986 18" Victorian (Velour) Mrs Santa 6855	Closed	1987	57.50	125
1993 18" Victorian Mr Santa 6850	Closed	1993	65.00	130
1987 18" Victorian Mr Santa Cardholder 6862	Closed	1987	50.00	145
1993 18" Victorian Mrs Santa 6855	Closed	1993	65.00	130
1987 18" Victorian Mrs Santa Cardholder 6864	Closed	1987	50.00	145
1987 18" Victorian Santa w/ Stocking 6860	Closed	1987	62.50	145
1988 18" Workshop Santa (Animated) 9900	Closed	1989	120.00	275
1981 18" Workshop Santa 5625	Closed	1990	44.00	65
1987 30" Mr & Mrs Tuckered w/ 2 18" PJ Kids 6205	Closed	1991	292.00	325

Thanksgiving - A. Thorndike

YEAR ISSUE	EDITION LIMIT	YEAR RETD.	ISSUE PRICE	*QUOTE U.S.$
1996 5" Teepee 9032	Closed	1997	20.00	35
1993 7" Girl Eating Turkey 3081	Yr.Iss.	1993	39.00	80
1993 7" Harvest Basket (Pilgrim) Mice 3074	Closed	1996	48.00	47-65
1987 7" Indian Boy & Indian Girl 3154, 3152	Closed	1996	62.00	30-95
1980 7" Indian Boy 3154	Closed	N/A	N/A	30-40
1987 7" Indian Girl 3152	Closed	1996	N/A	40
1992 7" Mouse in Cornucopia 3172	Closed	1995	26.00	45
1993 7" Pilgrim Boy w/ Fawn & Girl w/Pie 3159, 3157	Closed	1995	71.00	42-90
1994 7" Pilgrim Girl w/Pie (blue) 3157	Closed	1994	N/A	28-45
1987 7" Pilgrim Kids w/ Basket 3156	Closed	1992	54.00	75
1984 7" Pilgrim Mice Set w/ Basket 3050	Closed	1992	44.00	75-104
1994 7" Thanksgiving Boy 3200	Yr.Iss.	1994	40.00	60
1988 8" Boy Turkey (tan/brown body) 3160, 3161	Closed	1995	35.00	60-75
1993 8" Girl Turkey 3163	Closed	1995	37.00	75-80
1991 10" Indian Chief & Maiden 3168, 3170	Closed	1991	86.00	115
1995 10" Indian Chief & Maiden 3168, 3170	Closed	1996	86.00	140
1995 10" Indian Chief 3168	Closed	1996	43.00	80
1991 10" Indian Chief 3168	Closed	1991	43.00	65
1991 10" Indian Maiden 3170	Closed	1991	43.00	65
1995 10" Indian Maiden 3170	Closed	1996	43.00	80
1997 10" Medicine Man 3169	Closed	1997	48.00	95
1978 10" Pilgrim Boy & Girl A358, A357	Closed	1978	N/A	225
1991 10" Pilgrim Man w/ Basket & Woman w/ Turkey, set 3166, 3164	Closed	1992	90.00	45-140
1991 10" Pilgrim Woman w/ Turkey 3164	Closed	1992	45.00	75
1993 12" Indian Boy 3155	Closed	1993	36.00	80
1985 12" Indian Boy and Girl Mice 3095, 3100	Closed	1987	72.00	160
1985 12" Indian Boy Mice 3095	Closed	1987	36.00	115
1985 12" Indian Girl Mice 3100	Closed	1987	36.00	115
1991 12" Pilgrim Boy & Girl Mouse 3080, 3075	Closed	1991	86.00	140
1981 12" Pilgrim Boy & Girl Mice 3080, 3075	Closed	1989	74.00	175
1993 12" Pilgrim Boy w/Basket & Girl w/Pie 3083, 3084	Closed	1995	95.00	125
1996 12" Tommy Turkey 3162	Closed	1996	76.00	125-135
1988 12" Turkey (large) 3162	Closed	1992	58.00	110-125
1994 17" Tee Pee 9026	Closed	1996	38.00	55
1994 24" Turkey 3167	Yr.Iss.	1994	100.00	295-350

Valentine - A. Thorndike

YEAR ISSUE	EDITION LIMIT	YEAR RETD.	ISSUE PRICE	*QUOTE U.S.$
1987 3" Cupid in Heart Balloon 0302	Closed	1987	39.00	150
1990 5" Dragon 1990	4,135	1990	26.00	50
1984 7" Bunny 0335	Closed	1985	14.00	75
1984 7" Cupid Kid 0325	Closed	1985	16.00	50-55
1984 7" Cupid Kid in Hanging Heart 0330	Closed	1985	33.00	135
1986 7" Cupid Kid in Hot Air Balloon 0315	Closed	1986	55.00	185-200
1986 7" Cupid Mobile 0320	Closed	1987	17.00	60
1999 7" King of Hearts 9888	43	1999	80	325
1996 7" Sweetheart Boy & Girl Mouse 0341, 0340	Closed	1996	43.00	24-43
1993 7" Sweetheart Boy & Girl Mouse 2001, 2014	Closed	1993	40.00	43
1996 7" Sweetheart Boy 0391	Closed	1996	33.00	65-75
1991 7" Sweetheart Boy Mouse 2014	Closed	1991	24.00	25
1994 7" Sweetheart Girl 0390	Closed	1996	28.00	45-55
1997 10" Angel 1930	Closed	1997	45.00	45-70
1998 10" I'm All Heart Elf 037098	Yr.Iss.	1998	33.50	60
1986 10" Panda 0350	Yr.Iss.	1986	20.00	150-200
1998 10" Sweetheart Boy Elf 36698	Closed	1998	20.50	45
1998 10" Sweetheart Girl Elf 36598	Closed	1998	20.50	45
1999 10" Sweetheart Panda 350	47	1999	72.00	325
1985 18" Bear w/ Heart 0375	Closed	1986	42.00	150
1985 18" Cat w/ Heart 0380	Closed	1986	35.00	225

Various People - A. Thorndike

YEAR ISSUE	EDITION LIMIT	YEAR RETD.	ISSUE PRICE	*QUOTE U.S.$
1987 3" Baby in Basket 1960	Closed	1987	16.00	100
1987 3" Boy w/ Snowball 8040	Closed	1988	14.00	45
1987 3" Bride and Groom 0306	Closed	1987	39.00	40-200
1983 3" PJ Kid 7600	Closed	1983	11.00	175
1986 3" Skier 8025	Closed	1988	14.00	45
1991 3" Water Baby in Pond Lily 1677	Closed	1991	15.00	15-55
1995 3" Winken, Blynken & Nod 1919	Closed	1996	68.00	95
1987 5" Christmas Morning Kid w/ 3" Bear in Box 8018	Closed	1989	32.00	65
1992 5" Equestrian Kid on 10" Horse 9943	Closed	1992	75.00	75-130
1987 5" Monk 2500	Closed	1987	14.00	85
1994 5" Old World Caroller Boy & Girl 7251, 7252	Closed	1995	46.00	65
1995 5" Pixie Piccolo Player 1920	Closed	1996	30.00	45
1993 7" Arab Boy w/ Lamb 2349	Yr.Iss.	1993	36.00	60
1968 7" Baby "I'm Reading"	Closed	1968	N/A	275
1992 7" Baby New Year 8200	Closed	1993	27.00	30-55
1987 7" Baby w/ Blanket & Knit Sweater 1962	Closed	1989	22.00	50
1971 7" Baby w/ Wreath on Head	Closed	1971	N/A	175
1996 7" Baker Kid 2331	Yr.Iss.	1996	31.00	45
1993 7" Ballerina on Music Box 2345	Yr.Iss.	1993	42.00	95-100
1993 7" Bar Mitzuah Boy 2348	Yr.Iss.	1993	26.50	55
1993 7" Basketball Boy (black) 2352	Yr.Iss.	1993	26.00	50
1992 7" Beach Kid w/ Boat 2340	Yr.Iss.	1992	30.00	55
1993 7" Bedtime Kid 2350	Yr.Iss.	1993	26.00	50
1987 7" Boy on Victorian Sled 7258	Closed	1989	23.00	65
1984 7" Boy w/ Firecracker 1650	Yr.Iss.	1984	20.00	125
1984 7" Boy w/ Snowball 8005	Closed	1988	19.00	45
1988 7" Bunny Kid 1672	Closed	1990	24.00	55
1999 7" Chantel's Easter Basket 1599	42	1999	75.00	375
1994 7" Cheerleader Girl 2354	Yr.Iss.	1994	27.00	50
1993 7" Choir Boy & Girl 7249, 7248	Closed	1995	56.00	75
1993 7" Choir Boy 7249	Closed	1995	28.00	40
1994 7" Choir Boy w/ Black Eye 7247	Closed	1995	28.00	45
1993 7" Choir Girl 7248	Closed	1995	28.00	40
1994 7" Christa McAuliffe Skateboard Kid 9955	Closed	1994	N/A	75
1984 7" Christmas Morning Kid 8015	Closed	1986	22.00	45
1985 7" Dress-Up Boy & Girl 1670, 1665	Closed	1985	40.00	160
1989 7" Dress-Up Boy & Girl 1673, 1674	Closed	1990	56.00	80
1989 7" Dress-Up Boy 1673	Closed	1990	N/A	27-35
1993 7" Drummer Boy 7200	Closed	1995	29.00	40
1996 7" Drummer Boy 7200	Closed	1996	29.00	29-40
1985 7" Drummer Boy 7225	Closed	1992	29.00	40

YEAR ISSUE	EDITION LIMIT	YEAR RETD.	ISSUE PRICE	*QUOTE U.S.$
1995 7" Easter Bunny Kid 1672	Closed	1996	25.00	45-55
1988 7" Eskimo Boy 8022	Closed	1989	24.00	65
1993 7" Fishing Boy (black) 2347	Closed	1993	30.00	50
1983 7" Fishing Boy 1625	Closed	1984	N/A	75
1994 7" Girl Building Snowman (pink) 7231	Closed	1995	25.00	75
1984 7" Girl on Sled 8010	Closed	1986	19.00	75
1987 7" Graduate Girl 1662	Closed	1987	20.00	80-115
1994 7" Hershey Kid 9951	Closed	1996	40.00	65
1995 7" Hockey Kid 2361	Yr.Iss.	1995	31.00	50
1994 7" Hot Shot Business Girl 2355	Yr.Iss.	1994	37.00	55
1993 7" Hot Shot Businessman Kid 2351	Yr.Iss.	1993	36.00	55
1982 7" I'm a Ten G-555	Yr.Iss.	1982	13.00	75
1995 7" Joseph, Mary & Shepherd Child w/ Lamb 7070, 7071, 7072	Closed	1995	98.00	150
1993 7" Jump Rope Girl 2346	Closed	1993	26.00	50
1997 7" Karate Kid 2344	Closed	1997	27.00	45-50
1993 7" Kid Building Snowman (blue) 7230	Closed	1993	22.00	75
1994 7" Marbles Kid 9956	Closed	1994	N/A	75
1993 7" Pink Flower Kid 1597	Yr.Iss.	1993	26.00	26-55
1996 7" Powder Puff Baby 2332	Yr.Iss.	1996	21.00	21-45
1994 7" Scottish Lad 2356	Yr.Iss.	1994	30.00	55
1999 7" Shana in Leaf Pile 3242	30	1999	43.00	125
1992 7" Skateboard Kid 2330	Yr.Iss.	1992	30.00	45
1985 7" Skiing Kid 8020	Closed	1987	19.00	90
1996 7" Snowball Fight Kid 7233	Closed	1996	31.00	31-50
1996 7" St. Patricks Day Boy 1713	Closed	1997	32.00	45-55
1997 7" St. Patricks Day Girl 1714	Closed	1997	32.00	32-60
1982 8" Caroller Girl 7250	Closed	1986	20.00	40
1983 8" Monk w/ Jug 7915	Closed	1984	18.00	80
1984 10" Aerobic Girl 1950	Closed	1985	19.00	50
1989 10" Americana Couple w/ plaque 2445	Closed	1990	110.00	150
1990 10" Annalee Collector Doll w/ dome 2448	Closed	1991	150.00	245-350
1992 10" Baseball Batter 9941	Closed	1993	30.00	65-75
1994 10" Baseball Catcher 9946	Closed	1994	39.00	75
1993 10" Baseball Pitcher 9944	Closed	1993	36.00	75
1994 10" Basketball Player (black) 2601	Yr.Iss.	1994	32.00	60
1994 10" Basketball Player (white) 2601	Yr.Iss.	1994	32.00	60
1989 10" Bob Cratchet & 5" Tiny Tim w/ plaque 5462	Closed	1990	100.00	145-160
1984 10" Bride & Groom 2705, 2710	Closed	1985	63.00	50-300
1995 10" Bruins Hockey Player (signed by Chuck & S. Leech) 2610	Closed	1995	N/A	150
1995 10" Bruins Hockey Player 2610	Closed	1995	48.00	85-95
1994 10" Canadian Mountie on Horse (brass plaque) 9959	Closed	1995	130.00	275
1994 10" Canadian Mountie on Horse 9959	Closed	1995	130.00	175-250
1984 10" Caroller Boy 7255	Closed	1986	20.00	45
1975 10" Caroller Boy C-210	Closed	1976	N/A	125
1976 10" Caroller Girl C-209	Closed	1976	6.00	125
1967 10" Choir Boy	Closed	1969	N/A	225
1970 10" Choir Boy C-210	Closed	1973	N/A	150
1970 10" Choir Girl (red hair) C-209	Closed	1974	N/A	165
1994 10" Christa McAuliffe Ski Doll 9947	Yr.Iss.	1994	N/A	100
1992 10" Christmas Eve Bob Cratchet w/ plaque 5470	Yr.Iss.	1992	70.00	195-225
1992 10" Christmas Eve Scrooge w/ plaque 5468	Yr.Iss.	1992	60.00	195-225
1976 10" Colonial Drummer Boy A-304	Closed	1976	6.00	125-225
1975 10" Drummer Boy C-225	Closed	1975	6.00	175
1992 10" Father Time 8202	Closed	1993	55.00	100-105
1963 10" Friar (brown)	Closed	1965	3.00	375
1996 10" Ghost of Christmas Future 5457	Closed	1996	30.00	95-100
1996 10" Ghost of Christmas Past 5455	Closed	1996	40.00	95-100
1996 10" Ghost of Christmas Present 5456	Closed	1996	56.00	125
1996 10" Golfer Woman 2881	Closed	1996	44.00	75
1993 10" Headless Horseman w/ Horse 3070	Closed	1994	57.00	125-130
1987 10" Huck Finn w/ Dome 2550	Closed	1988	103.00	195-250
1990 10" Jacob Marley w/ plaque 5464	Closed	1992	90.00	150-175
1991 10" Man & Woman Skaters 7267, 7269	Closed	1992	92.00	46-165
1991 10" Martha Cratchet w/ plaque 5466	Closed	1992	60.00	125-150
1989 10" Merlin the Magician w/ brass plaque 3042	Closed	1990	70.00	95-150
1960 10" Monk	Closed	N/A	3.00	225
1996 10" Mr. Farmer 2883	Closed	1996	35.00	75
1996 10" Mr. Scrooge 5467	Closed	1996	38.00	85
2000 10" Music Box Skater 9727	200	2000	60.00	60
1990 10" N. H. Music Festival Conductor Doll w/ dome 9915	Closed	1991	110.00	295-450
1987 10" Nativity Set w/ dome & plaque 5420	Closed	1990	150.00	250-300
1994 10" Old World Caroller Man & Woman 7251, 7252	Closed	1995	58.00	30-100
1988 10" Scrooge w/ plaque 5460	Closed	1990	90.00	116-125
1988 10" Scrooge w/ plaque and dome 5460	Closed	1991	140.00	160
1988 10" Shepherd Boy & Lamb w/ plaque 5422	Closed	1990	90.00	175
1991 10" Skaters-Man 7267	Closed	1992	46.00	85
1991 10" Skaters-Woman 7269	Closed	1992	46.00	85
1984 10" Skier (cross country) 8160	Closed	1986	36.00	115-125
1984 10" Skier (downhill) 8150	Closed	1988	35.00	65-95
1992 10" Snow Queen 7008	Yr.Iss.	1992	40.00	80
1994 10" Soccer Player 9950	Closed	1994	36.00	60
1990 10" Spirit of 76 w/ dome 9646	Closed	1991	195.00	325-450
1987 10" State Trooper w/ dome	Closed	1987	134.00	325-395
1996 10" Tennis Player-Woman 2880	Yr.Iss.	1996	44.00	70
1990 10" Wiseman w/ Camel w/ plaque 5428	Closed	1991	110.00	175-250
1989 10" Wisemen (2) w/ plaque 5426	Closed	1990	110.00	175-240
1993 12" Drummer Boy 7225	Closed	1995	40.00	55
1985 12" Drummer Boy 7225	Closed	1992	50.00	55-65
1985 12" Kid w/ Sled 8050	Closed	1986	33.00	100
1992 12" P.J. Boy 7635	Closed	1993	30.00	60-70
1992 12" P.J. Girl 7630	Closed	1993	30.00	60-70
1991 12" P.J. Kid (blonde hair) 7644	Closed	1992	30.00	60
1991 12" P.J. Kid (red hair) 7642	Closed	1991	30.00	60-70
1991 12" P.J. Kid (brown hair) 7640	Closed	1992	30.00	60
1977 15" Drummer Boy C221	Closed	1977	14.00	125
1982 16" Caroller Girl 7275	Closed	1984	30.00	95
1983 16" Monk w/ Jug 7915	Closed	1984	35.00	140
1988 18" Americana Couple w/ plaque 2552	Closed	1988	170.00	325
1974 18" Bob Cratchet & 7" Tiny Tim /Mrs Cratchet C50-C51	Closed	1975	N/A	425
1987 18" Bottle Cover Monk 2502	Closed	1987	30.00	150
1990 18" Bunny Kid w/ Slippers 1671	Closed	1992	50.00	95-100
1976 18" Caroller Girl C-211	Closed	1976	13.00	150
1990 18" Choir Girl 5708	Closed	1991	58.00	90
1990 18" Christmas Morning Kid w/ Train 5702	Closed	1990	66.00	125
1976 18" Colonial Drummer Boy A305	Closed	1976	6.00	350
1983 18" Girl & Boy w/ Sleigh 7670	Closed	1983	80.00	195
1990 18" Girl on Sled 5706	Closed	1990	56.00	125
1990 18" Naughty Kid 2976	Closed	1991	75.00	125-140
1987 18" P.J. Kid 7650	Closed	1987	40.00	85
1989 18" P.J. Kid Hanging Stocking 7672	Closed	1991	47.00	95-105
1987 18" P.J. Kid w/ 2' Christmas Stocking 7658	Closed	1995	60.00	95
1993 18" Skater-Man 5476	Yr.Iss.	1993	45.00	95
1993 18" Skater-Woman 5477	Yr.Iss.	1993	45.00	125
1983 18" Sledding Boy 7665	Closed	1984	30.00	100
1983 18" Sledding Girl 7660	Closed	1984	30.00	100
1975 18" Yankee Doodle Dandy on 18" Horse A-306	Closed	1976	58.00	425

Annette Himstedt

Annette Himstedt Club - A. Himstedt

YEAR ISSUE	EDITION LIMIT	YEAR RETD.	ISSUE PRICE	*QUOTE U.S.$
1996 Morgana	Retrd.	1996	685.00	700-710
1996 Virpi	Retrd.	1996	N/A	N/A
1996 Copper Box w/Morgana & Virpi on top	Retrd.	1996	Gift	N/A
1997 Freeke w/Bibi	Retrd.	1997	860.00	900-920
1997 Keshia & Orjo	Retrd.	1997	N/A	N/A
1997 Klara & Paulinchen	Retrd.	1997	N/A	N/A
1997 Freeke w/Bibi Pendant	Retrd.	1997	Gift	N/A
1997 Sita Bust	Retrd.	1997	Gift	N/A
1998 Baby Lieschen	Retrd.	1998	698.00	698-750
1998 Baby Lieschen Miniature (Kleines Lieschen)	113	1998	Gift	N/A
1998 Sookja and Soonja	76	1998	N/A	N/A
1998 Jali and Jami	76	1998	N/A	N/A
1998 Jali and Jami baseball miniature	76	1998	N/A	N/A
1998 Sookja and Soonja miniature on box	76	1998	N/A	N/A
1999 Mirte	Yr.Iss.	1999	875.00	875-930
1999 Kleine (little) Mirte	Yr.Iss.	1999	Gift	N/A
2000 Skille	Yr.Iss.		840.00	840
2000 Kleine (little) Skille	Yr.Iss.		95.00	95

Puppen Kinder - A. Himstedt

YEAR ISSUE	EDITION LIMIT	YEAR RETD.	ISSUE PRICE	*QUOTE U.S.$
1989 Adrienne-France	2-Yr.	1991	560.00	900-950
1994 Alke-Norway	2-Yr.	1996	618.00	750
2000 Amber	1,013		1275.00	1275
1999 Anila	1-Yr.	1999	735.00	735
1997 AnMei-China	1-Yr.	1997	680.00	680
1998 Anna I-Germany	2-Yr.	1998	605.00	605
1998 Anna II-Germany	2-Yr.	1998	605.00	605
1990 Ännchen-Germay	2-Yr.	1992	560.00	840
1996 Aura-Spain	1,013	1996	1020.00	1020-1350
1989 Ayoka-Africa	2-Yr.	1991	560.00	1125-1150
2000 Baby Tri	2-Yr.		635.00	635
1987 Bastian-Germany	2-Yr.	1989	329.00	875
1987 Beckus-Nepal	2-Yr.	1989	329.00	1200-1500
1998 Catalina-Italy (Bolzano)	1-Yr.	1998	725.00	725
1996 Charly-Chicago	1-Yr.	1997	685.00	685
1999 Deda	1-Yr.	1999	698.00	698
1987 Ellen-Germany	2-Yr.	1989	329.00	975
2000 Emil	1-Yr.		695.00	695
1992 Enzo-Italy	2-Yr.	1994	582.00	675
1997 Esme-Scotland	1-Yr.	1997	725.00	725
1987 Fatou (Cornroll)-Senegal	2-Yr.	1989	329.00	1500
1987 Fatou-Senegal	2-Yr.	1989	329.00	950-1050
1990 Fiene-Belgium	2-Yr.	1992	560.00	1050
1988 Friederike-Alsace	2-Yr.	1990	525.00	1795-2175
1999 Georgi I	2-Yr.		635.00	635
1999 Georgi II	2-Yr.		635.00	635
1997 Irmi-Austria	1-Yr.	1997	690.00	690
1989 Janka-Hungry	2-Yr.	1991	560.00	950-1125
2000 Jette	1-Yr.		725.00	725
1992 Jule-Sweden	2-Yr.	1994	582.00	980
1989 Kai-Germany	2-Yr.	1991	560.00	900-1000
1988 Kasimir-Germany	2-Yr.	1990	525.00	1895-1975
1987 Käthe-Germany	2-Yr.	1989	329.00	1000
1998 Keri-Africa	1-Yr.	1998	690.00	690
1993 Kima-Greenland	2-Yr.	1995	582.00	690-720
1991 Liliane-Netherlands	2-Yr.	1993	569.00	695-725
1999 Lillwa	1-Yr.	1999	698.00	698
1996 Lina-Germany	1-Yr.	1997	680.00	680
1987 Lisa-Germany	2-Yr.	1989	329.00	975
1993 Lona-California	2-Yr.	1995	601.00	690
1998 Lonneke-Denmark	1-Yr.	1998	690.00	690
1995 Madino-Russia	2-Yr.	1997	640.00	640
1988 Makimura-Japan	2-Yr.	1990	525.00	1200-1295
1988 Malin-Sweden	2-Yr.	1990	525.00	1795
1996 Marlie-Germany	1-Yr.	1997	685.00	685
1994 Melvin-Ireland	2-Yr.	1996	618.00	550-618
1999 Mia Yin	1,013	1999	1275.00	1275
1988 Michiko-Japan	2-Yr.	1990	525.00	1390-1495
1995 Minou-Corsica	2-Yr.	1997	650.00	650
1990 Mo-USA	2-Yr.	1992	560.00	880
1991 Neblina-Switzerland	2-Yr.	1993	569.00	595-725
1998 Oscar-Ireland	1,013	1998	1250.00	1400
1994 Panchita-Mexico	2-Yr.	1996	618.00	550-620
1994 Pancho-Mexico	2-Yr.	1996	618.00	550-620
1987 Paula-Germany	2-Yr.	1989	329.00	1000
1992 Pemba-USA	2-Yr.	1994	569.00	575
2000 Reiki I	2-Yr.		635.00	635
2000 Reiki II	2-Yr.		635.00	635
2000 Sanfia	1-Yr.		795.00	795
1992 Sanga-USA	2-Yr.	1994	569.00	575
1991 Shireem-Bali	2-Yr.	1993	569.00	595-650
1990 Taki-Japan	2-Yr.	1992	560.00	840
1995 Takuma-Cheyenne Indian Boy	2-Yr.	1997	640.00	640
1995 Takumi-Cheyenne Indian Girl	2-Yr.	1997	650.00	650
1993 Tara-Germany	2-Yr.	1995	582.00	690
1988 Timi-Germany	2-Yr.	1990	329.00	400-500
1997 Tinka-Friesland	1,013	1997	1250.00	1250

ANRI

Disney Dolls - Disney Studios

YEAR ISSUE	EDITION LIMIT	YEAR RETD.	ISSUE PRICE	*QUOTE U.S.$
1990 Daisy Duck, 14"	2,500	1991	895.00	1089-1250
1990 Donald Duck, 14"	2,500	1991	895.00	1089-1250
1989 Mickey Mouse, 14"	2,500	1991	850.00	1000
1989 Minnie Mouse, 14"	2,500	1991	850.00	1000-1300
1989 Pinocchio, 14"	2,500	1991	850.00	8951513

Ferrandiz Dolls - J. Ferrandiz

YEAR ISSUE	EDITION LIMIT	YEAR RETD.	ISSUE PRICE	*QUOTE U.S.$
1991 Carmen, 14"	1,000	1992	730.00	730
1991 Fernando, 14"	1,000	1992	730.00	730
1989 Gabriel, 14"	1,000	1991	550.00	575
1991 Juanita, 7"	1,500	1992	300.00	300
1990 Margarite, 14"	1,000	1992	575.00	730
1989 Maria, 14"	1,000	1991	550.00	575
1991 Miguel, 7"	1,500	1992	300.00	300
1990 Philipe, 14"	1,000	1992	575.00	680

Sarah Kay Dolls - S. Kay

YEAR ISSUE	EDITION LIMIT	YEAR RETD.	ISSUE PRICE	*QUOTE U.S.$
1991 Annie, 7"	1,500	1993	300.00	300
1989 Bride to Love And To Cherish	750	1992	750.00	790
1989 Charlotte (Blue)	1,000	1991	550.00	575-715
1990 Christina, 14"	1,000	1993	575.00	730
1989 Eleanor (Floral)	1,000	1991	550.00	575
1989 Elizabeth (Patchwork)	1,000	1991	550.00	575
1988 Emily, 14"	Closed	1989	500.00	500
1990 Faith, 14"	1,000	1993	575.00	685
1989 Groom With This Ring Doll, 14"	750	1992	550.00	730
1989 Helen (Brown), 14"	1,000	1991	550.00	575
1989 Henry, 14"	1,000	1991	550.00	575
1991 Janine, 14"	1,000	1993	750.00	750
1988 Jennifer, 14"	Closed	1989	500.00	500-520
1991 Jessica, 7"	1,500	1993	300.00	300
1991 Julie, 7"	1,500	1993	300.00	300
1988 Katherine, 14"	Closed	1989	500.00	500-520
1988 Martha, 14"	Closed	1989	500.00	500
1989 Mary (Red)	1,000	1991	550.00	575
1991 Michelle, 7"	1,500	1993	300.00	300
1991 Patricia, 14"	1,000	1993	730.00	730
1991 Peggy, 7"	1,500	1993	300.00	300
1990 Polly, 14"	1,000	1993	575.00	680
1988 Rachael, 14"	Closed	1989	500.00	500-520
1988 Rebecca, 14"	Closed	1989	500.00	500-520
1988 Sarah, 14"	Closed	1989	500.00	500-514
1990 Sophie, 14"	1,000	1993	575.00	660
1991 Susan, 7"	1,500	1993	300.00	300
1988 Victoria, 14"	Closed	1989	500.00	500

Ashton-Drake Galleries

Age of Bear-ius/Plush - D. Henretty

YEAR ISSUE	EDITION LIMIT	YEAR RETD.	ISSUE PRICE	*QUOTE U.S.$
1999 Guthrie	Open		69.99	70
2000 Moonflower	Open		69.99	70
2000 Nash	Open		69.99	70
2000 Meadow	Open		69.99	70

All I Wish For You - J. Good-Krüger

YEAR ISSUE	EDITION LIMIT	YEAR RETD.	ISSUE PRICE	*QUOTE U.S.$
1994 I Wish You Love	Closed	1995	49.95	50
1995 I Wish You Faith	Closed	1998	49.95	50
1995 I Wish You Happiness	Closed	1998	49.95	50
1995 I Wish You Wisdom	Closed	1998	49.95	50
1996 I Wish You Charity	Closed	1999	49.95	50
1996 I Wish You Luck	Closed	1999	49.95	50

All Precious in His Sight - J. Ibarolle

YEAR ISSUE	EDITION LIMIT	YEAR RETD.	ISSUE PRICE	*QUOTE U.S.$
1998 Naomi	Closed	1999	72.99	73
1998 Kristina	Closed	1999	72.99	73
1998 Rosa	Closed	1999	72.99	73
1998 Su-Lee	Closed	1999	72.99	73

Amish Blessings - J. Good-Krüger

YEAR ISSUE	EDITION LIMIT	YEAR RETD.	ISSUE PRICE	*QUOTE U.S.$
1990 Rebeccah	Closed	1993	68.00	95-100
1991 Rachel	Closed	1993	69.00	125
1991 Adam	Closed	1993	75.00	125-150
1992 Ruth	Closed	1993	75.00	90-110
1992 Eli	Closed	1993	79.95	95-125
1993 Sarah	Closed	1994	79.95	125

Anne of Green Gables - J. Kovacik

YEAR ISSUE	EDITION LIMIT	YEAR RETD.	ISSUE PRICE	*QUOTE U.S.$
1995 Anne	Closed	1998	69.95	70
1996 Diana Barry	Closed	1999	69.95	70

*Quotes have been rounded up to nearest dollar

Year Issue	Edition Limit	Year Retd.	Issue Price	*Quote U.S.$
1996 Gilbert Blythe	Closed	1998	69.95	70
1996 Josie Pye	Closed	1998	69.95	70

As Cute As Can Be - D. Effner

Year Issue	Edition Limit	Year Retd.	Issue Price	*Quote U.S.$
1993 Sugar Plum	Closed	1994	49.95	75-95
1994 Puppy Love	Closed	1995	49.95	75-95
1994 Angel Face	Closed	1995	49.95	50-75
1995 Patty Cake	Closed	1998	49.95	50

Babies World of Wonder - K. Barry-Hippensteel

Year Issue	Edition Limit	Year Retd.	Issue Price	*Quote U.S.$
1996 Andrew	Closed	1999	59.95	60
1996 Sarah	Closed	1999	59.95	60
1997 Jason	Closed	1999	59.95	60
1997 Kristen	Closed	1999	69.95	70
1998 Alex	Closed	1999	69.95	70

Baby Book Treasures - K. Barry-Hippensteel

Year Issue	Edition Limit	Year Retd.	Issue Price	*Quote U.S.$
1990 Elizabeth's Homecoming	Closed	1993	58.00	58
1991 Catherine's Christening	Closed	1994	58.00	58
1991 Christopher's First Smile	Closed	1992	63.00	58-63

Baby Talk - J. Good-Krüger

Year Issue	Edition Limit	Year Retd.	Issue Price	*Quote U.S.$
1994 All Gone	Closed	1995	49.95	75
1994 Bye-Bye	Closed	1995	49.95	50-75
1994 Night, Night	Closed	1995	49.95	50-75

Baby's Own Book - E. Helland

Year Issue	Edition Limit	Year Retd.	Issue Price	*Quote U.S.$
1999 Hannah's Homecoming	Open		59.99	60

Backyard Pool Party - T. Tomescu

Year Issue	Edition Limit	Year Retd.	Issue Price	*Quote U.S.$
1999 Summer Lovin' Tweety	Open		79.99	80

Ballet Recital - P. Bomar

Year Issue	Edition Limit	Year Retd.	Issue Price	*Quote U.S.$
1996 Chloe	12/00		69.95	70
1996 Kylie	Closed	1999	69.95	70
1996 Heidi	Closed	1998	69.95	70

Barely Yours - T. Tomescu

Year Issue	Edition Limit	Year Retd.	Issue Price	*Quote U.S.$
1994 Cute as a Button	Closed	1994	69.95	95-125
1994 Snug as a Bug in a Rug	Closed	1995	75.00	75-125
1995 Clean as a Whistle	Closed	1996	75.00	75-125
1995 Pretty as a Picture	Closed	1996	75.00	75-125
1995 Good as Gold	Closed	1996	75.00	75-125
1996 Cool As A Cucumber	Closed	1999	75.00	75

Beach Babies - C. Jackson

Year Issue	Edition Limit	Year Retd.	Issue Price	*Quote U.S.$
1996 Carly	Closed	1998	79.95	80
1996 Kyle	Closed	1997	79.95	80
1997 Kellie	Closed	1999	79.95	80

Beach Babies - C. Marschner

Year Issue	Edition Limit	Year Retd.	Issue Price	*Quote U.S.$
1995 Sally	Closed	N/A	95.00	95
1996 Lacey	Closed	N/A	95.00	95-120
1997 Cassie	Closed	N/A	95.00	95

Bears of Memories/Plush - B. Ferrier

Year Issue	Edition Limit	Year Retd.	Issue Price	*Quote U.S.$
1997 Cinnamon Bear	Closed	N/A	79.99	80

Beautiful Dreamers - G. Rademann

Year Issue	Edition Limit	Year Retd.	Issue Price	*Quote U.S.$
1992 Katrina	Closed	1993	89.00	125-150
1992 Nicolette	Closed	1994	89.95	95-100
1993 Brigitte	Closed	1994	94.00	94
1993 Isabella	Closed	1994	94.00	94
1993 Gabrielle	Closed	1994	94.00	94-105

Beauty And Grace - B. Hanson

Year Issue	Edition Limit	Year Retd.	Issue Price	*Quote U.S.$
1997 Isabella	Closed	1999	99.95	100
1997 Patrice	Closed	1999	99.95	100
1998 Collette	Closed	2000	99.95	100
1998 Lara	Closed	1999	99.95	100

Bedtime for Bears/Plush - J. Davis

Year Issue	Edition Limit	Year Retd.	Issue Price	*Quote U.S.$
1998 Eliza	Closed	N/A	42.99	43
1998 Genie	Closed	N/A	42.99	43
1998 Jilly	Closed	N/A	42.99	43
1997 Sarah	Closed	N/A	42.99	43

The Bible Tells Me So - R. Miller

Year Issue	Edition Limit	Year Retd.	Issue Price	*Quote U.S.$
1998 Matthew	Open		72.99	73
1998 Mark	Closed	1999	72.99	73
1999 Luke	Open		72.99	73
1999 John	Open		72.99	73

Birthstone Bears/Plush - P. Blair

Year Issue	Edition Limit	Year Retd.	Issue Price	*Quote U.S.$
1997 January Garnet	Open		39.95	40
1997 February Amethyst	Open		39.95	40
1997 March Aquamarine	Open		39.95	40
1997 April Diamond	Open		39.95	40
1997 May Emerald	Open		39.95	40
1997 June Pearl	Open		39.95	40
1997 July Ruby	Open		39.95	40
1997 August Peridot	Open		39.95	40
1997 September Sapphire	Open		39.95	40
1997 October Opal	Open		39.95	40
1997 November Topaz	Open		39.95	40
1997 December Turquoise	Open		39.95	40

Blessed Are The Children - B. Deval

Year Issue	Edition Limit	Year Retd.	Issue Price	*Quote U.S.$
1996 Blessed Are The Peacemakers	Closed	1999	69.95	70
1996 Blessed Are The Pure of Heart	Closed	1998	69.95	70
1997 Blessed Are The Meek	Closed	1998	79.95	80
1997 Blessed Are The Merciful	Closed	1998	79.95	80

Blessings of the Great Spirit - J. Belle

Year Issue	Edition Limit	Year Retd.	Issue Price	*Quote U.S.$
1999 Miracle of the Spirit Wind	Open		99.99	100

Blessings of the Seasons - T. Tomescu

Year Issue	Edition Limit	Year Retd.	Issue Price	*Quote U.S.$
1999 Winter Wonder	Open		99.99	100
2000 The Glory of Summer	Open		99.99	100
2000 The Delight of Spring	Open		99.99	100
2000 The Bounty of Autumn	Open		99.99	100

Blossoming Belles - S. Freeman

Year Issue	Edition Limit	Year Retd.	Issue Price	*Quote U.S.$
1997 Yellow Rose	12/00		82.99	83
1998 Peach Blossom	Closed	1999	82.99	83
1998 Honeysuckle Rose	Closed	1999	82.99	83
1998 Magnolia Blossom	Closed	1999	82.99	83

Born To Be Famous - K. Barry-Hippensteel

Year Issue	Edition Limit	Year Retd.	Issue Price	*Quote U.S.$
1989 Little Sherlock	Closed	1991	87.00	90
1990 Little Florence Nightingale	Closed	1991	87.00	87-95
1991 Little Davey Crockett	Closed	1994	92.00	92
1992 Little Christopher Columbus	Closed	1993	95.00	95

Boys & Bears - A. Brown

Year Issue	Edition Limit	Year Retd.	Issue Price	*Quote U.S.$
1996 Cody and Cuddle Bear	Closed	1999	62.99	63
1997 Bobby and Buddy Bear	Closed	2000	62.99	63
1997 Nicky and Naptime Bear	12/01		62.99	63
1998 Sammy and Sharing Bear	Closed	1999	62.99	63

Boys Will Be Bears/Plush - P. Joho & E. Foran

Year Issue	Edition Limit	Year Retd.	Issue Price	*Quote U.S.$
1997 Charlie	Closed	1999	49.95	50
1998 Davey	Closed	1999	49.95	50
1998 Frankie	Open		49.95	50
1998 Jimmy	Closed	2000	49.95	50

Brides of the South - L. Dunsmore

Year Issue	Edition Limit	Year Retd.	Issue Price	*Quote U.S.$
1998 Charlotte	Open		132.99	133
1998 Savannah	Open		132.99	133
1999 Laurel	Open		132.99	133
1999 Florence	Open		132.99	133

Calendar Babies - Ashton-Drake

Year Issue	Edition Limit	Year Retd.	Issue Price	*Quote U.S.$
1995 New Year	Open		24.95	25
1995 Cupid	Open		24.95	25
1995 Leprechaun	Open		24.95	25
1995 April Showers	Open		24.95	25
1995 May Flowers	Open		24.95	25
1995 June Bride	Open		24.95	25
1995 Uncle Sam	Open		24.95	25
1995 Sun & Fun	Open		24.95	25
1995 Back to School	Open		24.95	25
1995 Happy Haunting	Open		24.95	25
1995 Thanksgiving Turkey	Open		24.95	25
1995 Jolly Santa	Open		24.95	25

Catch of the Day/Plush - A. Inman-Looms

Year Issue	Edition Limit	Year Retd.	Issue Price	*Quote U.S.$
1999 Any Minute Now	Open		49.99	50
1999 Early Bear Catches the Worm	Open		49.99	50
2000 The One That Got Away	Open		49.99	50
2000 A Good Day Fishing	Open		49.99	50

Caught In The Act - M. Tretter

Year Issue	Edition Limit	Year Retd.	Issue Price	*Quote U.S.$
1992 Stevie, Catch Me If You Can	Closed	1994	49.95	125-145
1993 Kelly, Don't I Look Pretty?	Closed	1994	49.95	60-95
1994 Mikey (Look It Floats)	Closed	1994	55.00	55
1994 Nickie (Cookie Jar)	Closed	1995	59.95	60
1994 Becky (Kleenex Box)	Closed	1995	59.95	60

Caught In The Act/Plush - M. Tretter

Year Issue	Edition Limit	Year Retd.	Issue Price	*Quote U.S.$
1994 Sandy	Closed	1995	59.95	60

Caught In The Act/Plush - S. Schutt

Year Issue	Edition Limit	Year Retd.	Issue Price	*Quote U.S.$
1995 Bailey	Closed	1999	39.95	40
1995 Bonnie	Closed	1998	39.95	40
1995 Katie	Closed	1999	39.95	40
1995 Nathaniel	Closed	1998	39.95	40

Century of Beautiful Brides - S. Bilotto

Year Issue	Edition Limit	Year Retd.	Issue Price	*Quote U.S.$
1997 Katherine	Closed	1997	62.99	63
1997 Grace	Closed	1998	62.99	63
1998 Donna	Closed	1999	62.99	63
1998 Heather	Closed	1999	62.99	63
1999 Joanna	Closed	1999	62.99	63

Charming Discoveries - S. Freeman

Year Issue	Edition Limit	Year Retd.	Issue Price	*Quote U.S.$
1996 Celeste	12/00		89.95	90
1996 Marie	12/00		89.95	90
1997 Cynthia	Closed	1998	89.95	90

A Child's Bedtime Prayer - M. Snyder

Year Issue	Edition Limit	Year Retd.	Issue Price	*Quote U.S.$
1997 Now I Lay Me Down To Sleep	Open		59.95	60
1998 I Pray The Lord My Soul To Keep	Open		59.95	60
1998 Keep Me Safe All Through The Night	Open		59.95	60
1998 Wake Me Up At Morning Light	Open		59.95	60

Children of Christmas - M. Sirko

Year Issue	Edition Limit	Year Retd.	Issue Price	*Quote U.S.$
1994 The Little Drummer Boy	Closed	1995	79.95	125-150
1994 The Littlest Angel	Closed	1995	79.95	80
1995 O Christmas Tree	Closed	1998	79.95	80
1995 Sugar Plum Fairy	Closed	1998	79.95	80

Children of Mother Goose - Y. Bello

Year Issue	Edition Limit	Year Retd.	Issue Price	*Quote U.S.$
1987 Little Bo Peep	Closed	1988	58.00	95-110
1987 Mary Had a Little Lamb	Closed	1989	58.00	110-175
1988 Little Jack Horner	Closed	1989	63.00	63
1989 Miss Muffet	Closed	1991	63.00	63-150

Children of the Great Spirit - S. Simon

Year Issue	Edition Limit	Year Retd.	Issue Price	*Quote U.S.$
1994 Meadowlark	Open		95.00	95
1995 Tashee	Open		95.00	95

Year Issue	Edition Limit	Year Retd.	Issue Price	*Quote U.S.$
1996 Star Dreamer	Open		95.00	95
1996 Sewanka	Open		95.00	95

A Children's Circus - J. McClelland

Year Issue	Edition Limit	Year Retd.	Issue Price	*Quote U.S.$
1990 Tommy The Clown	Closed	1993	78.00	70-125
1991 Katie The Tightrope Walker	Closed	1993	78.00	70-125
1991 Johnnie The Strongman	Closed	1994	83.00	83-125
1992 Maggie The Animal Trainer	Closed	1994	83.00	83-150

Christmas Cinderella 1998 - B. Deval

Year Issue	Edition Limit	Year Retd.	Issue Price	*Quote U.S.$
1998 1998 Christmas Cinderella	Closed	1998	114.99	115

Classic Brides of The Century - E. Williams

Year Issue	Edition Limit	Year Retd.	Issue Price	*Quote U.S.$
1990 Flora, The 1900s Bride	Closed	1993	145.00	195-300
1991 Jennifer, The 1980s Bride	Closed	1992	149.00	225-300
1993 Kathleen, The 1930s Bride	Closed	1993	149.95	150

Classic Collection - D. Effner

Year Issue	Edition Limit	Year Retd.	Issue Price	*Quote U.S.$
1996 Hillary	12/00		79.95	80
1996 Willow	12/00		79.95	80
1996 Emily	Closed	1998	79.95	80
1997 Jenny	12/01		79.95	80
1997 Schoolgirl Jenny	Closed	2000	79.95	80

Classic Pooh Storytime - C. McClure

Year Issue	Edition Limit	Year Retd.	Issue Price	*Quote U.S.$
1999 Storytime with Pooh	Open		172.99	173

Country Kids - C. Johnston

Year Issue	Edition Limit	Year Retd.	Issue Price	*Quote U.S.$
1994 Savannah	Closed	1998	79.00	95
1994 Skyler	Closed	1998	95.00	95
1995 Cheyene	Closed	1998	95.00	95
1995 Austin	Closed	1998	95.00	95

Country Sweethearts - M. Tretter

Year Issue	Edition Limit	Year Retd.	Issue Price	*Quote U.S.$
1996 Millie	Closed	1998	62.99	63

Cuddle Chums - K. Barry-Hippensteel

Year Issue	Edition Limit	Year Retd.	Issue Price	*Quote U.S.$
1995 Heather	Closed	1998	59.95	60
1995 Jeffrey	Closed	1998	59.95	60

Decorating The Tree - M. Tretter

Year Issue	Edition Limit	Year Retd.	Issue Price	*Quote U.S.$
1996 Trisha	12/00		59.95	60
1996 Patrick	12/00		59.95	60
1996 Ryan	12/00		59.95	60
1996 Melissa	12/00		59.95	60

Deval's Fairytale Princesses - B. Deval

Year Issue	Edition Limit	Year Retd.	Issue Price	*Quote U.S.$
1996 Cinderella	12/00		92.99	93
1996 Rapunzel	Closed	1999	92.99	93
1997 The Snow Queen	12/01		94.99	95
1997 Sleeping Beauty	Closed	1998	94.99	95
1997 Princess and the Frog	Closed	1999	94.99	95

Dianna Effner's Mother Goose - D. Effner

Year Issue	Edition Limit	Year Retd.	Issue Price	*Quote U.S.$
1990 Mary, Mary, Quite Contrary	Closed	1992	78.00	175-200
1991 The Little Girl With The Curl (Horrid)	Closed	1992	79.00	150-250
1991 The Little Girl With The Curl (Good)	Closed	1993	79.00	125-200
1992 Little Boy Blue	Closed	1993	85.00	75-85
1993 Snips & Snails	Closed	1994	85.00	125-150
1993 Sugar & Spice	Closed	1994	89.95	125-135
1993 Curly Locks	Closed	1995	89.95	90-100

Disney Babies in Dreamland - Y. Bello

Year Issue	Edition Limit	Year Retd.	Issue Price	*Quote U.S.$
1998 Baby Mickey	Open		62.99	63
1998 Baby Minnie	Open		62.99	63
1999 Baby Donald	Open		62.99	63
1999 Baby Pluto	Open		62.99	63
1999 Baby Daisy	Open		62.99	63
1999 Baby Goofy	Open		62.99	63

Down on the Beanbag Farm - R. Clark

Year Issue	Edition Limit	Year Retd.	Issue Price	*Quote U.S.$
1997 Janie	12/00		62.99	63
1998 Emma	Closed	1999	62.99	63
1998 Drew	Closed	1999	62.99	63

Emily Anne's Busy Day - A. Tsalikhan

Year Issue	Edition Limit	Year Retd.	Issue Price	*Quote U.S.$
1996 Emily Anne	Closed	1998	69.95	70
1997 Emily Anne Playing Mommy	Closed	1998	69.95	70
1997 Emily Anne Calling Grandma	Closed	1999	69.95	70
1997 Snacktime	Closed	1999	82.99	83

England's Rose/Plush - L. DeMent

Year Issue	Edition Limit	Year Retd.	Issue Price	*Quote U.S.$
1999 England's Rose	Open		62.99	63

Eternal Love - T. Tomescu

Year Issue	Edition Limit	Year Retd.	Issue Price	*Quote U.S.$
1997 Eternal Love	Closed	1997	92.99	93

European Fairytales - G. Rademann

Year Issue	Edition Limit	Year Retd.	Issue Price	*Quote U.S.$
1994 Little Red Riding Hood	Closed	1995	79.95	80-85
1995 Snow White	Closed	1996	79.95	80

Family Ties - M. Tretter

Year Issue	Edition Limit	Year Retd.	Issue Price	*Quote U.S.$
1994 Welcome Home Baby Brother	Closed	1995	79.95	80
1995 Kiss and Make it Better	Closed	1996	89.95	80-90
1995 Happily Ever Better	Closed	1996	89.95	80-90

First Day at Walt Disney World - T. Tomescu

Year Issue	Edition Limit	Year Retd.	Issue Price	*Quote U.S.$
1998 Disney Girl	Open		99.99	100
1998 Disney Boy	Open		99.99	100
1998 End of a Long Day	Open		99.99	100
1998 Just Being Goofy	Open		99.99	100

Flurry of Activity - T. Tomescu

Year Issue	Edition Limit	Year Retd.	Issue Price	*Quote U.S.$
1996 Making Snowflakes	Closed	1998	72.99	73
1997 Making Icicles	Closed	1997	72.99	73
1997 Making Sunshine	12/00		72.99	73

*Quotes have been rounded up to nearest dollar

YEAR ISSUE	EDITION LIMIT	YEAR RETD.	ISSUE PRICE	*QUOTE U.S.$
Forever Starts Today - C. McClure				
1996 Melody	Closed	2000	199.95	200
1997 Angelica	12/00		199.95	200
1997 Caroline	Closed	2000	199.95	200
1998 Monique	Open		199.95	200
Four Seasons Carousel - G. Rademann				
1998 Winter Splendor (with horse)	Open		124.99	125
1998 Spring Enchantment	Open		62.99	63
1999 Summer Glory	Open		62.99	63
1999 Autumn Radiance	Open		62.99	63
The Friendship Bouquet - P. Parkins				
1999 Everything's Coming Up Roses	Open		74.99	75
2000 Love Stems From Friendship	Open		74.99	75
2000 Bloom Where You Are Planted	Open		74.99	75
2000 Pick Your Friends & Love Them Bunches	Open		74.99	75
From This Day Forward - P. Tumminio				
1994 Elizabeth	Closed	1995	89.95	150-200
1995 Betty	Closed	1996	89.95	90-150
1995 Beth	Closed	1996	89.95	90-175
1995 Lisa	Closed	1996	89.95	90
Garden of Innocence - D. Richardson				
1996 Hope	Closed	1999	92.99	93
1996 Serenity	12/00		92.99	93
1997 Charity	12/01		92.99	93
1997 Grace	Closed	1998	92.99	93
1997 Kindness	12/01		92.99	93
Garden of Inspirations - B. Hanson				
1994 Gathering Violets	Closed	1995	69.95	75
1994 Daisy Chain	Closed	1995	69.95	70
1995 Heart's Bouquet	Closed	1996	74.95	75
1995 Garden Prayer	Closed	1996	74.95	75
Gentle Joys - J. Good-Krüger				
1997 A Day Filled With Hugs & Kisses	Closed	1998	49.99	50
Gibson Girl in Fashion - S. Bilotto				
1998 Garden Walk	12/01		132.99	133
1998 Evening at the Opera	12/01		132.99	133
1998 Derby Day	12/01		132.99	133
1998 The Masquerade Ball	12/01		132.99	133
Gifts For Mommy - M. Girard-Kassis				
1997 Mother's Day	12/01		62.99	63
1997 Christmas	12/01		62.99	63
1998 Be My Valentine	12/01		62.99	63
1998 Happy Birthday	12/01		62.99	63
Gingham & Bows - S. Freeman				
1995 Gwendolyn	Closed	1998	69.95	70
1996 Mallory	Closed	1999	69.95	70
1996 Ashleigh	Closed	1998	69.95	70
1996 Bridget	12/00		69.95	70
God Hears the Children - B. Conner				
1995 Now I Lay Me Down	Closed	1998	79.95	80
1996 God Is Great, God Is Good	Closed	1999	79.95	80
1996 We Give Thanks For Things We Have	Closed	1999	79.95	80
1996 All Creatures Great & Small	Closed	1998	79.95	80
God Sends an Angel - L. Tierney				
1999 Sleeping Like an Angel	Open		69.99	70
Growing Up Like Wildflowers - B. Madeja				
1996 Annie	Closed	1999	49.95	50
Happily Ever After - G. Rademann				
1998 Cinderella Bride	12/01		82.99	83
1998 Snow White Bride	12/01		82.99	83
1998 Rapunzel Bride	Open		82.99	83
1998 Beauty Bride	Open		82.99	83
Happiness Is Homemade - J. Good-Krüger				
1997 Hugs Made By Hand	Closed	1999	72.99	73
Happiness Is... - K. Barry-Hippensteel				
1991 Patricia (My First Tooth)	Closed	1993	69.00	125
1992 Crystal (Feeding Myself)	Closed	1994	69.95	100
1993 Brittany (Blowing Kisses)	Closed	1993	69.95	100
1993 Joy (My First Christmas)	Closed	1993	69.95	70-85
1994 Candy Cane (Holly)	Closed	1994	69.95	70
1994 Patrick (My First Playmate)	Closed	1994	69.95	70-85
Happy Meals World of Play - Y. Bello				
1997 McDonald's Express	Closed	1999	59.95	60
1997 McDonald's Old West	Closed	1998	64.99	65
Hats Off To The Seasons - L. Dunsmore				
1997 Christmas Carol	12/00		72.99	73
1997 Springtime Robin	Closed	1998	82.99	83
1998 Mary Sunshine	Closed	1999	82.99	83
1998 Autumn Joy	Closed	1999	82.99	83
Heavenly Blessings - C. Walser-Derek				
1998 Love's Gentle Kiss	Open		82.99	83
1999 Friendship's Warm Hug	Open		82.99	83
Heavenly Goodness/Plush - A. Inman-Looms				
1999 Purity	Open		49.99	50
Heavenly Inspirations - C. McClure				
1992 Every Cloud Has a Silver Lining	Closed	1994	59.95	48-75

YEAR ISSUE	EDITION LIMIT	YEAR RETD.	ISSUE PRICE	*QUOTE U.S.$
1993 Wish Upon A Star	Closed	1994	59.95	60-65
1994 Sweet Dreams	Closed	1994	65.00	65
1994 Luck at the End of Rainbow	Closed	1994	65.00	65
1994 Sunshine	Closed	1994	69.95	65-70
1994 Pennies From Heaven	Closed	1995	69.95	65-70
Here Comes Trouble - K. Barry-Hippensteel				
1999 Taz Made Me Do It	Open		79.99	80
2000 Loud but Lovable	Open		79.99	80
2000 Little Tornado	Open		79.99	80
2000 Too Tired for Trouble	Open		79.99	80
Heritage of American Quilting - J. Lundy				
1994 Eleanor	Closed	1995	79.95	80
1995 Abigail	Closed	1996	79.95	80
1995 Louisa	Closed	1996	84.95	85
1995 Ruth Anne	Closed	1996	84.95	85
Heroines from the Fairy Tale Forests - D. Effner				
1988 Little Red Riding Hood	Closed	1990	68.00	195-250
1989 Goldilocks	Closed	1991	68.00	68-95
1990 Snow White	Closed	1992	73.00	175
1991 Rapunzel	Closed	1993	79.00	175-250
1992 Cinderella	Closed	1993	79.00	175-295
1993 Cinderella (Ballgown)	Closed	1994	79.95	175-250
Honkytonk Gals Doll Collection - C. Johnston				
1996 Kendall	Open		95.00	95
I Love Tweety - L. Tierney				
1998 Tweety & Me	Open		74.99	75
1999 Sylvester's Surprise	Open		74.99	75
1999 A Snuggle With Tweety	Open		74.99	75
1999 Let's Have a Birdbath	Open		74.99	75
I Want Mommy - K. Barry-Hippensteel				
1993 Timmy (Mommy I'm Sleepy)	Closed	1994	59.95	145-150
1993 Tommy (Mommy I'm Sorry)	Closed	1994	59.95	125
1994 Up Mommy (Tammy)	Closed	1994	65.00	65
I'd Rather Be Fishin' - M. Tretter				
1996 What A Catch	12/00		72.99	73
1997 Fishin' Buddies	12/01		72.99	73
1997 Hooked on Fishin'	12/01		72.99	73
1997 Fish Story	12/01		72.99	73
I'm a Little Handyman - A. Tsalikhan				
1998 Tools Make the Man	Open		72.99	73
1999 Duct Tape Does it All	Open		72.99	73
1999 Brushing Up on the Job	Open		72.99	73
I'm Just Little - K. Barry-Hippensteel				
1995 I'm a Little Angel	Closed	1996	49.95	50
1995 I'm a Little Devil	Closed	1996	49.95	50
1996 I'm a Little Cutie	Closed	1999	49.95	50
I'm Tarzan Too - T. Tomescu				
1999 Jungle Buddies	Open		79.99	80
Imagine Where He'll Go - R. Miller				
1997 Adam	Closed	1998	62.99	63
In God's Garden - K. Barry-Hippensteel				
1998 Jessica Rose	Open		72.99	73
1998 Lil' Butterfly	Open		72.99	73
1999 Sweet Magnolia	Open		72.99	73
1999 Meadow Shade	Open		72.99	73
Innocence of Spring - C.W. Derek				
1997 Chelsea	Closed	2000	79.00	79
1999 Dori	Closed	1999	79.00	79
1999 Sidney	Open		79.00	79
1999 Leslie	Open		79.00	79
International Festival of Toys and Tots - K. Barry-Hippensteel				
1989 Chen, a Little Boy of China	Closed	1990	78.00	78-150
1989 Natasha	Closed	1992	78.00	78-150
1990 Molly	Closed	1993	83.00	75-99
1991 Hans	Closed	1993	88.00	88
1992 Miki, Eskimo	Closed	1994	88.00	88
It's So Much Friendlier With Pooh - C. McClure				
1998 You Need a Hug Pooh	12/01		72.99	73
1998 You Look Sleepy Pooh	12/01		72.99	73
1998 What's For Lunch Pooh?	Open		72.99	73
1998 Let's Play Pattycake Pooh	Open		72.99	73
1999 It's Our Bedtime Story, Pooh	Open		74.99	75
Joy Forever - C. McClure				
1996 Victorian Serenity	Closed	1998	129.95	130
1997 Victorian Bliss	Closed	1999	129.95	130
1997 Victorian Harmony	Closed	1998	129.95	130
1997 Victorian Peace	Closed	1998	129.95	130
Joys of Summer - K. Barry-Hippensteel				
1993 Tickles	Closed	1994	49.95	110-120
1993 Little Squirt	Closed	1994	49.95	65
1994 Yummy	Closed	1994	55.00	65
1994 Havin' A Ball	Closed	1994	55.00	65
1994 Lil' Scoop	Closed	1994	55.00	65
Just Caught Napping - A. Brown				
1996 Asleep in the Saddle	Closed	1999	69.95	70
1996 Oatmeal Dreams	Closed	1998	69.95	70
1997 Dog Tired	Closed	1998	69.95	70

YEAR ISSUE	EDITION LIMIT	YEAR RETD.	ISSUE PRICE	*QUOTE U.S.$
The King & I - P. Ryan Brooks				
1991 Shall We Dance	Closed	1992	175.00	395
La Quincenera - B. Hanson				
1998 La Quincenera	Open		92.99	93
The Language of Wedding Flowers - B. Hanson				
1998 White Roses	Open		99.99	100
2000 Calla Lilies	Open		99.99	100
2000 Gardenias	Open		99.99	100
2000 Camellias	Open		99.99	100
Lawton's Nursery Rhymes - W. Lawton				
1994 Little Bo Peep	Closed	1995	79.95	80-95
1994 Little Miss Muffet	Closed	1995	79.95	80
1994 Mary, Mary	Closed	1995	85.00	80-85
1994 Mary/Lamb	Closed	1995	85.00	80-85
The Legends of Baseball - Various				
1994 Babe Ruth - T. Tomescu	Closed	1995	79.95	140-175
1994 Lou Gehrig - T. Tomescu	Closed	1995	79.95	80-199
1995 Ty Cobb - E. Shelton	Closed	1996	79.95	80
Let's Play Mother Goose - K. Barry-Hippensteel				
1994 Cow Jumped Over the Moon	Closed	1995	69.95	70
1994 Hickory, Dickory, Dock	Closed	1995	69.95	95
Life's Little Blessings - R. Mattingly				
1997 Charity Is A Blessing	12/01		82.99	83
1997 Kindness Is A Blessing	Closed	1998	72.99	73
1998 Patience Is A Blessing	12/01		72.99	73
Little Ballerina Bears/Plush - A. Cranshaw				
1999 Gracie	Open		52.99	53
Little Girls of Classic Literature - W. Lawton				
1995 Pollyanna	Closed	1998	79.95	80
1996 Laura Ingalls	Closed	1999	79.95	80
1996 Rebecca of Sunnybrook Farm	Closed	1999	79.95	80
Little Gymnast - K. Barry-Hippensteel				
1996 Little Gymnast	Closed	1999	59.95	60
Little House On The Prairie - J. Ibarolle				
1992 Laura	Closed	1993	79.95	95
1993 Mary Ingalls	Closed	1993	79.95	300-395
1993 Nellie Olson	Closed	1994	85.00	145-150
1993 Almanzo	Closed	1994	85.00	95
1994 Carrie	Closed	1994	85.00	95-100
1994 Ma Ingalls	Closed	1995	85.00	85
1994 Pa Ingalls	Closed	1995	85.00	85
1995 Baby Grace	Closed	1996	69.95	75
Little Lacy Sleepyheads - J. Wolf				
1996 Jacqueline	Closed	N/A	99.99	100
The Little Performers - C. McClure				
1997 Joelle	Closed	1998	94.99	95
1997 Lauren	12/01		94.99	95
1998 Nicole	12/02		94.99	95
1998 Alyssa	Closed	1999	94.99	95
Little Rascals™ - S./J. Hoffman				
1992 Spanky	Closed	1999	75.00	150-200
1993 Alfalfa	Closed	1999	75.00	175
1994 Darla	Closed	1999	75.00	175-190
1994 Buckwheat	Closed	1999	75.00	100-150
1995 Stymie	Closed	1999	75.00	175
Little Women - W. Lawton				
1994 Jo	Closed	1995	59.95	75-150
1994 Meg	Closed	1995	59.95	60-125
1994 Beth	Closed	1996	59.95	125-175
1994 Amy	Closed	1996	59.95	175-250
1995 Marmie	Closed	1996	59.95	75-125
Looney Tunes Cuties - A. Tsalikhan				
1999 Pepe Le Pew	Open		74.99	75
1999 Marvin the Martian	Open		74.99	75
Lots Of Love - T. Menzenbach				
1993 Hannah Needs A Hug	Closed	1994	49.95	100
1993 Kaitlyn	Closed	1994	49.95	95
1994 Nicole	Closed	1995	55.00	55
1995 Felicia	Closed	1998	55.00	55
Love, Marriage, Baby Carriage/Plush - Various				
1996 Sam - B. Dewey	Open		49.95	50
1996 Katherine - M. Sibol	Closed	1999	49.95	50
1997 Carrie - D. Ortega	Closed	1999	49.95	50
The Loving Heart of the Irish Bride - J. Belle				
1999 Erin	Open		99.99	100
Lucky Charmers - C. McClure				
1995 Lucky Star	Closed	1998	69.95	70
1996 Bit O' Luck	Closed	N/A	69.95	70
Madonna & Child - B. Deval				
1996 Madonna & Child	Closed	1999	99.95	100
Magic Moments - K. Barry-Hippensteel				
1996 Birthday Boy	Closed	1999	69.95	70
Magical Moments of Summer - Y. Bello				
1995 Whitney	Closed	1998	59.95	48-60
1996 Zoe	Closed	1999	59.95	60

*Quotes have been rounded up to nearest dollar

YEAR ISSUE	EDITION LIMIT	YEAR RETD.	ISSUE PRICE	*QUOTE U.S.$
McDonald's And Me - D. Effner				
1996 You Deserve a Break Today	Closed	N/A	59.95	60
1997 Sharing a Good Time	Closed	N/A	59.95	60
McDonald's Future All Stars - B. Madeja				
1997 Joey	12/01		62.99	63
McDonald's Happy Times - K. Barry-Hippensteel				
1997 Ritchie	12/01		62.99	63
McDonald's Learning is Fun - T. Tomescu				
1996 Katie	Closed	1999	79.95	80
McDonald's Pillow Talk - B. Madeja				
1997 Sweet Dreams Ronald	12/00		62.99	63
McDonald's Treats For Tots - Y. Bello				
1996 Erik's First French Fry	12/00		59.95	60
1997 Nathan Picks a Pickle	12/01		59.95	60
1998 Krissy's Ice Cream Cone	12/01		59.95	60
Memories of Victorian Childhood - M. Girard-Kassis				
1998 Lydia	Closed	1998	82.99	83
1998 Paige	Closed	1999	82.99	83
1998 Olivia	Closed	1999	82.99	83
1998 Estelle	Closed	1999	82.99	83
Messages of Hope - T. Tomescu				
1994 Let the Little Children Come to Me	Closed	1995	129.95	175
1995 Good Shepherd	Closed	1996	129.95	130
1995 I Stand at the Door	Closed	1996	129.95	130
1996 Our Father	Closed	1999	129.95	130
Metropolitan Moments - V. Turner				
1998 Deirdre	Open		92.99	93
1998 Cecilia	Open		92.99	93
1999 Rosalind	Open		92.99	93
1999 Alexandra	Open		92.99	93
Miracle of Life - Y. Bello				
1996 Beautiful Newborn	Closed	1999	49.95	50
1996 Her Very First Smile	Closed	1999	49.95	50
1996 She's Sitting Pretty	Closed	1998	49.95	50
1996 Watch Her Crawl	Closed	1999	49.95	50
Miracles of Christ - T. Tomescu				
1996 Water Into Wine	12/00		99.95	100
1996 Multiplying the Loaves	Closed	1999	99.95	100
1997 Walking on Water	Closed	1999	99.95	100
1998 Ascension Into Heaven	Closed	1999	99.95	100
Moments To Remember - Y. Bello				
1991 Justin	Closed	1994	75.00	75
1992 Jill	Closed	1993	75.00	75-85
1993 Brandon (Ring Bearer)	Closed	1994	79.95	80-90
1993 Suzanne (Flower Girl)	Closed	1994	79.95	80
Mommy Can I Keep It?/Plush - P. Joho & E. Foran				
1995 Bartholomew & His Goldfish	Closed	1999	49.95	50
1995 Becky & Her Bunny	Closed	1999	49.95	50
1995 Belinda & Her Kitty	Closed	2000	49.95	50
1995 Benjamin & His Puppy	Retrd.	1997	49.95	50
Mommy Can You Fix It?/Plush - A. Cranshaw				
1997 Edgar	Open		49.95	50
1998 Edith	Open		49.95	50
1997 Emma	Open		49.95	50
1996 Emmett	Open		49.95	50
Morning Glories - B. Bambina				
1996 Rosebud	Closed	N/A	49.95	50
1996 Dew Drop	Closed	N/A	49.95	50
A Mother's Work Is Never Done - T. Menzenbach				
1995 Don't Forget To Wash Behind Your Ears	Closed	1998	59.95	60
1996 A Kiss Will Make It Better	Closed	1999	59.95	60
1996 Who Made This Mess	Closed	1999	59.95	60
My Closest Friend - J. Goodyear				
1991 Boo Bear 'N Me	Closed	1992	78.00	125-225
1991 Me and My Blankie	Closed	1993	79.00	95
1992 My Secret Pal (Robbie)	Closed	1993	85.00	85
1992 My Beary Softest Blanket	Closed	1993	79.95	85
My Fair Lady - P. Ryan Brooks				
1991 Eliza at Ascot	Closed	1992	125.00	395-450
My Little Ballerina - K. Barry-Hippensteel				
1994 My Little Ballerina	Closed	1995	59.95	60-75
Naturally Playful - S. Housely				
1997 Peek-A-Boo Bunny	Closed	1999	72.99	73
Noble Native Women - D. Wright				
1994 Sacajawea	Open		135.00	135
1994 Minnehaha	Open		135.00	135
1995 Pine Leaf	Open		135.00	135
1995 Lozen	Open		135.00	135
1997 White Rose	Open		135.00	135
1997 Falling Star	Closed	N/A	135.00	175-178
Nostalgic Toys - C. McClure				
1996 Amelia	Closed	1998	79.95	80
1996 Charlotte	Closed	1998	79.95	80
1997 Tess	Closed	1998	79.95	80
Nursery Newborns - J. Wolf				
1994 It's A Boy	Closed	1995	79.95	80
1994 It's A Girl	Closed	1995	79.95	80
Nursery Rhyme Favorites/Plush - J. Davis				
1995 Little Bo Peep	Closed	1997	39.95	40
1995 Little Miss Muffet	Open		39.95	40
1995 Mary, Mary	Open		39.95	40
1995 Little Lucy Locket	Open		39.95	40
Oh Holy Night - J. Good-Krüger				
1994 The Holy Family (Jesus, Mary, Joseph)	Closed	1995	129.95	130
1995 The Kneeling King	Closed	1995	59.95	60
1995 The Purple King	Closed	1995	59.95	60
1995 The Blue King	Closed	1995	59.95	60
1995 Shepherd with Pipes	Closed	1995	59.95	60
1995 Shepherd with Lamb	Closed	1995	59.95	60
1995 Angel	Closed	1995	59.95	60
Only At Grandma and Grandpa's - Y. Bello				
1996 I'll Finish The Story	Closed	1999	89.95	90
Our Own Ballet Recital - P. Bomar				
1996 Chloe	Closed	1999	69.95	70
Passports to Friendship - J. Ibarolle				
1995 Serena	Closed	1998	79.95	80
1996 Kali	Closed	1999	79.95	80
1996 Asha	Closed	1999	79.95	80
1996 Liliana	12/00		79.95	80
Patchwork of Love - J. Good-Krüger				
1995 Warmth of the Heart	Closed	1998	59.95	60
1996 Love One Another	Closed	1999	59.95	60
1996 Family Price	Closed	1999	59.95	60
1996 Simplicity Is Best	Closed	1999	59.95	60
1996 Fondest Memory	Closed	1999	59.95	60
1996 Hard Work Pays	Closed	1999	59.95	60
Peanuts Best Friends - L. Dunsmore				
1999 A Snuggle for Snoopy	Open		79.99	80
Perfect Companions/Plush - Various				
1998 Big Ears - B. Dewey	Open		59.99	60
1998 Big Hugs - A. Cranshaw	Open		59.99	60
Perfect Pairs - B. Bambina				
1995 Amber	Closed	1996	59.95	60
1995 Tiffany	Closed	1996	59.95	60
1995 Carmen	Closed	1996	59.95	60
1996 Susie	Closed	1999	59.95	60
Petting Zoo - Y. Bello				
1995 Andy	Closed	1996	59.95	60
1995 Kendra	Closed	1996	59.95	60
1995 Cory	Closed	1996	59.95	60
1995 Maddie	Closed	1996	59.95	60
Please Come To Tea - R. Miller				
1998 Abby	Closed	1999	62.99	63
1998 Clarissa	12/00		62.99	63
1999 Morgan	Open		62.99	63
1999 Robyn	Closed	2000	62.99	63
Portraits From the Past - C. Haase				
1999 Adele	Open		99.99	100
2000 Penelope	Open		99.99	100
2000 Celeste	Open		99.99	100
2000 Sophia	Open		99.99	100
Portraits of Diana - T. Tomescu				
1998 Diana, The Princess of Wales	Open		132.99	133
1998 Diana, The World's Beloved Rose	Open		132.99	133
1999 Diana, Visionary of Style	Closed	2000	132.99	133
1999 Diana, Emissary of Compassion	Open		132.99	133
Precious Memories of Motherhood - S. Kuck				
1989 Loving Steps	Closed	1991	125.00	125-225
1990 Lullaby	Closed	1993	125.00	130-200
1991 Expectant Moments	Closed	1993	149.00	130-250
1992 Bedtime	Closed	1993	150.00	150-200
Precious Moments - Baby Blessings - P. Archer				
1999 Jesus Loves Me	Open		74.99	75
1999 Heaven Bless You	Open		74.99	75
2000 Someone to Watch Over Me	Open		74.99	75
2000 The Lord is My Shepherd	Open		74.99	75
Precious Moments - Baby's First - S. Butcher				
1999 Baby's First Birthday	Open		74.99	75
1999 Baby's First Pet	Open		74.99	75
2000 Baby's First Christmas	Open		74.99	75
Precious Moments - S. Butcher				
1994 Tell Me the Story of Jesus	Open		79.00	79
1995 God Loveth a Cheerful Giver	Open		79.00	79
1995 Mother Sew Dear	Open		79.00	79
1996 You Are the Type I Love	Open		79.00	79
Precious Moments - Songs of the Spirit - S. Butcher				
1999 Hope is a Gentle Melody	Open		79.99	80
1999 Faith is Heaven's Sweet Song	Open		79.99	80
2000 Love is a Heavenly Song	Open		79.99	80
2000 Happiness is a Song From Heaven	Open		79.99	80
Precious Moments - Tender Twosomes - S. Butcher				
1999 I Love Ewe	Open		82.99	83
1999 You're My Hunny Bunny	Open		82.99	83
Precious Papooses - S. Housely				
1995 Sleeping Bear	Closed	1998	79.95	80
1996 Bright Feather	Closed	1999	79.95	80
1996 Cloud Chaser	Closed	1998	79.95	80
1996 Swift Fox	Closed	1998	79.95	80
Puppies Are People Too - M. Girard-Kassis				
1999 Dottie and Spots	Open		69.99	70
1999 Rusty and Red	Open		69.99	70
2000 Curly and Frenchy	Open		69.99	70
2000 Buster and Boxer	Open		69.99	70
Quiet Moments - S. Freeman				
1998 Her Mother's Voice	Open		74.99	75
Rainbow of Love - Y. Bello				
1994 Blue Sky	Closed	1995	59.95	60-80
1994 Yellow Sunshine	Closed	1995	59.95	60
1994 Green Earth	Closed	1995	59.95	60
1994 Pink Flower	Closed	1996	59.95	60
1994 Purple Mountain	Closed	1996	59.95	60
1994 Orange Sunset	Closed	1996	59.95	60
Recipe For Happiness - M. Girard-Kassis				
1999 A Cup of Love	Open		79.99	80
1999 Measure of Faith	Open		79.99	80
2000 Portion of Kindness	Open		79.99	80
2000 Dash of Laughter	Open		79.99	80
Ruffle & Ribbons, Buttons & Bows - B. Madeja				
1998 Ruffles For Rebecca	12/01		62.99	63
1998 Rachel in Ribbons	Closed	2000	62.99	63
1998 Betsy in Buttons	Open		62.99	63
1998 Bows for Belinda	Open		62.99	63
Seasons of Joy - J. Ibarolle				
1997 Nicholas	Closed	1998	74.99	75
1997 Kimberly	12/01		74.99	75
1998 Molly	12/01		74.99	75
1998 Brandon	Closed	1999	74.99	75
Secret Garden - J. Kovacik				
1994 Mary	Closed	1995	69.95	70
1995 Colin	Closed	1996	69.95	70
1995 Martha	Closed	1996	69.95	70
1995 Dickon	Closed	1996	69.95	70
A Sense of Discovery - K. Barry-Hippensteel				
1993 Sweetie (Sense of Discovery)	Closed	1994	59.95	60
Sense of Security - G. Rademann				
1996 Amy	Closed	1998	62.99	63
She Walks in Beauty - S. Bilotto				
1996 Winter Romance	12/00		92.99	93
1997 Spring Promise	12/01		92.99	93
1997 Summer Dream	12/01		92.99	93
1998 Autumn Reflection	12/01		92.99	93
Siblings Through Time - C. McClure				
1995 Alexandra	Closed	1996	69.95	70
1995 Gracie	Closed	1996	59.95	60
Simple Gifts - J. Good-Krüger				
1996 Roly Poly Harvest	Closed	1998	49.95	50
1997 Sweet Sensation	Closed	1998	49.95	50
1997 Papa's Helper	Closed	1998	49.95	50
1997 Naptime at Noon	Closed	1998	49.95	50
1997 Cuddly Companions	Closed	1999	49.95	50
Simple Pleasures, Special Days - J. Lundy				
1996 Gretchen	Closed	1999	79.95	80
1996 Molly	Closed	1999	79.95	80
1996 Adeline	Closed	N/A	79.95	80
1996 Eliza	Closed	N/A	79.95	80
Sing a Song of Childhood - J. Good-Krüger				
1999 I'm a Little Teapot	Open		79.99	80
Sleepytown Lullabies - P. Parkins				
1995 Nite, Nite Pony	Open		95.00	95
1996 Twice As Nice	Open		95.00	95
1996 Sleep Tight, Sweetheart	Open		95.00	95
1996 Cradled in Love	Open		95.00	95
Snow Babies - T. Tomescu				
1995 Beneath the Mistletoe	Closed	1995	69.95	70
1995 Follow the Leader	Closed	1996	75.00	75
1995 Snow Baby Express	Closed	1996	75.00	75
1996 Slip Slidn'	Closed	1998	75.00	75
1996 Learning To Fly	Closed	1998	75.00	75
1996 Catch of the Day	Closed	1999	75.00	75
Someone to Watch Over Me - K. Barry-Hippensteel				
1994 Sweet Dreams	Closed	1995	69.95	70
1995 Night-Night Angel	Closed	1995	24.95	25
1995 Lullaby Angel	Closed	1995	24.95	25
1995 Sleepyhead Angel	Closed	1996	24.95	25
1995 Stardust Angel	Closed	1996	24.95	25
1995 Tuck-Me-In Angel	Closed	1996	24.95	25

*Quotes have been rounded up to nearest dollar

Special Edition Tour 1993 - Y. Bello

YEAR ISSUE	EDITION LIMIT	YEAR RETD.	ISSUE PRICE	*QUOTE U.S.$
1993 Miguel	Closed	1993	69.95	70-150
1993 Rosa	Closed	1993	69.95	70-150

Spending Time With Grandparents/Plush - B. Conley & T. Roe

YEAR ISSUE	EDITION LIMIT	YEAR RETD.	ISSUE PRICE	*QUOTE U.S.$
1996 Grandma and Sam	Closed	1998	49.95	50

Spice of Life - Y. Bello

YEAR ISSUE	EDITION LIMIT	YEAR RETD.	ISSUE PRICE	*QUOTE U.S.$
1997 Ginny	Closed	1998	49.95	46
1997 Megan	Closed	1998	49.95	46
1997 Cindy	Closed	1999	49.95	46

Sunday's Best - C. Jackson

YEAR ISSUE	EDITION LIMIT	YEAR RETD.	ISSUE PRICE	*QUOTE U.S.$
1996 Brianne	Closed	1996	72.99	73
1997 Jacob	Closed	1999	72.99	73
1997 Tamara	Closed	2000	72.99	73
1997 Jacob	Closed	1999	72.99	73

Sweet Inspirations - V. Turner

YEAR ISSUE	EDITION LIMIT	YEAR RETD.	ISSUE PRICE	*QUOTE U.S.$
1998 Kathryn Rose	Open		82.99	83
1999 Lily Anne	Open		82.99	83
1999 Dahlia	Open		82.99	83
1999 Iris Diane	Open		82.99	83

Tales From the Nursery - T. Tomescu

YEAR ISSUE	EDITION LIMIT	YEAR RETD.	ISSUE PRICE	*QUOTE U.S.$
1997 Baby Bo Peep	12/00		82.99	83
1998 Baby Red Riding Hood	12/01		82.99	83
1998 Baby Goldilocks	Closed	1999	82.99	83
1998 Baby Miss Muffet	Closed	1999	82.99	83

To Have and To Hold - A. Brown

YEAR ISSUE	EDITION LIMIT	YEAR RETD.	ISSUE PRICE	*QUOTE U.S.$
1998 Paulette	Open		99.99	100

Together Forever - S. Krey

YEAR ISSUE	EDITION LIMIT	YEAR RETD.	ISSUE PRICE	*QUOTE U.S.$
1994 Kirsten	Closed	1995	59.95	60
1994 Courtney	Closed	1995	59.95	60
1994 Kim	Closed	1995	59.95	60

Too Cute to Resist - M. Girard-Kassis

YEAR ISSUE	EDITION LIMIT	YEAR RETD.	ISSUE PRICE	*QUOTE U.S.$
1997 Ally	12/00		49.99	50
1997 Kayla	Closed	2000	49.99	50
1998 Jennifer	12/01		49.99	50

Toy Chest Treasures/Plush - P. Joho & E. Foran

YEAR ISSUE	EDITION LIMIT	YEAR RETD.	ISSUE PRICE	*QUOTE U.S.$
1996 Tad	Closed	1998	49.95	50
1997 Theo	Closed	1998	49.95	50

Treasured Togetherness - M. Tretter

YEAR ISSUE	EDITION LIMIT	YEAR RETD.	ISSUE PRICE	*QUOTE U.S.$
1994 Tender Touch	Closed	1995	99.95	100
1994 Touch of Love	Closed	1995	99.95	100

Tumbling Tots - K. Barry-Hippensteel

YEAR ISSUE	EDITION LIMIT	YEAR RETD.	ISSUE PRICE	*QUOTE U.S.$
1993 Roly Poly Polly	Closed	1994	69.95	70
1994 Handstand Harry	Closed	1995	69.95	70

Twinkle Toes Recital - T. Tomescu

YEAR ISSUE	EDITION LIMIT	YEAR RETD.	ISSUE PRICE	*QUOTE U.S.$
1997 Little Carnation	12/00		72.99	73
1998 Little Daffodil	Closed	1998	72.99	73
1998 Little Violet	Closed	1998	72.99	73

Two Much To Handle - K. Barry-Hippensteel

YEAR ISSUE	EDITION LIMIT	YEAR RETD.	ISSUE PRICE	*QUOTE U.S.$
1993 Julie (Flowers For Mommy)	Closed	1994	59.95	60
1993 Kevin (Clean Hands)	Closed	1995	59.95	145

Under Her Wings - P. Bomar

YEAR ISSUE	EDITION LIMIT	YEAR RETD.	ISSUE PRICE	*QUOTE U.S.$
1995 Guardian Angel	Closed	1998	79.95	80

Victorian Dreamers - K. Barry-Hippensteel

YEAR ISSUE	EDITION LIMIT	YEAR RETD.	ISSUE PRICE	*QUOTE U.S.$
1995 Rock-A-Bye/Good Night	Closed	1996	49.95	55
1995 Victorian Storytime	Closed	1996	49.95	50

Victorian Lace - C. Layton

YEAR ISSUE	EDITION LIMIT	YEAR RETD.	ISSUE PRICE	*QUOTE U.S.$
1993 Alicia	Closed	1994	79.95	125
1994 Colleen	Closed	1995	79.95	85
1994 Olivia	Closed	1995	79.95	80

Victorian Nursery Heirloom - C. McClure

YEAR ISSUE	EDITION LIMIT	YEAR RETD.	ISSUE PRICE	*QUOTE U.S.$
1994 Victorian Lullaby	Closed	1995	129.95	130-150
1995 Victorian Highchair	Closed	1996	129.95	130-150
1995 Victorian Playtime	Closed	1996	139.95	140
1995 Victorian Bunny Buggy	Closed	1996	139.95	140

Victorian Vanity - S. Freeman

YEAR ISSUE	EDITION LIMIT	YEAR RETD.	ISSUE PRICE	*QUOTE U.S.$
1998 Melissa	Open		92.99	93
1998 Dorothea	Open		92.99	93
1998 Marianne	Open		92.99	93

Visions Of Our Lady - B. Deval

YEAR ISSUE	EDITION LIMIT	YEAR RETD.	ISSUE PRICE	*QUOTE U.S.$
1996 Our Lady of Grace	Closed	1999	99.95	100
1996 Our Lady of Lourdes	12/00		99.95	100
1997 Our Lady of Fatima	12/01		99.95	100
1997 Our Lady of Medjugorje	12/01		99.95	100

Wain, Wain Go Away - M. Girard-Kassis

YEAR ISSUE	EDITION LIMIT	YEAR RETD.	ISSUE PRICE	*QUOTE U.S.$
1999 Melinda	Open		69.99	70
1999 Lexi	Open		69.99	70
1999 Holly	Open		69.99	70

Warner Brothers Baby - A. Tsalikhan

YEAR ISSUE	EDITION LIMIT	YEAR RETD.	ISSUE PRICE	*QUOTE U.S.$
1998 Tweet Dreams	12/01		74.99	75
1998 Some Bunny Loves You	Open		74.99	75
1999 Mommy's Little Angel	Open		74.99	75
1999 Rock-a-Bye Puddy	Open		74.99	75

We Love The Homerun King - R. Miller

YEAR ISSUE	EDITION LIMIT	YEAR RETD.	ISSUE PRICE	*QUOTE U.S.$
1999 I Got His Autograph!	Open		79.99	80
1999 Hit It Here, Mark	Open		79.99	80

The Wee Wild West - J. Good-Krüger

YEAR ISSUE	EDITION LIMIT	YEAR RETD.	ISSUE PRICE	*QUOTE U.S.$
1999 Little Buckaroo	Open		72.99	73
1999 Little Card Shark	Open		72.99	73
1999 Little Lawman	Open		72.99	73
1999 Little Bandit	Open		72.99	73

What Little Girls Are Made Of - D. Effner

YEAR ISSUE	EDITION LIMIT	YEAR RETD.	ISSUE PRICE	*QUOTE U.S.$
1994 Peaches and Cream	Closed	1995	69.95	125-150
1995 Lavender & Lace	Closed	1998	69.95	70
1995 Sunshine & Lollipops	Closed	1998	69.95	115-135

Where Do Babies Come From - T. Tomescu

YEAR ISSUE	EDITION LIMIT	YEAR RETD.	ISSUE PRICE	*QUOTE U.S.$
1996 Special Delivery	Closed	1999	79.95	80
1996 Fresh From The Patch	12/00		79.95	80
1996 Just Hatched	Closed	1996	79.95	80
1997 Handle With Care	12/01		79.95	80

Winning Style - B. Hanson

YEAR ISSUE	EDITION LIMIT	YEAR RETD.	ISSUE PRICE	*QUOTE U.S.$
1998 Winning Style	Closed	1998	99.95	100

Winter Magic - M. Tretter

YEAR ISSUE	EDITION LIMIT	YEAR RETD.	ISSUE PRICE	*QUOTE U.S.$
1998 Lindsey	Open		64.99	65
1998 Bradley with Snowman	Open		64.99	65
1998 Tyler	Open		64.99	65
1998 Pamela	Open		64.99	65

The Wonderful Wizard of Oz - M. Tretter

YEAR ISSUE	EDITION LIMIT	YEAR RETD.	ISSUE PRICE	*QUOTE U.S.$
1994 Dorothy	Closed	1995	79.95	125
1994 Scarecrow	Closed	1995	79.95	80-125
1994 Tin Man	Closed	1995	79.95	80
1994 The Cowardly Lion	Closed	1996	79.95	80

A World of Romantic Weddings - T. Tomescu

YEAR ISSUE	EDITION LIMIT	YEAR RETD.	ISSUE PRICE	*QUOTE U.S.$
1999 Paris Bride	Open		129.99	130

Wreathed in Beauty - G. Rademann

YEAR ISSUE	EDITION LIMIT	YEAR RETD.	ISSUE PRICE	*QUOTE U.S.$
1996 Winter Elegance	Closed	1999	89.95	90
1997 Spring Promise	Closed	1999	99.99	100
1997 Summer Sweetness	Closed	1999	99.99	100
1997 Autumn Harmony	Closed	1999	99.99	100

A Year With Addie/Plush - B. Conley & T. Roe

YEAR ISSUE	EDITION LIMIT	YEAR RETD.	ISSUE PRICE	*QUOTE U.S.$
1995 January Ice Skating	Open		39.95	40
1995 February Valentine	Open		39.95	40
1995 March Kite Flying	Open		39.95	40
1995 April Easter Fun	Open		39.95	40
1995 May Gardening Time	Open		39.95	40
1995 June Dress Up	Open		39.95	40
1995 July Summer Fun	Open		39.95	40
1995 August Autumn Adventure	Open		39.95	40
1995 September Back to School	Open		39.95	40
1995 October Masquerade	Open		39.95	40
1995 November Give Thanks	Open		39.95	40
1995 December Trim a Tree	Open		39.95	40

Yesteryear's Bears/Plush - L. DeMent

YEAR ISSUE	EDITION LIMIT	YEAR RETD.	ISSUE PRICE	*QUOTE U.S.$
1998 Theodora	Open		62.99	63
1999 Jacob	Open		62.99	63
1999 Constance	Open		62.99	63
2000 Alexander	Open		62.99	63

Yolanda's Heaven Scent Babies - Y. Bello

YEAR ISSUE	EDITION LIMIT	YEAR RETD.	ISSUE PRICE	*QUOTE U.S.$
1993 Meagan Rose	Closed	1994	49.95	75-125
1993 Daisy Anne	Closed	1994	49.95	50
1993 Morning Glory	Closed	1995	49.95	50
1993 Sweet Carnation	Closed	1995	54.95	55
1993 Lily	Closed	1995	54.95	55
1993 Cherry Blossom	Closed	1995	54.95	55-60

Yolanda's Lullaby Babies - Y. Bello

YEAR ISSUE	EDITION LIMIT	YEAR RETD.	ISSUE PRICE	*QUOTE U.S.$
1991 Christy (Rock-a-Bye)	Closed	1993	69.00	75-105
1992 Joey (Twinkle, Twinkle)	Closed	1994	69.00	75
1993 Amy (Brahms Lullaby)	Closed	1994	75.00	75
1993 Eddie (Teddy Bear Lullaby)	Closed	1994	75.00	75
1993 Jacob (Silent Night)	Closed	1994	75.00	75
1994 Bonnie (You Are My Sunshine)	Closed	1994	80.00	80

Yolanda's Picture - Perfect Babies - Y. Bello

YEAR ISSUE	EDITION LIMIT	YEAR RETD.	ISSUE PRICE	*QUOTE U.S.$
1985 Jason	Closed	1988	48.00	650-695
1986 Heather	Closed	1988	48.00	225-250
1987 Jennifer	Closed	1989	58.00	200-225
1987 Matthew	Closed	1990	58.00	195-200
1987 Sarah	Closed	1990	58.00	95-175
1988 Amanda	Closed	1990	63.00	125-150
1989 Jessica	Closed	1993	63.00	63-85
1990 Michael	Closed	1992	63.00	120-150
1990 Lisa	Closed	1992	63.00	100-150
1991 Emily	Closed	1992	63.00	110-150
1991 Danielle	Closed	1993	69.00	125-250

Yolanda's Playtime Babies - Y. Bello

YEAR ISSUE	EDITION LIMIT	YEAR RETD.	ISSUE PRICE	*QUOTE U.S.$
1993 Todd	Closed	1994	59.95	60
1993 Lindsey	Closed	1994	59.95	65
1993 Shawna	Closed	1994	59.95	60-75

Yolanda's Precious Playmates - Y. Bello

YEAR ISSUE	EDITION LIMIT	YEAR RETD.	ISSUE PRICE	*QUOTE U.S.$
1992 David	Closed	1994	69.95	125-250
1993 Paul	Closed	1994	69.95	125
1994 Johnny	Closed	1994	69.95	70

BARBIE Collectibles by Hallmark/Hallmark Keepsake Collections

Be My Valentine Collector Series

YEAR ISSUE	EDITION LIMIT	YEAR RETD.	ISSUE PRICE	*QUOTE U.S.$
1995 Sweet Valentine Barbie®	Yr.Iss.	1995	45.00	45-75
1996 Sentimental Valentine Barbie®	Yr.Iss.	1996	50.00	50-65
1997 Fair Valentine Barbie®	Yr.Iss.	1997	50.00	50

Holiday Homecoming Collection

YEAR ISSUE	EDITION LIMIT	YEAR RETD.	ISSUE PRICE	*QUOTE U.S.$
1997 Holiday Traditions™ Barbie® QHB3402	Retrd.	1998	50.00	50
1998 Holiday Voyage™ Barbie® QHB6022	Retrd.	1999	50.00	50
1999 Holiday Sensation™ Barbie® QHB3403	Retrd.	1999	50.00	50

Special Edition Hallmark Barbie Dolls

YEAR ISSUE	EDITION LIMIT	YEAR RETD.	ISSUE PRICE	*QUOTE U.S.$
1994 Victorian Elegance™ Barbie®	Yr.Iss.	1994	40.00	120-150
1995 Holiday Memories™ Barbie®	Yr.Iss.	1995	45.00	45
1996 The Yuletide Romance™ Barbie®	Yr.Iss.	1996	50.00	50-75

Barbie/Mattel

Members Choice™-The Official Barbie Collectors Club℠ - Various

YEAR ISSUE	EDITION LIMIT	YEAR RETD.	ISSUE PRICE	*QUOTE U.S.$
1997 Grand Premiere™ Barbie® - A. Driskill	Retrd.	1997	59.00	200
1998 Café Society™ - C. Spencer	Yr.Iss.	1998	59.00	60-125
1999 Embassy Waltz™ - S. Zuckerman	Yr.Iss.	1999	59.00	60
1999 Holiday Treasures™ 1999 - K. Jimenez	Yr.Iss.	1999	59.00	60
2000 Club Couture Barbie® - R. Best	Yr.Iss.		59.00	60
2000 Holiday Treasures™ 2000 - S. Zuckerman	Yr.Iss.		49.99	50

35th Anniversary Dolls by Mattel - Mattel

YEAR ISSUE	EDITION LIMIT	YEAR RETD.	ISSUE PRICE	*QUOTE U.S.$
1994 Barbie® Gift Set	Retrd.	1994	79.97	140-150

40th Anniversary Collection - Mattel

YEAR ISSUE	EDITION LIMIT	YEAR RETD.	ISSUE PRICE	*QUOTE U.S.$
1999 40th Anniversary Barbie - Caucasian	Retrd.	1999	49.99	50
1999 40th Anniversary Barbie - African American	Retrd.	1999	49.99	50
1999 *Bob Mackie* LePapillon	Retrd.	1999	150.00	150

American Stories Series - Mattel

YEAR ISSUE	EDITION LIMIT	YEAR RETD.	ISSUE PRICE	*QUOTE U.S.$
1995 Colonial Barbie	Retrd.	1995	24.99	25
1995 Pilgrim Barbie	Retrd.	1995	24.99	25
1995 Pioneer Barbie	Retrd.	1995	24.99	25
1996 Civil War Nurse Barbie	Retrd.	1996	24.99	25
1996 Pioneer Shopkeeper Barbie	Retrd.	1996	24.99	25
1996 American Indian Barbie	Retrd.	1996	24.99	25-35
1997 Patriot Barbie	Retrd.	1997	24.99	25
1997 American Indian Barbie	Retrd.	1997	24.99	25

Angels of Music™ Collection - Mattel

YEAR ISSUE	EDITION LIMIT	YEAR RETD.	ISSUE PRICE	*QUOTE U.S.$
1998 Harpist Angel™ Barbie- Caucasian	Retrd.	1998	96.95	97
1998 Harpist Angel™ - African-American	Retrd.	1998	96.95	97
1999 Heartstring Angel - Caucasian	Retrd.	1998	89.00	89
1999 Heartstring Angel - African-American	Retrd.	1998	89.00	89

Artist Series - Mattel

YEAR ISSUE	EDITION LIMIT	YEAR RETD.	ISSUE PRICE	*QUOTE U.S.$
1997 Water Lily™ Barbie®	Retrd.	1997	75.00	75-125
1998 Sunflower	Retrd.	1998	80.00	80-125
1999 Reflections of Light™	Retrd.	1999	79.99	80

Barbie Milicent Roberts® Collection - Mattel

YEAR ISSUE	EDITION LIMIT	YEAR RETD.	ISSUE PRICE	*QUOTE U.S.$
1996 Picnic Perfect® fashion	Retrd.	1996	31.00	31
1996 Matinee Today® (doll & fashion)	Retrd.	1996	65.00	31
1996 Goin' to the Game fashion	Retrd.	1996	31.00	31
1997 Jet Set luggage	Retrd.	1997	31.00	31
1997 Final Touches® (4 asst.)	Retrd.	1997	15.00	31
1998 Pinstripe Power® (doll & fashion)	Retrd.	1998	65.00	31-65
1997 Perfectly Suited® Gift Set (doll & fashion)	Retrd.	1997	65.00	31-40
1997 Court Favorite® fashion	Retrd.	1997	31.00	31
1997 All Decked Out™ fashion	Retrd.	1997	31.00	31
1997 City Slicker® fashion	Retrd.	1997	31.00	31
1998 Snow Chic-So Chic fashion	Retrd.	1997	31.00	31
1998 Green Thumb fashion	Retrd.	1998	31.00	31

Barbie® Couture Collection - Mattel

YEAR ISSUE	EDITION LIMIT	YEAR RETD.	ISSUE PRICE	*QUOTE U.S.$
1996 Portrait in Taffeta® Barbie®	Retrd.	1996	135.00	135
1997 Serenade in Satin®	Retrd.	1997	135.00	90-135
1998 Symphony in Chiffon™ - Caucasian	Retrd.	1998	135.00	135
1998 Symphony in Chiffon™ - African-American	Retrd.	1999	135.00	135

Barbie® Fashion Model Collection - Mattel

YEAR ISSUE	EDITION LIMIT	YEAR RETD.	ISSUE PRICE	*QUOTE U.S.$
2000 Lunch at the Club™ fashion	Yr.Iss.		39.95	40
2000 Garden Party™ fashion	Yr.Iss.		39.95	40
2000 The Lingerie Barbie - blonde & brunette	Yr.Iss.		39.95	40
2000 Delphine™ Barbie	Yr.Iss.		39.95	40

Barbie® Loves Pop Culture - Mattel

YEAR ISSUE	EDITION LIMIT	YEAR RETD.	ISSUE PRICE	*QUOTE U.S.$
1996 Barbie and Ken Star Trek Gift Set	Retrd.	1996	74.99	40-75
1997 Barbie Loves Elvis® Gift Set	Retrd.	1997	79.96	80-90
1999 Barbie Loves Frankie	Retrd.	1999	80.00	80
2000 Barbie as Wonder Woman™	Yr.Iss.		49.95	50
2000 The Addams Family™ Gift Set	Yr.Iss.		79.95	80

Barbie® Loves Sports - Mattel

YEAR ISSUE	EDITION LIMIT	YEAR RETD.	ISSUE PRICE	*QUOTE U.S.$
1998 NASCAR® 50th Anniversary	Retrd.	1998	39.95	40
1999 Chicago Cubs™ - Caucasian	Retrd.	1999	39.95	35-40
1999 Chicago Cubs™ - African American	Retrd.	1999	39.95	40

310 Collectors' Information Bureau

*Quotes have been rounded up to nearest dollar

YEAR ISSUE	EDITION LIMIT	YEAR RETD.	ISSUE PRICE	*QUOTE U.S.$
1999 Los Angeles Dodgers™ - Caucasian	Retrd.	1999	39.95	35-40
1999 Los Angeles Dodgers™ - African American	Retrd.	1999	39.95	40
1999 New York Yankees™ - Caucasian	Retrd.	1999	39.95	35-40
1999 New York Yankees™ - African American	Retrd.	1999	39.95	40
1999 NASCAR® Official #94	Retrd.	1999	39.95	40
2000 Scuderia Ferrari	Yr.Iss.		39.95	40
2000 Bowling Champ™ Barbie®	Yr.Iss.		39.95	40

Birds of Beauty® Collection - Mattel

YEAR ISSUE	EDITION LIMIT	YEAR RETD.	ISSUE PRICE	*QUOTE U.S.$
1998 The Peacock™ Barbie®	Retrd.	1998	99.00	99
1999 The Flamingo Barbie®	Retrd.	1999	99.00	60-99
2000 The Swan Barbie®	Yr.Iss.		79.95	80

Birthday Series - Mattel

YEAR ISSUE	EDITION LIMIT	YEAR RETD.	ISSUE PRICE	*QUOTE U.S.$
1999 Birthday Wishes™ Barbie® - Caucasian	Yr.Iss.		34.99	35
1999 Birthday Wishes™ - African American	Yr.Iss.		34.99	35
2000 Birthday Wishes™ - Caucasian	Yr.Iss.		34.99	35
2000 Birthday Wishes ™- African American	Yr.Iss.		34.99	35

The Bridal Collection - Mattel

YEAR ISSUE	EDITION LIMIT	YEAR RETD.	ISSUE PRICE	*QUOTE U.S.$
2000 Millennium Wedding™ Barbie - Brunette	Yr.Iss.		49.98	50
2000 Millennium Wedding™ - Caucasian	Yr.Iss.		49.98	50
2000 Millennium Wedding™ - African American	Yr.Iss.		49.98	50

Celebrity Dolls - Mattel

YEAR ISSUE	EDITION LIMIT	YEAR RETD.	ISSUE PRICE	*QUOTE U.S.$
1998 Audrey Hepburn in Breakfast at Tiffany's	Retrd.	1998	79.99	80
1998 Elvis' 1968 TV Special	Retrd.	1998	49.98	50
1998 Lucy Does a TV Commercial	Retrd.	1998	39.99	40-69
1999 Audrey Hepburn Pink Princess™	Retrd.	1999	69.99	70
1999 Elvis® The Army Years™	Retrd.	1999	49.98	80
1999 Lucy in "Job Switching" ™	Retrd.	1999	39.98	80
2000 "Lucy's Italian Movie"™	Yr.Iss.		39.99	40
2000 Elizabeth Taylor in Father of the Bride™	Yr.Iss.		75.00	75
2000 Elizabeth Taylor in Cleopatra™	Yr.Iss.		75.00	75

The Celestial Collection™ - Mattel

YEAR ISSUE	EDITION LIMIT	YEAR RETD.	ISSUE PRICE	*QUOTE U.S.$
2000 Morning Star Princess™	Yr.Iss.		49.95	50
2000 Midnight Moon Princess™	Yr.Iss.		49.95	50
2000 Evening Star Princess™	Yr.Iss.		49.95	50

Children's Collector Series - Mattel

YEAR ISSUE	EDITION LIMIT	YEAR RETD.	ISSUE PRICE	*QUOTE U.S.$
1995 Barbie® as Rapunzel	Retrd.	1995	39.99	25-40
1996 Barbie® as Little Bo Peep	Retrd.	1996	39.99	40-150
1997 Barbie® as Cinderella	Retrd.	1997	39.99	30-40
1998 Barbie® as Sleeping Beauty	Retrd.	1998	39.99	35-40
1999 Barbie® as Snow White	Retrd.	1999	39.99	25-80

City Seasons™ Collection - Mattel

YEAR ISSUE	EDITION LIMIT	YEAR RETD.	ISSUE PRICE	*QUOTE U.S.$
1998 Summer in San Francisco™ (FAO Exclusive)	Retrd.	1998	50.00	50-175
1998 Winter in New York™	Retrd.	1998	49.99	50
1998 Autumn in Paris™	Retrd.	1998	49.99	40-50
1999 Winter in Montreal™	Retrd.	1999	49.98	40-50
1999 *Vintage* Spring in Tokyo™	Retrd.	1999	49.98	50-55
1999 Spring in Tokyo™	Retrd.	1999	49.98	40-50
1999 Summer in Rome™	Retrd.	1999	49.98	40-50
1999 Autumn in London™	Retrd.	1999	49.98	40-50

Classic Ballet Series® - Mattel

YEAR ISSUE	EDITION LIMIT	YEAR RETD.	ISSUE PRICE	*QUOTE U.S.$
1999 Barbie as Marzipan™ in The Nutcracker	Retrd.	1999	29.99	30
1997 Barbie as The Sugar Plum Fairy in The Nutcracker	Retrd.	1997	29.99	30
1998 Barbie as The Swan Queen in Swan Lake	Retrd.	1998	29.99	30
2000 Barbie as Snowflake in The Nutcracker	Yr.Iss.		29.99	30

Classique® Collection - Mattel

YEAR ISSUE	EDITION LIMIT	YEAR RETD.	ISSUE PRICE	*QUOTE U.S.$
1992 Benefit Ball™	Retrd.	1992	59.95	125-130
1993 Opening Night™	Retrd.	1993	59.95	80
1993 City Style®	Retrd.	1993	59.95	100
1994 Evening Extravaganza® - Caucasian	Retrd.	1994	59.95	90
1994 Evening Extravaganza® - African American	Retrd.	1994	59.95	60
1994 Uptown Chic Barbie®	Retrd.	1994	53.95	80-95
1995 Midnight Gala®	Retrd.	1996	59.99	55-75
1996 Starlight Dance® - Caucasian	Retrd.	1996	59.99	35-60
1996 Starlight Dance® - African American	Retrd.	1996	59.99	60
1997 Romantic Interlude® - Caucasian	Retrd.	1997	59.99	60
1997 Romantic Interlude® - African American	Retrd.	1997	59.99	60
1998 Evening Sophisticate®	Retrd.	1998	59.99	40-60

COCA-COLA® Barbie Series - Mattel

YEAR ISSUE	EDITION LIMIT	YEAR RETD.	ISSUE PRICE	*QUOTE U.S.$
1999 COCA-COLA® Barbie	Retrd.	1999	59.97	60
2000 COCA-COLA® Soda Fountain	Yr.Iss.		150.00	150
2000 COCA-COLA® Ken	Yr.Iss.		59.97	60
2000 COCA-COLA® Barbie #2	Yr.Iss.		59.97	60

COCA-COLA® Fashion Classic Series® - Mattel

YEAR ISSUE	EDITION LIMIT	YEAR RETD.	ISSUE PRICE	*QUOTE U.S.$
1996 Soda Fountain Sweetheart	Retrd.	1996	89.00	89-225
1997 After The Walk	Retrd.	1997	89.00	50-90
1998 Summer Daydreams	Retrd.	1998	96.95	50-97

Coca-Cola® Santa™ Doll - Mattel

YEAR ISSUE	EDITION LIMIT	YEAR RETD.	ISSUE PRICE	*QUOTE U.S.$
1999 Coca-Cola® Santa™ Doll	Retrd.	1999	99.75	40-100

Collector's Request™ Collection - Mattel

YEAR ISSUE	EDITION LIMIT	YEAR RETD.	ISSUE PRICE	*QUOTE U.S.$
1998 Twist 'n Turn® - brunette	Retrd.	1998	50.00	50-54
1999 Twist 'n Turn® - redhead	Retrd.	1999	50.00	50
1999 Commuter Set™	Retrd.	1999	50.00	50
2000 Sophisticated Lady®	Yr.Iss.		59.97	60

Designer Barbie Series - Mattel

YEAR ISSUE	EDITION LIMIT	YEAR RETD.	ISSUE PRICE	*QUOTE U.S.$
1990 Bob Mackie Gold Barbie	Retrd.	1990	120.00	400-700
1991 *Bob Mackie* Starlight Splendor™ Barbie 2704	Retrd.	1991	135.00	560-700
1991 Bob Mackie Platinum Barbie	Retrd.	1991	153.00	400-596
1992 Bob Mackie Empress Bride Barbie	Retrd.	1992	232.00	850-1000
1992 *Bob Mackie* Neptune Fantasy™ Barbie	Retrd.	1992	160.00	795-1000
1993 *Bob Mackie* Masquerade™ Ball	Retrd.	1993	175.00	300-400
1994 Bob Mackie Queen of Hearts	Retrd.	1994	178.00	225-300
1995 *Bob Mackie* Goddess of the Sun®	Retrd.	1995	198.00	135-180
1995 Christian Dior	Retrd.	1995	160.00	96-160
1996 Escada	Retrd.	1996	160.00	88-160
1996 *Bob Mackie* Moon Goddess®	Retrd.	1996	198.00	135-160
1997 Byron Lars in the Limelight	Retrd.	1997	79.00	79-295
1997 Bill Blass Barbie	Retrd.	1997	160.00	160-175
1997 Christian Dior 50th Anniversary	Retrd.	1997	160.00	175-375
1997 Bob Mackie Madame du Barbie	Retrd.	1997	259.00	190-280
1998 *Nolan Miller* Sheer Illusion®	Retrd.	1998	135.00	135
1998 Vera Wang Barbie #1	Retrd.	1998	135.00	135
1998 Oscar de la Renta Barbie	Retrd.	1998	90.00	75-90
1998 *Byron Lars* Cinnabar Sensation®	Retrd.	1998	79.00	79
1998 *Bob Mackie* Fantasy Goddess of Asia®	Retrd.	1998	240.00	100-240
1999 Vera Wang Barbie #2	15,000	1999	135.00	135
1999 Todd Oldham Barbie	Retrd.	1999	79.99	80
1999 *Nolan Miller* Evening Illusion™	20,000	1999	135.00	135
1999 *Byron Lars* Plum Royale™	Retrd.	1999	79.00	80-125
1999 Bob Mackie The Tango	Retrd.	1999	299.00	299
1999 *Bob Mackie* LePapillon™	Retrd.	1999	150.00	150
1999 *Bob Mackie* Fantasy Goddess of Africa™	Retrd.	1999	240.00	175-240
2000 Lady Liberty	Yr.Iss.		179.00	179
2000 Givenchy Barbie	Yr.Iss.		79.95	80
2000 *Bob Mackie* Fantasy Goddess of the Americas™	25,000		240.00	240

Dolls of the World® Collection - Mattel

YEAR ISSUE	EDITION LIMIT	YEAR RETD.	ISSUE PRICE	*QUOTE U.S.$
1980 Royal U.K.	Retrd.	1980	N/A	200
1980 Parisian - 1st Ed.	Retrd.	1980	N/A	150-200
1980 Italian - 1st Ed.	Retrd.	1980	N/A	200
1981 Scottish - 1st Ed.	Retrd.	1981	N/A	200
1981 Oriental	Retrd.	1981	N/A	100-125
1982 Eskimo - 1st Ed.	Retrd.	1982	N/A	90
1982 India	Retrd.	1982	N/A	75
1983 Swedish	Retrd.	1983	N/A	100
1983 Spanish - 1st Ed.	Retrd.	1983	N/A	75
1984 Swiss	Retrd.	1984	N/A	75-100
1984 Irish	Retrd.	1984	N/A	75-150
1985 Japanese - 1st Ed.	Retrd.	1985	N/A	75
1986 Peruvian - 1st Ed.	Retrd.	1986	N/A	75
1986 Greek	Retrd.	1986	N/A	75
1987 Icelandic	Retrd.	1987	N/A	75
1987 German - 1st Ed.	Retrd.	1987	N/A	75
1988 Korean	Retrd.	1988	N/A	75
1988 Canadian	Retrd.	1988	N/A	75-80
1989 Russian - 1st Ed.	Retrd.	1989	N/A	60-75
1989 Mexican - 1st Ed.	Retrd.	1989	N/A	45-75
1990 Nigerian	Retrd.	1990	N/A	50-75
1990 Brazilian	Retrd.	1990	N/A	60-75
1991 Scottish - 2nd Ed.	Retrd.	1991	N/A	75
1991 Parisian - 2nd Ed.	Retrd.	1991	N/A	60-75
1991 Malaysian	Retrd.	1991	N/A	75
1991 Eskimo - 2nd Ed.	Retrd.	1991	N/A	75
1991 Czechoslovakian	Retrd.	1991	N/A	75
1992 Spanish - 2nd Ed.	Retrd.	1992	N/A	50-75
1992 Jamaican	Retrd.	1992	N/A	50-75
1992 English	Retrd.	1992	N/A	50
1993 Native American - 1st Ed.	Retrd.	1993	19.99	20-75
1993 Italian - 2n Ed.	Retrd.	1993	19.99	20-90
1993 Australian	Retrd.	1993	19.99	20-60
1994 Native American - 2nd Ed.	Retrd.	1994	19.99	20-70
1994 Kenyan	Retrd.	1994	19.99	20-40
1994 Barbie Limited Edition Set	Retrd.	1994	N/A	N/A
1994 Dutch	Retrd.	1994	19.99	20
1994 Chinese	Retrd.	1994	19.99	20-45
1995 Polynesian	Retrd.	1995	19.99	20-40
1995 Native American - 3rd Ed.	Retrd.	1995	19.99	20-45
1995 Irish - 2nd Ed.	Retrd.	1995	19.99	20
1995 Barbie Limited Edition Gift Set	Retrd.	1995	59.99	60-80
1995 German - 2nd Ed.	Retrd.	1995	19.99	20
1996 Norwegian	Retrd.	1996	21.99	22-75
1996 Mexican - 2nd Ed.	Retrd.	1996	21.99	22
1996 Japanese - 2nd Ed.	Retrd.	1996	21.99	22-35
1996 Indian	Retrd.	1996	21.99	22
1996 Ghanian	Retrd.	1996	21.99	22
1996 Barbie Dolls of the World Gift Set	Retrd.	1996	66.00	66
1997 Russian - 2nd Ed.	Retrd.	1997	21.99	22-30
1997 Puerto Rican	Retrd.	1997	21.99	22-30
1997 French - 2nd Ed.	Retrd.	1997	21.99	20-22
1997 Arctic	Retrd.	1997	21.99	22-45
1998 Polish	Retrd.	1998	24.99	25-50
1998 Thai	Retrd.	1998	24.99	20-35
1998 Chilean	Retrd.	1998	24.99	25-35
1998 Native American	Retrd.	1998	24.99	25
1999 Moroccan	Retrd.	1999	24.99	25-30
1999 Peruvian - 2nd Ed.	Retrd.	1999	24.99	25-30
1999 Austrian	Retrd.	1999	24.99	20-35
2000 Swedish	Yr.Iss.		24.99	25
2000 Northwest Coast Native American	Yr.Iss.		24.99	25

Enchanted Seasons Collection® - Mattel

YEAR ISSUE	EDITION LIMIT	YEAR RETD.	ISSUE PRICE	*QUOTE U.S.$
1994 Snow Princess - brunette	Retrd.	1994	79.00	79-140
1994 Snow Princess - blonde	Retrd.	1994	79.00	79-195
1995 Spring Bouquet™	Retrd.	1995	79.00	79-100
1996 Autumn Glory®	Retrd.	1996	79.00	79
1997 Summer Splendor®	Retrd.	1997	79.00	50-79

The Enchanted World of Fairies™ - Mattel

YEAR ISSUE	EDITION LIMIT	YEAR RETD.	ISSUE PRICE	*QUOTE U.S.$
2000 Fairy of the Forest™	Yr.Iss.		49.95	50

Essence of Nature Collection® - Mattel

YEAR ISSUE	EDITION LIMIT	YEAR RETD.	ISSUE PRICE	*QUOTE U.S.$
1998 Water Rhapsody™	Retrd.	1998	80.00	80-100
1999 Whispering Wind™	Retrd.	1999	80.00	80
2000 Dancing Fire™	Yr.Iss.		79.96	80

Exclusives - Mattel

YEAR ISSUE	EDITION LIMIT	YEAR RETD.	ISSUE PRICE	*QUOTE U.S.$
1993 Tru Harley #1	Retrd.	1993	60.00	60
1994 *Nicole Miller* Savvy Shopper®	Retrd.	1994	65.00	65
1994 Victorian Elegance	Retrd.	1994	N/A	80
1995 Shopping Chic®	Retrd.	1995	65.00	65
1995 Holiday Memories®	Retrd.	1995	39.99	40
1995 DKNY Barbie	Retrd.	1995	65.00	65
1996 Yuletide Romance®	Retrd.	1996	45.00	45
1996 Calvin Klein Barbie	Retrd.	1996	70.00	35-70
1996 Sweet Valentine®	Retrd.	1996	45.00	45
1996 Barbie @ Bloomingdale's	Retrd.	1996	36.00	36-40
1996 Statue of Liberty Barbie	Retrd.	1996	75.00	36
1996 Summer Sophisticate®	Retrd.	1996	69.99	70
1996 Andalucia	Retrd.	1996	19.99	20
1996 Radiant Rose	Retrd.	1996	225.00	36
1996 Pink Ice®	Retrd.	1996	130.00	36-125
1996 *Nicole Miller* City Shopper®	Retrd.	1996	65.00	36
1996 Midnight Waltz® - brunette	Retrd.	1996	90.00	36
1996 Midnight Waltz®	Retrd.	1996	90.00	36-50
1996 Antique Rose®	Retrd.	1996	225.00	36-250
1996 Emerald Enchantment™	Retrd.	1996	50.00	50
1997 Mrs. P.F.E. Albee	Retrd.	1997	50.00	50
1997 Sentimental Valentine®	Retrd.	1997	49.99	50
1997 Ralph Lauren	Retrd.	1997	80.00	80
1997 Lily Barbie	Retrd.	1997	200.00	200-250
1997 Winner's Circle	Retrd.	1997	65.00	65
1997 Anne Klein	Retrd.	1997	70.00	70
1997 Harley-Davidson®	Retrd.	1997	60.00	45-60
1997 Moonlight Waltz®	Retrd.	1997	90.00	90-120
1997 George Washington	Retrd.	1997	80.00	80
1998 Harley-Davidson #2	Retrd.	1998	60.00	80-300
1998 Twist N' Turn®	Retrd.	1998	50.00	50
1998 Golden Qui Pao	Retrd.	1998	60.00	60-195
1998 Definitely Diamonds™	Retrd.	1998	70.00	70-195
1998 Phantom of the Opera Gift Set	Retrd.	1998	120.00	120
1999 Harley-Davidson #3 & Ken	Retrd.	1999	75.00	100
1999 Avon Representative	Retrd.	1999	45.00	35-45
1999 MGM Golden Hollywood	Retrd.	1999	70.00	70

Faberge™ - Mattel

YEAR ISSUE	EDITION LIMIT	YEAR RETD.	ISSUE PRICE	*QUOTE U.S.$
1998 Imperial Elegance®	15,000	1998	399.90	300-400
2000 Imperial Splendor™	10,000		399.90	400

Far Out™ Barbie® - Mattel

YEAR ISSUE	EDITION LIMIT	YEAR RETD.	ISSUE PRICE	*QUOTE U.S.$
1999 Far Out™ Barbie®	Retrd.	1999	39.99	40

Fashion Savvy Collection® - Mattel

YEAR ISSUE	EDITION LIMIT	YEAR RETD.	ISSUE PRICE	*QUOTE U.S.$
1998 Uptown Chic	Retrd.	1998	49.99	50
1998 Tangerine Twist®	Retrd.	1998	49.99	50

Francie® Series - Mattel

YEAR ISSUE	EDITION LIMIT	YEAR RETD.	ISSUE PRICE	*QUOTE U.S.$
1996 30th Anniversary Francie	Retrd.	1999	65.00	53-65
1997 The Wild Bunch Francie	Retrd.	1997	50.00	50

A Garden of Flowers™ Collection - Mattel

YEAR ISSUE	EDITION LIMIT	YEAR RETD.	ISSUE PRICE	*QUOTE U.S.$
1999 Rose	Retrd.	1999	49.98	40-50

Grand Ole Opry™ Collection - Mattel

YEAR ISSUE	EDITION LIMIT	YEAR RETD.	ISSUE PRICE	*QUOTE U.S.$
1999 Barbie and Kenny™ Country Duet	Retrd.	1999	99.00	90-99
1997 Country Rose®	Retrd.	1997	79.00	79-90
1998 Rising Star®	Retrd.	1998	89.00	60-80

The Great Eras® - Mattel

YEAR ISSUE	EDITION LIMIT	YEAR RETD.	ISSUE PRICE	*QUOTE U.S.$
1993 1920s Flapper	Retrd.	1993	53.99	195-225
1993 Gibson Girl	Retrd.	1993	53.99	130-140
1994 Southern Belle	Retrd.	1994	53.99	125
1994 Egyptian Queen®	Retrd.	1994	53.99	130-135
1995 Elizabethan Queen	Retrd.	1995	53.99	48
1995 Medieval Lady®	Retrd.	1995	53.99	60
1996 Victorian Lady®	Retrd.	1996	59.99	50-60
1996 Grecian Goddess	Retrd.	1996	59.99	60
1997 Chinese Empress®	Retrd.	1997	59.99	60
1997 French Lady®	Retrd.	1997	59.99	40-60

Great Fashions of the 20th Century Series - Mattel

YEAR ISSUE	EDITION LIMIT	YEAR RETD.	ISSUE PRICE	*QUOTE U.S.$
1998 Dance 'til Dawn®	Retrd.	1998	59.99	60
1998 Promenade in the Park™	Retrd.	1998	59.99	60
1999 Steppin' Out®	Retrd.	1998	59.99	50-60
2000 Nifty 50's™	Retrd.	1998	59.95	60
2000 Groovy 60's™	Retrd.	1998	59.95	60
2000 Fabulous Forties™	Retrd.	1998	59.95	60

Happy Holidays® Barbie® - Mattel

YEAR ISSUE	EDITION LIMIT	YEAR RETD.	ISSUE PRICE	*QUOTE U.S.$
1988 Happy Holidays® Barbie® - Caucasian	Retrd.	1990	24.95	800-1000
1989 Happy Holidays® Barbie® - Caucasian	Retrd.	1991	N/A	200-260
1990 Happy Holidays® Barbie® - Caucasian	Retrd.	1991	N/A	125-250

*Quotes have been rounded up to nearest dollar

YEAR ISSUE	EDITION LIMIT	YEAR RETD.	ISSUE PRICE	*QUOTE U.S.$
1990 Happy Holidays® Barbie® - African American	Retrd.	1991	N/A	N/A
1991 Happy Holidays® Barbie® - Caucasian	Retrd.	1993	N/A	125-200
1991 Happy Holidays® Barbie® - African American	Retrd.	1993	N/A	N/A
1992 Happy Holidays® Barbie® - Caucasian	Retrd.	1992	N/A	100-170
1992 Happy Holidays® Barbie® - African American	Retrd.	1992	N/A	N/A
1993 Happy Holidays® Barbie® - Caucasian	Retrd.	1993	N/A	125-150
1993 Happy Holidays® Barbie® - African American	Retrd.	1993	N/A	95
1994 Happy Holidays® Barbie® - Caucasian	Retrd.	1994	44.95	150-195
1994 Happy Holidays® Barbie® - African American	Retrd.	1994	44.95	NA
1995 Happy Holidays® Barbie® - Caucasian	Retrd.	1995	44.95	65-90
1995 Happy Holidays® Barbie® - African American	Retrd.	1995	44.95	90
1996 Happy Holidays® Barbie® - Caucasian	Retrd.	1996	34.95	40-110
1996 Happy Holidays® Barbie® - African American	Retrd.	1996	34.95	75
1997 Happy Holidays® Barbie® - Caucasian	Retrd.	1997	34.95	20-100
1997 Happy Holidays® Barbie® - African American	Retrd.	1997	34.95	35-45
1998 Happy Holidays® Barbie® - Caucasian	Retrd.	1998	34.95	29-50
1998 Happy Holidays® Barbie® - African American	Retrd.	1998	34.95	30-52

Holiday Angel Series - Mattel

YEAR ISSUE	EDITION LIMIT	YEAR RETD.	ISSUE PRICE	*QUOTE U.S.$
2000 Holiday Angel - African American	Yr.Iss.		49.95	40
2000 Holiday Angel - Caucasian	Yr.Iss.		49.95	40

Holiday Porcelain Barbie Collection - Mattel

YEAR ISSUE	EDITION LIMIT	YEAR RETD.	ISSUE PRICE	*QUOTE U.S.$
1995 Holiday Jewel®	Retrd.	1995	189.00	189
1996 Holiday Caroler®	Retrd.	1996	195.00	195
1997 Holiday Ball®	Retrd.	1997	195.00	195
1998 Porcelain Holiday Gift Barbie	Retrd.	1998	195.00	195

Hollywood Legends Collection® - Mattel

YEAR ISSUE	EDITION LIMIT	YEAR RETD.	ISSUE PRICE	*QUOTE U.S.$
1994 Barbie as Scarlett O' Hara from Gone With the Wind in Red Dress	Retrd.	1994	74.99	75-100
1994 Ken as Rhett Butler from Gone With the Wind	Retrd.	1994	74.99	75
1994 Barbie as Scarlett O' Hara from Gone With the Wind in Green Dress	Retrd.	1994	74.99	75-80
1994 Barbie as Scarlett O' Hara from Gone With the Wind in Black and White Dress	Retrd.	1994	74.99	75-85
1994 Barbie as Scarlett O' Hara from Gone With the Wind in Green and White Dress	Retrd.	1994	74.99	75-80
1995 Barbie as Dorothy™ from The Wizard of Oz™	Retrd.	1995	49.99	35-200
1995 Barbie as Maria from The Sound of Music	Retrd.	1995	49.99	50-65
1996 Ken as Professor Henry Higgins from My Fair Lady™	Retrd.	1996	74.99	45-75
1996 Barbie as Eliza Doolittle from My Fair Lady in Her Closing Scene	Retrd.	1996	74.99	65-75
1996 Barbie as Eliza Doolittle from My Fair Lady as The Flower Girl	Retrd.	1996	74.99	65-90
1996 Barbie as Eliza Doolittle from My Fair Lady at Ascot	Retrd.	1996	99.99	100
1996 Barbie as Eliza Doolittle from My Fair Lady at the Embassy Ball	Retrd.	1996	99.99	100
1996 Ken as The Tin Man from The Wizard of Oz	Retrd.	1996	74.99	50-75
1996 Barbie as Glinda the Good Witch from The Wizard of Oz	Retrd.	1996	74.99	75-135
1996 Ken as the Cowardly Lion from The Wizard of Oz	Retrd.	1996	74.99	75-275
1996 Ken as the Scarecrow from The Wizard of Oz	Retrd.	1996	74.99	75
1997 Barbie as Marilyn in Red Dress from Gentlemen Prefer Blondes™	Retrd.	1997	59.99	60-75
1997 Barbie as Marilyn in Pink Dress from Gentlemen Prefer Blondes	Retrd.	1997	59.99	60-75
1997 Barbie as Marilyn in White Dress from The Seven Year Itch™	Retrd.	1997	59.99	60-80

Hollywood Movie Star™ Collection - Mattel

YEAR ISSUE	EDITION LIMIT	YEAR RETD.	ISSUE PRICE	*QUOTE U.S.$
2000 Between Takes™	Yr.Iss.		49.95	50
2000 Hollywood Premiere™	Yr.Iss.		49.95	50

The Jewel Essence Collection® by Bob Mackie - Mattel

YEAR ISSUE	EDITION LIMIT	YEAR RETD.	ISSUE PRICE	*QUOTE U.S.$
1997 Amethyst Aura™	Retrd.	1997	85.00	85-190
1997 Diamond Dazzle	Retrd.	1997	85.00	100-190
1997 Emerald Embers®	Retrd.	1997	85.00	90-190
1997 Rudy Radiance®	Retrd.	1997	85.00	90-190
1997 Sapphire Splendor®	Retrd.	1997	85.00	90-190

Keepsake Treasures™ Collection - Mattel

YEAR ISSUE	EDITION LIMIT	YEAR RETD.	ISSUE PRICE	*QUOTE U.S.$
1998 Barbie and The Tale of Peter Rabbit	Retrd.	1998	39.99	40

Limited - Mattel

YEAR ISSUE	EDITION LIMIT	YEAR RETD.	ISSUE PRICE	*QUOTE U.S.$
1989 Pink Jubilee	Retrd.	1996	N/A	N/A
1994 Gold Jubilee®	Retrd.	1994	299.00	600-650
1995 Mattel's 50th Anniversary Barbie	Retrd.	1995	499.00	499
1996 Pink Splendor®	Retrd.	1996	900.00	550-600
1997 Billions of Dreams®	Retrd.	1997	299.00	300-320
1999 Gala 40th Anniversary Barbie	Retrd.	1999	49.99	50
1999 Crystal Jubilee®	Retrd.	1999	299.90	300
2000 Millennium Bride™	10,000		500.00	500

Magic & Mystery™ Series - Mattel

YEAR ISSUE	EDITION LIMIT	YEAR RETD.	ISSUE PRICE	*QUOTE U.S.$
2000 Ken & Barbie as Merlin and Morgan Le Fay™	Yr.Iss.		99.95	100

The Masquerade Gala Collection™ - Mattel

YEAR ISSUE	EDITION LIMIT	YEAR RETD.	ISSUE PRICE	*QUOTE U.S.$
1998 Illusion™	Retrd.	1998	99.00	99
1998 Rendezvous®	Retrd.	1998	99.00	99
2000 Venetian Opulence™	Yr.Iss.		99.00	99

Millennium Princess Barbie - Mattel

YEAR ISSUE	EDITION LIMIT	YEAR RETD.	ISSUE PRICE	*QUOTE U.S.$
1999 Millennium Princess Barbie	Retrd.	1999	39.98	40-125
1999 Millennium Princess Barbie - African American	Retrd.	1999	39.98	40

Nostalgic Porcelain Barbie Dolls - Mattel

YEAR ISSUE	EDITION LIMIT	YEAR RETD.	ISSUE PRICE	*QUOTE U.S.$
1988 Benefit Performance	Retrd.	1988	N/A	250-545
1986 Blue Rhapsody®	Retrd.	1986	N/A	260-750
1987 Enchanted Evening®	Retrd.	1987	N/A	225-500
1991 Gay Parisienne®	Retrd.	1991	N/A	150-260
1991 Plantation Belle™	Retrd.	1991	N/A	200-550
1992 Silken Flame®	Retrd.	1992	N/A	150-550
1990 Solo in the Spotlight® 7613	Retrd.	1990	198.00	200
1990 Sophisticated Lady® 5313	Retrd.	1990	198.00	125-220
1989 Wedding Day® Barbie 2641	Retrd.	1989	198.00	250-650

The Nursery Rhyme Collection - Mattel

YEAR ISSUE	EDITION LIMIT	YEAR RETD.	ISSUE PRICE	*QUOTE U.S.$
1999 Barbie Had a Little Lamb	Retrd.	1999	39.98	40

Presidential Porcelain Barbie Collection - Mattel

YEAR ISSUE	EDITION LIMIT	YEAR RETD.	ISSUE PRICE	*QUOTE U.S.$
1992 Crystal Rhapsody® - blonde	Retrd.	1992	N/A	250
1993 Royal Splendor®	Retrd.	1993	189.00	189
1996 Evening Pearl®	Retrd.	1996	194.00	194

Royal Houses of Europe - Mattel

YEAR ISSUE	EDITION LIMIT	YEAR RETD.	ISSUE PRICE	*QUOTE U.S.$
1996 Barbie as Empress Sissy	Retrd.	1996	160.00	100-160

Royal Jewels Collection™ - Mattel

YEAR ISSUE	EDITION LIMIT	YEAR RETD.	ISSUE PRICE	*QUOTE U.S.$
2000 Empress of Emeralds™	Yr.Iss.		99.00	99
2000 Queen of Sapphires™	Yr.Iss.		99.00	99

Storybook Favorites - Mattel

YEAR ISSUE	EDITION LIMIT	YEAR RETD.	ISSUE PRICE	*QUOTE U.S.$
2000 Kelly and Tommy™ as Raggedy Ann and Andy	Yr.Iss.		16.99	17

Timeless Sentiments® Collection - Mattel

YEAR ISSUE	EDITION LIMIT	YEAR RETD.	ISSUE PRICE	*QUOTE U.S.$
1998 Angel of Joy® - Caucasian	Retrd.	1998	49.99	50
1998 Angel of Joy® - African American	Retrd.	1998	49.99	50
1999 Angel of Peace™ - Caucasian	Retrd.	1999	49.99	50
1999 Angel of Peace™ - African American	Retrd.	1999	49.99	50

Together Forever® Series - Mattel

YEAR ISSUE	EDITION LIMIT	YEAR RETD.	ISSUE PRICE	*QUOTE U.S.$
1998 Ken & Barbie as Romeo & Juliet	Retrd.	1998	99.00	99
1999 Ken & Barbie as Arthur & Guinevere	Retrd.	1999	99.00	99

Trend Forecaster™ Barbie® - Mattel

YEAR ISSUE	EDITION LIMIT	YEAR RETD.	ISSUE PRICE	*QUOTE U.S.$
1999 Trend Forecaster™ Barbie®	Retrd.	1999	50.00	50

Victorian Tea Porcelain Collection - Mattel

YEAR ISSUE	EDITION LIMIT	YEAR RETD.	ISSUE PRICE	*QUOTE U.S.$
1999 Mint Memories®	Retrd.	1999	225.00	175-225
2000 Orange Pekoe™	Yr.Iss.		225.00	225

Vintage Reproductions Collection - Mattel

YEAR ISSUE	EDITION LIMIT	YEAR RETD.	ISSUE PRICE	*QUOTE U.S.$
1994 35th Anniversary - blonde	Retrd.	1994	24.99	25-52
1994 35th Anniversary - brunette	Retrd.	1994	24.99	25-75
1995 Solo in the Spotlight® - blonde	Retrd.	1995	24.99	25
1995 Solo in the Spotlight® - brunette	Retrd.	1995	24.99	25
1995 Busy Gal	Retrd.	1995	45.00	45
1996 Enchanted Evening® - blonde	Retrd.	1996	27.99	28-30
1996 Enchanted Evening® - brunette	Retrd.	1996	27.99	28-33
1996 Poodle Parade®	Retrd.	1996	50.00	28-50
1997 Wedding Day® - blonde	Retrd.	1997	34.99	35-50
1997 Wedding Day® - redhead	Retrd.	1997	34.99	35-50
1997 Fashion Luncheon®	Retrd.	1997	50.00	50
1998 Silken Flame® - blonde	Retrd.	1998	29.99	20-30
1998 Silken Flame® - brunette	Retrd.	1998	29.99	30
1999 Commuter Set™	Retrd.	1997	50.00	50

Wedding Flower Collection® - Mattel

YEAR ISSUE	EDITION LIMIT	YEAR RETD.	ISSUE PRICE	*QUOTE U.S.$
1995 Star Lily Bride®	Retrd.	1995	189.00	189-250
1996 Romantic Rose Bride®	Retrd.	1995	194.00	194-200
1997 Blushing Orchid Bride®	Retrd.	1995	189.00	125-189

The Winter Princess® Collection - Mattel

YEAR ISSUE	EDITION LIMIT	YEAR RETD.	ISSUE PRICE	*QUOTE U.S.$
1993 Winter Princess®	Retrd.	1993	59.95	325-495
1994 Evergreen Princess	Retrd.	1994	59.95	90-125
1994 Evergreen Princess - redhead	Retrd.	1994	59.95	350-575
1995 Peppermint Princess™	Retrd.	1995	79.00	44-65
1996 Jewel Princess®	Retrd.	1996	60.00	44-50
1997 Midnight Princess®	Retrd.	1997	60.00	60

Beanie Babies/Ty, Inc.

Beanie Babies - Ty

YEAR ISSUE	EDITION LIMIT	YEAR RETD.	ISSUE PRICE	*QUOTE U.S.$
1996 Ally the Alligator 4032	Retrd.	1997	5.00	30-50
1999 Almond the Beige Bear	Retrd.	1999	5.00	6-15
1999 Amber the Gold Tabby	Retrd.	1999	5.00	6-9
1998 Ants the Anteater 4195	Retrd.	1998	5.00	5-10
1997 Baldy the Eagle (76ers) 4074	Retrd.	1998	5.00	10-120
1997 Baldy the Eagle 4074	Retrd.	1998	5.00	7-15
1998 Batty the Bat (Brewers) 4105	Retrd.	1998	5.00	40-100
1998 Batty the Bat (Mets) 4105	Retrd.	1998	5.00	10-77
1996 Batty the Bat (pink) 4105	Retrd.	1996	5.00	10-15
1996 Batty the Bat 4105	Retrd.	1999	5.00	10-15
1998 Beak the ty-dye Kiwi Bird	Retrd.	1999	5.00	5-10
1997 Bernie the St. Bernard 4109	Retrd.	1998	5.00	6-10
1995 Bessie the Brown Cow 4009	Retrd.	1997	5.00	25-50
1995 Blackie the Black Bear 4011	Retrd.	1998	5.00	10-20
1998 Blizzard the White Tiger (White Sox) 4163	Retrd.	1998	5.00	50
1997 Blizzard the White Tiger 4163	Retrd.	1998	5.00	30-90
1998 Bones the Dog (Yankees) 4001	Retrd.	1998	5.00	10-137
1994 Bones the Dog 4001	Retrd.	1998	5.00	9-12
1998 Bongo the Monkey (Cavaliers) 4067	Retrd.	1998	5.00	122
1995 Bongo the Monkey (dark tail) 4067	Retrd.	1997	5.00	35
1995 Bongo the Monkey (light tail) 4067	Retrd.	1998	5.00	7-12
1997 Britannia the Bear (UK Exclusive) 4600	Retrd.	1998	5.00	157-250
1995 Bronty the Brontosaurus 4085	Retrd.	1996	5.00	650
1993 Brownie the Brown Bear	Retrd.	1997	5.00	2500-2748
1997 Bruno the Terrier 4183	Retrd.	1998	5.00	5-10
1995 Bubbles the Fish (yellow & black) 4078	Retrd.	1997	5.00	45-100
1996 Bucky the Beaver 4016	Retrd.	1997	5.00	18-40
1995 Bumble the Bee 4045	Retrd.	1996	5.00	375-575
1997 Bunny, set/3 (lilac, mint, pink)	Retrd.	1999	15.00	45-75
1998 Butch the Bull Terrier	Retrd.	1999	5.00	5-10
1998 Canyon the Couger	Retrd.	1999	5.00	6-15
1995 Caw the Crow 4071	Retrd.	1996	5.00	100-400
1999 Cheeks the Baboon	Retrd.	1999	5.00	5-10
1995 Chilly the Polar Bear 4012	Retrd.	1996	5.00	1000-1400
1997 Chip the Calico Cat 4121	Retrd.	1999	5.00	6-12
1999 Chipper the Chipmunk	Retrd.	1999	5.00	5
1998 Chocolate the Moose (Nuggets) 4015	Retrd.	1998	5.00	100
1994 Chocolate the Moose 4015	Retrd.	1998	5.00	7-15
1996 Chops the Lamb 4019	Retrd.	1997	5.00	90-150
1997 Claude the Crab 4083	Retrd.	1997	5.00	6-20
1998 Clubby (Club Bear)	Retrd.	1999	5.00	10-75
1996 Conga the Gorilla 4160	Retrd.	1997	5.00	5-10
1995 Coral the ty-dye Fish 4079	Retrd.	1997	5.00	110-130
1997 Crunch the Shark 4130	Retrd.	1998	5.00	5-10
1998 Cubbie the Brown Bear (Cubs 5/18/97) 4010	Retrd.	1998	5.00	175-179
1998 Cubbie the Brown Bear (Cubs 9/6/97) 4010	Retrd.	1998	5.00	150
1994 Cubbie the Brown Bear 4010	Retrd.	1997	5.00	15-30
1998 Curly the Bear (Spurs) 4052	Retrd.	1998	5.00	158
1996 Curly the Bear 4052	Retrd.	1998	5.00	8-25
1998 Daisy the Black & White Cow (Cubs-Harry Caray) 4006	Retrd.	1998	5.00	175
1994 Daisy the Black & White Cow 4006	Retrd.	1998	5.00	7-12
1995 Derby the Horse (Fine Mane) 4008	Retrd.	1995	5.00	10-50
1995 Derby the Horse (No Star) 4008	Retrd.	1997	5.00	10-27
1995 Derby the Horse w/Star 4008	Retrd.	1998	5.00	7-10
1994 Digger the Crab (orange) 4027	Retrd.	1995	5.00	400
1995 Digger the Crab (red) 4027	Retrd.	1997	5.00	60-90
1997 Doby the Doberman 4110	Retrd.	1997	5.00	6-10
1997 Doodle the ty-dye Rooster 4171	Retrd.	1997	5.00	15-20
1997 Dotty the Dalmatian 4100	Retrd.	1997	5.00	6-20
1998 Early the Robin	Retrd.	1999	5.00	5-15
1996 Ears the Bunny 4018	Retrd.	1998	5.00	8-25
1997 Echo the Dolphin 4180	Retrd.	1998	5.00	8-15
1998 Eggbert the Baby Chick	Retrd.	1999	5.00	7-15
1999 The End the Black Bear	Retrd.	1999	5.00	22-32
1997 Erin the Bear 4186	Retrd.	1997	5.00	10-30
1999 Eucalyptus the Koala	Retrd.	1999	5.00	5-10
1998 Ewey the Lamb	Retrd.	1999	5.00	7-15
1997 Fetch the Golden Retriever 4189	Retrd.	1998	5.00	10-12
1994 Flash the Dolphin 4021	Retrd.	1997	5.00	75-120
1997 Fleece the Lamb 4125	Retrd.	1997	5.00	7-20
1996 Flip the White Cat 4012	Retrd.	1997	5.00	28-45
1999 Flitter the Butterfly	Retrd.	1999	5.00	12-20
1997 Floppity the Lilac Bunny 4118	Retrd.	1998	5.00	10-25
1995 Flutter the ty-dye Butterfly 4043	Retrd.	1996	5.00	450-650
1997 Fortune the Panda 4196	Retrd.	1998	5.00	9-12
1996 Freckles the Leopard 4066	Retrd.	1997	5.00	9-12
1998 Fuzz the Bear	Retrd.	1999	5.00	5-30
1996 Garcia the ty-dye Bear 4051	Retrd.	1997	5.00	150-175
1990 Germania the Bear (Ty Europe Exclusive)	Retrd.	1999	5.00	175
1997 Gigi the Poodle 4191	Retrd.	1999	5.00	5-20
1998 Glory the Bear (98 All Star) 4188	Retrd.	1998	5.00	322
1998 Glory the Bear 4188	Retrd.	1998	5.00	23-40
1998 Goatee the Mountain Goat	Retrd.	1999	5.00	5-20
1996 Gobbles the Turkey 4034	Retrd.	1999	5.00	5-12
1995 Goldie the Goldfish 4023	Retrd.	1997	5.00	22-38
1998 Goochy the ty-dye Jellyfish	Retrd.	1999	5.00	5-9
1997 Gracie the Swan 4126	Retrd.	1998	5.00	7-10
1999 Groovy the Bear	Retrd.	1999	5.00	10-15
1996 Grunt the Razorback 4096	Retrd.	1997	5.00	110-130
1998 Halo the Angel Bear	Retrd.	1999	5.00	5-22
1995 Happy the Hippo (gray) 4061	Retrd.	1995	5.00	375-450
1994 Happy the Hippo (lavender) 4061	Retrd.	1998	5.00	15-20
1998 Hippie the ty-dye Bunny	Retrd.	1999	5.00	12-20
1997 Hippity the Mint Bunny 4119	Retrd.	1998	5.00	15-20
1998 Hissy the Snake (Razorbacks) 4185	Retrd.	1998	5.00	98
1997 Hissy the Snake 4185	Retrd.	1999	5.00	5-10
1999 Honks the Goose	Retrd.	1999	5.00	5-10
1996 Hoot the Owl 4073	Retrd.	1997	5.00	22-25
1998 Hope the Praying Bear	Retrd.	1999	5.00	5-10
1997 Hoppity the Pink Bunny 4117	Retrd.	1998	5.00	10-20
1994 Humphrey the Camel 4060	Retrd.	1996	5.00	1000-1300
1997 Iggy the Iguana 4038	Retrd.	1999	5.00	6-20
1996 Inch the Worm (felt antennas) 4044	Retrd.	1996	5.00	100
1996 Inch the Worm 4044	Retrd.	1998	5.00	18-20
1995 Inky the Octopus (pink) 4028	Retrd.	1998	5.00	12-20

*Quotes have been rounded up to nearest dollar

YEAR ISSUE	EDITION LIMIT	YEAR RETD.	ISSUE PRICE	*QUOTE U.S.$
1995 Inky the Octopus (tan w/mouth) 4028	Retrd.	1995	5.00	450
1994 Inky the Octopus (tan w/o mouth) 4028	Retrd.	1994	5.00	400-500
1997 Jabber the Parrot 4197	Retrd.	1999	5.00	5-10
1997 Jake the Mallard Duck 4199	Retrd.	1999	5.00	5-10
1997 Jolly the Walrus 4082	Retrd.	1998	5.00	7-10
1998 Kicks the Soccer Bear	Retrd.	1999	5.00	5-25
1995 Kiwi the Toucan 4070	Retrd.	1997	5.00	135
1999 Knuckles the Pig	Retrd.	1999	5.00	5-10
1997 Kuku the Cockatoo 4192	Retrd.	1999	5.00	5-10
1996 Lefty the Donkey (w/American flag) 4085	Retrd.	1997	5.00	175-300
1996 Lefty the Donkey (w/o American flag) 4085	Retrd.	1997	5.00	300-400
1994 Legs the Frog 4020	Retrd.	1997	5.00	10-20
1996 Libearty the Bear w/American Flag 4057	Retrd.	1997	5.00	275-280
1999 Lips the Fish	Retrd.	1999	5.00	10
1996 Lizzy the Lizard (blue/black) 4033	Retrd.	1997	5.00	15-33
1995 Lizzy the Lizard (tie-dyed) 4033	Retrd.	1995	5.00	500-600
1998 Loosy the Canadain Goose	Retrd.	1999	5.00	5-15
1996 Lucky the Ladybug (11 dots) 4040	Retrd.	1998	5.00	15-25
1996 Lucky the Ladybug (21 dots) 4040	Retrd.	1996	5.00	250-300
1994 Lucky the Ladybug (seven glued on spots) 4040	Retrd.	1996	5.00	100-188
1998 Luke the Lab	Retrd.	1999	5.00	6-20
1998 Mac the Cardinal	Retrd.	1999	5.00	6-10
1995 Magic the Dragon (hot pink lines) 4088	Retrd.	1997	5.00	100
1995 Magic the Dragon (light pink lines) 4088	Retrd.	1997	5.00	38-50
1996 Manny the Manatee 4081	Retrd.	1997	5.00	100-150
1997 Maple/Maple the Canadian Exclusive Bear 4600	Retrd.	1998	5.00	123-200
1997 Maple/Pride the Canadian Exclusive Bear 4600	Retrd.	1997	5.00	200-400
1997 Mel the Koala Bear 4162	Retrd.	1999	5.00	7-10
1998 Millenium the Bear	Retrd.	1999	5.00	13-44
1998 Mooch the Monkey	Retrd.	1999	5.00	5-9
1996 Mystic the Unicorn (coarse mane/iridescent horn) 4007	Retrd.	1999	5.00	7-20
1996 Mystic the Unicorn (coarse mane/tan horn) 4007	Retrd.	1997	5.00	10-20
1994 Mystic the Unicorn (fine mane) 4007	Retrd.	1995	5.00	195-200
1998 Nana the Monkey 4067	Retrd.	1998	5.00	1960
1997 Nanook the Husky 4104	Retrd.	1999	5.00	7-20
1999 Neon the ty-dye Seahorse	Retrd.	1999	5.00	5-10
1998 Nibbler the Rabbit	Retrd.	1999	5.00	7-20
1998 Nibbly the Rabbit	Retrd.	1999	5.00	7-20
1995 Nip the Cat (all gold) 4003	Retrd.	1995	5.00	250-375
1996 Nip the Cat (gold cat/white paws) 4003	Retrd.	1997	5.00	12-14
1995 Nip the Cat (white belly) 4003	Retrd.	1995	5.00	100
1997 Nuts the Squirrel 4114	Retrd.	1997	5.00	7-25
1999 Osito the Mexican Bear	Retrd.	1999	5.00	10-28
1996 Patti the Platypus (fuchsia) 4025	Retrd.	1999	5.00	15-23
1995 Patti the Platypus (magenta) 4025	Retrd.	1995	5.00	400-450
1994 Patti the Platypus (raspberry) 4025	Retrd.	1994	5.00	400-500
1999 Paul the Walrus	Retrd.	1999	5.00	5-10
1997 Peace the ty-dyed Bear (embroidered) 4053	Retrd.	1997	5.00	10-25
1996 Peanut the Elephant (light blue) 4062	Retrd.	1998	5.00	15-20
1995 Peanut the Elephant (royal blue) 4062	Retrd.	1995	5.00	2000-3000
1999 Pecan the Gold Bear	Retrd.	1999	5.00	5-10
1994 Peking the Panda Bear 4013	Retrd.	1996	5.00	1000
1994 Pinchers the Lobster (red) 4026	Retrd.	1998	5.00	10-20
1998 Pinky the Flamingo (Spurs) 4072	Retrd.	1998	5.00	140
1995 Pinky the Flamingo 4072	Retrd.	1999	5.00	5-20
1997 Pouch the Kangaroo 4161	Retrd.	1999	5.00	6-20
1997 Pounce the ty-dye Brown Cat 4122	Retrd.	1999	5.00	6-20
1997 Prance the Cat 4123	Retrd.	1999	5.00	6-20
1998 Prickles the Hedgehog	Retrd.	1999	5.00	6-20
1997 Princess the Bear (Princess Diana) (Non-Charity)	Retrd.	1997	5.00	15-48
1997 Princess the Bear (Princess Diana) (PE Pellets)	Retrd.	1997	5.00	15-38
1997 Princess the Bear (Princess Diana) (purple) (PVC Pellets)	Retrd.	1997	5.00	40-100
1997 Puffer the Puffin 4181	Retrd.	1998	5.00	5-10
1997 Pugsly the Pug Dog 4106	Retrd.	1998	5.00	6-10
1998 Pumkin' the Pumpkin	Retrd.	1998	5.00	18-35
1994 Punchers the Lobster (misprint)	Retrd.	1994	5.00	800-1020
1994 Quackers the Duck (w/o wings) 4024	Retrd.	1995	5.00	800-1350
1995 Quackers the Duck (w/wings) 4024	Retrd.	1995	5.00	7-20
1996 Radar the Bat 4091	Retrd.	1997	5.00	100-125
1997 Rainbow the Chameleon 4037	Retrd.	1999	5.00	20-60
1995 Rex the Tyrannosaurus 4086	Retrd.	1996	5.00	575-625
1996 Righty the Elephant 4086	Retrd.	1997	5.00	170-200
1996 Ringo the Racoon 4014	Retrd.	1998	5.00	8-20
1998 Roam the Buffalo	Retrd.	1999	5.00	5-9
1997 Roary the Lion (Royals) 4069	Retrd.	1998	5.00	10-100
1997 Roary the Lion 4069	Retrd.	1998	5.00	7-60
1998 Rocket the Blue Jay 4202	Retrd.	1999	5.00	5-9
1996 Rover the Red Dog 4101	Retrd.	1998	5.00	25
1998 Sammy the ty-dyed Bear Cub	Retrd.	1999	5.00	8-25
1998 Santa	Retrd.	1998	5.00	30-35
1999 Scaly the Lizard	Retrd.	1999	5.00	5-10
1998 Scat the Cat	Retrd.	1999	5.00	5-15
1999 Schweetheart the Orangutan	Retrd.	1999	5.00	5-10
1996 Scoop the Pelican 4107	Retrd.	1998	5.00	7-10
1998 Scorch the Dragon	Retrd.	1999	5.00	5-15
1996 Scottie the Black Terrier 4102	Retrd.	1998	5.00	13-29
1994 Seamore the White Seal 4029	Retrd.	1997	5.00	80-125
1996 Seaweed the Otter 4080	Retrd.	1998	5.00	10-15
1999 Sheets the Ghost	Retrd.	1999	5.00	5-15

YEAR ISSUE	EDITION LIMIT	YEAR RETD.	ISSUE PRICE	*QUOTE U.S.$
1999 Signature Bear	Retrd.	1999	5.00	9-15
1999 Silver the Grey Tabby	Retrd.	1999	5.00	5-10
1998 Slippery the Seal	Retrd.	1999	5.00	5-15
1994 Slither the Snake 4031	Retrd.	1996	5.00	1000
1999 Slowpoke the Sloth	Retrd.	1999	5.00	5-10
1996 Sly the Fox (brown belly) 4115	Retrd.	1996	5.00	50-100
1996 Sly the Fox (white belly) 4115	Retrd.	1998	5.00	7-10
1997 Smoochy the Frog 4039	Retrd.	1999	5.00	7-12
1997 Snip the Siamese Cat 4120	Retrd.	1998	5.00	6-12
1997 Snort the Bull 4002	Retrd.	1998	5.00	6-20
1996 Snowball the Snowman	Retrd.	1997	5.00	20-35
1999 Spangle the American Bear	Retrd.	1999	5.00	5-20
1996 Sparky the Dalmatian 4100	Retrd.	1997	5.00	85-100
1994 Speedy the Turtle 4030	Retrd.	1997	5.00	20-25
1996 Spike the Rhinoceros 4060	Retrd.	1997	5.00	6-12
1997 Spinner the Spider 4036	Retrd.	1998	5.00	6-12
1994 Splash the Orca Whale 4022	Retrd.	1997	5.00	75-90
1996 Spook the Ghost 4090	Retrd.	1997	5.00	325
1996 Spooky the Ghost 4090	Retrd.	1997	5.00	15-35
1994 Spot the Black & White Dog (black spot) 4000	Retrd.	1997	5.00	30-40
1994 Spot the Black & White Dog (no spot) 4000	Retrd.	1994	5.00	1000-1371
1997 Spunky the Cocker Spaniel 4184	Retrd.	1999	5.00	7-12
1994 Squealer the Pig 4005	Retrd.	1998	5.00	25
1995 Steg the Stegosaurus 4087	Retrd.	1996	5.00	780-800
1998 Stilts the Stork	Retrd.	1999	5.00	10-12
1995 Sting the Manta Ray 4077	Retrd.	1996	5.00	110-150
1997 Stinger the Scorpion 4193	Retrd.	1998	5.00	10
1995 Stinky the Skunk 4017	Retrd.	1998	5.00	7-15
1998 Stretch the Ostrich (Cardinals) 4182	Retrd.	1998	5.00	122
1997 Stretch the Ostrich 4182	Retrd.	1999	5.00	5-12
1996 Stripes the Tiger (black/tan) 4065	Retrd.	1998	5.00	10
1998 Stripes the Tiger (Detroit) 4065	Retrd.	1998	5.00	122-130
1995 Stripes the Tiger (orange/black) 4065	Retrd.	1996	5.00	200-320
1998 Strut the Rooster (Pacers) 4171	Retrd.	1998	5.00	100-147
1997 Strut the Rooster 4171	Retrd.	1999	5.00	6-15
1999 Swirly the Snail	Retrd.	1999	5.00	5-10
1995 Tabasco the Bull 4002	Retrd.	1997	5.00	110-150
1996 Tank the Armadillo (7 rib lines) 4031	Retrd.	1996	5.00	110-150
1996 Tank the Armadillo (7-9 rib lines w/shell) 4031	Retrd.	1997	5.00	40-80
1996 Tank the Armadillo (9 rib lines) 4031	Retrd.	1996	5.00	200-400
1998 Teddy (Holiday 98)	Retrd.	1998	5.00	40-50
1999 Teddy (Holiday 99)	Retrd.	1999	5.00	15-38
1997 Teddy the Brown Teddy Bear (Holiday 97) 4050	Retrd.	1997	5.00	15-50
1995 Teddy the Brown Teddy Bear (new face) 4050	Retrd.	1997	5.00	60-75
1994 Teddy the Brown Teddy Bear (old face) 4050	Retrd.	1994	5.00	1440-2200
1995 Teddy the Colored Teddies-Cranberry (new face) 4052	Retrd.	1996	5.00	1020-1200
1994 Teddy the Colored Teddies-Cranberry (old face) 4052	Retrd.	1994	5.00	1100-1400
1995 Teddy the Colored Teddies-Jade (new face) 4057	Retrd.	1996	5.00	1200-1540
1994 Teddy the Colored Teddies-Jade (old face) 4057	Retrd.	1994	5.00	1100-1470
1995 Teddy the Colored Teddies-Magenta (new face) 4056	Retrd.	1996	5.00	1200-1400
1994 Teddy the Colored Teddies-Magenta (old face) 4056	Retrd.	1994	5.00	1100
1995 Teddy the Colored Teddies-Teal (new face) 4051	Retrd.	1996	5.00	1200-1500
1994 Teddy the Colored Teddies-Teal (old face) 4051	Retrd.	1994	5.00	700-1100
1995 Teddy the Colored Teddies-Violet (new face) 4055	Retrd.	1996	5.00	1250-1400
1994 Teddy the Colored Teddies-Violet (old face) 4055	Retrd.	1994	5.00	1100-1300
1998 Tiny the Chihuahua	Retrd.	1999	5.00	5-10
1999 Tiptoe the Mouse	Retrd.	1999	5.00	7-15
1997 Tracker the Basset Hound 4198	Retrd.	1999	5.00	6-13
1994 Trap the Mouse 4042	Retrd.	1996	5.00	950-1000
1995 Tuck the Walrus (misprint)	Retrd.	1996	5.00	120-175
1997 Tuffy the Brown Terrier 4108	Retrd.	1997	5.00	7-10
1995 Tusk the Walrus 4076	Retrd.	1997	5.00	100-120
1996 Twigs the Giraffe 4068	Retrd.	1998	5.00	10-20
1999 Ty 2K the Bear	Retrd.	1999	5.00	10-30
1998 Valentina the Bear	Retrd.	1999	5.00	13-20
1996 Valentino the Bear (Toys For Tots) 4058	Retrd.	1997	5.00	227
1996 Valentino the Bear (Yankees) 4058	Retrd.	1997	5.00	150-168
1994 Valentino the Bear 4058	Retrd.	1997	5.00	13-20
1995 Velvet the Panther 4064	Retrd.	1997	5.00	15-20
1995 Waddle the Penguin 4075	Retrd.	1998	5.00	10-25
1999 Wallace the Bear	Retrd.	1999	5.00	5-20
1997 Waves the Orca Whale 4084	Retrd.	1998	5.00	7-10
1994 Web the Spider 4041	Retrd.	1996	5.00	750-1000
1996 Weenie the Dog 4013	Retrd.	1998	5.00	18-27
1997 Whisper the Deer 4187	Retrd.	1999	5.00	5
1997 Wise the Owl 4194	Retrd.	1998	5.00	6-30
1999 Wiser the Owl	Retrd.	1999	5.00	7-15
1996 Wrinkles the Bulldog 4103	Retrd.	1998	5.00	6-12
1998 Zero the Holiday Penguin	Retrd.	1998	5.00	25
1995 Ziggy the Zebra 4063	Retrd.	1998	5.00	10-15
1994 Zip the Black Cat (all black) 4004	Retrd.	1995	5.00	700-1100
1994 Zip the Black Cat (white face & belly) 4004	Retrd.	1995	5.00	250-400
1994 Zip the Black Cat (white paws) 4004	Retrd.	1998	5.00	21-40

McDonald Teenie Beanies - Ty

YEAR ISSUE	EDITION LIMIT	YEAR RETD.	ISSUE PRICE	*QUOTE U.S.$
1997 Chocolate Moose	Retrd.	1997	N/A	15-20
1997 Chops the Lamb	Retrd.	1997	N/A	20-25
1997 Goldie the Goldfish	Retrd.	1997	N/A	15-25
1997 Lizz the Lizard	Retrd.	1997	N/A	15-18
1997 Patti the Platypus	Retrd.	1997	N/A	20-25
1997 Pinky the Flamingo	Retrd.	1997	N/A	15-18
1997 Quacks the Duck	Retrd.	1997	N/A	15
1997 Seamore the Seal	Retrd.	1997	N/A	20
1997 Snort the Bull	Retrd.	1997	N/A	15-18
1997 Speedy the Turtle	Retrd.	1997	N/A	15
1997 Set of 10	Retrd.	1997	N/A	85-125
1998 Bones the Dog	Retrd.	1998	N/A	20-27
1998 Bongo the Monkey	Retrd.	1998	N/A	20-27
1998 Doby the Doberman	Retrd.	1998	N/A	20-27
1998 Happy the Hippo	Retrd.	1998	N/A	10
1998 Inch the Worm	Retrd.	1998	N/A	10
1998 Mel the Koala	Retrd.	1998	N/A	15
1998 Pinchers the Lobster	Retrd.	1998	N/A	10
1998 Scoop the Pelican	Retrd.	1998	N/A	10
1998 Twigs the Giraffe	Retrd.	1998	N/A	10
1998 Waddles the Penguin	Retrd.	1998	N/A	15
1998 Zip the Cat	Retrd.	1998	N/A	15
1999 Antsy the Anteater	Retrd.	1999	N/A	5
1999 Britannia the Bear (UK)	Retrd.	1999	2.49	3
1999 Chip the Calico Cat	Retrd.	1999	N/A	N/A
1999 Claude the Crab	Retrd.	1999	N/A	N/A
1999 Erin the Bear (Ireland)	Retrd.	1999	2.49	3
1999 Freckles the Leopard	Retrd.	1999	N/A	N/A
1999 Glory the Bear (USA)	Retrd.	1999	2.49	10
1999 Iggy the Iguana	Retrd.	1999	N/A	N/A
1999 Maple the Canadian Bear	Retrd.	1999	2.49	10
1999 Nook the Husky	Retrd.	1999	N/A	N/A
1999 Nuts the Squirrel	Retrd.	1999	N/A	N/A
1999 Rocket the Blue Jay	Retrd.	1999	N/A	N/A
1999 Smoochy the Frog	Retrd.	1999	N/A	N/A
1999 Spunky the Cocker Spaniel	Retrd.	1999	N/A	N/A
1999 Stretch the Ostrich	Retrd.	1999	N/A	N/A
1999 Strut the Rooster	Retrd.	1999	N/A	N/A

Boyds Collection Ltd.

Animal Menagerie™ - The Boyds Collection

YEAR ISSUE	EDITION LIMIT	YEAR RETD.	ISSUE PRICE	*QUOTE U.S.$
2000 Bandit Bushytail 55211	Open		12.00	12
2000 Elford Bullsworth 55330-05	Open		19.00	19
2000 I.M. Uproarius 55220	Open		16.00	16
2000 Matilda Baahead 55200-01	Open		14.00	14

The Archive Series™ - The Boyds Collection

YEAR ISSUE	EDITION LIMIT	YEAR RETD.	ISSUE PRICE	*QUOTE U.S.$
2000 Blake B. Wordsworth 5745-06	Open		7.50	8
2000 Bristol B. Windsor 57052-03	Open		13.00	13
2000 Cambridge Q. Bearrister 57003-08	Open		20.00	20
2000 Dickens Q. Wordsworth 5745-03	Open		7.50	8
2000 Dover D. Windsor 57051-03	Open		13.00	13
1990 Eden 5708	Retrd.	N/A	7.00	35
2000 Emerson T. Penworthy 57410-03	Open		12.00	12
2000 Hastings P. Bearsford 57250-11	Open		7.00	7
2000 Hayden T. Bearsford 57250-10	Open		7.00	7
2000 Milton R. Penworthy 57410-07	Open		12.00	12
2000 Natalie Nibblenose 573300-01	Open		7.00	7
2000 Nickie Nibblenose 573303-03	Open		7.00	7
2000 Rockwell B. Bruin 57211-05	Open		40.00	40
2000 Romano B. Grated 5755	Open		7.50	8
2000 Sinclair Bearsford 57150-03	Open		31.00	31
2000 Stellina Hopswell 573700-01	Open		14.00	14
2000 Sterling Hopswell 573701-06	Open		14.00	14

Baby Boyds™ - The Boyds Collection

YEAR ISSUE	EDITION LIMIT	YEAR RETD.	ISSUE PRICE	*QUOTE U.S.$
2000 Binky McFarkle 517050-03	Open		5.00	5
2000 Bundles B. Joy & Blankie 56391-04	Open		22.00	22
2000 Bunkie Hoppleby 51740-06	Open		7.50	8
2000 Callie Fuzzbucket 517020-06	Open		5.00	5
2000 Dipsey Baadoodle 51800-01	Open		7.50	8
2000 Kookie Snicklefritz 51770-12	Open		14.00	14
2000 Mudpuddle P. Piglet 51790-09	Open		7.50	8
2000 Poof Pufflebeary & Blankie 51780-03	Open		23.00	23
2000 Pookie C. Hoppleby 517040-01	Open		5.00	5
2000 Snookie Snicklefritz 51770-09	Open		14.00	14
2000 Wookie Snicklefritz 51770-06	Open		14.00	14

Bailey and Friends™ - The Boyds Collection

YEAR ISSUE	EDITION LIMIT	YEAR RETD.	ISSUE PRICE	*QUOTE U.S.$
2000 Bailey 9199-14	6-mon.		26.00	26
2000 Edmund 9175-14	6-mon.		25.00	25
2000 Emily Babbit 9150-14	6-mon.		26.00	26
2000 Indy 91757-14	6-mon.		12.00	12

Dressed Artisan Series™ - The Boyds Collection

YEAR ISSUE	EDITION LIMIT	YEAR RETD.	ISSUE PRICE	*QUOTE U.S.$
2000 Betsie B. Jodibear 92000-07	Open		20.50	21
2000 Ross G. Jodibear 92000-08	Open		20.50	21

J.B. Bean & Associates™ - The Boyds Collection

YEAR ISSUE	EDITION LIMIT	YEAR RETD.	ISSUE PRICE	*QUOTE U.S.$
1996 Bedford B. Bean 5121-08	Retrd.	N/A	14.00	88-94
2000 Buffie Bunnyhop 522700-03	Open		10.00	10
2000 Carson B. Barker 540300-05	Open		29.00	29
XX Daryl Bear 5114	Retrd.	N/A	27.00	313
2000 Fluffie Bunnyhop 522700-01	Open		10.00	10
2000 Hazlenut B. Bean 500100-05	Open		7.00	7
2000 Java B. Bean 500102-07	Open		7.00	7
2000 Patches B. Beariluved 51000	Open		18.00	18
XX Pop Bruin 5124	Retrd.	N/A	27.00	94
2000 Snuffy B. Barker 5405	Open		14.50	15
2000 T. Hopplewhite 52200-01	Open		19.00	19
2000 Tessa Fluffypaws 5309-01	Open		20.00	20
2000 Webber Vanguard 51100-07	Open		28.00	28

*Quotes have been rounded up to nearest dollar

The Mohair Bears™ - The Boyds Collection

YEAR ISSUE	EDITION LIMIT	YEAR RETD.	ISSUE PRICE	*QUOTE U.S.$
2000 Aunt Mamie Bearington 590104	Open		10.50	11
2000 Bamboo Bearington 590030	Retrd.	2000	50.00	50
2000 Dwight D. Bearington 590081-03	Retrd.	2000	14.00	14
2000 Edith Q. Harington II 5901600-03	Retrd.	2000	30.00	30
2000 Hampton T. Bearington 590052-08	Retrd.	2000	35.00	35
2000 Nantucket P. Bearington 590102	Open		10.50	11
2000 Rosalynn P. Harington II 5901400-01	Retrd.	2000	54.00	54
2000 Uncle Ben Bearington 590103	Open		10.50	11

T.J.'s Best Dressed™ - The Boyds Collection

YEAR ISSUE	EDITION LIMIT	YEAR RETD.	ISSUE PRICE	*QUOTE U.S.$
2000 Agatha Snoopstein 91870	Open		17.00	17
2000 Aissa Witebred 912070	Open		26.00	26
2000 Aubrey Tippeetoes 912054	Open		27.00	27
2000 Auntie Lavonne Higgenthorpe 918452	Open		24.00	24
2000 B.A. Blackbelt 917361	Open		21.00	21
2000 Billy Bob Bruin w/Froggie 912622	Open		30.00	30
2000 Brianna Tippeetoes 913959	Open		12.50	13
2000 Brooke B. Bearsley 917400	Open		20.00	20
2000 Bumble B. Buzzoff 91773	Open		17.00	17
2000 Cara Z. Bunnyhugs 914569	Open		14.00	14
2000 Caroline Mayflower 913958	Open		13.50	14
2000 Cathy J. Hiphop 917030	Open		12.00	12
2000 Clark S. Bearhugs 918055	Open		9.50	10
2000 Cori Beariburg 915211	Open		14.00	14
2000 Darby Bearibug 913960	Open		12.00	12
2000 Dorchester Catsworth w/Artie 919760	Open		29.00	29
2000 Eleanore Bearsevelt 912010	Open		56.00	56
2000 Elmer O. Bearroad 911931	Open		26.00	26
2000 Embraceable Ewe 913121	Open		11.00	11
2000 Ginnie Higgenthorpe 918442	Open		9.50	10
2000 Huney B. Keeper 91774	Retrd.	2000	23.00	23
2000 Hunter Bearsdale w/Greenspan 912625	Retrd.	2000	31.00	31
2000 Jenna d. Lapinne 916630	Open		16.00	16
2000 Juliana Hopkins II 911220	Open		15.00	15
2000 Juliet S. Bearlove 912651	Open		23.00	23
2000 Kevin G. Bearsley 917362	Open		22.00	22
2000 Kyle L. Berriman 917401	Open		20.00	20
2000 Lady B. Bug 91775	Open		20.00	20
2000 Lila Hopkins 91124	Open		18.00	18
2000 Lois B. Bearlove 913956	Open		12.50	13
2000 Lottie de Lopear 91648	Retrd.	2000	15.00	15
2000 Megan Berriman 912623	Open		31.00	31
2000 Melinda S. Willoughby 913961	Open		12.00	12
2000 Mikayla Springsbeary 912624	Open		31.00	31
2000 Mipsie Blumenshine 917040	Open		12.00	12
2000 Miss Prissy Fussybuns 912094	Open		29.00	29
2000 Momma McFuzz and Missy 910080	Open		29.00	29
2000 Mr. Bojingles 91264	Open		20.00	20
2000 Nanette DuBeary 918432	Open		9.50	10
2000 Naomi Bearlove 913957	Retrd.	2000	13.50	14
2000 Paige Willoughby 918351	Open		19.00	19
2000 Paula Hoppleby 91125	Open		18.00	18
2000 Phoebe Purrsmore 917101	Open		12.00	12
2000 Primrose IV 9160-04	Open		22.00	22
2000 Radcliffe Fitzbruin 912020	Retrd.	2000	43.00	43
2000 Regena Haresford 916490	Open		29.00	29
2000 Robyn Purrsmore 915600	Open		11.50	12
2000 Roslyn Hiphop 912080	Open		30.00	30
2000 Sally Quignapple and Annie 91009	Open		24.00	24
2000 Samuel Adams 915210	Open		14.00	14
2000 Savannah Buttercup 91650	Open		26.00	26
2000 Truffles O' Pigg 916010-01	Open		16.00	16

Cast Art Industries

Dreamsicles Angel Hugs™ - K. Haynes

YEAR ISSUE	EDITION LIMIT	YEAR RETD.	ISSUE PRICE	*QUOTE U.S.$
1999 Bluebeary (bear) (1st Generation)-08002	Retrd.	1999	8.00	8
1999 Bubbles (whale)-08013	Retrd.	1999	8.00	8
1999 Creampuff (cherub) (1st Generation)-08001	Retrd.	1999	8.00	8
1999 Cupcake (cherub) (1st Generation)-08003	Retrd.	1999	8.00	8
1999 Daisy (cow) (1st Generation)-08004	Retrd.	1999	8.00	8
1999 Dawn-Millennium Edition-08029	Open		8.00	8
1999 Faith (cherub)-08012	Retrd.	1999	8.00	8
1999 Honey Bunny-08041	Open		8.00	8
1999 Joy (cherub)-08014	Retrd.	1999	8.00	8
1999 Peaches (cherub) (1st Generation)-08005	Retrd.	1999	8.00	8
1999 Peanut (elephant) (1st Generation)-08006	Retrd.	1999	8.00	8
1999 Peg (horse)-08017	Retrd.	1999	8.00	8
1999 Rosebud (cherub)-08016	Retrd.	1999	8.00	8
1999 Rosie - Rosemont ICE Commemorative-08030	750	1999	Gift	N/A
1999 Smooches (cherub)-08039	Open		8.00	8
1999 Splash (frog)-08015	Retrd.	1999	8.00	8
1999 Sugar (cherub)-08038	Open		8.00	8
1999 Sunshine-08040	Open		8.00	8
1999 Sweetie (cherub)-08037	Open		8.00	8
1999 Tooth Fairy-08042	Open		8.00	8

Dreamsicles Angel Hugs™ Event - K. Haynes

YEAR ISSUE	EDITION LIMIT	YEAR RETD.	ISSUE PRICE	*QUOTE U.S.$
2000 I Love Dreamsicles-08057	Retrd.	2000	7.95	8

Dreamsicles Angel Hugs™ Holiday - K. Haynes

YEAR ISSUE	EDITION LIMIT	YEAR RETD.	ISSUE PRICE	*QUOTE U.S.$
1999 Candy (cherub)-08021	Retrd.	1999	8.00	8
1999 Crystal (cherub)-08025	Retrd.	1999	8.00	8
1999 Evergreen (bear)-08026	Retrd.	1999	8.00	8
1999 Holly (cherub)-08023	Retrd.	1999	8.00	8
1999 Mittens (snowman)-08022	Retrd.	1999	8.00	8
1999 Moose L. Toe (moose)-08024	Retrd.	1999	8.00	8

Dreamsicles Northern Lights Angel Hugs™ - K. Haynes

YEAR ISSUE	EDITION LIMIT	YEAR RETD.	ISSUE PRICE	*QUOTE U.S.$
1999 Loverboy (Moose)-08051	Open		8.00	8
1999 Shivers (Snowman)-08050	Open		8.00	8
1999 Sparkle (Snow Angel)-08047	Open		8.00	8
1999 Squeak (Penguin)-08049	Open		8.00	8
1999 Sweatheart (Snow Angel)-08046	Open		8.00	8
1999 Twinkle (Snow Angel)-08048	Open		8.00	8

Cavanagh Group Intl.

Coca-Cola Brand Bean Bag - CGI

YEAR ISSUE	EDITION LIMIT	YEAR RETD.	ISSUE PRICE	*QUOTE U.S.$
1997 #0101 Seal with Holiday Scarf	Yr.Iss.	1997	5.00	7-20
1997 #0102 Seal with Long Snowflake Cap	Yr.Iss.	1997	5.00	7-20
1997 #0103 Penguin with Snowflake Cap	Yr.Iss.	1997	5.00	7-20
1997 #0104 Polar Bear with Snowflake Cap	Yr.Iss.	1997	5.00	20
1997 #0105 Polar Bear with Plaid Bow Tie	Yr.Iss.	1997	5.00	15
1997 #0106 Polar Bear with Red Bow	Yr.Iss.	1997	5.00	15
1997 #0107 Seal with Baseball Cap	Yr.Iss.	1997	5.00	15
1997 #0108 Penguin with Delivery Cap	Yr.Iss.	1997	5.00	7-15
1997 #0109 Polar Bear with Coke Bottle	Yr.Iss.	1997	5.00	15
1997 #0110 Polar Bear with Pink Bow	Yr.Iss.	1997	5.00	15
1997 #0111 Polar Bear with Baseball Cap	Yr.Iss.	1997	5.00	20
1997 #0112 Polar Bear with Tee Shirt	Yr.Iss.	1997	5.00	7-20
1997 #0113 Polar Bear with Long Snowflake Cap (Musicland Exclusive)	Yr.Iss.	1997	5.00	25
1998 #0114 Seal with Red & Green Ski Cap	Yr.Iss.	1998	6.00	6
1998 #0116 Polar Bear with a Red & Green Sweater	Yr.Iss.	1998	6.00	6
1998 #0118 Polar Bear with Snowflake Hat	Yr.Iss.	1998	5.00	5
1998 #0120 Polar Bear with Long Red Scarf	Yr.Iss.	1998	5.00	5-7
1998 #0123 Seal with Long Green Scarf	Yr.Iss.	1998	5.00	5
1998 #0124 Walrus with a Snowflake Scarf	Yr.Iss.	1998	6.00	7
1998 #0127 Penguin with Chef's Hat	Yr.Iss.	1998	5.00	5
1998 #0131 Polar Bear in Argyle Shirt	Yr.Iss.	1998	5.00	5
1998 #0132 Coca-Cola Can Topped by a Cap & Sunglasses	Yr.Iss.	1998	6.00	7
1998 #0133 Reindeer in a Coca-Cola Tee Shirt	Yr.Iss.	1998	6.00	7
1998 #0135 Walrus	Yr.Iss.	1998	5.00	5
1998 #0136 Husky	Yr.Iss.	1998	5.00	5
1998 #0137 Whale	Yr.Iss.	1998	5.00	5
1998 #0140 Polar Bear with a Green Delivery Cap	Yr.Iss.	1998	6.00	7
1998 #0141 Walrus with Snowflake Hat	Yr.Iss.	1998	5.00	5
1998 #0142 Reindeer with Snowflake Scarf	Yr.Iss.	1998	5.00	7
1997 #0144 Polar Bear with Green Bow (Blockbuster Exclusive)	Yr.Iss.	1997	N/A	N/A
1997 #0145 Seal with Green Striped Scarf (Blockbuster Exclusive)	Yr.Iss.	1997	N/A	N/A
1997 #0146 Polar Bear in Driver's Cap (Blockbuster Exclusive)	Yr.Iss.	1997	N/A	N/A
1997 #0147 Seal with Long Snowflake Cap (Blockbuster Exclusive)	Yr.Iss.	1997	N/A	N/A
1997 #0148 Penguin with Snowflake Cap (Blockbuster Exclusive)	Yr.Iss.	1997	N/A	N/A
1997 #0149 Polar Bear with Red Vest and Black Bow Tie (Blockbuster Exclusive)	Yr.Iss.	1997	N/A	N/A
1998 #0152 Reindeer	Yr.Iss.	1998	5.00	5
1997 #0153 & 154 Kissing Bears (White's Guide to Collecting Figures Magazine Exclusive)	15,000	1997	15.00	22-25
1998 #0155 Penguin with Snowflake Scarf	Yr.Iss.	1998	5.00	5
1998 #0158 Seal with White Tee Shirt (Coca-Cola Exclusive)	Yr.Iss.	1998	6.00	6
1998 #0159 Polar Bear with Long Coca-Cola scarf (Coca-Cola Exclusive)	Yr.Iss.	1998	6.00	6
1999 #0161 Polar Bear-trademark Vest (Musicland Exclusive)	Yr.Iss.	1998	5.00	5
1998 #0162 Reindeer-trademark Shirt (Musicland Exclusive)	Yr.Iss.	1998	5.00	5
1998 #0163 Polar Bear-trademark Long Scarf (Musicland Exclusive)	Yr.Iss.	1998	5.00	5
1998 #0164 Seal-trademark Cap (Musicland Exclusive)	Yr.Iss.	1998	5.00	5
1998 #0165 Polar Bear-Blue & Green trademark Vest (Parade of Gifts Exclusive)	Yr.Iss.	1998	6.00	6
1998 #0166 Polar Bear-Blue & White Strip Hat & Vest (GCC Exclusive)	Yr.Iss.	1998	6.00	6
1998 #0167 Polar Bear-trademark Coca-Cola Cap and Red Scarf	Closed	1999	6.00	6
1998 #0168 Polar Bear-trademark Coca-Cola Vest & Beanie Hat	Closed	1999	6.00	6
1998 #0169 Polar Bear-trademark Coca-Cola Long Ski Cap	Closed	1999	6.00	6
1998 #0170 Seal-Blue Delivery Outfit	Closed	1999	6.00	6
1998 #0171 Polar Bear-Soda Fountain Outfit	Closed	1999	6.00	6
1998 #0172 Penguin-trademark Coca-Cola Vest and Bow Tie	Closed	1999	6.00	6
1998 #0177 Polar Bear with Red & Yellow Chinese Shirt (Manchu Wok Exclusive)	Yr.Iss.	1998	N/A	N/A
1998 #0182 &#0183 Kissing Bears-trademark Coca-Cola Vest & Jumper (White's Guide to Collecting Figures Magazine Exclusive)	Yr.Iss.	1998	14.95	15-20
1998 #0184 Polar Bear-Red Fleece Shirt/Collector Classic Logo Imprinted: "World of Coca-Cola, Atlanta, October 24, 1998" (Coca-Cola Exclusive)	1,800	1998	6.00	6
1998 #0191 Polar Bear-Atlanta (Exclusive to Coke Store in Atlanta)	Closed	1998	6.00	6
1998 #0192 Polar Bear-Las Vegas (Exclusive to Coke Store in Las Vegas)	Closed	1998	6.00	6
1999 #0193 & #0194 Polar Bear-Black & Red Vest & Red Bow Tie & Black & Red Bow and Red Bow Tie (Coca-Cola Exclusive)	Closed	1998	6.00	6
1999 #0195 Polar Bear-trademark Coca-Cola Vest & Bow Tie (Coca-Cola Exclusive)	Closed	2000	6.00	6
1999 #0196 Polar Bear-trademark Coca-Cola Jumper (Coca-Cola Exclusive)	Closed	2000	7.00	7
1999 #0197 Seal in Night Shirt and Cap (Coca-Cola Exclusive)	Closed	2000	6.00	6
1999 #0198 Polar Bear-trademark Coca-Cola Night Shirt & Long Cap (Coca-Cola Exclusive)	Closed	2000	7.00	7
1999 #0199 Polar Bear-trademark Coca-Cola Baseball Cap	Yr.Iss.	1999	5.00	5
1999 #0200 Polar Bear-trademark Coca-Cola Shirt	Yr.Iss.	1999	5.00	5
1999 #0201 Polar Bear-trademark Coca-Cola Scarf	Yr.Iss.	1999	5.00	5
1999 #0202 Penguin-trademark Coca-Cola Vest and Red Bow Tie	Yr.Iss.	1999	5.00	5
1999 #0203 Seal-trademark Coca-Cola Scarf	Yr.Iss.	1999	5.00	5
1999 #0204 Seal-trademark Coca-Cola Baseball Cap	Yr.Iss.	1999	5.00	5
1999 #0205 Penguin-trademark Coca-Cola Red Vest & Green Hat & Bow Tie	Yr.Iss.	1999	5.00	5
1999 #0206 Polar Bear-trademark Coca-Cola Long Cap and Green Scarf	Yr.Iss.	1999	5.00	5
1999 #0207 Seal-trademark Coca-Cola Blue Vest and Green Hat	Yr.Iss.	1999	5.00	5
1999 #0208 Polar Bear-trademark Coca-Cola Vest & Red Bow Tie & Hat	Yr.Iss.	1999	5.00	5
1999 #0209 Polar Bear-trademark Coca-Cola Shirt and Red Scarf	Yr.Iss.	1999	5.00	5
1999 #0210 Seal-trademark Coca-Cola Scarf and Red Hat	Yr.Iss.	1999	5.00	5
1999 #0249 Adam Petty #45	Yr.Iss.	1999	10.00	10
1999 #0261 Polar Bear in Baseball Jersey	Yr.Iss.	1999	7.00	7
1999 #0262 Polar Bear in Red Football Jersey	Yr.Iss.	1999	7.00	7
1999 #0263 Penquin in Red Hockey Shirt	Yr.Iss.	1999	7.00	7
1999 #0264 Polar Bear in Red Golf Shirt	Yr.Iss.	1999	7.00	7
1999 #0265 Polar Bear in Ski Outfit & Goggles	Yr.Iss.	1999	7.00	7
1999 #0266 Seal in Soccer Shirt	Yr.Iss.	1999	7.00	7
1999 #0267 Polar Bear-trademark Coca-Cola Romper (GCC Exclusive)	Closed	1999	7.00	7
1999 #0269 Polar Bear-"Property of Coca Cola" Sweatshirt (Coca-Cola Exclusive)	Closed	1999	7.00	7
1999 #0270 Polar Bear-Everything Coca Cola - New York (Exclusive to Coke Store in NY)	Closed	1999	7.00	7
1999 #0271 Polar Bear with Everything Coca- Cola - Atlanta (Exclusive to Coke Store in Atlanta)	Closed	1999	7.00	7
1999 #0273 Seal-Green Striped Jacket & Cap (Coca-Cola Exclusive)	Closed	1999	7.00	7
1999 #0274 Polar Bear-White Vest, Bowtie and Soda Cap (Coca-Cola Exclusive)	Closed	1999	7.00	7
1999 #0277 Polar Bear-Year 2000 Top Hat/Red Scarf	Closed	1999	9.95	10
1999 #0278 Polar Bear-Year 2000 Red Shirt/Bow	Closed	1999	9.95	10
1999 #0279 Seal-Year 2000 trademark Coca-Cola Vest/Soda Cap	Closed	1999	9.95	10
1999 #0280 Penguin-Year 2000 Green Hat/Scarf	Closed	1999	9.95	10
1999 #0287 Polar Bear-Red Vest/Soda Hat/Bow Tie (Musicland Exclusive)	Yr.Iss.	1999	7.00	7
1999 #0288 Polar Bear-Delivery Cap/Pants/Suspenders/Bow Tie (Musicland Exclusive)	Yr.Iss.	1999	7.00	7
1999 #0289 Polar Bear-Red Delivery Cap/Shirt/Black Bow Tie (Musicland Exclusive)	Yr.Iss.	1999	7.00	7
1999 #0295 Bobby LaBonte #18	Yr.Iss.	1999	10.00	10
1999 #0296 Tony Stewart #20	Yr.Iss.	1999	10.00	10
1999 #0297 Kenny Irwin #28	Yr.Iss.	1999	10.00	10
1999 #0298 Kyle Petty #44	Yr.Iss.	1999	10.00	10
1999 #0299 Dale Jarrett #88	Yr.Iss.	1999	10.00	10
1999 #0300 Bill Elliott #94	Yr.Iss.	1999	10.00	10
1999 #0301 Jeff Burton #99	Yr.Iss.	1999	10.00	10
1999 #0304 Polar Bear-Yellow Shirt/Collector Classic Logo Imprinted:"World of Coca-Cola, Atlanta, October 16,1999 (Coca-Cola Exclusive)	2,160	1999	9.95	10
2000 #0310 Polar Bear Fireman	Yr.Iss.		8.00	8
2000 #0311 Polar Bear Construction Worker	Yr.Iss.		8.00	8
2000 #0312 Reindeer Artist	Yr.Iss.		8.00	8
2000 #0313 Seal Chef	Yr.Iss.		8.00	8

*Quotes have been rounded up to nearest dollar

YEAR ISSUE	EDITION LIMIT	YEAR RETD.	ISSUE PRICE	*QUOTE U.S.$
2000 #0314 Penguin Pilot	Yr.Iss.		8.00	8
2000 #0315 Polar Bear Policeman	Yr.Iss.		8.00	8
2000 #0316 Penguin in Red Vest	Yr.Iss.		6.00	6
2000 #0317 Polar Bear in Red Jacket & Hat	Yr.Iss.		6.00	6
2000 #0318 Reindeer in Red & White Vest	Yr.Iss.		6.00	6
2000 #0319 Polar Bear in Red & Black Vest	Yr.Iss.		6.00	6
2000 #0320 Penguin in Green Jacket	Yr.Iss.		6.00	6
2000 #0321 Seal in Tan & Red Jacket	Yr.Iss.		6.00	6
2000 #0322 Coca-Cola Panda (Kroger Store Exclusive)	Yr.Iss.		5.00	5
2000 #0378 Dale Earnhardt, Jr. #8	Yr.Iss.		10.00	10
2000 #0379 Bill Elliott #94	Yr.Iss.		10.00	10
2000 #0380 Dale Jarrett #88	Yr.Iss.		10.00	10
2000 #0381 Tony Stewart #20	Yr.Iss.		10.00	10
2000 #0382 Steve Park #1	Yr.Iss.		10.00	10
2000 #0383 Jeff Burton #99	Yr.Iss.		10.00	10
2000 #0384 Kyle Petty #44	Yr.Iss.		10.00	10
2000 #0386 Bobby LaBonte #18	Yr.Iss.		10.00	10
2000 #0388 Dale Earnhardt #3	Yr.Iss.		10.00	10
1998 McDonald's Boy with Vest & Girl with Bow, set/2	Yr.Iss.	1998	Gift	N/A

Coca-Cola Brand Heritage Collection (Sundblom) - P. Hamel

YEAR ISSUE	EDITION LIMIT	YEAR RETD.	ISSUE PRICE	*QUOTE U.S.$
1997 Hospitality	3,000	1999	200.00	200

Coca-Cola Brand Heritage Soda Fountain Bears - CGI

YEAR ISSUE	EDITION LIMIT	YEAR RETD.	ISSUE PRICE	*QUOTE U.S.$
1998 Bearnard Bearansson	5,000		60.00	60
1998 Bearry Bearresford	5,000		50.00	50
2000 Cappy" Diaz	5,000		60.00	60
1998 Cubby Bearringer	5,000		50.00	50
1998 Dr. Pembearton	5,000		60.00	60
1998 Fra Bruinhilda Bearlinger	5,000		60.00	60
1998 George Bearton	5,000		50.00	50
2000 Herbeart Smartenuff	5,000		60.00	60
1998 Lillian Bearica	5,000		70.00	70
1998 Officer Zoltan Bearrezinski	5,000		70.00	70
1998 Tessie Bear Bearringer	5,000		50.00	50

Coca-Cola Brand International Bean Bag - CGI

YEAR ISSUE	EDITION LIMIT	YEAR RETD.	ISSUE PRICE	*QUOTE U.S.$
1999 #0211 Reegle - Bald Eagle (USA)	Yr.Iss.	1999	7.99	8
1999 #0212 Toolu the Toucan - Toucan (Honduras)	Yr.Iss.	1999	7.99	8
1999 #0213 Dover the Bulldog - Bulldog (England)	Yr.Iss.	1999	7.99	8
1999 #0214 Strudel - French Poodle (France)	Yr.Iss.	1999	7.99	8
1999 #0215 Toro - Bull (Spain)	Yr.Iss.	1999	7.99	8
1999 #0216 Curry - Bengal Tiger (India)	Yr.Iss.	1999	7.99	8
1999 #0217 Clomp the Elephant - Elephant (Kenya)	Yr.Iss.	1999	7.99	8
1999 #0218 Rilly - Gorilla (Rwanda)	Yr.Iss.	1999	7.99	8
1999 #0219 Masa - Lion (Mozambique)	Yr.Iss.	1999	7.99	8
1999 #0220 Quala - Koala Bear (Australia)	Yr.Iss.	1999	7.99	8-10
1999 #0221 Can Can - Pelican (Cuba)	Yr.Iss.	1999	7.99	8
1999 #0222 Baltic - Reindeer (Sweden)	Yr.Iss.	1999	7.99	8
1999 #0223 Paco - Iguana (Mexico)	Yr.Iss.	1999	7.99	8
1999 #0224 Rifraff - Giraffe (Somalia)	Yr.Iss.	1999	7.99	8
1999 #0225 Croon - Baboon (Pakistan)	Yr.Iss.	1999	7.99	8
1999 #0226 Salty - Sea Turtle (Bahamas)	Yr.Iss.	1999	7.99	8
1999 #0227 Vaca - Long Horn Cow (Argentina)	Yr.Iss.	1999	7.99	8
1999 #0228 Zongshi - Panda Bear (China)	Yr.Iss.	1999	7.99	8
1999 #0229 Barrot - Parrot (Brazil)	Yr.Iss.	1999	7.99	8
1999 #0230 Fannie the Fox - Red Fox (Germany)	Yr.Iss.	1999	7.99	8
1999 #0231 Taps - Tapir (Venezuela)	Yr.Iss.	1999	7.99	8
1999 #0232 Rhiny - Black Rhinoceros (Tanzania)	Yr.Iss.	1999	7.99	8
1999 #0233 Gourmand - Moose (Canada)	Yr.Iss.	1999	7.99	8
1999 #0234 Lors - Wild Boar (Italy)	Yr.Iss.	1999	7.99	8
1999 #0235 Barris the Bear - Brown Bear (Russia)	Yr.Iss.	1999	7.99	8
1999 #0236 Waks -Yak (Nepal)	Yr.Iss.	1999	7.99	8
1999 #0237 Key Key - Snow Monkey (Japan)	Yr.Iss.	1999	7.99	8
1999 #0238 Ramel - Camel (Egypt)	Yr.Iss.	1999	7.99	8
1999 #0239 Pock - Peacock (Sri Lanka)	Yr.Iss.	1999	7.99	8
1999 #0240 Badgey - Badger (Czech Republic)	Yr.Iss.	1999	7.99	8
1999 #0241 Topus - Zebra (Nigeria)	Yr.Iss.	1999	7.99	8
1999 #0242 Waller - Walrus (Greenland)	Yr.Iss.	1999	7.99	8
1999 #0243 Laffs - Llama (Bolivia)	Yr.Iss.	1999	7.99	8
1999 #0244 Woolsie - Sheep (Ireland)	Yr.Iss.	1999	7.99	8
1999 #0245 Crunch - Crocodile (Sudan)	Yr.Iss.	1999	7.99	8
1999 #0246 Howls - Wolf (Romania)	Yr.Iss.	1999	7.99	8
1999 #0247 Orany - Orangutan (Singapore)	Yr.Iss.	1999	7.99	8
1999 #0248 Ardie - Aardvark (Niger)	Yr.Iss.	1999	7.99	8
1999 #0249 Heeta - Cheetah (Namibia)	Yr.Iss.	1999	7.99	8
1999 #0250 Blubby - Pot Belly Pig (Viet Nam)	Yr.Iss.	1999	7.99	8
1999 #0251 Hopps - Coki Frog (Puerto Rico)	Yr.Iss.	1999	7.99	8-10
1999 #0252 Peng the Penguin - Penguin (Chile)	Yr.Iss.	1999	7.99	8
1999 #0253 Lochs - Rabbit (Scotland)	Yr.Iss.	1999	7.99	8
1999 #0254 Neppy - Proboscis Monkey (Thailand)	Yr.Iss.	1999	7.99	8
1999 #0255 Meeska - Hippopotamus (Zambia)	Yr.Iss.	1999	7.99	8
1999 #0256 Nardie - St. Bernard (Switzerland)	Yr.Iss.	1999	7.99	8
1999 #0257 Kelp - Kiwi (New Zealand)	Yr.Iss.	1999	7.99	8
1999 #0258 Oppy - Octopus (Greece)	Yr.Iss.	1999	7.99	8
1999 #0259 Streak - Jackal (Tunisia)	Yr.Iss.	1999	7.99	8
1999 #0260 Masha -Ostrich (South Africa)	Yr.Iss.	1999	7.99	8
2000 #0330 Sailor - Swan (Austria)	Yr.Iss.		8.99	9
2000 #0333 Duckles - Mandarin Duck (Taiwan)	Yr.Iss.		8.99	9
2000 #0343 Draco - Flying Dragon (Indonesia)	Yr.Iss.		8.99	9
2000 #0345 Tides - Killer Whale (Norway)	Yr.Iss.		8.99	9
2000 #0351 Jose - Jaguar (Peru)	Yr.Iss.		8.99	9
2000 #0365 Crooner - Raccoon (USA)	Yr.Iss.		8.99	9

Harley-Davidson Bean Bag - CGI

YEAR ISSUE	EDITION LIMIT	YEAR RETD.	ISSUE PRICE	*QUOTE U.S.$
1998 Baby Blue & Studs	Closed	1999	8.00	8
1999 Boot Hill Bob	Closed	1999	8.00	8
1999 Bravo	Closed	1999	8.00	8
1999 Bubba	Closed	1999	8.00	8
1998 Chopper	Closed	1998	8.00	8
1998 Clutch Carbo	Closed	1999	8.00	8
1999 Curly	Yr.Iss.	1999	8.00	8
1999 Duck	2,000		8.00	8
1997 Enforcer	Closed	1998	8.00	8
1998 Evo	Closed	1999	8.00	8
1998 Fat Bob	Closed	1999	8.00	8
1999 Frog	2,000		8.00	8
1999 Hog	Yr.Iss.	1999	8.00	8
1998 Kickstart	Closed	1999	8.00	8
1998 Manifold Max	Closed	1998	8.00	8
1997 Motorhead	Closed	1998	8.00	8
1997 Punky	Closed	1998	8.00	8
1997 Racer	Closed	1998	8.00	8
1997 Rachet	Closed	1998	8.00	8
1997 Roamer	Closed	1999	8.00	8
1999 Rocky	Yr.Iss.	1999	8.00	8
1998 Spike	Closed	1999	8.00	8
1999 Spotts	2,000		8.00	8
1999 Starke	2,000		8.00	8
1999 Stroker	2,000		8.00	8
1999 Tanker	Closed	1999	8.00	8
1999 Thunder	Closed	1999	8.00	8
1999 Torque	2,000		8.00	8
1999 Tusk	Closed	1999	8.00	8

Harley-Davidson Plush - B. Yaney

YEAR ISSUE	EDITION LIMIT	YEAR RETD.	ISSUE PRICE	*QUOTE U.S.$
1999 Babe	Closed	2000	60.00	60
1999 Bosco	Closed	2000	60.00	60
1998 Clutch Carbo	Closed	2000	50.00	50
1997 Cruiser	Closed	1999	50.00	50
1998 Curt Chrome	Closed	1999	50.00	50
1997 Panhead Pete	Closed	2000	50.00	50
1997 Sissy Bar	Closed	1998	50.00	50
1997 V-Twin	Closed	1998	50.00	50

Humbug Bean Bugs - T. Fraley

YEAR ISSUE	EDITION LIMIT	YEAR RETD.	ISSUE PRICE	*QUOTE U.S.$
1998 Humbug	Open		8.00	8
1999 Little Dickens	Open		8.00	8
1998 Santa Bug	Open		8.00	8
1998 Scroogy Bug	Open		8.00	8
1998 Sleepy Bug	Open		8.00	8
1999 Snoozy	Open		8.00	8

Save The Children Bean Bag Collection - Save The Children

YEAR ISSUE	EDITION LIMIT	YEAR RETD.	ISSUE PRICE	*QUOTE U.S.$
1999 Damita	Open		8.00	8
1999 Eric	Open		8.00	8
1998 Haruko	Open		8.00	8
1998 Juji	Open		8.00	8
1999 Jun	Open		8.00	8
1999 Kachina	Open		8.00	8
1998 Mackenzie	Open		8.00	8
1998 Patrick	Open		8.00	8
1998 Paz	Open		8.00	8
1998 Sila	Open		8.00	8
1999 Stella	Open		8.00	8
1999 Stephane	Open		8.00	8

Cherished Teddies/Enesco Group, Inc.

Collectible Plush - P. Hillman

YEAR ISSUE	EDITION LIMIT	YEAR RETD.	ISSUE PRICE	*QUOTE U.S.$
1999 Antique Toy Bear 662240	Open		17.50	18
1999 Antique Toy Bear/Boat 737380	Open		17.50	18
1999 Antique Toy Bear/Bunny 737399	Open		17.50	18
1999 Antique Toy Cow/Teddie 662259	Open		17.50	18
1999 Antique Toy Elephant/Teddie 622275	7,500		17.50	18
1999 Antique Toy Horse/Teddie 662267	Open		17.50	18
1999 Antique Toy Lamb/Teddie 742740	Open		17.50	18
1999 Bear w/Sweater, 2 asst. 649155	Yr.Iss.	1999	25.00	25
1999 Girls w/velvet Christmas Scarfs 644323	Open		15.00	15
1999 Spanky "Friendship Can Sometimes Be Bumpy But It's Worth It" 661597	Open		30.00	30
1999 Val 662291	Open		27.50	28
1999 Val 662291L	12,000		27.50	28

Holiday Occasions Plush - P. Hillman

YEAR ISSUE	EDITION LIMIT	YEAR RETD.	ISSUE PRICE	*QUOTE U.S.$
1999 4th of July 637998	Open		7.00	7
1999 Christmas 638021	Open		7.00	7
1999 Easter 637955	Open		7.00	7
1999 Halloween 638005	Open		7.00	7
1999 Mother's Day 637963	Open		7.00	7
1999 New Year's 637696	Open		7.00	7
1999 St. Patrick's Day 637947	Open		7.00	7
1999 Teacher 637971	Open		7.00	7
1999 Thanksgiving 638013	Open		7.00	7
1999 Valentine 637939	Open		7.00	7

Monthly Plush - P. Hillman

YEAR ISSUE	EDITION LIMIT	YEAR RETD.	ISSUE PRICE	*QUOTE U.S.$
1999 January 556165	Open		7.00	7
1999 February 556181	Open		7.00	7
1999 March 556203	Open		7.00	7
1999 April 556246	Open		7.00	7
1999 May 556270	Open		7.00	7
1999 June 556289	Open		7.00	7
1999 July 556327	Open		7.00	7
1999 August 556483	Open		7.00	7
1999 September 556688	Open		7.00	7
1999 October 556750	Open		7.00	7
1999 November 556785	Open		7.00	7
1999 December 556793	Open		7.00	7

Columbus International

HERMANN-Spielwaren Annual Bears - U. Hermann

YEAR ISSUE	EDITION LIMIT	YEAR RETD.	ISSUE PRICE	*QUOTE U.S.$
1992 Annual Bear Teddy Black & White	Yr.Iss.	1992	140.00	200
1993 Annual Bear Greeny	Yr.Iss.	1993	140.00	180
1994 Annual Bear Rosanna	Yr.Iss.	1994	140.00	175
1995 Annual Bear Symphonie	Yr.Iss.	1995	140.00	160
1996 Annual Bear Kir Royal	Yr.Iss.	1996	140.00	160
1997 Annual Bear Golden Blue	Yr.Iss.	1997	140.00	155-199
1998 Annual Bear Smoky	Yr.Iss.	1998	140.00	140-162
1999 Annual Bear True Love	Yr.Iss.	1999	145.00	145
2000 Annual Bear Green Leaves	Yr.Iss.		150.00	150

HERMANN-Spielwaren Annual Christmas Bears - U. Hermann

YEAR ISSUE	EDITION LIMIT	YEAR RETD.	ISSUE PRICE	*QUOTE U.S.$
1994 Annual Christmas Bear 1994	Yr.Iss.	1994	176.00	240
1995 Annual Christmas Bear 1995	Yr.Iss.	1995	176.00	230
1996 Annual Christmas Bear 1996	Yr.Iss.	1996	176.00	210
1997 Annual Christmas Bear 1997	Yr.Iss.	1997	176.00	200-235
1998 Annual Christmas Bear 1998	Yr.Iss.	1998	176.00	190
1999 Annual Christmas Bear 1999	Yr.Iss.	1999	197.00	197
2000 Annual Christmas Bear 2000	Yr.Iss.		199.00	199

HERMANN-Spielwaren Artline Bears - U. Hermann

YEAR ISSUE	EDITION LIMIT	YEAR RETD.	ISSUE PRICE	*QUOTE U.S.$
1996 Artline Bear Bleu	Closed	1996	260.00	415
1996 Artline Bear Rouge	Closed	1996	260.00	415
1996 Artline Bear Vert	Closed	1996	260.00	415

HERMANN-Spielwaren Collectible Bears - N/A, unless otherwise noted

YEAR ISSUE	EDITION LIMIT	YEAR RETD.	ISSUE PRICE	*QUOTE U.S.$
1960 Baby Bear, Dralon fabric, 26 cm	Closed	N/A	N/A	550
1998 Baby Panda - M. Hermann	500	1999	125.00	125
1998 Chester Bear Michael - M. Hermann	500	1999	159.00	159
1996 Chimney Sweep	500	1999	140.00	140
1998 Edelweiss - M. Hermann	1,000	1999	159.00	159
1954 Flexible Bear, tipped Mohair, 35 cm	Closed	N/A	N/A	3000
1999 Grand Panda	500	1999	160.00	160
2000 Hermann 80th Anniversary Bear - U. Hermann	1,000		150.00	150
1999 Hermann Euro Bear - M. Hermann	500	1999	159.00	300
2000 Hermann Golfer Bear - U. Hermann	2,000		250.00	250
1999 Hilde Hermann-Classic Birthday Bear - M. Hermann	500	1999	199.00	199
1998 Leopold, the little old music bear - M. Hermann	250	1999	150.00	150
1996 Little Old Max	500	1999	160.00	160
1999 Max III - U. Hermann	750	2000	220.00	220
1998 Millennium Bear - M. Hermann	2,000	1999	215.00	215-224
2000 Millennium Set, set/2 - U. Hermann	4-day		500.00	500
1999 New York Toy Fair, 1999 - M. Hermann	333	1999	99.00	99
1998 Papa Panda - M. Hermann	500	1999	140.00	140
1998 Phantom of the Opera - M. Hermann	500	1999	209.00	209
1999 Polar "Ice" Bear	1,000	1999	160.00	160-170
1998 Professor Higgins - M. Hermann	500	1999	198.00	198
2000 Red Baron - U. Hermann	500		260.00	260
1996 Robinhood	500	1999	210.00	210
1998 Small Jacob - M. Hermann	500	1999	106.00	106
1965 Speaking Bear, with speak mechanism, 45 cm	Closed	N/A	N/A	550
1940 Teddy, Cotton fabric, 50 cm	Closed	N/A	N/A	600
1950 Teddy, Mohair, 50 cm - M. Hermann	Closed	N/A	N/A	550
1950 Teddy, Mohair, 80 cm - M. Hermann	Closed	N/A	N/A	4250
1920 Teddy, Mohair, 50 cm - M. Hermann	Closed	N/A	N/A	2650
1954 Teddy, Mohair, 55 cm	Closed	N/A	N/A	900
1960 Teddy, short Mohair, 40 cm	Closed	N/A	N/A	900
1955 Teddy, synthetic	Closed	N/A	N/A	800
1955 Teddy, tipped Mohair, 50 cm	Closed	N/A	N/A	1000
1955 Teddy, tipped Mohair, 60 cm	Closed	N/A	N/A	1250
1955 Teddy, tipped Mohair, long nose, 70 cm	Closed	N/A	N/A	1500
1971 Teddybear, synthetic fabric with airbrush	Closed	N/A	N/A	400
1933 Trachtenbären, Artificial Silk, 18 cm - M. Hermann	Closed	N/A	N/A	1750
1998 Wolfgang Amadeus Mozart - M. Hermann	500	1999	225.00	225
2000 XXI - Twenty First Century Bear - U. Hermann	1,000		150.00	150

HERMANN-Spielwaren Columbus International "Columbus Collection™" - U. Hermann

YEAR ISSUE	EDITION LIMIT	YEAR RETD.	ISSUE PRICE	*QUOTE U.S.$
1998 Oktoberfest	250	1998	198.00	198-250
1998 Rosemont Special Edition, 1998	100	1998	199.00	250
1999 Oktoberfest	500	1999	220.00	220
1999 Rosemont Special Edition, 1999	191	1999	199.00	199
1999 Snowflake	250	1999	179.00	179
2000 Rosemont Special Edition, 2000	200		198.00	198
2000 Christopher Columbus	780		279.00	279

*Quotes have been rounded up to nearest dollar

HERMANN-Spielwaren Hennef Bears - U. Hermann

YEAR ISSUE	EDITION LIMIT	YEAR RETD.	ISSUE PRICE	*QUOTE U.S.$
1996 Hennef Bär 1996 Shooting Gallerie	85	1996	140.00	250
1997 Hennef Bär 1997 Bear Pocket	85	1997	160.00	200
1998 Hennef Bär 1998 Vario Bear	65	1998	140.00	400

HERMANN-Spielwaren Internet Bears - U. Hermann

YEAR ISSUE	EDITION LIMIT	YEAR RETD.	ISSUE PRICE	*QUOTE U.S.$
1996 HERMANN 1st Internet Bear	250	1997	225.00	800
1999 HERMANN 2nd Internet Bear -Y2K Bug Bear	1,000		198.00	198
1997 Internet Bear Miniature Edtion	500	1998	180.00	450

HERMANN-Spielwaren Neustadter Festival Bears - U. Hermann

YEAR ISSUE	EDITION LIMIT	YEAR RETD.	ISSUE PRICE	*QUOTE U.S.$
1992 Neustadter Festival Bear 1992	100	1992	130.00	1500
1993 Neustadter Festival Bear 1993	100	1993	160.00	1200
1994 Neustadter Festival Bear 1994	100	1994	180.00	1000
1995 Neustadter Festival Bear 1995	100	1995	190.00	800
1996 Neustadter Festival Bear 1996	100	1996	190.00	600
1997 Neustadter Festival Bear 1997	100	1997	190.00	700
1998 Neustadter Festival Bear 1998	100	1998	190.00	400

HERMANN-Spielwaren Sonneberger Kirmes Bears - U. Hermann

YEAR ISSUE	EDITION LIMIT	YEAR RETD.	ISSUE PRICE	*QUOTE U.S.$
1995 HERMANN Nachkriegsbär	50	1995	103.00	170
1995 Sonneberger Kirmesbär Adelbert	16	1995	103.00	300
1995 Sonneberger Kirmesbär Berta	8	1995	103.00	300
1995 Sonneberger Kirmesbär Casimier	100	1995	84.00	150
1995 Sonneberger Kirmesbär Dieter	100	1995	61.00	100
1995 Sonneberger Kirmesbär Erna	50	1995	57.00	90
1995 Sonneberger Kirmesbär Friedrich	150	1995	61.00	80
1995 Sonneberger Kirmesbär Gerda	25	1995	57.00	80
1995 Sonneberger Kirmesbär Heidi	25	1995	73.00	90
1995 Sonneberger Kirmesbär Inge	60	1995	73.00	90
1995 Sonneberger Kirmesbär Jan	25	1995	57.00	80
1995 Sonneberger Kirmesbär Kurt	25	1995	92.00	140
1995 Sonneberger Kirmesbär Ludwig	20	1995	73.00	100-160
1995 Sonneberger Kirmesbär Moritz	10	1995	73.00	300
1995 Sonneberger Kirmesbär Norbert	85	1995	61.00	100
1995 Sonneberger Kirmesbär Oskar	30	1995	92.00	130-150
1995 Sonneberger Kirmesbär Peter	40	1995	57.00	80
1995 Sonneberger Kirmesbär Quax	150	1996	57.00	80
1995 Sonneberger Kirmesbär Rudolf	250	1996	57.00	70
1995 Sonneberger Kirmesbär Sabine	250	1996	65.00	70
1995 Sonneberger Kirmesbär Tina	50	1995	65.00	100

HERMANN-Spielwaren Special Event Bears - U. Hermann, unless otherwise noted

YEAR ISSUE	EDITION LIMIT	YEAR RETD.	ISSUE PRICE	*QUOTE U.S.$
1994 Soccer Bear "WM 94 USA"	250	1995	400.00	500
1995 HERMANN Raritätenbär, 40 cm	50	1995	400.00	3000
1995 Der Verhüllte Bär (Covered Bear)	100	1995	300.00	650
1996 RGH Bear - Rolf G. Hermann	2,000	1996	235.00	800
1998 Pustefix Bear	1,000	1998	140.00	180

HERMANN-Spielwaren Yes-No Bear - M. Hermann

YEAR ISSUE	EDITION LIMIT	YEAR RETD.	ISSUE PRICE	*QUOTE U.S.$
1938 Nicky, Yes-No Bear, Mohair, 28 cm	Closed	1950	15.00	2750

Coyne's & Company

Bavarian Heritage Collection - Coyne's & Company

YEAR ISSUE	EDITION LIMIT	YEAR RETD.	ISSUE PRICE	*QUOTE U.S.$
1999 Bastien BH1101	Open		20.00	20

Daddy's Long Legs/KVK, Inc.

Daddy's Long Legs/1. Collectors Club Members Only - K. Germany

YEAR ISSUE	EDITION LIMIT	YEAR RETD.	ISSUE PRICE	*QUOTE U.S.$
1993 Faith	2,290	1993	65.00	250-450
1994 Bubby, w/Heart blanket	580	1994	65.00	295-385
1994 Bubby, w/Star blanket	1,537	1994	65.00	145-225
1994 Sissy	1,963	1995	65.00	225-375
1995 Bull Bishop	1,529	1995	65.00	130-220
1995 Cherry	1,010	1995	65.00	130-220
1995 Joy (Angel)	Closed	1995	Gift	100
1996 Jack	1,574	1996	65.00	98-200
1996 Jill	1,578	1996	65.00	98-200
1996 Carrie (Angel)	Closed	1996	Gift	50
1997 Joseph	1,397	1997	65.00	65-155
1997 Mary	1,342	1997	65.00	65-155
1997 Baby Jesus	Closed	1997	Gift	65
1998 Jeffy	934	1998	65.00	65-135
1998 Jenni	934	1998	65.00	65-135
1998 Boo	Closed	1998	Gift	N/A
1999 Meagan	Closed	1999	65.00	65
1999 Natalie	Closed	1999	65.00	65
1999 Weezie	Closed	1999	Gift	N/A
2000 Alyssa	Yr.Iss.		39.95	40
2000 Patti	Yr.Iss.		65.00	65
2000 Millie	Yr.Iss.		Gift	N/A

Daddy's Long Legs/Advertising - K. Germany

YEAR ISSUE	EDITION LIMIT	YEAR RETD.	ISSUE PRICE	*QUOTE U.S.$
1997 Boots	1,204	1997	90.00	180-225
1999 Brianna	362	1999	94.00	94-125
1996 Gigi	931	1996	90.00	150-210
1995 Gretchen	982	1995	80.00	150-200
1998 Jodi	732	1998	90.00	135-155
1995 Pistol	1,352	1995	80.00	200-285
1993 Priscilla	501	1993	70.00	375-475
1997 Skipper	1,016	1997	90.00	110-150
1998 Squirt	748	1998	94.00	94-135
1994 Ticker	1,714	1994	76.00	160-285
1994 Wendy	1,609	1994	80.00	120-160

Daddy's Long Legs/Angels - K. Germany

YEAR ISSUE	EDITION LIMIT	YEAR RETD.	ISSUE PRICE	*QUOTE U.S.$
1995 Demetria	1	1995	2500.00	N/A
1994 Glory	692	1994	118.00	265-350
1994 Hope	345	1994	118.00	203-350
1994 Kara	424	1994	76.00	160-275
1996 Monica	1,349	1998	150.00	185-165
1994 Precious	824	1994	76.00	215-275

Daddy's Long Legs/Animals - K. Germany

YEAR ISSUE	EDITION LIMIT	YEAR RETD.	ISSUE PRICE	*QUOTE U.S.$
1990 Abigail the Cow, blue	3,498	1995	62.00	270-285
1990 Abigail the Cow, red	1,063	1995	68.00	300-400
1990 Cat in Jump Suit	66	1990	60.00	700-1700
1990 Goat-boy	109	1991	62.00	1600-1700
1990 Goat-girl	154	1991	62.00	1600-1700
1990 Hugh Hoofner	1,453	1994	68.00	375-475
1991 Kitty Kat	527	1992	78.00	800-925
1991 Mamie the Pig, blue	425	1992	84.00	800-925
1990 Mamie the Pig, green	425	1992	68.00	800-925
1990 Pig-boy	124	1990	58.00	1500-1700
1990 Raccoon	123	1990	66.00	1600-1700
1990 Rachael Rabbit	377	1992	15.00	225-275
1990 Robby Rabbit	529	1992	44.00	675-775
1990 Rose Rabbit	684	1992	54.00	1200-1300
1990 Roxanne Rabbit	351	1992	52.00	675-800
1990 Rudy Rabbit	547	1992	54.00	1200-1300
1990 Wedding Rabbits	3	1990	240.00	3400-4500

Daddy's Long Legs/Arts & Theater - K. Germany

YEAR ISSUE	EDITION LIMIT	YEAR RETD.	ISSUE PRICE	*QUOTE U.S.$
1994 Margo	2,349	1996	126.00	150-300
1990 Mime	57	1990	58.00	1575-2500
1998 Simone	670	1999	98.00	98-175
1990 Witch Hazel	1,791	1995	86.00	275-450

Daddy's Long Legs/Babies & Toddlers - K. Germany

YEAR ISSUE	EDITION LIMIT	YEAR RETD.	ISSUE PRICE	*QUOTE U.S.$
1999 Annie Lee at 5 (convention ed.)	308	1999	175.00	175-275
1995 Annie Lee w/blanket	450	1995	150.00	320-400
1995 Annie Lee w/o blanket	100	1995	150.00	275-375
1996 Bunny	682	1996	80.00	175-350

Daddy's Long Legs/Children Around the World - K. Germany

YEAR ISSUE	EDITION LIMIT	YEAR RETD.	ISSUE PRICE	*QUOTE U.S.$
1994 Julie	873	1999	76.00	85-110
1996 Starr	1,237	1999	80.00	80-125
1995 Su	675	1999	76.00	100-125
1996 Teresa	2,072	1999	80.00	100-175
1996 Teresa	2,072	1999	80.00	80

Daddy's Long Legs/Clowns - K. Germany

YEAR ISSUE	EDITION LIMIT	YEAR RETD.	ISSUE PRICE	*QUOTE U.S.$
1996 Buttons	2,030	1996	80.00	190-260
1997 Dr. Tickles (convention ed.)	659	1997	125.00	280-400
1999 Magic (convention ed.)	Closed	1999	125.00	125-185
1995 Sugar (convention ed.)	475	1995	120.00	500-750

Daddy's Long Legs/Family - K. Germany

YEAR ISSUE	EDITION LIMIT	YEAR RETD.	ISSUE PRICE	*QUOTE U.S.$
1993 Abe	2,483	1995	94.00	195-285
1994 Aunt Fannie	1,475	1996	90.00	135-200
1992 Bessie	4,926	1996	94.00	175-275
1993 Billye	1,863	1995	98.00	150-340
1995 Camille	2,000	1997	184.00	275-350
1994 Charles Louis	1,184	1996	90.00	135-200
1992 Doc Moses	2,494	1993	98.00	350-425
1996 Earl	693	1996	98.00	375-475
1996 Ella	693	1996	98.00	375-475
1993 Esther	3,000	1993	158.00	395-450
1992 Gracie	3,133	1996	94.00	135-275
1993 Jackie	2,425	1995	98.00	175-300
1992 Jasmine	3,977	1994	90.00	175-425
1993 Judge	1,866	1995	98.00	180-340
1994 Maxine	1,538	1996	90.00	135-200
1992 Nurse Garnet	1,415	1993	90.00	350-400
1993 Sam	1,813	1995	94.00	150-285
1993 Slats	2,323	1995	98.00	175-350
1990 Sofie	5,548	1992	44.00	450-595
1994 Uncle Leon	1,547	1996	90.00	135-200

Daddy's Long Legs/Old West - K. Germany

YEAR ISSUE	EDITION LIMIT	YEAR RETD.	ISSUE PRICE	*QUOTE U.S.$
1997 Bullseye Billy	1,200	1992	90.00	375-600
1990 Cowboy Buck	1,824	1994	78.00	425-700
1990 Indian, 1st ed.	304	1990	78.00	1200-1700
1992 Lucky the Gambler	939	1992	90.00	850-925
1990 Miss Lilly	1,664	1994	78.00	450-700
1997 Morning Dove	1,700	1998	290.00	290-450
1997 Proud Eagle	1,500	1998	290.00	290-600
1991 Still River (Indian, 2nd ed.)	1,452	1995	98.00	275-550
1996 Sweet Savannah	2,000	1997	260.00	325-425
1999 Swiftwater Bill	400	1999	150.00	175-250
1996 Wildwood Will	1,000	1996	290.00	650-900

Daddy's Long Legs/Patriotic - K. Germany

YEAR ISSUE	EDITION LIMIT	YEAR RETD.	ISSUE PRICE	*QUOTE U.S.$
1992 Jeremiah	3,219	1994	90.00	175-425
1995 Uncle Sam, black	1,510	1997	120.00	225-250
1991 Uncle Sam, white	729	1991	150.00	1750-1850

Daddy's Long Legs/Santa Claus - K. Germany

YEAR ISSUE	EDITION LIMIT	YEAR RETD.	ISSUE PRICE	*QUOTE U.S.$
1990 Santa-1990, white	48	1990	64.00	1900-2300
1990 Santa-Red Velvet	25	1990	180.00	2000-3000
1990 Santa-Tapestry	25	1990	180.00	2000-3000
1991 Santa-1991, black	1,101	1991	98.00	450-700
1991 Santa-1991, white	311	1991	98.00	450-700
1992 Santa-1992, black	511	1993	158.00	375-475
1992 Santa-1992, special ed.	213	1993	158.00	400-500
1992 Santa-1992, white	166	1993	158.00	400-500
1993 Santa-1993, black	1,112	1994	178.00	240-385
1994 Santa-1994, Tubbin' Santa	1,859	1995	150.00	185-350
1994 Odessa Claus, 1st ed.	778	1995	144.00	275-300
1995 Santa-1995, black	1,010	1996	160.00	300-325
1995 Santa-1995, white	565	1996	160.00	300-345
1995 Odessa Claus, 2nd ed.	267	1998	144.00	175-250
1996 Santa-1996, black	985	1997	200.00	275-300
1997 Santa-1997, black	912	1998	250.00	250-275
1998 Santa-1998, black	Closed	1999	170.00	170
1999 Santa-1999, black - Cowboy	Closed	2000	190.00	190

Daddy's Long Legs/Schoolhouse Days - K. Germany

YEAR ISSUE	EDITION LIMIT	YEAR RETD.	ISSUE PRICE	*QUOTE U.S.$
1992 Choo-Choo	3,618	1993	56.00	135-190
1991 Daphne	1,060	1992	72.00	275-475
1993 Emily	1,278	1993	80.00	150-280
1991 Iris, Teacher	997	1992	90.00	375-575
1994 Jane	3,768	1994	70.00	95-125
1992 Josie	4,132	1993	56.00	135-195
1992 Katy	5,533	1996	64.00	98-185
1993 Lucy	1,946	1995	64.00	94-225
1995 Marcus	1,511	1995	76.00	115-225
1992 Micah	4,789	1996	64.00	95-185
1995 Molly	1,498	1995	76.00	115-225
1993 Phoebe	2,789	1995	64.00	125-225
1993 Priscilla	501	1993	70.00	280-475
1993 Timothy	750	1993	76.00	400-475

Daddy's Long Legs/Storybook - K. Germany

YEAR ISSUE	EDITION LIMIT	YEAR RETD.	ISSUE PRICE	*QUOTE U.S.$
1996 Little Miss Muffet	1,117	1996	90.00	175-200
1994 Little Red Riding Hood	1,824	1994	80.00	94-335
1995 Mary and her Lamb	1,627	1995	80.00	185-275

Daddy's Long Legs/Sunday School & Church - K. Germany

YEAR ISSUE	EDITION LIMIT	YEAR RETD.	ISSUE PRICE	*QUOTE U.S.$
1993 Cassie	1,521	1993	70.00	98-195
1993 Polly	1,523	1995	70.00	98-195
1993 Sister Carter	1,719	1995	94.00	140-240
1992 Sister Mary Kathleen	1,844	1994	98.00	150-400

Daddy's Long Legs/Wedding Party - K. Germany

YEAR ISSUE	EDITION LIMIT	YEAR RETD.	ISSUE PRICE	*QUOTE U.S.$
1992 James, Groom (originally sold as set/2)	1,295	1992	125.00	350-500
1992 Olivia, Bride (originally sold as set/2)	1,295	1992	125.00	350-500
1992 James, Groom & Olivia, Bride, set	Closed	1992	250.00	600-725
1996 Joshua, Ringbearer	2,500	1997	98.00	125-250
1994 Maggie, Flower Girl	2,500	1996	98.00	100-225
1996 Maurice, Groom	2,500	1997	118.00	118-400
1994 Victoria, Bride	2,500	1995	178.00	200-400

Daddy's Long Legs/Winter Collection - K. Germany

YEAR ISSUE	EDITION LIMIT	YEAR RETD.	ISSUE PRICE	*QUOTE U.S.$
1997 Lauren	445	1999	86.00	86-115
1997 Winter Lizabeth	637	1999	86.00	86-135
1997 Winter Lovie	600	1999	100.00	100-175
1997 Winter Sally	418	1999	86.00	86-135
1997 Winter Skeeter	547	1999	86.00	86-135

Deb Canham Artist Designs Inc.

DCAD Collector's Club - D. Canham

YEAR ISSUE	EDITION LIMIT	YEAR RETD.	ISSUE PRICE	*QUOTE U.S.$
1999 Binker	1,100	2000	80.00	80
1999 Santa on Holiday	940	2000	80.00	80
1999 Gift	750	2000	Gift	N/A
2000 Harvey	1,400	2000	80.00	80
2000 Molly & Jake	Yr.Iss.		80.00	80
2000 Together Forever	Yr.Iss.		150.00	150
2000 Pin	Yr.Iss.		Gift	N/A

Signing Events - D. Canham

YEAR ISSUE	EDITION LIMIT	YEAR RETD.	ISSUE PRICE	*QUOTE U.S.$
1999 Fluffy	200	2000	60.00	60-125
2000 Kasalopy	100	2000	100.00	150-225
2000 Silkie	100	2000	95.00	150-175
2000 Acorn	100	2000	95.00	95-100
2000 Blitz	400		95.00	95

Alice Collection - D. Canham

YEAR ISSUE	EDITION LIMIT	YEAR RETD.	ISSUE PRICE	*QUOTE U.S.$
2000 Alice	2,500		68.00	68
2000 Carpenter	2,500		56.00	56
2000 Cheshire Cat	2,500		56.00	56
2000 Dormouse	2,500		54.00	54
2000 Herald	2,500		56.00	56
2000 Madhatter	2,500		56.00	56
2000 March Hare	2,500		56.00	56
2000 Queen of Hearts	2,500		56.00	56
2000 Tweedle Dee	2,500		56.00	56
2000 Tweedle Dum	2,500		56.00	56
2000 Walrus	2,500		56.00	56
2000 White Rabbit	2,500		56.00	56

BIGger Bears (7-12") - D. Canham

YEAR ISSUE	EDITION LIMIT	YEAR RETD.	ISSUE PRICE	*QUOTE U.S.$
2000 Beau	500		110.00	110
2000 Big Carrot Top	150		199.00	199
2000 Big Columbine	500		110.00	110
2000 Big Cosmic Moonshine	100		280.00	280
2000 Big Gussie Galactica	100		280.00	280
2000 Big Jingle	150		199.00	199
2000 Big Pananini	150		199.00	199
2000 Big Plum	150		199.00	199
2000 Big Snowflake	500		90.00	90
2000 Blue Elephant	100	2000	100.00	90-100
2000 Cissie	500		102.00	102
2000 Fleur	500		110.00	110
2000 Hoppyrabbit	500		130.00	130
2000 J. Hunter	100	2000	150.00	150-225
1999 Judy	1,000		60.00	60
2000 Kenny	500		80.00	80
2000 Little Blue	500		80.00	80
2000 Pink Elephant	100	2000	100.00	90-100
2000 Prissie	150		199.00	199
1999 Punch	1,000		60.00	60

316 Collectors' Information Bureau

*Quotes have been rounded up to nearest dollar

YEAR ISSUE	EDITION LIMIT	YEAR RETD.	ISSUE PRICE	*QUOTE U.S.$
2000 Scruffy	500		90.00	90
2000 Sweetpea	500		130.00	130
2000 Tiny	100		270.00	270
2000 Toots	100		250.00	250
2000 Violet	500		105.00	105
2000 Wishi Washi	500		110.00	110

Brenda Power Animals - B. Power

YEAR ISSUE	EDITION LIMIT	YEAR RETD.	ISSUE PRICE	*QUOTE U.S.$
1999 Goosey	400	2000	54.00	54-75
1999 Ping	400	2000	54.00	54-75
1999 Pong	400	2000	54.00	54-75
1999 Quackers	400	2000	54.00	54-75

Brenda Power Collection - B. Power

YEAR ISSUE	EDITION LIMIT	YEAR RETD.	ISSUE PRICE	*QUOTE U.S.$
1998 Penguin	2,000		54.00	55
1998 Rabbit on Wheels	2,000	2000	54.00	54-75
1998 Racoon	2,000		54.00	55
1998 Standing Rabbit	2,000	2000	54.00	54-75

Camelot Collection - D. Canham, unless otherwise noted

YEAR ISSUE	EDITION LIMIT	YEAR RETD.	ISSUE PRICE	*QUOTE U.S.$
1998 Guinivere	2,500	2000	54.00	55-57
1998 Jester	2,500		54.00	55
1998 King Arthur	2,500	2000	54.00	55-75
1998 Merlin - L. Sasaki	2,500	1999	54.00	55-75
1998 Sir Dennis	2,500	2000	54.00	54-80
1998 Sir Lancelot	2,500	2000	54.00	54-60
1998 Slap-a-Roo	2,500	2000	54.00	65-80

Cloth Dolls (5") - J. Davis

YEAR ISSUE	EDITION LIMIT	YEAR RETD.	ISSUE PRICE	*QUOTE U.S.$
2000 Calico Clown	300		100.00	100
2000 Charlie Calico	300		110.00	110
2000 Tilly Twill	300		130.00	130

Country Collection - D. Canham

YEAR ISSUE	EDITION LIMIT	YEAR RETD.	ISSUE PRICE	*QUOTE U.S.$
1996 Annalee and Miss Goosey	3,000	1999	40.00	50-93
1996 Missi and Miss Moo	3,000	1999	40.00	50-78
1996 Tom and Mr. H	3,000	1999	40.00	50-67
1996 Zack and Mr. H	3,000	1999	40.00	50-85

Dappled Dragons - D. Canham

YEAR ISSUE	EDITION LIMIT	YEAR RETD.	ISSUE PRICE	*QUOTE U.S.$
2000 Bella the Ballerina	1,500		58.00	58
2000 Clarissa Style	1,500		58.00	58
2000 Custard	1,500	2000	55.00	55-70
1999 Dringle	1,500		58.00	58
2000 Drungo the Magnificent	1,500		58.00	58
1999 Stan	1,500	1999	58.00	58-65

Denizens of Honey Hills - D. Canham

YEAR ISSUE	EDITION LIMIT	YEAR RETD.	ISSUE PRICE	*QUOTE U.S.$
1996 Bratty Butchy	3,000	1999	60.00	60-90
1996 Gertie Lady of the Bag	3,000	1999	60.00	60-90
1996 Poppo the Wise	3,000	1999	60.00	60-90
1996 Simon the Curious	3,000	1999	60.00	60-90
1996 Willyum the Brave	3,000	1999	60.00	75-110

Gollies - D. Canham

YEAR ISSUE	EDITION LIMIT	YEAR RETD.	ISSUE PRICE	*QUOTE U.S.$
1999 Nosey	1,500		56.00	56
1997 Spangles	2,000	2000	52.00	60-70
1997 Spats	2,000	2000	52.00	60-70
1999 Sunshine	1,500		56.00	56

Good Old Day - D. Canham

YEAR ISSUE	EDITION LIMIT	YEAR RETD.	ISSUE PRICE	*QUOTE U.S.$
1999 Doodle	2,500	2000	58.00	58-65
1999 Ginger	2,500		58.00	58
1999 Old Soldier	2,500		58.00	58
1999 Peaches	2,500		58.00	58
1999 Prue	2,500		58.00	58

Have a Heart Collection - D. Canham

YEAR ISSUE	EDITION LIMIT	YEAR RETD.	ISSUE PRICE	*QUOTE U.S.$
1998 Angel	2,500	1999	52.00	60
1999 Blush	2,000		56.00	56
2000 Chi Chi	1,200		58.00	58
1998 Crispin	2,500	1999	52.00	54-65
1998 Gus	2,500	1999	52.00	54-65
2000 Kevin	1,200		60.00	60
1998 Lilac Lil	2,500	1999	52.00	65
1998 Mummy's Little Monster	2,500	1999	52.00	56-70
1998 Peppermint	2,500	1999	52.00	65
2000 Rose	1,200		60.00	60
2000 Ruby Red	800		60.00	60
1998 Susie	2,500	1999	52.00	52-60

Hermann (Red Tag) Exclusives - D. Canham

YEAR ISSUE	EDITION LIMIT	YEAR RETD.	ISSUE PRICE	*QUOTE U.S.$
1998 Belinda	Retrd.	2000	60.00	60-100
1998 Benji	Retrd.	2000	60.00	60-100

Mini Mices - D. Canham

YEAR ISSUE	EDITION LIMIT	YEAR RETD.	ISSUE PRICE	*QUOTE U.S.$
2000 Angelina	1,200		58.00	58
2000 Cuthbert	1,200		58.00	58
2000 Merry	1,200		58.00	58

Mohair Collection - D. Canham

YEAR ISSUE	EDITION LIMIT	YEAR RETD.	ISSUE PRICE	*QUOTE U.S.$
1996 A.J.	5,000	1998	40.00	70-87
1996 B.J.	5,000	1998	40.00	70-87
1996 Benjamin	3,000	1997	40.00	85-125
1996 Flore	3,000	1997	40.00	200-250
1996 Golly Gosh	3,000	1997	40.00	150-225
1996 Panda	5,000	1999	40.00	75-100
1996 Peter	3,000	1997	40.00	95-200
1996 Sorry	5,000	1997	40.00	90-125

Nutcracker Suite - D. Canham, unless otherwise noted

YEAR ISSUE	EDITION LIMIT	YEAR RETD.	ISSUE PRICE	*QUOTE U.S.$
1997 Columbine	2,000	1998	52.00	100-175
1997 Harlequin	2,000	1999	52.00	53-75
1997 Magician	2,000	1999	52.00	53-60
1997 Nutcracker Prince - L. Sasaki	2,000	1999	52.00	53-60
1997 Rat King - B. Windell	2,000	1999	52.00	53-60
1997 Snowflake	2,000	1998	52.00	85-150
1997 Sugar Plum	2,000	1999	52.00	55-65

Out of Towners - D. Canham

YEAR ISSUE	EDITION LIMIT	YEAR RETD.	ISSUE PRICE	*QUOTE U.S.$
2000 Galaxy	1,500		60.00	60
1997 Gussie Galactica	1,000	1998	54.00	130-238
1997 Moonshine Cosmic	1,000	1998	54.00	180-238
2000 Star Bright	1,500		60.00	60
2000 Twinkle	1,500		60.00	60

Rainy Days Collection - D. Canham

YEAR ISSUE	EDITION LIMIT	YEAR RETD.	ISSUE PRICE	*QUOTE U.S.$
1997 Chuckles	2,000	1999	48.00	55-100
1997 Hattie	2,000	1998	48.00	70-100
1997 Herschel	2,000	1997	48.00	70-125
1997 Lady Ascot	2,000	1999	48.00	50-60
1997 Pilgrim	2,000	1998	48.00	75-90
1997 Sticky Bun	2,000		48.00	50

Specials - D. Canham

YEAR ISSUE	EDITION LIMIT	YEAR RETD.	ISSUE PRICE	*QUOTE U.S.$
1999 Billie	39	1999	60.00	300
1998 Button Jester	200	1998	60.00	130-175
2000 Christmas	1,200		60.00	60
1999 Clementine	400		60.00	60
2000 Coco	400		60.00	60
2000 Happy Chap	800		60.00	60
1999 Lulu	99	1999	60.00	60-200
2000 Myrtle (Camp Canham Bear)	200	2000	80.00	80
1999 Old Punch	20	1999	80.00	300
2000 Popsicle	400		60.00	60
2000 Rusty	500		60.00	60
2000 Snowy	1,200		60.00	60
1998 Swat	27	1999	80.00	350
2000 Titania & Puck (Disney)	150	2000	150.00	150
1999 Topper	Retrd.	1999	60.00	100-175
1998 Tulip	400	1998	54.00	130-175
1997 Uncle Ernie	700	1997	48.00	75-130
1999 Winnie the Pooh	500	1999	95.00	95-180

Department 56

Heritage Village Doll Collection - Department 56

YEAR ISSUE	EDITION LIMIT	YEAR RETD.	ISSUE PRICE	*QUOTE U.S.$
1987 Christmas Carol Dolls 1000-6 set/4 (Tiny Tim, Bob Crachet, Mrs. Crachet, Scrooge)	250	1988	1500.00	900-1100
1987 Christmas Carol Dolls 5907-2 set/4 (Tiny Tim, Bob Crachet, Mrs. Crachet, Scrooge)	Closed	1993	250.00	150-315
1988 Mr. & Mrs. Fezziwig 5594-8 set/2	Closed	1995	172.00	125-200

Snowbabies Dolls - Department 56

YEAR ISSUE	EDITION LIMIT	YEAR RETD.	ISSUE PRICE	*QUOTE U.S.$
1988 Allison & Duncan-Set of 2, 7730-5	Closed	1989	200.00	486-1025

Snowbabies Plush - Department 56

YEAR ISSUE	EDITION LIMIT	YEAR RETD.	ISSUE PRICE	*QUOTE U.S.$
2000 Frosty Frolic Friends-Penguin 69002	Open		15.00	15
2000 Frosty Frolic Friends-Polar Bear, large 69000	Open		20.00	20
2000 Frosty Frolic Friends-Polar Bear, small 69001	Open		15.00	15
2000 Frosty Frolic Friends-Sled Dog 69003	Open		15.00	15

Elke's Originals, Ltd.

Elke Hutchens - E. Hutchens

YEAR ISSUE	EDITION LIMIT	YEAR RETD.	ISSUE PRICE	*QUOTE U.S.$
1991 Alicia	250	N/A	595.00	700-995
1989 Annabelle	250	N/A	575.00	1400-1500
1990 Aubra	250	N/A	575.00	900-1050
1990 Aurora	250	N/A	595.00	900-1050
1991 Bellinda	400	N/A	595.00	1010
1992 Bethany	400	N/A	595.00	1050-1100
1991 Braelyn	400	N/A	595.00	1525
1991 Brianna	400	N/A	595.00	1500
1992 Cecilia	435	N/A	635.00	1050
1992 Charles	435	N/A	635.00	975
1992 Cherie	435	N/A	635.00	1050
1992 Clarissa	435	N/A	635.00	1050
1993 Daphne	435	N/A	675.00	700-850
1993 Deidre	435	N/A	675.00	795
1993 Desirée	435	N/A	675.00	700-900
1990 Kricket	500	N/A	575.00	400
1992 Laurakaye	435	N/A	550.00	875
1990 Little Liebchen	250	N/A	475.00	1000
1990 Victoria	500	N/A	645.00	870

G. DeBrekht Artistic Studios/Russian Gift & Jewelry

Matryoshka Memories Celebrations - G. DeBrekht Artistic Studios

YEAR ISSUE	EDITION LIMIT	YEAR RETD.	ISSUE PRICE	*QUOTE U.S.$
1998 Easter	Open		99.00	99
1998 Romantic	Open		130.00	130

Matryoshka Memories Childhood Memories - G. DeBrekht Artistic Studios

YEAR ISSUE	EDITION LIMIT	YEAR RETD.	ISSUE PRICE	*QUOTE U.S.$
1998 Angel	250		330.00	330
1998 Angel of Love 16075	300		250.00	250
1998 Childhood Play	250		300.00	300
1998 Children Always Playing	250		250.00	250
1998 Frog Princess	100		1100.00	1100
1998 Guardian Angel 16025	100		830.00	830
1998 Nutcracker 18017	100		270.00	270
1998 Nutcracker 18018	100		270.00	270
1998 Nutcracker DA-10/10N	50	1999	1590.00	1590
1998 Russian Fairy-Tales	300		390.00	390
1998 Winter Pleasure	100		270.00	270

Matryoshka Memories Family Dolls - G. DeBrekht Artistic Studios

YEAR ISSUE	EDITION LIMIT	YEAR RETD.	ISSUE PRICE	*QUOTE U.S.$
1998 Captain	Open		49.00	49
1998 Family Man C/PE-3N	Open		35.00	35
1998 Family Man C/PE-5N	Open		49.00	49
1998 Family Women	Open		30.00	30
1998 Girl	Open		49.00	49
1998 Grandma	Open		49.00	49
1998 Merchant	Open		49.00	49
1998 Musician Man	Open		49.00	49
1998 Snow Maiden	Open		49.00	49

Matryoshka Memories Four Season - G. DeBrekht Artistic Studios

YEAR ISSUE	EDITION LIMIT	YEAR RETD.	ISSUE PRICE	*QUOTE U.S.$
1998 Spring	500		130.00	130
1998 Summer	500		99.00	99
1998 Winter	500		130.00	130

Matryoshka Memories Holiday Surprises - G. DeBrekht Artistic Studios

YEAR ISSUE	EDITION LIMIT	YEAR RETD.	ISSUE PRICE	*QUOTE U.S.$
1998 Doll with Ornaments	Open		59.00	59
1998 Egg-Santa	Open		45.00	45
1998 Girl	Open		45.00	45
1998 Samovar	Open		35.00	35
1998 Santa with Ornament	Open		59.00	59
1998 Santa with Samovar	Open		33.00	33

Matryoshka Memories Musical Roly-Poly - G. DeBrekht Artistic Studios

YEAR ISSUE	EDITION LIMIT	YEAR RETD.	ISSUE PRICE	*QUOTE U.S.$
1998 Angel	Open		35.00	35
1998 Animals	Open		35.00	35
1998 Animals	Open		35.00	35
1998 Girl	Open		35.00	35
1998 Indian	Open		35.00	35
1998 Santa	Open		35.00	35

Matryoshka Memories Nested Wood Dolls - G. DeBrekht Artistic Studios

YEAR ISSUE	EDITION LIMIT	YEAR RETD.	ISSUE PRICE	*QUOTE U.S.$
1998 Frog Princess Fairy Tale, set/10	250		1100.00	1100
1998 Guardian Angel, set/10	250		830.00	830
1998 Guardian Angel, set/5	750		250.00	250
1998 Nutcracker, set/10	50	2000	1590.00	1590
1998 Village Holidays, set/6	250		300.00	300

Matryoshka Memories Roly-Poly Dolls - G. DeBrekht Artistic Studios

YEAR ISSUE	EDITION LIMIT	YEAR RETD.	ISSUE PRICE	*QUOTE U.S.$
1998 Nutcracker #1	100		270.00	270
1998 Nutcracker #2	100		270.00	270
1998 Royal Couple, set/2	500		90.00	90
1998 Snowman's Time	100		270.00	270

Matryoshka Memories Russian Elegance - G. DeBrekht Artistic Studios

YEAR ISSUE	EDITION LIMIT	YEAR RETD.	ISSUE PRICE	*QUOTE U.S.$
1998 Holiday	Open		300.00	300
1998 Snowmaiden	Open		300.00	300

Matryoshka Memories Russian Traditions - G. DeBrekht Artistic Studios

YEAR ISSUE	EDITION LIMIT	YEAR RETD.	ISSUE PRICE	*QUOTE U.S.$
1998 Babushka with Bird (5N)	Open		150.00	150
1998 Babushka with Cat (5N)	Open		150.00	150
1998 Babushka with Children (5N)	Open		150.00	150
1998 Babushka with Troika (10N)	500		590.00	590
1998 Ballet (5N)	Open		90.00	90
1998 Fairy-Tale (5N)	Open		40.00	40
1998 Kitty Cats (5N)	Open		150.00	150
1998 Musical Girls (5N)	Open		130.00	130
1998 Royalty	750		90.00	90
1998 Snowmaiden (5N)	Open		130.00	130

Matryoshka Memories Santa Dolls - G. DeBrekht Artistic Studios

YEAR ISSUE	EDITION LIMIT	YEAR RETD.	ISSUE PRICE	*QUOTE U.S.$
1998 All Santas CS/5N#2	Open		49.00	49
1998 Family Santa	Open		49.00	49
1998 Santa 6SC/5N-CT/SM	Open		11.00	11
1998 Santa 6SE/LG	Open		15.00	15
1998 Santa Cone/Shape	Open		29.00	29
1998 Santa CS/3N#1	Open		35.00	35
1998 Santa CS/3N#3-SM	Open		23.00	23
1998 Santa CS/3N#4-LG	Open		37.00	37
1998 Santa with Teddy Bear	Open		31.00	31

Matryoshka Memories Special Friends - G. DeBrekht Artistic Studios

YEAR ISSUE	EDITION LIMIT	YEAR RETD.	ISSUE PRICE	*QUOTE U.S.$
1998 Cat 1CAT/5N-MD	Open		35.00	35
1998 Cat E/CAT-5N	Open		35.00	35
1998 Doll with Rabbit, Cat, Pig	Open		27.00	27
1998 Fairy-Tale	Open		35.00	35
1998 Holiday	Open		35.00	35

Matryoshka Memories Timeless Faith - G. DeBrekht Artistic Studios

YEAR ISSUE	EDITION LIMIT	YEAR RETD.	ISSUE PRICE	*QUOTE U.S.$
1998 Icon Doll D-21/5N	Open		150.00	150
1998 Icon Doll D-21/5N#2	Open		150.00	150

Matryoshka Memories Toy - G. DeBrekht Artistic Studios

YEAR ISSUE	EDITION LIMIT	YEAR RETD.	ISSUE PRICE	*QUOTE U.S.$
1998 Floral	Open		35.00	35
1998 Girl with Cats	2-Yr.		130.00	130
1998 Squirrel	2-Yr.		130.00	130
1998 Unusual	Open		55.00	55

Matryoshka Memories Toy Land - G. DeBrekht Artistic Studios

YEAR ISSUE	EDITION LIMIT	YEAR RETD.	ISSUE PRICE	*QUOTE U.S.$
1998 Abramtsevo	Open		99.00	99
1998 Girls & Boys	Open		130.00	130

*Quotes have been rounded up to nearest dollar

YEAR ISSUE	EDITION LIMIT	YEAR RETD.	ISSUE PRICE	*QUOTE U.S.$
1998 Santa with Children	3-Yr.		130.00	130
1998 Teddy Bear	3-Yr.		130.00	130

Gene/Ashton-Drake Galleries

Gene Accessories - J. Greene, unless otherwise noted

YEAR ISSUE	EDITION LIMIT	YEAR RETD.	ISSUE PRICE	*QUOTE U.S.$
1999 Birthday Accessory Set 76079 - N/A	Open		29.95	30
2000 Chaise Lounge 94661 - N/A	Open		74.95	75
1999 Director's Chair 76080 - N/A	Open		29.95	30
1996 Dress Form 94390	Open		19.95	20
1999 Dresser 76073 - N/A	Open		79.95	80
1999 Gene Patio Set 94679 - N/A	Open		49.95	50
2000 Gene's Croquet Set 76406 - D. Gibbons	Open		29.95	30
2000 Gene's Dressing Screen 92937 - N/A	Open		44.95	45
2000 Gene's Gazebo 92259 - N/A	Open		44.95	45
1999 Gene's Jewelry Set 92938 - N/A	Open		34.95	35
1999 Gene's Paper Doll Set #1 92931 - N/A	Open		12.95	13
1999 Gene's Paper Doll Set #2 92932 - N/A	Open		12.95	13
1999 Gene's Paper Doll Set #3 92933 - N/A	Open		12.95	13
1996 Gene's Trunk 93504	Open		69.95	70
2000 Gene's Wardrobe Rack 92256 - N/A	Open		44.95	45
2000 Hanger Set 76156 - N/A	Open		14.95	15
2000 Hat Stand 92255 - N/A	Open		14.95	15
2000 Hat/Purse Set #1 92940 - M. Tibbitts	Open		44.95	45
2000 Hat/Purse Set #2 92255 - M. Tibbitts	Open		44.95	45
2000 Hat/Purse Set #3 96314 - M. Tibbitts	Open		44.95	45
2000 Hat/Purse Set #4 96319 - M. Tibbitts	Open		44.95	45
2000 Hearts and Flowers 92939 - E. Foran	Open		34.95	35
1997 Hot Day in Hollywood 93548	Open		34.95	35
1999 Mirror 94678 - N/A	Open		19.95	20
1997 Out For a Stroll 93547 - E. Foran	Open		29.95	30
1999 Panther Lamp 94671 - N/A	Open		34.95	35
1999 Picnic Basket 76072 - N/A	Open		34.95	35
2000 Shoe Set #1 96317 - E. Foran	Open		19.95	20
2000 Shoe Set #2 96318 - E. Foran	Open		19.95	20
1999 Swan Bed 76087 - N/A	Open		89.95	90
2000 Swan Lamp 93322 - D. Gibbons	Open		49.95	50
2000 Undercover Story (Lingerie) 96316 - N/A	Open		29.95	30
1999 USO Accessory Pack 94677 - N/A	Open		34.95	35
1997 White Christmas 94398	Open		44.95	45

Gene Costumed Dolls by Mel Odom - Various

YEAR ISSUE	EDITION LIMIT	YEAR RETD.	ISSUE PRICE	*QUOTE U.S.$
1999 An American Countess (Parkwest /NALED Exclusive) 76082 - C. Curtis	Retrd.	1999	99.95	100-120
1997 Bird of Paradise 94397 - W. Long	Retrd.	1999	79.95	80
1996 Blue Goddess 93503 - T. Kennedy	Retrd.	1999	69.95	70
2000 Bon Voyage (Star Dealer Exclusive) 92266 - J. Ferrand	3,500		99.95	100
1999 Breathless (Retailer Exclusive) (YDA Winner) 76074 - S. Bruner	9,999	1999	99.95	100-110
1998 Broadway Medley (Convention Exclusive) 94665 - T. Kennedy	800	1998	N/A	350-695
1998 Champagne Supper 94662 - T. Kennedy	Open		79.95	80
1998 Covent Garden (Parkwest/NALED Exclusive) 94664 - T. Kennedy	Closed	1998	99.95	100-120
1998 Crème de Cassis 94685 - T. Alberts	Retrd.	1999	79.95	80-90
2000 Dance With Me 76154 - L. Day	5,000		84.95	85
1998 Daughter of the Nile 94667 - T. Alberts	Retrd.	2000	79.95	80-100
1998 Destiny (YDA Winner) 94656 - M. Esposito	Yr.Iss	1998	89.95	90-120
2000 Encore (Retailer Exclusive) 76529 - L. Day	5,000		99.95	100
2000 Heart of Hollywood (Parkwest/NALED Exclusive) 96376 - V. Nowell	3,500		99.95	100
1998 Hello Hollywood, Hello 94657 - D. James	Open		79.95	80
2000 I Do 96371 - T. Kennedy	5,000		84.95	85
1997 Iced Coffee 94396 - L. Meisner	Retrd.	1999	79.95	80
1998 Incognito 94659 - T. Alberts	Open		79.95	80
1997 The King's Daughter (Retailer Exclusive) (YDA Winner) 93525 - M. Gutierrez	5,000	1997	99.95	300-381
2000 Love At First Sight 76528 - D. Cipolla	5,000		84.95	85
1999 Love, Paris 76063 - J. Ferrand	Retrd.	2000	79.95	80-90
1999 Lucky Stripe 93529 - T. Kennedy	Open		79.95	80
2000 Meet Me In Paris (Paris Convention Doll) 93329 - V. Nowell	Closed	2000	N/A	N/A
1998 Midnight Gamble (Retailer Exclusive) 94666 - D. James	9,500	1998	99.95	100-130
1997 Midnight Romance (Parkwest/NALED Exclusive) 93550 - T. Alberts	Closed	1997	89.95	165-325
1995 Monaco 96403 - T. Alberts	Retrd.	1997	69.95	145-195
1999 Mood Music (Convention Exclusive) 76083 - L. Day	Closed	1999	N/A	N/A
1997 My Favorite Witch (Convention Exclusive) 93549 - T. Kennedy	350	1997	N/A	675-1500
1997 A Night At Versailles (FAO Schwarz Exclusive) 93551 - T. Alberts	5,000	1997	90.00	210-300
1998 On The Avenue (FAO Schwarz Spring Exclusive) 94668 - T. Kennedy	5,000	1998	90.00	213-250
1996 Pin-Up 93507 - T. Kennedy	Retrd.	1999	69.95	70-90
1995 Premiere 96401 - T. Kennedy	Retrd.	1996	69.95	700-800
1999 Priceless (FAO Schwarz Exclusive) 76081 - J. Ferrand	Retrd.	1999	110.00	110
1995 Red Venus 96402 - T. Kennedy	Open		69.95	70
1999 Savannah (YDA Winner) 76064 - K. McHale	Open		79.95	80
1999 She'd Rather Dance 76062 - T. Kennedy	Open		79.95	80
2000 Shooting Star 76402 - D. James	5,000		84.95	85
1999 Simply Gene (blond) 93527	Open		49.95	50
1999 Simply Gene (brunette) 93528	Open		49.95	50
2000 Simply Gene (platinum) 76157 - J. Greene	Open		54.95	55
1999 Simply Gene (red) 93526	Open		49.95	50
1999 Song of Spain 76065 - T. Kennedy	Yr.Iss.	1999	99.95	100
1997 Sparkling Seduction (YDA Winner) 94394 - S. Rinker	Open		79.95	80
2000 Spotted In The Park (FAO Exclusive) (YDA Winner) 93326 - V. Alvarado	3,500		99.95	100
2000 Symphony In G (Ashton-Drake Galleries Exclusive) (YDA Winner} 96379 - T. Butts	Open		99.95	100
1999 Tea Time (FAO Schwarz Exclusive) 76066 - L. Day	Closed	1999	100.00	100
2000 Twilight Rumba 93325 - D. James	Yr.Iss.		99.95	100
1999 Unforgettable (Ashton-Drake Galleries Exclusive) 76075 - D. Cipolla	Open		99.95	100
1999 USO 76061 - D. James	Open		79.95	80
1998 Warmest Wishes (FOA Schwarz Fall Exclusive) 94663 - T. Kennedy	Closed	1998	110.00	155
1997 White Hyacinth 94395 - D. James	Retrd.	1998	79.95	80-155

Gene Costumes - Various

YEAR ISSUE	EDITION LIMIT	YEAR RETD.	ISSUE PRICE	*QUOTE U.S.$
1996 Afternoon Off 93508 - D. James	Retrd.	1998	29.95	50-75
1999 At Home For The Holidays (Retailer Exclusive) 76084 - T. Kennedy	9,999	1999	49.95	50
1996 Atlantic City Beauty (Convention Exclusive) 94393 - D. James	250	1996	N/A	800-1250
1999 Avant Garde 76085 - J. Ferrand	Open		39.95	40
2000 Baking Cookies 76239 - T. Kennedy	5,000		34.95	35
1999 Black Ribbon 76088 - T. Kennedy	Open		39.95	40
1995 Blonde Lace 96404 - T. Kennedy	Retrd.	1998	29.95	30-70
1997 Blossoms in the Snow (Retailer Exclusive) 93544 - T. Kennedy	5,000	1997	44.95	125-200
1995 Blue Evening 96409 - T. Alberts	Retrd.	1999	29.95	30-60
2000 Bolera (YDA Winner) 76407 - D. Trejo	5,000		39.95	40
1999 Bridge Club 76069 - V. Nowell	Open		34.95	35
1998 Cameo (YDA Winner) 94655 - K. Johnson	Open		29.95	30
1999 Cognac Evening 76086 - J. Ferrand	Open		44.95	45
1996 Crescendo 93505 - D. James	Open		39.95	40
1995 Crimson Sun 93502 - D. James	Retrd.	1999	29.95	30-60
2000 Croquet Anyone? 76526 - L. Day	5,000		34.95	35
2000 Don't Fence Me In 76403 - V. Nowell	5,000		34.95	35
1996 El Morocco 93506 - T. Alberts	Retrd.	2000	29.95	30-35
1998 Embassy Luncheon 94652 - L. Meisner	Open		39.95	40
1999 Farewell, Golden Moon 76067 - T. Kennedy	Open		44.95	45
2000 First Close Up 76524 - T. Kennedy	5,000		39.95	40
2000 First Stop Chicago 76522 - L. Day	5,000		44.95	45
1998 Forget Me Not 94653 - T. Alberts	Open		39.95	40
2000 Friendly Connection (Ashton-Drake Galleries Exclusive) 76155 - G. Sarofeen	2,500		39.95	40
1995 Goodbye New York 93501 - D. James	Open		34.95	35
2000 Hacienda 76408 - L. Day	5,000		44.95	45
2000 Hearts Afire 76404 - L. Day	5,000		44.95	45
1998 Hi Fi 94669 - D. James	Open		34.95	35
1996 Holiday Magic (Retailer Exclusive) 94392 - T. Kennedy	2,000	1996	44.95	360-395
1999 Honeymoon 93524 - J. Ferrand	Open		44.95	45
2000 It's A Wrap 76274 - T. Kennedy	5,000		32.95	33
2000 Jazz Note 76273 - D. Cipolla	5,000		44.95	45
1995 The Kiss 96410 - T. Kennedy	Open		29.95	30
2000 Kiss Me, Gene 76271 - L. Day	5,000		44.95	45
2000 The Little Black Dress 93328 - T. Kennedy	5,000		49.95	50
1998 Love After Hours 94658 - T. Kennedy	Open		34.95	35
2000 Love Letters 93327 - J. Ferrand	5,000		39.95	40
1995 Love's Ghost 96406 - D. James	Open		29.95	30
1997 Mandarin Mood 93543 - T. Kennedy	Retrd.	1999	34.95	35
1998 Midnight Angel (YDA Winner) 94674 - N. Burke	Open		39.95	40
1998 My Favorite Bow 94686 - T. Kennedy	Retrd.	2000	39.95	40
1999 On The Veranda (NALED Exclusive) 76071 - L. Day	Closed	1999	49.95	50
2000 The Perfect Gift (YDA Winner) 92269 - R. Ganem	5,000		44.95	45
1997 Personal Secretary 93542 - T. Kennedy	Open		34.95	35
1999 Picnic In The Country 76077 - L. Day	Retrd.	2000	39.95	40
1995 Pink Lightening 96405 - T. Kennedy	Retrd.	1998	29.95	35-55
1999 Poolside 76078 - V. Nowell	Open		34.95	35
1999 Press Conference 76068 - D. Cipolla	Open		44.95	45
1997 Promenade 93541 - T. Kennedy	Retrd.	1998	29.95	30-50
1998 Rain Song 94675 - D. James	Open		29.95	30
1998 Ransom in Red (Retailer Exclusive) 94676 - T. Kennedy	7,500	1998	44.95	45-65
1998 Safari 94673 - T. Alberts	Open		39.95	40
1997 Sea Spree 93546 - T. Kennedy	Retrd.	1999	34.95	35
1999 Secret Sleuth 93523 - T. Kennedy	Open		39.95	40
2000 Shorts Story 76234 - V. Nowell	5,000		32.95	33
1998 Smart Set 94687 - D. James	Open		39.95	40
1999 Somewhere Summer 93522 - T. Kennedy	Open		44.95	45
2000 Spellbound (Retailer Exclusive) 76235 - T. Kennedy	5,000		44.95	45
2000 The Spirit of Truth (YDA Winner) 96313 - E. Machnica	5,000		44.95	45
2000 St. Moritz 92257 - L. Day	5,000		49.95	50
1999 Stand Up and Cheer 76070 - D. Cipolla	Open		44.95	45
1995 Striking Gold 96407 - T. Alberts	Retrd.	1998	29.95	30-55
1999 Sunday Afternoon (YDA Winner) 93521 - A. Haskell	Open		39.95	40
1999 Sunset Celebration 76076 - V. Nowell	Open		39.95	40
2000 Table For Two 93145 - J. Ferrand	5,000		34.95	35
1997 Tango 93545 - T. Kennedy	Retrd.	2000	39.95	40
1995 Usherette 96408 - T. Kennedy	Open		29.95	30
2000 Will You Marry Me? 96372 - G. Sarofeen	5,000		44.95	45

Madra Accessories - D. Gibbons

YEAR ISSUE	EDITION LIMIT	YEAR RETD.	ISSUE PRICE	*QUOTE U.S.$
2000 Madra's Dogs 92258 - D. Gibbons	Open		44.95	45

Madra Costumed Dolls by Mel Odom - Various

YEAR ISSUE	EDITION LIMIT	YEAR RETD.	ISSUE PRICE	*QUOTE U.S.$
2000 Black Widow 96312 - L. Day/J. Greene	2,500		125.00	125
2000 First Encounter 96311 - C. Curtis	Open		110.00	110

Madra Costumes - Various

YEAR ISSUE	EDITION LIMIT	YEAR RETD.	ISSUE PRICE	*QUOTE U.S.$
2000 Cat Walk 92285 - J. Ferrand	Open		39.95	40
2000 Devil May Care 92287 - L. Day	Open		49.95	50
2000 Dressed To Kill 92268 - T. Kennedy	Open		44.95	45
2000 Heartless 92288 - T. Kennedy	Open		44.95	45
2000 Highland Fling 92267 - T. Kennedy	3,500		59.95	60
2000 Pink With Envy 92286 - B. Lange	Open		44.95	45
2000 So Evil My Love 92289 - T. Kennedy	Open		49.95	50

Georgetown Collection, Inc./Ashton-Drake Galleries

Age of Romance - J. Reavey

YEAR ISSUE	EDITION LIMIT	YEAR RETD.	ISSUE PRICE	*QUOTE U.S.$
1994 Catherine	Closed	1998	150.00	150

American Diary Dolls - L. Mason

YEAR ISSUE	EDITION LIMIT	YEAR RETD.	ISSUE PRICE	*QUOTE U.S.$
1991 Bridget Quinn	Closed	1996	129.25	130
1991 Christina Merovina	Closed	1996	129.25	130
1990 Jennie Cooper	Closed	1996	129.25	130-155
1994 Lian Ying	Closed	1996	130.00	130
1991 Many Stars	Open		129.25	130
1992 Rachel Williams	Closed	1996	129.25	130
1993 Sarah Turner	Closed	1996	130.00	130
1992 Tulu	100-day		129.25	130

Baby Kisses - T. DeHetre

YEAR ISSUE	EDITION LIMIT	YEAR RETD.	ISSUE PRICE	*QUOTE U.S.$
1992 Michelle	Closed	1996	118.60	119

Blessed Are The Children - J. Reavey

YEAR ISSUE	EDITION LIMIT	YEAR RETD.	ISSUE PRICE	*QUOTE U.S.$
1994 Faith	Closed	2000	83.00	83

Boys Will Be Boys - J. Reavey

YEAR ISSUE	EDITION LIMIT	YEAR RETD.	ISSUE PRICE	*QUOTE U.S.$
1996 Just Like Dad	Closed	2000	96.00	96
1994 Mr. Mischief	100-day		96.00	96
1997 Tyler	100-day		96.80	97

Caught in the Act - J. Reavey

YEAR ISSUE	EDITION LIMIT	YEAR RETD.	ISSUE PRICE	*QUOTE U.S.$
1997 Nicholas	Closed	1998	115.00	121

Children of Main St. - G. Braun

YEAR ISSUE	EDITION LIMIT	YEAR RETD.	ISSUE PRICE	*QUOTE U.S.$
1996 Alice	Closed	2000	130.00	130
1997 Sara	Closed	2000	131.00	131

Children of the Great Spirit - C. Theroux

YEAR ISSUE	EDITION LIMIT	YEAR RETD.	ISSUE PRICE	*QUOTE U.S.$
1993 Buffalo Child	100-day		140.00	140
1994 Golden Flower	Closed	2000	130.00	130
1994 Little Fawn	Closed	1997	114.00	114
1993 Winter Baby	Closed	1997	160.00	160

The Christening Day - J. Reavey

YEAR ISSUE	EDITION LIMIT	YEAR RETD.	ISSUE PRICE	*QUOTE U.S.$
1998 Jasmine	100-day		131.00	131

Class Portraits - J. Kissling

YEAR ISSUE	EDITION LIMIT	YEAR RETD.	ISSUE PRICE	*QUOTE U.S.$
1995 Anna	Closed	1997	140.00	140

The Cottage Garden - P. Phillips

YEAR ISSUE	EDITION LIMIT	YEAR RETD.	ISSUE PRICE	*QUOTE U.S.$
1996 Emily	Closed	2000	131.00	131

Counting Our Blessings - N/A

YEAR ISSUE	EDITION LIMIT	YEAR RETD.	ISSUE PRICE	*QUOTE U.S.$
1998 Tama	100-day		121.00	121

Country Quilt Babies - B. Prusseit

YEAR ISSUE	EDITION LIMIT	YEAR RETD.	ISSUE PRICE	*QUOTE U.S.$
1996 Hannah	Closed	1998	104.00	104

Cultures of the World - M. Aldred

YEAR ISSUE	EDITION LIMIT	YEAR RETD.	ISSUE PRICE	*QUOTE U.S.$
1998 Maya	100-day		131.00	131

Dreams Come True - M. Sirko

YEAR ISSUE	EDITION LIMIT	YEAR RETD.	ISSUE PRICE	*QUOTE U.S.$
1995 Amanda	Closed	1996	120.00	120

Enchanted Garden - S. Blythe

YEAR ISSUE	EDITION LIMIT	YEAR RETD.	ISSUE PRICE	*QUOTE U.S.$
1998 Floral Whimsies	100-day		94.50	95

Enchanted Nursery - S. Lekven

YEAR ISSUE	EDITION LIMIT	YEAR RETD.	ISSUE PRICE	*QUOTE U.S.$
1998 Aria	100-day		131.00	131

Faerie Princess - B. Deval

YEAR ISSUE	EDITION LIMIT	YEAR RETD.	ISSUE PRICE	*QUOTE U.S.$
1989 Faerie Princess	Closed	1996	248.00	248

Fanciful Dreamers - A. Timmerman

YEAR ISSUE	EDITION LIMIT	YEAR RETD.	ISSUE PRICE	*QUOTE U.S.$
1995 Sweetdreams & Moonbeams	Closed	1997	130.00	130

Faraway Friends - S. Skille

YEAR ISSUE	EDITION LIMIT	YEAR RETD.	ISSUE PRICE	*QUOTE U.S.$
1994 Dara	Closed	2000	140.00	140
1993 Kristin	Closed	1996	140.00	140

*Quotes have been rounded up to nearest dollar

YEAR ISSUE	EDITION LIMIT	YEAR RETD.	ISSUE PRICE	*QUOTE U.S.$
1994 Mariama	100-day		140.00	140
Favorite Friends - K. Murawska				
1997 Brittany	100-day		131.00	131
1995 Christina	100-day		130.00	130
1996 Samantha	100-day		130.00	130
Friendships of the Heart - P. Erff				
1998 Kari & Danielle	100-day		156.00	156
Fuzzy Friends - A. DiMartino				
1996 Sandy & Sam	Closed	2000	130.00	130
Georgetown Collection - Various				
1995 Buffalo Boy - C. Theroux	Open		130.00	130
1993 Quick Fox - L. Mason	Closed	1996	138.95	139
1994 Silver Moon - L. Mason	100-day		140.00	140
Gifts From Heaven - B. Prusseit				
1994 Good as Gold	Closed	1998	88.00	88
1995 Sweet Pea	Closed	2000	88.00	88
Gifts of Endearment - J. Reavey				
1997 Katie	100-day		115.00	115
Hearts in Song - J. Galperin				
1994 Angelique	100-day		150.00	150
1992 Grace	100-day		149.60	150
1993 Michael	Closed	2000	150.00	150
Heavenly Messages - M. Sirko				
1996 David	100-day		104.00	104
1995 Gabrielle	Closed	1997	104.00	104
Hidden Realms - S. Lekven				
1998 Brianna	100-day		153.50	154
A House Just For Me - G. Braun				
1998 Anne	100-day		156.00	156
I Love It - K. Murawska				
1998 Jamila	100-day		131.00	131
Irish Traditions - L. Mason				
1998 Kathleen	100-day		151.00	151
Kindergarten Kids - V. Walker				
1992 Nikki	Closed	1996	129.60	130
Let There Be Light - K. Murawska				
1997 Charlotte	100-day		130.00	130
Let's Play - T. DeHetre				
1992 Eentsy Weentsy Willie	Closed	1996	118.60	119
1992 Peek-A-Boo Beckie	Closed	1996	118.60	119
Linda's Little Ladies - L. Mason				
1993 Shannon's Holiday	Closed	1997	169.95	170
Little Artists of Africa - C. Massey				
1997 Little Ashanti Weaver	100-day		125.00	125
1996 Oluwa Fumike	Closed	2000	131.00	131
Little Bit of Heaven - A. Timmerman				
1996 Adriana	Closed	2000	135.00	135
1994 Arielle	100-day		130.00	130
1995 Cupid	Closed	2000	135.00	135
1995 Noelle	100-day		130.00	130
Little Bloomers - J. Reavey				
1995 Darling Daisy	Closed	1997	99.00	99
Little Dreamers - A. DiMartino				
1994 Beautiful Buttercup	Closed	2000	130.00	130
1995 Julie	Closed	1997	130.00	130
1996 Nicole	Closed	2000	130.00	130
Little Loves - B. Deval				
1988 Emma	Closed	1996	139.20	140
1989 Katie	Closed	1996	139.20	140
1990 Laura	Closed	1996	139.20	140
1989 Megan	Closed	1996	138.00	160
Little Performers - M. Sirko				
1996 Tickled Pink	Closed	1997	100.00	100
Little Sweethearts - J. Reavey				
1997 Melanie & Michael	Closed	2000	152.50	153
Loving Moments - J. Reavey				
1998 A Hug Just Because	Closed	2000	181.00	181
Maud Humphrey's Little Victorians - M. Humphrey				
1996 Papa's Little Sailor	Closed	2000	130.00	130
Messengers of the Great Spirit - Various				
1994 Noatak - L. Mason	Closed	2000	150.00	150
1994 Prayer for the Buffalo - C. Theroux	Closed	2000	120.00	120
Miss Ashley - P. Thompson				
1989 Miss Ashley	Closed	1996	228.00	228
Mommy's World - A. Hollis				
1996 Julia	100-day		136.00	136
Moody Cuties - L. Randolph				
1997 Cece	100-day		130.00	130
1998 Tasha	100-day		136.00	136

YEAR ISSUE	EDITION LIMIT	YEAR RETD.	ISSUE PRICE	*QUOTE U.S.$
My Hero - C. Joniak				
1998 Matthew	Closed	2000	105.00	105
Naturally Curious Kids - A. Hollis				
1996 Jennifer	Closed	1997	100.00	100
Nursery Babies - T. DeHetre				
1990 Baby Bunting	Closed	1996	118.20	150
1991 Diddle, Diddle	Closed	1996	118.20	119
1991 Little Girl	Closed	1996	118.20	119
1990 Patty Cake	Closed	1996	118.20	119
1991 Rock-A-Bye Baby	Closed	1996	118.20	119
1991 This Little Piggy	Closed	1996	118.20	119
Nutcracker Sweethearts - S. Skille				
1995 Sugar Plum	Closed	2000	130.00	130
The Old Country - L. Mason				
1998 Elsa	100-day		136.00	136
Pictures of Innocence - J. Reavey				
1994 Clarissa	Closed	1997	135.00	135
Portraits From the Bible - T. Francirek				
1998 Madonna & Child	100-day		156.00	156
Portraits of a Perfect World - A. Timmerman				
1997 Cherry Pie	100-day		136.00	136
1998 Lemon Drop	100-day		136.00	136
1997 Orange Blossom	100-day		136.00	136
Portraits of Enchantment - A. Timmerman				
1996 Sleeping Beauty	Closed	2000	150.00	150
Portraits of Perfection - A. Timmerman				
1993 Apple Dumpling	100-day		149.60	150
1994 Blackberry Blossom	Closed	2000	149.60	150
1993 Peaches & Cream	100-day		149.60	150
1993 Sweet Strawberry	Closed	2000	149.60	150
Prayers From The Heart - S. Skille				
1995 Hope	Closed	1997	115.00	115
Proud Moments - P. Erff				
1996 Chelsea	100-day		126.00	126
Reflections of Childhood - L. Mason				
1996 Courtney	Closed	1997	152.50	153
Russian Fairy Tales Dolls - B. Deval				
1993 Vasilisa	Closed	N/A	190.00	190
Small Wonders - B. Deval				
1991 Abbey	Closed	1996	97.60	98
1990 Corey	Closed	1996	97.60	98
1992 Sarah	Closed	1996	97.60	98
A Song in My Heart - J. Reavey				
1998 Caitlyn	100-day		121.00	121
Songs of Innocence - J. Reavey				
1997 Andy	Closed	2000	99.00	99
1996 Eric	Closed	2000	105.00	105
1995 Kelsey	Closed	2000	104.00	104
1996 Meagan	Closed	2000	104.00	104
Sugar & Spice - L. Mason				
1992 Little Sunshine	Closed	1996	141.10	142
1991 Little Sweetheart	Closed	1996	118.25	119
1991 Red Hot Pepper	Closed	1996	118.25	119
Sweethearts of Summer - P. Phillips				
1997 Ashley	Closed	2000	135.00	135
1994 Caroline	Closed	2000	140.00	140
1995 Jessica	Closed	2000	140.00	140
1995 Madeleine & Harry	Closed	2000	140.00	140
Sweets For the Sweet - V. Ohms				
1996 Elise	Closed	2000	130.00	130
Tansie - P. Coffer				
1988 Tansie	Closed	1996	81.00	81
Victorian Fantasies - L. Mason				
1995 Amber Afternoon	Closed	2000	150.00	150
1997 Emerald Memories	100-day		145.00	145
1995 Lavender Dreams	Closed	2000	150.00	150
1996 Reflections of Rose	Closed	2000	150.00	150
Victorian Innocence - L. Mason				
1994 Annabelle	100-day		130.00	130
Victorian Splendor - J. Reavey				
1994 Emily	100-day		130.00	130
Warm Hearts in Winter - L. Mason				
1997 Claire	100-day		145.00	145
Warm World - A. Hollis				
1997 Alison & Angus	100-day		140.00	140
The Wedding Day - S. Sauer				
1997 Elizabeth	100-day		121.00	121
What a Beautiful World - R. Hockh				
1996 Marisa	100-day		130.00	130
1996 Mora	100-day		126.00	126
1996 Therese & Tino	100-day		155.00	155

YEAR ISSUE	EDITION LIMIT	YEAR RETD.	ISSUE PRICE	*QUOTE U.S.$
Wings of Love - L. Randolph				
1998 Angel Dreams	100-day		105.00	105
1998 Angel Hugs	100-day		105.00	105
1997 Angel Kisses	100-day		125.00	125
Yesterday's Dreams - P. Phillips				
1994 Mary Elizabeth	100-day		130.00	130
1996 Sophie	100-day		130.00	130

Goebel of North America

YEAR ISSUE	EDITION LIMIT	YEAR RETD.	ISSUE PRICE	*QUOTE U.S.$
Bob Timberlake Dolls - B. Ball				
1996 Abby Liz 911350	2,000	1997	195.00	195
1996 Ann 911352	2,000	1997	195.00	195
1996 Carter 911351	2,000	1997	195.00	195
1996 Kate 911353	2,000	1997	195.00	195
Cindy Guyer Romance Dolls - B. Ball				
1996 Cordelia 911824	1,000	1997	225.00	225
1996 Cynthia 911830	1,000	1997	225.00	225
1996 Mackenzie 911825	1,000	1997	225.00	225
Dolly Dingle - B. Ball				
1995 Melvis Bumps 911617	1,000	1997	99.00	99
Goebel Dolls - B. Ball				
1995 Brother Murphy 911100	2,000	1997	125.00	125
Hummel Dolls - B. Ball				
1998 Apple Tree Boy 911213	N/A		250.00	250
1998 Apple Tree Girl 911214	N/A		250.00	250
1998 Kiss Me 911216	N/A		200.00	200
1996 Little Scholar, 14" 911211	N/A		200.00	200
1997 School Girl, 14" 911212	N/A		200.00	200
Hummel Dolls - Goebel				
1998 Ride Into Christmas 911215	Open		195.00	195
United States Historical Society - B. Ball				
1995 Mary-911155	1,500	1997	195.00	195
Victoria Ashlea® Birthstone Dolls - K. Kennedy				
1995 January-Garnet-912471	2,500	1996	29.50	30
1995 February-Amethyst-912472	2,500	1996	29.50	30
1995 March-Aquamarine-912473	2,500	1996	29.50	30
1995 April-Diamond-912474	2,500	1996	29.50	30
1995 May-Emerald-912475	2,500	1996	29.50	30
1995 June -Lt. Amethyst-912476	2,500	1996	29.50	30
1995 July-Ruby-912477	2,500	1996	29.50	30
1995 August-Peridot-912478	2,500	1996	29.50	30
1995 September-Sapphire-912479	2,500	1996	29.50	30
1995 October-Rosestone-912480	2,500	1996	29.50	30
1995 November-Topaz-912481	2,500	1996	29.50	30
1995 December-Zircon-912482	2,500	1996	29.50	30
Victoria Ashlea® Originals - B. Ball, unless otherwise noted				
1985 Adele-901172	Closed	1989	145.00	275
1989 Alexa-912214	Closed	1991	195.00	195
1989 Alexandria-912273	Closed	1991	275.00	275
1987 Alice-901212	Closed	1991	95.00	135
1990 Alice-912296 - K. Kennedy	Closed	1992	65.00	65
1992 Alicia-912388	500	1994	135.00	135
1992 Allison-912358	Closed	1993	160.00	165
1987 Amanda Pouty-901209	Closed	1991	150.00	215
1988 Amanda-912246	Closed	1991	180.00	180
1993 Amanda-912409	2,000	1995	40.00	40
1984 Amelia-933006	Closed	1988	100.00	100
1990 Amie-912313 - K. Kennedy	Closed	1991	150.00	150
1990 Amy-901262	Closed	1993	110.00	110
1990 Angela-912324 - K. Kennedy	Closed	1994	130.00	135
1988 Angelica-912204	Closed	1991	150.00	150
1992 Angelica-912339	1,000	1995	145.00	145
1990 Annabelle-912278	Closed	1992	200.00	200
1988 Anne-912213	Closed	1991	130.00	150
1990 Annette-912333 - K. Kennedy	Closed	1993	85.00	85
1988 April-901239	Closed	1992	225.00	225
1989 Ashlea-901250	Closed	1992	550.00	550
1988 Ashley-901235	Closed	1991	110.00	110
1992 Ashley-911004	Closed	1994	99.00	105
1986 Ashley-912147	Closed	1989	125.00	125
1986 Baby Brook Beige Dress-912103	Closed	1989	60.00	60
1986 Baby Courtney-912124	Closed	1990	120.00	120
1988 Baby Daryl-912200	Closed	1991	85.00	85
1987 Baby Doll-912184	Closed	1990	75.00	75
1988 Baby Jennifer-912210	Closed	1992	75.00	75
1988 Baby Katie-912222	Closed	1993	70.00	70
1986 Baby Lauren Pink-912086	Closed	1991	120.00	120
1987 Baby Lindsay-912190	Closed	1990	80.00	80
1984 Barbara-901108	Closed	1987	57.00	110
1990 Baryshnicat-912298 - K. Kennedy	Closed	1991	25.00	25
1988 Bernice-901245	Closed	1991	90.00	90
1993 Beth-912430 - K. Kennedy	2,000	1996	45.00	45
1992 Betsy-912390	500	1994	150.00	150
1990 Bettina-912310	Closed	1993	100.00	105
1988 Betty Doll-912220	Closed	1993	90.00	90
1987 Bonnie Pouty-901207	Closed	1992	100.00	100
1988 Brandon-901234	Closed	1992	90.00	90
1990 Brandy-912304 - K. Kennedy	Closed	1992	150.00	150
1987 Bride Allison-901218	Closed	1993	180.00	180
1988 Brittany-912207	Closed	1990	130.00	145
1992 Brittany-912365 - K. Kennedy	Closed	1993	140.00	145
1987 Caitlin-901228	Closed	1991	260.00	260
1988 Campbell Kid-Boy-758701	Closed	1988	13.80	14
1988 Campbell Kid-Girl-758700	Closed	1988	13.80	14

*Quotes have been rounded up to nearest dollar

YEAR ISSUE	EDITION LIMIT	YEAR RETD.	ISSUE PRICE	*QUOTE U.S.$
1989 Candace-912288 - K. Kennedy	Closed	1992	70.00	70
1992 Carol-912387 - K. Kennedy	1,000	1996	140.00	140
1987 Caroline-912191	Closed	1990	80.00	80
1990 Carolyn-901261 - K. Kennedy	Closed	1993	200.00	200
1992 Cassandra-912355 - K. Kennedy	1,000	1996	165.00	165
1988 Cat Maude-901247	Closed	1993	85.00	85
1986 Cat/Kitty Cheerful Gr Dr-901179	Closed	1990	60.00	60
1987 Catanova-901227	Closed	1991	75.00	75
1988 Catherine-901242	Closed	1992	240.00	240
XX Charity-912244	Closed	1990	70.00	70
1982 Charleen-912094	Closed	1986	65.00	65
1985 Chauncey-912085	Closed	1988	75.00	110
1988 Christina-901229	Closed	1991	350.00	400
1987 Christine-912168	Closed	1989	75.00	75
1992 Cindy-912384	1,000	1994	185.00	190
1985 Claire-901158	Closed	1988	115.00	160
1984 Claude-901032	Closed	1987	110.00	225
1984 Claudette-901033	Closed	1987	110.00	225
1989 Claudia-901257 - K. Kennedy	Closed	1993	225.00	225
1987 Clementine-901226	Closed	1991	75.00	75
1986 Clown Calypso-912104	Closed	1990	70.00	70
1985 Clown Casey-912078	Closed	1988	40.00	40
1986 Clown Cat Cadwalader-912132	Closed	1988	55.00	55
1987 Clown Champagne-912180	Closed	1989	95.00	95
1986 Clown Christabel-912095	Closed	1988	100.00	150
1985 Clown Christie-912084	Closed	1988	60.00	90
1986 Clown Clarabella-912096	Closed	1989	80.00	80
1986 Clown Clarissa-912123	Closed	1990	75.00	110
1988 Clown Cotton Candy-912199	Closed	1990	67.00	67
1986 Clown Cyd-912093	Closed	1988	70.00	70
1985 Clown Jody-912079	Closed	1988	100.00	150
1982 Clown Jolly-912181	Closed	1991	70.00	70
1986 Clown Kitten-Cleo-912133	Closed	1989	50.00	50
1986 Clown Lollipop-912127	Closed	1989	125.00	225
1984 Clown-901136	Closed	1988	90.00	120
1988 Crystal-912226	Closed	1992	75.00	75
1983 Deborah-901107	Closed	1987	220.00	400
1990 Debra-912319 - K. Kennedy	Closed	1992	120.00	120
1992 Denise-912362 - K. Kennedy	1,000	1994	145.00	175-225
1989 Diana Bride-912277	Closed	1992	180.00	180
1984 Diana-901119	Closed	1987	55.00	135
1988 Diana-912218	Closed	1992	270.00	270
1987 Dominique-901219	Closed	1991	170.00	225
1987 Doreen-912198	Closed	1990	75.00	75
1985 Dorothy-901157	Closed	1988	130.00	275
1992 Dottie-912393 - K. Kennedy	1,000	1996	160.00	160
1988 Elizabeth-901214	Closed	1991	90.00	90
1988 Ellen-901246	Closed	1991	100.00	100
1990 Emily-912303	Closed	1992	150.00	150
1988 Erin-901241	Closed	1991	170.00	170
1990 Fluffer-912293	Closed	1994	135.00	150-225
1985 Garnet-901183	Closed	1988	160.00	295
1990 Gigi-912306 - K. Kennedy	Closed	1994	150.00	150
1986 Gina-901176	Closed	1989	300.00	300
1989 Ginny-912287 - K. Kennedy	Closed	1993	140.00	140
1986 Girl Frog Freda-912105	Closed	1989	20.00	20
1988 Goldilocks-912234 - K. Kennedy	Closed	1992	65.00	65
1986 Googley German Astrid-912109	Closed	1989	60.00	60
1988 Heather-912247	Closed	1990	135.00	150
1990 Heather-912322	Closed	1992	150.00	150
1990 Heidi-901266	2,000	1995	150.00	150
1990 Helene-901249 - K. Kennedy	Closed	1991	160.00	160
1990 Helga-912337	Closed	1994	325.00	325
1984 Henri-901035	Closed	1986	100.00	200
1984 Henrietta-901036	Closed	1986	100.00	200
1992 Hilary-912353	Closed	1993	130.00	135
1992 Holly Belle-912380	500	1994	125.00	125
1982 Holly-901233	Closed	1985	160.00	200
1989 Holly-901254	Closed	1992	180.00	180
1989 Hope Baby w/ Pillow-912292	Closed	1992	110.00	110
1992 Iris-912389 - K. Kennedy	500	1995	165.00	165
1987 Jacqueline-912192	Closed	1990	80.00	80
1990 Jacqueline-912329 - K. Kennedy	Closed	1993	136.00	150-225
1984 Jamie-912061	Closed	1987	65.00	100
1984 Jeannie-901062	Closed	1987	200.00	550
1988 Jennifer-901248	Closed	1991	150.00	150
1988 Jennifer-912221	Closed	1990	80.00	80
1992 Jenny-912374 - K. Kennedy	Closed	1993	150.00	150
1988 Jesse-912231	Closed	1994	110.00	115
1987 Jessica-912195	Closed	1990	120.00	135
1993 Jessica-912410	2,000	1994	40.00	40
1990 Jillian-912323	Closed	1993	150.00	150
1989 Jimmy Baby w/ Pillow-912291 - K. Kennedy	Closed	1992	165.00	165
1989 Jingles-912271	Closed	1991	60.00	60
1990 Joanne-912307 - K. Kennedy	Closed	1991	165.00	165
1987 Joy-912155	Closed	1989	50.00	50
1989 Joy-912289 - K. Kennedy	Closed	1992	110.00	110
1987 Julia-912174	Closed	1989	80.00	80
1990 Julia-912334 - K. Kennedy	Closed	1993	85.00	85
1993 Julie-912435 - K. Kennedy	2,000	1995	45.00	45
1990 Justine-901256	Closed	1992	200.00	200
1988 Karen-912205	Closed	1991	200.00	250
1993 Katie-912412	2,000	1996	40.00	40
1993 Kaylee-912433 - K. Kennedy	2,000	1994	45.00	45
1992 Kelli-912361	1,000	1995	160.00	165
1990 Kelly-912331	Closed	1991	95.00	95
1990 Kimberly-912341	1,000	1996	140.00	145
1987 Kittie Cat-912167	Closed	1989	55.00	55
1987 Kitty Cuddles-901201	Closed	1990	65.00	65
1992 Kris-912345 - K. Kennedy	Closed	1992	160.00	160
1989 Kristin-912285 - K. Kennedy	Closed	1994	90.00	95

YEAR ISSUE	EDITION LIMIT	YEAR RETD.	ISSUE PRICE	*QUOTE U.S.$
1984 Laura-901106	Closed	1987	300.00	575
1988 Laura-912225	Closed	1991	135.00	135
1988 Lauren-912212	Closed	1991	110.00	110
1992 Lauren-912363 - K. Kennedy	1,000	1996	190.00	195
1993 Lauren-912413	2,000	1996	40.00	40
1993 Leslie-912432 - K. Kennedy	2,000	1994	45.00	45
1989 Licorice-912290	Closed	1991	75.00	75
1987 Lillian-901199	Closed	1990	85.00	100
1989 Lindsey-901263	Closed	1991	100.00	100
1989 Lisa-912275	Closed	1991	160.00	160
1989 Loni-912276	Closed	1993	125.00	150-185
1985 Lynn-912144	Closed	1988	90.00	135
1992 Margaret-912354 - K. Kennedy	1,000	1994	150.00	150
1989 Margot-912269	Closed	1991	110.00	110
1989 Maria-912265	Closed	1990	90.00	90
1982 Marie-901231	Closed	1985	95.00	95
1989 Marissa-901252 - K. Kennedy	Closed	1993	225.00	225
1988 Maritta Spanish-912224	Closed	1990	140.00	140
1992 Marjorie-912357	Closed	1993	135.00	135
1990 Marshmallow-912294 - K. Kennedy	Closed	1992	75.00	75
1985 Mary-912126	Closed	1988	60.00	90
1990 Matthew-901251	Closed	1993	100.00	100
1989 Megan-901260	Closed	1993	120.00	120
1987 Megan-912148	Closed	1989	70.00	70
1989 Melanie-912284 - K. Kennedy	Closed	1992	135.00	135
1990 Melinda-912309 - K. Kennedy	Closed	1991	70.00	70
1988 Melissa-901230	Closed	1991	110.00	110
1988 Melissa-912208	Closed	1990	125.00	125
1989 Merry-912249	Closed	1990	200.00	200
1987 Michelle-901222	Closed	1991	90.00	90
1985 Michelle-912066	Closed	1989	100.00	225
1992 Michelle-912381 - K. Kennedy	Closed	1992	175.00	175
1985 Millie-912135	Closed	1988	70.00	125
1989 Missy-912283	Closed	1993	110.00	115
1988 Molly-912211 - K. Kennedy	Closed	1992	75.00	75
1990 Monica-912336 - K. Kennedy	Closed	1993	100.00	105
1990 Monique-912335 - K. Kennedy	Closed	1993	85.00	85
1988 Morgan-912239 - K. Kennedy	Closed	1992	75.00	75
1990 Mrs. Katz-912301	Closed	1993	140.00	145
1993 Nadine-912431 - K. Kennedy	2,000	1995	45.00	45
1989 Nancy-912266	Closed	1990	110.00	110
1987 Nicole-901225	Closed	1991	575.00	575
1993 Nicole-912411	2,000	1996	40.00	40
1987 Noel-912170	Closed	1989	125.00	125
1992 Noelle-912360 - K. Kennedy	1,000	1994	165.00	170
1990 Pamela-912302	Closed	1991	95.00	95
1986 Patty Artic Flower Print-901185	Closed	1990	140.00	140
1990 Paula-912316	Closed	1992	100.00	100
1988 Paulette-901244	Closed	1991	90.00	90
1990 Penny-912325 - K. Kennedy	Closed	1993	130.00	150-225
1986 Pepper Rust Dr/Appr-901184	Closed	1990	125.00	200
1985 Phyllis-912067	Closed	1989	60.00	60
1989 Pinky Clown-912268 - K. Kennedy	Closed	1993	70.00	75
1988 Polly-912206	Closed	1990	100.00	125
1990 Priscilla-912300	Closed	1993	185.00	190
1990 Rebecca-901258	Closed	1992	250.00	250
1988 Renae-912245	Closed	1990	120.00	120
1990 Robin-912321	Closed	1993	160.00	165
1985 Rosalind-912087	Closed	1988	145.00	225
1985 Roxanne-901174	Closed	1988	155.00	275
1984 Sabina-901155	Closed	1988	75.00	N/A
1990 Samantha-912314	Closed	1993	185.00	190
1988 Sandy-901240 - K. Kennedy	Closed	1993	115.00	115
1989 Sara-912279	Closed	1991	175.00	175
1988 Sarah w/Pillow-912219	Closed	1991	105.00	105
1987 Sarah-901220	Closed	1992	350.00	350
1993 Sarah-912408	2,000	1996	40.00	40
1993 Shannon-912434 - K. Kennedy	2,000	1996	45.00	45
1990 Sheena-912338	Closed	1992	115.00	115
1984 Sheila-912060	Closed	1988	75.00	135
1990 Sheri-912305 - K. Kennedy	Closed	1992	115.00	115
1992 Sherise-912383 - K. Kennedy	Closed	1992	145.00	145
1989 Sigrid-912282	Closed	1992	145.00	145
1988 Snow White-912235 - K. Kennedy	Closed	1992	65.00	65
1987 Sophia-912173	Closed	1989	40.00	40
1988 Stephanie-912238	Closed	1992	200.00	200
1990 Stephanie-912312	Closed	1993	150.00	150
1984 Stephanie-933012	Closed	1988	115.00	115
1988 Susan-901243	Closed	1991	100.00	100
1990 Susie-912328	Closed	1993	115.00	120
1987 Suzanne-901200	Closed	1990	85.00	100
1989 Suzanne-912286	Closed	1992	120.00	120
1989 Suzy-912295	Closed	1991	110.00	110
1992 Tamika-912382	500	1994	185.00	185
1989 Tammy-912264	Closed	1990	110.00	110
1987 Tasha-901221	Closed	1990	115.00	130
1990 Tasha-912299 - K. Kennedy	Closed	1992	25.00	25
1989 Terry-912281	Closed	1994	125.00	130
1987 Tiffany Pouty-901211	Closed	1991	120.00	160
1990 Tiffany-912326 - K. Kennedy	Closed	1992	180.00	180
1984 Tobie-912023	Closed	1987	30.00	30
1992 Toni-912367 - K. Kennedy	Closed	1993	120.00	120
1990 Tracie-912315	Closed	1993	125.00	125
1993 Trudie-912391	500	1996	135.00	135
1982 Trudy-901232	Closed	1985	100.00	100
1992 Tulip-912385 - K. Kennedy	500	1994	145.00	145
1989 Valerie-901255	Closed	1994	175.00	175
1989 Vanessa-912272	Closed	1991	110.00	110
1984 Victoria-901068	Closed	1987	200.00	1500
1992 Wendy-912330 - K. Kennedy	1,000	1995	125.00	130
1988 Whitney Blk-912232	Closed	1994	62.50	65

Victoria Ashlea® Originals-Birthday Babies - K. Kennedy

YEAR ISSUE	EDITION LIMIT	YEAR RETD.	ISSUE PRICE	*QUOTE U.S.$
1996 January-913017	2,500		30.00	30
1996 February-913018	2,500		30.00	30
1996 March-913019	2,500		30.00	30
1996 April-913020	2,500		30.00	30
1996 May-913021	2,500		30.00	30
1996 June-913022	2,500		30.00	30
1996 July-913023	2,500		30.00	30
1996 August-913024	2,500		30.00	30
1996 September-913025	2,500		30.00	30
1996 October-913026	2,500		30.00	30
1996 November-913027	2,500		30.00	30
1996 December-913028	2,500		30.00	30

Victoria Ashlea® Originals-Collectible Cats - K. Kennedy

YEAR ISSUE	EDITION LIMIT	YEAR RETD.	ISSUE PRICE	*QUOTE U.S.$
1996 Charmer-913005	2,000		39.50	40
1996 Copper-913006	2,000		39.50	40
1996 Cuddles-913007	2,000		39.50	40
1996 Fluffy-913008	2,000		39.50	40
1996 Lollipop-913009	2,000		39.50	40
1996 Mittens-913010	2,000		39.50	40
1996 Patches-913011	2,000		39.50	40
1996 Pebbles-913012	2,000		39.50	40
1996 Pepper-913013	2,000		39.50	40
1996 Ruffles-913014	2,000		39.50	40
1996 Tumbles-913015	2,000		39.50	40
1996 Whiskers-913016	2,000		39.50	40

Victoria Ashlea® Originals-Holiday Babies - K. Kennedy

YEAR ISSUE	EDITION LIMIT	YEAR RETD.	ISSUE PRICE	*QUOTE U.S.$
1996 Bool-913001	1,000		30.00	30
1996 Happy Easter-913002	1,000		30.00	30
1996 Happy Holidays-913003	1,000		30.00	30
1996 I Love You-913004	1,000		30.00	30

Victoria Ashlea® Originals-Tiny Tot Clowns - K. Kennedy

YEAR ISSUE	EDITION LIMIT	YEAR RETD.	ISSUE PRICE	*QUOTE U.S.$
1994 Danielle-912461	2,000	1996	45.00	45
1994 Lindsey-912463	2,000	1996	45.00	45
1994 Lisa-912458	2,000	1996	45.00	45
1994 Marie-912462	2,000	1996	45.00	45
1994 Megan-912460	2,000	1996	45.00	45
1994 Stacy-912459	2,000	1996	45.00	45

Victoria Ashlea® Originals-Tiny Tot School Girls - K. Kennedy

YEAR ISSUE	EDITION LIMIT	YEAR RETD.	ISSUE PRICE	*QUOTE U.S.$
1994 Andrea- 912456	2,000	1996	47.50	48
1994 Christine- 912450	2,000	1996	47.50	48
1994 Monique- 912455	2,000	1996	47.50	48
1994 Patricia- 912453	2,000	1996	47.50	48
1994 Shawna- 912449	2,000	1996	47.50	48
1994 Susan- 912457	2,000	1996	47.50	48

Goebel/M.I. Hummel

M. I. Hummel Collectible Dolls - M. I. Hummel

YEAR ISSUE	EDITION LIMIT	YEAR RETD.	ISSUE PRICE	*QUOTE U.S.$
1964 Chimney Sweep 1908	Closed	N/A	55.00	200
1964 For Father 1917	Closed	N/A	55.00	100-150
1964 Goose Girl 1914	Closed	N/A	55.00	390
1964 Gretel 1901	Closed	N/A	55.00	200
1964 Hansel 1902	Closed	N/A	55.00	200
1964 Little Knitter 1905	Closed	N/A	55.00	200
1964 Lost Stocking 1926	Closed	N/A	55.00	200
1964 Merry Wanderer 1906	Closed	N/A	55.00	200-390
1964 Merry Wanderer 1925	Closed	N/A	55.00	200-390
1964 On Secret Path 1928	Closed	N/A	55.00	200
1964 Rosa-Blue Baby 1904/B	Closed	N/A	45.00	150
1964 Rosa-Pink Baby 1904/P	Closed	N/A	45.00	150
1964 School Boy 1910	Closed	N/A	55.00	200
1964 School Girl 1909	Closed	N/A	55.00	200
1964 Visiting and Invalid 1927	Closed	N/A	55.00	200

M. I. Hummel Porcelain Dolls - M. I. Hummel

YEAR ISSUE	EDITION LIMIT	YEAR RETD.	ISSUE PRICE	*QUOTE U.S.$
1984 Birthday Serenade/Boy	Closed	N/A	225.00	300-325
1984 Birthday Serenade/Girl	Closed	N/A	225.00	300-325
1985 Carnival	Closed	N/A	225.00	300
1985 Easter Greetings	Closed	N/A	225.00	299-325
1998 Kiss Me 805	Open		200.00	200
1996 Little Scholar 522	Open		200.00	200
1985 Lost Sheep	Closed	N/A	225.00	300
1984 On Holiday	Closed	N/A	225.00	300
1984 Postman	Closed	N/A	225.00	390-520
1996 School Girl 521	Suspd.		200.00	200
1985 Signs of Spring	Closed	N/A	225.00	300

Good-Krüger

Limited Edition - J. Good-Krüger

YEAR ISSUE	EDITION LIMIT	YEAR RETD.	ISSUE PRICE	*QUOTE U.S.$
1990 Alice	Retrd.	1991	250.00	250
1992 Anne with an E	Retrd.	1992	240.00	400
1990 Annie-Rose	Retrd.	1990	219.00	425
1994 Christmas Carols	1,000	1995	240.00	240
1990 Christmas Cookie	Retrd.	1993	199.00	225
1995 Circus Trainer	500	1995	250.00	250
1990 Cozy	Retrd.	1992	179.00	275-375
1990 Daydream	Retrd.	1990	199.00	350
1993 Good Friends	1,000	1993	179.00	179
1994 Heidi	1,000	1994	250.00	250
1992 Jeepers Creepers (Porcelain)	Retrd.	1992	725.00	800
1992 Jody	500	1992	240.00	240
1991 Johnny-Lynn	Retrd.	1991	240.00	650-800
1992 Karen	500	1992	240.00	240
1995 Letter to Santa	1,000	1995	250.00	250
1995 Little Princess	1,500	1995	250.00	250
1991 Moppett	Retrd.	1991	179.00	275

*Quotes have been rounded up to nearest dollar

YEAR ISSUE	EDITION LIMIT	YEAR RETD.	ISSUE PRICE	*QUOTE U.S.$
1994 Mother's Love	1,000	1994	275.00	275
1992 Snuggle Ebony	750	1992	240.00	240
1994 Stuffed Animal Zoo	1,000	1994	189.00	189
1990 Sue-Lynn	Retrd.	1990	240.00	300
1991 Teachers Pet	Retrd.	1991	199.00	250
1995 Tiny Newborns	500	1995	225.00	225
1991 Victorian Christmas	Retrd.	1992	219.00	275

Gorham

Beverly Port Designer Collection - B. Port

YEAR ISSUE	EDITION LIMIT	YEAR RETD.	ISSUE PRICE	*QUOTE U.S.$
1988 The Amazing Calliope Merriweather 17"	Closed	1990	275.00	1000
1988 Baery Mab 9-1/2"	Closed	1990	110.00	250
1987 Christopher Paul Bearkin 10"	Closed	1990	95.00	400
1988 Hollybeary Kringle 15"	Closed	1990	350.00	450
1987 Kristobear Kringle 17"	Closed	1990	200.00	450
1988 Miss Emily 18"	Closed	1990	350.00	1400
1987 Molly Melinda Bearkin 10"	Closed	1990	95.00	300
1987 Silver Bell 17"	Closed	1990	175.00	400
1988 T.R. 28-1/2"	Closed	1990	400.00	700
1987 Tedward Jonathan Bearkin 10"	Closed	1990	95.00	350
1987 Tedwina Kimelina Bearkin 10"	Closed	1990	95.00	350
1988 Theodore B. Bear 14"	Closed	1990	175.00	550

Bonnets & Bows - B. Gerardi

YEAR ISSUE	EDITION LIMIT	YEAR RETD.	ISSUE PRICE	*QUOTE U.S.$
1988 Belinda	Closed	1990	195.00	450
1988 Annemarie	Closed	1990	195.00	450
1988 Allessandra	Closed	1990	195.00	350
1988 Lisette	Closed	1990	285.00	495
1988 Bettina	Closed	1994	285.00	495
1988 Ellie	Closed	1994	285.00	495
1988 Alicia	Closed	1994	385.00	700
1988 Bethany	Closed	1994	385.00	1350
1988 Jesse	Closed	1994	525.00	675
1988 Francie	Closed	1994	625.00	800

Celebrations Of Childhood - L. Di Leo

YEAR ISSUE	EDITION LIMIT	YEAR RETD.	ISSUE PRICE	*QUOTE U.S.$
1992 Happy Birthday Amy	Closed	1994	160.00	225

Children Of Christmas - S. Stone Aiken

YEAR ISSUE	EDITION LIMIT	YEAR RETD.	ISSUE PRICE	*QUOTE U.S.$
1989 Clara, 16"	Closed	1994	325.00	650
1990 Natalie, 16"	1,500	1994	350.00	500
1991 Emily	1,500	1994	375.00	400
1992 Virginia	1,500	1994	375.00	400

Dollie And Me - J. Pilallis

YEAR ISSUE	EDITION LIMIT	YEAR RETD.	ISSUE PRICE	*QUOTE U.S.$
1991 Dollie's First Steps	Closed	1994	160.00	225

Gifts of the Garden - S. Stone Aiken

YEAR ISSUE	EDITION LIMIT	YEAR RETD.	ISSUE PRICE	*QUOTE U.S.$
1991 Alisa	Closed	1994	125.00	250
1991 Deborah	Closed	1994	125.00	250
1991 Holly (Christmas)	Closed	1994	150.00	250
1991 Irene	Closed	1994	125.00	250
1991 Joelle (Christmas)	Closed	1994	150.00	250
1991 Lauren	Closed	1994	125.00	250
1991 Maria	Closed	1994	125.00	250
1991 Priscilla	Closed	1994	125.00	250
1991 Valerie	Closed	1994	125.00	250

Gorham Baby Doll Collection - Aiken/Matthews

YEAR ISSUE	EDITION LIMIT	YEAR RETD.	ISSUE PRICE	*QUOTE U.S.$
1987 Christening Day	Closed	1990	245.00	350
1987 Leslie	Closed	1990	245.00	350
1987 Matthew	Closed	1990	245.00	350

Gorham Dolls - S. Stone Aiken, unless otherwise noted

YEAR ISSUE	EDITION LIMIT	YEAR RETD.	ISSUE PRICE	*QUOTE U.S.$
1985 Alexander, 19"	Closed	1990	275.00	400
1981 Alexandria, 18"	Closed	1990	250.00	500
1986 Alissa	Closed	1990	245.00	300
1985 Amelia, 19"	Closed	1990	275.00	325
1982 Baby in Apricot Dress, 16"	Closed	1990	175.00	375
1982 Baby in Blue Dress, 12"	Closed	1990	150.00	300
1982 Baby in White Dress, 18" - Gorham	Closed	1990	250.00	350-395
1982 Benjamin, 18"	Closed	1990	200.00	600
1981 Cecile, 16"	Closed	1990	200.00	800
1981 Christina, 16"	Closed	1990	200.00	425
1981 Christopher, 19"	Closed	1990	250.00	500
1982 Corrine, 21"	Closed	1990	250.00	500
1981 Danielle, 14"	Closed	1990	150.00	300
1981 Elena, 14"	Closed	1990	150.00	650
1982 Ellice, 18"	Closed	1990	200.00	400
1986 Emily, 14"	Closed	1990	175.00	395
1986 Fleur, 19"	Closed	1990	300.00	450
1985 Gabrielle, 19"	Closed	1990	225.00	350
1983 Jennifer, 19" Bridal Doll	Closed	1990	325.00	750
1982 Jeremy, 23"	Closed	1990	300.00	700
1986 Jessica	Closed	1990	195.00	275
1981 Jillian, 16"	Closed	1990	200.00	400
1986 Julia, 16"	Closed	1990	225.00	350
1987 Juliet	Closed	1990	325.00	400
1982 Kristin, 23"	Closed	1990	300.00	575
1986 Lauren, 14"	Closed	1990	175.00	350
1985 Linda, 19"	Closed	1990	275.00	600
1982 M. Anton, 12" - Unknown	Closed	1990	125.00	175
1982 Melanie, 23"	Closed	1990	300.00	600
1981 Melinda, 14"	Closed	1990	150.00	300
1986 Meredith	Closed	1990	295.00	350
1982 Mlle. Jeanette, 12"	Closed	1990	125.00	175
1982 Mlle. Lucille, 12"	Closed	1990	125.00	375
1982 Mlle. Marsella, 12" - Unknown	Closed	1990	125.00	275
1982 Mlle. Monique, 12"	Closed	1990	125.00	275
1982 Mlle. Yvonne, 12" - Unknown	Closed	1990	125.00	375
1985 Nanette, 19"	Closed	1990	275.00	325
1985 Odette, 19"	Closed	1990	250.00	450
1981 Rosemond, 18"	Closed	1990	250.00	750
1981 Stephanie, 18"	Closed	1990	250.00	2000

Gorham Holly Hobbie Childhood Memories - Holly Hobbie

YEAR ISSUE	EDITION LIMIT	YEAR RETD.	ISSUE PRICE	*QUOTE U.S.$
1985 Mother's Helper	Closed	1990	45.00	175
1985 Best Friends	Closed	1994	45.00	175
1985 First Day of School	Closed	1994	45.00	175
1985 Christmas Wishes	Closed	1994	45.00	175

Gorham Holly Hobbie For All Seasons - Holly Hobbie

YEAR ISSUE	EDITION LIMIT	YEAR RETD.	ISSUE PRICE	*QUOTE U.S.$
1984 Summer Holly 12"	Closed	1994	42.50	195
1984 Fall Holly 12"	Closed	1994	42.50	195
1984 Winter Holly 12"	Closed	1994	42.50	195
1984 Spring Holly 12"	Closed	1994	42.50	195
1984 Set of 4	Closed	1994	170.00	750

Holly Hobbie - Holly Hobbie

YEAR ISSUE	EDITION LIMIT	YEAR RETD.	ISSUE PRICE	*QUOTE U.S.$
1983 Blue Girl, 14"	Closed	1994	80.00	245
1983 Blue Girl, 18"	Closed	1994	115.00	295
1983 Christmas Morning, 14"	Closed	1994	80.00	245
1983 Heather, 14"	Closed	1994	80.00	275
1983 Little Amy, 14"	Closed	1994	80.00	245
1983 Robbie, 14"	Closed	1994	80.00	275
1983 Sunday Best, 18"	Closed	1994	115.00	295
1983 Sweet Valentine, 16"	Closed	1994	100.00	295
1983 Yesterday's Memories, 18"	Closed	1994	125.00	375

Joyful Years - B. Gerardi

YEAR ISSUE	EDITION LIMIT	YEAR RETD.	ISSUE PRICE	*QUOTE U.S.$
1989 Katrina	Closed	1994	295.00	375
1989 William	Closed	1994	295.00	375

Kezi Doll For All Seasons - Kezi

YEAR ISSUE	EDITION LIMIT	YEAR RETD.	ISSUE PRICE	*QUOTE U.S.$
1985 Ariel 16"	Closed	1994	135.00	500
1985 Aubrey 16"	Closed	1994	135.00	500
1985 Amber 16"	Closed	1994	135.00	500
1985 Adrienne 16"	Closed	1994	135.00	500
1985 Set of 4	Closed	1994	540.00	1900

Kezi Golden Gifts - Kezi

YEAR ISSUE	EDITION LIMIT	YEAR RETD.	ISSUE PRICE	*QUOTE U.S.$
1984 Charity 16"	Closed	1990	85.00	175
1984 Faith 18"	Closed	1990	95.00	195
1984 Felicity 18"	Closed	1990	95.00	195
1984 Grace 16"	Closed	1990	85.00	175
1984 Hope 16"	Closed	1990	85.00	175
1984 Merrie 16"	Closed	1990	85.00	175
1984 Patience 18"	Closed	1990	95.00	195
1984 Prudence 18"	Closed	1990	85.00	195

Les Belles Bebes Collection - S. Stone Aiken

YEAR ISSUE	EDITION LIMIT	YEAR RETD.	ISSUE PRICE	*QUOTE U.S.$
1993 Camille	1,500	1994	375.00	395
1991 Cherie	Closed	1994	375.00	475
1991 Desiree	1,500	1994	375.00	395

Limited Edition Dolls - S. Stone Aiken

YEAR ISSUE	EDITION LIMIT	YEAR RETD.	ISSUE PRICE	*QUOTE U.S.$
1982 Allison, 19"	Closed	1990	300.00	4500-4900
1983 Ashley, 19"	Closed	1990	350.00	1000-1200
1984 Nicole, 19"	Closed	1990	350.00	875-1200
1984 Holly (Christmas), 19"	Closed	1990	300.00	850
1985 Lydia,19"	Closed	1990	550.00	1800
1985 Joy (Christmas), 19"	Closed	1990	350.00	695
1986 Noel (Christmas), 19"	Closed	1990	400.00	750
1987 Jacqueline, 19"	Closed	1990	500.00	700
1987 Merrie (Christmas), 19"	Closed	1994	500.00	750-795
1988 Andrew, 19"	Closed	1994	475.00	750
1988 Christa (Christmas), 19"	Closed	1994	550.00	1500
1990 Amey (10th Anniversary Edition)	Closed	1994	650.00	1100

Limited Edition Sister Set - S. Stone Aiken

YEAR ISSUE	EDITION LIMIT	YEAR RETD.	ISSUE PRICE	*QUOTE U.S.$
1988 Kathleen	Closed	1994	550.00	750
1988 Katelin	Set	1994	Set	Set

Little Women - S. Stone Aiken

YEAR ISSUE	EDITION LIMIT	YEAR RETD.	ISSUE PRICE	*QUOTE U.S.$
1983 Amy, 16"	Closed	1994	225.00	500
1983 Beth, 16"	Closed	1994	225.00	500
1983 Jo, 19"	Closed	1994	275.00	575
1983 Meg, 19"	Closed	1994	275.00	650

Precious as Pearls - S. Stone Aiken

YEAR ISSUE	EDITION LIMIT	YEAR RETD.	ISSUE PRICE	*QUOTE U.S.$
1986 Colette	Closed	1994	400.00	1500
1987 Charlotte	Closed	1994	425.00	750
1988 Chloe	Closed	1994	525.00	850-925
1989 Cassandra	Closed	1994	525.00	1250
XX Set	Closed	1994	1875.00	4000

Southern Belles - S. Stone Aiken

YEAR ISSUE	EDITION LIMIT	YEAR RETD.	ISSUE PRICE	*QUOTE U.S.$
1985 Amanda, 19"	Closed	1990	300.00	1400
1986 Veronica, 19"	Closed	1990	325.00	750
1987 Rachel, 19"	Closed	1990	375.00	800
1988 Cassie, 19"	Closed	1990	500.00	875

Special Moments - E. Worrell

YEAR ISSUE	EDITION LIMIT	YEAR RETD.	ISSUE PRICE	*QUOTE U.S.$
1991 Baby's First Christmas	Closed	1994	135.00	235
1992 Baby's First Steps	Closed	1994	135.00	135

Sporting Kids - R. Schrubbe

YEAR ISSUE	EDITION LIMIT	YEAR RETD.	ISSUE PRICE	*QUOTE U.S.$
1993 Up At Bat	Closed	1994	49.50	80

Times To Treasure - L. Di Leo

YEAR ISSUE	EDITION LIMIT	YEAR RETD.	ISSUE PRICE	*QUOTE U.S.$
1991 Bedtime	Closed	1994	195.00	250
1993 Playtime	Closed	1994	195.00	250
1990 Storytime	Closed	1994	195.00	250

Valentine Ladies - P. Valentine

YEAR ISSUE	EDITION LIMIT	YEAR RETD.	ISSUE PRICE	*QUOTE U.S.$
1987 Anabella	Closed	1994	145.00	395
1987 Elizabeth	Closed	1994	145.00	450
1988 Felicia	Closed	1994	225.00	325
1987 Jane	Closed	1994	145.00	350
1988 Judith Anne	Closed	1994	195.00	325
1989 Julianna	Closed	1994	225.00	275
1987 Lee Ann	Closed	1994	145.00	325
1988 Maria Theresa	Closed	1994	225.00	350
1987 Marianna	Closed	1994	160.00	400
1987 Patrice	Closed	1994	145.00	325
1988 Priscilla	Closed	1994	195.00	325
1987 Rebecca	Closed	1994	145.00	325
1987 Rosanne	Closed	1994	145.00	325
1989 Rose	Closed	1994	225.00	275
1987 Sylvia	Closed	1994	160.00	350

Victorian Cameo Collection - B. Gerardi

YEAR ISSUE	EDITION LIMIT	YEAR RETD.	ISSUE PRICE	*QUOTE U.S.$
1990 Victoria	1,500	1994	375.00	425
1991 Alexandra	Closed	1994	375.00	425

Victorian Children - S. Stone Aiken

YEAR ISSUE	EDITION LIMIT	YEAR RETD.	ISSUE PRICE	*QUOTE U.S.$
1992 Sara's Tea Time	1,000	1994	495.00	750
1993 Catching Butterflies	1,000	1994	495.00	495

The Victorian Collection - E. Woodhouse

YEAR ISSUE	EDITION LIMIT	YEAR RETD.	ISSUE PRICE	*QUOTE U.S.$
1992 Victoria's Jubilee	Yr.Iss.	1994	295.00	350

Hallmark Galleries

Mary Engelbreit's Friendship Garden - M. Engelbreit

YEAR ISSUE	EDITION LIMIT	YEAR RETD.	ISSUE PRICE	*QUOTE U.S.$
1993 Porcelain Doll-Josephine QHG5003	12,500	1995	60.00	60
1993 Porcelain Doll-Louisa QHG5002	12,500	1995	65.00	65
1993 Porcelain Doll-Margaret QHG5001	12,500	1995	60.00	60

Victorian Memories - J. Greene

YEAR ISSUE	EDITION LIMIT	YEAR RETD.	ISSUE PRICE	*QUOTE U.S.$
1992 Abigail QHG1019	4,500	1995	125.00	125
1992 Abner QHG1018	4,500	1995	110.00	110
1992 Alice QHG1020	4,500	1995	125.00	125
1993 Baby Doll Beatrice QHG1029	9,500	1994	20.00	20
1992 Bear-plush bear QHG1011	9,500	1995	35.00	35
1992 Bunny B-plush rabbit QHG1012	9,500	1995	35.00	35
1992 Daisy-plush bear QHG1009	2,500	1995	85.00	85
1992 Emma/miniature doll QHG1016	9,500	1995	25.00	25
1993 Hannah QHG1030	2,500	1995	130.00	130
1992 Katherine QHG1017	1,200	1995	150.00	150
1994 Mini Jointed Bear Jesse QHG1037	9,500	1995	12.00	12
1992 Olivia QHG1021	4,500	1995	125.00	125
1992 Seth-plush bear QHG1007	9,500	1995	40.00	40
1992 Teddy -plush bear QHG1008	9,500	1995	45.00	45

Hamilton Collection/Ashton-Drake Galleries

Abbie Williams Doll Collection - A. Williams

YEAR ISSUE	EDITION LIMIT	YEAR RETD.	ISSUE PRICE	*QUOTE U.S.$
1992 Molly	Closed	N/A	155.00	200

American Country Doll Collection - T. Tucker

YEAR ISSUE	EDITION LIMIT	YEAR RETD.	ISSUE PRICE	*QUOTE U.S.$
1995 Carson	Closed	1997	95.00	95-150
1995 Bonnie	Closed	1997	195.00	195-295
1996 Patsy	Closed	1997	95.00	95-150
1996 Delaney	Closed	1997	95.00	95-150
1996 Arizona	Closed	1997	95.00	95-150
1996 Kendra	Closed	1997	195.00	195-295

Annual Connossieur Doll - N/A

YEAR ISSUE	EDITION LIMIT	YEAR RETD.	ISSUE PRICE	*QUOTE U.S.$
1992 Lara	Closed	1997	295.00	295

The Antique Doll Collection - Unknown

YEAR ISSUE	EDITION LIMIT	YEAR RETD.	ISSUE PRICE	*QUOTE U.S.$
1989 Nicole	Closed	N/A	195.00	195-300
1990 Colette	Closed	1996	195.00	195
1991 Lisette	Closed	1996	195.00	225
1991 Katrina	Closed	1996	195.00	195

Baby Portrait Dolls - B. Parker

YEAR ISSUE	EDITION LIMIT	YEAR RETD.	ISSUE PRICE	*QUOTE U.S.$
1991 Melissa	Closed	1993	135.00	175-200
1992 Jenna	Closed	N/A	135.00	135-200
1992 Bethany	Closed	1996	135.00	150
1993 Mindy	Closed	1996	135.00	150-160

Belles of the Countryside - C. Heath Orange

YEAR ISSUE	EDITION LIMIT	YEAR RETD.	ISSUE PRICE	*QUOTE U.S.$
1992 Erin	Closed	1997	135.00	150
1992 Rose	Closed	1997	135.00	135
1993 Lorna	Closed	1997	135.00	150
1994 Gwyn	Closed	1997	135.00	135

The Bessie Pease Gutmann Doll Collection - B.P. Gutmann

YEAR ISSUE	EDITION LIMIT	YEAR RETD.	ISSUE PRICE	*QUOTE U.S.$
1989 Love is Blind	Closed	N/A	135.00	220
1989 He Won't Bite	Closed	N/A	135.00	135
1991 Virginia	Closed	1996	135.00	135
1991 First Dancing Lesson	Closed	1996	135.00	135
1991 Good Morning	Closed	1996	135.00	135
1991 Love At First Sight	Closed	1996	135.00	135

Best Buddies - C.M. Rolfe

YEAR ISSUE	EDITION LIMIT	YEAR RETD.	ISSUE PRICE	*QUOTE U.S.$
1994 Jodie	Closed	1997	69.00	69-90
1994 Brandy	Closed	1997	69.00	69
1995 Joey	Closed	1997	69.00	69-100
1996 Stacey	Closed	1997	69.00	69

Boehm Christening - Boehm Studio

YEAR ISSUE	EDITION LIMIT	YEAR RETD.	ISSUE PRICE	*QUOTE U.S.$
1994 Elena's First Portrait	Closed	1996	155.00	180-250
1994 Elena	Closed	1996	155.00	180-250

Bridal Elegance - Boehm

YEAR ISSUE	EDITION LIMIT	YEAR RETD.	ISSUE PRICE	*QUOTE U.S.$
1994 Camille	Closed	1996	195.00	225

Bride Dolls - Unknown

YEAR ISSUE	EDITION LIMIT	YEAR RETD.	ISSUE PRICE	*QUOTE U.S.$
1991 Portrait of Innocence	Closed	1996	195.00	210
1992 Portrait of Loveliness	Closed	1996	195.00	250

*Quotes have been rounded up to nearest dollar

YEAR ISSUE	EDITION LIMIT	YEAR RETD.	ISSUE PRICE	*QUOTE U.S.$
Brooker Tickler - Harris/Brooker				
1995 Nellie	Closed	1997	95.00	95
1996 Callie	Closed	1997	95.00	95
Brooks Wooden Dolls - P. Ryan Brooks				
1993 Waiting For Santa	15,000	1994	135.00	200-250
1993 Are You the Easter Bunny?	Closed	1997	135.00	135
1994 Be My Valentine	Closed	1997	135.00	135
1995 Shh! I Only Wanna Peek	Closed	1997	135.00	135
Byi Praying Dolls - C. Byi				
1996 Mark & Mary	Closed	1997	89.95	90-175
Catherine Mather Dolls - C. Mather				
1993 Justine	Closed	1997	155.00	155-200
Central Park Skaters - Unknown				
1991 Central Park Skaters	Closed	1996	245.00	245
A Child's Menagerie - B. Van Boxel				
1993 Becky	Closed	1996	69.00	69-100
1993 Carrie	Closed	1996	69.00	69
1994 Mandy	Closed	1996	69.00	69
1994 Terry	Closed	1996	69.00	69
Children To Cherish - Cybis				
1991 A Gift of Innocence	Yr.Iss.	1991	135.00	135
1991 A Gift of Beauty	Closed	1996	135.00	135
Ciambra - M. Ciambra				
1995 Chloe	Closed	1997	155.00	135-180
1996 Lydia	Closed	1997	155.00	155
Cindy Marschner Rolfe Dolls - C.M. Rolfe				
1993 Shannon	Closed	1996	95.00	95
1993 Julie	Closed	1997	95.00	95
1993 Kayla	Closed	1997	95.00	95
1994 Janey	Closed	1997	95.00	95
Cindy Marschner Rolfe Twins - C.M. Rolfe				
1995 Shelby & Sydney	Closed	1996	190.00	190-210
Connie Walser Derek Baby Dolls - C.W. Derek				
1990 Jessica	Closed	1993	155.00	350-500
1991 Sara	Closed	1995	155.00	200-250
1991 Andrew	Closed	1996	155.00	155-225
1991 Amanda	Closed	1996	155.00	155-180
1992 Samantha	Closed	1996	155.00	155-225
Connie Walser Derek Baby Dolls II - C.W. Derek				
1992 Stephanie	Closed	1996	95.00	200
1992 Beth	Closed	1996	95.00	160
Connie Walser Derek Baby Dolls III - C.W. Derek				
1994 Chelsea	Closed	1997	79.00	79
1995 Tina	Closed	1997	79.00	79
1995 Tabitha	Closed	1997	79.00	79
1995 Ginger	Closed	1997	79.00	79
Connie Walser Derek Dolls - C.W. Derek				
1992 Baby Jessica	Closed	1996	75.00	75
1993 Baby Sara	Closed	1996	75.00	75-95
Connie Walser Derek Toddlers - C.W. Derek				
1994 Jessie	Closed	1996	79.00	120
1994 Casey	Closed	1996	79.00	120
1995 Angie	Closed	1996	79.00	120
1995 Tori	Closed	1997	79.00	79
Daddy's Little Girls - M. Snyder				
1992 Lindsay	Closed	1996	95.00	95
1993 Cassie	Closed	1996	95.00	95
1993 Dana	Closed	1996	95.00	120
1994 Tara	Closed	1996	95.00	95
Dey Recital Dolls - P. Dey				
1996 Mallory	Closed	1997	195.00	225-250
Dolls by Autumn Berwick - A. Berwick				
1993 Laura	Closed	1995	135.00	150
Dolls By Kay McKee - K. McKee				
1992 Shy Violet	Closed	1993	135.00	300-320
1992 Robin	Closed	1995	135.00	135
1993 Katie Did It!	Closed	1995	135.00	135-150
1993 Ryan	Closed	1997	135.00	135-180
Dolls of America's Colonial Heritage - A. Elekfy				
1986 Katrina	Closed	1994	55.00	55
1986 Nicole	Closed	1994	55.00	55
1987 Maria	Closed	1994	55.00	55
1987 Priscilla	Closed	1994	55.00	55
1987 Colleen	Closed	1994	55.00	55
1988 Gretchen	Closed	1994	55.00	55
Dreamsicle Dolls - K. Haynes				
1997 Sweet Dreams Teddy	Closed	1997	49.95	50
1998 Story Time With Bunny	Closed	1997	49.95	50
Elaine Campbell Dolls - E. Campbell				
1994 Emma	Closed	1994	95.00	95-120
1995 Abby	Closed	1997	95.00	95
1995 Jana	Closed	1997	95.00	95
1995 Molly	Closed	1997	95.00	95
Eternal Friends Doll Collection - Precious Moments				
1996 Love One Another	Closed	1997	135.00	135
1997 Friendship Hits The Spot	Closed	1997	135.00	135
First Recital - N/A				
1993 Hillary	Closed	1998	135.00	135-195
1994 Olivia	Closed	1998	135.00	135
Grobben Ethnic Babies - J. Grobben				
1994 Jasmine	Closed	1996	135.00	180
1995 Taiya	Closed	1996	135.00	160-175
Grothedde Dolls - N. Grothedde				
1994 Cindy	Closed	1996	69.00	100
1995 Holly	Closed	1997	69.00	69
Hargrave Dolls - M. Hargrave				
1994 Angela	Closed	1997	79.00	79-110
1995 April	Closed	1997	79.00	79-100
Heath Babies - C. Heath Orange				
1995 Hayley	Closed	1997	95.00	95
1996 Ellie	Closed	1997	95.00	95
Heavenly Clowns Doll Collection - K. McKee				
1996 Blue Moon	Closed	1997	95.00	95
Helen Carr Dolls - H. Carr				
1994 Claudia	Closed	1997	135.00	135-185
1995 Jillian	Closed	1997	135.00	135-185
1996 Abigail	Closed	1997	135.00	135-185
1996 Rosalee	Closed	1997	135.00	135
Helen Kish II Dolls - H. Kish				
1992 Vanessa	Closed	1997	135.00	135-155
1994 Jordan	Closed	1997	95.00	95
Holiday Carollers - U. Lepp				
1992 Joy	Closed	1996	155.00	155
1993 Noel	Closed	1996	155.00	155
Huckleberry Hill Kids - B. Parker				
1994 Gabrielle	Closed	1997	95.00	95-125
1994 Alexandra	Closed	1997	95.00	95-135
1995 Jeremiah	Closed	1997	95.00	95-135
1996 Sarah	Closed	1997	95.00	95-135
I Love Lucy (Porcelain) - Unknown				
1990 Lucy	Closed	N/A	95.00	240-300
1991 Ricky	Closed	N/A	95.00	350
1992 Queen of the Gypsies	Closed	N/A	95.00	245-400
1992 Vitameatavegamin	Closed	N/A	95.00	300-400
I Love Lucy (Vinyl) - Unknown				
1988 Ethel	Closed	N/A	40.00	100
1988 Fred	Closed	N/A	40.00	100
1990 Lucy	Closed	N/A	40.00	100
1991 Ricky	Closed	N/A	40.00	150
1992 Queen of the Gypsies	Closed	1997	40.00	40
1992 Vitameatavegamin	Closed	1997	40.00	40
I'm So Proud Doll Collection - L. Cobabe				
1992 Christina	Closed	1996	95.00	95-125
1993 Jill	Closed	1996	95.00	120
1994 Tammy	Closed	1996	95.00	95-110
1994 Shelly	Closed	1996	95.00	115
Inga Manders - I. Manders				
1995 Miss Priss	Closed	1997	79.00	79
1995 Miss Hollywood	Closed	1997	79.00	79
1995 Miss Glamour	Closed	1997	79.00	79
1996 Miss Sweetheart	Closed	1997	79.00	79
International Children - C. Woodie				
1991 Miko	Closed	N/A	49.50	80
1991 Anastasia	Closed	1996	49.50	50
1991 Angelina	Closed	1996	49.50	50
1992 Lian	Closed	1996	49.50	50
1992 Monique	Closed	1996	49.50	50
1992 Lisa	Closed	1996	49.50	50
Jane Zidjunas Party Dolls - J. Zidjunas				
1991 Kelly	Closed	1994	135.00	135-150
1992 Katie	Closed	1994	135.00	135
1993 Meredith	Closed	1994	135.00	135-140
Jane Zidjunas Sleeping Dolls - J. Zidjunas				
1995 Annie	Closed	1997	79.00	79-110
1995 Jamie	Closed	1997	79.00	79-120
Jane Zidjunas Toddler Dolls - J. Zidjunas				
1991 Jennifer	Closed	1995	135.00	135
1991 Megan	Closed	1995	135.00	160
1992 Kimberly	Closed	1995	135.00	135
1992 Amy	Closed	1995	135.00	175-225
Jane Zidjunas Victorian - J. Zidjunas				
1996 Constance	Closed	1997	195.00	195-210
Jeanne Wilson Dolls - J. Wilson				
1994 Priscilla	Closed	1997	155.00	155
Join The Parade - N/A				
1992 Betsy	Closed	1996	49.50	50
1994 Peggy	Closed	1996	49.50	50
1994 Sandy	Closed	1996	49.50	50
1995 Brian	Closed	1996	49.50	50
Joke Grobben Dolls - J. Grobben				
1992 Heather	Closed	1995	69.00	69-100
1993 Kathleen	Closed	1995	69.00	69-110
1993 Brianna	Closed	1995	69.00	69-125
1994 Bridget	Closed	1995	69.00	69-125
Joke Grobben Tall Dolls - J. Grobben				
1995 Jade	Closed	1997	135.00	135-150
1996 Raven	Closed	1997	135.00	135-150
Just Like Mom - H. Kish				
1991 Ashley	Closed	1993	135.00	250-300
1992 Elizabeth	Closed	1994	135.00	160
1992 Hannah	Closed	1994	135.00	135
1993 Margaret	Closed	1994	135.00	135-145
Kay McKee Downsized Dolls - K. McKee				
1995 Kyle	Closed	1997	79.00	79
1996 Cody	Closed	1997	79.00	79
Kay McKee Klowns - K. McKee				
1993 The Dreamer	15,000	1995	155.00	155-295
1994 The Entertainer	15,000	1996	155.00	180
Kuck Fairy - S. Kuck				
1994 Tooth Fairy	Closed	1996	135.00	135
Laura Cobabe Dolls - L. Cobabe				
1992 Amber	Closed	1994	195.00	225-250
1992 Brooke	Closed	1994	195.00	195
Laura Cobabe Dolls II - L. Cobabe				
1993 Kristen	Closed	1994	75.00	75
Laura Cobabe Ethnic - L. Cobabe				
1995 Nica	Closed	1997	95.00	95-135
1996 Kenu	Closed	1997	95.00	95-135
Laura Cobabe Indians - L. Cobabe				
1994 Snowbird	Closed	1997	135.00	155-200
1995 Little Eagle	Closed	1997	135.00	135-175
1995 Desert Bloom	Closed	1997	135.00	135-185
1996 Call of the Coyote	Closed	1997	135.00	135-175
Laura Cobabe Tall Dolls - L. Cobabe				
1994 Cassandra	Closed	1997	195.00	250
1994 Taylor	Closed	1997	195.00	250
Laura Cobabe's Costume Kids - L. Cobabe				
1994 Lil' Punkin	Closed	1996	79.00	110-125
1994 Little Ladybug	Closed	1997	79.00	79
1995 Miss Dinomite	Closed	1997	79.00	79
1995 Miss Flutterby	Closed	1997	79.00	79
Little Gardners - J. Galperin				
1996 Daisy	Closed	1997	95.00	95
Littlest Members of the Wedding - J. Esteban				
1993 Matthew & Melanie	Closed	1995	195.00	195
Lucy Dolls - Unknown				
1996 Lucy	Closed	1997	95.00	118-135
Maud Humphrey Bogart Dolls - Unknown				
1992 Playing Bridesmaid	Closed	N/A	195.00	225
Maud Humphrey Bogart Doll Collection - M.H. Bogart				
1989 Playing Bride	Closed	N/A	135.00	225-250
1990 First Party	Closed	N/A	135.00	150
1990 The First Lesson	Closed	N/A	135.00	149
1991 Seamstress	Closed	N/A	135.00	149
1991 Little Captive	Closed	1996	135.00	135
1992 Kitty's Bath	Closed	1996	135.00	135
Mavis Snyder Dolls - M. Snyder				
1994 Tara	Closed	1995	95.00	95
Parker Carousel - B. Parker				
1996 Annelise's Musical Ride	Closed	1997	295.00	295
Parker Fairy Tale - B. Parker				
1995 Claire	Closed	1997	155.00	155-185
1996 Marissa	Closed	1997	155.00	155-195
Parker Levi Toddlers - B. Parker				
1992 Courtney	Closed	1994	135.00	200
1992 Melody	Closed	1994	135.00	135
Parkins Baby - P. Parkins				
1995 Baby Alyssa	Closed	1997	225.00	225
Parkins Connisseur - P. Parkins				
1993 Faith	Closed	1995	135.00	180
Parkins Portraits - P. Parkins				
1993 Lauren	Closed	1995	79.00	110-125
1993 Kelsey	Closed	1997	79.00	79-110
1994 Morgan	Closed	1997	79.00	79-100
1994 Cassidy	Closed	1996	79.00	100
Parkins Toddler Angels - P. Parkins				
1995 Celeste	Closed	1997	135.00	135-195
1996 Charity	Closed	1997	135.00	108-135
1996 Charisse	Closed	1997	135.00	135-175
1996 Chantelle	Closed	1997	135.00	135-150
Parkins Treasures - P. Parkins				
1992 Tiffany	Closed	1994	55.00	125-135
1992 Dorothy	Closed	1995	55.00	80
1993 Charlotte	Closed	1995	55.00	80-110

*Quotes have been rounded up to nearest dollar

YEAR ISSUE	EDITION LIMIT	YEAR RETD.	ISSUE PRICE	*QUOTE U.S.$
1993 Cynthia	Closed	1995	55.00	80

Phyllis Parkins Dolls - P. Parkins

YEAR ISSUE	EDITION LIMIT	YEAR RETD.	ISSUE PRICE	*QUOTE U.S.$
1992 Swan Princess	9,850	1995	195.00	220-250

Phyllis Parkins II Dolls - P. Parkins

YEAR ISSUE	EDITION LIMIT	YEAR RETD.	ISSUE PRICE	*QUOTE U.S.$
1995 Dakota	Closed	1997	135.00	135-160
1996 Kerrie	Closed	1997	135.00	135
1996 Ginny	Closed	1997	135.00	135
1996 Dixie	Closed	1997	135.00	135-150

Picnic In The Park - J. Esteban

YEAR ISSUE	EDITION LIMIT	YEAR RETD.	ISSUE PRICE	*QUOTE U.S.$
1991 Rebecca	Closed	1995	155.00	155-180
1992 Emily	Closed	1995	155.00	155
1992 Victoria	Closed	1995	155.00	155
1993 Benjamin	Closed	1995	155.00	155-180

Pitter Patter Doll Collection - C.W. Derek

YEAR ISSUE	EDITION LIMIT	YEAR RETD.	ISSUE PRICE	*QUOTE U.S.$
1996 Bobbie Jo	Closed	1997	79.00	79-100
1997 Mary Anne	Closed	1997	79.00	79

A Pocket Full of Love Doll Collection - S. Kuck

YEAR ISSUE	EDITION LIMIT	YEAR RETD.	ISSUE PRICE	*QUOTE U.S.$
1997 Gabriella	Closed	1997	29.95	30
1998 Tanya	Closed	1997	39.95	40

Precious Moments Christening - S. Butcher

YEAR ISSUE	EDITION LIMIT	YEAR RETD.	ISSUE PRICE	*QUOTE U.S.$
1996 Anna	Closed	1997	95.00	95
1996 Elise	Closed	1997	95.00	95

Proud Indian Nation - R. Swanson

YEAR ISSUE	EDITION LIMIT	YEAR RETD.	ISSUE PRICE	*QUOTE U.S.$
1992 Navajo Little One	Closed	1993	95.00	200-225
1993 Dressed Up For The Pow Wow	Closed	1996	95.00	95-150
1993 Autumn Treat	Closed	1997	95.00	115
1994 Out with Mama's Flock	Closed	1998	95.00	95-115

Rachel Cold Toddlers - R. Cold

YEAR ISSUE	EDITION LIMIT	YEAR RETD.	ISSUE PRICE	*QUOTE U.S.$
1995 Jenny	Closed	1997	95.00	95
1996 Trudy	Closed	1997	95.00	95

The Royal Beauty Dolls - Unknown

YEAR ISSUE	EDITION LIMIT	YEAR RETD.	ISSUE PRICE	*QUOTE U.S.$
1991 Chen Mai	Closed	1994	195.00	195-225

Russian Czarra Dolls - Unknown

YEAR ISSUE	EDITION LIMIT	YEAR RETD.	ISSUE PRICE	*QUOTE U.S.$
1991 Alexandra	Closed	N/A	295.00	350

Sandra Kuck Dolls - S. Kuck

YEAR ISSUE	EDITION LIMIT	YEAR RETD.	ISSUE PRICE	*QUOTE U.S.$
1993 A Kiss Goodnight	Closed	N/A	79.00	79-95
1994 Teaching Teddy	Closed	1997	79.00	79
1995 Reading With Teddy	Closed	1997	79.00	79
1996 Picnic With Teddy	Closed	N/A	79.00	79-95

Santa's Little Helpers - C.W. Derek

YEAR ISSUE	EDITION LIMIT	YEAR RETD.	ISSUE PRICE	*QUOTE U.S.$
1992 Nicholas	Closed	1996	155.00	155-250
1993 Hope	Closed	1996	155.00	155-225

Schmidt Babies - J. Schmidt

YEAR ISSUE	EDITION LIMIT	YEAR RETD.	ISSUE PRICE	*QUOTE U.S.$
1995 Baby	Closed	1997	79.00	79
1996 Snookums	Closed	1997	79.00	79

Schmidt Dolls - J. Schmidt

YEAR ISSUE	EDITION LIMIT	YEAR RETD.	ISSUE PRICE	*QUOTE U.S.$
1994 Kaitlyn	Closed	1995	79.00	120
1995 Kara	Closed	1995	79.00	79
1995 Kathy	Closed	1997	79.00	79
1996 Karla	Closed	1997	79.00	79

Schrubbe Santa Dolls - R. Schrubbe

YEAR ISSUE	EDITION LIMIT	YEAR RETD.	ISSUE PRICE	*QUOTE U.S.$
1994 Jolly Old St. Nick	Closed	1995	135.00	135-150

Sentiments From the Garden - M. Severino

YEAR ISSUE	EDITION LIMIT	YEAR RETD.	ISSUE PRICE	*QUOTE U.S.$
1996 Fairy of Innocence	Closed	1997	59.00	59
1997 Fairy of Loveliness	Closed	1997	59.00	59

Shelton II Doll - V. Shelton

YEAR ISSUE	EDITION LIMIT	YEAR RETD.	ISSUE PRICE	*QUOTE U.S.$
1996 Josie	Closed	1997	79.00	79

Shelton Indians - V. Shelton

YEAR ISSUE	EDITION LIMIT	YEAR RETD.	ISSUE PRICE	*QUOTE U.S.$
1995 Little Cloud	Closed	1997	95.00	120
1996 Little Basketweaver	Closed	1997	95.00	95-135
1996 Little Warrior	Closed	1997	95.00	95-135
1996 Little Skywatcher	Closed	1997	95.00	95-125

Songs of the Seasons Hakata Doll Collection - T. Murakami

YEAR ISSUE	EDITION LIMIT	YEAR RETD.	ISSUE PRICE	*QUOTE U.S.$
1985 Winter Song Maiden	9,800	1991	75.00	75
1985 Spring Song Maiden	9,800	1991	75.00	75
1985 Summer Song Maiden	9,800	1991	75.00	75
1985 Autumn Song Maiden	9,800	1991	75.00	75

Star Trek Doll Collection - E. Daub

YEAR ISSUE	EDITION LIMIT	YEAR RETD.	ISSUE PRICE	*QUOTE U.S.$
1988 Mr. Spock	Closed	N/A	75.00	150
1988 Captain Kirk	Closed	N/A	75.00	120
1989 Dr. Mc Coy	Closed	N/A	75.00	120
1989 Scotty	Closed	N/A	75.00	120
1990 Sulu	Closed	N/A	75.00	120
1990 Chekov	Closed	N/A	75.00	120
1991 Uhura	Closed	N/A	75.00	120

Storybook Dolls - L. Di Leo

YEAR ISSUE	EDITION LIMIT	YEAR RETD.	ISSUE PRICE	*QUOTE U.S.$
1991 Alice in Wonderland	Closed	1996	75.00	75

Through The Eyes of Virginia Turner - V. Turner

YEAR ISSUE	EDITION LIMIT	YEAR RETD.	ISSUE PRICE	*QUOTE U.S.$
1992 Michelle	Closed	1993	95.00	150-180
1992 Danielle	Closed	1997	95.00	113
1993 Wendy	Closed	1995	95.00	125
1994 Dawn	Closed	1996	95.00	95

Toddler Days Doll Collection - D. Schurig

YEAR ISSUE	EDITION LIMIT	YEAR RETD.	ISSUE PRICE	*QUOTE U.S.$
1992 Erica	Closed	1995	95.00	125
1993 Darlene	Closed	1995	95.00	95
1994 Karen	Closed	1995	95.00	95
1995 Penny	Closed	1995	95.00	95

Treasured Toddlers - V. Turner

YEAR ISSUE	EDITION LIMIT	YEAR RETD.	ISSUE PRICE	*QUOTE U.S.$
1992 Whitney	Closed	1996	95.00	200
1993 Natalie	Closed	1996	95.00	150

Vickie Walker 1st's - V. Walker

YEAR ISSUE	EDITION LIMIT	YEAR RETD.	ISSUE PRICE	*QUOTE U.S.$
1995 Leah	Closed	1998	79.00	79
1995 Leslie	Closed	1997	79.00	79
1995 Lily	Closed	1997	79.00	79
1995 Leanna	Closed	1997	79.00	79

Victorian Treasures - C.W. Derek

YEAR ISSUE	EDITION LIMIT	YEAR RETD.	ISSUE PRICE	*QUOTE U.S.$
1992 Katherine	Closed	1996	155.00	155
1993 Madeline	Closed	1996	155.00	155

Virginia Turner Dolls - V. Turner

YEAR ISSUE	EDITION LIMIT	YEAR RETD.	ISSUE PRICE	*QUOTE U.S.$
1995 Amelia	Closed	1997	95.00	95-135
1995 Mckenzie	Closed	1997	95.00	95-135
1996 Grace	Closed	1997	95.00	95-135
1996 Alexis	Closed	1997	95.00	95-135
1997 Felicia	Closed	1997	95.00	95
1997 Courtney	Closed	1997	95.00	95-135
1998 Miranda	Closed	1997	95.00	95

Virginia Turner Little Sisters - V. Turner

YEAR ISSUE	EDITION LIMIT	YEAR RETD.	ISSUE PRICE	*QUOTE U.S.$
1996 Allie	Closed	1997	95.00	95

Wooden Dolls - N/A

YEAR ISSUE	EDITION LIMIT	YEAR RETD.	ISSUE PRICE	*QUOTE U.S.$
1991 Gretchen	9,850	1995	225.00	280
1991 Heidi	9,850	1995	225.00	250

Year Round Fun - D. Schurig

YEAR ISSUE	EDITION LIMIT	YEAR RETD.	ISSUE PRICE	*QUOTE U.S.$
1992 Allison	Closed	1995	95.00	95
1993 Christy	Closed	1995	95.00	95
1993 Paula	Closed	1995	95.00	95
1994 Kaylie	Closed	1995	95.00	125

Zolan Dolls - D. Zolan

YEAR ISSUE	EDITION LIMIT	YEAR RETD.	ISSUE PRICE	*QUOTE U.S.$
1991 A Christmas Prayer	Closed	1993	95.00	250
1992 Winter Angel	Closed	1996	95.00	95-110
1992 Rainy Day Pals	Closed	1996	95.00	125
1992 Quiet Time	Closed	1996	95.00	125
1993 For You	Closed	1996	95.00	125
1993 The Thinker	Closed	1996	95.00	180

Zolan Double Dolls - D. Zolan

YEAR ISSUE	EDITION LIMIT	YEAR RETD.	ISSUE PRICE	*QUOTE U.S.$
1993 First Kiss	Closed	1995	155.00	180-295
1994 New Shoes	Closed	1995	155.00	155

Islandia International

Sonshine Promises - G. Clasby

YEAR ISSUE	EDITION LIMIT	YEAR RETD.	ISSUE PRICE	*QUOTE U.S.$
2000 The Best Seat in Life is Next to You 2007	Open		19.50	20
2000 Congratulations, You Earned Your Wings! 2006	Open		19.50	20
2000 Friends Are Tied Together With Ribbons of Love 2010	Open		19.50	20
2000 Let Your Star Shine 2001	Open		19.50	20
2000 Love From the Heart 2003	Open		19.50	20
2000 Mark the Positive, Erase the Negative 2009	Open		19.50	20
2000 A Scoop Full of Birthday Wishes 2004	Open		19.50	20
2000 Together We're Going Places-Bride 2011	Open		19.50	20
2000 Together We're Going Places-Groom 2012	Open		19.50	20
2000 A Tribute: For You Answer the Call 2013	Open		19.50	20
2000 You're a Bouquet of Joy 2005	Open		19.50	20
2000 You're An Angel To Me 2008	Open		19.50	20
2000 You're One in a Million 2002	Open		19.50	20

Jan Hagara Collectables

Jan Hagara Collector's Club - J. Hagara

YEAR ISSUE	EDITION LIMIT	YEAR RETD.	ISSUE PRICE	*QUOTE U.S.$
1987 Jan at Age 4 Plaque (Charter Member)	Closed	1988	Gift	50-125
1987 Jan at Age 4 Pin (Charter Member)	Closed	1988	Gift	25
1987 Mattie Print	Closed	1988	55.00	55-150
1988 Cloud Pin	Closed	1989	Gift	N/A
1988 Bonnie Print	Closed	1989	45.00	45-85
1988 Mattie Figurine	Closed	1989	47.50	65-75
1989 Mattie Doll	Closed	1990	550.00	550
1989 Cloud Figurine	Closed	1990	30.00	40
1989 Jan at Age 4 Miniature	Closed	1990	22.00	22-35
1989 Brandon Print	Closed	1990	45.00	50
1989 Bonnie Pin	Closed	1990	Gift	N/A
1990 Bonnie Figurine	Closed	1991	40.00	50
1990 Cloud Miniature	Closed	1991	20.00	20-30
1990 Brandon Pin	Closed	1991	Gift	N/A
1990 Tiffany Print	Closed	1991	55.00	55
1991 Tiffany Pin	Closed	1992	Gift	N/A
1991 Brandon Figurine	Closed	1992	40.00	55
1991 Bonnie Doll	Closed	1992	395.00	395-407
1991 Mattie Miniature	Closed	1992	22.50	23
1991 Cherished (Bonnie's Bear) Miniature	Closed	1992	Gift	15
1991 Peggy Sue Print	Closed	1992	Gift	48
1991 Peggy Sue Figurine (Charter Member)	Closed	1992	27.50	60
1991 Peggy Sue Pin (Charter Member)	Closed	1992	Gift	20
1991 Larka Print	Closed	1992	75.00	75
1992 Enya Print	Closed	1992	Gift	55
1992 Larka Pin	Closed	1993	Gift	N/A
1992 Tiffany Figurine	Closed	1993	50.00	50-55
1993 Audrey Print	Closed	1993	Gift	35
1993 Brandon Doll	Closed	1994	360.00	360
1993 Audrey Pin	Closed	1994	Gift	N/A
1993 Audrey Figurine	Closed	1994	55.00	47-55
1994 Tara Pin	Closed	1995	Gift	N/A
1994 Tara Print	Closed	1995	55.00	55
1994 Courtney Print	Closed	1994	Gift	20
1994 Larka Figurine	Closed	1996	115.00	99-115
1995 Daniet Print	Closed	1995	Gift	25
1995 Daniel Pin	Closed	1996	Gift	N/A
1995 Tara Figurine	Closed	1996	Gift	55-65
1995 Tara Figurine	Closed	1996	60.00	60-65
1995 Star's Buggy II	Closed	1996	27.00	27-35
1996 Sean Print (matted)	Closed	1997	40.00	40
1996 Sean Print (fr. canvas)	Closed	1997	165.00	165
1996 Sean Print (gallery-w/o frame)	Closed	1997	250.00	250
1996 Sean Print (gallery-w/frame)	Closed	1997	338.00	338
1996 Peggy Sue Doll	Closed	1997	395.00	395
1996 Courtney Figurine	Closed	1997	Gift	40
1996 Barbara Print (fr. canvas)	Closed	1997	144.00	144
1996 Barbara Print (unfr. canvas)	Closed	1997	99.00	99
1996 Barbara Print (matted)	Closed	1997	25.00	25
1996 Sean Figurine (Charter)	Closed	1999	47.50	45
1996 Sean Figurine	Closed	1999	52.00	52
1996 Larka's Toys	Closed	1997	27.00	27
1997 Barbara Figurine	Closed	1998	Gift	40-45
1997 Inya Figurine	Closed	1999	55.00	55-65
1997 Peppermint Print (gallery-w/o frame)	Closed	1998	85.00	85
1997 Peppermint Print (gallery-w/frame)	Closed	1998	143.00	143
1997 Peppermint Print	Closed	1998	Gift	N/A
1996 Star's Buggy Pin	Closed	1997	Gift	N/A
1997 Peppermint Figurine	Closed	1998	49.00	49-75
1997 Peppermint Pin	Closed	1998	Gift	N/A
1998 Debbie Pin	Closed	1999	Gift	N/A

B&J Co. - J. Hagara

YEAR ISSUE	EDITION LIMIT	YEAR RETD.	ISSUE PRICE	*QUOTE U.S.$
1995 Addie w/Princess 23"	85	1997	2000.00	2000
1988 Adrianne 14"	2-Yr.	1990	125.00	219-250
1987 Allegra 12"	250	1988	800.00	800-1000
1988 Amy 13"	2-Yr.	1990	160.00	160-250
1992 Ann Marie 14"	500	1993	425.00	425-495
1988 Ashley 13"	2-Yr.	1990	160.00	160-200
1992 Brianna 7 1/2"	300	1993	300.00	300
1990 Clara 18"	120	1990	375.00	375-795
1992 Dacy 18"	700	1995	495.00	495-595
1995 Debra 15"	250	1997	425.00	425
1993 Jackie 18"	300	1996	495.00	495
1993 Jamie 14"	350	1995	395.00	395-450
1990 Jessica 18"	350	1991	700.00	700
1995 Joseph 12" (blue)	150	1997	250.00	250-300
1995 Joseph 12" (pink)	150	1997	250.00	250-300
1995 June 12"	300	1997	250.00	250
1995 Kelton 7"	300	1997	250.00	250
1988 Lee 8"	100	1988	300.00	300
1995 May 12"	300	1997	250.00	250
1987 Meg 15"	2-Yr.	1989	250.00	219-250
1987 Michael 12"	250	1989	650.00	728-850
1986 Paige 12"	430	1988	195.00	195-800
1995 Princess 12"	100	1997	270.00	270-350
1994 Renny 18"	300	1996	495.00	495
1991 Renny 23"	50	1994	2500.00	2500
1993 Rosie 18"	300	1994	495.00	495
1992 Sheldon 18"	500	1995	495.00	495
1990 Shelley 18"	1,200	1992	550.00	550-595
1994 Star 18"	100	1994	800.00	800-1000
1992 Tina 14"	500	1994	425.00	425
1994 Tiny Lee 6"	900	1997	52.50	55
1994 Todd 14"	75	1995	425.00	425
1986 Tracy 12"	2-Yr.	1988	125.00	125-200
1994 Wendy 25"	60	1996	2500.00	2500

Danbury Mint - J. Hagara

YEAR ISSUE	EDITION LIMIT	YEAR RETD.	ISSUE PRICE	*QUOTE U.S.$
1991 Adell 19"	Yr.Iss.	1992	195.00	195
1990 Brook 19"	Yr.Iss.	1991	195.00	195
1990 Goldie 19"	Yr.Iss.	1991	195.00	195-295
1989 Sophie 19"	Yr.Iss.	1990	195.00	295

Effanbee Vinyl Dolls - J. Hagara

YEAR ISSUE	EDITION LIMIT	YEAR RETD.	ISSUE PRICE	*QUOTE U.S.$
1984 Belinda	2-Yr.	1986	55.00	55-65
1984 Beth	2-Yr.	1986	55.00	55-125
1984 Bobby	2-Yr.	1986	55.00	65

Heirloom Dolls - J. Hagara

YEAR ISSUE	EDITION LIMIT	YEAR RETD.	ISSUE PRICE	*QUOTE U.S.$
1985 Amanda 12"	2-Yr.	1987	125.00	250
1985 Carol 12"	2-Yr.	1987	85.00	125-250
1985 Jimmy 12"	2-Yr.	1987	125.00	125-250
1985 Lisa 12"	2-Yr.	1987	125.00	125-250
1985 Sharice 12"	2-Yr.	1987	125.00	125-250

Royal Orleans Porcelain Dolls - J. Hagara

YEAR ISSUE	EDITION LIMIT	YEAR RETD.	ISSUE PRICE	*QUOTE U.S.$
1984 Jenny & the Bye Lo 17"	2-Yr.	1986	375.00	375-750
1985 Jody & the Toy Horse 17"	2-Yr.	1987	375.00	375

Vinyl Dolls - J. Hagara

YEAR ISSUE	EDITION LIMIT	YEAR RETD.	ISSUE PRICE	*QUOTE U.S.$
1983 Cristina #1	2-Yr.	1985	65.00	100-227
1984 Larry #3	2-Yr.	1986	65.00	65-140
1984 Laurel #2	2-Yr.	1986	65.00	65-157
1984 Lesley #3	2-Yr.	1986	65.00	50-188
1985 Mary Ann #4	2-Yr.	1987	70.00	70-150
1985 Molly #4	2-Yr.	1987	50.00	50-100

*Quotes have been rounded up to nearest dollar

Jan McLean Originals

Flowers of the Heart Collection - J. McLean

YEAR ISSUE	EDITION LIMIT	YEAR RETD.	ISSUE PRICE	*QUOTE U.S.$
1991 Marigold	100	N/A	2400.00	2900-3200
1990 Pansy	100	N/A	2200.00	2800-2900
1990 Pansy (bobbed blonde)	Retrd.	N/A	2200.00	2800-3000
1990 Pansy, A/P	Retrd.	N/A	4300	4800
1990 Poppy	100	N/A	2200.00	2700
1991 Primrose	100	N/A	2500.00	2500-2600

Jan McLean Originals - J. McLean

YEAR ISSUE	EDITION LIMIT	YEAR RETD.	ISSUE PRICE	*QUOTE U.S.$
1991 Lucrezia	15		6000.00	6000
1990 Phoebe I	25	N/A	2700.00	3300-3600

Kurt S. Adler, Inc.

Fleur-dis-Lis Enchanted Garden - J. Mostrom

YEAR ISSUE	EDITION LIMIT	YEAR RETD.	ISSUE PRICE	*QUOTE U.S.$
1997 Alexandra in Plum W3340	Open		20.00	20
1998 Bethany with Flowers W3461	Retrd.	1999	21.00	21
1997 Bonnie in Ribbons W3343	Retrd.	1999	21.00	21
1997 Celeste the Garden Angel W3344	Retrd.	1997	45.00	45
1998 Jennifer Ballerina W3462	Retrd.	2000	18.00	18
1997 Jenny Lind W3336	Retrd.	1999	28.00	28
1997 Lilac Fairy W3342	Retrd.	1999	22.00	22
1997 Lily Fairy W3342	Retrd.	1999	22.00	22
1997 Marissa In Mauve W3340	Open		20.00	20
1997 Melissa in Lace W3343	Retrd.	1999	21.00	21
1998 Michael with Dog W3463	Retrd.	1999	22.00	22
1998 Monica Ballerina W3462	Retrd.	2000	18.00	18
1998 Natalie with Doll W3461	Retrd.	1999	21.00	21
1998 Pauline with Cat W3463	Retrd.	1999	22.00	22
1997 Rose Fairy W3342	Retrd.	1999	22.00	22
1998 Sarah with Present W3461	Retrd.	1999	21.00	21

Fleur-dis-Lis Sugar Plum - J. Mostrom

YEAR ISSUE	EDITION LIMIT	YEAR RETD.	ISSUE PRICE	*QUOTE U.S.$
2000 Bertie in Velvet/Natalie W3877	Open		20.00	20
2000 Etoile with Garland/Cherie with Dove W3878	Open		18.00	18
2000 Sugar Plum Babies W3879	Open		12.50	13

Fleur-dis-Lis Victorian Manor - J. Mostrom

YEAR ISSUE	EDITION LIMIT	YEAR RETD.	ISSUE PRICE	*QUOTE U.S.$
1997 Barbara With Muff W3348	Retrd.	1997	30.00	30
1997 Caroling Jane with Book W3338	Retrd.	1997	22.00	22
1997 Jonathan with Horn W3338	Retrd.	1997	22.00	22
1997 Kathryn with Cape W3338	Retrd.	1997	22.00	22
1997 Rebecca Burgundy Skater Lady W3337	Retrd.	1999	32.00	32

Fleur-dis-Lis Victorian Valentine - J. Mostrom

YEAR ISSUE	EDITION LIMIT	YEAR RETD.	ISSUE PRICE	*QUOTE U.S.$
2000 Jenny w/Teapot/Emma w/Doll W3867	Open		25.00	25

Fleur-dis-Lis Winter Dreams - J. Mostrom

YEAR ISSUE	EDITION LIMIT	YEAR RETD.	ISSUE PRICE	*QUOTE U.S.$
1997 Charlotte with Hat & Cape W3345	Retrd.	1997	22.00	22
1997 George with Box W3345	Retrd.	1997	22.00	22
1998 Jack Frost W3483	Open		21.00	21
1998 Joshua with Sled W3485	Retrd.	1999	25.00	25
1998 Kristen with Muff W3485	Retrd.	1999	25.00	25
1998 Patricia with Snowflake W3485	Retrd.	1999	25.00	25
1997 Sandra with Box W3345	Retrd.	1997	22.00	22
1998 Snow Fairy W3483	Open		21.00	21
1998 Snowflake Babies W3482	Retrd.	2000	18.00	18

Holly Bearies - H. Adler

YEAR ISSUE	EDITION LIMIT	YEAR RETD.	ISSUE PRICE	*QUOTE U.S.$
1998 Ashton, 10" K2032	Retrd.	1998	40.00	40
1999 Brittany, 24" K2036	Retrd.	2000	67.00	67
1999 Cedric, 20" K2040	Retrd.	2000	40.00	40
1997 Charlie, 6 1/2" H6006	Retrd.	1998	11.00	11
1997 Freemont, 15" K2027	Retrd.	1999	80.00	80
1999 Happy, 17" K2039	Open		33.50	34
1998 Holden, 18" K2031	Open		50.00	50
1999 Katerina, 16" K2038	Retrd.	2000	33.50	34
1998 Merry, Merry Holly Bearie, 12" K2030	Retrd.	1999	35.00	35
1999 Stefan, 20" K2037	Retrd.	2000	50.00	50
1997 Toby, 8" K2025	Retrd.	1999	18.00	18
1999 Tyler, 9 1/2" K2041	Retrd.	2000	27.00	27
1998 Zoe, 10" K2033	Retrd.	1999	28.00	28

Royal Heritage Collection - J. Mostrom

YEAR ISSUE	EDITION LIMIT	YEAR RETD.	ISSUE PRICE	*QUOTE U.S.$
1993 Anastasia J5746	3,000	1996	125.00	125
1993 Good King Wenceslas W2928	2,000	1996	130.00	130
1993 Medieval King of Christmas W2981	2,000	1994	390.00	390
1994 Nicholas on Skates J5750	3,000	1996	120.00	120
1994 Sasha on Skates J5749	3,000	1996	130.00	130

Small Wonders - J. Mostrom

YEAR ISSUE	EDITION LIMIT	YEAR RETD.	ISSUE PRICE	*QUOTE U.S.$
1995 America-Hollie Blue W3162	Retrd.	1999	30.00	30
1995 America-Texas Tyler W3162	Retrd.	1999	30.00	30
1995 Ireland-Cathleen W3082	Retrd.	1997	28.00	28
1995 Ireland-Michael W3082	Retrd.	1997	28.00	28
1995 Kwanzaa-Mufaro W3161	Retrd.	1996	28.00	28
1995 Kwanzaa-Shani W3161	Retrd.	1996	28.00	28

When I Grow Up - J. Mostrom

YEAR ISSUE	EDITION LIMIT	YEAR RETD.	ISSUE PRICE	*QUOTE U.S.$
1995 Dr. Brown W3079	Retrd.	1996	27.00	27
1995 Freddy the Fireman W3163	Open		28.00	28
1995 Melissa the Teacher W3081	Retrd.	1996	28.00	28
1995 Nurse Nancy W3079	Retrd.	1996	27.00	27
1995 Scott the Golfer W3080	Open	1996	28.00	28

Ladie and Friends

Lizzie High Society™ Members-Only Dolls - B.&P. Wisber

YEAR ISSUE	EDITION LIMIT	YEAR RETD.	ISSUE PRICE	*QUOTE U.S.$
1993 Audrey High -1301	Closed	1992	59.00	450-525
1993 Becky High -1330	Closed	1994	96.00	400-500
1994 Chloe Valentine -1351	Closed	1995	79.00	175-200
1996 Dottie Bowman -1371	Closed	1996	78.00	100-140
1997 Ellie Bowman -1396	Closed	1997	62.00	74-120
1998 Fiona High -1415	Closed	1998	67.00	80-110
1999 Gloria Valentine -1440	Closed	1999	67.95	68-100
2000 Heidi Bowman - 1470	Yr.Iss.		62.00	62

The Christmas Concert - B.&P. Wisber

YEAR ISSUE	EDITION LIMIT	YEAR RETD.	ISSUE PRICE	*QUOTE U.S.$
1990 Claire Valentine -1262	Closed	1997	56.00	58-68
1993 James Valentine -1310	Closed	1997	60.00	72
1992 Judith High -1292	Closed	1997	70.00	88
1996 Meredith High -1383	Closed	1999	79.50	80
1996 Phillip Valentine -1384	Closed	1999	79.50	80
1993 Stephanie Bowman -1309	Closed	1998	74.00	77-96

The Christmas Pageant™ - B.&P. Wisber

YEAR ISSUE	EDITION LIMIT	YEAR RETD.	ISSUE PRICE	*QUOTE U.S.$
1985 "Earth" Angel -1122	Closed	1989	30.00	110
1985 "Noel" Angel (1st ed.) -1126	Closed	1989	30.00	110
1989 "Noel" Angel (2nd ed.) -1126	Open		48.00	52
1985 "On" Angel -1121	Closed	1989	30.00	110-200
1985 "Peace" Angel (1st ed.) -1120	Closed	1989	30.00	110
1989 "Peace" Angel (2nd ed.) -1120	Open		48.00	52
1985 Christmas Wooly Lamb -1133	Closed	1991	11.00	35
1985 Joseph and Donkey -1119	Closed	2000	30.00	38-60
1985 Mary and Baby Jesus -1118	Closed	2000	30.00	38-60
1986 Shepherd -1193	Closed	2000	32.00	38-60
1985 Wiseman #1 -1123	Closed	1996	30.00	47-100
1985 Wiseman #2 -1124	Closed	1996	30.00	47-100
1985 Wiseman #3 -1125	Closed	1996	30.00	47-100
1985 Wooden Creche -1132	Closed	2000	28.00	32-50

The Grummels of Log Hollow™ - B.&P. Wisber

YEAR ISSUE	EDITION LIMIT	YEAR RETD.	ISSUE PRICE	*QUOTE U.S.$
1986 Aunt Gertie Grummel™ -1171	Closed	1988	34.00	115
1986 Aunt Hilda Grummel™ -1174	Closed	1988	34.00	115
1986 Aunt Polly Grummel™ -1169	Closed	1988	34.00	115
1986 Cousin Lottie Grummel™ -1170	Closed	1988	36.00	115
1986 Cousin Miranda Grummel™ -1165	Closed	1988	47.00	115
1986 Grandma Grummel™ -1173	Closed	1988	45.00	115
1986 Grandpa Grummel™ -1176	Closed	1988	36.00	180
1986 The Little Ones -Grummels™ (boy/girl) -1196	Closed	1988	15.00	40
1986 Ma Grummel™ -1167	Closed	1988	36.00	115
1986 Pa Grummel™ -1172	Closed	1988	34.00	115
1986 Sister Nora Grummel™ -1177	Closed	1988	34.00	115
1986 Teddy Bear Bed -1168	Closed	1988	15.00	115
1986 Uncle Hollis Grummel™ -1166	Closed	1988	34.00	115
1986 Washline -1175	Closed	1988	15.00	70-100

The Little Ones at Christmas™ - B.&P. Wisber

YEAR ISSUE	EDITION LIMIT	YEAR RETD.	ISSUE PRICE	*QUOTE U.S.$
1991 Boy (black) w/Santa Photo -1273A	Closed	1996	24.00	34-40
1991 Boy (white) w/Santa Photo -1273	Closed	1996	24.00	28-40
1993 Boy Peeking (Alone) -1314	Closed	1997	22.00	23-28
1993 Boy Peeking w/Tree -1313	Closed	1997	60.00	61-68
1996 Boy Tangled in Lights -1390	Closed	2000	31.00	31-38
1996 Boy w/Ornament -1388	Closed	1997	26.00	30
1990 Girl (black) w/Basket of Greens -1263	Closed	1996	22.00	28-32
1991 Girl (black) w/Santa Photo -1272A	Closed	1996	24.00	34-40
1990 Girl (white) w/Cookie -1264	Closed	1997	22.00	28-32
1990 Girl (white) w/Gift -1266	Closed	1997	22.00	28-32
1991 Girl (white) w/Santa Photo -1272	Closed	1996	24.00	28-40
1990 Girl (white) w/Tree Garland -1265	Closed	1997	22.00	28-32
1993 Girl Peeking (Alone) -1316	Closed	1997	22.00	23-30
1993 Girl Peeking w/Tree -1315	Closed	1997	60.00	61-68
1999 Girl Stringing Lights on Tree -1465	Open		47.50	48
1996 Girl Tangled in Lights -1389	Closed	2000	35.00	35-42
1993 Girl w/Baking Table -1317	Closed	1999	38.00	40-46
1999 Girl w/Basket -1467	Open		32.50	33
1999 Girl w/Birdhouses -1466	Open		29.95	30
1992 Girl w/Christmas Lights -1287	Closed	1998	34.00	36-42
1994 Girl w/Greens on Table -1337	Closed	2000	46.00	48-56
1993 Girl w/Note for Santa -1318	Closed	1999	36.00	38-44
1996 Girl w/Ornament -1387	Closed	1997	30.00	30-36
1999 Girl w/Snowman Wreath -1468	Open		33.50	34
1995 Little Santa -1364	Open		50.00	51
1998 Santa -1438	Open		29.95	30

The Little Ones™ - B.&P. Wisber

YEAR ISSUE	EDITION LIMIT	YEAR RETD.	ISSUE PRICE	*QUOTE U.S.$
1993 Ballerina -1321	Closed	2000	40.00	42-48
1996 Baseball (boy) -1399	Closed	2000	44.00	44-52
1996 Baseball (girl) -1398	Closed	2000	44.00	44-52
1995 Basketweaver -1363	Closed	2000	48.00	49-58
1994 Bonnie Valentine -1323	Closed	1998	35.00	36-42
1985 Boy (black) (1st ed.) -1130	Closed	1989	15.00	45-65
1989 Boy (black) (2nd ed.) -1130I	Closed	1994	20.00	26
1985 Boy (white) (1st ed.) -1130	Closed	1989	15.00	45-65
1989 Boy (white) (2nd ed.) -1130H	Closed	1994	20.00	26
1994 Boy Dyeing Eggs -1327	Closed	2000	30.00	32-36
1993 Boy w/Easter Flowers -1306	Closed	1999	30.00	32-36
1992 Clown -1290	Closed	1999	32.00	35
1986 Ghost Petey (1st ed.) 1197	Closed	1996	15.00	24-28
1998 Ghost Petey (2nd ed.) -1197	Open		23.50	24
1985 Girl (black) (1st ed.) -1130	Closed	1989	15.00	45-65
1989 Girl (black) -country color (2nd ed.) -1130G	Closed	1994	20.00	26
1989 Girl (black) -pastels (2nd ed.) -1130E	Closed	1994	20.00	26
1985 Girl (white) (1st ed.) -1130	Closed	1989	15.00	45-65
1989 Girl (white) -country color (2nd ed.) -1130F	Closed	1994	20.00	26
1989 Girl (white) -pastels (2nd ed.) -1130H	Closed	1994	20.00	26
1994 Girl Dyeing Eggs -1326	Closed	2000	30.00	32-36
1996 Girl Hopscotching -1385	Closed	1999	45.00	45-54
1992 Girl Reading -1286	Closed	1997	36.00	39
1996 Girl Rollerskating (black) -1377	Closed	1999	40.00	40-48
1996 Girl Rollerskating (white) -1376	Closed	1999	40.00	40-48
1992 Girl w/Beach Bucket -1275	Closed	1999	26.00	29-32
1993 Girl w/Easter Eggs -1276	Closed	1997	26.00	29
1993 Girl w/Easter Flowers -1296	Closed	1999	34.00	35-38
1992 Girl w/Kitten and Milk -1280	Closed	1997	32.00	35
1992 Girl w/Kitten and Yarn -1278	Closed	1997	34.00	37
1994 Girl w/Laundry Basket -1338	Closed	2000	38.00	40-46
1993 Girl w/Mop -1300	Closed	1999	36.00	38-42
1994 Girl w/Puppy in Tub -1339	Closed	1999	43.00	45-49
1993 Girl w/Spinning Wheel -1299	Closed	1999	36.00	38-42
1992 Girl w/Valentine -1291	Closed	1998	30.00	36
1993 Girl w/Violin -1319	Closed	2000	28.00	30-34
1994 Jamie Bowman -1324	Closed	1998	35.00	36-42
1995 June Fete (boy) -1350	Closed	1997	33.00	32-40
1995 June Fete (girl) -1349	Closed	1997	33.00	32-40

Lizzie High® Dolls - B.&P. Wisber

YEAR ISSUE	EDITION LIMIT	YEAR RETD.	ISSUE PRICE	*QUOTE U.S.$
1987 Abigail Bowman (1st ed.) -1199	Closed	1994	40.00	92-100
1997 Abigail Bowman (2nd ed.) -1199	Open		68.50	69
1996 Adam Valentine -1380	Closed	1999	69.50	70-82
1987 Addie High -1202	Closed	1996	37.00	50-72
1990 Albert Valentine -1260	Closed	1995	42.00	65-85
1986 Alice Valentine (1st ed.) -1148	Closed	1987	32.00	100
1995 Alice Valentine (2nd ed.) -1148	Closed	1998	56.00	68
1988 Allison Bowman -1229	Closed	1996	56.00	74-105
1985 Amanda High (1st ed.) -1111	Closed	1988	30.00	116
1990 Amanda High (2nd ed.) -1111	Closed	1995	54.00	65-85
1989 Amelia High -1248	Closed	2000	45.00	50-60
1987 Amy Bowman -1201	Closed	1994	37.00	82
1986 Andrew Brown -1157	Closed	1988	45.00	125
1991 Annabelle Bowman -1267	Closed	1997	68.00	72-82
1986 Annie Bowman (1st ed.) -1150	Closed	1989	32.00	100
1993 Annie Bowman (2nd ed.) -1150	Closed	1997	68.00	72-82
1993 Ashley Bowman -1304	Closed	1997	48.00	50-58
1992 Barbara Helen -1274	Closed	1996	58.00	74
1985 Benjamin Bowman (Santa) -1134	Closed	1996	34.00	42-50
1985 Benjamin Bowman -1129	Closed	1987	30.00	100
1988 Bess High (1st ed.) -1241	Closed	1996	45.00	60-100
1988 Bess High (2nd ed.) -1241	Open		72.95.	73
1996 Beth Bowman (2nd ed.) -1149A	Open		28.50	29
1988 Betsy Valentine -1245	Closed	1996	42.00	56-84
1996 Beverly Ann Bowman -1379	Closed	1999	69.50	70-82
1987 Bridget Bowman (1st ed.) -1222	Closed	1994	40.00	95
1996 Bridget Bowman (2nd ed.) -1222	Open		76.00	76
1992 Carol Anne Bowman -1282	Closed	1994	70.00	142
1986 Carrie High (1st ed.) -1190	Closed	1989	45.00	100
1989 Carrie High (2nd ed.) -1190	Closed	1997	46.00	50-56
1986 Cassie Yocum (1st ed.) -1179	Closed	1988	36.00	150
1993 Cassie Yocum (2nd ed.) -1179	Closed	1998	80.00	96
1987 Cat on Chair -1217	Closed	1991	16.00	45
1996 Cecelia Brown (alone) -1366A	Closed	1998	27.50	33
1996 Cecelia Brown (w/Mother) -1366	Closed	1998	101.00	118
1987 Charles Bowman (1st ed.) -1221	Closed	1990	34.00	100
1992 Charles Bowman (2nd ed.) -1221	Closed	1995	46.00	58
1996 Charlotte High -1370	Closed	2000	73.50	74-89
1985 Christian Bowman -1110	Closed	1987	30.00	100
1994 Christine Bowman -1332	Closed	1999	62.00	65-75
1986 Christopher High -1182	Closed	1992	34.00	80-100
1985 Cora High -1115	Closed	1987	30.00	115
1991 Cynthia High -1127A	Closed	1995	60.00	75-80
1996 Daniel Brown (alone) -1367A	Closed	1998	27.50	33
1996 Daniel Brown (w/Mother) -1367	Closed	1998	101.00	118
1988 Daphne Bowman -1235	Closed	1994	38.00	76
1996 Darlene Bowman -1368	Closed	1997	77.50	78-92
1986 David Yocum -1195	Closed	1995	33.00	66-85
1986 Delia Valentine (1st ed.) -1153	Closed	1988	32.00	100
1996 Delia Valentine (2nd ed.) -1153	Closed	2000	65.50	66-80
1991 The Department Store Santa -1270	Closed	1996	76.00	100-120
1986 Dora Valentine (1st ed.) -1152	Closed	1989	30.00	100
1992 Dora Valentine (2nd ed.) -1152	Open		48.00	51
1986 Edward Bowman (1st ed.) -1158	Closed	1988	45.00	125
1994 Edward Bowman (2nd ed.) -1158	Closed	1998	76.00	79-92
1992 Edwin Bowman -1281	Closed	1994	70.00	90
1985 Elizabeth Sweetland (1st ed.) -1109	Closed	1987	30.00	115
1991 Elizabeth Sweetland (2nd ed.) -1109	Closed	1996	56.00	72-85
1994 Elsie Bowman -1325	Closed	2000	64.00	67-80
1986 Emily Bowman (1st ed.) -1185	Closed	1990	34.00	115
1990 Emily Bowman (2nd ed.) -1185	Closed	1996	48.00	58-85
1985 Emma High (1st ed.) -1103	Closed	1988	30.00	100
1996 Emma High (2nd ed.) -1103	Closed	2000	69.50	70-84
1989 Emmy Lou Valentine -1251	Closed	1997	45.00	54-59
1985 Esther Dunn (1st ed.) -1127	Closed	1987	45.00	125
1991 Esther Dunn (2nd ed.) -1127	Closed	1995	60.00	80-95
1988 Eunice High -1240	Closed	1994	56.00	115-125
1997 Father Christmas -1409	2-Yr.	1999	84.00	80-100
1985 Flossie High (1st ed.) -1128	Closed	1988	45.00	125
1989 Flossie High (2nd ed.) -1128	Closed	1997	54.00	57-66
1987 The Flower Girl -1204	Closed	1995	17.00	50
1996 Francine Bowman -1381	Closed	2000	60.00	60
1993 Francis Bowman -1305	Closed	1997	48.00	49-58
1994 Gilbert High -1335	Closed	2000	65.00	68-82
1996 Glenda Brown -1382	Closed	2000	60.00	60-72
1986 Grace Valentine (1st ed.) -1146	Closed	1989	32.00	100
1991 Grace Valentine (2nd ed.) -1146	Closed	1999	48.00	58-68
1987 Gretchen High -1216	Closed	1994	40.00	88
1994 Gwendolyn High -1342	Closed	1999	56.00	59-68
1985 Hannah Brown -1131	Closed	1988	45.00	125
1988 Hattie Bowman -1239	Closed	1996	40.00	88
1985 Ida Valentine -1116	Closed	1988	30.00	100
1987 Imogene Bowman -1206	Closed	1994	37.00	90
1988 Jacob High -1230	Closed	1994	44.00	88-102
1988 Janie Valentine -1231	Closed	1996	37.00	52

*Quotes have been rounded up to nearest dollar

YEAR ISSUE	EDITION LIMIT	YEAR RETD.	ISSUE PRICE	*QUOTE U.S.$
1989 Jason High (alone) -1254A	Closed	1996	20.00	30-50
1989 Jason High (with Mother) -1254	Closed	1996	58.00	75-85
1986 Jenny Valentine (1st ed.) -1181	Closed	1989	34.00	110
1997 Jenny Valentine (2nd ed.) -1181	Open		52.00	52
1986 Jeremy Bowman -1192	Closed	1991	36.00	80
1989 Jessica High (alone) -1253A	Closed	1996	20.00	30-50
1989 Jessica High (with Mother) -1253	Closed	1996	58.00	75-85
1986 Jillian Bowman (1st ed.) -1180	Closed	1990	34.00	110
1995 Jillian Bowman (2nd ed.) -1180	Closed	1998	90.00	75
1992 Joanie Valentine -1295	Closed	1998	48.00	50
1989 Johann Bowman -1250	Closed	1997	40.00	48
1987 Johanna Valentine -1198	Closed	1988	37.00	100
1992 Joseph Valentine -1283	Closed	1995	62.00	75
1994 Josie Valentine -1322	Closed	1998	76.00	78-92
1986 Juliet Valentine (1st ed.) -1147	Closed	1988	32.00	100
1990 Juliet Valentine (2nd ed.) -1147	Closed	1996	48.00	62
1993 Justine Valentine -1302	Closed	1997	84.00	87
1986 Karl Valentine (1st ed.) -1161	Closed	1988	30.00	100
1994 Karl Valentine (2nd ed.) -1161	Closed	1999	54.00	57-65
1987 Katie and Barney (1st Costume)-1219	Closed	1996	38.00	43-80
1987 Katie and Barney (2nd Costume)-1219	Closed	1996	38.00	43-85
1986 Katie Bowman -1178	Closed	1994	36.00	96
1985 Katrina Valentine -1135	Closed	1989	30.00	125
1988 Kinch Bowman -1237	Closed	1996	47.00	62
1987 Laura Valentine -1223	Closed	1994	36.00	86-95
1995 Leona High -1355	Closed	1999	68.00	70-82
1987 Little Witch -1225	Closed	1996	17.00	23-32
1985 Lizzie High® (1st ed.) -1100	Closed	1995	30.00	100-115
1996 Lizzie High® (2nd ed.) -1100	Open		92.00	92
1985 Louella Valentine -1112	Closed	1991	30.00	100
1989 Lucy Bowman -1255	Closed	1997	45.00	48-54
1985 Luther Bowman (1st ed.) -1108	Closed	1987	30.00	100
1993 Luther Bowman (2nd ed.) -1108	Open		60.00	63
1995 Lydia Bowman -1347	Closed	1997	54.00	55-66
1986 Madaleine Valentine (1st ed.) -1187	Closed	1989	34.00	90
1989 Madaleine Valentine (2nd ed.) -1187	Closed	1997	37.00	40-60
1986 Maggie High -1160	Closed	1988	30.00	100
1987 Margaret Bowman -1213	Closed	1996	35.00	54-100
1986 Marie Valentine (1st ed.) -1184	Closed	1990	47.00	125
1992 Marie Valentine (2nd ed.) -1184	Closed	1996	68.00	82-86
1986 Marisa Valentine (alone) (1st ed.) -1194A	Closed	1996	33.00	66
1998 Marisa Valentine (alone) (2nd ed.) -1194A	Open		57.50	58
1986 Marisa Valentine (w/ Brother Petey) (1st ed.) -1194	Closed	1996	45.00	70-88
1998 Marisa Valentine (w/ Brother Petey) (2nd ed.) -1194	Open		79.95	80
1994 Marisa Valentine -1333	Open		58.00	61
1986 Marland Valentine -1183	Closed	1990	33.00	100-150
1990 Marlene Valentine -1259	Closed	1995	48.00	85-96
1986 Martha High -1151	Closed	1989	32.00	100
1985 Martin Bowman (1st ed.) -1117	Closed	1992	30.00	85-100
1996 Martin Bowman (2nd ed.) -1117	Open		64.00	64
1988 Mary Ellen Valentine -1236	Closed	1996	40.00	54
1985 Mary Valentine -1105	Closed	1988	30.00	100
1986 Matthew Yocum -1186	Closed	1988	33.00	100
1988 Megan Valentine -1227	Closed	1994	44.00	94
1987 Melanie Bowman (1st ed.) -1220	Closed	1990	36.00	125
1992 Melanie Bowman (2nd ed.) -1220	Closed	1995	46.00	56
1991 Michael Bowman -1268	Closed	1997	52.00	66-85
1994 Minnie Valentine -1336	Closed	2000	64.00	65-80
1989 Miriam High -1256	Closed	1997	46.00	60-75
1986 Molly Yocum (1st ed.) -1189	Closed	1989	34.00	42-47
1989 Molly Yocum (2nd ed.) -1189	Closed	1997	39.00	47
1993 Mommy -1312	Closed	1998	48.00	49-58
1989 Mrs. Claus -1258	Closed	1997	42.00	45-75
1990 Nancy Bowman -1261	Closed	1997	48.00	58
1987 Naomi Valentine -1200	Closed	1993	40.00	88
1992 Natalie Valentine -1284	Closed	1995	62.00	75-90
1995 Nathan Bowman -1354	Closed	1999	70.00	70-84
1985 Nettie Brown (1st ed.) -1102	Closed	1987	30.00	100
1988 Nettie Brown (2nd ed.) -1102	Closed	1995	36.00	72-85
1985 Nettie Brown (Christmas) (1st ed.) -1114	Closed	1987	30.00	100
1996 Nettie Brown (Christmas) (2nd ed.) -1114	Closed	1999	66.00	66-80
1996 Nicholas Valentine (alone) -1365A	Closed	1998	27.50	33
1996 Nicholas Valentine (w/Mother) -1365	Closed	1998	101.00	99-118
1987 Olivia High -1205	Closed	1997	37.00	45
1987 Patsy Bowman -1214	Closed	1995	50.00	110-115
1988 Pauline Bowman -1228	Closed	1996	44.00	58-75
1993 Pearl Bowman -1303	Closed	1998	56.00	57-68
1989 Peggy Bowman -1252	Closed	1995	58.00	95
1987 Penelope High -1208	Closed	1991	40.00	100
1985 Peter Valentine (1st ed.) -1113	Closed	1991	30.00	75
1995 Peter Valentine (2nd ed.) -1113	Closed	1999	55.00	57-66
1988 Phoebe High (1st ed.) -1246	Closed	1992	48.00	90
1997 Phoebe High (2nd ed.) -1246	Closed	1999	65.50	66-78
1987 Priscilla High -1226	Closed	1995	56.00	130-135
1986 Rachel Bowman (1st ed.) -1188	Closed	1989	34.00	100
1989 Rachel Bowman (2nd ed.) -1188	Closed	1997	34.00	38-60
1987 Ramona Brown -1215	Closed	1989	40.00	66
1985 Rebecca Bowman (1st ed.) -1104	Closed	1988	30.00	100
1989 Rebecca Bowman (2nd ed.) -1104	Closed	1997	56.00	66-74
1987 Rebecca's Mother (2nd ed.) -1207	Closed	1995	75.95	76
1987 Rebecca's Mother -1207	Closed	1995	37.00	76-92
1995 Regina Bowman -1353	Closed	1999	70.00	70-84
1995 Robert Bowman -1348	Closed	1997	64.00	64-80
1985 Russell Dunn -1107	Closed	1987	30.00	110
1988 Ruth Anne Bowman -1232	Closed	1994	44.00	92-100
1985 Sabina Valentine (1st ed.) -1101	Closed	1987	30.00	110
1988 Sabina Valentine (2nd ed.) -1101	Closed	1996	40.00	53-80
1986 Sadie Valentine -1163	Closed	1996	45.00	72-105
1986 Sally Bowman (1st ed.) -1155	Closed	1991	32.00	110
1996 Sally Bowman (2nd ed.) -1155	Open		75.50	76
1988 Samantha Bowman -1238	Closed	1996	47.00	61-85
1989 Santa (with Tub) -1257	Closed	1997	58.00	78-85
1999 Santa -1469	2-Yr.		69.95	70
1987 Santa Claus (sitting) -1224	Closed	1991	50.00	125-175
1993 Santa Claus -1311	Closed	1998	48.00	49-100
1991 Santa's Helper -1271	Closed	1996	52.00	75-80
1986 Sara Valentine -1154	Closed	1994	32.00	90
1994 Shirley Bowman -1334	Closed	2000	63.00	70-80
1986 Sophie Valentine (1st ed.) -1164	Closed	1991	45.00	125
1996 Sophie Valentine (alone) -1164A	Closed	1998	27.50	33
1996 Sophie Valentine (w/Mother) (2nd ed.) -1164	Closed	1998	101.00	118
1995 St. Nicholas -1356	2-Yr.	1997	98.00	100-250
1986 Susanna Bowman (1st ed.) -1149	Closed	1988	45.00	125
1996 Susanna Bowman (2nd ed.) -1149	Open		49.50	50
1997 Theodore Bowman -1408	Closed	2000	59.00	59-72
1986 Thomas Bowman (1st ed.)-1159	Closed	1987	30.00	100
1996 Thomas Bowman (2nd ed.) -1159	Closed	2000	59.50	60-72
1986 Tillie Brown -1156	Closed	1988	32.00	100
1992 Timothy Bowman -1294	Closed	1999	56.00	58-68
1991 Trudy Valentine -1269	Closed	1997	64.00	82-95
1996 Tucker Bowman -1369	Closed	1997	77.50	78-92
1989 Vanessa High -1247	Closed	1996	45.00	60
1989 Victoria Bowman -1249	Closed	1997	40.00	44-52
1987 The Wedding (Bride) -1203	Closed	1995	37.00	100
1987 The Wedding (Groom) -1203A	Closed	1995	34.00	75
1985 Wendel Bowman (1st ed.) -1106	Closed	1987	30.00	100
1992 Wendel Bowman (2nd ed.) -1106	Closed	1996	60.00	75
1992 Wendy Bowman -1293	Closed	1999	78.00	58-94
1986 William Valentine -1191	Closed	1992	36.00	80
1986 Willie Bowman -1162	Closed	1992	30.00	72

The Pawtuckets of Sweet Briar Lane™ - B.&P. Wisber

YEAR ISSUE	EDITION LIMIT	YEAR RETD.	ISSUE PRICE	*QUOTE U.S.$
1986 Aunt Lillian Pawtucket™ (1st ed.) -1141	Closed	1989	32.00	125
1994 Aunt Lillian Pawtucket™ (2nd ed.) -1141	Closed	1998	58.00	61-70
1987 Aunt Mabel Pawtucket™ -212	Closed	1989	45.00	140
1986 Aunt Minnie Pawtucket™ (w/Flossie) (1st ed.) -1136	Closed	1989	45.00	115
1994 Aunt Minnie Pawtucket™ (2nd ed.) -1136	Closed	1998	72.00	86
1986 Brother Noah Pawtucket™ -1140	Closed	1989	32.00	115
1987 Bunny Bed -1218	Closed	1989	16.00	115
1987 Cousin Alberta Pawtucket™ -1210	Closed	1989	36.00	115
1986 Cousin Clara Pawtucket™ (1st ed.) -1144	Closed	1989	32.00	115
1996 Cousin Clara Pawtucket™ (2nd ed.) -1144	Closed	1998	84.00	84-100
1987 Cousin Isabel Pawtucket™ -1209	Closed	1989	36.00	115
1988 Cousin Jed Pawtucket™ -1234	Closed	1990	34.00	115
1988 Cousin Winnie Pawtucket™ -1233	Closed	1990	49.00	115
1994 Flossie Pawtucket™ (2nd ed.) -1136A	Closed	1998	33.00	35-40
1986 Grammy Pawtucket™ (1st ed.) -1137	Closed	1989	32.00	150-200
1994 Grammy Pawtucket™ (2nd ed.) -1137	Closed	1998	68.00	71-82
1995 The Little One Bunnies (1995) -female w/ laundry basket -1211A	Closed	1998	33.00	34-40
1986 The Little One Bunnies -boy (1st ed.) -1145	Closed	1989	15.00	50
1994 The Little One Bunnies -boy (2nd ed.) -1145A	Closed	1998	33.00	35-40
1986 The Little One Bunnies -girl (1st ed.) -1145	Closed	1989	15.00	40-50
1994 The Little One Bunnies -girl (2nd ed.) -1145	Closed	1998	33.00	35-40
1986 Mama Pawtucket™ (1st ed.) -1142	Closed	1989	34.00	115
1994 Mama Pawtucket™ (2nd ed.) -1142	Closed	1998	86.00	100
1986 Pappy Pawtucket™ (1st ed.) -1143	Closed	1989	32.00	115
1995 Pappy Pawtucket™ (2nd ed.) -1143	Closed	1998	56.00	58-68
1994 Pawtucket™ Bunny Hutch -1141A	Closed	1998	38.00	46
1995 Pawtucket™ Wash Line -1211B	Closed	1998	20.00	22-30
1987 Sister Clemmie Pawtucket™ (1st ed.) -1211	Closed	1989	34.00	115
1995 Sister Clemmie Pawtucket™ (2nd ed.) -1211	Closed	1998	60.00	62-72
1986 Sister Flora Pawtucket™ (1st ed.) -1139	Closed	1989	32.00	115
1996 Sister Flora Pawtucket™ (2nd ed.) -1139	Closed	1998	63.50	62-75
1986 Uncle Harley Pawtucket™ (1st ed.) -1138	Closed	1989	32.00	115
1994 Uncle Harley Pawtucket™ (2nd ed.) -1138	Closed	1998	74.00	77-90

Special Editions - B.&P. Wisber

YEAR ISSUE	EDITION LIMIT	YEAR RETD.	ISSUE PRICE	*QUOTE U.S.$
1992 Kathryn Bowman™ -1992 -1285	3,000	1992	140.00	800
1994 Prudence Valentine™ -1994 -1331	4,000	1994	180.00	350-400
1995 Little Lizzie High® -Anniversary Special Event Edition	Yr.Iss.	1995	40.00	50-60
1995 Lizzie High® -10th Anniversary Signature Edition -1100A	Yr.Iss.	1995	90.00	120-200
1996 Little Rebecca Bowman™ -1996 Special Event Edition -1372	Yr.Iss.	1996	37.00	43-57
1996 Lizzie & The Pawtuckets™ -1378	3,000	1996	180.00	180-250
1997 Libby Bowman - One-of-a-Kind Auction Doll & Teddy Bear Expo West	1	1997	N/A	1500
1997 Michelle Valentine -1997 Doll & Teddy Bear Expo Show Special (East & West)	150	1997	59.00	275-300
1997 Little Amanda High -1997 Special Event Edition -1397	Closed	1997	36.00	40-44
1998 Caroline Rebecca High - Golden Goose Store Exclusive	750	1998	79.95	80
1998 Courtney Valentine -1431	3,000	1998	158.00	190-200
1998 Little Sally Bowman -1998 Special Event Edition -1416	Closed	1998	36.95	40-44
1998 Molly - Longaberger® Exclusive	Closed	1998	79.95	80
1998 Daisy Mae - Longaberger® Exclusive	Closed	1998	67.95	68
1999 Little Sara Valentine -1999 Special October Event Edition	Closed	1999	36.95	37-44
1999 Holly - Longaberger® Exclusive -1095	Open		89.95	90
1999 Jenny - Longaberger® Exclusive -1097	Open		79.95	80
1999 Katie - Longaberger® Exclusive -1094	Open		79.95	80

The Thanksgiving Play - B.&P. Wisber

YEAR ISSUE	EDITION LIMIT	YEAR RETD.	ISSUE PRICE	*QUOTE U.S.$
1998 Father Pilgrim (2nd ed.) -1242	Open		55.95	56
1999 Indian Boy (1st ed.) -1244A	Open		53.95	54
1988 Indian Squaw (1st ed.) -1244	Closed	1995	36.00	62-90
1999 Indian Squaw (2nd ed.) -1244	Open		53.95	54
1998 Mother Pilgrim (2nd ed.) -1243	Open		65.95	66
1988 Pilgrim Boy (1st ed.) -1242	Closed	1995	40.00	52-90
1998 Pilgrim Boy Little One (1st ed.) -1242A	Open		29.95	30
1988 Pilgrim Girl (1st ed.) -1243	Closed	1995	48.00	60-90
1998 Pilgrim Girl Little One (1st ed.) -1243A	Open		32.95	33

The Lawton Doll Co.

Guild Dolls - W. Lawton

YEAR ISSUE	EDITION LIMIT	YEAR RETD.	ISSUE PRICE	*QUOTE U.S.$
1989 Baa Baa Black Sheep	1,003	1989	395.00	650-700
1990 Lavender Blue	781	1990	395.00	400
1991 To Market, To Market	683	1991	495.00	600
1992 Little Boy Blue	510	1992	395.00	395
1993 Lawton Logo Doll	575	1993	350.00	500
1994 Wee Handful	540	1994	250.00	295
1995 Uniquely Yours	500	1995	395.00	395
1996 Teddy And Me	601	1996	450.00	450
1997 The Lawton Travel Doll	485	1997	695.00	695
1998 Baby Boutique Blue	Retrd.	1998	495.00	495
1998 Baby Boutique Pink	Retrd.	1998	495.00	495
1999 Dreaming of Dolly	Retrd.	1999	495.00	495
2000 September Sojourn	Yr.Iss.		495.00	495

Cherished Customs - W. Lawton

YEAR ISSUE	EDITION LIMIT	YEAR RETD.	ISSUE PRICE	*QUOTE U.S.$
1990 The Blessing/Mexico	500	1990	395.00	1000-1200
1992 Carnival/Brazil	750	1992	425.00	495
1992 Cradleboard/Navajo	750	1993	425.00	495
1991 Frolic/Amish	500	1991	395.00	395
1990 Girl's Day/Japan	500	1990	395.00	450
1990 High Tea/Great Britain	500	1990	395.00	500-550
1994 Kwanzaa/Africa	500	1994	425.00	495
1990 Midsommar/Sweden	500	1990	395.00	450
1993 Nalauqataq-Eskimo	500	1993	395.00	450
1991 Ndeko/Zaire	500	1991	395.00	550
1992 Pascha/Ukraine	750	1992	495.00	495
1995 Piping the Haggis	350	1995	495.00	550
1993 Topeng Klana-Java	250	1993	495.00	495

Childhood Classics® - W. Lawton

YEAR ISSUE	EDITION LIMIT	YEAR RETD.	ISSUE PRICE	*QUOTE U.S.$
1983 Alice In Wonderland	100	1983	225.00	2000
1986 Anne Of Green Gables	250	1986	325.00	1600-2400
1991 The Bobbsey Twins: Flossie	350	1991	364.50	500
1991 The Bobbsey Twins: Freddie	350	1991	364.50	500
1985 Hans Brinker	250	1985	325.00	1800
1984 Heidi	250	1984	325.00	650
1991 Hiawatha	500	1991	395.00	500
1989 Honey Bunch	250	1989	350.00	550
1987 Just David	250	1987	325.00	700
1986 Laura Ingalls	250	1986	325.00	500
1991 Little Black Sambo	500	1991	395.00	695
1988 Little Eva	250	1988	350.00	700-900
1989 Little Princess	250	1989	395.00	600
1990 Mary Frances	350	1990	350.00	350
1987 Mary Lennox	250	1987	325.00	550-600
1987 Polly Pepper	250	1987	325.00	450
1986 Pollyanna	250	1986	325.00	1600
1990 Poor Little Match Girl	350	1990	350.00	550
1988 Rebecca	250	1988	350.00	450
1988 Topsy	250	1988	350.00	750

The Children's Hour - W. Lawton

YEAR ISSUE	EDITION LIMIT	YEAR RETD.	ISSUE PRICE	*QUOTE U.S.$
1991 Edith With Golden Hair	500	1991	395.00	475
1991 Grave Alice	500	1991	395.00	475
1991 Laughing Allegra	500	1991	395.00	475

Christmas Dolls - W. Lawton

YEAR ISSUE	EDITION LIMIT	YEAR RETD.	ISSUE PRICE	*QUOTE U.S.$
1988 Christmas Joy	500	1988	325.00	800
1989 Noel	500	1989	325.00	450
1990 Christmas Angel	500	1990	325.00	450
1991 Yuletide Carole	500	1991	395.00	450
1996 The Bird's Christmas Carol	500	1996	450.00	450
1998 Yes, Virginia	350	1998	450.00	450
2000 Trinkets and Poppets	175	2000	595.00	595

Classic Children - W. Lawton

YEAR ISSUE	EDITION LIMIT	YEAR RETD.	ISSUE PRICE	*QUOTE U.S.$
1998 Fleurette 'n' Fifi	350	1998	595.00	595

Classic Literature - W. Lawton

YEAR ISSUE	EDITION LIMIT	YEAR RETD.	ISSUE PRICE	*QUOTE U.S.$
2000 Jane Austen's Emma	175	2000	995.00	995

*Quotes have been rounded up to nearest dollar

Classic Playthings - W. Lawton

YEAR ISSUE	EDITION LIMIT	YEAR RETD.	ISSUE PRICE	*QUOTE U.S.$
2000 Bertha and Her Baby Doll	250	2000	695.00	695
1998 Petra and Pinocchio	750	1998	595.00	595

Early American Portraits - W. Lawton

YEAR ISSUE	EDITION LIMIT	YEAR RETD.	ISSUE PRICE	*QUOTE U.S.$
2000 Clarissa Fields and Bangwell Putt	175	2000	1295.00	1295

Fables and Folktales - W. Lawton

YEAR ISSUE	EDITION LIMIT	YEAR RETD.	ISSUE PRICE	*QUOTE U.S.$
2000 The Red Shoes	225	2000	595.00	595
2000 Tattercoats	225	2000	595.00	595

Language of Flowers - W. Lawton

YEAR ISSUE	EDITION LIMIT	YEAR RETD.	ISSUE PRICE	*QUOTE U.S.$
1998 Daisy	350	1998	395.00	395
1998 Violet	350	1998	395.00	395

Lawton Library - W. Lawton

YEAR ISSUE	EDITION LIMIT	YEAR RETD.	ISSUE PRICE	*QUOTE U.S.$
2000 The Secret Garden	175	2000	895.00	895

Masquerade Collection - W. Lawton

YEAR ISSUE	EDITION LIMIT	YEAR RETD.	ISSUE PRICE	*QUOTE U.S.$
2000 Harlequin	250	2000	695.00	695

Merely Me - W. Lawton

YEAR ISSUE	EDITION LIMIT	YEAR RETD.	ISSUE PRICE	*QUOTE U.S.$
2000 Only Olivia	250	2000	495.00	495

Newcomer Collection - W. Lawton

YEAR ISSUE	EDITION LIMIT	YEAR RETD.	ISSUE PRICE	*QUOTE U.S.$
1987 Ellin Elizabeth, Eyes Closed	49	1987	335.00	750-1000
1987 Ellin Elizabeth, Eyes Open	19	1987	335.00	900-1200

Playthings Past - W. Lawton

YEAR ISSUE	EDITION LIMIT	YEAR RETD.	ISSUE PRICE	*QUOTE U.S.$
1989 Edward And Dobbin	500	1989	395.00	495-600
1989 Elizabeth And Baby	500	1989	395.00	495-650
1989 Victoria And Teddy	500	1989	395.00	395

Royalty Collection - W. Lawton

YEAR ISSUE	EDITION LIMIT	YEAR RETD.	ISSUE PRICE	*QUOTE U.S.$
1998 Grand Duchess Anastasia Nicholaievna	250	1998	795.00	795

Special Edition - W. Lawton

YEAR ISSUE	EDITION LIMIT	YEAR RETD.	ISSUE PRICE	*QUOTE U.S.$
1998 Beatrice Louise	310	1998	N/A	N/A
1993 Flora McFlimsey	250	1993	895.00	1000
1988 Marcella And Raggedy Ann	2,500	1988	395.00	800-950
1994 Mary Chilton	350	1994	395.00	395
1995 Through The Looking Glass	180	1995	N/A	1700

Special Occasion - W. Lawton

YEAR ISSUE	EDITION LIMIT	YEAR RETD.	ISSUE PRICE	*QUOTE U.S.$
1990 First Birthday	500	1990	295.00	350
1989 First Day Of School	500	1989	325.00	525
1988 Nanthy	500	1988	325.00	525

Sugar 'n' Spice - W. Lawton

YEAR ISSUE	EDITION LIMIT	YEAR RETD.	ISSUE PRICE	*QUOTE U.S.$
1987 Ginger	454	1987	275.00	395-550
1986 Jason	27	1986	250.00	800-1700
1986 Jessica	30	1986	250.00	800-1700
1986 Kersten	103	1986	250.00	550-800
1986 Kimberly	87	1986	250.00	550-800
1987 Marie	208	1987	275.00	450

Timeless Ballads® - W. Lawton

YEAR ISSUE	EDITION LIMIT	YEAR RETD.	ISSUE PRICE	*QUOTE U.S.$
1987 Annabel Lee	250	1987	550.00	600-695
1987 Highland Mary	250	1987	550.00	700-900
1988 She Walks In Beauty	250	1988	550.00	700-800
1987 Young Charlotte	250	1987	550.00	900-950

Wee Bits - W. Lawton

YEAR ISSUE	EDITION LIMIT	YEAR RETD.	ISSUE PRICE	*QUOTE U.S.$
1989 Wee Bit O'Bliss	250	1989	295.00	350
1988 Wee Bit O'Heaven	250	1988	295.00	350
1988 Wee Bit O'Sunshine	250	1988	295.00	350
1988 Wee Bit O'Woe	250	1988	295.00	350
1989 Wee Bit O'Wonder	250	1989	295.00	350

Lee Middleton Original Dolls

Our Doll Family - Various

YEAR ISSUE	EDITION LIMIT	YEAR RETD.	ISSUE PRICE	*QUOTE U.S.$
1997 Bye Baby Blessed Homecoming - Lee Middleton	Retrd.	1998	175.00	175-275
1998 Bye Baby To Grandmother's House We Go - Lee Middleton	Retrd.	1999	175.00	175-275
1999 Love & Prayers - R. Schick	Retrd.	1999	190.00	190-275
2000 Dressed For The Holidays - R. Schick	12/00		198.00	198
2000 Loving Sisters, set/2 (Convention) - R. Schick	Open		249.97	250
2000 Loving Sisters, African/American, set/2 (Convention) - R. Schick	Open		249.97	250

Birthday Babies - Lee Middleton

YEAR ISSUE	EDITION LIMIT	YEAR RETD.	ISSUE PRICE	*QUOTE U.S.$
1992 Winter	Retrd.	1994	180.00	180
1992 Fall	Retrd.	1994	170.00	170
1992 Summer	Retrd.	1994	160.00	160
1992 Spring	3,000	1994	170.00	170

Charity Piece - Reva Schick

YEAR ISSUE	EDITION LIMIT	YEAR RETD.	ISSUE PRICE	*QUOTE U.S.$
2000 Precious In His Sight (Baby Face)	Yr.Iss.		170.00	170
2000 Precious In His Sight (Small Wonder)	Yr.Iss.		170.00	170

Christmas Angel Collection - Lee Middleton

YEAR ISSUE	EDITION LIMIT	YEAR RETD.	ISSUE PRICE	*QUOTE U.S.$
1987 Christmas Angel 1987	4,174	1987	130.00	500-600
1988 Christmas Angel 1988	8,969	1988	130.00	250-300
1989 Christmas Angel 1989	7,500	1991	150.00	225
1990 Christmas Angel 1990	5,000	1991	150.00	200
1991 Christmas Angel 1991	5,000	1992	180.00	225
1992 Christmas Angel 1992	5,000	1995	190.00	200
1993 Christmas Angel 1993-Girl	3,144	1995	190.00	200
1993 Christmas Angel 1993 (set)	1,000	1993	390.00	500
1994 Christmas Angel 1994	5,000	1996	190.00	190
1995 Christmas Angel 1995 (white or black)	3,000	1996	190.00	225
1996 Christmas Angel 1996 (Shall I Play For You)	2,000	1997	250.00	250

Collector Series Vinyl - Lee Middleton

YEAR ISSUE	EDITION LIMIT	YEAR RETD.	ISSUE PRICE	*QUOTE U.S.$
1999 ABC - Look At Me	2,500		180.00	180
1997 Afternoon Nap-Honey Love - Awake Boy	5,000	1998	170.00	185-200
1997 Afternoon Nap-Honey Love - Awake Dark Boy	2,000	1998	170.00	185-200
1997 Afternoon Nap-Honey Love - Awake Dark Girl	2,000	1997	170.00	185-200
1997 Afternoon Nap-Honey Love - Awake Girl	5,000	1997	170.00	170-210
1997 Afternoon Nap-Honey Love - Dark Sleeping Boy	2,000	1998	170.00	140-170
1997 Afternoon Nap-Honey Love - Dark Sleeping Girl	2,000	1998	170.00	140-170
1997 Afternoon Nap-Honey Love - Sleeping Boy	5,000	1998	170.00	170-175
1997 Afternoon Nap-Honey Love - Sleeping Girl	5,000	1998	170.00	175-185
1998 All Dolled Up	5,000	1999	180.00	180
1987 Amanda - 1st Edition	3,778	1989	140.00	295
1993 Amanda Springtime	612	1994	180.00	225
1985 Angel Face	20,200	1989	90.00	150
1989 Angel Fancy	5,310	1992	120.00	195
1994 Angel Kisses Boy	Retrd.	1997	98.00	98-150
1994 Angel Kisses Girl	Retrd.	1997	98.00	98-150
1995 Angel Kisses-Belly Dancer	1,000	1995	139.00	139-165
1990 Angel Locks	8,140	1992	140.00	150
2000 Baby Beauty	2,000		184.00	184
1991 Baby Grace	4,862	1991	190.00	250
1996 Beloved Bedtime Story	1,500	1997	170.00	170
1996 Beloved Good Friends	1,500	1997	180.00	180-220
1997 Beloved Sunbeams and Flowers	2,500	1997	170.00	170-235
1994 Beloved-Happy Birthday (Blue)	1,000	1995	220.00	250
1994 Beloved-Happy Birthday (Pink)	1,000	1995	220.00	250
1992 Beth	1,414	1994	160.00	160-185
1995 Beth-Flapper	1,000	1995	119.00	140-150
1995 Bethie Bows	1,000	1996	150.00	150
1995 Bethie Buttons	1,000	1996	150.00	150
1996 Bitsy Sister	1,500	1997	130.00	130-145
1998 Bo Peep	2,000	1998	170.00	180-200
1995 The Bride	1,000	1995	250.00	250
1995 The Bride (Ruby Slipper Edition)	1,000	1995	250.00	250
1991 Bubba Batboy	3,925	1994	190.00	190-200
1986 Bubba Chubbs	5,550	1988	100.00	275-350
1996 Bubba Chubbs Bubba The Kid	1,000	1997	196.00	220-250
1988 Bubba Chubbs Railroader	7,925	1994	140.00	170
1999 Bunny Boo Boy	1,500		170.00	170
1999 Bunny Boo Girl	2,500		180.00	180
1997 Bunny Love	5,000	1998	180.00	190-200
1999 Buttercup	2,000		176.00	176
2000 Button Button	2,500		176.00	176
1998 Cat Nap	2,000	1998	170.00	170
1988 Cherish	14,790	1992	160.00	250
1996 Cherish - Hug A Bug	5,000	1999	170.00	170-195
1997 Cherish Little Guy	2,500	1998	170.00	185-220
1997 Christmas Surprise Asleep Red Stocking	Retrd.	1998	180.00	140-185
1997 Christmas Surprise Asleep White Stocking	Retrd.	1998	180.00	180-185
1997 Christmas Surprise Awake Red Stocking	Retrd.	1998	180.00	185-220
1997 Christmas Surprise Awake White Stocking	Retrd.	1998	180.00	185-220
1992 Cottontop Cherish	3,525	1994	180.00	180
1994 Country Boy	Retrd.	1996	118.00	118-140
1994 Country Boy (Dark Flesh)	Retrd.	1996	118.00	118-140
1998 Country Cozy	2,500	1998	170.00	180-200
1994 Country Girl	Retrd.	1996	118.00	118-140
1994 Country Girl (Dark Flesh)	Retrd.	1996	118.00	118-140
2000 Cuddle Time	1,500		184.00	184
1999 Cup of Tea	2,500	1999	176.00	176-190
1986 Dear One - 1st Edition	4,935	1988	90.00	250
1991 Dear One-Sunday Best	1,371	1994	140.00	140
1989 Devan	8,336	1991	170.00	200
1991 Devan Delightful	4,520	1994	170.00	160-295
1997 Devan Happy Birthday	2,500	1998	170.00	170
1993 Echo	Retrd.	1995	180.00	180-220
1996 Echo All Dressed Up	500	1996	180.00	180
1995 Echo Little Eagle	500	1997	180.00	180-250
2000 Faith	1,000		180.00	180
1997 Feelin' Froggy	2,000	1998	160.00	160-195
1998 First Born "Loving Memories" - Lee Middleton	1,000	1998	190.00	190
1997 First Born - Awake Beauty	2,500	1997	180.00	235-250
1997 First Born - Awake Berry Sweet	2,500	1997	170.00	235
1997 First Born - Berry Sweet	2,500	1998	170.00	170
1995 First Born - My Baby Boy	1,500	1995	160.00	160
1995 First Born - Newborn Twin Boy	2,000	1996	160.00	160-180
1995 First Born - Newborn Twin Girl	2,000	1996	160.00	160-180
1996 First Born - So Snuggly	1,000	1996	170.00	190
1996 First Born - Wee One	5,000	1998	170.00	170-185
1996 First Moments - Battenburg Christening	1,000	1997	238.00	238
1995 First Moments - Lullaby Time	1,000	1996	180.00	180
1996 First Moments - Toot Sweet	5,000	1998	170.00	170-200
1990 Forever Cherish	5,000	1991	170.00	200
2000 Garden Party	1,000		180.00	180
1995 Gordon-Growing Up	1,000	1995	220.00	220
1996 Grace Fresh As A Daisy	300	1996	176.00	176-200
1995 Grace-Growing Up	1,000	1995	220.00	220
1992 Gracie Mae (Blond Hair)	3,660	1995	250.00	250
1992 Gracie Mae (Brown Hair)	2,551	1994	250.00	250
1993 Gracie Mae (Red Velvet)	100	1993	250.00	250
1997 Heaven Sent Asleep	7,500	1998	180.00	180
1997 Heaven Sent Awake	7,500	1999	180.00	190-235
1999 Heavenly	Yr.Iss.	1999	200.00	200-235
1996 Hershey's Baker Girl	Retrd.	1997	130.00	130-165
1996 Hershey's Cake Kids Set (2)	Retrd.	1997	220.00	220-235
1996 Hershey's Chocolate Soldier	Retrd.	1997	130.00	130-165
1995 Hershey's Kisses - Gold	Retrd.	1996	99.50	130
1996 Hershey's Kisses - Green	Retrd.	1996	199.00	200
1996 Hershey's Kisses - Red	Retrd.	1996	199.00	200
1994 Hershey's Kisses - Silver	Retrd.	1997	99.50	140-150
1999 I Love You Beary Much	1,000	1999	180.00	180
1996 Joey Go Bye Bye	1,000	1998	190.00	190
1994 Joey-Newborn	1,000	1995	180.00	180
1991 Johanna	1,388	1994	190.00	250
1994 Johanna-Newborn	2,000	1994	180.00	180
1986 Little Angel - 3rd Edition	15,158	1992	90.00	110
1992 Little Angel Boy	Retrd.	1997	130.00	150
1992 Little Angel Girl	Retrd.	1997	130.00	150
1997 Little Angel Wish Finders Star Bright	Retrd.	1997	120.00	120-140
1997 Little Angel Wish Finders Twinkle Twinkle	Retrd.	1997	120.00	120-140
1995 Little Angel-Ballerina	1,000	1995	119.00	119-140
1985 Little Angel-King-2 (Hand Painted)	Retrd.	1985	40.00	200
1981 Little Angel-Kingdom (Hand Painted)	Retrd.	1981	40.00	300
1998 Little Big Guy	2,500	1999	180.00	185-210
2000 Little Blessings	2/01		200.00	200
1995 Little Blessings Awake Boy	1,000	1995	180.00	180
1995 Little Blessings Awake Girl	1,000	1995	180.00	180
1995 Little Blessings Blessed Event	1,500	1995	190.00	190
1996 Little Blessings Cuddle Up	1,000	1997	180.00	180-225
1996 Little Blessings Newborn Twins Awake Boy	1,500	1996	180.00	180
1996 Little Blessings Newborn Twins Awake Girl	1,500	1996	180.00	180
1996 Little Blessings Newborn Twins Sleeping Boy	1,000	1996	180.00	180
1996 Little Blessings Newborn Twins Sleeping Girl	1,000	1996	180.00	180
1995 Little Blessings Pretty in Pink	1,500	1997	190.00	190
1997 Little Blessings Ships Ahoy	2,500	1998	170.00	170-175
1995 Little Blessings Sleeping Boy	1,000	1995	180.00	180
1995 Little Blessings Sleeping Girl	1,000	1995	180.00	180
1998 Little Boy Blue	2,000		170.00	170
1999 Little Friends	2,000		180.00	180
1996 Little Love - Cuddle Bumps	5,000	1998	170.00	170-175
1997 Little Love - Peek A Boo Boy	2,500	1998	170.00	170-175
1997 Little Love - Peek A Boo Girl	2,500	1998	170.00	170-175
1996 Little Love - Such A Good Boy	1,000	1996	160.00	190
1995 Little Love - Violets	1,500	1995	160.00	160
1998 Little Patty Cake	2,800	1998	170.00	170
1998 Little Playmate	2,000	1998	170.00	170-180
1998 Loving Tribute	Yr.Iss.	1999	220.00	240-250
1997 Lullaby Baby Boy	5,000	1998	180.00	180-200
1997 Lullaby Baby Girl	5,000	1997	180.00	180-200
1998 Mary Mary	2,000	1999	170.00	170-185
1987 Missy	11,855	1991	100.00	120
1991 Missy- Buttercup	4,748	1994	160.00	200
1992 Molly Rose	2,981	1994	196.00	196
1996 Molly Rose Good Friends	1,500	1997	180.00	180-235
1996 My Darling Boy	2,000	1998	170.00	170
1996 My Darling Girl	2,000	1998	170.00	170-185
1989 My Lee	3,794	1991	170.00	275
1991 My Lee Candy Cane	2,240	1994	170.00	295
1993 Patty	4,000	1995	49.00	49
1998 Patty Cake	2,000	1998	170.00	170-185
1997 Picture Perfect	7,500	1999	190.00	190-220
1992 Polly Esther	2,137	1994	160.00	160
1995 Polly Esther "Sock Hop"	1,000	1995	119.00	150-165
1996 Polly Esther - Hershey's Country Girl	Retrd.	1997	130.00	150-165
2000 Pretty As A Rose	1,500		176.00	176
1996 Pretty Baby Sister	1,500	1997	170.00	170-195
1998 Proud Heritage/Boy	2,000		164.00	164
1998 Proud Heritage/Girl	2,000		164.00	164
1998 Quiet As A Mouse	Yr.Iss.	1999	180.00	180
1998 Santa's Little Helper/Boy	Yr.Iss.	1998	180.00	195-220
1998 Santa's Little Helper/Girl	Yr.Iss.	1998	180.00	195-220
1992 Serenity Berries & Bows	458	1993	250.00	250
2000 She's So Pretty	1,500		180.00	180
1988 Sincerity - Limited 1st Ed. - Nettie/Simplicity	3,711	1989	160.00	200-250
1992 Sincerity Petals & Plums	414	1993	250.00	250
1991 Sincerity-Apples n' Spice	1,608	1993	250.00	250
1991 Sincerity-Apricots n' Cream	1,789	1993	250.00	250
1989 Sincerity-Schoolgirl	6,622	1992	180.00	295
1998 Slumber Kisses	1,000	1998	170.00	170
1999 Snow Baby (African American Boy)	1,000		170.00	170
1999 Snow Baby (African American Girl)	1,500		170.00	170
1999 Snow Baby (Caucasian Boy)	2,000		170.00	170
1999 Snow Baby (Caucasian Girl)	2,000		170.00	170
1998 Softly Sleeping	2,000	1999	164.00	164-175
1998 Starry Night	2,500	1999	170.00	170-175
1997 Summerfun - Asleep Boy	5,000	1998	170.00	170-175
1997 Summerfun - Asleep Dark Boy	2,000	1998	170.00	170-175
1997 Summerfun - Asleep Dark Girl	2,000	1998	170.00	170-175
1997 Summerfun - Asleep Girl	5,000	1999	170.00	170-175
1997 Summerfun - Awake Boy	5,000	1998	170.00	175-185
1997 Summerfun - Awake Dark Boy	2,000	1998	170.00	175-185
1997 Summerfun - Awake Dark Girl	2,000	1999	170.00	180-185
1997 Summerfun - Awake Girl	5,000	1998	170.00	180-190
1999 Sweet Baby Boy	3,000		180.00	180

*Quotes have been rounded up to nearest dollar

YEAR ISSUE	EDITION LIMIT	YEAR RETD.	ISSUE PRICE	*QUOTE U.S.$
1999 Sweet Baby Boy (African American Girl)	1,500		170.00	170
1999 Sweet Baby Boy (Caucasian American Boy)	2,000		170.00	170
1982 Sweet Dreams	Retrd.	1994	39.00	39
2000 Sweet Memories	Yr.Iss.		220.00	220
1995 Sweetness-Newborn	Retrd.	1995	190.00	190
2000 Tender Moments	1,500		170.00	170
1995 Tenderness French BeBe	1,500	1997	220.00	235-250
1996 Tenderness So Brave	1,500	1997	170.00	190-220
1998 Touch of Velvet	2,500	1999	180.00	180-210
1998 Tough Guy	1,000		170.00	170
1994 Town Boy	Retrd.	1995	118.00	118-140
1994 Town Boy (Dark Flesh)	Retrd.	1995	118.00	118-140
1994 Town Girl	Retrd.	1995	118.00	118-140
1994 Town Girl (Dark Flesh)	Retrd.	1995	118.00	118-140
1997 Treasured Traditions	5,000	1998	170.00	170-195
1998 Warm & Cozy	350	1998	150.00	150
1998 Wee Willie Winkie	2,000	1999	170.00	170-200
1996 Young Lady Bride in White Satin	1,000	1997	250.00	250

Collector Series Vinyl - Reva Schick, unless otherwise noted

YEAR ISSUE	EDITION LIMIT	YEAR RETD.	ISSUE PRICE	*QUOTE U.S.$
2000 All Star	1,000		184.00	184
1999 Angel Baby	2,000		180.00	180
2000 Angel Bear (African-American)	1,000		184.00	184
2000 Angel Bear (Caucasian)	2,500		184.00	184
1998 Angel Love	2,000	1998	180.00	185-195
1999 Apple Dumpling	3,000		176.00	176
2000 Baby Blue	1,000	2000	180.00	180
2000 Baby Bows	1,500	2000	170.00	170
2000 Baby Girl	1,000		184.00	184
1998 Baby Mine	2,000	1999	164.00	164
1999 Baby Sister	2,500	1999	180.00	180
1999 Baby's First Christmas	1,000	1999	184.00	190-195
2000 Be My Baby	2,500		184.00	184
1998 Bear Hug/Boy	1,000	1998	180.00	190-210
1998 Bear Hug/Girl	1,000	1998	180.00	190-210
1999 Beary Cute Boy	5,000		180.00	180
1999 Beary Cute Girl	5,000		180.00	180
2000 Bedtime Babies Boy	1,500		180.00	180
2000 Bedtime Babies Girl	2,000		180.00	180
1998 Being Good	2,500	2000	190.00	190
2000 Best Buddies	1,000	2000	180.00	180
2000 Bundle of Love	1,000		170.00	170
1998 Bunny Dreams	2,000	1998	180.00	180-200
2000 Butterfly Kisses	Yr.Iss.		190.00	190
2000 By Gone Days Boy	1,000		180.00	180
2000 By Gone Days Girl	1,000		180.00	180
1999 Cat Bird	2,500		180.00	180
1998 Cherry Blossom	2,000	1998	180.00	180-220
2000 Chloe	500		350.00	350
1999 Cotton Candy	5,000		176.00	176
1998 Cuddle Cub	2,500		190.00	190
1998 Cute As Can Bee	2,500		180.00	180
2000 Cutie Pie	2,000		180.00	180
1999 Daisy Daisy	5,000		180.00	180
1999 Doggone Cute Boy	2,000	1999	184.00	184
1999 Doggone Cute Girl	3,000	2000	184.00	184
2000 Dolly & Me	Yr.Iss.		180.00	180
1998 Fine & Frilly	2,000	1998	174.00	185-220
1998 Forever Friend/Boy	1,500	1999	170.00	170-190
1998 Forever Friend/Girl	2,500	1998	170.00	170
1998 Friends Forever	1,500		160.00	160
1998 Frilly & Fancy	1,000	1998	190.00	190
1999 From The Heart	2,500	1999	180.00	180
2000 Fun In The Sun	1,000	2000	180.00	180
2000 Fuzzy Wuzzy	2,000		184.00	184
2000 Gentle Touch Baby	Yr.Iss.		190.00	190
1998 Gimme a Hug	2,000	1998	180.00	180
1999 Going to a Party	1,500	1999	190.00	190
1998 Grandmother's Dream	2,500	1999	198.00	198
1999 Growing Up	Open		210.00	210
1998 Hearts & Flowers	2,000	1999	170.00	170-220
2000 Hearts Desire	2,000		180.00	180
2000 Here Kitty Kitty - S. Housley	2,000		194.00	194
1999 Honey Pie	3,000	2000	180.00	180
1999 Hugs & Kisses	5,000		180.00	180
1998 Hunny Bunny	2,500		190.00	190
1999 I Love You Beary Much	1,000	1999	180.00	180
1999 I Wanna Play Baseball	2,000		190.00	190
1999 I Wanna Play Basketball	2,000		190.00	190
1999 I Wanna Play Football	2,000		190.00	190
2000 I'm a Big Girl Now	1,500		184.00	184
1999 I'm A Little Angel	2,000	1999	180.00	180-200
1999 I'm So Special	5,000		190.00	190
2000 I'm This Big - M. Snyder	2,000		184.00	184
1998 In The Pink	2,000	1998	180.00	210-225
2000 Irresistible	1,500	2000	190.00	190
1999 Jitterbug	1,500		176.00	176
1999 Just Ducky	3,000	1999	190.00	200-235
2000 Just So Sweet	2,000		180.00	180
2000 Lambie Pie	1,500		194.00	194
1999 Let It Rain Boy	2,000	1999	184.00	184-235
1999 Let It Rain Girl	2,000	1999	184.00	184-235
2000 Li'l Snowball - M. Snyder	2,000		184.00	184
1999 Lions & Tigers & Bears	2,000	2000	170.00	170
1999 Little Ballerina (Green)	1,000	1999	180.00	180
1999 Little Ballerina (Pink)	1,000	1999	180.00	180
1999 Little Ballerina, yellow	1,500		180.00	180
1999 Little Beauty	2,000		170.00	170
1999 Little Blue Eyes	2,500	1999	180.00	180
1998 Little Chickadee	2,000	1998	180.00	185-225
1999 Little Cowboy	1,500		190.00	190
2000 Little Lullaby	1,000		184.00	184
1998 Little Peanut	2,500	1998	180.00	190-225
1999 Little Princess (African)	Open		198.00	198
1999 Little Princess (Caucasian)	Open		198.00	198
1999 Little Princess (Hispanic)	Open		198.00	198
1998 Little Scottie/Boy	1,000	1998	180.00	190-210
1998 Little Scottie/Girl	1,000	1998	180.00	190-210
2000 Little Sunbeam	2,500		180.00	180
1999 Little Sweetheart	5,000		194.00	194
2000 Little Sweetie	1,500		184.00	184
2000 Little Treasure	2,500		184.00	184
2000 Look What I Found	2 ,500		180.00	180
1999 Love Bug Boy	1,500		176.00	176
1999 Love Bug Girl	2,500		176.00	176
1999 Love in Bloom	3,000		190.00	190
1999 Lovin' Gingerbread Boy	3,000		170.00	170
1999 Lovin' Gingerbread Girl	3,000		180.00	180
1999 Lovin' Stuff	2,500		194.00	194
2000 Lucky Ducky	Yr.Iss.		180.00	180
1999 Mittens Mittens	3,000		190.00	190
1999 Mommy's Good Girl	Open		180.00	180
1998 Oops A Daisy	2,000	1999	174.00	195-200
2000 Party Time	1,000		194.00	194
1999 Peaceful Slumber (African American)	2,000		170.00	170
1999 Peaceful Slumber (Caucasian)	2,000		170.00	170
1998 Pink & Playful	1,000	1998	190.00	190
1998 Playtime Boy	2,500		140.00	140
1998 Playtime Girl	2,500		140.00	140
2000 Pretty as a Picture	1,500		194.00	194
1999 Proud Heritage Boy	1,000		170.00	170
1999 Proud Heritage Girl	1,000		170.00	170
1998 Puppy Love	2,500	1999	190.00	190-200
2000 Rainy Day Play - S. Housley	1,000		194.00	194
2000 Ready To Go	2,000		190.00	190
1999 Ready to Play	3,000	1999	176.00	176
2000 Ribbons & Lace	1,000	2000	184.00	184
1999 Roses, Lace & Love	3,000	2000	180.00	180
1999 Say Cheese	3,000	2000	190.00	190
2000 Simply Sweet	3,000		184.00	184
1999 Sitting Pretty	2,500		170.00	170
1999 Snips & Snails	1,500		180.00	180
1998 Snoozy Bear	2,500	1999	190.00	190-200
1998 Snow Baby	1,000	1998	170.00	225-235
1998 Soft & Innocent	2,500	1999	180.00	180
2000 Soft & Sweet	1,000		184.00	184
2000 Special Occasion	1,000		200.00	200
1999 Spring Bouquet (green)	1,500		176.00	176
1999 Spring Bouquet (pink)	2,000		176.00	176
1999 Spring Bouquet (white)	3,000	1999	176.00	176-195
1999 Spring Bouquet (yellow)	2,000		176.00	176
2000 Spring in Bloom	1,500	2000	184.00	184
2000 Springtime Stroll	2,500		184.00	184
1998 Star Struck	2,000	1999	170.00	170
1999 Sugar & Spice	1,500	2000	180.00	180
1998 Sugar Plum	2,000	1999	170.00	180-200
1998 Surprise	2,500		180.00	180
2000 Sweet as a Sonnet - S. Housley	1,000		184.00	184
2000 Sweet Blue Birdie	1,000		184.00	184
2000 Sweet Flower	1,000		184.00	184
2000 Sweet Sis	1,500		170.00	170
1998 Sweetheart Boy	2,500		180.00	180
1998 Sweetheart Girl	2,500	1999	180.00	185-200
1999 Sweetly Sailing, Boy	2,000		170.00	170
1999 Sweetly Sailing, Girl	3,000		170.00	170
1999 Sweetly Sailing, Hispanic Boy	1,500		170.00	170
1999 Sweetly Sailing, Hispanic Girl	2,000		170.00	170
2000 Take Me Home	1,500		194.00	194
2000 Teddy Poo - S. Housley	2,000		184.00	184
2000 That's My Girl	1,000	2000	180.00	180
2000 Timeless Beauty	1,000		200.00	200
2000 True Pals	Yr.Iss.		190.00	190
2000 Tumbling Teddies	2,500		184.00	184
1998 Two Cute/Boy	2,500	1999	180.00	180-235
1998 Two Cute/Girl	2,500	1998	180.00	185-285
2000 Up, Up & Away	2,000		184.00	184
2000 Victoria	500		350.00	350
1999 Warm & Cuddly	3,000		190.00	190
1998 Yesterday's Dream/ Boy	1,500	1998	184.00	184-190
1998 Yesterday's Dream/ Girl	2,500	1999	184.00	184

FAO Exclusive - Reva Schick

YEAR ISSUE	EDITION LIMIT	YEAR RETD.	ISSUE PRICE	*QUOTE U.S.$
1999 Baby Love	1,000		170.00	170
2000 Sweet Angel	1,000		170.00	170

Fifties Series - Lee Middleton

YEAR ISSUE	EDITION LIMIT	YEAR RETD.	ISSUE PRICE	*QUOTE U.S.$
1996 Angel Kisses Earth Angel	1,500	1997	130.00	130-140
1996 Angel Kisses Splish Splash	1,500	1997	130.00	130-140
1996 Little Angel Leader of the Pack	1,500	1997	130.00	130-160
1996 Polly Esther Car Hop	1,500	1997	130.00	130-160
1996 Polly Esther Peggy Sue	1,500	1997	130.00	130-150

First Collectibles - Lee Middleton

YEAR ISSUE	EDITION LIMIT	YEAR RETD.	ISSUE PRICE	*QUOTE U.S.$
1990 Sweetest Little Dreamer (Asleep)	Retrd.	1993	40.00	40-59
1990 Day Dreamer (Awake)	Retrd.	1993	42.00	42-59
1991 Day Dreamer Sunshine	Retrd.	1993	49.00	49
1991 Teenie	Retrd.	1993	59.00	59

First Moments Series - Lee Middleton

YEAR ISSUE	EDITION LIMIT	YEAR RETD.	ISSUE PRICE	*QUOTE U.S.$
1984 First Moments (Sleeping)	40,861	1990	69.00	300
1992 First Moments Awake in Blue	1,230	1994	170.00	170-235
1992 First Moments Awake in Pink	856	1994	170.00	170
1986 First Moments Blue Eyes	14,494	1990	120.00	120-150
1987 First Moments Boy	6,075	1989	130.00	130-160
1986 First Moments Brown Eyes	5,324	1989	120.00	120-150
1987 First Moments Christening (Asleep)	9,377	1992	160.00	160-250
1987 First Moments Christening (Awake)	16,384	1992	160.00	160-180
1993 First Moments Heirloom	1,372	1995	190.00	190
1991 First Moments Sweetness	6,323	1995	180.00	180
1990 First Moments Twin Boy	2,971	1991	180.00	180
1990 First Moments Twin Girl	2,544	1991	180.00	180
1994 Sweetness-Newborn	Retrd.	1995	190.00	190

Home Shopping Network Series - Lee Middleton

YEAR ISSUE	EDITION LIMIT	YEAR RETD.	ISSUE PRICE	*QUOTE U.S.$
1996 Bye Baby Bundle of Joy	2,000	1996	129.00	129
1996 Cherish Ribbons and Bows	2,000	1996	129.00	129
1997 Cherish Sleeping Angels	2,000	1997	129.00	129
1996 First Born Dark Precious Baby Girl	1,000	1996	129.00	129
1997 First Born Dark Snug As A Bug	1,000	1997	129.00	129
1996 First Born Gingham and Lace	2,000	1996	129.00	129
1996 First Born Katie	2,000	1996	129.00	129
1997 First Born Mother's Dream	2,000	1997	129.00	129
1997 First Born Open Eye Bed of Roses	2,000	1997	129.00	129
1997 First Born Open Eye Dark Snug As A Bug	1,000	1997	129.00	129
1997 First Born Open Eye Precious Traditions	2,000	1997	129.00	129
1996 First Moments Open Eye Baseball Boy	2,000	1996	129.00	129
1997 Honey Love Answered Prayer Boy	2,000	1997	129.00	129
1997 Honey Love Answered Prayer Girl	2,000	1997	129.00	129
1997 Honey Love Dark Baby's Sleeping	1,000	1997	129.00	129
1997 Honey Love Open Eye Little Peep	2,000	1997	129.00	129
1996 Little Blessing Awake Grandma's Little Boy	2,000	1997	129.00	129
1997 Little Blessing Open Eye Bundle Up Boy	2,000	1997	129.00	129
1997 Little Blessing Open Eye Bundle Up Girl	2,000	1997	129.00	129
1997 Little Blessing Open Eye Mother's Little Sweetheart (blue)	2,000	1997	129.00	129
1997 Little Blessing Open Eye Mother's Little Sweetheart (pink)	2,000	1997	129.00	129
1997 Little Love Baby Brother	2,000	1997	129.00	129
1997 Little Love Baby Sister	2,000	1997	129.00	129
1996 Little Love Baby's First Book	2,000	1996	129.00	129
1997 Little Love Bunny Surprise	2,000	1997	129.00	129
1996 Little Love Sleepy Time	2,000	1996	129.00	129
2000 Pretty in Pastel Peach, Yellow and Green w/Cuddle Pack, set/3	1,000		300.00	300

I Wanna Play Series - Reva Schick

YEAR ISSUE	EDITION LIMIT	YEAR RETD.	ISSUE PRICE	*QUOTE U.S.$
2000 Peek A Boo	Yr.Iss.		180.00	180
2000 Ring Around the Rosy	Yr.Iss.		170.00	170
2000 Tic Tac Toe	500	2000	170.00	170

J.C. Penney Exclusive - Reva Schick

YEAR ISSUE	EDITION LIMIT	YEAR RETD.	ISSUE PRICE	*QUOTE U.S.$
1999 Baby Bear (My Own Baby)	Open		99.00	99
1999 Rudolph, My Own Baby	Open		120.00	120

J.C. Penney Exclusive Porcelain - Reva Schick

YEAR ISSUE	EDITION LIMIT	YEAR RETD.	ISSUE PRICE	*QUOTE U.S.$
2000 Small Wonder	2,500		204.00	204

J.C. Penney Series - Various

YEAR ISSUE	EDITION LIMIT	YEAR RETD.	ISSUE PRICE	*QUOTE U.S.$
1998 Little Love ABCs - Lee Middleton	Closed	1999	120.00	120

Kewpie Series - R. O'Neill

YEAR ISSUE	EDITION LIMIT	YEAR RETD.	ISSUE PRICE	*QUOTE U.S.$
1997 Almost Angelic	Retrd.	1998	42.00	50-55
1997 Breezy	Retrd.	1998	42.00	50-55
1997 Buddy	Retrd.	1998	52.00	55-65
1997 Rosebud	Retrd.	1998	52.00	55-85

Millennium Piece - Reva Schick

YEAR ISSUE	EDITION LIMIT	YEAR RETD.	ISSUE PRICE	*QUOTE U.S.$
2000 Bright New World	Yr.Iss.		220.00	220

Mohair Bear Edition - L. Henry

YEAR ISSUE	EDITION LIMIT	YEAR RETD.	ISSUE PRICE	*QUOTE U.S.$
1999 Alpha Bear Baby	Yr.Iss.		180.00	180
1999 Ginger Bear Baby	Yr.Iss.		180.00	180
1999 Honey Bear Baby Boy	Yr.Iss.		180.00	180
1999 Honey Bear Baby Girl	Yr.Iss.		180.00	180
1999 Hush-A-Bear Baby	Yr.Iss.		180.00	180
1999 Sleep Bear Baby	Yr.Iss.		180.00	180

My Own Baby Series - Lee Middleton, unless otherwise noted

YEAR ISSUE	EDITION LIMIT	YEAR RETD.	ISSUE PRICE	*QUOTE U.S.$
2000 Baby Face Boy - R. Schick	Open		99.00	99
2000 Baby Face Girl - R. Schick	Open		99.00	99
1999 Cuddle Me Boy - R. Schick	Open		99.00	99
1999 Cuddle Me Girl - R. Schick	Open		99.00	99
1996 First Born Asleep My Own Baby Boy	Retrd.	1999	120.00	120-125
1996 First Born Asleep My Own Baby Girl	Retrd.	1999	120.00	120-125
1997 First Born Awake My Own Baby Boy	Open		120.00	120
1997 First Born Awake My Own Baby Girl	Open		120.00	120
1996 First Born Dark My Own Baby Boy	Retrd.	1998	120.00	120-125
1996 First Born Dark My Own Baby Girl	Retrd.	1998	120.00	120-125
1997 First Moments Awake My Own Baby Boy	Retrd.	1997	120.00	120-125
1997 First Moments Awake My Own Baby Girl	Retrd.	1997	120.00	120-125
1997 First Moments My Own Baby Boy	Retrd.	1997	120.00	120-125
1997 First Moments My Own Baby Girl	Retrd.	1997	120.00	120-125
1998 Honey Love Asleep Boy Dark Skin My Own Baby	Retrd.	1999	120.00	120-125
1998 Honey Love Asleep Boy My Own Baby	Retrd.	2000	120.00	120
1998 Honey Love Asleep Girl Dark Skin My Own Baby	Retrd.	1999	120.00	120-125
1998 Honey Love Asleep Girl My Own Baby	Retrd.	2000	120.00	120

*Quotes have been rounded up to nearest dollar

YEAR ISSUE	EDITION LIMIT	YEAR RETD.	ISSUE PRICE	*QUOTE U.S.$
1998 Honey Love Awake Boy African/American My Own Baby	Open		120.00	120
1998 Honey Love Awake Boy My Own Baby	Open		120.00	120
1998 Honey Love Awake Girl My Own Baby	Open		120.00	120
1996 Little Blessings My Own Baby Asleep Boy	Retrd.	1998	120.00	120-125
1996 Little Blessings My Own Baby Asleep Girl	Retrd.	1998	120.00	120-125
1996 Little Blessings My Own Baby Awake Boy	Retrd.	1999	120.00	120-125
1996 Little Blessings My Own Baby Awake Girl	Retrd.	1999	120.00	120-125
1996 Little Love My Own Baby Boy	Open		120.00	120
1996 Little Love My Own Baby Girl	Open		120.00	120
1999 Little One Boy - R. Schick	Retrd.	2000	99.00	99
1999 Little One Girl - R. Schick	Retrd.	2000	99.00	99
1997 Newborn Taylor Bear - L. Henry	Retrd.	1998	120.00	125-155
1999 Small Wonder Boy - R. Schick	Open		99.00	99
1999 Small Wonder Girl - R. Schick	Open		99.00	99
1999 Special Delivery - R. Schick	Open		160.00	160
1999 Sweet Cheeks Boy - R. Schick	Retrd.	2000	99.00	99
1999 Sweet Cheeks Girl - R. Schick	Retrd.	2000	99.00	99

NALED Exclusive - Reva Schick

YEAR ISSUE	EDITION LIMIT	YEAR RETD.	ISSUE PRICE	*QUOTE U.S.$
1999 Forever Yours	1,500	2000	190.00	190
2000 Being Sweet	1,000		150.00	150

Porcelain Bears & Bunny - Lee Middleton

YEAR ISSUE	EDITION LIMIT	YEAR RETD.	ISSUE PRICE	*QUOTE U.S.$
1993 Buster Bear	Retrd.	1994	250.00	250
1993 Baby Buster	Retrd.	1994	230.00	230
1993 Bye Baby Bunting	Retrd.	1994	270.00	270

Porcelain Collector Series - Lee Middleton

YEAR ISSUE	EDITION LIMIT	YEAR RETD.	ISSUE PRICE	*QUOTE U.S.$
1992 Beloved & Bé Bé	362	1994	590.00	600-650
1993 Cherish - Lilac & Lace	141	1994	500.00	500
1992 Sencerity II - Country Fair	253	1994	500.00	500

Porcelain Limited Edition Series - Lee Middleton

YEAR ISSUE	EDITION LIMIT	YEAR RETD.	ISSUE PRICE	*QUOTE U.S.$
1999 All Dressed Up	2,500		220.00	220
1990 Baby Grace	500	1990	500.00	650-800
1994 Blossom	86	1995	500.00	500
1994 Bride	200	1994	1390.00	1500-2000
1988 Cherish -1st Edition	750	1988	350.00	550
1986 Dear One	750	1988	450.00	450
1989 Devan	543	1991	500.00	500-650
1995 Elise - 1860's Civil War	200	1996	1790.00	1800
1999 Having Fun	2,500		220.00	220
1991 Johanna	381	1992	500.00	500
1999 Just Precious	2,500		180.00	180
1999 Little Dreamer	2,500	1999	180.00	180
1999 Little Sweetheart	2,500		180.00	180
1991 Molly Rose	500	1991	500.00	850
1999 My Beloved	2,500		180.00	180
1989 My Lee	655	1991	500.00	650
1988 Sincerity -1st Edition - Nettie/Simplicity	750	1988	330.00	350-600
1995 Tenderness - Baby Clown	250	1996	590.00	590
1994 Tenderness - Petite Pierrot	250	1995	500.00	500

Porcelain Limited Edition Series - Reva Schick

YEAR ISSUE	EDITION LIMIT	YEAR RETD.	ISSUE PRICE	*QUOTE U.S.$
1999 Go Bye Bye	2,500	2000	200.00	200
1999 Little Lamb	2,500		200.00	200
1999 Something Special	2,500		200.00	200
1999 Sweet & Petite	2,500		200.00	200

Romper Series - Lee Middleton

YEAR ISSUE	EDITION LIMIT	YEAR RETD.	ISSUE PRICE	*QUOTE U.S.$
1996 First Born Dark Romper Boy	2,000	1998	160.00	180-195
1996 First Born Dark Romper Girl	2,000	1997	160.00	180-195
1996 First Born Romper Boy	2,000	1996	160.00	160-180
1996 First Born Romper Girl	2,000	1996	160.00	160-180
1996 Little Love Twin Boy	2,000	1996	160.00	160
1996 Little Love Twin Girl	2,000	1996	160.00	160

Scootles - R. O'Neill

YEAR ISSUE	EDITION LIMIT	YEAR RETD.	ISSUE PRICE	*QUOTE U.S.$
1997 Scootles	Retrd.	1998	50.00	60-85

Show Specials - Various

YEAR ISSUE	EDITION LIMIT	YEAR RETD.	ISSUE PRICE	*QUOTE U.S.$
1993 Molly Goes to Disneyland - L. Middleton	25	1993	125.00	125
1998 My Best Friend - R. Schick	25	1998	200.00	200
1999 Innocence - R. Schick	100	2000	200.00	200
2000 Love at First Sight - R. Schick	25	2000	200.00	200

Small Wonder/Play Babies - Reva Schick

YEAR ISSUE	EDITION LIMIT	YEAR RETD.	ISSUE PRICE	*QUOTE U.S.$
2000 Black Hair Girl	Open		49.95	50
2000 Blonde Hair Boy	Open		49.95	50
2000 Blonde Hair Girl	Open		49.95	50
2000 Brown Hair Girl	Open		49.95	50

Spiegel Exclusive Limited Edition Series - Reva Schick

YEAR ISSUE	EDITION LIMIT	YEAR RETD.	ISSUE PRICE	*QUOTE U.S.$
1999 Elegance	1,000		149.00	149

Spiegel MOB Series - Reva Schick

YEAR ISSUE	EDITION LIMIT	YEAR RETD.	ISSUE PRICE	*QUOTE U.S.$
1999 New Beginnings, pink	Open		100.00	100
1999 New Beginnings, white	Open		100.00	100
1998 Small Wonder	Open		120.00	120
1998 Sweet Cheeks	Open		120.00	120

Toys R Us Exclusive - Reva Schick

YEAR ISSUE	EDITION LIMIT	YEAR RETD.	ISSUE PRICE	*QUOTE U.S.$
1999 Happy Bear, My Own Baby	Open		100.00	100
1999 Very Good Baby, My Own Baby	Open		100.00	100

Wise Penny Collection - Lee Middleton

YEAR ISSUE	EDITION LIMIT	YEAR RETD.	ISSUE PRICE	*QUOTE U.S.$
1993 Jennifer (Peach Dress)	Retrd.	1995	140.00	140-185
1993 Jennifer (Print Dress)	Retrd.	1995	140.00	140-185
1993 Molly Jo	Retrd.	1995	140.00	140
1993 Gordon	Retrd.	1995	140.00	140
1993 Ashley (Brown Hair)	Retrd.	1995	120.00	120-195
1993 Merry	Retrd.	1995	140.00	140
1993 Grace	Retrd.	1995	140.00	200
1993 Ashley (Blond Hair)	Retrd.	1995	120.00	120-195
1993 Baby Devan	Retrd.	1995	140.00	140-195

Lenox Collections

Lenox China Dolls - J. Grammer

YEAR ISSUE	EDITION LIMIT	YEAR RETD.	ISSUE PRICE	*QUOTE U.S.$
1985 Abigail, 20"	Closed	1985	425.00	870
1985 Amanda, 16"	Closed	1985	425.00	770
1985 Amy, 14"	Closed	1985	250.00	650-700
1985 Annabelle, 14"	Closed	1985	250.00	650-700
1985 Elizabeth, 14"	Closed	1985	250.00	650-700
1985 Jennifer, 14"	Closed	1985	250.00	650-700
1985 Jessica, 20"	Closed	1985	475.00	1180
1985 Maggie, 16"	Closed	1985	400.00	770
1985 Mary Anne, 20"	Closed	1985	450.00	1200
1985 Miranda, 14"	Closed	1985	250.00	650-700
1985 Rebecca, 16"	Closed	1985	375.00	770
1985 Samantha, 16"	500	1985	500.00	1400
1985 Sarah, 14"	Closed	1985	250.00	650-700

Little Gem/Akira Trading Co.

Bloosom Bears - L. Mullins

YEAR ISSUE	EDITION LIMIT	YEAR RETD.	ISSUE PRICE	*QUOTE U.S.$
1999 Daisy	2,000		40.00	40
1999 Lily of the Valley	2,000		40.00	40
1999 Orchid	2,000		40.00	40
1999 Rose Petals	2,000		40.00	40
1999 Violet	2,000		40.00	40

Butterfly Boy - Chu-Ming Wu

YEAR ISSUE	EDITION LIMIT	YEAR RETD.	ISSUE PRICE	*QUOTE U.S.$
1999 Garden Boy	500		40.00	40

Christmas Collection - L. Lloyd

YEAR ISSUE	EDITION LIMIT	YEAR RETD.	ISSUE PRICE	*QUOTE U.S.$
1998 Elfie	2,000		40.00	40
1998 Kringle	2,000		40.00	40

Circus Collection - D. Canham

YEAR ISSUE	EDITION LIMIT	YEAR RETD.	ISSUE PRICE	*QUOTE U.S.$
1999 Bianca	2,000		40.00	40
1999 Boom	2,000		49.00	49
1998 Carrot Top	2,000		40.00	40
1998 Jingle	2,000		40.00	40
1999 Juggler	2,000		49.00	49
1999 Leopold and Larry	2,000		50.00	50
1999 Lulu, Patches and Spots	2,000		60.00	60
1999 Notsosilly	2,000		30.00	30
1998 Pananini	2,000		40.00	40
1998 Plum	2,000		40.00	40
1999 Ringmaster	2,000		40.00	40

Fairy Collection - S. Lambert

YEAR ISSUE	EDITION LIMIT	YEAR RETD.	ISSUE PRICE	*QUOTE U.S.$
1999 Blossom	2,000		40.00	40
1999 Bugsby	2,000		40.00	40
1999 Dragonfly	2,000		40.00	40
1999 Figis	2,000		40.00	40
1999 Firefly	2,000		40.00	40

Formosa Bear - Chu-Ming Wu

YEAR ISSUE	EDITION LIMIT	YEAR RETD.	ISSUE PRICE	*QUOTE U.S.$
1998 Formosa Green Bear	1,000	1999	65.00	65

Garden Harvest - L. Mullins, unless otherwise noted

YEAR ISSUE	EDITION LIMIT	YEAR RETD.	ISSUE PRICE	*QUOTE U.S.$
1999 Berry	2,000		40.00	40
1999 Lemon	2,000		40.00	40
1999 Lime Tart	2,000		40.00	40
1999 Plum Puddin	2,000		40.00	40
1999 Punkin	2,000		40.00	40

Golfer Collection - Chu-Ming Wu

YEAR ISSUE	EDITION LIMIT	YEAR RETD.	ISSUE PRICE	*QUOTE U.S.$
1999 Angus	2,000		40.00	40
1999 Master McGreen	2,000		40.00	40
1999 Miss Andrea	2,000		40.00	40
1999 Norman Putt	2,000		40.00	40

Little Gem Teddy Bears - Various

YEAR ISSUE	EDITION LIMIT	YEAR RETD.	ISSUE PRICE	*QUOTE U.S.$
2000 21st Century Bear - Chu-Ming Wu	2,000		50.00	50
1998 4th of July Boy - L. Lloyd	500	1999	40.00	40
1998 4th of July Girl - L. Lloyd	500	1999	40.00	40
1998 Alex (Open Mouth Bear) - C. Stewart	500		40.00	40
1995 Alex - D. Canham	3,000	1997	40.00	55-65
1995 Amelia Baby Blue - D. Canham	3,000	1997	40.00	85-100
2000 Amos - C. Stewart	2,000		40.00	40
1993 Annie - D. Canham	3,000	1995	40.00	45-65
1995 Banana & Chip - D. Canham	3,000	1997	40.00	90-140
1998 Bearfoot & Pregnant - L. Spiegel	2,000	1999	40.00	40-50
1996 Bilbo & Bruno - D. Canham	2,000		50.00	50
1993 Bonnie - D. Canham	3,000	1995	40.00	50-60
1995 Bosworth & Chichi - D. Canham	3,000	1997	40.00	80-110
1996 Bumble Bee - D. Canham	3,000	1998	40.00	60-70
1993 Cameo - Chu-Ming Wu	3,000	1996	40.00	90-105
1994 Caramel- Chu-Ming Wu	3,000	1996	40.00	70-80
1998 Chester I - C. Taylor	2,000		40.00	40
1998 Chester II - C. Taylor	2,000		40.00	40
1994 Chico - D. Canham	3,000	1996	40.00	55-65
1994 Chilly - D. Canham	3,000	1998	40.00	45-75
2000 Chimp - C. Starnes	2,000		30.00	30
1994 Chocolate - Chu-Ming Wu	500	1997	40.00	75-90
1994 Chu-Ming - S. Dotson	3,000	1995	40.00	85-105
2000 Coco - D. Canham	2,000		40.00	40
1993 Connie - Chu-Ming Wu	3,000	1995	40.00	60-65
2000 Court Jester - D. Allen	2,000		40.00	40
1999 Crazy Ike - L. Spiegel	2,000		30.00	30
1996 Cuddles - D. Canham	2,000		40.00	40
1994 Cupid - D. Canham	3,000	1995	40.00	60-65
1994 Darcy - Chu-Ming Wu	3,000	1997	40.00	40-50
1996 Dizzy - D. Canham	3,000	1998	40.00	40-45
1999 English Guard - C. Stewart	2,000		48.00	48
1999 Ethan & Edith - L. Lloyd	2,000		50.00	50
1998 Fibber - L. Spiegel	2,000		40.00	40
1999 Garden Boy II - Chu-Ming Wu	500		40.00	40
1999 Ginger & Snaps - D. Allen	2,000		40.00	40
1998 Gnomes - K. Kilby	2,000		40.00	40
1999 Harriet & Her Hedgehog - L. Lloyd	2,000		40.00	40
1998 Holland Boy - Lydarys/Gertenback	2,000		40.00	40
2000 Huggie - D. Canham	2,000		40.00	40
2000 Issie & Ice - D. Canham	2,000		50.00	50
1998 Jamie Jr. - Chu-Ming Wu	1,000		170.00	170
1994 Jester Blue - D. Canham	3,000	1995	40.00	60-80
1994 Jester Grey - D. Canham	3,000	1995	40.00	60-80
1994 Jester Pink - D. Canham	3,000	1995	40.00	60-70
1999 Johnny on the Pot - L. Spiegel	2,000		40.00	40
1994 Juliet (pin) - D. Canham	3,000	1998	40.00	40-50
1995 Kiki - D. Canham	3,000	1998	40.00	55-65
1996 Lady Bug - D. Canham	3,000	1998	40.00	55-65
1996 Latte - Chu-Ming Wu	3,000	1998	40.00	65-80
1998 Leona - C. Stewart	2,000		40.00	40
1998 Lester Jester - L. Lloyd	2,000		40.00	40
1994 Li-Ling - Chu-Ming Wu	3,000	1996	40.00	40-45
2000 Little Blue - C. Stewart	2,000		30.00	30
1994 Lopsy Blue - D. Canham	3,000	1995	40.00	65-75
1994 Lopsy Plum - D. Canham	3,000	1995	40.00	60-75
1999 Lucky Catch - L. Spiegel	2,000		49.00	49
1998 Lucky Locket - D. Allen	2,000		44.00	44
2000 Luv Bug - D. Canham	2,000		40.00	40
2000 Magical Jester Duo - D. Allen	2,000		40.00	40
1994 Marcy - Chu-Ming Wu	3,000	1997	40.00	40-45
1998 Mardi Gras - Chu-Ming Wu	2,000		40.00	40
1994 Max (Ceylon) - Chu-Ming Wu	3,000	1996	40.00	50-60
2000 Me & Golly - D. Canham	2,000		50.00	50
1994 Mei-Mei - Chu-Ming Wu	3,000	1995	40.00	50-65
1998 Mellie - D. Canham	2,000		40.00	40
1999 Millenium Milton - L. Lloyd	500		40.00	40
1995 Milly & Quackers - D. Canham	3,000	1997	40.00	85-95
1994 Mopsy - Chu-Ming Wu	3,000	1998	40.00	45-55
1999 Mr. Everything - L. Spiegel	2,000		30.00	30
1999 Mr. Golly - L. Lloyd	2,000		40.00	40
1999 Mukaluk & Seal - L. Spiegel	2,000		49.00	49
1998 Nester Jester - L. Lloyd	2,000		40.00	40
1995 Nicholas - D. Canham	3,000	1998	40.00	60-65
1996 No-No (Amber) - Chu-Ming Wu	3,000	1998	40.00	75-85
1998 Old Fashioned - C. Stewart	3,000		40.00	40
1993 Onyx - Chu-Ming Wu	3,000	1995	40.00	90-115
1993 Pearl - Chu-Ming Wu	3,000	1995	40.00	90-115
1996 Perfume Bottle - Chu-Ming Wu	3,000	1998	40.00	80-90
1994 Perky - D. Canham	3,000	1996	40.00	65-80
1999 Pete - L. Lloyd	2,000		49.00	49
1998 Philmore - A. Sison	2,000		40.00	40
2000 Pip - D. Canham	2,000		40.00	40
1998 Polar Bear - D. Shaw	2,000		49.00	49
1995 Rags - Chu-Ming Wu	3,000	1998	40.00	45-50
1998 Rainbow - C. Stewart	1,000	1998	40.00	40-45
1998 Rainbow II - C. Stewart	1,000	1999	40.00	40-45
1994 Razz - D. Canham	3,000	1997	40.00	80-90
2000 Rex & Rooster - D. Canham	2,000		50.00	50
1993 Rex - Chu-Ming Wu	3,000	1997	40.00	60-70
1995 Rhonda - Chu-Ming Wu	3,000	1997	40.00	55-65
1998 Ripley - A. Sison	2,000		49.00	49
1998 Robin Hood - Chu-Ming Wu	2,000		40.00	40
1994 Romeo (pin) - D. Canham	3,000	1998	40.00	40-45
1998 Rosanna - Chu-Ming Wu	2,000		40.00	40
1995 Rosie - Chu-Ming Wu	3,000	1996	40.00	45-50
1994 Rudolph - Chu-Ming Wu	3,000	1997	40.00	80-90
1998 Sailorboy - K. Kilby	2,000		40.00	40
1995 Samantha - S. Dotson	3,000	1997	40.00	95-115
1994 Santa - D. Canham	3,000	1998	40.00	75-80
1995 Saphire (honey) - Chu-Ming Wu	3,000	1996	40.00	45-50
1998 Sassie - L. Spiegel	2,000		40.00	40
1994 Scottie - D. Canham	3,000	1998	40.00	55-60
1998 See No Evil, Hear No Evil, Speak No Evil - L. Spiegel	2,000		100.00	100
2000 Shani - C. Starnes	2,000		30.00	30
1995 Sharon - D. Canham	3,000	1997	40.00	50-60
1995 Sophie - D. Canham	3,000	1998	40.00	50-60
1998 Spanky - L. Spiegel	2,000		49.00	49
1999 Spencer - L. Lloyd	2,000		40.00	40
2000 Star Bug - D. Canham	2,000		40.00	40
1994 Strawberry (Alpaca) - Chu-Ming Wu	500	1995	40.00	80-100
1998 Superteddy - K. Kilby	2,000		40.00	40
1996 Tabatha - D. Canham	3,000	1998	40.00	50-55
1996 Teddy's Bear - L. Mullin	3,000	1998	49.00	75-80
1995 Thai - Chu-Ming Wu	3,000	1996	40.00	65-70
1998 Tumbler - L. Mullins	2,000		40.00	40
1994 Vanilla - Chu-Ming Wu	500	1995	40.00	70-75
1996 Winter Sprite - D. Canham	3,000	1998	40.00	65-70
1998 Yo Yo Bear - L. Lloyd	2,000		40.00	40
1994 Zack - S. Dotson	3,000	1997	40.00	65-70
1998 Zeke - L. Spiegel	2,000		40.00	40
1994 Zev - Chu-Ming Wu	3,000	1998	40.00	50-55

Mohair Collection - Chu-Ming Wu, unless otherwise noted

YEAR ISSUE	EDITION LIMIT	YEAR RETD.	ISSUE PRICE	*QUOTE U.S.$
1998 Andy D.	1,000		40.00	40
1998 Baby Boo D.	450	1999	40.00	40
1998 Boomer - K. Mahanna	2,000		40.00	40

*Quotes have been rounded up to nearest dollar

YEAR ISSUE	EDITION LIMIT	YEAR RETD.	ISSUE PRICE	*QUOTE U.S.$
1998 Candy D.	200	1998	40.00	40-50
1995 Goldie	3,000	1998	40.00	40-50
1998 Midget & Sheep - C. Stewart	2,000		40.00	40
1998 Missy - L. Lloyd	2,000		40.00	40
1995 Priscilla	3,000	1999	40.00	40-50
1998 Stuart - S. Quinn	2,000		40.00	40

Walt Disney World Teddy Bear & Doll Convention - Chu-Ming Wu

YEAR ISSUE	EDITION LIMIT	YEAR RETD.	ISSUE PRICE	*QUOTE U.S.$
1999 Pooh & Bee	750		80.00	80
1998 Winnie the Pooh	500	1998	80.00	175

Mill Mountain

Chenille Collection - Team, unless otherwise noted

YEAR ISSUE	EDITION LIMIT	YEAR RETD.	ISSUE PRICE	*QUOTE U.S.$
1999 33-00-11288 12" Dressed Snowman	Open		15.00	15
1999 33-00-11292 8" Dressed Snowman	Open		8.00	8
1999 33-00-11293 10" Dressed Snowman	Open		10.00	10
1999 33-00-12745 3 pc.Snowmen Asst. 1 each, 8", 10" & 12"	Open		33.00	33
2000 33-00-13418 3" Pumpkin	Open		8.00	8
2000 33-00-13420 7" Pumpkin	Open		33.00	33
2000 33-00-13425 17" x 10" - Snowgirl Mini Door Stop	Open		25.00	25
2000 33-00-13426 17" x 10" - Snowboy Mini Door Stop	Open		25.00	25
2000 33-00-13429 5" - Ice Skating Snowman	Open		13.00	13
2000 33-00-13430 8" - Speed Skating Snowman	Open		13.00	13
2000 33-00-13435 9" x 14" - Shelf Sitter Snowman	Open		25.00	25
2000 33-00-13797 11" Snowgirl	Open		28.00	28
2000 33-00-13798 11" Angel with Silver Star	Open		16.00	16
2000 33-00-13799 9." Angel with Star Staff	Open		20.00	20
2000 33-00-13800 11" Santa with Wreath	Open		28.00	28
1999 33-05-11960 8" Shelf Sitter Angel - K. Drayne	Open		8.00	8
1999 33-05-11962 12" Shelf Sitter Angel - K. Drayne	Open		13.00	13
1999 33-05-11994 14" Santa with Accessories - K. Drayne	Open		18.00	18

From Grandma's Heart Plush 10" Beanies - K. Drayne

YEAR ISSUE	EDITION LIMIT	YEAR RETD.	ISSUE PRICE	*QUOTE U.S.$
2000 33-16-13371 Ramona - Pastel Pink Bear	Open		16.00	16
2000 33-16-13374 Richard - Pastel Yellow Bunny	Open		16.00	16
2000 33-16-13407 Rachel - Calico Cat with Mouse	Open		16.00	16
2000 33-16-13408 Morgan - White Lamb with Shepherd's Crook	Open		18.00	18
2000 33-16-13409 Grace - Pale Blue Bear with Butterflies	Open		18.00	18
2000 33-16-13410 Devin - Brown Bear with Bees	Open		18.00	18
2000 33-16-13411 Destiny - Antique Bear	Open		16.00	16
2000 33-16-13772 Roxanne - Pastel Pink Bunny	Open		16.00	16
2000 33-16-13773 Geoff - Pale Blue Bear	Open		16.00	16

From Grandma's Heart Plush 10" Bedspread Babies - K. Drayne

YEAR ISSUE	EDITION LIMIT	YEAR RETD.	ISSUE PRICE	*QUOTE U.S.$
2000 33-05-13338 Sarah - White Bunny with Chenille Jacket	Open		19.00	19
2000 33-05-13339 Jacob - Antique Bear with Chenille Turtleneck	Open		19.00	19
2000 33-05-13340 Allison - White Bear with Chenille Sweater	Open		19.00	19

From Grandma's Heart Plush 10" Poseable - K. Drayne

YEAR ISSUE	EDITION LIMIT	YEAR RETD.	ISSUE PRICE	*QUOTE U.S.$
1999 33-05-12438 Penny - Antique Bear with Blue Sweater	Open		15.00	15
1999 33-05-12439 Adam - White Bear with Plaid Vest	Open		15.00	15
1999 33-05-12442 Phoebe - White Cat with Floral Vest	Open		15.00	15
1999 33-05-12443 Nicholas - Brown Puppy with Yellow Jacket	Open		15.00	15
1999 33-05-12444 Kathy - Antique Bunny with Eyelet Vest	Open		15.00	15

From Grandma's Heart Plush 10" Shelf Sitter - K. Drayne

YEAR ISSUE	EDITION LIMIT	YEAR RETD.	ISSUE PRICE	*QUOTE U.S.$
1999 33-05-12393 Max - White Bear	Open		12.00	12
1999 33-05-12394 Brooke - Antique Bunny	Open		12.00	12
1999 33-05-12395 Emily - Antique Cat	Open		12.00	12
1999 33-05-12396 Erica - Antique Lamb	Open		12.00	12
1999 33-05-12397 Taylor - Brown Puppy	Open		12.00	12
1999 33-05-12398 Maxine - Antique Bear	Open		12.00	12
1999 33-05-12399 Steven - Brown Bear	Open		12.00	12

From Grandma's Heart Plush 12" Poseable - K. Drayne

YEAR ISSUE	EDITION LIMIT	YEAR RETD.	ISSUE PRICE	*QUOTE U.S.$
1999 33-05-12348 Joshua - White Bear with Corduroy Overalls	Open		17.00	17
1999 33-05-12436 Cynthia - Antique Cat with Plum Collar and Hat	Open		17.00	17
1999 33-05-12437 Randy - White Bunny with Red and White Star Jacket	Open		17.00	17
2000 33-05-13036 Brittany - Antique Lamb	Open		16.00	16
2000 33-05-13037 Ashley - Antique Bunny	Open		16.00	16
2000 33-05-13237 Kelly - Pastel Pink Bunny	Open		16.00	16
2000 33-05-13344 Alexis - White Bunny	Open		16.00	16

From Grandma's Heart Plush 3' Beanies - K. Drayne

YEAR ISSUE	EDITION LIMIT	YEAR RETD.	ISSUE PRICE	*QUOTE U.S.$
1999 33-05-12579 Benjamin - Antique Beanie Bear	Open		200.00	200
1999 33-05-12580 Shelby - White Beanie Bear	Open		200.00	200
2000 33-05-13118 Valentina - Antique Beanie Bear with Burgundy Check Heart	Open		200.00	200

From Grandma's Heart Plush 6" Beanies - K. Drayne

YEAR ISSUE	EDITION LIMIT	YEAR RETD.	ISSUE PRICE	*QUOTE U.S.$
1999 33-05-12450 Pastel Pink Bear	Open		6.00	6
1999 33-05-12454 Antique Bear	Open		6.00	6
1999 33-05-12455 Brown Bear	Open		6.00	6
1999 33-05-12456 White Bear	Open		6.00	6
1999 33-05-12457 White Cat	Open		6.00	6
1999 33-05-12458 Antique Puppy	Open		6.00	6
1999 33-05-12459 White Bunny	Open		6.00	6
1999 33-05-12460 White Lamb	Open		6.00	6
2000 33-05-13119 Brianna-Pastel Pink Bear	Open		6.00	6
2000 33-05-13138 Christian-Pastel Blue Bear	Open		6.00	6

From Grandma's Heart Plush 8" Beanies - K. Drayne

YEAR ISSUE	EDITION LIMIT	YEAR RETD.	ISSUE PRICE	*QUOTE U.S.$
1999 33-05-12461 Laura - Antique Bear	Open		9.00	9
1999 33-05-12462 Jeannie - Brown Bear	Open		9.00	9
1999 33-05-12463 Shelby - White Bear	Open		9.00	9
1999 33-05-12464 Julia - White Cat	Open		9.00	9
1999 33-05-12465 Brian - Antique Puppy	Open		9.00	9
1999 33-05-12466 Nicole - White Bunny	Open		9.00	9
1999 33-05-12467 Melinda - White Lamb	Open		9.00	9
2000 33-05-12752 Kyle - Pastel Blue Lamb	Open		9.00	9
2000 33-05-13145 Kayla - Pastel Pink Lamb	Open		9.00	9

From Grandma's Heart Plush 8" Cameo Beanies - K. Drayne

YEAR ISSUE	EDITION LIMIT	YEAR RETD.	ISSUE PRICE	*QUOTE U.S.$
2000 33-16-13453 Emma - Lt. Foliage Bunny with Pin	Open		13.00	13
2000 33-16-13454 Sydney - Peach Bunny with Pin	Open		13.00	13
2000 33-16-13455 Ethan - Red Bunny with Pin	Open		13.00	13
2000 33-16-13456 Angela - Dark Blue Angel Bear with Pin	Open		13.00	13
2000 33-16-13457 Olivia - Antique Bear with Cameo Pin	Open		13.00	13
2000 33-16-13458 Daniel - Antique Bear with Bear on Spool	Open		13.00	13
2000 33-16-13459 Shelby - White Bear with pin	Open		13.00	13
2000 33-16-13460 Logan - Antique & Red Bear with Pull Cart	Open		14.00	14

From Grandma's Heart Plush American Classic - K. Drayne

YEAR ISSUE	EDITION LIMIT	YEAR RETD.	ISSUE PRICE	*QUOTE U.S.$
1999 33-05-12340 Trudy - 12" Chambray Striped Bear w/ Heart Turtleneck	Open		20.00	20
1999 33-05-12341 Danielle - 12" Burgundy Check Bear w/ Heart Dress	Open		20.00	20
1999 33-05-12343 Molly - 12" Tan Felt Bear w/ Cherry Jacket	Open		20.00	20
1999 33-05-12698 Trudy - 8" Chambray Striped Bear w/ Star Sweater	Open		15.00	15
1999 33-05-12699 Danielle - 8" Burgundy Check Bear w/ Apple Coat	Open		15.00	15
1999 33-05-12700 Molly - 8" Tan Felt Bear w/ Butterfly Sweater	Open		15.00	15

From Grandma's Heart Plush Grandma's Gem - K. Drayne

YEAR ISSUE	EDITION LIMIT	YEAR RETD.	ISSUE PRICE	*QUOTE U.S.$
1999 33-05-12445 Christopher - 8" Antique Beanie in Sailor Suit	Open		12.00	12
1999 33-05-12446 Megan - 8" White Beanie Flower Bear	Open		12.00	12
1999 33-05-12447 Donnie - 8" Pastel Blue Beanie Bear	Open		12.00	12
1999 33-05-12448 Jeremy - 12" White Poseable Garden Bear	Open		20.00	20
1999 33-05-12449 Angel - 8" Pastel Blue Angel Bear with Heart Pillow	Open		12.00	12
1999 33-05-12451 Bethany - 7" Angel Bear in Dress	Open		12.00	12
1999 33-05-12453 Matthew - 10" Pumpkin Bear	Open		15.00	15
2000 33-05-12704 Brianna - 6" Pastel Pink Beanie Bear with Wings	Open		12.00	12
2000 33-16-13038 Michael - 20" Antique Poseable Bear	Open		56.00	56
2000 33-16-13124 Janet - 18" Antique Poseable Bunny	Open		56.00	56
2000 33-16-13130 Leah - 16" Blueish Lavender Poseable Bear	Open		40.00	40
2000 33-16-13336 Patty - 21" Pastel Patchwork Poseable Bunny	Open		60.00	60
2000 33-16-13369 Victoria - 16" Antique Poseable Reading Bear	2-Yr.		50.00	50
2000 33-16-13405 Nathaniel - 16" White Poseable Pig	Open		40.00	40
2000 33-16-13451 Betty - 18" White Poseable Nurse Bear	2-Yr.		60.00	60
2000 33-16-13452 Nathaniel - 12" White Poseable Pig	Open		25.00	25
2000 33-16-13788 Cole - 15" Poseable Clown Bear	Open		60.00	60

From Grandma's Heart Plush Grandma's Holiday Gem - K. Drayne

YEAR ISSUE	EDITION LIMIT	YEAR RETD.	ISSUE PRICE	*QUOTE U.S.$
2000 33-16-13404 Trevor - 13" Pale Blue Poseable Snow Bear	Open		30.00	30
2000 33-16-13406 Angel - 8" Antique & Red Holiday Angel Bear	Open		16.00	16
2000 33-16-13422 Luis - 8" Red Poseable Elf Bear	Open		16.00	16
2000 33-16-13423 Luis - 13" - Red Poseable Elf Bear	Open		36.00	36
2000 33-16-13720 Clementine - 18" White Poseable Polar Bear	Open		46.00	46
2000 33-16-13787 Charles - 29" Antique/Red Poseable Santa Bear	Open		150.00	150

Original Appalachian Artworks

Collectors Club Editions - X. Roberts

YEAR ISSUE	EDITION LIMIT	YEAR RETD.	ISSUE PRICE	*QUOTE U.S.$
1987 Baby Otis	1,275	1987	250.00	175-300
1989 Anna Ruby	693	1990	250.00	225-300
1990 Lee Ann	468	1991	250.00	250-300
1991 Richard Russell	490	1991	250.00	250-300
1992 Baby Dodd & 'Ittle Bitty	354	1993	250.00	250-300
1993 Patti w/ Cabbage Bud Boutonnier	358	1994	280.00	250-300
1994 Mother Cabbage	245	1995	150.00	150
1995 Rosie	322	1996	275.00	230-275
1996 Gabriella (Angel)	Closed	1997	265.00	260-265
1997 Robert London	Closed	1997	275.00	225-275
1998 Dexter (Anniversary)	Yr.Iss.	1998	395.00	395
1999 Harley	Yr.Iss.	1999	345.00	345
2000 Millie	Yr.Iss.		300.00	300

BabyLand Career - X. Roberts

YEAR ISSUE	EDITION LIMIT	YEAR RETD.	ISSUE PRICE	*QUOTE U.S.$
1992 BabyLand (Engineer -Career Kid)	Closed	1992	220.00	250-300
1993 BabyLand (Miss BLGH Career 'Kid)	240	1993	220.00	220-300
1994 BabyLand (Child Star Career 'Kid)	241	1994	220.00	260-265
1995 BabyLand (Career Nurse)	83	1995	210.00	210-250
1997 BabyLand (Ballerina)	Closed	1997	210.00	210

BabyLand General Hospital Convention Baby - X. Roberts

YEAR ISSUE	EDITION LIMIT	YEAR RETD.	ISSUE PRICE	*QUOTE U.S.$
1990 Charlie (Amber)	200	1990	175.00	175-300
1991 Nurse Payne (Garnet)	160	1991	210.00	225-275
1992 Princess Nacoochee (BabyLand)	160	1992	210.00	250
1993 Baby BeBop (BabyLand)	199	1993	210.00	260-300
1994 Norma Jean (BabyLand)	250	1994	225.00	375-500
1995 Delta (BabyLand)	200	1995	230.00	230
1996 Marlene (BabyLand)	200	1996	230.00	230
1997 Hayley (BabyLand)	200	1997	220.00	220
1998 Marisa (BabyLand)	200	1998	250.00	250
1999 Middle Name "Bea"	200	1999	255.00	255
2000 PJ	200	2000	235.00	235

BunnyBees - X. Roberts

YEAR ISSUE	EDITION LIMIT	YEAR RETD.	ISSUE PRICE	*QUOTE U.S.$
1986 Girl	Closed	N/A	13.00	25-50
1986 Boy	Closed	N/A	13.00	25-40
1994 Girl w/Squeaker	Closed	N/A	18.00	18
1994 Boy w/Squeaker	Closed	N/A	18.00	18

Cabbage Patch Kids (10 Character Kids) - X. Roberts

YEAR ISSUE	EDITION LIMIT	YEAR RETD.	ISSUE PRICE	*QUOTE U.S.$
1982 Amy L.	206	1982	125.00	500-700
1982 Bobbie J.	314	1982	125.00	450-600
1982 Billy B.	201	1982	125.00	450-600
1982 Dorothy J.	126	1982	125.00	550-700
1982 Gilda R.	105	1982	125.00	700-2500
1982 Marilyn S.	275	1982	125.00	595-800
1982 Otis L.	308	1982	125.00	700
1982 Rebecca R.	301	1982	125.00	500-700
1982 Sybil S.	502	1982	125.00	450-700
1982 Tyler B.	94	1982	125.00	2000-3000

Cabbage Patch Kids - X. Roberts

YEAR ISSUE	EDITION LIMIT	YEAR RETD.	ISSUE PRICE	*QUOTE U.S.$
1989 Amber (Reg. & Halloween)	1,356	1990	195.00	135-150
1989 Amber (Halloween, Asian)	654	1989	175.00	135-225
1989 Amber (Toddler)	272	1989	150.00	100-225
1986 Amethyst	9,250	1986	135.00	100-200
1988 Aquamarine	5,000	1988	150.00	150-200
1994 BabyLand (Bald)	Closed	1994	210.00	200-250
1994 BabyLand (Preemie)	Closed	1994	175.00	150-250
1995 BabyLand (Preemie)	Closed	1995	175.00	150-225
1997 BabyLand (Preemie)	Closed	1997	175.00	150-175
1991 BabyLand (Reg.)	969	1991	190.00	190-240
1992 BabyLand (Reg.)	770	1992	190.00	190-240
1994 BabyLand (Reg.)	Closed	1994	210.00	210-260
1995 BabyLand (Reg.)	Closed	1994	210.00	210-260
1994 BabyLand (Sweet Sixteen "Casey Ann")	191	1994	260.00	295-500
1993 Blackberry Preemie	438	1993	175.00	200
1999 Blue Creek Kid	Closed	1999	255.00	255
1999 Blue Creek (Newborn)	Closed	1999	235.00	235
1999 Blue Creek (Preemie)	Closed	1999	190.00	190
1992 Brass	321	1992	190.00	190
1992 Brass (Flower Girl Toddler)	Closed	1992	175.00	175-225
1992 Brass (Garden Party Girl)	Closed	1992	190.00	190-240
1992 Brass (Hispanic Girl Toddler)	Closed	1992	175.00	175-225
1992 Brass (Ring Bearer Boy Toddler)	Closed	1992	175.00	175-225
1992 Brass (Toddler)	424	1992	175.00	175-225
1995 Bucky (California Collectors Club)	105	1995	220.00	220
1983 Champagne (Andre)	1,000	1983	250.00	250-500
1983 Champagne (Madeira)	1,000	1983	250.00	250-500
1998 Chattahoochee Kid	Closed	1999	255.00	255
1998 Chattahoochee (Newborn)	Closed	1999	195.00	195
1998 Chattahoochee (Preemie)	Closed	1999	185.00	185
1983 Cleveland "Green"	2,000	1983	125.00	400
1999 Col. Casey Preemie (BLGH)	Closed	1999	170.00	170
2000 Col. Casey Preemie (BLGH)	Yr.Iss.		170.00	170
1991 Copper	241	1991	190.00	190
1991 Copper (Halloween)	273	1991	190.00	190-240
1991 Copper (Toddler)	241	1991	175.00	175-225
1986 Corporate 'Kid	2,000	1986	400.00	150-400
1991 Crystal	176	1991	190.00	190
1991 Crystal (Easter Fashions)	302	1991	190.00	185-210
1991 Crystal (Toddler)	41	1991	175.00	175-225
1991 Crystal (Valentine Fashions)	256	1991	190.00	190-240

*Quotes have been rounded up to nearest dollar

Original Appalachian Artworks
to Original Appalachian Artworks

DOLLS/PLUSH

YEAR ISSUE	EDITION LIMIT	YEAR RETD.	ISSUE PRICE	*QUOTE U.S.$
1991 Crystal (Valentine Toddler Fashions)	189	1991	175.00	175-225
1984 Daddy's Darlins' (Kitten)	500	1984	300.00	225-400
1984 Daddy's Darlins' (Princess)	500	1984	300.00	225-400
1984 Daddy's Darlins' (Pun'kin)	500	1983	300.00	225-400
1984 Daddy's Darlins' (Tootsie)	500	1984	300.00	225-400
1984 Daddy's Darlins', set/4	2,000	1984	1200.00	1200-2000
2000 Daddy's Lil' Darlin'	Yr.Iss.		199.00	199
1992 Diamond	360	1993	210.00	210
1992 Diamond (Choir Christmas)	54	1992	210.00	210-260
1992 Diamond (Thanksgiving Indian)	123	1992	210.00	210-260
1992 Diamond (Thanksgiving Toddler Indian)	55	1992	195.00	195-245
1992 Diamond (Toddler)	51	1993	195.00	195-245
1985 Emerald	35,000	1985	135.00	100-135
1985 Four Seasons (Autumn)	2,000	1985	160.00	100-160
1985 Four Seasons (Crystal)	2,000	1985	160.00	100-160
1985 Four Seasons (Morton)	2,000	1985	160.00	100-160
1985 Four Seasons (Sunny)	2,000	1985	160.00	100-160
1991 Garnet	376	1991	190.00	200-215
1991 Garnet (Father's Day Toddler)	85	1991	175	250
1991 Garnet (Father's Day)	173	1991	190.00	250
1991 Garnet (Mother's Day Girl)	259	1991	190.00	200
1991 Garnet (Mother's Day Toddler Girl)	364	1991	175.00	200
1991 Garnet (Toddler)	49	1991	175.00	175
1993 Georgia Power (Special Stork Delivery)	288	1993	230.00	250-350
1985 Gold	50,000	1985	135.00	130-135
1995 Graceland Elvis	500	1995	300.00	300
1993 Happily Ever After (Bride)	343	1993	230.00	230-275
1993 Happily Ever After (Groom)	343	1993	230.00	230-275
1994 House of Tyrol (Christina Marie)	1,000	1994	200.00	200
1994 House of Tyrol (Markus Michael)	1,000	1994	200.00	200
1987 Iddy Buds	750	1987	650.00	275-650
1986 Identical Twins, set/2	5,000	1987	150.00	200-350
1985 Ivory	45,000	1985	135.00	130-200
1989 Jade	Closed	1989	150.00	130-150
1989 Jade (4th of July Fashions)	Closed	1989	150.00	150-200
1989 Jade (Mother's Day Fashions)	338	1989	150.00	150-200
1989 Jade (Toddler)	Closed	1989	150.00	150-200
1992 JC Penney 1992 Catalog Exclusive (Cocoa-Girl)	245	1992	200.00	200-215
1992 JC Penney 1992 Catalog Exclusive (Lemon Girl)	248	1992	200.00	200
2000 Kellum Valley Kid	Yr.Iss.		255.00	255
2000 Kellum Valley (Newborn)	Yr.Iss.		195.00	195
2000 Kellum Valley (Preemie)	Yr.Iss.		190.00	190
1983 KP Darker Green	2,000	1983	125.00	195-400
1983 KPB Burgundy	10,000	1983	130.00	185-250
1984 KPF Turquoise	30,000	1984	130.00	130-140
1984 KPZ Bronze	30,000	1984	130.00	130-150
1984 KPG Coral	35,000	1984	130.00	125-135
1983 KPP Purple	20,000	1984	130.00	130-150
1983 KPR Red	2,000	1983	125.00	130-400
1989 Lapis (Swimsuit Fashions)	645	1989	150.00	135-150
1989 Lapis (Swimsuit Fashions-Toddler)	836	1989	150.00	120-150
1993 Little People 27" (Girl)	300	1993	325.00	500-800
1994 Little People 27" (Boy)	300	1994	325.00	300-500
1996 Little People Girls 27"	300	1996	375.00	300-375
1997 Little People 27" (Boy)	300	1997	395.00	395
2000 Little People (Girl)	300	2000	375.00	375
1994 Mt. Laurel (African Inspired Toddler)	Closed	1994	195.00	195
1994 Mt. Laurel (African Inspired) (Reg.)	Closed	1994	210.00	210
1994 Mt. Laurel (Mrs. Pauls)	Closed	1994	198.00	198
1994 Mt. Laurel (Mysterious Barry)	Closed	1994	225.00	225
1994 Mt. Laurel (Northern)	Closed	1995	210.00	210
1994 Mt. Laurel (Twins Baby Sidney & Baby Lanier)	100	1994	390.00	390
1994 Mt. Laurel (Western)	Closed	1994	210.00	210
1994 Mt. Laurel St. Patrick Boys	100	1994	210.00	210
1994 Mt. Laurel St. Patrick Girls	200	1994	210.00	210
1995 Mt. Yonah (Easter)	Closed	1995	215.00	215
1995 Mt. Yonah (Valentine)	Closed	1995	200.00	200-205
1996 Nacoochee Valley (Easter)	Closed	1996	215.00	215
1996 Nacoochee Valley (Halloween)	Closed	1996	210.00	210
1991 Newborn (BLGH)	909	1991	195.00	150-195
1992 Newborn (BLGH)	869	1992	195.00	150-195
1993 Newborn (BLGH)	1,136	1993	195.00	150-195
1994 Newborn (BLGH)	1,107	1994	195.00	150-195
1995 Newborn (BLGH)	1,042	1995	195.00	150-195
1996 Newborn (BLGH)	1,710	1996	195.00	150-195
1997 Newborn (BLGH)	Closed	1997	195.00	150-195
1998 Newborn (BLGH)	Closed	1998	195.00	150-195
1999 Newborn (BLGH)	Closed	1999	195.00	195
2000 Newborn (BLGH)	Yr.Iss.		195.00	195
1991 Onyx (Thanksgiving Pilgrim)	349	1991	190.00	220-240
1991 Onyx (Toddler)	297	1991	175.00	175-225
1991 Onyx 22"	297	1991	190.00	190
1990 Opal (Easter Toddler Fashions)	751	1989	175.00	125-175
1990 Opal (Garden Fashions)	Closed	1989	175.00	125-175
1990 Opal (Toddler)	Closed	1990	175.00	175
1990 Pearl	542	1990	190.00	190-240
1990 Pearl (Toddler)	226	1990	175.00	175-225
1990 Peridot	680	1990	190.00	170-225
1990 Peridot (Halloween Toddler Fashions)	588	1990	175.00	175-210
1990 Peridot (Toddler)	794	1990	175.00	220-320
1992 Platinum	Closed	1992	210.00	220-320
1992 Platinum (Best Man)	Closed	1992	220.00	320
1992 Platinum (Maid of Honor)	Closed	1992	220.00	320
1992 Platinum (Summertime 'Kids-Watermelon)	Closed	1992	210.00	210
1992 Platinum (Toddler)	19	1992	195.00	195
1985 Preemie (boy)	3,750	1985	150.00	110-145
1985 Preemie (girl)	11,250	1985	150.00	110-145
1985 Preemie Twins, set/2	1,500	1985	600.00	325-600
1990 Quartz (Toddler)	347	1989	175.00	175
1990 Quartz (Valentine Toddler Fashions)	708	1989	175.00	175-225
1992 QVC Exclusive (Janeen Sybil)	200	1992	275.00	275
1993 QVC Exclusive (Lauren Rose)	300	1993	335.00	300-800
1994 QVC Exclusive (Lee Ryan)	300	1994	348.00	600-1000
1992 QVC Exclusive (Preemie) (Celeste Diane)	500	1992	250.00	250
1992 QVC Exclusive (Toddler) (Abigail Sydney)	1,000	1992	225.00	225
1993 QVC Exclusive (Newborn)	187	1993	N/A	200
1985 Rose	40,000	1985	135.00	130-140
1989 Ruby	1,325	1989	150.00	150
1985 Sapphire	35,000	1985	135.00	135
1997 Sautee Valley	Closed	1997	210.00	210
1997 Sautee Valley (Festival Kid)	Closed	1997	220.00	220
1992 Silver	73	1992	190.00	190
1992 Silver (Asian Toddler)	219	1992	175.00	175-225
1992 Silver (Toddler)	59	1992	175.00	175
1992 Silver (Valentine Toddler)	283	1992	190.00	190-240
1995 Skitts Mountain	192	1995	210.00	210
1986 Southern Belle "Georgiana"	4,000	1990	160.00	120-160
1984 Sweetheart (Beau)	750	1984	150.00	150-300
1984 Sweetheart (Candi)	750	1984	150.00	150-300
1988 Tiger's Eye	3,653	1989	150.00	150-175
1988 Tiger's Eye (Easter)	788	1989	150.00	180-275
1989 Tiger's Eye (Mother's Day)	231	1989	150.00	175-275
1988 Tiger's Eye (Valentine's Day)	328	1989	150.00	175-275
1987 Topaz	5,000	1987	135.00	130-135
1993 Unicoi	Closed	1993	210.00	210
1993 Unicoi (Ballerina Toddler)	Closed	1993	195.00	195-260
1993 Unicoi (Spring Toddler)	Closed	1993	195.00	195-260
1993 Unicoi (Spring)	Closed	1993	210.00	210-260
1993 Unicoi (Summer Dinosaur)	Closed	1993	210.00	210-260
1993 Unicoi (Summer Toddler Dinosaur)	Closed	1993	210.00	210-260
1993 Unicoi (Toddler)	Closed	1993	210.00	210
1993 White Christmas - Regular Kids (only)	223	1993	210.00	210-260
1984 World Class	2,500	1984	150.00	150-400

Cabbage Patch Kids Anniversary - X. Roberts

YEAR ISSUE	EDITION LIMIT	YEAR RETD.	ISSUE PRICE	*QUOTE U.S.$
1998 Spring Sass	300		395.00	395
1998 Summer Mischief	300		395.00	395
1998 Autumn Scholar	300		395.00	395
1998 Winter Snuggles	300		395.00	395

Cabbage Patch Kids Baby Character - X. Roberts

YEAR ISSUE	EDITION LIMIT	YEAR RETD.	ISSUE PRICE	*QUOTE U.S.$
1990 Baby Amy Loretta Nursery	509	1990	200.00	130-200
1991 Baby Billy Badd Nursery	306	1991	200.00	130-225
1991 Baby Bobbie Jo Nursery	393	1991	200.00	130-225
1988 Baby Dorothy Jane Nursery	2,000	1992	165.00	130-225
1992 Baby Gilda Roxanne Nursery	351	1992	200.00	130-225
1988 Baby Marilyn Suzanne Nursery	2,000	1992	165.00	130-225
1992 Baby Rebecca Ruby Nursery	373	1992	200.00	130-225
1988 Baby Sybil Sadie Nursery	2,000	1992	165.00	130-225
1988 Baby Tyler Bo Nursery	2,000	1993	165.00	130-225

Cabbage Patch Kids Circus Parade - X. Roberts

YEAR ISSUE	EDITION LIMIT	YEAR RETD.	ISSUE PRICE	*QUOTE U.S.$
1987 Big Top Clown-Baby Cakes	2,000	1987	180.00	225-300
1991 Big Top Tot-Mitzi	1,000	1993	220.00	220-225
1989 Happy Hobo-Bashful Billy	1,000	1989	180.00	250-350
1997 Jingling Jester-Jacqueline	500	1997	275.00	275

Cabbage Patch Kids International - X. Roberts

YEAR ISSUE	EDITION LIMIT	YEAR RETD.	ISSUE PRICE	*QUOTE U.S.$
1983 American Indian/Pair	500	1983	300.00	1000-1200
1984 Bavarian/Pair	500	1984	300.00	350-800
1983 Hispanic/Pair	500	1983	300.00	375-450
1983 Irish/Pair	2,000	1985	320.00	225-320
1983 Oriental/Pair	500	1983	300.00	1000
1987 Polynesian (Lokelina)	1,000	1987	180.00	180
1987 Polynesian (Ohana)	1,000	1987	180.00	180

Cabbage Patch Kids OlympiKids™ - X. Roberts

YEAR ISSUE	EDITION LIMIT	YEAR RETD.	ISSUE PRICE	*QUOTE U.S.$
1996 Baseball Boy	159	1996	275.00	275-280
1996 Basketball Boy & Girl	199	1996	275.00	275
1996 Basketball Girl	302	1996	275.00	275
1996 Cyclist Boy	126	1996	275.00	275
1996 Equestrian Girl	350	1996	275.00	275-350
1995 Gymnastics Boy	241	1996	275.00	275
1995 Rowing Girl	205	1996	275.00	275
1995 Soccer Boy	162	1996	275.00	275
1995 Soccer Girl	262	1996	275.00	275
1996 Softball Girl	140	1996	275.00	275
1995 Track & Field Girl	422	1996	275.00	275
1995 Weight Lifting Boy	158	1996	275.00	275

Cabbage Patch Kids Porcelain - X. Roberts

YEAR ISSUE	EDITION LIMIT	YEAR RETD.	ISSUE PRICE	*QUOTE U.S.$
1994 Porcelain Angel (Angelica)	208	1994	160.00	160
1994 Porcelain Friends (Karen Lee)	59	1994	150.00	150
1994 Porcelain Friends (Kassie Lou)	58	1994	150.00	150
1994 Porcelain Friends (Katie Lyn)	61	1994	150.00	150
1995 Porcelain Peirrot (Sharri Starr)	198	1995	160.00	160

Cabbage Patch Kids Storybook - X. Roberts

YEAR ISSUE	EDITION LIMIT	YEAR RETD.	ISSUE PRICE	*QUOTE U.S.$
1986 Mark Twain (Becky Thatcher)	2,500	1986	160.00	150-170
1986 Mark Twain (Huck Finn)	2,500	1986	160.00	150-170
1986 Mark Twain (Tom Sawyer)	2,500	1986	160.00	150-170
1987 Sleeping Beauty (Prince Charming)	1,250	1991	180.00	150-170
1987 Sleeping Beauty (Sleeping Beauty)	1,250	1991	180.00	150-170

Christmas Collection - X. Roberts

YEAR ISSUE	EDITION LIMIT	YEAR RETD.	ISSUE PRICE	*QUOTE U.S.$
1979 X Christmas	1,000	1979	150.00	3000-5500
1980 Christmas-Nicholas/Noel	500	1980	400.00	900-1000
1982 Christmas-Baby Rudy/Christy Nicole	500	1982	400.00	1000-1600
1983 Christmas-Holly/Berry	1,000	1983	400.00	680-800
1984 Christmas-Carole/Chris	1,000	1984	400.00	425-600
1985 Christmas-Baby Sandy/Claude	2,500	1990	400.00	250-400
1986 Christmas-Hilliary/Nigel	2,000	1990	400.00	400-425
1987 Christmas-Katrina/Misha	2,000	1990	500.00	500
1988 Christmas-Kelly/Kane	2,000	1993	500.00	250-500
1989 Christmas-Joy	500	1989	250.00	300-400
1990 Christmas-Krystina	596	1991	250.00	210-260
1991 Christmas-Nick	700	1991	275.00	275
1992 Christmas-Christy Claus	700	1993	285.00	285
1993 Christmas-Rudolph	500	1993	275.00	275
1994 Christmas-Natalie	500	1994	275.00	225-275
1995 Christmas-Treena	500	1995	275.00	275
1996 Christmas-Sammy The Snowman	500	1996	275.00	245-275
1997 Christmas-Melody	300	1997	295.00	295-400
1998 Christmas-Ginger	300	1998	315.00	245-315
1999 Christmas-Arella	300	1999	320.00	250-320
2000 Christmas-Merry	300	2000	295.00	295

Convention Baby - X. Roberts

YEAR ISSUE	EDITION LIMIT	YEAR RETD.	ISSUE PRICE	*QUOTE U.S.$
1989 Ashley (Jade)	200	1989	250.00	250-500
1990 Bradley (Opal)	200	1990	175.00	300-600
1991 Caroline (Garnet)	200	1991	200.00	300
1992 Duke (Brass)	200	1992	225.00	375-400
1993 Ellen (Unicoi)	200	1993	225.00	300-400
1994 Justin (Mt. Laurel)	200	1994	225.00	300-400
1995 Fifi (Mt. Yonah)	200	1995	250.00	450-700
1996 Gina (Nacoochee Valley)	200	1996	275.00	275
1997 Hannah (Sautee Valley)	200	1997	275.00	300-350
1998 Ian (Chattahoochee)	200	1998	310.00	310-350
1999 Crystal (Blue Creek)	200	1999	255.00	255
2000 Sandy (Kellum Valley)	200	2000	275.00	275

Favorite Memories - X. Roberts

YEAR ISSUE	EDITION LIMIT	YEAR RETD.	ISSUE PRICE	*QUOTE U.S.$
1999 Terrific 30's	200		345.00	345
1999 Fabulous 40's	200		345.00	345
1999 Nifty 50's	200		345.00	345
1999 Super 70's	200		345.00	345

Furskins - X. Roberts

YEAR ISSUE	EDITION LIMIT	YEAR RETD.	ISSUE PRICE	*QUOTE U.S.$
1983 Humphrey Furskin	2,500	1993	75.00	90-100
1985 Boone (no letter)	25,000	1985	55.00	45-75
1985 Farrell (no letter)	25,000	1985	55.00	45-75
1985 Dudley (no letter)	25,000	1985	55.00	45-75
1985 Hattie (no letter)	25,000	1985	55.00	45-75
1985 Boone (A)	25,000	1985	55.00	45-55
1985 Farrell (A)	25,000	1985	55.00	45-55
1985 Dudley (A)	25,000	1985	55.00	45-55
1985 Hattie (A)	25,000	1985	55.00	45-55
1985 Boone (B)	75,000	1985	55.00	45-55
1985 Farrell (B)	75,000	1985	55.00	45-55
1985 Dudley (B)	75,000	1985	55.00	45-55
1985 Hattie (B)	75,000	1985	55.00	45-55
1985 Boone (C)	100,000	1985	55.00	45-55
1985 Farrell (C)	100,000	1985	55.00	45-55
1985 Dudley (C)	100,000	1985	55.00	45-55
1985 Hattie (C)	100,000	1985	55.00	45-55
1985 Boone (D)	125,000	1985	55.00	45-55
1985 Farrell (D)	125,000	1985	55.00	45-55
1985 Dudley (D)	125,000	1985	55.00	45-55
1985 Hattie (D)	125,000	1985	55.00	45-55
1986 Orville T. (no letter)	5,000	1986	55.00	75-125
1986 Jedgar (no letter)	5,000	1986	55.00	75-125
1986 Selma Jean (no letter)	5,000	1986	55.00	75-125
1986 Fannie Fay (no letter)	5,000	1986	55.00	75-125
1986 Orville T. (A)	5,000	1986	55.00	55-100
1986 Jedgar A)	5,000	1986	55.00	55
1986 Selma Jean (A)	5,000	1986	55.00	55
1986 Fannie Fay (A)	5,000	1986	55.00	55
1986 Bubba (licensed)	Closed	1986	30.00	40-45
1986 Cecelia ("CeCe") (licensed)	Closed	1986	30.00	40-45
1986 Hank "Spitball" (licensed)	Closed	1986	30.00	40-45
1986 J. Livingston Clayton ("Scout") (licensed)	Closed	1986	30.00	40-45
1986 Junie Mae (licensed)	Closed	1986	30.00	40-45
1986 Lila Claire (licensed)	Closed	1986	30.00	40-45
1986 Persimmon (licensed)	Closed	1986	30.00	40-45
1986 Thistle (licensed)	Closed	1986	30.00	75-125

Little People - X. Roberts

YEAR ISSUE	EDITION LIMIT	YEAR RETD.	ISSUE PRICE	*QUOTE U.S.$
1978 "A" Blue	1,000	1978	45.00	2000-5000
1978 "B" Red	1,000	1978	80.00	3200-5000
1979 "C" Burgundy	5,000	1979	80.00	1600-2300
1979 "D" Purple	10,000	1979	80.00	500-1000
1979 "E" Bronze	15,000	1980	80.00	450-700
1982 "PE" New 'Ears Preemie	5,000	1982	140.00	225-300
1981 "PR II" Preemie	10,000	1981	130.00	150-250
1980 "SP" Preemie	5,000	1980	100.00	180-400
1982 "U" Unsigned	21,000	1982	125.00	225-300
1980 "U" Unsigned (& 1980)	73,000	1981	125.00	250-300
1980 Celebrity	5,000	1980	200.00	300-400
1980 Grand Edition	1,000	1988	1000.00	700-800
1978 Helen Blue	Closed	1978	30.00	6000-10000
1981 Little People Pals 12"	10,000	N/A	75.00	165-350
1981 New 'Ears	15,000	1981	125.00	130-250
1981 Standing Edition	5,000	1988	300.00	250-300

Mobile Patch Babies - X. Roberts

YEAR ISSUE	EDITION LIMIT	YEAR RETD.	ISSUE PRICE	*QUOTE U.S.$
1992 Garden Party Sprout (Babyland "Miss Eula")	140	1992	250.00	350-500
1992 Garden Party Sprout (Chris' Corner Clown-Daisy)	110	1992	250.00	350-500
1992 Garden Party Sprout (Cottage of Memories Indian Girl)	80	1992	250.00	350-500

*Quotes have been rounded up to nearest dollar

YEAR ISSUE	EDITION LIMIT	YEAR RETD.	ISSUE PRICE	*QUOTE U.S.$
1992 Garden Party Sprout (Doll House Sweet Dreams)	82	1992	250.00	350-500
1992 Garden Party Sprout (Hobby City "Tinkerbell")	160	1992	250.00	350-500
1992 Garden Party Sprout (Wee Heather Victorian-Heather)	62	1992	250.00	350-500
1997 Sautee Valley (Mama's Babies & Bears)	Closed	1997	195.00	195
1997 Sautee Valley (Doll & Teddy Bear Expo)	Closed	1997	195.00	195
1997 Sautee Valley (Rainbow's End)	Closed	1997	195.00	195
1997 Sautee Valley (Roxanne's Doll Shoppe)	Closed	1997	195.00	195
1997 Sautee Valley (S.W. Randall Toys & Gifts)	Closed	1997	195.00	195
1997 Sautee Valley (Rainbow Connection)	Closed	1997	195.00	195
1997 Sautee Valley (Heirlooms of Tomorrow)	Closed	1997	195.00	195
1998 Chattahoochee Newborn (Rainbow Connection)	Closed	1998	225.00	225
1998 Chattahoochee Newborn (Hobby City)	Closed	1998	225.00	225
1998 Chattahoochee Newborn (Cape Art Mart)	Closed	1998	225.00	225
1998 Chattahoochee Newborn (Rainbow's End)	Closed	1998	225.00	225
1998 Chattahoochee Newborn (Black Gold Dolls)	Closed	1998	225.00	225
1998 Chattahoochee Newborn (Mama's Babies & Bears)	Closed	1998	225.00	225
1998 Chattahoochee Newborn (Puppenkinder)	Closed	1998	225.00	225
1998 Chattahoochee Newborn (Doll House)	Closed	1998	225.00	225
1998 Chattahoochee Newborn (Merry Christmas Shoppe)	Closed	1998	225.00	225
1998 Chattahoochee Newborn (Contemporary Dolls)	Closed	1998	225.00	225
1998 Chattahoochee Newborn (Roxanne's Doll Shoppe)	Closed	1998	225.00	225
1998 Chattahoochee Newborn (SW Randall)	Closed	1998	225.00	225
1998 Chattahoochee Newborn (Heirlooms of Tomorrow)	Closed	1998	225.00	225
1999 Blue Creek Newborn	Yr.Iss.		235.00	235

Show Specials - X. Roberts

YEAR ISSUE	EDITION LIMIT	YEAR RETD.	ISSUE PRICE	*QUOTE U.S.$
1985 Topaz (Iris)	1,500	1985	135.00	450-600
1986 Amethyst (Rusty)	250	1986	135.00	200-300
1986 Amethyst (Tiffy)	500	1986	135.00	200-400
1998 Chattahoochee Preemie (Aimee) (West Coast Expo)	20	1998	225.00	450-600
1998 Chattahoochee Preemie (Abigail) (East Coast Expo)	20	1998	225.00	225
1999 Blue Creek Newborn (Annabelle) (West Coast Booth Baby)	30	1999	225.00	225
1999 Blue Creek Newborn (Amanda) (West Coast Show Baby)	25	1999	225.00	225
2000 Kellum Valley Newborn (Laura Beth) (West Coast Show Baby)	25		225.00	225
2000 Kellum Valley Newborn (Prissy) (East Coast Show Baby)	25		225.00	225

Papel Giftware

Annette Funicello Collectible Bear Co./Angel Collection - Various

YEAR ISSUE	EDITION LIMIT	YEAR RETD.	ISSUE PRICE	*QUOTE U.S.$
2000 Coral - B. Cardwell	20,000		60.00	60
2000 Twyla - S. Payne	20,000		60.00	60

Annette Funicello Collectible Bear Co./Bear Buddies Collection - D. Rife

YEAR ISSUE	EDITION LIMIT	YEAR RETD.	ISSUE PRICE	*QUOTE U.S.$
2000 Piggy Bear Ride	3,000		50.00	50

Annette Funicello Collectible Bear Co./Beary'licious Collection - J. Fox

YEAR ISSUE	EDITION LIMIT	YEAR RETD.	ISSUE PRICE	*QUOTE U.S.$
2000 Peachbeary Fluff	2,500		60.00	60

Annette Funicello Collectible Bear Co./Dream Keeper Collection - K. Rundlett

YEAR ISSUE	EDITION LIMIT	YEAR RETD.	ISSUE PRICE	*QUOTE U.S.$
2000 Pillow Talk	5,000		70.00	70

Annette Funicello Collectible Bear Co./Flavorite Collection - K. Rundlett

YEAR ISSUE	EDITION LIMIT	YEAR RETD.	ISSUE PRICE	*QUOTE U.S.$
2000 Razzbeary Truffle	2,500		70.00	70

Annette Funicello Collectible Bear Co./Hat Box Collection - L. Medford

YEAR ISSUE	EDITION LIMIT	YEAR RETD.	ISSUE PRICE	*QUOTE U.S.$
2000 Olive	2,500		70.00	70

Annette Funicello Collectible Bear Co./Special Collection - Various

YEAR ISSUE	EDITION LIMIT	YEAR RETD.	ISSUE PRICE	*QUOTE U.S.$
2000 Rub A Dub Dub - D. Rife	3,000		50.00	50
2000 Sushi - K. Ruff	2,500		50.00	50

Annette Funicello Collectible Bear Co./Victorian Collection - Various

YEAR ISSUE	EDITION LIMIT	YEAR RETD.	ISSUE PRICE	*QUOTE U.S.$
2000 Elizabeth Grace - S. Knapp	1,500		90.00	90
2000 Paluma - A. Dana	1,500		90.00	90

Peanuts Gallery/Hallmark Keepsake Collections

Peanuts Gallery/Hallmark Keepsake Collections

YEAR ISSUE	EDITION LIMIT	YEAR RETD.	ISSUE PRICE	*QUOTE U.S.$
2000 Franklin QPC4037	Numbrd.		25.00	25
2000 Joe Cool QPC4034	Numbrd.		25.00	25
2000 Peppermint Patty QPC4036	Numbrd.		25.00	25

Precious Moments/Enesco Group, Inc.

Jack-In-The-Boxes - S. Butcher

YEAR ISSUE	EDITION LIMIT	YEAR RETD.	ISSUE PRICE	*QUOTE U.S.$
1991 You Have Touched So Many Hearts 422282	2-Yr.	1993	175.00	175
1991 May You Have An Old Fashioned Christmas 417777	2-Yr.	1993	200.00	200
1990 The Voice of Spring 408735	2-Yr.	1992	200.00	200
1990 Summer's Joy 408743	2-Yr.	1992	200.00	200
1990 Autumn's Praise 408751	2-Yr.	1992	200.00	200
1990 Winter's Song 408778	2-Yr.	1992	200.00	200

Precious Moments Dolls - S. Butcher

YEAR ISSUE	EDITION LIMIT	YEAR RETD.	ISSUE PRICE	*QUOTE U.S.$
1981 Mikey, 18" E-6214B	Suspd.		150.00	230
1981 Debbie, 18" E-6214G	Suspd.		150.00	260-286
1982 Cubby, 18" E-7267B	5,000		200.00	380
1982 Tammy, 18" E-7267G	5,000		300.00	450-500
1983 Katie Lynne, 16" E-0539	Suspd.		165.00	143-175
1984 Mother Sew Dear, 18" E-2850	Retrd.	1985	350.00	325-350
1984 Kristy, 12" E-2851	Suspd.		150.00	143-170
1984 Timmy, 12" E-5397	Suspd.		125.00	126-150
1985 Aaron, 12" 12424	Suspd.		135.00	160
1985 Bethany, 12" 12432	Suspd.		135.00	160
1985 P.D., 7" 12475	Suspd.		50.00	54-70
1985 Trish, 7" 12483	Suspd.		50.00	68-95
1986 Bong Bong, 13" 100455	12,000		150.00	225-265
1986 Candy, 13" 100463	12,000		150.00	280-300
1986 Connie, 12" 102253	7,500		160.00	203-240
1987 Angie, The Angel of Mercy 12491	12,500		160.00	253-275
1990 The Voice of Spring 408786	2-Yr.	1992	150.00	150
1990 Summer's Joy 408794	2-Yr.	1992	150.00	129-150
1990 Autumn's Praise 408808	2-Yr.	1992	150.00	129-150
1990 Winter's Song 408816	2-Yr.	1992	150.00	129-150
1991 You Have Touched So Many Hearts 427527	2-Yr.	1993	90.00	90
1991 May You Have An Old Fashioned Christmas 417785	2-Yr.	1993	150.00	175
1991 The Eyes Of The Lord Are Upon You (Boy Action Muscial) 429570	Suspd.		65.00	75
1991 The Eyes Of The Lord Are Upon You (Girl Action Musical) 429589	Suspd.		65.00	65

Precious Moments Plush - S. Butcher

YEAR ISSUE	EDITION LIMIT	YEAR RETD.	ISSUE PRICE	*QUOTE U.S.$
1999 Friendship Hits The Spot 729167	Open		35.00	35
1999 You Have Touched So Many Hearts 729175	Open		35.00	35
1999 Put On A Happy Face 729183	Open		35.00	35
1999 Lord Keep Me On My Toes 729191	Open		35.00	35
1999 God Loveth A Cheerful Giver 729205	Open		35.00	35
1999 Tell It To Jesus 729221	Open		35.00	35
2000 Make A Joyful Noise 752762	Open		35.00	35
2000 The Future Is In Our Hands 752789	Open		35.00	35
2000 Cheers To The Leader 752835	Open		35.00	35
2000 Jesus Loves Me 752894	Open		35.00	35

R. JOHN WRIGHT DOLLS

The R. JOHN WRIGHT Collectors' Club - R. John Wright

YEAR ISSUE	EDITION LIMIT	YEAR RETD.	ISSUE PRICE	*QUOTE U.S.$
1996 Golliwogg	1,498	1997	535.00	600
1997 Miss Golli	849	1998	535.00	600
1997 Teddy Bear	866	1998	375.00	400
1998 Periwinkle	Closed	1999	385.00	385
1999 Silly Old Bear	Closed	1999	325.00	325

Babes in Toyland Series II - R. John Wright

YEAR ISSUE	EDITION LIMIT	YEAR RETD.	ISSUE PRICE	*QUOTE U.S.$
1984 Lindsay & Michael	250	1985	750.00	1350-2350
1983 Timothy & Rosemary	50	1983	700.00	N/A

Character Dolls - R. John Wright

YEAR ISSUE	EDITION LIMIT	YEAR RETD.	ISSUE PRICE	*QUOTE U.S.$
1979 Bernard	N/A	1981	100.00	N/A
1979 Bridget	N/A	1981	100.00	2400
1979 Elsa	N/A	1981	100.00	N/A
1979 Emma	N/A	1981	100.00	N/A
1979 Erica	N/A	1981	100.00	N/A
1979 Gretchen	N/A	1981	100.00	2400
1979 Guido	N/A	1981	100.00	2400
1979 Jenny	N/A	1981	100.00	N/A
1979 Karl	N/A	1981	100.00	N/A
1979 Kate	N/A	1981	100.00	N/A
1979 Lina	N/A	1981	100.00	N/A
1979 MacTavish	N/A	1981	100.00	2400
1979 Marion	N/A	1981	100.00	N/A
1979 Paddy	N/A	1981	100.00	2400
1979 Seth	N/A	1981	100.00	2400
1979 St. Nicholas	N/A	1981	100.00	3500

Childhood Classics - R. John Wright

YEAR ISSUE	EDITION LIMIT	YEAR RETD.	ISSUE PRICE	*QUOTE U.S.$
1988 Little Red Riding Hood	500	1991	875.00	1200-1600

Children Dolls - R. John Wright

YEAR ISSUE	EDITION LIMIT	YEAR RETD.	ISSUE PRICE	*QUOTE U.S.$
1982 Captain Corey	50	1982	350.00	350
1985 Edward and His Drum	150	1985	425.00	1800
1984 Emily and the Enchanted Doll	150	1984	425.00	3500
1983 The Little Prince	250	1984	375.00	3995
1985 Max and His Pinocchio	150	1985	385.00	1800

Disneyana Convention - R. John Wright

YEAR ISSUE	EDITION LIMIT	YEAR RETD.	ISSUE PRICE	*QUOTE U.S.$
1992 Pinocchio	100	1992	750.00	1000-2000

Little Children - R. John Wright

YEAR ISSUE	EDITION LIMIT	YEAR RETD.	ISSUE PRICE	*QUOTE U.S.$
1981 Becky	250	1985	325.00	1500
1981 Elizabeth	250	1985	325.00	1200
1981 Hannah	250	1985	325.00	325
1981 Jesse	250	1985	325.00	1200
1981 Lillian	250	1985	325.00	900
1985 Lisa	250	1986	325.00	900
1981 Peter	250	1985	325.00	325
1985 Rachel -Sunday Best	250	1986	325.00	1800
1985 Scott	250	1986	325.00	900
1981 Tad	250	1985	325.00	325
1981 William	250	1985	325.00	1000

Pinocchio - R. John Wright

YEAR ISSUE	EDITION LIMIT	YEAR RETD.	ISSUE PRICE	*QUOTE U.S.$
1994 Geppetto & Pinocchio I (marionette)	500	1995	1800.00	2985
1994 Geppetto & Pinocchio II (traditional)	250	1994	1800.00	2750-3125
1992 Pleasure Island Pinocchio	250	1992	725.00	2000

Sewn Felt Dolls - R. John Wright

YEAR ISSUE	EDITION LIMIT	YEAR RETD.	ISSUE PRICE	*QUOTE U.S.$
1978 8" Elfs and Black Imps	N/A	1979	45.00	45

Snow White - R. John Wright

YEAR ISSUE	EDITION LIMIT	YEAR RETD.	ISSUE PRICE	*QUOTE U.S.$
1992 Frightened Dopey	Retrd.	1992	N/A	N/A
1989 Snow White & The Seven Dwarfs (8 pc. matched numbd. set)	1,000	1994	3000.00	2925-4925
1989 Snow White Princess, Snow White in Rags & Seven Dwarfs (matched numbd. set)	250	1994	3500.00	5500-6500
1989 •Snow White in Rags	Retrd.	1994	800.00	800

Winnie-the-Pooh - R. John Wright

YEAR ISSUE	EDITION LIMIT	YEAR RETD.	ISSUE PRICE	*QUOTE U.S.$
1985 Christopher Robin	Retrd.	N/A	595.00	895
1986 Christopher Robin I w/8" Pooh	1,000	1986	595.00	1325-3252
1986 Christopher Robin II Raincoat	500	1987	585.00	1750-3252
1985 Eeyore 6"	1,000	1988	95.00	450-650
1997 Holiday Winnie-the-Pooh	1,000	1997	585.00	750-895
1985 Kanga & Roo 10"	1,000	1988	95.00	695
1987 Lifesize Piglet 9"	1,000	1988	85.00	550
1987 Lifesize Pooh 18"	2,500	1988	190.00	1050-1400
1997 Party Tigger & Eeyore, set/2	100	N/A	440.00	590
1989 Piglet 10 1/2"	1,000	1989	145.00	675
1985 Piglet 5"	1,000	1988	45.00	290-650
1988 Piglet 7" w/Violets	2,500	1989	145.00	650
1985 Tigger 6"	1,000	1988	95.00	295-650
1988 Winnie-the-Pooh 20"	2,500	1988	165.00	1150-2150
1985 Winnie-the-Pooh 8"	1,500	1986	95.00	600-1200
1989 Winnie-the-Pooh and His Favorite Chair 10"	500	1989	595.00	2475
1987 Winnie-the-Pooh with Hunny Pot 14"	5,000	1989	145.00	675-1275

Winnie-the-Pooh Pocket Series - R. John Wright

YEAR ISSUE	EDITION LIMIT	YEAR RETD.	ISSUE PRICE	*QUOTE U.S.$
1997 Christopher Robin	Retrd.	1997	N/A	895
1994 Pocket Eeyore	3,500	N/A	95.00	250-350
1999 Pocket Kanga & Roo	3,500		310.00	310
1999 Pocket Owl	3,500		310.00	310
1994 Pocket Piglet	3,500	1994	135.00	250-350
1993 Pocket Pooh	3,500	1993	285.00	675-875
1996 Pocket Tigger	Retrd.	1996	N/A	295
1996 Wintertime Eeyore (FAO Schwarz Exclusive)	250	1996	725.00	895
1996 •Eeyore's Stickhouse (FAO Schwarz Exclusive)	250	1996	N/A	700-1400
1995 Wintertime Pooh & Piglet (FAO Schwarz Exclusive)	250	1995	725.00	1495-1650

Reco International

Childhood Doll Collection - S. Kuck

YEAR ISSUE	EDITION LIMIT	YEAR RETD.	ISSUE PRICE	*QUOTE U.S.$
1994 A Kiss Goodnight	Retrd.	1995	79.00	79-150
1995 Reading With Teddy	Retrd.	1995	79.00	125-130
1994 Teaching Teddy His Prayers	Retrd.	1997	79.00	125-130
1996 Teddy's Picnic	Retrd.	1997	79.00	79-125

Christmas Doll Collection - S. Kuck

YEAR ISSUE	EDITION LIMIT	YEAR RETD.	ISSUE PRICE	*QUOTE U.S.$
1996 Carol	Open		135.00	135
1997 Kristen	Open		135.00	135

Little Valentina - S. Kuck

YEAR ISSUE	EDITION LIMIT	YEAR RETD.	ISSUE PRICE	*QUOTE U.S.$
1998 Little Valentina	Open		99.00	99

Pocket Full of Love - S. Kuck

YEAR ISSUE	EDITION LIMIT	YEAR RETD.	ISSUE PRICE	*QUOTE U.S.$
1997 Gabriella	Open		30.00	30
1998 Tanya	Open		30.00	30
1999 Victoria	Open		30.00	30
1999 Natasha	Open		30.00	30

Precious Memories of Motherhood - S. Kuck

YEAR ISSUE	EDITION LIMIT	YEAR RETD.	ISSUE PRICE	*QUOTE U.S.$
1993 Bedtime	Retrd.	1994	149.00	90-149
1992 Expectant Moments	Retrd.	1993	149.00	90-149
1990 Loving Steps	Retrd.	1992	125.00	150-195
1991 Lullaby	Retrd.	1995	125.00	125-200

Wedding Doll - S. Kuck

YEAR ISSUE	EDITION LIMIT	YEAR RETD.	ISSUE PRICE	*QUOTE U.S.$
1997 Jennifer Rose	Open		195.00	195
1998 Audrey & Lindsey	Open		195.00	195

Roman, Inc.

Holiday Traditions Collection - Roman, Inc.

YEAR ISSUE	EDITION LIMIT	YEAR RETD.	ISSUE PRICE	*QUOTE U.S.$
1997 Claire, The Christmas Doll	Retrd.	1998	75.00	75
1997 Tatters the Bear	Retrd.	1998	17.50	18

Timeless Teddies Collection - Roman, Inc.

YEAR ISSUE	EDITION LIMIT	YEAR RETD.	ISSUE PRICE	*QUOTE U.S.$
2000 Teddy Bear	Open		15.00	15

Whitney Poppins Collection - B. Sargent

YEAR ISSUE	EDITION LIMIT	YEAR RETD.	ISSUE PRICE	*QUOTE U.S.$
2000 Bedtime Whitney	Open		50.00	50
2000 Playtime Whitney	Open		60.00	60
2000 Winter Whitney	Open		50.00	50

*Quotes have been rounded up to nearest dollar

San Francisco Music Box Company

Boyds Bears Musicals - G. M. Lowenthal

YEAR ISSUE	EDITION LIMIT	YEAR RETD.	ISSUE PRICE	*QUOTE U.S.$
1998 Abbey Ewe	Closed	1999	35.00	35
2000 Adrian Ornament	Open		12.00	12
1999 Alexis Berriman	Closed	1999	70.00	70
1997 Allison Babbit Hare	Closed	1997	24.95	25
1997 Ariel with Heart Ornament	Open		9.95	10
1997 Ashley Hare	Closed	1998	24.95	25
2000 Aubrey Tippietoes	Open		35.00	35
1998 Aunt Becky Bearchild	Closed	1999	50.00	50
1997 Benjamin Honey Bear with Sweater	Closed	1999	24.95	25
1998 Braxton B. Bear	Open		25.00	25
1998 Camomile w/Quilt	Closed	1999	27.00	27
1998 Clarissa Bear	Closed	1999	57.00	57
1997 Cleo P. Pussytoes	Closed	1999	39.95	40
1997 Eugenia Bear	Closed	1998	49.95	50
1998 Fidelity B. Morgan IV Bear	Closed	1999	35.00	35
1997 Guinevere Bear	Closed	1999	24.95	25
1999 Hayes R. Bearington	2,000		125.00	125
1998 Heranamous	Closed	1999	35.00	35
2000 Katie with Welby 12" Doll	Open		50.00	50
1999 Klaus von Fuzzner	Closed	1999	50.00	50
1998 Lady Pembrooke	Closed	1999	25.00	25
1998 Lavina V. Harriweather	Closed	1999	25.00	25
2000 Marissa P. Pussytoes	Open		40.00	40
1998 Momma McBear	Open		30.00	30
2000 Momma McFuzz and Missy	Open		35.00	35
1999 Mrs. Trumbull	Closed	1999	40.00	40
2000 Poof Puffleberry w/Blankie	Open		30.00	30
1999 Prudence Bearimore	Closed	1999	45.00	45
1997 Rosalind Bear	Closed	1997	39.95	40
1998 Rosalind II Bear	Closed	1998	40.00	40
1998 Rosie O'Pigg	Open		18.00	18
2000 Sally and Annie	Open		30.00	30
1997 Smith Witter II	Open		34.95	35
2000 Susan with Malcolm and Beau Bear Collectors	Open		85.00	85
1998 Winnie II in blue Romper	Closed	1999	35.00	35
1998 Zelda Fitzhare	Closed	1999	35.00	35

Katherine's Collection - W. Kleski

YEAR ISSUE	EDITION LIMIT	YEAR RETD.	ISSUE PRICE	*QUOTE U.S.$
1999 Bubbles Cat Doll Musical	Open		125.00	125
1999 Giggles Cat Doll Musical	Open		125.00	125
1999 Louisa Victorian Baby Doll Musical	Open		150.00	150

Musical Porcelain Dolls - San Francisco Music Box Company

YEAR ISSUE	EDITION LIMIT	YEAR RETD.	ISSUE PRICE	*QUOTE U.S.$
1998 Aerial Angel	2,500	1998	125.00	125
1999 Amanda and Baby Doll	2,500		150.00	150
1997 Angelica Angel	600	1997	200.00	200
1999 Anne Antique	2,500	1999	135.00	135
1999 Ballerina	2,500	1999	100.00	100
1999 Bride	2,500		200.00	200
1999 Brittany II Doll	Closed	2000	85.00	85
1999 Caitlyn Doll	2,500		150.00	150
1997 Christina Ballroom	1,500	1998	200.00	200
1999 Elise Fairy	2,500	1999	200.00	200
1998 Elizabeth Victorian	1,200	1998	200.00	200
1999 Fairy	2,500	2000	200.00	200
1999 Faith Christening Doll	2,500		150.00	150
1999 Genevieve	2,500	1999	99.00	99
1997 Julia Bride	1,600	1998	200.00	200
1998 Michelle with Baby	1,200	2000	200.00	200
1998 Mom & Baby	2,500	1998	150.00	150
1999 Mom & Daughter	2,500		150.00	150
1999 Mom & Toddler	2,500		200.00	200
1999 Nicole w/Rabbit	2,500	1999	150.00	150
1997 Priscilla Bride	600	1997	200.00	200
1999 Rapunzel	2,500	1999	100.00	100
1999 Rose Bride	2,500		200.00	200
1997 Therese Victorian	600	1998	200.00	200
1997 Tiffany Victorian	1,800	1998	200.00	200
1999 Victoria Antique	2,500	1999	135.00	135

Sandy USA Inc.

Angelic Maillé - G. Dy

YEAR ISSUE	EDITION LIMIT	YEAR RETD.	ISSUE PRICE	*QUOTE U.S.$
1998 Darielle	Retrd.	2000	75.00	75
1998 Deandra	Retrd.	2000	75.00	75
1998 Maribel	Retrd.	2000	75.00	75
1998 Moriah	Retrd.	2000	75.00	75

Angels of the Millennium - R. Tejada

YEAR ISSUE	EDITION LIMIT	YEAR RETD.	ISSUE PRICE	*QUOTE U.S.$
2000 Adela 2000	1,500		75.00	75
2000 Adela 2001	1,500		75.00	75
2000 Elisa 2000	1,500		75.00	75
2000 Elisa 2001	1,500		75.00	75

Della - Glory Collection - D. Reese

YEAR ISSUE	EDITION LIMIT	YEAR RETD.	ISSUE PRICE	*QUOTE U.S.$
2000 Amadi - African American Angel	Open		85.00	85
2000 Anna - Caucasian American Angel	Open		85.00	85
2000 Constanza - Latino American Angel	Open		85.00	85
2000 Mahala - Native American Angel	Open		85.00	85
2000 Zhin Gui - Asian American Angel	Open		85.00	85

Gentle Dreams Baby - R. Tejada

YEAR ISSUE	EDITION LIMIT	YEAR RETD.	ISSUE PRICE	*QUOTE U.S.$
1998 Gentle Blossom - Cherokee	Open		35.00	35
1999 Gentle Brook - Iroquois Girl	Open		35.00	35
1999 Gentle Butterfly - Kiowa Girl	Open		35.00	35
1998 Gentle Dewdrop - Sioux	Open		35.00	35
1999 Gentle Dove - Ute	Open		35.00	35
1999 Gentle Eagle - Tlingit Girl	Open		35.00	35
1998 Gentle Fawn - Cheyenne	Open		35.00	35
1998 Gentle Flower - Hopi	Open		35.00	35
2000 Gentle Heart - Chippewa Girl	Open		35.00	35
1999 Gentle Moon - Nez Perce	Open		35.00	35
1998 Gentle Night - Blackfoot	Open		35.00	35
1999 Gentle Rainbow - Comanche	Open		35.00	35
2000 Gentle Song - Crow Girl	Open		35.00	35
1999 Gentle Star - Pawnee	Open		35.00	35
2000 Gentle Sun - Arapaho Girl	Open		35.00	35
1998 Gentle Wind - Apache	Open		35.00	35

Kente Claus Collection® - K. Stafford

YEAR ISSUE	EDITION LIMIT	YEAR RETD.	ISSUE PRICE	*QUOTE U.S.$
2000 Kente Claus (gold) 12"	Open		37.50	38
2000 Kente Claus (gold) 14"	Open		50.00	50
2000 Kente Claus (red) 12"	Open		37.50	38
2000 Kente Claus (red) 14"	Open		50.00	50

Sarah's Gang - S. Schultz

YEAR ISSUE	EDITION LIMIT	YEAR RETD.	ISSUE PRICE	*QUOTE U.S.$
1996 Buddy	Retrd.	1999	25.00	25
1996 Katie	Retrd.	1999	25.00	25
1997 Maria	Retrd.	1999	25.00	25
1997 Miguel	Retrd.	1999	25.00	25
1997 Sammy	Retrd.	1999	25.00	25
1997 Shina	Retrd.	1999	25.00	25
1996 Tillie	Retrd.	1999	25.00	25
1996 Willie	Retrd.	1999	25.00	25

Sweet Spirit Baby - R. Tejada

YEAR ISSUE	EDITION LIMIT	YEAR RETD.	ISSUE PRICE	*QUOTE U.S.$
1996 Little Blossom	1,500	1996	65.00	65
1997 Little Moonbeam	2,500	1997	85.00	85
1997 Little Raindrop	2,500	1999	85.00	85
1998 Little Bear's Track	2,500	2000	85.00	85
1998 Little Sala	2,500		85.00	85
1999 Little Songbird	2,500		85.00	85
1999 Little Azziza	2,500		85.00	85

Tender Spirit Baby - R. Tejada

YEAR ISSUE	EDITION LIMIT	YEAR RETD.	ISSUE PRICE	*QUOTE U.S.$
2000 Tender Dancer - Pawnee	Open		10.00	10
2000 Tender Dawn - Nez Perce	Open		10.00	10
2000 Tender Dove - Ute	Open		12.00	12
2000 Tender Fawn - Comanche	Open		12.00	12
2000 Tender Flower - Iroquois	Open		10.00	10
2000 Tender Lily - Cherokee	Open		12.00	12
2000 Tender Moon - Pawnee	Open		12.00	12
2000 Tender Owl - Apache	Open		12.00	12
2000 Tender Rosebud - Cheyenne	Open		12.00	12
2000 Tender Shadow - Kiowa	Open		10.00	10
2000 Tender Sky - Arapaho	Open		10.00	10
2000 Tender Songbird - Lakota Sioux	Open		12.00	12
2000 Tender Willow - Kiowa	Open		12.00	12
2000 Tender Wind - Blackfoot	Open		10.00	10

Traditions - R. Tejada

YEAR ISSUE	EDITION LIMIT	YEAR RETD.	ISSUE PRICE	*QUOTE U.S.$
1996 Angeni - Spirit Angel	500	1998	175.00	175

Warrior & Princess - R. Tejada

YEAR ISSUE	EDITION LIMIT	YEAR RETD.	ISSUE PRICE	*QUOTE U.S.$
1995 Bear's Track - Fox	5,000	1999	37.50	38
1997 Evening Star - Ute	5,000	1999	37.50	38
1997 Flying Falcon - Assiniboine	5,000	1999	37.50	38
1997 Graceful Song - Cherokee	5,000	1999	37.50	38
1996 Growling Bear - Mohegan	5,000	1999	37.50	38
1995 Howling Dog - Cheyenne	5,000	1999	37.50	38
1995 Laughing Brook - Comanche	5,000	1999	37.50	38
1996 Leaping Water - Apache	5,000	1999	37.50	38
1995 Little Otter - Hupa	5,000	1999	37.50	38
1995 Pocahontas - Powhatan	5,000	1996	37.50	38
1996 Radiant Dove - Sioux	5,000	1999	37.50	38
1994 Shining Cloud - Cheyenne	5,000	1997	37.50	38
1994 Soaring Hawk - Comanche	5,000	1997	37.50	38
1995 Swaying Reed - Chippewa	5,000	1999	37.50	38
1997 White Stone - Cherokee	5,000	1999	37.50	38
1996 Wind Rider with Horse - Nez Perce	5,000	1998	60.00	60
1996 Wise Buffalo - Sioux	5,000	1999	37.50	38

Sarah's Attic, Inc.

Heirlooms from the Attic - Sarah's Attic

YEAR ISSUE	EDITION LIMIT	YEAR RETD.	ISSUE PRICE	*QUOTE U.S.$
1991 Adora 1823	500	1991	90.00	200
1991 All Cloth Muffin blk. Doll 1820	Closed	1991	90.00	200
1991 All Cloth Puffin blk. Doll 1821	Closed	1991	90.00	200
1992 Angelle Guardian Angel 3569	2,000	1993	170.00	400
1989 Becky 1461	150	1991	120.00	400
1989 Bobby 1462	150	1991	120.00	400
1991 Enos 1822	500	1991	90.00	200
1989 Freedom-Americana Clown 1472	500	1992	120.00	350
1993 Granny Quilting Lady Doll 3576	Closed	1993	130.00	150
1989 Harmony-Victorian Clown 1464	500	1992	120.00	250
1992 Harpster w/Banjo 3591	Closed	1992	250.00	350
1990 Hickory-Americana 1771	Closed	1993	150.00	400
1990 Hickory-Beachtime 1769	2,000	1993	140.00	150-175
1991 Hickory-Christmas 1810	2,000	1993	150.00	150-175
1990 Hickory-Playtime 1768	2,000	1993	140.00	175
1990 Hickory-School Days 1766	2,000	1993	140.00	325
1991 Hickory-Springtime 1814	2,000	1993	150.00	195
1990 Hickory-Sunday's Best 1770	2,000	1993	150.00	225
1990 Hickory-Sweet Dreams 1767	2,000	1993	140.00	175
1992 Hilary-Victorian 1831	500	1993	200.00	250
1986 Holly blk. Angel 0410	Retrd.	1986	34.00	200
1992 Kiah Guardian Angel 3570	2,000	1993	170.00	400
1989 Liberty Angel 1470	Closed	1991	50.00	250
1993 Lilla Quilting Lady Doll 3581	Closed	1993	130.00	200
1986 Maggie Cloth Doll 0012	Closed	1989	70.00	120
1986 Matt Cloth Doll 0011	Closed	1989	70.00	120
1989 Megan 1752	100	1990	70.00	200
1993 Millie Quilting Lady Doll 3586	Closed	1993	130.00	150
1988 Mrs. Claus 6284	500	1989	120.00	400
1989 Peace Angel 1465	500	1991	50.00	300
1992 Peace on Earth Santa 3564	200	1992	175.00	700
1986 Priscilla Doll 0030	Closed	1989	140.00	300
1988 Santa Claus 6337	500	1989	120.00	400
1990 Sassafras-Americana 1685	2,000	1993	150.00	400
1990 Sassafras-Beachtime 1683	2,000	1993	140.00	175
1991 Sassafras-Christmas 1809	2,000	1993	150.00	150-175
1990 Sassafras-Playtime 1682	2,000	1993	140.00	200
1989 Sassafras-School Days 1680	2,000	1993	140.00	325
1991 Sassafras-Springtime 1813	2,000	1993	150.00	195
1990 Sassafras-Sunday's Best 1684	2,000	1993	150.00	225
1990 Sassafras-Sweet Dreams 1681	2,000	1993	140.00	195
1989 Scott 1753	100	1990	70.00	200
1988 Smiley Clown Doll 3050	Closed	1988	126.00	1000
1989 Spirit of America Santa 1476	500	1993	120.00	400
1987 Sunshine 3003	Closed	1988	118.00	650
1989 Victoria Doll 1467	500	1990	120.00	650
1988 Victorian Boy 1192	Closed	1988	24.00	200

Seymour Mann, Inc.

Connossieur Doll Collection - E. Mann, unless otherwise noted

YEAR ISSUE	EDITION LIMIT	YEAR RETD.	ISSUE PRICE	*QUOTE U.S.$
1991 Abby 16" Pink Dress-C3145	Closed	1993	100.00	100
1995 Abby C-3229	2,500	1996	30.00	30
1994 Abby YK-4533	3,500	1995	135.00	135
1991 Abigail EP-3	Closed	1993	100.00	100
1991 Abigal WB-72WM	Closed	1993	75.00	75
1994 Adak PS-412	2,500	1995	150.00	150
1993 Adrienne C-3162	Closed	1994	135.00	135
1995 Aggie PS-435	2,500	1996	80.00	80
2000 Alexa CJC-225	1,200		95.00	95
2000 Alexander AWL-555	1,200		125.00	125
1991 Alexis 24" Beige Lace-EP32	Closed	1993	220.00	220
1994 Alice GU-32	2,500	1995	150.00	150
1994 Alice IND-508	2,500	1995	115.00	115
1992 Alice JNC-4013	Closed	1993	90.00	90
1998 Alicia AWL-522	2,500	1999	175.00	175
1995 Alicia C-3235	2,500	1996	65.00	65
1991 Alicia YK-4215	Closed	1993	90.00	90
1995 Allison CD-18183	2,500	1997	35.00	35
1995 Allison TR-92	2,500	1996	125.00	125
1994 Ally FH-556	2,500	1995	115.00	115
1994 Alyssa C-3201	2,500	1995	110.00	110
1994 Alyssa PP-1	2,500	1996	275.00	300
1991 Amanda Toast-OM-182	Closed	1993	260.00	260
1995 Amanda TR-96	2,500	1996	135.00	135
1989 Amber DOM-281A	Closed	1993	85.00	85
1991 Amelia-TR-47	Closed	1993	105.00	105
1991 Amy C-3147	Closed	1993	135.00	135
1995 Amy GU-300A	2,500	1995	30.00	30
1994 Amy OC-43M	2,500	1996	115.00	115
1990 Anabelle C-3080	Closed	1992	85.00	85
1990 Angel DOM-335	Closed	1992	105.00	105
1995 Angel FH-291DP	2,500	1996	70.00	70
1994 Angel LL-956	2,500	1996	90.00	90
1994 Angel SP-460	2,500	1996	140.00	140
1998 Angela AWL-518	2,400	1999	75.00	75
1990 Angela C-3084	Closed	1992	105.00	105
1990 Angela C-3084M	Closed	1992	115.00	115
1995 Angela Doll 556	2,500	1996	35.00	35
1998 Angela OM-174	1,200	2000	175.00	175
1995 Angela OM-87	2,500	1996	150.00	150
1995 Angelica FH-291B	2,500	1996	70.00	70-100
1995 Angelina FH-291S	2,500	1996	70.00	70-95
1994 Angelita FH-291G	2,500	1995	85.00	85
1994 Angelo OC-57	2,500	1996	135.00	135
1990 Anita FH-277G	Closed	1992	65.00	65
1991 Ann TR-52	Closed	1993	135.00	135
1995 Annette FH-635	2,500	1996	110.00	110
1991 Annette TR-59	Closed	1993	130.00	130
1996 Annie PS-462	2,500	1998	100.00	100
1991 Antoinette FH-452	Closed	1993	100.00	100
1997 Antonio FH-820	7,500	1998	150.00	150
1995 April CD-2212B	2,500	1997	50.00	50
1991 Arabella C-3163	Closed	1993	135.00	135
1991 Ariel 34" Blue/White-EP-33	Closed	1993	175.00	175
1994 Arilene LL-940	2,500	1994	90.00	90
1993 Arlene SP-421	Closed	1993	100.00	100
1989 Ashley C-278	Closed	1993	80.00	80
1990 Ashley FH-325	Closed	1993	75.00	75
1994 Atanak PS-414	2,500	1994	150.00	150
1991 Audrey FH-455	2,500	1993	125.00	125
1990 Audrey YK-4089	Closed	1992	125.00	125
1987 Audrina YK-200	Closed	1986	85.00	140-292
1991 Azure AM-15	2,500	1993	175.00	175
1994 Baby Belle C-3193	2,500	1994	150.00	150
1991 Baby Beth DOLL-406P	2,500	1993	27.50	28
1995 Baby Betsy Doll 336	2,500	1996	75.00	75
1990 Baby Betty YK-4087	Closed	1991	125.00	125
1990 Baby Bonnie SP-341	Closed	1991	55.00	55
1991 Baby Bonnie SP-341	Closed	1993	55.00	55
1991 Baby Brent EP-15	Closed	1993	85.00	110
1991 Baby Carrie DOLL-402P	2,500	1993	27.50	28
1990 Baby Ecru WB-17	Closed	1991	65.00	65
1991 Baby Ellie Ecru Musical DOLL-402E	2,500	1993	27.50	28
1991 Baby Gloria Black Baby PS-289	Closed	1993	75.00	75-110
1991 Baby John PS-498	Closed	1993	85.00	85

*Quotes have been rounded up to nearest dollar

YEAR ISSUE	EDITION LIMIT	YEAR RETD.	ISSUE PRICE	*QUOTE U.S.$
1989 Baby John PS-49B	Closed	1991	85.00	85
1990 Baby Kate WB-19	Closed	1991	85.00	85
1991 Baby Linda DOLL-406E	2,500	1993	27.50	28
1990 Baby Nelly PS-163	Closed	1991	95.00	95
1994 Baby Scarlet C-3194	2,500	1994	115.00	115
1991 Baby Sue DOLL-402B	2,500	1993	27.50	28
1990 Baby Sunshine C-3055	Closed	1992	90.00	90
1995 Barbara PS-439	2,500	1995	65.00	65
1991 Belinda C-3164	Closed	1993	150.00	150
1991 Bernetta EP-40	Closed	1993	115.00	115
1995 Beth OC-74	2,500	1995	40.00	40
1990 Beth YK-4099A/B	Closed	1992	125.00	125
1991 Betsy AM-6	Closed	1993	105.00	105
1997 Betsy AWL-506 - S. Mann	2,500	2000	25.00	25
1995 Betsy C-3224	2,500	1996	45.00	45
1990 Bettina TR-4	Closed	1991	125.00	125
1991 Bettina YK-4144	Closed	1993	105.00	105
1995 Betty LL-996	2,500	1996	115.00	115
1989 Betty PS27G	Closed	1993	65.00	125
1990 Billie YK-4056V	Closed	1992	65.00	65
1993 Blaine C-3167	Closed	1993	100.00	100
1994 Blair YK-4532	3,500	1994	150.00	150-175
1991 Blythe CH-15V	Closed	1993	135.00	135
1991 Bo-Peep w/Lamb C-3128	Closed	1993	105.00	105
1994 Bobbi NM-30	2,500	1994	135.00	135
1994 Brandy YK-4537	3,500	1995	165.00	165
1989 Brett PS27B	Closed	1992	65.00	125
1991 Bridget SP-379	2,500	1993	105.00	105
1995 Brie C-3230	2,500	1998	30.00	30
1995 Brittany Doll 558	2,500	1996	35.00	35
1989 Brittany TK-4	Closed	1990	150.00	150
1997 Brooke Ashley VL -154 - S. Mann	2,500	1998	135.00	159
1991 Brooke FH-461	2,500	1993	115.00	115
1994 Browyn IND-517	2,500	1994	140.00	140
1991 Bryna AM-100B	2,500	1993	70.00	70
1995 Bryna DOLL-555	2,500	1997	35.00	35
1995 Bunny TR-97	2,500	1997	85.00	85
1995 Burgundy Angel FH-291D	2,500	1995	75.00	75
1994 Cactus Flower Indian LL-944	2,500	1994	105.00	105
1990 Caillin DOLL-11PH	Closed	1992	60.00	60
1995 Caitlin LL-997	2,500	1996	115.00	115
1990 Caitlin YK-4051V	Closed	1992	90.00	90
1994 Callie TR-76	2,500	1994	140.00	140
1994 Calypso LL-942	2,500	1994	150.00	150
1991 Camellia FH-457	2,500	1993	100.00	100
1986 Camelot Fairy C-84	Closed	1988	75.00	225-265
1995 Candice TR-94	2,500	1995	135.00	135
1994 Carmen PS-408	2,500	1994	150.00	150
1990 Carole YK-4085W	Closed	1992	125.00	125
1991 Caroline LL-838	2,500	1993	110.00	110
1991 Caroline LL-905	2,500	1993	110.00	110
1997 Caroline RDK-838B - S. Mann	2,500	1999	80.00	125
1994 Casey C-3197	2,500	1995	140.00	140
1995 Catherine RDK-231	2,500	1995	30.00	30-62
1994 Cathy GU-41	2,500	1994	140.00	140
1995 Celene FH-618	2,500	1997	120.00	120
1995 Celestine LL-982	2,500	1996	100.00	100
1997 Charity & Joshua TEC-564B/G - S. Mann	2,500	1999	42.50	85
1990 Charlene YK-4112	Closed	1992	90.00	90
1992 Charlotte FH-484	2,500	1993	115.00	115
1992 Chelsea IND-397	Closed	1993	85.00	85
1995 Cherry FH-616	2,500	1997	62.50	100
1991 Cheryl TR-49	2,500	1993	120.00	120
1991 Chin Chin YK-4211	Closed	1993	85.00	85
1990 Chin Fa C-3061	Closed	1992	95.00	95
1990 Chinook WB-24	Closed	1992	85.00	85
1994 Chris FH-561	2,500	1994	85.00	85
1994 Chrissie FH-562	2,500	1994	85.00	85
1990 Chrissie WB-2	Closed	1992	75.00	75
1991 Christina PS-261	Closed	1993	115.00	115
1985 Christmas Cheer 125	Closed	1988	40.00	100
1995 Christmas Kitten IND-530	2,500	1997	100.00	140-159
1991 Cindy Lou FH-464	2,500	1993	85.00	85
1994 Cindy OC-58	2,500	1994	140.00	140-165
1993 Cinnamon JNC-4014	Closed	1993	90.00	90
1988 Cissie DOM263	Closed	1990	65.00	135-148
1991 Cissy EP-56	2,500	1993	95.00	95
1995 Clancy GU-54	2,500	1995	80.00	80
1994 Clara IND-518	2,500	1994	140.00	140
1994 Clara IND-524	2,500	1994	150.00	150
1991 Clare DOLL-465	Closed	1993	100.00	100-125
1993 Clare FH-497	2,500	1993	100.00	100
1994 Claudette TR-81	2,500	1995	150.00	150-180
1991 Claudine C-3146	Closed	1993	95.00	95
1993 Clothilde FH-469	2,500	1993	125.00	125
1995 Cody FH-629	2,500	1995	120.00	120
1991 Colette WB-7	Closed	1993	65.00	65
1991 Colleen YK-4163	Closed	1993	120.00	120
1991 Cookie GU-6	2,500	1993	110.00	110-182
1994 Copper YK-4546C	3,500	1995	150.00	150
1994 Cora FH-565	2,500	1996	140.00	140
1991 Courtney LL-859	2,500	1993	150.00	150
1991 Creole AM-17	2,500	1993	160.00	200-209
1989 Crying Courtney PS-75	Closed	1992	115.00	115
1999 Crystal SJ-887	1,200	2000	135.00	135
1991 Crystal YK-4237	3,500	1993	125.00	125
1997 Cute Kathy TEC-591	7,500	1998	30.00	30
1987 Cynthia DOM-211	Closed	1986	85.00	85
1995 Cynthia GU-300C	2,500	1996	30.00	30
1998 Cynthia TR-4240 - S. Mann	7,500	1998	105.00	105
1990 Daisy EP-6	Closed	1992	90.00	90
1994 Dallas PS-403	2,500	1994	150.00	150
1991 Danielle AM-5	Closed	1993	125.00	175
1995 Danielle MER-808	2,500	1996	65.00	65
1989 Daphne Ecru/Mint Green C3025	Closed	1992	85.00	85
1991 Darcy EP-47	Closed	1993	110.00	110
1991 Darcy FH-451	2,500	1993	105.00	105
1995 Darcy FH-636	2,500	1996	80.00	80
1991 Daria C-3122	Closed	1993	110.00	110
2000 Daria NY-310M	1,200	2000	150.00	150
1995 Darla LL-988	2,500	1996	100.00	100
1991 Darlene DOLL-444	2,500	1993	75.00	75
1994 Daryl LL-947	2,500	1994	150.00	150
1991 Dawn C-3135	Closed	1993	130.00	130
1987 Dawn C185	Closed	1986	75.00	175
1992 Debbie JNC-4006	Open	1993	90.00	90
1994 Dee LL-948	2,500	1994	110.00	110
1992 Deidre FH-473	2,500	1993	115.00	115-129
1992 Deidre YK-4083	Closed	1993	95.00	95
1994 Delilah C-3195	2,500	1994	150.00	150
1991 Delphine SP-308	Closed	1993	135.00	135
1991 Denise LL-852	2,500	1993	105.00	105-132
1995 Denise LL-994	2,500	1996	105.00	105
1991 Desiree LL-898	2,500	1993	120.00	120
1990 Diane FH-275	Closed	1992	90.00	90
1990 Dianna TK-31	Closed	1992	175.00	175
1988 Doll Oliver FH392	Closed	1990	100.00	100
1990 Domino C-3050	Closed	1992	145.00	200
1992 Dona FH-494	2,500	1993	100.00	100
1993 Donna DOLL-447	2,500	1993	85.00	85-105
1990 Dorothy TR-10	Closed	1992	135.00	150
1991 Duanane SP-366	Closed	1993	85.00	85
1991 Dulcie YK-4131V	Closed	1993	100.00	100
1991 Edie YK-4177	Closed	1993	115.00	115
2000 Edwina HH-221	1,200		55.00	55
1998 Edwina NY-134 - S. Mann	2,500	1998	85.00	85-112
1990 Eileen FH-367	Closed	1992	100.00	100
1991 Elisabeth and Lisa C-3095	2,500	1993	195.00	195
1989 Elisabeth OM-32	Closed	1990	120.00	120
1991 Elise PS-259	Closed	1993	105.00	105
1997 Elizabeth & Child VL-151 - S. Mann	2,500	2000	200.00	200-215
1991 Elizabeth AM-32	2,500	1993	105.00	105
1989 Elizabeth C-246P	Closed	1990	150.00	200
1993 Ellen YK-4223	3,500	1994	150.00	150
1995 Ellie FH-621	2,500	1996	125.00	125
2000 Emily AWL-553	1,200		105.00	105
1996 Emily DOLL-718E	7,500	1998	40.00	40
1989 Emily PS-48	Closed	1990	110.00	110
1988 Emily YK-243V	Closed	1990	70.00	70
1991 Emmy C-3099	Closed	1993	125.00	125
1991 Erin DOLL-4PH	Closed	1993	60.00	60
1991 Evalina C-3124	Closed	1993	135.00	135
1994 Faith IND-522	2,500	1994	135.00	135
1994 Faith OC-60	2,500	1994	115.00	115
1990 Felicia TR-9	Closed	1992	115.00	115
1991 Fifi AM-100F	Closed	1993	70.00	70
1995 Fleur C-16415	2,500		30.00	30
1991 Fleurette PS-286	2,500	1993	75.00	75
1994 Flora FH-583	2,500	1994	115.00	115
1991 Flora TR-46	Closed	1993	125.00	125
1994 Florette IND-519	2,500	1994	140.00	140
1998 Flower Fairie TEC-566 - S. Mann	5,000		45.00	45
1988 Frances C-233	Closed	1990	80.00	125
1991 Francesca AM-14	2,500	1993	175.00	175
1990 Francesca C-3021	Closed	1992	100.00	175
1994 Gardiner PS-405	2,500	1996	150.00	150
1994 Georgia IND-510	2,500	1995	220.00	220
1991 Georgia YK-4131	Closed	1993	100.00	100
1991 Georgia YK-4143	Closed	1993	150.00	150
1990 Gerri Beige YK4094	Closed	1992	95.00	140-153
1991 Gigi C-3107	Closed	1993	135.00	135
1991 Ginger LL-907	Closed	1993	115.00	115
1995 Ginnie FH-619	2,500	1996	110.00	125
1990 Ginny YK-4119	Closed	1995	100.00	100-150
1992 Giselle OM-02	Closed	1993	90.00	90
1988 Giselle on Goose FH176	Closed	1990	105.00	225-258
1991 Gloria AM-100G	2,500	1993	70.00	70-90
1991 Gloria YK-4166	Closed	1993	105.00	105
1995 Gold Angel FH-511G	2,500	1997	85.00	85
1995 Green Angel FH-511C	2,500	1997	85.00	85
1991 Gretchen DOLL-446	Open	1993	45.00	45
1995 Gretchen FH-620	2,500	1995	120.00	120
1991 Gretel DOLL-434	Closed	1993	60.00	60
1995 Guardian Angel TR-98	2,500	1997	85.00	85
1991 Hansel and Gretel DOLL-448V	Closed	1993	60.00	60
1989 Happy Birthday C3012	Closed	1990	80.00	125-144
1993 Happy FH-479	2,500	1994	105.00	105
1994 Hatty/Matty IND-514	2,500	1996	165.00	165-199
1993 Hedy FH-449	Closed	1994	95.00	95
1989 Heidi 260	Closed	1990	50.00	95
1991 Helene AM-29	2,500	1993	150.00	150
1991 Holly CH-6	Closed	1993	100.00	100
1991 Honey Bunny WB-9	Closed	1993	70.00	70
1991 Honey FH-401	Closed	1993	100.00	100
1994 Honey LL-945	2,500	1996	150.00	150-175
1991 Hope FH-434	2,500	1993	90.00	90
1996 Hope FH-800G	2,500	1998	75.00	75
1990 Hope YK-4118	Closed	1992	90.00	90
1995 Hyacinth C-3227	2,500		130.00	130
1990 Hyacinth DOLL-15PH	Closed	1992	85.00	85
1994 Hyacinth LL-941	2,500	1995	90.00	90
1990 Indian Doll FH-295	Closed	1992	60.00	60
1991 Indira AM-4	2,500	1993	125.00	125
1993 Iris FH-483	2,500	1994	95.00	95-105
1991 Iris TR-58	Closed	1993	120.00	120
1994 Ivy C-3203	2,500	1996	85.00	85
1991 Ivy PS-307	Closed	1993	75.00	75-105
1993 Jan Dress-Up OM-12	2,500	1994	135.00	175-202
1994 Jan FH-584R	2,500	1996	115.00	115
1992 Jan OM-012	9,200	1993	135.00	135
1991 Jane PS-243L	Closed	1993	115.00	115
1992 Janet FH-496	2,500	1993	120.00	120
1990 Janette DOLL-385	Closed	1992	85.00	85
1994 Janis FH-584B	2,500	1996	115.00	115
1989 Jaqueline DOLL-254M	Closed	1990	85.00	85
1998 Jasmine SJ-512	2,400	1998	60.00	75
1999 Jennifer in a Basket SJ-1035	2,400		45.00	45
1995 Jenny CD-16673B	2,500	1997	35.00	50-75
1988 Jessica DOM-267	Closed	1990	90.00	90
1991 Jessica FH-423	2,500	1993	95.00	95
1992 Jet FH-478	2,500	1993	115.00	150
1995 Jewel TR-100	2,500	1998	110.00	110
1994 Jillian C-3196	2,500	1997	150.00	150
1990 Jillian DOLL-41PH	Closed	1992	90.00	90
1993 Jillian SP-428	Closed	1994	165.00	165
1994 Jo YK-4539	3,500	1995	150.00	150-171
1988 Joanne Cry Baby PS-50	Closed	1990	100.00	100
1990 Joanne TR-12	Closed	1992	175.00	175
1992 Jodie FH-495	2,500	1993	115.00	115
1995 Joella CD-16779	2,500	1996	35.00	35
1988 Jolie C231	Closed	1990	65.00	150
1994 Jordan SP-455	2,500	1995	150.00	150
1991 Joy EP-23V	Closed	1993	130.00	130
1995 Joy TR-99	2,500	1997	85.00	135
1991 Joyce AM-100J	2,500	1993	35.00	35
1991 Julia C-3102	Closed	1993	135.00	135
1995 Julia C-3234	2,500	1996	100.00	100-132
1988 Julie C245A	Closed	1990	65.00	160
1990 Julie WB-35	Closed	1992	70.00	70
1988 Juliette Bride Musical C246LTM	Closed	1990	150.00	200
1995 June CD-2212	2,500	1996	50.00	50
2000 Kara AWL-551	1,200		75.00	75
1991 Karen EP-24	Closed	1993	115.00	115
1990 Karen PS-198	Closed	1992	150.00	150
1991 Karmela EP-57	2,500	1993	120.00	120
1990 Kate C-3060	Closed	1992	95.00	95
1997 Katherine VL-158 - S. Mann	2,500	1997	200.00	200-220
1990 Kathy w/Bear-TE1	Closed	1992	70.00	70
1994 Katie IND-511	2,500	1995	110.00	110
1989 Kayoko PS-24	Closed	1991	75.00	175
1991 Kelly AM-8	Closed	1993	125.00	125
1997 Kelly AWL-500 - S. Mann	2,500	1999	75.00	75
1993 Kendra FH-481	2,500	1994	115.00	115
1991 Kerry FH-396	Closed	1993	100.00	100
1994 Kevin MS-25	2,500	1996	150.00	150
1990 Kiku EP-4	Closed	1992	100.00	100
1991 Kinesha SP-402	2,500	1993	110.00	110-145
1989 Kirsten PS-40G	Closed	1991	70.00	70
1993 Kit SP-426	Closed	1994	55.00	55
1994 Kit YK-4547	3,500	1994	115.00	115
1994 Kitten IND-512	2,500	1996	110.00	110
1995 Kitty IND-527	2,500	1996	40.00	40
1991 Kristi FH-402	Closed	1993	100.00	100
1991 Kyla YK-4137	Closed	1993	95.00	150
1994 Lady Caroline LL-830	2,500	1995	120.00	120-145
1994 Lady Caroline LL-939	2,500	1995	120.00	120
1990 Laura DOLL-25PH	Closed	1992	55.00	55
1991 Laura WB-110P	Closed	1993	85.00	85
1990 Lauren SP-300	Closed	1992	85.00	85
1991 Leila AM-2	Closed	1993	125.00	125-165
1995 Lenore FH-617	2,500		120.00	120
1991 Lenore LL-911	2,500	1993	105.00	105
1991 Lenore YK-4218	3,500	1995	135.00	135-172
1995 Leslie LL-983	2,500	1995	105.00	105
1991 Libby EP-18	Closed	1993	85.00	85
1990 Lien Wha YK-4092	Closed	1992	100.00	150-177
1995 Lily FH-630	2,500	1996	120.00	175-201
1995 Lily in pink stripe IND-533	2,500	1995	85.00	85
1987 Linda C190	Closed	1986	60.00	120
1993 Linda SP-435	Closed	1994	95.00	95
1991 Lindsey C-3127	Closed	1993	135.00	175
1991 Linetta C-3166	Closed	1993	135.00	135
1990 Ling-Ling DOLL	Closed	1992	50.00	50
1989 Ling-Ling PS-87G	Closed	1991	90.00	90
1988 Lionel FH206B	Closed	1990	50.00	120-145
1990 Lisa Beige Accordion Pleat YK4093	Closed	1992	125.00	125
1990 Lisa FH-379	Closed	1992	100.00	100
1995 Lisette LL-993	2,500	1996	105.00	105
1991 Little Boy Blue C-3159	Closed	1993	100.00	100
1989 Liz YK-269	Closed	1991	70.00	100-125
1990 Liza C-3053	Closed	1992	100.00	100
1990 Lola SP-79	Closed	1992	105.00	105
1991 Lori EP-52	2,500	1993	95.00	95
1990 Lori WB-72BM	Closed	1992	75.00	75
1991 Louise LL-908	2,500	1993	105.00	105
1989 Lucinda DOM-293	Closed	1990	90.00	90
1988 Lucinda DOM-293	Closed	1990	90.00	90
1991 Lucy LL-853	Closed	1993	80.00	80
1990 Madame De Pompadour C-3088	Closed	1992	250.00	250-310
1991 Madeleine C-3106	Closed	1993	95.00	95
1992 Maggie FH-505	Closed	1993	125.00	125
1990 Maggie PS-151P	Closed	1992	90.00	90
1990 Maggie WB-51	Closed	1992	105.00	105
1989 Mai-Ling PS-79	2,500	1991	100.00	100
1994 Maiden PS-409	2,500	1995	150.00	150

*Quotes have been rounded up to nearest dollar

YEAR ISSUE	EDITION LIMIT	YEAR RETD.	ISSUE PRICE	*QUOTE U.S.$
1989 Marcey YK-4005	3,500	1995	90.00	90
1991 Marcy TR-55	Closed	1993	135.00	135
1987 Marcy YK122	Closed	1986	55.00	100-110
1989 Margaret 245	Closed	1991	100.00	150-175
1990 Maria YK-4116	Closed	1992	85.00	85
1993 Mariah LL-909	Closed	1993	135.00	135
1991 Mariel 18" Ivory-C-3119	Closed	1993	125.00	125
1995 Marielle PS-443	2,500	1997	175.00	175
1995 Martina RDK-232	2,500	1997	35.00	50-76
1995 Mary Ann FH-633	2,500	1996	110.00	110
1994 Mary Ann TR-79	2,500	1998	125.00	125
1995 Mary Elizabeth OC-51	2,500	1996	50.00	50
2000 Mary HH-222	1,200		45.00	45
1994 Mary Lou FH-565	2,500	1995	135.00	135
1994 Mary OC-56	2,500	1995	135.00	135
1991 Maude AM-100M	2,500	1993	70.00	70
1989 Maureen PS-84	Closed	1990	90.00	90
1995 Mc Kenzie LL-987	2,500	1997	100.00	100
2000 Megan AWL-550	1,200		55.00	55
1994 Megan C-3192	2,500	1997	150.00	150
1989 Meimei PS22	Closed	1990	75.00	225-270
1990 Melanie YK-4115	Closed	1992	80.00	80
1999 Melba CJC-104 - S. Mann	1,200	2000	55.00	55
1991 Melissa AM-9	Closed	1993	120.00	120
1991 Melissa CH-3	Closed	1993	110.00	110
1990 Melissa DOLL-390	Closed	1992	75.00	75
1989 Melissa LL-794	Closed	1990	95.00	95
1991 Melissa LL-901	Closed	1993	135.00	135
1997 Mercedes AWL-501 - S. Mann	2,500		75.00	75
1991 Meredith FH-391-P	Closed	1993	95.00	95
1995 Meredith MER-806	2,500	1996	65.00	65
1995 Merri MER-810	2,500	1996	65.00	65
1990 Merry Widow 20" C-3040M	Closed	1992	140.00	140
1991 Meryl FH-463	2,500	1993	95.00	95
1991 Michael w/School Books FH-439B	2,500	1993	95.00	95
1988 Michelle & Marcel YK176	Closed	1990	70.00	150-180
1991 Michelle Lilac/Green EP36	Closed	1993	95.00	95
1991 Michelle w/School Books FH-439G	Closed	1993	95.00	95
1995 Mindi PS-441	2,500	1995	125.00	125
1995 Miranda C16456B	2,500	1997	30.00	30
1991 Miranda DOLL-9PH	Closed	1993	75.00	75
1984 Miss Debutante Debi	Closed	1987	75.00	180-210
1989 Miss Kim PS-25	Closed	1990	75.00	175
1991 Missy DOLL-464	Closed	1993	70.00	70
1994 Missy FH-567	2,500	1996	140.00	140-165
1991 Missy PS-258	Closed	1993	90.00	90
1991 Mon Yun w/Parasol TR33	2,500	1993	115.00	150
1995 Monica TR-95	2,500	1997	135.00	135
1994 Morning Dew Indian PS-404	2,500	1995	150.00	150
1998 Musical Cathy TEC-591 - S. Mann	7,500	1998	30.00	30-45
1994 Musical Doll OC-45M	2,500	1996	140.00	140
1991 Nancy 21" Pink w/Rabbit EP-31	Closed	1993	165.00	165-195
1992 Nancy JNC-4001	Open	1993	90.00	90
1991 Nancy WB-73	2,500	1993	65.00	65
1990 Nanook WB-23	Closed	1992	75.00	75
1994 Natalie PP-2	2,500	1997	275.00	275-316
1990 Natasha PS-102	Closed	1992	100.00	100
1995 Natasha TR-90	2,500	1997	125.00	125-145
1991 Nellie EP-1B	Closed	1993	75.00	75
1996 Nicki MCC-501	2,500	1998	105.00	105
1991 Nicole AM-12	Closed	1993	135.00	135
1994 Nikki PS-401	2,500	1995	150.00	150
1993 Nina YK-4232	3,500	1993	135.00	135
1987 Nirmala YK-210	Closed	1995	50.00	50
1991 Noelle PS-239V	Closed	1993	95.00	95
1995 Norma C-3226	2,500	1998	135.00	135
1990 Odessa FH-362	Closed	1992	65.00	65
1994 Odetta IND-521	2,500	1995	140.00	140
2000 Olivia SJ-1181	1,200		75.00	75
1993 Oona TR-57	Closed	1993	135.00	135
1998 Orlando NL-131	2,500	1999	250.00	250
1998 Orlando VL131 - S. Mann	2,500	1999	250.00	250-315
1995 Our First Skates RDK-226/BG	2,500	1998	50.00	50-60
1994 Paige GU-33	2,500	1997	150.00	150
1994 Pamela LL-949	2,500	1996	115.00	115
1995 Pan Pan GU-52	2,500	1997	60.00	60
1994 Panama OM-43	2,500	1996	195.00	195
1989 Patricia/Patrick 215GBB	Closed	1990	105.00	135-262
1991 Patti DOLL-440	2,500	1993	65.00	65
1995 Patty C-3220	2,500	1997	60.00	60
1991 Patty YK-4221	3,500	1993	125.00	125
1989 Paula PS-56	Closed	1990	75.00	75
1995 Paulette PS-430	2,500	1995	80.00	80
1989 Pauline Bonaparte OM68	Closed	1990	120.00	120
1995 Pauline PS-440	2,500	1996	65.00	65
1988 Pauline YK-230	Closed	1990	90.00	90
1996 Pavlovia Ballerina TEC-560	7,500	1998	55.00	55-70
1994 Payton PS-407	2,500	1995	150.00	150
1995 Peaches IND-531	2,500	1996	80.00	80-110
1994 Pearl IND-523	2,500	1996	275.00	275-320
1994 Pegeen C-3205	2,500	1996	150.00	150
1991 Pepper PS-277	Closed	1993	130.00	150
1994 Petula C-3191	2,500	1996	140.00	140
1991 Pia-PS 246L	Closed	1993	115.00	115
1990 Ping-LingDOLL-363RV	Closed	1992	50.00	50
1990 Polly DOLL-22PH	Closed	1992	90.00	90
1996 Praying Pennie TEC-549	7,500	1998	50.00	50
1990 Princess Fair Skies FH-268B	Closed	1992	75.00	75
1994 Princess Foxfire PS-411	2,500	1997	150.00	150
1994 Princess Moonrise YK-4542	3,500	1996	140.00	140-175
1990 Princess Red Feather PS-189	Closed	1992	90.00	90
1994 Princess Snow Flower PS-402	2,500	1995	150.00	150-175

YEAR ISSUE	EDITION LIMIT	YEAR RETD.	ISSUE PRICE	*QUOTE U.S.$
1991 Princess Summer Winds FH-427	2,500	1993	120.00	120-138
1990 Priscilla WB-50	Closed	1992	105.00	105
1991 Prissy White/Blue C-3140	Closed	1993	100.00	100
2000 Rachel HH-220	1,200		75.00	75
1995 Rainie LL-984	2,500	1996	125.00	125
1989 Ramona PS-31B	Closed	1992	80.00	80
1991 Rapunzel C-3157	2,500	1993	150.00	150-200
1998 Rapunzel C-3276	2,400	1999	145.00	145
1987 Rapunzel C158	Closed	1986	95.00	165
1998 Rapunzel C3-276	2,500	1999	134.00	134
1993 Rebecca C-3177	2,500	1993	135.00	135
1989 Rebecca PS-34V	Closed	1992	45.00	45
1991 Red Wing AM-30	2,500	1993	165.00	165-200
1994 Rita FH-553	2,500	1996	115.00	115
1994 Robby NM-29	2,500	1995	135.00	135
1991 Robin AM-22	Closed	1993	120.00	120
1995 Robin C-3236	2,500	1997	60.00	60
1991 Rosalind C-3090	Closed	1992	150.00	150
1989 Rosie 290M	Closed	1992	55.00	85
1987 Sabrina C208	Closed	1986	65.00	95
1990 Sabrina C3050	Closed	1992	105.00	105
1987 Sailorette DOM217	Closed	1986	70.00	150
1992 Sally FH-492	2,500	1994	105.00	105
1990 Sally WB-20	Closed	1992	95.00	95
1991 Samantha GU-3	Closed	1992	100.00	100
2000 Samatha NY-312	1,200		100.00	100
1995 San San GU-53	2,500	1997	60.00	60
1991 Sandra DOLL-6-PHE	2,500	1992	65.00	65
1992 Sapphires OM-223	2,500	1993	250.00	250
1992 Sara Ann FH-474	2,500	1993	115.00	115
1993 Saretta SP-423	2,500	1993	100.00	100
1991 Scarlett FH-399	2,500	1992	100.00	100
1991 Scarlett FH-436	2,500	1992	135.00	135-160
1992 Scarlett FH-471	2,500	1993	120.00	120-135
1991 Shaka SP-401	2,500	1992	110.00	110-125
1994 Shaka TR-45	2,500	1996	100.00	100
1991 Sharon 21" Blue EP-34	Closed	1992	120.00	120
1991 Shau Chen GU-2	2,500	1992	85.00	85
1991 Shelley CH-1	2,500	1992	110.00	110
1995 Shimmering Caroline LL-992	2,500	1997	115.00	115-144
1990 Shirley WB-37	Closed	1992	65.00	65
1988 Sister Agnes 14" C250	Closed	1990	75.00	75
1988 Sister Ignatius Notre Dame FH184	Closed	1990	75.00	75
1989 Sister Mary C-249	Closed	1992	75.00	125
1990 Sister Mary WB-15	Closed	1992	70.00	70
1994 Sister Suzie IND-509	2,500	1995	95.00	95
1988 Sister Teresa FH187	Closed	1990	80.00	80
1992 Sonja FH-486	2,500	1994	125.00	125
1995 Sophia PS-445	2,500	1998	125.00	125
1991 Sophie TR-53	2,500	1992	135.00	135
1995 Southern Belle Bride FH-637	2,500		160.00	185
1994 Southern Belle FH-570	2,500		140.00	140
1991 Stacy DOLL-6PH	Closed	1992	65.00	65
1995 Stacy OC-75	2,500	1996	40.00	40
1990 Stacy TR-5	Closed	1992	105.00	105
1991 Stephanie AM-11	Closed	1992	105.00	105
1991 Stephanie FH-467	Closed	1992	95.00	95
1994 Stephie OC-41M	2,500	1995	115.00	115
1990 Sue Chuen C-3061G	Closed	1992	95.00	95
1992 Sue JNC-4003	Closed	1994	90.00	90
1994 Sue Kwei TR-73	2,500	1996	110.00	110
1991 Summer AM-33	Closed	1992	200.00	200
1990 Sunny FH-331	Closed	1992	70.00	70
1989 Sunny PS-59V	Closed	1992	71.00	71
1990 Susan DOLL-364MC	Closed	1992	75.00	75
1994 Suzanne LL-943	2,500	1996	105.00	105
1994 Suzie GU-38	2,500	1997	135.00	135
1995 Suzie OC-80	2,500	1997	50.00	50
1989 Suzie PS-32	Closed	1992	80.00	80
1993 Suzie SP-422	2,500	1993	164.00	164
1995 Sweet Pea LL-981	2,500	1996	90.00	90
1991 Sybil 20" Beige C-3131	Closed	1992	135.00	135
1991 Sybil Pink DOLL-12PHMC	2,500	1992	75.00	75
1994 Taffey TR-80	2,500	1994	150.00	150
1990 Tania DOLL-376P	Closed	1992	65.00	65
1989 Tatiana Pink Ballerina M-60	Closed	1991	120.00	175
1998 Taylor NY-132 - S. Mann	2,500	1999	75.00	75
1994 Teresa C-3198	2,500	1995	110.00	110-125
1995 Terri OM-78	2,500	1997	150.00	150
1989 Terri PS-104	Closed	1991	85.00	85
1991 Terri TR-62	Closed	1992	75.00	75
1991 Tessa AM-19	Closed	1992	135.00	135
1994 Tiffany OC-44M	2,500	1996	140.00	140
1991 Tina AM-16	Closed	1992	130.00	130
1990 Tina DOLL-371	Closed	1992	85.00	85
1990 Tina WB-32	Closed	1992	65.00	65
1994 Tippy LL-946	2,500	1995	110.00	110
1990 Tommy-C-3064	Closed	1992	75.00	75
1994 Topaz TR-74	2,500	1995	195.00	195-220
1997 Tracy AWL-519 - S. Mann	2,400		100.00	100
1988 Tracy C-3006	Closed	1990	95.00	150-172
1994 Trixie TR-77	2,500	1996	110.00	110
1991 Vanessa AM-34	Closed	1992	90.00	90
1991 Vicki C-3101	Closed	1992	200.00	200
1991 Violet EP-41	Closed	1992	135.00	135
1992 Violette FH-503	2,500	1994	120.00	120
1991 Virginia SP-359	Closed	1992	120.00	120
1994 Virginia TR-78	2,500	1998	195.00	195-215
1987 Vivian C-201P	Closed	1986	80.00	80
1991 Wah-Ching Watching Oriental Toddler YK-4175	Closed	1992	110.00	110
1995 Wei Lin GU-44	2,500	1998	70.00	70-90

YEAR ISSUE	EDITION LIMIT	YEAR RETD.	ISSUE PRICE	*QUOTE U.S.$
1994 Wendy MS-26	2,500	1996	150.00	150
1989 Wendy PS-51	Closed	1991	105.00	105
1990 Wendy TE-3	Closed	1992	75.00	75
1985 Wendy-C120	Closed	1987	45.00	150
1990 Wilma PS-174	Closed	1992	75.00	75
1995 Windy in Rose Print FH-626	2,500	1995	200.00	200-265
1995 Winnie LL-985	2,500	1996	75.00	75
1995 Yelena RDK-236	2,500	1996	35.00	35
1990 Yen Yen YK-4091	Closed	1992	95.00	95
1992 Yvette OM-015	2,500	1994	150.00	150

Signature Doll Series - Various

YEAR ISSUE	EDITION LIMIT	YEAR RETD.	ISSUE PRICE	*QUOTE U.S.$
1992 Abigail MS-11 - M. Severino	5,000	1994	125.00	125
1995 Adak PPA-21 - P. Phillips	5,000	1996	110.00	110
1998 Addy OM-174 - B.K. Lee	1,200	2000	175.00	175
1998 Agnesy VP-20 - V. Pike	1,200	1999	175.00	174-225
1998 Akia OM-208 - B.K. Lee	1,200	1999	175.00	149-220
1997 Alexandria MS-70 - M. Severino	5,000	1999	75.00	125
1999 Alexis JAY-149 - J.C. Lee	1,200	2000	75.00	95
1991 Alice MS-7- M. Severino	5,000	1996	120.00	120
1998 Alicia AWL-522 - S. Mann	2,500	1999	175.00	175
1999 Alison OM227 - B.K. Lee	1,200	1999	200.00	200-220
1999 Amber JAY-147 - J.C. Lee	1,200		100.00	100
1991 Amber MS-1 - M. Severino	Closed	1994	95.00	95
1999 Amelia CK-16 - C. Koch	1,200	2000	250.00	290
1992 Amy OM-06	2,500	1993	150.00	200-248
1995 Amy Rose HKHF-200 - H.K. Hyland	5,000	1997	125.00	150-265
2000 Angel of Autumn SEU-2 - S. Easton	1,200		300.00	300
2000 Angel of Music SEU-16 - S. Easton	1,200		125.00	125
2000 Angel of Spring SEU-4 - S. Easton	1,200		300.00	300
2000 Angel of Summer SEU-1 - S. Easton	1,200		300.00	300
2000 Angel of Winter SEU-3 - S. Easton	1,200		300.00	300
1995 Angeline OM-84	2,500	1998	100.00	100-120
1998 Antonia FH-820 - C.I. Lee	1,200	1998	150.00	150
1993 Antonia OM-227	2,500	2000	200.00	350
1998 April MCOM-104 - M. Costa	5,000	2000	174.00	174
1999 Ardith OM-260 - B.K. Lee	1,200	2000	165.00	165
1995 Ariel OM-81	2,500	1997	185.00	240-288
1998 Ashley DEA-205 - Heléne	5,000	1999	135.00	135
2000 Ashley MCNY-3 - M. Costa	1,200		150.00	150
1997 Audrey OM-197 - B.K. Lee	2,500	1999	150.00	150
1991 Aurora Gold 22"-OM-181	2,500	1993	260.00	260-312
1996 Aurora HKHO - H.K. Hyland	5,000	1999	250.00	250-375
1992 Baby Cakes Crumbs PK-CRUMBS - P. Kolesar	5,000	1994	17.50	35-42
1992 Baby Cakes Crumbs/Black PK-CRUMBS/B - P. Kolesar	5,000	1994	17.50	35-42
1997 The Bear Collector FH-853 - J. Sauerbrey	1,200		125.00	125
1997 Beauty TF-6 - T. Francirek	1,200	1998	150.00	150-175
1997 Bebe TF-8- T. Franciek	5,000	2000	150.00	150
1991 Becky MS-2 - M. Severino	5,000	1994	95.00	95
1992 Beth OM-05	Closed	1993	135.00	135
1997 Bette DALI-030 - E. Dali	1,200	1999	150.00	150
1992 Bette OM-01	2,500	1993	115.00	115-165
1999 Bianca MCU-1010 - M. Costa	1,200	2000	115.00	135-175
1997 Birth of Hope OM-140 - C. Wang	5,000	1998	175.00	175-225
2000 Bliss JSU-200 - J. Sauerbrey	1,200		125.00	125
1993 Bonnett Baby MS-17W - M. Severino	5,000	1996	175.00	175
2000 Brandy MCNY-5 - M. Costa	1,200		150.00	150
1997 Brett JS-3 - J. Sauerbrey	1,200	2000	175.00	175
1997 Briana OM-164 - C. Wang	2,500	1999	150.00	179
1998 Briana OM-199 - B.K. Lee	1,200	1999	195.00	225-350
1999 Butterfly Kisses MCU-1001 - M. Costa	1,200	2000	50.00	65-100
1999 Byrna JAY-130 - J.C. Lee	1,200	1999	125.00	125
1998 Camilla DEA-223 - Heléne	2,500	1999	175.00	175
1993 Camille OM-230	2,500	1994	250.00	250
1995 Cara DALI-1 - E. Dali	5,000	1997	400.00	400
1995 Casey PPA-23 - P. Phillips	5,000	1997	85.00	85-105
1992 Cassandra PAC-8 - P. Aprile	Closed	1994	450.00	450
1998 Cassidy MCOM-100 - M. Costa	5,000	2000	175.00	175-200
1992 Cassie Flower Girl PAC-9 - P. Aprile	Closed	1994	175.00	175
1997 Cathy Ann MCOM-105 - M. Costa	5,000	1998	200.00	200
1992 Celine PAC-11 - P. Aprile	5,000	1995	165.00	165
1999 Chelsea JAY-189 - J.C. Lee	1,200		150.00	150
1998 Cheyene OM-218 - B.K. Lee	1,200	1999	175.00	205
1998 Cheyenne OM-128 - B.K. Lee	2,500	1998	195.00	195-230
1998 Chloe Sofia GMN-205 - G. Mc Neill	1,200	2000	175.00	175
2000 Christina Christmas Fairy SENY-100 - S. Easton	1,200		120.00	120
1995 Christmas Alyssa - P. Phillips	5,000	1995	100.00	175-220
1997 Christmas Ashley - J. Sauerbrey	10,000	1997	96.00	150-177
1998 Christopher Daniel MHF-501 - M Hargrave	5,000	1999	149.00	149
1999 Cindy JAY-109 - J.C. Lee	1,200		125.00	125
1991 Clair-Ann PK-252 - P. Kolesar	5,000	1993	100.00	100-119
1998 Claire CK-102 - C. Koch	1,200	2000	350.00	350-475
1997 Claire, Princess Bride FH-864 - C.I. Lee	1,200	1999	175.00	175-205
1992 Clarissa PAC-3 - P. Aprile	5,000	1996	165.00	165
1999 Claudine JSU-14 - J. Sauerbrey	1,200	2000	175.00	175
1998 Colette MC-1 - M. Costa	5,000	2000	350.00	350
1999 Colleen JAY-102 - J.C. Lee	1,200	1999	80.00	80-100
1997 Consuelo CK-101 - C. Koch	1,200	1998	400.00	400-450
1992 Cordelia OM-09	2,500	1993	250.00	250-315
2000 Courtney JAY-183 - J.C. Lee	1,200		100.00	100
1998 Courtney MC-15 - M. Costa	1,200	2000	150.00	150
1999 Daisy JAY-132 - J.C. Lee	1,200	2000	150.00	150
1999 Delja MSF-500 - M. Severino	1,200	2000	160.00	160
1998 Delores DALI-034 - E. Dali	1,200		150.00	150
1998 Delphine OM-183 - B.K. Lee	2,500	1999	250.00	250
1999 Denise OM-235 - C. Wang	1,200	1999	150.00	150
1999 Destiny CK-107 - C. Koch	1,200	1999	300.00	450-495

*Quotes have been rounded up to nearest dollar

YEAR ISSUE	EDITION LIMIT	YEAR RETD.	ISSUE PRICE	*QUOTE U.S.$
2000 Dewela MCNY-2 - M. Costa	1,200		150.00	150
1992 Dulcie HP-200 - H. Payne	Closed	1993	250.00	250
1999 Eileen JAY-133 - J.C. Lee	1,200	2000	150.00	150
1998 Ella DEA-226 - Heléne	2,500	1998	175.00	175
1991 Emmaline Beige/Lilac OM-197	Closed	2000	150.00	150
1997 Emmy Lou CK-3 - C. Koch	5,000	2000	250.00	250-295
1998 Engrid OM-173 - B.K. Lee	1,200	1999	175.00	225-250
1991 Enoc PK-100 - P. Kolesar	5,000	1994	100.00	135
1992 Eugenie Bride PAC-1 - P. Aprile	5,000	1996	165.00	165
1992 Eugenie OM-225	2,500	1999	150.00	150
1998 Fiona DEA-230 - Heléne	2,500	2000	175.00	175
1997 Frenchie CK-100 - C. Koch	5,000	1999	300.00	300-325
1997 Gabriella OM-165 - C. Wang	5,000	1998	250.00	250-300
1997 Galena DALI-015 - E. Dali	1,200	1999	150.00	150
1993 Gena OM-229	1,200	2000	165.00	165
1997 Gigi MCC-508 - M. Costa	2,400	2000	75.00	95
1998 Gillian JAY-115 - J.C. Lee	2,500	2000	125.00	125-210
1999 Ginger JAY-125 - J.C. Lee	2,500		175.00	175
1993 Grace HKH-2 - H. Kahl-Hyland	5,000	1996	250.00	250-475
1995 Guardian Angel of Marriage OM-112 - K. Wang	1,500	1996	150.00	150-205
1995 Guardian Angel OM-91	2,500		150.00	150
1997 Hailey MCC-511 - M. Costa	5,000	1998	65.00	65-100
1999 Haley JAY-148 - J.C. Lee	1,200	2000	135.00	150
1996 Hali MC-11	2,500	1998	100.00	100
1997 Hanna's Enchanted Garden HKHT-10 - H. Hyland	5,000	2000	95.00	95
2000 Harmony JSU-201 - J. Sauerbrey	1,200	2000	125.00	125
1993 Helene HKH-1 - H. Kahl-Hyland	5,000	1996	250.00	250-325
1997 Jacqueline OM-137 - C. Wang	5,000	1998	300.00	300-325
1999 Jane JSU-11 - J. Sauerbrey	1,200	1999	175.00	175-300
1991 Janice OM-194	2,500	1999	165.00	165
1999 Jasmine OM-237 - Nora	1,200	2000	100.00	100-125
1998 Jason JAY-103 - J. Lee	1,200	1998	50.00	50-90
1997 Jean DALI-037 - E. Dali	1,200	1999	150.00	150
1997 Jennifer JS-5 - J. Sauerbrey	1,200	1998	125.00	125
1999 Jenny GAR-5 - G. Rademann	1,200	2000	85.00	85
1999 Joann & Larissa MCU-1000A/B - M. Costa	1,200	2000	200.00	255
2000 Jordan JAY-203 - J.C. Lee	1,200		150.00	150
1999 Jubilee GAR-1 - G. Rademann	1,200	1999	100.00	125
1997 Juliet HKRO-307 - H. Hyland	5,000	1999	175.00	175
1991 Juliette OM-192	2,500	2000	300.00	300
1992 Juliette OM-8	2,500	1994	175.00	175-272
1999 Kameesha OM-224 - B.K. Lee	1,200	1999	165.00	165
1999 Kara JAY-164 - J.C. Lee	1,200	2000	225.00	250
1997 Katerina OM-234	1,200	2000	250.00	305
1998 Katherine DEA-228 - Heléne	2,500	1999	175.00	175
1999 Keri JAY-138 - J.C. Lee	1,200	2000	95.00	95
1999 Kim OM-250 - B.K. Lee	1,200	1999	150.00	150-225
1997 Kirsten OM-172 - B.K. Lee	5,000	1999	175.00	175-350
1997 Kyla MC-9 - M. Costa	5,000	2000	100.00	100
2000 Kyoto VP-26 - V. Pike	1,200		125.00	125
1998 Laraline CK-10 - C. Koch	1,200	1999	300.00	300-365
1997 Latisha MS-97 - M. Severino	5,000	1998	40.00	40
1995 Latisha PPA-25 - P. Phillips	5,000	1996	110.00	110
1999 Laura CK-130 - C. Koch	1,200	2000	225.00	225
1995 Laurel HKH-17R - H.K. Hyland	5,000	1997	110.00	110
1995 Lauren HKH-202 - H.K. Hyland	5,000	1996	150.00	150-215
1999 Lenore CK-108 - C. Koch	1,200	1999	250.00	250
1997 Liliac Fairie OM-201 - B.K. Lee	2,500	1998	175.00	175
2000 Little Kelly JAY-195 - J.C. Lee	1,200		85.00	85
1995 Little Lisa OM-86	2,500	1997	125.00	125-162
2000 Little Lucy JAY-202 - J.C. Lee	1,200		175.00	175
1992 Little Match Girl HP-205 - H. Payne	Closed	1994	150.00	150-270
1999 Liu VPU-21 - V. Pike	1,200	2000	75.00	75
1998 Louisa DEA-227 - Heléne	2,500	2000	175.00	175
1995 Lucy HKH-14 - H.K. Hyland	2,500	1996	105.00	105
1998 Lureline CK-10 - C. Koch	1,200	2000	300.00	300
1999 Lydia JAY-142 - J.C. Lee	1,200	2000	125.00	125
1997 Lyndsey MCA-101 - M. Costa	5,000	1999	200.00	200
1999 Lysbeth JAY-139 - J.C. Lee	1,200	2000	100.00	115-130
1999 Mackenzie JAY-188 - J.C. Lee	1,200	2000	115.00	115
1997 Madame Charpentier TF-5 - T. Francirek	1,200	2000	150.00	150
1999 Mara JAY-124 - J.C. Lee	1,200	2000	165.00	165-205
1999 Margaret Anne GAR-5 - G. Rademann	1,200	1999	85.00	85
1999 Margaret OM-223 - M. Costa	1,200	2000	250.00	250
1999 Marinda & Mandy JAY-180 - J.C. Lee	1,200	2000	125.00	125
1998 Maritza OM-209 - C. Wang	5,000	1999	135.00	135-165
1997 Marlene DALI-031 - E. Dali	1,200		150.00	150
1999 Marley JAY-137 - J.C. Lee	1,200	2000	95.00	95
1997 Mary Ann JS-8 - J. Sauerbrey	5,000	1998	150.00	150
1999 Masquerade CK-105 - C. Koch	1,200	1999	350.00	450-475
1997 Maureen DALI-26B - E. Dali	1,200	1999	100.00	100
1999 Megan & Caitlan JAY140A/B - J.C. Lee	1,200	2000	200.00	200
1992 Megan MS-12 - M. Severino	5,000	1995	125.00	125
1997 Megan PP-112 - P. Phillips	5,000	1998	150.00	150-195
1999 Mei Ling OM225 - Nora	1,200	2000	150.00	150
1999 Mei Ping OM226 - B.K. Lee	1,200	2000	125.00	125
1997 Melissa Ann VP-10 - V. Pike	5,000	1998	325.00	325-406
1992 Melissa OM-03	2,500	1993	135.00	135-324
1999 Meredith JAY-141 - J.C. Lee	1,200	2000	105.00	125
1997 Mickey & Hanna BRU-600/3 - Bruny	5,000	1999	50.00	50
1991 Mikey MS-3 - M. Severino	5,000	1994	95.00	95
1997 Milou MAV-303 - M. Synder	5,000	2000	175.00	175
1997 Mme. De Champs TF-2 - T. Francirek	1,200	1999	150.00	150
1997 Mme. De Falaise TF-17 - T. Francirek	1,200	1999	150.00	150
1997 Mme. Fourtot TF-3 - T. Francirek	1,200	1999	150.00	150
1991 Mommy's Rays of Sunshine MS-9 - M. Severino	5,000	1994	165.00	185-221
1997 Monique OM-167 - C. Wang	5,000	1997	150.00	150
1998 Morgan MHVL-202 - M. Hargrave	1,200	1998	175.00	175
1999 The Murphy Kids JAY-135 - J.C. Lee	1,200	2000	200.00	225-235
1997 Myrna DALI-033 - E. Dali	1,200		150.00	150
1995 Natasha HKH-17P - H.K. Hyland	5,000		110.00	110
1996 Nichole PPA-39 - P. Phillips	1,200	1999	150.00	195
1998 Nicole DEA-204 - Heléne	1,200	1998	135.00	150
1997 Night & Day DALI-02/3 - E. Dali	1,200	1999	300.00	300
1998 Odette OM-210 - C. Wang	1,200	1999	135.00	135-150
1997 Odile OM-168 - C. Wang	1,200	2000	135.00	135-150
1998 Orchid CK-5 - C. Koch	1,200	1999	350.00	400-425
2000 Parker JAY-198A - J.C. Lee	1,200		115.00	115
1991 Paulette PAC-2 - P. Aprile	5,000	1996	250.00	300
1992 Pavlova PAC-17 - P. Aprile	5,000	1994	145.00	145-230
1998 Peekaboo Sue JAY-105 - J. Lee	1,200		125.00	125
1998 Penny CK-4 - C. Koch	5,000	2000	149.00	149
2000 Penny JAY-198B - J.C. Lee	1,200		115.00	115
1998 Penny Sue JAY-101 - J. Lee	1,200	1999	85.00	85-115
1998 Pia DALI-07 - E. Dali	1,200	1999	150.00	150
1991 Precious Baby SB-100 - S. Bilotto	5,000	1996	250.00	250-300
1991 Precious Pary Time SB-102 - S. Bilotto	5,000	1996	250.00	275
1998 Rapunzel's Wedding FH-866 - P. Phillips	5,000	1999	149.00	149-195
1992 Rebecca Beige Bonnet MS-17B - M. Severino	5,000	1995	175.00	175
1994 Regina OM-41	2,500	1996	150.00	150-195
1993 Reilly HKH-3 - H. Kahl-Hyland	5,000	1996	260.00	260
1997 Rosey GMNO-3 - G. McNeil	5,000	1998	250.00	300
1992 Ruby MS-18 - M. Severino	5,000	1993	135.00	135
1997 Sabrina MCC-507 - M. Costa	5,000	1999	65.00	65
2000 Samantha MCNY-4 - M. Costa	1,200		150.00	150
1998 Sapphire TF-18 - T. Francirek	1,200	1999	200.00	225-250
1998 Sarah (w/rug/bear/stool JAY-100 - J. Lee	1,200	1999	135.00	135
1999 Sarah HKHZ-102 - H.K. Hyland	1,200	2000	275.00	275-375
1997 Sarah OM-190 - B.K. Lee	1,200	1999	195.00	195-200
2000 Scarlett DALI-100 - E. Dali	1,200		200.00	200
1999 Schehrezade OM-229 - B.K. Lee	1,200	2000	175.00	175
1997 Scott & Becky BRU-601/5 - Bruny	5,000	1998	50.00	50-75
1998 Shadow DALI-01 - E. Dali	1,200	2000	150.00	150
2000 Shannon HKHN-5 - H.K. Hyland	1,200		175.00	175
1995 Shao Ling PPA-22 - P. Phillips	5,000	1996	110.00	110
1999 Sissy GAR-4 - G. Rademann	1,200	2000	85.00	85
2000 Skylar JSU-202 - J. Sauerbrey	1,200		125.00	125
2000 Skylar MCNY-6 - M. Costa	1,200		150.00	150
1995 Sleeping Beauty OM-88	2,500	1996	115.00	115
1990 Sophie OM-1	Closed	1992	65.00	65
1994 Sparkle OM-40	2,500	1996	150.00	150
1991 Sparkle PK-250 - P. Kolesar	5,000	1996	100.00	100-145
1998 Stacy MHVL-203 - M. Hargrave	5,000	2000	175.00	175
1992 Stacy MS-24 - M. Severino	Closed	1993	110.00	110
1997 Starr MSA-14 - M. Severino	5,000	2000	175.00	175
1999 Stephanie JAY-160 - J.C. Lee	1,200		135.00	135
1991 Stephanie Pink & White OM-196	Closed	1992	300.00	300-395
1991 Stephie MS-6 - M. Severino	Closed	1994	125.00	125
1991 Su Lin MS-5 - M. Severino	5,000	1994	105.00	105
1994 Sugar Plum Fairy OM-39	2,500	1996	150.00	150
1997 Suryah MS-88 - M. Severino	5,000	1998	40.00	40
1995 Suzie HKH-16 - H.K. Hyland	5,000		100.00	100
1991 Sweet Pea PK-251 - P. Kolesar	Closed		100.00	100
1994 Tallulah OM-44	2,500	1996	275.00	275
1997 Tam MSA-15 - M. Severino	5,000	2000	150.00	150
1998 Tara DEA-203 - Heléne	1,200	1999	95.00	95
1998 Taylor JAY-106 - J. Lee	1,200	2000	100.00	120
2000 Taylor JAY-196 - J.C. Lee	1,200		125.00	125
1998 Teacher's Pet MS-114 - M. Severino	5,000	1998	75.00	75
1998 Tiffany & Friends JAY-104	2,500	1999	135.00	135-195
1998 Tiffany & Friends JAY-104 - J. Lee	2,500	1999	135.00	135-202
1992 Tiffany OM-014	2,500	1994	150.00	150-160
1995 Tina OM-79	2,500	1997	150.00	150-185
1999 Tippi The Thumbsucker JAY-128 - J.C. Lee	1,200	2000	125.00	125
1994 Tracy JAG-111 - J. Grammer	5,000	1996	150.00	150
1994 Trevor JAG-112 - J. Grammer	5,000	1996	115.00	115
1999 Tricia HKHZ-104 - H. Hyland	1,200	1999	175.00	175-225
1992 Trina OM-011	Closed	1994	165.00	165-190
1999 Trista OM-254 - B.K. Lee	1,200	2000	135.00	135
1999 Turandot VP-23 - V. Pike	1,200	1999	175.00	255
1998 Venus CK-103 - C. Koch	1,200	1999	300.00	300-375
1997 Vicki FH-815 - C.I. Lee	5,000	1999	150.00	150
1999 Victoria OM236 - C. Wang	1,200	1999	150.00	150
1991 Violet OM-186	2,500	1992	270.00	270-275
1992 Violetta PAC-16 - P. Aprile	5,000	1994	165.00	165
1997 Willow DALI-05 - E. Dali	1,200	1999	150.00	150-205
1998 Woodland Fairie OM-200 - B.K. Lee	2,500	1999	175.00	175
1995 Woodland Sprite OM-90	2,500	1997	100.00	100
1997 Xena DALI-05 - E. Dali	1,200	1999	150.00	150
1991 Yawning Kate MS-4 - M. Severino	Closed	1994	105.00	105-145

Susan Wakeen Doll Co. Inc.

The Littlest Ballet Company - S. Wakeen

YEAR ISSUE	EDITION LIMIT	YEAR RETD.	ISSUE PRICE	*QUOTE U.S.$
1985 Cynthia	375		198.00	350
1987 Elizabeth	250		425.00	1000
1985 Jeanne	375		198.00	800
1985 Jennifer	250		750.00	750
1987 Marie Ann	50		1000.00	1000
1985 Patty	375		198.00	400-500

Zolan Fine Arts, LLC

Zolan Dolls - D. Zolan

YEAR ISSUE	EDITION LIMIT	YEAR RETD.	ISSUE PRICE	*QUOTE U.S.$
1995 A Child's Prayer	Retrd.	1998	119.00	100-119
1997 Little Rain Dancer	Open		168.00	168
1996 O Holy Night	Retrd.	1998	119.00	119
1997 Sunday School	Retrd.	1998	119.00	119
1995 Winter Wonder	Retrd.	1998	119.00	119

FIGURINES

All God's Children/Miss Martha Originals

Collectors' Club - M. Root

YEAR ISSUE	EDITION LIMIT	YEAR RETD.	ISSUE PRICE	*QUOTE U.S.$
1989 Molly -1524	Retrd.	1990	38.00	325-500
1990 Joey -1539	Retrd.	1991	32.00	330
1991 Mandy -1540	Retrd.	1992	36.00	215-288
1992 Olivia -1562	Retrd.	1993	36.00	175-236
1993 Garrett -1567	Retrd.	1994	36.00	232-275
1993 Peek-a-Boo	Retrd.	1994	Gift	88-95
1994 Alexandria -1575	Retrd.	1995	36.00	153-180
1994 Lindy	Retrd.	1995	Gift	75-87
1995 Zamika -1581	Retrd.	1996	36.00	80-92
1995 Zizi	Retrd.	1996	Gift	30-42
1996 Donnie -1585	Retrd.	1997	36.00	50-68
1996 Dinky	Retrd.	1997	Gift	32-39
1997 Daylon - 1586	Retrd.	1998	36.00	30-45
1997 Snuffles	Retrd.	1998	Gift	25-32
1998 Rebekka - 1600	Retrd.	1999	38.00	38
1998 Kat	Retrd.	1999	Gift	30-40
1999 Miquela - 1608	Retrd.	2000	35.00	35
1999 Evan	Retrd.	2000	Gift	N/A
2000 Daniel - 1611W	5/01		32.50	33
2000 Daniel - 1611B	5/01		32.50	33
2000 Hubcap	5/01		Gift	N/A

Event Piece - M. Root

YEAR ISSUE	EDITION LIMIT	YEAR RETD.	ISSUE PRICE	*QUOTE U.S.$
1994 Uriel - 2000	Yr.Iss.	1994	45.00	110-160
1995 Jane - 2001 (ten year Anniversary)	Yr.Iss.	1995	45.00	120-130
1996 Patti - 2002-Spring (rose colored dress for girl, green colored dress for doll)	Yr.Iss.	1996	45.00	80-100
1996 Patti - 2002-Fall (dark blue dress for girl, peach colored dress for doll)	Yr.Iss.	1996	45.00	80-100
1997 Shalisa - 2003	Yr.Iss.	1997	45.00	50-72

Signing Event - M. Root

YEAR ISSUE	EDITION LIMIT	YEAR RETD.	ISSUE PRICE	*QUOTE U.S.$
2000 Santa Claus	Yr.Iss.		32.50	33

All God's Children - M. Root

YEAR ISSUE	EDITION LIMIT	YEAR RETD.	ISSUE PRICE	*QUOTE U.S.$
1985 Abe - 1357	Retrd.	1988	25.00	1040-1450
1989 Adam - 1526	Open		36.00	44
1997 Alaysha (clock) - 2800	6,000	1997	59.50	95-120
1999 Albert - 1606	Open		44.00	44
1987 Amy - 1405W	Retrd.	1996	22.00	60-68
1987 Angel - 1401W	Retrd.	1995	20.00	74-95
1986 Annie Mae 6" -1311	Retrd.	1989	19.00	100-135
1986 Annie Mae 8 1/2" - 1310	Retrd.	1989	27.00	160-195
1987 Aunt Sarah - blue - 1440	Retrd.	1989	45.00	240-256
1987 Aunt Sarah - red - 1440	Retrd.	1989	45.00	300-400
2000 Barbara - 1607	Open		42.00	42
1992 Barney - 1557	Retrd.	1995	32.00	75-92
1988 Bean (Clear Water) - 1521	Retrd.	1992	36.00	200-276
1992 Bean (Painted Water) - 1521	Retrd.	1993	36.00	95-128
1987 Becky - 1402W	Retrd.	1995	22.00	74-85
1987 Becky with Patch - 1402W	Retrd.	1988	19.00	60-92
1987 Ben - 1504	Retrd.	1988	22.00	300-390
1991 Bessie & Corkie - 1547	Open		70.00	75
1992 Beth - 1558	Retrd.	1995	32.00	50-60
1988 Betsy (Clear Water) - 1513	Retrd.	1992	36.00	170-335
1992 Betsy (Painted Water) - 1513	Retrd.	1993	36.00	85-95
1999 Betty - 1610	Open		42.00	42
1989 Beverly (small) - 1525	Retrd.	1990	50.00	670-710
1991 Billy (lg. stars raised) - 1545	Retrd.	1993	36.00	115-166
1991 Billy (stars imprinted) - 1545	Retrd.	1993	36.00	140-175
1987 Blossom (blue) - 1500	Retrd.	1989	60.00	170-300
1987 Blossom (red) - 1500	Retrd.	1989	60.00	830-875
1989 Bo - 1530	Retrd.	1994	22.00	55-99
1987 Bonnie & Buttons - 150	Retrd.	1992	24.00	90-152
1985 Booker T - 1320	Retrd.	1988	19.00	500-1000
1987 Boone - 1510	Retrd.	1989	16.00	50-115
1989 Bootsie - 1529	Retrd.	1994	22.00	60
1992 Caitlin - 1554	Retrd.	1994	36.00	114-135
1985 Callie 2 1/4" - 1362	Retrd.	1988	12.00	280-300
1985 Callie 4 1/2" - 1361	Retrd.	1988	19.00	320-540
1988 Calvin - 777	Retrd.	1988	200.00	2195-2240
1998 Carmen - 1605	Open		48.00	48
1987 Cassie - 1503	Retrd.	1989	22.00	90-175
1994 Chantel - 1573	Suspd.		39.00	50-80
1987 Charity - 1408	Retrd.	1994	28.00	111-130
1996 Charles (nativity) - 1588	Open		36.00	40
1994 Cheri - 1574	Retrd.	1999	38.00	42
1989 David - 1528	Open		28.00	35
1996 Debi - 1584	Open		36.00	42
1998 Denise - 1596	Open		39.00	41
1991 Dori (green dress) - 1544	Retrd.	1991	30.00	200-425
1991 Dori (peach dress) - 1544	Open		28.00	36
1987 Eli - 1403W	Retrd.	2000	26.00	34
1985 Emma - 1322	Retrd.	1988	27.00	2045-2110
1992 Faith - 1555	Retrd.	1993	32.00	90-95
1995 Gina - 1579	Open		38.00	45
1987 Ginnie - 1508	Retrd.	1988	22.00	300-450

*Quotes have been rounded up to nearest dollar

YEAR ISSUE	EDITION LIMIT	YEAR RETD.	ISSUE PRICE	*QUOTE U.S.$
1986 Grandma - 1323	Retrd.	1987	30.00	3725-3765
1988 Hannah - 1515	Retrd.	1999	36.00	40-44
1988 Hope - 1519	Retrd.	1998	36.00	60-80
2000 Hosanna - 2301	Open		69.00	69
1987 Jacob - 1407W	Retrd.	1996	26.00	35-85
1998 James - 1599	Open		41.50	42
1997 Janae - 1594	Open		32.50	33
1989 Jeremy - 1523	800	1993	195.00	750-1000
1989 Jerome - 1532	Open		30.00	38
1989 Jessica - 1522	800	1993	195.00	700-1000
1989 Jessica and Jeremy -1522-1523	Retrd.	1993	390.00	2000-2150
1987 Jessie (no base) -1501W	Retrd.	1989	19.00	250-400
1989 Jessie - 1501	Retrd.	2000	30.00	39
1988 John - 1514	Retrd.	1990	30.00	180-217
1989 Joseph (nativity) - 1537	Open		30.00	35
1991 Joy (nativity) - 1548	Suspd.		30.00	40
1994 Justin - 1576	Open		37.00	42
1989 Kacie - 1533	Suspd.		38.00	40-80
1988 Kezia - 1518	Retrd.	1997	36.00	38-45
1998 Krishna - 1593	Retrd.	1999	40.00	44
1998 Leon - 1603	Open		45.00	45
1998 Leroy - 1597	Open		40.00	44
1986 Lil' Emmie 3 1/2" - 1345	Retrd.	1989	14.00	125
1986 Lil' Emmie 4 1/2" - 1344	Retrd.	1989	18.00	150-175
1988 Lisa - 1512	Retrd.	1991	36.00	250-275
1999 Lucinda - 1609	Open		42.00	42
1998 Marcy - 1602	Open		46.00	46
1997 Martin (nativity) - 1595	Open		38.00	40
1989 Mary (nativity) - 1536	Open		30.00	35
1988 Maya - 1520	Retrd.	1993	36.00	40-95
1987 Meg (beige dress) - 1505	Retrd.	1988	21.00	1240
1988 Meg (blue dress, long hair) - 1505	Retrd.	1988	21.00	400-450
1988 Meg (blue dress, short hair) - 1505	Retrd.	1988	21.00	900-950
1992 Melissa - 1556	Retrd.	1995	32.00	70-96
1992 Merci - 1559	Retrd.	1999	36.00	42
1986 Michael & Kim - 1517	Open		36.00	45
1988 Moe & Pokey - 1552	Retrd.	1993	16.00	55-75
1987 Moses - 1506	Retrd.	1992	30.00	90-159
1993 Nathaniel (nativity) - 1569	Open		36.00	40
1991 Nellie - 1546	Retrd.	1993	36.00	110-125
1994 Niambi (nativity) - 1577	Open		34.00	37
1987 Paddy Paw & Lucy - 1553	Suspd.		24.00	60-105
1987 Paddy Paw & Luke - 1551	Suspd.		24.00	45-60
1988 Peanut -1509	Retrd.	1990	16.00	164-175
1989 Preshus (nativity) - 1538	Open		24.00	29
1987 Primas Jones (w/base) - 1377	Retrd.	1988	40.00	800-860
1987 Primas Jones - 1377	Retrd.	1988	40.00	600-850
1986 Prissy (Bear) - 1348	Retrd.	1997	18.00	45-52
1986 Prissy (Moon Pie) - 1347	Open		20.00	39
1986 Prissy with Basket - 1346	Retrd.	1989	16.00	60-150
1986 Prissy with Yarn Hair (6 strands) - 1343	Retrd.	1989	19.00	120-250
1986 Prissy with Yarn Hair (9 strands) - 1343	Retrd.	1989	19.00	450-550
1987 Pud - 1550	Retrd.	1988	11.00	1300-1386
1987 Rachel - 1404W	Retrd.	1998	20.00	30-50
1992 Rakiya - 1561	Open		36.00	40
1992 Rakiya - 1561 (w/white tassel)	Retrd.	N/A	36.00	500
1997 Robert - 1591	Open		38.50	41
1988 Sally -1507	Retrd.	1989	19.00	165
1991 Samantha - 1542	Retrd.	1994	38.00	40-110
1991 Samuel - 1541	Retrd.	1994	32.00	95-176
1989 Sasha - 1531	Open		30.00	39
1986 Selina Jane (6 strands) - 1338	Retrd.	1989	21.95	120-295
1986 Selina Jane (9 strands) - 1338	Retrd.	1989	21.95	525-625
1999 Serenity - 2300	Open		69.00	69
1995 Shani - 1583	Open		33.00	39
1996 Shari - 1586	Open		38.00	46
1998 Sharon - 1604	Open		45.00	45
1998 Sissy - 1598	Open		41.00	41
1986 St. Nicholas-B - 1316	Retrd.	1990	30.00	90-142
1986 St. Nicholas-W - 1315	Retrd.	1990	30.00	142-150
1992 Stephen (Nativity Shepherd) - 1563	Open		36.00	40
1988 Sunshine - 1535	Retrd.	1997	38.00	58-68
1993 Sylvia - 1564	Open		36.00	42
1997 Tangie - 1590	Open		45.00	47
1988 Tansi & Tedi (green socks, collar, cuffs) - 1516	Retrd.	1988	30.00	338
1988 Tansy & Tedi - 1516	Retrd.	1998	N/A	45
1989 Tara - 1527	Open		36.00	44
1989 Tess - 1534	Retrd.	1998	30.00	35-40
1990 Thaliyah - 778	Retrd.	1990	200.00	1900
1991 Thomas - 1549	Retrd.	1998	30.00	38-50
1987 Tiffany - 1511	Open		32.00	40
1994 Tish - 1572	Retrd.	2000	38.00	41
1986 Toby 3 1/2" - 1332	Retrd.	1989	13.00	100-145
1986 Toby 4 1/2" - 1331	Retrd.	1989	16.00	225-231
1985 Tom - 1353	Retrd.	1988	16.00	475-485
1986 Uncle Bud 6"- 1304	Retrd.	1991	19.00	175-225
1986 Uncle Bud 8 1/2"- 1303	Retrd.	1991	27.00	225-325
1992 Valerie - 1560	Open		36.00	41
1995 William - 1580	Open		38.00	41
1987 Willie - 1406W	Retrd.	1996	22.00	68-77
1987 Willie - 1406W (no base)	Retrd.	1987	22.00	450-480
1993 Zack - 1566	Open		34.00	38

All God's Children Ragbabies - M. Root

YEAR ISSUE	EDITION LIMIT	YEAR RETD.	ISSUE PRICE	*QUOTE U.S.$
1995 Honey - 4005	Retrd.	1998	33.00	35
1995 Issie - 4004	Open		33.00	35
1995 Ivy - 4008	Open		33.00	35
1995 Josie - 4003	Retrd.	1997	33.00	60-84
1995 Mitzi - 4000	Retrd.	1999	33.00	35
1995 Muffin - 4001	Retrd.	1999	33.00	35
1995 Puddin - 4006	Open		33.00	35
1995 Punkin - 4007	Open		33.00	35
1995 Sweetie - 4002	Retrd.	1997	33.00	40-85

Angelic Messengers - M. Root

YEAR ISSUE	EDITION LIMIT	YEAR RETD.	ISSUE PRICE	*QUOTE U.S.$
1994 Cieara - 2500	Open		38.00	40
1996 Demetrious - 2503	Open		38.00	40
1994 Mariah - 2501	Open		38.00	40
1994 Mariah - 2501 (scratched in letters)	Retrd.	1996	38.00	100-120
1995 Sabrina - 2502	Open		38.00	40

Christmas - M. Root

YEAR ISSUE	EDITION LIMIT	YEAR RETD.	ISSUE PRICE	*QUOTE U.S.$
1987 1987 Father Christmas-W - 1750	Retrd.	1987	145.00	745-775
1987 1987 Father Christmas-B - 1751	Retrd.	1987	145.00	745-775
1988 1988 Father Christmas-W - 1757	Retrd.	1988	195.00	520-640
1988 1988 Father Christmas-B - 1758	Retrd.	1988	195.00	640-660
1988 Santa Claus-W - 1767	Retrd.	1989	185.00	665-670
1988 Santa Claus-B - 1768	Retrd.	1989	185.00	665-670
1989 1989 Father Christmas-W - 1769	Retrd.	1989	195.00	700-750
1989 1989 Father Christmas-B - 1770	Retrd.	1989	195.00	700-750
1990 1990-91 Father Christmas-W - 1771	Retrd.	1990	195.00	650-730
1990 1990-91 Father Christmas-B - 1772	Retrd.	1990	195.00	295-500
1991 1991-92 Father Christmas-W - 1773	Retrd.	1992	195.00	500-525
1991 1991-92 Father Christmas-B - 1774	Retrd.	1992	195.00	500-730
1992 Father Christmas Bust-W - 1775	Retrd.	1993	145.00	150-380
1992 Father Christmas Bust-B - 1776	Retrd.	1993	145.00	175-410

Count Your Blessings - M. Root

YEAR ISSUE	EDITION LIMIT	YEAR RETD.	ISSUE PRICE	*QUOTE U.S.$
1997 Anna - 2703	Open		24.50	26
1997 Asia - 2705	Open		24.50	26
1997 Baby Rei - 2700	Open		24.50	26
1997 Cece - 2701	Open		24.50	26
1997 Levi - 2702	Open		24.50	26
1997 Taci - 2704	Open		24.50	26
1997 Theo - 2706	Open		24.50	26

Historical Series - M. Root

YEAR ISSUE	EDITION LIMIT	YEAR RETD.	ISSUE PRICE	*QUOTE U.S.$
1994 Augustus Walley (Buffalo Soldier) - 1908	Retrd.	1995	95.00	160-175
1997 Bessie Coleman - 1913	Open		74.00	74
1998 Bessie Coleman, 9 1/4"	Open		71.50	74
1994 Bessie Smith - 1909	Open		70.00	74
1997 Clara Brown - 1912	Open		71.00	74
1992 Dr. Daniel Williams - 1903	Retrd.	1995	70.00	95-168
1998 Fannie Lou Hamer - 1914	Open		74.00	74
1992 Frances Harper - 1905	Retrd.	1998	70.00	74
1991 Frederick Douglass - 1902	Open		70.00	74
1992 George Washington Carver - 1907	Open		70.00	74
1989 Harriet Tubman - 1900	Retrd.	1994	65.00	230-268
1992 Ida B. Wells - 1906	Retrd.	1996	70.00	160-176
1992 Mary Bethune (misspelled) - 1904	Retrd.	1992	70.00	200-260
1992 Mary Bethune - 1904	Open		70.00	74
1995 Mary Mahoney - 1911	Retrd.	2000	65.00	74
1995 Richard Allen - 1910	Open		70.00	74
1990 Sojourner Truth - 1901	Retrd.	1997	65.00	100-120

Inspirational Series - M. Root

YEAR ISSUE	EDITION LIMIT	YEAR RETD.	ISSUE PRICE	*QUOTE U.S.$
1999 Addy 2907	Open		35.00	35
1999 Addy 2907W	Open		35.00	35
1999 Charlotte 2901	Open		35.00	35
1999 Charlotte 2901W	Open		35.00	35
1999 Hallie 2906	Open		35.00	35
1999 Hallie 2906W	Open		35.00	35
1999 Jana 2905	Open		35.00	35
1999 Jana 2905W	Open		35.00	35
1999 Nate 2902	Retrd.	2000	35.00	35
1999 Tina 2900	Open		35.00	35
1999 Tina 2900W	Open		35.00	35
1999 Vanessa 2904	Open		35.00	35
1999 Vanessa 2904W	Open		35.00	35

International Series - M. Root

YEAR ISSUE	EDITION LIMIT	YEAR RETD.	ISSUE PRICE	*QUOTE U.S.$
1987 Juan - 1807	Retrd.	1993	26.00	75-136
1987 Kameko - 1802	Open.		26.00	32
1987 Karl - 1808	Retrd.	1996	26.00	70-86
1987 Katrina - 1803	Retrd.	1993	26.00	148-181
1987 Kelli - 1805	Open		30.00	36
1987 Little Chief - 1804	Open		32.00	40
1993 Minnie - 1568	Open		36.00	40
1987 Pike - 1806	Retrd.	1997	30.00	30-60
1987 Tat - 1801	Retrd.	1996	30.00	30-47

Little Missionary Series - M. Root

YEAR ISSUE	EDITION LIMIT	YEAR RETD.	ISSUE PRICE	*QUOTE U.S.$
1994 Nakia - 3500	Retrd.	1995	40.00	85-100
1994 Nakia - 3500 (Mat.)	Retrd.	1995	40.00	110-125

Sugar And Spice - M. Root

YEAR ISSUE	EDITION LIMIT	YEAR RETD.	ISSUE PRICE	*QUOTE U.S.$
1987 Blessed are the Peacemakers (Eli} -1403	Retrd.	1988	22.00	550
1987 Friend Show Love (Becky) -1402	Retrd.	1988	22.00	550
1987 Friendship Warms the Heart (Jacob) -1407	Retrd.	1988	22.00	550
1987 God is Love (Angel) -1401	Retrd.	1988	22.00	550
1987 Jesus Loves Me (Amy) -1405	Retrd.	1989	22.00	550
1987 Old Friends are Best (Rachel) - 1404	Retrd.	1988	22.00	550
1987 Sharing with Friends (Willie) - 1406	Retrd.	1988	22.00	550

Through His Eyes - M. Root

YEAR ISSUE	EDITION LIMIT	YEAR RETD.	ISSUE PRICE	*QUOTE U.S.$
1993 Simon & Andrew - 1565	Open		45.00	51
1995 Jewel & Judy - 1582	Open		45.00	50

American Artists

Fred Stone Figurines - F. Stone

YEAR ISSUE	EDITION LIMIT	YEAR RETD.	ISSUE PRICE	*QUOTE U.S.$
1986 Arab Mare & Foal	2,500		150.00	225
1985 The Black Stallion, (bronze)	1,500		150.00	175
1985 The Black Stallion, (porcelain)	2,500		125.00	260
1987 Rearing Black Stallion, (bronze)	1,250		175.00	195
1987 Rearing Black Stallion, (porcelain)	3,500		150.00	175
1986 Tranquility	2,500		175.00	275

American Mint LLC

Pewter Locomotives - American Mint

YEAR ISSUE	EDITION LIMIT	YEAR RETD.	ISSUE PRICE	*QUOTE U.S.$
1998 Adler 1835	9,999		49.95	50
1998 Adler 1835 Miniature	9,999		10.00	10
1998 Barbelroth	9,999		49.95	50
1998 Bavaria	9,999		49.95	50
1998 Bayerische D VI - Bn 2 - Berg	9,999		49.95	50
1998 Best Friend	9,999		49.95	50
1998 Caledonian	9,999		49.95	50
1998 Dampflok 38.10 (pr P8)	9,999		49.95	50
1998 Dampfspeicherlokomotive - Oma	9,999		49.95	50
1998 Electrolok E 19 12	9,999		49.95	50
1998 Ernst August	9,999		49.95	50
1998 Krokodil	9,999		49.95	50
1998 Locomotive American Type 4-4-0	9,999		49.95	50
1998 Rocket	9,999		49.95	50
1998 Sächsische IV L. Locomotive	9,999		49.95	50
1998 Schnellzug - Dampflok 03.10	9,999		49.95	50
1998 Spanish Brötli	9,999		49.95	50

Reproductive Badges of America's Most Famous Lawmen - American Mint

YEAR ISSUE	EDITION LIMIT	YEAR RETD.	ISSUE PRICE	*QUOTE U.S.$
1998 Alaska Territory Police	9,999		39.95	40
1998 Apache Police San Carlos	9,999		39.95	40
1998 Arapahoe County Deputy Sheriff	9,999		39.95	40
1998 Big horn County Deputy Sheriff	9,999		29.95	30
1998 Denver & Rio Grande Railroad Deputy	9,999		29.95	30
1998 Deputy Sheriff of Montana	9,999		29.95	30
1998 Deputy Sheriff Ventura County	9,999		29.95	30
1998 Idaho US Deputy Marshall	9,999		39.95	40
1998 Kansas Abilene Deputy Marshall	9,999		29.95	30
1998 Marshal Deadwood	9,999		29.95	30
1998 Marshal Witchita	9,999		29.95	30
1998 Marshall of Dodge City (miniature)	9,999		10.00	10
1998 Marshall of El Passo	9,999		29.95	30
1998 Napoleon Police	9,999		39.95	40
1998 San Antonio Patrolman	9,999		39.95	40
1998 Sheriff Lincoln County	9,999		39.95	40
1998 Sheriff Lincoln County (miniature)	9,999		10.00	10
1998 South Dakota Mobridge Police	9,999		39.95	40
1998 Texas State Ranger	9,999		39.95	40
1998 Tombstone Arizona Sheriff	9,999		19.95	20
1998 US Deputy Marshall	9,999		29.95	30
1998 US Indian Police	9,999		29.95	30
1998 US Marshall (miniature)	9,999		10.00	10
1998 US Marshall - San Carlos	9,999		29.95	30
1998 US Marshall Tombstone	9,999		29.95	30

American Spirit Collection/Hallmark Keepsake Collections

American Spirit Collection/Hallmark Keepsake Collections

YEAR ISSUE	EDITION LIMIT	YEAR RETD.	ISSUE PRICE	*QUOTE U.S.$
1999 Delaware Coin and Figurine Set QMP9406	10,000		16.95	17
1999 Pennsylvania Coin and Figurine Set QMP9407	10,000		16.95	17
1999 New Jersey Coin and Figurine Set QMP9408	10,000		16.95	17
1999 Georgia Coin and Figurine Set QMP9409	10,000		16.95	17
1999 Connecticut Coin and Figurine Set QMP9410	10,000		16.95	17
2000 Massachusetts Coin and Figurine Set QMP9424	10,000		16.95	17
2000 Maryland Coin and Figurine Set QMP9427	19,500		18.95	19
2000 South Carolina Coin and Figurine Set QMP9430	19,500		18.95	19
2000 New Hampshire Coin and Figurine Set QMP9406	19,500		18.95	19
2000 Virginia Coin and Figurine Set QMP9441	19,500		18.95	19

Anchor Bay

Great Ships of the World - Staff

YEAR ISSUE	EDITION LIMIT	YEAR RETD.	ISSUE PRICE	*QUOTE U.S.$
1997 Lightship "Chesapeake"	Open		155.00	155
1997 Lightship "Chesapeake" (special ed.)	4,000	1997	170.00	170-250
1998 Lightship "Columbia"	4,000		154.00	154
1997 Lightship "Huron"	Retrd.	1998	155.00	155
1997 Lightship "Huron" (special ed.)	4,000		170.00	170
1998 Lightship "Portsmouth"	4,000		170.00	170
1997 Motor Yacht "Kim"	Retrd.	1998	139.00	139
1997 Motor Yacht "Kim" (special ed.)	4,000	1998	154.00	154
1998 Purse Seiner "The Tori Dawn"	4,000		154.00	154
1997 Sardine "Lori"	Retrd.	1998	159.00	159
1997 Sardine "Lori" (special ed.)	4,000		174.00	174
1997 Skipjack "Nancy"	Retrd.	1998	151.00	151
1997 Skipjack "Nancy" (special ed.)	4,000	1998	166.00	149-166
1997 Tugboat "Toledo"	Retrd.	1998	131.00	131
1997 Tugboat "Toledo" (special ed.)	4,000	1998	146.00	146
1999 U.S.C.G. 44 ft. Lifeboat	4,000		125.00	125

Anheuser-Busch, Inc.

Anheuser-Busch Collectible Figurines - A. Busch, Inc., unless otherwise noted

YEAR ISSUE	EDITION LIMIT	YEAR RETD.	ISSUE PRICE	*QUOTE U.S.$
1994 Buddies N4575 - M. Urdahl	7,500	1997	65.00	65

336

Collectors' Information Bureau

*Quotes have been rounded up to nearest dollar

YEAR ISSUE	EDITION LIMIT	YEAR RETD.	ISSUE PRICE	*QUOTE U.S.$
1995 Horseplay F1 - P. Radtke	7,500		65.00	65
1996 "Bud-weis-er Frogs" F4	Retrd.	1999	30.00	30
1996 Something Brewing F3	7,500		65.00	65
1997 "Gone Fishing" F5	7,500		65.00	65
1997 "Boy Meets Girl" Budweiser Frogs F7	Open		30.00	30
1998 "Free Ride" Budweiser Frogs F8	Open		35.00	35
1998 "Louie and Frank" Budweiser Lizards F9	Open		35.00	35

The Clydesdale Collection - A. Busch, Inc.

YEAR ISSUE	EDITION LIMIT	YEAR RETD.	ISSUE PRICE	*QUOTE U.S.$
1998 An Apple For King CLYD5	Open		60.00	60
1999 Braiding For Parade CLYD9	Open		75.00	75
1998 Clydesdale Football CLYD3	20,000		85.00	85
1999 Five-Horse Hitch CLYD10	20,000		120.00	120
1998 Full Parade Dress CLYD1	Open		50.00	50
1999 Getting Shod CLYD8	Open		80.00	80
2000 Holiday Scene CLYD15	5,000		235.00	235
1998 Mare & Foal CLYD4	Retrd.	2000	70.00	70
1998 Pals CLYD2	Open		65.00	65
2000 Running Free CLYD12	Open		60.00	60
1999 Scottish Farmer CLYD7	Open		60.00	60
2000 Separated At Birth CLYD11	Open		35.00	35
1999 Washington Scene CLYD6	5,000		230.00	230

ANRI

Club ANRI - Various

YEAR ISSUE	EDITION LIMIT	YEAR RETD.	ISSUE PRICE	*QUOTE U.S.$
1983 Welcome, 4" - J. Ferrandiz	Yr.Iss.	1984	110.00	254-350
1984 My Friend, 4" - J. Ferrandiz	Yr.Iss.	1985	110.00	195-350
1984 Apple of My Eye, 4 1/2" - S. Kay	Yr.Iss.	1985	135.00	163-300
1985 Harvest Time, 4" - J. Ferrandiz	Yr.Iss.	1986	125.00	260-358
1985 Dad's Helper, 4 1/2" - S. Kay	Yr.Iss.	1986	135.00	350-400
1986 Harvest's Helper, 4" - J. Ferrandiz	Yr.Iss.	1987	135.00	195-293
1986 Romantic Notions, 4" - S. Kay	Yr.Iss.	1987	135.00	156-310
1986 Celebration March, 5" - J. Ferrandiz	Yr.Iss.	1987	165.00	290-350
1987 Will You Be Mine, 4" - J. Ferrandiz	Yr.Iss.	1988	135.00	310-350
1987 Make A Wish, 4" - S. Kay	Yr.Iss.	1988	165.00	228-253
1987 A Young Man's Fancy, 4" - S. Kay	Yr.Iss.	1988	135.00	195-260
1988 Forever Yours, 4" - J. Ferrandiz	Yr.Iss.	1989	170.00	189-250
1988 I've Got a Secret, 4" - S. Kay	Yr.Iss.	1989	170.00	189-205
1988 Maestro Mickey, 4 1/2" - Disney Studio	Yr.Iss.	1989	170.00	228-293
1989 Diva Minnie, 4 1/2" - Disney Studio	Yr.Iss.	1990	190.00	228-293
1989 I'll Never Tell, 4" - S. Kay	Yr.Iss.	1990	190.00	156-190
1989 Twenty Years of Love, 4" - J. Ferrandiz	Yr.Iss.	1990	190.00	221
1990 You Are My Sunshine, 4" - J. Ferrandiz	Yr.Iss.	1991	220.00	220-275
1990 A Little Bashful, 4" - S. Kay	Yr.Iss.	1991	220.00	169-220
1990 Dapper Donald, 4" - Disney Studio	Yr.Iss.	1991	199.00	228-260
1991 With All My Heart, 4" - J. Ferrandiz	Yr.Iss.	1992	250.00	250-300
1991 Kiss Me, 4" - S. Kay	Yr.Iss.	1992	250.00	250-300
1991 Daisy Duck, 4 1/2" - Disney Studio	Yr.Iss.	1992	250.00	260

ANRI Club - Various

YEAR ISSUE	EDITION LIMIT	YEAR RETD.	ISSUE PRICE	*QUOTE U.S.$
1992 You Are My All, 4" - J. Ferrandiz	Yr.Iss.	1993	260.00	260
1992 My Present For You, 4" - S. Kay	Yr.Iss.	1993	270.00	270
1992 Gift of Love - S. Kay	Yr.Iss.	1993	Gift	65
1993 Truly Yours, 4" - J. Ferrandiz	Yr.Iss.	1994	290.00	290
1993 Sweet Thoughts, 4" - S. Kay	Yr.Iss.	1994	300.00	300
1993 Just For You - S. Kay	Yr.Iss.	1994	Gift	65
1994 Sweet 'N Shy, 4" - J. Ferrandiz	Yr.Iss.	1994	250.00	250
1994 Snuggle Up, 4" - S. Kay	Yr.Iss.	1994	300.00	300
1994 Dapper 'N Dear, 4" - J. Ferrandiz	Yr.Iss.	1994	250.00	250

ANRI Collectors' Society - Various

YEAR ISSUE	EDITION LIMIT	YEAR RETD.	ISSUE PRICE	*QUOTE U.S.$
1995 On My Own, 4" - S. Kay	Yr.Iss.	1996	175.00	175
1995 Sealed With A Kiss - J. Ferrandiz	Yr.Iss.	1997	275.00	275
1995 ANRI Artists' Tree House - ANRI	Yr.Iss.	1997	695.00	695
1996 On Cloud Nine - J. Ferrandiz	Yr.Iss.	1997	275.00	275
1996 Sweet Tooth - S. Kay	Yr.Iss.	1997	199.50	200
1997 Read Me A Story - S. Kay	Yr.Iss.	1998	395.00	395
1998 Little Leaguer - S. Kay	Yr.Iss.	1999	295.00	295
1999 Bearly Ready, 4"	Yr.Iss.	1999	336.00	336

ANRI Collectors' Society Gold Leaf Level - Various

YEAR ISSUE	EDITION LIMIT	YEAR RETD.	ISSUE PRICE	*QUOTE U.S.$
1996 Helping Mother, 6" - S. Kay	150	1996	595.00	494-595
1996 Little Gardner, 6" - J. Ferrandiz	150	1996	595.00	595
1997 La Moderna, 10" - Flavio	150	1997	815.00	815
1997 Talking To The Animals, 6" - J. Ferrandiz	150	1997	595.00	595
1997 Ballerina, 6" - S. Kay	150	1997	595.00	595
1998 Chimney Sweep Girl - S. Kay	150	1998	675.00	675
1998 The Artist - J. Ferrandiz	150	1998	595.00	595
1998 "Reflective Moment" Clown Blanc - M. Fujita	150	1998	595.00	595

Bernardi Reflections - U. Bernardi

YEAR ISSUE	EDITION LIMIT	YEAR RETD.	ISSUE PRICE	*QUOTE U.S.$
1996 Learning the Skills, 4"	500	1998	275.00	285
1996 Learning the Skills, 6"	250	1998	550.00	670
1994 Master Carver, 4"	500	1998	350.00	375
1994 Master Carver, 6"	250	1995	600.00	670
1995 Planning the Tour, 4"	500	1998	250.00	250
1995 Planning the Tour, 6"	250	1998	300.00	475

Christmas Eve Series - L. Gaither

YEAR ISSUE	EDITION LIMIT	YEAR RETD.	ISSUE PRICE	*QUOTE U.S.$
1998 First Gift of Christmas, Mr. Santa	500	1998	325.00	325
1998 First Gift of Christmas, Mrs. Santa	500	1998	325.00	325

Disney Studios Mickey Mouse Thru The Ages - Disney Studios

YEAR ISSUE	EDITION LIMIT	YEAR RETD.	ISSUE PRICE	*QUOTE U.S.$
1991 The Mad Dog, 4"	1,000	1991	500.00	600-750
1990 Steam Boat Willie, 4"	1,000	1991	295.00	600-900

Disney Woodcarving - Disney Studio

YEAR ISSUE	EDITION LIMIT	YEAR RETD.	ISSUE PRICE	*QUOTE U.S.$
1991 Bell Boy Donald, 4" 656029	Closed	1991	250.00	250
1991 Bell Boy Donald, 6" 656110	500	1991	400.00	450-600
1990 Chef Goofy, 2 1/2" 656222	Closed	1991	125.00	185-215
1990 Chef Goofy, 5" 656227	Closed	1991	265.00	350-520
1989 Daisy, 4" 656021	Closed	1991	190.00	260-295
1990 Donald & Daisy, 6" 656108	500	1991	700.00	850-900
1988 Donald Duck, 1 3/4" 656209	Closed	1990	80.00	170-215
1988 Donald Duck, 2" 656204	Closed	1990	85.00	195-225
1987 Donald Duck, 4" 656004	Closed	1989	150.00	350-375
1988 Donald Duck, 4" 656014	Closed	1990	180.00	350-375
1988 Donald Duck, 6" 656102	500	1988	350.00	525-625
1989 Donald, 4" 656020	Closed	1991	190.00	320-345
1988 Goofy, 1 3/4" 656210	Closed	1990	80.00	190-225
1988 Goofy, 2" 656205	Closed	1990	85.00	190-225
1987 Goofy, 4" 656005	Closed	1989	150.00	315-400
1988 Goofy, 4" 656015	Closed	1990	180.00	310-400
1989 Goofy, 4" 656022	Closed	1991	190.00	315-400
1988 Goofy, 6" 656103	500	1988	380.00	650-700
1989 Mickey & Minnie Set, 6" 656106	500	1991	700.00	1000-1650
1989 Mickey & Minnie, 20" matched set	50	1991	7000.00	7000
1987 Mickey & Minnie, 6" 656101	500	1987	625.00	1100-1950
1988 Mickey Mouse, 1 3/4" 656206	Closed	1990	80.00	315-345
1988 Mickey Mouse, 2" 656201	Closed	1990	85.00	215-315
1990 Mickey Mouse, 2" 656220	Closed	1991	100.00	350-375
1987 Mickey Mouse, 4" 656001	Closed	1989	150.00	225-275
1988 Mickey Mouse, 4" 656011	Closed	1990	180.00	250-275
1990 Mickey Mouse, 4" 656025	Closed	1991	199.00	350-375
1991 Mickey Skating, 2" 656224	Closed	1991	120.00	400-450
1991 Mickey Skating, 4" 656030	Closed	1991	250.00	400-450
1988 Mickey Sorcerer's Apprentice, 2" 656211	Closed	1991	80.00	420-450
1988 Mickey Sorcerer's Apprentice, 4" 656016	Closed	1991	180.00	275-350
1988 Mickey Sorcerer's Apprentice, 6" 656105	500	1991	350.00	725-825
1989 Mickey, 10" 656800	250	1991	700.00	950-1000
1989 Mickey, 20" 656850	50	1991	3500.00	3500
1989 Mickey, 4" 656018	Closed	1991	190.00	350-375
1988 Mini Donald, 1 3/4" 656204	Closed	1991	85.00	250-275
1989 Mini Donald, 2" 656215	Closed	1991	85.00	250-275
1988 Mini Goofy, 1 3/4" 656205	Closed	1991	85.00	220-275
1989 Mini Goofy, 2" 656217	Closed	1991	85.00	220-275
1988 Mini Mickey, 1 3/4" 656201	Closed	1991	85.00	220-275
1989 Mini Mickey, 2" 656213	Closed	1991	85.00	220-275
1988 Mini Minnie, 1 3/4" 656202	Closed	1991	85.00	220-275
1989 Mini Minnie, 2" 656214	Closed	1991	85.00	220-275
1989 Mini Pluto, 2" 656218	Closed	1991	85.00	220-275
1989 Minnie Daisy, 2" 656216	Closed	1991	85.00	220-275
1988 Minnie Mouse, 2" 656202	Closed	1990	85.00	220-275
1990 Minnie Mouse, 2" 656221	Closed	1991	100.00	220-275
1987 Minnie Mouse, 4" 656002	Closed	1989	150.00	300-325
1990 Minnie Mouse, 4" 656026	Closed	1991	199.00	300-325
1988 Minnie Pinocchio, 1 3/4" 656203	Closed	1991	85.00	370-400
1991 Minnie Skating, 2" 656225	Closed	1991	120.00	190-225
1991 Minnie Skating, 4" 656031	Closed	1991	250.00	375-400
1989 Minnie, 10" 656801	250	1991	700.00	900
1989 Minnie, 20" 656851	50	1991	3500.00	3500
1989 Minnie, 4" 656019	Closed	1991	190.00	205-300
1988 Pinocchio, 1 3/4" 656208	Closed	1990	80.00	200-300
1989 Pinocchio, 10" 656802	250	1991	700.00	1000
1988 Pinocchio, 2" 656203	Closed	1990	85.00	85
1989 Pinocchio, 2" 656219	Closed	1991	85.00	100
1989 Pinocchio, 20" 656851	50	1991	3500.00	3500
1987 Pinocchio, 4" 656003 (apple)	Closed	1989	150.00	400-450
1988 Pinocchio, 4" 656013	Closed	1990	180.00	225
1989 Pinocchio, 4" 656024	Closed	1991	190.00	199
1989 Pinocchio, 6" 656107	500	1991	350.00	500-550
1988 Pluto, 1 3/4" 656207	Closed	1990	80.00	125-195
1988 Pluto, 4" 656012	Closed	1990	180.00	350-375
1989 Pluto, 4" 656023	Closed	1991	190.00	300-325
1988 Pluto, 6" 656104	500	1991	350.00	500-550
1990 Sorcerer's Apprentice w/ crystal, 2" 656223	Closed	1991	125.00	870-900
1990 Sorcerer's Apprentice w/ crystal, 4" 656028	Closed	1991	265.00	600-650
1990 Sorcerer's Apprentice w/ crystal, 6" 656109	1,000	1991	475.00	750-775
1990 Sorcerer's Apprentice w/ crystal, 8" 656803	350	1991	790.00	900-950
1990 Sorcerer's Apprentice w/ crystal,16" 656853	100	1991	3500.00	3500

Ferrandiz 1998 Mini Nativity Set - J. Ferrandiz

YEAR ISSUE	EDITION LIMIT	YEAR RETD.	ISSUE PRICE	*QUOTE U.S.$
1998 Nativity Set, 14 figurines, 1 1/2" with stable & comet	Open		720.00	720

Ferrandiz 1999 Mini Nativity Set - J. Ferrandiz

YEAR ISSUE	EDITION LIMIT	YEAR RETD.	ISSUE PRICE	*QUOTE U.S.$
1999 Nativity Set, 6 figurines, 1 1/2"	Open		334.00	334

Ferrandiz Boy and Girl - J. Ferrandiz

YEAR ISSUE	EDITION LIMIT	YEAR RETD.	ISSUE PRICE	*QUOTE U.S.$
1983 Admiration, 6"	2,250	1983	220.00	260-295
1990 Alpine Friend, 3"	1,500	1990	225.00	365
1990 Alpine Friend, 6"	1,500	1990	450.00	610
1990 Alpine Music, 3"	1,500	1990	225.00	225
1990 Alpine Music, 6"	1,500	1990	450.00	580
1989 Baker Boy, 3"	1,500	1989	170.00	170
1989 Baker Boy, 6"	1,500	1989	340.00	340
1978 Basket of Joy, 6"	1,500	1978	140.00	220-350
1983 Bewildered, 6"	2,250	1983	196.00	260-295
1991 Catalonian Boy, 3"	1,500	1993	227.50	228
1991 Catalonian Boy, 6"	1,500	1993	500.00	500
1991 Catalonian Girl, 3"	1,500	1993	227.50	228
1991 Catalonian Girl, 6"	1,500	1993	500.00	500
1976 Cowboy, 6"	1,500	1976	75.00	500-600
1987 Dear Sweetheart, 3"	2,250	1989	130.00	130
1987 Dear Sweetheart, 6"	2,250	1989	250.00	250
1988 Extra, Extra!, 3"	1,500	1988	145.00	145
1988 Extra, Extra!, 6"	1,500	1988	320.00	320-325
1979 First Blossom, 6"	2,250	1979	135.00	200-345
1987 For My Sweetheart, 3"	2,250	1989	130.00	130
1987 For My Sweetheart, 6"	2,250	1989	250.00	250
1984 Friendly Faces, 3"	2,250	1984	93.00	110
1984 Friendly Faces, 6"	2,250	1984	210.00	225-295
1980 Friends, 6"	2,250	1980	200.00	260-300
1986 Golden Sheaves, 3"	2,250	1986	125.00	125
1986 Golden Sheaves, 6"	2,250	1986	245.00	245
1982 Guiding Light, 6"	2,250	1982	225.00	275-350
1979 Happy Strummer, 6"	2,250	1979	160.00	395
1976 Harvest Girl, 6"	1,500	1976	75.00	400-800
1977 Leading the Way, 6"	1,500	1977	100.00	300-375
1992 May I, Too?, 3"	1,000	1993	230.00	230
1992 May I, Too?, 6"	1,000	1993	440.00	440
1980 Melody for Two, 6"	2,250	1980	200.00	260-350
1981 Merry Melody, 6"	2,250	1981	210.00	300-350
1989 Pastry Girl, 3"	1,500	1989	170.00	170
1989 Pastry Girl, 6"	1,500	1989	340.00	340
1978 Peace Pipe, 6"	1,500	1978	140.00	450-520
1985 Peaceful Friends, 3"	2,250	1985	120.00	120
1985 Peaceful Friends, 6"	2,250	1985	250.00	295
1986 Season's Bounty, 3"	2,250	1986	125.00	125
1986 Season's Bounty, 6"	2,250	1986	245.00	245
1988 Sunny Skies, 3"	1,500	1988	145.00	145
1988 Sunny Skies, 6"	1,500	1988	320.00	320-325
1985 Tender Love, 3"	2,250	1985	100.00	125
1985 Tender Love, 6"	2,250	1985	225.00	250
1981 Tiny Sounds, 6"	2,250	1981	210.00	300-350
1982 To Market, 6"	1,500	1982	220.00	295
1977 Tracker, 6"	1,500	1977	100.00	400
1984 Wanderer's Return, 3"	2,250	1984	93.00	135
1984 Wanderer's Return, 6"	2,250	1984	196.00	250
1992 Waste Not, Want Not, 3"	1,000	1993	190.00	200
1992 Waste Not, Want Not, 6"	1,000	1993	430.00	430

Ferrandiz Children of the World - J. Ferrandiz

YEAR ISSUE	EDITION LIMIT	YEAR RETD.	ISSUE PRICE	*QUOTE U.S.$
1999 Island Feast, 4"	Open		270.00	270
1999 Island Welcome, 4"	Open		270.00	270
1998 Kareem	Open		285.00	285
1998 Keisha	Open		285.00	285
1999 Lighting the Way, 4"	Open		270.00	270
1997 Maria, 4"	Open		285.00	285
1997 Miguel, 4"	Open		285.00	285
1999 Tea for Two, 4"	Open		270.00	270

Ferrandiz Circus - J. Ferrandiz

YEAR ISSUE	EDITION LIMIT	YEAR RETD.	ISSUE PRICE	*QUOTE U.S.$
1986 Balancing Ballerina, 2 1/2"	Closed	1988	100.00	100
1986 Balancing Ballerina, 5"	3,000	1988	150.00	150
1986 Ballerina on Horse, 2 1/2"	Closed	1988	125.00	125
1986 Ballerina on Horse, 5"	3,000	1988	200.00	200
1986 Cat on Stool, 2 1/2"	Closed	1988	50.00	50
1986 Cat on Stool, 5"	3,000	1988	110.00	110
1986 Clown on Elephant, 2 1/2"	Closed	1988	125.00	125
1986 Clown on Elephant, 5"	3,000	1988	200.00	200
1986 Clown on Unicycle, 2 1/2"	Closed	1988	80.00	52-80
1986 Clown on Unicycle, 5"	3,000	1988	175.00	175
1987 Clown w/Bunny, 2 1/2"	Closed	1988	80.00	80
1987 Clown w/Bunny, 5"	3,000	1988	175.00	175
1986 Clown w/Sax, 2 1/2"	Closed	1988	80.00	80
1986 Clown w/Sax, 5"	3,000	1988	175.00	175
1987 Clown w/Umbrella, 2 1/2"	Closed	1988	80.00	80
1987 Clown w/Umbrella, 5"	3,000	1988	175.00	175
1986 Lion Tamer, 2 1/2"	Closed	1988	80.00	65-80
1986 Lion Tamer, 5"	3,000	1988	175.00	175
1986 Ring Master, 2 1/2"	Closed	1988	80.00	39-65
1986 Ring Master, 5"	3,000	1988	175.00	175

Ferrandiz Memorial - J. Ferrandiz

YEAR ISSUE	EDITION LIMIT	YEAR RETD.	ISSUE PRICE	*QUOTE U.S.$
1998 Peaceful Love, 3"	Open		225.00	225
1998 Peaceful Love, 6"	Open		450.00	450
1998 Peaceful Love, 10"	Open		950.00	950
1998 Peaceful Love, 20"	250		4500.00	4500
1998 Peaceful Love, 40"	12		11500.00	11500

Ferrandiz Message Collection - J. Ferrandiz

YEAR ISSUE	EDITION LIMIT	YEAR RETD.	ISSUE PRICE	*QUOTE U.S.$
1990 Christmas Carillon, 4 1/2"	2,500	1992	299.00	299
1990 Count Your Blessings, 4 1/2"	5,000	1992	300.00	300
1990 God's Creation, 4 1/2"	5,000	1992	300.00	300
1989 God's Miracle, 4 1/2"	5,000	1991	300.00	300
1989 God's Precious Gift, 4 1/2"	5,000	1991	300.00	300
1989 He Guides Us, 4 1/2"	5,000	1991	300.00	300
1989 He is the Light, 4 1/2"	5,000	1991	300.00	300
1989 He is the Light, 9"	5,000	1991	600.00	600
1989 Heaven Sent, 4 1/2"	5,000	1991	300.00	300
1989 Light From Within, 4 1/2"	5,000	1991	300.00	300
1989 Love Knows No Bounds, 4 1/2"	5,000	1991	300.00	300
1989 Love So Powerful, 4 1/2"	5,000	1991	300.00	300

Ferrandiz Mini Nativity Set - J. Ferrandiz

YEAR ISSUE	EDITION LIMIT	YEAR RETD.	ISSUE PRICE	*QUOTE U.S.$
1985 Baby Camel, 1 1/2"	Closed	1993	45.00	53-85
1985 Camel Guide, 1 1/2"	Closed	1993	45.00	53-85
1985 Camel, 1 1/2"	Closed	1993	45.00	53-85
1988 Devotion, 1 1/2"	Closed	1993	53.00	53-86
1985 Harmony, 1 1/2"	Closed	1993	45.00	53-86
1984 Infant, 1 1/2"	Closed	1993	Set	53-86
1988 Jolly Gift, 1 1/2"	Closed	1992	53.00	53-86
1984 Joseph, 1 1/2"	Closed	1993	Set	53-86
1984 Leading the Way, 1 1/2"	Closed	1993	Set	53-86
1988 Long Journey, 1 1/2"	Closed	1993	53.00	53-86
1984 Mary, 1 1/2"	Closed	1993	45.00	53-87

*Quotes have been rounded up to nearest dollar

FIGURINES

YEAR ISSUE	EDITION LIMIT	YEAR RETD.	ISSUE PRICE	*QUOTE U.S.$
1986 Mini Angel, 1 1/2"	Closed	1993	45.00	53-85
1986 Mini Balthasar, 1 1/2"	Closed	1993	45.00	53-85
1986 Mini Caspar, 1 1/2"	Closed	1993	45.00	53-85
1986 Mini Free Ride, plus Mini Lamb, 1 1/2"	Closed	1993	45.00	53-85
1986 Mini Melchoir, 1 1/2"	Closed	1993	45.00	53-85
1986 Mini Star Struck, 1 1/2"	Closed	1993	45.00	53-85
1986 Mini The Hiker, 1 1/2"	Closed	1993	45.00	53-85
1986 Mini The Stray, 1 1/2"	Closed	1993	45.00	53-85
1986 Mini Weary Traveller, 1 1/2"	Closed	1993	45.00	53-85
1984 Ox Donkey, 1 1/2"	Closed	1993	Set	53-85
1985 Rest, 1 1/2"	Closed	1993	45.00	53-85
1985 Reverence, 1 1/2"	Closed	1993	45.00	53-85
1984 Sheep Kneeling, 1 1/2"	Closed	1993	Set	53-85
1984 Sheep Standing, 1 1/2"	Closed	1993	Set	53-85
1985 Small Talk, 1 1/2"	Closed	1993	45.00	53-85
1988 Sweet Dreams, 1 1/2"	Closed	1993	53.00	53-85
1988 Sweet Inspiration, 1 1/2"	Closed	1992	53.00	53-85
1985 Thanksgiving, 1 1/2"	Closed	1993	45.00	53-85

Ferrandiz Shepherds of the Year - J. Ferrandiz

YEAR ISSUE	EDITION LIMIT	YEAR RETD.	ISSUE PRICE	*QUOTE U.S.$
1982 Companions, 6"	2,250	1982	220.00	195-275
1984 Devotion, 3"	2,250	1984	82.50	125
1984 Devotion, 6"	2,250	1984	180.00	200-250
1979 Drummer Boy, 3"	Yr.Iss.	1979	80.00	117-250
1979 Drummer Boy, 6"	Yr.Iss.	1979	220.00	260-400
1980 Freedom Bound, 3"	Yr.Iss.	1980	90.00	225
1980 Freedom Bound, 6"	Yr.Iss.	1980	225.00	400
1977 Friendship, 3"	Yr.Iss.	1977	53.50	330
1977 Friendship, 6"	Yr.Iss.	1977	110.00	293-350
1983 Good Samaritan, 6"	2,250	1983	220.00	300-320
1981 Jolly Piper, 6"	2,250	1981	225.00	375
1978 Spreading the Word, 3"	Yr.Iss.	1978	115.00	250-275
1978 Spreading the Word, 6"	Yr.Iss.	1978	270.50	500

Ferrandiz Woodcarvings - J. Ferrandiz

YEAR ISSUE	EDITION LIMIT	YEAR RETD.	ISSUE PRICE	*QUOTE U.S.$
1988 Abracadabra, 3"	1,500	1991	145.00	165
1988 Abracadabra, 6"	1,500	1991	315.00	345
1976 Adoration, 12"	Closed	1987	350.00	350
1981 Adoration, 20"	250	1987	3200.00	3200
1976 Adoration, 3"	Closed	1987	45.00	45-143
1976 Adoration, 6"	Closed	1987	100.00	195
1987 Among Friends, 3"	3,000	1990	125.00	151
1987 Among Friends, 6"	3,000	1990	245.00	291
1969 Angel Sugar Heart, 6"	Closed	1973	25.00	2500
1974 Artist, 3"	Closed	1981	30.00	195
1970 Artist, 6"	Closed	1981	25.00	350
1982 Bagpipe, 3"	Closed	1983	80.00	95
1982 Bagpipe, 6"	Closed	1983	175.00	190
1978 Basket of Joy, 3"	Closed	1984	65.00	120
1984 Bird's Eye View, 3"	Closed	1989	88.00	129
1984 Bird's Eye View, 6"	Closed	1989	216.00	700
1987 Black Forest Boy, 3"	3,000	1990	125.00	151
1987 Black Forest Boy, 6"	3,000	1990	250.00	295-301
1987 Black Forest Girl, 3"	3,000	1990	125.00	151
1987 Black Forest Girl, 6"	3,000	1990	250.00	293-300
1977 The Blessing, 3"	Closed	1982	45.00	106-150
1977 The Blessing, 6"	Closed	1982	125.00	250
1988 Bon Appetit, 3"	500	1991	175.00	195
1988 Bon Appetit, 6"	500	1991	395.00	440
1974 The Bouquet, 3"	Closed	1981	35.00	175
1974 The Bouquet, 6"	Closed	1981	75.00	325
1982 Bundle of Joy, 3"	Closed	1990	100.00	300
1982 Bundle of Joy, 6"	Closed	1990	225.00	323
1985 Butterfly Boy, 3"	Closed	1990	95.00	140
1985 Butterfly Boy, 6"	Closed	1990	220.00	322
1976 Catch a Falling Star, 3"	Closed	1983	35.00	150
1976 Catch a Falling Star, 6"	Closed	1983	75.00	250
1986 Celebration March, 11"	750	1987	495.00	495
1986 Celebration March, 20"	200	1987	2700.00	2700
1982 The Champion, 3"	Closed	1985	98.00	110
1982 The Champion, 6"	Closed	1985	225.00	250
1975 Cherub, 2"	Open		32.00	90
1975 Cherub, 4"	Open		32.00	275
1993 Christmas Time, 5"	750	1999	360.00	420
1982 Circus Serenade, 3"	Closed	1988	100.00	78-160
1982 Circus Serenade, 6"	Closed	1988	220.00	220-286
1982 Clarinet, 3"	Closed	1983	80.00	100
1982 Clarinet, 6"	Closed	1983	175.00	200
1982 Companions, 3"	Closed	1984	95.00	115
1975 Courting, 3"	Closed	1982	70.00	235
1975 Courting, 6"	Closed	1982	150.00	450
1984 Cowboy, 10"	Closed	1989	370.00	500
1983 Cowboy, 20"	250	1989	2100.00	2100
1976 Cowboy, 3"	Closed	1989	35.00	140-160
1994 Donkey Driver, 3"	Open		160.00	160
1994 Donkey Driver, 6"	Open		360.00	360
1994 Donkey, 3"	Open		200.00	200
1994 Donkey, 6"	Open		450.00	450
1980 Drummer Boy, 3"	Closed	1988	130.00	200
1980 Drummer Boy, 6"	Closed	1988	300.00	400
1970 Duet, 3"	Closed	1991	36.00	165
1970 Duet, 6"	Closed	1991	Unkn.	355
1986 Edelweiss, 10"	Open		500.00	1080
1986 Edelweiss, 20"	250		3300.00	5420
1983 Edelweiss, 3"	Open		95.00	245
1983 Edelweiss, 6"	Open		220.00	575
1982 Encore, 3"	Closed	1984	100.00	115
1982 Encore, 6"	Closed	1984	225.00	235
1979 First Blossom, 3"	Closed	1985	70.00	78-110
1974 Flight Into Egypt, 3"	Closed	1986	35.00	125
1974 Flight Into Egypt, 6"	Closed	1986	70.00	500
1976 Flower Girl, 3"	Closed	1988	40.00	40
1976 Flower Girl, 6"	Closed	1988	90.00	310
1982 Flute, 3"	Closed	1983	80.00	95
1982 Flute, 6"	Closed	1983	175.00	190-225
1976 Gardener, 3"	Closed	1984	32.00	195
1976 Gardener, 6"	Closed	1985	65.00	275-350
1975 The Gift, 3"	Closed	1982	40.00	195
1975 The Gift, 6"	Closed	1982	70.00	295
1973 Girl in the Egg, 3"	Closed	1988	30.00	127
1973 Girl in the Egg, 6"	Closed	1988	60.00	272
1973 Girl with Dove, 3"	Closed	1984	30.00	110
1973 Girl with Dove, 6"	Closed	1984	50.00	175-200
1976 Girl with Rooster, 3"	Closed	1982	32.50	175
1976 Girl with Rooster, 6"	Closed	1982	60.00	275
1986 God's Little Helper, 2"	3,500	1991	170.00	255
1986 God's Little Helper, 4"	2,000	1991	425.00	550
1975 Going Home, 3"	Closed	1988	40.00	175
1975 Going Home, 6"	Closed	1988	70.00	325
1986 Golden Blossom, 10"	Open		500.00	1060
1986 Golden Blossom, 20"	250		3300.00	5420
1983 Golden Blossom, 3"	Open		95.00	250
1986 Golden Blossom, 40"	50		8300.00	12950
1983 Golden Blossom, 6"	Open		220.00	550
1982 The Good Life, 3"	Closed	1984	100.00	200
1982 The Good Life, 6"	Closed	1984	225.00	295
1969 The Good Sheperd, 3"	Closed	1988	12.50	121
1971 The Good Shepherd, 10"	Closed	1988	90.00	90
1969 The Good Shepherd, 6"	Closed	1988	25.00	237
1974 Greetings, 3"	Closed	1976	30.00	300
1974 Greetings, 6"	Closed	1976	55.00	475
1982 Guiding Light, 3"	Closed	1984	100.00	115-140
1982 Guitar, 3"	Closed	1983	80.00	95
1982 Guitar, 6"	Closed	1983	175.00	190
1979 Happy Strummer, 3"	Closed	1986	75.00	110
1973 Happy Wanderer, 10"	Closed	1985	120.00	500
1974 Happy Wanderer, 3"	Closed	1986	40.00	74-105
1974 Happy Wanderer, 6"	Closed	1986	70.00	200
1982 Harmonica, 3"	Closed	1983	80.00	95
1982 Harmonica, 3"	Closed	1983	80.00	95
1982 Harmonica, 6"	Closed	1983	175.00	190
1978 Harvest Girl, 3"	Closed	1986	75.00	110-140
1975 Have You Heard, 3"	Closed	1987	50.00	112
1979 He's My Brother, 3"	Closed	1984	70.00	130
1979 He's My Brother, 6"	Closed	1984	155.00	240
1987 Heavenly Concert, 2"	3,000	1991	200.00	200
1987 Heavenly Concert, 4"	2,000	1991	450.00	550
1969 Heavenly Gardener, 6"	Closed	1973	25.00	2000
1969 Heavenly Quintet, 6"	Closed	1973	25.00	2000
1969 The Helper, 3"	Closed	1987	12.50	13
1969 The Helper, 5"	Closed	1987	25.00	25
1974 Helping Hands, 3"	Closed	1976	30.00	350
1974 Helping Hands, 6"	Closed	1976	55.00	700
1984 High Hopes, 3"	Closed	1986	81.00	81-100
1984 High Hopes, 6"	Closed	1986	170.00	255
1979 High Riding, 3"	Closed	1984	145.00	200
1979 High Riding, 6"	Closed	1984	340.00	475
1974 The Hiker, 3"	Closed	1993	36.00	36
1974 The Hiker, 6"	Closed	1993	80.00	80
1982 Hitchhiker, 3"	Closed	1986	98.00	85-110
1982 Hitchhiker, 6"	Closed	1986	125.00	230
1993 Holiday Greetings, 3"	1,000	1993	200.00	200
1993 Holiday Greetings, 6"	1,000	1993	450.00	450
1975 Holy Family, 3"	Closed	1988	75.00	250
1975 Holy Family, 6"	Closed	1988	200.00	670
1996 Homeward Bound, 3"	Open		155.00	155
1996 Homeward Bound, 6"	Open		410.00	410
1977 Hurdy Gurdy, 3"	Closed	1988	53.00	150
1977 Hurdy Gurdy, 6"	Closed	1988	112.00	390
1975 Inspector, 3"	Closed	1981	40.00	250
1975 Inspector, 6"	Closed	1981	80.00	395
1988 Jolly Gift, 3"	Closed	1991	129.00	129
1988 Jolly Gift, 6"	Closed	1991	296.00	296
1981 Jolly Piper, 3"	Closed	1984	100.00	120
1977 Journey, 3"	Closed	1983	67.50	143-175
1977 Journey, 6"	Closed	1983	120.00	400
1977 Leading the Way, 3"	Closed	1984	62.50	124
1976 The Letter, 3"	Closed	1988	40.00	40
1976 The Letter, 6"	Closed	1988	90.00	600
1982 Lighting the Way, 3"	Closed	1984	105.00	150
1982 Lighting the Way, 6"	Closed	1984	225.00	295
1974 Little Mother, 3"	Closed	1981	136.00	117-200
1974 Little Mother, 6"	Closed	1981	85.00	285
1989 Little Sheep Found, 3"	Open		120.00	180
1989 Little Sheep Found, 6"	Open		275.00	335
1993 Lots of Gifts, 3"	1,000	1993	200.00	200
1993 Lots of Gifts, 6"	1,000	1993	450.00	450
1975 Love Gift, 3"	Closed	1982	40.00	175
1975 Love Gift, 6"	Closed	1982	70.00	295
1969 Love Letter, 3"	Closed	1982	12.50	150
1969 Love Letter, 6"	Closed	1982	25.00	176-250
1983 Love Message, 3"	Closed	1990	105.00	151
1983 Love Message, 6"	Closed	1990	240.00	366
1969 Love's Messenger, 6"	Closed	1973	25.00	2000
1992 Madonna With Child, 3"	1,000	1994	190.00	190
1992 Madonna With Child, 6"	1,000	1994	370.00	370
1981 Merry Melody, 3"	Closed	1984	90.00	115
1989 Mexican Boy, 3"	1,500	1993	170.00	175
1989 Mexican Boy, 6"	1,500	1993	340.00	350
1989 Mexican Girl, 3"	1,500	1993	170.00	175
1989 Mexican Girl, 6"	1,500	1993	340.00	350
1975 Mother and Child, 3"	Closed	1983	45.00	150
1975 Mother and Child, 6"	Closed	1983	90.00	295
1981 Musical Basket, 3"	Closed	1984	90.00	115
1981 Musical Basket, 6"	Closed	1984	200.00	225
1986 A Musical Ride, 4"	Closed	1990	165.00	237
1986 A Musical Ride, 8"	Closed	1990	395.00	559
1973 Nature Girl, 3"	Closed	1988	30.00	30
1973 Nature Girl, 6"	Closed	1988	60.00	272-338
1987 Nature's Wonder, 3"	3,000	1990	125.00	151
1987 Nature's Wonder, 6"	3,000	1990	245.00	291
1974 New Friends, 3"	Closed	1976	30.00	275
1974 New Friends, 6"	Closed	1976	55.00	550
1977 Night Night, 3"	Closed	1983	45.00	120
1977 Night Night, 6"	Closed	1983	67.50	163-250
1992 Pascal Lamb, 3"	1,000	1993	210.00	210
1992 Pascal Lamb, 6"	1,000	1993	460.00	460
1988 Peace Maker, 3"	1,500	1991	180.00	200
1988 Peace Maker, 6"	1,500	1991	360.00	395
1983 Peace Pipe, 10"	Closed	1986	460.00	495
1984 Peace Pipe, 20"	250	1986	2200.00	3500
1979 Peace Pipe, 3"	Closed	1986	85.00	120-137
1988 Picnic for Two, 3"	500	1991	190.00	210
1988 Picnic for Two, 6"	500	1991	425.00	465
1982 Play It Again, 3"	Closed	1984	100.00	120
1982 Play It Again, 6"	Closed	1984	250.00	255
1977 Poor Boy, 3"	Closed	1986	50.00	110
1977 Poor Boy, 6"	Closed	1986	125.00	215
1977 Proud Mother, 3"	Closed	1988	52.50	150
1977 Proud Mother, 6"	Closed	1988	130.00	350
1971 The Quintet, 10"	Closed	1990	100.00	750
1971 The Quintet, 20"	Closed	1990	Unkn.	4750
1969 The Quintet, 3"	Closed	1990	12.50	156-175
1969 The Quintet, 6"	Closed	1990	25.00	247-395
1970 Reverance, 3"	Closed	1991	30.00	30
1970 Reverance, 6"	Closed	1991	56.00	56
1977 Riding Thru the Rain, 10"	Open		400.00	1190
1985 Riding Thru the Rain, 20"	100	1988	3950.00	3950
1977 Riding Thru the Rain, 5"	Open		145.00	470
1976 Rock A Bye, 3"	Closed	1987	60.00	60
1976 Rock A Bye, 6"	Closed	1987	125.00	125
1974 Romeo, 3"	Closed	1981	50.00	250
1974 Romeo, 6"	Closed	1981	85.00	275-395
1993 Santa and Teddy, 5"	750	1999	360.00	380
1994 Santa Resting on Bag, 5"	750	1999	400.00	400
1987 Serenity, 3"	3,000	1989	125.00	151
1987 Serenity, 6"	3,000	1989	245.00	291
1976 Sharing, 3"	Closed	1983	32.50	130-312
1976 Sharing, 6"	Closed	1983	32.50	225-275
1984 Shipmates, 3"	Closed	1989	81.00	119
1984 Shipmates, 6"	Closed	1989	170.00	248
1975 Small Talk, 3"	Closed	1987	35.00	90
1978 Spreading the Word, 3"	Closed	1989	115.00	117-194
1978 Spreading the Word, 6"	Closed	1989	270.00	495
1980 Spring Arrivals, 10"	Open		435.00	770
1980 Spring Arrivals, 20"	250	1998	2000.00	3360
1973 Spring Arrivals, 3"	Open		30.00	160
1973 Spring Arrivals, 6"	Open		50.00	350
1978 Spring Dance, 12"	Closed	1984	950.00	1750
1978 Spring Dance, 24"	Closed	1984	4750.00	6200
1974 Spring Outing, 3"	Closed	1976	30.00	625
1974 Spring Outing, 6"	Closed	1976	55.00	900
1982 Star Bright, 3"	Closed	1984	110.00	125
1982 Star Bright, 6"	Closed	1984	250.00	295
1982 Star Struck, 10"	Closed	1987	490.00	490
1982 Star Struck, 20"	250	1987	2400.00	2400
1974 Star Struck, 3"	Closed	1987	97.50	98-130
1974 Star Struck, 6"	Closed	1987	210.00	210-254
1981 Stepping Out, 3"	Closed	1984	95.00	110-145
1981 Stepping Out, 6"	Closed	1984	220.00	275
1979 Stitch in Time, 3"	Closed	1984	75.00	125
1979 Stitch in Time, 6"	Closed	1984	150.00	235
1975 Stolen Kiss, 3"	Closed	1987	80.00	80-143
1975 Stolen Kiss, 6"	Closed	1987	150.00	400-449
1969 Sugar Heart, 3"	Closed	1973	12.50	450
1969 Sugar Heart, 6"	Closed	1973	25.00	273-525
1975 Summertime, 3"	Closed	1989	35.00	35
1975 Summertime, 6"	Closed	1989	70.00	258
1982 Surprise, 3"	Closed	1988	100.00	78-150
1982 Surprise, 6"	Closed	1988	225.00	325-423
1973 Sweeper, 3"	Closed	1981	35.00	130
1973 Sweeper, 6"	Closed	1981	75.00	250-425
1981 Sweet Arrival Blue, 3"	Closed	1985	105.00	110
1981 Sweet Arrival Blue, 6"	Closed	1985	225.00	255
1981 Sweet Arrival Pink, 3"	Closed	1985	105.00	110
1981 Sweet Arrival Pink, 6"	Closed	1985	225.00	225
1982 Sweet Dreams, 3"	Closed	1990	100.00	140
1982 Sweet Dreams, 6"	Closed	1990	225.00	330
1989 Sweet Inspiration, 3"	Closed	1991	129.00	129
1989 Sweet Inspiration, 6"	Closed	1991	296.00	296
1982 Sweet Melody, 3"	Closed	1985	80.00	90
1982 Sweet Melody, 6"	Closed	1985	198.00	210
1986 Swiss Boy, 3"	Closed	1993	122.00	162
1989 Swiss Boy, 3"	Closed	1993	180.00	180
1986 Swiss Boy, 6"	Closed	1993	245.00	324
1989 Swiss Boy, 6"	Closed	1993	380.00	380
1986 Swiss Girl, 3"	Closed	1993	122.00	122
1989 Swiss Girl, 3"	Closed	1993	200.00	200
1986 Swiss Girl, 6"	Closed	1993	245.00	304
1989 Swiss Girl, 6"	Closed	1993	470.00	470
1971 Talking to Animals, 20"	Closed	1989	Unkn.	3000
1971 Talking to the Animals, 10"	Closed	1989	90.00	600
1969 Talking to the Animals, 3"	Closed	1989	12.50	155
1969 Talking to the Animals, 6"	Closed	1989	45.00	385
1995 Tender Care, 3" 55710/52	Open		125.00	150
1995 Tender Care, 6" 55700/52	Open		275.00	396
1974 Tender Moments, 3"	Closed	1976	30.00	375

*Quotes have been rounded up to nearest dollar

YEAR ISSUE	EDITION LIMIT	YEAR RETD.	ISSUE PRICE	*QUOTE U.S.$
1974 Tender Moments, 6"	Closed	1976	55.00	575
1981 Tiny Sounds, 3"	Closed	1984	90.00	105
1982 To Market, 3"	Closed	1984	95.00	115-325
1977 Tracker, 3"	Closed	1984	70.00	120-200
1982 Treasure Chest w/6 mini figurines	10,000	1984	300.00	300
1980 Trumpeter, 10"	Closed	1986	500.00	500
1984 Trumpeter, 20"	250	1986	2350.00	3050
1973 Trumpeter, 3"	Closed	1986	69.00	115
1973 Trumpeter, 6"	Closed	1986	120.00	240
1980 Umpapa, 4"	Closed	1984	125.00	140
1982 Violin, 3"	Closed	1983	80.00	95
1982 Violin, 6"	Closed	1983	175.00	195
1976 Wanderlust, 3"	Closed	1983	32.50	125-397
1975 Wanderlust, 6"	Closed	1983	70.00	450
1972 The Weary Traveler, 3"	Closed	1989	24.00	24
1972 The Weary Traveler, 6"	Closed	1989	48.00	48
1988 Winter Memories, 3"	1,500	1991	180.00	195
1988 Winter Memories, 6"	1,500	1991	398.00	440

Gunther Granget Animals - G. Granget

YEAR ISSUE	EDITION LIMIT	YEAR RETD.	ISSUE PRICE	*QUOTE U.S.$
1980 Barn Owl, 6 1/2"	Closed	1984	240.00	240
1974 Barn Owl, 10"	2,500	1984	800.00	800
1974 Barn Owl, 12 1/2"	1,500	1984	1050.00	1050
1974 Barn Owl, 20"	250	1984	3350.00	3350
1980 Black Grouse, 3 3/4"	Closed	1984	265.00	265
1972 Black Grouse, 6"	1,000		1150.00	3510
1972 Black Grouse, 11"	200		5600.00	16660
1998 Dolphin w/ Young	Open		450.00	450
1972 Female Fox w/Young	1,000	1984	1100.00	1100
1972 Female Fox w/Young	200	1984	4300.00	4300
1980 Fox, 3 3/4"	Closed	1984	180.00	180
1980 Golden Eagle, 5 3/4"	Closed	1985	265.00	265
1972 Golden Eagle, 8"	1,000		800.00	2390
1972 Golden Eagle, 15"	250		3600.00	10500
1976 The Green Woodpecker	1,500	1980	393.00	393
1976 The Green Woodpecker	750	1980	1132.00	1132
1976 The Jay	1,500	1980	393.00	393
1976 The Jay	750	1980	1132.00	1132
1998 Lioness	Open		595.00	595
1980 Lynx, 3 3/4"	Closed	1984	240.00	240
1972 Lynx	1,000	1980	600.00	600
1972 Lynx	250	1980	2900.00	2900
1980 Mallard, 4"	Closed	1985	265.00	265
1980 Partridge, 4 1/4"	Closed	1984	195.00	195
1980 Peregrine Falcon, 6"	Closed	1984	240.00	240
1974 Peregrine Falcon, 10"	2,500	1984	700.00	700
1974 Peregrine Falcon, 12 1/2"	1,500	1984	1000.00	1000
1974 Peregrine Falcon, 20"	250	1984	3350.00	3350
1980 Pheasant (Ringed neck), 6 1/2"	Closed	1985	280.00	280
1972 Pheasant (Ringed neck), 9"	1,000		800.00	2620
1972 Pheasant (Ringed neck), 17"	250		3700.00	10930
1980 Roadrunner, 6"	Closed	1984	300.00	300
1980 Roadrunner	1,000	1980	1750.00	1750
1980 Roadrunner	250	1980	6500.00	6500
1980 Rooster, 7"	Closed	1984	300.00	300
1974 Rooster, 11"	1,000		805.00	2800
1974 Rooster, 22"	250		3800.00	10500
1980 Shoveler, 4"	Closed	1984	240.00	240
1980 Shoveler	1,000	1980	1600.00	1600
1980 Shoveler	200	1980	8000.00	8000
1972 Wild Sow w/Young	1,000	1984	950.00	950
1972 Wild Sow w/Young	200	1984	4000.00	4000

Gunther Granget Animals Temporarily Withdrawn - G. Granget

YEAR ISSUE	EDITION LIMIT	YEAR RETD.	ISSUE PRICE	*QUOTE U.S.$
1972 Mallard, 5"	1,000		700.00	2200
1972 Mallard, 10"	250		3600.00	10800
1972 Partridges, 6"	1,000		800.00	2680
1972 Partridges, 13"	200		4200.00	13100

Ivano Colletion - Ivano

YEAR ISSUE	EDITION LIMIT	YEAR RETD.	ISSUE PRICE	*QUOTE U.S.$
1999 Spring, 9"	2,000		266.00	266
1999 Summer, 9"	2,000		266.00	266
1999 Autumn, 9"	2,000		266.00	266
1999 Winter, 9"	2,000		266.00	266
2000 Mountain Climber, 9"	2,000		300.00	300
2000 Fisherman, 9"	2,000		266.00	266

Limited Edition Couples - J. Ferrandiz

YEAR ISSUE	EDITION LIMIT	YEAR RETD.	ISSUE PRICE	*QUOTE U.S.$
1985 First Kiss, 8"	750	1985	590.00	950
1987 Heart to Heart, 8"	750	1991	590.00	850
1988 A Loving Hand, 8"	750	1991	795.00	850
1986 My Heart Is Yours, 8"	750	1991	590.00	850
1985 Springtime Stroll, 8"	750	1990	590.00	950
1986 A Tender Touch, 8"	750	1990	590.00	850

Lyndon Gaither Christmas Eve Series - L. Gaither

YEAR ISSUE	EDITION LIMIT	YEAR RETD.	ISSUE PRICE	*QUOTE U.S.$
1995 Hitching Prancer, 3 1/2" figurine & ornament	500	1998	499.00	525
1996 Getting Ready, 3 1/2" figurine & ornament	500	1998	499.00	525
1997 Time To go, 5" figurine & ornament	500	1998	595.00	595

Lyndon Gaither Religious - L. Gaither

YEAR ISSUE	EDITION LIMIT	YEAR RETD.	ISSUE PRICE	*QUOTE U.S.$
1998 Holy Family Plaque	Open		995.00	995
1998 Moses And The Ten Commandments	Closed	1999	995.00	995

Nativity "Block" Scene - R. Kostner

YEAR ISSUE	EDITION LIMIT	YEAR RETD.	ISSUE PRICE	*QUOTE U.S.$
2000 Holy Family w/Ox & Donkey, 6 1/2"	Open		990.00	990
1999 Millennium Triptych	500	1999	1390.00	1390
2000 Shepherd Group, 6 1/2"	Open		958.00	958
2000 The Three Wise Men, 6 1/2"	Open		998.00	998

Sarah Kay Figurines - S. Kay

YEAR ISSUE	EDITION LIMIT	YEAR RETD.	ISSUE PRICE	*QUOTE U.S.$
1985 Afternoon Tea, 11"	750	1993	650.00	770
1985 Afternoon Tea, 20"	100	1993	3100.00	3500
1985 Afternoon Tea, 4"	4,000	1990	95.00	185
1985 Afternoon Tea, 6"	4,000	1990	195.00	280-442
1987 All Aboard, 1 1/2"	7,500	1990	50.00	90
1987 All Aboard, 4"	4,000	1990	130.00	185-195
1987 All Aboard, 6"	2,000	1990	265.00	355
1987 All Mine, 1 1/2"	7,500	1988	49.50	95
1987 All Mine, 4"	4,000	1988	130.00	225
1987 All Mine, 6"	4,000	1988	245.00	465
1986 Always By My Side, 1 1/2"	7,500	1988	45.00	65-95
1986 Always By My Side, 4"	4,000	1988	95.00	195
1986 Always By My Side, 6"	4,000	1988	195.00	375
1999 Armfuls of Love, 4"	1,000		320.00	320
1999 Armfuls of Love, 6"	1,000		568.00	568
1990 Batter Up, 1 1/2"	3,750	1991	90.00	95
1990 Batter Up, 4"	2,000		220.00	280
1990 Batter Up, 6"	2,000		440.00	540
1983 Bedtime, 1 1/2"	7,500	1984	45.00	110
1983 Bedtime, 4"	Closed	1987	95.00	230-299
1983 Bedtime, 6"	4,000	1987	195.00	435
2000 Bridesmaid, 11"	750		840.00	840
2000 Bridesmaid, 20"	250		3900.00	3900
2000 Bridesmaid, 4"	1,000		270.00	270
2000 Bridesmaid, 6"	1,000		460.00	460
1986 Bunny Hug, 1 1/2"	7,500	1989	45.00	85
1986 Bunny Hug, 4"	4,000	1989	95.00	172
1986 Bunny Hug, 6"	2,000	1989	210.00	395-514
1989 Cherish, 1 1/2"	Closed	1991	80.00	95
1989 Cherish, 4"	2,000	1994	199.00	290
1989 Cherish, 6"	2,000	1994	398.00	560-748
1993 Christmas Basket, 4"	1,000		310.00	298
1993 Christmas Basket, 6"	1,000		600.00	590
1994 Clowning Around, 4"	1,000		300.00	300
1994 Clowning Around, 6"	1,000		550.00	600
1998 Coffee Break, 4"	2,000		295.00	295
1998 Coffee Break, 6"	1,000		575.00	575
1987 Cuddles, 1 1/2"	7,500	1988	49.50	95
1987 Cuddles, 4"	4,000	1988	130.00	225
1987 Cuddles, 6"	4,000	1988	245.00	465
1984 Daydreaming, 1 1/2"	7,500	1984	45.00	125
1984 Daydreaming, 4"	4,000	1988	95.00	235
1984 Daydreaming, 6"	4,000	1988	195.00	445
1991 Dress Up, 1 1/2"	3,750	1991	110.00	110
1991 Dress Up, 4"	2,000	1993	270.00	270
1991 Dress Up, 6"	2,000	1993	550.00	570
1983 Feeding the Chickens, 1 1/2"	7,500	1984	45.00	110
1983 Feeding the Chickens, 4"	Closed	1987	95.00	250
1983 Feeding the Chickens, 6"	4,000	1987	195.00	450
1991 Figure Eight, 1 1/2"	3,750	1991	110.00	110
1991 Figure Eight, 4"	2,000	1996	270.00	375
1991 Figure Eight, 6"	2,000	1996	550.00	740
1984 Finding Our Way, 1 1/2"	7,500	1984	45.00	135
1984 Finding Our Way, 4"	4,000	1988	95.00	245
1984 Finding Our Way, 6"	2,000	1984	210.00	449-650
1986 Finishing Touch, 1 1/2"	7,500	1989	45.00	85
1986 Finishing Touch, 4"	4,000	1989	95.00	172
1986 Finishing Touch, 6"	4,000	1989	195.00	312
1989 First School Day, 1 1/2"	Closed	1991	85.00	95
1989 First School Day, 4"	2,000	1993	290.00	350
1989 First School Day, 6"	2,000	1993	550.00	650
1989 Fisherboy, 1 1/2"	Closed	1991	85.00	95
1989 Fisherboy, 4"	2,000	1994	220.00	250
1989 Fisherboy, 6"	1,000	1994	440.00	475
1984 Flowers for You, 1 1/2"	7,500	1984	45.00	125
1984 Flowers for You, 4"	4,000	1988	95.00	250
1984 Flowers for You, 6"	4,000	1988	195.00	450
1991 Fore!!, 1 1/2"	3,750	1991	110.00	115
1991 Fore!!, 4"	2,000		270.00	325
1991 Fore!!, 6"	2,000		550.00	590
1983 From the Garden, 1 1/2"	7,500	1984	45.00	110
1983 From the Garden, 4"	Closed	1987	95.00	195-235
1983 From the Garden, 6"	4,000	1987	195.00	450
1989 Garden Party, 1 1/2"	Closed	1991	85.00	95
1989 Garden Party, 4"	2,000	1993	220.00	240
1989 Garden Party, 6"	2,000	1993	440.00	475
1985 Giddyap!, 4"	4,000	1990	95.00	250
1985 Giddyap!, 6"	4,000	1990	195.00	325
1988 Ginger Snap, 1 1/2"	Closed	1990	70.00	90
1988 Ginger Snap, 4"	2,000	1990	150.00	185
1988 Ginger Snap, 6"	1,000	1990	300.00	355
1986 Good As New, 1 1/2"	7,500	1991	45.00	90
1986 Good As New, 4"	4,000	1994	95.00	290
1986 Good As New, 6"	4,000	1994	195.00	500
1998 Having Fun, 4"	2,000		295.00	295
1998 Having Fun, 6"	1,000		575.00	575
2000 Hello, 11"	750		1020.00	1020
2000 Hello, 20"	250		4180.00	4180
2000 Hello, 4"	1,000		280.00	280
2000 Hello, 6"	1,000		520.00	520
1983 Helping Mother, 1 1/2"	7,500	1983	45.00	110
1983 Helping Mother, 4"	Closed	1983	95.00	300
1983 Helping Mother, 6"	2,000	1983	210.00	495
1988 Hidden Treasures, 1 1/2"	Closed	1990	70.00	90
1988 Hidden Treasures, 4"	2,000	1990	150.00	185
1988 Hidden Treasures, 6"	1,000	1990	300.00	355
1990 Holiday Cheer, 1 1/2"	3,750	1991	90.00	95
1990 Holiday Cheer, 4"	2,000		225.00	365
1990 Holiday Cheer, 6"	1,000		450.00	720
1989 House Call, 1 1/2"	Closed	1991	85.00	95
1989 House Call, 4"	2,000	1991	190.00	195
1989 House Call, 6"	2,000	1991	390.00	390
1993 Innocence, 4"	1,000		345.00	315
1993 Innocence, 6"	1,000		630.00	630
1994 Jolly Pair, 4"	1,000	1996	350.00	350
1994 Jolly Pair, 6"	1,000	1996	650.00	670
1993 Joy to the World, 4"	1,000		310.00	310
1993 Joy to the World, 6"	1,000		600.00	610
1987 Let's Play, 1 1/2"	7,500	1990	49.50	90
1987 Let's Play, 4"	4,000	1990	130.00	185
1987 Let's Play, 6"	2,000	1990	265.00	355
1994 Little Chimney Sweep, 4"	1,000	1996	300.00	350
1994 Little Chimney Sweep, 6"	1,000	1996	600.00	680
1987 Little Nanny, 1 1/2"	7,500	1990	49.50	90
1987 Little Nanny, 4"	4,000	1990	150.00	200
1987 Little Nanny, 6"	4,000	1990	295.00	400
2000 Looking For The Future, 11"	750		960.00	960
2000 Looking For The Future, 20"	250		4700.00	4700
2000 Looking For The Future, 4"	2,000		300.00	300
2000 Looking For The Future, 6"	2,000		580.00	580
1987 A Loving Spoonful, 1 1/2"	7,500	1991	49.50	90
1987 A Loving Spoonful, 4"	4,000	1994	150.00	234-290
1987 A Loving Spoonful, 6"	4,000	1994	295.00	550
1992 Merry Christmas, 1 1/2"	3,750	1994	110.00	115
1992 Merry Christmas, 4"	1,000	1994	350.00	350
1992 Merry Christmas, 6"	1,000	1994	580.00	580
1983 Morning Chores, 1 1/2"	7,500	1983	45.00	110
1983 Morning Chores, 4"	Closed	1983	95.00	208-300
1983 Morning Chores, 6"	2,000	1983	210.00	550
1993 Mr. Santa, 4"	750	1999	375.00	390
1993 Mr. Santa, 6"	750	1999	695.00	745
1993 Mrs. Santa, 4"	750	1999	375.00	390
1993 Mrs. Santa, 6"	750	1999	695.00	745
1993 My Favorite Doll, 4"	1,000		315.00	354
1993 My Favorite Doll, 6"	1,000		600.00	670
1988 My Little Brother, 1 1/2"	Closed	1991	70.00	90
1988 My Little Brother, 4"	2,000	1991	195.00	225
1988 My Little Brother, 6"	2,000	1991	375.00	450-598
1988 New Home, 1 1/2"	Closed	1991	70.00	90
1988 New Home, 4"	2,000	1991	185.00	208-240
1988 New Home, 6"	2,000	1991	365.00	500
1985 Nightie Night, 4"	4,000	1990	95.00	163-185
1985 Nightie Night, 6"	4,000	1990	195.00	325-436
1984 Off to School, 1 1/2"	7,500	1984	45.00	125
1984 Off to School, 11"	750		590.00	960
1984 Off to School, 20"	100	1998	2900.00	4200
1984 Off to School, 4"	4,000		95.00	270
1984 Off to School, 6"	4,000		195.00	510
1986 Our Puppy, 1 1/2"	7,500	1990	45.00	90
1986 Our Puppy, 4"	4,000	1990	95.00	185
1986 Our Puppy, 6"	2,000	1990	210.00	355-462
1988 Penny for Your Thoughts, 1 1/2"	Closed	1991	70.00	90
1988 Penny for Your Thoughts, 4"	2,000	1998	185.00	315
1988 Penny for Your Thoughts, 6"	2,000		365.00	635
1983 Playtime, 1 1/2"	7,500	1984	45.00	52-110
1983 Playtime, 4"	Closed	1987	95.00	250
1983 Playtime, 6"	4,000	1987	195.00	495
1999 Pretty as a Posey, 4"	1,000		306.00	306
1999 Pretty as a Posey, 6"	1,000		544.00	544
1988 Purrfect Day, 4"	2,000	1991	184.00	195-215
1988 Purrfect Day, 1 1/2"	Closed	1991	70.00	90
1988 Purrfect Day, 6"	2,000	1991	265.00	455
1992 Raindrops, 1 1/2"	3,750	1994	110.00	110
1992 Raindrops, 4"	1,000	1994	350.00	350
1992 Raindrops, 6"	1,000	1994	640.00	640
1988 School Marm, 6"	500	1988	398.00	398
1991 Season's Joy, 1 1/2"	3,750	1991	110.00	115
1991 Season's Joy, 4"	2,000		270.00	410
1991 Season's Joy, 6"	1,000		550.00	784
1990 Seasons Greetings, 1 1/2"	3,750	1991	90.00	95
1990 Seasons Greetings, 4"	2,000		225.00	335
1990 Seasons Greetings, 6"	1,000		450.00	650
1990 Shootin' Hoops, 4"	2,000	1993	220.00	250
1990 Shootin' Hoops, 6"	2,000	1993	440.00	450
1990 Shootin' Hoops,1 1/2"	3,750	1991	90.00	95
1985 A Special Day, 4"	4,000	1990	95.00	195
1985 A Special Day, 6"	4,000	1990	195.00	325
1984 Special Delivery, 1 1/2"	7,500	1984	45.00	125
1984 Special Delivery, 4"	4,000	1989	95.00	187
1984 Special Delivery, 6"	4,000	1989	195.00	312-350
1990 Spring Fever, 1 1/2"	3,750	1991	90.00	95
1990 Spring Fever, 4"	2,000		225.00	365
1990 Spring Fever, 6"	2,000		450.00	735
1983 Sweeping, 1 1/2"	7,500	1984	45.00	52-110
1983 Sweeping, 4"	Closed	1987	95.00	176-230
1983 Sweeping, 6"	4,000	1987	195.00	435
1986 Sweet Treat, 1 1/2"	7,500	1989	45.00	85
1986 Sweet Treat, 4"	4,000	1989	95.00	156-172
1986 Sweet Treat, 6"	4,000	1989	195.00	312
1984 Tag Along, 1 1/2"	7,500	1984	45.00	130
1984 Tag Along, 4"	4,000	1988	95.00	225
1984 Tag Along, 6"	4,000	1988	195.00	290
1989 Take Me Along, 1 1/2"	Closed	1991	85.00	95
1992 Take Me Along, 11"	400	1998	950.00	1050
1992 Take Me Along, 20"	100	1998	4550.00	4780
1989 Take Me Along, 4"	2,000	1998	220.00	315
1989 Take Me Along, 6"	1,000	1998	440.00	640
1993 Ten Roses For You, 4"	1,000		290.00	295
1993 Ten Roses For You, 6"	1,000		525.00	590
1990 Tender Loving Care, 1 1/2"	3,750	1991	90.00	95
1990 Tender Loving Care, 4"	2,000	1993	220.00	240
1990 Tender Loving Care, 6"	2,000	1993	440.00	475
1985 Tis the Season, 4"	4,000	1993	95.00	250

*Quotes have been rounded up to nearest dollar

YEAR ISSUE	EDITION LIMIT	YEAR RETD.	ISSUE PRICE	*QUOTE U.S.$
1985 Tis the Season, 6"	2,000	1985	210.00	425-553
1986 To Love And To Cherish, 1 1/2"	7,500	1989	45.00	85
1986 To Love and To Cherish, 11"	1,000	1989	Unkn.	350-667
1986 To Love and To Cherish, 20"	200	1989	Unkn.	3600
1986 To Love And To Cherish, 4"	4,000	1989	95.00	172
1986 To Love And To Cherish, 6"	4,000	1989	195.00	312
1991 Touch Down, 1 1/2"	3,750	1994	110.00	110
1991 Touch Down, 4"	2,000	1994	270.00	310
1991 Touch Down, 6"	2,000	1994	550.00	550
1992 Tulips For Mother, 4"	1,000		310.00	325
1992 Tulips For Mother, 6"	1,000		590.00	620
1983 Waiting for Mother, 1 1/2"	7,500	1984	45.00	65-110
1983 Waiting for Mother, 11"	750	1987	495.00	795
1983 Waiting for Mother, 4"	Closed	1987	95.00	208-299
1983 Waiting for Mother, 6"	4,000	1987	195.00	445
1984 Wake Up Kiss, 1 1/2"	7,500	1984	45.00	550
1984 Wake Up Kiss, 4"	4,000	1993	95.00	195
1983 Wake Up Kiss, 6"	2,000	1984	210.00	550
1984 Watchful Eye, 4"	4,000	1988	95.00	235
1984 Watchful Eye, 6"	4,000	1988	195.00	445
1984 Watchful Eye,1 1/2"	7,500	1984	45.00	125
1992 Winter Cheer, 4"	2,000	1993	300.00	300
1992 Winter Cheer, 6"	1,000	1993	580.00	580
1991 Winter Surprise, 1 1/2"	3,750	1994	110.00	110
1991 Winter Surprise, 4"	2,000	1994	270.00	290
1991 Winter Surprise, 6"	1,000	1994	550.00	570
1986 With This Ring, 1 1/2"	7,500	1989	45.00	85
1986 With This Ring, 11"	1,000	1989	Unkn.	330-668
1986 With This Ring, 20"	200	1989	Unkn.	3600
1986 With This Ring, 4"	4,000	1989	95.00	172
1986 With This Ring, 6"	4,000	1989	195.00	312
1989 Yearly Check-Up, 1 1/2"	Closed	1991	85.00	95
1989 Yearly Check-Up, 4"	2,000	1991	190.00	195
1989 Yearly Check-Up, 6"	2,000	1991	390.00	390
1985 Yuletide Cheer, 4"	4,000	1993	95.00	250
1985 Yuletide Cheer, 6"	Closed	1985	210.00	435-572

Sarah Kay Figurines Temporarily Withdrawn- S. Kay

YEAR ISSUE	EDITION LIMIT	YEAR RETD.	ISSUE PRICE	*QUOTE U.S.$
1994 Bubbles & Bows, 4"	1,000		300.00	310
1994 Bubbles & Bows, 6"	1,000		600.00	620
1994 Christmas Wonder, 4"	1,000		370.00	420
1994 Christmas Wonder, 6"	1,000		700.00	770
1992 Free Skating, 4"	1,000		310.00	325
1992 Free Skating, 6"	1,000		590.00	620

Sarah Kay Koalas - S. Kay

YEAR ISSUE	EDITION LIMIT	YEAR RETD.	ISSUE PRICE	*QUOTE U.S.$
1986 Green Thumb, 3"	3,500	1986	81.00	81
1985 Green Thumb, 5"	2,000	1986	165.00	165
1985 Honey Bunch, 3"	3,500	1986	75.00	75
1985 Honey Bunch, 5"	2,000	1986	165.00	165
1985 A Little Bird Told Me, 3"	3,500	1986	75.00	75
1985 A Little Bird Told Me, 5"	2,000	1986	165.00	165
1985 Party Time, 3"	3,500	1986	75.00	75
1985 Party Time, 5"	2,000	1986	165.00	165
1986 Scout About, 3"	3,500	1986	81.00	81
1986 Scout About, 5"	2,000	1986	178.00	178
1986 A Stitch with Love, 3"	3,500	1986	81.00	81
1986 A Stitch with Love, 5"	2,000	1986	178.00	178

Sarah Kay Mini Santas - S. Kay

YEAR ISSUE	EDITION LIMIT	YEAR RETD.	ISSUE PRICE	*QUOTE U.S.$
1992 Father Christmas, 1 1/2"	2,500	1993	110.00	110
1992 A Friend to All, 1 1/2"	2,500	1993	110.00	110
1991 Jolly Santa, 1 1/2"	2,500	1993	110.00	110
1991 Jolly St. Nick, 1 1/2"	2,500	1993	110.00	110
1991 Kris Kringle, 1 1/2"	2,500	1993	110.00	110
1991 Sarah Kay Santa, 1 1/2"	2,500	1993	110.00	110

Sarah Kay Santas - S. Kay

YEAR ISSUE	EDITION LIMIT	YEAR RETD.	ISSUE PRICE	*QUOTE U.S.$
1995 Checking It Twice, 4" 57709	500	1999	250.00	305
1995 Checking It Twice, 6" 57710	250	1998	395.00	580
1992 Father Christmas, 4"	750	1994	350.00	350
1992 Father Christmas, 6"	750	1994	590.00	590
1991 A Friend To All, 4"	750	1994	300.00	300
1991 A Friend To All, 6"	750	1994	590.00	590
1989 Jolly Santa, 12"	150	1990	1300.00	1300
1988 Jolly Santa, 4"	750	1989	235.00	300-350
1988 Jolly Santa, 6"	750	1989	480.00	600
1988 Jolly St. Nick, 4"	750	1989	199.00	300-550
1988 Jolly St. Nick, 6"	750	1989	398.00	850
1999 Joyful Giving, 4"	500	1999	414.00	414
1999 Joyful Giving, 6"	250	1999	708.00	708
1990 Kris Kringle Santa, 4"	750	1990	275.00	350
1990 Kris Kringle Santa, 6"	750	1990	550.00	550
1997 Santa's Helper, 4"	500	1999	350.00	350
1997 Santa's Helper, 6"	250	1999	630.00	630
1989 Santa, 4"	750	1990	235.00	350
1989 Santa, 6"	750	1990	480.00	480-520
1998 Up on the Rooftop, 4"	500	1999	295.00	295
1998 Up on the Rooftop, 6"	250	1999	695.00	695
1996 Workshop Santa, 4"	500	1999	295.00	320
1996 Workshop Santa, 6"	250	1999	495.00	610

Sarah Kay School Days - S. Kay

YEAR ISSUE	EDITION LIMIT	YEAR RETD.	ISSUE PRICE	*QUOTE U.S.$
1996 Head of the Class, 4"	500	1999	295.00	360
1996 Head of the Class, 6"	250	1999	495.00	610
1997 Homework, 4"	500	1999	315.00	315
1997 Homework, 6"	250	1999	520.00	520
1995 I Know, I Know, 4" 57701	500	1999	250.00	310
1995 I Know, I Know, 6" 57702	250	1998	395.00	565
1998 Straight A's, 4"	500		375.00	375
1998 Straight A's, 6"	250		650.00	650

Sarah Kay Tribute To Mother - S. Kay

YEAR ISSUE	EDITION LIMIT	YEAR RETD.	ISSUE PRICE	*QUOTE U.S.$
1998 Don't Forget, 7"	250	1999	650.00	650
1995 Mom's Joy, 5" 57902	250	1995	297.00	325
1997 Storytime, 5 1/2"	250	1998	650.00	650
1996 Sweets for My Sweet, 6"	250	1999	399.00	520
1999 Letting Go	250		554.00	554

Sarah Kay's First Christmas - S. Kay

YEAR ISSUE	EDITION LIMIT	YEAR RETD.	ISSUE PRICE	*QUOTE U.S.$
1994 Sarah Kay's First Christmas, 4"	500	1998	350.00	440
1994 Sarah Kay's First Christmas, 6"	250	1995	600.00	804
1995 First Christmas Stocking, 4" 57553	500	1999	250.00	335
1995 First Christmas Stocking, 6" 57554	250	1999	395.00	450
1996 All I Want For Christmas, 4" 57555	500	1998	325.00	360
1996 All I Want For Christmas, 6" 57556	250	1999	550.00	700
1997 Christmas Puppy, 4"	500	1999	375.00	375
1997 Christmas Puppy, 6"	250	1999	625.00	630

Armani

G. Armani Society Members Only Figurine - G. Armani

YEAR ISSUE	EDITION LIMIT	YEAR RETD.	ISSUE PRICE	*QUOTE U.S.$
1990 My Fine Feathered Friends (Bonus)122S	Closed	1990	175.00	163-560
1990 Awakening 591C	Closed	1991	137.50	975-1500
1991 Peace & Harmony (Bonus) 824C	7,500	1991	300.00	600-650
1991 Ruffles 745E	Closed	1991	139.00	139-585
1992 Ascent 866C	Closed	1992	195.00	195-650
1992 Julie (Bonus) 293P	Closed	1992	90.00	192-234
1992 Juliette (Bonus) 294P	Closed	1992	90.00	224-260
1993 Venus 881E	Closed	1993	225.00	345-390
1993 Lady Rose (Bonus) 197C	Closed	1993	125.00	125-600
1994 Harlequin 1994 Fifth Anniversary 490C	Closed	1994	300.00	300-625
1994 Flora 212C	Closed	1994	225.00	450-625
1994 Aquarius (Bonus) 248C	Closed	1994	125.00	241-500
1995 Melody 656C	Closed	1995	250.00	475
1995 Scarlette (Bonus) 698C	Closed	1995	200.00	450-500
1996 Allegra 345C	Closed	1996	250.00	400
1996 Arianna (Bonus) 400C	Closed	1996	125.00	125-225
1997 It's Mine (Bonus) 136C	Closed	1997	200.00	160-200
1997 Sabrina 110C	Closed	1997	275.00	250-395
1998 Beth (Bonus) 519C	Closed	1998	115.00	92-115
1998 Lucia 755C	Closed	1998	325.00	260-325
1999 Desiree 303C	Closed	1999	300.00	300-395
2000 Camille 1300C	Yr.Iss.		300.00	300

G. Armani Society Member Gift - G. Armani

YEAR ISSUE	EDITION LIMIT	YEAR RETD.	ISSUE PRICE	*QUOTE U.S.$
1993 Petite Maternity 939F	Closed	1993	Gift	60-98
1994 Lady w/Dogs 245F	Closed	1994	Gift	40-100
1995 Lady w/Doves mini 546F	Closed	1995	Gift	44-90
1996 Perfect Match 358F	Closed	1996	Gift	80-100
1997 Quiet Please 446F	Closed	1997	Gift	65-85
1998 Puppy Love 114F	Closed	1998	Gift	65-75
1999 Chantal	Closed	1999	Gift	75
2000 Starr	Yr.Iss.		Gift	N/A

G. Armani Society Sponsored Event - G. Armani

YEAR ISSUE	EDITION LIMIT	YEAR RETD.	ISSUE PRICE	*QUOTE U.S.$
1990 Pals (Boy w/ Dog) '90 & '91 409S	Closed	1991	200.00	360-450
1992 Springtime 961C	Closed	1992	250.00	286-390
1993 Loving Arms 880E	Closed	1993	250.00	325-390
1994 Daisy 202E	Closed	1994	250.00	293-450
1995 Iris 628E	Closed	1995	250.00	383-423
1996 Rose 678C	Closed	1997	250.00	250-520
1997 Marianne 135C	Closed	1997	275.00	222-275
1998 Victoria 525C	Closed	1998	275.00	220-275
1999 Heather 428C	Closed	1999	350.00	350
2000 Emma 1330C	Yr.Iss		275.00	275

G. Armani Society 10th Anniversary Event - G. Armani

YEAR ISSUE	EDITION LIMIT	YEAR RETD.	ISSUE PRICE	*QUOTE U.S.$
1999 Celebration 1260C	Closed	1999	199.00	210-250

Advantgarde - G. Armani

YEAR ISSUE	EDITION LIMIT	YEAR RETD.	ISSUE PRICE	*QUOTE U.S.$
1999 Born to Dance 1172C	3,000		475.00	475
1999 Joy Ride 1168C	3,000		575.00	575
1999 Lady Wynne 1173C	3,000		475.00	475
1999 On the Road 1169C	3,000		675.00	675
1999 Roseabelle 1171C	3,000		475.00	475
1999 So Pretty 1170C	3,000		475.00	475

Ashley Avery Collection - Armani

YEAR ISSUE	EDITION LIMIT	YEAR RETD.	ISSUE PRICE	*QUOTE U.S.$
1998 Aurora 884M	125		375.00	375
1997 Giselle 681M	100		425.00	425
1997 Juliette 682M	100		425.00	425
1998 Lilacs and Roses 882M	125		375.00	375

Cabaret - G. Armani

YEAR ISSUE	EDITION LIMIT	YEAR RETD.	ISSUE PRICE	*QUOTE U.S.$
2000 Jacqueline 1295C	3,000		850.00	850
2000 Josephine 1294C	3,000		900.00	900

Capodimonte - G. Armani

YEAR ISSUE	EDITION LIMIT	YEAR RETD.	ISSUE PRICE	*QUOTE U.S.$
1985 Boy Reading w/Dog 685C	Retrd.	1999	110.00	240-300
1995 Clear Water 381C	Retrd.	1999	300.00	315
1976 Country Girl (Little Shepherdess) 3153	Closed	1991	47.50	120-150
1997 Gallant Approach 146C	750	2000	1250.00	1250
1985 Girl Reading w/Cat 686C	Retrd.	1999	100.00	240-300
1993 Lady Golfer 911C	Retrd.	1999	325.00	335
1976 Lawyer 414	Retrd.	1986	60.00	48-60
1985 Little Vagabond 328C	Retrd.	1999	55.00	44-55
1998 Morning Ride 147C	5,000		770.00	770
1977 Napoleon (5464) 464C	Closed	1991	250.00	400-500
1980 Old Drunk (Richard's Night Out) 3243	Closed	1988	130.00	192-240
1978 Organ Grinder 3323	Closed	1989	140.00	280-350
1985 Peasant Group Clock 1115E	Retrd.	1990	320.00	320
1976 The Picture 441B	Retrd.	1983	N/A	N/A
1976 Shepherd 439	Retrd.	1988	N/A	N/A
1976 Shepherdess 440	Retrd.	1988	N/A	N/A
1977 Swing MIC#7471	Retrd.	1989	275.00	220-275
1980 The Tender Clown 217C	Suspd.		75.00	200-250
1984 Two on a Horse 625C	Retrd.	1999	350.00	670
1997 Venetian Night 125C	975		2000.00	2000
1995 Young Hearts 679C	1,500		900.00	1000

Clown Series - G. Armani

YEAR ISSUE	EDITION LIMIT	YEAR RETD.	ISSUE PRICE	*QUOTE U.S.$
1991 Bust of Clown (The Fiddler Clown) 725E	5,000		500.00	575
1984 Clown with Dog 653E	Closed	1991	135.00	100

Commemorative - G. Armani

YEAR ISSUE	EDITION LIMIT	YEAR RETD.	ISSUE PRICE	*QUOTE U.S.$
1992 Discovery of America - Columbus Plaque 867C	2,500	1994	400.00	340-425
1993 Mother's Day Plaque 899C	Closed	1993	100.00	80-104
1994 Mother's Day Plaque-The Swing 254C	Closed	1994	100.00	96-120
1995 Mother's Day Plaque-Love/Peace 538C	Closed	1995	125.00	88-125
1996 Mother's Day Plaque-Mother's Rosebud 341C	Closed	1996	150.00	150-250
1997 Mother's Day Figurine-Mother's Angel 155C	Closed	1997	175.00	123-175
1998 Mother's Day Figurine-Mother's Bouquet 799C	Closed	1998	175.00	100-175
1999 Mother's Day Figurine-Rosette 300C	Closed	1999	100.00	100
2000 Mother's Day Figurine-Babette 1328C	Closed	2000	100.00	100
2000 Dawn 1409	5,000		395.00	395

Disney - G. Armani

YEAR ISSUE	EDITION LIMIT	YEAR RETD.	ISSUE PRICE	*QUOTE U.S.$
2000 Cinderella & Fairy Godmother 14210	975		1250.00	1250

Disneyana - G. Armani

YEAR ISSUE	EDITION LIMIT	YEAR RETD.	ISSUE PRICE	*QUOTE U.S.$
1992 Cinderella '92 783C	500	1992	500.00	4130-4500
1993 Snow White '93 199C	2,000	1993	750.00	825-1550
1994 Ariel (Little Mermaid) '94 505C	1,500	1994	750.00	1200-1750
1995 Beauty and the Beast '95 543C	2,000	1995	975.00	1275-1430
1996 Jasmine & Rajah '96 410C	1,200	1996	800.00	990-1080
1997 Cinderella & Prince 107C	1,000	1997	825.00	825-1658
1998 Geppetto & Pinocchio 490C	1,075	1998	775.00	765-847
1999 Lady & The Tramp	750		750.00	750

Etrusca - G. Armani

YEAR ISSUE	EDITION LIMIT	YEAR RETD.	ISSUE PRICE	*QUOTE U.S.$
1993 Lady with Bag 2149E	Retrd.	1996	350.00	263-375

Figurine of the Year - G. Armani

YEAR ISSUE	EDITION LIMIT	YEAR RETD.	ISSUE PRICE	*QUOTE U.S.$
1996 Lady Jane 390C	Yr.Iss.	1996	200.00	350-500
1997 April 121C	Yr.Iss.	1997	250.00	175-250
1998 Violet 756C	Yr.Iss.	1998	250.00	175-250
1999 Elise 410C	Yr.Iss.	1999	230.00	230-250
2000 Celeste 1302C	Yr.Iss.		295.00	295

Florence/Disney - G. Armani

YEAR ISSUE	EDITION LIMIT	YEAR RETD.	ISSUE PRICE	*QUOTE U.S.$
1995 Jiminy Cricket "Special Backstamp" 379C	1,200	1995	300.00	520-650
1996 Jiminy Cricket 379C	Open		300.00	375
1996 Sleeping Beauty (Briar Rose) 106C	Open		650.00	675
1996 Pinocchio & Figaro 464C	Open		500.00	550
1995 Bashful 916C	Open		150.00	155
1995 Doc 326C	Open		150.00	155
1993 Dopey 200C	Open		105.00	155
1997 Fauna 609C	Retrd.	1999	200.00	200
1997 Flora 608C	Retrd.	1999	200.00	200
1995 Grumpy 917C	Open		145.00	155
1995 Happy 327C	Open		150.00	155
1997 Merryweather 607C	Retrd.	1999	200.00	200
1995 Sleepy 915C	Open		125.00	155
1995 Sneezy 914C	Open		125.00	155
1993 Snow White 209C	Open		400.00	450
1997 Tinkerbell 108C	Open		425.00	425

Florentine Gardens - G. Armani

YEAR ISSUE	EDITION LIMIT	YEAR RETD.	ISSUE PRICE	*QUOTE U.S.$
1992 Abundance 870C	10,000	1996	600.00	540-675
1994 Ambrosia 482C	5,000		435.00	550
1994 Angelica 484C	5,000		575.00	715
1998 Aphrodite 230C	3,000		1350.00	1350
1995 Aquarius 426C	5,000		600.00	650
1997 Artemis 126C	5,000		1750.00	1750
1993 Aurora-Lady With Doves 884C	7,500		370.00	400
1997 Bacchus & Arianna 419C	5,000		1500.00	1500
1999 Cancer 1239C	5,000		650.00	650
1998 Capricorn 699C	5,000		650.00	650
2000 Dance of the Flowers - Innocence 14240	5,000		395.00	395
2000 Dance of the Flowers - Love 14220	5,000		395.00	395
2000 Dance of the Flowers - Purity 14230	5,000		395.00	395
2000 Daphne 1353C	5,000		650.00	650
1992 Dawn 874C	10,000	1996	500.00	560-650
1995 Ebony 372C	5,000		550.00	600
1994 The Embrace 480C	3,000	1996	1450.00	3000-4000
1998 Flora 173C	5,000		600.00	600
2000 Fortuna 1322C	5,000		400.00	400
1993 Freedom-Man And Horse 906C	3,000	1996	850.00	1138-1200
1995 Gemini 426C	5,000		600.00	650
1998 Golden Nectar 212C	1,500		2000.00	2000
2000 Harmonie 1352C	5,000		600.00	600
1999 Heart and Soul 1254C	5,000		400.00	400
2000 Leda 1337C	5,000		400.00	400
1997 Leo 149C	5,000		650.00	650
1993 Liberty-Girl On Horse 903C	5,000	1996	750.00	1105-1268
1999 Libra 1238C	5,000		650.00	650
1993 Lilac & Roses-Girl w/Flowers 882C	7,500		410.00	440
1993 Lovers 191C	3,000	1996	450.00	900-1200
1997 Pisces 171C	5,000		650.00	650
1998 Pomona 174C	5,000		550.00	550

*Quotes have been rounded up to nearest dollar

YEAR ISSUE	EDITION LIMIT	YEAR RETD.	ISSUE PRICE	*QUOTE U.S.$
2000 Purity 1338C	5,000		400.00	400
1998 Sagittarius 698C	5,000		650.00	650
1999 Sea Breeze 864C	5,000		425.00	425
1999 Sea Song 863C	5,000		475.00	475
2000 Sky Riders 1324C	3,000		950.00	950
2000 Spring Blossoms 1323C	5,000		400.00	400
1994 Summertime-Lady on Swing 485C	5,000		650.00	775
2000 Swept Away 1267C	3,000		1000.00	1000
1997 Taurus 170C	5,000		650.00	650
1999 Three Graces 1256C	3,000		800.00	800
1992 Twilight 872C	10,000	1996	560.00	560-960
1992 Vanity 871C	10,000	1996	585.00	858-1170
1995 Virgo 425C	5,000		600.00	650
1993 Wind Song-Girl With Sail 904C	5,000		520.00	575
1994 Wisteria 626C	Retrd.	1999	375.00	425-650

Four Seasons - G. Armani

YEAR ISSUE	EDITION LIMIT	YEAR RETD.	ISSUE PRICE	*QUOTE U.S.$
1990 Skating-Winter 542P	Retrd.	1999	355.00	284-450

Galleria Collection - G. Armani

YEAR ISSUE	EDITION LIMIT	YEAR RETD.	ISSUE PRICE	*QUOTE U.S.$
1995 Eros 406T	1,500		750.00	775
1994 Grace 1029T	1,000	1999	465.00	485
1994 Joy 1028T	1,000	1999	465.00	485
1995 Pearl 1019T	1,000	1999	550.00	600
1993 Leda & The Swan 1012T	1,500	1996	550.00	1000-1500
1993 The Sea Wave 1006T	1,500	1996	500.00	506-633
1993 The Sea Wave, signed 1006T	Retrd.	1996	500.00	910-1008
1993 Spring Herald 1009T	1,500	1996	500.00	572-845
1993 Spring Herald, signed 1009T	Retrd.	1996	500.00	600
1993 Spring Water 1007T	1,500	1996	500.00	595-1300
1993 Zephyr 1010T	1,500	1996	500.00	600-1200
1993 Set (Sea Wave, Spring Water, Spring Herald, Leda & Swan, Zephyr)	Retrd.	1996	2550.00	3380-5500

Golden Age - G. Armani

YEAR ISSUE	EDITION LIMIT	YEAR RETD.	ISSUE PRICE	*QUOTE U.S.$
1995 Fragrance 340C	3,000	1999	500.00	560
1998 Lacey 645C	3,000		700.00	700
1999 Lady Anne 1159C	3,000		375.00	375
1997 Morning Ride 147C	5,000		770.00	770
1995 Promenade 339C	3,000	1999	600.00	650
1998 Reverie 646C	3,000		600.00	600
1999 Rosanna 794C	3,000		400.00	400
1995 Soiree 338C	3,000		600.00	630
1995 Spring Morning 337C	3,000	1998	600.00	800-900
1999 Wind Swept 795C	3,000		500.00	500

Gulliver's World - G. Armani

YEAR ISSUE	EDITION LIMIT	YEAR RETD.	ISSUE PRICE	*QUOTE U.S.$
1994 The Barrel 659T	1,000	1999	225.00	255
1981 Boy with Fish 185C	Retrd.	1985	45.00	36-45
1981 Boy with Pistol 191T (original "Cowboy")	Retrd.	1988	45.00	40-50
1981 Children in Shoe 309C	Retrd.	1983	300.00	240-300
1994 Cowboy 657T	1,000	1996	125.00	120-125
1981 Dice Game 305C	Retrd.	1985	265.00	212-265
1994 Getting Clean 661T	1,000	1998	130.00	120-150
1981 Indian Girl w/Dog 262C	Retrd.	1985	60.00	48-60
1994 Ray of Moon 658T	1,000	1998	100.00	80-100
1994 Serenade 660T	1,000	1998	200.00	188-235
1981 Serenade on Barrel 306C	Retrd.	1987	190.00	152-190
1976 Stealing Puppies 432C	Retrd.	1989	55.00	44-55
1981 Wine Curriers 199T	Retrd.	1983	130.00	104-130

Impressions - G. Armani

YEAR ISSUE	EDITION LIMIT	YEAR RETD.	ISSUE PRICE	*QUOTE U.S.$
1990 Bittersweet 528C	Retrd.	1993	400.00	910-1040
1990 Bittersweet 528P	Retrd.	1993	275.00	476-595
1990 Masquerade 527C	Retrd.	1993	400.00	344-430
1990 Masquerade 527P	Retrd.	1993	300.00	476-595
1990 Mystery 523C	Retrd.	1993	370.00	296-845
1990 Temptation 522C	Retrd.	1993	400.00	320-400

Masterworks - G. Armani

YEAR ISSUE	EDITION LIMIT	YEAR RETD.	ISSUE PRICE	*QUOTE U.S.$
1995 Aurora 680C	1,500	1996	3500.00	3600-5000
1998 Circle of Joy 760C	1,500	1999	2750.00	2750

Moonlight Masquerade - G. Armani

YEAR ISSUE	EDITION LIMIT	YEAR RETD.	ISSUE PRICE	*QUOTE U.S.$
1991 Lady Clown 742C	7,500	1995	390.00	650-795
1991 Lady Clown with Puppet 743C	7,500	1995	410.00	328-780
1991 Lady Harlequin 740C	7,500	1995	450.00	695-780
1991 Lady Pierrot 741C	7,500	1995	390.00	780-795
1991 Queen of Hearts 744C	7,500	1995	450.00	476-595
1991 Set	Retrd.	1995	2090.00	2090

My Fair Ladies™ - G. Armani

YEAR ISSUE	EDITION LIMIT	YEAR RETD.	ISSUE PRICE	*QUOTE U.S.$
1994 At Ease 634C	5,000		650.00	715
1998 Brief Encounter 167C	5,000		350.00	350
1990 Can-Can Dancer 589P	Retrd.	1991	460.00	453-520
1989 Can-Can Dancers 516C	Retrd.	1993	880.00	720-1100
1998 Charm 197C	3,000		850.00	850
1999 Cleo 801C	5,000		500.00	500
2000 Elegance 1180C	5,000		700.00	700
1993 Elegance 195C	5,000		525.00	660
2000 Enchanting 1181C	5,000		700.00	700
1993 Fascination 192C	5,000		500.00	633
1987 Flamenco Dancer 389C	5,000	1999	400.00	579-600
2000 The Flirt 1288C	3,000		400.00	400
1997 Garden Delight 157C	3,000	1999	1000.00	1000
1995 Georgia 414C	5,000		550.00	625
1996 Grace 383C	5,000		475.00	515
1995 In Love 382C	5,000		450.00	500
1998 In The Mood 164C	5,000		425.00	425
1994 Isadora 633C	3,000		920.00	1050
2000 Kelly 1290C	3,000		400.00	400
1990 Lady at Piano 449C	Retrd.	1999	370.00	440
1987 Lady with Book 384C	5,000	1999	300.00	475
1988 Lady with Chain 411C	Retrd.	1999	125.00	170
1987 Lady with Fan 387C	5,000	1999	300.00	395-455
1988 Lady with Great Dane 429C	5,000	1996	385.00	550-960
1987 Lady with Mirror (Compact) 386C	5,000	1993	300.00	300-943
1987 Lady with Muff 388C	5,000	1999	250.00	250-390
1988 Lady with Muff 408C	Retrd.	1999	135.00	175
1990 Lady with Parrot 616C	5,000	1995	460.00	1040-1395
1987 Lady with Peacock 385C	5,000	1992	380.00	380-3000
1987 Lady with Peacock 385F	Retrd.	1996	230.00	1675-1880
1987 Lady with Peacock 385P	Retrd.	1996	300.00	1000-1600
1993 Lady with Umbrella-Nellie 196C	5,000		370.00	450
1995 Lara 415C	5,000		450.00	500
1993 Mahogany 194C	5,000	1995	500.00	1680-2500
1998 Moonlight 151C	1,500		1250.00	1250
1993 Morning Rose 193C	5,000	2000	450.00	515
1998 Mystical Fountain 159C	3,000	2000	900.00	900
1998 Opal 758C	5,000		450.00	450
1987 The Parrot 393C	Retrd.	1999	175.00	270
1994 Promenade 630C	Retrd.	1999	185.00	215
1999 Samantha 800C	5,000		500.00	500
1998 Starlight 150C	1,500		1250.00	1250
1994 Starry Night 632C	Retrd.	1999	210.00	210
1997 Swans Lake 158C	3,000	2000	900.00	900
1999 Tamara 798C	5,000		500.00	500
1988 The Tango 431F	Retrd.	1983	330.00	264-330
1988 The Tango 441P	Retrd.	1993	550.00	728-910
1999 Tracy 797C	5,000		500.00	500
1989 Two Can-Can Dancers 516C	Retrd.	1993	880.00	1100-2000

Novecento - G. Armani

YEAR ISSUE	EDITION LIMIT	YEAR RETD.	ISSUE PRICE	*QUOTE U.S.$
2000 Charme 1317C	5,000		600.00	600

Pearls Of The Orient - G. Armani

YEAR ISSUE	EDITION LIMIT	YEAR RETD.	ISSUE PRICE	*QUOTE U.S.$
1990 Chu Chu San 612C	10,000	1994	550.00	572-910
1990 Lotus Blossom 613C	10,000	1994	475.00	380-475
1990 Madame Butterfly 610C	10,000	1994	500.00	572-910
1990 Turnadot 611C	10,000	1994	500.00	440-550
1990 Set	Retrd.	1994	2025.00	2025

Premiere Ballerinas - G. Armani

YEAR ISSUE	EDITION LIMIT	YEAR RETD.	ISSUE PRICE	*QUOTE U.S.$
1989 Ballerina 508C	10,000	1994	470.00	1326-1658
1989 Ballerina Group in Flight 518C	7,500	1994	780.00	960-1040
1989 Ballerina with Drape 504C	10,000	1994	500.00	500-650
1991 Dancer with Peacock 727C	Retrd.	1993	460.00	424-530
1989 Flying Ballerina 503C	10,000	1994	440.00	400-500
1989 Kneeling Ballerina 517C	10,000	1994	340.00	350-429
1989 Two Ballerinas 515C	7,500	1994	670.00	620-775

Religious - G. Armani

YEAR ISSUE	EDITION LIMIT	YEAR RETD.	ISSUE PRICE	*QUOTE U.S.$
1991 Angel with Flowers "Innocence" 772C	Retrd.	1999	135.00	140
1997 Angel with Harp "Heavenly Music" 1033C	Retrd.	1999	600.00	600
1997 Angel with Lute "Raphael" 1031C	Retrd.	1999	600.00	600
1991 Angel with Lyre "Peace 773C	Retrd.	1999	130.00	135
1997 Angel with Trumpet "Gabriel" 1032C	Retrd.	1999	600.00	600
1994 The Assumption 697C	5,000		650.00	725
1983 Choir Boys 900	5,000	1996	400.00	400-900
1994 Christ Child (Nativity) 1020C	1,000		175.00	195
1999 Come to Me 783C	5,000		1250.00	1250
1987 Crucifix 1158C	10,000	1990	155.00	650-850
1993 Crucifix 786C	7,500		285.00	315
1987 Crucifix 790C	15,000		160.00	250
1991 Crucifix Plaque 711C	15,000	1996	265.00	265-285
1995 The Crucifixion 780C	5,000		500.00	550
1994 Donkey (Nativity) 1027C	1,000		185.00	210
1995 The Holy Family 788C	5,000		1000.00	1100
1994 La Pieta 802C	5,000	1999	950.00	1100
1994 Madonna (Nativity) 1022C	1,000		365.00	430
1994 Magi King Gold (Nativity) 1023C	1,000		600.00	650
1994 Magi King Incense (Nativity) 1024C	1,000		600.00	650
1994 Magi King Myrrh (Nativity) 1025C	1,000		450.00	500
1995 Moses 606C	2,500	1999	365.00	400
1999 Moses 785C	5,000		1200.00	1200
1994 Ox (Nativity) 1026C	1,000		300.00	350
1994 Renaissance Crucifix 1017T	5,000		265.00	275
2000 The Sorrow 1325C	5,000		1500.00	1500
1994 St. Joseph (Nativity) 1021C	1,000		500.00	550

Siena Collection - G. Armani

YEAR ISSUE	EDITION LIMIT	YEAR RETD.	ISSUE PRICE	*QUOTE U.S.$
1993 Back From The Fields 1002T	1,000	1995	400.00	410-550
1994 Country Boy w/Mushrooms 1014T	2,500	1999	135.00	155
1993 Encountering 1003T	1,000	1995	350.00	480-780
1993 Fresh Fruit 1001T	2,500	1995	155.00	332
1993 The Happy Fiddler 1005T	1,000	1997	225.00	239-390
1993 Mother's Hand 1008T	2,500	1998	250.00	228-285
1993 Soft Kiss 1000T	2,500	1995	155.00	332-390
1993 Sound The Trumpet! 1004T	1,000	1995	225.00	280-390
1993 Set of 8	N/A	N/A	1895.00	1895

Special Events in a Life - G. Armani

YEAR ISSUE	EDITION LIMIT	YEAR RETD.	ISSUE PRICE	*QUOTE U.S.$
2000 Beloved 1319C	5,000		600.00	600
1994 Black Maternity 502C	3,000		535.00	650
1999 Bliss 386C	5,000		375.00	375
1984 Bride & Groom 641C	Retrd.	1994	125.00	990-1238
1994 Bride with Flower Vase 489C	Retrd.	1999	155.00	165
1993 Carriage Wedding 902C	2,500		1000.00	1100
1986 Enfance 694C	Retrd.	1992	380.00	308-380
1991 Just Married 827C	5,000	1998	1000.00	1100-2200
1999 Magic Touch 385C	5,000		500.00	500
1988 Maternity 405C	5,000	1998	415.00	500-570
1999 My Love 238C	5,000		575.00	575
1994 Perfect Love 652C	3,000		1200.00	1250
1999 Pride and Joy 104C	3,000		1000.00	1000
1995 Sweet Smile 366C	Suspd.		420.00	470
1995 Tenderness 418C	5,000		950.00	1000
1995 Tomorrow's Dream 336C	5,000		700.00	730
1991 Wedding Couple At Threshold 813C	7,500		400.00	475
1991 Wedding Couple Kissing 815C	7,500		500.00	575
1991 Wedding Couple With Bicycle 814C	7,500		600.00	665
1994 Wedding Waltz (black) 501C	3,000		750.00	875
1994 Wedding Waltz (white) 493C	3,000		750.00	875

Special Releases - G. Armani

YEAR ISSUE	EDITION LIMIT	YEAR RETD.	ISSUE PRICE	*QUOTE U.S.$
1989 Bust of Eve 590T	1,000	1991	250.00	566-1200
1993 Doctor in Car 848C	2,000	1996	800.00	660-825
1992 Girl in Car 861C	3,000	1995	900.00	740-925
1992 Lady with Dove (Dove Dancer) 858E	1,000	1994	320.00	360-845
1992 Old Couple in Car (Two Hearts Remember) 862C	5,000	1999	1000.00	1000

Spring Melodies - G. Armani

YEAR ISSUE	EDITION LIMIT	YEAR RETD.	ISSUE PRICE	*QUOTE U.S.$
1987 Lady with Wheelbarrow 960C	Retrd.	1999	165.00	230
2000 Spring Bluebell 1333C	3,000		550.00	550
2000 Spring Daisy 1335C	3,000		550.00	550
2000 Spring Iris 1336C	3,000		500.00	500
2000 Spring Rose 1334C	3,000		550.00	550

Valentine - G. Armani

YEAR ISSUE	EDITION LIMIT	YEAR RETD.	ISSUE PRICE	*QUOTE U.S.$
1983 Hoopla 107E	Retrd.	1996	190.00	160-200
1983 Little Nativity 115C	Retrd.	1991	270.00	216-270
1983 Soccer Boy 109C	Retrd.	1994	80.00	64-80

Vanity Fair - G. Armani

YEAR ISSUE	EDITION LIMIT	YEAR RETD.	ISSUE PRICE	*QUOTE U.S.$
1992 Beauty at the Mirror 850P	Retrd.	1996	300.00	280-350
1992 Beauty w/Perfume 853P	Retrd.	1996	330.00	296-370

Via Veneto - G. Armani

YEAR ISSUE	EDITION LIMIT	YEAR RETD.	ISSUE PRICE	*QUOTE U.S.$
1994 Alessandra 648C	5,000		355.00	400
1999 Be My Love 1248C	5,000		450.00	450
1997 Black Orchid 444C	5,000		1100.00	1100
1999 Claudia 1193C	5,000		375.00	375
1998 Cuddle Up 322C	3,000	2000	475.00	475
1999 Erika 1192C	5,000		475.00	475
1998 Free Spirit 321C	3,000	1999	825.00	825
1999 Isabella 1190C	5,000		375.00	375
1994 Marina 649C	5,000		450.00	530
1994 Nicole 651C	5,000		500.00	600
1998 Poetry 231C	5,000		600.00	600
1998 Roman Holiday 271C	3,000		1500.00	1500
1999 Silvia 1191C	5,000		450.00	450
1997 Summer Stroll 431C	5,000	1999	650.00	650
1997 Tiger Lily 244C	5,000		1200.00	1200
1994 Valentina 647C	5,000		400.00	440
1997 Whitney 432C	5,000		750.00	750

Wildlife - G. Armani

YEAR ISSUE	EDITION LIMIT	YEAR RETD.	ISSUE PRICE	*QUOTE U.S.$
1997 Alert (Irish Setters) 550S	975		900.00	900
1998 Back To The Barn 591S	3,000		400.00	400
1989 Bird of Paradise 454S	5,000		475.00	550
1991 Bird of Paradise 718S	5,000	1996	500.00	440-550
1998 Bonding 744S	3,000		3000.00	3000
1998 Brilliance 586S	1,500	1999	850.00	850
1982 Cardinal 546C	Retrd.	1989	100.00	80-100
1984 Cat & Kitten 618C	Retrd.	1999	77.50	190
1997 Collie 304S	975		500.00	500
1995 Companions (Two Collies) 302S	3,000		900.00	950
1991 Crane 713S	5,000		430.00	465
1998 Crystal Morning 597S	1,500	2000	900.00	900
1997 Dalmation 552S	975		600.00	600
1998 Descent 604S	3,000		500.00	500
1998 Early Arrivals 593S	1,500		600.00	600
1997 Early Days (Deer) 557S	975		1200.00	1200
1994 Elegance in Nature (Herons) 226S	3,000	2000	1000.00	1200
1998 Ever Watchful 602S	3,000		450.00	450
1994 The Falconer 224S	3,000	1999	1000.00	1200
1995 Feed Us! (Mother/Baby Owls) 305S	1,500	1998	950.00	800-1000
1997 First Days (Mare & Foal) 564S	1,500		800.00	800
1991 Flying Duck 839S	3,000		470.00	530
1993 Galloping Horse 905C	Retrd.	1999	425.00	475
1993 Galloping Horse 905S	7,500	1999	465.00	500
1998 Garden Delight 734S	1,500		500.00	500
1991 Great Argus Pheasant 717S	3,000	1996	625.00	520-650
1991 Hummingbird 719S	Retrd.	1996	300.00	296-370
1995 The Hunt (Falcon) 290S	3,000	2000	850.00	880
1991 Large Owl 842S	5,000		520.00	570
1995 Lone Wolf 285S	3,000		550.00	575
1995 Midnight 284S	3,000		600.00	630
1997 Monarch (Stag) 555S	1,500		1200.00	1200
1998 Moon Flight 603S	3,000	2000	600.00	600
1998 Morning Call 742S	3,000		465.00	465
1998 Morning Mist 737S	3,000		335.00	335
1997 Mother's Touch (Elephants) 579S	3,000	2000	700.00	700
1997 Nature's Colors (Pheasant) 582S	1,500		1350.00	1350
1997 Nature's Dance (Herons) 576S	750	1999	1750.00	1750
1995 Night Vigil (Owl) 306S	3,000	1999	650.00	675-1000
1995 Nocturne 976S	1,500	2000	1000.00	1100
1998 On Guard 605S	3,000	2000	475.00	475
1998 On Watch 589S	3,000	2000	400.00	400
1989 Peacock 455S	5,000		620.00	700
1989 Peacock 458S	5,000		650.00	730
1998 Peacock's Pride 733S	1,500	2000	400.00	400
1997 Please Play (Cocker Spaniels) 312S	975		600.00	600
1997 Pointer 554S	975		700.00	700
2000 Pride 1357C	1,500		1650.00	1650
1995 Proud Watch (Lion) 278S	1,500	1999	700.00	750
1993 Rearing Horse 907C	Retrd.	1999	515.00	530
1993 Rearing Horse 907S	7,500		550.00	585

*Quotes have been rounded up to nearest dollar

YEAR ISSUE	EDITION LIMIT	YEAR RETD.	ISSUE PRICE	*QUOTE U.S.$
1997 Royal Couple (Afghan Hounds) 310S	975		850.00	850
1994 Running Free (Greyhounds) 972S	3,000		850.00	930
1993 Running Horse 909C	Retrd.	1999	465.00	500
1993 Running Horse 909S	7,500		515.00	550
1997 Shepherd (Dog) 307S	975		450.00	450
2000 Sign of Spring 1356C	1,500		650.00	650
1998 Silent Flight 592S	3,000	2000	450.00	450
1995 Silent Watch (Mtn. Lion) 291S	1,500		700.00	750
1997 Sky Watch (Flying Eagle) 559S	3,000		1200.00	1200
1990 Soaring Eagle 970S	5,000	1996	620.00	620-950
1998 Spring Orchestra 584S	975	1999	1250.00	1250
1998 Stallions 572S	1,500		1100.00	1100
1997 Standing Tall (Heron) 577S	1,500		800.00	800
1998 Summer Song 585S	1,500	1999	750.00	750
1991 Swan 714S	5,000		550.00	600
1990 Three Doves 996S	5,000		690.00	750
1998 Tropical Gossip 726S	3,000		450.00	475
1998 Tropical Splendor 288S	1,500		1750.00	1750
1997 Trumpeting (Elephant) 578S	3,000	1999	850.00	850
1983 Unicorn 487C	Retrd.	1999	130.00	250
1995 Vantage Point (Eagle) 270S	3,000		600.00	650
1993 Vase with Doves 204S	3,000	1996	375.00	387-650
1993 Vase with Parrot 736S	3,000	1996	460.00	380-748
1993 Vase with Peacock 735S	3,000		450.00	500
1998 Wild Colors 727S	3,000		450.00	450
1995 Wild Hearts (Horses) 282S	3,000		2000.00	2100
1998 Winter's End 583S	1,500	1999	900.00	900
1995 Wisdom (Owl) 281S	3,000		1250.00	1300

Armstrong's

Armstrong's/Ron Lee - R. Skelton

YEAR ISSUE	EDITION LIMIT	YEAR RETD.	ISSUE PRICE	*QUOTE U.S.$
1984 Captain Freddie	7,500	N/A	85.00	350-450
1984 Freddie the Torchbearer	7,500	N/A	110.00	400-450

Happy Art - W. Lantz

YEAR ISSUE	EDITION LIMIT	YEAR RETD.	ISSUE PRICE	*QUOTE U.S.$
1982 Woody's Triple Self-Portrait	5,000	N/A	95.00	350

The Red Skelton Collection - R. Skelton

YEAR ISSUE	EDITION LIMIT	YEAR RETD.	ISSUE PRICE	*QUOTE U.S.$
1981 Clem Kadiddlehopper	Retrd.	N/A	75.00	145-165
1981 Freddie in the Bathtub	5,000	N/A	80.00	85-95
1981 Freddie on the Green	5,000	1997	80.00	120-125
1981 Freddie the Freeloader	Retrd.	N/A	70.00	150-195
1981 Jr., The Mean Widdle Kid	Retrd.	N/A	75.00	160-175
1981 San Fernando Red	Retrd.	N/A	75.00	125-150
1981 Sheriff Deadeye	Retrd.	N/A	75.00	145-150

Artaffects

Members Only Limited Edition Redemption Offerings - G. Perillo

YEAR ISSUE	EDITION LIMIT	YEAR RETD.	ISSUE PRICE	*QUOTE U.S.$
1983 Apache Brave (Bust)	Closed	N/A	50.00	150-195
1986 Painted Pony	Closed	N/A	125.00	175
1991 Chief Crazy Horse	Closed	N/A	195.00	250-300

Limited Edition Free Gifts to Members - G. Perillo

YEAR ISSUE	EDITION LIMIT	YEAR RETD.	ISSUE PRICE	*QUOTE U.S.$
1986 Dolls	Closed	N/A	Gift	35
1991 Sunbeam	Closed	N/A	Gift	35-49
1992 Little Shadow	Closed	N/A	Gift	35-49

The Chieftains - G. Perillo

YEAR ISSUE	EDITION LIMIT	YEAR RETD.	ISSUE PRICE	*QUOTE U.S.$
1983 Cochise	5,000	N/A	65.00	275
1983 Crazy Horse	5,000	N/A	65.00	200-250
1983 Geronimo	5,000	N/A	65.00	250-300
1983 Joseph	5,000	N/A	65.00	285-300
1983 Red Cloud	5,000	N/A	65.00	275-300
1983 Sitting Bull	5,000	N/A	65.00	200-300

Pride of America's Indians - G. Perillo

YEAR ISSUE	EDITION LIMIT	YEAR RETD.	ISSUE PRICE	*QUOTE U.S.$
1988 Brave and Free	10-day	N/A	50.00	150
1989 Dark Eyed Friends	10-day	N/A	45.00	75
1989 Kindred Spirits	10-day	N/A	45.00	50
1989 Loyal Alliance	10-day	N/A	45.00	75
1989 Noble Companions	10-day	N/A	45.00	50
1989 Peaceful Comrades	10-day	N/A	45.00	50
1989 Small & Wise	10-day	N/A	45.00	50
1989 Winter Scouts	10-day	N/A	45.00	50

Special Issue - G. Perillo

YEAR ISSUE	EDITION LIMIT	YEAR RETD.	ISSUE PRICE	*QUOTE U.S.$
1984 Apache Boy Bust	Closed	N/A	40.00	75-150
1984 Apache Girl Bust	Closed	N/A	40.00	75
1985 Lovers	Closed	N/A	70.00	125
1984 Papoose	325	N/A	500.00	500
1982 The Peaceable Kingdom	950	N/A	750.00	750

The Storybook Collection - G. Perillo

YEAR ISSUE	EDITION LIMIT	YEAR RETD.	ISSUE PRICE	*QUOTE U.S.$
1981 Cinderella	10,000	N/A	65.00	95
1982 Goldilocks & 3 Bears	10,000	N/A	80.00	110
1982 Hansel and Gretel	10,000	N/A	80.00	110
1980 Little Red Ridinghood	10,000	N/A	65.00	95

The Tribal Ponies - G. Perillo

YEAR ISSUE	EDITION LIMIT	YEAR RETD.	ISSUE PRICE	*QUOTE U.S.$
1984 Arapaho	1,500	N/A	65.00	175-200
1984 Comanche	1,500	N/A	65.00	175-200
1984 Crow	1,500	N/A	65.00	175-200

The War Pony - G. Perillo

YEAR ISSUE	EDITION LIMIT	YEAR RETD.	ISSUE PRICE	*QUOTE U.S.$
1983 Apache War Pony	495	N/A	150.00	175-200
1983 Nez Perce War Pony	495	N/A	150.00	175-200
1983 Sioux War Pony	495	N/A	150.00	175-200

Artesania Rinconada Collection/John J. Madison Co. Inc.

Artesania Rinconada Collector's Society - J. & J. Carbajales

YEAR ISSUE	EDITION LIMIT	YEAR RETD.	ISSUE PRICE	*QUOTE U.S.$
1998 White Cat	Closed	1999	Gift	350
1999 Horse	Closed	2000	Gift	N/A
2000 Walking Panda	6/01		Gift	N/A

Classic Collection - J. & J. Carbajales

YEAR ISSUE	EDITION LIMIT	YEAR RETD.	ISSUE PRICE	*QUOTE U.S.$
1972 01 Ostrich	Open		12.50	21
1970 2 Musk Ox	Closed	1990	8.00	75
1973 03 Horse	Open		8.00	17
1991 03A Clydesdale Horse	Open		22.00	23
1991 03B Baby Clydesdale	Open		16.00	19
1970 4 Kangaroo	Closed	1980	11.00	240
1991 04A Circus Elephant Sitting	Open		14.00	17
1991 04B Circus Elephant Standing	Open		14.00	17
1991 04C Circus Elephant	Open		14.00	17
1971 05 Ram	Open		13.00	23
1972 6 Pig	Open		6.00	12
1986 6A Baby Pig	Open		7.00	14
1986 06B Pig (black)	Open		7.00	15
1995 06BB Baby Pig (black)	Open		8.00	9
1984 06BW Pig (black & white)	Open		7.00	15
1987 6C Pig (White)	Open		7.00	14
1991 06D Pig In Tube	Open		12.00	15
1995 6R Pig (Rust)	Open		14.00	15
1995 06W Pig (white)	Open		14.00	15
1995 06RR Baby Pig (rust)	Open		8.00	9
1995 06WA Baby Pig (black & white)	Open		8.00	9
1995 06WW Baby Pig (white)	Open		8.00	9
1970 7 Large Elephant	Closed	1980	13.00	300-600
1970 7 Large Elephant w/ceramic tusks	Closed	1980	13.00	13
1979 07 Duck	Open		12.50	19
1993 07A Baby Duck	Closed	2000	14.00	22
1970 08 Middle Elephant	Open		10.00	19
1970 08 Middle Elephant w/ceramic tusks	Closed	N/A	10.00	19
1970 09 Small Elephant	Open		8.50	17
1970 09 Small Elephant w/ceramic tusks	Closed	N/A	8.50	17
1970 10 Rooster	Open		10.00	17
1970 11 Hen	Open		6.00	15
1971 12 Cat	Closed	1980	11.00	600
1980 12 Cat	Open		12.00	19
1990 12A Baby Cat	Open		13.00	15
1971 13 Gorilla	Closed	1984	13.00	60-80
1987 13 Barn Owl	Open		17.50	23
1971 14 Baby Gorilla	Closed	1984	5.50	40
1986 14 Baby Barn Owl	Open		14.00	19
1971 15 Hippo	Open		9.00	17
1971 16 Small Owl	Open		8.00	15
1972 17 Small Lion	Open		8.00	17
1971 18 Parrot	Closed	1987	8.00	60-110
1971 18 Parrot (red & yellow)	Closed	1987	8.00	60-110
1971 19 Llama (1)	Closed	1980	11.00	240
1980 19 Llama (2)	Closed	1984	11.00	150
1987 19 Llama (3)	Open		12.00	17
1989 19A Baby Llama	Open		5.00	13
1971 20 Baboon	Closed	1984	8.00	140-145
1972 21 Walrus	Open		10.00	17
1994 21A Baby Walrus	Open		12.00	14
1994 21B Baby Walrus	Open		12.00	14
1971 22 Calf	Closed	1984	7.00	60-80
1994 22A Sea Lion	Open		16.00	18
1994 22B Sea Lion	Open		16.00	18
1994 22C Sea Lion	Open		16.00	18
1972 23 Sheep	Closed	1999	7.00	25-45
1972 24 Toucan	Open		12.50	21
1972 25 High Turkey	Closed	1980	12.00	350-500
1979 25 Seal (white)	Closed	1999	11.50	30
1990 25A Seal (brown)	Open		14.50	17
1990 25B Seal (brown)	Closed	1999	14.50	15
1972 26 Flag Dog	Closed	1980	10.00	140-275
1979 26 Baby Seal	Open		9.50	15
1972 27 Fish	Closed	1984	10.00	60-80
1972 28 Whale	Open		10.00	19
1972 29 Rhino	Open		10.00	19
1972 30 Baby Rhino	Open		5.50	13
1972 31 Armadillo	Closed	1980	8.00	80-95
1982 31 New Armadillo	Closed	1998	12.50	42-43
1971 32 Tiger	Closed	1998	8.00	45
1987 32A Tiger Baby	Closed	1998	9.50	35
1972 33 Bull W/ Flower	Closed	1984	11.00	83-125
1992 33 Lg. Tiger	Open		18.00	21
1973 34 Turtle	Open		10.00	19
1972 35 Cow	Closed	1984	8.00	68-90
1972 36 Donkey	Closed	1990	8.00	72
1973 37 Goat	Closed	1980	9.00	240
1982 37 Goat	Closed	1999	19.00	19
1973 38 White Rabbit	Closed	1980	10.00	200
1985 38 Rabbit	Open		9.50	17
1972 39 Vicuna	Open		14.50	25
1973 40 Eagle (1)	Closed	1984	14.00	325-1000
1982 40 Eagle (2)	Closed	1987	18.00	165-235
1986 40 Eagle (3)	Open		20.00	23
1973 41 Carpincho	Closed	1980	8.00	240
1974 42 Wild Boar (1)	Closed	1984	10.00	350
1985 42 A Wild Boar (2)	Closed	1990	12.50	85
1971 43 Frog	Open		8.00	17
1972 44 Giraffe	Open		12.50	23
1973 45 Chimp w/Flowers	Open		10.00	17
1974 46 Chimp w/Bottle	Closed	1999	10.00	25-30
1982 47 Thinking Monkey	Closed	1990	13.00	60
1986 47 Zebra (Male)	Open		15.00	21
1972 48 Zebra	Open		10.00	21
1986 48A Baby Zebra	Open		10.00	15
1993 48B Baby Zebra	Open		13.00	15
1971 49 Crocodile	Open		12.50	21
1971 49 Crocodile	Closed	N/A	12.50	21
1974 50 Dog	Closed	1984	8.00	90
1993 50A Common Barn Owl	Open		19.00	21
1993 50B Common Barn Owl	Open		16.00	18
1993 50C Baby Barn Owl	Open		17.00	19
1976 51 Moose	Open		10.50	19
1995 51A Moose (Female)	Open		19.00	20
1974 52 Vampire Bat	Closed	1984	12.50	30-40
1979 52 Coyote Howling	Closed	1998	8.00	40
1976 53 Pheasant	Closed	1999	13.50	45
1976 54 Panda	Closed	1980	10.00	130
1985 54 Panda Bear	Open		12.50	19
1976 55 Brown Bear	Closed	1995	12.50	65
1976 56 Dolphin	Open		9.00	19
1976 57 Squirrel	Closed	1987	12.00	60-80
1993 57 Skunk in Cart	Open		19.00	21
1993 57A Baby Skunk in Cart	Open		13.00	15
1993 57B Baby Skunk in Cart	Open		13.00	15
1976 58 Large Owl	Closed	1995	16.00	40
1976 59 Penguin	Closed	1984	9.00	75
1976 60 Racoon	Open		9.50	17
1976 61 Large Lion	Open		12.00	21
1976 62 Shark	Open		9.50	17
1976 63 Papagayo	Open		9.00	19
1977 64 Camel	Open		13.50	25
1987 64A Baby Camel	Open		12.50	17
1977 65 Okapi	Closed	1980	10.50	150
1994 65 American Shorthair	Open		17.00	19
1994 65A Baby American Shorthair	Open		12.00	14
1994 65B Baby American Shorthair	Open		12.00	14
1977 66 Pelican	Open		12.00	21
1987 66A Baby Pelican	Open		10.50	13
1987 66B Baby Pelican	Open		10.50	13
1977 67 Sea Otter	Open		9.50	17
1987 67A Baby Sea Otter	Open		10.50	13
1987 67B Baby Sea Otter	Open		10.50	13
1977 68 Baby Vicuna	Open		9.50	19
1977 69 Baby Turtle	Open		7.50	15
1977 70 Anteater	Closed	1980	10.00	120
1987 70 Canada Goose	Closed	1995	14.00	50
1987 70A Baby Canada Goose	Closed	1995	8.50	30-40
1977 71 Beaver	Closed	1998	11.00	42
1994 72 Cats In A Basket	Open		16.00	18
1977 72 Condor	Closed	1984	10.00	130-140
1978 73 Mouse	Closed	1999	8.00	40
1990 73A Mouse On A Book	Open		15.50	19
1991 73B Mouse w/Photo	Closed	1999	16.00	22
1991 73C Mouse In Santa	Closed	1999	16.00	22
1993 73D Mouse In Pumpkin	Closed	1999	18.00	22
1994 73E Mouse In Cowboy Boot	Closed	1999	16.00	22
1994 73F Papa Mouse Eating Cheese	Closed	1999	15.00	22
1994 73G Baby Mouse Asleep	Closed	1999	15.00	35
1994 73H Baby Mouse Eating Cheese	Closed	1999	16.00	25
1994 73I Storyteller Mouse	Closed	1999	16.00	22
1994 73J Baby Mouse	Closed	1999	13.00	22
1994 73K Mice On Bench	Closed	1999	26.00	26-50
1978 74 Antelope	Closed	1999	11.50	35-40
1978 75 Orangutan	Closed	1999	11.50	55-145
1978 76 Gray Fox	Closed	1987	11.50	140
1994 77 Frog On Mushroom	Open		20.00	22
1978 77 Lynx	Closed	1984	10.00	90-120
1978 78 Koala	Open		10.50	19
1979 79 Polar Bear	Open		12.00	19
1987 79B Polar Bear (Male)	Open		15.00	19
1979 80 Mountain Lion	Closed	1987	12.00	80-120
1987 80 Mountain Lion (2)	Closed	1990	13.50	80
1980 81 Dove	Closed	1987	14.00	85
1980 82 Skunk	Closed	1987	13.00	60-80
1980 83 Persian Cat	Closed	1998	15.00	35
1987 84 Somali Cat	Open		9.00	19
1980 84 Vampire Bat	Closed	1984	12.50	45
1987 84A Somali Cat Female	Closed	1995	14.00	35
1987 84B Baby Somali	Open		10.00	13
1981 85 Cheetah	Closed	1998	12.00	45
1987 85A Baby Cheetah	Closed	2000	10.00	28
1987 85B Baby Cheetah	Closed	2000	10.00	28
1981 86 Wolf	Closed	1984	12.50	110
1981 87 Tree Frog	Open		11.00	17
1981 88 American Buffalo	Closed	1990	12.00	80
1981 88 American Buffalo	Closed	1998	12.00	35
1981 89 African Buffalo	Closed	1995	16.00	80-100
1981 90 Siamese Cat	Open		12.50	19
1981 91 Baby Camel	Closed	1984	11.00	100
1982 92 Orca Killer Whale	Open		16.50	21
1982 93 Quail	Open		13.50	19
1982 94 Goose	Closed	1999	14.00	35-40
1987 94A Baby Goose	Closed	1999	10.00	22-25
1987 94B Baby Goose	Closed	2000	10.00	13-22
1982 95 Middle Owl	Closed	2000	11.50	20-60
1982 96 Baby Ostrich	Open		13.00	19
1982 97 Baby Orca	Open		11.00	15
1982 98 Baby Gray Fox	Closed	1987	11.00	80
1987 98 Baby Red Fox	Closed	1995	12.00	60-70
1982 99 Baby Giraffe	Open		12.00	17
1982 100 Wild Rabbit	Closed	1995	12.00	100
1978 101 Pekingese	Closed	1995	12.50	52
1978 102 Bassethound	Closed	1995	12.00	55
1978 103 Scottish Terrier	Closed	1998	11.00	55

342
Collectors' Information Bureau

*Quotes have been rounded up to nearest dollar

YEAR ISSUE	EDITION LIMIT	YEAR RETD.	ISSUE PRICE	*QUOTE U.S.$
1978 104 Poodle	Closed	1987	17.00	220
1978 105 Bulldog	Closed	1998	11.50	55
1979 106 Collie	Closed	1995	12.50	60
1979 107 Duchshund	Closed	1998	13.50	55-60
1979 108 Husky	Closed	1998	13.50	60
1979 109 German Shephard	Closed	1995	13.50	55-60
1980 110 Boxer	Closed	1995	12.50	50-60
1980 111 Doberman	Closed	1995	13.00	50
1980 112 White Terrier	Closed	1998	12.00	45
1980 113 English Sheepdog	Open		13.50	19
1990 113A English Sheepdog Baby	Closed	1999	17.00	25-35
1980 114 Chihuahua	Closed	1998	9.50	10
1980 115 Dalmatian	Closed	1998	11.50	12
1980 116 Bloodhound	Closed	1990	10.50	30-40
1992 116 Dalmatian-Female	Open		17.00	19
1980 117 Fox Terrrier	Closed	1990	12.50	13
1981 118 St Bernard	Closed	1995	16.50	17
1981 119 Hunting Dog	Closed	1995	12.00	23
1981 120 Spaniel	Open		15.50	19
1982 121 Afghan	Closed	1998	15.00	15
1984 122 Cocker	Closed	1998	13.00	13
1994 123 Bassethound w/Bowl	Open		18.00	21
1993 124A Turtle (light green)	Open		15.00	17
1993 124B Turtle (blue)	Open		15.00	17
1993 124C Turtle (green)	Open		15.00	17
1993 124D Turtle (rose)	Open		15.00	17
1990 125 Galapagos	Closed	1999	20.00	22
1990 125A Baby Galapagos Turtle	Open		16.50	19
1990 126 Land Turtle	Closed	1999	15.50	50
1991 127 Box Turtle	Closed	1999	14.00	35-42
1990 128 Koala w/Baby	Open		22.00	25
1990 128A Baby Koala	Open		15.00	19
1991 129 Lg. Frog	Open		18.00	21
1994 135 Cameo Persian Cat	Closed	1999	15.00	20-35
1994 135A Kitten w/Sock A	Closed	1999	12.00	16-20
1994 135B Kitten w/Sock B	Closed	1999	12.00	16-20
1982 151 Lemur	Closed	1995	14.50	50-55
1982 152 Big Horn Sheep	Closed	1998	16.00	45-50
1983 153 Tabby Cat	Open		13.50	19
1983 154 Swan	Closed	1995	16.00	60
1983 155 Baby Wild Rabbit	Closed	1999	9.00	30
1983 156 Sea Turtle	Open		11.50	17
1983 157 Black Bear	Closed	1995	12.50	52
1983 158 Cockatoo	Closed	1995	14.50	65
1983 159 Lg. African Elephant	Open		13.00	19
1983 160 Baby African Elephant	Open		9.00	15
1983 161 Baby Polar Bear	Open		9.50	15
1987 161B Baby Polar Bear	Open		11.00	15
1984 162 Snow Owl	Open		13.50	19
1987 162A Baby Snow Owl	Closed	1999	10.50	22-23
1987 162B Baby Snow Owl	Closed	1999	10.50	22-23
1984 163 Baby Crocodile	Closed	1998	11.00	40
1984 164 Standing Raccoon	Closed	1999	14.50	30-40
1984 165 Kangaroo w/Baby	Open		13.50	19
1983 166 Kangaroo w/Flowers	Closed	1990	9.00	65
1984 167 Penguin	Open		12.50	17
1984 168A Baby Penguin	Open		7.50	13
1984 168B Baby Penguin	Open		7.50	13
1984 170 Lamb	Open		9.50	15
1984 171 Tabby Cat Female	Closed	1995	13.50	60
1984 172A Baby Tabby	Open		8.00	13
1984 172B Baby Tabby	Open		8.00	13
1984 173 Baby Fish	Closed	1987	8.50	50
1984 174 Flamingo	Open		16.50	21
1995 174A Flamingo Nesting	Open		20.00	21
1995 174B Baby Flamingo In Nest	Open		13.00	14
1984 175 Baby Moose	Open		11.00	15
1994 175A Baby Moose	Open		14.00	15
1984 176 Baby Cockatoo	Closed	1995	12.50	40
1984 177 Leopard	Open		13.50	19
1984 178 Chipmunk	Closed	1998	13.00	30
1984 179 Gorilla	Closed	1998	13.50	35
1984 180 Bull	Closed	1998	13.00	42
1987 180A Baby Bull	Closed	1998	6.00	25
1984 181 Crane	Closed	1990	14.50	60
1984 182 Water Buffalo	Closed	1990	13.50	65
1984 183 Baby Black Bears	Closed	1995	10.00	38
1984 184 Baby Black Bears	Closed	1995	10.00	45
1984 185 Sea Gull	Open		14.00	19
1985 186 Himlayan	Closed	1999	13.00	25-40
1985 187A Baby Himalayan	Closed	1999	7.50	16
1985 187B Baby Himalayan	Closed	1999	7.50	16
1985 188 Road Runner	Open		13.50	19
1985 189 Langur Monkey	Closed	1990	12.00	72
1985 190 Calico Cat	Open		14.00	19
1985 191A Baby Calico Cat	Open		10.00	13
1985 191B Baby Calico Cat	Open		10.50	13
1985 192 Baby Wild Boar	Closed	1990	8.00	45
1985 193 Burro	Open		14.00	19
1986 194 Cow (Holstein)	Open		13.50	17
1986 194A Baby Holstein Cow	Open		9.00	13
1985 195 Mouse	Closed	1999	10.50	25
1985 196 Baby Standing Racoon	Closed	1999	10.00	22-30
1985 197 Female African Elephant	Closed	1998	13.50	38-40
1986 198 Oriental Cat Male	Closed	1995	14.50	48
1986 199 Oriental Cat Female	Closed	1990	14.50	60
1979 202 Puppy Bassethound	Closed	1995	6.50	35
1979 203 Scottish Puppy	Closed	1998	6.50	42
1980 206 Puppy Colie	Closed	1995	6.50	35
1979 207 Dachshund Puppy	Closed	1998	6.50	42
1979 208 Husky Puppy	Closed	1998	6.50	25
1979 209 Puppy Shephard	Closed	1995	6.50	38-40

YEAR ISSUE	EDITION LIMIT	YEAR RETD.	ISSUE PRICE	*QUOTE U.S.$
1980 210 Puppy Boxer	Closed	1995	6.50	30
1980 211 Puppy Doberman	Closed	1995	6.50	30
1980 212 White Terrier Puppy	Closed	1998	6.50	30
1984 213 English Sheepdog Pup	Open		11.00	11
1980 215 Dalmatian Puppy	Closed	1998	8.00	30
1980 216 Bloodhound Puppy	Closed	1990	7.00	35-38
1992 216A Dalmatian w/Tray	Closed	1999	9.00	30
1992 216B Dalmatian Paw Up	Closed	1999	9.00	30
1992 216C Dalmatian Inclined	Closed	1999	9.00	30
1984 222 Cocker Puppy	Closed	1998	8.00	35
1995 223A Basset Puppy Lying Down	Open		14.00	15
1995 223B Basset Puppy Standing	Open		14.00	15
1994 235 Great White Shark	Closed	1999	16.00	30
1994 235A Baby Great White	Closed	1999	15.00	25
1994 236 Bottle-Nosed Dolphin	Open		17.00	19
1994 236A Baby Bottle-Nosed Dolphin	Open		12.00	14
1994 237 Killer Whale	Open		22.00	24
1994 237A Baby Killer Whale	Open		16.00	18
1995 241 Green Toad	Open		17.00	18
1995 244 Monkey With Book	Open		18.00	19
1995 247A Black Mouse	Open		7.00	8
1995 247B Ruby Mouse	Open		7.00	8
1995 247C Yellow Mouse	Open		7.00	8
1984 250A Unicorn (royal blue)	Closed	1999	18.00	23-40
1982 250B Unicorn (green)	Closed	1987	18.00	35-40
1982 250C Unicorn (black)	Closed	1987	18.00	135
1982 250D Unicorn (yellow)	Closed	1987	18.00	100-120
1984 250E Unicorn (maroon)	Closed	1999	18.00	22-40
1984 250F Unicorn (lt. blue)	Closed	1999	18.00	30-45
1984 251 Unicorn Sitting (gold horn)	Closed	1998	15.00	45-55
1983 252 Dragon	Closed	1998	16.00	45
1989 252A Baby Dragon	Closed	1995	12.00	30
1984 253A Baby Unicorn (royal blue)	Closed	1999	12.50	17-25
1983 253B Baby Unicorn (green)	Closed	1987	12.00	25
1983 253C Baby Unicorn (black)	Closed	1987	12.00	65
1983 253D Baby Unicorn (yellow)	Closed	1987	12.00	20
1984 253E Baby Unicorn (maroon)	Closed	1999	12.50	16-25
1984 253F Baby Unicorn (lt. blue)	Closed	1999	12.50	25-30
1989 254 Baby Dragon Pair	Closed	1995	16.00	30-40
1985 255A Pegasus (royal blue)	Closed	1998	11.00	45
1986 255B Pegasus (green)	Closed	1987	18.00	35
1986 255C Pegasus (brown)	Closed	1987	18.00	35
1986 255D Pegasus (yellow)	Closed	1987	18.00	35
1986 255E Pegasus (red)	Closed	1987	18.00	120
1986 255F Pegasus (grey)	Closed	1987	18.00	35
1985 256A Pegasus Female (royal blue)	Closed	1998	11.00	35
1986 256B Pegasus Sitting (green)	Closed	1987	18.00	35-40
1986 256C Pegasus Sitting (brown)	Closed	1987	18.00	40
1986 256D Pegasus Sitting (yellow)	Closed	1987	18.00	40
1986 256E Pegasus Sitting (red)	Closed	1987	18.00	40
1986 256F Pegasus Sitting (grey)	Closed	1987	18.00	40
1985 257A Baby Pegasus (royal blue)	Closed	1988	8.00	20
1986 257B Pegasus Baby Male (green)	Closed	1987	13.50	20
1986 257C Pegasus Baby Male (brown)	Closed	1987	13.50	20
1986 257D Pegasus Baby Male (yellow)	Closed	1987	13.50	20
1986 257E Pegasus Baby Male (red)	Closed	1987	13.50	20
1986 257F Pegasus Baby Male (grey)	Closed	1987	13.50	20
1985 258A Baby Pegasus (royal blue)	Closed	1998	8.00	20
1986 258B Pegasus Baby Female (green)	Closed	1987	13.50	20
1986 258C Pegasus Baby Female (brown)	Closed	1987	13.50	20
1986 258D Pegasus Baby Female (yellow)	Closed	1987	13.50	20
1986 258E Pegasus Baby Female (red)	Closed	1987	13.50	20
1986 258F Pegasus Baby Female (grey)	Closed	1987	13.50	20
1985 300 Butterfly Fish	Open		14.50	17
1985 301 Morish Idol Fish	Open		14.00	17
1985 302 Blue Tang Fish	Open		14.50	17
1986 303 Clown Fish (red)	Open		14.50	17
1986 304 Clown Fish (brown)	Closed	1990	14.00	55
1986 305 Clown Fish (orange)	Open		14.50	17
1986 306 Surgeon Fish	Open		14.00	17
1987 307 Long-Nosed Butterfly Fish	Open		15.00	19
1987 308 Butterfly Fish (orange)	Open		14.50	19
1986 310 Panda Male	Open		14.50	19
1986 311 Panda Female	Open		14.50	17
1986 312 Young Panda	Open		12.50	17
1986 313 Baby Panda	Open		11.00	15
1986 314 Persian (black & white)	Closed	1998	15.00	30
1986 315 Baby Persian	Closed	1998	9.50	20
1986 316 Mountain Goat	Closed	1998	15.00	42-44
1986 317 Baby Mountain Goat	Closed	1998	9.50	28-30
1986 318 Dolphin (blue)	Open		14.00	19
1986 318A Baby Dolphin (blue)	Open		9.50	13
1986 318B Baby Dolphin (blue)	Open		9.50	13
1986 319 Green Dolphin	Closed	1990	13.50	60
1986 319A Baby Dolphin (green)	Closed	1990	9.00	30
1986 319B Baby Dolphin (green)	Closed	1990	9.00	30
1986 320 Brown Dolphin	Closed	1990	13.50	60
1986 320A Baby Brown Dolphin	Closed	1990	9.00	30
1986 320B Baby Brown Dolphin	Closed	1990	9.00	30
1986 321 Yellow Dolphin	Closed	1990	13.50	60
1986 321A Baby Yellow Dolphin	Closed	1990	9.00	30
1986 321B Baby Yellow Dolphin	Closed	1990	9.00	30
1986 322 Dolphin (white)	Closed	1999	14.00	45
1986 322A Baby Dolphin	Closed	1999	9.50	25
1986 322B Baby Dolphin	Closed	1999	9.50	25
1987 323 Parrot (blue)	Open		16.00	19
1987 324 Parrot (green)	Open		16.00	19
1987 325 Parrot (red)	Open		16.00	19
1989 327 Baby Bear	Closed	1999	13.00	28-35
1989 327A Bear w/Baby	Closed	1999	16.50	35-45
1989 328A Baby Bear	Closed	1999	10.50	22
1989 328B Baby Bear	Closed	1999	10.50	18

YEAR ISSUE	EDITION LIMIT	YEAR RETD.	ISSUE PRICE	*QUOTE U.S.$
1989 328C Baby Bear	Closed	1999	10.50	18
1989 329 Owl	Closed	1999	16.50	35-40
1989 329A Baby Owl	Closed	1999	12.00	25-32
1992 330A Wise Bear A	Closed	1999	15.00	21-30
1992 330B Wise Bear B	Closed	1999	15.00	21-30
1992 330C Wise Bear C	Closed	1999	15.00	21-30
1993 331 Bear w/Pot Of Honey	Closed	1999	19.00	35
1993 331A Baby Bear w/Honey	Closed	1999	13.00	22
1993 331B Baby Bear w/Lid	Closed	1999	12.00	18
1992 332 Owls On Tree Trunk	Open		20.00	22
1993 333 Kiwi On Egg	Closed	2000	14.00	25
1993 334A Puffin (male)	Open		17.00	19
1993 334B Puffin (female)	Open		17.00	19
1993 335 Blue Persian Cat	Closed	1999	17.00	22
1993 335A Baby Persian On Pillow	Closed	1999	13.00	25
1993 335B Baby Persian (standing)	Closed	1999	10.00	16
1993 335C Baby Persian (sitting)	Closed	1999	10.00	16
1993 336 New Zealand Ram	Closed	1999	20.00	30-45
1993 336A New Zealand Sheep	Closed	1999	18.00	25
1993 336B New Zealand Ram (white)	Closed	1999	16.00	22
1993 336C New Zealand Lamb (black)	Closed	1999	16.00	22
1993 337 Camel (two humped)	Open		23.00	25
1994 337A Female Camel (two humped)	Open		21.00	23
1994 337B Baby Camel (standing)	Open		16.00	18
1994 337C Baby Camel (sitting)	Open		16.00	18
1993 338 Circus Bear (Papa)	Closed	1999	17.00	26
1993 338A Circus Bear (Mama)	Closed	1999	17.00	26
1993 338B Circus Bear (Baby)	Closed	1999	13.00	26
1993 338C Baby Bear On Bike	Closed	1999	13.00	20
1993 339 Hen Nesting in Cart	Open		20.00	22
1993 339A Rooster On Bucket	Open		20.00	22
1994 342 Mama Chimpance w/Baby	Closed	1999	25.00	35-65
1994 343 Baby Chimpance w/Sw.Cl.	Closed	1999	13.00	20-40
1993 344 White Tiger	Open		19.00	21
1993 344A White Tiger Cub	Open		13.00	15
1993 344B White Tiger Cub	Open		13.00	15
1995 350 Ostrich (new)	Open		22.00	23
1995 350A Ostrich (mother)	Open		21.00	27
1995 350B Baby Ostrich (standing)	Open		15.00	16
1995 350C Baby Ostrich In Egg	Open		13.00	14
1995 351 Emperor Penguin	Open		22.00	23
1995 351A Emperor Penguin w/Baby	Open		24.00	25
1995 351B Baby Emperor (sliding)	Open		12.00	13
1995 351C Baby Emperor (standing)	Open		14.00	15

Large Wildlife Collection - J. & J. Carbajales

YEAR ISSUE	EDITION LIMIT	YEAR RETD.	ISSUE PRICE	*QUOTE U.S.$
1986 401 Buffalo	Open		45.00	90
1986 402 Eagle	Open		45.00	100
1985 403 Elephant	Open		70.00	120
1986 404 Horse	Open		88.00	110
1987 405 Peacock	Open		85.00	150
1987 406 Iguana	Open		88.00	140
1987 407 Camel	Open		95.00	140
1990 408 Turtle	Open		96.00	110
1990 409 Tiger Cub	Open		100.00	120
1990 410 Persian Cat	Open		104.00	130
1990 411 Calico Cat	Open		110.00	130
1990 412 Tabby Cat	Open		104.00	120
1990 414 Owl	Open		96.00	110
1991 415 Ram	2,000		150.00	150
1994 416 Moose	3,000		180.00	200
1990 417 Polar Bear	Open		110.00	130
1992 419 Lion	2,500		150.00	180
1993 420 Unicorn	3,000		170.00	200
1993 421 Angora Cat	3,000		140.00	150
1993 424 Zebra	3,000		160.00	170
1994 426 Snowy Owl	3,000		160.00	180
1994 427 Panther	2,000		160.00	180
1994 428 Medieval Horse	2,000		240.00	250
1995 431 Loon	2,000		190.00	200
1994 432 Sea Turtle w/Turtles	3,000		220.00	250
1994 432A Sea Turtle w/Dolphins	3,000		220.00	250

Silver Anniversary Collection - J. & J. Carbajales

YEAR ISSUE	EDITION LIMIT	YEAR RETD.	ISSUE PRICE	*QUOTE U.S.$
1997 700 Ostrich (matte)	Closed	2000	29.00	32
2000 700 Ostrich (shiny black)	Open		29.00	32
1997 701 Ram (black)	Closed	2000	29.00	40-50
2000 701W Ram (white)	Open		29.00	32
1997 703 Duck	Open		29.00	32
1997 705 Turtle	Open		29.00	32
2000 706 Sea Turtle (blue shell)	Open		29.00	32
1997 706 Sea Turtle (white shell, blue dots)	Closed	2000	29.00	32
1997 707 Moose	Open		32.00	36
2000 708 Hippo (brown)	Open		36.00	36
1998 708 Hippo (purple)	Closed	2000	36.00	36
1997 709 Lion	Open		29.00	32
1997 711 Panther	Open		29.00	32
1997 712 Flamingo	Open		29.00	32
1997 713 Frog	Open		29.00	32
1997 714 Owl	Open		29.00	32
1997 715 Snowy Owl	Open		29.00	32
1997 717 Zebra	Open		29.00	32
1997 718 Camel	Open		32.00	36
1997 719 Elephant	Open		29.00	32
1997 721 Cat	Open		32.00	36
1997 723 Blue Owl	Open		32.00	36
1997 724 Spotted Owl	Open		32.00	36
1997 726 Loon	Open		32.00	36
1997 727 Tiger	Open		36.00	36
1997 728 African Elephant	Open		32.00	36
1998 731 Toad	Open		36.00	36
1998 732 Widgeon	Open		32.00	36

*Quotes have been rounded up to nearest dollar

Artesania Rinconada Collection/John J. Madison Co. Inc. to Boyds Collection Ltd.

FIGURINES

YEAR ISSUE	EDITION LIMIT	YEAR RETD.	ISSUE PRICE	*QUOTE U.S.$
1998 733 Turtle	Open		32.00	36
1998 734 Eagle	Open		32.00	36
1998 735 Dragon	Open		36.00	36
1999 736 Sea Otter	Open		36.00	36
1998 737 Calico Cat	Open		32.00	36
1999 738 Blue Duck	Open		36.00	36
1999 740 Trout	Open		40.00	40
2000 741 Rooster (cream neck)	Open		40.00	40
1999 741 Rooster (dark neck)	Closed	2000	40.00	40
1999 742 Pelican	Open		40.00	40
2000 743 Chicadee	Open		40.00	40
1999 744 Koala	Open		40.00	40
2000 746 Panda	Open		40.00	40
2000 747 Giraffe	Open		40.00	40
2000 748 Dolphin	Open		40.00	40
2000 749 Rhino	Open		40.00	40

Artists of the World

DeGrazia Annual Christmas Collection - T. DeGrazia

YEAR ISSUE	EDITION LIMIT	YEAR RETD.	ISSUE PRICE	*QUOTE U.S.$
1992 Feliz Navidad	1,992	N/A	195.00	200
1993 Fiesta Angels	1,993	1995	295.00	450-485
1994 Littlest Angel	1,994	N/A	165.00	150
1995 Bethlehem Bound	1,995	1996	195.00	200
1996 Christmas Serenade	1,996	N/A	145.00	145
1997 Christmas Bride	1,997		125.00	125
1998 Christmas Angel of Light	1,998	N/A	145.00	145
1999 Angel Love	1,999	N/A	145.00	145
2000 Blessed Child	2,000		135.00	135

DeGrazia Figurine - T. DeGrazia

YEAR ISSUE	EDITION LIMIT	YEAR RETD.	ISSUE PRICE	*QUOTE U.S.$
1990 Alone	7,500	1994	395.00	585-800
1995 Apache Mother	3,500	1996	165.00	225
1988 Beautiful Burden	Closed	1990	175.00	250-275
1990 Biggest Drum	Closed	1992	110.00	225
1996 Blessed Madonna	2,500	1997	195.00	200-225
1986 The Blue Boy	Suspd.		70.00	140
1992 Coming Home	3,500	1995	165.00	200-228
1990 Crucifixion	S/O	1995	295.00	350
1990 Desert Harvest	5,000	1993	135.00	150-200
1986 Festival Lights	Suspd.		75.00	125-150
1994 Festive Flowers	3,500	1996	145.00	150-300
1984 Flower Boy	Closed	1992	65.00	225-250
1988 Flower Boy Plaque	Closed	1990	80.00	170-190
1984 Flower Girl	Suspd.		65.00	175
1984 Flower Girl Plaque	Closed	1985	45.00	150
1999 Friendship	2,500	N/A	145.00	145
1999 Heavenly Madonna	2,500	N/A	165.00	165
1996 Homeward Bound	2,500	1997	195.00	195-200
1995 Little Helper	3,500	N/A	185.00	185
1985 Little Madonna	Closed	1993	80.00	200
1993 Little Medicine Man	Closed	1997	175.00	180-190
1988 Los Ninos	5,000	1989	595.00	900
1989 Los Ninos (Artist's Edition)	S/O	N/A	695.00	2000-3500
1987 Love Me	Closed	1992	95.00	250
1988 Merrily, Merrily, Merrily	Closed	1991	95.00	200-210
1986 Merry Little Indian	12,500	1989	175.00	300
1996 Mother's Warmth	950	1997	295.00	300
1989 My Beautiful Rocking Horse	Suspd.		225.00	325
1989 My First Arrow	Closed	1992	95.00	225
1984 My First Horse	Closed	1990	65.00	250
1990 Navajo Boy	Closed	1992	110.00	200-275
1992 Navajo Madonna	Closed	1993	135.00	275
1991 Navajo Mother	3,500	1995	295.00	300-423
1985 Pima Drummer Boy	Closed	1991	65.00	100-200
1998 Pueblo Sandpainter	950	N/A	295.00	295
1997 Resounding Joy	950	N/A	295.00	295
1993 Saddle Up	5,000	1995	195.00	200-280
1994 Saguaro Dance	2,500	N/A	495.00	495
1995 Spring Blossoms	5,000	N/A	170.00	170
1992 Sun Showers	5,000	N/A	195.00	195
1984 Sunflower Boy	Closed	1985	65.00	300
1990 Sunflower Girl	Closed	1993	95.00	149-300
1987 Wee Three	Closed	1990	180.00	275
1984 White Dove	Closed	1992	45.00	125
1984 Wondering	Closed	1987	85.00	225

DeGrazia Nativity Collection - T. DeGrazia

YEAR ISSUE	EDITION LIMIT	YEAR RETD.	ISSUE PRICE	*QUOTE U.S.$
1993 Balthasar	Closed	N/A	135.00	125-135
1988 Christmas Prayer Angel (red)	Closed	1991	70.00	150-293
1990 El Burrito	Closed	N/A	60.00	100
1999 El Camello	Closed	N/A	90.00	90
1993 El Toro	Closed	N/A	95.00	98
1999 Flowers For Baby Jesus	Closed	N/A	145.00	145
1993 Gaspar	Closed	N/A	135.00	125-135
1985 Jesus	Closed	N/A	35.00	65
1985 Joseph	Closed	N/A	50.00	110-125
1990 Little Prayer Angel (white)	Closed	1992	85.00	200-215
1985 Mary	Closed	N/A	40.00	125
1993 Melchoir	Closed	N/A	135.00	125
1996 Music For Baby Jesus	Closed	N/A	145.00	145
1997 My Gift For Baby Jesus	Closed	N/A	135.00	135
1998 My Guardian Angel	Closed	N/A	145.00	145
1985 Nativity Set-3 pc. (Mary, Joseph, Jesus)	Closed	N/A	275.00	270-290
1995 Pima Indian Drummer Boy	Closed	N/A	135.00	135
1991 Shepherd's Boy	Closed	N/A	95.00	100-135
1989 Two Little Lambs	Closed	1992	70.00	225

DeGrazia Pendants - R. Olszewski

YEAR ISSUE	EDITION LIMIT	YEAR RETD.	ISSUE PRICE	*QUOTE U.S.$
1987 Festival of Lights 562-P	Suspd.		90.00	225
1985 Flower Girl Pendant 561-P	Suspd.		125.00	150-291

DeGrazia Village Collection - T. DeGrazia

YEAR ISSUE	EDITION LIMIT	YEAR RETD.	ISSUE PRICE	*QUOTE U.S.$
1992 The Listener	Closed	1992	48.00	90-100
1992 Little Feather	Closed	1995	53.00	120
1992 Medicine Man	Closed	1995	75.00	100-150
1992 Standing Tall	Closed	1996	65.00	120
1992 Telling Tales	Closed	1992	48.00	75-90
1992 Tiny Treasure	Closed	1995	53.00	100-200
1993 Water Wagon	Closed	1995	295.00	295

DeGrazia: Goebel Miniatures - R. Olszewski

YEAR ISSUE	EDITION LIMIT	YEAR RETD.	ISSUE PRICE	*QUOTE U.S.$
1988 Adobe Display 948D	Closed	N/A	45.00	60-90
1990 Adobe Hacienda (large) Display 958-D	Closed	N/A	85.00	150-200
1989 Beautiful Burden 554-P	Closed	N/A	110.00	150
1990 Chapel Display 971-D	Closed	N/A	95.00	100-120
1986 Festival of Lights 507-P	Closed	N/A	85.00	225-250
1985 Flower Boy 502-P	Closed	N/A	85.00	110-200
1985 Flower Girl 501-P	Closed	N/A	85.00	110-200
1986 Little Madonna 552-P	Closed	N/A	93.00	150-225
1989 Merry Little Indian 508-P (new style)	Closed	N/A	110.00	175-200
1987 Merry Little Indian 508-P (old style)	Closed	N/A	95.00	200-300
1991 My Beautiful Rocking Horse 555-P	Closed	N/A	110.00	150-175
1985 My First Horse 503-P	Closed	N/A	85.00	150-165
1986 Pima Drummer Boy 506-P	Closed	N/A	85.00	250-300
1985 Sunflower Boy 551- P	Closed	N/A	93.00	135-195
1985 White Dove 504-P	Closed	N/A	80.00	110-125
1985 Wondering 505-P	Closed	N/A	93.00	175-200

BARBIE Collectibles by Hallmark/Hallmark Keepsake Collections

Holiday Homecoming Collection

YEAR ISSUE	EDITION LIMIT	YEAR RETD.	ISSUE PRICE	*QUOTE U.S.$
1997 Holiday Traditions™ Barbie® QHB6001	Retrd.	1998	45.00	45
1998 Holiday Voyage™ Barbie® QHB6017	Retrd.	1999	45.00	45

Barbie/Enesco Group, Inc.

Happy Holidays Musicals - Enesco

YEAR ISSUE	EDITION LIMIT	YEAR RETD.	ISSUE PRICE	*QUOTE U.S.$
1995 Happy Holidays Barbie, 1988 154199	Yr.Iss.	1995	100.00	100
1996 Holiday, 1989 188832	Yr.Iss.	1996	100.00	100
1996 Happy Holidays Barbie, 1996 274321	Yr.Iss.	1997	100.00	100
1997 Happy Holidays Barbie, 1990 274313	Yr.Iss.	1997	100.00	100

Bing & Grondahl

Centennial Anniversary Commemoratives - F.A. Hallin

YEAR ISSUE	EDITION LIMIT	YEAR RETD.	ISSUE PRICE	*QUOTE U.S.$
1995 Centennial Vase: Behind the Frozen Window	1,250	1995	295.00	295-300

Boyds Collection Ltd.

The Loyal Order of Friends of Boyds ("F.o.B.s" for Short) - G.M. Lowenthal

YEAR ISSUE	EDITION LIMIT	YEAR RETD.	ISSUE PRICE	*QUOTE U.S.$
1996 Raeburn (6" plush bear)	Retrd.	1997	Gift	44
1996 Uncle Elliot Pin	Retrd.	1997	Gift	75
1996 Uncle Elliot...The Head Bean Wants You	Retrd.	1997	Gift	50-90
1996 Velma Q. Berriweather...The Cookie Queen (11" plush)	Retrd.	1997	29.00	50-90
1996 Velma Q. Berriweather...The Cookie Queen (figurine)	Retrd.	1997	19.00	60-69
1998 Eleanor (6" plush bear)	Retrd.	1998	Gift	45
1998 Lady Libearty Patriotic Pin	Retrd.	1998	Gift	17-65
1998 Zelma G. Berriweather (11" plush bear)	Retrd.	1998	32.00	31-38
1998 Ms. Berriweather's Cottage (figurine)	Retrd.	1998	21.00	21-75
1999 Flora Mae Berriweather (6" plush bear)	Retrd.	1999	Gift	42-57
1999 I'm a Bloomin' F.o.B. Bearstone Pin	Retrd.	1999	Gift	N/A
1999 Blossum B. Berriweather...Bloom with Joy!	Retrd.	1999	Gift	38
1999 F.o.B. Mug	Retrd.	1999	7.50	8
1999 Hope, Love and Joy (plush bear)	Retrd.	1999	25.00	25
1999 Sunny and Sally	Retrd.	1999	23.00	23
2000 Caitlin Berriweather (6" plush bear)	12/00		Gift	N/A
2000 Catherine & Caitlin Berriweather...Fine Cup of Tea	12/00		Gift	N/A
2000 Tea for Three (poem)	12/00		Gift	N/A
2000 "Brewin F.o.B." Bearstone Pin	12/00		Gift	N/A
2000 Catherine and Caitlin w/Little Scruff	12/00		25.00	25
2000 Catherine w/Little Scruff	12/00		26.00	26
2000 Mini Tea Set	12/00		7.50	8
2000 Noah's Toolbox	12/00		12.00	12

Special Event - G.M. Lowenthal

YEAR ISSUE	EDITION LIMIT	YEAR RETD.	ISSUE PRICE	*QUOTE U.S.$
1997 Prince Hamalot	Retrd.	1997	30.00	45-62
1998 Elizabeth...I am the Queen	Retrd.	1998	34.00	44-69
1999 Victoria Regena Buzzbruin...So Many Flowers, So Little Time 01999-71	Retrd.	1999	26.00	26-46
1999 Matthew Bear (Anniversary Edition) 5000-1	Retrd.	1999	9.50	10-49
2000 Prissie, Sissie and Missie...Fixin' Tea For Three	Retrd.	2000	23.00	23-43

The Bearstone Collection Nativity™ - G.M. Lowenthal

YEAR ISSUE	EDITION LIMIT	YEAR RETD.	ISSUE PRICE	*QUOTE U.S.$
1997 Ariel & Clarence...As The Pair O' Angels 2411	Retrd.	1999	14.00	35-69
1995 Baldwin...as the Child 2403	Retrd.	1999	14.95	31-38
1997 Bruce...as the Shepherd 2410	Retrd.	1999	15.00	29-38
1998 Caledonia...as the Narrator 2412	Retrd.	1999	16.00	32-38
1997 Essex...as the Donkey 2408	Retrd.	1999	15.00	37-47
1996 Heath as Casper Bearing Frankincense 2405	Retrd.	1999	14.00	23-38
1998 Matthew...as the Drummer 2415	Retrd.	1999	16.00	32-50
1998 Ms. Bruin...as the Teacher 2414	Retrd.	1999	16.00	22-32
1995 Neville...as Joseph 2401	Retrd.	1999	14.95	23-32
1996 Raleigh as Balthasar Bearing Myrrh 2406	Retrd.	1999	14.00	23-32
1998 Serendipity...as the Guardian Angel 2416	Retrd.	1999	16.00	32-38
1995 The Stage...the School Pagent 2425	Retrd.	1999	34.50	35-75
1996 Thatcher & Eden as the Camel 2407	Retrd.	1999	17.00	20-32
1995 Theresa...as Mary 2402	Retrd.	1999	14.95	25-32
1996 Wilson as Melchior Bearing Gold 2404	Retrd.	1999	14.00	38-40
1996 Winkie & Dink as the Lambs 2409	Retrd.	1999	11.00	40-51

The Bearstone Collection™ - G.M. Lowenthal, unless otherwise noted

YEAR ISSUE	EDITION LIMIT	YEAR RETD.	ISSUE PRICE	*QUOTE U.S.$
1994 Agatha & Shelly-'Scardy Cat' 2246	Retrd.	1998	16.25	19-82
1999 Alexandra and Belle...Telephone Tied 227720	Open		18.50	29-82
1995 Amelia's Enterprise 'Carrot Juice' 2258	Retrd.	1998	16.25	19-69
1995 Angelica...'the Guardian' 2266	Retrd.	1999	17.95	31-69
1995 Angelica...the Guardian Angel (waterglobe) 2702	Retrd.	1998	37.50	50-69
1999 Arnold P. Bomber...The Duffer 227714	Open		21.00	21-40
1993 Arthur...with Red Scarf 2003-03	Retrd.	1994	10.50	88-213
1994 Bailey & Emily...'Forever Friends' 2018	Retrd.	1996	34.00	75-110
1994 Bailey & Wixie 'To Have and To Hold' 2017	Retrd.	1998	15.75	29-250
1994 Bailey at the Beach 2020-09	Retrd.	1995	15.75	80-175
1993 Bailey Bear with Suitcase (old version) 2000	Retrd.	1993	14.20	360-630
1993 Bailey Bear with Suitcase (revised version) 2000	Retrd.	2000	14.20	15-200
1994 Bailey's Birthday 2014	Retrd.	1999	15.95	45-238
1996 Bailey's Birthday 2763SF	Retrd.	1999	45.00	45
1995 Bailey...'The Baker with Sweetie Pie' 2254	Open		12.50	13-69
1995 Bailey...'The Baker with Sweetie Pie' 2254CL	3,600	1995	15.00	200-225
1995 Bailey...'the Cheerleader' 2268	Open		15.95	16-70
1995 Bailey...'The Honeybear' 2260	Open		15.75	16-88
1996 Bailey...Heart's Desire 2272	Retrd.	2000	15.00	29-69
1993 Bailey...in the Orchard 2006	Retrd.	1996	14.20	62-296
1997 Bailey..Poor Old Bear 227704	Retrd.	1997	14.00	14-77
1997 Bailey..The Graduate 227701-10	Open		16.50	17-44
1999 Bailey...The Bride 227712	Open		18.00	18-47
1998 Beatrice...We are always the Same Age Inside 227802	Yr.Iss.	1998	62.00	95-125
1999 Bernice as Mrs. Noah...the Chief Cook and Bottle Washer 2427	Open		11.00	11-38
1994 Bessie the Santa Cow 2239	Retrd.	1996	15.75	50-80
1999 Bumble B. Bee...Sweeter Than Honey 227718	Open		16.00	16-75
1997 Buzz...the flash 227706	Open		18.00	18
1993 Byron & Chedda w/Catmint 2010	Retrd.	1994	14.20	115-207
1999 Caren B. Bearlove 227722	Retrd.	1999	13.50	14-37
1994 Celeste...'The Angel Rabbit' 2230	Retrd.	1997	16.25	74-300
1998 Celestina 25710	Retrd.	1999	10.00	10
1994 Charlotte & Bebe...'The Gardeners' 2229	Retrd.	1995	15.75	32-98
2000 Chester Birdbreath...purrstone 371006	Open		17.00	17
1999 Chrissie...Game, Set, Match 227717	Retrd.	2000	16.50	25-44
1993 Christian by the Sea 2012	Retrd.	1998	14.20	15-125
1994 Christmas Big Pig, Little Pig BC2256	Retrd.	N/A	N/A	138-219
1996 Claire 25701	Retrd.	1998	11.00	11
1994 Clara...'The Nurse' 2231	Retrd.	1998	16.25	45-360
2000 Clara..the nurse Spoonful of Sugar 2777	Open		38.00	38
1994 Clarence Angel Bear (rust) 2029-11	Retrd.	1995	12.60	70-175
1995 Clarion 2254CL	Retrd.	N/A	13.00	13
1998 Clestina 25710	Retrd.	1999	10.00	10
1998 The Collector 227707	Open		21.00	21-50
1995 Cookie Catberg...'Knittin' Kitten' 2250	Retrd.	1997	18.75	39-75
1994 Cookie the Santa Cat 2237	Retrd.	1995	15.25	32-75
1999 Daphne And Eloise (musical) 270553	Open		35.00	35-57
1995 Daphne and Eloise...'Women's Work' 2251	Retrd.	1999	18.00	18-88
1993 Daphne Hare & Maisey Ewe 2011	Retrd.	1995	14.20	44-63
1994 Daphne...The Reader Hare 2226	Retrd.	1998	14.20	15-184
1998 Dean Newbearger 111...the Investor 227715	Retrd.	1998	16.00	16-52
2000 Dominique Surfoot w/coach colby 371052	Open		15.00	15
1998 Dr. Harrison Griz PHD & bud 228309	Open		15.00	15-53
1998 Eddie...Bear American 228312	Open		14.00	14-39
1994 Edmond & Bailey...'Gathering Holly' 2240	Retrd.	2000	24.25	39-232
1997 Edmond..The Graduate 227701-07	Open		16.50	17-44
1998 Edmund the Elf Christmas Carol 228311	Open		15.00	15-44
1996 Edmund-Claire-Winston 25700-25701-25702	Retrd.	1998	11.00	11
1994 Elgin the Elf Bear 2236	Retrd.	1997	14.20	32-119
1997 Elias The Elf Grizberg 3206	Retrd.	1999	10.00	19-150
1994 Elliot & Snowbeary 2242	Retrd.	1999	15.25	16-100

*Quotes have been rounded up to nearest dollar

YEAR ISSUE		EDITION LIMIT	YEAR RETD.	ISSUE PRICE	*QUOTE U.S.$
1994	Elliot & The Tree 2241	Retrd.	1999	16.25	17-252
1995	Elliot & the Tree Water Globe 2704	Retrd.	1997	35.00	63-94
1996	Elliot...the Hero 2280	Retrd.	2000	16.75	25-75
1998	Elvira & Chauncey Fitzbruin...Shipmates 227708	Retrd.	2000	19.00	29-69
1999	Elvira and Chauncey Fitzbruin...Shipmates (waterglobe) 270552	Open		37.00	37
1996	Emma & Bailey...Afternoon Tea 2277	Retrd.	N/A	18.00	47-75
1995	Emma...'the Witchy Bear' 2269	Open		16.75	17-69
1996	Ewell/Walton Manitoba Moosemen BC2228	12,000		24.99	25-76
1993	Father Chrisbear and Son 2008	Retrd.	1993	15.00	375-546
1998	Feldman D. Finklebearg & Dooley ..."Painless" & The Patient 227710	Retrd.	2000	20.00	20-59
1998	Filbert Q Foghorn 3208	Retrd.	1999	17.00	17
1999	Flash McBear and The Sitting 227721	Open		33.00	33-75
1997	The Flying Lesson (waterglobe) 270601	Retrd.	1997	62.00	55-100
1997	The Flying Lesson 227801	Yr.Iss.	1997	62.00	75-103
1999	G M Bearenthal...Happy Birthday you ole' bear 228321	Open		18.50	19-39
1999	Gary, Tina, Matt and Bailey...From Our Home to Yours 227804	Open		46.00	46-95
1996	Gertrude Gerty Grisberg 3201	Retrd.	1998	15.00	15
1996	Gladys-Grisberg Shoebox bear 3201-01	Retrd.	1996	15.00	15
2000	Goodfer U. Bear...Way to Go! 227729 - The Boyds Collection	Open		16.00	16-35
1997	Grace & Jonathan...Born to Shop 228306	Open		19.00	19-38
2000	Greg McBruin...the Wind Up 227732 - The Boyds Collection	Open		16.00	16-28
1994	Grenville & Beatrice...'Best Friends' 2016	Retrd.	1999	26.25	27-510
1996	Grenville & Beatrice...True Love 2274	Open		36.00	39-92
1995	Grenville & Knute...Football Buddies 2255	Retrd.	1998	19.95	32-125
1993	Grenville & Neville...'The Sign' (prototype) 2099	Retrd.	1993	15.75	13-94
1993	Grenville & Neville...'The Sign' 2099	Retrd.	1998	15.75	16-20
1994	Grenville the Santabear (musical waterball) 2700	Retrd.	1996	35.75	73-82
1994	Grenville the Santabear 2030	Retrd.	1996	14.20	88-480
1996	Grenville with Matthew & Bailey...Sunday Afternoon 2281	Retrd.	2000	34.50	42-69
1994	Grenville...'The Graduate' 2233	Retrd.	1996	16.25	50-63
1995	Grenville...'The Storyteller' 2265	Retrd.	1995	50.00	45-100
1993	Grenville...with Green Scarf 2003-04	Retrd.	1994	10.50	600-660
1993	Grenville...with Red Scarf 2003-08	Retrd.	1995	10.50	98-188
1998	Gwain....love is the master key 228317	Open		15.00	22-84
1998	The Head Bean & Co....Work is Love Made Visible (5th Anniversary) 227803	18,000	1998	61.00	63-94
1994	Homer on the Plate 2225	Retrd.	1999	15.75	16-88
1997	Homer on the Plate 270550	Retrd.	1999	36.00	36
1994	Homer on the Plate BC2210	Open		24.99	25-60
1995	Hop-a-Long...'The Deputy' 2247	Retrd.	2000	14.00	26-69
2000	Hsing Hsing & Ling Ling 2433	Open		12.00	12
2000	Huck w/Mandy, Zoe and Zack...Rollin' along 227727 - The Boyds Collection	Open		22.00	22-35
1997	Humboldt...the Simple Bear 227703	Open		12.00	12-19
2000	Ima Chillin'...Takin' it Easy 227728 - The Boyds Collection	Open		18.00	18-29
1997	Ingrid..Be Warm 25651	Retrd.	1998	12.00	12
1999	Ivan Mooselbeary 3216	Open		15.00	15
1998	Jean 25852	Retrd.	1999	10.00	10
1999	Jeremy as Noah...The Ark Builder 2426	Open		11.00	11-35
2000	Joey & Alice...outback 2432	Open		12.00	12
2000	Jonathon C. Tootsenwhistle w/Majorie Marchalong...one bear band 227806 - The Boyds Collection	120,000	2000	25.00	25-47
1997	Judge Griz...Hissonah 228303	Retrd.	1998	18.50	19-52
1998	Juliette 25712	Retrd.	1999	10.00	10
1994	Juliette Angel Bear (ivory) 2029-10	Retrd.	1995	12.60	76-125
1994	Justina & M. Harrison...'Sweetie Pie' 2015	Retrd.	1999	26.25	69-113
1996	Justina...The Message "Bearer" 2273	Open		16.00	16-22
1999	Justina...the choir singer 228324	Open		18.00	18-38
2000	Kandace Purrshop...hidden treasures 371054	Open		18.00	18
1994	Knute & The Gridiron 2245	Retrd.	1997	16.25	56-88
1998	Knute...half time 25705	Retrd.	1999	11.00	11
1994	Kringle & Bailey with List 2235	Retrd.	1999	14.20	15-120
1996	Kringle And Company 2283	Retrd.	1999	17.45	60-88
1998	Larry...Nutin But Net 25706	Retrd.	1999	11.00	11
1998	Lars...ski, ski, ski 25653	Open		12.00	12
1995	Lefty...'On the Mound' 2253	Retrd.	2000	15.00	15-57
1995	Lefty...'On the Mound' BC2056	Open		24.99	25-63
1999	Light a Candle for a Better World 227805	Retrd.	1999	53.00	53
1997	Louella and Hedda...The Secret 227705	Open		18.00	18-66
1994	Lucy Big Pig, Little Pig BC2250	Retrd.	1996	24.99	100-150
1996	M. Harrison's Birthday 2275	Retrd.	1999	17.00	17-38
1994	Manheim the 'Eco-Moose' 2243	Retrd.	1999	15.25	86-113
1998	Margot...The Ballerina 227709	Retrd.	2000	18.00	54-88
1999	Mario..Hat Trick 25718	Open		11.00	11
1994	Maynard the Santa Moose 2238	Retrd.	1997	15.25	32-144
1999	McDuffer...The 19th Hole 25719	Open		11.00	11
1999	McGuire...it's out of here 25717	Open		11.00	11
1998	Megan 25850	Retrd.	1999	10.00	10
1998	Miles Grizberg 3209-10	Retrd.	1999	17.00	17
1995	Miss Bruin & Bailey 'The Lesson' 2259	Open		18.45	19-150
1999	Momma & Ellie Grizberg 3211-12	Retrd.	2000	14.00	14
2000	Momma and Poppa McNewbear w/Baby Bundles 227731 - The Boyds Collection	Open		19.00	19-29
1998	Momma Mcbear & Caledonia...Quiet Time 227711	Open		20.00	20-69
1996	Momma Mcbear...Anticipation 2282	Open		14.95	15-48
2000	Momma Purrsmore & baby Belle 371053	Open		19.00	19
1993	Moriarty-'The Bear in the Cat Suit' 2005	Retrd.	1995	13.75	113-269
1999	Mrs. Fezziwig w/Marley-Bob & Caroline 371005	Retrd.	1999	27.00	27
1999	Mrs. Tuttle 228315	Open		15.00	15-26
1999	Ms Friday...take this jo! 228318	Open		17.00	17-35
1999	Ms. Bruin and Bailey...The Lesson (musical) 270554	Retrd.	2000	38.00	38-125
1996	Ms. Griz...Monday Morning 2276	Retrd.	1999	34.00	45-144
1996	Ms. Griz...Saturday Night GCC 2284	Retrd.	2000	15.00	40-87
1993	Neville...The 'Bedtime Bear' 2002	Retrd.	1996	14.20	61-132
1997	Neville...compubear 227702	Retrd.	2000	15.50	25-62
1997	Nickolas Uncle Nick Grizberg 3205	Retrd.	1999	20.00	20
1996	Noah & Co...Ark Builders 2278	Retrd.	1996	61.00	94-157
1996	Noah & Company (waterglobe) 2706	6,000	1996	50.95	88-275
1999	Noah's Genius at work...table 2429	Retrd.	1999	11.50	12
1999	Noah...And the Golden Rule (votive) 27754	Open		26.00	26-57
2000	Ol' Mother McBear...the More the Merrier 227733 - The Boyds Collection	Open		20.50	21-35
1997	Ola...let it snow 25650	Retrd.	1998	12.00	12
1998	Olivia...wishing you peace 25800	Retrd.	1999	12.00	12
2000	Opie Baithook w/Barney...catch of the day 371051	Open		19.00	19
1995	Otis...'Taxtime' 2262	Retrd.	1997	18.75	59-100
1995	Otis...'The Fisherman' 2249-06	Retrd.	1998	15.75	16-57
2000	Packy & Dermah 2431	Open		12.00	12
2000	Pokie Pawsworthy...bug inspector 371050	Open		20.50	21
1999	Princess Standingbear 3217	Open		15.00	15
1997	Puck...Slapshot 228305	Open		18.50	19-29
1998	Ray...Croccodopius (Desk Animals™) 380000	Retrd.	1999	11.00	11
1998	Regina...I am the queen 25709	Retrd.	1999	11.00	11
1998	Rocky Bruin...Score-Score-Score 228307	Open		19.00	19
1998	Rosemar...bearhugs 228316	Open		25.00	25-44
1999	S. Kringleberry...have a simple x-mas (QVC Exclusive) 228320	Retrd.	1999	15.00	15
1998	S.C. Northstar and Emmett 228310	Open		25.00	25
1999	S.S. Noah...The Ark 2450	Open		34.50	35-75
1999	Sage Buzzby...Bee Wis 25715	Open		10.00	10
1999	Santa Claws & Nibbles 371003	Open		17.00	17
1994	Sebastian's Prayer 2227	Retrd.	1996	16.25	59-112
1998	Serena 25711	Retrd.	1999	10.00	10
1998	Serendipity 25955	Retrd.	1998	21.00	21
1999	Sergeant Bookum O' Reilly 3214	Open		15.00	15
1994	Sherlock & Watson-In Disguise 2019	Retrd.	1996	15.75	82-175
1995	Simone & Bailey...'Helping Hands' 2267	Retrd.	1999	25.95	40-63
1996	Simone and Bailey...Helping Hands 2705	Retrd.	1998	34.80	45-57
1993	Simone De Bearvoire and Her Mom 2001	Retrd.	1996	14.20	140-450
1996	Sir Edmund... Persistence 2279	Retrd.	1999	20.75	53-63
1999	Sissie & Squirt...big helper lil' sipper 228323	Open		21.00	21-42
1999	Sparky & the box 227716	Open		20.00	20-48
1997	Stonewall the Rebel 228302	Retrd.	1999	19.00	19-52
1999	Stretch and Skye Longnecker...The Lookouts 2428	Open		11.00	11-48
1998	Tabitha w/Wolsey & Zip...flying high 228319	Retrd.	1999	26.00	26
1994	Ted & Teddy 2223	Retrd.	1997	15.75	52-138
1999	Tessa-Ben & Cissie...T.B.C...a sign of the times 2299	Open		19.00	19-32
1996	Thaddeus Bud Grisberg 3202	Retrd.	1998	10.00	10
2000	Tillie Hopgood...the Eggsitter 227734 - The Boyds Collection	Retrd.	2000	15.00	15-25
2000	Tweedle Bedeedle...Stop and Smell the Roses 227730 - The Boyds Collection	Open		16.00	16-36
1995	Union Jack...'Love Letters' 2263	Retrd.	1998	18.95	52-69
1993	Victoria...'The Lady' 2004	Retrd.	1999	18.40	19-306
1999	Wanda and Gert...A Little Off The Top 227719	Open		18.00	18-42
2000	Webster Grizberg 3219	Open		14.00	14
2000	Willie...as Noah's son 2430	Open		11.00	11
1996	Wilson 25702	Retrd.	1998	11.00	11
1994	Wilson at the Beach 2020-06	Retrd.	1997	15.75	52-132
1994	Wilson the "Perfesser" 2222	Retrd.	1997	16.25	32-75
1993	Wilson with Love Sonnets 2007	Retrd.	1997	12.60	88-550
1995	Wilson...'the Wonderful Wizard of Wuz' 2261	Retrd.	1999	15.95	16-75
1998	Winnie Hopkins & Bunnylove 3207	Retrd.	2000	20.00	20
1994	Xmas Bear Elf with List BC2051	1,865	1994	24.99	1250-1500
1997	Zoe...Angel of Life (GCC Exclusive) 2286	Retrd.	1997	15.00	32-44

The Dollstone Collection™ - G.M. Lowenthal, unless otherwise noted

YEAR ISSUE		EDITION LIMIT	YEAR RETD.	ISSUE PRICE	*QUOTE U.S.$
1996	Betsey and Edmund with Union Jack BC35031	Open		24.99	25-82
1995	Betsey & Edmund 3503PE	Retrd.	1995	19.50	27-75
1995	Katherine, Amanda & Edmund 3505PE	Retrd.	1995	19.50	32-119
1995	Meagan 3504PE	Retrd.	1995	19.50	200-300
1995	Victoria with Samantha 3502PE	Retrd.	1995	19.50	75-90
1995	Set of 4 PE	Retrd.	1995	78.00	312-400
1999	Alyssa With Caroline...A Stitch in Time 3539	Open		18.00	18-50
1997	The Amazing Bailey...'Magic Show' 3518	Yr.Iss.	1997	60.00	48-88
1998	Amy and Edmund...Momma's Clothes 3529	Retrd.	2000	29.50	50-63
1996	Anne...the Masterpiece 3599	Retrd.	1999	24.25	27-56
1996	Ashley with Chrissie...Dress Up 3506	Retrd.	1998	20.50	21-78
1998	Austin w/Allen...the firechief 3534	Retrd.	1999	20.00	20-37
2000	Barbara Ann w/Jodi and Annie...Stitched w/Love 3554 - The Boyds Collection	Open		23.00	23-38
1997	Benjamin with Mattew...The Speed Trap 3524	Retrd.	2000	30.00	35-69
1996	Betsey with Edmond...The Patriots 3503	Open		20.00	20-100
2000	Brooke w/Joshua...Puddle Jumpers 3551 - The Boyds Collection	Open		20.00	20-32
1997	Caitlin with Emma & Edmund...Diapering Baby 3525	Retrd.	1999	20.00	19-75
1996	Candice with Matthew...Gathering Apples 3514	Retrd.	1999	18.95	19-69
2000	Casey w/Baxter...Afternoon Stroll 3557 - The Boyds Collection	120,000		35.00	35-72
1999	Cheryl w/Ashlie...nighty night 3544	Open		20.00	20-39
1996	Christy w/Nicole...Mother's Presence GCC 3516	Open		26.00	26-60
2000	Cindy w/Collier...Dress Up 3555 - The Boyds Collection	Open		14.00	14-22
1996	Courtney with Phoebe...over the River and Thru the Woods (waterglobe) 3512	Retrd.	1997	24.25	28-43
1996	Emily with Kathleen & Otis...The Future 3508	Retrd.	2000	30.00	59-122
1999	Grace and Faith...I Have a Dream (musical) 272054	Retrd.	1999	36.00	36-47
1999	Heather With Lauren...Bunny Helpers 3538	Open		19.50	20-38
1998	Jamie and Thomasina...the Last One 3530	Open		20.00	20-57
1996	Jean with Elliot & Debbie...The Bakers 3510	Open		19.50	20-75
1996	Jennifer with Priscilla...The Doll in the Attic 3500	Retrd.	1997	20.50	32-50
1997	Julia with Emmy Lou...Garden Friends 3520	Open		19.00	19-65
1998	Jessica & Timmy...Animal Hospital 3532	72,000	1998	40.00	42-84
1996	Karen & Wilson..Skater's Waltz GCC 3515	Open		26.00	26-50
1997	Karen with Wilson and Eloise...Mother's Present 3515-01	Retrd.	1998	20.00	20-55
1996	Katherine with Amanda & Edmund...Kind Hearts 3505	Open		20.00	94-119
1999	Kelly and Company...The Bear Collector 3542	Open		35.00	35-76
1997	Kristi with Nicole...Skater's Waltz 3516	Retrd.	1999	22.00	26-87
1997	Laura with Jane...First Day of School 3522	Retrd.	2000	23.00	23-57
1998	Lindsey w/Louise...the recital 3535	Open		18.00	18-66
2000	Lisa w/Plato...Graduation Day 3550 - The Boyds Collection	Open		18.00	18-29
1999	Lucinda and Dawn...By the Sea (votive) 27951	Open		26.00	26-45
1999	Lucinda and Dawn...By the Sea 3536	Open		18.00	18-44
1996	Mallory w/Patsy & J.B....Trick or Treat 3517	Retrd.	1996	27.00	40-88
1999	Mark w/Luke...the prayer 3545	Retrd.	2000	14.00	14
1998	Mary and Paul...The Prayer 3531-01	Retrd.	1998	16.00	36-38
1996	Megan with Elliot & Annie...Christmas Carol 3504	Retrd.	1997	19.50	26-250
1996	Megan with Elliot...Christmas Carol (waterglobe) 2720	Retrd.	1997	39.45	60-65
1999	Melissa With Katie...The Ballet 3537	Open		18.00	18-53
1999	Meredith With Jacqueline...Daisy Chain 3541	Retrd.	1999	18.00	18-34
1999	Mia...the save 3549	Open		20.00	20
2000	Michael and Thayer...Waitin for Grandpa 3552 - The Boyds Collection	Open		24.00	24-35
1999	Michelle...Reading's Fun 25855	Retrd.	1999	11.00	11
1996	Michelle with Daisy...Reading is Fun 3511	Retrd.	2000	17.95	18-57
1999	Miranda w/Mary K....pretty as a picture 3548	Open		37.00	37-50
1997	Natalie w/Joy...Sunday School 3519	Retrd.	1999	22.00	22-44
1996	Patricia with Molly...Attic Treasures 3501	Retrd.	1998	14.00	14-89
1998	Rachel w/Barbara & Matthew 3526	Retrd.	1999	23.00	23-64
1996	Rebecca with Elliot...Birthday 3509	Retrd.	2000	20.50	21-40
1999	Ryan and Diane...Love is Forever 25856	Retrd.	1999	12.00	12
1999	Ryan and Diane...Love is Forever (waterglobe) 272053	Open		37.00	37-54
2000	Ryan and Diane w/Cory, Wesley and Carly...Love is Forever 3553 - The Boyds Collection	Open		29.00	29-48

*Quotes have been rounded up to nearest dollar

YEAR ISSUE	EDITION LIMIT	YEAR RETD.	ISSUE PRICE	*QUOTE U.S.$
1996 Sara & Heather with Elliot & Amelia...Tea for Four 3507	Retrd.	1997	46.00	99-144
1998 Shannon & Wilson...waiting for Grandma 3533	Open		34.00	34-85
1998 Shelby...Asleep in Teddy's Arms 3527	Retrd.	2000	15.00	15-62
1999 Stephanie With Jim...School Days 3540	Open		25.00	25-42
1999 Tami w/Doug...half time 3546	Retrd.	2000	20.00	20-39
1998 Teresa and John...The Prayer 3531	Retrd.	2000	14.00	28-50
1996 Victoria with Samantha...Victorian Ladies 3502	Retrd.	1999	20.00	69-75
1997 Wendy...Wash Day 3521	Retrd.	1998	22.00	22-70
1997 Whitney & Wilson...Tea Party 3523	Retrd.	2000	19.00	19-74
1997 Whitney w/Wilson 272001	Open		37.00	37

The Folkstone Collection™ - G.M. Lowenthal, unless otherwise noted

YEAR ISSUE	EDITION LIMIT	YEAR RETD.	ISSUE PRICE	*QUOTE U.S.$
1995 Abigail...Peaceable Kingdom 2829	Retrd.	1998	18.95	26-52
1998 Aerobics angel 28244v (GCC)	Retrd.	1999	20.00	20-50
1996 Alvin T. Mac Barker...Dogface 2872	Retrd.	1997	19.00	20-48
2000 Amber Faeriedreams 36107	Open		19.00	19-50
1997 Amy & Abby - Angel Stitch 36006	Retrd.	1999	26.00	26-43
1994 Angel of Freedom 2820	Retrd.	1996	16.75	42-58
1994 Angel of Love 2821	Retrd.	1996	16.75	37-100
1994 Angel of Peace 2822	Retrd.	1996	16.75	50-94
1997 Angelina - Smidge 36100	Retrd.	1999	16.00	16-44
1997 Astrid Isinglass...Snow Angel 28206-06	Yr.Iss.	1997	23.50	44-70
1996 Athena...The Wedding Angel 28202	Open		19.00	19-48
1999 Audubon P. Pussywillow...The Birdwatcher (votive) 27803	Retrd.	2000	26.00	30-42
1999 Audubon P. Pussywillow...The Birdwatcher 2868	Retrd.	2000	19.00	19
1998 Auntie Cocoa M. Maximus... Chocolate Angel (NQGA) 28242	Retrd.	2000	20.00	20-50
1999 Autumn L. Fairiefrost 36005	Open		18.00	18-38
1998 Barnaby JR 370101	Retrd.	1999	19.00	19-26
1997 Bearly Nick & Buddies 28001	Retrd.	1999	19.50	20-38
1994 Beatrice-Birthday Angel 2825	Retrd.	1998	20.00	20-38
1995 Beatrice...the Giftgiver 2836	Retrd.	1999	17.95	31-75
1996 Bernie... I Got Wat I wanted St. Bernard Santa 2873	Retrd.	1999	17.75	17-35
1996 Betty Biscuit 2870	Retrd.	1999	19.00	22-65
1998 Birdie Holeinone...NQGA of Golfers 28245	Retrd.	2000	20.00	20-40
1999 Birdie...fore! 25661	Retrd.	1999	11.00	11
1998 Bjorn w/Nils & Sven 25654	Open		12.00	12
1998 Bobby...the defender 36505	Retrd.	1999	19.00	19
1995 Boowinkle Vonhindenmoose...2831	Open		17.95	18-44
1998 Bridges...Scuba Frog 36751	Retrd.	1999	15.00	15
1997 Bristol...Just sweep in 28101 (GCC)	Retrd.	1997	17.00	17
1998 Burt JR 370102	Retrd.	1999	14.00	14
1998 Burt...Bundle Up 370002	Retrd.	1998	20.00	20
1996 Buster Goes A' Courtin' 2844	Retrd.	1998	19.00	27-32
1998 Caffeinata...coffee faerie 36304	Open		19.00	19
2000 Calliope Clipsalot...Guardian Angel of Pennies 28211 - The Boyds Collection	Open		19.50	20-29
1999 Cantwell Waddlewak & Peek 36802	Open		16.00	16
1998 Cerebella Smarty Faueriemogn 36201	Open		18.00	18
1998 Charles prince of Tales 36700	Retrd.	1999	13.00	13
1999 Chester Bigheart...Love Much 370053	Retrd.	1999	27.00	27
1999 Chilly & Millie...Starlights 28106	Open		19.00	19
1994 Chilly & Son with Dove 2811	Retrd.	1997	17.75	27-90
1996 Chilly with wreath 2564	Retrd.	1998	10.00	10
1998 Cicely & Juneau 36503	Open		16.00	16
1999 Cocoa M. Anglerich & Scoop Musical 271050	Retrd.	2000	28.00	28
1999 Confidentia...No tell 36105	Open		18.00	18
1997 Constance & Felicity 28205	14,000	1997	37.50	63-82
1996 Cosmos...The Gardening Angel 28201	Retrd.	2000	19.00	19-44
1994 December 26th 3003	Retrd.	1997	32.00	25-125
1997 Dentinata Flossie Tooth Fairy 36102	Retrd.	1999	16.00	16
1999 Domestica T. Whirlwind...NQGA of Supermoms 28249	Open		20.00	20-47
1999 Dr. R X Mooselberry...making rounds 28301	Retrd.	2000	19.00	19-45
1996 Egon...the Skier 2837	Retrd.	1999	17.75	18-59
1997 Electra Angelbyte 36300	Open		18.00	18
1999 Electronic & Splice ...The Surprise 28004	Open		19.00	19
1995 Elmer-Cow on Haystacks 2851	Retrd.	1998	19.00	19-38
1996 Elmo "Tex" Beefcake...On the Range 2853	Retrd.	1997	19.00	19-57
1995 Ernest Hemmingmoose...the Hunter 2835	Retrd.	1999	17.95	25-78
1995 Esmeralda...the Wonderful Witch 2860	Open		17.95	18-60
1997 Estudious – Cram 36301	Retrd.	1999	18.00	18
1998 Execunick...1st global businessman 28002	Retrd.	1999	21.00	21
2000 Farmer McHare 36601	Open		10.00	10
1999 Felicity...angelbliss 36103	Open		18.00	18
1999 Fergus Bogey MacDivot 36401	Retrd.	1999	18.00	18
1996 Fixit...Santa's Faerie 3600	Retrd.	1998	17.45	25-45
1998 Flakey...ice sculptor 36504	Retrd.	1999	19.00	19
1996 Flora & Amelia...The Gardeners 2843	Retrd.	1999	19.00	23-75
1996 Flora, Amelia & Eloise...The Tea Party 2846	Retrd.	1998	19.00	17-57
1999 Florence and Katerina 36511	Open		19.00	19
1994 Florence-Kitchen Angel 2824	Retrd.	1996	20.00	47-88
1998 Francoise & Suzanne...the Spree 2875	Retrd.	2000	20.00	20-55
1998 Frogmorton...fly fishjng 36701	Retrd.	2000	15.00	15
1999 Fuzznick s. Claws & Co. 28003	Open		19.00	19
1996 G.M.'s Choice, Etheral...Angel of Light 28203-06	7,200	1996	18.25	91-138
1997 Gabrielle "Gabby" Faeriejabber 36003	Retrd.	1998	18.50	27-35
1999 Gaston Coldfish 36801	Open		16.00	16
1999 Grandma Faeriehugs 36106	Open		15.00	15
1997 Half Pipe the hotdogger 36502	Retrd.	1999	14.50	15
1999 Harriet and Punch with Hermine...The Challenge 28402	Retrd.	2000	19.00	19-31
2000 Heather w/Chris...Guardian Angel of Volleyball 28210 - The Boyds Collection	Retrd.	2000	20.00	20-28
1998 Heavenly Sconce 65429	Open		21.00	21
1997 Helga with Ingrid & Anna ...Be Warm 2818	Retrd.	1999	19.00	19-50
1999 Henry K. Wallstreet...Luck 36402	Open		17.00	17
2000 Honker T. Flatfoot...Send in the Clowns 2887 - The Boyds Collection	Retrd.	2000	19.50	20-36
1998 I.B. Colman 28102	Retrd.	2000	20.00	20-50
1999 I.B. Freezin 36508	Open		19.00	19
1995 Icabod Mooselman...the Pilgrim 2833	Retrd.	1997	17.95	45-95
1994 Ida & Bessie-The Gardeners 2852	Retrd.	1998	19.00	25-60
1996 Illumina...Angel of Light 28203	Retrd.	1999	18.45	26-75
1998 Imin Payne 28244	Retrd.	1999	20.00	20
1997 Immaculata T Faeriburg 36302	Open		18.00	18
1998 Indulgenia Q. bluit 36305	Retrd.	2000	19.00	19
1997 Infiniti Faerielove...the Wedding Faerie 36101	Retrd.	1998	16.00	16-30
1998 Ingrid & Olaf 27801	Open		27.00	27
1997 Ingrid be warm 25651	Retrd.	1998	12.00	12
2000 Jack Hammer...Hard Hat 2885 - The Boyds Collection	Retrd.	2000	19.00	19-32
1998 Jacques...the wine tester 36702	Retrd.	1998	14.00	14
1996 Jean Claude & Jacque...the Skiers (waterglobe) 2710	Open		37.50	38-55
1995 Jean Claude & Jacques...the Skiers 2815	Retrd.	1999	16.95	17-34
1999 Jeremiah Jellybean Pondhopper 36704	Retrd.	1999	14.00	14
1999 Jester Q. Funnybones 370054	Retrd.	1999	27.00	27
1994 Jill-Language of Love 2842	Retrd.	1997	19.00	19-82
1994 Jingle Moose 2830	Retrd.	1996	17.75	62-120
1996 Jingle Nick & Stary Stary (QVC)	Retrd.	1996	N/A	N/A
1994 Jingles & Son with Wreath 2812	Retrd.	1996	17.75	26-125
1999 Ketchem & B. Quick..got one 36509	Open		19.00	19
1997 Kristabell Wee Faerie Frost 36002	Retrd.	1999	17.00	17
1997 Krystal Isinglass...Snow Angel 28206	Retrd.	1999	19.00	19-45
1999 Laverne B. Bowler...Strikes and Spares 28248	Retrd.	2000	18.00	18-29
1998 Liddy Pearl...How Does Your Garden Grow 2881	12,000	1998	40.00	59-115
1994 Lizzie Shopping Angel 2827	Retrd.	1998	20.00	22-58
1996 Loretta Moostein..."Yer Cheatin' Heart" 2854	Retrd.	1998	19.00	29-32
1996 Lucky McPlug 2871	Retrd.	1999	19.00	19-45
1998 Luna 28207	Retrd.	2000	19.00	19-50
1999 Madge....Magic Scissors 25658	Open		11.00	11
1997 Madge...The Magician/Beautician (NQGA) 28243	Open		19.00	19-48
1998 Mangianata...cooking faerie 36303	Open		18.00	18
2000 Mary Angelwish 36108	Open		19.00	19
1997 Mercy...Angel of Nurses (NQGA) 28240	Retrd.	2000	19.00	19-35
1999 Mercy...Night Shift Nurse 25656	Open		11.00	11
1998 Milken VHM...trees company 2832	Open		19.00	19
1994 Minerva-Baseball Angel 2826	Retrd.	1997	20.00	29-57
1998 Miss Prudence P. Carrotjuice...Multiplication 2848	Retrd.	2000	18.50	19
1997 Mistletoe & Holly Snowball 25900	Retrd.	1997	14.00	14
2000 Momma McHutch and Babies...Family Matters 28403 - The Boyds Collection	Open		19.50	20-31
2000 Mommie McHopple & babie 36600	Open		10.00	10
1997 Montague Von Hindenmoose...Surprise! 2839	Open		19.00	19-38
1999 Ms Fries...The Guardian Angel of Waitresses 28246	Retrd.	2000	19.00	19-31
1999 Ms Lilypond...Lesson #1 36705	Open		14.00	14
1999 Ms McFrazzle...Daycare Extraordinaire 2883	Open		20.00	20-49
1999 Ms McFrazzle...on the job 271002	Retrd.	2000	39.00	39-49
1997 Ms Patience...Angel of Teachers (NQGA) 28241	Retrd.	1998	19.00	28-38
1999 Ms Patience...Inspiration Teacher 25657	Open		11.00	11
1999 Ms Pickelsencream...Heaven Sent 36202	Open		18.00	18
1999 Ms Pleasant...May I help you? 28250	Open		19.00	19
1999 Murphy McFrost...Fire & ice 28105	Open		19.00	19
1999 Myron R. Fishmeister and Billy Bob...Angel of Fish Stories 28247	Open		21.00	21-44
1999 Myron...the Angler 25660	Retrd.	1999	11.00	11
1994 Myrtle-Believe 2840	Retrd.	1998	20.00	18-57
1995 Na-Nick of the North 2804	Retrd.	1999	17.95	18-57
1998 Nana Mchare...and the Love Gardeners 2849	Open		20.00	20-38
1996 Nanick & Siegfried the Plan 2807	10,000	1996	32.50	39-138
1996 Nanny...the Snowmom 2817	Open		17.95	18-34
1994 Nicholai with Tree 2800	Retrd.	1997	17.75	32-58
1994 Nicholas with Book 2802	Retrd.	1996	17.75	47-100
1994 Nick on Ice (1st ed. GCC) 3001	3,600	1995	49.95	25-65
1994 Nick on Ice 3001	Retrd.	1997	32.95	25-65
1996 Nick, Siegfried 2807	Yr.Iss.	1996	35.00	100-125
1996 Nicknoah...Santa with Ark 2806	Retrd.	1999	17.95	18-37
1994 Nikki with Candle 2801	Retrd.	1997	17.75	24-47
1996 No-No Nick...Bad Boy Santa 2805	Retrd.	1998	17.95	25-44
1995 Northbound Wille 2814	Retrd.	1997	16.95	24-44
1994 Oceana....Ocean Angel 2838	Retrd.	1998	16.00	27-100
1997 Olaf...Mogul Meister 2819	Open		16.50	17-43
1998 Olivia....Peace 25800	Retrd.	1999	12.00	12
1998 P.J. McSnoozin 2882	Open		19.00	19-39
1998 Peace nick Santa 2809	Retrd.	1999	20.00	20
1998 Peacenick...the Sixties	Open		20.00	20-32
1994 Peter-The Whopper 2841	Retrd.	1997	19.00	19-63
1997 Polaris & The North Star...on Ice 2880	Open		19.00	19-44
2000 Polly Pekoe...tee faerie 36109	Open		17.00	17
1997 Prudence & Daffodils 2847	Retrd.	2000	18.00	18-49
1995 Prudence Mooselmaid...the Pilgrim 2834	Retrd.	1997	17.95	40-88
1998 Purrscilla G. Pussenboots...Mitten Knitters 2865	Open		20.50	21-39
1998 Purrscilla...give thanks 2866	Open		19.00	19-49
1998 Rememberance Angleflyte 36004	Open		18.00	18
1996 Robin...the Snowbird Lover 2816	Retrd.	1999	17.95	18-32
1995 Rufus-Hoedown 2850	Retrd.	1998	19.00	17-38
1998 S.C. Ribbit...Hoppy Christmas 36750	Retrd.	1999	19.00	19
1999 Salem...Give thanks 2867	Open		19.00	19-39
2000 Sam, Libby and Ellis...Fife and Drum 2886 - The Boyds Collection	120,000	2000	40.00	40
1998 Santa & the final inspection 370003	Retrd.	1998	53.00	53
1998 Santa in the Nick of time 370000	Retrd.	1998	48.00	48
1998 Santa JR...nick of time 370100	Retrd.	1999	23.00	23
1998 Santa JR...quick as a flash 370104	Retrd.	1999	20.00	20
1998 Santa JR...the final inspection 370103	Retrd.	1999	24.00	24
1994 Santa's Challenge (1st ed. GCC) 3002	3,600	1995	49.95	25-65
1994 Santa's Challenge 3002	Retrd.	1997	32.95	25-65
1994 Santa's Flight Plan (1st ed. GCC) 3000	3,600	1995	49.95	25-73
1995 Santa's Flight Plan (waterglobe) 2703	Retrd.	1996	37.00	75-139
1994 Santa's Flight Plan 3000	Retrd.	1997	32.95	25-73
1996 Santa's Hobby 3004	Retrd.	1997	36.00	44-69
1998 Santa...Quick as a flash 370004	Retrd.	1998	42.00	42
1995 Seraphina with Jacob & Rachael...the Choir Angels 2828	Retrd.	1997	19.95	19-75
1996 Serenity...the Mother's Angel 28204	Retrd.	2000	18.25	19-32
1997 Sgt. Rex & Matt...The Runaway 2874	Retrd.	1999	19.50	20-48
1995 Siegfried and Egon...the Sign 2899	Retrd.	1998	18.95	29-58
1995 Sliknick the Chimney Sweep 2803	Retrd.	1998	17.95	18-50
1997 Slurp and the Snowcone stand 36500	Open		14.50	15
2000 Soltice Angeldance...Sunlight 28209 - The Boyds Collection	Retrd.	2000	19.00	19-29
1997 St. Nick...the Quest 2808	Retrd.	1999	19.00	29-50
2000 Sudsie Faerisock 36306	Open		19.00	19
1997 T H Bean...The Bearmaker Elf 36400	Retrd.	1999	20.00	20
1996 Too Loose Lapin...The Arteest 2845	Retrd.	1998	19.00	19-40
1999 Tu Tu C Ribbit...Fog Lake 36703	Open		14.00	14
1999 Tuxworth P Cummerbund 36104	Open		18.00	18
1999 Wainwright & Rudy Waddlesworth 36800	Open		16.00	16
1999 Walter T. Goodlife...Live Well 370052	Retrd.		27.00	27
1999 Wendy Willowhare...A Tisket A Tasket 28401	Retrd.	2000	19.50	20-48
1994 Windy with Book 2810	Retrd.	1996	17.75	63-138
1996 Windy with Tree 2563	Retrd.	1998	10.00	10
1997 Yukon, Kodiak & Nanuk...Nome Sweet Home (waterglobe) 271001	Retrd.	1999	38.50	39-44
1997 Ziggy...The Duffer 2838	Retrd.	1999	39.50	23-44
1999 Zip Shoveland...Got Snow/ 28104	Open		N/A	N/A

Byers' Choice Ltd.

Accessories - J. Byers

YEAR ISSUE	EDITION LIMIT	YEAR RETD.	ISSUE PRICE	*QUOTE U.S.$
1995 Cat in Hat	Closed	1995	10.00	18
1997 Cat with Milk	Closed	1997	18.50	20
1996 Dog with Hat	Closed	1996	18.50	19
1997 Dog with Lollipop	Closed	1997	18.50	19-21
1995 Dog with Sausages	Closed	1995	18.00	45-75
1996 Street Clock	Closed	1997	85.00	95-100

Carolers - J. Byers

YEAR ISSUE	EDITION LIMIT	YEAR RETD.	ISSUE PRICE	*QUOTE U.S.$
1978 Hilltown Traditional Lady	Closed	N/A	N/A	600
1976 Traditional Adult (1976-80)	Closed	1980	N/A	475
1981 Traditional Adult (1981-current)	Open		45.00	45-300
XX Traditional Adult (undated)	Closed	N/A	N/A	400-700
1978 Traditional Colonial Lady (w/ hands)	Closed	1978	N/A	1500
1982 Victorian Adult (1st ed.)	Closed	1982	32.00	400
1982 Victorian Adult (2nd ed./dressed alike)	Closed	1983	46.00	300-400
1983 Victorian Adult (assorted) (2nd ed.)	Open		35.00	49
1982 Victorian Child (1st ed. w/floppy hats)	Closed	1982	32.00	300-375
1983 Victorian Child (2nd ed./sailor suit)	Closed	1983	33.00	300-400
1983 Victorian Child (assorted) (2nd. ed.)	Open		33.00	49

Children of The World - J. Byers

YEAR ISSUE	EDITION LIMIT	YEAR RETD.	ISSUE PRICE	*QUOTE U.S.$
1993 Bavarian Boy	Closed	1993	50.00	150-210
1992 Dutch Boy	Closed	1992	50.00	173-300
1992 Dutch Girl	Closed	1992	50.00	115-300

*Quotes have been rounded up to nearest dollar

YEAR ISSUE	EDITION LIMIT	YEAR RETD.	ISSUE PRICE	*QUOTE U.S.$
1994 Irish Girl	Closed	1994	50.00	175-250
1997 Mexican Children	Closed	1997	50.00	65
1996 Saint Lucia	Closed	1998	52.00	52-60

Christmas Traditions - J. Byers

YEAR ISSUE	EDITION LIMIT	YEAR RETD.	ISSUE PRICE	*QUOTE U.S.$
1999 Children w/Pickles	Closed	1999	57.00	57

Cries Of London - J. Byers

YEAR ISSUE	EDITION LIMIT	YEAR RETD.	ISSUE PRICE	*QUOTE U.S.$
1991 Apple Lady (red stockings)	Closed	1991	80.00	750-1400
1991 Apple Lady (red/wh stockings)	Closed	1991	80.00	850
1992 Baker	Closed	1992	62.00	157-250
1998 Candlestick Maker	Closed	1998	72.00	125-275
1993 Chestnut Children (pair)	Closed	1993	42.00	115-150
1993 Chestnut Roaster	Closed	1993	64.00	195-250
1996 Children Buying Gingerbread	Closed	1996	46.00	115-220
1998 Children Holding Candles	Closed	1998	48.00	65-125
1999 Children Holding Fruit	Closed	1999	48.00	48
1995 Dollmaker	Closed	1995	64.00	85-125
1994 Flower Vendor	Closed	1994	64.00	95-120
1999 Fruit Vendor	Closed	1999	84.00	84
1996 Gingerbread Vendor	Closed	1996	75.00	95-150
1995 Girl Holding Doll	Closed	1995	48.00	45-75
1997 Milk Maid	Closed	1997	67.00	100

Dickens Series - J. Byers

YEAR ISSUE	EDITION LIMIT	YEAR RETD.	ISSUE PRICE	*QUOTE U.S.$
1990 Bob Cratchit & Tiny Tim (1st ed.)	Closed	1990	84.00	250-325
1991 Bob Cratchit & Tiny Tim (2nd ed.)	Open		86.00	90
1991 Happy Scrooge (1st ed.)	Closed	1991	50.00	160-225
1992 Happy Scrooge (2nd ed.)	Closed	1992	50.00	150-345
1986 Marley's Ghost (1st ed.)	Closed	1986	40.00	250-325
1987 Marley's Ghost (2nd ed.)	Closed	1992	42.00	200-225
1985 Mr. & Mrs. Fezziwig (1st ed.)	Closed	1985	86.00	900-1400
1985 Mr. Fezziwig (1st ed.)	Closed	1985	43.00	300-400
1986 Mr. Fezziwig (2nd ed.)	Closed	1990	43.00	200-400
1984 Mrs. Cratchit (1st ed.)	Closed	1984	38.00	500-700
1985 Mrs. Cratchit (2nd ed.)	Open		39.00	50
1985 Mrs. Fezziwig (1st ed.)	Closed	1985	43.00	300-400
1986 Mrs. Fezziwig (2nd ed.)	Closed	1990	43.00	200-350
1983 Scrooge (1st ed.)	Closed	1983	36.00	900
1984 Scrooge (2nd ed.)	Open		38.00	50
1989 Spirit of Christmas Future (1st ed.)	Closed	1989	46.00	250-295
1990 Spirit of Christmas Future (2nd ed.)	Closed	1991	48.00	300-345
1987 Spirit of Christmas Past (1st ed.)	Closed	1987	42.00	250-345
1988 Spirit of Christmas Past (2nd ed.)	Closed	1991	46.00	300-345
1988 Spirit of Christmas Present (1st ed.)	Closed	1988	44.00	250-345
1989 Spirit of Christmas Present (2nd ed.)	Closed	1991	48.00	200-250

Display Figures - J. Byers

YEAR ISSUE	EDITION LIMIT	YEAR RETD.	ISSUE PRICE	*QUOTE U.S.$
1998 20th Anniversary Santa in Sleigh	1,000		750.00	750
1986 Display Adults	Closed	1987	170.00	500-600
1983 Display Carolers	Closed	1983	200.00	500
1985 Display Children (Boy & Girl)	Closed	1987	140.00	1200-1500
1982 Display Drummer Boy-1st	Closed	1983	96.00	600-800
1985 Display Drummer Boy-2nd	Closed	1986	160.00	400-600
1981 Display Lady	Closed	1981	N/A	2000
1981 Display Man	Closed	1981	N/A	2000
1985 Display Old World Santa	Closed	1985	260.00	500-650
1982 Display Santa	Closed	1983	96.00	450-650
1990 Display Santa-bayberry	Closed	1990	250.00	450-650
1990 Display Santa-red	Closed	1990	250.00	600-650
1984 Display Working Santa	Closed	1985	260.00	500
1987 Mechanical Boy with Drum	Closed	1987	N/A	700-850
1987 Mechanical Girl with Bell	Closed	1987	N/A	450-800

Historical Figurines - J. Byers

YEAR ISSUE	EDITION LIMIT	YEAR RETD.	ISSUE PRICE	*QUOTE U.S.$
1998 Colonial Boy w/Recorder	Closed	1999	50.00	50
1998 Colonial Girl w/Hoop	Closed	1999	50.00	50
1998 Colonial Man w/Music Book	Closed	1999	50.00	50
1998 Colonial Woman w/Music Book	Closed	1999	50.00	50
1999 Plimoth Plantation Pilgrim Adults	Closed	1999	57.00	57

Lil' Dickens/Toddlers - J. Byers

YEAR ISSUE	EDITION LIMIT	YEAR RETD.	ISSUE PRICE	*QUOTE U.S.$
1998 Assorted Toddler Groups	Closed	1999	20.00	20
1996 Book - "Night Before Christmas"	Closed	1998	20.00	20
1996 Doll - "Night Before Christmas"	Closed	1998	20.00	20
1993 Gingerbread Boy	Closed	1994	18.50	27-35
1993 Package	Closed	1993	18.50	35
1992 Shovel	Closed	1993	17.00	35-50
1994 Skis (snowsuit)	Closed	1996	19.00	20
1994 Sled (black toddler)	Closed	1994	19.00	19
1992 Sled (white toddler)	Closed	1993	17.00	20
1995 Sled (white toddler-2nd ed.)	Closed	1995	19.00	20
1991 Sled with Dog/toddler	Closed	1991	30.00	95-125
1992 Snowball	Closed	1994	17.00	35
1994 Snowflake	Closed	1994	18.00	18-35
1993 Teddy Bear	Closed	1993	18.50	35
1997 Toddler Holding Merry Christmas Banner	Closed	1997	20.00	20
1997 Toddler in Sleigh	Closed	1998	27.50	30
1999 Toddler in Snow Saucer	Closed	1999	20.00	20
1997 Toddler on Rocking Horse	Closed	1998	27.50	30-35
1999 Toddler on Skates	Closed	1999	20.00	20
1997 Toddler with Skis (sweater)	Closed	1997	21.50	23-30
1997 Toddler with Tricycle (sweater)	Closed	1997	21.50	25-30
1994 Tree	Closed	1996	18.00	20
1996 Tricycle (snowsuit)	Closed	1996	20.00	20-25
1995 Victorian Boy Toddler	Closed	1995	19.50	20
1995 Victorian Girl Toddler	Closed	1995	19.50	20
1995 Wagon	Closed	1996	19.50	20

Musicians - J. Byers

YEAR ISSUE	EDITION LIMIT	YEAR RETD.	ISSUE PRICE	*QUOTE U.S.$
1991 Boy with Mandolin	Closed	1991	48.00	195-295
1985 Horn Player	Closed	1985	38.00	450
1985 Horn Player, chubby face	Closed	1985	37.00	500-900
1991 Musician with Accordian	Closed	1991	48.00	175-350
1989 Musician with Clarinet	Closed	1989	44.00	450-650
1992 Musician with French Horn	Closed	1992	52.00	115-250
1990 Musician with Mandolin	Closed	1990	46.00	240
1986 Victorian Girl with Violin	Closed	1986	39.00	325-330
1983 Violin Player Man (1st ed.)	Closed	1983	38.00	900
1984 Violin Player Man (2nd ed.)	Closed	1984	38.00	1500

Nativity - J. Byers

YEAR ISSUE	EDITION LIMIT	YEAR RETD.	ISSUE PRICE	*QUOTE U.S.$
1989 Angel Gabriel	Closed	1991	37.00	210-250
1987 Angel-Great Star (Blonde)	Closed	1991	40.00	125-150
1987 Angel-Great Star (Brunette)	Closed	1991	40.00	125-150
1987 Angel-Great Star (Red Head)	Closed	1991	40.00	125-150
1987 Black Angel	Closed	1987	36.00	250-350
1990 Holy Family with stable	Closed	1991	119.00	250-300
1989 King Balthasar	Closed	1991	40.00	95-150
1989 King Gaspar	Closed	1991	40.00	95-150
1989 King Melchior	Closed	1991	40.00	95-150
1988 Shepherds	Closed	1991	37.00	100-135

The Nutcracker - J. Byers, unless otherwise noted

YEAR ISSUE	EDITION LIMIT	YEAR RETD.	ISSUE PRICE	*QUOTE U.S.$
1996 Drosselmeier w/Music Box (1st ed.)	Closed	1996	83.00	83-96
1997 Drosselmeier w/Music Box (2nd ed.)	Closed	1999	83.00	83
1994 Fritz (1st ed.)	Closed	1994	56.00	65-175
1995 Fritz (2nd ed.)	Closed	1997	57.00	65-75
1995 Louise Playing Piano (1st ed.)	Closed	1995	82.00	100-200
1996 Louise Playing Piano (2nd ed.)	Closed	1996	83.00	83-150
1993 Marie (1st ed.)	Closed	1993	52.00	100-116
1994 Marie (2nd ed.)	Closed	1999	53.00	85
1997 Mouse King (1st ed.) - Jeff Byers	Closed	1997	70.00	71
1998 Mouse King (2nd ed.) - Jeff Byers	Closed	1999	70.00	70
1998 Prince (1st ed.)	Closed	1998	68.00	68-115
1999 Prince (2nd ed.)	Closed	1999	68.00	68

Salvation Army Band - J. Byers

YEAR ISSUE	EDITION LIMIT	YEAR RETD.	ISSUE PRICE	*QUOTE U.S.$
1994 Black Woman w/Tambourine	Closed	1994	58.00	400
1997 Boy with Flag	Closed	1999	57.00	57-61
1995 Girl with War Cry	Closed	1999	55.00	56
1996 Man with Bass Drum	Closed	1999	60.00	60
1993 Man with Cornet	Closed	1997	54.00	54-61
1999 Woman with Bible	Closed	1999	58.00	58
1992 Woman with Kettle (1st ed.)	Closed	1992	64.00	64-100
1993 Woman with Tambourine	Closed	1995	58.00	58-125

Santas/Christmas Figurines - J. Byers

YEAR ISSUE	EDITION LIMIT	YEAR RETD.	ISSUE PRICE	*QUOTE U.S.$
1998 Belsnickel	Closed	1998	64.00	118-250
1991 Father Christmas	Closed	1992	48.00	150-200
1988 Knecht Ruprecht (Black Peter)	Closed	1989	38.00	110-200
1996 Knickerbocker Santa	Closed	1998	58.00	58-65
1984 Mrs. Claus	Closed	1991	38.00	96-150
1992 Mrs. Claus (2nd ed.)	Closed	1993	50.00	60-140
1986 Mrs. Claus on Rocker	Closed	1986	73.00	600
1999 Mrs. Claus Trimming Tree	Closed	1999	92.00	92
1995 Mrs. Claus' Needlework	Closed	1995	70.00	70-135
1978 Old World Santa	Closed	1986	33.00	390-650
1989 Russian Santa	Closed	1989	85.00	475-650
1988 Saint Nicholas	Closed	1992	44.00	100-155
1997 Santa Feeding Reindeer	Closed	1997	64.50	65-95
1982 Santa in a Sleigh (1st ed.)	Closed	1983	46.00	800
1998 Santa in Gold Sleigh	400	1998	95.00	245-300
1984 Santa in Sleigh (2nd ed.)	Closed	1985	70.00	750
1996 Santa in Sleigh (in select stores)	Closed	1996	70.00	250
1998 Seated Santa with Toddler	Closed	1999	90.00	90
1997 Shopping Mrs. Claus	Closed	1997	59.50	55-75
1993 Skating Santa	Closed	1993	60.00	75-83
1978 Velvet Santa	Closed	1993	Unkn.	55-58
1994 Velvet Santa with Stocking (2nd ed.)	Open		47.00	52
1998 Velvet Santa with Toy	Closed	1999	55.00	55
1986 Victorian Santa	Closed	1989	39.00	310
1999 Victorian Santa (red)	Closed	1999	60.00	60
1990 Weihnachtsmann (German Santa)	Closed	1990	56.00	125-200
1992 Working Santa	Closed	1996	52.00	52-96
1983 Working Santa (1st yr. issue)	Closed	1991	38.00	170-310
1992 Working Santa (1st yr. issue)	Closed	1992	52.00	200-310

Shoppers - J. Byers

YEAR ISSUE	EDITION LIMIT	YEAR RETD.	ISSUE PRICE	*QUOTE U.S.$
1995 Shopper-Man	Closed	1995	56.00	60-65
1995 Shopper-Woman	Closed	1995	56.00	40-65
1995 Traditional Adult Shoppers (1st ed.)	Closed	1995	56.00	75-95

Special Characters - J. Byers

YEAR ISSUE	EDITION LIMIT	YEAR RETD.	ISSUE PRICE	*QUOTE U.S.$
1996 Actress	Closed	1996	52.00	52-71
1979 Adult Male "Icabod"	Closed	1979	32.00	2400-2600
1988 Angel Tree Top	100	1988	Unkn.	275-375
1994 Baby in Basket	Closed	1994	7.50	10-20
1989 Black Boy w/skates	Closed	N/A	N/A	400-450
1989 Black Drummer Boy	Closed	N/A	N/A	500
1989 Black Girl w/skates	Closed	N/A	N/A	400-450
1989 Black Mother w/Baby	Closed	1989	45.00	400
1983 Boy on Rocking Horse	300	1983	85.00	2400-2600
1987 Boy on Sled	Closed	1987	50.00	300-375
1991 Boy with Apple	Closed	1991	41.00	150-275
1994 Boy with Goose	Closed	1995	49.50	60-125
1996 Boy with Lamb	Closed	1999	52.00	150
1995 Boy with Skis	Closed	1999	49.50	51-75
1991 Boy with Tree	Closed	1994	49.00	69-125
1995 Butcher	Closed	1995	54.00	75-125
1987 Caroler with Lamp	Closed	1987	40.00	125-200
1998 Children with Toys	Closed	1999	57.00	57
1997 Children with Treats	Closed	1998	58.00	58-65
1984 Chimney Sweep-Adult	Closed	1984	36.00	1200-1500
1991 Chimney Sweep-Child	Closed	1994	50.00	120-175
1982 Choir Children, boy and girl set	Closed	1986	32.00	600-625
1993 Choir Director, lady/music stand	Closed	1995	56.00	60-100
1982 Conductor	Closed	1992	32.00	125-140
1994 Constable	Closed	1996	53.00	60-125
1995 Couple in Sleigh	Closed	1995	110.00	115-120
1996 Crabtree & Evelyn Man & Woman	Closed	1996	113.00	110-145
1997 Crabtree & Evelyn Man & Woman	Closed	1997	113.00	113-175
1999 Croquet Players (Adults)	Closed	1999	60.00	60
1982 Drummer Boy	Closed	1992	34.00	180-190
1982 Easter Boy	Closed	1983	32.00	550-1000
1982 Easter Girl	Closed	1983	32.00	550-1000
1997 Gardener	Closed	1998	69.50	70
1996 Girl Holding Holly Basket	Closed	1997	52.00	75-150
1991 Girl with Apple	Closed	1991	41.00	150
1991 Girl with Apple/coin purse	Closed	1991	41.00	250-335
1989 Girl with Hoop	Closed	1990	44.00	100-125
1995 Girl with Skis	Closed	1999	49.50	51-60
1982 Icabod	Closed	1982	32.00	1150-1500
1998 Indian Children	Closed	1999	53.50	54-95
1993 Lamplighter	Closed	1996	48.00	90-96
1993 Lamplighter (1st yr. issue)	Closed	1993	48.00	125-250
1982 Leprechauns	Closed	1982	34.00	1200-2000
1997 Man Feeding Birds on Bench	Closed	1997	83.00	85-105
1998 Man with Bicycle	Closed	1998	82.00	82-100
1988 Mother Holding Baby	Closed	1993	40.00	125-200
1987 Mother's Day	225	1987	125.00	325
1988 Mother's Day (Daughter)	Closed	1988	125.00	450
1993 Mother's Day (green)	Closed	1993	N/A	130
1988 Mother's Day (Son)	Closed	1988	125.00	450
1989 Mother's Day (with Carriage)	3,000	1989	75.00	350-465
1994 Nanny	Closed	1997	66.00	66-75
1989 Newsboy with Bike	Closed	1992	78.00	125-250
1998 Nurse	Closed	1998	60.00	60
1985 Pajama Children (painted flannel)	Closed	1989	35.00	245-275
1985 Pajama Children (red flannel)	Closed	1989	35.00	275-338
1990 Parson	Closed	1993	44.00	113-132
1998 Peddler	Closed	1998	120.00	116-120
1998 Photographer	Closed	1999	70.00	70
1990 Postman	Closed	1993	45.00	175-275
1994 Sandwich Board Man (red board)	Closed	1994	52.00	52-125
1994 Sandwich Board Man (white board)	Closed	1996	52.00	52-95
1993 School Kids	Closed	1994	48.00	75-104
1992 Schoolteacher	Closed	1994	48.00	100-120
1998 Seated Victorian Woman w/ Baby	Closed	1998	70.00	47-70
1999 Sign Painter	Closed	1999	68.00	68
1981 Thanksgiving Lady (Clay Hands)	Closed	1981	Unkn.	2000
1981 Thanksgiving Man (Clay Hands)	Closed	1981	Unkn.	2000
1994 Treetop Angel	Closed	1996	50.00	50-100
1982 Valentine Boy	Closed	1983	32.00	550-940
1982 Valentine Girl	Closed	1983	32.00	550-940
1990 Victorian Girl On Rocking Horse (blonde)	Closed	1991	70.00	140-180
1990 Victorian Girl On Rocking Horse (brunette)	Closed	1991	70.00	140-220
1992 Victorian Mother with Toddler (Fall/Win-green)	Closed	1993	60.00	125-130
1993 Victorian Mother with Toddler (Spr/Sum-blue)	Closed	1993	61.00	95-150
1992 Victorian Mother with Toddler (Spr/Sum-white)	Closed	1993	60.00	90-120
1998 Woman Selling Candles	Closed	1998	66.00	66-100
1997 Woman w/ Gingerbread House	Closed	1998	60.00	60-125

Store Exclusives-AOL Chat Group Exclusives - J. Byers

YEAR ISSUE	EDITION LIMIT	YEAR RETD.	ISSUE PRICE	*QUOTE U.S.$
1998 AOL Cat	Closed	1998	Gift	38

Store Exclusives-Christmas Dove - J. Byers

YEAR ISSUE	EDITION LIMIT	YEAR RETD.	ISSUE PRICE	*QUOTE U.S.$
1995 Dove Children (pr)	Closed	1996	96.00	365-450

Store Exclusives-Christmas Loft - J. Byers

YEAR ISSUE	EDITION LIMIT	YEAR RETD.	ISSUE PRICE	*QUOTE U.S.$
1991 Russian Santa	40	1991	100.00	425-650

Store Exclusives-Country Christmas - J. Byers

YEAR ISSUE	EDITION LIMIT	YEAR RETD.	ISSUE PRICE	*QUOTE U.S.$
1988 Toymaker	600	1988	59.00	850-1000

Store Exclusives-Foster's Exclusives - J. Byers

YEAR ISSUE	EDITION LIMIT	YEAR RETD.	ISSUE PRICE	*QUOTE U.S.$
1995 American Boy	100	1995	50.00	500

Store Exclusives-Log Gift Shop Exclusives - J. Byers

YEAR ISSUE	EDITION LIMIT	YEAR RETD.	ISSUE PRICE	*QUOTE U.S.$
1998 Shang Bailey	Closed	1998	50.00	153-200

Store Exclusives-Long's Jewelers - J. Byers

YEAR ISSUE	EDITION LIMIT	YEAR RETD.	ISSUE PRICE	*QUOTE U.S.$
1981 Leprechaun (with bucket)	Closed	N/A	N/A	2000

Store Exclusives-Nuance - J. Byers

YEAR ISSUE	EDITION LIMIT	YEAR RETD.	ISSUE PRICE	*QUOTE U.S.$
1995 Kids w/Mittens (pr)	Closed	1995	94.00	94

Store Exclusives-Paper Store Exclusives - J. Byers

YEAR ISSUE	EDITION LIMIT	YEAR RETD.	ISSUE PRICE	*QUOTE U.S.$
1998 Apple Harvest Couple	Closed	1998	92.00	203

Store Exclusives-Port-O-Call - J. Byers

YEAR ISSUE	EDITION LIMIT	YEAR RETD.	ISSUE PRICE	*QUOTE U.S.$
1986 Cherub Angel-blue	Closed	1987	N/A	275-400
1986 Cherub Angel-cream	Closed	1987	N/A	400
1986 Cherub Angel-pink	Closed	1987	N/A	275-400
1987 Cherub Angel-rose	Closed	1987	N/A	275-400

Store Exclusives-Snow Goose - J. Byers

YEAR ISSUE	EDITION LIMIT	YEAR RETD.	ISSUE PRICE	*QUOTE U.S.$
1988 Man with Goose	600	1988	60.00	400-650

Store Exclusives-Stacy's Gifts & Collectibles - J. Byers

YEAR ISSUE	EDITION LIMIT	YEAR RETD.	ISSUE PRICE	*QUOTE U.S.$
1987 Santa in Rocking Chair with Boy	100	1987	130.00	1000
1987 Santa in Rocking Chair with Girl	100	1987	130.00	1000

Store Exclusives-Talbots - J. Byers

YEAR ISSUE	EDITION LIMIT	YEAR RETD.	ISSUE PRICE	*QUOTE U.S.$
1990 Victorian Family of Four	Closed	N/A	N/A	400
1993 Skating Girl/Boy	Retrd.	N/A	N/A	280-400
1994 Man w/Log Carrier	Closed	N/A	N/A	130-150
1994 Family of Four/Sweaters	Retrd.	N/A	N/A	550

*Quotes have been rounded up to nearest dollar

YEAR ISSUE	EDITION LIMIT	YEAR RETD.	ISSUE PRICE	*QUOTE U.S.$
1995 Santa in Sleigh	1,625	1995	88.00	150-200
1995 Boy & Girl Skaters	Closed	1995	110.00	190-250

Store Exclusives-Truffles - J. Byers

YEAR ISSUE	EDITION LIMIT	YEAR RETD.	ISSUE PRICE	*QUOTE U.S.$
1997 Peddler	Closed	1997	110.00	116-300

Store Exclusives-Tudor Cottage Exclusives - J. Byers

YEAR ISSUE	EDITION LIMIT	YEAR RETD.	ISSUE PRICE	*QUOTE U.S.$
1993 Penny Children (boy/girl)	Closed	1993	42.00	500

Store Exclusives-Walt Disneyworld Exclusives - J. Byers

YEAR ISSUE	EDITION LIMIT	YEAR RETD.	ISSUE PRICE	*QUOTE U.S.$
1998 Disney Couple, set/2	Closed	1998	120.00	203-250

Store Exclusives-Wayside Country Store Exclusives - J. Byers

YEAR ISSUE	EDITION LIMIT	YEAR RETD.	ISSUE PRICE	*QUOTE U.S.$
1988 Colonial Lady s/n	600	1988	49.00	500-600
1986 Colonial Lamplighter s/n	600	1986	46.00	750
1987 Colonial Watchman s/n	600	1987	49.00	750
1995 Sunday School Boy	150	1995	55.00	250-300
1995 Sunday School Girl	150	1995	55.00	250-300
1995 Victorian Lady Centerpiece	50	1995	N/A	200-250
1996 Victorian Lady Centerpiece	50	1996	N/A	175-200

Store Exclusives-Wooden Soldier - J. Byers

YEAR ISSUE	EDITION LIMIT	YEAR RETD.	ISSUE PRICE	*QUOTE U.S.$
XX Victorian Lamp Lighter	Closed	N/A	N/A	175-200

Store Exclusives-Woodstock Inn - J. Byers

YEAR ISSUE	EDITION LIMIT	YEAR RETD.	ISSUE PRICE	*QUOTE U.S.$
1987 Skier Boy	200	1987	40.00	250-350
1987 Skier Girl	200	1987	40.00	250-350
1991 Sugarin Kids (Woodstock)	Closed	1991	41.00	300-350
1988 Woodstock Lady	Closed	1988	41.00	350
1988 Woodstock Man	Closed	1988	41.00	350
1988 Woodstock Man & Woman Set	Closed	1988	82.00	563

Store Exclusives-Yankee Craftsman Exclusives - J. Byers

YEAR ISSUE	EDITION LIMIT	YEAR RETD.	ISSUE PRICE	*QUOTE U.S.$
1999 Cape Cod Cranberry Couple	Closed	1999	115.00	550

Tour Pieces - J. Byers

YEAR ISSUE	EDITION LIMIT	YEAR RETD.	ISSUE PRICE	*QUOTE U.S.$
1996 Amish Boy (blue or purple)	Closed	1996	54.00	100-225
1997 Amish Girl (blue or purple)	Closed	1997	54.00	60-175
1998 Best of Times Lady	Closed	1998	49.00	125
1998 20th Anniversary Newsboy	Closed	1998	48.00	48-185
1999 Amish Man	Closed	1999	50.00	50

Winter Activities - J. Byers

YEAR ISSUE	EDITION LIMIT	YEAR RETD.	ISSUE PRICE	*QUOTE U.S.$
1991 Adult Skaters	Closed	1994	50.00	75-125
1991 Adult Skaters (1991 ed.)	Closed	1991	50.00	130-150
1993 Boy Skater on Log	Closed	1993	55.00	75-90
1992 Children Skaters (1992 ed.)	Closed	1992	50.00	150
1993 Grandparent Skaters	Closed	1993	50.00	65-100
1993 Grandparent Skaters (1993 ed.)	Closed	1993	50.00	145-153
1995 Man Holding Skates	Closed	1998	52.00	55
1995 Woman Holding Skates	Closed	1998	52.00	55

Calico Kittens/Enesco Group, Inc.

April Showers - P. Hillman

YEAR ISSUE	EDITION LIMIT	YEAR RETD.	ISSUE PRICE	*QUOTE U.S.$
1996 April Showers 155500	Retrd.	1998	17.50	18
1996 Friendship Grows When Shared 129321	Retrd.	1998	15.00	15
1996 Kite Tails 155497	Retrd.	1998	17.50	18

Birthstone Minis - P. Hillman

YEAR ISSUE	EDITION LIMIT	YEAR RETD.	ISSUE PRICE	*QUOTE U.S.$
2000 January 784788	Open		10.00	10
2000 February 784796	Open		10.00	10
2000 March 784818	Open		10.00	10
2000 April 784826	Open		10.00	10
2000 May 784834	Open		10.00	10
2000 June 784842	Open		10.00	10
2000 July 784850	Open		10.00	10
2000 August 784869	Open		10.00	10
2000 September 784877	Open		10.00	10
2000 October 784893	Open		10.00	10
2000 November 784907	Open		10.00	10
2000 December 784915	Open		10.00	10

Breed Apart Minis - P. Hillman

YEAR ISSUE	EDITION LIMIT	YEAR RETD.	ISSUE PRICE	*QUOTE U.S.$
1999 Calico 642274	Open		9.00	9
1999 Himalayan 642266	Open		9.00	9
1999 Persian 642258	Open		9.00	9
1999 Shorthair 642231	Open		9.00	9
1999 Siamese 642223	Open		9.00	9
1999 Tiffany 642215	Open		9.00	9

Calico Corner - P. Hillman

YEAR ISSUE	EDITION LIMIT	YEAR RETD.	ISSUE PRICE	*QUOTE U.S.$
1995 Buttoned Up with Love 104094	Retrd.	1996	13.50	14
1995 Grandma's Are Sew Full Of Love, set/2 104108	Retrd.	1996	13.50	14
1994 Hand Knitted With Love 626023	Retrd.	1998	13.50	27
1995 Nothing Is Sweeter Than Mom 104086	Retrd.	1996	13.50	14
1994 Our Friendship Is A Quilt Of Love 626015	Retrd.	1998	13.50	14
1994 Sew Happy It's Your Birthday 625965	Retrd.	1998	13.50	14
1994 Tea And You Hit The Spot 625981	Retrd.	1998	13.50	14
1994 You Always Top Off My Days 626007	Retrd.	1998	13.50	14
1994 Your Friendship Is My Silver Lining 625973	Retrd.	1998	13.50	14

Calico Kittens - P. Hillman

YEAR ISSUE	EDITION LIMIT	YEAR RETD.	ISSUE PRICE	*QUOTE U.S.$
1995 3 Asst. Kittens w/Candy Hearts 102199	Retrd.	1997	11.00	11
1994 3 Asst. mini cats 623520	Retrd.	1995	11.00	11
1994 6 Asst. Mini 651117	Retrd.	1997	12.00	12
1995 All About Angels 144215	5,000	1996	25.00	25-47
1998 Bet You're Kit N' Kaboodle We're Five 314579	Yr.Iss.	1998	50.00	50
1994 Blossoms Of Friendship 623555	Retrd.	1995	20.00	20
1999 Chatty Catty 546569	7,500		22.50	23
2000 Countryside Kitty (February Show Exclusive) 720852	Retrd.	2000	17.50	18
2000 Creature Comforts 720755	Yr.Iss.		17.50	18
1993 Dressed In Our Holiday Best 628190	Retrd.	1996	15.50	16
1994 Ewe Warm My Heart 628182	Retrd.	1996	17.50	18
1994 Extra Special 624624	Retrd.	1998	15.00	15
1999 Feel-ine Fine In The City (January Exclusive) 543500	Closed	1999	17.50	18
1999 Feel-ine Fine In The Country (Spring Fling Exclusive) 543519	Closed	1999	17.50	18
1993 Friends Are Cuddles Of Love 627976	Retrd.	1996	20.00	20
1999 Friends Of A Feather Flock Together (Special Exclusive) 505633	Closed	1999	22.50	23
1994 Friendship Cushions The Fall 651087	Retrd.	1999	18.50	19
1994 Friendship Is A Warm, Close Feeling 623598	Retrd.	1995	25.00	25
1994 Friendship Is The Best O'Luck 623601	Retrd.	1999	13.50	14
1993 A Good Friend Warms The Heart 627984	Retrd.	1996	15.00	15
2000 Handle With Care (Mother's Day) 785024	7,500		25.00	25
1996 Hey Diddle Diddle The Cat And The Fiddle 166456	7,500	1996	20.00	20
1994 Home Sweet Home 624705	Retrd.	1998	15.00	15
1993 I'm All Fur You 627968	Retrd.	1996	15.00	15
1996 I've Been A Good Kitty 178446	Yr.Iss.	1996	17.50	18
1994 Joy To The World "Joy" 625264	Retrd.	1997	22.50	23
2000 Just Hangin Around 720879	7,500		40.00	40
1994 Kitten On Quilt (musical) 620742	Retrd.	1997	40.00	40
1994 Kitten With Signage Plaque 699179	Retrd.	1996	15.00	15
1997 Kitty And Me 203963	Retrd.	1998	20.00	20
2000 Kosmopolitan Kitty (January Show Exclusive) 720844	Retrd.	2000	20.00	20
1994 Love 624721	Retrd.	1998	15.00	15
1995 Love Pours From My Heart 102210	Retrd.	1998	22.50	23
1994 A Loving Gift "Love" 625272	Retrd.	1997	22.50	25
1998 My Favorite Things 360295	Retrd.	1999	45.00	45
1994 My Heart Belongs To You (lg.) 771201	Retrd.	1996	50.00	50
1994 My Heart Belongs To You (sm.) 771236	Retrd.	1996	25.00	25
1993 Our Friendship Blossomed From The Heart 627887	Retrd.	1996	15.00	15
1997 Our Friendship Is A Magical Spell 274852	Retrd.	1999	13.50	14
1994 Peace On Earth "Peace" 625256	Retrd.	1997	22.50	23
1994 Planting The Seeds Of Friendship 623547	Retrd.	1996	20.00	20
1994 A Pocketful O'Luck For You 623628	Retrd.	1999	13.50	14
1994 Purr-fect Friends 624691	Retrd.	1998	15.00	15
1998 Santa Paws 359653	Yr.Iss.	1998	17.50	18
1995 Stitch In Time Saves Nine 129429	3,000	1995	35.00	35
2000 Surround Yourself With Your Favorite Things 676969	Yr.Iss.		40.00	40
1999 There Are No Ordinary Cats - Expect The Unexpected 686573	Yr.Iss.	1999	17.50	18
1994 There's No Friend Like You 625299	Retrd.	1999	18.50	19
1994 Thinking Of You 624713	Retrd.	1998	15.00	15
1998 Three Little Kittens Who Lost Their Mittens 359785	5,000	1998	25.00	25
1993 Waiting For A Friend Like You - 9" 628662	Retrd.	1998	100.00	100
1993 Waiting For A Friend Like You 627895	Retrd.	1996	30.00	30
1993 We're A Purr-fect Pair 627925	Retrd.	1996	25.00	25
1993 Wrapped In The Warmth Of Friendship 628174	Retrd.	1996	17.50	18
1994 You And Me 624748	Retrd.	1998	15.00	15
1993 You're A Friend Fur-ever 628018	Retrd.	1996	20.00	28-34
1994 You're A Special Aunt 651117	Retrd.	1997	12.00	12
1994 You're A Special Friend 651117	Retrd.	1997	12.00	12
1994 You're A Special Grandma 651117	Retrd.	1997	12.00	12
1994 You're A Special Mom 651117	Retrd.	1997	12.00	12
1994 You're A Special Niece 651117	Retrd.	1997	12.00	12
1994 You're A Special Sister 651117	Retrd.	1997	12.00	12
1999 You're the Best Gift of All 543470	Yr.Iss.	1999	20.00	20
1996 You've Earned Your Wings 178454	5,000	1996	35.00	35
1999 Your Friendship Takes The Prize Customer Appreciation 477877	Closed	1999	17.50	18

Carolling Kitties - P. Hillman

YEAR ISSUE	EDITION LIMIT	YEAR RETD.	ISSUE PRICE	*QUOTE U.S.$
1999 Dance Of The Sugar Plum Fairies 542555	Open		15.00	15
1999 Here Comes Santa Claus 542563	Open		15.00	15
1999 Jingle Bells 542539	Open		15.00	15
1999 O Christmas Tree 542571	Open		15.00	15
1999 Up On The Rooftop 542547	Open		15.00	15
1999 We Three Kings 542598	Open		25.00	25

Cat Astrology Collection - P. Hillman

YEAR ISSUE	EDITION LIMIT	YEAR RETD.	ISSUE PRICE	*QUOTE U.S.$
1999 Leo 542423	Open		12.50	13
1999 Aries 542385	Open		12.50	13
1999 Taurus 542393	Open		12.50	13
1999 Gemini 542407	Open		12.50	13
1999 Cancer 542415	Open		12.50	13
1999 Virgo 542431	Open		12.50	13
1999 Libra 542458	Open		12.50	13
1999 Scorpio 542466	Open		12.50	13
1999 Saguittaruis 542474	Open		12.50	13
1999 Capricorn 542482	Open		12.50	13
1999 Aquarius 542490	Open		12.50	13
1999 Pisces 542504	Open		12.50	13

The Cat's Out of the Bag - P. Hillman

YEAR ISSUE	EDITION LIMIT	YEAR RETD.	ISSUE PRICE	*QUOTE U.S.$
1997 Friendship Lets The Cat Out Of The Bag 210544	Retrd.	1999	17.50	18
1997 I'm Sending You A Bag Full Of Love 210587	Retrd.	1999	17.50	18
1997 Our Friendship Is Out Of The Bag 210536	Retrd.	1999	17.50	18

Christmas - P. Hillman

YEAR ISSUE	EDITION LIMIT	YEAR RETD.	ISSUE PRICE	*QUOTE U.S.$
1993 Girl Kitten w/Hat & Scarf (musical) 629162	Retrd.	1998	60.00	60
1994 Hark, The Herald Angels Sing (musical) 651397	Retrd.	1996	60.00	60
1994 Hark, The Herald Angels Sing (musical) 651397	Retrd.	1996	60.00	60
1995 Hark-A-Herald Angel 144193	Retrd.	1998	17.50	18
1994 Hold On To Friendship 651079	Retrd.	1998	20.00	20
1993 Tan Angel Kitten (musical) 628212	Retrd.	1998	40.00	40
1993 Tan kitten Holding a Snowman (musical waterball) 623806	Retrd.	1998	50.00	50
1994 Tis' The Season For Sharing (musical) 628166	Retrd.	1998	25.00	25
1993 We Wish You a Merry Christmas (musical) 627526	Retrd.	1997	50.00	50
1996 We Wish You A Merry Christmas 932418	Retrd.	1998	17.50	18

Cozy Kitties - P. Hillman

YEAR ISSUE	EDITION LIMIT	YEAR RETD.	ISSUE PRICE	*QUOTE U.S.$
1997 All Wrapped Up In Warmth 274879	Retrd.	1999	16.50	17
1997 Friendship Covers The Holidays 274887	Retrd.	1999	16.50	17
1997 Hats Off To Friendship 274909	Retrd.	1999	16.50	17
1997 A Purr-fect Fit 274917	Retrd.	1999	16.50	17
1997 You Hold The Strings To My Heart 274895	Retrd.	1999	16.50	17

Different Hats for Different Cats - P. Hillman

YEAR ISSUE	EDITION LIMIT	YEAR RETD.	ISSUE PRICE	*QUOTE U.S.$
2000 The Earth Blossoms For You 720674	Open		17.50	18
2000 Our Friendship Is The Real Deal 720666	Open		15.00	15
2000 Thanks For Guiding Us Towards Our Goal 720631	Open		15.00	15
2000 You Motivate The Rest of Us 720682	Open		15.00	15
2000 You Spice Up My Life 720712	Open		17.50	18
2000 Your Touch Heals Body and Soul 720690	Open		17.50	18

Everything I Know I Learned From My Cat - P. Hillman

YEAR ISSUE	EDITION LIMIT	YEAR RETD.	ISSUE PRICE	*QUOTE U.S.$
1999 Always Land On Your Feet 642320	Open		20.00	20
1999 Meow When You're Hungry 642290	Open		15.00	15
1999 Milk and Treats Are Good For You 642304	Open		15.00	15
1999 Nap Anywhere 642347	Open		17.50	18
1999 Play Hard 642312	Open		15.00	15
1999 Rubbing People the Right Way is a Sign of Affection 642339	Open		17.50	18

For You - P. Hillman

YEAR ISSUE	EDITION LIMIT	YEAR RETD.	ISSUE PRICE	*QUOTE U.S.$
1996 For You 178500	Retrd.	1998	12.50	13
1996 I Love Teacher 178519	Retrd.	1998	12.50	13
1996 Mom 178489	Retrd.	1998	12.50	13
1996 To My Grandma 178497	Retrd.	1998	12.50	13

Gallery of Kittens - P. Hillman

YEAR ISSUE	EDITION LIMIT	YEAR RETD.	ISSUE PRICE	*QUOTE U.S.$
1998 Antiqued Gold 489344	Closed	1999	10.00	10
1998 Black Ebony 489263	Closed	1999	10.00	10
1998 Blue White Porcelain 489271	Closed	1999	10.00	10
1998 Frosted Glass 489336	Closed	1999	10.00	10
1998 Gold Trim 489352	Closed	1999	10.00	10
1998 Granite 489298	Closed	1999	10.00	10
1998 Green Jade 48932	Closed	1999	10.00	10
1998 Ivory 489379	Closed	1999	10.00	10
1998 Marble 489360	Closed	1999	10.00	10
1998 Pewter 489417	Closed	1999	10.00	10
1998 Stitched Cat 489182	Closed	1999	10.00	10
1998 Wood Hand Carved 489190	Closed	1999	10.00	10

Green-Eyed Monsters - P. Hillman

YEAR ISSUE	EDITION LIMIT	YEAR RETD.	ISSUE PRICE	*QUOTE U.S.$
1999 Don't Be A Scaredy Cat 543527	Retrd.	1999	17.50	18
1999 Feel-ine Spooky 543535	Retrd.	1999	15.00	15
1999 Trick or Treat - Preferably Catnip! 543543	Retrd.	1999	17.50	18

Holiday Harmony - P. Hillman

YEAR ISSUE	EDITION LIMIT	YEAR RETD.	ISSUE PRICE	*QUOTE U.S.$
1995 The First Noel 144606	Yr.Iss.	1995	17.50	18
1995 I'll Be Home For Christmas 144614	Retrd.	1998	17.50	18
1995 Jolly Old St. Nicholas 144630	Retrd.	1998	17.50	18
1995 Oh, Tannenbaum 144428	Retrd.	1998	17.50	18
1995 Silent Night 144622	Retrd.	1998	17.50	18

Itty Bitty Christmas Kitties - P. Hillman

YEAR ISSUE	EDITION LIMIT	YEAR RETD.	ISSUE PRICE	*QUOTE U.S.$
1996 Mini Figurines, set/3 178462	Closed	1999	7.00	7

Itty Bitty Garden Kitties - P. Hillman

YEAR ISSUE	EDITION LIMIT	YEAR RETD.	ISSUE PRICE	*QUOTE U.S.$
1997 Mini Figurines, set/3 204048	Closed	1999	7.00	7

Itty Bitty Kitties - P. Hillman

YEAR ISSUE	EDITION LIMIT	YEAR RETD.	ISSUE PRICE	*QUOTE U.S.$
1996 Congratulations 167312	Retrd.	1998	7.50	8
1996 Get Well 167339	Retrd.	1998	7.50	8
1996 Graduation 167347	Retrd.	1998	7.50	8
1996 Happy Birthday 167320	Retrd.	1998	7.50	8
1996 I Love You 167304	Retrd.	1998	7.50	8
1996 Mini Figurines, set/3 155527	Retrd.	1999	7.00	7
1996 Mini Figurines, set/3 155578	Retrd.	1999	7.00	7
1996 New Baby 167355	Retrd.	1998	7.50	8

Itty Bitty Kitties-Cat's Got Your Tongue - P. Hillman

YEAR ISSUE	EDITION LIMIT	YEAR RETD.	ISSUE PRICE	*QUOTE U.S.$
1997 Alley Cat 255122	Retrd.	1998	7.50	8
1997 Cat Baskets, set/3 254924	Retrd.	1999	6.00	6
1997 Cat Tails 255106	Retrd.	1998	7.50	8

*Quotes have been rounded up to nearest dollar

YEAR ISSUE	EDITION LIMIT	YEAR RETD.	ISSUE PRICE	*QUOTE U.S.$
1997 Cool Cat 255084	Retrd.	1998	7.50	8
1997 Fat Cat 255076	Retrd.	1998	7.50	8
1997 House Cat 255114	Retrd.	1998	7.50	8
1997 Top Cat 255092	Retrd.	1998	7.50	8

Itty Bitty...Purr-fect Pairs - P. Hillman

YEAR ISSUE	EDITION LIMIT	YEAR RETD.	ISSUE PRICE	*QUOTE U.S.$
1997 Best Friends 203629	Retrd.	1999	14.00	14
1997 Mom And Me 204994	Retrd.	1999	14.00	14
1997 True Love 205001	Retrd.	1999	14.00	14

Kitchen Cuddles - P. Hillman

YEAR ISSUE	EDITION LIMIT	YEAR RETD.	ISSUE PRICE	*QUOTE U.S.$
1999 Calico Kitten in Pitcher 465658	Open		6.50	7
1999 Calico Kitten in Sugar Bowl 465623	Open		6.50	7
1999 Calico Kitten in Teacup 465666	Open		6.50	7
1999 Calico Kitten in Teapot 465615	Open		6.50	7

Kitty Capers - P. Hillman

YEAR ISSUE	EDITION LIMIT	YEAR RETD.	ISSUE PRICE	*QUOTE U.S.$
1996 Hats Off To The Holidays 178381	Retrd.	1999	12.50	13
1996 I'm All Yours 178373	Retrd.	1999	12.50	13
1996 Not Purr-fect, Just Purr-fectly Happy 178403	Retrd.	1999	12.50	13
1996 Wrapped Up In You 178411	Retrd.	1999	15.00	15
1996 You Brighten My Holidays 178365	Retrd.	1999	15.00	15

Life Through A Cat's Eyes - P. Hillman

YEAR ISSUE	EDITION LIMIT	YEAR RETD.	ISSUE PRICE	*QUOTE U.S.$
1999 A Cat Changes Coming Home To Any Empty House To Coming Home 686565	Open		17.50	18
1999 A Cat Must Be Loved On Its Own Terms 686557	Open		17.50	18
1999 Cats Believe The Best Things In Life Are Free 686603	Open		17.50	18
1999 Cats Like Doors Left Open In Case They Change Their Minds 686581	Open		17.50	18
1999 This House Under Feline Management 686611	Open		17.50	18

A Little Bird Told Me... - P. Hillman

YEAR ISSUE	EDITION LIMIT	YEAR RETD.	ISSUE PRICE	*QUOTE U.S.$
1997 A Little Bird Told Me You're Tweet 203998	Retrd.	1999	20.00	20

Look What The Cat Dragged In - P. Hillman

YEAR ISSUE	EDITION LIMIT	YEAR RETD.	ISSUE PRICE	*QUOTE U.S.$
1998 Friends Are a Feast Worth Sharing 360066	Open		15.00	15
1998 It's The Thought That Counts 360074	Open		15.00	15
1999 A Lobor of Love 295582	Retrd.	1999	15.00	15
1998 One Look From You Melts My Heart 360120	Open		15.00	15
1998 Sock Full of Love 360090	Open		15.00	15
1999 Some Bunny To Love You 295590	Retrd.	1999	15.00	15
1999 A Splash of Happiness 295566	Retrd.	1999	15.00	15
1999 A Sprinkle of Joy 295574	Retrd.	1999	15.00	15

Mommy's Little Helper - P. Hillman

YEAR ISSUE	EDITION LIMIT	YEAR RETD.	ISSUE PRICE	*QUOTE U.S.$
1999 Calico w/Kitten 642274	Open		9.00	9
1999 Himalayan w/Kitten 642266	Open		9.00	9
1999 Persian w/Kitten 642258	Open		9.00	9
1999 Shorthair Tabby w/Kitten 642231	Open		9.00	9
1999 Siamese w/Kitten 642223	Open		9.00	9
1999 Tiffany w/Kitten 642215	Open		9.00	9

My Heart Belongs To Kitty - P. Hillman

YEAR ISSUE	EDITION LIMIT	YEAR RETD.	ISSUE PRICE	*QUOTE U.S.$
1996 Hope All Your Dreams Come True 129356	Retrd.	1998	20.00	20
1996 My Funny Valentine 155454	Retrd.	1998	17.50	18

Nativity - P. Hillman

YEAR ISSUE	EDITION LIMIT	YEAR RETD.	ISSUE PRICE	*QUOTE U.S.$
1993 Creche 628441	Retrd.	1997	50.00	50
1994 Friends Come From Afar 625248	Retrd.	1997	17.50	18
1993 I'll Bring A Special Gift For You, Friendship Is The Best Gift Of All, Sharing The Gift Of Friendship, set/3 628476	Retrd.	1997	55.00	55
1993 A Purr-fect Angel From Above 628468	Retrd.	1997	15.00	15
1993 Sharing A Special Gift Of Love, Always Watching Over You, set/2 628484	Retrd.	1997	35.00	35

Nine Lives - P. Hillman

YEAR ISSUE	EDITION LIMIT	YEAR RETD.	ISSUE PRICE	*QUOTE U.S.$
2000 Discover Your World 682993	Open		10.00	10
2000 Fit For Life 683256	Open		10.00	10
2000 The Joy of Your Life 683205	Open		10.00	10
2000 Let Your Beauty Shine 683159	Open		10.00	10
2000 Reach For Your Goals 683167	Open		10.00	10
2000 Recharge Your Batteries 683272	Open		10.00	10
2000 Searching For Fulfillment 683213	Open		10.00	10
2000 Soulmates 682933	Open		10.00	10
2000 Treat Yourself 683183	Open		10.00	10

Picks of the Litter - P. Hillman

YEAR ISSUE	EDITION LIMIT	YEAR RETD.	ISSUE PRICE	*QUOTE U.S.$
1996 Hello, Little One 129410	Retrd.	1999	17.50	18
1996 A Little Litter Of Blessings 168602	Retrd.	1999	15.00	15
1996 New Kit On The Block 903140	Retrd.	1999	12.50	13
1996 Our Friendship Is Squeaky Clean 132713	Retrd.	1999	15.00	15
1996 Tummy Full Of Love For You 132721	Retrd.	1999	12.50	13
1996 Wagon Our Tails For You 172693	Retrd.	1999	17.50	18

Purr-fect Personalities - P. Hillman

YEAR ISSUE	EDITION LIMIT	YEAR RETD.	ISSUE PRICE	*QUOTE U.S.$
1995 Always Thinking Of You "Solitude" 112437	Retrd.	1998	14.50	15
1995 Fishing For A Friend "Mischievous" 112453	Retrd.	1998	14.50	15
1995 Good As New "Cleanliness" 113301	Retrd.	1998	14.50	15
1995 I'm Lost Without You "Observant" 112488	Retrd.	1998	14.50	15
1995 My Favorite Companion "Companionship" 112410	Retrd.	1998	14.50	15
1995 A Playful Afternoon "Playful" 112429	Retrd.	1998	14.50	15
1995 A Purr-fect Pair "Curiosity" 112445	Retrd.	1998	14.50	15
1995 Sweet Dreams "Catnap" 112461	Retrd.	1998	14.50	15
1995 An Unexpected Treat "Finicky" 112321	Retrd.	1998	14.50	15

Scaredy Cats - P. Hillman

YEAR ISSUE	EDITION LIMIT	YEAR RETD.	ISSUE PRICE	*QUOTE U.S.$
1997 Carving A Season Of Smiles 274828	Retrd.	1999	13.50	14
1997 Mummy Mischief 274836	Retrd.	1999	13.50	14
1997 Pussy Cat And The Queen 255157	5,000	1998	25.00	25
1997 You Can Always Spot A Friend 274844	Retrd.	1999	13.50	14

Seasonal Scenes - P. Hillman

YEAR ISSUE	EDITION LIMIT	YEAR RETD.	ISSUE PRICE	*QUOTE U.S.$
2000 Wintery Retreat 785075	Open		30.00	30

Sportin' An Attitude - P. Hillman

YEAR ISSUE	EDITION LIMIT	YEAR RETD.	ISSUE PRICE	*QUOTE U.S.$
1999 Friends Are A Goal Worth Saving 454648	Retrd.	2000	15.00	15
1999 Laughter Drives A Winning Friendship 454664	Retrd.	2000	15.00	15
1999 We're A Perfect Match 454656	Retrd.	2000	15.00	15
1999 You're an All-Star Friend 454621	Retrd.	2000	15.00	15

Springtime Friends - P. Hillman

YEAR ISSUE	EDITION LIMIT	YEAR RETD.	ISSUE PRICE	*QUOTE U.S.$
1995 3 Asst. Kittens w/eggs 102687	Retrd.	1998	11.00	11
1993 A Bundle Of Love 628433	Retrd.	1997	13.50	14-17
1995 Friendship Is The Best Blessing 102679	Retrd.	1997	20.00	20
1995 Furry And Feathered Friends 102636	Retrd.	1997	20.00	20
1995 Hats Off To A Perfect Friendship 129437	Retrd.	1997	20.00	20
1993 Just Thinking About You (musical) 620742	Retrd.	1997	40.00	40
1993 Just Thinking About You 627917	Retrd.	1997	20.00	20
1995 Love Blooms Fur-Ever 102644	Retrd.	1997	17.50	18
1993 Loves Special Delivery 628425	Retrd.	1997	13.50	14
1994 A Puff-fect Love "True Love" (musical) 622702	Retrd.	1996	60.00	60
1994 A Purr-fect Love Knot 626031	Retrd.	1997	50.00	50
1995 You Make Life Colorful 102601	Retrd.	1995	25.00	25
1993 You'll Always Be Close To My Heart 627909	Retrd.	1997	20.00	20
1993 You're Always There When I Need You 627992	Retrd.	1997	25.00	25
1995 Your Patchwork Charm Shows Through 129453	Retrd.	1997	17.50	18

Welcome to Whisker Way - P. Hillman

YEAR ISSUE	EDITION LIMIT	YEAR RETD.	ISSUE PRICE	*QUOTE U.S.$
1995 Blue Without You (Russian Blue) 129615	Retrd.	1998	17.50	18
1995 Friendship Has Many Riches (Persian) 129755	Retrd.	1998	17.50	18
1995 Great Scot, We're The Best Of Friends (Scottish Fold) 129593	Retrd.	1998	17.50	18
1996 I'd Never Desert You (Abyssinian) 903116	Retrd.	1998	17.50	18
1995 It's No Mystery We're Friends (British Shorthair) 129585	Retrd.	1998	17.50	18
1996 Tried And True For The Red, White And Blue (American Shorthair) 903086	Retrd.	1998	17.50	18
1995 We're Insep-purr-able Friends (Siamese) 129577	Retrd.	1998	17.50	18
1995 You're My All American Friend (Tabby) 129607	Retrd.	1998	17.50	18

You're The Cat's Meow - P. Hillman

YEAR ISSUE	EDITION LIMIT	YEAR RETD.	ISSUE PRICE	*QUOTE U.S.$
1997 A Dash Of Love Makes You Sweeter 276863	Yr.Iss.	1997	17.50	18
1998 Friendship Is Heavenly 274968	5,000	1998	20.00	20
1997 White kitten 275891	Yr.Iss.	1998	10.00	10

Cardew Design North America

"English Bettys" - P. Cardew

YEAR ISSUE	EDITION LIMIT	YEAR RETD.	ISSUE PRICE	*QUOTE U.S.$
1995 Cat Got the Cream-Brown Betty	Retrd.	1998	50.00	58
1996 Chess-Black Betty	Retrd.	1998	50.00	55
1996 Gardening-Green Betty	Retrd.	1999	50.00	60
1996 Golf-White Betty	Retrd.	1998	50.00	55
1995 Harvest Pies-Brown Betty	Retrd.	1998	50.00	60
1996 London Touring-Black Betty	Retrd.	1998	50.00	55
1996 Magician-Black Betty	Retrd.	1996	50.00	55
1995 Ploughman's Lunch-Brown Betty	Retrd.	1996	50.00	55
1995 Rise & "Shoe" Shine-Brown Betty	Retrd.	1996	50.00	55
1995 Summer Picnic-Brown Betty	Retrd.	1996	50.00	55
1995 Tea Table-Brown Betty	Retrd.	1999	50.00	60
1996 Teddy Bear's Picnic-Yellow Betty	Retrd.	1999	50.00	65

Cardew Collectors' Club - P. Cardew

YEAR ISSUE	EDITION LIMIT	YEAR RETD.	ISSUE PRICE	*QUOTE U.S.$
1995 Moving Day	5,000	1997	175.00	200
1995 Tiny Tea Chest	Retrd.	1997	Gift	N/A
1997 Willow Pattern Tea Cup Teapot	Yr.Iss.	1997	45.00	45
1997 Mug One-Cup	Yr.Iss.	1997	Gift	N/A
1998 Collectors Tea For Two/Victorian Tea Table	Yr.Iss.	1998	Gift	N/A
1998 Sewing Machine	5,000	1999	185.00	185

Disney Full Sized Teapots - P. Cardew

YEAR ISSUE	EDITION LIMIT	YEAR RETD.	ISSUE PRICE	*QUOTE U.S.$
1996 Donald in Mangle	5,000	1999	140.00	170-187
1997 Goofy - Baking Day	5,000	1999	225.00	225
1997 Mickey - Stove	5,000	1999	225.00	225
1997 Minnie - Dressing Table	5,000	1999	225.00	225
1998 Minnie/Mickey Piano - 70th Anniversary	5,000	1999	250.00	250
1998 Winnie The Pooh	5,000	1999	250.00	250

Disney One-Cup Teapots - P. Cardew

YEAR ISSUE	EDITION LIMIT	YEAR RETD.	ISSUE PRICE	*QUOTE U.S.$
1998 Donald Santa	5,000	1999	75.00	75
1998 Goofy Santa	5,000	1999	75.00	75

Disney Tiny Teapots - P. Cardew

YEAR ISSUE	EDITION LIMIT	YEAR RETD.	ISSUE PRICE	*QUOTE U.S.$
1998 Donald	10,000	1999	20.00	20
1998 Goofy	10,000	1999	20.00	20
1998 Mickey	10,000	1999	20.00	20
1996 Mickey Santa	5,000	1996	75.00	75

Disney Two-Cup Teapots - P. Cardew

YEAR ISSUE	EDITION LIMIT	YEAR RETD.	ISSUE PRICE	*QUOTE U.S.$
1996 101 Dalmatians	5,000	1999	110.00	110-182
1996 Beauty & The Beast	5,000	1999	80.00	80
1996 Cinderella's Dress	10,000	1998	80.00	110
1998 Jungle Book	5,000	1999	110.00	110
1997 Lady & Tramp	5,000	1999	95.00	95
1996 Madhatters Tea Party	5,000	1998	80.00	80
1998 Mickey Automobile	5,000	1999	225.00	225
1998 Mickey Aviator	5,000	1999	225.00	225
1997 Pooh Bear	5,000	1998	95.00	95
1998 Winnie The Pooh Hutch	5,000	1999	120.00	120

Event Piece - P. Cardew

YEAR ISSUE	EDITION LIMIT	YEAR RETD.	ISSUE PRICE	*QUOTE U.S.$
1996 "Travellers Return"	5,000	1996	45.00	75

Limited Edition Full Sized Teapots - P. Cardew

YEAR ISSUE	EDITION LIMIT	YEAR RETD.	ISSUE PRICE	*QUOTE U.S.$
1990 Allsorts of Liquorice	Retrd.	1993	60.00	405-450
1998 Blue Willow Tea Table	5,000	1999	185.00	185
1970 Cactus	Retrd.	1978	60.00	1080-1260
1997 Charles Atlas Stand	5,000	1999	250.00	375
1997 Classical Fireplace	5,000	1999	175.00	180
1998 Do-It-Yourself	5,000	1999	185.00	185
1997 Farmhouse Dresser	5,000	1999	175.00	188
1997 Farmhouse Fireplace	5,000	1999	175.00	180
1997 Gardener's Bench	5,000	1999	175.00	188
1996 Heart	Retrd.	N/A	N/A	315
1998 Kirvan's Tea Merchant	5,000	1999	225.00	229
1998 Kirvan's Tea Van	5,000	1999	225.00	229
1995 Kitchen Sink	5,000	1999	175.00	188
1995 Ladies Dressing Table	5,000	1998	175.00	175
1996 Lilliput Lane Market Stall	Retrd.	1996	250.00	250
1993 Punctualitea	Retrd.	1995	N/A	180
1995 Refrigerator	5,000	1999	175.00	180
1997 Rington's Tea Merchant	5,000	1997	250.00	250
1998 Sewing Machine II	5,000	1999	185.00	185
1995 Snowman	Retrd.	N/A	N/A	360-405
1995 Teapot Market Stall	5,000	1996	199.00	199
1996 Teapot Market Stall Mark II	5,000	1999	199.00	265
1996 Teddy Bear's Picnic	5,000	1999	175.00	229
1995 Washing Machine	5,000	1998	175.00	180
1996 Welsh Dresser	5,000	1996	175.00	175

Market Stall Series - P. Cardew

YEAR ISSUE	EDITION LIMIT	YEAR RETD.	ISSUE PRICE	*QUOTE U.S.$
1993 Antiques Market Stall	Retrd.	1996	160.00	160
1993 China Market Stall	Retrd.	1997	160.00	175
1993 Hardware Market Stall	5,000	1997	160.00	175
1995 Shoe Market Stall	5,000	1998	160.00	188

One-Cup Teapot Collection - P. Cardew

YEAR ISSUE	EDITION LIMIT	YEAR RETD.	ISSUE PRICE	*QUOTE U.S.$
1995 50's Stove	Retrd.	1996	45.00	45
1990 Allsorts of Liquorice	Retrd.	1995	N/A	85
1994 Baking Day	Retrd.	1995	45.00	45
1996 Bloomingdales	Retrd.	1997	45.00	45
1995 China Stall	Retrd.	1998	45.00	64
1995 Christmas Presents	Retrd.	1998	45.00	45
1996 Christmas Tree	Retrd.	1998	45.00	64
1994 Crimewriter's Desk	Retrd.	1996	45.00	45
1996 Egg Cup	Retrd.	1999	45.00	48
1996 Gardening	Retrd.	1999	45.00	70
1996 Golf Bag	Retrd.	1999	45.00	48
1996 Grandfather Clock	Retrd.	1999	45.00	48
1997 Hiker's Rest	Retrd.	1998	60.00	64
1995 Kitchen Sink	Retrd.	1996	45.00	45
1995 Lady's Dressing Table	Retrd.	1998	45.00	48
1995 Moving Day	Retrd.	1998	45.00	70
1995 Refrigerator	Retrd.	1998	45.00	64
1996 Romance/Heart/Valentine	Retrd.	1998	45.00	48
1996 Santa Claus	Retrd.	1998	45.00	64
1995 Sewing Machine	Retrd.	1999	45.00	64
1995 Snowman	Retrd.	1998	N/A	65
1995 Tea Scoop	Retrd.	1996	45.00	45
1995 Tea Shop Counter	Retrd.	1996	45.00	45
1995 Teddy Bear's Picnic	Retrd.	1999	45.00	70
1995 Toy Box	Retrd.	1996	45.00	45
1997 Victorian Fireplace	Retrd.	1999	45.00	64
1995 Victorian Tea Table	Retrd.	1996	45.00	45
1997 Victorian Washstand	Retrd.	1998	45.00	64
1995 Washing Machine	Retrd.	1998	45.00	64
1995 Washing Mangle	Retrd.	1996	45.00	45
1995 Welsh Dresser	Retrd.	1998	45.00	64

Standard Teapots - P. Cardew

YEAR ISSUE	EDITION LIMIT	YEAR RETD.	ISSUE PRICE	*QUOTE U.S.$
1991 50's Stove	Retrd.	1996	140.00	140
1992 Baking Day	Retrd.	1998	140.00	180
1992 Crime Writer's Desk	Retrd.	1999	140.00	180
1991 Cupid's Cloud & Pedestal	Retrd.	1994	125.00	1080-1440
1991 Mechanics Bench	Retrd.	1994	100.00	450-540
1991 Safe	Retrd.	1994	100.00	270
1992 Sewing Machine	Retrd.	1997	140.00	140
1993 Tea Shop Counter	Retrd.	1995	140.00	140
1991 Toy Box	Retrd.	1996	140.00	217-315
1992 Victorian Tea Table	Retrd.	1997	140.00	145
1993 Victorian Washstand	Retrd.	1995	140.00	140
1992 Washing Mangle	Retrd.	1996	140.00	140

*Quotes have been rounded up to nearest dollar

Tiny Teapots - P. Cardew

YEAR ISSUE	EDITION LIMIT	YEAR RETD.	ISSUE PRICE	*QUOTE U.S.$
1995 50's Stove	Retrd.	1997	10.00	10
1995 Baking Day	Retrd.	1996	10.00	10
1996 Bedside Table	Retrd.	1996	10.00	10
1995 Crime Writer's Desk	Retrd.	1996	10.00	12
1995 Kitchen Sink	Retrd.	1997	10.00	10
1995 Refrigerator	Retrd.	1996	10.00	10
1995 Sewing Machine	Retrd.	1997	10.00	10
1995 Tea Shop Counter	Retrd.	1996	10.00	12
1995 Teddy Bear's Picnic	Retrd.	1996	10.00	10
1995 Toy Box	Retrd.	1996	10.00	10
1995 Victorian Wash Stand	Retrd.	1996	10.00	10
1995 Washing Machine	Retrd.	1996	10.00	10
1995 Washing Mangle	Retrd.	1997	10.00	10
1996 Golf Trolley	Retrd.	1997	10.00	10
1996 Petrol Pump	Retrd.	1996	10.00	10
1996 Heart	Retrd.	1996	10.00	10
1996 Radio	Retrd.	1997	10.00	10
1996 Safe	Retrd.	1996	10.00	10
1996 50's TV	Retrd.	1997	10.00	10
1996 Fireplace	Retrd.	1997	10.00	10
1996 Grandfather's Clock	Retrd.	1997	10.00	10
1996 Lady's Dressing Table	Retrd.	1996	10.00	10
1996 Victorian Tea Table	Retrd.	1996	10.00	10
1996 Welsh Dresser	Retrd.	1997	10.00	10

Two-Cup Teapot Collection - P. Cardew

YEAR ISSUE	EDITION LIMIT	YEAR RETD.	ISSUE PRICE	*QUOTE U.S.$
1997 Anniversary Teatable	Retrd.	1998	75.00	75
1997 Birthday Teatable	Retrd.	1998	75.00	80
1997 Cats on Dresser/Colour Box Welsh Dresser	Retrd.	1998	75.00	75
1997 Christening Teatable	Retrd.	1998	75.00	80
1997 Jewelery Box	Retrd.	1999	75.00	87
1997 Safe	Retrd.	1998	75.00	87
1997 Sewing Machine	Retrd.	1999	75.00	80
1997 Tea Service Tea Table	Retrd.	1998	75.00	87
1997 Television	Retrd.	1998	75.00	80
1997 Welsh Dresser	Retrd.	1999	75.00	75
1997 Willow Pattern Teatable	Retrd.	1999	75.00	87

Cast Art Industries

Dreamsicles Club - K. Haynes

YEAR ISSUE	EDITION LIMIT	YEAR RETD.	ISSUE PRICE	*QUOTE U.S.$
1993 A Star is Born-CD001	Retrd.	1993	Gift	107-115
1994 Daydream Believer-CD100	Retrd.	1994	29.95	75-85
1994 Join The Fun-CD002	Retrd.	1994	Gift	40-50
1994 Makin' A List-CD101	Retrd.	1994	47.95	65-75
1995 Three Cheers-CD003	Retrd.	1995	Gift	45-60
1995 Town Crier-CD102	Retrd.	1995	24.95	25-45
1995 Snowbound-CD103	Retrd.	1996	24.95	35
1996 Star Shower-CD004	Retrd.	1996	Gift	35-39
1996 Heavenly Flowers-CD104	Retrd.	1997	24.95	25
1996 Bee-Friended-CD105	Retrd.	1999	24.95	25-45
1997 Free Spirit-CD005	Retrd.	1997	Gift	30
1997 Peaceable Kingdom-CD106	Retrd.	1999	14.75	15
1997 First Blush-CD109	12,000	1998	49.95	50
1997 Sweet Tooth (w/cookbook)-CD110	Retrd.	1998	19.95	20
1997 Editor's Choice (Newsletter Participation)-CD107	N/A		Gift	N/A
1997 Golden Halo ("Good Samaritan" award)-CD108	N/A		Gift	N/A
1998 Let's Get Together-CD006	Retrd.	1998	Gift	N/A
1997 Summertime Serenade-CD111	Open		14.75	15
1998 Above and Beyond (5th Anniversary Piece)-CD112	Retrd.	1999	29.95	30
1999 Share The Magic-CD007	Retrd.	1999	Gift	N/A
1999 Golden Memories-CD113	Open		20.00	20
1999 Snowflake Angel Hug™ (cherub)-08008	Retrd.	1999	Gift	N/A
1999 Ship of Dreams-CD117	Open		39.95	40
1999 Tic Tac Toe -CD116	Open		29.95	30
2000 Get On Board-CD008	Yr.Iss.		Gift	N/A
2000 Hugged By An Angel-08055	Yr.Iss.		Gift	N/A
2000 Threads of Love-CD128	Yr.Iss.		19.95	20

Dreamsicles - K. Haynes

YEAR ISSUE	EDITION LIMIT	YEAR RETD.	ISSUE PRICE	*QUOTE U.S.$
1997 Anticipation - ICE Commemorative Figurine-SP002	Retrd.	1997	29.95	30
1992 Baby Love-DC147	Retrd.	1995	7.00	10
1995 Best Buddies-DC159	Retrd.	1998	14.00	35
1991 Best Pals-DC103	Retrd.	1994	15.00	40
1992 Bluebird On My Shoulder-DC115	Retrd.	1995	19.00	30-40
1994 Born This Day-DC230	Retrd.	1998	16.00	16
1995 Brotherhood-DC307	Retrd.	1998	20.00	20
1996 Bubble Bath-DC416	Retrd.	1998	22.00	22-35
1992 Bundle of Joy-DC142	Retrd.	1995	7.00	145-295
1993 By the Silvery Moon-DC253	10,000	1994	100.00	150-175
1992 Caroler - Center Scroll-DC216	Retrd.	1995	19.00	28
1992 Caroler - Left Scroll-DC218	Retrd.	1995	19.00	25-28
1992 Caroler - Right Scroll-DC217	Retrd.	1995	19.00	25-28
1996 Carousel Ride-DS283	Retrd.	1998	150.00	150
1994 Carousel-DC174	Suspd.		35.00	58-60
2000 Castle in the Sky-11400	10,000		58.00	58
1993 Catch a Falling Star-DC166	Retrd.	1997	12.00	12-22
1991 Cherub and Child-DC100	Retrd.	1995	15.00	100
1994 Cherub Bowl-Stars-DC161	Suspd.		9.50	50
1992 Cherub For All Seasons-DC114	Retrd.	1995	23.00	45-75
1992 Cherub-DC111	10,000	1992	50.00	105-115
1992 Cherub-DC112	10,000	1993	50.00	200-225
1996 A Child Is Born-DC256	10,000	1996	95.00	95
1992 A Child's Prayer-DC145	Retrd.	1995	7.00	7
2000 A Collector's Delight - ICE Commemorative Figurine-SP002	Retrd.	2000	25.00	25
1996 Corona Centennial	Retrd.	1996	Gift	N/A
1996 Crossing Guardian-DC422	Retrd.	1998	40.00	40
1994 Cuddle Blanket-DC153	Retrd.	1995	6.50	7
1997 Cutie Pie-10241	12,500	1998	42.00	42
1996 Daffodil Days DC343 (American Cancer Society Figurine)	Retrd.	1998	15.00	30-35
1992 Dance Ballerina Dance-DC140	Retrd.	1995	37.00	42
1998 Daydreamin'-10332	Retrd.	1999	30.00	30
1991 Dimples DA-100	Retrd.	1991	5.50	6
1992 Dream A Little Dream-DC144	Retrd.	1995	7.00	10
1997 Dream Weaver-10159	Retrd.	1999	10.00	10
1997 Dreamboat-10060 (Sp. Ed.)	Retrd.	1998	90.00	90
1997 Dreamin' Of You-10030	Retrd.	1999	10.00	10
1998 Dreamsicles Ark-10564, set/7	Open		100.00	100
1994 Eager to Please-DC154	Retrd.	1995	6.50	10
1992 Flying Lesson-DC251	10,000	1993	80.00	850-875
1997 Follow Me-10050	Retrd.	1998	28.00	28
1991 Forever Friends-DC102	Retrd.	1994	15.00	35-40
1991 Forever Yours-DC110	Retrd.	1995	44.00	75
1996 Free Kittens-DK038	Retrd.	1998	18.00	18
1996 Free Puppies-DK039	Retrd.	1998	18.00	18
1994 Friendship Cherubs-DC-175	Retrd.	1999	20.00	20
1995 Get Well Soon-DC244	Retrd.	1997	11.00	11-18
1997 Goodness Me-10160	Retrd.	1999	10.00	10
1997 Handmade With Love-10324	10,000	1998	78.00	78
1997 Happy Landings-10156	5,000	1997	88.00	88
1997 Hear No Evil-10040	Open		18.00	18
1996 Heaven's Gate-DC257 (5th Anniversary piece)	15,000	1996	129.00	129
1991 Heavenly Dreamer-DC106	Retrd.	1996	11.50	12
1994 Here's Looking at You-DC172	Retrd.	1995	25.00	35
1997 Here's My Hand-10248	Retrd.	1999	20.00	20
1995 Hugabye Baby-DC701	Retrd.	1997	12.50	13-18
1991 Hunny Buns DA-101	Retrd.	1995	5.50	6
1994 I Can Read-DC151	Retrd.	1995	6.50	10
1997 Ice Dancing-10256	Retrd.	1999	17.00	17
1994 International Collectible Exposition Commemorative Figurine	Retrd.	1995	34.95	116-150
1997 It's Your Day-10220	Retrd.	1998	30.00	30
1992 Life Is Good-DC119	Retrd.	1996	10.00	15
1992 Little Darlin'-DC146	Retrd.	1995	7.00	10
1993 Little Dickens-DC127	Retrd.	1995	24.00	25
1992 Littlest Angel-DC143	Retrd.	1995	7.00	10
2000 Live, Love, Laugh-11061	10,000		55.00	55
1993 Long Fellow-DC126	Retrd.	1995	24.00	30-35
1995 Lots of Love-DC403	Retrd.	1999	16.00	16
1995 Love Me Do-DC194	Retrd.	1998	15.00	15
1993 Love My Kitty-DC130	Retrd.	1997	14.50	15-18
1993 Love My Puppy-DC131	Retrd.	1997	12.50	13-18
1993 Love My Teddy-DC132	Retrd.	1997	14.50	18-20
1998 Love You Sew-10263	Retrd.	1999	15.00	15
1998 Lullaby and Goodnight-10613 (musical)	Suspd.		45.00	45
1997 Lyrical Lute-10169	Retrd.	1998	29.00	29
2000 A Magical Beginning-11138	10,000		44.00	44
2000 Magical Merry Go Round-11481	7,500		150.00	150
1993 Me And My Shadow-DC116	Retrd.	1996	19.00	19-22
1997 Mellow Cello-10170	Retrd.	1998	39.00	39
1991 Mischief Maker-DC105	Retrd.	1996	10.00	10-25
1993 Miss Morningstar-DC141	Retrd.	1996	25.00	35-40
1994 Moon Dance-DC210	Retrd.	1997	29.00	29-38
1994 Moon Dance-DC210	Retrd.	1997	29.00	29-38
1991 Musician w/Cymbals-5154	Suspd.		22.00	22
1991 Musician w/Drums-5152	Suspd.		22.00	22
1991 Musician w/Flute-5153	Suspd.		22.00	22-75
1991 Musician w/Trumpet-5151	Suspd.		22.00	22
1992 My Funny Valentine-DC201	Suspd.		17.00	28
1995 Nursery Rhyme-DC229	Suspd.		42.00	50-70
1995 One World-DC306	Retrd.	1998	24.00	24
1993 P.S. I Love You-DC203	Retrd.	1997	7.50	8-18
1999 Passage of Time-10671 (millennium ed.)	Retrd.	1999	40.00	40
1998 Peaceful Dreams-10331	Retrd.	1999	17.00	17
1995 Picture Perfect-DC255	10,000	1995	100.00	89-125
1998 Please Be Mine-10259	Retrd.	1999	14.00	14
1995 Poetry In Motion-DC113 (Sp. Ed.)	Retrd.	1997	80.00	90-115
1996 Pull Toy-DK027	Retrd.	1998	18.00	18
1995 Range Rider-DC305	Retrd.	1998	15.00	15
1994 The Recital-DC254	10,000	1994	135.00	119-195
1997 See No Evil-10041	Open		18.00	18
1994 Side By Side-DC169	Retrd.	1995	31.50	40-45
1991 Sitting Pretty-DC101	Retrd.	1996	9.50	12
1996 Sleepover-DC421	Retrd.	1999	18.00	18
1994 Snowflake-DC117	Suspd.		10.00	14
1997 Speak No Evil-10042	Open		18.00	18
1997 Special Occasion-10167	Retrd.	1999	48.00	48
1997 Special Occasions-10167	Retrd.	1999	45.00	45
1999 Stairway to Heaven-10672	10,000	1999	78.00	78-82
1997 String Serenade-10168	Retrd.	1998	30.00	30
1994 Sucking My Thumb-DC156	Retrd.	1995	6.50	7-10
1996 Sugar 'N Spice-DC327	Retrd.	1999	10.00	10
1994 Sugarfoot-DC167	Retrd.	1998	25.00	25
1994 Surprise Gift-DC152	Retrd.	1995	6.50	10
1993 Sweet Dreams-DC125	Retrd.	1995	29.00	35-45
1996 Swimming For Hope-DC016	Retrd.	1996	75.00	75-100
1997 Taking Aim-DC432	Retrd.	1998	33.00	33
1996 Tea Party-DC015 (GCC event)	Retrd.	1996	19.00	20-40
1993 Teacher's Pet-DC124	Retrd.	1997	11.00	11
1993 Teeter Tots-DC252	10,000	1993	100.00	125-178
1993 Thinking of You-DC129	Retrd.	1997	42.00	44-55
1993 Tiny Dancer-DC165	Retrd.	1998	14.00	14
1995 Twinkle, Twinkle-DC700	Retrd.	1997	14.50	15
1994 Up All Night-DC155	Retrd.	1995	6.50	10
1998 We Are Winning-10380 (American Cancer Society)	Open		17.00	17
1991 Wild Flower-DC107	Retrd.	1996	10.00	10
1997 Wish You Were Here-10075	Retrd.	1999	14.00	14
1993 Wishin' On A Star-DC120	Retrd.	1998	10.00	10
1996 Wishing 'N Hoping-DC328	Retrd.	1999	10.00	10
1996 Wishing Well-DC423	Retrd.	1998	35.00	35
1995 Wistful Thinking-DC707	Retrd.	1998	7.00	7-20

Dreamsicles Animals - K. Haynes

YEAR ISSUE	EDITION LIMIT	YEAR RETD.	ISSUE PRICE	*QUOTE U.S.$
1991 Armadillo -5176	Suspd.		13.50	14-25
1992 Beach Baby-DA615	Retrd.	1994	24.00	35
1991 Buddy Bear-DA451	Retrd.	1994	6.00	17
1991 Carnation-DA379	Retrd.	1996	16.00	16-30
1993 Country Bear-DA458	Suspd.		14.00	14-29
1992 Fat Cat-DA555	Retrd.	1994	27.00	27
1991 Hambone-DA344	Retrd.	1996	10.75	20-25
1991 Hamlet-DA342	Retrd.	1996	10.75	20-25
1991 Hey Diddle Diddle-DA380	Retrd.	1996	16.00	16-30
1991 King Rabbit-DA124	Retrd.	1994	73.00	73-115
1991 Mama Bear-DA452	Retrd.	1994	7.00	18-25
1991 Mr. Bunny-DA107	Retrd.	1994	28.00	28
1996 Naptime-DA556	Suspd.		18.00	18
1992 Needlenose-DA610	Suspd.		8.00	8-28
1991 P.J. Mouse-DA476	Suspd.		10.00	10-28
1992 Papa Pelican-DA602	Retrd.	1994	22.50	35
1992 Pelican Jr.-DA601	Suspd.		9.00	9-30
1993 Pierre The Bear-DA453	Suspd.		14.00	14-32
1991 Piglet-DA343	Retrd.	1996	10.00	10
1991 Pigmalion-DA340	Retrd.	1995	6.25	20-30
1991 Pigtails-DA341	Retrd.	1995	6.25	18
1991 Ricky Raccoon -5170	Suspd.		28.00	28
1992 Sarge-DA111	Retrd.	1995	8.00	17
1992 Sir Hareold-DA123	Retrd.	1996	41.50	50-60
1991 Soap Box Bunny-DA551	Retrd.	1995	15.00	35
1991 Socrates The Sheep -5029	Suspd.		19.00	19
1993 Splash-DA616	Retrd.	1994	24.00	35
1991 Sweet Cream-DA382	Retrd.	1996	29.00	29-38
1991 Wooley Bully-DA327	Retrd.	1994	7.75	8

Dreamsicles Calendar Collection - K. Haynes

YEAR ISSUE	EDITION LIMIT	YEAR RETD.	ISSUE PRICE	*QUOTE U.S.$
1994 Winter Wonderland (January)-DC180	Retrd.	1995	24.00	30-45
1994 Special Delivery (February)-DC181	Retrd.	1995	24.00	30-45
1994 Ride Like The Wind (March)-DC182	Retrd.	1995	24.00	35-45
1994 Springtime Frolic (April)-DC183	Retrd.	1995	24.00	30
1994 Love In Bloom (May)-DC184	Retrd.	1995	24.00	30
1994 Among Friends (June)-DC185	Retrd.	1995	24.00	45-57
1994 Pool Pals (July)-DC186	Retrd.	1995	24.00	30-45
1994 Nature's Bounty (August)-DC187	Retrd.	1995	24.00	30-45
1994 School Days (September)-DC188	Retrd.	1995	24.00	30
1994 Autumn Leaves (October)-DC189	Retrd.	1995	24.00	30-45
1994 Now Give Thanks (November)-DC190	Retrd.	1995	24.00	30
1994 Holiday Magic (December)-DC191	Retrd.	1995	24.00	30-45

Dreamsicles Christmas - K. Haynes

YEAR ISSUE	EDITION LIMIT	YEAR RETD.	ISSUE PRICE	*QUOTE U.S.$
1998 All Aboard!-10364 (7th Ed.)	Retrd.	1998	78.00	78
1992 Baby Love-DX147	Retrd.	1995	7.00	30
1992 Bluebird On My Shoulder-DX115	Retrd.	1995	19.00	19-25
1992 Bundle of Joy-DX142	Retrd.	1995	7.00	7
1992 Caroler - Center Scroll-DX216	Retrd.	1995	19.00	30-45
1992 Caroler - Left Scroll-DX218	Retrd.	1995	19.00	30
1992 Caroler - Right Scroll-DX217	Retrd.	1995	19.00	30-45
1991 Cherub and Child-DX100	Retrd.	1995	14.00	30-70
1992 A Child's Prayer-DX145	Retrd.	1995	7.00	38
1999 A Christmas Carol-10844	5,000		40.00	40
1998 Christmas Eve-10429	5,000	1998	78.00	78
1999 Dash Away!-10791 (8th Ed.)	Yr.Iss		78.00	78
1992 Dream A Little Dream-DX144	Retrd.	1995	7.00	7
1993 Father Christmas-DX246	Suspd.		42.00	42
1993 The Finishing Touches-DX248 (2nd Ed.)	Retrd.	1994	85.00	125-179
1991 Forever Yours-DX110	Retrd.	1995	44.00	44-50
1991 Heavenly Dreamer-DX106	Retrd.	1996	11.00	11
1994 Here's Looking at You-DX172	Retrd.	1995	25.00	35-37
1994 Holiday on Ice-DX249 (3rd Ed.)	Retrd.	1995	85.00	130-175
1996 Homeward Bound-DX251 (5th Ed.)	Retrd.	1997	80.00	80
1995 Hugabye Baby-DX701	Retrd.	1997	12.50	13
1992 Life Is Good-DX119	Retrd.	1996	10.50	12
1992 Little Darlin'-DX146	Retrd.	1995	7.00	10
1993 Little Dickens-DX127	Retrd.	1995	24.00	25-35
1992 Littlest Angel-DX143	Retrd.	1995	7.00	7
1993 Long Fellow-DX126	Retrd.	1995	24.00	25
1996 Mall Santa-DX258	Retrd.	1998	35.00	35
1993 Me And My Shadow-DX116	Retrd.	1996	19.50	20-35
1991 Mischief Maker-DX105	Retrd.	1996	10.50	11-14
1993 Miss Morningstar-DX141	Retrd.	1996	25.50	40-50
1995 Poetry In Motion-DX113 (Sp. Ed.)	Retrd.	1996	80.00	85-105
1991 Santa Bunny-DX203	Retrd.	1994	32.00	32
1992 Santa In Dreamsicle Land-DX247 (1st Ed.)	Retrd.	1993	85.00	300-340
1991 Santa's Elf-DX240	Retrd.	1996	19.00	22
1995 Santa's Kingdom-DX250 (4th Ed.)	Retrd.	1995	80.00	90-100
1991 Santa's Little Helper-DX109	Retrd.	1998	9.50	10
1994 Share The Fun-DX178	Suspd.		14.00	14-25
1994 Side By Side-DX169	Retrd.	1995	31.50	45-50
1991 Sitting Pretty-DX101	Retrd.	1996	10.00	10-15
1997 Sleigh Bells Ring-10187	2,500	1997	48.00	48-95
1994 Stolen Kiss-DX162	Suspd.		12.50	14
1993 Sweet Dreams-DX125	Retrd.	1995	29.00	29
1997 Time To Dash-10184 (6th Ed.)	Retrd.	1998	78.00	78
1998 Tis Better to Give-10421	5,000	1998	38.00	38
1995 Twinkle Twinkle-DX700	Retrd.	1997	14.50	15
1991 Wildflower-DX107	Retrd.	1996	10.50	15

*Quotes have been rounded up to nearest dollar

Dreamsicles Day Event - K. Haynes

YEAR ISSUE	EDITION LIMIT	YEAR RETD.	ISSUE PRICE	*QUOTE U.S.$
1995 1995 Dreamsicles Event Figurine-DC075	Retrd.	1995	20.00	39-65
1996 Glad Tidings-DD100	Retrd.	1996	15.95	27-35
1996 Time to Retire-DD103	Retrd.	1996	15.95	30
1997 The Golden Rule-E9701	Retrd.	1997	19.95	30
1998 A Day of Fun-E9801	Retrd.	1998	18.00	18
1999 Yours Truly-E9901	Retrd.	1999	20.00	20
2000 With All My Heart-E0001	7,500		18.95	19

Dreamsicles Golden Halo - K. Haynes

YEAR ISSUE	EDITION LIMIT	YEAR RETD.	ISSUE PRICE	*QUOTE U.S.$
1999 The Flying Lesson Golden Halo Edition-10935	10,000		78.00	78
1998 Golden Best Pals-10659	Suspd.		16.00	16
1998 Golden Cherub & Child-10656	Open		15.00	15
1998 Golden Forever Friends-10658	Open		16.00	16
1998 Golden Heavenly Dreamer-10661	Open		12.00	12
1998 Golden Make A Wish-10663	Open		15.00	15
1998 Golden Mischief Maker-10660	Suspd.		12.00	12
1998 Golden Sitting Pretty-10657	Open		12.00	12
1999 Golden Thinking of You-10932	Open		44.00	44
1999 Golden Tiny Dancer-10934	Suspd.		16.00	16
1998 Golden Wildflower-10662	Open		12.00	12

Dreamsicles Heavenly Classics - K. Haynes & S. Hackett

YEAR ISSUE	EDITION LIMIT	YEAR RETD.	ISSUE PRICE	*QUOTE U.S.$
1996 Bundles of Love-HC370	327	1996	80.00	675-700
1995 The Dedication-DC351	10,000	1996	118.00	150-165
1997 Making Memories-10096 (spec. ed.)	Suspd.		100.00	100

Dreamsicles Northern Lights - K. Haynes

YEAR ISSUE	EDITION LIMIT	YEAR RETD.	ISSUE PRICE	*QUOTE U.S.$
1999 Northern Crossing-60013	10,000		38.00	38

Dreamsicles Nursery Rhymes - K. Haynes

YEAR ISSUE	EDITION LIMIT	YEAR RETD.	ISSUE PRICE	*QUOTE U.S.$
1999 The Frog Prince-10765	Suspd.		17.00	17
1998 Humpty Dumpty-10372	Suspd.		16.50	17
1998 Little Bo Peep-10375	Suspd.		17.50	18
1999 Mary Contrary-10766	Suspd.		17.00	17

Cavanagh Group Intl.

Coca-Cola Christmas Collectors Society Members' Only - Sundblom, unless otherwise noted

YEAR ISSUE	EDITION LIMIT	YEAR RETD.	ISSUE PRICE	*QUOTE U.S.$
1993 Ho Ho Ho (ornament)	Closed	1993	Gift	35-40
1994 Fishing Bear (ornament) - CGI	Closed	1994	Gift	30-35
1995 Hospitality (ornament)	Closed	1995	Gift	25
1996 Sprite (ornament)	Closed	1996	Gift	N/A
1996 Hollywood - CGI	Closed	1996	35.00	30-35
1997 Carousel Capers (ornament) - CGI	Closed	1997	Gift	N/A
1997 Always Friends - CGI	Closed	1997	35.00	30-35
1998 Passing The Day In A Special Way	Closed	1998	Gift	N/A
1998 I Belong - CGI	Closed	1998	35.00	35
1998 Polar Bear Bean Bag #0151	25,000	1998	Gift	10
1999 Hearing From You Is A Special Treat - CGI	Yr.Iss.	1999	Gift	N/A
1999 Polar Bear Bean Bag w/ Polka Dot Collar #0126	25,000	1999	Gift	10
1999 Atlanta's First Coca-Cola Bottling Plant - CGI	Yr.Iss.	1999	40.00	50-85
1999 Totonca Buffalo Bean Bag (USA) #0268	Yr.Iss.	1999	10.00	10
2000 Rewards of Membership	Yr.Iss.	2000	Gift	N/A
2000 Happy Holidays Ornament	Yr.Iss.	2000	Gift	N/A
2000 Gator The Alligator Bean Bag #HS0347-01	Yr.Iss.	2000	Gift	N/A
2000 Possy The Opposum Bean Bag #HS0367-01	Yr.Iss.	2000	10.00	10
2000 Family Time Is A Special Treat	Yr.Iss.	2000	35.00	35

Coca-Cola Brand Chrome-Plated Porcelain - CGI

YEAR ISSUE	EDITION LIMIT	YEAR RETD.	ISSUE PRICE	*QUOTE U.S.$
2000 Polar Bears & Penguins on Jukebox	Open		30.00	30
2000 Polar Bears & Penguins on Soda Fountain	Open		30.00	30
2000 Polar Bears, Penguin & Seal on Radio	Open		30.00	30
2000 Santa w/Bag of Toys	Open		30.00	30

Coca-Cola Brand Heritage Collection - Various

YEAR ISSUE	EDITION LIMIT	YEAR RETD.	ISSUE PRICE	*QUOTE U.S.$
1995 Always - CGI	Closed	1996	30.00	30
2000 Always Panda Friends - CGI	Open		30.00	30
2000 Always Truck'n with Refreshment - CGI	Open		30.00	30
2000 Always Truck'n with Refreshment-Snowglobe - CGI	Open		40.00	40
1995 Always-Musical - CGI	Closed	1996	50.00	50
1998 And Now the Gift For Thirst-Snowglobe - Sundblom	Closed	1999	40.00	40
1995 Boy at Well - N. Rockwell	5,000	1997	60.00	35-80
1995 Boy Fishing - N. Rockwell	5,000	1997	60.00	60-80
1996 Busy Man's Pause - Sundblom	Closed	1997	80.00	80
1998 C Is For Coca-Cola - CGI	10,000	1998	45.00	45
1994 Calendar Girl 1916-Music Box - CGI	500	1996	60.00	90-100
1996 Coca-Cola Stand - CGI	Closed	1998	45.00	45
1996 Cool Break - CGI	Closed	1998	40.00	45
1994 Dear Santa, Please Pause Here - Sundblom	2,500	1995	80.00	85
1994 Dear Santa, Please Pause Here-Musical - Sundblom	2,500	1995	100.00	100
1996 Decorating The Tree - CGI	Closed	1996	45.00	45
1997 Downhill Derby-CGI	10,000	1998	22.50	23
1994 Eight Polar Bears on Wood - CGI	15,000	1998	100.00	140
1994 Eight Polar Bears on Wood-Musical - CGI	15,000	1998	150.00	150
1995 Elaine - CGI	2,500	1996	100.00	90-100
1994 Extra Bright Refreshment -Snowglobe - Sundblom	2,500	1996	50.00	50
1996 For Me - Sundblom	Closed	1997	40.00	40
1997 For Me-Snowglobe - Sundblom	Closed	1997	25.00	25
1998 Friends Make the Job Easier - CGI	10,000	1999	40.00	40
1995 Girl on Swing - CGI	2,500	1996	100.00	100
1996 Gone Fishing - CGI	Closed	1997	60.00	45-60
1994 Good Boys and Girl - Sundblom	2,500	1995	80.00	80
1994 Good Boys and Girls-Musical - Sundblom	2,500	1995	100.00	100
1994 Good Boys and Girls-Snowglobe - Sundblom	2,000	1995	45.00	45
1994 Hilda Clark 1901-Music Box - CGI	500	1996	60.00	60-85
1994 Hilda Clark 1903-Music Box - CGI	500	1996	60.00	60
1996 Hollywood-Snowglobe - CGI	Closed	1997	50.00	50
1995 The Homecoming - S. Stearman	2,500	1995	125.00	100-125
1995 Hospitality - Sundblom	5,000	1997	35.00	35
1998 It Will Refresh You Too - Sundblom	10,000	1999	40.00	40
1998 It Will Refresh You Too-Musical - Sundblom	Closed	1999	60.00	60
1997 A Job Well Done Deserves a Coke - CGI	10,000	1999	22.50	23
1997 Mama Look! Is He a Bear Too? - CGI	10,000	1998	22.50	23
1999 Me Too - Sundblom	Open		40.00	40
1999 Me Too-Musical - Sundblom	Open		60.00	60
1999 Me Too-Snowglobe - Sundblom	Open		40.00	40
1998 On The Road to Adventure - CGI	10,000	1999	45.00	45
1999 The Perfect Refreshment - CGI	10,000	1999	40.00	40
1999 The Perfect Refreshment -Snowglobe - CGI	Closed	1999	50.00	50
1995 Playing with Dad - CGI	Closed	1996	40.00	40
2000 Polar Party-Snowglobe - CGI	Open		40.00	40
1996 A Refreshing Break - N. Rockwell	Closed	1997	60.00	60
1996 Refreshing Treat - CGI	Closed	1996	45.00	45
2000 A Refreshing Treat-Snowglobe - CGI	Open		40.00	40
1999 Refreshment on the Line-Musical - CGI	Closed	1999	50.00	50
1998 Rub-A-Dub-Dub - CGI	10,000	1998	45.00	45
1994 Santa at His Desk - Sundblom	5,000	1996	80.00	80
1994 Santa at His Desk-Musical - Sundblom	5,000	1996	100.00	100
1994 Santa at His Desk-Snowglobe - Sundblom	Closed	1996	45.00	45
1994 Santa at the Fireplace - Sundblom	5,000	1996	80.00	80-90
1994 Santa at the Fireplace-Musical - Sundblom	5,000	1996	100.00	100
1994 Santa at the Lamppost-Snowglobe - Sundblom	Closed	1996	50.00	50
1997 Santa with Deer - Sundblom	Closed	1998	100.00	100
1995 Santa with Polar Bear-Snowglobe - CGI	Closed	1997	50.00	50
1996 Say Uncle-Snowglobe - CGI	Closed	1997	50.00	50
2000 Service With a Smile - CGI	Open		30.00	30
2000 Serving Up Refreshment - CGI	Open		30.00	30
2000 Serving Up Refreshment-Snowglobe - CGI	Open		40.00	40
1999 Sharing Refreshment-Animated - CGI	Closed	1999	60.00	60
1994 Single Polar Bear on Ice-Snowglobe - CGI	Closed	1996	40.00	50
1999 A Special Treat - CGI	10,000	1999	40.00	40
1999 A Special Treat-Snowglobe- CGI	Closed	1999	40.00	40
1996 Sshh!-Musical - Sundblom	Closed	1997	55.00	55
1995 They Remember Me-Musical - Sundblom	5,000	1997	50.00	50
2000 Things Go Better with Coke - Sundblom	2,000		40.00	40
2000 Things Go Better with Coke-Musical - Sundblom	2,000		60.00	60
2000 Things Go Better with Coke-Snowglobe - Sundblom	2,000		45.00	45
1997 A Time to Share-Musical - Sundblom	5,000	1999	100.00	100
1997 Times With Dad are Special - CGI	10,000	1998	22.50	23
1999 Times with Dad are Special-Musical - CGI	Closed	1999	50.00	50
1998 Travel Refreshed-Snowglobe - Sundblom	Closed	1998	45.00	45
1994 Two Polar Bears on Ice - CGI	Closed	1998	25.00	25
1994 Two Polar Bears on Ice-Musical -CGI	Closed	1996	45.00	50
1999 Wherever Go-Animated - Sundblom	Open		60.00	60

Coca-Cola Brand Heritage Collection Ebon Memories - CGI

YEAR ISSUE	EDITION LIMIT	YEAR RETD.	ISSUE PRICE	*QUOTE U.S.$
2000 The Big Question	Open		50.00	50
2000 Coolin' Off	Open		10.00	10
2000 Sock Hop	Open		40.00	40
2000 Steppin' Out in Sisters Shoes	Open		40.00	40
2000 A Sunday Treat	Open		40.00	40

Coca-Cola Brand Heritage Collection Polar Bear Cubs - CGI

YEAR ISSUE	EDITION LIMIT	YEAR RETD.	ISSUE PRICE	*QUOTE U.S.$
1996 Balancing Act	Closed	1998	16.00	17
1996 The Bear Cub Club	Closed	1998	20.00	20
1996 Bearing Gifts of Love and Friendship	10,000	1998	30.00	30
1998 Birthday Surprise	Closed	1999	16.00	16
1997 Caring Is A Special Gift	Closed	1998	16.00	17
1996 A Christmas Wish	Closed	1998	10.00	10
1997 Dad Showed Me How-Musical	Closed	1998	35.00	35
1998 Dear Santa	Closed	1998	30.00	30
1999 Decorating For the Holidays	10,000	1999	25.00	25
2000 Delivering Refreshment to All	Open		10.00	10
1996 Enjoy!	Closed	1998	12.00	12
2000 Enjoying Friendship & Refreshment	Open		10.00	10
1997 Everybody Needs A Friend	Closed	1998	12.00	12
1997 Fire Chief	Closed	1998	16.00	17
1998 Friends are the Best Catch	Closed	1999	25.00	25
1997 Friends Double the Joy	Closed	1998	30.00	25-30
1997 Friends Make the Holiday Special	10,000	1998	30.00	30
1999 Friends Make the Journey More Fun	Closed	1999	16.00	16
2000 Friends Make the Task Easier	Open		10.00	10
1997 Friendship is A Hiddlen Treaure	Closed	1998	20.00	20
1997 Friendship is the Best Gift	Closed	1998	16.00	17
1997 Friendship is the Perfect Medicine	Closed	1998	20.00	20-22
1997 Friendship Makes Life Bearable	Closed	1998	16.00	17
1998 Giving Thanks for Friends & Family	10,000	1998	20.00	20
1996 Good Friends Stick Together	Closed	1998	16.00	16
1997 Graduation Day	Closed	1997	12.00	12-17
1997 Happy Birthday	Closed	1998	12.00	8-14
1997 I Can Do Anything with You By My Side-Snowglobe	Closed	1998	45.00	45
1999 I Can Tell You Everything	Closed	1999	25.00	25
1997 I Can't Bear To See You Sick	Closed	1998	20.00	20
1998 I Carved This Just for You	Closed	1998	16.00	16
1997 I Get A Kick Out of You	Closed	1998	16.00	16
1998 I'd Follow You Anywhere	Closed	1999	16.00	16
1998 I'd Follow You Anywhere-Snowglobe	Closed	1998	40.00	40
1996 I'm Not Sleepy...Really	Closed	1998	10.00	10
1996 I'm Sorry	Closed	1998	12.00	12
1998 Ice Skating -Snowglobe	Closed	1998	16.00	16
1996 It's My Turn to Hide	Closed	1998	12.00	12
1997 Just For You	Closed	1998	16.00	16-21
1997 Just Like My Dad	Closed	1998	16.00	16
1997 Little Boys are Best	Closed	1998	16.00	16
1997 Little Girls are Special	Closed	1998	16.00	16-45
1996 Look What I Can Do	Closed	1998	12.00	12
1998 Look What I Do-Snowglobe	Closed	1999	40.00	40
1997 Love Bears All Things	Closed	1998	12.00	13
1997 Lucky O'Bear and McPuffin	Closed	1998	16.00	17
1997 On The Road to Adventure-Musical - CGI	Closed	1998	15.00	15
1998 On Your Mark, Get Set, Go	Closed	1999	20.00	20
1996 Patience is a Virtue	Closed	1998	16.00	16
1998 Peek A Boo-Mini Musical	Closed	1998	30.00	30
1998 A Perfect Time for a Refreshing Treat-Snowglobe	Closed	1999	40.00	40
1997 Polar Bear Cub Sign	Closed	1998	16.00	16
1996 Puppy Love	Closed	1998	12.00	12
2000 Refreshing Friends Make Times Fun	Open		10.00	10
1996 Ride 'em Cowboy	Closed	1998	20.00	20
1999 Santa's Little Helper	Closed	1999	16.00	16
1997 Seeds of Friendship Grow with Caring	Closed	1998	16.00	16-40
2000 Service with a Smile	Open		10.00	10
1998 Singing in the Season w/Special Friends	Closed	1999	16.00	16
1997 Sled Racing-Snowglobe	Closed	1998	35.00	35
1996 Snowday Adventure	Closed	1998	12.00	12
1996 Sweet Dreams	Closed	1998	12.00	12
1999 Teamwork Makes Winners	Closed	1999	25.00	25
1998 Teamwork Wins Every Time	Closed	1999	20.00	20
1997 Thanks For All You Taught Me	Closed	1998	16.00	16
1996 Thanks For The Lift	Closed	1998	20.00	20
1998 There's No Place Like Home-Mini Musical	Closed	1998	30.00	30
1996 There's Nothing Like A Friend	Closed	1998	16.00	16
1996 To Grandmother's House We Go	Closed	1998	12.00	12
1997 Visits with You are Special	Closed	1998	20.00	20
1997 We Did It	Closed	1997	20.00	17-20
1996 Who Says Girls Can't Throw	Closed	1998	16.00	16
2000 Wishing You a Refreshing Holiday Season	Open		10.00	10
1997 With All My Heart	Closed	1998	16.00	16-21
1999 With All My Love	Closed	1999	25.00	25
1999 You Always Lift My Spirits	Closed	1999	16.00	16
1998 You Bring Out the Best in Me	Closed	1999	20.00	20
1997 You're the Greatest	Closed	1998	20.00	20-31
2000 You're Worth the Extra Effort	Open		10.00	10

Coca-Cola Brand Mercury Glass - CGI, unless otherwise noted

YEAR ISSUE	EDITION LIMIT	YEAR RETD.	ISSUE PRICE	*QUOTE U.S.$
1998 Hollywood	Closed	1998	29.50	30
1998 Hollywood (Target Stores Exclusive)	Closed	1998	29.50	30
2000 Polar Bear at Bottle Stand	Open		25.00	25
1998 Polar Bear at Vending Machine	Closed	1999	29.50	30
2000 Polar Bear in Delivery Truck	Open		25.00	25
2000 Polar Bears on Juke Box	Open		25.00	25
1998 Santa - Sundblom	Closed	1999	29.50	30
2000 Santa on Globe - Sundblom	Open		25.00	25
1999 Santa with Bag of Gifts - Sundblom	Closed	1999	29.50	30
1999 Soda Fountain Bear	Closed	1999	29.50	30
1998 Vending Machine	Closed	1999	29.50	30

Coca-Cola Brand Musical - Various

YEAR ISSUE	EDITION LIMIT	YEAR RETD.	ISSUE PRICE	*QUOTE U.S.$
1993 Dear Santa, Please Pause Here - Sundblom	Closed	1996	50.00	50
1994 Santa's Soda Shop - CGI	Closed	1996	50.00	50

Coca-Cola Brand Santa Animations - Sundblom

YEAR ISSUE	EDITION LIMIT	YEAR RETD.	ISSUE PRICE	*QUOTE U.S.$
1991 Ssshh! (1st Ed.)	Closed	1992	99.99	300-365
1992 Santa's Pause for Refreshment (2nd Ed.)	Closed	1993	99.99	265-295
1993 Trimming the Tree (3rd Ed.)	Closed	1994	99.99	235-265
1995 Santa at the Lamppost (4th Ed.)	Closed	1996	110.00	115-225

Harley-Davidson - CGI

YEAR ISSUE	EDITION LIMIT	YEAR RETD.	ISSUE PRICE	*QUOTE U.S.$
1997 The Age Old Urge to Run Away	10,000	1999	40.00	40
1999 American Legend-Snowglobe	Open		40.00	40
1997 Born to Ride	10,000	1998	50.00	50
1998 Born to Ride-Musical (San Francisco Music Box Exclusive)	6,000	1998	60.00	60
2000 Engine (Clear Resin)	Open		35.00	35
2000 Gas Tank (Clear Resin)	Open		35.00	35
1997 Harley Eagle (Harley Dealer Exclusive)	2,500	2000	50.00	50
2000 A Life Less Ordinary	10,000		50.00	50

*Quotes have been rounded up to nearest dollar

YEAR ISSUE	EDITION LIMIT	YEAR RETD.	ISSUE PRICE	*QUOTE U.S.$
2000 Mr. & Mrs. Claus-Snowglobe	Open		40.00	40
1999 Riding the Wind	10,000		50.00	50
2000 Salute to Officers in Blue	Open		50.00	50
1998 Santa in the Sky	Closed	1999	40.00	40
1999 Santa in the Sky-Musical (San Francisco Music Box Exclusive)	Closed	1999	60.00	60
1999 Santa's Bag-Snowglobe	Closed	1999	50.00	50
1999 Up Up and Away-Snowglobe	Open		40.00	40

Harley-Davidson Little Cruisers - CGI

YEAR ISSUE	EDITION LIMIT	YEAR RETD.	ISSUE PRICE	*QUOTE U.S.$
1999 The Adventure Begins	Closed	1999	16.00	16
1998 Can I Have A Harley	Closed	1999	25.00	25
1997 Daddy's Little Helper	Closed	1998	16.00	16
1997 Following in Mom's Footsteps	Closed	1998	16.00	16
1997 Free & Proud (Harley Dealer Exclusive)	Closed	1999	20.00	20
1997 Harley Club House	Closed	1998	25.00	25
1997 Here's Looking at You	Closed	1998	16.00	16
1998 Hide & Seek	Closed	1998	16.00	16
1997 I Wrapped It Myself	Closed	1998	16.00	16
1997 Just Like My Dad	Closed	1998	16.00	16
1999 Marching to a Different Drummer	Closed	1999	20.00	20
1998 The Mechanics	Closed	1999	20.00	20
1997 Mr. Fix-It	Closed	1999	16.00	16
1998 On the Open Road	Closed	1999	16.00	16
1997 On the Road to Adventure	Closed	1998	16.00	16
1999 A Perfect Fit	Closed	1999	16.00	16
1999 The Road Less Traveled	Closed	1999	20.00	20
1999 Road Warriors	Closed	1999	20.00	20
1998 Santa Bear Rides Again	Closed	1999	20.00	20
1999 Teamwork Makes Winners	Closed	1999	20.00	20
1997 Varoom	Closed	1998	16.00	16
1997 With You I Will Go Anywhere	Closed	1998	20.00	20

Humbug - T. Fraley

YEAR ISSUE	EDITION LIMIT	YEAR RETD.	ISSUE PRICE	*QUOTE U.S.$
1998 Holding Down the Fort	Open		20.00	20
1998 Let Me Call You Sweetheart	Open		20.00	20
1998 Let Me Call You Sweetheat-Musical	Open		35.00	35
1998 Making Faces	Open		20.00	20
1998 A Nutty Humbug-Musical	Open		35.00	35
1998 That's More Like It-Snowglobe	Open		35.00	35
1998 This "Was" For Santa	Open		20.00	20
1998 Where to Next?-Snowglobe	Open		35.00	35

Prince of Egypt - Dreamworks

YEAR ISSUE	EDITION LIMIT	YEAR RETD.	ISSUE PRICE	*QUOTE U.S.$
1998 The Bond of Love	5,000		50.00	50
1998 Chariot Race	5,000		100.00	100
1998 Deliver Us	5,000		30.00	30
1998 Destiny	5,000		45.00	45
1998 Exodus-Musical	5,000		70.00	70
1998 Friendly Competition-Waterball	5,000		60.00	60
1998 I Am Egypt	5,000		30.00	30
1998 Life of a Shepherd-Waterball	5,000		30.00	30
1998 Looming Power of Seti (bookends)	5,000		30.00	30
1998 New Beginnings	5,000		30.00	30
1998 Tender Welcome	5,000		50.00	50
1998 Tender Welcome-Waterball	5,000		40.00	40
1998 To Save a Son, To Find a Son-Musical	5,000		90.00	90

Charming Tails/Fitz and Floyd Collectibles

The Leaf & Acorn Club - D. Griff

YEAR ISSUE	EDITION LIMIT	YEAR RETD.	ISSUE PRICE	*QUOTE U.S.$
1997 Thank You 98/700	Closed	1998	Gift	25-32
1997 Maxine's Leaf Collection 98/701	Closed	1998	15.00	18-25
1998 A Growing Friendship 97/12	Closed	1998	17.00	17
1998 Sharing a Warm and Cozy Holiday 97/13	Closed	1998	22.00	22-35
1999 You Are My Shining Star 97/11	Closed	1999	Gift	N/A
1999 Nap Time Pin 97/14	Closed	1999	Gift	N/A
1999 Ring Around The Rosie 97/15	Closed	1999	23.00	23
1999 A Snowy Trio 97/16	Closed	1999	21.00	23
2000 You Hold The Key To My Heart 97/18	12/00		Gift	N/A
2000 This Is The Key 97/20	12/00		Gift	N/A
2000 Peek-A-Boo Bouquet 97/21	12/00		22.00	22
2000 Christmas Treasures 97/19	12/00		24.00	24

Charming Tails Event Piece - D. Griff

YEAR ISSUE	EDITION LIMIT	YEAR RETD.	ISSUE PRICE	*QUOTE U.S.$
1996 Take Me Home 87/691	Closed	1997	17.00	35-50
1997 I Picked This For You 98/197	Closed	1997	18.00	26-60
1998 Riding On The Wings of Friendship 98/207	4,500	1998	18.00	36-45
1999 This One Is Yours 98/208	Closed	1999	18.00	18-25
2000 A Treasure of Memories 98/224	Yr.Iss.		18.00	18

Charming Tails Autumn Harvest Figurines - D. Griff

YEAR ISSUE	EDITION LIMIT	YEAR RETD.	ISSUE PRICE	*QUOTE U.S.$
1993 Acorn Built For Two 85/403	Open		10.00	13
2000 Autumn Breezes 85/101	Open		17.00	17
1999 Autumn Harvest Music Box 93/100	Open		40.00	40
1999 Autumn Harvest Picture Frame 93/103	Open		25.00	25
1996 Bag of Tricks...Or Treats 87/436	Open		15.50	18
2000 Be Thankful For Friends 85/500	Open		20.00	20
1996 Binkey's Acorn Costume 87/429	Closed	2000	11.50	14
1998 Boooo! 85/417	Open		18.00	19
1995 Candy Apples 85/611	Closed	1998	16.00	38-48
1995 Candy Corn Vampire 85/607	Closed	1997	18.00	18-40
1993 Caps Off to You 85/402	Closed	1996	10.00	35-75
1996 Chauncey's Pear Costume 87/431	Closed	1998	12.00	13-20
1993 Cornfield Feast 85/399	Closed	1994	15.00	125-150
1993 Fall Frolicking (2 pc.) 85/401	Closed	1996	13.00	73-90
1994 Frosting Pumpkins 85/511	Closed	1996	16.00	35-65
1995 Garden Naptime 85/615	Closed	1997	18.00	32-40
1997 Ghost Stories 85/703	Open		18.50	20
1995 Giving Thanks 85/608	Open		16.00	19
1997 The Good Witch 85/704	Open		18.50	20
1993 Gourd Slide 85/398	Closed	1996	16.00	46-82
1994 Harvest Fruit (2 pc.) 85/507	Closed	1995	16.00	35-88
1999 Harvest Time Honeys 85/882	Open		18.50	19
1999 Haunted Hayride 85/883	Open		18.50	19
1999 Hocus Pocus 85/880	Open		18.00	18
1995 Horn of Plenty 85/610	Closed	1997	20.00	25-55
1996 Indian Impostor 87/446	Closed	2000	14.00	16
1998 Jack O'Lantern Jalopy 85/410	Closed	2000	18.00	18
1994 Jumpin' Jack O' Lanterns 85/512	Closed	1997	16.00	45-63
1995 Let's Get Cracking 85/776	Closed	1997	20.00	32-35
1996 Look! No Hands 87/428	Closed	1999	15.50	17
1999 Mackenzie's Putt-Putt Tractor 85/881	Open		17.50	18
1996 Maxine's Pumpkin Costume 87/430	Open		12.00	15
1993 Mouse Candleholder (2 pc.) 85/400	Closed	1995	13.00	100-238
1994 Mouse on Leaf Candleholder 87/503	Closed	1995	17.00	110
1996 Oops, I Missed 87/443	Closed	1998	16.00	20-30
1994 Open Pumpkin 85/508	Closed	1994	15.00	98-125
1994 Painting Leaves 85/514	Closed	1996	16.00	60-82
1994 Pear Candleholder 85/509	Closed	1995	14.00	94-122
1996 Pickin' Time 87/438	Closed	1997	16.00	18-32
1996 Pilgrim's Progress 87/445	Closed	2000	13.50	15
1999 Pumpkin and Squash Votive 93/101	Open		20.00	20
1995 Pumpkin Pie 85/606	Closed	1996	16.00	63-82
1994 Pumpkin Slide 85/513	Closed	1995	16.00	40-50
1994 Pumpkin Votive 85/510	Closed	1995	13.50	39-74
1998 Pumpkin's First Pumpkin 85/411	Open		17.00	18
2000 Put On A Happy Face 85/100	Open		17.00	17
1997 Reginald's Gourd Costume 85/701	Closed	2000	12.50	18-38
1995 Reginald's Hideaway 85/777	Closed	1997	14.00	32
1998 Stack O'Lanterns 85/416	Open		18.00	18
1997 Stewart's Apple Costume 85/700	Closed	2000	12.50	14
1994 Stump Candleholders (2 pc.) 85/516	Closed	1995	20.00	195-250
1997 Turkey Traveller 85/702	Closed	2000	18.50	20
1998 Turkey With Dressing 85/412	Closed	2000	18.00	19
2000 What A Hoot! 85/101	Open		17.00	17
1996 You're Not Scary 87/440	Closed	1998	14.00	15-75
1996 You're Nutty 87/451	Closed	1998	12.00	20-38

Charming Tails Easter Basket Figurines - D. Griff

YEAR ISSUE	EDITION LIMIT	YEAR RETD.	ISSUE PRICE	*QUOTE U.S.$
1995 After the Hunt 87/372	Closed	2000	18.00	19
1993 Animals in Eggs (4 asst.) 89/313	Closed	1996	11.00	140-200
1995 Binkey's Bouncing Bundle 87/422	7,500	1995	18.00	38-40
1994 Bunny Imposter 89/609	Closed	1998	12.00	25-30
1995 Bunny Love 87/424	Closed	2000	18.00	19
1998 Chickie Back Ride 88/700	Open		15.00	15
1999 Chickie Chariot Ride 88/100	Open		18.00	18
1993 Duckling in Egg with Mouse 89/316	Closed	1994	15.00	158-200
1999 Ducky Weather 88/101	Open		18.00	18
1995 Gathering Treats 87/377	Closed	1998	12.00	30-38
1994 Jelly Bean Feast 89/559	Closed	1996	14.00	30-45
1995 Look Out Below 87/373	Closed	1997	20.00	32
1999 Motoring Along 88/703	Open		16.50	17
1996 No Thanks, I'm Stuffed 88/603	Closed	2000	15.00	16
1998 Paint By Paws 88/701	Open		16.00	16
1999 Shhh, Don't Make a Peep 88/702	Open		16.50	17
1994 Wanna Play? 89/561	2,500	1994	15.00	110-125
1995 Want a Bite? 87/379	Closed	1997	18.00	38
1996 What's Hatchin' 88/600	Open		16.00	17

Charming Tails Everyday Figurines - D. Griff

YEAR ISSUE	EDITION LIMIT	YEAR RETD.	ISSUE PRICE	*QUOTE U.S.$
1994 After Lunch Snooze 89/558	Closed	1997	15.00	22-38
1996 Ahh-Choo, Get Well Soon 89/624	Closed	2000	12.00	14-21
1999 Along For The Ride 89/100	Open		18.50	19
2000 Apple of My Eye 89/110	Yr.Iss.		19.00	19
1996 The Berry Best 87/391	Closed	2000	16.00	18-25
1994 Binkey Growing Carrots 89/605	Closed	1995	15.00	69-94
1993 Binkey in a Lily 89/305	Closed	1996	16.00	36-69
1995 Binkey's First Cake 98/349	Closed	1997	16.00	44-55
1994 Binkey's New Pal 89/586	Closed	1996	14.00	14-24
2000 A Bubbly Personality 89/109	Open		17.00	17
1996 Bunny Buddies 89/619	Closed	2000	20.00	22
1994 Bunny w/Carrot Candleholder 89/317	Closed	1995	12.00	90-188
1994 Butterfly Smelling Zinnia 89/606	Closed	1995	15.00	63-75
1994 Can I Keep Him? 89/600	2,500	1994	13.00	300-360
1995 Catchin' Butterflies 87/423	Closed	1998	16.00	25-35
1996 Cattail Catapult 87/448	Closed	1998	16.00	25-30
1995 Charming Tails Display Sign 87/690	Open		20.00	22
1995 The Chase is On 87/386	Closed	1997	16.00	13-17
1994 Chauncey Growing Tomatoes 89/607	Closed	1995	15.00	48-50
1998 A Collection of Friends (Convention Piece) 98/206	7,500	1998	23.00	35-80
2000 Con-Graduations 89/106	Open		17.00	17
2000 Dandelion Wishes 89/107	Open		18.00	18
1994 Duckling Votive 89/315	Closed	1994	12.00	100-175
1998 Even The Ups And Downs Are Fun 89/705	Closed	2000	16.50	18
1995 Feeding Time 98/417	Closed	1996	16.00	59-100
1999 Floral Candleholder Mackenzie 93/202	Open		20.00	20
1999 Floral Candleholder Maxine 93/203	Open		20.00	20
1996 Flower Friends 89/608	Closed	1998	16.00	20-23
1996 Fragile...Handle with Care (no numbers on bottom)	Closed	1997	18.00	250-300
1996 Fragile...Handle with Care 89/601	15,000	1997	18.00	40-63
1996 Fragile...Handle with Love (mismarked) 89/601	Closed	1997	18.00	110-121
1995 Gardening Break 87/364	Closed	2000	16.00	17-25
1994 Get Well Soon 97/719	Closed	1997	15.00	27-49
1999 A Gift Of Love 89/102	Open		18.00	18
1994 Good Luck 97/716	Open		15.00	18
1997 Guess What? 89/714	Closed	1999	16.50	17
1997 Hang On (GCC Exclusive) 98/600	Closed	1997	18.00	18
1996 Hangin' Around 89/623	Open		18.00	20
1994 Happy Birthday 97/715	Open		15.00	18
1998 Hear, Speak and See No Evil 89/717	Open		17.50	19
1999 Hi Cookie 89/760	Open		17.50	18
1993 Hide and Seek 89/307	Closed	1997	13.50	113-250
1999 The Honeymoon's Over 89/763	Open		20.00	20
1994 Hope You're Feeling Better 97/723	Closed	1997	15.00	27-30
1996 Hoppity Hop 87/425	Closed	1997	16.00	15
1994 How Do You Measure Love 98/461	Closed	1996	15.00	35-100
1998 How Many Candles? 89/713	Open		16.50	18
1996 I Have a Question for You 89/603	Open		16.00	19
1994 I Love You 97/724	Closed	2000	15.00	17
1997 I Love You a Whole Bunch 89/715	Open		17.00	18
1999 I Miss You Already 89/756	Open		17.50	18
1996 I See Things Clearly Now 89/626	Closed	2000	14.00	16
1998 I'm A Winner 89/719	Open		16.00	17
1998 I'm Here For You 89/706	Open		17.50	19
1994 I'm So Sorry 97/720	Closed	1998	15.00	25-30
1997 I'm Thinking of You 89/701	Closed	1999	15.00	16
1999 In Every Life a Little Rain Must Fall 89/757	Open		20.00	20
1994 It's Not the Same Without You 97/721	Closed	1997	15.00	23
1998 It's Your Move 89/704	Closed	2000	17.00	18
1996 Just Plane Friends 89/627	Closed	2000	19.00	20
1997 Keeping Our Love Alive 89/710	Closed	2000	19.50	20
1993 King of the Mushroom 89/318	Closed	1996	16.00	29-35
1998 Life is a Bed of Roses (Special Ed. Artist Event) 98/198	7,000	1998	19.00	45-63
1998 A Little Birdie Told Me 89/720	Closed	2000	17.00	18
1996 Love Blooms (GCC Spring Exclusive) 87/862	Closed	1996	16.00	20-36
1996 Love me-Love Me Not 87/395	Closed	1999	16.00	18
1993 Love Mice 89/314	Closed	1994	15.00	100-150
1994 Mackenzie Growing Beans 89/604	Closed	1995	15.00	38-75
1997 Maxine Goes On-Line 89/702	Open		17.00	18
1994 Mender of Broken Hearts 98/460	Closed	1996	15.00	50-82
1996 Mid-day Snooze 89/617	Closed	1999	19.00	20
2000 Morning Hare 89/108	Open		16.00	16
1993 Mouse on a Grasshopper 89/321	Closed	1994	15.00	360-420
1994 New Arrival 97/717	Open		15.00	18
1999 Now I Lay Me Down To Sleep 89/758	Yr.Iss.	1999	18.00	20
1999 On The First Day of Christmas 98/210	Yr.Iss.	1999	17.50	18
1995 One for Me... 87/360	Closed	1997	16.00	41-45
1995 One for You... 87/361	Closed	1997	16.00	32-35
1997 One Mouse Open Sleigh (GCC Spring Exclusive) 98/195	Yr.Iss.	1997	17.50	18-50
1999 Party Animals 89/101	Open		22.00	22
1998 Picture Perfect 89/722	Open		18.50	19
1993 Rabbit/Daffodil Candleholder (2 pc.) 89/312	Closed	1995	13.50	180-252
1994 Reach for the Stars 97/718	Open		15.00	19
1999 Rose Votive 93/204	Open		20.00	20
2000 Sleepy Head 89/113	Open		19.00	19
1994 Slumber Party 89/560	Closed	1996	16.00	41-55
1993 Spring Flowers (2 pc.) 89/310	Closed	1996	16.00	88-200
1998 Steady Wins The Race 89/716	17,500	1998	20.00	20-30
1995 Surrounded By Friends 87/353	Closed	1997	16.00	16-24
1996 Taggin' Along 87/399	Closed	1997	14.00	12-15
1996 Take Time To Reflect 87/396	Closed	1997	16.00	16-24
1999 Take Time To Smell The Flowers 89/765	Open		18.00	18
1999 Take Two Aspirin... 89/103	Open		15.00	15
1997 Teacher's Pet 89/700	Closed	1999	19.50	20
1994 Thanks for Being There 89/754	Closed	1996	15.00	18-25
1998 There's No "US" Without "U" 89/703	Closed	2000	19.50	20-27
1999 Together Every Step OF The Way 89/104	Open		18.00	18
1996 Training Wings 87/398	Closed	1997	16.00	25-45
1995 Tuggin' Twosome 87/362	10,000	1997	18.00	20-27
1993 Two Peas in a Pod 89/306	Closed	1996	14.00	40-60
2000 Wash Away Those Worries 89/111	Open		17.00	17
1996 The Waterslide 87/384	Open		20.00	22
1994 We'll Weather the Storm Together 97/722	Open		15.00	18
1995 Why, Hello There! 87/357	Closed	1997	14.00	14-25
1999 Wishing You Well 98/930	Open		20.00	20
1999 You Are My Cup of Tea 89/762	Open		19.00	19
1995 You Are Not Alone 98/929	Closed	1996	20.00	30-45
1996 You Couldn't Be Sweeter 89/625	Open		17.00	18
1999 You Quack Me Up 89/105	Open		18.00	18
2000 You're Cute as a Button 89/115	Open		18.50	19
2000 You're Pretty as a Picture 89/112	Open		19.00	19

Charming Tails Everyday Lazy Days of Summer Figurines - D. Griff

YEAR ISSUE	EDITION LIMIT	YEAR RETD.	ISSUE PRICE	*QUOTE U.S.$
2000 Adventure Bound 83/100	Open		20.00	20
2000 Beach Bunnie 83/101	Open		16.00	16
1997 The Blossom Bounce 83/704	Closed	1999	20.00	20-25
1997 Building Castles 83/802	Closed	1999	17.00	17-20
1999 Buried Treasures 83/806	Open		19.00	19
1998 Camping Out 83/703	Open		18.50	20
2000 Catching Fireflies 83/102	Open		18.00	18
1998 Come On In -The Water's Fine! 83/804	Closed	2000	18.00	19
1998 A Day At The Lake 83/803	Open		18.50	19
1999 Friendship is Always a Great Bargain 83/810	Open		19.50	20
1997 Gone Fishin' 83/702	Closed	1999	16.00	14-16
2000 Hang Ten 83/103	Open		19.00	19
1997 Life's a Picnic With You 83/701	Closed	1999	18.00	16-18
1999 Mow, Mow, Mow the Lawn 83/809	Open		16.50	17
2000 A Real Lifesaver 83/104	Open		20.00	20
1997 Row Boat Romance 83/801	Open		15.00	17

*Quotes have been rounded up to nearest dollar

YEAR ISSUE	EDITION LIMIT	YEAR RETD.	ISSUE PRICE	*QUOTE U.S.$
1998 Stewart's Day In The Sun 83/805	Closed	2000	17.00	18
1998 Toasting Marshmallows 83/700	Closed	2000	20.00	21
1999 Triple Delight 83/807	Open		18.00	18

Charming Tails Love Is In The Air Figurines - D. Griff

YEAR ISSUE	EDITION LIMIT	YEAR RETD.	ISSUE PRICE	*QUOTE U.S.$
1999 An Abundance of Love 84/107	Open		18.00	18
1999 Candy Kisses 84/108	Open		17.00	17
1999 Give Love a Shot! 84/109	Open		15.00	15
1999 I'd Do It All Over Again 84/106	Open		17.50	18
1999 I'm Your Love Bunny 84/101	Open		16.00	16
1999 Love Birds 84/110	Open		20.00	20
1999 Love Is In The Air 84/100	Open		19.50	20
1999 Our Love Has Blossomed 84/103	Open		18.00	18
1999 We're a Perfect Fit 84/111	Open		17.00	17
1999 You Can't Run From Love 84/104	Closed	2000	17.50	18

Charming Tails Love Is In The Air Gifts - D. Griff

YEAR ISSUE	EDITION LIMIT	YEAR RETD.	ISSUE PRICE	*QUOTE U.S.$
2000 Dancin' Darlin's Musical 93/208	Open		20.00	20
1999 Heart Picture Frame 93/206	Open		25.00	25
1999 Love Bunny Music Box 93/200	Open		35.00	35
2000 Love Is In The Air Votive 93/205	Open		20.00	20
1999 Thinking Of You Picture Frame 93/207	Open		25.00	25
1999 Tunnel Of Love Music Box 93/201	Open		49.50	50

Charming Tails Musicals and Waterglobes - D. Griff

YEAR ISSUE	EDITION LIMIT	YEAR RETD.	ISSUE PRICE	*QUOTE U.S.$
1994 Jawbreakers Musical 87/542	Closed	1995	40.00	77-125
1994 Letter to Santa Waterglobe 87/518	Closed	1994	45.00	65-125
1994 Me Next! Musical 89/555	Closed	1995	45.00	198-240
1994 Mini Surprise Waterglobe 87/956	Closed	1994	22.00	54-125
1994 Mouse on Cheese, Waterglobe 92/224	Closed	1995	44.00	44
1994 Mouse on Rubber Duck, Waterglobe 92/225	Closed	1995	44.00	117-200
1994 My Hero! Waterglobe 89/557	Closed	1995	45.00	81-98
1995 Pumpkin Playtime Musical 85/778	Closed	1995	35.00	72-104
1993 Rocking Mice Musical 86/790	Closed	1994	65.00	150-202
1994 Sailing Away Waterglobe 87/200	Closed	1994	50.00	90-120
1994 Sharing the Warmth Waterglobe 87/517	Closed	1994	40.00	77-108
1993 Skating Mice Musical 87/511	Closed	1994	25.00	100-360
1994 Sweet Dreams Waterglobe 87/534	Closed	1994	40.00	40-48
1994 Together at Christmas, Mini Waterglobe 87/530	Closed	1995	30.00	54-80
1994 Trimmings for the Tree Waterglobe 87/516	Closed	1994	45.00	104-163
1994 Underwater Explorer Waterglobe 89/556	Closed	1995	45.00	99-250
1994 Up, Up and Away Musical 89/602	Closed	1995	70.00	190-360

Charming Tails Sports Series - D. Griff

YEAR ISSUE	EDITION LIMIT	YEAR RETD.	ISSUE PRICE	*QUOTE U.S.$
2000 Follow The Bouncing Ball 87/800	8,000		19.00	19
2000 Good Cheer 87/801	10,000		19.00	19
2000 I Get a Kick Out of You 87/802	8,600		19.00	19
2000 Keep Your Eye on the Birdie 87/803	6,600		19.00	19
2000 Ready to Take a Swing at it 87/804	10,000		19.00	19
2000 Spare Me 87/805	6,600		19.00	19
2000 Touchdown 87/806	8,000		19.00	19
2000 Two Love 87/807	6,600		22.00	22

Charming Tails Squashville Figurines - D. Griff

YEAR ISSUE	EDITION LIMIT	YEAR RETD.	ISSUE PRICE	*QUOTE U.S.$
1996 Airmail 87/698	Closed	1997	15.00	14-23
1996 All I Can Give You is Me 87/498	Closed	1996	15.00	16-38
1996 All Snug in Their Beds Waterglobe 87/476	Closed	1996	30.00	50
1997 All The Trimmings 87/703	Yr.Iss.	1997	15.00	15-30
1996 Angel of Light 87/481	Open		12.00	14
1997 Baby's 1st Christmas 1997 Annual 87/705	Closed	1997	18.50	20
1996 Baby's 1st Christmas Waterglobe 87/475	Closed	1996	28.00	35-75
1999 Baby's First Christmas 87/111	Closed	1999	16.50	20-44
1997 Bearing Gifts 87/600	Closed	2000	16.00	17
1996 Binkey in a Bed of Flowers 87/426	Closed	1996	15.00	40-44
1995 Binkey Snow Shoeing 87/580	Open		14.00	16
1995 Binkey's 1995 Ice Sculpture 87/572	Closed	1995	20.00	20-38
1996 Building a Snowbunny 87/692	Open		16.00	18
1998 The Building Blocks of Christmas 87/619	Closed	1998	17.00	17-35
1995 Charming Choo-Choo and Cabbose 87/579	Closed	1999	35.00	36
1997 Chauncey's Choo Choo Ride 87/707	Closed	1999	19.00	20
1996 Chauncey's Noisemakers 87/554	Closed	2000	12.00	14
1995 Christmas Pageant Stage 87/546	Open		30.00	32
1996 Christmas Stroll 87/575	Closed	2000	16.00	18
1997 Christmas Trio 87/713	Closed	2000	15.50	18
1998 Dashing Through The Snow 87/624	Open		16.50	18
1997 Decorating Binkey 87/714	Closed	2000	16.00	18-24
1996 Did I Do That? 87/469	Closed	1997	14.00	23-25
2000 Dive Into The Holidays 87/208	Open		22.00	22
1996 The Drum Major 87/556	Closed	2000	12.00	14
1999 Everybody Sing 87/102	Open		26.00	26
1996 Extra! Extra! 87/590	Closed	1997	14.00	17-35
1996 Farmer Mackenzie 87/695	Closed	2000	16.00	18
1996 The Float Driver 87/587	Closed	2000	12.00	14
1995 Flying Leaf Saucer 87/305	Open		16.00	18
1996 Follow in my Footsteps 87/473	Closed	2000	12.00	14
1996 Holiday Trumpeteer 87/555	Closed	2000	12.00	14
1995 Holy Family Players 87/547	Open		20.00	22
1994 Hot Doggin' 87/993	Closed	1995	20.00	25-60
1996 Jingle Bells 87/513	Closed	1997	15.00	23-40
2000 Just The Right Size 87/209	Open		20.00	20
2000 Kiss-Mas Lights 87/205	Yr.Iss.		19.00	19
1994 Lady Bug Express 87/188	Closed	1994	18.00	188-438
1994 Leaf Vine Ornament Hanger 87/519	Closed	1995	25.00	50-63
1996 Lil' Drummer Mouse 87/480	Open		12.00	14
1996 Little Drummer Boy 87/557	Closed	2000	12.00	14
2000 The Littlest Reindeer 87/207	Open		17.00	17
1994 Mackenzie Building a Snowmouse 87/203	7,500	1994	18.00	107-188
1996 Mackenzie Claus on Parade 87/576	Closed	2000	22.00	24
1998 Mackenzie's Wish List (NALED piece) 98/201	Retrd.	1998	17.00	19
1995 Mail Mouse 87/573	Closed	1996	12.00	24
1996 Manger Animals 87/482	Open		20.00	22
1994 Maxine and Mackenzie Caroling 87/925	Closed	1995	18.00	27-50
1994 Maxine Making Snow Angels 87/510	Open		20.00	22
1997 Maxine the Snowman (NALED piece) 98/196	Retrd.	1997	16.50	30-63
1996 Maxine's Snowmobile Ride 87/612	Closed	2000	16.00	18
1998 Merry Christmas From Our House To Yours 87/622	Open		23.00	24
1994 Mouse Candle Climber 87/189	Closed	1995	8.00	35-65
1994 Mouse Card Holder 87/501	Closed	1995	13.00	13-35
1994 Mouse in Tree Hole Candleholder 87/502	Closed	1995	17.00	69-77
1994 Mouse on Basket 87/529	Closed	1995	50.00	60-85
1994 Mouse on Vine Basket 87/506	Closed	1995	55.00	66
1994 Mouse on Vine Candleholder 87/504	Closed	1995	55.00	66-85
1994 Mouse on Vine Wreath 87/505	Closed	1995	55.00	66-150
2000 My Little Chick-A-Deer 87/206	Open		18.00	18
1996 My New Toy 87/500	Closed	1997	14.00	18-35
1998 My Spring Bonnet (NALED piece) 98/204	Retrd.	1998	18.50	19
1999 Nestled In For The Holidays (NALED piece) 87/101	Open		20.00	20
1997 Not a Creature Was Stirring 87/704	Closed	2000	17.00	18
2000 Oh Mackenzie Tree... 87/213	Open		17.00	17
1996 Parade Banner 87/543	Closed	2000	16.00	25
1995 Pear Taxi 87/565	Closed	1996	16.00	20-50
1996 Peeking at Presents 87/527	Closed	1997	13.00	14-40
1998 Please, Just One More... 87/625	Closed	2000	16.50	18
1994 Pyramid with Mice Candleholder 87/509	Closed	1995	40.00	48
1998 Reginald's Choo-Choo Ride 87/620	Closed	1999	19.00	19
1996 Reginald's Newsstand 87/591	Closed	1997	20.00	18-44
1997 The Santa Balloon 87/708	Closed	2000	25.00	26
1996 Sending A Little Snow Your Way 87/601	Retrd.	1996	15.00	25-45
1997 Shepherd's set 87/710	Open		12.50	14
2000 A Shoveling We Will Go 87/204	Open		18.00	18
1999 Skating Party (NALED piece) 87/103	Open		21.00	21
1995 Sleigh Ride 87/569	7,500	1995	16.00	45-68
1999 Sleigh Ride Sweeties 87/100	Closed	1999	23.00	25
1996 Snack for the Reindeer 87/512	Closed	1996	13.00	35-40
1995 Snow Plow 87/566	Closed	2000	16.00	18
1995 The Snowball Fight 87/570	Closed	1999	16.00	18
1998 Snowman Float 87/626	Closed	2000	23.00	25
1996 Stewart's Choo Choo Ride 87/694	Closed	1999	17.50	20
1999 The Stockings Were Hung By The Chimney 87/110	Open		18.50	19
1999 Sugar Time Band Float 87/104	Closed	2000	25.00	25
1999 Tea Party Train Ride 87/105	Closed	1999	26.00	26
1998 Team Igloo 87/623	Closed	1998	23.00	23-45
1995 Teamwork Helps 87/571	Open		16.00	18
1996 Testing the Lights 87/514	Closed	1997	14.00	18-30
1995 Three Wise Mice 87/548	Open		20.00	22
1996 Town Crier 87/696	Open		14.00	16
1997 Trimming A Tree 87/702	Open		27.50	28
2000 Wait For Us! 87/210	Closed	2000	20.00	20
1996 Waiting For Christmas 87/496	14,000	1997	16.00	36
1998 Who Put That Tree There? 87/621	Closed	2000	16.50	18
1996 You Melted My Heart 87/472	Closed	1997	20.00	21-25

Charming Tails Wedding Figurines - D. Griff

YEAR ISSUE	EDITION LIMIT	YEAR RETD.	ISSUE PRICE	*QUOTE U.S.$
1998 The Altar of Love 82/108	Closed	2000	25.00	25
1998 The Best...Bunny 82/103	Closed	2000	16.00	17
1998 The Get-Away Car 82/107	Open		22.00	23
1998 Here Comes The Bride 82/100	Closed	2000	17.00	18
1998 Maid of Honor 82/102	Closed	2000	16.00	17
1998 My Heart's All A-Flutter (Groom) 82/101	Closed	2000	17.00	18
1998 The Ring Bearer 82/104	Closed	2000	16.00	17
1998 Together Forever 82/109	Open		25.00	26
1998 Wedding Day Blossoms 82/105	Closed	2000	16.00	17

Moon & Star Nursery Gifts - D. Griff

YEAR ISSUE	EDITION LIMIT	YEAR RETD.	ISSUE PRICE	*QUOTE U.S.$
2000 Musical (pink) 93/601	Open		39.00	39
2000 Photo Frame (blue) 93/607	Open		25.00	25
2000 Photo Frame (pink) 93/604	Open		25.00	25
2000 Waterglobe (blue) 93/602	Open		45.00	45

Teeny Tiny Tails Squashville Country Fair Booths - D. Griff

YEAR ISSUE	EDITION LIMIT	YEAR RETD.	ISSUE PRICE	*QUOTE U.S.$
1998 Berry Toss 80/7	Closed	1999	14.00	14-20
1998 The Big Winner 80/10	Closed	1999	12.00	12-20
1998 Candy Apples 80/3	Closed	1999	12.00	12-27
1998 Off to the Fair 80/1	Closed	1999	16.00	16-20
1998 Test Your Strength 80/5	Closed	1999	14.00	14-20
1998 Ticket Seller Booth 80/2	Closed	1999	16.00	15-18

Teeny Tiny Tails Squashville Country Fair Musical Rides - D. Griff

YEAR ISSUE	EDITION LIMIT	YEAR RETD.	ISSUE PRICE	*QUOTE U.S.$
1998 Daffodil Twirl 80/4	Closed	1999	49.50	50-75
1998 Mushroom Carousel 80/6	Closed	1999	49.50	50-75
1998 Tulip Ferris Wheel 80/8	Closed	1999	49.50	50-75

Cherished Teddies/Enesco Group, Inc.

Cherished Teddies Club - P. Hillman

YEAR ISSUE	EDITION LIMIT	YEAR RETD.	ISSUE PRICE	*QUOTE U.S.$
1995 Cub E. Bear CT001	Yr.Iss.	1995	Gift	35-69
1995 Mayor Wilson T. Beary CT951	Yr.Iss.	1995	20.00	35-45
1995 Hilary Hugabear CT952	Yr.Iss.	1995	17.50	38-40
1996 R. Harrison Hartford-New Member (yellow pencil) CT002	Yr.Iss.	1996	Gift	25-38
1996 R. Harrison Hartford-Charter Member (red pencil) CT102	Yr.Iss.	1996	Gift	44-69
1996 Emily E. Claire CT962	Yr.Iss.	1996	17.50	25-40
1996 Kurtis D. Claw CT961	Yr.Iss.	1996	17.50	32-40
1996 Town Tattler Building CT953	Yr.Iss.	1996	50.00	40-45
1996 Club Flag 901350	Yr.Iss.	1996	20.00	20-40
1997 Lloyd, CT Town Railway Conductor -Membearship (red suitcase) CT003	Yr.Iss.	1997	Gift	30-38
1997 Lloyd, CT Town Railway Conductor-Charter Membear (green suitcase) CT103	Yr.Iss.	1997	Gift	30-38
1997 Bernard and Bernice CT972	Yr.Iss.	1997	17.50	30-32
1997 Eleanor P. Beary CT971	Yr.Iss.	1997	17.50	25-32
1997 Mary Jane "My Favorite Things" 277002 (Cherished Rewards)	Yr.Iss.	1997	Gift	94-110
1997 Amelia "You Make Me Smile" 273554 (Cherished Rewards)	Yr.Iss.	1997	Gift	55-63
1997 Benny "Let's Ride Through Life Together" 273198 (Cherished Rewards)	Yr.Iss.	1997	Gift	38-60
1997 Blaire Beary (mini figurine) 297550 (Member Get Member)	Yr.Iss.	1997	Gift	32-56
1998 Cherished Teddies Town Accessory Set CT983	Yr.Iss.	1998	17.50	18
1998 Lela Nightingale CT981	Yr.Iss.	1998	15.00	15-25
1998 Wade Weathersbee CT982	Yr.Iss.	1998	13.50	40-44
1998 Cherished Teddies Lithograph CRT608 (Cherished Rewards)	Yr.Iss.	1998	Gift	50
1998 Bubbie Waterton (mini figurine) 466808 (Member Get Member)	Yr.Iss.	1998	Gift	35
1998 Dr. Darlene Makebetter (orange bag) CT004	Yr.Iss.	1998	Gift	28
1998 Dr. Darlene Makebetter (pink bag) Charter Membear CT104	Yr.Iss.	1998	Gift	N/A
1999 Lanny CT005	Yr.Iss.	1999	Gift	N/A
1999 Lanny (red flag) Charter Membear CT105	Yr.Iss.	1999	Gift	N/A
1999 Letty CT993 (5th Anniversary)	Yr.Iss.	1999	22.50	23-32
1999 Vivienne CT992	Yr.Iss.	1999	17.50	18-25
1999 Walter CT991	Yr.Iss.	1999	17.50	18-25
2000 Julia Bearon as Gloria Growlette 685747	Yr.Iss.		Gift	N/A
2000 Brad Wheeler - Troy "Mac McBear" 685976	Yr.Iss.		25.00	25
2000 Marco Pawllini 685771	Yr.Iss.		20.00	20

Cherished Teddies - P. Hillman

YEAR ISSUE	EDITION LIMIT	YEAR RETD.	ISSUE PRICE	*QUOTE U.S.$
1993 Abigail "Inside We're All The Same" 900362	Suspd.		16.00	39-100
2000 Abraham "Embrace The Earth" 706876	7,500		45.00	45
1999 Alex "Cherish The Little Things" (Sculptor Tour Figurine) 368156	Retrd.	1999	17.50	43-57
2000 Alexis (Spring Catalog) 681113	Yr.Iss.	2000	22.50	23
1993 Alice "Cozy Warm Wishes Coming Your Way" (9") 903620	Suspd.		100.00	175-225
1993 Alice "Cozy Warm Wishes Coming Your Way" (Dated 1993) 912875	Yr.Iss.	1993	17.50	170-220
1995 Allison & Alexandria "Two Friends Mean Twice The Love" 127981	Retrd.	1999	25.00	25-35
1999 Alyssa "You Warm My Soul" 533866	Open		15.00	15
1995 Amanda "Here's Some Cheer to Last The Year" 141186	Yr.Iss.	1995	17.50	24-32
1993 Amy "Hearts Quilted With Love" 910732	Retrd.	1999	13.50	32
2000 Angela "Thanks For Helping Me Get My Wings 706809	Open		50.00	50
1999 "Anxiously Awaiting The Arrival" 476978	Open		15.00	15
1996 Andy "You Have A Special Place In My Heart" 176265	Retrd.	1998	18.50	19-36
1999 Anita "You're A Tulip To Treasure" (1999 Spring Catalog Exclusive) 477915	Yr.Iss.	1999	20.00	27-32
1992 Anna "Hooray For You" 950459	Retrd.	1997	22.50	30-100
1999 Anne "So Glad You're Here To Keep Me Warm 534234	Open		10.00	10
1997 Annie, Brittany, Colby, Danny, Ernie "Strike Up The Band And Give Five Cherished Years A Hand" (5th Anniversary) 205354	Yr.Iss.	1997	75.00	65-99
1999 Anthony "Friendship is a Work of Art" 476528R	Open		20.00	20
1999 Anthony "Friendship is a Work of Art" 476528	Open		20.00	20
1999 Archie "Through Ups and Downs, You're Still The Best Friend Around" 589977	Open		20.00	20
2000 Ariel "Everyone Needs A Little Help Learning To Fly" 706698	Yr.Iss.		17.50	18-28
1999 Arnold "You 'Putt' Me In A Great Mood" 476161	Open		17.50	18
2000 Awaiting The Arrival 743801	Open		20.00	20
1994 Baby Boy Jointed (musical-"Schubert's Lullaby") 699314	Suspd.		60.00	60
1994 Baby Girl Jointed (musical -"Schubert's Lullaby") 699322	Suspd.		60.00	60
1993 Baby in Cradle (musical-"Brahms' Lullaby") 914320	Open		60.00	60
1999 Bailey & Friends 662011	Open		22.50	23
1998 Ballerina in Jewelry Box (musical -"Music Box Dancer") 331473	Open		40.00	40

*Quotes have been rounded up to nearest dollar

Cherished Teddies/Enesco Group, Inc.
to Cherished Teddies/Enesco Group, Inc.

FIGURINES

YEAR ISSUE	EDITION LIMIT	YEAR RETD.	ISSUE PRICE	*QUOTE U.S.$
1997 Barry "I'm Batty Over You" 270016	Open		17.50	18
1999 Baxter 644358	Open		22.50	23
1995 Bea " 'Bee' My Friend" 141348	Retrd.	1998	15.00	18-35
1994 Bear as Bunny Jointed (musical-"Here Comes Peter Cottontail") 625302	Retrd.	1996	60.00	115-125
1995 Bear Cupid Girl "Love" "Be Mine" 2 Asst 103640	Suspd.		15.00	17-32
1994 Bear Holding Harp (musical-"Love Makes The World Go Round") 916323	Retrd.	1997	40.00	50-70
1996 Bear In Bunny Outfit Resin Egg Dated 1996 156507	Yr.Iss.	1996	8.50	17-21
1998 Bear in Crib "Tucked in Teddie" (musical-"Brahm's Lullaby") 335797	Closed	1999	75.00	75
1992 Bear on Rocking Reindeer (musical-"Jingle Bells") 950815	Suspd.		60.00	150-175
1998 Bear on Swing in Tree "Picnic in the Park" (musical-"That's What Friends Are For") 335827	Closed	1999	50.00	50
1993 Bear Playing w/Train (musical-"Santa Claus is Coming to Town") 912964	Open		40.00	40
1994 Bear w/Goose (musical-"Wind Beneath My Wings") 627445	Retrd.	1997	45.00	53-63
1994 Bear w/Horse (musical-"My Favorite Things") 628565	Retrd.	1996	150.00	165
1994 Bear w/Rocking Reindeer (musical-"Jingle Bells") 629618	Open		165.00	165
1994 Bear w/Toy Chest (musical-"My Favorite Things") 627453	Open		60.00	60
1995 Beary Scary Halloween House 152382	Open		20.00	20-30
2000 Beatrice "Honey, You're The Sweetest" 786837	Open		20.00	20
1994 Becky "Springtime Happiness" 916331	Suspd.		20.00	32-105
1992 Benji "Life Is Sweet, Enjoy" 950548	Retrd.	1995	13.50	34-100
2000 Bert "I'm Busy As A Bee Every Day Of The Week 790192	Open		20.00	20
1994 Bessie "Some Bunny Loves You" 916404	Suspd.		15.00	97-200
1995 The Best Is Yet To Come 127949	Open		12.50	14
1995 The Best Is Yet To Come 127957	Open		12.50	14
1992 Beth & Blossom "Friends Are Never Far Apart" 950564	Retrd.	1997	50.00	57-81
1992 Beth & Blossom "Friends Are Never Far Apart" w/butterfly 950564	Closed	1992	50.00	120-175
1992 Beth "Bear Hugs" 950637	Retrd.	1995	17.50	35-75
1992 Beth "Happy Holidays, Deer Friend" 950807	Suspd.		22.50	35-75
1999 Bette "You Are The Star Of The Show" (1999 Adoption Center Event) 533637	Yr.Iss.	1999	20.00	20-28
1994 Betty "Bubblin' Over With Love" 626066	Open		18.50	20-24
1999 Bianca "Sweet Dreams My Little One" 533297	Open		15.00	15
1994 Billy "Everyone Needs A Cuddle", Betsey "First Step To Love" Bobbie "A Little Friendship To Share" 624896	Retrd.	1999	12.50	13
1994 Billie (spelling error) "Everyone Needs A Cuddle", Betsey "First Step To Love" Bobbie "A Little Friendship To Share" 624896	Closed	N/A	12.50	43-46
1998 Bonnie & Harold "Ring in the Holidays with Me" 466301	Open		25.00	25
1995 Boy Bear Cupid "Sent With Love" 103551	Suspd.		17.50	28-35
1995 Boy Bear Flying Cupid "Sending You My Heart" 103608	Suspd.		13.00	13-27
1998 Boy in Train Car (musical-"Toyland") 331465	Open		40.00	50
1993 Boy Praying (musical-"Jesus Loves Me") 914304	Retrd.	1997	37.50	77
1994 Boy/Girl in Laundry Basket (musical-"Love Will Keep Us Together") 624926	Open		60.00	60
1994 Boy/Girl in Sled (musical-"Oh, What a Merry Christmas Day") 651435	Closed	1998	100.00	100
1998 Brandon "Friendship Is My Goal" 354252	Open		20.00	20
1994 Breanna "Pumpkin Patch Pals" 617180	Retrd.	1998	15.00	23-40
1994 Bride/Groom (musical-"Mendelssohn Wedding March") 699349	Open		50.00	50
1998 Brooke "Arriving With Love And Care" 302686	Open		25.00	25
2000 Bryce "I Scored A Strike When I Met You" 731870	Open		22.50	23
1993 Buckey & Brenda "How I Love Being Friends With You" 912816	Retrd.	1995	15.00	75-100
1993 • Brenda "How I Love Being Friends With You" 912816	Retrd.	1995	N/A	44-60
1993 • Buckey "How I Love Being Friends With You" 912816	Retrd.	1995	N/A	34-40
1995 Bunny "Just In Time For Spring" 103802	Retrd.	1998	13.50	14-44
1996 Butch "Can I Be Your Football Hero?" 156388	Retrd.	1999	15.00	15-28
2000 Caleb & Friends "When One Lacks Vision Another Must Provide Supervision" (Special Event) 661996	Yr.Iss.	2000	Gift	N/A
1992 Camille "I'd Be Lost Without You" 950424	Retrd.	1996	20.00	28-49
1997 Can't Bear To See You Under The Weather 215856	Open		15.00	15
1999 Carlin & Janay "When I Count My Blessings, I Count You Twice" 533874	Open		25.00	25
1998 Carol "Angels Snow How To Fly" 352969	Retrd.	2000	17.50	18-27
1993 Carolyn "Wishing You All Good Things" 912921	Retrd.	1996	22.50	32-48
1995 Carrie "The Future 'Beareth' All Things" 141321	Retrd.	1998	18.50	19-40
2000 Carter & Friends "Take Time For Others and Others Will Take Time For You" 706817	Open		25.00	25
2000 Cassandra "Ghostly Greetings" 706779	Open		25.00	25
1997 Cathy "An Autumn Breeze Blows Blessings To Please" 269980	Open		25.00	25
2000 Cecilia "You Pull At My Heartstrings" 662445 (Mother's Day Exclusive) 12 pc. 679089	Open		30.00	30
1999 Charissa & Ashylynn "Every Journey Begins With One Step" 601578	Open		25.00	25
1993 Charity "I Found A Friend In Ewe" 910678	Retrd.	1996	20.00	119-195
1992 Charlie "The Spirit of Friendship Warms The Heart" 950742	Retrd.	1996	22.50	50-110
1993 Chelsea "Good Friends Are A Blessing" 910694	Retrd.	1995	15.00	175-225
1999 Cherish "Reach Out To Someone Around You" 476633	Open		12.50	13
1996 Cheryl & Carl "Wishing You A Cozy Christmas" 141216	Retrd.	1998	25.00	35-39
1995 Christian "My Prayer Is For You" 103837	Open		18.50	19-34
1995 Christine "My Prayer Is For You" 103845	Open		18.50	19-32
1992 Christopher "Old Friends Are The Best Friends" 950483	Open		50.00	50-82
1998 Clown on Ball (musical-"You Are My Sunshine") 336459	Open		40.00	40
2000 Clement & Jodie "Try, Try And Try Again" 706744	Open		20.00	20
1998 Cole "We've Got a Lot To Be Thankful For" (Summer Show Exclusive) 476714	Closed	1998	12.50	36-48
2000 "Collecting Cherished Friends Along The Way" 759511	10,000		50.00	50
1999 Collector Starter Kit CRT675	Open		30.00	30
1993 Connie "You're A Sweet Treat" 912794	Retrd.	1996	15.00	24-75
1999 Corey "I Know How To Take Care of Business" 676942	Open		22.50	23
1992 Couple in Basket/Umbrella Friends Are Never Far Apart (musical-"Let Me Be Your Teddy Bear") 950645	Retrd.	1997	60.00	120-180
1994 Courtney "Springtime Is A Blessing From Above" 916390	Retrd.	1996	15.00	82-100
1999 Crystal "Hang On! We're In For A Wonderful Ride" 589942	Open		20.00	20
1999 Crystal "Hang On! We're In For A Wonderful Ride" 589942R	Open		20.00	20
1995 Cupid Baby on Pillow "Little Bundle of Joy", 2 Asst. 103659	Suspd.		13.50	28-37
1995 Cupid Boy Sitting "From My Heart", "Sealed With Love", 2 Asst. 869074	Suspd.		13.50	25-32
1995 Cupid Boy/Girl Double "Aiming For Your Heart" 103594	Suspd.		25.00	37-50
1995 Cupid Boy/Girl Double "Heart to Heart", "My Love", 2 Asst. 869082	Suspd.		18.50	30-34
2000 Dad, Drake & Dustee "You Have A Very Special Way Of Lifting Spirits" 661791	Open		25.00	25
1993 Daisy "Friendship Blossoms With Love" 910651	Retrd.	1996	15.00	313-499
1999 Daisy & Chelsea "Old Friends Always Find Their Way Back" (1999 Reunion Event) 597392	Open		20.00	20
1996 Daniel "You're My Little Pumpkin" 176214	Retrd.	1998	22.50	23-45
1997 Danielle, Sabrina, & Tiffany "We're Three Of A Kind" (1997 Adoption Center Only) 265780	Yr.Iss.	1997	35.00	45-63
1996 Debbie "Let's Hear It For Friendship!" 156361	Open		15.00	15-30
2000 Delia "You're The Beary Best Babysitter" 476536	Open		20.00	20
1999 Dennis "You Put The Spice In My Life" (1999 National Event) 510963	Yr.Iss.	1999	17.50	18
1999 Design Your Own Double /Raincoats Resin Figurine 726621	Yr.Iss.	1999	30.00	30
2000 Destiny & Kay "You've Never Looked More Beautiful Than You Do Today 789658	Open		25.00	25
1995 Donald "Friends Are Egg-ceptional Blessings" 103799	Retrd.	1998	20.00	25-32
1992 Douglas "Let's Be Friends" 950661	Retrd.	1995	20.00	35-49
1995 Earl "Warm Hearted Friends" 131873	Retrd.	1998	17.50	18-40
1999 Ed "There's A Patch In My Heart For You" 466220	Open		20.00	20
1994 Elizabeth & Ashley "My Beary Best Friend" 916277	Retrd.	1996	25.00	47-57
2000 Elmer & Friends "Friends Are The Thread That Holds The Quilt of Life Together" 786691	Open		30.00	30
1994 Eric "Bear Tidings Of Joy" 622796	Retrd.	1998	22.50	25-45
1996 Erica "Friends Are Always Pulling For You" 176028	Retrd.	2000	22.50	23
1998 Erin "My Irish Eyes Smile When You're Near" 203068	Open		15.00	15
2000 Ernestine & Regina "I've Never Been More Proud Of You Than I Am Today 789623	Open		25.00	25
1998 Evan "May Your Christmas Be Trimmed In Happiness" (Naled Catalog Exclusive) 484822	Open		27.50	28
1994 Faith "There's No Bunny Like You" 916412	Suspd.		20.00	30-60
1999 Flossie "I'd Stick My Neck Out For You Anytime" 589950	Open		20.00	20
1998 Frank & Helen "Snow One Like You" (Fall Catalog Exclusive) 352950	Yr.Iss.	1998	22.50	23
1993 Freda & Tina "Our Friendship Is A Perfect Blend" 911747	Open		35.00	35
1995 Gail "Catching the First Blooms of Friendship" 103772	Retrd.	1998	20.00	25-35
1993 Gary "True Friendships Are Scarce" 912786	Suspd.		18.50	25-55
1995 Girl Bear Cupid "Be My Bow" 103586	Suspd.		15.00	29-35
1995 Girl Bear Flying Cupid "Sending You My Heart" 103616	Suspd.		13.00	29-32
1995 Girl Bear on Ottoman (musical-"Au Clair De La Lune") 128058	Open		55.00	55-69
1998 Girl in Teacup with Saucer (musical-"My Favorite Things") 331457	Open		40.00	45
1993 Girl Praying (musical-"Jesus Loves Me") 914312	Retrd.	1997	37.50	75
1999 Glenn "By Land Or By Sea, Let's Go - Just You And Me" 477893	Yr.Iss.	1999	35.00	35
1993 Gretel "We Make Magic, Me And You" 912778	Retrd.	1998	18.50	24-33
1998 Growing Better Each Year 302651	Open		22.50	23
1993 Hans "Friends In Toyland" 912956	Retrd.	1995	20.00	65-100
1999 Harriet "You Make Me Feel Beautiful Inside" 476587	Open		22.50	23
1999 Hazel "I've Got A Notion To Give You A Potion!" 534129	Retrd.	1999	15.00	15
2000 Heather & Friends "Remembering The Simple Pleasures Of Childhood (Toys For Tots Figurine) 662038	Open		37.50	38
1993 Heidi & David "Special Friends" 910708	Suspd.		25.00	35-75
1993 Henrietta "A Basketful of Wishes" 910686	Suspd.		22.50	125-175
1994 Henry "Celebrating Spring With You" 916420	Suspd.		20.00	35-75
1999 Homer & Friends "Adventure Is Just Around The Corner" 662046	Open		35.00	35
1999 Honey "You're A Good Friend That Sticks Like Honey" 534099	Retrd.	1999	16.50	17
1995 Hope "Our Love Is Ever-Blooming" 103764	Retrd.	1998	20.00	20-45
1998 Humphrey "Just the Bear Facts, Ma'am" (1998 Regional Event Piece) 352977	Yr.Iss.	1998	15.00	40-82
1998 Hunter "Me Cavebear, You Friend" 354104	Retrd.	1999	15.00	15-26
2000 Isaac, Jeremiah & Temperance "Faith Of Our Fathers" 707031	Open		30.00	30
2000 Irmgard "Your Smile Can Melt Any Heart" 706728	Yr.Iss.		25.00	25
1994 Ingrid "Bundled-Up With Warm Wishes" Dated 1994 617237	Yr.Iss.	1994	20.00	35-65
1999 Irene "Time Leads Us Back To The Things We Love The Most" 476404	Open		20.00	20
1999 Ivan "I've Packed My Trunk And I'm Ready To Go" 589969	Open		20.00	20
1992 Jacob "Wishing For Love" 950734	Suspd		22.50	26-34
1996 Jamie & Ashley "I'm All Wrapped Up In Your Love" 141224	Retrd.	1998	25.00	35-45
1998 Janet "You're Sweet As A Rose" (Avon Exclusive) 336521	Open		9.00	9
1999 Jasmine "A Bouquet Of Blessings For You" (GCC Exclusive) 202940	Open		15.00	15
1992 Jasmine "You Have Touched My Heart" 950475	Suspd.		22.50	40-100
1997 Jean "Cup Full Of Peace" 269859	Open		25.00	25
1994 Jedediah "Giving Thanks For Friends" 617091	Retrd.	1997	17.50	19-75
1996 Jeffrey "Striking Up Another Year" Dated 1996 176044	Yr.Iss.	1996	17.50	18-35
1995 Jennifer "Gathering The Blooms of Friendship" 103810	Retrd.	1998	22.50	23-50
1992 Jeremy "Friends Like You Are Precious And Few" 950521	Retrd.	1995	15.00	25-110
1999 Jerrod "Don't Worry - It's Just Another Little Bump In The Road" 589926	Open		20.00	20
1997 Jessica "A Mother's Heart Is Full of Love" 155438	Retrd.	1997	25.00	41-48
1996 Jessica "A Mother's Heart Is Full of Love" (GCC Early Introduction) 155438A	Retrd.	1996	25.00	46-70
2000 Jessie 2000 National Convention 706655	Yr.Iss.	2000	175.00	175
1999 Joe "Love Only Gets Better With Age" 476412	Open		15.00	15
1999 John & William "When Friends Meet, Hearts Warm" 533858	Retrd.	1999	35.00	35
1993 Jointed Bear Christmas (musical-"Jingle Bells") 903337	Suspd.		60.00	80-110
1998 Joseph "Everyone Has Their 'Old Friends' to Hug" (Palmer Catalog Exclusive) 476471A	Open		25.00	25
1992 Joshua "Love Repairs All" 950556	Retrd.	1997	20.00	20-31

*Quotes have been rounded up to nearest dollar

FIGURINES

Cherished Teddies/Enesco Group, Inc. to Cherished Teddies/Enesco Group, Inc.

YEAR ISSUE		EDITION LIMIT	YEAR RETD.	ISSUE PRICE	*QUOTE U.S.$
2000	Jude "Love Is The Beary Best Bedtime Story" (St. Jude Philanthropic figurine) 506818	Open		17.50	18
1999	Junior "Everyone Is A Bear's Best Friend" 476641	Open		12.50	13
1999	Kayla "Big Hearts Come In Small Packages" (January Show Exclusive) 533815	Open		20.00	20
1997	Kara "You're A Honey Of A Friend" Adoption Center (1997 National Event) 265799	Yr.Iss.	1997	15.00	30-50
1994	Kathleen "Luck Found Me A Friend In You" 916447	Retrd.	1999	12.50	15-27
1992	Katie "A Friend Always Knows When You Need A Hug" 950440	Retrd.	1997	20.00	28-75
1999	Katie, Renee, Jessica, Matthew "I'm Surrounded By Hugs" 538299	Yr.Iss.	1999	25.00	25-38
1998	Keith & Deborah "The Holidays Are Twice As 'Ice'" 354244	Open		30.00	30
1994	Kelly "You're My One And Only" 916307	Suspd.		15.00	45-57
1999	Kent "Officer , I've Got a Warrant Out For Your Heart" 476560	Open		20.00	20
1999	Kent "Officer , I've Got a Warrant Out For Your Heart" 476560R	Open		20.00	20
1995	Kevin "Good Luck To You" 103896	Retrd.	1996	12.50	20-26
2000	Kim "Treat Yourself To Life's Little Pleasures" 661872	Open		17.50	18
1995	Kiss The Hurt And Make It Well 127965	Open		15.00	15
1996	Kittie "You Make Wishes Come True" (1996 Adoption Center Event) 131865	Yr.Iss.	1996	17.50	44-75
1995	Kristen "Hugs of Love And Friendship" 141194	Retrd.	1998	20.00	20-45
1998	Kyle "Even Though We're Far Apart, You'll Always Have A Place In My Heart" 476390	Open		15.00	15
1999	Lacey "Cherish the Little Things in Life" (Paint Your Own Resin Figurine) 662453A	Yr.Iss.	1999	25.00	25
1998	Lance "Come Fly With Me" (1998 National Event Piece) 337463	Yr.Iss.	1998	20.00	25-40
1997	Larry "You're My Shooting Star" 203440	Open		17.50	18-28
1996	Laura "Friendship Makes It All Better" 156396	Open		15.00	15
1997	Lee "You're A Bear's Best Friend" 272167	Yr.Iss.	1997	20.00	25-35
1998	Libby "My Country Tis Of Thee" 305979	Retrd.	1998	20.00	30-42
1997	Lily "Lilies Bloom With Petals of Hope" (Spring Catalog Exclusive) 202959A	Yr.Iss.	1997	15.00	27-31
1996	Linda "ABC And 1-2-3, You're A Friend To Me!" 156426	Open		15.00	15-25
1996	Lindsey & Lyndon "Walking In A Winter Wonderland" (Fall Catalog Exclusive) 141178A	Yr.Iss.	1996	30.00	30-75
1995	Lisa "My Best Is Always You" 103780	Retrd.	1998	20.00	25-32
1998	Lori "Those We Love Should Be Cherished" 476439	Open		17.50	18
1998	Lou "Take Me Out To The Ball Game" 203432	Open		15.00	15-25
1999	Lydia "You're the Bees Knees" 661929	Open		27.50	28
1997	Lynn "A Handmade Holiday Wish" (Fall Catalog Exclusive) 310735A	Yr.Iss.	1997	25.00	40-75
1998	Lynn "A Handmade Holiday Wish" 310735	Open		25.00	25-41
1995	Madeline "A Cup Full of Friendship" 135593	Retrd.	1999	20.00	27
1992	Mandy "I Love You Just The Way You Are" 950572	Retrd.	1995	15.00	28-32
1999	Marcus "There's Nobody I'd Rather Go 'Round With Than You" 589934	Open		20.00	20
1995	Margaret "A Cup Full of Love" 103667	Retrd.	1999	20.00	20-42
1998	Margy (Avon Exclusive) 475602	Retrd.	1998	19.99	35-40
1993	Marie "Friendship Is A Special Treat" 910767	Retrd.	1999	20.00	20-32
1995	Marilyn "A Cup Full of Cheer" 135682	Retrd.	1999	20.00	27-30
1998	Marlene and Marissa "Good Friends Are Always Beary Near" 368164	Closed	1998	Gift	94-115
1998	Marty "I'll Always Be There For You" (Summer Show Exclusive) 476722	Closed	1998	12.50	36-103
1993	Mary "A Special Friend Warms The Season" 912840	Retrd.	2000	25.00	25
1999	Matt And Vicki "Love Is The Best Thing Two Can Share" 476781	Yr.Iss.		35.00	35
1995	Maureen "Lucky Friend" 135690	Retrd.	1996	12.50	20-28
1995	Melissa "Every Bunny Needs A Friend" 103829	Retrd.	1998	20.00	22-32
1999	Merideth "You're As Cozy As A Pair of Mittens! 534226	Open		10.00	10
1993	Michael & Michelle "Friendship Is A Cozy Feeling" 910775	Suspd.		30.00	75-100
1998	Mike "I'm Sweet On You" (1998 Adoption Center Only) 356255	Yr.Iss.	1998	15.00	25-32
1993	Miles "I'm Thankful For A Friend Like You" 912751	Retrd.	1998	17.00	21-30
1995	Millie, Christy, Dorothy "A. Love Me Tender, B. Take Me To Your Heart, C. Love Me True" 128023	Retrd.	1996	37.50	24-30
1995	• Dorothy- "C. Love Me True" 128023	Retrd.	1996	N/A	35-75
1995	• Millie-"A. Love Me Tender 128023	Retrd.	1996	N/A	35-70

YEAR ISSUE		EDITION LIMIT	YEAR RETD.	ISSUE PRICE	*QUOTE U.S.$
1995	• Christy, " B. Take Me To Your Heart 128023	Retrd.	1996	N/A	32-70
1999	Milt & Garrett "A Haunting We Will Go" 534137	Retrd.	1999	20.00	20
1999	Milton "Wishing For A Future As Bright As The Stars" (Millennium Event) 542644	Open		20.00	20
1996	Mindy "Friendship Keeps Me On My Toes" 156418	Open		15.00	15
1998	Miranda "No Matter How Blue You Feel, A Hug Can Heal" (Summer Show Exclusive) 476706	Closed	1998	12.50	30-44
1993	Molly "Friendship Softens A Bumpy Ride" 910759	Retrd.	1996	30.00	34-40
1998	Mother Goose and Friends "Friends of a Feather Flock Together" 154016	Open		50.00	50
1994	Nancy "Your Friendship Makes My Heart Sing" 916315	Retrd.	1996	15.00	100-113
1999	Natalie "You Make Me Smile From Ear To Ear" 534110	Retrd.	1999	15.00	15
1998	Nathan "Leave Your Worries Behind" 176222	Open		17.50	18-27
1992	Nathaniel & Nellie "It's Twice As Nice With You" 950513	Retrd.	1996	30.00	27-35
1997	Newton "Ringing In The New Year With Cheer" 272361	Open		15.00	15-25
1999	Nikki "A Cold Winter's Day Won't Keep Me Away" 534218	Open		10.00	10
1994	Nils "Near And Deer For Christmas" 617245	Retrd.	1997	22.50	40-55
1997	Nina "Beary Happy Wishes" (1997 National Event Piece) 215864	Yr.Iss.	1997	17.50	27
1999	Norbit & Nyla "A Friend Is Someone Who Reaches For Your Hand And Touches Your Heart 534188	Yr.Iss.		25.00	25-50
1999	Norm "Patience Is A Fisherman's Virtue" 476765	Open		25.00	25
2000	Norma (2000 Regional Event Piece) 706639	Yr.Iss.	2000	65.00	65
1996	Olga "Feel The Peace...Hold The Joy...Share The Love" 182966	Yr.Iss.	1996	50.00	34-48
1994	Oliver & Olivia "Will You Be Mine?" 916641	Suspd.		25.00	75-113
1996	Our Hearts Are One (Artist Gallery) 186465	Yr.Iss.	1996	30.00	45
1996	Park Bench w/Bears "Heart to Heart" (1996 National Event Piece) CRT240	Yr.Iss.	1996	12.50	20
1995	Pat "Falling For You" 141313	Open		22.50	23-28
1994	Patience "Happiness Is Homemade" 617105	Retrd.	1997	17.50	35-65
1993	Patrice "Thank You For The Sky So Blue" 911429	Retrd.	1999	18.50	24-30
1993	Patrick "Thank You For A Friend That's True" 911410	Retrd.	1999	18.50	25-50
1999	Paul "Good Friends Warm The Heart With Many Blessings" (1999 Adoption Center Exclusive) 466328	Yr.Iss.	1999	22.50	25-40
1998	Penny, Chandler, Boots "We're Inseparable" (1998 Adoption Center Exclusive) 337579	Yr.Iss.	1998	25.00	50-69
1995	Peter "You're Some Bunny Special" 104973	Retrd.	1998	17.50	22-29
1994	Phoebe "A Little Friendship Is A Big Blessing" 617113	Retrd.	1995	13.50	22-29
1993	Priscilla "Love Surrounds Our Friendship" 910724	Retrd.	1997	15.00	27-31
1995	Priscilla & Greta "Our Hearts Belong to You" 128031	19,950	1998	50.00	62-82
1993	Prudence "A Friend To Be Thankful For" 912808	Retrd.	1998	17.00	23-31
1996	Pumpkins/Corn Stalk/Scarecrow Mini 3 Asst. 176206	Open		15.00	15
1999	Randy "You're Never Alone With Good Friends Around" 476498	Open		22.50	23
2000	Ralph "Bring Joy To Those You Hold Deer" 706841	Open		17.50	18
1997	Rex "Our Friendship Will Never Be Extinct" 269999	Open		17.50	18-28
1998	Rich "Always Paws For Holiday Treats" 352721	Yr.Iss.	1998	22.50	34-40
1999	Rita "Wishing You Love Straight From The Heart" (NALED Exclusive) 476617	Open		17.50	18
1993	Robbie & Rachel "Love Bears All Things" 911402	Retrd.	1999	27.50	30-48
1996	Robert "Love Keeps Me Afloat" 156272	Retrd.	1999	13.50	14
1999	Rodney "I'm Santa's Little Helper" 646504	Yr.Iss.	1999	25.00	25
2000	Roberta "Being Your Friend Is My Favorite Pastime" 789615	Open		15.00	15
2000	Ron "Enjoy The Simple Comforts Of Life" (2000 Adoption Center) 706647	25,000		20.00	20
2000	Rosemarie & Ronald "A Hug Is Worth A Thousand Words, A Friend Is Worth More" 706981	Open		27.50	28
1999	Roxie & Shelly "What A Story We Share!" 601586	Open		25.00	25
1998	Roy "I'm Your Country Cowboy" (Special Limited Edition) 466298	Closed	1998	17.50	30-40
1998	Roy "I'm Your Country Cowboy" 466298 & Sierra "You're My Partner" (Special Limited Edition) 466271, set/2	Closed	1998	25.00	28-30
2000	Russell & Ross "Thanks For Teaching Me About The Real World" 661783	Open		22.50	23

YEAR ISSUE		EDITION LIMIT	YEAR RETD.	ISSUE PRICE	*QUOTE U.S.$
1999	Ruth And Gene "Even When We Don't See Eye To Eye We're Always Heart To Heart" 476668	Open		25.00	25
1997	Ryan "I'm Green With Envy For You" 203041	Open		20.00	20-28
1999	Sally And Skip "We Make A Perfect Team" 1999 Adoption Center 510955	25,000		27.50	28
1998	Sam "I Want You...To Be My Friend" 302619	Retrd.	1998	17.50	30-40
1992	Sara "LoveYa", Jacki Hugs & Kisses", Karen "Best Buddy" 950432	Open		10.00	10-19
1999	Sarah "Memories To Wear And Share" 308676	Yr.Iss.	1999	30.00	30-45
1999	Sawyer & Friends "Hold On To The Past, But Look To The Future" 662003	Open		27.50	28
1994	Sean "Luck Found Me A Friend In You" 916439	Retrd.	1999	12.50	20-27
1999	Sedley "We've Turned Over A New Leaf On Our Friendship" 534102	Open		16.50	17
1998	Segrid, Justaf, Ingmar "The Spirit of Christmas Grows In Our Hearts" 352799	Yr.Iss.	1998	45.00	45-75
1995	Seth & Sarabeth "We're Beary Good Pals" 128015	Retrd.	1999	25.00	25-50
1998	Shannon "A Figure 8, Our Friendship Is Great!" 354260	Open		20.00	20-30
1998	Sierra "You're My Partner" (Special Limited Edtion) 466271	Closed	1998	17.50	30-45
1999	Simone & Jhodi "I've Always Believed In You" 601551	Open		25.00	25
1998	Sixteen Candles and Many More Wishes 302643	Open		22.50	23
1999	Skylar & Shana "When You Find A Sunbeam, Share The Warmth" 601594	Open		25.00	25
1994	Sonja "Holiday Cuddles" 622818	Retrd.	1998	20.00	26-32
1999	Spanky "Friendship Can Sometimes Be Bumpy But It's Worth It" (America's Promise) 644382	Open		27.50	28
1994	Stacie "You Lift My Spirit" 617148	Retrd.	1998	18.50	24-35
1999	Stanley & Valerie "Togetherness Is The Reason We Have Friends" 476676	Open		35.00	35
1999	Star "Cherish Yesterday, Dream Tomorrow, Live Today" 534250	Yr.Iss.		55.00	55
2000	Stella "Touches of Heaven Can Be Found On Earth" 706795	Open		22.50	23
1992	Steven "A Season Filled With Sweetness" 951129	Retrd.	1995	20.00	40-50
2000	Sullivan "The Most Important Truth Is To Be Your True Self" 706760	Open		17.50	18
1997	Sven & Liv "All Paths Lead To Kindness & Friendship" 272159	Yr.Iss.	1997	55.00	50-72
1997	Sylvia "A Picture Perfect Friendship" Regional Event Piece 265810	Yr.Iss.	1997	15.00	35-49
1996	Tabitha "You're The Cat's Meow" 176257	Retrd.	1998	15.00	25-30
1999	Tammy "Let's Go To The Hop" 1999 Regional Event 510947	Yr.Iss.	1999	15.00	63-70
1998	Tanna "When Your Hands Are Full, There's Still Room In Your Heart" (Summer Show Exclusive) 476595	Closed	1998	12.50	44-63
1996	Tasha "In Grandmother's Attic" (1996 Adoption Center Exclusive) 156353	19,960	1996	55.00	93-138
1994	Taylor "Sail The Seas With Me" 617156	Suspd.		15.00	19-25
1999	Teddy "Friends Give You Wings To Fly" 476757	Open		15.00	15
1999	Tess & Friends "Things Do Not Change, We Do" 661953	Open		27.50	28
1999	Terry Gift Set 686999	Open		30.00	30
1994	Thanksgiving Quilt 617075	Open		12.00	12-20
1992	Theadore, Samantha & Tyler "Friends Come In All Sizes" 950505	Open		20.00	20-35
1993	Theadore, Samantha & Tyler "Friendship Weathers All Storms" (9") 912883	Suspd.		160.00	160-200
1993	Theadore, Samantha & Tyler "Friendship Weathers All Storms" (musical-"Jingle Bells") 904546	Suspd.		170.00	250-300
1992	Theadore, Samantha & Tyler "Friendship Weathers All Storms" 950769	Retrd.	1997	20.00	38-65
1992	Theadore, Samantha & Tyler (9") "Friends Come In All Sizes" 951196	Retrd.	1999	130.00	130
1997	This Calls For A Celebration 215910	Open		15.00	15
1993	Thomas "Chuggin' Along", Jonathan "Sail With Me", Harrison "We're Going Places" 911739	Retrd.	1997	15.00	40
1993	• Thomas "Chuggin' Along" 911739	Retrd.	1997	N/A	25-40
1993	• Jonathan "Sail With Me" 911739	Retrd.	1997	N/A	30
1993	• Harrison "We're Going Places" 911739	Retrd.	1997	N/A	33
1993	Timothy "A Friend Is Forever" 910740	Retrd.	1996	15.00	25-34
2000	Todd & Friend "Share Life's Little Joys With Your Closest Friends" 786683	Open		25.00	25
1995	Town Tattler Sign 1995 National Event Piece CRT109	Yr.Iss.	1995	6.00	17-24

*Quotes have been rounded up to nearest dollar

YEAR ISSUE	EDITION LIMIT	YEAR RETD.	ISSUE PRICE	*QUOTE U.S.$
1998 Toy Cabinet "My Cherished Treasures" (musical-"My Favorite Things") 335681	Closed	1998	100.00	100
1993 Tracie & Nicole "Side By Side With Friends" 911372	Retrd.	1999	35.00	45-63
1998 Trevor "You Bring Out The Devil In Me" 354112	Open		17.50	18-27
1995 Tucker & Travis "We're in This Together" 127973	Open		25.00	25
1996 Two Boys By Lamp Post (musical-"The First Noel") 141089	Open		50.00	50
1995 UK Bears, Bertie "Friends Forever Near or Far" (International Exclusive) 163457	Open		17.50	35-63
1995 UK Bears, Duncan "Your Friendship Is Music To My Ears" (International Exclusive) 163473	Open		17.50	44-63
1995 UK Bears, Gordon "Keepin' A Watchful Eye on You" (International Exclusive) 163465	Open		17.50	32-63
1995 UK Bears, Sherlock "Good Friends Are Hard To Find" (International Exclusive) 163481	Open		17.50	125-157
1995 UK Bears, set/4 (Bertie 163457, Gordon 163465, Duncan 163473, Sherlock 163481)	Open		70.00	125
1999 Valentine Watch & Figurine Gift Set 738638	Retrd.	2000	30.00	30
1998 Veronica "You Make Happiness Bloom" (Spring Catalog Exclusive) 366854	Yr.Iss.	1998	15.00	22
1994 Victoria "From My Heart To Yours" 916293	Suspd.		16.50	75
1996 Violet "Blessings Bloom When You Are Near" 156280	Retrd.	1999	15.00	29-35
2000 Wanda "A Sprinkling Of Fairy Dust Will Make You Feel Better 786705	Open		20.00	20
1999 Wesley, Phillip, Fiona, Renee (1999 I.C.E. piece) 476846	Retrd.	1999	30.00	69
1998 Whitney "We Make A Winning Team" 302678	Open		15.00	25
1994 Willie "Bears Of A Feather Stay Together" 617164	Retrd.	1997	15.00	27-32
2000 Willow "Cherished Your Spirit" 661759	Open		35.00	35
1994 Winfield "Anything Is Possible When You Wish On A Star" (Millenium Edition) 476811	Open		50.00	27-33
1994 Winona "Little Fair Feather Friend" 617172	Retrd.	1997	15.00	25-50
1999 Woody "You Hold Everything in Place" 476544	Open		20.00	20
1994 Wyatt "I'm Called Little Running Bear" 629707	Retrd.	1998	15.00	20-45
1994 Wylie "I'm Called Little Friend" 617121	Retrd.	1998	15.00	20-45
1998 You're The Frosting on the Birthday Cake 306398	Open		22.50	23
1992 Zachary "Yesterday's Memories Are Today's Treasures" 950491	Retrd.	1997	30.00	32-40

Special Limited Edition - P. Hillman

YEAR ISSUE	EDITION LIMIT	YEAR RETD.	ISSUE PRICE	*QUOTE U.S.$
1993 Holding On To Someone Special -Collector Appreciation Fig. 916285	Yr.Iss.	1993	20.00	200
1994 Priscilla Ann "There's No One Like Hue" Collectible Exposition Exclusive available only at Secaucus and South Bend in 1994 and at Long Beach in 1995 CRT025	Yr.Iss.	1994	50.00	225
1993 Teddy & Roosevelt "The Book of Teddies 1903-1993" (90th Anniversary Commemorative) 624918	Yr.Iss.	1993	20.00	150

Across The Seas - P. Hillman

YEAR ISSUE	EDITION LIMIT	YEAR RETD.	ISSUE PRICE	*QUOTE U.S.$
1997 Bazza "I'm Lost Down Under Without You" 276995	Retrd.	1999	17.50	18
1996 Bob with Passport "Our Friendship Is From Sea To Shining Sea" 202444P	Retrd.	1999	17.50	30-35
1996 Carlos "I Found An Amigo In You" 202339	Retrd.	1999	17.50	49
1996 Claudette "Our Friendship Is Bon Appetit!" 197254	Retrd.	1999	17.50	18
1998 Colleen "The Luck Of The Irish To You" 373966	Retrd.	1999	17.50	49
1996 Fernando "You Make Everday A Fiesta" 202355	Retrd.	1999	17.50	49
1996 Franz "Our Friendship Knows No Boundaries" 202436	Retrd.	1999	17.50	30
1996 Katrien "Tulips Blossom With Friendship" 202401	Retrd.	1999	17.50	18
1996 Kerstin "You're The Swedish of Them All" 197289	Retrd.	1999	17.50	18
1998 Leilani "Tahiti - Sending You Warm And Friendly Island Breezes" 302627	Retrd.	1998	17.50	63
1996 Lian "Our Friendship Spans Many Miles" 202347	Retrd.	1998	17.50	18-35
1996 Lorna "Our Love Is In The Highlands" 202452	Retrd.	1999	17.50	18
1996 Machiko "Love Fans A Beautiful Friendship" 202312	Retrd.	1998	17.50	18-30
1996 Nadia "From Russia, With Love" 202320	Retrd.	1999	17.50	18
1996 Preston "Riding Across The Great White North" 216739	Retrd.	1998	17.50	18-49
1996 Rajul "You're The Jewel Of My Heart" 202398	Retrd.	1999	17.50	18
1997 Sophia "Like Grapes On The Vine, Our Friendship Is Divine" 276987	Retrd.	1999	17.50	18
1996 William "You're a Jolly Ol' Chap!" 202878	Retrd.	1999	17.50	18

American Classics Collection - P. Hillman

YEAR ISSUE	EDITION LIMIT	YEAR RETD.	ISSUE PRICE	*QUOTE U.S.$
2000 Jerald & Mary Ann "What Would Game Night Be Without You" 811742	Open		27.50	28

American Heroes Collection - P. Hillman

YEAR ISSUE	EDITION LIMIT	YEAR RETD.	ISSUE PRICE	*QUOTE U.S.$
2000 Daniel "You're The Finest Friend in the Forest" 676861	Open		22.50	23
2000 Paul "You Can Always Trust Me To Be There" 676888	Open		20.00	20

The Angel Series - P. Hillman

YEAR ISSUE	EDITION LIMIT	YEAR RETD.	ISSUE PRICE	*QUOTE U.S.$
1998 Angela "Peace On Earth And Mercy Mild" 175986	Yr.Iss.	1998	20.00	20-35
1997 Grace "Glory To The Newborn King" 175994	Yr.Iss.	1997	20.00	32
1996 Stormi "Hark The Herald Angels Sing" 176001	Yr.Iss.	1996	20.00	38

Anniversary Figurines - P. Hillman

YEAR ISSUE	EDITION LIMIT	YEAR RETD.	ISSUE PRICE	*QUOTE U.S.$
1997 You Grow More Dear With Each Passing Year 215880	Open		25.00	25
1998 A Decade of Teddy Bear Love 302694 (10 Yr. Anniversary)	Open		30.00	30
1998 25 Years To Treasure Together 302708 (25 Yr. Anniversary)	Open		30.00	30
1998 Forever Yours, Forever True 302716 (40 or 50 Yr. Anniversary)	Open		30.00	30

Antique Toy Minis - P. Hillman

YEAR ISSUE	EDITION LIMIT	YEAR RETD.	ISSUE PRICE	*QUOTE U.S.$
1999 A Big Hug From A Little Friend 537217	Open		12.50	13
1999 Everyone Needs An Occasional Hug 537187	Open		12.50	13
1999 Follow Your Heart Wherever It Takes You 537241	Open		12.50	13
1999 A Friend Is An Answered Prayer 537233	Open		12.50	13
1999 A Journey With You Is One To Remember 537268	Open		12.50	13
1999 Keep Good Friends Close To Your Heart 537195	Open		12.50	13
1999 Our Friendship Is An Adventure 537209	Open		12.50	13
1999 You Have The Biggest Heart of All 537225	Open		12.50	13

Beta Is For Bear - P. Hillman

YEAR ISSUE	EDITION LIMIT	YEAR RETD.	ISSUE PRICE	*QUOTE U.S.$
1998 Alpha 305995	Open		7.50	8
1998 Beta 306002	Open		7.50	8
1998 Gamma 306010	Open		7.50	8
1998 Delta 306037	Open		7.50	8
1998 Epsilon 306045	Open		7.50	8
1998 Zeta 306053	Open		7.50	8
1998 Eta 306088	Open		7.50	8
1998 Theta 306096	Open		7.50	8
1998 Iota 306118	Open		7.50	8
1998 Kappa 306126	Open		7.50	8
1998 Lambda 306134	Open		7.50	8
1998 Mu 306142	Open		7.50	8
1998 Nu 306150	Open		7.50	8
1998 Xi 306185	Open		7.50	8
1998 Omicron 306193	Open		7.50	8
1998 Pi 306207	Open		7.50	8
1998 Rho 306215	Open		7.50	8
1998 Sigma 306223	Open		7.50	8
1998 Tau 306231	Open		7.50	8
1998 Upsilon 306258	Open		7.50	8
1998 Phi 306266	Open		7.50	8
1998 Chi 306274	Open		7.50	8
1998 Psi 306282	Open		7.50	8
1998 Omega 306290	Open		7.50	8

Blossoms of Friendship - P. Hillman

YEAR ISSUE	EDITION LIMIT	YEAR RETD.	ISSUE PRICE	*QUOTE U.S.$
1997 Dahlia "You're The Best Pick of the Bunch" 202932	Retrd.	2000	15.00	15
1997 Iris "You're The Iris of My Eye" 202908	Retrd.	2000	15.00	15-20
1998 Lily "Lilies Bloom With Petals Of Hope" 202959	Retrd.	2000	15.00	15
1997 Rose "Everything's Coming Up Roses" 202886	Retrd.	2000	15.00	15
1997 Susan "Love Stems From Our Friendship" 202894	Retrd.	2000	15.00	15-22

By The Sea, By The Sea - P. Hillman

YEAR ISSUE	EDITION LIMIT	YEAR RETD.	ISSUE PRICE	*QUOTE U.S.$
1997 Gregg "Everything Pails in Comparison To Friends" 203505	Retrd.	2000	20.00	20-22
1997 Jerry "Ready To Make a Splash" 203475	Retrd.	2000	17.50	18
1997 Jim and Joey "Underneath It All We're Forever Friends" 203513	Retrd.	2000	25.00	25-28
1997 Judy "I'm Your Bathing Beauty" 203491	Retrd.	2000	35.00	35
1997 Sandy "There's Room In My Sand Castle For You" 203467	Retrd.	2000	20.00	20

Carousels - P. Hillman

YEAR ISSUE	EDITION LIMIT	YEAR RETD.	ISSUE PRICE	*QUOTE U.S.$
1999 Archie "Through Ups and Downs, You're Still The Best Friend Around" 589977	Open		20.00	20
1998 Bill "Friends Like You Are Always True Blue" 505552	Retrd.	2000	20.00	20
1998 Cody "I'll Cherish You For Many Moons" 505498	Retrd.	2000	20.00	20
1999 Crystal "Hang On! We're In For a Wonderful Ride" 589942	Open		20.00	20
1999 Flossie "I'd Stick My Neck Out For You Anytime" 589950	Open		20.00	20
1998 Gina "Where Friends Gather, Magic Blossoms" 502898	Retrd.	2000	20.00	20
1999 Ivan "I've Packed My Trunk And I'm Ready To Go" 589969	Open		20.00	20
1998 Jason "When It Comes To Friendship, You've Really Earned Your Stripes" 506214	Retrd.	2000	20.00	20
1998 Jenelle "A Friend is Somebunny to Cherish Forever" 505579	Retrd.	2000	20.00	20
1999 Jerrod "Don't Worry - It's Just Another Little Bump in the Road" 589926	Open		20.00	20
1999 Marcus "There's Nobody I'd Rather Go 'Round With Than You" 589934	Open		20.00	20
1998 Virginia "It's So Merry Going 'Round With You 506206	Retrd.	2000	20.00	20

The Cherished Seasons - P. Hillman

YEAR ISSUE	EDITION LIMIT	YEAR RETD.	ISSUE PRICE	*QUOTE U.S.$
1997 Megan "Spring Brings A Season Of Beauty" 203300	Open		20.00	20-28
1997 Kimberly "Summer Brings A Season Of Warmth" 203335	Open		22.50	23-28
1997 Hannah "Autumn Brings A Season Of Thanksgiving" 203343	Open		20.00	20-28
1997 Gretchen "Winter Brings A Season Of Joy" 203351	Open		25.00	25-28

Cherished Snowbears - P. Hillman

YEAR ISSUE	EDITION LIMIT	YEAR RETD.	ISSUE PRICE	*QUOTE U.S.$
2000 Buddy "And The North Wind Shall Blow" 706892	Open		25.00	25
2000 Merry "In The Meadow We Can Build A Snowman" 706906	Open		25.00	25

Childhood Memories - P. Hillman

YEAR ISSUE	EDITION LIMIT	YEAR RETD.	ISSUE PRICE	*QUOTE U.S.$
1999 Albert & Susann "When Life Hands You Lemons, Make Lemonade" 661848	Open		30.00	30
2000 Calvin "Life Is Filled With Ups And Downs" 706965	Open		17.50	18
1999 Dawn "Every Once In A While, There's A Bump In The Road " 661899	Open		17.50	18
1999 Fred "You're The Best Thing Since Sliced Bread" 661856	Open		27.50	28
1999 Lorraine "Don't Let It Get You Down" 661880	Open		17.50	18
1999 Melinda "I'm Only A Hop, Skip And A Jump Away If You Need Me" 661821	Open		17.50	18

A Christmas Carol - P. Hillman

YEAR ISSUE	EDITION LIMIT	YEAR RETD.	ISSUE PRICE	*QUOTE U.S.$
1994 Bear Cratchit "And A Very Merry Christmas To You Mr. Scrooge" 617326	Suspd.		17.50	18-35
1994 Counting House (Nite-Lite) 622788	Suspd.		75.00	75
1994 Cratchit's House (Nite-Lite) 651362	Suspd.		75.00	75-90
1994 Ebearnezer Scrooge "Bah Humbug!" 617296	Suspd.		17.50	18-38
1994 Gloria "I am the Ghost of Christmas Past", Garland "I am the Ghost Of Christmas Present", Gabriel "I am the Ghost of Christmas Yet To Come" 614807	Suspd.		55.00	67-88
1994 Jacob Bearly "You Will Be Haunted By Three Spirits" 614785	Suspd.		17.50	18-38
1994 Mrs. Cratchit "A Beary Christmas And Happy New Year!" 617318	Suspd.		18.50	19-32
1994 Tiny Ted-Bear "God Bless Us Every One" 614777	Suspd.		10.00	10-32

Circus Tent - P. Hillman

YEAR ISSUE	EDITION LIMIT	YEAR RETD.	ISSUE PRICE	*QUOTE U.S.$
1996 Bruno "Step Right Up And Smile" 103713	Retrd.	2000	17.50	18-22
1996 Claudia "You Take Center Ring With Me" 103721	Retrd.	2000	17.50	18-22
1996 Clown on Ball (musical-"Put on a Happy Face") 111430	Open		40.00	40
1997 Dudley "Just Clowning Around" 103748	Retrd.	2000	17.50	18-22
1996 Elephant-Trunk Full of Bear Hugs 103977	Retrd.	2000	22.50	23
1997 Lion-"You're My Mane Attraction" 203548	Retrd.	2000	12.50	13-18
1997 Logan "Love Is A Bear Necessity" 103756	Retrd.	2000	17.50	18
1996 Seal "Seal of Friendship" 137596	Retrd.	2000	10.00	10-15
1997 Shelby "Friendship Keeps You Popping" 203572	Retrd.	2000	17.50	18-22
1997 Tonya "Friends Are Bear Essentials" 103942	Retrd.	2000	20.00	20-22
1996 Wally "You're The Tops With Me" 103934	Retrd.	2000	17.50	18-22

Count on Me - P. Hillman

YEAR ISSUE	EDITION LIMIT	YEAR RETD.	ISSUE PRICE	*QUOTE U.S.$
1998 Bear w/number 0 302945	Open		5.00	5
1998 Bear w/number 1 302821	Open		5.00	5
1998 Bear w/number 2 302848	Open		5.00	5
1998 Bear w/number 3 302856	Open		5.00	5
1998 Bear w/number 4 302864	Open		5.00	5
1998 Bear w/number 5 302872	Open		5.00	5
1998 Bear w/number 6 302899	Open		5.00	5
1998 Bear w/number 7 302902	Open		5.00	5
1998 Bear w/number 8 302910	Open		5.00	5

*Quotes have been rounded up to nearest dollar

FIGURINES

Cherished Teddies/Enesco Group, Inc. to Cherished Teddies/Enesco Group, Inc.

YEAR ISSUE	EDITION LIMIT	YEAR RETD.	ISSUE PRICE	*QUOTE U.S.$
1998 Bear w/number 9 302929	Open		5.00	5

Down Strawberry Lane - P. Hillman

YEAR ISSUE	EDITION LIMIT	YEAR RETD.	ISSUE PRICE	*QUOTE U.S.$
1997 Diane "I Picked The Beary Best For You" 202991	Yr.Iss.	1997	25.00	28-45
1996 Ella "Love Grows in My Heart" 156329	Retrd.	2000	15.00	15-19
1996 Jenna "You're Berry Special To Me" 156337	Retrd.	2000	15.00	15-19
1996 Matthew "A Dash of Love Sweetens Any Day!" 156299	Retrd.	2000	15.00	15-19
1996 Tara "You're My Berry Best Friend!" 156310	Retrd.	2000	15.00	15-19
1996 Thelma "Cozy Tea For Two" 156302	Retrd.	2000	22.50	23-28
1996 Sign/Bunny/Basket of Strawberries Mini 3 Asst. 900931	Open		3.50	4

Fairy Tales - P. Hillman

YEAR ISSUE	EDITION LIMIT	YEAR RETD.	ISSUE PRICE	*QUOTE U.S.$
1999 Follow The Yellow Brick Road Collector Set: Scott "May Wisdom Follow You Wherever You Go", Tim "A Kind Heart Is The Best Gift". Leo "Courage Comes From Within", Dot "There's No Place Like Home" 476501	Yr.Iss.	1999	75.00	75-105
1999 Pinocchio "You've Got My Heart On A String" 476463	Open		30.00	30
1999 Winnie "You're My Perfect Prince" 481696	Retrd.	1999	17.50	18

Follow The Rainbow - P. Hillman

YEAR ISSUE	EDITION LIMIT	YEAR RETD.	ISSUE PRICE	*QUOTE U.S.$
1998 Carter & Elsie "We're Friends Rain Or Shine" 302791	Open		35.00	35
1998 Ellen "You Color My Rainbow" 302775	Open		20.00	20
1998 Joyce "Plant A Rainbow And Watch It Grow" 302767	Open		25.00	25

Happily Ever After - P. Hillman

YEAR ISSUE	EDITION LIMIT	YEAR RETD.	ISSUE PRICE	*QUOTE U.S.$
1998 Alicia "Through The Looking Glass, I See You!" 302465	Open		22.50	23
1998 Brett "Come To Neverland With Me" 302457	Retrd.	2000	22.50	23
1998 Christina "I Found My Prince In You" 302473	Open		22.50	23
1998 Harvey & Gigi "Finding The Path To Your Heart" 302481	Retrd.	2000	30.00	30
1998 Kelsie "Be The Apple Of My Eye" 302570	Retrd.	2000	20.00	20
1998 Lois "To Grandmother's House We Go" 302511	Open		22.50	23

Holiday Dangling - P. Hillman

YEAR ISSUE	EDITION LIMIT	YEAR RETD.	ISSUE PRICE	*QUOTE U.S.$
1996 Holden "Catchin' The Holiday Spirit!" 176095	Retrd.	1999	15.00	15
1996 Jolene "Dropping You A Holiday Greeting" 176133	Retrd.	1999	20.00	20
1996 Joy "You Always Bring Joy" 176087	Retrd.	1999	15.00	15
1996 Noel "An Old-Fashioned Noel To You" 176109	Retrd.	1999	15.00	15-17
1996 Nolan "A String Of Good Tidings" 176141	Retrd.	1999	20.00	20
1996 Santa Bear 2 asst. "Joy" "Ho Ho" 176168	Retrd.	1999	12.50	13-15

Just Between Friends - P. Hillman

YEAR ISSUE	EDITION LIMIT	YEAR RETD.	ISSUE PRICE	*QUOTE U.S.$
1998 Forgive Me 303100	Open		7.50	8
1998 Good Luck 303143	Open		7.50	8
1998 I Miss You 303127	Open		7.50	8
1998 I'm Sorry 303097	Open		7.50	8
1998 Please Smile 303135	Closed	1999	7.50	8
1998 "What A Day!" "Everything's O.K." 303119	Closed	1999	7.50	8

Let Heaven And Nature Sing - P. Hillman

YEAR ISSUE	EDITION LIMIT	YEAR RETD.	ISSUE PRICE	*QUOTE U.S.$
1999 Felicia "Joy to the World" 533890	Yr.Iss.	1999	20.00	20
2000 Emma "Let Earth Proclaim It's Peace 533904	Yr.Iss.		20.00	20

Little Sparkles - P. Hillman

YEAR ISSUE	EDITION LIMIT	YEAR RETD.	ISSUE PRICE	*QUOTE U.S.$
1997 Bear w/January Birthstone Mini Figurine 239720	Open		7.50	8-10
1997 Bear w/February Birthstone Mini Figurine 239747	Open		7.50	8-10
1997 Bear w/March Birthstone Mini Figurine 239763	Open		7.50	8-10
1997 Bear w/April Birthstone Mini Figurine 239771	Open		7.50	8-10
1997 Bear w/May Birthstone Mini Figurine 239798	Open		7.50	8-10
1997 Bear w/June Birthstone Mini Figurine 239801	Open		7.50	8-10
1997 Bear w/July Birthstone Mini Figurine 239828	Open		7.50	8-10
1997 Bear w/August Birthstone Mini Figurine 239836	Open		7.50	8-10
1997 Bear w/September Birthstone Mini Figurine 239844	Open		7.50	8-10
1997 Bear w/October Birthstone Mini Figurine 239852	Open		7.50	8-10
1997 Bear w/November Birthstone Mini Figurine 239860	Open		7.50	8-10
1997 Bear w/December Birthstone Mini Figurine 239933	Open		7.50	8-10

Love Letters From Teddie Mini - P. Hillman

YEAR ISSUE	EDITION LIMIT	YEAR RETD.	ISSUE PRICE	*QUOTE U.S.$
1997 Bear w/ "I Love Bears" Blocks 902950	Open		7.50	8-10
1997 Bear w/ "I Love Hugs" Blocks 902969	Open		7.50	8-10
1997 Bear w/ "I Love You" Blocks 156515	Open		7.50	8-10
1997 Bear w/Heart Dangling Blocks 203084	Open		7.50	8-10
1997 Bears w/ "Love" Double 203076	Open		13.50	14-16

Monthly Friends to Cherish - P. Hillman

YEAR ISSUE	EDITION LIMIT	YEAR RETD.	ISSUE PRICE	*QUOTE U.S.$
1993 Jack January Monthly "A New Year With Old Friends" 914754 (Also available through Hamilton Collection)	Retrd.	1999	15.00	15-25
1993 Phoebe February Monthly "Be Mine" 914762 (Also available through Hamilton Collection)	Retrd.	1999	15.00	15-25
1993 Mark March Monthly "Friendship Is In The Air" 914770 (Also available through Hamilton Collection)	Retrd.	1999	15.00	15-25
1993 Alan April Monthly "Showers of Friendship" 914789 (Also available through Hamilton Collection)	Retrd.	1999	15.00	15-25
1993 May May Monthly "Friendship Is In Bloom" 914797 (Also available through Hamilton Collection)	Retrd.	1999	15.00	15-45
1993 June June Monthly "Planting The Seed of Friendship" 914800 (Also available through Hamilton Collection)	Retrd.	1999	15.00	15-45
1993 Julie July Monthly "A Day in The Park" 914819 (Also available through Hamilton Collection)	Retrd.	1999	15.00	15-25
1993 Arthur August Monthly "Smooth Sailing" 914827 (Also available through Hamilton Collection)	Retrd.	1999	15.00	15-45
1993 Seth September Monthly "School Days" 914835 (Also available through Hamilton Collection)	Retrd.	1999	15.00	15-30
1993 Oscar October Monthly "Sweet Treats" 914843 (Also available through Hamilton Collection)	Retrd.	1999	15.00	15-45
1993 Nicole November Monthly "Thanks For Friends" 914851 (Also available through Hamilton Collection)	Retrd.	1999	15.00	15-25
1993 Denise December Monthly "Happy Holidays, Friend" 914878 (Also available through Hamilton Collection)	Retrd.	1999	15.00	15-25

Nativity - P. Hillman

YEAR ISSUE	EDITION LIMIT	YEAR RETD.	ISSUE PRICE	*QUOTE U.S.$
1993 "Friendship Pulls Us Through" & "Ewe Make Being Friends Special" 912867	Open		13.50	14-18
1992 Angie "I Brought The Star" 951137	Open		15.00	15-18
1995 Celeste "An Angel To Watch Over You" 141267	Open		20.00	20-28
1992 Creche & Quilt 951218	Open		50.00	50
1992 Maria, Baby & Josh "A Baby Is God's Gift of Love" "Everyone Needs a Daddy"- 950688	Open		35.00	35
1993 Nativity "Cherish The King" (musical-"O Little Town of Bethlehem") 912859	Suspd.		60.00	120-175
1993 Nativity Camel "Friends Like You Are Precious And True" 904309	Retrd.	1997	30.00	63
1994 Nativity Cow "That's What Friends Are For" 651095	Retrd.	1997	22.50	50
1993 Nativity Figurine Gift Set w/Creche 916684	Open		100.00	100
1996 Nativity Prayer Plaque "The Cherished One" 176362	Open		13.50	14
1993 Nativity w/ Creche (musical-"Silent Night") 903485	Suspd.		85.00	225-275
1994 Ronnie "I'll Play My Drum For You" 912905	Open		13.50	14-32
1992 Sammy "Little Lambs Are In My Care" 950726	Open		17.50	18
1992 Three Kings-Richard "My Gift Is Loving", Edward "My Gift Is Caring", Wilbur "My Gift Is Sharing" 950718	Open		55.00	55-75

Nursery Rhyme - P. Hillman

YEAR ISSUE	EDITION LIMIT	YEAR RETD.	ISSUE PRICE	*QUOTE U.S.$
1994 Jack & Jill "Our Friendship Will Never Tumble" 624772	Retrd.	1998	30.00	38
1994 Little Bo Peep "Looking For A Friend Like You" 624802	Retrd.	1998	22.50	30
1994 Little Jack Horner "I'm Plum Happy You're My Friend" 624780	Retrd.	1998	22.50	30
1994 Little Miss Muffet "I'm Never Afraid With You At My Side" 624799	Retrd.	1998	20.00	38
1994 Mary, Mary Quite Contrary "Friendship Blooms With Loving Care" 626074	Retrd.	1998	22.50	63
1994 Tom, Tom The Piper's Son "Wherever You Go I'll Follow" 624810	Retrd.	1998	20.00	27

Nutcracker Suite - P. Hillman

YEAR ISSUE	EDITION LIMIT	YEAR RETD.	ISSUE PRICE	*QUOTE U.S.$
1997 Collector's Set: Mouse King "Sugar Plum Dreams", Herr Drosselmeyer "Making Holiday Wishes Come True", Clara "Our Friendship Is Magical", & Boy Prince "I'll Keep You Beary Safe" 272388	Yr.Iss.	1997	70.00	85-100
1997 Nutcracker Suite Tree (musical "Dance of the Sugar-Plum Fairy") 292494	Open		45.00	45-50

Old Fashioned Country Christmas - P. Hillman

YEAR ISSUE	EDITION LIMIT	YEAR RETD.	ISSUE PRICE	*QUOTE U.S.$
1999 Annette "Tender Care Given Here" 533769	Retrd.	1999	20.00	20-25
1999 Brian "Look Out Snow! Here We Go!" 533807	Retrd.	1999	22.50	23-25
1999 Justin "We Share Forever, Whatever The Weather" 533793	Retrd.	1999	20.00	20-25
1999 Shirley "These Are The Best Kind of Days" 533777	Retrd.	1999	20.00	20-25
1999 Suzanne "Home Sweet Country Home" 533785	Retrd.	1999	20.00	20-25

Our Cherished Family - P. Hillman

YEAR ISSUE	EDITION LIMIT	YEAR RETD.	ISSUE PRICE	*QUOTE U.S.$
1994 Father "A Father Is The Bearer Of Strength" 624888	Open		13.50	14-18
1999 Fay And Arlene "Thanks For Always Being By My Side" 476684	Open		25.00	25
1998 A Gift To Behold (boy) 127922	Open		7.50	8
1998 A Gift To Behold (girl) 599352	Open		7.50	8
1998 Grandma Is God's Special Gift 127914	Open		17.50	18
1998 Grandpa Is God's Special Gift 127906	Open		17.50	18
1999 Haley and Logan "Sisters And Hugs Soothe The Soul" 534145	Open		25.00	25
1999 June And Jean "I've Always Wanted To Be Just Like You" 534153	Open		20.00	20
1999 Justine And Janice "Sisters And Friendship Are Crafted With Love" 537810	Open		25.00	25
1994 Mother "A Mother's Love Bears All Things" 624861	Open		20.00	20-25
1994 Older Daughter "Child Of Love" 624845	Open		10.00	10-15
1994 Older Son "Child Of Pride" 624829	Open		10.00	10-15
1994 Young Daughter "Child Of Kindness" 624853	Open		9.00	9-12
1994 Young Son "Child of Hope" 624837	Open		9.00	9-12

Santa - P. Hillman

YEAR ISSUE	EDITION LIMIT	YEAR RETD.	ISSUE PRICE	*QUOTE U.S.$
1995 Nickolas "You're At The Top Of My List" 141100	Yr.Iss.	1995	20.00	50
1996 Klaus "Bearer of Good Tidings" 176036	Yr.Iss.	1996	20.00	32
1997 Kris "Up On The Rooftop" 272140	Yr.Iss.	1997	22.50	32
1998 Santa "A Little Holiday R & R" 352713	Yr.Iss.	1998	22.50	30
1999 Sanford "Celebrate Family, Friends & Tradition" 534242	Yr.Iss.	1999	25.00	25-28
2000 Wolfgang "The Spirit of Christmas Is In Us All" 706701	Yr.Iss.		25.00	25

Santa Express - P. Hillman

YEAR ISSUE	EDITION LIMIT	YEAR RETD.	ISSUE PRICE	*QUOTE U.S.$
1996 Car of Toys "Rolling Along With Friends and Smiles" 219096	Retrd.	1998	17.50	18-35
1996 Casey "Friendship Is The Perfect End To The Holidays" 219525	Retrd.	1998	22.50	23-49
1997 Cindy "This Train Is Bound For Holiday Surprises!" 219177	Retrd.	1998	17.50	25-30
1996 Colin "He Knows If You've Been Bad or Good" 219088	Retrd.	1998	17.50	18-35
1997 Kirby "Heading Into The Holidays With Deer Friends" 219118	Retrd.	1998	17.50	25-30
1996 Lionel "All Aboard the Santa Express" 219061	Retrd.	1998	22.50	23-49
1997 Nick "Ho, Ho, Ho — To The Holidays We Go!" 219312	Retrd.	1998	17.50	25-30
1997 Snow Bear 269905	Closed	1999	12.50	13-20
1997 Street Lamp and Bear 269913	Retrd.	1999	15.00	15-19
1996 Tony "A First Class Delivery For You!" 219487	Retrd.	1998	17.50	18-26

Santa's Workshop - P. Hillman

YEAR ISSUE	EDITION LIMIT	YEAR RETD.	ISSUE PRICE	*QUOTE U.S.$
1995 Ginger "Painting Your Holidays With Love" 141127	Retrd.	1998	22.50	23
1995 Holly "A Cup of Homemade Love" 141119	Retrd.	1998	18.50	19-24
1995 Meri "Handsewn Holidays" 141135	Retrd.	1998	20.00	20
1996 Ornaments/Mailsack/North Pole Sign Mini 3 Asst. 176079	Closed	1999	15.00	15
1995 Santa's Workshop Nightlight 141925	Closed	1999	75.00	75
1995 Yule "Building a Sturdy Friendship" 141143	Retrd.	1998	22.50	23

The Springtime Angel Series - P. Hillman

YEAR ISSUE	EDITION LIMIT	YEAR RETD.	ISSUE PRICE	*QUOTE U.S.$
2000 Chantel & Fawn "We're Kindred Spirits" 661740	Yr.Iss.		45.00	45

The Springtime Teddies Collection - P. Hillman

YEAR ISSUE	EDITION LIMIT	YEAR RETD.	ISSUE PRICE	*QUOTE U.S.$
2000 Dawn "You Don't Have To Search Far To Find Your Rainbow" 739049	Open		20.00	20

Sugar & Spice - P. Hillman

YEAR ISSUE	EDITION LIMIT	YEAR RETD.	ISSUE PRICE	*QUOTE U.S.$
1998 Missy, Cookie, Riley "A Special Recipe For Our Friendship" 352586	Retrd.	2000	35.00	35
1998 Pamela & Grayson "A Dash of Love to Warm Your Heart" 352616	Retrd.	2000	22.50	23
1998 Sharon "Sweetness Pours From My Heart" 352594	Retrd.	2000	20.00	20
1998 Wayne "Spoonfuls of Sweetness" 352608	Retrd.	2000	20.00	20

Sweet Heart Ball - P. Hillman

YEAR ISSUE	EDITION LIMIT	YEAR RETD.	ISSUE PRICE	*QUOTE U.S.$
1996 Craig & Cheri "Sweethearts Forever" 156485	Retrd.	1999	25.00	25-28
1996 Darla "My Heart Wishes For You" 156469	Retrd.	1999	20.00	20-25
1996 Darrel "Love Unveils A Happy Heart" 156450	Retrd.	1999	17.50	18-20
1997 Harry & Katherine "You're The Queen/King Of My Heart" 302732	Yr.Iss.	1997	65.00	65-68
1996 Jilly "Won't You Be My Sweetheart?" 156477	Retrd.	1999	17.50	18-22
1996 Marian "You're The Hero Of My Heart" 156442	Retrd.	1999	20.00	20-25

*Quotes have been rounded up to nearest dollar

YEAR ISSUE	EDITION LIMIT	YEAR RETD.	ISSUE PRICE	*QUOTE U.S.$
1996 Robin "You Steal My Heart Away" 156434	Retrd.	1999	17.50	18-20
1997 Sweetheart Collector Set/3, (Balcony displayer, Romeo "There's No Sweeter Rose Than You" & Juliet "Wherefore Art Thou Romeo?" 203114	Yr.Iss.	1997	60.00	75

T Is For Teddies - P. Hillman

YEAR ISSUE	EDITION LIMIT	YEAR RETD.	ISSUE PRICE	*QUOTE U.S.$
1995 Bear w/"A" Block 158488A	Open		5.00	5-7
1995 Bear w/"B" Block 158488B	Open		5.00	5-7
1995 Bear w/"C" Block 158488C	Open		5.00	5-7
1995 Bear w/"D" Block 158488D	Open		5.00	5-7
1995 Bear w/"E" Block 158488E	Open		5.00	5-7
1995 Bear w/"F" Block 158488F	Open		5.00	5-7
1995 Bear w/"G" Block 158488G	Open		5.00	5-7
1995 Bear w/"H" Block 158488H	Open		5.00	5-7
1995 Bear w/"I" Block 158488I	Open		5.00	5-7
1995 Bear w/"J" Block 158488J	Open		5.00	5-7
1995 Bear w/"K" Block 158488K	Open		5.00	5-7
1995 Bear w/"L" Block 158488L	Open		5.00	5-7
1995 Bear w/"M" Block 158488M	Open		5.00	5-7
1995 Bear w/"N" Block 158488N	Open		5.00	5-7
1995 Bear w/"O" Block 158488O	Open		5.00	5-7
1995 Bear w/"P" Block 158488P	Open		5.00	5-7
1995 Bear w/"Q" Block 158488Q	Open		5.00	5-7
1995 Bear w/"R" Block 158488R	Open		5.00	5-7
1995 Bear w/"S" Block 158488S	Open		5.00	5-7
1995 Bear w/"T" Block 158488T	Open		5.00	5-7
1995 Bear w/"U" Block 158488U	Open		5.00	5-7
1995 Bear w/"V" Block 158488V	Open		5.00	5-7
1995 Bear w/"W" Block 158488W	Open		5.00	5-7
1995 Bear w/"X" Block 158488X	Open		5.00	5-7
1995 Bear w/"Y" Block 158488Y	Open		5.00	5-7
1995 Bear w/"Z" Block 158488Z	Open		5.00	5-7

Teddies in Motion - P. Hillman

YEAR ISSUE	EDITION LIMIT	YEAR RETD.	ISSUE PRICE	*QUOTE U.S.$
1999 Chad "With You My Spirits Soar" 477524	Open		20.00	20
1999 Dave "An Oldie But Goodie" 477494	Open		20.00	20
1999 Dustin and Austin "Hold On For The Ride Of Your Life" 477508	Open		30.00	30
1999 Ken "You Make My Heart Race" 477559	Open		20.00	20
1999 Roger "You Set My Heart in Motion" 477516	Open		20.00	20

Through The Years - P. Hillman

YEAR ISSUE	EDITION LIMIT	YEAR RETD.	ISSUE PRICE	*QUOTE U.S.$
1993 "Cradled With Love" Baby 911356	Open		16.50	17-25
1993 "Beary Special One" Age 1 911348	Open		13.50	14-20
1993 "Two Sweet Two Bear" Age 2 911321	Open		13.50	14-19
1993 "Three Cheers For You" Age 3 911313	Open		15.00	15-20
1993 "Unfolding Happy Wishes Four You" Age 4 911305	Open		15.00	15-22
1993 "Color Me Five" Age 5 911291	Open		15.00	15-23
1993 "Chalking Up Six Wishes" Age 6 911283	Open		16.50	17-24
1998 "Seven Is As Sweet As Honey" Age 7 466239	Open		16.50	17
1998 "Being Eight Is Really Great!" Age 8 466247	Open		16.50	17
1998 "Being Nine Is Really Fine!" Age 9 466255	Open		16.50	17
1998 "Count To Ten...and Celebrate!" Age 10 466263	Open		16.50	17

U.S. Military Bears - P. Hillman

YEAR ISSUE	EDITION LIMIT	YEAR RETD.	ISSUE PRICE	*QUOTE U.S.$
2000 Air Force 742988	Open		17.50	18
2000 Army 706930	Open		17.50	18
2000 Coast Guard 742961	Open		17.50	18
2000 Marines 706949	Open		17.50	18
2000 Navy 706957	Open		17.50	18

Up In The Attic - P. Hillman

YEAR ISSUE	EDITION LIMIT	YEAR RETD.	ISSUE PRICE	*QUOTE U.S.$
1998 Kaitlyn "Old Treasures, New Memories" 302600	Yr.Iss.	1998	50.00	50-65
2000 Lauren "Cherished Memories Never Fade" 308684	Yr.Iss.	2000	35.00	35-53
1999 Sarah "Memories To Wear And Share"308676	Yr.Iss.	1999	30.00	30-45

Victorian Bonnets & Bows - P. Hillman

YEAR ISSUE	EDITION LIMIT	YEAR RETD.	ISSUE PRICE	*QUOTE U.S.$
1999 Collette "Outer Beauty Is A Reflection Of Inner Beauty" 662518	Open		20.00	20
1999 Teresa "You Have Such Wonderful Grace" 662461	Open		20.00	20
1999 Vanessa "You're My Shelter From The Storm" 662437	Open		22.50	23
1999 Wilfred "A Lifetime Of Friendship...A Trunk Full Of Memories" 662496	Open		25.00	25

We Bear Thanks - P. Hillman

YEAR ISSUE	EDITION LIMIT	YEAR RETD.	ISSUE PRICE	*QUOTE U.S.$
1996 Barbara "Giving Thanks For Our Family" 141305	Retrd.	1997	12.50	13-29
1996 Dina "Bear In Mind, You're Special" 141275	Retrd.	1997	15.00	15-30
1996 John "Bear In Mind, You're Special" 141283	Retrd.	1997	15.00	15-33
1996 Rick "Suited Up For The Holidays" 141291	Retrd.	1997	12.50	38
1996 Table With Food / Dog " We Bear Thanks" 141542	Retrd.	1997	30.00	30

Wedding - P. Hillman

YEAR ISSUE	EDITION LIMIT	YEAR RETD.	ISSUE PRICE	*QUOTE U.S.$
1999 Bride "Beautiful And Bearly Blushing" 476285	Open		15.00	15
1999 Groom "A Beary Special Groom To Be" 476315	Open		15.00	15
1999 Bridesmaid "So Glad To Be Part Of Your Special Day" 476323	Open		10.00	10
1999 Groomsman "The Time Has Come For Wedded Bliss" 476366	Open		10.00	10
1999 Ringbearer "I've Got The Most Important Job!" 476382	Open		9.00	9
1999 Flower Girl "Sweet Flowers For The Bride" 476374	Open		9.00	9
1999 Wedding Collectors Set (3 pc.) 510254	Open		50.00	50

Winter Bear Festival - P. Hillman

YEAR ISSUE	EDITION LIMIT	YEAR RETD.	ISSUE PRICE	*QUOTE U.S.$
1997 Adam "It's A Holiday On Ice" 269751	Retrd.	2000	20.00	20-22
1997 Boy Waterball (musical-"White Christmas") 292575	Closed	1999	45.00	20-22
1997 Candace "Skating On Holiday Joy" 269778	Retrd.	2000	20.00	20-25
1997 Girl Waterball (musical-"Let It Snow") 272884	Closed	1998	45.00	45
1997 James "Going My Way For The Holidays" 269786	Retrd.	2000	25.00	25
1997 Lindsey & Lyndon "Walking In A Winter Wonderland" 141178	Retrd.	2000	30.00	30-40
1997 Mitch "Friendship Never Melts Away" 269735	Retrd.	2000	30.00	30-42
1997 Spencer "I'm Head Over Skis For You" 269743	Retrd.	2000	20.00	20-28
1997 Ted "Snow Fun When You're Not Around" 269727	Retrd.	2000	18.50	30

Chubby Charmers/Miss Martha Originals

Chubby Charmers - M. Root

YEAR ISSUE	EDITION LIMIT	YEAR RETD.	ISSUE PRICE	*QUOTE U.S.$
2000 Babette - 6003	Open		20.00	20
2000 Benny - 6008	Open		20.00	20
2000 Caroline - 6001	Open		27.50	28
2000 Georgette - 6004	Open		20.00	20
2000 Hazle - 6007	Open		20.00	20
2000 Mimi - 6002	Open		20.00	20
2000 Renee - 6005	Open		18.00	18
2000 Roxanne - 6006	Open		20.00	20
2000 Tallula - 6000	Open		20.00	20

Coyne's & Company

American Chestnut Folk Art - P. & D. Bretz

YEAR ISSUE	EDITION LIMIT	YEAR RETD.	ISSUE PRICE	*QUOTE U.S.$
1999 Amos AM1051	Open		65.00	65
2000 Belle AM1055	Open		30.00	30
2000 Chester AM2001	Open		40.00	40
1999 An Ernest Harvest AM1006	Open		50.00	50
1999 Ernest Isn't Hungry Anymore AM1003	Open		35.00	35
1999 Ernest Labors AM1001	Open		45.00	45
1999 Ernest Loves You AM1002	Open		35.00	35
1999 Everything's Just Ducky AM1075	Open		55.00	55
2000 Faith Makes It Grow AM1013	Open		25.00	25
2000 First Sign of Spring AM1012	Open		25.00	25
2000 Franklin AM2005	Open		55.00	55
1999 Friends Come in All Sizes AM1104	Open		50.00	50
1999 Gaggle of Garrulous Geese AM1077	Open		45.00	45
1999 Hannah AM1076	Open		40.00	40
1999 Isaac AM1052	Open		40.00	40
2000 Jenny AM1215	Open		35.00	35
2000 Julius AM1057	Open		27.50	28
1999 Junior Achievement AM1008	Open		25.00	25
1999 A Junior High AM1010	Open		20.00	20
1999 The Lettuce is Always Greener AM1007	3,500		70.00	70
1999 Lewis AM1004	Open		50.00	50
1999 Making New Friends AM1110	Open		25.00	25
2000 Nature's Small Miracles AM1011	Open		20.00	20
2000 Old Roy AM1054	Open		30.00	30
1999 Olive, This Little Piggy Went to Market AM1053	Open		55.00	55
1999 Open Water Expedition AM1112	Open		25.00	25
2000 Pearl and Chicks AM2003	Open		45.00	45
1999 Petey, Any for Me? AM1106	Open		25.00	25
1999 Petey, Look Out Bee-Low AM1105	Open		20.00	20
1999 Pixie Smells Sweet AM1009	Open		20.00	20
2000 Puddles, Dinky, & Webster AM1216	Open		10.00	10
2000 Raleigh AM2002	Open		35.00	35
2000 Roscoe AM1079	Open		25.00	25
2000 Rueben and Chicks AM2004	Open		55.00	55
1999 Satisfied Consumer, Full Belly Picnic Area AM1102	Open		65.00	65
2000 Sonny AM2006	Open		10.00	10
2000 Story Time AM1014	Open		60.00	60
2000 Sweet Dreams, Ernest AM1015	3,500		65.00	65
2000 Sweet Vidalia AM1078	Open		70.00	70
1999 Welcome, Open House AM1109	Open		25.00	25
1999 Wesley Hard at Work AM1108	Open		75.00	75
1999 Wesley Pleads Innocent AM1103	Open		65.00	65
1999 Wesley, Honey... AM1101	Open		45.00	45
1999 Where Friends Gather AM1111	Open		70.00	70

American Chestnut Folk Art Christmas - P. & D. Bretz

YEAR ISSUE	EDITION LIMIT	YEAR RETD.	ISSUE PRICE	*QUOTE U.S.$
1999 After Work AM1207	3,500		65.00	65
1999 Afternoon at Frozen Pond AM1203	3,500		65.00	65
1999 Dashing thru Snow AM1202	3,500		50.00	50
1999 Flight in the Starry Night AM1206	3,500		75.00	75
1999 Friends Help AM1201	3,500		60.00	60
1999 A Gift for the Giver AM1212	Open		30.00	30
1999 I Saved the Best for Last AM1211	Open		30.00	30
1999 A Little Help Please AM1205	3,500		65.00	65
1999 Oh, What Fun AM1213	Open		33.00	33
1999 Please Let Me Go, Too! AM1208	Open		30.00	30
1999 Practice for the Christmas Parade AM1214	Open		35.00	35
1999 Up, Up and Away AM1204	3,500		70.00	70

Ashland Studio Santas - J. McKenna

YEAR ISSUE	EDITION LIMIT	YEAR RETD.	ISSUE PRICE	*QUOTE U.S.$
2000 Americana Santa JM1029	Open		12.00	12
2000 Bears Galore JM1011	Open		35.00	35
2000 Bringing Home Christmas JM1001	Open		45.00	45
2000 Christmas Carols JM1026	Open		40.00	40
2000 Christmas Dreams JM1003	3,500		75.00	75
2000 Christmas Journey JM1012	Open		50.00	50
2000 Christmas Play JM1032	Open		12.00	12
2000 Fishing Santa JM1016	Open		25.00	25
2000 For Santa's Eyes Only JM1030	Open		12.00	12
2000 Golfing Santa JM1017	Open		35.00	35
2000 Lending a Hand JM1028	Open		45.00	45
2000 Patriotic Santa JM1019	Open		50.00	50
2000 Protective Guidance JM1010	3,500		50.00	50
2000 The Protector Fireman Santa JM1033	Open		12.00	12
2000 Reminiscing JM1008	Open		40.00	40
2000 Sergeant Santa JM1031	Open		12.00	12
2000 The Story Teller JM1027	Open		25.00	25
2000 Teaching Santa JM1015	Open		25.00	25
2000 Woodland Santa JM1002	Open		45.00	45

Ashland Studio Snow Angels - J. McKenna

YEAR ISSUE	EDITION LIMIT	YEAR RETD.	ISSUE PRICE	*QUOTE U.S.$
2000 First Time on Skis JM2013	Open		6.00	6
2000 A Helping Hand (mini) JM2017	Open		6.00	6
2000 A Helping Hand JM2003	Open		15.00	15
2000 I'm Going to Catch You JM2010	Open		6.00	6
2000 I'm Ready (mini) JM2018	Open		6.00	6
2000 I'm Ready JM2004	Open		15.00	15
2000 Ice Skating (mini) JM2020	Open		6.00	6
2000 Ice Skating JM2006	Open		17.00	17
2000 Let it Snow (mini) JM2021	Open		6.00	6
2000 Let it Snow JM2007	Open		15.00	15
2000 Let's Go Sleigh Riding JM2011	Open		6.00	6
2000 Let's Go Sleigh Riding JM2026	Open		25.00	25
2000 Making Do JM2001	Open		15.00	15
2000 Making Do JM2015	Open		6.00	6
2000 Making Snow Angels (mini) JM2016	Open		6.00	6
2000 Making Snow Angels JM2002	Open		15.00	15
2000 O' Christmas Tree (musical) JM2024M	Open		50.00	50
2000 O' Christmas Tree (musical) JM2025M	Open		36.00	36
2000 Snow Angel Mountain Display JM2022	Open		60.00	60
2000 Snow Coasting JM2008	Open		15.00	15
2000 Wait for Me JM2012	Open		6.00	6
2000 We're a Team (mini) JM2019	Open		6.00	6
2000 We're a Team JM2005	Open		15.00	15
2000 Welcome to Snow Mountain JM2014	Open		6.00	6
2000 Whoa...Here Goes JM2009	Open		6.00	6
2000 You're Too Cute! (musical) JM2023M	Open		30.00	30

Bavarian Heritage Collection - Coyne's & Company

YEAR ISSUE	EDITION LIMIT	YEAR RETD.	ISSUE PRICE	*QUOTE U.S.$
1999 Away We Go BH1005	Open		25.00	25
1999 Black Forest Santa BH1003	Open		35.00	35
1999 Boughs of Bounty BH1009	Open		25.00	25
1999 Checking it Twice BH1001	Open		35.00	35
1999 Christmas Cheer BH1010	Open		25.00	25
1999 Happy Home BH1006	Open		25.00	25
1999 Home for the Holidays BH1018	3,500		80.00	80
1999 A Hug for a Faithful Friend BH1019M	Open		75.00	75
1999 On Top of Old Smokey BH1017	Open		35.00	35
1999 Over Hill and Hollow Santa BH1016	Open		30.00	30
1999 Safe in Santa's Lap BH1015	Open		30.00	30
1999 Santa of Music BH1007	Open		25.00	25
1999 Santa's Sleigh of Wonder BH1012M	3,500		60.00	60
1999 Shepherd of Joy BH1002	Open		35.00	35
1999 Special Delivery BH1004	Open		35.00	35
1999 Tailor of Treasures Santa BH1020	Open		60.00	60
1999 Warm With Love BH1008	Open		25.00	25

David Frykman Arctic Fisherman - D. Frykman

YEAR ISSUE	EDITION LIMIT	YEAR RETD.	ISSUE PRICE	*QUOTE U.S.$
2000 Penguin's Best Friend DF1508	3,500		40.00	40

David Frykman Christmas Collection - D. Frykman

YEAR ISSUE	EDITION LIMIT	YEAR RETD.	ISSUE PRICE	*QUOTE U.S.$
1999 Arctic Armada, set/4 DF2060	5,000		69.95	70
1999 Arctic Express DF2027	3,000		70.00	70
2000 As Time Goes By DF2072	Yr.Iss.		30.00	30
1995 Bear Back Holiday DF2007	2,500	1996	65.00	65-70
1998 Bear Backin' DF2018	3,000		90.00	90
2000 Bear Necessities DF2031	3,500		60.00	60
1995 Caribou Christmas DF2008	2,500	1996	60.00	60-70
1999 Christmoose is Coming DF2026	3,000		77.00	77
1999 Cross-Country Christmas DF2025	3,000		77.00	77
1999 Father Time DF2028 (Millennium Piece)	Yr.Iss.	1999	50.00	50
1999 Father Time, signed DF2028 (Millennium Piece)	2,000	1999	50.00	50
1996 Follow That Sleigh DF2011	2,500	1997	100.00	100-125
1998 The Frosty Night Flyers DF2050	5,000	1998	69.95	70-80
1998 Go Faster DF2016	3,000		77.00	77
1998 Grand Casino Exclusive DF2041GC	Closed	1998	45.00	45
1996 Hang A Shining Star DF2020	5,000	1996	79.95	80
1997 Just Head South DF2015	2,500	1999	100.00	100
1997 Last Stop (musical) DF2014M	2,500	1998	70.00	70
1998 Making Spirits Bright DF2021	3,000		100.00	100
1997 Moosh DF2012	2,500	1998	70.00	70

*Quotes have been rounded up to nearest dollar

FIGURINES

Coyne's & Company to Crystal World

YEAR ISSUE	EDITION LIMIT	YEAR RETD.	ISSUE PRICE	*QUOTE U.S.$
1995 O Joyful Sound DF2006M	2,500		120.00	120
1996 Oh What Fun It Is To Ride DF2030	Yr.Iss.	1996	40.00	40
1998 On Top Of The World DF2017	3,000		100.00	100
2000 On, Blitzen DF2029	3,500		70.00	70
1994 Polar Bear Dance DF2003	2,400	1997	100.00	100-110
1997 Santa's Ark DF2013	2,500	1998	77.00	77
1999 Santa's Christmas Presence DF2024	3,000		60.00	60
1994 Santa's Flight DF2002	2,400	1997	120.00	120
1996 Special Delivery DF2010	2,500	1997	80.00	80-95
1997 Tannenbaum Express DF2040	5,000	1997	69.95	90-95
1999 Tannenbaum Timberwolf DF2023	3,000		100.00	100
2000 Times Are A Changing (musical) DF2071M	Yr.Iss.		50.00	50
1999 Tis The Season DF1306M (5th Anniversary)	Yr.Iss.	1999	30.00	30
1994 Toymaker's March DF2001	2,400	1997	80.00	80
1996 Winter Walk DF2009	2,500	1997	60.00	60

David Frykman Old Farmer - D. Frykman

YEAR ISSUE	EDITION LIMIT	YEAR RETD.	ISSUE PRICE	*QUOTE U.S.$
1997 Farmers Market, set/3 DF3010	3,000	1998	50.00	50

David Frykman Oldest Sailor - D. Frykman

YEAR ISSUE	EDITION LIMIT	YEAR RETD.	ISSUE PRICE	*QUOTE U.S.$
1999 Land Ho! DF3504	3,500		85.00	85

David Frykman Santa Crafted Musicals - D. Frykman

YEAR ISSUE	EDITION LIMIT	YEAR RETD.	ISSUE PRICE	*QUOTE U.S.$
1995 The Christmas Cart DF2004M	2,500	1997	80.00	80

David Frykman The Golfer - D. Frykman

YEAR ISSUE	EDITION LIMIT	YEAR RETD.	ISSUE PRICE	*QUOTE U.S.$
2000 A Eagle Time DF4601	3,500		50.00	50

Folkwoods Studio Christmas Series - A. Strom

YEAR ISSUE	EDITION LIMIT	YEAR RETD.	ISSUE PRICE	*QUOTE U.S.$
2000 Harvest Festival Santa	3,500		90.00	90
2000 Large Reindeer FW1010	Open		50.00	50
2000 Santa Holding Beehive & Birdhouse FW1009	Open		50.00	50
2000 Santa Holding Hobby Horse & Bear FW1001	Open		95.00	95
2000 Santa Holding Pocket Watch FW1004	Open		75.00	75
2000 Santa Holding Skates & Sled FW1008	Open		80.00	80
2000 Santa In Red Sweater Skiing FW1003	Open		90.00	90
2000 Santa w/Gifts In Red Robe Skiing FW1005	Open		55.00	55
2000 Santa w/Green Scarf Skiing FW1006	Open		40.00	40
2000 Santa w/Sack Of Fruit Holding Tree FW1007	Open		50.00	50
2000 Small Reindeer FW1011	Open		35.00	35

Folkwoods Studio Lodge Series - A. Strom

YEAR ISSUE	EDITION LIMIT	YEAR RETD.	ISSUE PRICE	*QUOTE U.S.$
2000 Evergreen Trees, Set/3 FW3007	Open		45.00	45
2000 Fisherman Holding Giant Fish FW2013	Open		55.00	55
2000 Fisherman Holding Stringer Of Fish FW2002	Open		60.00	60
2000 Fisherman w/Fishing Pole Holding Northern Pike Fw2001	Open		55.00	55
2000 Fishermen With Three Fish FW2015	Open		55.00	55
2000 Hunter w/Duck Decoys FW2016	Open		30.00	30
2000 Large Black Bear Walking FW2006	Open		35.00	35
2000 Large Box w/Reindeer On Top FW3003	Open		25.00	25
2000 Large Hinged Box w/Walleye On Cover FW2010	Open		40.00	40
2000 Medium Black Bear Standing FW2007	Open		23.00	23
2000 Moose w/Antlers FW2004	Open		30.00	30
2000 Reindeer w/Antlers FW2003	Open		40.00	40
2000 Small Black Bear Standing FW2008	Open		17.50	18
2000 Small Black Bear Walking FW2009	Open		13.00	13
2000 Small Box w/Animals On Top FW3004	Open		17.00	17
2000 Small Hinged Box w/Trout On Cover FW2011	Open		27.50	28
2000 Standing Black Bear Holding Pine Cone, Candle Holder FW2017	Open		35.00	35
2000 Standing Black Bear w/Birch Backpack Holding Friends "Northwoods Sojourner" FW2018	3,500		120.00	120
2000 Trimmed Evergreen Trees, Set Of 3 FW2005	Open		40.00	40
2000 Woodsman In Checkered Overcoat w/Black Bear FW2014	Open		55.00	55
2000 Woodsman w/Forest Friends FW2012	Open		45.00	45

The Little Street Christmas Collection™ - E. Watrus

YEAR ISSUE	EDITION LIMIT	YEAR RETD.	ISSUE PRICE	*QUOTE U.S.$
2000 An Angel For You EW2015	Open		12.00	12
2000 Are You Sure You Can Fly? EW2001	Open		12.00	12
2000 The Christmas Carolers EW2018	Open		15.00	15
2000 Christmas Morning EW2010	Open		15.00	15
2000 The Christmas Shepherd EW2008	Open		12.00	12
2000 Christmas Wishes EW2006	Open		12.00	12
2000 Delivering Joy To The World EW2020	Open		13.50	14
2000 The Elfin Express EW2017	Open		13.50	14
2000 The Good Neighbor EW2005	Open		12.00	12
2000 He'll Bearly Notice EW2013	Open		12.00	12
2000 Let's Make Another! EW2011	Open		15.00	15
2000 Look Mom, No Hands! EW2019	Open		12.00	12
2000 The Newborn King EW2003	Open		15.00	15
2000 Noel EW2016	Open		13.50	14
2000 Oh Christmas Tree EW2009	Open		10.00	10
2000 The Perfect Star! EW2021	Open		13.50	14
2000 Santa & His Helpers EW2007	Open		13.50	14
2000 A Stocking Full of Joy EW2002	Open		15.00	15
2000 Up, Up, And Away! EW2028	5,000		40.00	40
2000 We Can Do It! EW2022	Open		17.00	17
2000 Winter Wonderland EW2004	Open		13.50	14

The Little Street Everyday Collection™ - E. Watrus

YEAR ISSUE	EDITION LIMIT	YEAR RETD.	ISSUE PRICE	*QUOTE U.S.$
2000 Ballet Class EW1909	Open		10.00	10
2000 Cinderella EW1102	Open		30.00	30
2000 Dancin' The Night Away EW1402	Open		12.00	12
2000 Earth Angel EW1901	Open		10.00	10
2000 Forever Friends EW1903	Open		13.50	14
2000 Future Fish Stories EW1201	Open		15.00	15
2000 Goldilocks and the Three Bears EW1104	Open		15.00	15
2000 Got Spurs? EW1305	Open		10.00	10
2000 He's A Ringer EW1908	Open		10.00	10
2000 I Do EW1404	Open		12.00	12
2000 I Thought Flying Was For The Birds EW1306	Open		10.00	10
2000 I'll Give My Heart To You EW1403	Open		12.00	12
2000 Jack & Jill EW1105	Open		17.00	17
2000 Kitty Litter EW1302	Open		12.00	12
2000 Little Red Riding Hood EW1105	Open		12.00	12
2000 Mother's Little Helper EW1906	Open		12.00	12
2000 My Favorite Fairy EW1902	Open		8.00	8
2000 Noah's Ark EW1910	3,500		45.00	45
2000 Nurse Nightingale EW1001	Open		10.00	10
2000 Over The Moon EW1103	Open		13.50	14
2000 Piggy-Back Ride EW1304	Open		10.00	10
2000 Puppy Love EW1301	Open		12.00	12
2000 Queen of the Jungle EW1303	Open		10.00	10
2000 Shoot The Rapids EW1904	Open		15.00	15
2000 Sweethearts EW1401	Open		13.50	14
2000 The Teacher's Aide EW1004	Open		12.00	12
2000 Terri's Garden EW1905	Open		13.50	14
2000 The Three Little Pigs EW1101	Open		15.00	15
2000 Under The Sea EW1907	Open		10.00	10

Williraye Studio Christmas Collection - J.&B. Punzel-Schuknecht

YEAR ISSUE	EDITION LIMIT	YEAR RETD.	ISSUE PRICE	*QUOTE U.S.$
1997 Along for the Ride WW2006	2,500	1998	130.00	130
1996 Always Flying South WW2001	1,500	1997	75.00	75
1997 A Country Carol, set/4 WW2031	5,000	1998	60.00	60
1998 A Country Church, set/5 WW2051	5,000	1999	60.00	60
1996 Everything's Pointing North WW3051	1,500	1998	150.00	150
2000 Feline Express WW2366	Open		60.00	60
2000 Fowl Weather Flight WW2754	3,500		90.00	90
2000 Lean on Me WW2356	5,000		80.00	80
1998 Long Winter's Nap WW2217	3,500		80.00	80
2000 Master of Moguls WW2353	Open		35.00	35
1999 The Millennium Angel WW2231	Yr.Iss.	1999	35.00	35
1998 Moose-Stache WW3052	3,500		65.00	65
1999 Moory Christmas WW2286	3,500		100.00	100
1996 Risky Road Ahead WW2002	1,500	1998	150.00	150
2000 Skating Party WW2351	5,000		79.95	80
1999 A Snowman Serenade WW2280	3,500		90.00	90
1999 Starlight Flight WW2275	3,500		150.00	150
1997 When Pigs Fly? WW2009	3,000	1998	77.00	77
1997 ...Whoa WW2007	2,500	1998	100.00	100
1999 Winter Friends, set/4 WW2061	5,000	1999	59.95	60
1997 Wintery Flight WW2008	3,000	1997	77.00	77

Williraye Studio Spring Collection - J.&B. Punzel-Schuknecht

YEAR ISSUE	EDITION LIMIT	YEAR RETD.	ISSUE PRICE	*QUOTE U.S.$
1997 Blue Ribbon Bossy WW3021	2,500	1997	85.00	85
1999 Come Blow Your Horn WW3022	3,500	1999	85.00	85
1997 A Country Picnic WW2021	3,000	1997	80.00	80
1998 A Country School WW2041	5,000	1999	60.00	60
1998 Country Taxi WW3033	3,000		115.00	115
2000 Miss Liberty WW1308	3,500		80.00	80
1999 Uncle Sam WW1306	3,500		80.00	80

Crystal World

All God's Creatures - Various

YEAR ISSUE	EDITION LIMIT	YEAR RETD.	ISSUE PRICE	*QUOTE U.S.$
1997 Allie Gator - R. Nakai	Open		100.00	100
2000 American Eagle - T. Suzuki	Open		195.00	195
2000 Baby Deer - R. Takii	Open		110.00	110
1990 Baby Dinosaur - T. Suzuki	Closed	1992	50.00	50
1990 Betsy Bunny - T. Suzuki	Closed	1992	32.00	32
1997 Buffalo - Team	Open		350.00	350
2000 Charleston Charlie - T. Suzuki	Open		60.00	60
1990 Clara Cow - T. Suzuki	Closed	1991	32.00	32
1996 Freddy Frog - R. Nakai	Open		27.00	27
1996 Frieda Frog - R. Nakai	Open		35.00	35
1990 Georgie Giraffe - T. Suzuki	Closed	1992	32.00	32
1997 Giant Sea Turtle - Team	Closed	2000	250.00	250
1990 Henry Hippo - T. Suzuki	Closed	1992	32.00	32
1994 Hoot Owls - N. Mulargia	Closed	1998	45.00	45
1990 Jumbo Elephant - T. Suzuki	Open		32.00	32
1997 Junior (Elephant) - R. Nakai	Open		110.00	110
1995 Ling Ling - T. Suzuki	Closed	1997	53.00	53
1998 Little Owl - T. Suzuki	Open		100.00	100
1997 Mama Elephant - R. Nakai	Closed	2000	250.00	250
1990 Mikey Monkey - T. Suzuki	Closed	1991	32.00	32
2000 Mother and Cub - R. Takii	Open		175.00	175
1995 Percy Piglet - T. Suzuki	Closed	1996	19.00	19
1993 Pig - N. Mulargia	Closed	1995	50.00	50
1993 Playful Seal - T. Suzuki	Closed	1998	42.00	42
2000 Ponder - T. Suzuki	Open		55.00	55
1997 Proud Peacock - R. Nakai	Open		150.00	150
1994 Seal - R. Nakai	Closed	1996	46.00	46
1999 Thrills 'N Chills - R. Takii	Open		195.00	195
1992 Trumpeting Elephant - T. Suzuki	Closed	1996	50.00	50
1993 Turtle - R. Nakai	Closed	1996	65.00	65
1995 Wilbur in Love - N. Mulargia	Closed	1996	90.00	90
1994 Wilbur the Pig - T. Suzuki	Open		45.00	45

Bon Voyage Collection - Various

YEAR ISSUE	EDITION LIMIT	YEAR RETD.	ISSUE PRICE	*QUOTE U.S.$
1990 Airplane, sm. - T. Suzuki	Closed	1993	200.00	200
1995 Amish Buggy - R. Nakai	Closed	1997	160.00	160
1995 Amish Buggy w/Wood Base - R. Nakai	Closed	1997	190.00	190
1994 Bermuda Rig Sailboat - R. Nakai	Open		50.00	50
1998 Bi-Plane - T. Suzuki	Open		40.00	75
1992 Bi-Plane, mini - T. Suzuki	Closed	1998	65.00	65
1991 Cruise Ship -T. Suzuki	1,000		2000.00	2000
1997 Cruise Ship, med. - R. Nakai	Open		550.00	550
1995 Cruise Ship, mini - N. Mulargia	Open		100.00	100
1994 Cruise Ship, sm. - T. Suzuki	Open		250.00	250
1993 Express Train - N. Mulargia	Closed	1993	95.00	100
1998 Float Plane - T. Suzuki	Open		40.00	75
1994 Mainsail Sailboat - R. Nakai	Open		110.00	110
1990 Orbiting Space Shuttle - T. Suzuki	Closed	1997	300.00	300
1991 Orbiting Space Shuttle, sm. - T. Suzuki	Closed	1999	150.00	150
1991 The Rainbow Express - N. Mulargia	Closed	1993	125.00	130
1993 Sailboat - R. Nakai	Open		90.00	90
1992 Sailing Ship - N. Mulargia	Closed	1998	38.00	38
1991 Schooner - N. Mulargia	Closed	1995	95.00	95
1997 Schooner - R. Nakai	Closed	1998	60.00	60
1990 Space Shuttle Launch, sm. - T. Suzuki	Closed	1996	265.00	270
1994 Spinnaker Sailboat - R. Nakai	Open		130.00	130
1990 Square Rigger - R. Nakai	Open		250.00	270
1995 Tall Ship - R. Nakai	Closed	2000	395.00	395
1998 Titanic -T. Suzuki	1,912		175.00	175
1990 Train Set, lg. - T. Suzuki	Closed	1992	480.00	480
1990 Train Set, sm. - T. Suzuki	Open		100.00	170
1997 Truckin' - R. Nakai	Open		260.00	260

Castles and Legends - R. Nakai, unless otherwise noted

YEAR ISSUE	EDITION LIMIT	YEAR RETD.	ISSUE PRICE	*QUOTE U.S.$
1991 Castle In The Sky	Closed	1994	150.00	165
1994 Castle Rainbow Rainbow Mtn. Bs.	Closed	2000	1575.00	1600
1994 Castle Royale/Clear Mtn. Bs.	Open		1300.00	1350
2000 Delilah Shares a Secret - R. Takii	Open		70.00	70
2000 Delilah Welcomes Summer - R. Takii	Open		70.00	70
1989 Dream Castle	Closed	1999	9000.00	10000
1996 Emerald Castle	Closed	1998	105.00	105
1993 Enchanted Castle	750		800.00	850
1993 Fantasy Castle, lg.	Open		230.00	235
1993 Fantasy Castle, med.	Open		130.00	135
1992 Fantasy Castle, mini - N. Mulargia	Open		40.00	40
1992 Fantasy Castle, sm.	Open		85.00	90
1995 Fantasy Coach, lg. - N. Mulargia	Open		350.00	350
1995 Fantasy Coach, med. - N. Mulargia	Open		150.00	150
1995 Fantasy Coach, sm. - N. Mulargia	Open		95.00	95
1988 Imperial Castle	Closed	1998	320.00	320
1999 Legendary Unicorn - T. Suzuki	Open		125.00	125
1991 Majestic Castle - A. Kato	Closed	1998	390.00	390
1995 Mouse Coach, mini - N. Mulargia	Open		50.00	50
1995 Mouse Coach, sm. - N. Mulargia	Open		90.00	90
1988 Mystic Castle	Open		100.00	100
1987 Rainbow Castle	Open		150.00	190
1989 Rainbow Castle, mini	Open		60.00	60
1990 Rainbow Unicorn - N. Mulargia	Open		50.00	60

Celebration of Life - Various

YEAR ISSUE	EDITION LIMIT	YEAR RETD.	ISSUE PRICE	*QUOTE U.S.$
1998 Baby Booties - R. Nakai	Open		35.00	35
1997 Baby Boy Carriage - T. Suzuki	Closed	1998	50.00	50
1997 Baby Girl Carriage - T. Suzuki	Closed	1998	50.00	50
2000 First Dance - T. Suzuki	Open		90.00	90
1995 Happy Birthday Cake - R. Nakai	Open		60.00	60
XX Pacifier - Team	Open		30.00	30
1998 Wedding Bells - R. Nakai	Open		125.00	125
1989 Wedding Couple - N. Mulargia	Closed	2000	100.00	100
1995 Wedding Couple, med. - N. Mulargia	Closed	1998	63.00	63
1992 Wedding Couple, mini - N. Mulargia	Closed	1997	30.00	30

Crystal Concerto - Various

YEAR ISSUE	EDITION LIMIT	YEAR RETD.	ISSUE PRICE	*QUOTE U.S.$
1997 Clarinet - J. Makoto	Closed	1999	235.00	235
1998 Grand Piano with Bench - R. Nakai	Open		125.00	125
1999 Violin and Bow - T. Suzuki	Open		80.00	80

Disney Showcase Collection - Various

YEAR ISSUE	EDITION LIMIT	YEAR RETD.	ISSUE PRICE	*QUOTE U.S.$
1998 Cinderella's Castle - T. Suzuki	1,250		1495.00	1495
1999 Cinderella's Coach - R. Nakai	1,450		893.00	893
1998 Cinderella's Slipper - R. Nakai	9,750		49.50	50
1998 Dumbo & Timothy - T. Suzuki	2,750		279.00	279
1998 Gee, You're the Sweetest (Minnie) - R. Nakai	4,750		249.00	249
1998 Just For You (Mickey) - R. Nakai	4,750		249.00	249
1998 Pinocchio & Jiminy Cricket - T. Suzuki	2,750		299.00	299
2000 Sorcerer Mickey Makes Magic - T. Suzuki	2,000		299.00	299
1999 Steamboat Willie - T. Suzuki	2,000		299.00	299
1999 Tinker Bell - R. Nakai	3,750		193.00	193

The Gambler Collection - R. Nakai, unless otherwise noted

YEAR ISSUE	EDITION LIMIT	YEAR RETD.	ISSUE PRICE	*QUOTE U.S.$
1993 Black Jack Teddies - N. Mulargia	Open		97.00	97
1991 Dice, sm.	Closed	1997	27.00	27
1997 Jackpot Teddy - T. Suzuki	Open		62.50	63
1991 Lucky 7	Closed	1992	50.00	50
1997 Lucky Die	Closed	1998	70.00	70
1994 Lucky Roll	Closed	1998	95.00	95
1996 One Arm Bandit	Open		70.00	70
1991 Rolling Dice - T. Suzuki	Closed	N/A	110.00	110
1993 Rolling Dice, lg.	Closed	1997	60.00	60
1993 Rolling Dice, med.	Open		45.00	45
1992 Rolling Dice, mini	Open		32.00	32
1993 Rolling Dice, sm.	Closed	1996	40.00	40
1993 Slot Machine, lg. - T. Suzuki	Open		80.00	80
1991 Slot Machine, mini	Open		30.00	35

*Quotes have been rounded up to nearest dollar

YEAR ISSUE	EDITION LIMIT	YEAR RETD.	ISSUE PRICE	*QUOTE U.S.$
1991 Slot Machine, sm. - T. Suzuki	Open		60.00	60
1994 Super Slot Machine	Open		295.00	295
1999 Teddies on a Roll - R. Takii	Open		100.00	100

Holiday Treasures - R. Nakai, unless otherwise noted

YEAR ISSUE	EDITION LIMIT	YEAR RETD.	ISSUE PRICE	*QUOTE U.S.$
1999 Angel of Joy - T. Suzuki	Open		60.00	60
1999 Angel of Love - T. Suzuki	Open		60.00	60
1999 Angel of Peace - T. Suzuki	Open		60.00	60
1997 Angel with Heart - T. Suzuki	Closed	1998	30.00	30
1995 Angel, lg.	Closed	1998	50.00	50
1994 Angel, mini	Closed	1996	25.00	25
1995 Baby Bear's Christmas - T. Suzuki	Closed	1997	48.00	48
1994 Cathedral w/Rainbow Base	Closed	1996	99.00	99
1994 Christmas Tree, Extra lg.	Open		300.00	300
1985 Christmas Tree, lg.	Open		126.00	130
1985 Christmas Tree, mini	Open		45.00	45
1985 Christmas Tree, sm.	Open		50.00	70
1991 Christmas Wreath Teddy - T. Suzuki	Closed	1992	70.00	75
1994 Country Church	Closed	1997	53.00	53
1994 Country Church w/Rainbow Base	Open		60.00	60
2000 Drumming Toy Soldier - T. Suzuki	Open		60.00	60
1996 Frosty	Open		41.00	45
1991 Holy Angel Blowing A Trumpet - T. Suzuki	Closed	1997	38.00	38
1991 Holy Angel Holding A Candle - T. Suzuki	Closed	1998	38.00	38
1991 Holy Angel Playing A Harp - T. Suzuki	Closed	1996	38.00	38
2000 Marching Toy Soldier - T. Suzuki	Open		60.00	60
1991 Merry Christmas Teddy - T. Suzuki	Open		55.00	55
1986 Nativity - N. Mulargia	Open		150.00	170
1991 Nativity, sm. - T. Suzuki	Closed	1998	85.00	85
1991 Santa Bear Christmas - T. Suzuki	Closed	1997	70.00	70
2000 Santa Bear is Coming to Town - T. Suzuki	Open		55.00	55
1991 Santa Bear Sleighride - T. Suzuki	Closed	1997	70.00	70
2000 Santa's Buddy - T. Suzuki	Open		50.00	50
1987 Teddy Bear Christmas	Open		100.00	100
1991 Trim A Tree Teddy	Closed	1996	50.00	50
1990 Trumpeting Angel	Closed	1991	60.00	60
2000 Trumpeting Toy Soldier - T. Suzuki	Open		60.00	60

Imagination - Various

YEAR ISSUE	EDITION LIMIT	YEAR RETD.	ISSUE PRICE	*QUOTE U.S.$
1996 Bo-Bo The Clown - N. Mulargia	Open		50.00	50
1998 Carousel Horse - R. Nakai	Open		125.00	125
1992 Fire Engine - T. Suzuki	Closed	1998	80.00	80
1996 Friends Forever - R. Nakai	Closed	1998	75.00	75
1997 Frog Prince - R. Nakai	Open		55.00	55
1998 Glass Slipper - T. Suzuki	Open		30.00	30
1990 I Love You Unicorn - N. Mulargia	Closed	1992	58.00	58
1996 Merry-Go-Round - N. Mulargia	750	2000	265.00	265
1996 Merry-Go-Round, sm. - N. Mulargia	Open		150.00	150
1996 Noah and Friends - N. Mulargia	Open		150.00	150
1990 Pegasus - N. Mulargia	Closed	1991	50.00	50
1996 Pinocchio - T. Suzuki	Open		150.00	150
1999 Rocking Horse - T. Suzuki	Open		150.00	150
1990 Unicorn - N. Mulargia	Closed	1992	38.00	40
1998 Wishin' and a Hoppin' - T. Suzuki	Closed	2000	95.00	95

The Jitterbugs - T. Suzuki, unless otherwise noted

YEAR ISSUE	EDITION LIMIT	YEAR RETD.	ISSUE PRICE	*QUOTE U.S.$
1999 Buzz	Open		70.00	70
1999 Lady	Open		65.00	65
1999 Madame D - R. Takii	Open		65.00	65
1999 Mister G	Open		65.00	65

Limited Edition Collection Series - Various

YEAR ISSUE	EDITION LIMIT	YEAR RETD.	ISSUE PRICE	*QUOTE U.S.$
1993 Country Gristmill -T. Suzuki	1,250	1998	320.00	340
1991 Ellis Island - R. Nakai	Closed	1992	450.00	500
1992 Santa Maria - N. Mulargia	Closed	1993	1000.00	1050
1990 Tower Bridge -T. Suzuki	Closed	1992	600.00	650
1993 Victorian House - N. Mulargia	Closed	1996	190.00	190

New York Collection - R. Nakai, unless otherwise noted

YEAR ISSUE	EDITION LIMIT	YEAR RETD.	ISSUE PRICE	*QUOTE U.S.$
1993 Apple with Red Heart, med.	Closed	1997	37.00	37
1985 Apple, lg.	Open		44.00	65
1985 Apple, med.	Open		30.00	40
1987 Apple, mini	Open		12.50	13
1985 Apple, sm.	Open		15.00	20
1995 Chrysler Building	Closed	1996	275.00	275
1992 Contemp. Empire State Bldg., lg. - A. Kato	Closed	1996	475.00	475
1992 Contemp. Empire State Bldg., med.	Closed	1997	170.00	170
1992 Contemp. Empire State Bldg., sm.	Closed	1996	95.00	95
1992 Contemp. Empire State Bldg., sm. MV	Open		95.00	95
1996 The Empire State Bldg.	475		1315.00	1315
1992 Empire State Bldg. w/Windows, mini	Open		65.00	65
1987 Empire State Bldg., lg.	2,000		650.00	700
1987 Empire State Bldg., med.	Open		250.00	260
1991 Empire State Bldg., mini	Open		60.00	65
1987 Empire State Bldg., sm.	Open		120.00	120
1993 Holiday Empire State building - N. Mulargia	Open		170.00	170
2000 Lady Liberty - R. Takii	Open		89.00	89
2000 Lady Liberty w/colored base - R. Takii	Open		95.00	95
1989 Liberty Island - N. Mulargia	Open		75.00	80
1990 Manhattan Island	Open		240.00	240
1993 Manhattan Island, sm. - N. Mulargia	Open		80.00	80
1985 The Statue of Liberty	Open		250.00	350
1987 Statue of Liberty, med.	Closed	2000	120.00	155
2000 Statue of Liberty, med. - R. Takii	Open		165.00	165
1992 Statue Of Liberty, mini	Open		40.00	40
1987 Statue of Liberty, sm. - N. Mulargia	Open		50.00	65
1998 Twin Towers, lg.	Open		150.00	150
1992 Twin Towers, sm.	Open		90.00	90
2000 A View of New York - T. Suzuki	Open		450.00	450

North American Wildlife - R. Takii, unless otherwise noted

YEAR ISSUE	EDITION LIMIT	YEAR RETD.	ISSUE PRICE	*QUOTE U.S.$
1997 Majestic Bald Eagle - N. Mulargia	1,250		1100.00	1100
1999 Mountain Lion	Open		195.00	195
2000 Mustang	Open		185.00	185
1998 Timber Wolf - R. Nakai	1,250		175.00	175
1999 White-Tailed Deer	Open		195.00	195

Nostalgia Collection - Various

YEAR ISSUE	EDITION LIMIT	YEAR RETD.	ISSUE PRICE	*QUOTE U.S.$
2000 Antique Gramophone - T. Suzuki	Open		65.00	65
2000 Antique Telephone - T. Suzuki	Open		65.00	65
1991 Cable Car, lg. - T. Suzuki	Open		100.00	100
1992 Cable Car, mini - T. Suzuki	Closed	1996	40.00	40
1991 Cable Car, sm. - T. Suzuki	Closed	1997	70.00	70
1996 Classic Motorcycle -T. Suzuki	Closed	1999	400.00	400
1996 Classic Motorcycle, sm. - T. Suzuki	Open		200.00	200
1999 Engine No. 9 - T. Suzuki	Open		85.00	85
1996 Fabulous Fifties Jukebox - N. Mulargia	Open		80.00	80
1992 Fire Engine - T. Suzuki	Closed	1998	75.00	80
1997 Grand Cable Car - T. Suzuki	Closed	1998	150.00	150
1993 Riverboat - N. Mulargia	350	1999	570.00	600
1994 Riverboat, sm. - N. Mulargia	Open		100.00	100
1993 San Francisco Cable Car, lg. - R. Nakai	Open		60.00	60
1993 San Francisco Cable Car, sm. - R. Nakai	Open		40.00	40
2000 Tea For Two - T. Suzuki	Open		65.00	65

Raining Cats and Dogs (and occasional Mice) - T. Suzuki, unless otherwise noted

YEAR ISSUE	EDITION LIMIT	YEAR RETD.	ISSUE PRICE	*QUOTE U.S.$
1990 Barney Dog	Closed	1992	32.00	32
1991 Calamity Cat	Closed	1998	60.00	60
1990 Cat N Mouse	Closed	1996	45.00	45
1994 Cheese Mouse - R. Nakai	Closed	2000	50.00	50
1998 Coffee Break	Open		50.00	50
1992 Country Cat	Closed	1998	60.00	60
1990 The Curious Cat	Open		60.00	60
1991 Curious Cat, lg.	Closed	1998	90.00	90
1997 CyberMouse - N. Mulargia	Closed	1997	35.00	35
1995 Fido the Dog	Closed	1997	27.00	27
1995 Frisky Fido	Closed	1996	27.00	27
1998 Glamour Puss	Open		70.00	70
1991 Hello Birdie	Open		70.00	70
2000 Karma the Bulldog - R. Takii	Open		60.00	60
1992 Kitten in Basket - C. Kido	Closed	1997	35.00	40
1993 Kitty Kare	Closed	1994	70.00	70
1993 Kitty with Butterfly	Closed	1994	60.00	60
1991 Kitty with Heart	Open		30.00	30
1990 Moonlight Cats - R. Nakai	Closed	1992	100.00	110
1995 Moonlight Kitties	Closed	1997	83.00	83
1994 Mozart	Closed	2000	50.00	50
1991 Peek-A-Boo Kitties	Open		60.00	60
1993 Pinky	Closed	1996	50.00	50
1992 Playful Kitty	Open		32.00	32
1993 Playful Kitty, lg.	Closed	1996	50.00	50
1990 Playful Pup	Closed	N/A	85.00	85
1994 Playful Pup - T. Suzuki	Closed	1998	53.00	53
1990 Puppy Love	Closed	1992	45.00	45
1993 Puppy-Gram	Open		60.00	60
1991 Rock-A-Bye Kitty - R. Nakai	Open		80.00	80
1992 See Saw Pals - A. Kato	Closed	1999	40.00	40
1997 Sparkie	Closed	2000	60.00	60
1991 Sparkie - R. Nakai	Closed	1992	50.00	50
1991 Spike - R. Nakai	Closed	1992	50.00	50
1991 Spot	Closed	1992	50.00	50
1991 Strolling Kitties	Closed	1992	65.00	65
1994 Sweetie	Closed	2000	28.00	28
1995 Tea Time - R. Nakai	Closed	1998	50.00	50
1996 Wanna Play?	Closed	1999	65.00	65

Seaside Memories - R. Nakai, unless otherwise noted

YEAR ISSUE	EDITION LIMIT	YEAR RETD.	ISSUE PRICE	*QUOTE U.S.$
1992 Baby Seal - T. Suzuki	Closed	1998	21.00	21
1998 Barnegat Lighthouse-NJ	Open		80.00	80
1991 Beaver	Closed	1996	47.00	47
2000 Cape May Lighthouse	Open		110.00	110
1997 Coastal Lighthouse	Open		80.00	80
1996 Crabbie le Crab	Closed	1997	38.00	38
1992 Cute Crab - T. Suzuki	Closed	1997	27.00	27
1992 Dolphin Dreams	1,250		220.00	220
1990 Duck Family	Closed	1992	70.00	70
1993 Extra Large Oyster with Pearl	Closed	1996	75.00	78
1993 Harbor Lighthouse - N. Mulargia	Open		70.00	70
1988 Hatching Sea Turtle - T. Suzuki	Closed	1998	45.00	45
1998 Lobster - T. Suzuki	Open		125.00	135
1993 Manatee Paperweight - Team	Open		125.00	125
1999 Nubble Lighthouse-Maine	Open		125.00	125
1994 Oscar Otter - T. Suzuki	Closed	1996	105.00	105
1990 Pearl Oyster, lg.	Open		60.00	60
1990 Pearl Oyster, sm.	Open		25.00	25
1996 Pelican	Closed	1998	65.00	65
1991 Penguin On Cube	Closed	1995	40.00	40
1996 Penguin On Cube	Closed	1998	48.00	48
1996 Playful Dolphin	Closed	1999	125.00	125
1996 Playful Dolphin, sm.	Closed	1999	75.00	75
1992 Playful Dolphins - T. Suzuki	Closed	1996	60.00	60
1993 Playful Seal - T. Suzuki	Closed	1996	45.00	45
1998 Sea Turtle at Play - T. Suzuki	Open		85.00	85
1994 Seal	Closed	1996	47.00	50
1992 Seaside Pelican - T. Suzuki	Closed	1995	55.00	55
1998 Splash	Open		80.00	80
1995 Treasure Chest - R. Nakai	Open		60.00	60
1992 Tropical Fish	Closed	1995	95.00	95
1992 Tuxedo Penguin	Closed	1995	75.00	75
2000 Two To Tango - R. Takii	Open		100.00	100
1992 The Whales - T. Suzuki	Closed	1994	60.00	65

Spring Parade Collection - Various

YEAR ISSUE	EDITION LIMIT	YEAR RETD.	ISSUE PRICE	*QUOTE U.S.$
1990 African Violet - I. Nakamura	Open		32.00	32
1996 American Beauty Rose - N. Mulargia	Closed	1997	53.00	53
1992 Barrel Cactus - I. Nakamura	Closed	1995	45.00	45
1991 Blossom Bunny - T. Suzuki	Closed	1998	42.00	42
1991 Bunnies On Ice - T. Suzuki	Closed	1996	58.00	58
1991 Bunny Buddy with Carrot - T. Suzuki	Closed	2000	30.00	30
1992 Candleholder - N. Mulargia	Closed	1995	125.00	125
1991 Cheep Cheep - T. Suzuki	Closed	1998	35.00	35
1998 Cottontail - T. Suzuki	Open		70.00	70
1990 Crocus - R. Nakai	Closed	1991	45.00	45
1992 Cute Bunny - T. Suzuki	Closed	1995	38.00	38
1995 Desert Cactus - N. Mulargia	Closed	1996	48.00	48
1994 The Enchanted Rose - R. Nakai	Open		60.00	60
1992 Flowering Cactus - I. Nakamura	Closed	1996	58.00	58
2000 Golden Pineapple - R. Nakai	Open		40.00	40
1992 Half Dozen Flower Arrangement - N. Mulargia	Closed	1996	20.00	20
1992 Happy Heart - N. Mulargia	Closed	1996	25.00	25
1992 Hummingbird - T. Suzuki	Open		58.00	58
1992 Hummingbird, mini - T. Suzuki	Open		27.00	27
1990 Hyacinth - I. Nakamura	Closed	1996	50.00	50
1995 Long Stem Pink Rose in Vase - R. Nakai	Closed	1998	41.00	41
1992 Long Stem Rose - N. Mulargia	Open		35.00	40
1994 Long Stem Rose in Vase - R. Nakai	Open		40.00	40
1986 Love Swan - N. Mulargia	Closed	N/A	70.00	70
1995 Love Swans - N. Mulargia	Open		80.00	80
1996 Love Swans, lg. - N. Mulargia	Open		252.00	252
1992 Loving Hearts - N. Mulargia	Open		35.00	35
1996 Pineapple - R. Nakai	Closed	1998	50.00	50
1995 Pink Rose - R. Nakai	Closed	1997	53.00	53
1991 Rainbow Butterfly, mini - R. Nakai	Closed	1996	27.00	27
1994 Rainbow Rose - N. Mulargia	Closed	1996	82.00	82
1987 Red Rose - R. Nakai	Open		50.00	50
1990 Rose Basket - I. Nakamura	Closed	1992	52.00	52
1996 Rose Bouquet, sm. - R. Nakai	Closed	1998	45.00	45
1993 Songbirds - I. Nakamura	Open		90.00	100
1992 Spring Blossoms - T. Suzuki	Closed	1997	40.00	40
1995 Spring Butterfly - R. Nakai	Open		40.00	40
1989 Spring Chick - R. Nakai	Open		50.00	50
2000 Swallowtail Butterfly - R. Takii	Open		85.00	85
1990 Swan Family - T. Suzuki	Closed	N/A	70.00	70
1987 Swan, lg. - R. Nakai	Closed	1996	100.00	100
1987 Swan, med. - R. Nakai	Open		60.00	60
1987 Swan, mini - R. Nakai	Closed	2000	28.00	28
1987 Swan, sm. - R. Nakai	Open		32.00	45
1996 Water Lily, Medium, AB - R. Nakai	Open		200.00	200
1997 Water Lily, sm. AB - R. Nakai	Open		100.00	100
1992 Waterfront Village - N. Mulargia	Closed	1996	190.00	190
1992 Wedding Couple - N. Mulargia	Closed	2000	100.00	100
1991 Windmill, mini - R. Nakai	Closed	1992	63.00	63

Teddyland Collection - Various

YEAR ISSUE	EDITION LIMIT	YEAR RETD.	ISSUE PRICE	*QUOTE U.S.$
1990 Baron Von Teddy - T. Suzuki	Closed	1993	60.00	60
1987 Beach Teddies - N. Mulargia	Open		100.00	100
1992 Beach Teddies, sm. - N. Mulargia	Open		70.00	70
1992 Billard Buddies - T. Suzuki	Closed	1998	70.00	70
1988 Bouquet Teddy, sm. - N. Mulargia	Open		35.00	40
1998 Broadway Ted - R. Nakai	Open		45.00	45
1990 Choo Choo Teddy - T. Suzuki	Closed	1993	100.00	100
1995 CompuBear - N. Mulargia	Open		60.00	60
1996 Cuddly Bear - R. Nakai	Closed	1998	50.00	50
1993 Flower Teddy - T. Suzuki	Closed	1997	50.00	50
1995 Fly A Kite Teddy - T. Suzuki	Closed	1996	41.00	41
1995 Get Well Teddy - R. Nakai	Closed	1996	48.00	48
1989 Golfing Teddies - R. Nakai	Open		100.00	120
1991 Gumball Teddy - T. Suzuki	Closed	1996	63.00	63
1989 Happy Birthday Teddy - R. Nakai	Open		50.00	50
1991 Heart Bear - T. Suzuki	Open		28.00	28
1991 High Chair Teddy - T. Suzuki	Closed	1992	75.00	78
1988 I Love You Teddy - N. Mulargia	Open		40.00	40
1994 I Love You Teddy Couple - N. Mulargia	Open		45.00	45
1992 Ice Cream Teddies - N. Mulargia	Closed	1998	55.00	55
1987 Loving Teddies - N. Mulargia	Closed	1998	75.00	75
1990 Loving Teddies, sm. - N. Mulargia	Open		60.00	65
1991 Luck Of The Irish - R. Nakai	Closed	1992	60.00	60
1990 Mountaineer Teddy - N. Mulargia	Closed	1992	80.00	80
1991 My Favorite Picture - T. Suzuki	Open		45.00	45
1998 Mystic Teddy - R. Nakai	Open		70.00	70
1992 Patriotic Teddy - N. Mulargia	Open		30.00	30
1991 Play It Again Ted - T. Suzuki	Closed	1997	65.00	65
1991 Playground Teddy - R. Kido	Closed	1992	90.00	90
1990 Rainbow Teddies - N. Mulargia	Closed	1993	95.00	95
1990 Rocking Horse Teddy - N. Mulargia	Closed	1992	80.00	80
1991 School Bears - H. Serino	Closed	1992	75.00	75
1991 Scuba Bear - T. Suzuki	Closed	1992	65.00	65
1992 Singing Baby Bear - T. Suzuki	Closed	1993	55.00	55
1999 Sophie - T. Suzuki	Open		60.00	60
1989 Speedboat Teddies - R. Nakai	Closed	1998	90.00	90
1990 Storytime Teddies - T. Suzuki	Open		70.00	80
1991 Swinging Teddies - N. Mulargia	Closed	2000	100.00	120
1988 Teddies At Eight - N. Mulargia	Open		100.00	100
1988 Teddies with Heart - R. Nakai	Open		45.00	50
1994 Teddy Bear with Rainbow Base - R. Nakai	Closed	1996	75.00	75
1991 Teddy with Red Heart, mini - R. Nakai	Open		25.00	25
1995 Teddy's Self Portrait - T. Suzuki	Closed	1996	53.00	53

360 Collectors' Information Bureau

*Quotes have been rounded up to nearest dollar

YEAR ISSUE	EDITION LIMIT	YEAR RETD.	ISSUE PRICE	*QUOTE U.S.$
1999 Theodore - T. Suzuki	Open		55.00	60
1988 Touring Teddies - N. Mulargia	Open		90.00	100
1990 Tricycle Teddy - T. Suzuki	Closed	1993	40.00	40
1997 Up and Away - N. Mulargia	Open		80.00	80

Wonders of the World Collection - R. Nakai, unless otherwise noted

YEAR ISSUE	EDITION LIMIT	YEAR RETD.	ISSUE PRICE	*QUOTE U.S.$
1993 Capitol Building, sm. - N. Mulargia	Closed	1996	100.00	100
1997 Capitol Hill -T. Suzuki	350		1300.00	1300
1991 Chicago Water Tower w/base - T. Suzuki	Closed	1997	300.00	300
1986 The Eiffel Tower -T. Suzuki	2000		1000.00	1350
1988 Eiffel Tower, sm. -T. Suzuki	2000		500.00	625
1995 Independence Hall	750	1999	370.00	370
1990 Le Petit Eiffel -T. Suzuki	Open		240.00	250
1995 The Liberty Bell	Open		150.00	150
1999 Liberty Bell, sm.	Open		80.00	80
1993 Sears Tower	Closed	1997	150.00	150
1987 Taj Mahal - T. Suzuki	2,000		2000.00	2250
1995 Taj Mahal, med.	Open		790.00	790
1995 Taj Mahal, sm.	Open		210.00	210
1999 Totem Pole	Open		79.00	79
2000 Totem Pole, lg.	Open		145.00	145
2000 Totem Pole, sm.	Open		59.00	59
1987 U.S. Capitol Building	Open		250.00	300
1998 Washington Monument	Open		75.00	75
1992 The White House	Closed	1993	3000.00	3000
1994 White House w/Oct. Mirror, sm. - N. Mulargia	Open		175.00	175

Dave Grossman Creations

Button Box Kids - H. Payne

YEAR ISSUE	EDITION LIMIT	YEAR RETD.	ISSUE PRICE	*QUOTE U.S.$
1999 Arthur HP-3	2,400	2000	25.00	25
1999 Charity HP-4	2,400	2000	25.00	25
1999 Faith HP-12	2,400	2000	25.00	25
1999 First Love HP-5	2,400	2000	50.00	50
1999 First Star I See Tonight HP-10	2,400	2000	60.00	60
1999 Garland Makers HP-7	2,400	2000	90.00	90
1999 Jacob HP-2	2,400	2000	25.00	25
1999 Jodi HP-13	2,400	2000	25.00	25
1999 Ol' Fishin' Hole HP-8	2,400	2000	40.00	40
1999 Peek-A-Boo HP-9	2,400	2000	35.00	35
1999 Quilting Bee HP-11	2,400	2000	70.00	70
1999 Trim-A-Tree HP-6	2,400	2000	65.00	65

Embrace Series - T. Snyder

YEAR ISSUE	EDITION LIMIT	YEAR RETD.	ISSUE PRICE	*QUOTE U.S.$
1998 Bedtime Prayers (musical) ES-4538	Open		50.00	50
1998 Bedtime Prayers ES-4537	Open		45.00	45
1998 Bundle of Joy ES-4539	Open		50.00	50
1998 Embrace ES-4516	Open		40.00	40
1998 Generations ES-4530	Open		65.00	65
1998 Gospel Singers ES-4536	Open		65.00	65
1998 The Kiss ES-4526	Open		40.00	40
1998 Last Dance ES-4527	Open		45.00	45
1998 Mother's Love ES-4528	Open		65.00	65
1998 Mother's Touch ES-4532	Open		40.00	40
1998 Puppy Love ES-4541	Open		40.00	40
1998 Time Honored Wisdom ES-4535	Open		45.00	45
1998 Wedding Day ES-4540	Open		50.00	50

Emmett Kelly Sr. "The Original Emmett Kelly Circus Collection - B. Leighton-Jones

YEAR ISSUE	EDITION LIMIT	YEAR RETD.	ISSUE PRICE	*QUOTE U.S.$
1986 "Fore"	10,000		36.00	36
1998 100th Birthday!	10,000		50.00	60
1986 All Washed Up	10,000	1987	48.00	48
1987 Cabbage Routine	10,000	1988	30.00	30
1986 The Cheaters	10,000	1987	70.00	70
1986 Christmas Carol	10,000	1988	35.00	35
1996 The Christmas Tree	10,000	2000	50.00	50
1992 Christmas Tunes	10,000	1998	40.00	40
1989 Cotton Candy	10,000	1995	55.00	55
1993 Dear Emmett	10,000		45.00	45
1990 A Dog's Life	10,000		52.00	52
1988 Dressing Room	10,000		64.00	64
1992 Emmett At The Organ	10,000		50.00	50
1992 Emmett The Caddy	10,000		45.00	45
1991 Emmett The Snowman	10,000	2000	45.00	45
1988 Feather Act	10,000	1998	40.00	40
1986 Feels Like Rain	10,000	1987	34.00	34
1996 Fire Fighter	10,000		45.00	45
1987 Fisherman	10,000		44.00	44
1993 Hard Times	10,000		45.00	45
1995 Holiday Skater	10,000		55.00	55
1986 I Love You	10,000		36.00	36
1994 I've Got It	10,000		45.00	45
1986 Kelly Plaque	10,000		30.00	30
1993 The Lion Tamer	10,000		55.00	55
1992 Look At The Birdie	10,000		40.00	40
1995 Looking Out	10,000		45.00	45
1997 Missed	10,000	2000	50.00	50
1989 Missing Parents	10,000	1998	38.00	38
1997 Mystery Spotlight	10,000		40.00	40
1997 Off To the Races	10,000		85.00	85
1994 Parenthood	10,000		55.00	55
1995 Pierrot & Emmett	10,000	2000	50.00	50
1990 The Proposal	10,000	1993	65.00	65
1992 Self Portrait	2,400	2000	150.00	150
1987 Self-Portrait	10,000		60.00	60
1994 Stuck on Bowling	10,000		45.00	45
1993 Sunday Driver	10,000		55.00	55
1986 The Thinker	10,000		37.00	37
1986 Till Death Do Us Part	10,000	1987	48.00	48
1986 The Titanic	10,000	1987	50.00	50
1987 Wagon Wheel	10,000	1988	40.00	40
1986 Wallstreet	10,000	2000	40.00	40
1986 Where Did I Go Wrong	10,000	1987	80.00	80
1990 With This Ring	10,000	1993	65.00	65

Emmett Kelly Sr. Casino Series - Inspired by Emmett Kelly

YEAR ISSUE	EDITION LIMIT	YEAR RETD.	ISSUE PRICE	*QUOTE U.S.$
1994 Black Jack EK-721	10,000		65.00	65
1994 Dice Table EK-711	10,000		80.00	80
1994 Jackpot EK-700	10,000		70.00	70

Emmett Kelly Sr. Figurines - Inspired by Emmett Kelly Sr.

YEAR ISSUE	EDITION LIMIT	YEAR RETD.	ISSUE PRICE	*QUOTE U.S.$
1986 All Washed Up EK-607	15,000	1987	48.00	48
1991 Artful Dodger EK-627	15,000	1996	35.00	35
1987 Big Game Hunter EK-615	15,000	2000	38.00	38
1999 A Box of Love	15,000		40.00	40
1987 Cabbage Routine EK-613	15,000	1988	30.00	30
1986 The Cheaters EK-608	15,000	1987	70.00	70
1989 Choosing Sides EK-622	15,000	2000	55.00	55
1986 Christmas Carol (EKA-86) EK-612	15,000	1988	35.00	35
1992 Christmas Tunes EK-629	15,000	1994	40.00	40
1989 Cotton Candy EK-621	15,000		65.00	65
1993 Dear Emmett EK-637	15,000		45.00	45
1990 A Dog's Life EK-623	15,000		55.00	55
1988 Dressing Room EK-618	15,000		64.00	64
1991 Emmett At Bat EK-628	15,000		35.00	35
1992 Emmett At The Organ EK-631	15,000		50.00	50
1992 Emmett At Work EK-632	15,000	1996	45.00	45
1992 Emmett The Caddy EK-630	15,000		45.00	45
1991 Emmett The Snowman EK-626	15,000		45.00	45
1988 Feather Act EK-619	15,000	1994	40.00	40
1986 Feels Like Rain EK-605	15,000	1989	34.00	34
1996 Fire Fighter EK-644	15,000		45.00	45
1987 Fisherman EK-614	15,000		44.00	44
1986 Fore EK-611	15,000		36.00	36
1993 Hard Times EK-634	15,000		45.00	45
1994 Holiday Skater EK-641	15,000		55.00	55
1986 I Love You EK-601	15,000		36.00	36
1994 I've Got It EK-640	15,000		45.00	45
1987 Kelly Music Box EKB-1	Closed	1988	60.00	60
1986 Kelly Plaque KDP-1	15,000		30.00	30
1993 The Lion Tamer EK-635	15,000		55.00	55
1992 Look At The Bride EK-633	15,000		50.00	50
1996 Looking Out EK-642	15,000		45.00	45
1997 Missed EK-647	15,000		50.00	50
1989 Missing Parents EK-620	15,000	1994	38.00	38
1997 Mystery Spotlight EK-646	15,000		40.00	40
1997 Off To The Races EK-648	15,000		85.00	85
1994 Parenthood EK-639	15,000		55.00	55
1996 Pierrot & Emmett EK-643	15,000		50.00	50
1990 The Proposal EK-624	15,000	1993	65.00	65
1993 Self Portrait EKL-17	15,000		150.00	150
1987 Self-Portrait EK-617	15,000		60.00	60
1986 Spotlight EK-603	15,000	1994	36.00	36
1994 Stuck on Bowling EK-638	15,000		45.00	45
1993 Sunday Driver EK-636	15,000		55.00	55
1986 Thinker EK-604	15,000		37.00	37
1986 Till Death Do Us Part EK-609	15,000	1987	48.00	48
1986 The Titanic EK-606	15,000	1987	50.00	50
1987 Wagon Wheel EK-616	15,000	1988	40.00	40
1986 Wallstreet EK-602	15,000		40.00	40
1986 Where Did I Go Wrong EK-610	15,000	1987	80.00	80
1987 Wish You A Merry Christmas EKG-01 (waterglobe)	Closed	1998	28.00	28
1990 With This Ring EK-625	15,000	1993	65.00	65

Emmett Kelly Sr. Large Earthenware - Inspired by Emmett Kelly Sr.

YEAR ISSUE	EDITION LIMIT	YEAR RETD.	ISSUE PRICE	*QUOTE U.S.$
1987 Circus Days EK-102	15,000	1988	50.00	50
1987 Fore EK-101	15,000	1988	50.00	50
1987 Spotlight EK-100	15,000	1988	50.00	50
1987 Wallstreet EK-103	15,000	1988	50.00	50

Emmett Kelly Sr. Miniatures- Inspired by Emmett Kelly Sr.

YEAR ISSUE	EDITION LIMIT	YEAR RETD.	ISSUE PRICE	*QUOTE U.S.$
1987 Fore EK-311	15,000	1988	17.00	17
1987 I Love You EK-301	15,000	1989	16.00	16
1987 Looking For Love EK-305	15,000	1989	17.00	17
1987 Spotlight EK-303	15,000	1988	17.00	17
1987 Thinker EK-304	15,000	1989	16.00	16
1987 Wallstreet EK-302	15,000	1988	18.50	19

Emmett Kelly Sr. Professionals - Inspired by Emmett Kelly Sr.

YEAR ISSUE	EDITION LIMIT	YEAR RETD.	ISSUE PRICE	*QUOTE U.S.$
1988 Dentist EK-500	15,000	1989	36.00	36
1988 Doctor EK-501	15,000	1989	35.00	35
1988 Fireman EK-504	15,000	1989	36.00	36
1988 Lawyer EK-503	15,000	1989	36.00	36
1988 Pharmacist EK-502	15,000	1989	40.00	40
1988 Policeman EK-505	15,000	1989	36.00	36

Emmett Kelly Sr. Stiffened Cloth - Inspired by Emmett Kelly Sr.

YEAR ISSUE	EDITION LIMIT	YEAR RETD.	ISSUE PRICE	*QUOTE U.S.$
1991 Christmas Tunes EKC-29	5,000		100.00	100
1991 Emmett The Caddy EKC-30	5,000	1997	125.00	125
1991 I Love You EKC-1	5,000		80.00	80
1991 Self Portrait EKC-17	Retrd.	1997	100.00	100
1991 Spotlight EKC-3	5,000		80.00	80
1991 Sunday Driver EKC-36	Open		85.00	85
1991 Wallstreet EKC-2	5,000		125.00	125

Gone With The Wind Series - Inspired by Film

YEAR ISSUE	EDITION LIMIT	YEAR RETD.	ISSUE PRICE	*QUOTE U.S.$
1987 Ashley GWW-2	Retrd.	1989	65.00	195
1993 Belle Waiting GWW-10	Retrd.	N/A	70.00	95
1997 Bonnie GWW-21	Retrd.	2000	50.00	50
1994 Gerald O'Hara GWW-15	Retrd.	N/A	70.00	79-85
1988 Mammy GWW-6	Retrd.	2000	70.00	70
1995 Mrs. O'Hara GWW-16	Retrd.	1997	70.00	75
1991 Prissy GWW-8	Retrd.	2000	50.00	50
1993 Rhett & Bonnie GWW-11	Retrd.	N/A	80.00	80
1987 Rhett GWW-4	Retrd.	1989	65.00	249-270
1996 Rhett in Tuxedo GWW-19	Retrd.	2000	70.00	70
1993 Rhett in White Suit GWW-12	Retrd.	N/A	70.00	149-195
1998 Scarlett & Rhett GWW-22	Retrd.	2000	90.00	90
1990 Scarlett & Rhett on Stairs GWW-50	Retrd.	1992	130.00	130-249
1990 Scarlett (red dress) GWW-7	Retrd.	1992	70.00	149-195
1987 Scarlett GWW-1	Retrd.	1989	65.00	300
1997 Scarlett in Atlanta Dress GWW-20	Retrd.	2000	70.00	70
1994 Scarlett in Bar B Que Dress GWW-14	Retrd.	N/A	70.00	125-195
1996 Scarlett in Blue Dress GWW-18	Retrd.	2000	70.00	70
1992 Scarlett in Green Dress GWW-9	Retrd.	2000	70.00	70-129
1995 Suellen GWW-17	Retrd.	1997	70.00	95
1987 Tara GWW-5	Retrd.	N/A	70.00	90

Gone With The Wind Series 6" - Inspired by Film

YEAR ISSUE	EDITION LIMIT	YEAR RETD.	ISSUE PRICE	*QUOTE U.S.$
1994 Ashley GWW-102	Retrd.	2000	40.00	40
1995 Mammy GWW-106	Retrd.	2000	40.00	40
1994 Rhett GW-104	Retrd.	2000	40.00	40
1996 Scarlett (B-B-Q Dress) GWW-114	Retrd.	2000	40.00	40
1994 Scarlett GWW-101	Retrd.	2000	40.00	40
1995 Suellen GWW-105	Retrd.	2000	40.00	40

Gone With The Wind-Scarlett & Her Beaus - Inspired by Film

YEAR ISSUE	EDITION LIMIT	YEAR RETD.	ISSUE PRICE	*QUOTE U.S.$
1995 The Kiss GWWL-200	750	1995	150.00	300
1995 The Kiss GWWL-200AP	75	1995	180.00	180
1997 Scarlett & Ashley GWWL-202	750	2000	150.00	150
1997 Scarlett & Ashley GWWL-202AP	75	2000	180.00	180
1996 The Wedding GWWL-201	750	1996	150.00	150
1996 The Wedding GWWL-201AP	75	1996	180.00	180

I Love Lucy - Dave Grossman Creations

YEAR ISSUE	EDITION LIMIT	YEAR RETD.	ISSUE PRICE	*QUOTE U.S.$
1999 Chocolate Factory (globe) ILL-GL1	5,000		40.00	40
1999 Chocolate Factory (musical) ILL-101RM	5,000		40.00	40
1999 Ethel (musical) ILL-103M	5,000		30.00	30
1999 Ethel ILL-103	5,000		25.00	25
1999 Fred (musical) ILL-104M	5,000		30.00	30
1999 Fred ILL-104	5,000		25.00	25
2000 Lucy "Wine Stomping" (globe) ILL-GL3	10,000		40.00	40
2000 Lucy "Wine Stomping" (musical) ILL-102RM	10,000		40.00	40
2000 Lucy "Wine Stomping" ILL-105	10,000		25.00	25
2000 Lucy (musical) ILL-101M	10,000		35.00	35
1999 Lucy ILL-101	5,000		25.00	25
2000 Ricky (musical) ILL-102M	10,000		35.00	35
1999 Ricky ILL-102	5,000		25.00	25
1999 Vitameatavegamin (globe) ILL-GL2	5,000		40.00	40
1999 Vitameatavegamin (musical) ILL-101RM	5,000		40.00	40

Laurel & Hardy - Dave Grossman Creations

YEAR ISSUE	EDITION LIMIT	YEAR RETD.	ISSUE PRICE	*QUOTE U.S.$
2000 Black Suits (globe) LHDY-1	10,000		35.00	35
1999 Hardy	5,000		25.00	25
1999 Hardy (musical)	5,000		30.00	30
1999 Hardy Policeman	5,000		25.00	25
1999 Laurel	5,000		25.00	25
1999 Laurel (musical)	5,000		30.00	30
1999 Laurel Policeman	5,000		25.00	25
2000 Policemen (globe) LHDY-2	10,000		35.00	35

Legacy Series - T. Snyder

YEAR ISSUE	EDITION LIMIT	YEAR RETD.	ISSUE PRICE	*QUOTE U.S.$
1998 Dominion Lion LS-4549	Open		40.00	40
1998 Legacy LS-4546	Open		50.00	50
1998 Pride of Africa LS-4506	Open		130.00	130
1998 Quiet Strength LS-4533	Open		130.00	130
1998 Sambaru Elder LS-4514	Open		130.00	130
1998 Sebrina LS-4513	Open		130.00	130
1998 Solitary Runner LS-4547	Open		40.00	40

Lighthouse Keepers - T. Snyder

YEAR ISSUE	EDITION LIMIT	YEAR RETD.	ISSUE PRICE	*QUOTE U.S.$
1998 Abbie Burgess LK-102	2,500	2000	50.00	50
1998 Augustin-Jean Fresnal LK-106	2,500	2000	50.00	50
1998 Bob Gerloff LK-103	2,500	2000	50.00	50
1998 Dunbar Davis LK-104	2,400	2000	50.00	50
1998 Emily Fish LK-105	2,500	2000	50.00	50
1998 George G. Meade LK-101	2,500	2000	50.00	50
1998 Ida Lewis LK-109	2,500	2000	50.00	50
1998 Joseph Strout LK-107	2,500	2000	50.00	50
1998 Marcus Hanna LK-110	2,500	2000	50.00	50
1998 Orris "Pete" Young LK-108	2,500	2000	50.00	50

Lladró-Norman Rockwell Collection Series - Rockwell-Inspired

YEAR ISSUE	EDITION LIMIT	YEAR RETD.	ISSUE PRICE	*QUOTE U.S.$
1982 Court Jester RL-405G	5,000	N/A	600.00	1050-1250
1982 Daydreamer RL-404G	5,000	N/A	450.00	1100-1500
1982 Lladró Love Letter RL-400G	5,000	N/A	650.00	750-950
1982 Practice Makes Perfect RL-402G	5,000	N/A	725.00	725-995
1982 Springtime RL-406G	5,000	N/A	450.00	1200-1400
1982 Summer Stock RL-401G	5,000	N/A	750.00	850-900
1982 Young Love RL-403G	5,000	N/A	450.00	1200

Norman Rockwell America Collection - Rockwell-Inspired

YEAR ISSUE	EDITION LIMIT	YEAR RETD.	ISSUE PRICE	*QUOTE U.S.$
1989 Bottom of the Sixth NRC-607	Retrd.	N/A	140.00	140
1981 Breaking Home Ties NRV-300	Retrd.	N/A	2000.00	2300
1989 Doctor and Doll NRP-600	Retrd.	N/A	90.00	60

*Quotes have been rounded up to nearest dollar

FIGURINES

YEAR ISSUE	EDITION LIMIT	YEAR RETD.	ISSUE PRICE	*QUOTE U.S.$
1989 First Day Home NRC-606	Retrd.	N/A	80.00	80
1989 First Haircut NRC-604	Retrd.	N/A	75.00	100
1989 First Visit NRC-605	Retrd.	N/A	110.00	110
1982 Lincoln NRV-301	Retrd.	N/A	300.00	375
1989 Locomotive NRC-603	Retrd.	N/A	110.00	110-125
1989 Runaway NRP-610	Retrd.	N/A	140.00	190
1982 Thanksgiving NRV-302	Retrd.	N/A	2500.00	2650
1989 Weigh-In NRP-611	Retrd.	N/A	120.00	125-140

Norman Rockwell America Collection-Lg. Ltd. Edition - Rockwell-Inspired

YEAR ISSUE	EDITION LIMIT	YEAR RETD.	ISSUE PRICE	*QUOTE U.S.$
1975 Baseball NR-102	Retrd.	N/A	125.00	450
1989 Bottom of the Sixth NRP-307	Retrd.	N/A	190.00	190
1982 Circus NR-106	Retrd.	N/A	500.00	500-750
1974 Doctor and Doll NR-100	Retrd.	N/A	300.00	1400
1989 Doctor and Doll NRP-300	Retrd.	N/A	150.00	150
1981 Dreams of Long Ago NR-105	Retrd.	N/A	500.00	750
1979 Leapfrog NR-104	Retrd.	N/A	440.00	750
1984 Marble Players NR-107	Retrd.	N/A	500.00	650-750
1975 No Swimming NR-101	Retrd.	N/A	150.00	600-1200
1989 Runaway NRP-310	Retrd.	N/A	190.00	190
1974 See America First NR-103	Retrd.	N/A	100.00	550-1500
1989 Weigh-In NRP-311	Retrd.	N/A	160.00	140-175

Norman Rockwell Collection - Rockwell-Inspired

YEAR ISSUE	EDITION LIMIT	YEAR RETD.	ISSUE PRICE	*QUOTE U.S.$
1982 American Mother NRG-42	Retrd.	N/A	100.00	125
1978 At the Doctor NR-29	Retrd.	N/A	108.00	165-195
1979 Back From Camp NR-33	Retrd.	N/A	96.00	145
1973 Back To School NR-02	Retrd.	N/A	20.00	75
1975 Barbershop Quartet NR-23	Retrd.	N/A	100.00	650-1300
1974 Baseball NR-16	Retrd.	N/A	45.00	160-180
1975 Big Moment NR-21	Retrd.	N/A	60.00	130-150
1973 Caroller NR-03	Retrd.	N/A	22.50	75
1975 Circus NR-22	Retrd.	N/A	55.00	145
1983 Country Critic NR-43	Retrd.	N/A	75.00	125
1982 Croquet NR-41	Retrd.	N/A	100.00	150
1973 Daydreamer NR-04	Retrd.	N/A	22.50	45-75
1975 Discovery NR-20	Retrd.	N/A	55.00	170-650
1973 Doctor & Doll NR-12	Retrd.	N/A	65.00	285
1979 Dreams of Long Ago NR-31	Retrd.	N/A	100.00	125-156
1976 Drum For Tommy NRC-24	Retrd.	N/A	40.00	95
1980 Exasperated Nanny NR-35	Retrd.	N/A	96.00	100-160
1978 First Day of School NR-27	Retrd.	N/A	100.00	150
1974 Friends In Need NR-13	Retrd.	N/A	45.00	100
1983 Graduate NR-44	Retrd.	N/A	30.00	85
1979 Grandpa's Ballerina NR-32	Retrd.	N/A	100.00	130-140
1980 Hankerchief NR-36	Retrd.	N/A	110.00	125
1973 Lazybones NR-08	Retrd.	N/A	30.00	250-455
1973 Leapfrog NR-09	Retrd.	N/A	50.00	600-1040
1973 Love Letter NR-06	Retrd.	N/A	25.00	85-95
1973 Lovers NR-07	Retrd.	N/A	45.00	85-110
1978 Magic Potion NR-28	Retrd.	N/A	84.00	150-200
1973 Marble Players NR-11	Retrd.	N/A	60.00	390-425
1973 No Swimming NR-05	Retrd.	N/A	25.00	65-145
1977 Pals NR-25	Retrd.	N/A	60.00	120-150
1986 Red Cross NR-47	Retrd.	N/A	67.00	100
1973 Redhead NR-01	Retrd.	N/A	20.00	210
1980 Santa's Good Boys NR-37	Retrd.	N/A	90.00	100
1973 Schoolmaster NR-10	Retrd.	N/A	55.00	225
1984 Scotty's Home Plate NR-46	Retrd.	N/A	30.00	60
1983 Scotty's Surprise NRS-20	Retrd.	N/A	25.00	60-175
1974 See America First NR-17	Retrd.	N/A	50.00	150
1981 Spirit of Education NR-38	Retrd.	N/A	96.00	125
1974 Springtime '33 NR-14	Retrd.	N/A	30.00	75
1977 Springtime '35 NR-19	Retrd.	N/A	50.00	65-75
1974 Summertime '33 NR-15	Retrd.	N/A	45.00	75
1974 Take Your Medicine NR-18	Retrd.	N/A	50.00	150
1979 Teacher's Pet NRA-30	Retrd.	N/A	35.00	100
1980 The Toss NR-34	Retrd.	N/A	110.00	250
1982 A Visit With Rockwell NR-40	Retrd.	N/A	120.00	100-120
1988 Wedding March NR-49	Retrd.	N/A	110.00	175
1978 Young Doctor NRD-26	Retrd.	N/A	100.00	180
1987 Young Love NR-48	Retrd.	N/A	70.00	120-150

Norman Rockwell Collection-Boy Scout Series - Rockwell-Inspired

YEAR ISSUE	EDITION LIMIT	YEAR RETD.	ISSUE PRICE	*QUOTE U.S.$
1981 Can't Wait BSA-01	Retrd.	N/A	30.00	130
1981 Good Friends BSA-04	Retrd.	N/A	58.00	65-130
1981 Good Turn BSA-05	Retrd.	N/A	65.00	125-130
1982 Guiding Hand BSA-07	Retrd.	N/A	58.00	150
1981 Physically Strong BSA-03	Retrd.	N/A	56.00	150-160
1981 Scout Is Helpful BSA-02	Retrd.	N/A	38.00	150
1981 Scout Memories BSA-06	Retrd.	N/A	65.00	100
1983 Tomorrow's Leader BSA-08	Retrd.	N/A	45.00	55-150

Norman Rockwell Collection-Country Gentlemen Series - Rockwell-Inspired

YEAR ISSUE	EDITION LIMIT	YEAR RETD.	ISSUE PRICE	*QUOTE U.S.$
1982 Bringing Home the Tree CG-02	Retrd.	N/A	60.00	110
1982 The Catch CG-04	Retrd.	N/A	50.00	100
1982 On the Ice CG-05	Retrd.	N/A	50.00	60-75
1982 Pals CG-03	Retrd.	N/A	36.00	95
1982 Thin Ice CG-06	Retrd.	N/A	50.00	60
1982 Turkey Dinner CG-01	Retrd.	N/A	85.00	110

Norman Rockwell Collection-Huck Finn Series - Rockwell-Inspired

YEAR ISSUE	EDITION LIMIT	YEAR RETD.	ISSUE PRICE	*QUOTE U.S.$
1980 Listening HF-02	Retrd.	N/A	110.00	125-135
1980 No Kings HF-03	Retrd.	N/A	110.00	150
1979 The Secret HF-01	Retrd.	N/A	110.00	130
1980 Snake Escapes HF-04	Retrd.	N/A	110.00	135

Norman Rockwell Collection-Miniatures - Rockwell-Inspired

YEAR ISSUE	EDITION LIMIT	YEAR RETD.	ISSUE PRICE	*QUOTE U.S.$
1984 At the Doctor's NR-229	Retrd.	N/A	35.00	35
1979 Back To School NR-202	Retrd.	N/A	18.00	50
1982 Barbershop Quartet NR-223	Retrd.	N/A	40.00	50-85
1980 Baseball NR-216	Retrd.	N/A	40.00	50-65
1982 Big Moment NR-221	Retrd.	N/A	36.00	40
1979 Caroller NR-203	Retrd.	N/A	20.00	35-50
1982 Circus NR-222	Retrd.	N/A	35.00	40-75
1979 Daydreamer NR-204	Retrd.	N/A	20.00	45-50
1982 Discovery NR-220	Retrd.	N/A	35.00	65
1979 Doctor and Doll NR-212	Retrd.	N/A	40.00	75
1999 Doctor and the Doll NRR-610	7,500		30.00	30
1984 Dreams of Long Ago NR-231	Retrd.	N/A	30.00	30
1982 Drum For Tommy NRC-224	Retrd.	N/A	25.00	30
1989 First Day Home MRC-906	Retrd.	N/A	45.00	45
1984 First Day of School NR-227	Retrd.	N/A	35.00	35
1989 First Haircut MRC-904	Retrd.	N/A	45.00	45
1999 Fishing NRR-602	7,500		25.00	25
1980 Friends In Need NR-213	Retrd.	N/A	30.00	40
1999 Gramps at the Plate NRR-604	7,500		25.00	25
1999 Gramps at the Reins (musical) NRR-603M	7,500		40.00	40
1999 Gramps at the Reins NRR-609	7,500		30.00	30
1979 Lazybones NR-208	Retrd.	N/A	22.00	45-50
1979 Leapfrog NR-209	Retrd.	N/A	32.00	45-65
1979 Love Letter NR-206	Retrd.	N/A	26.00	45-65
1979 Lovers NR-207	Retrd.	N/A	28.00	60
1984 Magic Potion NR-228	Retrd.	N/A	30.00	40
2000 Marble Champs NRR-614	7,500		25.00	25
1979 Marble Players NR-211	Retrd.	N/A	36.00	75-80
1999 The Marriage License (musical) NRR-602M	7,500		40.00	40
1999 The Marriage License NRR-607	7,500		30.00	30
1979 No Swimming NR-205	Retrd.	N/A	22.00	60
1984 Pals NR-225	Retrd.	N/A	25.00	25-50
1999 The Pharmacist NRR-606	7,500		30.00	30
1999 Puppy Love NRR-611	7,500		30.00	30
1979 Redhead NR-201	Retrd.	N/A	18.00	50
1999 The Runaway NRR-605	7,500		30.00	30
2000 Santa at the Globe NRR-612	7,500		25.00	25
1983 Santa On the Train NR-245	Retrd.	N/A	35.00	55-65
2000 Saturday Night Out NRR-613	7,500		25.00	25
1979 Schoolmaster NR-210	Retrd.	N/A	34.00	45
1980 See America First NR-217	Retrd.	N/A	28.00	55-60
1999 Serenade (musical) NRR-601M	7,500		30.00	30
1999 Serenade NRR-601	7,500		20.00	20
1999 Skaters NRR-600	7,500		20.00	20
1980 Springtime '33 NR-214	Retrd.	N/A	24.00	80
1982 Springtime '35 NR-219	Retrd.	N/A	24.00	30
1999 Stilt Walker NRR-603	7,500		25.00	25
1980 Summertime '33 NR-215	Retrd.	N/A	22.00	50
1980 Take Your Medicine NR-218	Retrd.	N/A	36.00	40-50
1999 Triple Self Portrait NRR-608	7,500		30.00	30
1984 Young Doctor NRD-226	Retrd.	N/A	30.00	50

Norman Rockwell Collection-Pewter Figurines - Rockwell-Inspired

YEAR ISSUE	EDITION LIMIT	YEAR RETD.	ISSUE PRICE	*QUOTE U.S.$
1980 Back to School FP-02	Retrd.	N/A	25.00	25
1980 Barbershop Quartet FP-23	Retrd.	N/A	25.00	25
1980 Big Moment FP-21	Retrd.	N/A	25.00	25
1980 Caroller FP-03	Retrd.	N/A	25.00	25
1980 Circus FP-22	Retrd.	N/A	25.00	25
1980 Doctor and Doll FP-12	Retrd.	N/A	25.00	25
1980 Figurine Display Rack FDR-01	Retrd.	N/A	60.00	60
1980 Grandpa's Ballerina FP-32	Retrd.	N/A	25.00	25
1980 Lovers FP-07	Retrd.	N/A	25.00	25
1980 Magic Potion FP-28	Retrd.	N/A	25.00	25
1980 No Swimming FP-05	Retrd.	N/A	25.00	25
1980 See America First FP-17	Retrd.	N/A	25.00	25
1980 Take Your Medicine FP-18	Retrd.	N/A	25.00	25

Norman Rockwell Collection-Rockwell Club Series - Rockwell-Inspired

YEAR ISSUE	EDITION LIMIT	YEAR RETD.	ISSUE PRICE	*QUOTE U.S.$
1982 Diary RCC-02	Retrd.	N/A	35.00	75
1984 Gone Fishing RCC-04	Retrd.	N/A	30.00	55
1983 Runaway Pants RCC-03	Retrd.	N/A	65.00	75
1981 Young Artist RCC-01	Retrd.	N/A	96.00	130-179

Norman Rockwell Collection-Select Collection, Ltd. - Rockwell-Inspired

YEAR ISSUE	EDITION LIMIT	YEAR RETD.	ISSUE PRICE	*QUOTE U.S.$
1982 Boy & Mother With Puppies SC-1001	Retrd.	N/A	27.50	28
1982 Father With Child SC-1005	Retrd.	N/A	22.00	22
1982 Football Player SC-1004	Retrd.	N/A	22.00	22
1982 Girl Bathing Dog SC-1006	Retrd.	N/A	26.50	27
1982 Girl With Dolls In Crib SC-1002	Retrd.	N/A	26.50	27
1982 Helping Hand SC-1007	Retrd.	N/A	32.00	32
1982 Lemonade Stand SC-1008	Retrd.	N/A	32.00	32
1982 Save Me SC-1010	Retrd.	N/A	35.00	35
1982 Shaving Lesson SC-1009	Retrd.	N/A	30.00	30
1982 Young Couple SC-1003	Retrd.	N/A	27.50	28

Norman Rockwell Collection-Tom Sawyer Miniatures - Rockwell-Inspired

YEAR ISSUE	EDITION LIMIT	YEAR RETD.	ISSUE PRICE	*QUOTE U.S.$
1983 First Smoke TSM-02	Retrd.	N/A	40.00	75
1983 Lost In Cave TSM-05	Retrd.	N/A	40.00	75
1983 Take Your Medicine TSM-04	Retrd.	N/A	40.00	75
1983 Whitewashing the Fence TSM-01	Retrd.	N/A	40.00	75

Norman Rockwell Collection-Tom Sawyer Series - Rockwell-Inspired

YEAR ISSUE	EDITION LIMIT	YEAR RETD.	ISSUE PRICE	*QUOTE U.S.$
1976 First Smoke TS-02	Retrd.	N/A	60.00	235
1978 Lost In Cave TS-04	Retrd.	N/A	70.00	175
1977 Take Your Medicine TS-03	Retrd.	N/A	63.00	235
1975 Whitewashing the Fence TS-01	Retrd.	N/A	60.00	235

Norman Rockwell Saturday Evening Post - Rockwell-Inspired

YEAR ISSUE	EDITION LIMIT	YEAR RETD.	ISSUE PRICE	*QUOTE U.S.$
1992 After the Prom NRP-916	Retrd.	1997	75.00	75
1994 Almost Grown Up NRC-609	Open		75.00	75
1993 Baby's First Step NRC-604	Open		100.00	100
1993 Bed Time NRC-606	Retrd.	1997	100.00	100
1990 Bedside Manner NRP-904	Retrd.	1997	65.00	85
1990 Big Moment NRP-906	Retrd.	N/A	100.00	100
1990 Bottom of the Sixth NRP-908	Retrd.	1997	165.00	165
1993 Bride & Groom NRC-605	Open		100.00	100
1991 Catching The Big One NRP-909	Retrd.	1997	75.00	125
1992 Choosin Up NRP-912	Retrd.	N/A	110.00	130-150
1990 Daydreamer NRP-902	Retrd.	1997	55.00	55
1990 Doctor and Doll NRP-907	Retrd.	N/A	110.00	150
1995 First Down NRC-614	Retrd.	1999	130.00	130
1995 First Haircut NRC-610	Retrd.	1999	85.00	80-85
1994 For A Good Boy NRC-608	Retrd.	1999	100.00	100
1992 Gone Fishing NRP-915	Retrd.	1999	65.00	65
1991 Gramps NRP-910	Retrd.	1999	85.00	85
1994 Little Mother NRC-607	Retrd.	1999	75.00	75
1998 Marriage License NRP-917	Retrd.	1999	65.00	65
1997 Missed NRP-914	Retrd.	1999	110.00	110-130
1995 New Arrival NRC-612	Retrd.	1999	90.00	90
1990 No Swimming NRP-901	Retrd.	N/A	50.00	85
1991 The Pharmacist NRP-911	Retrd.	1997	70.00	70-85
1990 Prom Dress NRP-903	Retrd.	N/A	60.00	60
1990 Runaway NRP-905	Retrd.	1997	130.00	165
1995 Sweet Dreams NRC-611	Retrd.	1999	85.00	85
1994 A Visit with Rockwell (100th Anniversary)-NRP-100	1,994	1999	100.00	100

Norman Rockwell Saturday Evening Post-Miniatures - Rockwell-Inspired

YEAR ISSUE	EDITION LIMIT	YEAR RETD.	ISSUE PRICE	*QUOTE U.S.$
1991 A Boy Meets His Dog BMR-01	Retrd.	N/A	35.00	40
1991 Downhill Daring BMR-02	Retrd.	N/A	40.00	40
1991 Flowers in Tender Bloom BMR-03	Retrd.	N/A	32.00	40
1991 Fondly Do We Remember BMR-04	Retrd.	N/A	30.00	30
1991 In His Spirit BMR-05	Retrd.	N/A	30.00	30
1991 Pride of Parenthood BMR-06	Retrd.	N/A	35.00	40
1991 Sweet Serenade BMR-07	Retrd.	N/A	32.00	40
1991 Sweet Song So Young BMR-08	Retrd.	N/A	30.00	40

The Spirit of Remington - R. Brown

YEAR ISSUE	EDITION LIMIT	YEAR RETD.	ISSUE PRICE	*QUOTE U.S.$
1998 The Captive RBS-3	2,500	2000	35.00	35
1998 Conjuring Back the Buffalo RBS-4	2,500	2000	35.00	35
1998 Lt. Powhatan Clark RBS-1	2,500	2000	35.00	35
1998 The Puncher RBS-2	2,500	2000	70.00	70
1998 The Smoke Signal RBS-5	2,500	2000	70.00	70

Three Stooges Collection - Dave Grossman Creations

YEAR ISSUE	EDITION LIMIT	YEAR RETD.	ISSUE PRICE	*QUOTE U.S.$
1998 Curly (musical) TS-301	5,000	2000	30.00	30
1998 Curly Fireman TS-996	5,000	2000	20.00	20
1998 Curly Policeman TS-993	5,000	2000	20.00	20
1998 Curly TS-301	5,000	2000	20.00	20
1998 Larry (musical) TS-300	5,000	2000	30.00	30
1998 Larry Fireman TS-995	5,000	2000	20.00	20
1998 Larry Policeman TS-992	5,000	2000	20.00	20
1998 Larry TS-300	5,000	2000	20.00	20
1998 Moe (musical) TS-302	5,000	2000	30.00	30
1998 Moe Fireman TS-994	5,000	2000	20.00	20
1998 Moe Policeman TS-991	5,000	2000	20.00	20
1998 Moe TS-302	5,000	2000	20.00	20
1998 Scrooges Golfing Globe TSG-01	5,000	2000	30.00	30

Wizard of Oz - Dave Grossman Creations

YEAR ISSUE	EDITION LIMIT	YEAR RETD.	ISSUE PRICE	*QUOTE U.S.$
1996 Apple Tree (waterglobe) OZG-7	Retrd.	1999	40.00	40
1996 Cowardly Lion (musical) OZ-102M	5,000	1999	35.00	35
1996 Cowardly Lion OZ-102	5,000	1999	20.00	20
1997 Dorothy & Friends (lg. musical) OZM-3	Retrd.	1999	75.00	75
1996 Dorothy & Glinda (waterglobe) OZG-2	Retrd.	1999	45.00	45
1996 Dorothy & Munchkins (waterglobe) OZG-4	Retrd.	1999	55.00	55
1996 Dorothy (musical) OZ-101M	5,000	1999	35.00	35
1996 Dorothy OZ-101	5,000	1999	20.00	20
1996 Emerald City (lighted) (waterglobe)OZG-5	Retrd.	1999	60.00	60
1996 Flying Monkey OZ-110	5,000	1999	16.00	16
1996 Good Witch (musical) OZ-106M	5,000	1999	35.00	35
1996 Good Witch OZ-106	5,000	1999	32.00	32
1996 Mayor OZ-107	5,000	1999	30.00	30
1996 Mortician OZ-108	5,000	1999	20.00	20
1996 Poppy Field (waterglobe) OZG-1	Retrd.	1999	55.00	55
1997 Rainbow (lg. musical) OZM-4	Retrd.	1999	75.00	75
1996 Ruby Slippers (waterglobe) OZG-9	Retrd.	1999	40.00	40
1996 Scarecrow (musical) OZ-104M	5,000	1999	35.00	35
1996 Scarecrow OZ-104	5,000	1999	20.00	20
1996 Tin Man (musical) OZ-103M	5,000	1999	35.00	35
1996 Tin Man OZ-103	5,000	1999	20.00	20
1996 Wicked Witch (musical) OZ-105M	5,000	1999	35.00	35
1996 Wicked Witch (waterglobe) OZG-3	Retrd.	1999	65.00	65
1996 Wicked Witch OZ-105	5,000	1999	25.00	25
1996 Winkie-Guard OZ-111	5,000	1999	16.00	16
1997 Witch's Castle (lg. musical) OZM-2	Retrd.	1999	85.00	85
1996 Witch's Castle (waterglobe) OZG-6	Retrd.	1999	40.00	40
1996 Witch's Glass Ball (waterglobe) OZG-8	Retrd.	1999	50.00	50
1996 Wizard OZ-109	5,000	1999	16.00	16

DC Super Heroes - Hallmark

DC Super Heroes - Hallmark

YEAR ISSUE	EDITION LIMIT	YEAR RETD.	ISSUE PRICE	*QUOTE U.S.$
1996 Golden Age Batman™ and Robin™, the Boy Wonder "The Dynamic Duo" QHF3103	Retrd.	1997	70.00	70

*Quotes have been rounded up to nearest dollar

YEAR ISSUE	EDITION LIMIT	YEAR RETD.	ISSUE PRICE	*QUOTE U.S.$
1996 Golden Age Superman™ "Man of Steel" QHF3101	14,500	1997	80.00	80
1996 Golden Age WonderWoman™ "Champion of Freedom" QHF3107	Retrd.	1997	35.00	35
1996 Modern Era Batman™ "Guardian of Gotham City" QHF3104	Retrd.	1997	55.00	55
1996 Modern Era Robin™ "World's Bravest Teenager" QHF3105	Retrd.	1997	40.00	40
1996 Modern Era Superman™ "In A Single Bound" QHF3102	Retrd.	1997	60.00	60
1996 Modern Era WonderWoman™ "Warrior of Strength and Wisdom" QHF3106	Retrd.	1997	35.00	35

Department 56

All Through The House - Department 56

YEAR ISSUE	EDITION LIMIT	YEAR RETD.	ISSUE PRICE	*QUOTE U.S.$
1993 All Snug in Their Bed 9322-0	Closed	1997	48.00	58-69
1992 Aunt Martha With Turkey 9317-3	Closed	1995	27.50	66-70
1993 Away To The Window 9321-1	Closed	1997	42.00	78-88
1995 Carrie Feeds The Cardinals 93339	Closed	1997	18.00	30-32
1994 Children With New Tree 9330-0, set/4	Closed	1997	85.00	84-102
1991 Christmas Tree 9302-5	Closed	1997	25.00	35-55
1992 Christopher Tasting Cookies, Caroline Stringing Cranberries 9310-6, (2 asst.)	Closed	1997	15.00	28-30
1992 Christopher Tasting Cookies 9310-6	Closed	1997	15.00	15-22
1992 Caroline Stringing Cranberries 9310-6	Closed	1997	15.00	16-23
1992 Dinner Table 9313-0	Closed	1995	65.00	102-140
1991 Down the Chimney & Sugar Plum Chair 9300-9, set/2	Closed	1997	96.00	132-140
1993 Elizabeth Spies Santa, Emily Spies Santa 9325-4, (2 asst.)	Closed	1997	16.00	30-32
1993 Elizabeth Spies Santa 9325-4	Closed	1997	16.00	16-36
1993 Emily Spies Santa 9325-4	Closed	1997	16.00	16-20
1994 Fletcher Playing Flute, Kenneth & Katie Singing Carols 9327-0, (3 asst.)	Closed	1997	16.00	16-24
1992 Grandma & Kitchen Table 9308-4, set/2	Closed	1997	55.00	55-90
1994 I Saw Mama Kissing Santa Claus 9332-7, set/2	Closed	1997	45.00	90-110
1993 Johnny Riding His Pony, Judith and Her Jack-In-The-Box 9319-0, (2 asst.)	Closed	1997	15.00	20-30
1993 Johnny Riding His Pony 9319-0	Closed	1997	15.00	15-36
1993 Judith and Her Jack-In-The-Box 9319-0	Closed	1997	15.00	22-25
1991 Jolly Old Elf 9303-3	Closed	1997	25.00	27-36
1992 Kitchen 9307-6	Closed	1997	75.00	74-92
1995 Let's Sing "Here Comes Santa Claus" 93336, set/3	Closed	1997	96.00	90-120
1992 Madeline Making Cookies 9309-2	Closed	1997	24.00	24-35
1991 Mama in Her Kerchief, Papa in His Cap 9304-1	Closed	1997	30.00	19-40
1991 Mary Jo, Billy 9306-8 (2 asst.)	Closed	1997	15.00	32-36
1996 Michael Makes a Snowman 93340	Closed	1997	32.50	22-48
1992 Mr. & Mrs. Bell at Dinner 9314-9, set/2	Closed	1995	40.00	78-98
1992 Nicholas Hanging Coat 9311-4	Closed	1997	22.50	29-32
1992 Nicholas, Natalie, & Spot The Dog 9315-7, set/3	Closed	1995	45.00	34-58
1993 Not A Creature Was Stirring, Not Even a Mouse 9318-1	Closed	1997	37.50	40-54
1993 Pamela & Peter's Pillow Fight 9324-6, (2 asst.)	Closed	1997	16.00	24-32
1993 Pamela's Pillow Fight 9324-6	Closed	1997	16.00	16
1993 Peter's Pillow Fight 9324-6	Closed	1997	16.00	16
1993 Ruthan & Baby Patrick, Bradley Builds With Blocks 9320-3, (2 asst.)	Closed	1997	16.00	16-30
1991 Sarah Kate & Andy, Sue Ellen 9305-0 (2 asst.)	Closed	1997	28.00	48-55
1991 •Sarah Kate & Andy 9305-0	Closed	1997	16.00	21-30
1991 •Sue Ellen 9305-0	Closed	1997	16.00	9-28
1992 Sideboard 9316-5	Closed	1995	45.00	58-77
1994 Sleigh Full of Toys and St. Nicholas Too 9328-9	Closed	1997	75.00	165-210
1995 Sliding Down The Bannister 9333-5	Closed	1997	70.00	80-96
1994 Snowman with Plexi Sign 9874-4	Closed	1996	25.00	38-44
1991 Staircase 9301-7	Closed	1997	48.00	48-64
1995 Steven Skis on New-Fallen Snow 93338	Closed	1997	15.00	24-28
1995 Suzy and Spencer Making Snowballs 93337, set/2	Closed	1997	30.00	36-46
1992 Theodore Adjusting Time on Grandfather Clock 9312-2, set/2	Closed	1997	32.50	32-44
1994 To His Team Gave a Whistle 9329-7, (2 asst.)	Closed	1997	20.00	62
1996 Uncle John Takes a Family Portrait 93348, set/2	Closed	1997	72.00	96
1994 Under The Mistletoe 9331-9	Closed	1997	35.00	46
1994 Up On The Rooftop 9326-2	Closed	1997	85.00	82
1993 Visions of Sugarplums Danced in His Head 9323-8	Closed	1997	24.00	32-40

Brontë Candle Crown - Department 56

YEAR ISSUE	EDITION LIMIT	YEAR RETD.	ISSUE PRICE	*QUOTE U.S.$
1999 Alice in Wonderland Set 50000, set/11 plus book	2,500		4000.00	4000
1999 The Nutcracker Suite 50001, set/10 plus book	2,500		4000.00	4000
1999 The Wizard of Oz 50002, set/9 plus book	2,500		4000.00	4000

Candle Crown Collections - Department 56

YEAR ISSUE	EDITION LIMIT	YEAR RETD.	ISSUE PRICE	*QUOTE U.S.$
2000 Father Time - 2000 50036	Yr.Iss.		50.00	50

Candle Crown Collections-A Christmas Carol - Department 56

YEAR ISSUE	EDITION LIMIT	YEAR RETD.	ISSUE PRICE	*QUOTE U.S.$
2000 Bob Cratchit & Tiny Tim 50030	Open		45.00	45
2000 Ebenezer Scrooge 50029	Open		40.00	40
2000 Ghost of Christmas Present 50033	Open		40.00	40
2000 Ghost of Jacob Marley 50031	Open		40.00	40
2000 Mr. Fezziwig 50034	Open		40.00	40

Candle Crown Collections-African Safari Animals - Department 56

YEAR ISSUE	EDITION LIMIT	YEAR RETD.	ISSUE PRICE	*QUOTE U.S.$
2000 Enjoying Solitude (Cheetah) 50038	Open		37.50	38
2000 Learning To Play (Elephant) 50041	Open		37.50	38
2000 Loving Touch (Velvet Monkey) 50042	Open		37.50	38
2000 A Quiet Moment (Zebra) 50037	Open		37.50	38

Candle Crown Collections-Alice In Wonderland - Department 56

YEAR ISSUE	EDITION LIMIT	YEAR RETD.	ISSUE PRICE	*QUOTE U.S.$
1999 Alice 50003	Open		35.00	35
1999 Cheshire Cat 50007	Open		40.00	40
1999 King of Hearts 50004	Open		40.00	40
1999 Mad Hatter 50028	Open		40.00	40
1999 Queen of Hearts 50005	Open		40.00	40
1999 White Rabbit 50006	Open		35.00	35

Candle Crown Collections-The Nutcracker - Department 56

YEAR ISSUE	EDITION LIMIT	YEAR RETD.	ISSUE PRICE	*QUOTE U.S.$
1999 Clara & The Nutcracker Doll 50009	Open		45.00	45
1999 Drosselmeyer 50010	Open		40.00	40
1999 Nutcracker Prince 50011	Open		40.00	40
1999 Sugar Plum Fairy 50012	Open		40.00	40

Candle Crown Collections-The Wizard of Oz - Department 56

YEAR ISSUE	EDITION LIMIT	YEAR RETD.	ISSUE PRICE	*QUOTE U.S.$
1999 Cowardly Lion 50026	Open		45.00	45
1999 Dorothy 50025	Open		45.00	45
1999 Scarecrow 50014	Open		45.00	45
1999 Tin Man 50015	Open		45.00	45

Easter Collectibles - Department 56

YEAR ISSUE	EDITION LIMIT	YEAR RETD.	ISSUE PRICE	*QUOTE U.S.$
1991 Bisque Lamb, Large 4" 7392-0	Closed	1991	7.50	29-48
1991 Bisque Lamb, Small 2.5" 7393-8	Closed	1991	5.00	21-24
1991 Bisque Lamb, set	Closed	1991	12.50	39-78
1992 Bisque Rabbit, Large 5" 7498-5	Closed	1992	8.00	20-26
1992 Bisque Rabbit, Small 4" 7499-3	Closed	1992	6.00	18-29
1992 Bisque Rabbit, set	Closed	1992	14.00	42
1993 Bisque Duckling, Large 3.5" 7282-6	Closed	1993	8.50	10-15
1993 Bisque Duckling, Small 2.75" 7281-8	Closed	1993	6.50	10-20
1993 Bisque Duckling, set	Closed	1993	15.00	18-36
1994 Bisque Fledgling in Nest, Large 2.75" 2400-7	Closed	1994	6.00	6-18
1994 Bisque Fledgling in Nest, Small 2.5" 2401-5	Closed	1994	5.00	5-16
1995 Bisque Chick, Large 2464-3	Closed	1996	8.50	7-25
1995 Bisque Chick, Small 2465-1	Closed	1996	6.50	16-25
1995 Bisque Chick, Set	Closed	1996	6.50	29
1996 Bisque Rabbit, Large 2765-0	Closed	1996	8.50	12-18
1996 Bisque Rabbit, Small 2764-2	Closed	1996	7.50	12-18
1996 Bisque Rabbit, set	Closed	1996	16.00	29
1997 Bisque Rabbit, large 23700	Closed	1997	8.50	8-20
1997 Bisque Rabbit, small 23701	Closed	1997	7.50	7-15
1998 Bisque Pig, large 23773	Closed	1998	7.50	8
1998 Bisque Pig, small 23774	Closed	1998	6.50	7
1999 Bisque Kitten, large 23862	Closed	1999	7.00	7
1999 Bisque Kitten, small 23861	Closed	1999	6.00	6
2000 Bisque Duck, large 23901	Closed	2000	8.50	9
2000 Bisque Duck, small 23902	Closed	2000	7.50	8
2001 Bisque Squirrel, large 24056	Yr.Iss.		7.50	8
2001 Bisque Squirrel, small 24097	Yr.Iss.		6.50	7

Madeline™ Musicals - Department 56

YEAR ISSUE	EDITION LIMIT	YEAR RETD.	ISSUE PRICE	*QUOTE U.S.$
1999 Skater's Waltz Music Box 13100	Open		40.00	40
1999 We Wish You A Merry Christmas Music Box 13101	Open		40.00	40

Merry Makers - Department 56

YEAR ISSUE	EDITION LIMIT	YEAR RETD.	ISSUE PRICE	*QUOTE U.S.$
1995 Barnaby The Breadman 9361-0	Closed	1996	20.00	18-29
1992 Bartholomew The Baker w/Cart 9366-1	Closed	1996	35.00	60-70
1994 Bremwell The Bell-A-Ringer 9387-4	Closed	1996	22.00	32-36
1995 Brewster The Bird Feeder 93976	Closed	1996	25.00	24-60
1994 Calvin The Candycane Striper 93912	Closed	1996	22.00	24-32
1991 Charles The Cellist 9355-6	Closed	1995	19.00	32-36
1995 Chester The Tester & His Kettle 93972	Closed	1996	27.50	78-86
1993 Clarence the Concertinist (waterglobe/music box) 9377-7	Closed	1996	25.00	42-50
1991 Clarence The Concertinist 9353-0	Closed	1995	19.00	20-32
1991 Frederick The Flutist 9352-1	Closed	1995	19.00	25-32
1993 Garrison The Guzzler 9379-3	Closed	1996	20.00	26-44
1993 Godfrey The Gatherer 9380-7	Closed	1996	20.00	24-29
1995 Halsey The Stocking Hanger 93974	Closed	1996	32.50	28-48
1993 Heavenly Bakery Entrance 9371-8	Closed	1996	20.00	38-56
1991 Horatio The Hornblower 9351-3	Closed	1995	19.00	25-32
1994 Leo The Lamp-A-Lighter 9386-6	Closed	1996	22.00	28-32
1994 Leopold The Lollipopman 9390-4	Closed	1996	22.00	28-30
1994 Lollipop Shop Entrance 9389-0	Closed	1996	35.00	48-60
1993 Martin The Mandolinist (waterglobe/music box) 9377-7	Closed	1996	25.00	37-52
1991 Martin The Mandolinist 9350-5	Closed	1995	19.00	24-32
1993 Maxwell The Mixer at his Table, set/8 9372-6	Closed	1996	50.00	64-68
1994 Merrily We Roll Carolers & Gabriel The Goat 9382-3	Closed	1996	144.00	158-188
1992 Merry Makers Papier-Mache Church 9359-9	Closed	1995	95.00	99-105
1993 Merry Mountain Chapel, lighted 9370-0	Closed	1996	60.00	68-98
1995 Ollie The Optimist 93973	Closed	1996	25.00	46-48
1993 Otto The Ovenman at his Table, set/2 9373-4	Closed	1996	45.00	60
1994 The Peppermint Tree 9394-7	Closed	1996	18.00	24-29
1993 Percival The Puddingman (waterglobe/music box) 9376-9	Closed	1996	30.00	37-52
1992 Percival The Puddingman 9362-9	Closed	1996	20.00	16-29
1994 Percy The Pudding-A-Bringer 9388-2	Closed	1996	22.00	26-32
1994 Peter The Peppermint Maker 9393-9	Closed	1996	22.00	27-38
1993 Porter The Presser & His Press, set/2 9378-5	Closed	1996	65.00	60-74
1993 Samuel the Sampler & Cider Barrel, set/3 9381-5	Closed	1996	27.50	45-58
1992 Sebastian The Snowball Maker 9367-0	Closed	1996	20.00	24-29
1993 Seigfried & The Snowman (waterglobe/music box) 9374-2	Closed	1996	30.00	52-58
1992 Seymore, Seigfried & The Snowman9365-3	Closed	1996	45.00	50-58
1995 Sheridan Thinks Santa, set/2 93975	Closed	1996	27.50	66-76
1991 Sidney The Singer 9354-8	Closed	1995	19.00	24-30
1992 Sigmund The Snowshoer 9358-0	Closed	1996	20.00	24-30
1993 Simon The Pieman (waterglobe/music box) 9376-9	Closed	1996	25.00	37-52
1992 Simon The Pieman 9363-7	Closed	1996	30.00	27-29
1993 Solomon The Sledder (waterglobe/music box) 9385-8	Closed	1996	37.50	44-52
1992 Solomon The Sledder 9356-4	Closed	1996	24.00	28-35
1992 Sweet Treats Tree 9364-5	Closed	1996	18.00	29-32
1992 Thaddeus The Tobogganist (waterglobe/music box) 9375-0	Closed	1996	30.00	38
1993 Thaddeus The Tobogganist 9357-2	Closed	1996	24.00	24-35
1992 Timothy The Taffy Twister 9392-0	Closed	1996	22.00	27-36

Silhouette Santas (Winter Silhouette) - Department 56

YEAR ISSUE	EDITION LIMIT	YEAR RETD.	ISSUE PRICE	*QUOTE U.S.$
1995 Cat Nap Santa & Finishing Touches Santa Bookends/Stocking Hangers 78560, (2 asst.)	Closed	1997	16.50	24-26
1994 Cat Nap Santa 7855-7	Closed	1997	37.50	40-69
1995 Dog's Best Friend Santa 78558, set/2	Closed	1999	37.50	38-69
1995 Finishing Touches Santa 78559	Closed	1997	37.50	39-69
1998 I See You Santa 78553, set/2	Closed	1999	35.00	35
1996 I Spy Santa 78562, set/2	Closed	1999	45.00	45-75
1998 I Wuv You Santa 78554	Closed	1999	30.00	30
1994 Naughty Or Nice? Santa 78565	Closed	1999	37.50	38-65
1995 Naughty Or Nice? Santa waterglobe/music box 7859-0	Closed	1997	30.00	31
1997 String The Lights Santa 78550	Closed	1999	50.00	50-69
1998 Toys For Tots Santa 78552	Closed	1999	40.00	40
1997 What's New? Santa 78551, set/2	Closed	1999	37.50	38-64
1996 Your Move, Santa 78561, set/2	Closed	1998	37.50	36-64

Silhouette Treasures (Winter Silhouette) - Department 56

YEAR ISSUE	EDITION LIMIT	YEAR RETD.	ISSUE PRICE	*QUOTE U.S.$
1992 Accompanying A Carol 78352, set/2	Closed	1999	55.00	55-87
1991 Angel Candle Holder 7794-1	Closed	1997	95.00	104-118
1990 Angel Candle Holder w/Candle 6767-9	Closed	1992	32.50	35-38
1999 Angel of Peace 78617	Open		30.00	30
2000 Bar Mitzvah 78636	Open		30.00	30
2000 Bat Mitzvah 78637	Open		25.00	25
1991 Bedtime Stories 7792-5	Closed	1997	42.00	46-69
1992 Bedtime Stories Waterglobe 7838-7	Closed	1995	30.00	55-69
1993 A Bright Star on Christmas Eve 7843-3, set/2	Closed	1997	48.00	48-75
1989 Bringing Home The Tree 7790-9, set/4	Closed	1993	75.00	125-150
1989 Camel w/glass Votive 6766-0	Closed	1993	25.00	50-52
1987 Carolers 7774-7, set/4	Closed	1993	120.00	213-220
1990 Caroling Angel w/Brass Halo & Songbook 67709	Closed	1998	15.00	16-29
1991 Caroling Bells 7798-4, set/3	Closed	1997	60.00	60-85
1991 Chimney Sweep 7799-2	Closed	1993	37.50	58-64
1992 A Choir of Angels Candle Holder 78034	Closed	1998	13.50	14-33
1992 A Choir of Angels Votive Holder 78026	Closed	1998	18.00	20-28
1994 Christmas Concerto Cellist 78484, set/2	Closed	1998	35.00	18-49
1994 Christmas Concerto Harpist 78468, set/2	Closed	1999	40.00	40-48
1994 Christmas Concerto Violinist 78476	Closed	1998	32.50	18-49
1996 A Christmas Dollhouse Built By Grandfather 78587, set/2	Closed	1999	35.00	35
2000 Christmas in the Pines 78644	Open		68.00	68
1993 A Christmas Kiss 7845-0, set/2	Closed	1997	32.50	33-55
1992 Christmas Presents 7805-0, set/2	Closed	1997	35.00	35-64
1995 Christmas Tea 78575, set/3	Closed	1999	40.00	40-52
1999 Cooking With Grandmother 78623, set/2	Open		37.50	38
1990 Decorating The Mantel 77917, set/3	Closed	1999	60.00	60-87
1999 Does Santa Really Come Down The Chimney? (lighted) 78625	Open		75.00	75
1989 Father Christmas 7788-7	Closed	1993	50.00	90-104
1991 Grandfather Clock 7797-6	Closed	1995	27.50	52-68
1991 Hanging The Ornaments 7793-3, set/3	Closed	1997	30.00	38-58
2000 Happy Anniversary 78640	Open		45.00	45
1999 Helping Hands 78624, set/6	Open		45.00	45
2000 Home For Christmas (lighted) 78645	Open		68.00	68
2000 I Believe (boy) 78639	Open		20.00	20
2000 I Believe (girl) 78638	Open		20.00	20
1996 I Spy Santa 78562, set/2	Closed	1998	45.00	36-45
1988 Joy To The World "Carolers On Songbooks" 5595-6	Closed	1990	42.00	84-120
1995 Kneeling Angel With Mandolin 78585	Closed	1997	48.00	48-96
1999 Lighting the Menorah 78618	Open		85.00	85

*Quotes have been rounded up to nearest dollar

YEAR ISSUE	EDITION LIMIT	YEAR RETD.	ISSUE PRICE	*QUOTE U.S.$
2000 Love Is All Around 78643	Open		15.00	15
1994 Mantelpiece Santa 7854-9	Closed	1997	55.00	55-92
1992 The Marionette Performance 7807-7, set/3	Closed	1997	75.00	88-110
1999 Mother and Child 78620	Open		40.00	40
1999 O Holy Night Church 78627	Open		30.00	30
1990 Old World Santa 67725	Closed	1998	50.00	55-87
1999 Peace and Good Will To All 78616	4,000	1999	200.00	200
1989 Putting Up the Tree 7789-5, set/3	Closed	1997	90.00	161-195
2000 Reaching For the Stars 78641	Open		15.00	15
1999 Roses and Lace 78621	Open		15.00	15
1995 Santa Filling The Stockings (lighted) 78573	Closed	1999	55.00	55-78
1993 Santa Lucia 7844-1	Closed	1997	27.50	28-49
1991 Santa's Reindeer 7796-8, (2 asst.)	Closed	1997	14.00	26-30
1991 Santa's Sleigh & 4 Reindeer 77950, set/5	Closed	1998	125.00	155-184
1999 The Shepherds Watched 78629, set/2	Open		50.00	50
1994 Shiny Skates & A Brand New Sled 78522, set/2	Closed	1999	35.00	35-52
1988 Silver Bells Music Box "Corner Carolers" 8271-6	Closed	1990	75.00	135-150
1994 Skater's Waltz 78530, set/2	Closed	1998	42.00	58-63
1988 Skating Children 7773-9, set/2	Closed	1997	33.00	40-58
1988 Skating Couple 7772-0	Closed	1995	35.00	72
1988 Sleighride 77712	Closed	1998	60.00	65-104
1987 Snow Doves 8215-5, set/2	Closed	1992	60.00	68
1992 Snowy White Deer 7837-9, set/2	Closed	1995	55.00	115-135
1995 Standing Angel With Horn 78584	Closed	1997	48.00	46-75
1999 Thank Heaven For Little Girls 78635	Open		32.50	33
1989 Three Kings Candle Holder 6765-2, set/3	Closed	1992	85.00	172-180
1999 Tidings of Comfort And Joy 78626, set/3	Open		75.00	75
1999 To Have And To Hold 78630	Open		32.50	33
1999 To Honor Him 78622, set/6	Open		80.00	80
1991 Town Crier 7800-0	Closed	1994	37.50	58-84
1993 A Visit With Santa 78417, set/2	Closed	1999	55.00	55-75
1992 Winter Silhouette Church 78360 (lighted)	Closed	1999	48.00	48

Snowbabies Collectors' Club - Department 56

YEAR ISSUE	EDITION LIMIT	YEAR RETD.	ISSUE PRICE	*QUOTE U.S.$
1997 You Better Watch Out 68851	Closed	1998	Gift	35-45
1998 Together We Can Make The Season Bright 68852	Closed	1998	75.00	75-110
1998 Baby It's Cold Outside 68889	Closed	1999	Gift	35
1998 Nice To Meet You Little One 68898, set/2	Closed	1999	75.00	75
1999 Friendsship Charms, set/5	Closed	1999	Gift	N/A
1999 Storytime 68956	Closed	1999	60.00	60
2000 Ready to See The World 69051	Yr.Iss.		Gift	N/A
2000 I Think I Can, set/2 69052	Yr.Iss.		50.00	50

Snowbabies - Department 56

YEAR ISSUE	EDITION LIMIT	YEAR RETD.	ISSUE PRICE	*QUOTE U.S.$
1999 All Aboard Star Express, set/4 68943	Open		55.00	55
1989 All Fall Down, set/4 7984-7	Closed	1991	36.00	53-98
1997 All We Need Is Love (1998 Mother's Day Event Piece) 68860	Closed	1998	32.50	40-60
1998 ...And That Spells BABY, set/4 68923	Open		50.00	50
1988 Are All These Mine? 7977-4	Closed	1998	10.00	14-25
1995 Are You On My List? 6875-6	Closed	1998	25.00	28-45
2000 As Time Goes By (w/clock) 69053	Yr.Iss.		40.00	40
1999 Batter Up 68957	Closed	1999	16.50	17
1999 Batter Up (Starlight Games™) 69047	Open		16.50	17
1986 Best Friends 7958-8	Closed	1989	12.00	114-173
1997 Best Little Star 68842	Closed	1999	16.00	16
1997 Bisque Friendship Pin (Event Piece) 68849	Closed	1997	5.00	5-10
1994 Bringing Starry Pines 6862-4	Closed	1997	35.00	65
1992 Can I Help, Too? 6806-3	18,500	1992	48.00	54-75
1993 Can I Open it Now? (Event Piece) 6838-1	Closed	1994	15.00	29-38
1997 Candle Light...Season Bright (tree topper) 68863	Closed	1999	20.00	20
1997 Candlelight Trees, set/3 68861	Closed	1999	25.00	25
1999 Celebrate (1999 Winter Celebration Event Piece) 68941	Closed	1999	60.00	60
1997 Celebrating A Snowbabies Journey, 1987-1997..."Let's Go See Jack Frost" (Event Piece) 68850	Closed	1997	60.00	60-75
1996 Climb Every Mountain 68816	22,500	1996	75.00	82-125
1986 Climbing on Snowball, Bisque Votive w/Candle 7965-0	Closed	1989	15.00	90-140
1987 Climbing On Tree, set/2 7971-5	Closed	1989	25.00	906-1020
1998 Come Fly With Me 68920	22,500	1999	165.00	165
1999 Come Sail With Me 69019	Open		60.00	60
1993 Crossing Starry Skies 6834-9	Closed	1997	35.00	55-70
2000 Crown Me 69056	Open		35.00	35
1991 Dancing To a Tune, set/3 6808-0	Closed	1995	30.00	38-60
1987 Don't Fall Off 7968-5	Closed	1990	12.50	79-130
1987 Down The Hill We Go 7960-0	Open		20.00	23
2000 Dreams Do Come True 69058	Open		22.50	23
1999 Even A Small Light Shines In The Darkness 69017	Open		45.00	45
1999 Falling For You 69035	Open		18.00	18
1989 Finding Fallen Stars 7985-5	6,000	1990	32.50	150-208
2000 First To The Finish (Starlight Games™) 69930	Open		16.50	17
1991 Fishing For Dreams 6809-8	Closed	1994	28.00	40-60
1996 Five-Part Harmony 68824	Closed	1999	32.50	45
2000 Flag (Starlight Games™) 69933	Open		6.00	6
1999 Follow Me 68944	Yr.Iss.		17.50	18
1986 Forest Accessory "Frosty Forest", set/2 7963-4	Open		15.00	20
1988 Frosty Frolic 7981-2	4,800	1989	35.00	975-1095
1989 Frosty Fun 7983-9	Closed	1991	27.50	42-69
1995 Frosty Pines, set/3 76687	Closed	1998	12.50	20
1998 A Gift So Fine From Madeline (1999 Mother's Day Event) (Snowbabies Guest Collection™) 69901	Closed	1999	50.00	50
1986 Give Me A Push 7955-3	Closed	1990	12.00	70-85
1986 Hanging Pair (votive) 7966-9	Closed	1989	15.00	132-185
1997 Heigh-Ho, Heigh-Ho, To Frolic Land We Go! 68853	Open		48.00	48
1992 Help Me, I'm Stuck 6817-9	Closed	1994	32.50	44-65
1989 Helpful Friends 7982-0	Closed	1993	30.00	54-60
1999 Hit The Mark (Starlight Games™) 69005	Open		25.00	25
1986 Hold On Tight 7956-1	Closed	1999	12.00	28
1998 How Many Days 'Til Christmas? 68882	Closed	1999	36.00	36
2000 I Can Do That, Too! 69012	Open		37.50	38
1998 I Can Touch My Toes 68927, set/2	Open		30.00	30
1995 I Can't Find Him 68800	Closed	1998	37.50	40-60
1999 I Caribou You 68942	Open		50.00	50
1995 I Found The Biggest Star of All! 6874-8	Closed	1998	16.00	24-30
1993 I Found Your Mittens, set/2 6836-5	Closed	1996	30.00	32-40
1998 I Have A Feeling We're Not In Kansas Anymore (Snowbabies Guest Collection™) 69900	Open		50.00	50
1998 I Love You This Much! 68918	Open		16.50	17
1991 I Made This Just For You 6802-0	Closed	1998	15.00	22-30
1992 I Need A Hug 6813-6	Open		20.00	20
1995 I See You!, set/2 6878-0	Closed	1999	27.50	28
1999 I'll Love You Always (Discover Department 56® Spring Promotion) 69009	Open		30.00	30
1995 I'll Play A Christmas Tune 68801	Closed	1999	16.00	15-50
1991 I'll Put Up The Tree 6800-4	Closed	1995	24.00	28-35
1993 I'll Teach You A Trick 6835-7	Closed	1996	24.00	28
2000 I'm An Artist 69069, set/3	Open		22.50	23
1993 I'm Making an Ice Sculpture 6842-0	Closed	1996	30.00	42-60
1986 I'm Making Snowballs 7962-6	Closed	1992	12.00	33-58
1994 I'm Right Behind You! 6852-7	Closed	1997	60.00	60
1996 I'm So Sleepy 68810	Open		16.00	16
1997 I'm The Star Atop Your Tree! (tree topper) 68862	Closed	1999	20.00	20
1996 It's A Grand Old Flag 68822	Closed	1998	25.00	34-50
2000 It's A Wonderful World 69059	Open		32.50	33
1996 It's Snowing! 68821	Open		16.50	17
1989 Icy Igloo 7987-1	Open		37.50	38
1991 Is That For Me, set/2 6803-9	Closed	1993	32.50	48-65
1996 Jack Frost...A Sleighride Through the Stars, set/3 68811	Open		110.00	110
1999 Jack Frost...Through The Frosty Forest 69020	Open		150.00	150
1994 Jack Frost...A Touch of Winter's Magic 6854-3	Closed	1999	90.00	105-108
1997 Jingle Bell 68855	Open		16.00	16
1992 Join The Parade 6824-1	Closed	1994	37.50	50-75
1999 Jolly Friends Forevermore, set/11 69021	Open		50.00	50
1998 A Journey For Two By Caribou! 68881	Open		50.00	50
1999 Jumping For Joy 69036	Open		18.00	18
1998 Just Imagine (hinged photo frame box) 68929	Open		15.00	15
1992 Just One Little Candle 6823-3	Closed	1999	15.00	15
1999 A Kiss For You and 2000 Too (Snowbabies Guest Collection™) 69902	Open		50.00	50
1993 Let's All Chime In!, set/2 6845-4	Closed	1995	37.50	52-75
1998 Let's Be Friends (Disney Exclusive) 06850	Closed	1999	N/A	209-263
1994 Let's Go Skating 6860-8	Closed	1998	16.50	20-30
1992 Let's Go Skiing 6815-2	Closed	1999	15.00	15
1994 Lift Me Higher, I Can't Reach 6863-2	Closed	1998	75.00	80-100
1996 A Little Night Light 68823	Closed	1999	32.50	33
1996 A Little Night Light (lamp) 68836	Closed	1999	75.00	75
1999 The Littlest Angel 69011	Open		18.00	18
1992 Look What I Can Do! 6819-5	Closed	1996	16.50	30
1993 Look What I Found 6833-0	Closed	1997	45.00	59-90
2000 Love Is In The Air 69055	Open		18.00	18
1998 Make A Wish 68926	Open		30.00	30
1994 Mickey's New Friend (Disney Exclusive) 714-5	Closed	1995	60.00	540-620
1996 Moonbeams (Night Light) 68835	Closed	1999	20.00	20
1999 Music From The Highest, set/3 69016	Open		45.00	45
1995 Mush 68805	Closed	1999	48.00	48
1998 My Snowbaby Baby Dolls, set/2 68919	Open		32.50	33
1998 Nice To Meet You Little One, set/2 68898	Closed	1999	75.00	75
1993 Now I Lay Me Down to Sleep 6839-0	Open		13.50	14
1996 Once Upon A Time... (votive candleholder) 68815	Open		25.00	25
1997 One For You, One For Me 68858	Open		27.50	28
1992 Over the Milky Way 6828-4	Closed	1995	32.00	38-65
1999 Over the Top (Starlight Games™) 69004	Open		25.00	25
1995 Parade of Penguins, set/6 68804	Open		15.00	15
1989 Penguin Parade 7986-3	Closed	1992	25.00	54-65
1994 Pennies From Heaven 6864-0	Closed	1998	17.50	14-20
2000 Perfect Balance (Starlight Games™) 69932	Open		25.00	25
1990 Playing Games Is Fun 7947-2	Closed	1993	30.00	48-60
1988 Polar Express 7978-2	Closed	1992	22.00	77-132
1998 Pull Together 68924	Open		60.00	60
1999 Reach For The Moon (Avon Exclusive) 06852	Closed	1999	20.00	20
2000 Ready, Set...! (Starlight Games™) 69931	Open		16.50	17
1990 Read Me a Story! 7945-6	Open		25.00	25
2000 Ride The Wave (Discover Department 56® Holiday Program) 69057	12/00		50.00	50
1995 Ring The Bells...It's Christmas! 6876-4	Open		40.00	40
1997 Rock-A-Bye Baby (Event Piece) 68848	Closed	1997	15.00	15-20
1999 Score (Starlight Games™) 69007	Open		16.50	17
1992 Shall I Play For You? 6820-9	Closed	1998	16.50	20-30
1999 Shake It Up, Baby 69013	Open		20.00	20
1997 Ship O' Dreams, set/2 68859	Open		135.00	135
1998 Slip, Sliding Away (GCC Exclusive) 6808	Closed	1998	28.00	50
1998 Slip, Sliding Away 68934	Open		28.00	28
1995 Snowbabies Animated Skating Pond, set/14 7668-6	Closed	1998	60.00	85
1993 Snowbabies Picture Frame, Baby's First Smile 6846-2	Closed	1998	30.00	30-35
1996 Snowbaby Display Sled 6883-8	Open		45.00	45
1986 Snowbaby Holding Picture Frame, set/2 7970-7	Closed	1987	15.00	495-842
1986 Snowbaby Nite-Lite 7959-6	Closed	1989	15.00	327
1991 Snowbaby Polar Sign 6804-7	Closed	1996	20.00	40
1997 Snowbaby Shelf Unit 68874	Closed	1999	20.00	20
1993 So Much Work To Do 6837-3	Closed	1998	18.00	20-35
1993 Somewhere in Dreamland 6840-3	Closed	1997	85.00	125-185
1994 Somewhere in Dreamland (1 snowflake) 6840-3	Closed	1994	85.00	120-132
1995 Somewhere in Dreamland (2 snowflake) 6840-3	Closed	1995	85.00	95
1996 Somewhere in Dreamland (3 snowflake) 6840-3	Closed	1996	85.00	65-95
1997 Somewhere in Dreamland (4 snowflake) 6840-3	Closed	1997	85.00	95
1990 A Special Delivery 7948-0	Closed	1994	15.00	16-30
1998 Star Gazer's Castle 68925	Open		40.00	40
1995 Star Gazing (Starter Set) 7800	Open		40.00	40
1995 A Star in the Box (GCC exclusive) 68803	Closed	1996	18.00	42-65
1999 Star On The Top (tree topper) 68952	Open		12.50	13
1996 Stargazing, set/9 68817	Closed	1998	40.00	40-55
1997 Starlight Serenade 68856	Open		25.00	25
1999 Starlight, Starbright 69015	Open		25.00	25
1992 Starry Pines, set/2 6829-2	Closed	1998	17.50	25-30
1992 Stars-In-A-Row, Tic-Tac-Toe 6822-5	Closed	1995	32.50	47-66
1994 Stringing Fallen Stars 6861-6	Closed	1998	25.00	25-45
1998 Stuck In The Snow 68932	Open		30.00	30
1998 Stuck In The Snow (GCC Exclusive) 6806	Closed	1998	30.00	30-50
2000 Take Me With You (musical) 69068	Open		40.00	40
2000 Tea For Two (Snowbabies Guest Collection™) 69904, set/2	Open		50.00	50
1997 Thank You 68857	Open		32.50	33
1994 There's Another One!, 6853-5	Closed	1998	24.00	24-50
1996 There's No Place Like Home 68820	Open		16.50	17
1999 They're Coming From Oz, Oh My! (Snowbabies Guest Collection™) 69010	Open		55.00	55
1991 This Is Where We Live 6805-5	Closed	1994	60.00	66-100
1992 This Will Cheer You Up 6816-0	Closed	1994	30.00	48-60
1998 Three Tiny Trumpeters, set/2 (1998 Winter Celebration Event Piece) 68888,	Closed	1998	50.00	50-100
1988 Tiny Trio, set/3 7979-0	Closed	1990	20.00	168-215
1998 To My Friend 68917	Open		18.00	18
1999 Tower of Light 69022	Open		40.00	40
1987 Tumbling In the Snow, set/5 7957-0	Closed	1993	35.00	88-125
1990 Twinkle Little Stars, set/2 7942-1	Closed	1993	37.50	48-75
1997 Two Little Babies On The Go! 68840	Open		32.50	33
2000 Under The Midnight Moon With Barbie™ (Snowbabies Guest Collection™) 69903	Open		60.00	60
1992 Wait For Me 6812-8	Closed	1994	48.00	38-75
1991 Waiting For Christmas 6807-1	Closed	1993	27.50	50-56
1993 We Make a Great Pair 6843-8	Closed	1999	30.00	30
1990 We Will Make it Shine 7946-4	Closed	1992	45.00	50-98
1994 We'll Plant the Starry Pines, set/2 6865-9	Closed	1997	37.50	45-75
1995 We're Building An Icy Igloo 68802	Closed	1998	70.00	90-120
1995 What Shall We Do Today? 6877-2	Closed	1997	32.50	65-70
1996 When the Bough Breaks 68819	Open		30.00	30
1993 Where Did He Go? 6841-1	Open		35.00	35
1994 Where Did You Come From? 6856-0	Closed	1997	40.00	40-75
1996 Which Way's Up 68812	Closed	1997	30.00	30-60
1997 Whistle While You Work 68854	Closed	1999	32.50	33
1990 Who Are You? 7949-9	12,500	1991	32.50	77-130
1991 Why Don't You Talk To Me 6801-2	Open		24.00	24
1993 Will it Snow Today? 6844-6	Closed	1995	45.00	58-90
1992 Winken, Blinken, and Nod 6814-4	Closed	1998	60.00	70-110
1998 Winter Celebration Event Pin 68887	Closed	1998	5.00	10-20
1998 Winter Play On A Snowy Day, set/4 68880	Closed	1999	48.00	48

YEAR ISSUE	EDITION LIMIT	YEAR RETD.	ISSUE PRICE	*QUOTE U.S.$
1987 Winter Surprise 7974-0	Closed	1992	15.00	46-58
1997 Wish Upon a Falling Star 68839	Closed	1999	75.00	75
1990 Wishing on a Star 7943-0	Closed	1994	22.00	45-50
1997 Wishing You A Merry Christmas 68843	Closed	1998	40.00	40-60
1996 With Hugs & Kisses, set/2 68813	Closed	1998	32.50	35-55
1996 You Are My Lucky Star, set/2 68814	Closed	1999	35.00	35
1999 You Are My Starshine 68945	Open		17.50	18
1992 You Can't Find Me! 6818-7	Closed	1996	45.00	54-90
1992 You Didn't Forget Me 6821-7	Closed	1999	32.50	33
1996 You Need Wings Too! 68818	Open		25.00	25
1996 You're My Snowbaby (picture frame) 6883-4	Closed	1999	15.00	15
1998 You've Got The Cutest Little Baby Face 68933	Open		32.50	33
1998 You've Got The Cutest Little Baby Face (GCC Exclusive) 6809	Closed	1998	32.50	33

Snowbabies Pewter Miniatures - Department 56

YEAR ISSUE	EDITION LIMIT	YEAR RETD.	ISSUE PRICE	*QUOTE U.S.$
1998 All Aboard The Star Express, set/4 76739	Open		25.00	25
1989 All Fall Down, set/4 7617-1	Closed	1993	25.00	37-75
1998 All We Need Is Love, set/3 76722	Open		20.00	20
1989 Are All These Mine? 7605-8	Closed	1992	7.00	18-20
1995 Are You On My List?, set/2 7669-1	Closed	1997	9.00	20
1998 Baby, It's Cold Outside, set/2 76723	Open		8.50	9
1989 Best Friends 7604-0	Closed	1994	10.00	21-24
1997 Best Little Star 76718	Closed	1999	6.50	7
1994 Bringing Starry Pines, set/2 7666-0	Closed	1997	18.00	18-25
1992 Collector's Sign 76201	Closed	1999	7.00	7
1991 Dancing to a Tune, set/3 7630-9	Closed	1993	18.00	28
1989 Don't Fall Off! 7603-1	Closed	1994	7.00	18-24
1989 Finding Fallen Stars, set/2 7618-0	Closed	1992	12.50	24-32
1996 Five-Part Harmony, set/2 76710	Closed	1999	22.00	22
1998 Frosty Frolic Ice Palace 76729	Open		95.00	95
1989 Frosty Frolic Land, set/3 76198	Closed	1998	96.00	115-120
1989 Frosty Frolic, set/4 7613-9	Closed	1993	24.00	24-46
1989 Frosty Fun, set/2 7611-2	Closed	1997	13.50	18-20
1989 Give Me a Push! 7601-5	Closed	1994	7.00	18-20
1998 Heigh-Ho, Heigh-Ho, To Frolic Land We Go! 76711	Open		22.50	23
1992 Help Me, I'm Stuck, set/2 7638-4	Closed	1997	15.00	20
1989 Helpful Friends, set/4 7608-2	Closed	1992	13.50	24-30
1989 Hold On Tight! 76007	Closed	1998	7.00	7-25
1998 How Many Days 'Til Christmas? 76721	Open		18.00	18
1999 I Can Touch My Toes, set/2 76731	Open		13.50	14
1995 I Can't Find Him!, set/3 76695	Closed	1998	18.00	20
1995 I Found The Biggest Star Of All! 76690	Closed	1998	7.00	7-15
1998 I Love You This Much 76735	Open		7.00	7
1991 I Made This Just for You! 7628-7	Closed	1994	7.00	16-18
1992 I Need A Hug 7640-6	Closed	1997	10.00	10-15
1995 I See You!, set/2 76694	Closed	1999	13.50	14
1995 I'll Play A Christmas Tune 76696	Closed	1998	7.50	8-15
1991 I'll Put Up The Tree 7627-9	Closed	1996	9.00	16
1989 I'm Making Snowballs! 76023	Closed	1999	7.00	7
1994 I'm Right Behind You, set/5 7662-7	Closed	1997	27.50	32-35
1996 I'm So Sleepy 76700	Closed	1999	7.00	7
1989 Icy Igloo, w/tree, set/2 7610-4	Closed	1992	7.50	20-30
1991 Is That For Me?, set/2 7631-7	Closed	1993	12.50	24
1996 It's A Grand Old Flag 76705	Closed	1998	11.00	18-20
1997 Jack Frost...A Touch of Winter's Magic, set/3 76716	Open		27.50	28
1997 Jingle Bell 76713	Open		7.00	7
1992 Join the Parade, set/4 7645-7	Closed	1995	22.50	30-35
1998 A Journey For Two, By Caribou! 76720	Open		22.50	23
1992 Just One Little Candle 76449	Closed	1998	7.00	7-15
1993 Let's All Chime In! 76554	Closed	1998	20.00	20-30
1994 Let's Go Skating 76643	Closed	1999	7.00	7
1992 Let's Go Skiing 76368	Closed	1999	7.00	7
1994 Lift Me Highter, I Can't Reach!, set/5 7667-8	Closed	1997	25.00	30-40
1999 Make A Wish 76733	Open		15.00	15
1998 My Snowbaby Baby Dolls, set/2 76734	Open		15.00	15
1998 New Frosty Frolic Land 76728	Open		50.00	50
1998 One For You, One For Me 76724	Open		13.50	14
1989 Penguin Parade, set/4 7616-3	Closed	1993	12.50	25-30
1990 Playing Games is Fun!, set/2 7623-6	Closed	1993	13.50	30-58
1989 Polar Express, set/2 7609-0	Closed	1992	13.50	25-45
1998 Pull Together, set/4 79740	Open		25.00	25
1990 Read Me a Story 7622-8	Closed	1997	11.00	18-20
1992 Shall I Play For You? 76422	Closed	1998	7.00	7-15
1998 Ship O' Dreams, set/2 76726	Open		45.00	45
1998 Slip, Sliding Away 76737	Open		12.00	12
1993 Somewhere in Dreamland, set/5 7656-2	Closed	1997	30.00	35
1990 A Special Delivery 7624-4	Closed	1993	7.00	18-21
1995 A Star-In-The-Box 76698	Closed	1998	7.50	8-15
1997 Starlight Serenade 76714	Open		12.00	12
1994 Stringing Fallen Stars 76651	Closed	1998	8.00	8-15
1998 Stuck In The Snow 76738	Open		16.50	17
1997 Thank You, set/3 76715	Open		20.00	20
1994 There's Another One 7661-9	Closed	1997	10.00	15
1996 There's No Place Like Home 76708	Closed	1999	7.50	8
1992 This Will Cheer You Up 7639-2	Closed	1995	13.75	23
1998 Three Tiny Trumpeters, set/2 76725	Open		25.00	25
1989 Tiny Trio, set/3 7615-5	Closed	1993	18.00	65-68
1998 To My Friend 76736	Open		7.50	8
1989 Tumbling in the Snow!, set/5 7614-7	Closed	1992	30.00	75-80
1990 Twinkle Little Stars, set/2 7621-0	Closed	1993	15.00	28-30
1992 Wait For Me!, set/4 7641-4	Closed	1995	22.50	32-35
1991 Waiting for Christmas 7629-5	Closed	1993	12.50	21-24
1993 We Make a Great Pair 7652-0	Closed	1997	13.50	15
1994 We'll Plant The Starry Trees, set/4 7663-5	Closed	1997	22.00	22-25
1995 What Shall We Do Today?, set/2 76693	Closed	1999	17.00	17
1997 Whistle While You Work 76712	Open		18.00	18
1993 Will It Snow Today?, set/5 76538	Closed	1998	22.50	23-35
1993 Winken, Blinken & Nod, set/3 76589	Closed	1998	27.50	40
1998 Winter Play On A Snowy Day, set/4 76727	Open		27.50	28
1989 Winter Surprise! 7607-4	Closed	1994	13.50	21
1997 Wish Upon A Falling Star, set/4 76717	Open		25.00	25
1991 Wishing on a Star 7626-0	Closed	1995	10.00	9-25
1996 With Hugs And Kisses, set/2 76704	Closed	1998	15.00	15
1999 You Are My Starshine 76732	Open		7.50	8
1992 You Can't Find Me!, set/4 7637-6	Closed	1996	22.50	35
1992 You Didn't Forget Me!, set/3 7643-0	Closed	1995	17.50	17-20

Snowbabies-Waterglobes - Department 56

YEAR ISSUE	EDITION LIMIT	YEAR RETD.	ISSUE PRICE	*QUOTE U.S.$
1990 All Tired Out 7937-5	Closed	1992	55.00	58-100
1995 Are You On My List? 6879-7	Closed	1997	32.50	40-55
1986 Catch a Falling Star 7967-7	Closed	1987	18.00	528-780
1992 Fishing For Dreams 6832-2	Closed	1994	32.50	58
1997 Heigh-Ho 68872	Closed	1999	32.50	33
1995 I'll Hug You Goodnight 68798	Open		32.50	33
1997 Jingle Bell 68871	Closed	1999	32.50	33
1989 Let It Snow 7992-8	Closed	1993	25.00	50-54
1994 Look What I Found 6872-1	Closed	1997	32.50	35
1999 Make A Wish 69040	Open		32.50	33
1997 Moon Beams 68873	Closed	1999	32.50	33
1996 Now I Lay Me Down To Sleep 6883-1	Open		32.50	33
1991 Peek-A-Boo 7938-3	Closed	1993	50.00	85-100
1994 Planting Starry Pines 6870-5	Closed	1996	32.50	36
1991 Play Me a Tune 7936-7	Closed	1993	50.00	75-100
1996 Practice Makes Perfect 6883-0	Closed	1998	32.50	33-45
1992 Read Me a Story 6831-4	Closed	1996	32.50	60-65
1995 Skate With Me 68799	Closed	1998	32.50	35-45
1998 Ship Ahoy 68915	Open		37.50	38
1999 Ship O' Dreams 69039	Open		75.00	75
1986 Snowbaby Standing 7964-2	Closed	1987	7.50	313-500
1987 Snowbaby with Wings 7973-1	Closed	1988	20.00	416-675
1993 So Much Work To Do 6849-7	Closed	1995	32.50	24-35
1999 That's What Friends Are For 69041	Open		45.00	45
2000 Time To Dream 69067	Open		30.00	30
1993 You Didn't Forget Me 6850-0	Closed	1997	32.50	35
1990 What Are You Doing? 7935-9	Closed	1990	55.00	55
1987 Winter Wonderland 7975-8	Closed	1988	40.00	707-1000

Snowbunnies - Department 56

YEAR ISSUE	EDITION LIMIT	YEAR RETD.	ISSUE PRICE	*QUOTE U.S.$
1999 Afternoon in The Garden 26341	Open		32.50	33
2000 Airplane Ride 26359	Open		18.00	18
1997 All The Little Birdies Go Tweet, set/2 26288	Closed	2000	28.00	28
1999 Animals On Parade, set/4 26326	Open		17.50	18
1997 Are You My Momma? 26289	Closed	2000	18.00	18
2000 Birch Bench 26384	Open		15.00	15
1997 Bunny Express 26287	Closed	2000	22.50	23
1999 Bunny Hug 26327	Open		25.00	25
1999 Butterfly Kisses 26322	Open		20.00	20
1998 Can You Come Out & Play? 26309	Closed	1999	25.00	25
2000 Captain Of The Seas 26354	Open		20.00	20
2000 Chick Chat 26352	Open		16.50	17
2000 Come With Me, set/2 26357	Open		32.50	33
1996 Counting The Days 'Til Easter 26282	Yr.Iss.	1996	22.50	24-50
1995 Don't Get Lost! 26166	Closed	1998	32.50	35
1997 Double Yolk 26293	Yr.Iss.	1997	20.00	20-40
1994 Easter Delivery 26085	Closed	1997	27.50	30
1996 Easy Does It, set/2 26274	Closed	1998	30.00	30
1999 Ewe Haul 26324	Open		20.00	20
2000 Flower Basket 26364	Open		6.00	6
2000 For The Birds 26353	Open		16.50	17
1999 Full of Blooms, set/6 26329	Open		15.00	15
1999 Garden Park Bench 26328	Open		15.00	15
1999 Garden Picket Fence, set/4 26340	Open		30.00	30
1995 Goosey, Goosey, & Gander, set/2 26174	Closed	1997	30.00	30-41
1999 Guests Are Always Welcome 26325	Yr. Iss.	2000	25.00	25
1996 Happy Birthday To You, set/2 26273	Open		30.00	30
1994 Help Me Hide The Eggs 26077	Closed	1996	25.00	30-75
1998 Hop, Skip & A Melody, set/2 26301	Closed	2000	30.00	30
1995 I'll Color The Easter Egg 26212	Yr.Iss.	1995	20.00	22-50
1995 I'll Love You Forever 26158	Open		16.00	16
1994 I'll Paint The Top... 26034	Closed	1996	30.00	30-65
2000 I'll Pick You 26355	Open		16.50	17
1995 I'm Tweeter, You're Totter 26204	Closed	1998	30.00	30-60
1996 I've Got A Brand New Pair of Roller Skates 26272	Closed	1998	25.00	25-50
1994 I've Got A Surprise 26000	Closed	1997	15.00	16-35
1996 Is There Room For Me? 26275	Closed	1999	18.00	16-20
1995 It's Working...We're Going Faster! 26190	Closed	1999	35.00	27-35
1996 Just A Little Off The Top, set/3 26278	Closed	1998	25.00	25-55
1999 Just For You 26323	Open		16.50	17
1998 Just Start All Over Again 26304	Closed	2000	16.50	17
2000 Kiss Me?, set/2 26358	Open		28.00	28
1996 Let's All Sing Like The Birdies Sing, set/2 26276	Closed	1999	37.50	38-40
1994 Let's Do The Bunny Hop! 26096	Closed	2000	32.50	33
2000 Lily Pad 26365	Open		7.50	8
2000 Love Grows 26383	Open		18.00	18
1999 Master Gardener, set/4 26321	Open		20.00	20
2000 May Day Delivery 26382	Open		18.00	18
2000 May Luck Be With You 26381	Open		18.00	18
1995 My Woodland Wagon, At Dragonfly Hollow 26255	Closed	1997	32.50	34-65
1995 My Woodland Wagon, By Turtle Creek 26239	Closed	1996	32.50	40-65
1995 My Woodland Wagon, Parked In Robins Nest Thicket 26247	Closed	1999	35.00	32-70
1996 On A Trycle Built For Two 26283	17,500	1998	32.50	39-75
1994 Oops! I Dropped One! 26018	Closed	1998	16.00	18-35
2000 Picture Frames, 3 asst. 26366	Open		7.50	8
2000 Puddle Pals 26388	Open		24.00	24
1997 Rain, Rain, Go Away 26291	Closed	2000	45.00	45
1995 Rub-A-Dub-Dub, 3 Bunnies in a Tub 26115	Closed	1997	32.50	32-65
2000 Showers Brings Flowers (waterglobe) 26368	Open		20.00	20
1995 Shrubs-In-A-Tub, single, set/4 26123	Closed	1997	12.50	10-13
1995 Shrubs-In-A-Tub, tall, set/2 26140	Closed	1997	9.00	7-10
1995 Shrubs-In-A-Tub, triple 26131	Closed	1997	10.00	7-10
1996 Slow-Moving Vehicle 26280	Closed	1999	45.00	38-45
2000 Spring Topiaries, large, 3 asst. 26387	Open		95.00	95
2000 Spring Topiaries, medium, 3 asst. 26386	Open		30.00	30
2000 Spring Topiaries, small, 3 asst. 26385	Open		10.00	10
1999 Stop & Smell the Roses, set/2 26320	Open		20.00	20
1994 Surprise! It's Me! 26042	Closed	1998	25.00	25
2000 Swimming Lessons 26356	Open		20.00	20
2000 These Are For You 26360	Open		15.00	15
1998 This One's A Keeper 26307	Closed	2000	16.50	17
1994 A Tisket, A Tasket (waterglobe) 26107	Closed	1998	12.50	15-18
1994 A Tisket, A Tasket 26026	Closed	1996	15.00	17-35
1997 A Tisket, A Tasket Basket 26286	Open		45.00	45
1996 To Market, To Market, Delivering Eggs! 26281	Closed	1999	65.00	65
1994 Tra-La-La 26069	Closed	1997	37.50	38-42
1999 Trellis in Bloom 26330	Open		12.50	13
1996 Welcome To The Neighborhood 26277	Closed	1999	25.00	25-50
1995 Wishing You A Happy Easter 26182	Closed	1997	32.50	35-65
1995 You Better Watch Out Or I'll Catch You! 26220	Closed	1999	17.00	18-35
1997 You're Cute As A Bug's Ear 26292	Closed	2000	16.50	17

Disneyana

Disneyana Conventions - Various

YEAR ISSUE	EDITION LIMIT	YEAR RETD.	ISSUE PRICE	*QUOTE U.S.$
1992 1947 Mickey Mouse Plush J20967 - Gund	1,000	1992	50.00	303-3200
1992 Big Thunder Mountain A26648 - R. Lee	100	1992	1650.00	2360-2500
1992 Carousel Horse 022482 - PJ's	250	1992	125.00	404-455
1992 Cinderella 022076 - Armani	500	1992	500.00	4130-4500
1992 Cinderella Castle 022077 - John Hine Studios	500	1992	250.00	1100-1528
1992 Cruella DeVil Doll-porcelain 22554 - J. Wolf	25	1992	3000.00	3000-3500
1992 Disneyana Logo Charger - B. White	25	1992	600.00	2800
1992 Medallion	N/A	1992	Gift	121-165
1992 Nifty-Nineties Mickey & Minnie 022503 - House of Laurenz	250	1992	650.00	636-650
1992 Pinocchio - R. Wright	100	1992	750.00	1000-2000
1992 Steamboat Willie-Resin - M. Delle	500	1992	125.00	1452-1500
1992 Tinker Bell 022075 - Lladró	1,500	1992	350.00	2650-3380
1992 Two Merry Wanderers 022074 - Goebel/M.I. Hummel	1,500	1992	250.00	1050-1155
1992 Walt's Convertible (Cel) - Disney Art Ed.	500	1992	950.00	2300
1993 1947 Minnie Mouse Plush - Gund	1,000	1993	50.00	121-124
1993 Alice in Wonderland - Malvern	10	1993	8000.00	N/A
1993 Annette Doll - Alexander Doll	1,000	1993	395.00	605-780
1993 The Band Concert "Maestro Mickey" - Disney Art Ed.	275	1993	2950.00	N/A
1993 The Band Concert-Bronze - B. Toma	25	1993	650.00	2145-2904
1993 Bandleader (pewter)	N/A	1993	Gift	260-495
1993 Bandleader-Resin - M. Delle	1,500	1993	125.00	424-925
1993 Family Dinner Figurine - C. Boyer	1,000	1993	600.00	1210-1625
1993 Jumper from King Arthur Carousel - PJ's	250	1993	125.00	303-488
1993 Mickey & Pluto Charger - White/Rhodes	25	1993	850.00	2500-2750
1993 Mickey Mouse, the Bandleader - Arribas Bros.	25	1993	700.00	1568-2145
1993 Mickey's Dreams - R. Lee	250	1993	400.00	650-900
1993 Peter Pan - Lladró	2,000	1993	400.00	878-1200
1993 Sleeping Beauty Castle - John Hine Studios	500	1993	250.00	650-850
1993 Snow White - Armani	2,000	1993	750.00	825-1550
1993 Two Little Drummers - Goebel/M.I. Hummel	1,500	1993	325.00	725-750
1993 Walt's Train Celebration - Disney Art Ed.	950	1993	950.00	1800
1994 Ariel - Armani	1,500	1994	750.00	1200-1750
1994 Cinderella/Godmother - Lladró	2,500	1994	875.00	985-1175
1994 Cinderella's Slipper - Waterford	1,200	1994	250.00	380-550
1994 Euro Disney Castle - John Hine Studios	750	1994	250.00	350-845
1994 Jessica & Roger Charger - White/Rhodes	25	1994	2000.00	2750-3146
1994 Mickey Triple Self Portrait - Goebel Miniatures	500	1994	295.00	795-1235
1994 Minnie Be Patient - Goebel/M.I. Hummel	1,500	1994	395.00	450-725

*Quotes have been rounded up to nearest dollar

YEAR ISSUE	EDITION LIMIT	YEAR RETD.	ISSUE PRICE	*QUOTE U.S.$
1994 MM/MN w/House Kinetic - F. Prescott	10	1994	4000.00	N/A
1994 MM/MN/Goofy Limo (Stepin' Out) - Ron Lee	500	1994	500.00	750-1073
1994 Scrooge in Money Bin/Bronze - Carl Barks	100	1994	1800.00	4356-5445
1994 Sleeping Beauty - Malvern	10	1994	5500.00	N/A
1994 Sorcerer Mickey (bronze) - B. Toma	100	1994	1000.00	1900-2118
1994 Sorcerer Mickey (crystal) - Arribas Bros.	50	1994	1700.00	1650-1900
1994 Sorcerer Mickey (pewter)	N/A	1994	Gift	110-260
1994 Sorcerer Mickey (resin) - M. Delle	2,000	1994	125.00	209-390
1995 Ah, Venice - M. Pierson	100	1995	2600.00	2600-3025
1995 Ariel's Dolphin Ride - Wyland	250	1995	2500.00	2500
1995 Barbershop Quartet - Goebel Miniatures	750	1995	300.00	400-514
1995 Beauty and the Beast - Armani	2,000	1995	975.00	1275-1430
1995 Brave Little Tailor Charger - White/Rhodes	15	1995	2000.00	2000-3000
1995 Celebrating-Resin - M. Delle	1,500	1995	125.00	155-182
1995 Donald Duck Gong	N/A	1995	Gift	116
1995 Donald Duck Mini-Charger - White/Rhodes	1,000	1995	75.00	75
1995 Ear Force One - R. Lee	500	1995	600.00	635-1300
1995 Engine No. One - R. Lee	500	1995	650.00	726-765
1995 Fire Station #105 - Lilliput Lane	501	1995	195.00	350-595
1995 For Father - Goebel/M.I. Hummel	1,500	1995	450.00	450-485
1995 Grandpa's Boys - Goebel/M.I. Hummel	1,500	1995	340.00	413-424
1995 Mad Minnie Charger - White/Rhodes	10	1995	2000.00	4000-6050
1995 Memories - B. Toma	200	1995	1200.00	968-1029
1995 Neat & Pretty Mickey (crystal) - Arribas Bros.	50	1995	1700.00	1500-2057
1995 Neat & Pretty Mickey (resin) - M. Delle	2,000	1995	135.00	160-325
1995 Neat & Pretty Music Box	N/A	1994	Gift	110-260
1995 Plane Crazy - Arribas	50	1995	1750.00	1650-1815
1995 The Prince's Kiss - P Gordon	25	1995	250.00	1089-2175
1995 "Proud Pocahontas" Lithogragh - D. Struzan	500	1995	195.00	413
1995 Sheriff of Bullet Valley - Barks/Vought	200	1995	1800.00	2200-2420
1995 Showtime - B. Toma	200	1995	1400.00	1513-1694
1995 Simba - Bolae	200	1995	1500.00	1500
1995 Sleeping Beauty Castle Mirror - P. Gordon	250	1995	1200.00	1200
1995 Sleeping Beauty Dance - Lladró	1,000	1995	1280.00	1210-2275
1995 Sleeping Beauty's Tiara - Waterford	1,500	1995	250.00	374-550
1995 Snow White's Apple - Waterford	1,500	1995	225.00	420-495
1995 "Snow White & Friends" Brooch/Pendant - R. Viramontes	25	1995	1500.00	1500
1995 Thru the Mirror - Barks/Vought	200	1995	2600.00	2299-2420
1995 "Uncle Scrooge" Tile - Barks/Vought	50	1995	900.00	1595-1650
1996 Brave Little Taylor - Arribas Bros.	50	1996	1700.00	1870-2200
1996 Brave Little Taylor (pewter)	N/A	1996	Gift	80-163
1996 Brave Little Taylor (resin) - M. Delle	1,500	1996	125.00	121-325
1996 Brave Little Taylor Clock	N/A	1996	Gift	110-195
1996 Brave Little Taylor Inlaid Leather Box - P. Gordon	25	1996	300.00	300
1996 Breakfast of Tycoons-Scrooge (litho) - C. Barks	295	1996	295.00	385-473
1996 Cinderella's Castle (bronze) - B. Toma	100	1996	1400.00	2057
1996 Flying Dumbo (bronze) - Wolf's Head	N/A	1996	2000.00	2000-3630
1996 Hall of Presidents - Lilliput Lane	500	1996	225.00	330-715
1996 Heigh Ho - R. Lee	350	1996	500.00	605-726
1996 Jasmine & Rajah - Armani	N/A	1996	800.00	990-1080
1996 Mickey - Armani	N/A	1996	Gift	242-350
1996 Jasmine & Rajah w/Mickey - Armani	N/A	1996	800.00	823-1430
1996 Minnie for Mother - Goebel/M.I. Hummel	1,200	1996	470.00	470
1996 Proud Pongo (w/backstamp) - Walt Disney Classics	1,200	1996	175.00	295-350
1996 Puppy Love - Goebel Miniatures	750	1996	325.00	400-553
1996 Self Control-Donald Duck (bronze) - C. Barks	150	1996	1800.00	2600-3025
1996 Sorcerer - Waterford	1,200	1996	275.00	462-485
1996 Uncle Scrooge Charger Plate - B. White	25	1996	2500.00	2662-2723
1997 Chernabog Charger - B. White	15	1997	2000.00	3025-3328
1997 Chernabog - Walt Disney Classics	1,500	1997	750.00	1625-1750
1997 Cinderella & Prince - Armani	1,000	1997	825.00	825-1658
1997 Peg Leg Pete - M. Delle	1,000	1997	125.00	140-300
1997 Crocodile Clock	N/A	1997	Gift	110
1997 Cruella Car Box - P. Gordon	30	1997	500.00	1271-1331
1997 Disneyland's 40th (pewter)	N/A	1997	Gift	110
1997 Disney Villain Ornament set/6 - Walt Disney Classics	12,000	1997	40.00	94-130
1997 Dragon (Malificent) (pewter)	N/A	1997	Gift	110-228
1997 Grandma's Girl - Goebel/M.I. Hummel	1,000	1997	350.00	350-484
1997 Hands Off My Playthings (bronze) - C. Barks	176	1997	1950.00	2662-2723
1997 Haunted Mansion - Lilliput Lane	500	1997	250.00	605-655
1997 Lonesome Ghost - Arribas Bros.	50	1997	1700.00	1650-1815
1997 Magical Scrooge Serigraph - C. Barks	295	1997	395.00	555-589
1997 Mistletoe Mickey & Minnie - C. Radko	1,500	1997	250.00	350-514
1997 Mickey's 70th (bronze) - B. Toma	100	1997	1400.00	1815
1997 Mickey's 70th Sericel - Disney Art Ed.	1,500	1997	295.00	415
1997 Peg Leg Pete - Lynn Yi	1,000	1997	125.00	220-245
1997 Tinkerbell - Waterford Crystal	750	1997	250.00	415-425
1997 The Perfect Disguise - Goebel Miniatures	500	1997	300.00	330-375
1997 Walt's Railroad "Lilliebel" - Visions in Scale	75	1997	1600.00	1600-2294
1998 Ariel (Crystal) - Waterford Crystal	750	1998	275.00	363-396
1998 Bella Note - Goebel Miniatures	500	1998	295.00	400-457
1998 Best Friends - C. Radko	1,000	1998	70.00	121-215
1998 Best Pals	N/A	1998	Gift	127-165
1998 Casting Call Ornament set/6 - Disney Merchandise	1,500	1998	45.00	45-121
1998 Decades of Reel Memories - P. Gordon	50	1998	750.00	1452-1573
1998 Dopey Charger - B. White	25	1998	2000.00	2000
1998 Dumbo the Clown - Arribas Brothers	50	1998	1700.00	1700-2541
1998 Fond Memories w/Mickey & Friends Sericel - Disney Art Classics	1,998	1998	295.00	295
1998 A Friendly Day Poster - R. Souders	1,000	1998	25.00	25
1998 Friends Forever - Goebel/M.I. Hummel	350	1998	350.00	350-484
1998 Geppetto & Pinocchio - Armani	1,075	1998	775.00	765-847
1998 Heat Wave Serigraph - C. Barks	195	1998	295.00	295
1998 Jiminy Cricket - When Dreams Come True - B. Toma	75	1998	1400.00	2178-2450
1998 Mickey & Pluto (resin) - M. Delle	1,500	1998	125.00	200
1998 Snow White & Prince - Walt Disney Classics	1,650	1998	750.00	660-2035
1998 Tinkerbell Tile - M. Davis	75	1998	495.00	1650
1998 Tribute to Walt Disney Paperweight - Swarovski Crystal	25	1998	495.00	5000
1998 "Magic Kingdom Memories" - Lilliput Lane	400	1998	275.00	400-550
1998 Who's Out There (bronze) - C. Barks	131	1998	1950.00	2844-3200
1999 65 Feisty Years Lithograph - D. Williams	195	1999	195.00	385
1999 Bambi Scene (bronze) - M. Davis	100	1999	1895.00	2200-2500
1999 Bare Necessities Miniature - Goebel Miniatures	500		295.00	295
1999 Bella Note Double Tile - F. Thomas	75	1999	595.00	1210-1815
1999 Disney Adventure Eggs - J. Levasseur	36	1999	N/A	N/A
1999 Disney Safari Adventure - Liberty Mint Coin	750	1999	75.00	75
1999 Donald & Daisy - Goebel	350	1999	350.00	485-517
1999 Elmer & Tilly (pre registration)	600	1999	Gift	165
1999 Jiminy Cricket - Waterford Crystal	750		250.00	250
1999 Jungle Friends Photomosiac - R. Silvers	250	1999	50.00	125
1999 Kiss The Girl Chargers - E. Gomes	25	1999	750.00	1210
1999 Lady & The Tramp - Armani	750		750.00	750
1999 Lion King Ornament, set/7 - Disney	1,000	1999	45.00	110
1999 Main Street Cinema - Lilliput Lane	500	1999	275.00	325-415
1999 Maleficent as Dragon - Walt Disney Classics	1,350	1999	795.00	935-1350
1999 Maleficent Tile - M. Davis	75	1999	495.00	1100-1210
1999 Mickey & Friends Safari Jeep - Swarovski Crystal	50	1999	495.00	2200
1999 Mickey & Pluto w/ compass (check-in sculpture)	1,800	1999	Gift	165
1999 Mickey & The Treasure (pewter) (banquet gift)	2,000	1999	Gift	125
1999 Mickey Meteor Train - M. Trains	300	1999	595.00	820-1000
1999 Pinocchio (bronze) - B. Toma	50	1999	1600.00	2200
1999 The Pointer (resin) - R. King	1,500		150.00	150
1999 Safari Adventure - R. Souders	1,000	1999	25.00	100
1999 Safari Adventure Trunk - P. Gordon	50	1999	895.00	1210-1820
1999 Safari Surprise Sericel - Walt Disney Art. Ed.	1,000	1999	295.00	385
1999 Safari Trading Cards - Disney	250	1999	75.00	200
1999 Simba (The Pointer) (crystal) - Arribas Brothers	25	1999	1700.00	1700
1999 Simba Ornament - C. Radko	1,000	1999	50.00	50
1999 Song of the South Charger - B. White	15	1999	2000.00	2750

Doverdale Design

Adult Molenniums - Team

YEAR ISSUE	EDITION LIMIT	YEAR RETD.	ISSUE PRICE	*QUOTE U.S.$
1998 The 19th Mole	Open		10.00	10
1998 Able Seamole Jack	Open		10.00	10
1999 Been Moled Out	Open		10.00	10
1998 Demoleition	Open		10.00	10
1997 Double Mole Seven	Open		10.00	10
1998 Eskimole	Open		10.00	10
1997 First Moel	Retrd.	2000	10.00	10
1998 Formoler One	600	1999	100.00	100
1997 Geronemole	Retrd.	2000	10.00	10
1997 Hogmolenay	Open		10.00	10
1998 Holy Moley	Open		10.00	10
1997 Mole 'Ill	Open		10.00	10
1999 Mole Gibson	Open		10.00	10
1997 Mole Grip	Open		10.00	10
1997 Mole In One	Open		10.00	10
1997 Mole Miner	Open		10.00	10
1997 Mole Of Kintyre	Open		10.00	10
1997 Molearis Missile	Retrd.	2000	10.00	10
1997 Moleasses	Retrd.	2000	10.00	10
2000 Moled Age Pensioner	Open		10.00	10
1997 Moled Wine	Open		10.00	10
1998 Moledstream Guard	Open		10.00	10
1998 Molefanwy	Open		10.00	10
1997 Molein The Wizard	Open		10.00	10
1997 Moleinex The Chef	Open		10.00	10
1997 Moleionaire	Open		10.00	10
1997 Molemeal Bread	Retrd.	2000	10.00	10
1997 Molen Rouge	Retrd.	2000	10.00	10
1998 Molening All	Open		10.00	10
1999 The Molennium Bug	12/00		80.00	80
1999 The Molennium Party	2,000		100.00	100
1997 Moler The Dentist	Retrd.	2000	10.00	10
2000 Moletial Arts	Open		10.00	10
1997 Moleting	Open		10.00	10
2000 Moley Matrimony Bride	Open		10.00	10
2000 Moley Matrimony Groom	Open		10.00	10
1997 Moley Parton	Open		10.00	10
2000 Moley S' Kite Rescue	2,000		72.00	72
1998 Moley Smoke	Open		10.00	10
1999 Nurse Molearia	Open		10.00	10
1997 Paracetemole	Open		10.00	10
1999 Paramoledic	Open		10.00	10
1997 Pot Moleing	Open		10.00	10
1997 Ravels Molero	Open		10.00	10
1999 Roy L. Mole	Open		10.00	10
1997 Smoledering	Retrd.	2000	10.00	10
1997 Spaghetti Mole'ognese	Retrd.	2000	10.00	10
1997 Tobermoley	Open		10.00	10
1998 Yeomole Of The Guard	Open		10.00	10

Baby Infantesimoles - Team

YEAR ISSUE	EDITION LIMIT	YEAR RETD.	ISSUE PRICE	*QUOTE U.S.$
1998 Been Moled Off	Open		7.00	7
2000 Bridesmole	Open		7.00	7
1998 Footmole	Open		7.00	7
1998 I'm Mole Excited	Open		7.00	7
1998 I'm Mole'nly Dancing	Open		7.00	7
1997 I'm Mole'nly Dreaming	Open		7.00	7
1998 I'm Mole'nly Graduating	Open		7.00	7
2000 I'm Mole'nly Guiding	Open		7.00	7
1998 I'm Mole'nly Hitching	Open		7.00	7
1997 I'm Mole'nly In Love	Open		7.00	7
1997 I'm Mole'nly Little	Retrd.	2000	7.00	7
2000 I'm Mole'nly Scouting	Open		7.00	7
1997 I'm Mole'nly Sleepy	Open		7.00	7
2000 Mole'nly in a Mess	Open		7.00	7
1998 Mole'nly One More	Open		7.00	7
1999 Molecrochip	Open		7.00	7
1999 Molennium Bug Catcher	Open		7.00	7
1999 Molennium Bug Spotter	Open		7.00	7
2000 Molly - The Molennium Baby	Open		7.00	7
1999 Pick Mole Up	Open		7.00	7
1997 Potty Moleing	Open		7.00	7
1997 Roly Moley	Open		7.00	7
1997 Same Mole'd Prayers	Open		7.00	7
1997 Teddy Mole Broken	Retrd.	2000	7.00	7
1997 Wee Mole of Kintyre	Open		7.00	7
1997 Yummy Mole'k	Open		7.00	7

The Dr. Seuss™ Collection/Hallmark Keepsake Collections

The Dr. Seuss™ Collection/Hallmark Keepsake Collections

YEAR ISSUE	EDITION LIMIT	YEAR RETD.	ISSUE PRICE	*QUOTE U.S.$
2000 ABC Book QSU2057	Numbrd.		20.00	20
2000 The Cat in the Hat QSU2026	Numbrd.		12.00	12
2000 Cat in Tub QSU2062	Numbrd.		20.00	20
2000 Cindy Lou Who QSU2061	Numbrd.		18.00	18
2000 The Ends QSU2038	Numbrd.		45.00	45
2000 A Faithful Friend QSU2029	Numbrd.		12.00	12
2000 Fish in Teapot QSU2059	Numbrd.		15.00	15
2000 Funny Fish QSU2033	Numbrd.		20.00	20
2000 The Great Birthday Bird QSU2028	Numbrd.		12.00	12
2000 The Grinch QSU2055	Numbrd.		12.00	12
2000 A Grinchy Disguise QSU2054	Numbrd.		20.00	20
2000 Hat Tricks! QSU2027	Numbrd.		15.00	15
2000 Hop On Pop QSU2031	Numbrd.		20.00	20
2000 Horton the Elephant QSU2040	Numbrd.		12.00	12
2000 Lorax QSU2060	Numbrd.		18.00	18
2000 Max the Reindeer QSU2056	Numbrd.		18.00	18
2000 Merry Grinchmas! QSU2030	Numbrd.		20.00	20
2000 On A Train? QSU2036	Numbrd.		18.00	18
2000 On Top of the World QSU2034	Numbrd.		20.00	20
2000 Pup in Cup QSU2048	Numbrd.		15.00	15
2000 Rainy Day Games (Cat in the Hat) QSU2044	Numbrd.		20.00	20
2000 Sam and Ham QSU2032	Numbrd.		20.00	20
2000 A Seuss Safe QSU2037	Numbrd.		15.00	15
2000 Sneetches QSU2058	Numbrd.		18.00	18
2000 Socks and Blocks QSU2035	Numbrd.		20.00	20

Duncan Royale

Collector Club - Duncan Royale

YEAR ISSUE	EDITION LIMIT	YEAR RETD.	ISSUE PRICE	*QUOTE U.S.$
1991 Today's Nast	Retrd.	1993	80.00	150
1994 Winter Santa	Retrd.	1994	125.00	150
1995 Santa's Gift	Retrd.	1995	100.00	150
1996 Santa's Choir	Retrd.	1996	90.00	90
1996 Magi Pewter Bell	1,000	1996	Gift	30
1997 Angel Pewter Bell	1,000	1997	Gift	35

Special Event Piece - Duncan Royale

YEAR ISSUE	EDITION LIMIT	YEAR RETD.	ISSUE PRICE	*QUOTE U.S.$
1991 Nast & Music	Retrd.	1993	79.95	95-124

Duncan Royale Figurines - Duncan Royale

YEAR ISSUE	EDITION LIMIT	YEAR RETD.	ISSUE PRICE	*QUOTE U.S.$
1996 Guardian Angel	2,500	1996	150.00	150
1996 Peace & Harmony	2,500	1998	200.00	200

Ebony Collection - Duncan Royale

YEAR ISSUE	EDITION LIMIT	YEAR RETD.	ISSUE PRICE	*QUOTE U.S.$
1990 Banjo Man	5,000	1997	80.00	80
1993 Ebony Angel	5,000	1997	170.00	170
1991 Female Gospel Singer	5,000	1997	90.00	90
1990 The Fiddler	5,000	1997	90.00	90
1990 Harmonica Man	5,000	1997	80.00	80
1991 Jug Man	5,000	1997	90.00	90
1992 Jug Tooter	5,000	1997	90.00	90
1992 A Little Magic	5,000	1997	80.00	80
1991 Male Gospel Singer	5,000	1997	90.00	90
1996 O' Happy Day (Youth Gospel)	5,000	1997	70.00	71
1996 Pigskin (Youth Football)	5,000	1997	70.00	71
1991 Preacher	5,000	1997	90.00	90
1991 Spoons	5,000	1996	90.00	90

*Quotes have been rounded up to nearest dollar

Ebony Collection-Buckwheat - Duncan Royale

YEAR ISSUE	EDITION LIMIT	YEAR RETD.	ISSUE PRICE	*QUOTE U.S.$
1992 O'Tay	5,000	1997	70.00	90
1992 Painter	5,000	1997	80.00	90
1992 Petee & Friend	5,000	1997	90.00	90
1992 Smile For The Camera	5,000	1996	80.00	90

Ebony Collection-Friends & Family - Duncan Royale

YEAR ISSUE	EDITION LIMIT	YEAR RETD.	ISSUE PRICE	*QUOTE U.S.$
1994 Agnes	5,000		100.00	120
1994 Daddy	5,000	1997	120.00	125
1994 Lunchtime	5,000	1997	100.00	100
1994 Millie	5,000		100.00	100
1994 Mommie & Me	5,000		125.00	125

Ebony Collection-Jazzman - Duncan Royale

YEAR ISSUE	EDITION LIMIT	YEAR RETD.	ISSUE PRICE	*QUOTE U.S.$
1992 Bass	5,000	1997	90.00	110
1992 Bongo	5,000	1997	90.00	100
1992 Piano	5,000	1997	130.00	140
1992 Sax	5,000	1997	90.00	100
1992 Trumpet	5,000	1997	90.00	100

Ebony Collection-Jubilee Dancers - Duncan Royale

YEAR ISSUE	EDITION LIMIT	YEAR RETD.	ISSUE PRICE	*QUOTE U.S.$
1993 Bliss	5,000	1997	200.00	200
1993 Fallana	5,000	1997	100.00	100
1993 Keshia	5,000	1997	100.00	100
1993 Lamar	5,000	1997	100.00	100
1993 Lottie	5,000	1997	125.00	125
1993 Wilfred	5,000	1997	100.00	100

Ebony Collection-Special Releases - Duncan Royale

YEAR ISSUE	EDITION LIMIT	YEAR RETD.	ISSUE PRICE	*QUOTE U.S.$
1991 Signature Piece	Retrd.	1997	50.00	75

History of Classic Entertainers 12" - P. Apsit

YEAR ISSUE	EDITION LIMIT	YEAR RETD.	ISSUE PRICE	*QUOTE U.S.$
1987 American	Retrd.	1995	160.00	350
1987 Auguste	Retrd.	1995	220.00	350
1987 Greco-Roman	Retrd.	1995	180.00	350
1987 Grotesque	Retrd.	1995	230.00	350
1987 Harlequin	Retrd.	1995	250.00	350
1987 Jester	Retrd.	1995	410.00	800-1170
1987 Pantalone	Retrd.	1995	270.00	234-300
1987 Pierrot	Retrd.	1995	180.00	225
1987 Pulcinella	Retrd.	1995	220.00	350
1987 Russian	Retrd.	1995	190.00	325-455
1987 Slapstick	Retrd.	1995	250.00	300
1987 Uncle Sam	Retrd.	1995	160.00	325-350

History of Classic Entertainers II 12" - P. Apsit

YEAR ISSUE	EDITION LIMIT	YEAR RETD.	ISSUE PRICE	*QUOTE U.S.$
1988 Bob Hope	Retrd.	1995	250.00	250-295
1988 Feste	Retrd.	1995	250.00	250
1988 Goliard	Retrd.	1995	200.00	300
1988 Mime	Retrd.	1995	200.00	300
1988 Mountebank	Retrd.	1995	270.00	300
1988 Pedrolino	Retrd.	1995	200.00	300
1988 Tartaglia	Retrd.	1995	200.00	250
1988 Thomassi	Retrd.	1995	200.00	300
1988 Touchstone	Retrd.	1995	200.00	300
1988 Tramp	Retrd.	1995	200.00	300
1988 White Face	Retrd.	1995	250.00	300
1988 Zanni	Retrd.	1995	200.00	300

History of Classic Entertainers-Special Releases - Duncan Royale

YEAR ISSUE	EDITION LIMIT	YEAR RETD.	ISSUE PRICE	*QUOTE U.S.$
1990 Bob Hope-18"	Retrd.	1995	1500.00	1700
1990 Bob Hope-6" porcelain	Retrd.	1995	130.00	130
1990 Mime-18"	Retrd.	1995	1500.00	1500
1988 Signature Piece	Retrd.	1995	50.00	50

History of Santa Claus I (12") - P. Apsit

YEAR ISSUE	EDITION LIMIT	YEAR RETD.	ISSUE PRICE	*QUOTE U.S.$
1983 Black Peter	Retrd.	1991	145.00	195-228
1983 Civil War	Retrd.	1991	145.00	156-200
1983 Dedt Moroz	Retrd.	1989	145.00	228-300
1983 Kris Kringle	Retrd.	1988	165.00	600-943
1983 Medieval	Retrd.	1988	220.00	960-1300
1983 Nast	Retrd.	1987	90.00	1950-2145
1983 Pioneer	Retrd.	1989	145.00	195-241
1983 Russian	Retrd.	1989	145.00	288-488
1983 Soda Pop	Retrd.	1988	145.00	600-943
1983 St. Nicholas	Retrd.	1989	175.00	420-500
1983 Victorian	Retrd.	1990	120.00	137-280
1983 Wassail	Retrd.	1991	90.00	117-200

History of Santa Claus II (12") - P. Apsit

YEAR ISSUE	EDITION LIMIT	YEAR RETD.	ISSUE PRICE	*QUOTE U.S.$
1986 Alsace Angel	Retrd.	1997	250.00	250
1986 Babouska	Retrd.	1997	170.00	170-200
1986 Bavarian	Retrd.	1997	250.00	200-254
1986 Befana	Retrd.	1997	200.00	200-250
1986 Frau Holda	Retrd.	1997	160.00	91-160
1986 Lord of Misrule	Retrd.	1997	160.00	160-200
1986 The Magi	Retrd.	1997	350.00	267-350
1986 Mongolian/Asian	Retrd.	1997	240.00	240-350
1986 Odin	Retrd.	1996	200.00	200-300
1986 The Pixie	Retrd.	1997	140.00	124-140
1986 Sir Christmas	Retrd.	1997	150.00	150-175
1986 St. Lucia	Retrd.	1997	180.00	98-180

History of Santa Claus III (12") - Duncan Royale

YEAR ISSUE	EDITION LIMIT	YEAR RETD.	ISSUE PRICE	*QUOTE U.S.$
1990 Druid	Retrd.	1996	250.00	250
1991 Grandfather Frost & Snow Maiden	Retrd.	1997	400.00	400-500
1991 Hoteisho	Retrd.	1997	200.00	200
1991 Judah Maccabee	Retrd.	1997	300.00	300
1990 Julenisse	Retrd.	1997	200.00	200
1991 King Wenceslas	Retrd.	1997	300.00	300
1991 Knickerbocker	Retrd.	1997	300.00	300
1991 Samichlaus	Retrd.	1997	350.00	350-500
1991 Saturnalia King	Retrd.	1996	200.00	200
1990 St. Basil	Retrd.	1997	300.00	300
1990 Star Man	Retrd.	1997	300.00	300
1990 Ukko	Retrd.	1996	250.00	250

History of Santa Claus I (6") - Duncan Royale

YEAR ISSUE	EDITION LIMIT	YEAR RETD.	ISSUE PRICE	*QUOTE U.S.$
1988 Black Peter-6"	6,000/yr.	1997	80.00	80
1988 Civil War-6"	6,000/yr.	1997	80.00	80-104
1988 Dedt Moroz -6"	6,000/yr.	1997	80.00	80
1988 Kris Kringle-6"	6,000/yr.	1998	80.00	80
1988 Medieval-6"	6,000/yr.	1998	80.00	80
1988 Nast-6"	6,000/yr.	1998	80.00	80-104
1988 Pioneer-6"	6,000/yr.	1997	80.00	80
1988 Russian-6"	6,000/yr.	1997	80.00	80
1988 Soda Pop-6"	6,000/yr.	1998	80.00	80-85
1988 St. Nicholas-6"	6,000/yr.	1998	80.00	80
1988 Victorian-6"	6,000/yr.	1997	80.00	80-85
1988 Wassail-6"	6,000/yr.	1997	80.00	80

History of Santa Claus II (6") - Duncan Royale

YEAR ISSUE	EDITION LIMIT	YEAR RETD.	ISSUE PRICE	*QUOTE U.S.$
1988 Alsace Angel-6"	6,000/yr	1997	80.00	90
1988 Babouska-6"	6,000/yr	1998	80.00	80
1988 Bavarian-6"	6,000/yr	1998	90.00	100
1988 Befana-6"	6,000/yr	1997	80.00	80
1988 Frau Holda-6"	6,000/yr	1997	80.00	80
1988 Lord of Misrule-6"	6,000/yr	1997	80.00	80-91
1988 Magi-6"	6,000/yr	1997	130.00	150
1988 Mongolian/Asian-6"	6,000/yr	1998	80.00	90
1988 Odin-6"	6,000/yr	1997	80.00	90
1988 Pixie-6"	6,000/yr	1998	80.00	65-85
1988 Sir Christmas-6"	6,000/yr	1998	80.00	91
1988 St. Lucia-6"	6,000/yr	1998	80.00	80

History of Santa Claus I -Wood - Dolfi

YEAR ISSUE	EDITION LIMIT	YEAR RETD.	ISSUE PRICE	*QUOTE U.S.$
1987 Black Peter-8" wood	500	1993	450.00	450-700
1987 Civil War-8" wood	500	1993	450.00	450-700
1987 Dedt Moroz-8" wood	500	1993	450.00	450-750
1987 Kris Kringle-8" wood	500	1993	450.00	450-550
1987 Medieval-8" wood	500	1993	450.00	1200
1987 Nast-8" wood	500	1993	450.00	1500
1987 Pioneer-8" wood	500	1993	450.00	450-700
1987 Russian-8" wood	500	1993	450.00	450-700
1987 Soda Pop-8" wood	500	1993	450.00	850
1987 St. Nicholas-8" wood	500	1993	450.00	700
1987 Victorian-8" wood	500	1993	450.00	450
1987 Wassail-8" wood	500	1993	450.00	450-600

History Of Santa Claus -Special Releases - Duncan Royale

YEAR ISSUE	EDITION LIMIT	YEAR RETD.	ISSUE PRICE	*QUOTE U.S.$
1991 Signature Piece	Retrd.	1996	50.00	50-100
1992 Nast & Sleigh	5,000	1996	500.00	650

Enchantica

Enchantica Collectors Club - Various

YEAR ISSUE	EDITION LIMIT	YEAR RETD.	ISSUE PRICE	*QUOTE U.S.$
1991 Snappa on Mushroom-2101 - A. Hull	Retrd.	1991	Gift	200-285
1991 Rattajack with Snail-2102 - A. Bill	Retrd.	1991	60.00	300
1992 Jonquil-2103 - A. Hull	Retrd.	1992	Gift	40-200
1992 Ice Demon-2104 - K. Fallon	Retrd.	1992	85.00	100-400
1992 Sea Dragon-2106 - A. Bill	Retrd.	1993	99.00	300-825
1993 White Dragon-2107 - A. Bill	Retrd.	1993	Gift	100-160
1993 Jonquil's Flight-2108 - A. Bill	Retrd.	1993	140.00	145-350
1994 Verratus-2111 - A. Bill	Retrd.	1994	Gift	75
1994 Mimmer-Spring Fairy-2112 - A. Bill	Retrd.	1994	100.00	250
1994 Gorgoyle Cameo piece-2113 - K. Fallon	Retrd.	1994	Gift	25-50
1995 Destroyer-2116 - A. Hull	Retrd.	1995	100.00	115-200
1995 Cloudbreaker-2115 - J. Oliver	Retrd.	1995	Gift	50-100
1996 Sheylag's Trophy-2119	Retrd.	1996	125.00	80-125
1996 Jacarand-2118 - A. Hull	Retrd.	1996	Gift	40-99
1997 Dragonskeep-2126 - D. Mayer	Retrd.	1997	129.00	80-129
1997 Silverflame-2125 - A. Bill	Retrd.	1997	Gift	28-50
1998 Zemorga-2129 - A. Bill	Retrd.	1998	115.00	115
1998 Addax-2128 - A. Bill	Retrd.	1998	Gift	50
1999 Wyrmin & Geljade-2137 - A. Bill	Retrd.	1999	95.00	95
1999 Yorga-2136 - A. Bill	Retrd.	1999	Gift	50
2000 Nakach-2143 - J. Brierley	Yr.Iss.		90.00	90
2000 Baross-2142 - J. Brierley	Yr.Iss.		Gift	N/A

Retired Enchantica Collection - Various

YEAR ISSUE	EDITION LIMIT	YEAR RETD.	ISSUE PRICE	*QUOTE U.S.$
1998 The Adventure Begins-2130 - A. Bill	2,804	1998	385.00	385
1994 Anaxorg-Six Leg Dragon-2094 - A. Hull	Retrd.	1996	83.00	110-120
1996 Aramaan-2182 - A. Hull	4,950	1998	99.00	99-105
1993 Arangast-2073 - J. Bailey	9,500	1998	165.00	165-250
1989 Arangast-Summer Dragon-2026 - A. Bill	7,500	1992	165.00	205-450
1995 Avenger-2154 - A. Bill	450	1996	2700.00	3000-3200
1991 Bledderag, Goblin Twin-2048 - K. Fallon	8,532	1993	115.00	140-225
1988 Blick Scoops Crystals-2015 - A. Bill	Retrd.	1991	47.00	70-125
1993 Bloodstar-2078 - A. Hull	Retrd.	1998	35.00	35-43
1992 Breen-Carrier Dragon-2053 - K. Fallon	12,374	1993	156.00	175-199
1996 Bruntain-2189 - A. Hull	2,950	1998	210.00	210
1992 Cave Dragon-2065 - A. Bill	6,246	1995	200.00	200-285
1989 Cellandia-Summer Fairy-2029 - A. Bill	Retrd.	1992	115.00	150-225
1996 Changeling-2121 - A. Bill	1,250	1996	120.00	150-175
1997 Charlock-2201E - A. Bill	Retrd.	1997	150.00	150
1988 Chuckwalla-2021 - A. Bill	Retrd.	1994	43.00	47-80
1996 Cliffspringer, Snowhopper-2191 - A. Bill	Retrd.	1998	20.00	20-23
1996 Confrontation-2301 - A. Bill	1,950	1998	750.00	750
1994 Coracob-Cobra Dragon-2093 - A. Hull	Retrd.	1996	83.00	87-99
1995 Cormorin-2166 - J. Bailey	3,950	1998	156.00	156-173
1998 Custodian-2127 - A. Bill	Retrd.	1998	230.00	230
1994 Daggerback-2114 - K. Fallon	Retrd.	1995	95.00	95-100
1992 Desert Dragon-2064 - A. Bill	4,786	1995	175.00	200-225
1997 Dragonbrood-2174 - K. Fallon	2,950	1998	359.00	359
1995 Dragongorge Logo-2169 - J. Oliver	Retrd.	1998	50.00	40-55
1994 Dromelaid, Tunnel Serpent-2097 - A. Bill	Retrd.	1997	83.00	108-150
1994 Escape (5th Anniversary)-2110 - A. Bill	Retrd.	1994	250.00	350
1988 Fantazar- Spring Wizard-2016 - A. Bill	7,500	1991	132.50	220-900
1993 Fantazar-2069 - K. Fallon	9,500	1998	140.00	140-173
1991 Flight to Danger-2044 - A. Bill	450	1991	3000.00	5000-6500
1989 Fossfex - Autumn Fairy-2030 - A. Bill	Retrd.	1992	115.00	150-410
1996 Frostflier, Snowhopper-2194 - D. Mayer	Retrd.	1998	20.00	20
1991 Furza - Carrier Dragon-2050 - K. Fallon	10,024	1993	137.50	165-220
1996 Glostomorg-2122 - A. Bill	Retrd.	1996	250.00	165-275
1988 Gorgoyle - Spring Dragon-2017 - A. Bill	7,500	1991	132.50	410-450
1993 Gorgoyle-2070 - J. Bailey	9,500	1998	185.00	185
1991 Grawlfang '91 Winter Dragon-2046 - A. Bill	14,800	1995	295.00	330-350
1988 Grawlfang - Winter Dragon-2019 - A. Bill	7,500	1991	132.50	450-750
1993 Grawlfang-2068 - J. Bailey	9,500	1998	165.00	165
1994 Grogoda, She Troll-2150 - A. Bill	2,950	1997	220.00	220-250
1988 Hellbender, Goblin King-2022 - A. Bill	Retrd.	1998	69.00	69-110
1988 Hepna Pushes Truck-2014 - A. Bill	Retrd.	1994	47.00	57-125
1988 Hest Checks Crystals-2013 - A. Bill	Retrd.	1994	47.00	57-125
1988 Hobba, Hellbenders Twin Son-2023 - A. Bill	Retrd.	1992	69.00	105-150
1996 Hoolock-2177 - A. Bill	2,950	1997	250.00	170-270
1993 Ice Dragon-2109 - A. Bill	Retrd.	1994	95.00	95-225
1995 Infernos-2165 - A. Hull	3,950	1997	145.00	168-173
1996 JáQuara-2170 - K. Fallon	2,950	1998	240.00	240-250
1999 Jewel Dragon- 2135 - A. Bill	Retrd.	1999	230.00	230
1999 Jewel Thief-2138 - A. Bill	Retrd.	1999	200.00	200-230
1988 Jonquil & Rattajack "Safe"-2005 - A. Bill	Retrd.	1998	75.00	75-108
1993 Jonquil and Snappa-2055 - A. Hull	Retrd.	1996	83.00	83-99
1988 Jonquil- Dragons Footprint-2004 - A. Bill	Retrd.	1991	55.00	100
1997 Kellrass-2180 - C. Cooper	2,950	1998	400.00	400
1995 Kirrock of Dragon Duel-2159 - A. Bill	1,950	1996	400.00	435-550
1997 Leviathan-2123	Retrd.	1997	285.00	285
1995 Mai'terith-2164 - K. Fallon	2,950	1997	250.00	300
1992 Manu Manu-Peeper-2105 - A. Bill	Retrd.	1993	40.00	110-400
1994 Mezereon "Grand Corrupter"-2091 - A. Bill	5,100	1996	175.00	187-250
1996 Mezereon-2176 - A. Bill	2,950	1997	250.00	250-270
1998 Mini Vrost-2131 - R. Simpson	Retrd.	1999	49.00	49
1998 The Nalzarg-2133 - A. Bill	Retrd.	1998	145.00	145
1996 Naria-2181 - A. Hull	4,950	1998	99.00	99
1994 Necranon-Raptor Dragon-2095 - A. Bill	Retrd.	1996	105.00	75-120
1996 Nosfertus-2173 - J. Woodward	2,950	1998	290.00	297-350
1996 The Ocean Dragon-2172 - A. Bill	2,950	1998	240.00	240-255
1990 Ogrod-Ice Troll-2032 - A. Bill	Retrd.	1995	235.00	350
1990 Okra, Goblin Princess-2031 - A. Bill	Retrd.	1994	105.00	124-165
1988 Old Yargle-2020 - A. Bill	Retrd.	1993	55.00	68-300
1990 Olm & Sylphen, Mer-King & Queen-2059 - A. Bill	4,251	1994	350.00	400-450
1993 Orolan-2071 - K. Fallon	9,500	1998	140.00	140-173
1989 Orolan-Summer Wizard-2025 - A. Bill	7,500	1992	165.00	168-350
1992 Peeper "Burra Burra"-2057 - A. Hull	Retrd.	1997	50.00	40-70
1993 Peeper "Pia Pia"-2079 - A. Bill	Retrd.	1998	47.00	60-70
1993 Peeper "Rio Rio"-2080 - A. Bill	Retrd.	1998	53.00	40-68
1992 Peeper "Sollo Sollo"-2058 - A. Bill	Retrd.	1997	50.00	40-70
1996 Pendra, The Custodian-2184 - A. Hull	4,950	1998	99.00	99
1995 Piasharn-2162 - K. Fallon	2,950	1996	250.00	270-297
1996 Quicksilver, Snowhopper-2192 - D. Mayer	Retrd.	1998	20.00	20-23
1991 Quillion-Autumn Witch-2045 - A. Bill	13,891	1995	205.00	275-299
1993 Rattajack "All Alone"-2089 - A. Bill	Retrd.	1996	48.00	52
1991 Rattajack "Bowled Over"-2037 - A. Hull	Retrd.	1997	65.00	66-75
1993 Rattajack "Gone Fishing"-2090 - A. Bill	Retrd.	1996	70.00	85
1993 Rattajack "Lazybones"-2087 - A. Bill	Retrd.	1997	49.00	60-70
1993 Rattajack "Soft Landing"-2088 - A. Bill	Retrd.	1996	49.00	53-75
1993 Rattajack & Snappa-2056 - A. Hull	Retrd.	1996	70.00	73-99
1988 Rattajack - Circles-2003 - A. Bill	Retrd.	1993	40.00	66-100
1988 Rattajack - My Ball-2001 - A. Bill	Retrd.	1993	40.00	58-70
1988 Rattajack - Please-2000 - A. Bill	Retrd.	1993	40.00	58-87
1988 Rattajack - Terragon Dreams-2002 - A. Bill	Retrd.	1993	40.00	58-80
1991 Rattajack - Up & Under-2038 - A. Hull	Retrd.	1995	65.00	50-75
1999 Rogamar-2139 - D. Mayer	Retrd.	1999	75.00	75
1995 Saberath-2117 - K. Fallon	Retrd.	1996	100.00	100
1991 Samphire-Carrier Dragon-2049 - A. Bill	11,800	1995	137.50	165-199
1991 Snappa Caught Napping-2039 - A. Hull	Retrd.	1995	39.50	30-60
1988 Snappa Climbs High-2008 - A. Bill	Retrd.	1993	25.00	69
1988 Snappa Dozing-2011 - A. Bill	Retrd.	1993	25.00	75
1988 Snappa Finds a Collar-2009 - A. Bill	Retrd.	1991	25.00	65
1993 Snappa Flapping-2082 - A. Bill	Retrd.	1996	29.50	60-65
1988 Snappa Hatches Out-2006 - A. Bill	Retrd.	1991	25.00	60-125
1993 Snappa If The Cap Fits-2084 - A. Bill	Retrd.	1996	32.50	35
1991 Snappa in Pool "Splash"-2035 - A. Hull	Retrd.	1997	39.50	65
1993 Snappa Nature Watch-2086 - J. Oliver	Retrd.	1996	26.00	28
1991 Snappa Nods Off-2043 - A. Hull	Retrd.	1995	30.00	20-50

*Quotes have been rounded up to nearest dollar

FIGURINES

YEAR ISSUE	EDITION LIMIT	YEAR RETD.	ISSUE PRICE	*QUOTE U.S.$
1988 Snappa Plays Ball-2010 - A. Bill	Retrd.	1993	25.00	35-80
1991 Snappa Posing-2042 - A. Hull	Retrd.	1995	30.00	23-65
1993 Snappa Rollaball-2081 - A. Bill	Retrd.	1996	32.50	35
1991 Snappa Snowdrift-2041 - A. Hull	Retrd.	1995	30.00	30-40
1991 Snappa Tickled Pink-2036 - A. Hull	Retrd.	1997	39.50	30-48
1991 Snappa Tumbles-2047 - A. Hull	Retrd.	1995	30.00	23-40
1993 Snappa w/Enchantica Rose-2083 - A. Bill	Retrd.	1996	24.50	30
1993 Snappa What Ball-2085 - J. Oliver	Retrd.	1996	30.00	30-33
1988 Snappa's First Feast-2007 - A. Bill	Retrd.	1993	25.00	35-75
1990 Snarlgard - Autumn Dragon-2034 - A. Bill	7,500	1993	337.00	240-575
1993 Snarlgard-2074 - J. Bailey	9,500	1998	185.00	185-250
1993 Snow Dragon-2066 - A. Bill	7,500	1996	150.00	80-175
1995 Snowhawk of Dragon Duel-2160 - A. Bill	1,950	1996	400.00	435-550
1993 Snowstar-2075 - A. Hull	Retrd.	1999	39.50	40-50
1996 Snowswift, Snowhopper-2193 - D. Mayer	Retrd.	1998	20.00	20
1992 Snowthorn & Wargren-2062 - A. Bill	7,500	1997	570.00	570-650
1992 Sorren & Gart-2054 - K. Fallon	3,978	1994	220.00	220-300
1999 Spectyr-2141 - C. Davison	Retrd.	1999	165.00	165
1991 Spring Wizard and Yim-2060 - A. Bill	4,554	1993	410.00	410-450
1993 Sunfire-2077 - A. Hull	Retrd.	1998	35.00	35
1989 The Swamp Demon-2028 - A. Bill	Retrd.	1992	69.00	110-150
1988 Tarbet with Sack-2012 - A. Bill	Retrd.	1991	47.00	57-125
1992 Thrace-Gladiator-2061 - K. Fallon	3,751	1993	280.00	300-500
1992 The Throne Citadel-2063 - J. Woodward	539	1995	2000.00	2000
1998 Trea-2234 - J. Brierley	Retrd.	1999	79.00	79
1993 Treeflame-2076 - A. Hull	Retrd.	1999	39.50	40
1996 Triscall-2183 - A. Hull	4,950	1999	99.00	99
1997 Tsunamis-2200E - D. Mayer	Retrd.	1998	137.00	137
1997 Tuatara-2215 - A. Bill	2,950	1998	240.00	240-275
1989 Tuatara-Evil Witch-2027 - A. Bill	6,977	1995	174.00	300
1995 Valkaria-2161 - K. Fallon	2,950	1997	250.00	165-270
1995 Vestra-2167 - A. Hull	3,950	1998	130.00	160
1996 Vladdigor-2171 - A. Bill	2,950	1996	290.00	290-400
1989 Vrorst - The Ice Sorcerer-2018 - A. Bill	7,500	1991	155.00	550
1993 Vrorst-2067 - A. Bill	9,500	1998	140.00	140-173
1990 Vrorst-Ice Sorcerer on Throne-2040 - A. Bill	11,111	1996	500.00	600
1994 Vyzauga-Twin Headed Dragon-2092 - A. Bill	Retrd.	1996	83.00	87-125
1990 Waxifrade - Autumn Wizard-2033 - A. Bill	7,500	1993	265.00	325-400
1993 Waxifrade-2073 - A. Bill	9,500	1998	140.00	140-199
1995 Wolfarlis-2163 - K. Fallon	2,950	1996	250.00	297-400
1996 Woodwidger-2120 - A. Bill	Retrd.	1997	100.00	100-132
1994 Zadragul, Tunnel Serpent-2151 - A. Bill	Retrd.	1997	83.00	96-150
1995 Zadratus-2168 - J. Oliver	3,950	1998	156.00	185-199
1994 Zorganoid-Crab Dragon-2096 - K. Fallon	Retrd.	1996	93.00	75-120
1999 Zykryll-2140 - A. Hull	Retrd.	1999	90.00	90

The Encore Group

Santa and Snow Buddies™ - Encore

YEAR ISSUE	EDITION LIMIT	YEAR RETD.	ISSUE PRICE	*QUOTE U.S.$
1999 Ride 'Em Santa	Open		15.00	15
2000 Santa, 10" Skiing with Buddies on Back	Open		30.00	30
1999 Santa, 20" Skiing with Buddies on Back	Open		78.00	78
2000 Santa, 5" in Sleigh	Open		15.00	15
2000 Santa, 5" with Buddy and Street Lamp	Open		15.00	15
2000 Santa, 8" And Two Buddies Skiing	Open		19.00	19
1999 Santa, 8" at Desk	Open		30.00	30
2000 Santa, 8" Standing with Buddy On Train	Open		19.00	19
2000 Santa, 8" with Buddy and Reindeer	Open		19.00	19
1999 Santa, with Buddy Hanging in Bag	Open		9.00	9
1999 Santa, with Buddy Holding Tree	Open		9.00	9
1999 Santa, with Buddy in Bag	Open		9.00	9

Santa and Snow Buddies™ Musicals - Encore

YEAR ISSUE	EDITION LIMIT	YEAR RETD.	ISSUE PRICE	*QUOTE U.S.$
2000 Buddies Dancing Together	Yr.Iss.		25.00	25
1999 Buddies Musical with Harp	Retrd.	1999	19.00	19
1999 Buddies with Book	Yr.Iss.		19.00	19
2000 Buddy on Horse	Yr.Iss.		25.00	25
2000 Figure 8	Yr.Iss.		24.00	24
2000 Santa at Workbench	Yr.Iss.		19.00	19
2000 Skate with Me	Yr.Iss.		25.00	25

Snow Buddies™ - Encore

YEAR ISSUE	EDITION LIMIT	YEAR RETD.	ISSUE PRICE	*QUOTE U.S.$
1999 Around Tree	Open		19.00	19
1999 Blizzy 10"	Retrd.	1999	30.00	30
1999 Blizzy Reading	Retrd.	1999	5.00	5
1999 Buddies with Reindeer	Retrd.	1999	19.00	19
2000 Crash Landing	Open		19.00	19
2000 Display Sign	Open		9.00	9
2000 Family Portrait	Yr.Iss.		30.00	30
2000 Feeding Time (platinum dealers)	Yr.Iss.		19.00	19
1999 Flurry Walking	Retrd.	1999	5.00	5
2000 Hill Thrill	Yr.Iss.		9.00	9
2000 Holding Train, 10"	Open		30.00	30
2000 Holding Train, 19 1/2"	Open		78.00	78
1999 Holiday on Ice	Open		15.00	15
2000 The Impersonator	Yr.Iss.		19.00	19
2000 No Dumping (platinum dealers)	Yr.Iss.		19.00	19
2000 On Skis	Yr.Iss.		78.00	78
2000 Penguin Hockey	Open		15.00	15
2000 Polar Tea Party	Yr.Iss.		15.00	15
2000 Quiet Time	Yr.Iss.		9.00	9
1999 Ride 'Em Buddies	Open		9.00	9
1999 Santa in Sleigh	Retrd.	1999	30.00	30
1999 Santa w/Powder & Bag	Retrd.	1999	30.00	30
1999 Santa w/Powder & Sign	Retrd.	1999	19.00	19
1999 Santa w/Powder with Tree	Retrd.	1999	19.00	19
2000 Seal of Approval	Open		15.00	15
1999 Secret No Melt	Open		15.00	15
2000 Show Off	Yr.Iss.		15.00	15
2000 Snow Budds Only!	Open		19.00	19
1999 Snowboardin'	Open		6.00	6
1999 Special Friend	Open		6.00	6
1999 Toboggganin'	Open		6.00	6
2000 Tons O' Fun (platinum & gold dealers)	Yr.Iss.		19.00	19
1999 Totem with Pipe	Open		9.00	9
1999 Totem without Pipe	Open		9.00	9
2000 The Tree Trimming	Yr.Iss.		30.00	30
2000 Winter On Parade	Yr.Iss.		19.00	19
1999 Yummy	Open		30.00	30

Snow Buddies™ All Occasion - Encore

YEAR ISSUE	EDITION LIMIT	YEAR RETD.	ISSUE PRICE	*QUOTE U.S.$
2001 Be Mine	Open		9.00	9
2001 Bride and Groom	Open		9.00	9
2001 Congratulations	Open		9.00	9
2001 Get Well	Open		9.00	9
2001 Happy Anniversary	Open		9.00	9
2001 Happy Birthday	Open		9.00	9
2001 I Love You	Open		9.00	9
2001 I Miss You	Open		9.00	9
2001 Thinking of You	Open		9.00	9

Snow Buddies™ Avalanche - Encore

YEAR ISSUE	EDITION LIMIT	YEAR RETD.	ISSUE PRICE	*QUOTE U.S.$
2000 Avalanche, 11"	Open		30.00	30
2000 Avalanche, 5"	Open		9.00	9
2000 Oops!	Open		9.00	9
2000 Remodeling	Open		9.00	9

Snow Buddies™ Blizzy - Encore

YEAR ISSUE	EDITION LIMIT	YEAR RETD.	ISSUE PRICE	*QUOTE U.S.$
2000 Blizzy 11"	Open		30.00	30
2000 Blizzy 5"	Open		9.00	9
2000 Come N' Get It	Open		9.00	9
2000 Teacher	Open		9.00	9

Snow Buddies™ Boo Buddies - Encore

YEAR ISSUE	EDITION LIMIT	YEAR RETD.	ISSUE PRICE	*QUOTE U.S.$
2000 Boo Buddy Collection Sign	Open		15.00	15
2000 Ghostly Surprise	Open		5.00	5
2000 Ghostly Trio	Open		15.00	15
2000 Going Batty	Open		9.00	9
2000 The Great Pumpkin	Open		13.00	13
2000 It's Halloween Time	Open		5.00	5
2000 Mummified	Open		5.00	5
2000 My Scary Friend	Open		5.00	5
2000 Peek-A-Boo	Open		15.00	15
2000 Pumpkin Fun	Open		5.00	5
2000 Pumpkin S'Mor	Open		7.00	7
2000 Twin Grins	Open		9.00	9
2000 Witch-N-Ride	Open		14.00	14
2000 Witchly Attired	Open		5.00	5

Snow Buddies™ Character Train Set - Encore

YEAR ISSUE	EDITION LIMIT	YEAR RETD.	ISSUE PRICE	*QUOTE U.S.$
2000 Blizzy in Caboose	Yr.Iss.		10.00	10
2000 Cousin Slick in Boxcar with Gifts	Yr.Iss.		10.00	10
2000 Everest in Boxcar with Candy Canes	Yr.Iss.		10.00	10
2000 Mayor Blustery in Engine	Yr.Iss.		10.00	10

Snow Buddies™ Cousin Slick - Encore

YEAR ISSUE	EDITION LIMIT	YEAR RETD.	ISSUE PRICE	*QUOTE U.S.$
2000 Cousin Slick, 11"	Open		30.00	30
2000 Cousin Slick, 5"	Open		9.00	9
2000 Doin' An Ollie	Open		9.00	9
2000 Snowboardin'	Open		9.00	9

Snow Buddies™ Everest - Encore

YEAR ISSUE	EDITION LIMIT	YEAR RETD.	ISSUE PRICE	*QUOTE U.S.$
2000 Appetizers	Open		9.00	9
2000 Cracking Up	Open		9.00	9
2000 Everest, 11"	Open		30.00	30
2000 Everest, 5"	Open		9.00	9

Snow Buddies™ Grandpa Frostbite - Encore

YEAR ISSUE	EDITION LIMIT	YEAR RETD.	ISSUE PRICE	*QUOTE U.S.$
2000 Grandpa Frostbite, 11"	Open		30.00	30
2000 Grandpa Frostbite, 5"	Open		9.00	9
2000 In My Day	Open		9.00	9
2000 U Snooze, U Lose!	Open		9.00	9

Snow Buddies™ Snowballs- Encore

YEAR ISSUE	EDITION LIMIT	YEAR RETD.	ISSUE PRICE	*QUOTE U.S.$
2000 Buddy Knit Cap Skatin'	Open		45.00	45
2000 Buddy Knit Cap Skatin'	Open		20.00	20
2000 Buddy Knit Cap Sleddin'	Open		20.00	20
2000 Buddy Knit Cap Sleddin', musical	Open		20.00	20
2000 Buddy Skatin', sm.	Open		30.00	30
2000 Buddy Skiing, sm.	Open		30.00	30
2000 Buddy Sleddin', sm.	Open		30.00	30
2000 Buddy Snowboardin', sm.	Open		30.00	30
2000 Buddy Top Hat Skiing	Open		20.00	20
2000 Buddy Top Hat Skiing	Open		45.00	45
2000 Buddy Top Hat Snowboardin'	Open		20.00	20
2000 Buddy Top Hat Snowboardin', musical	Open		20.00	20

Snow Buddies™ Springtime - Encore

YEAR ISSUE	EDITION LIMIT	YEAR RETD.	ISSUE PRICE	*QUOTE U.S.$
2000 Better Hurry	Yr.Iss.		15.00	15
2000 Duckee Weather	Yr.Iss.		15.00	15
2000 Home Improvements	Yr.Iss.		15.00	15
2000 Just For You!	Yr.Iss.		15.00	15
2000 Life Preservers	Yr.Iss.		15.00	15
2000 A Rite of Spring	Yr.Iss.		15.00	15
2000 Spring Cleaning	Yr.Iss.		15.00	15
2000 Spring Harvest	Yr.Iss.		15.00	15
2000 Stayin' Cool	9,500		30.00	30
2000 Team Effort	Yr.Iss.		15.00	15

Snow Buddies™ Uncle Melty - Encore

YEAR ISSUE	EDITION LIMIT	YEAR RETD.	ISSUE PRICE	*QUOTE U.S.$
2000 Slippery When Wet	Open		9.00	9
2000 Splish Splash	Open		9.00	9
2000 Uncle Melty, 11"	Open		30.00	30
2000 Uncle Melty, 5"	Open		9.00	9

Snow Buddies™ Valentine Buddies Melt Your Heart - Encore

YEAR ISSUE	EDITION LIMIT	YEAR RETD.	ISSUE PRICE	*QUOTE U.S.$
2000 Aiming For Your Heart	Open		5.00	5
2000 Be My Valentine	Open		9.00	9
2000 Hearts-N-Flowers	Open		9.00	9
2000 Luv You This Much	Open		3.00	3
2000 My Love, My Life	Open		5.00	5
2000 Queen of Hearts	Open		3.00	3
2000 Sweet Surprise	Open		3.00	5
2000 Sweets For My Sweet	Open		9.00	9
2000 Together Forever	Open		15.00	15
2000 Valentine Display Sign	Open		15.00	15
2000 You Melt My Heart	Open		3.00	3

Snow Buddies™ Valentine's Day - Encore

YEAR ISSUE	EDITION LIMIT	YEAR RETD.	ISSUE PRICE	*QUOTE U.S.$
2001 Cloud 9	Open		14.00	14
2001 Making Snow Heart	Open		9.00	9
2001 Painting Red Heart	Open		9.00	9
2001 Ready to Kiss	Open		9.00	9
2001 Serenade	Open		14.00	14
2001 Snow Buddy By Mailbox	Open		9.00	9
2001 Snow Buddy Holding Key/Holding Heart	Open		9.00	9
2001 Snow Buddy with Chain of Hearts	Open		6.00	6
2001 Snow Buddy with Heart Shaped Cake	Open		6.00	6
2001 The Suitor	Open		17.00	17
2001 Tunnel of Love	Open		9.00	9
2001 Watering A Heart Garden	Open		9.00	9

Fenton Art Glass Company

Fenton Art Glass Collectors - Fenton

YEAR ISSUE	EDITION LIMIT	YEAR RETD.	ISSUE PRICE	*QUOTE U.S.$
1978 Cranberry Opalescent Baskets w/variety of spot moulds	Yr.Iss.	1978	20.00	175-225
1979 Vasa Murrhina Vases (Variety of colors)	Yr.Iss.	1979	25.00	150-175
1980 Velva Rose Bubble Optic "Melon" Vases	Yr.Iss.	1980	30.00	115-125
1981 Amethyst w/White Hanging Hearts Vases	Yr.Iss.	1981	37.50	195-250
1982 Overlay Baskets in pastel shades (Swirl Optic)	Yr.Iss.	1982	40.00	115-125
1983 Cranberry Opalescent 1 pc. Fairy Lights	Yr.Iss.	1983	40.00	295-350
1984 Blue Burmese w/peloton Treatment Vases	Yr.Iss.	1984	25.00	150-175
1985 Overlay Vases in Dusty Rose w/Mica Flecks	Yr.Iss.	1985	25.00	100-125
1986 Ruby Iridized Art Glass Vase	Yr.Iss.	1986	30.00	295-300
1987 Dusty Rose Overlay/Peach Blow Interior w/dark blue Crest Vase	Yr.Iss.	1987	38.00	110-150
1988 Teal Green and Milk marble Basket	Yr.Iss.	1988	30.00	110-125
1989 Mulberry Opalescent Basket w/Coin Dot Optic	Yr.Iss.	1989	37.50	250-295
1990 Sea Mist Green Opalescent Fern Optic Basket	Yr.Iss.	1990	40.00	75-95
1991 Rosalene Leaf Basket and Peacock & Dahlia Basket	Yr.Iss.	1991	65.00	95
1992 Blue Bubble Optic Vases	Yr.Iss.	1992	35.00	75-95
1993 Cranberry Opalescent "Jonquil" Basket	Yr.Iss.	1993	35.00	110-125
1994 Cranberry Opalescent Jacqueline Pitcher	Yr.Iss.	1994	55.00	125-150
1994 Rosalene Tulip Vase-1994 Convention Pc.	Yr.Iss.	1994	45.00	150-195
1995 Fairy Light-Blue Burmese-1995 Convention Pc.	Yr.Iss.	1995	45.00	295-325
1996 Temple Jar, Burmese-1996 Convention Pc.	Yr.Iss.	1996	65.00	195-225
1997 Mouthblown Egg, Topaz Opal Irid. Hndpt.	Yr.Iss.	1997	65.00	175-195

Collector's Club-Glass Messenger Subscribers Only - Various

YEAR ISSUE	EDITION LIMIT	YEAR RETD.	ISSUE PRICE	*QUOTE U.S.$
1996 Basket, Roselle on Cranberry - M. Reynolds	Yr.Iss.	1996	89.00	130
1997 Vase, French Rose on Rosalene - M. Reynolds	Yr.Iss.	1997	95.00	195-225
1998 Vase, Morning Glory on Burmese - F. Burton	Yr.Iss.	1998	95.00	95
1999 Vase, Blue Harmony - M. Reynolds & F. Burton	Yr.Iss.	1999	95.00	95
2000 Basket, Dancing Windflowers on Lotus Mist - M. Reynolds	Yr.Iss.		95.00	95

1983 Connoisseur Collection - Fenton

YEAR ISSUE	EDITION LIMIT	YEAR RETD.	ISSUE PRICE	*QUOTE U.S.$
1983 Basket, 9" Vasa Murrhina	1,000	1983	75.00	125-150
1983 Craftsman Stein, White Satin Carnival	1,500	1983	35.00	50-95
1983 Cruet/Stopper Vasa Murrhina	1,000	1983	75.00	250-295
1983 Epergne Set, 5 pc. Burmese	500	1983	200.00	995-1295
1983 Vase, 4 1/2" Sculptured Rose Quartz	2,000	1983	32.50	125-155
1983 Vase, 7" Sculptured Rose Quartz	1,500	1983	50.00	120-190
1983 Vase, 9" Sculptured Rose Quartz	850	1983	75.00	220-250

1984 Connoisseur Collection - Fenton, unless otherwise noted

YEAR ISSUE	EDITION LIMIT	YEAR RETD.	ISSUE PRICE	*QUOTE U.S.$
1984 Basket, 10" Plated Amberina Velvet	1,250	1984	85.00	250-295

*Quotes have been rounded up to nearest dollar

YEAR ISSUE		EDITION LIMIT	YEAR RETD.	ISSUE PRICE	*QUOTE U.S.$
1984	Candy Box w/cover, 3 pc. Blue Burmese	1,250	1984	75.00	250-295
1984	Cane, 18" Plated Amberina Velvet	Yr.Iss.	1984	35.00	195-225
1984	Top Hat, 8" Plated Amberina Velvet	1,500	1984	65.00	250-295
1984	Vase, 9" Rose Velvet Hndpt. Floral - L. Everson	750	1984	75.00	225-295
1984	Vase, 9" Rose Velvet-Mother/Child	750	1984	125.00	250-295
1984	Vase, Swan, 8" Gold Azure	1,500	1984	65.00	295-325

1985 Connoisseur Collection - Fenton, unless otherwise noted

YEAR ISSUE		EDITION LIMIT	YEAR RETD.	ISSUE PRICE	*QUOTE U.S.$
1985	Basket, 8 1/2" Burmese, Hndpt. - L. Everson	1,250	1985	95.00	250-295
1985	Epergne Set, 4 pc. Diamond Lace Green Opal.	1,000	1985	95.00	295-325
1985	Lamp, 22" Burmese-Butterfly, Hndpt. - L. Everson	350	1985	300.00	795-995
1985	Punch Set, 14 pc. Green Opalescent	500	1985	250.00	350-395
1985	Vase, 12" Gabrielle Scul. French Opal.	800	1985	150.00	250-295
1985	Vase, 7 1/2" Burmese-Shell - D. Barbour	950	1985	135.00	300-350
1985	Vase, 7 1/2" Chrysanthemums/Circlet, Hndpt. - L. Everson	1,000	1985	125.00	175-250

1986 Connoisseur Collection - Fenton, unless otherwise noted

YEAR ISSUE		EDITION LIMIT	YEAR RETD.	ISSUE PRICE	*QUOTE U.S.$
1986	Basket, Top hat Wild Rose/Teal Overlay	1,500	1986	49.00	110-125
1986	Boudoir Lamp, Cranberry Pearl	750	1986	145.00	295-350
1986	Cruet/Stopper, Cranberry Pearl	1,000	1986	75.00	295-350
1986	Handled Urn, 13" Cranberry Satin	1,000	1986	185.00	550-595
1986	Handled Vase, 7" French Royale	1,000	1986	100.00	175-195
1986	Lamp, 20" Burmese Shells Hndpt. - D. Barbour	500	1986	350.00	995
1986	Vanity Set, 4 pc. Blue Ridge	1,000	1986	125.00	225-395
1986	Vase 10 1/2" Danielle Sandcarved - R. Delaney	1,000	1986	95.00	195-225
1986	Vase, 10 1/2" Misty Morn, Hndpt. - L. Everson	1,000	1986	95.00	195-225

1987 Connoisseur Collection - Various

YEAR ISSUE		EDITION LIMIT	YEAR RETD.	ISSUE PRICE	*QUOTE U.S.$
1987	Pitcher, 8" Enameled Azure Hndpt. - L. Everson	950	1987	85.00	125-150
1987	Vase, 7 1/4" Blossom/Bows on Cranberry Hndpt.- D. Barbour	950	1987	95.00	195-225

1988 Connoisseur Collection - Fenton, unless otherwise noted

YEAR ISSUE		EDITION LIMIT	YEAR RETD.	ISSUE PRICE	*QUOTE U.S.$
1988	Basket, Irid. Teal Cased Vasa Murrhina	2,500	1988	65.00	125-150
1988	Candy, Wave Crest, CranberryHndpt. - L. Everson	2,000	1988	95.00	225-250
1988	Pitcher, Cased Cranberry/ Opal Teal Ring	3,500	1988	60.00	175-195
1988	Vase, 6" Cased Cranberry/Opal Teal/Irid.	3,500	1988	50.00	125-150

1989 Connoisseur Collection - Fenton, unless otherwise noted

YEAR ISSUE		EDITION LIMIT	YEAR RETD.	ISSUE PRICE	*QUOTE U.S.$
1989	Basket, 7" Cranberry w/Crystal Ring Hndpt.- L. Everson	2,500	1989	85.00	175-195
1989	Candy Box, w/cover, Cranberry, Hndpt. - L. Everson	2,500	1989	85.00	125-195
1989	Epergne Set 5 pc., Rosalene	2,000	1989	250.00	595-795
1989	Lamp, 21" Rosalene Satin Hndpt. - L. Everson	1,000	1989	250.00	550-695
1989	Pitcher, Diamond Optic, Rosalene	2,500	1989	55.00	110-125
1989	Vase, Basketweave, Rosalene	2,500	1989	45.00	85-95
1989	Vase, Pinch, 8" Vasa Murrhina	2,000	1989	65.00	110-125

1990-85th Anniversary Collection - Various

YEAR ISSUE		EDITION LIMIT	YEAR RETD.	ISSUE PRICE	*QUOTE U.S.$
1990	Basket, 5 1/2" Trees on Burmese, Hndpt. - Piper/F. Burton	Closed	1990	57.50	125
1990	Basket, 7" Raspberry on Burmese, Hndpt. - L. Everson	Closed	1990	75.00	150-195
1990	Cruet/Stopper Petite Floral on Burmese, Hndpt. - L. Everson	Closed	1990	85.00	195-250
1990	Epergne Set, 2 pc. Pt. Floral on Burmese, Hndpt. - L. Everson	Closed	1990	125.00	295-350
1990	Lamp, 20" Rose Burmese, Hndpt. - Piper/D. Barbour	Closed	1990	250.00	550-695
1990	Lamp, 21" Raspberry on Burmese, Hndpt. - L. Everson	Closed	1990	295.00	695-995
1990	Vase, 6 1/2" Rose Burmese, Hndpt. - Piper/D. Barbour	Closed	1990	45.00	100-110
1990	Vase, 9" Trees on Burmese, Hndpt. - Piper/F. Burton	Closed	1990	75.00	220-250
1990	Vase, Fan 6" Rose Burmese, Hndpt. - Piper/D. Barbour	Closed	1990	49.50	110-125
1990	Water Set, 7 pc. Raspberry on Burmese, Hndpt. - L. Everson	Closed	1990	275.00	895-995

1991 Connoisseur Collection - Various

YEAR ISSUE		EDITION LIMIT	YEAR RETD.	ISSUE PRICE	*QUOTE U.S.$
1991	Basket, Floral on Rosalene, Hndpt. - M. Reynolds	1,500	1991	64.00	130-150
1991	Candy Box, 3 pc. Favrene - Fenton	1,000	1991	90.00	250-295
1991	Fish, Paperweight, Rosalene - Fenton	2,000	1991	30.00	60-75
1991	Lamp, 20" Roses on Burmese, Hndpt. - Piper/F. Burton	500	1991	275.00	595-695
1991	Vase, 7 1/2" Raspberry on Burmese, Hndpt. - L. Everson	1,500	1991	65.00	110-125
1991	Vase, Floral on Favrene, Hndpt. - M. Reynolds	850	1991	125.00	350-395
1991	Vase, Fruit on Favrene, Hndpt. - F. Burton	850	1991	125.00	395-450

1992 Connoisseur Collection - Various

YEAR ISSUE		EDITION LIMIT	YEAR RETD.	ISSUE PRICE	*QUOTE U.S.$
1992	Covered Box, Poppy/Daisy, Hndpt. - F. Burton	1,250	1992	95.00	200-225
1992	Pitcher, 4 1/2" Berries on Burmese, Hndpt. - M. Reynolds	1,500	1992	65.00	150-195
1992	Pitcher, 9" Empire on Cranberry, Hndpt. - M. Reynolds	950	1992	110.00	225-250
1992	Vase, 6 1/2" Raspberry on Burmese, Hndpt. - L. Everson	1,500	1992	45.00	150-195
1992	Vase, 8" Seascape, Hndpt. - F. Burton	750	1992	150.00	225-295
1992	Vase, Twining Floral Rosalene Satin, Hndpt. - M. Reynolds	950	1992	110.00	175-195

1993 Connoisseur Collection - Various

YEAR ISSUE		EDITION LIMIT	YEAR RETD.	ISSUE PRICE	*QUOTE U.S.$
1993	Amphora w/Stand, Favrene, Hndpt. - M. Reynolds	850	1993	285.00	350-395
1993	Bowl, Ruby Stretch w/Gold Scrolls, Hndpt. - M. Reynolds	1,250	1993	95.00	150-195
1993	Lamp, Spring Woods Reverse Hndpt. - F. Burton	500	1993	595.00	595-795
1993	Owl Figurine, 6" Favrene - Fenton	1,500	1993	95.00	125-150
1993	Perfume/Stopper, Rose Trellis Rosalene, Hndpt. - F. Burton	1,250	1993	95.00	125
1993	Vase, 9" Gold Leaves Sandcarved on Plum Irid., - M. Reynolds	950	1993	175.00	250-295
1993	Vase, Victorian Roses Persian Blue Opal., Hndpt. - M. Reynolds	950	1993	125.00	150-195

1993 Family Signature Collection - Various

YEAR ISSUE		EDITION LIMIT	YEAR RETD.	ISSUE PRICE	*QUOTE U.S.$
1993	Basket, 8 1/2" Lilacs - Bill Fenton	3,240	1993	65.00	95-125
1993	Vase, 9" Alpine Thistle/Ruby Carnival - Frank M. Fenton	1,205	1993	105.00	195-250
1993	Vase, 9" Cottage Scene - Shelley Fenton	855	1993	90.00	150-195
1993	Vase, 10" Vintage on Plum - Don Fenton	1,614	1993	80.00	150-225
1993	Vase, 11" Cranberry Dec. - George Fenton	1,217	1993	110.00	140-225

1994 Connoisseur Collection - Various

YEAR ISSUE		EDITION LIMIT	YEAR RETD.	ISSUE PRICE	*QUOTE U.S.$
1994	Bowl, 14" Cranberry Cameo Sandcarved - Reynolds/Delaney	500	1994	390.00	390-450
1994	Clock, 4 1/2" Favrene, Hndpt. - F. Burton	850	1994	150.00	175-225
1994	Lamp, Hummingbird Reverse, Hndpt. - F. Burton	300	1994	590.00	600-750
1994	Pitcher, 10" Lattice on Burmese, Hndpt. - F. Burton	750	1994	165.00	225-295
1994	Vase, 7" Favrene, Hndpt. - M. Reynolds	850	1994	185.00	225-250
1994	Vase, 8" Plum Opalescent, Hndpt. - M. Reynolds	750	1994	165.00	175-225
1994	Vase, 11" Gold Amberina, Hndpt. - M. Reynolds	750	1994	175.00	350-395

1994 Family Signature Collection - Various

YEAR ISSUE		EDITION LIMIT	YEAR RETD.	ISSUE PRICE	*QUOTE U.S.$
1994	Basket, 7 1/2" Lilacs - Shelley Fenton	1,459	1994	65.00	95-125
1994	Basket, 8" Stiegel Green - Bill Fenton	Closed	1994	60.00	95-110
1994	Basket, 8 1/2" Ruby Carnival - Tom Fenton	1,499	1994	60.00	110-120
1994	Basket, 11" Autumn Gold Opal - Frank Fenton	1,001	1994	70.00	95-150
1994	Candy w/cover, 9 1/2" Autumn Leaves - Don Fenton	1,301	1994	60.00	75-95
1994	Pitcher, 6 1/2" Cranberry - Frank M. Fenton	Closed	1994	85.00	125-150
1994	Vase, 9 1/2" Pansies on Cranberry - Bill Fenton	1,698	1994	95.00	125
1994	Vase, 10" Fuchsia - George Fenton	1,497	1994	95.00	125-150

1995 Burmese Historic Collection - Various

YEAR ISSUE		EDITION LIMIT	YEAR RETD.	ISSUE PRICE	*QUOTE U.S.$
1995	Basket, 8" "Butterflies" - M Reynolds	790	1995	135.00	195-200
1995	Bowl, 10 1/4" Rolled Rim "Vintage" - M. Reynolds	790	1995	150.00	200-225
1995	Lamp, 33" "Daybreak" - F. Burton	300	1995	495.00	650-795
1995	Pitcher, 10" "Cherry Blossoms & Butterfly" - M. Reynolds	790	1995	175.00	250-295
1995	Vase, 9" "Hummingbird", 11 Family Signatures - M. Reynolds	790	1995	150.00	200-250

1995 Connoisseur Collection - M. Reynolds, unless otherwise noted

YEAR ISSUE		EDITION LIMIT	YEAR RETD.	ISSUE PRICE	*QUOTE U.S.$
1995	Amphora w/stand, 10 1/4" Royal Purple, Hndpt.	890	1995	195.00	300-350
1995	Ginger Jar, 3 Pc. 8 1/2" Favrene, Hndpt.	790	1995	275.00	400-425
1995	Lamp, 21" Butterfly/Floral Reverse, Hndpt. - F. Burton	300	1995	595.00	700-850
1995	Pitcher, 9 1/2" Victorian Art Glass, Hndpt.	490	1995	250.00	295-350
1995	Vase, 7" Aurora Wild Rose, Hndpt.	890	1995	125.00	175-195

1995 Family Signature Collection - Various

YEAR ISSUE		EDITION LIMIT	YEAR RETD.	ISSUE PRICE	*QUOTE U.S.$
1995	Basket, 8 1/2" Trellis - Lynn Fenton	Closed	1995	85.00	85-95
1995	Basket, 9 1/2" Coralene Floral - Frank M./Bill Fenton	Closed	1995	75.00	95-120
1995	Candy w/cover, 9" Red Carnival - Mike Fenton	Closed	1995	65.00	85-120
1995	Pitcher, 9 1/2" Thistle - Don Fenton	Closed	1995	125.00	125-150
1995	Vase, 7" Gold Pansies on Cranberry - George Fenton	Closed	1995	75.00	95-120
1995	Vase, 9" Summer Garden on Spruce - Don Fenton	Closed	1995	85.00	85-95
1995	Vase, 9 1/2" Golden Flax on Cobalt - Shelley Fenton	Closed	1995	95.00	95-110

1996 Connoisseur Collection - Various

YEAR ISSUE		EDITION LIMIT	YEAR RETD.	ISSUE PRICE	*QUOTE U.S.$
1996	Covered Box, 7" Mandarin Red, Hndpt. - K. Plauche	1,250	1996	150.00	150-195
1996	Lamp, 33" Reverse Painted Poppies, Hndpt. - F. Burton	400	1996	750.00	750-895
1996	Pitcher, 8" Dragonfly on Burmese, Hndpt. - F. Burton	1,450	1996	165.00	165-195
1996	Vase, 11" Berries on Wildrose, Hndpt. - M. Reynolds	1,250	1996	195.00	195-295
1996	Vase, 11" Queen's Bird on Burmese, Hndpt. - M. Reynolds	1,350	1996	250.00	250-395
1996	Vase, 7 1/2" Favrene Cut-Back Sandcarved - M. Reynolds	1,250	1996	195.00	250-295
1996	Vase, 8" Trout on Burmese, Hndpt. - R. Spindler	1,450	1996	135.00	135-195

1996 Family Signature Collection - Various

YEAR ISSUE		EDITION LIMIT	YEAR RETD.	ISSUE PRICE	*QUOTE U.S.$
1996	Basket, 7 1/2" Starflower on Cran. Pearl - M. Fenton	2,430	1996	75.00	75-95
1996	Basket, 8" Mountain Berry - Don Fenton	2,033	1996	85.00	85-95
1996	Candy Box w/cover Pansies - Shelley Fenton	2,074	1996	65.00	75-95
1996	Pitcher, 6 1/2" Asters - Lynn Fenton	2,769	1996	70.00	70-95
1996	Vase, 10" Magnolia & Berry on Spruce - Tom Fenton	2,820	1996	85.00	85-95
1996	Vase, 11" Meadow Beauty - Nancy Fenton	3,217	1996	95.00	95-125
1996	Vase, 8 1/2" Blush Rose on Opaline - George Fenton	2,358	1996	75.00	75-95

1996 Mulberry Historic Collection - Various

YEAR ISSUE		EDITION LIMIT	YEAR RETD.	ISSUE PRICE	*QUOTE U.S.$
1996	Basket, 8" "Hummingbird & Wildrose" - M. Reynolds	1,250	1996	95.00	150-195
1996	Lamp, 21" "Evening Blossom w/ Ladybug" - R. Spindler	500	1996	495.00	495-695
1996	Pitcher, 7 1/2" "Evening Blossom w/ Ladybug" - R. Spindler	1,250	1996	95.00	195-225
1996	Vase, 8" Melon Herringbone "Hummingbird" - M. Reynolds	1,250	1996	85.00	150-175
1996	Vase, 9 1/2" "Hummingbird & Wildrose" - M. Reynolds	1,250	1996	95.00	150-195

1997 Connoisseur Collection - Various

YEAR ISSUE		EDITION LIMIT	YEAR RETD.	ISSUE PRICE	*QUOTE U.S.$
1997	Basket, 11 1/2" Burmes Fenced Garden - R. Spindler	1,750	1997	160.00	160-195
1997	Lamp, 24 1/2" Reverse painted Scenic Floral - F. Burton	550	1997	750.00	795
1997	Pitcher, 6 1/2" Wildrose - K. Plauché	1,350	1997	175.00	195
1997	Vase, 8" French Opal, "Tranquility" - R. Spindler	1,500	1997	135.00	135
1997	Vase, 9" Faverne Daisy w/Lid - M. Reynolds	1,350	1997	295.00	295
1997	Vase, 9" Opaline Floral - M. Reynolds	1,500	1997	95.00	95
1997	Vase, 9 1/2" Trillium - R. Spindler	1,750	1997	195.00	195-225

1997 Family Signature Collection - Various

YEAR ISSUE		EDITION LIMIT	YEAR RETD.	ISSUE PRICE	*QUOTE U.S.$
1997	Basket, 9" Sweetbriar on Plum Overlay - L. Fenton	2,137	1997	85.00	85-120
1997	Fairy Light, 7 1/2" Hydrangeas on Topaz - F. Fenton	2,364	1997	125.00	125-250
1997	Pitcher, 7 1/2" Irises on Misty Blue - D. Fenton	3,043	1997	85.00	85
1997	Pitcher, 8 1/2", Showcase Only - B. Fenton	945	1997	95.00	95
1997	Urn, 13" Magnolia & Berry - G. Fenton	2,108	1997	84.00	84-125
1997	Vase, 6" Field Flowers on Champ. Satin - S. Fenton	4,181	1997	55.00	55-65
1997	Vase, 8" Hydrangeas on Topaz - T. Fenton	1,607	1997	70.00	70-95
1997	Vase, 8" Medallion Collect. Floral on Black - M. Fenton	1,395	1997	75.00	75

1997 Rubina Verde Historic Collection - M. Reynolds

YEAR ISSUE		EDITION LIMIT	YEAR RETD.	ISSUE PRICE	*QUOTE U.S.$
1997	Basket, 7 1/2" Melon	1,750	1997	99.00	125-150
1997	Box, 5 1/4" Melon	1,750	1997	135.00	150-175
1997	Lamp, 24"	650	1997	495.00	495-595
1997	Pitcher, 6"	1,750	1997	95.00	95-150
1997	Vase, 11" Melon	1,750	1997	135.00	135-190
1997	Vase, 8" Reverse Melon	1,750	1997	95.00	110-125

1998 Connoisseur Collection - Various

YEAR ISSUE		EDITION LIMIT	YEAR RETD.	ISSUE PRICE	*QUOTE U.S.$
1998	Basket, 7 1/2" Bouquet - K. Plauché	2,250	1998	135.00	135
1998	Lamp, 20" Trysting Place - F. Burton	750	1998	650.00	650
1998	Lamp, 23 1/2" Jacobean Floral - M. Reynolds	750	1998	495.00	495
1998	Pitcher, 7" Bountiful Harvest - R. Spindler	2,250	1998	155.00	155-195
1998	Vase, 10" Papillon - K. Plauché	2,250	1998	165.00	165-195
1998	Vase, 6" Alhambra - M. Reynolds	4,604	1998	145.00	145
1998	Vase, 9 1/2" Fields of Gold, Showcase Only - M. Reynolds	1,350	1998	150.00	150-195
1998	Vase, 9" Leaves & Vines - D. Fetty	950	1998	245.00	245-350
1998	Vase, 9" Seasons - M. Reynolds	1,350	1998	250.00	250

1998 Family Signature Collection - Various

YEAR ISSUE		EDITION LIMIT	YEAR RETD.	ISSUE PRICE	*QUOTE U.S.$
1998	Basket, 10 1/2" Topaz - S. Fenton	2,035	1998	135.00	125-135
1998	Basket, Hat 9" - T. Fenton	1,850	1998	95.00	95
1998	Bell, 6 1/2" Royal Purple - D. Fenton	3,068	1998	99.00	99
1998	Clock, 4 1/2" Misty Blue - L. Fenton	1,411	1998	95.00	95
1998	Sleigh, 7 1/2" Twining Berries - M. Fenton	Closed	1998	67.50	45-68
1998	Tulip Vase, Sea Green Satin - N. & G. Fenton	4,851	1998	99.00	99-125

*Quotes have been rounded up to nearest dollar

FIGURINES

YEAR ISSUE	EDITION LIMIT	YEAR RETD.	ISSUE PRICE	*QUOTE U.S.$
1998 Vase, 8" After The Rain - R. Spindler	2,250	1998	185.00	185

1998 Royal Purple Historic Collection - F. Burton, unless otherwise noted

YEAR ISSUE	EDITION LIMIT	YEAR RETD.	ISSUE PRICE	*QUOTE U.S.$
1998 Basket, 8" "Colonial Scroll"	2,250	1998	115.00	115
1998 Blown Bell, 6 1/2" "Colonial Scroll" - D. Fenton	3,068	1998	99.00	99
1998 Fairy Light, 7 1/2" "Colonial Scroll"	2,250	1998	175.00	175-250
1998 Lamp, 20" "Colonial Scroll"	750	1998	350.00	350
1998 Perfume 6 1/2" "Colonial Scroll"	2,250	1998	125.00	125
1998 Pitcher, 6 1/2" "Colonial Scroll"	2,250	1998	129.00	129
1998 Tumble Up, 6" "Colonial Scroll", Showcase Only	1,049	1998	179.00	179-250
1998 Vase, 6 1/2" "Colonial Scroll"	2,950	1998	145.00	145
1998 Vase, 9 1/2" "Colonial Scroll"	2,250	1998	125.00	125

1999 Connoisseur Collection - Various

YEAR ISSUE	EDITION LIMIT	YEAR RETD.	ISSUE PRICE	*QUOTE U.S.$
1999 Amphora, 14", Mulberry "Mystic Bird" - M. Reynolds	1,250	1999	129.00	129
1999 Basket, 7 1/2", Peach Crest "Roses" - K. Plauché	1,750	1999	170.00	170
1999 Basket, 9 1/2", Burmese "Bluebird" - R. Spindler	2,950	1999	150.00	150
1999 Ewer, 7", Burmese "Gourds" - M. Reynolds	2,500	1999	175.00	175
1999 Ginger Jar, 6", Favrene "Orchid" - K. Plauché	1,750	1999	160.00	160
1999 Lamp, 17", Burmese "Memories" - R. Spindler	950	1999	695.00	695
1999 Lamp, 26", Reverse Painted "Tulips" - F. Burton	750	1999	695.00	695
1999 Vase, 13", Burmese "Poppies" - M. Reynolds	2,500	1999	185.00	185

1999 Family Signature Collection - Various

YEAR ISSUE	EDITION LIMIT	YEAR RETD.	ISSUE PRICE	*QUOTE U.S.$
1999 Bellflowers on Tranquility, 9 1/2" - D. Fenton	2,692	1999	109.00	109
1999 Martha's Rose Vase, 8 1/2" - S. Fenton Ash	1,365	1999	89.00	89
1999 Morning Mist Pitcher, 6" - S. Fenton	1,890	1999	70.00	70
1999 Rosalene Basket, 8" - L. Fenton Erb	3,715	1999	99.00	99
1999 Violet Satin Covered Box, 5" - G. Fenton	1,706	1999	70.00	70
1999 Violet Satin Doll, 6 3/4", Showcase Only - N. Fenton	1,629	1999	49.00	49

1999 Gold Amberina Historic Offering - R. Spindler

YEAR ISSUE	EDITION LIMIT	YEAR RETD.	ISSUE PRICE	*QUOTE U.S.$
1999 Basket, Hex, 11"	2,500	1999	149.00	149
1999 Cruet, 7"	2,500	1999	129.00	129
1999 Lamp, 24"	950	1999	449.00	449
1999 Pitcher, 9 1/2"	2,500	1999	145.00	145
1999 Vase, 11"	2,500	1999	135.00	135
1999 Vase, 6 1/2"	2,500	1999	95.00	95

2000 Connoisseur Collection - Various

YEAR ISSUE	EDITION LIMIT	YEAR RETD.	ISSUE PRICE	*QUOTE U.S.$
2000 Lamp, 21", Reverse Painted "Emerald Meadow" - M. Reynolds	950		595.00	595
2000 Basket, 9 1/2", Mulberry "Plum Blossoms" - M. Reynolds	1,950		170.00	170
2000 Bowl w/stand, 10", Plum Opal "Botanical Cadence" - R. Spindler	1,950		135.00	135
2000 Ewer Burmese, 8 1/2" "Rose Bed" - F. Burton	2,750		160.00	160
2000 Ginger Jar Burmese, 8" "Daisy" - R. Spindler	2,500		250.00	250
2000 Lotus Mist Burmese, 11", "Coastal Waters" - M. Reynolds	1,950		295.00	295
2000 Pitcher, 7 3/4", Peach Crest "Asian Garden" - R. Spindler	1,850		185.00	185
2000 Vase, 11", Mulberry, (Showcase Only), D. Fenton - R. Spindler	2,950		120.00	120
2000 Vase, 7 1/2", Willow Green Opal "Hanging Hearts" -N/A	1,250		250.00	250

2000 Family Signature Collection - Various

YEAR ISSUE	EDITION LIMIT	YEAR RETD.	ISSUE PRICE	*QUOTE U.S.$
2000 Angel's Blush Perfume, 6" Willow Green - Lynn Fenton Erb	Closed	2000	89.00	89
2000 Butterfly Garden Pitcher, 5 1/2" Cobalt - D. Fenton	Closed	2000	75.00	75
2000 Butterfly Garden Vase, 8 1/2" Gold - N. Fenton	Closed	2000	95.00	95
2000 Lady Basket, 11" Lavender - T. & S. Fenton	Closed	2000	109.00	109
2000 Provincial Floral Basket, 7" Cranberry - B. Fenton	Closed	2000	85.00	85
2000 Sweet Harvest Ribbed Basket, 9" - M. Fenton	11/00		65.00	65

2000 Lotus Mist Burmese Historic Collection - M. Reynolds

YEAR ISSUE	EDITION LIMIT	YEAR RETD.	ISSUE PRICE	*QUOTE U.S.$
2000 Basket, 8 1/2"	2,950		95.00	95
2000 Cruet, 8" (Showcase Only), G. Fenton	2,950		120.00	120
2000 Epergne, 9 1/2"	2,950		150.00	150
2000 Lamp, 23"	1,250		450.00	450
2000 Pitcher, 7"	2,950		99.00	99
2000 Vase, 5"	2,950		65.00	65
2000 Vase, 9 1/2"	2,950		95.00	95

American Classic Series - M. Dickinson

YEAR ISSUE	EDITION LIMIT	YEAR RETD.	ISSUE PRICE	*QUOTE U.S.$
1986 Jupiter Train on Opal Satin, Lamp, 23"	1,000	1986	295.00	400-450
1986 Studebaker-Garford Car on Opal Satin, Lamp, 16"	1,000	1986	235.00	375-450

The Centennial Collection - F. Burton

YEAR ISSUE	EDITION LIMIT	YEAR RETD.	ISSUE PRICE	*QUOTE U.S.$
2000 Epergne Set, 16 1/2", Willow Green Opal	11/00		350.00	350
2000 Vase, 9", Burmese Hndpt. w/Poppies	11/00		175.00	175

Christmas - Various

YEAR ISSUE	EDITION LIMIT	YEAR RETD.	ISSUE PRICE	*QUOTE U.S.$
1978 Christmas Morn, Lamp, 16" - M. Dickinson	Yr.Iss.	1978	125.00	250-295
1978 Christmas Morn, Fairy Light - M. Dickinson	Yr.Iss.	1978	25.00	50-95
1979 Nature's Christmas, Lamp, 16" - K. Cunningham	Yr.Iss.	1979	150.00	250-295
1979 Nature's Christmas, Fairy Light - K. Cunningham	Yr.Iss.	1979	30.00	50-95
1980 Going Home, Lamp, 16" - D. Johnson	Yr.Iss.	1980	165.00	250-295
1980 Going Home, Fairy Light - D. Johnson	Yr.Iss.	1980	32.50	50-95
1981 All Is Calm, Lamp, 16" - D. Johnson	Yr.Iss.	1981	175.00	200-295
1981 All Is Calm, Lamp, 20" - D. Johnson	Yr.Iss.	1981	225.00	295-350
1981 All Is Calm, Fairy Light - D. Johnson	Yr.Iss.	1981	35.00	50-95
1982 Country Christmas, Lamp, 16" - R. Spindler	Yr.Iss.	1982	175.00	250-295
1982 Country Christmas, Lamp, 21" - R. Spindler	Yr.Iss.	1982	225.00	250-350
1982 Country Christmas, Fairy Light - R. Spindler	Yr.Iss.	1982	35.00	50-95
1983 Anticipation, Fairy Light - D. Johnson	7,500	1983	35.00	50-95
1984 Expectation, Lamp, 10 1/2" - D. Johnson	7,500	1984	75.00	275-295
1984 Expectation, Fairy Light - D. Johnson	7,500	1984	37.50	50-95
1985 Heart's Desire, Fairy Light - D. Johnson	7,500	1986	37.50	50-95
1987 Sharing The Spirit, Fairy Light - L. Everson	Yr.Iss.	1987	37.50	50-95
1987 Cardinal in the Churchyard, Lamp, 18 1/2" - D. Johnson	500	1987	250.00	295
1987 Cardinal in the Churchyard, Fairy Light - D. Johnson	4,500	1987	29.50	75-95
1988 A Chickadee Ballet, Lamp, 21" - D. Johnson	500	1988	274.00	295
1988 A Chickadee Ballet, Fairy Light - D. Johnson	4,500	1988	29.50	75-95
1989 Downy Pecker, Lamp, 16" - Chisled Song - D. Johnson	500	1989	250.00	295
1989 Downy Pecker, Fairy Light - Chisled Song - D. Johnson	4,500	1989	29.50	75-95
1990 A Blue Bird in Snowfall, Lamp, 21" - D. Johnson	500	1990	250.00	295
1990 A Blue Bird in Snowfall, Fairy Light - D. Johnson	4,500	1990	29.50	75-95
1990 Sleigh Ride, Lamp, 16" - F. Burton	1,000	1990	250.00	295-350
1990 Sleigh Ride, Fairy Light - F. Burton	3,500	1990	39.00	75-95
1991 Christmas Eve, Lamp, 16" - F. Burton	1,000	1991	250.00	295
1991 Christmas Eve, Fairy Light - F. Burton	3,500	1991	39.00	95
1992 Family Tradition, Lamp, 20" - F. Burton	1,000	1992	250.00	295-350
1992 Family Tradition, Fairy Light - F. Burton	3,500	1992	39.00	75-95
1993 Family Holiday, Lamp, 16" - F. Burton	1,000	1993	265.00	295
1993 Family Holiday, Fairy Light - F. Burton	3,500	1993	39.00	75-95
1994 Silent Night, Lamp, 16" - F. Burton	500	1994	275.00	325-350
1994 Silent Night, Fairy Light - F. Burton	1,500	1994	45.00	95-120
1994 Silent Night, Egg on Stand - F. Burton	1,500	1994	45.00	65-95
1995 Our Home Is Blessed, Lamp, 21" - F. Burton	500	1995	275.00	295-350
1995 Our Home Is Blessed, Egg - F. Burton	1,500	1995	45.00	85-95
1995 Our Home Is Blessed, Fairy Light - F. Burton	1,500	1995	45.00	95-120
1996 Star of Wonder, Lamp, 16" - F. Burton	750	1996	175.00	175-250
1996 Star of Wonder, Egg - F. Burton	1,750	1996	45.00	45-65
1996 Star of Wonder, Fairy Light - F. Burton	1,750	1996	48.00	65-95
1997 The Way Home, Lamp, 20" - F. Burton	750	1997	299.00	299-325
1997 The Way Home, Egg - F. Burton	1,750	1997	59.00	59
1997 The Way Home, Fairy Light - F. Burton	1,750	1997	65.00	65
1997 Holy Family Nativity, set/3 (1st ed.) - J. Saffell	Closed	1997	125.00	125
1997 Olde World Santa - M. Reynolds	3,750	1997	75.00	75
1998 Wise Men , set/3 (Melchoir, Caspar, Belthazar) (1st ed.) - J. Saffell	Closed	1998	155.00	155
1998 Santa, 8 1/2" Patriotic - M. Reynolds	4,750	1998	79.00	79
1998 Santa, 8" Northern Lights - R. Spindler	Closed	1998	75.00	75
1998 Angel Girl, 5 3/4" - K. Plauché	Closed	1998	47.50	50
1998 Radiant Angel, 7 1/2" - K. Plauché	Closed	1998	67.50	68
1998 The Arrival, Egg - F. Burton	2,500	1998	49.00	49
1998 The Arrival, Fairy Light - F. Burton	2,500	1998	55.00	36-55
1998 The Arrival, Lamp - F. Burton	850	1998	285.00	285
1999 Golden Age Santa, 8 1/2" - R.Spindler	Closed	1999	75.00	75
1999 Bejeweled Santa, 8" - K. Plauché	Closed	1999	75.00	75
1999 Enjantment Santa, 7" - M. Reynolds	4,750	1999	85.00	85
1999 Angel Bell, Girl, 5 3/4" - M. Reynolds	Closed	1999	47.50	48
1999 Radiant Angel 7 1/2" - M. Reynolds	Closed	1999	89.50	90
1999 The Announcement, Egg - F. Burton	2,500	1999	49.00	49
1999 The Announcement, Fairy Light - F. Burton	2,500	1999	59.00	59
1999 The Announcement, Hurricane Candle - F. Burton	1,750	1999	149.00	149
1999 Gloria Angel, Camel, Donkey - R. Spindler	Closed	1999	145.00	145
2000 Quilted Santa, 8" - M. Reynolds	11/00		85.00	85
2000 Tyrolean Santa, 8 1/2" - K. Plauché	11/00		85.00	85
2000 Americana Santa, 7" - R. Spindler	11/00		85.00	85
2000 Radiant Angel, 7 1/2", Northern Lights - R. Spindler	11/00		75.00	75
2000 Angel Bell, Girl 5 3/4", Northern Lights - R. Spindler	11/00		49.50	50
2000 The Journey, Egg - F. Burton	2,500		49.00	49
2000 The Journey, Fairy Light - F. Burton	2,500		65.00	65
2000 The Journey, Hurricane Candle - F. Burton	1,750		149.00	149
2000 Shepherds, set/3 - R. Spindler	11/00		135.00	135

Designer Series - Various

YEAR ISSUE	EDITION LIMIT	YEAR RETD.	ISSUE PRICE	*QUOTE U.S.$
1983 Lighthouse Point, Lamp, 23 1/2", - M. Dickinson	150	1983	350.00	450-550
1983 Lighthouse Point, Lamp, 25 1/2", - M. Dickinson	150	1983	350.00	575-695
1983 Down Home, Lamp, 21" - G. Finn	300	1983	300.00	450-495
1984 Smoke 'N Cinders, Lamp, 16" - M. Dickinson	250	1984	195.00	375-495
1984 Smoke 'N Cinders, Lamp, 23" - M. Dickinson	250	1984	350.00	450-595
1984 Majestic Flight, Lamp, 16" - B. Cumberledge	250	1984	195.00	395-495
1984 Majestic Flight, Lamp, 23 1/2" - B. Cumberledge	250	1984	350.00	495-595
1985 In Season, Lamp, 16" - M. Dickinson	250	1985	225.00	450-495
1985 In Season, Lamp, 23" - M. Dickinson	250	1985	295.00	495-550
1985 Nature's Grace, Lamp, 16" - B. Cumberledge	250	1985	225.00	325-450
1985 Nature's Grace, Lamp, 23" - B. Cumberledge	295	1985	295.00	400-495

Easter Series - M. Reynolds

YEAR ISSUE	EDITION LIMIT	YEAR RETD.	ISSUE PRICE	*QUOTE U.S.$
1995 Fairy Light	Closed	1995	49.00	55-95

Mary Gregory - M. Reynolds

YEAR ISSUE	EDITION LIMIT	YEAR RETD.	ISSUE PRICE	*QUOTE U.S.$
1994 Basket, 7 1/2" Oval	Closed	1994	59.00	125-150
1995 Basket, 7 1/2" Oval	Closed	1995	65.00	125-150
1995 Egg on stand, 4" - Butterfly Delight	Closed	1995	37.50	45-95
1996 Hat Basket on Cranberry, 6 1/2"	2,000	1996	95.00	95-150
1996 Vase on Cranberry, 9"	1,500	1996	135.00	135-150
1997 Guest Set, 7" Cranberry	1,500	1997	189.00	250-295
1997 Fairy Light, 5" Cranberry	1,500	1997	79.00	150-250
1997 Basket, 8" Cranberry	1,500	1997	115.00	225-250
1998 Basket, Hex 11 1/2" Cranberry	1,950	1998	150.00	155-195
1998 Pitcher, 6 1/2" Cranberry	1,950	1998	125.00	125-175
1998 Perfume, 5 1/2" Cranberry	1,950	1998	115.00	115-195
1999 Basket, 8"	2,250	1999	129.00	129
1999 Pitcher, 7 1/2"	2,250	1999	135.00	135
1999 Lamp, 13"	1,250	1999	259.00	259
1999 Vase, 5"	2,500	1999	69.00	69
2000 First Rain Basket, 9 1/2"	2,350		139.00	139
2000 Lamp, 18"	1,250		359.00	359
2000 Pillar Vase, 9"	2,350		139.00	139

Millennium Collection - R. Spindler

YEAR ISSUE	EDITION LIMIT	YEAR RETD.	ISSUE PRICE	*QUOTE U.S.$
1999 Circular Vase, 6 1/2"	Closed	1999	149.00	149
1999 Happiness Bird, 6"	Closed	1999	39.00	39
1999 Rolled Rim Bowl, 10"	Closed	1999	95.00	95

Miniatures - Fenton

YEAR ISSUE	EDITION LIMIT	YEAR RETD.	ISSUE PRICE	*QUOTE U.S.$
1999 English Daisy Table Set, 5 pc.	1,500	1999	159.00	159
1998 Epergne, 4 1/2" Champagne	Closed	1998	65.00	65
1996 Epergne, 4 1/2" Opaline	Closed	1996	35.00	35
1996 Punch Bowl Set, 3 3/4" Dusty Rose	Closed	1996	59.00	59
1997 Punch Bowl Set, 3 3/4" Seamist Green	Closed	1997	59.00	59
1998 Punch Set, 3 3/4" Champagne	Closed	1998	75.00	75
2000 Water Set, 2 3/4" Irid.	Closed	2000	69.00	69
1998 Water Set, 4 1/2" Champagne	Closed	1998	85.00	85

Mother's Day - J. Saffell

YEAR ISSUE	EDITION LIMIT	YEAR RETD.	ISSUE PRICE	*QUOTE U.S.$
1999 Mother and Child Pendent	Closed	1999	39.00	39

Valentine's Day Series - Fenton, unless otherwise noted

YEAR ISSUE	EDITION LIMIT	YEAR RETD.	ISSUE PRICE	*QUOTE U.S.$
1992 Basket, 6" Cranberry Opal/Heart Optic	Closed	1992	50.00	50-150
1992 Vase, 4" Cranberry Opal/Heart Optic	Closed	1992	35.00	95-125
1992 Perfume, w/oval stopper Cranberry Opal/Heart Optic	Closed	1992	60.00	145-150
1993 Basket, 7" Caprice Cranberry Opal/Heart Optic	Closed	1993	59.00	59-170
1993 Trinket Box, 5" Cranberry Opal/Heart Optic	Closed	1993	79.00	79-170
1993 Vase, 5 1/2" Melon Cranberry Opal/Heart Optic	Closed	1993	45.00	95-110
1993 Southern Girl, 8", Hndpt. Opal Satin - M. Reynolds	Closed	1993	49.00	75-95
1993 Southern Girl, 8", Rose Pearl Irid.	Closed	1993	45.00	75-95
1994 Basket, 7" Cranberry Opal/Heart Optic	Closed	1994	65.00	120-175
1994 Vase, 5 1/2" Ribbed Cranberry Opal/Heart Optic	Closed	1994	47.50	75-95
1994 Perfume, w/ stopper, 5" Cranberry Opal/Heart Optic	Closed	1994	75.00	75-150
1995 Basket, 8" Melon Cranberry Opal/Heart Optic	Closed	1995	69.00	69-110
1995 Pitcher, 5 1/2" Melon Cranberry Opal/Heart Optic	Closed	1995	69.00	69-110
1995 Perfume, w/ heart stopper, Kristen's Floral Hndpt. - M. Reynolds	2,500	1995	49.00	49-60
1995 Doll, 7", Kristen's Floral Hndpt. Ivory Satin - M. Reynolds	2,500	1995	49.00	49-60
1996 Basket, 8" Melon Cranberry Opalescent	Closed	1996	75.00	75-110
1996 Perfume, 5" Melon Cranberry Opalescent	Closed	1996	95.00	125-150
1996 Fairy Light, 3 pc. Cranberry Opalescent	Closed	1996	135.00	195-250

*Quotes have been rounded up to nearest dollar

FIGURINES

Fenton Art Glass Company to Flambro Imports

YEAR ISSUE	EDITION LIMIT	YEAR RETD.	ISSUE PRICE	*QUOTE U.S.$
1996 Vanity Set, 4 pc. Tea Rose - M. Reynolds	1,500	1996	250.00	250-295
1996 Doll, w/Musical Base Tea Rose - M. Reynolds	2,500	1996	55.00	55-95
1997 Pitcher, 6 1/2" Cranberry Opal/Heart Optic	Closed	1997	89.00	110-125
1997 Puff Box, 4" Cranberry Opal/Heart Optic	Closed	1997	79.00	120-125
1997 Hat Basket, 7" Cranberry Opal/Heart Optic	Closed	1997	79.00	110-125
1997 Vanity Set, 7" Burmese Floral & Butterfly Hndpt. - R. Spindler	2,000	1997	225.00	295-350
1997 Girl Figurine, 8" Burmese Floral Hndpt. - R. Spindler	2,000	1997	75.00	125-150
1997 Pendant & Trinket Box, Champagne Satin	2,500	1997	65.00	65-95
1998 Fairy Light, 5", Cranberry Opal/Heart Optic	Closed	1998	65.00	65-125
1998 Vase, 5", Cranberry Opal/Heart Optic	Closed	1998	39.50	40
1998 Covered Box, 4 1/2", Cranberry Opal/Heart Optic	Closed	1998	125.00	125
1998 "Natalie" Ballerina, 6 1/2", Rosalene - R. Spindler	Closed	1998	85.00	85
1998 Vase, 6", Rosebuds on Rosalene - R. Spindler	Closed	1998	69.50	70
1998 Perfume, 6 1/2", Rosebuds on Rosalene - R. Spindler	Closed	1998	85.00	85
1998 Puffbox, 4 1/2", Rosebuds on Rosalene - R. Spindler	Closed	1998	99.50	80-100
1998 Pendant & Earrings Box, Amethyst	Closed	1998	95.00	95
1999 Violets on Rosalene, Perfume, 5" - K. Plauché	Closed	1999	79.00	75-79
1999 Violets on Rosalene, Music Box, 5" - K. Plauché	Closed	1999	85.00	85
1999 Violets on Rosalene, Praying Children, 4" - K. Plauché	Closed	1999	75.00	75
1999 Violets on Rosalene, Doll, 7" - K. Plauché	Closed	1999	49.50	50
1999 Violets on Rosalene, Butterfly, 4 1/2" - K. Plauché	Closed	1999	49.50	50

Flambro Imports

Emmett Kelly Jr. 1. Members Only Figurine - Undisclosed

YEAR ISSUE	EDITION LIMIT	YEAR RETD.	ISSUE PRICE	*QUOTE U.S.$
1990 Merry-Go-Round	Closed	1990	125.00	313-688
1991 10 Years Of Collecting	Closed	1991	100.00	182-225
1992 All Aboard	Closed	1992	75.00	150-300
1993 Ringmaster	Closed	1993	125.00	154-219
1994 Birthday Mail	Closed	1994	100.00	224-350
1995 Salute To Our Vets	Closed	1995	75.00	195-200
1996 I Love You	Closed	1996	95.00	250-265
1997 Filet of Sole	Closed	1997	130.00	130-160
1998 Autographs	Closed	1998	100.00	100-175
1999 Birthday Bath	Closed	1999	125.00	125
2000 Little Parade	Yr.Iss.		120.00	120

Emmett Kelly Jr. Annual Figurine - Undisclosed

YEAR ISSUE	EDITION LIMIT	YEAR RETD.	ISSUE PRICE	*QUOTE U.S.$
1996 EKJ For President	Retrd.	1996	60.00	60-100
1997 Send in the Clowns	Retrd.	1997	70.00	70
1998 Smile and the World Smiles with You	Retrd.	1998	50.00	50
1999 Our National Treasure	Retrd.	1999	60.00	60
2000 Into The Millenium	Yr.Iss.		55.00	55

EKJ Professionals - Undisclosed

YEAR ISSUE	EDITION LIMIT	YEAR RETD.	ISSUE PRICE	*QUOTE U.S.$
1987 Accountant	Retrd.	1994	50.00	145-175
1991 Barber	Retrd.	1995	50.00	100-195
2000 Biker	Open		70.00	70
1996 Bowler	Open		55.00	55
1988 Bowler	Retrd.	1994	50.00	115-135
1991 Carpenter	Retrd.	1996	50.00	110-145
1991 The Chef	Retrd.	1994	50.00	145-175
1995 Coach	Open		55.00	55
1990 Computer Whiz	Retrd.	1998	50.00	60-100
1997 Computer Whiz (w/garbage can)	Open		55.00	55
2000 Country Western Singer	Open		50.00	50
1987 Dentist	Retrd.	1995	50.00	110-145
1996 Dentist	Open		55.00	55
1995 Doctor	Retrd.	1998	55.00	55-140
1987 Doctor	Retrd.	1995	50.00	100
1999 Doctor	Open		50.00	50
1987 Engineer	Retrd.	1995	50.00	100
1987 Executive	Retrd.	1998	50.00	52-65
1997 Executive (talking on phone)	Open		55.00	55
1996 Farmer	Open		55.00	55
1988 Fireman	Retrd.	1994	50.00	100-145
1995 Fireman	Open		55.00	55
1999 Fireman	Open		50.00	50
1990 Fisherman	Open		50.00	50
1997 Fisherman (w/fish & dog)	Open		55.00	55
1997 Fitness (runaway weight loss)	Open		55.00	55
1997 Gardener (w/rake)	Open		55.00	55
1988 Golfer	Retrd.	1996	50.00	100-195
1995 Golfer	Open		55.00	55
1999 Golfer	Open		50.00	50
1998 Graduate	Open		60.00	60
1990 Hunter	Open		50.00	50
1997 Hunter (w/orange camouflauge)	Open		55.00	55
1999 Lawyer	Open		50.00	50
1987 Lawyer	Retrd.	1995	50.00	120-195
1995 Lawyer	Retrd.	1998	55.00	55-120
1996 Mailman	Open		55.00	55
1988 Mailman	Retrd.	1996	50.00	110-145
2000 Mime	Open		50.00	50
1993 On Maneuvers	Open		50.00	50
1991 Painter	Retrd.	1998	50.00	50-135
1991 Pharmacist	Retrd.	1995	50.00	50
1990 Photographer	Retrd.	1998	50.00	50-125
1993 Pilot	Retrd.	1998	50.00	50-100
1991 Plumber	Retrd.	1994	50.00	100-110
1999 Policeman	Open		50.00	50
1995 Policeman	Open		55.00	55
1988 Policeman	Retrd.	1994	50.00	110-135
1990 The Putt	Retrd.	1998	50.00	65-100
1998 Race Fan	Open		60.00	60
1993 Realtor	Retrd.	1998	50.00	100-125
1998 Retirement	Open		65.00	65
1998 Salesman	Open		60.00	60
1988 Skier	Retrd.	1995	50.00	135-150
1996 Skier	Open		55.00	55
1987 Stockbrocker	Retrd.	1997	50.00	125-150
1999 Teacher	Open		50.00	50
1987 Teacher	Retrd.	1995	50.00	120-145
2000 Truck Driver	Open		70.00	70
1993 Veterinarian	Retrd.	1997	50.00	100-150

Emmett Kelly Jr. - Undisclosed, unless otherwise noted

YEAR ISSUE	EDITION LIMIT	YEAR RETD.	ISSUE PRICE	*QUOTE U.S.$
1995 20th Anniversary of All Star Circus	5,000	1995	240.00	240-250
1997 25th Anniversary of White House Appearance	5,000		240.00	240
1995 35 Years of Clowning	5,000	1995	240.00	240-250
1989 65th Birthday Commemorative	1,989	1989	300.00	625-969
1993 After The Parade	7,500	1998	190.00	190
1988 Amen	12,000	1991	120.00	282-688
1996 American Circus Extravaganza	5,000		240.00	240
1991 Artist At Work	7,500	1997	285.00	300-450
1992 Autumn - D. Rust	Retrd.	1996	60.00	175
1983 The Balancing Act	10,000	1985	75.00	407-1063
1983 Balloons For Sale	10,000	1985	75.00	300-688
1990 Balloons for Sale II	7,500	1998	250.00	188-390
1986 Bedtime	12,000	1991	98.00	125-407
1984 Big Business	9,500	1987	110.00	488-900
1997 Catch of the Day	5,000		240.00	240
2000 Circus Las Vegas	2,000		150.00	150
2000 Circus Parade (Block Set)	1,500		275.00	275
1990 Convention-Bound	7,500	1998	225.00	169-230
1986 Cotton Candy	12,000	1987	98.00	125-469
1996 Daredevil Thrill Motor Show	5,000		240.00	240
1988 Dining Out	12,000	1991	120.00	125-563
1984 Eating Cabbage	12,000	1986	75.00	200-594
1998 Economy Class (Block Set)	1,500	1998	275.00	275
1985 Emmett's Fan	12,000	1986	80.00	225-594
1986 The Entertainers	12,000	1991	120.00	113-250
1986 Fair Game	2,500	1987	450.00	782-1500
1991 Finishing Touch	7,500	1998	230.00	169-307
1991 Follow The Leader	7,500	1998	200.00	150-300
1994 Forest Friends	7,500	1997	190.00	190-325
1983 Hole In The Sole	10,000	1986	75.00	369-594
2000 Home For The Holidays (Christmas Ed.)	2,000		150.00	150
1989 Hurdy-Gurdy Man	9,500	1991	150.00	150-500
1985 In The Spotlight	12,000	1989	103.00	119-438
1993 Kittens For Sale	7,500	1998	190.00	190-200
2000 Kodak's Clown (Hospital Visit)	2,000		130.00	130
2000 Leaving Tombstone	2,000		100.00	100
1994 Let Him Eat Cake	3,500	1995	300.00	300-480
1994 The Lion Tamer	7,500	1997	190.00	200-350
1981 Looking Out To See	12,000	1982	75.00	1040-3500
1986 Making New Friends	9,500	1988	140.00	188-407
1989 Making Up	7,500	1995	200.00	188-563
1985 Man's Best Friend	9,500	1989	98.00	232-750
1990 Misfortune?	3,500	1990	350.00	250-700
1987 My Favorite Things	9,500	1988	109.00	275-750
1989 No Loitering	7,500	1994	200.00	219-500
1985 No Strings Attached	9,500	1991	98.00	132-300
1992 No Use Crying	7,500	1998	200.00	188-313
1987 On The Road Again	9,500	1991	109.00	200-600
1998 Our Perennial Favorite (Block Set)	1,500	1998	275.00	275
1988 Over a Barrel	9,500	1991	130.00	150-250
1992 Peanut Butter?	7,500	1998	200.00	188-313
1984 Piano Player	9,500	1988	160.00	313-750
1992 Ready-Set-Go	7,500	1998	200.00	150-313
1987 Saturday Night	7,500	1988	153.00	438-875
1983 Spirit of Christmas I	3,500	1984	125.00	2088-3500
1984 Spirit of Christmas II	3,500	1985	270.00	313-688
1985 Spirit of Christmas III	3,500	1989	220.00	407-975
1986 Spirit of Christmas IV	3,500	1989	150.00	187-400
1987 Spirit of Christmas V	2,400	1989	170.00	688-969
1988 Spirit of Christmas VI	2,400	1989	194.00	220-400
1990 Spirit of Christmas VII	3,500	1990	275.00	275-400
1991 Spirit of Christmas VIII	3,500	1992	250.00	294-470
1993 Spirit of Christmas IX	3,500	1998	200.00	250-313
1993 Spirit of Christmas X	3,500	1998	200.00	200-225
1994 Spirit of Christmas XI	3,500	1995	200.00	225-260
1995 Spirit of Christmas XII	3,500	1997	200.00	250-295
1996 Spirit of Christmas XIII	3,500	1998	200.00	200-275
1997 Spirit of Christmas XIV	3,500	1998	200.00	200-275
1998 Spirit of Christmas XV	1,500	1998	250.00	250
1992 Spring - D. Rust	Retrd.	1996	60.00	95
1992 Summer - D. Rust	Retrd.	1996	60.00	250-300
1981 Sweeping Up	12,000	1982	75.00	520-1000
2000 Sweeping Up	2,000		100.00	100
1982 The Thinker	15,000	1986	60.00	657-1032
1987 Toothache	12,000	1995	98.00	75-220
1990 Watch the Birdie	9,500	1998	200.00	194-257
1982 Wet Paint	15,000	1983	80.00	369-560
1988 Wheeler Dealer	7,500	1990	160.00	175-500
1982 Why Me?	15,000	1984	65.00	438-750
1992 Winter - D. Rust	Retrd.	1996	60.00	125-150
1983 Wishful Thinking	10,000	1985	65.00	207-750
1993 World Traveler	7,500	1997	190.00	225-300
2000 World's Fair (Block Set)	1,500		275.00	275

Emmett Kelly Jr. A Day At The Fair - Undisclosed

YEAR ISSUE	EDITION LIMIT	YEAR RETD.	ISSUE PRICE	*QUOTE U.S.$
1990 75¢ Please	Retrd.	1994	65.00	150-175
1991 Coin Toss	Retrd.	1994	65.00	125-175
1990 Look At You	Retrd.	1994	65.00	125-175
1991 Popcorn!	Retrd.	1994	65.00	125-175
1990 Ride The Wild Mouse	Retrd.	1994	65.00	95-175
1990 Step Right Up	Retrd.	1994	65.00	165-175
1990 The Stilt Man	Retrd.	1994	65.00	125-175
1990 Thanks Emmett	Retrd.	1994	65.00	125-175
1990 Three For A Dime	Retrd.	1994	65.00	125-175
1991 The Trouble With Hot Dogs	Retrd.	1994	65.00	175
1990 You Can Do It, Emmett	Retrd.	1994	65.00	125-175
1990 You Go First, Emmett	Retrd.	1994	65.00	175

Emmett Kelly Jr. Appearance Figurine - Undisclosed

YEAR ISSUE	EDITION LIMIT	YEAR RETD.	ISSUE PRICE	*QUOTE U.S.$
1992 Now Appearing	Retrd.	1994	100.00	123-188
1993 The Vigilante	Retrd.	1994	75.00	75
1996 Going My Way	Retrd.	1997	90.00	90

Emmett Kelly Jr. Diamond Jubilee Birthday Series - Undisclosed

YEAR ISSUE	EDITION LIMIT	YEAR RETD.	ISSUE PRICE	*QUOTE U.S.$
1999 Big Cake	1,999	1999	100.00	100-103
1999 Birthday Cleanup	1,999	1999	125.00	100-125
1998 Birthday Parade	1,999	1999	150.00	150-200
1999 Jazz (Block Set)	1,500	1999	275.00	275
1999 Oops! Another Birthday (Block Set)	1,500	1999	275.00	275
1999 Surprise	1,999	1999	125.00	125-129

Emmett Kelly Jr. Diamond Jubilee Celebration (Birthday Miniatures) - Undisclosed

YEAR ISSUE	EDITION LIMIT	YEAR RETD.	ISSUE PRICE	*QUOTE U.S.$
1999 Cabbage?	Retrd.	1999	60.00	60
1999 Cake For Two	Retrd.	1999	65.00	65
1999 The Ultimate Gift	Retrd.	1999	60.00	60

Emmett Kelly Jr. Images of Emmett - Undisclosed

YEAR ISSUE	EDITION LIMIT	YEAR RETD.	ISSUE PRICE	*QUOTE U.S.$
1994 Baby's First Christmas	Retrd.	1997	80.00	80-135
1994 Best of Friends	Retrd.	1997	55.00	55-110
1994 Healing Heart	Retrd.	1997	90.00	90-150
1994 Holding The Future	Retrd.	1996	65.00	125-135
1994 Learning Together	Retrd.	1997	85.00	100-135
1994 Tightrope	Retrd.	1997	70.00	85
1994 Why Me, Again?	Retrd.	1997	60.00	60-100

Emmett Kelly Jr. Miniatures - Undisclosed

YEAR ISSUE	EDITION LIMIT	YEAR RETD.	ISSUE PRICE	*QUOTE U.S.$
1994 65th Birthday	Retrd.	1994	70.00	100-150
1998 All Aboard	Open		30.00	30
1996 Amen	Retrd.	1998	35.00	35-100
1998 Artist at Work	Open		55.00	55
1986 Balancing Act	Retrd.	1992	25.00	125-200
1986 Balloons for Sale	Retrd.	1993	25.00	75-100
1997 Balloons for Sale II	Open		55.00	55
1995 Bedtime	Retrd.	1998	35.00	35-100
1997 Big Boss	Open		55.00	55
1988 Big Business	Retrd.	1995	35.00	75-125
1997 Convention Bound	Open		55.00	55
1989 Cotton Candy	Retrd.	1991	30.00	135-150
1995 Dining Out	Retrd.	1998	35.00	35-100
1987 Eating Cabbage	Retrd.	1990	30.00	35-90
1987 Emmett's Fan	Retrd.	1994	30.00	135-150
1995 The Entertainers	Retrd.	1998	45.00	45
1994 Fair Game	Open		75.00	75
1999 Forest Friends	Open		55.00	55
1986 Hole in the Sole	Retrd.	1989	25.00	140-150
1995 Hurdy Gurdy Man	Open		40.00	40
1991 In The Spotlight	Retrd.	1996	35.00	90-115
1999 Let Him Eat Cake	Open		65.00	65
1999 Lion Tamer	Open		60.00	60
1986 Looking Out To See	Retrd.	1987	25.00	200-225
1992 Making New Friends	Retrd.	1996	40.00	135-150
1996 Making Up	Open		55.00	55
1989 Man's Best Friend?	Retrd.	1994	35.00	100-130
1997 Merry Go Round	Open		65.00	65
1996 Misfortune	Open		60.00	60
1990 My Favorite Things	Retrd.	1995	45.00	100-125
1995 No Loitering	Open		50.00	50
1991 No Strings Attached	Retrd.	1996	35.00	125
1992 On the Road Again	Retrd.	1997	35.00	35
1994 Over a Barrel	Retrd.	1998	30.00	30-125
2000 Peanut Butter?	Open		50.00	50
1992 Piano Player	Retrd.	1997	50.00	50
2000 Ready Set Go	Open		55.00	55
1999 Ringmaster	Open		60.00	60
1990 Saturday Night	Retrd.	1995	50.00	75-150
1988 Spirit of Christmas I	Retrd.	1990	40.00	100-200
1992 Spirit of Christmas II	Retrd.	1995	50.00	125-160
1990 Spirit of Christmas III	Retrd.	1993	50.00	72-175
1993 Spirit of Christmas IV	Retrd.	1997	40.00	100-115
1994 Spirit of Christmas V	Retrd.	1996	50.00	100-145
1996 Spirit of Christmas VI	Retrd.	1998	55.00	55
1997 Spirit of Christmas VII	Retrd.	1998	50.00	50-100
1998 Spirit of Christmas IX	Open		55.00	55
1986 Sweeping Up	Retrd.	1987	25.00	94-250
1998 Take Good Care of Her	Retrd.	1999	50.00	50
1986 The Thinker	Retrd.	1991	25.00	150-163
1996 The Toothache	Open		35.00	35
1997 Watch the Birdie	Open		55.00	55
1986 Wet Paint	Retrd.	1993	25.00	65-125
1996 Wheeler Dealer	Open		65.00	65
2000 White House Appearance	Open		60.00	60

*Quotes have been rounded up to nearest dollar

YEAR ISSUE	EDITION LIMIT	YEAR RETD.	ISSUE PRICE	*QUOTE U.S.$
1986 Why Me?	Retrd.	1989	25.00	57-157
1986 Wishful Thinking	Retrd.	1988	25.00	50-142
1998 World Traveler	Open		55.00	55
2000 World's Fair	Open		55.00	55

Emmett Kelly Jr. Musical Waterglobes - Undisclosed

YEAR ISSUE	EDITION LIMIT	YEAR RETD.	ISSUE PRICE	*QUOTE U.S.$
1999 EKJ Birthday Mail	Open		50.00	50
1999 EKJ Catch of the Day	Open		55.00	55
1999 EKJ Filet of Sole	Open		50.00	50
1999 EKJ Golfer	Open		40.00	40
1999 EKJ Making New Friends	Open		35.00	35
1999 EKJ Misfortune	Open		40.00	40
1999 EKJ Race Fan	Open		40.00	40
1999 EKJ Teacher	Open		40.00	40
1999 EKJ World Traveler	Open		50.00	50

Emmett Kelly Jr. Real Rags Collection - Undisclosed

YEAR ISSUE	EDITION LIMIT	YEAR RETD.	ISSUE PRICE	*QUOTE U.S.$
1993 Big Business II	Retrd.	1996	140.00	200
1993 Checking His List	Closed	N/A	100.00	115-200
1994 Eating Cabbage II	3,000	1997	100.00	100-150
1994 A Good Likeness	3,000	1997	120.00	120-175
1993 Looking Out To See II	3,000	1996	100.00	165-230
1994 On in Two	3,000	1996	100.00	135-175
1994 Rudolph Has A Red Nose, Too	3,000	1996	135.00	135-350
1993 Sweeping Up II	3,000	1996	100.00	135-175
1993 Thinker II	3,000	1996	120.00	150-200

Hap Henriksen's Collectors Fellowship - H. Henriksen

YEAR ISSUE	EDITION LIMIT	YEAR RETD.	ISSUE PRICE	*QUOTE U.S.$
XX The Legend (Event Special)	Retrd.	N/A	N/A	N/A
1993 On The Road (Event Special)	Retrd.	1993	N/A	195
XX Orbis Terrigena	Retrd.	N/A	88.00	88
XX Phantom	Retrd.	N/A	88.00	88

Hap Henriksen's Dragons - H. Henriksen

YEAR ISSUE	EDITION LIMIT	YEAR RETD.	ISSUE PRICE	*QUOTE U.S.$
1992 Albenon the Forest Dragon	Retrd.	1993	75.00	198
1995 Atnanticus	Retrd.	1996	150.00	175-330
1996 The Awakening	Retrd.	1997	150.00	150-295
1998 Decemurius Dragon of the Frost	750		441.00	441
1991 Drac Terriblius	3,000	N/A	325.00	700
1989 Dragon of the Golden Hoard	Retrd.	N/A	N/A	500
1989 Guardian of the Keep	Retrd.	N/A	189.00	500
1989 Hatched	Retrd.	N/A	N/A	195
1997 The Hatchling	1,500	N/A	160.00	100-160
1997 Histra Rex	1,500		295.00	350
XX Ice Dragon	Retrd.	N/A	70.00	175-190
1992 Keeper of the Ruin	300	1994	1800.00	3000
1989 Let Sleeping Dragons Lie	3,000	1992	N/A	1100-2000
1989 Leviathan	Retrd.	N/A	N/A	425-650
1992 The Merchant of Dreams	350	1994	1800.00	3000
XX Night & Day	Retrd.	N/A	N/A	N/A
1998 Rewyne Protector of the Lost World	1,500		265.00	265
1997 Tallonous Wyvernous	1,500		150.00	160
1992 Treasure of the Lost Lands	1,500	1995	N/A	N/A
1998 World	1,500		265.00	265
1994 Wundor	2,500	N/A	N/A	310
1994 Wynd	2,500	1996	N/A	340
1989 Wyvern	1,500	1992	N/A	N/A
1992 Zornakk the Elder	Retrd.	N/A	N/A	N/A

Hap Henriksen's Jesters - H. Henriksen

YEAR ISSUE	EDITION LIMIT	YEAR RETD.	ISSUE PRICE	*QUOTE U.S.$
1989 His Majesty Bladrick The Incredibly Simple	Retrd.	1990	275.00	275
1989 Jockomo	Retrd.	1990	55.00	55
1989 Jollies Pitchbelly	Retrd.	1990	175.00	175
1989 La DiDa Toogoode	Retrd.	1990	165.00	165
1989 Merry Andrew	Retrd.	1990	125.00	125
1989 Puck	Retrd.	1990	55.00	55
1989 Smack Thickwit	Retrd.	1990	175.00	175-240
1989 Twit Coxcombe	Retrd.	1990	135.00	135
1989 Ursula	Retrd.	1990	90.00	90

Hap Henriksen's Wizards - H. Henriksen

YEAR ISSUE	EDITION LIMIT	YEAR RETD.	ISSUE PRICE	*QUOTE U.S.$
1995 Alkmyne	1,500		135.00	145
1996 Apothes	1,500		195.00	240
1996 Archimedes Lessons	1,500		195.00	240
1994 Astrol	2,500	1996	N/A	N/A
1992 Balador	Retrd.	1993	N/A	N/A
1990 Balance of Truth	2,500	N/A	220.00	440
1993 Bilanx The Grand Master (Utopian)	3,500	1994	150.00	150
1993 Compriez (S. American)	Retrd.	1994	61.00	61
1995 Confrontation	999		266.00	266
1996 Conversation	1,500		175.00	189
1989 Counter Sign	Retrd.	1991	90.00	250
1997 The Crystal Gazer	1,500		150.00	160
1997 Curiosity	1,500		189.00	189
1997 Dragon Lord	1,500		195.00	195
1991 Dragon Master	1,500	N/A	575.00	695
1997 The Elusive Potion	1,500		270.00	270
1994 Farundel The Weary Traveler	2,500	1996	150.00	150
1993 Fidem (African)	Retrd.	1994	71.00	71
1989 Foreshadow the Seer	Retrd.	1992	N/A	425
1998 Gallianaus	1,500		136.00	136
1993 Hopai (Oriental)	Retrd.	1994	71.00	71
1991 Howland the Wise	2,500	1993	245.00	425
1989 Hubble Bubble	Retrd.	1990	75.00	295-450
1992 Journeyman	2,500	1995	240.00	440
1993 Karojan (American Indian)	Retrd.	1994	71.00	71
1994 Knowe	2,500	1996	N/A	495
1989 Lackey The Apprentice	Retrd.	1990	N/A	130
1996 Laidley Worm	1,500		150.00	160
1997 The Magic Sword	1,500		150.00	160
1989 Merlin Wizard Watcher	2,500	1991	N/A	195
1992 Merlinus Ambrosius	2,500	1996	275.00	385-410
1989 Merryweather Sunlighter	3,000	1993	390.00	590-595
1989 Morgan Le Fay	2,500	N/A	150.00	350-450
1989 Moriah	Retrd.	1992	240.00	440
1989 Mydwynter	Retrd.	1996	190.00	425
1994 Nateur	2,500	1996	N/A	310
1993 Nemesis (Greek)	Retrd.	1994	61.00	61
1994 Noctiluca	2,500	1996	N/A	410
1992 Ommiad the Magi	2,500	1995	N/A	410
1991 Past, Present and Future	2,500	1996	300.00	495
1995 Pelryn	2,500		175.00	189
1991 Pondering the Quest	2,500	1993	210.00	410
1995 Rammis	2,500		150.00	160
1989 Repository of Magic	Retrd.	1990	150.00	360-395
1989 Rimbaugh	Retrd.	N/A	N/A	445
1997 Seeking Council	1,500		451.00	451
1993 Smalaz (Russian)	Retrd.	1994	55.00	55
1997 Solaris The Star Seeker	1,500		189.00	189
1993 The Soothsayer	2,500	1996	N/A	395-410
1996 Stormbringer	1,500		150.00	150
1994 Sturm	2,500	1996	N/A	345-410
1998 Taihun, Master of Council	1,500		160.00	300
1989 Thorbauld	Retrd.	N/A	N/A	350
1996 Thorlief Graybeard	1,500		250.00	270
1994 The Travellers	1,500		295.00	295
1993 Troewe (Germanic)	Retrd.	1994	61.00	61
1998 Trouth	1,500		136.00	136
1998 Twiggle Tanglefoot	1,500		136.00	136
1997 Well of Sorrows	1,500		270.00	270
1993 Wroth (Nordic)	Retrd.	1994	61.00	61

Kensington Bears- Bears of Character - Undisclosed

YEAR ISSUE	EDITION LIMIT	YEAR RETD.	ISSUE PRICE	*QUOTE U.S.$
1998 Bear Bell Boy	2,500		75.00	75
1998 Bear Clown	Open		55.00	55
1998 Bear Graduate	Open		35.00	35
1998 Bear Indian	Open		55.00	55
1998 Bear Sewing	Open		35.00	35
1998 Bear With Candle	Open		35.00	35

Kensington Bears- Cute Companions - Undisclosed

YEAR ISSUE	EDITION LIMIT	YEAR RETD.	ISSUE PRICE	*QUOTE U.S.$
1998 Bear	Open		10.00	10
1998 Elephant	Open		10.00	10
1998 Labrador	Open		10.00	10
1998 Rabbit	Open		10.00	10

Kensington Bears- Cute Companions Puppies - Undisclosed

YEAR ISSUE	EDITION LIMIT	YEAR RETD.	ISSUE PRICE	*QUOTE U.S.$
1998 Basset Hound	Open		10.00	10
1998 Boxer	Open		10.00	10
1998 Cocker Spaniel	Open		10.00	10
1998 Rottweiler	Open		10.00	10
1998 Westie Terrier	Open		10.00	10
1998 Yorkshire Terrier	Open		10.00	10

Kensington Bears-Brown Bears - Undisclosed

YEAR ISSUE	EDITION LIMIT	YEAR RETD.	ISSUE PRICE	*QUOTE U.S.$
1998 Baxter	Open		50.00	50
1998 Bobby	Open		30.00	30
1998 Chaplin	Open		30.00	30
1998 Johnny	Open		30.00	30
1998 Louie	Open		50.00	50
1998 Trimble	Open		60.00	60

Kensington Bears-Golden Bears - Undisclosed

YEAR ISSUE	EDITION LIMIT	YEAR RETD.	ISSUE PRICE	*QUOTE U.S.$
1998 Baxter	Open		50.00	50
1998 Bobby	Open		30.00	30
1998 Chaplin	Open		30.00	30
1998 Johnny	Open		30.00	30
1998 Louie	Open		50.00	50
1998 Trimble	Open		60.00	60

Little Emmetts - M. Wu

YEAR ISSUE	EDITION LIMIT	YEAR RETD.	ISSUE PRICE	*QUOTE U.S.$
1998 #1 Teacher	Open		10.00	10
1996 Balancing Act	Retrd.	1998	25.00	25
1996 Balloons for Sale	Retrd.	1998	25.00	25
1994 Birthday Haul	Open		30.00	30
1995 Dance Lessons	Retrd.	1995	50.00	50
1998 Get Well Soon	Open		10.00	10
1998 Happy Birthday	Open		10.00	10
1998 I Love You	Open		10.00	10
1994 Little Artist Picture Frame	Retrd.	1997	22.00	22
1994 Little Emmett Fishing	Retrd.	1997	35.00	35
1995 Little Emmett Noel, Noel	Open		40.00	40
1994 Little Emmett Shadow Show	Retrd.	1997	40.00	40
1995 Little Emmett Someday	Retrd.	1997	50.00	50
1994 Little Emmett w/Blackboard	Retrd.	1997	30.00	30
1994 Little Emmett, Counting Lession (Musical)	Retrd.	1996	30.00	30
1994 Little Emmett, Country Road (Musical)	Retrd.	1996	35.00	35
1994 Little Emmett, Raindrops (Musical)	Retrd.	1995	35.00	35
1994 Little Emmett, You've Got a Friend (Musical)	Retrd.	1996	33.00	33
1996 Long Distance	Open		50.00	50
1995 Looking Back Musical Waterglobe	Retrd.	1997	75.00	75
1995 Looking Forward Musical Waterglobe	Retrd.	1999	75.00	75
1996 Looking Out To See	Retrd.	1998	25.00	25
1998 Miss You	Open		10.00	10
1994 Playful Bookends	Open		40.00	40
1998 Sorry	Open		10.00	10
1996 Sweeping Up	Retrd.	1998	25.00	25
1996 Thinker	Retrd.	1998	25.00	25
1996 Wet Paint	Retrd.	1998	40.00	40
1994 EKJ, Age 1	Open		9.00	9
1994 EKJ, Age2	Open		9.50	10
1994 EKJ, Age 3	Open		12.00	12
1994 EKJ, Age 4	Open		12.00	12
1994 EKJ, Age 5	Open		15.00	15
1994 EKJ, Age 6	Open		15.00	15
1994 EKJ, Age 7	Open		17.00	17
1994 EKJ, Age 8	Open		21.00	21
1994 EKJ, Age 9	Open		22.00	22
1994 EKJ, Age 10	Open		25.00	25
1996 January-New Years	Open		35.00	35
1996 February-Valentine's Day	Open		35.00	35
1996 March-St. Patrick's Day	Open		35.00	35
1996 April-April Showers	Open		35.00	35
1996 May-May Flowers	Open		35.00	35
1996 June-School Is Out	Open		35.00	35
1996 July-Independence Day	Open		35.00	35
1996 August-Summer Picnic	Open		35.00	35
1996 September-School Is In	Open		35.00	35
1996 October-Pumpkins for Fall & Halloween	Open		35.00	35
1996 November-Thanksgiving	Open		35.00	35
1996 December-Snow Sledding w/Friends	Open		35.00	35

Peanuts - Undisclosed

YEAR ISSUE	EDITION LIMIT	YEAR RETD.	ISSUE PRICE	*QUOTE U.S.$
2000 A Day in the Park	1,500		85.00	85
1999 First Day of School	1,500		100.00	100
1999 Heroes	1,500		85.00	85
2000 Hors d' oeuvres	1,500		85.00	85
2000 Joe Cool	1,500		85.00	85
2000 Joe No-Pride	1,500		65.00	65

Forma Vitrum/Cavanagh Group Intl.

Sailboats - Cavanagh

YEAR ISSUE	EDITION LIMIT	YEAR RETD.	ISSUE PRICE	*QUOTE U.S.$
1999 10" 3 Sail, aqua, blue, white 7205	Closed	2000	25.00	25
1999 10" 3 Sail, blue, white, yellow 7206	Closed	2000	25.00	25
2000 10" 3 Sail, green, blue, white 7219	Open		25.00	25
2000 10" 3 Sail, lt. blue, white, yellow 7220	Open		25.00	25
1999 10" 3 Sail, red, white, blue 7204	Closed	2000	25.00	25
2000 10" 3 Sail, red, white, lt. blue 7218	Open		25.00	25
1999 15" 3 Sail, white blue 7211	Closed	2000	50.00	50
2000 15" 3 Sail, white, red, lt. blue 7224	Open		50.00	50
1999 7" 2 Sail, all white 7210	Closed	2000	18.00	18
1999 7" 2 Sail, blue, yellow 7208	Closed	2000	18.00	18
2000 7" 2 Sail, blue, yellow 7222	Open		18.00	18
2000 7" 2 Sail, lt. blue, red 7221	Open		18.00	18
1999 7" 2 Sail, purple, yellow 7209	Closed	2000	18.00	18
1999 9" 7 Sail, all white 7202	Closed	2000	30.00	30
1999 9" 7 Sail, aqua, blue, white 7203	Closed	2000	30.00	30
1999 9" 7 Sail, blue, yellow, white 7201	Closed	2000	30.00	30
2000 9" 7 Sail, dark blue, translucent, red 7216	Open		30.00	30
2000 9" 7 Sail, green, lt. blue, while 7217	Open		30.00	30
2000 9" 7 Sail, lt. blue, yellow, while 7215	Open		30.00	30

Franklin Mint

Joys of Childhood - N. Rockwell

YEAR ISSUE	EDITION LIMIT	YEAR RETD.	ISSUE PRICE	*QUOTE U.S.$
1976 Coasting Along	3,700		120.00	175
1976 Dressing Up	3,700		120.00	175
1976 The Fishing Hole	3,700		120.00	175
1976 Hopscotch	3,700		120.00	175
1976 The Marble Champ	3,700		120.00	175
1976 The Nurse	3,700		120.00	175
1976 Ride 'Em Cowboy	3,700		120.00	175
1976 The Stilt Walker	3,700		120.00	175
1976 Time Out	3,700		120.00	175
1976 Trick or Treat	3,700		120.00	175

G. DeBrekht Artistic Studios/Russian Gift & Jewelry

Derévo Celebration Santa Musicals - G. DeBrekht Artistic Studios

YEAR ISSUE	EDITION LIMIT	YEAR RETD.	ISSUE PRICE	*QUOTE U.S.$
2000 Forest Bear	2,000		79.00	79
2000 Santa in Blue	2,000		79.00	79
2000 Santa in Red	2,000		79.00	79

Derévo Elegant Santa - G. DeBrekht Artistic Studios

YEAR ISSUE	EDITION LIMIT	YEAR RETD.	ISSUE PRICE	*QUOTE U.S.$
2000 Majestic Santa	1,200		175.00	175

Derévo Royal Santa - G. DeBrekht Artistic Studios

YEAR ISSUE	EDITION LIMIT	YEAR RETD.	ISSUE PRICE	*QUOTE U.S.$
2000 Regal Santa	2,500		49.00	49
2000 Santa Mayor	2,500		49.00	49

Derévo Russian Fairytale Collection - G. DeBrekht Artistic Studios

YEAR ISSUE	EDITION LIMIT	YEAR RETD.	ISSUE PRICE	*QUOTE U.S.$
2000 Fisherman & Goldfish, 2 pc. Set	2-Yr.		75.00	75
2000 Frog Princess, 2 pc. Set	2-Yr.		75.00	75
2000 The Gift, 2 pc. Set	2-Yr.		75.00	75
2000 Gingerbread Boy, 2 pc. Set	2-Yr.		75.00	75
2000 Golden Egg, 2 pc. Set	2-Yr.		75.00	75
2000 Snow Maiden, 3 pc. Set	2-Yr.		89.00	89
2000 Village Maiden	2-Yr.		35.00	35

Derévo Russian Sleigh Ride - G. DeBrekht Artistic Studios

YEAR ISSUE	EDITION LIMIT	YEAR RETD.	ISSUE PRICE	*QUOTE U.S.$
2000 Hitchhiking Santa	2,500		49.00	49
2000 Joyful Ride	2,500		49.00	49
2000 Making Memories	2,500		49.00	49
2000 Santa on the Go	2,500		49.00	49
2000 Touring Snowman	2,500		49.00	49
2000 Traveling Together	2,500		49.00	49
2000 Winter Wandering	2,500		49.00	49
2000 Winter's Pleasure	2,500		49.00	49

*Quotes have been rounded up to nearest dollar

Derévo Working Snowman - G. DeBrekht Artistic Studios

Year Issue	Edition Limit	Year Retd.	Issue Price	*Quote U.S.$
2000 Snowman Cleaner	1,500		65.00	65
2000 Snowman Lamplighter	1,500		65.00	65
2000 Snowman Sweeper	1,500		65.00	65

Heritage Floral Fantasy (Eggs) - G. DeBrekht Artistic Studios

Year Issue	Edition Limit	Year Retd.	Issue Price	*Quote U.S.$
1999 Floral Beauty	2-Yr.		17.00	17
1999 Gifts of Spring	2-Yr.		35.00	35
1999 Spring's Sweet Song	2-Yr.		39.00	39

Heritage Magical Myths (Eggs) - G. DeBrekht Artistic Studios

Year Issue	Edition Limit	Year Retd.	Issue Price	*Quote U.S.$
1999 Fire-Bird E/10-MD#1	Open		59.00	59
1999 Fire-Bird E/10-MD#3	Open		59.00	59
1999 For a Water	Open		59.00	59
1999 Humpback Pony	Open		59.00	59
1999 Meeting	Open		59.00	59
1999 Morosko E/10-MD#1	Open		59.00	59
1999 Morosko E/10-MD#4	Open		59.00	59
1999 Snow Maiden	Open		59.00	59
1999 Summer Scene	Open		59.00	59
1999 Winter Scene	Open		59.00	59

Heritage Symbols of Faith (Wooden Eggs) - G. DeBrekht Artistic Studios

Year Issue	Edition Limit	Year Retd.	Issue Price	*Quote U.S.$
1998 Icon Eggs E21/XLG#1	150		700.00	700
1998 Icon Eggs E21/XLG#2	150		700.00	700
1998 Icon Eggs E21/XLG#3	150		700.00	700

Masterpiece Children's Santa - G. DeBrekht Artistic Studios

Year Issue	Edition Limit	Year Retd.	Issue Price	*Quote U.S.$
1999 Children on Sleigh	300		270.00	270
1999 Children with Angel	500		270.00	270
1999 Children with Snowman	300		150.00	150
1999 Fox and Dwarf	750		150.00	150
1998 Girl and Angel SA/03/LG#22	500		270.00	270
1999 Girl and Angel SA/03/SM#22	500		150.00	150
1999 Girls with Angel	500		150.00	150
1998 Hunting	250		270.00	270
1999 Kids With Snowman	300		270.00	270
1998 Looking for Gifts SA/03-LG#1	150		270.00	270
1998 Looking for Gifts SA/03-SM#1	150		150.00	150
1999 Skiing Children SA/03-LG#7	150		270.00	270
1999 Skiing Children SA/03-SM#7	500		150.00	150
1998 Winter Scene SA/03/LG#9	500		200.00	200
1998 Winter Scene SA/03/SM#9	500		130.00	130
1998 Winter Scene with Kids	300		270.00	270

Masterpiece Collection - G. DeBrekht Artistic Studios

Year Issue	Edition Limit	Year Retd.	Issue Price	*Quote U.S.$
1999 Forest Bear	750		150.00	150
1999 Honey Lover Bear	500		390.00	390
1998 Hunter	200		390.00	390
1999 Hunter with Dog	200		450.00	450
1999 Mushroom Picker Bear	750		450.00	450
1999 Peasant Beauty	250		370.00	370
1999 Peasant Man "Golden Fish", Fairy Tale	150		450.00	450
1998 Samovar Keeper	100		390.00	390
1999 Vacationing Bear	500		390.00	390

Masterpiece Fairy Tale Memories Santa - G. DeBrekht Artistic Studios

Year Issue	Edition Limit	Year Retd.	Issue Price	*Quote U.S.$
1999 Emelya & Pike Santa	2-Yr.		290.00	290
1998 Gossips Santa	2-Yr.		290.00	290
1998 Santa with Couple	2-Yr.		290.00	290
1998 Snow Maiden	2-Yr.		300.00	300

Masterpiece Forest Bears - G. DeBrekht Artistic Studios

Year Issue	Edition Limit	Year Retd.	Issue Price	*Quote U.S.$
2000 Happy Honey Bear (20")	75		1895.00	1895
2000 Happy Honey Bear (9")	150		450.00	450

Masterpiece Jeweled Santa - G. DeBrekht Artistic Studios

Year Issue	Edition Limit	Year Retd.	Issue Price	*Quote U.S.$
2000 The Golden Santa	150		590.00	590

Masterpiece Kris Kringle Santa - G. DeBrekht Artistic Studios

Year Issue	Edition Limit	Year Retd.	Issue Price	*Quote U.S.$
1998 Children With Angel	750		270.00	270
1998 Girl With Angel	750		270.00	270
1998 Hunter With Dog	500		270.00	270
1998 Looking For Gifts	500		270.00	270
1998 Peasant Woman	250		370.00	370
1998 Skiing Children	500		270.00	270
1998 Snowmaiden With Squirrel	300		390.00	390
2000 Tree of Light	400		175.00	175
1998 Winter Scene	500		200.00	200

Masterpiece Merchant Santa - G. DeBrekht Artistic Studios

Year Issue	Edition Limit	Year Retd.	Issue Price	*Quote U.S.$
1999 Bag of Happiness	500		390.00	390
1998 Bear of Joy	350		490.00	490
1998 Child of Hope	350		590.00	590
1999 Child of Hope (Ex. Lg.)	300		695.00	695
1998 Merchant with Children SA/12-LG#3	500	1999	490.00	490
1998 Night Before Christmas	500		900.00	900
1999 Santa ...Happy Holiday	750		390.00	390
1998 Santa Christmas Night	500		790.00	790

Masterpiece Old World Santa - G. DeBrekht Artistic Studios

Year Issue	Edition Limit	Year Retd.	Issue Price	*Quote U.S.$
2000 Bell Ringer	Open		89.00	89
2000 Lamp Lighter	Open		89.00	89

Masterpiece Santa w/Bear - G. DeBrekht Artistic Studios

Year Issue	Edition Limit	Year Retd.	Issue Price	*Quote U.S.$
1998 Night Before Christmas	250		900.00	900

Masterpiece Santa w/Children - G. DeBrekht Artistic Studios

Year Issue	Edition Limit	Year Retd.	Issue Price	*Quote U.S.$
1998 Christmas Night	750		790.00	790
1998 Nutcracker	750		900.00	900
1998 A Winter Tale	350		650.00	650

Masterpiece Santa's Journey - G. DeBrekht Artistic Studios

Year Issue	Edition Limit	Year Retd.	Issue Price	*Quote U.S.$
2000 The Journey Begins	250		590.00	590
2000 Time to Rest	250		590.00	590

Masterpiece Snowmaiden - G. DeBrekht Artistic Studios

Year Issue	Edition Limit	Year Retd.	Issue Price	*Quote U.S.$
1998 Snowmaiden w/Squirrel	300		390.00	390

Masterpiece Storybook Santa - G. DeBrekht Artistic Studios

Year Issue	Edition Limit	Year Retd.	Issue Price	*Quote U.S.$
1999 Christmas Night	100		1895.00	1895
2000 Hansel & Gretel	250		900.00	900
1999 Night Before Christmas	250		950.00	950
2000 Nutcracker	250		900.00	900
2000 Nutcracker Romance	250		950.00	950
2000 Nutcracker Surprise	150		900.00	900
2000 Snow Queen	250		900.00	900
1999 A Winter Tale	250		900.00	900

Masterpiece Time For Santa - G. DeBrekht Artistic Studios

Year Issue	Edition Limit	Year Retd.	Issue Price	*Quote U.S.$
2000 Almost Home	250		795.00	795
2000 Angel's Blessing	300		595.00	595
2000 Bringing Love	300		595.00	595
2000 Santa's Arrival	250		695.00	695

Masterpiece Village Santa - G. DeBrekht Artistic Studios

Year Issue	Edition Limit	Year Retd.	Issue Price	*Quote U.S.$
2000 Joyful Snowman	300		325.00	325
2000 Santa's Arrival	300		325.00	325
2000 Santa's Rest	250		350.00	350
2000 We Wish You A Merry Christmas	300		325.00	325
2000 Winter Troika	300		325.00	325

Gartlan USA

Members Only Figurine

Year Issue	Edition Limit	Year Retd.	Issue Price	*Quote U.S.$
1990 Wayne Gretzky-Home Uniform - L. Heyda	Closed	1991	75.00	275-400
1991 Joe Montana-Road Uniform - F. Barnum	Closed	1992	75.00	200-489
1991 Kareem Abdul-Jabbar - L. Heyda	Closed	1993	75.00	175-395
1992 Mike Schmidt - J. Slockbower	Closed	1993	79.00	100-495
1993 Hank Aaron - J. Slockbower	Closed	1994	79.00	100-195
1994 Shaquille O'Neal - L. Cella	Closed	1995	39.95	275-350
1997 Ringo Starr (bath silver) - J. Hoffman	1,000	1997	80.00	80-125
1998 John Lennon (bath silver), (4 1/2") A/P - J. Hoffman	1,000	1998	195.00	195
2000 Yellow Submarine - A. Workman	5,000		35.00	35

Brandon Lee-The Crow - W. Merklein

Year Issue	Edition Limit	Year Retd.	Issue Price	*Quote U.S.$
1996 Brandon Lee-The Crow, (9")	5,700		225.00	275

Jerry Garcia - S. Sun

Year Issue	Edition Limit	Year Retd.	Issue Price	*Quote U.S.$
1997 Jerry Garcia, (4")	10,000		50.00	50
1997 Jerry Garcia, (9")	1,995		195.00	195
1997 Jerry Garcia, A/P (9")	300		295.00	295
1997 Jerry Garcia, marquee (6")	5,000		125.00	125

John Lennon - J. Hoffman

Year Issue	Edition Limit	Year Retd.	Issue Price	*Quote U.S.$
1998 John Lennon, pewter (9")	2,000		495.00	495
1998 John Lennon, pewter (honed in silver), (9") A/P	250		895.00	895
1998 John Lennon, pewter, (4 1/2")	5,000		125.00	125

Kareem Abdul-Jabbar Sky-Hook Collection - L. Heyda

Year Issue	Edition Limit	Year Retd.	Issue Price	*Quote U.S.$
1989 Kareem Abdul-Jabbar "The Captain", signed	1,989	1990	175.00	320-450
1989 Kareem Abdul-Jabbar, A/P	100	1990	200.00	500
1989 Kareem Abdul-Jabbar, Commemorative	33	1990	275.00	3700-4000

Kiss "Psycho-Circus" - R. Hollis

Year Issue	Edition Limit	Year Retd.	Issue Price	*Quote U.S.$
1998 Kiss "Psycho-Circus" Baseball	Open		20.00	20

Kiss - M. Pascucci

Year Issue	Edition Limit	Year Retd.	Issue Price	*Quote U.S.$
1997 Kiss A/P, (10")	250		595.00	595
1998 Kiss, (10") pewter	500		750.00	750
1998 Kiss, (10") pewter, signed, AP (silver bath)	50		995.00	995
1997 Kiss, (10") signed	1,000		395.00	395
1997 Kiss, (5")	10,000		89.00	89

Leave It To Beaver - Noble Studio

Year Issue	Edition Limit	Year Retd.	Issue Price	*Quote U.S.$
1995 Jerry Mathers, (5")	5,000	1999	49.95	50
1995 Jerry Mathers, (7 1/2"), signed	1,963	1999	195.00	195

Magic Johnson Collection - R. Sun

Year Issue	Edition Limit	Year Retd.	Issue Price	*Quote U.S.$
1988 Magic Johnson -"Magic in Motion"	1,737	1989	125.00	195-275
1988 Magic Johnson A/P "Magic in Motion", signed	250	1989	175.00	2000-2300
1988 Magic Johnson Commemorative, signed	32	1989	275.00	5000-7500

Mike Schmidt "500th" Home Run Edition - R. Sun

Year Issue	Edition Limit	Year Retd.	Issue Price	*Quote U.S.$
1987 Mike Schmidt "500th" Home Run, A/P signed	20	1988	275.00	1200-1395
1987 Mike Schmidt "500th" Home Run, signed	1,987	1988	150.00	625-650

Neil Diamond - J. Hoffman

Year Issue	Edition Limit	Year Retd.	Issue Price	*Quote U.S.$
1998 Neil Diamond, (4")	5,000		30.00	30
1998 Neil Diamond, (4") Marquee™	5,000		30.00	30
1998 Neil Diamond, (9") A/P signed	250		395.00	400
1998 Neil Diamond, (9") signed	1,000		295.00	300

Ozzy Osbourne - Sun Studios

Year Issue	Edition Limit	Year Retd.	Issue Price	*Quote U.S.$
1999 Ozzy Osbourne (4 1/2")	10,000		35.00	35
1999 Ozzy Osbourne (8") A/P, signed	250		275.00	275
1999 Ozzy Osbourne (8"), signed	5,000		175.00	175

Ringo Starr - Various

Year Issue	Edition Limit	Year Retd.	Issue Price	*Quote U.S.$
1996 Ringo Starr with drums, (6") - J. Hoffman	5,000		150.00	150
1999 Ringo Starr, (4 1/2") pewter - M. Pascucci	5,000		125.00	125
1996 Ringo Starr, (4") - J. Hoffman	10,000		49.95	50
1996 Ringo Starr, (8 1/2") A/P signed - J. Hoffman	250		600.00	600
1996 Ringo Starr, (8 1/2") signed - J. Hoffman	1,000		350.00	350
1999 Ringo Starr, (9") signed pewter - M. Pascucci	500		495.00	495
2000 Ringo Starr, hanging 4 1/2" figurine with stand "Peace" - M. Pascucci	10,000		30.00	30
1999 Ringo Starr, signed pewter AP (bath silver) - M. Pascucci	50		895.00	895

Signed Figurines - Various

Year Issue	Edition Limit	Year Retd.	Issue Price	*Quote U.S.$
1991 Al Barlick - V. Bova	1,989	1995	195.00	250-295
1993 Bob Cousy - L. Heyda	950	1995	150.00	100-195
1991 Bobby Hull - The Golden Jet - L. Heyda	1,983	1995	250.00	150-225
1992 Bobby Hull, A/P - L. Heyda	300	1994	350.00	350-500
1991 Brett Hull - The Golden Brett - L. Heyda	1,986	1995	250.00	150-250
1992 Brett Hull, A/P - L. Heyda	300	1994	350.00	400-600
1989 Carl Yastrzemski-"Yaz" - L. Heyda	1,989	1990	150.00	175-375
1989 Carl Yastrzemski-"Yaz", A/P - L. Heyda	250	1990	150.00	400-700
1992 Carlton Fisk - J. Slockbower	1,972	1995	225.00	225-275
1990 Darryl Strawberry - L. Heyda	2,500	1995	225.00	150-350
1994 Eddie Matthews - R. Sun	1,978	1995	195.00	100-200
1994 Frank Thomas - D. Carroll	500	1995	225.00	350-390
1990 George Brett - F. Barnum	2,250	1995	225.00	175-275
1992 Gordie Howe - L. Heyda	2,358	1994	225.00	250-350
1990 Gordie Howe, signed A/P - L. Heyda	250	1994	395.00	395
1992 Hank Aaron - F. Barnum	1,982	1994	225.00	200-400
1992 Hank Aaron Commemorative w/displ. case - F. Barnum	755	1994	275.00	275-350
1991 Hull Matched Figurines - L. Heyda	950	1993	500.00	500
1989 Joe DiMaggio - L. Heyda	2,214	1990	275.00	995-1500
1990 Joe DiMaggio, signed matched numbered set - L. Heyda	56	1991	4600.00	4600-9200
1990 Joe DiMaggio- Pinstripe Yankee Clipper - L. Heyda	325	1990	695.00	1750-2300
1990 Joe DiMaggio- Pinstripe Yankee Clipper, A/P - L. Heyda	12	1990	1500.00	4000-8000
1991 Joe Montana - F. Barnum	2,250	1991	325.00	500-795
1991 Joe Montana, A/P - F. Barnum	250	1991	500.00	700-1100
1989 John Wooden-Coaching Classics - L. Heyda	1,975	1995	175.00	175
1989 John Wooden-Coaching Classics, A/P - L. Heyda	250	1995	350.00	350
1989 Johnny Bench - L. Heyda	1,989	1990	150.00	250-260
1989 Johnny Bench, A/P - L. Heyda	250	1990	150.00	400-500
1994 Ken Griffey Jr., - J. Slockbower	1,989	1995	225.00	300-400
1993 Kristi Yamaguchi - K. Ling Sun	950	1995	195.00	260-275
1990 Luis Aparicio - J. Slockbower	1,984	1995	225.00	150-295
1991 Monte Irvin - V. Bova	1,973	1995	195.00	195
1991 Negro League, Set/3	950	1995	500.00	650-750
1985 Pete Rose-"For the Record", signed - H. Reed	4,192	1987	125.00	950-1200
1992 Ralph Kiner - J. Slockbower	1,975	1995	225.00	225
1991 Rod Carew - Hitting Splendor - J. Slockbower	1,991	1995	225.00	225-250
1994 Sam Snead - L. Cella	950	1995	225.00	100-250
1994 Shaquille O'Neal - R. Sun	500	1995	225.00	500-795
1992 Stan Musial - J. Slockbower	1,969	1995	325.00	195-350
1992 Stan Musial, A/P - J. Slockbower	300	1995	425.00	250-425
1989 Steve Carlton - L. Heyda	3,290	1992	175.00	125-375
1989 Steve Carlton, A/P - L. Heyda	300	1992	350.00	400-500
1989 Ted Williams - L. Heyda	2,654	1990	295.00	475-495
1989 Ted Williams, A/P - L. Heyda	250	1990	650.00	595-700
1992 Tom Seaver - J. Slockbower	1,992	1995	225.00	325-400
1994 Troy Aikman - V. Davila	500	1995	225.00	350-500
1991 Warren Spahn - J. Slockbower	1,973	1995	225.00	250-275
1989 Wayne Gretzky - L. Heyda	1,851	1989	225.00	500-1000
1989 Wayne Gretzky, A/P - L. Heyda	300	1989	695.00	1000-1200
1990 Whitey Ford - S. Barnum	2,360	1995	225.00	100-350
1990 Whitey Ford, A/P - S. Barnum	250	1995	350.00	350
1989 Yogi Berra - F. Barnum	2,150	1994	225.00	250-350
1989 Yogi Berra, A/P - F. Barnum	250	1994	350.00	350

Yellow Submarine - M. Pascucci, unless otherwise noted

Year Issue	Edition Limit	Year Retd.	Issue Price	*Quote U.S.$
1999 Blue Meanie (4 1/2")	10,000		20.00	20
1999 Boob (2")	10,000		20.00	20
1999 Bulldogs (2")	10,000		20.00	20
1999 Fred (4")	10,000		20.00	20
1999 George Harrison (4")	10,000		25.00	25
1999 Glove (2")	10,000		20.00	20
1999 John Lennon (4")	10,000		25.00	25
1999 Lord Mayor (4")	10,000		20.00	20
1999 Max (3")	10,000		20.00	20
1999 Paul McCartney (4")	10,000		25.00	25
1999 Ringo Starr (4")	10,000		25.00	25
1999 Yellow Submarine, with Beatles (4 1/2") - A. Workman	5,000		70.00	70
1999 Yellow Submarine, with Beatles (8") - A. Workman	1,968		195.00	195
1999 Yellow Submarine, with Beatles A/P (8") - A. Workman	250		295.00	295

*Quotes have been rounded up to nearest dollar

Geo. Zoltan Lefton Company

Child Within - M. Garvin

YEAR ISSUE	EDITION LIMIT	YEAR RETD.	ISSUE PRICE	*QUOTE U.S.$
1998 Apples 11650	Open		15.00	15
1998 Bee 11641	Open		13.00	13
1998 Butterfly 11640	Open		15.00	15
1998 Chick 11638	Open		15.00	15
1998 Christmas Tree 11630	Open		15.00	15
1998 Cow 11635	Open		13.00	13
1998 Elephant 11633	Open		13.00	13
1998 Frog 11637	Open		13.00	13
1998 Grape 11631	Open		15.00	15
1998 Polar Bear 11636	Open		13.00	13
1998 Rabbit 11639	Open		13.00	13
1998 Reindeer 11634	Open		15.00	15
1998 Rose 11629	Open		15.00	15
1998 Snowman 11628	Open		15.00	15
1998 Strawberries 11651	Open		15.00	15
1998 Sunflower 11632	Open		15.00	15
1998 Watermelons 11649	Open		15.00	15

Gary Paterson Collections - G. Paterson

YEAR ISSUE	EDITION LIMIT	YEAR RETD.	ISSUE PRICE	*QUOTE U.S.$
1998 #1 Dad 11756	Open		25.00	25
1998 Art of Casting 11758	Open		40.00	40
1998 Fully Equiped 11760	Open		25.00	25
1998 Golf Lover 11759	Open		25.00	25
1998 It's Only A Game 11763	Open		40.00	40
1998 Mr. Fix It 11762	Open		40.00	40
1998 Now What 11752	Open		25.00	25
1998 Sports Fan 11751	Open		40.00	40
1998 Super Fan 11764	Open		25.00	25
1998 Super Mom 11757	Open		25.00	25
1998 Thrill of Victory 11753	Open		40.00	40
1998 Tips Up 11755	Open		25.00	25
1998 Up The Creek 11754	Open		40.00	40
1998 World's Greatest Golfer 11765	Open		25.00	25

The German Doll Company

Kewpie - Staff

YEAR ISSUE	EDITION LIMIT	YEAR RETD.	ISSUE PRICE	*QUOTE U.S.$
1999 Bellhop (red)	Yr.Iss.	1999	154.00	154
2000 Blunderboo	Open		110.00	110
1999 Classic, 16"	500		1500.00	1500
1999 Classic, 4"	Open		98.00	98
1999 German Soldier (gray/green helmet)	Yr.Iss.	1999	131.00	131
1999 Indian (brown & orange feathers)	Yr.Iss.	1999	154.00	154
2000 Kewpie with Elephant	Open		98.00	98
1999 Pin	Open		39.95	40
2000 Prussian Soldier	Open		130.00	130
1999 Sitting on Chamberpot with Blue Butterfly	Yr.Iss.	1999	84.00	84
2000 Sitting with Black Cat	Open		98.00	98
1999 Sunbonnet Girl (yellow hat/red dress)	Yr.Iss.	1999	150.00	150
1999 Thinker, 2 3/4"	Open		73.00	73
1999 Thinker, 4 1/2"	Open		105.00	105

Kewpie Riding Series - Staff

YEAR ISSUE	EDITION LIMIT	YEAR RETD.	ISSUE PRICE	*QUOTE U.S.$
1999 Confederate Soldier on Dachshund (light green base)	Yr.Iss.	1999	250.00	250
1999 Confederate Soldier on Dog (light green base)	Yr.Iss.	1999	250.00	250
1999 Confederate Soldier on Elephant (light green base)	Yr.Iss.	1999	250.00	250
1999 Confederate Soldier on Goat (light green base)	Yr.Iss.	1999	250.00	250
1999 Confederate Soldier on Rabbit (light green base)	Yr.Iss.	1999	250.00	250
1999 Confederate Soldier on Rocking Horse (light green base)	Yr.Iss.	1999	250.00	250
1999 Madeleine on Dachshund (light green base)	Yr.Iss.	1999	275.00	275
1999 Madeleine on Dog (light green base)	Yr.Iss.	1999	275.00	275
1999 Madeleine on Goat (light green base)	Yr.Iss.	1999	275.00	275
1999 Madeleine on Rabbit (light green base)	Yr.Iss.	1999	275.00	275
1999 Madeleine on Rocking Horse (light green base)	Yr.Iss.	1999	275.00	275
1999 Naked on Dachshund (light green base)	Yr.Iss.	1999	225.00	225
1999 Naked on Dog (light green base)	Yr.Iss.	1999	225.00	225
1999 Naked on Elephant (light green base)	Yr.Iss.	1999	250.00	250
1999 Naked on Goat (light green base)	Yr.Iss.	1999	250.00	250
1999 Naked on Rabbit (light green base)	Yr.Iss.	1999	225.00	225
1999 Naked on Rocking Horse (light green base)	Yr.Iss.	1999	250.00	250

Glynda Turley Prints

Turley - G. Turley

YEAR ISSUE	EDITION LIMIT	YEAR RETD.	ISSUE PRICE	*QUOTE U.S.$
1995 Circle of Friends	4,800	1997	67.00	67
1995 The Courtyard II	4,800	1997	99.00	99
1995 Flowers For Mommy	4,800	1997	85.00	85
1994 Old Mill Stream	4,800	1997	64.00	64
1995 Past Times	4,800	1997	78.00	78
1995 Playing Hookie Again	4,800	1997	83.00	83
1995 Secret Garden II	4,800	1997	95.00	95

Goebel of North America

Amerikids - H. Holt

YEAR ISSUE	EDITION LIMIT	YEAR RETD.	ISSUE PRICE	*QUOTE U.S.$
1983 Airborne	Closed	N/A	90.00	75-90
1983 Ball One	Closed	N/A	90.00	90
1983 Batter Up	Closed	N/A	90.00	90
1980 Benched	Closed	N/A	115.00	115
1983 Black Belt Champ	Closed	N/A	75.00	75
1980 Cactus Blues	Closed	N/A	100.00	100
1980 Curiosity	Closed	N/A	115.00	100-115
1983 End Run	Closed	N/A	75.00	75
1983 False Start	Closed	N/A	90.00	90
1980 Fish for Two	Closed	N/A	100.00	100
1983 Hot Shot	Closed	N/A	75.00	75
1983 Ice Nymph	Closed	N/A	35.00	35-55
1983 Icicle Treats	Closed	N/A	55.00	55
1980 Mom's Bridal Veil	Closed	N/A	100.00	100
1983 Peewee Dribbler	Closed	N/A	75.00	75
1980 Penny for a Tooth	Closed	N/A	80.00	80
1980 Please	Closed	N/A	80.00	80
1980 Rain Dance	Closed	N/A	115.00	115-125
1983 Ready to Fly	Closed	N/A	85.00	85
1980 Rodeo Cowboy	Closed	N/A	135.00	135
1983 The Signal	Closed	N/A	90.00	90
1983 Strategy	Closed	N/A	90.00	90
1980 The Suitor	Closed	N/A	80.00	75-80
1980 Swimming Hole	Closed	N/A	85.00	85-90
1983 Touchdown Flyer	Closed	N/A	75.00	75
1980 Who's Fish	Closed	N/A	135.00	135

Charlot Byj Blondes - C. Byj

YEAR ISSUE	EDITION LIMIT	YEAR RETD.	ISSUE PRICE	*QUOTE U.S.$
1968 Bless Us All	Closed	1987	6.00	20-55
1968 A Child's Prayer	Closed	1987	6.00	20-78
1968 Evening Prayer	Closed	1986	8.00	30-98
1969 Her Shining Hour	Closed	1988	14.00	60-170
1969 Little Prayers Are Best	Closed	1987	12.00	40-95
1972 Love Bugs	Closed	1986	38.00	130-210
XX Love Bugs (music box)	Closed	1986	80.00	325-400
1968 Madonna of the Doves	Closed	1993	25.00	160-240
1968 Mother Embracing Child	Closed	N/A	12.00	80-160
1968 Rock-A-Bye-Baby	Closed	N/A	7.50	50-130
XX Rock-A-Bye-Baby (music box)	Closed	1985	50.00	250-275
1968 Sitting Pretty	Closed	1983	9.00	50-110
1968 Sleepy Head	Closed	1986	9.00	50-95
1968 Tender Shepherd	Closed	1974	8.00	350-500
1968 The Way To Pray	Closed	1988	8.50	20-100

Charlot Byj Redheads - C. Byj

YEAR ISSUE	EDITION LIMIT	YEAR RETD.	ISSUE PRICE	*QUOTE U.S.$
1982 1-2 Ski-Doo	Closed	1986	75.00	140-150
1985 All Gone	Closed	1988	42.00	70-80
1987 Almost There	Closed	1988	45.00	95-125
1987 Always Fit	Closed	1988	45.00	100-150
1968 Atta Boy	Closed	1984	6.50	65-145
1972 Baby Sitter	Closed	1983	28.00	55-175
1972 Bachelor Degree	Closed	1986	18.00	40-145
1975 Barbeque	Closed	1983	55.00	140-208
1985 Bedtime Boy	Closed	1987	26.00	35-90
1985 Bedtime Girl	Closed	1987	26.00	35-75
1975 Bird Watcher	Closed	1983	48.00	105-170
1971 Bongo Beat	Closed	1980	18.50	60-190
1975 Camera Shy	Closed	1983	48.00	120-165
1984 Captive Audience	Closed	1988	55.00	100-150
1968 Cheer Up	Closed	1988	8.00	50-150
1987 Come Along	Closed	1988	47.50	100-125
1970 Copper Topper	Closed	1986	10.00	110-120
1968 Daisies Won't Tell	Closed	1986	6.00	50-145
1983 A Damper on the Camper	Closed	1986	75.00	160-170
1983 Dating and Skating	Closed	N/A	60.00	80-150
1983 Dear Sirs	Closed	1988	40.00	135-175
1968 Dropping In	Closed	1988	6.00	75-145
1968 E-e-eek	Closed	1986	8.00	50-160
1985 Farm Friends	Closed	1988	46.00	75-120
1987 Figurine Collector	Closed	1988	64.00	250-300
1972 First Degree	Closed	1986	18.00	50-145
1968 Forbidden Fruit	Closed	1978	7.00	50-125
1975 Fore	Closed	1983	48.00	90-150
1983 Four Letter Word For Ouch	Closed	1988	40.00	110-125
1983 A Funny Face From Outer Space	Closed	1987	65.00	170-300
1968 Gangway	Closed	1986	8.50	90-120
1968 Good News	Closed	1988	6.00	50-150
1988 Greetings	Closed	1988	55.00	125-198
1968 Guess Who	Closed	1979	8.50	100-145
1983 Heads or Tails	Closed	1986	60.00	135-175
1968 The Kibitzer	Closed	1983	7.50	50-150
1975 Lazy Day	Closed	1986	55.00	80-200
1969 Let It Rain	Closed	1988	26.00	90-220
1968 Little Miss Coy	Closed	1988	6.00	40-145
1968 Little Prayers Are Best	Closed	1969	13.00	75-91
1969 Little Shopper	Closed	1978	13.00	70-195
1968 Lucky Day	Closed	1986	5.50	50-140
1984 Not Yet a Vet	Closed	1988	65.00	150-175
1983 Nothing Beats a Pizza	Closed	1988	55.00	100-175
1971 The Nurse	Closed	1988	13.00	50-150
1968 O'Hair For President	Closed	1983	6.00	50-85
1968 Off Key	Closed	1986	7.50	50-155
1984 Once Upon a Time	Closed	1988	55.00	130
1984 One Puff's Enough (Yech)	Closed	1988	55.00	156-225
1968 Oops	Closed	1988	8.00	50-120
1987 Please Wait	Closed	1988	47.50	40-145
1968 Plenty of Nothing	Closed	1986	5.50	90
1987 The Practice	Closed	1988	64.00	150-250
1968 Putting on the Dog	Closed	1986	9.00	50-145
1968 The Roving Eye	Closed	1986	6.00	40-140
1972 Say A-a-a-aah	Closed	1986	19.00	60-175
1982 Sea Breeze	Closed	1986	65.00	70-170
1988 Shall We Dance?	Closed	1988	72.50	125-150
1985 Sharing Secrets	Closed	1988	44.00	60-125
1968 Shear Nonsense	Closed	1986	10.00	70-150
1970 Skater's Waltz	Closed	1986	15.00	120-150
XX Skater's Waltz (Musical)	Closed	1986	70.00	275
1983 Something Tells Me	Closed	1987	40.00	75-100
1988 A Special Friend (Black Angel)	Closed	1988	55.00	100-110
1968 Spellbound	Closed	1986	12.00	60-150
1968 Spring Time	Closed	1983	7.50	50-150
1968 The Stolen Kiss	Closed	1978	13.00	70-165
1968 Strike	Closed	1986	6.00	50-140
1968 Super Service	Closed	1979	9.00	70-150
1985 Sweet Snack	Closed	1988	40.00	60-90
1971 Swinger	Closed	1983	15.00	60-125
1969 Trim Lass	Closed	1978	14.00	80-150
1971 Trouble Shooter (This Won't Hurt)	Closed	1986	13.00	40-148
1975 Wash Day	Closed	1986	55.00	80-200
1984 Yeah Team	Closed	1987	65.00	229-250
1968 A Young Man's Fancy	Closed	1988	10.00	80-150

Co-Boy - G. Skrobek

YEAR ISSUE	EDITION LIMIT	YEAR RETD.	ISSUE PRICE	*QUOTE U.S.$
1981 Al the Trumpet Player	Closed	N/A	45.00	55-120
1987 Bank-Pete the Pirate	Closed	N/A	80.00	225-275
1987 Bank-Utz the Money Bank	Closed	N/A	80.00	120-225
1981 Ben the Blacksmith	Closed	N/A	45.00	63-70
XX Bert the Soccer Player	Closed	N/A	Unkn.	40-120
1971 Bit the Bachelor	Closed	N/A	16.00	30-82
1972 Bob the Bookworm	Closed	N/A	20.00	35-100
1984 Brad the Clockmaker	Closed	N/A	75.00	200-400
1972 Brum the Lawyer	Closed	N/A	20.00	75-120
XX Candy the Baker's Delight	Closed	N/A	Unkn.	45-75
1980 Carl the Chef	Closed	N/A	49.00	63-82
1984 Chris the Shoemaker	Closed	N/A	45.00	88-175
1987 Chuck on His Pig	Closed	N/A	75.00	250-300
1984 Chuck the Chimney Sweep	Closed	N/A	45.00	190-250
1987 Clock-Conny the Watchman	Closed	N/A	125.00	510-700
1987 Clock-Sepp and the Beer Keg	Closed	N/A	125.00	375-400
1972 Co-Boy Plaque (English)	Closed	N/A	20.00	120-200
1972 Co-Boy Plaque (German)	Closed	N/A	N/A	220-275
XX Conny the Night Watchman	Closed	N/A	Unkn.	100-125
1980 Doc the Doctor	Closed	N/A	49.00	75-125
XX Ed the Wine Cellar Steward	Closed	N/A	Unkn.	100-120
1984 Felix the Baker	Closed	N/A	45.00	75-120
1971 Fips the Foxy Fisherman	Closed	N/A	16.00	30-100
1971 Fritz the Happy Boozer	Closed	N/A	16.00	100-120
1981 George the Gourmand	Closed	N/A	45.00	125-150
1980 Gerd the Diver	Closed	N/A	49.00	125
1978 Gil the Goalie	Closed	N/A	34.00	100-120
1981 Greg the Gourmet	Closed	N/A	45.00	100-225
1981 Greta the Happy Housewife	Closed	N/A	45.00	50-75
1980 Herb the Horseman	Closed	N/A	49.00	63-120
1984 Herman the Butcher	Closed	N/A	45.00	45-170
1984 Homer the Driver	Closed	N/A	45.00	120-175
XX Jack the Village Pharmacist	Closed	N/A	Unkn.	35-125
XX Jim the Bowler	Closed	N/A	Unkn.	25-120
XX John the Hawkeye Hunter	Closed	N/A	Unkn.	63-113
1972 Kuni the Painter	Closed	N/A	20.00	35-120
XX Mark-Safety First	Closed	N/A	Unkn.	63-100
1984 Marthe the Nurse	Closed	N/A	45.00	95-250
XX Max the Boxing Champ	Closed	N/A	Unkn.	25-120
1971 Mike the Jam Maker	Closed	N/A	16.00	40-125
1980 Monty the Mountain Climber	Closed	N/A	49.00	75-100
1981 Nick the Nightclub Singer	Closed	N/A	45.00	45-125
1981 Niels the Strummer	Closed	N/A	45.00	55-120
1978 Pat the Pitcher	Closed	N/A	34.00	63-120
1984 Paul the Dentist	Closed	N/A	45.00	100-250
1981 Peter the Accordionist	Closed	N/A	45.00	55-120
XX Petrl the Village Angler	Closed	N/A	Unkn.	60-100
1971 Plum the Pastry Chef	Closed	N/A	16.00	35-100
1972 Porz the Mushroom Muncher	Closed	N/A	20.00	100-150
1984 Rick the Fireman	Closed	N/A	45.00	100-225
1971 Robby the Vegetarian	Closed	N/A	16.00	63-90
1984 Rudy the World Traveler	Closed	N/A	45.00	125-200
1971 Sam the Gourmet	Closed	N/A	16.00	63-110
1972 Sepp the Beer Buddy	Closed	N/A	20.00	63-100
1984 Sid the Vintner	Closed	N/A	45.00	70-120
1980 Ted the Tennis Player	Closed	N/A	49.00	63-90
1971 Tom the Honey Lover	Closed	N/A	16.00	63-100
1978 Tommy Touchdown	Closed	N/A	34.00	63-90
XX Toni the Skier	Closed	N/A	Unkn.	120-125
1972 Utz the Banker	Closed	N/A	20.00	63-120
1981 Walter the Jogger	Closed	N/A	45.00	63-120
1971 Wim the Court Supplier	Closed	N/A	16.00	63-120

Co-Boys-Culinary - Welling/Skrobek

YEAR ISSUE	EDITION LIMIT	YEAR RETD.	ISSUE PRICE	*QUOTE U.S.$
1994 Mike the Jam Maker 301050	Closed	N/A	25.00	30
1994 Plum the Sweets Maker 301052	Closed	N/A	25.00	30
1994 Robby the Vegetarian 301054	Closed	N/A	25.00	30
1994 Sepp the Drunkard 301051	Closed	N/A	25.00	30
1994 Tom the Sweet Tooth 301053	Closed	N/A	25.00	30

Co-Boys-Professionals - Welling/Skrobek

YEAR ISSUE	EDITION LIMIT	YEAR RETD.	ISSUE PRICE	*QUOTE U.S.$
1994 Brum the Lawyer 301060	Closed	N/A	25.00	30
1994 Conny the Nightwatchman 301062	Closed	N/A	25.00	30
1994 Doc the Doctor 301064	Closed	N/A	25.00	30
1994 John the Hunter 301063	Closed	N/A	25.00	30
1994 Utz the Banker 301061	Closed	N/A	25.00	30

Co-Boys-Sports - Welling/Skrobek

YEAR ISSUE	EDITION LIMIT	YEAR RETD.	ISSUE PRICE	*QUOTE U.S.$
1994 Bert the Soccer Player 301059	Closed	N/A	25.00	30
1994 Jim the Bowler 301057	Closed	N/A	25.00	30
1994 Petri the Fisherman 301055	Closed	N/A	25.00	30
1994 Ted the Tennis Player 301058	Closed	N/A	25.00	30
1994 Toni the Skier 301056	Closed	N/A	25.00	30

Fashions on Parade - G. Bochmann, unless otherwise noted

YEAR ISSUE	EDITION LIMIT	YEAR RETD.	ISSUE PRICE	*QUOTE U.S.$
1984 Afternoon Tea	Closed	1988	50.00	75-90
1980 At The Tea Dance	Closed	1988	50.00	75-90

*Quotes have been rounded up to nearest dollar

YEAR ISSUE	EDITION LIMIT	YEAR RETD.	ISSUE PRICE	*QUOTE U.S.$
1983 Center Court	Closed	1988	50.00	75-150
1987 Christina	Closed	1988	60.00	60
1980 The Cosmopolitan	Closed	1988	50.00	75-85
1982 Demure Elegance	Closed	1988	50.00	75-90
1986 Diana Viscountess	Closed	1988	55.00	75-90
1981 Edwardian Grace	Closed	1988	50.00	50-90
1987 Eleanor	Closed	1988	60.00	60
1987 Elisabeth	Closed	1988	60.00	60
1984 Equestrian	Closed	1988	50.00	50-75
1983 Fashions on Parade Plaque - K. Sauer	Closed	1988	12.50	13-60
1986 Forever & Always (Bride)	Closed	1988	55.00	55-85
1979 The Garden Fancier	Closed	1988	50.00	75-85
1984 Gentle Breezes	Closed	1988	50.00	75-85
1983 Gentle Moment - A. Gertloff	Closed	1988	50.00	50
1982 Gentle Thoughts	Closed	1988	50.00	75-90
1982 Her Treasured Day	Closed	1988	50.00	75-85
1982 Impatience	Closed	1988	50.00	85
1987 Isabella	Closed	1988	60.00	60-75
1983 A Lazy Day - A. Gertloff	Closed	1988	50.00	50
1987 Marie Antoinette	Closed	1988	60.00	60
1983 On the Fairway	Closed	1988	50.00	75-110
1986 Paris in Fall	Closed	1988	55.00	55-75
1986 Promenade at Nice	Closed	1988	55.00	55-100
1986 The Promise (Groom)	Closed	1988	55.00	55-85
1982 Reflection	Closed	1988	50.00	75-85
1984 River Outing	Closed	1988	50.00	75-90
1986 Say Please	Closed	1988	50.00	95-100
1986 Shepardess' Costume	Closed	1988	55.00	55-75
1986 Silver, Lace & Rhinestones	Closed	1988	55.00	55-95
1983 Skimming Gently	Closed	1988	50.00	75-90
1984 Southern Bell	Closed	1988	50.00	75-95
1980 Strolling On the Avenue	Closed	1988	50.00	75-90
1984 To the Hunt	Closed	1988	50.00	50-75
1979 The Visitor	Closed	1988	50.00	50-90
1982 Waiting For His Love	Closed	1988	50.00	75-85

Goebel Figurines - N. Rockwell

YEAR ISSUE	EDITION LIMIT	YEAR RETD.	ISSUE PRICE	*QUOTE U.S.$
1963 Advertising Plaque 218	Closed	N/A	Unkn.	750-1000
1963 Boyhood Dreams (Adventurers between Adventures) 202	Closed	N/A	12.00	350-400
1963 Buttercup Test (Beguiling Buttercup) 214	Closed	N/A	10.00	350-400
1963 First Love (A Scholarly Pace) 215	Closed	N/A	30.00	350-400
1963 His First Smoke 208	Closed	N/A	9.00	225-275
1963 Home Cure 211	Closed	N/A	16.00	350-400
1963 Little Veterinarian (Mysterious Malady) 201	Closed	N/A	15.00	350-400
1963 Mother's Helper (Pride of Parenthood) 203	Closed	N/A	15.00	350-400
1963 My New Pal (A Boy Meets His Dog) 204	Closed	N/A	12.00	200-365
1963 Patient Anglers (Fisherman's Paradise) 217	Closed	N/A	18.00	350-400
1963 She Loves Me (Day Dreamer) 213	Closed	N/A	8.00	350-400
1963 Timely Assistance (Love Aid) 212	Closed	N/A	16.00	350-400

Looney Tunes Spotlight Collection - Goebel

YEAR ISSUE	EDITION LIMIT	YEAR RETD.	ISSUE PRICE	*QUOTE U.S.$
1998 Accelleratti Incredibus	7,598		175.00	175
1997 And to All a Good Bite	15,098		75.00	75
1997 Bad Hare Day	10,098		110.00	110
1997 Bad Ol' Puddy Tat	5,098	1998	400.00	400-1200
1998 Carnivorous Vulgaris	7,598		175.00	175
1998 Dis Guy's a Pushover	10,098		175.00	175
1997 Duck Dodgers in the 24 1/2 TH Century ("Planet X")	10,098		80.00	80
1997 Gift Wrapped ("Christmas Morning")	10,098		80.00	80
1999 Grand Finale	7,500		195.00	195
1997 Hare-Do	10,098		80.00	80
1999 His Royal Hareness	5,000		70.00	70
1999 I Do?	10,000		175.00	175
1997 In the Name of Mars	10,098		110.00	110
1997 In the Name of the Earth	10,098		110.00	110
1997 Isn't She Wovewe	10,098		185.00	185
1997 Kiss the Little Birdie	10,098		100.00	100
1999 Laughing All The Way	1,200		995.00	995
1997 Looney Tunes Latest News-M.I. Hummel	7,598		320.00	320
1999 Lovelorn Lateral	10,000		100.00	100
1998 Michigan Rag	10,098		160.00	160
1997 Mine, Mine, Mine	7,598		245.00	245
1998 Monster Manicure	10,098		190.00	190
1999 Off Kilt-er	10,000		190.00	190
1999 Oh, Give Me A Home	Closed	1999	50.00	50
1999 The Only Way To Fly	5,000		80.00	80
1999 Paw De Deux	2,500		245.00	245
1997 Rabbit of Seville ("The Barbershop")	10,098		85.00	85
1998 Snowbird (Premier Edition)	Closed	1998	48.00	48-75
1998 That's All Folks!™ (75th Anniversary)	Closed	1999	48.00	48-73
2000 Them's Fightin Words & Yup	2,000		175.00	175
1999 Tweety Wreath	Open		25.00	25
1997 What a Present!	10,098		70.00	70
1997 Zie Broken Heart of Love	10,098		150.00	150

Miniatures-Americana Series - R. Olszewski

YEAR ISSUE	EDITION LIMIT	YEAR RETD.	ISSUE PRICE	*QUOTE U.S.$
1982 American Bald Eagle 661-B	Closed	1989	45.00	175-285
1986 Americana Display 951-D	Closed	1995	80.00	80-105
1989 Blacksmith 667-P	Closed	1989	55.00	95-150
1986 Carrousel Ride 665-B	Closed	1995	45.00	75-150
1985 Central Park Sunday 664-B	Closed	1995	45.00	95-125
1984 Eyes on the Horizon 663-B	Closed	1995	45.00	75-130
1981 The Plainsman 660-B	Closed	1989	45.00	200-295
1983 She Sounds the Deep 662-B	Closed	1995	45.00	75-150
1987 To The Bandstand 666-B	Closed	1995	45.00	75-125

Miniatures-Bob Timberlake Signature Series - B. Timberlake

YEAR ISSUE	EDITION LIMIT	YEAR RETD.	ISSUE PRICE	*QUOTE U.S.$
1996 Autumn Afternoons Vignette 818061	500		490.00	490

Miniatures-Children's Series - R. Olszewski

YEAR ISSUE	EDITION LIMIT	YEAR RETD.	ISSUE PRICE	*QUOTE U.S.$
1983 Backyard Frolic 633-P	Closed	1995	65.00	100-250
1980 Blumenkinder-Courting 630-P	Closed	1989	55.00	140-395
1990 Building Blocks Castle (large) 968-D	Closed	1995	75.00	100
1987 Carrousel Days (plain base) 637-P	Closed	1989	85.00	815-995
1987 Carrousel Days 637-P	Closed	1989	85.00	250-295
1988 Children's Display (small)	Closed	1995	45.00	60-65
1989 Clowning Around 636-P (new style)	Closed	1995	85.00	175-195
1986 Clowning Around 636-P (old style)	Closed	N/A	85.00	175-200
1984 Grandpa 634-P	Closed	1995	75.00	100-125
1988 Little Ballerina 638-P	Closed	1995	85.00	125-175
1982 Out and About 632-P	Closed	1989	85.00	375-385
1985 Snow Holiday 635-P	Closed	1995	75.00	100-245
1981 Summer Days 631-P	Closed	1989	65.00	300-375

Miniatures-Classic Clocks - Larsen

YEAR ISSUE	EDITION LIMIT	YEAR RETD.	ISSUE PRICE	*QUOTE U.S.$
1995 Alexis 818040	2,500		200.00	200
1995 Blinking Admiral 818042	2,500		200.00	200
1995 Play 818041	2,500		250.00	250

Miniatures-DeGrazia - R. Olszewski

YEAR ISSUE	EDITION LIMIT	YEAR RETD.	ISSUE PRICE	*QUOTE U.S.$
1988 Adobe Display 948D	Closed	N/A	45.00	100-125
1990 Adobe Hacienda (large) Display 958-D	Closed	N/A	85.00	150-200
1989 Beautiful Burden 554-P	Closed	N/A	110.00	110-250
1990 Chapel Display 971-D	Closed	N/A	95.00	100-120
1986 Festival of Lights 507-P	Closed	N/A	85.00	125-250
1985 Flower Boy 502-P	Closed	N/A	85.00	200-225
1985 Flower Girl 501-P	Closed	N/A	85.00	85-230
1986 Little Madonna 552-P	Closed	N/A	93.00	120-225
1989 Merry Little Indian 508-P (new style)	Closed	N/A	110.00	175-200
1987 Merry Little Indian 508-P (old style)	Closed	N/A	95.00	200-300
1991 My Beautiful Rocking Horse 555-P	Closed	N/A	110.00	100-232
1985 My First Horse 503-P	Closed	N/A	85.00	150-165
1986 Pima Drummer Boy 506-P	Closed	N/A	85.00	188-250
1985 Sunflower Boy 551- P	Closed	N/A	93.00	125-282
1985 White Dove 504-P	Closed	N/A	80.00	82-125
1985 Wondering 505-P	Closed	N/A	93.00	175-200

Miniatures-Disney-Cinderella - Disney

YEAR ISSUE	EDITION LIMIT	YEAR RETD.	ISSUE PRICE	*QUOTE U.S.$
1991 Anastasia 172-P	Suspd.		85.00	100-175
1991 Cinderella 176-P	Suspd.		85.00	144-238
1991 Cinderella's Coach Display 978-D	Suspd.		95.00	115-180
1991 Cinderella's Dream Castle 976-D	Suspd.		95.00	120-200
1991 Drizella 174-P	Suspd.		85.00	100-175
1991 Fairy Godmother 180-P	Suspd.		85.00	100-175
1991 Footman 181-P	Suspd.		85.00	100-175
1991 Gus 177-P	Suspd.		80.00	90-150
1991 Jaq 173-P	Suspd.		80.00	90-145
1991 Lucifer 175-P	Suspd.		80.00	90-165
1991 Prince Charming 179-P	Suspd.		85.00	100-200
1991 Stepmother 178-P	Suspd.		85.00	100-165

Miniatures-Disney-Peter Pan - Disney

YEAR ISSUE	EDITION LIMIT	YEAR RETD.	ISSUE PRICE	*QUOTE U.S.$
1994 Captain Hook 188-P	Suspd.		160.00	160-225
1992 John 186-P	Suspd.		90.00	110-180
1994 Lost Boy-Fox 191-P	Suspd.		130.00	130-225
1994 Lost Boy-Rabbit 192-P	Suspd.		130.00	130-225
1992 Michael 187-P	Suspd.		90.00	110-165
1992 Nana 189-P	Suspd.		95.00	110-165
1994 Neverland Display 997-D	Suspd.		150.00	150-215
1992 Peter Pan 184-P	Suspd.		90.00	125-375
1992 Peter Pan's London 986-D	Suspd.		125.00	135-215
1994 Smee 190-P	Suspd.		140.00	125-195
1992 Wendy 185-P	Suspd.		90.00	110-195

Miniatures-Disney-Pinocchio - Disney

YEAR ISSUE	EDITION LIMIT	YEAR RETD.	ISSUE PRICE	*QUOTE U.S.$
1991 Blue Fairy 693-P	Suspd.		95.00	120-125
1990 Geppetto's Toy Shop Display 965-D	Suspd.		95.00	120-200
1990 Geppetto/Figaro 682-P	Suspd.		90.00	110-180
1990 Gideon 683-P	Suspd.		75.00	100-165
1990 J. Worthington Foulfellow 684-P	Suspd.		95.00	115-195
1990 Jiminy Cricket 685-P	Suspd.		75.00	115-185
1991 Little Street Lamp Display 964-D	Suspd.		65.00	80-180
1992 Monstro The Whale 985-D	Suspd.		120.00	135-270
1990 Pinocchio 686-P	Suspd.		75.00	110-205
1991 Stromboli 694-P	Suspd.		95.00	120-185
1991 Stromboli's Street Wagon 979-D	Suspd.		105.00	125-210

Miniatures-Disney-Snow White - Disney

YEAR ISSUE	EDITION LIMIT	YEAR RETD.	ISSUE PRICE	*QUOTE U.S.$
1987 Bashful 165-P	Suspd.		60.00	95-116
1991 Castle Courtyard Display 981-D	Suspd.		105.00	125-155
1987 Cozy Cottage Display 941-D	Suspd.		35.00	300-345
1987 Doc 162-P	Suspd.		60.00	95-116
1987 Dopey 167-P	Suspd.		60.00	110-150
1987 Grumpy 166-P	Suspd.		60.00	95-100
1987 Happy 164-P	Suspd.		60.00	95-110
1988 House In The Woods Display 944-D	Suspd.		60.00	110-125
1992 Path In The Woods 996-D	Suspd.		140.00	150-225
1987 Sleepy 163-P	Suspd.		60.00	95-110
1987 Sneezy 161-P	Suspd.		60.00	95-100
1987 Snow White 168-P	Suspd.		60.00	154
1990 Snow White's Prince 170-P	Suspd.		80.00	115-130
1992 Snow White's Queen 182-P	Suspd.		100.00	115-125
1992 Snow White's Witch 183-P	Suspd.		100.00	115-150
1990 The Wishing Well Display 969-D	Suspd.		65.00	85-100

Miniatures-Disneyana Convention - P. Larsen

YEAR ISSUE	EDITION LIMIT	YEAR RETD.	ISSUE PRICE	*QUOTE U.S.$
1994 Mickey Self Portrait	500	1994	295.00	795-1235
1995 Barbershop Quartet	750	1995	325.00	400-514
1996 Puppy Love	750	1996	325.00	400-553
1997 The Perfect Disguise	500	1997	415.00	330-375
1998 Bella Note	500	1998	295.00	400-457
1999 Bare Necessities	500		295.00	295

Miniatures-Historical Series - R. Olszewski

YEAR ISSUE	EDITION LIMIT	YEAR RETD.	ISSUE PRICE	*QUOTE U.S.$
1985 Capodimonte 600-P (new style)	Closed	N/A	90.00	425-600
1980 Capodimonte 600-P (old style)	Closed	1987	90.00	355-425
1983 The Cherry Pickers 602-P	Closed	N/A	85.00	295-300
1990 English Country Garden 970-D	Closed	N/A	85.00	110
1989 Farmer w/Doves 607-P	Closed	N/A	85.00	82-169
1985 Floral Bouquet Pompadour 604-P	Closed	N/A	85.00	125-150
1990 Gentleman Fox Hunt 616-P	Closed	N/A	145.00	200-250
1988 Historical Display 943-D	Closed	1996	45.00	60-65
1981 Masquerade-St. Petersburg 601-P	Closed	1989	65.00	125-350
1987 Meissen Parrot 605-P	Closed	1996	85.00	125-150
1988 Minton Rooster 606-P	7,500		85.00	100
1984 Moor With Spanish Horse 603-P	Closed	1996	85.00	125-300
1992 Poultry Seller 608-G	1,500		200.00	200

Miniatures-Jack & The Beanstalk - R. Olszewski

YEAR ISSUE	EDITION LIMIT	YEAR RETD.	ISSUE PRICE	*QUOTE U.S.$
1994 Beanseller 742-P	5,000	N/A	200.00	225-235
1994 Jack & The Beanstalk Display 999-D	5,000	N/A	225.00	260-305
1994 Jack and the Cow 743-P	5,000	N/A	180.00	225-250
1994 Jack's Mom 741-P	5,000	N/A	145.00	180-225
1994 Set of 4	5,000	N/A	750.00	975-1200

Miniatures-Mickey Mouse - Disney

YEAR ISSUE	EDITION LIMIT	YEAR RETD.	ISSUE PRICE	*QUOTE U.S.$
1990 Fantasia Living Brooms 972-D	Suspd.		85.00	200-400
1990 The Sorcerer's Apprentice 171-P	Suspd.		80.00	157-563
1990 Set	Suspd.		165.00	532-850

Miniatures-Nativity Collection - R. Olszewski

YEAR ISSUE	EDITION LIMIT	YEAR RETD.	ISSUE PRICE	*QUOTE U.S.$
1992 3 Kings Display 987-D	Closed	1996	85.00	105-125
1992 Balthazar 405-P	Closed	1996	135.00	200
1994 Camel & Tender 819292	Closed	1996	380.00	375-395
1992 Caspar 406-P	Closed	1996	135.00	150-200
1994 Final Nativity Display 991-D	Closed	1996	260.00	275
1994 Guardian Angel 407-P	Closed	1996	200.00	225-295
1991 Holy Family Display 982-D	Closed	1996	85.00	95-100
1991 Joseph 401-P	Closed	1996	95.00	130-150
1991 Joyful Cherubs 403-P	Closed	1996	130.00	165-185
1992 Melchoir 404-P	Closed	1996	135.00	200
1991 Mother/Child 440-P	Closed	1996	120.00	155-165
1994 Sheep & Shepherd 819290	Closed	1996	230.00	240-295
1991 The Stable Donkey 402-P	Closed	1996	95.00	125-150

Miniatures-Night Before Christmas (1st Edition) - R. Olszewski

YEAR ISSUE	EDITION LIMIT	YEAR RETD.	ISSUE PRICE	*QUOTE U.S.$
1990 Eight Tiny Reindeer 691-P	5,000	N/A	110.00	135-145
1990 Mama & Papa 692-P	5,000	N/A	110.00	140-175
1990 St. Nicholas 690-P	5,000	N/A	95.00	125-150
1990 Sugar Plum Boy 687-P	5,000	N/A	70.00	100-125
1990 Sugar Plum Girl 689-P	5,000	N/A	70.00	100-125
1991 Up To The Housetop 966-D	5,000	N/A	95.00	115-135
1990 Yule Tree 688-P	5,000	N/A	90.00	110-160

Miniatures-Oriental Series - R. Olszewski

YEAR ISSUE	EDITION LIMIT	YEAR RETD.	ISSUE PRICE	*QUOTE U.S.$
1986 The Blind Men and the Elephant 643-P	Closed	N/A	70.00	150-207
1990 Chinese Temple Lion 646-P	Suspd.		90.00	135-150
1987 Chinese Water Dragon 644-P	Closed	N/A	70.00	150-195
1990 Empress' Garden Display 967-D	Suspd.		95.00	130-135
1982 The Geisha 641-P	Closed	N/A	65.00	128-219
1984 Kuan Yin 640-W (new style)	Closed	N/A	45.00	275
1980 Kuan Yin 640-W (old style)	Closed	1992	40.00	188-375
1987 Oriental Display (small) 945-D	Closed	N/A	45.00	70
1985 Tang Horse 642-P	Closed	N/A	65.00	95-175
1989 Tiger Hunt 645-P	Closed	N/A	85.00	125

Miniatures-Pendants - R. Olszewski

YEAR ISSUE	EDITION LIMIT	YEAR RETD.	ISSUE PRICE	*QUOTE U.S.$
1986 Camper Bialosky 151-P	Closed	1988	95.00	235-375
1991 Chrysanthemum Pendant 222-P	Closed	1996	135.00	155
1991 Daffodil Pendant 221-P	Closed	1996	135.00	100-250
1990 Hummingbird 697-P	Closed	1996	125.00	155-194
1988 Mickey Mouse 169-P	5,000	1989	92.00	265-357
1991 Poinsettia Pendant 223-P	Closed	1996	135.00	155-194
1991 Rose Pendant 220-P	Closed	1996	135.00	155

Miniatures-Portrait of America/Saturday Evening Post - N. Rockwell

YEAR ISSUE	EDITION LIMIT	YEAR RETD.	ISSUE PRICE	*QUOTE U.S.$
1989 Bottom Drawer 366-P	7,500	1996	85.00	55-95
1988 Bottom of the Sixth 365-P	Closed	1996	85.00	60-195
1988 Check-Up 363-P	Closed	1996	85.00	85-125
1988 The Doctor and the Doll 361-P	Closed	1996	85.00	100-200
1991 Home Coming Vignette-Soldier/Mother 990-D	2,000	1995	190.00	200-300
1988 Marbles Champion (Pewter) 362-P	Closed	1995	85.00	85-125
1988 No Swimming (Pewter) 360-P	Closed	1995	85.00	60-125
1988 Rockwell Display (Pewter) 952-D	Closed	1995	80.00	75-140
1988 Triple Self-Portrait (Pewter) 364-P	Closed	1996	85.00	175-275

Miniatures-Precious Moments Series I - Goebel

YEAR ISSUE	EDITION LIMIT	YEAR RETD.	ISSUE PRICE	*QUOTE U.S.$
1995 Fields of Friendship-Diorama (display)	Open		135.00	135
1995 God Loveth a Cheerful Giver	Open		70.00	70
1995 His Burden is Light	Open		70.00	70
1995 I'm Sending You a White Christmas	5,000		100.00	100
1995 Love Is Kind	Open		70.00	70
1995 Love One Another	Open		70.00	70
1995 Make a Joyful Noise	Open		70.00	70
1995 Praise the Lord Anyhow	Open		70.00	70
1995 Prayer Changes Things	Open		70.00	70

*Quotes have been rounded up to nearest dollar

FIGURINES

Miniatures-Precious Moments Series II - Goebel

YEAR ISSUE	EDITION LIMIT	YEAR RETD.	ISSUE PRICE	*QUOTE U.S.$
1996 Heart & Home-Diorama (display)	Open		150.00	150
1996 Jesus is the Answer	Open		70.00	70
1996 Jesus is the Light	Open		70.00	70
1996 Jesus Loves Me (boy)	Open		70.00	70
1996 Jesus Loves Me (girl)	Open		70.00	70
1996 Merry Christmas Deer	5,000		100.00	100
1996 O, How I Love Jesus	Open		70.00	70
1996 Smile, God Loves You	Open		70.00	70
1996 Unto Us A Child is born	Open		70.00	70

Miniatures-Precious Moments Series III - Goebel

YEAR ISSUE	EDITION LIMIT	YEAR RETD.	ISSUE PRICE	*QUOTE U.S.$
1997 Come Let Us Adore Him Cameo	Open		70.00	70
1997 God Understands Cameo	Open		70.00	70
1997 He Careth For You Cameo	Open		70.00	70
1997 He Leadeth Me Cameo	Open		70.00	70
1997 Jesus is Born Cameo	Open		70.00	70
1997 Love Lifted Me Cameo	Open		70.00	70
1997 Prayers of Peace Diorama	Open		150.00	150
1997 Process Stick: God Loveth A Cheerful Giver	Open		200.00	200
1997 Tell Me The Story of Jesus	5,000		100.00	100
1997 We Have Seen His Star Cameo	Open		70.00	70

Miniatures-Special Release-Alice in Wonderland - R. Olszewski

YEAR ISSUE	EDITION LIMIT	YEAR RETD.	ISSUE PRICE	*QUOTE U.S.$
1982 Alice In the Garden 670-P	Closed	1982	60.00	625-835
1984 The Cheshire Cat 672-P	Closed	1984	75.00	395-550
1983 Down the Rabbit Hole 671-P	Closed	1983	75.00	405-540

Miniatures-Special Release-Wizard of Oz - R. Olszewski

YEAR ISSUE	EDITION LIMIT	YEAR RETD.	ISSUE PRICE	*QUOTE U.S.$
1986 The Cowardly Lion 675-P	Closed	1987	85.00	185-438
1992 Dorothy/Glinda 695-P	Closed	1995	135.00	150-194
1992 Good-Bye to Oz Display 980-D	Closed	1996	110.00	200
1988 The Munchkins 677-P	Closed	1995	85.00	113-138
1987 Oz Display 942-D	Closed	1994	45.00	438-550
1984 Scarecrow 673-P	Closed	1985	75.00	395-455
1985 Tinman 674-P	Closed	1986	80.00	300-355
1987 The Wicked Witch 676-P	Closed	1995	85.00	94-150

Miniatures-Special Releases - R. Olszewski

YEAR ISSUE	EDITION LIMIT	YEAR RETD.	ISSUE PRICE	*QUOTE U.S.$
1994 Dresden Timepiece 450-P	750	N/A	1250.00	1250-1300
1991 Portrait Of The Artist (convention) 658-P	Closed	1991	195.00	525-750
1991 Portrait Of The Artist (promotion) 658-P	Closed	N/A	195.00	210-263
1992 Summer Days Collector Plaque 659-P	Closed	N/A	130.00	160-165

Miniatures-The American Frontier Collection - Various

YEAR ISSUE	EDITION LIMIT	YEAR RETD.	ISSUE PRICE	*QUOTE U.S.$
1987 American Frontier Museum Display 947-D - R. Olszewski	Closed	N/A	80.00	100-115
1987 The Bronco Buster 350-B - Remington	Closed	N/A	80.00	110-200
1987 Eight Count 310-B - Pounder	Closed	N/A	75.00	75-100
1987 The End of the Trail 340-B - Frazier	Closed	N/A	80.00	75-125
1987 The First Ride 330-B - Rogers	Closed	N/A	85.00	75-125
1987 Grizzly's Last Stand 320-B - Jonas	Closed	N/A	65.00	75-100
1987 Indian Scout and Buffalo 300-B - Bonheur	Closed	N/A	95.00	100-200

Miniatures-Three Little Pigs - R. Olszewski

YEAR ISSUE	EDITION LIMIT	YEAR RETD.	ISSUE PRICE	*QUOTE U.S.$
1991 The Hungry Wolf 681-P	7,500	N/A	80.00	80-110
1991 Little Bricks Pig 680-P	7,500	N/A	75.00	80-132
1989 Little Sticks Pig 678-P	7,500	N/A	75.00	80-132
1990 Little Straw Pig 679-P	7,500	N/A	75.00	80-132
1991 Three Little Pigs House 956-D	7,500	N/A	50.00	75-130

Miniatures-Wildlife Series - R. Olszewski

YEAR ISSUE	EDITION LIMIT	YEAR RETD.	ISSUE PRICE	*QUOTE U.S.$
1985 American Goldfinch 625-P	Closed	N/A	65.00	75-150
1986 Autumn Blue Jay 626-P	Closed	N/A	65.00	195-238
1992 Autumn Blue Jay 626-P (Archive release)	Closed	N/A	125.00	140-195
1980 Chipping Sparrow 620-P	Closed	N/A	55.00	100-520
1987 Country Display (small) 940-D	Closed	N/A	45.00	70
1990 Country Landscape (large) 957-D	Closed	N/A	85.00	115
1989 Hooded Oriole 629-P	Closed	N/A	80.00	125-175
1990 Hummingbird 696-P	Closed	N/A	85.00	175-200
1987 Mallard Duck 627-P	Closed	N/A	75.00	150-200
1981 Owl-Daylight Encounter 621-P	Closed	N/A	65.00	225-1275
1983 Red-Winged Blackbird 623-P	Closed	N/A	65.00	175-185
1988 Spring Robin 628-P	Closed	N/A	75.00	100-232
1982 Western Bluebird 622-P	Closed	N/A	65.00	100-220
1984 Winter Cardinal 624-P	Closed	N/A	65.00	150-400

Miniatures-Winter Lights - Norrgard

YEAR ISSUE	EDITION LIMIT	YEAR RETD.	ISSUE PRICE	*QUOTE U.S.$
1995 Once Upon a Winter Day	Closed	1996	275.00	275

Miniatures-Women's Series - R. Olszewski

YEAR ISSUE	EDITION LIMIT	YEAR RETD.	ISSUE PRICE	*QUOTE U.S.$
1980 Dresden Dancer 610-P	Closed	1989	55.00	200-550
1985 The Hunt With Hounds (new style) 611-P	Closed	N/A	75.00	225-375
1981 The Hunt With Hounds (old style) 611-P	Closed	1984	75.00	275-532
1986 I Do 615-P	Closed	N/A	85.00	300-425
1983 On The Avenue 613-P	Closed	1995	65.00	120-200
1982 Precious Years 612-P	Closed	N/A	65.00	170-320
1984 Roses 614-P	Closed	1995	65.00	80-150
1989 Women's Display (small) 950-D	Closed	1995	40.00	65-188

Pocket Dragon Land of Legends Collector Club - T. Raine

YEAR ISSUE	EDITION LIMIT	YEAR RETD.	ISSUE PRICE	*QUOTE U.S.$
1988 Sword in the Stone	Retrd.	1989	Gift	250-350

Pocket Dragon Land of Legends Members Only Pieces -Various

YEAR ISSUE	EDITION LIMIT	YEAR RETD.	ISSUE PRICE	*QUOTE U.S.$
1988 Hubble Bubble (LOL) - T. Raine	Retrd.	1989	95.00	275-350
1989 Self Taught (LOL) - H. Henriksen	Retrd.	1990	100.00	325-350
1989 Best Friends (LOL) - H. Henriksen	Retrd.	1990	95.00	205-225

Pocket Dragon Collector Club - R. Musgrave

YEAR ISSUE	EDITION LIMIT	YEAR RETD.	ISSUE PRICE	*QUOTE U.S.$
1989 Take a Chance	Retrd.	1990	Gift	300-350
1991 Collecting Butterflies	Retrd.	1992	Gift	195-205
1992 The Key to My Heart	Retrd.	1993	Gift	195
1993 Want A Bite?	Retrd.	1994	Gift	125-130
1993 Bitsy	Retrd.	1994	Gift	N/A
1994 Friendship Pin	Retrd.	1994	Gift	85
1994 Blue Ribbon Dragon	Retrd.	1995	Gift	75-125
1995 Making Time For You	Retrd.	1996	Gift	75-100
1996 Good News	Retrd.	1997	Gift	50-95
1997 Lollipop	Retrd.	1998	Gift	59-75
1998 Our Hero	Retrd.	1999	Gift	48
1999 Cook's Helper	Retrd.	2000	29.50	30
2000 Proud Gardener	5/01		29.50	30

Pocket Dragon Members Only Pieces - R. Musgrave

YEAR ISSUE	EDITION LIMIT	YEAR RETD.	ISSUE PRICE	*QUOTE U.S.$
1991 Won't You Join Us/A Spot of Tea (set)	Retrd.	1992	75.00	300-361
1991 Wizard's House Limited Print	Retrd.	1993	39.95	80-98
1992 Book Nook	Retrd.	1993	140.00	140-300
1993 Pen Pals	Retrd.	1994	90.00	90-165
1994 Best Seat in the House	Retrd.	1995	75.00	115-193
1995 Party Time	Retrd.	1996	75.00	75-110
1996 Looking For The Right Words	Retrd.	1997	80.00	80-105
1997 Sticking Together	Retrd.	1998	75.00	75-105
1998 The Merry Band	Retrd.	1999	75.00	75
1999 Chocolate Strawberry Avalanche Surprise	Retrd.	2000	65.00	65
2000 Gardening Basket	5/01		65.00	65

Pocket Dragon Annual Christmas Editions - R. Musgrave

YEAR ISSUE	EDITION LIMIT	YEAR RETD.	ISSUE PRICE	*QUOTE U.S.$
1989 Putting Me on the Tree	Retrd.	1990	52.50	52-156
1991 I've Been Very Good	Retrd.	1991	37.50	300-390
1992 A Pocket-Sized Tree	Retrd.	1992	18.95	108-170
1993 Christmas Angel	Retrd.	1993	45.00	95
1994 Dear Santa	Retrd.	1995	50.00	65-140
1995 Chasing Snowflakes	Retrd.	1995	35.00	85-120
1996 Christmas Skates	Retrd.	1996	36.00	75-80
1997 Deck The Halls	Retrd.	1997	39.00	50-60
1998 The Littlest Reindeer	Retrd.	1998	40.00	36-40
1999 All Wrapped Up	Retrd.	1999	33.00	33
2000 Under The Mistletoe	12/00		33.00	33

Pocket Dragon Event Figurines - R. Musgrave

YEAR ISSUE	EDITION LIMIT	YEAR RETD.	ISSUE PRICE	*QUOTE U.S.$
1993 A Big Hug	Retrd.	1994	35.00	105-115
1994 Packed and Ready	Retrd.	1995	47.00	70
1995 Attention to Detail	Retrd.	1996	24.00	40-65
1996 On The Road Again	Retrd.	1997	30.00	30-75
1998 In The Bag	Retrd.	1998	15.00	15
1999 Party Hat	Retrd.	1999	16.50	15-17
2000 Slipper Sleeper	12/00		18.00	18

Pocket Dragons - R. Musgrave

YEAR ISSUE	EDITION LIMIT	YEAR RETD.	ISSUE PRICE	*QUOTE U.S.$
1998 And I Won't Be Any Trouble	Open		20.00	23
1990 The Apprentice	Retrd.	1994	22.50	70-95
1989 Attack	Retrd.	1992	45.00	150-195
1989 Baby Brother	Retrd.	1992	19.50	95-163
1993 Bath Time	Retrd.	1995	90.00	120-130
2000 Best Friends	Open		28.00	28
1997 Big Heart	Open		21.50	18
2000 Big Splinter...Little Foot	Open		14.00	14
2000 Bird Watcher	Open		24.00	24
1993 The Book End	Retrd.	1996	90.00	93-110
1994 A Book My Size	Retrd.	1998	30.00	30-45
1999 Brave Explorer	Open		18.50	18
1992 Bubbles	Retrd.	1996	55.00	80-110
1995 But I am Too Little!	Open		14.50	14
1994 Butterfly Kisses	Retrd.	1999	29.50	30-33
1995 Bye...	Open		15.00	15
1999 Can You Hear Me Now?	Open		16.00	16
2000 Can't Catch Me	Open		14.00	14
1994 Candy Cane	Retrd.	1998	22.50	20-35
1997 A Choice of Ties	Retrd.	1999	38.00	38
2000 Christmas Sleigh (waterglobe)	Open		50.00	50
1995 Classical Dragon	Retrd.	1998	80.00	80
1997 Clean Hands	12/00		28.50	28
1994 Coffee Please	Retrd.	1999	24.00	24-50
2000 Cookie Jar (waterglobe)	Open		50.00	50
1989 Countersign	Retrd.	1991	50.00	375-425
1999 Counting The Days	Open		18.00	18
1996 D...Pressing	Retrd.	1999	28.00	28-45
1997 Daisy	Open		17.00	16
1994 Dance Partner	Retrd.	1998	23.00	23
1992 A Different Drummer	Retrd.	1994	32.50	55-60
1989 Do I Have To?	Retrd.	1996	45.00	45-90
1997 Doodles	Open		26.50	24
2000 Dr. Dragon	Open		24.00	24
1991 Dragons in the Attic	Retrd.	1995	120.00	125-200
1997 The Driver	Retrd.	2000	27.50	24
1989 Drowsy Dragon	Retrd.	1996	27.50	30-55
1995 Elementary My Dear	Retrd.	1999	35.00	35-49
1999 Fire Brigade	Open		28.00	28
1999 Flannel Nightie	Open		18.00	18
1989 Flowers For You	Retrd.	1992	42.50	125-195
1998 Frequent Flyer	Open		35.00	35
1991 Friends	Retrd.	1997	55.00	57-110
1993 Fuzzy Ears	Retrd.	1997	16.50	17-35
1989 The Gallant Defender	Retrd.	1992	36.50	175-205
1989 Gargoyle Hoping For Raspberry Teacakes	Retrd.	1990	139.50	1800-2500
1994 Gargoyles Just Wanna Have Fun	Retrd.	1997	30.00	30-32
1999 Giggles the Performing Gargoyle	Open		28.00	28
1989 A Good Egg	Retrd.	1991	36.50	200-295
1998 Grr I'm A Monster	Open		30.00	30
1998 Happy Birthday	Open		30.00	30
1998 Happy Camper	Open		24.00	24
1996 He Ain't Heavy...He's My Puffin	Retrd.	2000	34.00	30
1995 Hedgehog's Joke	Open		27.00	28
1995 Hi!	Open		15.00	15
1996 Hopalong Gargoyle	Retrd.	1999	42.00	38-42
1999 Hot! Hot! Hot!	Open		24.00	24
1993 I Ate the Whole Thing	Retrd.	1996	32.50	45-50
1991 I Didn't Mean To	Open		32.50	23
2000 I Don't See a Mess	Open		14.00	14
1995 I'll Be The Bride	Open		37.00	37
1995 I'll Be The Groom	Open		37.00	37
1995 I'll Fix It!	Open		23.50	24
1991 I'm A Kitty	Retrd.	1993	37.50	55-125
1999 I'm Cranky	Open		15.00	15
1999 I'm Not Listening	Open		13.00	14
1996 I'm So Pretty	Open		22.50	23
1997 I've Had a Hard Day	Open		23.50	23
1999 In The Library (waterglobe)	12/00		50.00	50
1994 In Trouble Again	Retrd.	1999	35.00	35
1995 It's a Present	Open		21.00	18
1994 It's Dark Out There	Retrd.	1998	45.00	45
1994 It's Magic	Retrd.	1998	31.00	31
1997 It's Me	Open		21.50	18
1998 It's Ok To Cry	Open		22.50	23
1994 Jingles	Retrd.	1998	22.50	30-35
1991 A Joyful Noise	Retrd.	1996	16.50	17-27
1992 The Juggler	Retrd.	1997	32.50	33
1993 Let's Make Cookies	Retrd.	1996	90.00	93-105
1992 The Library Cat	Retrd.	1994	38.50	75-80
1999 Life Is Good	Open		15.00	15
1993 Little Bit (pin)	Retrd.	1996	12.00	17-45
1993 Little Jewel (brooch)	Retrd.	1994	16.00	20-35
1994 A Little Security	Open		20.00	20
1989 Look at Me	Retrd.	1990	42.50	275-295
1992 Mitten Toes	Retrd.	1996	16.50	27-30
1994 My Big Cookie	Retrd.	1998	35.00	35-52
1992 Nap Time	Open		15.00	15
2000 Nature Lesson	Open		28.00	28
1997 The Navigator	Retrd.	2000	30.00	30
1989 New Bunny Shoes	Retrd.	1992	28.50	85-155
1989 No Ugly Monsters Allowed	Retrd.	1992	47.50	108-145
1999 Not Fair	Open		14.00	14
1993 Oh Goody!	Retrd.	1997	16.50	17
1996 Oh Happy Day	Open		22.00	23
1990 One-Size-Fits-All	Retrd.	1993	16.50	36-65
1992 Oops!	Retrd.	1996	16.50	17-30
1989 Opera Gargoyle	Retrd.	1991	85.00	300-425
1992 Percy	Retrd.	1994	70.00	100-165
1998 Perfect Fit	Open		17.50	18
1991 Pick Me Up	Retrd.	1995	16.50	17-30
1989 Pink 'n' Pretty	Retrd.	1992	23.90	80-155
1994 Playing Dress Up	Retrd.	1997	30.00	30-40
1991 Playing Footsie	Retrd.	1994	16.50	25-45
1998 Playtime	Open		15.00	16
1997 Pocket Cruise	Retrd.	2000	38.00	37
1989 The Pocket Minstrel	Retrd.	1991	36.50	225-254
2000 Pocket Money (bank)	Open		28.00	28
1996 Pocket Piper	Open		37.00	35
1992 Pocket Posey	Retrd.	1995	16.50	30-40
1993 Pocket Rider (brooch)	Retrd.	1995	19.50	30-45
1991 Practice Makes Perfect	Retrd.	1993	32.50	65-80
1999 Presents (waterglobe)	12/00		50.00	50
1997 Pretty Please	Open		17.00	15
1995 Purple	Retrd.	1999	24.00	24
1991 Putt Putt	Retrd.	1993	37.50	115
1996 Quartet	Open		80.00	80
1993 Reading the Good Parts	Retrd.	1997	70.00	100-120
2000 Really I've Grown	Open		25.00	25
1996 Red Ribbon	Open		16.50	16
1997 Rub My Tummy?	Open		17.00	15
1991 Scales of Injustice	Retrd.	1997	45.00	50
1998 The Scholar	Open		50.00	50
1999 Scooter	Open		33.00	33
1989 Scribbles	Retrd.	1994	32.50	60-65
1989 Sea Dragon	Retrd.	1991	45.00	200-385
1995 Sees All, Knows All	Retrd.	1999	35.00	35-39
2000 Shy	Open		14.00	14
1989 Sir Nigel Smythebe-Smoke	Retrd.	1993	120.00	240-385
1991 Sleepy Head	Retrd.	1995	37.50	50
1999 Smile	Open		30.00	30
1994 Snuggles	Retrd.	1998	35.00	34-52
1997 Spilt Milk	12/00		31.50	30
1999 Squish!	Open		28.00	28
1989 Stalking the Cookie Jar	Retrd.	1997	27.50	40-45
1997 Stars!	Open		85.00	85
1998 Superstar	Open		18.00	18
1996 Sweetie Pie	12/00		28.00	28
1990 Tag-A-Long	Retrd.	1993	15.00	65
1998 Take Your Medicine	Open		15.00	15
1997 The Teacher	Open		39.00	37
1989 Teddy Magic	Retrd.	1991	85.00	150-170
1995 Telling Secrets	Retrd.	1998	48.00	48-60
1991 Thimble Foot	Retrd.	1994	38.50	60-75
1991 Tickle	Retrd.	1996	27.50	40-50
1996 Tiny Bit Tired	Open		16.00	15
1989 Toady Goldtrayler	Retrd.	1993	55.00	150-225
1993 Treasure!	Retrd.	1997	90.00	90-93
1995 Tumbly	Retrd.	1999	21.00	19-21

*Quotes have been rounded up to nearest dollar

YEAR ISSUE	EDITION LIMIT	YEAR RETD.	ISSUE PRICE	*QUOTE U.S.$
2000 Tummy Ache	Open		14.00	14
1991 Twinkle Toes	Retrd.	1995	16.50	30
1997 Varoom!	Open		38.00	37
2000 A Very Good Sign (Countersign)	Open		39.00	39
1989 Walkies	Retrd.	1992	65.00	250
1998 Wash Behind Your Ears	Open		24.00	24
1996 Watcha Doin'?	Open		22.50	23
1995 Watson	Retrd.	1999	22.50	23
1993 We're Very Brave	Retrd.	1996	37.50	65-85
1989 What Cookie?	Retrd.	1997	38.50	60-70
1998 Why?	Open		15.00	15
2000 Will You Thread My Needle	Open		33.00	33
1999 Winged Messenger	Retrd.	2000	25.00	25
1993 You Can't Make Me	Open		15.00	14
1989 Your Paint is Stirred	Retrd.	1991	42.50	175-188
2000 Your Prince is Here	Open		28.00	28
1992 Zoom Zoom	Open		37.50	30

Pocket Dragons Anniversary Special - R. Musgrave

YEAR ISSUE	EDITION LIMIT	YEAR RETD.	ISSUE PRICE	*QUOTE U.S.$
1997 Jaunty	Yr.Iss.	1997	31.00	28-31
1998 Rise & Shine	Yr.Iss.	1998	20.00	18-30
1999 The Winner-10th Anniversary	Yr.Iss.	1999	42.00	42
2000 The Artist	Yr.Iss.		30.00	30

Pocket Dragons Limited Editions - R. Musgrave

YEAR ISSUE	EDITION LIMIT	YEAR RETD.	ISSUE PRICE	*QUOTE U.S.$
1997 Bathing the Gargoyle	3,000	1999	250.00	250-425
1999 Computer Wizard	4,000		375.00	375
2000 Magical Flying Airship	2,500		275.00	275
1996 Pillow Fight	3,500	1996	157.00	157-225
1994 Raiding the Cookie Jar	3,500	1995	200.00	250-325
2000 Scary Stories	5,000		175.00	175
1999 Seaside Castle	3,999		165.00	165
1989 Storytime at Wizard's House	3,000	1993	375.00	540-595
1998 Toy Box	3,999	1998	175.00	175
1992 Under the Bed	2,500	1995	450.00	575-750
1996 The Volunteer	2,500	1999	350.00	395-475
1989 Wizardry for Fun and Profit	2,500	1992	375.00	375-650

Goebel/M.I. Hummel

M.I. Hummel Collectors Club Exclusives - M.I. Hummel, unless otherwise noted

YEAR ISSUE	EDITION LIMIT	YEAR RETD.	ISSUE PRICE	*QUOTE U.S.$
1977 Valentine Gift 387	Closed	N/A	45.00	225-995
1978 Smiling Through Plaque 690	Closed	N/A	50.00	35-295
1979 Bust of Sister-M.I.Hummel HU-3 - G. Skrobek	Closed	N/A	75.00	186-350
1980 Valentine Joy 399	Closed	N/A	95.00	130-452
1981 Daisies Don't Tell 380	Closed	N/A	80.00	211-425
1982 It's Cold 421	Closed	N/A	80.00	125-425
1983 What Now? 422	Closed	N/A	90.00	125-425
1983 Valentine Gift Mini Pendant 248-P - R. Olszewski	Closed	N/A	85.00	175-695
1984 Coffee Break 409	Closed	N/A	90.00	142-425
1985 Smiling Through 408/0	Closed	N/A	125.00	185-425
1986 Birthday Candle 440	Closed	N/A	95.00	152-425
1986 What Now? Mini Pendant 249-P - R. Olszewski	Closed	N/A	125.00	136-325
1987 Morning Concert 447	Closed	N/A	98.00	117-350
1987 Little Cocopah Indian Girl - T. DeGrazia	Closed	N/A	140.00	350-625
1988 The Surprise 431	Closed	N/A	125.00	70-325
1989 Mickey and Minnie - H. Fischer	Closed	N/A	275.00	500-950
1989 Hello World 429	Closed	N/A	130.00	85-350
1989 I Brought You a Gift 479	Closed	N/A	Gift	75-120
1990 I Wonder 486	Closed	N/A	140.00	142-350
1991 Gift From A Friend 485	Closed	N/A	160.00	91-350
1991 Miniature Morning Concert w/ Display 269-P - R. Olszewski	Closed	N/A	175.00	131-175
1991 Two Hands, One Treat 493	Closed	1992	Gift	52-120
1992 My Wish Is Small 463/0	Closed	N/A	170.00	130-295
1992 Cheeky Fellow 554	Closed	N/A	120.00	96-160
1993 I Didn't Do It 626	Closed	1995	175.00	141-250
1993 Sweet As Can Be 541	Closed	1995	125.00	124-160
1994 Little Visitor 563/0	Closed	1996	180.00	180-215
1994 Little Troubadour 558	Closed	1996	130.00	117-160
1994 At Grandpa's 621	10,000	1996	1300.00	1025-1500
1994 Miniature Honey Lover Pendant 247-P	Closed	1996	165.00	125-250
1995 Country Suitor 760	Closed	1997	195.00	150-195
1995 Strum Along 557	Closed	1997	135.00	111-135
1995 A Story From Grandma 620	10,000	1996	1300.00	975-1500
1996 Valentine Gift Plaque 717	Closed	1996	250.00	275
1996 What's New 418	Closed	1997	310.00	240-310
1996 Celebrate with Song 790	Closed	1998	295.00	228-295
1996 One, Two, Three 555	Closed	1998	145.00	116-145
1997 What's That? 488	Closed	1999	150.00	100-157
1997 Playful Blessing 658	Closed	1999	260.00	208-260
1998 Garden Treasures 727	Closed	1999	85.00	75-85
1998 Forever Yours 793	Closed	1999	85.00	75-85
1998 Valentine Gift Doll 524	Closed	1999	200.00	200
1998 At Play 632	Closed	2000	260.00	260
1998 The Poet at the Podium 397/3/0	Closed	2000	150.00	150
2000 Wishes Come True 2025A	5/01		695.00	695
2000 Will It Sting? 450/0	5/01		260.00	260
2000 Sharpest Student 2087/A	5/01		95.00	95

Special Edition Anniversary Figurines For 5/10/15/20 Year Membership - M.I. Hummel

YEAR ISSUE	EDITION LIMIT	YEAR RETD.	ISSUE PRICE	*QUOTE U.S.$
1990 Flower Girl 548 (5 year)	Closed	2000	105.00	105-195
1990 The Little Pair 449 (10 year)	Closed	2000	170.00	125-170
1991 Honey Lover 312 (15 year)	Open		190.00	150-190
1996 Behave 339 (20 year)	Open		350.00	335-360
2000 Sunflower Friends 2104 (5 year)	Open		195.00	195

YEAR ISSUE	EDITION LIMIT	YEAR RETD.	ISSUE PRICE	*QUOTE U.S.$
2000 Miss Behaving 2105 (10 year)	Open		240.00	240

M.I. Hummel 60th Anniversary Figurines - M.I. Hummel

YEAR ISSUE	EDITION LIMIT	YEAR RETD.	ISSUE PRICE	*QUOTE U.S.$
1998 Heavenly Protection	Yr.Iss.	1998	495.00	500
1998 Angel Serenade w/Lamb	Yr.Iss.	1998	245.00	250
1998 Brother	Yr.Iss.	1998	230.00	235
1998 For Father	Yr.Iss.	1998	240.00	240-250
1998 Happiness	Yr.Iss.	1998	150.00	116-155
1999 Just Resting 112/I	Yr.Iss.	1999	320.00	310-320
1999 Let's Sing 110/0	Yr.Iss.	1999	149.00	140-149
1999 Let's Sing 110/I	Yr.Iss.	1999	190.00	185-190
1998 Little Cellist	Yr.Iss.	1998	240.00	250
1999 Little Thrifty 118	Yr.Iss.	1999	180.00	135-180
1999 Postman 119/0	Yr.Iss.	1999	230.00	225-230
1998 School Boy	Yr.Iss.	1998	225.00	150-230
1998 School Girl	Yr.Iss.	1998	225.00	162-230
1998 Sister	Yr.Iss.	1998	160.00	120-160
1999 Wayside Harmony 111/I	Yr.Iss.	1999	320.00	310-320
1998 Worship	Yr.Iss.	1998	180.00	150-180

M.I. Hummel Candleholders - M.I. Hummel

YEAR ISSUE	EDITION LIMIT	YEAR RETD.	ISSUE PRICE	*QUOTE U.S.$
XX Angel w/Accordian 1/39/0	Open		60.00	49-68
XX Angel w/Lute 1/38/0	Open		60.00	49-68
XX Angel w/Trumpet 1/40/0	Open		60.00	49-68
XX Boy w/Horse 117	Open		60.00	49-68
XX Girl w/Fir Tree 116	Open		60.00	49-68
XX Girl w/Nosegay 115	Open		60.00	49-68

M.I. Hummel Collectibles Century Collection - M.I. Hummel

YEAR ISSUE	EDITION LIMIT	YEAR RETD.	ISSUE PRICE	*QUOTE U.S.$
1986 Chapel Time 442	Closed	N/A	500.00	800-3500
1987 Pleasant Journey 406	Closed	N/A	500.00	1250-3000
1988 Call to Worship 441	Closed	N/A	600.00	700-1500
1989 Harmony in Four Parts 471	Closed	N/A	850.00	800-2500
1990 Let's Tell the World 487	Closed	N/A	875.00	650-1800
1991 We Wish You The Best 600	Closed	N/A	1300.00	719-1800
1992 On Our Way 472	Closed	N/A	950.00	777-1500
1993 Welcome Spring 635	Closed	N/A	1085.00	725-1800
1994 Rock-A-Bye 574	Closed	N/A	1150.00	1100-1500
1995 Strike Up the Band 668	Closed	N/A	1200.00	900-1500
1996 Love's Bounty 751	Yr.Iss.	1996	1200.00	900-1600
1997 Fond Goodbye 660	Yr.Iss.	1997	1450.00	1088-1192
1998 Here's My Heart 766	Yr.Iss.	1998	1375.00	1031-1375
1999 Fanfare 1999	Yr.Iss.	1999	1275.00	1275

M.I. Hummel Collectibles Christmas Angels - M.I. Hummel

YEAR ISSUE	EDITION LIMIT	YEAR RETD.	ISSUE PRICE	*QUOTE U.S.$
1993 Angel in Cloud 585	Open		25.00	35-40
1993 Angel with Lute 580	Open		25.00	36-40
1993 Angel with Trumpet 586	Open		25.00	36-40
1993 Celestial Musician 578	Open		25.00	36-40
1993 Festival Harmony with Flute 577	Open		25.00	35-40
1993 Festival Harmony with Mandolin 576	Open		25.00	36-40
1993 Gentle Song 582	Open		25.00	36-40
1993 Heavenly Angel 575	Open		25.00	35-40
1993 Prayer of Thanks 581	Open		25.00	36-40
1993 Song of Praise 579	Open		25.00	36-40

M.I. Hummel Collectibles Figurines - M.I. Hummel

YEAR ISSUE	EDITION LIMIT	YEAR RETD.	ISSUE PRICE	*QUOTE U.S.$
1988 The Accompanist 453	Open		Unkn.	91-124
XX Adoration 23/I	Open		Unkn.	380-507
XX Adventure Bound 347	Open		Unkn.	1800-4000
1997 All Smiles (Special Event)	25,000		175.00	175
XX Angel Duet 261	Open		Unkn.	208-255
XX Angel Serenade 214/D/I	Open		Unkn.	75-100
XX Angel Serenade with Lamb 83	Open		Unkn.	188-255
XX Angel with Accordion 238/B	Open		Unkn.	55-68
XX Angel with Lute 238/A	Open		Unkn.	45-68
XX Angel With Trumpet 238/C	Open		Unkn.	49-68
XX Angelic Song 144	Open		Unkn.	128-175
1995 The Angler 566	Open		Unkn.	270-370
1989 An Apple A Day 403	Open		Unkn.	240-310
XX Apple Tree Boy 142/3/0	Open		Unkn.	124-170
XX Apple Tree Boy 142/I	Open		Unkn.	240-310
XX Apple Tree Boy 142/V	Open		Unkn.	1350-1400
XX Apple Tree Boy 142/X	Open		Unkn.	25000
XX Apple Tree Girl 141/3/0	Open		Unkn.	124-170
XX Apple Tree Girl 141/I	Open		Unkn.	240-380
XX Apple Tree Girl 141/V	Open		Unkn.	1035-1400
XX Apple Tree Girl 141/X	Open		Unkn.	25000
XX Artist, The 304	Open		Unkn.	210-285
XX Auf Wiedersehen 153/0	12/00		Unkn.	280-285
XX Autumn Harvest 355	Open		Unkn.	196-235
XX Baker 128	Open		Unkn.	196-235
XX Band Leader 129/0	Open		Unkn.	196-335
XX Band Leader 129/4/0	Closed	1998	Unkn.	90-125
XX Barnyard Hero 195/2/0	Open		Unkn.	143-247
XX Bashful 377	Open		Unkn.	173-235
1990 Bath Time 412	Open		Unkn.	180-500
1999 Be Mine 2050/B	Open		85.00	64-88
XX Be Patient 197/2/0	Open		Unkn.	173-225
1997 Best Wishes (personalized) 540	Open		180.00	190
1997 Best Wishes (Special Event) 540	Open		180.00	180-185
XX Bird Duet 169	Open		Unkn.	124-175
2000 Bird Duet (50th Anniversary) 169	Yr.Iss.		175.00	175
XX Bird Duet (personalized)169	Open		Unkn.	165-180
XX Bird Watcher 300	Open		Unkn.	110-250
1994 Birthday Present 341/3/0	Open		140.00	131-170
XX Birthday Serenade 218/2/0	Open		Unkn.	146-200
XX Blessed Event 333	Open		Unkn.	270-380
1996 Blossom Time 608	Open		155.00	120-165
XX Bookworm 8	Open		Unkn.	155-255
XX Bookworm 3/I	Open		Unkn.	259-355
XX The Botanist 351	Open		Unkn.	200-205
1998 The Botanist w/Vase Sampler 151271	Open		210.00	150-210
XX Boy with Accordion 390	Open		Unkn.	75-100
XX Boy with Horse 239/C	Open		Unkn.	49-68
XX Boy with Toothache 217	Open		Unkn.	211-240
XX Brother 95	Open		Unkn.	176-305
XX The Builder 305	Open		Unkn.	210-285
XX Busy Student 367	Open		Unkn.	157-190
XX Call to Glory 739/I	Open		250.00	210-285
1996 Carefree 490	Open		120.00	94-128
XX Carnival 328	Open		Unkn.	208-245
2000 Catch of the Day (Collector's Set) 2031	Open		250.00	250
1993 Celestial Musician 188/4/0	Open		Unkn.	90-124
XX Celestial Musician 188/0	Open		Unkn.	188-255
1998 Cheeky Fellow 554	Open		120.00	96-135
XX Chick Girl 57/2/0	Open		Unkn.	128-175
XX Chick Girl 57/0	Open		Unkn.	274-748
XX Chicken-Licken 385/I	Open		Unkn.	330-964
XX Chicken-Licken 385/4/0	Closed	1998	Unkn.	90-125
XX Chimney Sweep 12/2/0	Open		Unkn.	101-140
XX Chimney Sweep 12/I	Open		Unkn.	188-355
1989 Christmas Angel 301	Open		Unkn.	210-290
1998 Christmas Delivery 2014/I	Open		485.00	371-475
1999 Christmas Gift 2074/A	Open		90.00	90
1996 Christmas Song 343/4/0	Open		110.00	90-124
XX Christmas Song 343/I	Open		Unkn.	188-255
XX Cinderella 337	Open		Unkn.	160-330
XX Close Harmony 336	Open		Unkn.	255-350
1995 Come Back Soon 545	Open		Unkn.	160-170
2000 Comfort & Care (Collector's Set) 2075	Open		250.00	250
1990 Crossroads (Commemorative) 331	20,000	N/A	360.00	710-725
XX Crossroads (Original) 331	Open		Unkn.	345-588
1998 Cuddles 2049/A	Open		80.00	64-85
XX Culprits 56/A	Open		Unkn.	285-435
1989 Daddy's Girls 371	Open		Unkn.	191-260
2000 Daydreamer Plaque 827	Open		140.00	140
1998 Dearly Beloved 2003	Open		450.00	345-475
1996 Delicious 435/3/0	Open		155.00	120-165
XX Doctor 127	Open		Unkn.	149-180
XX Doll Bath 319	Open		Unkn.	276-929
XX Doll Mother 67	Open		Unkn.	105-240
XX Easter Time 384	Open		Unkn.	238-285
2000 Easter's Coming (Collectors Set) 2027	5,000		230.00	230
1998 Echoes of Joy 642/4/0	Open		120.000	94-125
1998 Echoes of Joy 642/0	Open		180.00	139-190
1992 Evening Prayer 495	Open		Unkn.	94-128
XX Farm Boy 66	Open		Unkn.	199-270
1996 Fascination 649/0 (Special Event)	25,000	1996	190.00	143-198
XX Favorite Pet 361	Open		Unkn.	244-335
XX Feathered Friends 344	Open		Unkn.	150-330
XX Feeding Time 199/0	Open		Unkn.	173-299
XX Feeding Time 199/I	Open		Unkn.	315-325
2000 Fire Fighters (Collectors Set) 2030	Open		250.00	250
2000 First Bloom 2077/A	Open		85.00	85
XX Flower Vendor 381	Open		Unkn.	132-285
2000 A Flower For You 2077/B	Open		85.00	85
XX Follow the Leader 369	Open		Unkn.	1350-1560
1998 For Father (personalized) 87	Open		240.00	250-325
XX For Father 87	Open		Unkn.	188-255
XX For Mother 257/2/0	Open		Unkn.	105-145
XX For Mother 257/0	Open		Unkn.	124-336
1998 For Mother (gift set) 257/2/0	Open		165.00	170-200
1993 A Free Flight 569	Open		Unkn.	150-205
1997 A Free Flight (O Canada edition) 469	1,997	1997	210.00	158-210
1996 Free Spirit 564	Open		120.00	94-128
1991 Friend Or Foe 434	Open		Unkn.	189-255
XX Friends 136/I	Open		Unkn.	176-240
1993 Friends Together 662/0 (Commemorative)	Open		260.00	225-320
1993 Friends Together 662/I (Limited)	25,000		475.00	413-550
1997 From My Garden 795/0	Open		180.00	139-196
1996 From The Heart 761	Open		120.00	94-128
1999 Frosty Friends (Collectors Set) 2035/2036	20,000		598.00	598
2000 Garden Splendor 835	Open		185.00	185
XX Gay Adventure 356	Open		Unkn.	80-230
1995 Gentle Fellowship (Limited) 628	25,000		550.00	413-550
XX Girl with Doll 239/B	Open		Unkn.	49-68
XX Girl with Nosegay 239/A	Open		Unkn.	49-68
XX Girl with Sheet Music 389	Open		Unkn.	75-100
XX Girl with Trumpet 391	Open		Unkn.	67-100
XX Going Home 383	Open		Unkn.	270-370
XX Going to Grandma's 52/0	Open		Unkn.	205-285
XX Good Friends 182	Open		Unkn.	173-299
XX Good Hunting 307	Open		Unkn.	110-280
1997 Good News (personalized) 539	Open		180.00	180-200
XX Goose Girl 47/3/0	Open		Unkn.	143-249
XX Goose Girl 47/0	Open		Unkn.	199-420
1997 Goose Girl Sampler 47/3/0	Open		200.00	139-200
XX Grandma's Girl 561	Open		Unkn.	124-170
XX Grandpa's Boy 562	Open		Unkn.	124-170
1991 The Guardian 455	Open		Unkn.	139-190
1991 The Guardian (personalized) 455	Open		Unkn.	180-193
1998 The Guardian Gift Set 156017	Open		180.00	139-190
XX Guiding Angel 357	Open		Unkn.	75-100
2000 Halt (Collector's Set) 2039	Open		250.00	250
XX Happiness 86	Open		Unkn.	160-201
XX Happy Birthday 176/0	Open		Unkn.	184-260
XX Happy Days 150/2/0	Open		Unkn.	190-253
XX Happy Traveller 109/0	Open		Unkn.	145-175
XX Hear Ye! Hear Ye! 15/2/0	Open		Unkn.	131-180

*Quotes have been rounded up to nearest dollar

YEAR ISSUE	EDITION LIMIT	YEAR RETD.	ISSUE PRICE	*QUOTE U.S.$
1997 Hear Ye! Hear Ye! (Gift Set) 15/2/0	Open		170.00	170-180
XX Hear Ye! Hear Ye! 15/0	Open		Unkn.	173-299
1996 Heart and Soul 559	Open		120.00	94-128
1998 Heart's Delight (w/wooden chair) 698	Open		220.00	169-230
XX Heavenly Angel 21/0	Open		Unkn.	123-150
XX Heavenly Angel 21/0/6	Open		Unkn.	180-255
1999 Heavenly Prayer 815	Open		180.00	135-185
XX Heavenly Protection 88/I	Open		Unkn.	375-510
XX Hello 124/0	12/01		Unkn.	113-267
1997 Holy Child 70	Open		280.00	214-285
XX Home from Market 198/2/0	Open		Unkn.	131-180
1990 Horse Trainer 423	Open		Unkn.	188-255
1989 Hosanna 480	Open		Unkn.	94-128
2000 Icy Adventure (Collector's Set) 2058A/B	Open		375.00	375
1989 I'll Protect Him 483	Open		Unkn.	75-100
1994 I'm Carefree 633	Open		365.00	420-1040
1989 I'm Here 478	Open		Unkn.	94-130
1989 In D Major 430	Open		Unkn.	169-235
2000 In The Kitchen (Collectors Set) 2038	Open		250.00	250
XX In The Meadow 459	Open		Unkn.	173-235
XX Is It Raining? 420	Open		Unkn.	320-330
XX Joyful 53	Open		Unkn.	145-188
1995 Just Dozing 451	Open		Unkn.	184-250
XX Just Resting 112/31/0	Open		Unkn.	128-175
1999 Joyful Noise 643/0	Open		180.00	135-185
1999 Joyful Noise (mini) 643/4/0	Open		120.00	90-124
XX The Kindergartner 467	Open		Unkn.	173-235
XX Kiss Me 311	Open		Unkn.	130-335
XX Knit One, Purl One 432	Open		Unkn.	105-145
1991 Land in Sight 530	30,000		1600.00	1092-1800
XX Latest News 184	Open		Unkn.	200-400
XX Latest News (personalized) 184	Open		Unkn.	340-384
1997 Latest News ("Green Bay Wins") - Mader's Exclusive	Closed	1997	650.00	650
1998 Latest News ("Denver Wins")	45-day	1998	320.00	320
1998 Let's Play 2051/B	Open		80.00	64-88
XX Let's Sing 110/0	Open		Unkn.	150-188
XX Let's Sing 110/I	Open		Unkn.	162-195
XX Letter to Santa Claus 340	Open		Unkn.	175-380
2000 Light The Way 715/0	Open		180.00	180
2000 Light The Way (mini) 715/4/0	Open		120.00	120
1993 The Little Architect 410/I	Open		Unkn.	248-345
XX Little Bookkeeper 306	Open		Unkn.	130-335
XX Little Cellist 89/I	Open		Unkn.	255-403
XX Little Drummer 240	Open		Unkn.	128-175
XX Little Fiddler 4	Open		Unkn.	173-245
XX Little Fiddler 2/0	Open		Unkn.	188-325
XX Little Gardener 74	Open		Unkn.	140-175
XX Little Goat Herder 200/0	Open		Unkn.	235-299
XX Little Goat Herder 200/I	Open		Unkn.	199-370
XX Little Guardian 145	Open		Unkn.	128-175
XX Little Helper 73	Open		Unkn.	115-140
XX Little Hiker 16/2/0	Open		Unkn.	115-140
XX Little Nurse 376	Open		Unkn.	190-280
XX Little Pharmacist 322	Open		Unkn.	200-644
XX Little Scholar 80	Open		Unkn.	184-250
XX Little Shopper 96	Open		Unkn.	60-170
1988 Little Sweeper 171/0	Open		Unkn.	124-260
XX Little Tailor 308	Open		Unkn.	100-285
XX Little Thrifty 118	Open		Unkn.	80-185
1998 Little Troubadour 558	Open		130.00	98-135
XX Lost Stocking 374	Open		Unkn.	128-175
1998 Love In Bloom (w/wooden wagon) 699	Open		220.00	169-230
1995 Lucky Boy (Special Event) 335	25,000	1995	190.00	204-260
XX The Mail is Here 226	Open		Unkn.	450-1000
1996 Making New Friends 2002	Open		595.00	446-595
XX March Winds 43	Open		Unkn.	180-227
XX Max and Moritz 123	Open		Unkn.	188-255
2000 May Dance 791	Open		199.00	199
XX Meditation 13/2/0	Open		Unkn.	124-165
XX Meditation 13/0	Open		Unkn.	213-325
XX Merry Wanderer 11/2/0	Open		Unkn.	124-208
XX Merry Wanderer 11/0	Open		Unkn.	196-299
XX Merry Wanderer 7/0	Open		Unkn.	233-330
XX Merry Wanderer 7/X	Open		Unkn.	25000
1999 Messages of Love 2050/A	Open		85.00	64-88
2000 Millennium Bliss 2096/H	Yr.Iss.		140.00	140
1994 Morning Stroll 375/3/0	Open		170.00	95-205
XX Mother's Helper 133	Open		Unkn.	169-240
XX Mountaineer 315	Open		Unkn.	208-250
1998 My Best Friend 2049/B	Open		80.00	64-88
1991 A Nap 534	Open		Unkn.	60-140
1996 Nimble Fingers w/wooden bench 758	Open		225.00	173-240
1996 No Thank You 535	Open		120.00	90-128
XX Not For You 317	Open		Unkn.	100-280
XX On Holiday 350	Open		Unkn.	131-180
XX On Secret Path 386	Open		Unkn.	110-285
1998 Once Upon A Time 2051/A	Open		80.00	64-88
2000 One Coat or Two? (Collectors Set) 2040	Open		250.00	250
1989 One For You, One For Me 482	Open		Unkn.	94-125
1993 One Plus One 556	Open		Unkn.	113-155
XX Ooh My Tooth 533	Open		Unkn.	130-136
XX Out of Danger 56/B	Open		Unkn.	244-345
2000 Over The Horizon Plaque 828	Open		140.00	140
1993 Parade Of Lights 616	Open		Unkn.	210-285
1999 Pay Attention 426/3/0	Open		170.00	175-180
1999 Peaceful Blessing 814	Open		180.00	180-185
XX The Photographer 178	Open		Unkn.	130-335
1995 Pixie 768	Open		Unkn.	90-130
XX Playmates 58/2/0	Open		Unkn.	128-175
XX Playmates 58/0	Open		Unkn.	100-195
1989 Postman 119/2/0	Open		Unkn.	124-170
XX Postman Sampler 119/2/0	Open		Unkn.	165-170
XX Postman 119/0	Open		Unkn.	100-235
1997 Practice Makes Perfect (w/wooden rocker) 771	Open		250.00	191-260
XX Prayer Before Battle 20	Open		Unkn.	105-247
1996 Pretty Please 489	Open		120.00	90-128
2000 Pretzel Boy (Collectors Set) 2093	Open		185.00	185
1992 The Professor 320/0	Open		Unkn.	173-240
2000 Proud Moments 800	Open		300.00	300
1995 Puppy Love Display Plaque 767	Closed	1995	Unkn.	169-260
1997 Rainy Day (Gift Set) 71/2/0	Open		305.00	305
XX Retreat to Safety 201/2/0	Open		Unkn.	139-190
XX Ride into Christmas 396/2/0	Open		Unkn.	199-275
XX Ride into Christmas 396/I	Open		Unkn.	371-495
XX Ring Around the Rosie 348	Open		Unkn.	2000-3000
1998 Roses Are Red 762	Open		120.00	94-128
XX The Run-A-Way 327	Open		Unkn.	110-280
1997 Ruprecht 473	20,000		450.00	360-460
1992 Scamp 553	Open		Unkn.	94-128
XX School Boy 82/2/0	Open		Unkn.	50-170
XX School Boy 82/0	Open		Unkn.	173-299
XX School Boys 170/I	Open		Unkn.	1013-1400
XX School Girl 81/2/0	Open		Unkn.	112-214
XX School Girls 177/I	Open		Unkn.	990-1400
1997 School's Out 538	Open		170.00	131-180
XX Sensitive Hunter 6/0	Open		Unkn.	173-423
XX Serenade 85/0	Open		Unkn.	150-201
XX She Loves Me, She Loves Me Not 174	Open		Unkn.	191-240
1996 Shepherd Boy 395/0	Open		295.00	225-310
XX Shepherd's Boy 64	Open		Unkn.	110-351
XX Shining Light 358	Open		Unkn.	75-150
XX Singing Lesson 63	Open		Unkn.	50-182
XX Sister 98/2/0	Open		Unkn.	124-170
XX Skier 59	Open		Unkn.	173-460
1990 Sleep Tight 424	Open		Unkn.	135-255
XX Smart Little Sister 346	Open		Unkn.	210-758
XX Soloist 135/0	Open		Unkn.	116-200
1988 Song of Praise 454	Open		Unkn.	90-124
1988 Sound the Trumpet 457	Open		Unkn.	94-128
1988 Sounds of the Mandolin 438	Open		Unkn.	109-150
XX Spring Dance 353/0	Open		Unkn.	165-370
1997 St. Nicholas' Day 2012	20,000		650.00	650-800
XX Star Gazer 132	Open		Unkn.	200-305
2000 Star Gazer (60th Anniversary) 132	Yr.Iss.		245.00	245
XX Stormy Weather 71/2/0	Open		Unkn.	251-346
XX Stormy Weather 71/I	Open		Unkn.	225-510
1992 Storybook Time 458	Open		Unkn.	348-460
XX Street Singer 131	Open		Unkn.	156-292
1998 Strum Along 557	Open		135.00	101-145
1998 Summertime Surprise 428/3/0	Open		220.00	109-150
1997 Sunshower 634/2/0	10,000		360.00	274-375
XX Surprise 94/3/0	Open		Unkn.	131-180
2000 Swaying Lullaby (Collectors Set) 165	Open		325.00	325
1998 Sweet As Can Be Birthday Sampler 541	Open		150.00	116-160
XX Sweet Greetings 352	Open		Unkn.	150-205
XX Sweet Music 186	Open		Unkn.	173-299
XX Telling Her Secret 196/0	Open		Unkn.	255-350
1997 Thanksgiving Prayer 641/4/0	Open		120.00	86-125
1997 Thanksgiving Prayer 641/0	Open		180.00	135-190
XX Thoughtful 415	Open		Unkn.	188-255
XX Timid Little Sister 394	Open		Unkn.	250-495
1995 To Keep You Warm w/ Wooden Chair 759	Open		Unkn.	176-240
XX To Market 49/3/0	Open		Unkn.	185-234
1998 Traveling Trio 787	20,000		490.00	500-675
1997 Trio of Wishes 721	20,000		475.00	356-475
1989 Tuba Player 437	Open		Unkn.	233-320
XX Tuneful Angel 359	Open		Unkn.	75-100
2000 Tuneful Goodnight (Collector's Set) 180	Open		295.00	295
1996 A Tuneful Trio	20,000		450.00	364-675
XX Umbrella Boy 152/A/0	Open		Unkn.	265-675
XX Umbrella Boy 152/A/II	Open		Unkn.	1223-1650
XX Umbrella Girl 152/B/0	Open		Unkn.	495-675
XX Umbrella Girl 152/B/II	Open		Unkn.	1650-1775
XX Village Boy 51/3/0	Open		Unkn.	130-175
XX Village Boy 51/2/0	Open		Unkn.	145-175
XX Visiting an Invalid 382	Open		Unkn.	100-225
XX Volunteers 50/2/0	Open		Unkn.	188-325
XX Volunteers 50/0	Open		Unkn.	255-442
XX Waiter 154/0	Open		Unkn.	184-250
XX Wash Day 321/I	Open		Unkn.	150-345
XX Watchful Angel 194	Open		Unkn.	298-360
XX Wayside Devotion 28/II	Open		Unkn.	391-968
XX Wayside Harmony 111/3/0	Open		Unkn.	175-221
1993 We Come In Peace (Commemorative) 754	Open		385.00	289-385
XX We Congratulate 214/E/I	Open		Unkn.	139-190
XX We Congratulate 220	Open		Unkn.	143-190
1997 We Congratulate (Gift Set) 220	Open		170.00	131-190
1990 What's New? 418	Open		Unkn.	240-330
1999 Where Are You? 427/3/0	Open		170.00	130-180
XX Which Hand? 258	Open		Unkn.	136-235
1988 A Winter Song 476	Open		Unkn.	94-135
XX Worship 84/0	Open		Unkn.	157-190

M.I. Hummel Collectibles Figurines Retired - M.I. Hummel

YEAR ISSUE	EDITION LIMIT	YEAR RETD.	ISSUE PRICE	*QUOTE U.S.$
1947 Accordion Boy 185	Closed	1994	Unkn.	169-550
XX Boots 143/0	Closed	1998	Unkn.	216-400
XX Boots 143/I	Closed	1998	Unkn.	225-280
XX Congratulations 17/0	Closed	1999	Unkn.	173-280
1939 Duet 130	Closed	1995	Unkn.	250-600
1937 Farewell 65 TMK1-5	Closed	1993	Unkn.	100-550
1937 Globe Trotter 79 TMK1-7	Closed	1991	Unkn.	110-350
XX Happy Pastime 69	Closed	1996	Unkn.	143-475
1937 Lost Sheep 68/0 TMK1-7	Closed	1992	Unkn.	179-250
1955 Lost Sheep 68/2/0 TMK2-7	Closed	1992	7.50	116-350
XX Mother's Darling 175	Closed	1997	Unkn.	100-300
1935 Puppy Love I TMK1-6	Closed	1988	125.00	175-550
1948 Signs Of Spring 203/2/0 TMK2-6	Closed	1990	120.00	180-400
1948 Signs Of Spring 203/I TMK2-6	Closed	1990	155.00	206-450
1935 Strolling Along 5 TMK1-6	Closed	1989	115.00	200-400

M.I. Hummel Collectibles Madonna Figurines - M.I. Hummel

YEAR ISSUE	EDITION LIMIT	YEAR RETD.	ISSUE PRICE	*QUOTE U.S.$
1996 Flower Madonna, white 10 (Commemorative)	Closed	1996	225.00	169-225
XX Madonna with Halo, color 45/I/6	Open		Unkn.	109-150

M.I. Hummel Collectibles Nativity Components - M.I. Hummel, unless otherwise noted

YEAR ISSUE	EDITION LIMIT	YEAR RETD.	ISSUE PRICE	*QUOTE U.S.$
XX 12-Pc. Set Figs. only, Color, 214/A/M/I, B/I, A/K/I, F/I G/I J/I K/I, L/I, M/I, N/I, O/I, 366/I	Open		Unkn.	1680-1852
XX Angel Serenade 214/D/I	Open		Unkn.	100-150
XX Camel Kneeling - Goebel	Open		Unkn.	206-285
XX Camel Lying - Goebel	Open		Unkn.	206-285
XX Camel Standing - Goebel	Open		Unkn.	206-285
XX Donkey 214/J/0	Open		Unkn.	41-58
XX Donkey 214/J/I	Open		Unkn.	56-84
XX Flying Angel/color 366/I	Open		Unkn.	105-150
XX Good Night 214/C/I	Open		Unkn.	75-100
XX Holy Family, 3 Pcs., Color 214/A/M/0, B/0, A/K/0	Open		Unkn.	250-350
XX Holy Family, 3 Pcs., Color 214/A/M/I, B/I, A/K/I	Open		Unkn.	468-475
1997 Holy Family, 3 Pcs., White 214	Open		200.00	205-210
XX Infant Jesus 214/A/K/0	Open		Unkn.	34-50
XX Infant Jesus 214/A/K/I	Open		Unkn.	53-87
XX King, Kneeling 214/M/I	Open		Unkn.	149-200
XX King, Kneeling 214M/0	Open		Unkn.	120-165
XX King, Kneeling w/ Box 214/N/0	Open		Unkn.	116-160
XX King, Kneeling w/Box 214/N/I	Open		Unkn.	135-185
XX King, Moorish 214/L/0	Open		Unkn.	124-175
XX King, Moorish 214/L/I	Open		Unkn.	150-205
XX Lamb 214/O/0	Open		Unkn.	18-25
XX Lamb 214/O/I	Open		Unkn.	18-25
XX Little Tooter 214/H/I	Open		Unkn.	105-182
XX Little Tooter 214/H/O	Open		Unkn.	83-118
XX Madonna 214/A/M/0	Open		Unkn.	109-155
XX Madonna 214/A/M/I	Open		Unkn.	146-200
XX Ox 214/K/0	Open		Unkn.	42-58
XX Ox 214/K/I	Open		Unkn.	60-84
XX Shepherd Boy 214/G/I	Open		Unkn.	113-155
XX Shepherd Kneeling 214/G/0	Open		Unkn.	98-140
XX Shepherd Standing 214/F/0	Open		Unkn.	124-175
XX Shepherd with Sheep-1 piece 214/F/I	Open		Unkn.	149-200
XX Small Camel Kneeling - Goebel	Open		Unkn.	225-230
XX Small Camel Lying - Goebel	Open		Unkn.	225-230
XX Small Camel Standing - Goebel	Open		Unkn.	225-230
XX St. Joseph 214/B/0	Open		Unkn.	113-155
XX St. Joseph color 214/B/I	Open		Unkn.	146-200
XX Stable only fits12 or 16-pc. HUM214/II Set	Open		Unkn.	115
XX Stable only, fits 16-piece HUM260 Set	Open		Unkn.	400-450
XX Stable only, fits 3-pc. HUM214 Set	Open		Unkn.	50-83
XX We Congratulate 214/E/I	Open		Unkn.	180-185

M.I. Hummel Disneyana Figurines - M.I. Hummel

YEAR ISSUE	EDITION LIMIT	YEAR RETD.	ISSUE PRICE	*QUOTE U.S.$
1992 Two Merry Wanderers 022074	1,500	1992	250.00	1050-1155
1993 Two Little Drummers	1,500	1993	325.00	725-750
1994 Minnie Be Patient	1,500	1994	395.00	450-725
1995 For Father	1,500	1995	450.00	450-485
1995 Grandpa's Boys	1,500	1995	340.00	413-424
1996 Minnie For Mother	1,200	1996	470.00	470
1997 Grandma's Girl	1,000	1998	350.00	350-484
1998 Friends Forever	350	1998	350.00	350-484
1999 Donald & Daisy	350	1999	350.00	485-517

M.I. Hummel First Edition Miniatures - M.I. Hummel

YEAR ISSUE	EDITION LIMIT	YEAR RETD.	ISSUE PRICE	*QUOTE U.S.$
1991 Accordion Boy -37225	Suspd.		105.00	169-550
1989 Apple Tree Boy -37219	Suspd.		115.00	130-210
1990 Baker -37222	Suspd.		100.00	130-300
1992 Bavarian Church (Display) -37370	Closed	N/A	60.00	70-75
1988 Bavarian Cottage (Display) -37355	Closed	N/A	60.00	64-95
1990 Bavarian Marketsquare Bridge (Display) -37358	Closed	N/A	110.00	125-130
1988 Bavarian Village (Display) -37356	Closed	N/A	100.00	55-100
1991 Busy Student -37226	Suspd.		105.00	150-300
1990 Cinderella -37223	Suspd.		115.00	125-195
1991 Countryside School (Display) -37365	Closed	N/A	100.00	100-125
1989 Doll Bath -37214	Suspd.		95.00	105-185
1992 Goose Girl -37238	Suspd.		130.00	180-300
1989 Little Fiddler -37211	Suspd.		90.00	115-250
1989 Little Sweeper -37212	Suspd.		90.00	115-300
1990 Marketsquare Flower Stand (Display) -37360	Closed	N/A	35.00	50-80
1990 Marketsquare Hotel (Display)-37359	Closed	N/A	70.00	90-125
1989 Merry Wanderer -37213	Suspd.		95.00	250-300
1991 Merry Wanderer Dealer Plaque -37229	Closed	N/A	130.00	160-300
1989 Postman -37217	Suspd.		95.00	120-195

*Quotes have been rounded up to nearest dollar

YEAR ISSUE		EDITION LIMIT	YEAR RETD.	ISSUE PRICE	*QUOTE U.S.$
1991	Roadside Shrine (Display)-37366	Closed	N/A	60.00	60-85
1992	School Boy -37236	Suspd.		120.00	180-300
1991	Serenade -37228	Suspd.		105.00	120-275
1992	Snow-Covered Mountain (Display)-37371	Closed	N/A	100.00	100-125
1989	Stormy Weather -37215	Suspd.		115.00	150-350
1992	Trees (Display)-37369	Closed	N/A	40.00	50-55
1989	Visiting an Invalid -37218	Suspd.		105.00	130-175
1990	Waiter -37221	Suspd.		100.00	195-300
1992	Wayside Harmony -37237	Suspd.		140.00	180-300
1991	We Congratulate -37227	Suspd.		130.00	150-300

M.I. Hummel Fonts - M.I. Hummel

YEAR ISSUE		EDITION LIMIT	YEAR RETD.	ISSUE PRICE	*QUOTE U.S.$
XX	Angel Facing Left 91/A	Open		45.00	38-52
XX	Angel Facing Right 91/B	Open		45.00	34-52
XX	Angel Shrine 147	Open		55.00	44-62
XX	Angel Sitting 22/0	Open		45.00	51-52
XX	Angel w/Bird 167	Open		55.00	41-62
XX	Child w/Flowers 36/0	Open		45.00	43-52
XX	Good Shepherd 35/0	Open		45.00	38-52
XX	Heavenly Angel 207	Open		55.00	45-62
XX	Holy Family 246	Open		55.00	41-62
XX	Madonna & Child 243	Open		55.00	45-62
XX	Worship 164	Open		55.00	45-62

M.I. Hummel Hummel Scapes - M.I. Hummel

YEAR ISSUE		EDITION LIMIT	YEAR RETD.	ISSUE PRICE	*QUOTE U.S.$
1997	Around The Town	Open		75.00	56-75
1997	Castle On A Hill	Open		75.00	56-75
1997	Going To Church	Open		75.00	56-75
1996	Heavenly Harmonies	Open		100.00	100
1996	Home Sweet Home	Closed	1997	130.00	75-130
1996	Little Music Makers	Closed	1997	130.00	75-130
1997	Strolling Through The Park	Open		75.00	56-75

M.I. Hummel Pen Pals - M.I. Hummel

YEAR ISSUE		EDITION LIMIT	YEAR RETD.	ISSUE PRICE	*QUOTE U.S.$
1995	For Mother 257/5/0	Open		55.00	41-55
1995	March Winds 43/5/0	Open		55.00	55
1995	One For You, One For Me 482/5/0	Open		55.00	41-55
1995	Sister 98/5/0	Open		55.00	41-55
1995	Soloist 135/4/0	Open		55.00	41-55
1995	Village Boy 151/5/0	Open		55.00	41-55

M.I. Hummel Tree Toppers - M.I. Hummel

YEAR ISSUE		EDITION LIMIT	YEAR RETD.	ISSUE PRICE	*QUOTE U.S.$
1994	Heavenly Angel 755	Suspd.		450.00	375-500

M.I. Hummel Vignettes w/Solitary Domes - M.I. Hummel

YEAR ISSUE		EDITION LIMIT	YEAR RETD.	ISSUE PRICE	*QUOTE U.S.$
1992	Bakery Day w/Baker & Waiter 37726	3,000		225.00	169-230
1992	The Flower Market w/Cinderella 37729	3,000		135.00	101-135
1993	The Mail Is Here Clock Tower 826504	Open		495.00	431-575
1995	Ring Around the Rosie Musical 826101	10,000		675.00	506-675
1992	Winterfest w/Ride Into Christmas 37728	5,000		195.00	146-156

M.I. Hummel's Temporarily Out of Production (including trademarks) - M.I. Hummel

YEAR ISSUE		EDITION LIMIT	YEAR RETD.	ISSUE PRICE	*QUOTE U.S.$
XX	16-Pc. Set Figs. only, Color, 214/A/M/I, B/I, A/K/I, C/I, D/I, E/I, F/I, G/I, H/I, J/I, K/I, L/I, M/I, N/I, O/I, 366/I	Suspd.		Unkn.	1990
XX	17-Pc. Set Large Color 16 Figs.& Wooden Stable 260 A-R	Suspd.		Unkn.	4540
XX	Adoration 23/III	Suspd.		Unkn.	446-510
2000	African Wanderer 2062	Suspd.		250.00	250
2000	American Wanderer 2061	Suspd.		250.00	250
XX	Angel Cloud (font) 206	Suspd.		55.00	45-55
XX	Angel Duet (candleholder) 193	Suspd.		245.00	188-520
XX	Angel Duet (font) 146	Suspd.		55.00	45-65
XX	Angel Serenade 260/E	Suspd.		Unkn.	200-300
1935	Angelic Sleep Candleholder 25	Suspd.		Unkn.	139
1962	Apple Tree Boy & Girl Bookend 252A&B	Suspd.		Unkn.	225
XX	Apple Tree Boy 142/X	Suspd.		Unkn	15000-25000
XX	Apple Tree Girl 141/X	Suspd.		Unkn	15000-25000
1991	Art Critic 318	Suspd.		Unkn.	244-325
2000	Asian Wanderer 2063	Suspd.		250.00	250
XX	Auf Wiedersehen 153/I	Suspd.		Unkn.	255-340
2000	Australian Wanderer 2064	Suspd.		250.00	250
XX	Baking Day 330	Suspd.		Unkn.	140-320
XX	Barnyard Hero 195/I	Suspd.		Unkn.	140-360
XX	Be Patient 197/I	Suspd.		Unkn.	140-340
XX	Begging His Share 9	Suspd.		Unkn.	242-826
XX	Big Housecleaning 363	Suspd.		Unkn.	120-325
1989	Birthday Cake 338	Suspd.		Unkn.	124-170
XX	Birthday Serenade 218/0	Suspd.		Unkn.	255-366
XX	Blessed Child 78/0	Suspd.		Unkn.	73-179
XX	Blessed Child 78/I/83	Suspd.		Unkn.	35-40
XX	Blessed Child 78/II/83	Suspd.		Unkn.	41-60
XX	Blessed Child 78/III/83	Suspd.		Unkn.	49-75
XX	Bookworm 3/II	Suspd.		Unkn.	1100-1350
XX	Bookworm 3/III	Suspd.		Unkn.	1500-2000
1946	Boy With Bird, Ashtray 166	Suspd.		Unkn.	98
1988	A Budding Maestro 477	Suspd.		Unkn.	95-120
XX	Candlelight (candleholder) 192	Suspd.		255.00	230-473
XX	Celestial Musician 188/I	Suspd.		255.00	221-350
XX	Chick Girl 57/I	Suspd.		Unkn.	240-416
XX	Child in Bed Plaque 137	Suspd.		Unkn.	56-70
XX	Child Jesus (font) 56/0	Suspd.		45.00	38-45
XX	Christ Child 18	Suspd.		Unkn.	124-214
XX	Confidentially 314	Suspd.		Unkn.	200-423
XX	Coquettes 179	Suspd.		Unkn.	200-435
XX	Donkey 260/L	Suspd.		Unkn.	101-135
XX	Easter Greetings 378	Suspd.		Unkn.	196-270
2000	European Wanderer 2060	Suspd.		250.00	250
XX	Eventide 99	Suspd.		Unkn.	299-390
XX	A Fair Measure 345	Suspd.		Unkn.	251-753
XX	Festival Harmony, with Flute 173/0	Suspd.		Unkn.	263-360
XX	Festival Harmony, with Flute 173/4/0	Suspd.		Unkn.	90-200
XX	Festival Harmony, with Flute 173/II	Suspd.		Unkn.	800-1000
XX	Festival Harmony, with Mandolin 172/0	Suspd.		Unkn.	360-414
1994	Festival Harmony, with Mandolin 172/4/0	Suspd.		95.00	90-110
XX	Festival Harmony, with Mandolin 172/II	Suspd.		Unkn.	800-1000
XX	Fitting Butterfly Plaque 139	Suspd.		Unkn.	310
XX	Flower Madonna, color 10/I/II	Suspd.		Unkn.	360-462
XX	Flower Madonna, color 10/III/II	Suspd.		Unkn.	225-420
XX	Flower Madonna, white 10/I/W	Suspd.		Unkn.	420-450
XX	Flower Madonna, white 10/III/W	Suspd.		Unkn.	470-750
XX	Forest Shrine 183	Suspd.		Unkn.	450-650
XX	Friends 136/V	Suspd.		Unkn.	773-1380
XX	A Gentle Glow 439	Suspd.		Unkn.	100-230
XX	Going to Grandma's 52/I	Suspd.		Unkn.	300-500
XX	Good Night 260/D	Suspd.		Unkn.	105-145
XX	Good Shepherd 42	Suspd.		Unkn.	218-377
XX	Goose Girl 47/II	Suspd.		Unkn.	315-614
XX	Goose Girl 47/IIW	Suspd.		Unkn.	218
XX	Guardian Angel 248/0	Suspd.		55.00	41-55
XX	Happy Birthday 176/I	Suspd.		Unkn.	255-340
XX	Happy Days 150/0	Suspd.		Unkn.	255-442
XX	Happy Days 150/I	Suspd.		Unkn.	383-434
XX	Happy Traveler 109/II	Suspd.		Unkn.	800-950
XX	Hear Ye! Hear Ye! 15/I	Suspd.		Unkn.	131-370
XX	Hear Ye! Hear Ye! 15/II	Suspd.		Unkn.	338-500
XX	Hear Ye! Hear Ye! 15/IIW	Suspd.		Unkn.	218
XX	Heavenly Angel 21/I	Suspd.		Unkn.	221-300
XX	Heavenly Angel 21/II	Suspd.		Unkn.	361-500
XX	Heavenly Angel 21/IIW	Suspd.		Unkn.	218
XX	Heavenly Lullaby 262	Suspd.		Unkn.	183-233
XX	Heavenly Protection 88/II	Suspd.		Unkn.	600-900
1995	Hello (Perpetual Calendar) 788A	Suspd.		295.00	295-300
XX	Hello 124/I	Suspd.		Unkn.	206-275
XX	Holy Child 70	Suspd.		Unkn.	214-285
XX	Home from Market 198/I	Suspd.		Unkn.	184-318
XX	Homeward Bound 334	Suspd.		Unkn.	315-360
XX	Hummel Display Plaque 187	Suspd.		Unkn.	125-175
XX	In Tune 414	Suspd.		Unkn.	240-310
XX	Infant Jesus 260/C	Suspd.		Unkn.	79-120
XX	Joyous News 27/III	Suspd.		Unkn.	100-250
1985	Jubilee 416 TMK6	Suspd.		200.00	271-495
XX	Just Fishing 373	Suspd.		Unkn.	191-200
XX	Just Resting 112/I	Suspd.		Unkn.	288-330
XX	King, Kneeling 260/P	Suspd.		Unkn.	480
XX	King, Moorish 260/N	Suspd.		Unkn.	430-500
XX	King, Standing 260/O	Suspd.		Unkn.	300-500
XX	Knitting Lesson 256	Suspd.		Unkn.	455-550
XX	Little Band 392	Suspd.		Unkn.	206-234
1968	Little Band Candleholder 388	Suspd.		Unkn.	165-225
1968	Little Band Candleholder on Music Box 388M	Suspd.		Unkn.	248
1968	Little Band on Music Box 392M	Suspd.		Unkn.	270-467
XX	Little Cellist 89/II	Suspd.		Unkn.	270-500
XX	Little Cellist 89/IIW	Suspd.		Unkn.	218
XX	Little Fiddler 2/4/0	Suspd.		Unkn.	90-115
XX	Little Fiddler 2/I	Suspd.		Unkn.	212-340
XX	Little Fiddler 2/II	Suspd.		Unkn.	825-935
XX	Little Fiddler 2/III	Suspd.		Unkn.	900-1200
XX	Little Gabriel 32	Suspd.		Unkn.	92-170
XX	Little Hiker 16/I	Suspd.		Unkn.	188-325
XX	Little Sweeper 171/4/0	Suspd.		Unkn.	90-140
XX	Little Tooter 260/K	Suspd.		Unkn.	128-170
XX	Lullaby 24/I	Suspd.		210.00	158-390
XX	Lullaby 24/III	Suspd.		Unkn.	1000-1200
XX	Madonna 260/A	Suspd.		Unkn.	590
XX	Madonna Holding Child, color 151/II	Suspd.		Unkn.	115-135
XX	Madonna Holding Child, white 151/W	Suspd.		Unkn.	320-350
XX	Madonna Praying, color 46/III/6	Suspd.		Unkn.	400-425
XX	Madonna Praying, white 46/0/W	Suspd.		Unkn.	195-225
XX	Madonna Praying, white 46/I/W	Suspd.		Unkn.	175-185
XX	Madonna w/o Halo, color 46/I/6	Suspd.		Unkn.	300-315
XX	Madonna w/o Halo, white 45/I/W	Suspd.		Unkn.	175-185
XX	Madonna w/o Halo, white 46/I/W	Suspd.		Unkn.	175-185
1989	Make A Wish 475	Suspd.		Unkn.	169-230
XX	Meditation 13/V	Suspd.		Unkn.	1106-1200
XX	Meditation, color 13/II	Suspd.		Unkn.	1200-2500
XX	Merry Christmas Plaque 323	Suspd.		Unkn.	105-119
XX	Merry Wanderer 7/II	Suspd.		Unkn.	825-1250
XX	Merry Wanderer 7/III	Suspd.		Unkn.	975-1300
XX	Merry Wanderer 7/X	Suspd.		Unkn	12000-20000
XX	Merry Wanderer Stepbase 7/I	Suspd.		Unkn.	319-900
XX	Mischief Maker 342	Suspd.		Unkn.	240-320
1995	Ooh My Tooth (Special Event) 533	Suspd.		Unkn.	135-175
XX	Ox 260/M	Suspd.		Unkn.	113-135
XX	Playmates 58/I	Suspd.		Unkn.	240-320
1994	The Poet 397/I	Suspd.		220.00	191-260
XX	Retreat to Safety 201/I	Suspd.		Unkn.	194-468
XX	School Boy 82/II	Suspd.		Unkn.	296-510
XX	School Boys 170/III	Suspd.		Unkn.	1365-1850
XX	School Girl 81/0	Suspd.		Unkn.	196-230
XX	School Girls 177/III	Suspd.		Unkn.	1365-1850
XX	Searching Angel Plaque 310	Suspd.		Unkn.	101-135
XX	Sensitive Hunter 6/2/0	Suspd.		Unkn.	124-170
XX	Sensitive Hunter 6/I	Suspd.		Unkn.	137-285
XX	Sensitive Hunter 6/II	Suspd.		Unkn.	195-375
XX	Serenade 85/4/0	Suspd.		Unkn.	90-120
XX	Serenade 85/II	Suspd.		Unkn.	245-510
XX	Sheep (Lying) 260/R	Suspd.		Unkn.	50-100
XX	Sheep (Standing) w/ Lamb 260/H	Suspd.		Unkn.	110
XX	Shepherd Boy, Kneeling 260/J	Suspd.		Unkn.	221-300
XX	Shepherd, Standing 260/G	Suspd.		Unkn.	525
XX	Silent Night 54	Suspd.		360.00	185-370
XX	Sing Along 433	Suspd.		Unkn.	240-340
XX	Sing With Me 405	Suspd.		Unkn.	115-340
1995	Sister (Perpetual Calendar) 788B	Suspd.		295.00	225-300
XX	Sister 98/0	Suspd.		Unkn.	176-235
XX	Soldier Boy 332	Suspd.		Unkn.	168-281
XX	Soloist 135/4/0	Suspd.		Unkn.	90-140
XX	Spring Cheer 72	Suspd.		Unkn.	170-279
XX	Spring Dance 353/I	Suspd.		Unkn.	427-525
XX	St. George 55	Suspd.		Unkn.	263-375
XX	St. Joseph 260/B	Suspd.		Unkn.	390-520
XX	A Stitch in Time 255/4/0	Suspd.		Unkn.	90-120
XX	A Stitch in Time 255/I	Suspd.		Unkn.	181-301
1984	Supreme Protection 364 TMK6	Suspd.		150.00	281-395
XX	Surprise 94/I	Suspd.		Unkn.	325-435
1986	The Tally Plaque 460	Suspd.		Unkn.	116-410
XX	Telling Her Secret 196/I	Suspd.		Unkn.	300-400
XX	To Market 49/0	Suspd.		Unkn.	285-435
XX	To Market 49/I	Suspd.		Unkn.	326-500
XX	Trumpet Boy 97	Suspd.		Unkn.	113-201
XX	Village Boy 51/0	Suspd.		Unkn.	128-300
XX	Village Boy 51/I	Suspd.		Unkn.	138-225
XX	Volunteers 50/I	Suspd.		Unkn.	350-450
XX	Waiter 154/I	Suspd.		Unkn.	251-350
1989	Wash Day 321/4/0	Suspd.		Unkn.	90-140
XX	Wayside Devotion 28/III	Suspd.		Unkn.	510-897
XX	Wayside Harmony 111/I	Suspd.		Unkn.	272-416
XX	We Congratulate 260/F	Suspd.		Unkn.	278-400
XX	Weary Wanderer 204	Suspd.		Unkn.	115-370
1992	Whistler's Duet 413	Suspd.		Unkn.	240-330
XX	White Angel 75	Suspd.		45.00	34-45
XX	Whitsuntide 163	Suspd.		Unkn.	248-350
XX	With Loving Greetings 309	Suspd.		Unkn.	169-275
XX	Worship 84/V	Suspd.		Unkn.	825-1125

M.I. Hummel/Stieff - M.I. Hummel

YEAR ISSUE		EDITION LIMIT	YEAR RETD.	ISSUE PRICE	*QUOTE U.S.$
1999	Wonder of Christmas Collector's Set 2015	Closed	1999	575.00	463-575
2000	Little Maestro (Collector's Set) 826/I	Open		425.00	425

Gorham

(Four Seasons) A Boy And His Dog - N. Rockwell

YEAR ISSUE		EDITION LIMIT	YEAR RETD.	ISSUE PRICE	*QUOTE U.S.$
1972	A Boy Meets His Dog	2,500	1980	200.00	1300-1575
1972	Adventurers Between Adventures	2,500	1980	Set	Set
1972	The Mysterious Malady	2,500	1980	Set	Set
1972	Pride of Parenthood	2,500	1980	Set	Set

(Four Seasons) A Helping Hand - N. Rockwell

YEAR ISSUE		EDITION LIMIT	YEAR RETD.	ISSUE PRICE	*QUOTE U.S.$
1980	Year End Court	2,500	1980	650.00	900-1100
1980	Closed For Business	2,500	1980	Set	Set
1980	Swatter's Right	2,500	1980	Set	Set
1980	Coal Seasons Coming	2,500	1980	Set	Set

(Four Seasons) Dad's Boy - N. Rockwell

YEAR ISSUE		EDITION LIMIT	YEAR RETD.	ISSUE PRICE	*QUOTE U.S.$
1981	Ski Skills	2,500	1990	750.00	1000-1300
1981	In His Spirit	2,500	1990	Set	Set
1981	Trout Dinner	2,500	1990	Set	Set
1981	Careful Aim	2,500	1990	Set	Set

(Four Seasons) Four Ages of Love - N. Rockwell

YEAR ISSUE		EDITION LIMIT	YEAR RETD.	ISSUE PRICE	*QUOTE U.S.$
1974	Gaily Sharing Vintage Times	2,500	1980	300.00	600-1250
1974	Sweet Song So Young	2,500	1980	Set	Set
1974	Flowers In Tender Bloom	2,500	1980	Set	Set
1974	Fondly Do We Remember	2,500	1980	Set	Set

(Four Seasons) Going On Sixteen - N. Rockwell

YEAR ISSUE		EDITION LIMIT	YEAR RETD.	ISSUE PRICE	*QUOTE U.S.$
1978	Chilling Chore	2,500	1980	400.00	650-1200
1978	Sweet Serenade	2,500	1980	Set	Set
1978	Shear Agony	2,500	1980	Set	Set
1978	Pilgrimage	2,500	1980	Set	Set

(Four Seasons) Grand Pals - N. Rockwell

YEAR ISSUE		EDITION LIMIT	YEAR RETD.	ISSUE PRICE	*QUOTE U.S.$
1977	Snow Sculpturing	2,500	1980	350.00	1000-1200
1977	Soaring Spirits	2,500	1980	Set	Set
1977	Fish Finders	2,500	1980	Set	Set
1977	Ghostly Gourds	2,500	1980	Set	Set

(Four Seasons) Grandpa and Me - N. Rockwell

YEAR ISSUE		EDITION LIMIT	YEAR RETD.	ISSUE PRICE	*QUOTE U.S.$
1975	Gay Blades	2,500	1980	300.00	800-1000
1975	Day Dreamers	2,500	1980	Set	Set
1975	Goin' Fishing	2,500	1980	Set	Set
1975	Pensive Pals	2,500	1980	Set	Set

(Four Seasons) Life With Father - N. Rockwell

YEAR ISSUE		EDITION LIMIT	YEAR RETD.	ISSUE PRICE	*QUOTE U.S.$
1983	Big Decision	2,500	1990	250.00	250
1983	Blasting Out	2,500	1990	Set	Set
1983	Cheering The Champs	2,500	1990	Set	Set
1983	A Tough One	2,500	1990	Set	Set

(Four Seasons) Me and My Pal - N. Rockwell

YEAR ISSUE		EDITION LIMIT	YEAR RETD.	ISSUE PRICE	*QUOTE U.S.$
1976	A Licking Good Bath	2,500	1980	300.00	1200-1400
1976	Young Man's Fancy	2,500	1980	Set	Set
1976	Fisherman's Paradise	2,500	1980	Set	Set
1976	Disastrous Daring	2,500	1980	Set	Set

(Four Seasons) Old Buddies - N. Rockwell

YEAR ISSUE		EDITION LIMIT	YEAR RETD.	ISSUE PRICE	*QUOTE U.S.$
1984	Shared Success	2,500	1990	250.00	250
1984	Hasty Retreat	2,500	1990	Set	Set
1984	Final Speech	2,500	1990	Set	Set
1984	Endless Debate	2,500	1990	Set	Set

*Quotes have been rounded up to nearest dollar

FIGURINES

(Four Seasons) Old Timers - N. Rockwell

Year Issue		Edition Limit	Year Retd.	Issue Price	*Quote U.S.$
1982	Canine Solo	2,500	1990	250.00	250
1982	Sweet Surprise	2,500	1990	Set	Set
1982	Lazy Days	2,500	1990	Set	Set
1982	Fancy Footwork	2,500	1990	Set	Set

(Four Seasons) Tender Years - N. Rockwell

Year Issue		Edition Limit	Year Retd.	Issue Price	*Quote U.S.$
1979	New Year Look	2,500	1979	500.00	1200-1400
1979	Spring Tonic	2,500	1979	Set	Set
1979	Cool Aid	2,500	1979	Set	Set
1979	Chilly Reception	2,500	1979	Set	Set

(Four Seasons) Traveling Salesman - N. Rockwell

Year Issue		Edition Limit	Year Retd.	Issue Price	*Quote U.S.$
1985	Horse Trader	2,500	1985	275.00	250-275
1985	Expert Salesman	2,500	1985	Set	Set
1985	Traveling Salesman	2,500	1985	Set	Set
1985	Country Pedlar	2,500	1985	Set	Set

(Four Seasons) Young Love - N. Rockwell

Year Issue		Edition Limit	Year Retd.	Issue Price	*Quote U.S.$
1973	Downhill Daring	2,500	1973	250.00	1100
1973	Beguiling Buttercup	2,500	1973	Set	Set
1973	Flying High	2,500	1973	Set	Set
1973	A Scholarly Pace	2,500	1973	Set	Set

Miniature Christmas Figurines - Various

Year Issue		Edition Limit	Year Retd.	Issue Price	*Quote U.S.$
1979	Tiny Tim - N. Rockwell	Yr.Iss.	1979	15.00	20
1980	Santa Plans His Trip - N. Rockwell	Yr.Iss.	1980	15.00	15
1981	Yuletide Reckoning - N. Rockwell	Yr.Iss.	1981	20.00	20
1982	Checking Good Deeds - N. Rockwell	Yr.Iss.	1982	20.00	20
1983	Santa's Friend - N. Rockwell	Yr.Iss.	1983	20.00	20
1984	Downhill Daring - N. Rockwell	Yr.Iss.	1984	20.00	20
1985	Christmas Santa - T. Nast	Yr.Iss.	1985	20.00	20
1986	Christmas Santa - T. Nast	Yr.Iss.	1986	25.00	25
1987	Annual Thomas Nast Santa - T. Nast	Yr.Iss.	1987	25.00	25

Miniatures - N. Rockwell

Year Issue		Edition Limit	Year Retd.	Issue Price	*Quote U.S.$
1982	The Annual Visit	Closed	1990	50.00	50-75
1981	At the Vets	Closed	1990	27.50	50-75
1987	Babysitter	15,000	1990	75.00	75
1981	Beguiling Buttercup	Closed	1990	45.00	45
1985	Best Friends	Closed	1990	27.50	28
1987	Between The Acts	15,000	1990	60.00	60
1981	Boy Meets His Dog	Closed	1990	37.50	60
1984	Careful Aims	Closed	1990	55.00	55
1987	Cinderella	15,000	1990	70.00	75
1981	Downhill Daring	Closed	1990	45.00	75
1985	Engineer	Closed	1990	55.00	55
1981	Flowers in Tender Bloom	Closed	1990	60.00	60
1986	Football Season	Closed	1990	60.00	60
1981	Gay Blades	Closed	1990	45.00	75
1984	Ghostly Gourds	Closed	1990	60.00	60-80
1984	Goin Fishing	Closed	1990	60.00	60
1986	The Graduate	Closed	1990	30.00	40
1984	In His Spirit	Closed	1990	60.00	60
1984	Independence	Closed	1990	60.00	80-85
1986	Lemonade Stand	Closed	1990	60.00	60
1986	Little Angel	Closed	1990	50.00	60
1985	Little Red Truck	Closed	1990	25.00	25
1982	Marriage License	Closed	1990	60.00	75-125
1987	The Milkmaid	15,000	1990	80.00	85-110
1986	Morning Walk	Closed	1990	60.00	60
1985	Muscle Bound	Closed	1990	30.00	30
1985	New Arrival	Closed	1990	32.50	35-75
1984	The Oculist	Closed	1990	60.00	80
1986	The Old Sign Painter	Closed	1990	70.00	80
1984	Pride of Parenthood	Closed	1990	50.00	50
1987	The Prom Dress	15,000	1990	75.00	75
1982	The Runaway	Closed	1990	50.00	50-80
1984	Shear Agony	Closed	1990	60.00	60
1986	Shoulder Ride	Closed	1990	50.00	65-75
1981	Snow Sculpture	Closed	1990	45.00	70
1985	Spring Checkup	Closed	1990	60.00	60
1987	Springtime	15,000	1990	65.00	75-110
1987	Starstruck	15,000	1990	75.00	80-115
1981	Sweet Serenade	Closed	1990	45.00	45-80
1981	Sweet Song So Young	Closed	1990	55.00	55
1985	To Love & Cherish	Closed	1990	32.50	35
1982	Triple Self Portrait	Closed	1990	60.00	90-175
1983	Trout Dinner	15,000	1990	60.00	60-110
1982	Vintage Times	Closed	1990	50.00	50
1986	Welcome Mat	Closed	1990	70.00	75
1984	Years End Court	Closed	1990	60.00	60
1981	Young Man's Fancy	Closed	1990	55.00	55

Rockwell - N. Rockwell

Year Issue		Edition Limit	Year Retd.	Issue Price	*Quote U.S.$
1983	Antique Dealer RW48	7,500	1990	130.00	200
1982	April Fool's (At The Curiosity Shop) RW39	Closed	1990	55.00	100-110
1974	At The Vets RW4	Closed	1990	25.00	85-125
1974	Batter Up RW6	Closed	1990	40.00	150
1977	Beguiling Buttercup RW-19	Closed	1990	85.00	150
1978	Big Decision RW-25	Closed	1990	55.00	55
1975	Boy And His Dog RW9	Closed	1990	38.00	150
1974	Captain RW8	Closed	1990	45.00	95-130
1984	Card Tricks	7,500	1990	110.00	180
1978	Choosing Up RW24	Closed	1990	85.00	275
1981	Christmas Dancers RW37	7,500	1990	130.00	200-275
1988	Confrontation	15,000	1990	75.00	75
1988	Cramming	15,000	1990	80.00	80
1981	Day in the Life Boy II RW34	Closed	1990	75.00	95-115
1982	A Day in the Life Boy III RW40	Closed	1990	85.00	95
1982	A Day in the Life Girl III RW41	Closed	1990	85.00	115-150
1988	The Diary	15,000	1990	80.00	80-115
1988	Dolores & Eddie NRM59	15,000	1990	75.00	80
1986	Drum For Tommy RW53	Annual	1986	90.00	N/A
1983	Facts of Life RW45	7,500	1990	110.00	180
1974	Fishing RW5	Closed	1990	50.00	175
1977	Gaily Sharing Vintage Time RW-20	Closed	1990	60.00	165
1988	Gary Cooper in Hollywood	15,000	1990	90.00	90
1977	Gay Blades RW-21	Closed	1990	50.00	50-150
1976	God Rest Ye Merry Gentlemen RW13	Closed	1990	50.00	1000-1500
1988	Home for the Holidays	7,500	1990	100.00	100
1976	Independence RW15	Closed	1990	40.00	150
1980	Jolly Coachman RW33	7,500	1990	75.00	200
1982	Marriage License (10 3/4") RW38	5,000	1990	110.00	600
1976	Marriage License (6 1/4") RW16	Closed	1990	50.00	325
1982	Merrie Christmas RW43	7,500	1990	75.00	150
1978	Missed RW23	Closed	1990	85.00	275
1974	Missing Tooth RW2	Closed	1990	30.00	150
1975	No Swimming RW18	Closed	1990	35.00	150-175
1976	The Oculist RW17	Closed	1990	50.00	175
1978	Oh Yeah RW22	Closed	1990	85.00	275
1975	Old Mill Pond RW11	Closed	1990	45.00	145
1985	The Old Sign Painter	7,500	1990	130.00	210
1977	Pride of Parenthood RW18	Closed	1990	50.00	125
1985	Puppet Maker	7,500	1990	130.00	130-200
1987	Santa Planning His Annual Visit	7,500	1990	95.00	95
1984	Santa's Friend	7,500	1990	75.00	160
1976	Saying Grace (5 1/2") RW12	5,000	1990	75.00	265-275
1982	Saying Grace (8") RW42	Closed	1990	110.00	500-600
1984	Serenade	7,500	1990	95.00	165
1974	Skating RW7	Closed	1990	37.50	140
1976	Tackled (Ad Stand)	Closed	1990	35.00	125-150
1982	Tackled (Rockwell Name Signed) RW8662	Closed	1990	45.00	100
1974	Tiny Tim RW3	Closed	1990	30.00	125-135
1980	Triple Self Portrait (10 1/2") RW32	5,000	1990	300.00	600
1979	Triple Self Portrait (7 1/2") RW27	Closed	1990	125.00	425
1974	Weighing In RW1	Closed	1990	40.00	150
1981	Wet Sport RW36	Closed	1990	85.00	95-100

Great American Railways/Hallmark Keepsake Collections

Great American Railways - Hallmark Keepsake Collections

Year Issue		Edition Limit	Year Retd.	Issue Price	*Quote U.S.$
2000	Crossing Sign QHT3507	Retrd.	2000	10.00	10
2000	Crossing Sign With Gate QHT3508	Retrd.	2000	12.00	12
1998	Lionel® 2332 Pennsylvania GG-1 Electric Locomotive QHT7804	29,500	1998	95.00	95
1999	Lionel® 2333 New York Central F3A-A Diesel Locomotive QHT7802	29,500	2000	100.00	100
1999	Lionel® 3356 Horse Car QHT7805	29,500	2000	30.00	30
2000	Lionel® 3662 Refrigerated Milk Car QHT7808	29,500	2000	30.00	30
1999	Lionel® 671 Turbine Steam Locomotive 1QHT7806	29,500	2000	115.00	115
1998	Lionel® 726 Berkshire Steam Locomotive QHT7801	29,500	1999	120.00	120
1998	Lionel® 746 Norfolk and Western Steam Locomotive QHT7803	29,500	2000	90.00	90
1999	Lionel® 773 Hudson Steam Locomotive 1QHT7807	29,500	2000	125.00	125
2000	Lionel® Chessie Steam Special Locomotive QHT7822	24,500	2000	35.00	35
2000	Lionel® Santa Fe F3A Diesel Locomotive QHT7823	Numbrd.	2000	30.00	30
2000	Lionel® Soo Line SD60 Diesel Locomotive QHT7824	Numbrd.	2000	30.00	30
1999	Oceanside Depot QHT3501	29,500	2000	65.00	65

Greenwich Workshop

Bronze - Various

Year Issue		Edition Limit	Year Retd.	Issue Price	*Quote U.S.$
1994	Bird Hunters - J. Christensen	50	N/A	4500.00	4500
1990	The Candleman, AP - J. Christensen	100	N/A	2250.00	4500
1991	Comanche Raider - K. McCarthy	100	N/A	812.50	813
1989	The Fish Walker - J. Christensen	100	N/A	3200.00	4500
1999	A Lawyer More Than Adequately Attired in Fine Print - J. Christensen	200		6000.00	6000
1991	Pony Express - K. McCarthy	10	N/A	934.00	934
1994	Thunder of Hooves - K. McCarthy	10	N/A	875.00	875

The Greenwich Workshop Collection - Various

Year Issue		Edition Limit	Year Retd.	Issue Price	*Quote U.S.$
1998	The Ancient Angel - J. Christensen	1,750		195.00	195
1997	And The Wolf - S. Gustafson	945		350.00	350
1996	And They...Crooked House - J. Christensen	Retrd.	1998	295.00	295-350
1996	Another Fish Act - J. Christensen	2,500		350.00	350
1998	The Artist - W. Bullas	622	1998	95.00	95
1998	Baby Bear - S. Gustafson	1,950		50.00	50
1998	Back Quackers - W. Bullas	1,200		125.00	125
1997	Bassoonist - J. Christensen	1,500		395.00	395
1996	Bed Time Buddies - W. Bullas	Retrd.	1999	75.00	75
1998	Brother Avery - S. Gustafson	5,000		95.00	95
1997	Brother Folio Scrivner - S. Gustafson	2,364		95.00	95
1998	California Stylin - W. Bullas	Open		125.00	125
1996	Candleman - J. Christensen	2,500		295.00	295
1996	Christmas Angel - W. Bullas	1,996	1996	75.00	75-150
1996	Christmas Elf - W. Bullas	1,996	1996	75.00	150-180
1997	Consultant - W. Bullas	Retrd.	1999	95.00	95
1997	Crooked Cat, Crooked Mouse - J. Christensen	1,724	1998	60.00	60-90
1996	The Dare Devil - W. Bullas	Retrd.	1998	75.00	75-95
1998	Dressed for the Holidays - W. Bullas	1,500	N/A	95.00	95
1997	Duck Tape - W. Bullas	600		95.00	95
1996	Ductor - W. Bullas	Open		75.00	75
1997	Dust Bunnies - W. Bullas	500		75.00	75
1997	Fish Walker - J. Christensen	571		350.00	350
1999	The Fish Wizard - J. Christensen	1,500	N/A	160.00	160
1996	Fool and His Bunny - W. Bullas	Open		75.00	75
1998	Fool Moon - W. Bullas	1,750	1998	125.00	125
1997	Forest Fish Rider - J. Christensen	2,500		175.00	175
1998	Fowl Ball - W. Bullas	828		95.00	95
1997	Frog Horn - W. Bullas	2,028		85.00	85
1998	Froggy Goes A-Wooing - S. Gustafson	2,500		125.00	125
1999	Gift of Peace - J. Christensen	Retrd.	1999	85.00	85
1998	Goldilocks - S. Gustafson	1,950		130.00	130
1998	The Hare - S. Gustafson	1,950		95.00	95
1996	He Bought a Crooked Cat - J. Christensen	Retrd.	1998	60.00	60-75
1996	Head of the Class - W. Bullas	Retrd.	1998	75.00	75
1997	Hocus Pocus - W. Bullas	547		125.00	125
1997	How Many Angels Can Fit on Head - J. Christensen	536		215.00	215
1997	Humpty Dumpty - S. Gustafson	600		250.00	250
1996	Jack Be Nimble - J. Christensen	Retrd.	1999	295.00	295
1998	Jack Sprat Could Eat No Fat - J. Christensen	1,500	1999	175.00	175
1998	Jack's Wife Could Eat No Lean - J. Christensen	1,500	1999	185.00	185
1996	Jailbirds - W. Bullas	Retrd.	1999	75.00	75
1996	Lawrence Pretended Not to Notice... - J. Christensen	2,500	1998	350.00	350
1996	Levi Levitates a Stone Fish - J. Christensen	2,500		295.00	295
1996	Little Angel - W. Bullas	Retrd.	1996	75.00	75
1996	Little Elf - W. Bullas	Retrd.	1996	75.00	75
1999	Little Miss Muffet - S. Gustafson	1,950		245.00	245
1996	Little Red Riding Hood - S. Gustafson	2,500		150.00	150
1998	The Lute Player - J. Christensen	1,500		450.00	450
1998	Mama Bear - S. Gustafson	1,950		175.00	175
1996	Man Who Minds the Moon - J. Christensen	2,500	N/A	295.00	295
1999	Melchior - J. Christensen	Retrd.	1999	80.00	80
1998	The Miniature Artist - J. Christensen	1,500	1998	95.00	95
1996	Mother Goose - J. Christensen	Retrd.	1999	275.00	275
1998	Mrs. Claus - J. Christensen	2,500		295.00	295
1999	the mummy strikes! - W. Bullas	Open		95.00	95
1998	The Nurse - W. Bullas	2,500	N/A	95.00	95
1995	Olde World Santa - J. Christensen	950	1995	295.00	540-600
1996	The Oldest Angel - J. Christensen	2,500	1998	295.00	295
1998	Ottist - S. Gustafson	1,500	N/A	95.00	95
1998	Owl and the Pussycat - S. Gustafson	2,500		250.00	250
1998	Papa Bear - S. Gustafson	1,950		180.00	180
1999	Pear Balancer - J. Christensen	1,500		160.00	160
1997	Puppy Glove - W. Bullas	Open		95.00	95
1998	Puss in Boots - S. Gustafson	2,500		165.00	165
1998	Responsible Man - J. Christensen	1,950		450.00	450
1996	The Responsible Woman - J. Christensen	2,500		595.00	595
1997	Rudy - W. Bullas	2,553		125.00	125
1998	Sandtrap Pro - W. Bullas	828		95.00	95
1999	santa gets lit... - W. Bullas	1,500		95.00	95
1998	Santa's Belle - J. Christensen	Retrd.	1998	50.00	59
1998	Santa's Hopper - W. Bullas	1,250		85.00	85
1997	Santa's Other Helpers - J. Christensen	2,500	N/A	295.00	295
1997	The Scholar - J. Christensen	1,700		375.00	375
1999	secret agent - W. Bullas	Open		95.00	95
1998	Snow Buddies - W. Bullas	1,250		125.00	125
1998	Sock Hop - W. Bullas	Open		125.00	125
1999	Sometimes The Spirit Touches Us Through Our Weaknesses w/ graphic After Clouds, Sun - J. Christensen	1,950		275.00	275
1998	Space Cadet - W. Bullas	2,500		95.00	95
1999	superdad... - W. Bullas	Retrd.	N/A	95.00	95
1998	Supermom - W. Bullas	1,228	N/A	95.00	95
1996	There Was a Crooked Man... - J. Christensen	Retrd.	1998	225.00	225-275
1996	Three Blind Mice: Fluffy - J. Christensen	Retrd.	1998	75.00	75-90
1996	Three Blind Mice: Sniffer - J. Christensen	Retrd.	1998	75.00	75-90
1996	Three Blind Mice: Weevil - J. Christensen	Retrd.	1998	75.00	75-90
1997	Tommy Tucker - J. Christensen	1,250	1999	295.00	295
1999	the tooth faerie - W. Bullas	Open		95.00	95
1998	The Tortoise - S. Gustafson	1,950		125.00	125
1997	The Traveling Fish Salesman - J. Christensen	546	N/A	150.00	150
1996	Trick or Treat - W. Bullas	Retrd.	1998	75.00	75
1996	The Trick Rider - W. Bullas	Retrd.	1999	75.00	75
1996	Tweedle Dee - J. Christensen	1,250	1999	295.00	295
1996	Tweedle Dum - J. Christensen	1,250	1999	295.00	295
1998	Wetland Bird Hunter - J. Christensen	1,950		250.00	250
1996	Wolf - S. Gustafson	2,500		350.00	350
1996	Zippo...the Fire Eater - W. Bullas	Retrd.	1998	75.00	75-95

Pearl Bisque™ - Various

Year Issue		Edition Limit	Year Retd.	Issue Price	*Quote U.S.$
2000	bad to the bun - W. Bullas	Open		49.95	50
2000	ballet parking - W. Bullas	Open		24.98	25
2000	the cat burglar - W. Bullas	Open		22.48	23
2000	dog byte - W. Bullas	Open		19.98	20
2000	hogwash... - W. Bullas	Open		49.95	50
2000	life of the party - W. Bullas	Open		24.98	25
2000	the nerd dogs... - W. Bullas	Open		49.95	50
2000	please be mine... - W. Bullas	Open		49.95	50
2000	Queen Mab - W. Christensen	1,500		135.00	135
2000	Queen Mab's Fairies-Adeline - W. Christensen	1,500		75.00	75
2000	Queen Mab's Fairies-Cecily - W. Christensen	1,500		75.00	75

*Quotes have been rounded up to nearest dollar

YEAR ISSUE	EDITION LIMIT	YEAR RETD.	ISSUE PRICE	*QUOTE U.S.$
2000 Queen Mab's Fairies-Fiona - W. Christensen	1,500		75.00	75
2000 road hog - W. Bullas	Open		19.98	20

Porcelain Angels - W. Christensen

YEAR ISSUE	EDITION LIMIT	YEAR RETD.	ISSUE PRICE	*QUOTE U.S.$
2000 The Gift of Love	Open		85.00	85
2000 Leap of Faith	Open		112.50	113

Porcelain Wisemen - W. Christensen

YEAR ISSUE	EDITION LIMIT	YEAR RETD.	ISSUE PRICE	*QUOTE U.S.$
2000 Balthasar	Open		40.00	40
2000 Caspar	Open		40.00	40
2000 Melchoir	Open		40.00	40

Gzhel USA/Russian Gift & Jewelry

Fairy Tales - Gzhel USA, unless otherwise noted

YEAR ISSUE	EDITION LIMIT	YEAR RETD.	ISSUE PRICE	*QUOTE U.S.$
1998 Fire Bird 74301	Open		26.00	26
1998 Fishnet 74600 - Okulova	Open		27.00	27
1998 Goblin 75104 - Denissov	Open		35.00	35
1998 Ivan - Prince 74302	Open		13.00	13
1998 Magic Pike 75501	Open		24.00	24
1998 Nutcracker 75502 - Gordeyev	Open		35.00	35
1998 Old Man Mazai 73910	Open		13.00	13
1998 Under the Oak 74700 - Denissov	Open		57.00	57

Hallmark Galleries

Birds of North America - G.&G. Dooly

YEAR ISSUE	EDITION LIMIT	YEAR RETD.	ISSUE PRICE	*QUOTE U.S.$
1992 American Goldfinch QHG9887	2,500	1994	85.00	85
1992 American Robins QHG9878	2,500	1994	175.00	175
1992 Cardinal QHG9897	2,500	1994	110.00	110
1992 Cedar Waxwing QHG9889	2,500	1994	120.00	120
1992 Dark-eyed Junco QHG9899	2,500	1994	85.00	85
1992 House Wren QHG9801	2,500	1994	85.00	85
1992 Ovenbird QHG9837	2,500	1994	95.00	95
1992 Red-breasted Nuthatch QHG9802	2,500	1994	95.00	95

Days to Remember-The Art of Norman Rockwell - D. Unruh

YEAR ISSUE	EDITION LIMIT	YEAR RETD.	ISSUE PRICE	*QUOTE U.S.$
1993 A Child's Prayer QHG9722	7,500	1995	75.00	75
1992 The Fiddler QHG9708	4,500	1995	95.00	95
1992 The Fiddler-Musical Jewelry Box QHG9711	9,500	1994	48.00	48
1992 Little Spooner-Musical Jewelry Box QHG9712	9,500	1994	48.00	48
1992 Little Spooners QHG9705	4,500	1995	70.00	70
1992 Low and OutsideQHG9714	4,500	1995	95.00	95
1992 Marbles Champion QHG9704	4,500	1995	75.00	75
1994 No Swimming QHG9725	4,500	1995	70.00	70
1992 Santa and His Helpers QHG9702	7,500	1995	95.00	95
1992 Saying Grace QHG9719	1,500	1995	375.00	375
1993 Secrets QHG9721	7,500	1995	70.00	70
1992 Sleeping Children QHG9703	7,500	1995	105.00	105
1992 Springtime 1927 QHG9706	4,500	1995	95.00	95
1992 Springtime, 1927-Musical Jewelry Box QHG9713	9,500	1994	48.00	48
1992 The Truth About Santa QHG9720	7,500	1995	85.00	85

Eileen's Richardson's Enchanted Garden - E. Richardson

YEAR ISSUE	EDITION LIMIT	YEAR RETD.	ISSUE PRICE	*QUOTE U.S.$
1992 Baby Bunny Hop (bowl) QHG3004	9,500	1994	85.00	85
1992 Bunny Abundance (vase) QHG3005	9,500	1994	75.00	75
1992 Enchanted Garden (vase) QHG3006	1,200	1994	115.00	115
1992 Everybunny Can Fly (vase) QHG3007	9,500	1994	70.00	70
1992 Let Them Eat Carrots (pitcher) QHG3013	9,500	1994	70.00	70
1992 Milk Bath (vase) QHG3009	9,500	1994	80.00	80
1993 Peaceable Kingdom Lidded Box QHG3017	9,500	1994	38.00	38
1992 Promenade (bowl) QHG3002	9,500	1994	65.00	65

Innocent Wonders - T. Blackshear

YEAR ISSUE	EDITION LIMIT	YEAR RETD.	ISSUE PRICE	*QUOTE U.S.$
1992 Bobo Bipps QHG4005	2,500	1995	150.00	150
1992 Dinky Toot QHG4004	4,500	1995	125.00	125
1992 Pinkie Poo QHG4002	2,500	1995	135.00	135
1992 Pippy Lou QHG4006	4,500	1995	150.00	150
1992 Pockets QHG4018	4,500	1995	125.00	125
1992 Rectangular Music Box QHG4009	9,500	1995	60.00	60
1992 Square Music Box QHG4008	9,500	1995	45.00	45
1993 Twinky Wink QHG4021	4,500	1995	115.00	115
1992 Waggletag QHG4001	4,500	1995	125.00	125
1992 Waterdome-Dinky Toot QHG4020	9,500	1994	35.00	35
1992 Wood Base QHG4011	Retrd.	1995	20.00	20
1992 Zip Doodle QHG4010	4,500	1995	125.00	125

Little Creations - L. Rankin

YEAR ISSUE	EDITION LIMIT	YEAR RETD.	ISSUE PRICE	*QUOTE U.S.$
1993 Basset Hound-Happy Hound QEC1294	Retrd.	1995	10.00	10
1993 Beagle Daydreamin QEC1275	Retrd.	1995	8.50	9
1993 Bear Honey QEC1243	Retrd.	1995	12.00	12
1993 Bulldog-Bone Tired QEC1273	Retrd.	1995	8.50	9
1994 Cat Lookin' for Trouble QEC1227	Retrd.	1995	10.00	10
1993 Frog Ribbett QEC1285	Retrd.	1995	10.00	10
1994 Orangutan Peace & Quiet QEC1228	Retrd.	1995	12.00	12
1993 Otter-Water Sport QEC1245	Retrd.	1995	12.00	12
1993 Pig-Pee Wee Porker QEC1263	Retrd.	1995	7.50	8
1994 Polar Bear McKinley QEC1226	Retrd.	1995	18.00	18
1993 Reclining Terrier Dreamer QEC1265	Retrd.	1995	7.50	8
1993 Seated Rabbit Bashful QEC1253	Retrd.	1995	10.00	10
1993 Shih Tzu-Daddy's Girl QEC1293	Retrd.	1995	7.50	8
1994 Sitting Pig Li'l Piggy QEC1224	Retrd.	1995	10.00	10
1993 Spaniel & Beagle QEC1283	Retrd.	1995	12.00	12
1993 Squirrel-Cheeky QEC1223	Retrd.	1995	7.50	8
1993 Turtle-Tenderfoot QEC1225	Retrd.	1995	12.00	12
1993 White Seal Sea Baby QEC1235	Retrd.	1995	10.00	10

Lou Rankin's Creations - L. Rankin

YEAR ISSUE	EDITION LIMIT	YEAR RETD.	ISSUE PRICE	*QUOTE U.S.$
1993 Backyard Bandit Raccoon QHG9920	19,500	1995	30.00	30
1992 Basset Hound -Faithful Friend QHG9908	19,500	1995	38.00	38
1992 Bulldog and Beagle -Best Buddies QHG9906	9,500	1995	48.00	48
1994 Bulldog QHG9926	19,500	1995	38.00	38
1994 Cocker Spaniel Pal QHG9924	19,500	1995	35.00	35
1993 Fairbanks Polar Bear QHG9916	19,500	1995	70.00	70
1994 Frog Pucker Up Baby QHG9923	19,500	1995	35.00	35
1992 Happy Frog -Feelin' Fine QHG9918	19,500	1995	35.00	35
1993 Mini Paws Happy-Looking Cat QHG9922	19,500	1995	25.00	25
1992 Orangutan -The Thinker QHG9915	19,500	1995	38.00	38
1992 Pair of Pigs -Pork & Beans QHG9902	19,500	1995	38.00	38
1992 Pig with Head Raised - Fair Lady QHG9903	19,500	1995	35.00	35
1992 Reclining Bear QHG9901	19,500	1995	35.00	35
1992 Reclining Cat -Birdwatcher QHG9912	19,500	1995	30.00	30
1993 Seal Winsome QHG9921	19,500	1995	32.00	32
1992 Seated Bear QHG9905	19,500	1995	30.00	30
1992 Seated Rabbit QHG9911	19,500	1995	30.00	30
1992 Shih Tzu -The Sophisticate QHG9907	19,500	1995	30.00	30
1993 Slowpoke Turtle QHG9917	19,500	1995	30.00	30
1992 Squirrel I -Satisfied QHG9909	19,500	1995	25.00	25
1992 Squirrel II -Sassy QHG9910	19,500	1995	25.00	25
1992 Two Otters -Two's Company QHG9914	9,500	1995	45.00	45
1994 Two Pigs QHG9925	19,500	1995	45.00	45

Majestic Wilderness - M. Newman

YEAR ISSUE	EDITION LIMIT	YEAR RETD.	ISSUE PRICE	*QUOTE U.S.$
1992 American Bald Eagle QHG2009	1,200	1993	195.00	195
1993 American Wilderness Mini Environment Set QHG2029	2,500	1995	225.00	225
1992 American Wilderness Mini Environment With Dome QHG2019	Retrd.	1995	80.00	80
1994 Arctic Wolves QHG2031	4,500	1995	130.00	130
1992 Bighorn Sheep QHG2005	4,500	1995	125.00	125
1992 Bison QHG2016	4,500	1995	120.00	120
1994 Elk in Water QHG2032	4,500	1995	120.00	120
1992 Grizzly Mother with Cub QHG2004	2,500	1995	135.00	135
1992 Large Base QHG2028	Retrd.	1995	3.50	4
1992 The Launch QHG2025	2,500	1995	165.00	165
1992 Lidded Box/Deer QHG2010	9,500	1995	40.00	40
1992 Lidded Box/Wolves QHG2011	9,500	1995	40.00	40
1992 Male Grizzly QHG2001	2,500	1995	145.00	145
1992 Mini Black Bear QHG2020	14,500	1995	28.00	28
1992 Mini Cottontail Rabbits QHG2021	14,500	1995	20.00	20
1994 Mini Deer QHG2036	14,500	1995	25.00	25
1992 Mini Eagle QHG2026	14,500	1995	28.00	28
1992 Mini Mule Deer QHG2024	14,500	1995	28.00	28
1992 Mini Raccoons QHG2022	14,500	1995	20.00	20
1992 Mini Red Fox QHG2023	14,500	1995	20.00	20
1994 Mini Snow Owl QHG2034	14,500	1995	18.00	18
1994 Mini Snowshoe Rabbits QHG2037	14,500	1995	20.00	20
1994 Mini White Tailed Buck QHG2035	14,500	1995	25.00	25
1992 Mountain Lion QHG2006	4,500	1995	75.00	75
1992 Red Fox QHG2017	4,500	1995	75.00	75
1992 Small Base QHG2027	Retrd.	1995	2.50	3
1992 Snowshoe Rabbit QHG2007	4,500	1995	70.00	70
1992 Timber Wolves QHG2003	2,500	1995	135.00	135
1992 White-tailed Buck QHG2008	2,500	1995	135.00	135
1992 White-tailed Doe with Fawn QHG2002	2,500	1995	135.00	135
1994 Winter Environment QHG2033	Retrd.	1995	70.00	70
1994 Winter Environment Set QHG2038	2,500	1995	160.00	160

Mary Engelbreit Friendship Garden - M. Engelbreit

YEAR ISSUE	EDITION LIMIT	YEAR RETD.	ISSUE PRICE	*QUOTE U.S.$
1993 Birdhouse QHG5013	9,500	1995	45.00	45
1993 Blue Teapot QHG5004	9,500	1995	50.00	50
1993 Cherry Teapot QHG5005	9,500	1995	50.00	50
1993 Cookie Jar QHG5009	9,500	1995	50.00	50
1993 Mini Tea Set QHG5007	9,500	1995	45.00	45
1993 Teatime Table and Chairs QHG5014	12,500	1995	75.00	75
1993 Watering Can QHG5008	9,500	1994	30.00	30
1993 Yellow Teapot QHG5006	9,500	1995	50.00	50

Moustershire - D. Rhodus

YEAR ISSUE	EDITION LIMIT	YEAR RETD.	ISSUE PRICE	*QUOTE U.S.$
1992 Acorn Inn Customers QHG8020	9,500	1995	28.00	28
1992 Acorn Inn/Timothy Duzmuch QHG8009	9,500	1995	65.00	65
1992 Andrew Allsgood- Honorable Citizen QHG8001	Retrd.	1995	10.00	10
1992 Bakery/Dunne Eaton QHG8010	9,500	1994	55.00	55
1992 Bandstand/Cyrus & Cecilia Sunnyside QHG8011	9,500	1995	50.00	50
1992 Chelsea Goforth- Ingenue QHG8002	Retrd.	1995	10.00	10
1992 Claire Lovencare- Nanny QHG8014	19,500	1995	18.00	18
1992 Colin Tuneman- Musician of Note QHG8004	Retrd.	1995	10.00	10
1992 Hattie Chapeau- Milliner QHG8015	19,500	1995	15.00	15
1992 Henrietta Seaworthy QHG8026	19,500	1995	15.00	15
1992 Hillary Hemstitch- Seamstress QHG8006	Retrd.	1995	10.00	10
1992 Hyacinth House QHG8021	9,500	1995	65.00	65
1992 L.E. Hosten- Innkeeper QHG8007	Retrd.	1995	10.00	10
1992 Malcolm Cramwell- Mouserly Scholar QHG8008	Retrd.	1995	10.00	10
1993 Michael McFogg At Lighthouse QHG8025	9,500	1995	55.00	55
1992 Miles Fielding- Farmer QHG8003	Retrd.	1995	10.00	10
1992 Nigel Puffmore- Talented Tubist QHG8012	19,500	1995	10.00	10
1992 Olivia Puddingsby- Baker QHG8005	Retrd.	1994	10.00	10
1992 The Park Gate QHG8019	9,500	1995	60.00	60
1992 Peter Philpott- Gardener QHG8022	19,500	1995	12.00	12
1992 The Picnic/Tree QHG8017	9,500	1995	50.00	50
1992 Robin Ripengood- Grocer QHG8013	19,500	1995	28.00	28
1992 Tess Tellingtale/Well QHG8024	19,500	1995	28.00	28
1992 Trio QHG8016	19,500	1995	23.00	23
1992 Village/Bay Crossroads Sign QHG8023	19,500	1995	10.00	10

Tender Touches - E. Seale

YEAR ISSUE	EDITION LIMIT	YEAR RETD.	ISSUE PRICE	*QUOTE U.S.$
1990 Baby Bear in Backpack QEC9863	Retrd.	1991	16.00	45
1988 Baby Raccoon QHG7031	Retrd.	1992	20.00	40
1991 Baby's 1st Riding Rocking Bear QEC9349	Retrd.	1991	16.00	45
1989 Bear Decorating Tree QHG7050	Retrd.	1995	18.00	40
1992 Bear Family Christmas QHG7002	9,500	1995	45.00	90
1990 Bear Graduate QHG7043	Retrd.	1995	15.00	35
1988 Bear w/ Umbrella QHG7029	Retrd.	1994	16.00	35
1990 Bear's Easter Parade QHG7040	Retrd.	1995	23.00	23
1990 Bears Playing Baseball QHG7039	Retrd.	1994	20.00	20
1990 Bears w/ Gift QEC9461	Retrd.	1991	18.00	65
1992 Beaver Growth Chart QHG7007	19,500	1995	20.00	50
1992 Beaver w/ Double Bass QHG7058	Retrd.	1995	18.00	45
1990 Beavers w/Tree QHG7052	Retrd.	1994	23.00	23
1989 Birthday Mouse QHG7010	Retrd.	1993	16.00	45
1992 Breakfast in Bed QHG7059	Retrd.	1995	18.00	18
1989 Bride & Groom QHG7009	Retrd.	1994	20.00	40
1992 Building a Pumpkin Man QHG7061	Retrd.	1995	18.00	18
1990 Bunnies Eating Ice Cream QHG7038	Retrd.	1995	20.00	20
1990 Bunnies w/ Slide QHG7016	Retrd.	1994	20.00	55
1990 Bunny Cheerleader QHG7018	Retrd.	1994	16.00	35
1992 Bunny Clarinet QHG7063	Retrd.	1994	16.00	50
1990 Bunny Hiding Valentine QHG7035	Retrd.	1995	16.00	16
1990 Bunny in Boat QHG7021	Retrd.	1994	18.00	40
1989 Bunny in Flowers QHG7012	Retrd.	1992	16.00	49
1991 Bunny in High Chair QHG7054	Retrd.	1995	16.00	45
1990 Bunny Pulling Wagon QHG7008	Retrd.	1994	23.00	50
1990 Bunny w/ Ice Cream QHG7020	Retrd.	1993	15.00	50
1992 Bunny w/ Kite QHG7006	19,500	1995	19.00	40
1991 Bunny w/ Large Eggs QHG7056	Retrd.	1995	16.00	85
1990 Bunny w/ Stocking QEC9416	Retrd.	1990	15.00	35
1992 Chatting Mice QHG7003	19,500	1995	23.00	65
1989 Chipmunk Praying QEC9431	Retrd.	1991	18.00	75
1989 Chipmunk w/Roses QHG7023	Retrd.	1992	16.00	45
1992 Chipmunks w/Album QHG7057	Retrd.	1995	23.00	35
1991 Christmas Bunny Skiing QHG7046	Retrd.	1995	18.00	15-18
1990 Dad and Son Bears QHG7015	Retrd.	1992	23.00	33
1992 Delightful Fright QHG7067	19,500	1995	23.00	75
1993 Downhill Dash QHG7080	Retrd.	1995	23.00	20-23
1990 Easter Egg Hunt QEC9866	Retrd.	1991	18.00	275
1993 Easter Stroll QHG7084	Retrd.	1995	21.00	15-21
1993 Ensemble Chipmunk Kettledrum QHG7087	Retrd.	1994	18.00	45
1991 Father Bear Barbequing QHG7041	Retrd.	1995	23.00	15-23
1994 Fireman QHG7090	Retrd.	1995	23.00	50
1991 First Christmas Mice @ Piano QEC9357	Retrd.	1991	23.00	295
1992 Fitting Gift QHG7065	Retrd.	1995	23.00	15-23
1991 Foxes in Rowboat QHG7053	Retrd.	1995	23.00	23
1992 From Your Valentine QHG7071	Retrd.	1995	20.00	20
1993 Garden Capers QHG7078	Retrd.	1995	20.00	15-20
1994 Golfing QHG7091	Retrd.	1995	23.00	46
1994 Halloween QHG7093	Retrd.	1995	23.00	40
1989 Halloween Trio QEC9714	Retrd.	1990	18.00	150
1993 Handling a Big Thirst QHG7076	Retrd.	1995	21.00	21
1994 Happy Campers QHG7092	Retrd.	1995	25.00	45
1994 Jesus, Mary, Joseph QHG7094	Retrd.	1995	23.00	40
1993 Love at First Sight QHG7085	Retrd.	1995	23.00	55
1991 Love-American Gothic-Farmer Raccoons QHG7047	Retrd.	1995	20.00	15-20
1993 Making A Splash QHG7088	Retrd.	1995	20.00	20
1988 Mice at Tea Party QHG7028	Retrd.	1993	23.00	35
1991 Mice Couple Slow Waltzing QEC9437	Retrd.	1991	20.00	500
1990 Mice in Red Car QEC9886	Retrd.	1991	20.00	125
1988 Mice in Rocking Chair QHG7030	Retrd.	1994	18.00	50
1990 Mice w/Mistletoe QEC9423	Retrd.	1990	20.00	30
1990 Mice w/Quilt QHG7017	Retrd.	1994	20.00	45
1992 Mom's Easter Bonnet QHG7072	Retrd.	1995	18.00	18
1991 Mother Raccoon Reading Bible Stories QHG7042	Retrd.	1994	20.00	20
1989 Mouse at Desk QEC9434	Retrd.	1990	18.00	45
1991 Mouse Couple Sharing Soda QHG7055	Retrd.	1995	23.00	85
1990 Mouse in Pumpkin QEC9473	Retrd.	1991	18.00	295
1992 Mouse Matinee QHG7073	Retrd.	1995	22.00	22
1990 Mouse Nurse QHG7037	Retrd.	1995	15.00	15
1988 Mouse w/Heart QHG7024	Retrd.	1993	18.00	43
1989 Mouse w/Violin QHG7049	Retrd.	1992	16.00	30-50
1993 Mr. Repair Bear QHG7075	Retrd.	1995	18.00	18
1992 New World, Ahoy! QHG7068	Retrd.	1995	25.00	55
1992 Newsboy Bear QHG7060	Retrd.	1995	16.00	16
1993 The Old Swimming Hole QHG7086	9,500	1995	45.00	150
1990 Pilgrim Bear Praying QEC9466	Retrd.	1991	18.00	75
1989 Pilgrim Mouse QEC9721	Retrd.	1990	16.00	125
1993 Playground Go-Round QHG7089	Retrd.	1995	23.00	15-23
1989 Rabbit Painting Egg QHG7022	Retrd.	1994	18.00	45
1988 Rabbit w/Ribbon QHG7027	Retrd.	1994	15.00	35
1988 Rabbits at Juice Stand QHG7033	Retrd.	1994	23.00	45
1989 Rabbits Ice Skating QEC9391	Retrd.	1991	18.00	28
1988 Rabbits w/Cake QHG7025	Retrd.	1992	20.00	40
1992 Raccoon in Bath QHG7069	Retrd.	1993	18.00	75
1990 Raccoon Mail Carrier QHG7013	Retrd.	1995	16.00	16
1988 Raccoon w/Cake QEC9724	Retrd.	1991	18.00	45
1990 Raccoon Watering Roses QHG7036	Retrd.	1994	20.00	20
1991 Raccoon Witch QHG7045	Retrd.	1994	16.00	20

*Quotes have been rounded up to nearest dollar

FIGURINES

YEAR ISSUE	EDITION LIMIT	YEAR RETD.	ISSUE PRICE	*QUOTE U.S.$
1988 Raccoons Fishing QHG7034	Retrd.	1994	18.00	45
1992 Raccoons on Bridge QHG7004	19,500	1995	25.00	25
1988 Raccoons Playing Ball QEC9771	Retrd.	1991	18.00	40
1990 Raccoons w/Flag QHG7044	Retrd.	1994	23.00	45
1990 Raccoons w/Wagon QHG7014	Retrd.	1993	23.00	60
1990 Romeo & Juliet Mice QEC9903	Retrd.	1991	25.00	500
1990 Santa in Chimney QHG7051	Retrd.	1994	18.00	45
1989 Santa Mouse in Chair QEC9394	Retrd.	1990	20.00	135-150
1993 Sculpting Santa QHG7083	Retrd.	1995	20.00	20
1992 Soapbox Racer QHG7005	19,500	1995	23.00	23
1988 Squirrels w/Bandage QHG7032	Retrd.	1993	18.00	45
1992 Stealing a Kiss QHG7066	19,500	1995	23.00	55
1992 Sweet Sharing QHG7062	Retrd.	1995	20.00	15-20
1992 Swingtime Love QHG7070	Retrd.	1993	21.00	275
1990 Teacher & Student Chipmunks QHG7019	Retrd.	1992	20.00	30
1988 Teacher w/Student QHG7026	Retrd.	1995	18.00	18
1993 Teeter For Two QHG7077	Retrd.	1995	23.00	15-23
1992 Tender Touches Tree House QHG7001	9,500	1995	55.00	35-55
1992 Thanksgiving Family Around Table QHG7048	Retrd.	1995	25.00	25
1990 Tucking Baby in Bed QHG7011	Retrd.	1993	18.00	40-75
1992 Waiting for Santa QHG7064	Retrd.	1995	20.00	20
1993 Woodland Americana-Liberty Mouse QHG7081	Retrd.	1995	21.00	30
1993 Woodland Americana-Patriot George QHG7082	Retrd.	1995	25.00	50
1993 Woodland Americana-Stitching the Stars and Stripes QHG7079	Retrd.	1995	21.00	45
1992 Younger Than Springtime QHG7074	19,500	1995	35.00	60

Times to Cherish - Various

YEAR ISSUE	EDITION LIMIT	YEAR RETD.	ISSUE PRICE	*QUOTE U.S.$
1992 Beautiful Dreamer QHG6010 - T. Andrews	4,500	1994	65.00	65
1992 A Child's Prayer QHG6006 - T. Andrews	4,500	1994	35.00	35
1992 Daily Devotion QHG6005 - T. Andrews	4,500	1994	40.00	40
1992 Dancer's Dream QHG6009 - T. Andrews	4,500	1994	50.00	50
1992 The Embrace QHG6002 - T. Andrews	4,500	1994	60.00	60
1992 The Joys of Fatherhood QHG6001 - T. Andrews	4,500	1994	60.00	60
1992 Mother's Blessing QHG6008 - T. Andrews	4,500	1994	65.00	65
1992 A Mother's Touch QHG6007 - T. Andrews	4,500	1994	60.00	60
1993 Showing The Way QHG6011 - P. Andrews	4,500	1994	45.00	45
1992 Sister Time QHG6003 - T. Andrews	4,500	1994	55.00	55
1993 Spring Tulip Lidded Box QHG6012 - P. Andrews	4,500	1994	25.00	25

Victorian Memories - Various

YEAR ISSUE	EDITION LIMIT	YEAR RETD.	ISSUE PRICE	*QUOTE U.S.$
1992 Doll Trunk QHG1015 - J. Greene	7,500	1995	125.00	125
1993 Gloria Summer Figurine 6000QHG1032 - Greene/Lyle	9,500	1994	60.00	60
1993 Hobby Horse QHG1028 - J. Greene	9,500	1994	18.00	18
1992 Lillian-cold cast QHG1001 - J. Lyle	9,500	1994	55.00	55
1993 Mini Snow Globe QHG1031 - J. Greene	9,500	1995	18.00	18
1992 Music Box QHG1025 - J. Greene	9,500	1995	50.00	50
1992 Musical Jack-in-the Box QHG9502 - J. Greene	9,500	1995	20.00	20
1992 Rabbit (on wheels) QHG1022 - J. Greene	4,500	1995	65.00	65
1992 Rebecca-cold cast QHG1024 - J. Lyle	9,500	1994	60.00	60
1992 Sarah-cold cast QHG1003 - J. Lyle	9,500	1994	60.00	60
1993 Shoo-Fly Rocking Horse QHG1036 - J. Greene	9,500	1995	18.00	18
1992 Tea Set QHG1026 - J. Greene	9,500	1995	35.00	35
1993 Toy Cradle QHG1027 - J. Greene	9,500	1995	20.00	20
1993 Victorian Toy Cupboard QHG1038 - J. Greene	7,500	1995	75.00	75
1992 Wicker Rocker QHG9510 - J. Greene	4,500	1994	45.00	45
1992 Wooden Doll Carriage-miniature QHG9506 - J. Greene	9,500	1995	20.00	20
1992 Wooden Horse Pull Toy-miniature QHG9504 - J. Greene	9,500	1995	18.00	18
1992 Wooden Jewelry Box QHG9505 - J. Greene	9,500	1995	18.00	18
1992 Wooden Noah's Ark-miniature QHG9503 - J. Greene	9,500	1995	15.00	15
1992 Wooden Rocking Horse QHG9511 - J. Greene	4,500	1995	75.00	75
1992 Wooden Train-miniature QHG9501 - J. Greene	9,500	1995	15.00	15

Hamilton Collection

American Garden Flowers - D. Fryer

YEAR ISSUE	EDITION LIMIT	YEAR RETD.	ISSUE PRICE	*QUOTE U.S.$
1987 Azalea	15,000		75.00	75
1988 Calla Lilly	15,000		75.00	75
1987 Camelia	9,800		55.00	75
1988 Day Lily	15,000		75.00	75
1987 Gardenia	15,000		75.00	75
1989 Pansy	15,000		75.00	75
1988 Petunia	15,000		75.00	75
1987 Rose	15,000		75.00	75

American Wildlife Bronze Collection - H./N. Deaton

YEAR ISSUE	EDITION LIMIT	YEAR RETD.	ISSUE PRICE	*QUOTE U.S.$
1980 Beaver	7,500		60.00	65
1979 Bobcat	7,500		60.00	75
1979 Cougar	7,500		60.00	125
1980 Polar Bear	7,500		60.00	65
1980 Sea Otter	7,500		60.00	65
1979 White-Tailed Deer	7,500		60.00	105

Arctic Antics - N/A

YEAR ISSUE	EDITION LIMIT	YEAR RETD.	ISSUE PRICE	*QUOTE U.S.$
1998 Catching a Nap	Open		17.95	18
1998 Cool Slide	Open		17.95	18
1998 Delightful Dreams	Open		17.95	18
1998 Frisky Fun	Open		17.95	18
1998 Ice Fishing	Open		17.95	18
1998 Icy Romp	Open		17.95	18
1998 Strutting Along	Open		17.95	18
1998 Winter Song	Open		17.95	18

Arrowhead Spirits - M. Richter

YEAR ISSUE	EDITION LIMIT	YEAR RETD.	ISSUE PRICE	*QUOTE U.S.$
1997 Cry of the Full Moon	28-day		29.95	30
1997 In High Pursuit	28-day		29.95	30
1997 Nature's First Lesson	28-day		29.95	30
1996 Path of the Wolf	28-day		29.95	30
1996 Piercing The Night	28-day		29.95	30
1996 Soul of the Hunter	28-day		29.95	30

Birdhouses in Bloom - L. Yencho

YEAR ISSUE	EDITION LIMIT	YEAR RETD.	ISSUE PRICE	*QUOTE U.S.$
1996 Blackbird's Bower	Open		14.95	15
1996 Blue Jay's Minaret	Open		14.95	15
1996 Cardinal Cottage	Open		14.95	15
1996 Carriage House Perch	Open		14.95	15
1996 Country Morning	Open		14.95	15
1996 Dove Estate	Open		14.95	15
1996 Lilac Landing	Open		14.95	15
1996 Romantic Retreat	Open		14.95	15
1996 Rosebud Cottage	Open		14.95	15
1996 Springtime Victorian	Open		14.95	15
1996 Sweet Nectar Bed & Breakfast	Open		14.95	15
1996 Vineyard Villa	Open		14.95	15

Brrtown Bears - N/A

YEAR ISSUE	EDITION LIMIT	YEAR RETD.	ISSUE PRICE	*QUOTE U.S.$
1997 Brrtown Gliding Glee	Open		14.95	15
1997 Brrtown Journey	Open		14.95	15
1997 Brrtown School Days	Open		14.95	15
1997 The Brrtown Slide	Open		14.95	15
1997 Cool Splash	Open		14.95	15
1997 Fisherbear's Feast	Open		14.95	15
1997 Icy Encounter	Open		14.95	15
1997 Ski Breeze	Open		14.95	15

Camelot Frogs - S. Kerhli

YEAR ISSUE	EDITION LIMIT	YEAR RETD.	ISSUE PRICE	*QUOTE U.S.$
1997 The Aristocratic Actor	Closed	N/A	19.95	20-135
1997 The Country Cook	Closed	N/A	19.95	20-150
1997 Jumping Jester	Closed	N/A	19.95	20-135
1996 King Ribbit	Closed	N/A	19.95	20-135
1997 Knight of The Lily Pad	Closed	N/A	19.95	20-95
1996 Lady of The Lily Pad	Closed	N/A	19.95	20-135
1997 The Noble Artisan	Closed	N/A	19.95	20-135
1997 Queen Ribbit	Closed	N/A	19.95	20-135
1997 The Regal Tailor	Closed	N/A	19.95	20-135
1996 Royal Ribbiteer	Closed	N/A	19.95	20-135
1996 Sir Hop A Lot	Closed	N/A	19.95	20-135
1996 Wizard of Camelot	Closed	N/A	19.95	20-85

A Celebration of Roses - N/A

YEAR ISSUE	EDITION LIMIT	YEAR RETD.	ISSUE PRICE	*QUOTE U.S.$
1989 Brandy	Open		55.00	55
1989 Color Magic	Open		55.00	55
1989 Honor	Open		55.00	55
1989 Miss All-American Beauty	Open		55.00	55
1991 Ole'	Open		55.00	55
1990 Oregold	Open		55.00	55
1991 Paradise	Open		55.00	55
1989 Tiffany	Open		55.00	55

Cherished Teddies Miniature Nativity - P. Hillman

YEAR ISSUE	EDITION LIMIT	YEAR RETD.	ISSUE PRICE	*QUOTE U.S.$
2000 Bearing Good Tidings	Open		29.85	30
2000 A Beary Special Family	Open		29.85	30
2000 Beary Special Guardians	Open		29.85	30
2000 Creche	Open		29.85	30
2000 Wise Men Bearing Gifts	Open		29.85	30

Cherished Teddies Village - P. Hillman

YEAR ISSUE	EDITION LIMIT	YEAR RETD.	ISSUE PRICE	*QUOTE U.S.$
1997 Appletree Schoolhouse	Closed	1999	45.00	45
1997 Camille's Quilt Shop	Open		45.00	45
1995 A Picnic For Two	Open		45.00	45-75
1996 Sweet Treats For Teddie	Closed	1999	45.00	45
1996 Teddie's Boat Shop	Closed	1999	45.00	45-99
1997 Teddies Nursery	Open		45.00	45
1996 Toys For Teddies	Closed	1999	45.00	45-99
1996 The Wedding Gazebo	Closed	1999	45.00	44-99

Copy Cats - N/A

YEAR ISSUE	EDITION LIMIT	YEAR RETD.	ISSUE PRICE	*QUOTE U.S.$
1999 Hairdresser	Open		14.95	15
1998 Just A Spoonful	Open		14.95	15
1998 Kitty to the Rescue	Open		14.95	15
1999 Kitty Treats	Open		14.95	15
1998 Kitty's Special Delivery	Open		14.95	15
1999 Teacher's Pet	Open		14.95	15

Coral Reef Beauties - Everhart

YEAR ISSUE	EDITION LIMIT	YEAR RETD.	ISSUE PRICE	*QUOTE U.S.$
1996 Coral Paradise	Open		39.95	40
1996 Ocean's Bounty	Open		39.95	40
1996 Sentinel of the Sea	Open		39.95	40

Dale Earnhardt Good Ole Bears Figurines - B. Cleaver

YEAR ISSUE	EDITION LIMIT	YEAR RETD.	ISSUE PRICE	*QUOTE U.S.$
1999 Double Duty	Open		19.95	20
1999 Gassin' Around	Open		19.95	20
1999 The Intimidator	Open		19.95	20
1999 Need A Lift!	Open		19.95	20
1999 Rear Tire Changer	Open		19.95	20

Dreamsicles 12 Days of Chrismtas - K. Haynes

YEAR ISSUE	EDITION LIMIT	YEAR RETD.	ISSUE PRICE	*QUOTE U.S.$
1999 A Partridge in a Pear Tree, Two Turtle Doves, Three French Hens	Open		24.95	25

Dreamsicles Animal Pals - K. Haynes

YEAR ISSUE	EDITION LIMIT	YEAR RETD.	ISSUE PRICE	*QUOTE U.S.$
1998 African Pals	Open		19.90	20
1998 Frontier Friends	Open		19.90	20
1998 Outback Chums	Open		19.90	20
1998 Striped Companions	Open		19.90	20
1998 Underwater Buddies	Open		19.90	20
1998 Woodland Playmates	Open		19.90	20

Dreamsicles Anniversary Carousel Clock - K. Haynes

YEAR ISSUE	EDITION LIMIT	YEAR RETD.	ISSUE PRICE	*QUOTE U.S.$
1997 Dreamsicles Anniversary Carousel Clock	Open		95.00	95

Dreamsicles in Bloom - K. Haynes

YEAR ISSUE	EDITION LIMIT	YEAR RETD.	ISSUE PRICE	*QUOTE U.S.$
2000 Begonia & Marigold	Open		29.90	30
1998 Daisy & Rose	Open		29.90	30
1999 Gardenia & Azalea	Open		29.90	30
1999 Jasmine & Pansy	Open		29.90	30
1998 Sunflower & Poppy	Open		29.90	30
1998 Violet & Lily	Open		29.90	30

Dreamsicles International Friends Collection - K. Haynes

YEAR ISSUE	EDITION LIMIT	YEAR RETD.	ISSUE PRICE	*QUOTE U.S.$
1998 I'll Always Be Your Amigo	Open		14.95	15
1998 Your Friendship Is Wünderbar	Open		14.95	15
1998 Friendship Spans All Distances	Open		14.95	15
1998 Your Friendship Is A Home Run	Open		14.95	15

Dreamsicles Rainbow Express - K. Haynes

YEAR ISSUE	EDITION LIMIT	YEAR RETD.	ISSUE PRICE	*QUOTE U.S.$
1998 Full Steam Ahead	Open		14.95	15
1999 Happy Endings	Open		14.95	15
1999 Hearts-A-Plenty	Open		14.95	15
1999 Hold Tight	Open		14.95	15
1999 Moon Dreaming	Open		14.95	15
1999 Pretty Packages	Open		14.95	15
1999 Rainbow Ride	Open		14.95	15
1999 Shining Star	Open		14.95	15

Early Discoveries - Adams-Hart

YEAR ISSUE	EDITION LIMIT	YEAR RETD.	ISSUE PRICE	*QUOTE U.S.$
1997 Curious Encounters	Open		19.95	20-55
1997 Ducky Discoveries	Closed	1999	19.95	20-55
1996 First Recital	Closed	1999	19.95	20-55
1997 Friendly Encounters	Closed	1999	19.95	20
1997 Friendly Foes	Open		19.95	20
1997 Nature's Scent	Closed	1999	19.95	20
1997 New Explorers	Closed	1999	19.95	20
1996 New Friends	Closed	1999	19.95	20
1997 Peaceful Pals	Closed	1999	19.95	20
1997 Springtime Melodies	Closed	1999	19.95	20-95
1997 Strolling Along	Closed	1999	19.95	20
1996 Sweet Nature	Open		19.95	20

Elephant Tales - M. Adams

YEAR ISSUE	EDITION LIMIT	YEAR RETD.	ISSUE PRICE	*QUOTE U.S.$
1998 Cinderella	Open		17.95	18
1998 The Frog & Princess	Open		17.95	18
1998 Rapunzel	Open		17.95	18
1998 Rumpelstilskin	Open		17.95	18
1998 Sleeping Beauty	Open		17.95	18
1998 Snow White	Open		17.95	18

Exploring our Arctic World - N/A

YEAR ISSUE	EDITION LIMIT	YEAR RETD.	ISSUE PRICE	*QUOTE U.S.$
1998 Icy Rescue	Open		29.95	30
1998 Playful Antics	Open		29.95	30
1998 Frosty Kisses	Open		29.95	30
1998 Polar Playmates	Open		29.95	30
1998 It's Too Chilly	Open		29.95	30
1998 Snuggle Up	Open		29.95	30
1999 First Swim	Open		29.95	30

Farm Livin' - N/A

YEAR ISSUE	EDITION LIMIT	YEAR RETD.	ISSUE PRICE	*QUOTE U.S.$
1999 Hittin' the Hay	Open		17.95	18
1999 A Little Squirt	Open		17.95	18
1998 Squeaky Clean	Open		17.95	18
1999 Tight Squeeze	Open		17.95	18

First Loves - N/A

YEAR ISSUE	EDITION LIMIT	YEAR RETD.	ISSUE PRICE	*QUOTE U.S.$
1999 Bobbin' At The Hop	Open		19.95	20
1998 Our 1st Soda Together	Open		19.95	20
1999 Rainy Day Romance	Open		19.95	20
1998 To My Sweet	Open		19.95	20

First on Race Day Figurine Collection - N/A

YEAR ISSUE	EDITION LIMIT	YEAR RETD.	ISSUE PRICE	*QUOTE U.S.$
1996 Bill Elliott	Open		45.00	45
1996 Jeff Gordon	Open		45.00	45
1996 Sterling Marlin	Open		45.00	45

Freshwater Challenge - M. Wald

YEAR ISSUE	EDITION LIMIT	YEAR RETD.	ISSUE PRICE	*QUOTE U.S.$
1992 Prized Catch	Open		75.00	75
1991 Rainbow Lure	Open		75.00	75
1991 The Strike	Open		75.00	75
1991 Sun Catcher	Open		75.00	75

Garden Romances Are Forever - B. Cleaver

YEAR ISSUE	EDITION LIMIT	YEAR RETD.	ISSUE PRICE	*QUOTE U.S.$
1997 Bundles of Love	Open		14.95	15
1997 Endless Love Songs	Open		14.95	15
1997 Falling In Love	Closed	1999	14.95	15-55
1997 Flowered With Love	Open		14.95	15
1997 Fragrant Love	Open		14.95	15
1997 Fruits of Love	Open		14.95	15
1997 Heartfelt Love	Closed	1999	14.95	15
1997 Humming With Love	Open		14.95	15
1997 Love Buds	Open		14.95	15

*Quotes have been rounded up to nearest dollar

YEAR ISSUE	EDITION LIMIT	YEAR RETD.	ISSUE PRICE	*QUOTE U.S.$
1997 Love Has Its Ups and Downs	Open		14.95	15
1996 Love Is In The Air	Closed	1999	14.95	15
1997 Love Pecks	Closed	1999	14.95	15

Gifts of the Ancient Spirits - S. Kerhli

YEAR ISSUE	EDITION LIMIT	YEAR RETD.	ISSUE PRICE	*QUOTE U.S.$
1996 Talisman of Courage	Open		79.00	79
1996 Talisman of Strength	Closed	1999	79.00	79
1995 Talisman of the Bison	Closed	1999	79.00	79
1996 Talisman of the Buffalo	Open		79.00	79

Gone With The Wind-Porcelain Trading Cards - N/A

YEAR ISSUE	EDITION LIMIT	YEAR RETD.	ISSUE PRICE	*QUOTE U.S.$
1995 Fire and Passion	28-day		14.95	15
1995 Scarlett and Her Suitors	28-day		14.95	15
1996 Portrait of Scarlett	28-day		14.95	15
1996 Portrait of Rhett	28-day		14.95	15
1996 The Proposal	28-day		14.95	15
1996 Scarlett and Mammy	28-day		14.95	15
1996 Rhett at Twelve Oaks	28-day		14.95	15
1996 The Bold Entrance	28-day		14.95	15
1996 Sunset Embrace	28-day		14.95	15
1996 The Jail Scene	28-day		14.95	15
1996 The Exodus	28-day		14.95	15
1996 Anger Turns to Passion	28-day		14.95	15
1996 The Reunion	28-day		14.95	15
1997 Belle & Rhett	28-day		14.95	15
1997 Portrait of Ashley	28-day		14.95	15
1997 Rhett & Bonnie	28-day		14.95	15
1997 Scarlett & Ashley	28-day		14.95	15

Guardian of the Heavens - S. Kerhli

YEAR ISSUE	EDITION LIMIT	YEAR RETD.	ISSUE PRICE	*QUOTE U.S.$
1999 Dreamkeeper	Open		69.00	69
1998 Star Shooter	Open		69.00	69

Guardians of Vision - N. Rose

YEAR ISSUE	EDITION LIMIT	YEAR RETD.	ISSUE PRICE	*QUOTE U.S.$
1999 Guardian Spirit	Open		49.95	50
1999 Vision of the White Buffalo	Open		49.95	50

Happy Owlidays - W. Henry

YEAR ISSUE	EDITION LIMIT	YEAR RETD.	ISSUE PRICE	*QUOTE U.S.$
1998 Back to Schoo-owl	Open		17.95	18
1998 Easter Owlebration	Open		17.95	18
1998 Giving Owl Thanks	Open		17.95	18
1998 Happy Owloween	Open		17.95	18
1998 Luck of the Owlrish	Open		17.95	18
1998 Owl Be Home For Christmas	Open		17.95	18
1998 Owl Be Your Valentine	Open		17.95	18
1998 Owl Dependence Day	Open		17.95	18
1998 Owl Lang Syne	Open		17.95	18
1998 Owl What a Beautiful Day	Open		17.95	18
1998 Splashin-Owl Around	Open		17.95	18
1998 Suma Dependence Day	Open		17.95	18

Heart of Nature - S. Kerhli

YEAR ISSUE	EDITION LIMIT	YEAR RETD.	ISSUE PRICE	*QUOTE U.S.$
1999 Song of Devotion	Open		49.95	50
1999 Vision of Beauty	Open		49.95	50

Heaven's Messenger - S. Kerhli

YEAR ISSUE	EDITION LIMIT	YEAR RETD.	ISSUE PRICE	*QUOTE U.S.$
1999 My Spirit Soars	Open		69.95	70

Heavenly Gifts - S. Kuck

YEAR ISSUE	EDITION LIMIT	YEAR RETD.	ISSUE PRICE	*QUOTE U.S.$
1999 Melody	Open		24.95	25

Heroes of Baseball-Porcelain Baseball Cards - N/A

YEAR ISSUE	EDITION LIMIT	YEAR RETD.	ISSUE PRICE	*QUOTE U.S.$
1990 Brooks Robinson	Open		19.50	20
1991 Casey Stengel	Open		19.50	20
1990 Duke Snider	Open		19.50	20
1991 Ernie Banks	Open		19.50	20
1991 Gil Hodges	Open		19.50	20
1991 Jackie Robinson	Open		19.50	20
1991 Mickey Mantle	Open		19.50	20
1990 Roberto Clemente	Open		19.50	20
1991 Satchel Page	Open		19.50	20
1991 Whitey Ford	Open		19.50	20
1990 Willie Mays	Open		19.50	20
1991 Yogi Berra	Open		19.50	20

I Love Lucy Figurine Collection - N/A

YEAR ISSUE	EDITION LIMIT	YEAR RETD.	ISSUE PRICE	*QUOTE U.S.$
1999 Lucy's Rhumba	95-day		39.95	40

International Santa - N/A

YEAR ISSUE	EDITION LIMIT	YEAR RETD.	ISSUE PRICE	*QUOTE U.S.$
1995 Alpine Santa	Closed	1999	55.00	55
1993 Belsnickel	Closed	1999	55.00	55
1995 Dedushka Moroz	Closed	1999	55.00	55
1992 Father Christmas	Closed	1999	55.00	55
1992 Grandfather Frost	Closed	1999	55.00	55
1993 Jolly Old St. Nick	Closed	1999	55.00	55
1993 Kris Kringle	Closed	1999	55.00	55
1994 Pére Nöel	Closed	1999	55.00	55
1992 Santa Claus	Closed	1999	55.00	55
1994 Yuletide Santa	Closed	1999	55.00	55

Jeff Gordon Good Ole Bears Figurines - B. Cleaver

YEAR ISSUE	EDITION LIMIT	YEAR RETD.	ISSUE PRICE	*QUOTE U.S.$
1999 Double Duty	Open		19.95	20
1999 Gassin' Around	Open		19.95	20
1999 The Intimidator	Open		19.95	20
1999 Need A Lift!	Open		19.95	20
1999 Rear Tire Changer	Open		19.95	20

Jeweled Carousel - M. Griffin

YEAR ISSUE	EDITION LIMIT	YEAR RETD.	ISSUE PRICE	*QUOTE U.S.$
1996 Amethyst Jumper	Open		55.00	55
1996 Diamond Dancer	Open		55.00	55
1996 Emerald Stander	Open		55.00	55
1996 Ruby Prancer	Open		55.00	55
1995 Sapphire Jumper	Open		55.00	55
1997 Topaz Trotter	Open		55.00	55

Little Friends of the Arctic - M. Adams

YEAR ISSUE	EDITION LIMIT	YEAR RETD.	ISSUE PRICE	*QUOTE U.S.$
1995 The Young Prince	Open		37.50	38
1995 Princely Fishing	Closed	N/A	37.50	38-75
1996 Playful Prince	Closed	N/A	37.50	38-75
1996 Snoozing Prince	Open		37.50	38
1996 Princely Disguise	Closed	N/A	37.50	50-75
1996 Slippery Prince	Closed	N/A	37.50	38-75
1996 Prince Charming	Closed	N/A	37.50	50
1996 Prince of the Mountain	Closed	N/A	37.50	38-75
1996 Frisky Prince	Closed	N/A	37.50	38
1996 Dreamy Prince	Closed	N/A	37.50	38-75

Little Messengers - P. Parkins

YEAR ISSUE	EDITION LIMIT	YEAR RETD.	ISSUE PRICE	*QUOTE U.S.$
1997 Cleanliness Is Next To Godliness	Closed	N/A	29.95	30-135
1997 Let Your Light Shine Before All	Closed	N/A	29.95	30-125
1997 Love Is Contagious	Closed	N/A	29.95	30-135
1996 Love Is Happiness	Closed	N/A	29.95	30-135
1997 Love Is Harmony	Closed	N/A	29.95	30-150
1996 Love Is Kind	Closed	N/A	29.95	30-135
1997 Love Is Sharing	Closed	N/A	29.95	30-125
1997 Love Knows No Bounds	Closed	N/A	29.95	30-125
1996 Practice Makes Perfect	Closed	N/A	29.95	30-135
1996 Pretty Is As Pretty Does	Closed	N/A	29.95	30-135
1997 Seek And You Shall Find	Closed	N/A	29.95	30-135
1996 Love Is Patient	Closed	N/A	29.95	30-135

Little Messengers Heavenly Gardeners - P. Parkins

YEAR ISSUE	EDITION LIMIT	YEAR RETD.	ISSUE PRICE	*QUOTE U.S.$
1998 Enjoy The Fruits of Your Labors	Open		19.95	20
1997 He Showers Us With Blessings	Open		19.95	20
1998 His Love Gives Life	Open		19.95	20
1998 Plant the Seeds of Love	Open		19.95	20
1998 Sweet Rewards	Open		19.95	20
1998 We Reap What We Sow	Open		19.95	20

Little Night Owls - D.T. Lyttleton

YEAR ISSUE	EDITION LIMIT	YEAR RETD.	ISSUE PRICE	*QUOTE U.S.$
1990 Barn Owl	Open		45.00	45
1991 Barred Owl	Open		45.00	45
1991 Great Grey Owl	Open		45.00	45
1991 Great Horned Owl	Open		45.00	45
1991 Short-Eared Owl	Open		45.00	45
1990 Snowy Owl	Open		45.00	45
1990 Tawny Owl	Open		45.00	45
1991 White-Faced Owl	Open		45.00	45

A Maiden's Path - S. Kerhli

YEAR ISSUE	EDITION LIMIT	YEAR RETD.	ISSUE PRICE	*QUOTE U.S.$
1999 Dreams in the Wind	Open		39.95	40
1999 Gentle Winds of Love	Open		39.95	40

Makin' A Splash - B. Cleaver

YEAR ISSUE	EDITION LIMIT	YEAR RETD.	ISSUE PRICE	*QUOTE U.S.$
1998 Splashin' Around	N/A		17.95	18
1998 Chill'n Good Time	N/A		17.95	18
1998 Bathin' Time	Open		17.95	18
1998 Frolicin' Fun	Open		17.95	18
1998 Coolin' Off	Open		17.95	18
1998 Singin' in the Snow	Open		17.95	18
1998 A Sprinklin' of Fun	Open		17.95	18
1998 Catchin' A Wave	Open		17.95	18

Masters of the Evening Wilderness - N/A

YEAR ISSUE	EDITION LIMIT	YEAR RETD.	ISSUE PRICE	*QUOTE U.S.$
1994 The Great Snowy Owl	Open		37.50	38
1995 Autumn Barn Owls	Open		37.50	38
1995 Great Grey Owl	Open		37.50	38
1995 Great Horned Owl	Open		37.50	38
1996 Barred Owl	Open		37.50	38
1996 Screech Owl	Open		37.50	38
1996 Burrowing Owl	Open		37.50	38
1996 Eagle Owl	Open		37.50	38

Messenger of the Sky - S. Kerhli

YEAR ISSUE	EDITION LIMIT	YEAR RETD.	ISSUE PRICE	*QUOTE U.S.$
1999 Guardian of Dreams	95-day		49.95	50

Mickey Mantle Collector's Edition-Porcelain Baseball Cards - N/A

YEAR ISSUE	EDITION LIMIT	YEAR RETD.	ISSUE PRICE	*QUOTE U.S.$
1995 1952 Card #311/1969 Card #500	Open		39.90	40
1996 1956 Card #135/1965 Card #350	Open		39.90	40
1996 1953 Card #82/1964 Card #50	Open		39.90	40
1996 1957 Card #95/1959 Card #10	Open		39.90	40
1996 1958 Card #150/1962 Card #318	Open		39.90	40
1996 1959 Card #564/1961 Card #300	Open		39.90	40

Mickey Mantle Figurine Collection - N/A

YEAR ISSUE	EDITION LIMIT	YEAR RETD.	ISSUE PRICE	*QUOTE U.S.$
1995 Mickey Swings Home	Open		45.00	45-75
1996 The Switch Hitter Connects	Open		45.00	45
1996 The Ultimate Switch Hitter	Open		45.00	45
1996 On Deck	Open		45.00	45
1996 Bunting From the Left	Open		45.00	45

Mickey Mantle Sculpture - N/A

YEAR ISSUE	EDITION LIMIT	YEAR RETD.	ISSUE PRICE	*QUOTE U.S.$
1996 Tribute to a Yankee Legend	Open		195.00	195

Mother's Instinct - W. Henry

YEAR ISSUE	EDITION LIMIT	YEAR RETD.	ISSUE PRICE	*QUOTE U.S.$
1997 Mother's First Born	Closed	1999	17.95	18
1998 Mother's Guidance	Open		17.95	18
1997 Mother's Inspiration	Closed	1999	17.95	18
1998 Mother's Love	Open		17.95	18
1997 Mother's Warmth	Closed	1999	17.95	18
1997 Nourishing Mother	Open		17.95	18
1997 Picked Just For Mother	Closed	1999	17.95	18
1997 A Song For Mother	Closed	1999	17.95	18

Mystic Spirits - S. Douglas

YEAR ISSUE	EDITION LIMIT	YEAR RETD.	ISSUE PRICE	*QUOTE U.S.$
1995 Spirit of the Wolf	Closed	N/A	55.00	55-100
1995 Spirit of the Buffalo	Closed	N/A	55.00	55-100
1995 Spirit of the Golden Eagle	Closed	N/A	55.00	55
1996 Spirit of the Bear	Closed	N/A	55.00	55
1996 Spirit of the Mountain Lion	Closed	N/A	55.00	55-100
1996 Hawk Dancer	Open		55.00	55
1996 Wolf Scout	Closed	N/A	55.00	55
1996 Spirit of the Deer	Closed	N/A	55.00	55-99

Mystic Wolf Arrowhead - R. Koni

YEAR ISSUE	EDITION LIMIT	YEAR RETD.	ISSUE PRICE	*QUOTE U.S.$
1999 Twilight's Watch	Open		39.95	40
1999 Moonlit Run	Open		39.95	40
1999 Sunset Sentinel	Open		39.95	40
1999 Starlit Song	Open		39.95	40

Mystical Dreams - N/A

YEAR ISSUE	EDITION LIMIT	YEAR RETD.	ISSUE PRICE	*QUOTE U.S.$
1999 Maiden's Dream	Open		39.95	40
1999 Path of Hope	Open		39.95	40
1999 Promise of Love	Open		39.95	40

Nature's Beautiful Bonds - R. Roberts

YEAR ISSUE	EDITION LIMIT	YEAR RETD.	ISSUE PRICE	*QUOTE U.S.$
1996 A Mother's Vigil	Closed	N/A	29.95	30
1996 A Moment's Peace	Closed	N/A	29.95	30
1996 A Warm Embrace	Closed	N/A	29.95	30
1996 Safe By Mother's Side	Closed	N/A	29.95	30
1996 Curious Cub	Closed	N/A	29.95	30
1996 Under Mother's Watchful Eye	Closed	N/A	29.95	30-55
1996 Time To Rest	Closed	N/A	29.95	30
1996 Sheltered From Harm	Closed	N/A	29.95	30

Nature's Little Cherubs - J. Smith

YEAR ISSUE	EDITION LIMIT	YEAR RETD.	ISSUE PRICE	*QUOTE U.S.$
1997 Cherub of the Birds	Open		17.95	18
1997 Cherub of the Creatures	Open		17.95	18
1997 Cherub of the Flowers	Open		17.95	18
1997 Cherub of the Forest	Open		17.95	18
1997 Cherub of the Night	Open		17.95	18
1997 Cherub of the Stars	Open		17.95	18
1997 Cherub of the Sun	Open		17.95	18
1997 Cherub of the Waters	Open		17.95	18

Nature's Majestic Cats - D. Geenty

YEAR ISSUE	EDITION LIMIT	YEAR RETD.	ISSUE PRICE	*QUOTE U.S.$
1995 Tigress and Cubs	Closed	1999	55.00	55-99
1995 White Tiger & Cubs	Closed	1999	55.00	55
1996 Cougar and Cubs	Closed	1999	55.00	55-99
1996 Pride of the Lioness	Closed	1999	55.00	55-99
1996 Bobcat & Cubs	Closed	1999	55.00	55
1996 Jaguar & Cubs	Closed	1999	55.00	55
1996 Cheetah & Cubs	Closed	1999	55.00	55

Nature's Spiritual Realm - S. Kerhli

YEAR ISSUE	EDITION LIMIT	YEAR RETD.	ISSUE PRICE	*QUOTE U.S.$
1998 Spirit of the Earth	Open		69.00	69
1998 Spirit of the Fire	Open		69.00	69
1998 Spirit of the Water	Open		69.00	69
1997 Spirit of the Wind	Open		69.00	69

Nesting Instincts - R. Willis

YEAR ISSUE	EDITION LIMIT	YEAR RETD.	ISSUE PRICE	*QUOTE U.S.$
1995 By Mother's Side	Closed	1999	19.50	20
1995 Learning to Fly	Open		19.50	20
1995 Like Mother, Like Son	Closed	1999	19.50	20
1995 A Mother's Pride	Closed	1999	19.50	20
1997 Out on a Limb	Open		19.50	20
1995 Peaceful Perch	Closed	1999	19.50	20
1995 Safe and Sound	Open		19.50	20
1997 Two of a Kind	Closed	1999	19.50	20
1995 Under Mother's Wings	Closed	1999	19.50	20-55
1995 A Watchful Eye	Closed	1999	19.50	20-55

Noah's Endearing Mates - E. Harris

YEAR ISSUE	EDITION LIMIT	YEAR RETD.	ISSUE PRICE	*QUOTE U.S.$
1997 Chimpanzee Mates	Closed	1999	19.90	20-125
1997 Cow Mates	Closed	1999	19.90	20
1997 Elephant Mates	Open		19.90	20
1997 Giraffe Mates	Open		19.90	20
1997 Lion Mates	Closed	1999	19.90	55
1997 Panda Mates	Closed	1999	19.90	20-125
1997 Penguin Mates	Closed	1999	19.90	20
1997 Pig Mates	Closed	1999	19.90	20
1997 Polar Bear Mates	Closed	1999	19.90	20-125
1997 Tiger Mates	Open		19.90	20
1997 Wolf Mates	Closed	1999	19.90	20
1997 Zebra Mates	Closed	1999	19.90	20

Noble American Indian Women - N/A

YEAR ISSUE	EDITION LIMIT	YEAR RETD.	ISSUE PRICE	*QUOTE U.S.$
1994 Falling Star	Closed	1999	55.00	55
1995 Lily of the Mohawks	Closed	1999	55.00	55
1995 Lozen	Open		55.00	55
1994 Minnehaha	Closed	1999	55.00	55
1994 Pine Leaf	Closed	1999	55.00	55
1995 Pocahontas	Closed	1999	55.00	55
1993 Sacajawea	Closed	1999	55.00	55
1993 White Rose	Closed	1999	55.00	55-95

Noble Destiny - D. Geenty

YEAR ISSUE	EDITION LIMIT	YEAR RETD.	ISSUE PRICE	*QUOTE U.S.$
1999 Noble Destiny	Open		195.00	195

Noble Heritage - N/A

YEAR ISSUE	EDITION LIMIT	YEAR RETD.	ISSUE PRICE	*QUOTE U.S.$
1999 Tribal Guardians	Open		39.95	40

The Noble Swan - G. Granget

YEAR ISSUE	EDITION LIMIT	YEAR RETD.	ISSUE PRICE	*QUOTE U.S.$
1985 The Noble Swan	5,000		295.00	295

Noble Warriors - N/A

YEAR ISSUE	EDITION LIMIT	YEAR RETD.	ISSUE PRICE	*QUOTE U.S.$
1993 Deliverance	Open		135.00	135
1994 Spirit of the Plains	Open		135.00	135
1995 Top Gun	Open		135.00	135
1995 Windrider	Open		135.00	135

The Nolan Ryan Collectors Edition-Porcelain Baseball Cards - N/A

YEAR ISSUE	EDITION LIMIT	YEAR RETD.	ISSUE PRICE	*QUOTE U.S.$
1993 Angels 1972-C #595	Open		19.50	20
1993 Astros 1985-C #7	Open		19.50	20

*Quotes have been rounded up to nearest dollar

FIGURINES

YEAR ISSUE	EDITION LIMIT	YEAR RETD.	ISSUE PRICE	*QUOTE U.S.$
1993 Mets 1968-C #177	Open		19.50	20
1993 Mets 1969-C #533	Open		19.50	20
1993 Rangers 1990-C #1	Open		19.50	20
1993 Rangers 1992-C #1	Open		19.50	20
North Pole Bears - T. Newsom				
1996 All I Want For Christmas	Open		29.95	30
1996 Beary Best Snowman	Open		29.95	30
1996 Beary Started	Open		29.95	30
1996 Papa's Cozy Chair	Open		29.95	30
Ocean Odyssey - W. Youngstrom				
1995 Breaching the Waters	Closed	N/A	55.00	55-100
1995 Return to Paradise	Closed	N/A	55.00	55-95
1995 Riding the Waves	Closed	N/A	55.00	55
1996 Baja Bliss	Closed	N/A	55.00	55
1996 Arctic Blue	Closed	N/A	55.00	55
1996 Splashdown	Closed	N/A	55.00	55-95
1996 Free Spirit	Closed	N/A	55.00	55-95
1996 Beluga Belles	Closed	N/A	55.00	55
Owls in Your Big Back Yard - N/A				
1998 Autumn Harvest	Closed	2000	17.95	18
1998 Closed for the Season	Closed	2000	17.95	18
1998 Desert Watch	Closed	2000	17.95	18
1998 Harvest Splendor	Closed	2000	17.95	18
1998 Sandhill Lookout	Closed	2000	17.95	18
1998 Spirit of the Woods	Closed	2000	17.95	18
Pals of the Month - M. Adams				
1997 Back to School	Open		14.95	15
1997 Batter Up	Open		14.95	15
1997 Be Mine, Sweet Valentine	Open		14.95	15
1997 Bringing in the New Year	Open		14.95	15
1997 Have Yourself a Merry Xmas	Open		14.95	15
1997 July on Parade	Open		14.95	15
1997 Let's Give Thanks	Open		14.95	15
1997 Making the Grade	Open		14.95	15
1997 Singing in the Rain	Open		14.95	15
1997 Spring is Sprung	Open		14.95	15
1997 Trick or Treat	Open		14.95	15
1997 You're My Lucky Charm	Open		14.95	15
Peacemakers - S. Kerhli				
2000 Path of the Bear	Open		39.95	40
1999 Path of the Buffalo	Open		39.95	40
2000 Path of the Eagle	Open		39.95	40
1999 Path of the Wolf	Open		39.95	40
Peanut Pals - T. Newsom				
1996 All Aboard!	Open		19.95	20
1997 Feline Frolic	Closed	1999	19.95	20
1996 Having a Ball	Open		19.95	20
1997 The One That Got Away	Closed	1999	19.95	20
1997 Over The Bunny Slopes	Closed	1999	19.95	20
1997 Saturday Night	Closed	1999	19.95	20
1996 Shall I Pour?	Closed	1999	19.95	20-55
1997 Sidewalk Speedster	Open		19.95	20
1997 Sidewalk Surfin'	Closed	1999	19.95	20
1997 A Slice of Fun	Closed	1999	19.95	20
1996 Teeter Totter Fun!	Open		19.95	20
Polar Playmates - M. Adams				
1997 Belly Floppin'	Closed	1999	14.95	15
1997 Dreamin' Away	Closed	1999	14.95	15
1996 Goin' Fishin'	Closed	1999	14.95	15
1997 Hide'n & A Seek'n	Open		14.95	15
1997 Kickin' Back	Open		14.95	15
1996 Look Who's Nappin'	Closed	1999	14.95	15
1997 Lookin' Out	Open		14.95	15
1997 Reachin' for the Stars	Closed	1999	14.95	15-49
1996 Slip'n & Slide'n	Open		14.95	15
1997 Star Gazen'	Closed	1999	14.95	15-49
1997 Strollin' Along	Open		14.95	15
1997 Touchin' Toes	Open		14.95	15
Polar Playmates Playroom - N/A				
1998 Just Ducky	Open		17.95	18
1998 Lazy Days	Open		17.95	18
1998 Let's Have a Ball	Open		17.95	18
1998 Play Time	Open		17.95	18
1998 Snack Time	Open		17.95	18
1998 Sweet Rewards	Open		17.95	18
1998 Time Out With Teddy	Open		17.95	18
1998 Up, Up and Away	Open		17.95	18
Portraits of Christ - Inspired by the Art of Warner Saltman				
1997 Christ At Dawn	Closed	N/A	49.95	60
1996 His Presence	Closed	N/A	49.95	60-85
1997 Jesus, The Children's Friend	Closed	N/A	49.95	50-85
1997 Jesus, The Light of the World	Closed	N/A	49.95	50-85
1997 The Lord Is My Shepherd	Closed	N/A	49.95	75-99
1997 The Lord's Supper	Closed	N/A	49.95	50-100
Prayer of the Warrior - N/A				
1998 Buffalo Prayer	Closed	N/A	75.00	75
1997 Protector of Dreams	Closed	N/A	75.00	75
1997 Proud Dreamer	Closed	N/A	55.00	55
1997 Shield of Courage	Closed	N/A	75.00	75
1998 Victory of Prayer	Closed	N/A	75.00	75
Princess of the Plains - N/A				
1995 Mountain Princess	Open		55.00	55
1995 Nature's Guardian	Closed	2000	55.00	55
1995 Noble Beauty	Closed	2000	55.00	55

YEAR ISSUE	EDITION LIMIT	YEAR RETD.	ISSUE PRICE	*QUOTE U.S.$
1994 Noble Guardian	Closed	2000	55.00	55
1995 Proud Dreamer	Closed	2000	55.00	55
1994 Snow Princess	Closed	2000	55.00	55
1994 Wild Flower	Closed	2000	55.00	55
1995 Winter's Rose	Closed	2000	55.00	55
Protect Nature's Innocents I - R. Manning				
1995 African Elephant	Closed	1999	14.95	15
1995 Giant Panda	Closed	1999	14.95	15
1995 Snow Leopard	Closed	1999	14.95	15
1995 Rhinoceros	Open		14.95	15
1996 Orangutan	Open		14.95	15
1996 Key Deer	Open		14.95	15
1996 Bengal Tiger	Closed	1999	14.95	15
1996 Pygmy Hippo	Open		14.95	15
1996 Gray Wolf	Open		14.95	15
1996 Fur Seal	Closed	1999	14.95	15
1996 Gray Kangaroo	Closed	1999	14.95	15
1996 Sea Otter	Closed	1999	14.95	15
Protect Nature's Innocents II - R. Manning				
1998 Napping Time	Open		14.95	15
1998 Holding On	Open		14.95	15
1998 Wanna Ride?	Open		14.95	15
1999 Cooling Off	Closed	1999	14.95	15
1999 Butterfly Kisses	Open		14.95	15
1999 Mud Bath	Open		14.95	15
Proud Chieftains - N. Rose				
1999 Spirit Quest	Open		39.95	40
1999 Sacred Journey	Open		39.95	40
Puppy Playtime Sculpture Collection - J. Lamb				
1991 Cabin Fever	Closed	N/A	29.50	30
1991 Catch of the Day	Closed	N/A	29.50	30
1990 Double Take	Closed	N/A	29.50	30
1991 Fun and Games	Closed	N/A	29.50	30
1991 Getting Acquainted	Closed	N/A	29.50	30
1991 Hanging Out	Closed	N/A	29.50	30
1991 A New Leash on Life	Closed	N/A	29.50	30
1991 Weekend Gardner	Closed	N/A	29.50	30
Rainbow Dreams Lessons in Magic - T. Fabrizio				
1999 Flying Lesson	Open		24.95	25
1999 Moonstruck	Open		24.95	25
1999 Rising Star	Open		24.95	25
Rainbow Dreams Sweethearts - T. Fabrizio				
1999 The Courtship	Open		29.90	30
2000 Delicate Blossom	Open		31.90	32
1999 First Glance	Open		29.90	30
2000 Season of Love	Open		31.90	32
1999 Tender Love	Open		31.90	32
Rainbow Dreams Unicorn - T. Fabrizio				
1998 Butterflies and Rainbow Skies	Open		14.95	15
1998 Where Bluebirds Fly	Open		14.95	15
1998 Meadowland Dreams	Open		14.95	15
1999 Moonbeam Dreams	Open		17.95	18
1999 Dreams Come True	Open		17.95	18
1999 Dreams Take Flight	Open		19.95	20
1999 Field of Dreams	Open		19.95	20
1999 Lazy Day Dreaming	Open		19.95	20
1999 Run with Your Dreams	Open		19.95	20
Rainbow Reef - T. Fabrizio				
1998 Buried Treasure	Open		29.95	30
1999 Castles Under the Sea	Open		29.95	30
1999 Emerald Sea	Open		29.95	30
1999 Fantasy Ride	Open		29.95	30
1998 Friends of the Sea	Open		29.95	30
1998 Splash 'N Around	Open		29.95	30
1999 Twinkling Nights	Open		29.95	30
1999 Undersea Pals	Open		29.95	30
Realm of the Spirits - N/A				
1999 Vision from Above	Open		39.95	40
Ringling Bros. Circus Animals - P. Cozzolino				
1983 Acrobatic Seal	9,800	1999	49.50	50
1983 Baby Elephant	9,800	1999	49.50	55
1983 Miniature Show Horse	9,800	1999	49.50	68-75
1983 Mr. Chimpanzee	9,800	1999	49.50	50
1984 Parade Camel	9,800	1999	49.50	50
1983 Performing Poodles	9,800	1999	49.50	50
1984 Roaring Lion	9,800	1999	49.50	50
1983 Skating Bear	9,800	1999	49.50	50
Sacred Councils - S. Kerhli				
1999 Sacred Circle of the Wolf	Open		39.95	40
Sacred Crafts - N/A				
1999 Portrait of Power	Open		39.95	40
Sacred Cultures - S. Kerhli				
1998 Bravery	Open		39.95	40
1998 Courage	Open		39.95	40
1998 Protector	Open		39.95	40
1998 Strength	Open		39.95	40
1998 Vision	Open		39.95	40
1998 Wisdom	Open		39.95	40
The Sacred Village - S. Kerhli				
2000 Artist's Way	Open		39.95	40
1999 Chieftain's World	Open		39.95	40
1999 Hunter's Realm	Open		39.95	40

YEAR ISSUE	EDITION LIMIT	YEAR RETD.	ISSUE PRICE	*QUOTE U.S.$
2000 Shaman's Secrets	Open		39.95	40
Santa Clothtique - Possible Dreams				
1992 Checking His List	Open		95.00	95
1993 Last Minute Details	Open		95.00	95
1993 Twas the Nap Before Christmas	Open		95.00	95
1994 Upon the Rooftop	Open		95.00	95
1994 O Tannenbaum!	Open		95.00	95
1995 Baking Christmas Cheer	Open		95.00	95
1995 Santa to the Rescue	Open		95.00	95
1996 Toyshop Tally	Open		95.00	95
Seeing Spots - J. Smith				
1997 Spot Finds a Snowman	Open		19.95	20
1997 Spot Gets A Boo-Boo	Open		19.95	20
1997 Spot Gets Caught	Open		19.95	20
1997 Spot Goes Camping	Open		19.95	20
1997 Spot Goes On A Picnic	Open		19.95	20
1997 Spot Goes Sledding	Open		19.95	20
1997 Spot Plays With Fire Truck	Open		19.95	20
1997 Spot Sees A Crab	Open		19.95	20
1996 Spot Takes A Bath	Open		19.95	20
1997 Spot Takes A Nap	Open		19.95	20
1996 Spot Takes A Ride	Open		19.95	20
1997 Spot Visits Friends	Open		19.95	20
Shield of the Mighty Warrior - S. Kerhli				
1995 Spirit of the Grey Wolf	Closed	1999	45.00	45
1996 Spirit of the Bear	Open		45.00	45
1996 Protection of the Cougar	Open		45.00	45
1996 Protection of the Buffalo	Open		45.00	45
1996 Protection of the Bobcat	Open		45.00	45
1996 Protection of the Gray Wolf	Closed	1999	45.00	45
Snuggle - N/A				
1999 A Basket Full of Sweet Snuggles	Open		17.95	18
1999 Cleanliness is Next to Snuggliness	Open		17.95	18
1998 I Want to be Your Snuggle Bear	Open		14.95	15
1998 Peek-a-boo, Snuggle Loves You	Open		14.95	15
1999 Snuggle Hugs	Open		17.95	18
1999 Snuggle Loves Butterfly Kisses	Open		17.95	18
1999 Snuggle's Story Time	Open		17.95	18
1999 Sweet Dreams, Snuggle	Open		17.95	18
Soul of Nature - R. Sun				
1999 Eyes of Wisdom	Open		39.95	40
Spirit Messengers - S. Kerhli				
1999 Message of Hope	Open		59.95	60
Spirit of the Eagle - T. Sullivan				
1994 Spirit of Independence	Open		55.00	55
1995 Blazing Majestic Skies	Open		55.00	55
1995 Noble and Free	Open		55.00	55
1995 Proud Symbol of Freedom	Open		55.00	55
1996 Legacy of Freedom	Open		55.00	55
1996 Protector of Liberty	Open		55.00	55
Spirit of the Talisman - J. Pitcher				
1999 Dawn's Majesty	Open		39.95	40
2000 Sacred Flight	Open		39.95	40
2000 Soaring Spirits	Open		39.95	40
2000 Windswept	Open		39.95	40
STAR TREK®: First Contact: The Battle Begins - M.D. Ward				
1998 U.S.S. Defiant	Closed	1999	39.95	40
1998 Borg Cube	Closed	1999	39.95	40
1998 U.S.S. Enterprise NCC-1701E	Closed	1999	39.95	40
1998 Borg Sphere	Closed	1999	39.95	40
STAR TREK®: The Next Generation-Porcelain Cards - S. Hillios				
1996 Deanna Troi & Data	Closed	1998	39.90	40
1997 Inner Light & All Good Things	Closed	1998	39.90	40
1996 Jean-Luc Picard & Q	Closed	1998	39.90	40
1996 Ship In a Bottle & Best of Both Worlds	Closed	1998	39.90	40
1996 USS Enterprise NCC-1701-D & William T. Riker	Closed	1998	39.90	40
1997 Worf & Klingon Bird-of-Prey	Closed	1998	39.90	40
STAR TREK®: The Voyagers-Porcelain Cards - K. Birdsong				
1996 Klingon Bird-of-Prey & Cardassian Galor Warship	28-day	1998	39.90	40
1996 Triple Nacelled USS Enterprise & USS Excelsior	28-day	1998	39.90	40
1996 USS Enterprise NCC-1701 & Klingon Battlecruiser	28-day	1998	39.90	40
1996 USS Enterprise NCC-1701-A & Ferengi Marauder	28-day	1998	39.90	40
1996 USS Enterprise NCC-1701-D & Romulan Warbird	28-day	1998	39.90	40
1996 USS Voyager NCC-74656 & USS Defiant NX-74205	28-day	1998	39.90	40
Star Wars: A New Hope-Porcelain Cards - N/A				
1996 Good Versus Evil & Leia's Rescue	28-day	1999	39.90	40
1996 Hiding the Plans & Viewing the Hologram	28-day	1999	39.90	40
1996 In A Tight Spot & Millennium Falcon	28-day	1999	39.90	40
1996 Leia in Detention & Luke Skywalker	28-day	1999	39.90	40
1996 Millennium Falcon Cockpit & Capture of Leia's Ship	28-day	1999	39.90	40
1996 Obi Wan & Luke & A Daring Escape	28-day	1999	39.90	40
1996 Obi-wan Kenobi & C-3PO and R2-D2	28-day	1999	39.90	40
1996 Stormtroopers & X-Wing Attack	28-day	1999	39.90	40-100

*Quotes have been rounded up to nearest dollar

A Touch of Heaven - S. Kuck

YEAR ISSUE	EDITION LIMIT	YEAR RETD.	ISSUE PRICE	*QUOTE U.S.$
1997 Alexandra	Open		17.95	18
1998 Amanda	Open		17.95	18
1998 Brianna	Open		17.95	18
1998 Cassandra	Open		17.95	18
1998 Katherine	Open		17.95	18
1998 Miranda	Open		17.95	18
1998 Samantha	Open		17.95	18
1997 Victoria	Open		17.95	18

Tropical Treasures - M. Wald

YEAR ISSUE	EDITION LIMIT	YEAR RETD.	ISSUE PRICE	*QUOTE U.S.$
1990 Beaked Coral Butterfly Fish	Open		37.50	38
1990 Blue Girdled Angel Fish	Open		37.50	38
1989 Flag-tail Surgeonfish	Open		37.50	38
1989 Pennant Butterfly Fish	Open		37.50	38
1989 Sail-finned Surgeonfish	Open		37.50	38
1989 Sea Horse	Open		37.50	38
1990 Spotted Angel Fish	Open		37.50	38
1990 Zebra Turkey Fish	Open		37.50	38

Unbridled Spirits - C. DeHaan

YEAR ISSUE	EDITION LIMIT	YEAR RETD.	ISSUE PRICE	*QUOTE U.S.$
1994 Wild Fury	Open		135.00	135

Under The Sea Crystal Shell - R. Koni

YEAR ISSUE	EDITION LIMIT	YEAR RETD.	ISSUE PRICE	*QUOTE U.S.$
1997 Dolphin Dance	Open		29.95	30
1997 Fluid Grace	Open		29.95	30
1997 Manatee Minuet	Open		29.95	30
1997 Orca Ballet	Open		29.95	30
1997 Seahorse Samba	Open		29.95	30
1997 Slow Dance	Open		29.95	30
1997 Soft Serenade	Open		29.95	30
1997 Tropical Twist	Open		29.95	30

Visions of Christmas - M. Griffin

YEAR ISSUE	EDITION LIMIT	YEAR RETD.	ISSUE PRICE	*QUOTE U.S.$
1995 Gifts From St. Nick	Open		135.00	135
1994 Mrs. Claus' Kitchen	Open		135.00	135
1993 Santa's Delivery	Open		135.00	135
1993 Toys in Progress	Open		135.00	135

Warrior's Quest - S. Kerhli

YEAR ISSUE	EDITION LIMIT	YEAR RETD.	ISSUE PRICE	*QUOTE U.S.$
1996 Courage of the Bear	Open		95.00	95
1996 Cry of the Eagle	Open		95.00	95
1996 Power of the Buffalo	Open		95.00	95
1996 Strength of the Wolf	Open		95.00	95

Waterful Ways & Elephant Days - N/A

YEAR ISSUE	EDITION LIMIT	YEAR RETD.	ISSUE PRICE	*QUOTE U.S.$
1997 Back Splash	Closed	1999	17.95	18
1997 The Big Splash!	Open		19.95	20
1997 Catch of the Day	Open		19.95	20
1996 Clean Fun	Closed	1999	14.95	15
1997 How Does Your Garden Grow	Open		19.95	20
1997 Just Splashin' Ducky	Open		14.95	15
1997 Lazy Days	Open		19.95	20
1997 Merrily, Merrily	Open		19.95	20
1997 Rainy Day Splash	Closed	1999	19.95	20-45
1997 Sudsy Fun	Open		19.95	20
1997 Surfer Dude	Open		19.95	20
1997 Water Bathing Beauty	Open		17.95	18

The Way of the Warrior - J. Pyre

YEAR ISSUE	EDITION LIMIT	YEAR RETD.	ISSUE PRICE	*QUOTE U.S.$
1995 One With the Eagle	Open		45.00	45
1996 Star Shooter	Open		45.00	45
1996 Bear Warrior	Open		45.00	45
1996 Beckoning Back the Buffalo	Open		45.00	45
1996 Great Feather Warrior	Open		45.00	45
1996 Calling His Guardian	Open		45.00	45

Wild and Free - C. De Haan

YEAR ISSUE	EDITION LIMIT	YEAR RETD.	ISSUE PRICE	*QUOTE U.S.$
1996 Wild and Free	Open		195.00	195

The Wildlife Nursery - N/A

YEAR ISSUE	EDITION LIMIT	YEAR RETD.	ISSUE PRICE	*QUOTE U.S.$
1997 Go For A Ride, Mommy?	Open		14.95	15
1997 I Love My Doll, Mommy!	Open		14.95	15
1997 I'll Spell, Mommy!	Open		14.95	15
1997 I'm So Pretty, Mommy!	Open		14.95	15
1997 Mommy's Little Shaker	Open		14.95	15
1997 Mommy, Baby Go Boom	Open		14.95	15
1997 More Milk, Mommy	Open		14.95	15
1997 More Please, Mommy!	Open		14.95	15
1997 My Duck, Mommy!	Open		14.95	15
1997 Naptime, Mommy?	Open		14.95	15
1997 Pacify Me, Mommy!	Open		14.95	15
1997 Quiet Time, Mommy	Open		14.95	15

Wolf Spirit Crystal - A. Agnew

YEAR ISSUE	EDITION LIMIT	YEAR RETD.	ISSUE PRICE	*QUOTE U.S.$
1999 Eyes of Nature	Open		35.00	35
2000 Moonlit Cry	Open		35.00	35
2000 Noble Gaze	Open		35.00	35

Wolves of the Wilderness - D. Geenty

YEAR ISSUE	EDITION LIMIT	YEAR RETD.	ISSUE PRICE	*QUOTE U.S.$
1995 A Wolf's Pride	Open		55.00	55
1995 Mother's Watch	Open		55.00	55
1996 Time For Play	Open		55.00	55
1996 Morning Romp	Open		55.00	55
1996 First Adventure	Open		55.00	55
1996 Tumbling Twosome	Open		55.00	55
1997 Building Young Bonds	Open		55.00	55
1997 Timid Trio	Open		55.00	55
1997 Winter Hunter	Open		55.00	55

Harmony Kingdom

Teapots - P. Calvesbert & P. Cardew

YEAR ISSUE	EDITION LIMIT	YEAR RETD.	ISSUE PRICE	*QUOTE U.S.$
1999 Crackin' Brew	3,850	1999	225.00	250-453
1999 YT 42 HK	4,850	1999	250.00	250

Honeybourne Hollow/Fitz and Floyd Collectibles

Honeybourne Hollow - P. Sebern

YEAR ISSUE	EDITION LIMIT	YEAR RETD.	ISSUE PRICE	*QUOTE U.S.$
1999 B-e-e My Honey 27/108	Open		27.50	28
1999 Building Memories 27/107	Open		25.00	25
1999 Filled With Love 27/110	Open		27.50	28
2000 Filling Daddy's Shoes 27/115	Open		22.50	23
1999 Follow Your Dreams 27/100	5,000		25.00	25
1999 Friendship Keeps Us Warm 27/113	Open		25.00	25
2000 Happy Birthday (Musical) 27/120	Open		49.50	50
2000 Hush-A-Bye 27/117	Open		25.00	25
1999 I'd Follow You Anywhere 27/102	Open		22.50	23
1999 Moms Are Pretty Wonderful 27/103	Open		25.00	25
1999 Old Friends Are The Best Friends 27/106	Open		22.50	23
1999 Sending My Love 27/109	Open		25.00	25
1999 Sharing The Season 27/112	Open		25.00	25
1999 Sharing Warms The Heart 27/105	Open		25.00	25
1999 The Sky's The Limit 27/111	Open		22.50	23
2000 Special Friends Warm The Season 27/118	Open		25.00	25
1999 Time Is Precious (Millennium Ed.) 27/114	2,000		40.00	40
2000 Trick or Treat 27/116	Open		25.00	25
2000 We're Going Places (Musical) 27/119	Open		42.50	43
1999 Where Do We Go From Here? 27/101	Open		25.00	25
1999 You Take The Cake! 27/104	Open		22.50	23

Hot Wheels/Mattel

Channel Exclusives 1:64th Scale - Mattel

YEAR ISSUE	EDITION LIMIT	YEAR RETD.	ISSUE PRICE	*QUOTE U.S.$
2000 Car Craft Magazine 26266	Open		24.00	24
2000 Drive-In 27009	Open		36.00	36
2000 Gone in 60 Seconds 27838	Open		48.00	48
2000 Photo Finish 27839	Open		24.00	24

Channel Exclusives, 1:18th Scale - Mattel

YEAR ISSUE	EDITION LIMIT	YEAR RETD.	ISSUE PRICE	*QUOTE U.S.$
2000 Alt Channels 1969 Corvette (white & black) 27011	Open		40.00	40
2000 Alt Channels Custom 1957 Chevy (red w/white flames) 27010	Open		40.00	40

Ferrari Road Cars, 1:18th Scale - Mattel

YEAR ISSUE	EDITION LIMIT	YEAR RETD.	ISSUE PRICE	*QUOTE U.S.$
2000 1984 286 GTO 25731	Open		28.00	28
2000 Ferrari 1/18 Scale Millennium Asst. 25633	Open		50.00	50
2000 Ferrari 1984 Testarossa 25732	Open		28.00	28
2000 Ferrari 250 GT California Spider (burgundy) 25727	Open		28.00	28
2000 Ferrari 250 LM (yellow & #9) 25729	Open		28.00	28
2000 Ferrari 355 Berlinetta (recolor) 25735	Open		28.00	28
2000 Ferrari 360 Modena (yellow) 25736	Open		28.00	28
2000 Ferrari 360 Spider (red) 27774	Open		28.00	28
2000 Ferrari 365 GTS/4 (red) 25730	Open		28.00	28
2000 Ferrari 550 Maranello (dark red) 25734	Open		28.00	28
2000 Ferrari F 355 Spider (silver) 25733	Open		28.00	28
2000 Ferrari F50-Closed (yellow) 25728	Open		28.00	28

Ferrari Road Cars, 1:43rd Scale - Mattel

YEAR ISSUE	EDITION LIMIT	YEAR RETD.	ISSUE PRICE	*QUOTE U.S.$
2000 348 TB 25712	Open		16.00	16
2000 348 TS 25713	Open		16.00	16
2000 360 Medena 25720	Open		16.00	16
2000 365 GTS/4 25719	Open		16.00	16
2000 456 GT (red) 25711	Open		16.00	16
2000 F 335 GTS (dark silver) 25716	Open		16.00	16
2000 F 355 Berlinetta 25715	Open		16.00	16
2000 F 512M 25714	Open		16.00	16
2000 F40 (red) 25709	Open		16.00	16
2000 F40 Racing (yellow) 25710	Open		16.00	16
2000 F50-Coupe (silver) 25717	Open		16.00	16
2000 F50-Open 25718	Open		16.00	16

Hot Wheel Collectibles - Mattel

YEAR ISSUE	EDITION LIMIT	YEAR RETD.	ISSUE PRICE	*QUOTE U.S.$
1998 30th Anniversary of the Muscle Car Collection 18995	Retrd.	N/A	198.00	198
1997 40th Anniversary of 57 Chevy (4) 17401	Retrd.	N/A	48.00	48
1996 American Classics Giftset, set/3 16262	Retrd.	N/A	40.00	40
1997 Cadzilla Legends 17348	Retrd.	N/A	150.00	150
1998 Direct Marketing Hot Wheels Twin Mill 19305	Retrd.	N/A	150.00	150
1996 Hot Wheels Legends 1949 Mercury 14641	Retrd.	N/A	150.00	150
1996 Hot Wheels Legends Mongoose 18446	Retrd.	N/A	150.00	150
1997 Hot Wheels Legends Series Kellogg 17628	Retrd.	N/A	40.00	40
1998 Hot Wheels Legends to Life 18427	Retrd.	N/A	280.00	280
1997 JC Penney Hot Wheels 24 Caret Performance Pack 17221	Retrd.	N/A	89.98	90
1998 Legend to Life Twin Mill 19307	Retrd.	N/A	240.00	240
1997 Legends 40th Anniversary (4) 16452	Retrd.	N/A	150.00	150
1997 Pony Pack (3) 16986	Retrd.	N/A	36.00	36
1997 Snake Legends 17824	Retrd.	N/A	150.00	150
1997 Snake Legends To Life 17823	Retrd.	N/A	240.00	240
1997 Speigel Gold Plated Jet Propulsion Lab MarsRover 17987	Retrd.	N/A	49.98	50
1998 Vintage Signature Record Holders set/4 18621	Retrd.	N/A	150.00	150

Multi Car Sets 1:64th Scale - Mattel

YEAR ISSUE	EDITION LIMIT	YEAR RETD.	ISSUE PRICE	*QUOTE U.S.$
2000 30th Anniversary 1970 Muscle Cars, set/4 24887	Open		48.00	48
2000 Collectible Singles 20288	Open		10.00	10
2000 Cool N Custom, set/2 24553	Open		24.00	24
2000 Designer Dreamz, set/2 26079	Open		24.00	24
2000 Hard Rock II, set/3 27835	Open		36.00	36
2000 Harley Davidsons, set/4 25943	Open		24.00	24
2000 Holiday Hot Wheels, set/2	Open		24.00	24
2000 Hot Rod Magazine, set/4 24513	Open		48.00	48
2000 Night at the Races, set/2 24739	Open		24.00	24
2000 Xtreme Trucks, set/2 23787	Open		24.00	24

U.S. Road Cars, 1:18th Scale - Mattel

YEAR ISSUE	EDITION LIMIT	YEAR RETD.	ISSUE PRICE	*QUOTE U.S.$
2000 1950 Marc Woody (metallic burgundy) 26417	Open		28.00	28
2000 1950 Merc Woody (turquoise) 27806	Open		28.00	28
2000 1957 Chevy (purple & red flames) 27636	Open		28.00	28
2000 1965 Impala (white, red & green) 27635	Open		28.00	28
2000 1965 Impala Lowrider (purple & gold) 21354	Open		28.00	28
2000 1969 Corvette ZL1 (red) 27637	Open		28.00	28
2000 1969 Dodge Charger (orange) 27638	Open		28.00	28
2000 Corvette C5 (candy apple red) 25618	Open		28.00	28
2000 Harley Dyna Wide Glide (silver) 26442	Open		28.00	28
2000 Pantera 27809	Open		28.00	28
2000 VW Bus (white & blue w/flames) 26416	Open		28.00	28

U.S. Road Cars, 1:43rd Scale - Mattel

YEAR ISSUE	EDITION LIMIT	YEAR RETD.	ISSUE PRICE	*QUOTE U.S.$
2000 1932 Ford (red) 24783	Open		16.00	16
2000 1932 Ford (yellow) 27060	Open		16.00	16
2000 1955 Ford F-100 Hauler (blue & black/white/red) 25686	Open		16.00	16
2000 1955 Ford F-100 Panel Van (silver & red/blue) 25685	Open		16.00	16
2000 1955 Ford F-100 Pick-up Truck (red/purple) 25684	Open		16.00	16
2000 1965 Shelby GT350 (white & blue) 25559	Open		16.00	16
2000 1971 Plymouth GTX (green & black) 27062	Open		16.00	16
2000 1971 Plymouth GTX (orange & black) 25467	Open		16.00	16
2000 Shelby GT350 (red & white) 27061	Open		16.00	16
2000 Studebaker (blue w/white flames) 26398	Open		16.00	16
2000 Studebaker (white w/racing logos) 27063	Open		16.00	16

House of Hatten, Inc.

Amber Harvest - D. Calla

YEAR ISSUE	EDITION LIMIT	YEAR RETD.	ISSUE PRICE	*QUOTE U.S.$
1995 Elias Boy with Wild Turkey 15.5" 50550	Open		54.00	54
1995 Sarah Girl with Basket of Apples 14" 50551	Open		54.00	54
1995 Turkey 7" 50552	Open		35.00	35

American Folk Art - J. Bingham

YEAR ISSUE	EDITION LIMIT	YEAR RETD.	ISSUE PRICE	*QUOTE U.S.$
1995 Fireside Santa 36577	Retrd.	1995	210.00	210
1997 Ms. Jackie Lantern 13" 36785	Retrd.	1998	38.00	38
1995 Santa with Blocks 18" 36576	Retrd.	1996	180.00	180
1998 Santa with Coat of Red Stars 14" 36806	Retrd.	1998	70.00	70
1995 Santa with Train 20" 36575	Retrd.	1997	230.00	230
1998 Sleepy Santa with Red Reindeer 20" 36804	Retrd.	1998	74.00	74
1998 Sleepy Santa, green & red 15" 36807	Retrd.	1998	64.00	64
1995 Sleepytime Santa - Green 20" 36579	Retrd.	1996	130.00	130
1998 Snowman 18" 36808	Retrd.	1998	84.00	84
1995 Stars and Stripes Santa 16" 36581	Retrd.	1997	100.00	100
1995 Traditional Santa 17" 36583	Retrd.	1996	130.00	130
1995 Traditional Santa 26" 36578	Retrd.	1997	180.00	180
1995 Workshop Santa 16" 36580	Retrd.	1996	140.00	140

Angels Triumphant - D. Calla

YEAR ISSUE	EDITION LIMIT	YEAR RETD.	ISSUE PRICE	*QUOTE U.S.$
1998 Angel Cookie Wall Decoration 16"	Retrd.	1998	70.00	70
1998 Celestial Angel 21 1/2" 39851	5,000		150.00	150
1998 Keeper of the Christmas 12 1/2" 39855	Open		80.00	80
1998 Peaceable Kingdom 15 1/2" 39853	5,000		190.00	190
1998 Star Gazer Angel 7 1/2" 39859	Retrd.	1999	70.00	70
1998 Star Rider Angel 15" 39854	5,000	1999	180.00	180
1998 Star Struck Santa 18 1/2" 39852	Retrd.	1999	70.00	70

Belsnickle - D. Calla

YEAR ISSUE	EDITION LIMIT	YEAR RETD.	ISSUE PRICE	*QUOTE U.S.$
1995 Nick in Box 13.5" 31508	Retrd.	1997	130.00	130
1995 Santa in Red 9.5" 31514	Retrd.	1998	30.00	30
1995 Santa in Red 12.5" 31513	Retrd.	1998	36.00	36
1995 Santa in Red 15" 31512	Retrd.	1998	44.00	44
1995 Santa in White 9.5" 31519	Retrd.	1998	30.00	30
1995 Santa in White 12.5" 31518	Retrd.	1998	36.00	36
1995 Santa in White 15" 31517	Retrd.	1998	44.00	44
1995 Seated Musical Santa 31506	Retrd.	1995	130.00	130

Beyond the Garden Gate - D. Calla

YEAR ISSUE	EDITION LIMIT	YEAR RETD.	ISSUE PRICE	*QUOTE U.S.$
1994 Clover 9" 50402	Retrd.	1996	40.00	40
1994 Thistle 11.5" 50401	Open		40.00	40

The Bittersweets Harvest Collection - D. Calla

YEAR ISSUE	EDITION LIMIT	YEAR RETD.	ISSUE PRICE	*QUOTE U.S.$
2000 Bittersweet Acrobat 5.5" 50009	Open		12.00	12
2000 Bittersweet Broomhilda 11" 50001	Open		30.00	30

*Quotes have been rounded up to nearest dollar

YEAR ISSUE	EDITION LIMIT	YEAR RETD.	ISSUE PRICE	*QUOTE U.S.$
2000 Bittersweet Harvesting Pumpkins 7" 50003	Open		30.00	30
2000 Bittersweet in Pumpkin Wagon Ctrp. 7" 50002	Open		38.00	38
2000 Bittersweet Seated w/ Acorn 3" 50008	Open		10.00	10
2000 Bittersweet Standing 4" 5000+B207	Open		12.00	12
2000 Hob Goblin Shelf Sitter 6.5" 50005	Open		14.00	14
2000 Wee Bee Little Baby Pumpkin 4.5" 50004	Open		9.00	9

Bunny Pickin's - K.A. Walker

YEAR ISSUE	EDITION LIMIT	YEAR RETD.	ISSUE PRICE	*QUOTE U.S.$
1998 Albert Bunny 6" 54801	Retrd.	1999	6.00	6
1998 Bitsy Girl Bunny 3 1/2" 54804	Retrd.	1999	4.00	4

A Christmas Alphabet - V. & S. Rawson

YEAR ISSUE	EDITION LIMIT	YEAR RETD.	ISSUE PRICE	*QUOTE U.S.$
1998 Santa 15 1/2" 33800	Open		90.00	90

Christmas Messengers - V. & S. Rawson

YEAR ISSUE	EDITION LIMIT	YEAR RETD.	ISSUE PRICE	*QUOTE U.S.$
2000 Nursery Rhyme Sleigh 26965 6"	Open		14.00	14
1997 Patriotic Snowman 32756	Open		20.00	20
2000 Small Ark Centerpiece - Santa/Angel 27329 9"	Open		24.00	24
1998 Small Ark with Santa & Noah 4 1/4" 32850	Open		10.00	10
2000 Snowman Box - Blue 5" 27328	Open		10.00	10
2000 Snowman Box - Green 5" 27327	Open		10.00	10
2000 Snowman Box - Red 5" 27326	Open		10.00	10
2000 Snowman w/Toys Centerpiece 13" 27325	Open		50.00	50
1997 Snowman with Raccoon 32755	Retrd.	1999	20.00	20
1997 Snowman with Tree 32754	Retrd.	1999	20.00	20

Christmas Past - N. DeCamp

YEAR ISSUE	EDITION LIMIT	YEAR RETD.	ISSUE PRICE	*QUOTE U.S.$
1994 Burgundy Santa 20" 36450	Retrd.	1994	160.00	160
1994 Green Santa 16" 36451	Retrd.	1994	130.00	130
1998 Lace Santa 13" 36851	Retrd.	1999	160.00	160
1995 Lace Santa 20" 36552	Retrd.	1996	170.00	170
2000 Old Fashioned Santa w/child & Toys 27115 23"	Open		330.00	330
1995 Red Seated Santa 20" 36551	Retrd.	1995	130.00	130
1995 Santa in Car 15" 36553	Retrd.	1996	200.00	200
1999 Santa in Chimney 26781	Retrd.	1999	70.00	70
1996 Santa on Log with Children 13" 36657	Retrd.	1997	330.00	330
1999 Santa w/Children 26782	Open		220.00	220
1999 Santa w/Lantern 26780	Retrd.	1999	110.00	110
1995 Santa with Children Musical 22" 36550	Retrd.	1995	300.00	300
1996 Santa with Snowman 19" 36651	Retrd.	1996	250.00	250

Christmas Traditions - D.K. Wise

YEAR ISSUE	EDITION LIMIT	YEAR RETD.	ISSUE PRICE	*QUOTE U.S.$
1997 Father Christmas with Staff 12.5" 36751	Retrd.	1998	66.00	66
1997 North Pole Elf 13" 36752	Retrd.	1997	53.00	53
1997 Santa with Backpack 14" 36759	Retrd.	1998	82.50	83

Country Christmas - P.J. Hornberger

YEAR ISSUE	EDITION LIMIT	YEAR RETD.	ISSUE PRICE	*QUOTE U.S.$
1996 "Deliver What" Santa 13" 23651	Retrd.	1997	94.00	94
1996 "No Bows" Santa 14" 23652	Retrd.	1997	106.00	106
1997 Santa Riding Pig 33752	Retrd.	1997	110.00	110
1997 Santa Walking Pig 33753	Retrd.	1997	110.00	110
1997 Santa with Chicken and Sled 33751	Retrd.	1997	110.00	110

December Sky Spirit - D. Calla

YEAR ISSUE	EDITION LIMIT	YEAR RETD.	ISSUE PRICE	*QUOTE U.S.$
1991 Santa 16" 31153	Retrd.	1993	100.00	100

December's Bouquet - D. Calla

YEAR ISSUE	EDITION LIMIT	YEAR RETD.	ISSUE PRICE	*QUOTE U.S.$
2000 Candlebox w/ Acorns 14" x 4.5" x 6" 27554	Open		40.00	40
2000 Dove/Acorn Candlestick 10" 27553	Open		38.00	38
2000 Good Cheer Box w/ Acorns 3.5" x 3" x 1.5" 27555	Open		15.00	15
2000 Santa Centerpiece 19" 27550	Open		120.00	120
2000 St. Nick w/ Votive Centerpiece 16" 27552	Open		80.00	80

Easter - P. Bolinger

YEAR ISSUE	EDITION LIMIT	YEAR RETD.	ISSUE PRICE	*QUOTE U.S.$
2000 Bride Bunny 4.5" 50205	Open		10.00	10
2000 Carrot King Bunny w/ Cart 7" 50202	Open		20.00	20
2000 Groom Bunny 5" 50204	Open		10.00	10
2000 Hoe, Hoe, Hoe Bunny w/Seeds 8" 50200	Open		20.00	20
2000 Hop Til You Drop Bunny 8" 50203	Open		20.00	20
2000 Hop/Shop Bunny w/Stand Set/2 7" 50201	Open		20.00	20

Easter Parade - D. Calla

YEAR ISSUE	EDITION LIMIT	YEAR RETD.	ISSUE PRICE	*QUOTE U.S.$
1997 Bunny "Jack in the Box" 10" 52701	Retrd.	1999	58.00	58
1997 Bunny with Carrot 9" 52702	Retrd.	1998	32.00	32
1997 Eggstacy Bunny 10.5" 52710	Open		40.00	40
1997 Herb Farm Bunny 9" 52709	Retrd.	1999	45.00	45

Enchanted Forest - D. Calla

YEAR ISSUE	EDITION LIMIT	YEAR RETD.	ISSUE PRICE	*QUOTE U.S.$
1990 Christmas Comes 10" 31079	Retrd.	1992	170.00	170
1989 Elf with Goose Basket 31953	Retrd.	1993	46.00	46
1989 Good Cheer Elf 31956	Retrd.	1996	22.00	22
1993 Jolly Santa with Bear 16" 31354	Retrd.	1995	120.00	120
1990 Large Santa Tree 9" 31095	Retrd.	1999	12.00	12
1988 Nick in a Box 31851	Retrd.	1991	50.00	50
1990 Reindeer 9" 31081	Retrd.	1993	28.00	28
1988 Santa with Goose 9" 31852	Retrd.	1991	42.00	42
1988 Santa with Teddy 14" 31850	Open		95.00	95
1989 Seated Santa 9" 31955	Retrd.	1995	25.00	25
1990 Sleigh 10" 31080	Retrd.	1994	85.00	85
1990 Small Santa Tree 7" 31094	Retrd.	1999	9.00	9
1989 St. Nick and Forest Fawn 31951	Retrd.	1992	64.00	64
1989 St. Nick and Good Cheer Elf 31950	Retrd.	1991	80.00	80
1990 St. Nick on Reindeer 11" 31082	Retrd.	1992	66.00	66
1989 St. Nick with Goose Basket 31952	Retrd.	1997	55.00	55

Father Frost - D. Calla

YEAR ISSUE	EDITION LIMIT	YEAR RETD.	ISSUE PRICE	*QUOTE U.S.$
1991 Father Frost 14" 31131	Retrd.	1994	84.00	84

Fire & Ice - D. Calla

YEAR ISSUE	EDITION LIMIT	YEAR RETD.	ISSUE PRICE	*QUOTE U.S.$
1999 Fallen Skater Elf 26456	Open		40.00	40
1999 Gift Giver Snowman 26450	Open		70.00	70
1999 Good Cheer Enchanted Forest Santa 26466	Open		60.00	60
1999 Grateful Heart Angel Centerpiece 26467	Open		70.00	70
1999 Holly & Ivy Christmas Rabbit 26465	Open		100.00	100
1999 Jack Frost w/Votive 26451	Open		30.00	30
1999 Millenium Santa 26464	Open		110.00	110
1999 Snowman Skating 26459	Open		16.00	16
1999 Snowman-Feed the Birds 26457	Open		14.00	14
1999 Snowman-Wishing on a Star 26458	Open		14.00	14
1999 St. Nick in Skate 26453	Open		52.00	52
1999 St. Nick-Farewell Dear Friend 26455	Open		40.00	40
1999 St. Nick/Deer Reflections 26454	Open		40.00	40
1999 Winged Angel Mini Shelf Sitter 26468	Open		8.00	8
1999 Winged Santa Mini Shelf Sitter 26470	Open		8.00	8
1999 Winged Snowman Mini Shelf Sitter 26469	Open		8.00	8

Folk Art by P.J. - P.J. Hornberger

YEAR ISSUE	EDITION LIMIT	YEAR RETD.	ISSUE PRICE	*QUOTE U.S.$
1997 Bunny Gardener "It Could Happen" 56701	Retrd.	1997	56.00	56
1997 Colonel Sanders Bunny 56702	Retrd.	1997	56.00	56
1996 "Darn Rabbit" Chicken 53601	Retrd.	1998	40.00	40
1996 "Doin' My Part" Chicken 53604	Retrd.	1999	40.00	40
1996 "Good Day" Chicken 53602	Retrd.	1998	66.00	66
1997 "I Gotta Be Me" Chicken 56703	Retrd.	1999	40.00	40
1996 "Surely Not" Chicken 53603	Retrd.	1998	40.00	40
1997 "Texas Our Texas" Chicken 56704	Retrd.	1999	40.00	40

Four Seasons - D. Calla

YEAR ISSUE	EDITION LIMIT	YEAR RETD.	ISSUE PRICE	*QUOTE U.S.$
1996 Spring "Puddles" 50601	1,250	1999	90.00	90
1996 Summer "Melons" 50602	1,250	1999	90.00	90
1996 Fall "Cider" 50603	1,250		90.00	90
1996 Winter "Mistletoe" 50604	1,250		90.00	90

From Our House to Your House - D. Calla

YEAR ISSUE	EDITION LIMIT	YEAR RETD.	ISSUE PRICE	*QUOTE U.S.$
1991 Santa with Staff 11" 31106	Retrd.	1993	57.00	57

From Out of the North - R. Leeseberg

YEAR ISSUE	EDITION LIMIT	YEAR RETD.	ISSUE PRICE	*QUOTE U.S.$
1997 Adirondack Santa with Goose, set/2 34755	Retrd.	1998	50.00	50
2000 American West Santa 8 1/2" 34851	Retrd.	2000	20.00	20
1998 American West Santa 8 1/2" 34851	Retrd.	1999	18.00	18
1997 Bent Over Santa 8" 34753	Retrd.	1998	40.00	40
1998 Celestial Santa 13" 34850	Retrd.	1999	24.00	24
1997 Dream Catcher 7" 34754	Retrd.	1998	40.00	40
1999 Heart/Hand Santa 26548	Retrd.	1999	24.00	24
1998 HO Santa 7" 34857	Retrd.	2000	12.00	12
1998 Joy to the World, set/2 6 1/4" 34860	Retrd.	2000	12.00	12
1998 Keepsake Santa 7 1/2" 34852	Retrd.	1998	9.00	9
1999 Millenium Santa 26544	Retrd.	2000	38.00	38
1998 Moose 8 1/2" 34856	Retrd.	2000	15.00	15
1998 Moose Santa 7 1/2" 34855	Retrd.	2000	12.00	12
1997 Natureland Choir (set/8) 34771	Retrd.	1999	100.00	100
1998 Natureland Choir, set/5 34863	Retrd.	1999	15.00	15
1997 Noah's Ark, set/15 34770	Retrd.	2000	115.00	115
2000 Polar Bear/Santa 6" 27181	Retrd.	2000	16.00	16
1999 Red/White/Blue Santa w/Birdhouse 26543	Retrd.	2000	22.00	22
2000 Santa Has a Surprise 9" 27194	Retrd.	2000	20.00	20
1999 Santa Holding Moose 26551	Retrd.	2000	18.00	18
1999 Santa on Cardinal 26545	Retrd.	2000	38.00	38
1997 Santa Riding Fish 34756	Retrd.	1998	66.00	66
1997 Santa Riding Rooster 5.5" 34757	Retrd.	1999	44.00	44
2000 Santa w/Cardinal 12" 27176	Retrd.	2000	28.00	28
2000 Santa w/Cats 9.5" 27179	Retrd.	2000	18.00	18
2000 Santa w/Fox 14" 27177	Retrd.	2000	28.00	28
2000 Santa w/Gift 13" 27183	Retrd.	2000	39.00	39
2000 Santa w/Packages on Pedestal 14" 27178	Retrd.	2000	36.00	36
1999 Santa w/Pies 26540	Retrd.	2000	42.00	42
1999 Santa w/Rabbits 26542	Retrd.	2000	22.00	22
2000 Santa w/Stars/Wishes 9" 27175	Retrd.	2000	22.00	22
1997 Santa with Candle 7" 34758	Retrd.	1998	48.00	48
1997 Santa with Heart 11.25" 34751	Retrd.	1997	36.00	36
2000 Santa/Chicken w/Egg 8.5" 27180	Retrd.	2000	16.00	16
1998 Silent Night Santa 8" 34854	Retrd.	1999	12.00	12
2000 Small Santa on Cardinal 5" 27182	Retrd.	2000	12.00	12
2000 Snow Couple Lady w/Bow 6" 27185	Retrd.	2000	14.00	14
2000 Snow Couple Man w/Hat/Heart 6" 27184	Retrd.	2000	14.00	14
1998 Snowman 8 1/2" 34853	Retrd.	2000	15.00	15
1999 Snowman w/Birds/Sunflower Seeds 26541	Retrd.	2000	24.00	24
1999 Snowman w/Halo 26549	Retrd.	2000	30.00	30
1997 Snowman's Bad Day with Rabbit, set/2 34772	Retrd.	1998	36.00	36
2000 Squished Santa on Fish 7" 27193	Retrd.	2000	11.00	11
1999 Strawberry Santa 26547	Retrd.	1999	28.00	28
1997 Sunflower Santa 9" 34752	Retrd.	1997	44.00	44

Glad Tidings - D. Calla

YEAR ISSUE	EDITION LIMIT	YEAR RETD.	ISSUE PRICE	*QUOTE U.S.$
1999 Good Cheer Heart Gift Box 10" 27010	Open		40.00	40
1999 O' Snow Heart Gift Box 8" 27011	Open		36.00	36
1999 Warm Wishes Heart Gift Box 6" 27012	Open		28.00	28

Good Cheer - D. Calla

YEAR ISSUE	EDITION LIMIT	YEAR RETD.	ISSUE PRICE	*QUOTE U.S.$
1998 Aspen Snowman 7" 39808	Open		25.00	25
1998 Crested Butte Snowman 7" 39810	Open		15.00	15
1998 Jackson Hole Snowman 7" 39806	Open		50.00	50
1998 Killington Snowman 6 1/2" 39809	Open		24.00	24
1998 Noel Santa 17 1/2" 39801	Open		100.00	100
1998 Santa and Bird Weathervane 13" 39803	Retrd.	1998	90.00	90
1998 The Santa Collector 13 1/2" 39800	Open		170.00	170
1998 Santa Shelf Sitter 12 1/2" 39805	Retrd.	1999	60.00	60
1998 Santa with Collector Sign 9" 39804	Retrd.	1999	60.00	60
1998 Santa with Geese 13 1/2" 39802	Open		150.00	150
1998 Snowmass Snowman 11" 39807	Open		37.00	37
1998 Steamboat Snowman 4" 39811	Open		11.00	11

Grand Finale - P. Herrick

YEAR ISSUE	EDITION LIMIT	YEAR RETD.	ISSUE PRICE	*QUOTE U.S.$
1999 Apothecary Chest 26500	Open		250.00	250
1999 Bear Decorative Pedestal 26511	Retrd.	1999	120.00	120
2000 Bird Candlestick 10" 27151	Open		35.00	35
2000 Bird Candlestick 10" 27151	Open		38.00	38
1998 Ceramic Checkerboard Candlestick 38839	Open		34.00	34
1998 Ceramic Floral Black & White Candlestick 38841	Open		46.00	46
1998 Ceramic Green & Gold Check Candlestick 38840	Open		40.00	40
1998 Checkerboard Candlestick 10 3/4" 38813	Retrd.	1999	44.00	44
1999 Chick/Egg Dome Box 26513	Open		60.00	60
2000 Chicken Bowl 9.5" 27167	Open		70.00	70
1998 Floral Black & White Candlestick 14" 38811	Retrd.	1999	56.00	56
1999 Fox/Hare Pedestal Bowl 26501	Open		140.00	140
1998 Giraffe Candlestick 19" 38814	Open		60.00	60
1999 Goat Head Ceramic Box 26512	Open		40.00	40
1998 Green & Gold Candlestick 12" 38812	Retrd.	1999	50.00	50
1999 Hippo Candlestick 26506	Open		35.00	35
1998 Lion Candlestick 12 1/2" 38815	Open		44.00	44
1998 Monkey Candlestick 15 1/2" 38816	Open		60.00	60
1999 Pedestal Bowl 26514	Open		40.00	40
1999 Reindeer Ceramic Canister 26502	Open		70.00	70
2000 A Special Guest Teapot 9.5" 27149	Open		50.00	50
2000 A Tisket...Basket Bowl w/ Bunny 9.5" 27165	Open		100.00	100
1998 Tuffet 14 1/2" x 12" 38810	Open		250.00	250
2000 Waiting For Summer Teapot 10" 27164	Open		50.00	50

Halloween - D. Calla

YEAR ISSUE	EDITION LIMIT	YEAR RETD.	ISSUE PRICE	*QUOTE U.S.$
1994 Celeste - Harvest Witch with Stars 9.5" 50451	Retrd.	1999	24.00	24
1992 Harvest Witch on Pumpkin 50250	Open		40.00	40
1994 Harvest Witch Pumpkin Peddler 50450	Retrd.	1997	80.00	80
1993 Katrina and Friends 14" 50351	Retrd.	1998	55.00	55
1993 Treat Dish 50353	Retrd.	1999	55.00	55
1993 Winnie Witch 8" 50352	Retrd.	1998	30.00	30

Halloween - D. Gann

YEAR ISSUE	EDITION LIMIT	YEAR RETD.	ISSUE PRICE	*QUOTE U.S.$
1999 Esmiralda Witch 50101	Open		90.00	90
1999 Fredrika Witch 50102	Retrd.	1999	30.00	30
1999 Hanging Witch w/Bat Wings 50103	Retrd.	1999	30.00	30
1998 Henrietta Witch 18" 55850	Open		98.00	98
2000 Miss Punkin Witch 50171 9"	Open		55.00	55
2000 Petula Witch 50170 20"	Open		90.00	90
1998 Samantha Witch 15" 55851	Retrd.	1998	86.00	86
1999 Witch in Pumpkin Basket 50104	Open		26.00	26

Halloween - J. Bingham

YEAR ISSUE	EDITION LIMIT	YEAR RETD.	ISSUE PRICE	*QUOTE U.S.$
1998 Large Pumpkin Head Girl 23" 56801	Retrd.	1998	100.00	100
1998 Pumpkin Head Witch 24" 56800	Retrd.	1998	80.00	80
1998 Small Pumpkin Head Girl 14" 56802	Retrd.	1998	48.00	48
1998 Small Pumpkin Head Scarecrow 13" 56803	Retrd.	1998	40.00	40

Halloween - J. Crvich

YEAR ISSUE	EDITION LIMIT	YEAR RETD.	ISSUE PRICE	*QUOTE U.S.$
1995 Seated Ghost 51606	Retrd.	1998	26.00	26
1995 Witch Brew Pot 51604	Retrd.	1998	84.00	84

Halloween - P. Bolinger

YEAR ISSUE	EDITION LIMIT	YEAR RETD.	ISSUE PRICE	*QUOTE U.S.$
2000 Ghost w/pumpkins/black cat 50181 10"	Open		18.00	18

Halloween - P.J. Hornberger

YEAR ISSUE	EDITION LIMIT	YEAR RETD.	ISSUE PRICE	*QUOTE U.S.$
1997 Cat on Moon 17" 51732	Retrd.	1997	62.00	62
1997 Pumpkin with Black Cat 51731	Retrd.	1997	33.00	33
1997 Standing Witch with Cat 15.5" 51733	Retrd.	1997	80.00	80
1997 Witch Carriage 51730	Retrd.	1997	90.00	90

Halloween - R. Leeseberg

YEAR ISSUE	EDITION LIMIT	YEAR RETD.	ISSUE PRICE	*QUOTE U.S.$
1998 Guess What Witch 11" 54850	Retrd.	2000	15.00	15
1998 I Have Arrived Witch 6" 54852	Retrd.	2000	15.00	15
1999 Scarecrow Pumpkin 50110	Retrd.	2000	30.00	30
2000 What a Witch 50175 10"	Retrd.	2000	20.00	20
1999 Witch w/Pumpkin 50111	Retrd.	1999	20.00	20

Halloween - V. & S. Rawson

YEAR ISSUE	EDITION LIMIT	YEAR RETD.	ISSUE PRICE	*QUOTE U.S.$
1997 Scarecrow 11" 51725	Retrd.	1998	44.00	44
1997 Standing Witch 13.5" 51726	Retrd.	1998	50.00	50
1997 Witch and Harvest Moon 10.75" 51727	Retrd.	1998	35.00	35

*Quotes have been rounded up to nearest dollar

YEAR ISSUE	EDITION LIMIT	YEAR RETD.	ISSUE PRICE	*QUOTE U.S.$

Heart Beats - D. Calla

YEAR ISSUE	EDITION LIMIT	YEAR RETD.	ISSUE PRICE	*QUOTE U.S.$
1998 Baking Santa with Candy 3 3/4" 26314	5,000		12.00	12
1998 Caroling Angel, Santa & Snowman 26307	5,000		17.00	17
1998 Chasing Snowflakes 5" 26303	5,000		12.00	12
1998 Display Sign 4" 26302	5,000		17.00	17
1998 Dreaming Bear 2 1/2" 26311	5,000		12.00	12
1998 Giving Santa 3 1/2" 26306	5,000		16.00	16
1998 Glad Tidings Centerpiece 10 1/2" 26300	5,000		90.00	90
1998 Homecoming Santa 3 1/2" 26309	5,000		16.00	16
1998 Merry Christmas Santa 4" 26315	5,000		17.00	17
1998 Merry Making Elf 4 1/2" 26305	5,000		12.00	12
1998 Praying Angel 3 1/2" 26304	5,000		12.00	12
1998 Santa Centerpiece 10" 26301	5,000		28.00	28
1998 Star Gazing Santa & Snowman 3 1/2" 26313	5,000		12.00	12
1998 Story Telling Santa 4 1/2" 26308	5,000		12.00	12
1998 Tree Cutting Elf 3 1/2" 26310	5,000		12.00	12
1998 Tree Trimming 3 1/2" 26312	5,000		12.00	12

Heirloom Angels - S. Babin

YEAR ISSUE	EDITION LIMIT	YEAR RETD.	ISSUE PRICE	*QUOTE U.S.$
1997 Angel with Burgundy/Ecru Dress 22" 35776	Retrd.	1999	130.00	130
1997 Angel with Green/Pink Dress 20" 35777	Retrd.	1999	130.00	130
1997 Angel with Off-White/Gold Dress 18" 35775	Retrd.	1999	130.00	130
1997 Cherub with Pink Dress 16" 35778	Retrd.	1999	130.00	130

Heirloom Santas - J. Tasch

YEAR ISSUE	EDITION LIMIT	YEAR RETD.	ISSUE PRICE	*QUOTE U.S.$
1993 Green Victorian Santa 26" 35301	Retrd.	1993	300.00	300
1991 Large Santa in Patchwork Coat 24" 35100	Retrd.	1992	450.00	450
1992 Red Velvet Santa 18" 35202	Retrd.	1993	130.00	130
1993 Red Victorian Santa 18" 35308	Retrd.	1993	190.00	190
1992 Santa in Burgundy Coat 18" 35201	Retrd.	1993	200.00	200
1991 Santa in Green Coat 18" 35103	Retrd.	1993	270.00	270
1991 Santa in Patchwork Coat 18" 35102	Retrd.	1992	270.00	270
1992 Santa in Patchwork Coat 24" 35200	Retrd.	1993	350.00	350
1991 Santa in Red Coat 18" 35104	Retrd.	1993	270.00	270
1994 Santa in Sleigh Musical 19" 35402	Retrd.	1994	190.00	190
1991 Santa in White Coat 18" 35101	Retrd.	1992	270.00	270
1993 Santa with Musical Trunk 19" 35302	Retrd.	1993	270.00	270
1993 White Father Christmas 24" 35300	Retrd.	1994	300.00	300
1994 Woodland Santa 17" 35403	Retrd.	1994	100.00	100

Heritage Arts Studio - K. Stadelman

YEAR ISSUE	EDITION LIMIT	YEAR RETD.	ISSUE PRICE	*QUOTE U.S.$
1999 Apple Santa 26756	Open		34.00	34
2000 Fisher Santa 8" 27282	Open		22.00	22
1999 Flag Santa 26755	Open		26.00	26
1999 Gifts Galore Santa 26753	Open		34.00	34
2000 Holly/Bow Candlestick 9.5" 27284	Open		18.00	18
1999 Inspirational Santa 26752	Open		40.00	40
2000 Mr. Claus 8" 27280	Open		22.00	22
2000 Mrs. Claus 7.5" 27281	Open		22.00	22
1999 My Boys Santa 26750	Open		50.00	50
1999 Quilted Santa 26760	Retrd.	1999	24.00	24
1999 Rag Doll & Teddy Santa 26759	Open		30.00	30
2000 Santa Box 6" 27283	Open		18.00	18
2000 Santa Candlestick 9.5" 27285	Open		22.00	22
2000 Snow Nanny w/Baby 9.5" 27275	Open		22.00	22
2000 Snowman w/Bird in Nest 7" 27277	Open		22.00	22
2000 Snowman w/Broom 10.5" 27276	Open		22.00	22
2000 Snowman w/Snowshoes 5.5" 27278	Open		18.00	18
1999 Star & Moon Santa 26758	Open		26.00	26
1999 Stars & Stripes Santa 26754	Open		26.00	26
1999 Tree Santa 26757	Open		28.00	28
2000 Y2K Santa 9.5" 27279	Open		22.00	22

Holiday Post Santas - L. Clarkson

YEAR ISSUE	EDITION LIMIT	YEAR RETD.	ISSUE PRICE	*QUOTE U.S.$
1994 1950's American Santa 24" 36403	Retrd.	1994	190.00	190
1995 1950's Santa 25.5" 36501	Retrd.	1995	200.00	200
1994 Russian Santa 20" 36401	Retrd.	1994	170.00	170
1994 Santa and Sled 36402	Retrd.	1994	190.00	190
1995 Santa, Elf, and Sleigh 11" 36502	Retrd.	1996	100.00	100
1994 Skating Santa 17" 36404	Retrd.	1994	130.00	130

Holy Night - D. Calla

YEAR ISSUE	EDITION LIMIT	YEAR RETD.	ISSUE PRICE	*QUOTE U.S.$
1995 Holy Family, set/3 32576	Retrd.	1997	50.00	50
1995 Kings, set/3 32579	Retrd.	1996	90.00	90
1995 Shepherd and Sheep, set/3 32578	Retrd.	1997	50.00	50
1995 Stable 13" 32575	Retrd.	1997	90.00	90
1995 Stable Animals, set/3 32577	Retrd.	1997	46.00	46

Honey Bees - D. Calla

YEAR ISSUE	EDITION LIMIT	YEAR RETD.	ISSUE PRICE	*QUOTE U.S.$
2000 "Honey Bee" Garden Faery 9" 27073	Open		32.00	32
2000 "Honey Bee" Seated Garden Faery 4" 27074	Open		10.00	10
2000 "Dew Drop" Standing 4.5" 27076	Open		10.00	10
2000 "Dew Drop" Seated 2.5" 27077	Open		10.00	10

Lancaster - D. Calla

YEAR ISSUE	EDITION LIMIT	YEAR RETD.	ISSUE PRICE	*QUOTE U.S.$
1996 Barn 14" 52601	Retrd.	1997	72.00	72
1996 Levi Boy 11" 52602	Retrd.	1997	42.00	42
1996 Rachel Girl 11" 52603	Retrd.	1997	42.00	42

The Magic of Christmas - V. & S. Rawson

YEAR ISSUE	EDITION LIMIT	YEAR RETD.	ISSUE PRICE	*QUOTE U.S.$
1998 Elf Holding Lightbulb 5 1/2" 32807	Open		7.00	7
1998 Elf Holding Ornament 6" 32804	Open		7.00	7
1998 Elf with Boxes 6" 32808	Open		7.00	7
1998 Elf with List 5 1/2" 32805	Open		7.00	7
1998 Elf with Presents 6 1/2" 32809	Open		7.00	7
1998 Elf with Snowman 6" 32802	Retrd.	1999	7.00	7
1998 Elf with Tree 5 1/2" 32803	Retrd.	1999	7.00	7
1998 Elf Wrapping Package 4" 32806	Retrd.	1999	7.00	7
1998 Santa 8" 32801	Open		20.00	20
1998 Sleigh 10 1/2" 32800	Open		110.00	110

The Magic of Spring - J. Crvich

YEAR ISSUE	EDITION LIMIT	YEAR RETD.	ISSUE PRICE	*QUOTE U.S.$
1997 Bunny Magician with Egg 15" 54701	Retrd.	1997	64.00	64

Master Gardener - D. Calla

YEAR ISSUE	EDITION LIMIT	YEAR RETD.	ISSUE PRICE	*QUOTE U.S.$
1997 Master Gardener 14" 53701	Open		84.00	84
1997 "Rain" Weather Faery 6" 53703	Open		22.00	22
1997 "Sunshine" Weather Faery 6" 53704	Open		22.00	22
1997 "Wind" Weather Faery 6" 53702	Open		22.00	22

Merry Christmas - D. Calla

YEAR ISSUE	EDITION LIMIT	YEAR RETD.	ISSUE PRICE	*QUOTE U.S.$
1993 Santa with Girl 11" 31308	Retrd.	1995	100.00	100
1993 Santa with Heart 10" 31309	Retrd.	1995	50.00	50
1993 Snowman 9" 31313	Retrd.	1996	50.00	50

Nativity - V. & S. Rawson

YEAR ISSUE	EDITION LIMIT	YEAR RETD.	ISSUE PRICE	*QUOTE U.S.$
1996 Nativity Figurines, set/7 22660	Open		95.00	95
1996 Nativity Stable 10" x 19" 22650	Open		31.00	31

Night Before Christmas - D. Calla

YEAR ISSUE	EDITION LIMIT	YEAR RETD.	ISSUE PRICE	*QUOTE U.S.$
1994 Gent in Nightshirt 12" 31408	Retrd.	1996	60.00	60
1994 Santa 22" 31403	Retrd.	1995	120.00	120
1994 Sprite on Rocking Horse 14" 31409	Retrd.	1995	90.00	90
1994 St. Nick on Chimney 16" 31406	Retrd.	1995	100.00	100

North Star - D. Calla

YEAR ISSUE	EDITION LIMIT	YEAR RETD.	ISSUE PRICE	*QUOTE U.S.$
1995 Polar Bear 16" 32507	Retrd.	1997	90.00	90
1995 St. Nick 19" 32506	Retrd.	1997	100.00	100
1995 St. Nick Riding Polar Bear 15" 32505	Retrd.	1997	140.00	140

Old Fashioned Toys - P. Herrick

YEAR ISSUE	EDITION LIMIT	YEAR RETD.	ISSUE PRICE	*QUOTE U.S.$
1997 Bunny Kissing Santa 33702	Retrd.	1998	140.00	140
1997 Bunny Tricycle with Santa 33701	Retrd.	1998	120.00	120
1997 Santa on Frog Tricycle 33703	Retrd.	1998	120.00	120

On Christmas Day - D. Calla

YEAR ISSUE	EDITION LIMIT	YEAR RETD.	ISSUE PRICE	*QUOTE U.S.$
1991 Boy 8" 32111	Retrd.	1994	29.00	29
1991 Father 12" 32108	Retrd.	1994	46.00	46
1991 Girl 8" 32110	Retrd.	1994	29.00	29
1991 Mother 11" 32109	Retrd.	1994	46.00	46

Once Upon a Christmas - D. Calla

YEAR ISSUE	EDITION LIMIT	YEAR RETD.	ISSUE PRICE	*QUOTE U.S.$
1996 Baby Bear 9" 23621	Retrd.	1997	50.00	50
1996 House 10" 23618	Retrd.	1996	84.00	84
1996 Mama Bear 11" 23620	Retrd.	1997	70.00	70
1996 Papa Bear 11" 23619	Retrd.	1997	64.00	64
1996 "Read to Me Santa" 8" 23622	Retrd.	1996	60.00	60
1996 Santa Throwing Snowball 10" 23623	Retrd.	1997	60.00	60
1996 Tweedle Dee 8.5" 23624	Retrd.	1997	34.00	34

Patchwork Heart - J. Tasch

YEAR ISSUE	EDITION LIMIT	YEAR RETD.	ISSUE PRICE	*QUOTE U.S.$
1995 Father Christmas 23" 18508	Retrd.	1995	180.00	180
1995 Workbench Musical Santa 19" 18510	Retrd.	1995	200.00	200

Patriotic - D. Calla

YEAR ISSUE	EDITION LIMIT	YEAR RETD.	ISSUE PRICE	*QUOTE U.S.$
1992 Uncle Sam 50299	Open		60.00	60

Patriotic - P.J. Hornberger

YEAR ISSUE	EDITION LIMIT	YEAR RETD.	ISSUE PRICE	*QUOTE U.S.$
1997 Uncle Sam 17.5" 50730	Retrd.	1998	70.00	70

Patriotic - V. & S. Rawson

YEAR ISSUE	EDITION LIMIT	YEAR RETD.	ISSUE PRICE	*QUOTE U.S.$
1997 Banner Wave Angel 8.5" 50726	Retrd.	1998	33.00	33
1997 Broad Stripe Angel 11" 50725	Retrd.	1998	33.00	33
1997 "Oh Say Can You See" Angel 8" 50727	Retrd.	1998	33.00	33

Paul Bolinger Collection - P. Bolinger

YEAR ISSUE	EDITION LIMIT	YEAR RETD.	ISSUE PRICE	*QUOTE U.S.$
2000 Bear/Fishing Pole/Heart Shelf Sitter 7" 27203	Open		8.00	8
2000 Crawling Santa/Bell Shelf Sitter 3" x 7.5" 27201	Open		8.00	8
2000 Dancing Penguin 6" 27225	Open		12.00	12
2000 Home Sweet Snowbank Snowman 7" 27210	Open		8.00	8
1999 Love Rules Santa 7.5" 27092	Open		15.00	15
2000 Making New Friends Snowman 4.5" 27212	Open		9.00	9
2000 My Other Home...Snowman 7" 27211	Open		8.00	8
2000 Penguin - "Home Sweet Home" 5" 27227	Open		7.00	7
2000 Penguin w/Tree 5.5" 27226	Open		9.00	9
2000 Penguin/Baby 4.5" 27228	Open		7.00	7
2000 Reindeer/Bells Shelf Sitter 6" 27204	Open		8.00	8
2000 Santa - "Special - Cookies and Milk" 5" 27232	Open		7.00	7
2000 Santa and Reindeer-Loading Zone 4" 27214	Open		8.00	8
2000 Santa and Snowman w/Broom/Hat 4" 27213	Open		8.00	8
2000 Santa Fishing w/Heart 4" 27216	Open		8.00	8
2000 Santa Light Switch Cover 5.5" 27229	Open		7.00	7
2000 Santa w/ Club Motto 4.5" 27231	Open		7.00	7
2000 Santa w/Ark Centerpiece 10" 27236	Open		22.00	22
2000 Santa w/Gingerbread Cookies 9" 27238	Open		22.00	22
2000 Santa w/Polar Pals Centerpiece 10" 27237	Open		22.00	22
2000 Santa w/Star-Behold 6" 27217	Open		8.00	8
1999 Santa with Birdhouse 6" 27094	Open		15.00	15
1999 Santa with Cookie and Milk 6" 27095	Open		16.00	16
2000 Santa's Club House 5" 27230	Open		8.00	8
2000 Santa-Christmas is for Kids 4.5" 27219	Open		8.00	8
2000 Santa-Joy to the World 7" 27215	Open		9.00	9
2000 Santa-Peace on Earth 5" 27220	Open		8.00	8
2000 Santa/Chimney/Arc/Hearts Shelf Sitter 9" 27209	Open		12.00	12
2000 Santa/Fishing/Stocking Shelf Sitter 6" 27207	Open		8.00	8
2000 Santa/Joy Shelf Sitter 5.5" 27205	Open		8.00	8
2000 Santa/Snowman/Reindeer-Joy 4" 27218	Open		8.00	8
2000 Santa/Stars Shelf Sitter 7" 27206	Open		8.00	8
2000 Snowman - "Snowtime" 4.75" 27223	Open		9.00	9
2000 Snowman - "Spring" 6" 27222	Open		9.00	9
2000 Snowman Holding Heart 5" 27221	Open		8.00	8
2000 Snowman w/Bluebird 5" 27224	Open		8.00	8
2000 Snowman/ "Ice is Nice" Shelf Sitter 5.5" 27208	Open		8.00	8
2000 Snowman/Stars Shelf Sitter 5.5" 27202	Open		8.00	8
1999 Sunshine Diet Snowman 6" 27096	Open		16.00	16
1999 Up and Away Santa 5.25" 27093	Open		15.00	15
1999 Y2K Bug Off Santa 6.5" 27091	Open		16.00	16

Peace on Earth - D. Calla

YEAR ISSUE	EDITION LIMIT	YEAR RETD.	ISSUE PRICE	*QUOTE U.S.$
1994 Angel with Lamb 16" 32401	Retrd.	1997	90.00	90
1994 Lion, Lamb, and Angel 32402	Retrd.	1997	70.00	70
1993 St. Nicholas 20" 32355	Retrd.	1997	140.00	140

Reach for the Stars - D. Calla

YEAR ISSUE	EDITION LIMIT	YEAR RETD.	ISSUE PRICE	*QUOTE U.S.$
1992 Santa 19" 31256	Open		160.00	160

River Road - D. Calla

YEAR ISSUE	EDITION LIMIT	YEAR RETD.	ISSUE PRICE	*QUOTE U.S.$
2000 Blue Snowstorm Shelf Sitter 5" 27519	Open		18.00	18
2000 Cranberry Faery Reflection 5" 27536	Open		16.00	16
2000 Cranberry Faery Seated on Tree musical 8" 27535	Open		38.00	38
2000 Dear Old St. Nick 6" 27517	Open		44.00	44
2000 Elf on Tummy 3.5" 27520	Open		15.00	15
2000 Evergreen St. Nicholas 9" 27532	Open		30.00	30
2000 Feeding Goose 3" 27523	Open		10.00	10
2000 Honking Goose 4.5" 27522	Open		10.00	10
2000 Lighting the Way St. Nick w/lantern 7.5" 27534	Open		30.00	30
2000 Musical Santa/Deer Centerpiece 6" 27505	Open		40.00	40
2000 Musical Snowman Centerpiece 7" 27504	Open		40.00	40
2000 Northwind St. Nicholas 10" 27531	Open		35.00	35
2000 O Snow Snowman-musical 9" 27530	Open		50.00	50
2000 Santa Treasure Box 3.75" x 3" 27512	Open		15.00	15
2000 Santa/Deer/Tree Musical Centerpiece 10" 27502	Open		80.00	80
2000 Snowman Treasure Box 3.75" x 3" 27513	Open		15.00	15
2000 Snowstorm St. Nicholas 13" 27515	Open		55.00	55
2000 Spirit of St. Nicholas 18" 27514	Open		140.00	140
2000 St. Nicholas of the Forest w/ bluejay 13" 27529	Open		46.00	46
2000 St. Nicholas Riding Deer 15" 27516	Open		100.00	100
2000 St. Nicholas Shelf Sitter 7" 27533	Open		25.00	25
2000 St. Nick w/ Snowman 15" 27528	Open		70.00	70
2000 Standing Elf 8" 27521	Open		22.00	22
2000 Topiary Tree 10.5" 27518	Open		28.00	28

Santa's Kingdom - S. Smith

YEAR ISSUE	EDITION LIMIT	YEAR RETD.	ISSUE PRICE	*QUOTE U.S.$
1998 Cat-tastrophe 9 1/2" 37850	Open		16.00	16
1998 Panda-monium 9 1/2" 37851	Open		16.00	16
2000 Piggyback Santa/Bear 10" 27308	Open		16.00	16
1998 Santa & Penguin 3 1/4" 37853	Open		5.00	5
1998 Santa , Cat & Dog 6" 37852	Open		16.00	16
1996 Santa Fishing on Bear 37656	5,000		68.00	68
1999 Santa Fishing w/Loon 26815	Open		8.00	8
1997 Santa on Buffalo 37751	5,000	1998	72.00	72
1996 Santa on Deer 37660	5,000	1999	50.00	50
1996 Santa on Horse 37659	5,000	1998	68.00	68
1996 Santa on Moose 37657	5,000		66.00	66
1997 Santa on Polar Bear 37753	5,000		77.00	77
1997 Santa on Whale 37752	5,000		72.00	72
2000 Santa Sleeping on Loon 7" 27307	Open		26.00	26
1999 Santa w/Fawn 26816	Open		24.00	24
1996 Santa with Bear 37658	5,000		50.00	50
1999 Santa/Birdhouse 26813	Retrd.	1999	8.00	8
2000 Santa/Cow "Milk and Cookies" 7" 27300	Open		16.00	16
2000 Santa/Moon Fishing for Stars 8.5" 27301	Open		16.00	16
1999 Santa/Tortoise 26812	Open		9.00	9
2000 Skiing Santa 4" 27302	Open		4.00	4
1998 Special Delivery 6 1/4" 37854	Open		16.00	16

Santa's Legend - A. Schreck Moore

YEAR ISSUE	EDITION LIMIT	YEAR RETD.	ISSUE PRICE	*QUOTE U.S.$
1999 Elf with Green Coat 26772	Retrd.	1999	70.00	70
1999 Elf with Red Coat 26771	Retrd.	1999	70.00	70
1999 Elf with Tapestry Coat 26773	Retrd.	1999	70.00	70
1999 Santa on Sled 26770	Retrd.	1999	250.00	250
1998 Santa with Chair 20" 35802	Retrd.	1999	420.00	420
1998 Santa with Sled 22" 35801	Retrd.	1999	500.00	500
1998 Standing Santa with Green Coat 21" 35803	Retrd.	1999	330.00	330
1998 Standing Santa with Red Coat 22" 35800	Retrd.	1999	430.00	430

Seasonal Gift - V. Howard

YEAR ISSUE	EDITION LIMIT	YEAR RETD.	ISSUE PRICE	*QUOTE U.S.$
1997 Bear 5.5" 35729	Retrd.	1999	13.00	13
1997 Bunny 5.5" 35728	Retrd.	1999	13.00	13
1997 Santa 5.25" 35732	Retrd.	1998	13.00	13

*Quotes have been rounded up to nearest dollar

YEAR ISSUE	EDITION LIMIT	YEAR RETD.	ISSUE PRICE	*QUOTE U.S.$
1997 Santa Candleholder 5" 35725	Retrd.	1998	18.00	18
1997 Scarecrow 5.5" 35730	Retrd.	1999	13.00	13
1997 Scarecrow Candleholder 5.5" 35727	Retrd.	1999	18.00	18
1997 Snowlady 5" 35733	Retrd.	1998	13.00	13
1997 Witch 6.25" 35731	Retrd.	1998	13.00	13
1997 Witch Candleholder 6" 35726	Retrd.	1998	18.00	18

Silent Night - S. Smith

YEAR ISSUE	EDITION LIMIT	YEAR RETD.	ISSUE PRICE	*QUOTE U.S.$
1998 Cow and Donkey, set/2 37812	Retrd.	1998	40.00	40
1998 Mary, Joseph, Baby & Angel, set/4 37810	Retrd.	1998	60.00	60
1998 Shepherd, Boy & Two Lambs, set/4 37811	Retrd.	1998	55.00	55
1998 Silent Night, set/10 37814	Retrd.	1998	150.00	150
1998 Stable 12" 37813	Retrd.	1998	31.00	31

Simple Gifts - D. Calla

YEAR ISSUE	EDITION LIMIT	YEAR RETD.	ISSUE PRICE	*QUOTE U.S.$
1992 St. Nicholas 20" 32206	Retrd.	1994	60.00	60

Snow Meadow - D. Calla

YEAR ISSUE	EDITION LIMIT	YEAR RETD.	ISSUE PRICE	*QUOTE U.S.$
1992 Seated St. Nicholas 10" 31207	Retrd.	1995	30.00	30
1992 St. Nicholas 14" 31206	Retrd.	1996	70.00	70

Snowberries - D. Calla

YEAR ISSUE	EDITION LIMIT	YEAR RETD.	ISSUE PRICE	*QUOTE U.S.$
1990 Tall Angel 33002	Retrd.	1992	90.00	90

Snowbound - D. Calla

YEAR ISSUE	EDITION LIMIT	YEAR RETD.	ISSUE PRICE	*QUOTE U.S.$
1996 Nordic Skier 10.5" 27615	Retrd.	1997	80.00	80
1996 Ski Chalet 8" 27616	Retrd.	1997	140.00	140

SnowMa'am - D. Calla

YEAR ISSUE	EDITION LIMIT	YEAR RETD.	ISSUE PRICE	*QUOTE U.S.$
1997 SnowMa'am 14" 30752	Open		128.00	128

The Spirit of Giving - D. Calla

YEAR ISSUE	EDITION LIMIT	YEAR RETD.	ISSUE PRICE	*QUOTE U.S.$
1992 Babouschka - Russia 32253	Retrd.	1995	50.00	50
1992 Father Christmas - England 32251	Retrd.	1995	60.00	60
1992 Jule Nisse - Scandinavia 32254	Retrd.	1995	40.00	40
1992 Santa Claus - America 32255	Retrd.	1995	50.00	50
1992 St. Lucia - Sweden 32252	Retrd.	1995	30.00	30
1992 St. Nicholas - Netherlands 32250	Retrd.	1995	70.00	70

Spring - D. Calla

YEAR ISSUE	EDITION LIMIT	YEAR RETD.	ISSUE PRICE	*QUOTE U.S.$
1994 Beau Bunny 9" 50407	Retrd.	1997	25.00	25
1994 Belle Bunny 9" 50408	Retrd.	1997	25.00	25
1993 Boy Bunny 9" 50301	Open		30.00	30
1993 Girl Bunny 9" 50302	Open		30.00	30
1994 Mamma Beth Bunny 13" 50406	Retrd.	1995	50.00	50
1992 Spring Boy Bunny 13" 50201	Retrd.	1995	60.00	60
1992 Spring Girl Bunny 13" 50202	Retrd.	1995	60.00	60

Spring Harbinger - D. Calla

YEAR ISSUE	EDITION LIMIT	YEAR RETD.	ISSUE PRICE	*QUOTE U.S.$
1995 Harbinger Rabbit 20" 50521	Open		220.00	220

Ten Christmas - D. Calla

YEAR ISSUE	EDITION LIMIT	YEAR RETD.	ISSUE PRICE	*QUOTE U.S.$
1997 Santa 18" 30777	Open		190.00	190

Thanksgiving Kids - R. Morehead

YEAR ISSUE	EDITION LIMIT	YEAR RETD.	ISSUE PRICE	*QUOTE U.S.$
1997 Children Giving Thanks 6.5" 50750	Retrd.	1998	48.00	48
1997 Children with Basket and Squirrel 9" 50752	Retrd.	1998	66.00	66
1997 Children with Cornucopia 4.5" 50751	Retrd.	1998	54.00	54

Twelve Days of Christmas - D. Calla

YEAR ISSUE	EDITION LIMIT	YEAR RETD.	ISSUE PRICE	*QUOTE U.S.$
1990 Partridge 9" 32003	Retrd.	1993	49.00	49

Twelve Days of Christmas Anniversary Collection - D. Calla

YEAR ISSUE	EDITION LIMIT	YEAR RETD.	ISSUE PRICE	*QUOTE U.S.$
1999 Maid-a-Milking 14" 27030	Open		60.00	60
1999 Musical Maid-a-Milking 9" 27032	Open		42.00	42
1999 Piper Piping 14" 27029	Open		60.00	60
1999 Turtle Dove Candlesticks, set/2 8.5" 27031	Open		48.00	48

Twelve Days of Christmas Mantelpiece Collection - D. Calla

YEAR ISSUE	EDITION LIMIT	YEAR RETD.	ISSUE PRICE	*QUOTE U.S.$
2000 Partridge on Pear Mantelpiece 10.5" 27040	Open		32.00	32
2000 Turtle Doves/ Pear Mantelpiece 10.5" 27041	Open		34.00	34
2000 French Hen/Pear Mantelpiece 10.5" 27042	Open		32.00	32
2000 Calling Bird/Pear Mantelpiece 10" 27043	Open		32.00	32
2000 Five Gold Rings/Pear/Boy Mantelpiece 10" 27044	Open		36.00	36
2000 Goose/Nest/Pear Mantelpiece 11.5" 27045	Open		30.00	30
2000 Swan Swimming/Pear Mantelpiece 12" 27046	Open		32.00	32
2000 Drummer Drumming Mantelpiece 11.75" 27047	Open		50.00	50
2000 Lady Dancing Mantelpiece 14" 27048	Open		60.00	60
2000 Lord-a-Leaping Mantelpiece 13" 27049	Open		60.00	60

Two by Two - D. Calla

YEAR ISSUE	EDITION LIMIT	YEAR RETD.	ISSUE PRICE	*QUOTE U.S.$
1994 Noah's Ark 12" 32451	Retrd.	1997	120.00	120
1994 St. Nick 12" 32452	Retrd.	1997	90.00	90

Wings of Light - D. Calla

YEAR ISSUE	EDITION LIMIT	YEAR RETD.	ISSUE PRICE	*QUOTE U.S.$
1996 Angel 14" 21655	Retrd.	1997	60.00	60
1996 Angel with Dove 9.5" 21673	Retrd.	1999	42.00	42
1996 Seated Santa 9" 21676	Retrd.	1999	26.00	26
1996 St. Nick 15" 21672	Retrd.	1999	84.00	84

Ye Olde Santa Maker - D. Gann

YEAR ISSUE	EDITION LIMIT	YEAR RETD.	ISSUE PRICE	*QUOTE U.S.$
1993 From Santa with Love 21" 35355	Retrd.	1993	150.00	150
1993 Goodwill to All Santa 16" 35352	Retrd.	1993	160.00	160
1993 Hanzel - The Musical Elf 12" 35359	Retrd.	1994	75.00	75
1998 Lace Santa 19" 35867	Open		170.00	170
1997 Large Santa 25" 35767	Retrd.	1998	176.00	176
1999 Lion/Lamb Peace Santa 26720	Retrd.	1999	190.00	190
1993 Merry Ol' Santa 20" 35353	Retrd.	1994	190.00	190
2000 Millennium Santa 15" 27103	Open		95.00	95
1997 Musical "Merry Christmas" Santa 35766	Retrd.	1998	90.00	90
1995 Musical Santa in Chair 15.5" 35566	Retrd.	1995	160.00	160
1998 Nautical Santa 16" 35856	Open		90.00	90
1999 Patriotic Seated Santa 26722	Open		120.00	120
1999 Santa Baker 26724	Retrd.	1999	74.00	74
1998 Santa Holding Mirror 16" 35852	Retrd.	1998	110.00	110
1999 Santa on Donkey 26726	Retrd.	1999	70.00	70
1999 Santa on Polar Bear 26727	Open		70.00	70
1997 Santa on Rocking Horse 12" 35760	Retrd.	1997	80.00	80
2000 Santa on Rooster 12" 27104	Open		75.00	75
1996 Santa Riding Tricycle 13" 35669	Retrd.	1996	150.00	150
1995 Santa Riding Tricycle 16" 35565	Retrd.	1996	110.00	110
1998 Santa Riding Tricycle Cart 9 1/2" 35858	Retrd.	1999	130.00	130
1994 Santa with Angel 16" 35458	Retrd.	1994	160.00	160
1996 Santa with Angel and Bell 16.5" 35666	Retrd.	1997	76.00	76
1997 Santa with Basket 10" 35759	Retrd.	1997	57.00	57
1996 Santa with Fence and Toys 9" 35673	Open		76.00	76
1998 Santa with Toys 13" 35855	Retrd.	1998	70.00	70
1995 Seated Musical Santa 13" 35564	Retrd.	1998	100.00	100
2000 Seated Musical Santa with List 6" 27105	Open		90.00	90
1999 Seated Patchwork w/Rag Doll 26725	Retrd.	1999	44.00	44
1995 Seated Santa 21.5" 35556	Retrd.	1997	160.00	160
1993 Sleigh Ride Santa 16" 35350	Retrd.	1993	210.00	210
2000 St. Nicholas Antique Green Coat w/Basket 20" 27101	Open		160.00	160
2000 St. Nicholas in Green Coat w/ Toys 16" 26728	Open		110.00	110
2000 St. Nicholas in Red Coat w/ Toys 16" 26729	Open		80.00	80
2000 St. Nicholas in White Coat w/Angel & Bell 17" 27102	Open		90.00	90
1999 Stressed Out.com Santa 26723	Open		70.00	70
2000 Victorian Santa/Burgundy Coat 24" 27100	Open		190.00	190
1993 Winking Santa 20" 35354	Retrd.	1993	160.00	160
1994 Ye Olde Americana Santa 17" 35450	Retrd.	1994	130.00	130
1994 Ye Olde Dutch Santa 17" 35455	Retrd.	1994	130.00	130
1994 Ye Olde German Santa 17" 35451	Retrd.	1994	130.00	130
1994 Ye Olde Russian Santa 17" 35452	Retrd.	1994	130.00	130
1994 Ye Olde Scottish Santa 17" 35454	Retrd.	1994	130.00	130
1994 Ye Olde Swedish Santa 17" 35453	Retrd.	1994	130.00	130

Islandia International

Sonshine Promises - G. Clasby

YEAR ISSUE	EDITION LIMIT	YEAR RETD.	ISSUE PRICE	*QUOTE U.S.$
1999 After This Sundae, The Diet Starts on Monday 7063	15,000		25.00	25
1998 A Baby Boy - A Perfect Miracle 7008B	Numbrd.		22.50	23
1998 A Baby Girl - A Perfect Miracle 7008G	Numbrd.		22.50	23
1998 Baby's First Birthday 7034	Numbrd.		19.50	20
2000 Baked with Sweetness & Love 7066	Numbrd.		19.50	20
1998 Beginnings Offer the Gift of Promise 7032	Numbrd.		21.00	21
1999 Best Friends...Great Times! 7049	Numbrd.		25.00	25
1999 The Best Seat in Life is Next to You 7050	Numbrd.		25.00	25
1998 Bless This House With Joy and Love 7007	Numbrd.		22.50	23
1999 Bloom Where God Plants You 7072	Yr.Iss.	1999	24.00	24
1999 Celebrate - It's A Boy! (7061)	Yr.Iss.	1999	13.50	14
1999 Celebrate - It's A Girl! (7060)	Yr.Iss.	1999	13.50	14
1998 The Chorus of Life Brings Us All Together 7000	15,000		39.50	40
1999 Come Out From Under the Weather 7021	Numbrd.		23.50	24
1999 Congratulations, You Earned Your Wings! 7048	Numbrd.		23.00	23
2000 Differences Bond a Perfect Friendship 7058	Numbrd.		22.50	23
1998 Enjoy Your Special Day 7003	Numbrd.	1999	19.50	20
1999 Faith For The Future 7062	2,000		65.00	65
1999 Faith For The Future A/P 7062A/P	200		95.00	95
1999 Faith Promises a Safe Landing 7028	Numbrd.		21.00	21
2000 Fishing Calms the Soul 7075	Numbrd.		22.50	23
1998 Follow Your Dreams 7002	Numbrd.		19.50	20
1999 Forgiveness - The Lifting of Spirit 7043	Numbrd.		24.50	25
1999 Friends Are Tied Together With Ribbons of Joy 7070	Numbrd.		22.50	23
1998 God Blesses This House But He Doesn't Clean It 7009	Numbrd.		22.50	23
2000 God Never Gives You More Than You Can Handle 7071	Numbrd.		23.50	24
1999 Godparents Are Guardian Angels on Earth 7053	Numbrd.		29.50	30
1998 Golf is Not Life or Death - It's More Important 7015	Numbrd.		24.50	25
1998 Good Friends Will Lift Your Spirit 7017	Numbrd.		27.50	28
2000 The Greatest Gift is Your Friendship 7029	Numbrd.		24.00	24
1999 Happy Birthday - Savor Life's Magical Moments 7035	15,000		32.50	33
1999 Have Faith Through Life's Ups and Downs 7052	Numbrd.		32.50	33
2000 He Gives You Safe Passage 7073	Numbrd.		23.50	24
2000 A Healing Touch 7074	Numbrd.		22.50	23
1998 Hugs Make The World a Better Place 7013	Numbrd.	1999	22.50	23
1998 I Love You With All My Hearts 7004	Numbrd.		22.50	23
1999 It's No Surprise, Miracles do Happen! 7027	Numbrd.		22.50	23
1999 It's Your Time To Soar 7037	Numbrd.		23.50	24
1998 Joy to You Mini Lapel Pin 9001	Open		6.00	6
1998 A Joyful Wish 7033	Numbrd.		19.50	20
1999 Let Your Light Shine Mini Lapel Pin 9003	Open		6.00	6
1999 Let Your Star Shine 7056	Yr.Iss.	1999	15.00	15
2000 Mark the Positive, Erase the Negative 7067	Numbrd.		18.50	19
1998 May Love Always be in Full Bloom 7006	Numbrd.		29.50	30
1999 The Milk of Human Kindness Never Curdles 7030	Numbrd.		32.50	33
1999 The Miracle of God's Beauty is Everywhere 6002 (Special Event)	Yr.Iss.	1999	19.50	20
1999 My Trust in Your Light Shows Me the Way 7044	Numbrd.		24.00	24
1999 Nativity Pageant (13 pc. Set) 7500	Open		90.00	90
1999 A Nurse is Another Name for TLC 7025	Numbrd.		23.50	24
1999 One More In The Nest 7045	Numbrd.		23.50	24
1998 Ordinary Sisters - Extraordinary Friends 7011	Numbrd.		22.00	22
2000 Patience is a Virtue...Bedtime is a Godsend 7080	Numbrd.		23.50	24
1999 Progress at Any Speed is Better Than Standing Still 7022	Numbrd.		20.00	20
1998 Remember There's a Blue Sky Behind the Blackest Cloud 7010	Numbrd.		22.50	23
1999 Sail Into a Glorious Future 7023	Numbrd.		23.00	23
1999 A Scoop Full of Birthday Wishes 7019	Numbrd.		22.50	23
1999 Sending Sonshine Promises With Love 7020	Numbrd.		22.50	23
1998 Shared Love is Twice The Joy 7005	Numbrd.		22.50	23
2000 Shouting Good Cheer For All To Hear 7076	Numbrd.		23.50	24
1999 Sigh...We're Really Going to Miss You! 7031	Numbrd.		33.50	34
1999 The Sky's The Limit 7059	Yr.Iss.	1999	22.50	23
1999 The Sky's The Limit Pin 9005	2-Yr.		6.00	6
1998 Sonshine Promise Bluebird Figurine/Plaque 9000	Numbrd.		19.50	20
1999 Strengthened By The Warmth of the Family 7047	Numbrd.		40.00	40
1999 Thank You For the Seeds of Knowledge 7041	Numbrd.		20.00	20
1998 There's an Angel Watching Over You 7001	Numbrd.		22.50	23
2000 Together We're Going Places 7077	Numbrd.		24.50	25
1999 Traveling The Path Together 6001	Yr.Iss.	1999	22.50	23
2000 A Tribute: For You Answer the Call 7078	Numbrd.		23.50	24
1998 Wash Away The Blues 7016	Numbrd.	1999	23.50	24
1999 We Celebrate Our Differences 7042	Numbrd.		24.00	24
2000 Whatever You Sow...You Will Also Reap 7079	Numbrd.		23.50	24
1998 When Life Gives You Scraps, Make a Quilt 7012	Numbrd.		23.00	23
1999 You Are Like No Udder 7068	Yr.Iss.	1999	19.50	20
1998 You Are Special in my Life 7026	Numbrd.		27.50	28
1998 You Can Go Anywhere From Where You Are 7014	Numbrd.		24.00	24
1999 You're a Blooming Miracle! 7040	Numbrd.		20.00	20
1999 You're a Bouquet of Joy 7039	Numbrd.		23.50	24
1999 You're An Angel To Me 7054	Numbrd.		22.50	23
1999 You're An Angel To Me Pin 9004	Open		6.00	6
1999 You're One in a Million Mini Lapel Pin 9002	Open		6.00	6
1998 You're Worth The World to Me 7018	Numbrd.	1999	21.50	22
1999 Your Gift of Knowledge Will Last Forever 7024	Numbrd.		20.00	20

Sonshine Promises-Anniversary Collection - G. Clasby

YEAR ISSUE	EDITION LIMIT	YEAR RETD.	ISSUE PRICE	*QUOTE U.S.$
1999 Bless This House With Joy & Love 7007/2	5,000		55.00	55
1999 Blessed Are The Playful 3001/2	5,000		49.50	50
1999 Blessed Are The Spirited 3002/2	5,000		49.50	50
1999 God Blesses This House But He Doesn't Clean It 7009/2	5,000		49.50	50
1999 Remember There's a Blue Sky Behind the Blackest Cloud 7010/2	5,000		49.50	50
1999 There's an Angel Watching Over You 7001/2	5,000		49.50	50
1999 When Life Gives You Scraps, Make a Quilt 7012/2	5,000		49.50	50

Sonshine Promises-Blessed Are Cardinals - G. Clasby

YEAR ISSUE	EDITION LIMIT	YEAR RETD.	ISSUE PRICE	*QUOTE U.S.$
1999 Blessed Are Cardinal Lapel Pin 3000	Open		6.00	6
1999 Blessed are the Adventurous 3012	Numbrd.		23.50	24
1999 Blessed are the Cardinal Plaque 4000	Numbrd.		15.00	15
1999 Blessed are the Cheerful 3008	Numbrd.		23.50	24
1999 Blessed are the Contented 3004	Numbrd.		23.50	24
1999 Blessed are the Faithful 3013	Numbrd.		23.50	24
1999 Blessed are the Honest 3010	Numbrd.		23.50	24
1999 Blessed are the Hospitable 3009	Numbrd.		23.50	24
1999 Blessed are the Jubilant 3011	Numbrd.		23.50	24
1999 Blessed are the Optimistic 3005	Numbrd.		23.50	24

*Quotes have been rounded up to nearest dollar

YEAR ISSUE	EDITION LIMIT	YEAR RETD.	ISSUE PRICE	*QUOTE U.S.$
1999 Blessed are the Playful 3001	Numbrd.		23.50	24
1999 Blessed are the Spirited 3002	Numbrd.		23.50	24
1999 Blessed are the Trusting 3007	Numbrd.		23.50	24

Sonshine Promises-Collector Pins - G. Clasby

YEAR ISSUE	EDITION LIMIT	YEAR RETD.	ISSUE PRICE	*QUOTE U.S.$
2000 Let Your Star Shine 9016	Open		6.00	6
2000 Ordinary Sister - Extraordinary Friends 9006	Open		7.00	7
2000 A Scoop Full of Birthday Wishes 9009	Open		6.00	6
2000 Shared Love is Twice the Joy 9015	Open		7.00	7
2000 There's an Angel Watching Over You 9012	Open		7.00	7
2000 Traveling The Path Together 9010	Open		7.00	7
2000 When Life Gives You Scraps, Make a Quilt 9007	Open		6.00	6
2000 You're a Bouquet of Joy 9013	Open		6.00	6
2000 Collector set of 8 pins 9021	Open		45.00	45

African Wildlife - T. Swanson

YEAR ISSUE	EDITION LIMIT	YEAR RETD.	ISSUE PRICE	*QUOTE U.S.$
1998 Elephant	Numbrd.	1999	27.50	28
1998 Giraffe	Numbrd.	1999	27.50	28
1998 Lion	Numbrd.	1999	27.50	28
1998 Zebra	Numbrd.	1999	27.50	28

Collector Pins by Jonnié Chardonn - J. Chardonn

YEAR ISSUE	EDITION LIMIT	YEAR RETD.	ISSUE PRICE	*QUOTE U.S.$
1999 Seneca	Open		6.00	6
1999 Titichakyo	Open		6.00	6

Collector Pins by Trevor Swanson - T. Swanson

YEAR ISSUE	EDITION LIMIT	YEAR RETD.	ISSUE PRICE	*QUOTE U.S.$
1999 Catie the Cow	Open		6.00	6
1999 Rollie the Rooster	Open		6.00	6

International Fatcats - G. Pitt

YEAR ISSUE	EDITION LIMIT	YEAR RETD.	ISSUE PRICE	*QUOTE U.S.$
1998 Canada	Numbrd.		25.00	25
1998 France	Numbrd.		25.00	25
1998 Germany	Numbrd.		25.00	25
1998 Italy	Numbrd.		25.00	25
1998 Mexico	Numbrd.		25.00	25
1998 Spain	Numbrd.		25.00	25
1998 Switzerland	Numbrd.		25.00	25
1998 USA	Numbrd.		25.00	25

North American Wildlife - T. Swanson

YEAR ISSUE	EDITION LIMIT	YEAR RETD.	ISSUE PRICE	*QUOTE U.S.$
1998 Big Horn Sheep - "Mountain Gathering"	Numbrd.		30.00	33
1998 Buffalo - "Roaming The Plains"	Numbrd.		30.00	33
1998 Gamble Quail - "Family Gathering"	Numbrd.		30.00	33
1998 Mountain Goat - "Chilly Heights"	Numbrd.		30.00	33
1998 Mule Deer - "Trouble Ahead"	Numbrd.		30.00	33
1998 Red Fox - "Prey in Sight"	Numbrd.		30.00	33
1998 Whitetail Deer - "Regal Solitude"	Numbrd.		30.00	33
1998 Wolves - "Mist Morning Hunters"	Numbrd.		30.00	33

Rocky Mountain Wildlife - T. Swanson

YEAR ISSUE	EDITION LIMIT	YEAR RETD.	ISSUE PRICE	*QUOTE U.S.$
1998 Elk - "Storm King"	Numbrd.	1999	30.00	30
1998 Grizzly Bear - "Fishing in Still Water"	Numbrd.	1999	30.00	30
1998 Moose - "Evening Solitude"	Numbrd.	1999	30.00	30
1998 Mountain Lion - "Dangers Approach"	Numbrd.	1999	30.00	30

Trevor's Farm Friends - T. Swanson

YEAR ISSUE	EDITION LIMIT	YEAR RETD.	ISSUE PRICE	*QUOTE U.S.$
1998 Catie The Cow	Numbrd.		22.50	23
1998 Gerrie The Goat	Numbrd.		22.50	23
1998 Paulie The Pig	Numbrd.		22.50	23
1998 Rollie The Rooster	Numbrd.		22.50	23

Jan Hagara Collectables

Bust Series - J. Hagara

YEAR ISSUE	EDITION LIMIT	YEAR RETD.	ISSUE PRICE	*QUOTE U.S.$
1991 David	10,000	1997	120.00	60-120
1990 Hannah	10,000	1997	120.00	60-120
1990 Jamie	10,000	1997	120.00	60-120
1991 Violet	10,000	1997	120.00	60-120

Georgetown Series - J. Hagara

YEAR ISSUE	EDITION LIMIT	YEAR RETD.	ISSUE PRICE	*QUOTE U.S.$
1997 Ben	6,000	1997	69.00	69
1997 Cassie	6,000	1997	65.00	65
1996 Cathy II	6,000	1997	65.00	65
1996 Cynthia	6,000	1997	65.00	65
1998 Enya	6,000		65.00	65
1997 Faith	6,000	1997	65.00	65
1998 Judianna	6,000		55.00	55
1998 Miss Megan	6,000		69.00	69
1996 Ricky	6,000	1997	65.00	65

Legacy Series - J. Hagara

YEAR ISSUE	EDITION LIMIT	YEAR RETD.	ISSUE PRICE	*QUOTE U.S.$
1990 Rebecca	15,000	1997	95.00	65-95

Make Believe - J. Hagara

YEAR ISSUE	EDITION LIMIT	YEAR RETD.	ISSUE PRICE	*QUOTE U.S.$
1998 Brianna Rose	3,000		45.00	45
1998 Butchie & Oreo	3,000		45.00	45
1997 Emily	3,000		49.00	49
1997 Jasmine	3,000		49.00	49
1997 Jimmy Chuck	3,000		49.00	49
1997 Kayla	3,000		49.00	49
1996 Leah	3,000		49.00	49
1998 Mary Lou	3,000		49.00	49
1998 Peppermint	3,000		49.00	49

Musical Series - J. Hagara

YEAR ISSUE	EDITION LIMIT	YEAR RETD.	ISSUE PRICE	*QUOTE U.S.$
1985 Allison	2-Yr.	1987	45.00	300
1985 Cara	2-Yr.	1987	45.00	45-65
1985 Heather	2-Yr.	1987	45.00	300
1994 Jenny	10,000	1997	35.00	35
1985 JoJohn	2-Yr.	1987	45.00	150-250
1985 Michael	2-Yr.	1987	45.00	45-125
1985 Natalie	2-Yr.	1987	45.00	45-68
1985 Rachael	2-Yr.	1987	45.00	300
1985 Shannon	2-Yr.	1987	45.00	55-125

ShelfSitter Figurine - J. Hagara

YEAR ISSUE	EDITION LIMIT	YEAR RETD.	ISSUE PRICE	*QUOTE U.S.$
1995 Adrianne	7,500	1997	55.00	55
1990 Allegra	15,000	1994	40.00	40-45
1990 Chris	15,000	1994	40.00	55-65
1991 Crystal	15,000	1994	40.00	45-65
1996 Little Sharice w/Rocker	7,500	1997	71.50	72
1990 Matthew	15,000	1994	40.00	40-50
1991 Sally	15,000	1997	40.00	40
1990 Suzy	15,000	1996	40.00	40

Signature Musical Series - J. Hagara

YEAR ISSUE	EDITION LIMIT	YEAR RETD.	ISSUE PRICE	*QUOTE U.S.$
1985 Allegra	20,000	1989	65.00	150
1985 Mother & Child	17,500	1989	100.00	200
1985 Wendy	17,500	1989	65.00	135-300

Signature Series - J. Hagara

YEAR ISSUE	EDITION LIMIT	YEAR RETD.	ISSUE PRICE	*QUOTE U.S.$
1985 Alice & Andrew	20,000	1991	75.00	157
1985 Becky	20,000	1991	55.00	165-185
1988 Beth & Amy	10,000	1991	135.00	150-200
1992 Crista's Rabbit	800	1997	694.00	600-694
1985 Holly	20,000	1990	55.00	75-85
1985 In Line	10,000	1987	175.00	800-1000
1985 James	20,000	1988	55.00	75
1988 Jan & Sharice	7,500	1991	145.00	165-200
1985 Jessica	20,000	1990	55.00	75-90
1985 Julie	20,000	1990	55.00	55-75
1985 Kimmy	20,000	1990	55.00	235-250
1985 Linda	20,000	1988	55.00	75
1985 Mandy	20,000	1988	55.00	75
1985 Marc & Laurie	20,000	1990	55.00	213-250
1985 Memories	17,500	1991	75.00	225-300
1987 Nikki & Santa	5,000	1991	135.00	235-350
1989 Phillip's Cousins	7,500	1997	195.00	125-225
1990 Renny & Blueberry	1,200	1994	600.00	600
1992 Sophie	5,000	1995	125.00	150
1985 Storytime	17,500	1991	135.00	595
1985 Theresa	20,000	1991	55.00	135-200
1985 Todd	20,000	1990	55.00	125-250

Single Figurines - J. Hagara

YEAR ISSUE	EDITION LIMIT	YEAR RETD.	ISSUE PRICE	*QUOTE U.S.$
1988 Abby	15,000	1991	35.00	50-65
1989 Adell	15,000	1991	40.00	40-50
1984 Adrianne	6,000	1987	45.00	65-75
1984 Amanda	2-Yr.	1986	30.00	40-60
1986 Amy	2-Yr.	1988	30.00	60-85
1985 Angie & Honey	2-Yr.	1987	30.00	75-125
1983 Anne & The Bear	2-Yr.	1985	25.00	100-125
1989 April	15,000	1997	45.00	50
1986 Ashley (boy)	2-Yr.	1988	30.00	65
1994 Ashley (girl)	7,500	1997	60.00	60
1993 Baby Lee	7,500	1997	50.00	43-50
1991 Baby Sharice	15,000	1997	35.00	35
1983 Betsy & Jimmy	2-Yr.	1985	45.00	75
1990 Billy & Brenna	15,000	1992	55.00	65-75
1993 Blossom	7,500	1997	70.00	70-75
1984 Brian	2-Yr.	1986	30.00	50-68
1985 Brian & Cinnamon	2-Yr.	1987	30.00	250-350
1993 Brianna	7,500	1997	50.00	50
1990 Brooke	15,000	1997	42.50	39-43
1984 Carol	2-Yr.	1986	30.00	100-125
1987 Carrie	2-Yr.	1989	35.00	50
1990 Cathy	15,000	1997	42.50	45
1994 Chelsea	7,500	1997	90.00	90
1986 Chris	2-Yr.	1988	30.00	75-100
1984 Cristina	2-Yr.	1986	30.00	55-85
1991 Dacy	15,000	1994	45.00	45-65
1986 Daisies From Jimmy	2-Yr.	1988	45.00	75-125
1985 Daphanie & Unicorn	2-Yr.	1987	45.00	75-90
1992 Dee Dee	7,500	1997	50.00	50-60
1995 Elaina	7,500	1996	60.00	50-55
1984 Emily	2-Yr.	1986	30.00	50-65
1992 Erin	7,500	1997	70.00	50-70
1992 Fall (Megan)	7,500	1997	50.00	50
1987 Goldie	2-Yr.	1989	45.00	45
1987 Jeff	2-Yr.	1989	35.00	50
1994 Jennifer	7,500	1997	85.00	85
1983 Jenny & the Bye Lo	2-Yr.	1985	25.00	75-250
1983 Jody & Toy Horse	2-Yr.	1985	25.00	75-100
1994 Joy	7,500	1997	70.00	50-70
1986 Larry	2-Yr.	1988	30.00	50-70
1986 Laurel	2-Yr.	1988	30.00	75-85
1986 Lesley	2-Yr.	1988	30.00	58-65
1983 Lisa & Jumeau Doll	2-Yr.	1985	25.00	65-85
1994 Little Brian	7,500	1997	60.00	60
1983 Lydia & Shirley Temple	2-Yr.	1985	25.00	75-100
1991 Mary	15,000	1996	45.00	50
1988 Mary Ann & Molly	15,000	1991	50.00	65-85
1986 Meg	2-Yr.	1988	30.00	55-65
1986 Melanie & Scarlett	2-Yr.	1988	30.00	75-85
1984 Michelle	2-Yr.	1986	30.00	50-75
1984 Missy	2-Yr.	1986	30.00	75
1988 Nikki	15,000	1991	35.00	75
1986 Noel	2-Yr.	1988	30.00	100-200
1988 Paige	15,000	1991	35.00	75
1991 Paul	15,000	1994	45.00	45
1988 Sara Mae	15,000	1991	35.00	45-65
1989 Scott	15,000	1991	40.00	45
1990 Sharice	15,000	1993	42.50	43
1984 Sharice & Parry	2-Yr.	1986	50.00	55-85
1984 Spring & Lance	2-Yr.	1986	50.00	75
1993 Spring (Katy)	7,500	1997	60.00	50-60
1985 Stacy	2-Yr.	1987	30.00	75-85
1985 Stephen	2-Yr.	1987	30.00	75
1992 Summer	7,500	1997	50.00	60-70
1994 Tammy	7,500	1997	70.00	50-70
1994 Tommy	7,500	1997	70.00	60-70
1993 Twins	6,000	1997	75.00	55-75
1983 Victoria	2-Yr.	1985	25.00	65-125
1994 Winter (Aspen)	7,500	1997	60.00	50-60

June McKenna Collectibles, Inc.

Black Folk Art - J. McKenna

YEAR ISSUE	EDITION LIMIT	YEAR RETD.	ISSUE PRICE	*QUOTE U.S.$
1987 Aunt Bertha -3D	Closed	1991	36.00	100
1983 Black Boy With Watermelon, available in 3 colors	Closed	1988	12.00	75-125
1986 Black Butler	Closed	1989	13.00	75-100
1983 Black Girl With Watermelon, available in 3 colors	Closed	1988	12.00	125-145
1984 Black Man With Pig, available in 3 colors	Closed	1988	13.00	100-125
1984 Black Woman With Broom, available in 3 colors	Closed	1988	13.00	100-125
1989 Delia	Closed	1991	16.00	65-75
1992 Fishing John -3D	1,000	1997	160.00	160-175
1989 Jake	Closed	1991	16.00	65-75
1985 Kids in a Tub -3D	Closed	1990	30.00	110-125
1985 Kissing Cousins - sill sitter	Closed	1990	36.00	150-175
1990 Let's Play Ball -3D	Closed	1993	45.00	75-100
1987 Lil' Willie -3D	Closed	1991	36.00	75-100
1984 Mammie Cloth Doll	Closed	1988	90.00	500-590
1985 Mammie With Kids -3D	Closed	1990	90.00	175-250
1985 Mammie With Spoon	Closed	1989	13.00	175-225
1988 Netty	Closed	1991	16.00	65-75
1984 Remus Cloth Doll	Closed	1988	90.00	390-450
1988 Renty	Closed	1991	16.00	65-75
1990 Sunday's Best -3D	Closed	1993	45.00	75-100
1987 Sweet Prissy -3D	Closed	1991	36.00	75-100
1992 Sweet Sister Sue -3D	1,000	1997	160.00	160
1990 Tasha	Closed	1991	17.00	65-75
1985 Toaster Cover	Closed	1988	50.00	350
1990 Tyree	Closed	1991	17.00	65-75
1987 Uncle Jacob -3D	Closed	1991	36.00	75-100
1985 Watermelon Patch Kids	Closed	1990	24.00	150-175

Carolers - J. McKenna

YEAR ISSUE	EDITION LIMIT	YEAR RETD.	ISSUE PRICE	*QUOTE U.S.$
1985 Boy Caroler	Closed	1989	36.00	75-100
1992 Carolers, Grandparents	Closed	1994	70.00	85-125
1991 Carolers, Man With Girl	Closed	1994	50.00	85-100
1991 Carolers, Woman With Boy	Closed	1994	50.00	85-100
1994 Children Carolers	Closed	1997	90.00	90-100
1985 Girl Caroler	Closed	1989	36.00	75-100
1985 Man Caroler	Closed	1989	36.00	75-100
1985 Woman Caroler	Closed	1989	36.00	75-100

June McKenna Figurines - J. McKenna

YEAR ISSUE	EDITION LIMIT	YEAR RETD.	ISSUE PRICE	*QUOTE U.S.$
1989 16th Century Santa -3D, blue	Closed	1991	60.00	200-250
1989 16th Century Santa -3D, green	Closed	1989	60.00	300-450
1989 17th Century Santa -3D, red	Closed	1991	70.00	200-250
1993 Angel Name Plaque	Closed	1994	70.00	95-100
1983 Boy Rag Doll	Closed	1983	12.00	300-430
1985 Bride -3D	Closed	1987	25.00	200
1985 Bride w/o base -3D	Closed	1985	25.00	150-225
1993 Children Ice Skaters	Closed	1994	60.00	65-100
1992 Choir of Angels	Closed	1993	60.00	95-100
1992 Christmas Santa -3D	Closed	1993	60.00	100-150
1987 Country Rag Boy (sitting)	Closed	1990	40.00	175-200
1987 Country Rag Girl (sitting)	Closed	1990	40.00	250
1994 Decorating for Christmas -3D	Closed	1997	70.00	100-125
1985 Father Times -3D	Closed	1991	40.00	150-175
1983 Girl Rag Doll	Closed	1983	12.00	300-325
1993 A Good Night's Sleep -3D	Closed	1995	70.00	100-125
1985 Groom w/o base -3D	Closed	1985	25.00	175-235
1985 Groom-3D	Closed	1987	25.00	100-150
1989 Jolly Ole Santa -3D	Closed	1991	44.00	100-175
1992 Let It Snow	Closed	1997	70.00	90
1986 Little St. Nick -3D	Closed	1990	50.00	200-250
1986 Male Angel -3D	Closed	1986	44.00	1000-1300
1988 Mr. Santa -3D	Closed	1991	44.00	100-130
1993 Mr. Snowman	Closed	1994	40.00	65
1988 Mrs. Santa -3D	Closed	1989	50.00	250-300
1987 Name Plaque	Closed	1992	50.00	125-150
1990 Noel -3D	Closed	1992	50.00	120
1987 Patriotic Santa -3D	Closed	1989	50.00	300-350
1993 Santa and Friends -3D	Closed	1997	70.00	100-120
1993 Santa Name Plaque	Closed	1995	70.00	95-100
1993 The Snow Family	Closed	1994	40.00	65
1994 Snowman and Child	Closed	1997	70.00	85
1985 Soldier -3D	Closed	1988	40.00	200-250
1994 Star of Bethlehem-Angel	Closed	1997	40.00	40-45
1995 A Surprise For Joey -3D	Closed	1997	70.00	75-90
1992 Taking A Break -3D	Closed	1995	60.00	100
1995 Travel Plans	Closed	1997	70.00	70
1984 Tree Topper	Closed	1987	70.00	400-475

Limited Edition - J. McKenna

YEAR ISSUE	EDITION LIMIT	YEAR RETD.	ISSUE PRICE	*QUOTE U.S.$
1988 Bringing Home Christmas	4,000	1990	170.00	188-450
1987 Christmas Eve	4,000	1989	170.00	375-400
1992 Christmas Gathering	4,000	1997	220.00	300-325
1991 Coming to Town	4,000	1994	220.00	313-438
1983 Father Christmas	4,000	1986	90.00	1875-3000

*Quotes have been rounded up to nearest dollar

YEAR ISSUE	EDITION LIMIT	YEAR RETD.	ISSUE PRICE	*QUOTE U.S.$
1999 Feathered Friends	4,000		270.00	270
1987 Kris Kringle	4,000	1990	350.00	438-536
1997 Lighting The Way	4,000		270.00	270
1996 Magic of Christmas	4,000		270.00	270
1998 Memories of Christmas	4,000		270.00	270
1990 Night Before Christmas	1,500	1993	750.00	750-800
1984 Old Saint Nick	4,000	1986	100.00	938-1500
1993 The Patriot	4,000	1997	250.00	300
1995 Peaceful Journey	4,000	1998	270.00	270
1988 Remembrance of Christmas Past	4,000	1992	400.00	750
1991 Santa's Hot Air Balloon	1,500	1993	800.00	800-1000
1989 Santa's Wardrobe	1,500	1992	750.00	950
1989 Seasons Greetings	4,000	1992	200.00	188-394
1994 St. Nicholas	4,000	1998	250.00	250-275
1986 Victorian	4,000	1988	150.00	250-750
1990 Wilderness	4,000	1994	200.00	250-375
1985 Woodland	4,000	1987	140.00	313-1000

Limited Edition 7" - J. McKenna

YEAR ISSUE	EDITION LIMIT	YEAR RETD.	ISSUE PRICE	*QUOTE U.S.$
1991 Christmas Bishop	7,500	1993	110.00	175-250
1993 Christmas Cheer 1st ed.	7,500	1993	120.00	245-313
1993 Christmas Cheer 2nd. ed.	7,500	1995	120.00	150-200
1990 Christmas Delight	7,500	1992	100.00	150-250
1995 Christmas Lullaby, red	7,500	1996	120.00	150-350
1988 Christmas Memories	7,500	1991	90.00	125-244
1992 Christmas Wizard	7,500	1994	110.00	150-200
1990 Ethnic Santa	7,500	1992	100.00	200-225
1988 Joyful Christmas	7,500	1991	90.00	185-250
1994 Mrs. Claus, Dancing to the Tune	7,500	1997	120.00	120-200
1989 Old Fashioned Santa	7,500	1991	100.00	188
1996 Polar Bear Express	2,500	1999	120.00	120
1989 Santa's Bag of Surprises	7,500	1991	100.00	275-300
1994 Santa's One Man Band	7,500	1997	120.00	120-200

Limited Edition Flatback - J. McKenna

YEAR ISSUE	EDITION LIMIT	YEAR RETD.	ISSUE PRICE	*QUOTE U.S.$
1991 Bag of Stars	10,000	1993	34.00	65
1993 Bells of Christmas	10,000	1995	40.00	50
1989 Blue Christmas	10,000	1991	32.00	88-100
1992 Deck The Halls	10,000	1994	34.00	50
1991 Farewell Santa	10,000	1993	34.00	65-95
1992 Good Tidings	10,000	1994	34.00	45-65
1990 Medieval Santa	10,000	1992	34.00	65-75
1988 Mystical Santa	10,000	1991	30.00	100
1994 Not Once But Twice	10,000	1997	40.00	50-55
1990 Old Time Santa	10,000	1992	34.00	75-90
1994 Post Marked North Pole	10,000	1997	40.00	55
1993 Santa's Love	10,000	1995	40.00	60-75
1988 Toys of Joy	10,000	1991	30.00	65-70
1989 Victorian	10,000	1991	32.00	94-125

Nativity Set - J. McKenna

YEAR ISSUE	EDITION LIMIT	YEAR RETD.	ISSUE PRICE	*QUOTE U.S.$
1988 Nativity - 6/pc. (Mary, Joseph, Baby Jesus, Manger, Guardian Angel & creche)	Closed	1997	130.00	150
1990 Shepherds With Sheep - 2/pc.	Closed	1997	60.00	75-100
1989 Three Wise Men	Closed	1997	60.00	100-120

Personal Appearance Figurines - J. McKenna

YEAR ISSUE	EDITION LIMIT	YEAR RETD.	ISSUE PRICE	*QUOTE U.S.$
1989 Father Christmas	Closed	1993	30.00	188-200
1990 Old Saint Nick	Closed	1994	30.00	125-150
1991 Woodland	Closed	1995	35.00	57-125
1992 Victorian	Closed	1996	35.00	65-125
1993 Christmas Eve	Closed	1997	35.00	65-75
1994 Bringing Home Christmas	Closed	1998	35.00	65-75
1995 Seasons Greetings	Closed	1999	35.00	40-65
1996 Wilderness	4-Yr.		35.00	40
1997 Coming To town	4-Yr.		35.00	40
1998 Christmas Gathering	4-Yr.		35.00	40
1999 The Patriot Santa	4-Yr.		40.00	40

Registered Edition - J. McKenna

YEAR ISSUE	EDITION LIMIT	YEAR RETD.	ISSUE PRICE	*QUOTE U.S.$
1991 Checking His List	Closed	1994	230.00	288-350
1995 Christmas Down on the Farm	Closed	1998	260.00	260
1996 Christmas Overload	Closed	1999	260.00	260-270
1999 Christmas Rush	Open		280.00	280
1995 Christmas Treat for All	Closed	1998	260.00	260
1986 Colonial	Closed	1990	150.00	244-450
1997 Forest Friends	Open		280.00	280
1992 Forty Winks	Closed	1994	250.00	300
1988 Jolly Ole St. Nick	Closed	1996	170.00	350-600
1998 Lending A Hand	Open		280.00	280
1994 Say Cheese, Please	Closed	1997	250.00	250-300
1993 Tomorrow's Christmas	Closed	1995	250.00	275-300
1990 Toy Maker	Closed	1993	200.00	207-344
1989 Traditional	Closed	1991	180.00	221-228
1987 White Christmas	Closed	1987	170.00	900-1100

Special Limited Edition - J. McKenna

YEAR ISSUE	EDITION LIMIT	YEAR RETD.	ISSUE PRICE	*QUOTE U.S.$
1996 All Aboard-Logging Car	Yr.Iss.	1997	250.00	250
1995 All Aboard-Toy Car	Closed	1996	250.00	250-275
1993 Baking Cookies	2,000	1995	450.00	375-500
1991 Bedtime Stories	2,000	1994	500.00	438-560
1990 Christmas Dreams	4,000	1992	280.00	375-400
1990 Christmas Dreams (Hassock)	63	1990	280.00	2000
1996 International Santa-German Pelznichol	Yr.Iss.	1997	100.00	110-130
1989 Last Gentle Nudge	4,000	1991	280.00	324-350
1989 Santa & His Magic Sleigh	4,000	1992	280.00	363-450
1992 Santa's Arrival	2,000	1994	300.00	225-350
1990 Santa's Reindeer	1,500	1993	400.00	400-450
1990 Up On The Rooftop	4,000	1991	280.00	400-450
1994 Welcome to the World	2,000	1995	400.00	450

Victorian Limited Edition - J. McKenna

YEAR ISSUE	EDITION LIMIT	YEAR RETD.	ISSUE PRICE	*QUOTE U.S.$
1990 Edward -3D	1,000	1991	180.00	300-600
1990 Elizabeth -3D	1,000	1991	180.00	150-175
1990 Joseph -3D	Closed	1991	50.00	175-200
1990 Victoria -3D	Closed	1991	50.00	170-175

Kiddie Car Classics/Hallmark Keepsake Collections

Kiddie Car Classics - D. Palmiter

YEAR ISSUE	EDITION LIMIT	YEAR RETD.	ISSUE PRICE	*QUOTE U.S.$
2000 1924 Toledo Fire Engine #6 QHG9053	29,500		65.00	65
1999 1926 Speedster QHG9048	29,500		90.00	90
1998 1926 Steelcraft Speedster QHG9045	Retrd.	1998	90.00	90-157
2000 1927 Gillham™ "Honeymoon Special" QHG7111	Numbrd.		60.00	60
1998 1929 Steelcraft Roadster by Murray® QHG9040	39,500	1998	70.00	70
1998 1930 Custom Biplane QHG7104	Numbrd.		55.00	55
1998 1930 Spirit of Christmas Custom Biplane QHG7105	Retrd.	1998	60.00	60
1999 1934 Garton® Chrysler Airflow QHG9056	Open		50.00	50
1999 1934 Garton® Speed Demon QHG9046	Open		55.00	55
2000 1935 American Tandem QHG9058	29,500		100.00	100
2000 1935 Gillham™ Auburn QHG9059	29,500		90.00	90
2000 1935 Gillham™ Duesenberg QHG7116	14,500		90.00	90
1996 1935 Steelcraft Airplane by Murray® QHG9032	Retrd.	1997	50.00	69-90
1996 1935 Steelcraft by Murray® (Luxury Edition) QHG9029	24,500	1996	65.00	88-125
2000 1935 Timmy Racer QHG7118	14,500		50.00	50
2000 1935 Toledo Duesenberg Racer (5th in Winner's Circle Series) QHG9057	Open		55.00	55
2000 1936 Gillham™ Birthday Special QHG7115	14,500		20.00	20
1994 1936 Steelcraft Lincoln Zephyr by Murray® QHG9015	19,500	1996	50.00	78-119
1997 1937 Garton® Ford Luxury QHG9035	Retrd.	1997	65.00	75-88
1999 1937 Steelcraft "Junior" Streamliner QHG9047	39,500		70.00	70
1995 1937 Steelcraft Auburn Luxury Ed. QHG9021	24,500	1996	65.00	94-125
1995 1937 Steelcraft Chrysler Airflow by Murray® QHG9024	24,500	1996	65.00	75-119
2000 1938 American Graham Roadster QHG9060	29,500		75.00	75
1997 1938 Garton® Lincoln Zephyr Luxury Edition QHX9038	Retrd.	1997	65.00	95-125
2000 1938 Toledo Air King Airplane QHG9052	Numbrd.		50.00	50
1997 1939 Garton® Ford Station Wagon QHX9034	Retrd.	1999	55.00	55-100
1998 1940 Custom Roadster with Trailer QHG7106	39,500		75.00	75
1997 1940 Gendron "Red Hot" Roadster, (2nd in Winner's Circle Series) QHX9037	Retrd.	1999	55.00	55-100
1999 1941 Garton® Field Ambulance QHG9049	39,500		65.00	65
1999 1941 Garton® Roadster QHG9050	39,500		70.00	70
1999 1941 Garton® Speed Demon, (4th in Winner's Circle Series) QHG9046	Open		55.00	55
1992 1941 Murray® Airplane QHG9003	14,500	1993	50.00	300-390
1997 1941 Murray® Junior Service Truck QHG9031	Retrd.	1999	55.00	55-82
1998 1941 Steelcraft by Murray® Fire Truck QHG9042	Retrd.	2000	60.00	60
1998 1941 Steelcraft Chrysler by Murray® QHG9044	Retrd.	2000	55.00	55
1997 1941 Steelcraft Oldsmobile by Murray® QHG9036	Retrd.	1999	55.00	55
1994 1941 Steelcraft Spitfire Airplane QHG9009	19,500	1996	50.00	125-150
1995 1948 Murray® Pontiac QHG9026	Retrd.	1998	50.00	55-63
1999 1949 Gillham™ Special QHG7108	Numbrd.		50.00	50
1999 1949 Gillham™ Sport (with golf bag) QHG7109	Open		60.00	60
2000 1949 Gillham™ Sport QHG7109	Numbrd.		60.00	60
1999 1950 Holiday MURRAY® General QHG9054	Yr.Iss.	1999	60.00	60
1999 1950 Murray® General QHG9051	Numbrd.		50.00	50
1995 1950 Murray® Torpedo QHG9020	Retrd.	1996	50.00	99-125
1998 1950s Custom Convertible QHG7101	Retrd.	1999	60.00	60
1992 1953 Murray® Dump Truck QHG9012	14,500	1993	48.00	150-296
1998 1955 Custom Chevy® QHG7103	Retrd.	2000	50.00	50
1992 1955 Murray® Champion QHG9008	14,500	1993	45.00	275-360
1994 1955 Murray® Dump Truck QHG9011	19,500	1996	48.00	75-120
1993 1955 Murray® Fire Chief QHG9006	19,500	1996	45.00	125-219
1992 1955 Murray® Fire Truck QHG9001	14,500	1993	50.00	275-450
1994 1955 Murray® Fire Truck QHG9010	19,500	1996	50.00	340-375
1994 1955 Murray® Ranch Wagon QHG9007	24,500	1996	48.00	69-89
1994 1955 Murray® Red Champion QHG9002	19,500	1996	45.00	95-113
1995 1955 Murray® Royal Deluxe QHG9025	29,500	1999	55.00	55-69
1992 1955 Murray® Tractor and Trailer QHG9004	14,500	1993	55.00	270-350
1994 1956 Garton® Dragnet Police Car QHG9016	24,500	1997	50.00	60-75
1996 1956 Garton® Hot Rod Racer (1st in Winner's Circle Series) QHG9028	Retrd.	1999	55.00	55-75
1994 1956 Garton® Kidillac (Sp. Ed.) QHX9094	Retrd.	1994	50.00	40-63
1994 1956 Garton® Mark V QHG9022	24,500	1997	45.00	45-75
1997 1956 Murray® Golden Eagle QHG9033	29,500	1997	50.00	55-100
2000 1958 Custom Corvette QHG7112	39,500		65.00	65
1994 1958 Murray® Atomic Missile QHG9018	24,500	1997	55.00	75-100
1998 1958 Murray® Champion QHG9041	Retrd.	2000	55.00	55
1995 1959 Garton® Deluxe Kidillac QHG9017	Retrd.	1996	55.00	63-90
1998 1960 Eight Ball Racer (3rd in Winner's Circle Series) QHG9039	Retrd.	2000	55.00	55
1995 1961 Garton® Casey Jones Locomotive QHG9019	Retrd.	1996	55.00	32-88
1994 1961 Murray® Circus Car QHG9014	24,500	1997	48.00	53-69
1994 1961 Murray® Speedway Pace Car QHG9013	24,500	1997	45.00	60-75
1996 1961 Murray® Super Deluxe Tractor w/Trailer QHG9027	Retrd.	1998	55.00	82-90
1995 1962 Murray® Super Deluxe Fire Truck QHG9095	Retrd.	1997	55.00	55-100
1996 1964 1/2 Ford Mustang QHG9030	Retrd.	1999	55.00	55-75
1995 1964 Garton® Tin Lizzie QHG9023	Retrd.	1997	50.00	69-100
1993 1968 Murray® Boat Jolly Roger QHG9005	19,500	1996	50.00	50-75
1998 1998 NASCAR® 50th Anniversary Custom Champion QHG7110	Retrd.	2000	60.00	60
2000 Bill Elliott NASCAR® QHG7113	39,500		65.00	65
2000 Custom Chevy QHG7117	14,500		55.00	55
1998 Don's Street Rod QHG7102	Retrd.	1999	55.00	55
2000 Fire Truck #2 QHG9064	14,500		75.00	75
2000 Jingle Bell Express QHG9065	14,500		60.00	60
1998 NASCAR® Custom Murray® Champion QHG7110	Open		60.00	60
2000 Red Baron QHG7144	14,500		65.00	65

Kiddie Car Classics-minis - D. Palmiter

YEAR ISSUE	EDITION LIMIT	YEAR RETD.	ISSUE PRICE	*QUOTE U.S.$
2000 1937 Murray® Steelcraft Auburn QHG2211	14,500		30.00	30
1999 1941 Murray® Pursuit Airplane QHG2203	Numbrd.		25.00	25
2000 1941 Steelcraft Spitfire Airplane QHG2206	Numbrd.		25.00	25
2000 1950 Murray® Torpedo QHG2209	Numbrd.		25.00	25
1999 1953 Murray® Dump Truck QHG2201	Numbrd.		25.00	25
1999 1955 Murray® Champion QHG2202	Numbrd.		25.00	25
2000 1955 Murray® Fire Chief QHG2208	Numbrd.		25.00	25
1999 1955 Murray® Fire Truck QHG2204	Numbrd.		25.00	25
1999 1955 Murray® Tractor and Trailer QHG2205	Numbrd.		25.00	25
2000 1956 Garton® Kiddilac QHG2210	Numbrd.		25.00	25
2000 1968 Murray® Boat Jolly Roger QHG2207	Numbrd.		25.00	25

Sidewalk Cruisers - D. Palmiter

YEAR ISSUE	EDITION LIMIT	YEAR RETD.	ISSUE PRICE	*QUOTE U.S.$
1998 1932 Keystone Coast-to-Coast Bus QHG6320	Open		45.00	45
1998 1934 Mickey Mouse Velocipede QHG6316	Open		48.00	48
1996 1935 American Airflow Coaster QHG6310	Retrd.	1998	48.00	48-75
1996 1935 Sky King Velocipede QHG6311	Retrd.	1999	45.00	45-75
1995 1935 Steelcraft Streamline Velocipede by Murray® QHG6306	Retrd.	1999	45.00	45-50
1998 1937 De Luxe Velocipede QHG6319	Open		45.00	45
2000 1937 Mickey Mouse Streamline Express Coaster Wagon QHG6322	24,500		48.00	48
1997 1937 Scamp Wagon QHG6318	Open		48.00	48
1995 1937 Steelcraft Streamline Scooter by Murray® QHG6301	Retrd.	1997	35.00	35-57
1997 1939 American National Pedal Bike QHG6314	Retrd.	2000	38.00	38
1997 1939 Garton® Batwing Scooter QHG6317	Retrd.	2000	38.00	38
1995 1939 Mobo Horse QHG6304	Retrd.	1998	45.00	45-63
1995 1940 Garton® Aero Flight Wagon QHG6305	Retrd.	1998	48.00	48-63
1996 1940s (late) Mobo Sulky QHG6308	Retrd.	1999	48.00	48-119
1996 1941 Keystone Locomotive QHG6312	Retrd.	1998	38.00	25-38
1996 1950 Garton® Delivery Cycle QHG6309	Retrd.	1999	38.00	38-50
1999 1951 Hopalong Cassidy Velocipede QHG6325	24,500		48.00	48
1995 1958 Murray® Police Cycle QHG6307	Retrd.	1999	55.00	55-63
1997 1960 Murray® Blaze-O-Jet Tricycle QHG6313	Retrd.	2000	45.00	45
1998 1960s Sealtest Milk Truck QHG6315	Open		40.00	40
1995 1963 Garton® Speedster QHG6303	Retrd.	1999	38.00	38-57
1995 1966 Garton® Super-Sonda QHG6302	Retrd.	1997	45.00	45-60

Kurt S. Adler, Inc.

Angel Darlings - N. Bailey

YEAR ISSUE	EDITION LIMIT	YEAR RETD.	ISSUE PRICE	*QUOTE U.S.$
1996 Almost Fits H4765/1	Retrd.	1998	11.00	11
1996 Bottoms Up H4765/2	Retrd.	1998	11.00	11
1996 Buddies H4765/3	Retrd.	1998	11.00	11
1996 Cuddles H4765/5	Retrd.	1998	11.00	11
1996 Dream Builders H4765/4	Retrd.	1998	11.00	11
1997 For You W7951	Retrd.	1999	21.00	21
1996 Peek-A-Boo H4765/6	Retrd.	1998	11.00	11

*Quotes have been rounded up to nearest dollar

YEAR ISSUE	EDITION LIMIT	YEAR RETD.	ISSUE PRICE	*QUOTE U.S.$
1997 The Secret W7950	Retrd.	1999	19.00	19
1997 Sharing W7949	Retrd.	1998	21.00	21

Birthstone Bearies - H. Adler

YEAR ISSUE	EDITION LIMIT	YEAR RETD.	ISSUE PRICE	*QUOTE U.S.$
1998 Bearie w/Heart, 4 1/2" JAN Birthstone W6900/JAN	Retrd.	1999	12.00	12
1998 Bearie w/Heart, 4 1/2" FEB Birthstone W6900/FEB	Retrd.	1999	12.00	12
1998 Bearie w/Heart, 4 1/2" MAR Birthstone W6900/MAR	Retrd.	1999	12.00	12
1998 Bearie w/Heart, 4 1/2" APR Birthstone W6900/APR	Retrd.	1999	12.00	12
1998 Bearie w/Heart, 4 1/2" MAY Birthstone W6900/MAY	Retrd.	1999	12.00	12
1998 Bearie w/Heart, 4 1/2" JUN Birthstone W6900/JUN	Retrd.	1999	12.00	12
1998 Bearie w/Heart, 4 1/2" JUL Birthstone W6900/JUL	Retrd.	1999	12.00	12
1998 Bearie w/Heart, 4 1/2" AUG Birthstone W6900/AUG	Retrd.	1999	12.00	12
1998 Bearie w/Heart, 4 1/2" SEP Birthstone W6900/SEP	Retrd.	1999	12.00	12
1998 Bearie w/Heart, 4 1/2" OCT Birthstone W6900/OCT	Retrd.	1999	12.00	12
1998 Bearie w/Heart, 4 1/2" NOV Birthstone W6900/NOV	Retrd.	1999	12.00	12
1998 Bearie w/Heart, 4 1/2" DEC Birthstone W6900/DEC	Retrd.	1999	12.00	12

Christmas Legends - P.F. Bolinger

YEAR ISSUE	EDITION LIMIT	YEAR RETD.	ISSUE PRICE	*QUOTE U.S.$
1994 Aldwyn of the Greenwood J8196	Retrd.	1996	145.00	145
1994 Berwyn the Grand J8198	Retrd.	1996	175.00	175
1995 Bountiful J8234	Retrd.	1996	164.00	164
1994 Caradoc the Kind J8199	Retrd.	1999	70.00	70
1994 Florian of the Berry Bush J8199	Retrd.	1999	70.00	70
1994 Gustave the Gutsy J8199	Retrd.	1999	70.00	70
1998 Irish Santa J6623	Retrd.	1999	67.00	67
1998 Jolly Old St. Nick J6620	Retrd.	2000	50.00	50
1995 Luminatus J8241	Retrd.	1999	136.00	136
1998 Neptune Santa J3832	Retrd.	1999	60.00	60
1997 Peace Santa J6563	2,500	1999	80.00	80
1994 Silvanus the Cheerful J8197	Retrd.	1996	165.00	165

The Fabriché™ Bear & Friends Series - KSA Design Team

YEAR ISSUE	EDITION LIMIT	YEAR RETD.	ISSUE PRICE	*QUOTE U.S.$
1992 Laughing All The Way J1567	Retrd.	1994	83.00	83
1992 Not A Creature Was Stirring W1534	Retrd.	1996	67.00	67
1993 Teddy Bear Parade W1601	Retrd.	1996	73.00	73

Fabriché™ Angel Series - K.S. Adler

YEAR ISSUE	EDITION LIMIT	YEAR RETD.	ISSUE PRICE	*QUOTE U.S.$
1992 Heavenly Messenger W1584	Retrd.	1994	41.00	41

Fabriché™ Camelot Figure Series - P. Mauk

YEAR ISSUE	EDITION LIMIT	YEAR RETD.	ISSUE PRICE	*QUOTE U.S.$
1994 King Arthur J3372	7,500	1996	110.00	110
1993 Merlin the Magician J7966	7,500	1996	120.00	120
1993 Young Arthur J7967	7,500	1996	120.00	120

Fabriché™ Holiday Figurines - KSA Design Team, unless otherwise noted

YEAR ISSUE	EDITION LIMIT	YEAR RETD.	ISSUE PRICE	*QUOTE U.S.$
1998 African American Santa, 10" W1848 - A. Epton	Retrd.	2000	50.00	50
1995 All Aboard For Christmas W1679	Retrd.	1996	56.00	56
1994 All Star Santa W1652	Retrd.	1999	56.00	56
1993 All That Jazz W1620	Retrd.	1994	67.00	67
1992 An Apron Full of Love W1582 - M. Rothenberg	Retrd.	1996	75.00	75
1995 Armchair Quarterback W1693	Retrd.	1996	90.00	90
1998 Barbeque Santa W1850 - J. Adams	Retrd.	1999	72.00	72
1994 Basket of Goodies W1650	Retrd.	1996	60.00	60
1998 Believe Santa ME156 - M. Engelbreit	Retrd.	2000	56.00	56
1992 Bringing in the Yule Log W1589 - M. Rothenberg	5,000	1996	200.00	200
1993 Bringing the Gifts W1605	Retrd.	1996	60.00	60
1992 Bundles of Joy W1578	Retrd.	1994	78.00	78
1995 Captain Claus W1680	Retrd.	1999	56.00	56
2000 Captain Santa Holding Boat W5851	Open		30.00	30
2000 Chasmpion Golf Santa W5850	Open		30.00	30
1994 Checking His List W1643	Retrd.	1996	60.00	65
1993 Checking It Twice W1604	Retrd.	1997	56.00	56
1998 Chef Santa W1903 - J. Adams	Retrd.	2000	56.00	56
1992 Christmas is in the Air W1590	Retrd.	1995	110.00	125
1997 Christmas Wish List W1773	Retrd.	1999	40.00	40
2000 Coca Cola Santa in Rocking Chair W5862 - Coca Cola	Open		45.00	45
1995 Diet Starts Tomorrow W1691	Retrd.	1996	60.00	60
1997 Fan Mail W1804 - M. Rothenberg	Retrd.	1999	50.00	50
1995 Father Christmas W1687	Retrd.	1996	56.00	56
1994 Firefighting Friends W1654	Retrd.	1996	72.00	72
1997 For the Mrs. W1800 - V. Antonov	Retrd.	1999	42.00	42
1993 Forever Green W1607	Retrd.	1994	56.00	56
1994 Friendship W1642	Retrd.	1996	65.00	65
1997 Frosty Friends W1807	Retrd.	1997	40.00	40
1995 Gift From Heaven W1694	Retrd.	1996	60.00	60
1997 Gifts a Plenty W1775	Retrd.	1999	45.00	45
1992 He Did It Again J7944 - T. Rubel	Retrd.	1996	160.00	160
1993 Here Kitty W1618 - M. Rothenberg	Retrd.	1994	90.00	125
1994 Ho, Ho, Ho Santa W1632	Retrd.	1996	56.00	56
1994 Holiday Express W1636	Retrd.	1997	100.00	100
1997 Holiday on Ice W1805 - M. Rothenberg	Open		135.00	135
1992 Homeward Bound W1568	Retrd.	1996	61.00	65
1997 House Calls W1772	Retrd.	2000	40.00	40
1992 Hugs and Kisses W1531	Retrd.	1994	67.00	67
1992 I'm Late, I'm Late J7947 - T. Rubel	Retrd.	1995	100.00	100
2000 Irish Santa "When Irish Eyes Are Smiling" (musical) W5849 - M. Phelps	Open		45.00	45
1992 It's Time To Go J7943 - T. Rubel	Retrd.	1994	150.00	150
1995 Kris Kringle W1685	Retrd.	1996	55.00	55
1997 Labor of Love W1774	Retrd.	1999	45.00	45
1994 Mail Must Go Through W1667 - KSA/WRG	Retrd.	1996	110.00	110
1997 Making Waves W1806	Retrd.	1999	55.00	55
1992 Merry Kissmas W1548 - M. Rothenberg	Retrd.	1993	140.00	140
1995 Merry Memories W1735	Retrd.	1997	56.00	56
1994 Merry St. Nick W1641 - Giordano	Retrd.	2000	90.00	90
1995 Mrs. Santa Caroller W1690 - M. Rothenberg	Retrd.	1999	70.00	70
1997 My How You Have Grown W1803 - M. Rothenberg	Open		75.00	75
1995 Night Before Christmas W1692 - Wood River Gallery	Retrd.	1996	60.00	60
2000 Noah Santa W5856	Open		40.00	40
1994 Officer Claus W1677	Open		56.00	56
1997 One More Story W1796	Retrd.	1999	55.00	55
1997 Paperwork W1776	Retrd.	2000	56.00	56
1993 Par For The Claus W1603	Retrd.	2000	60.00	60
1994 Peace Santa W1631	Retrd.	1996	60.00	60
1995 Pere Noel W1686	Retrd.	1996	55.00	55
1995 Playtime For Santa W1619	Retrd.	1994	67.00	67
1997 Puppy Love W1808	Retrd.	1999	50.00	50
1994 Santa Calls W1678 - W. Joyce	Retrd.	1996	55.00	55
1995 Santa Caroller W1689 - M. Rothenberg	Retrd.	1999	70.00	70
2000 Santa Chef w/Gingerbread House W5821	Open		37.00	37
1991 Santa Fiddler W1549 - M. Rothenberg	Retrd.	1992	100.00	100
1998 Santa in Police Car W1849	Retrd.	1999	45.00	45
1997 Santa on Line W1799	Retrd.	1999	50.00	50
1992 Santa Steals A Kiss & A Cookie W1581 - M. Rothenberg	Retrd.	1994	150.00	175
1998 Santa w/Cats & Dogs W1853 - Giordano	Retrd.	1999	45.00	45
2000 Santa w/Dog W5823	Open		36.00	36
1992 Santa's Cat Nap W1504 - M. Rothenberg	Retrd.	1992	98.00	110
1994 Santa's Fishtales W1640	Retrd.	1999	60.00	60
1992 Santa's Ice Capades W1588 - M. Rothenberg	Retrd.	1995	110.00	110
1994 Schussing Claus W1651	Retrd.	1996	78.00	78
2000 Scottish Santa W5877	Open		37.00	37
1998 Someone Special W1917 - M. Rothenberg	Retrd.	2000	50.00	50
1992 St. Nicholas The Bishop W1532	Retrd.	1997	78.00	78
1998 St. Nicholas with Tree W1851	Retrd.	2000	50.00	50
2000 St. Patrick Bishop W5822	Open		45.00	45
1994 Star Gazing Santa W1656 - M. Rothenberg	Retrd.	1999	120.00	120
1993 Stocking Stuffer W1622	Retrd.	1994	56.00	56
1995 Strike Up The Band W1681	Retrd.	1996	55.00	55
1998 Tee For Two W1916 - M. Rothenberg	Open		95.00	95
1995 Tee Time W1734	Retrd.	1996	60.00	60
1997 Test Drive W1802	Open		45.00	45
1993 Top Brass W1630	Retrd.	1995	67.00	67
1998 Tourist Santa W1915 - V. Antonov	Open		60.00	60
1997 Up On The Roof W1783 - Giordano	Open		67.00	70
1997 What a Catch W1801	Retrd.	1997	45.00	45
1993 With All The Trimmings W1616	Retrd.	1999	76.00	76
1995 Woodland Santa W1731 - R. Volpi	Retrd.	1996	67.00	67

Fabriché™ Santa at Home Series - M. Rothenberg

YEAR ISSUE	EDITION LIMIT	YEAR RETD.	ISSUE PRICE	*QUOTE U.S.$
1995 Baby Burping Santa W1732	Retrd.	1996	80.00	80
1994 The Christmas Waltz 1635	Retrd.	1996	135.00	135
1995 Family Portrait W1727	Retrd.	1996	140.00	140
1993 Grandpa Santa's Piggyback Ride W1621	7,500	1996	84.00	84
1995 Santa's Horsey Ride W1728	Retrd.	1997	80.00	80
1994 Santa's New Friend W1655	Retrd.	1996	110.00	110

Fabriché™ Santa's Helpers Series - M. Rothenberg

YEAR ISSUE	EDITION LIMIT	YEAR RETD.	ISSUE PRICE	*QUOTE U.S.$
1993 Little Olde Clockmaker W1629	5,000	1996	134.00	134
1992 A Stitch in Time W1591	5,000	1997	135.00	135

Fabriché™ Smithsonian Museum Series - KSA/Smithsonian

YEAR ISSUE	EDITION LIMIT	YEAR RETD.	ISSUE PRICE	*QUOTE U.S.$
1992 Holiday Drive W1556	Retrd.	1995	155.00	155
1993 Holiday Flight W1617	Retrd.	1995	144.00	144
1992 Peace on Earth Angel Treetop W1583	Retrd.	1995	52.00	52
1992 Peace on Earth Flying Angel W1585	Retrd.	1995	49.00	49
1991 Santa On A Bicycle W1527	Retrd.	1994	150.00	150
1995 Toys For Good Boys and Girls W1696	Retrd.	1996	75.00	75

Fabriché™ Thomas Nast Figurines - KSA Design Team

YEAR ISSUE	EDITION LIMIT	YEAR RETD.	ISSUE PRICE	*QUOTE U.S.$
1992 Caught in the Act W1577	Retrd.	1993	133.00	133
1992 Christmas Sing-A-Long W1576	12,000	1996	110.00	110
1993 Dear Santa W1602	Retrd.	1993	110.00	110
1991 Hello! Little One W1552	12,000	1994	90.00	90

Gallery of Angels - KSA Design Team

YEAR ISSUE	EDITION LIMIT	YEAR RETD.	ISSUE PRICE	*QUOTE U.S.$
1994 Guardian Angel M1099	2,000	1996	150.00	150
1994 Unspoken Word M1100	2,000	1996	150.00	150

Halloween - P.F. Bolinger

YEAR ISSUE	EDITION LIMIT	YEAR RETD.	ISSUE PRICE	*QUOTE U.S.$
1996 Dr. Punkinstein HW535	Retrd.	1999	50.00	50
1996 Eat at Drac's HW493	Retrd.	1999	22.00	22
1996 Pumpkin Grumpkin HW494	Retrd.	1999	18.00	18
1996 Pumpkin Plumpkin HW494	Retrd.	1999	18.00	18
1996 Pumpkins Are Us HW534	Retrd.	1996	17.00	17

Helping Hand Santas - P.F. Bolinger

YEAR ISSUE	EDITION LIMIT	YEAR RETD.	ISSUE PRICE	*QUOTE U.S.$
1996 Harmonious J6509	Retrd.	1999	115.00	115
1996 Noah J6487	Retrd.	1999	56.00	56
1996 Uncle Sam J6488	Retrd.	1996	56.00	56

Ho Ho Ho Gang - P.F. Bolinger

YEAR ISSUE	EDITION LIMIT	YEAR RETD.	ISSUE PRICE	*QUOTE U.S.$
1997 Behavometer J6555	Retrd.	1999	25.00	25
1998 Born To Fish J3812	Retrd.	1999	22.00	22
1996 Box of Chocolate J6510	Retrd.	1997	33.00	33
1997 Boxers or Briefs J6559	Retrd.	1999	25.00	25
1997 Captain Noah J6550	Retrd.	1999	18.00	18
1998 Choo Choo Santa J3806	Retrd.	1999	20.00	20
1994 Christmas Goose J8201	Retrd.	1999	22.00	22
1996 Christmas Shopping Santa J6497	Retrd.	1999	22.00	22
1996 Claus-A-Lounger J6478	Retrd.	1997	33.00	33
1995 Cookie Claus J8286	Retrd.	1996	39.00	39
1995 Do Not Disturb J8233	Retrd.	1999	34.00	34
1996 Fire Department North Pole J6508	Retrd.	1999	50.00	50
1996 Fireman Santa J6476	Retrd.	1999	28.00	28
1997 Golf Heaven J6553	Retrd.	1999	25.00	25
1998 Good Luck Irish J3807	Retrd.	1999	14.00	14
1998 Good Tools J3814	Retrd.	1999	22.00	22
1994 Holy Mackerel J8201	Retrd.	1999	22.00	22
1998 I Clean Chimneys J3809	Retrd.	2000	20.00	20
1998 I Love Chocolate J6628	Open		25.00	25
1997 Java Jumpstart J6554	Retrd.	1999	15.00	15
1996 Joy of Cooking J6496	Retrd.	1999	28.00	28
1998 Joy Rider J3813	Open		23.00	23
1996 Love Santa J6493	Retrd.	1996	18.00	18
1997 Never Say Diet J6578	Retrd.	1997	15.00	15
1995 No Hair Day J8287	Retrd.	1996	50.00	50
1996 Noel Roly Poly J6489	Retrd.	1996	20.00	20
1995 North Pole (large) J8237	Retrd.	1997	56.00	56
1995 North Pole (small) J8238	Retrd.	1997	45.00	45
1997 North Pole Country Club J6557	Open		45.00	45
1996 North Pole Pro-Am J6479	Open		28.00	28
1996 On Strike For More Cookies J6506	Retrd.	1999	33.00	33
1996 Police Department North Pole J6507	Retrd.	1997	50.00	50
1996 Policeman Santa J6475	Retrd.	1999	28.00	28
1998 Psychic Santa J3810	Retrd.	1999	20.00	20
1998 Replace The Divots J3815	Retrd.	1999	22.00	22
1994 Santa Cob J8203	Retrd.	1995	28.00	28
1997 Santa With Bear J6556	Retrd.	1999	8.00	8
1997 Santa's Day Off J6558	Retrd.	1999	25.00	25
1996 Save The Reindeer J6498	Retrd.	1997	28.00	28
1997 Snowmen Are Cool J6551	Retrd.	1997	20.00	20
1996 Some Assembly Required J6477	Retrd.	1997	53.00	53
1997 Spring Sale Snowman J6549	Retrd.	1999	20.00	20
1994 Surprise J8201	Retrd.	1997	22.00	22
1998 Teddy Bear Santa J3816	Retrd.	1999	20.00	20
1998 Things Are Looking Up J3811	Retrd.	1999	14.00	14
1998 Tundra Runners J3808	Retrd.	1999	20.00	20
1998 Whoa Kitty J3805	Retrd.	1999	20.00	20
1994 Will He Make It? J8203	Retrd.	1995	28.00	28
1995 Will Work For Cookies J8235	Retrd.	1999	40.00	40
1997 Winter Fun J6552	Retrd.	1999	25.00	25
1995 Wishful Thinking J8239	Retrd.	1997	32.00	32

Holly Bearies - H. Adler

YEAR ISSUE	EDITION LIMIT	YEAR RETD.	ISSUE PRICE	*QUOTE U.S.$
1996 Angel Bear J7342	Retrd.	1998	14.00	18
1998 Angel Bear, 6 1/4" W6751	Retrd.	1998	19.00	19
1996 Angel Starcatcher (Starlight Foundation) J7222	Retrd.	1996	20.00	20
1997 Angel Starcatcher II (Starlight Foundation) W6457	Retrd.	1997	20.00	20
1998 Angel Starcatcher III (Starlight Foundation) W6912	Retrd.	1998	20.00	20
1999 Angel Starcatcher IV (Starlight Foundation) W7222	Retrd.	1999	23.00	23
1998 Barbeque Bear, 3 1/2" W6933	Retrd.	1999	10.00	10
1998 Bear Angel on Cloud W6935	Retrd.	1998	14.00	15
1998 Bearie in Red Heart Dress, 6" W6754	Retrd.	1998	17.00	17
1998 Bearie in Red PJs Sitting on Box W6787	Retrd.	1998	19.00	19
1997 Bearies Mailing Packages, 5 1/2" W6443	Retrd.	1998	28.00	28
1997 Charlie The Fisherman, 8 1/4" W6448	Yr.Iss.	1997	33.50	34
1998 Father Christmas, 4" W6930	Retrd.	1998	9.00	9
1998 Holly Bearie w/Blanket & Pull Rabbit, 8" W6753	Retrd.	1998	28.00	28
1998 Merry Merry Holly Bearie, 4" W6930	Retrd.	1998	9.00	9
1996 Mother's Day Bear J7318	Retrd.	1996	15.00	16
1997 Sledding Bearies W6445	Retrd.	1998	25.00	26
1996 Teddy Tower J7221	Retrd.	1998	23.00	23
1998 Wedding Couple, 3 1/4" W6926	Retrd.	1999	10.00	10

Holly Bearies Calendar Bears - H. Adler

YEAR ISSUE	EDITION LIMIT	YEAR RETD.	ISSUE PRICE	*QUOTE U.S.$
1996 Fergus & Fritzi's Frosty Frolic, 3 3/4" J7215/Jan	Open		16.00	16
1996 Pinky & Victoria Are Sweeties, 3 7/8" J7215/Feb	Open		16.00	16
1996 Philo's Pot O Gold, 3 3/4" J7215/Mar	Open		16.00	16
1996 Sunshine Catching Raindrops, 3 3/4" J7215/Apr	Open		16.00	16
1996 Petunia & Nathan Plant Posies, 4" J7215/May	Open		16.00	16
1996 Thorndike & Filbert Catch Fish, 4 1/4" J7215/Jun	Open		16.00	16
1996 Clairmont, Dempsey & Pete, 4 1/8" J7215/Jul	Open		16.00	16
1996 Nicole & Nicholas Sun Bearthing, 4 7/8" J7215/Aug	Open		16.00	16

*Quotes have been rounded up to nearest dollar

YEAR ISSUE	EDITION LIMIT	YEAR RETD.	ISSUE PRICE	*QUOTE U.S.$
1996 Skeeter & Sigourney Start School, 4 1/4" J7215/Sep	Open		16.00	16
1996 Clara & Carnation The Kitty, 4 1/4" J7215/Oct	Open		16.00	16
1996 Thorndike All Dressed Up, 4 1/4" J7215/Nov	Open		16.00	16
1996 Grandma Gladys, 4 3/8" J7215/Dec	Open		16.00	16

Holly Dearies - H. Adler

YEAR ISSUE	EDITION LIMIT	YEAR RETD.	ISSUE PRICE	*QUOTE U.S.$
1998 Dearie Sliding on Ice (2 asst.) H5447	Open		14.00	14
1997 Santa & Reindeer (Glass Ball) J9905	Retrd.	1998	21.00	21
1997 Santa & Reindeer (Musical Glass Ball) J9906	Retrd.	1998	40.00	40
1997 Santa at the North Pole, 8" H5401	5,000		155.00	155

Inspirational - P.F. Bolinger

YEAR ISSUE	EDITION LIMIT	YEAR RETD.	ISSUE PRICE	*QUOTE U.S.$
1997 Angel with Heart J6569	Retrd.	1999	20.00	20
1997 Noah J6487	Retrd.	1997	56.00	56
1997 Saint Francis J6585	Retrd.	1999	56.00	56

Old World Santa Series - J. Mostrom

YEAR ISSUE	EDITION LIMIT	YEAR RETD.	ISSUE PRICE	*QUOTE U.S.$
1992 Chelsea Garden Santa W2721	Retrd.	1994	33.50	34
1993 Good King Wenceslas W2928	3,000	1996	134.00	134
1992 Large Black Forest Santa W2717	Retrd.	1994	110.00	110
1992 Large Father Christmas W2719	Retrd.	1994	106.00	106
1993 Medieval King of Christmas W2881	3,000	1994	390.00	390
1992 Mrs. Claus W2714	5,000	1996	37.00	37
1992 Patriotic Santa W2720	3,000	1994	128.00	128
1992 Pere Noel W2723	Retrd.	1994	33.50	34
1992 Small Black Forest Santa W2712	Retrd.	1994	40.00	40
1992 Small Father Christmas W2712	Retrd.	1994	33.50	34
1992 Small Father Frost W2716	Retrd.	1994	43.00	43
1992 Small Grandfather Frost W2718	Retrd.	1994	106.00	106
1992 St. Nicholas W2713	Retrd.	1994	30.00	30
1992 Workshop Santa W2715	5,000	1997	43.00	43

Sesame Street Series - KSA/JHP

YEAR ISSUE	EDITION LIMIT	YEAR RETD.	ISSUE PRICE	*QUOTE U.S.$
1993 Big Bird Fabriche, Figurine J7928	Retrd.	1996	60.00	60
1993 Big Bird Nutcracker H1199	Retrd.	1994	60.00	60

Snow People - P.F. Bolinger

YEAR ISSUE	EDITION LIMIT	YEAR RETD.	ISSUE PRICE	*QUOTE U.S.$
1996 Coola Hula J6430	Retrd.	1996	20.00	20
1996 Snowpoke J6431	Retrd.	1997	28.00	28
1996 Snowy J6429	Retrd.	1997	28.00	28

Snowbearies - H. Adler

YEAR ISSUE	EDITION LIMIT	YEAR RETD.	ISSUE PRICE	*QUOTE U.S.$
1998 Snowbearie Couple Carrying Other Snowbearie, 3 1/4" W6878	Retrd.	1998	11.00	11
1998 Snowbearie Couple Dancing on Ice Block, 3 1/4" W6878	Retrd.	1998	11.00	11
1998 Snowbearie Couple Playing on Ice Block, 3 1/4" W6878	Retrd.	1998	11.00	11
1997 Snowbearie Pair Dancing & Playing Leapfrog W6451	Retrd.	1998	9.00	9
1997 Snowbearie Pair Dancing & Playing Leapfrog W6491	Retrd.	1998	9.00	9
1997 Snowbearie w/Heart, 4 1/2" W6490	Retrd.	1998	18.00	18
1997 Snowbearies at Play W6452	Open		5.50	6
1997 Snowbearies at Play W6492	Retrd.	1998	5.50	6
1997 Snowbearies Hugging, 5 1/4" W6494	Retrd.	1998	20.00	20
1998 Snowbearies on Sled, set/2 W6888	Retrd.	1999	20.00	20
1998 Snowbearies on Sled, set/3 W6887	Retrd.	1999	20.00	20
1998 Snowbearies on Sled, set/4 W6886	Retrd.	1998	21.00	21
1998 Snowbearies on Sled, set/5 W6885	Retrd.	1998	22.50	23
1997 White Bear w/Ribbon & Snowflake, 8 1/2" H5651	Retrd.	1998	10.00	10

Steinbach Camelot Smoking Figure Series - KSA/Steinbach

YEAR ISSUE	EDITION LIMIT	YEAR RETD.	ISSUE PRICE	*QUOTE U.S.$
1994 Chief Sitting Bull Smoker ES834	7,500	1998	150.00	149-190
1993 King Arthur ES832	7,500	1996	175.00	159-175
1992 Merlin The Magician ES830	7,500	1997	150.00	145-150
1994 Sir Lancelot Smoker ES833	7,500	1997	150.00	149-175

Vatican Library Collection - Vatican Library

YEAR ISSUE	EDITION LIMIT	YEAR RETD.	ISSUE PRICE	*QUOTE U.S.$
1999 3 Angels & Baby Jesus V39	Retrd.	2000	35.00	35
1997 Holy Family Set V29	Open		80.00	80
1997 Three Wise Men V30	Open		100.00	100

Visions Of Santa Series - KSA Design Team

YEAR ISSUE	EDITION LIMIT	YEAR RETD.	ISSUE PRICE	*QUOTE U.S.$
1992 Santa Coming Out Of Fireplace J1023	Retrd.	1993	29.00	29
1992 Santa Holding Child J826	Retrd.	1993	24.50	25
1992 Santa Spilling Bag Of Toys J1022	7,500	1994	25.50	26
1992 Santa With Little Girls On Lap J1024	7,500	1996	24.50	25
1992 Santa With Sack Holding Toy J827	7,500	1994	24.50	25
1992 Workshop Santa J825	7,500	1994	27.00	27

Lee Middleton Original Dolls

Times To Cherish - Reva Schick

YEAR ISSUE	EDITION LIMIT	YEAR RETD.	ISSUE PRICE	*QUOTE U.S.$
2000 All Tuckered Out	Open		39.95	40
2000 Blessing of Love	Open		39.95	40
2000 Just Teething	Open		39.95	40
2000 Snuggle Bug	Open		39.95	40
2000 This Little Piggie	Open		39.95	40
2000 What a Big Boy	Open		39.95	40

Legends

Annual Collectors Edition - C. Pardell

YEAR ISSUE	EDITION LIMIT	YEAR RETD.	ISSUE PRICE	*QUOTE U.S.$
1990 The Night Before	500	1991	990.00	1800-2535
1991 Medicine Gift of Manhood	500	1992	990.00	935-1300
1992 Spirit of the Wolf	500	1992	950.00	1073-2000
1993 Tomorrow's Warrior	500	1993	590.00	1200
1994 Guiding Hand	500	1994	590.00	875-1100
1995 Gift of the Sacred Calf	500	1995	650.00	650-900
1996 Spirit and Image	500		750.00	750

Collectors Only - Various

YEAR ISSUE	EDITION LIMIT	YEAR RETD.	ISSUE PRICE	*QUOTE U.S.$
1993 Give Us Peace - C. Pardell	1,250	1993	270.00	350-600
1994 First Born - C. Pardell	1,250	1994	350.00	400-600
1994 River Bandits - K. Cantrell	1,250	1995	350.00	425-514
1995 Sonata - K. Cantrell	1,250	1996	250.00	300-400
1995 Daydreams of Manhood - C. Pardell	2,500	1995	390.00	500
1996 Innocence Remembered - C. Pardell	Retrd.	1996	490.00	490

American Heritage - D. Edwards

YEAR ISSUE	EDITION LIMIT	YEAR RETD.	ISSUE PRICE	*QUOTE U.S.$
1987 Grizz Country (Bronze)	Retrd.	1990	350.00	350
1987 Grizz Country (Pewter)	Retrd.	1990	370.00	370-520
1987 Winter Provisions (Bronze)	Retrd.	1990	340.00	340
1987 Winter Provisions (Pewter)	Retrd.	1990	370.00	370
1987 Wrangler's Dare (Bronze)	Retrd.	1990	630.00	630
1987 Wrangler's Dare (Pewter)	Retrd.	1990	660.00	660

American Indian Dance Premier Edition - C. Pardell

YEAR ISSUE	EDITION LIMIT	YEAR RETD.	ISSUE PRICE	*QUOTE U.S.$
1996 Dancing Ground	750		2500.00	2500
1993 Drum Song	750	1995	2800.00	2000-3950
1994 Footprints of the Butterfly	750	1995	1800.00	1990
1994 Image of the Eagle	750	1997	1900.00	2100
1995 Spirit of the Mountain	750	1999	1750.00	1850

American West Premier Edition - C. Pardell

YEAR ISSUE	EDITION LIMIT	YEAR RETD.	ISSUE PRICE	*QUOTE U.S.$
1992 American Horse	950	1995	1300.00	1300
1992 Defending the People	950	1999	1350.00	1450
1991 First Coup	950	1993	1150.00	1170-1430
1993 Four Bears' Challenge	950	1996	990.00	1050
1994 Season of Victory	950	1997	1500.00	1580
1991 Unexpected Rescuer	950	1991	990.00	1170-1200

The Endangered Wildlife Collection - K. Cantrell

YEAR ISSUE	EDITION LIMIT	YEAR RETD.	ISSUE PRICE	*QUOTE U.S.$
1993 Big Pine Survivor	950	1998	390.00	390
1990 Forest Spirit	950	1991	290.00	1000
1991 Mountain Majesty	950	1997	350.00	390
1991 Old Tusker	950	1997	390.00	390
1992 Plains Monarch	950	1997	350.00	390
1994 Prairie Phantom	950	1997	370.00	390
1990 Savannah Prince	950	1997	290.00	290-350
1993 Silvertip	950	1997	370.00	390
1992 Songs of Autumn	950	1995	390.00	550
1992 Spirit Song	950	1992	350.00	500-700
1994 Twilight	950	1997	290.00	310
1992 Unchallenged	950	1996	350.00	390

Endangered Wildlife Eagle Series - K. Cantrell

YEAR ISSUE	EDITION LIMIT	YEAR RETD.	ISSUE PRICE	*QUOTE U.S.$
1989 Aquila Libre	2,500	1995	280.00	300-400
1993 Defiance	2,500	1999	350.00	350
1992 Food Fight	2,500		650.00	750
1989 Outpost	2,500	1995	280.00	320-350
1989 Sentinel	2,500	1993	280.00	400-500
1993 Spiral Flight	2,500		290.00	300
1992 Sunday Brunch	2,500		550.00	650
1989 Unbounded	2,500	1994	280.00	240-400

Gallery Editions - Various

YEAR ISSUE	EDITION LIMIT	YEAR RETD.	ISSUE PRICE	*QUOTE U.S.$
1994 Center Fire - W. Whitten	350		2500.00	2600
1994 Mountain Family - D. Lemon	150	1996	7900.00	8300
1996 On Wings of Eagles - D. Lemon	250		3700.00	3700
1993 Over the Rainbow - K. Cantrell	600	1995	2900.00	3850-4000
1993 Over the Rainbow AP - K. Cantrell	Retrd.	1996	4000.00	5000
1992 Resolute - C. Pardell	250	1992	7950.00	9100-12000
1993 Visionary - C. Pardell	350		7500.00	9000
1993 The Wanderer - K. Cantrell	350	1999	3500.00	3700
1996 Wind on Still Water - C. Pardell	350	1996	2500.00	4500

Hidden Images Collection - D. Lemon

YEAR ISSUE	EDITION LIMIT	YEAR RETD.	ISSUE PRICE	*QUOTE U.S.$
1994 In Search of Bear Rock	350	1995	1300.00	1500
1995 Sensed, But Unseen	350	1995	990.00	1200
1995 Spirit	350	1997	990.00	990

Indian Arts Collection - C. Pardell

YEAR ISSUE	EDITION LIMIT	YEAR RETD.	ISSUE PRICE	*QUOTE U.S.$
1990 Chief's Blanket	1,500	1992	350.00	600-700
1990 Indian Maiden	1,500	1997	240.00	240
1990 Indian Potter	1,500	1997	260.00	260
1990 Kachina Carver	1,500	1993	270.00	286-400
1990 Story Teller	1,500	1993	290.00	450-550

The Legacies Of The West Premier Edition - C. Pardell

YEAR ISSUE	EDITION LIMIT	YEAR RETD.	ISSUE PRICE	*QUOTE U.S.$
1991 Defiant Comanche	950	1991	1300.00	1000-2210
1993 Eminent Crow	950	1994	1500.00	1400-1755
1994 Enduring	950	1996	1250.00	1350
1992 Esteemed Warrior	950	1992	1750.00	1850-1950
1990 Mystic Vision	950	1990	990.00	1700-2080
1991 No More, Forever	950	1992	1500.00	1690-1800
1992 Rebellious	950	1996	1500.00	1600
1990 Victorious	950	1990	1275.00	1800-2200

The Legendary West Collection - C. Pardell

YEAR ISSUE	EDITION LIMIT	YEAR RETD.	ISSUE PRICE	*QUOTE U.S.$
1992 Beating Bad Odds	2,500		390.00	410
1989 Bustin' A Herd Quitter	2,500	1999	590.00	660
1993 Cliff Hanger	2,500	1996	990.00	1050
1992 Crazy Horse	2,500	1992	390.00	800-1100
1989 Eagle Dancer	2,500	1996	370.00	410
1993 Hunter's Brothers	2,500	1999	590.00	660
1989 Johnson's Last Fight	2,500	1991	590.00	750-1200
1990 Keeper of Eagles	2,500	1997	370.00	410
1987 Pony Express (Bronze)	2,500	N/A	320.00	320-450
1989 Pony Express (Mixed Media)	2,500		390.00	410
1987 Pony Express (Pewter)	2,500	N/A	320.00	320-450
1989 Sacajawea	2,500	1995	380.00	595
1990 Shhh	2,500		390.00	530
1990 Stand of the Sash Wearer	2,500	1996	390.00	295-410
1989 Tables Turned	2,500		680.00	750
1990 Unbridled	2,500	1996	290.00	290
1991 Warning	2,500	1997	390.00	410
1989 White Feather's Vision	2,500	1991	390.00	750

The Legendary West Premier Edition - C. Pardell

YEAR ISSUE	EDITION LIMIT	YEAR RETD.	ISSUE PRICE	*QUOTE U.S.$
1990 Crow Warrior	750	1990	1225.00	1235-2000
1992 The Final Charge	750	1992	1250.00	1300-1500
1989 Pursued	750	1989	750.00	2000-4000
1988 Red Cloud's Coup	750	1988	480.00	5000-5500
1989 Songs of Glory	750	1989	850.00	3500-3900
1991 Triumphant	750	1991	1150.00	2200-2600

Special Commissions - Various

YEAR ISSUE	EDITION LIMIT	YEAR RETD.	ISSUE PRICE	*QUOTE U.S.$
1988 Alpha Pair (Bronze) - C. Pardell	Retrd.	N/A	330.00	330
1988 Alpha Pair (Mixed Media) - C. Pardell	S/O	N/A	390.00	500-750
1988 Alpha Pair (Pewter) - C. Pardell	Retrd.	N/A	330.00	330
1991 American Allegiance - D. Edwards	1,250	1996	570.00	625
1995 Father-The Power Within - D. Medina	350		1500.00	1590
1990 Lakota Love Song - C. Pardell	Retrd.	1990	380.00	1950
1987 Mama's Joy (Bronze) - D. Edwards	Retrd.	N/A	200.00	200
1987 Mama's Joy (Pewter) - D. Edwards	Retrd.	N/A	250.00	250
1996 Proud Heritage - K. Cantrell	2,500		290.00	290
1995 Rapture - W. Whitten	350	1999	1750.00	1850
1995 Scent in the Air - K. Cantrell	750		990.00	1200
1991 Symbols of Freedom - K. Cantrell	2,500		490.00	550
1987 Wild Freedom (Bronze) - D. Edwards	Retrd.	N/A	320.00	320
1987 Wild Freedom (Pewter) - D. Edwards	Retrd.	N/A	330.00	330
1992 Yellowstone Bound - K. Cantrell	600	1994	2500.00	3120-3950

Way of the Cat Collection - K. Cantrell

YEAR ISSUE	EDITION LIMIT	YEAR RETD.	ISSUE PRICE	*QUOTE U.S.$
1996 Cat's Cradle	500	1997	790.00	790
1995 Encounter	500	1995	750.00	1100-1600

Way of the Warrior Collection - C. Pardell

YEAR ISSUE	EDITION LIMIT	YEAR RETD.	ISSUE PRICE	*QUOTE U.S.$
1991 Clan Leader	1,600	1994	170.00	195-225
1991 Elder Chief	1,600	1994	170.00	225
1991 Medicine Dancer	1,600	1994	170.00	195-225
1991 Rite of Manhood	1,600	1994	170.00	189-225
1991 Seeker of Visions	1,600	1994	170.00	195-225
1991 Tribal Defender	1,600	1994	170.00	195-225

Way of the Wolf Collection - K. Cantrell

YEAR ISSUE	EDITION LIMIT	YEAR RETD.	ISSUE PRICE	*QUOTE U.S.$
1993 Courtship	500	1993	590.00	1500
1995 Gossip Column	500	1999	1250.00	1250
1994 Missed by a Hare	500	1994	700.00	850-1100
1994 Renewal	500	1994	700.00	950-1500
1995 Stink Bomb	500	1995	750.00	750-970

Wild Realm Premier Edition - C. Pardell

YEAR ISSUE	EDITION LIMIT	YEAR RETD.	ISSUE PRICE	*QUOTE U.S.$
1989 High Spirit	1,600	1996	870.00	1000
1991 Speed Incarnate	1,600	1996	790.00	790

Legends in Flight/Hallmark Keepsake Collections

Legends in Flight - Hallmark Keepsake Collections

YEAR ISSUE	EDITION LIMIT	YEAR RETD.	ISSUE PRICE	*QUOTE U.S.$
2000 Blériot XI QHA1009	Numbrd.		25.00	25
1999 Curtiss P-40 Warhawk QHA1000	12/00		30.00	30
2000 Curtiss R3C-2 Seaplane QHA1002	Numbrd.		32.00	32
1999 F-14A Tomcat QHA1006	24,500		40.00	40
2000 F-86F Sabre QHA1010	Numbrd.		27.00	27
2000 F4U-1D Corsair QHA1008	24,500		32.00	32
1999 Fokker DR I "Red Baron" QHA1005	12/00		35.00	35
2000 Fokker DR I Jasta 6 QHA1021	12,500		30.00	30
2000 Gee Bee Racer Post W.W. I QHA1015	12,500		32.00	32
2000 Modern F14 Tomcat QHA1020	12,500		32.00	32
2000 P38Y Lightening W.W. II QHA1017	12,500		42.00	42
2000 P51D Mustang W.W. II QHA1016	12,500		30.00	30
2000 Ryan NYP "Spirit of St. Louis" QHA1004	Numbrd.		30.00	30
2000 SPAD XIII "Smith IV" QHA1003	24,500		40.00	40
2000 SPAD XIII Spa 3/W.W. I QHA1014	12,500		28.00	28
2000 Vega 5B QHA1007	24,500		30.00	30
1999 Wright Flyer QHA1001	Numbrd.		35.00	35

Lenox Classics

Lenox Classics-China Animal Sculptures - Lenox

YEAR ISSUE	EDITION LIMIT	YEAR RETD.	ISSUE PRICE	*QUOTE U.S.$
1998 Between Sea & Sky (Ivory Dolphins)	Retrd.	2000	136.00	136
1998 Eagle of Freedom (Ivory Eagle)	Retrd.	2000	160.00	160
1999 The Graceful Swan	Open		119.00	119
1999 The Lenox Ivory Elephant	Open		136.00	136
1998 The Majestic Elephant (Ivory Elephant)	Open		136.00	136
1999 Wave Dancers	Open		119.00	119

Lenox Classics-China Annual Angel - Lenox

YEAR ISSUE	EDITION LIMIT	YEAR RETD.	ISSUE PRICE	*QUOTE U.S.$
1997 Guardian of the Stars	2,500	1999	195.00	195
1998 Guardian of Light	2,500	2000	195.00	195
1999 Guardian of The Millennium	2,000		225.00	225

Lenox Classics-China Annual Santa - Lenox

YEAR ISSUE	EDITION LIMIT	YEAR RETD.	ISSUE PRICE	*QUOTE U.S.$
1997 Santa's Joy (Santa w/Elf & Ornament)	2,500	1999	195.00	195
1998 Santa's Journey	2,500	2000	195.00	195
1999 North Pole Express	2,500		195.00	195

Lenox Classics-China Away in a Manager - Lenox

YEAR ISSUE	EDITION LIMIT	YEAR RETD.	ISSUE PRICE	*QUOTE U.S.$
1996 Angel	Retrd.	1998	50.00	50
1997 Gaspar	Retrd.	1998	50.00	50
1997 Heralding Angel	Retrd.	1998	50.00	50
1996 Jesus	Retrd.	1998	40.00	40
1996 Joseph	Retrd.	1998	50.00	50

*Quotes have been rounded up to nearest dollar

YEAR ISSUE		EDITION LIMIT	YEAR RETD.	ISSUE PRICE	*QUOTE U.S.$
1996	Mary	Retrd.	1998	50.00	50

Lenox Classics-China Barefoot Blessings - Lenox

YEAR ISSUE		EDITION LIMIT	YEAR RETD.	ISSUE PRICE	*QUOTE U.S.$
1997	Bedtime Prayers (Girl Praying)	Retrd.	1999	60.00	60
1999	A Boy's Best Friend (African-American Boy w/Dog)	Open		60.00	60
1999	Chatterbox (Girl w/Telephone)	Open		60.00	60
1996	Cheerful Giver (Girl w/Vegetables)	Retrd.	1998	60.00	60
1999	First Recital	Open		60.00	60
1998	Friends Forever (Girl w/doll)	Open		60.00	60
1996	Gone Fishing (Boy w/Dog)	Open		60.00	60
1999	The Graduate (Graduation Boy)	Open		60.00	60
1998	Graduation Princess (Girl in cap & gown)	Open		60.00	60
1999	I Love Collecting	3,000		60.00	60
1997	Just Like Mommy (Girl w/Hat)	Open		60.00	60
1999	Little MVP (Soccer Boy)	Open		60.00	60
1997	Making Friends (Girl w/Butterfly)	Retrd.	1999	60.00	60
1996	Morning Chores (Boy w/Cat)	Retrd.	1999	60.00	60
1996	Sharing Secrets (Girl w/Doll)	Open		60.00	60
1996	Spring Surprise (Girl w/Chick)	Retrd.	1998	60.00	60
1997	With This Kiss (Girl Bride & Boy Groom)	Retrd.	2000	145.00	145

Lenox Classics-China Disney Showcase - Lenox

YEAR ISSUE		EDITION LIMIT	YEAR RETD.	ISSUE PRICE	*QUOTE U.S.$
2000	A Blustery Day Adventure	Open		136.00	136
1998	Cinderella	Numbrd.		125.00	125
2000	Debonair Donald Duck	Open		136.00	136
2000	Dumbo	Open		136.00	136
2000	Gentleman Mickey Mouse	Open		136.00	136
2000	Gus	Numbrd.		79.00	79
2000	Jaq	Numbrd.		79.00	79
2000	The Prince	Numbrd.		125.00	125
2000	Prince Charming	Numbrd.		125.00	125
1999	Bashful	Numbrd.		70.00	70
1999	Doc	Numbrd.		79.00	79
1998	Dopey	Numbrd.		70.00	70
1998	Grumpy	Numbrd.		70.00	70
1999	Happy	Numbrd.		79.00	79
2000	Sleepy	Numbrd.		79.00	79
2000	Sneezy	Numbrd.		70.00	70
1998	Snow White	Numbrd.		125.00	125
2000	Minnie Mouse's Elegant Evening	Open		136.00	136

Lenox Classics-China Ethnic - Lenox

YEAR ISSUE		EDITION LIMIT	YEAR RETD.	ISSUE PRICE	*QUOTE U.S.$
1999	Santa's List	2,500	2000	195.00	195

Lenox Classics-China Fantasia 2000 - Lenox

YEAR ISSUE		EDITION LIMIT	YEAR RETD.	ISSUE PRICE	*QUOTE U.S.$
2000	Sorcerer's Apprentice	2,000	2000	225.00	225

Lenox Classics-China Finishing Touches - Lenox

YEAR ISSUE		EDITION LIMIT	YEAR RETD.	ISSUE PRICE	*QUOTE U.S.$
1997	Checking the List (Elf w/List)	Retrd.	1999	70.00	70
1997	Hush Little Teddy (Elf w/Toy Bag)	Retrd.	1999	70.00	70
1997	Little Jingles (Elf w/Bells)	Retrd.	1999	70.00	70
1997	Loading the Sleigh (Elf w/Pkgs.)	Retrd.	1999	70.00	70
1997	Nap Time (Elf Sleeping)	Retrd.	1999	70.00	70
1997	Painting Stripes (Elf w/Brush)	Retrd.	1999	70.00	70

Lenox Classics-China Gala Fashion Figurines - Lenox

YEAR ISSUE		EDITION LIMIT	YEAR RETD.	ISSUE PRICE	*QUOTE U.S.$
1999	Belle of the Ball	Open		138.00	138
1999	Evening at the Opera	Open		138.00	138
2000	Ivory Centennial Ball	Open		138.00	138
2000	Ivory Debutante Ball	Open		138.00	138

Lenox Classics-China Inspirational - Lenox

YEAR ISSUE		EDITION LIMIT	YEAR RETD.	ISSUE PRICE	*QUOTE U.S.$
1999	The Children's Blessing (Jesus w/Two Children)	Open		136.00	136
2000	Classic Holy Family, set/3	Open		152.00	152
1998	Footprints (Ivory Footprints sculpt of Jesus w/Child)	Open		152.00	152

Lenox Classics-China Ivory Snowman - Lenox

YEAR ISSUE		EDITION LIMIT	YEAR RETD.	ISSUE PRICE	*QUOTE U.S.$
2000	Snowy Skier	Open		58.50	59

Lenox Classics-China Little Graces - Lenox

YEAR ISSUE		EDITION LIMIT	YEAR RETD.	ISSUE PRICE	*QUOTE U.S.$
1996	Enjoyment (Cherub w/Bell)	5,000	1999	95.00	95
1999	Enlightenment (African-American Cherub w/Torch)	5,000		95.00	95
1998	Faith (Cherub w/ cross & flowers)	5,000		95.00	95
1996	Guidance (Cherub w/Candle)	5,000	1999	95.00	95
1997	Happiness (Cherub Reclining)	5,000		95.00	95
1997	Harmony (Cherub w/ Lg. Harp)	5,000		95.00	95
1996	Hope (Cherub w/Star)	5,000	1999	95.00	95
1997	Innocence (Cherub w/Trumpet)	5,000		95.00	95
1996	Knowledge (Cherub w/Book)	5,000	1999	95.00	95
1997	Love (Cherub w/Heart)	5,000		95.00	95
1996	Peace (Cherub w/Dove)	5,000		95.00	95
1999	Peaceful Messenger	5,000		45.00	45
1996	Tranquility (Cherub w/Harp)	5,000	1999	95.00	95

Lenox Classics-China Mother & Child Sculpture - Lenox

YEAR ISSUE		EDITION LIMIT	YEAR RETD.	ISSUE PRICE	*QUOTE U.S.$
2000	Mother's Love	Open		138.00	138
1999	A Time To Cherish	Open		138.00	138

Lenox Classics-China Santa's Teddy Bear Collection - Lenox

YEAR ISSUE		EDITION LIMIT	YEAR RETD.	ISSUE PRICE	*QUOTE U.S.$
2000	First Mate	Open		45.00	45
2000	Sailor Girl	Open		45.00	45
2000	Santa's Route	2,500		195.00	195

Lenox Classics-China Seasonal - Lenox

YEAR ISSUE		EDITION LIMIT	YEAR RETD.	ISSUE PRICE	*QUOTE U.S.$
1999	Special Delivery	Open		58.50	59

Lenox Classics-China Statement Sculptures - Lenox

YEAR ISSUE		EDITION LIMIT	YEAR RETD.	ISSUE PRICE	*QUOTE U.S.$
1999	Glory of the Millennium	2,000		850.00	850

Lenox Classics-China Victorian Ladies of Fashion - Lenox

YEAR ISSUE		EDITION LIMIT	YEAR RETD.	ISSUE PRICE	*QUOTE U.S.$
1998	Grand Voyage	Retrd.	2000	138.00	138
1998	Morning Promenade	Open		138.00	138
1999	Picnic In The Park (Lady w/Fan)	Retrd.	2000	138.00	138
1999	Shopping on Fifth Avenue	Open		138.00	138
1998	Sunday Stroll	Open		138.00	138

Lenox Classics-Crystal Birds - Lenox

YEAR ISSUE		EDITION LIMIT	YEAR RETD.	ISSUE PRICE	*QUOTE U.S.$
2000	Love and Devotion	2,500		95.00	95

Lenox Classics-Crystal Cats - Lenox

YEAR ISSUE		EDITION LIMIT	YEAR RETD.	ISSUE PRICE	*QUOTE U.S.$
1997	Crystal Jaguar (Cat in Grass)	Retrd.	2000	160.00	175
1996	Fascination (Cat w/Butterfly)	Open		50.00	55
1998	Grace and Glamour (Crystal Cat Pair)	Open		79.00	79
1998	Hugs and Kisses (Crystal Cat Pair)	Retrd.	2000	79.00	79
2000	Majestic Tiger	Open		195.00	195
1997	Morning Stretch (Cat Stretching)	Open		136.00	145
1996	Playtime (Cat w/Ball)	Retrd.	2000	50.00	55
1996	Preen & Serene (Cat Pair)	Open		76.00	79
1998	Prim & Proper	Open		76.00	76
1997	Warm & Cozy (Cat & Kitten)	2,500		110.00	110

Lenox Classics-Crystal Collection - Lenox

YEAR ISSUE		EDITION LIMIT	YEAR RETD.	ISSUE PRICE	*QUOTE U.S.$
2000	Racing The Wind	2,500		136.00	136
2000	Sunset Sail	Open		136.00	136

Lenox Classics-Crystal Disney Showcase - Lenox

YEAR ISSUE		EDITION LIMIT	YEAR RETD.	ISSUE PRICE	*QUOTE U.S.$
2000	Flowers From Mickey	Open		80.00	80
2000	Hello Minnie!	Open		80.00	80
2000	Winnie the Pooh	Open		98.00	98

Lenox Classics-Crystal Eagles - Lenox

YEAR ISSUE		EDITION LIMIT	YEAR RETD.	ISSUE PRICE	*QUOTE U.S.$
1997	Protector of the Stars (Patriotic Eagle)	Open		115.00	125
1996	Soaring Majesty (Flying Eagle)	Open		195.00	195
1998	Wings of Brilliance (Eagle Taking Off)	Retrd.	2000	195.00	195
1996	Wings of the Sun (Eagle on Rock)	Open		195.00	195

Lenox Classics-Crystal Elephants - Lenox

YEAR ISSUE		EDITION LIMIT	YEAR RETD.	ISSUE PRICE	*QUOTE U.S.$
1999	Bashful & Bold	Open		79.00	79
1998	Cotton and Candy (Elephant Pair)	Open		79.00	79
1998	Crystal Dancer	Open		136.00	136
1997	Crystal Playmate (Elephant in Grass)	Open		136.00	136
1998	Crystal Repose	Open		136.00	136
1996	Peanuts & Popcorn (Elephant Pair)	Open		76.00	79
2000	Standing Elephant	Open		136.00	136
1999	Tender Embrace	2,500		195.00	195
1997	Touch of Love (Elephant Mother & Calf)	2,500		195.00	195

Lenox Classics-Crystal Inspirational - Lenox

YEAR ISSUE		EDITION LIMIT	YEAR RETD.	ISSUE PRICE	*QUOTE U.S.$
1999	The Ascension	2,500		195.00	195
1999	Footprints	2,500		195.00	195

Lenox Classics-Crystal Safari Animals - Lenox

YEAR ISSUE		EDITION LIMIT	YEAR RETD.	ISSUE PRICE	*QUOTE U.S.$
2000	Giraffe	2,500		154.00	154
2000	Zebra	2,500		136.00	136

Lenox Classics-Crystal Sea Animals - Lenox

YEAR ISSUE		EDITION LIMIT	YEAR RETD.	ISSUE PRICE	*QUOTE U.S.$
1998	Dolphin Duet (Crystal Dolphin pair)	Open		100.00	100
1996	Dolphin's Journey (Mother w/Child)	Retrd.	2000	76.00	100
1999	Dolphin's Love (Mother & Child Dolphin)	2,500		136.00	136
1996	Glorious Dolphin (Dolphin Jumping Up)	Retrd.	2000	76.00	100
1998	Majestic Dolpin	Open		100.00	100
1996	Radiant Dolphin (Dolphin Diving Down)	Retrd.	2000	76.00	100
1999	Sea Surrender (Diving Dolphin)	2,500	2000	125.00	125
1998	Swan King (Crystal Swan on Lake)	Open		65.00	65
1998	Trio of Light	Open		154.00	154
2000	Water Dance	2,500		136.00	136

Lenox Classics-Crystal Seasonal - Lenox

YEAR ISSUE		EDITION LIMIT	YEAR RETD.	ISSUE PRICE	*QUOTE U.S.$
1999	Jolly Santa Claus	2,500		136.00	136
1999	Winter Magic	2,500		60.00	60

Lenox Classics-Crystal Teddies - Lenox

YEAR ISSUE		EDITION LIMIT	YEAR RETD.	ISSUE PRICE	*QUOTE U.S.$
2000	Charming Teddy	2,500		65.00	65
1999	Cute 'N Cuddly (Teddy Bear Pair)	Open		100.00	100

Lenox Classics-Crystal Unicorns - Lenox

YEAR ISSUE		EDITION LIMIT	YEAR RETD.	ISSUE PRICE	*QUOTE U.S.$
1998	Unicorn	Open		136.00	136

Lenox Classics-Crystal Woodland Animals - Lenox

YEAR ISSUE		EDITION LIMIT	YEAR RETD.	ISSUE PRICE	*QUOTE U.S.$
1996	Lord & Lady (Wolf Pair)	Open		76.00	79
1997	Protector of the Wild (Wolf)	Open		100.00	100
1999	Regal Lion (Standing Lion)	2,500		195.00	195
1996	Satin & Silk (Bunny Pair)	Open		76.00	79
1999	Woodland Spirit (Wolf #2 Running)	2,500	2000	100.00	100

Lladró

Lladró Collectors Society - Lladró

YEAR ISSUE		EDITION LIMIT	YEAR RETD.	ISSUE PRICE	*QUOTE U.S.$
1985	Little Pals S7600	Closed	1986	95.00	2400-2900
1985	LCS Plaque w/blue writing S7601	Closed	1985	35.00	75-125
1986	Little Traveler S7602	Closed	1987	95.00	1150-1550
1987	Spring Bouquets S7603	Closed	1988	125.00	550-780
1988	School Days S7604	Closed	1989	125.00	500-750
1988	Flower Song S7607	Closed	1989	175.00	350-750
1989	My Buddy S7609	Closed	1990	145.00	455-800
1990	Can I Play? S7610	Closed	1991	150.00	320-495
1991	Summer Stroll S7611	Closed	1992	195.00	375-450
1991	Picture Perfect S7612	Closed	1991	350.00	450
1992	All Aboard S7619	Closed	1993	165.00	350-450
1992	The Voyage of Columbus LL5847	7,500	1994	1450.00	1450-1550
1993	Best Friend S7620	Closed	1994	195.00	295-325
1993	Jester's Serenade w/base LL5932	3,000	1994	1995.00	2400-2535
1994	Basket of Love S7622	Closed	1995	225.00	350-425
1994	Garden of Dreams 7634	Closed	1996	1250.00	1690-2250
1995	10 Year Society Anniversary - Ten and Growing S7635	Closed	1996	395.00	450-495
1995	Afternoon Promenade S7636	Closed	1996	240.00	325
1995	Now and Forever (10 year membership piece) S7642	Open		395.00	395-550
1996	Innocence In Bloom S7644	Closed	1997	250.00	300-345
1996	Where Love Begins w/base 7649	Closed	1996	895.00	1300-1500
1997	Guardian Angel 6352	Closed	1997	1300.00	1700
1997	Pocket Full of Wishes 7650	Yr.Iss.	1998	360.00	395-450
1998	Dolphins at Play 01007658	Yr.Iss.	1998	21.00	21
1998	Heaven and Earth 01001824	5,000	1998	725.00	725-895
1998	It Wasn't Me! 01007672	Yr.Iss.	1998	295.00	325-500
1999	Art Brings Us Together	Yr.Iss.	1999	Gift	N/A
1999	A Wish Come True 7676	Yr.Iss.	1999	340.00	340-395
1999	Scheherazade 7678	1,000	1999	975.00	975-1178
1999	Enchanted Lake 7679	4,000	1999	1225.00	1395-1600
2000	Pals Forever 7686	Yr.Iss.		350.00	350
2000	A Friend For Life 7685	Yr.Iss.		Gift	N/A
2000	Mystical Garden 6686	5,000		1100.00	1100

Lladró Event Figurines - Lladró

YEAR ISSUE		EDITION LIMIT	YEAR RETD.	ISSUE PRICE	*QUOTE U.S.$
1991	Garden Classic L7617G	Closed	1992	295.00	500-795
1992	Garden Song L7618G	Closed	1993	295.00	455-595
1993	Pick of the Litter L7621G	Closed	1994	350.00	525-585
1994	Little Riders L7623	Closed	1995	250.00	250-425
1995	For A Perfect Performance L7641	Closed	1995	310.00	500
1996	Destination Big Top L6245	Closed	1996	225.00	475-650
1997	Tailor Made (Event '97) L6489	Closed	1997	150.00	195-225
1997	Dreams of a Summer's Past (Event '97) L6401	Closed	1997	310.00	310-350
2000	Playing Mom 01006681	12/00		295.00	295

Capricho - Lladró

YEAR ISSUE		EDITION LIMIT	YEAR RETD.	ISSUE PRICE	*QUOTE U.S.$
1988	Bust w/ Black Veil & base C1538	Open		650.00	1390
1988	Small Bust w/ Veil & base C1539	Open		225.00	750
1987	Orchid Arrangement C1541	Closed	1991	500.00	1700-2100
1987	Iris Arrangement C1542	Closed	1991	500.00	1000-1500
1987	Fan C1546	Closed	1988	675.00	900-1600
1987	Fan C1546.3	Closed	1988	675.00	900-1600
1987	Iris with Vase C1551	Closed	1992	110.00	375
1987	Flowers Chest C1572	Open		550.00	1200
1987	Flat Basket with Flowers C1575	Closed	1991	450.00	750-850
1989	White Rosary C1647	Closed	1991	290.00	340-400
1989	Romantic Lady / Black Veil w/base C1666	Closed	1993	420.00	520
1988	White Bust w/ Veil & base C5927	Open		550.00	1150
XX	Special Museum Flower Basket C7606	Closed	1991	N/A	450-750

Crystal Sculptures - Lladró

YEAR ISSUE		EDITION LIMIT	YEAR RETD.	ISSUE PRICE	*QUOTE U.S.$
1983	Frosted Bear, Head Up L04502	Closed	1983	200.00	350
1983	Frosted Bear, Head Down L04503	Closed	1983	205.00	350
1983	Frosted Bear, Head Up L04504	Closed	1983	210.00	350
1983	Frosted Bear, Head Straight L04506	Closed	1983	200.00	350
1983	Frosted Angel w/Guitar L04507	Closed	1983	165.00	325-375
1983	Frosted Angel w/Cymbal L04508	Closed	1983	165.00	375
1983	Frosted Angel w/Violin L04509	Closed	1983	165.00	375-495
1983	Frosted Geisha, Praying L04510	Closed	1983	135.00	495
1983	Frosted Geishaw/Fan L04511	Closed	1983	135.00	375
1983	Frosted Geishaw/Flowers L04512	Closed	1983	135.00	375
1983	Clear Bear, Head Straight L04513	Closed	1983	220.00	400-450
1983	Clear Bear, Head Up L04514	Closed	1983	230.00	400-450
1983	Wedding Bell	Closed	1985	35.00	195

Disneyana Limited Edition - Lladró

YEAR ISSUE		EDITION LIMIT	YEAR RETD.	ISSUE PRICE	*QUOTE U.S.$
1992	Tinkerbell LL7518	1,500	1992	350.00	2650-3380
1993	Peter Pan LL7529	3,000	1993	400.00	878-1200
1994	Cinderella and Fairy Godmother LL7553G	2,500	1995	875.00	985-1175
1995	Sleeping Beauty Dance LL7560	1,000	1995	1280.00	1210-2275

Limited Edition - Lladró

YEAR ISSUE		EDITION LIMIT	YEAR RETD.	ISSUE PRICE	*QUOTE U.S.$
1971	Hamlet LL1144	750	1973	125.00	2800-5200
1971	Othello and Desdemona LL1145	750	1973	275.00	2500-3000
1971	Antique Auto LL1146	750	1975	1000.00	4900-6000
1971	Floral LL1184	200	1978	400.00	2200
1971	Floral LL1185	200	1974	475.00	1800
1971	Floral LL1186	200	1976	575.00	2200
1972	Eagles LL1189	750	1978	450.00	3200-4200
1972	Sea Birds with Nest LL1194	500	1975	300.00	2750
1972	Turkey Group LL1196	350	1982	325.00	1800
1972	Peace LL1202	150	1973	550.00	7500-9500
1972	Eagle Owl LL1223	750	1983	225.00	1000-1325
1972	Hansom Carriage LL1225	750	1975	1450.00	9000
1973	Buck Hunters LL1238	800	1976	400.00	3000
1973	Turtle Doves LL1240	850	1976	250.00	2500-3000
1973	The Forest LL1243	500	1976	625.00	3300
1974	Soccer Players LL1266	500	1983	1000.00	7500
1974	Man From LaMancha LL1269	1,500	1977	700.00	3700-4500
1974	Queen Elizabeth II LL1275	250	1985	3650.00	5200
1974	Judge LL1281	1,200	1978	325.00	1650-1800
1974	Partridge LL1290G	800	1974	700.00	1200-2000
1974	The Hunt LL1308	750	1984	4750.00	6900-8300
1974	Ducks at Pond LL1317	1,200	1984	4250.00	6250-6800
1976	Impossible Dream LL1318	1,000	1983	1200.00	4500-5380
1976	Comforting Baby LL1329	750	1978	350.00	1050
1976	Mountain Country Lady LL1330	750	1983	900.00	1700
1976	My Baby LL1331	1,000	1981	275.00	900
1978	Flight of Gazelles LL1352	1,500	1984	1225.00	3100
1978	Car in Trouble LL1375	1,500	1987	3000.00	6500-7800
1978	Fearful Flight LL1377	750		7000.00	20600
1978	Henry VIII LL 1384	1,200	1993	650.00	850-1000
1981	Venus and Cupid LL1392	750	1993	1100.00	1600-2100

*Quotes have been rounded up to nearest dollar

YEAR ISSUE	EDITION LIMIT	YEAR RETD.	ISSUE PRICE	*QUOTE U.S.$
1982 First Date w/base LL1393	1,500		3800.00	5900
1982 Columbus LL1432G	1,200	1988	535.00	1100-1300
1983 Venetian Serenade LL1433	750	1989	2600.00	3900-5000
1985 Festival in Valencia w/base LL1457	3,000	1994	1400.00	2350
1985 Camelot LL1458	3,000	1994	950.00	1500
1985 Napoleon Planning Battle w/base LL1459	1,500	1995	825.00	1450
1985 Youthful Beauty w/base LL1461	5,000		750.00	1200
1985 Flock of Birds w/base LL1462	1,500		1060.00	1750
1985 Classic Spring LL1465	1,500	1995	620.00	1100-1300
1985 Classic Fall LL1466	1,500	1995	620.00	975-1300
1985 Valencian Couple on Horse LL1472	3,000		885.00	1550
1985 Coach XVIII Century w/base LL1485	500		14000.00	31000
1986 The New World w/base LL1486	4,000	1997	700.00	750-1350
1986 Fantasia w/base LL1487	5,000		1500.00	2700
1986 Floral Offering w/base LL1490	3,000		2500.00	4450
1986 Oriental Music w/base LL1491	5,000		1350.00	2445
1986 Three Sisters w/base LL1492	3,000		1850.00	3250
1986 At the Stroke of Twelve w/base LL1493	1,500	1993	4250.00	7950-8500
1986 Hawaiian Festival w/base LL1496	4,000	1997	1850.00	3200
1987 A Sunday Drive w/base LL1510	1,000	1999	3400.00	5250
1987 Listen to Don Quixote w/base LL1520	750	1995	1800.00	2900-3200
1987 A Happy Encounter LL1523	1,500		2900.00	4900
1988 Japanese Vase LL1536	750	1989	2600.00	3450-3650
1988 Garden Party w/base LL1578	500	1999	5500.00	7250
1988 Blessed Lady w/base LL1579	1,000	1991	1150.00	3000
1988 Return to La Mancha w/base LL1580	500		6400.00	8350
1989 Southern Tea LL1597	1,000	1995	1775.00	2300-2900
1989 Kitakami Cruise w/base LL1605	500	1994	5800.00	7500-9000
1989 Mounted Warriors w/base LL1608	500		2850.00	3450
1989 Circus Parade w/base LL1609	1,000	1998	5200.00	6550
1989 "Jesus the Rock" w/base LL1615	1,000	1994	1175.00	1850-2100
1989 Hopeful Group LL1723	1,000	1993	1825.00	1825
1991 Valencian Cruise LL1731	1,000	1998	2700.00	2950
1991 Venice Vows LL1732	1,500	1998	3755.00	4100
1991 Liberty Eagle LL1738	1,500	1999	1000.00	1100
1991 Heavenly Swing LL1739	1,000		1900.00	2050
1991 Columbus, Two Routes LL1740	1,000	1995	1500.00	1650
1991 Columbus Reflecting LL1741	1,000	1994	1850.00	1995
1991 Onward! LL1742	1,000	1993	2500.00	2750-3100
1991 The Prophet LL1743	300	1997	800.00	950
1991 My Only Friend LL1744	200	1991	1400.00	1475-1700
1991 Dawn LL1745	200	1993	1200.00	2550-2637
1991 Champion LL1746	300	1994	1800.00	1950
1991 Nesting Doves LL1747	300	1994	800.00	875
1991 Comforting News LL1748	300	1997	1200.00	1345
1991 Baggy Pants LL1749	300	1994	1500.00	1650
1991 Circus Show LL1750	300	1994	1400.00	1525
1991 Maggie LL1751	300	1994	900.00	990
1991 Apple Seller LL1752	300	1994	900.00	1000-1075
1991 The Student LL1753	300	1998	1300.00	1425
1991 Tree Climbers LL1754	300	1994	1500.00	1650
1991 The Princess And The Unicorn LL1755	1,500	1994	1750.00	1950-2150
1991 Outing In Seville LL1756	500		23000.00	24500
1992 Hawaiian Ceremony LL1757	1,000		9800.00	10250
1992 Circus Time LL1758	2,500		9200.00	9650
1992 Tea In The Garden LL1759	2,000		9500.00	9750
1993 Paella Valenciano w/base LL1762	500		10000.00	10000
1993 Trusting Friends w/base LL1763	350		1200.00	1200
1993 He's My Brother w/base LL1764	350		1500.00	1500
1993 The Course of Adventure LL1765	250		1625.00	1625
1993 Ties That Bind LL1766	250		1700.00	1700
1993 Motherly Love LL1767	250		1330.00	1330
1993 Travellers' Respite w/base LL1768	250		1825.00	1960
1993 Fruitful Harvest LL1769	350	1996	1300.00	1300
1993 Gypsy Dancers LL1770	250	1995	2250.00	2500-2750
1993 Country Doctor w/base LL1771	250	1998	1475.00	1700
1993 Back To Back LL1772	350		1450.00	1700
1993 Mischevous Musician LL1773	350		975.00	1045
1993 A Treasured Moment w/base LL1774	350		950.00	965
1993 Oriental Garden w/base LL1775	750		22500.00	22500
1994 Conquered by Love w/base LL1776	2,500		2850.00	3000
1994 Farewell Of The Samurai w/base LL1777	2,500		3950.00	3950
1994 Pegasus w/base LL1778	1,500		1950.00	1950
1994 High Speed w/base LL1779	1,500	1998	3830.00	3830
1994 Indian Princess w/base LL1780	3,000		1630.00	1630
1994 Allegory of Time LL1781	5,000	1998	1290.00	1290
1994 Circus Fanfare w/base LL1783	1,500	1998	14240.00	14240
1994 Flower Wagon w/base LL1784	3,000		3290.00	3290
1994 Cinderella's Arrival w/base LL1785	1,500		25950.00	26400
1994 Floral Figure w/base LL1788	300		2198.00	2200
1994 Natural Beauty LL1795	500		650.00	650
1994 Floral Enchantment w/base LL1796	300	1999	2990.00	3080
1995 Enchanted Outing w/base LL1797	3,000		3950.00	3950
1995 Far Away Thoughts LL1798	1,500	1997	3600.00	3600
1995 Immaculate Virgin w/base LL1799	2,000		2250.00	2250
1995 To the Rim w/base LL1800	1,500		2475.00	2475
1995 Vision of Peace w/base LL1803	1,500		1895.00	1895
1995 Portrait of a Family w/base LL1805	2,500		1750.00	1975
1995 A Family of Love w/base LL1806	2,500		1750.00	1975
1995 A Dream of Peace w/base LL1807	2,000	1998	1160.00	1160
1995 Virgin of the Pillar LL1808	3,000	1998	650.00	650
1996 Noah w/base LL1809	1,200	1998	1720.00	1720
1996 Easter Fantasy w/base LL1810	1,000		3500.00	3500
1996 Moses & The Ten Commandments w/base LL1811	1,200		1860.00	1950
1996 La Menina w/base LL1812	1,000		3850.00	3850
1997 Christmas Journey LL1813	1,000	1999	1295.00	1295
1997 Call of the Sea LL1814	500		4250.00	4250
1997 Young Beethoven LL1815	2,500		875.00	875
1997 Venetian Carnival LL1816	1,000		3400.00	3500
1997 The Burial of Christ LL1817	1,250		5300.00	6400
1997 Spring Courtship LL1818	1,500		2350.00	2400
1997 Loving Couple 01001823	1,000		600.00	700
1998 Pope John Paul II 01001825	2,500		600.00	650
1998 On The Balcony 01001826	1,000		3000.00	3200
1999 A Day With Mom 01011834	1,000		3450.00	3450
1999 Dance 01011836	2,000		1200.00	1200
1999 Bridal Bouquet 01011837	2,000		875.00	875
1999 The Awakening of Spring 01011838	500		1500.00	1500
2000 Poetry 01011839	2,000		975.00	975
1999 Promises of Love 01011840	1,000		1500.00	1500
1999 Dance of the Nymphs 01001844	1,000		1450.00	1450
1999 Bumblebee Fantasy 01001845	2,000		725.00	725
1999 Butterfly Fantasy 01001846	2,000		725.00	725
1999 Celestial Journey 01001848	1,500		3900.00	3900
1999 The Annunciation 01001849	1,000		1550.00	1550
1999 Fairy of the Butterflies 01001850	1,500		2150.00	2150
2000 Celestial Ascent 01001851	1,500		1300.00	1300
2000 Lozania 01001852	1,500		1900.00	1900
2000 Eros 01001853	1,000		1350.00	1350
2000 Spring's New Arrivals 01001854	1,000		1050.00	1050
2000 Summer in Saint Tropez 01001856	1,500		1250.00	1250
2000 In the Emperor's Forest 01001858	1,000		5350.00	5350
2000 Father Sun 01001859 (Millennium Collection)	500		1750.00	1750
2000 Free as the Wind 01001860	1,500		2900.00	2900
2000 Mother Earth 01001861 (Millennium Collection)	500		5450.00	5450
2000 Love's First Light 01001862	1,500		2100.00	2100
2000 A Heavenly Christmas 01001863	2,500		850.00	850
1970 Girl with Guitar LL2016	750	1982	325.00	1800-2350
1970 Madonna with Child LL2018	300	1974	450.00	1750
1971 Oriental Man LL2021	500	1983	500.00	1850
1971 The Three Graces LL2028	500	1976	950.00	6000
1971 Eve at Tree LL2029	600	1976	450.00	4000
1971 Oriental Horse LL2030	350	1983	1100.00	4000
1971 Lyric Muse LL2031	400	1982	750.00	3000
1971 Madonna and Child LL2043	300	1974	400.00	1500
1973 Peasant Woman LL2049	750	1977	200.00	1300
1973 Passionate Dance LL2051	500	1975	375.00	4500
1977 St. Theresa LL2061	1,200	1987	387.50	1600
1977 Concerto LL2063	1,200	1988	500.00	1235
1977 Flying Partridges LL2064	1,200	1987	1750.00	4300
1987 Christopher Columbus w/base LL2176	1,000	1995	1000.00	1350
1990 Invincible w/base LL2188	300		1100.00	1250
1993 Flight of Fancy w/base LL2243	300	1995	1400.00	1400
1993 The Awakening w/base LL2244	300		1200.00	1200
1993 Inspired Voyage w/base LL2245	1,000	1998	4800.00	4800
1993 Days of Yore w/base LL2248	1,000		1950.00	2050
1993 Holiday Glow w/base LL2249	1,500	1998	750.00	750
1993 Autumn Glow w/base LL2250	1,500	1998	750.00	750
1993 Humble Grace w/base LL2255	2,000		2150.00	2150
1983 Dawn w/base LL3000	300	1994	325.00	550
1983 Monks w/base LL3001	300	1993	1675.00	2550
1983 Waiting w/base LL3002	125	1990	1550.00	1900
1983 Indolence LL3003	150	1993	1465.00	2100
1983 Venus in the Bath LL3005	200	1991	1175.00	1450
1987 Classic Beauty w/base LL3012	500		1300.00	1900
1987 Youthful Innocence w/base LL3013	500	1998	1300.00	2300
1987 The Nymph w/base LL3014	250		1000.00	1450
1987 Dignity w/base LL3015	150		1400.00	1900
1988 Passion w/base LL3016	750	1998	865.00	1250
1988 Muse w/base LL3017	300	1993	650.00	875
1988 Cellist w/base LL3018	300	1993	650.00	875
1988 True Affection w/base LL3019	300	1998	750.00	1100-1155
1989 Demureness w/base LL3020	300	1993	400.00	700-825
1990 Daydreaming w/base LL3022	500		550.00	775
1990 After The Bath w/base LL3023	300	1991	350.00	975-1450
1990 Discoveries w/Base LL3024	100	1994	1500.00	1750
1991 Resting Nude LL3025	200	1993	650.00	1000-1500
1991 Unadorned Beauty LL3026	200		1700.00	1850
1994 Ebony w/base LL3027	300	1998	1295.00	1295
1994 Modesty w/base LL3028	300		1295.00	1295
1994 Danae LL3029	300		2880.00	3900
1995 Nude Kneeling LL3030	300		975.00	975
1995 Resting LL3031	300	1998	975.00	995
1982 Elk LL3501	500	1987	950.00	1200
1978 Nude with Dove LL3503	1,500	1981	250.00	700-1250
1978 The Rescue LL3504	1,500	1987	2900.00	3500-5000
1978 St. Michael w/base LL3515	1,500	1998	2200.00	4900
1980 Turtle Dove Nest w/base LL3519	1,200	1995	3600.00	6100
1980 Turtle Dove Group w/base LL3520	750	1998	6800.00	11900
1981 Philippine Folklore LL3522	1,500	1995	1450.00	2400
1981 Nest of Eagles w/base LL3523	300	1994	6900.00	11500
1981 Drum Beats/Watusi Queen w/base LL3524	1,500	1994	1875.00	3100
1982 Togetherness LL3527	75	1987	375.00	1100
1982 Wrestling LL3528	50	1987	950.00	1125-1850
1982 Companionship w/base LL3529	65	1995	1000.00	1790
1982 Anxiety w/base LL3530	125	1993	1075.00	1875
1982 Victory LL3531	90	1984	1500.00	1800
1982 Plentitude LL3532	50	1984	1000.00	1375
1982 The Observer w/base LL3533	115	1993	900.00	1700
1982 In the Distance LL3534	75	1986	525.00	1300
1982 Slave LL3535	50	1986	950.00	1200
1982 Relaxation LL3536	100	1983	525.00	1100
1982 Dreaming w/base LL3537	250	1993	475.00	1475
1982 Youth LL3538	250	1988	525.00	1000
1982 Dantiness LL3539	100	1983	1000.00	1400
1982 Pose LL3540	100	1986	1250.00	1450
1982 Tranquility LL3541	75	1983	1000.00	1400
1982 Yoga LL3542	125	1991	650.00	1000
1982 Demure LL3543	100	1986	1250.00	1700
1982 Reflections w/base LL3544	75	1995	650.00	1050
1982 Adoration LL3545	150	1990	1050.00	1600
1982 African Woman LL3546	50	1983	1300.00	3500
1982 Reclining Nude LL3547	75	1983	650.00	975
1982 Serenity w/base LL3548	300	1993	925.00	925-1550
1982 Reposing LL3549	300	1986	425.00	575
1982 Boxer w/base LL3550	300	1993	850.00	1450
1982 Bather LL3551	300	1988	975.00	1300
1982 Blue God LL3552	1,500	1994	900.00	1575
1982 Fire Bird LL3553	1,500	1994	800.00	1350
1982 Desert People w/base LL3555	750	1986	1680.00	3100
1982 Road to Mandalay LL3556	750	1989	1390.00	2100
1982 Jesus in Tiberias w/base LL3557	1,200		2600.00	5450
1992 The Reader LL3560	200		2650.00	2815
1993 Trail Boss LL3561M	1,500	1998	2450.00	2595
1993 Indian Brave LL3562M	1,500	1998	2250.00	2250
1994 Saint James The Apostle w/base LL3563	1,000		950.00	950
1994 Gentle Moment w/base LL3564	1,000		1795.00	1835
1994 At Peace w/base LL3565	1,000		1650.00	1750
1994 Indian Chief w/base LL3566	3,000	1998	1095.00	1095
1994 Trapper w/base LL3567	3,000	1998	950.00	950
1994 American Cowboy w/base LL3568	3,000	1998	950.00	950
1994 A Moment's Pause w/base LL3569	3,500		1495.00	1635
1994 Ethereal Music w/base LL3570	1,000		2450.00	2500
1994 At The Helm w/base LL3571	3,500	1998	1495.00	1495
1995 Proud Warrior w/base LL3572	3,000	1998	995.00	995
1995 Golgotha w/base LL3773	1, 000		1650.00	1650
1996 Playing the Blues w/base LL3576	1,000		2160.00	2160
1997 Man of the Sea LL3577	1,000		1850.00	1850
1999 A Soft Refrain LL3578	1,000		1330.00	1330
1999 Intermezzo LL3580	1,000		1300.00	1330
2000 My Special Garden LL3582	1,000		1900.00	1900
1997 The Journey LL3700	500		700.00	700
1997 In Concert LL3701	350		1050.00	1050
1997 Pensive Journey LL3702	500		700.00	700
1997 Imagination LL3703	500		750.00	750
1985 Napoleon Bonaparte LL5338	5,000	1994	275.00	650
1985 Beethoven w/base LL5339	3,000	1993	760.00	1300
1985 Thoroughbred Horse w/base LL5340	1,000	1993	625.00	1000-1150
1985 I Have Found Thee, Dulcinea LL5341	750	1990	1460.00	3000
1985 Pack of Hunting Dogs w/base LL5342	3,000	1994	925.00	1200-2000
1985 Love Boat w/base LL5343	3,000	1997	825.00	1350
1986 Fox Hunt w/base LL5362	1,000		5200.00	8750
1986 Rey De Copas w/base LL5366	2,000	1993	325.00	600
1986 Rey De Oros w/base LL5367	2,000	1993	325.00	600
1986 Rey De Espadas w/base LL5368	2,000	1993	325.00	600
1986 Rey De Bastos w/base LL5369	2,000	1993	325.00	600
1986 Pastoral Scene w/base LL5386	750	1995	1100.00	2300-2350
1987 Inspiration LL5413	500	1993	1200.00	2100
1987 Carnival Time w/base LL5423	1,000	1993	2400.00	3900
1989 "Pious" LL5541	1,000	1991	1075.00	1560-1700
1989 Freedom LL5602	1,500	1989	875.00	1100-1300
1990 A Ride In The Park LL5718	1,000	1994	3200.00	4500-4700
1991 Youth LL5800	500	1993	650.00	725
1991 Charm LL5801	500	1994	650.00	725
1991 New World Medallion LL5808	5,000	1994	200.00	225
1992 Sorrowful Mother LL5849	1,500	1999	1750.00	925-1850
1992 Justice Eagle LL5863	1,500		1700.00	1840
1992 Maternal Joy LL5864	1,500	1998	1600.00	1700-1750
1992 Motoring In Style LL5884	1,500	1998	3700.00	3850
1992 The Way Of The Cross LL5890	2,000	1998	975.00	1050
1992 Presenting Credentials LL5911	1,500	1999	19500.00	20500
1992 Young Mozart LL5915	2,500	1992	500.00	1495-1575
1993 Infant of Cebu LL5937	1,500	1998	N/A	1390
1993 The Blessing w/base LL5942	2,000		1345.00	1345
1993 Our Lady of Rocio w/base LL5951	2,000		3500.00	3500
1993 Where to Sir? w/base LL5952	1,500	1998	5250.00	5250
1993 Discovery Mug LL5967	1,992	1994	90.00	90-95
1993 Graceful Moment w/base LL6033	3,000		1475.00	1475
1993 The Hand of Justice w/base LL6035	1,000	1998	1250.00	1250-1300
1997 Royal Slumber 01006385	750		1390	1425
1998 Goddess of Youth 01006449	2,500		1150.00	1500
1998 The Pelicans 01006478	1,000		990.00	1200
1998 Melody 01006513	2,000		870.00	950
1999 Ovation 01006614	3,000		525.00	550
2000 Tranquility 01006677	2,000		1340.00	1340
1995 Abraham Lincoln w/base LL7554	2,500		2190.00	2190
1996 Statue of Liberty w/base LL7563	2,000		1620.00	1620
1997 George Washington LL7575	2,000		1390.00	1390

Lladró - Lladró

YEAR ISSUE	EDITION LIMIT	YEAR RETD.	ISSUE PRICE	*QUOTE U.S.$
1963 Hunting Dog 308.13	Closed	N/A	N/A	2000
1966 Poodle 325.13	Closed	N/A	N/A	2300
1970 Girl with Pigtails L357.13G	Closed	N/A	N/A	1100
1969 Shepherdess with Goats L1001G	Closed	1987	67.50	550-675
1969 Shepherdess with Goats L1001M	Closed	1987	67.50	450
1969 Girl's Head L1003G	Closed	1985	150.00	675
1969 Girl's Head L1003M	Closed	1985	150.00	800
1969 Pan with Cymbals L1006	Closed	1975	45.00	400-550
1969 Pan with Pipes L1007	Closed	1975	45.00	400-700
1969 Satyrs Group L1008G	Closed	1976	N/A	750-1000
1969 Girl With Lamb L1010G	Closed	1993	26.00	202-250
1969 Girl With Pig L1011G	Open		13.00	100
1969 Centaur Girl L1012G	Closed	1989	45.00	455-550
1969 Centaur Girl L1012M	Closed	1989	45.00	400
1969 Centaur Boy L1013G	Closed	1989	45.00	400-425
1973 Christmas Carols L1239G	Closed	1981	125.00	750
1969 Centaur Boy L1013M	Closed	1989	45.00	425-455
1969 Two Women with Water Jugs L1014G	Closed	1985	85.00	550
1969 Dove L1015 G	Closed	1994	21.00	150

*Quotes have been rounded up to nearest dollar

YEAR ISSUE	EDITION LIMIT	YEAR RETD.	ISSUE PRICE	*QUOTE U.S.$
1969 Dove L1016 G	Closed	1995	36.00	190-250
1969 Idyl L1017G	Closed	1991	115.00	750
1969 Idyl L1017M	Closed	1991	115.00	625
1969 King Gaspar L1018M	Open		345.00	1895
1969 King Melchior L1019M	Open		345.00	1850
1969 King Baltasar L1020M	Open		345.00	1850
1969 Horse Group L1021G	Open		950.00	2465
1969 Horse Group/All White L1022M	Open		465.00	2150
1969 Flute Player L1025G	Closed	1978	73.00	750
1969 Clown with Concertina L1027G	Closed	1993	95.00	625-800
1969 Girl w/Heart L1028G	Closed	1970	37.50	650
1969 Boy w/Bowler L1029G	Closed	1970	37.50	550
1969 Don Quixote w/Stand L1030G	Open		225.00	1450
1969 Sancho Panza L1031G	Closed	1989	65.00	600
1969 Old Folks L1033G	Closed	1985	140.00	1100-1400
1969 Old Folks L1033M	Closed	1985	140.00	1500
1969 Shepherdess with Dog L1034	Closed	1989	30.00	250-275
1969 Girl with Geese L1035G	Closed	1995	37.50	225-275
1969 Girl With Geese L1035M	Closed	1992	37.50	165
1969 Horseman L1037G	Closed	1970	170.00	2500
1969 Girl with Turkeys L1038G	Closed	1978	95.00	400-550
1969 Violinist and Girl L1039G	Closed	1991	120.00	850-1100
1969 Violinist and Girl L1039M	Closed	1991	120.00	1000
1969 Hen L1041G	Closed	1975	13.00	350
1969 Hen L1042G	Closed	1975	13.00	350
1969 Cock L1043G	Closed	1975	13.00	350
1969 Small Hippo L1045G	Closed	1970	9.50	350-400
1969 Hunters L1048	Closed	1986	115.00	1420
1969 Del Monte (Boy) L1050	Closed	1978	65.00	N/A
1969 Girl with Duck L1052G	Closed	1998	30.00	205-275
1969 Girl with Duck L1052M	Closed	1992	30.00	190
1969 Bird L1053G	Closed	1985	13.00	100
1969 Bird L1054G	Closed	1985	14.00	135-220
1969 Duck L1056G	Closed	1978	19.00	275
1969 Girl with Pheasant L1055G	Closed	1978	105.00	N/A
1969 Panchito L1059	Closed	1980	28.00	100
1969 Bull w/Head Up L1063	Closed	1975	90.00	1100
1969 Deer L1064	Closed	1986	27.50	325-425
1969 Fox and Cub L1065G	Closed	1985	17.50	425
1969 Basset L1066G	Closed	1981	23.50	600
1969 Old Dog L1067G	Closed	1978	40.00	625
1969 Great Dane L1068G	Closed	1989	55.00	500-600
1969 Afghan (sitting) L1069G	Closed	1985	36.00	625
1969 Beagle Puppy L1070G	Closed	1991	16.50	275-350
1969 Beagle Puppy L1071G	Closed	1992	16.50	275-500
1969 Beagle Puppy L1071M	Closed	1992	16.50	250
1969 Beagle Puppy L1072G	Closed	1991	16.50	275
1969 Dutch Girl L1077G	Closed	1981	57.50	363-525
1969 Herald L1078G	Closed	1971	110.00	1100
1969 Boy with Lyre L1079M	Closed	1970	20.00	500
1969 Girl with Water Can L1080M	Closed	1970	20.00	500
1969 Girl With Brush L1081G	Closed	1985	14.50	320-325
1969 Girl Manicuring L1082G	Closed	1985	14.50	275-320
1969 Girl With Doll L1083G	Closed	1985	14.50	300-320
1969 Girl with Mother's Shoe L1084G	Closed	1985	14.50	275-320
1969 Musical 19th Century L1085G	Closed	1973	180.00	2500
1969 Pregonero L1086G	Closed	1975	120.00	1500
1969 Little Green-Grocer L1087G	Closed	1981	40.00	385-450
1969 Girl Seated with Flowers L1088G	Closed	1989	45.00	700-750
1971 Lawyer (Face) L1089G	Closed	1973	35.00	850-950
1971 Girl and Gazelle L1091G	Closed	1975	225.00	1200
1971 Satyr with Snail L1092G	Closed	1975	30.00	650
1971 Satyr with Frog L1093G	Closed	1975	50.00	700
1969 Beggar L1094G	Closed	1981	65.00	650-675
1971 Girl With Hens L1103G	Closed	1981	50.00	375-455
1971 Boy With Cornet 1105G	Closed	1973	30.00	350
1971 Byzantine Head L1106G	Closed	1975	105.00	950
1971 Pups in Box L1121G	Closed	1978	33.00	1500-1750
1971 La Tarantela L1123G	Closed	1975	550.00	2250
1971 Pelusa Clown L1125G	Closed	1978	70.00	1000-1700
1971 Pelusa Clown L1125M	Closed	1978	70.00	2250
1971 Clown with Violin L1126G	Closed	1978	71.00	1850
1971 Puppy Love L1127G	Closed	1997	50.00	330-350
1971 Dog in the Basket L1128G	Closed	1985	17.50	425-450
1971 Faun L1131G	Closed	1972	155.00	1500
1971 Carriage of Baccus L1132G	Closed	1972	160.00	2200
1971 Horse L1133G	Closed	1972	115.00	900
1971 Bull L1134G	Closed	1972	130.00	1500
1971 Dog and Snail L1139G	Closed	1981	40.00	845
1971 Girl with Bonnet L1147G	Closed	1985	20.00	275-325
1971 Girl Shampooing L1148G	Closed	1985	20.00	275-310
1971 Dog's Head L1149G	Closed	1981	27.50	450
1971 Elephants (3) L1150G	Open		100.00	795
1971 Elephants (2) L1151G	Closed	1999	45.00	440
1971 Dog Playing Guitar L1152G	Closed	1978	32.50	375-550
1971 Dog Playing Guitar L1153G	Closed	1978	32.50	400-550
1971 Dog Playing Bass Fiddle L1154G	Closed	1978	36.50	400-550
1971 Dog w/Microphone L1155G	Closed	1978	35.00	400-550
1971 Dog Playing Bongos L1156	Closed	1978	32.50	400-550
1971 Seated Torero L1162G	Closed	1973	35.00	700
1971 Soldier with Gun L1164G	Closed	1978	27.50	400
1971 Soldier with Flag L1165G	Closed	1978	27.50	500
1971 Soldier with Cornet L1166G	Closed	1978	27.50	500
1971 Soldier with Drum L1167G	Closed	1978	27.50	500
1971 Kissing Doves L1169G	Open		32.00	155
1971 Kissing Doves L1169M	Closed	1992	32.00	155
1971 Kissing Doves L1170G	Closed	1988	25.00	250
1971 Girl With Flowers L1172G	Closed	1993	27.00	375
1971 Girl With Domino L1175G	Closed	1981	34.00	350
1971 Girl With Dice L1176G	Closed	1981	25.00	363
1971 Girl With Ball L1177G	Closed	1981	27.50	450
1971 Girl With Accordian L1178G	Closed	1981	34.00	400
1971 Boy With Concertina L1179G	Closed	1981	34.00	375
1971 Little Girl w/Turkeys L1180G	Closed	1981	55.00	450
1971 Platero and Marcelino L1181G	Closed	1981	50.00	238-455
1971 Girl From Manchuria L1182G	Closed	1975	60.00	750
1972 Little Girl with Cat L1187G	Closed	1989	37.00	337
1972 Boy Meets Girl L1188G	Closed	1989	310.00	425
1972 Eskimo L1195G	Open		30.00	135
1972 Horse Resting L1203G	Closed	1981	40.00	600
1972 Attentive Bear, brown L1204G	Closed	1989	16.00	125
1972 Good Bear, brown L1205G	Closed	1989	16.00	125
1972 Bear Seated, brown L1206G	Closed	1989	16.00	125
1972 Attentive Polar Bear, white L1207G	Open		16.00	75
1972 Bear, white L1208G	Open		16.00	75
1972 Bear, white L1209G	Open		16.00	75
1972 Round Fish L1210G	Closed	1981	35.00	625
1972 Girl With Doll L1211G	Closed	1993	72.00	352-440
1972 Woman Carrying Water L1212G	Closed	1983	100.00	475
1972 Little Jug Magno L1222.3G	Closed	1979	35.00	300
1972 Young Harlequin L1229G	Closed	1999	70.00	520
1972 Young Harlequin L1229M	Closed	1991	70.00	550
1972 Friendship L1230G	Closed	1991	68.00	450-475
1972 Friendship L1230M	Closed	1991	68.00	404
1972 Angel with Lute L1231G	Closed	1988	60.00	425-450
1972 Angel with Clarinet L1232G	Closed	1988	60.00	450-475
1972 Angel with Flute L1233G	Closed	1988	60.00	450-475
1972 Little Jesus of Prag L1234G	Closed	1978	70.00	725
1973 Country Flirt L1241G	Closed	1980	110.00	650
1973 Lady at Dressing Table L1242G	Closed	1978	320.00	2500-3650
1973 Fluttering Nightingale L1244G	Closed	1981	44.00	375
1973 The Cart L1245G	Closed	1981	75.00	500-650
1974 Caress and Rest L1246G	Closed	1990	50.00	320-350
1974 Happy Harlequin L1247M	Closed	1983	220.00	1150
1974 Sweety L1248G	Closed	1990	100.00	525-550
1974 The Race L1249G	Closed	1988	450.00	2250
1974 Lovers from Verona L 1250G	Closed	1990	330.00	1250
1974 Pony Ride L1251G	Closed	1979	220.00	1400
1974 Shepherd's Rest L1252G	Closed	1981	100.00	500
1974 Sad Chimney Sweep L1253G	Closed	1983	180.00	1200-1250
1974 Hamlet and Yorick L1254G	Closed	1983	325.00	1200-1275
1974 Seesaw L1255G	Closed	1993	110.00	700-847
1974 Mother with Pups L1257G	Closed	1981	50.00	650
1974 Playing Poodles L1258G	Closed	1981	47.50	800
1974 Poodle L1259G	Closed	1985	27.50	488-500
1974 Dalmatian L1260G	Closed	1981	25.00	325-350
1974 Dalmatian L1261G	Closed	1981	25.00	350
1974 Dalmatian L1262G	Closed	1981	25.00	325-350
1974 Flying Duck L1263G	Closed	1998	20.00	77-140
1974 Flying Duck L1264G	Closed	1998	20.00	75-110
1974 Flying Duck L1265G	Closed	1998	20.00	77-110
1974 Girl with Ducks L1267G	Closed	1993	55.00	260-300
1974 Reminiscing L1270G	Closed	1988	975.00	1375
1974 Thoughts L1272G	Closed	1998	87.50	3490
1974 Lovers in the Park L1274G	Closed	1993	450.00	1365-1400
1974 Christmas Seller L1276G	Closed	1981	120.00	700
1974 Feeding Time L1277G	Closed	1994	120.00	323-350
1974 Feeding Time L1277M	Closed	1993	120.00	450
1974 Devotion L1278G	Closed	1990	140.00	475
1974 The Wind L1279M	Open		250.00	830
1974 Child's Play L1280G	Closed	1983	110.00	494-700
1974 Afghan Standing L1282G	Closed	1985	45.00	500
1974 Little Gardener L1283G	Open		250.00	785
1974 "My Flowers" L1284G	Open		200.00	550
1974 "My Goodness" L1285G	Closed	1995	190.00	307-450
1974 Flower Harvest L1286G	Closed	1998	200.00	421-550
1974 Picking Flowers L1287G	Closed	1998	170.00	440-495
1974 Aggressive Duck L1288G	Closed	1995	170.00	489-575
1974 Good Puppy L1289G	Closed	1985	16.60	225-250
1974 Victorian Girl on Swing L1297G	Closed	1990	520.00	1850-1950
1974 Birds Resting L1298G	Closed	1985	235.00	975
1974 Birds in Nest L1299G	Closed	1985	120.00	750
1974 Little Bird L1301G	Closed	1983	72.50	550
1974 Blue Creeper L1302G	Closed	1985	110.00	650
1974 Bird on Cactus L1303G	Closed	1983	150.00	800
1974 Valencian Lady with Flowers L1304G	Open		200.00	625
1974 "On the Farm" L1306G	Closed	1990	130.00	400-425
1974 Ducklings L1307G	Open		47.50	150
1974 Girl with Cats L1309G	Open		120.00	310
1974 Girl with Puppies in Basket L1311G	Closed	1997	120.00	325-375
1974 Exquisite Scent L1313G	Closed	1990	201.00	650
1974 Girl From Scotland L1315G	Closed	1979	450.00	2800
1976 Collie L1316G	Closed	1981	45.00	500
1976 Herons L1319G	Open		1550.00	2625
1977 Angel with Tamborine L1320G	Closed	1985	125.00	450-500
1977 Angel with Lyre L1321G	Closed	1985	125.00	450-475
1977 Angel Recital L1322G	Closed	1985	125.00	475
1977 Angel with Accordian L1323G	Closed	1985	125.00	400
1977 Angel with Violin L1324G	Closed	1985	125.00	400-500
1976 The Helmsman L1325M	Closed	1988	600.00	1220
1976 Playing Cards L1327 M, numbd. series	Open		3800.00	6600
1977 Chow Time L1334G	Closed	1981	135.00	625-650
1977 Dove Group L1335G	Closed	1990	950.00	1600
1977 Girl With Watering Can L1339G	Closed	1988	325.00	550-575
1977 Male Jockey L1341G	Closed	1979	120.00	550
1977 Wrath of Don Quixote L1343G	Closed	1990	250.00	875-990
1977 Derby L1344G	Closed	1985	1125.00	2500
1978 Sacristan L1345G	Closed	1979	385.00	2200-2300
1978 Under the Willow L1346G	Closed	1990	1600.00	1950-2150
1978 Mermaid on Wave L1347G	Closed	1983	425.00	1600-1850
1978 Pearl Mermaid L1348G	Closed	1983	225.00	1850
1978 Mermaids Playing L1349G	Closed	1983	425.00	2250-2700
1978 In the Gondola L1350G, numbd. series	Open		1850.00	3250
1978 Lady with Girl L1353G	Closed	1985	175.00	575-780
1978 Girl Watering L1354G	Closed	1988	485.00	635
1978 Phyllis L1356G	Closed	1993	75.00	225-275
1978 Shelley L1357G	Closed	1993	75.00	225-250
1978 Beth L1358G	Closed	1993	75.00	225
1978 Heather L1359G	Closed	1993	75.00	225
1978 Laura L1360G	Closed	1993	75.00	225-250
1978 Julia L1361G	Closed	1993	75.00	240-275
1978 Girls in the Swing L1366G	Closed	1988	825.00	1425-1900
1978 Playful Dogs L1367	Closed	1982	160.00	710-900
1978 Spring Birds L1368G	Closed	1990	1600.00	2500
1978 Anniversary Waltz L1372G	Open		260.00	570
1978 Chestnut Seller L1373G	Closed	1981	800.00	750-900
1978 Waiting in the Park L1374G	Closed	1993	235.00	450-600
1978 Watering Flowers L1376G	Closed	1990	400.00	748-1150
1978 Suzy and Her Doll L1378G	Closed	1985	215.00	600-650
1978 Debbie and Her Doll L1379G	Closed	1985	215.00	800
1978 Cathy and Her Doll L1380G	Closed	1985	215.00	650
1978 Medieval Girl L1381G	Closed	1985	11.80	400-600
1978 Medieval Boy L1382G	Closed	1985	235.00	700
1978 A Rickshaw Ride L1383G	Open		1500.00	2150
1978 Quixote on Guard L1385G	Closed	1988	350.00	850-975
1981 St. Joseph L1386G	Open		250.00	385
1981 Mary L1387G	Open		240.00	385
1981 Baby Jesus L1388G	Open		85.00	140
1981 Donkey L1389G	Open		95.00	215
1981 Cow L1390G	Open		95.00	215
1982 Holy Mary L1394G, numbd. series	Open		1000.00	1475
1982 Full of Mischief L1395G	Closed	1998	420.00	865
1982 Appreciation L1396G	Closed	1998	420.00	584-860
1982 Second Thoughts L1397G	Closed	1998	420.00	880-925
1982 Reverie L1398G	Closed	1998	490.00	970-1075
1982 Dutch Girl L1399G	Closed	1988	750.00	725-775
1982 Valencian Boy L1400G	Closed	1988	298.00	500-560
1982 Butterfly Girl L1401G	Closed	1988	210.00	600-750
1982 Butterfly Girl L1402G	Closed	1988	210.00	595-750
1982 Butterfly Girl L1403G	Closed	1988	210.00	642-750
1982 Matrimony L1404G	Closed	1998	320.00	585-625
1982 Illusion L1413G	Open		115.00	260
1982 Fantasy L1414G	Open		115.00	260
1982 Mirage L1415G	Open		115.00	260
1982 From My Garden L1416G	Closed	1998	140.00	315-365
1982 Nature's Bounty L1417G	Closed	1995	160.00	400
1982 Flower Harmony L1418G	Closed	1995	130.00	400
1982 A Barrow of Blossoms L1419G	Open		390.00	675
1982 Born Free w/base L1420G	Open		1520.00	3250
1982 Mariko w/base L1421G	Closed	1995	860.00	1300-1625
1982 Miss Valencia L1422G	Closed	1998	175.00	415
1982 King Melchior L1423G	Open		225.00	440
1982 King Gaspar L1424G	Open		265.00	475
1982 King Balthasar L1425G	Open		315.00	585
1982 Male Tennis Player L1426M	Closed	1988	200.00	400
1982 Female Tennis Player L1427M	Closed	1988	200.00	400-475
1982 Afternoon Tea L1428G	Closed	1998	115.00	300-350
1982 Afternoon Tea L1428M	Closed	1998	115.00	300
1982 Winter Wonderland w/base L1429G	Open		1025.00	2230
1982 High Society L1430G	Closed	1993	305.00	585-695
1982 The Debutante L1431G	Closed	1998	115.00	300-375
1982 The Debutante L1431M	Closed	1998	115.00	300
1983 Vows L1434G	Closed	1991	600.00	425
1983 Blue Moon L1435G	Closed	1988	98.00	355-400
1983 Moon Glow L1436G	Closed	1988	98.00	405-500
1983 Moon Light L1437G	Closed	1988	98.00	450-575
1983 Full Moon L1438G	Closed	1988	115.00	575-675
1983 "How Do You Do!" L1439G	Open		185.00	295
1983 Pleasantries L1440G	Closed	1991	960.00	1700-2300
1983 A Litter of Love L1441G	Open		385.00	645
1983 Kitty Confrontation L1442G	Open		155.00	285
1983 Bearly Love L1443G	Closed	1999	55.00	140
1983 Purr-Fect L1444G	Open		350.00	615
1983 Springtime in Japan L1445G	Open		965.00	1800
1983 "Here Comes the Bride" L1446G	Closed	1998	518.00	995-1145
1983 Michiko L1447G	Open		235.00	515
1983 Yuki L1448G	Closed	1998	285.00	550-625
1983 Mayumi L1449G	Closed	1998	235.00	525-600
1983 Kiyoko L1450G	Closed	1998	235.00	550-575
1983 Teruko L1451G	Open		235.00	550
1983 On the Town L1452G	Closed	1993	220.00	500-595
1983 Golfing Couple L1453G	Open		248.00	545
1983 Flowers of the Season L1454G	Open		1460.00	2550
1983 Reflections of Hamlet L1455G	Closed	1988	1000.00	1650
1983 Cranes w/base L1456G	Open		1000.00	1950
1985 A Boy and His Pony L1460G	Closed	1988	285.00	800
1985 Carefree Angel with Flute L1463G	Closed	1988	220.00	650
1985 Carefree Angel with Lyre L1464G	Closed	1988	220.00	650-675
1985 Girl on Carousel Horse L1469G	12/00		470.00	945
1985 Boy on Carousel Horse L1470G	12/00		470.00	945
1985 Wishing On A Star L1475G	Closed	1988	130.00	495-520
1985 Star Light Star Bright L1476G	Closed	1988	130.00	350-400
1985 Star Gazing L1477G	Closed	1988	130.00	375-400
1985 Hawaiian Dancer/Aloha! L1478G	Open		230.00	440
1985 In a Tropical Garden L1479G	Closed	1995	230.00	450-525
1985 Aroma of the Islands L1480G	Open		260.00	480
1985 Sunning L1481G	Closed	1988	145.00	575
1985 Eve L1482	Closed	1988	145.00	700
1985 Free As a Butterfly L1483G	Closed	1988	145.00	550
1986 Lady of the East w/base L1488G	Closed	1993	625.00	1100-1250
1986 Valencian Children L1489G	Open		700.00	1225
1986 My Wedding Day L1494G	Closed	1998	800.00	1495-1650
1986 A Lady of Taste L1495G	Open		575.00	1495
1986 Don Quixote & The Windmill L1497G	Closed	1997	1100.00	2050-2150
1986 Tahitian Dancing Girls L1498G	Closed	1995	750.00	1450-1550
1986 Blessed Family L1499G	Closed	1998	200.00	395

*Quotes have been rounded up to nearest dollar

FIGURINES

YEAR ISSUE	EDITION LIMIT	YEAR RETD.	ISSUE PRICE	*QUOTE U.S.$
1986 Ragamuffin L1500G	Closed	1991	125.00	400-425
1986 Ragamuffin L1500M	Closed	1991	125.00	300
1986 Rag Doll L1501G	Closed	1991	125.00	300
1986 Rag Doll L1501M	Closed	1991	125.00	300
1986 Forgotten L1502G	Closed	1991	125.00	300
1986 Forgotten L1502M	Closed	1991	125.00	300
1986 Neglected L1503G	Closed	1991	125.00	425-550
1986 Neglected L1503M	Closed	1991	125.00	325
1986 The Reception L1504G	Closed	1990	625.00	1040-1100
1986 Nature Boy L1505G	Closed	1991	100.00	250-300
1986 Nature Boy L1505M	Closed	1991	100.00	300
1986 A New Friend L1506G	Closed	1991	110.00	325-350
1986 A New Friend L1506M	Closed	1991	110.00	275
1986 Boy & His Bunny L1507G	Closed	1991	90.00	275
1986 Boy & His Bunny L1507M	Closed	1991	90.00	160-275
1986 In the Meadow L1508G	Closed	1991	100.00	195-325
1986 In the Meadow L1508M	Closed	1991	100.00	195-310
1986 Spring Flowers L1509G	Closed	1991	100.00	310
1986 Spring Flowers L1509M	Closed	1991	100.00	295
1987 Cafe De Paris L1511G	Closed	1995	1900.00	2950
1987 Hawaiian Beauty L1512G	Closed	1990	575.00	850-1200
1987 A Flower for My Lady L1513G	Closed	1990	1150.00	1750
1987 Gaspar 's Page L1514G	Closed	1990	275.00	475-550
1987 Melchior's Page L1515G	Closed	1990	290.00	495-550
1987 Balthasar's Page L1516G	Closed	1990	275.00	850
1987 Circus Train L1517G	Closed	1994	2900.00	4350
1987 Valencian Garden L1518G	Closed	1991	1100.00	1795
1987 Stroll in the Park L1519G	Closed	1998	1600.00	2600
1987 The Landau Carriage L1521G	Closed	1998	2500.00	3109-3850
1987 I am Don Quixote! L1522G	Open		2600.00	3950
1987 Valencian Bouquet L1524G	Closed	1991	250.00	400
1987 Valencian Dreams L1525G	Closed	1991	240.00	400
1987 Valencian Flowers L1526G	Closed	1991	375.00	550
1987 Tenderness L1527G	Open		260.00	430
1987 I Love You Truly L1528G	Open		375.00	595
1987 Momi L1529G	Closed	1990	275.00	550
1987 Leilani L1530G	Closed	1990	275.00	550
1987 Malia L1531G	Closed	1990	275.00	500-550
1987 Lehua L1532G	Closed	1990	275.00	550-600
1987 Not So Fast! L1533G	Closed	1996	175.00	214-325
1988 Little Sister L1534G	Open		180.00	240
1988 Sweet Dreams L1535G	Open		150.00	240
1988 Stepping Out L1537G	12/00		230.00	335
1988 Pink Ballet Slippers L1540	Closed	1991	275.00	450-500
1988 White Ballet Slippers L1540.3	Closed	1991	275.00	395-465
1987 Light Blue Spoon L1548G	Closed	1991	70.00	150
1987 Dark Blue Spoon L1548.1	Closed	1991	70.00	150
1987 White Spoon L1548.3	Closed	1991	70.00	150
1987 Flower Basket L1552	Closed	1991	115.00	213-280
1987 Small Pink Broad Brimmed Hat L1563.3M	Closed	1991	45.00	125
1987 Wild Stallions w/base L1566G	Closed	1993	1100.00	1465
1987 Running Free w/base L1567G	Closed	1998	1500.00	1600
1987 Grand Dame L1568G	12/00		290.00	515
1989 Fluttering Crane L1598G	Closed	1998	115.00	145-175
1989 Nesting Crane L1599G	Closed	1998	95.00	98-115
1989 Landing Crane L1600G	Closed	1998	115.00	145
1989 Rock Nymph L1601G	Closed	1995	665.00	825-950
1989 Spring Nymph L1602G	Closed	1995	665.00	825-950
1989 Latest Addition L1606G	Open		385.00	480
1989 Flight Into Egypt w/base L1610G	12/00		885.00	1150
1989 Courting Cranes L1611G	Open		565.00	695
1989 Preening Crane L1612G	Closed	1998	385.00	485-525
1989 Bowing Crane L1613G	Closed	1998	385.00	485
1989 Dancing Crane L1614G	12/00		385.00	485
1989 Snow Queen Mask No.11 L1645G	Closed	1991	390.00	450
1989 Medieval Cross No.4 L1652G	Closed	1991	250.00	350
1989 Lavender Lady L1667M	Closed	1991	385.00	550
1989 Lacy Butterfly #1 L1673M	Closed	1991	95.00	200
1989 Beautiful Butterfly #2 L1674M	Closed	1991	100.00	195
1989 Black Butterfly #3 L1675M	Closed	1991	120.00	195
1989 Pink & White Butterfly #4 L1676M	Closed	1991	100.00	195
1989 Black & White Butterfly #5 L1677M	Closed	1991	100.00	195
1989 Large Pink Butterfly #6 L1678M	Closed	1991	100.00	175
1989 Pink & Blue Butterfly #7 L1679M	Closed	1991	80.00	150
1989 Small Pink Butterfly #8 L1680M	Closed	1991	72.50	125
1989 Blue Butterfly #9 L1681M	Closed	1991	185.00	275
1989 Pretty Butterfly #10 L1682M	Closed	1991	185.00	275
1989 Spotted Butterfly #11 L1683M	Closed	1991	175.00	260
1989 Leopard Butterfly #12 L1684M	Closed	1991	165.00	250
1989 Great Butterfly #13 L1685M	Closed	1991	150.00	225
1989 Queen Butterfly #14 L1686M	Closed	1991	125.00	200
1988 Cellist L1700M	Closed	1993	1200.00	1813
1988 Saxophone Player L1701M	Closed	1993	835.00	1840
1988 Boy at the Fair (Decorated) L1708M	Closed	1993	650.00	650
1988 Exodus L1709M	Closed	1993	875.00	875
1988 School Boy L1710M	Closed	1993	750.00	750
1988 School Girl L1711M	Closed	1993	950.00	950
1988 Nanny L1714M	Closed	1993	575.00	700
1988 On Our Way Home (decorated) L1715M	Closed	1993	2000.00	2000
1988 Harlequin with Puppy L1716M	Closed	1993	825.00	1000
1988 Harlequin with Dove L1717M	Closed	1993	900.00	1000
1988 Dress Rehearsal L1718M	Closed	1993	1150.00	1150
1989 Back From the Fair L1719M	Closed	1993	1825.00	1825
1990 Sprite w/base L1720G, numbd. series	Open		1200.00	1400
1990 Leprechaun w/base L1721G, numbd. series	Open		1200.00	1400
1989 Group Discussion L1722M	Closed	1993	1500.00	1500
1989 Hopeful Group L1723M	Closed	1993	1825.00	1825
1989 Belle Epoque L1724M	Closed	1993	700.00	700
1989 Young Lady with Parasol L1725M	Closed	1993	950.00	950
1989 Young Lady with Fan L1726M	Closed	1993	750.00	750
1989 Pose L1727M	Closed	1993	725.00	725
1991 Nativity L1730M	Closed	1997	725.00	725
1970 Monkey L2000M	Closed	1975	35.00	500
1970 Cat L2001G	Closed	1975	27.50	625
1970 Gothic King L2002G	Closed	1975	25.00	450
1970 Gothic Queen L2003G	Closed	1975	25.00	450
1970 Shepherdess Sleeping L2005M	Closed	1981	100.00	710
1970 Water Carrier Girl Lamp L2006M	Closed	1975	30.00	600
1970 Mounted Harlequin L2012M	Closed	1981	200	2200
1971 Girl with Dog L2013M	Closed	1975	300.00	2350
1971 Little Eagle Owl L2020M	Closed	1985	15.00	425-618
1971 Boy/Girl Eskimo L2038.3M	Closed	1994	100.00	450
1971 Aida L2039M	Closed	1979	65.00	1200
1974 Setter's Head L2045M	Closed	1981	42.50	550
1974 Magistrates L2052M	Closed	1981	135.00	950-1200
1974 Oriental L2056M	Open		35.00	105
1974 Oriental L2057M	Open		30.00	105
1974 Thailandia L2058M	Open		650.00	1885
1974 Muskateer L2059M	Closed	1981	900.00	2000-3000
1977 Monk L2060M	Closed	1998	60.00	155-195
1977 Day Dream L2062M	Closed	1985	400.00	1300
1977 Chinese Farmer w/Staff L2065M	Closed	1985	340.00	1800
1977 Dogs-Bust L2067M	Closed	1979	280.00	800
1977 Thai Dancers L2069M	Closed	1999	300.00	745
1977 A New Hairdo L2070M	Open		1060.00	1525
1977 Graceful Duo L2073M	Closed	1994	775.00	1650
1977 Nuns L2075M	12/00		90.00	250
1978 Lonely L2076M	Closed	1999	72.50	185
1978 Rain in Spain L2077M	Closed	1990	190.00	475-550
1978 Lola L2078M	Closed	1981	250.00	650
1978 Woman L2080M	Closed	1985	625.00	625
1978 Fisherwoman L2081M	Closed	1985	550.00	1450
1978 Carmen L2083M	Closed	1981	275.00	625
1978 Don Quixote Dreaming L2084M	Closed	1985	550.00	2100
1978 The Little Kiss L2086M	Closed	1985	180.00	500
1978 Girl in Rocking Chair L2089	Closed	1981	235.00	600
1978 Saint Francis L2090	Closed	1981	565.00	765-1400
1978 Holy Virgin L2092M	Closed	1981	260.00	N/A
1978 Girl Waiting L2093M	Closed	1995	90.00	148
1978 Tenderness L2094M	12/00		100.00	205
1978 Duck Pulling Pigtail L2095M	Closed	1998	110.00	275-295
1978 Nosy Puppy L2096M	Closed	1993	190.00	349-400
1978 Laundress and Water Carrier L2109M	Closed	1983	325.00	600-650
1978 Charity L2112M	Closed	1981	360.00	1200-1500
1980 My Little Duckling L2113M	Closed	1993	240.00	295
1980 Kissing Father L2114M	Closed	1981	575.00	575
1980 Mother's Kiss L2115M	Closed	1981	575.00	700
1980 The Whaler L2121M	Closed	1988	820.00	1050
1981 Lost in Thought L2125M	Closed	1990	210.00	300
1983 Indian Chief L2127M	Closed	1988	525.00	700-750
1983 Venus L2128M	Open		650.00	1330
1983 Waiting for Sailor L2129M	Closed	1985	325.00	600
1983 Egyptian Cat L2130M	Closed	1985	75.00	450
1983 Mother & Son L2131M, numbd. series	Closed	1998	850.00	1550
1983 Spring Sheperdess L2132M	Closed	1985	450.00	1250
1983 Autumn Sheperdess L2133M	Closed	1985	285.00	1250
1984 Nautical Watch L2134M	Closed	1988	450.00	800
1984 Mystical Joseph L2135M	Closed	1988	428.00	750
1984 The King L2136M	Closed	1988	570.00	710
1984 Fairy Ballerina L2137M	Closed	1988	500.00	1250
1984 Friar Juniper L2138M	Closed	1993	160.00	400-475
1984 Aztec Indian L2139M	Closed	1988	553.00	600
1984 Pepita wth Sombrero L2140M	Open		97.50	200
1984 Pedro with Jug L2141M	Open		100.00	205
1984 Sea Harvest L2142M	Closed	1990	535.00	725
1984 Aztec Dancer L2143M	Closed	1988	463.00	650
1984 Leticia L2144M	Closed	1995	100.00	225
1984 Gabriela L2145M	Closed	1994	100.00	250
1984 Desiree L2146M	Closed	1995	100.00	225
1984 Alida L2147M	Closed	1994	100.00	250
1984 Head of Congolese Woman L2148M	Closed	1988	55.00	695-700
1985 Young Madonna L2149M	Closed	1988	400.00	675
1985 A Tribute to Peace w/base L2150M	Open		470.00	930
1985 A Bird on Hand L2151M	Closed	1999	118.00	255
1985 Chinese Girl L2152M	Closed	1990	90.00	250-275
1985 Chinese Boy L2153	Closed	1990	90.00	250-275
1985 Hawaiian Flower Vendor L2154M	12/00		245.00	460
1985 Arctic inter L2156M	Open		75.00	145
1985 Eskimo Girl with Cold Feet L2157M	Open		140.00	285
1985 Pensive Eskimo Girl L2158M	Open		100.00	210
1985 Pensive Eskimo Boy L2159M	Open		100.00	210
1985 Flower Vendor L2160M	Closed	1995	110.00	215
1985 Fruit Vendor L2161M	Closed	1994	120.00	230
1985 Fish Vendor L2162M	Closed	1994	110.00	205
1987 Mountain Shepherd L2163M	Closed	1999	120.00	210
1987 My Lost Lamb L2164M	Closed	1999	100.00	175
1987 Chiquita L2165M	Closed	1993	100.00	170
1987 Paco L2166M	Closed	1993	100.00	170
1987 Fernando L2167M	Closed	1993	100.00	153-200
1987 Julio L2168M	Closed	1993	100.00	225
1987 Repose L2169M	Open		120.00	195
1987 Spanish Dancer L2170M	Open		190.00	400
1987 Ahoy Tere L2173M	Open		190.00	325
1987 Andean Flute Player L2174M	Closed	1990	250.00	350
1988 Harvest Helpers L2178M	Open		190.00	265
1988 Sharing the Harvest L2179M	Open		190.00	265
1988 Dreams of Peace w/base L2180M	Open		880.00	1450
1988 Bathing Nymph w/base L2181M	Open		560.00	795
1988 Daydreamer w/base L2182M	Open		560.00	795
1989 Wakeup Kitty L2183M	Closed	1993	225.00	285-325
1989 Angel and Friend L2184M	Closed	1994	150.00	185
1989 Devoted Reader L2185M	Closed	1994	125.00	195-200
1989 The Greatest Love L2186M	Closed	1998	235.00	320
1989 Jealous Friend L2187M	Closed	1995	275.00	365-400
1990 Mother's Pride L2189M	Closed	1999	300.00	375
1990 To The Well L2190M	Open		250.00	295
1990 Forest Born L2191M	Closed	1991	230.00	336-475
1990 King Of The Forest L2192M	Closed	1992	290.00	325
1990 Heavenly Strings L2194M	Closed	1993	170.00	250
1990 Heavenly Sounds L2195M	Closed	1993	170.00	250
1990 Heavenly Solo L2196M	Closed	1993	170.00	250
1990 Heavenly Song L2197M	Closed	1993	175.00	195-250
1990 A King is Born w/base L2198M	Open		750.00	895
1990 Devoted Friends w/base L2199M	Closed	1995	700.00	895
1990 A Big Hug! L2200M	Closed	1998	250.00	310
1990 Our Daily Bread L2201M	Closed	1994	150.00	275-300
1990 A Helping Hand L2202M	Closed	1993	150.00	250
1990 Afternoon Chores L2203M	Closed	1994	150.00	185-250
1990 Farmyard Grace L2204M	Closed	1993	180.00	300
1990 Prayerful Stitch L2205M	Closed	1994	160.00	179-250
1990 Sisterly Love L2206M	Open		300.00	375
1990 What A Day! L2207M	Open		550.00	640
1990 Let's Rest L2208M	Open		550.00	665
1991 Long Dy L2209M	Open		295.00	340
1991 Lazy Day L2210M	Open		240.00	260
1991 Patrol Leader L2212M	Closed	1993	390.00	425
1991 Nature's Friend L2213M	Closed	1993	390.00	425
1991 Seaside Angel L2214M	Open		150.00	165
1991 Friends in Flight L2215M	Open		165.00	180
1991 Laundry Day L2216M	Open		350.00	400
1991 Gentle Play L2217M	Closed	1993	380.00	425
1991 Costumed Couple L2218M	Closed	1993	680.00	750
1992 Underfoot L2219M	Open		360.00	410
1992 Free Spirit L2220M	Closed	1994	235.00	245
1992 Spring Beauty L2221M	Closed	1994	285.00	295-350
1992 Tender Moment L2222M	Closed	1999	400.00	450
1992 New Lamb L2223M	Closed	1999	365.00	385
1992 Cherish L2224M	Open		1750.00	1850
1992 Friendly Sparrow L2225M	Open		295.00	325
1992 Boy's Best Friend L2226M	Open		390.00	410
1992 Artic Allies L2227M	Open		585.00	615
1992 Snowy Sunday L2228M	Open		550.00	625
1992 Seasonal Gifts L2229M	Open		450.00	475
1992 Mary's Child L2230M	Closed	1994	525.00	550
1992 Afternoon Verse L2231M	Open		580.00	595
1992 Poor Little Bear L2232M	Open		250.00	265
1992 Guess What I Have L2233M	Open		340.00	375
1992 Playful Push L2234M	12/00		850.00	875
1993 Adoring Mother L2235M	Closed	1999	405.00	440
1993 Frosty Outing L2236M	Closed	1998	375.00	410
1993 The Old Fishing Hole L2237M	Open		625.00	640
1993 Learning Together L2238M	Closed	1998	500.00	500
1993 Valencian Courtship L2239M	Open		880.00	895
1993 Winged Love L2240M	Closed	1995	285.00	310
1993 Winged Harmony L2241M	Closed	1995	285.00	310-350
1993 Away to School L2242M	Open		465.00	465
1993 Lion Tamer L2246M	Closed	1995	375.00	375-400
1993 Just Us L2247M	Closed	1995	650.00	650
1993 Noella L2251M	Open		405.00	420
1993 Waiting For Father L2252M	Closed	1999	660.00	660
1993 Noisy Friend L2253M	Closed	1998	280.00	280
1993 Step Aside L2254M	Open		280.00	280
1994 Solitude L2256M	Closed	1998	398.00	435
1994 Constant Companions L2257M	Closed	1997	575.00	625
1994 Family Love L2258M	12/00		450.00	485
1994 Little Fisherman L2259M	Closed	1999	298.00	330
1994 Artic Friends L2260M	Closed	1997	345.00	380
1989 Latest Addition L2262M	Closed	1998	495.00	495
1994 Mother and Child L2263	Closed	1998	285.00	285
1994 Madonna Head L2264	12/00		210.00	220
1994 Little Friskies L2266	Closed	1998	250.00	260
1994 Playful Kittens L2268	Closed	1998	285.00	300
1994 The Wanderer L2271	Closed	1998	245.00	245
1994 My Best Friend L2272	Closed	1998	240.00	240
1994 May Flowers L2274	Closed	1998	195.00	195
1994 Musical Muse L2285	Closed	1998	465.00	465
1994 Barnyard Scene L2286	Closed	1998	260.00	230-270
1994 Dog's Best Friend L2287	12/00		310.00	310
1994 Carefree L2288	Closed	1998	325.00	325
1994 Dressing The Baby L2289	Closed	1998	325.00	325
1994 Surprise L2290	12/00		335.00	335
1994 World of Fantasy L2292	Closed	1998	325.00	335
1995 Jesus and Joseph L2294M	Closed	1999	550.00	550
1995 Peaceful Rest L2295M	Closed	1998	390.00	390
1995 Life's Small Wonders L2296M	Open		370.00	370
1995 Elephants L2297M	Open		875.00	875
1995 Hindu Children L2298M	12/00		450.00	450
1995 Poetic Moment L2299M	Open		465.00	465
1995 Emperor L2300M	Closed	1999	765.00	765
1995 Empress L2301M	Closed	1999	795.00	795
1995 Twilight Years L2302M	Closed	1998	385.00	385-425
1995 Not So Fast L2303M	Closed	1998	350.00	350
1995 Love in Bloom L2304M	Open		420.00	420
1995 Fragrant Bouquet L2305M	Open		330.00	330
1995 Hurry Now L2306M	12/00		310.00	310
1995 Happy Birthday L2307M	Closed	1998	150.00	150
1995 Let's Make Up L2308M	Closed	1998	265.00	265
1995 Sea Breeze (Windblown Girl) L2309M	Closed	1998	320.00	320
1995 Chit-Chat L2310M	Closed	1998	270.00	270
1995 Good Night L2311M	Closed	1998	280.00	280
1995 Goose Trying to Eat L2312M	Closed	1998	325.00	325
1995 Who's the Fairest L2313M	Closed	1998	230.00	230
1995 Breezy Afternoon L2314M	Closed	1998	220.00	220

*Quotes have been rounded up to nearest dollar

YEAR ISSUE	EDITION LIMIT	YEAR RETD.	ISSUE PRICE	*QUOTE U.S.$
1995 On the Green L2315M	12/00		575.00	575
1995 Closing Scene L2316M	Closed	1998	560.00	560
1995 Talk to Me L2317M	Closed	1998	175.00	175
1995 Taking Time L2318M	Closed	1998	175.00	175
1995 A Lesson Shared L2319M	Closed	1997	215.00	215
1995 Cat Nap L2320M	Closed	1999	265.00	265
1995 All Tuckered Out L2321M	Open		275.00	275
1995 Naptime L2322M	Open		275.00	275
1995 Water Girl L2323M	Open		245.00	245
1995 A Basket of Fun L2324M	Open		320.00	320
1995 Spring Splendor L2325M	Open		440.00	440
1995 Physician L2326M	Closed	1998	350.00	350
1995 Sad Sax L2327M	Open		225.00	225
1995 Circus Sam L2328M	Open		225.00	225
1995 Daily Chores L2329M	Closed	1999	345.00	345
1996 The Shepherdess L2330	Closed	1999	410.00	410
1996 Little Peasant Girl (pink) L2331	Open		155.00	155
1996 Little Peasant Girl (blue) L2332	Open		155.00	155
1996 Little Peasant Girl (white) L2333	Open		155.00	155
1996 Asian Melody L2334	Closed	1998	690.00	690
1996 Young Fisherman L2335	Open		225.00	225
1996 Young Water Girl L2336	Open		315.00	315
1996 Virgin of Montserrat w/base L2337	Open		1000.00	1000
1996 Sultan's Dream L2338	Open		700.00	700
1996 The Sultan L2339	Open		480.00	480
1996 Oriental Fantasy w/bow L2340	12/00		1350.00	1350
1996 Oriental Fantasy w/brooch L2341	12/00		1350.00	1350
1996 Returning From the Well w/base L2342	12/00		1800.00	1800
1996 Care and Tenderness w/base L2343	Closed	1999	860.00	860
1996 Oration L2344	Open		295.00	295
1996 Bedtime Story L2345	Closed	1999	360.00	360
1996 Feeding the Ducks L2346	Closed	1999	305.00	305
1996 Meditation (blue) L2347	Closed	1999	145.00	145
1996 Prayerful Moment (blue) L2348	Closed	1999	145.00	145
1996 Sleigh Ride w/base L2349	Closed	1998	1520.00	1520
1996 Pensive Clown w/base L2350	Closed	1999	680.00	680
1996 Fishing With Gramps w/base L2351	Open		1025.00	1025
1996 Under My Spell L2352	Closed	1998	225.00	225
1996 Shot on Goal w/base L2353	Closed	1998	935.00	935
1997 Waiting For Spring L2354	12/00		385.00	400
1997 Gabriela L2355	Open		740.00	740
1997 Country Joy L2356	Closed	1999	310.00	310
1997 In Search of Water L2357	Open		410.00	425
1997 I'm Sleepy L2358	12/00		360.00	360
1997 First Crush L2359	Open		945.00	990
1997 Hunting Butterflies L2360	12/00		465.00	465
1997 Cold Weather Companions L2361	Open		380.00	380
1997 Braving The Storm L2362	Closed	1999	470.00	470
1997 Pampered Puppy L2363	12/00		345.00	375
1997 Melodies L2364	Open		590.00	660
1997 Holy Mother L2365	Open		230.00	230
1997 Bread of Life L2366	Open		230.00	230
1997 Pensive Harlequin L2367	Open		560.00	560
1997 Colombina L2368	Closed	1999	585.00	585
1998 Early Awakening 01012369	Closed	1999	595.00	700
1998 It's Magic! 01012372	12/00		1045.00	1100
1998 Spring Inspiration 01012374	12/00		635.00	725
1998 Emperor 01012375	12/00		695.00	695
1998 Empress 01012376	12/00		735.00	750
1998 Arctic Explorer 01012379	12/00		550.00	580
1998 A Comforting Friend 01012380	Open		330.00	360
1998 Island Beauty 01012382	Open		180.00	185
1998 Pacific Jewel 01012383	Open		170.00	185
1998 What About Me? 01012384	12/00		790.00	925
1998 Tropical Flower 01012385	Open		190.00	190
1998 Low Tide 01012386	12/00		560.00	675
1998 Karina 01012387	Open		390.00	415
1998 Ready To Go 01012388	Open		350.00	350
1998 Time To Go 01012389	Open		330.00	360
1999 Joelia 01012390	Open		1300.00	1300
1998 Loyal Companions 01012391	Open		400.00	475
1998 My Memories 01012392	Open		345.00	400
1998 A Girl in Love 01012393	Open		465.00	525
1999 Island Breeze 01012394	Open		550.00	550
1999 Serenity 01012395	Open		1450.00	1450
1999 From The Spring 01012396	Open		475.00	475
1999 Little Chief 01012397	Open		325.00	325
1999 Conversing With Nature 01012398	Open		370.00	370
1999 Little Brave Resting 01012399	Open		325.00	325
1999 Waiting at the Beach 01012400	12/00		900.00	900
1999 Little Shepherd 01012401	12/00		275.00	275
1999 Africa 01012402	Open		700.00	750
1999 Pacific Beauty 01012403	Open		850.00	850
1999 Sunset 01012404	Open		440.00	440
1999 Midday 01012405	Open		535.00	535
1999 Dawn 01012406	Open		550.00	550
2000 Memories of Tuscany 01012407	Open		995.00	995
2000 Deep in Thought 01012408	Open		1325.00	1325
2000 Loving Mother 01012409	Open		1090.00	1090
2000 Poetic Interlude 01012410	Open		460.00	460
2000 In the Country 01012411	Open		525.00	525
2000 Thoughts of Peace 01012412	Open		1000.00	1000
2000 Grace 01012413	Open		250.00	250
2000 Beauty 01012414	Open		250.00	250
2000 Youth 01012415	Open		245.00	245
2000 In Mother's Arms 01012416	Open		990.00	990
2000 Young Mary 01012417	Open		340.00	340
1978 Native L3502M	Open		700.00	2450
1978 Letters to Dulcinea L3509M, numbd. series	Closed	1998	875.00	2175
1978 Horse Heads L3511M	Closed	1990	260.00	650
1978 Girl With Pails L3512M	Open		140.00	285
1978 A Wintry Day L3513M	Closed	1988	525.00	1100
1978 Pensive w/ base L3514M	Open		500.00	1050
1978 Jesus Christ L3516M	Closed	1988	1050.00	1500
1978 Nude with Rose w/ base L3517M	Open		225.00	780
1980 Lady Macbeth L3518M	Closed	1981	385.00	700-1350
1981 Weary w/ base L3525M	Open		360.00	685
1980 Mother's Love L3521M	Closed	1990	1000.00	1100
1982 Contemplation w/ base L3526M	Open		265.00	590
1982 Stormy Sea w/base L3554M	Open		675.00	1650
1984 Innocence w/base/green L3558M	Closed	1991	960.00	1650
1984 Innocence w/base/red L3558.3M	Closed	1987	960.00	1200
1985 Peace Offering w/base L3559M	Open		397.00	850
1969 Marketing Day L4502G	Closed	1985	40.00	400
1969 Girl with Lamb L4505G	Open		20.00	130
1969 Boy with Kid L4506M	Closed	1985	22.50	400
1969 Boy with Lambs L4509G	Closed	1981	37.50	275
1969 Girl with Parasol and Geese L4510G	Closed	1993	40.00	300-350
1969 Nude L4511M	Closed	1985	45.00	700
1969 Nude L4512G	Closed	1985	44.00	450
1969 Diana L4514G	Closed	1981	65.00	650-750
1969 Man on Horse L4515G	Closed	1985	180.00	1100
1969 Female Equestrian L4516G	Open		170.00	745
1969 Boy Student L4517G	Closed	1978	57.50	475-495
1969 Girl Student L4518G	Closed	1978	57.50	475
1969 Flamenco Dancers L4519G	Closed	1993	150.00	1200-1400
1970 Boy With Dog L4522M	Closed	1992	25.00	170-180
1970 Boy With Dog L4522G	Closed	1998	25.00	180-250
1969 Girl With Slippers L4523G	Closed	1993	17.00	125
1969 Girl With Slippers L4523M	Closed	1993	17.00	125
1969 Donkey in Love L4524G	Closed	1985	15.00	375
1969 Donkey in Love L4524M	Closed	1985	15.00	350
1969 Violinist Lamp L4527G	Closed	1985	75.00	500
1969 Ballet Lamp L4528G	Closed	1985	120.00	750-850
1969 Joseph L4533G	Closed	1996	60.00	110
1969 Joseph L4533M	Closed	1996	60.00	110
1969 Mary L4534G	Open		60.00	85
1969 Mary L4534M	Open		60.00	85
1971 Baby Jesus L4535.3G	Open		60.00	70
1969 Baby Jesus L4535.3M	Open		60.00	70
1969 Angel, Chinese L4536G	Open		45.00	95
1969 Angel, Chinese L4536M	Open		45.00	95
1969 Angel, Black L4537G	Open		13.00	95
1969 Angel, Black L4537M	Open		13.00	95
1969 Angel, Praying L4538G	Open		13.00	95
1969 Angel, Praying L4538M	Open		13.00	95
1969 Angel, Thinking L4539G	Open		13.00	95
1969 Angel, Thinking L4539M	Open		13.00	95
1969 Angel with Horn L4540G	Open		13.00	95
1969 Angel with Horn L4540M	Open		13.00	95
1969 Angel Reclining L4541G	Open		13.00	95
1969 Angel Reclining L4541M	Open		13.00	95
1969 Group of Angels L4542G	Open		31.00	200
1969 Group of Angels L4542M	Open		31.00	200
1969 Troubador L4548G	Closed	1978	67.50	750
1969 Geese Group L4549G	Closed	1997	28.50	245-275
1969 Geese Group L4549M	Closed	1992	28.50	245-275
1969 Flying Dove L4550G	Closed	1998	47.50	265-295
1969 Turtle Dove L4550M	Closed	1992	47.50	265
1969 Ducks, Set/3 asst. L4551-3G	Open		18.00	140
1969 Shepherd w/Girl & Lamb L4554	Closed	1972	69.00	N/A
1969 Sad Harlequin L4558G	Closed	1993	110.00	600-845
1969 Ballerina L4559G	Closed	1993	110.00	500-550
1970 Llama Group 4561G	Closed	1970	55.00	1600
1969 Couple with Parasol L4563G	Closed	1985	180.00	850-900
1969 Girl with Geese L4568G	Closed	1993	45.00	358-375
1969 Girl With Turkey L4569G	Closed	1981	28.50	375
1969 Shepherd Resting L4571G	Closed	1981	60.00	475
1969 Girl with Piglets L4572G	Closed	1985	70.00	425
1969 Girl with Piglets L4572M	Closed	1985	70.00	400
1969 Mother & Child L4575G	Closed	1998	50.00	295-325
1969 New Shepherdess L4576G	Closed	1985	37.50	315
1969 New Shepherd L4577G	Closed	1983	35.00	550
1969 Mardi Gras L4580G	Closed	1975	57.50	1800
1969 Mardi Gras L4580M	Closed	1975	57.50	1800
1969 Setter L4583G	Closed	1981	21.00	600
1969 Girl with Sheep L4584G	Closed	1993	27.00	170
1969 Girl with Sheep L4584M	Closed	1993	27.00	210
1969 Holy Family L4585G	Open		18.00	135
1969 Holy Family L4585M	Closed	1994	18.00	135
1969 Madonna L4586G	Closed	1979	32.50	350
1969 White Cockeral L4588G	Closed	1979	17.50	300
1969 Girl with Pitcher L4590G	Closed	1981	47.50	400
1969 Girl with Cockerel L4591G	Closed	1993	20.00	275
1969 Lady with Greyhound L4594G	Closed	1981	60.00	700-850
1969 Fairy L4595G	Closed	1994	27.50	200-245
1969 Girl With Flower L4596G	Closed	1980	25.00	275
1969 Two Horses L4597	Closed	1990	240.00	1000
1969 Doctor L4602.3G	Closed	1999	33.00	230-295
1969 Nurse-L4603.3G	Closed	N/A	35.00	225
1969 Magic L4605	Closed	1985	160.00	900-1100
1969 Accordian Player L4606	Closed	1978	60.00	650
1969 Cupid L4607G	Closed	1980	15.00	800
1969 Cook in Trouble L4608	Closed	1985	27.50	600-650
1969 Nuns L4611G	Open		37.50	155
1969 Nuns L4611M	Open		37.50	155
1969 Girl Singer L4612G	Closed	1979	14.00	375-450
1969 Boy with Cymbals L4613G	Closed	1979	14.00	400
1969 Boy with Guitar L4614G	Closed	1979	19.50	400
1969 Boy with Double Bass L4615G	Closed	1979	22.50	400-553
1969 Boy with Drum L4616G	Closed	1979	16.50	350
1969 Group of Musicians L4617G	Closed	1979	33.00	500
1969 Clown L4618G	Open		70.00	415
1969 Seminarist L4619G	Closed	1972	18.50	650
1969 Policeman L4620G	Closed	1972	16.00	500
1969 Sea Captain L4621G	Closed	1993	45.00	325-350
1969 Sea Captain L4621M	Closed	1989	42.50	300
1969 Old Man with Violin L4622G	Closed	1982	45.00	700-750
1969 Velazquez Bookend L4626G	Closed	1975	90.00	950
1969 Columbus Bookend L4627G	Closed	1975	90.00	950
1969 Angel with Child L4635G	Open		15.00	130
1969 Honey Peddler L4638G	Closed	1978	60.00	575
1969 Cow With Pig L4640G	Closed	1981	42.50	650-750
1969 Cow With Pig L4640M	Closed	1981	42.50	750
1969 Pekinese L4641G	Closed	1985	20.00	375-450
1969 Dog L4642	Closed	1981	22.50	390-500
1969 Skye Terrier L4643G	Closed	1985	15.00	500
1969 Pierrot w/Mandolin L4646M	Closed	1970	60.00	1950
1969 Andalucians Group L4647G	Closed	1990	412.00	1400
1969 Valencian Couple on Horseback L4648	Closed	1990	900.00	1400
1969 Madonna Head L4649G	Open		25.00	185
1969 Madonna Head L4649M	Open		25.00	170
1969 Girl with Calla Lillies L4650G	Closed	1998	16.50	155-195
1969 Cellist L4651G	Closed	1978	70.00	600-750
1969 Happy Travelers L4652	Closed	1978	115.00	650
1969 Orchestra Conductor L4653G	Closed	1979	95.00	750-950
1969 The Grandfather L4654G	Closed	1979	75.00	1200
1969 Horses L4655G	12/00		110.00	760
1969 Woodcutter L4656G	Closed	1978	80.00	600
1969 Shepherdess L4660G	Closed	1993	21.00	300
1969 Countryman L4664M	Closed	1979	50.00	500
1969 Girl with Basket L4665G	Closed	1979	50.00	450
1969 Girl with Basket L4665M	Closed	1979	50.00	550
1969 Birds L4667G	Closed	1985	25.00	250-750
1969 Maja Head L4668G	Closed	1985	50.00	750-787
1969 Pastoral Couple L4669G	Closed	1978	100.00	850
1969 Baby Jesus L4670BG	Open		6.00	55
1969 Mary L4671G	Open		70.00	75
1969 St. Joseph L4672G	Closed	1998	70.50	90
1969 King Melchior L4673G	Closed	1998	11.00	95
1969 King Gaspar L4674G	Open		11.00	95
1969 King Balthasar L4675G	Open		11.00	95
1969 Shepherd with Lamb L4676G	Open		14.00	110
1969 Shepherd with Lamb L4676M	Closed	N/A	14.00	150
1969 Girl with Rooster L4677G	Open		14.00	90
1969 Girl with Rooster L4677M	Closed	N/A	14.00	150
1969 Shepherdess with Basket L4678G	Open		13.00	90
1969 Shepherdess with Basket L4678M	Closed	N/A	13.00	150
1969 Donkey L4679G	Open		11.50	100
1969 Cow L4680G	Open		12.00	90
1970 Girl with Milkpail L4682G	Closed	1991	28.00	300-375
1970 Girl with Milkpail L4682M	Closed	1991	28.00	275
1970 Hebrew Student L4684G	Closed	1985	33.00	750-975
1970 Hebrew Student L4684M	Closed	1985	33.00	620
1970 Girl's Head w/Cap L4686G	Closed	1984	25.00	750
1970 Gothic Queen L4689	Closed	1975	20.00	700
1970 Troubadour in Love L4699	Closed	1975	60.00	1000
1970 Dressmaker L4700G	Closed	1993	45.00	425-488
1970 Mother & Child L4701G	Closed	1998	45.00	295-325
1970 Girl Jewelry Dish L4713G	Closed	1978	30.00	550
1970 Girl Jewelry Dish L4713M	Closed	1978	30.00	550
1970 Boy Jewelry Dish L4714G	Closed	1978	30.00	600
1970 Lady Empire L4719G	Closed	1979	150.00	990-1100
1970 Girl With Tulips L4720G	Closed	1978	65.00	500-600
1970 Girl With Tulips L4720M	Closed	1978	65.00	450
1970 Hamlet L4729G	Closed	1980	85.00	800-875
1970 Bird Watcher L4730	Closed	1985	35.00	520-1000
1970 German Shepherd w/Pup L4731	Closed	1975	40.00	950
1971 Small Dog L4749	Closed	1985	5.50	190-200
1971 Romeo and Juliet L4750G	Open		150.00	1250
1971 Boy w/Dog L4755G	Closed	1978	50.00	400
1971 Doncel With Roses L4757G	Closed	1979	35.00	500
1974 Woman L4761G	Closed	1993	60.00	400-500
1971 Dentist L4762	Closed	1978	36.00	550
1971 Dentist (Reduced) L4762.3G	Closed	1985	30.00	550
1971 Obstetrician L4763G	Closed	1973	47.50	255-450
1971 Obstetrician L4763.3G	Closed	1973	40.00	300-325
1971 Obstetrician L4763M	Closed	1998	47.50	255
1971 Maternal Elephant L4765G	Closed	1975	50.00	700
1971 Don Quixote Vase L4770G	Closed	1975	25.00	750
1971 Don Quixote Vase L4770M	Closed	1975	25.00	750
1971 Rabbit L4772G	Closed	1998	17.50	135
1971 Rabbit L4773G	Closed	1998	17.50	130
1971 Dormouse L4774	Closed	1983	30.00	375
1971 Children, Praying L4779G	Closed	1998	36.00	187-260
1971 Children, Praying L4779M	Closed	1992	36.00	210-225
1971 Boy with Goat L4780	Closed	1978	80.00	300-600
1972 Girl Tennis Player L4798	Closed	1981	50.00	450
1972 Japanese Woman L4799	Closed	1975	45.00	425-500
1972 Gypsy with Brother L4800G	Closed	1979	36.00	400-450
1972 The Teacher L4801G	Closed	1978	45.00	500
1972 Fisherman L4802G	Closed	1979	70.00	550-700
1972 Woman with Umbrella L4805G	Closed	1981	100.00	800
1972 Girl with Dog L4806G	Closed	1981	80.00	500
1972 Geisha L4807G	Closed	1993	190.00	495-600
1972 Wedding L4808G	Open		50.00	190
1972 Wedding L4808M	Open		50.00	190
1972 Going Fishing L4809G	Open		33.00	160
1972 Boy w/Yacht L4810G	Closed	1998	33.00	195-210
1972 Boy w/Yacht L4810M	Closed	1998	33.00	225
1972 Dutch Boy L4811	Closed	1988	30.00	350-400
1972 Little Girl w/Goat L4812G	Closed	1988	55.00	450-525
1972 Girl with Calf L4813	Closed	1981	50.00	550-650

*Quotes have been rounded up to nearest dollar

FIGURINES

YEAR ISSUE	EDITION LIMIT	YEAR RETD.	ISSUE PRICE	*QUOTE U.S.$
1972 Little Girl with Turkey L4814	Closed	1981	45.00	475
1972 Girl with Goose L4815G	Closed	1991	72.00	354-400
1972 Girl with Goose L4815M	Closed	1991	72.00	295
1972 Little Shepherd with Goat L4817M	Closed	1981	50.00	475
1972 Burro L4821G	Closed	1979	24.00	450
1974 Peruvian Girl with Baby L4822	Closed	1981	65.00	775
1974 Legionary L4823	Closed	1978	55.00	500-625
1972 Male Golfer L4824G	Open		66.00	295
1972 Veterinarian L4825	Closed	1985	48.00	500-550
1972 Rabbit's Food L4826G	Closed	1993	40.00	300-325
1972 Rabbit's Food L4826M	Closed	1993	40.00	225
1972 Caressing Calf L4827G	Closed	1981	55.00	475
1972 Cinderella L4828G	Closed	1998	47.00	275-295
1975 Swan L4829G	Closed	1983	16.00	400
1972 You and Me L4830G	Closed	1979	112.50	1100-1150
1972 Romance L4831G	Closed	1981	175.00	1350-1500
1972 Chess Set Pieces L4833.3G	Closed	1985	410	2300
1972 Girl w/Lamb L4835G	Closed	1991	42.00	350
1973 Clean Up Time L4838G	Closed	1993	36.00	250-295
1973 Clean Up Time L4838M	Closed	1992	36.00	250
1973 Oriental Flower Arranger/Girl L4840G	Closed	1998	90.00	575-600
1973 Oriental Flower Arranger/Girl L4840M	Closed	1998	90.00	515-600
1974 Girl from Valencia L4841G	Open		35.00	240
1973 Viola Lesson L4842G	Closed	1981	66.00	375-450
1973 Donkey Ride L4843	Closed	1981	86.00	650
1973 Pharmacist L4844G	Closed	1985	70.00	1200-1350
1973 Classic Dance L4847G	Closed	1985	80.00	575-600
1973 Charm L4848G	Closed	1985	45.00	350
1973 Feeding The Ducks L4849G	Closed	1995	60.00	425-700
1973 Feeding The Ducks L4849M	Closed	1992	60.00	250
1973 Aesthetic Pose L4850G	Closed	1985	110.00	650
1973 Lady Golfer L4851M	Closed	1992	70.00	500
1973 Gardner in Trouble L4852	Closed	1981	65.00	550
1974 Cobbler L4853G	Closed	1985	100.00	550-600
1973 Don Quixote L4854G	Open		40.00	205
1973 Death of the Swan L4855G	12/00		45.00	330
1983 Death of the Swan, white L4855.3	Closed	1987	110.00	250
1974 Waltz Time L4856G	Closed	1985	65.00	450-560
1974 Dog L4857G	Closed	1979	40.00	550
1974 Pleasant Encounter L4858M	Closed	1981	60.00	450
1974 Peddler L4859G	Closed	1985	180.00	750
1974 Dutch Girl L4860G	Closed	1985	45.00	363-425
1974 Horse L4861	Closed	1978	55.00	500
1974 Horse L4862	Closed	1978	55.00	500
1974 Horse L4863	Closed	1978	55.00	400
1974 Mother L4864G	Closed	1979	190.00	1100
1974 Embroiderer L4865G	Closed	1994	115.00	725-765
1974 Girl with Goose and Dog L4866G	Closed	1993	26.00	205-225
1974 Seesaw L4867G	Closed	1997	55.00	375-650
1974 Girl with Candle L4868G	12/00		13.00	90
1974 Girl with Candle L4868M	Closed	1992	13.00	80
1974 Boy Kissing L4869G	Closed	1998	13.00	95-125
1974 Boy Kissing L4869M	Closed	1992	13.00	180
1974 Boy Yawning L4870G	Closed	1999	13.00	90-110
1974 Boy Yawning L4870M	Closed	1992	13.00	180
1974 Girl with Guitar L4871G	12/00		13.00	90
1974 Girl with Guitar L4871M	Closed	1992	13.00	90
1974 Girl Stretching L4872G	Closed	1992	13.00	90-125
1974 Girl Stretching L4872M	Closed	1992	13.00	90
1974 Girl Kissing L4873G	Closed	1998	13.00	90-135
1974 Girl Kissing L4873M	Closed	1992	13.00	90
1974 Boy & Girl L4874G	Closed	1998	25.00	165-200
1974 Boy & Girl L4874M	Closed	1992	25.00	150
1974 The Jug Carrier L4875G	Closed	1985	40.00	300
1974 Boy Thinking L4876G	Closed	1993	20.00	135-170
1974 Boy Thinking L4876M	Closed	1992	20.00	120
1974 Boy with Flute L4877G	Closed	1981	60.00	450-475
1974 Aranjuez Little Lady L4879G	Closed	1997	48.00	325-375
1974 Carnival Couple L4882G	Closed	1995	60.00	375-425
1974 Carnival Couple L4882M	Closed	1991	60.00	361-375
1974 Lady w/ Young Harlequin L4883G	Closed	1975	100.00	1750-2350
1974 Seraph's Head No.1 L4884	Closed	1985	10.00	150-160
1974 Seraph's Head No.2 L4885	Closed	1985	10.00	150-175
1974 Seraph's Head No.3 L4886	Closed	1985	10.00	150
1974 The Kiss L4888G	Closed	1983	150.00	700
1974 Spanish Policeman L4889G	Open		55.00	310
1974 Watching the Pigs L4892G	Closed	1978	160.00	1250
1976 "My Dog" L4893G	Open		85.00	240
1974 Tennis Player Boy L4894	Closed	1980	75.00	500
1974 Ducks L4895G	Open		45.00	95
1974 Ducks L4895M	Closed	1992	45.00	95
1974 Boy with Snails L4896G	Closed	1979	50.00	400
1974 Mechanic L4897G	Closed	1985	45.00	325-350
1974 Boy From Madrid L4898G	Closed	1998	55.00	150-200
1974 Boy From Madrid L4898M	Closed	1992	55.00	150
1974 Boy with Smoking Jacket L4900	Closed	1983	45.00	200
1974 Vagabond Dog L4901G	Closed	1979	25.00	300
1974 Moping Dog L4902G	Closed	1979	35.00	375
1974 Santa Claus L4904G	Closed	1978	100.00	1150
1974 Admiration/Florinda L4907G	Closed	1985	165.00	650
1974 Barrister L4908G	Closed	1985	100.00	400-625
1974 Girl With Dove L4909G	Closed	1982	70.00	425-450
1974 Girl With Lantern L4910G	Closed	1990	85.00	320-375
1974 Shepherd L4911G	Closed	1979	175.00	750
1974 Young Lady in Trouble L4912G	Closed	1985	110.00	450-520
1974 Lesson in the Country L4913G	Closed	1978	240.00	1250
1975 Lady with Shawl L4914G	Closed	1998	220.00	484-800
1975 Girl with Pigeons L4915	Closed	1990	110.00	370-400
1976 Chinese Noblewoman L4916G	Closed	1978	300.00	2000-2145
1974 Dog and Butterfly L4917G	Closed	1981	50.00	800-850
1974 A Girl at the Pond L4918G	Closed	1985	85.00	425
1976 Gypsy Woman L4919G	Closed	1981	165.00	1400-1820

YEAR ISSUE	EDITION LIMIT	YEAR RETD.	ISSUE PRICE	*QUOTE U.S.$
1974 Country Lass with Dog L4920G	Closed	1995	185.00	520-650
1974 Country Lass with Dog L4920M	Closed	1992	185.00	495
1974 Chinese Nobleman L4921G	Closed	1978	325.00	2000-2405
1974 Windblown Girl L4922G	Open		150.00	375
1974 Lanquid Clown L4924G	Closed	1983	200.00	1500
1974 Milk For the Lamb L4926G	Closed	1980	185.00	1300
1974 Medieval Lady L4928G	Closed	1980	275.00	410
1974 Sisters L4930	Closed	1981	250.00	625-650
1974 Children with Fruits L4931G	Closed	1981	210.00	500
1974 Dainty Lady L4934G	Closed	1985	60.00	500
1974 "Closing Scene" L4935G	Closed	1997	180.00	520-546
1983 "Closing Scene"/white L4935.3M	Closed	1987	213.00	275
1974 Spring Breeze L4936G	Open		145.00	410
1976 Golden Wedding L4937M	Closed	1981	285.00	600
1976 Baby's Outing L4938G	12/00		250.00	775
1976 Milk Maid L4939G	Closed	1981	70.00	371-400
1977 Missy L4951M	Closed	1985	300.00	850
1977 Meditation L4952M	Closed	1979	200.00	1600
1977 Tavern Drinkers L4956G	Closed	1985	1125.00	3500
1977 Attentive Dogs L4957G	Closed	1981	350.00	1750
1977 Cherub, Puzzled L4959G	Open		40.00	135
1977 Cherub, Smiling L4960G	Open		40.00	135
1977 Cherub, Dreaming L4961G	Open		40.00	135
1977 Cherub, Wondering L4962G	Open		40.00	135
1977 Cherub, Wondering L4962M	Closed	1992	40.00	114-195
1977 Infantile Candour L4963G	Closed	1979	285.00	1250
1977 Little Red Riding Hood L4965G	Closed	1983	210.00	575
1977 Tennis Player Puppet L4966G	Closed	1985	60.00	525
1977 Soccer Puppet L4967G	Closed	1985	65.00	425
1977 Oympic Puppet L4968	Closed	1983	65.00	800
1977 Sheriff Puppet L4969G	Closed	1985	85.00	600-780
1977 Skier Puppet L4970G	Closed	1983	85.00	500-900
1977 Hunter Puppet L4971G	Closed	1985	95.00	968
1977 Girl with Calla Lillies sitting L4972G	Closed	1998	65.00	190
1977 Choir Lesson L4973G	Closed	1981	350.00	1500
1977 Dutch Children L4974G	Closed	1981	375.00	1150
1977 Augustina of Aragon L4976G	Closed	1979	475.00	1500-1800
1977 Harlequin Serenade L4977	Closed	1979	185.00	1250
1977 Milkmaid with Wheelbarrow L4979G	Closed	1981	220.00	950
1977 Ironing Time L4981G	Closed	1985	80.00	375-400
1978 Naughty Dog L4982G	Closed	1995	130.00	275-350
1978 Gossip L4984G	Closed	1985	260.00	1000
1978 Mimi L4985G	Closed	1980	110.00	650
1978 Attentive Lady L4986G	Closed	1981	635.00	2200
1978 Oriental Spring L4988G	Closed	1997	125.00	325-375
1978 Sayonara L4989G	Closed	1997	125.00	300-350
1978 Chrysanthemum L4990G	Closed	1998	125.00	310-375
1978 Butterfly L4991G	Closed	1998	125.00	295-375
1978 Dancers Resting L4992G	Closed	1983	350.00	750-850
1978 Gypsy Venders L4993G	Closed	1985	165.00	475
1978 Ready to Go L4996G	Closed	1981	425.00	1500-1700
1978 Don Quixote & Sancho L4998G	Closed	1983	875.00	2900
1978 Reading L5000G	Open		150.00	275
1978 Elk Family L5001G	Closed	1981	550.00	850
1978 Sunny Day L5003G	Closed	1993	193.00	425
1978 Eloise L5005G	Closed	1978	175.00	555
1978 Naughty L5006G	Closed	1998	55.00	195-225
1978 Bashful L5007G	Closed	1998	55.00	225-275
1978 Dreamer-Girl w/Straw Hat L5008G	Closed	1999	55.00	155-195
1978 Curious-Girl w/Straw Hat L5009G	Open		55.00	155
1978 Prissy L5010G	Closed	1998	55.00	195-250
1978 Trying on a Straw Hat L5011G	Closed	1998	55.00	195-225
1978 Daughters L5013G	Closed	1991	425.00	900
1978 Genteel L5014G	Closed	1981	725.00	2300
1978 Painful Monkey L5018	Closed	1981	135.00	750-850
1978 Painful Giraffe L5019	Closed	1981	115.00	850
1978 Painful Elephant L5020	Closed	1981	85.00	850
1978 Painful Bear L5021	Closed	1981	75.00	800
1978 Painful Lion L5022G	Closed	1981	95.00	800
1978 Painful Kangaroo L5023G	Closed	1981	150.00	900-950
1978 Woman With Scarf L5024G	Closed	1985	141.00	650-726
1980 A Clean Sweep L5025G	Closed	1985	100.00	450
1980 Planning the Day L5026G	Closed	1985	90.00	275
1979 Flower Curtsy L5027G	Open		230.00	470
1980 Flowers in Pot L5028G	Closed	1985	325.00	575
1980 The Flower Peddler L5029G	Closed	1985	675.00	1350
1980 Wildflower L5030G	Closed	1994	360.00	591-850
1979 Little Friskies L5032G	Closed	1998	108.00	220-300
1980 Avoiding the Goose L5033G	Closed	1993	160.00	350-600
1980 Goose Trying To Eat L5034G	Closed	1997	135.00	315-350
1980 Act II w/base L5035G	Open		700.00	1425
1979 Jockey with Lass L5036G	12/00		950.00	2590
1980 Sleighride w/base L5037G	Closed	1997	585.00	1050-1300
1979 Girl Bowing L5038G	Closed	1981	185.00	750
1980 Candid L5039G	Closed	1981	145.00	400
1979 Girl Walking L5040G	Closed	1981	150.00	400-1105
1980 Tulips in my Basket L5041G	Closed	1981	160.00	850
1980 Friends L5042G	Closed	1983	385.00	1000
1980 Hind and Baby Deer L5043G	Closed	1981	650.00	2600
1980 Girl with Toy Wagon L5044G	Closed	1998	115.00	249-260
1980 Belinda with Doll L5045G	Closed	1995	115.00	215
1980 Organ Grinder L5046G	Closed	1981	328.00	1650
1980 Teacher Woman L5048G	Closed	1981	115.00	600-625
1980 Dancer L5050G	Open		85.00	205
1980 Samson and Delilah L5051G	Closed	1981	350.00	1600
1980 At the Circus L5052G	Closed	1985	525.00	1250
1980 Festival Time L5053G	Closed	1985	250.00	375
1980 Little Senorita L5054G	Closed	1985	235.00	180-400
1980 Apprentice Seaman L5055G	Closed	1985	140.00	450
1980 Boy Clown with Clock L5056G	Closed	1985	290.00	750-850
1980 Clown with Violin L5057G	Closed	1985	270.00	850
1980 Clown with Concertina L5058G	Closed	1985	290.00	600

YEAR ISSUE	EDITION LIMIT	YEAR RETD.	ISSUE PRICE	*QUOTE U.S.$
1980 Clown with Saxaphone L5059G	Closed	1985	320.00	700
1980 Clown with Trumpet L5060G	Closed	1985	290.00	550
1980 March Wind L5061G	Closed	1983	370.00	600
1980 Kristina L5062G	Closed	1985	225.00	400
1980 Margaretta/Dutch Girl With Braids L5063G	Closed	1985	265.00	450
1980 Gretel/Dutch Girl, Hands Akimbo L5064G	Closed	1990	255.00	400-425
1980 Ingrid L5065G	Closed	1990	370.00	650-726
1980 Ilsa L5066G	Closed	1990	275.00	400
1981 Halloween L5067G	Closed	1983	450.00	1400-1500
1980 Fairy Queen L5068G	Closed	1983	625.00	1600
1980 Napping L5070G	Closed	1983	240.00	850
1980 Nostalgia L5071G	Closed	1993	185.00	450-520
1980 Courtship L5072	Closed	1990	327.00	660-750
1980 Country Flowers L5073	Closed	1985	315.00	750
1980 My Hungry Brood L5074G	Closed	1998	295.00	350-400
1980 Little Harlequin "A" L5075G	Closed	1985	217.50	415
1980 Little Harlequin "B" L5076G	Closed	1985	185.00	415
1980 Little Harlequin "C" L5077G	Closed	1985	185.00	500
1980 Teasing the Dog L5078G	Closed	1985	300.00	600
1980 Woman Painting Vase L5079G	Closed	1985	300.00	750
1980 Boy Pottery Seller L5080G	Closed	1985	320.00	600-780
1980 Girl Pottery Seller L5081G	Closed	1985	300.00	600-650
1980 Little Flower Seller L5082G	Closed	1985	750.00	2360-2850
1980 Dutch Mother L5083G	Closed	1983	485.00	1100
1980 A Good Book L5084G	Closed	1985	175.00	525
1980 Mother Amabilis L5086G	Closed	1983	275.00	550
1980 Roses for My Mom L5088G	Closed	1988	645.00	1150-1350
1980 Scare-Dy Cat/Playful Cat L5091G	Closed	1998	65.00	95-145
1980 After the Dance L5092G	Closed	1983	165.00	350-475
1980 A Dancing Partner L5093G	Closed	1983	165.00	400-500
1980 Ballet First Step L5094G	Closed	1983	165.00	363-400
1980 Ballet Bowing L5095G	Closed	1983	165.00	300-400
1989 Her Ladyship, L5097G	Closed	1991	5900.00	6700
1980 Successful Hunt L5098	Closed	1993	5200.00	5200
1982 Playful Tot L5099G	Closed	1985	58.00	275-295
1982 Cry Baby L5100G	Closed	1985	58.00	300
1982 Learning to Crawl L5101G	Closed	1985	58.00	300
1982 Teething L5102G	Closed	1985	58.00	300
1982 Time for a Nap L5103G	Closed	1985	58.00	275
1982 Little Ballet Girl L5105G	Closed	1985	85.00	350-375
1982 Natalia L5106G	Closed	1985	85.00	350
1982 Little Ballet Girl L5108G	Closed	1985	85.00	375-400
1982 Little Ballet Girl L5109G	Closed	1985	85.00	400
1982 Dog Sniffing L5110G	Closed	1985	50.00	625
1982 Timid Dog L5111G	Closed	1985	44.00	600
1982 Play with Me L5112G	12/00		40.00	80
1982 Feed Me L5113G	Open		40.00	80
1982 Pet Me L5114G	Closed	1999	40.00	80-110
1982 Little Boy Bullfighter L5115G	Closed	1985	123.00	400
1982 A Victory L5116G	Closed	1985	123.00	500
1982 Proud Matador L5117G	Closed	1985	123.00	500
1982 Girl in Green Dress L5118G	Closed	1985	170.00	650
1982 Girl in Bluish Dress L5119G	Closed	1985	170.00	675
1982 Girl in Pink Dress L5120G	Closed	1985	170.00	650
1982 August Moon L5122G	Closed	1993	185.00	350
1982 My Precious Bundle L5123G	Closed	1998	150.00	245-275
1982 Dutch Couple with Tulips L5124G	Closed	1985	310.00	1150-1200
1982 Amparo L5125G	Closed	1990	130.00	350
1982 Sewing A Trousseau L5126G	Closed	1990	185.00	425-600
1982 Marcelina L5127G	Closed	1985	255.00	275
1982 Lost Love L5128G	Closed	1988	400.00	700
1982 Jester w/base L5129G	12/00		220.00	455
1982 Pensive Clown w/base L5130G	12/00		250.00	475
1982 Cervantes L5132G	Closed	1988	925.00	1200-1600
1982 Trophy with Base L5133G	Closed	1983	250.00	650
1982 Girl Soccer Player L5134G	Closed	1983	140.00	500-600
1982 Billy Football Player L5135G	Closed	1983	140.00	600
1982 Billy Skier L5136G	Closed	1983	140.00	800-850
1982 Billy Baseball Player L5137G	Closed	1983	140.00	700
1982 Billy Golfer L5138G	Closed	1983	140.00	750-1000
1982 A New Doll House L5139G	Closed	1983	185.00	850
1982 Feed Her Son L5140G	Closed	1991	170.00	300
1982 Balloons for Sale L5141G	Closed	1997	145.00	295
1982 Comforting Daughter L5142G	Closed	1991	195.00	350-560
1982 Scooting L5143G	Closed	1988	575.00	1500-1950
1982 Amy L5145G	Closed	1985	110.00	1400-1500
1982 "E" is for Ellen L5146G	Closed	1985	110.00	1250
1982 Ivez L5147G	Closed	1985	100.00	600
1982 Olivia L5148G	Closed	1985	100.00	400
1982 Ursula L5149G	Closed	1985	100.00	400-425
1982 Girl's Head L5150G	Closed	1983	435.00	1300
1982 Girl's Head L5151G	Closed	1983	380.00	1400
1982 Girl's Head L5152G	Closed	1983	535.00	2000
1982 Girl's Head L5153G	Closed	1983	475.00	1350
1982 First Prize L5154G	Closed	1985	90.00	300
1982 Monks at Prayer L5155M	Open		130.00	275
1982 Susan and the Doves L5156G	Closed	1991	203.00	350-595
1982 Bongo Beat L5157G	Closed	1998	135.00	230
1982 A Step In Time L5158G	Closed	1998	90.00	200-250
1982 Harmony L5159G	Closed	1998	270.00	495-550
1982 Rhumba L5160G	Closed	1998	113.00	185-225
1982 Cycling To A Picnic L5161G	Closed	1985	2000.00	2800
1982 Mouse Girl/Mindy L5162G	Closed	1985	125.00	272-500
1982 Bunny Girl/Bunny L5163G	Closed	1985	125.00	442-450
1982 Cat Girl/Kitty L5164G	Closed	1985	125.00	375-510
1982 Sancho with Bottle L5165	Closed	1990	100.00	475
1982 Sea Fever L5166M	Closed	1993	130.00	260-306
1982 Sea Fever L5166G	Closed	1993	130.00	350
1982 Jesus L5167G	Open		130.00	265
1982 King Solomon L5168G	Closed	1985	205.00	950

*Quotes have been rounded up to nearest dollar

YEAR ISSUE	EDITION LIMIT	YEAR RETD.	ISSUE PRICE	*QUOTE U.S.$
1982 Abraham L5169G	Closed	1985	155.00	750
1982 Moses L5170G	12/00		175.00	410
1982 Madonna with Flowers L5171G	Open		173.00	310
1982 Fish A'Plenty L5172G	Closed	1994	190.00	425-475
1982 Pondering L5173G	Closed	1993	300.00	495-700
1982 Roaring 20's L5174G	Closed	1993	173.00	425-650
1982 Flapper L5175G	Closed	1995	185.00	450-475
1982 Rhapsody in Blue L5176G	Closed	1985	325.00	1450-1850
1982 Dante L5177G	Closed	1983	263.00	750
1982 Stubborn Mule L5178G	Closed	1993	250.00	495-500
1983 Three Pink Roses w/base L5179M	Closed	1990	70.00	300
1983 Dahlia L5180M	Closed	1990	65.00	150-250
1983 Japanese Camelia w/base L5181M	Closed	1990	60.00	100
1983 White Peony L5182M	Closed	1990	85.00	150
1983 Two Yellow Roses L5183M	Closed	1990	57.50	100
1983 White Carnation L5184M	Closed	1990	65.00	100
1983 Lactiflora Peony L5185M	Closed	1990	65.00	100
1983 Begonia L5186M	Closed	1990	67.50	100
1983 Rhododendrom L5187M	Closed	1990	67.50	190
1983 Miniature Begonia L5188M	Closed	1990	80.00	130
1983 Chrysanthemum L5189M	Closed	1990	100.00	150
1983 California Poppy L5190M	Closed	1990	97.50	190
1985 Predicting the Future L5191G	Closed	1985	135.00	450
1984 Lolita L5192G	Open		80.00	165
1984 Juanita L5193G	Open		80.00	165
1984 Roving Photographer L5194G	Closed	1985	145.00	1450-1500
1983 Say "Cheese!" L5195G	Closed	1990	170.00	520-600
1983 "Maestro, Music Please!" L5196G	Closed	1988	135.00	395-425
1983 Female Physician L5197	Open		120.00	275
1984 Boy Graduate L5198G	Open		160.00	290
1984 Girl Graduate L5199G	Open		160.00	285
1984 Male Soccer Player L5200G	Closed	1988	155.00	500
1984 Special Male Soccer Player L5200.3G	Closed	1988	150.00	525
1983 Josefa Feeding Duck L5201G	Closed	1991	125.00	295-350
1983 Aracely with Ducks L5202G	Closed	1991	125.00	295-350
1984 Little Jester L5203G	Closed	1993	75.00	350-455
1984 Little Jester L5203M	Closed	1992	75.00	300
1983 Sharpening the Cutlery L5204	Closed	1988	210.00	975
1983 Lamplighter L5205G	Open		170.00	425
1983 Yachtsman L5206G	Closed	1994	110.00	210-250
1983 A Tall Yarn L5207G	Open		260.00	570
1983 Professor L5208G	Closed	1990	205.00	600-650
1983 School Marm L5209G	Closed	1990	205.00	800-850
1984 Jolie L5210G	Open		105.00	255
1984 Angela L5211G	Open		105.00	255
1984 Evita L5212G	Closed	1998	105.00	245-250
1984 Lawyer L5213G	Closed	1998	250.00	620-650
1984 Architect L5214G	Closed	1990	140.00	500
1984 Fishing with Gramps w/base L5215G	Open		410.00	895
1984 On the Lake L5216G	Closed	1988	660.00	1100
1984 Spring L5217G	Open		90.00	215
1984 Spring L5217M	Open		90.00	215
1984 Autumn L5218G	Closed	1999	90.00	200-225
1984 Autumn L5218M	Closed	1999	90.00	200
1984 Summer L5219G	Closed	1999	90.00	185
1984 Summer L5219M	Closed	1999	90.00	185-225
1984 Winter L5220G	Open		90.00	195
1984 Winter L5220M	Open		90.00	195
1984 Sweet Scent L5221G	Open		80.00	180
1984 Sweet Scent L5221M	Open		80.00	180
1984 Pretty Pickings L5222G	Open		80.00	180
1984 Pretty Pickings L5222M	Open		80.00	180
1984 Spring is Here L5223G	Open		80.00	180
1984 Spring is Here L5223M	Open		80.00	180
1984 The Quest L5224G	Closed	1998	125.00	350-375
1984 Male Candleholder L5226	Closed	1985	660.00	1200
1984 Playful Piglets L5228G	Closed	1998	80.00	165-225
1984 Storytime L5229G	Closed	1990	245.00	850-1100
1984 Graceful Swan L5230G	12/00		35.00	115
1984 Swan with Wings Spread L5231G	Open		50.00	150
1984 Playful Kittens L5232G	Open		130.00	300
1984 Charlie the Tramp L5233G	Closed	1991	150.00	850-950
1984 Artistic Endeavor L5234G	Closed	1988	225.00	650
1984 Ballet Trio L5235G	Closed	1998	785.00	1675-1800
1984 Cat and Mouse L5236G	Open		55.00	98
1984 Cat and Mouse L5236M	Closed	1992	55.00	98-130
1984 School Chums L5237G	Closed	1997	225.00	485-550
1984 Eskimo Boy with Pet L5238G	Open		55.00	115
1984 Eskimo Boy with Pet L5238M	Closed	1992	55.00	95
1984 Wine Taster L5239G	Open		190.00	465
1984 Lady from Majorca L5240G	Closed	1990	120.00	475-488
1984 Best Wishes L5244G	Closed	1986	185.00	225-330
1984 A Thought for Today L5245	Closed	1986	180.00	250
1984 St. Cristobal L5246	Closed	1988	265.00	650
1984 Penguin L5247G	Closed	1988	70.00	225-250
1984 Penguin L5248G	Closed	1988	70.00	200-250
1984 Penguin L5249G	Closed	1988	70.00	200-275
1984 Exam Day L5250G	Closed	1994	115.00	165-295
1984 Torch Bearer L5251G	Closed	1988	100.00	400-500
1984 Dancing the Polka L5252G	Closed	1994	205.00	525
1984 Cadet L5253G	Closed	1984	150.00	650-700
1984 Making Paella L5254G	Closed	1993	215.00	500-575
1984 Spanish Soldier L5255G	Closed	1988	185.00	475-575
1984 Folk Dancing L5256G	Closed	1990	205.00	525
1984 Vase L5257.30	Closed	1988	55.00	200
1984 Vase L5258.30	Closed	1988	55.00	175
1984 Vase L5261.30	Closed	1988	70.00	150
1984 Vase L5262.30	Closed	1988	70.00	150
1984 Centerpiece-Decorated L5265M	Closed	1990	50.00	175
1985 Bust of Lady from Elche L5269M	Closed	1988	432.00	750
1985 Racing Motor Cyclist L5270G	Closed	1988	360.00	850
1985 Gazelle L5271G	Closed	1988	205.00	550
1985 Biking in the Country L5272G	Closed	1990	295.00	795-850
1985 Civil Guard at Attention L5273G	Closed	1988	170.00	520
1985 Wedding Day L5274G	Closed	1999	240.00	435
1985 Weary Ballerina L5275G	Closed	1995	175.00	310-375
1985 Weary Ballerina L5275M	Closed	1992	175.00	310
1985 Sailor Serenades His Girl L5276G	Closed	1988	315.00	950
1985 Pierrot with Puppy L5277G	Open		95.00	160
1985 Pierrot with Puppy and Ball L5278G	Open		95.00	160
1985 Pierrot with Concertina L5279G	Open		95.00	160
1985 Hiker L5280G	Closed	1988	195.00	385-425
1985 Nativity Scene "Haute Relief" L5281M	Closed	1988	210.00	450
1985 Over the Threshold L5282G	Open		150.00	290
1985 Socialite of the Twenties L5283G	Open		175.00	345
1985 Glorious Spring L5284G	Open		355.00	720
1985 Summer on the Farm L5285G	Open		235.00	455
1985 Fall Clean-up L5286G	Open		295.00	565
1985 Winter Frost L5287G	Open		270.00	520
1985 Mallard Duck L5288G	Closed	1994	310.00	525-600
1985 Little Leaguer Exercising L5289	Closed	1990	150.00	450-585
1985 Little Leaguer, Catcher L5290	Closed	1990	150.00	475-550
1985 Little Leaguer on Bench L5291	Closed	1990	150.00	450-480
1985 Love in Bloom L5292G	Closed	1998	225.00	435
1985 Mother and Child and Lamb L5299G	Closed	1988	180.00	750
1985 Medieval Courtship L5300G	Closed	1990	735.00	800
1985 Waiting to Tee Off L5301G	Closed	1999	145.00	295-325
1985 Antelope Drinking L5302	Closed	1988	215.00	550
1985 Playing with Ducks at the Pond L5303G	Closed	1990	425.00	875
1985 Children at Play L5304	Closed	1990	220.00	475-550
1985 A Visit with Granny L5305G	Closed	1993	275.00	550-600
1985 Young Street Musicians L5306G	Closed	1988	300.00	975-1650
1985 Mini Kitten L5307G	Closed	1993	35.00	100-175
1985 Mini Cat L5308G	Closed	1993	35.00	100-150
1985 Mini Cocker Spaniel Pup L5309G	Closed	1993	35.00	125-150
1985 Mini Cocker Spaniel L5310G	Closed	1993	35.00	150
1985 Mini Puppies L5311G	Closed	1990	65.00	225
1985 Mini Bison Resting L5312G	Closed	1990	50.00	150
1985 Mini Bison Attacking L5313G	Closed	1990	57.50	225
1985 Mini Deer L5314G	Closed	1990	40.00	175
1985 Mini Dromedary L5315G	Closed	1990	45.00	150-175
1985 Mini Giraffe L5316G	Closed	1990	50.00	225-250
1985 Mini Lamb L5317G	Closed	1990	30.00	200
1985 Mini Seal Family L5318G	Closed	1990	77.50	250-280
1985 Wistful Centaur Girl L5319G	Closed	1990	157.00	375-450
1985 Demure Centaur Girl L5320	Closed	1990	157.00	375-425
1985 Parisian Lady L5321G	Closed	1995	193.00	325-350
1985 Viennese Lady L5322G	Closed	1994	160.00	300-370
1985 Milanese Lady L5323G	Closed	1994	180.00	375-400
1985 English Lady L5324G	Closed	1994	225.00	410-495
1985 Ice Cream Vendor L5325G	Closed	1995	380.00	750
1985 The Tailor L5326G	Closed	1988	335.00	800-1000
1985 Nippon Lady L5327G	12/00		325.00	595
1985 Lady Equestrian L5328G	Closed	1988	160.00	475
1985 Gentleman Equestrian L5329G	Closed	1988	160.00	425-525
1985 Concert Violinist L5330G	Closed	1988	220.00	400-450
1985 Gymnast with Ring L5331	Closed	1988	95.00	395
1985 Gymnast Balancing Ball L5332	Closed	1988	95.00	276-375
1985 Gymnast Exercising with Ball L5333G	Closed	1988	95.00	285-350
1985 Aerobics Push-Up L5334G	Closed	1988	110.00	295-425
1985 Aerobics Floor Exercies L5335G	Closed	1988	110.00	250-300
1985 Aerobics Scissor L5336G	Closed	1988	110.00	110-319
1985 "La Giaconda" L5337G	Closed	1988	110.00	400-600
1986 A Stitch in Time L5344G	Closed	1998	425.00	810-850
1986 A New Hat L5345G	Closed	1990	200.00	375
1986 Nature Girl L5346G	Closed	1988	450.00	775
1986 Bedtime L5347G	Closed	1998	300.00	445-600
1986 On The Scent L5348G	Closed	1990	47.50	300
1986 Relaxing L5349G	Closed	1990	47.50	200
1986 On Guard L5350G	Closed	1990	50.00	300
1986 Woe is Me L5351G	Closed	1990	45.00	200
1986 Hindu Children L5352G	Open		250.00	445
1986 Eskimo Riders L5353G	Open		150.00	270
1986 Eskimo Riders L5353M	Open		150.00	160
1986 A Ride in the Country L5354G	Closed	1993	225.00	450-488
1986 Consideration L5355M	Closed	1988	100.00	250
1986 Wolf Hound L5356G	Closed	1990	45.00	250
1986 Oration L5357G	Open		170.00	300
1986 Little Sculptor L5358G	Closed	1990	160.00	400
1986 El Greco L5359G	Closed	1990	300.00	650-750
1986 Sewing Circle L5360G	Closed	1990	600.00	1200-1400
1986 Try This One L5361G	Closed	1998	225.00	385
1986 Still Life L5363G	Closed	1998	180.00	425-553
1986 Litter of Fun L5364G	12/00		275.00	465
1986 Sunday in the Park L5365G	Closed	1997	375.00	625-675
1986 Can Can L5370G	Closed	1990	700.00	1400
1986 Family Roots L5371G	Open		575.00	935
1986 Lolita L5372G	Closed	1993	120.00	250-275
1986 Carmencita L5373G	Closed	1993	120.00	200-275
1986 Pepita L5374G	Closed	1993	120.00	250-275
1986 Teresita L5375G	Closed	1993	120.00	250-275
1986 This One's Mine L5376G	Closed	1995	300.00	300-600
1986 A Touch of Class L5377G	12/00		475.00	795
1986 Time for Reflection L5378G	Open		425.00	745
1986 Children's Games L5379G	Closed	1991	325.00	585-750
1986 Sweet Harvest L5380G	Closed	1990	450.00	850-875
1986 Serenade L5381	Closed	1990	450.00	650
1986 Lovers Serenade L5382G	Closed	1990	350.00	850
1986 Petite Maiden L5383	Closed	1990	110.00	265-400
1986 Petite Pair L5384	Closed	1990	225.00	425
1986 Scarecrow & the Lady L5385G	Closed	1997	350.00	680-725
1986 St. Vincent L5387	Closed	1990	190.00	400
1986 Sidewalk Serenade L5388G	Closed	1988	750.00	1300
1986 Deep in Thought L5389G	Closed	1990	170.00	350-450
1986 Spanish Dancer L5390G	Closed	1990	170.00	400-450
1986 A Time to Rest L5391G	Closed	1990	170.00	375-442
1986 Balancing Act L5392G	Closed	1990	35.00	119-200
1986 Curiosity L5393G	Closed	1990	25.00	150
1986 Poor Puppy L5394G	Closed	1990	25.00	250
1986 Valencian Boy L5395G	Closed	1991	200.00	400
1986 The Puppet Painter L5396G	Open		500.00	850
1986 The Poet L5397G	Closed	1988	425.00	900
1986 At the Ball L5398G	Closed	1991	375.00	750-910
1987 Time To Rest L5399G	Closed	1993	175.00	295
1987 Time To Rest L5399M	Closed	1991	175.00	350
1987 The Wanderer L5400G	Closed	1998	150.00	245
1987 My Best Friend L5401G	Closed	1998	150.00	275-312
1987 Desert Tour L5402G	Closed	1990	950.00	1150-1425
1987 The Drummer Boy L5403G	Closed	1990	225.00	400-450
1987 Cadet Captain L5404G	Closed	1990	175.00	375
1987 The Flag Bearer L5405G	Closed	1990	200.00	450
1987 The Bugler L5406G	Closed	1990	175.00	375
1987 At Attention L5407G	Closed	1990	175.00	325
1987 Courting Time L5409	Closed	1990	425.00	500-550
1987 Sunday Stroll L5408G	Closed	1990	250.00	600
1987 Pilar L5410G	Closed	1990	200.00	400
1987 Teresa L5411G	Closed	1990	225.00	375-430
1987 Isabel L5412G	Closed	1990	225.00	350
1987 Mexican Dancers L5415G	Open		800.00	1195
1987 In the Garden L5416G	Closed	1997	200.00	350
1987 Artist's Model L5417	Closed	1990	425.00	475
1987 Short Eared Owl L5418G	Closed	1990	200.00	280-375
1987 Great Gray Owl L5419G	Closed	1990	190.00	200-230
1987 Horned Owl L5420G	Closed	1990	150.00	230-340
1987 Barn Owl L5421G	Closed	1990	120.00	185
1987 Hawk Owl L5422G	Closed	1990	120.00	250
1987 Intermezzo L5424	Closed	1990	325.00	550
1987 Studying in the Park L5425G	Closed	1991	675.00	950
1987 Studying in the Park L5425M	Closed	1989	675.00	600
1987 One, Two, Three L5426G	Closed	1995	240.00	400
1987 Saint Nicholas L5427G	Closed	1991	425.00	700-795
1987 Feeding the Pigeons L5428	Closed	1990	490.00	568-700
1987 Happy Birthday L5429G	Open		100.00	155
1987 Music Time L5430G	Closed	1990	500.00	700
1987 Midwife L5431G	Closed	1990	175.00	650
1987 Midwife L5431M	Closed	1990	175.00	525
1987 Monkey L5432G	Closed	1990	60.00	200
1987 Kangaroo L5433G	Closed	1990	65.00	175-300
1987 Miniature Polar Bear L5434G	12/00		65.00	115
1987 Cougar L5435G	Closed	1990	65.00	275
1987 Lion L5436G	Closed	1990	50.00	300
1987 Rhino L5437G	Closed	1990	50.00	175
1987 Elephant L5438G	Closed	1990	50.00	250
1987 The Bride L5439G	Closed	1995	250.00	525-553
1987 Poetry of Love L5442G	Closed	1998	500.00	875
1987 Sleepy Trio L5443G	Closed	1997	190.00	350
1987 Will You Marry Me? L5447G	Closed	1994	750.00	1250
1987 Naptime L5448G	Open		135.00	260
1987 Naptime L5448M	Open		135.00	260
1987 Goodnight L5449	Open		225.00	375
1987 I Hope She Does L5450G	Closed	1998	190.00	279-350
1988 Study Buddies L5451G	Open		225.00	295
1988 Masquerade Ball L5452G	Closed	1993	220.00	545
1988 Masquerade Ball L5452M	Closed	1992	220.00	350
1988 For You L5453G	Closed	1998	450.00	640-700
1988 For Me? L5454G	Closed	1998	290.00	395
1988 Bashful Bather L5455G	Open		150.00	190
1988 Bashful Bather L5455M	Closed	1992	150.00	180
1988 New Playmates L5456G	Open		160.00	255
1988 New Playmates L5456M	Closed	1992	160.00	190
1988 Bedtime Story L5457G	Open		275.00	355
1988 Bedtime Story L5457M	Closed	1992	275.00	330
1988 A Barrow of Fun L5460G	Open		370.00	650
1988 A Barrow of Fun L5460M	Closed	1992	370.00	450
1988 Koala Love L5461G	Closed	1993	115.00	225-325
1988 Practice Makes Perfect L5462G	Closed	1998	375.00	500-625
1988 Look At Me! L5465G	Open		375.00	545
1988 Look At Me! L5465M	Closed	1992	375.00	455
1988 "Chit-Chat" L5466G	Open		150.00	220
1988 "Chit-Chat" L5466M	Closed	1992	150.00	220
1988 May Flowers L5467G	Open		160.00	245
1988 May Flowers L5467M	Closed	1992	160.00	200
1988 "Who's The Fairest?" L5468G	12/00		150.00	205
1988 "Who's The Fairest?" L5468M	Closed	1992	150.00	200
1988 Lambkins L5469G	Closed	1993	150.00	250
1988 Lambkins L5469M	Closed	1989	150.00	200
1988 Tea Time L5470G	Closed	1998	280.00	410-475
1988 Sad Sax L5471G	Open		175.00	205
1988 Circus Sam L5472G	Open		175.00	205
1988 How You've Grown! L5474G	Closed	1998	180.00	270
1988 How You've Grown! L5474M	Closed	1992	180.00	250
1988 A Lesson Shared L5475G	Closed	1998	150.00	195-240
1988 A Lesson Shared L5475M	Closed	1992	150.00	195
1988 St. Joseph L5476G	Open		210.00	295
1988 Mary L5477G	Open		130.00	165
1988 Baby Jesus L5478G	Open		55.00	75
1988 King Melchior L5479G	Open		210.00	265
1988 King Gaspar L5480G	Open		210.00	265
1988 King Balthasar L5481G	Open		210.00	265
1988 Ox L5482G	Open		125.00	175
1988 Donkey L5483G	Open		125.00	175
1988 Lost Lamb L5484G	Open		100.00	140
1988 Shepherd Boy L5485G	Open		140.00	215
1988 Debutantes L5486G	Closed	1998	490.00	650-745
1988 Debutantes L5486M	Closed	1992	490.00	655-695
1988 Ingenue L5487G	Open		110.00	145

*Quotes have been rounded up to nearest dollar

FIGURINES

YEAR ISSUE	EDITION LIMIT	YEAR RETD.	ISSUE PRICE	*QUOTE U.S.$
1988 Ingenue L5487M	Closed	1992	110.00	150-185
1988 Sandcastles L5488G	Closed	1993	160.00	300-325
1988 Sandcastles L5488M	Closed	1992	160.00	200
1988 Justice L5489G	Closed	1993	675.00	900-950
1988 Flor Maria L5490G	Open		500.00	635
1988 Heavenly Strings L5491G	Closed	1993	140.00	250
1988 Heavenly Cellist L5492G	Closed	1993	240.00	350
1988 Angel with Lute L5493G	Closed	1993	140.00	150-175
1988 Angel with Clarinet L5494G	Closed	1993	140.00	175-250
1988 Angelic Choir L5495G	Closed	1993	300.00	550-575
1988 Recital L5496G	Open		190.00	285
1988 Dress Rehearsal L5497G	Open		290.00	420
1988 Opening Night L5498G	Open		190.00	285
1988 Pretty Ballerina L5499G	Closed	1998	190.00	285
1988 Prayerful Moment (blue) L5500G	Open		90.00	110
1988 Time to Sew (blue) L5501G	Open		90.00	110
1988 Time to Sew (white) L5501.3	Closed	1991	90.00	250-275
1988 Meditation (blue) L5502G	Open		90.00	110
1988 Hurry Now L5503G	Open		180.00	270
1988 Hurry Now L5503M	Closed	1992	180.00	250
1988 Silver Vase No. 20 L5531.4	Closed	1991	135.00	300
1989 Flowers for Sale L5537G	12/00		1200.00	1550
1989 Puppy Dog Tails L5539G	Open		1200.00	1675
1989 An Evening Out L5540G	Closed	1991	350.00	650
1989 Melancholy w/base L5542G	12/00		375.00	455
1989 "Hello, Flowers" L5543G	Closed	1993	385.00	485-845
1989 Reaching the Goal L5546G	Closed	1998	215.00	234-375
1989 Only the Beginning L5547G	Closed	1997	215.00	275-300
1989 Pretty Posies L5548G	Closed	1994	425.00	530-575
1989 My New Pet L5549G	Closed	1998	150.00	185
1989 Serene Moment (blue) L5550G	Closed	1993	115.00	200-375
1989 Serene Moment (white) L5550.3G	Closed	1991	115.00	250-300
1989 Serene Moment (white) L5550.3M	Closed	1991	115.00	250
1989 Call to Prayer (blue) L5551G	Closed	1993	100.00	200-375
1989 Call to Prayer (white) L5551.3G	Closed	1991	100.00	250-350
1989 Call to Prayer (white) L5551.3M	Closed	1991	100.00	250
1989 Morning Chores (blue) L5552G	Closed	1993	115.00	200-300
1989 Morning Chores (white) L5552G	Closed	1991	115.00	250-300
1989 Wild Goose Chase L5553G	Closed	1998	175.00	196-230
1989 Pretty and Prim L5554G	Closed	1998	215.00	143-320
1989 "Let's Make Up" L5555G	Open		215.00	265
1989 Wide Tulip Vase L5560G	Closed	1990	110.00	300
1989 Green Clover Vase L5561G	Closed	1991	130.00	225
1989 Sad Parting L5583G	Closed	1991	375.00	525
1989 Daddy's Girl/Father's Day L5584G	Closed	1997	315.00	395-450
1989 Fine Melody w/base L5585G	Closed	1993	225.00	325-350
1989 Sad Note w/base L5586G	Closed	1993	185.00	225
1989 Wedding Cake L5587G	Closed	1997	595.00	750-850
1989 Blustery Day L5588G	Closed	1993	185.00	230-325
1989 Pretty Pose L5589G	Closed	1993	185.00	230-260
1989 Spring Breeze L5590G	Closed	1993	185.00	230-275
1989 Garden Treasures L5591G	Closed	1993	185.00	230-260
1989 Male Siamese Dancer L5592G	Closed	1993	345.00	449-480
1989 Siamese Dancer L5593G	Closed	1993	345.00	420
1989 Playful Romp L5594G	Closed	1997	215.00	270
1989 Joy in a Basket L5595G	Closed	1998	215.00	230-300
1989 A Gift of Love L5596G	Closed	1998	400.00	495-600
1989 Summer Soiree L5597G	Closed	1998	150.00	180-195
1989 Bridesmaid L5598G	Open		150.00	180
1989 Coquette L5599G	Open		150.00	180
1989 The Blues w/base L5600G	Closed	1993	265.00	395
1989 "Ole" L5601G	Open		365.00	460
1989 Close To My Heart L5603G	Closed	1998	125.00	165-215
1989 Spring Token L5604G	Open		175.00	140-165
1989 Floral Treasures L5605G	Open		195.00	250
1989 Quiet Evening L5606G	Closed	1993	125.00	200-215
1989 Calling A Friend L5607G	Closed	1998	125.00	165-210
1989 Baby Doll L5608G	Closed	1998	150.00	180-225
1989 Playful Friends L5609G	Closed	1995	135.00	170
1989 Star Struck w/base L5610G	Closed	1998	335.00	420-450
1989 Sad Clown w/base L5611G	Closed	1998	335.00	336-400
1989 Reflecting w/base L5612G	Closed	1994	335.00	336-420
1989 Sealore Pipe L5613G	Closed	1993	125.00	175
1989 Startled L5614G	Closed	1991	265.00	265-425
1989 Bathing Beauty L5615G	Closed	1991	265.00	350-475
1989 Candleholder L5625G	Closed	1990	105.00	125
1989 Candleholder L5626	Closed	1990	90.00	125
1989 Lladró Vase L5631G	Closed	1990	150.00	225-395
1990 Water Dreamer Vase L5633G	Closed	1990	150.00	400
1990 Cat Nap L5640G	Open		125.00	145
1990 The King's Guard w/base L5642G	Closed	1993	950.00	1100
1990 Cathy L5643G	Closed	1998	200.00	235-275
1990 Susan L5644G	Open		190.00	215
1990 Elizabeth L5645G	Closed	1998	190.00	225-250
1990 Cindy L5646G	Closed	1998	190.00	215-225
1990 Sarah L5647G	Closed	1998	200.00	196-250
1990 Courtney L5648G	Open		200.00	230
1990 Nothing To Do L5649G	Closed	1998	190.00	220
1990 Anticipation L5650G	Closed	1993	300.00	340-575
1990 Musical Muse L5651G	Closed	1997	375.00	440-500
1989 Marbella Clock L5652	Closed	1994	125.00	132-235
1989 Avila Clock L5653	Closed	1995	135.00	135
1990 Venetian Carnival L5658G	Closed	1993	500.00	625
1990 Barnyard Scene L5659G	Closed	1998	200.00	245-295
1990 Sunning In Ipanema L5660G	Closed	1993	370.00	525-600
1990 Traveling Artist L5661G	Closed	1994	250.00	290
1990 May Dance L5662G	Open		170.00	210
1990 Spring Dance L5663G	12/00		170.00	210
1990 Giddy Up L5664G	Closed	1994	190.00	230
1990 Hang On! L5665G	Closed	1995	225.00	285-325
1990 Trino At The Beach L5666G	Closed	1995	390.00	500-550
1990 Valencian Harvest L5668G	Closed	1993	175.00	350-400

YEAR ISSUE	EDITION LIMIT	YEAR RETD.	ISSUE PRICE	*QUOTE U.S.$
1990 Valencian FLowers L5669G	Closed	1993	370.00	375
1990 Valencian Beauty L5670G	Closed	1993	175.00	175-325
1990 Little Dutch Gardener L5671G	Closed	1993	400.00	475
1990 Hi There! L5672G	Closed	1997	450.00	520-570
1990 A Quiet Moment L5673G	Closed	1998	450.00	520-575
1990 A Faun And A Friend L5674G	Closed	1997	450.00	550-600
1990 Tee Time L5675G	Closed	1993	280.00	315
1990 Wandering Minstrel L5676G	Closed	1993	270.00	248-310
1990 Twilight Years L5677G	Closed	1998	370.00	500-550
1990 I Feel Pretty L5678G	Closed	1998	190.00	230
1990 In No Hurry L5679G	Closed	1994	550.00	640-695
1990 Traveling In Style L5680G	Closed	1994	425.00	495-550
1990 On The Road L5681G	Closed	1991	320.00	550
1990 Breezy Afternoon L5682G	Open		180.00	195
1990 Breezy Afternoon L5682M	Open		180.00	195
1990 Beautiful Burro L5683G	Closed	1993	280.00	325-435
1990 Barnyard Reflections L5684G	Closed	1993	460.00	650
1990 Promenade L5685G	Closed	1994	275.00	325-375
1990 On The Avenue L5686G	Closed	1994	275.00	325-375
1990 Afternoon Stroll L5687G	Closed	1994	275.00	350-375
1990 Dog's Best Friend L5688G	Open		250.00	295
1990 Can I Help? L5689G	Closed	1998	250.00	335
1990 Marshland Mates w/base L5691G	Open		950.00	1200
1990 Street Harmonies w/base L5692G	Closed	1993	3200.00	3750
1990 Circus Serenade L5694G	Closed	1994	300.00	375
1990 Concertina L5695G	Closed	1994	300.00	360
1990 Mandolin Serenade L5696G	Closed	1994	300.00	360
1990 Over The Clouds L5697G	Open		275.00	310
1990 Don't Look Down L5698G	Open		330.00	405
1990 Sitting Pretty L5699G	Closed	1998	300.00	340
1990 Southern Charm L5700G	Closed	1998	675.00	1050-1095
1990 Just A Little Kiss L5701G	Closed	1998	320.00	375
1990 Back To School L5702G	Closed	1993	350.00	350-405
1990 Behave! L5703G	Closed	1994	230.00	363
1990 Swan Song L5704G	Closed	1995	350.00	410-450
1990 The Swan And The Princess L5705G	Closed	1994	350.00	410-495
1990 We Can't Play L5706G	Closed	1998	200.00	235-250
1990 After School L5707G	Closed	1993	280.00	315
1990 My First Class L5708G	Closed	1993	280.00	315
1990 Between Classes L5709G	Closed	1993	280.00	315
1990 Fantasy Friend L5710G	Closed	1993	420.00	495
1990 A Christmas Wish L5711G	Closed	1998	350.00	349-410
1990 Sleepy Kitten L5712G	Open		110.00	130
1990 The Snow Man L5713G	Open		300.00	350
1990 First Ballet L5714G	Open		370.00	420
1990 Mommy, it's Cold! L5715G	Closed	1994	360.00	450-500
1990 Land of The Giants L5716G	Closed	1994	275.00	315-425
1990 Rock A Bye Baby L5717G	Closed	1999	300.00	365
1990 Sharing Secrets L5720G	Closed	1998	290.00	335-375
1990 Once Upon A Time L5721G	Closed	1998	550.00	700-750
1990 Follow Me L5722G	Open		140.00	160
1990 Heavenly Chimes L5723G	Open		100.00	120
1990 Angelic Voice L5724G	Open		125.00	145
1990 Making A Wish L5725G	Open		125.00	145
1990 Sweep Away The Clouds L5726G	Open		125.00	145
1990 Angel Care L5727G	12/00		185.00	210
1990 Heavenly Dreamer L5728G	12/00		100.00	120
1991 Carousel Charm L5731G	Closed	1994	1700.00	2100
1991 Carousel Canter L5732G	Closed	1994	1700.00	1482-1850
1991 Horticulturist L5733G	Closed	1993	450.00	495
1991 Pilgrim Couple L5734G	Closed	1993	490.00	525
1991 Big Sister L5735G	Open		650.00	685
1991 Puppet Show L5736G	Closed	1997	280.00	295-375
1991 Little Prince L5737G	Closed	1993	295.00	315
1991 Best Foot Forward L5738G	Closed	1994	280.00	244-305
1991 Lap Full Of Love L5739G	Closed	1995	275.00	295
1991 Alice In Wonderland L5740G	Closed	1997	440.00	495-550
1991 Dancing Class L5741G	Closed	N/A	340.00	365
1991 Bridal Portrait L5742G	Closed	1995	480.00	560-748
1991 Don't Forget Me L5743G	Open		150.00	160
1991 Bull & Donkey L5744G	Closed	1997	250.00	275-295
1991 Baby Jesus L5745G	Closed	1997	170.00	185
1991 St. Joseph L5746G	Closed	1997	350.00	375-400
1991 Mary L5747G	Closed	1997	275.00	285-295
1991 Shepherd Girl L5748G	Closed	1997	150.00	165
1991 Shepherd Boy L5749G	Closed	1997	225.00	245
1991 Little Lamb L5750G	Closed	1997	40.00	42-75
1991 Walk With Father L5751G	Closed	1994	375.00	410-440
1991 Little Virgin L5752G	Closed	1994	295.00	320-325
1991 Hold Her Still L5753G	Closed	1993	650.00	695-725
1991 Singapore Dancers L5754G	Closed	1993	950.00	1150-1195
1991 Claudette L5755G	Closed	1993	265.00	285-350
1991 Ashley L5756G	Closed	1993	265.00	300-350
1991 Beautiful Tresses L5757G	Closed	1993	725.00	785-875
1991 Sunday Best L5758G	Closed	1998	725.00	620-785
1991 Presto! L5759G	Closed	1993	275.00	325-455
1991 Interrupted Nap L5760G	Closed	1995	325.00	280-425
1991 Out For A Romp L5761G	Closed	1995	375.00	410-533
1991 Checking The Time L5762G	Closed	1995	560.00	595-750
1991 Musical Partners L5763G	Closed	1995	625.00	675
1991 Seeds Of Laughter L5764G	Closed	1995	525.00	600-695
1991 Hats Off To Fun L5765G	Closed	1995	475.00	510
1991 Charming Duet L5766G	Closed	1997	575.00	625-725
1991 First Sampler L5767G	Closed	1995	625.00	680-750
1991 Academy Days L5768G	Closed	1993	280.00	310
1991 Faithful Steed L5769G	Closed	1994	370.00	375-395
1991 Out For A Spin L5770G	Closed	1994	390.00	420-495
1991 The Magic Of Laughter L5771G	Closed	1997	950.00	1065-1250
1991 Little Dreamers L5772G	Open		230.00	240
1991 Little Dreamers L5772M	Open		230.00	240
1991 Graceful Offering L5773G	Closed	1995	850.00	900-1100
1991 Nature's Gifts L5774G	Closed	1994	900.00	900-975

YEAR ISSUE	EDITION LIMIT	YEAR RETD.	ISSUE PRICE	*QUOTE U.S.$
1991 Gift Of Beauty L5775G	Closed	1995	850.00	900-1100
1991 Lover's Paradise L5779G	Closed	1998	2250.00	2450-2500
1991 Walking The Fields L5780G	Closed	1993	725.00	795-850
1991 Not Too Close L5781G	Closed	1994	365.00	365-450
1991 My Chores L5782G	Closed	1995	325.00	355-400
1991 Special Delivery L5783G	Closed	1994	525.00	550-650
1991 A Cradle Of Kittens L5784G	Closed	1998	360.00	360-385
1991 Ocean Beauty L5785G	Open		625.00	665
1991 Story Hour L5786G	Closed	1998	550.00	625
1991 Sophisticate L5787G	Closed	1998	185.00	195
1991 Talk Of The Town L5788G	Closed	1998	185.00	195
1991 The Flirt L5789G	Closed	1998	185.00	195-215
1991 Carefree L5790G	Open		300.00	325
1991 Fairy Godmother L5791G	Closed	1994	375.00	403-600
1991 Reverent Moment L5792G	Closed	1994	295.00	320
1991 Precocious Ballerina L5793G	Closed	1995	575.00	625
1991 Precious Cargo L5794G	Closed	1994	460.00	495-550
1991 Floral Getaway L5795G	Closed	1993	625.00	695-745
1991 Holy Night L5796G	Closed	1994	330.00	360-400
1991 Come Out And Play L5797G	Closed	1994	275.00	295-375
1991 Milkmaid L5798G	Closed	1993	450.00	485
1991 Shall We Dance? L5799G	Closed	1993	600.00	700-750
1991 Elegant Promenade L5802G	Open		775.00	825
1991 Playing Tag L5804G	Closed	1993	170.00	190
1991 Tumbling L5805G	Closed	1993	130.00	175
1991 Tumbling L5805M	Closed	1992	130.00	140
1991 Tickling L5806G	Closed	1993	130.00	145
1991 Tickling L5806M	Closed	1992	130.00	145
1991 My Puppies L5807G	Closed	1993	325.00	325-360
1991 Musically Inclined L5810G	Closed	1993	235.00	235-250
1991 Littlest Clown L5811G	Open		225.00	240
1991 Tired Friend L5812G	Open		225.00	245
1991 Having A Ball L5813G	Open		225.00	240
1991 Curtain Call L5814G	Closed	1994	490.00	520-825
1991 Curtain Call L5814M	Closed	1994	490.00	520
1991 In Full Relave L5815G	Closed	1994	490.00	520-825
1991 In Full Relave L5815M	Closed	1994	490.00	520
1991 Prima Ballerina L5816G	Closed	1994	490.00	520
1991 Prima Ballerina L5816M	Closed	1994	490.00	520
1991 Backstage Preparation L5817G	Closed	1994	490.00	520-525
1991 Backstage Preparation L5817M	Closed	1994	490.00	650
1991 On Her Toes L5818G	Closed	1994	490.00	490-520
1991 On Her Toes L5818M	Closed	1994	490.00	520
1991 Allegory Of Liberty L5819G	Open		1950.00	2100
1991 Dance Of Love L5820G	Closed	1993	575.00	625
1991 Minstrel's Love L5821G	Closed	1993	525.00	575
1991 Little Unicorn L5826G	Closed	1998	275.00	275-375
1991 Little Unicorn L5826M	Closed	1998	275.00	295
1991 I've Got It L5827G	Closed	1995	170.00	180-250
1991 Next At Bat L5828G	Closed	1998	170.00	180-230
1991 Heavenly Harpist L5830	Yr.Iss.	1991	135.00	195-250
1991 Jazz Horn L5832G	Open		295.00	310
1991 Jazz Sax L5833G	Open		295.00	315
1991 Jazz Bass L5834G	Open		395.00	425
1991 I Do L5835G	Open		165.00	190
1991 Sharing Sweets L5836G	Closed	1998	220.00	245
1991 Sing With Me L5837G	Closed	1998	240.00	250
1991 On The Move L5838G	Closed	1998	340.00	395
1992 A Quiet Afternoon L5843G	Closed	1995	1050.00	1125
1992 Flirtatious Jester L5844G	Closed	1998	890.00	890-925
1992 Dressing The Baby L5845G	Open		295.00	295
1992 All Tuckered Out L5846G	Open		220.00	255
1992 All Tuckered Out L5846M	Open		220.00	255
1992 The Loving Family L5848G	Closed	1994	950.00	985
1992 Inspiring Muse L5850G	Closed	1994	1200.00	1250-1650
1992 Feathered Fantasy L5851G	Closed	1997	1200.00	1200-1250
1992 Easter Bonnets L5852G	Closed	1993	265.00	400
1992 Floral Admiration L5853G	Closed	1994	690.00	825
1992 Floral Fantasy L5854G	Closed	1995	690.00	745-890
1992 Afternoon Jaunt L5855G	Closed	1993	420.00	440-500
1992 Circus Concert L5856G	Closed	1997	570.00	585-600
1992 Grand Entrance L5857G	Closed	1994	265.00	275
1992 Waiting to Dance L5858G	Closed	1995	295.00	335
1992 At The Ball L5859G	Open		295.00	330
1992 Fairy Garland L5860G	Closed	1995	630.00	750-850
1992 Fairy Flowers L5861G	Closed	1995	630.00	750-850
1992 Fragrant Bouquet L5862G	Open		350.00	370
1992 Dressing For The Ballet L5865G	Closed	1995	395.00	415
1992 Final Touches L5866G	Closed	1995	395.00	415
1992 Serene Valenciana L5867G	Closed	1994	365.00	385
1992 Loving Valenciana L5868G	Closed	1995	365.00	385
1992 Fallas Queen L5869G	Closed	1995	420.00	440
1992 Olympic Torch w/Fantasy Logo L5870G	Closed	1994	165.00	145
1992 Olympic Champion w/Fantasy Logo L5871G	Closed	1994	165.00	145
1992 Olympic Pride w/Fantasy Logo L5872G	Closed	1994	165.00	225-495
1992 Modern Mother L5873G	Closed	1997	325.00	276-375
1992 Off We Go L5874G	Closed	1994	365.00	385
1992 Angelic Cymbalist L5876	Yr.Iss.	1992	140.00	195-250
1992 Guest Of Honor L5877G	Closed	1997	195.00	195-200
1992 Sister's Pride L5878G	Closed	1997	595.00	615-695
1992 Shot On Goal L5879G	Closed	1997	1100.00	1150-1250
1992 Playful Unicorn L5880G	Closed	1998	295.00	320-475
1992 Playful Unicorn L5880M	Closed	1998	295.00	320
1992 Mischievous Mouse L5881G	Closed	1998	285.00	295-345
1992 Restful Mouse L5882G	Closed	1997	285.00	295-325
1992 Loving Mouse L5883G	Closed	1997	285.00	295-325
1992 From This Day Forward L5885G	Open		265.00	285
1992 Hippity Hop L5886G	Closed	1995	95.00	95-125
1992 Washing Up L5887G	Closed	1995	95.00	95

400 Collectors' Information Bureau

*Quotes have been rounded up to nearest dollar

YEAR ISSUE	EDITION LIMIT	YEAR RETD.	ISSUE PRICE	*QUOTE U.S.$
1992 That Tickles! L5888G	Closed	1995	95.00	105-165
1992 Snack Time L5889G	Closed	1995	95.00	105-150
1992 The Aviator L5891G	Closed	1998	375.00	450-600
1992 Circus Magic L5892G	Closed	1998	470.00	495
1992 Friendship In Bloom L5893G	Closed	1995	650.00	685
1992 Precious Petals L5894G	Closed	1997	395.00	415
1992 Bouquet of Blossoms L5895G	Closed	1998	295.00	295
1992 The Loaves & Fishes L5896G	Closed	1998	695.00	760-900
1992 Trimming The Tree L5897G	Open		900.00	925
1992 Spring Splendor L5898G	Open		440.00	450
1992 Just One More L5899G	Closed	1998	450.00	495-550
1992 Sleep Tight L5900G	Closed	1998	450.00	500-550
1992 Surprise L5901G	Open		325.00	335
1992 Easter Bunnies L5902G	Closed	1997	240.00	250
1992 Down The Aisle L5903G	Closed	1997	295.00	251-345
1992 Sleeping Bunny L5904G	Closed	1998	75.00	75
1992 Attentive Bunny L5905G	Closed	1998	75.00	75-100
1992 Preening Bunny L5906G	Closed	1998	75.00	80-105
1992 Sitting Bunny L5907G	Closed	1998	75.00	80
1992 Just A Little More L5908G	Closed	1998	370.00	323-380
1992 All Dressed Up L5909G	Closed	1998	440.00	450-525
1992 Making A Wish L5910G	Closed	1998	790.00	825
1992 Swans Take Flight L5912G	Open		2850.00	2950
1992 Rose Ballet L5919G	Open		210.00	215
1992 Swan Ballet L5920G	Open		210.00	215
1992 Take Your Medicine L5921G	Closed	1998	360.00	370-450
1990 Floral Clock L5924	Closed	1995	N/A	165
1990 Garland Quartz Clock L5926	Closed	1995	195.00	195
1992 Jazz Clarinet L5928G	Open		295.00	295
1992 Jazz Drums L5929G	Open		595.00	610
1992 Jazz Duo L5930G	Open		795.00	900
1993 The Ten Commandments w/Base L5933G	Closed	1997	930.00	930
1993 The Holy Teacher L5934G	Closed	1997	375.00	375-425
1993 Nutcracker Suite L5935G	Closed	1998	620.00	620-675
1993 Little Skipper L5936G	Closed	1997	320.00	289-390
1993 Riding The Waves L5941G	Closed	1998	405.00	425-575
1993 World of Fantasy L5943G	Closed	1995	295.00	295
1993 The Great Adventurer L5944G	Closed	1994	325.00	325
1993 A Mother's Way L5946G	Closed	1997	1350.00	1350-1400
1993 General Practitioner L5947G	Closed	1998	360.00	315-370
1993 Physician L5948G	Open		360.00	360
1993 Angel Candleholder w/Lyre L5949G	Closed	1998	295.00	315-365
1993 Angel Candleholder w/Tambourine L5950G	Closed	1998	295.00	315-365
1993 Sounds of Summer L5953G	Open		150.00	150
1993 Sounds of Winter L5954G	Open		150.00	150
1993 Sounds of Fall L5955G	Open		150.00	150
1993 Sounds of Spring L5956G	Open		150.00	150
1993 The Glass Slipper L5957G	Open		475.00	475
1993 Country Ride w/base L5958G	Open		2850.00	2875
1993 It's Your Turn L5959G	Closed	1997	365.00	365
1993 On Patrol L5960G	Closed	1998	395.00	378-550
1993 The Great Teacher w/base L5961G	Closed	1997	850.00	850
1993 Angelic Melody L5963	Yr.Iss.	1993	145.00	175-275
1993 The Great Voyage L5964G	Closed	1994	50.00	50
1993 The Clipper Ship w/base L5965M	Closed	1997	240.00	250
1993 Flowers Forever w/base L5966G	Open		4150.00	4150
1993 Honeymoon Ride w/base L5968G	Closed	1995	2750.00	2795
1993 A Special Toy L5971G	Closed	1997	815.00	815-850
1993 Before the Dance w/base L5972G	Open		3550.00	3550
1993 Before the Dance w/base L5972M	Open		3550.00	3550
1993 Family Outing w/base L5974G	Closed	1998	4275.00	4275
1993 Up and Away w/base L5975G	Closed	1997	2850.00	2850
1993 The Fireman L5976G	Closed	1998	395.00	465-500
1993 Revelation w/base (white) L5977G	Closed	1995	325.00	325
1993 Revelation w/base (black) L5978M	Closed	1995	325.00	325
1993 Revelation w/base (sand) L5979M	Closed	1995	325.00	325
1993 The Past w/base (white) L5980G	Closed	1995	325.00	325
1993 The Past w/base (black) L5981M	Closed	1995	325.00	325
1993 The Past w/base (sand) L5982M	Closed	1995	325.00	325
1993 Beauty w/base (white) L5983G	Closed	1995	325.00	325
1993 Beauty w/base (black) L5984M	Closed	1995	325.00	325
1993 Beauty w/base (sand) L5985M	Closed	1995	325.00	325
1993 Sunday Sermon L5986G	Open		425.00	425
1993 Talk to Me L5987G	Closed	1998	145.00	175
1993 Taking Time L5988G	Closed	1998	145.00	145-175
1993 A Mother's Touch L5989G	Closed	1997	470.00	470
1993 Thoughtful Caress L5990G	Closed	1997	225.00	225
1993 Love Story L5991G	12/00		2800.00	2800
1993 Unicorn and Friend L5993G	Closed	1998	355.00	355-425
1993 Unicorn and Friend L5993M	Closed	1998	355.00	355
1993 Meet My Friend L5994G	Closed	1997	695.00	695
1993 Soft Meow L5995G	Closed	1998	480.00	515-575
1993 Bless the Child L5996G	Closed	1994	465.00	465
1993 One More Try L5997G	Closed	1997	715.00	795-850
1993 My Dad L6001G	Closed	1995	550.00	575
1993 Down You Go L6002G	Closed	1998	815.00	815-865
1993 Ready To Learn L6003G	Closed	1999	650.00	650
1993 Bar Mitzvah Day L6004G	Open		395.00	430
1993 Christening Day w/base L6005G	Closed	1995	1425.00	1425
1993 Oriental Colonade w/base L6006G	Closed	1995	1875.00	1875
1993 The Goddess & Unicorn w/base L6007G	Open		1675.00	1675
1993 Joyful Event L6008G	Open		825.00	825
1993 Monday's Child (Boy) L6011G	Closed	1998	245.00	200-352
1993 Monday's Child (Girl) L6012G	Closed	1998	260.00	290-350
1993 Tuesday's Child (Boy) L6013G	Closed	1998	225.00	175-300
1993 Tuesday's Child (Girl) L6014G	Closed	1998	245.00	285-350
1993 Wednesday's Child (Boy) L6015G	Closed	1998	245.00	242-325
1993 Wednesday's Child (Girl) L6016G	Closed	1998	245.00	350
1993 Thursday's Child (Boy) L6017G	Closed	1998	225.00	175-300
1993 Thursday's Child (Girl) L6018G	Closed	1998	245.00	250-325
1993 Friday's Child (Boy) L6019G	Closed	1998	225.00	213-320
1993 Friday's Child (Girl) L6020G	Closed	1998	225.00	250-350
1993 Saturday's Child (Boy) L6021G	Closed	1998	245.00	242-285
1993 Saturday's Child (Girl) L6022G	Closed	1998	245.00	285-325
1993 Sunday's Child (Boy) L6023G	Closed	1998	225.00	213-300
1993 Sunday's Child (Girl) L6024G	Closed	1998	225.00	300-325
1993 Barnyard See Saw L6025G	Closed	1998	500.00	425-550
1993 My Turn L6026G	Closed	1998	515.00	515
1993 Hanukah Lights L6027G	Closed	1999	345.00	395
1993 Mazel Tov! L6028G	Open		380.00	395
1993 Hebrew Scholar L6029G	Closed	1997	225.00	245-295
1993 On The Go L6031G	Closed	1995	475.00	412-631
1993 On The Green L6032G	Open		645.00	645
1993 Monkey Business L6034G	Closed	1994	745.00	800-850
1993 Young Princess L6036G	Closed	1997	240.00	240
1994 Saint James L6084G	Closed	1998	310.00	310-400
1994 Angelic Harmony L6085G	Closed	1998	495.00	575
1994 Allow Me L6086G	Closed	1998	1625.00	1625
1994 Loving Care L6087G	Closed	1999	250.00	270-295
1994 Communion Prayer (Boy) L6088G	Open		194.00	200
1994 Communion Prayer (Girl) L6089G	Open		198.00	225
1994 Baseball Player L6090G	Closed	1998	295.00	310-400
1994 Basketball Player L6091G	Closed	1998	295.00	310-350
1994 The Prince L6092G	Closed	1998	325.00	325
1994 Songbird L6093G	Open		395.00	395
1994 The Sportsman L6096G	Closed	1998	495.00	540
1994 Sleeping Bunny With Flowers L6097G	Closed	1998	110.00	110-195
1994 Attentive Bunny With Flowers L6098G	Open		140.00	140
1994 Preening Bunny With Flowers L6099G	Closed	1998	140.00	140-175
1994 Sitting Bunny With Flowers L6100G	Open		110.00	110
1994 Follow Us L6101G	Closed	1998	198.00	183-215
1994 Mother's Little Helper L6102G	Closed	1998	275.00	242-325
1994 Beautiful Ballerina L6103G	Closed	1999	250.00	285-325
1994 Finishing Touches L6104	Closed	1999	240.00	250-295
1994 Spring Joy L6106G	Open		795.00	795
1994 Football Player L6107	Closed	1998	295.00	310-375
1994 Hockey Player L6108G	Closed	1998	295.00	310-550
1994 Meal Time L6109G	12/00		495.00	525
1994 Medieval Maiden L6110G	Closed	1997	150.00	145-220
1994 Medieval Soldier L6111G	Closed	1997	225.00	245
1994 Medieval Lord L6112G	Closed	1997	285.00	300
1994 Medieval Lady L6113G	Closed	1997	225.00	225
1994 Medieval Princess L6114G	Closed	1997	245.00	310-350
1994 Medieval Prince L6115G	Closed	1997	295.00	315-325
1994 Medieval Majesty L6116G	Closed	1997	315.00	315-325
1994 Constance L6117G	Closed	1997	195.00	205
1994 Constance L6117M	Closed	1998	195.00	205-225
1994 Musketeer Portos L6118G	Closed	1997	220.00	230-250
1994 Musketeer Aramis L6119G	Closed	1997	275.00	275-295
1994 Musketeer Dartagnan L6120G	Closed	1997	245.00	242-285
1994 Musketeer Athos L6121G	Closed	1997	245.00	245-290
1994 A Great Adventure L6122	Closed	1998	198.00	183-215
1994 Out For a Stroll L6123G	Closed	1998	198.00	161-250
1994 Travelers Rest L6124G	Closed	1998	275.00	250-295
1994 Angelic Violinist L6126G	Yr.Iss.	1994	150.00	140-250
1994 Sweet Dreamers L6127G	Open		280.00	290
1994 Christmas Melodies L6128G	Closed	1998	375.00	385
1994 Little Friends L6129G	Closed	1998	225.00	235
1996 Spring Enchantment L6130G	Open		245.00	245
1994 Angel of Peace L6131G	Open		345.00	370
1994 Angel with Garland L6133G	Closed	1999	345.00	315-370
1994 Birthday Party L6134G	Closed	1998	395.00	450-575
1994 Football Star L6135	Closed	1998	295.00	251-295
1994 Basketball Star L6136G	Closed	1998	295.00	251-295
1994 Baseball Star L6137G	Closed	1998	295.00	221-295
1994 Globe Paperweight L6138M	Closed	1997	95.00	95
1994 Springtime Friends L6140G	Open		485.00	485
1994 Kitty Cart L6141G	Open		750.00	795
1994 Indian Pose L6142G	Closed	1998	475.00	475-550
1994 Indian Dancer L6143G	Closed	1998	475.00	475
1995 Caribbean Kiss L6144G	Closed	1999	340.00	289-340
1994 Heavenly Prayer L6145	Closed	1998	675.00	695
1994 Spring Angel L6146G	Closed	1998	250.00	265-325
1994 Fall Angel L6147G	Closed	1998	250.00	265-300
1994 Summer Angel L6148G	Closed	1998	220.00	220-295
1994 Winter Angel L6149G	Closed	1998	250.00	265
1994 Playing The Flute L6150G	Closed	1999	175.00	190-215
1994 Bearing Flowers L6151G	Closed	1998	175.00	190-220
1994 Flower Gazer L6152G	Closed	1999	175.00	190-220
1994 American Love L6153G	Closed	1998	225.00	235-285
1994 African Love L6154G	Closed	1998	225.00	235-250
1994 European Love L6155G	Closed	1998	225.00	235
1994 Asian Love L6156G	Closed	1998	225.00	235
1994 Polynesian Love L6157G	Closed	1998	225.00	235
1995 Fiesta Dancer L6163G	Closed	1998	285.00	305-345
1994 Wedding Bells L6164G	Open		175.00	195
1995 Pretty Cargo L6165G	Closed	1998	500.00	500
1995 Dear Santa L6166G	Closed	1999	250.00	260
1995 Delicate Bundle L6167G	Closed	1999	275.00	275
1994 The Apollo Landing L6168G	Closed	1995	450.00	525-550
1995 Seesaw Friends L6169G	12/00		795.00	795
1995 Under My Spell L6170G	Closed	1999	195.00	200-250
1995 Magical Moment L6171G	Closed	1999	180.00	200
1995 Coming of Age L6172G	Closed	1998	345.00	345
1995 A Moment's Rest L6173G	Open		130.00	140
1995 Graceful Pose L6174G	Open		195.00	195
1995 Graceful Pose L6174M	Open		195.00	195
1995 White Swan L6175G	Open		90.00	90
1995 Communion Bell L6176G	Open		85.00	85
1995 Asian Scholar L6177G	Open		315.00	315
1995 Little Matador L6178G	Open		245.00	245
1995 Peaceful Moment L6179G	Open		385.00	385
1995 Sharia L6180G	Open		235.00	235
1995 Velisa L6181G	Open		180.00	180
1996 Wanda L6182	Open		205.00	220
1995 Preparing For The Sabbath L6183G	Closed	1999	385.00	385
1995 For a Better World L6186G	Closed	1998	575.00	489-575
1995 European Boy L6187G	Closed	1998	185.00	185
1995 Asian Boy L6188G	Closed	1998	225.00	225-275
1995 African Boy L6189G	Closed	1998	195.00	195-275
1995 Polynesian Boy L6190G	Closed	1998	250.00	250-275
1995 All American L6191G	Closed	1998	225.00	225-275
1995 American Indian Boy L6192G	Closed	1998	225.00	225-275
1995 Summer Serenade L6193G	Open		375.00	385
1995 Summer Serenade L6193M	Open		375.00	385
1996 Christmas Wishes L6194	Closed	1998	245.00	208-295
1995 Carnival Companions L6195G	Closed	1998	650.00	582-685
1995 Seaside Companions L6196G	Closed	1998	230.00	230
1995 Seaside Serenade L6197G	Closed	1998	275.00	275
1995 Soccer Practice L6198G	Open		195.00	195
1995 In The Procession L6199G	Closed	1998	250.00	250-295
1995 In The Procession L6199M	Closed	1998	250.00	250
1995 Bridal Bell L6200G	Open		125.00	125
1995 Cuddly Kitten L6201G	Closed	1999	270.00	270
1995 Daddy's Little Sweetheart L6202G	Open		595.00	595
1995 Grace and Beauty L6204G	Closed	1998	325.00	276-325
1995 Grace and Beauty L6204M	Closed	1998	325.00	325
1995 Graceful Dance L6205G	Closed	1998	340.00	340-395
1995 Graceful Dance L6205M	Closed	1998	340.00	340-395
1995 Reading the Torah L6208G	12/00		535.00	535
1995 The Rabbi L6209G	Closed	1998	250.00	250-300
1995 Gentle Surprise L6210G	Open		125.00	125
1995 New Friend L6211G	Open		120.00	120
1995 Little Hunter L6212G	12/00		115.00	115
1995 Lady Of Nice L6213G	Closed	1999	198.00	210-220
1995 Lady Of Nice L6213M	Closed	1999	198.00	210
1995 Leo L6214G	Closed	1998	198.00	179-275
1995 Virgo L6215G	Closed	1998	198.00	210-300
1995 Aquarius L6216G	Closed	1998	198.00	210-275
1995 Sagittarius L6217G	Closed	1998	198.00	210-275
1995 Taurus L6218G	Closed	1998	198.00	210-275
1995 Gemini L6219G	Closed	1998	198.00	210-275
1995 Libra L6220G	Closed	1998	198.00	210-300
1995 Aries L6221G	Closed	1998	198.00	210-275
1995 Capricorn L6222G	Closed	1998	198.00	210-275
1995 Pisces L6223G	Closed	1998	198.00	210-275
1995 Cancer L6224G	Closed	1998	198.00	210-300
1995 Scorpio L6225G	Closed	1998	198.00	235-300
1995 Snuggle Up L6226G	12/00		170.00	170
1995 Trick or Treat L6227G	Closed	1998	250.00	250-300
1995 Special Gift L6228G	Open		265.00	265
1995 Contented Companion L6229G	12/00		195.00	195
1995 Oriental Dance L6230G	Open		198.00	210
1995 Oriental Lantern L6231G	Open		198.00	210
1995 Oriental Beauty L6232G	12/00		198.00	210
1995 Chef's Apprentice L6233G	Closed	1998	260.00	260-285
1995 Chef's Apprentice L6233M	Closed	1998	260.00	260
1995 The Great Chef L6234G	Closed	1998	195.00	195-225
1995 The Great Chef L6234M	Closed	1998	195.00	195
1995 Dinner is Served L6235G	Closed	1998	185.00	157-225
1995 Dinner is Served L6235M	Closed	1998	185.00	185
1995 Lady of Monaco L6236G	Closed	1999	250.00	260
1995 Lady of Monaco L6236M	Closed	1999	250.00	260-300
1995 The Young Jester-Mandolin L6237G	Closed	1998	235.00	235-275
1995 The Young Jester-Mandolin L6237M	Closed	1998	235.00	235
1995 The Young Jester-Trumpet L6238G	Closed	1998	235.00	235
1995 The Young Jester-Trumpet L6238M	Closed	1998	235.00	235
1995 The Young Jester-Singer L6239G	Closed	1998	235.00	235
1995 The Young Jester-Singer L6239M	Closed	1998	235.00	235
1995 Graceful Ballet L6240G	Closed	1998	795.00	815
1995 Graceful Ballet L6240M	Closed	1998	795.00	815
1995 Allegory of Spring L6241G	12/00		735.00	735
1995 Allegory of Spring L6241M	12/00		735.00	735
1996 Winged Companions L6242G	Closed	1999	270.00	270-300
1996 Winged Companions L6242M	Closed	1999	270.00	270
1996 Sweet Symphony L6243	Open		450.00	450
1996 Pumpkin Ride L6244	Closed	1999	695.00	695
1996 Sunday's Best L6246	Closed	1999	370.00	370
1995 Challenge L6247M	Closed	1997	350.00	350-400
1995 Regatta L6248G	Closed	1997	695.00	695-750
1995 Delphica w/base L6249	Open		1200.00	1200
1996 Springtime Harvest L6250	Open		760.00	760
1997 Wind of Peace L6251	Closed	1999	310.00	310
1996 Nature's Beauty w/base L6252	Closed	1999	770.00	770
1996 Making Rounds L6256	Open		295.00	295
1996 Pierrot in Preparation L6257	Closed	1999	195.00	195
1996 Pierrot in Love L6258	Closed	1999	195.00	166-195
1996 Pierrot Rehearsing L6259	Closed	1999	195.00	166-195
1996 Our Lady "Caridid Del Cobre" w/base L6268	Closed	1998	1355.00	1355
1996 Diana Goddess of the Hunt w/base L6269	12/00		1550.00	1550
1996 Commencement L6270	Open		200.00	200
1996 Cap and Gown L6271	Open		200.00	200
1996 Going Forth L6272	Closed	1999	200.00	200
1996 Pharmacist L6273	12/00		290.00	290
1996 Daisy L6274	Open		150.00	150
1996 Rose L6275	Open		150.00	150
1996 Iris L6276	Open		150.00	150
1996 Young Mandolin Player L6278	12/00		330.00	330
1996 Flowers of Paris L6279	Closed	1999	525.00	525
1996 Paris in Bloom L6280	Closed	1999	525.00	525

*Quotes have been rounded up to nearest dollar

YEAR ISSUE	EDITION LIMIT	YEAR RETD.	ISSUE PRICE	*QUOTE U.S.$
1996 Coqueta L6281G	Closed	1998	435.00	435
1996 Coqueta L6281M	Closed	1998	435.00	435
1996 Medic L6282G	Closed	1999	225.00	191-225
1996 Medic L6282M	Closed	1999	225.00	225
1996 Temis L6283G	Closed	1998	435.00	435
1996 Temis L6283M	Closed	1998	435.00	435
1996 Quione L6284G	Closed	1998	435.00	435
1996 Quione L6284M	Closed	1998	435.00	435
1996 Dreams of Aladdin w/base L6285	Closed	1999	1440.00	1440
1996 Tennis Champion w/base L6286G	Closed	1999	350.00	350
1996 Tennis Champion w/base L6286M	Closed	1999	350.00	332-350
1996 Restless Dove L6287G	Closed	1998	105.00	105
1996 Restless Dove L6287M	Closed	1998	105.00	105
1996 Taking Flight L6288G	Closed	1999	150.00	150
1996 Taking Flight L6288M	Closed	1999	150.00	150
1996 Peaceful Dove L6289G	Closed	1999	105.00	105
1996 Peaceful Dove L6289M	Closed	1999	105.00	105
1996 Proud Dove L6290G	Closed	1999	105.00	105
1996 Proud Dove L6290M	Closed	1999	105.00	105
1996 Love Nest L6291G	Open		260.00	285
1996 Love Nest L6291M	Open		260.00	260
1997 Summer Egg L6293	Open		365.00	365
1998 Autumn Egg 01006294	Open		365.00	365
1999 Winter Egg 01006295	Open		365.00	365
1996 Sweethearts L6296	Closed	1999	900.00	900
1996 Little Bear L6299	Closed	1999	285.00	285
1996 Rubber Ducky L6300	12/00		285.00	285
1996 Care and Tenderness w/base L6301	Open		850.00	850
1996 Thena L6302G	Closed	1998	485.00	485
1996 Thena L6302M	Closed	1998	485.00	485
1996 Tuba Player L6303	Closed	1998	315.00	252-375
1996 Bass Drummer L6304	Closed	1998	400.00	340-400
1996 Trumpet Player L6305	Closed	1998	270.00	230-270
1996 Majorette L6306	Closed	1998	310.00	248-310
1996 Young Nurse L6307	Open		185.00	185
1996 Natural Wonder L6308	Closed	1999	220.00	220-250
1996 Nature's Treasures L6309	Closed	1998	220.00	220
1996 Nature's Song L6310	Closed	1998	230.00	230
1996 Cupid L6311	Open		200.00	200
1996 The Harpist L6312	Closed	1999	820.00	820
1996 Lost in Dreams L6313	Open		420.00	420
1996 Little Sailor Boy L6314	Closed	1999	225.00	225
1996 Dreaming of You L6315	Closed	1999	1280.00	1280
1996 Carnevale L6316	Closed	1998	840.00	840-950
1996 Making House Calls L6317	Closed	1998	260.00	260
1996 Little Distraction L6318	Closed	1999	350.00	298-350
1996 Beautiful Rhapsody L6319	Open		450.00	450
1996 Architect L6320	Closed	1999	330.00	281-330
1996 Serenading Colombina L6322	Closed	1998	415.00	353-415
1996 Stage Presence L6323	12/00		355.00	355
1996 Princess of Peace L6324	12/00		830.00	830
1996 Curtains Up L6325	Closed	1999	255.00	217-255
1996 Virgin of Carmen w/base L6326	Closed	1999	1270.00	1270-1350
1996 Medieval Romance w/base L6327	Closed	1999	2250.00	1645-2250
1996 Venice Festival w/base L6328	Closed	1999	5350.00	5350
1996 Blushing Bride L6329G	Closed	1999	370.00	370
1996 Blushing Bride L6329M	Closed	1999	370.00	370
1996 Refreshing Pause L6330	Open		170.00	170
1996 Bridal Bell L6331	Open		155.00	155
1996 Concerto L6332	Open		490.00	490
1996 Medieval Chess Set L6333	Open		2120.00	2120
1997 Little Fireman L6334	12/00		185.00	185
1997 Home Sweet Home L6336	Closed	1998	85.00	85
1997 Poodle L6337	12/00		150.00	150
1997 I'm Sleepy L6338	12/00		360.00	375
1996 Country Sounds L6339	Closed	1998	750.00	638-750
1996 Sweet Country L6340	Closed	1998	750.00	638-750
1998 Petals of Love 01006346	Open		350.00	350
1997 Little Veterinarian L6348	Closed	1999	210.00	179-210
1997 Little Maestro L6349	12/00		165.00	165
1997 Hunting Butterflies L6350	12/00		425.00	475
1997 Tokens of Love L6351	12/00		385.00	425
1997 A World of Love L6353	Open		450.00	450
1997 Attentive Polar Bear w/Flowers L6354	Open		100.00	100
1997 Polar Bear Resting w/Flowers L6355	Open		100.00	100
1997 Polar Bear Seated w/Flowers L6356	Open		100.00	100
1997 Kissing Doves w/Flowers L6359	Open		225.00	225
1997 St. Joseph The Carpenter L6363	Closed	1999	1050.00	1050
1997 A Dream Come True L6364	12/00		550.00	550
1997 Spring Flirtation L6365	Open		395.00	395
1998 Summer Infatuation 01006366	Open		325.00	325
1997 Little Policeman L6367	12/00		185.00	185
1997 Little Artist L6368	12/00		175.00	175
1997 Indian Maiden L6369	Closed	1999	600.00	600
1997 Country Chores L6370	12/00		260.00	260
1997 En Pointe L6371	12/00		390.00	390
1997 Palace Dance L6373	Closed	1999	700.00	700
1997 Pas De Deux L6374	12/00		725.00	745
1997 Pierrot's Proposal L6375	12/00		1425.00	1475
1997 Light and Life L6376G	12/00		220.00	220
1997 Light and Life L6376M	12/00		220.00	220
1997 Unity L6377G	Closed	1999	220.00	220-250
1997 Unity L6377M	Closed	1999	220.00	220
1997 Beginning and End L6378G	Closed	1999	220.00	220
1997 Beginning and End L6378M	Closed	1999	220.00	220
1997 Love L6379G	12/00		220.00	220
1997 Love L6379M	12/00		220.00	220
1997 King Gaspar L6380	Closed	1998	75.00	75-90
1997 Little Roadster L6381	Closed	1998	79.00	79-98
1997 New Arrival L6382	Open		265.00	265
1997 The Ascension L6383	Closed	1999	775.00	775
1997 A Quiet Moment L6384	Closed	1999	270.00	270

YEAR ISSUE	EDITION LIMIT	YEAR RETD.	ISSUE PRICE	*QUOTE U.S.$
1997 Royal Slumber L6385	Open		1390.00	1425
1997 Little Harlequin L6386	Closed	1998	79.00	79-98
1997 A Passionate Dance L6387	Closed	1998	890.00	960
1997 Circus Star L6388	Closed	1998	79.00	79-98
1997 The Bouquet L6389	Closed	1998	95.00	95
1997 The Encounter L6391	Closed	1998	150.00	150
1997 The Kiss L6392	Closed	1998	150.00	150-170
1997 Heavenly Flutist L6393	Closed	1998	98.00	98
1997 Seraph with Holly L6394	Closed	1998	79.00	79-98
1997 Through the Park L6395	Open		2350.00	2350
1997 Oriental Forest L6396	Open		565.00	565
1997 In Neptune's Waves L6397	Closed	1999	1030.00	1030
1997 Seraph w/Holly L6394	Open		79.00	79
1997 Morning Delivery L6398	Open		160.00	160
1997 Generous Gesture L6399	12/00		345.00	345
1997 Daydreams L6400	Open		325.00	325
1997 Little Ballerina L6402	Open		200.00	200
1997 Breathless L6403	12/00		235.00	235
1997 Sister w/Sax L6404G	Closed	1999	180.00	180
1997 Sister w/Sax L6404M	Closed	1999	180.00	180
1997 Sister Singing L6405G	Closed	1999	165.00	165
1997 Sister Singing L6405M	Closed	1999	165.00	165
1997 Sister w/Guitar L6406G	Closed	1999	200.00	200-220
1997 Sister w/Guitar L6406M	Closed	1999	200.00	200
1997 Sister w/Tambourine L6407G	Closed	1999	185.00	185
1997 Sister w/Tambourine L6407M	Closed	1999	185.00	185
1997 Sweet Song L6408	Open		480.00	480
1997 A Surprise Visit L6409	12/00		190.00	190
1997 Would You Be Mine? L6410	12/00		190.00	190
1997 Bath Time L6411	Open		195.00	195
1997 Joy of Life L6412	Open		215.00	220
1997 Spirit of Youth L6413	Open		215.00	220
1997 Hello Friend L6414	12/00		235.00	235
1997 It's A Boy! L6415	Open		125.00	125
1997 It's A Girl! L6416	Open		125.00	125
1997 Unlikely Friends L6417	Open		125.00	125
1997 So Beautiful! L6418G	12/00		325.00	325
1997 So Beautiful! L6418M	12/00		325.00	325
1997 Arms Full of Love L6419	Open		180.00	180
1997 My Favorite Slippers L6420	Closed	1999	145.00	145-175
1997 Off To Bed L6421	Closed	1999	145.00	145-175
1997 My Chubby Kitty L6422	Open		135.00	140
1997 Precious Papoose L6423	Closed	1999	240.00	240-275
1997 Ceremonial Princess L6424	12/00		240.00	240
1997 Female Attorney L6425	12/00		300.00	320
1997 Male Attorney L6426	12/00		300.00	320
1997 A Flower For You L6427	12/00		320.00	320
1997 My First Step L6428	Open		165.00	165
1997 Ready To Roll L6429	Open		165.00	165
1997 Pony Ride L6430	12/00		825.00	825
1997 Little Lawyer L6431	Closed	1999	210.00	210-250
1997 Sea of Love L6432	12/00		1190.00	1290
1997 Cranes in Flight L6433	Open		1390.00	1390
1997 Pensive Harlequin L6434	Closed	1998	495.00	495
1997 Colombina L6435	Closed	1998	525.00	525
1997 The Dolphins L6436	Open		965.00	1090
1997 Timid Torero L6437	Closed	1999	195.00	195
1997 Young Torero L6438	Open		240.00	240
1998 Caught In The Act 01006439	12/00		260.00	260
1997 Time For Bed L6440	Closed	1999	160.00	160
1997 Spanish Dance L6444	12/00		445.00	545
1997 Surrounded by Love L6446	Open		315.00	320
1997 Dentist L6450	12/00		225.00	250
1997 Little Pilot L6451	Open		170.00	180
1998 Spring Recital 01006452	Open		685.00	725
1997 German Shepherd with Puppies 01006454	12/00		475.00	510
1997 Collie 01006455	12/00		295.00	300
1997 Dance of the Dolphins 01006456	Open		315.00	375
1997 Bathing Beauties 01006457	Open		240.00	245
1998 Fountain of Love 01006458	Open		395.00	425
1997 Collie with Puppy 01006459	12/00		350.00	355
1997 My Cuddly Puppy 01006463	Open		110.00	115
1997 Who's There? 01006464	Open		115.00	120
1997 Bedtime Prayers 01006465	Open		105.00	110
1998 A Prize Catch 01006466	12/00		340.00	355
1998 A Father's Pride 01006467	Open		475.00	520
2000 A Fishing Lesson 01006468	Open		530.00	530
1997 Our Cozy Home 01006469	Open		195.00	205
1997 A Swimming Lesson 01006470	Open		260.00	275
1997 My Pretty Flowers 01006471	Open		160.00	170
1997 Gardening Buddies 01006472	Open		195.00	200
1998 Sounds of Peace 01006473	Open		98.00	105
1998 Sounds of Love 01006474	Open		98.00	105
1998 Happy Anniversary 01006475	Open		300.00	330
1998 A Symbol of Pride 01006476	Open		695.00	740
1997 Heavenly Slumber 01006479	Open		185.00	210
1998 A Perfect Day 01006480	Open		495.00	510
1997 Just Resting 01006481	12/00		125.00	145
1997 Just Resting 01016481	12/00		125.00	145
1997 Little Sleepwalker 01006482	Open		110.00	120
1997 Little Sleepwalker 01016482	Open		110.00	120
1997 It's Morning Already? 01006483	Open		105.00	110
1997 It's Morning Already? 01016483	Open		105.00	110
1998 After the Show 01006484	12/00		350.00	375
1998 In Admiration 01006485	12/00		370.00	400
1998 Posing For a Portrait 01006486	12/00		380.00	410
1998 New Shoes 01006487	Open		150.00	170
1998 Gone Shopping 01006488	Open		150.00	185
1998 Your Special Angel 01006492	Open		92.00	95
1998 Filled With Joy 01006493	Open		92.00	95
1998 Onward and Upward 01006494	Open		170.00	170

YEAR ISSUE	EDITION LIMIT	YEAR RETD.	ISSUE PRICE	*QUOTE U.S.$
1998 The Road To Success 01006495	Open		155.00	170
1998 A Child's Prayer 01006496	Open		89.00	90
1998 Sleepy Time 01006497	Open		89.00	90
1998 Heavenly Musician 01006498	Closed	1999	100.00	100
1998 White Swan with Flowers 01006499	Open		110.00	110
1998 Jolly Santa 01006500	Closed	1998	180.00	180-230
1999 Please Come Home! 01006502	Open		695.00	750
1998 My Little Treasure 01006503	Open		295.00	350
1998 Daddy's Blessing 01006504	Open		340.00	350
1998 On The Farm 01006505	12/00		325.00	345
1998 Guess Who? 01006506	12/00		430.00	490
1998 Pierrot's Proposal 01006508	Open		1350.00	1600
1998 King Balthasar 01006509	Closed	1999	75.00	75-90
1998 An Unexpected Gift 01006510	12/00		260.00	265
1998 A Birthday Surprise 01006511	12/00		230.00	230
1998 How Skillful! 01006517	Open		390.00	395
1998 A Lovely Thought 01006518	12/00		580.00	580
1998 Love's Tender Tokens 01006521	Open		895.00	925
1998 Through The Clouds 01006522	Open		440.00	450
1998 Flying High 01006523	12/00		635.00	635
1998 Up And Away 01006524	Open		560.00	560
1998 Hindu Dancer 01006527	12/00		700.00	795
1998 Little Angel with Lyre 01006528	Open		120.00	120
1998 Little Angel with Violin 01006529	Open		120.00	120
1998 Little Angel with Tambourine 01006530	Open		120.00	120
1998 A New Life 01006531	12/00		490.00	530
1998 A Christmas Song 01006532	12/00		198.00	200
1998 The Christmas Caroler 01006533	12/00		175.00	175
1998 The Spirit of Christmas 01006534	12/00		198.00	200
1998 Cozy Companions 01006540	Open		195.00	200
1998 Bedtime Buddies 01006541	Open		195.00	200
1998 A Stroll In The Sun 01006542	Open		450.00	500
1998 On Our Way 01006544	Open		340.00	375
2000 On The Boulevard 01006545	Open		585.00	585
1998 Baby Boy Lamb 01006546	12/00		105.00	120
1998 Baby Girl Lamb 01006547	12/00		105.00	120
1998 Love Poems 01006548	Open		470.00	495
1998 Naptime Friends 01006549	Open		200.00	215
1998 Shhh...They're Sleeping 01006550	Open		200.00	215
1998 Pretty Posies 01006551	Open		180.00	180
1998 Pretty Pinwheel 01006552	Open		145.00	150
1998 Grandparent's Joy 01006553	12/00		645.00	700
1999 Treasures of the Heart 01006554	Open		215.00	215
1999 Springtime Scent 01006555	Open		255.00	255
1998 Playful Poodle 01006557	Open		579.00	630
1998 Great Dane 01006558	12/00		890.00	935
1999 A Wish For Love 01006562	Open		1875.00	1875
1999 A Day's Work 01006563	Open		615.00	615
1998 Gabriel The Archangel 01006565	12/00		475.00	475
1999 Want A Lift? 01006564	Open		515.00	515
1999 Dreamy Kitten 01006567	Open		250.00	255
1999 Kitten Patrol 01006568	Open		180.00	180
1999 The Milky Way 01006569 (Millennium Collection)	12/00		725.00	750
1999 New Horizons 01006570 (Millennium Collection)	12/00		560.00	560
2000 Rebirth 01006571 (Millennium Collection)	12/00		1270.00	1270
1999 In Touch With Nature 01006572	Open		625.00	625
1998 Parading Donkey 01006573	12/00		220.00	275
2000 Take Me Home! 01006574	Open		295.00	295
1999 A Gift From Santa 01006575	Closed	1999	200.00	170-220
1999 Autumn Romance 01006576	Open		345.00	375
2000 Afternoon Snack 01006577	Open		335.00	335
1999 Graceful Tune 01006578	Open		480.00	480
1999 Petals of Peace 01006579	Open		350.00	350
1998 Nightime Blessing 01006581	Open		136.00	160
1998 Bless Us All 01006582	Open		170.00	195
1998 Heaven's Lullabye 01006583	Open		186.00	210
1998 Sunday Prayer 01006584	Open		200.00	230
1999 Endless Love 01006585	Open		175.00	175
1998 Angelic Light Candleholder 01006586	Open		198.00	250
1998 Morning Calm 01006589	Open		130.00	130
1999 Elegant Trio 01006591	Open		675.00	675
1999 An Expression of Love 01006592	Open		295.00	295
1999 My Bar Mitzvah 01006593	Open		345.00	345
1999 A Night Out 01006594	Open		135.00	135
1999 On The Runway 01006595	Open		135.00	135
2000 Cupid's Arrow 01006596	Open		230.00	230
1999 Declaration of Love 01006597	Open		550.00	550
1999 The Enchanted Forest 01006598	Open		440.00	440
1999 Bosom Buddies 01006599	Open		235.00	235
1999 Like Father, Like Son 01006609	Open		440.00	440
1999 Faithful Companion 01006610	Open		675.00	675
1999 A Flight of Fantasy 01006611	Open		490.00	490
1999 Heaven's Gift (Boy) 01006612	Open		135.00	135
1999 Heaven's Gift (Boy-blank card) 01006613	Open		135.00	135
1999 Kitty Surprise 01006616	Open		280.00	280
1999 Puppy Surprise 01006617	Open		280.00	280
1999 Fawn Surprise 01006618	Open		280.00	280
1999 Holiday Light Candleholder 01006619	Open		225.00	250
1999 A Kiss to Remember 01006620	Open		250.00	250
1999 A Sunny Afternoon 01006622	Open		675.00	675
1999 The Master Chef 01006625	Open		240.00	240
1999 Heaven's Gift (Girl) 01006626	Open		135.00	135
1999 Heaven's Gift (Girl-blank card) 01006627	Open		135.00	135
1999 Adagio 01006628	Open		160.00	160
1999 Allegro 01006629	Open		160.00	160
1999 A Little Romance 01006630	Open		695.00	695
1999 Sweet Mary 01006631	Open		220.00	220

402 Collectors' Information Bureau

*Quotes have been rounded up to nearest dollar

YEAR ISSUE	EDITION LIMIT	YEAR RETD.	ISSUE PRICE	*QUOTE U.S.$
1999 A Birthday Kiss 01006632	Open		575.00	575
1999 Sancho 01006633	Open		255.00	255
1999 A Mother's Love 01006634	Open		335.00	335
1999 My Pretty Puppy 01006635	Open		295.00	295
1999 A Quiet Evening 01006638	Open		495.00	495
1999 Sunday Stroll 01006639	Open		925.00	925
1999 Little Explorer 01006640	12/00		430.00	430
1999 The Flamingos 01006641	Open		495.00	495
2000 Little Stowaway 01006642	Open		155.00	155
2000 Lakeside Daydream 01006644	Open		495.00	495
2000 Lillypad Love 01006645	Open		495.00	495
1999 Floral Path 01006646	Open		495.00	495
1999 Wildflowers 01006647	Open		525.00	525
2000 Flowers in Bloom 01006648	Open		545.00	545
2000 Allegory of Youth 01006649	Open		635.00	635
2000 Quinceañera 01006650	Open		450.00	450
2000 Wings of Fantasy 01006651	Open		775.00	775
2000 Kitty Care 01006652	Open		255.00	255
2000 Elegance on Ice 01006653	Open		365.00	365
2000 On Shore Leave 01006654	Open		285.00	285
2000 On Shore Leave 01016654	Open		285.00	285
2000 Cocktail Party 01006655	Open		265.00	265
2000 Cocktail Party 01016655	Open		265.00	265
2000 Tender Dreams 01006656	Open		150.00	150
2000 Tender Dreams 01016656	Open		150.00	150
2000 Santa's List 01016657	Open		210.00	210
2000 Morning Song 01006658	Open		885.00	885
2000 Today's Lesson 01006659	Open		265.00	265
2000 Let's Fly Away 01006665	Open		155.00	155
2000 Christmas is Here! 01006670	Open		495.00	495
2000 Ringing in the Season 01006671	Open		245.00	245
2000 I Love Christmas! 01006672	Open		245.00	245
2000 Thank You Santa! 01006674	Open		335.00	335
2000 Dreidel with Dove 01006678	Open		95.00	95
2000 Dreidel 01006679	Open		115.00	115
2000 Ocean Offering 01006682	Open		470.00	470
2000 Romance 01006683	Open		195.00	195
2000 Dreams 01006684	Open		195.00	195
2000 Happiness 01006685	Open		195.00	195
2000 Sweet Sixteen 01006687	Open		450.00	450
2000 Looking Pretty 0100688	Open		245.00	245
2000 A Perfect Drive 0100689	Open		335.00	335
2000 A Perfect Drive 0101689	Open		335.00	335
2000 Rosy Posey 01006690	Open		300.00	300
2000 Oopsy Daisy 010066991	Open		300.00	300
2000 Computing Companions 01006692	Open		290.00	290
2000 Programming Pals 01006693	Open		290.00	290
2000 Petals of Hope 01006701	Open		575.00	575
2000 Nature's Observer 01006702	Open		160.00	160
2000 From Nature's Palette 01006703	Open		140.00	140
2000 Love's Embrace 01006704	12/00		485.00	485
2000 One For You, One For Me 01006705	Open		370.00	370
2000 Menorah 01006706	Open		325.00	325
2000 Peace and Liberty 01006707	Open		1500.00	1500
2000 Serene Moment 01006708	Open		585.00	585
2000 Pensive Traveler 01006709	Open		400.00	400
2000 Comforting Dreams 01006710	Open		150.00	150
2000 Comforting Dreams 01016710	Open		150.00	150
2000 Lady in Love 01016712	Open		330.00	330
2000 An Embroidery Lesson 01016713	Open		545.00	545
2000 A Christmas Duet 01016714	Open		315.00	315
2000 Dragon with Base 01006715	Open		395.00	395
2000 Underwater Explorers 01006742	Open		655.00	655
2000 An Angel's Wish 01006788	Open		125.00	125
2000 An Angel's Song 01006789	Open		125.00	125
2000 A Child's Prayer w/Musical Base 71070036	Open		125.00	125
2000 Heavenly Slumber w/Musical Base 71070037	Open		245.00	245
2000 Heaven's Lullaby w/Musical Base 71070038	Open		245.00	245
1992 Special Torch L7513G	Closed	1997	165.00	175-225
1992 Special Champion L7514G	Closed	1997	165.00	175-196
1992 Special Pride L7515G	Closed	1997	165.00	175-195
1985 Lladró Plaque L7116	Open		17.50	18
1985 Lladró Plaque L7118	Closed	N/A	17.00	18
1993 Courage L7522G	Closed	1997	195.00	235-250
1994 Dr. Martin Luther King, Jr. L7528G	Open		345.00	375
1994 Doc 7533	Closed	1998	195.00	195-375
1995 Dopey 7534	Closed	1998	175.00	175-350
1995 Sneezy 7535	Closed	1998	175.00	225-450
1994 Bashful 7536	Closed	1998	175.00	175-395
1994 Happy 7537	Closed	1998	195.00	295-375
1994 Grumpy 7538	Closed	1998	175.00	250-450
1994 Sleepy 7539	Closed	1998	175.00	175-375
1994 Spike L7543G	Closed	1998	95.00	105-165
1994 Brutus L7544G	Closed	1998	125.00	140-210
1994 Rocky L7545G	Closed	1998	110.00	120-175
1994 Stretch L7546G	Closed	1998	125.00	140-195
1994 Rex L7547G	Closed	1998	125.00	140-210
1995 16th Century Globe Paperweight L7551	Open		105.00	105
1994 Snow White L7555G (Disney-back stamp Theme Park issue)	Closed	N/A	295.00	545-675
1994 Snow White L7555G	Closed	1998	295.00	295-475
1995 Snow White Wishing Well L7558	Closed	1998	1500.00	1500-1800
2000 Heaven's Gift (Boy-2000 card) 01007586	12/00		140.00	140
2000 Heaven's Gift (It's a Boy) 01007587	Open		140.00	140
2000 Heaven's Gift (Girl-2000 card) 01007588	12/00		140.00	140
2000 Heaven's Gift (It's a Girl) 01007589	Open		140.00	140
1989 Starting Forward/Lolo L7605G	Open		190.00	190
1996 By My Side L7645	Closed	1999	250.00	250
1996 Chess Board L8036	Open		145.00	145

Lladró Limited Edition Egg Series - Lladró

YEAR ISSUE	EDITION LIMIT	YEAR RETD.	ISSUE PRICE	*QUOTE U.S.$
1993 1993 Limited Edition Egg L6083M	Closed	1993	145.00	250-350
1994 1994 Limited Edition Egg L7532M	Closed	1994	150.00	150-250
1995 1995 Limited Edition Egg L7548M	Closed	1995	150.00	175-195
1996 1996 Limited Edition Egg L7550M	Closed	1996	155.00	136-175
1997 1997 Limited Edition Egg L7552M	Closed	1997	155.00	155-160
1998 Garden Stroll 01016590	Closed	1998	150.00	150
2000 Parsian Afternoon 01016698	Yr.Iss.		150.00	150

The Night Before Christmas - Lladró

YEAR ISSUE	EDITION LIMIT	YEAR RETD.	ISSUE PRICE	*QUOTE U.S.$
1999 Visions of Sugarplums 01006667	Open		260.00	260
1999 Up The Chimney He Rose 01006668	Open		370.00	370
1999 A Stocking For Kitty 01006669	Open		235.00	235
1999 Cookies For Santa 01006675	Open		325.00	325

Norman Rockwell Collection - Rockwell-Inspired

YEAR ISSUE	EDITION LIMIT	YEAR RETD.	ISSUE PRICE	*QUOTE U.S.$
1982 Lladró Love Letter L1406 (RL-400G)	5,000	N/A	650.00	750-950
1982 Summer Stock L1407 (RL-401G)	5,000	N/A	750.00	850-900
1982 Practice Makes Perfect L1408 (RL-402G)	5,000	N/A	725.00	725-995
1982 Young Love L1409 (RL-403G)	5,000	N/A	450.00	1200
1982 Daydreamer L1411 (RL-404G)	5,000	N/A	450.00	1100-1500
1982 Court Jester L1405 (RL-405G)	5,000	N/A	600.00	1050-1250
1982 Springtime L1410 (RL-406G)	5,000	N/A	450.00	1200-1400

Lowell Davis Farm Club

Lowell Davis Farm Club - L. Davis

YEAR ISSUE	EDITION LIMIT	YEAR RETD.	ISSUE PRICE	*QUOTE U.S.$
1985 The Bride 221001 / 20993	Yr.Iss.	1985	45.00	400-553
1987 The Party's Over 221002 / 20994	Yr.Iss.	1987	50.00	260
1988 Chow Time 221003 / 20995	Yr.Iss.	1988	55.00	59-111
1989 Can't Wait 221004 / 20996	Yr.Iss.	1989	75.00	59-75
1990 Pit Stop 221005 / 20997	Yr.Iss.	1990	75.00	150-195
1991 Arrival Of Stanley 221006 / 20998	Yr.Iss.	1991	100.00	85-100
1991 Don't Pick The Flowers 221007 / 21007	Yr.Iss.	1991	100.00	72-100
1992 Hog Wild	Yr.Iss.	1992	100.00	100-130
1992 Check's in the Mail	Yr.Iss.	1992	100.00	120-130
1993 The Survivor 25371	Yr.Iss.	1993	70.00	70-130
1994 Summer Days	Yr.Iss.	1994	100.00	130-195
1995 Dutch Treat	Yr.Iss.	1995	100.00	100
1995 Free Kittens	Yr.Iss.	1995	40.00	40
1996 Sunnyside Up	Yr.Iss.	1997	55.00	55
1997 Grandpa's Ole Tom	Yr.Iss.	1997	80.00	70-80

Lowell Davis Farm Club Renewal Figurine - L. Davis

YEAR ISSUE	EDITION LIMIT	YEAR RETD.	ISSUE PRICE	*QUOTE U.S.$
1986 Thirsty? 892050 / 92050	Yr.Iss.	1987	Gift	46-78
1987 Cackle Berries 892051 / 92051	Yr.Iss.	1989	Gift	78-85
1988 Ice Cream Churn 892052 / 92052	Yr.Iss.	1990	Gift	39-78
1990 Not A Sharing Soul 892053 / 92053	Yr.Iss.	1991	Gift	50-72
1991 New Arrival 892054 / 92054	Yr.Iss.	1992	Gift	30-78
1992 Garden Toad 92055	Yr.Iss.	1993	Gift	30-78
1993 Luke 12:6 25372	Yr.Iss.	1994	Gift	40-78
1994 Feathering Her Nest	Yr.Iss.	1995	Gift	40-50
1995 After the Rain	Yr.Iss.	1996	Gift	40-50
1996 A Gift For You	Retrd.	1997	Gift	25
1997 One in the Hand 97011	Retrd.	1998	Gift	N/A

Davis Cat Tales Figurines - L. Davis

YEAR ISSUE	EDITION LIMIT	YEAR RETD.	ISSUE PRICE	*QUOTE U.S.$
1982 Company's Coming 25205	Closed	1986	60.00	125
1982 Flew the Coop 25207	Closed	1986	60.00	98-125
1982 On the Move 25206	Closed	1986	70.00	650
1982 Right Church, Wrong Pew 25204	Closed	1986	70.00	250-325

Davis Country Christmas Figurines - L. Davis

YEAR ISSUE	EDITION LIMIT	YEAR RETD.	ISSUE PRICE	*QUOTE U.S.$
1983 Hooker at Mailbox with Presents 23550	Closed	1984	80.00	750
1984 Country Christmas 23551	Closed	1985	80.00	250-350
1985 Christmas at Fox Fire Farm 23552	Closed	1986	80.00	275
1986 Christmas at Red Oak 23553	Closed	1987	80.00	225-250
1987 Blossom's Gift 23554	Closed	1988	150.00	400-475
1988 Cutting the Family Christmas Tree 23555	Closed	1989	80.00	350
1989 Peter and the Wren 23556	Closed	1990	165.00	450
1990 Wintering Deer 23557	Closed	1991	165.00	150-165
1991 Christmas At Red Oak II 23558	Closed	1992	250.00	150-250
1992 Born on a Starry Night 23559	2,500	1993	225.00	234-254
1993 Waiting For Mr. Lowell 23606	2,500	1994	250.00	250
1994 Visions of Sugar Plums	2,500	1995	250.00	200-250
1995 Bah Humbug	2,500	1996	200.00	250-275

Davis Country Pride - L. Davis

YEAR ISSUE	EDITION LIMIT	YEAR RETD.	ISSUE PRICE	*QUOTE U.S.$
1981 Bustin' with Pride 25202	Closed	1985	100.00	250
1981 Duke's Mixture 25203	Closed	1985	100.00	450
1981 Plum Tuckered Out 25201	Closed	1985	100.00	520-585
1981 Surprise in the Cellar 25200	Closed	1985	100.00	1040-1170

Davis Friends of Mine - L. Davis

YEAR ISSUE	EDITION LIMIT	YEAR RETD.	ISSUE PRICE	*QUOTE U.S.$
1992 Cat and Jenny Wren 23633	5,000	1993	170.00	15-175
1992 Cat and Jenny Wren Mini 23634	Closed	1993	35.00	40
1989 Sun Worshippers 23620	5,000	1993	120.00	156-163
1989 Sun Worshippers Mini 23621	5,000	1993	32.50	34-40
1990 Sunday Afternoon Treat 23625	5,000	1993	120.00	130
1990 Sunday Afternoon Treat Mini 23626	Closed	1993	32.50	40-50
1991 Warm Milk 23629	Closed	1993	120.00	156-200
1991 Warm Milk Mini 23630	5,000	1993	32.50	40

Davis Little Critters - L. Davis

YEAR ISSUE	EDITION LIMIT	YEAR RETD.	ISSUE PRICE	*QUOTE U.S.$
1992 Charivari 25707	950	1993	250.00	273-345
1991 Christopher Critter 25514	1,192	1993	150.00	65-150
1992 Double Yolker 25516	Yr.Iss.	1993	70.00	75
1989 Gittin' a Nibble 25294	Closed	1993	50.00	46-75
1991 Great American Chicken Race 25500	2,500	1993	225.00	208-225
1991 Hittin' The Sack 25510	Closed	1993	70.00	70-75
1990 Home Squeezins 25504	Closed	1993	90.00	90-100
1991 Itiskit, Itasket 25511	Closed	1993	45.00	45-50
1991 Milk Mouse 25503	2,500	1993	175.00	175-182
1992 Miss Private Time 25517	Yr.Iss.	1993	35.00	35
1990 Outing With Grandpa 25502	2,500	1993	200.00	169-200
1990 Private Time 25506	Closed	1993	18.00	25-35
1990 Punkin' Pig 25505	2,500	1993	250.00	189-455
1991 Punkin' Wine 25501	Closed	1993	100.00	125
1991 Toad Strangler 25509	Closed	1993	57.00	75
1991 When Coffee Never Tasted So Good (Music box) 809225	1,250	1993	800.00	800
1991 When Coffee Never Tasted So Good 25507	1,250	1993	800.00	800
1992 A Wolf in Sheep's Clothing 25518	Yr.Iss.	1993	110.00	110

Davis Pen Pals - L. Davis

YEAR ISSUE	EDITION LIMIT	YEAR RETD.	ISSUE PRICE	*QUOTE U.S.$
1993 The Old Home Place (mini) 25801	Closed	1995	25.00	25
1993 The Old Home Place 25802	1,200	1995	200.00	200-228

Davis Promotional Figurine - L. Davis

YEAR ISSUE	EDITION LIMIT	YEAR RETD.	ISSUE PRICE	*QUOTE U.S.$
1991 Leavin' The Rat Race 225512	Yr.Iss.	1991	80.00	85-98
1992 Hen Scratch Prom 225968	Yr.Iss.	1992	90.00	82
1993 Leapin' Lizard 225969	Yr.Iss.	1993	80.00	59-80
1994 Don't Forget Me 227130	Yr.Iss.	1994	70.00	70
1995 Nasty Stuff 95103	Yr.Iss.	1995	40.00	50-75

Davis RFD America - L. Davis

YEAR ISSUE	EDITION LIMIT	YEAR RETD.	ISSUE PRICE	*QUOTE U.S.$
1984 Anybody Home 25239	Closed	1987	35.00	100
1994 Attic Antics	Closed	1995	100.00	150
1982 Baby Blossom 25227	Closed	1984	40.00	325
1982 Baby Bobs 25222	Closed	1984	47.50	200-254
1985 Barn Cats 25257	Closed	1990	39.50	90
1993 Be My Valentine 27561	Closed	1997	35.00	40
1986 Bit Off More Than He Could Chew 25279	Closed	1992	15.00	55
1979 Blossom 25032	Closed	1983	180.00	1560-1800
1993 Blossom 96846 (15th Anniversary)	Closed	1993	80.00	80
1982 Blossom and Calf 25326	Closed	1986	250.00	850
1995 Blossom's Best	750	1995	300.00	300-500
1987 Bottoms Up 25270	Closed	1992	80.00	105-124
1989 Boy's Night Out 25339	1,500	1992	190.00	250
1982 Brand New Day 25226	Closed	1984	23.50	169-228
1979 Broken Dreams 25035	Closed	1983	165.00	1200-1300
1993 Broken Dreams 96847 (15th Anniversary)	Closed	1993	80.00	80
1988 Brothers 25286	Closed	1990	55.00	65-111
1984 Catnapping Too? 25247	Closed	1991	70.00	104-111
1987 Chicken Thief 25338	Closed	1988	200.00	325-375
1983 City Slicker 25329	Closed	1990	150.00	270
1991 Cock Of The Walk 25347	2,500	1993	300.00	300-423
1986 Comfy? 25273	Closed	1997	40.00	80
1994 Companion pc. And Down the Hatch	Closed	1994	135.00	145
1994 Companion pc. Open The Lid	Closed	1994	135.00	145
1989 Coon Capers 25291	Closed	1997	67.50	90
1990 Corn Crib Mouse 25295	Closed	1993	35.00	31-45
1983 Counting the Days 25233	Closed	1992	40.00	60
1981 Country Boy 25213	Closed	1984	37.50	375-390
1985 Country Cousins 25266	Closed	1995	42.50	90
1982 Country Crook 25280	Closed	1984	37.50	330
1985 Country Crooner 25256	Closed	1995	25.00	50
1984 Country Kitty 25246	Closed	1987	52.00	65-125
1979 Country Road 25030	Closed	1983	100.00	675
1993 Country Road 96842 (15th Anniversary)	Closed	1993	65.00	65
1984 Courtin' 25220	Closed	1986	45.00	125
1980 Creek Bank Bandit 25038	Closed	1985	37.50	400-455
1995 Cussin' Up a Storm	Closed	1995	45.00	45
1993 Don't Open Till Christmas 27562	Closed	1997	35.00	35
1992 Don't Play With Fire 25319	Closed	1997	120.00	120-189
1985 Don't Play With Your Food 25258	Closed	1992	28.50	36-50
1981 Double Trouble 25211	Closed	1984	35.00	200-475
1981 Dry as a Bone 25216	Closed	1984	45.00	300-325
1993 Dry Hole 25374	Closed	1995	30.00	35
1987 Easy Pickins 25269	Closed	1990	45.00	52-85
1993 End of the Trail 81000A	100	1993	100.00	332
1983 Fair Weather Friend 25236	Closed	1987	25.00	85
1983 False Alarm 25237	Closed	1985	65.00	185
1989 Family Outing 25289	Closed	1995	45.00	60
1997 Farm Club Sign	Open		40.00	40
1996 Farm Club Sign	Open		40.00	40
1994 Favorite Sport 25381	Closed	1995	230.00	230
1985 Feelin' His Oats 25275	1,500	1990	150.00	273-300
1990 Finder's Keepers 25299	Closed	1997	39.50	39-45
1991 First Offense 25304	Closed	1993	70.00	80
1994 First Outing	Closed	1997	65.00	75
1988 Fleas 25272	Closed	1997	20.00	23-30
1980 Forbidden Fruit 25022	Closed	1985	25.00	90-150
1990 Foreplay 25300	Closed	1993	59.50	80-128
1979 Fowl Play 25033	Closed	1983	100.00	275-325
1993 Fowl Play 96845 (15th Anniversary)	Closed	1993	60.00	60
1992 Free Lunch 25321	Closed	1997	85.00	85
1993 The Freeloaders 95042	1,250	1995	230.00	221-228
1985 Furs Gonna Fly 25335	1,500	1989	145.00	228
1994 Get Well 96902	Closed	1997	35.00	40
1987 Glutton for Punishment 25268	Closed	1991	95.00	160
1988 Goldie and Her Peeps 25283	Closed	1991	25.00	29-37
1984 Gonna Pay for His Sins 25243	Closed	1989	27.50	46-55
1980 Good, Clean Fun 25020	Closed	1989	40.00	78-143
1984 Gossips 25248	Closed	1987	110.00	250-265
1992 The Grass is Always Greener 25367	Closed	1995	195.00	195

YEAR ISSUE	EDITION LIMIT	YEAR RETD.	ISSUE PRICE	*QUOTE U.S.$
1991 Gun Shy 25305	Closed	1993	70.00	70
1990 Hanky Panky 25298	Closed	1993	65.00	85-100
1994 Happy Anniversary 95089	Closed	1997	35.00	40
1993 Happy Birthday My Sweet 27560	Closed	1997	35.00	35-40
1988 Happy Hour 25287	Closed	1997	57.50	91-100
1983 Happy Hunting Ground 25330	Closed	1990	160.00	189-221
1984 Headed Home 25240	Closed	1991	25.00	46-59
1992 Headed South 25327	Closed	1995	45.00	45
1991 Heading For The Persimmon Grove 25306	Closed	1993	80.00	80
1994 Helpin Himself	Closed	1995	65.00	75
1983 Hi Girls, The Name's Big Jack 25328	Closed	1987	200.00	300-420
1981 Hightailing It 25214	Closed	1984	50.00	400-423
1983 His Eyes Are Bigger Than His Stomach 25332	Closed	1989	235.00	312-350
1984 His Master's Dog 25244	Closed	1988	45.00	75-150
1994 Hittin The Trail	1,250	1995	250.00	250
1985 Hog Heaven 25336	1,500	1988	165.00	350-400
1996 Homebodies	Yr.Iss.	1996	120.00	120
1992 The Honeymoon's Over 25370	1,950	1994	300.00	300-390
1995 Hook, Line & Sinker 25382	Closed	1997	35.00	35
1984 Huh? 25242	Closed	1989	40.00	72-150
1993 I'm Thankful For You 27563	Closed	1997	35.00	40
1982 Idle Hours 25230	Closed	1985	37.50	150-450
1993 If You Can't Beat Em Join Em 25379	1,750	1995	250.00	250-455
1979 Ignorance is Bliss 25031	Closed	1983	165.00	550-1000
1993 Ignorance is Bliss 96843 (15th Anniversary)	Closed	1993	75.00	75
1988 In a Pickle 25284	Closed	1995	40.00	40-50
1980 Itching Post 25037	Closed	1988	30.00	65-115
1993 King of The Mountain 25380	750	1995	500.00	400-500
1991 Kissin' Cousins 25307	Closed	1993	80.00	80
1990 The Last Straw 25301	Closed	1993	125.00	165-195
1989 Left Overs 25290	Closed	1997	90.00	95-104
1983 Licking Good 25234	Closed	1985	35.00	175-225
1990 Little Black Lamb (Baba) 25297	Closed	1993	30.00	34
1990 Long Days, Cold Nights 25344	2,500	1993	175.00	163-208
1991 Long, Hot Summer 25343	1,950	1995	250.00	250
1985 Love at First Sight 25267	Closed	1992	70.00	91-104
1992 Lowell Davis Profile 25366	Closed	1997	75.00	65
1984 Mad As A Wet Hen 25334	Closed	1986	185.00	700-800
1987 Mail Order Bride 25263	Closed	1991	150.00	163-325
1983 Makin' Tracks 25238	Closed	1989	70.00	117-143
1988 Making a Bee Line 25274	Closed	1990	75.00	72-125
1994 Mama Can Willie Stay For Supper	1,250	1995	200.00	220
1983 Mama's Prize Leghorn 25235	Closed	1988	55.00	65-135
1986 Mama? 25277	Closed	1991	15.00	46-78
1989 Meeting of Sheldon 25293	Closed	1992	120.00	125
1980 Milking Time 25023	Closed	1985	20.00	240
1988 Missouri Spring 25278	Closed	1992	115.00	130
1982 Moon Raider 25325	Closed	1986	190.00	390
1995 The Morning After 10000	Closed	1995	60.00	120-124
1989 Mother Hen 25292	Closed	1997	37.50	50
1993 Mother's Day 95088	Closed	1997	35.00	40
1982 Moving Day 25225	Closed	1984	43.50	115-250
1992 My Favorite Chores 25362	1,500	1994	750.00	750-845
1980 New Day 25025	Closed	1980	20.00	165
1989 New Friend 25288	Closed	1994	45.00	60
1993 No Hunting 25375	1,000	1995	95.00	105-150
1988 No Private Time 25316	Closed	1992	200.00	215-300
1994 Not a Happy Camper	Closed	1997	75.00	75
1994 Oh Mother What is it?	1,000	1995	250.00	250
1992 OH Sheeeit . . . 25363	Closed	1995	120.00	130
1993 Oh Where is He Now 95041	1,250	1995	250.00	250-260
1984 One for the Road 25241	Closed	1988	37.50	59-70
1987 The Orphans 25271	Closed	1992	50.00	130-260
1985 Out-of-Step 25259	Closed	1989	45.00	78-90
1985 Ozark Belle 25264	Closed	1990	35.00	65-130
1992 Ozark's Vittles 25318	Closed	1997	60.00	70
1984 Pasture Pals 25245	Closed	1990	52.00	65-91
1993 Peep Show 25376	Closed	1997	35.00	35
1988 Perfect Ten 25282	Closed	1990	95.00	124-180
1990 Piggin' Out 25345	Closed	1993	190.00	250-455
1994 Pollywogs 25617	750	1994	750.00	715-750
1984 Prairie Chorus 25333	Closed	1986	135.00	1200
1996 Proud Papa 96002	Yr.Iss.	1996	250.00	250
1981 Punkin' Seeds 25219	Closed	1984	225.00	1550-1750
1994 Qu'est - Ceque C'est?	Closed	1995	200.00	220
1985 Renoir 25261	Closed	1991	45.00	91-98
1981 Rooted Out 25217	Closed	1989	45.00	78-117
1992 Safe Haven 25320	Closed	1994	95.00	95
1988 Sawin' Logs 25260	Closed	1993	85.00	105
1981 Scallawags 25221	Closed	1987	65.00	124
1992 School Yard Dogs 25369	Closed	1994	100.00	100
1996 See Ya There 96002	Yr.Iss.	1996	330.00	330
1990 Seein' Red (Gus w/shoes) 25296	Closed	1993	35.00	47
1992 She Lay Low 25364	Closed	1995	120.00	120
1993 Sheep Sheerin Time 25388	1,200	1995	500.00	500-520
1982 A Shoe to Fill 25229	Closed	1986	37.50	150-175
1979 Slim Pickins 25034	Closed	1983	165.00	320-750
1993 Slim Pickins 96846 (15th Anniversary)	Closed	1993	75.00	85
1992 Snake Doctor 25365	Closed	1995	70.00	70
1991 Sooieee 25360	1,500	1994	350.00	358-1105
1981 Split Decision 25210	Closed	1984	45.00	195-325
1995 Sticks and Stones	Closed	1997	30.00	30
1983 Stirring Up Trouble 25331	Closed	1988	160.00	228-260
1980 Strawberry Patch 25021	Closed	1989	25.00	46-85
1982 Stray Dog 25223	Closed	1988	35.00	75-91
1981 Studio Mouse 25215	Closed	1984	60.00	360-520
1980 Sunday Afternoon 25024	Closed	1985	22.50	175-225
1993 Sweet Tooth 25373	Closed	1995	60.00	75
1982 Thinking Big 25231	Closed	1988	35.00	65-100
1985 Too Good to Waste on Kids 25262	Closed	1989	70.00	130
1982 Treed 25327	Closed	1988	155.00	300-320
1989 A Tribute to Hooker 25340	Closed	1992	180.00	124-150
1993 Trick or Treat 27565	Closed	1997	35.00	50
1990 Tricks Of The Trade 25346	Closed	1994	300.00	350-375
1987 Two in the Bush 25337	Closed	1988	150.00	300-320
1994 Two Timer	Closed	1995	95.00	95
1982 Two's Company 25224	Closed	1986	43.50	215
1981 Under the Weather 25212	Closed	1991	25.00	52-59
1995 Uninvited Caller	Closed	1995	35.00	35
1981 Up To No Good 25218	Closed	1984	200.00	450-850
1982 Waiting for His Master 25281	Closed	1986	50.00	300
1994 Warmin' Their Buns	1,250	1995	270.00	225-270
1991 Washed Ashore 25308	Closed	1993	70.00	60-70
1982 When Mama Gets Mad 25228	Closed	1986	37.50	200-350
1987 When the Cat's Away 25276	Closed	1990	40.00	60
1988 When Three Foot's a Mile 25315	Closed	1991	230.00	286
1980 Wilbur 25029	Closed	1985	100.00	585-715
1985 Will You Still Respect Me in the Morning 25265	Closed	1993	35.00	75
1988 Wintering Lamb 25317	Closed	1990	200.00	234-254
1988 Wishful Thinking 25285	Closed	1990	55.00	70
1983 Woman's Work 25232	Closed	1989	35.00	60-80
1989 Woodscolt 25342	Closed	1992	300.00	358-481
1997 You Snooze, You Lose	Open		120.00	120
1993 You're a Basket Full of Fun 27564	Open		35.00	35

Davis Route 66 - L. Davis

YEAR ISSUE	EDITION LIMIT	YEAR RETD.	ISSUE PRICE	*QUOTE U.S.$
1992 Fresh Squeezed? (w/ wooden base) 25609	350	1995	600.00	700
1992 Fresh Squeezed? 25608	2,500	1995	450.00	390-494
1992 Going To Grandma's 25619	Closed	1995	80.00	80
1993 Home For Christmas 25621	Closed	1995	80.00	80
1991 Just Check The Air 25600	350	1995	700.00	750
1991 Just Check The Air 25603	2,500	1995	550.00	410-423
1993 Kickin' Himself 25622	Closed	1995	80.00	80
1991 Little Bit Of Shade 25602	Closed	1995	100.00	100
1991 Nel's Diner 25601	350	1995	700.00	700
1991 Nel's Diner 25604	2,500	1995	550.00	390-520
1992 Quiet Day at Maple Grove 25618	Closed	1995	130.00	130
1992 Relief 25605	Closed	1995	80.00	80
1993 Summer Days 25607	Yr.Iss.	1995	100.00	100
1992 Welcome Mat (w/ wooden base) 25606	1,500	1995	400.00	400-455
1992 What Are Pals For? 25620	Closed	1995	100.00	100

Davis Special Edition Figurines - L. Davis

YEAR ISSUE	EDITION LIMIT	YEAR RETD.	ISSUE PRICE	*QUOTE U.S.$
1983 The Critics 23600	Closed	1986	400.00	1200-1600
1989 From A Friend To A Friend 23602	1,200	1990	750.00	780-1200
1985 Home from Market 23601	Closed	1988	400.00	688-1200
1992 Last Laff 23604	1,200	1994	900.00	650-900
1990 What Rat Race? 23603	1,200	1994	800.00	540-910

Davis Uncle Remus - L. Davis

YEAR ISSUE	EDITION LIMIT	YEAR RETD.	ISSUE PRICE	*QUOTE U.S.$
1981 Brer Bear 25251	Closed	1984	80.00	1000-1200
1981 Brer Coyote 25255	Closed	1984	80.00	500
1981 Brer Fox 25250	Closed	1984	70.00	513-900
1981 Brer Rabbit 25252	Closed	1984	85.00	2000
1981 Brer Weasel 25254	Closed	1984	80.00	384-700
1981 Brer Wolf 25253	Closed	1984	85.00	514

Lucy & Me/Enesco Group, Inc.

Christmas Lucy & Me - L. Riggs

YEAR ISSUE	EDITION LIMIT	YEAR RETD.	ISSUE PRICE	*QUOTE U.S.$
1985 Bear Holding Candle 16845	Retrd.	1989	9.00	39
1979 Bear Holding Candle E-2817	Retrd.	1983	9.00	52
1985 Bear Holding Candy Canes 16845	Retrd.	1989	9.00	27
1984 Bear Holding Doll & Lollipop E-5411	Retrd.	1989	10.00	27
1984 Bear Holding Jack in Box E-5411	Retrd.	1989	10.00	25
1984 Bear Holding Rocking Horse E-5411	Retrd.	1989	10.00	27
1985 Bear Holding Tree 16845	Retrd.	1989	9.00	25
1983 Bear Mailing Letter to Santa E-0555	Retrd.	1986	9.00	63
1983 Boy Bear Pulls Girl Bear on Sled E-0557	Retrd.	1989	15.00	30-63
1987 Boy in Blue Coat Pulling Tree in Wagon 110477	Retrd.	1989	12.00	39
1989 A Christmas Carol - Scrooge 222100	Yr.Iss.	1989	10.00	39
1987 Clown Juggler 110299	Retrd.	1989	10.00	33
1988 Couple Kissing Under the Mistletoe 510319	Retrd.	1989	15.00	31-45
1982 Dad E-5417	Retrd.	1989	9.00	N/A
1986 Dad Sleeping in Chair 105961	Retrd.	1989	10.00	39
1983 Girl Holding Teddy and Package E-0556	Retrd.	1986	10.00	25-27
1987 Girl in Nightgown Holds Stocking 110337	Retrd.	1989	10.00	30
1985 Girl Kneeling Next to Doll House 16675	Retrd.	1989	12.00	39
1987 Girl w/ Nightie and Cap 110310	Retrd.	1989	9.00	33
1989 Gnome Skiing 222062	Retrd.	1990	9.00	27
1982 Grandma E-5417	Retrd.	1989	9.00	39
1982 Grandpa E-5417	Retrd.	1989	9.00	34
1982 Mom E-5417	Retrd.	1989	9.00	N/A
1987 Mrs. Bear Strings Cranberry Garland 110957	Retrd.	1989	N/A	27
1988 Nutcracker Clara 510246	Retrd.	1989	11.00	39
1990 Red Skier 228141	Retrd.	1994	12.00	33
1985 Santa w/List of Good Girls and Boys 16640	Retrd.	1989	10.00	30-39
1987 Shoemaker Repairs Shoes 110485	Retrd.	1988	50.00	33-39
1989 Skier in Yellow & Blue Outfit 222038	Retrd.	1990	10.00	20
1986 Three Bears on a Toboggan 104981	Retrd.	N/A	20.00	57
1985 Tumbling Santa Claus (3 poses) 16039	Retrd.	1989	10.00	39-45
1987 Two Bears Dressed as Reindeer, set/2 110639	Retrd.	1990	10.00	33

Lucy & Me "Childs" - L. Riggs

YEAR ISSUE	EDITION LIMIT	YEAR RETD.	ISSUE PRICE	*QUOTE U.S.$
1986 Sunday's Child - Girl Goes to Church 107824	Retrd.	1989	11.00	40
1986 Monday's Child - Girl in Long Dress & Hat 107751	Retrd.	1989	11.00	N/A
1986 Tuesday's Child - Girl Ballerina 107778	Retrd.	1989	11.00	40
1986 Wednesday's Child - Girl w/ Handkerchief 107786	Retrd.	1989	11.00	40
1986 Thursday's Child - Girl Dressed in Hat/Coat 107794	Retrd.	1989	11.00	27
1986 Friday's Child - Bear Girl Holding Baby 107808	Retrd.	1989	11.00	40
1986 Saturday's Child - Girl as Nurse 107816	Retrd.	1989	11.00	27

Lucy & Me - L. Riggs

YEAR ISSUE	EDITION LIMIT	YEAR RETD.	ISSUE PRICE	*QUOTE U.S.$
1986 Angel Kissing 105767	Retrd.	1989	20.00	27
1985 Baby Boy Nap on Pillow 102156	Retrd.	1989	9.00	30
1988 Baby on Goose 114081	Retrd.	1988	9.50	33
1982 Baby w/Bear E-9341	Retrd.	1990	10.00	25
1987 Bear Dressed as Bunny with Carrot 111619	Retrd.	1990	11.00	39
1979 Bear in Bunny Ears w/blue Basket E-4731	Retrd.	1985	N/A	39
1985 Bear in Duck Inner Tube 101575	Retrd.	1989	8.00	45
1984 Bear in Red and White Clown Jester Suit 10170	Retrd.	1989	11.00	39
1981 Bear on Rocking Horse E-7135	Retrd.	1987	15.00	153
1986 Bear on Sandpile 107107	Retrd.	1989	9.50	39
1987 Bear Sitting w/honey Pot 112992	Retrd.	1989	8.00	20
1985 Bear w/Broken Leg 101621	Retrd.	1988	9.00	39
1985 Boy as Easter Egg 101370	Retrd.	1990	13.00	27
1983 Boy Bowler E-3079	Retrd.	1990	10.50	33
1979 Boy Gardener in Blue E4727	Retrd.	1985	2.30	27
1986 Boy w/Geese 106585	Retrd.	1989	9.50	39
1986 Boy w/Pail & Shovel 107107	Retrd.	1989	9.50	39
1987 Boy with Pacifier 114227	Retrd.	1991	9.50	33
1987 Canadian Bear as a Mountie 510491	Retrd.	1991	9.50	29
1990 Cavebears, Boy & Girl, set/2 228184	Retrd.	N/A	10.00	40
1985 Cookie Cutter Bear Skating 19618	Retrd.	1987	N/A	65
1989 Cow 224596	Retrd.	1992	10.00	15
1986 Dad and Son Fishing 104337	Retrd.	1989	10.00	33
1985 Dad w/Cub on Shoulders 101613	Retrd.	1991	15.00	30-39
1985 Dancing Bears in Irish Outfits 102032	Retrd.	1989	7.50	45
1986 Devil Kissing 105767	Retrd.	1989	20.00	27
1990 Elf Hammering Toy 568635	Retrd.	1992	33.30	69
1986 Family Going to Church (set/4) 106267	Retrd.	1992	11.00	65
1984 Fireman 11940	Retrd.	1989	11.00	20
1984 Four Seated Bears & Picnic Basket, set/6 12912	Retrd.	1988	N/A	123
1988 Gardener w/Cart 509353	Retrd.	1991	15.00	27
1987 Gardener w/Rake 111856	Retrd.	1990	11.00	39
1989 Gardner (w/o Flower Pot) 223659	Retrd.	1992	N/A	15
1987 German Bear w/ Bear Stein 510505	Retrd.	1991	9.50	23-33
1983 Get Well Bear E-3079	Retrd.	1990	10.50	33
1986 Girl Getting Ready For Bed 106941	Retrd.	1989	9.50	39
1984 Girl Pilgrim E-5414	Retrd.	1989	N/A	33
1987 Girl w/Coffee Pot 111635	Retrd.	1989	8.00	39
1986 Girl w/Yellow Dress w/Steno Pad 106968	Retrd.	1989	8.00	23
1987 Girl with Pacifier 114227	Retrd.	1991	9.50	27
1986 Graduate on School Books 106038	Retrd.	1991	10.00	25
1981 Hairdresser E-7137	Retrd.	1985	10.00	160
1981 Hugging Couple w/Valentine Hearts E-4729	Retrd.	1988	8.92	45-57
1987 John Hancock Bear 109681	Retrd.	1989	9.50	27
1988 Kissing Couple E-3197	Retrd.	1985	N/A	45
1989 Lamaze Couple, set/2 224537	Retrd.	N/A	20.00	45
1988 Little Red Riding Hood 510971	Retrd.	1989	9.50	30-39
1987 Mexican Bear in Sombrero Serape 510513	Retrd.	1991	9.50	33
1988 Mom w/Baby Diaper and Bag 114057	Retrd.	1988	10.00	39
1987 Mother and Child Carrying Laundry 111619	Retrd.	1989	11.00	39
1987 Party Animal 113018	Retrd.	1989	8.00	27
1986 Pilot with Plane 107018	Retrd.	1988	9.50	20-27
1985 Pregnant Mom (yellow) w/Baby Care Book (3 pc.) 101605	Retrd.	1992	12.00	27
1988 Queen of Hearts With Tarts 111791	Retrd.	1992	12.00	18
1988 Roller-skating Waitress 510602	Retrd.	1990	10.00	30-39
1979 Sailor Bear E3128	Retrd.	1989	9.00	27
1984 Sailor Bear w/Lollipop 11886	Retrd.	1988	10.50	33
1988 Sitting Bear w/Daisy 111953	Retrd.	1988	20.00	45
1984 Sitting Bear w/Heart 10715	Retrd.	1988	12.50	27
1986 Teddy Bear University 109541	Retrd.	1992	9.50	33
1982 Tennis Girl E-9342	Retrd.	1989	10.50	33
1983 Thank You Bear E-3079	Retrd.	1990	10.50	33
1982 Three Easter Bears E-9345	Retrd.	1990	N/A	75-93
1988 Turkey 510327	Retrd.	N/A	10.00	15
1985 Two Bears Playing Hearts, set/2 111538	Retrd.	1989	11.00	25-35
1986 Two Clowns Juggling Hearts 105775	Retrd.	1991	12.00	33
1979 Two Moms Hugging Cubs E-4733	Retrd.	1988	15.00	30-39
1982 Two Tumbling Bears E-8676	Retrd.	1990	10.00	45
1986 Vampire 103438	Retrd.	1989	10.00	25-33
1979 Wedding Couple E-4728	Retrd.	N/A	14.00	27

*Quotes have been rounded up to nearest dollar

YEAR ISSUE	EDITION LIMIT	YEAR RETD.	ISSUE PRICE	*QUOTE U.S.$
1986 Woman Holding Baby, set/2 105988	Retrd.	1988	10.00	66

Lucy & Me Alice in Wonderland - L. Riggs

YEAR ISSUE	EDITION LIMIT	YEAR RETD.	ISSUE PRICE	*QUOTE U.S.$
1988 Alice in Wonderland w/White Rabbit 510661	Retrd.	1990	35.00	123
1987 Alice in Wonderland Bear 111473	Retrd.	1989	9.00	25
1987 Mad Hatter Bear 111481	Retrd.	1989	9.00	25
1987 Tweedle-dee Bear 111503	Retrd.	1989	9.00	25
1987 Tweedle-dum Bear 111503	Retrd.	1989	9.00	25
1987 White Rabbit 111511	Retrd.	1989	9.50	25
1987 Two Bears Playing Cards 111538	Retrd.	1989	11.00	25-31
1987 March Hare 111545	Retrd.	1989	11.50	25

Lucy & Me Goldilocks - L. Riggs

YEAR ISSUE	EDITION LIMIT	YEAR RETD.	ISSUE PRICE	*QUOTE U.S.$
1986 Lucylocks Sleeping in Baby Bear's Cradle 107840	Retrd.	1989	40.00	123
1986 Lucylocks - Bear as Goldilocks 106976	Retrd.	1989	9.50	27
1986 3 Bears -Mama, Papa, Baby Table/Porridge, set/4 107034	Retrd.	1989	30.00	N/A
1986 3 Bears -Mama 107034	Retrd.	1989	30.00	27
1986 3 Bears -Papa 107034	Retrd.	1989	30.00	27
1986 3 Bears -Table 107034	Retrd.	1989	30.00	27
1986 3 Bears -Baby 107034	Retrd.	1989	30.00	27
1986 Lucylocks in Baby Bear's Chair 107875	Retrd.	1989	13.50	27
1986 Lucylocks in Mama Bear's Chair 107883	Retrd.	1989	16.50	27
1986 Lucylocks in Papa Bear's Chair 107891	Retrd.	1989	16.50	27

Margaret Furlong Designs

Home Décor - M. Furlong

YEAR ISSUE	EDITION LIMIT	YEAR RETD.	ISSUE PRICE	*QUOTE U.S.$
2000 Sea Urchin Tea Light Holder	Open		24.00	24
2000 Shell & Sea Horse Wall Sconce	Open		25.00	25
2000 Shell Button Wall Sconce	Open		20.00	20
2000 True Nautilus Vase	Open		36.00	36
2000 Urchin & Sea Horse Wall Sconce	Open		25.00	25

Home Décor/Wedding - M. Furlong

YEAR ISSUE	EDITION LIMIT	YEAR RETD.	ISSUE PRICE	*QUOTE U.S.$
1999 3 1/4" Small Vase & Place Card Holder	Open		12.00	12
1999 5 1/2" Paper Nautilus Candle Holder	Open		24.00	24
1999 5 1/4" Forever Love	Open		25.00	25
1999 8" Paper Nautilus Large Vase	Open		48.00	48

Maruri USA

African Safari Animals - W. Gaither

YEAR ISSUE	EDITION LIMIT	YEAR RETD.	ISSUE PRICE	*QUOTE U.S.$
1983 African Elephant	150	1996	3500.00	3500
1983 Black Maned Lion	300	1994	1450.00	1450
1983 Cape Buffalo	300	1994	2200.00	2200
1983 Grant's Zebras, pair	500	1995	1200.00	1200
1981 Nyala	300	1995	1450.00	1450
1983 Sable	500	1994	1200.00	1200
1983 Southern Greater Kudu	300	1994	1800.00	1800
1983 Southern Impala	300	1994	1200.00	1200
1983 Southern Leopard	300	1994	1450.00	1450
1983 Southern White Rhino	150	1997	3200.00	3200

America The Beautiful - W. Whitten

YEAR ISSUE	EDITION LIMIT	YEAR RETD.	ISSUE PRICE	*QUOTE U.S.$
2000 Autumn Serenity AB-2064	Open		48.00	48
2000 Charm of the South AB-2062	Open		48.00	48
2000 Lighting the Way AB-2063	Open		48.00	48
2000 Nature's Grandeur AB-2065	Open		90.00	90
2000 Northern Wilderness AB-2061	Open		48.00	48

American Eagle Gallery - Maruri Studios

YEAR ISSUE	EDITION LIMIT	YEAR RETD.	ISSUE PRICE	*QUOTE U.S.$
1985 E-8501	Closed	1989	45.00	75
1985 E-8502	Open		55.00	65
1985 E-8503	Open		60.00	65
1985 E-8504	Open		65.00	75
1985 E-8505	Closed	1989	65.00	150
1985 E-8506	Open		75.00	90
1985 E-8507	Closed	1997	75.00	90
1985 E-8508	Closed	1989	75.00	85
1985 E-8509	Closed	1989	85.00	125
1985 E-8510	Open		85.00	95
1985 E-8511	Closed	1989	85.00	125
1985 E-8512	Closed	1997	295.00	260-325
1987 E-8721	Open		40.00	50
1987 E-8722	Open		45.00	55
1987 E-8723	Closed	1989	55.00	55
1987 E-8724	Open		175.00	195
1989 E-8931	Open		55.00	60
1989 E-8932	Open		75.00	80
1989 E-8933	Open		95.00	95
1989 E-8934	Open		135.00	140
1989 E-8935	Open		175.00	185
1989 E-8936	Open		185.00	195
1991 E-9141 Eagle Landing	Open		60.00	60
1991 E-9142 Eagle w/ Totem Pole	Closed	1997	75.00	75
1991 E-9143 Pair in Flight	Open		95.00	95
1991 E-9144 Eagle w/Salmon	Open		110.00	110
1991 E-9145 Eagle w/Snow	Closed	1997	135.00	135
1991 E-9146 Eagle w/Babies	Open		145.00	145
1995 E-9551 Eagle	Open		60.00	60
1995 E-9552 Eagle	Open		65.00	65
1995 E-9553 Eagle	Open		75.00	75
1995 E-9554 Eagle	Open		80.00	80
1995 E-9555 Eagle	Open		90.00	90
1995 E-9556 Eagle	Open		110.00	110

Americana - W. Gaither

YEAR ISSUE	EDITION LIMIT	YEAR RETD.	ISSUE PRICE	*QUOTE U.S.$
1981 Grizzley Bear and Indian	300	1985	650.00	650
1982 Sioux Brave and Bison	300	1985	985.00	985

Baby Animals - W. Gaither

YEAR ISSUE	EDITION LIMIT	YEAR RETD.	ISSUE PRICE	*QUOTE U.S.$
1981 African Lion Cubs	1,500	1995	195.00	195
1981 Black Bear Cubs	1,500	1995	195.00	195
1981 Wolf Cubs	1,500	1995	195.00	195

Birds of Prey - W. Gaither

YEAR ISSUE	EDITION LIMIT	YEAR RETD.	ISSUE PRICE	*QUOTE U.S.$
1981 Screech Owl	300	1995	960.00	960
1981 American Bald Eagle I	950	1986	165.00	585-1750
1982 American Bald Eagle II	950	1986	245.00	2750
1983 American Bald Eagle III	950	1987	445.00	650-1750
1984 American Bald Eagle IV	950	1988	360.00	1750
1986 American Bald Eagle V	950	1989	325.00	1250

Eyes Of The Night - Maruri Studios

YEAR ISSUE	EDITION LIMIT	YEAR RETD.	ISSUE PRICE	*QUOTE U.S.$
1988 Double Barn Owl O-8807	Closed	1993	125.00	130
1988 Double Snowy Owl O-8809	Closed	1993	245.00	250
1988 Single Great Horned Owl O-8803	Closed	1993	60.00	65
1988 Single Great Horned Owl O-8808	Closed	1993	145.00	150
1988 Single Screech Owl O-8801	Closed	1993	50.00	55
1988 Single Screech Owl O-8806	Closed	1993	90.00	95
1988 Single Snowy Owl O-8802	Closed	1993	50.00	55
1988 Single Snowy Owl O-8805	Closed	1993	80.00	85
1988 Single Tawny Owl O-8804	Closed	1993	60.00	65

Gentle Giants - Maruri Studios

YEAR ISSUE	EDITION LIMIT	YEAR RETD.	ISSUE PRICE	*QUOTE U.S.$
1992 Baby Elephant Sitting GG-9252	Closed	1997	65.00	65
1992 Baby Elephant Standing GG-9251	Closed	1997	50.00	50
1992 Elephant Pair GG-9255	Closed	1997	220.00	220
1992 Elephant Pair Playing GG-9253	Closed	1997	80.00	80
1992 Mother & Baby Elephant GG-9254	Closed	1997	160.00	160

Graceful Reflections - Maruri Studios

YEAR ISSUE	EDITION LIMIT	YEAR RETD.	ISSUE PRICE	*QUOTE U.S.$
1991 Mute Swan w/Baby SW-9152	Closed	1993	95.00	95
1991 Pair-Mute Swan SW-9153	Closed	1993	145.00	145
1991 Pair-Mute Swan SW-9154	Closed	1993	195.00	195
1991 Single Mute Swan SW-9151	Closed	1993	85.00	85

Horses Of The World - Maruri Studios

YEAR ISSUE	EDITION LIMIT	YEAR RETD.	ISSUE PRICE	*QUOTE U.S.$
1993 Arabian HW-9356	Closed	1995	175.00	175
1993 Camargue HW-9354	Closed	1995	150.00	150
1993 Clydesdale HW-9351	Closed	1995	145.00	145
1993 Paint Horse HW-9355	Closed	1995	160.00	160
1993 Quarter Horse HW-9353	Closed	1995	145.00	145
1993 Thoroughbred HW-9352	Closed	1995	145.00	145

Hummingbirds - Maruri Studios

YEAR ISSUE	EDITION LIMIT	YEAR RETD.	ISSUE PRICE	*QUOTE U.S.$
1995 Allen's & Babies w/Rose H-9523	Open		120.00	120
1995 Allen's w/Easter Lily H-9522	Open		95.00	95
1999 Allen's w/Fuchsia H-9931	Open		75.00	75
1989 Allen's w/Hibiscus H-8906	Open		195.00	195
1989 Anna's w/Lily H-8905	Open		160.00	160
1999 Anna's w/Rhododendron H-9935	Open		95.00	95
1995 Anna's w/Trumpet Creeper H-9524	Open		130.00	130
1995 Broad-Billed w/Amaryllis H-9526	Open		150.00	150
1999 Broad-billed w/Regal Lily H-9932	Open		75.00	75
1989 Calliope w/Azalea H-8904	Open		120.00	120
1999 Ruby-throated and Babies H-9934	Open		85.00	85
1989 Ruby-Throated w/Azalea H-8911	Open		75.00	75
1989 Ruby-Throated w/Orchid H-8914	Open		150.00	150
1999 Ruby-topaz w/Cattleya H-9936	Open		95.00	95
1999 Rufous w/Morning Glory H-9933	Open		85.00	85
1989 Rufous w/Trumpet Creeper H-8901	Open		70.00	75
1989 Violet-crowned w/Gentian H-8903	Open		90.00	90
1989 Violet-Crowned w/Gentian H-8913	Open		75.00	75
1995 Violet-Crowned w/Iris H-9521	Open		95.00	95
1989 White-eared w/Morning Glory H-8902	Open		85.00	85
1989 White-Eared w/Morning Glory H-8912	Open		75.00	75
1995 White-Eared w/Tulip H-9525	Open		145.00	145

In A Nutshell - J. Trenholm

YEAR ISSUE	EDITION LIMIT	YEAR RETD.	ISSUE PRICE	*QUOTE U.S.$
1999 Baby's First Birthday NS-9974	Open		18.00	18
1999 Bright Smile for a Bright Day NS-9972	Open		15.00	15
1999 Coloring Eggs for Easter NS-9977	Open		20.00	20
1999 The Daydreamer NS-9975	Open		20.00	20
2000 Graduation Day NS-2002	Open		15.00	15
2000 Hedgehog Birthday NS-2005	Open		20.00	20
2000 Hudson's Halloween Party NS-2014	Open		29.50	30
2000 Johnny Sees the Nurse NS-2004	Open		20.00	20
1999 Keeping Your Marbles NS-9979	Open		24.50	25
2000 A Little Hug NS-2001	Open		10.00	10
1999 Love's Serenade NS-9978	Open		24.50	25
1999 Night Before Christmas NS-9981	Open		29.50	30
2000 The Nutivity Scene NS-2015	Open		29.50	30
2000 Opossum Picnic NS-2006	Open		22.00	22
1999 Paw Print in Plaster NS-9976	Open		20.00	20
1999 The Runaway Balloon NS-9971	Open		15.00	15
2000 Shhh...Momma's Asleep NS-2013	Open		29.50	30
2000 Sidewalk Sailors NS-2009	Open		24.50	25
2000 Skunk Bath NS-2007	Open		22.00	22
2000 Slumber Party NS-2008	Open		24.50	25
1999 Sneaking a Peek NS-9980	Open		24.50	25
2000 Surfing the Innernut NS-2003	Open		15.00	15
2000 The Swimming Hole	Open		24.50	25
2000 We Love Our Teacher NS-2011	Open		24.50	25
1999 The Wedding Day NS-9982	Open		29.50	30
2000 Welcome to Our World NS-2012	Open		24.50	25
1999 You're Super! NS-9973	Open		15.00	15

Kingdom of Cats - Maruri Studios

YEAR ISSUE	EDITION LIMIT	YEAR RETD.	ISSUE PRICE	*QUOTE U.S.$
1997 Baby Cougar w/Icicles KC-9701	Closed	1999	50.00	50
1997 Bobcat w/Cactus KC-9705	Closed	1999	70.00	70
1997 Female Lions w/Cub KC-9709	Closed	1999	95.00	95
1997 Female Mountain Lion w/Cubs KC-9708	Closed	1999	90.00	90
1997 Male Lion on Rocks KC-9707	Closed	1999	85.00	85
1997 Male Tiger Jumping KC-9703	Closed	1999	60.00	60
1997 Mountain Lion on Rocks KC-9704	Closed	1999	65.00	65
1997 Mountain Lion on Trees KC-9706	Closed	1999	75.00	75
1997 Tiger Cubs Playing KC-9702	Closed	1999	55.00	55

Legendary Flowers of the Orient - Ito

YEAR ISSUE	EDITION LIMIT	YEAR RETD.	ISSUE PRICE	*QUOTE U.S.$
1985 Cherry Blossom	15,000		45.00	55
1985 Chinese Peony	15,000		45.00	55
1985 Chrysanthemum	15,000		45.00	55
1985 Iris	15,000		45.00	55
1985 Lily	15,000		45.00	55
1985 Lotus	15,000		45.00	45
1985 Orchid	15,000		45.00	55
1985 Wisteria	15,000		45.00	55

Majestic Owls of the Night - D. Littleton

YEAR ISSUE	EDITION LIMIT	YEAR RETD.	ISSUE PRICE	*QUOTE U.S.$
1988 Barred Owl	15,000		55.00	55
1987 Burrowing Owl	15,000		55.00	55
1988 Elf Owl	15,000		55.00	55

National Parks - Maruri Studios

YEAR ISSUE	EDITION LIMIT	YEAR RETD.	ISSUE PRICE	*QUOTE U.S.$
1993 Baby Bear NP-9301	Closed	1996	60.00	60
1993 Bear Family NP-9304	Closed	1996	160.00	160
1993 Buffalo NP-9306	Closed	1996	170.00	170
1993 Cougar Cubs NP-9302	Closed	1996	70.00	70
1993 Deer Family NP-9303	Closed	1996	120.00	120
1993 Eagle NP-9307	Closed	1996	180.00	180
1993 Falcon NP-9308	Closed	1996	195.00	195
1993 Howling Wolves NP-9305	Closed	1996	165.00	165

North American Game Animals - W. Gaither

YEAR ISSUE	EDITION LIMIT	YEAR RETD.	ISSUE PRICE	*QUOTE U.S.$
1984 White Tail Deer	950		285.00	285

North American Game Birds - W. Gaither

YEAR ISSUE	EDITION LIMIT	YEAR RETD.	ISSUE PRICE	*QUOTE U.S.$
1983 Bobtail Quail, female	600	1990	375.00	375
1983 Bobtail Quail, male	600	1990	375.00	375
1981 Canadian Geese, pair	5	1990	20000.00	20000
1981 Eastern Wild Turkey	1,500	1990	300.00	300
1982 Ruffed Grouse	200	1990	1745.00	1745
1983 Wild Turkey Hen with Chicks	480	1990	300.00	300

North American Songbirds - W. Gaither

YEAR ISSUE	EDITION LIMIT	YEAR RETD.	ISSUE PRICE	*QUOTE U.S.$
1982 Bluebird	2,500	1986	95.00	95
1983 Cardinal, female	2,500	1986	95.00	95
1982 Cardinal, male	2,500	1986	95.00	95
1982 Carolina Wren	2,500	1986	95.00	95
1982 Chickadee	2,500	1986	95.00	95
1982 Mockingbird	2,500	1986	95.00	95
1983 Robin	2,500	1986	95.00	95

North American Waterfowl I - W. Gaither

YEAR ISSUE	EDITION LIMIT	YEAR RETD.	ISSUE PRICE	*QUOTE U.S.$
1981 Blue Winged Teal	200	1996	980.00	980
1981 Canvasback Ducks	300	1994	780.00	780
1981 Flying Wood Ducks	300	1994	880.00	880
1981 Mallard Drake	200	1994	2380.00	2380
1981 Wood Duck, decoy	950	1997	480.00	480

North American Waterfowl II - W. Gaither

YEAR ISSUE	EDITION LIMIT	YEAR RETD.	ISSUE PRICE	*QUOTE U.S.$
1982 Bufflehead Ducks Pair	1,500	1997	225.00	225
1982 Goldeneye Ducks Pair	1,500	1989	225.00	225
1983 Loon	1,500	1989	245.00	245
1981 Mallard Ducks Pair	1,500	1997	225.00	225
1982 Pintail Ducks Pair	1,500	1994	225.00	225
1982 Widgeon, female	1,500	1989	225.00	225
1982 Widgeon, male	1,500	1989	225.00	225

Polar Expedition - Maruri Studios

YEAR ISSUE	EDITION LIMIT	YEAR RETD.	ISSUE PRICE	*QUOTE U.S.$
1992 Arctic Fox Cubs Playing-P-9223	Closed	1999	65.00	65
1990 Baby Arctic Fox-P-9002	Closed	1999	50.00	55
1990 Baby Emperor Penguin-P-9001	Closed	1999	45.00	50
1992 Baby Harp Seal-P-9221	Closed	1999	55.00	55
1990 Baby Harp Seals-P-9005	Closed	1999	65.00	70
1992 Emperor Penguins-P-9222	Closed	1999	60.00	60
1990 Mother & Baby Emperor Penguins-P-9006	Closed	1999	80.00	85
1990 Mother & Baby Harp Seals-P-9007	Closed	1999	90.00	95
1990 Mother & Baby Polar Bears-P-9008	Closed	1999	125.00	130
1990 Polar Bear Cub Sliding-P-9003	Closed	1999	50.00	55
1990 Polar Bear Cubs Playing-P-9004	Closed	1999	60.00	65
1992 Polar Bear Family-P-9224	Closed	1999	90.00	90
1990 Polar Expedition Sign-PES-001	Closed	1999	18.00	18

Precious Panda - Maruri Studios

YEAR ISSUE	EDITION LIMIT	YEAR RETD.	ISSUE PRICE	*QUOTE U.S.$
1992 Lazy Lunch PP-9202	Closed	1999	60.00	60
1992 Mother's Cuddle-PP-9204	Closed	1999	120.00	120
1992 Snack Time PP-9201	Closed	1999	60.00	60
1992 Tug Of War PP-9203	Closed	1999	70.00	70

Premier Collection - Birds - Maruri Studios

YEAR ISSUE	EDITION LIMIT	YEAR RETD.	ISSUE PRICE	*QUOTE U.S.$
1999 American Goldfinch PB-9904	Open		24.95	25
2000 Baltimore Oriole PB-2021	Open		24.95	25
1999 Barn Swallow PB-9910	Open		24.95	25
1999 Black-capped Chickadee PB-9901	Open		24.95	25
2000 Blue Jay PB-2026	Open		24.95	25
2000 Bluebird PB-2022	Open		24.95	25
2000 Cardinal PB-2024	Open		24.95	25
1999 Golden-crowned Kinglet PB-9903	Open		24.95	25
1999 House Wren PB-9902	Open		24.95	25
1999 Northern Parula PB-9911	Open		24.95	25
1999 Pine Warbler PB-9907	Open		24.95	25

*Quotes have been rounded up to nearest dollar

YEAR ISSUE	EDITION LIMIT	YEAR RETD.	ISSUE PRICE	*QUOTE U.S.$
1999 Red-breasted Nuthatch PB-9909	Open		24.95	25
2000 Robin PB-2025	Open		24.95	25
1999 Savannah Sparrow PB-9908	Open		24.95	25
1999 Tufted Titmouse PB-9905	Open		24.95	25
1999 Yellow Warbler PB-9906	Open		24.95	25
2000 Yellow-bellied Sapsucker PB-2023	Open		24.95	25
1999 Yellow-throated Warbler PB-9912	Open		24.95	25

Premier Collection - Hummingbirds - Maruri Studios

YEAR ISSUE	EDITION LIMIT	YEAR RETD.	ISSUE PRICE	*QUOTE U.S.$
2000 Allen's w/ Azalea PH-2036	Open		20.00	20
2000 Anna's w/ Morning Glory PH-2032	Open		20.00	20
2000 Costa's w/ Primrose PH-2034	Open		20.00	20
2000 Ruby-throated w/ Trumpet Creeper PH-2033	Open		20.00	20
2000 Rufous w/ Hibiscus PH-2031	Open		20.00	20
2000 Violet-crowned w/ Gentian PH-2035	Open		20.00	20

Premier Collection - Kittens - Maruri Studios

YEAR ISSUE	EDITION LIMIT	YEAR RETD.	ISSUE PRICE	*QUOTE U.S.$
1999 Kitten Inside Teapot PK-9917	Open		25.00	25
1999 Kitten Looking Into Mirror PK-9920	Open		25.00	25
1999 Kitten Looking Out Window PK-9919	Open		25.00	25
1999 Kitten Napping in Ballet Shoes PK-9913	Open		25.00	25
1999 Kitten Under Hat PK-9914	Open		25.00	25
1999 Kitten w/ Fishbowl PK-9918	Open		25.00	25
1999 Kitten w/Christmas Ornaments PK-9916	Open		25.00	25
1999 Kitten w/Ragdoll PK-9915	Open		25.00	25

Santa's World Travels - Maruri Studios

YEAR ISSUE	EDITION LIMIT	YEAR RETD.	ISSUE PRICE	*QUOTE U.S.$
1999 Bringing Joy to the World SWT-9941	Open		25.00	25
1996 Cat Nap SWT-9603	7,500		85.00	85
1999 Clydesdale Christmas SWT-9945	3,500		195.00	195
1996 Crossing the Tundra SWT-9605	7,500		145.00	145
1996 Desert Trip SWT-9604	7,500		95.00	95
1999 Fill'er Up SWT-9943	5,000		60.00	60
1998 Frosty Penguins SWT-9821	7,500		60.00	60
1998 Guiding Tiger SWT-9824	7,500		95.00	95
1997 Polar Express SWT-9710	7,500		85.00	85
1998 Pouch Full of Dreams SWT-9822	7,500		70.00	70
1997 Rapid Delivery SWT-9711	7,500		85.00	85
1997 S. S. World Travels SWT-9713	5,000		175.00	175
1996 Santa's Safari SWT-9600	5,000		225.00	225
1997 A Special Gift SWT-9712	7,500		95.00	95
1999 Tall Order for Christmas SWT-9944	5,000		80.00	80
1998 Tea Time SWT-9823	7,500		70.00	70
1996 Trusted Friend SWT-9602	7,500		85.00	85
1996 Wild Ride SWT-9601	7,500		75.00	75
1999 Winter's Bear Necessities SWT-9942	5,000		60.00	60

Shore Birds - W. Gaither

YEAR ISSUE	EDITION LIMIT	YEAR RETD.	ISSUE PRICE	*QUOTE U.S.$
1984 Pelican	1,500	1989	260.00	260
1984 Sand Piper	1,500	1989	285.00	285

Signature Collection - W. Gaither

YEAR ISSUE	EDITION LIMIT	YEAR RETD.	ISSUE PRICE	*QUOTE U.S.$
1985 American Bald Eagle	Closed	1989	60.00	60
1985 Canada Goose	Closed	1989	60.00	60
1985 Hawk	Closed	1989	60.00	60
1985 Pintail Duck	Closed	1989	60.00	60
1985 Snow Goose	Closed	1989	60.00	60
1985 Swallow	Closed	1989	60.00	60

Songbird Serenade - Maruri Studios

YEAR ISSUE	EDITION LIMIT	YEAR RETD.	ISSUE PRICE	*QUOTE U.S.$
1998 Black Capped Chickadee w/Daffodil SBS-9833	Open		65.00	65
1997 Blue Jay w/Oak SBS-9723	Open		70.00	70
1997 Bluebird Family w/Apple Blossom SBS-9729	Open		95.00	95
1998 Bluebird w/Poppy SBS-9836	Open		65.00	65
1997 Cardinal Family w/Rose SBS-9728	Open		90.00	90
1998 Cardinal w/Wild Grape SBS-9835	Open		65.00	65
1998 Carolina Wren w/Snow Drops SBS-9831	Open		65.00	65
1997 Cedar Waxwing Pair w/Berries SBS-9726	Open		80.00	80
1997 Chickadee Pair w/Holly & Berries SBS-9727	Open		85.00	85
1997 Goldfinch w/Violets SBS-9721	Open		65.00	65
1998 Mockingbirds w/Prarie Rose SBS-9837	Open		85.00	85
1998 Northern Baltimore Oriole w/Dogwood SBS-9834	Open		65.00	65
1998 Robin and Nest w/Hawthorn SBS-9838	Open		85.00	85
1997 Robin w/Blackberry SBS-9724	Open		70.00	70
1997 Robin w/Lily SBS-9722	Open		70.00	70
1997 Wren Pair w/Cactus SBS-9725	Open		80.00	80
1998 Yellow Warbler w/Morning Glory SBS-9832	Open		65.00	65

Songbirds Of Beauty - Maruri Studios

YEAR ISSUE	EDITION LIMIT	YEAR RETD.	ISSUE PRICE	*QUOTE U.S.$
1991 Bluebird w/ Apple Blossom SB-9105	Closed	1994	85.00	85
1991 Cardinal w/ Cherry Blossom SB-9103	Closed	1994	85.00	85
1991 Chickadee w/ Roses SB-9101	Closed	1994	85.00	85
1991 Dbl. Bluebird w/ Peach Blossom SB-9107	Closed	1994	145.00	145
1991 Dbl. Cardinal w/ Dogwood SB-9108	Closed	1994	145.00	145
1991 Goldfinch w/ Hawthorne SB-9102	Closed	1994	85.00	85
1991 Robin & Baby w/ Azalea SB-9106	Closed	1994	115.00	115
1991 Robin w/ Lilies SB-9104	Closed	1994	85.00	85

Special Commissions - W. Gaither

YEAR ISSUE	EDITION LIMIT	YEAR RETD.	ISSUE PRICE	*QUOTE U.S.$
1982 Cheetah	200	1996	995.00	995-1560
1983 Orange Bengal Tiger	240	1998	340.00	340
1981 White Bengal Tiger	240	1998	340.00	340

Studio Collection - Maruri Studios

YEAR ISSUE	EDITION LIMIT	YEAR RETD.	ISSUE PRICE	*QUOTE U.S.$
1990 Majestic Eagles-MS-100	Closed	1994	350.00	800
1991 Delicate Motion-MS-200	3,500	1997	325.00	325
1992 Imperial Panda-MS-300	3,500	1997	350.00	350
1993 Wild Wings-MS-400	3,500	1997	395.00	395-450
1994 Waltz of the Dolphins-MS-500	3,500		300.00	300
1995 "Independent Spirit" MS-600	3,500		395.00	395
1998 Fantasy in Flight MS-700	3,500		295.00	295

Stump Animals - W. Gaither

YEAR ISSUE	EDITION LIMIT	YEAR RETD.	ISSUE PRICE	*QUOTE U.S.$
1984 Bobcat	1,200	1996	175.00	175
1984 Chipmunk	1,200	1996	175.00	175
1984 Gray Squirrel	1,200	1995	175.00	175
1983 Owl	1,200	1996	175.00	175
1983 Raccoon	1,200	1989	175.00	175
1982 Red Fox	1,200	1996	175.00	175

Tribal Spirits - Maruri Studios

YEAR ISSUE	EDITION LIMIT	YEAR RETD.	ISSUE PRICE	*QUOTE U.S.$
1996 Bear Healer TS-9653	5,000		140.00	140
1996 Buffalo Hunter TS-9651	5,000		130.00	130
1996 Eagle Messenger TS-9652	5,000		140.00	140
1996 Wolf Guide TS-9654	5,000		150.00	150

The Tropics - W. Whitten

YEAR ISSUE	EDITION LIMIT	YEAR RETD.	ISSUE PRICE	*QUOTE U.S.$
1999 Baja Surfer TR-9921	Open		40.00	40
1999 Hana Hideaway TR-9922	Open		50.00	50
1999 Happy Hut TR-9924	Open		70.00	70
1999 Shaman Hut TR-9926	Open		85.00	85
1999 Tahiti Dream TR-9925	Open		75.00	75
1999 Tiki Hut TR-9923	Open		60.00	60
1999 Tropic Counter Sign	Open		5.00	5

Upland Birds - W. Gaither

YEAR ISSUE	EDITION LIMIT	YEAR RETD.	ISSUE PRICE	*QUOTE U.S.$
1981 Mourning Doves	350	1997	780.00	780

Wings of Love Doves - Maruri Studios

YEAR ISSUE	EDITION LIMIT	YEAR RETD.	ISSUE PRICE	*QUOTE U.S.$
1987 D-8701 Single Dove w/ Forget-Me-Not	Closed	1994	45.00	55
1987 D-8702 Double Dove w/ Primrose	Open		55.00	65
1987 D-8703 Single Dove w/Buttercup	Closed	1994	65.00	70
1987 D-8704 Double Dove w/Daisy	Open		75.00	85
1987 D-8705 Single Dove w/Blue Flax	Closed	1994	95.00	95
1987 D-8706 Double Dove w/Cherry Blossom	Open		175.00	195
1990 D-9021 Double Dove w/Gentian	Open		50.00	55
1990 D-9022 Double Dove w/Azalea	Open		75.00	75
1990 D-9023 Double Dove w/Apple Blossom	Open		115.00	120
1990 D-9024 Double Dove w/Morning Glory	Closed	1997	150.00	160

Wonders of the Sea - Maruri Studios

YEAR ISSUE	EDITION LIMIT	YEAR RETD.	ISSUE PRICE	*QUOTE U.S.$
1994 Dolphin WS-9401	Open		70.00	70
1994 Great White Shark WS-9406	Open		90.00	90
1994 Green Sea Turtle WS-9405	Open		85.00	85
1994 Humpback Mother & Baby WS-9409	Open		150.00	150
1994 Manatee & Baby WS-9403	Open		75.00	75
1994 Manta Ray WS-9404	Open		80.00	80
1994 Orca Mother & Baby WS-9410	Open		150.00	150
1994 Sea Otter & Baby WS-9402	Open		75.00	75
1994 Three Dolphins WS-9408	Open		135.00	135
1994 Two Dolphins WS-9407	Open		120.00	120

Matchbox Collectibles/Mattel

Matchbox Collectors Guild

YEAR ISSUE	EDITION LIMIT	YEAR RETD.	ISSUE PRICE	*QUOTE U.S.$
1998 1920 Mack AC YY052/B-M	Retrd.	2000	Gift	N/A
2000 1948 GMC C.O.E.	Open		Gift	N/A

1930's & 1940's Pick-Ups - Mattel

YEAR ISSUE	EDITION LIMIT	YEAR RETD.	ISSUE PRICE	*QUOTE U.S.$
1999 1938 Studebaker YTC05-M	Open		29.95	30
1999 1939 REO YTC04-M	Open		29.95	30
1999 1940 Ford Pick-Up YTC03-M	Open		29.95	30
1999 1941 Chevy YTC01-M	Open		29.95	30
1999 1943 International YTC06-M	Open		29.95	30
1999 1946 Dodge YTC02-M	Open		29.95	30

1957 Chevy Collection - Mattel

YEAR ISSUE	EDITION LIMIT	YEAR RETD.	ISSUE PRICE	*QUOTE U.S.$
1997 1957 Chevy Bel-Air DYG02/SA-M	Open		24.95	25
1997 1957 Chevy Convertible DY027/SB-M	Open		24.95	25
1997 1957 Chevy Corvette CCV03/SA-M	Open		24.95	25
1997 1957 Chevy Nomad VCV01-M	Open		24.95	25
1997 1957 Chevy Pick-Up YRS05/SA-M	Open		24.95	25

Ambulance Series I - Mattel

YEAR ISSUE	EDITION LIMIT	YEAR RETD.	ISSUE PRICE	*QUOTE U.S.$
2000 1912 Ford Model T Van YYM38057	Open		29.95	30
2000 1937 GMC Van YYM38058	Open		29.95	30
2000 1947 Citroen Type H Van YYM38059	Open		29.95	30
2000 1950 Ford E83W 10CWT Van YYM38060	Open		29.95	30
2000 1955 Holden FJ Van YYM38061	Open		29.95	30
2000 1959 Mercedes L408 YYM38062	Open		29.95	30

American Giants - Mattel

YEAR ISSUE	EDITION LIMIT	YEAR RETD.	ISSUE PRICE	*QUOTE U.S.$
1998 1953 Ford F-100 Pick-Up Truck - Ford PartsYIS06-M	Open		29.95	30
1998 1954 Ford F-100 Pick-Up Truck Pennsylvania Railroad YIS05-M	Open		29.95	30
1998 1955 Chevy 3100 Pick-Up Truck - Harley Davidson YIS01-M	Open		29.95	30
1998 1955 Ford F-100 Pick-Up Truck - Caterpillar YIS02-M	Open		29.95	30
1998 1956 Chevy 3100 Pick-Up Truck - General Motor Parts YIS03-M	Open		29.95	30
1998 1957 Chevy 3100 Pick-Up Truck - American Airlines YIS04-M	Open		29.95	30

American Muscle Cars I - Mattel

YEAR ISSUE	EDITION LIMIT	YEAR RETD.	ISSUE PRICE	*QUOTE U.S.$
1997 1967 Pontiac GTO YMC03-M	Open		29.95	30
1997 1968 Chevy Camaro SS 396 YMC06-M	Open		29.95	30
1997 1970 Chevy Chevelle SS454 YMC01-M	Open		29.95	30
1997 1970 Mustang Boss 429 YMC05-M	Open		29.95	30
1997 1970 Road Runner Hemi YMC04-M	Open		29.95	30
1997 1971 Cuda 440 6-Pack YMC02-M	Open		29.95	30

American Muscle Cars II - Mattel

YEAR ISSUE	EDITION LIMIT	YEAR RETD.	ISSUE PRICE	*QUOTE U.S.$
1998 1966 Chevy Chevelle 396 SS YMC08-M	Open		29.95	30
1998 1967 Ford Fairlane 500XL YMC09-M	Open		29.95	30
1998 1969 Dodge Charger YMC10-M	Open		29.95	30
1998 1970 Oldsmobile YMC11-M	Open		29.95	30
1998 1970 Plymouth GTX YMC07-M	Open		29.95	30
1998 1971 Dodge Challenger YMC12-M	Open		29.95	30

Anheuser Busch Tractor Trailers - Mattel

YEAR ISSUE	EDITION LIMIT	YEAR RETD.	ISSUE PRICE	*QUOTE U.S.$
1998 Ford Aeromax - O'Doul's DYM36674	Open		24.95	25
1998 Kenworth - Michelob DYM36671	Open		24.95	25
1998 Kenworth Aerodyne - Busch DYM36675	Open		24.95	25
1998 Mack CH600 - Bud Lite DYM36672	Open		24.95	25
1998 Peterbilt - Bud Ice DYM36677	Open		24.95	25
1998 Peterbilt - Budweiser DYM36670	Open		24.95	25

Anniversary Collection - Mattel

YEAR ISSUE	EDITION LIMIT	YEAR RETD.	ISSUE PRICE	*QUOTE U.S.$
1995 1909 Opel Coupe YMS03-M	Retrd.	1999	19.95	20
1995 1910 Mercedes Benz Limousine YMS02-M	Retrd.	1999	19.95	20
1995 1911 Daimler YMS05-M	Retrd.	1999	19.95	20
1995 1911 Ford Model T YMS01-M	Retrd.	1999	19.95	20
1995 1911 Maxwell Roadster YMS06-M	Retrd.	1999	19.95	20
1995 1911 Packard Laundaulet YMS04-M	Retrd.	1999	19.95	20
1995 1912 Simplex YMS08-M	Retrd.	1999	19.95	20
1995 1914 Prince Henry Vauxhall YMS07-M	Retrd.	1999	19.95	20

Austin Powers - Mattel

YEAR ISSUE	EDITION LIMIT	YEAR RETD.	ISSUE PRICE	*QUOTE U.S.$
1999 Jaguar E-Type DYM37905	Open		37.95	38
1999 Volkswagen Beetle Concept Convertible DYM38094	Open		37.95	38

Best of Britain / 2 Seaters - Mattel

YEAR ISSUE	EDITION LIMIT	YEAR RETD.	ISSUE PRICE	*QUOTE U.S.$
1998 1955 Morgan DYB03-M	Retrd.	1998	29.95	30
1998 1956 Austin Healey DYB04-M	Retrd.	1998	29.95	30
1998 1959 Triumph TRS DYB01-M	Retrd.	1998	29.95	30
1998 1961 Aston Martin DB4 DYB06-M	Retrd.	1998	29.95	30
1998 1965 MGB DYB05-M	Retrd.	1998	29.95	30
1998 1967 Jaguar E-Type DYB02-M	Retrd.	1998	29.95	30
1998 Lotus Super 7 DYB07-M	Retrd.	1998	29.95	30

Best of Scotland - Mattel

YEAR ISSUE	EDITION LIMIT	YEAR RETD.	ISSUE PRICE	*QUOTE U.S.$
1997 1912 Sheep Dip YWG05-M	Retrd.	1998	19.95	20
1997 1926 Ford TT - Long John YWG02-M	Retrd.	1998	19.95	20
1997 1929 Morris - Cutty Sark YWG03-M	Retrd.	1998	19.95	20
1997 1930 Ford AA - Ballentines YWG01-M	Retrd.	1998	19.95	20
1997 1932 Ford AA - Teachers YWG06-M	Retrd.	1998	19.95	20
1997 1937 GMC - Laphroaig YWG04-M	Retrd.	1998	19.95	20

Budweiser Sports Cars - Mattel

YEAR ISSUE	EDITION LIMIT	YEAR RETD.	ISSUE PRICE	*QUOTE U.S.$
1999 1957 Chevy Bel-Air - Boxing DYM37600	Open		29.95	30
1999 1959 Cadillac Coupe Deville - Golf DYM37597	Open		29.95	30
1999 1964 Mustang - Rodeo DYM37619	Open		29.95	30
1999 1968 Volkswagen Beetle - Bowling DYM37622	Open		29.95	30
1999 1969 Dodge Charger - Racing DYM37598	Open		29.95	30
1999 1971 Barracuda - Fly Fishing DYM37599	Open		29.95	30

Budweiser Vintage Trucks - Mattel

YEAR ISSUE	EDITION LIMIT	YEAR RETD.	ISSUE PRICE	*QUOTE U.S.$
1998 1926 Ford Model TT YVT03-M	Open		29.95	30
1998 1932 Diamond T YVT01-M	Open		29.95	30
1998 1937 Dodge Airflow YVT02-M	Open		29.95	30
1998 1940 Ford Pick-Up YVT05-M	Open		29.95	30
1998 1948 GMC Cab Over YVT06-M	Open		29.95	30
1998 1955 Chevy Pick-Up YVT04-M	Open		29.95	30

Cars of the Rich & Infamous - Mattel

YEAR ISSUE	EDITION LIMIT	YEAR RETD.	ISSUE PRICE	*QUOTE U.S.$
1999 1930 Duesenberg Model J Town Car DYM35182	Open		29.95	30
1999 1931 Mercedes Benz 770 DYM35185	Open		29.95	30
1999 1931 Stutz Bearcat DYM35179	Open		29.95	30
1999 1933 Cadillac 452 V16 Town Car DYM35181	Open		29.95	30
1999 1937 Cord 812 Supercharged Viton DYM35178	Open		29.95	30
1999 1938 Lincoln Zephyr DYM35180	Open		29.95	30

Christmas Themes - Mattel

YEAR ISSUE	EDITION LIMIT	YEAR RETD.	ISSUE PRICE	*QUOTE U.S.$
1995 1880 Merryweather Horsedrawn Fire Engine w/Plinth YSFE05-M	Retrd.	1998	59.90	27
1997 1912 Ford Model T Ambulance YY012/SB-M	5,000		29.95	30
1997 1920 Mack Truck YY030A/SA-M	Open		24.95	25
1995 1922 Scania Vabis Bus YSC01-M	Retrd.	1997	29.50	30

*Quotes have been rounded up to nearest dollar

YEAR ISSUE	EDITION LIMIT	YEAR RETD.	ISSUE PRICE	*QUOTE U.S.$
1998 1930 Ahrens Fox Fire Engine YYM35193	Open		89.95	90
1997 1930 Duesenberg Model J YY004/C-M	Open		27.95	28
1996 1932 Ford Woody Van - Pepsi YY21A/SA-M	Retrd.	1996	19.95	20
1997 1937 GMC Van Ambulance YY034/SC-M	5,000	1997	29.95	30
1996 1955 Chevy Pick-Up YSC02-M	7,500		29.95	30
1995 1957 Chevy Nomad YM92088	Retrd.	1995	39.90	40
1997 1967 Ford Mustang Fastback DY016/D-M	Open		29.95	30
1997 1968 Ford Mustang Cobra MB298/SC-M	5,000		19.95	20
1996 1970 Pontiac GTO w/Plinth MB289/SA-M	5,000		19.95	20
1996 1995 Hummer VMM01-M	Open		24.95	25
1996 Ford AA w/Santa YSC03-M	5,000		39.00	39
1997 Ford Model AA 1 1/2 Ton Truck YSC04-M	9,500		39.90	40
1997 Ford Model AA 1 1/2 Ton Truck YY062A/B-M	9,500		39.90	40
1997 Kenworth w/Plinth KS188SB1-M	12,500		49.90	50
1997 Mack Tractor Trailer CCY05/B-M	Open		24.95	25
1995 MBC Christmas Train Set YSTS01/1	Retrd.	1996	125.00	125
1996 MBC Christmas Train Set YSTS02/1	Retrd.	1997	125.00	125
1997 Peterbilt Tractor Trailer - Jim Beam CCY06/SA-M	Open		29.95	30
1996 Willy's Jeep VMM02/A-M	Retrd.	1997	19.95	20

Classic 1950's Automobilia Collection - Mattel

YEAR ISSUE	EDITION LIMIT	YEAR RETD.	ISSUE PRICE	*QUOTE U.S.$
1999 1939 Peterbilt - Michelin DYM35269	Open		29.95	30
1999 1939 Peterbilt - Pep Boys DYM35267	Open		29.95	30
1999 1939 Peterbilt - Sinclair DYM35270	Open		29.95	30
1999 1956 Mack - Champion DYM35268	Open		29.95	30
1999 1956 Mack - Texaco DYM35266	Open		29.95	30
1999 1956 Mack B - Pennzoil DYM35265	Open		29.95	30

Coca-Cola Series I - Mattel

YEAR ISSUE	EDITION LIMIT	YEAR RETD.	ISSUE PRICE	*QUOTE U.S.$
1997 1912 Ford Model T YPC04-M	Open		29.95	30
1997 1920 Mack AC YPC03-M	Open		29.95	30
1997 1930 Ford Model A Pickup YPC05-M	Open		29.95	30
1997 1932 Ford Model AA Pickup YPC06-M	Open		29.95	30
1997 1937 GMC Van YPC02-M	Open		29.95	30
1997 1957 Chevy Pickup YPC01-M	Open		29.95	30

Coca-Cola Series II - Mattel

YEAR ISSUE	EDITION LIMIT	YEAR RETD.	ISSUE PRICE	*QUOTE U.S.$
2000 1932 Mercedes Benz L5 YYM96506	Open		29.95	30
2000 1937 Dodge Airflow YYM96505	Open		29.95	30
2000 1948 GMC COE YYM96504	Open		29.95	30
2000 Ford Model AA YYM96507	Open		29.95	30
2000 Ford Model TT YYM96509	Open		29.95	30
2000 Morris Light Van YYM96508	Open		29.95	30

Coke Cruisers - Mattel

YEAR ISSUE	EDITION LIMIT	YEAR RETD.	ISSUE PRICE	*QUOTE U.S.$
1998 1953 Corvette CCV06/B-M	Open		29.95	30
1998 1955 Thunderbird DYG08/B-M	Open		29.95	30
1998 1957 Chevy Bel-Air DYG02/B-M	Open		29.95	30
1998 1967 Pontiac GTO YMC03/B-M	Open		29.95	30
1998 1968 Camaro YMC06/B-M	Open		29.95	30
1998 1970 Mustang YMC05/B-M	Open		29.95	30

Coke Vintage Small TT's - Mattel

YEAR ISSUE	EDITION LIMIT	YEAR RETD.	ISSUE PRICE	*QUOTE U.S.$
2000 1939 Peterbilt - Baseball DYM96656	Open		29.95	30
2000 1939 Peterbilt - Bowling DYM96654	Open		29.95	30
2000 1939 Peterbilt - Sprite Boy DYM96658	Open		29.95	30

Corvette Collection - Mattel

YEAR ISSUE	EDITION LIMIT	YEAR RETD.	ISSUE PRICE	*QUOTE U.S.$
1997 1953 Corvette CCV06-M	Open		29.95	30
1997 1957 Corvette CCV03-M	Open		29.95	30
1997 1963 Stingray CCV05-M	Open		29.95	30
1997 1969 Corvette Convertible 427 CCV01-M	Open		29.95	30
1997 1993 Corvette 40th Anniversary CCV02-M	Open		29.95	30
1997 1997 Corvette Coupe CCV04-M	Open		29.95	30

European Economy Cars - Mattel

YEAR ISSUE	EDITION LIMIT	YEAR RETD.	ISSUE PRICE	*QUOTE U.S.$
1997 1949 Citroen 2CV VEM03-M	Retrd.	1999	19.95	20
1997 1949 Volkswagen Cabriolet VEM01-M	Retrd.	1999	19.95	20
1997 1959 Austin 7 VEM02-M	Retrd.	1999	19.95	20
1997 1959 Messerschmitt KR200 VEM04-M	Retrd.	1999	19.95	20
1997 1962 Renault 4L VEM07-M	Retrd.	1999	19.95	20
1997 1962 Wolseley Hornet VEM05-M	Retrd.	1999	19.95	20
1997 1966 Fiat 500 VEM06-M	Retrd.	1999	19.95	20

Evolution of the 4 X 4 - Mattel

YEAR ISSUE	EDITION LIMIT	YEAR RETD.	ISSUE PRICE	*QUOTE U.S.$
1999 1947 Jeep CJ2A YYM35055	Open		29.95	30
1999 1948 Dodge Power Wagon YYM35053	Open		29.95	30
1999 1948 Land Rover YYM35054	Open		29.95	30
1999 1961 International Scout 80 YYM35056	Open		29.95	30
1999 1966 Ford Bronco YYM35057	Open		29.95	30
1999 1969 Chevy K/5 Blazer YYM35058	Open		29.95	30

Gas & Oil Tankers - Mattel

YEAR ISSUE	EDITION LIMIT	YEAR RETD.	ISSUE PRICE	*QUOTE U.S.$
1998 DAF - BP CCY13-M	Open		24.95	25
1998 Ford Aeromax - Sunoco CCY10-M	Open		24.95	25
1998 Kenworth - Mobil CCY12-M	Open		24.95	25
1998 Mack - Citgo CCY11-M	Open		24.95	25
1998 Mack - Shell CCY11/B-M	Open		24.95	25
1998 Peterbilt - Texaco CCY09-M	Open		24.95	25

Golden Age of Sports Cars - Mattel

YEAR ISSUE	EDITION LIMIT	YEAR RETD.	ISSUE PRICE	*QUOTE U.S.$
1996 1957 Jaguar XK 150 DY036/A-M	Retrd.	1998	19.95	20
1996 1962 Mercedes Benz 300 SL DY033/A-M	Retrd.	1998	19.95	20
1996 1967 Jaguar E-Type DY001/C-M	Retrd.	1998	19.95	20
1996 1968 Volkswagen Karmann Ghia Convertible DY035/A-M	Retrd.	1998	19.95	20
1996 1969 Triumph Stag DY028/B-M	Retrd.	1997	19.95	20
1996 1973 MGB - GT V8 DY019/B-M	Retrd.	1997	19.95	20

Grand Classics - Mattel

YEAR ISSUE	EDITION LIMIT	YEAR RETD.	ISSUE PRICE	*QUOTE U.S.$
1993 1926 Rolls Royce Phantom I YY36-M	Open		14.95	15
1993 1930 Bugatti Royale YY45-M	Open		14.95	15
1993 1930 Duesenberg Model J YY4-M	Open		14.95	15
1993 1931 Mercedes 770 YY40-M	Retrd.	1997	14.95	15
1993 1933 Cadillac YY34-M	Retrd.	1997	14.95	15
1993 1936 Jaguar SS100 YY1-M	Retrd.	1997	14.95	15

Grand Marquis - Mattel

YEAR ISSUE	EDITION LIMIT	YEAR RETD.	ISSUE PRICE	*QUOTE U.S.$
1996 1928 Bugatti Type 44 YY024AD-M	Retrd.	1997	19.50	20
1996 1931 Stutz Bearcat YY014AC-M	Open		19.50	20
1996 1937 Cord 812 YY018AC-M	Retrd.	1997	19.50	20
1996 1938 Hispano Suiza YY017AD-M	Open		19.50	20
1996 1938 Lincoln Zephyr YY064/B-M	Open		19.50	20
1996 1939 Mercedes 540K YY020A/C	Open		19.50	20

Great American Microbreweries I - Mattel

YEAR ISSUE	EDITION LIMIT	YEAR RETD.	ISSUE PRICE	*QUOTE U.S.$
1996 Boulder Beer, Red Tail Ale, Fat Tire/Red Mountain MGB06-M	Open		29.95	30
1996 Fish Tail/Weidman's/Blue Whale/Gator Light MGB04-M	Open		29.95	30
1996 Left Hand/Holy Cow/Ozark/Dubuque Star MGB03-M	Open		29.95	30
1996 Lexington/No. Coast/Sun Valley/San Andreas MGB01-M	Open		29.95	30
1996 Rogue/Anderson Valley /Alaskan/Samuel Adams MGB05-M	Open		29.95	30
1996 Shipyard/Firehouse/Wild Goose/Blue Ridge MGB02-M	Open		29.95	30

Great American Microbreweries II - Mattel

YEAR ISSUE	EDITION LIMIT	YEAR RETD.	ISSUE PRICE	*QUOTE U.S.$
1997 Black Mntn/Crown City (Set of 2) MGB09/A-M	Open		15.90	16
1997 Catamnt/Great Divide (Set of 2) MGB07/B-M	Open		15.90	16
1997 Flossmoor/Pony Express (Set of 2) MGB09/B-M	Open		15.90	16
1997 Pennsylvania/Dixie (Set of 2) MGB08/B-M	Open		15.90	16
1997 River Horse/Snake River (Set of 2) MGB08/A-M	Open		15.90	16
1997 Woodstock/Seadog (Set of 2) MGB07/A-M	Open		15.90	16

Great Beers of the World I - Mattel

YEAR ISSUE	EDITION LIMIT	YEAR RETD.	ISSUE PRICE	*QUOTE U.S.$
1995 1918 Atkinson Steam - Swan YGB03-M	Open		14.95	15
1995 1926 Ford Model TT - Becks YGB02-M	Open		14.95	15
1995 1929 Morris Van - Fullers YGB04-M	Open		14.95	15
1995 1930 Ford - XXXX YGB01-M	Open		14.95	15
1995 1932 Ford Model AA - Carlsberg YGB05-M	Open		14.95	15
1995 1932 Mercedes L5 - Holsten YGB06-M	Open		14.95	15

Great Beers of the World II - Mattel

YEAR ISSUE	EDITION LIMIT	YEAR RETD.	ISSUE PRICE	*QUOTE U.S.$
1996 1910 Renault - Kronenbourg YGB07-M	Open		14.95	15
1996 1917 Yorkshire - Lowenbrau YGB12-M	Open		14.95	15
1996 1922 Foden Steam - Whitbread YGB11-M	Open		14.95	15
1996 1927 Talbot Van - South Pacific YGB10-M	Open		14.95	15
1996 1933 Mack Truck - Moosehead YGB09-M	Open		14.95	15
1996 1937 GMC Van - Steinlager YGB08-M	Open		14.95	15

Great Beers of the World III - Mattel

YEAR ISSUE	EDITION LIMIT	YEAR RETD.	ISSUE PRICE	*QUOTE U.S.$
1996 1912 Ford Model T - Kirin YGB14-M	Open		14.95	15
1996 1926 Ford Model TT - Anchor Steam YGB13-M	Open		14.95	15
1996 1929 Garrett Steam - Flowers YGB15-M	Open		14.95	15
1996 1931 Morris Van - Cascade YGB18-M	Open		14.95	15
1996 1932 Ford Model AA - Corona YGB16-M	Open		14.95	15
1996 1932 Mercedes - Henninger YGB17-M	Open		14.95	15

Great Beers of the World IV - Mattel

YEAR ISSUE	EDITION LIMIT	YEAR RETD.	ISSUE PRICE	*QUOTE U.S.$
1997 1912 Ford Model T - Yuengling YGB19-M	Open		14.95	15
1997 1918 Atkinson Steam Wagon - Beamish YGB22-M	Open		14.95	15
1997 1920 Mack AC - Tsingtao YGB23-M	Open		14.95	15
1997 1932 Ford AA Van - Stroh's YGB20-M	Retrd.	N/A	14.95	15
1997 1932 Mercedes - DAB YGB21-M	Open		14.95	15
1997 1939 Bedford Truck - Toohey's YGB24-M	Open		14.95	15

Great Outdoors - Mattel

YEAR ISSUE	EDITION LIMIT	YEAR RETD.	ISSUE PRICE	*QUOTE U.S.$
2000 1946 Dodge Power Wagon YYM38051	Open		29.95	30
2000 1947 Jeep CJ2A YYM38053	Open		29.95	30
2000 1948 Landrover YYM38052	Open		29.95	30
2000 1961 International Scout 80 YYM38054	Open		29.95	30
2000 1965 Ford Bronco YYM38055	Open		29.95	30
2000 1969 Chevrolet K/5 Blazer YYM38056	Open		29.95	30

Great Spirits - Mattel

YEAR ISSUE	EDITION LIMIT	YEAR RETD.	ISSUE PRICE	*QUOTE U.S.$
2000 1910 Renault AG - Dewars YYM37792	Open		29.95	30
2000 1926 Ford Model TT - Bacardi YYM37789	Open		29.95	30
2000 1929 Morris Light Courier Van - Cutty Sark YYM37791	Open		29.95	30
2000 1929 Morris Lisght Courier Van - Beefeater YYM37793	Open		29.95	30
2000 1937 Dodge Airflow - Jack Daniels YYM37790	Open		29.95	30
2000 1948 GMC COE - Jim Beam YYM37788	Open		29.95	30

Great Tanks of World War II - Mattel

YEAR ISSUE	EDITION LIMIT	YEAR RETD.	ISSUE PRICE	*QUOTE U.S.$
1999 Churchill MK IV DYM37584	Open		29.95	30
1999 Panther Type A DYM37581	Open		29.95	30
1999 Panzer IV Type F1 DYM37580	Open		29.95	30
1999 Panzer IV Type H/J DYM37586	Open		29.95	30
1999 Sherman M4A3 105MM DYM37585	Open		29.95	30
1999 Sherman M4A3 76MM DYM37579	Open		29.95	30
1999 T-34/76 DYM37583	Open		29.95	30
1999 Wirbelwind Flak PZ IV DYM37582	Open		29.95	30

Harley Davidson 95th Anniversary - Mattel

YEAR ISSUE	EDITION LIMIT	YEAR RETD.	ISSUE PRICE	*QUOTE U.S.$
1998 Ford Aeromax - 1957 Sportster CCY02/HA-M	Open		29.95	30
1998 Kenworth - 1929 WL 45" Twin CCY04/HA-M	Open		29.95	30
1998 Kenworth COE - 1909 V-Twin CCY03/HA-M	Open		29.95	30
1998 Mack - 1948 74 OHV-Twin (Panhead) CCY05/HA-M	Open		29.95	30
1998 Peterbilt - 1937 61 OHV Twin (Knucklehead) CCY06/HA-M	Open		29.95	30
1998 Peterbilt - 1966 Electra Glide (Shovelhead) CCY14/HA-M	Open		29.95	30

Hershey's Small Tractor Trailers - Mattel

YEAR ISSUE	EDITION LIMIT	YEAR RETD.	ISSUE PRICE	*QUOTE U.S.$
2000 Halloween DYM92172	Open		29.95	30
2000 Happy Easter DYM92168	Open		29.95	30
2000 Independence Day DYM92171	Open		29.95	30
2000 Mother's Day DYM92169	Open		29.95	30
2000 Season Greetings DYM92173	Open		29.95	30
2000 Valentine Greetings DYM92167	Open		29.95	30

Highway Commanders - Mattel

YEAR ISSUE	EDITION LIMIT	YEAR RETD.	ISSUE PRICE	*QUOTE U.S.$
1998 Freightliner Cab KS195/A-M	Open		37.95	38
1998 Kenworth Cab KS194/A-M	Open		37.95	38
1998 Mack Cab KS196/A-M	Open		37.95	38
1998 Peterbilt Cab KS193/A-M	Open		37.95	38

Horse Drawn Vehicles - Mattel

YEAR ISSUE	EDITION LIMIT	YEAR RETD.	ISSUE PRICE	*QUOTE U.S.$
1998 1875 Wells Fargo Stagecoach YSH03	Retrd.	1998	49.00	49
1998 1886 London Omnibus YSH02	Open		49.00	49
1998 1900 Gypsy Caravan YSH01	Open		49.00	49

Household Brands - Mattel

YEAR ISSUE	EDITION LIMIT	YEAR RETD.	ISSUE PRICE	*QUOTE U.S.$
1995 1920 Mack AC Truck - Kiwi Polish Y30	Open		14.95	15
1995 1922 A.E.C. Omnibus - Lifebuoy YY023A/F	Retrd.	1997	14.95	15
1995 1926 Ford Model TT Van Y21	Retrd.	1997	14.95	15
1995 1929 Morris Courier Van - Brasso YY019C/A	Retrd.	1997	14.95	15
1995 1929 Morris Cowley Light Van - Lindt Chocolate Y47	Retrd.	1997	14.95	15
1995 1930 Mack Truck - Goodyear YY33	Retrd.	1997	14.95	15

International Brewmasters - Mattel

YEAR ISSUE	EDITION LIMIT	YEAR RETD.	ISSUE PRICE	*QUOTE U.S.$
1997 DAF TT - Holsten Pils CCY08-M	Open		24.95	25
1997 Ford Aeromax - Dos Equis CCY02/B-M	Open		24.95	25
1997 Mack CH600 - Labatts CCY05/C-M	Open		24.95	25
1997 Peterbilt - Budweiser CCY06/B-M	Open		24.95	25
1997 Scania TT - Castlemaine XXXX CCY07/B-M	Open		24.95	25
1997 Scania TT - SKOL Lager CCY07-M	Open		24.95	25

International Fire Engine Collection I - Mattel

YEAR ISSUE	EDITION LIMIT	YEAR RETD.	ISSUE PRICE	*QUOTE U.S.$
1996 1920 Mack Fire Engine YFE01-M	Retrd.	2000	24.50	25
1996 1932 Ford Model AA Fire Engine YFE06-M	Retrd.	2000	24.50	25
1996 1932 Mercedes Ladder Truck YFE05-M	Retrd.	2000	24.50	25
1996 1933 Cadillac V16 Fire Engine YFE03-M	Retrd.	2000	24.50	25
1996 1939 Bedford Tanker Truck YFE04-M	Retrd.	2000	24.50	25
1996 1953 Land Rover w/Trailer YFE02-M	Retrd.	2000	24.50	25

International Fire Engine Collection II - Mattel

YEAR ISSUE	EDITION LIMIT	YEAR RETD.	ISSUE PRICE	*QUOTE U.S.$
1997 1923 Mack AC Water Tanker YFE11-M	Retrd.	2000	24.50	25
1997 1930 Ford Model A Battalion Chief Vehicle YFE12-M	Retrd.	2000	24.50	25
1997 1932 Ford Model AA Open Cab Fire Truck YFE09-M	Retrd.	2000	24.50	25
1997 1936 Leyland Cub Fire Engine YFE08	Retrd.	2000	24.50	25

*Quotes have been rounded up to nearest dollar

YEAR ISSUE	EDITION LIMIT	YEAR RETD.	ISSUE PRICE	*QUOTE U.S.$
1997 1937 GMC Rescue Squad Van YFE10-M	Retrd.	2000	24.50	25
1997 1938 Mercedes Fire Wagon YFE07-M	Retrd.	2000	24.50	25

International Fire Engine Collection III - Mattel

YEAR ISSUE	EDITION LIMIT	YEAR RETD.	ISSUE PRICE	*QUOTE U.S.$
1998 1935 Mack Fire Engine YFE15-M	Open		27.95	28
1998 1939 Bedford Truck YFE17-M	Open		27.95	28
1998 1947 Citroen Van YFE13-M	Open		27.95	28
1998 1948 Dodge Route Canteen Van YFE16-M	Open		27.95	28
1998 1950 Ford E83W Pumper Unit YFE18-M	Open		27.95	28
1998 1953 Ford Pick-Up YFE14-M	Open		27.95	28

International Fire Engine Collection IV - Mattel

YEAR ISSUE	EDITION LIMIT	YEAR RETD.	ISSUE PRICE	*QUOTE U.S.$
1998 1904 Merryweather YFE19-M	Open		37.95	38
1998 1906 Waterous YFE23-M	Open		37.95	38
1998 1907 Seagrave AC53 YFE21-M	Open		37.95	38
1998 1911 Mack YFE24-M	Open		37.95	38
1998 1912 Benz YFE20-M	Open		37.95	38
1998 1920 Ford Model T Truck YFE22-M	Open		37.95	38

International Fire Engine Collection V - Mattel

YEAR ISSUE	EDITION LIMIT	YEAR RETD.	ISSUE PRICE	*QUOTE U.S.$
1999 1932 Ford Model AA 1 1/2 Ton - US Forest Service YYM35190	Open		37.95	38
1999 1937 GMC Ambulance YYM35192	Open		37.95	38
1999 1938 Bedford - Airport Rescue YYM35191	Open		37.95	38
1999 1941 Chevy Pick-Up - US Army YYM35189	Open		37.95	38
1999 1952 Landrover - Royal Navy Rescue YYM35188	Open		37.95	38
1999 1954 Ford F-100 Pick-Up - Civil Defense YYM35187	Open		37.95	38

International Fire Engine Collection VI - Mattel

YEAR ISSUE	EDITION LIMIT	YEAR RETD.	ISSUE PRICE	*QUOTE U.S.$
1999 1920 Mack AC Water Tower Truck YYM37633	Open		37.95	38
1999 1932 Ford AA High Pressure Truck YYM37634	Open		37.95	38
1999 1932 Mercedes L5 Light Truck YYM37632	Open		37.95	38
1999 1936 Leyland Cub Open Top Ladder YYM37635	Open		37.95	38
1999 1946 Dodge Power Wagon Brush/Field Truck YYM37636	Open		37.95	38
1999 1948 GMC COE Tanker/Pumper YYM37631	Open		37.95	38

International Work Horses - Mattel

YEAR ISSUE	EDITION LIMIT	YEAR RETD.	ISSUE PRICE	*QUOTE U.S.$
1999 1920 Mack AC - 3M YYM36832	Open		29.95	30
1999 1929 Scammell 100 Ton Low Loader-Great Western Rail YYM36831	Open		29.95	30
1999 1937 Diamond T Low Wall - Caterpillar YYM36835	Open		29.95	30
1999 1937 Dodge Airflow Tanker - Texaco YYM36834	Open		29.95	30
1999 1937 International Stake Bed - Harley Davidson YYM36833	Open		29.95	30
1999 1948 GMC Dump Truck - US Steel YYM36836	Open		29.95	30

Kings of the Road - Mattel

YEAR ISSUE	EDITION LIMIT	YEAR RETD.	ISSUE PRICE	*QUOTE U.S.$
1999 Ford Aeromax - Consolidated Freight DYM38008	Open		29.95	30
1999 Ford Aeromax - Overnite DYM38009	Open		29.95	30
1999 Ford Aeromax - Roadway DYM38007	Open		29.95	30
1999 Kenworth Aerodyne - Yellow Freight DYM38010	Open		29.95	30

Limited Editions - Mattel

YEAR ISSUE	EDITION LIMIT	YEAR RETD.	ISSUE PRICE	*QUOTE U.S.$
1999 1889 Horsedrawn Wagon - Budweiser YYM36791	7,500		49.95	50
1997 1913 Ford Model TT - Jack Daniel's YY039/SF-M	12,500	1997	37.95	38
1997 1913 Fowler B6 Showman's Engine YY019B/SC-M	9,500		37.95	38
1997 1918 Atkinson Steam Lorry YY018E/SA-M	9,500		37.95	38
1998 1918 Crossley YY013/SA-M	9,500		37.95	38
1998 1920 Mack AC - Fisherman's Wharf YY030A/SB-M	9,500		29.95	30
1999 1920 Mack Fire Engine YYM38259	9,500		37.50	38
1997 1921 Scania Vabis Bus YY035/SB-M	5,000	1997	37.95	38
1999 1922 Scania Vabis Postbus YYM36793	5,000		37.95	38
1999 1929 Fowler Crane YYM36837	9,500		29.95	30
1999 1931 Diddler Tram - Coke YYM37797	12,500		44.95	45
1998 1931 Mercedes Benz 770 YY053/SA-M	12,500		29.95	30
1997 1932 Mercedes L5 Truck YY032A/SA-M	12,500		37.95	38
1999 1935 Auburn Speedster 851 DYM38179	5,000		29.95	30
1997 1937 Mercedes Benz 540K YY020A/SA-M	7,500		27.95	28
1997 1938 Hispano Suiza YY017A/SA-M	9,500		29.95	30
1998 1946 Delahaye Type-145 DY014/SA-M	7,500		44.95	45
1998 1948 Tucker DY011/SA-M	7,500		29.95	30
1997 1955 Ford Pick-Up YRS06/SA-M	9,500		37.95	38
1998 1956 Ford F-100 Pick-Up Truck MB300/SC	4,000		10.00	10
1998 1957 BMW 507 YY033/SB-M	7,500		29.95	30
1997 1957 Chevy Bel-Air Coupe DY002/SA-M	7,500	1997	29.95	30
1997 Foden Steam YY027/SC-M	5,000	1997	37.95	38
1999 Ford Aeromax - Jack Daniel's DYM36097	9,500		37.95	38
1999 Ford F-100 Pick-Up 50th Anniversary YRS07/SA-M	9,500		44.95	45
1998 Freightliner COE Tractor Trailer - Stars & Stripes KS191SA-M	6,000		119.85	120
1999 Mack CH600 Tractor Trailer - Matchbox DYM37796	7,500		119.85	120
1998 Peterbilt CCY06/SB-M	12,500		39.95	40
1998 Peterbilt Tractor Trailer - Matchbox KS186SC-M	3,500	1999	119.85	120

Military Planes - Mattel

YEAR ISSUE	EDITION LIMIT	YEAR RETD.	ISSUE PRICE	*QUOTE U.S.$
2000 F-4-U Corsair DYM92099	Open		29.95	30
2000 Grumman Hellcat DYM92101	Open		29.95	30
2000 P-38 Lightening DYM92108	Open		29.95	30
2000 P-40 Curtiss DYM92107	Open		29.95	30
2000 P-51 Mustang DYM92098	Open		29.95	30
2000 Spitfire DYM92106	Open		29.95	30

NASCAR - Victory Lane Collection - Mattel

YEAR ISSUE	EDITION LIMIT	YEAR RETD.	ISSUE PRICE	*QUOTE U.S.$
1995 1995 Burger King / Goodwrench (Set of 2) NC03-M	Open		19.90	20
1995 1995 Dupont / Texaco (Set of 2) NC01-M	Open		19.90	20
1995 1995 Interstate / Raybestos (Set of 2) NC02-M	Open		19.90	20
1995 1995 Kellogg's / Straightarrow (Set of 2) NC06-M	Open		19.90	20
1995 1995 McDonalds / Exide (Set of 2) NC05-M	Open		19.90	20
1995 1995 Valvoline / Lowes (Set of 2) NC04-M	Open		19.90	20

NBA Micro - Mattel

YEAR ISSUE	EDITION LIMIT	YEAR RETD.	ISSUE PRICE	*QUOTE U.S.$
1999 NBA (Set of 4) YYM36880	Open		39.95	40
1999 NBA (Set of 4) YYM36885	Open		39.95	40
1999 NBA (Set of 4) YYM36890	Open		39.95	40
1999 NBA (Set of 4) YYM36895	Open		39.95	40
1999 NBA (Set of 4) YYM36900	Open		39.95	40
1999 NBA (Set of 4) YYM36906	Open		39.95	40
1999 NBA (Set of 4) YYM36912	Open		39.95	40
1999 NBA (Set of 4) YYM36918	Open		39.95	40

North American Brewmasters - Mattel

YEAR ISSUE	EDITION LIMIT	YEAR RETD.	ISSUE PRICE	*QUOTE U.S.$
1996 Ford TT - Red Dog CCY02-M	Open		19.95	20
1996 Kenworth TT - Corona CCY04-M	Open		19.95	20
1996 Kenworth TT - Moosehead CCY03-M	Open		19.95	20
1996 Mack TT - Honey Brown CCY05-M	Open		19.95	20
1996 Peterbilt TT - Miller CCY01-M	Open		19.95	20
1996 Peterbilt TT - Pabst CCY06-M	Open		19.95	20

Oldies but Goodies I - Mattel

YEAR ISSUE	EDITION LIMIT	YEAR RETD.	ISSUE PRICE	*QUOTE U.S.$
1997 1948 Tucker Torpedo DYG07-M	Open		19.95	20
1997 1953 Buick Skylark DYG04-M	Open		19.95	20
1997 1955 Ford Thunderbird DYG08-M	Open		19.95	20
1997 1956 Chevy Corvette DYG06-M	Open		19.95	20
1997 1957 Chevy Bel-Air Coupe DYG02-M	Open		19.95	20
1997 1957 Studebaker Golden Hawk DYG03-M	Open		19.95	20
1997 1959 Cadillac Coupe Deville DYG05-M	Open		19.95	20
1997 1967 Ford Mustang Fastback DYG01-M	Open		19.95	20

Oldies but Goodies II - Mattel

YEAR ISSUE	EDITION LIMIT	YEAR RETD.	ISSUE PRICE	*QUOTE U.S.$
1998 1947 Chrysler Town & Country DYG10-M	Retrd.		19.95	20
1998 1948 Desoto Sedan DYG14-M	Retrd.		19.95	20
1998 1953 Cadillac Eldorado DYG13-M	Retrd.		19.95	20
1998 1955 Chevy Bel-Air DYG16-M	Retrd.		19.95	20
1998 1956 Ford Fairlane DYG12-M	Retrd.		19.95	20
1998 1958 Buick Special DYG11-M	Retrd.		19.95	20
1998 1958 Nash Metropolitan DYG15-M	Retrd.		19.95	20
1998 1959 Chevy Impala DYG09-M	Retrd.		19.95	20

Police Interceptors - Mattel

YEAR ISSUE	EDITION LIMIT	YEAR RETD.	ISSUE PRICE	*QUOTE U.S.$
2000 1957 Chevorlet Bel Air - Ohio DYM96666	Open		29.95	30
2000 1966 Chevy Chevelle - Arizona DYM96659	Open		29.95	30
2000 1966 Ford Fairlane - Florida DYM96665	Open		29.95	30
2000 1970 Dodge Challanger - Texas DYM96663	Open		29.95	30
2000 1970 Ford Boss 429 Mustang - Nevada DYM96667	Open		29.95	30
2000 1970 Plymouth Road Runner - New York DYM96664	Open		29.95	30

Power of the Press - Mattel

YEAR ISSUE	EDITION LIMIT	YEAR RETD.	ISSUE PRICE	*QUOTE U.S.$
1997 1910 Renault - Le Figaro YPP01-M	Retrd.		16.50	17
1997 1923 Mack AC - Pravda YPP06-M	Retrd.		16.50	17
1997 1930 Ford Model A - Washington Post YPP08-M	Retrd.		16.50	17
1997 1932 Ford Model AA - Las Angeles Times YPP05-M	Retrd.		16.50	17
1997 1932 Mercedes L5 - Berliner YPP03-M	Retrd.		16.50	17
1997 1935 Morris Van - London Times YPP02-M	Retrd.		16.50	17
1997 1937 GMC Van - Australian YPP07-M	Retrd.		16.50	17
1997 1948 Dodge Route Van - New York Times YPP04-M	Retrd.		16.50	17

Road Service Collection - Mattel

YEAR ISSUE	EDITION LIMIT	YEAR RETD.	ISSUE PRICE	*QUOTE U.S.$
1996 1953 Ford Tire Service YRS02-M	Open		29.95	30
1996 1954 Ford Snow Plough YRS04-M	Open		29.95	30
1996 1955 Chevy Tow Truck YRS01-M	Open		29.95	30
1996 1955 Ford F-100 Pick-Up - Red Crown Route 66 YRS06-M	Open		29.95	30
1996 1955 Ford F-100 Pick-Up - Red Crown Route 84 YRS06/B-M	Open		29.95	30
1996 1956 Chevy Battery Service YRS03-M	Open		29.95	30
1996 1957 Chevy Gas Station Truck YRS05-M	Open		29.95	30

Single Items - Mattel

YEAR ISSUE	EDITION LIMIT	YEAR RETD.	ISSUE PRICE	*QUOTE U.S.$
1991 1880 Merryweather Fire Engine YY46	Retrd.	1998	41.00	41
1997 1905 Busch Fire Engine YSFE03-M	Open		59.00	59
1994 1907 Unic Taxi Y28	Open		14.95	15
1990 1920 Rolls Royce Armored Car Y38	Retrd.	1996	14.95	15
1995 1925 Southern Crescent Limited Locomotive YSLO01	Retrd.	1999	195.00	195
1999 1926 Ford Model TT Truck YYM38030	Open		29.95	30
1998 1927 Ahrens Fox N-S-4 Fire Engine YSFE04-M	Open		69.90	70
1992 1929 Garrett Steam Wagon - Milkmaid Brand Milk Y37/92	Open		14.95	15
1995 1930 Ahrens Fox YSFE01	Retrd.	1999	88.50	89
1994 1930 Mack Tanker - Conoco YY23	Open		14.95	15
1995 1936 Leyland Cub YSFE02	Open		39.00	39
1994 1939 Triumph Dolomite DY17	Retrd.	1999	24.50	25
1999 1952 Landrover w/Trailer YYM36400	Open		59.00	59
1999 1955 Chevy 3100 Pick-Up Truck YYM37799	Open		30.00	30
1999 1956 Mack B-95 Pumper Fire Truck YYM35810	Open		64.90	65
1994 1967 Jaguar E-Type (pewter) DY921	Retrd.	1996	29.95	30
1997 1996 Mazda RX7 Gold Coin Car MB251/ZE	Open		19.95	20
1997 1997 Chrysler Atlantic Web Car MB306/ZZ	Open		10.00	10
1996 Australian Vintage Collection (Set of 6)) MB913	Open		27.95	28
1995 Circuses of the World Collection (Set of 6)) MB915	Retrd.	1998	24.50	25
1992 Dinky Triple Pack DY903	Retrd.	1998	29.95	30
1994 Ford Pilot DY05/92	Retrd.	1998	14.95	15
1996 International Postal Vehicles (Set of 6) MB916	Open		24.50	25
1995 Jaguar XJ220 LS003	Retrd.	1998	39.00	39
1997 Lamborghini Countach Gold Coin Car MB154/SL	Open		19.95	20
1995 Lamborghini Diablo LS002	Open		39.00	39
1995 Pills, Powders & Potions (Set of 6)) MB914	Open		24.50	25
1995 Porsche 911 Turbo LS001	Retrd.	1998	39.00	39

Small Town Pick-Ups - Mattel

YEAR ISSUE	EDITION LIMIT	YEAR RETD.	ISSUE PRICE	*QUOTE U.S.$
2000 1934 International - Wilson's Grain & Feed YYM38039	Open		29.95	30
2000 1939 REO - Forgione Stone & Brick Mason YYM38041	Open		29.95	30
2000 1940 Ford Pick-Up - Murdock Lumber Millwork YYM38040	Open		29.95	30
2000 1941 Chevy Pick-Up - Kent's Dairy YYM38042	Open		29.95	30
2000 1951 Holden FX Pick-Up - Mr. Fix It YYM38035	Open		29.95	30
2000 1953 Ford F-100 Pick-Up - Custer Dry Goods YYM38038	Open		29.95	30

Stars of the Silver Screen - Mattel

YEAR ISSUE	EDITION LIMIT	YEAR RETD.	ISSUE PRICE	*QUOTE U.S.$
1994 1948 Tucker Torpedo DY011/C-M	Retrd.	1998	19.95	20
1994 1953 Buick Skylark DY029/B-M	Retrd.	1998	19.95	20
1994 1955 Ford Thunderbird DY031/B-M	Retrd.	1998	19.95	20
1994 1956 Chevy Corvette DY023/A-M	Retrd.	1998	19.95	20
1994 1957 Chevy Bel-Air Convertible DY027/B-M	Retrd.	1998	19.95	20
1994 1958 Studebaker Golden Hawk DY026/B-M	Retrd.	1998	19.95	20
1994 1959 Cadillac Coupe Deville DY007/C-M	Retrd.	1998	19.95	20
1994 1967 Mustang Fastback DY016/C-M	Retrd.	1998	19.95	20

Steam Powered Vehicles I - Mattel

YEAR ISSUE	EDITION LIMIT	YEAR RETD.	ISSUE PRICE	*QUOTE U.S.$
1996 1829 Stephenson's Rocket YAS01-M	Open		27.95	28
1996 1894 Aveling & Porter Steam Roller YAS03-M	Open		27.95	28
1996 1905 Fowler B6 Showman's Engine YAS05-M	Open		27.95	28
1996 1917 Yorkshire Steam Wagon YAS04-M	Open		27.95	28
1996 1918 Atkinson Model D Steam Wagon YAS06-M	Open		27.95	28
1996 1922 Foden Steam Wagon YAS02-M	Open		27.95	28

Steam Powered Vehicles II - Mattel

YEAR ISSUE	EDITION LIMIT	YEAR RETD.	ISSUE PRICE	*QUOTE U.S.$
1997 1912 Burrel Traction Engine YAS08-M	Open		27.95	28
1997 1917 Yorkshire Steam Lorry w/Load YAS11-M	Open		27.95	28
1997 1918 Atkinson Steam Wagon w/Load YAS10-M	Open		27.95	28
1997 1922 Foden Steam Wagon w/Load YAS12-M	Open		27.95	28
1997 1929 Fowler Crane Engine YAS07-M	Open		27.95	28
1997 1930 Garrett Steam w/Barrels YAS09-M	Open		27.95	28

*Quotes have been rounded up to nearest dollar

Taste of France - Mattel

YEAR ISSUE	EDITION LIMIT	YEAR RETD.	ISSUE PRICE	*QUOTE U.S.$
1994 Citroen - Evian YTF1	Open		14.95	15
1994 Citroen - Marcillat YTF4	Open		14.95	15
1994 Citroen - Martell YTF2	Open		14.95	15
1994 Citroen - Pommery Mustard YTF6	Open		14.95	15
1994 Citroen - Tattinger Champagne YTF5	Open		14.95	15
1994 Citroen - Yoplait YTF3	Open		14.95	15

Tractor Trailers - Mattel

YEAR ISSUE	EDITION LIMIT	YEAR RETD.	ISSUE PRICE	*QUOTE U.S.$
2000 Campbells Soup Vintage TT DYM38337	Open		89.85	90
2000 Freightliner - Hershey's Modern TT DYM38277	Open		74.85	75
2000 Freightliner - McDonald's Modern TT DYM38314	Open		89.85	90
2000 Hershey's Vintage TT DYM92058	Open		89.85	90
1999 1938 Peterbilt Tractor Trailer - Coke DYM38050	Open		74.85	75
1999 1948 Diamond T Tractor Trailer - Budweiser DYM38233	Open		74.85	75
1996 Freightliner Tractor Trailer - Beefeater KS187SA-M	Open		59.00	59
1998 Freightliner Tractor Trailer - Budweiser KS201/A-M	Open		89.95	90
1997 Freightliner Tractor Trailer - J&B Christmas KS190SA-M	Open		74.85	75
1997 Kenworth Tractor Trailer - Harley Davidson KS188SA-M	Open		74.85	75
1998 Kenworth Tractor Trailer - J&B Christmas KS188/A-M	Open		74.85	75
1999 Kenworth Tractor Trailer - Jack Daniel's DYM37904	Open		74.85	75
1998 Kenworth Tractor Trailer - Shell KS200/A-M	Open		89.95	90
1999 Mack B - McDonalds DYM34577	Open		89.95	90
1999 Peterbilt - Budweiser DYM38258	Open		125.00	125
1998 Peterbilt 359 Tractor Trailer w/Flatbed KS192/SA-M	Open		74.85	75
1998 Peterbilt Tractor Trailer - Coke KS199/A-M	Open		74.85	75
1999 Peterbilt Tractor Trailer - Harley Davidson DYM37040	Open		74.85	75
1997 Peterbilt Tractor Trailer - Jack Daniel's KS189SA-M	Retrd.	2000	74.85	75
1996 Peterbilt Tractor Trailer - Jim Beam KS186SA-M	Retrd.	1999	59.00	59

Trolleys, Trams & Buses - Mattel

YEAR ISSUE	EDITION LIMIT	YEAR RETD.	ISSUE PRICE	*QUOTE U.S.$
1995 1910 Renault Bus YET06-M	Retrd.	1999	19.50	20
1995 1920 Preston Tram Car YET01-M	Retrd.	1999	19.50	20
1995 1922 A.E.C. Omnibus YET05-M	Retrd.	1999	19.50	20
1995 1922 Scania Bus YET04-M	Retrd.	1999	19.50	20
1995 1930 Leyland Titan Bus YET02-M	Retrd.	1999	19.50	20
1995 1931 Diddler Trolley Bus YET03-M	Retrd.	1999	19.50	20

U.S. Postal Vehicles - Mattel

YEAR ISSUE	EDITION LIMIT	YEAR RETD.	ISSUE PRICE	*QUOTE U.S.$
1999 1912 Ford Model T Truck YYM38237	Open		29.95	30
1999 1920 Mack AC Drop Side YYM38238	Open		29.95	30
1999 1932 Ford Model AA 1 1/2 Ton Truck YYM38239	Open		29.95	30
1999 1937 GMC Postal Van YYM38240	Open		29.95	30
1999 1948 Dodge Route Van YYM38241	Open		29.95	30
1999 1961 International Scout 80 YYM38242	Open		29.95	30

Ultimate Dream Machines - Mattel

YEAR ISSUE	EDITION LIMIT	YEAR RETD.	ISSUE PRICE	*QUOTE U.S.$
1995 1987 Ferrari F40 CDC150	Retrd.	1999	24.50	25
1995 1993 Corvette ZR1 Coupe CDC213	Open		24.50	25
1995 1993 Jaguar XJ220 CDC173	Open		24.50	25
1995 1993 Lamborghini Diablo Roadster CDC112	Open		24.50	25
1995 1994 Mercedes Benz 320SL CDC232	Open		24.50	25

Vintage Big Rig Cabs - Mattel

YEAR ISSUE	EDITION LIMIT	YEAR RETD.	ISSUE PRICE	*QUOTE U.S.$
1999 1939 Peterbilt DYM35217	Open		37.95	38
1999 1948 Diamond T DYM35216	Open		37.95	38
1999 1956 Mack B DYM35214	Open		37.95	38

Vintage City Police - Mattel

YEAR ISSUE	EDITION LIMIT	YEAR RETD.	ISSUE PRICE	*QUOTE U.S.$
1999 1912 Ford Model T Van - Dallas DYM38019	Open		29.95	30
1999 1926 Ford Model TT Van - Miami DYM38020	Open		29.95	30
1999 1933 Cadillac - Salt Lake City DYM38021	Open		29.95	30
1999 1957 Chevrolet Bel-Air - Atlanta DYM38023	Open		29.95	30
1999 1966 Ford Fairlane - New York City DYM38024	Open		29.95	30
1999 1970 Plymouth GTX - Denver DYM38022	Open		29.95	30

Worlds Greatest Automakers - Mattel

YEAR ISSUE	EDITION LIMIT	YEAR RETD.	ISSUE PRICE	*QUOTE U.S.$
1997 Cadillac / Aston Martin (Set of 2) CPM06-M	Open		19.95	20
1997 Corvette / BMW (Set of 2) CPM02-M	Open		19.95	20
1997 Jaguar / Mercedes (Set of 2) CPM01-M	Open		19.95	20
1997 Lincoln / Lamborghini (Set of 2) CPM03-M	Open		19.95	20
1997 Porsche / Saab (Set of 2) CPM04-M	Open		19.95	20
1997 Volvo / Ferrari (Set of 2) CPM05-M	Open		19.95	20

Maud Humphrey Bogart/Enesco Group, Inc.

Maud Humphrey Bogart Collectors' Club Members Only - M. Humphrey

YEAR ISSUE	EDITION LIMIT	YEAR RETD.	ISSUE PRICE	*QUOTE U.S.$
1991 Friends For Life MH911	Closed	N/A	60.00	130
1992 Nature's Little Helper MH921	Closed	N/A	65.00	82-94
1993 Sitting Pretty MH931	Closed	N/A	60.00	60-78

Maud Humphrey Bogart - Symbol Of Membership Figurines - M. Humphrey

YEAR ISSUE	EDITION LIMIT	YEAR RETD.	ISSUE PRICE	*QUOTE U.S.$
1991 A Flower For You H5596	Closed	N/A	Unkn.	35-65
1992 Sunday Best M0002	Closed	N/A	Unkn.	57-75
1993 Playful Companions M0003	Closed	N/A	Unkn.	57-91

Maud Humphrey Bogart - M. Humphrey

YEAR ISSUE	EDITION LIMIT	YEAR RETD.	ISSUE PRICE	*QUOTE U.S.$
1991 All Bundled Up -910015	19,500	N/A	85.00	75
1990 Autumn Days H1348	24,500	N/A	45.00	38-65
1992 Autumn's Child 910260	24,500	N/A	50.00	50-63
1989 The Bride-Porcelain H1388	15,000	N/A	125.00	119-125
1990 A Chance Acquaintance H5589	19,500	N/A	70.00	119-125
1992 The Christmas Carol 915823	24,500	N/A	75.00	69-75
1988 Cleaning House H1303	Retrd.	N/A	60.00	44-90
1991 Doubles -910023	19,500	N/A	70.00	82
1993 The Entertainer 910562	19,500	N/A	60.00	75-82
1993 Flying Lessons 910139	15,000	N/A	50.00	63-69
1988 Gift Of Love H1319	Retrd.	N/A	65.00	38-65
1994 Good As New 914924	5,000	N/A	100.00	88
1991 The Graduate H5559	19,500	N/A	75.00	219-225
1994 A Hidden Treasure - 914940	5,000	N/A	60.00	94
1990 Holiday Surprise H5551	24,500	N/A	50.00	30-75
1991 Hush A Bye Baby H5695	19,500	N/A	62.00	82
1989 In The Orchard H1373	24,500	N/A	33.00	32-44
1990 Kitty's Bath H1384	19,500	N/A	103.00	144
1989 Kitty's Lunch H1355	19,500	N/A	60.00	30-69
1989 Little Bo Peep H1382	Retrd.	N/A	45.00	32-50
1989 The Little Captive H1374	19,500	N/A	55.00	32-75
1988 Little Chickadees H1306	Retrd.	N/A	65.00	32-50
1989 Little Red Riding Hood H1381	24,500	N/A	42.50	57-65
1990 A Little Robin H1347	19,500	N/A	55.00	32-55
1994 Love To Last A Lifetime - 655627	5,000	N/A	45.00	50-63
1993 Love's First Bloom 910120	15,000	N/A	50.00	63-69
1988 The Magic Kitten H1308	Retrd.	N/A	66.00	38-85
1994 Marie-Childhood Memories 869619	5,000	N/A	35.00	35-44
1988 My 1st Birthday H1320	Retrd.	N/A	47.00	57-65
1988 My First Dance H1311	Retrd.	N/A	60.00	150-188
1990 My Winter Hat H5554	24,500	N/A	40.00	69
1989 No More Tears H1351	24,500	N/A	44.00	38-88
1991 The Pinwheel H5600	24,500	N/A	45.00	50
1989 Playing Bridesmaid H5500	19,500	N/A	125.00	120-125
1993 Playing Mama 5th Anniv. Figurine 915963	Retrd.	N/A	80.00	140-160
1993 Playing Mama Event Figurine 915963R	Retrd.	N/A	80.00	110-120
1988 A Pleasure To Meet You H1310	Retrd.	N/A	65.00	78-91
1988 Sarah H1312	Retrd.	N/A	60.00	188-358
1988 School Days H1318	Retrd.	N/A	42.50	46-50
1990 School Lesson H1356	19,500	N/A	77.00	77-188
1988 Sealed With A Kiss H1316	Retrd.	N/A	45.00	44-50
1988 Seamstress H1309	Retrd.	N/A	66.00	90-195
1988 Special Friends H1317	Retrd.	N/A	66.00	52-82
1990 A Special Gift H5550	19,500	N/A	70.00	57-88
1989 Springtime Gathering H1385	7,500	N/A	295.00	295
1992 Stars and Stripes Forever 910201	Retrd.	N/A	75.00	90-113
1992 Summer's Child 910252	24,500	N/A	50.00	50-57
1989 A Sunday Outing H1386	15,000	N/A	135.00	75-119
1988 Susanna H1305	Retrd.	N/A	60.00	132-144
1988 Tea And Gossip H1301	Retrd.	N/A	65.00	75-104
1989 Winter Fun H1354	Retrd.	N/A	46.00	46-75
1991 Winter Ride 910066	Retrd.	N/A	60.00	60-65

Maud Humphrey Bogart Gallery Figurines - M. Humphrey

YEAR ISSUE	EDITION LIMIT	YEAR RETD.	ISSUE PRICE	*QUOTE U.S.$
1991 Mother's Treasures H5619	15,000	N/A	118.00	88-118

Maud Humphrey Bogart Linen and Lace - M. Humphrey

YEAR ISSUE	EDITION LIMIT	YEAR RETD.	ISSUE PRICE	*QUOTE U.S.$
1994 Artist of Her Time 916722	2,500	N/A	60.00	60-69
1994 Capture the Moment 912654	2,500	N/A	125.00	125

Melody in Motion/Desert Specialties Ltd.

Melody In Motion/Collector's Society - S. Nakane, unless otherwise noted

YEAR ISSUE	EDITION LIMIT	YEAR RETD.	ISSUE PRICE	*QUOTE U.S.$
1992 Amazing Willie the One-Man Band 07152	Retrd.	1994	130.00	400
1992 Willie The Conductor	Retrd.	1994	Gift	150
1993 Charmed Bunnies	Retrd.	1993	Gift	40-45
1993 Willie The Collector 07170	Retrd.	1995	200.00	200-250
1994 Springtime	Retrd.	1994	Gift	30-50
1995 Best Friends	Retrd.	1995	Gift	30-50
1996 Willie The Entertainer 07199	Retrd.	1996	200.00	300-350
1996 '86 Santa Replica - K. Maeda	Retrd.	1997	Gift	50-80
1997 Willie on Parade/Drum 07214 - K. Maeda	Retrd.	1997	220.00	200-220
1997 Willie Sez - K. Maeda	Retrd.	1997	Gift	28-40
1998 Willie & Jumbo 07224 - K. Maeda	Retrd.	1998	180.00	170-180
1998 Purr-Fect Harmony 07307 - L. Miquez	Retrd.	1998	Gift	28-40
1999 Cheers 07240 - K. Maeda	Retrd.	1999	170.00	170
1999 Nocturne 07308 - T. Nomura	Retrd.	1999	Gift	45
2000 Y2K Willie 07309 - T. Nomura	Yr.Iss.		Gift	N/A

Melody In Motion - S. Nakane, unless otherwise noted

YEAR ISSUE	EDITION LIMIT	YEAR RETD.	ISSUE PRICE	*QUOTE U.S.$
1985 Willie The Trumpeter 07000	Open		90.00	175
1985 Willie The Hobo (Memories) 07001	2,500	1985	90.00	175-195
1985 Willie The Hobo (Show Me...) 07001	Retrd.	1996	90.00	200-275
1985 Willie The Whistler (Show Me...) 07002	2,500	1985	90.00	200-225
1985 Willie The Whistler (Memories) 07002	Retrd.	1998	90.00	200-250
1985 Salty 'N' Pepper 07010	Retrd.	1992	90.00	300-400
1986 The Cellist 07011	Retrd.	1995	100.00	200-350
1986 Santa Claus 1986 07012	20,000	1986	100.00	1800-2000
1986 The Guitarist 07013	Retrd.	1994	100.00	200-250
1986 The Fiddler 07014	Retrd.	1995	100.00	200-250
1987 Lamppost Willie 07051	Open		85.00	150
1987 The Organ Grinder 07053	Retrd.	1994	100.00	200-250
1987 Violin Clown 07055	Retrd.	1992	85.00	200-250
1987 Clarinet Clown 07056	Retrd.	1991	85.00	175-200
1987 Saxophone Clown 07057	Retrd.	1991	85.00	175-200
1987 Accordion Clown 07058	Retrd.	1991	85.00	175-200
1987 Santa Claus 1987 07060	16,000	1987	110.00	600-1200
1987 Balloon Clown 07061	Open		85.00	160
1987 The Carousel (1st Edition) 07065	Retrd.	1993	190.00	200-350
1987 Madame Violin 07075	Retrd.	1991	130.00	200-350
1987 Madame Mandolin 07076	Retrd.	1994	130.00	200-400
1987 Madame Cello 07077	Retrd.	1991	130.00	200-350
1987 Madame Flute 07078	Retrd.	1992	130.00	200-400
1987 Madame Harpsichord 07080	Retrd.	1991	130.00	200-400
1987 Madame Lyre 07081	Retrd.	1994	130.00	150-300
1988 Madame Harp 07079	Retrd.	1998	130.00	150-250
1988 Spotlight Clown Cornet 07082	Retrd.	1992	120	150-200
1988 Spotlight Clown Banjo 07083	Retrd.	1992	120.00	150-250
1988 Spotlight Clown Trombone 07084	Retrd.	1992	120.00	150-200
1988 Spotlight Clown Bingo 07085	Retrd.	1996	130.00	150
1988 Spotlight Clown Tuba 07086	Retrd.	1992	120.00	150-250
1988 Spotlight Clown Bass 07087	Retrd.	1994	130.00	200-275
1988 Peanut Vendor 07088	Retrd.	1994	140.00	200-350
1988 Ice Cream Vendor 07089	Retrd.	1994	140.00	200-225
1988 Santa Claus 1988 07090	12,000	1988	130.00	700-1000
1989 Clockpost Willie 07091	Open		150.00	230
1989 Santa Claus 1989 (Willie) 07092	12,000	1989	130.00	400-600
1989 Lull'aby Willie 07093	Retrd.	1992	170.00	400-500
1989 The Grand Carousel 07094	Retrd.	1995	3000.00	3000-4000
1989 Grandfather's Clock 07096	Retrd.	1994	200.00	220-325
1990 Santa Claus 1990 07097	12,000	1990	150.00	300-325
1990 Shoemaker 07130	3,700	1993	110.00	150-200
1990 Blacksmith 07131	3,700	1993	110.00	150-200
1990 Woodchopper 07132	3,700	1993	110.00	150-200
1990 Accordion Boy 07133	4,100	1992	120.00	150-200
1990 Hunter 07134	Retrd.	1994	110.00	150-250
1990 Robin Hood 07135 - C. Johnson	2,000	1991	180.00	300-400
1990 Little John 07136 - C. Johnson	2,000	1992	180.00	250-300
1990 Clockpost Willie II (European) 07140	Retrd.	1990	N/A	2000
1990 Clockpost Clown 07141	Retrd.	1999	220.00	220
1990 Lull' A Bye Willie II (European) 07142	Retrd.	1990	N/A	300-450
1991 The Carousel (2nd Edition) 07065	Retrd.	1995	240.00	300-400
1991 Victoria Park Carousel 07143	Retrd.	1999	300.00	360
1991 Hunter Timepiece 07144	Retrd.	1994	250.00	200-350
1991 Santa Claus 1991 07146	7,000	1991	150.00	300-400
1991 Willie The Fisherman 07148	Retrd.	1998	150.00	200
1992 King of Clowns Carousel 07149	Retrd.	1998	740.00	800-1200
1992 Golden Mountain Clock 07150	Retrd.	1995	250.00	250-280
1992 Santa Claus 1992 07151	11,000	1992	160.00	150-200
1992 Dockside Willie 07153	Retrd.	1998	160.00	150-250
1992 Wall Street Willie 07147	Open		180.00	250
1993 Wild West Willie 07154	Retrd.	1995	175.00	200-250
1993 Alarm Clock Post 07155 (Willie European)	Retrd.	1996	240.00	350-450
1993 Lamplight Willie 07156	Retrd.	1996	220.00	200-350
1993 Madame Cello Player, glaze 07157	200	1993	170.00	400
1993 Madame Flute, glaze 07158	200	1993	170.00	400
1993 Madame Harpsichord, glaze	200	1993	170.00	400
1993 Madame Harp, glaze	150	1993	190.00	400
1993 Santa Claus 1993 Coke 07161	6,000	1993	180.00	250-475
1993 Wall Street (Japanese) 07162	Retrd.	1993	N/A	350-450
1993 Santa Claus 1993 (European) 07163	1,000	1993	N/A	375-450
1993 When I Grow Up 07171	Retrd.	1996	200.00	200-400
1993 Willie The Golfer - Alarm 07164	Retrd.	1995	240.00	200-240
1993 The Artist 07165	Retrd.	1996	240.00	200-240
1993 Heartbreak Willie 07166	Retrd.	1998	180.00	190-200
1993 South of the Border 07167	Retrd.	1996	180.00	200-250
1994 Low Pressure Job-Alarm 07168	Retrd.	1995	240.00	200-240
1994 Day's End-Alarm 07169	Retrd.	1996	240.00	200-300
1994 Santa '94 Coca-Cola 07174	9,000	1994	190.00	200-250
1994 Smooth Sailing 07175	Retrd.	1996	200.00	250-300
1994 Santa Claus 1994 (European) 07176	700	1994	N/A	300-400
1994 The Longest Drive 07177	Open		150.00	160
1994 Happy Birthday Willie 07178	Open		170.00	170
1994 Chattanooga Choo Choo 07179	Open		180.00	200
1994 Jackpot Willie 07180	Open		180.00	200
1994 Caroler Boy 07189	10,000	1998	172.00	100-172
1994 Caroler Girl 07190	10,000	1998	172.00	100-172
1994 Day's End-Clock 07269	Retrd.	1997	240.00	200-240
1994 Willie the Yodeler 07192	Open		158.00	170
1994 Willie the Golfer- Clock 07264	Open		240.00	255
1995 Blue Danube Carousel 07173	Open		280.00	315
1995 Campfire Cowboy 07172	Retrd.	1995	180.00	200-300
1995 Coca-Cola Norman Rockwell 07194	Retrd.	1998	194.00	200
1995 Santa Claus '95 07195	6,000	1995	190.00	175-250
1995 Gaslight Willie 07197	Open		190.00	190
1995 Low Pressure Job-Clock 07268	Retrd.	1997	240.00	170-250
1995 Coca Cola Polar Bear 07198	6,000	1998	180.00	120-180
1995 Willie the Conductor (10th Anniversary) 07181	10,000	1999	220.00	220
1995 Willie The Fireman 07271	1,500	1996	200.00	200-300
1996 The Candy Factory-I Love Lucy 07203 - Willingham/Maeda	Retrd.	1998	250.00	200-250

YEAR ISSUE	EDITION LIMIT	YEAR RETD.	ISSUE PRICE	*QUOTE U.S.$
1996 Willie On The Road 07204 - K. Maeda	Open		180.00	190
1996 Marionette Clown 07205 - K. Maeda	Open		200.00	210
1996 Willie the Racer 07206 - K. Maeda	Open		180.00	210
1996 Willie the Organ Grinder 07207	3,000		200.00	210
1996 Santa Claus '96 07208 - K. Maeda	7,000		220.00	220
1996 Willie the Champion 07209 - K. Maeda	Open		180.00	190
1996 Willie the Photographer 07211 - K. Maeda	Open		220.00	235
1997 Willie on Parade/Trumpet 07212 - K. Maeda	Open		220.00	220
1997 Willie on Parade/Sousaphone 07213 - K. Maeda	Open		220.00	220
1997 Willie on Parade/Trombone 07215 - K. Maeda	Open		220.00	220
1997 I Love Lucy/Vitameatavegamin 07216 - K. Maeda	4,000	1998	250.00	150-250
1997 Santa Claus 1997 07217 - K. Maeda	4,000	1997	220.00	150-255
1997 Side Street Circus/Balancing Dog 07230	Closed	1998	110.00	50-110
1997 Side Street Circus/Juggling 07231	Closed	1998	110.00	50-110
1997 Side Street Circus/Accordian 07232	Closed	1998	110.00	50-110
1997 Side Street Circus/Clarinet 07233	Closed	1998	110.00	50-110
1997 Side Street Circus/Plate Spinning 07234	Closed	1998	110.00	50-110
1998 Coca Cola Santa Claus Clock 07223 - K. Maeda	3,000	1998	250.00	250-350
1998 Wedding Couple, white 07220 - K. Maeda	Open		196.00	210
1998 Willie The Wanderer 07221 - K. Maeda	Open		170.00	180
1998 Santa Claus 1998 07222 - K. Maeda	4,000	1998	220.00	220-300
1999 Balloon Clown (Europe) 07062 - K. Maeda	Open		150.00	160
1999 Willie The Entertainer ("As Time Goes By") 07199	360	1999	200.00	210
1999 Just For You (Europe) 07239 - K. Maeda	Retrd.	1999	170.00	170
1999 Wedding Couple, colors 07220 - K. Maeda	300	1999	196.00	200
1999 Willie the Hunter (Europe) 07241 - K. Maeda	Open		170.00	180
1999 Clock Post Clown (Europe) 07242 - K. Maeda	Open		200.00	200
1999 Santa Claus 1999 07243 - K. Maeda	3,000	1999	220.00	220
2000 Santa Claus 2000 07244 - K. Maeda	3,000		250.00	250
2000 Santa Claus Clock 07245 - K. Maeda	600		260.00	260
2000 Rail Road Cart Willie 07246 - K. Maeda	Open		200.00	200

Memories of Yesterday/Enesco Group, Inc.

Memories of Yesterday Society Figurines - M. Attwell

YEAR ISSUE	EDITION LIMIT	YEAR RETD.	ISSUE PRICE	*QUOTE U.S.$
1991 Welcome To Your New Home MY911	Yr.Iss.	1991	30.00	48
1992 I Love My Friends MY921	Yr.Iss.	1992	32.50	35
1993 Now I'm The Fairest Of Them All MY931	Yr.Iss.	1993	35.00	35
1993 A Little Love Song for You MY941	Yr.Iss.	1993	35.00	35
1994 Wot's All This Talk About Love MY942	Yr.Iss.	1994	27.50	28-40
1995 Sharing the Common Thread of Love MY951	Yr.Iss.	1995	100.00	100
1995 A Song For You From One That's True MY952	Yr.Iss.	1995	37.50	38
1996 You've Got My Vote MY961	Yr.Iss.	1996	40.00	40
1996 Peace, Heavenly Peace MY962	Yr.Iss.	1996	30.00	30
1997 We Take Care of One Another MY971	Yr.Iss.	1997	45.00	45
1997 You Mean the World to Me MY972	Yr.Iss.	1997	40.00	40
1998 A Little Caring Makes Everything Better MY981	Yr.Iss.	1998	45.00	45
1998 No Worries Here MY982	Yr.Iss.	1998	40.00	40
1999 She Loves Me MY991	Yr.Iss.	1999	30.00	55

Memories of Yesterday Exclusive Membership Figurine - M. Attwell

YEAR ISSUE	EDITION LIMIT	YEAR RETD.	ISSUE PRICE	*QUOTE U.S.$
1991 We Belong Together S0001	Yr.Iss.	1991	Gift	37
1992 Waiting For The Sunshine S0002	Yr.Iss.	1992	Gift	25-35
1993 I'm The Girl For You S0003	Yr.Iss.	1993	Gift	40-50
1994 Blowing a Kiss to a Dear I Miss S0004	Yr.Iss.	1994	Gift	N/A
1995 Time to Celebrate S0005	Yr.Iss.	1995	Gift	N/A
1996 Forget-Me-Not! S0006	Yr.Iss.	1996	Gift	N/A
1997 Holding On To Childhood Memories S0007	Yr.Iss.	1997	Gift	N/A
1998 I'll Never Leave Your Side S0008	Yr.Iss.	1998	Gift	N/A
1999 He Loves Me S0009	Yr.Iss.	1999	Gift	50

Memories of Yesterday Exclusive Charter Membership Figurine - M. Attwell

YEAR ISSUE	EDITION LIMIT	YEAR RETD.	ISSUE PRICE	*QUOTE U.S.$
1992 Waiting For The Sunshine S0102	Yr.Iss.	1992	Gift	N/A
1993 I'm The Girl For You S0103	Yr.Iss.	1993	Gift	N/A
1994 Blowing a Kiss to a Dear I Miss S0104	Yr.Iss.	1994	Gift	N/A
1995 Time to Celebrate S0105	Yr.Iss.	1995	Gift	N/A
1996 Forget-Me-Not! S0106	Yr.Iss.	1996	Gift	N/A
1997 Holding On To Childhood Memories S0107	Yr.Iss.	1997	Gift	N/A
1998 I'll Never Leave Your Side S0108	Yr.Iss.	1998	Gift	N/A

Memories of Yesterday 10th Anniversary Celebration - M. Attwell

YEAR ISSUE	EDITION LIMIT	YEAR RETD.	ISSUE PRICE	*QUOTE U.S.$
1997 Meeting Friends Along The Way Figurine 270407	Yr.Iss.	1997	85.00	85
1997 Meeting Friends Along The Way Covered Box 277746	Yr.Iss.	1997	14.00	14

Memories of Yesterday - M. Attwell

YEAR ISSUE	EDITION LIMIT	YEAR RETD.	ISSUE PRICE	*QUOTE U.S.$
1995 A Friend Like You Is Hard To Find 101176	Retrd.	1999	45.00	45-55
1995 A Helping Hand For You 101192	Retrd.	1997	40.00	40
1998 Good Morning Sunshine 115258	5,000	1999	30.00	30
1998 Have A Little Christmas Cheer 134856	Retrd.	1999	30.00	30-45
1995 Won't You Skate With Me? 134864	5,000	1999	35.00	35
1995 Dear Old Dear, Wish You Were Here 134872	5,000	1999	37.50	38
1998 Make a Little Garden 137618	5,000	1999	40.00	40
1995 You're My Sunshine On A Rainy Day 137626	Retrd.	1998	37.50	38
1995 Boo-Boo's Band Set/5 137758	Retrd.	1999	25.00	25
1996 We're In Trouble Now! 162299	7,500	1999	37.50	38
1998 Daddy's Little Shaver 162507	5,000	1999	30.00	30
1998 Night, Night Dollie 162566	Retrd.	1999	35.00	35
1996 A Basket Full of Love 162582	Retrd.	1999	50.00	50
1997 You're My Bouquet of Blessings 162604	5,000	1999	30.00	30
1996 Just Longing To See You 162620	7,500	1999	27.50	28
1996 We Are All His Children 162639	Retrd.	1999	30.00	30
1998 I'm A Little Lady 162655	5,000	1999	30.00	30
1996 Just Like Daddy 162698	7,500	1999	27.50	28
1998 Wishin You A Jolly Holiday 162736	Retrd.	1999	35.00	35
1998 Over The River And Through The Woods 162752	Retrd.	1999	65.00	65-85
1998 This Is The Life 162817	5,000	1999	32.50	33
1998 Hard Work Reaps Many Blessings 162841	5,000	1999	40.00	40
1996 How Good of God To Make Us All 164135	5,000	1999	50.00	50
1997 I Know You Can Do It 209821	5,000	1999	35.00	35
1997 In the Hands of a Guardian Angel 209856	5,000	1999	50.00	50
1997 There's Always a Rainbow 209864	5,000	1999	37.50	38
1997 Bringing Gifts of Friendship To Share 209872	5,000	1999	37.50	38
1997 Let Me Be Your Guardian Angel 279722	Retrd.	1999	25.00	25
1997 How 'Bout a Little Kiss 279730	Retrd.	1999	25.00	25
1997 Hoping To See You Soon 279706	Retrd.	1999	25.00	25
1997 I Pray Thee Lord My Soul To Keep 279714	Retrd.	1999	25.00	25
1997 Now I Lay Me Down To Sleep 279749	Retrd.	1999	25.00	25
1997 Time For Bed 279765	Retrd.	1999	25.00	25
1998 Fit For A Day 306509	5,000	1999	30.00	30
1990 Collection Sign 513156	Closed	1993	7.00	7
1989 Blow Wind, Blow 520012	Retrd.	1997	40.00	40
1990 Hold It! You're Just Swell 520020	Retrd.	1999	50.00	50
1990 Kiss The Place And Make It Well 520039	Retrd.	1999	50.00	50
1989 Let's Be Nice Like We Was Before 520047	Retrd.	1999	50.00	35-50
1991 Who Ever Told Mother To Order Twins? 520063	Retrd.	1999	33.50	34
1989 I'se Spoken For 520071	Retrd.	1991	30.00	30-50
1993 You Do Make Me Happy 520098	Retrd.	1999	27.50	28
1990 Where's Muvver? 520101	Retrd.	1994	30.00	30
1990 Here Comes The Bride And Groom God Bless 'Em! (musical) 520136	Retrd.	1999	80.00	80
1989 Daddy, I Can Never Fill Your Shoes 520187	Retrd.	1997	30.00	30
1989 This One's For You, Dear 520195	Retrd.	1999	50.00	50
1989 Should I . . . ? 520209	Retrd.	1999	50.00	50
1990 Luck At Last! He Loves Me 520217	Retrd.	1992	35.00	36-58
1989 Here Comes The Bride-God Bless Her! 9" 520527	Retrd.	1990	95.00	60-95
1989 We's Happy! How's Yourself? (musical) 520616	Retrd.	1991	70.00	85-150
1989 Here Comes The Bride & Groom (musical) God Bless 'Em 520896	Retrd.	1999	50.00	50
1989 The Long and Short of It 522384	Retrd.	1994	32.50	33
1989 As Good As His Mother Ever Made 522392	Retrd.	1997	32.50	32-40
1989 Must Feed Them Over Christmas 522406	Retrd.	1996	38.50	39
1989 Knitting You A Warm & Cozy Winter 522414	Retrd.	1999	37.50	38
1989 Joy To You At Christmas 522449	Retrd.	1996	45.00	45
1989 For Fido And Me (musical) 522457	Retrd.	1999	70.00	70
1991 Wishful Thinking 522597	Retrd.	1999	45.00	45
1991 Why Don't You Sing Along? 522600	Retrd.	1995	55.00	55
1995 You Brighten My Day With A Smile 522627	Retrd.	1998	30.00	30
1991 I Must Be Somebody's Darling 522635	Retrd.	1993	30.00	30
1991 Tying The Knot 522678	Retrd.	1998	60.00	60
1991 Wherever I Am, I'm Dreaming of You 522686	Retrd.	1999	40.00	40
1993 Will You Be Mine? 522694	Retrd.	1997	30.00	30
1991 Sitting Pretty 522708	Retrd.	1993	40.00	50
1993 Here's A Little Song From Me To You (musical) 522716	Retrd.	1999	70.00	70
1992 A Whole Bunch of Love For You 522732	Retrd.	1996	40.00	40
1992 I'se Such A Good Little Girl Sometimes 522759	Retrd.	1999	30.00	30
1992 Things Are Rather Upside Down 522775	Retrd.	1999	30.00	30
1991 Pull Yourselves Together Girls, Waists Are In 522783	Retrd.	1997	30.00	30
1993 Bringing Good Luck To You 522791	Retrd.	1996	30.00	30
1995 I Comfort Fido And Fido Comforts Me 522813	5,000	1999	50.00	50
1992 A Kiss From Fido 523119	Retrd.	1999	35.00	35
1994 Bless 'Em! 523127	Retrd.	1998	35.00	35
1994 Bless 'Em! 523232	Retrd.	1998	35.00	35
1990 I'm Not As Backwards As I Looks 523240	Retrd.	1997	32.50	33
1990 I Pray The Lord My Soul To Keep 523259	Retrd.	1999	25.00	25
1990 He Hasn't Forgotten Me 523267	Retrd.	1999	30.00	30
1990 Time For Bed 9" 523275	Yr.Iss.	1991	95.00	73-125
1991 Just Thinking 'bout You (musical) 523461	Retrd.	1999	70.00	70
1992 Now Be A Good Dog Fido 524581	Retrd.	1997	45.00	45
1991 Them Dishes Nearly Done 524611	Retrd.	1999	50.00	50
1995 Join Me For A Little Song 524654	5,000	1999	37.50	38
1990 Let Me Be Your Guardian Angel 524670	Retrd.	1999	32.50	33
1990 A Lapful Of Luck 524689	Retrd.	1999	30.00	30
1990 Not A Creature Was Stirrin' 524697	Retrd.	1999	45.00	45
1990 I'se Been Painting 524700	Retrd.	1999	37.50	38
1992 The Future-God Bless "Em! 524719	Retrd.	1998	37.50	38
1990 A Dash of Something With Something For the Pot 524727	Retrd.	1997	55.00	55
1991 Opening Presents Is Much Fun! 524735	Retrd.	1999	37.50	38
1992 You'll Always Be My Hero 524743	Retrd.	1997	50.00	50
1990 Got To Get Home For The Holidays (musical) 524751	Retrd.	1994	100.00	100
1990 Hush-A-Bye Baby (musical) 524778	Retrd.	1997	80.00	80
1990 The Greatest Treasure The World Can Hold 524808	Retrd.	1997	50.00	50
1994 With A Heart That's True, I'll Wait For You 524816	Retrd.	1996	50.00	50
1990 Hoping To See You Soon 524824	Retrd.	1999	30.00	30
1991 We All Loves A Cuddle 524832	Retrd.	1992	30.00	35
1991 He Loves Me 9" 525022	Retrd.	1992	100.00	50-100
1993 Now I Lay Me Down To Sleep (musical) 525413	Retrd.	1999	65.00	65
1992 Making Something Special For You 525472	Retrd.	1999	45.00	45
1991 I'm As Comfy As Can Be 525480	Retrd.	1999	50.00	50
1992 I'm Hopin' You're Missing Me Too 525499	Retrd.	1999	55.00	55
1992 A Friendly Chat & A Cup of Tea 525510	Yr.Iss.	1992	50.00	69-75
1993 The Jolly Ole Sun Will Shine Again 525502	Retrd.	1994	55.00	55
1997 May I Have This Dance? 525529	5,000	1999	50.00	50
1991 Friendship Has No Boundaries (Special Understamp) 525545	Yr.Iss.	1991	30.00	30-50
1992 Home's A Grand Place To Get Back To (musical) 525553	Retrd.	1995	100.00	100
1991 Give It Your Best Shot 525561	Retrd.	1999	35.00	35
1992 I Pray the Lord My Soul To Keep (musical) 525596	Retrd.	1999	65.00	65
1991 Could You Love Me For Myself Alone? 525618	Retrd.	1994	30.00	30
1996 Whenever I Get A Moment-I Think of You 525626	7,500	1999	37.50	38
1992 Good Night and God Bless You In Every Way! 525634	Retrd.	1999	50.00	50
1992 Five Years Of Memories (Five Year Anniversary Figurine) 525669	Yr.Iss.	1992	50.00	50-65
1992 Five Years Of Memories Celebrating Our Five Years 1992 525669A	Yr.Iss.	1992	N/A	N/A
1996 Loving You One Stitch At A Time 525677	5,000	1999	50.00	50
1993 May Your Flowers Be Even Better Than The Pictures On The Packets 525685	Retrd.	1997	37.50	38
1995 Let's Sail Away Together 525707	Retrd.	1999	32.50	33
1993 You Won't Catch Me Being A Golf Widow 525715	Retrd.	1998	30.00	30
1995 Good Friends Are Great Gifts 525723	Retrd.	1999	50.00	50
1994 Taking After Mother 525731	Retrd.	1999	40.00	40
1994 Too Shy For Words 525758	Retrd.	1996	50.00	50
1991 Good Morning, Little Boo-Boo 525766	Retrd.	1996	40.00	40
1997 Dreams Are Sweeter With Friends 525774	5,000	1999	37.50	38
1992 Hurry Up For the Last Train to Fairyland 525863	Retrd.	1999	40.00	40
1992 I'se So Happy You Called 9" 526401	Yr.Iss.	1993	100.00	100
1994 Pleasant Dreams and Sweet Repose-(musical) 526592	Retrd.	1999	80.00	80
1998 Always Getting Stronger 526606	5,000	1999	35.00	35
1998 Just A Ring To Say Hello 526975	5,000	1999	30.00	30
1996 Put Your Best Foot Forward 526983	5,000	1999	50.00	50
1994 Bobbed 526991	Retrd.	1995	32.50	33
1996 Can I Keep Her, Mommy? 527025	Retrd.	1999	13.50	14
1992 Time For Bed 527076	Retrd.	1999	30.00	30
1991 S'no Use Lookin' Back Now! 527203	Yr.Iss.	1991	75.00	75
1992 Collection Sign 527300	Retrd.	1999	30.00	30
1993 Having A Wash And Brush Up 527424	Retrd.	1999	35.00	35
1994 Having a Good Ole Laugh 527432	Retrd.	1999	50.00	50
1993 A Bit Tied Up Just Now-But Cheerio 527467	Retrd.	1999	45.00	45
1992 Send All Life's Little Worries Skipping 527505	Retrd.	1997	30.00	30
1994 Don't Wait For Wishes to Come True-Go Get Them! 527645	Retrd.	1999	37.50	38
1993 Hullo! Did You Come By Underground? 527653	Yr.Iss.	1993	40.00	40
1993 Hullo! Did You Come By Underground? Commemorative Issue: 1913 1993 527653A	500	1999	N/A	N/A

YEAR ISSUE	EDITION LIMIT	YEAR RETD.	ISSUE PRICE	*QUOTE U.S.$
1993 Look Out-Something Good Is Coming Your Way! 528781	Retrd.	1999	37.50	38-50
1992 Merry Christmas, Little Boo-Boo 528803	Retrd.	1999	37.50	38
1994 Do Be Friends With Me 529117	Retrd.	1999	40.00	40
1994 Good Morning From One Cheery Soul To Another 529141	Retrd.	1999	30.00	30
1994 May Your Birthday Be Bright And Happy 529575	Retrd.	1998	35.00	35
1996 God Bless Our Future 529583	5,000	1999	45.00	45
1993 Strikes Me, I'm Your Match 529656	Retrd.	1999	27.50	28
1993 Wot's All This Talk About Love? 9" 529737	Yr.Iss.	1994	100.00	100
1994 Thank God For Fido 9" 529753	Yr.Iss.	1994	100.00	100
1994 Making the Right Connection 529907	Yr.Iss.	1994	32.50	33
1994 Still Going Strong 530344	Retrd.	1998	27.50	28
1997 Let Your Light Shine 530360	5,000	1999	30.00	30
1993 Do You Know The Way To Fairyland? 530379	Retrd.	1996	50.00	50-75
1996 We'd Do Anything For You, Dear 530905	5,000	1999	50.00	50
1994 Comforting Thoughts 531367	Retrd.	1998	32.50	33
1995 Love To You Always 602752	Retrd.	1999	30.00	30
1995 Wherever You Go, I'll Keep In Touch 602760	Retrd.	1996	30.00	30
1995 Love Begins With Friendship 602914	Retrd.	1997	50.00	50
1994 The Nativity Pageant 602949	Retrd.	1999	90.00	90
1995 May You Have A Big Smile For A Long While 602965	Retrd.	1999	30.00	30
1995 Love To You Today 602973	Retrd.	1999	30.00	30
1998 Did I Hear You Say You Like Me 602981	5,000	1999	30.00	30
1996 You Warm My Heart 603007	7,500	1999	35.00	35

Memories of Yesterday Charter 1988 - M. Attwell

YEAR ISSUE	EDITION LIMIT	YEAR RETD.	ISSUE PRICE	*QUOTE U.S.$
1988 Mommy, I Teared It 114480	Retrd.	1999	27.50	40-143
1988 Now I Lay Me Down To Sleep 114499	Retrd.	1999	25.00	25-65
1988 We's Happy! How's Yourself? 114502	Retrd.	1996	45.00	33-60
1988 Hang On To Your Luck! 114510	Retrd.	1999	27.50	27-70
1988 How Do You Spell S-O-R-R-Y? 114529	Retrd.	1990	27.50	40-50
1988 What Will I Grow Up To Be? 114537	Retrd.	1999	45.00	45
1988 Can I Keep Her Mommy? 114545	Retrd.	1995	27.50	27-70
1988 Hush! 114553	Retrd.	1990	50.00	80-125
1988 It Hurts When Fido Hurts 114561	Retrd.	1992	32.50	32-75
1988 Anyway, Fido Loves Me 114588	Retrd.	1999	32.50	32-75
1988 If You Can't Be Good, Be Careful 114596	Retrd.	1993	55.00	55-90
1988 Welcome Santa 114960	Retrd.	1999	50.00	50-100
1988 Special Delivery 114979	Retrd.	1991	32.50	32-70
1988 How 'bout A Little Kiss? 114987	Retrd.	1995	27.50	75-85
1988 Waiting For Santa 114995	Retrd.	1999	45.00	32-50
1988 Dear Santa. . . 115002	Retrd.	1999	55.00	50-150
1988 I Hope Santa Is Home . . . 115010	Retrd.	1999	32.50	30-45
1988 It's The Thought That Counts 115029	Retrd.	1999	27.50	29-75
1988 Is It Really Santa? 115347	Retrd.	1996	55.00	55-60
1988 He Knows If You've Been Bad Or Good 115355	Retrd.	1999	45.00	45-75
1988 Now He Can Be Your Friend, Too! 115363	Retrd.	1999	50.00	50-70
1988 We Wish You A Merry Christmas 115371 (musical)	Retrd.	1999	75.00	75
1988 Good Morning Mr. Snowman 115401	Retrd.	1992	80.50	80-170
1988 Mommy, I Teared It, 9" 115924	Yr.Iss.	1990	95.00	125

Memories of Yesterday Event Item Only - M. Attwell

YEAR ISSUE	EDITION LIMIT	YEAR RETD.	ISSUE PRICE	*QUOTE U.S.$
1994 I'll Always Be Your Truly Friend 525693	Yr.Iss.	1994	30.00	30
1995 Wrapped In Love And Happiness 602930	Yr.Iss.	1995	35.00	35
1996 A Sweet Treat For You 115126	Yr.Iss.	1996	30.00	30
1997 Mommy, I Teared It 114480A	Yr.Iss.	1997	27.50	28
1998 A Circle of Friends 525030	Yr.Iss.	1998	30.00	30

Alice in Wonderland - M. Attwell

YEAR ISSUE	EDITION LIMIT	YEAR RETD.	ISSUE PRICE	*QUOTE U.S.$
1997 Alice in Wonderland Collector Set 255254	3,000	1999	150.00	150

Cinderella - M. Attwell

YEAR ISSUE	EDITION LIMIT	YEAR RETD.	ISSUE PRICE	*QUOTE U.S.$
1998 Cinderella Collector Set 314854	3,000	1999	150.00	150

Comforting Thoughts - M. Attwell

YEAR ISSUE	EDITION LIMIT	YEAR RETD.	ISSUE PRICE	*QUOTE U.S.$
1997 You Make My Heart Feel Glad 209880	5,000	1999	30.00	30

Exclusive Heritage Dealer Figurine - M. Attwell

YEAR ISSUE	EDITION LIMIT	YEAR RETD.	ISSUE PRICE	*QUOTE U.S.$
1991 A Friendly Chat and a Cup of Tea 525510	Yr.Iss.	1991	50.00	69-100
1993 I'm Always Looking Out For You 527440	Yr.Iss.	1993	55.00	55
1994 Loving Each Other Is The Nicest Thing We've Got 522430	Yr.Iss.	1994	60.00	60
1995 A Little Help From Fairyland 529133	1,995	1995	55.00	55
1995 Friendship Is Meant To Be Shared 602922	Yr.Iss.	1995	50.00	50
1995 Bedtime Tales-set 153400	2,000	1996	60.00	60
1996 Tucking My Dears All Safe Away 130095	Yr.Iss.	1996	50.00	50
1996 I Do Like My Holiday Crews 522805	1,996	1999	100.00	100
1996 Peter Pan Collector's Set 174564	1,000	1999	150.00	150
1997 Every Stitch is Sewn With Kindness 209910	Yr.Iss.	1997	50.00	50
1997 We're Going to Be Great Friends 525537	1,997	1999	50.00	50

Friendship - M. Attwell

YEAR ISSUE	EDITION LIMIT	YEAR RETD.	ISSUE PRICE	*QUOTE U.S.$
1996 I'll Miss You 179183	Retrd.	1999	20.00	25
1996 I Love You This Much! 179191	Retrd.	1999	20.00	25
1996 Thinking of You 179213	Retrd.	1999	20.00	25
1996 You And Me 179205	Retrd.	1999	20.00	25

Holiday Snapshots - M. Attwell

YEAR ISSUE	EDITION LIMIT	YEAR RETD.	ISSUE PRICE	*QUOTE U.S.$
1995 I'll Help You Mommy 144673	Retrd.	1999	20.00	25
1995 Isn't She Pretty? 144681	Retrd.	1999	20.00	25
1995 I Didn't Mean To Do It 144703	Retrd.	1999	20.00	25
1995 Can I Open Just One? 144711	Retrd.	1999	20.00	25

A Loving Wish For You - M. Attwell

YEAR ISSUE	EDITION LIMIT	YEAR RETD.	ISSUE PRICE	*QUOTE U.S.$
1995 Happiness Is Our Wedding Wish 135178	Retrd.	1999	20.00	25
1995 A Blessed Day For You 135186	Retrd.	1999	20.00	25
1995 Wishing You A Bright Future 135194	Retrd.	1999	20.00	25
1995 An Anniversary Is Love 135208	Retrd.	1999	25.00	25
1995 A Birthday Wish For You 135216	Retrd.	1999	20.00	25
1995 Bless You, Little One 135224	Retrd.	1999	20.00	25
1996 You Are My Shining Star 164585	Retrd.	1999	20.00	25
1996 You Brighten My Days 164615	Retrd.	1999	20.00	25

Memories Of A Special Day - M. Attwell

YEAR ISSUE	EDITION LIMIT	YEAR RETD.	ISSUE PRICE	*QUOTE U.S.$
1994 Monday's Child... 531421	Retrd.	1999	35.00	35
1994 Tuesday's Child... 531448	Retrd.	1999	35.00	35
1994 Wednesday's Child... 531405	Retrd.	1999	35.00	35
1994 Thursday's Child... 531413	Retrd.	1999	35.00	35
1994 Friday's Child... 531391	Retrd.	1999	35.00	35
1994 Saturday's Child... 531383	Retrd.	1999	35.00	35
1994 Sunday's Child... 531480	Retrd.	1999	35.00	35
1994 Collector's Commemorative Edition Set of 7, Hand-numbered 528056	1,994	1994	250.00	250

Nativity - M. Attwell

YEAR ISSUE	EDITION LIMIT	YEAR RETD.	ISSUE PRICE	*QUOTE U.S.$
1994 Nativity Set of 4 602949	Retrd.	1999	90.00	90
1995 Innkeeper 602892	Retrd.	1999	27.50	28
1996 Shepherd 602906	Retrd.	1999	27.50	28

Once Upon A Fairy Tale™... - M. Attwell

YEAR ISSUE	EDITION LIMIT	YEAR RETD.	ISSUE PRICE	*QUOTE U.S.$
1992 Mother Goose 526428	18,000	1999	50.00	50
1993 Mary, Mary Quite Contrary 526436	18,000	1999	45.00	45
1993 Little Miss Muffett 526444	18,000	1999	50.00	50
1992 Simple Simon 526452	18,000	1999	35.00	35
1992 Mary Had A Little Lamb 526479	18,000	1999	45.00	45
1994 Tweedle Dum & Tweedle Dee 526460	10,000	1999	50.00	50

A Penny For Your Thoughts - M. Attwell

YEAR ISSUE	EDITION LIMIT	YEAR RETD.	ISSUE PRICE	*QUOTE U.S.$
1997 You're Nice 204722	Retrd.	1999	20.00	20
1997 Now Do You Love Me Or Do You Don't 204730	Retrd.	1999	20.00	20
1997 Roses Are Red, Violets Are Blue -Violets Are Sweet, An' So Are You 204757	Retrd.	1999	20.00	20

Peter Pan - M. Attwell

YEAR ISSUE	EDITION LIMIT	YEAR RETD.	ISSUE PRICE	*QUOTE U.S.$
1996 John 165441	Retrd.	1999	20.00	25
1996 Michael and Nana 165425	Retrd.	1999	25.00	30
1996 Peter Pan 164666	Retrd.	1999	20.00	25
1996 Wendy 164674	Retrd.	1999	20.00	25

Special Edition - M. Attwell

YEAR ISSUE	EDITION LIMIT	YEAR RETD.	ISSUE PRICE	*QUOTE U.S.$
1989 As Good As His Mother Ever Made 523925	Yr.Iss.	1989	32.50	44-150
1988 Mommy, I Teared It 523488	Yr.Iss.	1988	25.00	175-325
1990 A Lapful of Luck 525014	Yr.Iss.	1990	30.00	32-180
1990 Set of Three	Retrd.	N/A	87.50	735

When I Grow Up - M. Attwell

YEAR ISSUE	EDITION LIMIT	YEAR RETD.	ISSUE PRICE	*QUOTE U.S.$
1995 When I Grow Up, I Want To Be A Doctor 102997	Retrd.	1999	20.00	25
1995 When I Grow Up, I Want To Be A Mother 103195	Retrd.	1999	20.00	25
1995 When I Grow Up, I Want To Be A Ballerina 103209	Retrd.	1999	20.00	25
1995 When I Grow Up, I Want To Be A Teacher 103357	Retrd.	1999	20.00	25
1995 When I Grow Up, I Want To Be A Fireman 103462	Retrd.	1999	20.00	25
1995 When I Grow Up, I Want To Be A Nurse 103535	Retrd.	1999	20.00	25
1996 When I Grow Up, I Want To Be A Businessman 164623	Retrd.	1999	20.00	25
1996 When I Grow Up, I Want To Be A Businesswoman 164631	Retrd.	1999	20.00	25

Merry Miniatures/Hallmark Keepsake Collections

1974 Christmas - Hallmark Keepsake Collections

YEAR ISSUE	EDITION LIMIT	YEAR RETD.	ISSUE PRICE	*QUOTE U.S.$
1974 Christmas, set/4 (Angel XPF506, Snowman XPF473, Santa XPF486, Reindeer XPF493)	Retrd.	1974	1.25	N/A

1974 Easter - Hallmark Keepsake Collections

YEAR ISSUE	EDITION LIMIT	YEAR RETD.	ISSUE PRICE	*QUOTE U.S.$
1974 Bunny EPF186	Retrd.	1974	.59	N/A
1974 Chick EPF206	Retrd.	1974	1.59	N/A
1974 Child EPF193	Retrd.	1974	.50	N/A

1974 Everyday - Hallmark Keepsake Collections

YEAR ISSUE	EDITION LIMIT	YEAR RETD.	ISSUE PRICE	*QUOTE U.S.$
1974 Raggedy Andy PF1433	Retrd.	1974	1.25	116
1974 Raggedy Ann PF1432	Retrd.	1974	1.25	N/A

1974 Halloween - Hallmark Keepsake Collections

YEAR ISSUE	EDITION LIMIT	YEAR RETD.	ISSUE PRICE	*QUOTE U.S.$
1974 Jack-O-Lantern HPF502	Retrd.	1974	.75	43
1974 Scarecrow HPF	Retrd.	1974	1.00	N/A

1974 Thanksgiving - Hallmark Keepsake Collections

YEAR ISSUE	EDITION LIMIT	YEAR RETD.	ISSUE PRICE	*QUOTE U.S.$
1974 Pilgrims TPF13	Retrd.	1974	1.00	N/A
1974 Turkey TPF13	Retrd.	1974	.75	N/A

1975 Christmas - Hallmark Keepsake Collections

YEAR ISSUE	EDITION LIMIT	YEAR RETD.	ISSUE PRICE	*QUOTE U.S.$
1975 Santa XPF49	Retrd.	1975	1.25	N/A

1975 Easter - Hallmark Keepsake Collections

YEAR ISSUE	EDITION LIMIT	YEAR RETD.	ISSUE PRICE	*QUOTE U.S.$
1975 Bunny EPF49	Retrd.	1975	1.25	N/A
1975 Duck EPF69	Retrd.	1975	1.25	N/A
1975 Girl EPF57	Retrd.	1975	1.25	N/A

1975 Halloween - Hallmark Keepsake Collections

YEAR ISSUE	EDITION LIMIT	YEAR RETD.	ISSUE PRICE	*QUOTE U.S.$
1975 Devil HPF29	Retrd.	1975	1.25	200

1975 Thanksgiving - Hallmark Keepsake Collections

YEAR ISSUE	EDITION LIMIT	YEAR RETD.	ISSUE PRICE	*QUOTE U.S.$
1975 Indian TPF29	Retrd.	1975	1.25	60

1976 Christmas - Hallmark Keepsake Collections

YEAR ISSUE	EDITION LIMIT	YEAR RETD.	ISSUE PRICE	*QUOTE U.S.$
1976 Betsey Clark XPF151	Retrd.	1976	1.25	295
1976 Drummer XPF144	Retrd.	1976	1.25	275
1976 Santa XPF131	Retrd.	1976	1.25	77-85
1976 Snowman XPF44	Retrd.	1976	1.25	60-66

1976 Halloween - Hallmark Keepsake Collections

YEAR ISSUE	EDITION LIMIT	YEAR RETD.	ISSUE PRICE	*QUOTE U.S.$
1976 Owl HPF515	Retrd.	1976	1.00	N/A
1976 Scarecrow HPF522	Retrd.	1976	1.00	267

1976 St. Patrick - Hallmark Keepsake Collections

YEAR ISSUE	EDITION LIMIT	YEAR RETD.	ISSUE PRICE	*QUOTE U.S.$
1976 Pipe SPF266	Retrd.	1976	.89	150

1976 Thanksgiving - Hallmark Keepsake Collections

YEAR ISSUE	EDITION LIMIT	YEAR RETD.	ISSUE PRICE	*QUOTE U.S.$
1976 Pilgrims TPF502	Retrd.	1976	1.00	203-225
1976 Turkey TPF512	Retrd.	1976	1.00	160

1977 Christmas - Hallmark Keepsake Collections

YEAR ISSUE	EDITION LIMIT	YEAR RETD.	ISSUE PRICE	*QUOTE U.S.$
1977 Mouse XPF122	Retrd.	1977	1.25	85-125

1977 Easter - Hallmark Keepsake Collections

YEAR ISSUE	EDITION LIMIT	YEAR RETD.	ISSUE PRICE	*QUOTE U.S.$
1977 Barnaby EPF12	Retrd.	1977	1.25	203-250
1977 Bernadette EPF25	Retrd.	1977	1.25	225
1977 Chick EPF32	Retrd.	1977	1.25	225

1977 Halloween - Hallmark Keepsake Collections

YEAR ISSUE	EDITION LIMIT	YEAR RETD.	ISSUE PRICE	*QUOTE U.S.$
1977 Witch HPF32	Retrd.	1977	1.25	170-225

1977 Thanksgiving - Hallmark Keepsake Collections

YEAR ISSUE	EDITION LIMIT	YEAR RETD.	ISSUE PRICE	*QUOTE U.S.$
1977 Pilgrims TPF502	Retrd.	1977	1.50	250

1978 Christmas - Hallmark Keepsake Collections

YEAR ISSUE	EDITION LIMIT	YEAR RETD.	ISSUE PRICE	*QUOTE U.S.$
1978 Joy Elf XPF1003	Retrd.	1978	1.50	80-110
1978 Mrs. Snowman XPF23	Retrd.	1978	1.50	99
1978 Snowman XPF33	Retrd.	1978	1.50	N/A

1978 Halloween - Hallmark Keepsake Collections

YEAR ISSUE	EDITION LIMIT	YEAR RETD.	ISSUE PRICE	*QUOTE U.S.$
1978 Kitten HPF1013	Retrd.	1978	1.50	24

1978 Thanksgiving - Hallmark Keepsake Collections

YEAR ISSUE	EDITION LIMIT	YEAR RETD.	ISSUE PRICE	*QUOTE U.S.$
1978 Pilgrim Boy TPF1003	Retrd.	1978	1.50	26-30
1978 Pilgrim Girl TPF1016	Retrd.	1978	1.50	27-30
1978 Turkey TPF12	Retrd.	1978	1.50	79-85

1979 Christmas - Hallmark Keepsake Collections

YEAR ISSUE	EDITION LIMIT	YEAR RETD.	ISSUE PRICE	*QUOTE U.S.$
1979 Mouse XPF1017	Retrd.	1979	1.50	113-125

1979 Easter - Hallmark Keepsake Collections

YEAR ISSUE	EDITION LIMIT	YEAR RETD.	ISSUE PRICE	*QUOTE U.S.$
1979 Bunny EPF377	Retrd.	1979	2.00	70-93
1979 Duck EPF397	Retrd.	1979	2.00	60

1979 Valentine - Hallmark Keepsake Collections

YEAR ISSUE	EDITION LIMIT	YEAR RETD.	ISSUE PRICE	*QUOTE U.S.$
1979 Love VPF1007	Retrd.	1979	1.50	110-125

1980 Christmas - Hallmark Keepsake Collections

YEAR ISSUE	EDITION LIMIT	YEAR RETD.	ISSUE PRICE	*QUOTE U.S.$
1980 Angel XPF3471	Retrd.	1980	3.00	40
1980 Kitten XPF3421	Retrd.	1980	3.00	34-40
1980 Reindeer XPF3464	Retrd.	1980	3.00	95
1980 Santa XPF39	Retrd.	1980	3.00	28-33
1980 Sleigh XPF3451	Retrd.	1980	3.00	42-50

1980 St. Patrick - Hallmark Keepsake Collections

YEAR ISSUE	EDITION LIMIT	YEAR RETD.	ISSUE PRICE	*QUOTE U.S.$
1980 Pipe SPF1017	Retrd.	1980	.75	59-65

1980 Thanksgiving - Hallmark Keepsake Collections

YEAR ISSUE	EDITION LIMIT	YEAR RETD.	ISSUE PRICE	*QUOTE U.S.$
1980 Turkey TPF3441	Retrd.	1980	2.00	44-85

1980 Valentine - Hallmark Keepsake Collections

YEAR ISSUE	EDITION LIMIT	YEAR RETD.	ISSUE PRICE	*QUOTE U.S.$
1980 Turtle VPF3451	Retrd.	1980	2.00	50

1981 Christmas - Hallmark Keepsake Collections

YEAR ISSUE	EDITION LIMIT	YEAR RETD.	ISSUE PRICE	*QUOTE U.S.$
1981 Penguin XHA3412	Retrd.	1981	3.00	95-99
1981 Redbird XHA3405	Retrd.	1981	3.00	33-40

1981 Easter - Hallmark Keepsake Collections

YEAR ISSUE	EDITION LIMIT	YEAR RETD.	ISSUE PRICE	*QUOTE U.S.$
1981 Lamb EPF402	Retrd.	1981	3.00	28-30

1981 Halloween - Hallmark Keepsake Collections

YEAR ISSUE	EDITION LIMIT	YEAR RETD.	ISSUE PRICE	*QUOTE U.S.$
1981 Ghost HHA3402	Retrd.	1981	3.00	295

1981 St. Patrick - Hallmark Keepsake Collections

YEAR ISSUE	EDITION LIMIT	YEAR RETD.	ISSUE PRICE	*QUOTE U.S.$
1981 Leprechaun SHA3415	Retrd.	1981	3.00	48

1981 Thanksgiving - Hallmark Keepsake Collections

YEAR ISSUE	EDITION LIMIT	YEAR RETD.	ISSUE PRICE	*QUOTE U.S.$
1981 Raccoon Pilgrim THA3402	Retrd.	1981	3.00	41-50
1981 Squirrel Indian THA3415	Retrd.	1981	3.00	50
1981 Turkey THA22	Retrd.	1981	3.00	53

1981 Valentine - Hallmark Keepsake Collections

YEAR ISSUE	EDITION LIMIT	YEAR RETD.	ISSUE PRICE	*QUOTE U.S.$
1981 Cupid VPF3465	Retrd.	1981	3.00	60

*Quotes have been rounded up to nearest dollar

FIGURINES

YEAR ISSUE	EDITION LIMIT	YEAR RETD.	ISSUE PRICE	*QUOTE U.S.$
1982 Christmas - Hallmark Keepsake Collections				
1982 Mouse XHA5023	Retrd.	1982	4.50	57-65
1982 Rocking Horse XHA5003	Retrd.	1982	4.50	83-95
1982 Santa XHA5016	Retrd.	1982	4.50	189
1982 Tree XHA5006	Retrd.	1982	4.50	135-150
1982 Easter - Hallmark Keepsake Collections				
1982 Ceramic Bunny EPF3702	Retrd.	1982	3.00	50
1982 Duck EPF3403	Retrd.	1982	3.00	26-30
1982 Halloween - Hallmark Keepsake Collections				
1982 Jack-O-Lantern HHA3446	Retrd.	1982	3.95	81-95
1982 Kitten HHA3466	Retrd.	1982	3.95	55
1982 Witch HHA3456	Retrd.	1982	3.95	N/A
1982 Thanksgiving - Hallmark Keepsake Collections				
1982 Pilgrim Mouse THA3433	Retrd.	1982	2.95	225
1982 Valentine - Hallmark Keepsake Collections				
1982 Kermit VHA3403	Retrd.	1982	3.95	26-40
1982 Miss Piggy VHA3416	Retrd.	1982	3.95	26-40
1983 Christmas - Hallmark Keepsake Collections				
1983 Angel XHA3467	Retrd.	1983	2.00	50
1983 Animals XHA3487	Retrd.	1983	7.50	37-40
1983 Deer XHA3419	Retrd.	1983	3.50	53
1983 Kitten XHA3447	Retrd.	1983	2.00	25-45
1983 Mouse XHA3459	Retrd.	1983	2.00	35-43
1983 Penguin XHA3439	Retrd.	1983	2.95	65
1983 Polar Bear XHA3407	Retrd.	1983	3.50	225
1983 Santa XHA3427	Retrd.	1983	2.95	35-43
1983 Snowman XHA3479	Retrd.	1983	3.00	36-40
1983 Easter - Hallmark Keepsake Collections				
1983 Betsey Clark EHA2429	Retrd.	1983	3.50	27-33
1983 Bunny EHA3457	Retrd.	1983	2.50	13-15
1983 Chick EHA3469	Retrd.	1983	2.50	N/A
1983 Duck EHA3477	Retrd.	1983	2.50	N/A
1983 Flocked Bunny EHA3417	Retrd.	1983	3.50	15
1983 Halloween - Hallmark Keepsake Collections				
1983 Shirt Tales HHA3437	Retrd.	1983	2.95	40
1983 St. Patrick - Hallmark Keepsake Collections				
1983 Mouse SHA3407	Retrd.	1983	3.50	8-20
1983 Thanksgiving - Hallmark Keepsake Collections				
1983 Turkey THA207	Retrd.	1983	2.95	37-43
1983 Valentine - Hallmark Keepsake Collections				
1983 Cherub VHA3497	Retrd.	1983	3.50	23-25
1983 Cupid VHA4099	Retrd.	1983	5.50	N/A
1983 Kitten VHA3489	Retrd.	1983	3.50	125
1984 Christmas - Hallmark Keepsake Collections				
1984 Koala XHA3401	Retrd.	1984	2.95	24-30
1984 Puppy XHA3494	Retrd.	1984	2.00	50-55
1984 Redbird XHA3501	Retrd.	1984	2.00	40-48
1984 Rodney XHA3391	Retrd.	1984	2.95	35-38
1984 Soldier XHA3481	Retrd.	1984	2.00	33-40
1984 Easter - Hallmark Keepsake Collections				
1984 Brown Bunny EHA3401	Retrd.	1984	3.50	13-15
1984 Chick EHA3461	Retrd.	1984	2.00	26-30
1984 Duck EHA3434	Retrd.	1984	3.50	20-23
1984 Duck EHA3474	Retrd.	1984	2.00	15-33
1984 Halloween - Hallmark Keepsake Collections				
1984 Jack-O-Lantern HHA3454	Retrd.	1984	2.00	21-25
1984 Kitten HHA3441	Retrd.	1984	2.00	20-23
1984 Thanksgiving - Hallmark Keepsake Collections				
1984 Hedgehog THA3444	Retrd.	1984	2.00	20
1984 Mouse THA3451	Retrd.	1984	2.00	N/A
1984 Valentine - Hallmark Keepsake Collections				
1984 Dog VHA3451	Retrd.	1984	2.00	55
1984 Panda VHA3471	Retrd.	1984	2.00	21-25
1984 Penguin VHA3464	Retrd.	1984	2.00	25-30
1985 Christmas - Hallmark Keepsake Collections				
1985 Bears XHA3392	Retrd.	1985	4.50	30
1985 Cat XHA3482	Retrd.	1985	2.00	30
1985 Goose XHA3522	Retrd.	1985	2.50	15-18
1985 Horse XHA3412	Retrd.	1985	3.50	9
1985 Mouse XHA3405	Retrd.	1985	3.50	20-25
1985 Mr. Santa XHA3495	Retrd.	1985	2.00	18-20
1985 Mrs. Santa XHA3502	Retrd.	1985	2.00	21
1985 Rocking Horse XHA3515	Retrd.	1985	2.00	26-30
1985 Easter - Hallmark Keepsake Collections				
1985 Basket EHA3495	Retrd.	1985	2.00	35-43
1985 Bunny EHA3482	Retrd.	1985	2.00	33-37
1985 Ceramic Bunny EPR3701	Retrd.	1985	N/A	12
1985 Lamb EHA3442	Retrd.	1985	3.50	16-20
1985 Mouse EHA3455	Retrd.	1985	3.50	25
1985 St. Patrick - Hallmark Keepsake Collections				
1985 Shamrock SHA3452	Retrd.	1985	2.00	18
1985 Thanksgiving - Hallmark Keepsake Collections				
1985 Turkey THA3395	Retrd.	1985	2.95	20
1985 Valentine - Hallmark Keepsake Collections				
1985 Kitten VHA3495	Retrd.	1985	2.00	25-30
1985 Skunk VHA3482	Retrd.	1985	2.00	18-25
1986 Christmas - Hallmark Keepsake Collections				
1986 Katybeth XHA3666	Retrd.	1986	2.00	43
1986 Mouse XHA3533	Retrd.	1986	2.00	59-65
1986 Mr. Mouse XHA3573	Retrd.	1986	2.00	24-30
1986 Mrs. Mouse XHA3653	Retrd.	1986	2.00	27-30
1986 Penguin XHA4413	Retrd.	1986	2.95	19-25
1986 Rhonda XHA3553	Retrd.	1986	3.50	33-43
1986 Rodney XHA3546	Retrd.	1986	3.50	21-27
1986 Santa XHA3673	Retrd.	1986	3.50	43
1986 Sebastian XHA3566	Retrd.	1986	2.00	90-95
1986 Easter - Hallmark Keepsake Collections				
1986 Basket EHA4143	Retrd.	1986	3.50	11-15
1986 Boy Bunny EHA4133	Retrd.	1986	2.95	19
1986 Bunny EHA3476	Retrd.	1986	3.50	20
1986 Bunny Girl EHA4106	Retrd.	1986	2.95	19
1986 Duck EHA3463	Retrd.	1986	2.95	12-15
1986 Duck Sailor EHA4113	Retrd.	1986	2.95	15
1986 Egg EHA4156	Retrd.	1986	3.50	22-25
1986 Girl Bunny EHA3503	Retrd.	1986	2.00	27-30
1986 Goose EHA3516	Retrd.	1986	2.00	13
1986 Sheep & Bell EHA4126	Retrd.	1986	2.95	11-15
1986 Graduation - Hallmark Keepsake Collections				
1986 Owl GHA3456	Retrd.	1986	2.00	12-15
1986 Halloween - Hallmark Keepsake Collections				
1986 Cat HHA3486	Retrd.	1986	2.00	15-20
1986 Witch HHA3473	Retrd.	1986	3.00	95
1986 Thanksgiving - Hallmark Keepsake Collections				
1986 Mr. Squirrel THA3403	Retrd.	1986	2.00	16-20
1986 Mrs. Squirrel THA3416	Retrd.	1986	2.00	16-20
1986 Valentine - Hallmark Keepsake Collections				
1986 Pandas VHA3523	Retrd.	1986	3.50	20
1986 Sebastian VHA3516	Retrd.	1986	2.00	72-80
1986 Unicorn VHA3503	Retrd.	1986	2.00	13-16
1987 Christmas - Hallmark Keepsake Collections				
1987 Bear XHA3709	Retrd.	1987	4.50	19-29
1987 Bunny Boy XHA3737	Retrd.	1987	2.50	18-20
1987 Bunny Girl XHA3749	Retrd.	1987	2.50	15-20
1987 Bunny XHA3729	Retrd.	1987	2.50	13-15
1987 Fawn XHA3757	Retrd.	1987	2.00	18-20
1987 Ginger Bear XHA207	Retrd.	1987	2.00	23
1987 Puppy XHA3769	Retrd.	1987	2.00	18-20
1987 Santa XHA3717	Retrd.	1987	3.50	33-40
1987 Easter - Hallmark Keepsake Collections				
1987 Boy Lamb EHA4197	Retrd.	1987	2.95	15-20
1987 Bunny EHA4179	Retrd.	1987	2.00	150
1987 Chick/Egg EHA4199	Retrd.	1987	3.50	11-15
1987 Girl Lamb EHA4187	Retrd.	1987	2.95	18-20
1987 Sebastian EHA4167	Retrd.	1987	2.00	50
1987 Halloween - Hallmark Keepsake Collections				
1987 Raccoon Witch HHA3487	Retrd.	1987	2.00	20
1987 St. Patrick - Hallmark Keepsake Collections				
1987 Mouse SHA3467	Retrd.	1987	2.00	15-17
1987 Thanksgiving - Hallmark Keepsake Collections				
1987 Turkey THA49	Retrd.	1987	3.75	15-20
1987 Valentine - Hallmark Keepsake Collections				
1987 Clown Teddy VHA3507	Retrd.	1987	2.00	13-17
1987 Giraffe VHA3519	Retrd.	1987	3.50	95
1987 Mouse VHA3527	Retrd.	1987	2.95	25-30
1988 Christmas - Hallmark Keepsake Collections				
1988 Donkey QFM1581	Retrd.	1988	2.25	8-10
1988 Jesus QFM1564	Retrd.	1988	2.50	15-23
1988 Joseph QFM1561	Retrd.	1988	2.50	11
1988 Kitten in Slipper QFM1544	Retrd.	1988	2.50	15-20
1988 Lamb QFM1574	Retrd.	1988	2.25	28
1988 Mary QFM1554	Retrd.	1988	2.50	13-15
1988 Mouse Angel QFM1551	Retrd.	1988	2.50	23-30
1988 Penguin QFM1541	Retrd.	1988	3.75	18-23
1988 Santa QFM1521	Retrd.	1988	3.75	33-40
1988 Shepherd QFM1571	Retrd.	1988	2.50	11
1988 Snowman QFM1534	Retrd.	1988	3.50	15-20
1988 Stable QFM1584	Retrd.	1988	14.00	15
1988 Tank Car QFM1591	Retrd.	1988	3.00	23-25
1988 Train Engine QFM1531	Retrd.	1988	3.00	8-12
1988 Unicorn QFM1524	Retrd.	1988	3.50	27-33
1988 Graduation - Hallmark Keepsake Collections				
1988 Dog GHA3524	Retrd.	1988	2.00	12-15
1988 Halloween - Hallmark Keepsake Collections				
1988 Mouse/Pumpkin QFM1501	Retrd.	1988	2.25	40
1988 Owl QFM1504	Retrd.	1988	2.25	13-18
1988 Thanksgiving - Hallmark Keepsake Collections				
1988 Indian Bear QFM1511	Retrd.	1988	3.25	14-18
1988 Mouse in Cornucopia QFM1514	Retrd.	1988	2.25	13-20
1988 Valentine - Hallmark Keepsake Collections				
1988 Koala & Hearts VHA3531	Retrd.	1988	2.00	8-12
1988 Koala & Lollipop VHA3651	Retrd.	1988	2.00	20
1988 Koala & Ruffled Heart VHA3631	Retrd.	1988	2.00	N/A
1988 Koala with Bow & Arrow VHA3624	Retrd.	1988	2.00	11
1989 Christmas - Hallmark Keepsake Collections				
1989 Baby's 1st QFM1615	Retrd.	1989	3.00	5-15
1989 Blue King QFM1632	Retrd.	1989	3.00	23-27
1989 Bunny Caroler QFM1662	Retrd.	1989	3.00	17-23
1989 Elf QFM1622	Retrd.	1989	3.00	5-17
1989 Joy Elf QFM1605	Retrd.	1989	3.00	5-13
1989 Mouse Caroler QFM1655	Retrd.	1989	2.50	17-23
1989 Mr. Claus QFM1595	Retrd.	1989	3.50	12-15
1989 Mrs. Claus QFM1602	Retrd.	1989	3.50	12
1989 Pink King QFM1642	Retrd.	1989	3.00	12-18
1989 Raccoon Caroler QFM1652	Retrd.	1989	3.50	16-20
1989 Teacher Elf QFM1612	Retrd.	1989	3.00	12-15
1989 Train Car QFM1562	Retrd.	1989	3.50	16
1989 Yellow King QFM1635	Retrd.	1989	3.00	12-18
1989 Easter - Hallmark Keepsake Collections				
1989 Bunny & Skateboard QSM3092	Retrd.	1989	3.50	19-23
1989 Bunny QSM1552	Retrd.	1989	3.50	11-17
1989 Lamb QSM1545	Retrd.	1989	3.50	17-20
1989 Graduation - Hallmark Keepsake Collections				
1989 Owl QSM1555	Retrd.	1989	2.50	15-16
1989 Halloween - Hallmark Keepsake Collections				
1989 Bunny QFM1565	Retrd.	1989	3.00	11-13
1989 Mouse QFM1572	Retrd.	1989	2.50	15-20
1989 Raccoon QFM1575	Retrd.	1989	3.50	13-15
1989 St. Patrick - Hallmark Keepsake Collections				
1989 Bear QSM1525	Retrd.	1989	2.50	12-15
1989 Thanksgiving - Hallmark Keepsake Collections				
1989 Baby Boy QFM1585	Retrd.	1989	3.00	15-20
1989 Baby Girl QFM1592	Retrd.	1989	3.00	15-20
1989 Momma Bear QFM1582	Retrd.	1989	3.50	12-18
1989 Valentine - Hallmark Keepsake Collections				
1989 Bear Baker QSM1522	Retrd.	1989	3.50	15-20
1989 Bunny QSM1512	Retrd.	1989	2.50	15-20
1989 Dog & Kitten QSM1515	Retrd.	1989	3.50	23-30
1989 Grey Mouse QSM1502	Retrd.	1989	2.50	17-23
1989 Kitten QSM1505	Retrd.	1989	2.50	20-25
1990 Christmas - Hallmark Keepsake Collections				
1990 1st Christmas QFM1686	Retrd.	1990	3.50	12-42
1990 Baby's 1st Polar Bear QFM1683	Retrd.	1990	2.50	8-15
1990 Candy Caboose QFM1693	Retrd.	1990	3.50	15
1990 Gentle Pal-Lamb QFM1656	Retrd.	1990	3.50	14-20
1990 Jingle Bell Santa QFM1663	Retrd.	1990	3.50	19-25
1990 Kangaroo QFM1653	Retrd.	1990	3.50	8-11
1990 Mama Polar Bear QFM1666	Retrd.	1990	3.00	12
1990 Papa Polar Bear & Child QFM1673	Retrd.	1990	3.50	13
1990 Snowman QFM1646	Retrd.	1990	2.50	11-13
1990 Squirrel Caroler QFM1696	Retrd.	1990	3.00	15-20
1990 Teacher Mouse QFM1676	Retrd.	1990	3.00	8
1990 Walrus QFM1643	Retrd.	1990	2.50	10-13
1990 Easter - Hallmark Keepsake Collections				
1990 Artist Raccoon QSM1543	Retrd.	1990	3.50	12-15
1990 Baby's 1st Easter QSM1536	Retrd.	1990	3.00	13-15
1990 Boy Bunny QSM1682	Retrd.	1990	3.50	13
1990 E-Bunny QSM1726	Retrd.	1990	3.00	15
1990 Girl Bunny QSM1675	Retrd.	1990	3.50	13
1990 Mouse & Bunny QSM1546	Retrd.	1990	3.50	15
1990 Squirrel QSM1553	Retrd.	1990	2.50	16-20
1990 Everyday - Hallmark Keepsake Collections				
1990 Baseball Bunny QSM1576	Retrd.	1990	2.50	10
1990 Puppy QSM1583	Retrd.	1990	2.50	7-13
1990 Everyday/Fall - Hallmark Keepsake Collections				
1990 Bear & Balloon QFM1716	Retrd.	1990	3.00	9-12
1990 Birthday Clown QFM1706	Retrd.	1990	3.50	17-20
1990 Bunny in Tux QFM1713	Retrd.	1990	3.00	9-13
1990 Get Well Puppy QFM1703	Retrd.	1990	3.00	10-13
1990 Everyday/Spring - Hallmark Keepsake Collections				
1990 Alligator QSM1573	Retrd.	1990	3.00	7-11
1990 Bunny QSM1593	Retrd.	1990	3.00	11
1990 Elephant QSM1566	Retrd.	1990	3.50	10-14
1990 Mouse QSM1603	Retrd.	1990	2.50	11-13
1990 Raccoon QSM1586	Retrd.	1990	3.50	9-13
1990 Graduation - Hallmark Keepsake Collections				
1990 Owl QSM1563	Retrd.	1990	3.00	15-19
1990 Halloween - Hallmark Keepsake Collections				
1990 Green Monster QFM1613	Retrd.	1990	3.50	8-14
1990 Scarecrow QFM1616	Retrd.	1990	3.50	12-14
1990 Squirrel Hobo QFM1606	Retrd.	1990	3.00	11-13
1990 Thanksgiving - Hallmark Keepsake Collections				
1990 Indian Chipmunk QFM1626	Retrd.	1990	3.00	15
1990 Pilgrim Mouse QFM1636	Retrd.	1990	2.50	6-14
1990 Pilgrim Squirrel QFM1633	Retrd.	1990	3.00	7-15
1990 Thankful Turkey QFM1623	Retrd.	1990	3.50	19-23
1990 Valentine - Hallmark Keepsake Collections				
1990 Grey Mouse QSM1533	Retrd.	1990	2.50	12-15
1990 Hippo Cupid QSM1513	Retrd.	1990	3.50	15-19
1990 Kitten QSM1516	Retrd.	1990	3.00	11-15
1990 Pig QSM1526	Retrd.	1990	3.00	13-17
1990 Stitched Teddy QSM1506	Retrd.	1990	3.50	22-25
1991 Christmas - Hallmark Keepsake Collections				
1991 1st Together QFM1799	Retrd.	1991	3.50	10
1991 Baby's 1st QFM1797	Retrd.	1991	3.00	11
1991 Bunny QFM1719	Retrd.	1991	3.00	9-12

*Quotes have been rounded up to nearest dollar

YEAR ISSUE	EDITION LIMIT	YEAR RETD.	ISSUE PRICE	*QUOTE U.S.$
1991 Cookie Elf QFM1769	Retrd.	1991	3.00	13
1991 Cookie Reindeer QFM1777	Retrd.	1991	3.00	10-13
1991 Cookie Santa QFM1767	Retrd.	1991	3.00	9-12
1991 Frog QFM1729	Retrd.	1991	3.00	9-12
1991 Gentle Pals Kitten QFM1709	Retrd.	1991	3.50	12-18
1991 Jingle Bell Santa QFM1717	Retrd.	1991	3.50	19-23
1991 Kitten QFM1737	Retrd.	1991	3.00	10-12
1991 Mouse QFM1789	Retrd.	1991	2.50	10-17
1991 Music Makers Bear QFM1779	Retrd.	1991	3.00	15-23
1991 Pig QFM1739	Retrd.	1991	3.00	11-15
1991 Puppy QFM1727	Retrd.	1991	3.00	9-14
1991 Puppy QFM1787	Retrd.	1991	3.00	15
1991 Snow Bunny QFM1749	Retrd.	1991	2.50	10-12
1991 Snow Lamb QFM1759	Retrd.	1991	2.50	10-12
1991 Snow Mice QFM1757	Retrd.	1991	2.50	10-12
1991 Teacher Raccoon QFM1807	Retrd.	1991	3.50	9
1991 Turtle QFM1747	Retrd.	1991	3.00	11-13

1991 Easter - Hallmark Keepsake Collections

YEAR ISSUE	EDITION LIMIT	YEAR RETD.	ISSUE PRICE	*QUOTE U.S.$
1991 Baby's 1st-Bunny QSM1557	Retrd.	1991	3.00	11-15
1991 Bunny Praying QSM1597	Retrd.	1991	2.50	14-18
1991 Daughter Bunny QSM1587	Retrd.	1991	2.50	10-15
1991 Duck QSM1549	Retrd.	1991	3.00	15-20
1991 Lamb & Duck QSM1569	Retrd.	1991	3.50	10
1991 Mother Bunny QSM1577	Retrd.	1991	3.00	10-15

1991 Everyday - Hallmark Keepsake Collections

YEAR ISSUE	EDITION LIMIT	YEAR RETD.	ISSUE PRICE	*QUOTE U.S.$
1991 Baby Bunny QSM1619	Retrd.	1991	3.50	9-12
1991 Bears Hugging QSM1609	Retrd.	1991	3.50	20-25
1991 Birthday Clown QSM1617	Retrd.	1991	3.50	16-20
1991 I Love Dad QSM1657	Retrd.	1991	2.50	14
1991 I Love Mom QSM1659	Retrd.	1991	2.50	13
1991 Bear QSM1637	Retrd.	1991	3.00	9-13
1991 Camel QSM1629	Retrd.	1991	3.00	13
1991 Elephant QSM1647	Retrd.	1991	3.00	14
1991 Horse QSM1649	Retrd.	1991	3.00	N/A
1991 Lion QSM1639	Retrd.	1991	3.00	10-15
1991 Carousel Set QSM1667	Retrd.	1991	20.00	53
1991 Carousel Display QSM1627	Retrd.	1991	5.00	N/A

1991 Everyday/Fall - Hallmark Keepsake Collections

YEAR ISSUE	EDITION LIMIT	YEAR RETD.	ISSUE PRICE	*QUOTE U.S.$
1991 Aerobic Bunny QFM1817	Retrd.	1991	2.50	16-22
1991 Backpack Chipmunk QFM1809	Retrd.	1991	2.50	14-18
1991 Baseball Bear QFM1827	Retrd.	1991	3.00	17-22
1991 Football Beaver QFM1829	Retrd.	1991	3.50	18-23
1991 Skating Raccoon QFM1837	Retrd.	1991	3.50	18-23
1991 Soccer Skunk QFM1819	Retrd.	1991	3.00	18-22

1991 Graduation - Hallmark Keepsake Collections

YEAR ISSUE	EDITION LIMIT	YEAR RETD.	ISSUE PRICE	*QUOTE U.S.$
1991 Dog & Cap & Gown QSM1607	Retrd.	1991	2.50	10-15

1991 Halloween - Hallmark Keepsake Collections

YEAR ISSUE	EDITION LIMIT	YEAR RETD.	ISSUE PRICE	*QUOTE U.S.$
1991 Bear QFM1669	Retrd.	1991	2.50	20
1991 Cat Witch QFM1677	Retrd.	1991	3.00	11-15
1991 Mummy QFM1679	Retrd.	1991	2.50	11-15

1991 St. Patrick - Hallmark Keepsake Collections

YEAR ISSUE	EDITION LIMIT	YEAR RETD.	ISSUE PRICE	*QUOTE U.S.$
1991 Irish Frog QSM1539	Retrd.	1991	3.50	11-15

1991 Thanksgiving - Hallmark Keepsake Collections

YEAR ISSUE	EDITION LIMIT	YEAR RETD.	ISSUE PRICE	*QUOTE U.S.$
1991 Fox QFM1689	Retrd.	1991	3.50	9-13
1991 Indian Maiden QFM1687	Retrd.	1991	2.50	9-12
1991 Turkey QFM1697	Retrd.	1991	3.50	18-25

1991 Valentine - Hallmark Keepsake Collections

YEAR ISSUE	EDITION LIMIT	YEAR RETD.	ISSUE PRICE	*QUOTE U.S.$
1991 Artist Mouse QSM1519	Retrd.	1991	2.50	11-15
1991 Bear QSM1509	Retrd.	1991	3.50	9-23
1991 Bunny QSM1537	Retrd.	1991	3.00	11-15
1991 Puppy QSM1529	Retrd.	1991	3.00	19-25
1991 Raccoon Thief QSM1517	Retrd.	1991	3.50	9-12

1992 Christmas - Hallmark Keepsake Collections

YEAR ISSUE	EDITION LIMIT	YEAR RETD.	ISSUE PRICE	*QUOTE U.S.$
1992 Bear With Drum QFM9134	Retrd.	1992	3.50	18-20
1992 Bear with Wheelbarrow QFM9111	Retrd.	1992	3.50	N/A
1992 Cat in P.J.'s QFM9084	Retrd.	1992	3.50	10-14
1992 Chipmunk QFM9144	Retrd.	1992	2.50	6-9
1992 Crab QFM9174	Retrd.	1992	3.00	7-10
1992 Dog in P.J.'s QFM9081	Retrd.	1992	3.50	9-12
1992 Giraffe as Tree QFM9141	Retrd.	1992	3.00	10-15
1992 Goldfish QFM9181	Retrd.	1992	3.00	9-12
1992 Mouse in Car QFM9114	Retrd.	1992	3.00	10-13
1992 Nina Ship QFM9154	Retrd.	1992	3.50	10-12
1992 Octopus QFM9171	Retrd.	1992	3.00	8-12
1992 Penguin Skating QFM9091	Retrd.	1992	3.50	14
1992 Pinta Ship QFM9161	Retrd.	1992	3.50	12
1992 Rabbit on Sled QFM9151	Retrd.	1992	3.00	9-12
1992 Santa Bee QFM9061	Retrd.	1992	3.00	9-12
1992 Santa Bell QFM9131	Retrd.	1992	3.50	18-19
1992 Santa Maria Ship QFM9164	Retrd.	1992	3.50	12
1992 Snow Bunny QFM9071	Retrd.	1992	4.00	8-12
1992 Squirrel Pal QFM9094	Retrd.	1992	3.50	12-20
1992 Squirrels in Nutshell QFM9064	Retrd.	1992	3.50	9-12
1992 Sweet Angel QFM9124	Retrd.	1992	3.00	12-15
1992 Teacher Cat QFM9074	Retrd.	1992	3.50	9
1992 Walrus & Bird QFM9054	Retrd.	1992	3.50	11-15
1992 Waving Reindeer QFM9121	Retrd.	1992	3.00	14

1992 Easter - Hallmark Keepsake Collections

YEAR ISSUE	EDITION LIMIT	YEAR RETD.	ISSUE PRICE	*QUOTE U.S.$
1992 Baby's 1st QSM9777	Retrd.	1992	3.50	10
1992 Bunny & Carrot QSM9799	Retrd.	1992	2.50	13
1992 Goose in Bonnet QSM9789	Retrd.	1992	3.00	10-11
1992 Lamb QSM9787	Retrd.	1992	3.50	10-12
1992 Praying Chipmunk QSM9797	Retrd.	1992	3.00	10-12
1992 Sweatshirt Bunny QSM9779	Retrd.	1992	3.50	12-13

1992 Everyday/Fall - Hallmark Keepsake Collections

YEAR ISSUE	EDITION LIMIT	YEAR RETD.	ISSUE PRICE	*QUOTE U.S.$
1992 Cow QFM9034	Retrd.	1992	3.00	12-15
1992 Horse QFM9051	Retrd.	1992	3.00	13-19
1992 Lamb QFM9044	Retrd.	1992	2.50	13-17
1992 Party Dog QFM9191	Retrd.	1992	3.00	14
1992 Pig QFM9041	Retrd.	1992	2.50	6-20
1992 Rabbit Holding Heart Carrot QFM9201	Retrd.	1992	3.50	15
1992 Skunk with Butterfly QFM9184	Retrd.	1992	3.50	14
1992 Teddy Bear QFM9194	Retrd.	1992	2.50	15

1992 Everyday/Summer - Hallmark Keepsake Collections

YEAR ISSUE	EDITION LIMIT	YEAR RETD.	ISSUE PRICE	*QUOTE U.S.$
1992 Clown QSM9819	Retrd.	1992	3.50	12-17
1992 Dog QSM9847	Retrd.	1992	3.00	13-20
1992 Hedgehog QSM9859	Retrd.	1992	2.50	11-13
1992 Kitten for Dad QSM9839	Retrd.	1992	3.50	11-15
1992 Kitten for Mom QSM9837	Retrd.	1992	3.50	10-15
1992 Kitten in Bib QSM9829	Retrd.	1992	3.50	13
1992 Rabbit & Squirrel QSM9827	Retrd.	1992	3.50	15-20
1992 Seal QSM9849	Retrd.	1992	3.00	10-13
1992 Turtle & Mouse QSM9857	Retrd.	1992	3.00	18-28

1992 Graduation - Hallmark Keepsake Collections

YEAR ISSUE	EDITION LIMIT	YEAR RETD.	ISSUE PRICE	*QUOTE U.S.$
1992 Grad Dog QSM9817	Retrd.	1992	2.50	12-18

1992 Halloween - Hallmark Keepsake Collections

YEAR ISSUE	EDITION LIMIT	YEAR RETD.	ISSUE PRICE	*QUOTE U.S.$
1992 Clown Mouse QFM9031	Retrd.	1992	2.50	10-13
1992 Ghost with Corn Candy QFM9014	Retrd.	1992	3.00	10-15
1992 Haunted House QFM9024	Retrd.	1992	3.50	12-15
1992 Pumpkin QFM9021	Retrd.	1992	3.00	10-14

1992 St. Patrick - Hallmark Keepsake Collections

YEAR ISSUE	EDITION LIMIT	YEAR RETD.	ISSUE PRICE	*QUOTE U.S.$
1992 Mouse QSM9769	Retrd.	1992	3.00	9-11

1992 Thanksgiving - Hallmark Keepsake Collections

YEAR ISSUE	EDITION LIMIT	YEAR RETD.	ISSUE PRICE	*QUOTE U.S.$
1992 Indian Bunnies QFM9004	Retrd.	1992	3.50	7-15
1992 Pilgrim Beaver QFM9011	Retrd.	1992	3.00	13-16
1992 Thankful Turkey QFM9001	Retrd.	1992	3.50	19-22

1992 Valentine - Hallmark Keepsake Collections

YEAR ISSUE	EDITION LIMIT	YEAR RETD.	ISSUE PRICE	*QUOTE U.S.$
1992 Ballet Pig QSM9759	Retrd.	1992	2.50	13-15
1992 Bear QSM9717	Retrd.	1992	3.50	16-20
1992 Lion QSM9719	Retrd.	1992	3.50	10-13
1992 Penguin in Tux QSM9757	Retrd.	1992	3.00	13-15
1992 Puppy QSM9767	Retrd.	1992	2.50	15

1993 Christmas - Hallmark Keepsake Collections

YEAR ISSUE	EDITION LIMIT	YEAR RETD.	ISSUE PRICE	*QUOTE U.S.$
1993 Arctic Fox QFM8242	Retrd.	1993	3.50	6-15
1993 Baby Walrus QFM8232	Retrd.	1993	3.00	6-15
1993 Baby Whale QFM8222	Retrd.	1993	3.50	5-15
1993 Bunny with Scarf QFM8235	Retrd.	1993	2.50	10-14
1993 Eskimo Child QFM8215	Retrd.	1993	3.00	6-20
1993 Husky Puppy QFM8245	Retrd.	1993	3.50	6-17
1993 Igloo QFM8252	Retrd.	1993	3.00	6-18
1993 Penguin in Hat QFM8212	Retrd.	1993	3.00	7-12
1993 Polar Bear QFM8265	Retrd.	1993	3.50	6-18
1993 Santa Eskimo QFM8262	Retrd.	1993	3.50	30
1993 Seal with Earmuffs QFM8272	Retrd.	1993	2.50	6-15

1993 Easter - Hallmark Keepsake Collections

YEAR ISSUE	EDITION LIMIT	YEAR RETD.	ISSUE PRICE	*QUOTE U.S.$
1993 Bunny Painting Egg QSM8115	Retrd.	1993	3.50	7
1993 Bunny with Basket QSM8142	Retrd.	1993	2.50	9
1993 Bunny with Egg QSM8125	Retrd.	1993	3.00	8
1993 Duck with Egg QSM8135	Retrd.	1993	3.00	5-8
1993 Easter Basket QSM8145	Retrd.	1993	2.50	4-10
1993 Lamb QSM8112	Retrd.	1993	3.50	9
1993 Sherlock Duck QSM8122	Retrd.	1993	3.00	5-9

1993 Everyday/Summer - Hallmark Keepsake Collections

YEAR ISSUE	EDITION LIMIT	YEAR RETD.	ISSUE PRICE	*QUOTE U.S.$
1993 Bear with Surfboard QSM8015	Retrd.	1993	3.50	13-18
1993 Bunny with Seashell QSM8005	Retrd.	1993	3.50	17-20
1993 Chipmunk QSM8002	Retrd.	1993	3.50	7-15
1993 Hedgehog QSM8026	Retrd.	1993	3.00	7-15
1993 Hippo QSM8032	Retrd.	1993	3.00	11-15
1993 Mouse in Sunglasses QSM8035	Retrd.	1993	2.50	10-15
1993 Pig in Blanket QSM8022	Retrd.	1993	3.00	20
1993 Prairie Dog QSM8012	Retrd.	1993	3.50	16-20
1993 Sandcastle QSM8045	Retrd.	1993	3.00	7-17

1993 Halloween - Hallmark Keepsake Collections

YEAR ISSUE	EDITION LIMIT	YEAR RETD.	ISSUE PRICE	*QUOTE U.S.$
1993 Animated Cauldron QFM8425	Retrd.	1993	2.50	6-15
1993 Bear Dressed as Bat QFM8285	Retrd.	1993	3.00	7-15
1993 Dragon Dog QFM8295	Retrd.	1993	3.00	6-14
1993 Ghost on Tombstone QFM8282	Retrd.	1993	2.50	5-12
1993 Mouse Witch QFM8292	Retrd.	1993	3.00	7-16
1993 Owl and Pumpkin QFM8302	Retrd.	1993	3.00	11-17
1993 Princess Cat QFM8305	Retrd.	1993	3.50	14-18
1993 Super Hero Bunny QFM8422	Retrd.	1993	3.00	5-26

1993 Independence Day - Hallmark Keepsake Collections

YEAR ISSUE	EDITION LIMIT	YEAR RETD.	ISSUE PRICE	*QUOTE U.S.$
1993 Betsey Ross Lamb QSM8482	Retrd.	1993	3.50	5-20
1993 Goat Uncle Sam QSM8472	Retrd.	1993	3.00	5-17
1993 Hedgehog Patriot QSM8492	Retrd.	1993	3.50	6-15
1993 Liberty Bell QSM8465	Retrd.	1993	2.50	14-16
1993 Liberty Mouse QSM8475	Retrd.	1993	3.00	6-19

1993 Thanksgiving - Hallmark Keepsake Collections

YEAR ISSUE	EDITION LIMIT	YEAR RETD.	ISSUE PRICE	*QUOTE U.S.$
1993 Bobcat Pilgrim QFM8172	Retrd.	1993	3.50	7-15
1993 Indian Bear QFM8162	Retrd.	1993	3.50	5-15
1993 Indian Squirrel QFM8182	Retrd.	1993	3.00	7-15
1993 Indian Turkey QFM8165	Retrd.	1993	3.50	7-15
1993 Pilgrim Chipmunk QFM8185	Retrd.	1993	3.00	11-15
1993 Pilgrim Mouse QFM8175	Retrd.	1993	3.00	7-18
1993 Plymouth Rock QFM8192	Retrd.	1993	2.50	6-18

1993 Valentine - Hallmark Keepsake Collections

YEAR ISSUE	EDITION LIMIT	YEAR RETD.	ISSUE PRICE	*QUOTE U.S.$
1993 Box of Candy QSM8095	Retrd.	1993	2.50	7-20
1993 Cat & Mouse QSM8102	Retrd.	1993	3.50	11-15
1993 Dog with Balloon QSM8092	Retrd.	1993	2.50	7-10
1993 Fox with Heart QSM8065	Retrd.	1993	3.50	6-10
1993 Panda QSM8105	Retrd.	1993	3.50	15
1993 Raccoon with Heart QSM8062	Retrd.	1993	3.50	7-10
1993 Skunk with Heart QSM8072	Retrd.	1993	3.00	6-10
1993 Stump & Can QSM8075	Retrd.	1993	3.00	5-12

1994 Christmas - Hallmark Keepsake Collections

YEAR ISSUE	EDITION LIMIT	YEAR RETD.	ISSUE PRICE	*QUOTE U.S.$
1994 Bear on Skates QFM8293	Retrd.	1994	3.75	5-17
1994 Fox on Skates QFM8303	Retrd.	1994	3.75	5-15
1994 Mrs. Claus QFM8286	Retrd.	1994	3.75	5-19
1994 North Pole Sign QFM8333	Retrd.	1994	6.75	15-25
1994 Penguin QFM8313	Retrd.	1994	2.75	13
1994 Polar Bears QFM8323	Retrd.	1994	3.25	5-11
1994 Seal with Earmuffs QFM8272	Retrd.	1994	2.50	15
1994 Sled Dog QFM8306	Retrd.	1994	3.25	10
1994 Snowman QFM8316	Retrd.	1994	2.75	5-9
1994 Tree QFM8326	Retrd.	1994	2.75	10

1994 Easter - Hallmark Keepsake Collections

YEAR ISSUE	EDITION LIMIT	YEAR RETD.	ISSUE PRICE	*QUOTE U.S.$
1994 Birds in Nest QSM8116	Retrd.	1994	3.75	7-10
1994 Chick in Wagon QSM8123	Retrd.	1994	3.75	6-15
1994 Lamb QSM8132	Retrd.	1994	3.25	9
1994 Mouse with Flower QSM8243	Retrd.	1994	2.75	5-12
1994 Rabbit with Can QSM8083	Retrd.	1994	3.25	5-10
1994 Rabbit with Croquet QSM8113	Retrd.	1994	3.75	6-7
1994 Wishing Well QSM8033	Retrd.	1994	6.75	15

1994 Everyday/Summer - Hallmark Keepsake Collections

YEAR ISSUE	EDITION LIMIT	YEAR RETD.	ISSUE PRICE	*QUOTE U.S.$
1994 Dock QSM8076	Retrd.	1994	6.75	17-25
1994 Pail of Seashells QSM8052	Retrd.	1994	2.75	13-15
1994 Rabbit QSM8066	Retrd.	1995	2.75	8-17
1994 Raccoon QSM8063	Retrd.	1994	3.75	15-20

1994 Halloween - Hallmark Keepsake Collections

YEAR ISSUE	EDITION LIMIT	YEAR RETD.	ISSUE PRICE	*QUOTE U.S.$
1994 Black Kitten QFM8273	Retrd.	1994	3.25	11-15
1994 Bunny Alien QFM8266	Retrd.	1994	3.75	6-15
1994 Fence with Lantern QFM8283	Retrd.	1994	6.75	16-20
1994 Pumpkin with Hat QFM8276	Retrd.	1994	2.75	5
1994 Squirrel as Clown QFM8263	Retrd.	1994	3.75	6-15

1994 Independence Day - Hallmark Keepsake Collections

YEAR ISSUE	EDITION LIMIT	YEAR RETD.	ISSUE PRICE	*QUOTE U.S.$
1994 Bear with Flag QSM8043	Retrd.	1994	3.75	17-29
1994 Document QSM8053	Retrd.	1994	2.75	5-14
1994 Eagle with Hat QSM8036	Retrd.	1994	3.75	7-18
1994 Flag QSM8056	Retrd.	1994	6.75	19-27

1994 Thanksgiving - Hallmark Keepsake Collections

YEAR ISSUE	EDITION LIMIT	YEAR RETD.	ISSUE PRICE	*QUOTE U.S.$
1994 Indian Bunny QFM8353	Retrd.	1994	2.75	5-15
1994 Basket of Apples QFM8356	Retrd.	1994	2.75	5-14
1994 Beaver QFM8336	Retrd.	1994	3.75	5-15
1994 Corn Stalk QFM8363	Retrd.	1994	6.75	15-20
1994 Indian Chickadee QFM8346	Retrd.	1994	3.25	11-18
1994 Pilgrim Bunny QFM8343	Retrd.	1994	3.75	10-15

1994 Valentine - Hallmark Keepsake Collections

YEAR ISSUE	EDITION LIMIT	YEAR RETD.	ISSUE PRICE	*QUOTE U.S.$
1994 Bear Letter Carrier QSM8006	Retrd.	1994	3.75	6-13
1994 Beaver QSM8013	Retrd.	1994	3.75	5-13
1994 Chipmunk With Kite QSM8003	Retrd.	1994	3.00	11-15
1994 Mailbox QSM8023	Retrd.	1994	6.75	12-15
1994 Owl in Stump QSM8243	Retrd.	1994	2.75	9-12
1994 Rabbit QSM8016	Retrd.	1994	3.25	5-12

1995 Christmas - Hallmark Keepsake Collections

YEAR ISSUE	EDITION LIMIT	YEAR RETD.	ISSUE PRICE	*QUOTE U.S.$
1995 Cameron on Sled QFM8199	Retrd.	1995	3.75	10-15
1995 Caroling Bear QFM8307	Retrd.	1995	3.25	5-14
1995 Caroling Bunny QFM8309	Retrd.	1995	3.25	5-14
1995 Caroling Mouse QFM8317	Retrd.	1995	3.00	5-13
1995 Christmas Tree QFM8197	Retrd.	1995	6.75	8-18
1995 Hamster With Cookies QFM8319	Retrd.	1995	3.25	6-17
1995 Lion and Lamb QFM8287	Retrd.	1995	4.00	5-15
1995 Nutcracker QFM8297	Retrd.	1995	3.75	8-15
1995 Santa QFM8299	Retrd.	1995	3.75	8-15
1995 Toymaker Beaver QFM8289	Retrd.	1995	3.75	6-15

1995 Easter - Hallmark Keepsake Collections

YEAR ISSUE	EDITION LIMIT	YEAR RETD.	ISSUE PRICE	*QUOTE U.S.$
1995 Beauregard QSM8047	Retrd.	1995	3.00	N/A
1995 Cameron/ Bunny QSM8029	Retrd.	1995	3.75	17
1995 Cottage QSM8027	Retrd.	1995	6.75	10-18
1995 Prince Charming QSM8049	Retrd.	1995	4.00	15-30
1995 Selby QSM8039	Retrd.	1995	3.00	5-11
1995 Stylish Rabbit QSM8037	Retrd.	1995	3.75	5-11

1995 Halloween - Hallmark Keepsake Collections

YEAR ISSUE	EDITION LIMIT	YEAR RETD.	ISSUE PRICE	*QUOTE U.S.$
1995 Cameron in Pumpkin Costume QFM8147	Retrd.	1995	3.75	10-19
1995 Cute Witch QFM8157	Retrd.	1995	3.00	6-15
1995 Friendly Monster QFM8159	Retrd.	1995	3.00	12-15
1995 Haunted House QFM8139	Retrd.	1995	6.75	10-20
1995 Rhino Mummy QFM8149	Retrd.	1995	3.75	6-15
1995 Stepmother QFM8099	Retrd.	1995	4.00	10-13

1995 St. Patrick's - Hallmark Keepsake Collections

YEAR ISSUE	EDITION LIMIT	YEAR RETD.	ISSUE PRICE	*QUOTE U.S.$
1995 Leprechaun QSM8119	Retrd.	1995	3.50	6-15

1995 Summer/Everyday - Hallmark Keepsake Collections

YEAR ISSUE	EDITION LIMIT	YEAR RETD.	ISSUE PRICE	*QUOTE U.S.$
1995 Birthday Bear QSM8057	Retrd.	1995	3.75	5-15
1995 Bride and Groom Bears QSM8067	Retrd.	1995	3.75	12-16
1995 Cameron With Camera QSM8077	Retrd.	1995	3.75	12-20
1995 Fairy Godmother QSM8089	Retrd.	1995	4.00	10-18
1995 Ground Hog QSM8079	Retrd.	1995	3.00	6-15
1995 Raccoon and Flower QSM8087	Retrd.	1995	3.00	6-13

*Quotes have been rounded up to nearest dollar

1995 Thanksgiving - Hallmark Keepsake Collections

YEAR ISSUE	EDITION LIMIT	YEAR RETD.	ISSUE PRICE	*QUOTE U.S.$
1995 Cameron in Pilgrim Costume QFM8169	Retrd.	1995	3.75	10-17
1995 Chipmunk With Corn QFM8179	Retrd.	1995	3.75	6-15
1995 Mouse With Cranberries QFM8189	Retrd.	1995	3.00	6-12
1995 Mouse With Pumpkin QFM8187	Retrd.	1995	3.00	13
1995 Pilgrim Turkey QFM8177	Retrd.	1995	3.75	7-15
1995 Pumpkin Coach QFM8127	Retrd.	1995	5.00	8-15
1995 Thanksgiving Feast QFM8167	Retrd.	1995	4.75	6-15

1995 Valentine - Hallmark Keepsake Collections

YEAR ISSUE	EDITION LIMIT	YEAR RETD.	ISSUE PRICE	*QUOTE U.S.$
1995 Bashful Boy QSM8107	Retrd.	1995	3.00	10-16
1995 Bashful Girl QSM8109	Retrd.	1995	3.00	13-16
1995 Cameron QSM8009	Retrd.	1995	3.75	17-20
1995 Cinderella QSM8117	Retrd.	1995	4.00	15-35
1995 Koala Bear QSM8019	Retrd.	1995	3.75	6-15
1995 St. Bernard QSM8017	Retrd.	1995	3.75	6-15
1995 Tree QSM8007	Retrd.	1995	6.75	10-20

1996 Christmas - Hallmark Keepsake Collections

YEAR ISSUE	EDITION LIMIT	YEAR RETD.	ISSUE PRICE	*QUOTE U.S.$
1996 Busy Bakers, set/2 QFM8121	Retrd.	1996	7.95	7-18
1996 Mr. & Mrs. Claus Bears, set/2 QFM8044	Retrd.	1996	7.95	8-20
1996 Santa's Helpers, set/3 QFM8051	Retrd.	1996	12.95	12-26
1996 The Sewing Club, set/3 QFM8061	Retrd.	1996	12.95	12-29

1996 Easter - Hallmark Keepsake Collections

YEAR ISSUE	EDITION LIMIT	YEAR RETD.	ISSUE PRICE	*QUOTE U.S.$
1996 Blue Ribbon Bunny QSM8064	Retrd.	1996	4.95	5-13
1996 Easter Egg Hunt QSM8024	Retrd.	1996	4.95	5-14
1996 Happy Birthday Clowns, set/2 QSM8114	Retrd.	1996	7.95	6-13
1996 Noah and Friends, set/5 QSM8111	Retrd.	1996	19.95	19-33

1996 Halloween - Hallmark Keepsake Collections

YEAR ISSUE	EDITION LIMIT	YEAR RETD.	ISSUE PRICE	*QUOTE U.S.$
1996 Happy Haunting, set/2 QFM8124	Retrd.	1996	12.95	18-33
1996 Peanuts® Pumpkin Patch, set/5 QFM8131	Retrd.	1996	19.95	30-66

1996 Premiere - Hallmark Keepsake Collections

YEAR ISSUE	EDITION LIMIT	YEAR RETD.	ISSUE PRICE	*QUOTE U.S.$
1996 Bashful Mistletoe, set/3 QFM8319	Retrd.	1996	12.95	N/A

1996 St. Patrick's - Hallmark Keepsake Collections

YEAR ISSUE	EDITION LIMIT	YEAR RETD.	ISSUE PRICE	*QUOTE U.S.$
1996 Lucky Cameron, set/2 QSM8021	Retrd.	1996	7.95	8-17

1996 Thanksgiving - Hallmark Keepsake Collections

YEAR ISSUE	EDITION LIMIT	YEAR RETD.	ISSUE PRICE	*QUOTE U.S.$
1996 Cowboy Cameron, set/3 QFM8041	Retrd.	1996	12.95	10-25
1996 Giving Thanks, set/3 QFM8134	Retrd.	1996	12.95	12-24

1996 Valentine - Hallmark Keepsake Collections

YEAR ISSUE	EDITION LIMIT	YEAR RETD.	ISSUE PRICE	*QUOTE U.S.$
1996 Alice in Wonderland, set/5 QSM8014	Retrd.	1996	19.95	18-30
1996 Panda Kids, set/2 QSM8011	Retrd.	1996	7.95	8-10
1996 Sweetheart Cruise, set/3 QSM8004	Retrd.	1996	12.95	13-22

1997 Christmas - Hallmark Keepsake Collections

YEAR ISSUE	EDITION LIMIT	YEAR RETD.	ISSUE PRICE	*QUOTE U.S.$
1997 HERSHEY'S™, set/2 QFM8625	Retrd.	1997	12.95	13
1997 Holiday Harmony, set/3 QFM8612	Retrd.	1997	12.95	13-25
1997 The Nativity, set/2 QFM8615	Retrd.	1997	7.95	8-29
1997 Santa Cameron, set/3 QFM8622	Retrd.	1997	4.95	5-12
1997 Six Dwarfs, set/3 QFM8685	Retrd.	1997	12.95	13-30
1997 Three Wee Kings, set/3 QFM8692	Retrd.	1997	12.95	13-27

1997 Easter - Hallmark Keepsake Collections

YEAR ISSUE	EDITION LIMIT	YEAR RETD.	ISSUE PRICE	*QUOTE U.S.$
1997 Easter Parade, set/2 QSM8562	Retrd.	1997	7.95	8
1997 Getting Ready For Spring, set/3 QSM8575	Retrd.	1997	12.95	13
1997 Happy Birthday Clowns QSM8565	Retrd.	1997	4.95	5
1997 Noah's Friends, set/2 QSM8572	Retrd.	1997	7.95	8

1997 Halloween - Hallmark Keepsake Collections

YEAR ISSUE	EDITION LIMIT	YEAR RETD.	ISSUE PRICE	*QUOTE U.S.$
1997 Bashful Visitors, set/3 QFM8582	Retrd.	1997	12.95	29
1997 Snow White and Dancing Dwarf, set/2 QFM8535	Retrd.	1997	7.95	20

1997 Peter Pan - Hallmark Keepsake Collections

YEAR ISSUE	EDITION LIMIT	YEAR RETD.	ISSUE PRICE	*QUOTE U.S.$
1997 Peter Pan, set/5 QSM8605	Retrd.	1997	19.95	20-34

1997 Premiere - Hallmark Keepsake Collections

YEAR ISSUE	EDITION LIMIT	YEAR RETD.	ISSUE PRICE	*QUOTE U.S.$
1997 Snowbear Season, set/3 QFM8602	Retrd.	1997	12.95	13

1997 Thanksgiving - Hallmark Keepsake Collections

YEAR ISSUE	EDITION LIMIT	YEAR RETD.	ISSUE PRICE	*QUOTE U.S.$
1997 Apple Harvest - Mary's Bears, set/3 QFM8585	Retrd.	1997	12.95	13-26
1997 Making a Wish, set/2 QFM8592	Retrd.	1997	7.95	8-17

1997 Valentine - Hallmark Keepsake Collections

YEAR ISSUE	EDITION LIMIT	YEAR RETD.	ISSUE PRICE	*QUOTE U.S.$
1997 Cupid Cameron QSM8552	Retrd.	1997	4.95	5
1997 Sule and Sara - PendaKids™, set/2 QSM8545	Retrd.	1997	7.95	8
1997 Tea Time - Mary's Bears, set/3 QSM8542	Retrd.	1997	12.95	9-13

1998 A Collection of Charm - Hallmark Keepsake Collections

YEAR ISSUE	EDITION LIMIT	YEAR RETD.	ISSUE PRICE	*QUOTE U.S.$
1998 Donald's Passenger Car QRP8513	Retrd.	1998	5.95	6-15
1998 Goofy's Caboose QRP8516	Retrd.	1998	5.95	6-15
1998 Mickey's Locomotive QRP8496	Retrd.	1998	5.95	6-15
1998 Minnie's Luggage Car QRP8506	Retrd.	1998	5.95	6-15
1998 Pluto's Coal Car QRP8503	Retrd.	1998	5.95	6-15

1998 Premiere - Hallmark Keepsake Collections

YEAR ISSUE	EDITION LIMIT	YEAR RETD.	ISSUE PRICE	*QUOTE U.S.$
1998 Bride and Groom QFM8486	Retrd.	1998	12.95	13
1998 HERSHEY'S™ (2nd Ed.) QFM8493	Retrd.	1998	10.95	11

1998 Spring Preview - Hallmark Keepsake Collections

YEAR ISSUE	EDITION LIMIT	YEAR RETD.	ISSUE PRICE	*QUOTE U.S.$
1998 Rapunzel, set/2 QSM8483	Retrd.	1998	12.95	13

1999 A Collection of Charm - Hallmark Keepsake Collections

YEAR ISSUE	EDITION LIMIT	YEAR RETD.	ISSUE PRICE	*QUOTE U.S.$
1999 Anniversary Edition, set/2 QRP8529	Retrd.	1999	12.95	13
1999 Bashful Friends, set/3	Retrd.	1999	2.95	3
1999 Eeyore QRP8519	Retrd.	1999	4.95	5
1999 Favorite Friends, set/2 QRP8537	Retrd.	1999	8.95	9
1999 A Kiss for You-HERSHEY'S™, set/3 (3rd Ed.) QRP8527	Retrd.	1999	12.95	13-15
1999 Piglet QRP8507	Retrd.	1999	4.95	5
1999 Tigger QRP8527	Retrd.	1999	4.95	5
1999 Winnie the Pooh QRP8509	Retrd.	1999	4.95	5

1999 Premiere Event - Keepsake

YEAR ISSUE	EDITION LIMIT	YEAR RETD.	ISSUE PRICE	*QUOTE U.S.$
1999 Park Avenue Wendy & Alex the Bellhop QFM8499	Yr.Iss.	1999	12.95	13

1999 Spring Preview - Hallmark Keepsake Collections

YEAR ISSUE	EDITION LIMIT	YEAR RETD.	ISSUE PRICE	*QUOTE U.S.$
1999 Bashful Boy and Girl at Garden Gate, set/2 QSM8459	Retrd.	1999	12.95	13

2000 A Collection of Charm - Hallmark Keepsake Collections

YEAR ISSUE	EDITION LIMIT	YEAR RETD.	ISSUE PRICE	*QUOTE U.S.$
2000 2000 Happy Hatters Collection Display Base QMM7003	Open		4.95	5
2000 B.B. Capps QMM7008	Open		4.95	5
2000 Bonnie Bonnet QMM7006	Open		4.95	5
2000 Booker Beanie QMM7017	Open		4.95	5
2000 Candy Capper QMM7022	Open		4.95	5
2000 Cora Copia QMM7023	Open		4.95	5
2000 Fire Fighter Wendy – 1997 QMM7010	Open		6.95	7
2000 Hattie Boxx QMM7024	Open		4.95	5
2000 Libby Crown QMM7015	Open		4.95	5
2000 Mary Had a Little Lamb-1996 QMM7014	Open		6.95	7
2000 Missy Milliner QMM7007	Open		4.95	5
2000 Mop Top Billy - 1996 QMM7005	Open		6.95	7
2000 Mop Top Wendy - 1996 QMM7004	Open		6.95	7
2000 Mother Goose-1997 QMM7013	Open		6.95	7
2000 Paddy O'Hatty QMM7002	Open		4.95	5
2000 Panama Pete QMM7016	Open		4.95	5
2000 Pink Pristine Angel – 1997 QMM7020	Open		6.95	7
2000 Rosie Chapeauzie QMM7001	Open		4.95	5
2000 Santa's Little Helper – 1998 QMM7021	Open		6.95	7
2000 Tiny Topper QMM7000	Open		4.95	5

2000 Way To Bees - Hallmark Keepsake Collections

YEAR ISSUE	EDITION LIMIT	YEAR RETD.	ISSUE PRICE	*QUOTE U.S.$
2000 January Bee QMM7035	Open		4.95	5
2000 February Bee QMM7036	Open		4.95	5
2000 March Bee QMM7037	Open		4.95	5
2000 April Bee QMM7039	Open		4.95	5
2000 May Bee QMM7040	Open		4.95	5
2000 June Bee QMM7041	Open		4.95	5
2000 July Bee QMM7046	Open		4.95	5
2000 August Bee QMM7047	Open		4.95	5
2000 September Bee QMM7048	Open		4.95	5
2000 October Bee QMM7051	Open		4.95	5
2000 November Bee QMM7052	Open		4.95	5
2000 December Bee QMM7053	Open		4.95	5

Kids! Collection - Hallmark Keepsake Collections

YEAR ISSUE	EDITION LIMIT	YEAR RETD.	ISSUE PRICE	*QUOTE U.S.$
2000 Baseball Boy 7045	Open		4.95	5
2000 Basketball Boy 7055	Open		4.95	5
2000 Basketball Girl 7054	Open		4.95	5
2000 Birthday Boy 7050	Open		4.95	5
2000 Birthday Girl 7059	Open		4.95	5
2000 Camping/Hiking Boy 7058	Open		4.95	5
2000 Camping/Hiking Girl 7049	Open		4.95	5
2000 Girl Gymnast 7044	Open		4.95	5
2000 Hockey Boy 7056	Open		4.95	5
2000 Ice Skating Girl 7057	Open		4.95	5
2000 Soccer Boy 7043	Open		4.95	5
2000 Soccer Girl 7042	Open		4.95	5

Madame Alexander - Hallmark Keepsake Collections

YEAR ISSUE	EDITION LIMIT	YEAR RETD.	ISSUE PRICE	*QUOTE U.S.$
2000 Artist Wendy 7032	Open		6.95	7
2000 Christmas Holly 7031	Open		6.95	7
2000 Empire Bride 7027	Open		6.95	7
2000 Glistening Angel 7030	Open		6.95	7
2000 Little Miss Muffet 7029	Open		6.95	7
2000 Little Red Riding Hood	Open		6.95	7
2000 Sleeping Beauty 7034	Open		6.95	7
2000 Sleeping Beauty's Prince 7033	Open		6.95	7
2000 Tooth Fairy 7028	Open		6.95	7

Midwest of Cannon Falls

Eddie Walker Collection - E. Walker

YEAR ISSUE	EDITION LIMIT	YEAR RETD.	ISSUE PRICE	*QUOTE U.S.$
1999 Fortune Teller Witch, set/2 31551-4	Yr.Iss.	1999	40.00	40
2000 Halloween Tour 38274-5	Yr.Iss.		35.00	35
2000 Ho, Ho, Ho Santa 37484-9	Yr.Iss.		40.00	40
1998 Holly Jolly Santa 27552-8	Yr.Iss.	1998	30.00	30
1995 Noah's Ark Set 15155-6	2,500	1996	175.00	225-350
1997 North Pole Express Train Set 21569-2	7,500	1997	200.00	200-300
2000 North Pole Noah 36941-8	5,000	2000	125.00	125
1998 Santa at Tree Farm, set/5 24941-3	7,500	1999	200.00	200
1999 Santa by Fireplace, set/4 32367-0	5,000		125.00	125
1996 Santa in Sleigh with Reindeer 17803-4	6,000	1996	180.00	460
1998 Santa on Holiday Plane 26141-5	Yr.Iss.	1998	55.00	70-80
1999 Santa on Motorcycle 32364-9	Yr.Iss.	1999	45.00	45
1997 Signature Santa-1997 21919-5	Yr.Iss.	1997	50.00	50
1999 Snowman with Birdhouse 33845-2	Yr.Iss.	2000	30.00	30
1998 Witch on Pumpkin 24360-2	Yr.Iss.	1998	40.00	40-45

Heaven and Nature Sings Millennium Edition Nativity Set - Midwest

YEAR ISSUE	EDITION LIMIT	YEAR RETD.	ISSUE PRICE	*QUOTE U.S.$
2000 Donkey 37976-9	2,000		80.00	80
2000 Elephant 37971-4	2,000		350.00	350
2000 Holy Family, set/3 37969-1	2,000		250.00	250
2000 Ox 37973-8	2,000		70.00	70
2000 Shepherd & Sheep, set/4 37968-4	2,000		250.00	250
2000 Sitting Camel 37974-5	2,000		130.00	130
2000 Standing Angel 37970-7	2,000		100.00	100
2000 Standing Camel 37972-1	2,000		170.00	170
2000 Wisemen, set/3 37967-7	2,000		250.00	250
2000 Nativity Backdrop, set/3 37975-2	2,000		500.00	500

Jolly Follies - S. Gore Evans

YEAR ISSUE	EDITION LIMIT	YEAR RETD.	ISSUE PRICE	*QUOTE U.S.$
2000 Do You See What I See 36811-4	Yr.Iss.	2000	35.00	35
1999 Snowlady with Hot Cocoa 33493-5	Yr.Iss.	1999	30.00	30
1999 Snowman Partiers 32910-8	Yr.Iss.	1999	32.00	32

Leo R. Smith III Collection - L. R. Smith

YEAR ISSUE	EDITION LIMIT	YEAR RETD.	ISSUE PRICE	*QUOTE U.S.$
1997 American Heritage Santa 21318-6	750	1999	110.00	110
1996 Angel of the Morning 18232-1	1,000	1999	48.00	50
1995 Angel with Lion and Lamb 13990-5	1,500	1995	125.00	175-232
1995 Circle of Nature Wreath 16120-3	500	1996	200.00	200
1991 Cossack Santa 01092-1	1,700	1993	103.00	185-200
1993 Dancing Santa 09042-8	5,000	1995	170.00	170
1992 Dreams of Night Buffalo 07999-7	1,062	1996	250.00	270-300
1991 Fisherman Santa 03311-1	4,000	1995	270.00	300-350
1993 Folk Angel 05444-4	2,095	1995	145.00	225-250
1995 Gardening Angel 16118-0	2,500	1996	130.00	175
1997 Gardening Santa 21320-9	1,000	1998	110.00	110
1994 Gift Giver Santa 12056-9	1,500	1996	180.00	180-225
1993 Gnome Santa on Deer 05206-8	1,463	1996	270.00	280-350
1992 Great Plains Santa 08049-8	5,000	1994	270.00	400-500
1995 Hare Leaping Over the Garden 16121-0	750	1996	100.00	100-150
1996 Jolly Boatman Santa 17794-5	1,500	1998	180.00	180
1992 Leo Smith Name Plaque 07881-5	5,000	1998	12.00	12
1995 Maize Maiden Angel 13992-9	2,500	1996	45.00	50
1991 Milkmaker 03541-2	5,000	1994	170.00	184-250
1992 Ms. Liberty 07866-2	5,000	1994	190.00	300
1998 Nature Santa 10" 25148-5	750	1998	120.00	120
1998 Northwoods Santa in Canoe 7" 25147-8	1,000	1998	140.00	140
1994 Old-World Santa 12053-8	1,500	1994	75.00	200-250
1995 Orchard Santa 13989-9	1,500	1996	125.00	125
1995 Otter Wall Hanging 16122-7	750	1996	150.00	250-300
1995 Owl Lady 13988-2	1,000	1995	100.00	200
1991 Pilgrim Man 03313-5	5,000	1994	84.00	200
1991 Pilgrim Riding Turkey 03312-8	1,811	1994	230.00	500-1000
1991 Pilgrim Woman 03315-9	5,000	1995	84.00	200
1996 Prairie Moon Market 17793-8	750	1999	300.00	300
1993 Santa Fisherman 08979-8	1,800	1997	250.00	400
1998 Santa Fisherman 8" 25145-4	1,000	1998	90.00	90
1996 Santa in Red Convertible 17790-7	2,000	1998	100.00	100-110
1995 Santa in Sleigh 13987-5	1,500	1996	125.00	250
1992 Santa of Peace 07328-5	5,000	1994	250.00	275-350
1997 Santa on Horse 21327-8	1,000	1997	150.00	160
1998 Santa on Moose 7" 25149-2	750	1998	150.00	150
1994 Santa Skier 12054-5	1,500	1995	190.00	195
1997 Snow King 21319-3	1,000	1998	100.00	100
1996 Snowflake in Nature Santa 17791-4	1,500	1999	125.00	125
1998 Snowshoe Santa 9" 25146-1	1,000	1998	120.00	120-150
1994 Star of the Roundup Cowboy 11966-1	1,500	1996	100.00	100
1991 Stars and Stripes Santa 01743-2	5,000	1994	190.00	350-400
1995 Sunbringer Santa 13991-2	1,500	1996	125.00	135-185
1996 SW Bach Santa 17792-1	1,500	1998	125.00	125
1991 Tis a Witching Time 03544-3	609	1991	140.00	1500-2000
1991 Toymaker 03540-5	5,000	1995	120.00	175-200
1997 Victorian Santa 21317-9	1,000	1998	130.00	130
1993 Voyageur 09043-5	788	1996	170.00	170
1994 Weatherwise Angel 12055-2	1,500	1996	150.00	150-175
1995 Wee Willie Santa 13993-6	2,500	1995	50.00	50
1997 White Nite Nick 21316-2	1,000	1998	130.00	130-150
1992 Woodland Brave 07867-9	1,500	1993	87.00	350-450
1991 Woodsman Santa 03310-4	5,000	1995	230.00	300-350

Rafterville - Midwest

YEAR ISSUE	EDITION LIMIT	YEAR RETD.	ISSUE PRICE	*QUOTE U.S.$
2000 Coach Braun w/Whistle, set/2 39513-4	Open		20.00	20
2000 Coach Braun's Helmet 39503-5	Open		20.00	20
2000 Edgerr Deux-Paws Paint Studio 39505-9	Open		25.00	25
2000 Edgerr Deux-Paws w/Tube of Paint, set/2 39497-7	Open		20.00	20
2000 Francesca Furrington w/Purse, set/2 39500-4	Open		20.00	20
2000 Francesca Furrington's Dollhouse 39504-2	Open		25.00	25
2000 The Greenpaw's Flower Pot 39510-3	Open		25.00	25
2000 Hans' Cookie Jar 39616-2	Open		25.00	25
2000 Hans, the Baker Bean w/Chocolate, set/2 39917-0	Open		20.00	20
2000 Madmoiselle Mischa w/Rose, set/2 39501-1	Open		20.00	20
2000 Madmoiselle Mischa's Jewelry Box 39567-3	Open		25.00	25
2000 Mayor Von Burin w/Key, set/2 39502-8	Open		20.00	20
2000 Mayor Von Burin's Mantel Clock 39509-7	Open		25.00	25
2000 Millicent w/Pin Cushion, set/2 39499-1	Open		20.00	20
2000 Millicent's Hat Box 39506-6	Open		25.00	25
2000 Miss Fern's Schoolhouse 39617-9	Open		25.00	25
2000 Miss Fern, Teacher w/Chalkboard, set/2 39918-7	Open		20.00	20
2000 Mr. Greenpaws w/Thimble, set/2 39511-0	Open		20.00	20

*Quotes have been rounded up to nearest dollar

YEAR ISSUE	EDITION LIMIT	YEAR RETD.	ISSUE PRICE	*QUOTE U.S.$
2000 Mrs. Greenpaws w/Bunny Twins, set/2 39512-7	Open		20.00	20
2000 Sip-Sum Broo w/Fan, set/2 39498-4	Open		20.00	20
2000 Sip-Sum Broo's Teapot 39508-0	Open		25.00	25

Miss Martha's Collection/Enesco Group, Inc.

Miss Martha's Collection - M. Root

YEAR ISSUE	EDITION LIMIT	YEAR RETD.	ISSUE PRICE	*QUOTE U.S.$
1993 Erin-Don't Worry Santa Won't Forget Us 307246	Retrd.	1994	55.00	110
1993 Amber-Mr. Snowman! (waterglobe) 310476	Closed	1994	50.00	100-115
1993 Kekisha-Heavenly Peace Musical 310484	Closed	1994	60.00	120
1993 Whitney-Let's Have Another Party 321559	Closed	1994	45.00	85-90
1993 Megan-My Birthday Cake! 321567	Closed	1994	60.00	115-120
1993 Doug-I'm Not Showin' Off 321575	Closed	1994	40.00	75-80
1993 Francie-Such A Precious Gift! 321583	Closed	1994	50.00	95-100
1993 Alicia-A Blessing From God 321591	Closed	1994	40.00	75-80
1993 Anita-It's For You, Mama! 321605	Closed	1994	45.00	85-90
1994 Jeffrey-Bein' A Fireman Sure Is Hot & Thirsty Work 350206	Closed	1994	40.00	80
1993 Jess-I Can Fly 350516	Retrd.	1994	45.00	90
1993 Ruth-Littlest Angel Figurine 350524	Closed	1994	40.00	80
1993 Stephen-I'll Be The Best Shepherd In The World! 350540	Closed	1994	40.00	80
1993 Jonathon-Maybe I Can Be Like Santa 350559	Closed	1994	45.00	90
1994 Charlotte-You Can Be Whatever You Dream 353191	Closed	1994	40.00	80
1992 Lillie-Christmas Dinner! 369373	Retrd.	1993	55.00	105-110
1992 Eddie-What A Nice Surprise! 369381	Retrd.	1994	50.00	95-100
1992 Kekisha-Heavenly Peace 421456	Closed	1994	40.00	75-80
1992 Angela-I Have Wings 421464	Closed	1994	45.00	90
1992 Amber-Mr. Snowman 421472	Retrd.	1993	60.00	120
1992 Mar/Jsh/Christopher-Hush Baby! It's Your B-day! Musical 431362	Closed	1994	80.00	105-160
1992 Carrie-God Bless America 440035	Closed	1994	45.00	90
1993 Hallie-Sing Praises To The Lord 443166	Retrd.	1993	60.00	120
1991 Jana-Plant With Love 443174	Closed	1994	40.00	80
1991 Hallie-Sing Praises To The Lord 443182	Closed	1994	37.50	75
1992 Belle/Maize-Not Now, Muffin 443204	Retrd.	1993	50.00	100
1991 Sammy/Leisha-Sister's First Day Of School 443190	Retrd.	1993	55.00	110
1991 Nate-Hope You Hear My Prayer, Lord 443212	Closed	1994	17.50	55
1991 Sadie-They Can't Find Us Here 443220	Retrd.	1993	45.00	90
1992 Patsy-Clean Clothes For Dolly 443239	Retrd.	1993	50.00	100
1991 Dawn-Pretty Please, Mama 443247	Closed	1994	40.00	80
1991 Tonya-Hush, Puppy Dear 443255	Closed	1994	50.00	100
1991 Jenny/Jeremiah-Birthday Biscuits, With Love... 443263	Retrd.	1993	60.00	150
1991 Suzi-Mama, Watch Me! 443271	Retrd.	1993	35.00	70
1992 Mattie-Sweet Child 443298	Retrd.	1993	30.00	60
1992 Sara Lou-Here, Lammie 443301	Retrd.	1993	50.00	100
1992 Angel Tree Topper 446521	Closed	1994	80.00	155-225
1992 Mar/Jsh/Christopher-Hush, Baby! It's Your B-day Figurine 448354	Closed	1994	55.00	110

Museum Collections, Inc.

American Family I - N. Rockwell

YEAR ISSUE	EDITION LIMIT	YEAR RETD.	ISSUE PRICE	*QUOTE U.S.$
1979 Baby's First Step	22,500	N/A	90.00	195-225
1980 Birthday Party	22,500	N/A	110.00	150
1981 Bride and Groom	22,500	N/A	110.00	125
1980 First Haircut	22,500	N/A	90.00	150-175
1980 First Prom	22,500	N/A	90.00	110-135
1980 Happy Birthday, Dear Mother	22,500	N/A	90.00	135
1980 Little Mother	22,500	N/A	110.00	125
1981 Mother's Little Helpers	22,500	N/A	110.00	135
1980 The Student	22,500	N/A	110.00	175
1980 Sweet Sixteen	22,500	N/A	90.00	125-175
1980 Washing Our Dog	22,500	N/A	110.00	125-150
1980 Wrapping Christmas Presents	22,500	N/A	90.00	125-130

Christmas - N. Rockwell

YEAR ISSUE	EDITION LIMIT	YEAR RETD.	ISSUE PRICE	*QUOTE U.S.$
1980 Checking His List	Yr.Iss.	1980	65.00	110
1983 High Hopes	Yr.Iss.	1983	95.00	175
1981 Ringing in Good Cheer	Yr.Iss.	1981	95.00	100
1984 Space Age Santa	Yr.Iss.	1984	65.00	100-110
1982 Waiting for Santa	Yr.Iss.	1982	95.00	110

Classic - N. Rockwell

YEAR ISSUE	EDITION LIMIT	YEAR RETD.	ISSUE PRICE	*QUOTE U.S.$
1984 All Wrapped Up	Closed	N/A	65.00	100
1980 Bedtime	Closed	N/A	65.00	125-150
1984 The Big Race	Closed	N/A	65.00	90-95
1983 Bored of Education	Closed	N/A	65.00	95-110
1983 Braving the Storm	Closed	N/A	65.00	135-150
1980 The Cobbler	Closed	N/A	65.00	95-125
1982 The Country Doctor	Closed	N/A	65.00	95-125
1981 A Dollhouse for Sis	Closed	N/A	65.00	90-95
1982 Dreams in the Antique Shop	Closed	N/A	65.00	90-95
1983 A Final Touch	Closed	N/A	65.00	90-95
1980 For A Good Boy	Closed	N/A	65.00	145-200
1984 Goin' Fishin'	Closed	N/A	65.00	90-95
1983 High Stepping	Closed	N/A	65.00	100-115
1982 The Kite Maker	Closed	N/A	65.00	100-110
1980 Lighthouse Keeper's Daughter	Closed	N/A	65.00	110-135
1980 Memories	Closed	N/A	65.00	110-150
1981 The Music Lesson	Closed	N/A	65.00	125-135
1981 Music Master	Closed	N/A	65.00	125
1981 Off to School	Closed	N/A	65.00	95-125
1981 Puppy Love	Closed	N/A	65.00	90-95
1984 Saturday's Hero	Closed	N/A	65.00	95-115
1983 A Special Treat	Closed	N/A	65.00	90-95
1982 Spring Fever	Closed	N/A	65.00	90-95
1980 The Toymaker	Closed	N/A	65.00	110-125
1981 While The Audience Waits	Closed	N/A	65.00	100-110
1983 Winter Fun	Closed	N/A	65.00	90-95
1982 Words of Wisdom	Closed	N/A	65.00	110-125

Commemorative - N. Rockwell

YEAR ISSUE	EDITION LIMIT	YEAR RETD.	ISSUE PRICE	*QUOTE U.S.$
1985 Another Masterpiece by Norman Rockwell	5,000	N/A	125.00	250-275
1981 Norman Rockwell Display	5,000	N/A	125.00	200-250
1983 Norman Rockwell, America's Artist	5,000	N/A	125.00	225
1984 Outward Bound	5,000	N/A	125.00	225-250
1986 The Painter and the Pups	5,000	N/A	125.00	250
1982 Spirit of America	5,000	N/A	125.00	225-275

North Light Ltd.

Crufts Champions - North Light Team

YEAR ISSUE	EDITION LIMIT	YEAR RETD.	ISSUE PRICE	*QUOTE U.S.$
1987 Airedale Bitch LE1986	350		200.00	200
1988 Afghan Hound LE1987	1,000		200.00	200
1989 English Setter LE1988	1,000		200.00	200
1990 Bearded Collie LE1989	1,000		200.00	200
1991 West Highland LE1990	1,000		200.00	200
1992 Clumber Spaniel LE1991	1,000		200.00	200
1993 Whippet LE1992	1,000		200.00	200
1994 Irish Setter LE1993	1,000		200.00	200
1995 Welsh Terrier LE1994	1,000		200.00	200
1996 Irish Setter LE1995	1,000		200.00	200
1997 Cocker Spaniel LE1996	1,000		200.00	200
1998 Yorkshire Terrier LE1997	1,000		200.00	200
1999 Welsh Terrier LE1998	1,000		200.00	200

Dogs - North Light Team

YEAR ISSUE	EDITION LIMIT	YEAR RETD.	ISSUE PRICE	*QUOTE U.S.$
1985 Beagle LE5001	350		240.00	240
1993 Boxer C E LE5067	1,000		220.00	220
1993 Boxer LE5074	1,000		220.00	220
1985 Bull Terrier Bust LE5021	350		100.00	100
1985 Bull Terrier LE5008	350		290.00	290
1987 Bull Terrier Std. Bitch 'Athena' LE5033	350		580.00	580
1985 Bull Terrier Trot Brin	350	1995	290.00	290
1985 Bull Terrier Trot LE5009	350		290.00	290
1985 Bull Terrier Trot White	350	1988	290.00	290
1985 Bulldog Bust LE5020	350		100.00	100
1985 Bulldog LE5010	350		430.00	430
1993 Bulldog Std. LE5068	1,000		280.00	280
1994 Cavalier KC Family LE5078	1,000		210.00	210
1990 Cavalier KC Std. LE5063	1,000		250.00	250
1990 Cocker Spaniel Std. LE5054	1,000		240.00	240
1990 Dachshund Sm-H LE5051	1,000		240.00	240
1996 English Mastiff LE5089	1,000		200.00	200
1989 Golden Retriever LE5038	1,000		250.00	250
1985 Great Dane LE5006	350		160.00	160
1993 Great Dane S/S LE5082	1,000		230.00	230
1986 Jack Russel Ben LE5024	350		290.00	290
1986 Jack Russel Ben Tri	350	1993	290.00	290
1986 Jack Russel Bitch LE5022	350		250.00	250
1989 Labrador LE5035	1,000		300.00	300
1996 Lancashire Heeler LE5088	1,000		200.00	200
1985 Lurcher LE5011	350		100.00	100
1988 Miniature Pinscher LE5032	1,000		190.00	190
1999 Munsterlander LE5098	250		410.00	410
1985 Newfoundland LE5016	350		140.00	140
1990 Papillon Std. LE5050	1,000		250.00	250
1990 Parson J R Jill LE5066	1,000		240.00	240
1987 Pug 'Joe' LE5029	350		280.00	280
1991 Pug Std. Facing Left LE5063	1,000		180.00	180
1991 Pug Std. Facing Right LE5064	1,000		180.00	180
1986 Rottweiler 'Hugo' LE5030	350		560.00	560
1986 Rottweiler 'Otto' LE5023	350		300.00	300
1989 Schnauzer C E LE5034	1,000		280.00	280
1989 Schnauzer LE5037	1,000		280.00	280
1987 Springer Spaniel LE5028	350		190.00	190
1995 Staffies at Home LE5081	1,000		410.00	410
1985 Staffordshire Bull Brin	350	1988	270.00	270
1985 Staffordshire Bull LE5007	350		270.00	270
1985 Staffordshire Bull Red	350	1999	270.00	270
1988 Staffs Bull 'Jason' LE5027	350		350.00	350
1987 Staffs Bull 'Jess' LE5031	350		1300.00	1300
1985 Staffs Bull Bust LE5019	350		140.00	140
1990 Staffs Bull Playing LE5045	350		270.00	270
1990 Staffs Bull Stand LE5055	1,000		300.00	300
1990 Staffs Bull Std. LE5056	1,000		220.00	220
1994 Whippet Std. Bitch LE5084	1,000		200.00	200
1994 Whippet Std. Dog LE5083	1,000		200.00	200
1991 Yorkshire Terrier Std. LE5058	1,000		280.00	280

Horses - North Light Team

YEAR ISSUE	EDITION LIMIT	YEAR RETD.	ISSUE PRICE	*QUOTE U.S.$
1998 All Creatures Great & Small LE5094	1,000		350.00	350
1993 Andalusian Valoroso LE5069	1,000		400.00	400
1993 Arab Head "Shadeed" LE5072	1,000		220.00	220
1988 Beagle Bay LE5012	1,000		130.00	130
1993 Cavort LE5071	1,000		410.00	410
1996 Eventer LE5085	1,000		630.00	630
1994 Friesian LE5074	1,000		200.00	200
1997 Homeward Bound LE5092	1,000		400.00	400
1987 Kings Troop LE5057	350		410.00	410
1991 Knight LE5086	1,000		900.00	900
1996 Lady LE5087	1,000		900.00	900
1997 Levade with Rider LE5091	1,000		350.00	350
1993 Lipizzaner 'Levade' LE5076	1,000		320.00	320
1993 Lipizzaner 'Piaffe' LE5077	1,000		350.00	350
1996 Lipizzaner Long Rein LE5090	1,000		420.00	420
1994 Rolling Horse LE5075	2,000		400.00	400
1993 Thoroughbred Head LE5073	1,000		210.00	210
1993 Thoroughbred on base LE5070	1,000		410.00	410

Limited Editions - North Light Team

YEAR ISSUE	EDITION LIMIT	YEAR RETD.	ISSUE PRICE	*QUOTE U.S.$
1982 Black Cock LE5005	350		420.00	420
1989 Blue Fronted Amazon LE5039	1,000		420.00	420
1991 Campbell Duck LE5062	1,000		310.00	310
1985 Cat Looking Left LE5003	350		240.00	240
1985 Cat Looking Left Tabby	350	1990	240.00	240
1990 Cat Reclining Looking Right 'Tabatha' LE5044	1,000		240.00	240
1985 Eagle Owl LE5018	350		660.00	660
1986 Grouse LE5026	350		320.00	320
1990 Koi Carp LE5052	1,000		500.00	500
1986 Pheasant LE5025	350		740.00	740
1989 Red Breasted Goose LE5041	1,000		180.00	180
1985 Siamese Cat Std. LE5004	350		230.00	230
1988 St. Vincent LE5013	1,000		420.00	420

Zoological - North Light Team

YEAR ISSUE	EDITION LIMIT	YEAR RETD.	ISSUE PRICE	*QUOTE U.S.$
1990 Bactrian Camel LE5048	350		340.00	340
1985 Bison LE5017	350		230.00	230
1998 Crocodile LE5093	100		700.00	700
1985 Elephant African LE5014	350		290.00	290
1990 Elephant Indian LE5042	1,000		260.00	260
1990 Gorilla LE5043	1,000		660.00	660
1991 Grizzly Bear LE5061	1,000		660.00	660
1985 Hippopotamus LE5002	350		230.00	230
1989 Leopard in Tree LE5040	1,000		230.00	230
1985 Leopard on Fork LE5000	1,000	1988	230.00	230
1985 Panther on Fork LE5036	350		210.00	210
1991 Polar Bear Female LE5060	1,000		400.00	400
1991 Polar Bear Male LE5059	1,000		400.00	400
1985 Rhinoceros, black & Calf LE5065	1,000		270.00	270
1994 Rhinocerous LE5015	350		230.00	230

The Oliver Weber Jeweled Collection

Jewels of Africa - O. Weber

YEAR ISSUE	EDITION LIMIT	YEAR RETD.	ISSUE PRICE	*QUOTE U.S.$
1999 Elephant, lg.	Open		115.00	115
1999 Elephant, sm.	Open		80.00	80

Jewels of the Arctic - O. Weber

YEAR ISSUE	EDITION LIMIT	YEAR RETD.	ISSUE PRICE	*QUOTE U.S.$
1999 Polar Bear	Open		105.00	105

Jewels of the Imagination - O. Weber

YEAR ISSUE	EDITION LIMIT	YEAR RETD.	ISSUE PRICE	*QUOTE U.S.$
1999 Dragon	Open		225.00	225
1999 Snow Man	Open		75.00	75

Jewels of the Sea - O. Weber

YEAR ISSUE	EDITION LIMIT	YEAR RETD.	ISSUE PRICE	*QUOTE U.S.$
1999 Dolphin Boy	Open		75.00	75
1999 Dolphin Father w/stand	Open		110.00	110
1999 Dolphin Girl	Open		75.00	75
1999 Dolphin Mother w/stand	Open		110.00	110
1999 Dolphin Set (8 pc.)	Open		495.00	495

Jewels of the Symphony - O. Weber

YEAR ISSUE	EDITION LIMIT	YEAR RETD.	ISSUE PRICE	*QUOTE U.S.$
1999 Guitar w/stand	Open		58.00	58
1999 Harp	Closed	2000	60.00	60
1999 Piano	Open		73.00	73
1999 Saxophone w/stand	Open		58.00	58
1999 Violin w/stand	Open		58.00	58

Olszewski Studios

Olszewski Studios - R. Olszewski

YEAR ISSUE	EDITION LIMIT	YEAR RETD.	ISSUE PRICE	*QUOTE U.S.$
1994 The Grand Entrance SM1	1,500	1994	225.00	225-325
1994 The Grand Entrance A/P SM1	120	1994	450.00	450-500
1994 Tinker's Treasure Chest SM2	750	1994	235.00	450-495
1994 Tinker's Treasure Chest A/P SM2	120	1994	470.00	470
1994 To Be... (included w/Treasure Chest) SM3	750	1994	Set	285-495
1994 To Be... (included w/Treasure Chest) A/P SM3	120	1994	Set	Set
1994 The Little Tinker SM4	750	1995	235.00	235-295
1994 The Little Tinker A/P SM4	100	1995	470.00	470
1995 Special Treat SM5	800	1995	220.00	220
1995 Special Treat A/P SM5	100	1995	440.00	440
1995 Mocking Bird with Peach Blossoms SM6	800	1995	230.00	230
1995 Mocking Bird with Peach Blossoms A/P SM6	100	1995	460.00	460
1995 Lady With An Urn (brown dress) SM7	250	1995	235.00	275-325
1995 Lady With An Urn (brown dress) A/P SM7	36	1995	470.00	470
1995 Lady With An Urn (green dress) SM7	250	1995	235.00	250-295
1995 Lady With An Urn (green dress) A/P SM7	36	1995	470.00	470
1995 Lady With An Urn (pink dress) SM7	250	1995	235.00	250-295
1995 Lady With An Urn (pink dress) A/P SM7	36	1995	470.00	470
1995 Lady With An Urn (blue dress) SM7	250	1995	235.00	235-295
1995 Lady With An Urn (blue dress) A/P SM7	36	1995	470.00	470
1995 Castle of Gleaming White Porcelain SM8	750	1995	285.00	300-350
1995 Castle of Gleaming White Porcelain A/P SM8	100	1995	570.00	570

*Quotes have been rounded up to nearest dollar

YEAR ISSUE	EDITION LIMIT	YEAR RETD.	ISSUE PRICE	*QUOTE U.S.$
1995 ...Not to Be Lapel Pin SM10	750	1995	110.00	110
1995 ...Not to Be Lapel Pin A/P SM10	100	1995	220.00	220
1996 Spring Dance SM9	750	1996	205.00	210-225
1996 Spring Dance A/P SM9	100	1996	410.00	410
1996 Oriental Lovers SM11	750	1996	240.00	240-290
1996 Oriental Lovers A/P SM11	100	1996	480.00	480
1996 Dashing Through the Snow SM12	500	1996	480.00	480
1996 Dashing Through the Snow A/P SM12	100	1996	960.00	960
1996 The Viceroy SM13	750	1996	235.00	250-350
1996 The Viceroy A/P SM13	100	1996	470.00	470
1996 Little Red Riding Hood SM14	750	1996	235.00	235-295
1996 Little Red Riding Hood A/P SM14	100	1996	470.00	470
1996 The Departure (Sterling) SM1S	375	1996	325.00	325-395
1996 The Departure (Sterling) A/P SM1S	27	1996	650.00	650
1997 American Beauty SM15	750	1997	225.00	225
1997 American Beauty A/P SM15	100	1997	450.00	450
1997 Summer: Picking Apples SM16	750	1997	240.00	240
1997 Summer: Picking Apples A/P SM16	100	1997	480.00	480
1997 The Fox Hunt SM17	500	1997	480.00	480
1997 The Fox Hunt A/P SM17	100	1997	960.00	960
1997 Winter: Tracking the Rabbit SM18	750	1997	225.00	225
1997 Winter: Tracking the Rabbit A/P SM18	100	1997	450.00	450
1998 Dollhouse Dreams SM20	750	1997	235.00	235
1998 Dollhouse Dreams A/P SM20	100	1997	470.00	470
1997 Spring Dance with Floral Dress SM9	100	1997	275.00	300-400
1998 Autumn: Going South SM19	750	1998	230.00	230-235
1998 Autumn: Going South A/P SM19	100	1998	460.00	460
1998 Victorians - Mother's Pride (girl) SM21	250	1998	480.00	480
1998 Victorians - Dad's Joy (girl) SM23	250	1998	set	set
1998 Victorians - First Curl Box (girl) SM24	250	1998	set	set
1998 Victorians - Mother's Pride (girl) A/P SM21	50	1998	960.00	960
1998 Victorians - Dad's Joy (girl) A/P SM23	50	1998	set	set
1998 Victorians - First Curl Box (girl) A/P SM24	50	1998	set	set
1998 Victorians - Mother's Pride (boy) SM21	250	1998	480.00	480
1998 Victorians - Dad's Joy (boy) SM23	250	1998	set	set
1998 Victorians - First Curl Box (boy) SM24	250	1998	set	set
1998 Victorians - Mother's Pride (boy) A/P SM21	50	1998	960.00	960
1998 Victorians - Dad's Joy (boy) A/P SM23	50	1998	set	set
1998 Victorians - First Curl Box (boy) A/P SM24	50	1998	set	set
1998 Spring: Nature's Awakening SM22	750	1998	240.00	240
1998 Spring: Nature's Awakening A/P SM22	100	1998	480.00	480
1998 Cedar Waxwing SM25	750	1998	230.00	230-295
1998 Cedar Waxwing A/P SM25	100	1998	460.00	460
1998 Trick or Treat SM26	750	1998	235.00	235-295
1998 Trick or Treat A/P SM26	100	1998	470.00	470
1998 The Scholars SM27	375	1998	185.00	185
1998 The Scholars A/P SM27	37	1998	370.00	370

Original Appalachian Artworks

Extra Special - X. Roberts

YEAR ISSUE	EDITION LIMIT	YEAR RETD.	ISSUE PRICE	*QUOTE U.S.$
1985 Baby's First Step	Closed	N/A	18.00	40
1984 Bedtime Story	Closed	N/A	15.00	25
1984 Birthday Party	Closed	N/A	26.50	40-45
1984 The Building Block	Closed	N/A	8.00	12
1985 Carousel (musical)	Closed	N/A	90.00	200
1984 CPK Clubhouse	Closed	N/A	26.50	45-50
1984 Daydreams	Closed	N/A	8.00	15
1984 Deer Friends	Closed	N/A	26.50	45
1984 Discovering New Life	Closed	N/A	16.00	25
1985 The Entertainers	30,000	N/A	50.00	85-100
1984 Getting Acquainted	Closed	N/A	20.00	40
1984 I Can Do It	Closed	N/A	8.00	15
1984 Just Being Silly	Closed	N/A	8.00	15
1984 The Little Drummer	Closed	N/A	8.00	15
1985 Lovely Ladies	Closed	N/A	26.50	50-60
1984 Noel, Noel	Closed	N/A	20.00	40-45
1984 Playtime	Closed	N/A	8.00	25
1985 Rainbow Sweetheart	Closed	N/A	15.00	15
1985 Sandcastles	Closed	N/A	26.50	45-55
1984 Sharing a Soda Cream	Closed	N/A	15.00	30
1984 Sleigh Ride	Closed	N/A	18.50	30
1985 Special Delivery	25,000	N/A	50.00	100
1985 A Special Gift	Closed	N/A	15.00	35
1984 Tea For Two	Closed	N/A	16.50	30
1984 Waiting Patiently	Closed	N/A	8.00	15

Extra Special Easter Collection - X. Roberts

YEAR ISSUE	EDITION LIMIT	YEAR RETD.	ISSUE PRICE	*QUOTE U.S.$
1985 Easter Artists	Closed	N/A	40.00	50-55
1985 Findin' Easter Treats	Closed	N/A	26.50	50-55
1985 In Your Easter Bonnet	Closed	N/A	8.00	15
1985 Our Easter Bunny	Closed	N/A	8.00	15

Extra Special Valentine Collection - X. Roberts

YEAR ISSUE	EDITION LIMIT	YEAR RETD.	ISSUE PRICE	*QUOTE U.S.$
1985 Hugs and Kisses	Closed	N/A	18.00	30
1985 I Love You	Closed	N/A	14.50	30
1985 Rainbow Sweetheart	Closed	N/A	15.00	30

Papel Giftware

The Windsor Bears of Cranbury Commons - Team

YEAR ISSUE	EDITION LIMIT	YEAR RETD.	ISSUE PRICE	*QUOTE U.S.$
1998 Alexander "I'll Be There"	Open		22.50	23
1998 Alyssa "Time to Hit the Slopes"	Open		18.50	19
2000 Amanda "Building Your Dreams"	Open		22.50	23
1996 Amanda "Sew Happy"	Retrd.	1997	14.50	15
1998 Amber "Thinking of You"	Open		16.50	17
1997 Amy "Roses are Red"	Retrd.	1999	16.00	16
2000 Andrea "The Maid of Honor"	Open		16.50	17
1997 Andrew & Allison "Love Is In the Air"	Open		30.00	30
1998 Andy "Reach for the Stars"	Open		22.50	23
1997 Angela "My Lil' Angel"	Suspd.		16.00	16
1998 Ann & Me "And the Stockings Were Hung By the Chimney with Care"	Open		30.00	30
1997 Arnold "Breakin' Par"	Open		18.00	18
1996 Ashley & Tyler "Skater's Waltz"	Retrd.	1997	25.00	25
1998 Becky "I'm Sweet on You"	Open		18.00	18
2000 Beth & Ben "America on Parade"	Open		30.00	30
1997 Betsy "Stars and Stripes Forever"	Open		16.00	16
1996 Brandon "Soft Landing"	Retrd.	1997	17.50	18
2000 Brannon "Hang In There"	Open		22.50	23
1999 Brett "Thinking of You at Christmas"	Suspd.		22.50	23
2000 Brianna "My Favorite Time of Year"	Open		22.50	23
1996 Brittany "All Things Grow With Love"	Retrd.	1997	14.50	15
2000 Bruce "Just Put Your Mind to It"	Open		16.50	17
2000 Caitlin "Your Secret Pal"	Open		18.00	18
1998 Cameron "Soccer Star"	Open		16.50	17
1999 Carey "Congratulations"	Open		18.00	18
1998 Casey "Welcome to Cranbury Commons"	Open		16.50	17
2000 Charles "The Best Man"	Open		16.50	17
1997 Charlie "The Littlest Christmas Tree"	Open		20.00	20
1998 Chris & Cody "We Made It!"	Open		30.00	30
1996 Christopher "Sweet Surprise"	Retrd.	1997	14.50	15
1996 Coleen "Luck O' the Irish"	Retrd.	1997	16.00	16
1998 Connor "Follow Your Dreams"	Open		22.50	23
1997 Courtney "How Does Your Garden Grow?"	Retrd.	1999	16.00	16
1998 Dad & Cory "Dad, How much Longer?"	Open		16.50	17
1996 Daddy & Junior "Once Upon A Time"	Retrd.	1997	14.50	15
1998 Daddy & Steven "Daddy, Can I Do It?"	Open		30.00	30
2000 Daddy and Me "Don't Worry, I Got You"	Open		27.50	28
2000 Daisy "How Do I Love Thee...?"	Open		18.00	18
1998 Dan "Let's Play"	Open		16.50	17
1998 Danielle & Derek "Sunday's Best"	Open		32.50	33
1997 David "Graduation Day"	Open		14.50	15
1999 Dennis & Doug "A Friend Is Always There In A Time of Need"	Open		30.00	30
1997 Dora & Her Little Sister "Halloween Surprise"	Retrd.	1999	16.00	16
1998 Dr. Jonathon Windsor "TLC...Tender Loving Care"	Open		16.50	17
2000 Dr. Windsor & Me "Smile"	Open		25.00	25
1998 Elizabeth & Evan "Hugs & Kisses"	Open		30.00	30
1996 Emily "Sleepy Head"	Retrd.	1997	14.50	15
1997 Eric "Bloomin' With Love"	Retrd.	1999	16.50	17
2000 Erica "Planting Seeds of Happiness"	Open		22.50	23
2000 Erin "The Sweetest Sounds of Harmony"	Open		18.00	18
2000 Ethan "Learning New Things Everyday"	Open		22.50	23
1997 Florence "Feeling Better?"	Open		14.50	15
1999 George "We Are Grateful"	Open		18.00	18
1999 Grace "We Are Grateful"	Open		18.00	18
1998 Grandma & Timothy "Can I Lick the Spoon?"	Open		30.00	30
1999 Grandpa & Me "Grandpa, Can You Teach Me"	Open		27.50	28
1998 Greg "Wow, Look At All these Treats"	Open		22.50	23
2000 Heather "A Brush of Happiness"	Open		25.00	25
1997 Jack "It's Time for Pumpkin Pickin'"	Open		16.00	16
2000 James "My Favorite Present"	Open		22.50	23
1998 Jamie "Baby's First Christmas"	Open		22.50	23
1999 Jason "It's Not the Same Without You"	Open		20.00	20
1999 Jean "Congratulations"	Open		18.00	18
1999 Jenna & Debbie "Our Friendship is the Best Bargin"	Open		30.00	30
1998 Jennifer "Happy Birthday"	Open		16.50	17
1999 Jeremy "The Ring Bearer"	Open		12.50	13
1996 Jessica "Homework Helper"	Retrd.	1997	14.50	15
2000 Jessica "Now I Lay Me Down to Sleep"	Open		30.00	30
1999 Jessie "Baby's 1st Birthday"	Open		12.50	13
1997 Jimmy "Fool for Love"	Retrd.	1999	16.00	16
2000 Joe "Leading the Team to Excellence"	Open		16.50	17
1998 John "Happy Birthday"	Open		16.50	17
2000 Jordan "Don't Worry, Be Happy"	Open		16.50	17
1996 Jordan "First Day"	Retrd.	1997	14.50	15
1997 Justin "Still Life with Flowers"	Retrd.	1999	22.50	23
1998 Kathleen & Me "Spending Time With You"	Suspd.		27.50	28
1996 Katie & Dolly "Best Friends"	Retrd.	1997	14.50	15
1998 Kelly "Love, Loyalty, & Friendship"	Open		18.00	18
1999 Keri "You Can Do It"	Open		16.50	17
1998 Kevin & Nicole "Will You Marry Me?"	Open		30.00	30
1997 Kimberly "Graduation Day"	Open		14.50	15
2000 Kristen "Everything Is Under Control"	Open		25.00	25
1997 Kyle "Look What Santa Brought Me"	Open		22.50	23
2000 Laura "A Caring Heart"	Open		18.00	18
1996 Lauren "Homemade with Love"	Retrd.	1997	14.50	15
1999 Lindsay & Louis "Childhood Sweethearts"	Open		30.00	30
1999 Lisa "Get Well Soon"	Open		18.00	18
1999 Lynn "You're As Sweet As Pie"	Open		25.00	25
2000 Maria & Nick "Bon Voyage"	Open		30.00	30
1999 Mark "Go For the Goal"	Open		18.00	18
1998 Mary "Miracle of Love"	Open		16.50	17
1996 Matthew "Bringing Home the Tree"	Retrd.	1997	16.50	17
1997 Maureen & Sean "Top O' the Morning"	Open		30.00	30
1997 Meghan & Daniel "Forever Yours"	Open		30.00	30
1997 Melissa "My Egg-stra Special Day"	Open		16.50	17
1999 Michael "Go For It"	Open		18.00	18
1997 Michael & Stephanie "Bee Mine"	Retrd.	1999	30.00	30
1999 Michelle "Have I Told You Lately"	Open		18.00	18
1999 Michelle & Todd "Together We Can Go Anywhere"	Open		30.00	30
1997 Mickey "Play Ball"	Open		16.00	16
1998 Miss Windsor & Brian "School Days"	Open		27.50	28
1998 Mommy & Me "Bundle of Joy"	Open		20.00	20
1999 Mommy & Me "You Always See the Best in Me"	Open		25.00	25
1998 Mommy, Daddy, & Me "Baby's First Step"	Open		32.50	33
2000 Monica "Tennis Anyone?"	Open		20.00	20
1999 Mr. & Mrs. Windsor "The Anniversary Waltz" Happy 50th Anniversary	Open		25.00	25
1999 Mr. & Mrs. Windsor "Through the Years" Happy 25th Anniversary	Open		25.00	25
1998 Mr. Thomas "World Class Teacher"	Open		16.50	17
2000 Mrs. Windsor and Dad "The First Dance"	Open		25.00	25
1997 Nancy "Fore"	Open		18.00	18
1999 The New Mr. & Mrs. Windsor "And the Bride Cuts the Cake"	Open		30.00	30
1997 The New Mr. & Mrs. Windsor "Dearly Beloved"	Open		25.00	25
1998 The New Mr. & Mrs. Windsor "Over the Theshold"	Open		25.00	25
1996 Nicholas "Santa's Little Helper"	Retrd.	1999	16.50	17
1999 Officer Bob "To Serve and Protect"	Open		20.00	20
2000 Officer Windsor and Me "Welcome Home"	Open		20.00	20
1996 Patrick "At the End of the Rainbow"	Retrd.	1997	16.00	16
1998 Paul "Just For You"	Open		18.00	18
1997 Peter "Where Did They Go?"	Suspd.		16.50	17
1999 Rachel "The Flower Girl"	Open		12.50	13
1999 Randy "All Bundled Up"	Open		18.00	18
1998 Rebecca "Thank You"	Open		16.50	17
1999 Redd "Courageous Hero"	Open		20.00	20
1998 Richard "Gone Fishing"	Open		22.50	23
1998 Riley "Kiss Me I'm Irish"	Open		18.00	18
1996 Robert "Sunny Morning"	Retrd.	1997	16.50	17
1997 Ryan "Watch Your Step"	Open		20.00	20
1997 Sam "Yankee Doodle Dandy"	Open		16.00	16
1998 Samantha "Prima Ballerina"	Open		16.50	17
1999 Sammy "Take Me Out to the Ball Game"	Open		50.00	50
1997 Sarah "Uh Oh!"	Open		22.50	23
1998 Scott "Halloween Traditions"	Open		16.50	17
1999 Tiffany "I'm Cheering for You"	Suspd.		16.50	17
1998 Tyler "Lil' Conductor"	Open		18.00	18
1997 William "Lil' Drummer Bear"	Open		20.00	20
1998 The Windsor Family "A Time to Remember"	2,750		100.00	100
2000 The Windsor Family "Christmas Morning"	2,750		75.00	75
1999 The Windsor Family "Sweet Dreams"	2,750		75.00	75
1997 Zachary "Winter Buddies"	Open		25.00	25

The Windsor Bears of Cranbury Commons Accessories - Team

YEAR ISSUE	EDITION LIMIT	YEAR RETD.	ISSUE PRICE	*QUOTE U.S.$
1999 Decorated Christmas Tree	Open		16.00	16
1999 Holiday Fireplace	Open		14.50	15
1999 Snowy Tree, lg.	Open		12.50	13
1999 Snowy Tree, med.	Open		10.00	10
1999 Snowy Tree, sm.	Open		7.50	8

Peanuts Gallery/Hallmark Keepsake Collections

Peanuts Gallery/Hallmark Keepsake Collections

YEAR ISSUE	EDITION LIMIT	YEAR RETD.	ISSUE PRICE	*QUOTE U.S.$
2000 An Ace in Action, Snoopy QPC4032	Numbrd.		15.00	15
2000 Being There QPC4005	Yr.Iss.		15.00	15
2000 Campfire Friends QPC4030	Numbrd.		20.00	20
2000 Celebrate! QPC4015	Yr.Iss.		12.95	13
2000 Charlie Brown QPC4025	24,500		25.00	25
2000 Cyber Chuck QPC4062	Numbrd.		18.00	18
2000 Fall Ball QPC4010	Numbrd.		20.00	20
2000 Fire Fighter Pig-Pen QPC4051	Numbrd.		15.00	15
2000 Five Decades of Charlie Brown QPC4002	Yr.Iss.		13.00	13
2000 Five Decades of Lucy QPC4003	Yr.Iss.		13.00	13
2000 Five Decades of Snoopy QPC4001	Yr.Iss.		13.00	13
2000 The Flock, Snoopy Shepherd QPC4050	Numbrd.		10.00	10
2000 Flying High QPC4004	Yr.Iss.		15.00	15
2000 Golf Is Life! QPC4012	Yr.Iss.		12.95	13
2000 A Good Man - Charlie Brown & Gang QPC4044	Numbrd.		35.00	35
2000 The Great Pumpkin QPC4022	Yr.Iss.		20.00	20
2000 Great Times! - Snoopy & Charlie Brown QPC4042	Numbrd.		20.00	20
2000 Hanging On! QPC4014	Yr.Iss.		12.95	13
2000 Hugs QPC4007	Numbrd.		15.00	15
2000 It Takes All Kinds! QPC4013	Yr.Iss.		12.95	13
2000 Joe Cool and Friend QPC4011	Numbrd.		15.00	15
2000 Jointed Woodstock QPC4035	Numbrd.		25.00	25
2000 Jolly Holidays QPC4023	Yr.Iss.		20.00	20
2000 A Joyful Song QPC4024	24,500		25.00	25
2000 King of the Sandbox, Linus QPC4027	Numbrd.		15.00	15
2000 Linus as M.D. QPC4046	Numbrd.		15.00	15
2000 Linus QPC4019	24,500		25.00	25
2000 A Little Rest QPC4016	Yr.Iss.		12.95	13
2000 Lucy QPC4018	24,500		25.00	25

416

Collectors' Information Bureau

*Quotes have been rounded up to nearest dollar

YEAR ISSUE	EDITION LIMIT	YEAR RETD.	ISSUE PRICE	*QUOTE U.S.$
2000 Mary, Joseph, and Baby Jesus QPC4049	Numbrd.		12.00	12
2000 Mood Booth QPC4031	Numbrd.		20.00	20
2000 Ms. Van Pelt - Lucy as Teacher QPC4028	Numbrd.		18.00	18
2000 Nurse Sally QPC4060	Numbrd.		15.00	15
2000 On the Course QPC4008	Numbrd.		20.00	20
2000 The Peanut Cracker - Snoopy Nutcracker QPC4041	Numbrd.		15.00	15
2000 A Perfect Angel (Sally) and Pageant Base QPC4048	Numbrd.		12.00	12
2000 Sally QPC4020	24,500		25.00	25
2000 Seventh Inning Stretch QPC4009	Numbrd.		15.00	15
2000 Snoopy QPC4021	24,500		25.00	25
2000 Snoopy, Business Beagle QPC4026	Numbrd.		15.00	15
2000 Special Blessings QPC4047	Numbrd.		15.00	15
2000 The Winning Team QPC4006	24,500		30.00	30
2000 Winter Games - Snoopy & Woodstock Hockey Snowglobe QPC4043	Numbrd.		20.00	20
2000 A Wise Man, Linus QPC4063	Numbrd.		10.00	10

Pemberton & Oakes

Zolan's Children - D. Zolan

1982 Erik and the Dandelion	17,000	1981	48.00	48-85
1983 Sabina in the Grass	6,800	1982	48.00	48-99
1985 Tender Moment	10,000	1985	29.00	75-85
1984 Winter Angel	8,000	1984	28.00	28-99

PenDelfin

PenDelfin Family Circle Collectors' Club - J. Heap, unless otherwise noted

1993 Herald	Closed	1993	Gift	249-290
1993 Bosun PD600	Closed	1993	50.00	120-200
1994 Buttons	Closed	1994	Gift	80-160
1994 Puffer PD601	Closed	1995	85.00	210-250
1995 Bellman PD502	Closed	1995	Gift	100-231
1995 Georgie and the Dragon PD602	Closed	1995	125.00	175
1996 Newsie PD534	Closed	1996	Gift	60-100
1996 Delia PD536	Closed	1996	125.00	210
1997 Little Tom PD556	Closed	1997	Gift	75-112
1997 Woody PD556	Closed	1997	125.00	125-165
1998 Tidy Patch PD574	Closed	1998	Gift	70
1998 Gramps PD576	Closed	1998	125.00	125
1999 Trove PD596	Closed	1999	Gift	N/A
1999 Treasure PD598 - D. Roberts	Closed	1999	130.00	130
2000 Little Hero PD618	Yr.Iss.		Gift	N/A
2000 Gran PD620	Yr.Iss.		120.00	120

40th Anniversary Piece - PenDelfin

1994 Aunt Ruby	10,000		275.00	351

Event Piece - J. Heap, unless otherwise noted

1994 Walmsley PD252	Retrd.	1995	75.00	175-250
1995 Runaway PD254	Retrd.	1995	90.00	90-125
1996 Bodgit PD544	Retrd.	1996	85.00	98-150
1997 Sylvana PD564 - D. Roberts	Retrd.	1997	85.00	75-105
1998 Rockafella PD584	Retrd.	1998	85.00	85
1999 Gentleman Jack PD610	Retrd.	1999	85.00	85
2000 Event Piece PD624	Yr.Iss.		N/A	N/A

Nursery Rhymes - Various

1956 Little Bo Peep - J. Heap	Retrd.	1959	2.00	N/A
1956 Little Jack Horner - J. Heap	Retrd.	1959	2.00	N/A
1956 Mary Mary Quite Contrary - J. Heap	Retrd.	1959	2.00	N/A
1956 Miss Muffet - J. Heap	Retrd.	1959	2.00	N/A
1956 Tom Tom the Piper's Son - J. Heap	Retrd.	1959	2.00	N/A
1956 Wee Willie Winkie - J. Heap	Retrd.	1959	2.00	N/A

Retired Figurines - Various

1990 Angelo - J. Heap	Retrd.	2000	90.00	97
1985 Apple Barrel - J. Heap	Retrd.	1992	N/A	20-83
1963 Aunt Agatha - J. Heap	Retrd.	1965	N/A	1400-3000
1982 Balcony's Scene - D. Roberts	Retrd.	1998	200.00	200
1955 Balloon Woman - J. Heap	Retrd.	1956	1.00	990-1200
1964 Bandstand (mold 1) - J. Heap	Retrd.	1973	70.00	495
1967 The Bath Tub - J. Heap	Retrd.	1975	4.50	83-125
1955 Bell Man - J. Heap	Retrd.	1956	1.00	800-1200
1996 Big Spender - D. Roberts	Retrd.	2000	53.00	53
1984 Blossom - D. Roberts	Retrd.	1989	35.00	85-205
1955 Bobbin Woman - J. Heap	2	1959	N/A	5000
1964 Bongo - D. Roberts	Retrd.	1987	31.00	115-150
1966 Cakestand - J. Heap	Retrd.	1972	2.00	495-595
1993 Campfire - D. Roberts	Retrd.	1999	30.00	30
1982 Casanova - J. Heap	Retrd.	1998	44.00	44
1953 Cauldron Witch - J. Heap	Retrd.	1959	3.50	990-1250
1959 Cha Cha - J. Heap	Retrd.	1961	N/A	1485-2000
1990 Charlotte - D. Roberts	Retrd.	1992	25.00	96-205
1996 Cheeky - D. Roberts	Retrd.	1998	53.00	53
1989 Chirpy - D. Roberts	Retrd.	1992	31.50	85-125
1985 Christmas Set - D. Roberts	2,000	1986	N/A	550-1150
1983 Clanger - J. Heap	Retrd.	1998	44.00	44
1983 Clinger - J. Heap	Retrd.	1997	38.00	38
1962 Cornish Prayer (Corny) - J. Heap	Retrd.	1965	N/A	990-1200
1993 Cousin Beau - D. Roberts	Retrd.	1999	55.00	55
1980 Crocker - D. Roberts	Retrd.	1989	20.00	126-164
1963 Cyril Squirrel - J. Heap	Retrd.	1965	N/A	1300-2000
1955 Daisy Duck - J. Heap	Retrd.	1958	N/A	1650-2500
1956 Desmond Duck - J. Heap	Retrd.	1958	2.50	1650-2500
1964 Dodger - J. Heap	Retrd.	1996	24.00	42-95
1955 Dungaree Father - N/A	Retrd.	1960	N/A	1073-1240
1955 Elf - J. Heap	Retrd.	1956	1.00	990
1954 Fairy Jardiniere - N/A	Retrd.	1958	N/A	1000-3000
1953 The Fairy Shop - J. Heap	Retrd.	1958	N/A	1000-3000
1961 Father Mouse (grey) - J. Heap	Retrd.	1966	N/A	372-743
1958 Father/Mother Book Ends - N/A	Retrd.	1965	N/A	824
1955 Flying Witch - J. Heap	Retrd.	1956	1.00	825
1993 Forty Winks - D. Roberts	Retrd.	1996	57.00	99-206
1969 Gallery Pieface - J. Heap	Retrd.	1971	N/A	575
1969 The Gallery Series: Wakey, Pieface, Poppet, Robert, Dodger - J. Heap	Retrd.	1971	N/A	400-600
1961 Grand Stand (mold 1) - J. Heap	Retrd.	1969	35.00	660-775
1992 Grand Stand (mold 2)- J. Heap	Retrd.	1996	150.00	108-150
1960 Gussie - J. Heap	Retrd.	1968	N/A	454-800
1989 Honey - D. Roberts	Retrd.	1993	40.00	115-132
1988 Humphrey Go-Kart - J. Heap	Retrd.	1994	70.00	120-165
1986 Jim-Lad - D. Roberts	Retrd.	1992	22.50	207-230
1985 Jingle - D. Roberts	Retrd.	1992	11.25	125-165
1960 Kipper Tie Father - N/A	Retrd.	1970	N/A	660
1986 Little Mo - D. Roberts	Retrd.	1994	35.00	85-150
1961 Lollipop (grey) (Mouse) - J. Heap	Retrd.	1966	N/A	700-825
1960 Lucy Pocket - J. Heap	Retrd.	1967	4.20	164-300
1956 Manx Kitten - J. Heap	Retrd.	1958	2.00	33
1955 Margot - J. Heap	Retrd.	1961	2.00	329-500
1967 Maud - J. Heap	Retrd.	1970	N/A	330-400
1961 Megan - J. Heap	Retrd.	1967	3.00	454-800
1956 Midge (Replaced by Picnic Midge) - J. Heap	Retrd.	1965	2.00	400-800
1966 Milk Jug Stand - J. Heap	Retrd.	1972	2.00	500-910
1960 Model Stand - J. Heap	Retrd.	1964	4.00	371-750
1961 Mother Mouse (grey) - J. Heap	Retrd.	1966	N/A	655-800
1965 Mouse House (bronze) - J. Heap	Retrd.	1969	N/A	288-400
1965 Mouse House (stoneware) - J. Heap	Retrd.	N/A	N/A	700-990
1965 Muncher - D. Roberts	Retrd.	1983	26.00	99-200
1990 New Boy - D. Roberts	Retrd.	1999	55.00	55-66
1981 Nipper - D. Roberts	Retrd.	1989	20.50	164-210
1955 Old Adam - J. Heap	Retrd.	1956	4.00	1980
1955 Old Father (remodeled)- J. Heap	Retrd.	1970	50.	700-1000
1956 Old Mother (thin neck) - J. Heap	Retrd.	1956	6.25	410
1957 Old Mother - J. Heap	Retrd.	1978	6.25	330-400
1984 Oliver - D. Roberts	Retrd.	1995	25.00	99-132
1955 Original Father - J. Heap	Retrd.	1960	50.00	750-1450
1956 Original Robert - J. Heap	Retrd.	1967	2.50	200-454
1953 Pendle Witch (stoneware) - J. Heap	Retrd.	1957	4.00	1645-1980
1967 Phumf - J. Heap	Retrd.	1985	24.00	99-160
1955 Phynnodderee (Commissioned-Exclusive) - J. Heap	Retrd.	1956	1.00	990
1966 Picnic Basket - J. Heap	Retrd.	1968	2.00	400-495
1965 Picnic Midge - J. Heap	Retrd.	1999	25.00	40
1965 Picnic Stand - J. Heap	Retrd.	1985	62.50	132-245
1967 Picnic Table - J. Heap	Retrd.	1972	N/A	250-600
1966 Pieface - D. Roberts	Retrd.	1987	31.00	66-100
1965 Pixie Bods - J. Heap	Retrd.	1967	N/A	400
1953 Pixie House - J. Heap	Retrd.	1958	N/A	N/A
1962 Pooch - D. Roberts	Retrd.	1987	24.50	83-125
1958 Rabbit Book Ends - J. Heap	Retrd.	1965	10.00	1500-2000
1983 The Raft - J. Heap	Retrd.	1997	70.00	60-132
1954 Rhinegold Lamp - J. Heap	Retrd.	1956	21.00	N/A
1967 Robert w/lollipop - D. Roberts	Retrd.	1979	12.00	132-400
1985 Robin's Cave - D. Roberts	Retrd.	1999	285.00	240-285
1978 Rocky (mold 2) - J. Heap	Retrd.	1997	N/A	22-50
1959 Rocky - J. Heap	Retrd.	1978	32.00	50-100
1959 Rolly - J. Heap	Retrd.	1997	17.50	22-66
1957 Romeo & Juliet - J. Heap	Retrd.	1959	11.00	N/A
1982 Rosa - J. Heap	Retrd.	1997	40.00	100-200
1960 Shiner w/black eye - J. Heap	Retrd.	1967	2.50	400-578
1981 Shrimp Stand - D. Roberts	Retrd.	1994	70.00	125-165
1985 Solo - D. Roberts	Retrd.	1993	40.00	99-125
1960 Squeezy - J. Heap	Retrd.	1970	2.50	329-495
1980 Sun Flower Plinth - N/A	Retrd.	1985	N/A	249
1957 Tammy - D. Roberts	Retrd.	1987	24.50	83-100
1987 Tennyson - D. Roberts	Retrd.	1994	35.00	120-132
1956 Timber Stand - J. Heap	Retrd.	1982	35.00	132-165
1995 Tippit - J. Heap	Retrd.	2000	55.00	55
1953 Tipsy Witch - J. Heap	Retrd.	1959	3.50	N/A
1955 Toper - J. Heap	Retrd.	1956	1.00	N/A
1971 Totty - J. Heap	Retrd.	1981	21.00	132-150
1959 Uncle Soames (brown trousers) - J. Heap	Retrd.	1985	105.00	105
1959 Uncle Soames - J. Heap	Retrd.	1985	105.00	289-500
1991 Wordsworth - D. Roberts	Retrd.	1993	60.00	119-200

Polland Studios

Collector Society - D. Polland

1987 I Come In Peace	Closed	1987	35.00	400-600
1987 Silent Trail	Closed	1987	300.00	1300
1987 I Come In Peace, Silent Trail-Matched Numbered Set	Closed	1987	335.00	15-1895
1988 The Hunter	Closed	1988	35.00	545
1988 Disputed Trail	Closed	1988	300.00	700-1045
1988 The Hunter, Disputed Trail-Matched Numbered Set	Closed	1988	335.00	11-1450
1989 Crazy Horse	Closed	1989	35.00	300-470
1989 Apache Birdman	Closed	1989	300.00	700-970
1989 Crazy Horse, Apache Birdman-Matched Numbered Set	Closed	1989	335.00	13-1700
1990 Chief Pontiac	Closed	1990	35.00	420
1990 Buffalo Pony	Closed	1990	300.00	600-800
1990 Chief Pontiac, Buffalo Pony-Matched Numbered Set	Closed	1990	335.00	900-1350
1991 War Drummer	Closed	1991	35.00	330
1991 The Signal	Closed	1991	350.00	730
1991 War Drummer, The Signal-Matched Numbered Set	Closed	1991	385.00	900-1150
1992 Cabinet Sign	Closed	1992	35.00	125
1992 Warrior's Farewell	Closed	1992	350.00	400
1992 Cabinet Sign, Warrior's Farewell-Matched Numbered Set	Closed	1992	385.00	465
1993 Mountain Man	Closed	1993	35.00	125
1993 Blue Bonnets & Yellow Ribbon	Closed	1993	350.00	350-400
1993 Mountain Man, Blue Bonnets & Yellow Ribbon-Matched Numbered Set	Closed	1993	385.00	385
1994 The Wedding Robe	Closed	1995	45.00	45
1994 The Courtship Race	Closed	1995	375.00	375
1994 The Wedding Robe, The Courtside Race-Matched Numbered Set	Closed	1995	385.00	420
1995 Thunder Pipe	Closed	1996	395.00	395
1995 Mystic Medicine Man	Closed	1996	Gift	N/A
1996 Two For the Price of One	Closed	1997	260.00	260
1996 Training Session	Closed	1997	Gift	N/A

Possible Dreams

Santa Claus Network® Collectors Club - Staff

1992 The Gift Giver 805001	Retrd.	1993	Gift	40
1993 Santa's Special Friend 805050	Retrd.	1993	59.00	59
1993 Special Delivery 805002	Retrd.	1994	Gift	N/A
1994 On a Winter's Eve 805051	Retrd.	1994	65.00	65
1994 Jolly St. Nick 805003	Retrd.	1995	Gift	N/A
1995 Marionette Santa 805052	Retrd.	1995	50.00	50
1995 Checking His List 805004	Retrd.	1996	Gift	40
1995 A Frosty Friend 805053	Retrd.	1996	48.00	48
1996 A Tree For the Children 805054	Retrd.	1996	40.00	40-48
1996 A Cookie From Santa 805005	Retrd.	1996	Gift	25
1997 Santa's Rocking Horse 805055	Retrd.	1997	40.00	48
1997 Santa's Handiwork 805006	Retrd.	1997	Gift	25
1998 Cross Country Crinkle	Retrd.	1998	18.50	19
1998 Wish Upon a Star 805056	Retrd.	1998	Gift	44
1999 North Pole Nanny 805057	Retrd.	1999	45.00	45
1999 Santa & Friends 805008	Retrd.	1999	Gift	25
1999 Right on Time 805007	Retrd.	1999	Gift	N/A
1999 A Child's Delight 713200 (Special Event Piece)	Retrd.	2000	40.00	40
2000 Fuzzy Friends 805009	Yr.Iss.		Gift	N/A
2000 Santa Express 805058	Yr.Iss.		65.00	65
2000 Holiday Treasures 713259 (Special Event Piece)	Yr.Iss.		50.00	50

African Spirit® - W. Still

1997 Bororo Man 347003	Open		119.50	120
1998 Bushman and Son 347008	Open		139.60	140
1997 Fulani Woman 347004	Open		100.00	100
1997 Hausa Man 347001	Open		100.00	100
1997 Maasai Warrior 347005	Open		115.00	115
1997 Peul Woman 347002	Open		100.00	100
1998 Rendille Woman & Child 347007	Open		136.00	136

The Citizens of Londonshire® - Unknown

1990 Admiral Waldo 713407	Open		65.00	68
1992 Albert 713426	Retrd.	1994	65.00	68
1991 Bernie 713414	Open		68.00	71
1992 Beth 713417	Open		35.00	37
1992 Christopher 713418	Open		35.00	37
1992 Countess of Hamlett 713419	Open		65.00	68
1992 David 713423	Open		37.50	39
1992 Debbie 713422	Open		37.50	39
1990 Dianne 713413	Open		33.00	35
1990 Dr. Isaac 713409	Retrd.	1995	65.00	68
1989 Earl of Hamlett 713400	Retrd.	1994	65.00	68
1992 Jean Claude 713421	Open		35.00	37
1989 Lady Ashley 713405	Open		65.00	68
1989 Lord Nicholas 713402	Open		72.00	76
1989 Lord Winston of Riverside 713403	Retrd.	1994	65.00	68
1994 Maggie 713428	Retrd.	1994	57.00	57
1990 Margaret of Foxcroft 713408	Open		65.00	68
1992 Nicole 713420	Open		35.00	37
1993 Nigel As Santa 713427	Open		53.50	56
1990 Officer Kevin 713406	Retrd.	1994	65.00	68
1990 Phillip 713412	Open		33.00	35
1992 Rebecca 713424	Open		35.00	37
1992 Richard 713425	Open		35.00	37
1989 Rodney 713404	Open		65.00	68
1991 Sir Red 713415	Retrd.	1994	72.00	76
1989 Sir Robert 713401	Open		65.00	68
1992 Tiffany Sorbet 713416	Open		65.00	68
1990 Walter 713410	Retrd.	1994	33.00	35
1990 Wendy 713411	Retrd.	1994	33.00	35

Clothtique® American Artist Collection™ - Various

1996 The 12 Days of Christmas 15052 - M. Monterio	Retrd.	1997	48.00	50
1991 Alpine Christmas 15003 - J. Brett	Retrd.	1994	129.00	135
1992 An Angel's Kiss 15008 - J. Griffith	Retrd.	1995	85.00	125
1993 A Beacon of Light 15022 - J. Vaillancourt	Retrd.	1996	60.00	65
1998 Bone Appetit! 15067 - G. Benvenuti	Open		53.50	54
2000 Bourbon Street Santa 15096 - J. Beury	Open		72.00	72
1993 A Brighter Day 15024 - J. St. Denis	Retrd.	1997	67.50	70
1994 Captain Claus 15030 - M. Monteiro	Retrd.	1996	77.00	77
1999 Celtic Father Christmas 15089	Open		46.70	47
1995 Christmas Caller 15035 - J. Vaillancourt	Retrd.	1999	57.50	58
1992 Christmas Company 15011 - T. Browning	Retrd.	1995	77.00	125

*Quotes have been rounded up to nearest dollar

Possible Dreams
to Possible Dreams

FIGURINES

YEAR ISSUE	EDITION LIMIT	YEAR RETD.	ISSUE PRICE	*QUOTE U.S.$
1996 Christmas Light 15055 - D. Wenzel	Retrd.	1997	53.50	54
1996 Christmas Stories 15054 - T. Browning	Open		63.50	64
1994 Christmas Surprise 15033 - M. Alvin	Retrd.	1997	88.00	88
1998 Clean Sweep 15071 - M. Humphries	Retrd.	2000	47.00	47
2000 A Coastline Christmas 15200 - B. Stebleton	Open		38.00	38
1999 Cookie Break 15081 - L. Fletcher	Open		49.00	49
1997 Cookie Maker 15063 - T. Browning	Retrd.	1998	55.00	55-65
1995 Country Sounds 15042 - M. Monteiro	Retrd.	1998	74.00	74
2000 Crystal Christmas 15093 - D. Selter	Open		50.00	50
1999 December 26th 15079 - L. Fletcher	Open		46.00	46
1997 Downhill Thrills 15058 - T. Browning	Retrd.	1998	49.00	49
1998 Dreams Come True 15065 - T. Browning	Open		69.00	69
1998 Dress Rehearsal 15075 - L. Fletcher	Open		50.00	50
1996 Dressed For the Holidays 15050 - J. Vaillancourt	Retrd.	2000	27.00	27
1993 Easy Putt 15018 - T. Browning	Retrd.	1996	110.00	115-135
1991 Father Christmas 15007 - J. Vaillancourt	Retrd.	1995	59.50	75-90
1993 Father Earth 15017 - M. Monteiro	Open		77.00	80
1998 Felice Natale! 15068 - G. Benvenuti	Retrd.	2000	45.90	46
1995 Fresh From The Oven 15051 - M. Alvin	Retrd.	1997	49.00	49
1991 A Friendly Visit 15005 - T. Browning	Retrd.	1994	99.50	105
2000 Frontier Cheer 15090 - L. Fletcher	Open		70.00	70
1997 The Fun Seekers 15064 - T. Browning	Retrd.	1998	48.00	48-54
1994 The Gentle Craftsman 15031 - J. Griffith	Retrd.	1996	81.00	99
1994 Gifts from the Garden 15032 - J. Griffith	Retrd.	1996	77.00	92
1995 Giving Thanks 15045 - M. Alvin	Open		45.50	46
1995 A Good Round 15041 - T. Browning	Retrd.	1997	73.00	73
1992 Heralding the Way 15014 - J. Griffith	Retrd.	1995	72.00	75
1999 Holiday Hiker 15085 - J. Beury	Open		53.00	53
1993 Ice Capers 15025 - T. Browning	Retrd.	1996	99.50	129
1999 Journey to Christmas 15083 - J. Vaillancourt	Open		44.00	44
1993 Just Scooting Along 15023 - J. Vaillancourt	Retrd.	1998	79.50	83
2000 Lamplighter Santa 15097 - J. Beury	Open		42.00	42
1997 Last Minute Prep 15060 - D. Wenzel	Retrd.	1998	52.50	53
1992 Lighting the Way 15012 - L. Bywaters	Retrd.	1996	85.00	106
1991 The Magic of Christmas 15001 - L. Bywaters	Retrd.	1994	132.00	139
2000 A Merry Musician 15094 - T. Browning	Open		58.00	58
1997 Morning Brew 15056 - J. Cleveland	Retrd.	1998	44.50	45
1992 Music Makers 15010 - T. Browning	Retrd.	1995	135.00	155
1993 Nature's Love 15016 - M. Alvin	Retrd.	1996	75.00	75-79
1998 New Arrival 15069 - S. Rusinko	Open		48.00	48
1995 A New Suit For Santa 15053 - T. Browning	Retrd.	1998	90.00	90
1997 North Country Weather 15057 - J. Cleveland	Open		40.00	40
1996 Not a Creature Was Stirring 15046 - J. Cleveland	Retrd.	1998	44.00	55
1992 Out of the Forest 15013 - J. Vaillancourt	Retrd.	1995	60.00	68
1995 Patchwork Santa 15039 - J. Cleveland	Retrd.	1999	67.50	68
2000 Peace 15092 - D. Selter	Open		43.00	43
1992 Peace on Earth 15009 - M. Alvin	Retrd.	1995	87.50	92
1997 Peaceable Kingdom 15061 - J. Griffith	Retrd.	2000	78.80	79
1991 A Peaceful Eve 15002 - L. Bywaters	Retrd.	1994	99.50	105
1999 Pedal Power 15088 - T. Browning	Open		84.00	84
1999 A Pinch of Cheer 15084 - T. Browning	Open		70.80	71
1998 Playing Through 15066 - T. Browning	Open		49.30	50
1995 Ready For Christmas 15049 - T. Browning	Retrd.	1997	95.00	99
1995 Refuge From The Storm15047 - M. Monterio	Retrd.	1997	49.00	49
1995 Riding High 15040 - L. Nillson	Retrd.	1997	115.00	115-125
1999 A Sack Full of Wishes 15082 - J. Vaillancourt	Open		53.00	53
1994 Santa and Feathered Friend 15026 - D. Wenzel	Retrd.	1999	84.00	84
1995 Santa and the Ark 15038 - J. Griffith	Retrd.	1997	71.50	75
1999 Santa Be Good 15086 - L. Fletcher	Open		54.00	54
1992 Santa in Rocking Chair 713090 - M. Monteiro	Retrd.	1995	85.00	100
1997 Santa on the Green 15062 - T. Browning	Open		41.00	41
1991 Santa's Cuisine 15006 - T. Browning	Retrd.	1994	138.00	148
1998 Santa's On A Roll 15072 - W. Still	Open		41.80	42
2000 Santa's Vineyard 15095 - T. Browning	Open		55.00	55
1998 Scandinavian Father Christmas 15078 - J. Vaillancourt	Open		40.00	40
1995 Southwest Santa 15043 - V. Wiseman	Retrd.	1996	65.00	89
1999 Speeding Through the Snow 15087 - J. Beury	Open		58.00	58
1994 Spirit of Christmas Past 15036 - J. Vaillancourt	Open		79.00	79
1994 Spirit of Santa 15028 - T. Browning	Retrd.	1996	68.00	75
1995 The Storyteller 15029 - T. Browning	Open		76.00	76
1993 Strumming the Lute 15015 - M. Alvin	Retrd.	1998	79.00	83
1999 Sun, Surf & Santa 15080 - T. Browning	Open		36.00	36
1995 Sunflower Santa 15044 - J. Griffith	Retrd.	1997	75.00	75
1994 Tea Time 15034 - M. Alvin	Retrd.	1997	90.00	90
1994 Teddy Love 15037 - J. Griffith	Retrd.	1999	89.00	89
1994 A Touch of Magic 15027 - T. Browning	Retrd.	1998	95.00	64-95
1991 Traditions 15004 - T. Blackshear	Retrd.	1994	50.00	75
1998 Trailside Prayer 15074 - L. Fletcher	Open		59.80	60
1993 The Tree Planter 15020 - J. Griffith	Open		79.50	84
2000 Unbearably Delicious 15098 - D. Wenzel	Open		44.00	44
1995 Visions of Sugar Plums 15048 - J. Griffith	Retrd.	1997	50.00	50
2000 Winter Green 15091 - L. Fletcher	Open		52.00	52
1998 The Woman Behind Christmas 15073 - L. Fletcher	Open		57.70	58
1993 The Workshop 15019 - T. Browning	Retrd.	1995	140.00	175
1997 Yuletide Gardner 15059 - J. Griffith	Retrd.	2000	50.00	50
1998 Yuletide Round Up 15070 - J. Sorenson	Open		43.00	43

Clothtique® Angels-Elves

YEAR ISSUE	EDITION LIMIT	YEAR RETD.	ISSUE PRICE	*QUOTE U.S.$
1997 Irish Angel 714167	Open		29.30	30
1997 Irish Lass 713677	Open		26.80	27

Clothtique® Champion Collection - Staff, unless otherwise noted

YEAR ISSUE	EDITION LIMIT	YEAR RETD.	ISSUE PRICE	*QUOTE U.S.$
2000 Female Basketball Player 711113	Open		24.00	24
2000 Female Soccer Player 711111	Open		24.00	24
2000 Female Softball Player 711112	Open		24.00	24
2000 Male Baseball Player 711114	Open		24.00	24
2000 Male Football Player 711115	Open		24.00	24
2000 Male Hockey Player 711117	Open		24.00	24
2000 Male Soccer Player 711116	Open		24.00	24

Clothtique® Couture Collection - Staff, unless otherwise noted

YEAR ISSUE	EDITION LIMIT	YEAR RETD.	ISSUE PRICE	*QUOTE U.S.$
2000 Alice, Circa 1910 711123	Open		40.00	40
2000 Diane, Circa 1920 711124	Open		36.00	36
2000 Dorothy, Circa 1950 711127	Open		40.00	40
2000 Irene, Circa 1930 711125	Open		38.00	38
2000 Joanne, Circa 1960 711128	Open		36.00	36
2000 Lauren, Circa 1970 711129	Open		36.00	36
2000 Margaret, Circa 1940 711126	Open		38.00	38
2000 Victoria, Circa 1900 711122	Open		40.00	40

Clothtique® Fine Arts Collection - Staff

YEAR ISSUE	EDITION LIMIT	YEAR RETD.	ISSUE PRICE	*QUOTE U.S.$
2000 Best Friends 711132	Open		70.00	70
2000 Mademoiselle 711133	Open		54.00	54
2000 Mother & Child 711131	Open		72.00	72
2000 Romance 711134	Open		80.00	80
2000 Sisters 711130	Open		65.00	65

Clothtique® Garfield® Collection - Staff

YEAR ISSUE	EDITION LIMIT	YEAR RETD.	ISSUE PRICE	*QUOTE U.S.$
1997 Countdown to Christmas 275003	Open		41.60	42
1996 Love Me, Love My Teddy Bear 275002	Open		51.60	52
1997 Private Stash 275004	Open		50.20	51
1996 Return to Sender 275001	Open		58.00	58

Clothtique® Historical Collection - Staff

YEAR ISSUE	EDITION LIMIT	YEAR RETD.	ISSUE PRICE	*QUOTE U.S.$
2000 Catherine the Great (Russia) 711120	Open		72.00	72
2000 Elizabeth (England) 711118	Open		84.00	84
2000 Mary Queen of Scots (Scotland) 711119	Open		68.00	68
2000 Queen Isabella (Spain) 711121	Open		56.00	56

Clothtique® Limited Edition Santas - Unknown

YEAR ISSUE	EDITION LIMIT	YEAR RETD.	ISSUE PRICE	*QUOTE U.S.$
1988 Father Christmas 3001	10,000	1993	240.00	550-650
1988 Kris Kringle 3002	10,000	1992	240.00	550-650
1988 Patriotic Santa 3000	10,000	1994	240.00	550-650
1989 Traditional Santa 40's 3003	10,000	1994	240.00	550-650

Clothtique® Looney Tunes® Collection - Staff

YEAR ISSUE	EDITION LIMIT	YEAR RETD.	ISSUE PRICE	*QUOTE U.S.$
1995 Bugs Bunny's 14 Carot Santa 3402	Open		57.50	58
1996 Merry Master of Ceremonies 3404	Open		55.40	56
1996 Pepe's Christmas Serenade 3406	Open		42.80	43
1996 Selfish Elfish Daffy Duck 3405	Open		46.90	47
1995 Sylvester's Holiday High Jinks 3403	Open		65.00	65
1996 Tasmanian Rhapsody 3407	Open		47.30	48
1995 Yosemite Sam's Rootin' Tootin' Christmas 3401	Open		59.00	59

Clothtique® Santas Collection - Staff, unless otherwise noted

YEAR ISSUE	EDITION LIMIT	YEAR RETD.	ISSUE PRICE	*QUOTE U.S.$
1992 1940's Traditional Santa 713049	Retrd.	1994	44.00	65
1992 African American Santa 713056	Retrd.	1995	65.00	68
1993 African-American Santa w/ Doll 713102	Open		40.00	42
1998 Angel w/Tree Topper 713678	Open		24.00	24
1997 Autograph For a Fan 713143	Retrd.	2000	39.00	39
1989 Baby's First Christmas 713042	Retrd.	1992	42.00	46
1995 Baby's First Noel 713120	Retrd.	1997	62.00	65
1998 Baseball Santa 713682	Open		19.80	20
1998 Basketball Santa 713681	Open		19.80	20
2000 Bringing Home the Tree 713230	Open		64.00	64
1988 Carpenter Santa 713033	Retrd.	1992	38.00	44
1999 Catching Some Zs 713197	Open		40.50	41
1997 Celtic Sounds 713162	Retrd.	2000	46.00	46
2000 Christmas 101 713232	Open		36.00	36
1994 Christmas Cheer 713109	Retrd.	1997	58.00	58
1999 A Christmas Dance 713211	Open		42.00	42
1994 A Christmas Guest 713112	Retrd.	1997	79.00	79
1998 Christmas in the Alps 713171	Open		48.00	48
1994 Christmas is for Children 713115	Open		62.00	62
1986 Christmas Man 713027	Retrd.	1989	34.50	35
2000 Christmas on the Farm?? 713245	Open		62.00	62
1999 Christmas Orbit 713202	Open		38.80	39
2000 Christmas Piper 713226	Open		48.00	48
1998 Christmas Spruce 713172	Open		42.00	42
1987 Colonial Santa 713032	Retrd.	1990	38.00	40
2000 Cross Country Santa 713250	Open		24.00	24
1999 December Descent 713188	Open		47.50	48
1997 Deck The Halls 713161	Retrd.	1998	39.70	38
1997 Doctor Claus 713157	Retrd.	1999	35.00	39
1995 Down Hill Santa 713123	Retrd.	1999	66.50	67
1997 Down the Chimney He Came 713154	Retrd.	2000	42.50	43
2000 Dressed for Success 713246	Open		38.00	38
1997 Easy Ridin' Santa 713159	Retrd.	2000	37.50	38
1992 Engineer Santa 713057	Retrd.	1995	130.00	137
1993 European Santa 713095	Retrd.	1996	53.00	48-69
2000 Evergreen Traveler 713237	Open		85.00	85
1989 Exhausted Santa 713043	Retrd.	1992	60.00	65
1991 Father Christmas 713087	Retrd.	1993	43.00	47
1995 Finishing Touch 713121	Retrd.	1998	54.70	55
1993 Fireman & Child 713106	Retrd.	1998	55.00	60
1992 Fireman Santa 713053	Retrd.	1996	60.00	70
1998 Football Santa 713679	Open		19.80	20
1998 For A Special Little Girl 713179	Open		44.00	44
1996 For Someone Special 713142	Retrd.	1998	39.00	39
1995 Frisky Friend 713130	Retrd.	1997	45.50	55
1988 Frontier Santa 713034	Retrd.	1991	40.00	42
1999 Getting in Shape 713201	Open		34.80	35
1999 Gift of Hope 713206	Open		53.00	53
1999 A Gifted Fellow 713199	Open		41.00	41
1995 Ginger Bread Baker 713135	Retrd.	1997	35.00	35
2000 Glassworks 713218	Open		64.00	64
1998 Gloria In Cielo 713674 - G. Benvenuti	Open		33.80	34
1994 Good Tidings 713107	Retrd.	1996	51.00	60
1997 Grampa Claus 713146	Retrd.	1998	41.40	42
2000 Greeting The Millennium 713213	Open		48.00	48
1990 Harlem Santa 713046	Retrd.	1994	46.00	55
2000 Hawaii or Bust 713241	Open		37.50	38
1995 Heaven Sent 713138	Retrd.	1997	50.00	50-56
1998 Highland Santa 713169	Retrd.	2000	42.50	43
1993 His Favorite Color 713098	Retrd.	1996	48.00	50
1999 His Littlest Fan 713195	Open		60.00	60
1995 Ho: Ho-Hole in One 713131	Retrd.	1999	43.00	48
2000 Hockey Holiday 713251	Open		24.00	24
1999 A Holiday Built for Two 713212	Open		56.00	56
1994 Holiday Friend 713110	Retrd.	1998	104.00	104
1997 Holiday Gourmet 713147	Retrd.	1999	39.10	45
1999 Holiday Hero 713198	Open		36.50	37
2000 Holiday Hoopster 713262	Open		44.00	44
1999 Holiday Thunder 713190	Open		34.70	35
1997 Holiday Traffic 713148	Retrd.	1998	47.50	50
1995 Home Spun Holidays 713128	Retrd.	1998	49.50	50
2000 Homerun For The Holidays 713260	Open		44.00	44
1995 Hook Line and Santa 713129	Retrd.	1998	49.70	50-55
1999 An Irish Gentleman 713185	Open		45.00	45
2000 Irish Melody Maker 713240	Open		42.00	42
1999 Irish Santa 713185	Open		45.00	45
2000 An Irish Toast 713254	Open		38.00	38
1998 Italian Angel Tree Topper 713673 - G. Benvenuti	Open		33.30	34
1999 A Jolly Old Saint 713191	Open		38.50	39
1996 Jumping Jack Santa 713139	Retrd.	1998	45.50	46
1991 Kris Kringle 713088	Retrd.	1993	43.00	48
1998 Landing Beacon 713181	Open		43.40	44
2000 Leading the Way 713258	Open		55.00	55
1997 Leprechaun 713153	Open		18.50	19
1999 Letters From Santa 713192	Open		37.20	38
2000 A Long Drive 713231	Open		38.00	38
1993 A Long Trip 713105	Open		95.00	100
1998 Mariachi Santa 713174	Open		48.80	49
1996 Master Toy Maker 713141	Retrd.	1998	44.80	45
1993 May Your Wishes Come True 713096	Retrd.	1996	59.00	65
2000 Millennium Angel 714228	Open		38.00	38
1993 The Modern Shopper 713103	Retrd.	1996	40.00	62
1995 A Modern Skier 713123	Retrd.	1998	59.50	60
1994 A Most Welcome Visitor 713113	Retrd.	1999	63.00	63
1994 Mrs. Claus 713118	Retrd.	1997	58.00	58
1991 Mrs. Claus in Coat 713078	Retrd.	1995	47.00	71
1989 Mrs. Claus w/doll 713041	Retrd.	1992	42.00	43
2000 Mrs. O' Claus 713257	Open		42.00	42
1992 Nicholas 713052	Retrd.	1994	57.50	60
1999 No. Pole Nanny 805057	Open		36.90	37
1998 North Pole 500 713180	Open		38.80	39
1998 North Pole Party Line 713167	Open		44.90	45
1999 North Pole Patrol 713196	Open		54.50	55
2000 North Pole Pizza 713219	Open		50.00	50
1997 North Pole Polka 713163	Retrd.	1998	46.00	48
1997 North Pole Prescription 713164	Retrd.	1998	65.60	66
2000 North Pole Volunteer 713247	Open		56.00	56
1998 Officer Claus 713119	Retrd.	1999	37.80	38
1997 On Christmas Pond 713156	Open		52.30	53
1994 Our Hero 713116	Retrd.	1999	62.00	62
2000 Out For a Ride 713242	Open		62.00	62
1989 Pelze Nichol 713039	Retrd.	1993	40.00	47
2000 Peppermint Twist 713217	Open		56.00	56
2000 Picture Perfect Christmas 713204	Open		52.00	52
1994 Playmates 713111	Retrd.	1996	104.00	104
1994 Puppy Love 713117	Retrd.	1997	62.00	62
1998 A Purry Friend 713168	Open		42.50	43
2000 Reel Good Time 713249	Open		56.00	56
1995 Rooftop Santa 659006	Retrd.	1998	28.50	29
2000 Rub-A-Dub Santa 713248	Open		47.00	47
1988 Russian St. Nicholas 713036	Retrd.	1996	40.00	43
2000 Russian Treasure 713228	Open		49.00	49
2000 Salty Claus 713244	Open		35.00	35
1990 Santa "Please Stop Here" 713045	Retrd.	1992	63.00	72
2000 Santa 'The IceBox' Claus 713261	Open		44.00	44
1991 Santa Decorating Christmas Tree 713079	Retrd.	1992	60.00	60
2000 Santa Express 713253	Open		64.00	64

*Quotes have been rounded up to nearest dollar

YEAR ISSUE	EDITION LIMIT	YEAR RETD.	ISSUE PRICE	*QUOTE U.S.$
1991 Santa in Bed 713076	Retrd.	1994	76.00	139
1997 Santa O' Claus 713165	Retrd.	2000	41.50	175
1992 Santa on Motorbike 713054	Retrd.	1994	115.00	130-135
1992 Santa on Reindeer 713058	Retrd.	1995	75.00	83
1992 Santa on Sled 713050	Retrd.	1994	75.00	79
1992 Santa on Sleigh 713091	Retrd.	1995	79.00	83
1997 Santa Online 713151	Retrd.	1998	55.20	56
1991 Santa Shelf Sitter 713089	Retrd.	1995	55.50	60
1999 Santa Strikes Again 713205	Open		36.00	36
1990 Santa w/Blue Robe 713048	Retrd.	1992	46.00	69
1989 Santa w/Embroidered Coat 713040	Retrd.	1991	43.00	43
1993 Santa w/Groceries 713099	Retrd.	1996	47.50	50
1997 Santa w/Nativity 713150	Retrd.	1999	36.00	36
1986 Santa w/Pack 713026	Retrd.	1989	34.50	35
1993 Santa with Doll 713102	Open		40.00	40
1998 Santa with Tree 713183	Open		38.50	39
1997 Santa's Better Half 713155	Retrd.	2000	35.80	36
1998 Santa's Check Up 713175	Open		37.00	37
1999 Santa's Favorite Pastime 713194	Open		37.60	38
1998 Santa's Flying Machines 713176	Open		39.60	37
1997 Santa's Grab Bag 713158	Retrd.	2000	47.50	48
1998 Santa's New List 713178	Open		44.90	45
1995 Santa's Pet Project 713134 - L. Craven	Retrd.	1999	37.00	37
2000 Santa's Shillelagh 713236	Open		44.00	44
2000 Santa's Snow Day 713256	Open		48.00	48
2000 Santa's Toy 713229	Open		47.00	47
1998 Santa's Tree 713182	Retrd.	2000	36.40	37
1996 Shamrock Santa 713140	Open		41.50	42
1991 Siberian Santa 713077	Retrd.	1993	49.00	96
2000 Skating Lesson 713227	Open		56.00	56
1990 Skiing Santa 713047	Retrd.	1993	62.00	65
1998 A Snack For Santa 713177	Open		37.00	37
1998 Soccer Santa 713683	Open		19.80	20
1995 Sounds of Christmas 713127	Retrd.	1996	57.50	58
1999 A Special Place 713207	Open		36.90	37
1995 A Special Treat 713122	Retrd.	1998	50.50	51
1988 St. Nicholas 713035	Retrd.	1991	40.00	170
1999 Stargazer 713186	Open		44.90	45
1995 The Stockings Were Hung 713126	Retrd.	1997	N/A	65
1999 Tee-Ball Instructor 713210	Open		44.00	44
1998 Tennis Santa 713680	Open		19.80	20
1997 Test Ride 713149	Open		47.10	48
1995 Three Alarm Santa 713137	Open		42.50	43
1998 Top O' The Mornin' 713173	Retrd.	2000	41.50	42
1987 Traditional Deluxe Santa 713030	Retrd.	1990	38.00	38
1986 Traditional Santa 713028	Retrd.	1989	34.50	125
1989 Traditional Santa 713038	Retrd.	1992	42.00	43
1991 The True Spirit of Christmas 713075	Retrd.	1992	97.00	97
1987 Ukko 713031	Retrd.	1990	38.00	38
1995 Victorian Evergreen 713125	Retrd.	1998	49.00	49
1995 Victorian Puppeteer 713124	Retrd.	1997	51.50	52
1993 Victorian Santa 713097	Retrd.	1996	55.50	58
2000 Vincent Van Claus 713264	Open		55.00	55
1998 Visitor From The North 713170	Retrd.	2000	39.50	40
1988 Weihnachtsman 713037	Retrd.	1991	40.00	43
2000 Welcome 2000 713263	Open		48.00	48
1994 A Welcome Visit 713114	Retrd.	1996	62.00	65
1999 While Santa's Away 713203	Open		36.00	36
2000 Winter Pals 713216	Open		50.00	50
1997 Winter Wanderer 713152	Retrd.	1998	56.90	57-64
1990 Workbench Santa 713044	Retrd.	1993	72.00	95
1999 Yankee Doodle Santa 713193	Open		39.00	39
2000 Yuletide Goal 713209	Open		34.00	34
1994 Yuletide Journey 713108	Retrd.	1998	58.00	58
1999 Yuletide Nibble 713208	Open		36.90	37

Clothtique® Saturday Evening Post J. C. Leyendecker - J. Leyendecker

YEAR ISSUE	EDITION LIMIT	YEAR RETD.	ISSUE PRICE	*QUOTE U.S.$
1991 Hugging Santa 3599	Retrd.	1994	129.00	150
1996 Hugging Santa 3650 (smaller re-issue)	Retrd.	1998	52.50	53-65
1992 Santa on Ladder 3598	Retrd.	1995	135.00	150
1996 Santa on Ladder 3651 (smaller re-issue)	Retrd.	1998	59.00	59-65
1991 Traditional Santa 3600	Retrd.	1992	100.00	125
1996 Traditional Santa 3652 (smaller re-issue)	Retrd.	1997	66.00	66

Clothtique® Saturday Evening Post Norman Rockwell - N. Rockwell

YEAR ISSUE	EDITION LIMIT	YEAR RETD.	ISSUE PRICE	*QUOTE U.S.$
1992 Balancing the Budget 3064	Retrd.	1998	120.00	126
1989 Christmas "Dear Santa" 3102	Retrd.	1992	160.00	180
1996 Christmas "Dear Santa" 3050 (smaller re-issue)	Retrd.	1998	70.50	71
1989 Christmas "Santa with Globe" 3051	Retrd.	1992	154.00	184
1996 Santa With Globe 3101 (smaller re-issue)	Retrd.	1998	73.00	73
1991 Doctor and Doll 3055	Retrd.	1995	196.00	206
1991 The Gift 3057	Retrd.	1996	160.00	195
1991 Gone Fishing 3054	Retrd.	1995	250.00	263
1997 Gone Fishing 3104 (smaller re-issue)	Open		67.70	68
1991 Gramps at the Reins 3058	Open		290.00	305
1990 Hobo 3052	Open		159.00	167
1990 Love Letters 3053	Open		172.00	180
1991 Man with Geese 3059	Open		120.00	126
1992 Marriage License 3062	Open		195.00	205
1996 Not a Creature was Stirring (smaller re-issue)	Open		44.00	44
1991 Santa Plotting His Course 3060	Retrd.	1998	160.00	168
1992 Santa's Helpers 3063	Retrd.	1994	170.00	179
1997 Santa's Helpers 3103 (smaller re-issue)	Retrd.	1998	64.90	65
1991 Springtime 3056	Retrd.	1996	130.00	137
1992 Triple Self Portrait 3061	Retrd.	1995	230.00	250
1997 Triple Self Portrait 3105 (smaller re-issue)	Open		65.70	66

Clothtique® Signature Series® - Stanley/Chang

YEAR ISSUE	EDITION LIMIT	YEAR RETD.	ISSUE PRICE	*QUOTE U.S.$
1995 Department Store Santa, USA/Circa 1940s 721001	Retrd.	1995	108.00	108
1995 Father Christmas, England/Circa 1890s 721002	Retrd.	2000	90.00	90
1996 St. Nicholas, Myra/Circa 1300s 721004	Retrd.	1996	99.00	99
1996 Kriss Kringle, USA/Circa 1840s 721005	Retrd.	2000	99.00	99
1997 Union Santa, USA/Circa 1863 721007	Retrd.	1998	79.00	79-100
1998 Romanov Santa, Russia/Circa 1890s 721008	Retrd.	1998	83.50	84

Clothtique® TLC Collection - Staff

YEAR ISSUE	EDITION LIMIT	YEAR RETD.	ISSUE PRICE	*QUOTE U.S.$
2000 The Good Doctor 711139	Open		40.00	40
2000 Loving Sisters 711143	Open		40.00	40
2000 Officer Friendly 711136	Open		40.00	40
2000 Save The Day 711137	Open		40.00	40
2000 Sew Sweet 711141	Open		50.00	50
2000 Special Delivery 711140	Open		48.00	48
2000 Take Care Bear 711138	Open		40.00	40
2000 Warm Hearts 711135	Open		44.00	44

Coca-Cola Brand Clothtique® Santas - H. Sundblom

YEAR ISSUE	EDITION LIMIT	YEAR RETD.	ISSUE PRICE	*QUOTE U.S.$
1998 Busy Man's Pause 468002	Retrd.	1999	49.00	49
1999 Greetings From Coca-Cola 468004	Retrd.	2000	62.80	63
1997 Hospitality 468001	Retrd.	1999	50.00	50
1999 It Will Refresh You Too 468007	Retrd.	1999	69.00	69
1998 Santa's Greetings 468005	Retrd.	1999	46.00	46
1999 Santa's Pause 468008	Retrd.	1999	47.00	47
1998 Step Up To Refreshment 468006	Retrd.	1999	47.00	47
1998 Thanks For the Pause That Refreshes 468003	Retrd.	1999	47.00	47

Crinkle Angels - Staff

YEAR ISSUE	EDITION LIMIT	YEAR RETD.	ISSUE PRICE	*QUOTE U.S.$
1996 Crinkle Angel w/Candle 659405	Open		19.80	20
1996 Crinkle Angel w/Dove 659403	Open		19.80	20
1996 Crinkle Angel w/Harp 659402	Open		19.80	20
1996 Crinkle Angel w/Lamb 659401	Open		19.80	20
1996 Crinkle Angel w/Lantern 659400	Open		19.80	20
1996 Crinkle Angel w/Mandolin 659404	Open		19.80	20

Crinkle Carousel - Staff

YEAR ISSUE	EDITION LIMIT	YEAR RETD.	ISSUE PRICE	*QUOTE U.S.$
1999 American Eagle 659816	Open		14.30	15
1999 Black Mane Crinkle 659819	Open		14.30	15
1998 Checkmate Crinkle 659807	Open		9.00	9
1998 Crinkle Antlers 659814	Open		16.00	16
1998 Crinkle Champion 659803	Open		10.50	11
1999 Crinkle Champion 659820	Open		14.30	15
1998 Crinkle Doodle-Doo 659810	Open		15.00	15
1998 Crinkle Filly 659801	Open		16.00	16
1998 Crinkle Pony (muscial) Waterdome 659881	Open		40.00	40
1998 Crinkle Stallion (musical) Waterdome 659880	Open		40.00	40
1998 Frisky Crinkle 659806	Open		12.00	12
1998 Galloping Crinkle 659804	Open		16.00	16
1999 Golden Mane Crinkle 659815	Open		14.30	15
1998 Happy Hog Crinkle 659808	Open		15.00	15
1998 Hippity-Hop Crinkle 659811	Open		15.00	15
1998 Honey Bear Crinkle 659809	Open		15.00	15
1998 Laughing Lion Crinkle 659812	Open		15.40	16
1999 Leopard Spot Crinkle 659820	Open		14.30	15
1998 Merry-Go Crinkle (lighted) 659860	Open		34.00	34
1998 Pachyderm Crinkle 659813	Open		15.40	16
1998 Parosol Crinkle 659805	Open		13.30	14
1998 Prancing Crinkle (muscial) 659850	Open		30.00	30
1999 Purple Palomino Crinkle 659817	Open		14.30	15
1998 Surf Rider Crinkle 659802	Open		16.00	16
1999 Three Ring Crinkle 659818	Open		14.30	15

Crinkle Claus - Staff

YEAR ISSUE	EDITION LIMIT	YEAR RETD.	ISSUE PRICE	*QUOTE U.S.$
1995 American Santa 657224	Retrd.	1998	15.50	16-20
1997 Appalachian Light 659030	Open		8.30	9
1995 Arctic Santa 659107	Retrd.	1998	15.70	16
1999 Arriving by Ram 659918	5,000		18.30	19
1995 Austrian Santa 659103	Retrd.	1998	15.80	16
1997 Bavarian Crinkle 659029	Open		8.30	9
1998 Bavarian Om-Pah Crinkle (musical) 659605	Open		38.80	39
1997 Bedtime Story 659910	Open		31.40	32
1995 Bell Shape Santa 659008	Retrd.	1996	23.50	25
1996 Bishop of Maya 659111	Open		19.90	20
1996 Bishop of Maya Plaque 659306	Open		19.90	20
1996 Black Forest Gift Giver 659114	Open		19.90	20
1996 Black Forest Gift Giver Plaque 659302	Open		19.90	20
1997 Blarney Stone Crinkle 659125	Open		13.40	14
1999 Bobbing Bell Crinkle 659154	Open		17.00	17
1999 Bobbing Tree Crinkle 659155	Open		18.90	19
1998 Bottle Crinkle 659052	Open		15.90	16
1997 Brazilian Fiesta 659028	Open		8.30	9
1997 British Jubilee 659027	Open		8.30	9
1996 Buckets of Fruit for Good Girls & Boys 659903	5,000	1997	45.00	45
1997 Buckingham Crinkle 659126	Open		13.40	14
1995 Candle Stick Santa 659121	Open		15.80	16
1999 Candy Cane Crinkle 659136	Open		13.60	14
1999 Candy Cane Crinkle 659150	Open		13.60	14
1996 Carrying The Torch	Open		19.80	20
1999 Cartwheel Crinkle 659161	Open		13.50	14
2000 Catch O' The Day Crinkle 659174	Open		14.00	14
1996 Catch of The Day 659504	Open		19.90	20
2000 Celtic Keepsake Crinkle 659172	Open		14.00	14
1996 Celtic Santa 659110	Retrd.	1997	19.90	20
1996 Celtic Santa Plaque 659305	Retrd.	1997	19.90	20
1996 Choo-Choo For The Children 659904	5,000		25.00	25
1998 Christmas Expedition 659914	5,000		26.90	27
1997 Christmas King Crinkle 659123	Open		13.40	14
1997 Christmas Tree Crinkle 659036	Open		16.30	17
1995 Christmas Tree Santa 659117	Open		19.90	20
1997 Christmas Wilderness Waterdome 659603	Retrd.	1998	46.80	47
1998 Clickety-Clack Crinkle 659044	Open		17.20	18
1995 Crescent Moon Santa 659119	Retrd.	1998	19.00	20
1997 Crinkle Ark (lighted) 660301	Open		57.00	57
1997 Crinkle Bears 660303	Open		14.90	15
1999 Crinkle Candle 659139	Open		10.50	11
1998 Crinkle Cello 659054	Open		14.80	15
1999 Crinkle Celtic Golfer 659163	Open		13.10	14
1998 Crinkle Christmas Eve 659252	Open		28.50	29
1999 Crinkle Claddaugh 659166	Open		12.50	13
1998 Crinkle Claus Cruise 659055	Open		17.20	18
1995 Crinkle Claus w/Dome-German Santa 659601	Retrd.	1998	45.00	45
1996 Crinkle Claus w/Dome-Santa/Chimney 659600	Retrd.	1998	45.00	45
1996 Crinkle Claus w/Dome-St. Nicholas 659602	Retrd.	1998	45.00	45
1999 Crinkle Clocker 659153	Open		12.20	13
1999 Crinkle Cone Santa 659148	Open		12.80	13
1998 Crinkle Cross 659053	Open		15.00	15
1999 Crinkle Elephants 660308	Open		14.50	15
1998 Crinkle Elf Carpenter 659060	Open		8.50	9
1998 Crinkle Elf Chef 659059	Open		8.50	9
1998 Crinkle Elf Fireman 659062	Open		8.50	9
1998 Crinkle Elf Postman 659056	Open		8.50	9
1998 Crinkle Elf Toymaker 659058	Open		8.50	9
1998 Crinkle Elf w/Jester 659063	Open		8.50	9
1998 Crinkle Elf w/Snowman 659061	Open		8.50	9
1998 Crinkle Elf w/Teddy 659057	Open		8.50	9
2000 Crinkle Engineer 659173	Open		20.00	20
1998 Crinkle Flag Bearer 659049	Open		12.40	13
1999 Crinkle Giraffes 660310	Open		12.40	13
1997 Crinkle Horses 660305	Open		13.30	14
1999 Crinkle House 659142	Open		13.50	14
1999 Crinkle Lions 660309	Open		11.90	12
1997 Crinkle Locomotive & Coal Car 660201	Open		42.00	42
1998 Crinkle Lyre 659051	Open		16.70	17
1998 Crinkle Mail Car 660202	Open		18.80	19
1997 Crinkle Noah 660302	Open		10.30	11
1999 Crinkle on the Green 659162	Open		13.10	14
1999 Crinkle Pitcher 659137	Open		14.00	14
1999 Crinkle Pot O' Gold 659168	Open		13.70	14
1997 Crinkle Reindeer 660306	Open		13.30	14
1997 Crinkle Sheep 660304	Open		10.80	11
1998 Crinkle Spirit of Giving 659253	Open		23.50	24
1999 Crinkle Tall Tales 659169	Open		13.70	14
1998 Crinkle Uncle Sam 659045	Open		13.50	14
1999 Crinkle Zebras 660307	Open		12.00	12
1996 A Crown of Antlers	Open		19.70	20
1996 Dashing Through The Snow 659902	5,000	1997	45.00	45
1998 Department Store Crinkle 659250	Open		23.50	24
1998 Ding Dong Crinkle 659046	Open		16.60	17
1996 Display Figurine-965003	Open		11.00	11
1997 Down The Chimney 659911	Open		31.10	32
1998 Dutch Treat Crinkle (musical) 659604	Open		38.80	39
1998 Emerald Isle Crinkle 659040	Open		13.40	14
1998 English Crinkle at Westminster Abbey 659355	Open		28.50	29
1995 English Santa 659100	Retrd.	1998	15.80	16
1999 Fairway Crinkle 659164	Open		13.10	14
1996 Feeding His Forest Friends 659905	5,000	1997	27.50	30-35
1998 Fine Feathered Friends 659915	5,000		25.40	26
1998 Firecracker Crinkle 659047	Open		14.60	15
1997 Fjord Crinkle 659124	Open		13.40	14
1997 Flickering Crinkle 659035	Open		14.00	14
1995 Forest Santa 657225	Open		15.50	16
1999 Four Leaf Crinkle 659165	Open		13.10	14
1995 French Santa 659108	Retrd.	1998	15.70	16
1998 German Crinkle at Rothenburg 659352	Open		28.50	29
1995 German Santa 659105	Retrd.	1998	15.80	16
1999 Gift Giver Crinkle 659143	Open		17.80	18
1999 Gravy Boat Crinkle 659138	Open		14.00	14
1998 Grizzly Bear Helper 659912	5,000		25.90	26
1999 Handstand Crinkle 659159	Open		13.50	14
1995 Hard Boiled Santa 659115	Retrd.	1997	13.70	17
1998 High Flying Crinkle 659251	Open		32.50	33
1995 High Hat Santa 657134	Retrd.	1998	13.40	14-17
1997 High Ho 659025	Open		13.20	14
1997 High Note 659023	Open		13.20	14
1997 Highland Piper 659026	Open		8.30	9
1997 Holiday Cane Crinkle 659034	Open		14.00	14
1999 Holiday Spokes-Man 659916	5,000		19.10	20
1995 Hour Glass Santa 659118	Open		15.00	15
2000 I Love The Irish 659175	Open		14.00	14
1996 Iceland Visitor 659112	Open		19.90	20
1996 Iceland Visitor Plaque 659303	Open		19.90	20
1998 Irish Crinkle at St. Patrick's Cathedral 659354	Open		28.50	29
1995 Italian Santa 659106	Retrd.	1998	15.70	16
1995 Jolly St. Nick 659012	Retrd.	1998	15.00	15

*Quotes have been rounded up to nearest dollar

FIGURINES

YEAR ISSUE	EDITION LIMIT	YEAR RETD.	ISSUE PRICE	*QUOTE U.S.$
1997 Kelly Crinkle 659132	Open		16.00	16
1997 Kelly Crinkle 659712	Open		7.80	8
2000 Kilted Crinkle 659171	Open		14.00	14
1998 Kremlin Crinkle (musical) 659606	Open		38.80	39
1996 Learned Gentleman	Open		19.80	20
1998 Liberty Crinkle 659048	Open		12.40	13
1996 Lighting The Way	Open		19.80	20
1997 Lisbon Traveler 659033	Open		8.30	9
1996 Low & Behold	Open		13.90	14
1999 Lucky Crinkle 659170	Open		10.60	11
1997 Madrid Crinkle 659131	Open		16.00	16
1997 Madrid Crinkle 659708	Open		7.80	8
1997 Mediterranean Treasure 659032	Open		8.30	9
1996 Merry Old England 659113	Retrd.	1997	19.90	20
1996 Merry Old England Plaque 659301	Open		19.90	20
1997 Moscow Crinkle 659128	Retrd.	1998	16.00	16
1997 Moscow Crinkle 659711	Retrd.	1998	7.80	10
1997 Munich Crinkle 659130	Retrd.	1998	16.00	16
1997 Munich Crinkle 659710	Open		7.80	8
1996 The Music Man	Open		19.80	20
1995 Netherlands Santa 659102	Retrd.	1998	15.70	16
1997 North Pole Artisan 659907	Open		30.00	30
1999 North Pole Caboose 660203	Open		19.30	20
1996 Northland Santa 659109	Retrd.	1998	19.90	20
1996 Northland Santa Plaque 659304	Open		19.90	20
1998 A Nutty Noel 659913	5,000		25.90	26
1998 Old Glory Crinkle 659050	Open		12.40	13
1997 Pamplona Crinkle 659122	Open		13.40	14
1997 Paris Crinkle 659129	Retrd.	1998	7.80	10-16
1995 Pine Cone Santa 657226	Retrd.	1997	15.50	16
1999 Pipe Dream Crinkle 659144	Open		14.10	15
2000 Pour on the Luck 659176	Open		16.00	16
1996 Rag/Doll Delivery 659906	5,000	1997	34.50	35-45
1997 Rocking Crinkle 659039	Open		17.60	18
1995 Roly Poly Santa 3.5" 657138	Retrd.	1996	12.50	18-22
1995 Roly Poly Santa 4" 659009	Retrd.	1996	23.00	23-27
1995 Rooftop Santa 659006	Retrd.	1998	28.50	29
1998 Royal Crinkle (musical) 659607	Open		38.80	39
1996 Running Down The List 659901	5,000	1997	33.00	35-45
1998 Russian Crinkle at St. Basil's 659353	Open		28.50	29
1995 Russian Santa 3.5" 659101	Retrd.	1998	15.70	16
1995 Russian Santa 4" 657228	Retrd.	1996	15.50	16
1995 Santa on Bag 657508	Retrd.	1996	15.00	15
1995 Santa Sitting Pretty 659116	Open		13.90	14
1995 Santa w/Book 659010	Retrd.	1997	13.80	14
1995 Santa w/Candy Cane 4.5" 657139	Retrd.	1996	13.00	13
1996 Santa w/Candy Cane 5" 657142	Retrd.	1996	27.00	27
1996 Santa w/Candy Cane 6.5" 657135	Retrd.	1996	17.50	18
1995 Santa w/Cane & Bag 657230	Retrd.	1996	12.00	12
1995 Santa w/Gifts 657143	Retrd.	1996	27.00	27
1995 Santa w/Lantern & Bag 657229	Retrd.	1996	15.50	16
1995 Santa w/Lantern 5" 657136	Retrd.	1996	12.50	13
1995 Santa w/Lantern 5" 657144	Retrd.	1996	27.00	27
1995 Santa w/Noah's Ark 657227	Retrd.	1998	15.50	16
1995 Santa w/Patchwork Bag 657232	Retrd.	1997	19.00	19
1995 Santa w/Stars 657140	Retrd.	1996	14.00	14
1995 Santa w/Teddy Bear 657231	Retrd.	1997	16.00	16
1995 Santa w/Tree 659011	Retrd.	1996	14.20	15
1995 Santa w/Wreath 657141	Retrd.	1996	16.30	19
1995 Santa's Candy Surprise	Open		27.00	27
1999 Santas Polar Delivery 659917	5,000		21.20	22
1995 Scandinavian Santa 659104	Retrd.	1998	15.80	17
1998 Scottish Crinkle at Glamis 659350	Open		28.50	29
1998 Shamrock Crinkle 659041	Open		13.40	14
1999 Sit-Down Crinkle 659156	Open		13.50	14
1997 Slavic Crinkle 659133	Open		16.00	16
1997 Slavic Crinkle 659713	Open		7.80	8
1997 Sled Filled With Joy 659908	Open		31.00	31
1995 Slimline Santa 657137	Retrd.	1996	12.00	18
1999 Somersault Crinkle 659160	Open		13.50	14
1997 Something For Everyone 659909	Open		31.10	32
1999 Special Postcard 659167	Open		13.10	14
1999 Stand-up Crinkle 659158	Open		13.50	14
1997 Starburst Crinkle 659038	Open		14.20	15
1995 Tall Santa	Open		17.50	18
1999 Tassel Top Crinkle 659147	Open		12.80	13
1999 Teapot Crinkle 659146	Open		10.50	11
1998 Teddy Beefeater Crinkle 659072	Open		20.00	20
1998 Teddy Crinkle Italiano 659071	Open		20.00	20
1998 Teddy Dutch Crinkle 659070	Open		20.00	20
1998 Teddy Mc Crinkle 659076	Open		24.80	25
1998 Teddy O' Crinkle 659075	Open		24.80	25
1998 Teddy Russian Crinkle 659073	Open		20.00	20
1998 Teddy Von Crinkle 659074	Open		20.00	20
1995 Tick Tock Santa 659120	Retrd.	1998	15.00	17
1995 Tip Top Santa 659007	Retrd.	1996	23.50	26
1999 Tippity Top Crinkle 659149	Open		13.60	14
1996 To The Rescue	Open		19.90	20
1997 Top of the List 659022	Open		13.20	14
1997 Top of the Tree 659024	Open		13.20	14
1997 Top Spin Crinkle 659037	Retrd.	1998	13.70	14
1999 Topsy Turvy Crinkle 659157	Open		13.50	14
1999 Toychest Crinkle 659152	Open		12.60	13
1998 US Crinkle at The Capitol 659351	Open		28.50	29
1997 Vatican Crinkle 659127	Open		13.40	14
1996 Well Rounded Santa	Open		13.70	14
1997 West Coast Beat 659031	Open		8.30	9

Crinkle Claus Agriclaus - Staff

YEAR ISSUE	EDITION LIMIT	YEAR RETD.	ISSUE PRICE	*QUOTE U.S.$
2000 Santa at Water Pump 659181	Open		16.00	16
2000 Santa on Tractor 659179	Open		24.00	24
2000 Santa with Cow 659178	Open		16.00	16
2000 Santa with Rooster 659182	Open		16.00	16
2000 Santa with Sheep and Pig 659180	Open		16.00	16
2000 Santa with Wheelbarrow 659177	Open		18.00	18

Crinkle Claus Candle Cuffs - Staff

YEAR ISSUE	EDITION LIMIT	YEAR RETD.	ISSUE PRICE	*QUOTE U.S.$
2000 Santa at Fireplace 22438	Open		24.50	25
2000 Santa in Sleigh 22415	Open		29.10	30
2000 Santa on Sled 22414	Open		29.10	30

Crinkle Cousins - Staff

YEAR ISSUE	EDITION LIMIT	YEAR RETD.	ISSUE PRICE	*QUOTE U.S.$
1995 Crinkle Cousin w/Clock 659002	Retrd.	1997	15.50	16
1995 Crinkle Cousin w/Clown 659004	Retrd.	1997	15.50	16
1995 Crinkle Cousin w/Dolls 659003	Retrd.	1997	15.50	16
1995 Crinkle Cousin w/Lantern 659001	Retrd.	1997	15.50	16
1995 Crinkle Cousin w/Teddy 659005	Retrd.	1997	15.50	16

Crinkle Crackers - Staff

YEAR ISSUE	EDITION LIMIT	YEAR RETD.	ISSUE PRICE	*QUOTE U.S.$
1995 Admiral Crinkle Cracker 659212	Retrd.	1997	18.50	19
1995 Captain Crinkle Cracker 659211	Retrd.	1996	13.00	13
1995 Corporal Crinkle Cracker 659214	Retrd.	1996	14.60	15
1995 French Crinkle Cracker 659203	Open		22.00	22
1995 French Lieutenant Crinkle Cracker 659205	Open		13.50	14
1995 General Crinkle Cracker 659213	Retrd.	1996	15.50	16
1995 Lieutenant Crinkle Cracker 659209	Open		26.50	27
1995 Major Crinkle Cracker 659215	Open		14.50	15
1995 Private Crinkle Cracker 659210	Retrd.	1996	15.00	15
1995 Roly Poly French Crinkle Cracker 659204	Open		13.90	14
1995 Roly Poly Russian Crinkle Cracker 659207	Open		13.50	14
1995 Roly Poly Sergeant Crinkle Cracker 659216	Open		13.50	14
1995 Roly Poly U.S. Crinkle Cracker 659201	Open		13.90	14
1995 Russian Crinkle Cracker 4" 659208	Open		13.50	14
1995 Russian Crinkle Cracker 7.75" 659206	Open		29.50	30
1995 U.S. Crinkle Cracker 3.75" 659202	Open		13.50	14
1995 U.S.Crinkle Cracker 7.5" 659200	Open		29.00	29

Crinkle Professionals - Staff

YEAR ISSUE	EDITION LIMIT	YEAR RETD.	ISSUE PRICE	*QUOTE U.S.$
1996 Baseball Player 659507	Retrd.	1998	19.50	22-25
1996 Doctor 659500	Retrd.	1998	19.50	22-25
1996 Fireman 659503	Retrd.	1998	19.50	22-25
1996 Fisherman 659504	Retrd.	1998	19.50	22-25
1996 Football Player 659506	Retrd.	1997	19.50	22-25
1996 Golfer 659505	Open		19.50	20
1996 Hockey Player 659508	Retrd.	1997	19.50	22
1997 Lawyer 659511	Open		19.50	20
1996 Policeman 659502	Open		19.50	20
1996 Postman 659501	Open		19.50	20
1996 Soccer Player 659509	Retrd.	1997	19.50	25
1997 Teacher 659510	Retrd.	1998	19.50	22
1997 Tennis Player 659512	Retrd.	1998	19.50	22

Floristine Angels® - B. Sargent

YEAR ISSUE	EDITION LIMIT	YEAR RETD.	ISSUE PRICE	*QUOTE U.S.$
1996 Angel of Happiness 668002	Open		100.00	100
1996 An Angel's Prayer 668003	Open		98.00	98
1997 Blissful Ballet 668008	Open		72.40	73
1996 Celestial Garden 668001	Open		98.00	98
1996 Heavenly Harmony 668006	Open		100.00	100
1996 Lessons From Above 668005	Open		100.00	100
1996 My Guardian Angel 668004	Open		112.00	112
1997 My Inspiration 668007	Open		37.70	38
1997 Sacred Virgil 668009	Open		47.10	48

Ingrid's Clowns - I. White

YEAR ISSUE	EDITION LIMIT	YEAR RETD.	ISSUE PRICE	*QUOTE U.S.$
1998 Bobo 317003	Open		11.80	12
1998 Carrot Top 317004	Open		11.80	12
1998 Harley 317001	Open		11.80	12
1998 Jester 317006	Open		11.80	12
1998 Pinky 317002	Open		11.80	12
1998 Popcorn 317005	Open		11.80	12
1998 Slapstick 317007	Open		11.80	12

McDonald's Santa - Staff

YEAR ISSUE	EDITION LIMIT	YEAR RETD.	ISSUE PRICE	*QUOTE U.S.$
1999 Down the Chimney, Down the Hatch 132003	Retrd.	2000	57.00	57
1998 Happy Holiday 132002	Retrd.	2000	50.00	50
1998 Midnight Break 132001	Retrd.	2000	54.00	54
1999 Working Up An Appetite 132004	Retrd.	2000	46.00	46

Poultry Power - B. Stebleton

YEAR ISSUE	EDITION LIMIT	YEAR RETD.	ISSUE PRICE	*QUOTE U.S.$
2000 Cheep! Cheep! Cheap! 194150	Open		20.00	20
2000 Ham & Eggs 194148	Open		18.00	18
2000 A Mother's Work is Never Done 194149	Open		24.00	24
2000 Motherhood is Exhausting 194146	Open		18.00	18
2000 Which Came First 194147	Open		13.00	13

Spanglers Realm® - R. Spangler

YEAR ISSUE	EDITION LIMIT	YEAR RETD.	ISSUE PRICE	*QUOTE U.S.$
1997 'Twas The Night Before 191003	Open		19.90	20
1997 Bath Time 191019	Open		15.50	16
1997 Best Friends 191020	Open		18.10	19
1997 Cherish The Small Wonders of Life 191005	Open		15.00	15
1997 Chocolate Treat 191018	Open		17.30	18
1998 Christmas Cookie Express 191004	Open		27.80	28
1997 Christmas Treasures 191021	Open		18.10	19
1997 Delicious Discovery 191001	Open		35.70	36
1997 Downhill Racer 191013	Open		18.90	19
1997 Draggin' In The Morning 191009	Open		21.90	22
1998 Dragling on the Scale 191007	Open		35.60	36
1997 A Dragon's Work Is Never Done 191006	Open		19.80	20
1997 Equal Partners Stocking Holder 191150	Open		25.20	26
1997 Fishin' Chips 191017	Open		16.30	17
1997 A Flour Just For You 191016	Open		18.10	19
1997 From Dagmar, To Dewey 191015	Open		18.30	19
1997 Guardian Angel 191010	Open		15.40	16
1997 Hole In One 191014	Open		18.50	19
1997 Home Is Where The Magic Is 191101	Open		144.50	145
1998 No Smoking Sign 191002	Open		31.30	32
1997 Santa's Surprise 191008	Open		17.10	18
1998 Sleepy Time 191022	Open		18.50	19
1997 Story Time 191012	Open		21.20	22
1997 To The Rescue 191011	Open		15.90	16

Stebleton Folk Art - B. Stebleton

YEAR ISSUE	EDITION LIMIT	YEAR RETD.	ISSUE PRICE	*QUOTE U.S.$
1998 Bearly Balanced 194050	Open		25.20	26
1999 Celestial Santa (lg.) 194053	Open		34.00	34
1999 Celestial Santa (sm.) 194054	Open		19.00	19
1998 Jolly Jurassic Christmas 194051	Open		32.00	32
1998 Scuba Claus 194052	Open		39.00	39

Stebleton's Cagey Critters - B. Stebleton

YEAR ISSUE	EDITION LIMIT	YEAR RETD.	ISSUE PRICE	*QUOTE U.S.$
2000 Angel Kitty 194140	Open		26.00	26
1998 Beach Belly 194106	Open		15.60	16
2000 Cleared For Take-Off 194139	Open		24.00	24
1999 Curly-Q 194113	Open		15.40	16
1999 Derby Day Duo 194117	Open		15.40	16
2000 Devil's Food Feline 194138	Open		25.00	25
1999 Dream Team 194114	Open		15.40	16
1998 Finger Food 194105	Open		14.00	14
1999 Furry Yellow Fellow 194115	Open		15.50	16
1999 Kitty Court Jester 194116	Open		15.80	16
1998 Liberty Kitty 194103	Open		15.60	16
1998 Lunch is on Me 194107	Open		17.70	18
2000 Pool Pals 194142	Open		25.00	25
1998 Randolph The Red Nose Cat 194108	Open		17.50	18
1998 Simply Red 194101	Open		11.30	12
1999 Skateboard Buddies 194118	Open		17.20	18
2000 Sun Tan Tabby 194141	Open		20.00	20
1998 Sushi Cat 194102	Open		14.00	14
2000 Welcoming Committee 194144	Open		25.00	25
1998 Yokes on You 194104	Open		17.90	18

The Thickets at Sweetbriar® - B. Ross

YEAR ISSUE	EDITION LIMIT	YEAR RETD.	ISSUE PRICE	*QUOTE U.S.$
1997 Amber Twinkle 350140	Open		26.80	27
1995 Angel Dear 350123	Open		32.00	32
1996 Autumn Peppergrass 350135	Open		31.00	31
1997 Berty Cosgrove 350137	Open		27.50	28
1993 The Bride-Emily Feathers 350112	Open		30.00	30
1995 Buttercup 350121	Open		32.00	32
1995 Cecily Pickwick 350125	Open		32.00	32
1998 Celeste 350146	Open		26.40	27
1998 Chip Weezley 350418	Open		10.50	11
1995 Clem Jingles 350130	Open		37.00	37
1993 Clovis Buttons 350101	Retrd.	1996	24.15	25
1996 Dainty Whiskers 350136	Open		30.00	30
1997 Divinity 350142	Open		27.30	28
1998 Dottie Crispin 350149	Open		26.80	27
1998 Erin Penny 350145	Open		25.50	26
1996 Goody Pringle 350134	Open		31.00	31
1993 The Groom-Oliver Doone 350111	Retrd.	1996	30.00	30
1997 Herman Noodles 350141	Open		27.50	28
1993 Jewel Blossom 350106	Open		36.75	37
1995 Katy Hollyberry 350124	Retrd.	1996	35.00	35
1997 Kitty Glitter 350143	Open		27.50	28
1995 Kris Krinkle 350414	Open		12.50	13
1994 Lady Slipper 350116	Open		20.00	20
1993 Lily Blossom 350105	Retrd.	1996	36.75	37
1996 Lily Blossom 350201 (musical)	Retrd.	1996	59.50	60
1998 Marie Periwinkle 350148	Open		25.50	26
1997 Mary Pawpins 350138	Open		26.80	27
1993 Maude Tweedy 350100	Retrd.	1994	26.25	27
1998 Maybelle Pudding 350144	Open		25.90	26
1996 Merry Heart 350131	Open		30.00	30
1994 Morning Dew 350113	Open		30.00	30
1993 Morning Glory 350104	Open		30.45	31
1993 Mr. Claws 350109	Retrd.	1996	34.00	34
1993 Mrs. Claws 350110	Retrd.	1996	34.00	34
1993 Orchid Beasley 350103	Retrd.	1996	26.25	27
1995 Parsley Divine 350129	Open		37.00	37
1996 Patience Finney 350133	Open		31.00	31
1993 Peablossom Thorndike 350102	Retrd.	1994	26.25	27
1995 Penny Pringle 350128	Open		32.00	32
1995 Pittypat 350122	Open		32.00	32
1994 Precious Petals 350115	Open		34.00	34
1993 Raindrop 350108	Retrd.	1996	47.25	48
1995 Riley Pickens 350127	Open		32.00	32
1993 Rose Blossom 350107	Open		36.75	37
1998 Samuel Goodley 350147	Open		21.00	21
1997 Smokey Longwood 350139	Open		27.50	28
1994 Sunshine 350118	Open		33.00	33
1994 Sweetie Flowers 350114	Retrd.	1996	33.00	33
1995 Tillie Lilly 350120	Open		32.00	32
1995 Timmy Evergreen 350126	Open		29.00	29
1996 Velvet Winterberry 350132	Open		30.00	30
1995 Violet Wiggles 350119	Open		32.00	32

Precious Art/Panton

Krystonia Collector's Club - Panton

YEAR ISSUE	EDITION LIMIT	YEAR RETD.	ISSUE PRICE	*QUOTE U.S.$
1989 Pultzr	Retrd.	1990	55.00	300-600

*Quotes have been rounded up to nearest dollar

YEAR ISSUE	EDITION LIMIT	YEAR RETD.	ISSUE PRICE	*QUOTE U.S.$
1989 Key	Retrd.	1990	Gift	135-188
1991 Dragons Play	Retrd.	1992	65.00	238-438
1991 Kephrens Chest	Retrd.	1992	Gift	113-219
1992 Vaaston	Retrd.	1993	65.00	185-200
1992 Lantern	Retrd.	1993	Gift	100-169
1993 Sneaking A Peak	Retrd.	1994	Gift	113-125
1993 Spreading His Wings	Retrd.	1994	60.00	72-135
1994 All Tuckered Out	Retrd.	1995	65.00	100-124
1994 Filler-Up	Retrd.	1995	Gift	75-82
1995 Twingnuk	Retrd.	1996	55.00	95-143
1995 Kappah Krystal	Retrd.	1996	Gift	45-100
1996 Quinzet	Retrd.	1997	38.00	38-68
1996 Holy Dragons	Retrd.	1997	65.00	65-98
1996 Frobbit	Retrd.	1997	Gift	65-104
1996 Glowing Mashal	Retrd.	1998	Gift	30-50
1997 Almost There	Retrd.	1998	75.00	75
1998 Cauldron	Retrd.	1999	Gift	45
1998 The Bahl 510	Retrd.	1999	55.00	55
1999 Which Way?	Retrd.	1999	Gift	N/A
1999 Krystonia This Way	Retrd.	2000	60.00	60
2000 Flopple	Yr.Iss.		Gift	N/A
2000 Why 2000?	5/01		60.00	60

Fair Maidens - Panton

YEAR ISSUE	EDITION LIMIT	YEAR RETD.	ISSUE PRICE	*QUOTE U.S.$
1994 Faithful Companion	1,000	1994	325.00	350-400
1995 Safe Passage	1,000	1996	350.00	350
1996 Serenity 1002	1,000	1999	350.00	350
1998 Forever Friends 1003	1,000		300.00	300

World of Krystonia - Panton

YEAR ISSUE	EDITION LIMIT	YEAR RETD.	ISSUE PRICE	*QUOTE U.S.$
1993 All Mine - 3903	Retrd.	1998	38.00	38-57
1992 Azael - 3811	Retrd.	1995	85.00	100
1989 Babul - 1402	Retrd.	1995	25.00	30-45
1989 Bags-Large - 703	Retrd.	1996	12.00	12-18
1989 Bags-Small - 704	Retrd.	1996	4.00	12-18
1994 Boll - 3912	Retrd.	1994	52.00	165
1994 Boll - 3912R	250	1994	52.00	52-185
1989 Caught At Last! - 1107	Retrd.	1992	150.00	147-188
1999 Challon - 3954	Retrd.	2000	50.00	50
1991 Charcoal Cookie - 3451	Retrd.	1996	38.00	50
1994 Checkin It Out - 3914	15,000	1998	46.00	46-50
1993 Cuda Tree - 705	Retrd.	1997	35.00	46-50
1991 Culpy - 3441	Retrd.	1996	38.00	45-50
1992 Dubious Alliance - 1109	Retrd.	1995	195.00	195-200
1998 The Encounter - 1116	Retrd.	2000	100.00	100
1995 Enough Is Enough - 1114	1,500	1996	250.00	250
1992 Escublar (Classic Moment) - 1110	7,500	1997	170.00	170
1991 Flayla w/Fumbly - 1105	Retrd.	1995	104.00	104-125
1980 Gateway to Krystonia - 3301	Retrd.	1994	35.00	40-125
1989 Gorph In Bucket - 2801	Retrd.	1996	20.00	26-39
1989 Gorphylia - 2802	Retrd.	1996	18.00	58-163
1987 Grackene (with legs) - 1051	Retrd.	N/A	50.00	450
1987 Grackene - 1051	Retrd.	1995	50.00	125-150
1987 Graffyn on Grumblypeg Grunch-Large -1011	Retrd.	1992	52.00	107-110
1987 Graffyn on Grumblypeg Grunch-Small - 1012	Retrd.	1989	45.00	225-250
1989 Graffyn on Grunch (waterglobe) - 9006	Retrd.	1992	42.00	65-85
1987 Graffyn w/Green Coat - 1011	Retrd.	1987	52.00	52
1988 Grazzi - 2301	Retrd.	1998	32.00	80-85
1987 Groc - 1041	Retrd.	1995	50.00	55
1987 Groc-Small - 1042B	Retrd.	1987	24.00	3000-3495
1991 Groosh-Large - 3601	15,000	1997	65.00	80-98
1991 Groosh-Small - 3602	Retrd.	1998	36.00	36
1987 Grumblypeg Grunch - 1081	Retrd.	1992	52.00	160-175
1991 Grunch's Toothache-Large - 1082	Retrd.	1994	76.00	90-105
1989 Grunch's Toothache-Small - 1083	15,000	1998	52.00	75
1997 Grunchie - 3938	Retrd.	1999	35.00	35
1989 Gurneyfoot & Shadra - 1106	15,000	1998	90.00	110-117
1987 Haapf-Large - 1901	Retrd.	1991	38.00	125-350
1994 Hagga-Beast - 3908	Retrd.	1999	130.00	130-150
1990 Hottlepottle - 3501	Retrd.	1997	60.00	66-80
1993 Hulbert - 3905	Retrd.	1999	35.00	35-45
1994 Ikshar - 3916	Retrd.	1998	46.00	46-63
1997 Jasu - 3940	Retrd.	1998	27.00	27
1990 Jumbly - 3411	Retrd.	1994	32.00	32-36
1996 Just a Pinch - 3930	Retrd.	1999	35.00	35
1989 Kephren - 2702	Retrd.	1994	56.00	62-110
1988 Koozl - 2901	Retrd.	1998	36.00	55-78
1987 Krak N' Borg-Small - 3003	Retrd.	1993	60.00	132-250
1987 Krak N'Borg-Large - 3001	Retrd.	1990	240.00	500-750
1987 Krak N'Borg-Med. - 3002	Retrd.	1997	200.00	200-325
1989 Krystonia Sign - 701	Retrd.	1993	10.00	50-120
1989 Lands of Krystonia	1,500	1998	240.00	300-325
1994 Learning is Gweat - 3910	Retrd.	1998	48.00	50
1997 Lubyn - 3942	Retrd.	1998	27.00	27
1991 Mahouhda - 3701	Retrd.	1998	36.00	40
1991 Maj-Dron Migration - 1108	Retrd.	1994	145.00	155-188
1992 Mini N' Grall - 611	Retrd.	1995	27.00	27
1987 Moplos-Large - 1021	Retrd.	1991	90.00	250
1987 Moplos-Small - 1022	15,000	1998	80.00	96-100
1987 Mos - 1031	15,000	1998	90.00	130
1991 Muffler - 3901	Retrd.	2000	24.00	24
1990 Myzer's Barrel 706	Retrd.	2000	45.00	45
1987 Myzer-Large - 1201	Retrd.	1991	50.00	65-119
1987 Myzer-Small - 1202	15,000	1997	40.00	48-59
1987 N' Chakk-Large - 2101	Retrd.	1995	140.00	140-228
1989 N' Grall-Small - 2203	Retrd.	1997	32.00	40-85
1992 N' Leila - 3801	Retrd.	1994	60.00	113-155
1987 N' Tormet-Small - 2602	Retrd.	1993	44.00	50-100
1989 N'Borg on Throne-Large - 1093	15,000	1997	90.00	110-293
1989 N'Borg on Throne-Small - 1094	15,000	1998	60.00	70
1987 N'Borg-Large - 1092	Retrd.	1994	98.00	200-250
1991 N'Borg-Mini - 609	Retrd.	1994	29.00	34-40
1987 N'Borg-Small - 1091	Retrd.	1989	50.00	250-300
1990 N'Chakk-Mini - 607	Retrd.	1994	29.00	40-60
1988 N'Chakk-Small - 2102	15,000	1998	48.00	45-55
1988 N'Grall-Large - 2201	Retrd.	1990	108.00	250
1988 N'Grall-Med. - 2202	Retrd.	1994	70.00	250-275
1988 N'Grall-Small - 2203	Retrd.	1997	30.00	30-75
1989 N'Tormet - 2601	15,000	1996	60.00	75-78
1992 Off We Go - 3926	Retrd.	2000	60.00	60
1994 Oh Sweet Dreams - 3911	Retrd.	1998	36.00	36
1994 Okinawathe - 1111	15,000	1998	90.00	90-125
1994 One Unhappy Ride - 1112	Retrd.	1999	125.00	125-175
1991 Oops - 3907	Retrd.	2000	36.00	35-40
1996 Ottho - 3928	15,000	1998	48.00	48
1990 Owhey (waterglobe) - 9004	Retrd.	1995	42.00	150-250
1987 Owhey - 1071	Retrd.	1990	32.00	125
1997 Ploot - 3936	7,500	1998	67.00	67
1997 Ploot - 3936B	250	1997	67.00	85-95
1987 Poffles - 1401	Retrd.	1998	16.00	34-45
1991 Pooter - 3721	Retrd.	2000	40.00	40
1989 Puffles (waterball) - 9001	Retrd.	1998	36.00	36
1997 Pultz - 3939	Retrd.	1998	35.00	35
1996 Reamon - 3927B	250	1996	70.00	70-145
1995 Remmon - 3937	Retrd.	1999	65.00	65
1994 Root - 3922	Retrd.	1999	80.00	80
1995 Root - 3922R	250	1995	85.00	140-260
1987 Rueggan-Large - 1701	Retrd.	1989	55.00	175
1988 Rueggan-Med. - 1702	Retrd.	1993	48.00	125
1988 Rueggan-Small - 1703	Retrd.	1995	42.00	63-75
1994 Schnoogles - 3915	Retrd.	1998	42.00	42
1989 Scrolls-Small - 702	Retrd.	1996	4.00	4-12
1998 Seer - 3944B	250		70.00	70
1990 Shadra - 3401	Retrd.	1994	30.00	55-90
1997 Shanu - 3941	Retrd.	1998	27.00	27
1989 Shepf (waterball) - 9005	Retrd.	1998	40.00	40
1987 Shepf - 1151	15,000	1997	70.00	100
1987 Shepf-Small - 1152	Retrd.	1990	40.00	120
1987 Shigger - 1801	Retrd.	1998	30.00	35-98
1987 Spyke - 1061	Retrd.	1993	50.00	63-107
1995 Spyke - 615	Retrd.	1998	20.00	20
1997 Spyster - 3937	Retrd.	1999	35.00	35
1989 Stoope (waterglobe) - 9003	Retrd.	1991	40.00	150-260
1994 Stoope - 613	Retrd.	1998	23.00	23
1987 Stoope-Large - 1103	15,000	1996	98.00	160-180
1987 Stoope-Med. - 1101	Retrd.	1990	52.00	225
1987 Stoope-Small - 1102	Retrd.	1995	46.00	46-85
1997 Storyteller - 1115	3,500	1998	145.00	145-155
1993 Tag - 3909R	250	1993	48.00	450
1996 Tallac - 3934	Retrd.	1998	65.00	65-75
1988 Tarnhold-Large - 3201	Retrd.	1997	200.00	250
1988 Tarnhold-Med. - 3202	Retrd.	1992	120.00	175-250
1987 Tarnhold-Small - 3203	Retrd.	1995	60.00	75-117
1988 Tokkel - 2401	Retrd.	1995	42.00	60
1989 Trumph (waterball) - 9002	Retrd.	1998	36.00	36
1987 Trumph - 1501	Retrd.	1998	20.00	31-65
1989 Tulan - 2501	15,000	1996	60.00	75-96
1988 Tulan Captain-Small - 2502	Retrd.	1991	44.00	95-100
1987 Turfen-Large - 1601	Retrd.	1991	50.00	100
1991 Twilyght - 3421	Retrd.	1998	32.00	40
1990 Vena - 3101	15,000	1997	40.00	75-110
1990 Vena w/Blond Hair 3101	Retrd.	1990	40.00	40
1996 Waldurgan - 3933	3,500	1998	195.00	195
1994 Welcome to Krystonia - 3913	15,000	1998	60.00	65
1996 What's Cookin' - 3931	Retrd.	1999	35.00	35
1997 Woby - 3943	Retrd.	1998	27.00	30
1987 Wodema-Large - 1301	Retrd.	1990	50.00	156-325
1987 Wodema-Med. - 1302	Retrd.	1993	44.00	70-95
1987 Wodema-Small - 1303	Retrd.	1998	22.00	32-78
1990 Zygmund - 3511	Retrd.	1997	50.00	60

World of Krystonia-Timeless Treasures - Panton

YEAR ISSUE	EDITION LIMIT	YEAR RETD.	ISSUE PRICE	*QUOTE U.S.$
1998 On Watch - 4001	3,500		100.00	100
1997 Recorder	3,500	1998	100.00	300
1999 Shigger's Dilemma - 4002	3,500		125.00	125

Precious Moments/Enesco Group, Inc.

Precious Moments Collectors Club Welcome Gift - S. Butcher

YEAR ISSUE	EDITION LIMIT	YEAR RETD.	ISSUE PRICE	*QUOTE U.S.$
1982 But Love Goes On Forever-Plaque E-0202	Yr.Iss.	1982	N/A	45-102
1983 Let Us Call the Club to Order E-0303	Yr.Iss.	1983	21.00	39-60
1984 Join in on the Blessings E-0404	Yr.Iss.	1984	N/A	27-111
1985 Seek and Ye Shall Find E-0005	Yr.Iss.	1985	N/A	25-41
1986 Birds of a Feather Collect Together E-0006	Yr.Iss.	1986	N/A	26-46
1987 Sharing Is Universal E-0007	Yr.Iss.	1987	N/A	22-30
1988 A Growing Love E-0008	Yr.Iss.	1988	N/A	22-50
1989 Always Room For One More C-0009	Yr.Iss.	1989	N/A	21-40
1990 My Happiness C-0010	Yr.Iss.	1990	N/A	22-50
1991 Sharing the Good News Together C-0011	Yr.Iss.	1991	N/A	21-29
1992 The Club That's Out Of This World C-0012	Yr.Iss.	1992	N/A	23-36
1993 Loving, Caring, and Sharing Along the Way C-0013	Yr.Iss.	1993	N/A	23-30
1994 You Are the End of My Rainbow C-0014	Yr.Iss.	1994	N/A	23-30
1995 You're The Sweetest Cookie In The Batch C-0015	Yr.Iss.	1995	N/A	16-22
1996 You're As Pretty As A Picture C-0016	Yr.Iss.	1996	N/A	19-35
1997 A Special Toast To Precious Moments C-0017	Yr.Iss.	1997	N/A	10-35
1998 Focusing In On Those Precious Moments C-0018	Yr.Iss.	1998	N/A	19-35
1999 Wishing You a World of Peace C-0019	Yr.Iss.	1999	N/A	N/A
2000 Thanks A Bunch C-0020	Yr.Iss.		N/A	N/A

Precious Moments Inscribed Charter Member Renewal Gift - S. Butcher

YEAR ISSUE	EDITION LIMIT	YEAR RETD.	ISSUE PRICE	*QUOTE U.S.$
1981 But Love Goes on Forever E-0001	Yr.Iss.	1981	17.00	98-130
1982 But Love Goes on Forever-Plaque E-0102	Yr.Iss.	1982	N/A	24-99
1983 Let Us Call the Club to Order E-0103	Yr.Iss.	1983	25.00	45-65
1984 Join in on the Blessings E-0104	Yr.Iss.	1984	25.00	32-50
1985 Seek and Ye Shall Find E-0105	Yr.Iss.	1985	25.00	41-50
1986 Birds of a Feather Collect Together E-0106	Yr.Iss.	1986	25.00	26-48
1987 Sharing Is Universal E-0107	Yr.Iss.	1987	25.00	24-40
1988 A Growing Love E-0108	Yr.Iss.	1988	25.00	23-35
1989 Always Room For One More C-0109	Yr.Iss.	1989	35.00	35-45
1990 My Happiness C-0110	Yr.Iss.	1990	N/A	23-40
1991 Sharing The Good News Together C-0111	Yr.Iss.	1991	N/A	35-50
1992 The Club That's Out Of This World C-0112	Yr.Iss.	1992	N/A	23-40
1993 Loving, Caring, and Sharing Along the Way C-0113	Yr.Iss.	1993	N/A	35-40
1994 You Are the End of My Rainbow C-0114	Yr.Iss.	1994	N/A	15-26
1995 You're The Sweetest Cookie In The Batch C-0115	Yr.Iss.	1995	N/A	26-35
1996 You're As Pretty As A Picture C-0116	Yr.Iss.	1996	N/A	33-35
1997 A Special Toast To Precious Moments C-0117	Yr.Iss.	1997	N/A	35
1998 Focusing In On Those Precious Moments C-0118	Yr.Iss.	1998	N/A	39
1999 Wishing You a World of Peace C-0119	Yr.Iss.	1999	N/A	N/A
2000 Thanks A Bunch C-0120	Yr.Iss.		N/A	N/A

Precious Moments Special Edition Members' Only - S. Butcher

YEAR ISSUE	EDITION LIMIT	YEAR RETD.	ISSUE PRICE	*QUOTE U.S.$
1981 Hello, Lord, It's Me Again PM-811	Yr.Iss.	1981	25.00	275-520
1982 Smile, God Loves You PM-821	Yr.Iss.	1982	25.00	122-260
1983 Put on a Happy Face PM-822	Yr.Iss.	1983	25.00	129-221
1983 Dawn's Early Light PM-831	Yr.Iss.	1983	27.50	48-70
1984 God's Ray of Mercy PM-841	Yr.Iss.	1984	25.00	38-95
1984 Trust in the Lord to the Finish PM-842	Yr.Iss.	1984	25.00	53-68
1985 The Lord is My Shepherd PM-851	Yr.Iss.	1985	25.00	53-70
1985 I Love to Tell the Story PM-852	Yr.Iss.	1985	27.50	35-65
1986 Grandma's Prayer PM-861	Yr.Iss.	1986	25.00	59-90
1986 I'm Following Jesus PM-862	Yr.Iss.	1986	25.00	56-68
1987 Feed My Sheep PM-871	Yr.Iss.	1987	25.00	45-92
1987 In His Time PM-872	Yr.Iss.	1987	25.00	30-58
1987 Loving You Dear Valentine PM-873	Yr.Iss.	1987	25.00	30-45
1987 Loving You Dear Valentine PM-874	Yr.Iss.	1987	25.00	30-49
1988 God Bless You for Touching My Life PM-881	Yr.Iss.	1988	27.50	34-67
1988 You Just Can't Chuck A Good Friendship PM-882	Yr.Iss.	1988	27.50	30-54
1989 You Will Always Be My Choice PM-891	Yr.Iss.	1989	27.50	35-52
1989 Mow Power To Ya PM-892	Yr.Iss.	1989	27.50	35-72
1990 Ten Years And Still Going Strong PM-901	Yr.Iss.	1990	30.00	33-52
1990 You Are A Blessing To Me PM-902	Yr.Iss.	1990	30.00	27-58
1991 One Step At A Time PM-911	Yr.Iss.	1991	33.00	40-55
1991 Lord, Keep Me In TeePee Top Shape PM-912	Yr.Iss.	1991	33.00	45-58
1992 Only Love Can Make A Home PM-921	Yr.Iss.	1992	30.00	49-60
1992 Sowing The Seeds of Love PM-922	Yr.Iss.	1992	30.00	26-39
1993 His Little Treasure PM-931	Yr.Iss.	1993	30.00	28-48
1993 Loving PM-932	Yr.Iss.	1993	30.00	45-80
1994 Caring PM-941	Yr.Iss.	1994	35.00	38-43
1994 Sharing PM-942	Yr.Iss.	1994	35.00	30-40
1995 You Fill The Pages of My Life (figurine/book) 530980	Yr.Iss.	1994	37.50	50-76
1995 You're One In A Million To Me PM-951	Yr.Iss.	1995	35.00	28-35
1995 Always Take Time To Pray PM-952	Yr.Iss.	1995	35.00	35-57
1996 Teach Us To Love One Another PM-961	Yr.Iss.	1996	40.00	43-57
1996 Our Club Is Soda-licious PM-962	Yr.Iss.	1996	35.00	42-58
1997 You Will Always Be A Treasure To Me PM971	Yr.Iss.	1997	50.00	50-55
1997 Blessed Are The Merciful PM972	Yr.Iss.	1997	40.00	35-48
1998 Happy Trails PM981	Yr.Iss.	1998	50.00	50
1998 Lord Please Don't Put Me On Hold PM982	Yr.Iss.	1998	40.00	40
1998 How Can Two Work Together Except They Agree PM983	Yr.Iss.	1998	125.00	125
1999 Jumping For Joy PM991	Yr.Iss.	1999	30.00	30
1999 God Speed PM992	Yr.Iss.	1999	30.00	30
1999 He Watches Over Us All PM993	Yr.Iss.	1999	225.00	225
2000 My Collection PM001	Yr.Iss.		20.00	20
2000 Collecting Friends Along The Way PM002	Yr.Iss.		100.00	100

Precious Moments Club 5th Anniversary Commemorative Edition - S. Butcher

YEAR ISSUE	EDITION LIMIT	YEAR RETD.	ISSUE PRICE	*QUOTE U.S.$
1985 God Bless Our Years Together 12440	Yr.Iss.	1985	175.00	247-300

*Quotes have been rounded up to nearest dollar

Precious Moments/Enesco Group, Inc. to Precious Moments/Enesco Group, Inc.

FIGURINES

Precious Moments Club 10th Anniversary Commemorative Edition - S. Butcher

YEAR ISSUE	EDITION LIMIT	YEAR RETD.	ISSUE PRICE	*QUOTE U.S.$
1988 The Good Lord Has Blessed Us Tenfold 114022	Yr.Iss.	1988	90.00	100-188

Precious Moments Club 15th Anniversary Commemorative Edition - S. Butcher

YEAR ISSUE	EDITION LIMIT	YEAR RETD.	ISSUE PRICE	*QUOTE U.S.$
1993 15 Happy Years Together: What A Tweet 530786	Yr.Iss.	1993	100.00	100-274
1995 A Perfect Display of 15 Happy Years 127817	Yr.Iss.	1995	100.00	100-150

Precious Moments Club 20th Anniversary Commemorative Edition - S. Butcher

YEAR ISSUE	EDITION LIMIT	YEAR RETD.	ISSUE PRICE	*QUOTE U.S.$
1998 20 Years And The Vision's Still The Same 306843	Yr.Iss.	1998	55.00	45-55

Precious Moments - S. Butcher

YEAR ISSUE	EDITION LIMIT	YEAR RETD.	ISSUE PRICE	*QUOTE U.S.$
1983 Sharing Our Season Together E-0501	Suspd.		50.00	112-128
1983 Jesus is the Light that Shines E-0502	Suspd.		23.00	44-50
1983 Blessings from My House to Yours E-0503	Suspd.		27.00	60-73
1983 Christmastime Is for Sharing E-0504	Retrd.	1989	37.00	61-80
1983 Surrounded with Joy E-0506	Retrd.	1987	21.00	50-104
1983 God Sent His Son E-0507	Suspd.		32.50	58-80
1983 Prepare Ye the Way of the Lord E-0508	Suspd.		75.00	122-138
1983 Bringing God's Blessing to You E-0509	Suspd.		35.00	54-90
1983 Tubby's First Christmas E-0511	Suspd.		12.00	15-26
1983 It's a Perfect Boy E-0512	Suspd.		18.50	19-47
1983 Onward Christian Soldiers E-0523	Open		24.00	28-65
1983 You Can't Run Away from God E-0525	Retrd.	1989	28.50	50-175
1983 He Upholdeth Those Who Fall E-0526	Suspd.		35.00	58-112
1987 His Eye Is On The Sparrow E-0530	Retrd.	1987	28.50	30-150
1979 Jesus Loves Me E-1372B	Retrd.	1998	7.00	30-130
1979 Jesus Loves Me E-1372G	Open		7.00	21-39
1979 Smile, God Loves You E-1373B	Retrd.	1984	7.00	33-125
1979 Jesus is the Light E-1373G	Retrd.	1988	7.00	33-104
1979 Praise the Lord Anyhow E-1374B	Retrd.	1982	8.00	26-92
1979 Make a Joyful Noise E-1374G	Retrd.	2000	8.00	30-106
1979 Love Lifted Me E-1375A	Retrd.	1993	11.00	35-175
1979 Prayer Changes Things E-1375B	Suspd.		11.00	80-126
1979 Love One Another E-1376	Open		10.00	30-98
1979 He Leadeth Me E-1377A	Suspd.		9.00	40-135
1979 He Careth For You E-1377B	Suspd.		9.00	75-140
1979 God Loveth a Cheerful Giver E-1378	Retrd.	1981	11.00	625-1050
1979 Love is Kind E-1379A	Suspd.		8.00	15-88
1979 God Understands E-1379B	Suspd.		8.00	72-135
1979 O, How I Love Jesus E-1380B	Retrd.	1984	8.00	55-175
1979 His Burden Is Light E-1380G	Retrd.	1984	8.00	40-175
1979 Jesus is the Answer E-1381	Suspd.		11.50	104-170
1992 Jesus is the Answer E-1381R	Retrd.	1996	55.00	45-128
1979 We Have Seen His Star E-2010	Suspd.		8.00	50-120
1979 Come Let Us Adore Him E-2011	Retrd.	1981	10.00	143-290
1979 Jesus is Born E-2012	Suspd.		12.00	85-260
1979 Unto Us a Child is Born E-2013	Suspd.		12.00	32-111
1982 May Your Christmas Be Cozy E-2345	Suspd.		23.00	51-100
1982 May Your Christmas Be Warm E-2348	Suspd.		30.00	82-140
1983 Tell Me the Story of Jesus E-2349	Suspd.		30.00	75-150
1982 Dropping in for Christmas E-2350	Suspd.		18.00	42-115
1982 Holy Smokes E-2351	Retrd.	1987	27.00	52-120
1983 O Come All Ye Faithful E-2353	Retrd.	1986	27.50	51-105
1982 I'll Play My Drum for Him E-2356	Suspd.		30.00	39-115
1982 I'll Play My Drum for Him E-2360	Open		16.00	28-48
1982 Christmas Joy from Head to Toe E-2361	Suspd.		25.00	44-80
1982 Camel Figurine E-2363	Open		20.00	35-42
1982 Goat Figurine E-2364	Suspd.		10.00	45-80
1982 The First Noel E-2365	Suspd.		16.00	40-80
1982 The First Noel E-2366	Suspd.		16.00	44-100
1982 Bundles of Joy E-2374	Retrd.	1993	27.50	30-125
1982 Dropping Over for Christmas E-2375	Retrd.	1991	30.00	45-140
1982 Our First Christmas Together E-2377	Suspd.		35.00	49-100
1982 3 Mini Nativity Houses & Palm Tree E-2387	Open		45.00	75-78
1982 Come Let Us Adore Him E-2395 (11pc. set)	Open		80.00	104-224
1980 Come Let Us Adore Him E-2800 (9 pc. set)	Open		70.00	110-175
1980 Jesus is Born E-2801	Suspd.		37.00	245-293
1980 Christmas is a Time to Share E-2802	Suspd.		20.00	53-110
1980 Crown Him Lord of All E-2803	Suspd.		20.00	41-120
1980 Peace on Earth E-2804	Suspd.		20.00	104-155
1980 Wishing You a Season Filled w/ Joy E-2805	Retrd.	1985	20.00	61-115
1984 You Have Touched So Many Hearts E-2821	Suspd.		25.00	33-90
1984 This is Your Day to Shine E-2822	Retrd.	1988	37.50	71-155
1984 To God Be the Glory E-2823	Suspd.		40.00	58-155
1984 To a Very Special Mom E-2824	Open		27.50	35-62
1984 To a Very Special Sister E-2825	Open		37.50	50-75
1984 May Your Birthday Be a Blessing E-2826	Suspd.		37.50	38-150
1984 I Get a Kick Out of You E-2827	Suspd.		50.00	149-205
1984 Precious Memories E-2828	Retrd.	1999	45.00	43-115
1984 I'm Sending You a White Christmas E-2829	Retrd.	2000	37.50	41-77
1984 God Bless the Bride E-2832	Open		35.00	42-60
1986 Sharing Our Joy Together E-2834	Suspd.		30.00	34-85
1984 Baby Figurines (set of 6) E-2852	Closed	N/A	15.00	63-140

YEAR ISSUE	EDITION LIMIT	YEAR RETD.	ISSUE PRICE	*QUOTE U.S.$
1984 Boy Standing E-2852A	Suspd.		13.50	17-27
1984 Girl Standing E-2852B	Suspd.		13.50	19-22
1984 Boy & Girl Standing, set E-2852A&B	Suspd.		27.00	125-228
1984 Boy Sitting Up E-2852C	Suspd.		13.50	17-32
1984 Girl Sitting Clapping E-2852D	Suspd.		13.50	17-22
1984 Boy Crawling E-2852E	Suspd.		13.50	14-25
1984 Girl Laying Down E-2852F	Suspd.		13.50	17-36
1980 Blessed Are the Pure in Heart E-3104	Suspd.		9.00	21-60
1980 He Watches Over Us All E-3105	Suspd.		11.00	30-105
1980 Mother Sew Dear E-3106	Open		13.00	33-80
1980 Blessed are the Peacemakers E-3107	Retrd.	1985	13.00	57-91
1980 The Hand that Rocks the Future E-3108	Suspd.		13.00	45-78
1980 The Purr-fect Grandma E-3109	Open		13.00	33-59
1980 Loving is Sharing E-3110B	Retrd.	1993	13.00	55-145
1980 Loving is Sharing E-3110G	Open		13.00	33-105
1980 Be Not Weary In Well Doing E-3111	Retrd.	1985	14.00	43-144
1980 God's Speed E-3112	Retrd.	1983	14.00	33-120
1980 Thou Art Mine E-3113	Open		16.00	32-90
1980 The Lord Bless You and Keep You E-3114	Open		16.00	50-85
1980 But Love Goes on Forever E-3115	Open		16.50	40-100
1980 Thee I Love E-3116	Retrd.	1994	16.50	40-145
1980 Walking By Faith E-3117	Retrd.	2000	35.00	64-130
1980 Eggs Over Easy E-3118	Retrd.	1983	12.00	45-125
1980 It's What's Inside that Counts E-3119	Suspd.		13.00	50-130
1980 To Thee With Love E-3120	Suspd.		13.00	42-125
1981 The Lord Bless You and Keep You E-4720	Suspd.		14.00	34-38
1981 The Lord Bless You and Keep You E-4721	Open		14.00	35-115
2000 The Lord Bless You and Keep You E-4721B	Open		37.00	37
2000 The Lord Bless You and Keep You E-4721DB	Open		37.00	37
1981 Love Cannot Break a True Friendship E-4722	Suspd.		22.50	67-200
1981 Peace Amid the Storm E-4723	Suspd.		22.50	60-125
1981 Rejoicing with You E-4724	Open		25.00	34-67
1981 Peace on Earth E-4725	Suspd.		25.00	52-62
1981 Bear Ye One Another's Burdens E-5200	Suspd.		20.00	56-110
1981 Love Lifted Me E-5201	Suspd.		25.00	48-110
1981 Thank You for Coming to My Ade E-5202	Suspd.		22.50	84-125
1981 Let Not the Sun Go Down Upon Your Wrath E-5203	Suspd.		22.50	117-250
1981 To A Special Dad E-5212	Suspd.		20.00	30-75
1981 God is Love E-5213	Suspd.		17.00	44-88
1981 Prayer Changes Things E-5214	Suspd.		35.00	80-220
1984 May Your Christmas Be Blessed E-5376	Suspd.		37.50	56-80
1984 Love is Kind E-5377	Retrd.	1987	27.50	62-85
1984 Joy to the World E-5378	Suspd.		18.00	34-42
1984 Isn't He Precious? E-5379	Retrd.	2000	20.00	21-33
1984 A Monarch is Born E-5380	Suspd.		33.00	56-76
1984 His Name is Jesus E-5381	Suspd.		45.00	75-98
1984 For God So Loved the World E-5382	Suspd.		70.00	104-110
1984 Wishing You a Merry Christmas E-5383	Yr.Iss.	1984	17.00	29-45
1984 I'll Play My Drum for Him E-5384	Open		10.00	15-35
1984 Oh Worship the Lord (B) E-5385	Suspd.		10.00	40-46
1984 Oh Worship the Lord (G) E-5386	Suspd.		10.00	53-70
1981 Come Let Us Adore Him E-5619	Suspd.		10.00	13-33
1981 Donkey Figurine E-5621	Open		6.00	15-25
1981 They Followed the Star E-5624	Open		130.00	225-275
1981 We Three Kings E-5635	Open		40.00	40-78
1981 Rejoice O Earth E-5636	Retrd.	1999	15.00	26-78
1981 The Heavenly Light E-5637	Open		15.00	30-76
1981 Cow with Bell Figurine E-5638	Open		16.00	36-40
1981 Isn't He Wonderful (B) E-5639	Suspd.		12.00	35-50
1981 Isn't He Wonderful (G) E-5640	Suspd.		12.00	56-100
1981 They Followed the Star E-5641	Suspd.		75.00	144-156
1981 Nativity Wall (2 pc. set) E-5644	Open		60.00	120-160
1984 God Sends the Gift of His Love E-6613	Suspd.		22.50	50-70
1982 God is Love, Dear Valentine E-7153	Suspd.		16.00	17-65
1982 God is Love, Dear Valentine E-7154	Suspd.		16.00	17-65
1982 Thanking Him for You E-7155	Suspd.		16.00	26-60
1982 I Believe in Miracles E-7156	Suspd.		17.00	37-120
1988 I Believe In Miracles E-7156R	Retrd.	1992	22.50	44-156
1982 There is Joy in Serving Jesus E-7157	Retrd.	1986	17.00	29-110
1982 Love Beareth All Things E-7158	Open		25.00	36-46
1982 Lord Give Me Patience E-7159	Suspd.		25.00	27-65
1982 The Perfect Grandpa E-7160	Suspd.		25.00	48-71
1982 His Sheep Am I E-7161	Suspd.		25.00	52-70
1982 Love is Sharing E-7162	Suspd.		25.00	125-170
1982 God is Watching Over You E-7163	Suspd.		27.50	68-80
1982 Bless This House E-7164	Suspd.		45.00	130-250
1982 Let the Whole World Know E-7165	Suspd.		45.00	82-165
1981 The Lord Bless You And Keep You E-7167	Suspd.		25.00	25-48
1983 Love is Patient E-9251	Suspd.		35.00	64-100
1983 Forgiving is Forgetting E-9252	Suspd.		37.50	58-110
1983 The End is in Sight E-9253	Suspd.		25.00	43-100
1983 Praise the Lord Anyhow E-9254	Retrd.	1994	35.00	40-152
1983 Bless You Two E-9255	Open		21.00	42-55
1983 We are God's Workmanship E-9258	Open		19.00	30-58
1983 We're In It Together E-9259	Suspd.		24.00	43-104
1983 God's Promises are Sure E-9260	Suspd.		30.00	57-86
1983 Seek Ye the Lord E-9261	Suspd.		21.00	24-52

YEAR ISSUE	EDITION LIMIT	YEAR RETD.	ISSUE PRICE	*QUOTE U.S.$
1983 Seek Ye the Lord E-9262	Suspd.		21.00	48-70
1983 How Can Two Walk Together Except They Agree E-9263	Suspd.		35.00	119-200
1983 Press On E-9265	Retrd.	1999	40.00	53-70
1983 I'm Falling For Some Bunny/Our Love Is Heaven-scent E-9266	Suspd.		18.50	19-22
1983 Animal Collection, Teddy Bear E-9267A	Suspd.		6.50	15-22
1983 Animal Collection, Dog W/ Slippers E-9267B	Suspd.		6.50	10-20
1983 Animal Collection, Bunny W/ Carrot E-9267C	Suspd.		6.50	15-22
1983 Animal Collection, Kitty With Bow E-9267D	Suspd.		6.50	15-22
1983 Animal Collection, Lamb With Bird E-9267E	Suspd.		6.50	12-18
1983 Animal Collection, Pig W/ Patches E-9267F	Suspd.		6.50	12-18
1983 Nobody's Perfect E-9268	Retrd.	1990	21.00	50-100
1983 Nobody's Perfect (smiling) E-9268	Retrd.	1990	21.00	398
1983 Let Love Reign E-9273	Retrd.	1987	27.50	53-110
1983 Taste and See that the Lord is Good E-9274	Retrd.	1986	22.50	45-75
1983 Jesus Loves Me E-9278	Retrd.	1998	9.00	16-31
1983 Jesus Loves Me E-9279	Retrd.	2000	9.00	17-33
1983 To Some Bunny Special E-9282A	Suspd.		8.00	15-32
1983 You're Worth Your Weight In Gold E-9282B	Suspd.		8.00	15-30
1983 Especially For Ewe E-9282C	Suspd.		8.00	15-24
1983 Set of Three Animals E-9282A,B,C	Suspd.		24.00	41-72
1983 If God Be for Us, Who Can Be Against Us E-9285	Suspd.		27.50	70-80
1983 Peace on Earth E-9287	Suspd.		37.50	108-200
1997 And A Child Shall Lead Them E-9287R	Open		50.00	45-55
1983 Sending You a Rainbow E-9288	Suspd.		22.50	68-120
1983 Trust in the Lord E-9289	Suspd.		21.00	53-100
1985 Love Covers All 12009	Suspd.		27.50	45-68
1985 Part of Me Wants to be Good 12149	Suspd.		19.00	48-110
1987 This Is The Day Which The Lord Has Made 12157	Suspd.		20.00	30-60
1985 Get into the Habit of Prayer 12203	Suspd.		19.00	24-52
1985 Miniature Clown 12238A	Suspd.		13.50	29-49
1985 Miniature Clown 12238B	Suspd.		13.50	20-59
1985 Miniature Clown 12238C	Suspd.		13.50	29-49
1985 Miniature Clown 12238D	Suspd.		13.50	21-49
1985 It is Better to Give than to Receive 12297	Suspd.		19.00	95-178
1985 Love Never Fails 12300	Retrd.	2000	25.00	34-70
1985 God Bless Our Home 12319	Retrd.	1998	40.00	48-69
1986 You Can Fly 12335	Suspd.		25.00	52-60
1985 Jesus is Coming Soon 12343	Suspd.		22.50	34-45
1985 Halo, and Merry Christmas 12351	Suspd.		40.00	114-170
1985 May Your Christmas Be Delightful 15482	Suspd.		25.00	33-55
1985 Honk if You Love Jesus 15490	Open		13.00	18-30
1985 Baby's First Christmas 15539	Yr.Iss.	1985	13.00	23-38
1985 Baby's First Christmas 15547	Yr.Iss.	1985	13.00	18-38
1985 God Sent His Love 15881	Yr.Iss.	1985	17.00	24-45
1985 God Bless You With Rainbows 16020	Suspd.		57.50	115
1986 To My Favorite Paw 100021	Suspd.		22.50	33-50
1987 To My Deer Friend 100048	Open		33.00	42-70
1986 Sending My Love 100056	Suspd.		22.50	36-51
1986 O Worship the Lord 100064	Open		24.00	34-55
1986 To My Forever Friend 100072	Open		33.00	46-70
1987 He's The Healer Of Broken Hearts 100080	Retrd.	1999	33.00	42-62
1987 Make Me A Blessing 100102	Retrd.	1990	35.00	43-82
1986 Lord I'm Coming Home 100110	Open		22.50	30-50
1986 Lord, Keep Me On My Toes 100129	Retrd.	1988	22.50	56-85
1986 The Joy of the Lord is My Strength 100137	Open		35.00	46-125
1986 God Bless the Day We Found You 100145	Suspd.		37.50	62-120
1995 God Bless the Day We Found You (Girl) 100145R	Open		60.00	51-60
1986 God Bless the Day We Found You 100153	Suspd.		37.50	55-115
1995 God Bless the Day We Found You (Boy) 100153R	Open		60.00	51-60
1986 Serving the Lord 100161	Suspd.		19.00	46-82
1986 I'm a Possibility 100188	Retrd.	1993	21.00	44-68
1987 The Spirit Is Willing But The Flesh Is Weak 100196	Retrd.	1991	19.00	35-85
1987 The Lord Giveth & the Lord Taketh Away 100226	Retrd.	1995	33.50	50-85
1986 Friends Never Drift Apart 100250	Retrd.	2000	35.00	49-65
1986 Help, Lord, I'm In a Spot 100269	Retrd.	1989	18.50	47-60
1986 He Cleansed My Soul 100277	Open		24.00	34-50
1986 Serving the Lord 100293	Suspd.		19.00	26-62
1987 Scent From Above 100528	Retrd.	1991	19.00	48-64
1987 I Picked A Very Special Mom 100536	Yr.Iss.	1987	40.00	50-75
1986 Brotherly Love 100544	Suspd.		37.00	65-78
1987 No Tears Past The Gate 101826	Open		40.00	59-95
1987 Smile Along The Way 101842	Retrd.	1991	30.00	131-150
1987 Lord, Help Us Keep Our Act Together 101850	Retrd.	1991	35.00	82-148
1986 O Worship the Lord 102229	Open		24.00	34-40
1986 Shepherd of Love 102261	Open		10.00	15-32
1986 Three Mini Animals 102296	Suspd.		13.50	21-25
1986 Wishing You a Cozy Christmas 102342	Yr.Iss.	1986	17.00	30-48
1986 Love Rescued Me 102393	Retrd.	1999	21.00	32-40

*Quotes have been rounded up to nearest dollar

FIGURINES

Precious Moments/Enesco Group, Inc. to Precious Moments/Enesco Group, Inc.

YEAR ISSUE	EDITION LIMIT	YEAR RETD.	ISSUE PRICE	*QUOTE U.S.$
1986 Angel of Mercy 102482	Open		19.00	26-33
1986 Sharing our Christmas Together 102490	Suspd.		35.00	60-80
1987 We Are All Precious In His Sight 102903	Yr.Iss.	1987	30.00	60-80
1986 God Bless America 102938	Yr.Iss.	1986	30.00	35-91
1986 It's the Birthday of a King 102962	Suspd.		18.50	32-57
1987 I Would Be Sunk Without You 102970	Open		15.00	16-28
1986 We Belong To The Lord 103004	Retrd.	1986	50.00	169-200
1987 My Love Will Never Let You Go 103497	Open		25.00	34-42
1986 I Believe in the Old Rugged Cross 103632	Open		25.00	30-55
1986 Come Let Us Adore Him 104000 (9 pc. set w/cassette)	Open		95.00	110-140
1987 With this Ring I... 104019	Open		40.00	55-80
1987 Love Is The Glue That Mends 104027	Suspd.		33.50	49-68
1987 Cheers To The Leader 104035	Retrd.	1997	22.50	28-75
1987 Happy Days Are Here Again 104396	Suspd.		25.00	47-82
1986 Come Let Us Adore Him 9 pc. 104523	Suspd.		350.00	350-550
1987 A Tub Full of Love 104817	Suspd.		22.50	23-35
1987 Sitting Pretty 104825	Suspd.		22.50	42-68
1987 Have I Got News For You 105635	Suspd.		22.50	39-52
1988 Something's Missing When You're Not Around 105643	Suspd.		32.50	50
1987 To Tell The Tooth You're Special 105813	Suspd.		38.50	140-275
1988 Hallelujah Country 105821	Retrd.	2000	35.00	38-163
1987 We're Pulling For You 106151	Suspd.		40.00	46-55
1987 God Bless You Graduate 106194	Open		20.00	30-55
1987 Congratulations Princess 106208	Open		20.00	30-65
1987 Lord Help Me Make the Grade 106216	Suspd.		25.00	43-50
1988 Heaven Bless Your Togetherness 106755	Retrd.	1999	65.00	77-100
1988 Precious Memories 106763	Open		37.50	45-75
1988 Puppy Love Is From Above 106798	Retrd.	1995	45.00	45-70
1988 Happy Birthday Poppy 106836	Suspd.		27.50	33-72
1988 Sew In Love 106844	Retrd.	1997	45.00	52-110
1987 They Followed The Star 108243	Open		75.00	96-144
1987 The Greatest Gift Is A Friend 109231	Retrd.	1999	30.00	33-55
1988 Believe the Impossible 109487	Suspd.		35.00	36-88
1988 Happiness Divine 109584	Retrd.	1992	25.00	33-82
1987 Wishing You A Yummy Christmas 109754	Suspd.		35.00	42-75
1987 We Gather Together To Ask The Lord's Blessing 109762	Retrd.	1995	130.00	250-345
1988 Meowie Christmas 109800	Retrd.	2000	30.00	30-53
1987 Oh What Fun It Is To Ride 109819	Retrd.	1998	85.00	92-110
1988 Wishing You A Happy Easter 109886	Retrd.	1999	23.00	30-35
1988 Wishing You A Basket Full Of Blessings 109924	Retrd.	1999	23.00	30-35
1988 Sending You My Love 109967	Open		35.00	38-45
1988 Mommy, I Love You 109975	Open		22.50	26-30
1987 Love Is The Best Gift of All 110930	Yr.Iss.	1987	22.50	30-42
1988 Faith Takes The Plunge 111155	Suspd.		27.50	28-38
1988 Tis the Season 111163	Suspd.		27.50	30-80
1987 O Come Let Us Adore Him (4 pc. 9" Nativity) 111333	Suspd.		200.00	176-220
1988 Mommy, I Love You 112143	Open		22.50	26-45
1987 A Tub Full of Love 112313	Open		22.50	28-33
1988 This Too Shall Pass 114014	Retrd.	1999	23.00	23-38
1988 Some Bunny's Sleeping 115274	Suspd.		15.00	16-23
1988 Our First Christmas Together 115290	Suspd.		50.00	66-70
1988 Time to Wish You a Merry Christmas 115339	Yr.Iss.	1988	24.00	24-42
1995 Love Blooms Eternal 127019 (1st in dated cross series)	Yr.Iss.	1995	35.00	30-60
2000 He Shall Lead The Children Into the 21st Century (Millennium Event) 127930A	Open		160.00	160
2000 He Shall Lead The Children Into the 21st Century (Millennium Event) 127930	Open		160.00	160
1995 Dreams Really Do Come True 128309	Open		37.50	40
1995 Another Year More Grey Hares 128686	Open		17.50	17-19
1995 Happy Hula Days 128694	Open		30.00	26-35
1995 I Give You My Love Forever True 129100	Open		70.00	59-85
1997 Love Letters in The Sand 129488	Open		35.00	30-35
2000 He Is My Salvation (Salvation Army) 135984	Yr.Iss.		45.00	45
1995 Love Makes The World Go 'Round 139475	15,000		200.00	360-438
1995 He Covers the Earth With His Beauty 142654	Yr.Iss.	1995	30.00	26-30
1995 Come Let Us Adore Him 142735-Large Nativity	Open		50.00	50-55
1995 Come Let Us Adore Him 142743-Small Nativity	Open		35.00	35
1995 Making A Trail to Bethlehem 142751	Retrd.	1998	30.00	25-35
1995 I'll Give Him My Heart 150088	Retrd.	1998	40.00	32-45
1995 Soot Yourself To A Merry Christmas 150096	Retrd.	1999	35.00	30-37
1995 Making Spirits Bright 150118	Retrd.	1998	37.50	28-38
1998 Even The Heavens Shall Praise Him 150312	15,000		125.00	125
1999 Blessed Are They With A Caring Heart (Century Circle) 163724	Open		55.00	55
1996 Standing In The Presence Of The Lord 163732 (2nd in dated cross series)	Yr.Iss.	1996	37.50	32-60
1996 Take It To The Lord In Prayer 163767	Open		30.00	26-30
1996 The Sun Is Always Shining Somewhere 163775	Retrd.	1999	37.50	33-40
1996 Sowing Seeds of Kindness 163856 (1st in Growing In God's Garden Of Love Series)	Open		37.50	33-38
1996 It May Be Greener, But It's Just As Hard to Cut 163899	Open		37.50	33-38
1996 God's Love Is Reflected In You 175277	15,000		150.00	163-267
1996 Some Plant, Some Water, But God Giveth The Increase 176958 (2nd in Growing In God's Garden Of Love Series)	Open		37.50	34-40
1996 Peace On Earth...Anyway 183342	Yr.Iss.	1996	32.50	28-50
1996 Angels On Earth-Boy Making Snow Angel 183776	Open		40.00	38-45
1996 Snowbunny Loves You Like I Do 183792	Open		18.50	17-19
1997 The Most Precious Gift of All 183814	Open		37.50	40-46
1996 Sing In Excelsis Deo Tree Topper 183830	Retrd.	1999	125.00	125
1997 You're Just Too Sweet To Be Scary 183849	Open		55.00	55
1996 Color Your World With Thanksgiving 183857	Retrd.	1998	50.00	42-65
1996 Shepard/Standing White Lamb/Sitting Black Lamb 3pc. Nativity set 183954	Open		40.00	33-40
1997 Shepard with Lambs 3pc. Nativity set 183962	Open		40.00	34-40
1996 Making a Trail to Bethlehem-Mini Nativity 184004	Open		18.50	17-19
1996 All Sing His Praises-Large Nativity 184012	Open		32.50	29-42
1996 Love Makes The World Go 'Round 184209	Yr.Iss.	1996	22.50	42
1997 A Bouquet From God's Garden Of Love 184268 (3rd in God's Garden of Love series)	Open		37.50	40
1997 You're A Life Saver To Me 204854	Retrd.	2000	35.00	30-35
1996 Shepherd with Sheep-Mini Nativity 2-pc. 213616	Open		22.50	23
1996 Wee Three Kings-Mini Nativity set 213624	Open		55.00	47-55
1997 Lead Me To Calvary 260916 (3rd in dated cross series)	Yr.Iss.	1997	37.50	33-40
1997 Friends From The Very Beginning 261068	Retrd.	2000	50.00	45-55
1997 You Have Touched So Many Hearts 261084	Open		37.50	40
1997 Lettuce Pray 261122	Retrd.	1999	17.50	12-18
1997 Have You Any Room For Jesus 261130	Open		35.00	30-35
1997 Say I Do 261149	Open		35.00	48-60
1997 We All Have Our Bad Hair Days 261157	Open		35.00	35
1997 The Lord Is the Hope Of Our Future 261564	Open		40.00	34-40
2000 The Lord Is the Hope Of Our Future 261564B	Open		42.00	42
2000 The Lord Is the Hope Of Our Future 261564G	Open		42.00	42
1998 In God's Beautiful Garden Of Love 261629	15,000		150.00	150-197
1997 Happy Birthday Jesus 272523	Open		35.00	30-35
1997 Sharing The Light of Love 272531	Open		35.00	30-35
1997 I Think You're Just Divine 272558	Open		40.00	34-40
1997 Nativity Enhancement Set 4pc. 272582	Open		60.00	51-60
1997 I'm Dreaming Of A White Christmas 272590	Open		25.00	22-25
1997 Cane You Join Us For A Merry Christmas 272671	Open		30.00	26-30
1997 And You Shall See a Star-Large Nativity 272787	Open		32.50	33
1998 My Love Will Keep You Warm 272957	Open		37.50	33-38
1997 Animal Additions-Mini Nativity 3-pc. 279323	Open		30.00	30
1997 Lighted Inn-Large Nativity 283428	Open		100.00	80-100
1997 Mini- Nativity Wall 283436	Open		40.00	34-40
1997 For An Angel You're So Down To Earth-Mini Nativity 283444	Open		17.50	18
1997 For An Angel You're So Down To Earth-Mini Nativity 283444	Open		17.50	18
1997 For An Angel You're So Down To Earth-Mini Nativity 283444	Open		17.50	18
1997 For An Angel You're So Down To Earth-Mini Nativity 283444	Open		17.50	18
1997 Cats With Kittens Mini-Nativity 291293	Open		18.50	17-19
1997 Wishing Well 292753	Open		30.00	26-30
1998 He Shall Cover You With His Wings 306935	Yr.Iss.	1998	37.50	38
1998 For The Sweetest Tu-Lips In Town 306959	Open		30.00	27-33
1998 You Are Always On My Mind 306967	Retrd.	2000	37.50	34-40
1998 Missum You 306991	Open		45.00	38-50
1997 Charity Begins In The Heart 307009	Retrd.	1998	50.00	40-60
2000 Wait Patiently On The Lord 325279	Open		30.00	30
1998 Only One Life To Offer 325309	Open		35.00	33-35
1998 The Good Lord Will Always Uphold Us 325325	Open		50.00	42-50
2000 By Grace We Have Communion With God 325333C	Open		75.00	75
1998 There Are Two Sides To Every Story 325368	Open		15.00	15
1999 Mom, You're My Special-Tea 325473	Retrd.	1999	25.00	25
1998 Marvelous Grace 325503	Yr.Iss.	1998	50.00	50-60
1998 Well, Blow Me Down It's Yer Birthday 325538	Open		50.00	42-50
1998 I'm Sending You a Merry Christmas 455601	Yr.Iss.	1998	30.00	26-30
1998 Mornin' Pumpkin 455687	Retrd.	1999	45.00	37-45
1998 Praise God From Whom All Blessings Flow 455695	Open		40.00	33-40
1998 Praise The Lord And Dosie-Do 455733	Open		50.00	41-50
1998 Peas On Earth 455768	Open		32.50	35
1998 Alaska Once More, How's Yer Christmas? 455784	Open		35.00	35
1998 You Can Always Fudge A Little During the Season 455792	Open		35.00	35
2000 Wishing You An Old Fashioned Christmas 455806	Open		45.00	45
1998 Wishing You A Yummy Christmas 455814	Open		30.00	26-30
1998 I Saw Mommy Kissing Santa Claus 455822	Open		65.00	53-65
1999 Warmest Wishes For The Holidays 455830	Open		50.00	50
1998 Time For A Holy Holiday 455849	Open		35.00	29-35
1998 Have A Cozy Country Christmas 455873	Open		50.00	41-50
1998 Friends Are Forever, Sew Bee It 455903	Open		60.00	50-60
1998 I Now Pronounce You Man And Wife 455938	Open		30.00	26-30
1998 The Light Of The World Is Jesus-Large Nativity 455954	Open		30.00	30
1998 Hang On To That Holiday Feeling-Mini Nativity 455962	Open		17.50	15-18
1999 Sharing Our Time Is So Precious (Century Circle) 456349	Open		110.00	110
1999 My Universe Is You 487902	Retrd.	1999	45.00	37-45
1999 Believe It Or Knot I Luv You 487910	Open		35.00	35
1999 You're My Honey Bee 487929	Open		20.00	17-20
1999 Jesus Is My Lighthouse (January Show) 487945	Open		75.00	64-75
1999 You Can Always Count On Me 487953	Open		35.00	29-35
1999 What Better To Give Than Yourself 487988	Open		30.00	25-30
1999 Mom, You've Given Me So Much 488046	Open		35.00	29-35
1999 You Just Can't Replace A Good Friendship 488054	Open		35.00	35
2000 He'll Carry Me Through 488089	Open		45.00	45
1999 Confirmed In The Lord 488178	Open		30.00	25-30
1999 A Very Special Bond 488240	Open		70.00	70
2000 You'll Always Be Daddy's Little Girl 488224	Open		50.00	50
1998 Victorian Girlw/Umbrella (1998 Summer Show Exclusive) 488259	Yr.Iss.	1998	70.00	58-70
1999 You Can't Take It With You 488321	Open		25.00	21-25
1999 Always Listen To Your Heart 488356	Open		25.00	21-25
1999 You Count 488372	Open		25.00	21-25
1999 You Always Stand Behind Me 492140	Open		50.00	41-50
2000 Have Faith in God 505153	Open		50.00	50
1988 Rejoice O Earth 520268	Open		13.00	19-30
1988 Jesus the Savior Is Born 520357	Suspd.		25.00	36-65
1992 The Lord Turned My Life Around 520535	Suspd.		35.00	25-50
1991 In The Spotlight Of His Grace 520543	Suspd.		35.00	33-40
1990 Lord, Turn My Life Around 520551	Suspd.		35.00	24-75
1992 You Deserve An Ovation 520578	Open		35.00	33-38
1989 My Heart Is Exposed With Love 520624	Retrd.	1999	45.00	42-78
1989 A Friend Is Someone Who Cares 520632	Retrd.	1995	30.00	44-100
1989 I'm So Glad You Fluttered Into My Life 520640	Retrd.	1991	40.00	149-395
1989 Eggspecially For You 520667	Retrd.	1999	45.00	38-65
1989 Puppy Love 520764	Retrd.	1999	12.50	14-24
1989 Your Love Is So Uplifting 520675	Retrd.	1998	60.00	57-75
1989 Sending You Showers Of Blessings 520683	Retrd.	1992	32.50	45-85
1989 Just A Line To Wish You A Happy Day 520721	Suspd.		65.00	45-125
1989 Friendship Hits The Spot 520748	Retrd.	2000	55.00	59-90
1989 Jesus Is The Only Way 520756	Suspd.		40.00	42-75
1989 Many Moons In Same Canoe, Blessum You 520772	Retrd.	1990	50.00	200-361
1989 Wishing You Roads Of Happiness 520780	Open		60.00	64-93
1989 Someday My Love 520799	Retrd.	1992	40.00	40-88
1989 My Days Are Blue Without You 520802	Suspd.		65.00	71-100
1989 We Need A Good Friend Through The Ruff Times 520810	Suspd.		35.00	40-45
1989 You Are My Number One 520829	Suspd.		25.00	30-35
1989 The Lord Is Your Light To Happiness 520837	Open		50.00	52-72
1989 Wishing You A Perfect Choice 520845	Open		55.00	56-70
1989 I Belong To The Lord 520853	Suspd.		25.00	27-48
1990 Heaven Bless You 520934	Open		35.00	30-42
1993 There Is No Greater Treasure Than To Have A Friend Like You 521000	Retrd.	1998	30.00	26-40
1990 That's What Friends Are For 521183	Open		45.00	42-62
1997 Lord, Spare Me 521191	Open		37.50	34-58
1990 Hope You're Up And OnThe Trail Again 521205	Suspd.		35.00	30-65
1993 The Fruit of the Spirit is Love 521213	Retrd.	1999	30.00	28-35

*Quotes have been rounded up to nearest dollar

Precious Moments/Enesco Group, Inc.
to Precious Moments/Enesco Group, Inc.

FIGURINES

YEAR ISSUE	EDITION LIMIT	YEAR RETD.	ISSUE PRICE	*QUOTE U.S.$
1996 Enter His Court With Thanksgiving 521221	Open		35.00	30-40
1991 Take Heed When You Stand 521272	Suspd.		55.00	51-65
1990 Happy Trip 521280	Suspd.		35.00	33-80
1991 Hug One Another 521299	Retrd.	1995	45.00	42-100
1990 Yield Not To Temptation 521310	Suspd.		27.50	30-55
1998 Heaven Must Have Sent You 521388	Open		60.00	65
1990 Faith Is A Victory 521396	Retrd.	1993	25.00	25-160
1990 I'll Never Stop Loving You 521418	Retrd.	1996	37.50	40-100
1991 To A Very Special Mom & Dad 521434	Suspd.		35.00	30-50
1990 Lord, Help Me Stick To My Job 521450	Retrd.	1997	30.00	28-85
1989 Tell It To Jesus 521477	Open		35.00	34-78
1991 There's A Light At The End Of The Tunnel 521485	Suspd.		55.00	35-85
1991 A Special Delivery 521493	Open		30.00	28-38
1998 Water-Melancholy Day Without You 521515	Open		35.00	30-35
1991 Thumb-body Loves You 521698	Suspd.		55.00	51-100
1996 My Love Blooms For You 521728	Open		50.00	42-55
1990 Sweep All Your Worries Away 521779	Retrd.	1996	40.00	34-150
1990 Good Friends Are Forever 521817	Open		50.00	46-70
1990 Love Is From Above 521841	Suspd.		45.00	42-100
1989 The Greatest of These Is Love 521868	Suspd.		27.50	34-39
1997 Pizza On Earth 521884	Open		55.00	46-55
1990 Easter's On Its Way 521892	Retrd.	1999	60.00	55-85
1991 Hoppy Easter Friend 521906	Retrd.	1999	40.00	34-40
1994 Perfect Harmony 521914	Retrd.	1999	55.00	46-55
1993 Safe In The Arms Of Jesus 521922	Open		30.00	30-35
1989 Wishing You A Cozy Season 521949	Suspd.		42.50	38-57
1990 High Hopes 521957	Suspd.		30.00	30-55
1991 To A Special Mum 521965	Retrd.	1999	30.00	28-45
1999 Caught Up In Sweet Thoughts Of You 521973	Open		30.00	25-30
1996 Marching To The Beat of Freedom's Drum 521981	Open		35.00	30-35
1993 To The Apple Of God's Eye 522015	Retrd.	1999	32.50	27-35
1989 May Your Life Be Blessed With Touchdowns 522023	Retrd.	1998	45.00	40-60
1989 Thank You Lord For Everything 522031	Suspd.		55.00	48-95
1994 Now I Lay Me Down To Sleep 522058	Retrd.	1997	30.00	28-70
1991 May Your World Be Trimmed With Joy 522082	Suspd.		55.00	35-95
1990 There Shall Be Showers Of Blessings 522090	Retrd.	1999	60.00	49-80
1992 It's No Yolk When I Say I Love You 522104	Suspd.		60.00	65-81
1989 Don't Let the Holidays Get You Down 522112	Retrd.	1993	42.50	60-100
1989 Wishing You A Very Successful Season 522120	Retrd.	1999	60.00	60-70
1989 Bon Voyage! 522201	Suspd.		75.00	110-157
1989 He Is The Star Of The Morning 522252	Suspd.		55.00	60-88
1989 To Be With You Is Uplifting 522260	Retrd.	1994	20.00	20-60
1991 A Reflection Of His Love 522279	Retrd.	1999	50.00	41-50
1990 Thinking Of You Is What I Really Like To Do 522287	Suspd.		30.00	28-40
1989 Merry Christmas Deer 522317	Retrd.	1997	50.00	41-120
1996 Sweeter As The Years Go By 522333	Retrd.	1998	60.00	60-70
1989 Oh Holy Night 522546	Yr.Iss.	1989	25.00	28-45
1995 Just A Line To Say You're Special 522864	Retrd.	1999	50.00	42-60
1997 On My Way To A Perfect Day 522872	Open		45.00	38-45
1989 Isn't He Precious 522988	Suspd.		15.00	19-27
1990 Some Bunny's Sleeping 522996	Suspd.		12.00	27
1989 Jesus Is The Sweetest Name I Know 523097	Suspd.		22.50	30-40
1991 Joy On Arrival 523178	Open		50.00	46-60
1990 The Good Lord Always Delivers 523453	Open		27.50	30
1990 This Day Has Been Made In Heaven 523496	Open		30.00	30-42
1990 God Is Love Dear Valentine 523518	Retrd.	1999	27.50	23-30
1991 I Will Cherish The Old Rugged Cross 523534	Yr.Iss.	1991	27.50	24-39
1992 You Are The Type I Love 523542	Open		40.00	38-50
1993 The Lord Will Provide 523593	Yr.Iss.	1993	40.00	40-75
1991 Good News Is So Uplifting 523615	Retrd.	1999	60.00	59-70
1992 I'm So Glad That God Has Blessed Me With A Friend Like You 523623	Retrd.	1995	50.00	50-135
1994 I Will Always Be Thinking Of You 523631	Retrd.	1996	45.00	43-90
1990 Time Heals 523739	Retrd.	2000	37.50	34-40
1990 Blessings From Above 523747	Retrd.	1994	45.00	63-72
1994 Just Poppin' In To Say Halo 523755	Retrd.	1999	45.00	38-45
1991 I Can't Spell Success Without You 523763	Suspd.		40.00	44-150
1990 Once Upon A Holy Night 523836	Yr.Iss.	1990	25.00	27-45
1996 Love Never Leaves A Mother's Arms 523941	Open		40.00	40
1992 My Warmest Thoughts Are You 524085	Retrd.	1996	55.00	51-95
1991 Good Friends Are For Always 524123	Retrd.	1999	27.50	28-40
1994 Lord Teach Us to Pray 524158	Yr.Iss.	1994	35.00	30-40
1991 May Your Christmas Be Merry 524166	Yr.Iss.	1991	27.50	20-35
1995 Walk In The Sonshine 524212	Open		35.00	30-37
1991 He Loves Me 524263	Yr.Iss.	1991	35.00	30-50
1992 Friendship Grows When You Plant A Seed 524271	Retrd.	1994	40.00	78-120
1993 May Your Every Wish Come True 524298	Open		50.00	42-50
1991 May Your Birthday Be A Blessing 524301	Open		30.00	30-35
1992 Our Friendship Is Soda-Licious 524336	Retrd.	1999	70.00	70
1992 What The World Needs Now 524352	Retrd.	1997	50.00	42-100
1997 Something Precious From Above 524360	Open		50.00	45-55
1993 You Are Such A Purr-fect Friend 524395	Open		35.00	30-53
1991 May Only Good Things Come Your Way 524425	Retrd.	1998	30.00	33-48
1993 Sealed With A Kiss 524441	Retrd.	1996	50.00	45-100
1993 A Special Chime For Jesus 524468	Retrd.	1997	32.50	27-70
1994 God Cared Enough To Send His Best 524476	Retrd.	1996	50.00	42-125
1990 Happy Birthday Dear Jesus 524875	Suspd.		13.50	12-20
1992 It's So Uplifting To Have A Friend Like You 524905	Retrd.	1999	40.00	38-45
1990 We're Going To Miss You 524913	Open		50.00	48-69
1991 Angels We Have Heard On High 524921	Retrd.	1996	60.00	60-70
1992 Tubby's First Christmas 525278	Retrd.	1999	10.00	10-15
1991 It's A Perfect Boy 525286	Retrd.	1999	16.50	19-28
1993 May Your Future Be Blessed 525316	Open		35.00	34-40
1992 Ring Those Christmas Bells 525898	Retrd.	1996	95.00	111-138
1998 Let's Put The Pieces Together 525928	Open		60.00	51-60
1992 Going Home 525979	Open		60.00	60
1996 A Prince Of A Guy 526037	Retrd.	2000	35.00	24-35
1996 Pretty As A Princess 526053	Open		35.00	30-40
1998 The Pearl Of A Great Price 526061	Open		50.00	50-65
2000 I'm Completely Suspended With Love 526096	Open		28.50	29
1992 I Would Be Lost Without You 526142	Retrd.	1999	27.50	21-100
1993 Friends To The Very End 526150	Retrd.	1997	45.00	45-53
1992 You Are My Happiness 526185	Yr.Iss.	1992	37.50	45-85
1994 You Suit Me to a Tee 526193	Retrd.	1999	35.00	30-36
1994 Sharing Sweet Moments Together 526487	Retrd.	1999	45.00	45-62
1996 The Lord Is With You 526835	Retrd.	1999	27.50	24-28
1991 We Have Come From Afar 526959	Suspd.		17.50	16-25
1993 Bless-Um You 527335	Retrd.	1998	35.00	30-40
1992 You Are My Favorite Star 527378	Retrd.	1997	55.00	66-90
1992 Bring The Little Ones To Jesus 527556	Open		90.00	77-90
1992 God Bless The U.S.A. 527564	Yr.Iss.	1992	32.50	28-42
1993 Tied Up For The Holidays 527580	Suspd.		40.00	34-75
1993 Bringing You A Merry Christmas 527599	Retrd.	1995	45.00	60-77
1992 Wishing You A Ho Ho Ho 527629	Open		40.00	45-50
2000 Waiting For A Merry Christmas (April Shows) 527637	Retrd.	2000	65.00	65
1991 You Have Touched So Many Hearts w/personalization kit 527661	Suspd.		37.50	33-44
1992 But The Greatest of These Is Love 527688	Yr.Iss.	1992	27.50	28-35
1992 Wishing You A Comfy Christmas 527750	Retrd.	1999	30.00	30-35
1993 I Only Have Arms For You 527769	Retrd.	1998	15.00	14-25
1992 This Land Is Our Land 527777	Yr.Iss.	1992	35.00	26-70
1994 Nativity Cart 528072	Open		16.00	19
1999 He Came As The Gift Of God's Love 528129	Open		30.00	30
1994 Have I Got News For You 528137	Retrd.	1999	16.00	14-19
1994 To a Very Special Sister 528633	Open		60.00	52-65
1993 America You're Beautiful 528862	Yr.Iss.	1993	35.00	33-100
1996 My True Love Gave To Me 529273	Open		40.00	34-40
1993 Happiness Is At Our Fingertips (Spring Catalog) 529931	Open		35.00	35-47
1993 Ring Out The Good News 529966	Retrd.	1997	27.50	26-80
1999 Wishes For The World (Millennium Event) 530018	Open		35.00	35
1993 Wishing You the Sweetest Christmas 530166	Yr.Iss.	1993	27.50	30-45
1994 You're As Pretty As A Christmas Tree 530425	Yr.Iss.	1994	27.50	24-40
1994 Serenity Prayer Girl 530697	Open		35.00	33-38
1994 Serenity Prayer Boy 530700	Open		35.00	33-40
1995 We Have Come From Afar 530913	Open		12.00	11-15
1995 I Only Have Ice For You 530956	Retrd.	1999	27.50	40-100
1997 Sometimes You're Next To Impossible 530964	Open		50.00	50
1998 My World's Upside Down Without You 531014	Open		15.00	15
1997 Potty Time 531022	Open		25.00	22-25
1998 You Are My Once In A Lifetime 531030	Retrd.	2000	45.00	45
1995 What The World Needs Is Love 531065	Retrd.	1999	45.00	38-53
1994 Money's Not The Only Green Thing Worth Saving 531073	Retrd.	1996	50.00	42-64
1996 What A Difference You've Made In My Life 531138	Open		50.00	42-55
1995 Vaya Con Dios (To Go With God) 531146	Open		32.50	30-40
1995 Bless Your Soul 531162	Open		25.00	24-42
1997 Who's Gonna Fill You're Shoes 531634	Open		37.50	38-42
1996 You Deserve a Halo—Thank You 531693	Retrd.	1998	55.00	46-60
1994 The Lord is Counting on You 531707	Open		32.50	30-35
1994 Sharing Our Christmas Together 531944	Open		35.00	30-35
1994 Dropping In For The Holidays 531952	Retrd.	1998	40.00	40-45
1999 Lord Speak To Me 531987	Open		45.00	37-45
1995 Hallelujah For The Cross 532002	Retrd.	1999	35.00	30-37
1995 Sending You Oceans Of Love 532010	Retrd.	1996	35.00	33-75
1995 I Can't Bear To Let You Go 532037	Retrd.	1999	50.00	35-58
1998 Who's Gonna Fill Your Shoes 532061	Open		37.50	40
1995 Lord Help Me To Stay On Course 532096	Open		35.00	35-59
1994 The Lord Bless You and Keep You 532118	Open		40.00	42-50
1994 The Lord Bless You and Keep You 532126	Open		30.00	30-35
1994 The Lord Bless You and Keep You 532134	Open		30.00	30-35
1994 Luke 2:10 11 532916	Retrd.	1999	35.00	25-38
1999 Lord, Police Protect Us 539953	Open		45.00	36-45
1999 Sharing Our Winter Wonderland 539988	Open		75.00	75
1991 May Your World Be Trimmed... 552082	Suspd.		55.00	55-68
1999 Slide Into The Next Millenium With Joy 587761	Open		35.00	35
1999 Witch Way Do You Spell Love? 587869	Open		25.00	20-25
1999 May Your Seasons Be Jelly And Bright 587885	Open		37.50	30-38
1999 My Life Is A Vacuum Without You 587907	Open		37.50	30-38
1999 RV Haven' Fun Or What 587915	Open		45.00	36-45
1999 Thank You Sew Much 587923	Open		25.00	20-25
1999 Behold The Lamb of God 588164	Open		45.00	36-45
1994 Nothing Can Dampen The Spirit of Caring 603864	Open		35.00	30-35
1997 May Your Christmas Be Delightful 604135	Open		40.00	34-40
1995 A Poppy For You 604208	Suspd.		35.00	25-45
2000 Life's Beary Precious With You 642673	Open		25.00	25
2000 My Heart's Cut Out To Be Yours 650013	Open		40.00	40
1999 I Will Love You Always 679701S	Retrd.	2000	26.00	26
2000 Life Is Worth Fighting For 680982 (NABCO)	Open		30.00	30
2000 God Gives Us Memories So That We Might Have Roses In December (Compassionate Friends) 680990	Open		45.00	45
2000 Precious Moments Will Last Forever (Gene Freedman World Tour) 681008	Open		35.00	35
2000 Let Freedom Ring 681059E	Open		45.00	45
1999 A Love Like No Other 681075	Open		45.00	45
1999 Alleluia, He Is Risen 692409	Open		30.00	30
2000 The Future Is In Our Hands 730068	Yr.Iss.		30.00	30
2000 We're A Family That Sticks Together (Spring Fling) 730114	Retrd.	2000	40.00	40
2000 There's Sno-boredom With You 730122	Open		45.00	45
2000 Raisin' Cane On The Holidays 730130	Open		35.00	35
2000 Home Made of Love 730211	Open		45.00	45
2000 The Fun Is Being Together (Century Circle Exclusive) 730262	Open		200.00	200
2000 Squeaky Clean (Century Circle Event) 731048	Open		45.00	45
2000 Take Thyme For Yourself 731064	Open		32.50	33
2000 I'll Never Let You Down 731065	Open		45.00	45
2000 Grandma I'll Never Outgrow You 731587	Open		25.00	25
2000 Grandpa I'll Never Outgrow You 731595	Open		25.00	25
2000 Fall Festival 732494	Open		150.00	150
2000 You Should Be As Proud As A Peacock-Congratulations 733008	Open		27.50	28
2000 You Have A Special Place In My Heart (June Show) 737534	Retrd.	2000	55.00	55
2000 Cradle Large Nativity 737607	Open		25.00	25
2000 Auntie, You Make Beauty Blossom 737623	Open		40.00	40
2000 To The Sweetest Girl In The Cast 742880	Open		35.00	35
2000 Collection of Precious Moments 745510	Open		27.00	27
2000 Eat Turkey 763225	Open		25.00	25
2000 You Are The Queen Of Hearts 795151	Yr.Iss.		50.00	50
2000 You Will Always Be Mine 795186	Open		45.00	45
2000 You Can't Hide From God 795194	Open		18.50	19
2000 The Lord Can Dew Anything 795208	Open		35.00	35
2000 It's A Banner Day-Congratulations 795259	Open		25.00	25
2000 You Are The Wind Beneath My Wings 795267	Open		35.00	35
2000 You're As Sweet As Apple Pie 795275	Open		35.00	35
2000 You're A Honey 795283	Open		32.50	33
2000 O' Fish-Aly Friends For A Lifetime 795305	Open		50.00	50
2000 Wishing You A Birthday Full of Surprises 795313	Open		40.00	40
2000 I Give You My Heart 801313C	Open		30.00	30
2000 A Winning Spirit Comes From Within (Special Olympics) 813044	Open		35.00	35
2000 I Will Make My Country Proud (Canadian Exclusive) 820423	Open		37.50	38

Anniversary Figurines - S. Butcher

YEAR ISSUE	EDITION LIMIT	YEAR RETD.	ISSUE PRICE	*QUOTE U.S.$
1984 God Blessed Our Years Together With So Much Love And Happiness E-2853	Open		35.00	42-66
1984 God Blessed Our Year Together With So Much Love And Happiness (1st) E-2854	Retrd.	2000	35.00	42-65

*Quotes have been rounded up to nearest dollar

FIGURINES

Precious Moments/Enesco Group, Inc.
to Precious Moments/Enesco Group, Inc.

YEAR ISSUE	EDITION LIMIT	YEAR RETD.	ISSUE PRICE	*QUOTE U.S.$
1984 God Blessed Our Years Together With So Much Love And Happiness (5th) E-2855	Suspd.		35.00	60-75
1984 God Blessed Our Years Together With So Much Love And Happiness (10th) E-2856	Suspd.		35.00	67-78
1984 God Blessed Our Years Together With So Much Love And Happiness (25th) E-2857	Open		35.00	42-65
1984 God Blessed Our Years Together With So Much Love And Happiness (40th) E-2859	Suspd.		35.00	42-80
1984 God Blessed Our Years Together With So Much Love And Happiness (50th) E-2860	Open		35.00	42-78
1994 I Still Do 530999	Open		30.00	26-50
1994 I Still Do 531006	Open		30.00	26-50

Baby Classics - S. Butcher

YEAR ISSUE	EDITION LIMIT	YEAR RETD.	ISSUE PRICE	*QUOTE U.S.$
1997 Good Friends Are Forever 272422	Open		30.00	26-30
1997 Make A Joyful Noise 272450	Open		30.00	26-30
1997 We Are God's Workmanship 272434	Open		25.00	22-25
1997 I Believe In Miracles 272469	Open		25.00	22-25
1997 God Loveth A Cheerful Giver 272477	Retrd.	1998	25.00	22-25
1997 Love Is Sharing 272493	Open		25.00	22-25
1997 You Have Touched So Many Hearts 272485	Open		25.00	22-25
1997 Love One Another 272507	Open		30.00	24-30
1998 Friendship Hits The Spot 306916	Open		30.00	30
1998 Loving You Dear Valentine 306932	Open		25.00	22-25
1998 He Cleansed My Soul 306940	Open		25.00	25

Baby's First - S. Butcher

YEAR ISSUE	EDITION LIMIT	YEAR RETD.	ISSUE PRICE	*QUOTE U.S.$
1984 Baby's First Step E-2840	Suspd.		35.00	60-105
1984 Baby's First Picture E-2841	Retrd.	1986	45.00	129-175
1985 Baby's First Haircut 12211	Suspd.		32.50	117-185
1986 Baby's First Trip 16012	Suspd.		32.50	195-240
1989 Baby's First Pet 520705	Suspd.		45.00	45-85
1990 Baby's First Meal 524077	Retrd.	1999	35.00	25-45
1992 Baby's First Word 527238	Retrd.	1999	24.00	21-35
1993 Baby's First Birthday 524069	Open		25.00	25-35

Birthday Club Figurines - S. Butcher

YEAR ISSUE	EDITION LIMIT	YEAR RETD.	ISSUE PRICE	*QUOTE U.S.$
1986 Fishing For Friends BC-861	Yr.Iss.	1986	10.00	94-130
1987 Hi Sugar BC-871	Yr.Iss.	1987	11.00	65-100
1988 Somebunny Cares BC-881	Yr.Iss.	1988	13.50	35-80
1989 Can't Bee Hive Myself Without You BC-891	Yr.Iss.	1989	13.50	35-55
1990 Collecting Makes Good Scents BC-901	Yr.Iss.	1990	15.00	29-35
1990 I'm Nuts Over My Collection BC-902	Yr.Iss.	1990	15.00	26-35
1991 Love Pacifies BC-911	Yr.Iss.	1991	15.00	24-36
1991 True Blue Friends BC-912	Yr.Iss.	1991	15.00	24-73
1992 Every Man's Home Is His Castle BC-921	Yr.Iss.	1992	16.50	14-30
1992 I Got You Under My Skin BC-922	Yr.Iss.	1992	16.00	30-35
1993 Put a Little Punch In Your Birthday BC-931	Yr.Iss.	1993	15.00	14-24
1993 Owl Always Be Your Friend BC-932	Yr.Iss.	1993	16.00	24-30
1994 God Bless Our Home BC-941	Yr.Iss.	1994	16.00	26-36
1994 Yer A Pel-I-Can Count On BC-942	Yr.Iss.	1994	16.00	17-26
1995 Making A Point To Say You're Special BC-951	Yr.Iss.	1995	15.00	21-32
1995 10 Wonderful Years Of Wishes BC-952	Yr.Iss.	1995	50.00	50-58
1996 There's A Spot In My Heart For You BC-961	Yr.Iss.	1996	15.00	15-30
1996 You're First In My Heart BC-962	Yr.Iss.	1996	15.00	19-28
1997 Hare's To The Birthday Club BC-971	Yr.Iss.	1997	16.00	16-20
1998 Holy Tweet BC-972	Yr.Iss.	1997	18.50	19-23
1998 Slide Into The Celebration BC-981	Yr.Iss.	1998	15.00	15-18

Birthday Club Inscribed Charter Membership Renewal Gift - S. Butcher

YEAR ISSUE	EDITION LIMIT	YEAR RETD.	ISSUE PRICE	*QUOTE U.S.$
1987 A Smile's the Cymbal of Joy B-0102	Yr.Iss.	1987	Unkn.	53-80
1988 The Sweetest Club Around B-0103	Yr.Iss.	1988	Unkn.	30-50
1989 Have A Beary Special Birthday B-0104	Yr.Iss.	1989	Unkn.	26-55
1990 Our Club Is A Tough Act To Follow B-0105	Yr.Iss.	1990	Unkn.	26-38
1991 Jest To Let You Know You're Tops B-0106	Yr.Iss.	1991	Unkn.	24-40
1992 All Aboard For Birthday Club Fun B-0107	Yr.Iss.	1992	Unkn.	25-35
1993 Happiness is Belonging B-0108	Yr.Iss.	1993	Unkn.	17-34
1994 Can't Get Enough of Our Club B-0109	Yr.Iss.	1994	Unkn.	19-25
1995 Hoppy Birthday B-0110	Yr.Iss.	1995	Unkn.	14-35
1996 Scootin' By Just To Say Hi! B-0111	Yr.Iss.	1996	Unkn.	21-32
1997 The Fun Starts Here B-0112	Yr.Iss.	1997	Unkn.	21-25

Birthday Club Welcome Gift - S. Butcher

YEAR ISSUE	EDITION LIMIT	YEAR RETD.	ISSUE PRICE	*QUOTE U.S.$
1986 Our Club Can't Be Beat B-0001	Yr.Iss.	1986	Unkn.	64-90
1987 A Smile's The Cymbal of Joy B-0002	Yr.Iss.	1987	Unkn.	44-70
1988 The Sweetest Club Around B-0003	Yr.Iss.	1988	Unkn.	32-50
1989 Have A Beary Special Birthday B-0004	Yr.Iss.	1989	Unkn.	21-35
1990 Our Club Is A Tough Act To Follow B-0005	Yr.Iss.	1990	Unkn.	25-35
1991 Jest To Let You Know You're Tops B-0006	Yr.Iss.	1991	Unkn.	20-32
1992 All Aboard For Birthday Club Fun B-0007	Yr.Iss.	1992	Unkn.	23-30
1993 Happiness Is Belonging B-0008	Yr.Iss.	1993	Unkn.	16-24
1994 Can't Get Enough of Our Club B-0009	Yr.Iss.	1994	Unkn.	16-25
1995 Hoppy Birthday B-0010	Yr.Iss.	1995	Unkn.	14-28
1996 Scootin' By Just To Say Hi! B-0011	Yr.Iss.	1996	Unkn.	16-28
1997 The Fun Starts Here B-0012	Closed	1998	Unkn.	16

Fun Club - S. Butcher

YEAR ISSUE	EDITION LIMIT	YEAR RETD.	ISSUE PRICE	*QUOTE U.S.$
1999 You Are My Mane Inspiration B-0014	Yr.Iss.	1999	Unkn.	18
1999 Chester BC-992	Yr.Iss.	1999	7.00	7
1999 Ewe Are So Special to Me (Buttercup) BC-993	Yr.Iss.	1999	15.00	15
2000 Hold On To The Moment FC003	Yr.Iss.		7.00	7
2000 Reed The Centipede FC001	Yr.Iss.		7.00	7
2000 Don't Fret, We'll Get You There Yet (Charter) F0012	Yr.Iss.		Gift	N/A
2000 Don't Fret, We'll Get You There Yet F0002	Yr.Iss.		Gift	N/A
2000 Ronnie The Rhino FC002	Yr.Iss.		25.00	25

Birthday Series - S. Butcher

YEAR ISSUE	EDITION LIMIT	YEAR RETD.	ISSUE PRICE	*QUOTE U.S.$
1988 Friends To The End 104418	Suspd.		15.00	17-32
1987 Showers Of Blessings 105945	Retrd.	1993	16.00	21-31
1987 Brighten Someone's Day 105953	Suspd.		12.50	15-34
1990 To My Favorite Fan 521043	Suspd.		16.00	16-43
1989 Hello World! 521175	Retrd.	1999	13.50	16-21
1993 Hope You're Over The Hump 521671	Suspd.		16.00	17-30
1990 Not A Creature Was Stirring 524484	Suspd.		17.00	17-25
1991 Can't Be Without You 524492	Retrd.	1999	16.00	18
1991 How Can I Ever Forget You 526924	Open		15.00	16-18
1992 Let's Be Friends 527270	Retrd.	1996	15.00	15-35
1992 Happy Birdie 527343	Suspd.		8.00	8-30
1993 Happy Birthday Jesus 530492	Retrd.	1999	20.00	16-25
1994 Oinky Birthday 524506	Retrd.	1999	13.50	14-18
1995 Wishing You A Happy Bear Hug 520659	Suspd.		27.50	24-45
1996 I Haven't Seen Much of You Lately 531057	Open		13.50	12-14
1997 From The First Time I Spotted You I Knew We'd Be Friends 260940	Retrd.	2000	18.50	18-55

Birthday Train Figurines - S. Butcher

YEAR ISSUE	EDITION LIMIT	YEAR RETD.	ISSUE PRICE	*QUOTE U.S.$
1985 Bless The Days Of Our Youth 16004	Open		15.00	20-48
1985 May Your Birthday Be Warm 15938	Open		10.00	14-15
1985 Happy Birthday Little Lamb 15946	Open		10.00	14-45
1985 God Bless You On Your Birthday 15962	Open		11.00	16-45
1985 Heaven Bless Your Special Day 15954	Open		11.00	16-38
1985 May Your Birthday Be Gigantic 15970	Open		12.50	18-30
1985 This Day Is Something To Roar About 15989	Open		13.50	20-25
1985 Keep Looking Up 15997	Open		13.50	20-42
1988 Wishing You Grr-eatness 109479	Open		18.50	19-32
1988 Isn't Eight Just Great 109460	Open		18.50	19-29
1998 May Your Christmas Be Warm 470279	Open		15.00	13-15
1991 Being Nine Is Just Divine 521833	Open		25.00	23-32
1991 May Your Birthday Be Mammoth 521825	Open		25.00	23-25
1999 Take Your Time It's Your Birthday 488003	Open		25.00	25
2000 Give A Grin & Let The Fun Begin 488011	Open		25.00	25
2000 You Mean The Moose To Me 488038	Open		25.00	25

Bless Those Who Serve Their Country - S. Butcher

YEAR ISSUE	EDITION LIMIT	YEAR RETD.	ISSUE PRICE	*QUOTE U.S.$
1991 Bless Those Who Serve Their Country (Navy) 526568	Suspd.		32.50	109-165
1991 Bless Those Who Serve Their Country (Army) 526576	Suspd.		32.50	38-82
1991 Bless Those Who Serve Their Country (Air Force) 526584	Suspd.		32.50	38-60
1991 Bless Those Who Serve Their Country (Girl Soldier) 527289	Suspd.		32.50	30-48
1991 Bless Those Who Serve Their Country (Soldier) 527297	Suspd.		32.50	30-45
1991 Bless Those Who Serve Their Country (Marine) 527521	Suspd.		32.50	37-94
1995 You Will Always Be Our Hero 136271	Yr.Iss.	1995	40.00	34-46

Boys & Girls Club - S. Butcher

YEAR ISSUE	EDITION LIMIT	YEAR RETD.	ISSUE PRICE	*QUOTE U.S.$
1996 Shoot For The Stars And You'll Never Strike Out 521701	Open		60.00	51-65
1997 He Is Our Shelter From The Storm 523550	Open		75.00	63-75
1998 Love Is Color Blind 524204	Open		60.00	50-60
1999 I Couldn't Make It Without You 635030	Open		60.00	60
2000 You Tug On My Heart Strings 795526	Open		60.00	60

Bridal Party - S. Butcher

YEAR ISSUE	EDITION LIMIT	YEAR RETD.	ISSUE PRICE	*QUOTE U.S.$
1984 Bridesmaid E-2831	Open		13.50	22-35
1985 Ringbearer E-2833	Open		11.00	17-23
1985 Flower Girl E-2835	Open		11.00	17-32
1984 Best Man E-2836	Open		13.50	22-35
1986 Groom E-2837	Open		13.50	24-38
1987 This is the Day That the Lord Hath Made E-2838	Yr.Iss.	1987	185.00	181-225
1985 Junior Bridesmaid E-2845	Open		12.50	20-23
1987 Bride E-2846	Open		18.00	24-30
1987 God Bless Our Family (Parents of the Groom) 100498	Retrd.	1999	35.00	42-50
1987 God Bless Our Family (Parents of the Bride) 100501	Retrd.	1999	35.00	42-50
1987 Wedding Arch 102369	Suspd.		22.50	26-40

Calendar Girl - S. Butcher

YEAR ISSUE	EDITION LIMIT	YEAR RETD.	ISSUE PRICE	*QUOTE U.S.$
1988 January 109983	Open		37.50	38-45
1988 February 109991	Open		27.50	33-50
1988 March 110019	Open		27.50	34-40
1988 April 110027	Open		30.00	34-110
1988 May 110035	Open		25.00	25-35
1988 June 110043	Open		40.00	55-62
1988 July 110051	Open		35.00	40-45
1988 August 110078	Open		40.00	40-55
1988 September 110086	Open		27.50	33-52
1988 October 110094	Open		35.00	35-52
1988 November 110108	Open		32.50	33-52
1988 December 110116	Open		27.50	30-45
1997 Garnet-Color of Boldness January 335533	Open		25.00	25
1997 Amethyst-Color of Faith February 335541	Open		25.00	25
1997 Aquamarine-Color of Kindness March 335568	Open		25.00	25
1997 Diamond-Color of Purity April 335576	Open		25.00	25
1997 Emerald-Color of Patience May 335584	Open		25.00	25
1997 Pearl-Color of Love June 335592	Open		25.00	25
1997 Ruby-Color of Joy July 335606	Open		25.00	25
1997 Peridot-Color of Pride August 335614	Open		25.00	25
1997 Sapphire-Color of Confidence September 335622	Open		25.00	25
1997 Opal-Color of Happiness October 335657	Open		25.00	25
1997 Topaz-Color of Truth November 335665	Open		25.00	25
1997 Turquoise-Color of Loyalty December 335673	Open		25.00	25

Care-A-Van Tour - S. Butcher

YEAR ISSUE	EDITION LIMIT	YEAR RETD.	ISSUE PRICE	*QUOTE U.S.$
1998 Have a Heavenly Journey 12416R	Yr.Iss.	1998	25.00	19-35
1998 How Can Two Work Together Except They Agree (ornament) 456268	Yr.Iss.	1998	25.00	18-25
1999 Scootin Your Way To A Perfect Day 634999	Yr.Iss.	1999	25.00	19-25
2000 Believe the Impossible 109487R	Yr.Iss.	2000	45.00	45
2000 Care-Van 2000 Die Cast Truck 817546	Yr.Iss.	2000	30.00	30

Chapel Exclusives - S. Butcher

YEAR ISSUE	EDITION LIMIT	YEAR RETD.	ISSUE PRICE	*QUOTE U.S.$
1996 His Presence Is Felt In The Chapel 163872	Retrd.	1998	25.00	25
1995 Lighting The Way To A Happy Holiday 129267	Retrd.	1998	30.00	23-30
1989 There's A Christian Welcome Here 523011	Suspd.		45.00	47-125
1991 He Is My Inspiration 523038	Retrd.	N/A	60.00	60-87
1991 Blessed Are...Shall Obtain Mercy 523291	Retrd.	N/A	55.00	55-59
1991 Blessed Are The Meek, They Shall Inherit The Earth 523313	Retrd.	N/A	55.00	55-59
1991 Blessed Are They That Hunger... 523321	Retrd.	N/A	55.00	55-59
1991 Blessed Are The Poor In Spirit... 523347	Retrd.	N/A	55.00	55-100
1991 Blessed Are The Peacemakers... 523348	Retrd.	N/A	55.00	55-152
1991 Blessed Are They That Mourn... 523380	Retrd.	N/A	55.00	55-59
1991 Blessed Are The Pure in Heart... 523399	Retrd.	N/A	55.00	55

Christmas Remembered - S. Butcher

YEAR ISSUE	EDITION LIMIT	YEAR RETD.	ISSUE PRICE	*QUOTE U.S.$
2000 Sure Good Use Less Hustle & Bustle 737550	Open		37.50	38

Clown - S. Butcher

YEAR ISSUE	EDITION LIMIT	YEAR RETD.	ISSUE PRICE	*QUOTE U.S.$
1985 I Get a Bang Out of You 12262	Retrd.	1997	30.00	33-65
1986 Lord Keep Me On the Ball 12270	Suspd.		30.00	38-45
1985 Waddle I Do Without You 12459	Retrd.	1989	30.00	48-95
1986 The Lord Will Carry You Through 12467	Retrd.	1988	30.00	55-72

Commemorative 500th Columbus Anniversary - S. Butcher

YEAR ISSUE	EDITION LIMIT	YEAR RETD.	ISSUE PRICE	*QUOTE U.S.$
1992 This Land Is Our Land 527386	Yr.Iss.	1992	350.00	318-375

Commemorative Easter Seal - S. Butcher

YEAR ISSUE	EDITION LIMIT	YEAR RETD.	ISSUE PRICE	*QUOTE U.S.$
1988 Jesus Loves Me 9" fig. 104531	1,000		500.00	1400-1750
1987 He Walks With Me 107999	Yr.Iss.	1987	25.00	30-45
1988 Blessed Are They That Overcome 115479	Yr.Iss.	1988	27.50	25-32
1989 Make A Joyful Noise 9" fig. 520322	1,500		N/A	745-937
1989 His Love Will Shine On You 522376	Yr.Iss.	1989	30.00	37-55
1990 You Have Touched So Many Hearts 9" fig. 523283	2,000		500.00	561-775
1991 We Are God's Workmanship 9" fig. 523879	2,000		N/A	683-725
1990 Always In His Care 524522	Yr.Iss.	1990	30.00	29-40
1992 You Are Such A Purr-fect Friend 9" fig. 526010	2,000		N/A	582-700
1991 Sharing A Gift Of Love 527114	Yr.Iss.	1991	30.00	43-50
1992 A Universal Love 527173	Yr.Iss.	1992	32.50	75-105
1993 Gather Your Dreams 9" fig. 529680	2,000		500.00	575-625
1993 You're My Number One Friend 530026	Yr.Iss.	1993	30.00	26-55
1994 It's No Secret What God Can Do 531111	Yr.Iss.	1994	30.00	30-50
1994 You Are The Rose of His Creation 9" fig. 531243	2,000		N/A	500-555
1995 Take Time To Smell the Flowers 524387	Yr.Iss.	1995	30.00	26-48
1995 He's Got The Whole World In His Hands 9" fig. 526886	Yr.Iss.	1995	500.00	N/A
1996 He Loves Me 9" fig. 152277	2,000		500.00	N/A

*Quotes have been rounded up to nearest dollar

Precious Moments/Enesco Group, Inc.
to Precious Moments/Enesco Group, Inc.

FIGURINES

YEAR ISSUE	EDITION LIMIT	YEAR RETD.	ISSUE PRICE	*QUOTE U.S.$
1996 You Can Always Count on Me 526827	Yr.Iss.	1996	30.00	26-38
1997 Love Is Universal 9" fig. 192376	2,000		N/A	446-500
1997 Give Ability A Chance 192368	Yr.Iss.	1997	30.00	26-30
1998 Love Grows Here 9" fig. 272981	2,000		N/A	N/A
1998 Somebody Cares 522325	Yr.Iss.	1998	40.00	32-45
1999 We Are All Precious In His Sight 475068	1,500		N/A	N/A
1999 Heaven Bless You Easter Seal 456314	Yr.Iss.	1999	35.00	29-35
2000 Jesus Loves Me 9" ES2000	1,500		500.00	500
2000 Give Your Whole Heart 490245	Yr.Iss.		30.00	30

Country Lane - S. Butcher

YEAR ISSUE	EDITION LIMIT	YEAR RETD.	ISSUE PRICE	*QUOTE U.S.$
1999 Hogs & Kisses 261106	Open		50.00	41-50
1998 You're Just As Sweet As Pie 307017	Open		45.00	37-45
1998 Oh Taste And See That The Lord Is Good 307025	Open		55.00	45-55
1998 Fork Over Those Blessings 307033	Open		45.00	37-45
1998 Nobody Likes To Be Dumped 307041	Retrd.	1999	65.00	65
1998 I'll Never Tire of You 307068	Retrd.	1999	50.00	41-50
1998 Peas Pass The Carrots 307076	Retrd.	2000	35.00	29-35
1998 Bringing In The Sheaves (Musical) 307084	Yr.Iss.	1998	90.00	90-195
1999 Moo-ie Christmas 455856	Open		60.00	48-60
1999 Shear Happiness and Hare Cuts 539910	Open		40.00	32-40
1999 Eat Ham 587842	Open		25.00	20-25
1999 You Brighten My Field of Dreams 587850	Open		55.00	44-55
1999 Dear Jon, I Will Never Leave You-JESUS 588091	Open		50.00	40-50
2000 Life Would Be the Pits Without Friends 795356	Open		40.00	40

Cruise - S. Butcher

YEAR ISSUE	EDITION LIMIT	YEAR RETD.	ISSUE PRICE	*QUOTE U.S.$
1993 15 Year Tweet Music Together (15th Anniversary Collection Convention Medallion) 529087	Yr.Iss.	1993	Gift	58-86
1993 Friends Never Drift Apart (15th Anniversary Cruise Medallion) 529079	Yr.Iss.	1993	Gift	N/A
1995 Sailabration (15th Anniversary Collectors Club Cruise Figurine) 150061	Yr.Iss.	1995	Gift	507
1998 Our Future Is Looking Much Brighter (20th Anniversary Collection Cruise Figurine) 325511	Yr.Iss.	1998	Gift	N/A
2000 Whale Have Oceans Of Fun 748412	Yr.Iss.		Gift	N/A

Events Figurines - S. Butcher

YEAR ISSUE	EDITION LIMIT	YEAR RETD.	ISSUE PRICE	*QUOTE U.S.$
1988 You Are My Main Event 115231	Yr.Iss.	1988	30.00	36-72
1989 Sharing Begins In The Heart 520861	Yr.Iss.	1989	25.00	30-80
1990 I'm A Precious Moments Fan 523526	Yr.Iss.	1990	25.00	23-48
1990 Good Friends Are Forever 525049	Yr.Iss.	1990	25.00	625
1991 You Can Always Bring A Friend 527122	Yr.Iss.	1991	27.50	28-55
1992 An Event Worth Wading For 527319	Yr.Iss.	1992	32.50	28-62
1993 An Event For All Seasons 530158	Yr.Iss.	1993	30.00	31-62
1994 Memories Are Made of This 529982	Yr.Iss.	1994	30.00	29-45
1995 Follow Your Heart 528080	Yr.Iss.	1995	30.00	36-55
1996 Hallelujah Hoedown 163864	Yr.Iss.	1996	32.50	33-58
1996 May The Sun Always Shine On You 184217	Yr.Iss.	1996	37.50	58-68
1997 We're So Hoppy You're Here 261351	Yr.Iss.	1997	32.50	28-35
1998 Love Is Kind E1379R	Yr.Iss.	1998	8.00	8-17
1999 You Oughta Be in Pictures 490327	Yr.Iss.	1999	32.50	26-38
1999 You Color Our World With Loving, Caring and Sharing 644463 (September Event)	Retrd.	1999	19.00	19
1999 He Leadeth Me E1377R	Yr.Iss.	1999	19.00	19
2000 Scoopin' Up Some Love 635049	Retrd.	2000	35.00	35
2000 Mr. Fujioka 781851	Retrd.	2000	Gift	N/A
2000 To God Be the Glory E-2823R	11/00		45.00	45

Family Christmas Scene - S. Butcher

YEAR ISSUE	EDITION LIMIT	YEAR RETD.	ISSUE PRICE	*QUOTE U.S.$
1985 May You Have the Sweetest Christmas 15776	Suspd.		17.00	27-60
1985 The Story of God's Love 15784	Suspd.		22.50	33-60
1985 Tell Me a Story 15792	Suspd.		10.00	27-35
1985 God Gave His Best 15806	Suspd.		13.00	23-50
1985 Silent Night 15814	Suspd.		37.50	63-87
1986 Sharing Our Christmas Together 102490	Suspd.		40.00	50-90
1989 Have A Beary Merry Christmas 522856	Suspd.		15.00	18-45
1990 Christmas Fireplace 524883	Suspd.		37.50	37-62
1999 Wishing You An Old Fashioned Christmas 634778	Yr.Iss.	1999	175.00	140-170

Four Seasons - S. Butcher

YEAR ISSUE	EDITION LIMIT	YEAR RETD.	ISSUE PRICE	*QUOTE U.S.$
1985 The Voice of Spring 12068	Yr.Iss.	1985	30.00	150-400
1985 Summer's Joy 12076	Yr.Iss.	1985	30.00	78-95
1986 Autumn's Praise 12084	Yr.Iss.	1986	30.00	44-75
1986 Winter's Song 12092	Yr.Iss.	1986	30.00	92-108
1986 Set	Yr.Iss.	1986	120.00	250-550
1999 He Graces The Earth With Abundance (Fall) 129119	Open		50.00	50
1999 He Covers The Earth With His Glory (Winter) 129135	Open		50.00	50
1999 The Beauty Of God Blooms Forever (Spring) 129143	Open		50.00	50
1999 Beside The Still Waters (Summer) 129127	Open		50.00	50

Growing In Grace - S. Butcher

YEAR ISSUE	EDITION LIMIT	YEAR RETD.	ISSUE PRICE	*QUOTE U.S.$
1995 Infant Angel With Newspaper 136204	Open		22.50	21-28
1995 Age 1 Baby With Cake 136190	Open		25.00	22-25
1995 Age 2 Girl With Blocks 136212	Open		25.00	22-25
1995 Age 3 Girl With Flowers 136220	Open		25.00	22-28
1995 Age 4 Girl With Doll 136239	Open		27.50	24-28
1995 Age 5 Girl With Lunch Box 136247	Open		27.50	24-33
1995 Age 6 Girl On Bicycle 136255	Open		30.00	26-30
1996 Age 7 Girl Dressed As Nurse 163740	Open		32.50	28-33
1996 Age 8 Girl Shooting Marbles 163759	Open		32.50	28-33
1996 Age 9 Girl With Charm Bracelet 183865	Open		30.00	26-30
1996 Age 10 Girl Bowling 183873	Open		37.50	33-38
1997 Age 11 Girl With Ice Cream Cone 260924	Open		37.50	33-38
1997 Age 12 Girl/Puppy Holding Clock 260932	Open		37.50	33-38
1997 Age 13 Girl/Turtle Race 272647	Open		40.00	34-40
1997 Age 14 Girl With Diary 272655	Open		35.00	30-35
1997 Age 15 Girl With List 272663	Open		40.00	34-40
1995 Age 16 Sweet Sixteen Girl Holding Sixteen Roses 136263	Open		45.00	38-52

Japanese Figurines Exclusives - S. Butcher

YEAR ISSUE	EDITION LIMIT	YEAR RETD.	ISSUE PRICE	*QUOTE U.S.$
2000 On Our Way To A Special Day - Kindergarten Boy 481602	Open		17.50	18
2000 On Our Way To A Special Day - Kindergarten Girl 481610	Open		17.50	18
2000 Shiny New And Ready For School - Elem. Girl 481629	Open		20.00	20
2000 Shiny New And Ready For School - Elem. Boy 481637	Open		20.00	20
2000 Growing In Wisdom - Jr. High Boy 481645	Open		22.50	23
2000 Growing In Wisdom - Jr. High Girl 481653	Open		22.50	23
2000 All Girls Are Beautiful - St/4 Girls Festival 481661	Open		55.00	55
2000 Make Me Strong - St/4 Boys Festival 481688	Open		55.00	55
2000 Everybody Has A Part - St/3 Summer Festival 731625	Open		50.00	50
2000 Good Fortune 731633	Open		17.50	18

Little Moments - S. Butcher

YEAR ISSUE	EDITION LIMIT	YEAR RETD.	ISSUE PRICE	*QUOTE U.S.$
1996 Where Would I Be Without You 139491	Open		20.00	20
1996 All Things Grow With Love 139505	Open		20.00	20
1996 You're The Berry Best 139513	Open		20.00	20
1996 You Make The World A Sweeter Place 139521	Open		20.00	20
1996 You're Forever In My Heart 139548	Open		20.00	20-25
1996 Birthday Wishes With Hugs & Kisses 139556	Open		20.00	20
1996 You Make My Spirit Soar 139564	Open		20.00	20
1997 Bless Your Little Tutu 261173	Open		20.00	20
1997 January 261203	Open		20.00	20
1997 February 261246	Open		20.00	20
1997 April 261300	Open		20.00	20
1997 March 261270	Open		20.00	20
1997 May 261211	Open		20.00	20
1997 June 261254	Open		20.00	20
1997 July 261289	Open		20.00	20
1997 August 261319	Open		20.00	20
1997 September 261238	Open		20.00	20
1997 October 261262	Open		20.00	20
1997 November 261297	Open		20.00	20
1997 December 261327	Open		20.00	20
1997 You Will Always Be A Winner To Me (Boy) 272612	Open		20.00	20
1997 It's Ruff To Always Be Cheery 272639	Open		20.00	20
1997 You Will Always Be A Winner To Me (Girl) 283460	Open		20.00	20
1997 Holiday Wishes Sweetie Pie 312444	Open		20.00	20
1997 You're Just Perfect In My Book 320560	Open		25.00	20-22
1997 Loving Is Caring 320579	Open		20.00	20
1997 Loving Is Caring 320595	Open		20.00	18-20
1997 You Set My Heart Ablaze 320625	Open		20.00	20
1997 Just The Facts...You're Terrific 320668	Open		20.00	20
1997 You Have Such A Special Way Of Caring Each And Every Day 320706	Open		25.00	25
1997 What Would I Do Without You? 320714	Open		25.00	25
1998 Thank You For The Time We Share (Avon) 384836	Retrd.	1998	19.99	25
1999 World's Greatest Student (Boy) 491586	Open		20.00	20
1999 World's Greatest Student (Girl) 491616	Open		25.00	25
1999 World's Sweetest Girl 491594	Open		25.00	25
1999 World's Best Helper (Girl) 491608	Open		25.00	25
1999 You're No. 1 (Girl) 491624	Open		25.00	25
1999 You're No. 1 (Boy) 491640	Open		25.00	25
2000 Sharing Sweet Moments Together 731579	Open		20.00	20

Little Moments Bible Stories - S. Butcher

YEAR ISSUE	EDITION LIMIT	YEAR RETD.	ISSUE PRICE	*QUOTE U.S.$
1999 Jonah And The Whale 488283	Open		25.00	25
1999 Daniel And The Lion's Den 488291	Open		25.00	25
1999 Joseph's Special Coat 488305	Open		25.00	25
1999 Baby Moses 649953	Open		25.00	25
1999 The Good Samaritan 649988	Open		25.00	25
1999 The Great Pearl 649996	Open		20.00	20

Little Moments Days of the Week - S. Butcher

YEAR ISSUE	EDITION LIMIT	YEAR RETD.	ISSUE PRICE	*QUOTE U.S.$
2000 The Child That's Born On The Sabbath Day...692077	Open		20.00	20
2000 Monday's Child Is Fair Of Face 692085	Open		20.00	20
2000 Tueday's Child Is Full Of Grace 692093	Open		20.00	20
2000 Wednesday's Child Is Full Of Woe 692107	Open		20.00	20
2000 Thursday's Child Has Far To Go 692115	Open		20.00	20
2000 Friday's Child Is Loving And Giving 692123	Open		20.00	20
2000 Saturday's Child Works Hard For A Living 692131	Open		20.00	20

Little Moments Highway To Happiness - S. Butcher

YEAR ISSUE	EDITION LIMIT	YEAR RETD.	ISSUE PRICE	*QUOTE U.S.$
1999 Cross Walk 649511	Open		20.00	20
1999 Go 4 It 649438	Open		20.00	20
1999 God's Children At Play 649481	Open		20.00	20
1999 Highway To Happiness 649457	Open		20.00	20
1999 I'll Never Stop Loving You 649465	Open		20.00	20
1999 There's No Wrong Way With You 649473	Open		20.00	20

Little Moments Internationals - S. Butcher

YEAR ISSUE	EDITION LIMIT	YEAR RETD.	ISSUE PRICE	*QUOTE U.S.$
1998 You Are a Dutch-ess To Me 456373	Open		20.00	20
1998 Life Is A Fiesta 456381	Open		20.00	20
1998 Don't Rome Too Far From Home 456403	Open		20.00	20
1998 You Can't Beat The Red, White And Blue 456411	Open		20.00	20
1998 Love's Russian Into My Heart 456446	Open		20.00	20
1998 Hola, Amigo 456454	Open		20.00	20
1998 Afri-can Be There For You, Then I Will Be 456462	Open		20.00	20
1998 I'd Travel The Highlands To Be With You 456470	Open		20.00	20
1998 Sure Would Love To Squeeze You 456896	Open		20.00	20
1998 You Are My Amour 456918	Open		20.00	20
1998 Our Friendship Is Always In Bloom 456926	Open		20.00	20
1998 My Love Will Stand Guard Over You 456934	Open		20.00	20

Military - S. Butcher

YEAR ISSUE	EDITION LIMIT	YEAR RETD.	ISSUE PRICE	*QUOTE U.S.$
1999 Army Boy-Caucasian "I'm Proud To Be An American" 588105	Open		32.50	33
1999 Marine Boy-Caucasian "I'm Proud To Be An American" 588113	Open		32.50	33
1999 Navy Boy-Caucasian "I'm Proud To Be An American" 588121	Open		32.50	33
1999 Coast Guard Boy-Caucasian "I'm Proud To Be An American" 588148	Open		32.50	33
1999 Air Force Boy-Caucasian "I'm Proud To Be An American" 588156	Open		32.50	33
1999 Army Girl-Caucasian "I'm Proud To Be An American" 729876	Open		32.50	33
1999 Marine Girl-Caucasian "I'm Proud To Be An American" 729884	Open		32.50	33
1999 Navy Girl-Caucasian "I'm Proud To Be An American" 729892	Open		32.50	33
1999 Coast Guard Girl-Caucasian "I'm Proud To Be An American" 729906	Open		32.50	33
1999 Air Force Girl-Caucasian "I'm Proud To Be An American" 729914	Open		32.50	33
1999 Army Boy-African American "I'm Proud To Be An American" 729973	Open		32.50	33
1999 Marine Boy-African American "I'm Proud To Be An American" 730009	Open		32.50	33
1999 Navy Boy-African American "I'm Proud To Be An American" 730017	Open		32.50	33
1999 Coast Guard Boy-African American "I'm Proud To Be An American" 730025	Open		32.50	33
1999 Air Force Boy-African American "I'm Proud To Be An American" 730033	Open		32.50	33
1999 Army Girl-African American "I'm Proud To Be An American" 729922	Open		32.50	33
1999 Marine Girl-African American "I'm Proud To Be An American" 729930	Open		32.50	33
1999 Navy Girl-African American "I'm Proud To Be An American" 729949	Open		32.50	33
1999 Coast Guard Girl-African American "I'm Proud To Be An American" 729957	Open		32.50	33
1999 Air Force Girl-African American "I'm Proud To Be An American" 729965	Open		32.50	33

Musical Figurines - S. Butcher

YEAR ISSUE	EDITION LIMIT	YEAR RETD.	ISSUE PRICE	*QUOTE U.S.$
1983 Sharing Our Season Together E-0519	Retrd.	1986	70.00	112-138
1983 Wee Three Kings E-0520	Suspd.		60.00	108-125
1983 Let Heaven And Nature Sing E-2346	Suspd.		55.00	100-170
1982 O Come All Ye Faithful E-2352	Suspd.		50.00	124-152
1982 I'll Play My Drum For Him E-2355	Suspd.		45.00	136-205
1980 Christmas Is A Time To Share E-2806	Retrd.	1984	35.00	90-180
1980 Crown Him Lord Of All E-2807	Suspd.		35.00	80-130
1980 Unto Us A Child Is Born E-2808	Suspd.		35.00	84-140
1980 Jesus Is Born E-2809	Suspd.		35.00	96-170
1980 Come Let Us Adore Him E-2810	Suspd.		45.00	83-155
1980 Peace On Earth E-4726	Suspd.		45.00	100-125
1981 The Hand That Rocks The Future E-5204	Open		30.00	54-100
1981 My Guardian Angel E-5205	Suspd.		22.50	88-118
1981 My Guardian Angel E-5206	Suspd.		22.50	64-110
1984 Wishing You A Merry Christmas E-5394	Suspd.		55.00	88-120
1981 Silent Knight E-5642	Suspd.		45.00	268-475

*Quotes have been rounded up to nearest dollar

YEAR ISSUE	EDITION LIMIT	YEAR RETD.	ISSUE PRICE	*QUOTE U.S.$
1981 Rejoice O Earth E-5645	Retrd.	1988	35.00	64-130
1982 The Lord Bless You And Keep You E-7180	Open		55.00	85-135
1982 Mother Sew Dear E-7182	Open		35.00	65-100
1982 The Purr-fect Grandma E-7184	Suspd.		35.00	53-98
1982 Love Is Sharing E-7185	Retrd.	1985	40.00	122-175
1982 Let the Whole World Know E-7186	Suspd.		60.00	96-165
1985 Lord Keep My Life In Tune (B) (2/set) 12165	Suspd.		50.00	94-150
1985 We Saw A Star 12408	Suspd.		50.00	75-104
1987 Lord Keep My Life In Tune (G) (2/set) 12580	Suspd.		50.00	218-285
1985 God Sent You Just In Time 15504	Retrd.	1989	60.00	81-138
1986 Heaven Bless You 100285	Suspd.		45.00	57-75
1986 Our 1st Christmas Together 101702	Retrd.	1992	50.00	70-100
1986 Let's Keep In Touch 102520	Retrd.	1999	85.00	45-95
1988 Peace On Earth 109746	Suspd.		120.00	116-130
1987 I'm Sending You A White Christmas 112402	Retrd.	1993	55.00	82-150
1988 You Have Touched So Many Hearts 112577	Suspd.		50.00	52-65
1991 Lord Keep My Life In Balance 520691	Suspd.		60.00	55-88
1989 The Light Of The World Is Jesus 521507	Retrd.	1999	65.00	59-70
1992 Do Not Open Till Christmas 522244	Suspd.		75.00	70-85
1992 This Day Has Been Made In Heaven 523682	Open		60.00	55-65
1993 Wishing You Were Here 526916	Suspd.		100.00	83-100

Rejoice in the Lord - S. Butcher

YEAR ISSUE	EDITION LIMIT	YEAR RETD.	ISSUE PRICE	*QUOTE U.S.$
1985 There's a Song in My Heart 12173	Suspd.		11.00	34-58
1985 Happiness is the Lord 12378	Suspd.		15.00	30-54
1985 Lord Give Me a Song 12386	Suspd.		15.00	34-54
1985 He is My Song 12394	Suspd.		17.50	33-50

Salvation Army - S. Butcher

YEAR ISSUE	EDITION LIMIT	YEAR RETD.	ISSUE PRICE	*QUOTE U.S.$
2000 He Is My Salvation 135984	Open		45.00	45

Sammy's Circus - S. Butcher

YEAR ISSUE	EDITION LIMIT	YEAR RETD.	ISSUE PRICE	*QUOTE U.S.$
1994 Markie 528099	Suspd.		18.50	15-19
1994 Dusty 529176	Suspd.		22.50	17-23
1994 Katie 529184	Suspd.		17.00	17-22
1994 Tippy 529192	Suspd.		12.00	12-15
1994 Collin 529214	Suspd.		20.00	20-25
1994 Sammy 529222	Yr.Iss.	1994	20.00	20-45
1994 Circus Tent 528196 (Nite-Lite)	Suspd.		90.00	45-90
1995 Jordan 529168	Suspd.		20.00	20-26
1996 Jennifer 163708	Suspd.		20.00	20-25

Spring Catalog - S. Butcher

YEAR ISSUE	EDITION LIMIT	YEAR RETD.	ISSUE PRICE	*QUOTE U.S.$
1993 Happiness Is At Our Fingertips 529931	Yr.Iss.	1993	35.00	42-90
1994 So Glad I Picked You As A Friend 524379	Yr.Iss.	1994	40.00	45-53
1995 Sending My Love Your Way 528609	Yr.Iss.	1995	40.00	40-62
1996 Have I Toad You Lately I Love You 521329	Yr.Iss.	1996	30.00	30-45
1997 Happiness To The Core 261378	Yr.Iss.	1997	37.50	38-50
1998 Mom, You Always Make Our House A Home 325465	Yr.Iss.	1998	37.50	38

Sugartown - S. Butcher

YEAR ISSUE	EDITION LIMIT	YEAR RETD.	ISSUE PRICE	*QUOTE U.S.$
1992 Chapel Night Light 529621	Retrd.	1994	85.00	89-160
1992 Christmas Tree 528684	Retrd.	1994	15.00	25-35
1992 Grandfather 529516	Retrd.	1994	15.00	25-36
1992 Nativity 529508	Retrd.	1994	20.00	41-55
1992 Philip 529494	Retrd.	1994	17.00	19-27
1992 Aunt Ruth & Aunt Dorothy 529486	Retrd.	1994	20.00	20-43
1992 Sam Butcher 529567 (1st sign)	Yr.Iss.	1992	22.50	100-169
1993 7 pc. Sam's House Collector's Set 531774	Retrd.	1997	189.00	189
1993 Sam's House Night Light 529605	Retrd.	1997	80.00	71-85
1993 Fence 529796	Retrd.	1997	10.00	10-18
1993 Sammy 528668	Retrd.	1997	17.00	16-28
1993 Katy Lynne 529524	Retrd.	1997	20.00	20-42
1993 Sam Butcher 529842 (2nd sign)	Yr.Iss.	1993	22.50	35-70
1993 Dusty 529435	Retrd.	1997	17.00	17-32
1993 Sam's Car 529443	Retrd.	1997	22.50	23-25
1994 Dr. Sam Sugar 529850	Retrd.	1997	17.00	17-34
1994 Doctor's Office Night Light 529869	Retrd.	1997	80.00	69-85
1994 Sam's House 530468	Yr.Iss.	1994	17.50	18-75
1994 Jan 529826	Retrd.	1997	17.00	17-20
1994 Sugar & Her Dog House 533165	Retrd.	1997	20.00	20-32
1994 Stork With Baby Sam 529788	Yr.Iss.	1994	22.50	18-48
1994 Free Christmas Puppies 528064	Retrd.	1997	18.50	11-23
1994 7 pc. Doctor's Office Collectors Set 529281	Yr.Iss.	1994	189.00	167-189
1994 Leon & Evelyn Mae 529818	Retrd.	1997	20.00	20-30
1995 Sam the Conductor 150169	Yr.Iss.	1995	20.00	20-38
1995 Train Station Night Light 150150	Retrd.	1997	50.00	58-125
1995 Railroad Crossing Sign 150177	Retrd.	1997	12.00	12-20
1995 Tammy and Debbie 531812	Retrd.	1997	22.50	20-25
1995 Donny 531871	Retrd.	1997	22.50	18-25
1995 Luggage Cart With Kitten And Tag 150185	Retrd.	1997	13.00	12-23
1995 6 pc. Train Station Collector Set 750193	Yr.Iss.	1995	190.00	156-190
1996 Sugar Town Skating Sign 184020	Yr.Iss.	1996	15.00	12-26
1996 Skating Pond 184047	Retrd.	1997	40.00	34-45
1996 Mazie 184055	Retrd.	1997	18.50	19-32
1996 Cocoa 184063	Retrd.	1997	7.50	8-15
1996 Leroy 184071	Retrd.	1997	18.50	19-25
1996 Hank and Sharon 184098	Retrd.	1997	25.00	19-33
1996 Lighted Warming Hut 192341	Retrd.	1997	60.00	60
1997 Lighted Schoolhouse 272795	Retrd.	1997	80.00	80-100
1997 Chuck 272809	Retrd.	1997	22.50	20-30
1997 Aunt Cleo 272817	Retrd.	1997	18.50	17-19
1997 Aunt Bulah & Uncle Sam 272825	Retrd.	1997	22.50	20-23
1997 Heather 272833	Retrd.	1997	20.00	18-20
1997 Merry-Go-Round 272841	Retrd.	1997	20.00	18-20
1997 Schoolhouse Collector's Set-6-pc. 272876	Retrd.	1997	183.50	153-184
1997 Sugar Town Accessories 212725	Retrd.	1997	20.00	20
1997 Sugar Town Train Cargo Car 273007	Yr.Iss.	1997	27.50	28
1998 Post Office Collector's Set 456217	Yr.Iss.	1998	250.00	199-250

Sugartown Enhancements - S. Butcher

YEAR ISSUE	EDITION LIMIT	YEAR RETD.	ISSUE PRICE	*QUOTE U.S.$
1995 Bus Stop 150207	Retrd.	1997	8.50	8-13
1995 Fire Hydrant 150215	Retrd.	1997	5.00	5-9
1995 Bird Bath 150223	Retrd.	1997	8.50	8-13
1995 Sugartown Enhancement Pack, set/5 152269	Retrd.	1997	45.00	38-45
1996 Tree Night Light 184039	Retrd.	1997	45.00	45-75
1996 Flag Pole w/Kitten 184136	Retrd.	1997	15.00	14-20
1996 Wooden Barrel Hot Cocoa Stand 184144	Retrd.	1997	15.00	15
1996 Bonfire with Bunnies 184152	Retrd.	1997	10.00	9-17
1997 Bike Rack 272906	Retrd.	1997	15.00	15
1997 Garbage Can 272914	Retrd.	1997	20.00	18-20
1997 Enhancements 3-pc. 273015	Retrd.	1997	43.50	37-44
1995 Dog And Kitten On Park Bench 529540	Retrd.	1997	13.00	13-21
1994 Lamp Post 529559	Retrd.	1997	8.00	8-13
1997 Bunnies Caroling 531804	Retrd.	1997	10.00	10
1994 Mailbox 531847	Retrd.	1997	5.00	5-12
1995 Street Sign 532185	Retrd.	1997	5.00	5-18
1994 Village Town Hall Clock 532908	Retrd.	1997	80.00	85
1994 Curved Sidewalk 533149	Retrd.	1997	10.00	10-15
1994 Straight Sidewalk 533157	Retrd.	1997	10.00	10-13
1994 Single Tree 533173	Retrd.	1997	10.00	10-23
1994 Double Tree 533181	Retrd.	1997	10.00	10-14
1994 Cobble Stone Bridge 533203	Retrd.	1997	17.00	17-25

To Have And To Hold - S. Butcher

YEAR ISSUE	EDITION LIMIT	YEAR RETD.	ISSUE PRICE	*QUOTE U.S.$
1996 Love Vows To Always Bloom 1st Anniversary Couple With Flowers 129097	Open		70.00	70-75
1996 A Year Of Blessings-1st Anniversary Couple With Cake 163783	Open		70.00	70-75
1996 Each Hour Is Precious With You-5th Anniversary Couple With Clock 163791	Open		70.00	70-75
1996 Ten Years Heart To Heart-10th Anniversary Couple With Pillow 163805	Open		70.00	70-75
1996 A Silver Celebration To Share-25th Anniversary Couple With Silver Platter 163813	Open		70.00	70-75
1996 Sharing The Gift of 40 Precious Years-40th Anniversary Couple With Gift Box 163821	Open		70.00	70-75
1996 Precious Moments To Remember-50th Anniversary Couple With Photo Album 163848	Open		70.00	70-75

Two By Two - S. Butcher

YEAR ISSUE	EDITION LIMIT	YEAR RETD.	ISSUE PRICE	*QUOTE U.S.$
1993 Noah, Noah's Wife, & Noah's Ark (lighted) 530042	Open		125.00	125-150
1993 Sheep (mini double fig.) 530077	Open		10.00	10-25
1993 Pigs (mini double fig.) 530085	Open		12.00	12-18
1993 Giraffes (mini double fig.) 530115	Open		16.00	16-22
1993 Bunnies (mini double fig.) 530123	Open		9.00	9-15
1993 Elephants (mini double fig.) 530131	Open		18.00	18-25
1993 Eight Piece Collector's Set 530948	Open		190.00	190
1994 Llamas 531375	Open		15.00	15-20
1995 Congratulations You Earned Your Stripes 127809	Open		15.00	15
1996 I'd Goat Anywhere With You 163694	Open		10.00	10-15

You Are Always There For Me - S. Butcher

YEAR ISSUE	EDITION LIMIT	YEAR RETD.	ISSUE PRICE	*QUOTE U.S.$
1996 Mother Kissing Daughter's Owie 163600	Open		50.00	55-57
1996 Father Helping Son Bat 163627	Open		50.00	50
1996 Sister Consoling Sister 163635	Open		50.00	50
1997 Mother Kissing Son's Owie 163619	Open		50.00	55
1997 Father Bandaging Daughter's Doll 163597	Open		50.00	50-53

Prizm, Inc./Pipka

Pipka's Memories of Christmas Collector's Club - Pipka

YEAR ISSUE	EDITION LIMIT	YEAR RETD.	ISSUE PRICE	*QUOTE U.S.$
1998 Knock, Knock Santa Figurine 13923	3,300	1999	95.00	95-135
1998 Knock, Knock Santa Ornament 11418	3,950	1999	Gift	N/A
1999 Knock, Knock Santa Door 13702	1,650	1999	75.00	75-110
1999 Knock, Knock Small Door 13703	3,950	1999	Gift	75
2000 Christmas Ark 13941	Yr.Iss.		95.00	95
2000 Christmas Ark Ornament 11433	Yr.Iss.		Gift	N/A
2000 Two by Two Santa 11330	Yr.Iss.		Gift	N/A

Pipka's Artist Choice Santa - Pipka

YEAR ISSUE	EDITION LIMIT	YEAR RETD.	ISSUE PRICE	*QUOTE U.S.$
1999 Laplander Santa 13922	7,180	2000	130.00	130
2000 Chef Claus 13938	6/01		110.00	110

Pipka's Displays - Pipka

YEAR ISSUE	EDITION LIMIT	YEAR RETD.	ISSUE PRICE	*QUOTE U.S.$
2000 Angel Garden Backdrop 13725	Open		N/A	N/A
2000 German Village Backdrop 13724	Open		N/A	N/A

Pipka's Earth Angels - Pipka

YEAR ISSUE	EDITION LIMIT	YEAR RETD.	ISSUE PRICE	*QUOTE U.S.$
1996 Angel of Hearts 13801	3,400	1999	85.00	85-90
1997 Angel of Roses 13804	5,400		85.00	85
2000 Carolyn- Angel of Contemplation 13820	2,500		65.00	65
1998 Celeste-Angel of Stars 13807	5,400		90.00	90
1998 Christine-The Christmas Angel 13808	5,400		90.00	90
1996 Cottage Angel 13800	3,400	1999	85.00	85-90
1998 Elizabeth-Forget-Me-Not Angel 13809	5,400		90.00	90
2000 Eric- The Leader Angel 13821	2,500		30.00	30
1996 Gardening Angel 13802	3,400	1999	85.00	85-90
1997 Guardian Angel 13805	5,400		85.00	85
2000 Jessica- The Bell Ringer 13822	2,500		35.00	35
1999 Kim & Lee-Baby Angel 13816	1,000		40.00	40
2000 Lindsey- The Baby Angel 13823	2,500		20.00	20
1997 Messenger Angel 13803	5,400		85.00	85
1999 Michele-The Snow Angel 13813	1,000	2000	95.00	95
1998 Mikaela-Angel of Innocence 13810	5,400		40.00	40
2000 Pauline- The Poinsettia Angel 13819	2,500		65.00	65
1998 Samantha-The Playful Angel 13811	5,400		40.00	40
1999 Sang-The Teddy Bear Angel 13815	1,000	2000	90.00	90
1998 Sarah-The Littlest Angel 13812	5,400		40.00	40
1999 Sissy-The Little Helper 13814	1,000		40.00	40
1999 Sylvia- The Song Angel 13817	1,000	2000	95.00	95
2000 Whitney- The Wedding Angel 13818	2,500		65.00	65

Pipka's Fifth Year Anniversary Santa - Pipka

YEAR ISSUE	EDITION LIMIT	YEAR RETD.	ISSUE PRICE	*QUOTE U.S.$
1999 Irish Santa 13926	2,100	2000	100.00	100

Pipka's Gallery Collection - Pipka

YEAR ISSUE	EDITION LIMIT	YEAR RETD.	ISSUE PRICE	*QUOTE U.S.$
2000 Caribbean Santa 13934	Yr.Iss.		105.00	105
2000 Jul-Tomte 13713	Open		20.00	20
2000 Julbock 13712	Open		30.00	30
2000 Little Helper - Jul-To 13714	Open		20.00	20
2000 St. Lucia 13711	Open		45.00	45
2000 Starlight Santa 13932	2-Yr.		100.00	100
2000 Starlight Sleigh 13710	Open		45.00	45
2000 Swedish Father Christmas 13931	Yr.Iss.		110.00	110

Pipka's Kinder Christmas - Pipka

YEAR ISSUE	EDITION LIMIT	YEAR RETD.	ISSUE PRICE	*QUOTE U.S.$
2000 Best Friends 13717	6,500		40.00	40
2000 His New Train 13718	6,500		40.00	40
1999 Jakub's Tree 13700	6,500		55.00	55
2000 Muffy's Tea Party 13719	6,500		45.00	45
1999 Playful Pals 13701	6,500		55.00	55
2000 Snow Gentleman 13716	6,500		50.00	50

Pipka's Madonna Collection - Pipka

YEAR ISSUE	EDITION LIMIT	YEAR RETD.	ISSUE PRICE	*QUOTE U.S.$
2000 Black Wooden Display Base 13737	Open		10.00	10
1998 Decorative Displayer 12001	1,000	1999	30.00	30
2000 Mary, Mother of All Children 12004	5,400		110.00	110
1998 Queen of Roses 12000	5,400		90.00	90
1999 Renaissance Madonna 12002	5,400		90.00	90

Pipka's Memories of Christmas - Pipka

YEAR ISSUE	EDITION LIMIT	YEAR RETD.	ISSUE PRICE	*QUOTE U.S.$
1995 Czechoslovakian Santa 13905	3,600	1996	85.00	435-895
1995 Gingerbread Santa 13903	3,600	1996	85.00	200-395
1995 Midnight Visitor 13902	3,600	1996	85.00	625-1500
1995 Santa's Ark 13901	3,600	1997	85.00	200-395
1995 Star Catcher Santa 13904	3,600	1996	85.00	250-510
1995 Starcoat Santa 13900	3,600	1996	85.00	325-510
1995 Set of 1995 Santas (13900-13905)	Closed	N/A	510.00	2400
1996 Aussie Santa & Boomer 13906	3,600	1997	85.00	200-450
1996 Good News Santa 13908	3,600	1997	85.00	235-300
1996 Storytime Santa 13909	3,600	1997	85.00	175-300
1996 Ukrainian Santa 13907	3,600	1997	85.00	175-300
1997 Norwegian/Julenisse Santa 13911	3,600	1997	90.00	200-500
1997 Polish Father Christmas 13917	3,600	1997	90.00	195-225
1997 Russian Santa 13916	3,600	1998	90.00	150-300
1997 Santa's Spotted Grey 13914	3,600	1998	90.00	175-350
1997 St. Nicholas 13912	3,600	1998	90.00	185-300
1997 Where's Rudolph? 13915	3,600	1997	90.00	200-310
1998 Father Christmas 13919	3,600	1998	95.00	150-300
1998 Peace Maker 13918	3,600	1998	95.00	110-160
1998 San Nicolas 13921	3,600	1998	95.00	95-225
1998 Teddy Bear Santa 13920	3,600	1998	95.00	225-350
1999 Door County Santa 13924	3,600	1999	110.00	110-250
1999 Yes Virginia 13925	4,500	1999	105.00	105-195
1999 Winterman 13927	4,500	1999	95.00	95-150
1999 German St. Nick 13928	4,500	1999	100.00	100
1999 Santa & His Snow Friend 13929	4,500	1999	95.00	95-100
1999 The Christmas Traveler 13930	4,500	1999	95.00	95-100
2000 Old Father Christmas 13939	4,500		95.00	95
2000 Santa with Toys 13940	4,500		95.00	95
2000 St. Nicholas and the Christkind 13937	4,500		150.00	150
2000 Victorian Father Christmas 13933	4,500		100.00	100

Pipka's Millennium Santa - Pipka

YEAR ISSUE	EDITION LIMIT	YEAR RETD.	ISSUE PRICE	*QUOTE U.S.$
2000 Carpenter Santa 13936	6,216	2000	100.00	100

Pipka's Reflections of Christmas - Pipka

YEAR ISSUE	EDITION LIMIT	YEAR RETD.	ISSUE PRICE	*QUOTE U.S.$
1997 Amish Country Santa 11305	4,330	1999	40.00	40-45
1998 Aussie Santa & Boomer 11306	4,330	2000	40.00	40
1997 Better Watch Out Santa 11304	4,330	1999	40.00	40-45
2000 The Christmas Traveler 11327	9,700		40.00	40
1997 Czechoslovakian Santa 11301	4,330	1999	40.00	40-45
1998 Dear Santa 11311	9,700		40.00	40
2000 The Door County Santa 11324	9,700		40.00	40
1999 Father Christmas 11319	9,700		40.00	40
1999 German St. Nick 11321	9,700		40.00	40
1998 Gingerbread Santa 11309	9,700		40.00	40
1998 Good News Santa 11307	3,760	2000	40.00	40
1999 Irish Santa 11320	9,700		40.00	40
1997 Midnight Visitor 11300	4,330	1999	40.00	40-50

*Quotes have been rounded up to nearest dollar

YEAR ISSUE	EDITION LIMIT	YEAR RETD.	ISSUE PRICE	*QUOTE U.S.$
1998 Norwegian Julenisse 11313	9,700		40.00	40
1999 Peace Make 11322	9,700		40.00	40
1998 Polish Father Christmas 11312	9,700		40.00	40
1999 Russian Santa 11317	9,700		40.00	40
2000 Santa & Snow Friend 11326	9,700		40.00	40
1999 Santa's Spotted Grey 11316	9,700		40.00	40
1999 St. Nicholas 11314	9,700		40.00	40
1997 Star Catcher Santa 11303	4,330	1999	40.00	40-45
1997 Starcoat Santa 11302	4,330	1999	40.00	40-50
2000 Starlight Santa 11329	9,700		40.00	40
2000 Starlight Sleigh 11331	Open		N/A	N/A
1998 Storytime Santa 11308	3,760	2000	40.00	40
2000 Swedish Father Christmas 11328	9,700		40.00	40
1998 Teddy Bear Santa 11318	9,700		40.00	40
1998 Ukrainian Santa 11310	9,700		40.00	40
1998 Where's Rudolph? 11315	9,700		40.00	40
2000 The Winterman 11325	9,700		40.00	40
1999 Yes Virginia 11323	9,700		40.00	40

Pipka's Signs - Pipka

1996 Angel's Gate 13806	Open		35.00	35
1996 Memories Sign 13910	2,100		35.00	35

Pulaski Furniture, Inc.

PFC Collectors' Club

1996 Jack Russell Terrier (figurine)	Closed	1997	19.95	20
1998 Rembrandt Russell - Self Pawtrait (graphic)	500		Gift	30

Reco International

Fancy Footwork - J. Everett

1999 Everything's Coming Up Rosy	Open		20.00	20
1999 Family Ties	Open		20.00	20
1999 Head Over Heals	Open		20.00	20
1999 Hook Shot	Open		20.00	20
1999 Just Desserts	Open		20.00	20
1999 Life's a Beach	Open		20.00	20
1999 Ski Bunnies	Open		20.00	20
1999 Splish, Splash	Open		20.00	20
1999 This Boot Is Made For Working	Open		20.00	20

Forever In His Love - G. Olsen

2000 Alpha & Omega	Open		60.00	60
2000 Be Not Afraid	Open		75.00	75
2000 Forever and Ever	Open		60.00	60
2000 The Good Shepherd	Open		65.00	65

Legends of The Old West (bookends) - G. Perillo

1999 Crazy Horse & George Armstrong Custer	900		80.00	80
1999 Indian Brave & Pony Express	900		90.00	90

Masquerade - Lakeland Studios, unless otherwise noted

1998 Aviator	Open		30.00	30
1998 Chef	Open		30.00	30
1998 Conductor	Open		30.00	30
1998 Drover	Open		30.00	30
1998 Engineer	Open		30.00	30
1998 Fireman	Open		30.00	30
1998 Fish Merchant - A. Brindley	Open		30.00	30
1998 Fisherman	Open		30.00	30
1998 Josephine - A. Brindley	Open		30.00	30
1998 Lifeboatman	Open		30.00	30
1998 Long Shoreman	Open		30.00	30
1998 Miner	Open		30.00	30
1998 Napoleon - A. Brindley	Open		30.00	30
1998 Nurse	Open		30.00	30
1998 Pharmacist	Open		30.00	30
1998 Policeman	Open		30.00	30
1998 Sailor - A. Brindley	Open		30.00	30
1998 Sea Captain	Open		30.00	30
1998 Seamen - A. Brindley	Open		30.00	30
1998 Sherlock Holmes - A. Brindley	Open		30.00	30
1998 Skipper - A. Brindley	Open		30.00	30
1998 Trainer	Open		30.00	30
1998 Trawlerman - A. Brindley	Open		30.00	30
1998 Yachtsman - A. Brindley	Open		30.00	30

Pure Potential - J. Claybrooks

1999 Chocolate Drop	Open		17.50	18
1999 Gospel Truth	Open		19.00	19
1999 More Bubbles	Open		22.50	23
1999 Pure Potential	Open		19.00	19

Reco Creche Collection - J. McClelland

1988 Cow	Open		15.00	15
1988 Donkey	Open		16.50	17
1987 Holy Family (3 Pieces)	Open		49.00	49
1988 King/Frankincense	Open		22.50	23
1988 King/Gold	Open		22.50	23
1988 King/Myrrh	Open		22.50	23
1987 Lamb	Open		9.50	10
1987 Shepherd-Kneeling	Open		22.50	23
1987 Shepherd-Standing	Open		22.50	23

The Roaring Adventures of Rip Squeak™ - L. Filgate

2000 Balancing Act	Open		30.00	30
2000 Harmony	Open		70.00	70
2000 The Hug	Open		20.00	20
2000 Sports Fan	Open		25.00	25
2000 Storyteller	Open		30.00	30
2000 Sweet Dreams	Open		39.00	39

Sandra Kuck's Treasures - S. Kuck

YEAR ISSUE	EDITION LIMIT	YEAR RETD.	ISSUE PRICE	*QUOTE U.S.$
1997 Baby Bunnies	Open		20.00	20
1997 Be Good	Open		20.00	20
2000 Birthday Wishes	Open		25.00	25
1998 Bridge of Love	Open		27.50	28
1999 Bundle of Joy	Open		25.00	25
1999 Cherub Fountain	Open		35.00	35
1997 Christmas Morning	1,200		Gift	N/A
1997 Fishin' Buddies	Open		25.00	25
1997 For Mom	Open		20.00	20
1998 Friendship & Sharing	Open		50.00	50
1998 Gift of Love	Open		30.00	30
1998 Giving Thanks	Open		30.00	30
1999 Grandma's Trunk	Open		30.00	30
1998 Happy Birthday	Open		25.00	25
2000 Happy Bubbles	Open		20.00	20
1999 Kitty Did It	Open		20.00	20
2000 Little Blessings	Open		25.00	25
1998 Little Cowboy	Open		27.50	28
1999 Little Miss Sunshine	Open		30.00	30
2000 Look What I Found	Open		20.00	20
2000 Lost & Found	Open		20.00	20
1997 Love and Kisses	Open		20.00	20
1998 Make Believe	Open		30.00	30
1999 Morning Prayers	Open		30.00	30
2000 My New Friend	Open		25.00	25
1997 Playful Kitten	Open		20.00	20
1998 Pretty Kitty	Open		30.00	30
1999 Rose Gazebo	Open		50.00	50
1998 Schooldays	Open		25.00	25
1998 Sisters	Open		30.00	30
1999 Storybook Dreams	Open		20.00	20
1997 Sunday Stroll	Open		20.00	20
1998 Sweet Dreams	Open		20.00	20
1997 Swing For Two	Open		25.00	25
1997 Tea With Kitty	Open		20.00	20
1997 Teacher's Pet	Open		20.00	20
1997 Teddy & Me	Open		20.00	20
1998 Thank You So Much	Open		20.00	20
1999 To Grandma's House	Open		30.00	30
1997 Victoria's Garden	Open		20.00	20
1998 Winter Fun	Open		30.00	30

Victorian Home Collection - S. Kuck

1999 Gift of Knowledge Bookends	Open		85.00	85
1999 Gift of Peace Candlestick	Open		40.00	40
1999 Unity Candlestick	Open		40.00	40

River Shore

Rockwell Single Issues - N. Rockwell

1982 Grandpa's Guardian	9,500	N/A	125.00	195
1981 Looking Out To Sea	9,500	N/A	85.00	195

Roman, Inc.

Animal Kingdom - D. Griff

1994 Cat w/Mice Inside Waterball	Closed	N/A	19.50	20
1994 Cat w/Mouse on Tail	Closed	N/A	15.00	15
1994 Chipmunk w/Mice Musical	Closed	N/A	35.00	35
1995 Glitterdome Musical	Closed	N/A	45.00	45
1994 Lounging Cat on Pillow	Closed	N/A	13.50	14
1994 Two Kittens in Basket	Closed	N/A	15.00	15
1995 Yawning Chipmunks Waterglobe	Closed	N/A	45.00	45

Bouncing Baby Bunnies - D. Griff

1996 Bunnies on Block	Closed	N/A	7.00	7
1996 Bunnies on Carrot	Closed	N/A	6.50	7
1996 Bunnies on Flowers	Closed	N/A	6.00	6
1996 Bunnies w/Carrot Slippers	Closed	N/A	6.00	6
1996 Bunnies w/Crayons	Closed	N/A	4.00	4
1996 Bunnies w/White Diapers	Closed	N/A	4.50	5
1996 Bunny Bubble Bath in Teacup	Closed	N/A	10.00	10
1996 Bunny Bubble Bath in Teacup Musical	Closed	N/A	27.50	28
1996 Bunny Cowboy	Closed	N/A	8.00	8
1996 Bunny Doctor	Closed	N/A	7.00	7
1996 Bunny Fireman	Closed	N/A	7.00	7
1996 Bunny Policeman	Closed	N/A	8.00	8
1996 Bunny Sliding on Easter Egg	Closed	N/A	7.50	8
1996 Ring-Around-The-Rosie	Closed	N/A	10.00	10
1996 Three Bunnies in an Easter Basket	Closed	N/A	9.00	9
1996 Two Bunnies w/egg Cup	Closed	N/A	9.00	9

A Child's World 1st Edition - F. Hook

1980 Beach Buddies, signed	15,000	N/A	29.00	600
1980 Beach Buddies, unsigned	15,000	N/A	29.00	450
1980 Helping Hands	Closed	N/A	45.00	85
1980 Kiss Me Good Night	15,000	N/A	29.00	40
1980 My Big Brother	Closed	N/A	39.00	200
1980 Nighttime Thoughts	Closed	N/A	25.00	65
1980 Sounds of the Sea	15,000	N/A	45.00	150

A Child's World 2nd Edition - F. Hook

1981 All Dressed Up	15,000	N/A	36.00	70
1981 Cat Nap	15,000	N/A	42.00	125
1981 I'll Be Good	15,000	N/A	36.00	80
1981 Making Friends	15,000	N/A	42.00	46
1981 The Sea and Me	15,000	N/A	39.00	80
1981 Sunday School	15,000	N/A	39.00	70

A Child's World 3rd Edition - F. Hook

1981 Bear Hug	15,000	N/A	42.00	45
1981 Pathway to Dreams	15,000	N/A	47.00	50
1981 Road to Adventure	15,000	N/A	47.00	50
1981 Sisters	15,000	N/A	64.00	75
1981 Spring Breeze	15,000	N/A	37.50	50
1981 Youth	15,000	N/A	37.50	40

A Child's World 4th Edition - F. Hook

1982 All Bundled Up	15,000	N/A	37.50	40
1982 Bedtime	15,000	N/A	35.00	38
1982 Birdie	15,000	N/A	37.50	40
1982 Flower Girl	15,000	N/A	42.00	45
1982 My Dolly!	15,000	N/A	39.00	40
1982 Ring Bearer	15,000	N/A	39.00	40

A Child's World 5th Edition - F. Hook

1983 Brothers	15,000	N/A	64.00	70
1983 Finish Line	15,000	N/A	39.00	42
1983 Handful of Happiness	15,000	N/A	36.00	40
1983 He Loves Me...	15,000	N/A	49.00	55
1983 Puppy's Pal	15,000	N/A	39.00	42
1983 Ring Around the Rosie	15,000	N/A	99.00	105

A Child's World 6th Edition - F. Hook

1984 Can I Help?	15,000	N/A	37.50	40
1984 Future Artist	15,000	N/A	42.00	45
1984 Good Doggie	15,000	N/A	47.00	50
1984 Let's Play Catch	15,000	N/A	33.00	35
1984 Nature's Wonders	15,000	N/A	29.00	31
1984 Sand Castles	15,000	N/A	37.50	40

A Child's World 7th Edition - F. Hook

1985 Art Class	15,000	N/A	99.00	105
1985 Don't Tell Anyone	15,000	N/A	49.00	50
1985 Look at Me!	15,000	N/A	42.00	45
1985 Mother's Helper	15,000	N/A	45.00	50
1985 Please Hear Me	15,000	N/A	29.00	30
1985 Yummm!	15,000	N/A	36.00	39

A Child's World 8th Edition - F. Hook

1985 Chance of Showers	15,000	N/A	33.00	35
1985 Dress Rehearsal	15,000	N/A	33.00	35
1985 Engine	15,000	N/A	36.00	40
1985 Just Stopped By	15,000	N/A	36.00	40
1985 Private Ocean	15,000	N/A	29.00	31
1985 Puzzling	15,000	N/A	36.00	40

A Child's World 9th Edition - F. Hook

1987 Hopscotch	15,000	N/A	67.50	70
1987 Li'l Brother	15,000	N/A	60.00	65

Classic Brides of the Century - E. Williams

1989 1900-Flora	5,000	N/A	175.00	175
1989 1910-Elizabeth Grace	5,000	N/A	175.00	175
1989 1920-Mary Claire	5,000	N/A	175.00	175
1989 1930-Kathleen	5,000	N/A	175.00	175
1989 1940-Margaret	5,000	N/A	175.00	175
1989 1950-Barbara Ann	5,000	N/A	175.00	175
1989 1960-Dianne	5,000	N/A	175.00	175
1989 1970-Heather	5,000	N/A	175.00	175
1989 1980-Jennifer	5,000	N/A	175.00	175
1992 1990-Stephanie Helen	5,000	N/A	175.00	175-199

Fontanini Club Members' Only - E. Simonetti

1990 The Pilgrimage	Closed	1994	24.00	200
1992 She Rescued Me	Yr.Iss.	1992	23.50	150
1993 Christmas Symphony	Yr.Iss.	1993	13.50	150
1994 Sweet Harmony	Yr.Iss.	1994	13.50	150
1995 Faith: The Fifth Angel	Yr.Iss.	1995	22.50	150

Fontanini Club Members' Only Nativity Preview - E. Simonetti

1996 Mara	Yr.Iss.	1996	12.50	55-75
1997 Benjamin	Yr.Iss.	1997	15.00	60
1998 Hannah	Yr.Iss.	1998	15.00	15
1999 Obediah, The Teacher	Yr.Iss.	1999	15.00	15
2000 Jacob	Yr.Iss.		19.50	20

Fontanini Club Renewal Gift - E. Simonetti

1993 He Comforts Me	Yr.Iss.	1993	Gift	225
1994 I'm Heaven Bound	Yr.Iss.	1994	Gift	150
1995 Gift of Joy	Yr.Iss.	1995	Gift	150

Fontanini Club Symbol of Membership - E. Simonetti

1990 I Found Him	Closed	1995	Gift	25-75
1996 Rosannah - Angel of The Roses	Yr.Iss.	1996	Gift	50-65
1997 Leah - Angel of Light	Yr.Iss.	1997	Gift	50
1998 Candace - The Caregiver	Yr.Iss.	1998	Gift	40
1999 Lemuel, The Lord's Herald	Yr.Iss.	1999	Gift	N/A
2000 Temira	Yr.Iss.		Gift	N/A

Fontanini 5" Collection - E. Simonetti

1978 3 Kings on Camels	Retrd.	1996	52.00	125
1994 Aaron	Open		11.50	12
1967 Aaron	Retrd.	1993	5.50	13
1987 Abraham	Open		7.00	7
1998 Alexander	Open		15.00	15
1998 Andrew	Open		15.00	15
1995 Angel, Standing Angel	Open		11.50	12
1979 Angels, Gloria Angel	Open		7.00	7
1966 Angels, Heraldic Angels	Retrd.	2000	27.50	28
1995 Angels, Kneeling Angel	Open		11.50	12
1998 Anthony	Open		15.00	15
1967 Asa	Retrd.	2000	13.50	14
1996 Azzan	Retrd.	1999	15.00	15
1992 Baby Jesus	Open		11.50	12
1966 Baby Jesus	Retrd.	1991	5.50	12

YEAR ISSUE	EDITION LIMIT	YEAR RETD.	ISSUE PRICE	*QUOTE U.S.$
1993 Balthazar	Open		11.50	12
1966 Balthazar	Retrd.	1992	5.50	30
1993 Balthazar on Camel	Open		32.50	33
2000 Benjamin	Open		17.50	18
1998 Birds, Barnyard Birds	Open		29.50	30
1989 Birds, Bethlehem Birds	Open		12.50	13
2000 Birds, Dove Set	Open		9.00	9
1968 Caleb	Open		7.00	7
1993 Camel with Saddle Blanket	Open		17.50	18
1967 Camel, Seated	Open		7.00	7
1967 Camel, Standing	Open		7.00	7
2000 Carmi	Open		19.50	20
1996 Cornelius, King's Steward	Open		12.50	13
1968 Daniel	Open		7.00	7
1987 David	Open		7.00	7
1968 Deborah	Open		7.00	7
1967 Dog	Open		2.30	3
1966 Donkey, Seated	Open		7.00	7
1966 Donkey, Standing	Open		6.00	6
1993 Elephant with Saddle Blanket	Open		29.50	30
1987 Eli	Open		7.00	7
1996 Elisabeth	Open		12.50	13
1968 Ephraim	Open		7.00	7
1997 Esau	Open		15.00	15
1997 Eva	Open		15.00	15
1968 Ezra	Open		7.00	7
1997 Flavius	Open		15.00	15
1967 Gabriel	Retrd.	1992	5.50	12
1993 Gabriel	Open		11.50	12
1966 Gaspar	Retrd.	1992	5.50	25
1993 Gaspar	Open		11.50	12
1993 Gaspar on Elephant	Open		45.00	45
1996 Gilead, King's Servant	Open		12.50	13
1966 Gloria Angel	Retrd.	1979	3.00	3
1967 Goat	Open		2.30	3
1998 Horse, Black with Saddle Blanket	Open		22.50	23
1998 Horse, Brown with Saddle Blanket	Open		22.50	23
1993 Horse, White with Saddle Blanket	Open		17.50	18
1996 Issak	Retrd.	1999	13.50	14
1989 Jareth	Open		12.50	13
1994 Jeremiah	Open		11.50	12
1994 Jethro, Tamar & Saul	Retrd.	2000	24.00	24
1968 Joel	Retrd.	1998	5.50	14-17
1997 John	Open		15.00	15
1966 Joseph	Retrd.	1991	5.50	12
1992 Joseph	Open		11.50	12
1997 Joshua	Retrd.	1999	13.50	14
1994 Josiah	Open		11.50	12
1967 Josiah	Retrd.	1993	5.50	12
1968 Judith	Retrd.	1998	5.50	13-17
2000 Kenan	Open		22.50	23
1967 Kneeling Angel	Retrd.	1994	5.50	13-45
1967 Levi	Retrd.	1993	5.50	13
1994 Levi	Open		11.50	12
1968 Malachi, Camel Driver	Open		7.00	7
1998 Marcus	Open		15.00	15
1997 Mariel	Open		19.50	20
1966 Mary	Retrd.	1991	5.50	12
1992 Mary	Open		11.50	12
1997 Maya	Open		15.00	15
1966 Melchior	Retrd.	1992	5.50	12-25
1993 Melchoir	Open		11.50	12
1993 Melchoir on Horse	Open		32.50	33
1983 Micah	Retrd.	1995	5.50	14
1996 Micah	Open		12.50	13
1968 Michael	Retrd.	1998	5.50	13-17
1967 Miriam	Retrd.	1993	5.50	12
1994 Miriam	Open		11.50	12
1967 Mordecai	Retrd.	1995	5.50	13-29
1996 Mordecai	Open		12.50	13
1996 Naomi	Retrd.	1999	15.00	15
1987 Nathan	Open		7.00	7
1966 Ox, Seated	Open		7.00	7
1966 Ox, Standing	Open		6.00	6
1998 Priscilla	Open		15.00	15
1994 Rachel	Open		11.50	12
2000 Rebekah, Aram and Adel	Open		29.50	30
1967 Reuben	Retrd.	1998	5.50	17-29
1968 Samuel	Open		7.00	7
1987 Seth	Open		7.00	7
2000 Sharon	Open		19.50	20
1966 Sheep Set, Brown	Open		13.50	14
1998 Sheep, White	Open		17.50	18
1990 Shepherd Choir	Open		24.00	24
1995 St. Francis of Assisi	Open		24.00	24
1967 Standing Angel	Retrd.	1994	5.50	13-42
1996 Thaddeus	Open		12.50	13
1997 Three King's on Camels	Open		75.00	75
1966 Zachariah	Open		7.00	7

Fontanini 5" Life of Christ Collection - E. Simonetti

YEAR ISSUE	EDITION LIMIT	YEAR RETD.	ISSUE PRICE	*QUOTE U.S.$
2000 Angel at the Resurrection	Open		22.50	23
1999 John, the Apostle	Open		17.50	18
2000 Mary Magdalene	Open		17.50	18
1999 Mary, Mother of Christ	Open		17.50	18
2000 Risen Christ	Open		17.50	18

Fontanini Special Event Figurine - E. Simonetti

YEAR ISSUE	EDITION LIMIT	YEAR RETD.	ISSUE PRICE	*QUOTE U.S.$
1994 Susanna	Yr.Iss.	1994	15.00	30-65
1995 Dominica	Yr.Iss.	1995	15.00	30-50
1996 Sarah	Yr.Iss.	1996	15.00	30-65
1997 Martha	Yr.Iss.	1997	15.00	30-50
1998 Phoebe, Perfume Maker	Yr.Iss.	1998	15.00	18
1999 Herschel, The Carpenter's Apprentice	Yr.Iss.	1999	17.50	18
2000 Leora	Yr.Iss.		19.50	20

Fontanini Personal Tour Exclusive - E. Simonetti

YEAR ISSUE	EDITION LIMIT	YEAR RETD.	ISSUE PRICE	*QUOTE U.S.$
1990 Gideon	Closed	1995	8.00	30-70
1995 Luke	Closed	1998	15.00	30-55
1998 Emanuele, The Founder	Closed	1999	15.00	45

Fontanini Heirloom Nativity Limited Edition Figurines - E. Simonetti

YEAR ISSUE	EDITION LIMIT	YEAR RETD.	ISSUE PRICE	*QUOTE U.S.$
1992 Ariel	Closed	1992	29.50	30-65
1993 Jeshua & Adin	Closed	1996	29.50	50-90
1994 Abigail & Peter	Closed	1996	29.50	60-80
1994 14 pc. Golden Edition Heirloom Nativity Set	2,500	1999	375.00	375
1995 Gabriela	25,000	1995	18.00	30-60
1996 Raphael	Closed	1996	18.00	30-50
1997 Judah	Closed	1997	19.50	30-35
1998 Celeste, Angel w/Dove	Yr.Iss.	1998	19.50	20-29
1998 90th Anniversary Nativity Set, (10 pc.), includes Charis, 90th Anniversary Ltd. Ed. Angel	Closed	1999	300.00	300
1998 Charis, 90th Anniversary Angel	Yr.Iss.	1998	29.50	30
1999 Tiras & Lena	Yr.Iss.	1999	27.50	30
2000 Erela	Yr.Iss.		19.50	20

Fontanini Millennium Edition Nativity - E. Simonetti

YEAR ISSUE	EDITION LIMIT	YEAR RETD.	ISSUE PRICE	*QUOTE U.S.$
1999 12 pc. Figure Set	3-Yr.		300.00	300
1999 12 pc. Figure Set with Creche	3-Yr.		475.00	475
1999 3 pc. Angel & Stable Animals Figure Set	3-Yr.		75.00	75
1999 3 pc. Holy Family Figure Set	3-Yr.		75.00	75
1999 3 pc. Holy Family Figure Set w/ Creche	3-Yr.		250.00	250
1999 3 pc. Shepherds Figure Set	3-Yr.		75.00	75
1999 3 pc. Three Kings Figure Set	3-Yr.		75.00	75
1999 Millennium Edition Nativity Creche	3-Yr.		175.00	175

Fontanini Retired 7.5" Collection - E. Simonetti

YEAR ISSUE	EDITION LIMIT	YEAR RETD.	ISSUE PRICE	*QUOTE U.S.$
1968 Baby Jesus	Retrd.	1993	6.00	25
1968 Balthazar	Retrd.	1994	6.00	6
1979 Daniel	Retrd.	1996	13.00	13
1979 Gabriel	Retrd.	1993	13.00	25
1968 Gaspar	Retrd.	1994	6.00	6
1985 Isaac	Retrd.	1998	15.00	28-30
1968 Joseph	Retrd.	1993	6.00	25
1979 Josiah	Retrd.	1998	13.00	13
1985 Judith	Retrd.	1996	15.00	15
1968 Kneeling Angel	Retrd.	1995	6.00	25
1968 Mary	Retrd.	1993	6.00	25
1968 Melchoir	Retrd.	1994	6.00	6
1979 Reuben	Retrd.	1996	13.00	13
1968 Standing Angel	Retrd.	1995	6.00	25

Frances Hook's Four Seasons - F. Hook

YEAR ISSUE	EDITION LIMIT	YEAR RETD.	ISSUE PRICE	*QUOTE U.S.$
1984 Winter	12,500	N/A	95.00	100
1985 Spring	12,500	N/A	95.00	100
1985 Summer	12,500	N/A	95.00	100
1985 Fall	12,500	N/A	95.00	100

Holiday Traditions Collection - Roman, Inc.

YEAR ISSUE	EDITION LIMIT	YEAR RETD.	ISSUE PRICE	*QUOTE U.S.$
1997 Angel of Peace	Retrd.	1999	12.00	12
1997 Blessed by an Angel (waterglobe)	Retrd.	1998	20.00	20
2000 Bluebird of Happiness	Open		25.00	25
1997 Christmas Gargoyle	Retrd.	1997	7.50	8
1997 Christmas Lighthouse	Retrd.	1998	26.00	26
1999 Christmas Poinsettia	Open		22.50	23
1997 Christmas Rose	Open		22.50	23
1998 Tradition of the Easter Lily	Open		25.00	25
1998 Tradition of the Egg	Open		10.00	10
1998 Tradition of the Shamrock	Open		15.00	15
1998 Tradition of the Valentine	Open		15.00	15

Hook - F. Hook

YEAR ISSUE	EDITION LIMIT	YEAR RETD.	ISSUE PRICE	*QUOTE U.S.$
1986 Carpenter Bust	Retrd.	1986	95.00	95
1986 Carpenter Bust-Heirloom Edition	Retrd.	1986	95.00	95
1987 Little Children, Come to Me	15,000	N/A	45.00	45
1987 Madonna and Child	15,000	N/A	39.50	40
1982 Sailor Mates	2,000	N/A	290.00	315
1982 Sun Shy	2,000	N/A	290.00	315

The Magic of Christmas - D. Morgan

YEAR ISSUE	EDITION LIMIT	YEAR RETD.	ISSUE PRICE	*QUOTE U.S.$
2000 Christmas Past	Open		65.00	65
2000 Christmas Present	Open		65.00	65
1999 Magic of Christmas	Open		65.00	65
2000 Magic of Christmas Musical Glitterdome	Open		47.50	48
1999 The Magic of Giving	Open		65.00	65
1999 Santa's Magic	Open		65.00	65

The Millenium™ Collection - Sr. Mary Jean Dorcy

YEAR ISSUE	EDITION LIMIT	YEAR RETD.	ISSUE PRICE	*QUOTE U.S.$
1996 The Annunciation	Open		29.50	30
1997 Gentle Love	Open		29.50	30
1999 Heaven's Blessing	Open		29.50	30
1999 Joy	Open		35.00	35
1999 Joyful Promise	Open		29.50	30
1996 Prince of Peace	Retrd.	1998	29.50	30-50
1998 Rejoice	Open		29.50	30
1994 Silent Night	Open		29.50	30

The Museum Collection by Angela Tripi - A. Tripi

YEAR ISSUE	EDITION LIMIT	YEAR RETD.	ISSUE PRICE	*QUOTE U.S.$
1994 The Batter	1,000	N/A	95.00	95
1993 Be a Clown	1,000	N/A	95.00	95
1994 Blackfoot Woman with Baby	1,000	N/A	95.00	95
1990 The Caddie	1,000	N/A	135.00	135
1992 Checking It Twice	2,500	N/A	95.00	95
1990 Christopher Columbus	1,000	N/A	250.00	250
1994 Crow Warrior	1,000	N/A	195.00	195
1990 The Fiddler	1,000	N/A	175.00	176
1992 Flying Ace	1,000	N/A	95.00	95
1993 For My Next Trick	1,000	N/A	95.00	95
1992 Fore!	1,000	N/A	175.00	175
1992 The Fur Trapper	1,000	N/A	175.00	175
1991 A Gentleman's Game	1,000	N/A	175.00	175
1992 The Gift Giver	2,500	N/A	95.00	95
1994 Iroquois Warrior	1,000	N/A	95.00	95
1994 Jesus in Gethsemane	1,000	N/A	75.00	75
1993 Jesus, The Good Shepherd	1,000	N/A	95.00	95
1992 Justice for All	1,000	N/A	95.00	95
1992 Ladies' Day	1,000	N/A	175.00	175
1992 Ladies' Tee	1,000	N/A	250.00	250
1990 The Mentor	1,000	N/A	290.00	291
1993 Native American Woman-Cherokee Maiden	1,000	N/A	110.00	110
1992 Nativity Set-8 pc.	2,500	N/A	425.00	425
1994 Nurse	1,000	N/A	95.00	95
1993 One Man Band Clown	1,000	N/A	95.00	95
1992 Our Family Doctor	1,000	N/A	95.00	95
1994 The Pitcher	1,000	N/A	95.00	95
1993 Preacher of Peace	1,000	N/A	175.00	175
1992 Prince of the Plains	1,000	N/A	175.00	175
1993 Public Protector	1,000	N/A	95.00	95
1993 Rhapsody	1,000	N/A	95.00	95
1993 Right on Schedule	1,000	N/A	95.00	95
1993 Road Show	1,000	N/A	95.00	95
1995 The Runner	1,000	N/A	95.00	95
1993 Serenade	1,000	N/A	95.00	95
1995 Sioux Chief	1,000	N/A	95.00	95
1993 Sonata	1,000	N/A	95.00	95
1990 St. Francis of Assisi	1,000	N/A	175.00	175
1992 The Tannenbaum Santa	2,500	N/A	95.00	95
1992 The Tap In	1,000	N/A	175.00	175
1994 Teacher	1,000	N/A	95.00	95
1990 Tee Time at St. Andrew's	1,000	N/A	175.00	175
1992 This Way, Santa	2,500	N/A	95.00	95
1992 To Serve and Protect	1,000	N/A	150.00	150
1993 Tripi Crucifix-Large	Open		59.00	59
1993 Tripi Crucifix-Medium	Open		35.00	35
1993 Tripi Crucifix-Small	Open		27.50	28

On Angel's Wings - G.G. Santiago

YEAR ISSUE	EDITION LIMIT	YEAR RETD.	ISSUE PRICE	*QUOTE U.S.$
1999 Angel of Dance	Open		65.00	65
1999 Angel of Dreams	Open		65.00	65
1999 Angel of Joy	Open		65.00	65
1999 Angel of Knowledge	Open		65.00	65
1999 Angel of Love	Open		65.00	65
1999 Angel of Music	Open		65.00	65
1999 Angel of Peace	Open		65.00	65
1999 Angel of Song	Open		65.00	65

Remember When by Frances Hook - F. Hook

YEAR ISSUE	EDITION LIMIT	YEAR RETD.	ISSUE PRICE	*QUOTE U.S.$
1999 Beach Buddies	Open		30.00	30
1999 Bear Hug	Open		30.00	30
1999 Can I Help?	Open		30.00	30
1999 Finish Line	Open		30.00	30
1999 Handful of Happiness	Open		30.00	30
1999 Sand Castles	Open		30.00	30
1999 The Sea and Me	Open		30.00	30
1999 Sounds of the Sea	Open		30.00	30

Seraphim Classics® Club Members' Only - G. Ho

YEAR ISSUE	EDITION LIMIT	YEAR RETD.	ISSUE PRICE	*QUOTE U.S.$
1998 Lillian - Nurturing Life	Closed	1998	65.00	125-300
1999 Josephine-Celebration of Peace	Closed	1999	65.00	65-75
1999 Heavenly Reflections Block Set	Closed	1999	500.00	500
2000 Sierra - Nature's Haven	Yr.Iss.		75.00	75
2000 Jacquelyn - Happiness Abounds	Yr.Iss.		175.00	175

Seraphim Classics® Club Symbol of Membership - G. Ho

YEAR ISSUE	EDITION LIMIT	YEAR RETD.	ISSUE PRICE	*QUOTE U.S.$
1997 Tess - Tender One	Closed	1998	55.00	85-100
1999 Eve-Tender Heart	Closed	1999	59.50	70-94
2000 Cassidy - Blessings From Above	Yr.Iss.		59.50	60

Seraphim Classics® 12" Limited Edition - G. Ho

YEAR ISSUE	EDITION LIMIT	YEAR RETD.	ISSUE PRICE	*QUOTE U.S.$
1995 Alyssa - Nature's Angel	Closed	1995	145.00	1200-1895
1996 Vanessa - Heavenly Maiden	Closed	1996	150.00	185-244
1997 Chloe - Nature's Gift	Closed	1997	159.00	165-200
1997 Ariel - Heaven's Shining Star	Closed	1997	159.00	125-200
1998 Hope - Light in the Distance	2-Yr.	1999	175.00	175-200
1998 Avalon - Free Spirit	Yr.Iss.	1998	175.00	175
1998 Annalisa - Celebrating The Millennium	2-Yr.	2000	175.00	175
1999 Nina-Heavenly Harvest	Yr.Iss.	1999	175.00	175
2000 Jillian - Cherish The Day	Yr.Iss.		195.00	195

Seraphim Classics® 27" - G. Ho

YEAR ISSUE	EDITION LIMIT	YEAR RETD.	ISSUE PRICE	*QUOTE U.S.$
2000 Alyssa - Nature's Angel	Open		750.00	750

Seraphim Classics® 4" - G. Ho

YEAR ISSUE	EDITION LIMIT	YEAR RETD.	ISSUE PRICE	*QUOTE U.S.$
1999 Celine - The Morning Star	Open		19.50	20
1995 Cymbeline - Peacemaker	Retrd.	1999	19.50	20-125
1995 Evangeline - Angel of Mercy	Retrd.	1999	19.50	20-50
2000 Faith - The Easter Angel	Open		19.50	20
1995 Felicia - Adoring Maiden	Retrd.	1999	19.50	20-100
1999 Gabriel - Celestial Messenger	Open		19.50	20
2000 Harmony - Love's Guardian	Open		19.50	20
1995 Iris - Rainbow's End	Retrd.	1999	19.50	20-50
1995 Isabel - Gentle Spirit	Retrd.	1999	19.50	20-57
1995 Laurice - Wisdom's Child	Retrd.	1999	19.50	20
1995 Lydia - Winged Poet	Retrd.	1999	19.50	20-60
2000 Mariah - Heavenly Joy	Open		19.50	20

*Quotes have been rounded up to nearest dollar

YEAR ISSUE	EDITION LIMIT	YEAR RETD.	ISSUE PRICE	*QUOTE U.S.$
2000 Melody - Heaven's Song	Open		19.50	20
1995 Ophelia - Heart Seeker	Retrd.	1999	19.50	20-65
1995 Priscilla - Benevolent Guide	Retrd.	1999	19.50	20
2000 Rachel - Children's Joy	Open		19.50	20
1999 Rosalie - Nature's Delight	Open		19.50	20
1995 Seraphina - Heaven's Helper	Retrd.	1999	19.50	20-119
1999 Serena - Angel of Peace	Open		19.50	20

Seraphim Classics® 7" - G. Ho

YEAR ISSUE	EDITION LIMIT	YEAR RETD.	ISSUE PRICE	*QUOTE U.S.$
1998 Amelia - Eternal Bloom	Closed	1998	65.00	65-76
2000 Amy - Paradise Found	Open		125.00	125
2000 Andrea - Creation Praise	Open		65.00	65
1999 Angel's Touch - The Dedication Angel Musical	Retrd.	2000	75.00	75
1998 Angels' Touch - The Dedication Angel	Open		59.50	60
1998 Annabella - Announcement of Joy	Closed	1998	59.50	60-125
1999 April - Spring's Blossom	Open		59.50	60
1999 Arianna - Winter's Warmth	Retrd.	2000	59.50	60
1999 Audra - Embraced By Love	Retrd.	2000	59.50	60
2000 Bethany - Lighting the Way	Open		59.50	60
2000 Caring Touch Angel with Medical Professional	Open		87.50	60
1999 Caroline-Garden Song	Retrd.	2000	75.00	75
1999 Cassandra - Heavenly Beauty, 5th Anniversary Figurine	Yr.Iss.	1999	100.00	100-120
2000 Celebration - Rejoice in Life	Open		100.00	60
2000 Celeste - Light of the World	Open		65.00	60
1996 Celine - The Morning Star	Retrd.	2000	55.00	55
1999 Charisse-Bloom From Heaven	Retrd.	2000	65.00	65
1997 Chelsea - Summer's Delight	Retrd.	2000	55.00	55
1999 Clarissa-Celestial Sounds	2-Yr.		65.00	65
1996 Constance-Gentle Keeper	Closed	1996	55.00	153-225
1994 Cymbeline - Peacemaker	Retrd.	1997	49.50	75-100
1999 Danielle - Messenger of Love	Open		75.00	75
1998 Diana - Heaven's Rose	Retrd.	2000	59.50	60
2000 Dominique - Simple Pleasures	Open		65.00	65
1999 Eden - Beautiful Haven Fountain	Open		175.00	175
1999 Elizabeth - Heaven's Victory	Open		59.50	60
1999 Erin - Irish Blessing	Open		59.50	60
1994 Evangeline - Angel of Mercy	Retrd.	2000	49.50	55
1998 Evangeline - Angel of Mercy Musical	Open		75.00	75
1996 Faith - The Easter Angel	Retrd.	1999	55.00	55-75
1995 Felicia - Adoring Maiden	Retrd.	1998	49.50	65-155
1996 Francesca - Loving Guardian	Retrd.	1998	65.00	65
1994 Francesca - Loving Guardian Musical	Retrd.	1998	75.00	75-80
1995 Francesca - Loving Guardian -Glitterdome® Musical	Open		50.00	50
1996 Gabriel - Celestial Messenger	Retrd.	2000	59.50	60
1997 Grace - Born Anew	Retrd.	2000	55.00	55
1997 Hannah - Always Near	Retrd.	2000	55.00	55
2000 Hannah - Always Near Musical	Open		50.00	60
1997 Harmony - Love's Guardian	Retrd.	2000	55.00	55
1999 Harmony - Love's Guardian Musical	Open		75.00	60
1997 Heather - Autumn Beauty	Retrd.	2000	55.00	55
1999 Heavenly Guardian with Little Boy Musical	Open		49.50	50
1999 Heavenly Guardian with Little Girl Musical	Open		49.50	50
1994 Iris - Rainbow's End	Retrd.	1999	49.50	55
1996 Iris - Rainbow's End Musical	Open		65.00	65
1997 Iris - Rainbow's End-Glitterdome® Musical	Open		50.00	50
1994 Isabel - Gentle Spirit	Retrd.	2000	49.50	55
1999 Joelle - Nature's Spirit	Yr.Iss.	1999	59.50	75
1999 Joy-Gift of Heaven	Retrd.	2000	65.00	65
1999 Juliette - Music's Gift	2-Yr.		65.00	65
1999 Katherine-Angel of Knowledge	Retrd.	2000	59.50	60
1999 Kristina - Song of Joy	2-Yr.		85.00	85
1999 Laurel-Nature's Harmony	Retrd.	2000	65.00	65
1995 Laurice - Wisdom's Child	Retrd.	1997	49.50	55-75
2000 Leah - Bless Our Home	Yr.Iss.		59.50	60
1994 Lydia - Winged Poet	Retrd.	1997	49.50	54-70
1996 Mariah - Heavenly Joy	Retrd.	2000	59.50	59-70
1999 Mariah-Heavenly Joy Musical	Open		80.00	80
1997 Melody - Heaven's Song	Retrd.	2000	55.00	55
1999 Michael - Victorious	Open		59.50	60
1999 Naomi - Nurturing Spirit	Retrd.	2000	59.50	60
1998 Noelle - Giving Spirit	Retrd.	1999	59.50	59-75
1999 Olivia-Loving Heart	Retrd.	2000	65.00	65
1994 Ophelia - Heart Seeker	Retrd.	1996	49.50	115-125
1999 Patrice-Delight in the Day	Yr.Iss.	1999	59.50	60-90
1995 Priscilla - Benevolent Guide	Retrd.	1998	49.50	55
1997 Rachel - Children's Joy	Retrd.	1999	55.00	55-65
1996 Rosalie - Nature's Delight	Retrd.	2000	55.00	55
1997 Sabrina - Eternal Guide	Closed	1997	55.00	54-65
1998 Samantha - Blessed At Birth	Open		59.50	60
2000 Sarah - Peaceful Reflections	Open		59.50	60
1995 Seraphina - Heaven's Helper	Retrd.	1996	49.50	116-120
1996 Serena - Angel of Peace	Retrd.	2000	65.00	65
1999 Serena-Angel of Peace Glitterdome® Musical	Open		50.00	50
1999 Serenity - Trusting Soul	Open		65.00	65
1998 Simone - Nature's Own	Open		100.00	100
1999 Sisters-Heart and Soul	Retrd.	2000	115.00	115
1997 Tamara - Blessed Guardian	Open		65.00	65
2000 Victoria - Embrace Life	Open		65.00	65

Seraphim Classics® Angels To Watch Over Me - G. Ho

YEAR ISSUE	EDITION LIMIT	YEAR RETD.	ISSUE PRICE	*QUOTE U.S.$
1996 Newborn - Blonde	Open		39.50	40
1996 Newborn - Brunette	Open		39.50	40
1996 First Year - Girl	Open		39.50	40
1996 Second Year - Girl	Open		39.50	40
1996 Third Year - Girl	Open		39.50	40
1996 Fourth Year - Girl	Open		39.50	40
1996 Fifth Year - Girl	Open		39.50	40
1997 Sixth Year - Girl	Open		39.50	40
1997 Seventh Year - Girl	Open		39.50	40
1998 Eighth Year - Girl	Open		45.00	45
1998 Ninth Year - Girl	Open		45.00	45
1999 Tenth Year - Girl	Open		45.00	45
1999 Sixteenth Year - Girl	Open		50.00	50
1997 Newborn - Boy	Open		39.50	40
1997 First Year - Boy	Open		39.50	40
1997 Second Year - Boy	Open		39.50	40
1997 Third Year - Boy	Open		39.50	40
1997 Fourth Year - Boy	Open		39.50	40
1997 Fifth Year - Boy	Open		39.50	40
1997 Sixth Year - Boy	Open		39.50	40
1998 Seventh Year - Boy	Open		45.00	45

Seraphim Classics® Heaven Sent - Seraphim Studios

YEAR ISSUE	EDITION LIMIT	YEAR RETD.	ISSUE PRICE	*QUOTE U.S.$
1997 Hope Eternal Musical	Retrd.	2000	37.50	38
1997 Loving Spirit Musical	Open	-	37.50	38
1998 Peaceful Embrace Musical	Open		85.00	85
1997 Pure At Heart Musical	Retrd.	2000	37.50	38

Seraphim Classics® Nativity - G. Ho

YEAR ISSUE	EDITION LIMIT	YEAR RETD.	ISSUE PRICE	*QUOTE U.S.$
2000 Camel	Open		25.00	25
1998 Gloria Angel	Open		59.50	60
2000 Holy Family Musical Glitterdome	Open		55.00	55
1996 Nativity Set - 5 pc. set	Open		125.00	125
1999 Natvity Animals	Open		40.00	40
1998 Shepherds - 2 pc. Set	Open		65.00	65
2000 Stable	Open		50.00	50
1997 Three Kings - 3 pc. set	Open		125.00	125

Seraphim Classics® Special Event - G. Ho

YEAR ISSUE	EDITION LIMIT	YEAR RETD.	ISSUE PRICE	*QUOTE U.S.$
1996 Dawn - Sunshine's Guardian Angel	Closed	1997	55.00	125-200
1997 Monica - Under Love's Wing	Closed	1997	55.00	55-150
1998 Alexandra - Endless Dreams	Closed	1998	65.00	85-94
1999 Rebecca-Beautiful Dreamer	Yr.Iss.	1999	125.00	125-150
2000 Amanda - Sharing The Spirit	Yr.Iss.		65.00	65

The Valencia Collection - G. Ho

YEAR ISSUE	EDITION LIMIT	YEAR RETD.	ISSUE PRICE	*QUOTE U.S.$
1998 The Annunciation	Open		59.50	60
1998 Christ in the Garden of Gethsemane	Open		45.00	45
1998 Crucifix	Open		39.50	40
1998 Flight into Egypt	Open		90.00	90
1998 The Good Shepard	Open		45.00	45
1997 Guardian Angel w/boy	Open		49.50	50
1997 Guardian Angel w/girl	Open		49.50	50
1997 Holy Family	Open		59.50	60
1997 Jesus	Open		39.50	40
1998 Jesus with Children	Open		45.00	45
1997 Last Supper	Open		125.00	125
1997 Madonna and Child	Open		39.50	40
1997 Madonna with Flowers	Open		39.50	40
1997 Seated Angel	Open		49.50	50
1997 St. Francis	Open		39.50	40
1997 St. Joseph	Open		39.50	40
1999 Valencia Nativity (11 pc.)	Open		285.00	285
1998 Way of the Cross	Open		59.50	60

Ron Lee's World of Clowns

The Ron Lee Collector's Club Gifts - R. Lee

YEAR ISSUE	EDITION LIMIT	YEAR RETD.	ISSUE PRICE	*QUOTE U.S.$
1987 Doggin' Along CC1	Yr.Iss.	1987	75.00	125-138
1988 Midsummer's Dream CC2	Yr.Iss.	1988	97.00	168
1989 Peek-A-Boo Charlie CC3	Yr.Iss.	1989	65.00	150
1990 Get The Message CC4	Yr.Iss.	1990	65.00	100-150
1991 I'm So Pretty CC5	Yr.Iss.	1991	65.00	100-150
1992 It's For You CC6	Yr.Iss.	1992	65.00	95
1993 My Son Keven CC7	Yr.Iss.	1993	70.00	95-100

The Ron Lee Collector's Club Renewal Sculptures - R. Lee

YEAR ISSUE	EDITION LIMIT	YEAR RETD.	ISSUE PRICE	*QUOTE U.S.$
1987 Hooping It Up CCG1	Closed	1987	Gift	145
1988 Pudge CCG2	Closed	1988	Gift	95
1989 Pals CCG3	Closed	1989	Gift	95
1990 Potsie CCG4	Closed	1990	Gift	95
1991 Hi! Ya! CCG5	Closed	1991	Gift	95
1992 Bashful Beau CCG6	Closed	1992	Gift	95
1993 Lit'l Mate CCG7	Closed	1993	Gift	95
1994 Chip Off the Old Block CCG8	Closed	1994	Gift	65
1995 Rock-A-Billy CCG9	Closed	1995	Gift	65-72
1995 Rascal CCG1	Closed	1997	Gift	72
1996 Hey There CCG10	Closed	1996	Gift	65
1997 Thumbs Up CCG-11	Yr. Iss.	1997	Gift	N/A
1998 Adorable Lara CCG12	Yr.Iss.	1998	Gift	N/A
1999 Spiffy CCG13	Yr.Iss.	1999	Gift	N/A
2000 Kix CCG14	Yr.Iss.		Gift	N/A
2000 Baggy Pant CCNMS100	Yr.Iss.		Gift	N/A

The Ron Lee Collector's Club Specials - R. Lee

YEAR ISSUE	EDITION LIMIT	YEAR RETD.	ISSUE PRICE	*QUOTE U.S.$
1995 Welcome CCGIVE	500	1997	85.00	105
1995 Have a Ball CCS100	3,500		45.00	45
1995 Two Bagger CCS105	3,500		45.00	45
1995 Skate Freighter CCS110	3,500		45.00	45
1995 Lit'l Thinker CCS115	3,500		45.00	45
1995 Mop of My Heart CCS120	3,500		45.00	45
1995 Dreamin' CCS125	3,500		45.00	45
1995 Ground Breaking Celebration LV ONE	10,000		92.50	93
1995 Scissors LV TWO	500	1997	120.00	120-145
1996 Lara's Glorious Ride CCS130	350		325.00	325
1996 Hear Ye! Hear Ye! CCGIVE2	500	1997	75.00	75-90
1996 Extra! Extra! LV THREE	500		110.00	110
1996 Ride That Horse CCS135	2,500		65.00	65
1996 Pickles CCS140	2,500		59.50	60
1996 Gingerbread Man CCS145	1,500		47.50	48
1996 Top Hat and Tail CCS150	1,500		47.50	48
1996 A Doll Story CCS155	1,500		47.50	48
1996 Hats All Folks CCS160	1,500		47.50	48
1996 All Day Sucker CCS165	1,500		47.50	48

Around the World With Hobo Joe - R. Lee

YEAR ISSUE	EDITION LIMIT	YEAR RETD.	ISSUE PRICE	*QUOTE U.S.$
1994 Hobo Joe in Caribbean L412	750	1995	110.00	110-177
1994 Hobo Joe in Egypt L415	750	1995	110.00	110-177
1994 Hobo Joe in England L411	750	1995	110.00	110-177
1994 Hobo Joe in France L407	750	1995	110.00	110-177
1994 Hobo Joe in Italy L406	750	1995	110.00	110-177
1994 Hobo Joe in Japan L408	750	1995	110.00	110-177
1994 Hobo Joe in Norway L413	750	1995	110.00	110-177
1994 Hobo Joe in Spain L414	750	1995	110.00	110-177
1994 Hobo Joe in Tahiti L410	750	1995	110.00	110-177
1994 Hobo Joe in the U.S.A L409	750	1995	110.00	110-177

The Betty Boop Collection - R. Lee

YEAR ISSUE	EDITION LIMIT	YEAR RETD.	ISSUE PRICE	*QUOTE U.S.$
1992 Bamboo Isle BB715	1,500		240.00	240
1992 Boop Oop A Doop BB705	1,500		97.00	97
1992 Harvest Moon BB700	1,500		93.00	93
1992 Max's Cafe BB720	1,500		99.00	99
1992 Spicy Dish BB710	1,500		215.00	215

Center Ring - R. Lee

YEAR ISSUE	EDITION LIMIT	YEAR RETD.	ISSUE PRICE	*QUOTE U.S.$
1994 According To L431SE	750	1995	125.00	125-140
1994 Aristocrat L424SE	750	1995	125.00	125-140
1994 Barella L423SE	750	1995	125.00	125-140
1994 Belt-a-Loon L427SE	750	1995	125.00	125-140
1994 Boo-Boo L430SE	750	1995	125.00	125-140
1994 Bubbles L422SE	750	1995	125.00	125-140
1994 Carpetbagger L421SE	750	1995	125.00	125-140
1994 Daisy L417SE	750	1995	125.00	125-140
1994 Forget-Me-Not L428SE	750	1995	125.00	125-140
1994 Glamour Boy L433SE	750	1995	125.00	125-140
1994 Hoop-De-Doo L434SE	750	1995	125.00	125-140
1994 Hot Dog L418SE	750	1995	125.00	125-140
1994 Kandy L419SE	750	1995	125.00	125-140
1994 Maid in the USA L432SE	750	1995	125.00	135-140
1994 Mal-Lett L426SE	750	1995	125.00	125-140
1994 Poodles L420SE	750	1995	125.00	125-140
1994 Puddles L416SE	750	1995	125.00	125-140
1994 Rabbit's Foot L429SE	750	1995	125.00	125-140
1994 Ruffles L435SE	750	1995	125.00	125-140
1994 Snacks L-425SE	750	1995	125.00	125-140

The Classics - R. Lee

YEAR ISSUE	EDITION LIMIT	YEAR RETD.	ISSUE PRICE	*QUOTE U.S.$
1991 Huckleberry Hound HB815	2,750	1995	90.00	108-130
1991 Quick Draw McGraw HB805	2,750	1995	90.00	108-130
1991 Scooby Doo & Shaggy HB810	2,750	1995	114.00	137-200
1991 Yogi Bear & Boo Boo HB800	2,750	1995	95.00	114-140

The Commemorative Collection - R. Lee

YEAR ISSUE	EDITION LIMIT	YEAR RETD.	ISSUE PRICE	*QUOTE U.S.$
1995 April 12th L455	2,500		180.00	180
1995 Between Shows L456	2,500		250.00	250
1995 Filet of Sole L460	2,500		180.00	200
1995 The Highwayman L457	2,500		165.00	165
1995 Just Plain Tired L459	2,500		195.00	225
1995 Practice Swing...Not!! L458	2,500		180.00	205

The E.T. Collection - R. Lee

YEAR ISSUE	EDITION LIMIT	YEAR RETD.	ISSUE PRICE	*QUOTE U.S.$
1992 E.T. ET100	1,500	1995	94.00	113-140
1993 Flight ET115	1,500	1995	325.00	390-475
1993 Friends ET110	1,500	1995	125.00	150-180
1992 It's Mee...E.T. ET105	1,500	1995	94.00	113-140

The Flintstones - R. Lee

YEAR ISSUE	EDITION LIMIT	YEAR RETD.	ISSUE PRICE	*QUOTE U.S.$
1991 Bedrock Serenade HB130	2,750		250.00	250
1991 Bogey Buddies HB150	2,750		143.00	143
1991 Buffalo Brothers HB170	2,750		134.00	134
1991 The Flintstones HB100	2,750		410.00	410
1991 Joyride-A-Saurus HB140	2,750		107.00	107
1991 Saturday Blues HB120	2,750		105.00	105
1991 Vac-A-Saurus HB160	2,750		105.00	110
1991 Yabba-Dabba-Doo HB110	2,750		230.00	230

History of Golf - R. Lee

YEAR ISSUE	EDITION LIMIT	YEAR RETD.	ISSUE PRICE	*QUOTE U.S.$
1994 20th Century GTA700	10,000		150.00	150
1994 Age of Chivalry GTA400	10,000		150.00	150
1994 Caesar GTA300	10,000		150.00	150
1994 Dawn of Man GTA100	10,000		150.00	150
1994 New Frontiers GTA800	10,000		150.00	150
1994 Old West GTA600	10,000		150.00	150
1994 The Pharaoh GTA200	10,000		150.00	150
1994 Plymouth GTA500	10,000		150.00	150

Holiday Special - R. Lee

YEAR ISSUE	EDITION LIMIT	YEAR RETD.	ISSUE PRICE	*QUOTE U.S.$
1995 Bells, Stars, and Angels XMAS-4	N/A		39.00	39
1999 Bummin' A Ride w/Santa L586	1,500		235.00	235
1995 Gifts From Santa XMAS-5	N/A		39.00	39
1996 Happy Chanukah L489	950		190.00	190
1995 Holiday on Ice XMAS-3	N/A		39.00	39
1996 How Big! So Big! L490	950		197.00	197
1995 Santa's Other Sleigh L461	750		195.00	195
1995 Snowflake XMAS-6	N/A		35.00	35
1999 World of Clowns Menorah L585	1,500		325.00	325

Jerry Lewis Collection - R. Lee

YEAR ISSUE	EDITION LIMIT	YEAR RETD.	ISSUE PRICE	*QUOTE U.S.$
1990 The Accidental Tourist JL015	5,000	1998	330.00	675
1990 Angel's Lucky Day JL009	5,000	1996	205.00	325
1990 Angel, My Foot JL004	5,000	1997	205.00	325
1990 The Caddy JL020	5,000	1996	290.00	425
1990 Coming Attractions JL016	5,000	1995	280.00	675

*Quotes have been rounded up to nearest dollar

YEAR ISSUE	EDITION LIMIT	YEAR RETD.	ISSUE PRICE	*QUOTE U.S.$
1990 Curtain in 5 JL017	5,000	1998	310.00	425
1990 Hare Raising Experience JL012	5,000	1996	276.00	400
1990 I Shall Return JL007	5,000	1995	320.00	675
1990 I Wasn't Fishing, Honest! JL011	5,000	1998	320.00	450
1990 Mush! Andole! Moch Schnell JL014	5,000	1998	276.00	400
1990 Nutty! Love! JL001	5,000	1997	192.00	325
1990 Out To Lunch JL018	5,000	1995	470.00	1000
1990 Roll 'Em JL006	5,000	1996	285.00	500
1990 Steppin' Out JL002	5,000	1998	395.00	650
1990 Sugar and Spice JL005	5,000	1996	240.00	400
1990 Take it From the Top JL008	5,000	1995	225.00	325
1990 That's My Boy JL003	5,000	1997	370.00	675
1990 Vegas and Bust JL013	5,000	1997	210.00	325
1990 Who's Walking Who JL219	5,000	1995	460.00	1000

The Jetsons - R. Lee

YEAR ISSUE	EDITION LIMIT	YEAR RETD.	ISSUE PRICE	*QUOTE U.S.$
1991 4 O'Clock Tea HB550	2,750	1995	203.00	247
1991 Astro: Cosmic Canine HB520	2,750	1995	275.00	330-400
1991 The Cosmic Couple HB510	2,750	1995	105.00	126-150
1991 I Rove Roo HB530	2,750	1995	105.00	127-150
1991 The Jetsons HB500	2,750	1995	500.00	600-730
1991 Scare-D-Dog HB540	2,750	1995	160.00	192-235

Lance Burton - R. Lee

YEAR ISSUE	EDITION LIMIT	YEAR RETD.	ISSUE PRICE	*QUOTE U.S.$
1996 Levitation LB100	950		425.00	425

The Millennium Collection - R. Lee

YEAR ISSUE	EDITION LIMIT	YEAR RETD.	ISSUE PRICE	*QUOTE U.S.$
1999 Ching-Ching MS2006	950		225.00	225
1999 Ching-Ching w/Dixie MS2006A	950		295.00	295
1999 Congo Chango MS2000	950		355.00	355
1999 Har-Peggio MS2003	950		270.00	270
1999 Mal-Cello MS2004	950		295.00	295
1999 Ooom-Pa-Pa MS2001	950		325.00	325
1999 Ron-Tovin MS2002	950		495.00	495
1999 Senorita Ballerina MS2005	950		225.00	225
1999 Sheriff Ron MS2007	950		250.00	250
1999 Side Kicks MS2008	950		825.00	825

Musical Clowns in Harmony - R. Lee

YEAR ISSUE	EDITION LIMIT	YEAR RETD.	ISSUE PRICE	*QUOTE U.S.$
1994 Aristocrat L-424	750	1995	125.00	125-180
1994 Barella L-423	750	1995	125.00	125-180
1994 Bubbles L-422	750	1995	125.00	125-180
1994 Carpet Bagger L-421	750	1995	125.00	125-180
1994 Daisy L-417	750	1995	125.00	125-180
1994 Hot Dog L-418	750	1995	125.00	125-180
1994 Kandy L-419	750	1995	125.00	125-180
1994 Poodles L-420	750	1995	125.00	125-180
1994 Puddles L-416	750	1995	125.00	125-180
1994 Snacks L-425	750	1995	125.00	125-180

The Original Ron Lee Collection-1976 - R. Lee

YEAR ISSUE	EDITION LIMIT	YEAR RETD.	ISSUE PRICE	*QUOTE U.S.$
1976 Alligator Bowling 504	Closed	N/A	15.00	75-94
1976 Bear Fishing 511	Closed	N/A	15.00	75-94
1976 Clown and Dog Act 101	Closed	N/A	48.00	100-168
1976 Clown and Elephant Act 107	Closed	N/A	56.00	100-168
1976 Clown Tightrope Walker 104	Closed	N/A	50.00	125-186
1976 Dog Fishing 512	Closed	N/A	15.00	75-94
1976 Frog Surfing 502	Closed	N/A	15.00	75-94
1976 Hippo on Scooter 505	Closed	N/A	15.00	75-94
1976 Hobo Joe Hitchiking 116	Closed	N/A	55.00	78-150
1976 Hobo Joe with Balloons 120	Closed	N/A	63.00	150
1976 Hobo Joe with Pal 115	Closed	N/A	63.00	175-200
1976 Hobo Joe with Umbrella 117	Closed	N/A	58.00	150-192
1976 Kangaroos Boxing 508	Closed	N/A	15.00	75-94
1976 Owl With Guitar 500	Closed	N/A	15.00	75-94
1976 Penguin on Snowskis 503	Closed	N/A	15.00	75-94
1976 Pig Playing Violin 510	Closed	N/A	15.00	75-94
1976 Pinky Lying Down 112	Closed	N/A	25.00	150-250
1976 Pinky Sitting 119	Closed	N/A	25.00	150-170
1976 Pinky Standing 118	Closed	N/A	25.00	125-270
1976 Pinky Upside Down 111	Closed	N/A	25.00	150
1976 Rabbit Playing Tennis 507	Closed	N/A	15.00	75-94
1976 Turtle On Skateboard 501	Closed	N/A	15.00	75-94

The Original Ron Lee Collection-1977 - R. Lee

YEAR ISSUE	EDITION LIMIT	YEAR RETD.	ISSUE PRICE	*QUOTE U.S.$
1977 Bear On Rock 523	Closed	N/A	18.00	75-96
1977 Billie with Flowers 123	Closed	N/A	N/A	275
1977 Bingo 301A	Closed	N/A	N/A	N/A
1977 Bongo 300A	Closed	N/A	N/A	N/A
1977 Jumbo, the Elephant 121	Closed	N/A	175.00	175
1977 Koala Bear In Tree 514	Closed	N/A	15.00	50-94
1977 Koala Bear On Log 516	Closed	N/A	15.00	50-94
1977 Koala Bear With Baby 515	Closed	N/A	15.00	50-94
1977 Monkey With Banana 521	Closed	N/A	18.00	75-96
1977 Mouse and Cheese 520	Closed	N/A	18.00	75-96
1977 Mr. Penguin 518	Closed	N/A	18.00	75-102
1977 Owl Graduate 519	Closed	N/A	22.00	60-96
1977 Pelican and Python 522	Closed	N/A	18.00	70-96

The Original Ron Lee Collection-1978 - R. Lee

YEAR ISSUE	EDITION LIMIT	YEAR RETD.	ISSUE PRICE	*QUOTE U.S.$
1978 Bobbi on Unicycle 204	Closed	N/A	45.00	118-190
1978 Bow Tie 222	Closed	N/A	67.50	200-258
1978 Butterfly and Flower 529	Closed	N/A	22.00	40
1978 Clancy, the Cop 210	Closed	N/A	55.00	165-190
1978 Clara-Bow 205	Closed	N/A	52.00	148-190
1978 Coco-Hands on Hips 218	Closed	N/A	70.00	85-250
1978 Corky, the Drummer Boy 202	Closed	N/A	53.00	130-175
1978 Cuddles 208	Closed	N/A	37.00	110-140
1978 Dolphins 525	Closed	N/A	22.00	40-85
1978 Driver the Golfer 211	Closed	N/A	55.00	200-250
1978 Elephant on Ball 214	Closed	N/A	26.00	42-80
1978 Elephant on Stand 213	Closed	N/A	26.00	42-80
1978 Elephant Sitting 215	Closed	N/A	26.00	42-80
1978 Fancy Pants 224	Closed	N/A	55.00	120-220
1978 Fireman with Hose 216	Closed	N/A	62.00	170-190
1978 Hey Rube 220	Closed	N/A	35.00	92-125
1978 Hummingbird 528	Closed	N/A	22.00	40-85
1978 Jeri In a Barrel 219	Closed	N/A	75.00	175-190
1978 Jocko with Lollipop 221	Closed	N/A	67.50	93-215
1978 Oscar On Stilts 223	Closed	N/A	55.00	120-190
1978 Pierrot Painting 207	Closed	N/A	50.00	170-190
1978 Polly, the Parrot & Crackers 201	Closed	N/A	63.00	170-190
1978 Poppy with Puppet 209	Closed	N/A	60.00	75-140
1978 Prince Frog 526	Closed	N/A	22.00	40-85
1978 Sad Sack 212	Closed	N/A	48.00	62-210
1978 Sailfish 524	Closed	N/A	18.00	40-95
1978 Sea Otter on Back 531	Closed	N/A	22.00	40-85
1978 Sea Otter on Rock 532	Closed	N/A	22.00	40-85
1978 Seagull 527	Closed	N/A	22.00	40-85
1978 Skippy Swinging 239	Closed	N/A	52.00	65-85
1978 Sparky Skating 206	Closed	N/A	55.00	72-260
1978 Tinker Bowing 203	Closed	N/A	37.00	110-140
1978 Tobi-Hands Outstretched 217	Closed	N/A	70.00	98-260
1978 Turtle on Rock 530	Closed	N/A	22.00	40-85

The Original Ron Lee Collection-1979 - R. Lee

YEAR ISSUE	EDITION LIMIT	YEAR RETD.	ISSUE PRICE	*QUOTE U.S.$
1979 Buttons Bicycling 229	Closed	N/A	75.00	150-300
1979 Carousel Horse 232	Closed	N/A	119.00	130-225
1979 Darby Tipping Hat 238	Closed	N/A	35.00	75-140
1979 Darby with Flower 235	Closed	N/A	35.00	60-140
1979 Darby with Umbrella 236	Closed	N/A	35.00	60-140
1979 Darby With Violin 237	Closed	N/A	35.00	75-140
1979 Doctor Sawbones 228	Closed	N/A	75.00	150-250
1979 Fearless Fred in Cannon 234	Closed	N/A	80.00	105-300
1979 Gnome Playing Flute 600	Closed	N/A	N/A	N/A
1979 Gnome Reading 602	Closed	N/A	N/A	N/A
1979 Gnome Skiing 601	Closed	N/A	N/A	N/A
1979 Gnome with Pot O' Gold 603	Closed	N/A	N/A	N/A
1979 Harry and the Hare 233	Closed	N/A	69.00	180-225
1979 Kelly at the Piano 241	Closed	N/A	185.00	375
1979 Kelly in Kar 230	Closed	N/A	164.00	375
1979 Kelly's Kar 231	Closed	N/A	75.00	90-280
1979 Lilli 227	Closed	N/A	75.00	125
1979 Timmy Tooting 225	Closed	N/A	35.00	52-85
1979 Tubby Tuba 226	Closed	N/A	35.00	50-95

The Original Ron Lee Collection-1980 - R. Lee

YEAR ISSUE	EDITION LIMIT	YEAR RETD.	ISSUE PRICE	*QUOTE U.S.$
1980 Alexander's One Man Band 261	Closed	N/A	N/A	350
1980 Banjo Willie 258	Closed	N/A	68.00	85-195
1980 Carousel Horse 248	Closed	N/A	88.00	115-285
1980 Carousel Horse 249	Closed	N/A	88.00	115-285
1980 Chuckles Juggling 244	Closed	N/A	98.00	150-275
1980 Cubby Holding Balloon 240	Closed	N/A	50.00	70-95
1980 Dennis Playing Tennis 252	Closed	N/A	74.00	95-185
1980 Doctor Jawbones 260	Closed	N/A	85.00	250
1980 Donkey What 243	Closed	N/A	60.00	92-250
1980 Emile 257	Closed	N/A	43.00	82-190
1980 Happy Waving 255	Closed	N/A	43.00	75-125
1980 Hobo Joe in Tub 259	Closed	N/A	96.00	225
1980 Horse Drawn Chariot 263	Closed	N/A	N/A	720
1980 Jaque Downhill Racer 253	Closed	N/A	74.00	90-210
1980 Jingles Telling Time 242	Closed	N/A	75.00	150
1980 Jo-Jo at Make-up Mirror 250	Closed	N/A	86.00	125-185
1980 The Menagerie 262	Closed	N/A	N/A	N/A
1980 Monkey 251	Closed	N/A	60.00	85-210
1980 P. T. Dinghy 245	Closed	N/A	65.00	190-300
1980 Peanuts Playing Concertina 247	Closed	N/A	65.00	150-285
1980 Roni Riding Horse 246	Closed	N/A	115.00	290-375
1980 Ruford 254	Closed	N/A	43.00	75-100
1980 Zach 256	Closed	N/A	43.00	82-190

The Original Ron Lee Collection-1981 - R. Lee

YEAR ISSUE	EDITION LIMIT	YEAR RETD.	ISSUE PRICE	*QUOTE U.S.$
1981 Al at the Bass 284	Closed	N/A	48.00	90
1981 Barbella 273	Closed	N/A	76.00	190
1981 Bojangles 276	Closed	N/A	N/A	190
1981 Bosom Buddies 299	Closed	N/A	135.00	280-325
1981 Bozo On Unicycle 279	Closed	N/A	28.00	99-185
1981 Bozo Playing Cymbols 277	Closed	N/A	28.00	90-110
1981 Bozo Riding Car 278	Closed	N/A	28.00	99-185
1981 Carney and Seal Act 300	Closed	N/A	63.00	120
1981 Carousel Horse 280	Closed	N/A	88.00	125-290
1981 Carousel Horse 281	Closed	N/A	88.00	125-290
1981 Cashew On One Knee 275	Closed	N/A	N/A	N/A
1981 Elephant Reading 271	Closed	N/A	N/A	N/A
1981 Executive Hitchiking 267	Closed	N/A	23.00	75
1981 Executive Reading 264	Closed	N/A	23.00	75
1981 Executive Resting 266	Closed	N/A	23.00	75
1981 Executive with Umbrella 265	Closed	N/A	23.00	75
1981 Harpo 296	Closed	N/A	120.00	220
1981 Hobo Joe Praying 298	Closed	N/A	57.00	85-120
1981 Kevin at the Drums 283	Closed	N/A	50.00	90-120
1981 Larry and His Hotdogs 274	Closed	N/A	76.00	200-225
1981 Louie Hitching A Ride 269	Closed	N/A	47.00	120
1981 Louie on Park Bench 268	Closed	N/A	56.00	120
1981 Louie On Railroad Car 270	Closed	N/A	77.00	140-160
1981 Mickey With Umbrella 291	Closed	N/A	50.00	75-140
1981 Mickey Tightrope Walker 292	Closed	N/A	50.00	75-140
1981 Mickey Upside Down 293	Closed	N/A	50.00	75-140
1981 My Son Darren 295	Closed	N/A	57.00	72-140
1981 Nicky Sitting on Ball 289	Closed	N/A	39.00	48-92
1981 Nicky Standing on Ball 290	Closed	N/A	39.00	48-92
1981 Perry Sitting With Balloon 287	Closed	N/A	37.00	50-95
1981 Perry Standing With Balloon 288	Closed	N/A	37.00	50-95
1981 Pickles and Pooch 297	Closed	N/A	90.00	220
1981 Pistol Pete 272	Closed	N/A	76.00	180-210
1981 Rocketman 294	Closed	N/A	77.00	150-240
1981 Ron at the Piano 285	Closed	N/A	46.00	90
1981 Ron Lee Trio 282	Closed	N/A	144.00	275-300
1981 Timothy In Big Shoes 286	Closed	N/A	37.00	50-95

The Original Ron Lee Collection-1982 - R. Lee

YEAR ISSUE	EDITION LIMIT	YEAR RETD.	ISSUE PRICE	*QUOTE U.S.$
1982 Ali on His Magic Carpet 335	Closed	N/A	105.00	150-350
1982 Barnum Feeding Bacon 315	Closed	N/A	120.00	160-295
1982 Beaver Playing Accordian 807	Closed	N/A	23.00	65
1982 Benny Pulling Car 310	Closed	N/A	190.00	290
1982 Burrito Bandito 334	Closed	N/A	150.00	190-260
1982 Buster in Barrel 308	Closed	N/A	85.00	120-190
1982 Camel 818	Closed	N/A	57.00	75-150
1982 Captain Cranberry 320	Closed	N/A	115.00	175
1982 Captain Mis-Adventure 703	Closed	N/A	250.00	300-550
1982 Carney and Dog Act 301	Closed	N/A	63.00	120
1982 Charlie Chaplain 406	Closed	N/A	230.00	285-650
1982 Charlie in the Rain 321	Closed	N/A	80.00	90-160
1982 Chico Playing Guitar 336	Closed	N/A	70.00	95-180
1982 Clancy, the Cop and Dog 333	Closed	N/A	115.00	175-250
1982 Clarence - The Lawyer 331	Closed	N/A	100.00	140-230
1982 Denny Eating Ice Cream 305	Closed	N/A	39.00	50-170
1982 Denny Holding Gift Box 306	Closed	N/A	39.00	50-170
1982 Denny Juggling Ball 307	Closed	N/A	39.00	50-170
1982 Dog Playing Guitar 805	Closed	N/A	23.00	65
1982 Dr. Painless and Patient 311	Closed	N/A	195.00	350
1982 Fireman Watering House 303	Closed	N/A	99.00	99-180
1982 Fish With Shoe 803	Closed	N/A	23.00	65
1982 Fox In An Airplane 806	Closed	N/A	23.00	65
1982 Georgie Going Anywhere 302	Closed	N/A	95.00	220-375
1982 Giraffe 816	Closed	N/A	57.00	75-150
1982 Herbie Balancing Hat 327	Closed	N/A	26.00	40-110
1982 Herbie Dancing 325	Closed	N/A	26.00	40-110
1982 Herbie Hands Outstretched 326	Closed	N/A	26.00	40-110
1982 Herbie Legs in Air 329	Closed	N/A	26.00	60
1982 Herbie Lying Down 328	Closed	N/A	26.00	60
1982 Herbie Touching Ground 330	Closed	N/A	26.00	60
1982 Hobo Joe on Cycle 322	Closed	N/A	125.00	170-459
1982 Horse 819	Closed	N/A	57.00	75-150
1982 Kukla and Friend 316	Closed	N/A	100.00	210-240
1982 Laurel & Hardy 700	Closed	N/A	225.00	290-500
1982 Limousine Service 705	Closed	N/A	330.00	750-1500
1982 Lion 817	Closed	N/A	57.00	75-150
1982 Marion With Marrionette 317	Closed	N/A	105.00	225-240
1982 Murphy On Unicycle 337	Closed	N/A	115.00	160-288
1982 Nappy Snoozing 346	Closed	N/A	110.00	125-210
1982 Norman Painting Dumbo 314	Closed	N/A	126.00	210-250
1982 Ostrich 813	Closed	N/A	57.00	75-150
1982 Parrot Rollerskating 809	Closed	N/A	23.00	35-92
1982 Pig Brick Layer 800	Closed	N/A	23.00	65
1982 Pinball Pal 332	Closed	N/A	150.00	275
1982 Quincy Lying Down 304	Closed	N/A	80.00	92-210
1982 Rabbit With Egg 801	Closed	N/A	23.00	65
1982 Reindeer 812	Closed	N/A	57.00	75-150
1982 Robin Resting 338	Closed	N/A	110.00	125-210
1982 Ron Lee Carousel	Closed	N/A	1000.00	12500
1982 Rooster 815	Closed	N/A	57.00	65-110
1982 Rooster With Barbell 808	Closed	N/A	23.00	35-92
1982 Sammy Riding Elephant 309	Closed	N/A	90.00	125-250
1982 Seal Blowing His Horns 804	Closed	N/A	23.00	35-92
1982 Self Portrait 702	Closed	N/A	355.00	2500
1982 Slim Charging Bull 313	Closed	N/A	195.00	290
1982 Smokey, the Bear 802	Closed	N/A	23.00	65
1982 Steppin' Out 704	Closed	N/A	325.00	390-700
1982 Three Man Valentinos 319	Closed	N/A	55.00	110
1982 Tiger 814	Closed	N/A	57.00	75-150
1982 Too Loose-L'Artiste 312	Closed	N/A	150.00	290-325
1982 Tou Tou 323	Closed	N/A	70.00	90-190
1982 Toy Soldier 324	Closed	N/A	95.00	250
1982 Turtle With Gun 811	Closed	N/A	57.00	65-110
1982 Two Man Valentinos 318	Closed	N/A	45.00	110
1982 Walrus With Umbrella 810	Closed	N/A	23.00	65

The Original Ron Lee Collection-1983 - R. Lee

YEAR ISSUE	EDITION LIMIT	YEAR RETD.	ISSUE PRICE	*QUOTE U.S.$
1983 The Bandwagon 707	Closed	N/A	900.00	3700
1983 Beethoven's Fourth Paws 358	Closed	N/A	59.00	120
1983 Black Carousel Horse 1001	Closed	N/A	450.00	450-600
1983 Bumbles Selling Balloons 353	Closed	N/A	80.00	170-240
1983 Buster and His Balloons 363	Closed	N/A	47.00	90-125
1983 Captain Freddy 375	Closed	N/A	85.00	450
1983 Casey Cruising 351	Closed	N/A	57.00	95-170
1983 Catch the Brass Ring 708	Closed	N/A	510.00	900-1350
1983 Cecil and Sausage 354	Closed	N/A	90.00	120-200
1983 Chef's Cuisine 361	Closed	N/A	57.00	100-110
1983 Chestnut Carousel Horse 1002	Closed	N/A	450.00	700-1100
1983 Cimba the Elephant 706	Closed	N/A	225.00	300-550
1983 Clyde Juggling 339	Closed	N/A	39.00	65-100
1983 Clyde Upside Down 340	Closed	N/A	39.00	65-100
1983 Coco and His Compact 369	Closed	N/A	55.00	75-150
1983 Cotton Candy 377	Closed	N/A	150.00	250
1983 Daring Dudley 367	Closed	N/A	65.00	120
1983 Door to Door Dabney 373	Closed	N/A	100.00	240
1983 Engineer Billie 356	Closed	N/A	190.00	275-550
1983 Flipper Diving 345	Closed	N/A	115.00	225-300
1983 Gazebo 1004	Closed	N/A	750.00	1300-1750
1983 Gilbert Tee'd Off 376	Closed	N/A	60.00	120-200
1983 Hobi in His Hammock 344	Closed	N/A	85.00	175
1983 I Love You From My Heart 360	Closed	N/A	35.00	65-125
1983 The Jogger 372	Closed	N/A	75.00	120-220
1983 Josephine 370	Closed	N/A	55.00	90-125
1983 Knickers Balancing Feather 366	Closed	N/A	47.00	90-120
1983 The Last Scoop 379	Closed	N/A	175.00	350-600
1983 The Last Scoop 900	Closed	N/A	325.00	300-725
1983 Little Horse - Head Down 342	Closed	N/A	29.00	72
1983 Little Horse - Head Up 341	Closed	N/A	29.00	65-72

*Quotes have been rounded up to nearest dollar

YEAR ISSUE	EDITION LIMIT	YEAR RETD.	ISSUE PRICE	*QUOTE U.S.$
1983 Little Saturday Night 348	Closed	N/A	53.00	90-120
1983 Lou Proposing 365	Closed	N/A	57.00	90-120
1983 Matinee Jitters 378	Closed	N/A	175.00	200-450
1983 Matinee Jitters 901	Closed	N/A	325.00	350-425
1983 My Daughter Deborah 357	Closed	N/A	63.00	125-185
1983 No Camping or Fishing 902	Closed	N/A	325.00	350-450
1983 On The Road Again 355	Closed	N/A	220.00	300-650
1983 Riches to Rags 374	Closed	N/A	108.00	225
1983 Ride 'em Roni 347	Closed	N/A	125.00	200-375
1983 Rufus and His Refuse 343	Closed	N/A	65.00	120-192
1983 Say It With Flowers 359	Closed	N/A	35.00	65-95
1983 Singin' In The Rain 362	Closed	N/A	105.00	350-420
1983 Tatters and Balloons 352	Closed	N/A	65.00	150-162
1983 Teeter Tottie Scottie 350	Closed	N/A	55.00	105-165
1983 Tottie Scottie 349	Closed	N/A	39.00	75-115
1983 Up, Up and Away 364	Closed	N/A	50.00	300
1983 White Carousel Horse 1003	Closed	N/A	450.00	700-1100
1983 Wilt the Stilt 368	Closed	N/A	49.00	100-110

The Original Ron Lee Collection-1984 - R. Lee

YEAR ISSUE	EDITION LIMIT	YEAR RETD.	ISSUE PRICE	*QUOTE U.S.$
1984 40 Love 727	Closed	N/A	110.00	110
1984 Baggy Pants 387	Closed	N/A	98.00	250-300
1984 A Ballon for Muffin 396	Closed	N/A	148.00	148
1984 Barney Bowling 728	Closed	N/A	115.00	115
1984 Bear-Lee 398	Closed	N/A	118.00	118-140
1984 Beginner's Run 726	Closed	N/A	165.00	165
1984 Ben-Him 404	Closed	N/A	184.00	184-300
1984 Black Circus Horse 711A	Closed	N/A	305.00	350-520
1984 A Bozo Lunch 390	Closed	N/A	148.00	265-300
1984 Bozo's Seal of Approval 389	Closed	N/A	138.00	240-300
1984 Bust 716	Closed	N/A	100.00	100-300
1984 Bust 717	Closed	N/A	100.00	100-300
1984 Bust 718	Closed	N/A	100.00	100-300
1984 Buttons of Love 712	Closed	N/A	N/A	360
1984 Candy Sitting 736	Closed	N/A	135.00	135
1984 Carousel Horse 403	Closed	N/A	113.00	113
1984 Charlie at the Computer 406	Closed	N/A	140.00	140-210
1984 Chestnut Circus Horse 710A	Closed	N/A	305.00	350-520
1984 Coco Sitting 735	Closed	N/A	165.00	165
1984 Deli Dan 402	Closed	N/A	93.00	93
1984 Dragging My Ass 401	Closed	N/A	168.00	168
1984 Floyd Fishing 729	Closed	N/A	115.00	115
1984 Give a Dog a Bone 383	Closed	N/A	95.00	182-220
1984 Happy Birthday to Me 394	Closed	N/A	68.00	68-125
1984 Here Kitty-Kitty 397	Closed	N/A	78.00	78-125
1984 Hobo Hal at Slot Machine 732	Closed	N/A	178.00	178-275
1984 Hobo Hal at Violin 733	Closed	N/A	140.00	140-275
1984 Hobo Joe's Masterpiece 405	Closed	N/A	184.00	184-325
1984 It's Showtime 400	Closed	N/A	108.00	108-250
1984 Just For You 386	Closed	N/A	110.00	190
1984 Kittens For Sale 399	Closed	N/A	108.00	108-125
1984 Large Circus Horse 723	Closed	N/A	355.00	850
1984 Little Boy Blue 710	Closed	N/A	305.00	305
1984 Look at the Birdy 388	Closed	N/A	138.00	225
1984 The Mime 715	Closed	N/A	150.00	150
1984 Mortimer Fishing 382	Closed	N/A	78.00	94
1984 My Fellow Americans 391	Closed	N/A	138.00	240-300
1984 The Ninth Hole 725	Closed	N/A	110.00	110
1984 No Camping or Fishing 380	Closed	N/A	175.00	275-450
1984 No Loitering 392	Closed	N/A	113.00	150-250
1984 Penny For a Song 395	Closed	N/A	153.00	153-250
1984 The Peppermints 384	Closed	N/A	150.00	180-250
1984 Poke 'N Along 720	Closed	N/A	175.00	425
1984 Poke 'N Beans 719	Closed	N/A	175.00	425
1984 Poke 'N Park Bench 721	Closed	N/A	175.00	425
1984 Poke 'N Tub 722	Closed	N/A	175.00	400
1984 Rocky Roller Skating 730	Closed	N/A	N/A	N/A
1984 Rub-A-Dub Tub 737	Closed	N/A	355.00	1500
1984 Rudy Holding Balloons 713	Closed	N/A	230.00	450
1984 Saturday Night 714	Closed	N/A	250.00	750
1984 T.K. and OH!! 385	Closed	N/A	85.00	200-325
1984 Tara, The Elephant 724	Closed	N/A	355.00	355
1984 Tisket and Tasket 393	Closed	N/A	93.00	150-250
1984 Tobi Juggling 734	Closed	N/A	125.00	125-240
1984 Wheeler Sheila 381	Closed	N/A	75.00	175-225
1984 White Circus Horse 709	Closed	N/A	305.00	350-520
1984 Wimp Weighing 731	Closed	N/A	N/A	N/A

The Original Ron Lee Collection-1985 - R. Lee

YEAR ISSUE	EDITION LIMIT	YEAR RETD.	ISSUE PRICE	*QUOTE U.S.$
1985 Bareback Rider 429	Closed	N/A	155.00	155
1985 Bear-Lee Hitchhiking B-203	Closed	N/A	47.00	47-90
1985 Bear-Lee Raining B-201	Closed	N/A	47.00	47-90
1985 Bear-Lee with Balloon B-202	Closed	N/A	47.00	47-90
1985 Black Horse 425	Closed	N/A	75.00	75-90
1985 Bosco's Buddies 754	Closed	N/A	246.00	246-450
1985 Bozo Conducting 418	Closed	N/A	75.00	75-90
1985 Bozo Drumming 417	Closed	N/A	75.00	75-90
1985 Bozo Holding Balloons 419	Closed	N/A	75.00	75-90
1985 Bozo's Love of Balloons 751	Closed	N/A	235.00	235-450
1985 Brown Horse 424	Closed	N/A	75.00	75-90
1985 Bull-Can-Rear-You 422	Closed	N/A	120.00	245
1985 Cannonball 466	Closed	N/A	43.00	100
1985 Catch of the Day 441	Closed	N/A	170.00	365
1985 Clown Playing Bass 738	Closed	N/A	135.00	135
1985 Clown Playing Scrubboard 740	Closed	N/A	135.00	135
1985 Clown Playing Washbucket 739	Closed	N/A	135.00	135
1985 Clowns of the Caribbean PS101	Closed	N/A	1250.00	2800-3700
1985 Debbiedoo with Balloon 742	Closed	N/A	125.00	125
1985 Denny Playing Music M-102	Closed	N/A	129.00	129
1985 Dr. Sigmund Fraud 457	Closed	N/A	98.00	140-190
1985 Dr. Timothy DeCay 459	Closed	N/A	98.00	185
1985 Eat at Joe's 760	Closed	N/A	251.00	251
1985 The Finishing Touch 409	Closed	N/A	178.00	305-325
1985 First Down 756	Closed	N/A	425.00	425
1985 Fred Figures 903	Closed	N/A	175.00	300-595
1985 Freddie, The Torchbearer 407	Closed	N/A	113.00	250-450
1985 Friendly Gesture 762	Closed	N/A	255.00	255
1985 Frosty's Cool Treat 753	Closed	N/A	285.00	285-450
1985 Frosty's Precious Love 752	Closed	N/A	255.00	255-450
1985 Frosty's Reflections 423	Closed	N/A	160.00	160
1985 Gilbert Teed OFF 376	Closed	N/A	63.00	63-120
1985 Giraffe Getting a Bath 428	Closed	N/A	160.00	350-450
1985 Grandy Old Opry 741	Closed	N/A	N/A	N/A
1985 Great Escape 430	Closed	N/A	150.00	150-250
1985 Grey Horse 426	Closed	N/A	75.00	75-90
1985 He's Not Heavy - He's My Friend 759	Closed	N/A	275.00	275
1985 Jillee - The Mime 743	Closed	N/A	110.00	110-225
1985 Knickers Eating Lunch 414	Closed	N/A	100.00	100-220
1985 Knickers Golfing 416	Closed	N/A	90.00	90
1985 Knickers Hitchhiking 415	Closed	N/A	95.00	95
1985 Knickers with Balloons 413	Closed	N/A	85.00	85
1985 The Last Balloon 763	Closed	N/A	255.00	255
1985 Lee-Birace 757	Closed	N/A	450.00	450
1985 Munchkin Happy Birthday 410	Closed	N/A	55.00	55-75
1985 Munchkin I Love You 410	Closed	N/A	55.00	55-75
1985 Munchkin I'm All Yours 413	Closed	N/A	55.00	55
1985 Oscar on Stilts 748	Closed	N/A	N/A	110
1985 Outnumbered 423	Closed	N/A	97.00	240
1985 Pee Wee With Balloons 435	Closed	N/A	50.00	100-140
1985 Pee Wee With Umbrella 434	Closed	N/A	50.00	100
1985 Pepper's Fine Feathered Friend 755	Closed	N/A	195.00	195
1985 Perry Playing Music M-101	Closed	N/A	129.00	110-129
1985 Pinky Playing Music M-103	Closed	N/A	129.00	129
1985 Policy Paul 904	Closed	N/A	175.00	190-300
1985 Rosebuds 433	Closed	N/A	155.00	315
1985 Southern Exposure 420	Closed	N/A	80.00	210-300
1985 Tasty Punishment 421	Closed	N/A	115.00	115-240
1985 Tomorrow is Soon Enough 758	Closed	N/A	300.00	950
1985 Twas the Night Before 408	Closed	N/A	235.00	325-405
1985 The Virtuoso 761	Closed	N/A	265.00	950
1985 Whiskers Bathing 749	Closed	N/A	305.00	1000-1500
1985 Whiskers Hitchhiking 745	Closed	N/A	240.00	800
1985 Whiskers Holding Balloons 746	Closed	N/A	265.00	700-800
1985 Whiskers Holding Umbrella 747	Closed	N/A	265.00	500-800
1985 Whiskers On The Bench 750	Closed	N/A	230.00	695-895
1985 Whiskers Sweeping 744	Closed	N/A	240.00	700-850
1985 White Horse 427	Closed	N/A	65.00	65-90
1985 Winning a Peel 764	Closed	N/A	190.00	190
1985 Yo Yo Stravinsky-Attoney at Law 458	Closed	N/A	98.00	200
1985 You Want It When 431	Closed	N/A	155.00	155-220

The Original Ron Lee Collection-1986 - R. Lee

YEAR ISSUE	EDITION LIMIT	YEAR RETD.	ISSUE PRICE	*QUOTE U.S.$
1986 Automatic Starter 453	Closed	N/A	125.00	125-150
1986 Bag Lady 445	Closed	N/A	80.00	80-110
1986 Bathing Buddies 450	Closed	N/A	145.00	375
1986 Birds to You 471	Closed	N/A	143.00	143
1986 Bobo the Clown 455	Closed	N/A	60.00	60-75
1986 Bucki Lying Down 476	Closed	N/A	43.00	43-75
1986 Bucki Sitting 474	Closed	N/A	43.00	43
1986 Bucki Standing 475	Closed	N/A	43.00	43-75
1986 Bucki Upside Down 473	Closed	N/A	43.00	43
1986 Bum Mitzvah 470	Closed	N/A	130.00	300
1986 Bums Day at the Beach L105	Closed	N/A	97.00	97-120
1986 Cannon Ball 466	Closed	N/A	47.00	47
1986 Captain Cranberry 469	Closed	N/A	140.00	175-335
1986 Catch of the Day 441	Closed	N/A	187.00	187-250
1986 Caution, No Snow 438	Closed	N/A	106.00	106-210
1986 Childhood Fantasy 449	Closed	N/A	70.00	70
1986 Christmas Morning Magic L107	Closed	N/A	99.00	95
1986 Corky Sitting 452	Closed	N/A	62.00	62-72
1986 Danny Dentures 902	Closed	N/A	192.00	300
1986 Duster Buster 461	Closed	N/A	47.00	47-65
1986 Fly Me, I'm Maggie 446	Closed	N/A	N/A	120
1986 Get The Picture 456	Closed	N/A	77.00	77
1986 Get The Point 440	Closed	N/A	166.00	166-275
1986 Getting Even 485	Closed	N/A	85.00	140
1986 Ham Track 451	Closed	N/A	264.00	264
1986 Hari and Hare 454	Closed	N/A	57.00	90-120
1986 Have a Seat 481	Closed	N/A	43.00	43
1986 Have Bag, Will Travel 478	Closed	N/A	43.00	43-75
1986 Hi Ho Blinky 462	Closed	N/A	58.00	58-75
1986 High Above the Big Top L112	Closed	1997	162.00	220-475
1986 Hobo Joe in Concert 460	Closed	N/A	170.00	170
1986 Horsin Around 447	Closed	N/A	65.00	65
1986 Matinee Jitters 472	Closed	N/A	189.00	189
1986 Mini-Go-Round 465	Closed	N/A	50.00	50-65
1986 Morning Edition 480	Closed	N/A	43.00	43-65
1986 Most Requested Toy L108	Closed	1991	264.00	300
1986 One Wheel Winky 464	Closed	N/A	87.00	87
1986 Pee Wee Overflowing Generosity 437	Closed	N/A	146.00	146-225
1986 Pete Peddler 901	Closed	N/A	176.00	300
1986 Pockets 467	Closed	N/A	47.00	47-65
1986 Puppy Love's Portrait L113	Closed	1995	168.00	210-325
1986 Ride 'Em Peanuts 463	Closed	N/A	55.00	110
1986 Room with a View 477	Closed	N/A	43.00	43-65
1986 Sid Spectacle 900	Closed	N/A	166.00	166
1986 Squeeze-O 448	Closed	N/A	70.00	70-120
1986 Taggin' Along 479	Closed	N/A	43.00	43
1986 Things Look Fishy 439	Closed	N/A	192.00	192-275
1986 Tomorrow's Next President 444	Closed	N/A	75.00	75-110
1986 Two Weiner Willie 443	Closed	N/A	95.00	95
1986 Wet Paint 436	Closed	N/A	80.00	135-210
1986 Yes Dear!!! 468	Closed	N/A	140.00	140-240

The Original Ron Lee Collection-1987 - R. Lee

YEAR ISSUE	EDITION LIMIT	YEAR RETD.	ISSUE PRICE	*QUOTE U.S.$
1987 Balloons Balloons H-201	Closed	N/A	79.00	79-140
1987 Be It Ever So Humble L-111	1,750	1991	900.00	1900
1987 Beat It! Elephant 482	Closed	N/A	43.00	43
1987 Bulldog 484	Closed	N/A	150.00	150
1987 Bums Day at PGA L-105	4,500	1992	107.00	107-190
1987 First & Main L110	1,900	1997	368.00	350-500
1987 Going My Way H-202	Closed	N/A	66.00	66-140
1987 Happines Is L116	4,500	1992	155.00	185
1987 Hawaii or Bust H-208	Closed	N/A	143.00	143-210
1987 Heartbroken Harry L101	8,500	1992	63.00	125-225
1987 In Concert H-210	Closed	N/A	187.00	187-225
1987 The Last Stop L106	Closed	1995	108.00	108
1987 Lefty 483	Closed	N/A	150.00	150-225
1987 Lovable Luke L102	8,500	1997	70.00	150
1987 The Masterpiece H-207	Closed	N/A	202.00	202-250
1987 My Prayer H-205	Closed	N/A	69.00	69
1987 No Vacancy H-204	Closed	N/A	114.00	114-150
1987 Puppy Love L103	8,500	1998	71.00	150
1987 Rainy Day Blues H-203	Closed	N/A	70.00	70-140
1987 Ron Lee Sign S-100	Closed	N/A	40.00	40
1987 Sharing H-209	Closed	N/A	79.00	79-150
1987 Show of Shows L115	Closed	1990	175.00	245
1987 Sugarland Express L109	Closed	1996	342.00	400-600
1987 Traveling in Style H-206	Closed	N/A	136.00	136-240
1987 Wishful Thinking L114	1,911	1991	230.00	2000-3000
1987 Would You Like To Ride? L104	5,500	1990	246.00	350
1987 Xmas Morning Magic L107	Closed	1990	108.00	108-175

The Original Ron Lee Collection-1988 - R. Lee

YEAR ISSUE	EDITION LIMIT	YEAR RETD.	ISSUE PRICE	*QUOTE U.S.$
1988 Anchors-A-Way L120	1,500	1992	195.00	240
1988 Boulder Bay L124	1,250	1991	700.00	700-950
1988 Bozorina L118	Closed	1995	95.00	150
1988 Cactus Pete L125	1,500	1995	495.00	750
1988 Dinner for Two L119	1,500	1992	140.00	140-225
1988 The Fifth Wheel L117	1,950	1990	250.00	375
1988 Fore! L122	2,500	1992	135.00	175-210
1988 New Ron Lee Carousel	Closed	N/A	7000.00	9500
1988 Pumpkuns Galore L121	2,500	1995	135.00	160-245
1988 To The Rescue L127	1,750	1991	130.00	160-550
1988 Together Again L126	3,750	1995	130.00	160-210
1988 Tunnel of Love L123	1,500	1993	490.00	490-600
1988 When You're Hot, You're Hot! L128	1,750	1991	221.00	295-375

The Original Ron Lee Collection-1989 - R. Lee

YEAR ISSUE	EDITION LIMIT	YEAR RETD.	ISSUE PRICE	*QUOTE U.S.$
1989 The Accountant L173	7,500	1992	68.00	95-110
1989 The Baseball Player L189	7,500	1997	72.00	110
1989 The Basketball Player L187	7,500	1992	68.00	95-110
1989 Be Happy L198	2,500	1995	160.00	195-240
1989 Be It Ever So Humble L111	1,750	1991	900.00	1250-1500
1989 The Beautician L183	7,500	1995	68.00	150-200
1989 Beauty Is In The Eye Of L140	2,250	1996	190.00	250-400
1989 Birdbrain L206	3,500	1997	110.00	190-250
1989 The Bowler L191	7,500	1997	68.00	110
1989 Butt-R-Fly L151	2,750	1996	47.00	80
1989 Butterflies Are Free L204	2,250	1996	225.00	250
1989 Candy Apple L155	2,750	1995	47.00	80
1989 Candy Man L217	2,750	1995	350.00	400
1989 Catch A Falling Star L148	2,750	1996	57.00	80
1989 The Chef L178	7,500	1995	65.00	150-200
1989 The Chiropractor L180	7,500	1996	68.00	150-200
1989 Circus Little L143	750	1995	990.00	1250-1500
1989 Craps L212	3,500	1994	530.00	895-1000
1989 Dang It L200	7,500	1995	47.00	65
1989 The Dentist L175	7,500	1996	65.00	150-200
1989 The Doctor L170	7,500	1996	65.00	95-110
1989 Eye Love You L136	2,750	1995	68.00	140
1989 The Fireman L169	7,500	1997	68.00	95-110
1989 The Fisherman L194	7,500	1994	72.00	110
1989 The Football Player L186	7,500	1996	65.00	150-200
1989 Get Well L131	3,750	1996	79.00	96-149
1989 The Golfer L188	7,500	1997	72.00	95-110
1989 The Greatest Little Shoe On Earth L210	1,250	1996	165.00	250
1989 Happy Chanakah L162	1,250	1991	106.00	125-175
1989 Hi! Ho! Bingo L129	3,500	1995	116.00	190
1989 Hot Diggity Dog L201	7,500	1993	47.00	65
1989 The Housewife L181	7,500	1996	75.00	95-110
1989 Hughie Mungus L144	750	1996	250.00	425-600
1989 I Ain't Got No Money L195	2,250	1992	325.00	900
1989 I Just Called! L153	2,750	1996	47.00	80
1989 I Pledge Allegiance L134	3,750	1996	131.00	150-250
1989 I Should've When I Could've L196	2,250	1996	325.00	900
1989 I-D-D-D-Do! L215	3,500	1994	180.00	240
1989 If I Were A Rich Man L133	2,750	1996	315.00	695-900
1989 If That's Your Drive How's Your Putts L164	1,250	1995	260.00	420
1989 In Over My Head L135	3,750	1995	95.00	190-250
1989 Jingles Hitchhiking L209	2,750	1995	90.00	200
1989 Jingles Holding Balloon L208	2,750	1993	90.00	190
1989 Jingles With Umbrella L207	2,750	1995	90.00	210
1989 Just Carried Away L138	2,500	1995	135.00	225
1989 Just Go! L156	2,750	1992	47.00	75
1989 The Lawyer 171	7,500	1995	68.00	150-200
1989 Maestro L132	2,750	1992	173.00	200
1989 Marcelle L150	2,750	1995	47.00	80
1989 The Mechanic L184	7,500	1993	68.00	95-110
1989 Memories L197	2,250	1993	325.00	900
1989 Merry Xmas L159	1,250	1993	94.00	175
1989 My Affections L157	2,750	1995	47.00	75
1989 My First Tree L161	1,250	1995	92.00	150
1989 My Heart Beats For You L137	2,750	1995	74.00	135
1989 My Last Chip L213	3,500	1994	550.00	900
1989 My Money's OnThe Bull L142	1,750	1995	187.00	295-350
1989 The New Self Portrait L218	1,750	1995	800.00	2000-3000

*Quotes have been rounded up to nearest dollar

YEAR ISSUE	EDITION LIMIT	YEAR RETD.	ISSUE PRICE	*QUOTE U.S.$
1989 No Fishing L130	1,250	1995	247.00	795
1989 Not A Ghost Of A Chance L145	2,250	1996	195.00	275-350
1989 The Nurse L168	7,500	1995	65.00	95
1989 O' Solo Mia L139	2,750	1995	85.00	120
1989 The Optometrist L174	7,500	1997	65.00	95-110
1989 Over 21 L214	3,500	1994	550.00	N/A
1989 Perilous Journey PC-102	Closed	N/A	1250.00	1250
1989 The Pharmacist L166	7,500	1994	65.00	95
1989 The Photographer L172	7,500	1996	68.00	95-110
1989 The Plumber L176	7,500	1996	65.00	150-200
1989 The Policeman L165	7,500	1997	68.00	95-110
1989 Rain Bugs Me L203	2,250	1996	225.00	N/A
1989 The Real Estate Lady L185	7,500	1996	70.00	95-110
1989 The Real Estate Man L177	7,500	1996	65.00	95-110
1989 Rest Stop L149	2,750	1996	47.00	80
1989 The Salesman L167	7,500	1997	68.00	N/A
1989 Santa's Dilemma L160	1,250	1995	97.00	150-250
1989 The Secretary L179	7,500	1997	65.00	95
1989 The Serenade L202	7,500	1995	47.00	65
1989 Sh-h-h-h! L146	2,250	1996	210.00	350-450
1989 She Loves Me Not L205	2,250	1996	225.00	250
1989 The Skier L193	7,500	1994	75.00	110
1989 Slots Of Luck L211	3,500	1997	90.00	300-375
1989 Snowdrifter L163	750	1992	230.00	395-500
1989 Stormy Weathers L152	2,750	1996	47.00	80
1989 Sunflower L154	2,750	1995	47.00	80
1989 The Surfer L192	7,500	1995	72.00	150-200
1989 Tee for Two L141	2,500	1995	125.00	190
1989 The Tennis Player L190	7,500	1997	72.00	150-200
1989 Today's Catch L147	2,700	1995	230.00	360
1989 Two a.m. Blues L199	2,500	1995	125.00	190
1989 The Veterinarian L182	7,500	1993	72.00	95-110
1989 Wintertime Pals L158	1,250	1993	90.00	150
1989 You Must Be Kidding L216	1,750	1993	N/A	800

The Original Ron Lee Collection-1990 - R. Lee

YEAR ISSUE	EDITION LIMIT	YEAR RETD.	ISSUE PRICE	*QUOTE U.S.$
1990 All Show No Go L238	1,500		285.00	795
1990 The Big Wheel L236	2,750	1996	240.00	450
1990 Carousel Horse L219	3,500	1992	150.00	N/A
1990 Carousel Horse L220	3,500	1996	150.00	N/A
1990 Carousel Horse L221	3,500	1992	150.00	N/A
1990 Carousel Horse L222	3,500	1997	150.00	210
1990 Fill'er Up L248	2,250	N/A	280.00	300
1990 Flapper Riding Carousel L223	3,500	1992	190.00	N/A
1990 Heart of My Heart L246	5,500	1995	55.00	55
1990 Heartbroken Hobo L233	2,750	N/A	116.00	195
1990 Henry 8-3/4 L260	2,750	N/A	37.00	50
1990 Horsin' Around L262	2,750	1997	37.00	50-65
1990 I Love You L242	5,500	1995	55.00	55
1990 I.Q. Two L253	2,750	1995	33.00	50
1990 Jo-Jo Riding Carousel L226	3,500	1995	190.00	240
1990 Kiss! Kiss! L251	2,750	N/A	37.00	44-50
1990 L-O-V-E L245	5,500	1995	55.00	66
1990 Loving You L244	5,500	1996	55.00	66
1990 Me Too!! L231	3,500	1995	70.00	90
1990 My Heart's on for You L240	5,500	1995	55.00	66
1990 Na! Na! L252	2,750	1997	33.00	65
1990 New Pinky Lying Down L228	8,500		42.00	50
1990 New Pinky Sitting L230	8,500		42.00	50
1990 New Pinky Standing L229	8,500		42.00	50
1990 New Pinky Upside Down L227	8,500		42.00	50
1990 The New Self Portrait L218	1,750	1995	800.00	800
1990 Paddle L259	2,750	1995	33.00	50-65
1990 Par Three L232	2,750	1995	144.00	125-144
1990 Peaches Riding Carousel L224	3,500	1992	190.00	225
1990 Pitch L261	2,750	1995	35.00	50
1990 Push and Pull L249	2,250	N/A	260.00	280
1990 Q.T. Pie L257	2,750	1995	37.00	50
1990 Rascal Riding Carousel L225	3,500	1992	190.00	210
1990 Same To "U" L255	2,750	1995	37.00	50
1990 Scooter L234	2,750	1995	240.00	295-450
1990 Skiing My Way L239	2,500	1995	400.00	895
1990 Snowdrifter II L250	1,250	1996	340.00	895-925
1990 Squirt L258	2,750	1995	37.00	50
1990 Stuck on Me L243	5,500	1995	55.00	55
1990 Swinging on a Star L241	5,500	1995	55.00	55
1990 Tandem Mania L235	2,750	1995	360.00	650
1990 Uni-Cycle L237	2,750	1993	240.00	450
1990 Watch Your Step L247	2,500	1996	78.00	78
1990 Yo Mama L256	2,750	1995	35.00	50
1990 Your Heaviness L254	2,750	1995	37.00	65

The Original Ron Lee Collection-1991 - R. Lee

YEAR ISSUE	EDITION LIMIT	YEAR RETD.	ISSUE PRICE	*QUOTE U.S.$
1991 Ain't No Havana L315	500	1995	230.00	425
1991 Anywhere? L269	1,500	N/A	125.00	245
1991 Banjo Willie L293	1,750	1996	90.00	90-110
1991 Business is Business L266	1,500	1995	110.00	190-225
1991 Clarence Clarinet L289	1,750	1995	42.00	65
1991 Cruising L265	Closed	N/A	170.00	175-225
1991 Droopy Drummer L290	1,750	1995	42.00	65
1991 Eight Ball-Corner Pocket L311	1,750		224.00	250
1991 Fall L282	1,500		120.00	124
1991 Geronimo L304	1,750		127.00	127
1991 Gilbert's Dilemma L270	1,750	1997	90.00	125
1991 Give Me Liberty L313	1,776	1993	155.00	165-200
1991 Happy Birthday Puppy Love L278	1,750	1997	73.00	100-150
1991 Harley Horn L291	1,750	1995	42.00	50
1991 Hobi Daydreaming L299	1,750	1996	112.00	112
1991 Hook, Line and Sinker L303	1,750		100.00	100
1991 Hot Dawg! L316	500	1995	255.00	255
1991 I'm Singin' In The Rain L268	1,500	1997	135.00	195-225
1991 IRS or Bust L285	1,500	1995	122.00	90-122
1991 Lit'l Snowdrifter L298	1,750	1996	70.00	150
1991 Makin Tracks L283	1,500	1995	142.00	142-190
1991 Marcelle I L271	2,250	1995	50.00	50-90
1991 Marcelle II L272	2,250	1995	50.00	90-100
1991 Marcelle III L273	2,250	1995	50.00	50
1991 Marcelle IV L274	2,250	1995	50.00	50
1991 The New Circus Wagon L292	1,750	1991	N/A	N/A
1991 New Darby Tipping Hat L310	1,250	1995	57.00	59
1991 New Darby with Flower L307	1,250	1995	57.00	59
1991 New Darby with Umbrella L308	1,250	1995	57.00	59
1991 New Darby with Violin L309	1,250	1995	57.00	57
1991 New Harpo L305	1,250	1995	130.00	130
1991 New Toy Soldier L306	1,250	1995	115.00	125
1991 Our Nation's Pride L312	1,776	1996	150.00	150
1991 Puppy Love Scootin' L275	1,750	1997	73.00	100-125
1991 Puppy Love's Free Ride L276	1,750	1996	73.00	125-150
1991 Puppy Love's Treat L277	1,750	1996	73.00	125-150
1991 Refugee L267	1,750	1995	88.00	125
1991 Sand Trap L301	1,750		100.00	100
1991 Soap Suds Serenade L284	1,750	1996	85.00	85-136
1991 Spring L280	1,500		95.00	100
1991 Strike!!! L302	1,750		76.00	76
1991 Summer L281	1,500		95.00	100
1991 Surf's Up L300	1,750		80.00	80
1991 TA DA L294	1,500	1997	220.00	200-295
1991 Tender-Lee L264	1,750	1995	96.00	96
1991 This Won't Hurt L296	1,750	1995	110.00	110-190
1991 Tootie Tuba L286	1,750	1995	42.00	50
1991 Trash Can Sam L295	1,750	1995	118.00	118-190
1991 Truly Trumpet L287	1,750	1995	42.00	50
1991 Trusty Trombone L288	1,750	1995	42.00	50
1991 Two For Fore L297	1,750	1996	120.00	120-138
1991 United We Stand L314	1,776	1996	150.00	150
1991 The Visit L263	1,750	1995	100.00	100
1991 Winter L279	1,500		115.00	118

The Original Ron Lee Collection-1992 - R. Lee

YEAR ISSUE	EDITION LIMIT	YEAR RETD.	ISSUE PRICE	*QUOTE U.S.$
1992 Baloony L350	2,500		26.00	28
1992 Beats Nothin' L357	1,500	1997	145.00	145-175
1992 Beau Regards L342	2,500		26.00	28
1992 Big Wheel Kop RLC1005	1,750	1995	65.00	99
1992 Birdy The Hard Way L352	1,750		85.00	85
1992 Bo-Bo Balancing RLC1003	1,750	1995	75.00	75-84
1992 Break Point L335	2,500		26.00	28
1992 Brokenhearted Huey RLC1006	1,750	1995	65.00	65-95
1992 Buster Too PC100	1,500	1995	65.00	65-99
1992 Cannonball RLC1009	1,750	1995	95.00	125
1992 Clar-A-Bow L336	2,500		26.00	28
1992 Cyclin' Around L322	2,500		26.00	28
1992 Dreams L332	2,500		26.00	28
1992 Dudley's Dog Act RLC1010	1,750	1995	75.00	75-102
1992 Dunkin' L328	2,500		26.00	28
1992 Fish in Pail L358	1,500	1996	130.00	235
1992 Flyin' High L340	2,500		26.00	28
1992 Forget Me Not L341	2,500		26.00	28
1992 Gassing Up RLC1004	1,750	1995	70.00	99-102
1992 Go Man Go L344	2,500		26.00	28
1992 Handy Standy L321	2,500		26.00	28
1992 Heel's Up L329	2,500		26.00	28
1992 Hi-Five L339	2,500		26.00	28
1992 Hippolong Cassidy L320	1,250	N/A	166.00	140-175
1992 Howdy L325	2,500		26.00	28
1992 Jo-Jo Juggling RLC1002	1,750	1995	70.00	70
1992 Juggles L347	2,500		26.00	28
1992 Little Pard L349	2,500		26.00	28
1992 Lolly L326	2,500		26.00	28
1992 Love Ya' Baby L355	1,250		190.00	190
1992 Miles PC105	1,500	1995	65.00	65
1992 My Pal L334	2,500		26.00	28
1992 My Portrait L354	1,250	1996	315.00	595
1992 Myak Kyak L337	2,500		26.00	28
1992 On My Way L348	2,500		26.00	28
1992 Penny Saver L333	2,500		26.00	28
1992 Popcorn & Cotton Candy RLC1001	1,750	1995	70.00	70-102
1992 Scrub-A- Dub-Dub L319	1,250	1996	185.00	195
1992 Seven's Up L356	1,250		165.00	165
1992 Shake Jake L324	2,500		26.00	28
1992 Ship Ahoy L345	2,500		26.00	28
1992 Shufflin' L343	2,500		26.00	28
1992 Snowdrifter Blowin' In Wind L317	1,750		77.50	78
1992 Snowdrifter's Special Delivery L318	1,750		136.00	136
1992 Steamer L338	2,500		26.00	28
1992 Stop Cop L331	2,500		26.00	28
1992 Strike Out L323	2,500		26.00	28
1992 Struttin' L346	2,500		26.00	28
1992 Sure-Footed Freddie RLC1007	1,750	1995	80.00	80
1992 To-Tee L327	2,500		26.00	28
1992 Topper PC110	1,500	1995	65.00	65-95
1992 Twirp Chirp L330	2,500		26.00	28
1992 Vincent Van Clown L353	1,500	1996	160.00	160-210
1992 Walking A Fine Line RMB7000	1,750	1995	65.00	65-95
1992 Webb-ster PC115	1,500	1995	65.00	65-95
1992 Wrong Hole Clown L351	1,750		125.00	125

The Original Ron Lee Collection-1993 - R. Lee

YEAR ISSUE	EDITION LIMIT	YEAR RETD.	ISSUE PRICE	*QUOTE U.S.$
1993 Andy Jackson L364	950	1995	87.00	115
1993 Anywhere Warm L398	950		90.00	90
1993 Bellboy L390	950	1995	80.00	80-115
1993 Blinky Lying Down L384	1,200		45.00	45
1993 Blinky Sitting L383	1,200		45.00	45
1993 Blinky Standing L382	1,200		45.00	45
1993 Blinky Upside Down L385	1,200		45.00	45
1993 Bo-Bo L365	950	1995	95.00	95-135
1993 Britches L377	750		205.00	205
1993 Bumper Fun L403	750		330.00	330
1993 Buster L368	950	1995	87.00	115
1993 Charkles L381	750	1995	220.00	220
1993 Chattanooga Choo-Choo L374	750		420.00	420
1993 Dave Bomber L360	950	1995	90.00	90-115
1993 Happy Trails L369	950	1995	90.00	90-115
1993 Honk Honk L370	950	1995	90.00	90-115
1993 Hot Buns L376	750		175.00	175
1993 Lollipop L363	950	1995	87.00	120
1993 Merry Go Clown L405	750		375.00	375
1993 Moto Kris L380	750		255.00	255
1993 North Pole L396	950	1995	75.00	75
1993 Piggy Backin' L379	750		205.00	205
1993 Pretzels L372	750		195.00	195
1993 Sailin' L366	950	1995	95.00	95
1993 Scrubs L361	950	1995	87.00	115
1993 Sho-Sho L373	750		230.00	230
1993 Shriner Cop L404	750		175.00	175
1993 Skittles L367	950	1995	95.00	95-135
1993 Snoozin' L399	950		90.00	90
1993 Soft Shoe L400	750		275.00	295
1993 Sole-Full L375	750		250.00	250
1993 Special Occasion L402	750		280.00	295
1993 Taxi L378	750		470.00	470
1993 Tinker And Toy L359	950	1995	95.00	95
1993 Wagonetts L371	750		210.00	210
1993 Wanderer L401	750		255.00	295
1993 Yo-Yo L362	950	1995	87.00	115

The Original Ron Lee Collection-1995 - R. Lee

YEAR ISSUE	EDITION LIMIT	YEAR RETD.	ISSUE PRICE	*QUOTE U.S.$
1995 Bar Mitzvah L463	950		216.00	216
1995 Bat Mitzvah L462	950		216.00	216
1995 Batter Up L465	500		270.00	270
1995 Cimba's Last Stand L466	950		165.00	165
1995 Fillet of Sole L460	750		180.00	180
1995 Fore! Anyone! L464	500		275.00	275
1995 Santa's Other Sleigh L461	750		195.00	195

The Original Ron Lee Collection-1996 - R. Lee

YEAR ISSUE	EDITION LIMIT	YEAR RETD.	ISSUE PRICE	*QUOTE U.S.$
1996 7-7-7 L486	1,200		420.00	450
1996 The Bass Drum L478	950		47.00	47
1996 Bunches L482	950		215.00	215
1996 The Clarinet L476	950		47.00	47
1996 Craps L488	1,200		380.00	395
1996 The Cymbols L477	950		47.00	47
1996 Fabulous Las Vegas L491	1,200		187.50	230
1996 Frankie L480	750		95.00	95
1996 The Grand Bandwagon L470	750		895.00	895
1996 Hit Me L487	1,200		340.00	375
1996 Jocko KL105	500		375.00	375
1996 Johnnie L481	750		95.00	95
1996 The Juggler KL100	500		350.00	390
1996 Juggling Joel L484	950		150.00	150
1996 Pastime Pals L469	950		135.00	135
1996 Pepe L485	950		220.00	220
1996 Portrait Pals L468	950		135.00	135
1996 Rajah, The Elephant KL110	500		295.00	295
1996 Sleepytime Pals L467	950		115.00	115
1996 The Snare Drum L472	950		47.00	47
1996 The Sousaphone L471	950		47.00	47
1996 Strike It Rich L479	950		110.00	110
1996 Tim-Tim L483	950		125.00	125
1996 The Trombone L475	950		47.00	47
1996 The Trumpet L474	950		47.00	47
1996 The Tuba L473	950		47.00	47

The Original Ron Lee Collection-1997 - R. Lee

YEAR ISSUE	EDITION LIMIT	YEAR RETD.	ISSUE PRICE	*QUOTE U.S.$
1997 Dr. Painless L492	950		165.00	165
1997 A Pyramid of Elephants L493	950		135.00	135

The Original Ron Lee Collection-1998 - R. Lee

YEAR ISSUE	EDITION LIMIT	YEAR RETD.	ISSUE PRICE	*QUOTE U.S.$
1998 A Apple A Day L540	2,500		45.00	45
1998 Blast Off L532	2,500		43.00	43
1998 Blue Moon L494	950		165.00	165
1998 Breaking Out L518	950		89.00	89
1998 The Camel L506	950		48.00	48
1998 Captain Cranberry L507	950		99.00	99
1998 Ceslee L529	500		225.00	225
1998 Chico Playing Guitar L524	950		70.00	70
1998 Cotton Candy L523	950		125.00	125
1998 The Deer L502	950		48.00	48
1998 Four Tips L539	2,500		45.00	45
1998 The Giraffe L505	950		48.00	48
1998 Gnome Playing Flute L512	950		55.00	55
1998 Gnome Reading L514	950		62.00	62
1998 Gnome Skiing L513	950		62.00	62
1998 Gnome with Pot-O-Gold L515	950		62.00	62
1998 Goin' South L536	2,500		43.00	43
1998 Horse L501A	950		48.00	48
1998 It's Me L535	2,500		35.00	35
1998 Josephine L511	950		75.00	75
1998 Kick'n Back L527	500		150.00	150
1998 Kisses L541	2,500		35.00	35
1998 The Last Drop L530	950		825.00	825
1998 The Lion L503	950		48.00	48
1998 Look! No Hands L543	2,500		35.00	35
1998 Mobil Mania L496	950		142.50	165
1998 Nappy, Snoozing L517	950		125.00	125
1998 On The Road Again L510	950		225.00	295
1998 Oops! L533	2,500		42.00	42
1998 Playin' Hooky L531	950		495.00	595
1998 The Portrait L500	950		425.00	425
1998 Raindrops L509	950		80.00	92

*Quotes have been rounded up to nearest dollar

YEAR ISSUE	EDITION LIMIT	YEAR RETD.	ISSUE PRICE	*QUOTE U.S.$
1998 Ride 'Em Sunny L520	950		145.00	145
1998 Ruffles L528	500		225.00	225
1998 The Snooze L501	950		330.00	330
1998 Sparky L534	2,500		35.00	35
1998 Sunny Jetskiing L498	950		98.50	99
1998 Sunny Waterskiing L499	950		90.50	91
1998 Sunny Windsurfing L497	950		108.50	109
1998 Sunny's Catch L521	950		165.00	165
1998 Sunny's Snack L519	950		190.00	190
1998 A Swinging Par-Tee L525	750		210.00	210
1998 The Tiger L504	950		48.00	48
1998 Tom & Tammy L526	950		210.00	210
1998 Tomorrow is Soon Enough L522	950		350.00	350
1998 Top This L542	2,500		38.00	38
1998 Tou Tou L508	950		85.00	92
1998 Tubby L538	2,500		43.00	43
1998 Up, Up, and Away L516	950		75.00	75
1998 Yank and File L495	950		275.00	275
1998 Yipes L537	2,500		35.00	35

The Original Ron Lee Collection-1999 - R. Lee

YEAR ISSUE	EDITION LIMIT	YEAR RETD.	ISSUE PRICE	*QUOTE U.S.$
1999 Arrowhead L559	950		295.00	295
1999 Bathin Buddy L558	950		258.00	258
1999 Bobby L554	950		280.00	280
1999 Bucky L544	950		110.00	110
1999 Cheerio Tipping Hat L566	950		72.00	72
1999 Chef Boy R Lee L571	950		240.00	275
1999 Clown Juggling Marbles L578	1,200		67.00	67
1999 Clown Sitting on Suitcase L577	1,200		79.00	79
1999 Dainty Puffs L565	1,200		72.00	72
1999 A Dog Day L550	950		257.00	257
1999 Domestic Goddess L574	950		295.00	295
1999 Dreamin L552	950		395.00	395
1999 Fish'n Chips L570	950		270.00	295
1999 Gotta Have Heart L547	950		390.00	390
1999 Hamming It Up L548	950		195.00	195
1999 Hit'n The Road L557	950		595.00	595
1999 Hobo Joe in Go-Cart L560	950		198.00	198
1999 Hobo Joe in Scooter L561	950		225.00	225
1999 Hobo Joe on Bicycle L572	950		173.00	173
1999 Hobo Joe on Unicycle L573	950		168.00	168
1999 Hoop Du Jour L567	950		258.00	258
1999 Kix Kicking L562	1,200		72.00	72
1999 Lazy Dayz L568	950		258.00	258
1999 Lil Darlin Curtsey L580	2,500		59.00	59
1999 Lil Darlin Dog Trick L582	2,500		59.00	59
1999 Lil Darlin on CannonL583	2,500		62.00	62
1999 Lil Darlin Playing Accordian L579	2,500		59.00	59
1999 Lil Darlin Ringmaster L581	2,500		59.00	59
1999 Lil Darlin with Umbrella L584	2,500		65.00	65
1999 Little Biker Boy L596	3,500		39.00	39
1999 Little Bowler L597	3,500		37.00	37
1999 Little Cyclist L598	3,500		39.00	39
1999 Little Fisherman L587	3,500		36.00	36
1999 Little Golfer Boy L589	3,500		35.00	35
1999 Little Golfer Girl L588	3,500		35.00	35
1999 Little Hobo L592	3,500		36.00	36
1999 Little Skier L590	3,500		35.00	35
1999 Little Slot Machine L594	3,500		35.00	35
1999 Little Swinger L595	3,500		39.00	39
1999 Little Umbrella Boy L593	3,500		37.00	37
1999 Little Weightlifter L599	3,500		36.00	36
1999 Little Whistler with Balloon L591	3,500		36.00	36
1999 Mae East L575	950		435.00	495
1999 Maurice L545	950		295.00	295
1999 Not! Solo! L551	950		390.00	390
1999 Precious L556	950		280.00	280
1999 Rocky The Lawyer L546	950		185.00	185
1999 Sach L553	950		295.00	295
1999 Tinkle and Water St. L576	950		360.00	395
1999 Toto L555	950		280.00	280
1999 Trix Puffing Hair L563	1,200		72.00	72
1999 Where's Waldo L549	950		245.00	245
1999 Y 2 K L569	950		398.00	398

The Original Ron Lee Collection-2000 - R. Lee

YEAR ISSUE	EDITION LIMIT	YEAR RETD.	ISSUE PRICE	*QUOTE U.S.$
2000 Angel with Book L604	1,500		85.00	85
2000 Angel with Flowers L607	1,500		85.00	85
2000 Angel with Flute L605	1,500		85.00	85
2000 Angel with Harp L608	1,500		85.00	85
2000 Angel with Mandolin L606	1,500		85.00	85
2000 Angels with Heart L603	1,500		139.00	139
2000 Boy with Hat L600	1,500		77.00	77
2000 Carousel Horse L609	200		300.00	300
2000 Clown on High-Wire L618	950		99.00	99
2000 Corvette L625	500		535.00	535
2000 Cubby with Balloon L611	1,500		92.00	92
2000 Frolicking '50's L614	950		215.00	215
2000 Harlequin L601	950		202.00	202
2000 Hobo Joe in London L620	750		225.00	225
2000 Hobo Joe in London Sp. Ed. L620SE	500		598.00	598
2000 Hot Stuff L624	950		195.00	195
2000 Joyride L615	950		215.00	215
2000 Little Las Vegas Sign L616	1,500		68.00	68
2000 Lucky Me L613	1,500		275.00	275
2000 Mini Playing Hookey L617	950		299.00	299
2000 Mount Rushmore 2000 L621	750		189.00	189
2000 P.J. L612	1,500		259.00	259
2000 Road Race L623	750		595.00	595
2000 Stringbean L610	1,500		85.00	85
2000 To Protect and Serve L602	950		275.00	275
2000 Video Poker L622	950		275.00	275
2000 Viper L626	500		535.00	535

The Popeye Collection - R. Lee

YEAR ISSUE	EDITION LIMIT	YEAR RETD.	ISSUE PRICE	*QUOTE U.S.$
1992 Liberty P001	1,750	1995	184.00	184-228
1992 Men!!! P002	1,750	1995	230.00	230
1992 Oh Popeye P005	1,750	1995	230.00	230-276
1992 Par Excellence P006	1,750	1995	220.00	220
1992 Strong to The Finish P003	1,750	1995	95.00	95
1992 That's My Boy P004	1,750	1995	145.00	145-228

Premier Dealer Collection - R. Lee

YEAR ISSUE	EDITION LIMIT	YEAR RETD.	ISSUE PRICE	*QUOTE U.S.$
1992 Dream On PD002	Closed	N/A	125.00	170
1992 Framed Again PD001	Closed	N/A	110.00	140
1993 Jake-A-Juggling Balls PD008	500		85.00	90
1993 Jake-A-Juggling Clubs PD007	500		85.00	90
1993 Jake-A-Juggling Cylinder PD006	500		85.00	90
1994 Joe's Feline Friend PD009	500		105.00	105
1994 Just Big Enough PD010	500		115.00	115
1992 Moonlighting PD004	Closed	N/A	125.00	125
1992 Nest to Nothing PD003	Closed	N/A	110.00	125
1994 Off The Toe PD011	500		105.00	120
1993 Pockets PD005	500		175.00	175
1994 Storm Warning PD012	500		115.00	115
1994 Trading Places PD013	500		190.00	190

Ringling Bros. & Barnum & Bailey - R. Lee

YEAR ISSUE	EDITION LIMIT	YEAR RETD.	ISSUE PRICE	*QUOTE U.S.$
1996 It's About Time R105	500		308.00	308
1996 Paddlin' R100	500		396.00	396
1996 Scootin' R115	500		420.00	420
1996 Ups & Downs R110	500		440.00	440

Rocky & Bullwinkle And Friends Collection - R. Lee

YEAR ISSUE	EDITION LIMIT	YEAR RETD.	ISSUE PRICE	*QUOTE U.S.$
1992 Dudley Do-Right RB610	1,750	1995	175.00	250
1992 KA-BOOM! RB620	1,750	1995	175.00	250
1992 My Hero RB615	1,750	1995	275.00	400
1992 Rocky & Bullwinkle RB600	1,750	1995	120.00	175
1992 The Swami RB605	1,750	1995	175.00	250

The Ron Lee Disney Collection Exclusives - R. Lee

YEAR ISSUE	EDITION LIMIT	YEAR RETD.	ISSUE PRICE	*QUOTE U.S.$
1998 70 Years Mick & Min Sweethearts MM1210	1,500		125.00	125
1993 Aladdin MM560	500	1996	550.00	550
1996 Alice In Wonderland MM840	750		295.00	295
1997 Ariel MM1120	5,000		47.00	47
1999 Aurora MM1517	1,500		65.00	65
1999 Aurora in Pink Dress MM1517a	250		65.00	65
1995 Autopia MM770	750		220.00	220
1992 Bambi MM330	2,750		195.00	195
1996 Bambi and Thumper MM990	750		130.00	130
1990 The Bandleader MM100	Closed	N/A	75.00	110-121
1998 Bashful MM1330	2,500		49.00	49
1992 Beauty & The Beast (shadow box) DIS100	500	1994	1650.00	1650
1994 Beauty & The Beast MM610	800	1996	170.00	170-500
1999 Beauty and the Beast MM1509	1,200		120.00	120
1999 Belle MM1516	1,500		65.00	65
1998 Bug's Life MM1503	500		320.00	320
1996 Buzz Light Year MM960	950		135.00	135
1992 Captain Hook MM320	2,750		175.00	175
1995 The Carousel MM730	750		125.00	125
1992 Christmas '92 MM420	1,500		145.00	145
1999 Cinderella MM1515	1,500		65.00	65
1999 Cinderella Coach MM1506	1,200		280.00	280
1993 Cinderella's Slipper MM510	1,750	1995	115.00	150-165
1998 Cindy's Dress MM1250	2,500		156.00	156
1999 Cogsworth MM1507	1,500		55.00	55
1999 Cruella MM1532	1,500		N/A	N/A
1996 Cruella and Pups MM1030	750		135.00	135
1997 Cruisin' MM1090	750		247.50	248
1996 A Dalmation Christmas MM970	750		98.00	98
1993 Darkwing Duck MM470	1,750		105.00	105
1991 Decorating Donald MM210	2,750		60.00	60
1992 The Dinosaurs MM370	2,750		195.00	195
1998 Disney 75th MM1400	750		320.00	320
1997 Disney's "5"th Anniversary MM1050	555	1998	200.00	200
1998 Doc MM1320	2,500		49.00	49
1991 Dopey MM120	2,750	1995	80.00	135-143
1998 Dopey MM1310	2,500		49.00	49
1996 Dumbo & The Ringmaster MM860	750		195.00	195
1990 Dumbo MM600	2,750	1996	110.00	110
1998 A Eeyore Christmas MM1470	1,500		49.00	49
1999 Evil Queen MM1531	1,500		N/A	N/A
1995 Fantasyland MM780	750		285.00	285
1992 Finishing Touch MM440	1,500		85.00	85
1993 Flying With Dumbo MM530	1,000		330.00	330
1995 Frontierland MM740	750		160.00	160
1992 Genie MM450	2,750		110.00	330
1998 Goofy Golfing MM1230	950		130.00	130
1999 Goofy in Mirror MM1518	1.500		N/A	N/A
1991 Goofy MM110	2,750		115.00	115
1991 Goofy's Gift MM230	2,750		70.00	70
1998 Grumpy MM1360	2,500		49.00	49
1994 Grumpy Playing Organ MM590	800	1995	150.00	242-275
1998 Happy MM1370	2,500		49.00	49
1999 Hawaiian Holiday-1937 MM1526	1,000		70.00	70
1995 Home Improvements MM820	750	1996	170.00	170
1996 Hunchback of Notre Dame MM910	950		185.00	185
1999 Jiminy Cricket MM1520	750		250.00	250
1998 Jiminy Cricket MM1270	2,500		50.00	50
1991 Jiminy's List MM250	2,750		60.00	60
1991 Lady and the Tramp MM280	1,500	1995	295.00	295
1996 Lady and Tramp MM1010	750	1999	150.00	150
1999 Lady in Hat Box MM1529	1,000		70.00	70
1993 Letters to Santa MM550	1,500		170.00	170
1997 Liberty Minnie MM1130	5,000		47.00	47
1991 Lion Around MM270	2,750		140.00	140
1994 The Lion King MM640	1,750	1996	170.00	250
1992 Litt'l Sorcerer MM340	2,750	1998	57.00	57
1992 Little Mermaid MM310	2,750		230.00	212
1997 Little Steamboat Willie MM1180	2,500	1998	51.00	51
1999 Lumiere MM1508	1,500		55.00	55
1992 Lumiere & Cogsworth MM350	2,750		145.00	145
1995 Main Street MM710	750		120.00	120
1995 The Matterhorn MM750	750		240.00	240
1991 Mickey & Minnie at the Piano MM180	2,750		195.00	195
1999 Mickey & Minnie in Plane MM1524	1,000		115.00	115
1999 Mickey & Minnie Valentine MM1513	1,500		125.00	125
1997 Mickey & Pluto's Gifts MM1110	1,000		95.00	95
1996 Mickey & The Caddie MM890	1,250		195.00	195
1998 Mickey Mouse 75th MM1380	2,500		55.00	55
1997 Mickey with Flowers MM1170	2,500		51.00	51
1997 Mickey with Scissors MM1190	2,500		51.00	51
1991 Mickey's Adventure MM150	2,750		195.00	195
1997 Mickey's Broom MM1150	1,500		120.00	120
1990 Mickey's Christmas MM400	2,750		95.00	95
1991 Mickey's Delivery MM220	2,750		70.00	70
1994 Mickey, Brave Little Tailor MM570	1,750	1995	72.00	100
1997 Mickey, The King MM1160	2,500		51.00	51
1998 Minnie and Mickey Mistletoe MM1500	1,250		127.50	128
1991 Minnie Mouse MM170	2,750		80.00	80
1994 Minnie, Brave Little Tailor MM580	1,750	1995	72.00	72
1999 Mr. Duck Steps Out-1940 MM1527	1,000		70.00	70
1999 Mrs. Potts & Chip MM1512	1,500		70.00	70
1992 Mrs. Potts & Chip MM360	2,750		125.00	125
1991 Mt. Mickey MM900	2,750		175.00	175
1998 New Genie MM1290	N/A		55.00	55
1998 New Sorcerer MM1220	2,500		52.00	52
1999 New Steamboat MM1533	1,500		N/A	N/A
1994 New Tinkerbell MM680	300	1995	99.00	99
1994 Official Conscience MM620	300	1995	65.00	65
1999 Old Hag MM1530	1,500		N/A	N/A
1995 The People Mover MM760	750		190.00	190
1998 A Piglet Christmas MM1460	1,500		49.00	49
1998 Pinocchio & Jiminy Cricket MM1280	950		115.00	115
1990 Pinocchio MM500	2,750	1995	85.00	85
1991 Pluto's Treat MM240	2,750		60.00	60
1994 Pongo & Pups MM670	800	1995	124.00	124
1998 Pooh & Family MM1501	1,250		132.00	132
1995 Pooh & The Cookie Jar MM830	750		190.00	190
1996 Pooh & The Honey Pot MM870	1,250		120.00	120
1998 Pooh & Tigger Hugging MM1502	1,200		125.00	125
1998 A Pooh Christmas MM1440	1,500		49.00	49
1998 Pooh Family on a Log MM1505	1,200		160.00	160
1996 Pooh In The Honey Tree MM850	750		300.00	300
1996 Pooh Musical MM950	950		150.00	150
1999 Pooh Valentine MM1511	1,500		55.00	55
1999 Pooh w/Piglet Flower Base MM1522	1,000		N/A	N/A
1997 Pooh with Flower MM1070	2,500		70.00	70
1997 Pooh's Honey Pot MM1100	5,000		47.00	47
1996 Pooh, Eeyore & Piglet MM880	1,250		150.00	150
1995 Reflections MM810	750	1996	99.00	99
1993 Santa's Workshop MM540	1,500		170.00	170
1998 Sir Goofy MM1260	950		80.00	80
1998 Sleepy MM1350	2,500		49.00	49
1998 Sneezy MM1340	2,500		49.00	49
1999 Snow White MM1514	1,500		N/A	N/A
1994 Snow White & Doc MM630	800		135.00	135
1990 Snow White & Grumpy MM800	2,750	1996	140.00	140
1993 Snow White & The Seven Dwarfs (shadow box) DIS200	250		1800.00	1800
1996 Snow White's 60th Anniversary MM980	750		495.00	495
1999 Sorcerer MM1519	750		250.00	250
1990 The Sorcerer MM200	Closed	N/A	85.00	120
1992 Sorcerer's Apprentice MM290	2,750	1996	125.00	125
1997 The Spaghetti Scene MM1200	950		125.00	125
1999 Steamboat Willie MM1521	750		350.00	350
1990 Steamboat Willie MM300	2,750	1995	95.00	95
1992 Stocking Stuffer MM410	1,500	1996	63.00	63
1991 The Tea Cup Ride (Disneyland Exclusive) MM260	1,250	1996	225.00	225
1999 Three Tiggers MM1528	950		140.00	140
1996 Tigger and Eyeore MM1000	750		135.00	135
1997 Tigger and Pooh MM1060	1,500		125.00	125
1998 A Tigger Christmas MM1450	1,500		49.00	49
1997 Tigger MM1140	5,000		47.00	47
1994 Tigger on Rabbit MM660	800	1995	110.00	110
1993 Tinker Bell MM490	1,750	1995	85.00	85
1999 Tinkerbell MM1523	750		N/A	N/A
1998 Tinkerbell 75th MM1390	2,500		59.00	59
1997 Tinkerbell in Lamp MM1020	500		179.00	179
1998 Tinkerbell on Lily Pad MM1240	1,500		120.00	120
1997 Tinkerbell on Spool MM1080	5,000		47.00	47
1995 The Topiary MM720	750		145.00	145
1996 Toy Story MM930	950		197.00	197
1991 Tugboat Mickey MM160	2,750		180.00	180
1996 TV Buddies MM920	1,250		199.00	199
1991 Two Gun Mickey MM140	2,750	1998	115.00	115
1990 Uncle Scrooge MM700	2,750	1998	110.00	110
1999 Valentine Tigger MM1510	1,500		55.00	55
1998 Walt's Car with Fab Five MM1420	1,500		200.00	200
1993 Winnie The Pooh MM480	1,750	1996	125.00	150-200
1992 Winnie The Pooh & Tigger MM390	2,750	1995	105.00	105
1999 The Wise Little Hen-1934 MM1525	1,000		70.00	70
1992 Wish Upon A Star MM430	1,500	1998	80.00	80
1991 The Witch MM130	2,750		115.00	115
1992 Workin' Out MM380	2,750		95.00	95

*Quotes have been rounded up to nearest dollar

The Ron Lee Disneyana Collection Exclusives - R. Lee

YEAR ISSUE	EDITION LIMIT	YEAR RETD.	ISSUE PRICE	*QUOTE U.S.$
1992 Big Thunder Mountain MM460	250	1995	1650.00	2360-2500
1993 Mickey's Dream MM520	250	1993	400.00	650-900
1994 MM/MN/Goofy Limo MM650	500	1994	500.00	750-1073
1995 Ear Force One MM790	500	1995	600.00	635-1300
1995 Engine Number One MM690	500	1995	650.00	726-765
1996 Heigh Ho MM940	350	1996	500.00	605-726

The Ron Lee Emmett Kelly, Sr. Collection - R. Lee

YEAR ISSUE	EDITION LIMIT	YEAR RETD.	ISSUE PRICE	*QUOTE U.S.$
1997 An Emmett Christmas EK315	950		195.00	195
1998 Emmett Golfing EK335	950		160.00	160
1998 Emmett Holding Umbrella EK330	950		142.00	142
1998 Emmett in Tub EK345	950	N/A	175.00	175
1991 Emmett Kelly, Sr. Sign E208	Closed	1995	110.00	125
1998 Emmett Lying on Bench EK325	950		175.00	175
1998 Emmett with Balloons EK320	950		142.00	142
1998 Emmett's Self Portrait EK340	950		215.00	215
1991 God Bless America EK206	1,750	1995	130.00	275
1991 Help Yourself EK202	1,750	1995	145.00	295
1991 Love at First Sight EK204	1,750	1996	197.00	300
1991 My Protege EK207	1,750	1995	160.00	295
1997 Playing Cello EK310	950		175.00	175
1997 Playing Piano EK305	950		175.00	175
1991 Spike's Uninvited Guest EK203	1,750	1995	165.00	295
1997 Sweeping EK300	950		145.00	145
1991 That-A-Way EK201	1,750	1995	125.00	275
1991 Time for a Change EK205	1,750	1995	190.00	325

The Ron Lee Gallery Collection - R. Lee

YEAR ISSUE	EDITION LIMIT	YEAR RETD.	ISSUE PRICE	*QUOTE U.S.$
1996 Toad Bo Joe KL300	500		195.00	195

The Ron Lee Looney Tunes Collection - R. Lee

YEAR ISSUE	EDITION LIMIT	YEAR RETD.	ISSUE PRICE	*QUOTE U.S.$
1991 1940 Bugs Bunny LT165	2,750	1998	85.00	120-150
1991 Bugs Bunny LT150	2,750	1996	123.00	135-155
1991 Daffy Duck LT140	2,750	1997	80.00	80-85
1991 Elmer Fudd LT125	2,750	1998	87.00	102-150
1991 Foghorn Leghorn & Henry Hawk LT160	2,750	1996	115.00	115
1991 Marvin the Martian LT170	2,750	1997	75.00	75
1991 Michigan J. Frog LT110	2,750	1998	115.00	115-138
1991 Mt. Yosemite LT180	850		160.00	160-300
1991 Pepe LePew & Penelope LT145	2,750	1998	115.00	115-145
1991 Porky Pig LT115	2,750	1998	97.00	163
1991 Sylvester & Tweety LT135	2,750	1998	110.00	115-176
1991 Tasmanian Devil LT120	2,750	1996	105.00	105
1991 Tweety LT155	2,750	1996	110.00	115-139
1991 Western Daffy Duck LT105	2,750	1998	87.00	90-132
1991 Wile E. Coyote & Roadrunner LT175	2,750		165.00	175
1991 Yosemite Sam LT130	2,750	1998	110.00	110-142

The Ron Lee Looney Tunes Collection - R. Lee

YEAR ISSUE	EDITION LIMIT	YEAR RETD.	ISSUE PRICE	*QUOTE U.S.$
1992 Beep Beep LT220	1,500		115.00	283
1992 Ditty Up LT200	2,750		110.00	110
1992 For Better or Worse LT190	1,500		285.00	285
1992 Leopold & Giovanni LT205	1,500		225.00	285
1992 No Pain No Gain LT210	950		270.00	270
1992 Rackin' Frackin' Varmint LT225	950		260.00	340
1992 Speedy Gonzales LT185	2,750		73.00	73
1992 Van Duck LT230	950		335.00	440
1992 The Virtuosos LT235	950		350.00	460
1992 What The ...? LT195	1,500		240.00	240
1992 What's up Doc? LT215	950		270.00	354

The Ron Lee Looney Tunes Collection - R. Lee

YEAR ISSUE	EDITION LIMIT	YEAR RETD.	ISSUE PRICE	*QUOTE U.S.$
1992 Bugs Bunny w/ Horse LT245	1,500		105.00	105
1992 Cowboy Bugs LT290	1,500		70.00	70
1992 Daffy Duck w/ Horse LT275	1,500		105.00	105
1992 Elmer Fudd w/ Horse LT270	1,500		105.00	105
1992 Pepe Le Pew w/ Horse LT285	1,500		105.00	105
1992 Porky Pig w/ Horse LT260	1,500		105.00	105
1992 Sylvester w/ Horse LT250	1,500		105.00	105
1992 Tasmanian Devil w/ Horse LT255	1,500		105.00	105
1992 Wile E. Coyote w/ Horse LT280	1,500		105.00	105
1992 Yosemite Sam w/ Horse LT265	1,500		105.00	105

The Ron Lee Looney Tunes Collection - R. Lee

YEAR ISSUE	EDITION LIMIT	YEAR RETD.	ISSUE PRICE	*QUOTE U.S.$
1993 Bugs LT330	1,200		79.00	79
1993 A Christmas Carrot LT320	1,200		175.00	175
1993 The Essence of Love LT310	1,200	1998	145.00	145
1993 Martian's Best Friend LT305	1,200		140.00	140
1993 Me Deliver LT295	1,200		110.00	110
1993 Puttin' on the Glitz LT325	1,200		79.00	79
1993 The Rookie LT315	1,200		75.00	75
1993 Yo-Ho-Ho- LT300	1,200		105.00	105

The Ron Lee Looney Tunes Collection - R. Lee

YEAR ISSUE	EDITION LIMIT	YEAR RETD.	ISSUE PRICE	*QUOTE U.S.$
1994 Bugs LT330	1,200		79.00	79
1994 A Carrot a Day LT350	1,200		85.00	85
1994 Guilty LT345	1,200		80.00	80
1994 Ma Cherie LT340	1,200		185.00	185
1994 No H20 LT355	1,200		160.00	160
1994 Puttin' on the Glitz LT325	1,200		79.00	79
1994 Smashing LT335	1,200		80.00	80
1994 Taz On Ice LT360	1,200	1998	115.00	115

The Ron Lee Looney Tunes Collection - R. Lee

YEAR ISSUE	EDITION LIMIT	YEAR RETD.	ISSUE PRICE	*QUOTE U.S.$
1994 Bugs Pharoah LT370	500	1996	130.00	150
1994 Cleopatra's Barge LT400	500	1996	550.00	660
1994 Cruising Down the Nile LT385	500	1996	295.00	410
1994 King Bugs and Friends LT395	500	1996	480.00	550
1994 Ramases & Son LT380	500	1996	230.00	260
1994 Tweety Pharoah LT365	500	1996	110.00	140
1994 Warrior Taz LT375	500	1996	140.00	170
1994 Yosemite's Chariot LT390	500	1996	310.00	360

The Ron Lee Looney Tunes Collection - R. Lee

YEAR ISSUE	EDITION LIMIT	YEAR RETD.	ISSUE PRICE	*QUOTE U.S.$
1995 The Baron LT475	750		235.00	235
1995 Daffy Scuba Diving LT470	750		170.00	170
1995 Drive..Drive!! Putt..Putt!! LT450	750	1997	120.00	120
1995 The Great Chase LT485	750		385.00	385
1995 Highway My Way LT460	750	1998	280.00	280
1995 The Hustler LT465	750		397.00	397
1995 Ice Dancing LT440	750	1998	180.00	180
1995 King Pin LT445	750		165.00	165
1995 Slam Dunk LT455	750		190.00	190
1995 Speedy Tweety LT480	750		225.00	225

The Ron Lee Looney Tunes Collection - R. Lee

YEAR ISSUE	EDITION LIMIT	YEAR RETD.	ISSUE PRICE	*QUOTE U.S.$
1996 Bugs Bunny LT490	1,500	1998	49.00	49
1996 Daffy Duck LT520	1,500	1998	49.00	49
1996 Daffy's New York Bistro LT575	750		350.00	350
1996 Foghorn Leghorn LT500	1,500	1999	49.00	49
1996 Liberty Bugs LT590	750		285.00	285
1996 Marvin the Martian LT525	1,500	1998	49.00	49
1996 Michigan J. Frog LT560	1,500	1998	49.00	49
1996 Michigan on Broadway LT585	750		330.00	330
1996 Penelope LT555	1,500	1999	49.00	49
1996 Pepe Le Pew LT550	1,500	1999	49.00	49
1996 Porky Pig LT515	1,500		49.00	49
1996 Roadrunner LT545	1,500	1999	49.00	49
1996 She-Devil LT530	1,500		49.00	49
1996 Speedy Gonzales LT505	1,500		49.00	49
1996 Sylvester LT565	1,500	1999	49.00	49
1996 Tasmanian Devil LT495	1,500	1998	49.00	49
1996 Taz and the Big Apple LT570	750		130.00	130
1996 Taz on Empire State LT580	750		170.00	170
1996 Tweety LT535	1,500	1998	49.00	49
1996 Wile E. Coyote LT540	1,500	1998	49.00	49
1996 Yosemite Sam LT510	1,500	1998	49.00	49

The Ron Lee Looney Tunes Collection - R. Lee

YEAR ISSUE	EDITION LIMIT	YEAR RETD.	ISSUE PRICE	*QUOTE U.S.$
1997 The Backstroke LT640	2,500		115.00	115
1997 Down Hill LT645	2,500		157.50	158
1997 The Eighteenth Hole LT615	2,500		95.00	95
1997 I Got Me Covered LT620	2,500		80.00	80
1997 Martian Canine LT625	2,500		80.00	80
1997 Marvin LT630	2,500		125.00	125
1997 Penelope Mini #2 LT655	2,500		49.00	49
1997 Pepe Mini #2 LT650	2,500		49.00	49
1997 Pumping Iron LT610	2,500		99.00	99
1997 Senior M. J. Frog LT635	2,500		125.00	125
1997 Tornado Taz LT605	2,500		85.00	85
1997 Tweety Mini #2 LT660	2,500		49.00	49

The Ron Lee Looney Tunes Sports Collection - R. Lee

YEAR ISSUE	EDITION LIMIT	YEAR RETD.	ISSUE PRICE	*QUOTE U.S.$
1996 The Baron LT475	750		235.00	235
1996 The Chase LT485	750		385.00	385
1996 Daffy Scuba Diving LT470	750		170.00	170
1996 The Hustler LT465	750		397.00	397
1996 Ice Dancing LT440	750		180.00	180
1996 King Pin LT445	750		165.00	165
1996 Slam Dunk LT455	750		190.00	190
1996 Speedy Tweety LT480	750		225.00	225

The Ron Lee Looney Tunes Western Collection - R. Lee

YEAR ISSUE	EDITION LIMIT	YEAR RETD.	ISSUE PRICE	*QUOTE U.S.$
1995 Acme Junction LT435	500		290.00	290
1995 Bwanding Iron LT420	500		210.00	210
1995 Heap Big Chief LT415	500		230.00	230
1995 Lit'l Trooper LT405	500		157.00	157
1995 Roadrunner Express LT425	500		240.00	240
1995 Saturday Serenade LT430	500		255.00	255
1995 Whoa!! LT410	500		215.00	215

The Ron Lee Warner Bros. Collection - R. Lee

YEAR ISSUE	EDITION LIMIT	YEAR RETD.	ISSUE PRICE	*QUOTE U.S.$
2000 8-Ball Bunny WB634	1,500		160.00	160
1995 Animaniacs WBA100	750		170.00	170
1999 Bat Girl WB603	2,500		65.00	65
1999 Batman & Robin WB625	1,500		275.00	275
1998 Batman WB012	1,250		100.00	100
1998 Batman WB027	2,500		50.00	50
1998 Bugs and Carrot WB025	2,500		49.00	49
1996 Bugs At The Door WB007	500		98.00	98
1998 Bugs Bunny Presents WB026	300	1998	80.00	80
1998 Bugs Conducting WB021	2,500		260.00	260
1999 Bugs Golfing WB604	950		65.00	65
2000 Bugs in Las Vegas WB631	950		215.00	215
1997 Bugs Playing Hockey WB016	750		103.00	103
1996 Bugs Playing Hockey WBSF100	750		106.00	106
1999 Cat Woman WB600	2,500		65.00	65
2000 China WB630	1,500		825.00	825
1993 Courtly Gent WB003	1,000		102.00	102
1992 Dickens' Christmas WB400	850		198.00	198
1993 Duck Dodgers WB005	1,000		300.00	300
2000 Egypt WB627	1,200		312.50	313
1998 The Flash WB031	2,500		50.00	50
1999 Foghorn WB607	2,500		55.00	55
1998 Gossamer WB020	2,500		49.00	49
1998 Green Lantern WB030	2,500		50.00	50
1993 Gridiron Glory WB002	1,000		102.00	102
1993 Hair-Raising Hare WB006	1,000		300.00	300
1993 Hare Under Par WB001	1,000	1995	102.00	102
1999 Harley Quinn WB601	2,500		65.00	65
1999 Harley Quinn WB615	1,500		140.00	140
1993 Home Plate Heroes WB004	1,000	1998	102.00	102
2000 Leaving Arizona WB636	950		400.00	400
1998 Lit'l Thinker WB018	2,500		49.00	49
1998 Lola Bunny WB011	750		88.00	88
2000 London WB626	1,200		225.00	225
1998 Looner Tune WB019	2,500		49.00	49
1991 The Maltese Falcon WB100	Closed	N/A	175.00	190
1999 Marvin & Daffy Space Scene WB621	1,500		140.00	195
2000 Marvin and Landrover WB633	950		540.00	540
1996 Marvin and The Maggott WB008	750		140.00	140
1999 Marvin Martian WB610	2,500		55.00	55
1999 Michigan J. Frog WB605	950		65.00	65
1998 Michigan J. Mini #2 WB024	2,500		49.00	49
2000 Paris WB629	1,200		225.00	225
1999 Pepe & Penelope on Candy Box WB612	1,500		195.00	195
1995 Pinky And The Brain WBA105	750		170.00	170
2000 Pirates WB638	500		625.00	625
1998 Poison Ivy WB013	1,250		90.00	90
1999 Poison Ivy WB602	2,500		65.00	65
1991 Robin Hood Bugs WB200	1,000		190.00	190
1999 Scooby WB609	2,500		55.00	55
2000 Scooby with Hamburger WB639	1,500		95.00	95
1998 Speechless WB022	2,500		390.00	390
1996 Speedy Playing Soccer WB009	750		135.00	135
1996 Spokesphibian WB500	750		205.00	205
1998 Superman WB028	2,500		50.00	50
1997 Sylvester Playing Basketball WB014	750		106.00	106
1996 Sylvester Playing Basketball WBSF150	750		106.00	106
2000 Taz on Motorcycle WB632	950		365.00	365
1997 Taz Playing Football WB017	750		106.00	106
1996 Taz Playing Football WBSF125	750		106.00	106
1998 Taz With Fist WB023	2,500		49.00	49
2000 Taz Working Out WB640	950		300.00	300
1998 Tuxedo Bugs WB010	750		88.00	88
1999 Tweety Angel WB611	2,500		85.00	85
1999 Tweety in Wagon WB606	950		65.00	65
1999 Tweety Mini #3 WB614	2,500		55.00	55
2000 Tweety on Telephone WB635	1,500		140.00	140
2000 Tweety Taking a Bath WB637	1,500		170.00	170
2000 Venice WB628	1,200		350.00	350
1997 Wile E. Coyote Playing Baseball WB015	750		106.00	106
1996 Wile E. Coyote Playing Basketball WBSF175	750		106.00	106
1998 Wonder Woman WB029	2,500		50.00	50
1992 Yankee Doodle Bugs WB300	850		195.00	195
1999 Yosemite Sam WB608	2,500		55.00	55

Shriner Clowns - R. Lee

YEAR ISSUE	EDITION LIMIT	YEAR RETD.	ISSUE PRICE	*QUOTE U.S.$
1994 Bubbles L437	1,750		120.00	120
1994 Helping Hand L436	1,750		145.00	145

Sports & Professionals - R. Lee

YEAR ISSUE	EDITION LIMIT	YEAR RETD.	ISSUE PRICE	*QUOTE U.S.$
1994 The Baseball Player L448	2,500		77.00	77
1994 The Basketball Player L450	2,500		74.00	74
1994 The Chef L441	2,500		74.00	74
1994 The Dentist L446	2,500		70.00	70
1994 The Doctor L439	2,500		70.00	70
1994 The Fireman L444	2,500		90.00	90
1994 The Fisherman L452	2,500		77.00	77
1994 The Football Player L449	2,500		74.00	74
1994 The Golfer L447	2,500		77.00	77
1994 The Hockey Player L454	2,500		80.00	80
1994 The Lawyer L445	2,500		70.00	70
1994 The Nurse L443	2,500		74.00	74
1994 The Pilot L440	2,500		74.00	74
1994 The Policeman L442	2,500		77.00	77
1994 The Skier L453	2,500		77.00	77
1994 The Teacher L438	2,500		70.00	70
1994 The Tennis Player L451	2,500		74.00	74

Superman I - R. Lee

YEAR ISSUE	EDITION LIMIT	YEAR RETD.	ISSUE PRICE	*QUOTE U.S.$
1993 Help Is On The Way SP100	750	1995	280.00	280-400
1993 Meteor Moment SP115	750	1995	314.00	314-460
1993 Metropolis SP110	750	1995	320.00	320-460
1993 Proudly We Wave SP105	750	1995	185.00	185-270

Superman II - R. Lee

YEAR ISSUE	EDITION LIMIT	YEAR RETD.	ISSUE PRICE	*QUOTE U.S.$
1994 Good and Evil SP135	750	1995	190.00	190
1994 More Powerful SP130	750	1995	420.00	420
1994 Quick Change SP120	750	1995	125.00	125
1994 To The Rescue SP125	750	1995	195.00	195

The Wizard of Oz Collection - R. Lee

YEAR ISSUE	EDITION LIMIT	YEAR RETD.	ISSUE PRICE	*QUOTE U.S.$
1992 The Cowardly Lion WZ425	750	1996	620.00	620-650
1992 Kansas WZ400	750	1996	550.00	550-660
1992 The Munchkins WZ405	750	1996	620.00	650-675
1992 The Ruby Slippers WZ410	750	1996	620.00	620
1992 The Scarecrow WZ415	750	1996	510.00	620
1992 The Tin Man WZ420	750	1996	530.00	600

Wizard of Oz II - R. Lee

YEAR ISSUE	EDITION LIMIT	YEAR RETD.	ISSUE PRICE	*QUOTE U.S.$
1998 Bad Witch WZ480	2,500		50.00	50
1994 The Cowardly Lion WZ445	500	1997	130.00	130
1998 The Cowardly Lion WZ470	2,500		50.00	50
1994 Dorothy WZ430	500	1997	150.00	150
1998 Dorothy WZ485	2,500		50.00	50
1994 Glinda WZ455	500	1998	225.00	225
1998 Good Witch WZ475	2,500		54.00	54
1994 The Scarecrow WZ435	500	1997	130.00	130
1998 Scarecrow WZ460	2,500		50.00	50
1998 Tin Man WZ465	2,500		50.00	50
1994 The Tinman WZ440	500	1997	110.00	110
1994 The Wicked Witch WZ450	500	1998	125.00	125

*Quotes have been rounded up to nearest dollar

Wizard of Oz III - R. Lee

YEAR ISSUE	EDITION LIMIT	YEAR RETD.	ISSUE PRICE	*QUOTE U.S.$
1999 Bad Witch WB622	500		225.00	250
1999 Cowardly Lion WB619	500		225.00	225
1999 Dorothy WB623	500		325.00	325
1999 Flying Monkey WB616	500		225.00	225
1999 The Good Witch WB624	500		325.00	325
1999 Scarecrow WB620	500		225.00	225
1999 Tin Man WB618	500		225.00	225
1999 Toto WB617	500		175.00	175

The Woody Woodpecker And Friends Collection - R. Lee

YEAR ISSUE	EDITION LIMIT	YEAR RETD.	ISSUE PRICE	*QUOTE U.S.$
1992 1940 Woody Woodpecker WL020	1,750	1996	73.00	75-89
1992 Andy and Miranda Panda WL025	1,750	1996	140.00	140
1992 Birdy for Woody WL005	1,750	1996	117.00	125-140
1992 Pals WL030	1,750	1996	179.00	179
1992 Peck of My Heart WL010	1,750	1996	370.00	495
1992 Woody Woodpecker WL015	1,750	1996	73.00	73-89

Royal Doulton

Royal Doulton International Collectors' Club - Various

YEAR ISSUE	EDITION LIMIT	YEAR RETD.	ISSUE PRICE	*QUOTE U.S.$
1980 John Doulton Jug (8 O'Clock) D6656 - E. Griffiths	Yr.Iss.	1981	70.00	350-369
1981 Sleepy Darling Figure HN2953 - P. Parsons	Yr.Iss.	1982	100.00	195-250
1982 Dog of Fo-Flambe - N/A	Yr.Iss.	1983	50.00	175
1982 Prized Possessions Figure HN2942 - R. Tabbenor	Yr.Iss.	1983	125.00	450-555
1983 Loving Cup - N/A	Yr.Iss.	1984	75.00	350-395
1983 Springtime HN3033 - A. Hughes	Yr.Iss.	1984	125.00	325-450
1984 Sir Henry Doulton Jug D6703 - E. Griffiths	Yr.Iss.	1985	50.00	200-300
1984 Pride & Joy Figure HN2945 - R. Tabbenor	Yr.Iss.	1985	125.00	350-400
1985 Top of the Hill HN2126 - P. Gee	Yr.Iss.	1986	35.00	175-300
1985 Wintertime Figure HN3060 - A. Hughes	Yr.Iss.	1986	125.00	250-465
1986 Albert Sagger Toby Jug - W. Harper	Yr.Iss.	1987	35.00	85
1986 Auctioneer Figure HN2988 - R. Tabbenor	Yr.Iss.	1987	150.00	400-500
1987 Collector Bunnykins DB54 - D. Lyttleton	Yr.Iss.	1988	40.00	695-850
1987 Summertime Figurine HN3137 - P. Parsons	Yr.Iss.	1988	140.00	300-450
1988 Top of the Hill Miniature Figurine HN2126 - P. Gee	Yr.Iss.	1989	95.00	125-225
1988 Beefeater Tiny Jug - R. Tabbenor	Yr.Iss.	1989	25.00	125-225
1988 Old Salt Tea Pot - N/A	Yr.Iss.	1989	135.00	200-275
1989 Geisha Flambe Figure HN3229 - P. Parsons	Yr.Iss.	1990	195.00	195
1989 Flower Sellers Children Plate - N/A	Yr.Iss.	1990	65.00	70-100
1990 Autumntime Figure HN3231 - P. Parsons	Yr.Iss.	1991	190.00	195-450
1990 Jester Mini Figure HN3335 - C.J. Noke	Yr.Iss.	1991	115.00	115
1990 Old King Cole Tiny Jug - H. Fenton	Yr.Iss.	1991	35.00	100-125
1991 Bunny's Bedtime Figure HN3370 - N. Pedley	9,500	1992	195.00	200-260
1991 Charles Dickens Jug D6901 - W. Harper	Yr.Iss.	1992	100.00	125-150
1991 L'Ambiteuse Figure (Tissot Lady) HN3359 - V. Annand	5,000	1992	295.00	350-375
1991 Christopher Columbus Jug D6911 - S. Taylor	Yr.Iss.	1992	95.00	125-175
1992 Discovery Figure HN3428 - A. Munslow	Yr.Iss.	1993	160.00	100
1992 King Edward Jug D6923 - W. Harper	Yr.Iss.	1993	250.00	295-310
1992 Master Potter Bunnykins DB131 - W. Platt	Yr.Iss.	1993	50.00	125-195
1992 Eliza Farren Prestige Figure HN3442 - N/A	Yr.Iss.	1993	335.00	325-400
1993 Barbara Figure - N/A	Yr.Iss.	1994	285.00	450-510
1993 Lord Mountbatten L/S Jug - S. Taylor	5,000	1994	225.00	225-269
1993 Punch & Judy Double Sided Jug - S. Taylor	2,500	1994	400.00	465
1993 Flambe Dragon HN3552 - N/A	Retrd.	1994	260.00	260-415
1994 Diane HN3604 - N/A	Retrd.	1995	250.00	300-400
1995 Le Bal HN3702 - N/A	Retrd.	1996	350.00	350
1995 George Tinworth Jug, sm. D7000 - W. Harper	Retrd.	1996	99.00	175
1995 Partners in Collecting Bunnykins DB151	Retrd.	1996	45.00	45-85
1996 Special Delivery Plate - N/A	Retrd.	1996	45.00	60-100
1996 Welcome - N/A	Retrd.	1996	80.00	150
1996 Pamela HN3756 - T. Potts	Retrd.	1996	275.00	310
1996 Mr. Pickwick Jug, sm. D7025 - M. Alcock	Retrd.	1996	138.00	150-250
1996 Winter's Day HN3769 - N. Pedley	Retrd.	1997	325.00	325-450
1996 Gifts For All plate - N. Pedley	Retrd.	1997	40.00	40
1997 Susan HN3871 - N. Pedley	Retrd.	1997	345.00	345-400
1997 Joy - (1997 membership gift) - N. Pedley	Retrd.	1997	85.00	85-140
1997 Sir Henry Doulton S/S - W. Harper	Retrd.	1997	157.50	165
1998 Janet figure HN4042 - V. Annand	Retrd.	1998	275.00	275-375
1998 Richard III Jug - R. Tabbenor	Retrd.	1998	275.00	275-450
1998 Bunnykins Builds a Snowman plate - N/A	Retrd.	1998	60.00	60
1999 Nicole HN4112 - N. Pedley	Yr.Iss.	1999	295.00	295
1999 Melody HN4117 - N. Pedley	Yr.Iss.	1999	50.00	50
1999 Judge Bunnykins DB188 - S. Ridge	Yr.Iss.	1999	50.00	50
1999 Tourist Bunnykin DB190 - M. Alcock	Yr.Iss.	1999	50.00	50
1999 King John - R. Tabbenor	Yr.Iss.	1999	310.00	310
1999 The Moor - Colorway - C. Noke	99	1999	5865.00	5865
2000 Lawyer Bunnykins DB214 - M. Alcock	Yr.Iss.		50.00	50
2000 Sightseer Bunnykins DB215 - M. Alcock	Yr.Iss.		50.00	50
2000 The Collector D7147 - R. Tabbenor	Yr.Iss.		145.00	145
2000 Sweet Lilac HN3792 - J. Bromley	Yr.Iss.		295.00	295
2000 Greetings HN4250 - A. Maslankowski	Yr.Iss.		50.00	50
2000 Lido Lady HN4247 - N. Pedley	Yr.Iss.		395.00	395

Age of Innocence - N. Pedley

YEAR ISSUE	EDITION LIMIT	YEAR RETD.	ISSUE PRICE	*QUOTE U.S.$
1991 Feeding Time HN3373	9,500	1994	245.00	300-400
1992 First Outing HN3377	9,500	1994	275.00	300-390
1991 Making Friends HN3372	9,500	1994	270.00	250-325
1991 Puppy Love HN3371	9,500	1994	270.00	300-390

Angels Of Harmony - Royal Doulton

YEAR ISSUE	EDITION LIMIT	YEAR RETD.	ISSUE PRICE	*QUOTE U.S.$
1998 Angel of Autumn	Retrd.	1999	80.00	80
1998 Angel of Friendship	Retrd.	1999	80.00	80
1998 Angel of Love	Retrd.	1999	80.00	80
1998 Angel of Peace	Retrd.	1999	80.00	80
1998 Angel of Spring	Retrd.	1999	80.00	80
1998 Angel of Summer	Retrd.	1999	80.00	80
1998 Angel of Winter	Retrd.	1999	80.00	80
1998 Guardian Angel	Retrd.	1999	80.00	80

Archive Collection - A. Maslankowski

YEAR ISSUE	EDITION LIMIT	YEAR RETD.	ISSUE PRICE	*QUOTE U.S.$
2000 Artemis HN4081	250		1465.00	1465
2000 Aurora HN4078	250		2935.00	2935
2000 Ceres HN4080	250		1465.00	1465
2000 Erato HN4082	250		1465.00	1465
2000 Hebe HN4079	250		1465.00	1465

Art Deco - T. Potts

YEAR ISSUE	EDITION LIMIT	YEAR RETD.	ISSUE PRICE	*QUOTE U.S.$
2000 Destiny HN4164	500		1160.00	1160
2000 Ecstasy HN4163	500		1160.00	1160
2000 Optimism HN4165	500		1160.00	1160
2000 Wisdom HN4166	500		1160.00	1160

Art Is Life - A. Maslankowski

YEAR ISSUE	EDITION LIMIT	YEAR RETD.	ISSUE PRICE	*QUOTE U.S.$
2000 Eagle AIL5	1,500		340.00	340
2000 Girl on Rock AIL8	2,000		245.00	245
2000 Girl Stretching AIL6	2,000		305.00	305
2000 Girl w/Ponytail AIL7	2,000		305.00	305
2000 Horses AIL4	1,500		340.00	340
2000 Kiss AIL1	950		380.00	380
2000 Love AIL2	950		380.00	380
2000 Wolves AIL3	1,500		360.00	360

Beatrix Potter Figures - Various

YEAR ISSUE	EDITION LIMIT	YEAR RETD.	ISSUE PRICE	*QUOTE U.S.$
1967 Amiable Guinea Pig P2061 - A. Hallam	Retrd.	1983	29.95	325-450
2000 Amiable Guinea Pig P4031 - W. Platt	Open		48.00	48
1992 And This Pig Had None P3319 - M. Alcock	Retrd.	1998	29.95	38-60
1963 Anna Maria P1851 - A. Hallam	Retrd.	1983	29.95	395-450
1971 Appley Dapply P2333 - A. Hallam	Open		29.95	36
1970 Aunt Pettitoes P2276 - A. Hallam	Retrd.	1993	29.95	55-115
1989 Babbity Bumble P2971 - W. Platt	Retrd.	1993	29.95	145-165
1992 Benjamin Ate a Lettuce Leaf P3317 - M. Alcock	Retrd.	1998	29.95	36-58
1948 Benjamin Bunny P1105 - A. Gredington	Retrd.	1997	29.95	55-100
1983 Benjamin Bunny Sat on a Bank P2803 - D. Lyttleton	Retrd.	1997	29.95	45-55
1975 Benjamin Bunny with Peter Rabbit P2509 - A. Maslankowski	Retrd.	1995	39.95	95
1995 Benjamin Bunny, lg. P3403 - M. Alcock	Retrd.	1997	65.00	75
1991 Benjamin Wakes Up P3234 - A. Hughes-Lubeck	Retrd.	1997	29.95	35
1965 Cecily Parsley P1941 - A. Gredington	Retrd.	1993	29.95	95-125
1979 Chippy Hackee P2627 - D. Lyttleton	Retrd.	1993	29.95	55-65
1991 Christmas Stocking P3257 - M. Alcock	Retrd.	1994	65.00	180-195
1985 Cottontail at Lunchtime P2878 - D. Lyttleton	Retrd.	1996	29.95	35-45
1970 Cousin Ribby P2284 - A. Hallam	Retrd.	1993	29.95	55-75
1982 Diggory Diggory Delvet P2713 - D. Lyttleton	Retrd.	1997	29.95	45
1955 Dutchess w/Pie P1355 - G. Orwell	Retrd.	1967	29.95	200-350
1995 F.W. Gent, lg. P3450 - M. Alcock	Open		65.00	73
1977 Fierce Bad Rabbit P2586 - D. Lyttleton	Retrd.	1997	29.95	35
1954 Flopsy Mopsy and Cottontail P1274 - A. Gredington	Retrd.	1997	29.95	45-100
2000 Former Potatoes P4014 - S. Ridge	Open		60.00	60
1990 Foxy Reading Country News P3219 - A. Hughes-Lubeck	Retrd.	1997	49.95	58-75
1954 Foxy Whiskered Gentleman P1277 - A. Gredington	Open		29.95	36
1990 Gentleman Mouse Made a Bow P3200 - T. Chawner	Retrd.	1996	29.95	33-45
1976 Ginger P2559 - D. Lyttleton	Retrd.	1982	29.95	550-695
1986 Goody and Timmy Tiptoes P2957 - D. Lyttleton	Retrd.	1996	49.95	65
1961 Goody Tiptoes P1675 - A. Gredington	Retrd.	1997	29.95	45
1998 Hiding From the Cat P3766 - G. Tongue	3,500	1998	195.00	195
1951 Hunca Munca P1198 - A. Gredington	Retrd.	2000	29.95	36
1992 Hunca Munca Spills the Beads P3288 - M. Alcock	Retrd.	1996	29.95	85-95
1977 Hunca Munca Sweeping P2584 - D. Lyttleton	Open		29.95	36
1990 Jemema Puddleduck-Foxy Whiskered Gentleman P3193 - T. Chawner	Retrd.	1999	55.00	60-80
1998 Jemima Puddleduck and her Ducklings P3786 - M. Alcock	Open		60.00	60
1983 Jemima Puddleduck Made a Feather Nest-P2823 - D. Lyttleton	Retrd.	1997	29.95	36
1948 Jemima Puddleduck P1092 - A. Gredington	Open		29.95	36
1993 Jemima Puddleduck, lg. P3373 - M. Alcock	Retrd.	1997	49.95	75-95
1999 Jeremy Fisher Catches A Fish P3919 - M. Alcock	Open		37.00	37
1988 Jeremy Fisher Digging P3090 - T. Chawner	Retrd.	1994	50.00	175
1995 Jeremy Fisher lg. P3372 - M. Alcock	Retrd.	1997	65.00	75
1950 Jeremy Fisher P1157 - A. Gredington	Open		29.95	36
1990 John Joiner P2965 - G. Tongue	Retrd.	1997	29.95	55
2000 Johnny Townmouse Eating Corn P3931 - M. Alcock	Open		48.00	48
1954 Johnny Townmouse P1276 - A. Gredington	Retrd.	1993	29.95	35-75
1988 Johnny Townmouse w/Bag P3094 - T. Chawner	Retrd.	1994	50.00	250
1990 Lady Mouse Made a Curtsy P3220 - A. Hughes-Lubeck	Retrd.	1997	29.95	35-65
1950 Lady Mouse P1183 - A. Gredington	Retrd.	2000	29.95	36
1977 Little Black Rabbit P2585 - D. Lyttleton	Retrd.	1997	29.95	36
1987 Little Pig Robinson Spying P3031 - T. Chawner	Retrd.	1993	29.95	150
1991 Miss Dormouse P3251 - M. Alcock	Retrd.	1995	29.95	75-95
1978 Miss Moppet P1275 - A. Gredington	Open		32.50	36
1990 Mittens & Moppet P3197 - T. Chawner	Retrd.	1994	50.00	100-175
1999 Mittens, Tom Kitten & Moppet (Tableau) P3792 - A. Hughes-Lubeck	Yr.Iss.	1999	205.00	205
1989 Mother Ladybird P2966 - W. Platt	Retrd.	1996	29.95	33-55
1973 Mr. Alderman Ptolemy P2424 - G. Tongue	Retrd.	1997	29.95	35-65
1965 Mr. Benjamin Bunny P1940 - A. Gredington	Retrd.	2000	29.95	36-40
1979 Mr. Drake Puddleduck P2628 - D. Lyttleton	Retrd.	2000	29.95	36-50
1974 Mr. Jackson P2453 - A. Hallam	Retrd.	1997	29.95	36
1995 Mr. McGregor P3506 - M. Alcock	Open		42.50	45
1988 Mr. Tod P3091 - T. Chawner	Retrd.	1993	29.95	110-165
1965 Mrs. Flopsy Bunny P1942 - A. Gredington	Retrd.	1999	29.95	36
1997 Mrs. Rabbit and Peter P3646 - W. Platt	Open		67.50	68
1997 Mrs. Rabbit and the Four Bunnies P3672 - S. Ridge	1,997	1997	275.00	275-295
1992 Mrs. Rabbit Cooking P3278 - M. Alcock	Retrd.	1999	29.95	36
1951 Mrs. Rabbit P1200 - A. Gredington	Open		29.95	36
1976 Mrs. Rabbit with Bunnies P2543 - D. Lyttleton	Retrd.	1997	29.95	35
1995 Mrs. Rabbit, lg. P3398 - M. Alcock	Retrd.	1997	65.00	75
1951 Mrs. Ribby P1199 - A. Gredington	Retrd.	2000	29.95	36
1998 Mrs. Tiggy-winkle Washing P3789 - W. Platt	Retrd.	2000	38.00	38
1997 Mrs. Tiggywinkle, lg. P3437 - M. Alcock	Retrd.	1997	75.00	75
1948 Mrs. Tittlemouse P1103 - A. Gredington	Retrd.	1993	29.95	50-95
2000 Mrs. Tittlemouse P4015 - S. Ridge	Open		48.00	48
1992 No More Twist P3325 - M. Alcock	Retrd.	1997	29.95	35-65
1986 Old Mr. Bouncer P2956 - D. Lyttleton	Retrd.	1995	29.95	55
1963 Old Mr. Brown P1796 - A. Hallam	Retrd.	1999	29.95	36
1983 Old Mr. Pricklepin P2767 - D. Lyttleton	Retrd.	1982	29.95	95-195
1959 Old Woman Who Lived in a Shoe P1545 - C. Melbourne	Retrd.	1997	29.95	35
1983 Old Woman Who Lived in a Shoe, Knitting P2804 - D. Lyttleton	Open		29.95	36
2000 Peter & Benjamin Picking Onions P3930 - M. Alcock	Open		215.00	215
1991 Peter & The Red Handkerchief P3242 - M. Alcock	Retrd.	1997	39.95	45
1995 Peter in Bed P3473 - M. Alcock	Open		39.95	45
1999 Peter in the Watering Can P3940 - W. Platt	Open		39.00	39
1989 Peter Rabbit in the Gooseberry Net P3157 - D. Lyttleton	Retrd.	1995	39.95	60-75
1948 Peter Rabbit P1098 - A. Gredington	Open		29.95	36
1993 Peter Rabbit, lg. P3356 - M. Alcock	Retrd.	1997	65.00	75
1996 Peter with Daffodils P3597 - A. Hughes-Lubeck	Open		42.50	45
1996 Peter with Postbag P3591 - A. Hughes-Lubeck	Retrd.	1999	42.50	48
1996 Peter with Red Pocket Handkerchief, lg. P3592 - A. Hughes-Lubeck	Retrd.	1999	75.00	75
1971 Pickles P2334 - A. Hallam	Retrd.	1982	29.95	450-500
1948 Pig Robinson P1104 - A. Gredington	Retrd.	1999	29.95	36
1972 Pig Wig P2381 - A. Hallam	Retrd.	1982	29.95	450-500
1955 Pigling Bland P1365 - G. Orwell	Retrd.	1999	29.95	36
1991 Pigling Eats Porridge P3252 - M. Alcock	Retrd.	1994	50.00	50-95
1976 Poorly Peter Rabbit P2560 - D. Lyttleton	Retrd.	1997	29.95	45-75
1981 Rebeccah Puddleduck P2647 - D. Lyttleton	Retrd.	2000	29.95	36-65
1992 Ribby and the Patty Pan P3280 - M. Alcock	Retrd.	1998	29.95	36-65
1974 Sally Henry Penney P2452 - A. Hallam	Retrd.	1993	29.95	95-125
1948 Samuel Whiskers P1106 - A. Gredington	Retrd.	1995	29.95	45-95
1975 Simpkin P2508 - A. Maslankowski	Retrd.	1983	29.95	650-695

*Quotes have been rounded up to nearest dollar

YEAR ISSUE		EDITION LIMIT	YEAR RETD.	ISSUE PRICE	*QUOTE U.S.$
1973	Sir Isaac Newton P2425 - G. Tongue	Retrd.	1984	29.95	350-450
1948	Squirrel Nutkin P1102 - A. Gredington	Retrd.	2000	29.95	36
1961	Tabitha Twitchitt P1676 - A. Gredington	Retrd.	1995	29.95	45-50
1976	Tabitha Twitchitt with Miss Moppett P2544 - D. Lyttleton	Retrd.	1993	29.95	150-175
1949	Tailor of Gloucester P1108 - A. Gredington	Open		29.95	36
1995	Tailor of Gloucester, lg. P3449 - M. Alcock	Retrd.	1997	65.00	75
1948	Tiggy Winkle P1107 - A. Gredington	Retrd.	2000	29.95	36
1985	Tiggy Winkle Takes Tea P2877 - D. Lyttleton	Open		29.95	36
1948	Timmy Tiptoes P1101 - A. Gredington	Retrd.	1997	29.95	35
2000	Timmy Willie Fetching Milk P3976 - W. Platt	Open		36.00	36
1949	Timmy Willie P1109 - A. Gredington	Retrd.	1993	29.95	45-65
1986	Timmy Willie Sleeping P2996 - G. Tongue	Retrd.	1996	29.95	33-95
1998	Tom Kitten in the Rockery P3719 - W. Platt	Open		36.00	36
1948	Tom Kitten P1100 - A. Gredington	Retrd.	1999	29.95	36
1995	Tom Kitten, lg. P3405 - M. Alcock	Retrd.	1997	65.00	75
1987	Tom Kittten and Butterfly P3030 - T. Chawner	Retrd.	1994	50.00	195-225
1987	Tom Thumb P2989 - W. Platt	Retrd.	1997	29.95	50-55
1955	Tommy Brock P1348 - G. Orwell	Open		29.95	36
2000	Yock Yock in Tub P3946 - W. Platt	Open		60.00	60

Birthday Figure of the Year - N. Pedley

YEAR ISSUE		EDITION LIMIT	YEAR RETD.	ISSUE PRICE	*QUOTE U.S.$
2000	Happy Birthday 2000 HN4215	Yr.Iss.		195.00	195

Brambly Hedge - Various

YEAR ISSUE		EDITION LIMIT	YEAR RETD.	ISSUE PRICE	*QUOTE U.S.$
2000	Ice Ball DBH30 - S. Ridge	Open		240.00	240
2000	Lady Woodmouse DBH32 - W. Platt	Open		80.00	80
2000	Lord Woodmouse DBH31 - S. Ridge	Open		80.00	80
2000	Primrose Woodmouse DBH33 - S. Ridge	Open		60.00	60
2000	Toy Chest Moneybox - M. Alcock	Open		100.00	100
2000	Wilfred Toadflax DBH34 - S. Ridge	Open		60.00	60

British Sporting Heritage - V. Annand

YEAR ISSUE		EDITION LIMIT	YEAR RETD.	ISSUE PRICE	*QUOTE U.S.$
1994	Ascot HN3471	5,000	1997	475.00	475-497
1996	Croquet HN3470	5,000	1997	475.00	475-497
1993	Henley HN3367	5,000	1997	475.00	475-497
1995	Wimbledon HN3366	5,000	1997	475.00	475-497

Bunnykins - Various

YEAR ISSUE		EDITION LIMIT	YEAR RETD.	ISSUE PRICE	*QUOTE U.S.$
1999	Airman DB199 - M. Alcock	5,000	2000	60.00	60
1999	Angel DB196 - M. Alcock	Open		39.00	39
1995	Bathtime DB148 - M. Alcock	Retrd.	1997	40.00	49-65
1987	Be Prepared DB56 - D. Lyttleton	Retrd.	1995	40.00	40-75
1987	Bed Time DB55 - D. Lyttleton	Retrd.	1998	40.00	45-50
1995	Boy Skater DB152 - M. Alcock	Retrd.	1998	40.00	42-68
1991	Bride DB101 - A. Hughes	Open		40.00	45
1987	Brownie DB61 - W. Platt	Retrd.	1993	39.00	75-95
1999	Businessman DB203 - M. Alcock	5,000	2000	60.00	60-116
1994	Christmas Surprise DB146 - W. Platt	Open		50.00	55
1990	Cook DB85 - W. Platt	Retrd.	1994	35.00	75-85
1998	Doctor Bunnykins DB181 - M. Alcock	Open		45.00	45
1984	Drummer Bunnykins (Golden Jubilee) DB26A	Yr.Iss.	1984	N/A	95
1995	Easter Greetings - M. Alcock	Retrd.	1999	50.00	55
1996	Father Bunnykin DB154 - M. Alcock	Retrd.	1996	50.00	55-85
1988	Father, Mother, Victoria DB68 - M. Alcock	Retrd.	1995	40.00	45-75
1989	Fireman DB75 - M. Alcock	Open		40.00	45
1998	Fisherman - S. Ridge	Retrd.	2000	52.50	52
1990	Fisherman DB84 - W. Platt	Retrd.	1993	39.00	95-125
2000	Fortune Teller DB218 - W. Platt	Retrd.	2000	60.00	60
1996	Gardener DB156 - W. Platt	Retrd.	1998	40.00	55-80
1995	Girl Skater DB153 - M. Alcock	Retrd.	1997	40.00	58-65
1995	Goodnight DB157 - S. Ridge	Retrd.	1999	40.00	42-45
1991	Groom DB102 - M. Alcock	Open		40.00	45
1993	Halloween Bunnykin DB132 - M. Alcock	Retrd.	1997	50.00	53-125
1983	Happy Birthday DB21 - G. Tongue	Retrd.	1997	40.00	45-50
1988	Harry DB73 - M. Alcock	Retrd.	1993	34.00	55-95
1972	Helping Mother DB2 - A. Hallam	Retrd.	1993	34.00	75-95
1986	Home Run DB43 - D. Lyttleton	Retrd.	1993	39.00	125-130
1990	Ice Cream DB82 - W. Platt	Retrd.	1993	39.00	75-95
2000	Jack and Jill DB222 - M. Alcock	Open		120.00	120
2000	Little Bo Peep DB220 - M. Alcock	Open		60.00	60
2000	Little Jack Horner DB221 - M. Alcock	Open		60.00	60
2000	Morris Dancer DB204 - S. Ridge	Yr.Iss.		70.00	70
1997	Mother and Baby DB167 - S. Ridge	Open		42.00	45
1996	Mother's Day DB155 - S. Ridge	Open		42.00	45
1986	Mr. Bunnykins "At The Easter Parade" (maroon jacket) DB51 - D. Lyttleton	Yr.Iss.	1986	40.00	700-1125
1982	Mr. Bunnykins "At The Easter Parade" (red jacket) DB18 - G. Tongue	Retrd.	1993	39.00	85-95
1982	Mrs. Bunnykins "At The Easter Parade" (blue dress) DB19 - D. Lyttleton	Retrd.	1996	40.00	85-95
1982	Mrs. Bunnykins "At The Easter Parade" (pink dress) DB52 - D. Lyttleton	Yr.Iss.	1986	40.00	700-1500
1999	Mystic DB197 - M. Alcock	Yr.Iss.		59.00	59
1995	New Baby DB158 - G. Tongue	Retrd.	1999	40.00	43-70
1989	Nurse DB74 - M. Alcock	Open		35.00	45
1989	Paper Boy DB77 - M. Alcock	Retrd.	1993	39.00	65-85
1972	Playtime DB8 - A. Hallam	Retrd.	1993	34.00	55-75
1988	Policeman DB69 - M. Alcock	Retrd.	2000	40.00	45
1988	Polly DB71 - M. Alcock	Retrd.	1993	34.00	60-85
1995	Rainy Day DB147 - M. Alcock	Retrd.	1997	40.00	55-65
1997	Sailor Bunnykins DB166 - S. Ridge	Yr.Iss.	1997	52.50	53-70
1981	Santa Bunnykins DB17 - D. Lyttleton	Retrd.	1995	40.00	85-125
1987	School Days DB57 - D. Lyttleton	Retrd.	1994	40.00	75
1982	School Master DB60 - W. Platt	Retrd.	1995	40.00	65-80
1974	Sleepytime DB15 - A. Maslankowski	Retrd.	1993	39.00	55-65
1972	Sleigh Ride DB4 - A. Hallam	Retrd.	1997	40.00	80-85
1972	Story Time DB9 - A. Hallam	Retrd.	1997	35.00	42-70
1988	Susan DB70 - M. Alcock	Retrd.	1993	34.00	60-75
1992	Sweetheart Bunnykin DB130 - W. Platt	Retrd.	1997	40.00	55-65
1988	Tom DB72 - M. Alcock	Retrd.	1993	34.00	60-75
1986	Uncle Sam DB50 - D. Lyttleton	Open		40.00	45
1988	William DB69 - M. Alcock	Retrd.	1993	34.00	85

Bunnykins-Figure of the Year - M. Alcock

YEAR ISSUE		EDITION LIMIT	YEAR RETD.	ISSUE PRICE	*QUOTE U.S.$
1998	Seaside Bunnykins	Yr.Iss.	1998	55.00	55-70
1999	Mother Bunnykins DB189	Yr.Iss.	1999	42.50	43
2000	Sundial DB213 - W. Platt	Yr.Iss.		50.00	50

Burslem Artwares - C. Noke

YEAR ISSUE		EDITION LIMIT	YEAR RETD.	ISSUE PRICE	*QUOTE U.S.$
1999	Aquatic Bowl	150	1999	1565.00	1565
1999	Bird of Paradise Vase	150	1999	1075.00	1075
1999	Canton Ginger Jar	250	1999	585.00	585
1999	Chengdu Bowl	250	1999	780.00	780
1999	Fanling Vase	250	1999	685.00	685
2000	Fanling Vase, Sung	350		525.00	525
1999	Foshon Jade Vase	250	1999	585.00	585
2000	Fuyang Dragon Vase	200		1325.00	1325
1999	Kowloon Dragon Vase	150	1999	1175.00	1175
2000	Kunshan Bowl	300		785.00	785
2000	Lantao Vase, Sung	350		525.00	525
1999	Lontao Vase, Flambe	250	1999	685.00	685
1999	Osprey Vase	75	1999	3900.00	3900
2000	Sanming Dragon Vase	125		4485.00	4485
2000	Wenzhou Bowl, Chang	250		1125.00	1125
1999	Wuhan Jade Vase	250	1999	685.00	685

Character Sculptures - Various

YEAR ISSUE		EDITION LIMIT	YEAR RETD.	ISSUE PRICE	*QUOTE U.S.$
1996	Bill Sikes HN3785 - A. Dobson	Retrd.	1996	306.25	307
1996	Bowls Player HN3780 - J. Jones	Retrd.	1996	137.50	138
1993	Captain Hook - R. Tabbenor	Retrd.	1996	250.00	270-325
1995	Cyrano de Bergerac HN3751 - D. Biggs	Retrd.	1996	268.75	269
1994	D' Artagnan - R. Tabbenor	Retrd.	1996	260.00	269
1993	Dick Turpin - R. Tabbenor	Retrd.	1996	250.00	269
1995	Fagin HN3752 - A. Dobson	Retrd.	1996	268.75	269
1995	Gulliver - D. Biggs	Retrd.	1996	285.00	307
1993	Long John Silver - A. Maslankowski	Retrd.	1996	250.00	269
1996	Oliver Twist and Artful Dodger HN3786 - A. Dobson	Retrd.	1996	275.00	275
1994	Pied Piper - A. Maslankowski	Retrd.	1996	260.00	269
1993	Robin Hood - A. Maslankowski	Retrd.	1996	250.00	269
2000	Santa Claus HN4175 - R. Tabbenor	Open		340.00	340
1995	Sherlock Holmes HN3639 - R. Tabbenor	Retrd.	1996	268.75	269
1996	Sir Francis Drake HN3770 - D. Biggs	Retrd.	1996	275.00	275
2000	Sorcerer HN4252 - A. Maslankowski	Open		450.00	450
2000	Sorceress HN4253 - A. Maslankowski	Open		395.00	395
1995	Wizard HN3722 - A. Maslankowski	Retrd.	1996	306.25	330-405

Charity Figure of the Year - N. Pedley

YEAR ISSUE		EDITION LIMIT	YEAR RETD.	ISSUE PRICE	*QUOTE U.S.$
1998	Hope	Yr.Iss.	1998	225.00	225-315
1999	Faith HN4151	Yr.Iss.	1999	235.00	235
2000	Charity HN4243	Yr.Iss.		235.00	235

Chelsea - V. Annand

YEAR ISSUE		EDITION LIMIT	YEAR RETD.	ISSUE PRICE	*QUOTE U.S.$
2000	Melinda HN4209	Open		165.00	165
2000	Zoe HN4208	Open		165.00	165

Christmas Figure of the Year - N. Pedley

YEAR ISSUE		EDITION LIMIT	YEAR RETD.	ISSUE PRICE	*QUOTE U.S.$
1999	Christmas Day HN4214	Yr.Iss.	1999	295.00	295
2000	Christmas Day 2000 HN4242	Yr.Iss.		295.00	295

Classique - Royal Doulton, unless otherwise noted

YEAR ISSUE		EDITION LIMIT	YEAR RETD.	ISSUE PRICE	*QUOTE U.S.$
1999	Anyone For Tennis CL4007 - T. Potts	Open		185.00	185
1999	Bernadette CL4005 - T. Potts	Open		245.00	245
2000	Celebration CL4011- T. Potts	Open		195.00	195
1998	Christina	Open		195.00	195
2000	Elizabeth CL4009 - T. Potts	Open		195.00	195
1999	Eve CL4002 - T. Potts	Open		175.00	175
1998	Faye CL3984	Open		175.00	175
1998	Felicity CL3986	Retrd.	1999	175.00	175
1998	From This Day Forth CL3990	Retrd.	1999	175.00	175
2000	Gabrielle CL4012- T. Potts	Open		185.00	185
1998	Helena	Open		175.00	175
1998	Isobel CL3890	Retrd.	1999	175.00	175
1999	Lorna CL3997 - T. Potts	Retrd.	2000	175.00	175
1998	Lucinda CL3983	Open		175.00	175
1998	Naomi	Open		225.00	225
1999	Nicola CL4000 - T. Potts	Retrd.	2000	175.00	175
2000	Philippa CL4010 - T. Potts	Open		185.00	185
1999	Simone CL4004 - T. Potts	Open		175.00	175
1999	Tanya CL4006 - T. Potts	Open		195.00	195
1999	To Love and Cherish CL4003 - T. Potts	Open		175.00	175
1999	To The Fairway CL4008 - T. Potts	Open		245.00	245
1998	Vanessa CL3989	Open		175.00	175

Country Maid Collection - N. Pedley

YEAR ISSUE		EDITION LIMIT	YEAR RETD.	ISSUE PRICE	*QUOTE U.S.$
2000	Dairy Maid HN4249	Open		225.00	225
2000	Fair Maid HN4222	Open		225.00	225
2000	Susannah HN4221	Open		225.00	225

Diamond Anniversary Tinies - Various

YEAR ISSUE		EDITION LIMIT	YEAR RETD.	ISSUE PRICE	*QUOTE U.S.$
1994	John Barleycorn - C. Noke	2,500	1994	350.00	450-500
1994	Simon The Cellarer - Noke/Fenton	2,500	1994	set	Set
1994	Dick Turpin - W. Harper	2,500	1994	set	Set
1994	Granny - W. Harper	2,500	1994	set	Set
1994	Jester - C. Noke	2,500	1994	set	Set
1994	Parson Brown - W. Harper	2,500	1994	set	Set

Femmes Fatales - P. Davies

YEAR ISSUE		EDITION LIMIT	YEAR RETD.	ISSUE PRICE	*QUOTE U.S.$
1979	Cleopatra HN2868	750	1995	750.00	1350
1984	Eve HN2466	750	1995	1250.00	1300-1500
1981	Helen of Troy HN2387	750	1993	1250.00	1400-1600
1985	Lucrezia Borgia HN2342	750	1993	1250.00	1300-1500
1982	Queen of Sheba HN2328	750	1996	1250.00	1300-1600
1983	Tz'u-Hsi HN2391	750	1996	1250.00	1300-1500

Figure of the Year - Various

YEAR ISSUE		EDITION LIMIT	YEAR RETD.	ISSUE PRICE	*QUOTE U.S.$
1991	Amy HN3316 - P. Gee	Closed	1991	195.00	695
1992	Mary HN3375 - P. Gee	Closed	1992	225.00	375-475
1993	Patricia HN3365 - V. Annand	Closed	1993	250.00	425-475
1994	Jennifer HN3447 - P. Gee	Closed	1994	250.00	300-400
1995	Deborah - HN3644 - N. Pedley	Closed	1995	225.00	225
1996	Belle HN3703 - V. Annand	Closed	1996	231.25	235
1997	Jessica HN3850 - N. Pedley	Closed	1997	245.00	245-400
1998	Rebecca HN4041 - V. Annand	Closed	1998	195.00	195-315
1999	Lauren HN3975 - D. Hughes	Yr.Iss.	1999	215.00	215
2000	Rachel HN3976 - D. Hughes	Yr.Iss.		215.00	215

The Four Seasons - V. Annand

YEAR ISSUE		EDITION LIMIT	YEAR RETD.	ISSUE PRICE	*QUOTE U.S.$
1993	Springtime HN3477	Retrd.	1996	325.00	395-445
1994	Summertime HN3478	Retrd.	1996	325.00	350-465
1993	Autumntime HN3621	Retrd.	1996	325.00	350
1993	Wintertime HN3622	Retrd.	1996	325.00	350

Gainsborough Ladies - P. Gee

YEAR ISSUE		EDITION LIMIT	YEAR RETD.	ISSUE PRICE	*QUOTE U.S.$
1991	Countess of Sefton HN3010	5,000	1996	650.00	700
1991	Hon Frances Duncombe HN3009	5,000	1996	650.00	700
1991	Lady Sheffield HN3008	5,000	1996	650.00	700
1990	Mary, Countess Howe HN3007	5,000	1996	650.00	700

Great Lovers - R. Jefferson

YEAR ISSUE		EDITION LIMIT	YEAR RETD.	ISSUE PRICE	*QUOTE U.S.$
1995	Antony and Cleopatra HN3114	150	1997	5250.00	5250
1996	Lancelot and Guinevere HN3112	150	1997	5250.00	5250
1994	Robin Hood and Maid Marian HN3111	150	1997	5250.00	5250
1993	Romeo and Juliet HN3113	150	1997	5250.00	5250

Image of the Year - D. Tootle, unless otherwise noted

YEAR ISSUE		EDITION LIMIT	YEAR RETD.	ISSUE PRICE	*QUOTE U.S.$
1998	Best Friends HN4026	Yr.Iss.	1998	125.00	125
1999	The Promise HN4033	Yr.Iss.	1999	150.00	150-205
2000	Kindred Spirits HN4077 - R. Tabbenor	Yr.Iss.		145.00	145

Images - Various

YEAR ISSUE		EDITION LIMIT	YEAR RETD.	ISSUE PRICE	*QUOTE U.S.$
1997	Amen HN4021 - D. Tootle	Open		55.00	55
1997	Angel HN3940 - A. Maslankowski	Retrd.	1999	125.00	125
1997	The Ballerina HN3828 - D. Tootle	Open		95.00	95
1998	The Ballet Dancer HN4027 - D. Tootle	Retrd.	2000	110.00	110
1998	Ballet Lesson HN4028 - D. Tootle	Open		110.00	110
1991	Bride & Groom HN3281 - R. Tabbenor	Retrd.	2000	85.00	99
1991	Bridesmaid HN3280 - R. Tabbenor	Retrd.	1999	85.00	99
1993	Brother & Sister HN3460 - A. Hughes	Open		52.50	112
1991	Brothers HN3191 - E. Griffiths	Open		90.00	112
1981	Family HN2720 - E. Griffiths	Open		187.50	215
1988	First Love HN2747 - D. Tootle	Retrd.	1997	170.00	215
1991	First Steps HN3282 - R. Tabbenor	Open		142.00	215
1993	Gift of Freedom HN3443 - N/A	Open		90.00	112
1997	Graduation HN3942 - A. Maslankowski	Open		125.00	125
1989	Happy Anniversary HN3254 - D. Tootle	Open		187.50	215
1997	Happy Birthday HN3829 - D. Tootle	Open		95.00	95
1999	Leap Frog HN4030 - D. Tootle	Open		150.00	150
2000	Love Everlasting HN4280 - A. Hughes	Open		90.00	90
1981	Lovers HN2762 - D. Tootle	Retrd.	1997	187.50	215-346
1997	The Messiah HN3952 - A. Maslankowski	Retrd.	1999	145.00	145
1980	Mother & Daughter HN2841 - E. Griffiths	Retrd.	1997	187.50	215
1997	Mother and Child HN3938 - A. Maslankowski	Open		125.00	125
1998	Night Watch (Owls) HN3895 - R. Tabbenor	Open		70.00	70
1993	Our First Christmas HN3452 - N/A	Retrd.	1998	185.00	215
1989	Over the Threshold HN3274 - R. Tabbenor	Retrd.	1998	187.50	215
1997	The Performance HN3827 - D. Tootle	Open		235.00	235
1983	Sisters HN3018 - P. Parson	Open		90.00	112
2000	Sweetheart Boy HN4351 - A. Maslankowski	Open		70.00	70
2000	Sweetheart Girl HN4352 - A. Maslankowski	Open		70.00	70
1987	Wedding Day HN2748 - D. Tootle	Open		187.50	215

Images of Nature - R. Tabbenor, unless otherwise noted

YEAR ISSUE		EDITION LIMIT	YEAR RETD.	ISSUE PRICE	*QUOTE U.S.$
2000	Dedication (Polar Bears) HN4173	Open		145.00	145
2000	Running Wild (Cheetahs) HN4172	Open		99.00	99
2000	Soaring High (Eagles) HN4087 - A. Maslankowski	Open		99.00	99
2000	Standing Tall (Giraffes) HN3898	Open		99.00	99
1999	Running Free HN3896	Open		99.00	99

Impressions - P. Parsons, unless otherwise noted

YEAR ISSUE		EDITION LIMIT	YEAR RETD.	ISSUE PRICE	*QUOTE U.S.$
2000	Daybreak HN4196	Open		245.00	245
2000	Loving Arms HN4262	Open		265.00	265

*Quotes have been rounded up to nearest dollar

YEAR ISSUE	EDITION LIMIT	YEAR RETD.	ISSUE PRICE	*QUOTE U.S.$
2000 Secret Thoughts HN4197	Open		245.00	245
2000 Summer Blooms HN4194	Open		245.00	245
2000 Summer Fragrance HN4195	Open		245.00	245
2000 Sunrise HN4199	Open		245.00	245
2000 Sunset HN4198	Open		245.00	245
2000 Sweet Dreams HN4193	Open		245.00	245
2000 Tender Greetings HN4261	Open		265.00	265
2000 Tender Moment HN4192 - A. Maslankowski	Open		245.00	245

In Vogue Collection - V. Annand

YEAR ISSUE	EDITION LIMIT	YEAR RETD.	ISSUE PRICE	*QUOTE U.S.$
2000 Claudia HN4230	Open		225.00	225
2000 Joanne HN4202	Open		225.00	225
2000 Rebecca HN4203	Open		225.00	225

Jody's Dreamkeepers - J. Bergsma

YEAR ISSUE	EDITION LIMIT	YEAR RETD.	ISSUE PRICE	*QUOTE U.S.$
1998 The Best Thing About Mom Is Everything	Retrd.	1999	20.00	20
1998 Happiness Is Made To Be Shared	Retrd.	1999	25.00	25
1998 Home Is Where The Heart Is	Retrd.	1999	30.00	30
1998 A Home Without A Dog Is Just A House	Retrd.	1999	15.00	15
1998 Life Is Best...Just Putting Around!	Retrd.	1999	20.00	20
1998 May All Our Hearts Beat As One	Retrd.	1999	35.00	35
1998 May Your Heart Be Filled With Simple Joys	Retrd.	1999	20.00	20
1998 The Memories Of Christmas	Retrd.	1999	40.00	40
1998 Never Let Go Of Your Dreams	Retrd.	1999	20.00	20
1998 Of All The Treasures In Life, Friendship Is The Greatest	Retrd.	1999	30.00	30
1998 The Purpose Of Life Is To Celebrate Living	Retrd.	1999	50.00	50
1998 Reach Out For The Impossible	Retrd.	1999	75.00	75
1998 Simple Pleasures Are The Treasures Of Life	Retrd.	1999	20.00	20
1998 There Are Very Few...As Special As You	Retrd.	1999	30.00	30
1998 To Be A Child Is To Know The Joy Of Living	Retrd.	1999	50.00	50
1998 We Are Always On Our Way To A Miracle	Retrd.	1999	20.00	20
1998 We Never Outgrow Our Need For Hugs	Retrd.	1999	15.00	15
1998 When I Count My Blessings, I Count You Twice	Retrd.	1999	20.00	20
1998 When You Need A Friend You Can Count On Me	Retrd.	1999	25.00	25
1998 The Work Is Hard, But The Reward Is Great	Retrd.	1999	15.00	15

Limited Edition Figurines - Various

YEAR ISSUE	EDITION LIMIT	YEAR RETD.	ISSUE PRICE	*QUOTE U.S.$
2000 The Bather HN4244 - N. Pedley	2,000		440.00	440
1992 Christopher Columbus HN3392 - A. Maslankowski	1,492	1995	1950.00	1950
1993 Duke of Wellington HN3432 - A. Maslankowski	1,500	1998	1750.00	1750
1996 Eastern Grace Flambe HN3683 - P. Parsons	2,500	1996	493.75	520
1994 Field Marshal Montgomery HN3405 - N/A	1,944	1996	1100.00	1100
1993 General Robert E. Lee HN3404 - R. Tabbenor	5,000	1995	1175.00	1175
2000 HM Queen Elizabeth (Queen Mother) HN4086 - A. Maslankowski	2,000		395.00	395
1997 HM Queen Elizabeth, The Queen Mother HN3944 - A. Maslankowski	5,000	1998	635.00	635
1993 Lt. General Ulysses S. Grant HN3403 - R. Tabbenor	5,000	1995	1175.00	1175
1992 Napoleon at Waterloo HN3429 - A. Maslankowski	1,500	1994	1900.00	1900
1992 Samurai Warrior HN3402 - R. Tabbenor	950	1995	500.00	500-600
1997 Sir Henry Doulton HN3891 - R. Tabbenor	1,997	1997	430.00	450
2000 Sunshine Girl HN4245 - N. Pedley	2,000		440.00	440
2000 The Swimmer HN4246 - N. Pedley	2,000		440.00	440
1997 Top o' the Hill Blue HN 3735 - L. Harradine	3,500	1997	370.00	370
1993 Vice Admiral Lord Nelson HN3489 - A. Maslankowski	950	1996	1750.00	1750
1993 Winston S. Churchill HN3433 - A. Maslankowski	5,000	1994	595.00	595-650

Literary Heroines - P. Parsons

YEAR ISSUE	EDITION LIMIT	YEAR RETD.	ISSUE PRICE	*QUOTE U.S.$
1998 Elizabeth Bennet	3,500	1999	350.00	350
1998 Emma	3,500	1999	375.00	375
1998 Jane Eyre	3,500	1999	375.00	375
1999 Moll Flanders HN3849	3,500		395.00	395
1998 Tess of the D'Urbervilles	3,500	1999	350.00	350

Literary Loves - A. Maslankowski

YEAR ISSUE	EDITION LIMIT	YEAR RETD.	ISSUE PRICE	*QUOTE U.S.$
1999 Heathcliff and Cathy HN4071	750		1275.00	1275

Michael Doulton Figure - J. Bromley

YEAR ISSUE	EDITION LIMIT	YEAR RETD.	ISSUE PRICE	*QUOTE U.S.$
2000 Susan HN4230	Yr.Iss.		255.00	255

Movie Classics - V. Annand

YEAR ISSUE	EDITION LIMIT	YEAR RETD.	ISSUE PRICE	*QUOTE U.S.$
2000 Scarlett O' Hara (Gone With The Wind) HN4200	Retrd.	2000	350.00	350

Myths & Maidens - R. Jefferson

YEAR ISSUE	EDITION LIMIT	YEAR RETD.	ISSUE PRICE	*QUOTE U.S.$
1986 Diana The Huntress HN2829	300	1990	2950.00	3000
1985 Europa & Bull HN2828	300	1990	2950.00	3000
1984 Juno & Peacock HN2827	300	1990	2950.00	3000
1982 Lady & Unicorn HN2825	300	1990	2500.00	2500
1983 Leda & Swan HN2826	300	1990	2950.00	3000

Name Your Own Figure - N. Pedley

YEAR ISSUE	EDITION LIMIT	YEAR RETD.	ISSUE PRICE	*QUOTE U.S.$
2000 Congratulations To You HN4306	Open		225.00	225
2000 Wedding Celebration, white HN4229	Open		215.00	215

Old Bear And Friends - J. Hissey

YEAR ISSUE	EDITION LIMIT	YEAR RETD.	ISSUE PRICE	*QUOTE U.S.$
1998 Bramwell Brown Has a Good Idea	Retrd.	1999	20.00	20
1998 Don't Worry Rabbit	Retrd.	1999	20.00	20
1998 Long Red Scarf	Retrd.	1999	29.00	29
1998 Old Bear	Retrd.	1999	15.00	15
1998 Ruff's Price	Retrd.	1999	21.50	22
1998 Snowflake Biscuits	Retrd.	1999	29.00	29
1998 Time For A Cuddle, Hug Me Tight	Retrd.	1999	20.00	20
1998 Time For Bed	Retrd.	1999	25.00	25
1998 Waiting For Snow	Retrd.	1999	25.00	25
1998 Welcome Home, Old Bear	Retrd.	1999	21.50	22

Prestige Figures - Various

YEAR ISSUE	EDITION LIMIT	YEAR RETD.	ISSUE PRICE	*QUOTE U.S.$
1996 Charge of the Light Brigade HN3718 - A. Maslankowski	Open		17500.00	17500
1982 Columbine HN2738 - D. Tootle	Retrd.	1999	1250.00	1375
1982 Harlequin HN2737 - D. Tootle	Retrd.	1999	1250.00	1375
1964 Indian Brave HN2376 - M. Davis	500	1993	2500.00	5500
1952 Jack Point HN2080 - C.J. Noke	Open		2900.00	3400
1950 King Charles HN2084 - C.J. Noke	Retrd.	1992	2500.00	2500
1964 Matador and Bull HN2324 - M. Davis	Open		21500.00	25200
1952 The Moor HN2082 - C.J. Noke	Retrd.	1998	2500.00	3000
1964 The Palio HN2428 - M. Davis	500	1993	2500.00	6500
1952 Princess Badoura HN2081 - H. Stanton	Open		28000.00	33000
1999 Romeo & Juliet HN4057 - D. Tootle	300		2900.00	2900
1978 St George and Dragon HN2856 - W.K. Harper	Retrd.	1999	13600.00	14500

Pretty Ladies - N. Pedley, unless otherwise noted

YEAR ISSUE	EDITION LIMIT	YEAR RETD.	ISSUE PRICE	*QUOTE U.S.$
1999 Beth HN4156	Open		215.00	215
2000 Camilla HN4220	Open		235.00	235
2000 Ellen HN4231- J. Bromley	Open		285.00	285
1999 Hannah HN4052 - V. Annand	Open		245.00	245
2000 Jennifer HN4248	Open		235.00	235
1999 Kelly HN4157	Open		185.00	185
2000 Lorraine HN4301	Open		185.00	185
1999 Lynne HN4155	Open		225.00	225
1999 Madeline HN4152	Open		225.00	225
1999 Marianne HN4153	Open		235.00	235
1999 Mary HN4114	Open		230.00	230
1999 Michelle HN4158	Open		185.00	185
1999 Natasha HN4154	Open		225.00	225
1999 The Open Road HN4161 - T. Potts	Open		245.00	245
2000 Specially For You HN4232 - J. Bromley	Open		315.00	315
1999 Sweet Poetry HN4113	Open		205.00	205

Queens of Realm - P. Parsons

YEAR ISSUE	EDITION LIMIT	YEAR RETD.	ISSUE PRICE	*QUOTE U.S.$
1989 Mary, Queen of Scots HN3142	S/O	1992	550.00	850-900
1988 Queen Anne HN3141	S/O	1992	525.00	600-800
1986 Queen Elizabeth I HN3099	S/O	1992	495.00	650-1100
1987 Queen Victoria HN3125	S/O	1992	495.00	1500-1750
1987 Set of 4	S/O	1992	2065.00	3000-3450

Reynolds Collection - P. Gee

YEAR ISSUE	EDITION LIMIT	YEAR RETD.	ISSUE PRICE	*QUOTE U.S.$
1992 Countess Harrington HN3317	5,000	1995	550.00	595
1993 Countess Spencer HN3320	5,000	1995	595.00	550-595
1991 Lady Worsley HN3318	5,000	1995	550.00	595
1992 Mrs. Hugh Bonfoy HN3319	5,000	1995	550.00	595

Royal Crown Derby Guild - Various

YEAR ISSUE	EDITION LIMIT	YEAR RETD.	ISSUE PRICE	*QUOTE U.S.$
2000 Firecrest - R. Jefferson/S. Rowe	Yr.Iss.		50.00	50
2000 Orchard Hedgehog - J. Ablitt	Yr.Iss.		125.00	125

Royal Crown Derby Paperweights - Various

YEAR ISSUE	EDITION LIMIT	YEAR RETD.	ISSUE PRICE	*QUOTE U.S.$
1990 Angel Fish - R. Jefferson/J. Ledger	Retrd.	1995	140.00	140
1996 Armadillo - J. Ablitt	Retrd.	1999	140.00	140-196
1995 Ashbourne Hedgehog - R. Jefferson/J. Ablitt	500	1995	118.00	118
1986 Badger - R. Jefferson/B. Branscombe	Retrd.	1994	110.00	110
1995 Bakewell Duck - R. Jefferson/J. Ablitt	500	1995	110.00	110
1994 Beaver - R. Jefferson/J. Ledger	Retrd.	1997	125.00	125
1994 Bengal Tiger - J. Ablitt	Retrd.	1999	435.00	435
1995 Bengal Tiger Cub - J. Ablitt	Retrd.	1999	200.00	200
1995 Blue Jay - J. Ablitt	Retrd.	1999	155.00	155
1991 Bulldog - R. Jefferson/J. Ledger	Retrd.	1997	175.00	175-225
1996 Buxton Badger - R. Jefferson/J. Ablitt	500	1996	130.00	130
1997 Catnip Kitten - R. Jefferson/L. Adams	Retrd.	1997	50.00	196
1996 Cheshire Cat - R. Jefferson/J. Ablitt	500	1996	170.00	170
1991 Chevroned Butterfly Fish - R. Jefferson/J. Ledger	Retrd.	1995	140.00	140
1986 Chipmunk - R. Jefferson /B. Branscombe	Retrd.	1997	85.00	135
1992 Cockerel - R. Jefferson/J. Ledger	Retrd.	1999	95.00	95-150
1995 Contented Cat - J. Ablitt	Retrd.	1998	155.00	135-155
1996 Contented Kitten - J. Ablitt	Retrd.	1998	75.00	75-80
1995 Coot - J. Ablitt	Retrd.	1997	110.00	110-120
2000 Country Mouse - J. Ablitt	Open		90.00	90
1988 Crab - R. Jefferson/B. Branscombe	Retrd.	1991	120.00	210
1990 Crown - R. Jefferson/J. Ledger	Retrd.	1998	160.00	160
2000 Dappled Quail - R. Jefferson/C. Adams	Open		145.00	145
1998 Debonair Bear - J. Ablitt	Retrd.	1998	130.00	130-228
1994 Deer - J. Ablitt	Retrd.	1994	250.00	250
1998 Derby Wren - R. Jefferson/S. Rowe	Retrd.	1998	50.00	50
1987 Dolphin - R. Jefferson /B. & J. Branscombe	Retrd.	1993	120.00	136
1991 Dormouse - R. Jefferson/J. Ledger	Retrd.	1995	80.00	101
1995 Dove - Gold Backstamp - J. Branscombe	50	1995	860.00	860
1995 Dove - J. Branscombe	100	1995	760.00	760
1988 Dragon - R. Jefferson/B. Branscombe	Retrd.	1992	120.00	210
1999 Drummer Bear - J. Ablitt	Open		165.00	165
1981 Duck - R. Jefferson/B. Branscombe	Retrd.	1997	95.00	95-135
1999 Duck-Billed Platypus	Open		135.00	135
1996 Fawn - J. Ablitt	Retrd.	1996	200.00	250
1983 Fox (Arctic) - R. Jefferson /B. Branscombe	Retrd.	1987	75.00	75
1983 Fox - R. Jefferson/B. Branscombe	Retrd.	1987	75.00	75
1983 Frog - R. Jefferson/B. Branscombe	Retrd.	1997	95.00	118
1999 Garden Snail - Tien Manh-Dinh /R. Jefferson	Yr.Iss.	1999	180.00	180
1990 Ginger Cat - R. Jefferson /B. Branscombe	Retrd.	1994	125.00	125
1986 Golden Carp - R. Jefferson /B. Branscombe	Retrd.	1991	125.00	125
1990 Gourami - R. Jefferson/J. Ledger	Retrd.	1995	140.00	140
1995 Grey Kitten - R. Jefferson /B. Branscombe	Retrd.	1995	95.00	95
1990 Gumps Large Elephant - R. Tabbenor/J. Ledger	100	1990	1000.00	1000
1990 Guppy - R. Jefferson/J. Ledger	Retrd.	1995	140.00	140
1989 Hamster - R. Jefferson/J. Ledger	Retrd.	1992	100.00	162
1985 Harvest Mouse - R. Jefferson /B. Branscombe	Retrd.	1994	75.00	80
1983 Hedgehog - R. Jefferson /B. Branscombe	Retrd.	1987	75.00	75
1994 Honey Bear - R. Jefferson/J. Ledger	Retrd.	1997	175.00	220-250
1990 Horse - R. Jefferson/J. Ledger	Retrd.	1993	140.00	140
1991 Imari Dormouse - R. Jefferson /J. Ledger	Retrd.	1994	80.00	80
1999 Kangaroo - J. Ablitt	Open		265.00	265
1993 King Charles Spaniel R. Jefferson/J. Ledger	Retrd.	1995	125.00	125
1999 Koala & Baby - J. Ablitt	Open		190.00	190
1988 Koala - R. Jefferson/B. Branscombe	Retrd.	1993	120.00	120
1991 Koran - R. Jefferson/J. Ledger	Retrd.	1995	140.00	140
1997 Ladybug - Two Spot - J. Ablitt	Retrd.	1998	70.00	70
1992 Lamb - J. Branscombe	Retrd.	1996	75.00	158
1997 Majestic Cat - R. Jefferson/C. Roome	3,500	1997	180.00	180
2000 Millennium Bug - Scarab - J. Ablitt	Yr.Iss.		95.00	95
1995 Mole - R. Jefferson/S. Rowe	Retrd.	1995	90.00	90
1992 Monkey & Baby - R. Jefferson /J. Ledger	Retrd.	1994	230.00	230
1997 Mulberry Hall Elephant - R. Tabbenor/L. Adams	500	1997	1190.00	1190
1996 Mulberry Hall Frog - R. Jefferson /S. Rowe	Retrd.	500	180.00	180
1997 Nesting Bullfinch - J. Ablitt	Retrd.	1999	135.00	135
1997 Nesting Chaffinch - J. Ablitt	Retrd.	1997	135.00	135
1997 Nesting Goldfinch - J. Ablitt	Retrd.	1999	135.00	135
1999 Nuthatch - J. Ablitt	Open		115.00	115
1998 Old Imari Frog - R. Jefferson/S. Rowe	4,500	1998	160.00	160
1981 Owl - R. Jefferson/B. Branscombe	Retrd.	1992	95.00	135
1999 Pelican - J. Ablitt	Open		155.00	155
1981 Penguin - R. Jefferson/B. Branscombe	Retrd.	1992	95.00	95
1983 Pheasant - R. Jefferson/B. Branscombe	Retrd.	1998	75.00	128
1985 Pig - R. Jefferson/B. Branscombe	Retrd.	1991	95.00	95
1996 Piglet - R. Jefferson/S. Rowe	Retrd.	1999	65.00	112
1988 Platypus - R. Jefferson/B. Branscombe	Retrd.	1992	120.00	120
1993 Playful Kitten - R. Tabbenor/J. Ledger	Retrd.	1996	110.00	110
1996 Poppy Mouse - R. Jefferson/S. Rowe	Retrd.	1996	50.00	50
1981 Quail - R. Jefferson/B. Branscombe	Retrd.	1991	95.00	139
1989 Ram - B. Branscombe/J. Branscombe	Retrd.	1993	250.00	250
1990 Red Fox - R. Jefferson/B. Branscombe	Retrd.	1993	85.00	85
1999 Red Squirrel - J. Ablitt	Open		135.00	135
1997 Regal Goldie Bear - J. Ablitt	1,000	1997	120.00	120
1999 Rocky Mountain Bear - R. Jefferson/S. Rowe	Open		195.00	195
1997 Rowsley Rabbit - R. Jefferson/S. Rowe	Retrd.	1997	118.00	118
1991 Russian Bear - R. Jefferson/J. Ledger	Retrd.	1998	85.00	123
1999 Santa and Sleigh - J. Ablitt	Open		160.00	160
1991 Seahorse - J. Branscombe	Retrd.	1994	170.00	170
1983 Seal - R. Jefferson/B. Branscombe	Retrd.	1987	95.00	95
1991 Sheep - J. Branscombe	Retrd.	1995	140.00	140
1999 Sitting Duckling - J. Ablitt	Open		105.00	105
1999 Sitting Piglet - J. Ablitt	Open		100.00	100
1999 Sleeping Piglet - J. Ablitt	Open		100.00	100
1985 Snail - R. Jefferson/B. Branscombe	Retrd.	1991	95.00	95
1989 Snake - R. Jefferson/B. Branscombe	Retrd.	1991	175.00	210
1991 Squirrel - R. Jefferson/J. Ledger	Retrd.	1996	100.00	100
2000 Striped Dolphin - R. Jefferson/S. Rowe	Open		175.00	175
1996 Swan - M. Delf	Retrd.	1999	150.00	183
1990 Swee - R. Jefferson/J. Ledger	Retrd.	1995	140.00	140
1990 Sweetlips - R. Jefferson/J. Ledger	Retrd.	1995	140.00	145
1999 Swimming Duckling - J. Ablitt	Open		105.00	105
1997 Teddy Bear - Red Bow Tie - J. Ablitt	950	1997	120.00	140
1993 Tiger Cub - R. Jefferson/J. Ledger	Retrd.	1995	105.00	105
1983 Turtle - R. Jefferson/B. Branscombe	Retrd.	1998	75.00	75-115
1993 Twin Lambs - J. Branscombe	Retrd.	1997	130.00	130
1987 Walrus - R. Jefferson/B. Branscombe	Retrd.	1991	70.00	210
1995 Waxwing - R. Jefferson/J. Ledger	Retrd.	1998	110.00	115-154
1995 Zebra - J. Ablitt	Retrd.	1998	375.00	392

Royal Doulton Figurines - Various

YEAR ISSUE	EDITION LIMIT	YEAR RETD.	ISSUE PRICE	*QUOTE U.S.$
1989 The Balloon Seller (mini) HN2130 - L. Harradine	Retrd.	1992	140.00	149
1933 Beethoven HN1778 - R. Garbe	25	1935	N/A	6500
1975 The Jersey Milkmaid HN2057A - L. Harradine	Closed	1981	N/A	225
1987 Life Boatman HN2764 - W. Harper	Closed	1991	N/A	350-400
1986 The Newsvendor HN2891 - W.K. Harper	2,500	N/A	225.00	349
1929 Old Balloon Seller HN1315 - L. Harradine	Retrd.	1998	250.00	270-299

YEAR	ISSUE	EDITION LIMIT	YEAR RETD.	ISSUE PRICE	*QUOTE U.S.$
1924	Tony Weller HN684 - C. Noke	Closed	1938	N/A	1800

Royalty - Various

YEAR	ISSUE	EDITION LIMIT	YEAR RETD.	ISSUE PRICE	*QUOTE U.S.$
1986	Duchess Of York HN3086 - E. Griffiths	1,500	1987	495.00	650
1981	Duke Of Edinburgh HN2386 - P. Davis	750	1982	395.00	450
1982	Lady Diana Spencer HN2885 - E. Griffiths	1,500	1982	395.00	2000-2300
1981	Prince Of Wales HN2883 - E. Griffiths	1,500	1982	395.00	450-650
1981	Prince Of Wales HN2884 - E. Griffiths	1,500	1982	750.00	1000
1982	Princess Of Wales HN2887 - E. Griffiths	1,500	1982	750.00	1700-2650
1997	Queen Elizabeth II & Duke of Edinburgh HN3836 - P. Parsons	750	1997	650.00	650
1973	Queen Elizabeth II HN2502 - P. Davis	750	1975	N/A	1800
1982	Queen Elizabeth II HN2878 - E. Griffiths	2,500	1984	N/A	450-800
1992	Queen Elizabeth II, 2nd. Version HN3440 - P. Gee	3,500	1994	460.00	460
1989	Queen Elizabeth, the Queen Mother as the Duchess of York HN3230 - P. Parsons	9,500	1990	N/A	450
1990	Queen Elizabeth, the Queen Mother HN3189 - E. Griffiths	2,500	1992	N/A	450-700
1980	Queen Mother HN2882 - E. Griffiths	1,500	1983	650.00	1250

Sentiments - A. Maslankowski

YEAR	ISSUE	EDITION LIMIT	YEAR RETD.	ISSUE PRICE	*QUOTE U.S.$
1999	Good Luck HN4070	Open		82.50	83
2000	Happy Christmas HN4255	Open		85.00	85
2000	Many Happy Returns HN4254	Open		85.00	85
1999	Missing You HN4076	Open		80.00	80
2000	Remembering You HN4085	Open		85.00	85

Triumphs Of The Heart - J. Griffin

YEAR	ISSUE	EDITION LIMIT	YEAR RETD.	ISSUE PRICE	*QUOTE U.S.$
1998	Forever Yours	Retrd.	1999	150.00	150
1998	Love Conquers All	Retrd.	1999	150.00	150
1998	Loveswept	Retrd.	1999	150.00	150
1998	My Beloved	Retrd.	1999	150.00	150
1998	Only You	Retrd.	1999	150.00	150
1998	Sweet Embrace	Retrd.	1999	150.00	150

Vanity Fair - N. Pedley

YEAR	ISSUE	EDITION LIMIT	YEAR RETD.	ISSUE PRICE	*QUOTE U.S.$
2000	Josephine HN4223	Open		175.00	175

San Francisco Music Box Company

Collector's Club - G. Ho

YEAR	ISSUE	EDITION LIMIT	YEAR RETD.	ISSUE PRICE	*QUOTE U.S.$
1998	Hanna w/Baby Waterglobe	Open		30.00	30

American Treasures Historical Reproduction Musical Carousel Collection - San Francisco Music Box Company

YEAR	ISSUE	EDITION LIMIT	YEAR RETD.	ISSUE PRICE	*QUOTE U.S.$
1997	Dentzel Tiger	4,500	1998	59.95	60
1997	Dentzel/Cernigliaro Giraffe	4,500	1998	59.95	60
1997	Dentzel/Cernigliaro Lion	4,500	1998	59.95	60
1997	Herschell-Spillman Hop Toad	4,500	1998	59.95	60
1997	Looff Jumper Horse	4,500	1998	84.95	85
1997	M.C. Illions American Beauty Horse	4,500	1998	84.95	85
1997	Muller Eagle Horse	4,500	1998	84.95	85
1997	PTC Armored Horse	4,500	1998	84.95	85

Boyds Bears Musical Bearstone Figurines - G.M. Lowenthal

YEAR	ISSUE	EDITION LIMIT	YEAR RETD.	ISSUE PRICE	*QUOTE U.S.$
1998	20th Anniversary Grace & Jonathon Born to Shop (1st ed.)	3,600	1998	45.00	45
1998	20th Anniversary Grace & Jonathon Born to Shop (2nd ed.)	3,600	1998	45.00	45
1998	20th Anniversary Grace & Jonathon Born to Shop (3rd ed.)	3,600	1998	45.00	45
1998	20th Anniversary Grace & Jonathon Born to Shop (4th ed.)	3,600	1998	45.00	45
1997	Amelia's Enterprise (1st ed.)	3,600	1998	44.95	58-69
1997	Amelia's Enterprise (2nd ed.)	3,600	1998	44.95	45
1995	Arthur on Trunk (1st ed.)	3,600	1997	39.95	67-75
1995	Arthur on Trunk (2nd ed.)	3,600	1997	39.95	47-94
1996	Bailey & Emily (1st ed.)	3,600	1997	44.95	58-65
1996	Bailey & Emily (2nd ed.)	3,600	1997	44.95	45
1998	Bailey Honey Bear (1st ed.)	3,600	1998	44.95	45-69
1998	Bailey Honey Bear (2nd ed.)	3,600	1998	44.95	45
1996	Bailey with Suitcase (1st ed.)	3,600	1997	39.95	58-79
1996	Bailey with Suitcase (2nd ed.)	3,600	1997	39.95	40
1997	Bailey's Birthday (1st ed.)	3,600	1998	44.95	45-63
1997	Bailey's Birthday (2nd ed.)	3,600	1998	44.95	45
1998	Bailey's Heart Desire (1st ed.)	3,600	1998	45.00	45-72
1998	Bailey's Heart Desire (2nd ed.)	3,600	1998	45.00	45
2000	Bud Buzzby Honey Bear	6,000	2000	45.00	45-88
1999	Checkers Waterglobe (1st ed.)	3,600	1999	55.00	55
1999	Checkers Waterglobe (2nd ed.)	3,600	1999	55.00	55
2000	Christmas Helper Waterglobe	6,000	2000	45.00	45
1999	Clara Nurse (1st ed.)	3,600	1999	45.00	45-85
1999	Clara Nurse (2nd ed.)	3,600	1999	45.00	45
1996	Clarence Angel (1st ed.)	3,600	1998	39.95	40-58
1996	Clarence Angel (2nd ed.)	3,600	1998	39.95	40
1997	The Collector (1st ed.)	3,600	1998	49.95	50-85
1997	The Collector (2nd ed.)	3,600	1998	49.95	50
1997	Daphne & Eloise (1st ed.)	3,600	1998	44.95	45-70
1997	Daphne & Eloise (2nd ed.)	3,600	1998	44.95	45
1999	Elliot... Hero Waterglobe (1st ed.)	3,600	1999	45.00	45
1999	Elliot... Hero Waterglobe (2nd ed.)	3,600	1999	50.00	50
1996	Emma & Bailey Tea Party Waterglobe (1st ed.)	3,600	1997	44.95	58-69
1996	Emma & Bailey Tea Party Waterglobe (2nd ed.)	3,600	1997	44.95	45
1998	Grenville & Beatrice True Love Waterglobe (1st ed.)	3,600	1998	44.95	45
1998	Grenville & Beatrice True Love Waterglobe (2nd ed.)	3,600	1998	44.95	45
1997	Homer on Plate Waterglobe (1st ed.)	3,600	1998	44.95	45
1997	Homer on Plate Waterglobe (2nd ed.)	3,600	1998	44.95	45
1998	Justina Message Bearer (1st ed.)	3,600	1998	44.95	47
1998	Justina Message Bearer (2nd ed.)	3,600	1998	44.95	45
1998	Kringle & Co. Waterglobe (1st ed.)	3,600	1999	45.00	45
1998	Kringle & Co. Waterglobe (2nd ed.)	3,600	1999	50.00	50
1999	Love Is The Master Key Waterglobe (1st ed.)	3,600	1999	45.00	45
1999	Love Is The Master Key Waterglobe (2nd ed.)	3,600	1999	45.00	45
2000	McNew Bear Waterglobe	6,000	2000	45.00	45
1996	Miss Bruin & Bailey (1st ed.)	3,600	1998	44.95	45-75
1996	Miss Bruin & Bailey (2nd ed.)	3,600	1998	44.95	45
1996	Nelville Bedtime (1st ed.)	3,600	1998	39.95	58-69
1996	Nelville Bedtime (2nd ed.)	3,600	1998	39.95	40
1998	Neville Compubear (1st ed.)	3,600	1998	44.95	47
1998	Neville Compubear (2nd ed.)	3,600	1998	44.95	45-79
1999	Quiet Time (1st ed.)	3,600	1999	40.00	40
1999	Quiet Time (2nd ed.)	3,600	1999	40.00	40
2000	Rosemary Bearhugs	6,000	2000	45.00	45
1997	The Secret (1st ed.)	3,600	1998	49.95	50
1997	The Secret (2nd ed.)	3,600	1998	49.95	50
2000	Shipmates	6,000	2000	45.00	45
1995	Ted & Teddy Waterglobe (1st ed.)	3,600	1997	39.95	45-86
1995	Ted & Teddy Waterglobe (2nd ed.)	3,600	1997	39.95	40
1999	Telephone Tied (1st ed.)	3,600	1999	45.00	45-94
1999	Telephone Tied (2nd ed.)	3,600	1999	45.00	45
1995	Wilson with Love Sonnets (1st ed.)	3,600	1995	39.95	45-86
1995	Wilson with Love Sonnets (2nd ed.)	3,600	1997	39.95	40-52

Boyds Bears Musical Dollstone Figurines - G.M. Lowenthal

YEAR	ISSUE	EDITION LIMIT	YEAR RETD.	ISSUE PRICE	*QUOTE U.S.$
2000	Ballerina Waterglobe	6,000		45.00	45
2000	By The Sea Waterglobe	6,000	2000	45.00	45
1999	Garden Friends Waterglobe (1st ed.)	4,800	1999	45.00	45
1999	Goin' to Grandma's (1st ed.)	4,800	1999	45.00	45
1999	Momma's Clothes (1st ed.)	4,800	1999	45.00	45
1999	School Days (1st ed.)	4,800	1999	40.00	40-59
2000	Stitched With Love	6,000	2000	45.00	45
1998	Wendy Wash Day (1st ed.)	4,800	1998	45.00	45-72
1998	Wendy Wash Day (2nd ed.)	4,800	1998	45.00	45

Charming Tails Musicals - D. Griff

YEAR	ISSUE	EDITION LIMIT	YEAR RETD.	ISSUE PRICE	*QUOTE U.S.$
1996	After Lunch Snooze	Closed	1996	40.00	56
1996	Getting To Know You	Closed	1996	40.00	55
1996	Spring Flowers	Closed	1996	40.00	57
1996	That's What Friends Are For	Closed	1996	40.00	55

Cherish The Thought - San Francisco Music Box Company

YEAR	ISSUE	EDITION LIMIT	YEAR RETD.	ISSUE PRICE	*QUOTE U.S.$
1994	Friendship Waterglobe	Closed	2000	45.95	46

Christmas - C. Radko

YEAR	ISSUE	EDITION LIMIT	YEAR RETD.	ISSUE PRICE	*QUOTE U.S.$
1999	Carlton Snowman Waterglobe	7,500		115.00	115
1999	Elves Waterglobe	7,500		115.00	115
1999	Gold Balmoral Santa Waterglobe	5,000		95.00	95
1999	Rooftop of London Waterglobe	7,500		115.00	115
1999	Sneak-a-Peak Waterglobe	5,000		95.00	95
1999	Vintage Santa Waterglobe	7,500		95.00	95
1999	Woodland Santa Waterglobe	7,500		115.00	115

Crystal Vision - M. Sarnat

YEAR	ISSUE	EDITION LIMIT	YEAR RETD.	ISSUE PRICE	*QUOTE U.S.$
1999	Hourglass Waterglobe	Open		100.00	100
1994	Hourglass Waterglobe	Closed	1997	150.00	150
1994	Merlin's Library	Closed	1996	150.00	150
2000	Merlin/Dragon Chess	Open		70.00	70
1999	Millenium Zodiac Hourglass Waterglobe	9,500		100.00	100

Dreamsicles - C. Hayes

YEAR	ISSUE	EDITION LIMIT	YEAR RETD.	ISSUE PRICE	*QUOTE U.S.$
1997	Butterfly Waterglobe	10,000	1998	70.00	70
1998	Dolphins Searching for Hope Waterglobe	10,000		40.00	40
1998	Flying Lesson Waterglobe	10,000	1999	70.00	70
1998	Handmade with Love Waterglobe	10,000	1999	70.00	70
1998	Heart to Heart Waterglobe	10,000	1999	70.00	70
1999	Love Waterglobe	10,000		70.00	70
1998	Time to Dash Waterglobe	10,000	1998	70.00	70

Gone With The Wind - San Francisco Music Box Company

YEAR	ISSUE	EDITION LIMIT	YEAR RETD.	ISSUE PRICE	*QUOTE U.S.$
2000	Gone With the Wind™ Rhett & Scarlett 120mm Waterglobe	Open		50.00	50
2000	Gone With the Wind™ Rhett & Scarlett Carriage	Open		80.00	80
2000	Gone With the Wind™ Scarlett & Rhett Lacquer Box	Open		45.00	45
2000	Gone With the Wind™ Scarlett & Rhett Stairs	Open		75.00	75
2000	Gone With the Wind™ Scarlett & Tara 120mm Waterglobe	Open		50.00	50
2000	Gone With the Wind™ Scarlett Ceramic Box	Open		35.00	35
2000	Gone With the Wind™ Scarlett Figurine	Open		50.00	50
2000	Gone With the Wind™ Scarlett on Bench	Open		70.00	70

Heart Tugs Musical Collection - M. Danko

YEAR	ISSUE	EDITION LIMIT	YEAR RETD.	ISSUE PRICE	*QUOTE U.S.$
1998	20th Anniversary - "Old Friendships are the Best"	2,500	1998	35.00	35
1998	Pie Safe - "Friendship is Homemade"	6,000	1998	49.95	50
1997	Tea Time - "Forever Friends"	6,000	1997	49.95	50

Musical Goose Eggs - V. Damann, unless otherwise noted

YEAR	ISSUE	EDITION LIMIT	YEAR RETD.	ISSUE PRICE	*QUOTE U.S.$
1998	20th Anniversary	300		200.00	200
1998	Blue Pansies	300		165.00	165
1999	Celestial Pendant	500		310.00	310
1999	Cinderella Crystal Slipper Coach	750		495.00	495
1997	Coach	300	1998	450.00	450
1998	Coach with Crown - R. Egg	700		495.00	495
1999	Crystal Flower Coach Egg	500		550.00	550
1999	Crystal Millenium Angel Egg	750		575.00	575
1999	Emeralds Jewel Egg	750		295.00	295
1997	Mauve Cherub	300	1998	195.00	195
1997	Purple Pansies	300	1998	160.00	160
1997	Roses	300	1998	160.00	160
1998	Silvery Blue	500		200.00	200
1997	Velvet Romance Carousel - K. Johnson	1,000	1998	240.00	240

Musical Merry-Go-Round Collection - Various

YEAR	ISSUE	EDITION LIMIT	YEAR RETD.	ISSUE PRICE	*QUOTE U.S.$
1998	The American Treasures™ 12-Animal Merry-Go-Round - Team	5,000	1999	500.00	500
1998	The American Treasures™ 6-Animal Merry-Go-Round - Team	5,000	1999	299.00	299
1999	Angel Flight 8" Horse	4,500		90.00	90
1999	Angel Flight Double Horse	4,500		110.00	110
1999	Arabesque Horse, 8" - E. Kamysz	4,500	1999	85.00	85
1998	Baroque Horse - P. Fulton	4,500	1999	85.00	85
1998	Baroque Horse with Canopy - P. Fulton	5,000	1999	65.00	65
1999	Chinese Double Horse with Canopy	4,000		110.00	110
1999	Cloisonne Merry-Go-Round - Scheherazade	500		1500.00	1500
2000	Elizabeth 6-Horse Merry-Go-Round	5,000		325.00	325
1999	Florentine Horse, 8"	4,500	1999	85.00	85
1999	Florentine Single Horse with Canopy	5,000	1999	85.00	85
1998	Four Season Merry-Go-Round - E. Kamysz	5,000		225.00	225
1997	Gardenia 10" Horse - M. Drdak	3,000	1998	87.50	88
1997	Gardenia 8" Horse - M. Drdak	4,500	1998	85.00	85
1997	Gardenia Horse with Canopy	4,000	1998	99.95	100
1998	Jewels of the Empire Jade Porcelain 6-horse Merry-Go-Round	5,000	1999	199.00	199
1997	Les Fleurs D'Amour 6-horse Merry-Go-Round - Team	5,000	1999	299.00	299
1999	Lily Double Horse with Canopy	4,000	1999	100.00	100
1999	Lily Horse, 8"	4,500	1999	85.00	85
1999	Lily Single Horse with Canopy	5,000	1999	85.00	85
1999	Millenium 12-Horse Merry-Go-Round	5,000	2000	499.00	499
1999	Neptune 8" Horse - M. Drdak	4,500		90.00	90
1999	Neptune Double Horse with Canopy - M. Drdak	4,500		110.00	110
1999	Neptune Merry-Go-Round	5,000		225.00	225
1998	Renaissance Horse with Canopy	5,000	1999	85.00	85
1999	Royal Crest Double 6-Horse Merry-Go-Round - Team	5,000	1999	299.00	299
1999	Royal Crest Double Horse with Canopy - Team	4,000	1999	100.00	100
1999	Royal Crest Horse, 10" - Team	3,000	1999	100.00	100
1997	Savannah Horse with Canopy - N. Bailey	5,000	1998	84.95	85
1998	Sultan's Dream 6-Horse Merry-Go-Round	5,000	1999	299.00	299
1998	Sultan's Dream Double Horse with Canopy	4,000	1999	100.00	100
1998	Sultan's Dream Horse, 12"	2,500	1999	125.00	125
1998	Sultan's Dream Horse, 8"	4,500	1999	85.00	85
2000	Venetian Rose 12-Horse Merry-Go-Round	2,500		525.00	525
1997	Venetian Rose Horse	4,500	1998	84.95	85
1997	Venetian Rose Horse with Canopy	5,000	1998	84.95	85

National Geographic Musical Figurines - M. Adams

YEAR	ISSUE	EDITION LIMIT	YEAR RETD.	ISSUE PRICE	*QUOTE U.S.$
1998	African Lion Family	7,500		125.00	125
1999	Appaloosa	7,500		85.00	85
1998	Baby Chickadee	7,500		55.00	55
1998	Bald Eagle	7,500		125.00	125
1999	Dolphin	7,500		75.00	75
1999	Double Eagle	7,500		125.00	125
1998	Gray Wolf Pup	Open		55.00	55
1998	Gray Wolves	7,500		85.00	85
1999	Hummingbirds	7,500		70.00	70
1998	Lion Cub	Open		50.00	50
1999	Mallards	7,500		85.00	85
1998	Mayan Jaguar	7,500		90.00	90
1998	Mom & Baby Giraffe	Open		55.00	55
1998	Mom & Baby Panda	Open		55.00	55
1998	Mom & Baby Seal	Open		55.00	55
1998	Mother & Baby Elephant	7,500		100.00	100
1998	Mother Zebra & Baby	7,500		100.00	100
1999	Mustang	7,500		125.00	125
1999	Mustang Rearing	7,500		85.00	85
1998	Polar Cub	Open		55.00	55
1998	Red Eyed Tree Frog	7,500		85.00	85
1998	Scarlet Macaw	7,500		100.00	100

Rainbow Visions - San Francisco Music Box Company

YEAR	ISSUE	EDITION LIMIT	YEAR RETD.	ISSUE PRICE	*QUOTE U.S.$
1993	Castle Hourglass Waterglobe	Closed	1997	150.00	150

Santa - Harley Davidson

YEAR	ISSUE	EDITION LIMIT	YEAR RETD.	ISSUE PRICE	*QUOTE U.S.$
1998	Born to Ride Santa Waterglobe	10,000		55.00	55
1999	Mr. & Mrs. Claus	15,000		65.00	65
1998	Santa in the Sky	10,000		65.00	65
1999	Santa Waterglobe	10,000		50.00	50

*Quotes have been rounded up to nearest dollar

Santa - L. Haney

YEAR ISSUE	EDITION LIMIT	YEAR RETD.	ISSUE PRICE	*QUOTE U.S.$
1999 "Bear Hugs"	250	1999	350.00	350
1998 Jolly Santa	300	1998	300.00	300
1999 Santa for a New Century	250	1999	300.00	300
1997 "Splendor of Christmas"	350	1997	300.00	300
1998 Winterfrost Santa	300	1998	300.00	300

Seraphim Angel Musical Figurines - Seraphim Studios

YEAR ISSUE	EDITION LIMIT	YEAR RETD.	ISSUE PRICE	*QUOTE U.S.$
1999 Ana Lisa	2,000	2000	210.00	210
1997 Ariel	1,202	1997	179.95	180-225
1998 Avalon	1,410	1998	195.00	195
1998 Hope	1,773	1999	179.95	180
1998 Monica - 20th Anniversary Special Edition	Closed	1999	60.00	60-95
1999 Nina	Closed	1999	195.00	195-225

Snow Magic Collection - San Francisco Music Box Company

YEAR ISSUE	EDITION LIMIT	YEAR RETD.	ISSUE PRICE	*QUOTE U.S.$
2000 Believe in Magic Waterglobe	Open		40.00	40
2000 Celebrate The Magic	Open		50.00	50
2000 Celebrate Winterstar Angel	Open		55.00	55
2000 Cold Nose, Warm Heart	Open		35.00	35
2000 Faith Gives Wishes Their Wings Waterglobe	Open		50.00	50
2000 Forever Friends Waterglobe	Open		45.00	45
2000 A Happy Wish or Two	Open		35.00	35
2000 Hope Upon A Star	9,500		60.00	60
2000 Jack Frost in Sleigh	Open		60.00	60
2000 Jack Frost Plate	Open		45.00	45
2000 Jack Frost Waterglobe	Open		85.00	85
2000 Jingle Bell Rock Waterglobe	Open		35.00	35
2000 Love Lights the Season	9,500		35.00	35
2000 May the Miracle of Christmas Waterglobe	Open		40.00	40
2000 May Your Heart Be Light	Open		50.00	50
2000 Peace and Joy	Open		30.00	30
2000 Winterstar Angel "Rejoice"	9,500		50.00	50
2000 Winterstar Angel with Harp	Open		45.00	45

Teddy Hugs Musical Collection - M. Danko

YEAR ISSUE	EDITION LIMIT	YEAR RETD.	ISSUE PRICE	*QUOTE U.S.$
1998 Praying Bears - "Now I Lay me Down to Sleep" (1st ed.)	3,600	1999	35.00	35
1998 Toy Hutch - "Hugs are for Sharing"	6,000	1999	45.00	45

Wizard of Oz - San Francisco Music Box Company

YEAR ISSUE	EDITION LIMIT	YEAR RETD.	ISSUE PRICE	*QUOTE U.S.$
1999 Dorothy	Open		45.00	45
1999 Emerald City Waterglobe	Open		60.00	60
1999 Glinda and Dorothy	Open		55.00	55
1999 Lion	Open		45.00	45
1999 No Place Like Home Waterglobe	Open		60.00	60
1999 Oz Hourglass Waterglobe	Open		125.00	125
1999 Oz Lacquer Box	Open		45.00	45
1999 Ruby Shoes Waterglobe	Open		45.00	45
1999 Scarecrow	Open		45.00	45
1999 Tinman	Open		45.00	45
1999 Witch Ball Waterglobe	Open		75.00	75

Sandy USA Inc.

Birthstone Baby - S. Bedard

YEAR ISSUE	EDITION LIMIT	YEAR RETD.	ISSUE PRICE	*QUOTE U.S.$
1996 January	Retrd.	1997	15.00	15
1996 February	Retrd.	1997	15.00	15
1996 March	Retrd.	1997	15.00	15
1996 April	Retrd.	1997	15.00	15
1996 May	Retrd.	1997	15.00	15
1996 June	Retrd.	1997	15.00	15
1996 July	Retrd.	1997	15.00	15
1996 August	Retrd.	1997	15.00	15
1996 September	Retrd.	1997	15.00	15
1996 October	Retrd.	1997	15.00	15
1996 November	Retrd.	1997	15.00	15
1996 December	Retrd.	1997	15.00	15
1999 January - 2nd release	Retrd.	2000	15.00	15
1999 February - 2nd release	Retrd.	2000	15.00	15
1999 March - 2nd release	Retrd.	2000	15.00	15
1999 April - 2nd release	Retrd.	2000	15.00	15
1999 May - 2nd release	Retrd.	2000	15.00	15
1999 June - 2nd release	Retrd.	2000	15.00	15
1999 July - 2nd release	Retrd.	2000	15.00	15
1999 August - 2nd release	Retrd.	2000	15.00	15
1999 September - 2nd release	Retrd.	2000	15.00	15
1999 October - 2nd release	Retrd.	2000	15.00	15
1999 November - 2nd release	Retrd.	2000	15.00	15
1999 December - 2nd release	Retrd.	2000	15.00	15

Della - Legacy Collection - D. Reese

YEAR ISSUE	EDITION LIMIT	YEAR RETD.	ISSUE PRICE	*QUOTE U.S.$
2000 Courage	Open		75.00	75
2000 Faith	Open		110.00	110
2000 Love	Open		85.00	85
2000 Perseverance	Open		85.00	85

Sass 'n Class by Annie Lee - A. Lee

YEAR ISSUE	EDITION LIMIT	YEAR RETD.	ISSUE PRICE	*QUOTE U.S.$
1998 5th Grade Substitute	Open		40.00	40
1998 8 1/2 Narrow	Open		40.00	40
1998 The Babysitter	Open		55.00	55
1998 Blue Monday	Open		40.00	40
1998 Blues Highway	Open		85.00	85
1998 Burn You Baby?	Open		55.00	55
1999 Cultured Pearls	Open		35.00	35
1998 Daily Snooze	Open		55.00	55
2000 Disappointed Again	Open		60.00	60
1998 First Mother	Open		35.00	35
1997 Gimme Dat Gum	5,000	1999	70.00	200-300
1999 Heat of the Beat	Open		50.00	50
1997 Holy Ghost	5,000	1998	40.00	100-350
1998 Jumping the Broom	Open		75.00	75
1999 Love Song	Open		60.00	60
1998 Loving Arms	Open		35.00	35
1998 Metamorphosis	Retrd.	2000	60.00	60
2000 Misdeal	Open		75.00	75
1999 Mississippi Samsonite	Open		40.00	40
1997 Mother Board	5,000	1999	85.00	215-300
1999 Primpin'	Open		55.00	55
2000 Sadie's Relief	Open		45.00	45
2000 Sassy Solo	Open		37.50	38
1999 Six-No-Uptown	Open		75.00	75
1999 Sixty Pounds	7,500	2000	75.00	75-95
1999 Spin Cycle	Open		75.00	75
2000 Sprinklin' and Pressin'	Retrd.	1999	55.00	55-120
2000 Sunday Evening Radio	10,000		85.00	85
2000 White Tie Only - Scene Four	Open		45.00	45
2000 White Tie Only - Scene One	Open		55.00	55
2000 White Tie Only - Scene Three	Open		75.00	75
2000 White Tie Only - Scene Two	Open		65.00	65
2000 White Tie Only - Shelves	Open		20.00	20
2000 White Tie Only - Window	Open		15.00	15

Voices by Howard Marshall - H. Marshall

YEAR ISSUE	EDITION LIMIT	YEAR RETD.	ISSUE PRICE	*QUOTE U.S.$
2000 Elizabeth	Open		30.00	30
2000 Francis	Open		25.00	25
2000 Harriet and Hattie	Open		30.00	30
2000 Helen and Child	Open		30.00	30
2000 Janet with Doll	Open		25.00	25
2000 Mary	Open		30.00	30

Sarah's Attic, Inc.

Collector's Club Promotion - Sarah's Attic

YEAR ISSUE	EDITION LIMIT	YEAR RETD.	ISSUE PRICE	*QUOTE U.S.$
1991 Diamond 3497	Closed	1992	36.00	100-150
1991 Ruby 3498	Closed	1992	42.00	98-150
1992 Christmas Love Santa 3522	Closed	1992	45.00	65
1992 Forever Frolicking Friends 3523	Closed	1992	Gift	75
1992 Love One Another 3561	Closed	1992	60.00	46-60
1992 Sharing Dreams 3562	Closed	1993	75.00	100
1992 Life Time Friends 3563	Closed	1993	75.00	125
1992 Love Starts With Children 3607	Closed	1993	Gift	75
1993 First Forever Friend Celebration 3903	Closed	1993	50.00	50
1993 Pledge of Allegiance 3749	Closed	1993	45.00	90
1993 Love Starts With Children II 3837	Closed	1994	Gift	65
1993 Gem wh. Girl w/Basket 3842	Closed	1994	33.00	150
1993 Rocky blk. Boy w/Marbles 3843	Closed	1994	25.00	65
1994 America Boy 4191	Closed	1994	25.00	25
1994 America Girl 4192	Closed	1994	25.00	25
1994 Forever Friends 4286	Closed	1994	45.00	45
1994 Saturday Night Round Up 4232	Closed	1995	Gift	25
1994 Billy Bob 4233	Closed	1995	38.00	38
1994 Jimmy Dean 4234	Closed	1995	38.00	38
1994 Sally/Jack 4235	Closed	1995	55.00	55
1994 Ellie/T.J. 4236	Closed	1995	55.00	55
1995 Flags in Heaven 4386	Closed	1995	45.00	45
1995 Friends Forever 4444	Closed	1996	60.00	60
1995 Playtime Pals 4446	Closed	1997	65.00	70
1995 Horsin' around 4445	Closed	1997	65.00	65
1996 Abigail 4543	Closed	1996	36.00	36
1996 Aretha 4542	Closed	1996	36.00	36
1997 Basket of Memories 4827	Closed	1997	35.00	35
1997 Sharing Memories 4828	Closed	1998	85.00	85
1997 Basket of Treasures 4829	Closed	1997	35.00	35
1997 Treasured Moments 4830	Closed	1998	85.00	85
1999 Angel Schugar Bear	Closed	2000	Gift	N/A
1999 Angel Schmoochie	Closed	2000	20.00	20
1999 Angel Schweetie	Closed	2000	20.00	20

Angels In The Attic - Sarah's Attic

YEAR ISSUE	EDITION LIMIT	YEAR RETD.	ISSUE PRICE	*QUOTE U.S.$
1989 Abbee-Angel-2336	Closed	1991	10.00	20
1990 Adora Girl Angel Standing 3276	4,000	1990	35.00	111-125
1991 Angel Adora With Bunny 3390	Closed	1993	50.00	65
1991 Angel Enos With Frog 3391	10,000	1993	50.00	65
1989 Ashbee-Angel-2337	Closed	1991	10.00	25
1991 Bert Angel 3416	1,000	1992	60.00	120
1990 Billi-Angel 3295	Closed	1991	18.00	22
1990 Cindi-Angel 3296	Closed	1991	18.00	22
1989 Clyde-Angel 2329	Closed	1991	17.00	20
1992 Contentment 3500	500	1992	100.00	200
1992 Enos & Adora-Small 3671	5,000	1993	35.00	60-125
1990 Enos Boy Angel Sitting 3275	4,000	1990	33.00	100-111
1989 Floppy-Angel 2330	Closed	1990	10.00	20
1990 Flossy-Angel 3301	Closed	1991	15.00	24
1989 Gramps Angel 2357	Closed	1990	17.00	40
1989 Grams Angel 2356	Closed	1990	17.00	40
1992 Heavenly Caring 3661	2,500	1993	70.00	90
1992 Heavenly Giving 3663	Closed	1993	70.00	90
1992 Heavenly Loving 3664	2,500	1993	70.00	90
1993 Heavenly Peace 3833	2,500	1994	47.00	50
1992 Heavenly Sharing 3662	2,500	1993	70.00	90
1990 Lena Angel 3297	Closed	1991	36.00	40
1992 Love 3501	500	1992	80.00	200
1992 Priscilla Angel 3511	5,000	1993	46.00	60
1989 Saint Willie Bill 2360	Closed	1991	30.00	40
1989 St. Anne 2323	Closed	1991	29.00	40
1989 St. Gabbe 2322	Closed	1991	30.00	33
1990 Trapper-Angel 3299	Closed	1991	17.00	40
1989 Wendall-Angel 2324	Closed	1991	10.00	45
1989 Wilbur-Angel 2327	Closed	1991	10.00	25

Black Heritage Collection - Sarah's Attic

YEAR ISSUE	EDITION LIMIT	YEAR RETD.	ISSUE PRICE	*QUOTE U.S.$
1991 Baby Tansy blk.3388	Closed	1993	40.00	50-60
1995 Bessie Coleman 4313	2,500	1998	50.00	50
1993 Bessie Gospel Singer 3754	Closed	1996	40.00	40-50
1995 Bill Pickett 4281	2,500	1998	56.00	56-85
1993 Blessed is He 3952	1,994	1994	48.00	150-225
1992 Booker T. Washington 3648	3,000	1993	80.00	100-150
1992 Boys Night Out 3660	2,000	1994	350.00	695-750
1990 Brotherly Love 3336	5,000	1991	80.00	175
1992 Buffalo Soldier 3524	5,000	1993	80.00	150-260
1991 Caleb w/ Football 3485	6,000	1993	40.00	55
1990 Caleb-Lying Down 3232	Closed	1994	23.00	35
1992 Calvin Prayer Time 3510	5,000	1993	46.00	55
1991 Corporal Pervis 3366	8,000	1993	60.00	80-125
1993 George Washington Carver 3848	3,000	1998	45.00	45
1987 Gramps 5104	Closed	1988	16.00	100
1987 Grams 5105	Closed	1988	16.00	100
1992 Granny Wynne & Olivia 3535	5,000	1994	85.00	95
1990 Harpster w/Banjo 3257	4,000	1990	60.00	111-250
1991 Harpster w/Harmonica II 3384	8,000	1993	60.00	125
1992 Harriet Tubman 3687	3,000	1993	60.00	125-150
1991 Hattie Quilting 3483	6,000	1993	60.00	125
1990 Hattie-Knitting 3233	4,000	1990	40.00	75-100
1992 Ida B. Wells & Frederick Douglass 3642	3,000	1993	160.00	250-295
1993 Jesse Gospel Singer 3755	Closed	1996	40.00	40-50
1994 Kitty w/Microphone 4141	Closed	1996	50.00	50-75
1990 Libby w/Overalls 3259	4,000	1990	36.00	175-195
1991 Libby w/Puppy 3386	10,000	1993	50.00	100
1991 Lucas w/Dog 3387	10,000	1993	50.00	100
1990 Lucas w/Overalls 3260	4,000	1990	36.00	175
1995 Martin Luther King Wedding 4406	Closed	1996	85.00	85
1994 Martin Luther King, Jr. 4179	Closed	1996	65.00	65-90
1996 Mary Eliza Mahoney 4501	1,000	1996	50.00	50-100
1993 Mary McLeod Bethune 3847	3,000	1998	45.00	45-60
1993 Miles Boy Angel 3752	2,500	1995	27.00	40
1993 Moriah Girl Angel 3759	2,500	1994	27.00	45
1992 Muffy-Prayer Time 3509	5,000	1993	46.00	55
1992 Music Masters 3533	1,000	1992	300.00	350-400
1992 Music Masters II 3621	1,000	1994	250.00	300-350
1994 Music Masters III 4142	Closed	1996	80.00	80-125
1993 Nat Love Cowboy (Isom Dart) 3792	2,500	1993	45.00	300-395
1994 Nat Love w/Saddle 4121	2,500	1998	60.00	60
1991 Nighttime Pearl 3362	Closed	1993	50.00	65
1991 Nighttime Percy 3363	Closed	1993	50.00	65
1995 Olivia A. D. Washington 4404	2,500	1998	51.00	51
1993 Otis Redding 3793	Closed	1994	70.00	250-300
1989 Pappy Jake 3100	Closed	1990	40.00	65-100
1990 Pearl-Blk. Girl Dancing 3291	5,000	1992	45.00	100
1990 Percy-Blk. Boy Dancing 3292	5,000	1993	45.00	100
1993 Phillis Wheatley 3846	3,000	1998	45.00	45-60
1992 Porter 3525	5,000	1993	80.00	125
1990 Portia Reading Book 3256	Closed	1991	30.00	45-65
1990 Praise the Lord I (Preacher I) 3277	4,000	1991	55.00	150-195
1991 Praise the Lord II w/Kids 3376	5,000	1994	100.00	100
1993 Praise the Lord III 3753	2,500	1994	44.00	55-60
1995 Praise the Lord IV 4369	5,000	1997	55.00	55-75
1989 Quilting Ladies 3099	Closed	1991	90.00	400
1995 Rosa Parks 4401	Closed	1997	65.00	65-90
1992 Sojourner Truth 3629	3,000	1993	80.00	125-150
1995 Tuskegee Airman W.W. II 4405	2,500	1996	60.00	60-120
1991 Uncle Reuben 3389	8,000	1993	70.00	95
1993 Vanessa Gospel Singer (Upside down book) 3756	Closed	1996	40.00	100
1994 W.E.B. DuBois 4123	2,500	1998	60.00	60-85
1990 Whoopie & Wooster 3255	4,000	1990	50.00	235-350
1991 Whoopie & Wooster II 3385	8,000	1993	70.00	111-125

Santas Of The Month-Series A - Sarah's Attic

YEAR ISSUE	EDITION LIMIT	YEAR RETD.	ISSUE PRICE	*QUOTE U.S.$
1988 January wh. Santa	Closed	1990	50.00	135-150
1988 January blk. Santa	Closed	1990	50.00	300-395
1988 February wh. Santa	Closed	1990	50.00	135-150
1988 February blk. Santa	Closed	1990	50.00	200-300
1988 March wh. Santa	Closed	1990	50.00	135-150
1988 March blk. Santa	Closed	1990	50.00	200-300
1988 April wh. Santa	Closed	1990	50.00	135-150
1988 April blk. Santa	Closed	1990	50.00	200-350
1988 May wh. Santa	Closed	1990	50.00	135-150
1988 May blk. Santa	Closed	1990	50.00	200-300
1988 June wh. Santa	Closed	1990	50.00	135-150
1988 June blk. Santa	Closed	1990	50.00	200-300
1988 July wh. Santa	Closed	1990	50.00	130-175
1988 July blk. Santa	Closed	1990	50.00	200-300
1988 August wh. Santa	Closed	1990	50.00	135-150
1988 August blk. Santa	Closed	1990	50.00	200-300
1988 September wh. Santa	Closed	1990	50.00	135-150
1988 September blk. Santa	Closed	1990	50.00	300-375
1988 October wh. Santa	Closed	1990	50.00	135-150
1988 October blk. Santa	Closed	1990	50.00	300-395
1988 November wh. Santa	Closed	1990	50.00	135-150
1988 November blk. Santa	Closed	1990	50.00	200-300
1988 December wh. Santa	Closed	1990	50.00	135-150
1988 December blk. Santa	Closed	1990	50.00	375-395
1988 Mini January wh. Santa	Closed	1990	14.00	33-35
1988 Mini January blk. Santa	Closed	1990	14.00	35-50
1988 Mini February wh. Santa	Closed	1990	14.00	33-35
1988 Mini February blk. Santa	Closed	1990	14.00	35-50
1988 Mini March wh. Santa	Closed	1990	14.00	33-35
1988 Mini March blk. Santa	Closed	1990	14.00	35
1988 Mini April wh. Santa	Closed	1990	14.00	33-35
1988 Mini April blk. Santa	Closed	1990	14.00	35
1988 Mini May wh. Santa	Closed	1990	14.00	33-35
1988 Mini May blk. Santa	Closed	1990	14.00	35
1988 Mini June wh. Santa	Closed	1990	14.00	33-35
1988 Mini June blk. Santa	Closed	1990	14.00	35
1988 Mini July wh. Santa	Closed	1990	14.00	40

*Quotes have been rounded up to nearest dollar

YEAR ISSUE	EDITION LIMIT	YEAR RETD.	ISSUE PRICE	*QUOTE U.S.$
1988 Mini July blk. Santa	Closed	1990	14.00	50
1988 Mini August wh. Santa	Closed	1990	14.00	33-35
1988 Mini August blk. Santa	Closed	1990	14.00	35
1988 Mini September wh. Santa	Closed	1990	14.00	33-35
1988 Mini September blk. Santa	Closed	1990	14.00	35-50
1988 Mini October wh. Santa	Closed	1990	14.00	33-35
1988 Mini October blk. Santa	Closed	1990	14.00	35-40
1988 Mini November wh. Santa	Closed	1990	14.00	33-35
1988 Mini November blk. Santa	Closed	1990	14.00	35
1988 Mini December wh. Santa	Closed	1990	14.00	33-35
1988 Mini December blk. Santa	Closed	1990	14.00	35-50

Santas Of The Month-Series B - Sarah's Attic

YEAR ISSUE	EDITION LIMIT	YEAR RETD.	ISSUE PRICE	*QUOTE U.S.$
1990 Jan. Santa Winter Fun 7135	Closed	1991	80.00	100
1990 Feb. Santa Cupids Help 7136	Closed	1991	120.00	120
1990 Mar. Santa Irish Delight 7137	Closed	1991	120.00	150
1990 Apr. Santa Spring/Joy 7138	Closed	1991	150.00	150
1990 May Santa Par For Course 7139	Closed	1991	100.00	125
1990 June Santa Graduation 7140	Closed	1991	70.00	70
1990 July Santa God Bless 7141	Closed	1991	100.00	175
1990 Aug. Santa Summers Tranquility 7142	Closed	1991	110.00	130
1990 Sept. Santa Touchdown 7143	Closed	1991	90.00	90
1990 Oct. Santa Seasons Plenty 7144	Closed	1991	120.00	120
1990 Nov. Santa Give Thanks 7145	Closed	1991	100.00	125
1990 Dec. Santa Peace 7146	Closed	1991	120.00	125
1990 Jan. Mrs. Winter Fun 7147	Closed	1991	80.00	100
1990 Feb. Mrs. Cupid's Helper 7148	Closed	1991	110.00	110
1990 March Mrs. Irish Delight7149	Closed	1991	80.00	100
1990 April Mrs. Spring Joy 7150	Closed	1991	110.00	110
1990 May Mrs. Par for the Course 7151	Closed	1991	80.00	100
1990 June Mrs. Graduate 7152	Closed	1991	70.00	100
1990 July Mrs. God Bless America 7153	Closed	1991	100.00	125
1990 Aug. Mrs. Summer Tranquility 7154	Closed	1991	90.00	112
1990 Sept. Mrs. Touchdown 7155	Closed	1991	90.00	100
1990 Oct. Mrs. Seasons of Plenty 7156	Closed	1991	90.00	112
1990 Nov. Mrs. Give Thanks 7157	Closed	1991	90.00	112
1990 Dec. Mrs. Peace 7158	Closed	1991	110.00	137

Sarah's Gang Collection - Sarah's Attic

YEAR ISSUE	EDITION LIMIT	YEAR RETD.	ISSUE PRICE	*QUOTE U.S.$
1989 Baby Rachel 2306	Closed	1994	20.00	30
1990 Baby Rachel-Beachtime 3248	Closed	1992	35.00	50
1988 Cupcake 4027	Closed	1994	20.00	25
1989 Cupcake Clown 3144	Closed	1989	21.00	35
1993 Cupcake on Bench 3766	Closed	1994	28.00	28
1987 Cupcake on Heart 5140	Closed	1989	9.00	28
1993 Cupcake w/Snowman 3822	2,500	1994	35.00	40
1989 Cupcake-Americana 2304	Closed	1993	21.00	30
1990 Cupcake-Beachtime 3244	Closed	1992	35.00	53
1986 Cupcake-Original 2034	Closed	1988	14.00	20-75
1989 Cupcake-Small School 2309	Closed	1990	11.00	20
1990 Katie & Whimpy-Beachtime 3243	Closed	1992	60.00	60-75
1987 Katie On Heart 5141	Closed	1989	9.00	28
1987 Katie Sitting 2002	Closed	1987	14.00	20
1989 Katie-Americana 2302	Closed	1993	21.00	25
1991 Katie-Bride 3431	Closed	1994	47.00	52
1986 Katie-Original 2032	Closed	1988	14.00	20
1989 Katie-Small Sailor 2307	Closed	1990	14.00	20
1990 Katie-Witch 3312	Closed	1992	40.00	50
1991 Percy-Minister 3440	Closed	1994	50.00	55
1991 Pug-Ringbearer 3439	Closed	1994	40.00	44
1991 Rachel-Flower Girl 3432	Closed	1994	40.00	43
1990 Rachel-Pumpkin 3318	Closed	1992	40.00	50
1991 Rachel-Thanksgiving 3474	10,000	1993	32.00	35
1988 Tillie 4032	Closed	1994	20.00	25
1991 Tillie Masquerade 3412	Closed	1993	45.00	50
1987 Tillie On Heart 5150	Closed	1989	9.00	40
1989 Tillie-Americana 2301	Closed	1993	21.00	25
1990 Tillie-Beachtime 3247	Closed	1992	35.00	53
1990 Tillie-Clown 3316	Closed	1992	40.00	50
1986 Tillie-Original 2027	Closed	1988	14.00	20
1989 Tillie-Small Country 2312	Closed	1992	18.00	26
1989 Twinkie Clown 3145	Closed	1989	19.00	35
1987 Twinkie On Heart 5143	Closed	1989	9.00	28
1989 Twinkie-Americana 2305	Closed	1993	21.00	25
1990 Twinkie-Beachtime 3245	Closed	1992	35.00	53
1990 Twinkie-Devil 3315	Closed	1992	40.00	50
1986 Twinkie-Original 2033	Closed	1988	14.00	20
1989 Twinkie-Small School 2310	Closed	1990	11.00	20
1991 Tyler-Ring Bearer 3433	Closed	1994	40.00	44
1988 Whimpy 4030	Closed	1994	20.00	25
1987 Whimpy on Heart 5142	Closed	1989	9.00	28
1987 Whimpy Sitting 2001	Closed	1987	14.00	20
1989 Whimpy-Americana 2303	Closed	1993	21.00	25
1991 Whimpy-Groom 3430	Closed	1994	47.00	52
1986 Whimpy-Original 2031	Closed	1988	14.00	20
1989 Whimpy-Small Sailor 2308	Closed	1990	14.00	20
1988 Willie 4031	Closed	1994	20.00	25
1993 Willie Lying w/Pillow 3768	Closed	1994	28.00	28
1987 Willie On Heart 5151	Closed	1989	9.00	40
1989 Willie-Americana 2300	Closed	1993	21.00	30
1990 Willie-Beachtime 3246	Closed	1992	35.00	53
1990 Willie-Clown 3317	Closed	1992	40.00	50
1986 Willie-Original 2028	Closed	1988	14.00	20-75
1989 Willie-Small Country 2311	Closed	1992	18.00	26

Seymour Mann, Inc.

Christmas Collection - Various

YEAR ISSUE	EDITION LIMIT	YEAR RETD.	ISSUE PRICE	*QUOTE U.S.$
1991 Reindeer Barn Lite Up House CJ-421 - Jaimy	Closed	1993	55.00	55

Doll Art™ Collection - E. Mann

YEAR ISSUE	EDITION LIMIT	YEAR RETD.	ISSUE PRICE	*QUOTE U.S.$
1996 Hope CLT-604P	25,000		30.00	60

Wizard Of Oz - 40th Anniversary - E. Mann

YEAR ISSUE	EDITION LIMIT	YEAR RETD.	ISSUE PRICE	*QUOTE U.S.$
1979 Dorothy, Scarecrow, Lion, Tinman	Closed	1981	7.50	45
1979 Dorothy, Scarecrow, Lion, Tinman, Musical	Closed	1981	12.50	75

Shenandoah Designs

Keeper Klub - Jack Weaver

YEAR ISSUE	EDITION LIMIT	YEAR RETD.	ISSUE PRICE	*QUOTE U.S.$
1996 Keeper of Collectors	Retrd.	1998	35.00	35-60
1996 Keeper Shelf	Retrd.	1998	Gift	N/A

Keeper Christmas Series - Jack Weaver

YEAR ISSUE	EDITION LIMIT	YEAR RETD.	ISSUE PRICE	*QUOTE U.S.$
1995 Keeper of Christmas 1995	6,000	1995	39.95	195-240
1996 Keeper of Christmas 1996	6,000	1996	39.95	150-175
1997 Keeper of Christmas 1997	6,000	1997	39.95	80
1998 Keeper of Christmas 1998	6,000	1998	39.95	40
1999 Keeper of Christmas 1999	6,000		39.95	40

Keeper Series #1 - Jack Weaver

YEAR ISSUE	EDITION LIMIT	YEAR RETD.	ISSUE PRICE	*QUOTE U.S.$
1993 Keeper of The Bath	9,000		34.95	35
1993 Keeper of The Bedchamber	9,000		34.95	35
1993 Keeper of The Entry	9,000		34.95	35
1993 Keeper of The Hearth	9,000		34.95	35
1993 Keeper of The Kitchen	Retrd.	1997	34.95	75-100
1993 Keeper of The Laundry	9,000		34.95	35
1993 Keeper of The Library	Retrd.	1996	34.95	75-105
1993 Keeper of The Nursery	Retrd.	1998	34.95	40

Keeper Series #2 - Jack Weaver

YEAR ISSUE	EDITION LIMIT	YEAR RETD.	ISSUE PRICE	*QUOTE U.S.$
1994 Keeper of The Cowboy Spirit	9,000		34.95	35
1994 Keeper of The Home Office	9,000		34.95	35
1994 Keeper of The Home Workshop	9,000		34.95	35
1994 Keeper of Love	9,000		34.95	35
1994 Keeper of Mothers	Retrd.	1998	34.95	40
1994 Keeper of Native Americans	Retrd.	1996	34.95	100-150
1994 Keeper of The Sunroom	9,000		34.95	35
1994 Keeper of The Time	9,000		34.95	35

Keeper Series #3 - Jack Weaver

YEAR ISSUE	EDITION LIMIT	YEAR RETD.	ISSUE PRICE	*QUOTE U.S.$
1995 Keeper of Bears	9,000		34.95	35
1995 Keeper of The Catch	9,000		34.95	35
1995 Keeper of Fathers	9,000		34.95	35
1995 Keeper of Flight	9,000		34.95	35
1995 Keeper of Rails	9,000		34.95	35
1995 Keeper of Thanksgiving	7,500	1997	34.95	55-60

Keeper Series #4 - Jack Weaver

YEAR ISSUE	EDITION LIMIT	YEAR RETD.	ISSUE PRICE	*QUOTE U.S.$
1995 Keeper of Birthdays	9,000		34.95	35
1995 Keeper of Faith	9,000		34.95	35
1995 Keeper of Firefighters	9,000		34.95	35
1995 Keeper of The Garden	9,000		34.95	35
1995 Keeper of Golfing	9,000		34.95	35
1995 Keeper of Music	9,000		34.95	35
1995 Keeper of The Sea	9,000		34.95	35
1995 Keeper of Trails	9,000		34.95	35
1995 Keeper of Woodland Animals	9,000		34.95	35

Keeper Series #5 - Jack Weaver

YEAR ISSUE	EDITION LIMIT	YEAR RETD.	ISSUE PRICE	*QUOTE U.S.$
1996 Keeper of The Checkered Flag	9,000		34.95	35
1996 Keeper of Friendship	9,000		34.95	35
1996 Keeper of Peace	9,000		34.95	35
1996 Keeper of Photography	9,000		34.95	35
1996 Keeper of Secrets	9,000		34.95	35
1996 Keeper of Teachers	9,000		34.95	35

Keeper Series #6 - Jack Weaver

YEAR ISSUE	EDITION LIMIT	YEAR RETD.	ISSUE PRICE	*QUOTE U.S.$
1997 Keeper of Cats	9,000		34.95	35
1997 Keeper of The Crown Jewels	6,000		39.95	40
1997 Keeper of The Galaxy	9,000		34.95	35
1997 Keeper of Halloween	3,500	1997	45.00	45-49
1997 Keeper of Pubs	9,000		34.95	35

Spoonful of Stars by Becky Kelly/Hallmark Keepsake Collections

Spoonful of Stars by Becky Kelly - Hallmark Keepsake Collections

YEAR ISSUE	EDITION LIMIT	YEAR RETD.	ISSUE PRICE	*QUOTE U.S.$
1998 Christmas Caring QHC8251	Numbrd.	1999	18.00	18
1998 Dreams and Wishes QHC8250	Numbrd.	1999	25.00	25
1998 Splendid Days QHC8216	Retrd.	1999	18.00	18
1998 Thoughtful Ways QHC8215	Retrd.	1999	18.00	18
1998 Together Days QHC8217	Retrd.	1999	18.00	18

Sports Impressions/Enesco Group, Inc.

Collectors' Club Members Only - Various

YEAR ISSUE	EDITION LIMIT	YEAR RETD.	ISSUE PRICE	*QUOTE U.S.$
1990 The Mick-Mickey Mantle 5000-1	Yr.Iss.	N/A	75.00	40-75
1991 Rickey Henderson-Born to Run 5001-11	Yr.Iss.	N/A	49.95	50
1991 Nolan Ryan-300 Wins 5002-01	Yr.Iss.	N/A	125.00	125
1991 Willie, Mickey & Duke plate 5003-04	Yr.Iss.	N/A	39.95	50
1992 Babe Ruth 5006-11	Yr.Iss.	N/A	40.00	38-40
1992 Walter Payton 5015-01	Yr.Iss.	N/A	50.00	38-50
1993 The 1927 Yankees plate - R.Tanenbaum	Yr.Iss.	N/A	60.00	35-60

Collectors' Club Symbol of Membership - Sports Impressions

YEAR ISSUE	EDITION LIMIT	YEAR RETD.	ISSUE PRICE	*QUOTE U.S.$
1991 Mick/7 plate 5001-02	Yr.Iss.	N/A	Gift	25-50
1992 USA Basketball team plate 5008-30	Yr.Iss.	N/A	Gift	25
1993 Nolan Ryan porcelain card	Yr.Iss.	N/A	Gift	25

Baseball Superstar Figurines - Sports Impressions

YEAR ISSUE	EDITION LIMIT	YEAR RETD.	ISSUE PRICE	*QUOTE U.S.$
1988 Al Kaline	2,500	N/A	90.00	90
1988 Andre Dawson	2,500	N/A	90.00	50-100
1988 Bob Feller	2,500	N/A	90.00	50-100
1992 Cubs Ryne Sandberg Home (signed) 1118-23	975	1993	150.00	250
1987 Don Mattingly	Closed	N/A	90.00	225-250
1987 Don Mattingly (Franklin glove variation)	Closed	N/A	90.00	350-600
1989 Duke Snider	2,500	N/A	90.00	50-100
1994 Giants Barry Bonds (signed) 1160-46	975	1995	150.00	100-150
1992 Johnny Bench (hand signed) 1126-23	975	1994	150.00	225
1988 Jose Canseco	Closed	N/A	90.00	50-100
1987 Keith Hernandez	2,500	N/A	90.00	50-100
1989 Kirk Gibson	Closed	N/A	90.00	50-100
1991 Mark McGwire 10" (Oakland As) 1039-12	1,900	N/A	295.00	295
1987 Mickey Mantle	Closed	N/A	90.00	150-195
1996 Mickey Mantle "The Greatest Switch Hitter" (hand signed) 1228-46 - T. Treadway	975	1995	395.00	495-600
1992 Nolan Ryan Figurine/plate/stand 1134-31	500	1994	260.00	260
1990 Nolan Ryan Kings of K	Closed	N/A	125.00	89-125
1990 Nolan Ryan Mini	Closed	N/A	50.00	50
1990 Nolan Ryan Supersize	Closed	N/A	250.00	225-250
1993 Oakland A's Reggie Jackson (signed) 1048-46	975	1994	150.00	150-275
1993 Rangers Nolan Ryan (signed) 1127-46	975	1994	175.00	225-250
1994 Rangers Nolan Ryan (signed) Farewell 1161-49	975	1994	150.00	225-250
1990 Ted Williams	Closed	N/A	90.00	90-125
1994 Tom Glavine (signed) 1163-46	975	N/A	150.00	90-150
1987 Wade Boggs	Closed	N/A	90.00	50-100
1989 Will Clark	Closed	N/A	90.00	50-100
1993 Yankees Mickey Mantle (signed) 1038-46	975	1993	195.00	350

Basketball Superstar Figurines - Sports Impressions

YEAR ISSUE	EDITION LIMIT	YEAR RETD.	ISSUE PRICE	*QUOTE U.S.$
1993 Julius Erving 76ers (hand signed) 4102-46	975	1994	150.00	150-250
1995 Larry Bird (hand signed) 4086-46	975	N/A	195.00	150-250

Swarovski Consumer Goods Ltd.

Swarovski Crystal Memories-Celebrations

YEAR ISSUE	EDITION LIMIT	YEAR RETD.	ISSUE PRICE	*QUOTE U.S.$
1995 Balloons	Open		32.50	33
1996 Bells	Open		32.50	33
1995 Birthday Cake	Open		32.50	33
1996 Bouquet	Open		40.00	40
1996 Champagne	Open		32.50	33
1995 Champagne Bucket w/2 flutes	Open		49.50	50
1995 Present	Open		32.50	33
1999 Wedding Bouquet	Open		49.50	50
1999 Wedding Cale	Open		65.00	65

Swarovski Crystal Memories-Childhood Dreams

YEAR ISSUE	EDITION LIMIT	YEAR RETD.	ISSUE PRICE	*QUOTE U.S.$
1993 Baby Carriage	Open		40.00	40
1997 Baby Shoes	Open		25.00	25
1998 Baby's Rattle	Open		17.50	18
2000 Ballet Shoes	Open		37.50	38
2000 Cradle	Open		45.00	45
1998 Doll	Open		49.50	50
1998 Freight Car	Open		32.50	33
1993 Merry-Go-Round	Open		32.50	33
1993 Pacifier	Open		17.50	18
1998 Passenger Car	Open		32.50	33
1996 Rocking Horse	Open		40.00	40
1997 Toy Train	Open		49.50	50
1998 Tricycle	Open		40.00	40

Swarovski Crystal Memories-Crystal Garden

YEAR ISSUE	EDITION LIMIT	YEAR RETD.	ISSUE PRICE	*QUOTE U.S.$
1999 Cactus, Blue Zircon	Open		49.50	50
1999 Cactus, Light Topaz	Open		49.50	50
1999 Cactus, Rosaline	Open		40.00	40

Swarovski Crystal Memories-Dedicated to Music

YEAR ISSUE	EDITION LIMIT	YEAR RETD.	ISSUE PRICE	*QUOTE U.S.$
1995 Flute	Open		40.00	40
1993 Guitar	12/00		32.50	33
1993 Piano	Open		40.00	40
1995 Saxophone	Open		40.00	40
1993 Violin	Open		25.00	25

Swarovski Crystal Memories-In a Class of Their Own

YEAR ISSUE	EDITION LIMIT	YEAR RETD.	ISSUE PRICE	*QUOTE U.S.$
2000 Binoculars	Open		45.00	45
1997 Camera	Open		32.50	33
1993 Golf Bag	Open		40.00	40
2000 In-Line Skate	Open		40.00	40
1994 Sailboat	Open		40.00	40

Swarovski Crystal Memories-In Familiar Surroundings

YEAR ISSUE	EDITION LIMIT	YEAR RETD.	ISSUE PRICE	*QUOTE U.S.$
1993 Piece of Cake	12/00		25.00	25
1993 Tea Set	Open		49.50	50
1999 Wine Set (5 pc.)	Open		65.00	65

Swarovski Crystal Memories-Times Past

YEAR ISSUE	EDITION LIMIT	YEAR RETD.	ISSUE PRICE	*QUOTE U.S.$
1998 Alarm Clock	Open		40.00	40
1998 Film Camera	Open		49.50	50
1996 Globe	Open		32.50	33
1995 Gramophone	Open		40.00	40
1993 Hourglass	Open		25.00	25
2000 Juke Box	Open		45.00	45
1996 Mantel Clock	Open		32.50	33
1998 Radio	Open		32.50	33
2000 Rocking Chair	Open		40.00	40
1994 Telephone	Open		32.50	33

*Quotes have been rounded up to nearest dollar

YEAR ISSUE	EDITION LIMIT	YEAR RETD.	ISSUE PRICE	*QUOTE U.S.$
1997 Typewriter	Open		40.00	40

Swarovski Crystal Memories-Your Special Treasures

YEAR ISSUE	EDITION LIMIT	YEAR RETD.	ISSUE PRICE	*QUOTE U.S.$
1993 Atomizer	Open		17.50	18
1993 Flower Basket	Open		40.00	40
1997 Flower Pot	Open		32.50	33
1993 High-Heeled Shoe	Open		32.50	33
1994 Inkwell with Quill	Open		17.50	18
1999 Sewing Machine	Open		49.50	50

Swarovski Crystal Memories-Journeys

YEAR ISSUE	EDITION LIMIT	YEAR RETD.	ISSUE PRICE	*QUOTE U.S.$
1999 Airplane	Open		95.00	95
1999 Carriage	Open		125.00	125
2000 Castle	Open		107.00	107
2000 Cathedral	Open		107.00	107
2000 Greek Temple	Open		95.00	95
1999 Hot Air Balloon	Open		85.00	85
2000 Japanese Temple	Open		107.00	107
2000 Lighthouse	Open		65.00	65
1999 Limousine	Open		95.00	95
1999 Locomotive	Open		125.00	125
2000 Mosque	Open		107.00	107

Swarovski Crystal Memories-Secrets

YEAR ISSUE	EDITION LIMIT	YEAR RETD.	ISSUE PRICE	*QUOTE U.S.$
1997 Beauty Case/Jewelry Box	Open		85.00	85
1999 Book/Clock	Open		95.00	95
1999 Cactus/Flacon	Open		85.00	85
2000 Egg with Garland	Open		90.00	90
1999 Flower Basket/Jewelry Box	Open		95.00	95
1997 Gift/Clock	Open		95.00	95
1997 Gift/Jewelry Box	Open		85.00	85
1997 Globe/Clock	Open		95.00	95
1997 Handbag/Clock	Open		95.00	95
1997 Rose Vase/Flacon	Open		65.00	65
1997 Spring Flower Vase/Flacon	12/00		65.00	65
1997 Suitcase/Picture Frame	Open		75.00	75
1997 Tulip Vase/Flacon	Open		75.00	75

Swarovski Crystal Memories-Retired

YEAR ISSUE	EDITION LIMIT	YEAR RETD.	ISSUE PRICE	*QUOTE U.S.$
1993 Anchor 9460NR000030	Retrd.	1996	32.50	33-68
1993 Baby's Bottle 9460NR000009	Retrd.	1998	17.50	18-23
1993 Beer Mug 9460NR000022	Retrd.	1997	25.00	25-59
1993 Coffee Mill 9460NR000001	Retrd.	1998	32.50	33-50
1994 Diary 9460NR000055	Retrd.	1999	40.00	35-40
1994 Dinner Bell 9460NR000047	Retrd.	1998	17.50	18-55
1996 Fruit Bowl 9460NR000069	Retrd.	1999	40.00	30-40
1993 Greek Vase 9460NR000006	Retrd.	1996	32.50	35-70
1993 Handbag 9460NR000013	Retrd.	1998	32.50	33-50
1994 Ice Cream Sundae 9460NR000046	Retrd.	1998	25.00	25
1994 Ice Skate 9460NR000051	Retrd.	1999	32.50	33-35
1993 Iron 9460NR000002	Retrd.	1996	25.00	30-61
1994 Kettledrum 9460NR000054	Retrd.	1997	32.50	33-69
1994 Knapsack 9460NR000049	Retrd.	1997	32.50	33-69
1993 Knitting Needles and Wool 9460NR000016	Retrd.	1996	32.50	30-67
1993 Lamp 9460NR000039	Retrd.	1997	25.00	30-59
1993 Lantern 9460NR000023	Retrd.	1997	40.00	40-79
1994 Penny Farthing Bicycle 9460NR000043	Retrd.	1998	32.50	33-40
1994 Row Boat 9460NR000034	Retrd.	1999	40.00	30-40
1993 Salt & Pepper 9460NR000045	Retrd.	1996	25.00	30-45
1993 Ski 9460NR000029	Retrd.	1999	25.00	20-25
1994 Spinning Wheel 9460NR000035	Retrd.	1997	40.00	40-76
1994 Tennis Racket 9460NR000048	Retrd.	1998	32.50	33-40
1993 Treasure Chest 9460NR000004	Retrd.	1996	40.00	35-76
1993 Treasure Island 9460NR000025	Retrd.	1996	32.50	35-69
1994 Trophy 9460NR000052	Retrd.	1998	40.00	40-50
1993 Umbrella 9460NR000008	Retrd.	1996	32.50	33-69
1993 Watering Can 9460NR000007	Retrd.	1998	32.50	33
1993 Wine Set 9460NR000038	Retrd.	1999	49.50	50

Swarovski Selection - Various

YEAR ISSUE	EDITION LIMIT	YEAR RETD.	ISSUE PRICE	*QUOTE U.S.$
2000 Allegra Table Clock - S. Weinberg	Open		590.00	590
1996 Apollo Bowl - B. Sipek	Open		650.00	650
2000 Arcadia Picture Frame - S. Weinberg	Open		280.00	280
1997 Astro Box - A. Putman	Open		355.00	355
1996 Calix Vase - B. Sipek	Open		650.00	650
1995 Cleo Picture Frame - M. Zendron	12/00		440.00	440
1995 Colorado Bowl - J. Desgrippes	Open		355.00	355
1995 Curaçao Tableclock - E. Mair	12/00		440.00	440
1992 Euclid Caviar Bowl - L. Redl	Open		650.00	650
2000 Galeo Card Holder - J. Desgrippes	Open		180.00	180
1996 Gemini Vase - B. Sipek	Open		440.00	440
1992 Helios Tableclock - B. Sipek	Open		355.00	355
2000 Medea Vase - J. Desgrippes	Open		315.00	315
1992 Petit Vase - J. Desgrippes	Open		650.00	650
1998 Providence Tableclock - S. Weinberg	Open		850.00	850
1998 Ren Candleholder - K. Nagai	Open		525.00	525
1996 Saturn Candleholder - B. Sipek	Open		440.00	440
1993 Shiva Bowl - L. Redl	Open		440.00	440
1992 Soliflor Vase - J. Desgrippes	Open		440.00	440
1994 Stalactite Candleholder - A. Putman	Open		620.00	620
1999 Toh Vase - K. Nagai	Open		650.00	650
1997 Wa Bowl - K. Nagai	Open		850.00	850
1999 Yin Yang Candleholder - Tao Ho	Open		620.00	620

Swarovski Selection-Retired

YEAR ISSUE	EDITION LIMIT	YEAR RETD.	ISSUE PRICE	*QUOTE U.S.$
1992 Boite meli-melo (bowl) 0168008	Retrd.	1995	210.00	210-273
1994 Buchstützen (bookends) 0168342	Retrd.	1996	385.00	360-462
1992 Cendrier (ashtray) 0168007	Retrd.	1995	190.00	175-190
1994 Coupe-papier (letter opener) 0172756	Retrd.	1997	190.00	185-225
1992 Enigma Tableclock 0168002 - L. Redl	Retrd.	1998	355.00	275-355
1992 Federhalter (pen holder) 0168006	Retrd.	1995	385.00	360-385
1992 Grand Contenitore (bowl) 0167997	Retrd.	1995	620.00	600-720
1997 Hong Kong 0222859 - Mae Tsang	1,997	1997	1100.00	1200-2900
1993 Porte-cartes imago (card holder) 0170199	Retrd.	1995	190.00	150-190
1992 Scatola Piccola con tappo (bowl) 0167998	Retrd.	1995	515.00	480-515
1992 Schmuckdose (jewel box) 0168005	Retrd.	1995	515.00	420-515
1994 Stalagmite Ringholder 0182484 - A. Putman	Retrd.	1998	355.00	355-495
1992 Uranus Candleholder 0168004 - B. Sipek	Retrd.	1998	385.00	360-385

Swarovski Collectors Society - Various

YEAR ISSUE	EDITION LIMIT	YEAR RETD.	ISSUE PRICE	*QUOTE U.S.$
1987 Togetherness-The Lovebirds - M. Schreck	Yr.Iss.	1987	150.00	4000-5400
1988 Sharing-The Woodpeckers - A. Stocker	Yr.Iss.	1988	165.00	1500-2200
1988 Mini Cactus	Yr.Iss.	1988	Gift	157-236
1989 Amour-The Turtledoves - A. Stocker	Yr.Iss.	1989	195.00	900-1200
1989 The Lovebirds, The Woodpeckers, The Turtledoves	Closed	1989	510.00	4800-7440
1989 SCS Key Chain	Yr.Iss.	1989	Gift	50-125
1990 Lead Me-The Dolphins - M. Stamey	Yr.Iss.	1990	225.00	900-1075
1990 Mini Chaton	Yr.Iss.	1990	Gift	110-125
1991 Save Me-The Seals - M. Stamey	Yr.Iss.	1991	225.00	375-650
1991 Dolphin Brooch	Yr.Iss.	1991	75.00	100-150
1991 SCS Pin	Yr.Iss.	1991	Gift	75-135
1992 Care For Me - The Whales - M. Stamey	Yr.Iss.	1992	265.00	450-650
1992 The Dolphins, The Seals, The Whales - M. Stamey	Closed	1992	715.00	1500-2760
1992 SCS Pen	Yr.Iss.	1992	Gift	35-75
1992 5th Anniversary Edition-The Birthday Cake - G. Stamey	Yr.Iss.	1992	85.00	200-300
1993 Inspiration Africa-The Elephant - M. Zendron	Yr.Iss.	1993	325.00	1200-1500
1993 Elephant Brooch	Yr.Iss.	1993	85.00	85-195
1993 Leather Luggage Tag	Yr.Iss.	1993	Gift	35-55
1994 Inspiration Africa-The Kudu - M. Stamey	Yr.Iss.	1994	295.00	500-600
1994 Leather Double Picture Frame	Yr.Iss.	1994	Gift	50-85
1995 Inspiration Africa-The Lion - A. Stocker	Yr.Iss.	1995	325.00	400-550
1995 Centenary Swan Brooch	Yr.Iss.	1995	125.00	100-185
1995 The Elephant, The Kudu, The Lion	Closed	1995	945.00	1440-2375
1995 Miniature Crystal Swan	Yr.Iss.	1995	Gift	55-130
1996 Fabulous Creatures-The Unicorn - M. Zendron	Yr.Iss.	1996	325.00	450-750
1996 Clear Crystal Heart	Yr.Iss.	1996	Gift	100-185
1996 Bag of Hearts (3 Yr. Renewal) SCMR10	Retrd.	1998	Gift	20-75
1997 Fabulous Creatures-The Dragon - G. Stamey	Yr.Iss.	1997	325.00	400-450
1997 SCS 10th Anniversary Edition - The Squirrel - A. Hirzinger	Yr.Iss.	1997	140.00	95-185
1997 Blue Crystal Heart	Yr.Iss.	1997	Gift	60-80
1998 Fabulous Creatures-The Pegasus - A. Stocker	Yr.Iss.	1998	350.00	250-500
1998 Red Crystal Heart	Yr.Iss.	1998	Gift	55-80
1999 "Masquerade"-Pierrot	Yr.Iss.	1999	350.00	300-350
2000 "Masquerade"-Columbine - G. Stamey	Yr.Iss.		350.00	350

Swarovski Silver Crystal-Worldwide Limited Editions - A. Stocker

YEAR ISSUE	EDITION LIMIT	YEAR RETD.	ISSUE PRICE	*QUOTE U.S.$
1995 Eagle	10,000	1995	1750.00	4800-7000
1998 Peacock	10,000	1998	1800.00	3600-5500

Swarovski Silver Crystal-Annual Editions - A. Hirzinger

YEAR ISSUE	EDITION LIMIT	YEAR RETD.	ISSUE PRICE	*QUOTE U.S.$
1995 Centenary Swan	Yr.Iss.	1995	150.00	95-250
2000 Crystal Planet	Yr.Iss.		275.00	275

Swarovski Silver Crystal-Commemorative Single Issues - Team

YEAR ISSUE	EDITION LIMIT	YEAR RETD.	ISSUE PRICE	*QUOTE U.S.$
1990 Elephant, 7640NR100 (Introduced by Swarovski America as a commemorative item for Design Celebration/January '90 in Walt Disney World)	Closed	1990	125.00	900-1085
1993 Elephant, 7640NR100001 (Introduced by Swarovski America as a commemorative item for Design Celebration/January '93 in Walt Disney World)	Closed	1993	150.00	480-506

Swarovski Silver Crystal-Special Walt Disney Theme Park Specials - Team

YEAR ISSUE	EDITION LIMIT	YEAR RETD.	ISSUE PRICE	*QUOTE U.S.$
1987 Elephant (small tusks, small ears) - A. Stocker	Closed	1987	95.00	2799-4800
1987 Elephant (large tusks, small ears) - A. Stocker	Closed	1987	95.00	2799
1987 Elephant (no tusks, small ears) - A. Stocker	Closed	1987	95.00	2615
1988 Elephant (no tusks, large ears) - A. Stocker	Closed	1988	95.00	3105
1988 Elephant (large tusks, large ears) - A. Stocker	Closed	1988	95.00	3429

Swarovski Silver Crystal-African Wildlife - Various

YEAR ISSUE	EDITION LIMIT	YEAR RETD.	ISSUE PRICE	*QUOTE U.S.$
1995 Baby Elephant - M. Zendron	Open		155.00	155
1999 Baby Giraffe - M. Stamey	Open		260.00	260
2000 Camel - H. Tabertshofer	Open		375.00	375
1994 Cheetah - M. Stamey	Open		275.00	275
1998 Chimpanzee - E. Mair	Open		125.00	125
2000 Cobra - H. Tabertshofer	Open		140.00	140
1989 Elephant-Small - A. Stocker	Open		50.00	65
1997 Leopard - M. Stamey	Open		260.00	260
1997 Lion Cub - A. Stocker	Open		125.00	125

Swarovski Silver Crystal-Among Flowers And Foliage - Various

YEAR ISSUE	EDITION LIMIT	YEAR RETD.	ISSUE PRICE	*QUOTE U.S.$
1994 Butterfly on Leaf - C. Schneiderbauer	Open		75.00	85
1995 Dragonfly - C. Schneiderbauer	Open		85.00	85
1992 Hummingbird - C. Schneiderbauer	Open		195.00	210
1996 Snail on Vine-Leaf - E. Mair	Open		65.00	65

Swarovski Silver Crystal-Barnyard Friends - Various

YEAR ISSUE	EDITION LIMIT	YEAR RETD.	ISSUE PRICE	*QUOTE U.S.$
2000 Cockerel - M. Stamey	Open		75.00	75
1984 Medium Pig - M. Schreck	Open		35.00	55
1988 Miniature-Chickens (Set/3) - G. Stamey	Open		35.00	45
1987 Miniature-Hen - G. Stamey	Open		35.00	45
1982 Miniature-Pig - M. Schreck	Open		16.00	30
1987 Miniature-Rooster - G. Stamey	12/00		35.00	55

Swarovski Silver Crystal-Beauties of the Lake - Various

YEAR ISSUE	EDITION LIMIT	YEAR RETD.	ISSUE PRICE	*QUOTE U.S.$
1997 Baby Carp - M. Stamey	Open		49.50	50
1994 Frog - G. Stamey	Open		49.50	50
1996 Goldfish-Mini - M. Stamey	12/00		45.00	45
1989 Mallard-Giant - M. Stamey	Open		2000.00	4500
1984 Standing Drake-Mini - M. Schreck	Open		20.00	45
1987 Standing Duck-Mini - A. Stocker	Open		22.00	38
2000 Swan Family - A. Stocker	Open		185.00	185
1981 Swan-Large - M. Schreck	Open		55.00	95
1995 Swan-Maxi - A. Hirzinger	Open		4500.00	4500
1981 Swan-Medium - M. Schreck	Open		44.00	85
1982 Swan-Small - M. Schreck	Open		35.00	50
1986 Swimming Duck-Mini - A. Stocker	Open		16.00	38

Swarovski Silver Crystal-Crystal Melodies - Various

YEAR ISSUE	EDITION LIMIT	YEAR RETD.	ISSUE PRICE	*QUOTE U.S.$
1993 Grand Piano - M. Zendron	Open		250.00	260
1997 Saxophone - M. Zendron	Open		125.00	125
1996 Violin - G. Stamey	Open		140.00	140

Swarovski Silver Crystal-Decorative Items For The Desk (Paperweights) - Various

YEAR ISSUE	EDITION LIMIT	YEAR RETD.	ISSUE PRICE	*QUOTE U.S.$
1999 Chaton - Team	Open		185.00	185
1990 Chaton-Giant - M. Schreck	Open		4500.00	4500

Swarovski Silver Crystal-Endangered Species - Various

YEAR ISSUE	EDITION LIMIT	YEAR RETD.	ISSUE PRICE	*QUOTE U.S.$
1993 Baby Panda - A. Stocker	Open		24.50	25
2000 Bald Eagle - A. Stocker	Open		275.00	275
1993 Mother Panda - A. Stocker	Open		120.00	125
1987 Koala-Large - A. Stocker	Open		50.00	65
1989 Miniature-Koala - A. Stocker	12/00		35.00	45
1993 Mother Kangaroo with Baby - G. Stamey	Open		95.00	95
1998 Baby Sea Lion - M. Stamey	Open		49.50	50
1998 Miniature-Alligator - M. Stamey	Open		75.00	75
1998 Baby Tortoises (Set/2) - E. Mair	Open		45.00	45
1997 Tortoise - E. Mair	Open		55.00	55
1998 Tiger - M. Stamey	Open		275.00	275
1983 Turtle-Giant - M. Schreck	Open		2500.00	4500

Swarovski Silver Crystal-Exquisite Accents - Various

YEAR ISSUE	EDITION LIMIT	YEAR RETD.	ISSUE PRICE	*QUOTE U.S.$
1995 Angel - A. Stocker	Open		210.00	210
1981 Birdbath - M. Schreck	Open		150.00	210
1996 Blue Flower Jewel Box - G. Stamey	12/00		210.00	210
1996 Blue Flower Picture Frame - G. Stamey	12/00		260.00	260
1999 Comet Candleholder - M. Zendron	Open		185.00	185
2000 Flacon Napoleon - A. Hirzinger	Open		185.00	185
1997 Kris Bear Picture Frame - M. Zendron	Open		95.00	95
1997 Kris Bear Table Clock - M. Zendron	Open		210.00	210
1999 Nutcracker - A. Hirzinger	Open		155.00	155
1996 The Orchid-pink - M. Stamey	Open		140.00	140
1996 The Orchid-yellow - M. Stamey	12/00		140.00	140
1997 Oriental Flacon - M. Zendron	Open		185.00	185
1997 Picture Frame w/Butterfly - C. Schneiderbauer	Open		85.00	85
1997 Picture Frame w/Ladybug - E. Mair	12/00		55.00	55
1997 Reindeer - A. Hirzinger	Open		185.00	185
1993 The Rose - M. Stamey	Open		150.00	155
1999 Rose Flacon - M. Zendron	Open		185.00	185
1998 Santa Claus - M. Zendron	Open		155.00	155
1996 Sleigh - M. Zendron	Open		295.00	295
1999 Solaris Table Bell - A. Hirzinger	Open		185.00	185
1998 Solaris Table Clock - A. Stocker	Open		375.00	375
1997 Sweet Heart - E. Mair	Open		110.00	110
1997 Sweet Heart Jewel Box - E. Mair	Open		140.00	140

Swarovski Silver Crystal-Fairy Tales - E. Mair, unless otherwise noted

YEAR ISSUE	EDITION LIMIT	YEAR RETD.	ISSUE PRICE	*QUOTE U.S.$
1999 Dragon - G. Stamey	Open		325.00	325
1996 Red Riding Hood	Open		185.00	185
1996 Wolf	Open		155.00	155

Swarovski Silver Crystal-Feathered Friends - Various

YEAR ISSUE	EDITION LIMIT	YEAR RETD.	ISSUE PRICE	*QUOTE U.S.$
1996 Baby Lovebirds - A. Stocker	Open		155.00	155
1995 Dove - E. Mair	Open		55.00	55
1993 Pelican - A. Hirzinger	Open		37.50	38
1999 Toucan - M. Stamey	Open		155.00	155
1998 Silver Heron - A. Stocker	Open		275.00	275

Swarovski Silver Crystal-Game of Kings - M. Schreck

YEAR ISSUE	EDITION LIMIT	YEAR RETD.	ISSUE PRICE	*QUOTE U.S.$
1985 Chess Set	Open		950.00	1375

Swarovski Silver Crystal-Horses on Parade - M. Zendron

YEAR ISSUE	EDITION LIMIT	YEAR RETD.	ISSUE PRICE	*QUOTE U.S.$
1998 Arabian Stallion	Open		260.00	260
1993 White Stallion	Open		250.00	260

Swarovski Silver Crystal-In A Summer Meadow - Various

YEAR ISSUE	EDITION LIMIT	YEAR RETD.	ISSUE PRICE	*QUOTE U.S.$
1997 Bunny Rabbit - E. Mair	Open		55.00	55
1983 Butterfly-Large - Team	Open		44.00	85

*Quotes have been rounded up to nearest dollar

YEAR ISSUE	EDITION LIMIT	YEAR RETD.	ISSUE PRICE	*QUOTE U.S.$
1994 Field Mice (Set/3) - A. Stocker	Open		42.50	45
1991 Field Mouse - A. Stocker	Open		47.50	50
1997 Four-Leaf Clover - A. Hirzinger	Open		49.50	50
1988 Hedgehog-Medium - M. Schreck	Open		70.00	85
1988 Hedgehog-Small - M. Schreck	Open		50.00	55
1995 Ladybug - E. Mair	Open		29.50	30
1986 Miniature-Butterfly - Team	Open		16.00	45
1988 Miniature-Rabbit, sitting - A. Stocker	Open		35.00	45
1988 Mother Rabbit - A. Stocker	Open		60.00	75

Swarovski Silver Crystal-Kingdom Of Ice And Snow - Various

YEAR ISSUE	EDITION LIMIT	YEAR RETD.	ISSUE PRICE	*QUOTE U.S.$
1997 Baby Penguins (Set/3) - A. Stocker	Open		75.00	75
1985 Miniature-Penguin - M. Schreck	Open		16.00	38
1985 Miniature-Seal - A. Stocker	Open		30.00	45
1995 Sir Penguin - A. Stocker	12/00		85.00	85

Swarovski Silver Crystal-Our Candleholders - Various

YEAR ISSUE	EDITION LIMIT	YEAR RETD.	ISSUE PRICE	*QUOTE U.S.$
1996 Blue Flower - G. Stamey	Open		260.00	260
1999 Solaris Candleholder - A. Stocker	Open		350.00	350
1989 Star-Medium 7600NR143001 - Team	Open		200.00	260
1985 Water Lily-Large 7600NR125 - M. Schreck	Open		200.00	375
1984 Water Lily-Medium 7600NR123 - M. Schreck	Open		150.00	260
1985 Water Lily-Small 7600NR124 - M. Schreck	Open		100.00	175

Swarovski Silver Crystal-Pets' Corner - Various

YEAR ISSUE	EDITION LIMIT	YEAR RETD.	ISSUE PRICE	*QUOTE U.S.$
1990 Beagle - A. Stocker	Open		40.00	50
1993 Beagle Playing - A. Stocker	Open		49.50	50
1999 German Shepherd - H. Tabertshofer	Open		140.00	140
2000 Mini Cat - M. Schreck	Open		29.50	30
1991 Sitting Cat - M. Stamey	Open		75.00	85
1993 Sitting Poodle - A. Stocker	Open		85.00	85
1996 St. Bernard - E. Mair	Open		95.00	95
1996 Tomcat - A. Hirzinger	Open		45.00	45

Swarovski Silver Crystal-South Sea - Various

YEAR ISSUE	EDITION LIMIT	YEAR RETD.	ISSUE PRICE	*QUOTE U.S.$
1996 Miniature-Crab - M. Stamey	Open		65.00	65
1987 Miniature-Blowfish - Team	Open		22.00	30
1987 Blowfish-Small - Team	Open		35.00	55
1995 Dolphin - M. Stamey	Open		210.00	210
1998 Maxi Dolphin - M. Stamey	Open		880.00	880
1993 Sea Horse - M. Stamey	Open		85.00	85
1999 Siamese Fighting Fish - H. Tabertshofer	Open		125.00	125
1987 Shell w/Pearl - M. Stamey	Open		120.00	175
1995 Shell - M. Stamey	Open		45.00	45
1995 Starfish - M. Stamey	Open		29.50	30
1995 Conch - M. Stamey	Open		29.50	30
1995 Maritime Trio (Shell, Starfish, Conch) - M. Stamey	Open		104.00	104

Swarovski Silver Crystal-Sparkling Fruit - Various

YEAR ISSUE	EDITION LIMIT	YEAR RETD.	ISSUE PRICE	*QUOTE U.S.$
1995 Grapes - Team	Open		375.00	375
1983 Pineapple-Giant /Gold - M. Schreck	Open		1750.00	3250
1982 Pineapple-Large /Gold - M. Schreck	Open		150.00	260
1987 Pineapple-Small /Gold - M. Schreck	Open		55.00	85

Swarovski Silver Crystal-When We Were Young - Various

YEAR ISSUE	EDITION LIMIT	YEAR RETD.	ISSUE PRICE	*QUOTE U.S.$
1999 Ballerina - M. Zendron	Open		325.00	325
1999 Celebration Kris Bear - M. Zendron	Open		85.00	85
1999 Fawn - M. Zendron	Open		125.00	125
1993 Kris Bear - M. Zendron	Open		75.00	75
1995 Kris Bear on Skates - M. Zendron	Open		75.00	75
1997 Kris Bear with Honey Pot - M. Zendron	Open		75.00	75
1999 Kris Bear with Skis - M. Zendron	Open		85.00	85
1988 Locomotive - G. Stamey	Open		150.00	155
1995 Miniature-Train - G. Stamey	Open		125.00	125
1990 Petrol Wagon - G. Stamey	Open		75.00	95
1997 Puppet - G. Stamey	Open		125.00	125
1994 Replica Cat - Team	Open		37.50	38
1994 Replica Hedgehog - Team	Open		37.50	38
1994 Replica Mouse - Team	Open		37.50	38
1994 Rocking Horse - G. Stamey	Open		125.00	125
1994 Sailboat - G. Stamey	Open		195.00	210
1991 Santa Maria - G. Stamey	Open		375.00	375
1994 Starter Set - Team	Open		112.50	113
1998 Tank Wagon - G. Stamey	Open		95.00	95
1988 Tender - G. Stamey	Open		55.00	55
1993 Tipping Wagon - G. Stamey	Open		95.00	95
1988 Wagon - G. Stamey	Open		85.00	95

Swarovski Silver Crystal-Woodland Friends - Various

YEAR ISSUE	EDITION LIMIT	YEAR RETD.	ISSUE PRICE	*QUOTE U.S.$
1981 Bear-Large - M. Schreck	Open		75.00	95
2000 Doe - M. Zendron	Open		260.00	260
1999 Fawn - M. Zendron	Open		125.00	125
1983 Giant Owl- M. Schreck	Open		1200.00	2000
2000 Grizzly - H. Tabertshofer	Open		325.00	325
1988 Mini Sitting Fox - A. Stocker	Open		35.00	45
1985 Miniature-Bear - M. Schreck	Open		16.00	55
1981 Miniature-Owl - M. Schreck	Open		16.00	30
1996 Night Owl - A. Hirzinger	Open		85.00	85
1981 Owl-Large - M. Schreck	Open		90.00	125
1995 Owlet - A. Hirzinger	12/00		45.00	45
2000 Snowman - E. Mair	Open		95.00	95
1985 Squirrel - M. Schreck	Open		35.00	55

Swarovski Silver Crystal-Retired Candleholders - Team, unless otherwise noted

YEAR ISSUE	EDITION LIMIT	YEAR RETD.	ISSUE PRICE	*QUOTE U.S.$
1981 Candleholder 7600NR101	Retrd.	1981	28.00	88-275
1981 Candleholder 7600NR102 (hole) - H. Koch	Retrd.	1986	40.00	147-500
1981 Candleholder 7600NR102 (pin) - H. Koch	Retrd.	1986	40.00	140-313
1976 Candleholder 7600NR102T (smoked) (pin) - H. Koch	Retrd.	N/A	44.00	468-520
1986 Candleholder 7600NR103 (hole)	Retrd.	1988	40.00	112-225
1976 Candleholder 7600NR103 (pin) (European)	Retrd.	1983	N/A	416-719
1986 Candleholder 7600NR103 (pin)	Retrd.	1988	40.00	462
1986 Candleholder 7600NR104 (hole)	Retrd.	1988	95.00	217-650
1976 Candleholder 7600NR104 (pin) (European)	Retrd.	1989	N/A	438-650
1981 Candleholder 7600NR106 (hole)	Retrd.	1986	100.00	459-784
1981 Candleholder 7600NR106 (pin)	Retrd.	1986	100.00	364-590
1981 Candleholder 7600NR107 (hole)	Retrd.	1985	120.00	480-700
1981 Candleholder 7600NR107 (pin)	Retrd.	1985	120.00	284-391
1976 Candleholder 7600NR108 (pin) (European)	Retrd.	1987	N/A	625-756
1981 Candleholder 7600NR109 (hole)	Retrd.	1985	40.00	155-194
1981 Candleholder 7600NR109 (pin)	Retrd.	1985	40.00	158-250
1981 Candleholder 7600NR110 (hole)	Retrd.	1986	45.00	194-375
1981 Candleholder 7600NR110 (pin)	Retrd.	1986	45.00	163-375
1981 Candleholder 7600NR111 (hole)	Retrd.	1985	100.00	457-888
1981 Candleholder 7600NR111 (pin)	Retrd.	1985	100.00	700-813
1981 Candleholder 7600NR112 (hole)	Retrd.	1985	80.00	370-750
1981 Candleholder 7600NR112 (pin)	Retrd.	1985	80.00	237-310
1976 Candleholder 7600NR112T (pin)	Retrd.	N/A	N/A	1940-3450
1976 Candleholder 7600NR113 (Euopean) (pin)	Retrd.	1981	N/A	642-1313
1981 Candleholder 7600NR114 (hole)	Retrd.	1985	40.00	221-469
1981 Candleholder 7600NR114 (pin)	Retrd.	1985	40.00	173-272
1981 Candleholder 7600NR115 (hole)	Retrd.	1986	200.00	800-938
1981 Candleholder 7600NR115 (pin)	Retrd.	1986	200.00	438-588
1981 Candleholder 7600NR116 (hole)	Retrd.	1985	350.00	1638-3100
1981 Candleholder 7600NR116 (pin)	Retrd.	1985	350.00	1610-2750
XX Candleholder 7600NR118 (European) (pin)	Retrd.	N/A	N/A	3500-4000
1977 Candleholder 7600NR119 (European)	Retrd.	1989	N/A	232-532
1986 Candleholder 7600NR122	Retrd.	1986	85.00	625-1250
1985 Candleholder 7600NR125 (with floweret)	Retrd.	N/A	250.00	253-360
1985 Candleholder 7600NR127	Retrd.	1987	65.00	375-775
1985 Candleholder 7600NR128	Retrd.	1987	100.00	422-919
1985 Candleholder 7600NR129	Retrd.	1987	120.00	450-750
1981 Candleholder 7600NR130	Retrd.	1985	300.00	1890-2268
1978 Candleholder 7600NR131, set/6 (European)	Retrd.	1989	N/A	325-750
1986 Candleholder 7600NR138	Retrd.	1986	160.00	750-938
1986 Candleholder 7600NR139	Retrd.	1986	140.00	1063-1200
1986 Candleholder 7600NR140	Retrd.	1986	120.00	1000-1875
1986 Candleholder 7600NR141 (European) - M. Schreck	Retrd.	1991	N/A	750-1500
1986 Candleholder 7600NR142 (European) - M. Schreck	Retrd.	1990	N/A	282-688
1994 Candleholder 7600NR145	Retrd.	N/A	N/A	3000-5880
1982 Candleholder-Baroque 7600NR121	Retrd.	1986	150.00	625-1313
1981 Candleholder-Global-Kg. Sz. 7600NR135	Retrd.	1988	50.00	257-282
1981 Candleholder-Global-Lg. 7600NR134	Retrd.	1990	40.00	100-313
1981 Candleholder-Global-Med. (2) 7600NR133	Retrd.	1990	40.00	94-250
1981 Candleholder-Global-Sm. (4) 7600NR132	Retrd.	1989	60.00	60-244
1988 Candleholder-Neo-Classic-Lg. 7600NR144090 - A. Stocker	Retrd.	1992	220.00	400-750
1990 Candleholder-Neo-Classic-Med. 7600NR144080 - A. Stocker	Retrd.	1992	190.00	250-382
1990 Candleholder-Neo-Classic-Sm. 7600NR144070 - A. Stocker	Retrd.	1992	170.00	182-282
1985 Candleholder-Pineapple-Gold 7600NR136 - M. Schreck	Retrd.	1986	150.00	394-690
1984 Candleholder-Pineapple-Rhodium 7600NR136 - M. Schreck	Retrd.	1986	150.00	500-750
1987 Candleholder-Star-Lg. 7600NR143000	Retrd.	1996	250.00	375-525
1984 Candleholder-w/Flowers-Lg. 7600NR137	Retrd.	1990	150.00	312-407
1986 Candleholder-w/Flowers-Sm. 7600NR120	Retrd.	1987	60.00	450-500
1986 Candleholder-w/Leaves-Sm. 7600NR126	Retrd.	1987	100.00	750-844

Swarovski Silver Crystal-Retired Paperweights - Team, unless otherwise noted

YEAR ISSUE	EDITION LIMIT	YEAR RETD.	ISSUE PRICE	*QUOTE U.S.$
1981 Pprwgt-Atomic-Crystal Cal 7454NR60095 - M. Schreck	Retrd.	1985	80.00	720-1500
1981 Pprwgt-Atomic-Vitrl Med. 7454NR60087 - M. Schreck	Retrd.	1985	80.00	760-1875
1981 Pprwgt-Barrel-Crystal Cal 7453NR60095 - M. Schreck	Retrd.	1988	80.00	302-938
1981 Pprwgt-Barrel-Vitrl Med. 7453NR60087 - M. Schreck	Retrd.	1988	80.00	375-532
1981 Pprwgt-Carousel-Crystal Cal 7451NR60095 - M. Schreck	Retrd.	1985	80.00	950-1500
1981 Pprwgt-Carousel-Vitrl Med. 7451NR60087 - M. Schreck	Retrd.	1985	80.00	1250-2000
1976 Pprwgt-Cone Bermuda Blue 7452NR60088 - M. Schreck	Retrd.	1992	N/A	500
1982 Pprwgt-Cone Crystal Cal 7452NR60095 - M. Schreck	Retrd.	1982	80.00	235-625
1982 Pprwgt-Cone Vitrl Med. 7452NR60087 - M. Schreck	Retrd.	1982	80.00	250-875
1981 Pprwgt-Egg 7458NR63069 - M. Schreck	Retrd.	1982	60.00	165-313
1987 Pprwgt-Geometric 7432NR57002	Retrd.	1990	75.00	219-313
1987 Pprwgt-Octron-Bermuda Blue 7456NR41088	Retrd.	1991	N/A	313-332
1987 Pprwgt-Octron-Crystal Cal 7456NR41	Retrd.	1991	75.00	115-232
1987 Pprwgt-Octron-Crystal Cal 7456NR41095	Retrd.	1991	95.00	115-200
1988 Pprwgt-Octron-Vitrl Med. 7456NR41087	Retrd.	1991	90.00	121-250
1987 Pprwgt-One Ton 7495NR65	Retrd.	1990	75.00	127-438
1981 Pprwgt-Rd.-Berm Blue 7404NR30	Retrd.	1982	15.00	250
1981 Pprwgt-Rd.-Berm Blue 7404NR40	Retrd.	1981	20.00	82-150
1981 Pprwgt-Rd.-Berm Blue 7404NR50	Retrd.	1982	40.00	94-302
1981 Pprwgt-Rd.-Crystal Cal 7404NR30095/30	Retrd.	1989	15.00	63-125
1981 Pprwgt-Rd.-Crystal Cal 7404NR40095/40	Retrd.	1989	20.00	95-100
1981 Pprwgt-Rd.-Crystal Cal 7404NR50095/50	Retrd.	1989	40.00	125-175
1981 Pprwgt-Rd.-Crystal Cal 7404NR60095/60	Retrd.	1989	50.00	200-319
1981 Pprwgt-Rd.-Green 7404NR30	Retrd.	1982	15.00	100-250
1981 Pprwgt-Rd.-Green 7404NR40	Retrd.	1981	20.00	150-240
1981 Pprwgt-Rd.-Green 7404NR50	Retrd.	1982	40.00	255
1981 Pprwgt-Rd.-Sahara 7404NR30	Retrd.	1982	15.00	195-200
1981 Pprwgt-Rd.-Sahara 7404NR40	Retrd.	1981	20.00	115-195
1981 Pprwgt-Rd.-Sahara 7404NR50	Retrd.	1982	40.00	208-313
1981 Pprwgt-Rd.-Vitrl Med. 7404NR30087	Retrd.	1989	15.00	63-113
1981 Pprwgt-Rd.-Vitrl Med. 7404NR40087	Retrd.	1989	20.00	94-113
1981 Pprwgt-Rd.-Vitrl Med. 7404NR50087	Retrd.	1989	40.00	125-244
1981 Pprwgt-Rd.-Vitrl Med. 7404NR60087	Retrd.	1989	50.00	100-344

Swarovski Silver Crystal-Retired - Various

YEAR ISSUE	EDITION LIMIT	YEAR RETD.	ISSUE PRICE	*QUOTE U.S.$
1990 Airplane 7473NR000002 - A. Stocker	Retrd.	1999	135.00	135-182
1991 Apple 7476NR000001- M. Stamey	Retrd.	1996	175.00	240-438
1984 Apple Photo Stand-Kg. Sz. (Gold) 7504NR060G - M. Schreck	Retrd.	1988	120.00	394-681
1981 Apple Photo Stand-Kg. Sz. (Rhodium) 7504NR060R - M. Schreck	Retrd.	1988	120.00	473-750
1983 Apple Photo Stand-Lg. (Gold) 7504NR050G - M. Schreck	Retrd.	1990	80.00	244-425
1981 Apple Photo Stand-Lg. (Rhodium) 7504NR050R - M. Schreck	Retrd.	1986	80.00	373-500
1983 Apple Photo Stand-Sm. (Gold) 7504NR030G - M. Schreck	Retrd.	1990	40.00	150-282
1981 Apple Photo Stand-Sm. (Rhodium) 7504NR030R - M. Schreck	Retrd.	1986	40.00	240-275
1982 Ashtray 7461NR100 - M. Schreck	Retrd.	1990	150.00	185-325
1981 Ashtray 7501NR061 - Team	Retrd.	1981	45.00	580-1063
1996 Baby Carriage 7473NR000005 - G. Stamey	Retrd.	1999	140.00	124-188
1983 Bear-Giant Size 7637NR112 - M. Schreck	Retrd.	1988	125.00	2250-3125
1983 Bear-King Size (no tail) 7637NR92 - M. Schreck	Retrd.	1987	95.00	1875-2900
1985 Bear-Mini 7670NR32 - M. Schreck	Retrd.	1989	16.00	150-375
1982 Bear-Sm 7637NR054000 - M. Schreck	Retrd.	1995	44.00	80-150
1992 Beaver-Baby Lying 7616NR000003 - A. Stocker	Retrd.	1995	47.50	75-118
1992 Beaver-Baby Sitting 7616NR000002 - A. Stocker	Retrd.	1999	47.50	50-80
1985 Bee (Gold) 7553NR100 - Team	Retrd.	1988	200.00	1813-2471
1985 Bee (Rhodium) 7553NR200 - Team	Retrd.	1986	200.00	1990-4380
1983 Beetle Bottle Opener (Gold) 7505NR76 - Team	Retrd.	1983	80.00	750-1875
1981 Beetle Bottle Opener (Rhodium) 7505NR76 - Team	Retrd.	1983	80.00	540-1688
1987 Birds' Nest 7470NR050000 - Team	Retrd.	1996	90.00	169-225
1985 Blowfish-Lg. 7644NR41 - Team	Retrd.	1991	40.00	135-375
1992 Bumblebee 7615NR000002 - C. Schneiderbauer	Retrd.	1997	85.00	109-150
1982 Butterfly (gold antenna) 7551NR55000 - Team	Retrd.	N/A	85.00	85-330
1985 Butterfly (Gold) 7551NR100 - Team	Retrd.	1988	200.00	1063-1375
1985 Butterfly (Rhodium) 7551NR200 - Team	Retrd.	1986	200.00	2750-4200
1991 Butterfly Fish 7644NR077000 - M. Stamey	Retrd.	1998	150.00	150-212
1985 Butterfly-Mini (black tips/rhodium antenna) 7671NR30 - Team	Retrd.	1988	16.00	172-216
1985 Butterfly-Mini (crystal tips/gold antenna) 7671NR30 - Team	Retrd.	1988	16.00	182-313
1981 Cardholders-Lg., Set/4 -7403NR30095 - K. Mignon	Retrd.	1989	43.00	231-439
1981 Cardholders-Sm., Set/4-7403NR20095 - K. Mignon	Retrd.	1989	25.00	180-250
1981 Cardholders-Sm., Set/6-7403NR20095 - K. Mignon (European)	Retrd.	1989	25.00	116-375
1984 Cat-Lg 7634NR70 - M. Schreck	Retrd.	1991	44.00	125-280
1983 Cat-Medium 7634NR52 - M. Schreck	Retrd.	1987	38.00	482-650
1983 Cat-Mini (Retired in U.S. only) 7659NR31 - M. Schreck	Retrd.	1991	16.00	38-125
1987 Chaton-Large 7433NR080000 - M. Schreck	Retrd.	1998	190.00	211-300
1987 Chaton-Small 7433NR050000 - M. Schreck	Retrd.	1998	50.00	85-130
1985 Chess Board (mirror) 7700345006 - M. Schreck	Retrd.	1986	N/A	221
1985 Chess Carrying Case - Team	Retrd.	1986	N/A	99
1985 Chess Men 7469100000 - M. Schreck	Retrd.	1986	N/A	337
1985 Chess Set/Wooden Board 7550NR432032 - M. Schreck	Retrd.	1986	950.00	1188-3000

*Quotes have been rounded up to nearest dollar

YEAR ISSUE		EDITION LIMIT	YEAR RETD.	ISSUE PRICE	*QUOTE U.S.$
1981	Chicken-Mini 7651NR20 - M. Schreck	Retrd.	1988	16.00	57-125
1978	Cigarette Box 7503NR050 (European)	Retrd.	1983	N/A	2100-3000
1982	Cigarette Holder 7463NR062 - M. Schreck	Retrd.	1990	85.00	115-192
1977	Cigarette Holder Rhodium 7503NR50	Retrd.	1982	160.00	512-1680
1977	Cigarette Lighter Rhodium 7500NR50	Retrd.	1982	130.00	1134-1400
1987	Clock, Athena 9280NR102	Retrd.	1992	330.00	350-430
1987	Clock, Belle Epoque 9280NR104	Retrd.	1992	N/A	782-1000
1987	Clock, Colosseum 9280NR105	Retrd.	1992	N/A	536-679
1987	Clock, El Dorado 9280NR106	Retrd.	1992	N/A	509-536
1987	Clock, Napoleon 9280NR101	Retrd.	1992	N/A	300-475
1987	Clock, Polar Star 9280NR103	Retrd.	1992	N/A	419-500
1990	Coin Box no hinge 7400090001	Retrd.	1991	N/A	1008
1991	Coin Box w/hinge 7400090001	Retrd.	1995	N/A	313-420
1985	Dachshund-Lg. 7641NR75 - M. Schreck	Retrd.	1991	48.00	113-400
1985	Dachshund-Mini (wire tail) 7672NR42 - M. Schreck	Retrd.	1988	20.00	155-250
1987	Dachshund-Mini (frosted tail) 7672NR042000 - A. Stocker	Retrd.	1995	20.00	85-190
1993	Dick Gosling 7613NR000004 - A. Stocker	Retrd.	1999	37.50	38-70
1982	Dinner Bell-Lg. 7467NR71 - M. Schreck	Retrd.	1991	80.00	135-290
1987	Dinner Bell-Medium 7467NR54 - M. Schreck	Retrd.	1997	80.00	90-175
1981	Dog (Pluto) 7635NR70 - M. Schreck	Retrd.	1990	44.00	115-219
1983	Duck-Lg. 7653NR75 - M. Schreck	Retrd.	1987	44.00	563-750
1983	Duck-Med. 7653NR55 - M. Schreck	Retrd.	1988	38.00	181-375
1981	Duck-Mini 7653NR45 - M. Schreck	Retrd.	1988	16.00	67-115
1983	Elephant-Lg. 7640NR55 - M. Schreck	Retrd.	1989	90.00	150-360
1988	Elephant-Sm. 7640NR60 - A. Stocker	Retrd.	1995	70.00	105-180
1985	Falcon Head-Lg. 7645NR100 - M. Schreck	Retrd.	1991	600.00	1940-4000
1987	Falcon Head-Sm. 7645NR45 - M. Schreck	Retrd.	1991	60.00	175-313
1987	Fox-Lg. (black nose) 7629NR70 - A. Stocker	Retrd.	1999	50.00	75-157
1987	Fox-Lg. (frosted nose) 7629NR70 - A. Stocker	Retrd.	1988	50.00	125-207
1988	Fox-Mini Running 7677NR055 - A. Stocker	Retrd.	1996	35.00	57-95
1985	Frog (black eyes) 7642NR48 - M. Schreck	Retrd.	1991	30.00	151-225
1984	Frog (clear eyes) 7642NR48 - M. Schreck	Retrd.	1985	30.00	285-420
1985	Grapes (European) 7550NR150070 - Team	Retrd.	1989	N/A	1008-1600
1983	Grapes-Lg. 7550NR30015 - Team	Retrd.	1988	250.00	2000-2620
1983	Grapes-Med. (gold & rhodium) 7550NR20029 - Team	Retrd.	1985	N/A	1016-1400
1983	Grapes-Med. (gold) 7550NR20029 - Team	Retrd.	1995	300.00	352-640
1983	Grapes-Med. (rhodium) 7550NR20029 - Team	Retrd.	1985	N/A	1629-1810
1983	Grapes-Sm. (gold & rhodium) 7550NR20015 - Team	Retrd.	1985	N/A	1278-1420
1983	Grapes-Sm. (gold) 7550NR20015 - Team	Retrd.	1995	200.00	313-475
1983	Grapes-Sm. (rhodium) 7550NR20015 - Team	Retrd.	1985	N/A	1449-1610
1992	Harp 7477NR000003 - M. Zendron	Retrd.	1998	175.00	175-282
1993	Harry Gosling 7613NR000003 - A. Stocker	Retrd.	1999	37.50	38-70
1982	Hedgehog-Kg. Sz. 7630NR60 - Team	Retrd.	1987	98.00	938-1000
1981	Hedgehog-Lg. 7630NR50 - M. Schreck	Retrd.	1987	65.00	175-420
1988	Hedgehog-Lg. 7630NR70 - M. Schreck	Retrd.	1996	120.00	174-244
1981	Hedgehog-Med. 7630NR40 - M. Schreck	Retrd.	1987	44.00	155-260
1982	Hedgehog-Sm. 7630NR30 - Team	Retrd.	1987	38.00	464-563
1988	Hippopotamus 7626NR65 - A. Stocker	Retrd.	1992	70.00	140-170
1989	Hippopotamus-Sm. 7626NR055000 - A. Stocker	Retrd.	1995	70.00	88-140
1985	Hummingbird (Gold) 7552NR100 - Team	Retrd.	1988	200.00	1080-2100
1985	Hummingbird (Rhodium) 7552NR200 - Team	Retrd.	1986	200.00	5200-6000
1990	Kingfisher 7621NR000001 - M. Stamey	Retrd.	1992	75.00	144-210
1991	Kitten 7634NR028000 - M. Stamey	Retrd.	1995	47.50	63-110
1991	Kiwi 7617NR043000 - M. Stamey	Retrd.	1996	37.50	60-100
1987	Koala (right) 7673NR40 - A. Stocker	Retrd.	1993	65.00	95-150
1989	Koala-Mini (left) 7673NR30 - A. Stocker	Retrd.	1993	45.00	55-172
1977	Lighter (European) 7500NR050	Retrd.	1983	N/A	1400-3000
1982	Lighter 7462NR062 - M. Schreck	Retrd.	1990	160.00	275-471
1992	Lute 7477NR000004 - M. Zendron	Retrd.	1997	125.00	125-195
1996	Madame Penguin 7661NR000002 - A. Stocker	Retrd.	1999	85.00	90-100
1986	Mallard 7647NR80 - M. Schreck	Retrd.	1994	80.00	161-225
1992	Mother Beaver 7616NR000001 - A. Stocker	Retrd.	1996	110.00	124-200
1993	Mother Goose 7613NR000001 - A. Stocker	Retrd.	1999	75.00	75-105
1982	Mouse-Kg. Sz. 7631NR60 - M. Schreck	Retrd.	1987	95.00	1540-2500
1982	Mouse-Lg. 7631NR50 - M. Schreck	Retrd.	1987	69.00	907-1500
1976	Mouse-Med. (coil tail) 7631NR040 - M. Schreck	Retrd.	1995	85.00	105-180
1976	Mouse-Med. (floppy tail) 7631NR040 - M. Schreck	Retrd.	1995	60.00	126-150
1976	Mouse-Med. (leather tail) 7631NR040 - M. Schreck	Retrd.	1995	60.00	1397-1552
1976	Mouse-Med. (stone cut ears) 7631NR040 - M. Schreck	Retrd.	1995	60.00	455-505
1981	Mouse-Mini 7655NR23 - M. Schreck	Retrd.	1988	16.00	53-138
1976	Mouse-Sm. (coil tail) 7631NR30 - M. Schreck	Retrd.	1991	42.50	82-161
1976	Mouse-Sm. (flexible tail) 7631NR30 - M. Schreck	Retrd.	1978	40.00	145-161
1976	Mouse-Sm. (leather tail) 7631NR30 - M. Schreck	Retrd.	1991	40.00	279-310
1989	Mushrooms 7472NR030000 - A. Stocker	Retrd.	1998	35.00	35-105
1992	Nativity Angel 7475NR000009 - Team	Retrd.	1993	65.00	150-200
1991	Nativity Arch 7475NR0010 - Team	Retrd.	1993	N/A	123-245
1991	Nativity Holy Family 7475NR001 - Team	Retrd.	1993	N/A	114-175
1991	Nativity Holy Family w/Arch 7475NR001 - Team	Retrd.	1993	N/A	325-395
1992	Nativity Set (European) 6475NR0000099 - Team	Retrd.	1993	N/A	650-1000
1992	Nativity Shepherd 7475NR000007 - Team	Retrd.	1993	65.00	90-175
1992	Nativity Wise Men (Set/3) 7475NR200000 - Team	Retrd.	1993	175.00	219-360
1989	Old Timer Automobile 7473NR000001 - G. Stamey	Retrd.	1995	130.00	211-263
1989	Owl 7621NR000003 - M. Stamey	Retrd.	1992	70.00	175-313
1989	Owl, Parrot, Kingfisher, Toucan - M. Stamey	Retrd.	N/A	285.00	600-1063
1981	Owl-Sm. 7636NR046000 - M. Schreck	Retrd.	1995	59.00	69-140
1989	Parrot 7621NR000004 - M. Stamey	Retrd.	1992	70.00	163-250
1988	Partridge 7625NR50 - A. Stocker	Retrd.	1990	85.00	119-182
1991	Pear 7476NR000002 - M. Stamey	Retrd.	1997	175.00	169-340
1984	Penguin-Lg. 7643NR085000 - M. Schreck	Retrd.	1995	44.00	133-200
1986	Picture Frame/Oval 7505NR75G - Team	Retrd.	1989	90.00	293-445
1984	Picture Frame/Square 7506NR60G - M. Schreck	Retrd.	1989	100.00	214-425
1983	Picture Frame/Square 7506NR60R - M. Schreck	Retrd.	1987	N/A	211-234
1982	Pig-Lg. 7638NR65 - M. Schreck	Retrd.	1987	50.00	423-550
1984	Pig-Med. (crystal tail) 7638NR50 - M. Schreck	Retrd.	N/A	42.50	268-476
1982	Pig-Mini (crystal tail) 7657NR27 - M. Schreck	Retrd.	1994	29.50	85-125
XX	Pillbox 7506NR030	Retrd.	1983	N/A	194
XX	Pillbox 7506NR050	Retrd.	1983	N/A	257-543
1983	Pineapple/Rhodium-Giant 7507NR26002 - M. Schreck	Retrd.	1986	1750.00	2115-3750
1982	Pineapple/Rhodium-Lg. 7507NR105002 - M. Schreck	Retrd.	1986	150.00	350-657
1986	Pineapple/Rhodium-Sm. 7507NR060002 - M. Schreck	Retrd.	1986	55.00	188-360
1987	Polar Bear-Large 7649NR85 - A. Stocker	Retrd.	1997	140.00	175-295
1992	Poodle 7619NR000003 - A. Stocker	Retrd.	1997	125.00	150-188
1981	Pyramid-Lg.-Crystal Cal 7450NR50095 - M. Schreck	Retrd.	1993	90.00	200-250
1976	Pyramid-Lg.-Helio 7450NR50 - M. Schreck	Retrd.	1990	N/A	520
1981	Pyramid-Lg.-Vitrl Med. 7450NR50087 - M. Schreck	Retrd.	1993	90.00	180-295
1986	Pyramid-Small-Bermuda Blue 7450NR40088 - M. Schreck	Retrd.	1992	N/A	165-214
1987	Pyramid-Small-Crystal Cal. 7450NR40095 - M. Schreck	Retrd.	1997	100.00	140-210
1986	Pyramid-Small-Vitrail Light 7450NR400 - M. Schreck	Retrd.	1990	N/A	500-549
1987	Pyramid-Small-Vitrail Med. 7450NR40087 - M. Schreck	Retrd.	1997	100.00	140-175
1983	Rabbit-Lg. 7652NR45 - M. Schreck	Retrd.	1988	38.00	396-531
1981	Rabbit-Mini 7652NR20 - M. Schreck	Retrd.	1988	16.00	100-125
1988	Rabbit-Mini Lying 7678NR030000 - A. Stocker	Retrd.	1995	35.00	67-125
1988	Rhinoceros-Lg. 7622NR70 - A. Stocker	Retrd.	1992	70.00	144-180
1990	Rhinoceros-Sm. 7622NR060000 - A. Stocker	Retrd.	1995	70.00	64-150
1994	Roe Deer Fawn 7608NR000001 - E. Mair	Retrd.	1998	75.00	74-150
1982	Salt & Pepper 7508NR068034	Retrd.	1988	100.00	367-530
XX	Salt & Pepper Rhodium Cruet Set 7502NR030-031-032	Retrd.	1983	N/A	2394-2660
1984	Salt and Pepper Shakers 7508NR068034 - Team	Retrd.	1988	80.00	271-400
1982	Schnapps Glasses, Set/3 7468NR039000 - Team (European)	Retrd.	1990	N/A	225-250
1982	Schnapps Glasses, Set/6 7468NR039000 - Team	Retrd.	1990	150.00	480-518
1990	Scotch Terrier 7619NR000002 - A. Stocker	Retrd.	1996	60.00	88-135
1985	Seal-Large (black nose) 7646NR085000 - M. Schreck	Retrd.	1995	85.00	125-282
1985	Seal-Large (black whiskers-left) 7646NR085000 - M. Schreck	Retrd.	1995	85.00	119-157
1985	Seal-Large (black whiskers-right) 7646NR085000 - M. Schreck	Retrd.	1995	85.00	531
1985	Seal-Large (black whiskers-straight) 7646NR085000 - M. Schreck	Retrd.	1995	85.00	150-300
1985	Seal-Large (silver whiskers) 7646NR085000 - M. Schreck	Retrd.	1995	85.00	135-250
1986	Seal-Mini (black nose) 7663NR46 - A. Stocker	Retrd.	N/A	45.00	205-275
1986	Seal-Mini (silver whiskers) 7663NR46 - A. Stocker	Retrd.	N/A	45.00	60-350
XX	Silver Crystal City Espositore, set/8 9097422 - G. Stamey/M. Parma	4,999	1993	N/A	1055-2040
1990	Silver Crystal City-Cathedral 7474NR000021 - G. Stamey	Retrd.	1994	95.00	138-250
1991	Silver Crystal City-City Gates 7474NR000023 - G. Stamey	Retrd.	1994	95.00	113-163
1991	Silver Crystal City-City Tower 7474NR000022 - G. Stamey	Retrd.	1994	37.50	50-185
1990	Silver Crystal City-Houses I & II (Set/2) 7474NR100000 - G. Stamey	Retrd.	1994	75.00	85-150
1990	Silver Crystal City-Houses III & IV (Set/2) 7474NR200000 - G. Stamey	Retrd.	1994	75.00	85-150
1990	Silver Crystal City-Poplars (Set/3) 7474NR020003 - G. Stamey	Retrd.	1994	40.00	120-157
1993	Silver Crystal City-Town Hall 7474NR000027 - G. Stamey	Retrd.	1994	135.00	185-319
1986	Snail 7648NR030000 - M. Stamey	Retrd.	1995	35.00	78-125
1991	South Sea Shell 7624NR72000 - M. Stamey	Retrd.	1994	110.00	113-200
1992	Sparrow 7650NR000001 - C. Schneiderbauer	Retrd.	1997	29.50	40-85
1983	Sparrow-Lg. 7650NR32 - M. Schreck	Retrd.	1988	38.00	181-313
1981	Sparrow-Mini 7650NR20 - M. Schreck	Retrd.	1991	16.00	61-125
1985	Squirrel (black nut) 7662NR42 - M. Schreck	Retrd.	N/A	55.00	397-441
1985	Squirrel (small ears) 7662NR42 - M. Schreck	Retrd.	1994	55.00	125-188
1977	Swan-Lg. (chandlier) 7633NR63 - M. Schreck	Retrd.	N/A	75.00	75-140
1983	Swan-Mini 7658NR27 - M. Schreck	Retrd.	1988	16.00	125-200
1982	Swan-Small 7633NR38V1 - M. Schreck	Retrd.	1988	35.00	35-80
1989	Swan-Small 7633NR38V2 - M. Schreck	Retrd.	1995	35.00	50
1987	Table Bell-Small 7467NR039000 - M. Schreck	Retrd.	1999	60.00	65
XX	Table Magnifier (gold chain) 7800NR026	Retrd.	1984	N/A	1015-1200
1981	Table Magnifier (no chain) 7510NR01G	Retrd.	1984	70.00	961-1200
1981	Table Magnifier (no chain) 7510NR01R	Retrd.	1984	80.00	914-1800
XX	Table Magnifier (rhodium chain) 7800NR026	Retrd.	1984	N/A	787-875
1981	Table Magnifier (with chain) 7510NR01R	Retrd.	1984	80.00	914-1200
1993	Three South Sea Fish 7644NR057000 - M. Stamey	Retrd.	1998	135.00	137-194
1993	Tom Gosling 7613NR000002 - A. Stocker	Retrd.	1999	37.50	38-70
1989	Toucan 7621NR000002 - M. Stamey	Retrd.	1992	70.00	157-225
1982	Treasure Box (Heart/Butterfly) 7465NR52/100 - M. Schreck	Retrd.	1990	80.00	325-438
1982	Treasure Box (Heart/Flower) 7465NR52 - M. Schreck	Retrd.	1988	80.00	220-525
1982	Treasure Box (Oval/Butterfly) 7466NR063100 - M. Schreck	Retrd.	1988	80.00	270-360
1982	Treasure Box (Oval/Flower) 7466NR063000 - M. Schreck	Retrd.	1990	80.00	282-360
1982	Treasure Box (Round/Butterfly) 7464NR50/100 - M. Schreck	Retrd.	1988	80.00	290-375
1982	Treasure Box (Round/Flower) 7464NR50 - M. Schreck	Retrd.	1990	80.00	256-438
1983	Turtle-King Sz. 7632NR75 - M. Schreck	Retrd.	1988	58.00	375-600
1981	Turtle-Large 7632NR045000 - M. Schreck	Retrd.	1998	48.00	65-113
1981	Turtle-Small 7632NR030000 - M. Schreck	Retrd.	1996	35.00	57-105
1986	Vase 7511NR70 - Team	Retrd.	1990	50.00	169-250
1989	Walrus 7620NR100000 - M. Stamey	Retrd.	1993	120.00	181-230
1987	Whale 7628NR80 - M. Stamey	Retrd.	1991	70.00	250-313
1981	Zoo-Mini (Set/6) 7656NR006 - Team	Retrd.	1982	90.00	872-1250

United Design Corp.

Angels Collection - D. Newburn, unless otherwise noted

YEAR ISSUE		EDITION LIMIT	YEAR RETD.	ISSUE PRICE	*QUOTE U.S.$
2000	AA-Arch Angel w/Lion & Lamb AA-184 - J. Beasely	7,500		70.00	70
1999	Angel in Flight AA-178 - G.G. Santiago	5,000		N/A	N/A
1993	Angel of Flight AA-032 - K. Memoli	10,000		100.00	110
1993	Angel w/ Birds AA-034	10,000	1995	75.00	75
1994	Angel w/ Book AA-058	10,000	1998	84.00	90
1994	Angel w/ Christ Child AA-061 - K. Memoli	10,000		84.00	90
1993	Angel w/ Lilies AA-033	10,000	1998	80.00	84
1993	Angel w/ Lilies, Crimson AA-040	10,000	1996	80.00	80
1992	Angel, Lamb & Critters AA-021 - S. Bradford	10,000	1998	90.00	95
1996	Angel, Lion & Fawn AA-093 - K. Memoli	20,000		280.00	280
1992	Angel, Lion & Lamb AA-020 - K. Memoli	10,000	1994	135.00	195-300
1994	Angel, Roses and Bluebirds AA-054	10,000		65.00	84
1996	Angels, Roses & Doves AA-112	10,000	1999	75.00	84
1993	Autumn Angel AA-035	10,000	1996	70.00	70-80
1993	Autumn Angel, Emerald AA-041	10,000	1996	70.00	70
1995	Celestial Guardian Angel AA-069 - S. Bradford	10,000	1997	120.00	120
1991	Christmas Angel AA-003 - S. Bradford	10,000	1994	125.00	125
1991	Classical Angel AA-005 - S. Bradford	10,000	1998	79.00	79

*Quotes have been rounded up to nearest dollar

YEAR ISSUE	EDITION LIMIT	YEAR RETD.	ISSUE PRICE	*QUOTE U.S.$
1994 Dreaming of Angels AA-060 - K. Memoli	10,000		120.00	130
1996 Dreaming of Angels, pastel AA-111 - K. Memoli	10,000		120.00	130
1994 Earth Angel AA-059 - S. Bradford	10,000	1997	84.00	84
1997 Eyes Toward Heaven AA-132 - K. Memoli	10,000	1999	130.00	130
1991 The Gift AA-009 - S. Bradford	2,500	1991	135.00	550-665
1992 The Gift '92 AA-018 - S. Bradford	3,500	1992	140.00	325-350
1993 The Gift '93 AA-037 - S. Bradford	3,500	1993	120.00	225-235
1994 The Gift '94 AA-057	5,000	1994	140.00	165-175
1995 The Gift '95 AA-067	5,000	1995	140.00	140-180
1996 The Gift '96 AA-094	5,000	1996	140.00	140
1997 The Gift '97 AA-128 - P.J. Jonas	7,500	1997	150.00	150
1998 The Gift '98 AA-147 - P.J. Jonas-Pendergast	5,000		150.00	150
1999 The Gift '99 AA-176 - K. Memoli	5,000		N/A	N/A
2000 The Gift 2000 AA-187 - C. Smith	7,500		75.00	75
1995 Guardian Angel, Lion & Lamb AA-083 - S. Bradford	10,000	1998	165.00	170-195
1995 Guardian Angel, Lion & Lamb, lt. AA-068 - S. Bradford	10,000		165.00	170
1994 Harvest Angel AA-063 - S. Bradford	10,000	1997	84.00	84
1991 Heavenly Shepherdess AA-008 - S. Bradford	10,000	1999	99.00	99
1992 Joy To The World AA-016	10,000	1996	90.00	95
1995 A Little Closer to Heaven AA-081 - K. Memoli	10,000	1998	230.00	245
1995 A Little Closer to Heaven, lt. AA-085 - K. Memoli	10,000		230.00	230
1993 Madonna AA-031 - K. Memoli	10,000	1999	100.00	100
1991 Messenger of Peace AA-006 - S. Bradford	10,000	1997	75.00	79
1999 Musical Motion AA-174 - P.J. Couch	5,000		55.00	55
1992 Peaceful Encounter AA-017	10,000		100.00	100
1997 Rejoice AA-130 - K. Memoli	10,000		90.00	90
1997 Rejoice, silver AA-143 - K. Memoli	10,000	1997	90.00	90
1997 Serenity AA-131 - K. Memoli	10,000	1999	90.00	90
1997 Serenity, silver AA-144 - K. Memoli	10,000	1997	90.00	90
1998 Spirit of Autumn AA-158 - G.G. Santiago	15,000		200.00	200
1998 Spirit of Spring AA-146 - G.G. Santiago	15,000		200.00	200
1999 Spirit of Summer AA-170 - G.G. Santiago	15,000		200.00	200
1997 Spirit of Winter AA-142 - G.G. Santiago	15,000		200.00	200
1995 Starlight Starbright AA-066	10,000	1998	70.00	80
1991 Trumpeter Angel AA-004 - S. Bradford	10,000	1997	99.00	99
1992 Winter Angel AA-019	10,000		75.00	75
2000 Winter Flight AA-183 - P.J. Couch	2,000		250.00	250
1991 Winter Rose Angel AA-007 - S. Bradford	10,000	1994	65.00	65

Backyard Birds™ - Various

YEAR ISSUE	EDITION LIMIT	YEAR RETD.	ISSUE PRICE	*QUOTE U.S.$
1994 Allen's on Pink Flowers BB-044 - P.J. Jonas	Retrd.	1999	22.00	22
1994 Allen's on Purple Morning Glory BB-051 - P.J. Jonas	Retrd.	1999	22.00	22
1989 Baltimore Oriole BB-024 - S. Bradford	Retrd.	1996	19.50	22
1989 Blue Jay BB-026 - S. Bradford	Open		19.50	22
1989 Blue Jay, Baby BB-027 - S. Bradford	Retrd.	1996	15.00	15
1990 Bluebird (Upright) BB-031 - S. Bradford	Retrd.	1997	20.00	20
1988 Bluebird BB-009 - S. Bradford	Open		15.00	21
1988 Bluebird Hanging BB-017 - S. Bradford	Retrd.	1990	11.00	17
1988 Bluebird, Small BB-001 - S. Bradford	Retrd.	1999	10.00	11
1994 Broadbill on Blue Morning Glory BB-053 - P.J. Jonas	Retrd.	1999	22.00	22
1994 Broadbill on Trumpet Vine BB-043 - P.J. Jonas	Retrd.	1999	22.00	22
1994 Broadbill on Yellow Fuscia BB-055 - P.J. Jonas	Retrd.	1997	22.00	22
1994 Broadbill Pair on Yellow Flowers BB-048 - P.J. Jonas	Retrd.	1997	30.00	30
1988 Cardinal Hanging BB-018 - S. Bradford	Retrd.	1990	11.00	11
1988 Cardinal, Female BB-011 - S. Bradford	Retrd.	1999	15.00	17
1988 Cardinal, Male BB-013 - S. Bradford	Open		15.00	18
1988 Cardinal, Small BB-002 - S. Bradford	Open		10.00	11
1990 Cedar Waxwing Babies BB-033 - S. Bradford	Retrd.	1996	22.00	22
1990 Cedar Waxwing BB-032 - S. Bradford	Retrd.	1996	20.00	20
1988 Chickadee BB-010 - S. Bradford	Retrd.	1999	15.00	18
1988 Chickadee Hanging BB-019 - S. Bradford	Retrd.	1990	11.00	11
1988 Chickadee, Small BB-003 - S. Bradford	Retrd.	1999	10.00	11
1990 Evening Grosbeak BB-034 - S. Bradford	Retrd.	1996	22.00	22
1989 Goldfinch BB-028 - S. Bradford	Open		16.50	20
1989 Hoot Owl BB-025 - S. Bradford	Retrd.	1997	15.00	20
1988 Hummingbird BB-012 - S. Bradford	Open		15.00	18
1988 Hummingbird Female, Small BB-005 - S. Bradford	Retrd.	1991	10.00	10
1988 Hummingbird Flying, Small BB-004 - S. Bradford	Retrd.	1999	10.00	11
1988 Hummingbird Sm., Hanging BB-022 - S. Bradford	Retrd.	1990	11.00	11
1988 Hummingbird, Lg., Hanging BB-023 - S. Bradford	Retrd.	1990	15.00	15
1990 Indigo Bunting BB-036 - S. Bradford	Retrd.	1996	20.00	20
1990 Indigo Bunting, Female BB-039 - S. Bradford	Retrd.	1996	20.00	20
1994 Magnificent Pair on Trumpet Vine BB-046 - P.J. Jonas	Retrd.	1997	30.00	30
1990 Nuthatch, White-throated BB-037 - S. Bradford	Retrd.	1996	20.00	20
1990 Painted Bunting BB-040 - S. Bradford	Retrd.	1996	20.00	20
1990 Painted Bunting, Female BB-041 - S. Bradford	Retrd.	1996	20.00	20
1990 Purple Finch BB-038 - S. Bradford	Retrd.	1996	20.00	20
1988 Red-winged Blackbird BB-014 - S. Bradford	Retrd.	1991	15.00	17
1988 Robin Babies BB-008 - S. Bradford	Retrd.	1999	15.00	19
1988 Robin Baby, Small BB-006 - S. Bradford	Retrd.	1999	10.00	11
1988 Robin BB-015 - S. Bradford	Open		15.00	21
1988 Robin Hanging BB-020 - S. Bradford	Retrd.	1990	11.00	11
1990 Rose Breasted Grosbeak BB-042 - S. Bradford	Retrd.	1996	20.00	20
1994 Rubythroat on Pink Fuscia BB-054 - P.J. Jonas	Retrd.	1997	22.00	22
1994 Rubythroat on Red Morning Glory BB-052 - P.J. Jonas	Open		22.00	22
1994 Rubythroat on Thistle BB-049 - P.J. Jonas	Open		16.50	17
1994 Rubythroat on Yellow Flowers BB-045 - P.J. Jonas	Retrd.	1997	22.00	22
1994 Rubythroat Pair on Pink Flowers BB-047 - P.J. Jonas	Retrd.	1999	30.00	30
1989 Saw-Whet Owl BB-029 - S. Bradford	Retrd.	1999	15.00	18
1988 Sparrow BB-016 - S. Bradford	Open		15.00	17
1988 Sparrow Hanging BB-021 - S. Bradford	Retrd.	1990	11.00	11
1988 Sparrow, Small BB-007 - S. Bradford	Retrd.	1996	10.00	11
1989 Woodpecker BB-030 - S. Bradford	Retrd.	1997	16.50	20

Easter Bunny Family™ - D. Kennicutt

YEAR ISSUE	EDITION LIMIT	YEAR RETD.	ISSUE PRICE	*QUOTE U.S.$
1994 All Hidden SEC-045	Retrd.	1996	24.50	25
1989 Auntie Bunny SEC-008	Retrd.	1992	20.00	23
1992 Auntie Bunny w/Cake SEC-033R	Retrd.	1994	20.00	22
1991 Baby in Buggy, Boy SEC-027R	Retrd.	1994	20.00	22
1991 Baby in Buggy, Girl SEC-029R	Retrd.	1994	20.00	22
1994 Babysitter SEC-049	Retrd.	1999	24.50	25
1999 Baseball Buddies SEC-075	Open		18.00	18
1999 Baskets to Fill SEC-074	Open		18.00	18
1994 Bath Time SEC-044	Retrd.	1997	24.50	25
1995 Bed Time SEC-057	Retrd.	1999	24.00	24
1992 Boy Bunny w/Large Egg SEC-034R	Retrd.	1994	20.00	22
1991 Bubba In Wheelbarrow SEC-021	Retrd.	1993	20.00	20
1990 Bubba w/Wagon SEC-016	Retrd.	1993	16.50	18
1988 Bunnies, Basket Of SEC-001	Retrd.	1991	13.00	18
1991 Bunny Boy w/Basket SEC-025	Retrd.	1993	20.00	20
1988 Bunny Boy w/Duck SEC-002	Retrd.	1991	13.00	18
1997 Bunny Express SEC-070	Open		27.00	27
1988 Bunny Girl w/Hen SEC-004	Retrd.	1991	13.00	18
2000 Bunny Tea Party - SEC-079	Retrd.	2000	20.00	20
1989 Bunny w/Prize Egg SEC-010	Retrd.	1993	19.50	20
1988 Bunny, Easter SEC-003	Retrd.	1991	15.00	18
1993 Christening Day SEC-040	Retrd.	1995	20.00	22
1998 Doll Buggy, 1998 SEC-071	Yr.Iss.	1999	15.00	15
1989 Ducky w/Bonnet, Blue SEC-015	Retrd.	1992	10.00	12
1989 Ducky w/Bonnet, Pink SEC-014	Retrd.	1992	10.00	12
1996 Easter Bunny In Evening Clothes-SEC-064	Retrd.	1998	20.00	20
1992 Easter Bunny w/Back Pack SEC-030	Retrd.	1999	20.00	22
1990 Easter Bunny w/Crystal SEC-017	Retrd.	1995	23.00	25
1993 Easter Bunny, Chocolate Egg SEC-041	Retrd.	1996	23.00	25
1995 Easter Cookies SEC-052	Open		24.00	25
1997 Easter Dress SEC-067	Retrd.	1999	22.00	22
1989 Easter Egg Hunt SEC-012	Retrd.	1995	16.50	22
1996 Easter Pageant - SEC-059	Retrd.	1999	17.00	17
1996 Easter Parade - SEC-063	Retrd.	1998	25.00	25
1998 Egg Paint Design SEC-072	Open		18.00	18
1993 Egg Roll SEC-036	Open		23.00	25
1991 Fancy Find SEC-028	Retrd.	1995	20.00	22
1996 First Kiss - SEC-061	Retrd.	2000	20.00	20
1995 First Outing SEC-054	Retrd.	1998	19.00	20
1994 First Steps SEC-048	Retrd.	1998	24.50	25
1997 Friendship, 1997 SEC-068	Yr.Iss.	1997	22.00	22
1997 The Gardener SEC-069	Retrd.	2000	22.00	22
1994 Gift Carrot SEC-046	Retrd.	2000	22.00	22
1993 Girl Bunny w/Basket SEC-039	Retrd.	1999	20.00	22
1992 Girl Bunny w/Large Egg SEC-035R	Retrd.	1994	20.00	22
1993 Grandma & Quilt SEC-037	Retrd.	1997	23.00	25
1992 Grandma w/ Bible SEC-031	Retrd.	1996	20.00	22
1996 Grandma's Dress Makers Form-1996-SEC-066	Yr.Iss.	1996	25.00	25
1992 Grandpa w/Carrots SEC-032R	Retrd.	1994	20.00	22
1996 Grandpa w/Sunflowers - SEC-065	Retrd.	1999	20.00	20
1999 Happy Spring SEC-077	Open		18.00	18
1990 Hen w/Chick SEC-018	Retrd.	1992	23.00	23
1994 Large Prize Egg SEC-047	Retrd.	1999	22.00	22
1989 Little Sis w/Lolly SEC-009	Retrd.	1992	14.50	18
1993 Lop Ear Dying Eggs SEC-042	Retrd.	1997	23.00	25
1996 Lop Girl w/Gift Box - SEC-060	Retrd.	1999	20.00	20
1991 Lop-Ear w/Crystal SEC-022	Retrd.	1999	23.00	25
1993 Mom Storytime SEC-043	Retrd.	1999	20.00	22
1996 Mom w/Chocolate Egg - SEC-062	Retrd.	1998	25.00	25
1990 Momma Making Basket SEC-019	Retrd.	1992	23.00	23
1990 Mother Goose SEC-020	Retrd.	1992	16.50	20
1991 Nest of Bunny Eggs SEC-023	Retrd.	1998	17.50	22
1995 Painting Lessons SEC-053	Retrd.	1998	19.00	20
2000 Potter's Bench - SEC-080	Yr. Iss.		25.00	25
1995 Quality Inspector SEC-055	Retrd.	1998	19.00	20
1988 Rabbit, Grandma SEC-005	Retrd.	1991	15.00	20
1988 Rabbit, Grandpa SEC-006	Retrd.	1991	15.00	20
1988 Rabbit, Momma w/Bonnet SEC-007	Retrd.	1991	15.00	20
1989 Rock-A-Bye Bunny SEC-013	Retrd.	1995	20.00	25
1993 Rocking Horse SEC-038	Retrd.	1996	20.00	22
1989 Sis & Bubba Sharing SEC-011	Retrd.	1996	22.50	25
2000 Slam Dunk Hares - SEC-078	Retrd.	2000	25.00	25
1999 Smile (1999 Coll. Piece) SEC-076	Yr.Iss.	1999	18.00	18
1998 Spring Break SEC-073	Open		15.00	15
1995 Spring Flying SEC-058	Retrd.	1997	19.00	19
1995 Team Work SEC-051	Open		24.00	24
1995 Two in a Basket SEC-056	Retrd.	1997	24.00	25
1991 Victorian Auntie Bunny SEC-026	Retrd.	1993	20.00	20
1991 Victorian Momma SEC-024	Retrd.	1993	20.00	20
1994 Wheelbarrow Full SEC-050	Retrd.	2000	24.50	25

Easter Bunny Family™ Babies - D. Kennicutt

YEAR ISSUE	EDITION LIMIT	YEAR RETD.	ISSUE PRICE	*QUOTE U.S.$
1995 Baby in Basket SEC-815	Open		8.00	8
1994 Baby on Blanket, Naptime SEC-807	Retrd.	1999	6.50	7
1996 Baby w/Diaper & Bottle, Blue - SEC-825	Retrd.	1999	8.00	8
1996 Baby w/Diaper & Bottle, Pink - SEC-817	Retrd.	1999	8.00	8
1996 Baby w/Diaper & Bottle, Yellow - SEC-824	Retrd.	1999	8.00	8
1995 Basket of Carrots SEC-812	Open		8.00	8
1994 Boy Baby w/Blocks SEC-805	Open		6.50	7
1994 Boy w/Baseball Bat SEC-801	Open		6.50	7
1996 Boy w/Baseball Mitt - SEC-822	Open		8.00	8
1994 Boy w/Basket and Egg SEC-802	Open		6.50	7
1996 Boy w/Big Teddy - SEC-819	Retrd.	1999	8.00	8
1995 Boy w/Butterfly SEC-814	Open		8.00	8
1994 Boy w/Stick Horse SEC-803	Retrd.	1999	6.50	7
1996 Boy w/Train Engine - SEC-816	Retrd.	1999	8.00	8
1997 Bubble Bath SEC-828	Retrd.	1999	8.50	9
1998 Bunny & Birdhouse SEC-831	Open		8.50	9
1996 Dress Up Girl - SEC-821	Retrd.	1999	8.00	8
1996 Egg Delivery - SEC-823	Retrd.	1999	8.00	8
1995 Gift Egg SEC-808	Retrd.	1999	8.00	8
1996 Girl w/Apron Full - SEC-820	Open		8.00	8
1994 Girl w/Big Egg SEC-806	Open		6.50	7
1994 Girl w/Blanket SEC-800	Retrd.	1999	6.50	7
1996 Girl w/Book - SEC-818	Retrd.	1999	8.00	8
1994 Girl w/Toy Rabbit SEC-804	Retrd.	1999	6.50	7
1999 Grandma's Girl SEC-833	Open		8.50	9
1997 Grandpa's Boy SEC-826	Open		8.50	9
1999 H.M.S. Springtime SEC-835	Open		8.50	9
1995 Hostess SEC-810	Open		8.00	8
1995 Lop Ear & Flower Pot SEC-809	Open		8.00	8
1999 Mary's Lamb SEC-834	Open		8.50	9
1998 The Rocking Chair SEC-832	Open		8.50	9
1997 Soccer Player SEC-829	Open		8.50	9
1999 Special Delivery SEC-836	Open		8.50	9
1995 Spring Flowers SEC-813	Retrd.	1999	8.00	8
1998 Spring Showers SEC-830	Open		8.50	9
1995 Tea Party SEC-811	Open		8.00	8
1997 Thank You SEC-827	Retrd.	1999	8.50	9

Kooky Cats™ - D. Wentzel

YEAR ISSUE	EDITION LIMIT	YEAR RETD.	ISSUE PRICE	*QUOTE U.S.$
2000 Kooky Cat Chef ND-0092	2,500		90.00	90
2000 Kooky Basket Case ND-0091	2,500		90.00	90
2000 Kooky Cupholder ND-0093	2,500		90.00	90
2000 Kooky Mouse Slide ND-0094	2,500		140.00	140
2000 Kooky Waiter ND-0095	2,500		90.00	90

Legend of Santa Claus™ - L. Miller, unless otherwise noted

YEAR ISSUE	EDITION LIMIT	YEAR RETD.	ISSUE PRICE	*QUOTE U.S.$
1992 Arctic Santa CF-035 - S. Bradford	7,500	1997	90.00	150-165
1988 Assembly Required CF-017	7,500	1994	79.00	130
1997 Bells of Christmas Morn CF-074 - K. Memoli	7,500		190.00	190
1997 Bells of Christmas Morn, Victorian CF-075 - K. Memoli	7,500		190.00	190
1991 Blessed Flight CF-032 - K. Memoli	7,500	1994	159.00	325-350
1996 Blessing Santa CF-066 - K. Memoli	10,000		160.00	170
1987 Checking His List CF-009	15,000	1994	75.00	155-170
1997 A Christmas Galleon CF-073 - K. Memoli	7,500		150.00	150
1989 Christmas Harmony CF-020 - S. Bradford	7,500	1992	85.00	119-130
1998 Christmas Sharing CF-080 - K. Memoli	10,000		150.00	150
1992 The Christmas Tree CF-038	7,500	1995	90.00	125-165
2000 Come an' Get It Cowboy Santa CF-086 - J. Littlejohn	7,500		130.00	130
1993 Dear Santa CF-046 - K. Memoli	7,500	1996	170.00	225-230
1995 Dear Santa, Vict. CF-063	10,000		170.00	180
1987 Dreaming Of Santa CF-008 - S. Bradford	15,000	1988	65.00	325
1998 Drifts & Gifts CF-079 - K. Memoli	10,000		140.00	140
1992 Earth Home Santa CF-040 - S. Bradford	7,500	1997	135.00	140
1986 Elf Pair CF-005	10,000	1992	60.00	135-151
1988 Father Christmas CF-018 - S. Bradford	7,500	1993	75.00	115-135
1991 For Santa CF-029	7,500	1997	99.00	160
1990 Forest Friends CF-025	7,500	1993	90.00	110-125
1998 Friends of the North Santa CF-077 - J. Littlejohn	10,000		100.00	100
1995 Getting Santa Ready CF-056	10,000	1998	170.00	190
1996 High Country Santa CF-064	15,000		190.00	200
1989 Hitching Up CF-021	7,500	1993	90.00	110
1995 Into the Wind CF-061	10,000		140.00	150
1995 Into the Wind, Vict. CF-062	10,000		140.00	150
1993 Jolly St. Nick CF-045 - K. Memoli	7,500	1999	130.00	140
1993 Jolly St. Nick, Victorian CF-050 - K. Memoli	7,500	1999	120.00	140
1986 Kris Kringle CF-002	10,000	1991	60.00	155-160
1992 Letters to Santa CF-036	7,500	1995	125.00	210
1997 A Light on the Roof CF-072 - K. Memoli	7,500		160.00	160
1997 A Light on the Roof, Victorian CF-076 - K. Memoli	7,500		160.00	160

*Quotes have been rounded up to nearest dollar

YEAR ISSUE	EDITION LIMIT	YEAR RETD.	ISSUE PRICE	*QUOTE U.S.$
1988 Load 'Em Up CF-016 - S. Bradford	7,500	1990	79.00	350-400
1987 Loading Santa's Sleigh CF-010	15,000	1993	100.00	90-110
1992 Loads of Happiness CF-041 - K. Memoli	7,500	1996	100.00	135-165
1994 Long Stocking Dilemma, Victorian CF-055 - K. Memoli	7,500	1999	170.00	190
1994 Longstocking Dilemma CF-052 - K. Memoli	7,500		170.00	190
1987 Mrs. Santa CF-006 - S. Bradford	15,000	1991	60.00	235
1993 The Night Before Christmas CF-043	7,500	1996	100.00	135-165
1993 Northwoods Santa CF-047 - S. Bradford	7,500	1996	100.00	100
1987 On Santa's Knee-CF007 - S. Bradford	15,000	1994	65.00	120-135
1996 Pause For a Tale CF-065	10,000		190.00	200
1996 Pause For a Tale, Victorian CF-069 - K. Memoli	10,000		190.00	200
1998 Prince of Giving CF-078 - K. Memoli	10,000		180.00	180
1998 Prince of Giving, Victorian CF-082 - K. Memoli	10,000		180.00	180
1990 Puppy Love CF-024	7,500	1994	100.00	195-220
1989 A Purrr-Fect Christmas CF-019 - S. Bradford	7,500	1994	95.00	135
1991 Reindeer Walk CF-031 - K. Memoli	7,500	1997	150.00	170
1995 The Ride CF-057	10,000	1998	130.00	140
1986 Rooftop Santa CF-004 - S. Bradford	10,000	1991	65.00	200-225
1990 Safe Arrival CF-027 - Memoli/Jonas	7,500	1996	150.00	175
1996 Santa & Blitzen CF-067 - K. Memoli	10,000		140.00	190
1996 Santa & Blitzen, Victorian CF-070 - K. Memoli	10,000		140.00	190
1992 Santa and Comet CF-037	7,500	1995	110.00	135-165
1992 Santa and Mrs. Claus CF-039 - K. Memoli	7,500		150.00	160
1992 Santa and Mrs. Claus, Victorian CF-042 - K. Memoli	7,500		135.00	160
1986 Santa At Rest CF-001	10,000	1988	70.00	600
1991 Santa At Work CF-030	7,500	1995	99.00	175
1987 Santa On Horseback CF-011 - S. Bradford	15,000	1990	75.00	350-375
1994 Santa Riding Dove CF-053	7,500	1998	120.00	135-140
1986 Santa With Pups CF-003 - S. Bradford	10,000	1988	65.00	570-575
1993 Santa's Friends CF-044	7,500	1996	100.00	100
1995 Santa, Dusk & Dawn CF-060	10,000		150.00	160
1988 St. Nicholas CF-015	7,500	1992	75.00	125-135
1994 Star Santa w/ Polar Bear CF-054 - S. Bradford	7,500	1998	130.00	140
1995 Starlight Express CF-059	10,000	1999	170.00	180
1994 The Story of Christmas CF-051 - K. Memoli	10,000	1996	180.00	250-300
1996 The Story of Christmas, Victorian CF-068 - K. Memoli	10,000		180.00	190
1998 Totem Gathering CF-081 - J. Littlejohn	10,000		120.00	120
1999 Up on the Rooftop CF-083 - J. Littlejohn	5,000		190.00	190
1993 Victorian Lion & Lamb Santa CF-048 - S. Bradford	7,500	1997	100.00	100-120
1990 Victorian Santa CF-028 - S. Bradford	7,500	1992	125.00	295-325
1991 Victorian Santa w/ Teddy CF-033 - S. Bradford	7,500	1997	150.00	160
1990 Waiting For Santa CF-026 - S. Bradford	7,500	1995	100.00	225-250
1999 Warm & Fuzzy Christmas CF-084 - K. Memoli	5,000		150.00	150
1997 Wilderness Santa CF-071	10,000		300.00	300
1999 Woodland Santa CF-085 - D. Vaughan	7,500		120.00	120

Legend Of The Little People™ - L. Miller

YEAR ISSUE	EDITION LIMIT	YEAR RETD.	ISSUE PRICE	*QUOTE U.S.$
1989 Adventure Bound LL-002	Retrd.	1993	35.00	50
1989 Caddy's Helper LL-007	Retrd.	1993	35.00	50
1991 The Easter Bunny's Cart LL-020	Retrd.	1994	45.00	50
1991 Fire it Up LL-023	Retrd.	1994	50.00	55
1990 Fishin' Hole LL-012	Retrd.	1994	35.00	50
1989 A Friendly Toast LL-003	Retrd.	1993	35.00	50
1990 Gathering Acorns LL-014	Retrd.	1994	100.00	100
1991 Got It LL-021	Retrd.	1994	45.00	50
1990 Hedgehog In Harness LL-010	Retrd.	1994	45.00	50
1990 Husking Acorns LL-008	Retrd.	1994	60.00	65
1991 It's About Time LL-022	Retrd.	1994	55.00	60
1990 A Little Jig LL-018	Retrd.	1994	45.00	50
1990 A Look Through The Spyglass LL-015	Retrd.	1994	40.00	50
1989 Magical Discovery LL-005	Retrd.	1993	45.00	50
1990 Ministral Magic LL-017	Retrd.	1994	45.00	50
1990 A Proclamation LL-013	Retrd.	1994	45.00	55
1989 Spring Water Scrub LL-006	Retrd.	1993	35.00	50
1990 Traveling Fast LL-009	Retrd.	1994	45.00	50
1989 Treasure Hunt LL-004	Retrd.	1993	45.00	50
1991 Viking LL-019	Retrd.	1994	45.00	50
1989 Woodland Cache LL-001	Retrd.	1993	35.00	50
1990 Woodland Scout LL-011	Retrd.	1994	40.00	50
1990 Writing The Legend LL-016	Retrd.	1994	35.00	65

Lil' Doll™ - Various

YEAR ISSUE	EDITION LIMIT	YEAR RETD.	ISSUE PRICE	*QUOTE U.S.$
1992 Clara & The Nutcracker LD-017 - D. Newburn	Retrd.	1994	35.00	35
1991 The Nutcracker LD-006 - P.J. Jonas	Retrd.	1994	35.00	35

Music Makers™ - Various

YEAR ISSUE	EDITION LIMIT	YEAR RETD.	ISSUE PRICE	*QUOTE U.S.$
1991 A Christmas Gift MM-015 - D. Kennicutt	Retrd.	1993	59.00	59
1991 Crystal Angel MM-017 - D. Kennicutt	Retrd.	1993	59.00	59
1991 Dashing Through The Snow MM-013 - D. Kennicutt	Retrd.	1993	59.00	59
1989 Evening Carolers MM-005 - D. Kennicutt	Retrd.	1993	69.00	69
1989 Herald Angel MM-011 - S. Bradford	Retrd.	1993	79.00	79
1991 Nutcracker MM-024 - P.J. Jonas	Retrd.	1994	69.00	69
1991 Peace Descending MM-025 - P.J. Jonas	Retrd.	1993	69.00	69
1991 Renaissance Angel MM-028 - P.J. Jonas	Retrd.	1994	69.00	69
1989 Santa's Sleigh MM-004 - L. Miller	Retrd.	1993	69.00	69
1991 Teddy Bear Band #2 MM-023 - D. Kennicutt	Retrd.	1994	90.00	90
1989 Teddy Bear Band MM-012 - S. Bradford	Retrd.	1993	99.00	100
1989 Teddy Drummers MM-009 - D. Kennicutt	Retrd.	1993	69.00	69
1991 Teddy Soldiers MM-018 - D. Kennicutt	Retrd.	1994	69.00	84
1991 Victorian Santa MM-026 - L. Miller	Retrd.	1993	69.00	69

Party Animals™ - L. Miller, unless otherwise noted

YEAR ISSUE	EDITION LIMIT	YEAR RETD.	ISSUE PRICE	*QUOTE U.S.$
1992 Democratic Donkey ('92) - K. Memoli	Retrd.	1994	20.00	20
1984 Democratic Donkey ('84) - D. Kennicutt	Retrd.	1986	14.50	16
1986 Democratic Donkey ('86)	Retrd.	1988	14.50	15
1988 Democratic Donkey ('88)	Retrd.	1990	14.50	16
1990 Democratic Donkey ('90) D. Kennicutt	Retrd.	1992	16.00	16
1984 GOP Elephant ('84)	Retrd.	1986	14.50	16
1986 GOP Elephant ('86)	Retrd.	1988	14.50	15
1988 GOP Elephant ('88)	Retrd.	1990	14.50	16
1990 GOP Elephant ('90) - D. Kennicutt	Retrd.	1992	16.00	16
1992 GOP Elephant ('92) - K. Memoli	Retrd.	1994	20.00	20

PenniBears™ - P.J. Jonas

YEAR ISSUE	EDITION LIMIT	YEAR RETD.	ISSUE PRICE	*QUOTE U.S.$
1992 After Every Meal PB-058	Retrd.	1994	22.00	22
1992 Apple For Teacher PB-069	Retrd.	1994	24.00	24
1989 Attic Fun PB-019	Retrd.	1992	20.00	40
1989 Baby Hugs PB-007	Retrd.	1992	20.00	35
1991 Baking Goodies PB-043	Retrd.	1993	26.00	30
1989 Bathtime Buddies PB-023	Retrd.	1992	20.00	25
1992 Batter Up PB-066	Retrd.	1994	22.00	22
1991 Bear Footin' it PB-037	Retrd.	1993	24.00	24
1992 Bear-Capade PB-073	Retrd.	1994	22.00	22
1991 Bearly Awake PB-033	Retrd.	1993	22.00	25
1989 Beautiful Bride PB-004	Retrd.	1992	20.00	35
1993 Big Chief Little Bear PB-088	Retrd.	1996	28.00	28
1989 Birthday Bear PB-018	Retrd.	1992	20.00	40
1991 Boo Hoo Bear PB-050	Retrd.	1994	22.00	22
1990 Boooo Bear PB-025	Retrd.	1993	20.00	22
1991 Bountiful Harvest PB-045	Retrd.	1994	24.00	24
1989 Bouquet Boy PB-003	Retrd.	1992	20.00	45
1989 Bouquet Girl PB-001	Retrd.	1992	20.00	45
1991 Bump-bear-Crop PB-035	Retrd.	1993	26.00	30
1991 Bunny Buddies PB-042	Retrd.	1993	22.00	25
1989 Butterfly Bear PB-005	Retrd.	1992	20.00	45-50
1990 Buttons & Bows PB-012	Retrd.	1992	20.00	45
1992 Christmas Cookies PB-075	Retrd.	1994	22.00	22
1991 Christmas Reinbear PB-046	Retrd.	1994	28.00	28
1992 Cinderella PB-056	Retrd.	1994	22.00	22
1992 Clowning Around PB-065	Retrd.	1994	22.00	22
1989 Cookie Bandit PB-006	Retrd.	1992	20.00	30
1990 Count Bearacula PB-027	Retrd.	1993	22.00	24
1991 Country Lullabye PB-036	Retrd.	1993	24.00	25
1990 Country Quilter PB-030	Retrd.	1993	22.00	30
1990 Country Spring PB-013	Retrd.	1992	20.00	45
1991 Curtain Call PB-049	Retrd.	1994	24.00	24
1992 Decorating The Wreath PB-076	Retrd.	1994	22.00	22
1989 Doctor Bear PB-008	Retrd.	1992	20.00	30
1992 Downhill Thrills PB-070	Retrd.	1994	24.00	24
1990 Dress Up Fun PB-028	Retrd.	1993	22.00	30
1992 Dust Bunny Roundup PB-062	Retrd.	1994	22.00	22
1992 First Prom PB-064	Retrd.	1994	22.00	22
1990 Garden Path PB-014	Retrd.	1992	20.00	45-50
1993 Getting 'Round On My Own PB-085	Retrd.	1996	26.00	26
1990 Giddiap Teddy PB-011	Retrd.	1992	20.00	35
1991 Goodnight Little Prince PB-041	Retrd.	1993	26.00	30
1991 Goodnight Sweet Princess PB-040	Retrd.	1993	26.00	30
1993 Gotta Try Again PB-082	Retrd.	1996	24.00	24
1989 Handsome Groom PB-015	Retrd.	1992	20.00	40
1993 Happy Birthday PB-084	Retrd.	1996	26.00	26
1993 A Happy Camper PB-077	Retrd.	1996	28.00	28
1991 Happy Hobo PB-051	Retrd.	1994	26.00	26
1989 Honey Bear PB-002	Retrd.	1992	20.00	45
1992 I Made It Boy PB-061	Retrd.	1994	22.00	22
1992 I Made It Girl PB-060	Retrd.	1994	22.00	22
1989 Lazy Days PB-009	Retrd.	1992	20.00	25
1992 Lil' Devil PB-071	Retrd.	1994	24.00	24
1991 Lil' Mer-teddy PB-034	Retrd.	1993	24.00	24
1992 Lil' Sis Makes Up PB-074	Retrd.	1994	22.00	22
1993 Little Bear Peep PB-083	Retrd.	1996	24.00	24
1993 Making It Better PB-087	Retrd.	1996	24.00	24
1993 May Joy Be Yours PB-080	Retrd.	1996	24.00	24
1993 My Forever Love PB-078	Retrd.	1996	28.00	28
1989 Nap Time PB-016	Retrd.	1992	20.00	22
1989 Nurse Bear PB-017	Retrd.	1992	20.00	35
1992 On Your Toes PB-068	Retrd.	1994	24.00	24
1989 Petite Mademoiselle PB-010	Retrd.	1992	20.00	40
1991 Pilgrim Provider PB-047	Retrd.	1994	32.00	32
1992 Pot O' Gold PB-059	Retrd.	1994	22.00	22
1992 Puddle Jumper PB-057	Retrd.	1994	24.00	24
1989 Puppy Bath PB-020	Retrd.	1992	20.00	25
1989 Puppy Love PB-021	Retrd.	1992	20.00	25
1993 Rest Stop PB-079	Retrd.	1996	24.00	24
1992 Sandbox Fun PB-063	Retrd.	1994	22.00	22
1990 Santa Bear-ing Gifts PB-031	Retrd.	1993	24.00	30
1993 Santa's Helper PB-081	Retrd.	1996	28.00	28
1990 Scarecrow Teddy PB-029	Retrd.	1993	24.00	25
1992 Smokey's Nephew PB-055	Retrd.	1994	22.00	22
1990 Sneaky Snowball PB-026	Retrd.	1993	20.00	25
1989 Southern Belle PB-024	Retrd.	1992	20.00	35
1992 Spanish Rose PB-053	Retrd.	1994	24.00	24
1990 Stocking Surprise PB-032	Retrd.	1993	22.00	26
1993 Summer Belle PB-086	Retrd.	1996	24.00	24
1991 Summer Sailing PB-039	Retrd.	1993	26.00	30
1991 Sweet Lil 'Sis PB-048	Retrd.	1994	22.00	22
1991 Sweetheart Bears PB-044	Retrd.	1993	28.00	30
1992 Tally Ho! PB-054	Retrd.	1994	22.00	22
1992 Touchdown PB-072	Retrd.	1994	22.00	22
1989 Tubby Teddy PB-022	Retrd.	1992	20.00	22
1991 A Wild Ride PB-052	Retrd.	1994	26.00	26
1992 Will You Be Mine? PB-067	Retrd.	1994	22.00	22
1991 Windy Day PB-038	Retrd.	1993	24.00	24

PenniBears™ Collector's Club Members Only Editions - P.J. Jonas

YEAR ISSUE	EDITION LIMIT	YEAR RETD.	ISSUE PRICE	*QUOTE U.S.$
1990 1990 First Collection PB-C90	Retrd.	1990	26.00	125
1991 1991 Collecting Makes Cents PB-C91	Retrd.	1991	26.00	150
1992 1992 Today's Pleasures, Tomorrow's Treasures PB-C92	Retrd.	1992	26.00	100
1993 1993 Chalkin Up Another Year PB-C93	Retrd.	1993	26.00	35
1994 1994 Artist's Touch-Collector's Treasure PB-C94	Retrd.	1994	26.00	26

Reasons to Believe Santas™ - D. Brown/S. Schultz

YEAR ISSUE	EDITION LIMIT	YEAR RETD.	ISSUE PRICE	*QUOTE U.S.$
2000 Captain Claus CF-402	3,500		47.50	48
2000 Christmas Dance CF-405	3,500		35.00	35
2000 High Country Excursion CF-410	3,500		39.50	40
2000 Making Dreams Come True CF-407	3,500		47.50	48
2000 North Pole Aviary CF-401	3,500		42.50	43
2000 Polar Express CF-409	3,500		145.00	145
2000 Santa In Toyland CF-404	3,500		32.50	33
2000 Santa's Chair CF-400	3,500		62.50	63
2000 Seaside Santa CF-411	3,500		47.50	48
2000 Southwest Santa CF-406	3,500		60.00	60
2000 Sweet Talkin' Santa CF-403	3,500		27.50	28
2000 Windswept Santa CF-408	3,500		37.50	38

Storytime Rhymes & Tales - H. Henriksen

YEAR ISSUE	EDITION LIMIT	YEAR RETD.	ISSUE PRICE	*QUOTE U.S.$
1991 Humpty Dumpty SL-008	Retrd.	1993	64.00	64
1991 Little Jack Horner SL-007	Retrd.	1993	50.00	50
1991 Little Miss Muffet SL-006	Retrd.	1993	64.00	64
1991 Mistress Mary SL-002	Retrd.	1993	64.00	64
1991 Mother Goose SL-001	Retrd.	1993	64.00	64
1991 Owl & Pussy Cat SL-004	Retrd.	1993	100.00	100
1991 Simple Simon SL-003	Retrd.	1993	90.00	90
1991 Three Little Pigs SL-005	Retrd.	1993	100.00	100

Teddy Angels™ - P.J. Jonas

YEAR ISSUE	EDITION LIMIT	YEAR RETD.	ISSUE PRICE	*QUOTE U.S.$
1995 Bruin & Bluebirds "Nurture nature." BA-013	Open		19.00	19
1995 Bruin Making Valentines "Holidays start within the heart." BA-012	Open		15.00	15
1995 Bruin With Harp Seal "Make your corner of the world a little warmer." BA-021	Open		15.00	15
1995 Bunny's Picnic "Make a feast of friendship." BA-007	Open		19.00	19
1995 Casey & Honey Reading "Friends are the best recipe for relaxation." BA-023	Open		15.00	15
1995 Casey Tucking Honey In "There is magic in the simplest things we do." BA-008	Open		19.00	19
1995 Cowboy Murray "Have a Doo Da Day." BA-002	Open		19.00	19
1995 Honey "Love gives our hearts wings." BA-014	Open		13.00	13
1995 Ivy & Blankie "Nothing is as comfortable as an old friend." BA-003	Open		13.00	13
1995 Ivy In Garden "Celebrate the little things." BA-009	Open		15.00	15
1995 Ivy With Locket "You're always close at heart." BA-028	Open		13.00	13
1995 Murray & Little Bit "Imagination can take you anywhere." BA-004	Open		19.00	19
1995 Murray Mending Bruin "Everybody needs a helping hand." BA-005	Open		15.00	15
1995 Murray With Angel "I believe in you, too." BA-022	Open		22.00	22
1995 Nicholas With Stars "Dreams are never too far away to catch." BA-024	Open		15.00	15
1995 Old Bear "Always remember your way home." BA-011	Open		19.00	19
1995 Old Bear & Little Bit Gardening "The well-watered garden produces a great harvest." BA-026	Open		15.00	15
1995 Old Bear & Little Bit Reading "Love to learn and learn to love." BA-006	Open		15.00	15
1995 Rufus Helps Bird "We could all use a little lift." BA-027	Open		15.00	15
1995 Sweetie "Come tell me all about it." BA-001	Open		15.00	15
1995 Sweetie With Kitty Cats "Always close-knit." BA-025	Open		15.00	15
1995 Tilli & Murray "Friendship is a bridge between hearts." BA-010	Open		15.00	15

Teddy Angels™ Christmas - P.J. Jonas

YEAR ISSUE	EDITION LIMIT	YEAR RETD.	ISSUE PRICE	*QUOTE U.S.$
1997 Angel & Sweetie BA-029	Open		22.00	22

*Quotes have been rounded up to nearest dollar

YEAR ISSUE	EDITION LIMIT	YEAR RETD.	ISSUE PRICE	*QUOTE U.S.$
1995 Casey "You're a bright & shining star." BA-019	Open		13.00	13
1995 Ivy "Enchantment glows in winter snows." BA-020	Open		13.00	13
1995 Sweetie & Santa Bear "Tis the season of surprises." BA-016	Open		22.00	22
1995 Tilli & Doves "A wreath is a circle of love." BA-015	Open		19.00	19

Tyber Katz™ - P. & P. Tyber

YEAR ISSUE	EDITION LIMIT	YEAR RETD.	ISSUE PRICE	*QUOTE U.S.$
2000 Cha Cha & Rumba TK-4004	2,500		45.00	45
1999 Fanbelt & Squeaky TK-2001	2,500		45.00	45
1999 Fuzzhead & Friend TK-2000	2,500		45.00	45
2000 Hoochie & Koochie TK-4003	2,500		45.00	45
2000 Hugs & Kisses TK-4000	2,500		45.00	45
2000 Kit & Caboodle TK-4006	2,500		45.00	45
1999 Kozmo & Blue Willow TK-3002	2,500		42.00	42
1999 Kozmo & Indigo TK-2005	2,500		45.00	45
2000 Lovey & Dovey TK-4001	2,500		45.00	45
1999 Lying 'Round TK-1002	2,500		29.00	29
1999 Mr. Dude & Chirper TK-2004	2,500		45.00	45
1999 Mr. Dude & Majolica TK-3001	2,500		42.00	42
1999 Pooker & Flutterby TK-2003	2,500		45.00	45
2000 Rhythm & Blue TK-2006	2,500		45.00	45
2000 Rock & Roll TK-2007	2,500		45.00	45
1999 Sitting Pretty TK-1000	2,500		29.00	29
2000 Smoochie & Woochie TK-4002	2,500		45.00	45
2000 Stanley & Livingstone TK-4007	2,500		45.00	45
1999 Tasha & Blue Jasper TK-3000	2,500		42.00	42
2000 Tiki & Squeaky TK-4005	2,500		45.00	45
1999 Tux & Redhead TK-2002	2,500		45.00	45

Wacky Dogs™ - D. Wentzel

YEAR ISSUE	EDITION LIMIT	YEAR RETD.	ISSUE PRICE	*QUOTE U.S.$
1999 Senor Wacky ND-0022	Open		100.00	100
2000 Senor Wacky, Small ND-0053	Open		65.00	65
1999 Wacky Chef ND-0021	Open		100.00	100
2000 Wacky Chef, Small ND-0052	Open		50.00	50
1999 Wacky Floral Friend ND-0019	Open		100.00	100
2000 Wacky Floral Friend, Small ND-0050	Open		50.00	50
1999 Wacky Go-Getter ND-0020	Open		120.00	120
2000 Wacky Go-Getter, Small ND-0051	Open		60.00	60
2000 Wacky Hipster ND-0061	2,500		100.00	100
2000 Wacky Lantern Holder ND-0054	2,500		120.00	120
1999 Wacky Lightbearer ND-0017	Open		100.00	100
2000 Wacky Racer ND-0060	2,500		100.00	100
1999 Wacky Retriever, Small ND-0048	Open		50.00	50
1999 Wacky Thoroughbred ND-0018	Open		120.00	120
1999 Wacky Thoroughbred, Small ND-0049	Open		60.00	60
2000 Wacky Timekeeper ND-0055	2,500		120.00	120

United Treasures

Angels of Inspiration - K. Stafford

YEAR ISSUE	EDITION LIMIT	YEAR RETD.	ISSUE PRICE	*QUOTE U.S.$
2000 Faith 71001	Open		29.95	30
2000 Happiness 71006	Open		29.95	30
2000 Joy 71000	Open		29.95	30
2000 Kente Claus® 78000	Open		39.95	40
2000 Love 71002	Open		29.95	30
2000 Mercy 71005	Open		29.95	30
2000 Peace 71003	Open		29.95	30
2000 Unity 71004	Open		29.95	30

Billy Dee Williams Romance - B. D. Williams

YEAR ISSUE	EDITION LIMIT	YEAR RETD.	ISSUE PRICE	*QUOTE U.S.$
1999 Dancers 68002	5,000		125.00	125
1999 Gardenia 68001	5,000		95.00	95
1999 Passion 68000	5,000		95.00	95

Black Legend Series - N. Hughes

YEAR ISSUE	EDITION LIMIT	YEAR RETD.	ISSUE PRICE	*QUOTE U.S.$
1994 Bill Pickett 60404	Open		50.00	50
1994 George Washington Carver 60405	Open		50.00	50
1994 Ida B. Wells 60402	Open		60.00	60
1994 Mahalia Jackson 60401	Open		50.00	50

Classic Positive Image - N. Hughes

YEAR ISSUE	EDITION LIMIT	YEAR RETD.	ISSUE PRICE	*QUOTE U.S.$
1991 Boy in Chair 60301	Open		25.00	25
1992 Buffalo Soldier 60311	Open		50.00	50
1996 Civil War Soldier 60310	Open		50.00	50
1991 Girl in Chair 60302	Open		25.00	25
XX Madonna With Child 60600	Open		75.00	75
XX Old Fashion Santa 61201	Open		50.00	50
1997 Praying Slave 60328	Open		75.00	75
1994 Sailor Going Home On Leave 60326	Open		50.00	50
XX Santa's Treat 61202	Open		75.00	75
1992 Tuskegee Airman 60323	Open		50.00	50
1996 Tuskegee Bust 60601	Open		75.00	75
1995 Vietnam Field Nurse 60330	Open		50.00	50
1995 Vietnam Soldier 60329	Open		50.00	50

Emma Jane's Children - E.J. Watkins

YEAR ISSUE	EDITION LIMIT	YEAR RETD.	ISSUE PRICE	*QUOTE U.S.$
1997 Baby Lexie Wore Her First "Sunday Go To Meeting Dress" 62008	5,000		75.00	75
1997 Bertie May Watched Over Little Hattie 62000	5,000		95.00	95
1997 Booker Found the Lost Puppy Under the Old Barn 62002	5,000		75.00	75
2000 Calbert's dreamin' 'bout Maizie	5,000		75.00	75
1997 Calvin Held His Momma's Picture Close to His Heart 62006	5,000		75.00	75
1997 Chloe Gave Her Momma a Rose for Christmas 62004	5,000		75.00	75
1997 Cissie Didn't Want Her Picture Taken "No Way, No How" 62003	5,000		75.00	75
1997 Eubie Just Stood There and Grinned 62001	5,000		75.00	75
1997 Maizie Daydreamed About her Boyfriend All Afternoon 62007	5,000		75.00	75
1997 Nate's Pa Took Him to His First Day of School 62005	5,000		75.00	75

Rolling Round Heaven - N. Hughes

YEAR ISSUE	EDITION LIMIT	YEAR RETD.	ISSUE PRICE	*QUOTE U.S.$
1994 Daydreamer Susie 60507	Open		15.00	15
1994 Dress Up Angel Desiree 60502	Open		15.00	15
1994 Praying Angel Leroy 60505	Open		15.00	15
1994 Reach For A Star Mary 60504	Open		15.00	15
1994 Rolling Round Heaven Display Piece 60500	Open		15.00	15
1994 Why Me Lord Buster 60506	Open		15.00	15

Sankofa - N. Hughes

YEAR ISSUE	EDITION LIMIT	YEAR RETD.	ISSUE PRICE	*QUOTE U.S.$
1998 Akoko Nan "Mother and Child" 60703	5,000		60.00	60
1998 Akomo Ntoaso "The Family" 60701	5,000		85.00	85
1998 Donno Ntoaso "The Drummer" 60709	5,000		95.00	95
1998 Dono "The Dancer" 60707	5,000		85.00	85
1998 Fie Kwan "Lovers" 60708	5,000		95.00	95
1998 Nyame Dua "Joy" 60710	5,000		100.00	100
1998 Se Ne Tekrema "Father and Son" 60702	5,000		85.00	85
1998 Sun Sum "Woman with Bucket" 60704	5,000		60.00	60
1998 Wo Soro "Woman with Gourd" 60706	5,000		75.00	75

Walnut Ridge Collectibles

Americana Collection - K. Bejma

YEAR ISSUE	EDITION LIMIT	YEAR RETD.	ISSUE PRICE	*QUOTE U.S.$
1999 Liberty Egg w/Stand A103	Open		40.00	40
1999 Miss Liberty A100	Open		90.00	90
1999 Uncle Sam Rabbit A101	Open		32.00	32
1999 Uncle Sam, sm. A102	Open		38.00	38

Cat Figurines - K. Bejma

YEAR ISSUE	EDITION LIMIT	YEAR RETD.	ISSUE PRICE	*QUOTE U.S.$
1993 Basket of Kittens 309	Open		70.00	112
1991 Calico Cat 306	Open		40.00	46
1991 Goodrich Cat 300	Retrd.	1998	50.00	56
1997 Gypsy 313	Open		62.00	64
1997 Small Striped Cat 312	Open		36.00	40
1997 Striped Cat, sm. 312	Open		30.00	36
1994 Tabby Cat 310	Open		50.00	60
1991 Tiny Cat 304	Open		24.00	30
1997 White Kitten 311	Open		56.00	46

Fall & Halloween Figurines - K. Bejma

YEAR ISSUE	EDITION LIMIT	YEAR RETD.	ISSUE PRICE	*QUOTE U.S.$
1996 Black Cat 410	Open		24.00	30
1997 Cat Mask, paper mache 425	Retrd.	1999	30.00	30
1997 Ghost on Pumpkin 423	Open		34.00	36
1996 Ghost with Pumpkin 417	Open		30.00	44
1997 Halloween Mask, paper mache 426	Retrd.	1997	32.00	32
1998 Happy Pumpkin 433	Open		44.00	48
1996 Jack-O-Lantern 414	Open		28.00	36
1996 Jack-O-Lantern Man 416	Open		40.00	48
1998 Little Cat 430	Open		30.00	32
1998 Little Witch 429	Open		30.00	32
1996 Oak Leaf, set/2 420	Open		28.00	44
1996 Owl 411	Open		22.00	28
1996 Pilgrim Set 400	Open		80.00	92
1998 Pumpkin 433	Open		44.00	48
1999 Pumpkin Face w/cutout 435	Open		50.00	52
1996 Pumpkin Kids, set/3 415	Open		56.00	64
1998 Pumpkin Man 431	Open		46.00	50
1997 Pumpkin with Black Cat 422	Open		72.00	76
2000 Pumpkin With Cornstalk, lg. 437	Open		88.00	88
1996 Pumpkin, lg. 412	Open		48.00	54
1997 Pumpkin, lg. paper mache 427	Retrd.	1999	36.00	36
1991 Pumpkin, set/3 404	Open		22.00	32
1997 Pumpkin, sm. paper mache 424	Retrd.	1997	32.00	32
1996 Pumpkin,sm. 413	Open		28.00	34
2000 Scarecrow 438	Open		44.00	44
1996 Turkey, lg. 419	Open		44.00	52
1996 Turkey, med. 418	Open		36.00	48
1991 Turkey, sm. 401	Open		20.00	32
1998 Witch on broom, lg. 428	Open		78.00	80
1998 Witch on Gourd 432	Open		46.00	50
1999 Witch w/ Sky, lg. 434	Open		150.00	150
2000 Witch With Cauldron 436	Open		150.00	150
1997 Witch with Pumpkins 421	Open		56.00	60
1996 Witch, lg. 407	Open		68.00	84
1996 Witch, med. 408	Open		48.00	56
1996 Witch, sm. 409	Open		44.00	50

Gossamer Wings - K. Bejma

YEAR ISSUE	EDITION LIMIT	YEAR RETD.	ISSUE PRICE	*QUOTE U.S.$
1994 Addie 167	Open		40.00	48
1995 Alexandra 183	Open		54.00	72
1998 Cecelia 1011	Open		90.00	98
1999 Charlene 1029	Open		84.00	90
1997 Choirs 1010	Open		76.00	90
1996 Deborah 192	Open		50.00	66
1994 Elizabeth 170	Retrd.	1999	52.00	58
1997 Elysia 1005	Open		54.00	68
1997 Emma 1006	Retrd.	2000	50.00	62
1998 Felicia 1020	Open		76.00	80
1996 Gabriella 194	Open		64.00	80
1994 Hannah 169	Open		50.00	60
1998 Harmony 1018	Open		84.00	86
1997 Helena 1009	Open		56.00	70
1995 Julia 184	Retrd.	1998	38.00	46
1996 Kathleen 193	Retrd.	2000	56.00	90
1995 Lucia 187	Retrd.	1998	62.00	80
1995 Lydia 185	Retrd.	1999	58.00	70
1994 Meghan 168	Open		46.00	56
1998 Michael 1017	Open		120.00	120
1997 Noel 1008	Open		40.00	48
1996 Olivia 196	Retrd.	1999	56.00	62
1998 Peace 1019	Open		84.00	90
1997 Sarah 1007	Open		32.00	42
1995 Tatiana 186	Retrd.	1998	58.00	66
1996 Thomas 195	Open		64.00	80
1996 Victoria 191	Retrd.	1999	54.00	64
2000 Hope 1036	Open		76.00	76

Herr Belsnickle Collection - K. Bejma

YEAR ISSUE	EDITION LIMIT	YEAR RETD.	ISSUE PRICE	*QUOTE U.S.$
1993 Herr Dieter 807	Open		90.00	100
1993 Herr Franz 805	Open		90.00	100
1993 Herr Fritz 803	Open		100.00	116
1993 Herr Gottfried 806	Open		90.00	100
1994 Herr Gregor 818	Open		90.00	100
1993 Herr Gunther 809	Open		70.00	80
1993 Herr Heinrich 810	Open		60.00	68
1993 Herr Hermann 813	Open		48.00	54
1995 Herr Hobart 824	Open		68.00	72
1995 Herr Johann 820	Open		230.00	260
1993 Herr Karl 801	Open		150.00	168
1993 Herr Klaus 800	Open		180.00	200
1993 Herr Ludwig 811	Open		60.00	68
1993 Herr Nicholas 802	Open		130.00	150
1993 Herr Oskar 816	Open		44.00	50
1993 Herr Peter 815	Open		44.00	50
1993 Herr Reiner 812	Open		60.00	68
1995 Herr Roland 823	Open		64.00	68
1994 Herr Rudolph 819	Open		230.00	260
1995 Herr Rutger 822	Open		150.00	168
1995 Herr Sebastian 821	Open		70.00	80
1994 Herr Viktor 817	Open		64.00	74
1993 Herr Wilhelm 804	Open		100.00	116
1993 Herr Willi 814	Open		44.00	50
1993 Herr Wolfgang 808	Open		70.00	80

Holiday Collection - K. Bejma

YEAR ISSUE	EDITION LIMIT	YEAR RETD.	ISSUE PRICE	*QUOTE U.S.$
1996 Alpine Tree 1001	Open		24.00	26
1999 Angel Snowchildren 1028	Open		44.00	46
2000 Bald Snowman 1030	Open		28.00	28
1988 Belsnickle 102	Retrd.	1997	32.00	36
1988 Belsnickle 104	Retrd.	1996	48.00	48
1988 Belsnickle 105	Retrd.	1996	32.00	32
1989 Belsnickle 124	Retrd.	1996	30.00	30
1991 Belsnickle 140	Retrd.	1996	40.00	40
1994 Belsnickle 176	Retrd.	1996	28.00	32
1988 Belsnickle, mini 116	Retrd.	1997	22.00	24
1994 Belsnickle/Tree 174	Retrd.	1997	32.00	38
1994 Children on Sled 172	Retrd.	1998	48.00	58
1995 Crying Snowman 189	Open		44.00	52
1994 Father Christmas 175	Retrd.	1997	28.00	32
1992 Father Christmas, lg. 161	Retrd.	1997	270.00	300
1988 Father Christmas/Apples 122	Retrd.	1996	48.00	51
1988 Father Christmas/Bag 114	Retrd.	1996	34.00	34
1993 Father Christmas/Bag 163	Retrd.	1996	38.00	42
1994 Father Christmas/Bag 166	Retrd.	1997	30.00	40
1994 Father Christmas/Bag 178	Retrd.	1996	42.00	42
1988 Father Christmas/Basket 100R	Retrd.	1996	120.00	120
1988 Father Christmas/Basket 100W	Retrd.	1996	120.00	120
1994 Father Christmas/Girl/Doll 165	Retrd.	1998	52.00	62
1993 Father Christmas/Holly 164	Retrd.	1997	52.00	58
1990 Father Christmas/Toys/Switch 136	Retrd.	1996	120.00	120
1991 Gnome/Rabbit 148	Retrd.	1996	32.00	42
1999 Jolly Snowman 1026	Open		36.00	36
1990 Jolly St. Nick 135	Retrd.	1996	52.00	52
2000 Let it Snow (3rd Ed.) 1031	250	2000	140.00	140
1999 Let it Snow Snowman (2nd Ed.) 1027	100	1999	380.00	380
1998 Let it Snow Snowman 1023	100	1999	480.00	480
1997 Magnolia 1016	Open		24.00	26
2000 Patriotic Bear 1035	Open		32.00	32
1994 Primitive Snowman 173	Open		32.00	40
1990 Rocking Santa 129	Retrd.	1996	36.00	40
1992 Santa/Horse, sm. 158	Retrd.	1997	24.00	28
1991 Santa/Walking Stick 152	Retrd.	1996	56.00	60
1998 Snow Angel 1022	Open		62.00	64
1996 Snow Children 1002	Open		56.00	70
2000 Snow Kitty 1038	Open		44.00	44
1999 Snowboy with Twig Arms 1024	Open		56.00	58
1994 Snowflake Belsnickle 177	Retrd.	1998	36.00	44
1999 Snowlady with Twig Arms 1025	Open		64.00	66
1994 Snowman & Boy 181	Open		34.00	40
1997 Snowman 1013	Open		50.00	50
1990 Snowman 127	Retrd.	1996	32.00	35
1996 Snowman in Forest 1003	Open		70.00	82
2000 Snowman with Broom 1032	Open		46.00	46
1993 Snowman with Scarf 162	Retrd.	1998	28.00	34
1998 Snowman with twig arms 1021	Open		74.00	76
1995 Snowman with Twig Arms 188	Open		32.00	40
1994 Snowman, lg. 182	Open		44.00	54
1990 Snowman, med. 131	Retrd.	1997	28.00	34
1991 Snowman, sm. 139	Retrd.	1996	22.00	28
1996 Snowman/Snowflake Scarf 1004	Open		44.00	52
1992 Snowman/Twigs 156	Retrd.	1998	30.00	34
1997 Snowy Tree, lg. 1014	Open		26.00	28
1997 Snowy Tree, sm. 1015	Open		24.00	26
1995 Tall Tree 190	Open		28.00	36
1996 Tree 197	Open		26.00	36
1996 Tree 198	Open		22.00	28
1996 Tree 199	Retrd.	1999	18.00	20
1992 Tree Set 160	Retrd.	1998	44.00	52
1994 Walking Santa 180	Retrd.	1996	90.00	90
2000 White Bears (Two) 1034	Open		42.00	42

*Quotes have been rounded up to nearest dollar

Collectors' Information Bureau

447

Home Accents - K. Bejma

YEAR ISSUE	EDITION LIMIT	YEAR RETD.	ISSUE PRICE	*QUOTE U.S.$
1998 Paper Mache Angel 9002	Retrd.	1998	80.00	80
1998 Paper Mache Snowman 9000	Retrd.	2000	30.00	30
1998 Paper Mache Witch 9001	Retrd.	1998	90.00	90

Lamps - K. Bejma

YEAR ISSUE	EDITION LIMIT	YEAR RETD.	ISSUE PRICE	*QUOTE U.S.$
1995 Angel 510	Retrd.	1999	160.00	160
1988 Belsnickle, lg. 500	Open		220.00	220
1988 Belsnickle, sm. 501	Retrd.	1996	170.00	170
1993 Belsnickle, sm. 508	Retrd.	1999	160.00	160
1997 Bunny, lg. 512	Open		190.00	190
1990 Cat 503	Retrd.	1999	180.00	180
1992 Father Christmas 507	Open		280.00	280
1990 Rabbit 502	Retrd.	1996	170.00	170
1997 Santa, lg. 511	Open		220.00	220
1992 Sheep 506	Retrd.	1994	150.00	150
1994 Snowman 509	Retrd.	1999	280.00	280
1998 Snowman, sm 513	Open		90.00	96
1992 Spaniel 504	Retrd.	1994	170.00	170
1992 Spaniel, set 505	Retrd.	1994	330.00	330

Limited Edition Christmas Figurines - K. Bejma

YEAR ISSUE	EDITION LIMIT	YEAR RETD.	ISSUE PRICE	*QUOTE U.S.$
1993 Naughty Otto 700	Yr.Iss.	1993	70.00	70
1994 Father Christmas 701	Yr.Iss.	1994	60.00	60
1995 Sinter Klaas 702	Yr.Iss.	1995	60.00	60
1996 Snowy, Snowy Night 703	Yr.Iss.	1996	56.00	56
1997 Glad Tidings 704	Yr.Iss.	1997	60.00	60
1998 1998 Limited Edition 705	Yr.Iss.	1998	60.00	60
1998 10th Anniversary Edition 706	Yr.Iss.	1998	64.00	64
1999 Snowy Christmas 707	Yr.Iss.	1999	60.00	60
2000 Christmas Piece 2000 708	Yr.Iss.		60.00	60

Limited Edition Collector's Series - K. Bejma

YEAR ISSUE	EDITION LIMIT	YEAR RETD.	ISSUE PRICE	*QUOTE U.S.$
1997 Bearing Gifts 650	500		72.00	76
1997 Bring Yuletide Cheer 657	350		250.00	260
2000 Buddies 680	750		52.00	52
2000 Bunny Trail 681	750		72.00	72
1997 Cabbages & Violets 639	350	2000	64.00	74
1998 Carrot Cruiser 642	750		84.00	84
1996 Christkindl 635	2,000		68.00	86
1996 Christmas Aglow 629	1,000		36.00	36
2000 Christmas Elegance 683	700		170.00	170
2000 Christmas Posies (Gold Star Dealers) 689	Yr.Iss.		50.00	50
2000 Christmas Splendor 686	350	2000	74.00	74
1998 Crystal Cottage 641	1,000		96.00	74
1996 Dash Away All 628	1,500		108.00	120
1995 Downhill Racer 618	2,500		48.00	64
2000 Ear-Resistible 682	500		86.00	86
1994 Egg Cottage 603	1,500	1997	80.00	90
1994 Egyptian Egg/Rabbits 600	1,500	1997	48.00	54
1997 Field of Flowers 636	750		56.00	64
1997 Forever Friends 638	500		52.00	64
1998 From The Chimney He Rose 659	2,500		66.00	70
1997 The Garden Gate 637	350		56.00	68
1998 Garden Party 671	2,500		54.00	58
2000 Giddy Up 678	1,500		46.00	46
1998 Goin' on a Ride 670	750		48.00	56
1995 Happy Christmas 622	2,000		50.00	64
1998 Hare Hansel 645	1,500		50.00	52
1995 Hareratio 613	1,500		42.00	48
1994 Hemlocks And Holly 610	750		260.00	300
1998 Hi! 668	2,000		18.00	20
1996 Hitching a Ride 625	750	2000	44.00	58
1996 Holiday Rider 631	1,000		48.00	50
1995 Holiday Sledding 620	2,500		52.00	68
1994 Holy Night 612	750	1999	250.00	280
1998 Humphrey 648	100		600.00	600
1998 Jack 647	750	2000	30.00	34
1995 Jacqueline 614	1,500		48.00	54
1995 Jeffrey 615	1,500		48.00	54
1998 Jumpin' for Joy 666	1,500		24.00	26
1994 Keeping Secrets 605	3,500		52.00	64
1994 Kimbra 609	10,000	1999	24.00	36
2000 Leapfrog 679	2,500		18.00	18
1996 Life is but a Dream 627	1,000		42.00	52
1994 Lite The Way 604	3,500		52.00	58
1998 Littlest Helper 660	1,500		66.00	70
1995 Magnolias in Bloom 616	1,500	1999	90.00	110
1997 Memorable Journey 655	1,500		70.00	74
1996 A Merry Christmas Santa 100A	100		600.00	770
1998 A Merry Olde Gent 663	2,500		72.00	76
1996 A Midnight Clear 634	1,250		52.00	82
1994 Miles To Go 607	10,000		52.00	64
1997 Noel, Noel 651	750		70.00	70
1995 O' Tannenbaum 621	1,500		56.00	82
2000 On A Snowy Night 685	500		70.00	70
1998 Pair O' Hares 644	500		96.00	90
2000 Patches 677	1,500		50.00	50
1995 Père Noel 619	1,500		90.00	116
1998 Pocketful of Posies 646	750		38.00	40
1994 Rabbits At Home Egg 602	1,500	1997	80.00	90
1996 Robin Tracks 624	1,000		48.00	60
1998 Rock-A-Bunny 669	1,500		20.00	22
2000 Rooster Ride (Gold Star Dealers) 690	Yr.Iss.		48.00	48
1998 Round About Rabbit 643	1,000		60.00	62
1995 Santa Express 617	2,000		56.00	66
2000 Santa Hugs (Gold Star Dealers) 688	Yr.Iss.		96.00	96
1997 Santa's Helper 658	500		48.00	48
1997 Scooter Claus 649	500		92.00	96
1998 Season's Greetings 664	750		160.00	164
1996 Sharing The Spirit 630	1,000		90.00	104
1998 Shedding A Tear 667	1,500		24.00	26
1994 Shhh... 606	5,000		36.00	36
1994 Silent Night 611	750	1999	120.00	140
2000 Snowmen Melt Your Heart 687	750		96.00	96
1997 Snowy Ride 656	2,500		108.00	112
1998 Special Delivery 661	750		104.00	110
1995 St. Nick's Visit 623	750		380.00	430
1996 The Stocking Was Hung 633	1,500		68.00	76
1994 Strolling Rabbits Egg 601	1,500	1997	80.00	90
1997 Sweet Dreams 653	750		70.00	70
1996 Sweet Messenger 632	1,500		52.00	66
1998 A Tisket, A Tasket 665	2,500		30.00	32
1997 To All A Good Night 654	500		72.00	76
1997 To Market, To Market 640	500		50.00	64
1994 Up On The Rooftop 608	5,000		56.00	64
1996 Violets for Mary 626	500		64.00	76
2000 Violets for Mary 626	Retrd.	2000	60.00	60
1997 A Walk In The Woods 652	750		56.00	58
2000 Who Needs a Reindeer? 684	350		130.00	130
1998 Winter Wonderland 662	1,500		76.00	80

Nativity Collection - K. Bejma

YEAR ISSUE	EDITION LIMIT	YEAR RETD.	ISSUE PRICE	*QUOTE U.S.$
1995 Elephant	Open		160.00	160
1995 Group I Stable, Joseph, Mary, Baby Jesus, Angel	Open		240.00	240
1995 Group II Wise Men, set/3	Open		180.00	180
1995 Group III Shepards and Wanderer, set/4	Open		190.00	190
1995 Group IV Farm Animals, Sheep/2, Goat, Donkey, Cow	Open		160.00	160
1995 Laying Camel	Open		170.00	170
1995 Standing Camel	Open		180.00	180

Outdoors Collection - K. Bejma

YEAR ISSUE	EDITION LIMIT	YEAR RETD.	ISSUE PRICE	*QUOTE U.S.$
1998 Acorn Birdhouse 7004	Retrd.	1998	64.00	76
1998 Copper Garden Angel/birdseed tray 7001C	Retrd.	1998	320.00	320
1998 Copper Garden Angel/flowers 7000C	Retrd.	1998	320.00	320
1998 Copper Praying Garden Angel 7002C	Retrd.	1998	320.00	320
1998 Garden Angel w/Child 7009	Retrd.	1998	240.00	240
1998 Garden Angel w/Roses 7008	Retrd.	1998	240.00	240
1998 Garden Angel w/Shell 7007	Retrd.	1998	240.00	240
1998 Pansy Birdhouse 7005	Retrd.	1998	64.00	64
1998 Rust Garden Angel/birdseed tray 7001R	Retrd.	1998	320.00	320
1998 Rust Garden Angel/flowers 7000R	Retrd.	1998	320.00	320
1998 Rust Praying Garden Angel 7002R	Retrd.	1998	320.00	320
1998 Sunflower Birdhouse 7006	Retrd.	1998	64.00	64
1998 Tabletop Angel Fountain 7003	Retrd.	1998	300.00	300

Romance Collection - K. Bejma

YEAR ISSUE	EDITION LIMIT	YEAR RETD.	ISSUE PRICE	*QUOTE U.S.$
1998 "Be Mine" Cherub 6000	Open		40.00	40
2000 Boy/Bunny Box 6005	Open		70.00	70
2000 Bride & Groom 6003	Open		84.00	84
1998 Cherub Bud Vase 6001	Open		36.00	36
2000 Cherub w/Heart 6004	Open		66.00	66
1998 Heart Vase w/Cherub 6002	Open		60.00	60

Spring Figurines - K. Bejma

YEAR ISSUE	EDITION LIMIT	YEAR RETD.	ISSUE PRICE	*QUOTE U.S.$
1991 Bavarian Rabbit Set 226	Retrd.	1999	90.00	110
1996 Bunny in Shamrocks 268	Retrd.	2000	52.00	60
1996 Bunny with Carrots on Base 272	Retrd.	1998	48.00	55
1995 Bunny with Colored Eggs 263	Retrd.	1999	28.00	36
1990 Bunny/Acorns/Carrots 202	Retrd.	2000	32.00	38
1991 Bunny/Basket 227	Retrd.	1996	26.00	26
1993 Bunny/Cabbage 233	Open		24.00	28
1997 Cherub on Rabbit 282	Open		44.00	40
1997 Cherub, lg. 283	Open		120.00	150
1994 Chick with Egg 257	Open		48.00	60
1994 Chicks, set/3 260	Open		64.00	76
1995 Country Rabbit, lg. 265	Open		70.00	96
1996 Egg Wagon 275	Open		44.00	48
1996 Farmer Rabbit w/Carrots 270	Retrd.	1999	56.00	80
1992 Folksy/Rabbit 231	Retrd.	1999	48.00	52
1994 Hatching Chick 259	Open		20.00	38
1993 Hatching Rabbit 234	Open		34.00	44
1995 Hiking Bunny w/Egg Basket 262	Retrd.	1998	28.00	36
1994 Lady Vendor Rabbit 256	Retrd.	1999	42.00	50
1994 Laying Sheep 245	Retrd.	1997	44.00	50
1995 Meadow Rabbit 266	Open		90.00	100
1991 Mother Rabbit/Basket 215	Retrd.	1996	48.00	48
1990 Mother Rabbit/Six Babies 200	Open		120.00	130
1990 Mother/Bowl of Eggs 207	Retrd.	1996	30.00	32
1993 Mr. Rabbit/Two Children 244	Retrd.	1996	44.00	44
1994 Professor Rabbit/Chicks 236	Retrd.	1997	30.00	44
1990 Rabbit Holding Basket 220	Retrd.	1996	50.00	54
1994 Rabbit Holding Carrot 253	Open		52.00	60
1994 Rabbit in Flower Garden 246	Retrd.	1998	64.00	76
1996 Rabbit on Scooter 271	Retrd.	1999	44.00	50
1991 Rabbit Riding Rooster 209	Retrd.	1997	36.00	48
1996 Rabbit w/Ferns and Lillies 269	Open		120.00	140
1997 Rabbit w/Paw Up 281	Open		32.00	38
1994 Rabbit with Basket 255	Retrd.	1998	52.00	60
1994 Rabbit with Vest 254	Retrd.	1997	38.00	44
1991 Rabbit/Basket Eggs 224	Retrd.	1999	46.00	52
1991 Rabbit/Basket/Bow 225	Retrd.	1997	46.00	52
1994 Rabbit/Hat/Stick 239	Retrd.	1997	28.00	36
1990 Rabbit/Holding Basket 203	Retrd.	1997	30.00	34
1990 Rabbit/Umbrella 208	Retrd.	1996	30.00	30
1994 Rabbits on See-Saw 252	Retrd.	1998	44.00	50
1990 Running Rabbit 205	Open		32.00	38
1996 Shamrock Cart 273	Open		36.00	48
1990 Sitting Bunny 204	Retrd.	1996	24.00	25
1995 Sitting Bunny 261	Open		24.00	32
1990 Sitting Bunny, lg. 216	Open		68.00	76
1994 Sitting Rabbit 251	Retrd.	1999	36.00	42
1993 Sitting Rabbit, lg. 235	Retrd.	1997	44.00	62
1994 Squirrel on Pinecone 249	Open		40.00	48
1996 Squirrel, lg. 276	Open		48.00	56
1996 Squirrel, med. 277	Open		44.00	52
1994 Standing Chick 258	Open		24.00	30
1994 Standing Rabbit 237	Retrd.	1996	44.00	44
1990 Standing Sheep 211	Retrd.	1996	36.00	40
1996 Tan Rabbit w/Basket on Back 267	Open		90.00	104
1990 Two Rabbits/Basket 219	Retrd.	2000	52.00	72
1996 Wheelbarrow Egg 274	Open		48.00	48
1994 Wheelbarrow Rabbit 250	Retrd.	1998	44.00	50
1997 White Rabbit, lg. 278	Open		36.00	56
1997 White Rabbit, med. 279	Open		30.00	56
1997 White Rabbit, sm. 280	Open		24.00	52
1995 Woodland Rabbit 264	Open		48.00	60

Walnut Ridge Everyday Collection - K. Bejma

YEAR ISSUE	EDITION LIMIT	YEAR RETD.	ISSUE PRICE	*QUOTE U.S.$
1997 Bunch of Violets 5009	Open		30.00	40
1997 Cone Topiary 5013	Retrd.	1999	80.00	80
1997 Fantail Rooster 5005	Open		64.00	80
1997 Flower Wall Basket 5003	Open		48.00	70
1997 Fruit Topiary, lg. 5000	Open		150.00	180
1997 Fruit Topiary, med. 5001	Open		120.00	160
1997 Fruit Topiary, sm. 5002	Open		60.00	90
1997 Hen in Basket 5006	Open		48.00	60
1997 Hen w/Shamrocks 5008	Open		36.00	44
1997 Rooster w/Shamrocks 5007	Open		36.00	44
1997 Rooster, lg. 5004	Open		120.00	150
1997 Rose Topiary 5012	Retrd.	1999	150.00	150
1997 Summer Flowers 5010	Open		80.00	100
1997 Victorian Vase w/Roses 5011	Retrd.	1999	70.00	70

Walt Disney

Walt Disney Collectors Society - Disney Studios

YEAR ISSUE	EDITION LIMIT	YEAR RETD.	ISSUE PRICE	*QUOTE U.S.$
1993 Jiminy Cricket Members Only Gift Piece (Kit)	Closed	1993	Gift	140-250
1993 Jiminy Cricket 4"	Closed	1993	Gift	200-275
1993 Brave Little Tailor 7 1/4" "I Let em' Have It!" (Animator's Choice)	Closed	1994	160.00	135-275
1994 Cheshire Cat 4 3/4"	Closed	1994	Gift	95-145
1994 Pecos Bill and Widowmaker 9 1/2"	Closed	1994	650.00	550-800
1994 Admiral Duck 6 1/4" (Animator's Choice)	Closed	1995	165.00	175-275
1995 Dumbo	Closed	1995	Gift	95-150
1995 Cruella De Vil 10 1/4" "Anita, Daahling" (Animator's Choice)	Closed	1995	250.00	265-395
1995 Dumbo Ornament "Simply Adorable"	Closed	1995	20.00	40
1995 Slue Foot Sue 41075	Closed	1995	695.00	350-750
1996 Winnie the Pooh "Time for something sweet" 41091	Closed	1996	Gift	85-125
1996 Winnie the Pooh Ornament "Time for something sweet" 41096	Closed	1996	25.00	40
1996 Princess Minnie 41095 (Animator's Choice)	Closed	1996	165.00	120-295
1996 Casey at the Bat 41107	Closed	1996	395.00	250-395
1997 Magician Mickey "On with the show" 41134	Closed	1997	Gift	55-60
1997 Magician Mickey "On with the show" Ornament 41135	Closed	1997	25.00	65-75
1997 Mickey's Debut (Steamboat Willie) (5th Anniversary) (Charter member backstamp) 41136	Yr.Iss.	1997	175.00	175-325
1997 Mickey's Debut (Steamboat Willie) (5th Anniversary) (Non-Charter member) 41255	Open		175.00	175
1997 Goofy-Moving Day "Oh The World Owes Me A Livin.'" 41138 (Animator's Choice)	Yr.Iss.	1997	185.00	100-210
1997 Maleficent: "The Mistress of all Evil" 41177	Yr.Iss.	1997	450.00	350-545
1997 Chernabog: Night on Bald Mountain, A/P	25	1997	750.00	1120-1200
1998 Timon: "Luau!" 41197	Yr.Iss.	1998	Gift	50-75
1998 Timon: "Luau!" Ornament 41262	Yr.Iss.	1998	25.00	25
1998 Timothy Mouse: "Friendship Offering" Ornament 41179	Yr.Iss.	1998	55.00	55-60
1998 Autumn Fairy: The Touch of an Autumn Fairy 41281	Yr.Iss.	1998	495.00	495-568
1998 Pluto: Sticky Situation 41199 (Animator's Choice)	Yr.Iss.	1998	150.00	150-190
1998 Jafar: "Oh Mighty Evil One" 41280	Yr.Iss.	1998	395.00	395-450
1998 Snow White and Prince, A/P "A Kiss Brings Love Anew"	75	1998	750.00	795-1000
1999 Lady: A Perfectly Beautiful Little Lady	Yr.Iss.	1999	Gift	50
1999 White Rabbit Figural Ornament "No Time to Say Hello-Goodbye" 41373	Yr.Iss.	1999	59.00	59
1999 "Tinker Bell Pauses to Reflect" 41366 (Animator's Choice)	Yr.Iss.	1999	240.00	275
1999 Cruella in Bed "It's That De Vil Woman" 41405	Yr.Iss.	1999	450.00	450
1999 Pumbaa & Timon: "Double Trouble" 41416	Yr.Iss.	1999	135.00	135
2000 Footman: Presenting The Glass Slipper 1204011	Yr.Iss.		125.00	125
2000 Millennium Midway: "On Top of the World"	Yr.Iss.		50.00	50
2000 Pinocchio: "I'll Never Lie Again" 1202881 (Animator's Choice)	Yr.Iss.		240.00	240
2000 Fantasia Fairy:: "Pretty in Pink" Ornament 1202880	Yr.Iss.		59.00	59

*Quotes have been rounded up to nearest dollar

YEAR ISSUE	EDITION LIMIT	YEAR RETD.	ISSUE PRICE	*QUOTE U.S.$
2000 Evil Queen: "Enthroned Evil" 1205544	Yr.Iss.		395.00	395

Walt Disney Classics Collection-Special Event - Disney Studios

YEAR ISSUE	EDITION LIMIT	YEAR RETD.	ISSUE PRICE	*QUOTE U.S.$
1993 Flight of Fancy 3" 41051	Closed	1994	35.00	60-95
1994 Mr. Smee 5" "Oh, dear, dear, dear."41062	Closed	1995	90.00	100-150
1994 Mr. Smee 5" 41062 (teal stamp)	Closed	1995	90.00	95-125
1995 Lucky 41080	Closed	1995	40.00	50-65
1995 Wicked Witch "Take the apple, dearie." 41084	Closed	1996	130.00	450-500
1996 Tinkerbell Ornament	Closed	1996	50.00	75-90
1996 Fairy Godmother "Bibbidi, Bobbidi, Boo" 41108	Closed	1996	125.00	125-215
1997 Evil Queen "Bring back her heart...." 41165	Closed	1997	150.00	135-225
1997 Winnie the Pooh Ornament 41176	Closed	1997	59.00	59-95
1997 Hercules and Pegasus: A gift from the Gods Ornament 41167	Closed	1997	55.00	55
1997 Blue Fairy: Making Dreams Come True 41139	Closed	1997	150.00	113-150
1998 Shere Khan: Everyone Runs From Shere Kahn 41254	Closed	1998	145.00	145-195
1998 Ursula: "We Made a Deal" 41285	Closed	1998	165.00	165-195
2000 Bambi & Mother: My Little Bambi 1204799	Closed	2000	195.00	195
2000 Jiminy Cricket: "Let Your Conscience Be Your Guide" 1210986	Open		85.00	85

Disney's Enchanted Places - Disney Studios

YEAR ISSUE	EDITION LIMIT	YEAR RETD.	ISSUE PRICE	*QUOTE U.S.$
1998 Alice in Wonderland: A Tea Party in Wonderland 41295	4,500		395.00	395
1997 Ariel's Secret Grotto: The Little Mermaid 41235	Open		175.00	175
1996 The Beast's Castle: Beauty & The Beast 41225	Open		245.00	245
1997 A Castle For Cinderella: Cinderella	Retrd.	1997	225.00	225-300
1997 Cruella's Car: 101 Dalmatians 41230	Retrd.	1999	165.00	165
1996 An Elegant Coach For Cinderella: Cinderella 41208	Retrd.	1999	265.00	265
1996 Fiddler Pig's Stick House: Three Little Pigs 41204	Retrd.	1998	85.00	85-90
1996 Fifer Pig's Straw House: Three Little Pigs 41205	Retrd.	1998	85.00	85-90
1996 Geppetto's Toy Shop: Pinocchio 41207	Retrd.	1998	150.00	150
1998 Geppettos Toy Creation: Pinocchio 41315	Closed	1998	125.00	125-195
1996 Grandpa's House: Peter & The Wolf 41211	Closed	1996	125.00	125
1997 Hade's Chariot: Hercules 41246	Retrd.	1997	125.00	125
1996 The Jolly Roger: Peter Pan 41209	10,000		475.00	475
1997 King Louie's Temple: Jungle Book	Yr.Iss.	1997	125.00	125
1997 Pastoral Setting: Fantasia 41232	3,000	1997	195.00	195-210
1997 Pooh Bear's House: Winnie the Pooh & The Honey Tree 41231	Open		150.00	150
1996 Practical Pig's Brick House: Three Little Pigs 41206	Retrd.	1998	115.00	85-115
1999 Rose and Table:The Enchanted Rose: Beauty & The Beast 41343	Open		100.00	100
1995 Seven Dwarf's Cottage: Snow White 41200	Retrd.	2000	180.00	180
1995 Seven Dwarf's Jewel Mine: Snow White 41203	Retrd.	2000	190.00	190
1998 Sleeping Beauty's Castle 41263	Open		225.00	225
1997 Snow White's Wishing Well: Snow White 41248	Open		160.00	160
1998 Steamboat Willie's Steamboat 41264	Yr.Iss.	1998	160.00	160
1995 White Rabbit's House: Alice in Wonderland 41202	Open		175.00	175
1995 Woodcutter's Cottage: Sleeping Beauty 41201	Retrd.	1999	170.00	170

Disney's Enchanted Places Miniatures - Disney Studios

YEAR ISSUE	EDITION LIMIT	YEAR RETD.	ISSUE PRICE	*QUOTE U.S.$
1997 Ariel 41240	Retrd.	1999	50.00	50
1998 Bashful 41273	Retrd.	2000	50.00	50
1996 Briar Rose 41214	Retrd.	1999	50.00	50
1996 Captain Hook 41219	Retrd.	1998	50.00	50
1998 Doc 41271	Retrd.	2000	50.00	50
1996 Dopey 41215	Retrd.	2000	50.00	50
1999 Eeyore 41319	Open		50.00	50
1996 Fiddler Pig 41224	Retrd.	1998	50.00	50
1996 Fifer Pig 41223	Retrd.	1998	50.00	50
1997 Grumpy 41239	Retrd.	2000	50.00	50
1996 Gus 41218	Retrd.	1999	50.00	50
1998 Happy 41272	Retrd.	2000	50.00	50
1996 Jaq 41242	Retrd.	1999	50.00	50
1998 Jiminy Cricket 41335	Closed	1998	50.00	50
1999 Kanga & Roo 1201838	Open		50.00	50
1998 Mickey Mouse 41265	Closed	1998	50.00	50
1997 Pain 41247	Retrd.	1997	50.00	50
1997 Panic 41250	Retrd.	1997	50.00	50
1996 Peter 41221	Yr.Iss.	1996	50.00	50
1999 Piglet 41337	Open		50.00	50
1996 Pinocchio 41217	Retrd.	1998	50.00	50
1996 Practical Pig 41216	Retrd.	1998	50.00	50
1999 Sleepy 41411	Retrd.	2000	50.00	50
1998 Sneezy 41318	Retrd.	2000	50.00	50
1996 Snow White 41212	Retrd.	2000	50.00	50
1998 Tigger 41274	Open		50.00	50
1997 Unicorn 41237	Retrd.	1998	50.00	50
1996 White Rabbit 41213	Open		50.00	50

YEAR ISSUE	EDITION LIMIT	YEAR RETD.	ISSUE PRICE	*QUOTE U.S.$
1997 Winnie the Pooh 41238	Open		50.00	50
1999 Witch 1201785	Retrd.	2000	50.00	50

Disneyana - Disney Studios

YEAR ISSUE	EDITION LIMIT	YEAR RETD.	ISSUE PRICE	*QUOTE U.S.$
1996 Proud Pongo (w/backstamp)	1,200	1996	175.00	295-350
1997 Chernabog: Night on Bald Mountain	1,500	1997	750.00	1625-1750
1997 Disney Villain Ornament, set/6	12,000	1997	40.00	94-130
1998 Snow White & Prince	1,650	1998	750.00	660-2035
1999 Lion King Ornament, set/7	1,000	1999	45.00	110
1999 Maleficent as Dragon	1,350	1999	795.00	935-1350

Walt Disney Classics Collection-101 Dalmatians - Disney Studios

YEAR ISSUE	EDITION LIMIT	YEAR RETD.	ISSUE PRICE	*QUOTE U.S.$
1996 "Go get him thunder!" Two Puppies on Newspaper 41129	Retrd.	1999	120.00	120-143
1996 Lucky and Television "Come on Lucky..." 41131	Retrd.	1999	150.00	135-150
1996 Patient Perdita Perdita with Patch and Puppy 41133	Retrd.	1999	175.00	130-175
1996 Proud Pongo Pongo with Pepper and Penny 41132	Retrd.	1999	175.00	130-190
1996 Rolly "I'm hungry, Mother" 41130	Retrd.	1999	65.00	65-77
1996 Opening Title 41169	Open		29.00	29

Walt Disney Classics Collection-Alice in Wonderland - Disney Studios

YEAR ISSUE	EDITION LIMIT	YEAR RETD.	ISSUE PRICE	*QUOTE U.S.$
1999 Alice: "Yes, Your Majesty" 41375	Open		145.00	145
1999 Card Player: "Playing Card" 41414	Open		120.00	120
1999 King of Hearts: "...and the King" 41419	Open		90.00	90
1999 Queen of Hearts" "Let the Game Begin!" 41413	Yr.Iss.	1999	175.00	175
1999 Opening Title 41378	Open		29.00	29

Walt Disney Classics Collection-Bambi - Disney Studios

YEAR ISSUE	EDITION LIMIT	YEAR RETD.	ISSUE PRICE	*QUOTE U.S.$
1992 Bambi "Purty Flower" 6" 41033	Retrd.	1998	195.00	195
1992 Bambi & Flower "He can call me a flower if he wants to" 6" 41010	10,000	1992	298.00	375-800
1992 Field Mouse-not touching "Little April Shower" 5 3/5" 41012	Closed	1993	195.00	825-980
1992 Field Mouse-touching "Little April Shower" 5 3/5" 41012	Closed	1993	195.00	875-946
1992 Flower "Oh...gosh!" 3" 41034	Retrd.	1998	78.00	85-160
1992 Friend Owl "What's going on around here?" 8 3/5" 41011	Retrd.	1998	195.00	110-225
1992 Thumper "Hee! Hee! Hee!" 3" 41013	Retrd.	1998	55.00	65-75
1992 Thumper's Sisters "Hello, hello there!" 3 3/5" 41014	Retrd.	1998	69.00	70-115
1992 Opening Title 41015	Retrd.	1998	29.00	25-45

Walt Disney Classics Collection-Beauty & The Beast - Disney Studios

YEAR ISSUE	EDITION LIMIT	YEAR RETD.	ISSUE PRICE	*QUOTE U.S.$
2000 Belle and Beast: "She Didn't Shudder at My Paw" (2000 Gold Circle Exclusive) 1209684	1,991		395.00	395
1997 Lumiere: Vive L'amour! 41181	Open		115.00	115
1997 Cogsworth: Just in Time 41182	Open		120.00	120
1997 Mrs. Potts and Chip: "Good Night, Luv" 41183	Open		125.00	125
1997 Tale as Old as Time-Belle and the Beast Dancing 41156	Open		295.00	295
1997 Opening Title 41189	Open		29	29

Walt Disney Classics Collection-Cinderella - Disney Studios

YEAR ISSUE	EDITION LIMIT	YEAR RETD.	ISSUE PRICE	*QUOTE U.S.$
1993 A Lovely Dress For Cinderelly 41030/ wheel & clef	5,000	1993	800.00	1875-1900
2000 Anastasia: Awful Anastasia 1202883	Open		145.00	145
1993 Birds "We'll tie a sash around it" 6 2/5" 41005	Retrd.	1994	149.00	90-250
1992 Bruno "Just learn to like cats" 4 2/5" 41002	Retrd.	1993	69.00	145-195
1992 Chalk Mouse "No time for dilly-dally" 3 2/5" 41006	Retrd.	1994	65.00	125-170
1992 Cinderella "They can't stop me from dreaming" 6" 41000	Retrd.	1992	195.00	500-695
2000 Cinderella: Fit For a Princess 1202882	Open		225.00	225
1995 Cinderella & Prince Charming "So this is love" 41079	Open		275.00	275
1998 Cinderella & Prince Wedding Sculpture: Fairy Tale Wedding 41267	Open		195.00	195
2000 Drizella: Dreadful Drizella 1202885	Open		145.00	145
2000 Grand Duke: Royal Fitting 1202884	Open		150.00	150
1992 Gus "You go get some trimmin'" 3 2/5" 41007	Retrd.	1994	65.00	110-195
1992 Jaq "You go get some trimmin'" 4 1/5" 41008	Retrd.	1994	65.00	74-120
2000 Lady Termaine: Spiteful Stepmother 1204798	Open		165.00	165
1992 Lucifer "Meany, sneaky, roos-a-fee" 2 3/5" 41001	Retrd.	1993	69.00	100-195
1992 Needle Mouse "Hey, we can do it!" 5 4/5" 41004	Retrd.	1993	69.00	150-250
1992 Sewing Book 41003	Retrd.	1994	69.00	39-74
1992 Opening Title 41009	Open		29.00	29
1992 Opening Title-Technicolor 41009	Closed	1993	29.00	25-80

Walt Disney Classics Collection-Delivery Boy - Disney Studios

YEAR ISSUE	EDITION LIMIT	YEAR RETD.	ISSUE PRICE	*QUOTE U.S.$
1992 Mickey "Hey Minnie, wanna go steppin'?" 6" 41020	Retrd.	1997	125.00	99-182
1992 Minnie "I'm a Jazz Baby" 6" 41021	Retrd.	1996	125.00	90-150
1992 Pluto Dynamite Dog 3 3/5" 41022	Retrd.	1993	125.00	125-185
1992 Pluto Dynamite Dog- 1st version (raised letters) 3 3/5" 41022/ wheel	Closed	1993	125.00	270-402

YEAR ISSUE	EDITION LIMIT	YEAR RETD.	ISSUE PRICE	*QUOTE U.S.$
1992 Opening Title 41019	Retrd.	1993	29.00	20-35

Walt Disney Classics Collection-Don Donald - Disney Studios

YEAR ISSUE	EDITION LIMIT	YEAR RETD.	ISSUE PRICE	*QUOTE U.S.$
1999 Daisy Duck: Daisy's Debut (Gold Circle Dealer's Exclusive) 1028770	Closed	1999	130.00	130

Walt Disney Classics Collection-Donald's Better Self - Disney Studios

YEAR ISSUE	EDITION LIMIT	YEAR RETD.	ISSUE PRICE	*QUOTE U.S.$
1998 Donald Duck: Donald's Decision 41296	Retrd.	1999	145.00	110-145
1998 Donald Duck: Little Devil 41309	Retrd.	1999	145.00	145-180
1998 Donald Duck: What An Angel 41297	Retrd.	1999	145.00	145-180
1998 Opening Title 41298	Retrd.	1999	29.00	29

Walt Disney Classics Collection-Fantasia - Disney Studios

YEAR ISSUE	EDITION LIMIT	YEAR RETD.	ISSUE PRICE	*QUOTE U.S.$
1993 Blue Centaurette-Beauty in Bloom 7 1/2" 41041	Retrd.	1995	195.00	100-260
1992 Broom, Bucket Brigade 5 4/5" 41017	Retrd.	1995	75.00	90-150
1992 Broom, Bucket Brigade w/water spots 5 4/5" 41017/ wheel	Retrd.	1992	75.00	190-220
1996 Ben Ali Gator 7 1/2" 41118	Retrd.	1999	185.00	148-190
1996 Hyacinth Hippo 5 1/2" 41117	Retrd.	1999	195.00	200-225
1993 Love's Little Helpers Cupids 8" 41042	Retrd.	1995	290.00	175-300
1994 Small Mushroom: Hop Low 41067	Retrd.	1999	35.00	30-55
1994 Mushroom Dancer-Medium 4 1/4" 41068	Retrd.	1999	50.00	60
1994 Mushroom Dancer-Large 4 3/4" 41058	Retrd.	1999	60.00	70-90
1993 Pink Centaurette-Romantic Reflections 7 1/2" 41040	Retrd.	1995	175.00	175-210
1992 Mickey Mouse: Mischievous Apprentice 5 1/8" 41016	Retrd.	1993	195.00	225-300
1997 Mademoiselle Upanova: Prima Ballerina 41178	Retrd.	1999	165.00	165
1992 Opening Title 41018	Open		29.00	29-50
1992 Opening Title-Technicolor 41018	Closed	1993	29.00	25-35

Walt Disney Classics Collection-Holiday Series - Disney Studios

YEAR ISSUE	EDITION LIMIT	YEAR RETD.	ISSUE PRICE	*QUOTE U.S.$
1995 Mickey Mouse: "Presents For My Pals" 41086	Closed	1995	150.00	150-195
1996 Pluto: Pluto Helps Decorate 41112	Closed	1996	150.00	55-180
1997 Chip 'n Dale: Little Mischief Makers 41163	Closed	1997	150.00	90-150
1997 Holiday Base 41140	Closed	1997	25.00	25
1997 Santa Candle 41172	Closed	1997	40.00	40
1998 Minnie Mouse: Caroler Minnie 41308	Closed	1998	150.00	150
1999 Goofy: "Tis the Season to Be Jolly" 41367	Closed	1999	175.00	175
2000 Donald Duck: "Fa La La..." 1207741	Yr.Iss.		150.00	150
2000 Lampost Base Lighted 1209688	Open		100.00	100
2000 Opening Title 1205736	Open		29.00	29

Walt Disney Classics Collection-Jungle Book - Disney Studios

YEAR ISSUE	EDITION LIMIT	YEAR RETD.	ISSUE PRICE	*QUOTE U.S.$
1997 King of the Swingers (King Louie) 41158	Retrd.	1999	175.00	175-195
1997 Monkeying Around (Flunky Monkey) 41159	Closed	1997	135.00	135-175
1997 Hula Baloo (Baloo) 41160	Retrd.	1999	185.00	185
1997 Mancub (Mowgli) 41161	Retrd.	1999	115.00	115
1997 Bagheera: Mowgli's Protector 41162	Retrd.	1999	135.00	135
1997 Opening Title 41171	Open		29.00	29

Walt Disney Classics Collection-Lady and The Tramp - Disney Studios

YEAR ISSUE	EDITION LIMIT	YEAR RETD.	ISSUE PRICE	*QUOTE U.S.$
1996 Lady: Lady in Love 4 1/2" 41089	Retrd.	1997	120.00	135-195
1996 Tramp: Tramp in Love 5 1/2" 41090	Retrd.	1996	100.00	149-185
1998 Lady and Tramp: Spaghetti Scene Base 41403	Open		75.00	75
1998 Lady and Tramp: "Bella Notte" (Matched Numbered - 3 Sculpture Set) 41284	5,000	1999	795.00	795-864
1996 Opening Title 41099	Open		29.00	29-35

Walt Disney Classics Collection-Little Mermaid - Disney Studios

YEAR ISSUE	EDITION LIMIT	YEAR RETD.	ISSUE PRICE	*QUOTE U.S.$
1997 Ariel: Seahorse Surprise 41184	Retrd.	1999	275.00	275
1997 Ariel: Seahorse Surprise-1st version (Bandstand) 41184	Closed	1997	275.00	347-380
1997 Blackfish: Deep Sea Diva 41195	Retrd.	1999	95.00	95-150
1998 Carp: Classic Carp (Gold Circle Dealer's Exclusive) 41194	Closed	1998	150.00	150
1997 Flounder: Flounder's Fandango 41198	Retrd.	1999	150.00	150
1998 Fluke: The Duke of Soul 41191	Retrd.	1999	120.00	120
1998 Newt: Newt's Nautical Note 41193	Retrd.	1999	135.00	135-150
1998 Sebastian: Calypso Crustacean 41187	Retrd.	1999	130.00	130
1998 Snails: Sing-Along Snails 41196	Retrd.	1999	135.00	135
1997 Turtle: Twistin' Turtle 41192	Retrd.	1999	85.00	85
1997 Opening Title 41188	Retrd.	1999	29.00	29

Walt Disney Classics Collection-Mr. Duck Steps Out - Disney Studios

YEAR ISSUE	EDITION LIMIT	YEAR RETD.	ISSUE PRICE	*QUOTE U.S.$
1993 Donald & Daisy "Oh boy, what a jitterbug!" 6 3/5" 41024	5,000	1996	295.00	365-465
1994 Donald Duck: "With love from Daisy" 6 1/4" 41060	Retrd.	1996	180.00	180
1993 Dewey: "I got somethin for ya" 4" 41025	Retrd.	1996	65.00	65

*Quotes have been rounded up to nearest dollar

YEAR ISSUE	EDITION LIMIT	YEAR RETD.	ISSUE PRICE	*QUOTE U.S.$
1993 Huey: Tag-Along Trouble 4" 41049	Retrd.	1996	65.00	65
1993 Nephew Duck-Louie 4" 41050	Retrd.	1994	65.00	65
1993 Opening Title 41023	Retrd.	1996	29.00	29-38

Walt Disney Classics Collection-Peter Pan - Disney Studios

YEAR ISSUE	EDITION LIMIT	YEAR RETD.	ISSUE PRICE	*QUOTE U.S.$
1993 Captain Hook: "I've got you this time!" 8" 41044	Suspd.		275.00	400-495
1993 Crocodile: "Tick-tock, tick-tock" 6 1/4" 41054	Suspd.		315.00	315-360
1993 Peter Pan: "Nobody calls Pan a coward!" 7 1/2" 41043	Suspd.		165.00	175-400
1993 Tinkerbell: A firefly! A pixie! Amazing!" 5" 41045	12,500	1993	215.00	320-395
1993 Opening Title 41047	Suspd.		29.00	22-35

Walt Disney Classics Collection-Pinocchio - Disney Studios

YEAR ISSUE	EDITION LIMIT	YEAR RETD.	ISSUE PRICE	*QUOTE U.S.$
1996 Figaro "Say hello to Figaro" 41111	Retrd.	1998	55.00	55-94
1996 Geppetto "Good-bye, Son" 41114	Retrd.	1998	145.00	155-170
1996 Jiminy Cricket "Wait for me, Pinoke!" 41109	Retrd.	1998	85.00	85-115
1996 Pinocchio "Good-bye Father" 41110	Retrd.	1998	125.00	140-195
1996 Opening Title 41116	Retrd.	1998	29.00	29

Walt Disney Classics Collection-Puppy Love - Disney Studios

YEAR ISSUE	EDITION LIMIT	YEAR RETD.	ISSUE PRICE	*QUOTE U.S.$
1998 Mickey Mouse: "Brought You Something" 41324	Retrd.	2000	135.00	135
1998 Minnie Mouse: "Oh, It's Swell!" 41325	Retrd.	2000	135.00	135
1998 Fifi: Flirtatious Fifi 41336	Retrd.	2000	95.00	95
1998 Opening Title 41326	Retrd.	2000	29.00	29

Walt Disney Classics Collection-Reluctant Dragon - Disney Studios

YEAR ISSUE	EDITION LIMIT	YEAR RETD.	ISSUE PRICE	*QUOTE U.S.$
1996 The Reluctant Dragon "The more the merrier" 7" 41072	7,500	1996	695.00	489-695

Walt Disney Classics Collection-Sleeping Beauty - Disney Studios

YEAR ISSUE	EDITION LIMIT	YEAR RETD.	ISSUE PRICE	*QUOTE U.S.$
1997 Briar Rose: "Once upon a dream" 41157	12,500		345.00	345-415
1998 Aurora & Phillip: A Dance in the Clouds 1028723 (blue dress)	Open		295.00	295
1998 Aurora & Phillip: A Dance in the Clouds 1028581 (pink dress)	2,000	1998	295.00	740-875
1998 Fauna: A Little Bit of Both 41259	Open		100.00	100
1998 Flora: A Little Bit of Pink 41258	Open		100.00	100
1998 Merryweather: A Little Bit of Blue 41260	Open		95.00	95
1998 Opening Title 41275	Open		29.00	29

Walt Disney Classics Collection-Song of the South - Disney Studios

YEAR ISSUE	EDITION LIMIT	YEAR RETD.	ISSUE PRICE	*QUOTE U.S.$
1996 Brer Bear "Duh" 7 1/2" 41112	Retrd.	1997	175.00	132-175
1996 Brer Fox "I got cha, Brer Rabbit" 4" 41101	Retrd.	1997	120.00	100-190
1996 Brer Rabbit: Born and Bred in a Briar Patch 4 3/4" 41103	Retrd.	1997	150.00	120-280
1996 Opening Title 41104	Retrd.	1997	29.00	29

Walt Disney Classics Collection-Symphony Hour - Disney Studios

YEAR ISSUE	EDITION LIMIT	YEAR RETD.	ISSUE PRICE	*QUOTE U.S.$
1993 Clarabelle Cow: Clarabella's Crescendo 6 4/5" 41027/ wheel	Retrd.	1993	198.00	198-204
1994 Clara Cluck: Bravo Bravissimo 41061	Retrd.	1997	185.00	185-210
1996 Donald Duck: Donald's Drum Beat 8 1/4" 41105/ hat	Retrd.	1996	225.00	185-450
1993 Goofy: Goofy's Grace Notes 6 4/5" 41026/wheel	Retrd.	1993	198.00	1150-2700
1993 Goofy: Goofy's Grace Notes 6 4/5" 41026	Retrd.	1997	198.00	118-275
1993 Horace Horsecollar: Horace's High Notes 6 4/5" 41028	Retrd.	1997	198.00	124-275
1996 Donald Duck: Donald's Drum Beat 8 1/4" 41105	Retrd.	1997	225.00	375-407
1993 Mickey Mouse Conductor: Maestro Michael Mouse 7 3/8" 41029	Retrd.	1997	185.00	185-250
1996 Sylvester Macaroni 41106	12,500	1997	395.00	395
1993 Opening Title 41031	Retrd.	1997	29.00	29

Walt Disney Classics Collection-Three Caballeros - Disney Studios

YEAR ISSUE	EDITION LIMIT	YEAR RETD.	ISSUE PRICE	*QUOTE U.S.$
1995 Amigo Donald 7" 41076	Retrd.	1996	180.00	180
1995 Amigo Jose 7" 41077	Retrd.	1996	180.00	180
1995 Amigo Panchito 7" 41078	Retrd.	1996	180.00	180
1995 Opening Title 41070	Retrd.	1996	29.00	15-33

Walt Disney Classics Collection-Three Little Pigs - Disney Studios

YEAR ISSUE	EDITION LIMIT	YEAR RETD.	ISSUE PRICE	*QUOTE U.S.$
1993 Big Bad Wolf "Who's afraid of the Big Bad Wolf?" 41039 (short straight teeth/cone base) 1st version	S/O	1993	295.00	715-995
1993 Big Bad Wolf "Who's afraid of the Big Bad Wolf?" 41039 (short straight teeth/flat base) 2nd version	S/O	1994	295.00	380-495
1993 Big Bad Wolf "Who's afraid of the Big Bad Wolf?" 41039 (long/short curved teeth) 3rd version	S/O	1994	295.00	373-895
1996 Big Bad Wolf "I'm a poor little sheep..." 41094	Open		225.00	225
1993 Fiddler Pig "Hey diddle, diddle, I play my fiddle" 4 1/2" 41038	Open		75.00	75-111
1993 Fifer Pig "I toot my flute, I don't give a hoot" 4 1/2" 41037	Open		75.00	75-111
1993 Practical Pig "Work and play don't mix" 4 1/2" 41036	Open		75.00	75-111
1993 Opening Title 41046	Open		29.00	28-46

Walt Disney Classics Collection-Toy Story - Disney Studios

YEAR ISSUE	EDITION LIMIT	YEAR RETD.	ISSUE PRICE	*QUOTE U.S.$
1998 Bo Peep: "I Found My Moving Buddy" 41320	Open		150.00	150
1998 Buzz 41304	Open		175.00	175
1998 Hamm: "It's Showtime" 41321	Open		90.00	90
1999 Mr. Potato Head: "That's Mr. Potato Head To You" 1201782	Open		115.00	115
1999 Rex: "I'm So Glad You're Not a Dinosaur" 41334	Yr.Iss.	1999	140.00	140-182
1998 Woody 41305	Open		175.00	175
1998 Opening Title 41306	Open		29.00	29

Walt Disney Classics Collection-Tribute Series - Disney Studios

YEAR ISSUE	EDITION LIMIT	YEAR RETD.	ISSUE PRICE	*QUOTE U.S.$
1995 Simba & Mufasa: Pals Forever 41085	Closed	1995	175.00	225-295
1996 Pocahontas "Listen With Your Heart" 6 1/2" 41098	Closed	1996	225.00	225-275
1997 Quasimodo and Esmeralda "Not a single monster line" 41143	Closed	1997	195.00	195
1998 Hercules: "From Zero To Hero" 41253	Closed	1998	250.00	250-286
1999 Mulan: Honorable Decision 41374	Yr.Iss.	1999	175.00	175

Walt Disney Classics Collection-Wise Little Hen - Disney Studios

YEAR ISSUE	EDITION LIMIT	YEAR RETD.	ISSUE PRICE	*QUOTE U.S.$
1997 Donald Duck: Donald's Debut (Gold Circle Dealer's Exclusive) 41175	Closed	1997	110.00	138-185

Wee Forest Folk

Animals - A. Petersen, unless otherwise noted

YEAR ISSUE	EDITION LIMIT	YEAR RETD.	ISSUE PRICE	*QUOTE U.S.$
1974 Baby Hippo H-2	Closed	1977	7.00	N/A
1978 Beaver Wood Cutter BV-1 - W. Petersen	Closed	1980	8.00	500-800
1974 Miss and Baby Hippo H-3	Closed	1977	15.00	960-1200
1973 Miss Ducky D-1	Closed	1977	6.00	N/A
1974 Miss Hippo H-1	Closed	1977	8.00	N/A
1977 Nutsy Squirrel SQ-1 - W. Petersen	Closed	1977	3.00	N/A
1979 Turtle Jogger TS-1	Closed	1980	4.00	600

Bears - A. Petersen

YEAR ISSUE	EDITION LIMIT	YEAR RETD.	ISSUE PRICE	*QUOTE U.S.$
1978 Big Lady Bear BR-4	Closed	1980	7.50	1000-1200
1977 Blueberry Bears BR-1	Closed	1982	8.75	375-500
1977 Boy Blueberry Bear BR-3	Closed	1982	4.50	300
1977 Girl Blueberry Bear BR-2	Closed	1982	4.25	300
1995 Good Pickin's BB-4	Closed	1997	64.00	88-95
1978 Traveling Bear BR-5	Closed	1980	8.00	425-500

Book / Figurine - W. Petersen

YEAR ISSUE	EDITION LIMIT	YEAR RETD.	ISSUE PRICE	*QUOTE U.S.$
1988 Tom & Eon BK-1	Suspd.	1991	45.00	280-358

Bunnies - A. Petersen, unless otherwise noted

YEAR ISSUE	EDITION LIMIT	YEAR RETD.	ISSUE PRICE	*QUOTE U.S.$
1977 Batter Bunny B-9	Closed	1982	4.50	275-350
1973 Broom Bunny B-6	Closed	1978	9.50	N/A
1972 Double Bunnies B-1	Closed	1980	4.25	1675
1972 Housekeeping Bunny B-2	Closed	1980	4.50	N/A
1973 Market Bunny B-8	Closed	1977	9.00	N/A
1973 Muff Bunny B-7	Closed	1977	9.00	N/A
1973 The Professor B-4	Closed	1980	4.75	1100
1980 Professor Rabbit B-11 - W. Petersen	Closed	1981	14.00	500-600
1973 Sir Rabbit B-3 - W. Petersen	Closed	1980	4.50	400-500
1973 Sunday Bunny B-5	Closed	1978	4.75	N/A
1977 Tennis Bunny BS-1	Closed	1980	3.75	500-540
1985 Tiny Easter Bunny B-12 - D. Petersen	Closed	1992	25.00	25-90
1978 Wedding Bunnies B-10 - W. Petersen	Closed	1981	12.50	1000-1800
1992 Windy Day! B-13 - D. Petersen	Closed	1998	37.00	50-65

Christmas Carol Series - A. Petersen

YEAR ISSUE	EDITION LIMIT	YEAR RETD.	ISSUE PRICE	*QUOTE U.S.$
1988 The Fezziwigs CC-7	Closed	1996	65.00	88-195

Cinderella Series - A. Petersen

YEAR ISSUE	EDITION LIMIT	YEAR RETD.	ISSUE PRICE	*QUOTE U.S.$
1988 Cinderella's Slipper (with Prince) C-1	Closed	1989	62.00	125-200
1989 Cinderella's Slipper C-1a	Closed	1994	32.00	94-125
1988 Cinderella's Wedding C-5	Closed	1994	62.00	150-215
1989 The Fairy Godmother C-7	Closed	1994	69.00	125-293
1988 Flower Girl C-6	Closed	1994	22.00	65-100
1988 The Flower Girls C-4	Closed	1994	42.00	85-150
1988 The Mean Stepmother C-3	Closed	1994	32.00	80-90
1988 The Ugly Stepsisters C-2	Closed	1994	62.00	90-115
1988 Set	Closed	1994	383.00	725

Fairy Tale Series - A. Petersen

YEAR ISSUE	EDITION LIMIT	YEAR RETD.	ISSUE PRICE	*QUOTE U.S.$
1980 Red Riding Hood & Wolf FT-1	Closed	1982	29.00	960-1250
1980 Red Riding Hood FT-2	Closed	1982	13.00	400-500

Forest Scene - W. Petersen

YEAR ISSUE	EDITION LIMIT	YEAR RETD.	ISSUE PRICE	*QUOTE U.S.$
1989 Hearts and Flowers FS-2 - W. Petersen	Closed	1998	110.00	145-155
1992 Love Letter FS-5	Closed	1997	98.00	145-312
1990 Mousie Comes A-Calling FS-3	Closed	1996	128.00	290-300
1993 Picnic on the Riverbank FS-6	Closed	2000	150.00	150-180
1988 Woodland Serenade FS-1	Closed	1995	125.00	125-200

Foxes - A. Petersen

YEAR ISSUE	EDITION LIMIT	YEAR RETD.	ISSUE PRICE	*QUOTE U.S.$
1978 Barrister Fox FX-3	Closed	1980	7.50	700-900
1977 Dandy Fox FX-2	Closed	1979	6.00	500-1200
1977 Fancy Fox FX-1	Closed	1979	4.75	350-700

Frogs - A. Petersen, unless otherwise noted

YEAR ISSUE	EDITION LIMIT	YEAR RETD.	ISSUE PRICE	*QUOTE U.S.$
1997 Flirty Frog F7	Closed	1999	46.00	45
1997 Freddy Frog F8	Closed	1999	46.00	46
1977 Frog Friends F-3 - W. Petersen	Closed	1981	5.75	500-1200
1974 Frog on Rock F-2	Closed	1977	6.00	N/A
1977 Grampa Frog F-5 - W. Petersen	Closed	1981	6.00	700-1100
1974 Prince Charming F-1 - W. Petersen	Closed	1977	7.50	N/A
1978 Singing Frog F-6	Closed	1979	5.50	1500
1977 Spring Peepers F-4	Closed	1979	3.50	N/A

Limited Edition - A. Petersen, unless otherwise noted

YEAR ISSUE	EDITION LIMIT	YEAR RETD.	ISSUE PRICE	*QUOTE U.S.$
1997 At the Mouseum LTD-5	Closed	1998	220.00	180-220
1981 Beauty and the Beast (color variations) BB-1 - W. Petersen	Closed	1981	89.00	8000-12000
1985 Helping Hand LTD-2	Closed	1985	62.00	650-750
1984 Postmouster LTD-1 - W. Petersen	Closed	1984	46.00	750-900
1987 Statue in the Park LTD-3 - W. Petersen	Closed	1987	93.00	625-1200
1988 Uncle Sammy LTD-4	Closed	1988	85.00	250-325

Mice - A. Petersen, unless otherwise noted

YEAR ISSUE	EDITION LIMIT	YEAR RETD.	ISSUE PRICE	*QUOTE U.S.$
1988 Aloha! M-158	Closed	1994	32.00	75-150
1982 Arty Mouse M-71	Closed	1991	19.00	94-163
1985 Attic Treasure M-126	Closed	1995	42.00	95-182
1977 Baby Sitter M-19	Closed	1981	5.75	300-350
1982 Baby Sitter M-66	Closed	1993	23.50	120-176
1987 Band Mice, set/3 M-153a-c - W. Petersen	Closed	1989	87.00	150-250
1981 Barrister Mouse M-57	Closed	1982	16.00	900
1987 Bat Mouse M-154	Closed	1994	25.00	70-125
1982 Beach Mousey M-76	Closed	1993	19.00	100-125
1983 Birthday Girl M-99 - W. Petersen	Closed	1997	18.50	70-120
1981 Blue Devil M-61	Closed	N/A	12.50	350-450
1982 Boy Sweetheart M-81	Closed	1982	13.50	350-600
1975 Bride Mouse M-9	Closed	1978	4.00	N/A
1978 Bridge Club Mouse M-20	Closed	1979	6.00	600-1625
1978 Bridge Club Mouse Partner M-21	Closed	1979	6.00	450-1625
1984 Campfire Mouse M-109 - W. Petersen	Closed	1986	26.00	250-450
1981 The Carolers M-63	Closed	1981	29.00	900-1250
1980 Carpenter Mouse M-49	Closed	1981	15.00	800
1983 Chief Geronimouse M-107a	Closed	1995	21.00	65-130
1994 Chief Mouse-asoit M-197	Closed	1997	90.00	90-150
1978 Chief Nip-a-Way Mouse M-26	Closed	1981	7.00	900-1000
1987 Choir Mouse M-147 - W. Petersen	Closed	1990	23.00	65-111
1979 Chris-Miss M-32	Closed	1982	9.00	200-300
1979 Chris-Mouse M-33	Closed	1982	9.00	250-400
1990 Chris-Mouse Slipper M-166	Closed	1999	35.00	42-80
1985 Chris-Mouse Tree M-124	Closed	1998	28.00	49-80
1983 Christmas Morning M-92	Closed	1987	35.00	200-225
1983 Clown Mouse M-98	Closed	1984	22.00	350-450
1986 Come & Get It! M-141	Closed	1988	34.00	158-225
1985 Come Play! M-131	Closed	1991	18.00	100-143
1989 Commencement Day M-161 - W. Petersen	Closed	1996	28.00	91-100
1980 Commo-Dormouse M-42 - W. Petersen	Closed	1981	14.00	900-1200
1978 Cowboy Mouse M-25	Closed	1981	6.00	500-700
1983 Cupid Mouse M-94 - W. Petersen	Closed	1997	22.00	80-100
1981 Doc Mouse & Patient M-55 - W. Petersen	Closed	1981	14.00	750-1100
1987 Don't Cry! M-149	Closed	1990	33.00	110-200
1986 Down the Chimney M-143	Closed	1988	48.00	200-300
1987 Drummer M-153b - W. Petersen	Closed	1989	29.00	50-75
1996 Early Riser M-217 - W. Petersen	Closed	2000	68.00	68
1989 Elf Tales M-163	Closed	1995	48.00	150-400
1985 Family Portrait M-127	Closed	1987	54.00	250-350
1976 Fan Mouse M-10	Closed	1979	5.75	N/A
1974 Farmer Mouse M-5	Closed	1979	3.75	N/A
1983 First Christmas M-93	Closed	1986	16.00	220-250
1984 First Day of School M-112	Closed	1985	27.00	375-450
1986 First Haircut M-137 - W. Petersen	Closed	1992	58.00	134-273
1993 First Kiss! M-192	Closed	1996	65.00	125-200
1980 Fisher Mouse M-41	Closed	1981	16.00	750-1000
1981 Flower Girl M-53	Closed	1983	15.00	375-525
1988 Forty Winks M-159 - W. Petersen	Closed	1996	36.00	65-130
1979 Gardener Mouse M-37	Closed	1981	12.00	600-900
1983 Get Well Soon! M-96	Closed	1983	15.00	600-900
1982 Girl Sweetheart M-80	Closed	2000	13.50	28
1974 Good Knight Mouse M-4 - W. Petersen	Closed	1977	7.50	N/A
1981 Graduate Mouse M-58	Closed	1988	15.00	115-225
1991 Grammy-Phone M-176	Closed	1996	75.00	88-175
1992 Greta M-169b	Closed	1993	35.00	50-65
1992 Hans M-169a	Closed	1993	35.00	50-80
1990 Hans & Greta M-169	Closed	1992	64.00	150-175
1982 Happy Birthday! M-83	Closed	1997	17.50	70-90
1983 Harvest Mouse M-104 - W. Petersen	Closed	1984	23.00	400-500
1995 Heavenly Slumber M-210	Closed	1999	49.00	49
1995 High Flyer M-207 - W. Petersen	Closed	2000	88.00	88
1992 High on the Hog M-186	Closed	1995	52.00	125-150
1982 Holly Mouse M-87	Closed	1997	13.50	90-100
1976 June Belle M-13	Closed	1979	4.25	400-600
1986 Just Checking M-140	Closed	2000	34.00	42-44
1977 King "Tut" Mouse TM-1	Closed	1979	4.50	1000-1400
1995 Lady Mousebatten M-195b	Closed	1996	46.00	100-250
1982 Lamplight Carolers M-86	Closed	1987	35.00	275-350
1982 Little Fire Chief M-77 - W. Petersen	Closed	1984	29.00	500
1982 Little Sledders M-85	Closed	1985	24.00	300-400
1982 Littlest Angel M-88	Closed	1986	15.00	125-165
1987 Littlest Witch M-156	Closed	1993	24.00	50-100
1981 Lone Caroler M-64	Closed	1981	15.50	800-1000
1993 Lord & Lady Mousebatten M-195	Closed	1995	85.00	150-300
1995 Lord Mousebatten M-195a	Closed	1996	46.00	75-100
1976 Mama Mouse with Baby M-18	Closed	1979	6.00	450-500
1987 Market Mouse M-150 - W. Petersen	Closed	1993	49.00	125-145
1972 Market Mouse M-1a	Closed	1978	4.25	N/A
1976 May Belle M-12	Closed	1980	4.25	350-600

*Quotes have been rounded up to nearest dollar

YEAR ISSUE	EDITION LIMIT	YEAR RETD.	ISSUE PRICE	*QUOTE U.S.$
1982 Me and Raggedy Ann M-70	Closed	1999	18.50	37
1983 Merry Chris-Miss M-90	Closed	1985	17.00	219-300
1983 Merry Chris-Mouse M-91	Closed	1985	16.00	250-325
1972 Miss Mouse M-1	Closed	1978	4.25	N/A
1972 Miss Mousey M-2	Closed	1978	4.00	N/A
1972 Miss Mousey w/ Bow Hat M-2b	Closed	1979	4.25	350-1100
1972 Miss Mousey w/ Straw Hat M-2a	Closed	1980	4.25	350-450
1973 Miss Nursey Mouse M-3	Closed	1980	4.00	400-500
1980 Miss Polly Mouse M-46	Closed	1984	23.00	325-480
1982 Miss Teach & Pupil M-73	Closed	1984	29.50	413-500
1980 Miss Teach M-45	Closed	1980	18.00	700-900
1984 Mom & Ginger Baker M-115 - W. Petersen	Closed	1998	38.00	65-125
1982 Moon Mouse M-78	Closed	1984	15.50	450-650
1981 Mother's Helper M-52	Closed	1983	11.00	225-400
1979 Mouse Artiste M-39	Closed	1981	12.50	350-550
1979 Mouse Ballerina M-38	Closed	1979	12.50	900-1100
1983 Mouse Call M-97 - W. Petersen	Closed	1983	24.00	500-800
1979 Mouse Duet M-29	Closed	1982	25.00	600-900
1986 Mouse on Campus M-139 - W. Petersen	Closed	1988	25.00	100-350
1979 Mouse Pianist M-30	Closed	1984	17.00	250-480
1985 Mouse Talk M-130	Closed	1993	44.00	100-260
1979 Mouse Violinist M-31	Closed	1984	9.00	250-300
1976 Mouse with Muff M-16	Closed	1977	9.00	N/A
1979 Mousey Baby M-34	Closed	1982	9.50	300-400
1981 Mousey Express M-65	Closed	1993	22.00	106-163
1983 Mousey's Cone M-100	Closed	1994	22.00	65-111
1983 Mousey's Dollhouse M-102	Closed	1985	30.00	300-425
1988 Mousey's Easter Basket M-160	Closed	N/A	32.00	110-180
1982 Mousey's Teddy M-75	Closed	1985	29.00	313-350
1983 Mousey's Tricycle M-101	Closed	1995	24.00	49
1976 Mrs. Mousey M-15	Closed	1978	4.00	N/A
1976 Mrs. Mousey w/ Hat M-15a	Closed	1979	4.25	N/A
1992 Mrs. Mousey's Studio M-184 - W. Petersen	Closed	1997	150.00	195-200
1980 Mrs. Tidy M-51	Closed	1981	19.50	500-650
1980 Mrs. Tidy and Helper M-50	Closed	1981	24.00	650-700
1976 Nightie Mouse M-14	Closed	1979	4.75	400-500
1981 Nurse Mousey M-54	Closed	1982	14.00	350-500
1982 Office Mousey M-68	Closed	1984	23.00	375-450
1993 One-Mouse Band M-196	Closed	1999	95.00	104
1983 Pack Mouse M-106 - W. Petersen	Closed	1984	19.00	400-450
1985 Pageant Shepherds M-122	Closed	1985	35.00	163-200
1985 Pageant Wiseman M-121	Closed	1985	58.00	241
1981 Pearl Knit Mouse M-59	Closed	1985	20.00	295-350
1992 Peekaboo! M-183 - D. Petersen	Closed	1998	52.00	58-115
1984 Pen Pal Mousey M-114	Closed	1985	26.00	395-450
1993 Peter Pumpkin Eater M-190	Closed	1995	98.00	175-200
1984 Peter's Pumpkin M-118	Closed	1992	19.00	70-125
1980 Photographer Mouse M-48 - W. Petersen	Closed	1981	23.00	1200
1978 Picnic Mice M-23 - W. Petersen	Closed	1979	7.25	900-1000
1985 Piggy-Back Mousey M-129 - W. Petersen	Closed	1986	28.00	325-350
1994 Pilgrim's Welcome M-198	Closed	1997	55.00	80-100
1978 Pirate Mouse M-27	Closed	1979	6.50	800-1200
1980 Pirate Mouse M-47 - W. Petersen	Closed	1981	16.00	500-700
1990 Polly's Parasol M-170	Closed	1993	39.00	73-150
1982 Poorest Angel M-89	Closed	1986	15.00	145-165
1989 Prima Ballerina M-162	Closed	1996	35.00	44-130
1984 Prudence Pie Maker M-119	Closed	1992	18.50	70-130
1977 Queen "Tut" Mouse TM-2	Closed	1979	4.50	1000-1400
1985 Quilting Bee M-125 - W. Petersen	Closed	1998	30.00	90-250
1979 Raggedy and Mouse M-36	Closed	1981	12.00	400-425
1987 The Red Wagon M-151 - W. Petersen	Closed	1991	54.00	160-293
1997 Ring Around the Rosie M-228 - W. Petersen	Closed	2000	24.00	25-150
1979 Rock-a-bye Baby Mouse M-35	Closed	1981	17.00	450-950
1983 Rocking Tot M-103	Closed	1990	19.00	130-150
1983 Rope 'em Mousey M-108	Closed	1984	19.00	400-650
1983 Running Doe/Little Deer M-107b	Closed	1997	35.00	94-130
1980 Santa Mouse M-43	Closed	1985	12.00	200-455
1984 Santa's Trainee M-116 - W. Petersen	Closed	1984	36.50	450-800
1982 Say "Cheese" M-72 - W. Petersen	Closed	1983	15.50	400-500
1981 School Marm Mouse M-56	Closed	1981	19.50	600-900
1987 Scooter Mouse M-152 - W. Petersen	Closed	1996	34.00	75-98
1978 Secretary Miss Pell M-22	Closed	1981	4.50	550-600
1996 Settin' a Spell M-213 - D. Petersen	Closed	1999	62.00	62
1976 Shawl Mouse M-17	Closed	1977	9.00	N/A
1987 Skeleton Mousey M-157	Closed	1993	27.00	75-100
1992 Snow Buddies M-188 - D. Petersen	Closed	2000	58.00	58
1982 Snowmouse & Friend M-84	Closed	1985	23.50	350
1996 Spotted Sea Horse M-219 - W. Petersen	Closed	1999	52.00	52
1990 Stars & Stripes M-168	Closed	1996	34.00	98-300
1997 String of Hearts M-221 - D. Petersen	Closed	2000	45.00	45
1985 Strolling with Baby M-128	Closed	1997	42.00	61-150
1985 Sunday Drivers (yellow) M-132 - W. Petersen	Closed	1994	58.00	1200-1500
1985 Sunday Drivers M-132 - W. Petersen	Closed	1994	58.00	325-375
1986 Sweet Dreams M-136	Closed	1992	58.00	225-325
1982 Sweethearts M-79	Closed	1982	26.00	400-600
1982 Tea for Two M-74	Closed	1984	26.00	360-500
1976 Tea Mouse M-11	Closed	1979	5.75	500-800
1984 Tidy Mouse M-113	Closed	1985	38.00	420-720
1978 Town Crier Mouse M-28	Closed	1979	10.50	900-1200
1984 Traveling Mouse M-110	Closed	1987	28.00	350
1987 Trumpeter M-153a - W. Petersen	Closed	1989	29.00	50-75
1987 Tuba Player M-153c - W. Petersen	Closed	1989	29.00	50-75
1992 Tuckered Out! M-136a	Closed	1993	46.00	200-260
1975 Two Mice with Candle M-7	Closed	1979	4.50	450-550
1975 Two Tiny Mice M-8	Closed	1979	4.50	450-600
1985 Under the Chris-Mouse Tree M-123	Closed	1998	48.00	125-195
1986 Waltzing Matilda M-135 - W. Petersen	Closed	1993	48.00	169-200
1983 Wash Day M-105	Closed	1984	23.00	300-500
1994 We Gather Together M-199	Closed	1997	90.00	150
1978 Wedding Mice M-24 - W. Petersen	Closed	1981	7.50	450-600
1982 Wedding Mice M-67 - W. Petersen	Closed	1993	29.50	157-200
1993 Welcome Chick! M-193	Closed	2000	64.00	70
1980 Witch Mouse M-44	Closed	1983	12.00	200-325
1984 Witchy Boo! M-120	Closed	1995	21.00	124-150
1974 Wood Sprite M-6a	Closed	1978	4.00	N/A
1974 Wood Sprite M-6b	Closed	1978	4.00	N/A
1974 Wood Sprite M-6c	Closed	1978	4.00	N/A
1974 Wood Sprite M-6d	Closed	1978	4.00	N/A

Minutemice - A. Petersen, unless otherwise noted

YEAR ISSUE	EDITION LIMIT	YEAR RETD.	ISSUE PRICE	*QUOTE U.S.$
1974 Concordian On Drum with Glasses MM-4	Closed	1977	9.00	1950
1974 Concordian Wood Base w/Hat MM-4b	Closed	1977	8.00	N/A
1974 Concordian Wood Base w/Tan Coat MM-4a	Closed	1977	7.50	N/A
1974 Little Fifer on Drum MM-5b	Closed	1977	8.00	N/A
1974 Little Fifer on Drum with Fife MM-5	Closed	1977	8.00	N/A
1974 Little Fifer on Wood Base MM-5a	Closed	1977	8.00	N/A
1974 Mouse Carrying Large Drum MM-3	Closed	1977	8.00	1950
1974 Mouse on Drum with Black Hat MM-2	Closed	1977	9.00	N/A
1974 Mouse on Drum with Fife MM-1	Closed	1977	9.00	N/A
1974 Mouse on Drum with Fife Wood Base MM-1a	Closed	1977	9.00	N/A

Moles - A. Petersen

YEAR ISSUE	EDITION LIMIT	YEAR RETD.	ISSUE PRICE	*QUOTE U.S.$
1997 Jackie O. Mole MO-5	Closed	1999	49.00	49
1978 Mole Scout MO-1	Closed	1980	4.25	310-500
1996 Mole's "Belly Whopper" MO-4b	Closed	1999	44.00	44
1996 Mole's First Snow MO-4a	Closed	2000	44.00	44
1995 Mole's Red Sled MO-3	Closed	1999	59.00	59

Mouse Sports - A. Petersen, unless otherwise noted

YEAR ISSUE	EDITION LIMIT	YEAR RETD.	ISSUE PRICE	*QUOTE U.S.$
1975 Bobsled Three MS-1	Closed	1977	12.00	N/A
1985 Fishin' Chip MS-14 - W. Petersen	Closed	1992	46.00	250-350
1981 Golfer Mouse MS-10	Closed	1984	15.50	325-480
1977 Golfer Mouse MS-7	Closed	1980	5.25	400-750
1984 Land Ho! MS-12	Closed	1987	36.50	250-350
1976 Mouse Skier MS-3	Closed	1979	4.25	350-500
1975 Skater Mouse MS-2	Closed	1980	4.50	450-600
1980 Skater Mouse MS-8	Closed	1983	16.50	400-650
1977 Skating Star Mouse MS-6	Closed	1979	3.75	250-350
1980 Skier Mouse (Early Colors) MS-9	Closed	1983	13.00	200-250
1997 Surf's Up! MS-19 - W. Petersen	Closed	2000	72.00	72
1984 Tennis Anyone? MS-13	Closed	1988	18.00	182-300
1976 Tennis Star MS-4	Closed	1978	3.75	300-450
1976 Tennis Star MS-5	Closed	1981	3.75	250-300
1982 Two in a Canoe MS-11 - W. Petersen	Closed	1999	29.00	62
1996 Victor! MS-18	Closed	1999	49.00	49

Owls - A. Petersen, unless otherwise noted

YEAR ISSUE	EDITION LIMIT	YEAR RETD.	ISSUE PRICE	*QUOTE U.S.$
1975 Colonial Owls O-4	Closed	1977	11.50	N/A
1979 Grad Owl O-5 - W. Petersen	Closed	1979	4.25	400-600
1980 Graduate Owl (On Books) O-6 - W. Petersen	Closed	1980	12.00	550
1974 Mr. and Mrs. Owl O-1	Closed	1981	6.00	500-600
1974 Mr. Owl O-3	Closed	1981	3.25	400
1974 Mrs. Owl O-2	Closed	1981	3.00	350-400

Piggies - A. Petersen

YEAR ISSUE	EDITION LIMIT	YEAR RETD.	ISSUE PRICE	*QUOTE U.S.$
1978 Boy Piglet/ Picnic Piggy P-6	Closed	1981	4.00	300-400
1978 Girl Piglet/Picnic Piggy P-5	Closed	1981	4.00	300-400
1981 Holly Hog P-11	Closed	1981	25.00	600
1978 Jolly Tar Piggy P-3	Closed	1979	4.50	350-400
1978 Miss Piggy School Marm P-1	Closed	1979	4.50	300-600
1980 Nurse Piggy P-10	Closed	1981	15.50	300-400
1978 Picnic Piggies P-4	Closed	1981	7.75	400-600
1980 Pig O' My Heart P-9	Closed	1981	12.00	400-750
1978 Piggy Baker P-2	Closed	1981	4.50	300-400
1980 Piggy Ballerina P-7	Closed	1981	15.50	300-400
1978 Piggy Jogger PS-1	Closed	1981	4.50	400-700
1980 Piggy Policeman P-8	Closed	1981	17.50	300-500

Raccoons - A. Petersen

YEAR ISSUE	EDITION LIMIT	YEAR RETD.	ISSUE PRICE	*QUOTE U.S.$
1978 Bird Watcher Raccoon RC-3	Closed	1981	6.50	500-600
1977 Hiker Raccoon RC-2	Closed	1980	4.50	500-600
1977 Mother Raccoon RC-1	Closed	1980	4.50	400-600
1978 Raccoon Skater RCS-1	Closed	1980	4.75	400-600
1978 Raccoon Skier RCS-2	Closed	1980	6.00	600-900

Rats - A. Petersen, unless otherwise noted

YEAR ISSUE	EDITION LIMIT	YEAR RETD.	ISSUE PRICE	*QUOTE U.S.$
1975 Doc Rat R-2 - W. Petersen	Closed	1980	5.25	500-700
1975 Seedy Rat R-1	Closed	1977	5.25	N/A

Robin Hood Series - A. Petersen

YEAR ISSUE	EDITION LIMIT	YEAR RETD.	ISSUE PRICE	*QUOTE U.S.$
1990 Friar Tuck RH-3	Closed	1994	32.00	75-130
1990 Maid Marion RH-2	Closed	1994	32.00	75-117
1990 Robin Hood RH-1	Closed	1994	37.00	75-273

Single Issues - A. Petersen, unless otherwise noted

YEAR ISSUE	EDITION LIMIT	YEAR RETD.	ISSUE PRICE	*QUOTE U.S.$
1980 Cave Mice - W. Petersen	Closed	N/A	N/A	550-800
1972 Party Mouse in Plain Dress	Closed	N/A	N/A	N/A
1972 Party Mouse in Polka-Dot Dress	Closed	N/A	N/A	N/A
1972 Party Mouse in Sailor Suit	Closed	N/A	N/A	N/A
1972 Party Mouse with Bow Tie	Closed	N/A	N/A	N/A
1980 Screech Owl - W. Petersen	Closed	1982	N/A	N/A

Tiny Teddies - D. Petersen

YEAR ISSUE	EDITION LIMIT	YEAR RETD.	ISSUE PRICE	*QUOTE U.S.$
1984 Boo Bear T-3	Closed	N/A	20.00	143-150
1987 Christmas Teddy T-10	Closed	N/A	26.00	69-175
1984 Drummer Bear T-4	Closed	N/A	22.00	63-125
1988 Hansel & Gretel Bears @ Witch's House T-11	Closed	2000	175.00	175
1986 Huggy Bear T-8	Closed	N/A	26.00	150-195
1984 Little Teddy T-1	Closed	1986	20.00	175-200
1989 Momma Bear T-12	Closed	N/A	27.00	95-110
1985 Ride 'em Teddy! T-6	Closed	N/A	32.00	150-175
1984 Sailor Teddy T-2	Closed	N/A	20.00	60-150
1984 Santa Bear T-5	Closed	N/A	27.00	125-150
1985 Seaside Teddy T-7	Closed	N/A	28.00	75-125
1983 Tiny Teddy TT-1	Closed	1983	16.00	500-700
1987 Wedding Bears T-9	Suspd.		54.00	165-200

Wind in the Willows - A. Petersen, unless otherwise noted

YEAR ISSUE	EDITION LIMIT	YEAR RETD.	ISSUE PRICE	*QUOTE U.S.$
1982 Badger WW-2	Closed	1983	18.00	375-400
1982 Mole WW-1	Closed	1983	18.00	300-400
1982 Ratty WW-4	Closed	1983	18.00	350-400
1982 Toad WW-3 - W. Petersen	Closed	1983	18.00	300-400

Willitts Designs

Carousel Classics/Carousel Memories - A. Dezendorf

YEAR ISSUE	EDITION LIMIT	YEAR RETD.	ISSUE PRICE	*QUOTE U.S.$
1998 American Musical Carousel	9,500	1999	100.00	100
1997 Armoured Lead Horse	9,500	1999	75.00	75
1997 Eagle-Back Stander	9,500	1999	65.00	65
1998 English Musical Carousel	9,500	1999	100.00	100
1998 French Musical Carousel	9,500	1999	100.00	100
1998 German Musical Karussell	9,500	1999	100.00	100
1997 Indian Pony Stander	9,500	1999	75.00	75
1998 Lion with Cherub	9,500	1999	75.00	75
1998 Middle Row Jumper w/Dog	9,500	1999	70.00	70
1997 Outside Row Jumper w/Parrot	9,500	1999	70.00	70
1998 Outside Row Stander w/ Scalloped Saddle	9,500	1999	70.00	70
1997 Outside Row Stander w/Cherub	9,500	1999	70.00	70
1997 Outside Row Stander w/Gold Mane	9,500	1999	75.00	75
1998 Outside Row Zebra Stander	9,500	1999	75.00	75
1997 Patriotic Outside Row Jumper	9,500	1999	70.00	70
1997 Stander "King" Horse	9,500	1999	70.00	70
1998 Stander w/Roached Mane	9,500	1999	70.00	70

Just The Right Club - Raine

YEAR ISSUE	EDITION LIMIT	YEAR RETD.	ISSUE PRICE	*QUOTE U.S.$
1999 Ribeting	12/00		16.00	16
1999 The Wave	12/00		20.00	20
1999 Touch of Lace	12/00		20.00	20

Just The Right Shoe/Accessories - Raine

YEAR ISSUE	EDITION LIMIT	YEAR RETD.	ISSUE PRICE	*QUOTE U.S.$
1999 All That Glitters (purse Musical)	Open		30.00	30
1999 Arabesque (musical)	Open		37.50	38
1999 Bayou (purse Musical)	Open		28.00	28
2000 Carved Heel (purse)	Open		13.50	14
1999 Chic Plastique (purse box)	Open		16.00	16
1999 Cotillion (purse)	Open		15.50	16
1999 Devoted to You (musical)	Open		35.00	35
1999 Fanfare (hat box)	Open		17.50	18
1999 Feather Flair (hat box)	Open		17.50	18
1999 Fedora (hat box)	Open		17.50	18
1999 From the Sea (purse box)	Open		16.00	16
1999 Frosted Fantasy (purse box)	Open		23.50	24
1999 Girl's Best Friend (musical)	Open		40.00	40
1999 I Do (box)	Open		27.50	28
2000 In Scale (purse)	Open		12.00	12
1999 Ingenue (box)	Open		15.50	16
1999 Majestic (purse)	Open		16.50	17
2000 Midnight Promises (purse)	Open		14.50	15
1999 Minuet (musical)	Open		37.50	38
1999 Pas de Deux (shoe Musical)	Open		37.50	38
1999 Pink Frost (hat w/mannequin)	Open		28.50	29
1999 Raine (purse box)	Open		14.00	14
1999 Sea of Pearls (hat w/mannequin)	Open		29.50	30
1999 Seregeti (purse boxl)	Open		15.50	16
1999 Silver Kitten (musical)	Open		37.50	38
1999 Sweet Surprise (box)	Open		16.50	17
1999 Tapestry (purse box)	Open		17.50	18
1999 Traveler (purse box)	Open		13.00	13
1999 Tweed (hat box)	Open		17.50	18
1999 Velvet Crush (purse Musical)	Open		28.00	28
2000 You Animal You (purse)	Open		16.00	16

Just The Right Shoe/Children - Raine

YEAR ISSUE	EDITION LIMIT	YEAR RETD.	ISSUE PRICE	*QUOTE U.S.$
1999 Baby Quilt (shoe musical)	Open		35.00	35
1999 Beach Time (box)	Open		16.50	17
1999 Blue Lullabye (box)	Open		14.00	14
1999 Mary Jane (box)	Open		14.50	15
1999 Pink Lullabye (box)	Open		14.00	14
1999 Rough 'n Tumble (box)	Open		14.00	14
1999 Sleepy Time (shoe musical)	Open		38.50	39

Just The Right Shoe/Classic Collection - Raine

YEAR ISSUE	EDITION LIMIT	YEAR RETD.	ISSUE PRICE	*QUOTE U.S.$
1998 Afternoon Tea	Open		24.00	24
1999 Aladdin's Delight	Open		16.00	16
2000 Aristocrat	Open		15.50	16
2000 Baroness	Open		16.00	16
1999 Blush	Retrd.	1999	13.50	20-32
1999 Bordeaux	Retrd.	1999	16.00	20-35
1999 Bovine Bliss	Open		14.00	14
2000 Brave Warrior	Open		12.00	12
1998 Brocade Court	Retrd.	1999	16.00	23-32
2000 Calla Lily	Open		16.50	17
2000 Carved Heel	Open		13.00	13
2000 Check It Out!	Open		15.00	15
2000 Cork Wedge	Open		14.00	14
1998 Deco Boot	Retrd.	1999	25.00	25-38
1999 Edwardian Grace	Open		18.00	18

*Quotes have been rounded up to nearest dollar

Willitts Designs
to Willitts Designs

FIGURINES

YEAR ISSUE	EDITION LIMIT	YEAR RETD.	ISSUE PRICE	*QUOTE U.S.$
1998 The Empress	Retrd.	2000	18.00	18
1998 En Pointe	Open		17.50	18
1998 Frosted Fantasy	Open		20.00	20
1999 Geometrika	Open		12.50	13
2000 Golden Leaf	Open		15.00	15
1999 High-Buttoned Boot	Open		17.50	18
2000 Home on the Range	Open		15.00	15
1999 I Do	Open		16.00	16
2000 In Scale	Open		13.00	13
1999 Ingenue	Open		14.50	15
1998 Italian Racer	Retrd.	1999	13.50	20-31
1998 Jeweled Heel Pump	Open		24.00	24
2000 Lavish Tapestry	Open		14.50	15
1998 Leopard Stiletto	Open		15.00	15
1999 Magnetic Allure	Open		14.00	14
1999 Majestic	Open		17.50	18
2000 Midori	Open		20.00	20
1999 New Heights	Retrd.	2000	12.00	12
1998 Opera Boot	Open		25.00	25
1998 Pavé	Retrd.	2000	22.00	22
1998 Pearl Mule	Retrd.	2000	17.00	17
1998 Promenade	Open		20.00	20
1999 Purple Dream	Open		15.00	15
1998 Ravishing Red	Open		12.00	12
1998 Rose Court	Retrd.	2000	15.00	15
1999 Serengeti	Open		15.00	15
1999 Shimmering Night	Open		16.00	16
1999 Shower of Flowers	Open		14.00	14
1998 Silver Cloud	Retrd.	1999	14.50	15-31
1999 Sneaking By	Open		15.00	15
2000 Spectate This	Open		13.00	13
1998 Sumptuous Quilt	Retrd.	1999	13.50	18-28
2000 Sunray	Open		13.50	14
2000 Tassles	Open		17.50	18
1998 Teetering Court	Retrd.	1999	18.00	21-33
2000 Treads	Open		12.50	13
2000 Truffles	Open		12.50	13
1998 Tying the Knot	Open		15.00	15
1999 Va-Va-Voom	Open		14.50	15
1999 Versailles	Retrd.	1999	15.00	15
2000 Victorian Ankle Boot	Open		17.50	18
2000 Victorian Wedding Boot	Open		16.00	16
2000 You Animal You!	Open		17.00	17

Just The Right Shoe/Designer Collection - Raine

YEAR ISSUE	EDITION LIMIT	YEAR RETD.	ISSUE PRICE	*QUOTE U.S.$
2000 Bow Me	Open		14.50	15
2000 Espadrille "Pasha"	Open		17.00	17
2000 Fruity	Open		14.50	15
2000 Fruity Purse	Open		15.50	16
2000 La Rosa	Open		18.50	19
2000 Mostly Matisse	Open		17.50	18
2000 Queen of Hearts	Open		14.00	14
2000 Queen of Hearts Purse	Open		16.00	16
2000 Sparkle Purse	Open		15.50	16
2000 Sparkle Shoe	Open		15.50	16

Just The Right Shoe/Exclusives - Raine

YEAR ISSUE	EDITION LIMIT	YEAR RETD.	ISSUE PRICE	*QUOTE U.S.$
2000 Celebration (Exclusive Color) (Parkwest)	Open		13.00	13
2000 Courageous Rose (FFANY)	Open		N/A	N/A
2000 Denim Blues (GCC)	Open		14.00	14
1999 Frosted Fantasy (Exclusive Color)	Open		20.00	20
2000 Opulent Purse (QVC)	Open		20.00	20
1998 Opulent Shoe (QVC)	Open		20.00	20
1999 Tuxedo (Exclusive Color) (GCC)	Open		16.50	17
1999 Victoria (Exclusive Color) (QVC)	Open		18.00	18
1998 Victorious (Exclusive Color) (POG)	Open		17.00	17

Just The Right Shoe/Men's Collection - Raine

YEAR ISSUE	EDITION LIMIT	YEAR RETD.	ISSUE PRICE	*QUOTE U.S.$
1999 Cowboy Boot	Open		14.00	14
1999 Golf Shoe	Open		12.50	13
1999 Military Boot	Open		13.00	13
1999 Motorcycle Boot	Open		14.00	14
1999 Penny Loafer	Open		12.00	12
1999 Tassle Loafer	Open		12.00	12

Just The Right Shoe/Museum-Biltmore Estate Collection - Raine

YEAR ISSUE	EDITION LIMIT	YEAR RETD.	ISSUE PRICE	*QUOTE U.S.$
2000 Brogue Ballyhoo	Open		13.00	13
2000 Charisma	Open		15.00	15
2000 Something Blue	Open		16.00	16
2000 Starry Night	Open		15.50	16
2000 Sweet Elegance	Open		14.00	14

Just The Right Shoe/Museum-Mt. Vernon Collection - Raine

YEAR ISSUE	EDITION LIMIT	YEAR RETD.	ISSUE PRICE	*QUOTE U.S.$
2000 First Lady Slipper	Open		13.00	13
2000 George Washington Dress Shoe	Open		13.00	13
2000 George Washington Riding Boot	Open		17.00	17
2000 Martha Washington Dress Shoe	Open		14.00	14
2000 Martha Washington Wedding Shoe	Open		15.00	15

Just The Right Shoe/Raine Originals - Raine

YEAR ISSUE	EDITION LIMIT	YEAR RETD.	ISSUE PRICE	*QUOTE U.S.$
2000 Autumn	Open		13.00	13
2000 Crocus	Open		14.50	15
2000 Forever Yours	Open		20.00	20
2000 Groovy Baby	Open		24.50	25
2000 Later Gator	Open		13.50	14
2000 Mardi Gras	Open		22.50	23
2000 Midnight Promises	Open		16.00	16
2000 Pretty Penny	Open		13.50	14
2000 Red Devil	Open		18.50	19
2000 Rio	Open		15.00	15
2000 Sea of Pearls	Open		20.00	20
2000 Snake Skin Wrap	Open		16.00	16

YEAR ISSUE	EDITION LIMIT	YEAR RETD.	ISSUE PRICE	*QUOTE U.S.$
2000 Spring Raine	Open		16.00	16
2000 Tux Shoe (silver)	Open		16.50	17
2000 Venus of Pearls	Open		15.00	15
2000 Zap	Open		14.50	15

Just The Right Shoe/Shoes of the Century - Raine

YEAR ISSUE	EDITION LIMIT	YEAR RETD.	ISSUE PRICE	*QUOTE U.S.$
1999 Class Act	Open		13.00	13
1999 Courtly Riches	Open		14.00	14
1999 Elegant Affair	Open		14.00	14
1999 Golden Stiletto	Open		15.00	15
1999 Ladylike	Open		12.50	13
1999 Pastiche	Open		13.00	13
1999 Patently Perfect	Open		13.00	13
1999 Rising Star	Open		16.00	16
1999 Struttin'	Open		13.50	14
1999 Suffrogette	Open		15.00	15

The Latest Thing/After Dark - S. Bayne

YEAR ISSUE	EDITION LIMIT	YEAR RETD.	ISSUE PRICE	*QUOTE U.S.$
2000 After Eight	Open		29.50	30
2000 Debutante	Open		29.50	30
2000 Eastern Promise	Open		29.50	30
2000 Glitz and Glamour	Open		29.50	30
2000 Hollywood Nights	Open		29.50	30
2000 Midnight Desire	Open		29.50	30
2000 Moonstruck	Open		29.50	30
2000 Premiere	Open		29.50	30
2000 Putting on the Ritz	Open		29.50	30
2000 Rendezvous	Open		29.50	30
2000 Sheer Elegance	Open		29.50	30
2000 Soiree	Open		29.50	30

The Latest Thing/Fashion Showcase - S. Bayne

YEAR ISSUE	EDITION LIMIT	YEAR RETD.	ISSUE PRICE	*QUOTE U.S.$
2000 All the Rage	Open		17.50	18
2000 Contemporary Grace	Open		26.50	27
2000 Dress for Success	Open		22.50	23
2000 Fabulous Folds	Open		26.50	27
2000 Girl Power	Open		17.50	18
2000 Happy Days	Open		20.00	20
2000 High Society	Open		22.50	23
2000 Illusion	Open		22.50	23
2000 Silver Lady	Open		22.50	23
2000 Tailored to Perfection	Open		26.50	27

The Latest Thing/Silhouettes - S. Bayne

YEAR ISSUE	EDITION LIMIT	YEAR RETD.	ISSUE PRICE	*QUOTE U.S.$
2000 Black Magic	Open		20.00	20
2000 Breathless	Open		22.50	23
2000 Groovy Baby	Open		16.50	17
2000 In Full Bloom	Open		26.50	27
2000 Satin and Lace	Open		17.50	18
2000 Scarlet Fever	Open		16.50	17
2000 Second Skin	Open		16.50	17
2000 Soft to the Touch	Open		17.50	18
2000 Taboo	Open		20.00	20
2000 Vital Statistics	Open		17.50	18
2000 Welcome Home	Open		20.00	20
2000 What a Waist!	Open		17.50	18

The Latest Thing/Style Sensations - S. Bayne

YEAR ISSUE	EDITION LIMIT	YEAR RETD.	ISSUE PRICE	*QUOTE U.S.$
2000 Afternoon Stroll	Open		26.50	27
2000 Animal Instinct	Open		17.50	18
2000 Bathing Belle	Open		22.50	23
2000 Decadence	Open		26.50	27
2000 Decked Out	Open		22.50	23
2000 Diva	Open		20.00	20
2000 Dolce Vida	Open		22.50	23
2000 Dolly Bird	Open		17.50	18
2000 Drama!	Open		20.00	20
2000 English Rose	Open		26.50	27
2000 The Eyes Have It	Open		17.50	18
2000 Feel the Vibe	Open		20.00	20
2000 High Impact	Open		17.50	18
2000 Hot to Go	Open		15.00	15
2000 In the Swim	Open		17.50	18
2000 Jazzing it Up	Open		22.50	23
2000 Liberation	Open		22.50	23
2000 Living Doll	Open		30.00	30
2000 Making a Splash	Open		15.00	15
2000 Mix and Match	Open		20.00	20
2000 On Parade	Open		23.50	24
2000 On the Fairway	Open		22.50	23
2000 Opulence	Open		29.50	30
2000 Out of this World	Open		15.00	15
2000 Perfect Skin	Open		15.00	15
2000 Slender Lines	Open		23.50	24
2000 Socialite	Open		25.50	26
2000 Suitably Sophisticated	Open		22.50	23
2000 Summer of Love	Open		20.00	20
2000 Sweet Dreams	Open		20.00	20
2000 Taking the Plunge	Open		17.50	18
2000 That Certain Something	Open		23.50	24
2000 Unashamed Luxury	Open		29.50	30

MasterPeace Collection - Various

YEAR ISSUE	EDITION LIMIT	YEAR RETD.	ISSUE PRICE	*QUOTE U.S.$
1999 Coat of Many Colors - T. Blackshear	Open		180.00	180
1999 Coat of Many Colors A/P - T. Blackshear	25		216.00	216
1998 Forgiven - T. Blackshear	Open		200.00	200
1998 Forgiven A/P - T. Blackshear	100		240.00	240
1998 The Invitation - M. Weistling	Retrd.	1999	250.00	250
1998 The Invitation A/P - M. Weistling	100	1999	300.00	300
1998 Victorious Lion of Judah - M. Dudash	Retrd.	1999	175.00	175
1998 Victorious Lion of Judah A/P - M. Dudash	100	1999	210.00	210
1998 Watchers in the Night - T. Blackshear	Retrd.	1999	300.00	300
1998 Watchers in the Night A/P - T. Blackshear	100	1999	360.00	360

Our Song - B. Joysmith

YEAR ISSUE	EDITION LIMIT	YEAR RETD.	ISSUE PRICE	*QUOTE U.S.$
1999 Barefoot Dreams	Open		25.00	25
1999 Bedtime Story	Open		75.00	75
2000 Big Brother	Open		40.00	40
1999 Bumpin'	Open		42.50	43
1999 Country Mouse	Open		32.50	33
2000 Delta Girls's	Open		90.00	90
2000 Developing a Winner	7,500		150.00	150
2000 Dreaming	Open		55.00	55
1999 He's My Brother	Open		35.00	35
2000 Joyful Noise	Open		60.00	60
1999 Men of the Bench	7,500		225.00	225
2000 Mother and Child	Open		47.50	48
1999 Open Gate	Open		37.50	38
1999 Part of Growing	Open		60.00	60
2000 Roses and Sunshine	Open		45.00	45
1999 Sisters & Secrets	Open		47.50	48
2000 Summer Dress	Open		40.00	40
2000 Summer's Song	Open		35.00	35
2000 Tricycle	Open		50.00	50

Rainbow Babies - A. Blackshear

YEAR ISSUE	EDITION LIMIT	YEAR RETD.	ISSUE PRICE	*QUOTE U.S.$
1998 Beloved	Retrd.	1999	31.50	32
1997 Bright Eyes	Retrd.	1999	27.50	28
1997 Cuddles	Retrd.	1999	39.50	40
1998 Lil' Blossom	Retrd.	1999	34.50	35
1999 Lil' Wonder	Retrd.	1999	28.00	28
1998 Peek-A-Boo Pals	Retrd.	1999	47.50	48
1997 Peewee & Peeper	Retrd.	1999	39.50	40
1997 Pookie	Retrd.	1999	24.50	25
1997 Precious	Retrd.	1999	29.50	30
1999 Sleepyhead	Retrd.	1999	34.50	35
1999 SnuggleBunnies	Retrd.	1999	35.00	35
1997 Sunshine	Retrd.	1999	32.50	33

Take A Seat - Raine

YEAR ISSUE	EDITION LIMIT	YEAR RETD.	ISSUE PRICE	*QUOTE U.S.$
2000 Adirondack	Open		11.00	11
2000 Art Nouveau	Open		11.50	12
2000 Billiard Room	Open		15.00	15
2000 Corner	Open		13.00	13
2000 Cow	Open		13.00	13
2000 Folkloric	Open		13.00	13
2000 Form & Function	Open		12.00	12
2000 Giltwood Rococo	Open		12.00	12
2000 Graphite	Open		17.00	17
2000 Leather & Chrome	Open		14.00	14
2000 Leather Recliner w/Ottoman	Open		12.50	13
2000 Longhorn	Open		13.00	13
2000 Louis XVI	Open		13.50	14
2000 Mexican Leather	Open		12.00	12
2000 Mission Style	Open		14.00	14
2000 Mr. Vanderbilt's	Open		16.00	16
2000 Mrs. Vanderbilt's	Open		15.00	15
2000 Music Room	Open		16.00	16
2000 Pati	Open		13.00	13
2000 Pearwood	Open		12.00	12
2000 Red Heart	Open		12.00	12
2000 Regency Leopard	Open		14.00	14
2000 Ribbon	Open		12.00	12
2000 San Demas	Open		15.00	15
2000 Screaming Red	Open		13.50	14
2000 Slipper	Open		14.50	15
2000 Slope Wingback	Open		13.00	13
2000 Stenciled	Open		14.50	15
2000 Viridian	Open		13.00	13
2000 Wicker w/Ottoman	Open		13.00	13
2000 Zebra	Open		16.00	16

The Blackshear Circle Collector Club - T. Blackshear

YEAR ISSUE	EDITION LIMIT	YEAR RETD.	ISSUE PRICE	*QUOTE U.S.$
1997 A Child Shall Lead Them	5,900	1998	225.00	400-500
1999 Spring	6,250	1999	150.00	225
2000 Summer	Yr.Iss.	2000	140.00	140

The Blackshear Jamboree Parade - T. Blackshear

YEAR ISSUE	EDITION LIMIT	YEAR RETD.	ISSUE PRICE	*QUOTE U.S.$
2000 Gypsy	Open		60.00	60
2000 Gypsy A/P	50		72.00	72
2000 Gypsy G/P	50		78.00	78
2000 Jay Jay and Cluck	Open		60.00	60
2000 Jay Jay and Cluck A/P	50		72.00	72
2000 Jay Jay and Cluck G/P	50		78.00	78
2000 Skeeter	Open		65.00	65
2000 Skeeter A/P	50		78.00	78
2000 Skeeter G/P	50		84.50	85
2000 Tootie	Open		60.00	60
2000 Tootie A/P	50		72.00	72
2000 Tootie G/P	50		78.00	78

Thomas Blackshear's Ebony Visions Event - T. Blackshear

YEAR ISSUE	EDITION LIMIT	YEAR RETD.	ISSUE PRICE	*QUOTE U.S.$
2000 Rudy Toot	Yr.Iss.	2000	50.00	50

Thomas Blackshear's Ebony Visions - T. Blackshear

YEAR ISSUE	EDITION LIMIT	YEAR RETD.	ISSUE PRICE	*QUOTE U.S.$
2000 Bundle of Joy	Open		175.00	175
2000 Bundle of Joy A/P	50		210.00	210
2000 Bundle of Joy G/P	50		227.50	228
1998 Catching The Eye	Retrd.	1999	235.00	235
1997 Catching The Eye (Parkwest/NALED exclusive)	1,000	1997	225.00	225
1998 Catching The Eye A/P	50	1999	282.00	282
1998 Catching The Eye G/P	50	1999	305.50	325
1999 Cherished	Open		160.00	160

*Quotes have been rounded up to nearest dollar

YEAR ISSUE	EDITION LIMIT	YEAR RETD.	ISSUE PRICE	*QUOTE U.S.$
1999 Cherished A/P	50		192.00	192
1999 Cherished G/P	50		208.00	208
1998 The Comforter	Open		250.00	250
1998 The Comforter A/P	50		300.00	300
1998 The ComforterG/P	50		325.00	325
2000 Commitment	Open		190.00	190
2000 Commitment A/P	50		228.00	228
2000 Commitment G/P	50		247.00	247
1999 Daddy's Girl	Open		160.00	160
1999 Daddy's Girl A/P	50		192.00	192
1999 Daddy's Girl G/P	50		208.00	208
1996 The Dreamer	11,500	1997	135.00	180-210
1996 The Dreamer A/P	50	1997	162.00	225
1996 The Dreamer G/P	50	1997	175.50	176
1997 Ebony Visions in Bas Relief	4,000	1998	150.00	150
1997 Ebony Visions in Bas Relief A/P	50	1998	180.00	180
1997 Ebony Visions in Bas Relief G/P	50	1998	195.00	200
1997 The Family	11,200	1999	225.00	225
1997 The Family A/P	50	1999	270.00	270
1997 The Family G/P	50	1999	292.50	300
1999 First Step	Open		150.00	150
1999 First Step A/P	50		180.00	180
1999 First Step G/P	50		195.00	195
1997 The Flower Girl	12,350	2000	100.00	100
1997 The Flower Girl A/P	50	2000	120.00	120
1997 The Flower Girl G/P	50	2000	130.00	130
1999 Forever Friends	Open		100.00	100
1999 Forever Friends A/P	50		120.00	120
1999 Forever Friends G/P	50		130.00	130
1998 The Fruits of Friendship	Retrd.	2000	115.00	115
1998 The Fruits of Friendship A/P	50	2000	138.00	138
1998 The Fruits of Friendship G/P	50	2000	149.50	150
1999 Grandmama	Open		175.00	175
1999 Grandmama A/P	50		210.00	210
1999 Grandmama G/P	50		227.00	227
1996 The Guardian	25,600	1999	300.00	500-600
1996 The Guardian A/P	50	1999	360.00	360
1996 The Guardian G/P	50	1999	390.00	390
1997 The Heirs	13,175	1999	125.00	125
1997 The Heirs A/P	50	1999	150.00	150
1997 The Heirs G/P	50	1999	162.50	195
1998 Hero	Open		200.00	200
1998 Hero A/P	50		240.00	240
1998 Hero G/P	50		260.00	260
1997 Hopes & Dreams	2,500	1997	225.00	225-400
1997 Hopes & Dreams A/P	50	1997	270.00	270
1997 Hopes & Dreams G/P	50	1997	292.50	325
2000 Intimacy	Open		165.00	165
2000 Intimacy A/P	50		198.00	198
2000 Intimacy G/P	50		214.50	215
1998 Joyful Noise	Open		150.00	150
1998 Joyful Noise A/P	50		180.00	180
1998 Joyful Noise G/P	50		195.00	195
1997 The Kiss	9,100	1999	225.00	225
1997 The Kiss A/P	50	1999	270.00	270
1997 The Kiss G/P	50	1999	292.50	293
1999 Leap of Faith	Open		170.00	170
1999 Leap of Faith A/P	50		204.00	204
1999 Leap of Faith G/P	50		221.00	221
1995 The Madonna	13,325	1997	160.00	250-300
1995 The Madonna A/P	50	1997	192.00	192-230
1995 The Madonna G/P	50	1997	208.00	208
2000 Message to God	Open		90.00	90
2000 Message to God A/P	50		108.00	108
2000 Message to God G/P	50		117.00	117
1997 Midnight	9,825	2000	250.00	250
1997 Midnight A/P	50	2000	300.00	300
1997 Midnight G/P	50	2000	325.00	325
1996 The Music Maker	12,375	1998	195.00	195-203
1996 The Music Maker A/P	50	1998	234.00	250
1996 The Music Maker G/P	50	1998	253.50	295
1998 Night in Day	Open		225.00	225
1998 Night in Day A/P	50		270.00	270
1998 Night in Day G/P	50		292.50	293
1995 The Nurturer	16,923	1998	160.00	250-351
1995 The Nurturer A/P	50	1998	192.00	192-290
1995 The Nurturer G/P	50	1998	208.00	208
2000 Oh No She Didn't	4,500		300.00	300
2000 Oh No She Didn't A/P	50		36.00	360
2000 Oh No She Didn't G/P	50		390.00	390
1997 The Prayer	Retrd.	2000	150.00	150
1997 The Prayer A/P	50	2000	180.00	180
1997 The Prayer G/P	50	2000	195.00	195
1995 The Protector	7,900	1996	195.00	700-800
1995 The Protector A/P	50	1996	234.00	600-650
1995 The Protector G/P	50	1996	253.50	600-650
1999 Serenity	Open		190.00	190
1999 Serenity A/P	50		228.00	228
1999 Serenity G/P	50		247.00	247
1995 Siblings	8,800	1996	120.00	300-330
1995 Siblings A/P	50	1996	144.00	275-300
1995 Siblings G/P	50	1996	156.00	345-395
1998 Sisters Fover: In Childhood	Open		140.00	140
1998 Sisters Fover: In Childhood A/P	50		168.00	168
1998 Sisters Fover: In Childhood G/P	50		182.00	182
1995 The Storyteller	2,500	1996	410.00	2500-4000
1995 The Storyteller A/P	50	1996	492.00	2900
1995 The Tender Touch	16,900	1997	185.00	300-345
1995 The Tender Touch A/P	50	1997	222.00	222
1995 The Tender Touch G/P	50	1997	240.50	280
1996 A Time To Dream	10,500	1997	120.00	120-210
1996 A Time To Dream A/P	50	1997	144.00	150
1996 A Time To Dream G/P	50	1997	156.00	195

Legends Edition - T. Blackshear

YEAR ISSUE	EDITION LIMIT	YEAR RETD.	ISSUE PRICE	*QUOTE U.S.$
2000 The Guardian	300		2200.00	2200
2000 The Guardian - Walter Payton Tribute	36		3400.00	3400
2000 The Guardian A/P	50		2640.00	2640
2000 The Guardian G/P	50		2860.00	2860
1998 The Madonna	550	1999	1075.00	1075
1998 The Madonna A/P	50	1999	1290.00	1290
1998 The Madonna G/P	50	1999	1397.50	1398
1997 The Protector	950		1450.00	1450
1997 The Protector A/P	50		1740.00	1740
1997 The Protector G/P	50		1885.00	1885
1996 The Storyteller	650	1996	1900.00	1900-2100
1996 The Storyteller A/P	50	1996	2300.00	2300-2490
1996 The Storyteller G/P	50	1996	2470.00	2470

Woodland Winds/Christopher Radko

Woodland Winds Musicals - C. Radko

YEAR ISSUE	EDITION LIMIT	YEAR RETD.	ISSUE PRICE	*QUOTE U.S.$
2000 Blustery Bunny Band Musical 00-802-0	Open		40.00	40
2000 Burl's Hat Party Musical 00-802-0	Open		40.00	40
1998 Carlton The Snowman 98-704-0	Retrd.	1999	60.00	60
2000 Forest Friends 00-701-0	Open		30.00	30
1998 Frosty Leaf Santa 98-703-0	Retrd.	1999	60.00	60
1998 Is This the Way to Make Figure 8's? 98-841-0	Retrd.	1999	40.00	40
1998 Snow Tunes Bunny Carolers 98-802-0	Retrd.	1999	35.00	35
1999 Snowflake Ornament Holder 99-861-0	Open		35.00	35
1998 Stardust Santa w/Scepter 98-804-0	Retrd.	1999	50.00	50
1998 Stardust Santa w/Snowflakes 98-806-0	Retrd.	1999	50.00	50

Woodland Winds Porcelain Figurines - C. Radko

YEAR ISSUE	EDITION LIMIT	YEAR RETD.	ISSUE PRICE	*QUOTE U.S.$
1999 Afternoon Stroll 99-858-0	Open		25.00	25
1998 All Tuckered Out 98-847-0	Retrd.	1999	20.00	20
1999 Blizzard's Big Day 99-851-0	Open		25.00	25
2000 Blustery Bunny Bonfire Votive 00-872-0	Open		25.00	25
2000 Burl Dressed for the Holidays 00-858-0	Open		25.00	25
1999 Carlton the Snowman Jr. 99-925-0	Open		26.00	26
1999 Carlton's Day 99-755-0	Open		22.50	23
2000 Catching Snowflakes 00-854-0	Open		15.00	15
1998 Dashing Thru The Snow 98-852-0	Retrd.	1999	25.00	25
1999 Dressed For The Holidays 99-855-0	Open		20.00	20
2000 Frosty Leaf Santa Snooze Votive 00-772-0	Open		25.00	25
1999 Frosty Love 99-753-0	Open		25.00	25
1999 Gift Giving 99-857-0	Open		27.50	28
1999 Harvest Frost 99-754-0	Retrd.	1999	30.00	30
2000 Hello Hudson 00-751-0	Open		15.00	15
1999 Holiday Hideaway 99-730-0	Open		17.50	18
2000 Home Sweet Home 00-871-0	Open		25.00	25
1999 I'm Still Standing 99-832-0	Open		22.50	23
2000 Joy to the World 00-855-0	Open		25.00	25
1999 Measuring Snowflakes 99-852-0	Open		27.50	28
1998 Meet Our New Friend Burl 98-849-0	Retrd.	1999	22.00	22
2000 Nice to Meet You...I'm A Sprig 00-750-0	Open		15.00	15
2000 Paddy Cake Sprigs 00-754-0	Open		19.50	20
1999 Petite Nana Leaf 99-927-0	Open		28.00	28
1999 Pleasant Dreams 99-751-0	Open		25.00	25
1998 Santa w/Bubble Bear 98-743-0	Open		30.00	30
1999 A Season For Giving 99-752-0	Open		27.50	28
1999 Silver Bells 99-850	Open		22.50	23
1998 Skiing My Way To You 98-844-0	Retrd.	1999	22.50	23
1998 Sled Express 98-850-0	Retrd.	1999	20.00	20
1999 Snow Angels 99-856-0	Open		22.50	23
1999 Snow Showers 99-853-0	Retrd.	1999	17.50	18
2000 Snow Tunes Metal Candleholder 00-877-0	Open		20.00	20
1999 Snowflower 99-826-0	Open		22.50	23
1998 Starburst Santa w/Flakes 98-803-0	Open		35.00	35
1999 Stardust Sleigh Ride 99-854-0	Open		27.50	28
1998 Surrounded By Friends 98-851-0	Retrd.	1999	30.00	30
2000 Travel Plans 00-859-0	Open		50.00	50
1999 A Tree For All 99-750-0	Open		20.00	20
2000 Warm and Cozy 00-752-0	Open		25.00	25

Woodland Winds Porcelain Lighting/Candles - C. Radko

YEAR ISSUE	EDITION LIMIT	YEAR RETD.	ISSUE PRICE	*QUOTE U.S.$
1999 Carlton Candle 99-589-0	Open		18.00	18
1998 Cold Hands Warm Heart 98-853-0	Open		25.00	25
1999 Frosty Leaf Candle 99-588-0	Open		18.00	18
1998 Snowball Snooze Candleholder 98-846-0	Retrd.	1999	18.00	18

Woodland Winds Snowglobes - C. Radko

YEAR ISSUE	EDITION LIMIT	YEAR RETD.	ISSUE PRICE	*QUOTE U.S.$
2000 Burl's Forest Friends 00-805-0	Open		100.00	100
1998 Carlton The Snowman 98-702-0	7,500		110.00	110
2000 The Country Cottage 00-700-0	Open		110.00	110
1998 Frosty Leaf Santa 98-700-0	7,500	1999	110.00	110
1998 Happy Holidays 98-701-0	7,500		110.00	110
2000 Snow Sailors 00-801-0	Open		100.00	100
2000 Travel Plans 00-800-0	Open		125.00	125

Woodland Winds Tabletop Figurines - C. Radko

YEAR ISSUE	EDITION LIMIT	YEAR RETD.	ISSUE PRICE	*QUOTE U.S.$
1998 Carved Carlton 98-746-0	Open		40.00	40
1998 Carved Frosty Leaf Santa 98-747-0	Open		50.00	50
1999 Carved Nana Leaf 99-761-0	Open		50.00	50
1998 Frosty Leaf Santa 98-744-0	5,000		125.00	125
1999 Frosty's Cookies 99-774-0	Open		65.00	65
1999 Nana Leaf 99-760-0	2,500		125.00	125

GRAPHICS

American Artists

Fred Stone - F. Stone

YEAR ISSUE	EDITION LIMIT	YEAR RETD.	ISSUE PRICE	*QUOTE U.S.$
1979 Affirmed, Steve Cauthen Up	750	N/A	100.00	600
1988 Alysheba	950	N/A	195.00	650
1992 The American Triple Crown I, 1948-1978	1,500		325.00	325
1993 The American Triple Crown II, 1937-1946	1,500		325.00	325
1993 The American Triple Crown III, 1919-1935	1,500		225.00	225
1983 The Andalusian	750	N/A	150.00	350
1981 The Arabians	750	N/A	115.00	525
1989 Battle For The Triple Crown	950	N/A	225.00	550-650
1980 The Belmont-Bold Forbes	500	N/A	100.00	375
1991 Black Stallion	1,500		225.00	250
1988 Cam-Fella	950	N/A	175.00	250-350
1996 Cigar, canvas	250	1997	295.00	295
1996 Cigar, litho	1,200	1997	150.00	150
1981 Contentment	750	N/A	115.00	525
1992 Dance Smartly-Pat Day Up	950	N/A	225.00	275-325
1995 Dancers, canvas litho	350		375.00	375
1995 Dancers, print	Open		60.00	60
1983 The Duel	750	N/A	150.00	400
1985 Eternal Legacy	950	N/A	175.00	950
1980 Exceller-Bill Shoemaker	500	N/A	90.00	800
1990 Final Tribute- Secretariat	1,150	N/A	265.00	1200-1300
1987 The First Day	950	N/A	175.00	225
1991 Forego	1,150		225.00	250
1986 Forever Friends	950	N/A	175.00	725
1985 Fred Stone Paints the Sport of Kings (Book)	750	N/A	265.00	750
1980 Genuine Risk	500	N/A	100.00	700
1991 Go For Wand-A Candle in the Wind	1,150		225.00	225
1986 Great Match Race-Ruffian & Foolish Pleasure	950	N/A	175.00	350-375
1995 Holy Bull, canvas litho	350		375.00	375
1995 Holy Bull, litho	1,150		225.00	225
1996 In Pursuit of Greatness-Cigar, canvas	250	1997	295.00	295
1996 In Pursuit of Greatness-Cigar, litho	1,500	1997	90.00	90
1981 John Henry-Bill Shoemaker Up	595	N/A	160.00	1500
1985 John Henry-McCarron Up	750	N/A	175.00	500-750
1995 Julie Krone - Colonial Affair	1,150		225.00	225
1985 Kelso	950	N/A	175.00	750
1980 The Kentucky Derby	750	N/A	100.00	650
1980 Kidnapped Mare-Franfreluche	750	N/A	115.00	575
1987 Lady's Secret	950	N/A	175.00	425
1982 Man O'War "Final Thunder"	750	N/A	175.00	2500-3100
1979 Mare and Foal	500	N/A	90.00	500
1979 The Moment After	500	N/A	90.00	350
1986 Nijinski II	950	N/A	175.00	250-275
1984 Northern Dancer	950	N/A	175.00	625
1982 Off and Running	750	N/A	125.00	250-350
1990 Old Warriors Shoemaker-John Henry	1,950	N/A	265.00	595-650
1979 One, Two, Three	500	N/A	100.00	1000
1980 The Pasture Pest	500	N/A	100.00	875
1979 Patience	1,000	N/A	90.00	1200
1989 Phar Lap	950	N/A	195.00	275
1982 The Power Horses	750	N/A	125.00	250
1997 Preakness-Silver Charm, canvas	250		295.00	295
1997 Preakness-Silver Charm, litho	1,150		195.00	195
1987 The Rivalry-Alysheba and Bet Twice	950	N/A	195.00	500-550
1979 The Rivals-Affirmed & Alydar	500	N/A	90.00	500
1983 Ruffian-For Only a Moment	750	N/A	175.00	1100
1983 Secretariat	950	N/A	175.00	995-1200
1989 Shoe Bald Eagle	950	N/A	195.00	675
1981 The Shoe-8,000 Wins	395	N/A	200.00	7000
1980 Spectacular Bid	500	N/A	65.00	350-400
1995 Summer Days, canvas litho	350		375.00	375
1995 Summer Days, litho	1,150		225.00	225
XX Sunday Silence	950	N/A	195.00	425
1981 The Thoroughbreds	750	N/A	115.00	425
1983 Tranquility	750	N/A	150.00	525
1984 Turning For Home	750	N/A	150.00	425
1982 The Water Trough	750	N/A	125.00	575

Anheuser-Busch, Inc.

Anheuser-Busch - H. Droog

YEAR ISSUE	EDITION LIMIT	YEAR RETD.	ISSUE PRICE	*QUOTE U.S.$
1994 Gray Wolf Mirror N4570	2,500	1999	135.00	125-160

Endangered Species Fine Art Prints - B. Kemper

YEAR ISSUE	EDITION LIMIT	YEAR RETD.	ISSUE PRICE	*QUOTE U.S.$
1996 Bald Eagle Print, framed N9995	2,500	1997	159.00	135-159
1996 Bald Eagle, unframed N9995U	2,500	1997	79.00	79
1996 Cougar Print, framed N9993	2,500	1997	159.00	135-159
1996 Cougar Print, unframed N9993U	2,500	1997	79.00	79
1996 Gray Wolf Print, framed N9992	2,500	1997	159.00	135-159
1996 Gray Wolf Print, unframed N9992U	2,500	1997	79.00	79
1996 Panda Print, framed N9994	2,500	1997	159.00	135-159
1996 Panda Print, unframed N9994U	2,500	1997	79.00	79

Arts Uniq', Inc.

Fincher - K. Andrews Fincher

YEAR ISSUE	EDITION LIMIT	YEAR RETD.	ISSUE PRICE	*QUOTE U.S.$
1996 The Angel's Promise (lg.)	2,950		30.00	30
1996 The Best Gift (lg.)	2,950		35.00	35
1998 The Blessing	Open		22.00	22
1997 Butterflies	Open		20.00	20

*Quotes have been rounded up to nearest dollar

Arts Uniq', Inc.
to Arts Uniq', Inc.

GRAPHICS

YEAR ISSUE	EDITION LIMIT	YEAR RETD.	ISSUE PRICE	*QUOTE U.S.$
1997 Charm School (lg.)	2,950		40.00	40
1995 The Children's Table (lg.) A/P	195	1998	48.00	48
1995 The Children's Table (lg.) A/P	1,950		28.00	28
1997 Doin' Chores	2,950		30.00	30
1997 Firefly	2,950		30.00	30
1995 First Look (lg.)	1,950		28.00	28
1995 First Look (lg.) A/P	195	1998	28.00	28
1995 Glimpse Of Glory I	1,950		60.00	60
1995 Glimpse Of Glory I A/P	195	1998	80.00	80
1995 Glimpse Of Glory II	1,950		60.00	60
1995 Glimpse Of Glory II A/P	195	1998	80.00	80
1999 God's Treasure	Open		15.00	15
1999 God's Treasure (Mini)	Open		2.40	3
1997 Grandma's Treasures	Closed	2000	15.00	15
1997 Howdy Partner	Open		15.00	15
1994 If Time Could Stand Still	950	2000	65.00	65
1993 Ladybug (lg.)	1,950		45.00	45
1997 Light On Learning	Open		20.00	20
1994 Lightplay	1,950		25.00	25
1996 Look Into My World (lg.)	2,950		30.00	30
1996 Mom Said Share (lg.)	2,950		35.00	35
1997 Mom Will Be Proud	Open		28.00	28
1995 Mom Will Be Proud	1,950	1997	55.00	55
1995 Mom Will Be Proud A/P	195	1997	75.00	75
1993 Mom Won't Mind	1,950	1995	55.00	55
1996 Mom Won't Mind (sm.)	Open		24.00	24
1995 Mom Won't Mind A/P	Closed	1996	55.00	55
1994 A Morning Visit	1,950	1997	45.00	45
1993 My Moment, My Child	1,950		45.00	45
1993 Path To The Meadow	1,950		45.00	45
1993 A Place To Dream	1,950	2000	45.00	45
1993 Seasons Of Color	1,950		40.00	40
1994 Seek And Find	1,950		40.00	40
1997 Shucks	2,950		30.00	30
1993 Siblings	1,950		55.00	55
1993 This Moment Is Mine	1,950		65.00	65
1997 Three Wishes	2,950		35.00	35
1997 Time Out	Open		28.00	28
1999 Together We Build	Open		15.00	15
1993 Together We'll See The World	950		65.00	65
1994 When You Get Big Like Me	1,950		12.00	12
1993 Where Dreams Begin	1,950		35.00	35
1997 Wings	Closed	1999	15.00	15

Morgan - D. Morgan

YEAR ISSUE	EDITION LIMIT	YEAR RETD.	ISSUE PRICE	*QUOTE U.S.$
1993 Acquainted With The Night	950		24.00	24
1993 Across The Moon	950		24.00	24
1993 Again With You	Closed	1995	40.00	40
XX Again With You A/P	Closed	1995	40.00	40
2000 Again with You II	Open		39.00	39
1994 Alabama	Open		17.00	17
2000 Amazing Grace	Open		15.00	15
1997 Ambrosia	Open		27.00	27
1993 American Pie	Open		16.00	16
1993 Angels All Around	Open		17.00	17
1993 An Anniversary	Open		17.00	17
1994 Arkansas	Open		17.00	17
1997 At My Grandmother's House	Open		22.00	22
1993 At My Table	Open		22.00	22
1999 Autumn Comes Along	Open		16.00	16
1996 Back In My Home Town	3,950		48.00	48
1991 Bear Creek Junction	950	1995	65.00	65
1999 Bear Creek Junction (sm.)	Open		27.00	27
1990 A Better Friend	Open		17.00	17
1997 A Bit Old Fashioned	3,950		48.00	48
XX A Bit Old Fashioned A/P	Closed	1998	68.00	68
1989 Bless This House	Open		17.00	17
1991 Blue Ridge	Closed	1998	31.00	31
1990 Bluebird Of Happiness	Open		17.00	17
1997 Candlelight For Two	Open		42.00	42
1993 Carolina By The Sea	Open		22.00	22
1990 Carolina In The Morning	Closed	1999	22.00	22
XX Carousel	1,950		30.00	30
1990 Chambered Nautilus	Open		18.00	18
1993 Chestnuts Roasting	Closed	1998	17.00	17
2000 Childhood December	Open		14.00	14
2000 Christmas Future S/N	2,950		55.00	55
1991 Christmas Keepsakes	950		55.00	55
1999 Christmas Keepsakes (sm.)	Open		16.00	16
1998 Christmas Past	2,950		55.00	55
XX Christmas Past A/P	295		75.00	75
1999 Christmas Present	2,950		55.00	55
1995 Colorado	Open		17.00	17
1994 Cottage By The Lake	Open		18.00	18
XX Count My Blessings	Open		39.00	39
1990 Daddy	Open		22.00	22
1989 Dark Hair My Little Girl (lg.)	Closed	1996	27.00	27
1991 Dark Hair My Little Girl (sm.)	Open		17.00	17
1995 Dark Haired Little Girl II	Closed	1998	27.00	27
1993 Darling Chosen One	Open		20.00	20
1990 Daughter's Husband	Open		17.00	17
1989 Dear Grandson	Closed	1995	20.00	20
2000 Dear Santa	Open		27.00	27
1991 Dear Santa II	1,950	1995	35.00	35
1994 Dear Santa II	Closed	1997	22.00	22
1993 Dear Sister	Open		17.00	17
1992 Dear To My Heart	Open		14.00	14
1998 Different Drummmer	Open		27.00	27
1998 Down To The Sea	Open		18.00	18
1994 Each Day	Open		11.00	11
1996 Each New Sunrise	Open		17.00	17
1990 Each New Wave	Open		22.00	22

YEAR ISSUE	EDITION LIMIT	YEAR RETD.	ISSUE PRICE	*QUOTE U.S.$
1990 Eternal Sea	1,000	1998	40.00	40
1998 Every Christmas Card	Open		17.00	17
1992 Every Star	Open		17.00	17
1994 A Favorite Christmas Memory (Gold)	1,950		65.00	65
1994 Florida	Closed	1999	17.00	17
1995 Folks Dressed Up	Open		17.00	17
1989 Footsteps	Open		17.00	17
1993 Footsteps On The Pathway	Open		33.00	33
1993 Friend And Guest	Closed	1999	18.00	18
1989 Friends All True	Open		17.00	17
1996 Friends We'll Always Be	Open		17.00	17
2000 Friendship Cottage	Open		17.00	17
1994 From Far Away	Open		17.00	17
1994 From Morning Light	Open		17.00	17
1997 From This Day	Open		17.00	17
1992 Georgia	Open		17.00	17
1996 Georgia On My Mind II	Open		17.00	17
2000 Give A Child A Dream	Open		16.00	16
1992 God Bless Me	Open		18.00	18
1989 Good Morning Miss Opie	1,950		50.00	50
1989 Grandmother's House	Open		22.00	22
1990 Guardian Angel	Closed	1995	17.00	17
1997 Guardian Angels	Open		17.00	17
1993 Guardian Angels From Above	Closed	1998	17.00	17
1990 Guide Our Children	Open		39.00	39
2000 Harbour Town Lighthouse	Open		22.00	22
2000 Hatteras Lighthouse	Open		15.00	15
1993 He's Always There	Open		17.00	17
2000 Heceta Head Lighthouse	Open		15.00	15
2000 Highland Lighthouse	Open		15.00	15
1997 His Rhapsody	Open		27.00	27
1997 His Symphony	Open		27.00	27
1997 Home Fires	Closed	1999	28.00	28
1992 Homecoming Christmas Eve (Gold)	1,950		65.00	65
2000 The Horse Knows II	Open		5.00	5
1990 House By The Sea	Open		22.00	22
1995 How Far I Roam	2,950	1997	48.00	48
1995 How Far I Roam A/P	295	1997	68.00	68
2000 How Far I Roam II	Open		45.00	45
2000 How Great Thou Art	Open		15.00	15
1995 I Believe In Angels II	Open		17.00	17
1996 I Had A Dad	Open		17.00	17
1992 If God Would Grant (lg.)	Closed	1996	17.00	17
1996 The Impossible Dream III	Closed	1999	17.00	17
1993 In A Bungalow	Open		22.00	22
1993 In His Keeping	Open		17.00	17
XX In The Name Of Love	Closed	1995	15.00	15
1991 Indiana	Open		17.00	17
1994 Jack Frost	Open		17.00	17
1993 Joy Of Living	Open		22.00	22
1993 Keep A Candle	Open		17.00	17
1990 The Keeper	Open		22.00	22
2000 Keeper To Eternity	Open		27.00	27
1993 Kettle's On	295		18.00	18
2000 Key To Paradise	Open		27.00	27
1993 Kris Kringle	2,950	1995	45.00	45
XX Kris Kringle A/P	295		65.00	65
1998 Learn By Going (lg.)	Open		12.00	12
1996 Let It Snow	Open		27.00	27
1996 Life Begins Anew	Open		24.00	24
1994 Light The Candles On The Tree	Open		27.00	27
1994 Lighthouse Beacon	Open		17.00	17
1996 Linger By The Sea	Open		17.00	17
2000 A Little Bit of Heaven	Open		45.00	45
2000 Love Endures	Open		24.00	24
1992 Love Is A Circle (lg.)	Open		17.00	17
2000 Love Someone	Open		45.00	45
1993 Lover's Knot	Closed	1996	16.00	16
1991 Loving You	Open		18.00	18
1993 Magic In The Night (Gold)	1,950	1997	65.00	65
1994 The Magic Never Ends	4,500	1997	48.00	48
XX The Magic Never Ends A/P	Closed	1998	68.00	68
1995 The Magic Of Christmas	3,950		50.00	50
1995 The Magic Of Christmas A/P	395		70.00	70
1997 The Magic Of Giving	3,950		50.00	50
1997 The Magic Of Giving A/P	395		70.00	70
1990 Man And Wife	Open		22.00	22
2000 May All Your Christmases	Open		16.00	16
1994 May The Sunshine	Open		18.00	18
1994 May You Always	Open		18.00	18
1993 May You Dream	Open		18.00	18
1994 May You Follow	Open		18.00	18
1991 May Your Journey	Open		22.00	22
1997 Memories Everafter	Open		17.00	17
1997 Memories You Give	Closed	1999	27.00	27
1999 Merry and Bright	Open		17.00	17
1994 Michigan	Closed	1997	17.00	17
1992 Missouri	Closed	N/A	17.00	17
1990 Mom And Dad	Open		22.00	22
1995 A Mom Like You	Open		17.00	17
1990 Mother	Open		22.00	22
1992 Mother-In-Law	Open		17.00	17
1992 Mountain Greenery III	Closed	1996	31.00	31
1997 Mountain Greenery IV	Open		24.00	24
2000 Mountain Magic	Open		45.00	45
1992 Moutain Magic (Gold)	950	1998	75.00	75
1992 My Blue Heaven III	1,950	1995	40.00	40
XX My Blue Heaven III A/P	Closed	1996	40.00	40
XX My Brother	Closed	1995	15.00	15
1992 My Daughter	Open		27.00	27
1997 My Dearest Daughter	Open		27.00	27
1997 My Dearest Sister	Open		14.00	14

YEAR ISSUE	EDITION LIMIT	YEAR RETD.	ISSUE PRICE	*QUOTE U.S.$
1992 My Favorite Place	1,950	1997	40.00	40
2000 My Favorite Place	Open		39.00	39
1997 My Favorite Place A/P	122	1998	40.00	40
1996 My Front Door	3,950		48.00	48
1994 My Husband Dear	Open		22.00	22
XX My Impossible Dream	Open		17.00	17
XX My Little Boy (lg.)	Open		27.00	27
1991 My Little Boy (sm.)	Open		17.00	17
XX My Little Girl (lg.)	Open		27.00	27
1991 My Little Girl (sm.)	Open		17.00	17
1995 My Little Girl II	Closed	1999	27.00	27
1993 My Precious Friend	Open		18.00	18
1993 My Safety Harbour	Open		17.00	17
1989 My Sister	Open		17.00	17
1990 My Son	Open		27.00	27
1993 My Special Friend	Open		11.00	11
2000 My True Friend	Open		7.00	7
1990 Near The Ocean	1,000	1997	40.00	40
1995 Near The Ocean A/P	Closed	1995	40.00	40
1994 Never Too Far	Open		18.00	18
1995 New England	Open		17.00	17
1995 New York	Open		17.00	17
2000 No Place on Earth	Open		35.00	35
1989 No Place On Earth II	1,950	1995	40.00	40
XX No Place On Earth II A/P	Closed	1996	40.00	40
1996 Nothing Could Be Finer	Open		22.00	22
1995 Nothing Happens II	Open		17.00	17
1989 Nothing Happens Without A Dream	Open		17.00	17
1995 Nutcracker King	3,950		28.00	28
1995 Nutcracker King A/P	195		40.00	40
1995 Nutcracker Queen	3,950		28.00	28
1995 Nutcracker Queen A/P	195		40.00	40
1992 October Afternoon	1,950		45.00	45
1990 Old Love Letters	Open		31.00	31
1996 One Hundred Years Together	3,950	1997	48.00	48
1997 One Hundred Years Together A/P	Closed	1998	68.00	68
1999 One Hundred Years Together II	Open		45.00	45
1997 Our Cup Is Full	3,950		48.00	48
1996 Our Family (lg.)	Open		18.00	18
1996 Our Family (sm.)	Open		17.00	17
1995 Paradise On Earth	2,950		48.00	48
1995 Paradise On Earth A/P	295		68.00	68
1997 Paradise On Earth II	Open		24.00	24
XX Path Of Ribbons	1,950	1995	22.00	22
1994 Peaceful Nights	Open		11.00	11
1990 Pink Conch	Closed	N/A	18.00	18
2000 Places in My Heart	Open		17.00	17
2000 Point Bonita Lighthouse	Open		15.00	15
1993 Power Of A Dream	Open		17.00	17
1993 Quittin' Time	Closed	1995	18.00	18
1994 Reminders Of Carefree Days	Open		11.00	11
1993 Ribbons In The Sky	950		35.00	35
1997 Romance With The Sea (lg.)	Open		30.00	30
1997 Romance With The Sea (sm.)	Open		14.00	14
2000 Sable Point Lighthouse	Open		22.00	22
XX Safe Crossing	Closed	1999	20.00	20
1990 Salty Air	Closed	N/A	17.00	17
1990 Sand Dollar	Closed	1998	18.00	18
1995 Santa's Magic	3,950		50.00	50
1995 Santa's Magic A/P	395		70.00	70
1993 Seldom An Evening	Open		17.00	17
1999 Sentimental Journal (sm.)	Open		22.00	22
1993 Sentimental Journey	950	1999	75.00	75
1989 Shangri-La	1,950		50.00	50
1993 The Sharecroppers	Closed	1998	17.00	17
1990 Shell Miracle	Open		22.00	22
1990 Shell Trio	Closed	N/A	18.00	18
1992 Sinterklaus	Closed	1996	22.00	22
1995 Sleigh Ride	Open		24.00	24
1989 Snow Job	1,950	1999	50.00	50
2000 Softly and Tenderly	Open		15.00	15
2000 Song of Summer	Open		22.00	22
1993 Song Of The Sea	Open		22.00	22
2000 Split Rock Lighthouse	Open		22.00	22
1997 Spring Is Coming Soon	Open		16.00	16
2000 St. Augustine Lighthouse	Open		22.00	22
1995 Starlight Twinkling	Open		17.00	17
XX Stars Like Diamonds	Closed	1995	12.00	12
1999 Summer Song	Open		16.00	16
1999 Tender Yesterdays	Open		22.00	22
1995 Texas	Open		17.00	17
XX Thanks For The Memory	Closed	1995	50.00	50
XX Thanks For The Memory III	1,950	1995	38.00	38
1999 That Little Country Church	Open		22.00	22
2000 That Old Rugged Cross	Open		15.00	15
1997 That Precious Little Boy	Open		27.00	27
1993 There'll Be No Goodbyes	Open		17.00	17
XX There's A Little Cottage	Closed	1996	14.00	14
1993 There's A Season	Open		11.00	11
1994 These Tiny Shells	Closed	1999	11.00	11
2000 This Heart of Mine	Open		45.00	45
1997 Those Who Teach	Open		17.00	17
2000 Those Who Teach II	Open		11.00	11
1994 Those Wonder Years	Closed	1999	42.00	42
1990 Through The Storm	Open		14.00	14
1990 Through The Storm - Snow	Open		20.00	20
1991 Through The Storm - Winter	Closed	1996	17.00	17
1993 Through Your Darkest Hour	Open		17.00	17
1996 Time Changes Many Things	Open		22.00	22
1995 Tiny Tots	Open		17.00	17
1990 Underwater	Closed	1998	33.00	33
1994 Walk Along The Beach	Closed	1996	18.00	18

*Quotes have been rounded up to nearest dollar

YEAR ISSUE	EDITION LIMIT	YEAR RETD.	ISSUE PRICE	*QUOTE U.S.$
1989 Welcome Friend	Open		17.00	17
1992 What Would Life Be	Open		18.00	18
1998 Where Winter Ends	Open		17.00	17
1997 White Christmas	Open		17.00	17
1990 Wife For My Son	Open		17.00	17
1997 Winter Longs To Linger	Open		16.00	16
1998 Winterset	Open		27.00	27
1993 Wish Upon A Star	Open		17.00	17
1994 With Every Step	Closed	1998	17.00	17
1993 You're A Treasure	Open		16.00	16
XX Your Friend	Open		18.00	18
1993 Your Wedding Day	Closed	1998	17.00	17

Morgan/Talbott-Boassy - D. Morgan/G. Talbott-Boassy

YEAR ISSUE	EDITION LIMIT	YEAR RETD.	ISSUE PRICE	*QUOTE U.S.$
2000 Changing Times	Open		17.00	17
2000 It Was Springtime	Open		15.00	15

Talbott-Boassy - G. Talbott-Boassy

YEAR ISSUE	EDITION LIMIT	YEAR RETD.	ISSUE PRICE	*QUOTE U.S.$
1998 Among My Favorite Memories	Open		22.00	22
1998 Angelic Innocence	Open		20.00	20
1997 Angels In The Garden	Closed	1999	15.00	15
XX Attic Angel	1,000		25.00	25
XX Attic Beauties	Closed	1995	25.00	25
1993 Best Wishes - Mother	Open		15.00	15
1993 Best Wishes - Sister	Open		15.00	15
2000 Breath Of Romance	Open		9.00	9
1999 Clean and Neat	Open		4.80	5
1999 Clean And Neat	Open		4.80	5
1994 Curl Up With A Book	Open		12.00	12
XX Dresses I	Closed	1995	11.00	11
1999 Earth And Flowers	Open		4.80	5
1991 Empty Nest	1,950		18.00	18
1993 First Christmas	Open		12.00	12
1992 Free As A Melody	Closed	N/A	12.00	12
1996 A Garden Wedding	Open		12.00	12
2000 Green Glide	Open		4.80	5
1995 Heaven's Treasures	Closed	2000	22.00	22
1990 Her Guardian Angel	1,950	1997	30.00	30
1991 His Favorite Season	1,950	1999	25.00	25
XX I Sing	1,950	1996	35.00	35
2000 I Will Honor Christmas	Open		9.00	9
XX In Service Of Our Country (lg.)	Open		15.00	15
1990 Keepsakes	Closed	1998	22.00	22
1991 Letters Of Love	1,950	1997	28.00	28
1995 Love Me Tender	Closed	2000	15.00	15
1990 Me And Mommy	1,950		30.00	30
XX Mi' Ladies	1,950		25.00	25
1999 Misty Early Morning	Open		9.00	9
1991 Mother's Love	Open		12.00	12
1999 Nice Clean Fun	Open		2.40	3
2000 An Old Flame	Open		4.80	5
1999 Paradise On Earth	Open		9.00	9
1997 Peanut Butter Picnic	Open		22.00	22
1997 Poetry Bouquet	Open		15.00	15
1995 Precious Gifts	Open		22.00	22
1995 Pretty As A Pitcher	1,950		35.00	35
1995 Pretty As A Pitcher A/P	195	1998	50.00	50
2000 Red Racer	Open		4.80	5
1999 Relaxing In Your Tub	Open		2.40	3
XX Remember Me	1,950	1999	25.00	25
2000 Santa	Open		15.00	15
2000 Santa (mini)	Open		2.40	3
XX Scarlet Ribbons	1,950		28.00	28
1997 Shared Moments	Closed	2000	28.00	28
1997 Shared Moments - Sister	Open	1999	28.00	28
1999 A Shovel And A Hose	Open		4.80	5
1990 Sincerely Yours - Single Rose	Closed	1996	12.00	12
XX Sincerely Yours-Best Friend	Closed	1995	12.00	12
1999 Sunny Hours	Open		9.00	9
1990 Sweet Dreams	1,950	1997	25.00	25
XX Tea Party	Closed	1995	26.00	26
1990 Tea Party	Open		22.00	22
1997 Tea Party - Ethnic	Open		22.00	22
1995 Teacups And Tassels	Open		15.00	15
1994 They Had Wings	Open		24.00	24
XX Those Who Have Suffered	Open		12.00	12
XX Three Sisters	1,000		20.00	20
1992 Timeless Treasures	Open		12.00	12
2000 True Blue	Open		4.80	5
1997 Waiting In The Attic (sm.)	Open		15.00	15
1995 Waiting In The Attic A/P	1,950		35.00	35
1995 Waiting In The Attic A/P	175	1998	45.00	45
XX When The Party Is Over	1,950		18.00	18
XX Wilt Thou Go	Closed	1998	12.00	12
1990 Your Love Keeps Me Warm	Closed	1998	24.00	24

Terry - J. Terry

YEAR ISSUE	EDITION LIMIT	YEAR RETD.	ISSUE PRICE	*QUOTE U.S.$
2000 Courtyard Fountain	Open		28.00	28
2000 Courtyard Garden	Open		28.00	28
2000 Duck Hunter's Dream	Open		28.00	28
2000 Misty Trail	950		150.00	150
2000 Spring Bouquet I	Open		28.00	28
2000 Spring Bouquet II	Open		28.00	28
2000 Tranquil Refuge	Open		28.00	28
2000 Winter Home	Open		28.00	28

Wright - C. Shores

YEAR ISSUE	EDITION LIMIT	YEAR RETD.	ISSUE PRICE	*QUOTE U.S.$
1996 Anna's Hummingbird With Roses I	Open		12.00	12
1994 Anna's Hummingbird With Salvia	Open		12.00	12
1994 Anna's With Azaleas	Open		12.00	12
1999 Anna's With Trumpet Vine	Open		4.80	5
XX Apartments	Open		12.00	12
XX Backyard Chef	Closed	1995	14.00	14
1997 Barn Swallows With Dawn Flowers	Open		15.00	15
1995 Berry Hill Fruit I	Closed	1998	12.00	12
1995 Berry Hill Fruit II	Closed	N/A	12.00	12
1995 Birdhouse Row	Open		12.00	12
1994 Birdhouse With Bluebirds	Open		12.00	12
1994 Birdhouse With Chickadee	Open		12.00	12
1996 Birdhouse With Roses	Open		12.00	12
1994 Birdhouse With Wren	Open		12.00	12
1994 Birdhouse With Yellow Throats	Open		12.00	12
1990 Bits And Pieces	1,950		12.00	12
XX Box Of Bunnies	Closed	1995	12.00	12
XX Break Point	1,950	1995	15.00	15
XX Briarpatch Bunny	1,000	1995	15.00	15
1999 Broad-Billed with Salvia	Open		4.80	5
XX Bunny Band	1,000	1995	15.00	15
1995 Butterfly Inn I	Open		12.00	12
1995 Butterfly Inn II	Open		12.00	12
1999 Calliope and Chorisia	Open		4.80	5
1990 Cardinal Female	Open		11.00	11
1994 Cardinal On A Flowering Branch	2,950		38.00	38
1999 Carnival I	Open		15.00	15
1999 Carnival II	Open		15.00	15
1992 Cascade	950	1995	45.00	45
1991 Cherries	Open		11.00	11
1994 Cherub Choir	Open		12.00	12
1993 Chickadee And Fledglings	1,950	1996	15.00	15
1997 Chickadees And Dogwood	Open		12.00	12
1992 Classic	950	1995	45.00	45
2000 Cookies with a Friend	Open		4.80	5
XX Cuddled Pair	1,950		10.00	10
1993 The Day's Catch (Premat)	Open		12.00	12
1994 Dynasty	Open		12.00	12
1992 Eastern Bluebirds	1,950	1999	38.00	38
1994 Embassy	Open		12.00	12
1995 Emperor	Open		12.00	12
1993 Evening Stroll	950		15.00	15
1995 Exotic Blooms I (Deckled)	Open		13.00	13
1995 Exotic Blooms II (Deckled)	Open		13.00	13
1996 Exotic Blooms III (Deckled)	Open		13.00	13
1996 Exotic Blooms IV (Deckled)	Open		13.00	13
1994 Fancy Flight	2,950		38.00	38
XX Farm House	Closed	1995	12.00	12
XX Father's Pride	1,950	1995	12.00	12
1990 Featherdo	1,950		12.00	12
XX Feeding Time-N/S	500		14.00	14
1999 Festival	Open		34.00	34
1989 Five Of A Kind A/P	1,950	1998	15.00	15
1992 Flowering Season I	950		15.00	15
1992 Flowering Season II	950		15.00	15
1992 Flowering Season III	950		15.00	15
XX Four Little Birds	1,950	1995	15.00	15
XX Friends	Closed	1995	12.00	12
1995 Fruit Fiesta	Closed	2000	15.00	15
1994 Garden Cherub	Open		12.00	12
1994 Geranium (lg.)	Open		12.00	12
1997 Goldfinch And Apple Blossoms	Open		12.00	12
1996 Goldfinch And Clematis	Open		12.00	12
XX Grandmother I	1,000		15.00	15
XX Grandmother II	1,000		15.00	15
1989 Grandmother's Darlings	1,950		15.00	15
1993 Grandmother's Little Man	950		15.00	15
1999 Harvest Home	Open		2.40	3
2000 He Will Shield You	Open		4.80	5
XX High Fashion	Closed	1995	15.00	15
1989 Holiday Cruise	1,950	1999	12.00	12
1999 Holly House	Open		2.40	3
2000 A House Made by God	Open		4.80	5
XX Hula Hoop	1,950		12.00	12
1994 Impromptu	Closed	1998	12.00	12
1995 Ivy Topiary I	Open		15.00	15
1995 Ivy Topiary II	Open		15.00	15
XX Joyful I	1,950	1997	15.00	15
XX Just A Swingin'	1,950		15.00	15
1991 Lavender Blue	1,950	1995	20.00	20
1998 Lemon Tree	Open		15.00	15
1992 Little Hummer IV	2,950	1995	20.00	20
1995 Little Hummer IX	9,950	1998	20.00	20
1993 Little Hummer V	2,950	1995	20.00	20
1993 Little Hummer VI	2,950	1995	20.00	20
1993 Little Hummer VII	9,950		20.00	20
XX Little Hummer VII A/P	Closed	1998	30.00	30
1993 Little Hummer VIII	9,950	1995	20.00	20
XX Little Hummer VIII A/P	Closed	1995	30.00	30
1995 Little Hummer X	9,950		20.00	20
1998 Little Hummer XI	9,950		20.00	20
1998 Little Hummer XII	9,950		20.00	20
1994 A Little Sun I	Open		12.00	12
1994 A Little Sun II	Open		12.00	12
2000 Love	Open		4.80	5
2000 Love One Another	Open		4.80	5
1996 Magnolia Memory (Deckled)	Open		25.00	25
1997 Magnolia Topiary I	Open		15.00	15
1997 Magnolia Topiary II	Open		15.00	15
2000 Making Music	Open		4.80	5
XX Mama's Bunch	Closed	1995	15.00	15
1995 May Day	Open		12.00	12
1999 Moon Shell with Border	Closed	1999	4.80	5
XX Mother's Joy	1,950	1995	12.00	12
1989 Nature's Harmony	1,950		35.00	35
1999 Nature's Sampler I	Open		20.00	20
1999 Nature's Sampler II	Open		20.00	20
1999 Nature's Sampler III	Open		20.00	20
2000 A New Song	Open		4.80	5
1994 Noah's Boat	Open		12.00	12
1997 Nuthatches With Morning Glories	Open		12.00	12
1999 Operetta Plate with Border	Closed	1999	9.00	9
1998 Orange Tree	Open		15.00	15
XX Out To Lunch	1,000		12.00	12
1999 Pacific Scallop Shell with Border	Closed	1999	4.80	5
XX Pals	Closed	1995	12.00	12
1997 Pansy Morning	Open		15.00	15
1993 Paurla Warblers	1,950	1996	15.00	15
1992 Peonies	1,950	1995	25.00	25
1990 Petals And Patches	1,950		12.00	12
1994 Petunia	Open		12.00	12
1997 Porch Visitor I	Open		20.00	20
1997 Porch Visitor II	Open		20.00	20
1997 Portrait	Open		15.00	15
2000 Precious Place	Open		4.80	5
1994 Princess	Closed	1998	12.00	12
1992 Promises Ii	2,950		12.00	12
1997 Purple Martin With Trumpet Vine	Open		15.00	15
1994 Quilt Patterns I	Open		12.00	12
1996 Radiant Blooms I (Deckled)	Open		13.00	13
1996 Radiant Blooms II (Deckled)	Open		13.00	13
1989 Retirement Benefits	1,950		15.00	15
1994 Romance	Open		12.00	12
1994 Rose Basket Cherubs	Open		12.00	12
1993 Rose Parade (Premat)	Open		20.00	20
1995 Rosemont	Open		12.00	12
XX Round Ball	Closed	1995	15.00	15
1996 Ruby Throated Humingbird W/Roses II	Open		12.00	12
1994 Ruby Throated With Geranium	Open		12.00	12
1994 Ruby Throated With Hibiscus	Open		12.00	12
1990 Sampler I	Open		15.00	15
1990 Sampler II	Open		15.00	15
1990 Sampler III	Open		15.00	15
1990 Sampler IV	Closed	1998	15.00	15
1999 Scallop Shell with Border	Open		4.80	5
1997 Scarlet Finches With Mock Orange	Open		12.00	12
XX Set Point	1,950	1995	15.00	15
2000 Sharing a Dream	Open		4.80	5
2000 Sisters Share	Open		4.80	5
XX Soft Feathers	1,950		10.00	10
1993 A Special Friend	950		15.00	15
XX Spring Fantasy (lg.)	1,950	1995	40.00	40
XX Spring Magic II	Closed	1995	20.00	20
XX Spring Song	Closed	1995	12.00	12
1995 St Nicholas II A/P	195	1998	36.00	36
1995 St. Nicholas I	1,950		16.00	16
1995 St. Nicholas I A/P	195	1998	36.00	36
1995 St. Nicholas II	1,950		16.00	16
1991 Strawberries	Open		11.00	11
1993 Sugarplums (Premat)	Open		15.00	15
2000 Summer Time I	Open		4.80	5
2000 Summer Time II	Open		4.80	5
2000 Sweetest Memories	Open		4.80	5
1992 Sweethearts	1,950	1995	15.00	15
1990 Tabby Tangle	Open		14.00	14
1998 Tapestry	Open		28.00	28
XX Tea Party	Open		12.00	12
1997 Three Owls	Open		15.00	15
1996 Timeless	2,950		48.00	48
1999 Top Shell with Border	Closed	1999	4.80	5
1994 Topiary I	Open		15.00	15
1994 Topiary II	Closed	1999	15.00	15
1993 Touch Of Blue (Premat)	1,950		20.00	20
2000 A True Friend	Open		4.80	5
2000 Tuscan Companion I	Open		15.00	15
2000 Tuscan Companion II	Open		15.00	15
2000 Tuscan Orchids	Open		28.00	28
XX Two Step	Closed	1995	12.00	12
1989 Warbler's Spring	1,950	1996	40.00	40
1993 Western Still Life	Open		15.00	15
1999 White-Eared with Freshia	Open		4.80	5
1993 Winter Rural	Open		11.00	11
1997 Winter Rural (S)	Open		15.00	15

Circle Fine Art

Rockwell - N. Rockwell

YEAR ISSUE	EDITION LIMIT	YEAR RETD.	ISSUE PRICE	*QUOTE U.S.$
XX American Family Folio	200		Unkn.	17500
XX The Artist at Work	130		Unkn.	3500
XX At the Barber	200		Unkn.	4900
XX Autumn	200		Unkn.	3500
XX Autumn/Japon	25		Unkn.	3600
XX Aviary	200		Unkn.	4200
XX Barbershop Quartet	200		Unkn.	4200
XX Baseball	200		Unkn.	3600
XX Ben Franklin's Philadelphia	200		Unkn.	3600
XX Ben's Belles	200		Unkn.	3500
XX The Big Day	200		Unkn.	3400
XX The Big Top	148		Unkn.	2800
XX Blacksmith Shop	200		Unkn.	6300
XX Bookseller	200		Unkn.	2700
XX Bookseller/Japon	25		Unkn.	2750
XX The Bridge	200		Unkn.	3100
XX Cat	200		Unkn.	3400
XX Cat/Collotype	200		Unkn.	4000
XX Cheering	200		Unkn.	3600
XX Children at Window	200		Unkn.	3600
XX Church	200		Unkn.	3400

*Quotes have been rounded up to nearest dollar

GRAPHICS

YEAR ISSUE	EDITION LIMIT	YEAR RETD.	ISSUE PRICE	*QUOTE U.S.$
XX Church/Collotype	200		Unkn.	4000
XX Circus	200		Unkn.	2650
XX County Agricultural Agent	200		Unkn.	3900
XX The Critic	200		Unkn.	4650
XX Day in the Life of a Boy	200		Unkn.	6200
XX Day in the Life of a Boy/Japon	25		Unkn.	6500
XX Debut	200		Unkn.	3600
XX Discovery	200		Unkn.	5900
XX Doctor and Boy	200		Unkn.	9400
XX Doctor and Doll-Signed	200		Unkn.	11900
XX Dressing Up/Ink	60		Unkn.	4400
XX Dressing Up/Pencil	200		Unkn.	3700
XX The Drunkard	200		Unkn.	3600
XX The Expected and Unexpected	200		Unkn.	3700
XX Family Tree	200		Unkn.	5900
XX Fido's House	200		Unkn.	3600
XX Football Mascot	200		Unkn.	3700
XX Four Seasons Folio	200		Unkn.	13500
XX Four Seasons Folio/Japon	25		Unkn.	14000
XX Freedom from Fear-Signed	200		Unkn.	6400
XX Freedom from Want-Signed	200		Unkn.	6400
XX Freedom of Religion-Signed	200		Unkn.	6400
XX Freedom of Speech-Signed	200		Unkn.	6400
XX Gaiety Dance Team	200		Unkn.	4300
XX Girl at Mirror-Signed	200		Unkn.	8400
XX The Golden Age	200		Unkn.	3500
XX Golden Rule-Signed	200		Unkn.	4400
XX Golf	200		Unkn.	3600
XX Gossips	200		Unkn.	5000
XX Gossips/Japon	25		Unkn.	5100
XX Grotto	200		Unkn.	3400
XX Grotto/Collotype	200		Unkn.	4000
XX High Dive	200		Unkn.	3400
XX The Homecoming	200		Unkn.	3700
XX The House	200		Unkn.	3700
XX Huck Finn Folio	200		Unkn.	35000
XX Ichabod Crane	200		Unkn.	6700
XX The Inventor	200		Unkn.	4100
XX Jerry	200		Unkn.	4700
XX Jim Got Down on His Knees	200		Unkn.	4500
XX Lincoln	200		Unkn.	11400
XX Lobsterman	200		Unkn.	5500
XX Lobsterman/Japon	25		Unkn.	5750
XX Marriage License	200		Unkn.	6900
XX Medicine	200		Unkn.	3400
XX Medicine/Color Litho	200		Unkn.	4000
XX Miss Mary Jane	200		Unkn.	4500
XX Moving Day	200		Unkn.	3900
XX Music Hath Charms	200		Unkn.	4200
XX My Hand Shook	200		Unkn.	4500
XX Out the Window	200		Unkn.	3400
XX Out the Window/ Collotype	200		Unkn.	4000
XX Outward Bound-Signed	200		Unkn.	7900
XX Poor Richard's Almanac	200		Unkn.	24000
XX Prescription	200		Unkn.	4900
XX Prescription/Japon	25		Unkn.	5000
XX The Problem We All Live With	200		Unkn.	4500
XX Puppies	200		Unkn.	3700
XX Raliegh the Dog	200		Unkn.	3900
XX Rocket Ship	200		Unkn.	3650
XX The Royal Crown	200		Unkn.	3500
XX Runaway	200		Unkn.	3800
XX Runaway/Japon	200		Unkn.	5700
XX Safe and Sound	200		Unkn.	3800
XX Saturday People	200		Unkn.	3300
XX Save Me	200		Unkn.	3600
XX Saying Grace-Signed	200		Unkn.	7400
XX School Days Folio	200		Unkn.	14000
XX Schoolhouse	200		Unkn.	4500
XX Schoolhouse/Japon	25		Unkn.	4650
XX See America First	200		Unkn.	5650
XX See America First/Japon	25		Unkn.	6100
XX Settling In	200		Unkn.	3600
XX Shuffelton's Barbershop	200		Unkn.	7400
XX Smoking	200		Unkn.	3400
XX Smoking/Collotype	200		Unkn.	4000
XX Spanking	200		Unkn.	3400
XX Spanking/ Collotype	200		Unkn.	4000
XX Spelling Bee	200		Unkn.	6500
XX Spring	200		Unkn.	3500
XX Spring Flowers	200		Unkn.	5200
XX Spring/Japon	25		Unkn.	3600
XX Study for the Doctor's Office	200		Unkn.	6000
XX Studying	200		Unkn.	3600
XX Summer	200		Unkn.	3500
XX Summer Stock	200		Unkn.	4900
XX Summer Stock/Japon	25		Unkn.	5000
XX Summer/Japon	25		Unkn.	3600
XX The Teacher	200		Unkn.	3400
XX Teacher's Pet	200		Unkn.	3600
XX The Teacher/Japon	25		Unkn.	3500
XX The Texan	200		Unkn.	3700
XX Then For Three Minutes	200		Unkn.	4500
XX Then Miss Watson	200		Unkn.	4500
XX There Warn't No Harm	200		Unkn.	4500
XX Three Farmers	200		Unkn.	3600
XX Ticketseller	200		Unkn.	4200
XX Ticketseller/Japon	25		Unkn.	4400
XX Tom Sawyer Color Suite	200		Unkn.	30000
XX Tom Sawyer Folio	200		Unkn.	26500
XX Top of the World	200		Unkn.	4200
XX Trumpeter	200		Unkn.	3900
XX Trumpeter/Japon	25		Unkn.	4100
XX Two O'Clock Feeding	200		Unkn.	3600
XX The Village Smithy	200		Unkn.	3500
XX Welcome	200		Unkn.	3500
XX Wet Paint	200		Unkn.	3800
XX When I Lit My Candle	200		Unkn.	4500
XX White Washing	200		Unkn.	3400
XX Whitewashing the Fence/Collotype	200		Unkn.	4000
XX Window Washer	200		Unkn.	4800
XX Winter	200		Unkn.	3500
XX Winter/Japon	25		Unkn.	3600
XX Ye Old Print Shoppe	200		Unkn.	3500
XX Your Eyes is Lookin'	200		Unkn.	4500

Cross Gallery, Inc.

Bandits & Bounty Hunters - P.A. Cross

YEAR ISSUE	EDITION LIMIT	YEAR RETD.	ISSUE PRICE	*QUOTE U.S.$
1994 Bounty Hunter	865		225.00	225

The Gift - P.A. Cross

YEAR ISSUE	EDITION LIMIT	YEAR RETD.	ISSUE PRICE	*QUOTE U.S.$
1989 B' Achua Dlubh-bia Bii Noskiiyahi The Gift, Part II	S/O	1989	225.00	650
1993 The Gift, Part III	S/O	1993	225.00	350-1000

Half Breed Series - P.A. Cross

YEAR ISSUE	EDITION LIMIT	YEAR RETD.	ISSUE PRICE	*QUOTE U.S.$
1989 Ach-hua Dlubh: (Body Two), Half Breed	S/O	1989	190.00	1450
1990 Ach-hua Dlubh: (Body Two), Half Breed II	S/O	1990	225.00	800-1100
1991 Ach-hua Dlubh: (Body Two), Half Breed III	S/O	1991	225.00	850
1995 Ach-hua Dlubh: (Body Two), Half Breed IV	865		225.00	225
2000 Ach-hua Dlubh: (Body Two), Half Breed V	475		225.00	225
2000 Iiluupkaabsúum Iichiilum Áakeenuuk (Riding Double)	475		225.00	225

Limited Edition Original Graphics - P.A. Cross

YEAR ISSUE	EDITION LIMIT	YEAR RETD.	ISSUE PRICE	*QUOTE U.S.$
1991 Bia-A-Hoosh (A Very Special Woman), Stone Lithograph	S/O	1991	500.00	500
1987 Caroline, Stone Lithograph	S/O	1987	300.00	600
1988 Maidenhood Hopi, Stone Lithograph	S/O	1988	950.00	1150
1990 Nighteyes I, Serigraph	S/O	1990	225.00	425
1989 The Red Capote, Serigraph	S/O	1989	750.00	1150
1989 Rosapina, Etching	74		1200.00	1200
1991 Wooltalkers, Serigraph	275		750.00	750

Limited Edition Prints - P.A. Cross

YEAR ISSUE	EDITION LIMIT	YEAR RETD.	ISSUE PRICE	*QUOTE U.S.$
1991 Ashpahdua Hagay Ashae-Gyoke (My Home & Heart Is Crow)	S/O	1991	225.00	225-350
1983 Ayla-Sah-Xuh-Xah (Pretty Colours, Many Designs)	S/O	1983	150.00	450
1990 Baape Ochia (Night Wind, Turquoise)	S/O	1990	185.00	370
1990 Biaachee-itah Bah-achbeh (Medicine Woman Scout)	S/O	1990	225.00	525
1984 Blue Beaded Hair Ties	S/O	1984	85.00	330
1991 The Blue Shawl	S/O	1991	185.00	275
1987 Caroline	S/O	1987	45.00	145
1989 Chey-ayjeh: Prey	S/O	1989	190.00	325-600
1988 Dance Apache	S/O	1988	190.00	360
1987 Dii-tah-shteh Ee-wihza-ahook (A Coat of much Value)	S/O	1987	90.00	740
1989 The Dreamer	S/O	1989	190.00	600
1987 The Elkskin Robe	S/O	1987	190.00	640
1990 Eshte	S/O	1990	185.00	200
1986 Grand Entry	S/O	1986	85.00	85
1983 Isbaaloo Eetshiileehcheek (Sorting Her Beads)	S/O	1983	150.00	1750
1990 Ishia-Kahda #1 (Quiet One)	S/O	1990	185.00	400
1988 Ma-a-luppis-she-La-dus (She is above everything, nothing can touch her)	S/O	1988	190.00	525
1984 Profile of Caroline	S/O	1984	85.00	185
1986 The Red Capote	S/O	1986	150.00	850
1987 The Red Necklace	S/O	1987	90.00	210
1989 Teesa Waits To Dance	S/O	1989	135.00	180
1984 Thick Lodge Clan Boy: Crow Indian	475		85.00	85
1987 Tina	S/O	1987	45.00	110
1985 The Water Vision	S/O	1985	150.00	325
1984 Whistling Water Clan Girl: Crow Indian	S/O	1984	85.00	85
1993 Winter Girl Bride	1,730		225.00	225
1986 Winter Morning	S/O	1986	185.00	1450
1986 The Winter Shawl	S/O	1986	150.00	1600

Miniature Line - P.A. Cross

YEAR ISSUE	EDITION LIMIT	YEAR RETD.	ISSUE PRICE	*QUOTE U.S.$
1991 BJ	S/O	1995	80.00	80
1993 Braids	447		80.00	80
1993 Daybreak	447		80.00	80
1991 The Floral Shawl	S/O	1995	80.00	80
1991 Kendra	S/O	1995	80.00	80
1993 Ponytails	447		80.00	80
1993 Sundown	447		80.00	80
1991 Watercolour Study #2 For Half Breed	S/O	1995	80.00	80

No Vacancy Series - P.A. Cross

YEAR ISSUE	EDITION LIMIT	YEAR RETD.	ISSUE PRICE	*QUOTE U.S.$
1999 LaMoza (canvas)	75		795.00	795
1999 No Vacancy (canvas)	75		N/A	N/A
1999 No Vacancy (paper)	475		225.00	225
1999 Sombrero (canvas)	75		795.00	795

The Painted Ladies' Series - P.A. Cross

YEAR ISSUE	EDITION LIMIT	YEAR RETD.	ISSUE PRICE	*QUOTE U.S.$
1992 Acoria (Crow; Seat of Honor)	S/O	1995	185.00	185
1992 Avisola	S/O	1995	185.00	185
1992 Dah-say (Crow; Heart)	S/O	1995	185.00	185
1992 Itza-chu (Apache; The Eagle)	S/O	1995	185.00	185
1992 Kel'hoya (Hopi; Little Sparrow Hawk)	S/O	1995	185.00	185
1992 The Painted Ladies	S/O	1992	225.00	1200
2000 Sus(h)gah-daydus(h) (Crow; Quick)	447		185.00	185
2000 Tze-go-juni (Chiricahua Apache)	447		185.00	185

Star Quilt Series - P.A. Cross

YEAR ISSUE	EDITION LIMIT	YEAR RETD.	ISSUE PRICE	*QUOTE U.S.$
1988 The Quilt Makers	S/O	1988	190.00	1200
1986 Reflections	S/O	1986	185.00	865
1985 Winter Warmth	S/O	1985	150.00	900-1215

Wolf Series - P.A. Cross

YEAR ISSUE	EDITION LIMIT	YEAR RETD.	ISSUE PRICE	*QUOTE U.S.$
1990 Agnjnaug Amaguut;Inupiag (Woman With Her Wolves)	S/O	1993	325.00	350-750
1993 Ahmah-ghut, Tuhtu-loo; Eelahn-nuht Kah-auhk (Wolves and Caribou; My Furs and My Friends)	1,050		255.00	255
1989 Biagoht Eecuebeh Hehsheesh-Checah: (Red Ridinghood and Her Wolves), Gift I	S/O	1989	225.00	1500-2500
1997 Cheedé Bilaxpáake Áashe Áakeeshdak (Wolf People Crossing the River)	S/O	1998	225.00	225
1985 Dii-tah-shteh Bii-wik; Chedah-bah Iiidah (My Very Own Protective Covering; Walks w/ Wolf Woman)	S/O	1985	185.00	3275
1987 The Morning Star Gives Long Otter His Hoop Medicine Power	S/O	1987	190.00	1800-2500

Flambro Imports

Emmett Kelly Jr. Lithographs - B. Leighton-Jones

YEAR ISSUE	EDITION LIMIT	YEAR RETD.	ISSUE PRICE	*QUOTE U.S.$
1995 All Star Circus	2 Yr.	1997	150.00	150
1994 EKJ 70th Birthday Commemorative	1,994	1997	150.00	150
1994 I Love You	2 Yr.	1996	90.00	90-150
1994 Joyful Noise	2 Yr.	1996	90.00	90-150
1994 Picture Worth 1,000 Words	2 Yr.	1996	90.00	90-150

Gartlan USA

Lithograph - Various

YEAR ISSUE	EDITION LIMIT	YEAR RETD.	ISSUE PRICE	*QUOTE U.S.$
1986 George Brett-"The Swing" - J. Martin	2,000	1990	85.00	200-250
1991 Joe Montana - M. Taylor	500	1994	495.00	600-700
1989 Kareem Abdul Jabbar-The Record Setter - M. Taylor	1,989	1993	85.00	275-395
1991 Negro League 1st World Series (print) - Unknown	1,924	1993	109.00	125
1987 Roger Staubach - C. Soileau	1,979	1992	85.00	200-300

Ringo Starr - B. Forbes

YEAR ISSUE	EDITION LIMIT	YEAR RETD.	ISSUE PRICE	*QUOTE U.S.$
2000 Ringo Starr, A/P signed framed lithograph "Retrospect"	50		595.00	595
2000 Ringo Starr, signed framed lithograph "Retrospect"	500		495.00	495
1998 Signed Drum Sticks & Lithograph	500	1999	495.00	695
1998 Signed Drum Sticks & Lithograph A/P	50	1998	595.00	895

Glynda Turley Prints

Turley - Canvas - G. Turley

YEAR ISSUE	EDITION LIMIT	YEAR RETD.	ISSUE PRICE	*QUOTE U.S.$
1996 Abundance III	350		190.00	190
1997 Abundance IV	350		190.00	190
1999 Abundance V	350		249.00	249
1997 Black-eyed Susans and Blackberries	350	1999	140.00	140
1996 Chrysanthemums and Apples	350	1999	140.00	140
1998 Cottage Garden	350		286.00	286
1992 Courtyard II	200	1996	140.00	140
1994 Courtyard III	350	1999	140.00	140
1988 Elegance	350	1999	130.00	130
1991 Floral Fancy	150	1999	130.00	130
1992 Flower Garden	350	1999	130.00	130
1998 Garden Favorites III	350		286.00	286
1990 Garden Room	250		130.00	130
1992 The Garden Wreath II	200	1996	130.00	130
1994 The Garden Wreath III	350		140.00	140
1994 Georgia Sweet	350	1999	140.00	140
1992 Grand Glory I	350	1999	160.00	160
1992 Grand Glory II	350	1999	160.00	160
1995 Grand Glory III	350		160.00	160
1995 Grand Glory IV	350		160.00	160
1997 Hand in Hand	350		160.00	160
1999 Heavenly Hydrageas	350		249.00	249
1992 In Full Bloom	200	N/A	160.00	160
1994 In Full Bloom II	350		160.00	160
1995 In Full Bloom III	350		140.00	140
1988 Iris Basket II	350	1999	130.00	130
1990 Iris Basket III	50	1997	130.00	130
1991 Iris Basket IV	25	1999	130.00	130
1989 Iris Parade	350	1996	130.00	130
2000 Ivy and Roses III	350		249.00	249
1997 Keeping Watch	350	1999	214.00	214
1988 La Belle IV	25	1999	130.00	130
1999 Lily Pond	350		232.00	232
1995 Little Red River	350		190.00	190
1995 Mabry In Spring	350		160.00	160
1992 Old Mill Stream	350	N/A	130.00	130
1993 Old Mill Stream II	350	1996	130.00	130
1994 Old Mill Stream III	350		190.00	190
1996 Old Mill Stream IV	350		190.00	190
1988 Once Upon A Time	200	1999	130.00	130
1996 Pears and Roses	350	1999	140.00	140

456 Collectors' Information Bureau

*Quotes have been rounded up to nearest dollar

YEAR ISSUE	EDITION LIMIT	YEAR RETD.	ISSUE PRICE	*QUOTE U.S.$
1989 Petals In Pink	100	1999	190.00	190
1997 Plums and Pansies	350	1999	140.00	140
1989 Pretty Pickings I	350	1999	130.00	130
1989 Pretty Pickings II	300	1999	130.00	130
1989 Pretty Pickings III	100	1999	130.00	130
1993 Primrose Lane II	300	1999	130.00	130
1995 Remember When	350	1999	190.00	190
1998 Ring Around The Rosy	350		232.00	232
1991 Secret Garden	350		130.00	130
1994 Secret Garden II	350		130.00	130
1996 Secret Garden III	350		160.00	160
1991 Simply Southern	350	1996	160.00	160
1998 Southern Elegance III	350		190.00	190
1992 Southern Sunday	200	1999	140.00	140
1995 Southern Sunday II	350		190.00	190
1993 A Southern Tradition II	350		190.00	190
1994 A Southern Tradition IV	350		190.00	190
1995 A Southern Tradition V	350		190.00	190
1998 Spring Flora III	350		190.00	190
1993 Spring's Promise II	300	1999	130.00	130
1988 Spring's Return	350	1999	130.00	130
1995 Summer in Victoria	350	1999	130.00	130
1994 Summer Stroll	350	1997	160.00	160
1990 Sweet Nothings	350	1999	130.00	130
1997 Wading at the Bridge	350		214.00	214
1996 Wreath of Spring	350	1999	140.00	140

Turley - Print - G. Turley

YEAR ISSUE	EDITION LIMIT	YEAR RETD.	ISSUE PRICE	*QUOTE U.S.$
1996 Abundance III	7,500		73.00	73
1996 Abundance III A/P	50		109.50	110
1997 Abundance IV	3,500		73.00	73
1997 Abundance IV A/P	50		109.50	110
1999 Abundance V	2,500		104.00	104
1999 Abundance V A/P	50		156.00	156
1995 Almost An Angel	7,500	1999	56.00	56
1995 Almost An Angel A/P	50	1999	84.00	84
1986 Attic Curiosity	2,000	N/A	15.00	15
1986 Attic Curiosity A/P	50	N/A	25.00	25
1997 Black-eyed Susans and Blackberries	7,500	1999	64.00	64
1997 Black-eyed Susans and Blackberries A/P	50	1999	96.00	96
1986 Busy Bodies I	2,000	N/A	25.00	25
1986 Busy Bodies I A/P	50	N/A	40.00	40
1986 Busy Bodies II	2,000	N/A	25.00	25
1986 Busy Bodies II A/P	50	N/A	40.00	40
1986 Callie And Company I	2,000	N/A	30.00	30
1986 Callie And Company I A/P	50	N/A	50.00	50
1987 Callie And Company II	3,000	N/A	30.00	30
1987 Callie And Company II A/P	50	N/A	50.00	50
1988 Calling On Callie	5,000	1996	30.00	30
1988 Calling On Callie A/P	50	1999	45.00	45
1990 Childhood Memories I	3,500	1999	30.00	30
1990 Childhood Memories I A/P	50	1999	45.00	45
1990 Childhood Memories II	3,500	1999	30.00	30
1990 Childhood Memories II A/P	50	1999	45.00	45
1996 Chrysanthemums and Apples	7,500	1999	64.00	64
1996 Chrysanthemums and Apples A/P	50	1999	96.00	96
1988 Circle of Friends	5,000	1996	25.00	25
1988 Circle Of Friends A/P	50	N/A	40.00	40
1990 The Coming Out Party	3,500	1999	35.00	35
1998 Cottage Garden	2,500		108.00	108
1998 Cottage Garden A/P	50		162.00	162
1991 The Courtyard I	2,500	N/A	47.00	47
1991 The Courtyard I A/P	50	N/A	70.50	71
1992 The Courtyard II	2,500	N/A	50.00	50
1992 The Courtyard II A/P	50		75.00	75
1994 The Courtyard III A/P	50	1999	91.50	92
1990 Dear To My Heart	3,500	1999	35.00	35
1990 Dear To My Heart A/P	50	1999	52.50	53
1988 Elegance	5,000	1999	30.00	30
1988 Elegance A/P	50	1999	45.00	45
1986 A Family Affair	2,500	N/A	25.00	25
1986 A Family Affair A/P	50	N/A	40.00	40
1984 Feeding Time I	1,000	N/A	50.00	50
1984 Feeding Time I A/P	50	N/A	75.00	75
1984 Feeding Time II	1,000	N/A	25.00	25
1984 Feeding Time II A/P	50	N/A	40.00	40
1987 Fence Row Gathering I	3,000	N/A	30.00	30
1987 Fence Row Gathering I A/P	50	N/A	50.00	50
1988 Fence Row Gathering II	5,000	N/A	30.00	60-145
1988 Fence Row Gathering II A/P	50	N/A	50.00	50
1991 Floral Fancy	3,500	N/A	40.00	40
1991 Floral Fancy A/P	50	1999	60.00	60
1992 The Flower Garden	2,500	1996	43.00	43
1992 The Flower Garden A/P	50	1999	64.50	65
1986 Flowers And Lace	3,000	N/A	25.00	25
1986 Flowers And Lace A/P	50	N/A	40.00	40
1988 Flowers For Mommy	5,000	N/A	25.00	25
1988 Flowers For Mommy A/P	50	N/A	40.00	40
1990 Forever Roses	3,500	1999	30.00	30
1990 Forever Roses A/P	50	1999	45.00	45
1998 Garden Favorites III	2,500		108.00	108
1998 Garden Favorites III A/P	50		162.00	162
1987 The Garden Gate	3,000	N/A	30.00	30
1987 The Garden Gate A/P	50	N/A	50.00	50
1990 Garden Room	3,500	N/A	40.00	40
1991 The Garden Wreath I	2,500	N/A	47.00	47
1991 The Garden Wreath I A/P	50	N/A	60.00	60
1992 The Garden Wreath II	2,500	N/A	50.00	50
1992 The Garden Wreath II A/P	50	N/A	75.00	75
1994 The Garden Wreath III	5,000		61.00	61
1994 The Garden Wreath III A/P	50		91.50	92
1994 Georgia Sweet	2,500	1999	50.00	50
1994 Georgia Sweet A/P	50	1999	75.00	75
1995 Glynda's Garden	7,500		73.00	73
1995 Glynda's Garden A/P	50		109.50	110
1993 Grand Glory I	2,500	N/A	53.00	53
1992 Grand Glory I A/P	50	1999	79.50	80
1993 Grand Glory II	2,500	N/A	53.00	53
1992 Grand Glory II A/P	50	1999	79.50	80
1995 Grand Glory III	7,500		65.00	65
1995 Grand Glory III A/P	50		97.50	98
1995 Grand Glory IV	7,500		65.00	65
1995 Grand Glory IV A/P	50		97.50	98
1997 Hand in Hand	3,500		69.00	69
1997 Hand in Hand A/P	50		103.50	104
1984 Heading Home I	1,000	N/A	25.00	25
1984 Heading Home I A/P	50	N/A	40.00	40
1984 Heading Home II	1,000	N/A	25.00	25
1984 Heading Home II A/P	50	N/A	40.00	40
1984 Heading Home III	1,000	N/A	25.00	25
1984 Heading Home III A/P	50	N/A	40.00	40
1987 Heart Wreath I	3,000	N/A	25.00	25
1987 Heart Wreath I A/P	50	N/A	40.00	40
1988 Heart Wreath II	3,500	N/A	25.00	25
1988 Heart Wreath II A/P	50	N/A	40.00	40
1989 Heart Wreath III	3,500	N/A	25.00	25
1989 Heart Wreath III A/P	50	N/A	40.00	40
1999 Heavenly Hydrageas	2,500		104.00	104
1999 Heavenly Hydrageas A/P	50		156.00	156
1987 Hollyhocks I	3,000	N/A	30.00	30
1987 Hollyhocks I A/P	50	N/A	50.00	50
1990 Hollyhocks II	3,500	N/A	25.00	25
1990 Hollyhocks II A/P	50	N/A	60.00	60
1995 Hollyhocks III	7,500		69.00	69
1995 Hollyhocks III A/P	50		103.50	104
1992 In Full Bloom I	2,500	N/A	53.00	53
1992 In Full Bloom I A/P	50	N/A	79.50	80
1994 In Full Bloom II	3,500	N/A	65.00	65
1994 In Full Bloom II A/P	50		97.50	98
1995 In Full Bloom III	7,500		64.00	64
1995 In Full Bloom III A/P	50		96.00	96
1984 In One Ear And Out The Other	950	N/A	50.00	50-165
1984 In One Ear And Out The Other A/P	50	N/A	75.00	75
1987 Iris Basket I	3,000	N/A	30.00	30
1987 Iris Basket I A/P	50	N/A	50.00	50
1988 Iris Basket II	3,500	N/A	30.00	30
1988 Iris Basket II A/P	50	N/A	50.00	50
1990 Iris Basket III	3,500	N/A	35.00	35
1990 Iris Basket III A/P	50	N/A	52.50	53
1991 Iris Basket IV	2,500	1999	35.00	35
1991 Iris Basket IV A/P	50	1999	52.50	53
1989 Iris Parade	3,500	1996	35.00	148
1989 Iris Parade A/P	50	1999	52.50	53
2000 Ivy & Roses III	2,500		104.00	104
2000 Ivy & Roses III A/P	50		156.00	156
1997 Keeping Watch	7,500	1999	77.00	77
1997 Keeping Watch A/P	50	1999	115.50	116
1985 La Belle I	750	N/A	25.00	25
1985 La Belle I A/P	50	N/A	40.00	40
1986 La Belle II	2,000	N/A	25.00	25
1986 La Belle II A/P	50	N/A	40.00	40
1986 La Belle III	3,500	N/A	25.00	25
1986 La Belle III A/P	50	N/A	40.00	40
1988 La Belle IV	5,000	N/A	30.00	30
1988 La Belle IV A/P	50	N/A	50.00	50
1999 Lily Pond	2,500		100.00	100
1999 Lily Pond A/P	50		150.00	150
1995 Little Red River	7,500		73.00	73
1995 Little Red River A/P	50		109.50	110
1995 Mabry In Spring	7,500		65.00	65
1995 Mabry In Spring A/P	50		97.50	98
1987 Mauve Iris I	3,000	N/A	10.00	10
1987 Mauve Iris I A/P	50	N/A	25.00	25
1987 Mauve Iris II	3,000	N/A	10.00	10
1987 Mauve Iris II A/P	50	N/A	25.00	25
1983 Now I Lay Me	1,000	N/A	50.00	50
1983 Now I Lay Me A/P	50	N/A	75.00	75
1989 Old Favorites	3,500	N/A	35.00	35
1989 Old Favorites A/P	50	N/A	52.50	53
1988 Old Friends	5,000	N/A	30.00	30
1988 Old Friends A/P	50	N/A	50.00	50
1992 Old Mill Stream I	2,500	N/A	40.00	40
1992 Old Mill Stream I A/P	50		60.00	60
1993 Old Mill Stream II	2,500	N/A	43.00	43
1993 Old Mill Stream II A/P	50		64.50	65
1994 Old Mill Stream III	3,500	N/A	69.00	69
1994 Old Mill Stream III A/P	50		103.50	104
1996 Old Mill Stream IV	7,500		73.00	73
1996 Old Mill Stream IV A/P	50		109.50	110
1988 Once Upon A Time	5,000	N/A	30.00	30
1988 Once Upon A Time A/P	50	1999	45.00	45
1988 Past Times	5,000	N/A	30.00	30
1988 Past Times A/P	50	N/A	50.00	50
1996 Pears and Roses	7,500	1999	64.00	64
1996 Pears and Roses A/P	50	1999	96.00	96
1988 Peeping Tom	5,000	N/A	35.00	35
1988 Peeping Tom A/P	50	N/A	55.00	55
1989 Petals In Pink	3,500	N/A	30.00	30-85
1989 Petals In Pink A/P	50	N/A	79.50	80
1987 Playing Hookie	3,000	N/A	30.00	30
1987 Playing Hookie A/P	50	N/A	50.00	50
1988 Playing Hookie Again	5,000	N/A	30.00	30
1988 Playing Hookie Again A/P	50	N/A	50.00	50
1997 Plums and Pansies	7,500	1999	64.00	64
1997 Plums and Pansies A/P	50	1999	96.00	96
1988 The Porch	5,000	N/A	30.00	30
1988 The Porch A/P	50	N/A	50.00	50
1989 Pretty Pickings I	3,500	N/A	30.00	130
1989 Pretty Pickings I A/P	50	1999	45.00	45
1989 Pretty Pickings II	3,500	1999	35.00	35
1989 Pretty Pickings II A/P	50	1999	52.50	53
1989 Pretty Pickings III	3,500	1999	30.00	30
1989 Pretty Pickings III A/P	50	1999	45.00	45
1991 Primrose Lane I	3,500	N/A	40.00	40
1991 Primrose Lane I A/P	50	N/A	60.00	60
1993 Primrose Lane II	2,500	N/A	43.00	43
1993 Primrose Lane II A/P	50	1999	64.50	65
1995 Remember When	7,500	1999	73.00	73
1995 Remember When A/P	50	1999	109.50	110
1998 Ring Around The Rosy	2,500		100.00	100
1998 Ring Around The Rosy A/P	50		150.00	150
1983 Sad Face Clown	950	N/A	50.00	50
1983 Sad Face Clown A/P	50	N/A	75.00	75
1991 Secret Garden I	3,500	N/A	40.00	40
1991 Secret Garden I A/P	50		60.00	60
1994 Secret Garden II A/P	50		79.50	80
1996 Secret Garden III	7,500		65.00	65
1996 Secret Garden III A/P	50		97.50	98
1991 Simply Southern	3,500	N/A	53.00	53
1991 Simply Southern A/P	50	N/A	79.50	80
1985 Snips N Snails	750	N/A	25.00	25
1985 Snips N Snails A/P	50	N/A	40.00	40
1998 Southern Elegance III	3,500		73.00	73
1998 Southern Elegance III A/P	50		109.50	110
1992 Southern Sunday I	2,500	N/A	50.00	50
1992 Southern Sunday I A/P	50	1999	75.00	75
1995 Southern Sunday II	7,500		73.00	73
1995 Southern Sunday II A/P	50		109.50	110
1993 A Southern Tradition II	3,500	N/A	60.00	60
1993 A Southern Tradition II A/P	50	N/A	90.00	90
1994 A Southern Tradition IV	5,000	N/A	69.00	69
1994 A Southern Tradition IV A/P	50		103.50	104
1995 A Southern Tradition V	7,500		73.00	73
1995 A Southern Tradition V A/P	50		109.50	110
1988 A Special Time	5,000	N/A	30.00	30
1988 A Special Time A/P	50		45.00	45
1998 Spring Flora III	3,500		73.00	73
1998 Spring Flora III A/P	50		109.50	110
1993 Spring's Promise II	2,500		43.00	43
1993 Spring's Promise III A/P	50		64.50	65
1988 Spring's Return	5,000		35.00	35
1988 Spring's Return A/P	50		52.50	53
1983 Stepping Out	1,000	N/A	50.00	50
1983 Stepping Out A/P	50	N/A	75.00	75
1985 Sugar N Spice	750	N/A	25.00	25
1985 Sugar N Spice A/P	50	N/A	40.00	40
1987 A Summer Day	3,000	N/A	30.00	30
1987 A Summer Day A/P	50	N/A	50.00	50
1995 Summer In Victoria	7,500		53.00	53
1995 Summer In Victoria A/P	50		79.50	80
1994 Summer Stroll	3,500	N/A	65.00	65
1994 Summer Stroll A/P	50	1997	97.50	98
1990 Sweet Nothings	3,500		40.00	40
1990 Sweet Nothings A/P	50		60.00	60
1987 Victorian Bouquet I	3,500	N/A	25.00	25
1987 Victorian Bouquet I A/P	50	N/A	40.00	40
1989 Victorian Bouquet II	3,500	N/A	25.00	25
1997 Wading at the Bridge	7,500		77.00	77
1997 Wading at the Bridge A/P	50		115.50	116
1986 White Iris	2,000	N/A	25.00	25
1986 White Iris A/P	50	N/A	40.00	40
1987 Wild Roses I	3,000	N/A	30.00	30
1987 Wild Roses I A/P	50	N/A	50.00	50
1990 Wild Roses II	3,500		35.00	35
1990 Wild Roses II A/P	50		52.50	53
1996 Wreath of Spring	7,500		64.00	64
1996 Wreath of Spring A/P	50		96.00	96

Greenwich Workshop

Austin - C. Austin

YEAR ISSUE	EDITION LIMIT	YEAR RETD.	ISSUE PRICE	*QUOTE U.S.$
1997 Saturday Near Sunset	850		150.00	150
1996 The Storm	850		165.00	165
1996 Wheat Field	850		125.00	125

Ballantyne - Ballantyne

YEAR ISSUE	EDITION LIMIT	YEAR RETD.	ISSUE PRICE	*QUOTE U.S.$
1995 John's New Pup	850		150.00	150
1995 Kate and Her Fiddle	850		150.00	150
1996 Partners	850		150.00	150

Bama - J. Bama

YEAR ISSUE	EDITION LIMIT	YEAR RETD.	ISSUE PRICE	*QUOTE U.S.$
1993 Art of James Bama Book with Chester Medicine Crow Fathers Flag Print	2,500	N/A	345.00	351-365
1981 At a Mountain Man Wedding	1,500	N/A	145.00	145-200
1981 At Burial Gallager and Blind Bill	1,650	N/A	135.00	150-350
1988 Bittin' Up-Rimrock Ranch	1,250	N/A	195.00	630-1250
1992 Blackfeet War Robe	1,000		195.00	195
1995 Blackfoot Ceremonial Headdress (Iris Print)	200		850.00	850
1987 Buck Norris-Crossed Sabres Ranch	1,000	N/A	195.00	790-1023
1990 Buffalo Bill	1,250	N/A	210.00	165-210
1993 The Buffalo Dance	1,000		195.00	195
1991 Ceremonial Lance	1,250		225.00	225
1996 Cheyene Split Horn Headdress (Iris Print)	200		850.00	850
1994 Cheyenne Dog Soldier	1,000		225.00	225

*Quotes have been rounded up to nearest dollar

GRAPHICS

YEAR ISSUE	EDITION LIMIT	YEAR RETD.	ISSUE PRICE	*QUOTE U.S.$
1991 Chuck Wagon	1,000		225.00	225
1975 Chuck Wagon in the Snow	1,000	N/A	50.00	1200-1520
1992 Coming' Round the Bend	1,000		195.00	195
1978 Contemporary Sioux Indian	1,000	N/A	75.00	1450-1600
1995 A Cowboy Named Anne	1,000		185.00	185
1992 Crow Cavalry Scout	1,000		195.00	195
1977 A Crow Indian	1,000	N/A	65.00	243-468
1982 Crow Indian Dancer	1,250		150.00	150
1988 Crow Indian From Lodge Grass	1,250		225.00	225
1988 Dan-Mountain Man	1,250	N/A	195.00	195-211
1983 The Davilla Brothers-Bronc Riders	1,250		145.00	145
1983 Don Walker-Bareback Rider	1,250	N/A	85.00	126-175
1991 The Drift on Skull Creek Pass	1,500		225.00	225
1979 Heritage	1,500	N/A	75.00	274-425
1978 Indian at Crow Fair	1,500	N/A	75.00	118-125
1988 Indian Wearing War Medicine Bonnet	1,000	N/A	225.00	225
1980 Ken Blackbird	1,500	N/A	95.00	125-150
1974 Ken Hunder, Working Cowboy	1,000	N/A	55.00	695-1105
1989 Little Fawn-Cree Indian Girl	1,250	N/A	195.00	165-195
1979 Little Star	1,500	N/A	80.00	1325-1650
1993 Magua-"The Last of the Mohicans"	1,000		225.00	225
1993 Making Horse Medicine	1,000		225.00	225
1978 Mountain Man	1,000	N/A	75.00	350-469
1980 Mountain Man 1820-1840 Period	1,500	N/A	115.00	395-808
1979 Mountain Man and His Fox	1,500	N/A	90.00	350-457
1982 Mountain Man with Rifle	1,250	N/A	135.00	195-200
1978 A Mountain Ute	1,000	N/A	75.00	700-787
1992 Northern Cheyene Wolf Scout	1,000		195.00	195
1981 Old Arapaho Story-Teller	1,500	N/A	135.00	135-175
1980 Old Saddle in the Snow	1,500	N/A	75.00	525-638
1980 Old Sod House	1,500	N/A	80.00	425-551
1981 Oldest Living Crow Indian	1,500	N/A	135.00	135-150
1993 On the North Fork of the Shoshoni	1,000		195.00	195
1990 Paul Newman as Butch Cassidy & Video	2,000		250.00	250
1981 Portrait of a Sioux	1,500	N/A	135.00	135-150
1979 Pre-Columbian Indian with Atlatl	1,500	N/A	75.00	165-195
1991 Ready to Rendezvous	1,000		225.00	225
1995 Ready to Ride	1,000		185.00	185
1990 Ridin' the Rims	1,250	N/A	210.00	215-281
1991 Riding the High Country	1,250		225.00	225
1978 Rookie Bronc Rider	1,000	N/A	75.00	188-315
1976 Sage Grinder	1,000	N/A	65.00	995-1397
1980 Sheep Skull in Drift	1,500	N/A	75.00	116-160
1974 Shoshone Chief	1,000	N/A	65.00	1200-1272
1982 Sioux Indian with Eagle Feather	1,250	N/A	150.00	150
1992 Sioux Subchief	1,000		195.00	195
1994 Slim Warren, The Old Cowboy	1,000		125.00	125
1983 Southwest Indian Father & Son	1,250		145.00	145
1977 Timber Jack Joe	1,000	N/A	65.00	975-1357
1988 The Volunteer	1,500		225.00	225
1996 The Warrior (Iris Print)	200		550.00	550
1987 Winter on Trout Creek	1,000	N/A	150.00	300-490
1981 Winter Trapping	1,500	N/A	150.00	595-779
1980 Young Plains Indian	1,500	N/A	125.00	1500-1992
1990 Young Sheepherder	1,500		225.00	225

Bastin - M. Bastin

YEAR ISSUE	EDITION LIMIT	YEAR RETD.	ISSUE PRICE	*QUOTE U.S.$
1997 Autumn Celebration	1,950		95.00	95
1997 Dinner Guests	2,500	1998	95.00	195-215
1997 Dinner Guests (framed)	34		277.00	277
1998 Garden Party	1,950		110.00	110

Bean - A. Bean

YEAR ISSUE	EDITION LIMIT	YEAR RETD.	ISSUE PRICE	*QUOTE U.S.$
1998 Apollo: An Eyewitness Account & Kissing the Earth	650	N/A	345.00	345
1993 Conrad Gordon and Bean: The Fantasy	1,000		385.00	500
2000 The Hammer and the Feather	650		315.00	315
1997 Heavenly Reflections	850		275.00	275
1987 Helping Hands	850	N/A	150.00	150
1998 Homeward Bound	550		215.00	215
1995 Houston, We Have a Problem	1,000	1998	500.00	500
1988 How It Felt to Walk on the Moon	850	N/A	150.00	150
1992 In Flight	850	1998	385.00	385
1994 In The Beginning Apollo 25 C/S	1,000	N/A	450.00	550
1999 Moon Rovers	550		215.00	215
1997 Reaching For the Stars (canvas)	1,500		2200.00	2200
1999 Straightening Our Stripes	550		195.00	195

Beecham - G. Beecham

YEAR ISSUE	EDITION LIMIT	YEAR RETD.	ISSUE PRICE	*QUOTE U.S.$
1999 The Boys of December	550		185.00	185
1998 Bustin' Through	750		150.00	150
2000 The Cascades (Giclée on canvas)	75		795.00	795
1998 Ferdinand	750		150.00	150
1999 Mystic Warrior	550		185.00	185
1999 Step Into The Light	550		185.00	185
1998 Tag Team	750		150.00	150

Blackshear - T. Blackshear

YEAR ISSUE	EDITION LIMIT	YEAR RETD.	ISSUE PRICE	*QUOTE U.S.$
1994 Beauty and the Beast	1,000	1998	225.00	225-350
1996 Dance of the Wind & Storm	850		195.00	195
1996 Golden Breeze	850		225.00	225
1993 Hero Frederick Douglass	746		20.00	20
1993 Hero Harriet Tubman	753		20.00	20
1993 Hero Martin Luther King, Jr.	762		20.00	20
1993 Heroes of Our Heritage Portfolio	5,000	N/A	35.00	35
1995 Intimacy	550		850.00	1200
1995 Night in Day	850	N/A	195.00	195
1994 Swansong	1,000		175.00	175

Blake - B. Blake

YEAR ISSUE	EDITION LIMIT	YEAR RETD.	ISSUE PRICE	*QUOTE U.S.$
1995 The Old Double Diamond	850		175.00	175
1994 West of the Moon	650		195.00	195

Blish - C. Blish

YEAR ISSUE	EDITION LIMIT	YEAR RETD.	ISSUE PRICE	*QUOTE U.S.$
1997 A Change in the Air w/book	950		195.00	195
1998 Father The Hour Has Come (framed)	559		95.00	95
1998 Father The Hour Has Come (gold frame)	621		150.00	150
1998 Father The Hour Has Come (unframed)	4,186		70.00	70
1997 Gathering Sea Oats	550		135.00	135
1998 He Stills the Sea (cherry frame)	Open		150.00	150
1998 He Stills the Sea (gold frame)	Open		150.00	150
1998 He Stills the Sea (unframed)	Open		110.00	110
1997 Island Church (framed)	149		95.00	95
1997 Jennifer (framed)	150		95.00	95
1997 Skywatcher (framed)	148		95.00	95
1997 The Swan (framed)	149		95.00	95
1997 Trinity (framed)	148		95.00	95
1997 Windswept Headlands (framed)	144		95.00	95

Blossom - C. Blossom

YEAR ISSUE	EDITION LIMIT	YEAR RETD.	ISSUE PRICE	*QUOTE U.S.$
1987 After the Last Drift	950	N/A	145.00	145
1984 Ah Your Majesty (poster)	N/A	N/A	45.00	45
1985 Allerton on the East River	650	N/A	145.00	145
1996 Arthur James Heading Out	850		150.00	150
1988 Black Rock	950	N/A	150.00	150
1984 December Moonrise	650	N/A	135.00	135-150
1984 December Moonrise, remarque	25	N/A	175.00	175
1990 Ebb Tide	950	N/A	175.00	175
1983 First Out	450	N/A	90.00	600-750
1983 First Out, remarque	25	N/A	190.00	800-1000
1987 Gloucester Mackeral Seiners	950	N/A	145.00	145
1998 Gold Rush Twilight	450		195.00	195
1998 Gold Rush Twilight, remarque	100		395.00	395
1989 Harbor Light	950	N/A	165.00	165
1988 Heading Home	950	N/A	150.00	250
1998 Morning Set	450		195.00	195
1985 Off Palmer Land	850	N/A	145.00	145
1995 Onshore Breeze	850		175.00	175
1992 Port of Call	850		175.00	175
1986 Potomac By Moonlight	950	N/A	145.00	145
1987 San Francisco-Eve of the Gold Rush	950	N/A	150.00	150
1992 Silhouette	850		175.00	175
1986 Southport @ Twilight	950	N/A	145.00	145
1985 Tranquil Dawn	650	N/A	95.00	95
1994 Traveling in Company	850		175.00	175
1994 Traveling in Company, Remarque	100		415.00	415
1992 Windward	950		175.00	175
1986 Winter Dawn @ Boston Wharf	850	N/A	85.00	85

Boren - N. Boren

YEAR ISSUE	EDITION LIMIT	YEAR RETD.	ISSUE PRICE	*QUOTE U.S.$
1999 "She Love Me...?"	150		850.00	850
1999 Cowboy Romance	350		295.00	295
1999 Sittin' Pretty	450		345.00	345

Bralds - B. Bralds

YEAR ISSUE	EDITION LIMIT	YEAR RETD.	ISSUE PRICE	*QUOTE U.S.$
1997 Abyssinian	175		195.00	195
1998 American Shorthair	175	N/A	195.00	195
1995 Bag Ladies	2,500	1995	150.00	675-725
1996 Basket Cases	2,500	1996	150.00	175-225
1997 British Blue Short Hair (Nine Lives)	175		195.00	195
1999 A Bushel and a Peck	1,250		145.00	145
1996 Cabinet Meeting	2,000	1996	150.00	195-225
2000 Cat-as-trophy	1,500	N/A	165.00	165
1996 Cheese	2,000		150.00	150
1997 Chocolate Point Siamese	175	N/A	195.00	195
1997 Cinnamon Tabby Maine Coon	175		195.00	195
1999 Diane's Broken Heart	1,500		125.00	125
2000 Heart to Heart	950		135.00	135
1998 Miss Kitty	2,500		125.00	125
1998 A Mixed Bag	2,500		125.00	125
1997 Nine Lives Suite - (Brit., Snowshoe, Persian)	1,750		150.00	150
1998 Nine Lives Suite - (Sho/Bur/Tabby)	1,750		150.00	150
1997 Nine Lives Suite - (Siamese, Abyssinian, Coon)	1,750		150.00	150
1997 Persian (Nine Lives)	175		195.00	195
1999 Rainbow Whiskers	1,250		155.00	155
1997 Siamese Twins	2,250		150.00	150
1997 Snowshoe (Nine Lives)	175		195.00	195
1998 Table Manners	1,950		175.00	175

Bullas - W. Bullas

YEAR ISSUE	EDITION LIMIT	YEAR RETD.	ISSUE PRICE	*QUOTE U.S.$
2000 the bad doggies...	750		135.00	135
1999 bad to the bun	750		95.00	95
1998 Ballet Parking	750		110.00	110
1995 The Big Game	1,500		95.00	95
1993 Billy the Pig	850		95.00	172
1997 A Chick Off The Old Block (framed)	57		125.00	125
1995 The Chimp Shot	1,000		95.00	95
1994 Clucks Unlimited	850		95.00	95
1995 The Consultant	1,000	N/A	95.00	95
1994 Court of Appeals	850	1995	95.00	275-395
1995 Dog Byte	1,000	1998	95.00	175-195
1997 Duck Tape (framed)	296	1998	125.00	125
1994 Ductor	850	1998	95.00	95
1997 Federal Duck Stump	1,250		95.00	95
1998 A Fool And His Bunny	950		95.00	95
1998 A Fool And His Bunny (framed)	Open		150.00	150
1998 A Fool Moon Collectors' Edition Book & Porcelain	900	1998	165.00	165
1995 fowl ball...	1,500		95.00	95
1994 Fridays After Five	850		95.00	95
1998 The House Swine	950		125.00	125
1998 Jingle This....	950		125.00	125
1995 Legal Eagles	1,000		95.00	95
1999 a little sangria	750		110.00	110
1993 Mr. Harry Buns	850	N/A	95.00	95
1996 The Nerd Dogs	1,500		95.00	95
1997 No Assembly Required	99		125.00	125
1993 Our Ladies of the Front Lawn	850		95.00	95
1997 Our of the Woods (framed)	320		125.00	125
1993 The Pale Prince	850		110.00	110
1993 Sand Trap Pro	850	1998	95.00	95-195
1997 Sock Hop (framed)	211	N/A	125.00	125
1993 Some Set of Buns	850		95.00	95
1997 Supermom (framed)	100		125.00	125
1995 tennis, anyone?	1,000		95.00	95
1993 Wine-Oceros	850	1998	95.00	595
1993 You Rang, Madam?	850		95.00	114
1996 Zippo...The Fire Eater	850		95.00	95

Buxton - J. Buxton

YEAR ISSUE	EDITION LIMIT	YEAR RETD.	ISSUE PRICE	*QUOTE U.S.$
1999 God's Gift	550		165.00	165

Christensen - J. Christensen

YEAR ISSUE	EDITION LIMIT	YEAR RETD.	ISSUE PRICE	*QUOTE U.S.$
1989 The Annunciation	850	N/A	175.00	150-215
1995 Balancing Act	3,500	N/A	185.00	195-215
1996 The Bassonist	2,500		125.00	125
1996 The Believer's Etching Edition	1,000		795.00	795
1998 Benediction	950	N/A	150.00	150
1990 The Burden of the Responsible Man	850	N/A	145.00	1000-1650
1991 The Candleman	850	N/A	160.00	350-375
1993 College of Magical Knowledge	4,500	N/A	185.00	325
1993 College of Magical Knowledge, remarque	500	N/A	252.50	450-500
1996 Court of the Faeries	3,500	N/A	245.00	245
1991 Diggery Diggery Dare-Etching	75	N/A	210.00	600-1100
1994 Evening Angels	4,000	N/A	195.00	195
1994 Evening Angels w/Art Furnishings Frame	200	N/A	800.00	800
1989 Fantasies of the Sea-poster	Open		35.00	35
1995 Fishing	2,500	N/A	145.00	175-190
1999 Flight of the Fablemaker	2,500		195.00	195
1998 Gerome Spent His Free Time Daydreaming of Being Reincarnated as a Snake	1,250		295.00	295
1998 Gethsemane	Open		125.00	125
1993 Getting it Right	4,000	N/A	185.00	100-185
1985 The Gift For Mrs. Claus	3,500	N/A	80.00	550-600
1998 The Great Garibaldi (serigraph)	450		800.00	800
1999 Icarus Bound	950		135.00	135
1991 Jack Be Nimble-Etching	75	N/A	210.00	1425
1986 Jonah	850	N/A	95.00	375-395
1991 Lawrence and a Bear	850	N/A	145.00	400-600
1998 Lawyer More Than Adequately Attired	950	1998	150.00	150
1998 Levi Levitates a Stonefish (serigraph)	450		800.00	800
1987 Low Tech-Poster	Open		35.00	35
1999 A Man and His Dog	950	N/A	225.00	225
1991 Man in the Moon-Etching	75	N/A	210.00	650-700
1988 The Man Who Minds the Moon	850	N/A	145.00	600-650
1991 Mother Goose-Etching	75	N/A	210.00	875-1200
2000 The Oath	2,950		160.00	160
1987 Old Man with a Lot on His Mind	850	N/A	85.00	725-850
1986 Olde World Santa	3,500	N/A	80.00	650-695
1992 The Oldest Angel	850	N/A	125.00	1000-1225
1992 The Oldest Angel-Etching	75	N/A	210.00	1550
1991 Once Upon a Time	1,500	N/A	175.00	1100-1650
1991 Once Upon a Time, remarque	500	N/A	220.00	1550-1600
1996 One Light	1,500		125.00	125
1999 Parables	1,500	N/A	150.00	150
1991 Pelican King	850	N/A	115.00	350-600
1991 Peter Peter Pumpkin Eater-Etching	75	N/A	210.00	600-1100
1995 Piscatorial Percussionist	3,000	N/A	125.00	95-125
2000 Queen Mab in the Ruins	1,950	N/A	185.00	185-350
1992 The Reponsible Woman	2,500	N/A	175.00	600-825
1990 Rhymes & Reasons w/Booklet	Open		150.00	150
1990 Rhymes & Reasons w/Booklet, remarque	500	N/A	208.00	350-595
1993 The Royal Music Barque	2,750	N/A	375.00	375
1992 The Royal Processional	1,500	N/A	185.00	425-450
1992 The Royal Processional, remarque	500	N/A	252.50	475-595
1997 Santa's Other Helpers	1,950		125.00	125
1993 The Scholar	3,250	N/A	125.00	125-215
1995 Serenade For an Orange Cat	3,000	N/A	125.00	125-130
1987 The Shakespearean Poster	Open		35.00	35
1995 Sisters of the Sea	2,000	N/A	195.00	175-195
1994 Six Bird Hunters-Full Camouflage 3	4,662	N/A	165.00	165-195
1994 Sometimes the Spirit Touches w/book	3,600	N/A	195.00	195-285
1998 Superstitious w/Booket/Key	2,500	1998	195.00	195
1998 Superstitious, remarque	200	1998	395.00	395
1991 Three Blind Mice-Etching	75	N/A	210.00	2200-3100
1991 Three Wise Men of Gotham-Etching	75	N/A	210.00	600-1100
1991 Tweedle Dee & Tweedle Dum-Etching	75	N/A	210.00	600-1400
1994 Two Angels Discussing Botticelli	2,950	N/A	145.00	125-150
1990 Two Sisters	650	N/A	325.00	350-375
1996 The Voyage of the Basset Collector's Edition Book & The Oldest Professor	2,500		195.00	195
1987 Voyage of the Basset w/Journal	850	N/A	225.00	1100-1250
1993 Waiting for the Tide	2,250	N/A	150.00	150-185
1997 Wendall Realized He Had A Dilemma	950	1998	125.00	125
1988 The Widows Mite	850	N/A	145.00	2900-3400
1986 Your Place, or Mine?	850	N/A	125.00	150-250

*Quotes have been rounded up to nearest dollar

Combes - S. Combes

YEAR ISSUE	EDITION LIMIT	YEAR RETD.	ISSUE PRICE	*QUOTE U.S.$
1992 African Oasis	650	N/A	375.00	795-850
1981 Alert	1,000	N/A	95.00	95
1987 The Angry One	850	N/A	95.00	95
1988 Bushwhacker	850	N/A	145.00	145
1983 Chui	275	N/A	250.00	250
1988 Confrontation	850	N/A	145.00	145
1988 The Crossing	1,250	N/A	245.00	245
1994 Disdain	850		110.00	110
1999 Drought, Dust and Danger (canvas)	75		1700.00	1700
1980 Facing the Wind	1,500	N/A	75.00	75-125
1993 Fearful Symmetry	850	N/A	110.00	110-215
1997 From The Shadows (canvas)	250		395.00	395
1995 Golden Silhouette	950		175.00	175
1994 Great Cats Masterwork & 9 prints with Journals	500		1900.000	1900
1998 Great Cats: Stories & Art From A World Traveler & Prowler	450		195.00	195
1990 The Guardian (Silverback)	1,000	N/A	185.00	185
1997 Heavy Drinkers	550		425.00	425
1999 Hot Lions	250		795.00	795
1992 The Hypnotist	1,250		145.00	145
1999 Imminent Pursuit	550		150.00	150
1994 Indian Summer	950		175.00	175
1980 Interlude	1,500	N/A	85.00	95-115
1995 Jungle Phantom	950		175.00	175
1991 Kilimanjaro Morning	850	N/A	185.00	185
1981 Leopard Cubs	1,000	N/A	95.00	315
1992 Lookout	1,250		95.00	95
1980 Manyara Afternoon	1,500	N/A	75.00	325-425
1989 Masai-Longonot, Kenya	850		145.00	145
1992 Midday Sun (Lioness & Cubs)	850	N/A	125.00	125
1989 Mountain Gorillas	550	N/A	135.00	135-150
1995 Mountain Myth	950		175.00	175
1995 Pride	950		175.00	175
1998 Sentinels	550		125.00	125
1980 Serengeti Monarch	1,500	N/A	85.00	275
1995 Serious Intent	950		175.00	175
1995 Siberian Winter	950		175.00	175
1996 The Siberians	850		175.00	175
1988 Simba	850	1998	125.00	125
1997 Snow Pack	550		175.00	175
1995 Snow Tracker	950		175.00	175
1980 Solitary Hunter	1,500	N/A	75.00	75
1990 Standoff	850	N/A	375.00	550-695
1991 Study in Concentration	850	N/A	185.00	395
1987 Tall Shadows	850	N/A	150.00	450-825
1985 Tension at Dawn	825	N/A	145.00	900-1100
1985 Tension at Dawn, remarque	25	N/A	275.00	1150-1295
1998 There Was A Time, One of Two	250		975.00	975
1998 There Was A Time, Two of Two	250		975.00	975
1989 The Watering Hole	850	N/A	225.00	225
1986 The Wildebeest Migration	450	N/A	350.00	1500-2150

Crowley - D. Crowley

YEAR ISSUE	EDITION LIMIT	YEAR RETD.	ISSUE PRICE	*QUOTE U.S.$
1981 Afterglow	1,500	N/A	110.00	110
1992 Anna Thorne	650	N/A	160.00	160
1980 Apache in White	1,500	N/A	85.00	85-125
1979 Arizona Mountain Man	1,500	N/A	85.00	85-125
1980 Beauty and the Beast	1,500	N/A	85.00	85-135
1992 Colors of the Sunset	650	N/A	175.00	175
1979 Desert Sunset	1,500	N/A	75.00	75-125
1978 Dorena	1,000	N/A	75.00	75-115
1995 The Dreamer	650		150.00	150
1981 Eagle Feathers	1,500	N/A	95.00	95-125
1988 Ermine and Beads	550	N/A	85.00	215
1989 The Gunfighters	3,000	N/A	35.00	35
1981 The Heirloom	1,000	N/A	125.00	125
1982 Hopi Butterfly	275	N/A	350.00	350
1978 Hudson's Bay Blanket	1,000	N/A	75.00	75-125
1980 The Littlest Apache	275	N/A	325.00	325-850
1997 Morning Fire (Canvas)	650		495.00	495
1994 Plumes and Ribbons	650		160.00	160
1979 Security Blanket	1,500	N/A	65.00	65-175
1981 Shannandoah	275	N/A	325.00	275-325
1978 The Starquilt	1,000	N/A	65.00	500-525
1986 The Trapper	550	N/A	75.00	75
1997 Water in the Draw	550		160.00	160

Dawson - J. Dawson

YEAR ISSUE	EDITION LIMIT	YEAR RETD.	ISSUE PRICE	*QUOTE U.S.$
1992 The Attack (Cougars)	850		175.00	175
1993 Berry Contented	850		150.00	150
1993 Berry Contented, remarque	100		235.00	235
1994 The Face Off (Right & Left Panel)	850		150.00	150
1993 Looking Back	850		110.00	110
1993 Otter Wise	850		150.00	150
1993 Taking a Break	850	N/A	150.00	150

Doolittle - B. Doolittle

YEAR ISSUE	EDITION LIMIT	YEAR RETD.	ISSUE PRICE	*QUOTE U.S.$
1983 Art of Camouflage, signed	2,000	1983	55.00	395-450
2000 Blue Mesa (poster)	Open		30.00	30
1980 Bugged Bear	1,000	1980	85.00	1575-3700
1987 Calling the Buffalo	8,500	1987	245.00	550-975
1983 Christmas Day, Give or Take a Week	4,581	1983	80.00	1650-3000
1988 Doubled Back	15,000	1988	245.00	750-1200
1996 Drawn From the Heart-Etching Suite	349	1996	750.00	1775-2100
1992 Eagle Heart	48,000	1992	285.00	225-285
1982 Eagle's Flight	1,500	1982	185.00	2900-3600
1999 The Earth Is My Mother Collector's Ed. Book w/print	12,500		295.00	295
1983 Escape by a Hare	1,500	1983	80.00	595-850
1984 The Forest Has Eyes	8,544	1984	175.00	2950-4200
2000 Fox Haven	Open		35.00	35
1980 Good Omen, The	1,000	1980	85.00	1650-3000
1987 Guardian Spirits	13,238	1987	295.00	595-862
1990 Hide and Seek (Composite & Video)	25,000	1990	1200.00	850-900
1984 Let My Spirit Soar	1,500	1984	195.00	4000-4800
2000 Mesa Ruins	Open		35.00	35
1997 Music in the Wind	43,500	1998	330.00	850-1350
1998 No Respect	25,000		195.00	195
2000 Painted Ladies	Open		35.00	35
1979 Pintos	1,000	1979	65.00	2295
1993 Prayer for the Wild Things	65,000	1993	325.00	1650-1775
1983 Runs With Thunder	1,500	1983	150.00	695-795
1983 Rushing War Eagle	1,500	1983	150.00	975-1075
1991 Sacred Circle (Print & Video)	40,192	1991	325.00	2350
1989 Sacred Ground	69,996	1989	265.00	700-750
1987 Season of the Eagle	36,548	1987	245.00	650-675
1991 The Sentinel	35,000	1991	275.00	550
1981 Spirit of the Grizzly	1,500	1981	150.00	650
1995 Spirit Takes Flight	48,000		225.00	225
1996 Three More for Breakfast	20,000	1996	245.00	1650-1775
1986 Two Bears of the Blackfeet	2,650	1986	225.00	1650-1775
1985 Two Indian Horses	12,253	1985	225.00	1650-1775
1995 Two More Indian Horses	48,000	1995	225.00	1650-1775
1981 Unknown Presence	1,500	1981	135.00	1650-1775
1992 Walk Softly (Chapbook)	40,192	1992	225.00	225-295
2000 West Fork Pintos	Open		35.00	35
1994 When The Wind Had Wings	57,500		325.00	325
1986 Where Silence Speaks, Doolittle The Art of Bev Doolittle	3,500	1986	650.00	1100-1200
1980 Whoo !?	1,000	1980	75.00	1200-1295
1993 Wilderness? Wilderness!	50,000		65.00	65
1985 Wolves of the Crow	2,650	1985	225.00	450-1100
1981 Woodland Encounter	1,500	1981	145.00	1575-1775

Dubowski - E. Dubowski

YEAR ISSUE	EDITION LIMIT	YEAR RETD.	ISSUE PRICE	*QUOTE U.S.$
1996 Aspen Flowers	850		145.00	145
1998 The Errand	550		125.00	125
1996 Fresh From the Garden	850		145.00	145
1998 Open For Business	550		125.00	125
1998 The Readers	550		125.00	125
1997 Reflections	850		175.00	175

Entz - L. Entz

YEAR ISSUE	EDITION LIMIT	YEAR RETD.	ISSUE PRICE	*QUOTE U.S.$
1996 Apple Pie	850		150.00	150
1995 Life's a Dance	850		150.00	150
1996 New Shoes	850		150.00	150
1997 A Plot of Her Own	650		175.00	175

Ferris - K. Ferris

YEAR ISSUE	EDITION LIMIT	YEAR RETD.	ISSUE PRICE	*QUOTE U.S.$
1990 The Circus Outbound	1,000		225.00	225
1991 Farmer's Nightmare	850		185.00	185
1991 Linebacker in the Buff	1,000		225.00	225
1983 Little Willie Coming Home	1,000	N/A	145.00	1750-1850
1994 Real Trouble	1,000		195.00	195
1995 Schweinfurt Again	1,000		195.00	195
1982 Sunrise Encounter	1,000	N/A	145.00	145-195
1993 A Test of Courage	850		185.00	185
1991 Too Little, Too Late w/Video	1,000		245.00	245

Frazier - L. Frazier

YEAR ISSUE	EDITION LIMIT	YEAR RETD.	ISSUE PRICE	*QUOTE U.S.$
1999 Bows on the String	550		170.00	170
1998 The Concubine	750		150.00	150
1998 Constant Traveler	750		150.00	150
1998 The Nomad	750		150.00	150
1997 Pay Dirt	450		425.00	425
1997 Royal Escort	450		395.00	395
1999 Search For Oneself	550		185.00	185
2000 Slack Water Buddies (canvas)	150		650.00	650

Frederick - R. Frederick

YEAR ISSUE	EDITION LIMIT	YEAR RETD.	ISSUE PRICE	*QUOTE U.S.$
1990 Autumn Leaves	1,250	N/A	175.00	125-175
1996 Autumn Trail	850		195.00	195
1989 Barely Spring	1,500		165.00	165
1994 Beeline (C)	1,000		195.00	195
1987 Before the Storm (Diptych)	550	N/A	350.00	550-675
1991 Breaking the Ice	2,750	N/A	235.00	195-235
1997 Cascade Gold	650		175.00	175
1989 Colors of Home	1,500	N/A	165.00	295-425
1995 Drifters	850		175.00	175
1985 Early Evening Gathering	475	N/A	325.00	435-495
1992 An Early Light Breakfast	1,750	N/A	235.00	295-300
1990 Echoes of Sunset	1,750	N/A	235.00	725-775
1987 Evening Shadows (White-Tail Deer)	1,500	N/A	125.00	95-125
1992 Fast Break	2,250		235.00	235
1992 Fire and Ice (Suite of 2)	1,750		175.00	175
1984 First Moments of Gold	825	N/A	145.00	225
1984 First Moments of Gold, remarque	25	N/A	172.50	265
1984 From Timber's Edge	850	N/A	125.00	140-165
1996 Geyser Basin	850		175.00	175
1989 Gifts of the Land #2	500	N/A	150.00	150
1988 Gifts of the Land w/Wine & Wine Label	500	N/A	150.00	150
1988 Glimmer of Solitude	1,500	N/A	145.00	145
1993 Glory Days	1,750		115.00	115
1986 Great Horned Owl	1,250	N/A	115.00	135
1995 High Country Harem	1,000		185.00	185
1985 High Society	950	N/A	115.00	425
1995 Jaywalkers	850		175.00	175
1991 The Long Run	1,750	N/A	235.00	250-295
1991 The Long Run, AP	200	N/A	167.50	495
1985 Los Colores De Chiapas	950	N/A	85.00	85
1994 The Lost World	1,000		175.00	175
1985 Misty Morning Lookout	950	N/A	145.00	145
1984 Misty Morning Sentinel	850	N/A	125.00	145
1989 Monarch of the North	2,000		150.00	150
1990 Morning Surprise	1,750	N/A	165.00	165
1991 Morning Thunder	1,750	N/A	185.00	200
1988 The Nesting Call	2,500	N/A	150.00	150
1988 The Nesting Call, remarque	1,000	N/A	165.00	165
1993 New Heights	1,950		195.00	195
1987 Northern Light	1,500	N/A	165.00	165
1986 Out on a Limb	1,250	N/A	145.00	300-375
1993 Point of View	1,000		235.00	235
1992 Rain Forest Rendezvous	1,500	N/A	225.00	225
1988 Rim Walk	1,500	N/A	90.00	90
1988 Shadows of Dusk	1,500	N/A	165.00	165
1990 Silent Watch (High Desert Museum)	2,000	N/A	35.00	35
1994 Snow Pack	1,000		175.00	175
1992 Snowstorm	1,750		195.00	195
1990 Snowy Reflections (Snowy Egret)	1,500	N/A	150.00	150
1986 Sounds of Twilight	1,500	N/A	135.00	250-295
1991 Summer's Song (Triptych)	2,500		225.00	225
1993 Temple of the Jaguar	1,500		225.00	225
1988 Timber Ghost w/Mini Wine Label	3,000	N/A	150.00	150
1994 Tropic Moon	850		165.00	165
1987 Tundra Watch (Snowy Owl)	1,500	N/A	145.00	145
1994 Way of the Caribou	1,235		235.00	235
1987 Winter's Brilliance (Cardinal)	1,500	N/A	135.00	135
1986 Winter's Call	1,250	N/A	165.00	550
1986 Winter's Call Raptor, AP	100	N/A	165.00	600
1987 Woodland Crossing (Caribou)	1,500	N/A	145.00	145
1988 World of White	2,500	N/A	150.00	150

Gurney - J. Gurney

YEAR ISSUE	EDITION LIMIT	YEAR RETD.	ISSUE PRICE	*QUOTE U.S.$
1992 Birthday Pageant	2,500	N/A	60.00	60
1992 Birthday Pageant, remarque	300	N/A	275.00	250-295
1991 Dinosaur Boulevard	2,000	N/A	125.00	125-150
1991 Dinosaur Boulevard, remarque	250	N/A	196.00	425
1990 Dinosaur Parade	1,995	1995	125.00	125-175
1990 Dinosaur Parade, remarque	150	N/A	130.00	2500-2800
1992 Dream Canyon	N/A	N/A	125.00	125
1992 Dream Canyon, remarque	150	N/A	196.00	395
1993 The Excursion	3,500		175.00	175
1993 Garden of Hope	3,500		175.00	175
1990 Morning in Treetown	1,500	N/A	175.00	275-325
1993 Palace in the Clouds	3,500	N/A	175.00	175
1993 Ring Riders	2,500	N/A	175.00	175
1995 Rumble & Mist	2,500		175.00	175
1995 Santa Claus	2,000		95.00	95
1990 Seaside Romp	1,000	N/A	175.00	395
1992 Skyback Print w/Dinotopia Book	3,500	N/A	295.00	295
1994 Small Wonder	3,299	N/A	75.00	75
1994 Steep Street	3,500		95.00	95
1995 Twilight in Bonaba	3,000		195.00	195
1991 Waterfall City	3,000	N/A	125.00	125
1991 Waterfall City, remarque	250	N/A	186.00	395
1995 The World Beneath Collectors' Book w/print	3,000		195.00	195

Gustafson - S. Gustafson

YEAR ISSUE	EDITION LIMIT	YEAR RETD.	ISSUE PRICE	*QUOTE U.S.$
1995 The Alice in Wonderland Suite	4,000		195.00	195
1999 Don Quixote	950		150.00	150
1994 Frog Prince	3,500	1994	125.00	150
1993 Goldilocks and the Three Bears	3,500	1993	125.00	300-400
1995 Hansel & Gretel	3,000		125.00	125
1993 Humpty Dumpty	3,500	1993	125.00	125
1995 Jack in the Beanstalk	3,500		125.00	125
1998 Little Bo Peep	950		125.00	125
1998 Little Miss Muffet	950		125.00	125
1993 Little Red Riding Hood	3,500	1993	125.00	125
2000 The Maiden and the Unicorn	1,250		185.00	185
1999 Mary, Mary, Quite Contrary	950		125.00	125
1998 Merlin and Arthur	1,250	N/A	185.00	185
1996 Old King Cole	2,750		125.00	125
1997 The Owl and the Pussycat	950		125.00	125
1994 Pat-A-Cake	4,000	1998	125.00	100-125
1997 Peter Peter Pumpkin Eater	950		125.00	125
1996 Puss in Boots	2,750		145.00	145
1995 Rumplestiltskin	2,750		125.00	125
1993 Snow White and the Seven Dwarfs	3,500	1993	165.00	225
1997 Tom Thumb	950	1998	125.00	125
1995 Touched by Magic	4,000		185.00	185
1999 The Wizard of Oz	2,000		185.00	185

Hartough - L. Hartough

YEAR ISSUE	EDITION LIMIT	YEAR RETD.	ISSUE PRICE	*QUOTE U.S.$
1995 7th Hole, Pebble Beach Golf Links	850	1998	225.00	225
1999 The 8th Hole, Pebble Beach Golf Links	350		950.00	950
1996 Postage Stamp 8th Royal Troon	154	N/A	210.00	210
1996 10th Hole, West Course Winged Foot	657	N/A	210.00	210
1996 11th Hole, "White Dogwood", Augusta National Golf Club	850	1998	225.00	225
1995 The 13th Hole, "Azalea"	25	N/A	225.00	225
1996 13th Hole, Augusta National	430	N/A	225.00	225
1999 14th and 4th Holes, Carnoustie Golf Links	850		225.00	225
1995 14th Hole, St. Andrews	850	1995	225.00	225
1996 15th Hole, "Firethorn", Augusta National Golf Club	850	N/A	325.00	325
1996 15th Hole, Haig Point Rees Jones	226		210.00	210
1996 17th Hole Clubhouse, Royal Troon	522		165.00	165
1996 17th Hole, Royal Dornoch	86	N/A	210.00	210
1996 17th Hole, Royal St. George, 1993 Bristish Open	153		225.00	225
1996 The Ultimate 18th Eden Royal H.K.	634		210.00	210
1997 18th Hole, 1997 Royal Troon	345		225.00	225
1997 18th Hole, Harbourtown Links	850	N/A	250.00	250
1996 18th Hole, Muirfield Village	780		210.00	210

*Quotes have been rounded up to nearest dollar

GRAPHICS

YEAR ISSUE	EDITION LIMIT	YEAR RETD.	ISSUE PRICE	*QUOTE U.S.$
1996 18th Hole, Royal Birkdale, 1991 British Open	245		210.00	210
1996 18th Hole, Royal Lytham & St. Annes Golf Club	850	N/A	225.00	225

Holm - J. Holm

YEAR ISSUE	EDITION LIMIT	YEAR RETD.	ISSUE PRICE	*QUOTE U.S.$
1998 Five Persians	550		130.00	130
1997 I Spy Summer	850		95.00	95
1998 The Sentry	550		125.00	125
1996 Slipper Thief	850		95.00	95

Howell-Sickles - D. Howell-Sickles

YEAR ISSUE	EDITION LIMIT	YEAR RETD.	ISSUE PRICE	*QUOTE U.S.$
1997 Cowgirl Rising w/And the Cowgirl Jumped Over the Moon print	1,000		245.00	245
1999 A Family Tradition	650		295.00	295
1998 Legends	650		295.00	295

Hurley - W. Hurley

YEAR ISSUE	EDITION LIMIT	YEAR RETD.	ISSUE PRICE	*QUOTE U.S.$
1998 Late Summer Sunset	550		225.00	225
1998 The Utah Suite - Monument Valley	550		1495.00	1495
1998 The Wyoming Suite (center panel 1/3)	550		500.00	500
1998 The Wyoming Suite (left panel 2/3)	550		500.00	500
1998 The Wyoming Suite (right panel 3/3)	550		495.00	495

Johnson - J. Johnson

YEAR ISSUE	EDITION LIMIT	YEAR RETD.	ISSUE PRICE	*QUOTE U.S.$
1994 Moose River	650		175.00	175
1994 Sea Treasures	650		125.00	125
1994 Winter Thaw	650		150.00	150
1993 Wolf Creek	550	N/A	165.00	200

Kennedy - S. Kennedy

YEAR ISSUE	EDITION LIMIT	YEAR RETD.	ISSUE PRICE	*QUOTE U.S.$
1988 After Dinner Music	2,500	N/A	175.00	230
1995 Alaskan Malamute	1,000		125.00	125
1992 Aurora	2,250	N/A	195.00	195
1991 A Breed Apart	2,750	N/A	225.00	225
1992 Cabin Fever	2,250		175.00	175
1995 Cliff Dwellers	850		175.00	175
1998 Crossing Over	750		135.00	135
1997 Curious Encounter & New Generation	850		125.00	125
1988 Distant Relations	950	N/A	200.00	300
1988 Eager to Run	950	N/A	200.00	1400-1790
1990 Fish Tales	5,500	N/A	225.00	225
1997 Fishing Buddies	1,000		165.00	165
1991 In Training	3,350	N/A	165.00	150-295
1991 In Training, remarque	150	N/A	215.50	345
1996 Keeping Watch	850		150.00	150
1995 The Lesson	1,000		125.00	125
1996 Looking For Trouble	850		125.00	125
1993 Midnight Eyes	1,750		125.00	125
1997 Miracle Mile	750		145.00	145
1993 Never Alone	2,250		225.00	225
1993 Never Alone, remarque	250	N/A	272.50	273
1997 The New Kitten	850		125.00	125
1990 On the Edge	4,000		225.00	225
1995 On the Heights	850		175.00	175
1994 Quiet Time Companions-Samoyed	1,000	1998	125.00	125
1994 Quiet Time Companions-Siberian Husky	1,000	N/A	125.00	125
1998 Rocky Mountain Gold	550		175.00	175
1998 Samoyed Pup	1,250		95.00	95
1998 Scouting the Trail	750		150.00	150
1994 Silent Observers	1,250	N/A	165.00	165
1996 Snow Buddies	850		125.00	125
1989 Snowshoes	4,000	N/A	185.00	185
1994 Spruce and Fur	1,500		165.00	165
1995 Standing Watch	850		175.00	175
1993 The Touch	1,500		115.00	115
1989 Up a Creek	2,500	N/A	185.00	185
1997 White Christmas	750		95.00	95

Kodera - C. Kodera

YEAR ISSUE	EDITION LIMIT	YEAR RETD.	ISSUE PRICE	*QUOTE U.S.$
1986 The A Team (K10)	850	N/A	145.00	145
1995 A.M. Sortie	1,000		225.00	225
1996 Canyon Starliner	850		185.00	185
1991 Darkness Visible (Stealth)	2,671	N/A	40.00	40
1987 Fifty Years a Lady	550	N/A	150.00	450-500
1988 The Great Greenwich Balloon Race	1,000		145.00	145
1990 Green Light-Jump!	650	N/A	145.00	200
1992 Halsey's Surprise	850		95.00	95
1997 Hitting the Kwai w/Artifact	850		265.00	265
1994 Last to Fight	1,000		225.00	225
1995 Lonely Flight to Destiny	1,000	1995	347.00	895-1000
1992 Looking For Nagumo	1,000		225.00	225
1996 The Lost Squadron	850		275.00	275
1992 Memphis Belle/Dauntless Dotty	1,250		245.00	245
1990 A Moment's Peace	1,250	N/A	150.00	150
1988 Moonlight Intruders	1,000	N/A	125.00	125
1995 Only One Survived	1,000		245.00	245
1989 Springtime Flying in the Rockies	550	N/A	95.00	95
1996 Stratojet Shakedown	1,000		265.00	265
1992 Thirty Seconds Over Tokyo	1,000	N/A	275.00	275
1991 This is No Drill w/Video	1,000		225.00	225
1994 This is No Time to Lose an Engine	850		150.00	150
1994 Tiger's Bite	850		150.00	150
1987 Voyager: The Skies Yield	1,500	N/A	225.00	225

Landry - P. Landry

YEAR ISSUE	EDITION LIMIT	YEAR RETD.	ISSUE PRICE	*QUOTE U.S.$
1996 Afternoon Tea (canvas)	450	1996	495.00	495
1993 The Antique Shop	1,250	N/A	125.00	125
1992 Apple Orchard	1,250		150.00	150
1999 Apple Valley Orchard	850		165.00	165
1992 Aunt Martha's Country Farm	1,500	N/A	185.00	300
1996 Autumn Hayride	550		165.00	165
1995 Autumn Market	1,000	N/A	185.00	185
1987 Bluenose Country	550	N/A	115.00	175
1992 Boardwalk Promenade	1,250		175.00	175
1989 A Canadian Christmas	1,250	N/A	125.00	125
1989 Cape Cod Welcome Cameo	850	N/A	75.00	275
1990 The Captain's Garden	1,000	N/A	165.00	425
1993 Christmas at Mystic Seaport	2,000		125.00	125
1992 Christmas at the Flower Market	2,500		125.00	125
1994 Christmas Carousel Pony	2,000		125.00	125
1997 Christmas Door	850		95.00	95
1997 Christmas Door, remarque	S/O	N/A	95.00	95
1998 A Christmas Morning	550		145.00	145
1990 Christmas Treasures	2,500	N/A	165.00	165
1992 Cottage Garden	1,250	N/A	160.00	160
1995 Cottage Reflections	850		135.00	135
1998 Country Garden	850		185.00	185
1994 An English Cottage	850		150.00	150
1994 Flower Barn	1,000	N/A	175.00	175
1988 Flower Boxes	550	N/A	75.00	250
1991 Flower Market	1,500	N/A	185.00	1000
1990 Flower Wagon	1,500	N/A	165.00	165
1994 Flowers For Mary Hope	1,250		165.00	165
1999 Garden Suite - Climbing Roses	Open		30.00	30
1999 Garden Suite - Memories	Open		30.00	30
1999 Garden Suite - Nestled In	Open		30.00	30
1997 A Gardener's Pride	950		95.00	95
1995 Harbor Garden	1,000		160.00	160
1993 Hometown Parade	1,250		165.00	165
1996 It's a Wonderful Christmas	1,250		165.00	165
1996 Joseph's Corner (canvas)	450		495.00	495
1996 Joseph's Corner, Artist Touch (canvas)	100		795.00	795
1995 Lantern Skaters	1,500		135.00	135
2000 Moonlight and Roses	850	N/A	110.00	110
1990 Morning Papers	1,250	N/A	135.00	145
1994 Morning Walk	850		135.00	135
1998 Mother's Day (Watercolor Sketch)	200		180.00	180
1991 Nantucket Colors	1,500		150.00	150
1998 New England Classic	850		150.00	150
1993 Paper Boy	1,500		150.00	150
1993 A Place in the Park	1,500		185.00	185
1984 Regatta	500	N/A	75.00	150
1984 Regatta, remarque	50	N/A	97.50	145
1990 Seaside Carousel	1,500	N/A	165.00	200
1988 Seaside Cottage	550	N/A	125.00	125
1986 Seaside Mist	450	N/A	85.00	200
1985 The Skaters	500	N/A	75.00	75
1985 The Skaters, remarque	50	N/A	97.50	98
1998 Southport (mixed media)	350		600.00	600
1995 Spring Song	2,500		145.00	145
1997 Springtime Garden	850		185.00	185
1996 Summer Buddies	950		135.00	135
1991 Summer Concert	1,500		195.00	195
1989 Summer Garden	850	N/A	125.00	400
1997 Summer Hill	850		165.00	165
1995 Summer Mist (Fine Art Original Lithograph)	550		750.00	850
1998 Summer Potpourri (mixed media)	350		600.00	600
1992 Sunflowers	1,250	N/A	125.00	125
1991 The Toymaker	1,500	N/A	165.00	165
1999 Verandah (canvas)	450		450.00	450
1991 Victorian Memories	1,500	N/A	150.00	150
1996 Winter Memories w/The Captain's Garden Collector's Edition Book	2,000		195.00	195

Lovell - T. Lovell

YEAR ISSUE	EDITION LIMIT	YEAR RETD.	ISSUE PRICE	*QUOTE U.S.$
1988 The Battle of the Crater	1,500	N/A	225.00	225
1988 Berdan's Sharpshooters -Gettysburg	1,500		225.00	225
1986 Blackfeet Wall	450	N/A	325.00	1195-1500
1981 Carson's Boatyard	1,000		150.00	150
1985 Chiricahua Scout	650		90.00	90
1981 The Deceiver	1,000		150.00	150
1990 Dry Goods and Molasses	1,000		225.00	225
1981 Fires Along the Oregon Trail	1,000	N/A	150.00	295
1993 The Handwarmer	1,000		225.00	225
1978 The Hunter	1,000		150.00	150
1982 Invitation to Trade	1,000	N/A	150.00	150
1989 The Lost Rag Doll	1,000		225.00	225
1988 Mr. Bodmer's Music Box	5,000		40.00	40
1975 The Mud Owl's Warning	1,000	N/A	150.00	175-250
1988 North Country Rider	2,500		95.00	95
1976 Quicksand at Horsehead	1,000		150.00	150
1976 Shotgun Toll	1,000		150.00	150
1983 Sugar in The Coffee	650	N/A	165.00	165
1987 Surrender at Appomattox	1,000	N/A	225.00	1695
1992 Target Practice	2,000		25.00	25
1976 Time of Cold-Maker	1,000		150.00	150
1989 Union Fleet Passing Vicksburg	1,500		225.00	225
1982 Walking Coyote & Buffalo Orphans	650	N/A	165.00	195-225
1982 The Wheelsoakers	1,000		150.00	150
1984 Winter Holiday	850		95.00	95
1989 Youth's Hour of Glory	1,500		175.00	175

Lyman - S. Lyman

YEAR ISSUE	EDITION LIMIT	YEAR RETD.	ISSUE PRICE	*QUOTE U.S.$
1997 Ahwahnee-The Deep Grassy Valley	1,500	1998	225.00	225-450
1990 Among The Wild Brambles	1,750	1990	185.00	600-625
1985 Autumn Gathering	850	N/A	115.00	850-1350
1996 Beach Bonfire	6,500	1996	225.00	175-225
1985 Bear & Blossoms (C)	850	N/A	75.00	600-665
1987 Canadian Autumn	1,500	1987	165.00	275-350
1995 Cathedral Snow	4,000	1996	245.00	245-265
1989 Color In The Snow (Pheasant)	1,500	N/A	165.00	350-500
1996 The Crossing	2,500	1996	195.00	215-225
1991 Dance of Cloud and Cliff	1,500	1991	225.00	495
1991 Dance of Water and Light	3,000	1991	225.00	225-245
1983 Early Winter In The Mountains	850	N/A	95.00	695-750
1987 An Elegant Couple (Wood Ducks)	1,000	N/A	125.00	295
1991 Embers at Dawn	3,500	1991	225.00	1500-1800
1983 End Of The Ridge	850	N/A	95.00	575-695
1990 Evening Light	2,500	1990	225.00	3000-3200
1995 Evening Star w/collector's edition book	9,500	1995	195.00	225-245
1993 Fire Dance	8,500	1993	235.00	540-600
1984 Free Flight	850	N/A	70.00	150
1999 Handsome (canvas)	1,250		295.00	295
1987 High Creek Crossing	1,000	N/A	165.00	1350-1400
1989 High Light	1,250	1989	165.00	475-550
1986 High Trail At Sunset	1,000	N/A	125.00	700-750
1988 The Intruder	1,500	N/A	150.00	250
1993 Lake of the Shining Rocks	2,250	1993	235.00	400-625
1992 Lantern Light Print w Firelight Chapbook	10,000	1993	195.00	195
1989 Last Light of Winter	1,500	1989	175.00	1050-1250
1998 Last Touch of Light	975		595.00	595
1999 A Light in the Wilderness (A Limited Ed. Liuve de Luxe)	2,250		750.00	750
1995 Midnight Fire	8,500	1996	245.00	195-225
1994 Moon Fire	7,500	1994	245.00	500-895
1987 Moon Shadows	1,500	N/A	135.00	150-185
1998 Moonbear Listens to the Earth	1,250	N/A	175.00	175
1994 Moonlit Flight on Christmas Night	2,750	1994	165.00	195
1996 Morning Light	8,000	1996	245.00	450-475
1986 Morning Solitude	850	N/A	115.00	595-700
1990 A Mountain Campfire	1,500	1990	195.00	3100-3200
1994 New Kid on the Rock	2,250	1996	185.00	215-225
1987 New Territory (Grizzly & Cubs)	1,000	N/A	135.00	495-550
1984 Noisy Neighbors	675	N/A	95.00	1395-1450
1984 Noisy Neighbors, remarque	25	N/A	127.50	1800
1994 North Country Shores	3,000	1994	225.00	325-525
1999 October Flight	950	N/A	195.00	195
1983 The Pass	850	N/A	95.00	750-1000
1989 Quiet Rain	1,500	N/A	165.00	900-995
1988 The Raptor's Watch	1,500	N/A	150.00	600-1000
1988 Return Of The Falcon	1,500	N/A	150.00	300-450
1993 Riparian Riches	2,500	1993	235.00	215-235
1992 River of Light (Geese)	2,950	N/A	225.00	225-235
1991 Secret Watch (Lynx)	2,250	N/A	150.00	150-165
1997 Sentinel of the Grove	450		195.00	195
1990 Silent Snows	1,750	N/A	210.00	400-450
1988 Snow Hunter	1,500	N/A	135.00	195-400
1986 Snowy Throne (C)	850	N/A	85.00	575-795
2000 Sounds of Sunset (canvas)	250		695.00	695
1993 The Spirit of Christmas	2,750	1993	165.00	495-550
1998 Steller Autumn	1,250	N/A	225.00	225
1998 Sunrise in the Wallowas	950	1998	450.00	575-675
1996 Sunset Fire (PC)	N/A	1996	245.00	215-300
1995 Thunderbolt	7,000	N/A	235.00	695
1987 Twilight Snow (C)	950	N/A	85.00	450-600
1988 Uzumati: Great Bear of Yosemite	1,750	N/A	150.00	250
1992 Warmed by the View	8,500	1992	235.00	395-425
1992 Wilderness Welcome	8,500	N/A	235.00	800-1200
1992 Wildflower Suite (Hummingbird)	2,250	N/A	175.00	225-325
1997 Winter Shadows	2,500	1997	225.00	195-225
1992 Woodland Haven	2,500	N/A	195.00	240-250
1999 Yosemite Alpenglow	950		270.00	270

Marris - B. Marris

YEAR ISSUE	EDITION LIMIT	YEAR RETD.	ISSUE PRICE	*QUOTE U.S.$
1987 Above the Glacier	850	N/A	145.00	145
1986 Best Friends	850	N/A	85.00	235-295
1994 Big Gray's Barn and Bistro	1,000		125.00	125
1989 Bittersweet	1,000	N/A	135.00	135
1990 Bugles and Trumpets!	1,000	N/A	175.00	175
1996 Catch The Wind	850		165.00	165
1992 The Comeback	1,250		175.00	175
1991 Cops & Robbers	1,000	N/A	165.00	165
1988 Courtship	850	N/A	145.00	145
1995 Dairy Queens	1,000		125.00	125
1995 The Dartmoor Ponies	1,000		165.00	165
1987 Desperados	850	N/A	135.00	135
1996 Dog Days	1,000	N/A	165.00	165
1991 End of the Season	1,000	1998	165.00	165
1985 The Fishing Lesson	1,000		145.00	145
1997 For the Love of Pete	950		130.00	130
1995 The Gift	1,000		125.00	125
2000 The Gifts of Spring (canvas)	150		695.00	695
1999 The Gold Thread	550		150.00	150
1987 Honey Creek Whitetales	850	N/A	145.00	145
1985 Kenai Dusk	1,000	N/A	145.00	800
1994 Lady Marmalade's Bed & Breakfast	1,000	N/A	125.00	125
1996 A Little Pig with a Big Heart	1,000	1996	95.00	95
1990 Mom's Shadow	1,000	N/A	165.00	165
1994 Moonshine	1,000		95.00	95
1989 New Beginnings	1,000	N/A	175.00	375
1990 Of Myth and Magic	1,500	N/A	175.00	175
1998 Old Faithful	750		125.00	125
1986 Other Footsteps	950	N/A	75.00	75
1989 The Playgroud Showoff	850	N/A	165.00	165
1992 Security Blanket	1,250		175.00	175
1993 Spring Fever	1,000		165.00	165
1991 The Stillness (Grizzly & Cubs)	1,000	N/A	165.00	165
1992 Sun Bath	1,000		95.00	95
1997 Sun Splashed	750		130.00	130
1992 To Stand and Endure	1,000	N/A	195.00	275-395
1991 Under the Morning Star	1,500		175.00	175
1998 Undercover	750		145.00	145
1988 Waiting For the Freeze	1,000	N/A	125.00	125
1995 Where Best Friends Are Welcome	850	1996	95.00	195

*Quotes have been rounded up to nearest dollar

YEAR ISSUE	EDITION LIMIT	YEAR RETD.	ISSUE PRICE	*QUOTE U.S.$
1999 Wolfsong	550		165.00	165

McCarthy - F. McCarthy

YEAR ISSUE	EDITION LIMIT	YEAR RETD.	ISSUE PRICE	*QUOTE U.S.$
1996 After the Council	550		850.00	850
1996 After the Council	1,000		195.00	195
1984 After the Dust Storm	1,000	N/A	145.00	295
1982 Alert	1,000	N/A	135.00	135
1984 Along the West Fork	1,000	N/A	175.00	225
1998 Ambush	750		195.00	195
1995 Ambush at the Ancient Rocks	1,000	1998	225.00	225
1978 Ambush, The	1,000	N/A	125.00	300
1982 Apache Scout	1,000	N/A	165.00	165
1988 Apache Trackers (C)	1,000	N/A	95.00	95
1992 The Art of Frank McCarthy	10,418	N/A	60.00	60
1982 Attack on the Wagon Train	1,400	N/A	150.00	150
1977 The Beaver Men	1,000	N/A	75.00	350
1980 Before the Charge	1,000	N/A	115.00	150
1978 Before the Norther	1,000	N/A	90.00	325
1990 Below The Breaking Dawn	1,250	N/A	225.00	225
1994 Beneath the Cliff (Petraglyphs)	1,500		295.00	295
1989 Big Medicine	1,000	N/A	225.00	350
1983 Blackfeet Raiders	1,000	N/A	90.00	200
1992 Breaking the Moonlit Silence	650	N/A	375.00	375
1986 The Buffalo Runners	1,000	N/A	195.00	170
1997 Buffalo Soldier Advance	1,500		225.00	225
1980 Burning the Way Station	1,000	N/A	125.00	250
1993 By the Ancient Trails They Passed	1,000	N/A	245.00	245
1989 Canyon Lands	1,250	N/A	225.00	225
1982 The Challenge	1,000	N/A	175.00	275-450
1995 Charge of the Buffalo Soldiers	1,000	1995	195.00	285
1985 Charging the Challenger	1,000	N/A	150.00	425
1991 The Chase	1,000		225.00	225
1986 Children of the Raven	1,000	N/A	185.00	550
1987 Chiricahua Raiders	1,000	N/A	165.00	225
1977 Comanche Moon	1,000	N/A	75.00	235
1992 Comanche Raider-Bronze	100		812.50	813
1986 Comanche War Trail	1,000	N/A	165.00	170
1989 The Coming Of The Iron Horse	1,500	N/A	225.00	225
1989 The Coming Of The Iron Horse (Print/Pewter Train Special Pub. Ed.)	100	N/A	1500.00	1600-2150
1981 The Coup	1,000	N/A	125.00	500
1998 The Crossing	850		185.00	185
1981 Crossing the Divide (The Old West)	1,500	N/A	850.00	450-750
1984 The Decoys	450	N/A	325.00	500
1977 Distant Thunder	1,500	N/A	75.00	500
1989 Down From The Mountains	1,500	N/A	245.00	245
1986 The Drive (C)	1,000	N/A	95.00	95-175
1977 Dust Stained Posse	1,000	N/A	75.00	650
1985 The Fireboat	1,000	N/A	175.00	175
1994 Flashes of Lighting-Thunder of Hooves	550		435.00	435
1987 Following the Herds	1,000	N/A	195.00	265-475
1980 Forbidden Land	1,000	N/A	125.00	125
1978 The Fording	1,000	N/A	75.00	250
1987 From the Rim	1,000	N/A	225.00	225
1981 Headed North	1,000	N/A	150.00	275
1992 Heading Back	1,000		225.00	225
1995 His Wealth	850		225.00	225
1990 Hoka Hey: Sioux War Cry	1,250	N/A	225.00	225
1987 The Hostile Land	1,000	N/A	225.00	235
1976 The Hostiles	1,000	N/A	75.00	475
1984 Hostiles, signed	1,000	N/A	55.00	55
1974 The Hunt	1,000	N/A	75.00	450
1988 In Pursuit of the White Buffalo	1,500	N/A	225.00	425-525
1992 In the Land of the Ancient Ones	1,250	N/A	245.00	265
1983 In The Land Of The Sparrow Hawk People	1,000	N/A	165.00	175
1987 In The Land Of The Winter Hawk	1,000	N/A	225.00	300
1978 In The Pass	1,500	N/A	90.00	265
1997 In The Shallows	1,000		185.00	185
1985 The Last Crossing	550	N/A	350.00	350
1989 The Last Stand: Little Big Horn	1,500	N/A	225.00	225
1984 Leading the Charge, signed	1,000	N/A	55.00	80
1974 Lone Sentinel	1,000	N/A	55.00	1100
1979 The Loner	1,000	N/A	75.00	225
1974 Long Column	1,000	N/A	75.00	400
1985 The Long Knives	1,000	N/A	175.00	350
1989 Los Diablos	1,250	N/A	225.00	225
1995 Medicine Man	850	1996	165.00	165
1983 Moonlit Trail	1,000	N/A	90.00	295
1992 Navajo Ponies Comanchie Warriors	1,000		225.00	225
1978 Night Crossing	1,000	N/A	75.00	200
1974 The Night They Needed a Good Ribbon Man	1,000	N/A	65.00	300
1977 An Old Time Mountain Man	1,000	N/A	65.00	200
1990 On The Old North Trail (Triptych)	650	N/A	550.00	675
1979 On the Warpath	1,000	N/A	75.00	150-175
1983 Out Of The Mist They Came	1,000	N/A	165.00	235
1990 Out Of The Windswept Ramparts	1,250	N/A	225.00	225
1976 Packing In	1,000	N/A	65.00	400
1998 Patrol at Broken Finger	750		165.00	165
1991 Pony Express	1,000		225.00	225
1979 The Prayer	1,500	N/A	90.00	450
1991 The Pursuit	650	N/A	550.00	550
1981 Race with the Hostiles	1,000	N/A	135.00	135
1987 Red Bull's War Party	1,000	N/A	165.00	165
1979 Retreat to Higher Ground	2,000	N/A	90.00	240-360
1975 Returning Raiders	1,000	N/A	75.00	300
1997 The Roar of the Falls	950		195.00	195
1980 Roar of the Norther	1,000	N/A	90.00	200
1977 Robe Signal	850	N/A	60.00	375
1988 Saber Charge	2,250	N/A	225.00	225-250
1984 The Savage Taunt	1,000	N/A	225.00	275
1985 Scouting The Long Knives	1,400	N/A	195.00	270
1993 Shadows of Warriors (3 Print Suite)	1,000		225.00	225
1994 Show of Defiance	1,000		195.00	195
1993 Sighting the Intruders	1,000		225.00	225
1978 Single File	1,000	N/A	75.00	850
1976 Sioux Warriors	650	N/A	55.00	250
1975 Smoke Was Their Ally	1,000	N/A	75.00	225
1980 Snow Moon	1,000	N/A	115.00	225
1995 Splitting the Herd	550		465.00	465
1986 Spooked	1,400	N/A	195.00	195
1981 Surrounded	1,000	N/A	150.00	350-395
1975 The Survivor	1,000	N/A	65.00	275
1980 A Time Of Decision	1,150	N/A	125.00	225
1978 To Battle	1,000	N/A	75.00	350-400
1985 The Traders	1,000	N/A	195.00	195
1996 The Trek	850		175.00	175
1980 The Trooper	1,000	N/A	90.00	165
1988 Turning The Leaders	1,500	N/A	225.00	225
1983 Under Attack	5,676	N/A	125.00	375-500
1981 Under Hostile Fire	1,000	N/A	150.00	160
1975 Waiting for the Escort	1,000	N/A	75.00	100
1976 The Warrior	650	N/A	55.00	350
1982 The Warriors	1,000	N/A	150.00	150
1984 Watching the Wagons	1,400	N/A	175.00	750
1995 The Way of the Ancient Migrations	1,250		245.00	245
1987 When Omens Turn Bad	1,000	N/A	165.00	425-500
1992 When the Land Was Theirs	1,000		225.00	225
1992 Where Ancient Ones Had Hunted	1,000	N/A	245.00	245
1992 Where Others Had Passed	1,000	N/A	245.00	245
1986 Where Tracks Will Be Lost	550	N/A	350.00	350
1982 Whirling He Raced to Meet the Challenge	1,000	N/A	175.00	400-525
1991 The Wild Ones	1,000	N/A	225.00	225
1990 Winter Trail	1,500	N/A	235.00	235
1993 With Pistols Drawn	1,000		195.00	195

Mitchell - D. Mitchell

YEAR ISSUE	EDITION LIMIT	YEAR RETD.	ISSUE PRICE	*QUOTE U.S.$
1994 Bonding Years	550		175.00	175
1993 Country Church	550		175.00	175
1997 Fort Scott Soldier	850	N/A	150.00	150
1995 Innocence	1,000		150.00	150
1995 Let Us Pray	850		175.00	175
1993 Psalms 4:1	550	N/A	195.00	195
1996 Return For Honor	850		150.00	150
1992 Rowena	550	N/A	195.00	300

Mo Da-Feng - M. Da-Feng

YEAR ISSUE	EDITION LIMIT	YEAR RETD.	ISSUE PRICE	*QUOTE U.S.$
1990 Family Boat	888		235.00	235
1993 First Journey	650		150.00	150
1989 Fishing Hut	888		235.00	235
1994 Ocean Mist	850		150.00	150

Morrissey - D. Morrissey

YEAR ISSUE	EDITION LIMIT	YEAR RETD.	ISSUE PRICE	*QUOTE U.S.$
2000 The Magic Door	950		175.00	175

Parker, Ed. - E. Parker

YEAR ISSUE	EDITION LIMIT	YEAR RETD.	ISSUE PRICE	*QUOTE U.S.$
1996 Acadia Tea and Tennis Society	850		135.00	135
1995 The Glorious 4th	850		150.00	150
1996 St. Duffer's Golf Club	850		135.00	135
1995 A Visit From St. Nicholas	850		125.00	125
1997 Windjammer Days	850		125.00	125

Parker, Ron. - R. Parker

YEAR ISSUE	EDITION LIMIT	YEAR RETD.	ISSUE PRICE	*QUOTE U.S.$
1995 The Breakfast Club	850		125.00	125
1995 Coastal Morning	850		195.00	195
1995 Evening Solitude	850		195.00	195
1994 Forest Flight	850		195.00	195
1997 Gliding Swan	650		145.00	145
1994 Grizzlies at the Falls	850		225.00	225
1994 Morning Flight	4,000		20.00	20
1996 Summer Memories	850		125.00	125
1996 Summer Reading	850		125.00	125
1995 Tea For Two	850		125.00	125

Phillips - W. Phillips

YEAR ISSUE	EDITION LIMIT	YEAR RETD.	ISSUE PRICE	*QUOTE U.S.$
1982 Advantage Eagle	1,000	N/A	135.00	300
1992 Alone No More	850		195.00	195
1988 America on the Move	1,500	N/A	185.00	150-185
1994 Among the Columns of Thor	1,000		295.00	295
1993 And Now the Trap	850		175.00	175
1999 And The Light Shall Prevail	950		195.00	195
1998 The Beginning of the End	1,000		365.00	365
1999 Cape Neddick Dawn	950	N/A	195.00	195
1997 Caping the Tico	950		275.00	275
1986 Changing of the Guard	500	N/A	100.00	100
1993 Chasing the Daylight	850	N/A	185.00	185
1994 Christmas Leave When Dreams Come True	1,500	N/A	185.00	185-220
1996 Clipper at the Gate	850		185.00	185
1986 Confrontation at Beachy Head	1,000	N/A	150.00	150
1999 Courtyard	950		165.00	165
1991 Dauntless Against a Rising Sun	850	N/A	195.00	195
1995 Dawn The World Forever Changed	1,000	1996	347.50	348
1998 December of '45	1,500		195.00	195
1995 The Dream Fulfilled	1,750	N/A	195.00	200
1998 Dust Off: Angels of Mercy Book	1,450		265.00	265
1997 Early Morning Visitors	1,250		195.00	195
1999 Evening Song (canvas)	550	N/A	595.00	595-1400
1991 Fifty Miles Out	1,000		175.00	175
1983 The Giant Begins to Stir	1,250	N/A	185.00	1100-1400
1990 Going in Hot w/Book	1,500		250.00	250
1985 Heading For Trouble	1,000	N/A	125.00	250
1984 Hellfire Corner	1,225	N/A	185.00	600
1984 Hellfire Corner, remarque	25	N/A	225.80	800
1998 Hill Country Homecoming	1,250		195.00	195
1990 Hunter Becomes the Hunted w/video	1,500	N/A	265.00	265
1992 I Could Never Be So Lucky Again	850	N/A	295.00	750
1993 If Only in My Dreams	1,000	N/A	175.00	750-1000
1984 Into the Teeth of the Tiger	975	N/A	135.00	925
1984 Into the Teeth of the Tiger, remarque	25	N/A	167.50	2000
1994 Into the Throne Room of God w/book "The Glory of Flight"	750	N/A	195.00	600
1991 Intruder Outbound	1,000		225.00	225
1991 Last Chance	1,000	N/A	165.00	350
1985 Lest We Forget	1,250	N/A	195.00	250
1994 Lethal Encounter	1,000		225.00	225
1996 The Lightkeepers Gift	1,000	N/A	175.00	175
1988 The Long Green Line	3,500	N/A	185.00	185
1992 The Long Ride Home (P-51D)	850	N/A	195.00	195
1991 Low Pass For the Home Folks, BP	1,000	N/A	175.00	175
1996 The Moonwatchers	1,750	1998	185.00	185-400
1986 Next Time Get 'Em All	1,500	N/A	225.00	275
1989 No Empty Bunks Tonight	1,500	N/A	165.00	165
1989 No Flying Today	1,500		185.00	185
1999 On Wings and a Prayer	950		175.00	175
1989 Over the Top	1,000		165.00	165
1985 The Phantoms and the Wizard	850	N/A	145.00	800
1992 Ploesti: Into the Fire and Fury	850		195.00	195
1987 Range Wars	1,000	N/A	160.00	160
2000 Rejoice	750		175.00	175
2000 Rejoice (canvas)	550		695.00	695
1996 Return of the Red Gremlin	1,000		350.00	350
1987 Shore Birds at Point Lobos	1,250	N/A	175.00	175
1989 Sierra Hotel	1,250	N/A	175.00	175
1997 Spring Fling	1,250		195.00	195
1998 The Storm Watchers	1,250		195.00	195
1995 Summer of '45	1,750	1998	195.00	1000
1998 Sunset Sentinels	550		695.00	695
1987 Sunward We Climb	1,000	N/A	175.00	175
1983 Those Clouds Won't Help You Now	625	N/A	135.00	500
1983 Those Clouds Won't Help You Now, remarque	25	N/A	275.00	675
1987 Those Last Critical Moments	1,250	N/A	185.00	300
1993 Threading the Eye of the Needle	1,000		195.00	195
1996 Thunder and Lightning	850		185.00	185
1986 Thunder in the Canyon	1,000	N/A	165.00	600
1990 A Time of Eagles	1,250	1996	245.00	245
1989 Time to Head Home	1,500	N/A	165.00	165
1986 Top Cover for the Straggler	1,000	N/A	145.00	325
1983 Two Down, One to Go	3,000	N/A	15.00	15
1982 Welcome Home Yank	1,000	N/A	135.00	800
1993 When Prayers are Answered	850		245.00	245
1991 When You See Zeros, Fight Em'	1,500	N/A	245.00	245

Pomm - Pomm

YEAR ISSUE	EDITION LIMIT	YEAR RETD.	ISSUE PRICE	*QUOTE U.S.$
1999 Above It All	150		395.00	395
1999 A Perfect Moment	450		200.00	200

Poskas - P. Poskas

YEAR ISSUE	EDITION LIMIT	YEAR RETD.	ISSUE PRICE	*QUOTE U.S.$
1997 Island Sea	650		175.00	175
1996 Yellow Moon Rising	850		175.00	175

Presse - H. Presse

YEAR ISSUE	EDITION LIMIT	YEAR RETD.	ISSUE PRICE	*QUOTE U.S.$
1998 Dance of the Sun	550		125.00	125
1999 The Flower Girl	550		145.00	145
1999 The Gardeners	550		150.00	150
1998 Oliver's Porch	550		125.00	125
1998 Stay This Moment	550		125.00	125
1998 The Victorian	550		125.00	125

Prosek - J. Prosek

YEAR ISSUE	EDITION LIMIT	YEAR RETD.	ISSUE PRICE	*QUOTE U.S.$
1996 Alaskan Rainbow Trout	1,000		125.00	125
1996 Brook Trout	1,000		125.00	125
1997 Yellowstone Cutthroat Trout	1,000		125.00	125

Reynolds - J. Reynolds

YEAR ISSUE	EDITION LIMIT	YEAR RETD.	ISSUE PRICE	*QUOTE U.S.$
1994 Arizona Cowboys	850	N/A	195.00	245
1994 Cold Country, Hot Coffee	1,000		185.00	185
1994 The Henry	850	N/A	195.00	195
1995 Mystic of the Plains	1,000		195.00	195
1994 Quiet Place	1,000	N/A	185.00	195
1994 Spring Showers	1,000		225.00	225
1996 A Strange Sign (canvas)	550		750.00	750
1996 The Summit	950		195.00	195
1998 Swing Shift	450		495.00	495

Riddick - R. Riddick

YEAR ISSUE	EDITION LIMIT	YEAR RETD.	ISSUE PRICE	*QUOTE U.S.$
1999 Early to Bed, Early to Rise	550		185.00	185
1998 The Muddy Arbuckle Café	550		185.00	185
1998 Prelude to the Dance	550		185.00	185

Riley - K. Riley

YEAR ISSUE	EDITION LIMIT	YEAR RETD.	ISSUE PRICE	*QUOTE U.S.$
1997 As One (Canvas print)	550		395.00	395
1997 Ceremonial Regalia	550		495.00	495
1999 Crow Fair	550		185.00	185
1998 Legend of the Mandan (serlith)	250		750.00	750
1998 The Red Flute (serlith)	250		750.00	750
1998 Split Horn Bonnet	550		425.00	425

Simpkins - J. Simpkins

YEAR ISSUE	EDITION LIMIT	YEAR RETD.	ISSUE PRICE	*QUOTE U.S.$
1994 All My Love	850		125.00	125
1993 Angels	850		225.00	225
1994 Gold Falls	1,750		195.00	195
1995 Mrs. Tenderhart	1,000		175.00	175
1995 Pavane in Gold	2,500		175.00	175
1996 Pavane von Khint	1,000		195.00	195
1994 Reverence For Life w/border & card	750	N/A	175.00	335
1994 Reverence For Life w/frame	100	N/A	600.00	600

*Quotes have been rounded up to nearest dollar

Greenwich Workshop
to Hadley House

GRAPHICS

YEAR ISSUE	EDITION LIMIT	YEAR RETD.	ISSUE PRICE	*QUOTE U.S.$
1995 Where Love Resides (Premiere Ed.)	1,000		450.00	450
1995 Where Love Resides (Studio Ed.)	1,000		225.00	225

Smith - T. Smith

YEAR ISSUE	EDITION LIMIT	YEAR RETD.	ISSUE PRICE	*QUOTE U.S.$
1992 The Challenger	1,300		185.00	185
1995 The Refuge	1,000		245.00	245

Solberg - M. Solberg

YEAR ISSUE	EDITION LIMIT	YEAR RETD.	ISSUE PRICE	*QUOTE U.S.$
1997 Rufous and Roses	550		150.00	150

Spirin - G. Spirin

YEAR ISSUE	EDITION LIMIT	YEAR RETD.	ISSUE PRICE	*QUOTE U.S.$
1997 Carnival in Venice (Inkjet)	200		395.00	395
1997 Tournament of Honor	200		395.00	395

Swindle - L. Swindle

YEAR ISSUE	EDITION LIMIT	YEAR RETD.	ISSUE PRICE	*QUOTE U.S.$
2000 Be It Unto Me	950	N/A	135.00	135-195

Terpning - H. Terpning

YEAR ISSUE	EDITION LIMIT	YEAR RETD.	ISSUE PRICE	*QUOTE U.S.$
1992 Against the Coldmaker	1,000	1992	195.00	195
1993 The Apache Fire Makers	1,000	1993	235.00	235
1993 Army Regulations	1,000		235.00	235
1997 Before the Little Big Horn	1,000		195.00	195
1987 Blackfeet Among the Aspen	1,000	1987	225.00	250
1985 Blackfeet Spectators	475	1985	350.00	1200-2250
1988 Blood Man	1,250	1988	95.00	300
1982 CA Set Pony Soldiers/Warriors	1,000	1982	200.00	450-650
1985 The Cache	1,000	N/A	175.00	175
1992 Capture of the Horse Bundle	1,250	1998	235.00	395
2000 Cheyenne Mother (canvas)	600		695.00	695
1982 Chief Joseph Rides to Surrender	1,000	1982	150.00	2600-3000
1996 Color of Sun	1,000	1998	175.00	175-350
1986 Comanche Spoilers	1,000	N/A	195.00	195
1990 Cree Finery	1,000	1998	225.00	375
1996 Crossing Below the Falls	1,000	1996	245.00	245
1983 Crossing Medicine Lodge Creek	1,000	1983	150.00	200-300
1994 Crow Camp, 1864	1,000	1994	235.00	235
1997 Crow Pipe Ceremony	975	1998	895.00	895-2200
1984 Crow Pipe Holder	1,000	N/A	150.00	150
1991 Digging in at Sappa Creek MW	650	1991	375.00	375
1994 The Feast	1,850	1994	245.00	285
1992 Four Sacred Drummers	1,000	1992	225.00	225
1997 Gold Seekers to the Black Hills'	1,000	1997	245.00	245
1999 Grandfather Speaks (canvas)	975		875.00	875
1998 Holy Man of the Blackfoot	975	1998	895.00	800-895
1988 Hope Springs Eternal-Ghost Dance	2,250	N/A	225.00	475-800
1998 Horse Feathers	975		495.00	495
1994 Isdzan-Apache Woman	1,000	1994	175.00	195
1991 The Last Buffalo	1,000		225.00	225
1991 Leader of Men	1,250	1991	235.00	300-500
1984 The Long Shot, signed	1,000	1984	55.00	75
1984 Medicine Man of the Cheyene	450	1984	350.00	2895-3195
1993 Medicine Pipe	1,000	1993	150.00	185
1999 Offerings to the Little People	975		875.00	875
1985 One Man's Castle	1,000	N/A	150.00	150
1995 Opening the Sacred Bundle (canvas)	550	1995	850.00	2295-3000
1983 Paints	1,000	1983	140.00	200
1992 Passing Into Womanhood	650	1992	375.00	400-1950
1987 The Ploy	1,000	1987	195.00	600-695
1992 Prairie Knights	1,000	1992	225.00	225
1996 Prairie Shade	1,000		225.00	225
1987 Preparing for the Sun Dance	1,000	1987	175.00	300-375
1988 Pride of the Cheyene	1,250	N/A	195.00	195
1993 Profile of Wisdom	1,000		175.00	175
1989 Scout's Report	1,250	N/A	225.00	225
1985 The Scouts of General Crook	1,000	1985	175.00	250-275
1988 Search For the Pass	1,000	1988	225.00	250
1982 Search For the Renegades	1,000	1982	150.00	195
1989 Shepherd of the Plains Cameo	1,250	N/A	125.00	125
1982 Shield of Her Husband	1,000	1982	150.00	600-900
1983 Shoshonis	1,250	1983	85.00	200-225
1985 The Signal	1,250	1985	90.00	400-600
1999 Signals in the Wind	750		225.00	225
1981 Sioux Flag Carrier	1,000	1981	125.00	165
1981 Small Comfort	1,000	1981	135.00	400-450
1993 Soldier Hat	1,000	N/A	235.00	235
1981 The Spectators	1,000	1981	135.00	195-295
1994 Spirit of the Rainmaker	1,500		235.00	235
1983 Staff Carrier	1,250	1983	90.00	550
1986 Status Symbols	1,000	1986	185.00	1250-1600
1981 Stones that Speak	1,000	1981	150.00	950-1200
1989 The Storyteller w/Video & Book	1,500	1989	950.00	1150-1500
1992 The Strength of Eagles	1,250	N/A	235.00	235
1988 Sunday Best	1,250	N/A	195.00	195
1995 Talking Robe	1,250		235.00	235
1990 Telling of the Legends	1,250	1990	225.00	900-1200
1986 Thunderpipe and the Holy Man	550	1986	350.00	500-800
1997 To Capture Enemy Horses	950		225.00	225
1995 Trading Post at Chadron Creek	1,000		225.00	225
1991 Transferring the Medicine Shield	850	1991	375.00	1300-1800
1996 The Trophy (canvas)	1,000	N/A	925.00	925
1981 The Victors	1,000	1981	150.00	825-1100
1985 The Warning	1,650	1985	175.00	550-750
1986 Watching the Column	1,250	1986	90.00	400
1998 The Weather Dancer Dream	1,000		225.00	225
1990 When Careless Spelled Disaster	1,000	1990	225.00	350
1987 Winter Coat	1,250	1987	95.00	175
1996 With Mother Earth	1,250	N/A	245.00	245
1984 Woman of the Sioux	1,000	1984	165.00	925-1200

Townsend - B. Townsend

YEAR ISSUE	EDITION LIMIT	YEAR RETD.	ISSUE PRICE	*QUOTE U.S.$
1994 Autumn Hillside	1,000		175.00	175
1993 Dusk	1,250		195.00	195
1995 Gathering of the Herd	1,000		195.00	195
1993 Hailstorm Creek	1,250		195.00	195
1994 Mountain Light	1,000		195.00	195
1992 Open Ridge	1,500	N/A	225.00	179-225
1993 Out of the Shadows	1,500	1998	195.00	195
1996 Out of the Valley	850		185.00	185
1992 Riverbend	1,000	N/A	185.00	300

Weiss - J. Weiss

YEAR ISSUE	EDITION LIMIT	YEAR RETD.	ISSUE PRICE	*QUOTE U.S.$
1995 All Is Well	1,250		165.00	165
1984 Basset Hound Puppies	1,000	N/A	65.00	200-300
1988 Black Labrador Head Study Cameo	1,000		90.00	90
1984 Cocker Spaniel Puppies	1,000	N/A	75.00	200-295
1999 Cold Nose, Warm Heart	950		125.00	125
1992 Cuddle Time	850		95.00	95
1998 Double Trouble	1,450		95.00	95
1999 Facing The Storm Together	950		125.00	125
1993 A Feeling of Warmth	1,000	N/A	165.00	475
1994 Forever Friends	1,000	1994	95.00	255
1998 Golden Moments	750		125.00	125
1983 Golden Retriever Puppies	1,000	N/A	65.00	900
1988 Goldens at the Shore	850	N/A	145.00	525-725
1997 Good As Gold	1,250	1998	95.00	95-150
1995 I Didn't Do It	1,250	1998	125.00	125
1982 Lab Puppies	1,000	N/A	65.00	195-250
1996 New Friends	1,000	1996	125.00	195
1992 No Swimming Lessons Today	1,000	1998	140.00	140
1984 Old English Sheepdog Puppies	1,000	N/A	65.00	200-250
1993 Old Friends	1,000	1993	95.00	700-800
1986 One Morning in October	850	N/A	125.00	525-650
1985 Persian Kitten	1,000	N/A	65.00	80-95
1999 Pick of the Litter	1,250		95.00	95
1982 Rebel & Soda	1,000	N/A	45.00	135
1999 Retrievers	950		110.00	110
1997 Storytime	850		95.00	95
1998 Three's Company	1,250		95.00	95
1991 Wake Up Call	850		165.00	165
1988 Yellow Labrador Head Study Cameo	1,000		90.00	90

Williams - B.D. Williams

YEAR ISSUE	EDITION LIMIT	YEAR RETD.	ISSUE PRICE	*QUOTE U.S.$
1993 Avant Garde S&N	500	N/A	60.00	60
1993 Avant Garde unsigned	2,603	N/A	30.00	30

Wootton - F. Wootton

YEAR ISSUE	EDITION LIMIT	YEAR RETD.	ISSUE PRICE	*QUOTE U.S.$
1990 Adlertag, 15 August 1940 & Video	1,500	N/A	245.00	245
1993 April Morning:France, 1918	850		245.00	245
1983 The Battle of Britain	850	N/A	150.00	300
1988 Encounter with the Red Baron	850	N/A	165.00	200
1985 Huntsmen and Hounds	650		115.00	115
1982 Knights of the Sky	850	N/A	165.00	375
1993 Last Combat of the Red Baron	850		185.00	185
1992 The Last of the First F. Wooten	850		235.00	235
1994 Peenemunde	850		245.00	245
1986 The Spitfire Legend	850	N/A	195.00	195

Wysocki - C. Wysocki

YEAR ISSUE	EDITION LIMIT	YEAR RETD.	ISSUE PRICE	*QUOTE U.S.$
1987 'Twas the Twilight Before Christmas	7,500	N/A	95.00	150-195
1988 The Americana Bowl	3,500		295.00	295
1983 Amish Neighbors	1,000	N/A	150.00	1100-1200
1989 Another Year At Sea	2,500	N/A	175.00	450-900
1983 Applebutter Makers	1,000	N/A	135.00	1200-1350
1987 Bach's Magnificat in D Minor	2,250	N/A	150.00	800-825
1991 Beauty And The Beast	2,000	N/A	125.00	125-175
1990 Belly Warmers	2,500	N/A	150.00	195
1984 Bird House Cameo	1,000	N/A	85.00	275-295
1985 Birds of a Feather	1,250	N/A	145.00	950-1150
1989 Bostonians And Beans (PC)	6,711	N/A	225.00	625-650
1979 Butternut Farms	1,000	N/A	75.00	1350-1450
1980 Caleb's Buggy Barn	1,000	N/A	80.00	395-435
1984 Cape Cod Cold Fish Party	1,000	N/A	150.00	150-195
1986 Carnival Capers	620	N/A	200.00	200
1981 Carver Coggins	1,000	N/A	145.00	1050-1150
1989 Christmas Greeting	11,000	N/A	125.00	100-125
1982 Christmas Print, 1982	2,000	N/A	80.00	500
1984 Chumbuddies, signed	1,000		55.00	55
1985 Clammers at Hodge's Horn	1,000	N/A	150.00	1200-1250
1983 Commemorative Print, 1983	2,000	N/A	55.00	55
1984 Commemorative Print, 1984	2,000	N/A	55.00	55
1984 Commemorative Print, 1985	2,000		55.00	55
1985 Commemorative Print, 1986	2,000		55.00	55
1984 Cotton Country	1,000	N/A	150.00	350-375
1983 Country Race	1,000	N/A	150.00	235-350
1997 Cow (framed)	150		135.00	135
1986 Daddy's Coming Home	1,250	N/A	150.00	875-895
1987 Dahalia Dinalhaven Makes a Dory Deal	2,250	N/A	150.00	425-475
1986 Dancing Pheasant Farms	1,750	N/A	165.00	405-525
1980 Derby Square	1,000	N/A	90.00	1000-1100
1986 Devilbelly Bay	1,000	N/A	145.00	250-395
1986 Devilstone Harbor/An American Celebration (Print & Book)	3,500	N/A	195.00	375-400
1989 Dreamers	3,000	N/A	175.00	425-450
1992 Ethel the Gourmet	10,179	N/A	150.00	500-700
1979 Fairhaven by the Sea	1,000	N/A	75.00	700-750
1988 Feathered Critics	2,500	N/A	150.00	150
1997 Fox Hill Farms (framed)	150		135.00	135
1979 Fox Run	1,000	N/A	75.00	950-1100
1984 The Foxy Fox Outfoxes the Fox Hunters	1,500	N/A	150.00	395-425
1992 Frederick the Literate	6,500	N/A	150.00	2500
1989 Fun Lovin' Silly Folks	3,000	N/A	185.00	475-495
1984 The Gang's All Here	Open		65.00	65
1984 The Gang's All Here, remarque	250		90.00	90
1992 Gay Head Light	2,500		165.00	165
1997 Hawk River Hollow (framed)	150		135.00	135
1986 Hickory Haven Canal	1,500	N/A	165.00	650-900
1988 Home Is My Sailor	2,500	N/A	150.00	150
1985 I Love America	2,000		20.00	20
1990 Jingle Bell Teddy and Friends	5,000		125.00	125
1980 Jolly Hill Farms	1,000	N/A	75.00	650-850
1997 Kitty Treat (framed)	150		135.00	135
1986 Lady Liberty's Independence Day Enterprising Immigrants	1,500	N/A	140.00	375-525
1992 Love Letter From Laramie	1,500		150.00	150
1989 The Memory Maker	2,500	1998	165.00	165-195
1985 Merrymakers Serenade	1,250	N/A	135.00	135-175
1986 Mr. Swallobark	2,000	N/A	145.00	1300-1550
1982 The Nantucket	1,000	N/A	145.00	275
1997 Nantucket Winds (framed)	150		135.00	135
1981 Olde America	1,500	N/A	125.00	450-500
1981 Page's Bake Shoppe	1,000	N/A	115.00	275-350
1997 Peppercricket Farms (framed)	150		135.00	135
1997 Pickwick Cottage (framed)	150		135.00	135
1983 Plum Island Sound, signed	1,000	N/A	55.00	675
1983 Plum Island Sound, unsigned	Open	N/A	40.00	40
1981 Prairie Wind Flowers	1,000	N/A	125.00	1375-1495
1992 Proud Little Angler	2,750	N/A	150.00	200
1994 Remington w/Book-Heartland	15,000	1998	195.00	250-300
1990 Robin Hood	2,000		165.00	165
1991 Rockland Breakwater Light	2,500	N/A	165.00	165-235
1985 Salty Witch Bay	475	N/A	350.00	2400
1991 Sea Captain's Wife Abiding	1,500	N/A	150.00	150-165
1979 Shall We?	1,000	N/A	75.00	1200-1450
1982 Sleepy Town West	1,500	N/A	150.00	600-650
1984 Storin' Up	450	N/A	325.00	700-750
1982 Sunset Hills, Texas Wildcatters	1,000	N/A	125.00	150-175
1984 Sweetheart Chessmate	1,000	N/A	95.00	1200
1983 Tea by the Sea	1,000	N/A	145.00	1000-1350
1997 Teddy Bear Express (framed)	150		135.00	135
1993 The Three Sisters of Nauset, 1880	2,500	N/A	165.00	165-195
1984 A Warm Christmas Love	3,951	N/A	80.00	200-375
1990 Wednesday Night Checkers	2,500	1998	175.00	215-295
1991 West Quoddy Head Light, Maine	2,500	1998	165.00	165
1990 Where The Bouys Are	2,750	N/A	175.00	175-195
1991 Whistle Stop Christmas	5,000		125.00	125
1980 Yankee Wink Hollow	1,000	N/A	95.00	1000-1200
1987 Yearning For My Captain	2,000	N/A	150.00	225-325
1987 You've Been So Long at Sea, Horatio	2,500	N/A	150.00	215-295

Young - C. Young

YEAR ISSUE	EDITION LIMIT	YEAR RETD.	ISSUE PRICE	*QUOTE U.S.$
1999 Japanese Apples	550		145.00	145
2000 Tuscan Cloud	550		175.00	175
1999 Tuscan Primrose	550		145.00	145

Hadley House

Agnew - A. Agnew

YEAR ISSUE	EDITION LIMIT	YEAR RETD.	ISSUE PRICE	*QUOTE U.S.$
1997 American Odyssey	750		125.00	125
1997 Birds of a Feather	999		50.00	50
1997 Quick Silver	999	1998	75.00	235
1997 Time Well Spent	999		150.00	150

Barnhouse - D. Barnhouse

YEAR ISSUE	EDITION LIMIT	YEAR RETD.	ISSUE PRICE	*QUOTE U.S.$
1997 Every Boys' Dream	1,950		150.00	150
1997 A Finishing Touch	1,950		150.00	150
1997 Horsepower	1,950		150.00	150
1997 Spring Cleaning	1,950	1997	150.00	220-265
1997 Sunset Strip	1,950		150.00	150
1997 The Warmth of Home	1,950		150.00	150

Bogle - C. Bogle

YEAR ISSUE	EDITION LIMIT	YEAR RETD.	ISSUE PRICE	*QUOTE U.S.$
1997 The Colors of Autumn	999	1997	75.00	75
1997 Crossing Paths	999		125.00	125
1997 A Golden Moment	999	1998	100.00	350

Bush - D. Bush

YEAR ISSUE	EDITION LIMIT	YEAR RETD.	ISSUE PRICE	*QUOTE U.S.$
1997 Cabin Fever	1,250		125.00	125
1997 Evening Run	999	1997	125.00	125-295
1997 Legends of The Lake	1,250	1998	125.00	125
1994 Moondance	999	1995	125.00	220-315
1997 Once In a Life Time	999		125.00	125
1996 Still of the Night	1,250	1997	125.00	195-215
1997 Time Flies	1,250		125.00	125
1997 Winter Colors	Open		35.00	35

Capser - M. Capser

YEAR ISSUE	EDITION LIMIT	YEAR RETD.	ISSUE PRICE	*QUOTE U.S.$
1997 Blossoms and Promises	999		100.00	100
1993 Briar and Brambles	999	1996	100.00	100
1992 Comes the Dawn	600		100.00	100
1994 Dashing Through the Snow	999		100.00	100
1994 Down the Lane	Retrd.	1998	30.00	30
1995 Enchanted Waters	999		100.00	100
1997 Grandma's Garden	999	1999	100.00	100
1995 Grapevine Estates	999	1998	100.00	100
1997 Guiding The Sails	999	1998	100.00	100
1994 The Lifting Fog	Retrd.	1997	30.00	30
1995 Mariner's Point	999	1996	100.00	100
1994 Nappin'	999		100.00	100
1994 A Night's Quiet	999		100.00	100
1995 On Gentle Wings	999		100.00	100
1993 Pickets & Vines	999	1994	100.00	100
1992 Reflections	600	1993	100.00	100
1993 Rock Creek Spring	999		80.00	80
1994 September Blush	999	1996	100.00	100
1992 Silence Unbroken	600	1996	100.00	100
1993 Skyline Serenade	600	1993	100.00	100
1995 Spring Creek Fever	999	1996	100.00	100

*Quotes have been rounded up to nearest dollar

YEAR ISSUE	EDITION LIMIT	YEAR RETD.	ISSUE PRICE	*QUOTE U.S.$
1993 A Summer's Glow	999	1997	60.00	60
1997 Sunrise Symphony	999		100.00	100
1994 A Time For Us	999		125.00	125
1994 To Search Again	Open		30.00	30
1992 The Watch	600	1993	100.00	150-517
1994 The Way Home	Retrd.	1998	30.00	30
1993 Whispering Wings	1,500	1994	100.00	100
1997 Woodland Warmth	999		125.00	125

Franca - O. Franca

YEAR ISSUE	EDITION LIMIT	YEAR RETD.	ISSUE PRICE	*QUOTE U.S.$
1988 The Apache	950	1990	70.00	175
1990 Blue Navajo	1,500	1991	125.00	179-319
1990 Blue Tranquility	999	1990	100.00	450-776
1988 Cacique	950	1990	70.00	150-216
1990 Cecy	1,500	1992	125.00	225-305
1990 Destiny	999	1990	100.00	100-345
1991 Early Morning	3,600	1994	125.00	225
1993 Evening In Taos	4,000	1994	80.00	80
1988 Feathered Hair Ties	600	1988	80.00	1198-1595
1990 Feathered Hair Ties II	999	1990	100.00	259-300
1991 The Lovers	2,400	1991	125.00	1224-1800
1991 The Model	1,500	1991	125.00	469-495
1992 Navajo Daydream	3,600	1993	175.00	450-480
1989 Navajo Fantasy	999	1989	80.00	150-302
1992 Navajo Meditating	4,000	1994	80.00	125
1992 Navajo Reflection	4,000	1992	80.00	100-225
1990 Navajo Summer	999	1988	100.00	175-345
1991 Olympia	1,500	1991	125.00	390
1989 Pink Navajo	999	1989	80.00	250-345
1988 The Red Shawl	600	1990	80.00	300
1991 Red Wolf	1,500	1991	125.00	125-130
1990 Santa Fe	1,500	1991	125.00	150-300
1988 Sitting Bull	950	1990	70.00	200-259
1988 Slow Bull	950	1990	70.00	200
1990 Turqoise Necklace	999	1990	100.00	200-317
1990 Wind Song	999	1990	100.00	195-345
1992 Wind Song II	4,000	1992	80.00	150-175
1989 Winter	999	1989	80.00	175
1989 Young Warrior	999	1989	80.00	450-560

Hanks - S. Hanks

YEAR ISSUE	EDITION LIMIT	YEAR RETD.	ISSUE PRICE	*QUOTE U.S.$
1994 All Gone Awry	2,000		150.00	150
1994 All In a Row	2,000	1994	150.00	164-200
1997 Being Perfect Angels	1,500	1997	150.00	150-175
1995 A Captive Audience	1,500	1997	150.00	150
1995 Cat's Lair	1,500		150.00	150
1993 Catching The Sun	999	1993	150.00	495
1992 Conferring With the Sea	999	1993	125.00	495
1995 Contemplation	999	1997	100.00	150
1995 Country Comfort	999	1997	100.00	100
1995 Drip Castles	4,000		30.00	30
1991 Duet	999	1993	150.00	150-600
1990 Emotional Appeal	999	1998	150.00	225
1993 Gathering Thoughts	1,500	1995	150.00	345
1996 Her Side	1,500	1997	100.00	100
1992 An Innocent View	999	1992	150.00	315-450
1994 The Journey Is The Goal	1,500	1995	150.00	495
1995 Kali	Open		25.00	25
1996 Little Angels	999	1996	125.00	250-395
1993 Little Black Crow	1,500		150.00	150
1994 Michaela and Friends/Book	2,500		200.00	200
1997 The Music Room	1,500	1997	150.00	150
1993 The New Arrival	1,500	1995	150.00	150-200
1995 Pacific Sanctuary	1,500	1998	150.00	275
1993 Peeking Out	Open		40.00	40
1993 Places I Remember	1,500		150.00	150
1990 Quiet Rapport	999	1997	150.00	300
1996 Sending Flowers	1,500	1997	150.00	180-225
1993 A Sense of Belonging	1,500	1997	150.00	150
1995 Small Miracle	1,500		125.00	125
1992 Sometimes It's the Little Things	999	1995	125.00	225
1994 Southwestern Bedroom	999	1997	150.00	180-225
1992 Stepping Stones	999	1993	150.00	295
1991 Sunday Afternoon	Open		40.00	40
1997 Sunshine Across The Sheets	1,500	1998	100.00	100
1992 Things Worth Keeping	999	1991	125.00	1100-1450
1993 The Thinkers	1,500		150.00	150
1994 Water Lilies In Bloom	750		295.00	295
1993 When Her Blue Eyes Close	999		100.00	100
1994 Where The Light Shines Brightest	1,500		150.00	150
1991 A World For Our Children	999	1992	125.00	1595

Hulings - C. Hulings

YEAR ISSUE	EDITION LIMIT	YEAR RETD.	ISSUE PRICE	*QUOTE U.S.$
1990 Ancient French Farmhouse	999		150.00	225
1989 Chechaquene-Morocco Market Square	999	1993	150.00	250
1992 Cuernavaca Flower Market	580		225.00	225
1988 Ile de la Cite-Paris	580	1990	150.00	225
1990 The Lonely Man	999	1993	150.00	150
1988 Onteniente	580	1989	150.00	425-457
1991 Place des Ternes	580	1991	195.00	700
1989 Portuguese Vegetable Woman	999	1993	85.00	216
1994 The Red Raincoat	580		225.00	225
1990 Spanish Shawl	999	1994	125.00	125-169
1993 Spring Flowers	580		225.00	225
1992 Sunday Afternoon	580		195.00	275
1988 Three Cats on a Grapevine	580	1989	65.00	225
1993 Washday In Provence	580		225.00	225

Redlin - T. Redlin

YEAR ISSUE	EDITION LIMIT	YEAR RETD.	ISSUE PRICE	*QUOTE U.S.$
1981 1981 MN Duck Stamp Print	7,800	1981	125.00	150
1982 1982 MN Trout Stamp Print	960	1982	125.00	600
1983 1983 ND Duck Stamp Print	3,438	1983	135.00	150
1984 1984 Quail Conservation	1,500	1984	135.00	135
1985 1985 MN Duck Stamp	4,385	1985	135.00	135
1985 Afternoon Glow	960	1985	150.00	1095-1475
1979 Ageing Shoreline	960	1979	40.00	395-733
1981 All Clear	960	1981	150.00	395
1994 America, America	29,500		250.00	250
1994 And Crown Thy Good w/Brotherhood	29,500		250.00	250
1977 Apple River Mallards	Retrd.	1977	10.00	100
1981 April Snow	960	1981	100.00	595-776
1989 Aroma of Fall	6,800	1989	200.00	1700-1800
1987 Autumn Afternoon	4,800	1987	100.00	795
1993 Autumn Evening	29,500		250.00	250
1980 Autumn Run	960	1980	60.00	375
1983 Autumn Shoreline	Retrd.	1983	50.00	450-776
1997 Autumn Traditions	1,950		275.00	275
1978 Back from the Fields	720	1978	40.00	250
1985 Back to the Sanctuary	960	1986	150.00	350-475
1978 Backwater Mallards	720	1978	40.00	945
1983 Backwoods Cabin	960	1983	150.00	965
1990 Best Friends (AP)	570	1993	1000.00	1895
1982 The Birch Line	960	1982	100.00	1295-1681
1984 Bluebill Point (AP)	240	1984	300.00	785
1988 Boulder Ridge	4,800		150.00	150
1997 Bountiful Harvest	19,500		275.00	275
1980 Breaking Away	960	1980	60.00	430
1985 Breaking Cover	960	1985	150.00	400-862
1981 Broken Covey	960	1981	100.00	525-664
1985 Brousing	960	1985	150.00	895
1994 Campfire Tales	29,500		250.00	250
1988 Catching the Scent	2,400		200.00	200
1986 Changing Seasons-Autumn	960	1986	150.00	450-503
1987 Changing Seasons-Spring	960	1987	200.00	475-845
1984 Changing Seasons-Summer	960	1984	150.00	1400
1986 Changing Seasons-Winter	960	1986	200.00	600
1985 Clear View	1,500	1985	300.00	1195-1552
1980 Clearing the Rail	960	1980	60.00	850-1034
1984 Closed for the Season	960	1984	150.00	450-495
1979 Colorful Trio	960	1979	40.00	800
1991 Comforts of Home	22,900	N/A	175.00	300-400
1986 Coming Home	2,400	1986	100.00	2400-2600
1992 The Conservationists	29,500		175.00	175
1988 Country Neighbors	4,800	1988	150.00	600
1980 Country Road	960	1980	60.00	650-745
1987 Deer Crossing	2,400	1987	200.00	1200
1985 Delayed Departure	1,500	1985	150.00	500-1000
1980 Drifting	960	1980	60.00	400
1987 Evening Chores (print & book)	2,400	1988	400.00	1000-1121
1985 Evening Company	960	1985	150.00	500-1300
1983 Evening Glow	960	1983	150.00	2250
1987 Evening Harvest	960	1987	200.00	1350-2155
1982 Evening Retreat (AP)	300	1982	400.00	3000
1990 Evening Solitude	9,500	1990	200.00	600
1983 Evening Surprise	960	1983	150.00	1000-3300
1990 Evening With Friends	19,500	1991	225.00	1500
1990 Family Traditions	Retrd.	1993	80.00	240-250
1979 Fighting a Headwind	960	1979	30.00	350
1991 Flying Free	14,500		200.00	200
1993 For Amber Waves of Grain	29,500		250.00	250
1993 For Purple Mountains Majesty	29,500		250.00	250
1995 From Sea to Shining Sea	29,500		250.00	250
1994 God Shed His Grace on Thee	29,500		250.00	250
1987 Golden Retreat (AP)	500	1986	800.00	2000
1995 Harvest Moon Ball	9,500	1995	275.00	275-350
1986 Hazy Afternoon	2,560	1986	200.00	850
1990 Heading Home	Retrd.	1993	80.00	135-200
1997 A Helping Hand	9,500		275.00	275
1983 Hidden Point	960	1983	150.00	600
1981 High Country	960	1981	100.00	600
1981 Hightailing	960	1981	75.00	350
1980 The Homestead	960	1980	60.00	640
1989 Homeward Bound	Retrd.	1994	80.00	250
1988 Homeward Bound	Retrd.	1993	70.00	150
1988 House Call	6,800	1990	175.00	1000
1991 Hunter's Haven (A/P)	1,000	N/A	175.00	1000
1989 Indian Summer	4,800	1989	200.00	725-905
1980 Intruders	960	1980	60.00	320
1982 The Landing	Retrd.	1982	30.00	80
1981 The Landmark	960	1981	100.00	400
1984 Leaving the Sanctuary	960	1984	150.00	475
1994 Lifetime Companions	29,500		250.00	250
1988 Lights of Home	9,500	1988	125.00	650-675
1979 The Loner	960	1979	40.00	300
1990 Master of the Valley	6,800		200.00	200
1988 The Master's Domain	2,400	1988	225.00	800-850
1988 Moonlight Retreat (A/P)	530	N/A	1000.00	1600
1979 Morning Chores	960	1979	40.00	1350
1984 Morning Glow	960	1984	150.00	1400-1879
1981 Morning Retreat (AP)	240	N/A	400.00	3000
1989 Morning Rounds	6,800	1992	175.00	595
1991 Morning Solitude	12,107	1991	250.00	405-600
1984 Night Harvest	960	1984	150.00	1795
1985 Night Light	1,500	1985	300.00	1195
1986 Night Mapling	960	1986	200.00	650-1000
1995 A Night on the Town	29,500		150.00	150
1980 Night Watch	2,400	1980	60.00	1000
1984 Nightflight (AP)	360	1984	600.00	2200
1982 October Evening	960	1982	100.00	1000
1989 Office Hours	6,800	1991	175.00	948
1992 Oh Beautiful for Spacious Skies	29,500		250.00	250
1978 Old Loggers Trail	720	1978	40.00	950-1200
1983 On the Alert	960	1983	125.00	400
1977 Over the Blowdown	Retrd.	1977	20.00	400-690
1978 Over the Rushes	720	1978	40.00	450
1981 Passing Through	960	1981	100.00	225
1983 Peaceful Evening	960	1983	100.00	1595
1991 Pleasures of Winter	24,500	1992	150.00	221-245
1986 Prairie Monuments	960	1986	200.00	795
1988 Prairie Morning	4,800	1988	150.00	450-550
1984 Prairie Skyline	960	1984	150.00	2328
1983 Prairie Springs	960	1983	150.00	595
1987 Prepared for the Season	Retrd.	1994	70.00	160
1990 Pure Contentment	9,500	1989	150.00	475-500
1978 Quiet Afternoon	720	1978	40.00	695
1988 Quiet of the Evening	4,800	1988	150.00	450-595
1982 Reflections	960	1982	100.00	600
1985 Riverside Pond	960	1985	150.00	525
1984 Rural Route	960	1984	150.00	395
1983 Rushing Rapids	960	1983	125.00	750
1980 Rusty Refuge I	960	1980	60.00	295
1981 Rusty Refuge II	960	1980	100.00	495
1984 Rusty Refuge III	960	1984	150.00	595
1985 Rusty Refuge IV	960	1985	150.00	695
1980 Secluded Pond	960	1980	60.00	295
1982 Seed Hunters	960	1982	100.00	575
1985 Sharing Season I	Retrd.	1993	60.00	150-225
1986 Sharing Season II	Retrd.	1993	60.00	225-240
1981 Sharing the Bounty	960	1981	100.00	1500
1994 Sharing the Evening	29,500		175.00	175
1987 Sharing the Solitude	2,400	1987	125.00	800-850
1986 Silent Flight	960	1986	150.00	335-400
1980 Silent Sunset	960	1980	60.00	780-1121
1984 Silent Wings Suite (set of 4)	960	1984	200.00	750
1981 Soft Shadows	960	1984	100.00	325
1989 Special Memories (AP)	570		1000.00	1000
1982 Spring Mapling	960	1982	100.00	975
1981 Spring Run-Off	1,700	1981	125.00	695-991
1980 Spring Thaw	960	1980	60.00	460
1980 Squall Line	960	1980	60.00	300
1978 Startled	720	1978	30.00	995-1336
1986 Stormy Weather	1,500	1986	200.00	550
1992 Summertime	24,900	1999	225.00	225
1997 Sunday Morning	9,500		275.00	275
1984 Sundown	960	1984	300.00	575
1986 Sunlit Trail	960	1986	150.00	150-200
1984 Sunny Afternoon	960	1984	150.00	700
1987 That Special Time	2,400	1987	125.00	825-850
1987 Together for the Season	Open		70.00	100
1995 Total Comfort	9,500	1995	275.00	275
1986 Twilight Glow	960	1986	200.00	700-1500
1988 Wednesday Afternoon	6,800	1989	175.00	900
1990 Welcome to Paradise	14,500	1990	150.00	700-974
1985 Whistle Stop	960	1985	150.00	785
1979 Whitecaps	960	1979	40.00	445
1982 Whitewater	960	1982	100.00	400
1982 Winter Haven	500	1982	85.00	800
1977 Winter Snows	Retrd.	1977	20.00	595-690
1984 Winter Windbreak	960	1984	150.00	750
1992 Winter Wonderland	29,500	1993	150.00	250

Hallmark Galleries

Innocent Wonders - T. Blackshear

YEAR ISSUE	EDITION LIMIT	YEAR RETD.	ISSUE PRICE	*QUOTE U.S.$
1992 Pinkie Poo QHG4016	9,500	1995	75.00	75

Majestic Wilderness - M. Newman

YEAR ISSUE	EDITION LIMIT	YEAR RETD.	ISSUE PRICE	*QUOTE U.S.$
1992 Timber Wolves QHG2013	9,500	1995	75.00	75
1992 White-tailed Deer QHG2014	9,500	1995	75.00	75

Hamilton Collection

Grateful Dead Autographed Prints - S. Mouse

YEAR ISSUE	EDITION LIMIT	YEAR RETD.	ISSUE PRICE	*QUOTE U.S.$
1999 Family Album	Open		49.95	50
1999 Icecream Kid	Open		49.95	50
1999 Mars Hotel	Open		49.95	50
1999 One More Saturday Night	Open		49.95	50
1999 Skelton and Roses	Open		49.95	50
1999 Workingman's Dead	Open		49.95	50

Mickey Mantle - R. Tanenbaum

YEAR ISSUE	EDITION LIMIT	YEAR RETD.	ISSUE PRICE	*QUOTE U.S.$
1996 An All American Legend-The Mick	Open		95.00	95

Imperial Graphics, Ltd.

Chang - L. Chang

YEAR ISSUE	EDITION LIMIT	YEAR RETD.	ISSUE PRICE	*QUOTE U.S.$
1988 Egrets with Lotus S/N	1,950		10.00	10
1988 Flamingos with Catail S/N	1,950		10.00	10

Irvine - G. Irvine

YEAR ISSUE	EDITION LIMIT	YEAR RETD.	ISSUE PRICE	*QUOTE U.S.$
1995 Pansies	Open		8.00	8
1995 Violets	Open		8.00	8

Lee - H.C. Lee

YEAR ISSUE	EDITION LIMIT	YEAR RETD.	ISSUE PRICE	*QUOTE U.S.$
1988 Blue Bird of Paradise S/N	950	1999	35.00	35
1988 Cat & Callas S/N	1,950	1999	30.00	30
1990 Double Red Hibiscus S/N	1,950	1999	16.00	16
1988 Hummingbird I S/N	1,950	1999	16.00	16
1988 Hummingbird II S/N	1,950	1999	16.00	16
1990 Maroon & Mauve Peonies S/N	950	1999	60.00	60
1990 Maroon & Peach Peonies S/N	950	1999	60.00	60
1990 Maroon Peony S/N	2,950		20.00	20
1990 Peacock w/Tulip & Peony S/N	1,950		105.00	105
1990 Peonies & Butterflies S/N	2,950		40.00	40
1990 Pink Peony S/N	2,950		20.00	20
1990 Single Red Hibiscus S/N	1,950		16.00	16
1988 White Bird of Paradise S/N	950	1999	35.00	35

*Quotes have been rounded up to nearest dollar

GRAPHICS

YEAR ISSUE	EDITION LIMIT	YEAR RETD.	ISSUE PRICE	*QUOTE U.S.$
1988 White Peacocks w/Peonies S/N	950	1999	65.00	65

Liu - Angels Among Us - L. Liu

YEAR ISSUE	EDITION LIMIT	YEAR RETD.	ISSUE PRICE	*QUOTE U.S.$
1997 Angel of Light S/N	3,500		125.00	125
1997 Angel of Love S/N	3,500		80.00	80
1996 Angel with Harp S/N	5,500		40.00	40
1996 Angel with Trumpet S/N	5,500		40.00	40
1996 Guardian Angel S/N	5,500		125.00	125
1997 Urn with Irises S/N	3,500		45.00	45
1997 Urn with Tulips S/N	3,500		45.00	45

Liu - Celestial Symphony Series - L. Liu

YEAR ISSUE	EDITION LIMIT	YEAR RETD.	ISSUE PRICE	*QUOTE U.S.$
1995 Flute Interlude S/N	5,500		40.00	40
1995 French Horn Melody S/N	5,500		40.00	40
1995 Piano Sonata S/N	5,500		40.00	40
1995 Violin Concerto S/N	5,500		40.00	40

Liu - Garden of Paradise - L. Liu

YEAR ISSUE	EDITION LIMIT	YEAR RETD.	ISSUE PRICE	*QUOTE U.S.$
1999 Majestic Peacock	2,950		135.00	135
1999 Majestic Peacock - Canvas	300		395.00	395
1999 Royal Peahen	2,950		135.00	135
1999 Royal Peahen - Canvas	300		395.00	395
1999 Swan Duet	2,950		135.00	135
1999 Swan Duet - Canvas	300		395.00	395

Liu - L. Liu

YEAR ISSUE	EDITION LIMIT	YEAR RETD.	ISSUE PRICE	*QUOTE U.S.$
1989 Abundance of Lilies (poster)	Closed	1993	25.00	30
1998 Abundant Blessings S/N	3,500		125.00	125
XX Afternoon Nap S/N	1,000		45.00	45
1994 Allen's Hummingbird w/Columbine S/N	3,300	1994	30.00	70-90
1987 Amaryllis S/N	1,950	N/A	16.00	60
2000 Angel of Purity S/N	2,500		50.00	50
2000 Angel of Wishes S/N	2,500		50.00	50
1993 Anna's Hummingbird w/Fuchsia S/N	3,300	1993	30.00	30
1998 Autumn Glory S/N	2,950		145.00	145
1989 Autumn Melody S/N	1,950	1993	45.00	45
1990 Azalea Path S/N	2,500	N/A	85.00	85
1990 Azalea w/Dogwood S/N	2,500	N/A	55.00	55
1988 Baby Bluebirds S/N	1,950	N/A	18.00	30
1990 Baby Bluebirds w/Plum Tree S/N	2,500	N/A	18.00	90-100
1988 Baby Chickadees S/N	1,950	N/A	16.00	215
1990 Baby Chickadees w/Pine Tree S/N	2,500	N/A	18.00	70-90
1999 Bamboo (9 x 15)	3,300		28.00	28
XX Basket of Begonias S/N	2,500	N/A	40.00	40
1993 Basket of Calla Lilies S/N	3,300	1994	50.00	88-100
1991 Basket of Grapes & Raspberries S/N	2,500	N/A	25.00	30
1993 Basket of Hydrangra S/N	3,300	1995	50.00	93-116
1989 Basket of Irises & Lilacs S/N	1,950	N/A	45.00	45
1993 Basket of Magnolias S/N	3,300	1993	50.00	100-235
1993 Basket of Orchids S/N	3,300	N/A	50.00	72-90
1992 Basket of Pansies & Lilacs S/N	2,950	N/A	50.00	50
1991 Basket of Pansies S/N	2,500	N/A	40.00	40
1991 Basket of Peonies S/N	2,500	N/A	40.00	40
1992 Basket of Roses & Hydrangeas S/N	2,950	N/A	50.00	50
1991 Basket of Roses S/N	2,500	N/A	40.00	40
1991 Basket of Strawberries & Grapes S/N	2,500	N/A	25.00	50-70
1991 Basket of Sweet Peas S/N	2,500	N/A	25.00	50-75
1989 Basket of Tulips & Lilacs S/N	1,950	N/A	45.00	45
1991 Basket of Wild Roses S/N	2,500	N/A	25.00	75-120
1991 Baskets of Primroses S/N	2,500	N/A	25.00	50-75
1986 Bearded Irises S/N	1,950	N/A	45.00	45
1994 Berries & Cherries S/N	3,500	1998	30.00	80-100
1990 Bluebirds & Dandelion S/N	2,500	N/A	40.00	64-80
1986 Bluebirds w/Plum Blossoms S/N	1,950	N/A	35.00	35
1988 Bluebirds w/Rhododendrons S/N	1,950	N/A	40.00	144-180
1990 Bouquet of Peonies S/N	2,500	N/A	50.00	50
1990 Bouquet of Poppies S/N	2,500	N/A	50.00	50
1992 Bouquet of Roses S/N	2,950	1994	20.00	20
1992 Breath of Spring S/N	2,950	N/A	135.00	135
1993 Broad-Billed HB w/Petunias S/N	3,300	N/A	30.00	64-80
1995 Burgundy Irises w/Foxgloves S/N	5,500	N/A	60.00	91-114
1995 Butterfly Garden I S/N	5,500		50.00	50
1995 Butterfly Garden II S/N	5,500		50.00	50
1994 Butterfly Kisses S/N	3,500	1998	50.00	67-125
1998 Butterfly Paradise S/N	3,500	N/A	80.00	80
1990 Butterfly w/Clematis S/N	2,500	1994	40.00	165-225
1990 Butterfly w/Wild Rose S/N	2,500	1993	40.00	50
1987 Calla Lily S/N	1,950	N/A	35.00	35
1994 Calliope Hummingbird w/Trumpet Vine S/N	3,300	N/A	30.00	64-80
1999 Camellia (12 x 12) S/N	2,950		28.00	28
1990 Cardinal & Queen Anne's Lace S/N	2,500	1994	40.00	225
XX Cat & Hummer S/N	1,000		45.00	45
1989 Cherries & Summer Bouquet S/N	2,500	N/A	45.00	45
1993 Cherub Orchestra S/N	3,300	1994	80.00	123-300
1991 Cherubim w/Ivy S/N	2,500	1993	20.00	20
1988 Chickadees w/Cherry Blossoms S/N	1,950	N/A	40.00	144-180
2000 The Chirp Inn S/N	2,500		45.00	45
1992 Conservatory S/N	2,950	1994	80.00	235-250
1999 Cymbidium w/White Butterfly S/N	1,950		40.00	40
1987 Daylily S/N	1,950	N/A	35.00	35
1989 Daylily w/Hummingbird S/N	2,500	N/A	18.00	18
1998 The Delights of Spring S/N	3,500		80.00	80
1987 Dogwood S/N	1,950	N/A	30.00	30
1986 The Dreamer S/N	950		65.00	65
1991 Dried-Floral Bouquet S/N	2,500	N/A	25.00	40-50
1991 The Drying Room S/N	2,500	N/A	75.00	112-140
1992 Early Spring S/N	2,950	1993	85.00	85
1988 Eastern Black Swallowtail w/Milkweed S/N	1,950	N/A	45.00	80-100
1991 Egret's w/Queen Anne's Lace S/N	2,500	1995	60.00	80-100
1992 Entryway S/N	2,950		40.00	40
1997 Evening Reflections S/N	5,500		135.00	135
1993 Fairy Ballet S/N	3,300	N/A	80.00	80
1986 Fall S/N	950	N/A	35.00	35
1988 Feathered Harmony S/N	1,950	N/A	60.00	295
1991 Field of Irises S/N	2,500	1994	85.00	120-150
1999 Fireside Solitude S/N	1,950		105.00	105
1989 First Landing S/N	1,950	N/A	16.00	25
1991 Floral Arch S/N	2,500	1996	25.00	25
1988 Floral Symphony S/N	1,950	N/A	95.00	95
1990 Forest Azalea S/N	2,500	N/A	55.00	225-250
1992 Forest Stream S/N	2,950	1995	85.00	218-261
1992 Fountain S/N	2,950		40.00	40
1986 Free Flight I -Rust Butterfly S/N	950		60.00	60
1986 Free Flight II -Pink Butterfly S/N	950		60.00	60
1989 Fritillaries w/ Violet S/N	2,500		18.00	18
1989 Fruit & Spring Basket S/N	1,500	N/A	45.00	225-250
1988 Garden Blossoms I S/N	1,950	N/A	35.00	35
1988 Garden Blossoms II S/N	1,950	N/A	35.00	35
1997 Garden Gate S/N	5,500		80.00	80
1991 Garden Peonies S/N	2,500	1997	60.00	88-110
1997 Garden Pleasure S/N	5,500		80.00	80
1986 Garden Poppies S/N	2,000	N/A	45.00	88-110
1991 Garden Poppies S/N	2,500	N/A	60.00	60
1992 Garden Seat S/N	2,950		40.00	40
1991 The Gathering S/N	2,500	N/A	75.00	75
1988 Harmonious Flight S/N	1,950	N/A	50.00	100-150
1994 Heavenly Tulips S/N	3,300	1994	80.00	250
1987 Herons & Irises S/N	1,950	N/A	65.00	130-150
1987 Hibiscus & Hummer S/N	1,950	1995	45.00	45
1988 Hummingbird & Hollyhock S/N	1,950	N/A	40.00	40
1989 Hummingbird & Floral I S/N	2,500	1994	35.00	35
1989 Hummingbird & Floral II S/N	2,500	1994	35.00	2500
1996 Hummingbird with Lilac S/N	5,500	2000	50.00	50
1988 Hummingbirds & Iris S/N	1,950	N/A	40.00	40
2000 Hummingbirds with Azaleas S/N	2,500		40.00	40
1996 Hummingbirds with Fuchsia S/N	5,500		50.00	50
2000 Hummingbirds with Roses S/N	2,500		40.00	40
1999 Hydrangea (12 x 12) S/N	2,950		28.00	28
1989 Hydrangea Bouquet S/N	2,500	N/A	30.00	96-120
1989 Innocents S/N	1,950	N/A	16.00	50-75
1993 Iris Garden II S/N	3,300	1994	105.00	400-510
1989 Iris Profusion (poster)	Closed	1995	30.00	60-80
1987 Iris S/N	1,950	N/A	16.00	16
1991 Irises in Bloom S/N	2,500	N/A	85.00	85
1992 Ivy & Fragrant Flowers S/N	3,300	1993	60.00	225-250
1992 Ivy & Honeysuckle S/N	3,300	1993	50.00	75
1992 Ivy & Sweetpea S/N	3,300	1994	50.00	75
1988 Kingfisher & Iris S/N	1,950	N/A	45.00	67-84
1986 Kingfisher S/N	950	1998	35.00	35
1999 Lilac (12 x 12) S/N	2,950		28.00	28
1995 Lilac Breezes S/N	5,500		80.00	80
1986 Lily Pond S/N	950	1998	35.00	35
1987 Lily S/N	1,950	N/A	16.00	16
1999 Magnolia (12 x 12) S/N	2,950		28.00	28
1998 Magnolia Bouquet S/N	3,500	N/A	50.00	80-100
1995 Magnolia Path S/N	5,500		135.00	135
1987 Magnolia S/N	1,950	N/A	30.00	30
1999 Magnolia Serenade S/N	1,950		105.00	105
1995 Magnolias & Day Lilies S/N	5,500		80.00	80
1995 Magnolias & Hydrangeas S/N	5,500		80.00	80
2000 The Manor House S/N	2,500		45.00	45
1986 Mauve Veiltail S/N	1,000	N/A	35.00	35
1994 Mermaid Callas S/N	5,500	N/A	80.00	194-232
1996 Messengers of Love S/N	5,500		60.00	60
XX Misty Valley S/N	1,950	N/A	45.00	45
1990 Mixed Irises I S/N	2,500	N/A	50.00	50
1990 Mixed Irises II S/N	2,500	N/A	50.00	50
1988 Moonlight Splendor S/N	1,950	N/A	60.00	60
1987 Morning Glories & Hummer S/N	1,950	N/A	45.00	45
1989 The Morning Room S/N	2,500	N/A	95.00	325-395
1987 Motherlove S/N	1,950	N/A	45.00	265
1987 Motif Orientale S/N	1,950	N/A	95.00	95
1994 Mystic Bouquet S/N	3,300	N/A	80.00	120-150
1995 Nature's Retreat S/N	5,500	N/A	145.00	176-211
1998 Nature's Tranquility S/N	2,950		125.00	125
1986 Nuthatch w/Dogwood S/N	1,950	N/A	35.00	35
1992 Old Stone House S/N	2,950	1996	50.00	72-90
1986 Opera Lady S/N	950	N/A	95.00	95
1989 Orange Tip & Blossoms S/N	2,500		18.00	18
1989 Oriental Screen S/N	2,500	N/A	95.00	325-350
1996 Oriental Splendor S/N	5,500	1999	145.00	210-252
1988 Painted Lady w/Thistle S/N	1,950	N/A	45.00	88-110
1988 Pair of Finches S/N	1,950	N/A	35.00	35
1992 Palladian Windows S/N	2,950	1993	80.00	80
1990 Pansies & Ivy S/N	2,500	N/A	18.00	18
1992 Pansies & Lilies of the Valley S/N	2,950	1993	20.00	20
1991 Pansies in a Basket S/N	2,500	N/A	25.00	25
1993 Pansies w/Blue Stardrift S/N	2,950	1995	25.00	40-50
1993 Pansies w/Daisies S/N	2,950	N/A	25.00	34-46
1992 Pansies w/Sweet Peas S/N	2,950	1994	20.00	20
1991 Pansies w/Violets S/N	2,500	N/A	16.00	16
1987 Parenthood S/N	1,950	N/A	45.00	45
1992 Patio S/N	2,950		40.00	40
1993 Peach & Purple Irises S/N	3,300	1994	50.00	50-100
1993 Peach & Yellow Roses S/N	3,300	N/A	50.00	50-80
1986 Peach Veiltail S/N	1,000	1998	35.00	35
1994 Peaches & Fruits S/N	3,500	N/A	30.00	80-110
1991 Peacock Duet-Serigraph S/N	325		550.00	550
1987 Peacock Fantasy S/N	950	N/A	65.00	65
1991 Peacock Solo-Serigraph S/N	325		550.00	550
1988 Peonies & Azaleas S/N	1,950	N/A	35.00	35
1988 Peonies & Forsythia S/N	1,950	N/A	35.00	35
1988 Peonies & Waterfall S/N	1,950	N/A	65.00	65
1993 Peonies S/N	3,300	1995	30.00	140
1990 Petunias & Ivy S/N	2,500	N/A	18.00	18
1999 Phalaenopsis w/Blue Butterflies S/N	1,950		40.00	40
1989 Phlox w/Hummingbird S/N	2,500	N/A	18.00	18
1999 Poetic Melody S/N	1,950		150.00	150
1990 Potted Beauties S/N	2,500	1997	105.00	152-190
1996 Potted Pansies S/N	5,500	N/A	40.00	64-80
1996 Potted Petunias S/N	5,500		40.00	40
1996 Protectors of Peace S/N	5,500		60.00	60
1995 Purple Irises w/Foxgloves S/N	5,500		60.00	60
1991 Putti w/Column S/N	2,500	N/A	20.00	20
1990 Quiet Moment S/N	2,500	N/A	105.00	450-525
1998 Rhapsody in Yellow & Blue S/N	3,500		45.00	45
1989 Romantic Abundance S/N	1,950	N/A	95.00	95
1989 Romantic Garden (poster)	Open		35.00	35
1994 Romantic Reflection S/N	5,950	1996	145.00	399-485
1998 Romantic Reverie S/N	3,500		45.00	45
1997 Rose Arbor S/N	5,500		80.00	80
1993 Rose Bouquet w/Tassel S/N	3,300	1995	25.00	25
1994 Rose Fairies S/N	5,500	1996	80.00	195
1996 Rose Memories S/N	5,500		80.00	80
1989 Roses & Lilacs S/N	2,500	N/A	30.00	96-120
1992 Roses & Violets S/N	2,950	1993	20.00	40-50
1999 Roses (14 x 14) S/N	2,950		36.00	36
1993 Roses in Bloom S/N	3,300	1995	105.00	210-250
1990 Royal Garden S/N	1,950		95.00	95
1990 Royal Retreat S/N	1,950	N/A	95.00	450
1995 Ruby Throated Hummingbird w/Hibiscus S/N	5,800		40.00	40
1993 Rufous Hummingbird w/Foxgloves S/N	3,300	1993	30.00	30
1998 Seasonal Flowers I	Open		20.00	20
1998 Seasonal Flowers II	Open		20.00	20
1998 Seasonal Flowers III	Open		20.00	20
1998 Seasonal Flowers IV	Open		20.00	20
1988 Snapdragon S/N	1,950	N/A	16.00	16
1987 Solitude S/N	1,950	N/A	60.00	295
1993 Southern Magnolia S/N	3,300	1995	30.00	65-85
1987 Spring Blossoms I S/N	1,950	N/A	45.00	45
1987 Spring Blossoms II S/N	1,950	N/A	45.00	45
1989 Spring Bouquet (poster)	Open		30.00	30
1989 Spring Bouquet (poster-signed)	Open		45.00	45
1996 Spring Bulbs S/N	5,500		50.00	50
1994 Spring Conservatory S/N	3,300		105.00	105
1986 Spring Fairy S/N	950	1998	35.00	35
1990 Spring Floral S/N	2,500	N/A	105.00	105
1995 Spring Garden S/N	5,500		125.00	125
1986 Spring S/N	950	N/A	35.00	35
1987 Spring Song S/N	1,950	N/A	60.00	120-140
1986 Spring Tulips S/N	1,950	N/A	45.00	45
1989 Spring Tulips S/N	2,500	N/A	45.00	45
1987 Stream w/Blossoms S/N	1,950	N/A	45.00	90-120
1992 Study for a Breath of Spring S/N	2,950	N/A	105.00	105
1996 Summer Bouquet S/N	5,500		50.00	50
1986 Summer Glads S/N	1,950	N/A	45.00	45
1988 Summer Lace w/Blue Chicory S/N	1,950	1991	45.00	45
1987 Summer Lace w/Chicadees S/N	950	N/A	65.00	170
1988 Summer Lace w/Chickadees II S/N	1,950	1991	65.00	65
1988 Summer Lace w/Daisies S/N	1,950	1991	45.00	45
1987 Summer Lace w/Dragon Fly S/N	950	N/A	45.00	45
1987 Summer Lace w/Lady Bug S/N	950	N/A	45.00	45
1989 Summer Rose S/N	2,500	N/A	45.00	45
1986 Summer S/N	950	N/A	35.00	35
1998 Sunflower Bouquet S/N	3,500		50.00	50
1987 Swans & Callas S/N	1,950	1994	65.00	65
1991 Swans w/Daylilies S/N	2,500	1993	60.00	60
1989 Swans w/Dogwood S/N	1,950	N/A	65.00	65
1995 Sweet Bounty S/N	5,500		80.00	80
1994 Sweet Delight S/N	3,500	1998	50.00	80-110
1988 Sweet Pea Floral S/N	1,950	N/A	16.00	16
1986 Three Little Deer S/N	950	1998	35.00	35
1987 Togetherness S/N	1,950	N/A	60.00	60
1988 Trio of Sparrows S/N	1,950	N/A	35.00	35
1993 Tulip Bouquet w/Tassel S/N	3,300	1995	25.00	30
1999 Tulips (14 x 14) S/N	2,950		36.00	36
1987 Tulips S/N	1,950	N/A	16.00	16
1993 Two Burgundy Irises S/N	3,300	1994	50.00	50
1990 Two White Irises S/N	2,500	N/A	40.00	40
1992 Victorian Pavilion S/N	2,950	N/A	50.00	80-100
1992 Vintage Bouquet S/N	2,950	1994	135.00	250-265
1993 Violet Crowned HB w/Morning Glories S/N	3,300	1996	30.00	46-60
1989 Waterfall w/Dogwood S/N	1,950	N/A	45.00	45
1989 Waterfall w/White & Pink Dogwood S/N	1,950	N/A	45.00	45
1990 White & Blue Irises S/N	2,500	N/A	40.00	40
1993 White & Burgundy Roses S/N	3,300	1995	50.00	64-80
1995 White Eared Hummingbird w/Hydrangea S/N	5,800		40.00	40
1991 Wild Flowers w/Single Butterfly S/N	2,500	1998	50.00	80-100
1991 Wild Flowers w/Two Butterflies S/N	2,500	1998	50.00	80-100
1986 Winter S/N	950	N/A	35.00	35
1996 Wisteria Dreams S/N	5,500		80.00	80
1993 Woodland Path S/N	3,300	1994	135.00	325-450
1993 Woodland Steps S/N	3,300	1995	85.00	85
1993 Woodland View S/N	3,300	1995	85.00	160-180
1995 Wreath of Lilies S/N	5,500		55.00	55
1995 Wreath of Pansies S/N	5,500		55.00	55
1994 Wreath of Peonies S/N	3,500	1998	55.00	80-100
1994 Wreath of Roses S/N	3,500	1995	55.00	210-252

Liu - The Music Room - L. Liu

YEAR ISSUE	EDITION LIMIT	YEAR RETD.	ISSUE PRICE	*QUOTE U.S.$
1994 Clarinet Ensemble S/N	5,500		115.00	115

*Quotes have been rounded up to nearest dollar

YEAR ISSUE	EDITION LIMIT	YEAR RETD.	ISSUE PRICE	*QUOTE U.S.$
1996 Concerto with Guitar S/N	5,500		45.00	45
1996 Concerto with Violin S/N	5,500		45.00	45
1994 Fancy Fiddle S/N	5,500	1994	80.00	114-142
1996 Harmonic Duet S/N	5,500		55.00	55
1999 Homage to Beethoven-Symphony No. 9 S/N	2,950		80.00	80
1999 Homage to Mozart-The Marriage of Figaro S/N	2,950		80.00	80
1994 Love Notes S/N	5,500	1994	80.00	120-150
1991 The Music Room I S/N	2,500	1992	135.00	2300-2400
1992 The Music Room II-Nutcracker S/N	4,500	1993	200.00	627-762
1994 The Music Room III-Composer's Retreat S/N	5,500	1994	145.00	358-435
1995 The Music Room IV-Swan Melody S/N	6,500	1997	150.00	206-247
1996 The Music Room V-Morning Serenade S/N	5,500		145.00	145
1997 The Music Room VI-Romantic Overture S/N	5,500		150.00	150
1999 The Music Room VII-Afternoon Repose S/N	5,500		150.00	150
1996 Musical Trio S/N	5,500		55.00	55

Liu - Unframed Canvas Transfers - L. Liu

YEAR ISSUE	EDITION LIMIT	YEAR RETD.	ISSUE PRICE	*QUOTE U.S.$
1998 Abundant Blessings S/N	300		395.00	395
2000 Angel of Purity S/N	300		195.00	195
2000 Angel of Wishes S/N	300		195.00	195
1996 Angel with Harp S/N	300		145.00	145
1996 Angel with Trumpet S/N	300		145.00	145
1998 Autumn Glory S/N	300		395.00	395
1993 Basket of Calla Lilies S/N	300	1995	195.00	195
1993 Basket of Magnolias S/N	300	1997	195.00	195
1998 Butterfly Paradise S/N	300		295.00	295
1999 Camellia (12 x 12) S/N	300		125.00	125
1993 Cherub Orchestra S/N	300	1995	295.00	400-550
2000 The Chip Inn S/N	300		195.00	195
1992 Conservatory S/N	300	1995	295.00	295
1999 Cymbidium w/White Butterfly S/N	300		145.00	145
1998 The Delights of Spring S/N	300		295.00	295
1997 Evening Reflections S/N	300		395.00	395
1993 Fairy Ballet S/N	300	1997	295.00	295
1994 Fancy Fiddle S/N	300		295.00	295
1999 Fireside Solitude S/N	300		365.00	365
1997 Garden Gate S/N	300		295.00	295
1997 Garden Pleasure S/N	300		295.00	295
1996 Hummingbird with Fuchsia S/N	300		195.00	195
1996 Hummingbird with Lilac S/N	300		195.00	195
1999 Hydrangea (12 x 12) S/N	300		125.00	125
1993 Iris Garden II S/N	300	1995	395.00	395-475
1999 Lilac (12 x 12) S/N	300		125.00	125
1995 Lilac Breezes S/N	300		295.00	295
1994 Love Notes S/N	300		295.00	295
1999 Magnolia (12 x 12) S/N	300		125.00	125
1998 Magnolia Bouquet S/N	300		195.00	195
1995 Magnolia Path S/N	300	1996	395.00	395
1999 Magnolia Serenade S/N	300		365.00	365
2000 The Manor House S/N	300		195.00	195
1994 Mermaid Callas S/N	300	1997	295.00	295-450
1995 Nature's Retreat S/N	300	1999	395.00	395
1998 Nature's Tranquility S/N	300		365.00	365
1992 Old Stone House S/N	300	1997	195.00	195
1996 Oriental Splendor S/N	300	1998	395.00	395
1992 Palladian Windows S/N	300	1995	295.00	295-395
1999 Phalaenopsis w/Blue Butterflies S/N	300		145.00	145
1999 Poetic Melody S/N	300		425.00	425
1996 Potted Pansies S/N	300		145.00	145
1996 Potted Petunias S/N	300		145.00	145
1998 Rhaposdy in Yellow & Blue S/N	300		195.00	195
1994 Romantic Reflection S/N	300	1997	395.00	395-450
1998 Romantic Reverie S/N	300		195.00	195
1997 Rose Arbor S/N	300		295.00	295
1994 Rose Fairies S/N	300	1997	295.00	295
1996 Rose Memories S/N	300		295.00	295
1999 Roses (13 x 13) S/N	300		145.00	145
1993 Roses in Bloom S/N	300	1995	395.00	395
1996 Spring Bulbs S/N	300		195.00	195
1994 Spring Conservatory S/N	300	1997	395.00	395
1995 Spring Garden S/N	300		395.00	395
1996 Summer Bouquet S/N	300		195.00	195
1998 Sunflower Bouquet S/N	300		195.00	195
1995 Sweet Bounty S/N	300		295.00	295
1999 Tulips (13 x 13) S/N	300		145.00	145
1992 Victorian Pavillion S/N	300	1997	195.00	195
1992 Vintage Bouquet S/N	300	1995	395.00	395
1996 Wisteria Dreams S/N	300		295.00	295
1993 Woodland Path S/N	300		495.00	495

Liu - Unframed Canvas Transfers Angels Among Us - L. Liu

YEAR ISSUE	EDITION LIMIT	YEAR RETD.	ISSUE PRICE	*QUOTE U.S.$
1997 Angel of Light S/N	300		395.00	395
1997 Angel of Love S/N	300		395.00	395
1996 Guardian Angel S/N	300		395.00	395
1996 Messengers of Love S/N	300		250.00	250
1996 Protectors of Peace S/N	300		250.00	250

Liu - Unframed Canvas Transfers Celestial Symphony Series - L. Liu

YEAR ISSUE	EDITION LIMIT	YEAR RETD.	ISSUE PRICE	*QUOTE U.S.$
1995 Flute Interlude S/N	300		145.00	145
1995 French Horn Melody S/N	300		145.00	145
1995 Piano Sonata S/N	300		145.00	145
1995 Violin Concerto S/N	300	1998	145.00	76-145

Liu - Unframed Canvas Transfers The Music Room Series - L. Liu

YEAR ISSUE	EDITION LIMIT	YEAR RETD.	ISSUE PRICE	*QUOTE U.S.$
1991 The Music Room S/N	300	1992	395.00	700-900
1992 The Music Room II-Nutcracker S/N	300	1993	395.00	600
1994 The Music Room III-Composer's Retreat S/N	300	1994	395.00	500
1995 The Music Room IV-Swan Melody S/N	300		425.00	425
1996 The Music Room V-Morning Serenade S/N	300		395.00	395
1999 Homage to Beethoven-Symphony No. 9 S/N	300		205.00	205
1999 Homage to Mozart-The Marriage of Figaro S/N	300		295.00	295
1997 The Music Room VI-Romantic Overture S/N	300		425.00	425
1999 The Music Room VII-Afternoon Repose S/N	300		425.00	425
1997 Clarinet Ensemble S/N	300		395.00	395
1996 Harmonic Duet S/N	300		195.00	195
1996 Musical Trio S/N	300		195.00	195

McDonald - M. McDonald

YEAR ISSUE	EDITION LIMIT	YEAR RETD.	ISSUE PRICE	*QUOTE U.S.$
1988 Amaryllis Dancer S/N	1,000	1999	55.00	55
1988 Lily Queen S/N	1,000	1999	55.00	55

Islandia International

Single Issues - S. Etem

YEAR ISSUE	EDITION LIMIT	YEAR RETD.	ISSUE PRICE	*QUOTE U.S.$
1998 Bluebird of Happiness	1,500		95.00	95
1998 The Miracle of Life	1,500		95.00	95

Lightpost Publishing

Kinkade Member's Only Collectors' Society - T. Kinkade

YEAR ISSUE	EDITION LIMIT	YEAR RETD.	ISSUE PRICE	*QUOTE U.S.$
1992 Skater's Pond	Closed	N/A	295.00	995-1045
1992 Morning Lane	Closed	N/A	Gift	595
1994 Collector's Cottage I	Closed	1995	315.00	550-775
1994 Painter of Light Book	Closed	1995	Gift	100-125
1995 Lochavan Cottage	Closed	1995	295.00	595-895
1995 Gardens Beyond Autumn Gate-pencil sketch	Closed	1995	Gift	110-125
1996 Julianne's Cottage-Keepsake Box	Closed	1996	Gift	50-69
1996 Skater's Pond Sketch Portfolio Edition	Closed	1997	75.00	89
1996 Julianne's Cottage Library Print	Closed	1997	50.00	75-95
1996 Meadowood Cottage (canvas framed)	4,950	1997	375.00	650-775
1996 Meadowood Cottage (paper unframed)	950	1997	150.00	225-345
1997 Simpler Times are Better Times	Closed	1997	Gift	50
1997 The Village Inn Library Print	Closed	1998	65.00	95
1997 Collectors' Cottages Portfolio Edition	Closed	1998	175.00	195-275
1997 Home is Where the Heart Is	Closed	1998	295.00	500-1000
1998 Let Your Light Shine	Closed	1998	Gift	50
1998 A Light In The Storm	Closed	1998	295.00	295
1998 Clearing Storms	Closed	1999	49.50	50
1999 Open Gate, Sussex	Closed	1999	Gift	N/A
1999 Teacup Cottage	Closed	1999	95.00	95
1999 Olde Porterfield Tea Room	Closed	1999	295.00	295
2000 Pye Corner Cottage	Yr.Iss.		Gift	N/A
2000 Teacup Cottage Classic (9 x 12)	Yr.Iss.		199.00	199
2000 Teacup Cottage Classic (12 x 16)	Yr.Iss.		299.00	299
2000 Teacup Cottage Teapot	2,950		100.00	100
2000 Beacon of Hope	Yr.Iss.		49.50	50
2000 The Sea of Tranquility	Yr.Iss.		49.50	50
2000 Light In The Storm	Yr.Iss.		49.50	50

Kinkade-Event Pieces - T. Kinkade

YEAR ISSUE	EDITION LIMIT	YEAR RETD.	ISSUE PRICE	*QUOTE U.S.$
1996 Candlelight Cottage (canvas framed)	Closed	1997	375.00	525-823
1996 Candlelight Cottage (canvas unframed)	Closed	1997	275.00	395-415
1996 Candlelight Cottage (paper framed)	Closed	1997	325.00	325-445
1996 Candlelight Cottage (paper unframed)	Closed	1997	150.00	150-195
1996 Lamplight Village	Closed	1997	Gift	80-125
1996 We Wish You a Merry Christmas	Closed	1997	70.00	70-125
1997 Chandler's Cottage Inspirational Print (Mother's Day Event)	Closed	1997	80.00	75-125

Kinkade-Archival Paper/Canvas-Combined Edition-Framed - T. Kinkade

YEAR ISSUE	EDITION LIMIT	YEAR RETD.	ISSUE PRICE	*QUOTE U.S.$
1989 Blue Cottage (Paper)	Retrd.	1993	125.00	295-461
1989 Blue Cottage (Canvas)	Retrd.	1993	495.00	1695
1990 Moonlit Village (Paper)	Closed	1992	225.00	695-1795
1990 Moonlit Village (Canvas)	Closed	1992	595.00	2950-4795
1986 New York, 1932 (Paper)	Closed	N/A	225.00	750-2395
1986 New York, 1932 (Canvas)	Closed	N/A	595.00	2950-5095
1989 Skating in the Park (Paper) S/N	750	1994	225.00	1295-1895
1989 Skating in the Park (Canvas) S/N	750	1994	595.00	3595

Kinkade-Canvas Editions-Framed - T. Kinkade

YEAR ISSUE	EDITION LIMIT	YEAR RETD.	ISSUE PRICE	*QUOTE U.S.$
1991 Afternoon Light, Dogwood A/P	98	1991	615.00	2350-2900
1991 Afternoon Light, Dogwood P/P	100	N/A	795.00	795-3275
1991 Afternoon Light, Dogwood R/P	200	N/A	N/A	3525
1991 Afternoon Light, Dogwood S/N	980	N/A	515.00	1500-2995
1992 Amber Afternoon A/P	200	1992	715.00	2295-2385
1992 Amber Afternoon G/P	200	1992	765.00	1795-2365
1992 Amber Afternoon P/P	100	1992	815.00	2350-2555
1992 Amber Afternoon S/N	980	N/A	615.00	2468-2495
1994 Autumn at Ashley's Cottage A/P	395	1999	590.00	695-777
1994 Autumn at Ashley's Cottage G/P	990		590.00	750
1994 Autumn at Ashley's Cottage P/P	315		640.00	800
1994 Autumn at Ashley's Cottage S/N	3,950		440.00	600
1991 The Autumn Gate A/P	200	N/A	695.00	3995-5155
1991 The Autumn Gate P/P	100	N/A	795.00	5765
1991 The Autumn Gate R/E	Closed	1992	695.00	4000-5000
1991 The Autumn Gate R/P	200	N/A	N/A	6105-6255
1991 The Autumn Gate S/N	980	N/A	595.00	4395-5095
1995 Autumn Lane A/P	295	1998	800.00	775-1005
1995 Autumn Lane G/P	740	2000	750.00	1005
1995 Autumn Lane P/P	240		850.00	1005
1995 Autumn Lane S/N	2,950		650.00	855
1994 Beacon of Hope A/P	275	1994	765.00	1450-2005
1994 Beacon of Hope G/P	685	1994	765.00	1893-2005
1994 Beacon of Hope P/P	220	N/A	815.00	1945-2055
1994 Beacon of Hope S/N	2,750	1994	615.00	1395-1663
1996 Beginning of a Perfect Day A/P	295	1996	1240.00	2095-2695
1996 Beginning of a Perfect Day G/P	740	1998	1240.00	2075-2145
1996 Beginning of a Perfect Day P/P	240	1999	1290.00	1860-2145
1996 Beginning of a Perfect Day S/N	2,950	1998	1090.00	2095-2180
1996 Beginning of a Perfect Day S/P	95	N/A	3270.00	8900-11000
1993 Beside Still Waters A/P	400	N/A	615.00	3500-3595
1993 Beside Still Waters G/P	490	N/A	665.00	3500-3595
1993 Beside Still Waters P/P	100	N/A	715.00	3295-3700
1993 Beside Still Waters S/N	980	N/A	515.00	3095-3495
1995 Beside Still Waters S/P	95	N/A	2325.00	9500-10351
1993 Beyond Autumn Gate A/P	600	1993	915.00	3468-4995
1993 Beyond Autumn Gate G/P	500	N/A	965.00	3490-5100
1995 Beyond Autumn Gate P/P	100	N/A	1045.00	3400-5500
1993 Beyond Autumn Gate S/N	1,750	N/A	815.00	2200-3850
1995 Beyond Autumn Gate S/P	95	N/A	N/A	8000-13000
1997 Beyond Spring Gate A/P	345	1997	1300.00	3850-4505
1997 Beyond Spring Gate G/P	865	1997	1300.00	3850-4505
1997 Beyond Spring Gate P/P	280	1997	1350.00	3995-4705
1997 Beyond Spring Gate S/N	3,450	1997	1150.00	3695-3995
1997 Beyond Spring Gate S/P	95	1997	3450.00	6995-13500
1993 The Blessings of Autumn A/P	300	1994	715.00	2295-2305
1993 The Blessings of Autumn G/P	250	1994	765.00	1495-2605
1993 The Blessings of Autumn P/P	100	1994	815.00	2150-2845
1993 The Blessings of Autumn S/N	1,250	1994	615.00	2195-2698
1993 The Blessings of Autumn S/P	95	1999	3750.00	7550
1994 The Blessings of Spring A/P	275	1994	665.00	1210-1282
1994 The Blessings of Spring G/P	685		665.00	1210
1994 The Blessings of Spring P/P	220		715.00	1305
1994 The Blessings of Spring S/N	2,750	1994	515.00	750-1055
1995 Blessings of Summer A/P	495		1015.00	1285
1995 Blessings of Summer G/P	1,240		965.00	1285
1995 Blessings of Summer P/P	400		1065.00	1335
1995 Blessings of Summer S/N	4,950		865.00	1135
1998 Block Island A/P (12 x 18)	490		775.00	800
1998 Block Island A/P (18 x 27)	490		940.00	1005
1998 Block Island G/P (12 x 18)	860		775.00	800
1998 Block Island G/P (18 x 27)	860		940.00	1005
1998 Block Island P/P (12 x 18)	300		825.00	850
1998 Block Island P/P (18 x 27)	300		990.00	1055
1998 Block Island R/E (12 x 18)	200		1800.00	1950
1998 Block Island R/E (18 x 27)	200		2250.00	2565
1998 Block Island S/N (12 x 18)	2,450		625.00	650
1998 Block Island S/N (18 x 27)	2,450		790.00	855
1998 Block Island S/P (18 x 27)	100		3750.00	4275
1995 Blossom Bridge A/P	295		730.00	865
1995 Blossom Bridge G/P	740		680.00	865
1995 Blossom Bridge P/P	240		780.00	915
1995 Blossom Bridge S/N	2,950		580.00	715
1995 Blossom Bridge S/P	95		1740.00	3575
1992 Blossom Hill Church A/P	200	1994	715.00	2455-2595
1992 Blossom Hill Church P/P	100	1999	815.00	22416-2695
1992 Blossom Hill Church R/E	Closed	1993	695.00	1600-2495
1992 Blossom Hill Church R/P	Closed	1993	N/A	2905-3195
1992 Blossom Hill Church S/N	980	1994	615.00	1650-2238
1991 Boston A/P	50	N/A	615.00	2095-4150
1991 Boston P/P	25	N/A	715.00	2495-4350
1991 Boston S/N	550	N/A	515.00	3195-3503
1999 Boulevard Lights, Paris A/P (18 x 27)	590		1005.00	1005
1999 Boulevard Lights, Paris A/P (24 x 36)	590		1510.00	1510
1999 Boulevard Lights, Paris G/P (18 x 27)	1,100		1005.00	1005
1999 Boulevard Lights, Paris G/P (24 x 36)	1,100		1510.00	1510
1999 Boulevard Lights, Paris P/P (18 x 27)	530		1055.00	1055
1999 Boulevard Lights, Paris P/P (24 x 36)	530		1560.00	1560
1999 Boulevard Lights, Paris R/E (18 x 27)	240		2565.00	2565
1999 Boulevard Lights, Paris R/E (24 x 36)	240		4080.00	4080
1999 Boulevard Lights, Paris S/N (18 x 27)	2,950		855.00	855
1999 Boulevard Lights, Paris S/N (24 x 36)	2,950		1360.00	1360
1999 Boulevard Lights, Paris S/P (18 x 27)	120		4275.00	4275
1999 Boulevard Lights, Paris S/P (24 x 36)	120		6800.00	6800
1997 Bridge of Faith A/P	395	1997	1300.00	3795-4716
1997 Bridge of Faith G/P	990	1997	1300.00	3895-4295
1997 Bridge of Faith P/P	320	1997	1350.00	3555-3995
1997 Bridge of Faith S/N	3,950	1997	1150.00	3000-4256
1997 Bridge of Faith S/P	95	1997	3450.00	6000-13950
1992 Broadwater Bridge A/P	200	N/A	615.00	2195-3575
1992 Broadwater Bridge G/P	200	N/A	665.00	2350-3725
1992 Broadwater Bridge P/P	100	N/A	715.00	3795-4075
1992 Broadwater Bridge S/N	980	N/A	495.00	2250-3195
1995 Brookside Hideaway A/P	395	1995	695.00	1195-1475
1995 Brookside Hideaway G/P	990	1998	695.00	995-1050
1995 Brookside Hideaway P/P	320		745.00	1745
1995 Brookside Hideaway S/N	3,950	1996	545.00	850-1065
1991 Carmel, Delores Street and the Tuck Box Tea Room A/P	200	1992	745.00	2950-4545
1991 Carmel, Delores Street and the Tuck Box Tea Room P/P	100	1992	845.00	4805-5105
1991 Carmel, Delores Street and the Tuck Box Tea Room R/P	Closed	1992	745.00	3950
1991 Carmel, Delores Street and the Tuck Box Tea Room S/N	980	1992	645.00	3995-4445
1989 Carmel, Ocean Avenue A/P	50	N/A	795.00	4200-6995
1989 Carmel, Ocean Avenue P/P	25	N/A	N/A	6825-7295
1989 Carmel, Ocean Avenue S/N	935	N/A	595.00	5222-5995
1999 Carmel, Sunset on Ocean Ave. A/P (18 x 27)	990		940.00	1005
1999 Carmel, Sunset on Ocean Ave. A/P (24 x 36)	990		1410.00	1510
1999 Carmel, Sunset on Ocean Ave. A/P (28 x 42)	990		2100.00	2145

*Quotes have been rounded up to nearest dollar

GRAPHICS

YEAR ISSUE	EDITION LIMIT	YEAR RETD.	ISSUE PRICE	*QUOTE U.S.$
1999 Carmel, Sunset on Ocean Ave. E/P (24 x 36)	980	1999	1410.00	1410-1510
1999 Carmel, Sunset on Ocean Ave. G/P (18 x 27)	1,750		940.00	1005
1999 Carmel, Sunset on Ocean Ave. G/P (24 x 36)	1,750		1410.00	1510
1999 Carmel, Sunset on Ocean Ave. G/P (28 x 42)	1,750		2100.00	2145
1999 Carmel, Sunset on Ocean Ave. P/P (18 x 27)	880		990.00	1055
1999 Carmel, Sunset on Ocean Ave. P/P (24 x 36)	880		1460.00	1560
1999 Carmel, Sunset on Ocean Ave. P/P (28 x 42)	880		2150.00	2195
1999 Carmel, Sunset on Ocean Ave. R/E (18 x 27)	400		2250.00	2565
1999 Carmel, Sunset on Ocean Ave. R/E (24 x 36)	400		3600.00	4080
1999 Carmel, Sunset on Ocean Ave. R/E (28 x 42)	400		5850.00	5985
1999 Carmel, Sunset on Ocean Ave. S/N (18 x 27)	4,950		790.00	855
1999 Carmel, Sunset on Ocean Ave. S/N (24 x 36)	4,950		1260.00	1360
1999 Carmel, Sunset on Ocean Ave. S/N (28 x 42)	4,950		1950.00	1995
1999 Carmel, Sunset on Ocean Ave. S/P (18 x 27)	200	2000	3750.00	4275
1999 Carmel, Sunset on Ocean Ave. S/P (24 x 36)	200	2000	6000.00	6450-6800
1999 Carmel, Sunset on Ocean Ave. S/P (28 x 42)	200		9750.00	9975
1991 Cedar Nook Cottage A/P	200	1991	315.00	595-1100
1991 Cedar Nook Cottage P/P	100	1991	515.00	945-1200
1991 Cedar Nook Cottage R/E	200	1991	315.00	700-1015
1991 Cedar Nook Cottage R/P	Closed	1991	N/A	1045-1300
1991 Cedar Nook Cottage S/N	1,960	1991	195.00	785-892
1990 Chandler's Cottage A/P	100	N/A	N/A	2775-4750
1990 Chandler's Cottage P/P	50	N/A	N/A	4895-5050
1990 Chandler's Cottage S/N	550	N/A	495.00	2350-2995
1992 Christmas At the Ahwahnee A/P	200	1999	615.00	885-1025
1992 Christmas At the Ahwahnee G/P	200	1998	665.00	880-1045
1992 Christmas At the Ahwahnee P/P	100	N/A	715.00	985-1888
1992 Christmas At the Ahwahnee S/N	980	1999	515.00	875-895
XX Christmas at the Courthouse S/N	2,950	N/A	N/A	2445-3500
1990 Christmas Cottage 1990 A/P	100	N/A	295.00	1595-3100
1990 Christmas Cottage 1990 P/P	50	N/A	N/A	3145-3445
1990 Christmas Cottage 1990 S/N	550	N/A	N/A	2123-2265
1991 Christmas Eve A/P	200	1991	515.00	1295-1841
1991 Christmas Eve P/P	100	1991	615.00	2545-2950
1991 Christmas Eve R/E	Retrd.	1991	495.00	2186-2595
1991 Christmas Eve R/P	Closed	1991	N/A	2645-3050
1991 Christmas Eve S/N	980	N/A	415.00	1195-1582
1994 Christmas Memories A/P	345	1996	695.00	895-1145
1994 Christmas Memories G/P	860		695.00	1145
1994 Christmas Memories P/P	275		745.00	1245
1994 Christmas Memories S/N	3,450	1995	545.00	650-823
1994 Christmas Tree Cottage A/P	395		590.00	750
1994 Christmas Tree Cottage G/P	990		590.00	750
1994 Christmas Tree Cottage P/P	315		640.00	800
1994 Christmas Tree Cottage S/N	3,950		440.00	600
1996 A Christmas Welcome A/P	295	1996	675.00	725-750
1996 A Christmas Welcome G/P	740		675.00	750
1996 A Christmas Welcome P/P	240		725.00	800
1996 A Christmas Welcome S/N	2,950		525.00	600
1996 A Christmas Welcome S/P	95		2750.00	3000
1997 Clearing Storms A/P (18 x 27)	590	1998	875.00	1695-1795
1997 Clearing Storms A/P (24 x 36)	590	1998	1300.00	1975-2301
1997 Clearing Storms G/P (18 x 27)	740	1998	875.00	1495-1893
1997 Clearing Storms G/P (24 x 36)	740	1998	1300.00	1995-2495
1997 Clearing Storms P/P (18 x 27)	360	1999	925.00	1705-1805
1997 Clearing Storms P/P (24 x 36)	360	1998	1350.00	1895-2595
1997 Clearing Storms R/E (18 x 27)	240	1998	2175.00	2895-3195
1997 Clearing Storms R/E (24 x 36)	240	1998	3450.00	3895-4595
1997 Clearing Storms S/N (18 x 27)	2,950	1998	725.00	1395-1628
1997 Clearing Storms S/N (24 x 36)	2,950	1998	1150.00	1875-2008
1997 Clearing Storms S/P (18 x 27)	120	N/A	3625.00	5200-9000
1997 Clearing Storms S/P (24 x 36)	120	N/A	5750.00	6000-10500
1997 Cobblestone Brooke A/P	495	1998	1300.00	1495-2045
1997 Cobblestone Brooke G/P	1,240	1998	1300.00	1495-2045
1997 Cobblestone Brooke P/P	400	1998	1350.00	1510-2095
1997 Cobblestone Brooke S/N	4,950	1997	1150.00	1360-1622
1997 Cobblestone Brooke S/P	95	1998	3450.00	6500-9000
1996 Cobblestone Lane A/P	295	1996	1125.00	2450-2876
1996 Cobblestone Lane G/P	740	1996	1125.00	2195-3895
1996 Cobblestone Lane P/P	240	1996	1175.00	2350-2195
1996 Cobblestone Lane S/N	2,950	1996	975.00	2350-2795
1996 Cobblestone Lane S/P	95	1996	2925.00	7900-9500
1998 Cobblestone Village A/P (18 x 24)	1,190		940.00	1005
1998 Cobblestone Village A/P (25 1/2 x 34)	1,190		1410.00	1510
1998 Cobblestone Village A/P (30 x 40)	990		2100.00	2145
1998 Cobblestone Village G/P (18 x 24)	2,100		940.00	1005
1998 Cobblestone Village G/P (25 1/2 x 34)	2,100		1410.00	1510
1998 Cobblestone Village G/P (30 x 40)	1,750		2100.00	2145
1998 Cobblestone Village P/P (18 x 24)	1,100		990.00	1055
1998 Cobblestone Village P/P (25 1/2 x 34)	1,100		1460.00	1560
1998 Cobblestone Village P/P (30 x 40)	900		2150.00	2195
1998 Cobblestone Village R/E (18 x 24)	480		2250.00	2565
1998 Cobblestone Village R/E (25 1/2 x 34)	480		3600.00	4080
1998 Cobblestone Village R/E (30 x 40)	400		5850.00	5985
1998 Cobblestone Village S/N (18 x 24)	5,950		790.00	855
1998 Cobblestone Village S/N (25 1/2 x 34)	5,950		1260.00	1360
1998 Cobblestone Village S/N (30 x 40)	4,950		1950.00	1995
1998 Cobblestone Village S/P (18 x 24)	240		3750.00	4275
1998 Cobblestone Village S/P (25 1/2 x 34)	240		6000.00	6800
1998 Cobblestone Village S/P (30 x 40)	200		9750.00	9975
1999 Conquering the Storms A/P (18 x 27)	590		940.00	1005
1999 Conquering the Storms A/P (24 x 36)	590		1410.00	1510
1999 Conquering the Storms A/P (28 x 42)	590		2100.00	2145
1999 Conquering the Storms E/P (24 x 36)	Closed	1999	1410.00	1550
1999 Conquering the Storms G/P (18 x 27)	1,100		940.00	1005
1999 Conquering the Storms G/P (24 x 36)	1,100	1999	1410.00	1410-1510
1999 Conquering the Storms G/P (28 x 42)	1,100		2100.00	2145
1999 Conquering the Storms P/P (18 x 27)	530		990.00	1005
1999 Conquering the Storms P/P (24 x 36)	530		1460.00	1560
1999 Conquering the Storms P/P (28 x 42)	530		2150.00	2195
1999 Conquering the Storms R/E (18 x 27)	240		2250.00	2565
1999 Conquering the Storms R/E (24 x 36)	240		3600.00	4080
1999 Conquering the Storms R/E (28 x 42)	240		5850.00	5985
1999 Conquering the Storms S/N (18 x 27)	2,950	2000	790.00	775-855
1999 Conquering the Storms S/N (24 x 36)	2,950		1260.00	1360
1999 Conquering the Storms S/N (28 x 42)	2,950		1950.00	1995
1999 Conquering the Storms S/P (18 x 27)	120	1999	3750.00	3750-4250
1999 Conquering the Storms S/P (24 x 36)	120	1998	6000.00	6000-6800
1999 Conquering the Storms S/P (28 x 42)	120		9750.00	9975
1992 Cottage-By-The-Sea A/P	200	1992	715.00	2395-3005
1992 Cottage-By-The-Sea G/P	200	N/A	765.00	2250-3155
1992 Cottage-By-The-Sea P/P	100	1992	815.00	3345-3455
1992 Cottage-By-The-Sea S/N	980	N/A	615.00	2150-2845
1992 Country Memories A/P	200	1992	515.00	1425-1595
1992 Country Memories G/P	200	1997	565.00	1295-1695
1992 Country Memories P/P	100	1999	615.00	1600-1745
1992 Country Memories S/N	980	1994	395.00	1095-1395
1994 Creekside Trail A/P	198	1999	840.00	985-1005
1994 Creekside Trail G/P	500	1999	840.00	965-1005
1994 Creekside Trail P/P	160	2000	890.00	1015
1994 Creekside Trail S/N	1,984		690.00	815
1994 Days of Peace A/P	198	1999	840.00	940-1005
1994 Days of Peace G/P	496	1999	840.00	940-1005
1994 Days of Peace P/P	160	2000	890.00	1055
1994 Days of Peace S/N	1,984		690.00	855
1995 Deer Creek Cottage A/P	295	1996	615.00	800-970
1995 Deer Creek Cottage G/P	740	1999	565.00	800-970
1995 Deer Creek Cottage P/P	240	1999	665.00	950-1020
1995 Deer Creek Cottage S/N	2,950	1998	465.00	820-900
1995 Deer Creek Cottage S/P	95	1999	1395.00	3000
1994 Dusk in the Valley A/P	198		840.00	1005
1994 Dusk in the Valley G/P	500		840.00	1005
1994 Dusk in the Valley P/P	160		890.00	1055
1994 Dusk in the Valley S/N	1,984		690.00	855
1994 Emerald Isle Cottage A/P	275	1994	665.00	995-1225
1994 Emerald Isle Cottage G/P	685	1998	665.00	1195-1225
1994 Emerald Isle Cottage P/P	220	2000	715.00	1250-1375
1994 Emerald Isle Cottage S/N	2,750	1998	515.00	1150
1993 End of a Perfect Day I A/P	400	1994	615.00	2695-3395
1993 End of a Perfect Day I G/P	300	N/A	665.00	2895-3595
1993 End of a Perfect Day I P/P	100	N/A	715.00	2800-3895
1993 End of a Perfect Day I S/N	1,250	1994	515.00	2495-3095
1995 End of a Perfect Day I S/P	95	1996	2325	8800-13050
1994 End of a Perfect Day II A/P	495	1994	965.00	3795-3945
1994 End of a Perfect Day II G/P	1,240	1994	965.00	3095-3935
1994 End of a Perfect Day II P/P	400	N/A	1015.00	4105-4195
1994 End of a Perfect Day II S/N	4,950	1995	815.00	2300-3695
1995 End of a Perfect Day III A/P	495	1995	1145.00	1825-2595
1995 End of a Perfect Day III G/P	1,240	1998	1145.00	1995-2595
1995 End of a Perfect Day III P/P	400	1998	1195.00	2095-2695
1995 End of a Perfect Day III S/N	4,950	1996	995.00	1795-2395
1989 Entrance to the Manor House A/P	50	1996	595.00	2325-2365
1989 Entrance to the Manor House P/P	25	N/A	N/A	2495-2665
1989 Entrance to the Manor House S/N	550	N/A	495.00	3500
1989 Evening at Merritt's Cottage A/P	50	N/A	595.00	2495-4150
1989 Evening at Merritt's Cottage P/P	25	N/A	N/A	4350-4395
1989 Evening at Merritt's Cottage S/N	Closed	N/A	495.00	1095-2295
1992 Evening at Swanbrooke Cottage Thomashire A/P	200	N/A	715.00	2650-4095
1992 Evening at Swanbrooke Cottage Thomashire G/P	200	N/A	765.00	2650-4195
1992 Evening at Swanbrooke Cottage Thomashire P/P	100	N/A	815.00	4330-4395
1992 Evening at Swanbrooke Cottage Thomashire S/N	980	N/A	615.00	2575-3795
1992 Evening Carolers A/P	200	1999	415.00	580
1992 Evening Carolers G/P	200	1998	465.00	570-580
1992 Evening Carolers P/P	100	2000	515.00	630
1992 Evening Carolers S/N	1,960		315.00	430
1999 Evening Glow A/P (12 x 16)	590		750.00	750
1999 Evening Glow A/P (16 x 20)	590		865.00	865
1999 Evening Glow G/P (12 x 16)	1,110		750.00	750
1999 Evening Glow G/P (16 x 20)	1,110		865.00	965
1999 Evening Glow P/P (12 x 16)	530		800.00	800
1999 Evening Glow P/P (16 x 20)	530		915.00	915
1999 Evening Glow R/E (12 x 16)	240		1650.00	1650
1999 Evening Glow R/E (16 X 20)	240		2145.00	2145
1999 Evening Glow S/N (12 x 16)	2,950		600.00	600
1999 Evening Glow S/N (16 x 20)	2,950		715.00	715
1999 Evening Glow S/P (12 x 16)	120		3000.00	3000
1999 Evening Glow S/P (16 x 20)	120		3575.00	3575
1995 Evening in the Forest A/P	495		695.00	865
1995 Evening in the Forest G/P	1,240		645.00	865
1995 Evening in the Forest P/P	400		745.00	915
1995 Evening in the Forest S/N	4,950		545.00	715
1999 Evening Majesty A/P (18 x 27)	990		1005.00	1005
1999 Evening Majesty A/P (24 x 36)	990		1510.00	1510
1999 Evening Majesty A/P (28 x 42)	990		2145.00	2145
1999 Evening Majesty G/P (18 x 27)	1,750		1005.00	1005
1999 Evening Majesty G/P (24 x 36)	1,750		1510.00	1510
1999 Evening Majesty G/P (28 x 42)	1,750		2145.00	2145
1999 Evening Majesty P/P (18 x 27)	900		1055.00	1055
1999 Evening Majesty P/P (24 x 36)	900		1560.00	1560
1999 Evening Majesty P/P (28 x 42)	900		2195.00	2195
1999 Evening Majesty R/E (18 x 27)	400		2565.00	2565
1999 Evening Majesty R/E (24 x 36)	400		4080.00	4080
1999 Evening Majesty R/E (28 x 42)	400		5985.00	5985
1999 Evening Majesty S/N (18 x 27)	4,950		855.00	855
1999 Evening Majesty S/N (24 x 36)	4,950		1360.00	1360
1999 Evening Majesty S/N (28 x 42)	4,950		1995.00	1995
1999 Evening Majesty S/P (18 x 27)	200		4275.00	4275
1999 Evening Majesty S/P (24 x 36)	200		6800.00	6800
1999 Evening Majesty S/P (28 x 42)	200		9975.00	9975
1998 Everett's Cottage A/P (16 x 20)	1,190		800.00	865
1998 Everett's Cottage A/P (20 x 24)	1,190		900.00	1005
1998 Everett's Cottage A/P (24 x 30)	990		1150.00	1285
1998 Everett's Cottage G/P (16 x 20)	2,100		835.00	865
1998 Everett's Cottage G/P (20 x 24)	2,100		940.00	1005
1998 Everett's Cottage G/P (24 x 30)	1,750		1200.00	1285
1998 Everett's Cottage P/P (16 x 20)	1,100		885.00	915
1998 Everett's Cottage P/P (20 x 24)	1,100		990.00	1005
1998 Everett's Cottage P/P (24 x 30)	600		1250.00	1335
1998 Everett's Cottage R/E (16 x 20)	480		1950.00	2145
1998 Everett's Cottage R/E (20 x 24)	480		2250.00	2565
1998 Everett's Cottage R/E (24 x 30)	400		3000.00	3405
1998 Everett's Cottage S/N (16 x 20)	5,950		650.00	715
1998 Everett's Cottage S/N (20 x 24)	5,950		750.00	855
1998 Everett's Cottage S/N (24 x 30)	4,950		1000.00	1135
1998 Everett's Cottage S/P (16 x 20)	240		3260.00	3575
1998 Everett's Cottage S/P (20 x 24)	240		3750.00	4275
1998 Everett's Cottage S/P (24 x 30)	200		5000.00	5675
1993 Fisherman's Wharf San Francisco A/P	275	1993	1065.00	1750-2520
1993 Fisherman's Wharf San Francisco G/P	550	N/A	1115.00	1410-2520
1993 Fisherman's Wharf San Francisco P/P	230	1998	1165.00	2000-2295
1993 Fisherman's Wharf San Francisco S/N	2,750	1995	965.00	1145-1595
1991 Flags Over The Capitol A/P	200	1999	715.00	1500
1991 Flags Over The Capitol P/P	100	1999	815.00	1195-1395
1991 Flags Over The Capitol R/E	Retrd.	N/A	695.00	1000-1345
1991 Flags Over The Capitol R/P	200	N/A	N/A	1395-1560
1991 Flags Over The Capitol S/N	980	1998	615.00	1195-1350
1999 The Forest Chapel A/P (20 x 24)	590	2000	940.00	1205-1495
1999 The Forest Chapel A/P (24 x 30)	590	2000	1200.00	1700-1750
1999 The Forest Chapel G/P (20 x 24)	1,100	1999	940.00	1455-1495
1999 The Forest Chapel G/P (24 x 30)	1,100	1999	1200.00	1735-1795
1999 The Forest Chapel P/P (20 x 24)	530	2000	990.00	1505-1595
1999 The Forest Chapel P/P (24 x 30)	530	2000	1250.00	1785-1895
1999 The Forest Chapel R/E (20 x 24)	240	2000	2250.00	3215-3295
1999 The Forest Chapel R/E (24 x 30)	240	2000	3000.00	3495-4195
1999 The Forest Chapel S/N (20 x 24)	2,950	1999	790.00	1055-1305
1999 The Forest Chapel S/N (24 x 30)	2,950	2000	1050.00	1135-1595
1999 The Forest Chapel S/P (20 x 24)	120	2000	3750.00	4500-4795
1999 The Forest Chapel S/P (24 x 30)	120	2000	5000.00	5600-6375
1999 Foxglove Cottage A/P (16 x 20)	790		835.00	865
1999 Foxglove Cottage A/P (20 x 24)	790		940.00	1005
1999 Foxglove Cottage A/P (24 x 30)	790		1200.00	1285
1999 Foxglove Cottage G/P (16 x 20)	1,400		835.00	865
1999 Foxglove Cottage G/P (20 x 24)	1,400		940.00	1005
1999 Foxglove Cottage G/P (24 x 30)	1,400		1200.00	1285
1999 Foxglove Cottage P/P (16 x 20)	710		885.00	915
1999 Foxglove Cottage P/P (20 x 24)	710		990.00	1055
1999 Foxglove Cottage P/P (24 x 30)	710		1250.00	1335
1999 Foxglove Cottage R/E (16 x 20)	320		1950.00	2145
1999 Foxglove Cottage R/E (20 x 24)	320		2250.00	2565
1999 Foxglove Cottage R/E (24 x 30)	320		3000.00	3405
1999 Foxglove Cottage S/N (16 x 20)	3,950		685.00	715
1999 Foxglove Cottage S/N (20 x 24)	3,950		790.00	855
1999 Foxglove Cottage S/N (24 x 30)	3,950		1050.00	1135
1999 Foxglove Cottage S/P (16 x 20)	160		3250.00	3575
1999 Foxglove Cottage S/P (20 x 24)	160		3750.00	4275
1999 Foxglove Cottage S/P (24 x 30)	160		5000.00	5675
1994 Garden Beyond Autumn Gate S/N	Closed	1996	1025.00	2195-2495
1997 Garden of Prayer A/P (18 x 24)	990	1998	900.00	1795-1995
1997 Garden of Prayer A/P (25 1/2 x 34)	990	1998	1350.00	2595-2845
1997 Garden of Prayer A/P (30 x 40)	790	1999	2100.00	2995-3095
1997 Garden of Prayer G/P (18 x 24)	1,750	1998	900.00	1140-1995
1997 Garden of Prayer G/P (25 1/2 x 34)	1,750	1998	1350.00	2595-2895
1997 Garden of Prayer G/P (30 x 40)	1,400	1999	2100.00	2895-3095
1997 Garden of Prayer P/P (18 x 24)	600	1999	950.00	1190-2045
1997 Garden of Prayer P/P (25 1/2 x 34)	600	1998	1400.00	1710-2895
1997 Garden of Prayer P/P (30 x 40)	480	1999	2150.00	2350-3145
1997 Garden of Prayer R/E (18 x 24)	400	1999	2250.00	3295-3950
1997 Garden of Prayer R/E (25 1/2 x 34)	400	1999	3600.00	5950-6495
1997 Garden of Prayer R/E (30 x 40)	320	1999	5850.00	6250-7995
1997 Garden of Prayer S/N (18 x 24)	4,950	1998	750.00	1495-1795
1997 Garden of Prayer S/N (25 1/2 x 34)	4,950	1998	1200.00	2350-2995
1997 Garden of Prayer S/N (30 x 40)	3,950	1999	1950.00	2595-2895
1997 Garden of Prayer S/P (18 x 24)	200	1998	3750.00	6400-6500
1997 Garden of Prayer S/P (25 1/2 x 34)	200	1998	6000.00	9400-10950
1997 Garden of Prayer S/P (30 x 40)	160	1999	9750.00	9750-12950
1993 The Garden of Promise A/P	400	N/A	715.00	2695-3445
1993 The Garden of Promise G/P	300	N/A	765.00	2795-3544
1993 The Garden of Promise P/P	100	N/A	815.00	3495-3745
1993 The Garden of Promise S/N	1,250	1994	615.00	2700-3200
1993 The Garden of Promise S/P	95	N/A	2800.00	8600-11600
1992 The Garden Party A/P	200		615.00	865
1992 The Garden Party G/P	200	1999	665.00	750-865
1992 The Garden Party P/P	100		715.00	915
1992 The Garden Party S/N	980		515.00	715
1998 Gardens Beyond Spring Gate A/P (18 x 24)	1,190		900.00	1005
1998 Gardens Beyond Spring Gate A/P (25 1/2 x 34)	1,190	1999	1350.00	1495-1825

*Quotes have been rounded up to nearest dollar

YEAR ISSUE	EDITION LIMIT	YEAR RETD.	ISSUE PRICE	*QUOTE U.S.$
1998 Gardens Beyond Spring Gate A/P (30 x 40)	1,190		2100.00	2145
1998 Gardens Beyond Spring Gate G/P (18 x 24)	2,100		900.00	1005
1998 Gardens Beyond Spring Gate G/P (25 1/2 x 34)	2,100	1999	1350.00	1525-1825
1998 Gardens Beyond Spring Gate G/P (30 x 40)	2,100		2100.00	2145
1998 Gardens Beyond Spring Gate P/P (18 x 24)	710		950.00	1055
1998 Gardens Beyond Spring Gate P/P (25 1/2 x 34)	710	1999	1400.00	1875-1950
1998 Gardens Beyond Spring Gate P/P (30 x 40)	710		2150.00	2195
1998 Gardens Beyond Spring Gate R/E (18 x 24)	480		2250.00	2565
1998 Gardens Beyond Spring Gate R/E (25 1/2 x 34)	480		3600.00	3775
1998 Gardens Beyond Spring Gate R/E (30 x 40)	480		5850.00	5985
1998 Gardens Beyond Spring Gate S/N (18 x 24)	5,950		750.00	855
1998 Gardens Beyond Spring Gate S/N (25 1/2 x 34)	5,950	1998	1200.00	1335-1645
1998 Gardens Beyond Spring Gate S/N (30 x 40)	5,950		1950.00	1995
1998 Gardens Beyond Spring Gate S/P (18 x 24)	240		3750.00	4275
1998 Gardens Beyond Spring Gate S/P (25 1/2 x 34)	240	1999	6000.00	5700-6995
1998 Gardens Beyond Spring Gate S/P (30 x 40)	240		9750.00	9975
1993 Glory of Evening A/P	400	1993	365.00	900-2535
1993 Glory of Evening G/P	490	N/A	365.00	695-2635
1993 Glory of Evening P/P	100	1994	830.00	1300-2835
1993 Glory of Evening S/N	1,980	1994	315.00	1850-2235
1993 Glory of Evening S/P	95	1994	2000.00	4000-9500
1993 Glory of Morning A/P	400	1993	365.00	730-2535
1993 Glory of Morning G/P	490	1993	365.00	875-2635
1993 Glory of Morning P/P	100	1993	830.00	1300-2835
1993 Glory of Morning S/N	1,980	1994	315.00	1850-2235
1993 Glory of Morning S/P	95	1993	2000.00	4000-9500
1993 Glory of Winter A/P	300		715.00	1005
1993 Glory of Winter G/P	250	1999	715.00	695-1005
1993 Glory of Winter P/P	175		815.00	1055
1993 Glory of Winter S/N	1,250		615.00	855
1995 Golden Gate Bridge, San Francisco A/P	395	1996	1240.00	2495-2620
1995 Golden Gate Bridge, San Francisco G/P	990	N/A	1190.00	1995-2620
1995 Golden Gate Bridge, San Francisco P/P	320	1996	1290.00	2395-2845
1995 Golden Gate Bridge, San Francisco S/N	3,950	1996	1090.00	1795-2395
1995 Golden Gate Bridge, San Francisco S/P	95	1996	3270.00	7995-13950
1994 Guardian Castle A/P	475		1015.00	1285
1994 Guardian Castle G/P	1,190		1015.00	1285
1994 Guardian Castle P/P	380		1065.00	1335
1994 Guardian Castle S/N	4,750		865.00	1135
1993 Heather's Hutch A/P	400	1993	515.00	1150-1350
1993 Heather's Hutch G/P	300	N/A	565.00	995-1450
1993 Heather's Hutch P/P	100	1999	615.00	1600
1993 Heather's Hutch S/N	1,250	N/A	415.00	995-1195
1994 Hidden Arbor A/P	375		665.00	865
1994 Hidden Arbor G/P	940		665.00	865
1994 Hidden Arbor P/P	300		715.00	915
1994 Hidden Arbor S/N	3,750		515.00	715
1990 Hidden Cottage I A/P	100	N/A	595.00	1995-5000
1990 Hidden Cottage I P/P	50	N/A	N/A	2295-5645
1990 Hidden Cottage I S/N	550	N/A	495.00	2150-2500
1993 Hidden Cottage II A/P	400	1993	615.00	1050-1550
1993 Hidden Cottage II G/P	400	1995	665.00	1150-1645
1993 Hidden Cottage II P/P	100	1995	715.00	1695-1800
1993 Hidden Cottage II S/N	1,480	1994	515.00	950-1395
1993 Hidden Cottage II S/P	95	1995	3250.00	4025-6950
1994 Hidden Gazebo A/P	240	1994	665.00	1175-1645
1994 Hidden Gazebo G/P	600	1994	665.00	1025-1645
1994 Hidden Gazebo P/P	190	1999	715.00	1725-1795
1994 Hidden Gazebo S/N	2,400	1994	515.00	1050-1365
1998 A Holiday Gathering A/P (12 x 16)	1,390		725.00	750
1998 A Holiday Gathering A/P (18 x 24)	1,390		940.00	1005
1998 A Holiday Gathering A/P (25 1/2 x 34)	1,390		1410.00	1510
1998 A Holiday Gathering G/P (12 x 16)	2,450		725.00	750
1998 A Holiday Gathering G/P (18 x 24)	2,450		940.00	1005
1998 A Holiday Gathering G/P (25 1/2 x 34)	2,450		1410.00	1510
1998 A Holiday Gathering P/P (12 x 16)	1,250		775.00	800
1998 A Holiday Gathering P/P (18 x 24)	1,250		990.00	1055
1998 A Holiday Gathering P/P (25 1/2 x 34)	1,250		1460.00	1560
1998 A Holiday Gathering R/E (12 x 16)	550		1650.00	1800
1998 A Holiday Gathering R/E (18 x 24)	550		2250.00	2565
1998 A Holiday Gathering R/E (25 1/2 x 34)	550		3600.00	4080
1998 A Holiday Gathering S/N (12 x 16)	6,950		575.00	600
1998 A Holiday Gathering S/N (18 x 24)	6,950		790.00	855
1998 A Holiday Gathering S/N (25 1/2 x 34)	6,950		1260.00	1360
1998 A Holiday Gathering S/P (12 x 16)	280		2750.00	3000
1998 A Holiday Gathering S/P (18 x 24)	280		3750.00	4276
1998 A Holiday Gathering S/P (25 1/2 x 34)	280		6000.00	6800
1996 Hollyhock House A/P	395	1999	730.00	835-865
1996 Hollyhock House G/P	990		730.00	865
1996 Hollyhock House P/P	320		780.00	915
1996 Hollyhock House S/N	3,950		580.00	715
1996 Hollyhock House S/P	95	1998	1740.00	4400-5950
1991 Home For The Evening A/P	200	1994	315.00	875-1225
1991 Home For The Evening P/P	100	N/A	415.00	1485-1525
1991 Home For The Evening S/N	980	N/A	215.00	850-995
1991 Home For The Holidays A/P	200	1991	715.00	2495-4055
1991 Home For The Holidays P/P	100	1991	815.00	4195-4355
1991 Home For The Holidays R/E	N/A	1991	695.00	3995-4195
1991 Home For The Holidays S/N	980	N/A	615.00	1995-3895
1992 Home is Where the Heart Is I A/P	200	N/A	715.00	2050-3545
1992 Home is Where the Heart Is I G/P	200	N/A	765.00	1165-3645
1992 Home is Where the Heart Is I P/P	100	N/A	815.00	2695-3805
1992 Home is Where the Heart Is I S/N	980	N/A	615.00	2295-3205
1996 Home is Where the Heart Is II A/P	495	1997	840.00	1165-1495
1996 Home is Where the Heart Is II G/P	1,240		840.00	1165
1996 Home is Where the Heart Is II P/P	400		890.00	1215
1996 Home is Where the Heart Is II S/N	Closed	1997	690.00	1015-1495
1996 Home is Where the Heart Is II S/P	95	1997	2070.00	5570-6995
1993 Homestead House A/P	300	1996	715.00	940-1675
1993 Homestead House G/P	250	N/A	765.00	1100-1775
1993 Homestead House P/P	100	1999	815.00	1895
1993 Homestead House S/N	1,250	1996	615.00	995-1495
1998 Hometown Bridge A/P (18 x 27)	1,190		940.00	1005
1998 Hometown Bridge A/P (24 x 36)	1,190		1410.00	1510
1998 Hometown Bridge A/P (28 x 42)	990		2100.00	2145
1998 Hometown Bridge G/P (18 x 27)	2,100		940.00	1005
1998 Hometown Bridge G/P (24 x 36)	2,100		1410.00	1510
1998 Hometown Bridge G/P (28 x 42)	1,750		2100.00	2145
1998 Hometown Bridge P/P (18 x 27)	1,100		990.00	1005
1998 Hometown Bridge P/P (24 x 36)	1,100		1460.00	1560
1998 Hometown Bridge P/P (28 x 42)	900		2150.00	2195
1998 Hometown Bridge R/E (18 x 27)	480		2250.00	2565
1998 Hometown Bridge R/E (24 x 36)	480		3600.00	4080
1998 Hometown Bridge R/E (28 x 42)	400		5850.00	5985
1998 Hometown Bridge S/N (18 x 27)	5,950		790.00	855
1998 Hometown Bridge S/N (24 x 36)	5,950		1260.00	1360
1998 Hometown Bridge S/N (28 x 42)	4,950		1950.00	1995
1998 Hometown Bridge S/P (18 x 27)	240		3750.00	4275
1998 Hometown Bridge S/P (24 x 36)	240		6000.00	6800
1998 Hometown Bridge S/P (28 x 42)	200		9750.00	9975
1995 Hometown Chapel A/P	495	1999	1045.00	1285
1995 Hometown Chapel G/P	1,240	1999	995.00	1200-1285
1995 Hometown Chapel P/P	400		1095.00	1335
1995 Hometown Chapel S/N	4,950		895.00	1135
1996 Hometown Evening A/P	295	1996	1070.00	3255-3595
1996 Hometown Evening G/P	740	1996	1070.00	2895-3595
1996 Hometown Evening P/P	240	1996	1120.00	3455-3795
1996 Hometown Evening S/N	2,950	1996	920.00	2695-3495
1996 Hometown Evening S/P	95	1996	2760.00	8950-13050
1997 Hometown Lake A/P	495	1998	1125.00	2550-2895
1997 Hometown Lake G/P	1,240	1998	1125.00	2625-2895
1997 Hometown Lake P/P	400	1998	1175.00	2405-3045
1997 Hometown Lake S/N	4,950	1998	975.00	2250-2645
1997 Hometown Lake S/P	125	1998	3900.00	8800-12050
1995 Hometown Memories I A/P	495	1995	1015.00	2395-2995
1995 Hometown Memories I G/P	1,240	N/A	1015.00	2830-2995
1995 Hometown Memories I P/P	400	N/A	1065.00	2850-3195
1995 Hometown Memories I S/N	4,950	1996	865.00	2250-2695
2000 Hometown Morning A/P (24 x 30)	790		1285.00	1285
2000 Hometown Morning A/P (25 1/2 x 34)	790		1510.00	1510
2000 Hometown Morning A/P (30 x 40)	790		2145.00	2145
2000 Hometown Morning G/P (24 x 30)	1,400		1285.00	1285
2000 Hometown Morning G/P (25 1/2 x 34)	1,400		1510.00	1510
2000 Hometown Morning G/P (30 x 40)	1,400		2145.00	2145
2000 Hometown Morning P/P (24 x 30)	710		1335.00	1335
2000 Hometown Morning P/P (25 1/2 x 34)	710		1560.00	1560
2000 Hometown Morning P/P (30 x 40)	710		2195.00	2195
2000 Hometown Morning R/E (25 1/2 x 34)	320		4080.00	4080
2000 Hometown Morning R/E (30 x 40)	320		N/A	N/A
2000 Hometown Morning S/N (24 x 30)	3,950		1135.00	1135
2000 Hometown Morning S/N (25 1/2 x 34)	3,950		1360.00	1360
2000 Hometown Morning S/N (30 x 40)	3,950		1995.00	1995
2000 Hometown Morning S/P (25 1/2 x 34)	160		6800.00	6800
1996 Hyde Street and the Bay, SF A/P	395	1996	1125.00	2695-3045
1996 Hyde Street and the Bay, SF G/P	980	1996	1125.00	2595-3045
1996 Hyde Street and the Bay, SF P/P	320	1996	1175.00	2705-3195
1996 Hyde Street and the Bay, SF S/N	3,950	1996	975.00	2495-2795
1996 Hyde Street and the Bay, SF S/P	95	1996	2925.00	5250-15500
1992 Julianne's Cottage A/P	200	N/A	515.00	2600-3375
1992 Julianne's Cottage G/P	200	N/A	565.00	2400-3575
1992 Julianne's Cottage P/P	100	N/A	615.00	3595-3875
1992 Julianne's Cottage S/N	980	N/A	415.00	2250-2995
1999 Lakeside Hideaway A/P (12 x 16)	590		725.00	750
1999 Lakeside Hideaway A/P (16 x 20)	590		835.00	865
1999 Lakeside Hideaway A/P (18 x 24)	590		940.00	1005
1999 Lakeside Hideaway G/P (12 x 16)	1,100		725.00	750
1999 Lakeside Hideaway G/P (16 x 20)	1,100		835.00	865
1999 Lakeside Hideaway G/P (18 x 24)	1,100		940.00	1005
1999 Lakeside Hideaway P/P (12 x 16)	530		775.00	800
1999 Lakeside Hideaway P/P (16 x 20)	530		885.00	915
1999 Lakeside Hideaway P/P (18 x 24)	530		990.00	1055
1999 Lakeside Hideaway R/E (12 x 16)	240		1650.00	1800
1999 Lakeside Hideaway R/E (16 x 20)	240		1950.00	2145
1999 Lakeside Hideaway R/E (18 x 24)	240		2250.00	2565
1999 Lakeside Hideaway S/N (12 x 16)	2,950		575.00	600
1999 Lakeside Hideaway S/N (16 x 20)	2,950		685.00	715
1999 Lakeside Hideaway S/N (18 x 24)	2,950		790.00	855
1999 Lakeside Hideaway S/P (12 x 16)	120		2750.00	3000
1999 Lakeside Hideaway S/P (16 x 20)	120		3250.00	3575
1999 Lakeside Hideaway S/P (18 x 24)	120		3750.00	4275
1996 Lamplight Bridge A/P	295	1996	730.00	950-1495
1996 Lamplight Bridge G/P	740	N/A	730.00	1395-1450
1996 Lamplight Bridge P/P	240	1999	780.00	1495-1545
1996 Lamplight Bridge S/N	2,950	1996	580.00	895-1295
1996 Lamplight Bridge S/P	95	1996	1740.00	3250-6950
1993 Lamplight Brooke A/P	400	1994	715.00	1095-3255
1993 Lamplight Brooke G/P	330	1994	765.00	1950-3405
1993 Lamplight Brooke P/P	230	1999	815.00	3555-3595
1993 Lamplight Brooke S/N	1,650	1994	615.00	1750-2995
1994 Lamplight Inn A/P	275	1994	765.00	940-1530
1994 Lamplight Inn G/P	685	1998	765.00	940-1530
1994 Lamplight Inn P/P	220	1999	815.00	1055-1645
1994 Lamplight Inn S/N	2,750	1994	615.00	855-1345
1993 Lamplight Lane A/P	200	N/A	715.00	3195-4855
1993 Lamplight Lane G/P	200	1994	765.00	3195-4955
1995 Lamplight Lane P/P	100	N/A	815.00	2995-5155
1993 Lamplight Lane S/N	980	N/A	615.00	2795-4595
1995 Lamplight Lane S/P	Closed	N/A	N/A	9000-13950
2000 Lamplight Manor A/P (18 x 27)	990		1005.00	1005
2000 Lamplight Manor A/P (24 x 36)	990		1510.00	1510
2000 Lamplight Manor A/P (28 x 42)	990		2145.00	2145
2000 Lamplight Manor G/P (18 x 27)	1,750		1005.00	1005
2000 Lamplight Manor G/P (24 x 36)	1,750		1510.00	1510
2000 Lamplight Manor G/P (28 x 42)	1,750		2145.00	2145
2000 Lamplight Manor P/P (18 x 27)	900		1055.00	1055
2000 Lamplight Manor P/P (24 x 36)	900		1560.00	1560
2000 Lamplight Manor P/P (28 x 42)	900		2195.00	2195
2000 Lamplight Manor R/E (24 x 36)	400		4080.00	4080
2000 Lamplight Manor S/N (18 x 27)	4,950		855.00	855
2000 Lamplight Manor S/N (24 x 36)	4,950		1360.00	1360
2000 Lamplight Manor S/N (28 x 42)	4,950		1995.00	1995
2000 Lamplight Manor S/P (24 x 36)	200		6800.00	6800
1995 Lamplight Village A/P	495	1995	800.00	1266-1855
1995 Lamplight Village G/P	1,210	N/A	800.00	1381-1855
1995 Lamplight Village P/P	400	1999	850.00	1496-2095
1995 Lamplight Village S/N	4,950	1995	650.00	1395-1695
1995 A Light in the Storm A/P	395	1995	800.00	1295-1595
1995 A Light in the Storm G/P	990	1998	750.00	1295-1595
1995 A Light in the Storm P/P	320	1999	850.00	1325-1695
1995 A Light in the Storm S/N	3,950	1996	650.00	1095-1355
1995 A Light in the Storm S/P	95	N/A	2070.00	6400-10950
1996 The Light of Peace A/P	345	1996	1300.00	3855-4350
1996 The Light of Peace G/P	865	1996	1300.00	3855-4195
1996 The Light of Peace P/P	280	1996	1350.00	4195-4345
1996 The Light of Peace S/N	3,450	1996	1150.00	3450-3950
1996 The Light of Peace S/P	95	1996	3450.00	12500-13950
1995 The Lights of Home S/N (8x10)	2,500	N/A	195.00	625-945
1996 Lilac Gazebo A/P	295	1997	615.00	725-750
1996 Lilac Gazebo G/P	740		615.00	750
1996 Lilac Gazebo P/P	240		665.00	800
1996 Lilac Gazebo S/N	2,950		465.00	600
1996 Lilac Gazebo S/P	95	1998	1395.00	2750-3510
1998 Lingering Dusk A/P (16 x 20)	790		800.00	865
1998 Lingering Dusk A/P (20 x 24)	790		900.00	1005
1998 Lingering Dusk G/P (16 x 20)	1,400		800.00	865
1998 Lingering Dusk G/P (20 x 24)	1,400		900.00	1005
1998 Lingering Dusk P/P (16 x 20)	480		850.00	915
1998 Lingering Dusk P/P (20 x 24))	480		950.00	1005
1998 Lingering Dusk R/E (16 x 20)	320		1950.00	2145
1998 Lingering Dusk R/E (20 x 24)	320		2250.00	2565
1998 Lingering Dusk S/N (16 x 20)	3,950		650.00	715
1998 Lingering Dusk S/N (20 x 24)	3,950		750.00	855
1998 Lingering Dusk S/P (16 x 20)	160		3250.00	3575
1998 Lingering Dusk S/P (20 x 24)	160		3750.00	4275
1991 The Lit Path A/P	200	1991	315.00	595-975
1991 The Lit Path P/P	100	1998	415.00	895-1025
1991 The Lit Path R/E	Closed	1991	395.00	495-1095
1991 The Lit Path S/N	1,960	1994	215.00	550-795
1995 Main Street Celebration A/P	125		800.00	1005
1995 Main Street Celebration P/P	400		850.00	1055
1995 Main Street Celebration S/N	1,250		650.00	855
1995 Main Street Courthouse A/P	125		800.00	1005
1995 Main Street Courthouse P/P	400		850.00	1055
1995 Main Street Courthouse S/N	1,250		650.00	855
1995 Main Street Matinee A/P	125		800.00	1005
1995 Main Street Matinee P/P	400		850.00	1005
1995 Main Street Matinee S/N	1,250		650.00	855
1995 Main Street Trolley A/P	125		800.00	1005
1995 Main Street Trolley P/P	400		850.00	1055
1995 Main Street Trolley S/N	1,250		650.00	855
1991 McKenna's Cottage A/P	200	N/A	615.00	835-1365
1991 McKenna's Cottage P/P	100	1998	715.00	1395-1515
1991 McKenna's Cottage R/E	200	N/A	615.00	700-2045
1991 McKenna's Cottage S/N	980	1995	515.00	750-1125
1992 Miller's Cottage, Thomashire A/P	200	N/A	615.00	2250-2300
1992 Miller's Cottage, Thomashire G/P	200	N/A	665.00	1495-2400
1992 Miller's Cottage, Thomashire P/P	100	1998	715.00	2645
1992 Miller's Cottage, Thomashire S/N	980	1994	515.00	1950-2045
1994 Moonlight Lane I A/P	240	1995	665.00	695-895
1994 Moonlight Lane I G/P	600	1999	665.00	835-895
1994 Moonlight Lane I P/P	190		715.00	1045
1994 Moonlight Lane I S/N	2,400	1998	515.00	500-745
1985 Moonlight on the Riverfront S/N	260	N/A	715.00	1250-2645
1992 Moonlit Sleigh Ride A/P	200	1995	415.00	850-1015
1992 Moonlit Sleigh Ride G/P	200	1995	465.00	590-1105
1992 Moonlit Sleigh Ride P/P	100	2000	515.00	1115
1992 Moonlit Sleigh Ride S/N	1,960	1995	315.00	695-845
1995 Morning Dogwood A/P	495	1999	645.00	800
1995 Morning Dogwood G/P	1,240		645.00	800
1995 Morning Dogwood P/P	400		695.00	850
1995 Morning Dogwood S/N	4,950		495.00	650
1995 Morning Glory Cottage A/P	495	1997	695.00	795-1095
1995 Morning Glory Cottage G/P	1,240	1999	645.00	885-1095
1995 Morning Glory Cottage P/P	400		745.00	1195
1995 Morning Glory Cottage S/N	4,950	1998	545.00	715-895
1992 Morning Lane I A/P	Closed	N/A	N/A	2095-2135
1990 Morning Light A/P	N/A	N/A	695.00	2095-2895

*Quotes have been rounded up to nearest dollar

Lightpost Publishing
to Lightpost Publishing

GRAPHICS

YEAR ISSUE	EDITION LIMIT	YEAR RETD.	ISSUE PRICE	*QUOTE U.S.$
1998 Mountain Chapel A/P (16 x 20)	1,190		800.00	865
1998 Mountain Chapel A/P (24 x 30)	1,190		1150.00	1285
1998 Mountain Chapel A/P (32 x 40)	990		2100.00	2145
1998 Mountain Chapel G/P (16 x 20)	2,100		835.00	865
1998 Mountain Chapel G/P (24 x 30)	2,100	2000	1200.00	1285
1998 Mountain Chapel G/P (32 x 40)	1,750		2100.00	2145
1998 Mountain Chapel P/P (16 x 20)	1,100		885.00	915
1998 Mountain Chapel P/P (24 x 30)	1,100		1250.00	1335
1998 Mountain Chapel P/P (32 x 40)	600		2150.00	2195
1998 Mountain Chapel R/E (16 x 20)	480		1950.00	2145
1998 Mountain Chapel R/E (24 x 30)	480		3000.00	3405
1998 Mountain Chapel R/E (32 x 40)	400		5850.00	5985
1998 Mountain Chapel S/N (16 x 20)	5,950		650.00	715
1998 Mountain Chapel S/N (24 x 30)	5,950		1000.00	1135
1998 Mountain Chapel S/N (32 x 40)	4,950		1950.00	1995
1998 Mountain Chapel S/P (16 x 20)	240		3250.00	3575
1998 Mountain Chapel S/P (24 x 30)	240		5000.00	5000
1998 Mountain Chapel S/P (32 x 40)	200		9750.00	9975
1998 Mountain Majesty A/P (18 x 24)	790		990.00	1040
1998 Mountain Majesty A/P (25 1/2 x 34)	790	1999	1460.00	1510
1998 Mountain Majesty A/P (30 x 40)	790		2100.00	2145
1998 Mountain Majesty G/P (18 x 24)	1,400	2000	990.00	1040-1055
1998 Mountain Majesty G/P (25 1/2 x 34)	1,400	1999	1460.00	1510
1998 Mountain Majesty G/P (30 x 40)	1,400		2100.00	2145
1998 Mountain Majesty P/P (18 x 24)	710		1040.00	1090
1998 Mountain Majesty P/P (25 1/2 x 34)	710	2000	1510.00	1560
1998 Mountain Majesty P/P (30 x 40)	710		2150.00	2195
1998 Mountain Majesty R/E (18 x 24)	320		2250.00	2565
1998 Mountain Majesty R/E (25 1/2 x 34)	320		3600.00	4080
1998 Mountain Majesty R/E (30 x 40)	320		5850.00	5985
1998 Mountain Majesty S/N (18 x 24)	3,950	2000	840.00	775-890
1998 Mountain Majesty S/N (25 1/2 x 34)	3,950	1999	1310.00	1190-1360
1998 Mountain Majesty S/N (30 x 40)	3,950		1950.00	1995
1998 Mountain Majesty S/P (18 x 24)	160		3750.00	4275
1998 Mountain Majesty S/P (25 1/2 x 34)	160	1999	6000.00	5800-6800
1998 Mountain Majesty S/P (30 x 40)	160		9750.00	9975
1997 A New Day Dawning A/P	395	1997	1300.00	2405-3195
1997 A New Day Dawning G/P	990	1997	1300.00	3495-3618
1997 A New Day Dawning P/P	320	1998	1350.00	3495-4078
1997 A New Day Dawning S/N	3,950	1998	1150.00	1960-2945
1997 A New Day Dawning S/P	95	1997	3450.00	8800-11950
1992 Olde Porterfield Gift Shoppe A/P	200	1995	615.00	895-1295
1992 Olde Porterfield Gift Shoppe G/P	200	N/A	665.00	1150-1345
1992 Olde Porterfield Gift Shoppe P/P	100	2000	715.00	1445
1992 Olde Porterfield Gift Shoppe S/N	980	1994	515.00	895-1095
1991 Olde Porterfield Tea Room A/P	200	N/A	615.00	1495-2400
1991 Olde Porterfield Tea Room P/P	100	1998	715.00	2395-2600
1991 Olde Porterfield Tea Room R/E	Closed	1991	595.00	1500-2695
1991 Olde Porterfield Tea Room S/N	980	N/A	515.00	1295-2245
1999 Open Gate A/P (12 x 16)	790		725.00	750
1999 Open Gate A/P (16 x 20)	790		835.00	865
1999 Open Gate A/P (18 x 24)	790		940.00	1005
1999 Open Gate G/P (12 x 16)	1,400		725.00	750
1999 Open Gate G/P (16 x 20)	1,400		835.00	865
1999 Open Gate G/P (18 x 24)	1,400		940.00	1005
1999 Open Gate P/P (12 x 16)	710		775.00	800
1999 Open Gate P/P (16 x 20)	710		885.00	915
1999 Open Gate P/P (18 x 24)	710		990.00	1055
1999 Open Gate R/E (12 x 16)	320		1650.00	1800
1999 Open Gate R/E (16 x 20)	320		1950.00	2145
1999 Open Gate R/E (18 x 24)	320		2250.00	2565
1999 Open Gate S/N (12 x 16)	3,950		575.00	600
1999 Open Gate S/N (16 x 20)	3,950		685.00	715
1999 Open Gate S/N (18 x 24)	3,950		790.00	855
1999 Open Gate S/P (12 x 16)	160		2750.00	3000
1999 Open Gate S/P (16 x 20)	160		3250.00	3575
1999 Open Gate S/P (18 x 24)	160		3750.00	4275
1991 Open Gate, Sussex A/P	100	1994	315.00	750-1050
1991 Open Gate, Sussex P/P	100	1994	415.00	1105
1991 Open Gate, Sussex R/E	Closed	1992	295.00	595-1175
1991 Open Gate, Sussex S/N	980	1994	215.00	625-875
1993 Paris, City of Lights A/P	600	1994	715.00	2395-3595
1993 Paris, City of Lights G/P	600	N/A	765.00	2695-3595
1993 Paris, City of Lights P/P	200	1994	815.00	2895-3895
1993 Paris, City of Lights S/N	1,980	N/A	615.00	2195-3295
1993 Paris, City of Lights S/P	190	1994	3750.00	6500-13950
1994 Paris, Eiffel Tower A/P	275	1994	945.00	1395-2105
1994 Paris, Eiffel Tower G/P	685	1995	945.00	1825-2145
1994 Paris, Eiffel Tower P/P	220	1998	995.00	1525-2355
1994 Paris, Eiffel Tower S/N	2,750	1994	795.00	1595-1795
2000 A Peaceful Time A/P (12 x 16)	590		750.00	750
2000 A Peaceful Time A/P (16 x 20)	590		865.00	865
2000 A Peaceful Time A/P (18 x 24)	590		1005.00	1005
2000 A Peaceful Time G/P (12 x 16)	1,110		750.00	750
2000 A Peaceful Time G/P (16 x 20)	1,110		865.00	865
2000 A Peaceful Time G/P (18 x 24)	1,110		1005.00	1005
2000 A Peaceful Time P/P (12 x 16)	530		800.00	800
2000 A Peaceful Time P/P (16 x 20)	530		915.00	915
2000 A Peaceful Time P/P (18 x 24)	530		1055.00	1055
2000 A Peaceful Time R/E (18 x 24)	240		2565.00	2565
2000 A Peaceful Time S/N (12 x 16)	2,950		600.00	600
2000 A Peaceful Time S/N (16 x 20)	2,950		715.00	715
2000 A Peaceful Time S/N (18 x 24)	2,950		855.00	855
2000 A Peaceful Time S/P (18 x 24)	120		4275.00	4275
1995 Petals of Hope A/P	395	1998	730.00	855-1015
1995 Petals of Hope G/P	990	1998	680.00	1015-1195
1995 Petals of Hope P/P	320	1999	780.00	3350-3575
1995 Petals of Hope S/N	3,950	1999	580.00	835-995
1995 Petals of Hope S/P	95	1999	1740.00	3350-3575
1996 Pine Cove Cottage A/P	495		840.00	1005
1996 Pine Cove Cottage G/P	1,240		840.00	1005
1996 Pine Cove Cottage P/P	400		890.00	1055
1996 Pine Cove Cottage S/N	4,950		690.00	855
1996 Pine Cove Cottage S/P	95		2070.00	4275
1999 Pools of Serenity A/P (20 x 24)	990		1005.00	1005
1999 Pools of Serenity A/P (24 x 30)	990		1285.00	1285
1999 Pools of Serenity A/P (32 x 40)	990		2145.00	2145
1999 Pools of Serenity G/P (20 x 24)	1,750		1005.00	1005
1999 Pools of Serenity G/P (24 x 30)	1,750		1285.00	1285
1999 Pools of Serenity G/P (32 x 40)	1,750		2145.00	2145
1999 Pools of Serenity P/P (20 x 24)	900		1055.00	1055
1999 Pools of Serenity P/P (24 x 30)	900		1335.00	1335
1999 Pools of Serenity P/P (32 x 40)	900		2195.00	2195
1999 Pools of Serenity R/E (20 x 24)	400		2565.00	2565
1999 Pools of Serenity R/E (24 x 30)	400		3405.00	3405
1999 Pools of Serenity R/E (32 x 40)	400		5985.00	5985
1999 Pools of Serenity S/N (20 x 24)	4,950		855.00	855
1999 Pools of Serenity S/N (24 x 30)	4,950		1135.00	1135
1999 Pools of Serenity S/N (32 x 40)	4,950		1995.00	1995
1999 Pools of Serenity S/P (20 x 24)	200		4275.00	4275
1999 Pools of Serenity S/P (24 x 30)	200		5675.00	5675
1999 Pools of Serenity S/P (32 x 40)	200		9975.00	9975
1994 The Power & The Majesty A/P	275		765.00	1005
1994 The Power & The Majesty G/P	685		765.00	1005
1994 The Power & The Majesty P/P	220		815.00	1055
1994 The Power & The Majesty S/N	2,750		615.00	855
1999 Prince of Peace A/P (18 x 24)	390	2000	800.00	800
1999 Prince of Peace G/P (18 x 24)	700	1999	800.00	800-1295
1999 Prince of Peace P/P (18 x 24)	350	2000	850.00	850
1999 Prince of Peace S/N (18 x 24)	1,950	1999	650.00	1055-1200
1991 Pye Corner Cottage A/P	200	N/A	315.00	595-845
1991 Pye Corner Cottage P/P	100	1999	415.00	910-945
1991 Pye Corner Cottage R/E	Closed	N/A	295.00	695-1045
1991 Pye Corner Cottage R/P	200	N/A	N/A	1110-1145
1991 Pye Corner Cottage S/N	1,960	1996	215.00	645
1998 Quiet Evening A/P (16 x 20)	790		835.00	865
1998 Quiet Evening A/P (20 x 24)	790	2000	940.00	1005
1998 Quiet Evening A/P (24 x 30)	790		1200.00	1285
1998 Quiet Evening G/P (16 x 20)	1,400		835.00	865
1998 Quiet Evening G/P (20 x 24)	1,400	1999	940.00	790-1005
1998 Quiet Evening G/P (24 x 30)	1,400	1999	1200.00	1050-1285
1998 Quiet Evening P/P (16 x 20)	710		885.00	915
1998 Quiet Evening P/P (20 x 24)	710		990.00	1055
1998 Quiet Evening P/P (24 x 30)	710		1250.00	1335
1998 Quiet Evening R/E (16 x 20)	320		1950.00	2145
1998 Quiet Evening R/E (20 x 24)	320	2000	2250.00	2565
1998 Quiet Evening R/E (24 x 30)	320		3000.00	3405
1998 Quiet Evening S/N (16 x 20)	3,950		685.00	715
1998 Quiet Evening S/N (20 x 24)	3,950	2000	790.00	855-995
1998 Quiet Evening S/N (24 x 30)	3,950		1050.00	1135
1998 Quiet Evening S/P (16 x 20)	160		3250.00	3575
1998 Quiet Evening S/P (20 x 24)	160	2000	3750.00	3650-4275
1998 Quiet Evening S/P (24 x 30)	160		5000.00	5675
1988 Room with a View S/N	N/A	N/A	795.00	1750-2295
1990 Rose Arbor A/P	98	N/A	595.00	2100-2550
1990 Rose Arbor S/N	935	N/A	495.00	1695-2250
1996 Rose Gate A/P	295	1996	615.00	725-775
1996 Rose Gate G/P	740	1999	615.00	775
1996 Rose Gate P/P	230		665.00	825
1996 Rose Gate S/N	2,950	1999	465.00	625-750
1996 Rose Gate S/P	95	1998	1395.00	2750-4500
1994 San Francisco Market Street A/P	750		945.00	1015
1994 San Francisco Market Street G/P	1,875		945.00	1015
1994 San Francisco Market Street P/P	600		995.00	1065
1994 San Francisco Market Street S/N	7,500		795.00	865
1992 San Francisco, Nob Hill (California St.) A/P	Closed	N/A	715.00	6200-7115
1992 San Francisco, Nob Hill (California St.) G/P	200	N/A	765.00	6100-7145
1992 San Francisco, Nob Hill (California St.) P/P	100	N/A	815.00	5700-7965
1992 San Francisco, Nob Hill (California St.) S/N	980	N/A	615.00	5900-6945
1989 San Francisco, Union Square A/P	50	N/A	795.00	4500-7155
1989 San Francisco, Union Square P/P	25	N/A	N/A	7705
1989 San Francisco, Union Square S/N	935	N/A	595.00	4000-6605
1998 The Sea of Tranquility A/P (18 x 27)	1,190		940.00	1005
1998 The Sea of Tranquility A/P (24 x 36)	1,190		1410.00	1510
1998 The Sea of Tranquility A/P (28 x 42)	1,190		2100.00	2145
1998 The Sea of Tranquility G/P (18 x 27)	2,100		940.00	1005
1998 The Sea of Tranquility G/P (24 x 36)	2,100		1410.00	1510
1998 The Sea of Tranquility G/P (28 x 42)	2,100		2100.00	2145
1998 The Sea of Tranquility P/P (18 x 27)	1,100		990.00	1055
1998 The Sea of Tranquility P/P (24 x 36)	1,100		1460.00	1560
1998 The Sea of Tranquility P/P (28 x 42)	1,100		2150.00	2195
1998 The Sea of Tranquility R/E (18 x 27)	480		2250.00	2565
1998 The Sea of Tranquility R/E (24 x 36)	480		3600.00	4080
1998 The Sea of Tranquility R/E (28 x 42)	480		5850.00	5985
1998 The Sea of Tranquility S/N (18 x 27)	5,950		790.00	855
1998 The Sea of Tranquility S/N (24 x 36)	5,950		1260.00	1360
1998 The Sea of Tranquility S/N (28 x 42)	5,950		1950.00	1995
1998 The Sea of Tranquility S/P (18 x 27)	240		3750.00	4275
1998 The Sea of Tranquility S/P (24 x 36)	240		6000.00	6800
1998 The Sea of Tranquility S/P (28 x 42)	200		9750.00	9975
2000 Seaside Village A/P (18 x 24)	400		1005.00	1005
2000 Seaside Village A/P (24 x 30)	400		1285.00	1285
2000 Seaside Village G/P (18 x 24)	700		1005.00	1005
2000 Seaside Village G/P (24 x 30)	700		1285.00	1285
2000 Seaside Village P/P (18 x 24)	360		1055.00	1055
2000 Seaside Village P/P (24 x 30)	360		1335.00	1335
2000 Seaside Village S/N (18 x 24)	2,000		855.00	855
2000 Seaside Village S/N (24 x 30)	2,000		1135.00	1135
1992 Silent Night A/P	200	N/A	515.00	1495-2100
1992 Silent Night G/P	200	N/A	565.00	1495-2150
1992 Silent Night P/P	100	N/A	615.00	1750-2295
1992 Silent Night S/N	980	N/A	415.00	1295-2150
1995 Simpler Times I A/P	345	1998	840.00	940-1005
1995 Simpler Times I G/P	870		790.00	1005
1995 Simpler Times I P/P	280		890.00	1055
1995 Simpler Times I S/N	3,450		690.00	855
1995 Simpler Times I S/P	95		2070.00	4275
1990 Spring At Stonegate A/P	100	N/A	515.00	1150-1325
1990 Spring At Stonegate P/P	50	N/A	615.00	1345-1425
1990 Spring At Stonegate S/N	550	1995	415.00	795-1095
1996 Spring Gate A/P	395	1997	1240.00	2495-2835
1996 Spring Gate G/P	990	1998	1240.00	2195-2935
1996 Spring Gate P/P	320	1997	1290.00	2645-3255
1996 Spring Gate S/N	3,950	1998	1090.00	2485-2695
1996 Spring Gate S/P	95	1997	3270.00	6000-12950
1994 Spring in the Alps A/P	198		725.00	865
1994 Spring in the Alps G/P	500		725.00	865
1994 Spring in the Alps P/P	160		775.00	915
1994 Spring in the Alps S/N	1,984		575.00	715
1993 St. Nicholas Circle A/P	420	1995	715.00	1795-2070
1993 St. Nicholas Circle G/P	350	1995	765.00	2195-2220
1993 St. Nicholas Circle P/P	100	1995	815.00	2145-2405
1993 St. Nicholas Circle S/N	1,750	1994	615.00	1850
1993 St. Nicholas Circle S/P	95	1999	3750.00	5250-8950
1998 Stairway to Paradise A/P (18 x 24)	790		940.00	1005
1998 Stairway to Paradise A/P (25 1/2 x 34)	790		1410.00	1510
1998 Stairway to Paradise A/P (30 x 40)	790		2100.00	2145
1998 Stairway to Paradise G/P (18 x 24)	1,400	1999	940.00	940-1005
1998 Stairway to Paradise G/P (25 1/2 x 34)	1,400	1999	1410.00	1410-1510
1998 Stairway to Paradise G/P (30 x 40)	1,400		2100.00	2145
1998 Stairway to Paradise P/P (18 x 24)	710		990.00	1055
1998 Stairway to Paradise P/P (25 1/2 x 34)	710		1460.00	1560
1998 Stairway to Paradise P/P (30 x 40)	710		2150.00	2195
1998 Stairway to Paradise R/E (18 x 24)	320		2250.00	2565
1998 Stairway to Paradise R/E (25 1/2 x 34)	320		3600.00	4080
1998 Stairway to Paradise R/E (30 x 40)	320		5850.00	5985
1998 Stairway to Paradise S/N (18 x 24)	3,950		790.00	855
1998 Stairway to Paradise S/N (25 1/2 x 34)	3,950		1260.00	1360
1998 Stairway to Paradise S/N (30 x 40)	3,950		1950.00	1975
1998 Stairway to Paradise S/P (18 x 24)	160		3750.00	4275
1998 Stairway to Paradise S/P (25 1/2 x 34)	160	2000	6000.00	5800-6800
1998 Stairway to Paradise S/P (30 x 40)	N/A		9750.00	9975
1995 Stepping Stone Cottage A/P	295	1996	840.00	1245-1395
1995 Stepping Stone Cottage G/P	740	1998	790.00	1245-1525
1995 Stepping Stone Cottage P/P	240	2000	890.00	1345
1995 Stepping Stone Cottage S/N	2,950	1996	690.00	1055-1295
1995 Stepping Stone Cottage S/P	95	1998	2070.00	5295-6950
1998 Stillwater Bridge A/P (12 x 16)	990		700.00	750
1998 Stillwater Bridge A/P (18 x 24)	790		900.00	1005
1998 Stillwater Bridge G/P (12 x 16)	1,750		700.00	750
1998 Stillwater Bridge G/P (18 x 24)	1,400		900.00	1005
1998 Stillwater Bridge P/P (12 x 16)	600		750.00	800
1998 Stillwater Bridge P/P (18 x 24)	480		950.00	1055
1998 Stillwater Bridge R/E (12 x 16)	400		1650.00	1800
1998 Stillwater Bridge R/E (18 x 24)	320		2250.00	2565
1998 Stillwater Bridge S/N (12 x 16)	4,950		550.00	600
1998 Stillwater Bridge S/N (18 x 24)	3,950		750.00	855
1998 Stillwater Bridge S/P (12 x 16)	200		2750.00	3000
1998 Stillwater Bridge S/P (18 x 24)	160		3750.00	4275
1993 Stonehearth Hutch A/P	400	N/A	515.00	995-1455
1993 Stonehearth Hutch G/P	300	1994	565.00	1300-1525
1993 Stonehearth Hutch P/P	150	1999	615.00	1425-1600
1993 Stonehearth Hutch S/N	1,650	N/A	415.00	995-1195
1993 Stonehearth Hutch S/P	95	1999	2750.00	3750-3950
1993 Studio in the Garden A/P	400	1998	515.00	950-1195
1993 Studio in the Garden G/P	600	1999	565.00	725-1195
1993 Studio in the Garden P/P	100	1998	615.00	950-1345
1993 Studio in the Garden S/N	1,480	1996	415.00	825-995
1993 Studio in the Garden S/P	95	1995	N/A	2750-3000
1999 Summer Gate A/P (18 x 24)	1,190		940.00	1005
1999 Summer Gate A/P (25 1/2 x 34)	1,190		1410.00	1510
1999 Summer Gate A/P (30 x 40)	1,190		2100.00	2145
1999 Summer Gate G/P (18 x 24)	2,100		940.00	1005
1999 Summer Gate G/P (25 1/2 x 34)	2,100		1410.00	1510
1999 Summer Gate G/P (30 x 40)	2,100		2100.00	2145
1999 Summer Gate P/P (18 x 24)	1,100		990.00	1055
1999 Summer Gate P/P (25 1/2 x 34)	1,100		1460.00	1560
1999 Summer Gate P/P (30 x 40)	1,100		2150.00	2195
1999 Summer Gate R/E (18 x 24)	480		2250.00	2565
1999 Summer Gate R/E (25 1/2 x 34)	480		3600.00	4080
1999 Summer Gate R/E (30 x 40)	480		5850.00	5985
1999 Summer Gate S/N (18 x 24)	5,950		790.00	855
1999 Summer Gate S/N (25 1/2 x 34)	5,950		1260.00	1360
1999 Summer Gate S/N (30 x 40)	5,950		1950.00	1995
1999 Summer Gate S/P (18 x 24)	240		3750.00	4275
1999 Summer Gate S/P (25 1/2 x 34)	240		6000.00	6800
1999 Summer Gate S/P (30 x 40)	240		9750.00	9975
1992 Sunday at Apple Hill A/P	200	1993	615.00	1750-2245
1992 Sunday at Apple Hill G/P	200	N/A	665.00	1895-2315
1992 Sunday at Apple Hill P/P	100	N/A	715.00	2095-2575
1992 Sunday at Apple Hill S/N	980	1993	515.00	1695-1995
1996 Sunday Evening Sleigh Ride A/P	298	1996	875.00	1295-1595
1996 Sunday Evening Sleigh Ride G/P	740	1998	875.00	1595-2500
1996 Sunday Evening Sleigh Ride P/P	240	2000	925.00	1405
1996 Sunday Evening Sleigh Ride S/N	2,950	1997	725.00	1250-1395
1996 Sunday Evening Sleigh Ride S/P	95	1998	2175.00	3760-6950
1993 Sunday Outing A/P	200	N/A	615.00	1795-2385
1993 Sunday Outing G/P	200	N/A	665.00	1595-2498
1993 Sunday Outing P/P	100	N/A	715.00	2345-2615
1993 Sunday Outing S/N	980	N/A	515.00	1695-2145
1993 Sunday Outing S/P	95		3250.00	6950
1999 Sunrise A/P (20 x 24)	590		1005.00	1005
1999 Sunrise A/P (24 x 30)	590		1285.00	1285

*Quotes have been rounded up to nearest dollar

YEAR ISSUE	EDITION LIMIT	YEAR RETD.	ISSUE PRICE	*QUOTE U.S.$
1999 Sunrise A/P (32 x 40)	400		2145.00	2145
1999 Sunrise G/P (20 x 24)	1,110		1005.00	1005
1999 Sunrise G/P (24 x 30)	1,110		1285.00	1285
1999 Sunrise G/P (32 x 40)	700		2145.00	2145
1999 Sunrise P/P (20 x 24)	530		1005.00	1005
1999 Sunrise P/P (24 x 30)	530		1335.00	1335
1999 Sunrise P/P (32 x 40)	360		2195.00	2195
1999 Sunrise R/E (20 x 24)	240		2565.00	2565
1999 Sunrise R/E (24 x 30)	240		3405.00	3405
1999 Sunrise R/E (32 x 40)	160		5985.00	5985
1999 Sunrise S/N (20 x 24)	2,950		855.00	855
1999 Sunrise S/N (24 x 30)	2,950		1135.00	1135
1999 Sunrise S/N (32 x 40)	2,000		1995.00	1995
1999 Sunrise S/P (20 x 24)	120		4275.00	4275
1999 Sunrise S/P (24 x 30)	120		5675.00	5675
1999 Sunrise S/P (32 x 40)	80		9975.00	9975
1996 Sunset on Riverbend Farm A/P	495	1998	840.00	940-1005
1996 Sunset on Riverbend Farm G/P	1,240		840.00	1005
1996 Sunset on Riverbend Farm P/P	400		890.00	1055
1996 Sunset on Riverbend Farm S/N	4,950		690.00	855
1996 Sunset on Riverbend Farm S/P	95	1998	2070.00	4250-4950
1992 Sweetheart Cottage I A/P	200	1992	615.00	1595-1945
1992 Sweetheart Cottage I G/P	200	N/A	665.00	1595-1945
1992 Sweetheart Cottage I P/P	100	2000	715.00	1650-2055
1992 Sweetheart Cottage I S/N	980	N/A	515.00	1450-1695
1993 Sweetheart Cottage II A/P	400	1993	515.00	2195-3395
1993 Sweetheart Cottage II G/P	490	N/A	665.00	2750-2925
1993 Sweetheart Cottage II P/P	100	N/A	715.00	1995-3055
1993 Sweetheart Cottage II S/N	980	N/A	515.00	1995-2595
1993 Sweetheart Cottage II S/P	95	N/A	3250.00	8500-11450
1994 Sweetheart Cottage III A/P	165	1994	765.00	1005-1520
1994 Sweetheart Cottage III G/P	410	1998	765.00	940-1520
1994 Sweetheart Cottage III P/P	130	2000	815.00	1195-1665
1994 Sweetheart Cottage III S/N	1,650	1994	615.00	950-1295
1996 Teacup Cottage A/P	295	1997	875.00	1140-1325
1996 Teacup Cottage G/P	740	1998	875.00	1140-1325
1996 Teacup Cottage P/P	240	1999	925.00	1395
1996 Teacup Cottage S/N	2,950	1998	725.00	1025-1145
1999 Town Square A/P (18 x 27)	790		940.00	1005
1999 Town Square G/P (18 x 27)	1,400		940.00	1005
1999 Town Square P/P (18 x 27)	710		990.00	1055
1999 Town Square S/N (18 x 27)	3,950		790.00	855
1997 Twilight Cottage A/P	495	1998	N/A	860-1115
1997 Twilight Cottage G/P	1,240	1999	N/A	1115-1695
1997 Twilight Cottage P/P	400	1999	775.00	1195-1895
1997 Twilight Cottage S/N	4,950	1999	625.00	945-1345
1997 Twilight Cottage S/P	95	1997	3250.00	3700-4950
1999 Twilight Vista A/P (24 x 36)	790		1410.00	1510
1999 Twilight Vista G/P (24 x 36)	1,400		1410.00	1510
1999 Twilight Vista P/P (24 x 36)	480		1460.00	1560
1999 Twilight Vista R/E (24 x 36)	320		3600.00	4080
1999 Twilight Vista S/N (24 x 36)	3,950		1260.00	1360
1999 Twilight Vista S/P (24 x 36)	160		6000.00	6800
1997 Valley of Peace A/P	395	1997	1300.00	3695-3995
1997 Valley of Peace G/P	990	1997	1300.00	2655-3345
1997 Valley of Peace P/P	320	1998	1350.00	2855-3545
1997 Valley of Peace S/N	3,950	1998	1150.00	3045-3495
1997 Valley of Peace S/P	95	1997	3450.00	6000-13950
1996 Venice A/P	495		1240.00	1510
1996 Venice G/P	1,240		1240.00	1510
1996 Venice P/P	400		1290.00	1560
1996 Venice S/N	4,950		1090.00	1360
1996 Venice S/P	95		3270.00	6800
1992 Victorian Christmas I A/P	200	1992	715.00	3150-4255
1992 Victorian Christmas I G/P	200	1992	765.00	3095-4325
1992 Victorian Christmas I P/P	100	1992	815.00	4145-4550
1992 Victorian Christmas I S/N	980	1992	615.00	2895-3695
1993 Victorian Christmas II A/P	400	1994	715.00	2095-3425
1993 Victorian Christmas II G/P	300	1994	765.00	2095-3425
1993 Victorian Christmas II P/P	150	1994	815.00	3295-3755
1993 Victorian Christmas II S/N	980	1994	615.00	2395-3095
1993 Victorian Christmas II S/P	95	1994	3750.00	8200-12950
1994 Victorian Christmas III A/P	395	1994	800.00	940-1465
1994 Victorian Christmas III G/P	990	1998	800.00	1195-1465
1994 Victorian Christmas III P/P	300	1999	850.00	1250-1590
1994 Victorian Christmas III S/N	3,950	1997	650.00	855-1235
1995 Victorian Christmas IV S/N	2,330	1995	650.00	790-1295
1991 Victorian Evening A/P	200	1993	N/A	1795-1965
1991 Victorian Evening P/P	100	1993	N/A	1995-2165
1991 Victorian Evening S/N	980	1993	495.00	850-1765
1992 Victorian Garden I A/P	200	1993	915.00	3195-3765
1992 Victorian Garden I G/P	200	1993	965.00	2450-3865
1992 Victorian Garden I P/P	100	1993	1015.00	3845-4095
1992 Victorian Garden I S/N	980	1993	815.00	3195-3335
1997 Victorian Garden II A/P	395	1998	875.00	950-1005
1997 Victorian Garden II G/P	990	2000	875.00	950-1005
1997 Victorian Garden II P/P	320		925.00	1005
1997 Victorian Garden II S/N	3,950		725.00	855
1997 Victorian Garden II S/P	95	N/A	2175.00	4250-6950
1997 Village Christmas A/P (18 x 24)	990		900.00	1065
1997 Village Christmas A/P (25 1/2 x 34)	390	1998	1350.00	1585-1875
1997 Village Christmas G/P (18 x 24)	1,240	1999	900.00	1065
1997 Village Christmas G/P (25 1/2 x 34)	490	1998	1350.00	1585-1875
1997 Village Christmas P/P (18 x 24)	600		950.00	1140
1997 Village Christmas P/P (25 1/2 x 34)	240	1999	1400.00	1660-1955
1997 Village Christmas R/E (18 x 24)	325	1999	2250.00	2750-3600
1997 Village Christmas R/E (25 1/2 x 34)	150	1998	3600.00	3600-4450
1997 Village Christmas S/N (12 x 16)	2,450	1999	630.00	550-745
1997 Village Christmas S/N (18 x 24)	4,950	1999	750.00	775-890
1997 Village Christmas S/N (25 1/2 x 34)	1,950	1999	1200.00	1495-1695
1997 Village Christmas S/P (18 x 24)	155	1998	3750.00	3750-5950
1997 Village Christmas S/P (25 1/2 x 34)	80	1998	6000.00	6000-12950
1993 Village Inn A/P	400	1996	615.00	1050-1335
1993 Village Inn G/P	400	N/A	665.00	995-1385
1993 Village Inn P/P	100	1999	715.00	1300-1510
1993 Village Inn S/N	1,200	1994	515.00	925-1105
1994 The Warmth of Home A/P	345		590.00	750
1994 The Warmth of Home G/P	860		590.00	750
1994 The Warmth of Home P/P	275		640.00	800
1994 The Warmth of Home S/N	3,450		440.00	600
1992 Weathervane Hutch A/P	200	1995	515.00	895-1065
1992 Weathervane Hutch G/P	200	N/A	565.00	615-1145
1992 Weathervane Hutch P/P	100	1999	615.00	1295
1992 Weathervane Hutch S/N	1,960	1995	415.00	715-895
1998 The Wind of the Spirit A/P (18 x 27)	1,190		940.00	1005
1998 The Wind of the Spirit A/P (24 x 36)	1,190		1410.00	1510
1998 The Wind of the Spirit A/P (28 x 42)	990		2100.00	2145
1998 The Wind of the Spirit G/P (18 x 27)	2,100		940.00	1005
1998 The Wind of the Spirit G/P (24 x 36)	2,100		1410.00	1510
1998 The Wind of the Spirit G/P (28 x 42)	1,750		2100.00	2145
1998 The Wind of the Spirit P/P (18 x 27)	1,100		990.00	1056
1998 The Wind of the Spirit P/P (24 x 36)	1,100		1460.00	1560
1998 The Wind of the Spirit P/P (28 x 42)	900		2150.00	2195
1998 The Wind of the Spirit R/E (18 x 27)	480		2250.00	2565
1998 The Wind of the Spirit R/E (24 x 36)	480		3600.00	4080
1998 The Wind of the Spirit R/E (28 x 42)	400		5850.00	5985
1998 The Wind of the Spirit S/N (18 x 27)	5,950		790.00	855
1998 The Wind of the Spirit S/N (24 x 36)	5,950		1260.00	1360
1998 The Wind of the Spirit S/N (28 x 42)	4,950		1950.00	1995
1998 The Wind of the Spirit S/P (18 x 27)	240		3750.00	4275
1998 The Wind of the Spirit S/P (24 x 36)	240		6000.00	6800
1998 The Wind of the Spirit S/P (28 x 42)	200		9750.00	9975
1996 Winsor Manor A/P	395		1070.00	1285
1996 Winsor Manor G/P	990		1070.00	1285
1996 Winsor Manor P/P	320		1120.00	1335
1996 Winsor Manor S/N	3,950		920.00	1135
1996 Winsor Manor S/P	95	1999	2760.00	7500
1999 Winter Chapel A/P (12x18)	790		775.00	800
1999 Winter Chapel A/P (18x27)	590		940.00	1005
1999 Winter Chapel G/P (12x18)	1,400		775.00	800
1999 Winter Chapel G/P (18x27)	1,100		940.00	1005
1999 Winter Chapel P/P (12x18)	480		825.00	850
1999 Winter Chapel P/P (18x27)	530		990.00	1055
1999 Winter Chapel R/E (12x18)	320		1800.00	1950
1999 Winter Chapel R/E (18x27)	240		2250.00	2565
1999 Winter Chapel S/N (12x18)	3,950		625.00	650
1999 Winter Chapel S/N (18x27)	2,950		790.00	855
1999 Winter Chapel S/P (12x18)	160		3000.00	3250
1999 Winter Chapel S/P (18x27)	120		3750.00	4275
1999 Winter Glen A/P (24 x 36)	390		1510	1510
1999 Winter Glen G/P (24 x 36)	700		1510.00	1510
1999 Winter Glen P/P (24 x 36)	350		1560.00	1560
1999 Winter Glen S/N (24 x 36)	1,950		1360.00	1360
1993 Winter's End A/P	400	1999	715.00	995-1180
1993 Winter's End G/P	490	1999	765.00	955-1180
1993 Winter's End P/P	100	1998	815.00	975-1240
1993 Winter's End S/N	1,450	1999	615.00	895-1020
1991 Woodman's Thatch A/P	200	1995	315.00	850-895
1991 Woodman's Thatch P/P	100	1995	415.00	650-995
1991 Woodman's Thatch R/E	200	N/A	295.00	695-1175
1991 Woodman's Thatch S/N	1,960	1994	215.00	450-735
1992 Yosemite A/P	200	1998	715.00	1775-2495
1992 Yosemite G/P	200	1998	765.00	1395-2045
1992 Yosemite P/P	100	1998	815.00	1295-2395
1992 Yosemite S/N	980	1997	615.00	1625-2295

Kinkade-Premium Paper-Unframed - T. Kinkade

YEAR ISSUE	EDITION LIMIT	YEAR RETD.	ISSUE PRICE	*QUOTE U.S.$
1991 Afternoon Light, Dogwood A/P	98	N/A	295.00	1895-2200
1991 Afternoon Light, Dogwood S/N	980	N/A	185.00	495-1395
1992 Amber Afternoon	980	1998	225.00	495-995
1994 Autumn at Ashley's Cottage A/P	245		335.00	390
1994 Autumn at Ashley's Cottage S/N	2,450		185.00	240
1991 The Autumn Gate S/N	980	1994	225.00	1785-2195
1995 Autumn Lane A/P	285		400.00	460
1995 Autumn Lane S/N	2,850		250.00	310
1994 Beacon of Hope A/P	275		400.00	460
1994 Beacon of Hope S/N	2,750	1999	235.00	310-650
1996 Beginning of a Perfect Day A/P	285		475.00	550
1996 Beginning of a Perfect Day S/N	2,850		325.00	400
1993 Beside Still Waters S/N	980	1994	185.00	1036-2495
1993 Beyond Autumn Gate S/N	1,750	1994	285.00	495-675
1997 Beyond Spring Gate A/P	335		475.00	550
1997 Beyond Spring Gate S/N	3,350	1999	325.00	400
1985 Birth of a City S/N	750	N/A	150.00	250-295
1993 The Blessings of Autumn S/N	1,250		235.00	310
1994 The Blessings of Spring A/P	275		345.00	410
1994 The Blessings of Spring S/N	2,750		195.00	260
1995 Blessings of Summer A/P	485		450.00	530
1995 Blessings of Summer S/N	4,850		300.00	380
1998 Block Island A/P (12 x 18)	470		380.00	390
1998 Block Island A/P (18 x 27)	470		435.00	460
1998 Block Island S/N (12 x 18)	2,350		230.00	240
1998 Block Island S/N (18 x 27)	2,350		285.00	310
1995 Blossom Bridge A/P	285		375.00	410
1995 Blossom Bridge S/N	2,850		205.00	260
1992 Blossom Hill Church S/N	980		225.00	335
1991 Boston A/P	100	N/A	245.00	1845
1991 Boston S/N	550	1994	175.00	1295-1795
1999 Boulevard Lights, Paris S/N (24 x 36)	2,850		400.00	400
1997 Bridge of Faith A/P	385		475.00	550
1997 Bridge of Faith S/N	3,850		325.00	400
1992 Broadwater Bridge S/N	980	1994	225.00	450-1395
1995 Brookside Hideaway A/P	385		355.00	410
1995 Brookside Hideaway S/N	3,850		205.00	260
1996 Candlelight Cottage S/N	Closed	1997	150.00	195-365
1991 Carmel, Delores Street and the Tuck Box Tea Room S/N	980	1994	275.00	685-2195
1989 Carmel, Ocean Avenue S/N	935	N/A	225.00	1550-2845
1999 Carmel, Sunset on Ocean Ave. A/P (18 x 27)	970		435.00	460
1999 Carmel, Sunset on Ocean Ave. A/P (24 x 36)	970		520.00	550
1999 Carmel, Sunset on Ocean Ave. A/P (28 x 42)	970		650.00	665
1999 Carmel, Sunset on Ocean Ave. S/N (18 x 27)	485		285.00	310
1999 Carmel, Sunset on Ocean Ave. S/N (24 x 36)	485		370.00	400
1999 Carmel, Sunset on Ocean Ave. S/N (28 x 42)	485		500.00	515
1990 Chandler's Cottage S/N	550	N/A	125.00	1415-1745
1992 Christmas At the Ahwahnee S/N	980		175.00	260
XX Christmas At the Courthouse S/N	Closed	N/A	N/A	595
1990 Christmas Cottage 1990 S/N	550	N/A	95.00	595-1595
1991 Christmas Eve S/N	980	1998	125.00	425-1095
1994 Christmas Memories A/P	245		375.00	410
1994 Christmas Memories S/N	2,450		225.00	260
1994 Christmas Tree Cottage A/P	295		335.00	390
1994 Christmas Tree Cottage S/N	2,950		185.00	240
1996 A Christmas Welcome A/P	285		350.00	390
1996 A Christmas Welcome S/N	2,850		200.00	240
1997 Clearing Storms A/P (18 x 27)	570		420.00	460
1997 Clearing Storms A/P (24 x 36)	570		500.00	550
1997 Clearing Storms S/N (18 x 27)	2,850		270.00	310
1997 Clearing Storms S/N (24 x 36)	2,850		350.00	400
1997 Cobblestone Brooke A/P	485		475.00	550
1997 Cobblestone Brooke S/N	4,850		325.00	400
1996 Cobblestone Lane A/P	285		450.00	530
1996 Cobblestone Lane S/N	2,850		300.00	380
1998 Cobblestone Village A/P (18 x 24)	1,170		435.00	460
1998 Cobblestone Village A/P (25 1/2 x 34)	1,170		520.00	550
1998 Cobblestone Village A/P (30 x 40)	970		650.00	665
1998 Cobblestone Village S/N (18 x 24)	5,850		285.00	310
1998 Cobblestone Village S/N (25 1/2 x 34)	5,850		370.00	400
1998 Cobblestone Village S/N (30 x 40)	4,850		500.00	515
1999 Conquering The Storms A/P (18 x 27)	570		435.00	435
1999 Conquering The Storms A/P (24 x 36)	570		520.00	520
1999 Conquering The Storms A/P (28 x 42)	570		650.00	650
1999 Conquering The Storms S/N (18 x 27)	2,850		285.00	285
1999 Conquering The Storms S/N (24 x 36)	2,850		370.00	370
1999 Conquering The Storms S/N (28 x 42)	2,850		500.00	500
1992 Cottage-By-The-Sea S/N	980	N/A	250.00	450-1325
1992 Country Memories A/P	200		N/A	395
1992 Country Memories S/N	980	1999	185.00	450-515
1994 Creekside Trail A/P	198		400.00	460
1994 Creekside Trail S/N	1,984		250.00	310
1984 Dawson S/N	750	N/A	150.00	750-2750
1994 Days of Peace A/P	198		400.00	460
1994 Days of Peace S/N	1,984		250.00	310
1995 Deer Creek Cottage A/P	285		335.00	390
1995 Deer Creek Cottage S/N	2,850		185.00	240
1994 Dusk in the Valley A/P	198		400.00	460
1994 Dusk in the Valley S/N	1,984		250.00	310
1994 Emerald Isle Cottage A/P	275		345.00	410
1994 Emerald Isle Cottage S/N	2,750		195.00	260
1993 End of a Perfect Day I S/N	1,250	1994	195.00	495-1495
1994 End of a Perfect Day II A/P	275	1998	385.00	550-1125
1994 End of a Perfect Day II S/N	2,750	1996	235.00	500-895
1995 End of a Perfect Day III A/P	485		475.00	545
1995 End of a Perfect Day III S/N	4,850		325.00	420
1989 Entrance to the Manor House S/N	550	N/A	125.00	750-1395
1989 Evening at Merritt's Cottage S/N	N/A	N/A	125.00	1095-1795
1992 Evening at Swanbrooke Cottage S/N	980	1994	250.00	475-1495
1999 Evening Glow A/P (16 X 20)	570		400.00	410
1999 Evening Glow S/N (16 X 20)	2,850		250.00	260
1995 Evening in the Forest A/P	485		355.00	410
1995 Evening in the Forest S/N	4,850		205.00	260
1999 Evening Majesty A/P (24 x 36)	970		550.00	550
1999 Evening Majesty S/N (24 x 36)	4,850		400.00	400
1985 Evening Service S/N	Closed	N/A	90.00	390-450
1998 Everett's Cottage A/P (16 x 20)	1,170		390.00	410
1998 Everett's Cottage A/P (20 x 24)	1,170		420.00	460
1998 Everett's Cottage A/P (24 x 30)	970		480.00	530
1998 Everett's Cottage S/N (16 x 20)	5,850		240.00	260
1998 Everett's Cottage S/N (20 x 24)	5,850		270.00	310
1998 Everett's Cottage S/N (24 x 30)	4,850		330.00	380
1993 Fisherman's Wharf, San Francisco S/N	2,750		305.00	370
1991 Flags Over The Capitol S/N	980		195.00	310
1999 The Forest Chapel A/P (24 x 30)	570		500.00	530
1999 The Forest Chapel S/N (24 x 30)	2,850		350.00	380
1999 Foxglove Cottage A/P (16 x 20)	770		400.00	410
1999 Foxglove Cottage A/P (20 x 24)	770		435.00	460
1999 Foxglove Cottage A/P (24 x 30)	770		500.00	530
1999 Foxglove Cottage S/N (16 x 20)	3,850		250.00	260
1999 Foxglove Cottage S/N (20 x 24)	3,850		285.00	310
1999 Foxglove Cottage S/N (24 x 30)	3,850		350.00	360
1997 Garden of Prayer A/P (18 x 24)	870		420.00	460
1997 Garden of Prayer A/P (25 1/2 x 34)	870		500.00	550
1997 Garden of Prayer A/P (30 x 40)	770		650.00	665
1997 Garden of Prayer S/N (18 x 24)	4,850		270.00	310
1997 Garden of Prayer S/N (25 1/2 x 34)	4,850		350.00	400
1997 Garden of Prayer S/N (30 x 40)	3,850		500.00	515
1993 The Garden of Promise S/N	1,250	1994	235.00	1205-2995
1992 The Garden Party S/N	980		175.00	260

*Quotes have been rounded up to nearest dollar

GRAPHICS

YEAR ISSUE	EDITION LIMIT	YEAR RETD.	ISSUE PRICE	*QUOTE U.S.$
1994 Gardens Beyond Autumn Gate S/N	789	1996	325.00	700-1195
1998 Gardens Beyond Spring Gate A/P (18 x 24)	1,170		435.00	460
1998 Gardens Beyond Spring Gate A/P (25 1/2 x 34)	1,170		520.00	550
1998 Gardens Beyond Spring Gate A/P (30 x 40)	1,170		650.00	665
1998 Gardens Beyond Spring Gate S/N (18 x 24)	5,850		270.00	310
1998 Gardens Beyond Spring Gate S/N (25 1/2 x 34)	5,850		350.00	400
1998 Gardens Beyond Spring Gate S/N (30 x 40)	5,850		500.00	515
1993 Glory of Winter S/N	1,250		235.00	395
1995 Golden Gate Bridge, San Francisco A/P	385		475.00	520
1995 Golden Gate Bridge, San Francisco S/N	3,850		325.00	370
1994 Guardian Castle A/P	275		450.00	530
1994 Guardian Castle S/N	2,750		300.00	380
1993 Heather's Hutch S/N	1,250	1999	175.00	230-545
1994 Hidden Arbor A/P	275		345.00	410
1994 Hidden Arbor S/N	2,750		195.00	260
1990 Hidden Cottage I S/N	550	N/A	125.00	1000-1945
1993 Hidden Cottage II S/N	1,480	1998	195.00	395-695
1994 Hidden Gazebo A/P	240		345.00	410
1994 Hidden Gazebo, S/N	2,400	1998	195.00	250-575
1998 A Holiday Gathering A/P (12 x 16)	1,370		380.00	390
1998 A Holiday Gathering A/P (18 x 24)	1,370		435.00	460
1998 A Holiday Gathering A/P (25 1/2 x 34)	1,370		520.00	550
1998 A Holiday Gathering S/N (12 x 16)	6,850		230.00	240
1998 A Holiday Gathering S/N (18 x 24)	6,850		285.00	310
1998 A Holiday Gathering S/N (25 1/2 x 34)	6,850		370.00	400
1996 Hollyhock House A/P	385		355.00	410
1996 Hollyhock House S/N	3,850		205.00	260
1991 Home For The Evening S/N	980	N/A	100.00	195-545
1991 Home For The Holidays S/N	980	1994	225.00	495-1395
1992 Home is Where the Heart Is I S/N	980	1994	225.00	750-1395
1996 Home is Where the Heart Is II A/P	485		400.00	490
1996 Home is Where the Heart Is II S/N	Closed	1997	250.00	285-655
1993 Homestead House S/N	1,250		235.00	310
1998 Hometown Bridge A/P (18 x 27)	1,170		435.00	460
1998 Hometown Bridge A/P (24 x 36)	1,170		520.00	550
1998 Hometown Bridge A/P (28 x 42)	970		650.00	665
1998 Hometown Bridge S/N (18 x 27)	5,850		285.00	310
1998 Hometown Bridge S/N (24 x 36)	5,850		370.00	400
1998 Hometown Bridge S/N (28 x 42)	4,850		500.00	515
1996 Hometown Evening A/P	285		450.00	530
1996 Hometown Evening S/N	2,850		300.00	380
1997 Hometown Lake A/P	485		480.00	530
1997 Hometown Lake S/N	4,850		330.00	380
1995 Hometown Memories I A/P	485		480.00	530
1995 Hometown Memories I S/N	4,850		300.00	380
2000 Hometown Morning A/P (25 1/2 x 34)	770		550.00	550
2000 Hometown Morning S/N (25 1/2 x 34)	3,850		400.00	400
1996 Hyde Street and the Bay A/P	385		450.00	500
1996 Hyde Street and the Bay S/N	3,850		300.00	350
1992 Julianne's Cottage S/N	980	N/A	185.00	500-1125
1999 Lakeside Hideaway A/P (12 x 16)	570		380.00	390
1999 Lakeside Hideaway A/P (16 x 20)	570		400.00	410
1999 Lakeside Hideaway A/P (18 x 24)	570		435.00	460
1999 Lakeside Hideaway S/N (12 x 16)	2,850		230.00	240
1999 Lakeside Hideaway S/N (16 x 20)	2,850		250.00	260
1999 Lakeside Hideaway S/N (18 x 24)	2,850		285.00	310
1996 Lamplight Bridge A/P	285		355.00	410
1996 Lamplight Bridge S/N	2,850		205.00	260
1993 Lamplight Brooke S/N	1,650	1995	235.00	395-1325
1994 Lamplight Inn A/P	275		385.00	460
1994 Lamplight Inn S/N	2,750		235.00	310
1993 Lamplight Lane S/N	980	N/A	225.00	695-1100
2000 Lamplight Manor A/P (24 x 36)	970		550.00	550
2000 Lamplight Manor S/N (24 x 36)	4,850		400.00	400
1995 Lamplight Village A/P	485		400.00	460
1995 Lamplight Village S/N	4,850		250.00	310
1995 A Light in the Storm A/P	385		400.00	460
1995 A Light in the Storm S/N	3,850		250.00	310
1996 The Light of Peace A/P	335		475.00	550
1996 The Light of Peace S/N	3,350	2000	325.00	400
1995 The Lights of Home A/P	250	1996	225.00	250-375
1996 Lilac Gazebo A/P	285		335.00	390
1996 Lilac Gazebo S/N	2,850		185.00	240
1998 Lingering Dusk A/P (16 x 20)	770		390.00	410
1998 Lingering Dusk A/P (20 x 24)	770		420.00	460
1998 Lingering Dusk S/N (16 x 20)	3,850		240.00	260
1998 Lingering Dusk S/N (20 x 24)	3,850		270.00	310
1995 Main Street Celebration A/P	195		400.00	460
1995 Main Street Celebration S/N	1,950		250.00	310
1995 Main Street Courthouse A/P	195		400.00	460
1995 Main Street Courthouse S/N	1,950		250.00	310
1995 Main Street Matinee A/P	195		400.00	460
1995 Main Street Matinee S/N	1,950		250.00	310
1995 Main Street Trolley A/P	195		400.00	460
1995 Main Street Trolley S/N	1,950		250.00	310
1991 McKenna's Cottage S/N	980	1999	150.00	325-725
1992 Miller's Cottage S/N	980	1995	175.00	495-795
1994 Moonlight Lane I A/P	240		345.00	410
1994 Moonlight Lane I S/N	2,400		195.00	260
1985 Moonlight on the Riverfront S/N	260	N/A	150.00	295-795
1995 Morning Dogwood A/P	485		345.00	390
1995 Morning Dogwood S/N	4,850		195.00	240
1995 Morning Glory Cottage A/P	485		355.00	410
1995 Morning Glory Cottage S/N	4,850		205.00	260
1992 Morning Lane S/N	Closed	N/A	N/A	285-400

YEAR ISSUE	EDITION LIMIT	YEAR RETD.	ISSUE PRICE	*QUOTE U.S.$
1998 Mountain Chapel A/P (16 x 20)	585		390.00	410
1998 Mountain Chapel A/P (24 x 30)	585		480.00	530
1998 Mountain Chapel A/P (32 x 40)	485		650.00	665
1998 Mountain Chapel S/N (16 x 20)	5,850		240.00	260
1998 Mountain Chapel S/N (24 x 30)	5,850		330.00	380
1998 Mountain Chapel S/N (32 x 40)	4,850		500.00	515
1998 Mountain Majesty A/P (18 x 24)	770		435.00	460
1998 Mountain Majesty A/P (25 1/2 x 34)	770		520.00	550
1998 Mountain Majesty A/P (30 x 40)	N/A		650.00	665
1998 Mountain Majesty S/N (18 x 24)	3,850		285.00	310
1998 Mountain Majesty S/N (25 1/2 x 34)	3,850		370.00	400
1998 Mountain Majesty S/N (30 x 40)	N/A		500.00	515
1997 A New Day Dawning A/P	385		475.00	550
1997 A New Day Dawning S/N	3,850		325.00	400
1986 New York, 6th Avenue S/N	950	N/A	150.00	1500-2795
1992 Olde Porterfield Gift Shoppe S/N	980		175.00	260
1991 Olde Porterfield Tea Room S/N	980	1998	150.00	395-480
1999 Open Gate A/P (12 x 16)	770		380.00	390
1999 Open Gate A/P (16 x 20)	770		400.00	410
1999 Open Gate A/P (18 x 24)	770		435.00	460
1999 Open Gate S/N (12 x 16)	3,850		230.00	240
1999 Open Gate S/N (16 x 20)	3,850		250.00	260
1999 Open Gate S/N (18 x 24)	3,850		285.00	310
1991 Open Gate, Sussex S/N	980		100.00	170
1993 Paris, City of Lights S/N	1,980		250.00	450
1994 Paris, Eiffel Tower A/P	275		400.00	460
1994 Paris, Eiffel Tower S/N	2,750		250.00	310
2000 A Peaceful Time A/P (16 x 20)	570		400.00	400
2000 A Peaceful Time S/N (16 x 20)	2,850		250.00	250
1995 Petals of Hope A/P	385		355.00	410
1995 Petals of Hope S/N	3,850		205.00	260
1996 Pine Cove Cottage A/P	485		400.00	460
1996 Pine Cove Cottage S/N	4,850		250.00	310
1984 Placerville, 1916 S/N	950	N/A	90.00	2495-3445
1999 Pools of Serenity A/P (24 x 30)	N/A		530.00	530
1999 Pools of Serenity S/N (24 x 30)	4,850		380.00	380
1994 The Power & The Majesty A/P	275		385.00	460
1994 The Power & The Majesty S/N	2,750		235.00	310
1999 Prince of Peace A/P	370		670.00	670
1999 Prince of Peace S/N	1,850		520.00	520
1998 Quiet Evening A/P (16 x 20)	770		400.00	410
1998 Quiet Evening A/P (20 x 24)	770		435.00	750
1998 Quiet Evening A/P (24 x 30)	770		500.00	500
1998 Quiet Evening S/N (16 x 20)	3,850		250.00	260
1998 Quiet Evening S/N (20 x 24)	3,850		285.00	285
1998 Quiet Evening S/N (24 x 30)	3,850		350.00	350
1988 Room with a View S/N	N/A	N/A	150.00	550-1350
1990 Rose Arbor S/N	935	1994	125.00	750-1495
1996 Rose Gate A/P	285		335.00	380
1996 Rose Gate S/N	2,850		185.00	230
1994 San Francisco Market Street A/P	750		250	285
1994 San Francisco Market Street S/N	7,500		375.00	435
1986 San Francisco, 1909 S/N	950	N/A	150.00	1800-2695
1992 San Francisco, Nob Hill (California St.) S/N	980	N/A	275.00	1275-3195
1989 San Francisco, Union Square S/N	Closed	N/A	225.00	2100-3025
1998 The Sea of Tranquility A/P (18 x 27)	1,170		435.00	435
1998 The Sea of Tranquility A/P (24 x 36)	1,170		520.00	520
1998 The Sea of Tranquility A/P (28 x 42)	1,170		650.00	650
1998 The Sea of Tranquility S/N (18 x 27)	5,850		285.00	285
1998 The Sea of Tranquility S/N (24 x 36)	5,850		370.00	370
1998 The Sea of Tranquility S/N (28 x 42)	5,850		500.00	500
1992 Silent Night S/N	980	1999	175.00	350-735
1995 Simpler Times I A/P	335		400.00	435
1995 Simpler Times I S/N	3,895		250.00	285
1990 Spring At Stonegate S/N	550	1996	200.00	265-865
1996 Spring Gate A/P	385		475.00	520
1996 Spring Gate S/N	3,850		325.00	370
1994 Spring in the Alps A/P	198		375.00	400
1994 Spring in the Alps S/N	1,984		225.00	250
1993 St. Nicholas Circle S/N	1,750		235.00	285
1998 Stairway to Paradise A/P (18 x 24)	770		435.00	435
1998 Stairway to Paradise A/P (25 1/2 x 34)	770		520.00	520
1998 Stairway to Paradise A/P (30 x 40)	N/A		650.00	650
1998 Stairway to Paradise S/N (18 x 24)	3,850		285.00	285
1998 Stairway to Paradise S/N (25 1/2 x 34)	3,850		370.00	370
1998 Stairway to Paradise S/N (30 x 40)	N/A		500.00	500
1995 Stepping Stone Cottage A/P	285		400.00	435
1995 Stepping Stone Cottage S/N	2,850		250.00	285
1998 Stillwater Bridge A/P (12 x 16)	570		370.00	380
1998 Stillwater Bridge A/P (18 x 24)	770		420.00	435
1998 Stillwater Bridge S/N (12 x 16)	2,850	2000	220.00	230
1998 Stillwater Bridge S/N (18 x 24)	3,850		270.00	285
1993 Stonehearth Hutch S/N	1,650		175.00	245
1993 Studio in the Garden S/N	980	1995	175.00	230-535
1999 Summer Gate A/P (18 x 24)	1,170		435.00	435
1999 Summer Gate A/P (25 1/2 x 34)	1,170		520.00	520
1999 Summer Gate A/P (30 x 40)	1,170		650.00	650
1999 Summer Gate S/N (18 x 24)	5,850		285.00	285
1999 Summer Gate S/N (25 1/2 x 34)	5,850		370.00	370
1999 Summer Gate S/N (30 x 40)	5,850		500.00	500
1992 Sunday At Apple Hill S/N	980	1994	175.00	395-805
1996 Sunday Evening Sleigh Ride A/P	285		400.00	435
1996 Sunday Evening Sleigh Ride S/N	2,850		250.00	285
1993 Sunday Outing S/N	980	1995	175.00	375-695
1999 Sunrise A/P (24 x 30)	570		530.00	530
1999 Sunrise S/N (24 x 30)	2,850		380.00	380
1996 Sunset at Riverbend Farm A/P	485		400.00	435
1996 Sunset at Riverbend Farm S/N	4,850		250.00	285
1992 Sweetheart Cottage I S/N	980	1995	150.00	310-695
1993 Sweetheart Cottage II S/N	980	1994	150.00	795
1993 Sweetheart Cottage III A/P	165		385.00	435

YEAR ISSUE	EDITION LIMIT	YEAR RETD.	ISSUE PRICE	*QUOTE U.S.$
1993 Sweetheart Cottage III S/N	1,650		235.00	285
1996 Teacup Cottage A/P	285		400.00	435
1996 Teacup Cottage S/N	2,850		250.00	285
1999 Town Square A/P	770		435.00	435
1999 Town Square S/N	3,850		285.00	285
1997 Twilight Cottage A/P	395		375.00	400
1997 Twilight Cottage S/N	3,950		225.00	250
1999 Twilight Vista A/P	770		500.00	500
1999 Twilight Vista S/N	3,850		350.00	350
1997 Valley of Peace A/P	385		475.00	520
1997 Valley of Peace S/N	3,850		325.00	370
1996 Venice A/P	485		475.00	520
1996 Venice S/N	4,850		325.00	370
1992 Victorian Christmas I S/N	980	N/A	235.00	750-1545
1993 Victorian Christmas II S/N	1,650	1996	235.00	345-695
1994 Victorian Christmas III A/P	295		400.00	435
1994 Victorian Christmas III S/N	2,950		250.00	285
1995 Victorian Christmas IV S/N	756	1995	250.00	300-695
1991 Victorian Evening S/N	980	1993	150.00	500-1025
1992 Victorian Garden I S/N	980	1994	275.00	750-1695
1997 Victorian Garden II A/P	385		400.00	435
1997 Victorian Garden II S/N	3,850		250.00	285
1997 Village Christmas A/P (18 x 24)	970		420.00	435
1997 Village Christmas A/P (25 1/2 x 34)	370		500.00	520
1997 Village Christmas S/N (18 x 24)	4,850		270.00	285
1997 Village Christmas S/N (25 1/2 x 34)	1,850		350.00	370
1993 Village Inn S/N	1,200		195.00	250
1994 The Warmth of Home A/P	245		335.00	380
1994 The Warmth of Home S/N	2,450		185.00	230
1998 The Wind of the Spirit A/P (18 x 27)	1,170		420.00	420
1998 The Wind of the Spirit A/P (24 x 36)	1,170		500.00	500
1998 The Wind of the Spirit A/P (28 x 42)	970		650.00	650
1998 The Wind of the Spirit S/N (18 x 27)	5,850		270.00	270
1998 The Wind of the Spirit S/N (24 x 36)	5,850		350.00	350
1998 The Wind of the Spirit S/N (28 x 42)	4,850		500.00	500
1996 Winsor Manor A/P	385		450.00	500
1996 Winsor Manor S/N	3,850		300.00	350
1999 Winter Chapel A/P (12 x 18)	770		380.00	380
1999 Winter Chapel A/P (18 x 27)	570		435.00	435
1999 Winter Chapel S/N (12 x 18)	3,850		230.00	230
1999 Winter Chapel S/N (18 x 27)	2,850		285.00	285
1993 Winter's End S/N	875		235.00	285
1992 Yosemite S/N	980	1996	225.00	705-1795

Lightpost Publishing/Recollections by Lightpost

American Heroes Collection-Framed - Recollections

YEAR ISSUE	EDITION LIMIT	YEAR RETD.	ISSUE PRICE	*QUOTE U.S.$
1992 Abraham Lincoln	7,500	1997	150.00	150
1993 Babe Ruth	2,250	1996	95.00	95
1993 Ben Franklin	1,000	1997	95.00	95-125
1994 Dwight D. Eisenhower	Closed	1997	30.00	30
1994 Eternal Love (Civil War)	1,861	1997	195.00	195
1994 Franklin D. Roosevelt	Closed	1997	30.00	30
1992 George Washington	7,500	1997	150.00	150-225
1994 George Washington	Closed	1997	30.00	30
1992 John F. Kennedy	7,500	1997	150.00	150
1994 John F. Kennedy	Closed	1997	30.00	30
1992 Mark Twain	7,500	1997	150.00	150
1994 A Nation Divided	1,000	1997	150.00	150
1993 A Nation United	1,000	1997	150.00	150

Cinema Classics Collection - Recollections

YEAR ISSUE	EDITION LIMIT	YEAR RETD.	ISSUE PRICE	*QUOTE U.S.$
1993 As God As My Witness Classic Clip	Closed	1995	40.00	40
1994 Attempted Deception Classic Clip	Closed	1997	30.00	30
1994 A Chance Meeting Classic Clip	Closed	1997	30.00	30
1993 A Dream Remembered Classic Clip	Closed	1995	40.00	40
1993 The Emerald City Classic Clip	Closed	1995	40.00	40
1993 Follow the Yellow Brick Road Classic Clip	Closed	1995	40.00	40
1993 Frankly My Dear Classic Clip	Closed	1995	40.00	40
1994 The Gift Classic Clip	Closed	1997	30.00	30
1993 Gone With the Wind-Movie Ticket Classic Clip	2,000	1997	40.00	40
1994 If I Only Had a Brain Classic Clip	Closed	1997	30.00	30
1994 If I Only Had a Heart Classic Clip	Closed	1997	30.00	30
1994 If I Only Had the Nerve Classic Clip	Closed	1997	30.00	30
1993 The Kiss Classic Clip	Closed	1995	40.00	40
1993 Not A Marrying Man	12,500	1997	150.00	150
1993 Over The Rainbow	7,500	1997	150.00	150
1994 The Proposal Classic Clip	Closed	1997	30.00	30
1993 The Ruby Slippers Classic Clip	Closed	1995	40.00	40
1993 Scarlett & Her Beaux	12,500	1997	150.00	150
1994 There's No Place Like Home Classic Clip	Closed	1997	30.00	30
1993 We're Off to See the Wizard Classic Clip	Closed	1995	40.00	40
1993 You Do Waltz Divinely	12,500	1997	195.00	195
1993 You Need Kissing	12,500	1997	195.00	195

The Elvis Collection - Recollections

YEAR ISSUE	EDITION LIMIT	YEAR RETD.	ISSUE PRICE	*QUOTE U.S.$
1994 Celebrity Soldier/Regular G.I.	Closed	1997	30.00	30
1994 Dreams Remembered/Dreams Realized	Closed	1997	30.00	30
1994 Elvis the King	2,750	1997	195.00	195
1994 Elvis the Pelvis	2,750	1997	195.00	195
1994 The King/The Servant	Closed	1997	30.00	30
1994 Lavish Spender/Generous Giver	Closed	1997	30.00	30
1994 Professional Artist/Practical Joker	Closed	1997	30.00	30
1994 Public Image/Private Man	Closed	1997	30.00	30
1994 Sex Symbol/Boy Next Door	Closed	1997	30.00	30
1994 To Elvis with Love	2,750	1997	195.00	195
1994 Vulgar Showman/Serious Musician	Closed	1997	30.00	30

*Quotes have been rounded up to nearest dollar

Gone With the Wind - Recollections

YEAR ISSUE	EDITION LIMIT	YEAR RETD.	ISSUE PRICE	*QUOTE U.S.$
1995 Final Parting Classic Clip	Closed	1997	30.00	30
1995 A Parting Kiss Classic Clip	Closed	1997	30.00	30
1995 The Red Dress Classic Clip	Closed	1997	30.00	30
1995 Sweet Revenge Classic Clip	Closed	1997	30.00	30

The Wizard of Oz - Recollections

YEAR ISSUE	EDITION LIMIT	YEAR RETD.	ISSUE PRICE	*QUOTE U.S.$
1995 Glinda the Good Witch	Closed	1997	30.00	30
1995 Toto	Closed	1997	30.00	30
1995 The Wicked Witch	Closed	1997	30.00	30
1995 The Wizard	Closed	1997	30.00	30

Little Angel Publishing

Gelsinger - Framed Canvas - D. Gelsinger

YEAR ISSUE	EDITION LIMIT	YEAR RETD.	ISSUE PRICE	*QUOTE U.S.$
1995 Alexandria's Teddy A/P	25		352.50	353
1995 Alexandria's Teddy S/N	250		295.00	295
1997 An Angel's Touch A/P	50		169.00	169
1997 An Angel's Touch S/N	500		137.50	138
1997 The Broadwalk A/P	5	1997	660.00	660-710
1997 The Broadwalk S/N	45		560.00	560
1997 Farewell Bend A/P	5	1997	675.00	675-725
1997 Farewell Bend S/N	40		575.00	575
1995 Fire Light A/P	30	1996	595.00	595-650
1995 Fire Light S/N	300		520.00	520
1994 A Flower For Baby A/P	25		585.00	585
1994 A Flower For Baby S/N	250		510.00	510
1999 Garden Miracle (5 x 7)	Open		99.00	99
1999 Gentle Guardian (5 x 7)	Open		99.00	99
1997 Gentle Guidance A/P	50		169.00	169
1997 Gentle Guidance S/N	500		137.50	138
1995 Golden Gate A/P	20		795.00	795
1995 Golden Gate S/N	200		695.00	695
1998 Heceta Head Lighthouse (18 x 24) A/P	20		699.00	699
1998 Heceta Head Lighthouse (18 x 24) S/N	200		599.00	599
1998 Heceta Head Lighthouse (8 x 10) A/P	20		238.00	238
1998 Heceta Head Lighthouse (8 x 10) S/N	200		188.00	188
1997 A Joyous Feast A/P	6	1998	370.00	370-470
1997 A Joyous Feast S/N	54	1998	290.00	290-390
1995 Life's Little Tangles A/P	35	1996	595.00	595-650
1995 Life's Little Tangles S/N	350		520.00	520
1996 The Lighthouse Keeper A/P	10	1997	625.00	625-825
1996 The Lighthouse Keeper S/N	50	1997	525.00	525-725
1999 A Little Faith (12 x 16)	Open		242.00	242
1999 A Little Faith (5 x 7)	Open		99.00	99
1999 A Little Hope (12 x 16)	Open		242.00	242
1999 A Little Hope (5 X 7)	Open		99.00	99
1995 Motherly Love A/P	30		525.00	525
1995 Motherly Love S/N	300		450.00	450
1995 The Perfect Tree A/P	25		352.50	353
1995 The Perfect Tree S/N	250		295.00	295
1996 Sugar & Spice A/P	20		352.50	353
1996 Sugar & Spice S/N	200		295.00	295
1998 Tender Love A/P	50		699.00	699
1998 Tender Love S/N	500		599.00	599
1994 The Toy Box A/P	25		525.00	525
1994 The Toy Box S/N	250		450.00	450

Gelsinger - Unframed Paper - D. Gelsinger

YEAR ISSUE	EDITION LIMIT	YEAR RETD.	ISSUE PRICE	*QUOTE U.S.$
1995 Alexandria's Teddy A/P	15		120.00	120
1995 Alexandria's Teddy S/N	150		80.00	80
1997 An Angel's Touch A/P	30		87.00	87
1997 An Angel's Touch S/N	300		57.00	57
1995 Fire Light A/P	15		200.00	200
1995 Fire Light S/N	150		150.00	150
1994 A Flower For Baby A/P	15		190.00	190
1994 A Flower For Baby S/N	150		140.00	140
1999 Garden Miracle (5 x 7)	Open		16.00	16
1999 Gentle Guardian (5 x 7)	Open		16.00	16
1997 Gentle Guidance A/P	30		87.00	87
1997 Gentle Guidance S/N	300		57.00	57
1995 Golden Gate A/P	10		230.00	230
1995 Golden Gate S/N	100		180.00	180
1998 Heceta Head Lighthouse (18 x 24) A/P	20		200.00	200
1998 Heceta Head Lighthouse (18 x 24) S/N	200		150.00	150
1998 Heceta Head Lighthouse (8 x 10) A/P	20		87.00	87
1998 Heceta Head Lighthouse (8 x 10) S/N	200		57.00	57
1995 Life's Little Tangles A/P	15		200.00	200
1995 Life's Little Tangles S/N	150		150.00	150
1999 A Little Faith (12 x 16)	Open		36.00	36
1999 A Little Faith (5 x 7)	Open		16.00	16
1999 A Little Hope (12 x 16)	Open		36.00	36
1999 A Little Hope (5 x 7)	Open		16.00	16
1995 Motherly Love A/P	15		170.00	170
1995 Motherly Love S/N	150		120.00	120
1995 The Perfect Tree A/P	15		120.00	120
1995 The Perfect Tree S/N	150		80.00	80
1996 Sugar & Spice A/P	5		120.00	120
1996 Sugar & Spice S/N	50		80.00	80
1998 Tender Love A/P	50		200.00	200
1998 Tender Love S/N	500		150.00	150
1994 The Toy Box A/P	15		170.00	170
1994 The Toy Box S/N	150		120.00	120

The Seasons of Angels - Framed Canvas - D. Gelsinger

YEAR ISSUE	EDITION LIMIT	YEAR RETD.	ISSUE PRICE	*QUOTE U.S.$
1996 Spring Angel A/P	12	1999	234.00	234
1996 Spring Angel S/N	125		184.00	184
1996 Winter Angel A/P	12	1999	234.00	234
1996 Winter Angel S/N	125		184.00	184

The Seasons of Angels - Unframed Paper - D. Gelsinger

YEAR ISSUE	EDITION LIMIT	YEAR RETD.	ISSUE PRICE	*QUOTE U.S.$
1996 Spring Angel A/P	12		87.00	87
1996 Spring Angel S/N	125		57.00	57
1996 Winter Angel A/P	12		87.00	87
1996 Winter Angel S/N	125		57.00	57

Marty Bell

Members Only Collectors Club - M. Bell

YEAR ISSUE	EDITION LIMIT	YEAR RETD.	ISSUE PRICE	*QUOTE U.S.$
1991 Little Thatch Twilight	Closed	1992	288.00	475
1991 Charter Rose, The	Closed	1992	Gift	300
1992 Candle At Eventide	Closed	1993	Gift	N/A
1992 Blossom Lane	Closed	1993	288.00	400
1993 Laverstoke Lodge	Closed	1994	328.00	328
1993 Chideock Gate	Closed	1994	Gift	N/A
1994 Hummingbird Hill	Closed	1995	320.00	450-495
1994 The Hummingbird	Closed	1995	Gift	N/A
1995 The Bluebird Victorian	Closed	1996	320.00	340-495
1995 The Bluebird	Closed	1996	Gift	N/A
1996 Goldfinch Garden	Closed	1997	220.00	275-325
1996 The Goldfinch	Closed	1997	Gift	N/A
1997 Wishing Well Garden	Closed	1998	180.00	180
1997 The Dove	Closed	1998	Gift	N/A
1998 Lovebirds Cottage	Closed	1999	190.00	190
1998 The Lovebirds	Closed	1999	Gift	N/A
1999 Millrun Cottage	Closed	2000	190.00	190
1999 The Swans	Closed	2000	Gift	N/A
2000 Gillian's Garden	Yr.Iss.		190.00	190
2000 The Cardinals	Yr.Iss.		Gift	N/A

America the Beautiful - M. Bell

YEAR ISSUE	EDITION LIMIT	YEAR RETD.	ISSUE PRICE	*QUOTE U.S.$
1998 Brenda's Porch	250	1998	235.00	295
1993 Jones Victorian	750	1994	400.00	1300
1998 Lemonade Afternoon	286	1998	220.00	220
1995 The Tuck Box Tea Room, Carmel	500	1995	456.00	1295-1495
1993 Turlock Spring	114	1995	700.00	850

Christmas - M. Bell

YEAR ISSUE	EDITION LIMIT	YEAR RETD.	ISSUE PRICE	*QUOTE U.S.$
1989 Fireside Christmas	500	1989	136.00	750
1990 Ready For Christmas	700	1990	148.00	495
1991 Christmas in Rochester	900	1991	148.00	350
1992 McCoy's Toy Shoppe	900	1992	148.00	350
1993 Christmas Treasures	900	1993	200.00	200
1995 Tuck Box Christmas	750	1995	250.00	500-550
1996 Sing A Song Of Christmas	750		225.00	225
1997 Bell Cottage Christmas	750		225.00	225
1998 Winter Holiday	500		220.00	220
1999 Home With the Tree	250		220.00	220

England - M. Bell

YEAR ISSUE	EDITION LIMIT	YEAR RETD.	ISSUE PRICE	*QUOTE U.S.$
1993 The Abbey	320	1998	400.00	424
1987 Alderton Village	500	1988	235.00	650
1988 Allington Castle Kent	646	1998	540.00	540-948
1990 Arbor Cottage	900	1990	130.00	150-250
1993 Arundel Row	282	1995	130.00	138
1981 Bibury Cottage	500	1988	280.00	800-1000
1981 Big Daddy's Shoe	700	1989	64.00	325-495
1988 The Bishop's Roses	900	1989	220.00	695-795
1989 Blush of Spring	1,200	1990	96.00	120-160
1995 Blyton Cottage	750	1999	100.00	100
1988 Bodiam Twilight	900	1991	520.00	900-1100
1995 Bower Roses	500	2000	100.00	100
1988 Brendon Hills Lane	860	1995	304.00	318
1992 Briarwood	217	1993	220.00	220-300
1993 Broadway Cottage	122	1995	330.00	350
1987 Broughton Village	900	1988	128.00	400-500
1984 Brown Eyes	312	1993	296.00	400-450
1990 Bryants Puddle Thatch	900	1990	130.00	150-295
1986 Burford Village Store	500	1988	106.00	595
1993 Byfleet	623	1998	180.00	180
1981 Castle Combe Cottage	500	1988	230.00	895
1993 The Castle Tearoom	900	1993	88.00	200
1987 The Chaplains Garden	500	1987	235.00	1100
1991 Childswickham Morning	305	1993	396.00	396-410
1987 Chippenham Farm	500	1988	120.00	300-900
1988 Clove Cottage	900	1988	128.00	500
1988 Clover Lane Cottage	1,800	1988	272.00	600-650
1991 Cobblestone Cottage	652	1995	374.00	404-1200
1993 Coln St. Aldwyn's	1,000	1995	730.00	850-1295
1986 Cotswold Parish Church	500	1988	98.00	1500-2000
1988 Cotswold Twilight	900	1988	128.00	395-495
1995 Cottage Roses	500	2000	100.00	100
1991 Cozy Cottage	900	1991	130.00	130
1993 Craigton Cottage	371	1998	130.00	130
1982 Crossroads Cottage	S/O	1987	38.00	350-460
1992 Devon Cottage	472	1995	374.00	404
1991 Devon Roses	1,200	1991	96.00	195-500
1991 Dorset Roses	1,200	1991	96.00	250
1987 Dove Cottage Garden	900	1990	260.00	304-495
1987 Driftstone Manor	500	1988	440.00	1500-1800
1987 Ducksbridge Cottage	500	1988	400.00	2000
1987 Eashing Cottage	900	1988	120.00	200-400
1992 East Sussex Roses (Archival)	1,200	1993	96.00	96
1985 Fiddleford Cottage	500	1986	78.00	1950
1993 The Flower Box	292	1998	300.00	300
1988 Friday Street Lane	1,800	1992	280.00	600
2000 Friendship Bouquet	350	2000	150.00	150
1989 The Game Keeper's Cottage	900	1989	560.00	1850
1992 Garlands Flower Shop	900	1992	220.00	350-450
1988 Ginger Cottage	1,800	1988	320.00	650
1989 Glory Cottage	911	1993	96.00	96
1989 Goater's Cottage	900	1991	368.00	560
1990 Gomshall Flower Shop	900	1990	396.00	1500-1800
1993 Graffam House	534	1998	180.00	180
1987 Halfway Cottage	900	1988	260.00	300-500
1992 Happy Heart Cottage	636	1998	368.00	400
1996 Holly Cottage	750	2000	100.00	100
1992 Hollybush	1,200	1994	560.00	795
1991 Horsham Farmhouse	593	1995	180.00	200-265
1986 Housewives Choice	500	1987	98.00	750-1000
1988 Icomb Village Garden	900	1988	620.00	1300-1500
1993 Idaho Hideaway	508	1998	400.00	400-450
1988 Jasmine Thatch	900	1991	272.00	495
1989 Larkspur Cottage	900	1989	220.00	495
1985 Little Boxford	500	1987	78.00	300-900
1991 Little Bromley Lodge	1,058	1998	456.00	456-500
1991 Little Timbers	900	1992	130.00	130
1987 Little Tulip Thatch	500	1988	120.00	400-700
1990 Little Well Thatch	950	1990	130.00	150-250
1990 Longparish Cottage	900	1991	368.00	650
1990 Longstock Lane	900	1990	130.00	295
1986 Lorna Doone Cottage	500	1987	380.00	3500-4000
1990 Lower Brockhampton Manor	900	1990	640.00	1800
1988 Lullabye Cottage	900	1988	220.00	300-400
1987 May Cottage	900	1988	120.00	200-699
1988 Meadow School	816	1993	220.00	350
1985 Meadowlark Cottage	500	1987	78.00	450-699
1987 Millpond, Stockbridge, The	500	1987	120.00	1100
1992 Miss Hathaway's Garden	1,349	1998	694.00	694
1987 Morning Glory Cottage	500	1988	120.00	450-599
1988 Morning's Glow	1,800	1989	280.00	320-650
1994 Mother Hubbard's Garden	2-Yr.	1996	230.00	244
1988 Murrle Cottage	1,800	1988	320.00	650
1983 Nestlewood	500	1987	300.00	2500
1989 Northcote Lane	1,160	1993	88.00	88
1989 Old Beams Cottage	900	1990	368.00	650
1988 Old Bridge, Grasmere	453	1993	640.00	640
1990 Old Hertfordshire Thatch	900	1990	396.00	2000
1993 Old Mother Hubbard's Cottage	2-Yr.	1995	230.00	250
1989 Overbrook	827	1993	220.00	350
1992 Pangbourne on Thames	900	1994	304.00	675-695
1984 Penshurst Tea Rooms (Archival)	1,000	1988	335.00	950
1984 Penshurst Tea Rooms (Canvas)	500	1987	335.00	2995
1989 The Periwinkle Tea Rooms	1,988	1998	694.00	694
1989 Pride of Spring	1,200	1990	96.00	200-400
1988 Rodway Cottage	900	1989	694.00	700-1500
1989 Rose Bedroom, The	515	1993	388.00	388
1995 Rose Bower Cottage	500	1997	320.00	320
1990 Sanctuary	900	1992	220.00	450
1982 Sandhills Cottage	S/O	1987	38.00	38
1988 Sandy Lane Thatch	375	1993	380.00	500
1982 School Lane Cottage	S/O	1987	38.00	38
1993 Selborne Cottage	750	1995	300.00	318
1992 Sheffield Roses	750	1998	298.00	298
1988 Shere Village Antiques	900	1988	272.00	304-699
1995 Sissinghurst Garden	88	1998	488.00	488
1991 Somerset Inn	766	1998	180.00	180
1993 Speldhurst Farms	363	1998	248.00	265
1981 Spring in the Santa Ynez	500	1991	400.00	1100
1991 Springtime at Scotney	1,200	1992	730.00	750-1500
1989 St. Martin's Ashurst	243	1993	344.00	344
1997 Staplewood	43	1998	200.00	200
1990 Summer's Garden	900	1991	78.00	400-800
1985 Summers Glow	500	1987	98.00	600-1000
1987 Sunrise Thatch	900	1988	120.00	260
1996 Sunshine Cottage	99	1998	200.00	200
1996 Sunshine Lodge	88	1998	200.00	200
1985 Surrey Garden House	500	1986	98.00	850-1499
1985 Sweet Pine Cottage	500	1987	78.00	350-1499
1988 Sweet Twilight	900	1988	220.00	350-600
1990 Sweetheart Thatch	900	1993	220.00	375-500
1991 Tea Time	900	1991	130.00	300
1994 Tea With Miss Teddy	350	1995	128.00	128
1982 Thatchcolm Cottage	S/O	1987	38.00	38
1989 The Thimble Pub	641	1993	344.00	344
1993 Tithe Barn Cottage	308	1995	368.00	398
1995 Tulip Time	500	1998	456.00	456
1993 Umbrella Cottage	515	1998	176.00	176
1991 Upper Chute	900	1991	496.00	1200
1992 Valentine Cottage	526	1998	176.00	176
1987 The Vicar's Gate	500	1988	110.00	700-900
1987 Wakehurst Place	900	1988	480.00	1750
1987 Well Cottage, Sandy Lane	500	1988	440.00	650-1500
1991 Wepham Cottage	1,200	1991	396.00	1050-1200
1984 West Kington Dell	500	1988	215.00	650-800
1992 West Sussex Roses (Archival)	1,200	1993	96.00	96
1990 Weston Manor	900	1995	694.00	760
1987 White Lilac Thatch	900	1988	260.00	400-700
1992 Wild Rose Cottage	155	1993	248.00	248-422
1985 Windsong Cottage	500	1987	156.00	350-799
1986 York Garden Shop	500	1988	98.00	450

England-Rye - M. Bell

YEAR ISSUE	EDITION LIMIT	YEAR RETD.	ISSUE PRICE	*QUOTE U.S.$
1992 Antiques of Rye	1,100	1996	220.00	260-300
1991 Bay Tree Cottage, Rye	1,100	1992	230.00	230-520
1990 Martin's Market, Rye	962	1998	304.00	400
1990 The Mermaid Inn, Rye	851	1998	560.00	600
1993 Simon the Pieman, Rye	497	1998	240.00	240
1992 The Strand Quay, Rye	771	1998	248.00	248
1991 Swan Cottage Tea Room, Rye	933	1998	176.00	176
1991 Windward Cottage, Rye	1,100	1991	228.00	800-895
1991 Ye Olde Bell, Rye	542	1998	196.00	196

Gardens of the Heart - M. Bell

YEAR ISSUE	EDITION LIMIT	YEAR RETD.	ISSUE PRICE	*QUOTE U.S.$
1995 Cloister Garden	250	1996	488.00	488-695

*Quotes have been rounded up to nearest dollar

YEAR ISSUE	EDITION LIMIT	YEAR RETD.	ISSUE PRICE	*QUOTE U.S.$
1998 Morningsong	250	1999	275.00	275
1994 My Garden	750	1998	430.00	430-785
1996 Sweetheart's Gate	750	1999	225.00	225

Mill Pond Press

Bateman - R. Bateman

YEAR ISSUE	EDITION LIMIT	YEAR RETD.	ISSUE PRICE	*QUOTE U.S.$
1982 Above the River-Trumpeter Swans	950	1984	200.00	850-1035
1984 Across the Sky-Snow Geese	950	1985	220.00	800-905
1980 African Amber-Lioness Pair	950	1980	175.00	475
1979 Afternoon Glow-Snowy Owl	950	1979	125.00	525-603
1990 Air, The Forest and The Watch	42,558	N/A	325.00	325-681
1984 Along the Ridge-Grizzly Bears	950	1984	200.00	700-900
1984 American Goldfinch-Winter Dress	950	1984	75.00	165-207
1979 Among the Leaves-Cottontail Rabbit	950	1980	75.00	1000
1980 Antarctic Elements	950	1980	125.00	160-216
1995 Approach-Bald Eagle	N/A		1295.00	1295
1991 Arctic Cliff-White Wolves	13,000	1991	325.00	600
1982 Arctic Evening-White Wolf	950	1982	185.00	1050-1700
1980 Arctic Family-Polar Bears	950	1980	150.00	1150-2200
1992 Arctic Landscape-Polar Bear	5,000	N/A	345.00	195
1992 Arctic Landscape-Polar Bear-Premier Ed.	450	1992	800.00	800
1982 Arctic Portrait-White Gyrfalcon	950	1982	175.00	325
1985 Arctic Tern Pair	950	1985	175.00	185
1981 Artist and His Dog	950	1983	150.00	550
1980 Asleep on Hemlock-Screech Owl	950	1980	125.00	575-825
1991 At the Cliff-Bobcat	12,500	1991	325.00	300-325
1992 At the Feeder-Cardinal	950	1992	125.00	200-475
1987 At the Nest-Secretary Birds	950	1987	290.00	290
1982 At the Roadside-Red-Tailed Hawk	950	1984	185.00	875
1980 Autumn Overture-Moose	950	1980	245.00	2000
1980 Awesome Land-American Elk	950	1980	245.00	2350
1989 Backlight-Mute Swan	950	1989	275.00	450
1983 Bald Eagle Portrait	950	1983	185.00	300-390
1982 Baobab Tree and Impala	950	1986	245.00	300
1980 Barn Owl in the Churchyard	950	1981	125.00	690-800
1989 Barn Swallow and Horse Collar	950	N/A	225.00	225
1982 Barn Swallows in August	950	N/A	245.00	350
1992 Beach Grass and Tree Frog	1,250		345.00	345
1985 Beaver Pond Reflections	950	1985	185.00	265
1984 Big Country, Pronghorn Antelope	950	1985	185.00	185
1986 Black Eagle	950	1986	200.00	200-250
1993 Black Jaguar-Premier Edition	450	N/A	850.00	1000
1986 Black-Tailed Deer in the Olympics	950	1986	245.00	245
1986 Blacksmith Plover	950	1986	185.00	185
1991 Bluebird and Blossoms	4,500		235.00	235
1991 Bluebird and Blossoms-Prestige Ed.	450		625.00	625
1980 Bluffing Bull-African Elephant	950	1981	135.00	1100-1450
1981 Bright Day-Atlantic Puffins	950	1985	175.00	875-1300
1989 Broad-Tailed Hummingbird Pair	950	1989	225.00	225
1980 Brown Pelican and Pilings	950	1980	165.00	1550
1979 Bull Moose	950	1979	125.00	650
1978 By the Tracks-Killdeer	950	1980	75.00	825-1025
1983 Call of the Wild-Bald Eagle	950	1983	200.00	200-250
1985 Canada Geese Family(stone lithograph)	260	1985	350.00	795-895
1985 Canada Geese Over the Escarpment	950	1985	135.00	225
1986 Canada Geese With Young	950	1986	195.00	200-265
1981 Canada Geese-Nesting	950	1981	295.00	1395-1595
1993 Cardinal and Sumac	2,510	N/A	235.00	235
1988 Cardinal and Wild Apples	12,183	1988	235.00	235
1989 Catching The Light-Barn Owl	2,000	1990	295.00	295
1988 Cattails, Fireweed and Yellowthroat	950	1988	235.00	275
1989 Centennial Farm	950	1989	295.00	295
1988 The Challenge-Bull Moose	10,671	1989	325.00	325
1980 Chapel Doors	950	1985	135.00	700-850
1986 Charging Rhino	950	1986	325.00	475-575
1982 Cheetah Profile	950	1985	245.00	365
1978 Cheetah With Cubs	950	1980	95.00	365
1988 Cherrywood with Juncos	950	1988	245.00	245
1990 Chinstrap Penguin	810	1991	150.00	150
1992 Clan of the Raven	950	1992	235.00	345-425
1981 Clear Night-Wolves	950	1981	245.00	4400-4600
1988 Colonial Garden	950	1988	245.00	400-525
1987 Continuing Generations-Spotted Owls	950	1987	525.00	475-550
1991 Cottage Lane-Red Fox	950	1991	285.00	250
1984 Cougar Portrait	950	1984	95.00	290
1979 Country Lane-Pheasants	950	1981	85.00	600
1981 Courting Pair-Whistling Swans	950	1981	245.00	275
1981 Courtship Display-Wild Turkey	950	1981	175.00	225
1980 Coyote in Winter Sage	950	1980	245.00	2250-2500
1992 Cries of Courtship-Red Crowned Cranes	950	1992	350.00	395-550
1980 Curious Glance-Red Fox	950	1980	135.00	995-1450
1986 Dark Gyrfalcon	950	1986	225.00	300
1993 Day Lilies and Dragonflies	1,250		345.00	345
1982 Dipper By the Waterfall	950	1985	165.00	475-485
1989 Dispute Over Prey	950		325.00	325
1989 Distant Danger-Raccoon	1,600	1989	225.00	225
1984 Down for a Drink-Morning Dove	950	1985	135.00	260
1978 Downy Woodpecker on Goldenrod Gall	950	1979	50.00	1000-1300
1988 Dozing Lynx	950	1988	335.00	1300-1500
1986 Driftwood Perch-Striped Swallows	950	1986	195.00	195
1983 Early Snowfall-Ruffed Grouse	950	1985	195.00	195-225
1983 Early Spring-Bluebird	950	1984	185.00	625-750
1981 Edge of the Ice-Ermine	950	1981	175.00	400
1982 Edge of the Woods-Whitetail Deer, w/Book	950	1983	745.00	925-1075
1991 Elephant Cow and Calf	950	1991	300.00	400
1986 Elephant Herd and Sandgrouse	950	1986	235.00	320
1991 Encounter in the Bush-African Lions	950	1991	295.00	345
1987 End of Season-Grizzly	950	1987	325.00	595-625
1991 Endangered Spaces-Grizzly	4,008	1991	325.00	325
1985 Entering the Water-Common Gulls	950	1986	195.00	195
1986 European Robin and Hydrangeas	950	1986	130.00	200-295
1989 Evening Call-Common Loon	950	1989	235.00	495-625
1980 Evening Grosbeak	950	1980	125.00	695
1983 Evening Idyll-Mute Swans	950	1984	245.00	675
1981 Evening Light-White Gyrfalcon	950	1981	245.00	775-975
1979 Evening Snowfall-American Elk	950	1980	150.00	950-1150
1987 Everglades	950	1987	360.00	360
1980 Fallen Willow-Snowy Owl	950	1980	200.00	515-600
1987 Farm Lane and Blue Jays	950	1987	225.00	300-400
1986 Fence Post and Burdock	950	1987	130.00	275
1991 Fluid Power-Orca	290		2500.00	2500
1980 Flying High-Golden Eagle	950	1980	150.00	1000
1982 Fox at the Granary	950	1985	165.00	300
1982 Frosty Morning-Blue Jay	950	1982	185.00	800-900
1982 Gallinule Family	950		135.00	135
1981 Galloping Herd-Giraffes	950	1981	175.00	950-1200
1985 Gambel's Quail Pair	950	1985	95.00	325
1982 Gentoo Penguins and Whale Bones	950	1986	205.00	550-600
1983 Ghost of the North-Great Gray Owl	950	1983	200.00	1700-3950
1982 Golden Crowned Kinglet and Rhododendron	950	1982	150.00	1800-2700
1979 Golden Eagle	950	1981	150.00	250
1985 Golden Eagle Portrait	950	1987	115.00	175
1989 Goldfinch In the Meadow	1,600	1989	150.00	250
1983 Goshawk and Ruffed Grouse	950	1984	185.00	500
1988 Grassy Bank-Great Blue Heron	950	1988	285.00	225
1981 Gray Squirrel	950	1981	180.00	685-1015
1979 Great Blue Heron	950	1980	125.00	800-1400
1987 Great Blue Heron in Flight	950	1987	295.00	295-395
1988 Great Crested Grebe	950	1988	135.00	135
1987 Great Egret Preening	950	1987	315.00	600-725
1983 Great Horned Owl in the White Pine	950	1983	225.00	450
1987 Greater Kudu Bull	950	1987	145.00	145
1993 Grizzly and Cubs	2,250	1993	335.00	400
1991 Gulls on Pilings	1,950	N/A	265.00	265
1988 Hardwood Forest-White-Tailed Buck	630	1988	300.00	1600-1950
1988 Harlequin Duck-Bull Kelp -Executive Ed.	623	1988	550.00	550
1988 Harlequin Duck-Bull Kelp-Gold Plated	950	1988	300.00	300
1980 Heron on the Rocks	950	1980	75.00	500-800
1981 High Camp at Dusk	950	1985	245.00	465-1100
1979 High Country-Stone Sheep	950	1982	125.00	600-900
1987 High Kingdom-Snow Leopard	950	1987	325.00	550-800
1990 Homage to Ahmed	290	N/A	3300.00	3500
1984 Hooded Mergansers in Winter	950	1984	210.00	400-500
1984 House Finch and Yucca	950	1984	95.00	195
1986 House Sparrow	950	1986	125.00	160-225
1987 House Sparrows and Bittersweet	950	1987	220.00	300-370
1986 Hummingbird Pair Diptych	950	1986	330.00	550-625
1987 Hurricane Lake-Wood Ducks	950	1987	135.00	200
1981 In for the Evening	950	1981	150.00	1750-2500
1994 In His Prime-Mallard	950	N/A	195.00	250-295
1984 In the Brier Patch-Cottontail	950	1985	165.00	350-400
1986 In the Grass-Lioness	950	1986	245.00	245
1985 In the Highlands-Golden Eagle	950	1985	235.00	350
1985 In the Mountains-Osprey	950	1987	95.00	200
1992 Intrusion-Mountain Gorilla	2,250	1996	325.00	325-550
1990 Ireland House	950	1990	265.00	265-295
1985 Irish Cottage and Wagtail	950	1990	175.00	200-300
1992 Junco in Winter	1,250	1992	185.00	215-280
1990 Keeper of the Land	290		3300.00	3300
1993 Kestrel and Grasshopper	1,250		335.00	335
1979 King of the Realm	950	1979	125.00	575-690
1987 King Penguins	950	1987	130.00	140-195
1981 Kingfisher and Aspen	950	1981	225.00	855-900
1980 Kingfisher in Winter	950	1981	175.00	825-1000
1980 Kittiwake Greeting	950	1980	75.00	365
1981 Last Look-Bighorn Sheep	950	1986	195.00	129-225
1987 Late Winter-Black Squirrel	950	1987	165.00	165
1981 Laughing Gull and Horseshoe Crab	950	1981	125.00	125
1982 Leopard Ambush	950	1986	245.00	395-625
1988 Leopard and Thomson Gazelle Kill	950	1988	275.00	275
1985 Leopard at Seronera	950	1985	175.00	290
1980 Leopard in a Sausage Tree	950	1980	150.00	1695-2195
1984 Lily Pads and Loon	950	1984	200.00	1250-1716
1987 Lion and Wildebeest	950	1987	265.00	265
1980 Lion at Tsavo	950	1983	150.00	350
1978 Lion Cubs	950	1981	125.00	259
1987 Lioness at Serengeti	950	1987	325.00	325
1985 Lions in the Grass	950	1985	265.00	700-825
1981 Little Blue Heron	950	1981	95.00	225
1982 Lively Pair-Chickadees	950	1982	160.00	362
1983 Loon Family	950	1983	200.00	850
1990 Lunging Heron	1,250	1990	225.00	225
1978 Majesty on the Wing-Bald Eagle	950	1979	150.00	2500-3395
1988 Mallard Family at Sunset	950	1988	235.00	235
1986 Mallard Family-Misty Marsh	950	1986	130.00	130
1986 Mallard Pair-Early Winter	41,740	1986	135.00	200
1985 Mallard Pair-Early Winter 24K Gold	950	1986	1650.00	2000
1986 Mallard Pair-Early Winter Gold Plated	7,691	1986	250.00	375
1989 Mangrove Morning-Roseate Spoonbills	2,000	1989	325.00	414
1991 Mangrove Shadow-Common Egret	1,250		285.00	285
1993 Marbled Murrelet	55	1993	1200.00	1200-1900
1986 Marginal Meadow	950	1986	220.00	220-250
1979 Master of the Herd-African Buffalo	950	1980	150.00	1895-3150
1984 May Maple-Scarlet Tanager	950	1984	175.00	625-725
1982 Meadow's Edge-Mallard	950	1982	175.00	600
1982 Merganser Family in Hiding	950	1982	200.00	575
1994 Meru Dusk-Lesser Kudu	950		135.00	135
1989 Midnight-Black Wolf	25,352	1989	325.00	1395-1983
1980 Mischief on the Prowl-Raccoon	950	1980	85.00	150-195
1980 Misty Coast-Gulls	950	1980	135.00	420
1984 Misty Lake-Osprey	950	1985	95.00	150-225
1981 Misty Morning-Loons	950	1981	150.00	1100-1300
1986 Moose at Water's Edge	950	1986	130.00	285
1990 Morning Cove-Common Loon	950	1990	165.00	185
1985 Morning Dew-Roe Deer	950	1985	175.00	175-230
1983 Morning on the Flats-Bison	950	1983	200.00	300
1984 Morning on the River-Trumpeter Swans	950	1984	185.00	320
1990 Mossy Branches-Spotted Owl	4,500	1990	300.00	475-700
1990 Mowed Meadow	950	1990	190.00	190
1986 Mule Deer in Aspen	950	1986	175.00	175
1983 Mule Deer in Winter	950	1983	200.00	275
1988 Muskoka Lake-Common Loons	2,500	1988	265.00	300-500
1989 Near Glenburnie	950		265.00	265
1983 New Season-American Robin	950	1983	200.00	325
1986 Northern Reflections-Loon Family	8,631	1986	255.00	1897-2550
1985 Old Whaling Base and Fur Seals	950	1985	195.00	300
1987 Old Willow and Mallards	950	1987	325.00	325
1980 On the Alert-Chipmunk	950	1980	60.00	350
1993 On the Brink-River Otters	1,250	1994	345.00	345-500
1985 On the Garden Wall	950	1985	115.00	300
1985 Orca Procession	950	1985	245.00	2475-4000
1981 Osprey Family	950	1981	245.00	245
1983 Osprey in the Rain	950	1983	110.00	500-600
1987 Otter Study	950	1987	235.00	360-475
1981 Pair of Skimmers	950	1981	150.00	195-220
1988 Panda's At Play (stone lithograph)	160	1988	400.00	1200-1379
1994 Path of the Panther	1,950	1997	295.00	295
1984 Peregrine and Ruddy Turnstones	950	1985	200.00	425-500
1985 Peregrine Falcon and White-Throated Swifts	950	1985	245.00	765-850
1987 Peregrine Falcon on the Cliff-Stone Litho	525	1988	350.00	780-1300
1983 Pheasant in Cornfield	950	1983	200.00	325
1988 Pheasants at Dusk	950	1988	325.00	550-724
1982 Pileated Woodpecker on Beech Tree	950	1982	175.00	825-900
1990 Pintails in Spring	9,651	1989	135.00	300
1982 Pioneer Memories-Magpie Pair	950	1982	175.00	175
1987 Plowed Field-Snowy Owl	950	1987	145.00	280-300
1990 Polar Bear	290	1990	3300.00	3300
1982 Polar Bear Profile	950	1982	210.00	1900-2586
1982 Polar Bears at Bafin Island	950	1982	245.00	875-1300
1990 Power Play-Rhinoceros	950	1990	320.00	320-500
1980 Prairie Evening-Short-Eared Owl	950	1983	150.00	293-325
1994 Predator Portfolio/Black Bear	950		475.00	475
1992 Predator Portfolio/Cougar	950		465.00	465
1993 Predator Portfolio/Grizzly	950		475.00	475
1993 Predator Portfolio/Polar Bear	950		485.00	485
1993 Predator Portfolio/Wolf	950		475.00	475
1994 Predator Portfolio/Wolverine	950		275.00	275
1988 Preening Pair-Canada Geese	950	1988	235.00	235
1987 Pride of Autumn-Canada Goose	15,294	1987	135.00	245-325
1986 Proud Swimmer-Snow Goose	950	1986	185.00	185
1989 Pumpkin Time	950		195.00	195
1982 Queen Anne's Lace and American Goldfinch	950	1982	150.00	700-900
1984 Ready for Flight-Peregrine Falcon	950	1984	185.00	470
1982 Ready for the Hunt-Snowy Owl	950	1982	245.00	650-770
1993 Reclining Snow Leopard	1,250		335.00	335
1988 Red Crossbills	950	1988	125.00	175
1984 Red Fox on the Prowl	950	1984	245.00	665-938
1982 Red Squirrel	950	1982	175.00	325
1986 Red Wolf	950	1986	250.00	275-395
1981 Red-Tailed Hawk by the Cliff	950	1981	245.00	425-655
1981 Red-Winged Blackbird and Rail Fence	950	1981	195.00	315
1984 Reeds	950	1984	185.00	388-415
1986 A Resting Place-Cape Buffalo	950	1986	265.00	265
1987 Rhino at Ngoro Ngoro	950	1988	325.00	171-325
1993 River Otter-North American Wilderness	350	N/A	325.00	800
1993 River Otters	290		1500.00	1500
1986 Robins at the Nest	950	1986	185.00	138-195
1987 Rocky Point-October	950	1987	195.00	420
1980 Rocky Wilderness-Cougar	950	1980	175.00	975-1600
1990 Rolling Waves-Greater Scaup	3,330	N/A	125.00	135
1993 Rose-breasted Grosbeak	290		450.00	450
1981 Rough-Legged Hawk in the Elm	950	1991	175.00	175-200
1981 Royal Family-Mute Swans	950	1981	245.00	715-950
1983 Ruby Throat and Columbine	950	1983	150.00	2000
1987 Ruddy Turnstones	950	1987	175.00	175
1994 Salt Spring Sheep	1,250		235.00	235
1981 Sarah E. with Gulls	950	1981	245.00	2500-5500
1993 Saw Whet Owl and Wild Grapes	950	N/A	185.00	185
1991 The Scolding-Chickadees & Screech Owl	12,500	1992	235.00	235
1991 Sea Otter Study	950	1991	150.00	245
1993 Shadow of the Rain Forest	9,000	1993	345.00	475-825
1981 Sheer Drop-Mountain Goats	950	1981	245.00	1900
1988 Shelter	950	1988	325.00	750-875
1992 Siberian Tiger	4,500	1992	325.00	325
1984 Smallwood	950	1985	200.00	700-925
1990 Snow Leopard	290	1990	2500.00	2200-2600
1985 Snowy Hemlock-Barred Owl	950	1985	245.00	245
1994 Snowy Nap-Tiger	950	1994	185.00	1034-1825
1994 Snowy Owl	150	N/A	265.00	600-750
1987 Snowy Owl and Milkweed	950	1987	235.00	575-845
1983 Snowy Owl on Driftwood	950	1983	245.00	650
1983 Spirits of the Forest	950	1984	170.00	2000
1986 Split Rails-Snow Buntings	950	1986	220.00	220
1980 Spring Cardinal	950	1980	125.00	512-625

*Quotes have been rounded up to nearest dollar

YEAR ISSUE	EDITION LIMIT	YEAR RETD.	ISSUE PRICE	*QUOTE U.S.$
1982 Spring Marsh-Pintail Pair	950	1982	200.00	302
1980 Spring Thaw-Killdeer	950	1980	85.00	121-245
1982 Still Morning-Herring Gulls	950	1982	200.00	200
1987 Stone Sheep Ram	950	1987	175.00	175
1985 Stream Bank June	950	1986	160.00	175
1984 Stretching-Canada Goose	950	1984	225.00	2300-4000
1985 Strutting-Ring-Necked Pheasant	950	1985	225.00	450-575
1985 Sudden Blizzard-Red-Tailed Hawk	950	1985	245.00	400-645
1990 Summer Morning Pasture	950	1990	175.00	175
1984 Summer Morning-Loon	950	1984	185.00	1000-1500
1986 Summertime-Polar Bears	950	1986	225.00	225
1979 Surf and Sanderlings	950	1980	65.00	1600-2000
1981 Swift Fox	950	1981	175.00	175-259
1986 Swift Fox Study	950	1986	115.00	200
1987 Sylvan Stream-Mute Swans	950	1987	125.00	175
1984 Tadpole Time	950	1985	135.00	400-500
1988 Tawny Owl In Beech	950	1988	325.00	325
1992 Tembo (African Elephant)	1,550	1992	350.00	350
1984 Tiger at Dawn	950	1984	225.00	1700-2600
1983 Tiger Portrait	950	1983	130.00	425-625
1988 Tree Swallow over Pond	950	1988	290.00	150-290
1991 Trumpeter Swan Family	290		2500.00	2500
1985 Trumpeter Swans and Aspen	950	1985	245.00	450-500
1979 Up in the Pine-Great Horned Owl	950	1981	150.00	675-795
1980 Vantage Point	950	1980	245.00	795-1121
1993 Vigilance	9,500		330.00	330
1989 Vulture And Wildebeest	550		295.00	295
1981 Watchful Repose-Black Bear	950	1981	245.00	475
1985 Weathered Branch-Bald Eagle	950	1985	115.00	300
1991 Whistling Swan-Lake Erie	1,950		325.00	375
1980 White Encounter-Polar Bear	950	1980	245.00	2950-4300
1990 White on White-Snowshoe Hare	950	1990	195.00	425
1982 White World-Dall Sheep	950	1982	200.00	600
1985 White-Breasted Nuthatch on a Beech Tree	950	1985	175.00	300
1980 White-Footed Mouse in Wintergreen	950	1980	60.00	650
1982 White-Footed Mouse on Aspen	950	1983	90.00	150-225
1992 White-Tailed Deer Through the Birches	10,000		335.00	335
1984 White-Throated Sparrow and Pussy Willow	950	1984	150.00	575-645
1991 Wide Horizon-Tundra Swans	2,862	1991	325.00	350
1991 Wide Horizon-Tundra Swans Companion	2,862		325.00	325
1986 Wildbeest	950		185.00	185
1982 Willet on the Shore	950	N/A	125.00	195-280
1979 Wily and Wary-Red Fox	950	1979	125.00	1075
1984 Window into Ontario	950	1984	265.00	1275
1983 Winter Barn	950	1984	170.00	420
1979 Winter Cardinal	950	1979	75.00	2250
1992 Winter Coat	1,250		245.00	575
1985 Winter Companion	950	1985	175.00	895
1980 Winter Elm-American Kestrel	950	1980	135.00	800-1000
1986 Winter in the Mountains-Raven	950	1987	200.00	200
1981 Winter Mist-Great Horned Owl	950	1981	245.00	500-722
1980 Winter Song-Chickadees	950	1980	95.00	550-776
1984 Winter Sunset-Moose	950	1984	245.00	1600
1992 Winter Trackers	4,500	1992	335.00	335
1981 Winter Wren	950	1981	135.00	450
1983 Winter-Lady Cardinal	950	1983	200.00	1025
1979 Winter-Snowshoe Hare	950	1980	95.00	1100-2300
1987 Wise One, The	950	1987	325.00	1800
1979 Wolf Pack in Moonlight	950	1979	95.00	1552-2150
1994 Wolf Pair in Winter	290	1994	795.00	1600
1983 Wolves on the Trail	950	1983	225.00	425-488
1985 Wood Bison Portrait	950	1985	165.00	225
1983 Woodland Drummer-Ruffed Grouse	950	1984	185.00	235
1981 Wrangler's Campsite-Gray Jay	950	1981	195.00	725
1979 Yellow-Rumped Warbler	950	1980	50.00	435
1978 Young Barn Swallow	950	1979	75.00	575-700
1983 Young Elf Owl-Old Saguaro	950	1983	95.00	325
1991 Young Giraffe	290	1997	850.00	2500
1989 Young Kittiwake	950		195.00	195
1988 Young Sandhill-Cranes	950	1988	325.00	325
1989 Young Snowy Owl	950	1990	195.00	112-195

Brenders - C. Brenders

YEAR ISSUE	EDITION LIMIT	YEAR RETD.	ISSUE PRICE	*QUOTE U.S.$
1986 The Acrobat's Meal-Red Squirrel	950	1989	65.00	475-603
1996 Amber Gaze-Snowy Owl	1,950		175.00	175
1988 Apple Harvest	950	1989	115.00	525
1989 The Apple Lover	1,500	1990	125.00	250
1987 Autumn Lady	950	1989	150.00	825-1207
1991 The Balance of Nature	1,950		225.00	225
1993 Black Sphinx	950		235.00	235
1986 Black-Capped Chickadees	950	1989	40.00	625-931
1990 Blond Beauty	1,950	1990	185.00	185
1986 Bluebirds	950	1989	40.00	150-250
1988 California Quail	950	1989	95.00	462-600
1991 Calm Before the Challenge-Moose	1,950	1991	225.00	225
1987 Close to Mom	950	1988	150.00	1095-2100
1993 Collectors Group (Butterfly Collections)	290		375.00	375
1986 Colorful Playground-Cottontails	950	1989	75.00	625-819
1989 The Companions	18,036	1989	200.00	525-600
1994 Dall Sheep Portrait	950		115.00	115
1992 Den Mother-Pencil Sketch	2,500	1992	135.00	135
1992 Den Mother-Wolf Family	25,000	1992	250.00	250-350
1986 Disturbed Daydreams	950	1989	95.00	425
1987 Double Trouble-Raccoons	950	1988	120.00	700-1550
1993 European Group (Butterfly Collections)	290		375.00	375
1993 Exotic Group (Butterfly Collections)	290		375.00	375

YEAR ISSUE	EDITION LIMIT	YEAR RETD.	ISSUE PRICE	*QUOTE U.S.$
1989 Forager's Reward-Red Squirrel	1,250	1989	135.00	135
1988 Forest Sentinel-Bobcat	950	1988	135.00	425-550
1990 Full House-Fox Family	20,106	1990	235.00	500
1990 Ghostly Quiet-Spanish Lynx	1,950	1990	200.00	200
1986 Golden Season-Gray Squirrel	950	1987	85.00	600-700
1986 Harvest Time-Chipmunk	950	1989	65.00	216
1988 Hidden In the Pines-Immature Great Hor	950	1988	175.00	1000-1125
1988 High Adventure-Black Bear Cubs	950	1989	105.00	415-860
1988 A Hunter's Dream	950	1988	165.00	1000
1993 In Northern Hunting Grounds	1,750		375.00	375
1992 Island Shores-Snowy Egret	2,500		250.00	250
1987 Ivory-Billed Woodpecker	950	1989	95.00	775
1988 Long Distance Hunters	950	1988	175.00	895-1095
1989 Lord of the Marshes	1,250	1989	135.00	175-447
1986 Meadowlark	950	1989	40.00	170-285
1989 Merlins at the Nest	1,250	1989	165.00	235-300
1985 Mighty Intruder	950	1989	95.00	265
1987 Migration Fever-Barn Swallows	950	1989	150.00	465-776
1990 The Monarch is Alive	4,071	1990	265.00	295
1993 Mother of Pearls	5,000		275.00	275
1990 Mountain Baby-Bighorn Sheep	1,950		165.00	195
1987 Mysterious Visitor-Barn Owl	950	1989	150.00	325-500
1993 Narrow Escape-Chipmunk	1,750		150.00	150
1991 The Nesting Season-House Sparrow	1,950	1991	195.00	200-295
1989 Northern Cousins-Black Squirrels	950	1989	150.00	290
1984 On the Alert-Red Fox	950	1986	95.00	350-397
1990 On the Old Farm Door	1,500	1990	225.00	225
1991 One to One-Gray Wolf	10,000	1991	245.00	425-602
1992 Pathfinder-Red Fox	5,000	1992	245.00	245-300
1984 Playful Pair-Chipmunks	950	1987	60.00	628-695
1994 Power and Grace	2,500	1994	265.00	600
1989 The Predator's Walk	1,250	1989	150.00	175-293
1992 Red Fox Study	1,250	1992	125.00	125
1994 Riverbank Kestrel	2,500	1995	225.00	300-350
1988 Roaming the Plains-Pronghorns	950	1989	150.00	195
1986 Robins	950	1989	40.00	175-431
1993 Rocky Camp-Cougar Family	5,000	1995	275.00	350
1993 Rocky Camp-Cubs	950		225.00	225
1992 Rocky Kingdom-Bighorn Sheep	1,750	1997	255.00	255-300
1991 Shadows in the Grass-Young Cougars	1,950	1991	235.00	235
1990 Shoreline Quartet-White Ibis	1,950	1995	265.00	265-340
1984 Silent Hunter-Great Horned Owl	950	1987	95.00	450-560
1984 Silent Passage	950	1988	150.00	350-475
1990 Small Talk	1,500	1990	125.00	140
1992 Snow Leopard Portrait	1,750	1993	150.00	150-172
1990 Spring Fawn	1,500	1990	125.00	275
1990 Squirrel's Dish	1,950		110.00	110
1989 Steller's Jay	1,250	1989	135.00	150-175
1993 Summer Roses-Winter Wren	1,500	1993	250.00	595-690
1989 The Survivors-Canada Geese	1,500	1989	225.00	400
1994 Take Five-Canadian Lynx	1,500	N/A	245.00	475-500
1988 Talk on the Old Fence	950	1988	165.00	825-975
1990 A Threatened Symbol	1,950	1990	145.00	160-175
1994 Tundra Summit-Arctic Wolves	6,061	1994	265.00	432-450
1984 Waterside Encounter	950	1987	95.00	1000-1500
1987 White Elegance-Trumpeter Swans	950	1989	115.00	500
1988 Witness of a Past-Bison	950	1990	110.00	95-135
1992 Wolf Scout #1	2,500	1992	105.00	78-150
1992 Wolf Scout #2	2,500	1992	105.00	135-160
1991 Wolf Study	950	1991	125.00	75-150
1987 Yellow-Bellied Marmot	950	1989	95.00	335-595
1989 A Young Generation	1,250	1989	165.00	175-295

Calle - P. Calle

YEAR ISSUE	EDITION LIMIT	YEAR RETD.	ISSUE PRICE	*QUOTE U.S.$
1981 Almost Home	950	1981	150.00	150
1991 Almost There	950	1991	165.00	165
1989 And A Good Book For Company	950	1990	135.00	435
1993 And A Grizzly Claw Necklace	750		150.00	150
1981 And Still Miles to Go	950	1981	245.00	400
1981 Andrew At The Falls	950	1981	150.00	150
1989 The Beaver Men	950		125.00	125
1984 A Brace for the Spit	950	1985	110.00	275-300
1980 Caring for the Herd	950	1981	110.00	110
1985 The Carrying Place	950	1990	195.00	195
1984 Chance Encounter	950	1986	225.00	325
1981 Chief High Pipe (Color)	950	1981	265.00	265
1980 Chief High Pipe (Pencil)	950	1980	75.00	175
1980 Chief Joseph-Man of Peace	950	1980	135.00	165
1990 Children of Walpi	350		160.00	160
1990 The Doll Maker	950		95.00	95
1982 Emerging from the Woods	950	1987	110.00	110
1981 End of a Long Day	950	1981	150.00	225
1984 Fate of the Late Migrant	950	1985	110.00	375
1983 Free Spirits	950	1985	195.00	475
1983 Free Trapper Study	550	1985	75.00	125-300
1981 Fresh Tracks	950	1981	150.00	150
1981 Friend or Foe	950		125.00	125
1981 Friends	950	1987	150.00	150
1985 The Frontier Blacksmith	950		245.00	245
1989 The Fur Trapper	550		75.00	175
1982 Generations in the Valley	950	1987	245.00	245
1985 The Grandmother	950	1987	400.00	400
1989 The Great Moment	950		350.00	350
1992 Hunter of Geese	950		125.00	125
1993 I Call Him Friend	950		235.00	235
1983 In Search of Beaver	950	1983	225.00	600
1991 In the Beginning . . . Friends	1,250	1993	250.00	275
1987 In the Land of the Giants	950	1988	245.00	900
1990 Interrupted Journey	1,750	1991	265.00	265
1990 Interrupted Journey-Prestige Ed.	290	1991	465.00	465
1987 Into the Great Alone	950	1988	245.00	700-850

YEAR ISSUE	EDITION LIMIT	YEAR RETD.	ISSUE PRICE	*QUOTE U.S.$
1981 Just Over the Ridge	950	1982	245.00	245
1980 Landmark Tree	950	1980	125.00	225
1991 Man of the Fur Trade	550		110.00	110
1984 Mountain Man	550	1988	95.00	225-395
1993 Mountain Man-North American Wilderness Portfolio	350		325.00	N/A
1989 The Mountain Men	300	1989	400.00	400
1989 Navajo Madonna	650		95.00	95
1988 A New Day	950		150.00	150
1981 One With The Land	950	1981	245.00	250
1992 Out of the Silence	2,500		265.00	265
1992 Out of the Silence-Prestige	290		465.00	465
1981 Pause at the Lower Falls	950	1981	110.00	250
1980 Prayer to the Great Mystery	950	1980	245.00	245
1982 Return to Camp	950	1982	245.00	500
1991 The Silenced Honkers	1,250	1993	250.00	250
1980 Sioux Chief	950	1980	85.00	140
1986 Snow Hunter	950	1988	150.00	225
1980 Something for the Pot	950	1980	175.00	1100
1990 Son of Sitting Bull	950		95.00	675
1985 Storyteller of the Mountains	950	1985	225.00	675-960
1983 Strays From the Flyway	950	1983	195.00	225
1981 Teton Friends	950	1981	150.00	225
1991 They Call Me Matthew	950		125.00	125
1992 Through the Tall Grass	950		175.00	175
1988 Trapper at Rest	550		95.00	95
1982 Two from the Flock	950	1982	245.00	500
1980 View from the Heights	950	1980	245.00	245
1988 Voyageurs and Waterfowl...Constant	950	1988	265.00	700-900
1980 When Snow Came Early	950	1980	85.00	250-340
1984 When Trails Cross	950	1984	245.00	750
1991 When Trails Grow Cold	2,500		265.00	265
1991 When Trails Grow Cold-Prestige Ed.	290	1991	465.00	465
1994 When Trappers Meet	750		165.00	165
1989 Where Eagles Fly	1,250	1990	265.00	350-570
1989 A Winter Feast	1,250	1989	265.00	375
1989 A Winter Feast-Prestige Ed.	290	1989	465.00	465
1981 Winter Hunter (Color)	950	1981	245.00	800
1980 Winter Hunter (Pencil)	950	1980	65.00	450
1983 A Winter Surprise	950	1984	195.00	500

Cross - T. Cross

YEAR ISSUE	EDITION LIMIT	YEAR RETD.	ISSUE PRICE	*QUOTE U.S.$
1994 April	750		55.00	55
1994 August	750		55.00	55
1993 Ever Green	750		135.00	135
1993 Flame Catcher	750	1993	185.00	185
1993 Flicker, Flash and Twirl	525		165.00	165
1994 July	750		55.00	55
1994 June	750		55.00	55
1994 March	750		55.00	55
1994 May	750		55.00	55
1992 Shell Caster	750	1993	150.00	150-391
1993 Sheperds of Magic	750	N/A	135.00	135
1993 Spellbound	750	N/A	85.00	85-115
1994 Spring Forth	750		145.00	145
1992 Star Weaver	750	1993	150.00	150-195
1994 Summer Musings	750		145.00	145
1993 The Summons...And Then They Are One	750	1993	195.00	195
1994 When Water Takes to Air	750		135.00	135
1993 Wind Sifter	750	1993	150.00	515

Daly - J. Daly

YEAR ISSUE	EDITION LIMIT	YEAR RETD.	ISSUE PRICE	*QUOTE U.S.$
1994 All Aboard	950		145.00	145
1990 The Big Moment	1,500		125.00	125
1991 Cat's Cradle-Prestige Ed.	950		450.00	450
1994 Catch of My Dreams	4,500		45.00	45
1994 Childhood Friends	950	1997	110.00	110-270
1990 Confrontation	1,500	1992	85.00	97-150
1990 Contentment	1,500	1990	95.00	275-450
1992 Dominoes	1,500		155.00	155
1992 Favorite Gift	2,500	1992	175.00	175
1987 Favorite Reader	950	1990	85.00	130-250
1986 Flying High	950	1988	50.00	525-603
1992 The Flying Horse	950		325.00	325
1993 Good Company	1,500		155.00	155
1992 Her Secret Place	1,500	1992	135.00	200-509
1991 Home Team: Zero	1,500	1998	150.00	150
1991 Homemade	1,500	1992	125.00	125
1990 Honor and Allegiance	1,500	1993	110.00	110
1990 The Ice Man	1,500	1992	125.00	135-265
1992 The Immigrant Spirit	5,000		125.00	125
1992 The Immigrant Spirit-Prestige Ed.	950		125.00	125
1989 In the Doghouse	1,500	1990	75.00	425-589
1990 It's That Time Again	1,500		120.00	120
1992 Left Out	1,500		110.00	110
1989 Let's Play Ball	1,500	1991	75.00	125-135
1990 Make Believe	1,500	1990	75.00	400-457
1994 Mud Mates	950		150.00	150
1994 My Best Friends	950	1995	85.00	365-450
1991 A New Beginning	5,000		125.00	125
1993 The New Citizen	5,000		125.00	125
1993 The New Citizen-Prestige Ed.	950		125.00	125
1987 Odd Man Out	950	1988	85.00	85
1988 On Thin Ice	950	1993	95.00	345-389
1991 Pillars of a Nation-Charter Ed.	20,000		175.00	175
1992 Playmates	1,500	1992	155.00	395-595
1990 Radio Daze	1,500		150.00	150
1983 Saturday Night	950	1985	85.00	1125
1990 The Scholar	1,500	N/A	110.00	112
1993 Secret Admirer	1,500		150.00	150
1994 Slugger	950		75.00	75

*Quotes have been rounded up to nearest dollar

GRAPHICS

YEAR ISSUE	EDITION LIMIT	YEAR RETD.	ISSUE PRICE	*QUOTE U.S.$
1982 Spring Fever	950	1988	85.00	600-759
1993 Sunday Afternoon	1,500		150.00	150
1988 Territorial Rights	950	1990	85.00	350
1989 The Thief	1,500	1990	95.00	250-379
1989 The Thorn	1,500	1990	125.00	350-688
1988 Tie Breaker	950	1990	95.00	293-350
1991 Time-Out	1,500	1993	125.00	125
1993 To All a Good Night	1,500		160.00	160
1992 Walking the Rails	1,500		175.00	175
1993 When I Grow Up	1,500		175.00	175
1994 The Wind-Up	950	1998	75.00	75-119
1988 Wiped Out	1,250	1990	125.00	500-579

Morrissey - D. Morrissey

YEAR ISSUE	EDITION LIMIT	YEAR RETD.	ISSUE PRICE	*QUOTE U.S.$
1994 The Amazing Time Elevator	950	1994	195.00	195
1993 Charting the Skies	1,250	1993	195.00	195-219
1993 Charting the Skies-Caprice Edition	550	1993	375.00	375
1993 Draft of a Dream	175	1993	250.00	195-250
1994 The Dreamer's Trunk	1,500	1997	195.00	195-276
1993 Drifting Closer	1,250		175.00	175
1994 Father Time Flying Past	450		195.00	195
1993 The Mystic Mariner	750	1993	150.00	150-175
1993 The Redd Rocket	1,250	1993	175.00	375-400
1994 The Redd Rocket-Pre-Flight	950	1993	110.00	110-155
1992 The Sandman's Ship of Dreams	750	1993	150.00	300-340
1994 Sighting off the Stern	950		135.00	135
1993 Sleeper Flight	1,250	1993	195.00	175-195
1993 The Telescope of Time	5,000		195.00	195

Olsen - G. Olsen

YEAR ISSUE	EDITION LIMIT	YEAR RETD.	ISSUE PRICE	*QUOTE U.S.$
1993 Airship Adventures	750		150.00	150
1993 Angels of Christmas	750	1993	135.00	135
1993 Dress Rehearseal	750	1993	165.00	2600
1993 The Fraternity Tree	750		195.00	195
1994 Little Girls Will Mothers Be	750	N/A	135.00	135
1994 Mother's Love	750	1994	165.00	165
1995 O Jerusalem	5,000	N/A	165.00	1250-2700
1994 Summerhouse	750	N/A	165.00	165

Seerey-Lester - J. Seerey-Lester

YEAR ISSUE	EDITION LIMIT	YEAR RETD.	ISSUE PRICE	*QUOTE U.S.$
1994 Abandoned	950		175.00	175
1986 Above the Treeline-Cougar	950	1986	130.00	130
1986 After the Fire-Grizzly	950	1990	95.00	95
1986 Along the Ice Floe-Polar Bears	950		200.00	200
1987 Alpenglow-Artic Wolf	950	1987	200.00	200
1987 Amboseli Child-African Elephant	950		160.00	160
1984 Among the Cattails-Canada Geese	950	1985	130.00	375
1984 Artic Procession-Willow Ptarmigan	950	1988	220.00	500-789
1990 Artic Wolf Pups	290		500.00	500
1987 Autumn Mist-Barred Owl	950	1987	160.00	160
1987 Autumn Thunder-Muskoxen	950		150.00	150
1985 Awakening Meadow-Cottontail	950		50.00	50
1992 Banyan Ambush- Black Panther	950	1992	235.00	235-300
1984 Basking-Brown Pelicans	950	1988	115.00	125
1988 Bathing-Blue Jay	950		95.00	95
1987 Bathing-Mute Swan	950	1992	175.00	275-299
1989 Before The Freeze-Beaver	950		165.00	165
1990 Bittersweet Winter-Cardinal	1,250	1990	150.00	175-186
1992 Black Jade	1,950	1992	275.00	350
1992 Black Magic-Panther	750	1992	195.00	225-579
1984 Breaking Cover-Black Bear	950	N/A	130.00	150-200
1987 Canyon Creek-Cougar	950	1987	195.00	435-965
1992 The Chase-Snow Leopard	950		200.00	200
1994 Child of the Outback	950		175.00	175
1985 Children of the Forest-Red Fox Kits	950	1985	110.00	325
1985 Children of the Tundra-Artic Wolf Pup	950	1985	110.00	325-395
1988 Cliff Hanger-Bobcat	950		200.00	200
1984 Close Encounter-Bobcat	950	1989	130.00	130
1988 Coastal Clique-Harbor Seals	950		160.00	160
1986 Conflict at Dawn-Heron and Osprey	950	1989	130.00	325
1983 Cool Retreat-Lynx	950	1988	85.00	125-200
1986 Cottonwood Gold-Baltimore Oriole	950		85.00	85
1985 Cougar Head Study	950		60.00	60
1989 Cougar Run	950	1989	185.00	225
1994 The Courtship	950		175.00	175
1993 Dark Encounter	3,500	N/A	200.00	200-365
1990 Dawn Majesty	1,250	1991	185.00	225-275
1987 Dawn on the Marsh-Coyote	950		200.00	200
1985 Daybreak-Moose	950		135.00	135
1991 Denali Family-Grizzly Bear	950	1991	195.00	235-550
1986 Early Arrivals-Snow Buntings	950		75.00	75
1983 Early Windfall-Gray Squirrels	950		85.00	85
1988 Edge of the Forest-Timber Wolves	950	1988	500.00	500-700
1989 Evening Duet-Snowy Egrets	1,250		185.00	185
1991 Evening Encounter-Grizzly & Wolf	1,250		185.00	185
1988 Evening Meadow-American Goldfinch	950		150.00	150
1991 Face to Face	1,250		200.00	200
1985 Fallen Birch-Chipmunk	950	1985	60.00	375-415
1985 First Light-Gray Jays	950	1985	130.00	175
1983 First Snow-Grizzly Bears	950	1984	95.00	325-395
1987 First Tracks-Cougar	950		150.00	150
1989 Fluke Sighting-Humback Whales	950	1989	185.00	185
1993 Freedom I	350		500.00	500
1993 Frozen Moonlight	2,500	1993	225.00	200-215
1985 Gathering-Gray Wolves, The	950	1987	165.00	250
1989 Gorilla	290	1989	400.00	450
1993 Grizzly Impact	950	N/A	225.00	300-385
1990 Grizzly Litho	290	1990	400.00	400-600
1989 Heavy Going-Grizzly	950	1989	175.00	240
1986 Hidden Admirer-Moose	950	1986	165.00	275
1988 Hiding Place-Saw-Whet Owl	950		95.00	95
1989 High and Mighty-Gorilla	950	1989	185.00	185
1986 High Country Champion-Grizzly	950	1986	175.00	375-465
1984 High Ground-Wolves	950	1984	130.00	225
1987 High Refuge-Red Squirrel	950		120.00	120
1984 Icy Outcrop-White Gyrfalcon	950	1986	115.00	200
1987 In Deep-Black Bear Cub	950		135.00	135
1990 In Their Presence	1,250		200.00	200
1985 Island Sanctuary-Mallards	950	1987	95.00	150-315
1986 Kenyan Family-Cheetahs	950		130.00	130
1986 Lakeside Family-Canada Geese	950		75.00	75
1988 Last Sanctuary-Florida Panther	950	1993	175.00	350
1983 Lone Fisherman-Great Blue Heron	950	1985	85.00	375
1993 Loonlight	1,500		225.00	225
1986 Low Tide-Bald Eagles	950		130.00	130
1987 Lying in Wait-Arctic Fox	950		175.00	175
1984 Lying Low-Cougar	950	1986	85.00	550
1991 Monsoon-White Tiger	950	1994	195.00	195-345
1991 Moonlight Chase-Cougar	1,250		195.00	195
1988 Moonlight Fishermen-Raccoons	950	1990	175.00	175-305
1988 Moose Hair	950	N/A	165.00	225-385
1988 Morning Display-Common Loons	3,395	1988	135.00	135
1986 Morning Forage-Ground Squirrel	950		75.00	75
1993 Morning Glory-Bald Eagle	1,250		225.00	225
1984 Morning Mist-Snowy Owl	950	1988	95.00	180-225
1990 Mountain Cradle	1,250	N/A	200.00	200
1988 Night Moves-African Elephants	950		150.00	150
1990 Night Run-Artic Wolves	1,250	1990	200.00	200-415
1993 Night Specter	1,250		195.00	195
1986 Northwoods Family-Moose	950		75.00	75
1987 Out of the Blizzard-Timber Wolves	950	1987	215.00	450-500
1992 Out of the Darkness	290		200.00	200
1987 Out of the Mist-Grizzly	950	1990	200.00	375
1991 Out on a Limb-Young Barred Owl	950		185.00	185
1991 Panda Trilogy	950	N/A	375.00	375
1993 Phantoms of the Tundra	950		235.00	235
1984 Plains Hunter-Prairie Falcon	950		95.00	95
1990 The Plunge-Northern Sea Lions	1,250		200.00	200
1986 Racing the Storm-Artic Wolves	950	1986	200.00	300
1987 Rain Watch-Belted Kingfisher	950		125.00	125
1993 The Rains-Tiger	950		225.00	225
1992 Ranthambhore Rush	950		225.00	225
1983 The Refuge-Raccoon	950	1983	85.00	275
1992 Regal Majesty	290		200.00	200
1985 Return to Winter-Pintails	950	1990	135.00	200-229
1983 River Watch-Peregrine Falcon	950		85.00	85
1988 Savana Siesta-African Lions	950		165.00	165
1990 Seasonal Greeting-Cardinal	1,250	1993	150.00	150-250
1993 Seeking Attention	950		200.00	200
1991 Sisters-Artic Wolves	1,250		185.00	185
1989 Sneak Peak	950		185.00	185
1986 Snowy Excursion-Red Squirrel	950		75.00	75
1988 Snowy Watch-Great Gray Owl	950		175.00	175
1989 Softly, Softly-White Tiger	950	1989	220.00	395-450
1991 Something Stirred (Bengal Tiger)	950		195.00	195
1988 Spanish Mist-Young Barred-Owl	950		175.00	175
1984 Spirit of the North-White Wolf	950	1986	130.00	185
1990 Spout	290		500.00	500
1989 Spring Flurry-Adelie Penguins	950		185.00	185
1986 Spring Mist-Chickadees	950	1986	105.00	1160
1990 Suitors-Wood Ducks	3,313	1989	135.00	135-160
1990 Summer Rain-Common Loons	4,500	1990	200.00	200
1990 Summer Rain-Common Loons (Prestige)	450		425.00	425
1987 Sundown Alert-Bobcat	950	N/A	150.00	195
1985 Sundown Reflections-Wood Ducks	950		85.00	85
1990 Their First Season	1,250	1990	200.00	200
1990 Togetherness	1,250		125.00	185
1986 Treading Thin Ice-Chipmunk	950		75.00	75
1988 Tundra Family-Arctic Wolves	950		200.00	200
1985 Under the Pines-Bobcat	950	1986	95.00	275-318
1989 Water Sport-Bobcat	950	1989	185.00	185-219
1990 Whitetail Spring	1,250	1990	185.00	185
1988 Winter Grazing-Bison	950		185.00	185
1986 Winter Hiding-Cottontail	950		75.00	75
1983 Winter Lookout-Cougar	950	1985	85.00	600-700
1986 Winter Perch-Cardinal	950	1986	85.00	150
1985 Winter Rendezvous-Coyotes	950	1985	140.00	140
1988 Winter Spirit-Gray Wolf	950		200.00	200
1987 Winter Vigil-Great Horned Owl	950	1990	175.00	175
1993 Wolong Whiteout	950		225.00	225
1986 The Young Explorer-Red Fox Kit	950	N/A	75.00	95
1992 Young Predator-Leopard	950		200.00	200

Smith - D. Smith

YEAR ISSUE	EDITION LIMIT	YEAR RETD.	ISSUE PRICE	*QUOTE U.S.$
1993 African Ebony-Black Leopard	1,250	1994	195.00	195
1997 Ancient Mariner	950		165.00	165
1992 Armada	950	N/A	195.00	195
1998 Brother Wolf	950	1998	125.00	249
1993 Catching the Scent-Polar Bear	950	1993	175.00	175
1994 Curious Presence-Whitetail Deer	950	1996	195.00	195-300
1991 Dawn's Early Light-Bald Eagles	950	1997	185.00	185
1993 Echo Bay-Loon Family	1,150	1993	185.00	185-400
1992 Eyes of the North	2,500	1996	225.00	225
1994 Forest Veil-Cougar	950	1994	195.00	376
1993 Guardians of the Den	1,500	N/A	195.00	195
1991 Icy Reflections-Pintails	500		250.00	250
1992 Night Moves-Cougar	950	1994	185.00	185
1994 Parting Reflections	950		185.00	185
1993 Shrouded Forest-Bald Eagle	950	N/A	150.00	650-1100
1991 Twilight's Calling-Common Loons	950	1991	175.00	250
1993 What's Bruin	1,750	1993	185.00	185-349

New Masters Publishing

Bannister - P. Bannister

YEAR ISSUE	EDITION LIMIT	YEAR RETD.	ISSUE PRICE	*QUOTE U.S.$
1982 Amaryllis	500	N/A	285.00	2000
1988 Apples and Oranges	485	N/A	265.00	650-675
1982 April	300	N/A	200.00	1200
1984 April Light	950	N/A	150.00	650-675
1987 Autumn Fields	950	N/A	150.00	300-350
1978 Bandstand	250	N/A	75.00	600-625
1992 Bed of Roses	663	N/A	265.00	525-575
1995 Bridesmaids	950	N/A	265.00	530-600
1991 Celebration	662	N/A	350.00	800-825
1989 Chapter One	485	N/A	265.00	1700-1875
1982 Cinderella	500	N/A	285.00	580-620
1991 Crossroads	485	N/A	295.00	600-625
1993 Crowning Glory	485	N/A	265.00	600-650
1981 Crystal	300	N/A	300.00	300-600
1992 Crystal Bowl	485	N/A	265.00	600-675
1989 Daydreams	485	N/A	265.00	625
1993 Deja Vu	663	N/A	265.00	1400-1500
1983 The Duchess	500	N/A	250.00	2000
1980 Dust of Autumn	200	N/A	200.00	1225
1981 Easter	300	N/A	260.00	1200
1982 Emily	500	N/A	285.00	1200-1225
1980 Faded Glory	200	N/A	200.00	1225
1984 The Fan Window	950	N/A	195.00	600-675
1987 First Prize	950	N/A	115.00	275-350
1988 Floribunda	485	N/A	265.00	675-750
1994 Fountain	485	N/A	265.00	600-725
1994 From Russia With Love	950	N/A	165.00	400-550
1980 Gift of Happiness	200	N/A	200.00	2050
1980 Girl on the Beach	200	N/A	200.00	1400-1500
1990 Good Friends	485	N/A	265.00	750-825
1988 Guinevere	485	N/A	265.00	1300-1375
1993 Into The Woods	485	N/A	265.00	500-600
1982 Ivy	500	N/A	285.00	750-800
1982 Jasmine	500	N/A	285.00	725-775
1981 Juliet	300	N/A	260.00	5050
1990 Lavender Hill	485	N/A	265.00	775-800
1992 Love Letters	485	N/A	265.00	550-650
1988 Love Seat	485	N/A	230.00	500-525
1989 Low Tide	485	N/A	265.00	650
1995 Magnolias	950	N/A	265.00	1000-1200
1982 Mail Order Brides	500	N/A	325.00	2400
1984 Make Believe	950	N/A	150.00	775-800
1989 March Winds	485	N/A	265.00	530-550
1983 Mementos	950	N/A	150.00	1500
1982 Memories	500	N/A	235.00	500-575
1992 Morning Mist	485	N/A	265.00	500-600
1981 My Special Place	300	N/A	260.00	2150
1995 Now and Then	950	N/A	265.00	265-550
1982 Nuance	500	N/A	235.00	500-580
1994 Once Upon A Time	950	N/A	265.00	600-700
1983 Ophelia	950	N/A	150.00	700-750
1996 Paradise Cove	950	N/A	265.00	865-950
1989 Peace	485	N/A	265.00	1200-1300
1981 Porcelain Rose	300	N/A	260.00	2100
1982 The Present	500	N/A	260.00	950
1986 Pride & Joy	950	N/A	150.00	325
1991 Puddings & Pies	485	N/A	265.00	500-575
1987 Quiet Corner	950	N/A	115.00	625-675
1989 The Quilt	485	N/A	265.00	950-975
1993 Rambling Rose	485	N/A	265.00	500-575
1981 Rehearsal	300	N/A	260.00	1950
1990 Rendezvous	485	N/A	265.00	650
1984 Scarlet Ribbons	950	N/A	150.00	350
1980 Sea Haven	300	N/A	260.00	1200-1350
1990 Seascapes	485	N/A	265.00	550
1987 September Harvest	950	N/A	150.00	400-500
1980 The Silver Bell	200	N/A	200.00	2000-2200
1990 Sisters	485	N/A	265.00	1250
1990 Songbird	485	N/A	265.00	550
1996 Southern Belle	950	N/A	265.00	850-950
1991 String of Pearls	485	N/A	265.00	850
1988 Summer Choices	300	N/A	250.00	850-900
1991 Teatime	485	N/A	295.00	650-700
1980 Titania	350	N/A	260.00	950-1125
1991 Wildflowers	485	N/A	295.00	725
1983 Window Seat	950	N/A	150.00	700-800

Past Impressions

Limited Edition Canvas Transfers - A. Maley

YEAR ISSUE	EDITION LIMIT	YEAR RETD.	ISSUE PRICE	*QUOTE U.S.$
1990 Cafe Royale	100	N/A	665.00	665
1992 Circle of Love	250	N/A	445.00	550-850
1992 An Elegant Affair	250	N/A	595.00	1095
1992 Evening Performance	100	N/A	295.00	1050
1990 Festive Occasion	100	N/A	595.00	250-300
1990 Gracious Era	100	N/A	645.00	1500-1700
1995 The Letter	250	N/A	465.00	600
1987 Love Letter	75	N/A	445.00	1250
1994 New Years Eve	250	N/A	445.00	600-800
1994 Parisian Beauties	250	N/A	645.00	750
1993 Rags and Riches	250	N/A	445.00	550-625
1993 The Recital	250	N/A	595.00	900-1400
1990 Romantic Engagement	100	N/A	445.00	1225
1993 Sleigh Bells	250	N/A	595.00	600
1991 Summer Carousel	250	N/A	345.00	500-600
1994 Summer Elegance	250	N/A	595.00	950
1995 Summer Romance	250	N/A	465.00	575-750
1993 Visiting The Nursery	250	N/A	445.00	1400

*Quotes have been rounded up to nearest dollar

YEAR ISSUE	EDITION LIMIT	YEAR RETD.	ISSUE PRICE	*QUOTE U.S.$
1992 A Walk in the Park	250	N/A	595.00	650-1000
1989 Winter Impressions	100	N/A	595.00	775-1100

Limited Edition Paper Prints - A. Maley

YEAR ISSUE	EDITION LIMIT	YEAR RETD.	ISSUE PRICE	*QUOTE U.S.$
1989 Alexandra	750	1994	125.00	125
1989 Beth	750	1994	125.00	125
1988 The Boardwalk	500	N/A	250.00	395
1989 Catherine	750	1994	125.00	200
1987 Day Dreams	500	N/A	200.00	325
1989 English Rose	750	N/A	250.00	400
1990 Festive Occasion	750	N/A	250.00	500-900
1984 Glorious Summer	350	N/A	150.00	600
1989 In Harmony	750	1995	250.00	250
1988 Joys of Childhood	500	N/A	250.00	320
1987 Love Letter	450	N/A	200.00	200
1988 Opening Night	500	N/A	250.00	2000
1985 Passing Elegance	350	N/A	150.00	900
1987 The Promise	450	N/A	200.00	525
1984 Secluded Garden	350	N/A	150.00	970
1985 Secret Thoughts	350	N/A	150.00	850
1990 Summer Pastime	750	N/A	250.00	375
1986 Tell Me	450	N/A	150.00	800
1988 Tranquil Moment	500	N/A	250.00	325
1989 Victoria	750	1994	125.00	125
1988 Victorian Trio	500	N/A	250.00	325-350
1986 Winter Romance	450	N/A	150.00	1000

Pemberton & Oakes

Membership-Miniature Lithographs - D. Zolan

YEAR ISSUE	EDITION LIMIT	YEAR RETD.	ISSUE PRICE	*QUOTE U.S.$
1992 Brotherly Love	Retrd.	1992	18.00	59
1993 New Shoes	Retrd.	1993	18.00	28-42
1993 Country Walk	Retrd.	1993	22.00	20-39
1994 Enchanted Forest	Retrd.	1994	22.00	35-40

Zolan's Children-Lithographs - D. Zolan

YEAR ISSUE	EDITION LIMIT	YEAR RETD.	ISSUE PRICE	*QUOTE U.S.$
1989 Almost Home	Retrd.	1989	98.00	135-150
1991 Autumn Leaves	Retrd.	1991	98.00	115-120
1993 The Big Catch	Retrd.	1993	98.00	98-130
1989 Brotherly Love	Retrd.	1989	98.00	295
1982 By Myself	Retrd.	1982	98.00	230
1989 Christmas Prayer	Retrd.	1989	98.00	100-145
1990 Colors of Spring	Retrd.	1990	98.00	200-375
1990 Crystal's Creek	Retrd.	1990	98.00	175-225
1989 Daddy's Home	Retrd.	1989	98.00	292-310
1988 Day Dreamer	Retrd.	1988	35.00	130
1992 Enchanted Forest	Retrd.	1992	98.00	110-125
1982 Erik and the Dandelion	Retrd.	1982	98.00	350-400
1990 First Kiss	Retrd.	1990	98.00	229-249
1991 Flowers for Mother	Retrd.	1991	98.00	160-195
1993 Grandma's Garden	Retrd.	1993	98.00	100-135
1989 Grandma's Mirror	Retrd.	1989	98.00	175
1990 Laurie and the Creche	Retrd.	1990	98.00	95-115
1989 Mother's Angels	Retrd.	1989	98.00	295-349
1992 New Shoes	Retrd.	1992	98.00	150-175
1989 Rodeo Girl	Retrd.	1989	98.00	125-225
1984 Sabina in the Grass	Retrd.	1984	98.00	625
1988 Small Wonder	Retrd.	1988	98.00	250
1989 Snowy Adventure	Retrd.	1989	98.00	205-225
1991 Summer Suds	Retrd.	1991	98.00	140-175
1989 Summer's Child	Retrd.	1989	98.00	90-165
1986 Tender Moment	Retrd.	1986	98.00	275
1988 Tiny Treasures	Retrd.	1988	150.00	215
1987 Touching the Sky	Retrd.	1987	98.00	225-245
1988 Waiting to Play	Retrd.	1988	35.00	135
1988 Winter Angel	Retrd.	1988	98.00	230-300

Porterfield's

Mini Prints - R. Anders

YEAR ISSUE	EDITION LIMIT	YEAR RETD.	ISSUE PRICE	*QUOTE U.S.$
1997 Time Out	5,000	1998	26.60	36-80
1997 Safe Harbor	5,000	1998	26.60	27-45
1997 Digging In	5,000	1998	26.60	27-45
1997 Two Bites To Go	5,000	1998	26.60	27-45

Prizm, Inc./Pipka

Pipka Collectibles - Pipka

YEAR ISSUE	EDITION LIMIT	YEAR RETD.	ISSUE PRICE	*QUOTE U.S.$
1999 Christmas Ark 10004 (framed)	750		240.00	240
1999 Christmas Ark 10006 (unframed)	—		60	60
1999 Gardening Angel Print 10003 (framed)	750		240.00	240
1999 Gardening Angel Print 10005 (unframed)	—		60.00	60
1998 Knock, Knock Santa Print 10001 (framed)	750	1999	180.00	180-300
1998 Knock, Knock Santa Print 10002 (unframed)	—	1999	50.00	50

Reco International

Fine Art Canvas Reproduction - J. McClelland

YEAR ISSUE	EDITION LIMIT	YEAR RETD.	ISSUE PRICE	*QUOTE U.S.$
1990 Beach Play	350	1998	80.00	80
1991 Flower Swing	350	1998	100.00	100
1991 Summer Conversation	350	1998	80.00	80

Limited Edition Print - S. Kuck

YEAR ISSUE	EDITION LIMIT	YEAR RETD.	ISSUE PRICE	*QUOTE U.S.$
1986 Ashley	500	1998	85.00	150
1985 Heather	Retrd.	1987	75.00	150
1984 Jessica	Retrd.	1986	60.00	400

McClelland - J. McClelland

YEAR ISSUE	EDITION LIMIT	YEAR RETD.	ISSUE PRICE	*QUOTE U.S.$
XX I Love Tammy	500	1998	75.00	100
XX Just for You	300	1998	155.00	155
XX Olivia	300	1998	175.00	175
XX Reverie	300	1998	110.00	110
XX Sweet Dreams	300	1998	145.00	145

Roman, Inc.

Hook - F. Hook

YEAR ISSUE	EDITION LIMIT	YEAR RETD.	ISSUE PRICE	*QUOTE U.S.$
1982 Bouquet	Closed	1994	70.00	350
1981 The Carpenter	Closed	1981	100.00	1000
1981 The Carpenter (remarque)	Closed	1981	100.00	3000
1982 Frolicking	Closed	1994	60.00	350
1982 Gathering	Closed	1994	60.00	350-450
1982 Little Children, Come to Me	Closed	1994	50.00	500
1982 Little Children, Come to Me, remarque	50	N/A	100.00	500
1982 Posing	Closed	1987	70.00	350
1982 Poulets	Closed	1994	60.00	350
1982 Surprise	Closed	1988	50.00	350

Portraits of Love - F. Hook

YEAR ISSUE	EDITION LIMIT	YEAR RETD.	ISSUE PRICE	*QUOTE U.S.$
1988 Expectation	Closed	1991	25.00	25
1988 In Mother's Arms	Closed	1990	25.00	25
1988 My Kitty	Closed	1992	25.00	25
1988 Remember When...	Closed	1991	25.00	25
1988 Sharing	Closed	1991	25.00	25
1988 Sunkissed Afternoon	Closed	1991	25.00	25

V.F. Fine Arts

Kuck - S. Kuck

YEAR ISSUE	EDITION LIMIT	YEAR RETD.	ISSUE PRICE	*QUOTE U.S.$
1994 '95 Angel Collection, S/N	750	1995	198.00	198
1995 '96 Angel Collection, S/N	750		198.00	198
1997 '98 Angel Collection	750		135.00	135
1997 '98 Angel Collection, canvas	150		330.00	330
1998 Afternoon Tea	1,250		95.00	95
1998 Afternoon Tea, Canvas	395		240.00	240
1993 Best Friend, proof	250	N/A	175.00	225
1993 Best Friends, canvas transfer	250	N/A	500.00	600
1993 Best Friends, S/N	2,500	N/A	145.00	150
1994 Best of Days, S/N	750	1994	160.00	175
1989 Bundle of Joy, S/N	1,000	1989	125.00	250
1993 Buttons & Bows, proof	95	N/A	125.00	150
1993 Buttons & Bows, S/N	950	N/A	95.00	125
1990 Chopsticks, proof	150	1991	120.00	150
1990 Chopsticks, remarque	25	1991	160.00	200
1990 Chopsticks, S/N	1,500	1990	80.00	95
1995 Christmas Magic, S/N	950		80.00	80
1987 The Daisy, proof	90	1988	40.00	175
1987 The Daisy, S/N	900	1988	30.00	125
1989 Day Dreaming, proof	90	1989	225.00	250
1989 Day Dreaming, remarque	50	1989	300.00	395
1989 Day Dreaming, S/N	900	1989	150.00	200
1994 Dear Santa, S/N	950	1994	95.00	125-225
1992 Duet, canvas framed	500	1994	255.00	325
1992 Duet, proof	95	N/A	175.00	200
1992 Duet, S/N	950	N/A	125.00	135
1998 Enchanted Garden	950		95.00	95
1998 Enchanted Garden, canvas	295		240.00	240
1988 First Recital, proof	25	1988	250.00	750
1988 First Recital, remarque	25	1988	400.00	1000
1988 First Recital, S/N	150	1988	200.00	500
1990 First Snow, proof	50	1990	150.00	250
1990 First Snow, remarque	25	1990	200.00	350
1990 First Snow, S/N	500	1990	95.00	150
1987 The Flower Girl, proof	90	1987	50.00	125
1987 The Flower Girl, S/N	900	1987	40.00	95
1994 Garden Memories, canvas transfer	250	N/A	500.00	500
1994 Garden Memories, S/N	2,500	N/A	145.00	175
1997 Gift From Angel	950		74.50	75
1997 Gift From Angel, AP	95		82.00	82
1997 Gift From Angel, canvas	295		119.50	120
1991 God's Gift, proof	150	N/A	150.00	175
1991 God's Gift, S/N	1,500	1993	95.00	125
1997 Golden Days	950		75.00	75
1997 Golden Days, canvas	295		120.00	120
1997 Gone Fishing	950		75.00	75
1997 Gone Fishing, canvas	495		120.00	120
1993 Good Morning, canvas	250	1993	500.00	500
1993 Good Morning, proof	50	N/A	175.00	200
1993 Good Morning, S/N	2,500	N/A	145.00	165
1997 Heavenly Whisper	950		74.50	75
1997 Heavenly Whisper, AP	95		82.00	82
1997 Heavenly Whisper, canvas	295		119.50	120
1996 Hidden Garden, canvas transfer	395		379.00	379
1996 Hidden Garden, S/N	950	1996	95.00	95
1995 Homecoming, proof	95	1995	172.50	173
1995 Homecoming, S/N	1,150	1995	125.00	125
1989 Innocence, proof	90	1989	225.00	275
1989 Innocence, remarque	50	1989	300.00	395
1989 Innocence, S/N	900	1989	150.00	220
1997 Interlude	500	1997	145.00	145
1997 Interlude, AP	50		175.00	175
1997 Interlude, canvas	200		300.00	300
1992 Joyous Day, canvas transfer	250	N/A	250.00	295
1992 Joyous Day, proof	120	N/A	175.00	200
1992 Joyous Day, S/N	1,200	1993	125.00	150
1997 Kate & Oliver	3,000		80.00	80
1997 Kate & Oliver, canvas	1,000		90.00	90
1997 Kitten Tails	950		75.00	75
1997 Kitten Tails, canvas	495		120.00	120
1988 The Kitten, proof	50	1988	150.00	1000
1988 The Kitten, remarque	25	1988	250.00	1200
1988 The Kitten, S/N	350	1988	120.00	1000
1990 Le Beau, proof	150	1990	120.00	225
1990 Le Beau, remarque	25	1990	160.00	275
1990 Le Beau, S/N	1,500	1990	80.00	175
1987 Le Papillion, proof	35	1990	110.00	175
1987 Le Papillion, remarque	7	1990	150.00	250
1987 Le Papillion, S/N	350	1990	90.00	150
1990 Lilly Pond, color remarque	125	1990	500.00	500
1990 Lilly Pond, proof	75	1990	200.00	200
1990 Lilly Pond, S/N	750	1990	150.00	150
1997 Lily Pond, canvas	295		135.00	135
1988 Little Ballerina, proof	25	1988	150.00	350
1988 Little Ballerina, remarque	25	1988	225.00	450
1988 Little Ballerina, S/N	150	1988	110.00	275
1987 The Loveseat, proof	90	1987	40.00	150
1987 The Loveseat, S/N	900	1987	30.00	100
1991 Memories, S/N	5,000	1991	195.00	250
1997 Merry Christmas	950		95.00	95
1997 Merry Christmas, canvas	495		240.00	240
1987 Mother's Love, proof	12	1987	225.00	1200
1987 Mother's Love, S/N	150	1987	195.00	750
1988 My Dearest, proof	50	1988	200.00	900
1988 My Dearest, remarque	25	1988	325.00	1200
1988 My Dearest, S/N	350	1988	160.00	700
1995 Night Before Christmas, S/N	1,150		95.00	95
1995 Playful Kitten	950	1995	95.00	95
1997 Precious	950		95.00	95
1997 Precious, canvas	395		265.00	265
1997 Puppy Love	950	1997	75.00	75
1997 Puppy Love, canvas	495	1997	120	120
1989 Puppy, proof	50	1989	180.00	500
1989 Puppy, remarque	50	1989	240.00	750
1989 Puppy, S/N	500	1989	120.00	400
1997 Quiet Garden	950		109.00	109
1997 Quiet Garden, AP	95		139.00	139
1997 Quiet Garden, canvas	295		249.00	249
1987 A Quiet Time, proof	90	1987	50.00	100
1987 A Quiet Time, S/N	900	1987	40.00	75
1987 The Reading Lesson, proof	90	1987	70.00	200
1987 The Reading Lesson, S/N	900	1987	60.00	150
1997 Rehearsal	950	1998	75.00	75
1997 Rehearsal, canvas	495		120.00	120
1995 Rhapsody & Lace	1,150		95.00	100
1989 Rose Garden, proof	50	1989	150.00	400
1989 Rose Garden, remarque	50	1989	200.00	500
1989 Rose Garden, S/N	500	1989	95.00	390
1986 Silhouette, proof	25	1987	90.00	250
1986 Silhouette, S/N	250	1987	80.00	200
1997 Sisters	950		75.00	75
1997 Sisters, canvas	495		120.00	120
1989 Sisters, proof	90	1989	150.00	550
1989 Sisters, remarque	50	1989	200.00	650
1989 Sisters, S/N	900	1988	95.00	300
1989 Sonatina, proof	90	1989	225.00	700
1989 Sonatina, remarque	50	1989	300.00	850
1989 Sonatina, S/N	900	1989	150.00	400
1986 Summer Reflections, proof	90	1987	70.00	300
1986 Summer Reflections, S/N	900	1987	60.00	250
1997 Take Me Home	950		125.00	125
1997 Take Me Home, canvas	295		295.00	295
1997 Tea With Kitty	950		80.00	80
1997 Tea With Kitty, canvas	295		200.00	200
1986 Tender Moments, proof	50	1986	80.00	300
1986 Tender Moments, S/N	500	1986	70.00	200
1993 Thinking of You, canvas transfer	250	1993	500.00	500
1993 Thinking of You, S/N	2,500	N/A	145.00	175
1988 Wild Flowers, proof	50	1988	175.00	300
1988 Wild Flowers, remarque	25	1988	250.00	400
1988 Wild Flowers, S/N	350	1988	160.00	250
1992 Yesterday, canvas framed	550	N/A	195.00	200
1992 Yesterday, proof	95	N/A	150.00	150
1992 Yesterday, S/N	950	N/A	95.00	95

Walnut Ridge Collectibles

Home Accents - K. Bejma

YEAR ISSUE	EDITION LIMIT	YEAR RETD.	ISSUE PRICE	*QUOTE U.S.$
1998 Alexandra 9005	Retrd.	1999	300.00	300
1998 Belsnickle 9006	Retrd.	1999	300.00	300
1999 Cat 9017	Retrd.	1999	300.00	300
1998 Snowman 9013	Retrd.	1999	300.00	300
1999 St. Nick's Visit 9021	Retrd.	1999	500.00	500

Willitts Designs

Cooperstown Film Cels - Willitts Designs

YEAR ISSUE	EDITION LIMIT	YEAR RETD.	ISSUE PRICE	*QUOTE U.S.$
1997 Babe Ruth	Retrd.	1999	25.00	25
1997 Hank Aaron	Retrd.	1999	25.00	25
1997 Lou Gehrig	Retrd.	1999	25.00	25
1997 Ted Williams	Retrd.	1999	25.00	25

Cooperstown Lithograph w/Lighted Film Cel - Willitts Designs

YEAR ISSUE	EDITION LIMIT	YEAR RETD.	ISSUE PRICE	*QUOTE U.S.$
1997 Babe Ruth/Lou Gehrig	700	1999	250.00	250
1997 Hank Aaron	2,500	1999	200.00	200
1997 Jackie Robinson	2,500	1999	200.00	200
1998 Mickey Mantle	2,500	1999	200.00	200
1997 Ted Williams	2,500	1999	200.00	200

Cooperstown Motion Cels - Willitts Designs

YEAR ISSUE	EDITION LIMIT	YEAR RETD.	ISSUE PRICE	*QUOTE U.S.$
1997 Babe Ruth	14,500	1999	25.00	25
1997 Hank Aaron	14,500	1999	25.00	25

*Quotes have been rounded up to nearest dollar

YEAR ISSUE	EDITION LIMIT	YEAR RETD.	ISSUE PRICE	*QUOTE U.S.$
1997 Jackie Robinson	14,500	1999	25.00	25
1997 Lou Gehrig	14,500	1999	25.00	25
1997 Stan Musial	14,500	1999	25.00	25
1997 Ted Williams	14,500	1999	25.00	25

Disney Showcase Collection Film Cels - Willitts Designs

YEAR ISSUE	EDITION LIMIT	YEAR RETD.	ISSUE PRICE	*QUOTE U.S.$
1998 Beauty and the Beast: Beast	Retrd.	1999	25.00	25
1998 Beauty and the Beast: Belle	Retrd.	1999	25.00	25
1998 Beauty and the Beast: Enchanted Objects	Retrd.	1999	25.00	25
1998 Beauty and the Beast: Gaston	Retrd.	1999	25.00	25
1998 Cinderella	Retrd.	1999	25.00	25
1998 Cinderella: Menagerie	Retrd.	1999	25.00	25
1998 Cinderella: Royals	Retrd.	1999	25.00	25
1998 Cinderella: Stepfamily	Retrd.	1999	25.00	25
1998 Magician Mickey	Retrd.	1999	25.00	25
1998 Mickey Mouse: Brave Little Tailor	Retrd.	1999	25.00	25
1998 Mickey Mouse: Prince and the Pauper	Retrd.	1999	25.00	25
1998 Mickey Mouse: Runaway Brain	Retrd.	1999	25.00	25
1998 Peter Pan	Retrd.	1999	25.00	25
1998 Peter Pan: Captain Hook	Retrd.	1999	25.00	25
1998 Peter Pan: Citizens of Neverland	Retrd.	1999	25.00	25
1998 Peter Pan: Tinkerbell	Retrd.	1999	25.00	25
1998 Peter Pan: Wendy, Michael, John	Retrd.	1999	25.00	25
1998 Snow White	Retrd.	1999	25.00	25
1998 Snow White Commemorative	Retrd.	1999	25.00	25
1998 Snow White: Seven Dwarfs	Retrd.	1999	25.00	25
1998 Snow White: Wicked Queen	Retrd.	1999	25.00	25

Disney Showcase Collection Motion Cels - Willitts Designs

YEAR ISSUE	EDITION LIMIT	YEAR RETD.	ISSUE PRICE	*QUOTE U.S.$
1998 Beauty and the Beast	Retrd.	1999	25.00	25
1998 Cinderella	Retrd.	1999	25.00	25
1998 Mickey Mouse (Brave Little Tailor)	Retrd.	1999	25.00	25
1998 Peter Pan	Retrd.	1999	25.00	25
1998 Snow White	Retrd.	1999	25.00	25

Disney Showcase Lithograph w/Lighted Film Cel - Willitts Designs

YEAR ISSUE	EDITION LIMIT	YEAR RETD.	ISSUE PRICE	*QUOTE U.S.$
1998 Beauty & the Beast	2,500	1999	200.00	200
1998 Cinderella	2,500	1999	200.00	200
1998 Mickey Mouse	5,000	1999	200.00	200
1998 Peter Pan	2,500	1999	200.00	200
1998 Snow White	2,500	1999	200.00	200

MasterPeace Collection - Various

YEAR ISSUE	EDITION LIMIT	YEAR RETD.	ISSUE PRICE	*QUOTE U.S.$
1998 Forgiven - T. Blackshear	Retrd.	1999	40.00	40
1998 The Invitation - M. Weistling	Retrd.	1999	99.00	99
1998 Victorious Lion of Judah - M. Dudash	Retrd.	1999	99.00	99
1998 Watchers in the Night - T. Blackshear	Retrd.	1999	50.00	50

Thomas Blackshear's Ebony Visions - T. Blackshear

YEAR ISSUE	EDITION LIMIT	YEAR RETD.	ISSUE PRICE	*QUOTE U.S.$
1997 Ebony Visions-Canvas Transfer (framed)	950	1998	575.00	575
1997 Ebony Visions-Canvas Transfer A/P (framed)	100	1998	690.00	690
1997 Ebony Visions-Canvas Transfer G/P (framed)	100	1998	747.50	748
1998 Ebony Visions-Lithograph (framed)	1,950	2000	275.00	275
1998 Ebony Visions-Lithograph A/P (framed)	50	2000	330.00	330
1998 Ebony Visions-Lithograph G/P (framed)	50	2000	357.00	357

Titanic Film Cels - Willitts Designs

YEAR ISSUE	EDITION LIMIT	YEAR RETD.	ISSUE PRICE	*QUOTE U.S.$
1998 Cal and Love Joy	Retrd.	1999	25.00	25
1998 Crew	Retrd.	1999	25.00	25
1998 Eternal Romance	2,500	1999	25.00	25
1998 Jack & Rose	Retrd.	1999	25.00	25
1998 Jack Dawson	Retrd.	1999	25.00	25
1998 Passengers	Retrd.	1999	25.00	25
1998 Rose DeWitt Bukater	Retrd.	1999	25.00	25
1998 Titanic	Retrd.	1999	25.00	25

Titanic Lithograph w/Lighted Film Cel - Willitts Designs

YEAR ISSUE	EDITION LIMIT	YEAR RETD.	ISSUE PRICE	*QUOTE U.S.$
1998 Domestic	5,000	1999	200	200
1998 I'm Flying	5,000	1999	200	200
1998 International	2,500	1999	200	200
1998 Titanic	2,500	1999	200	200

Zolan Fine Arts, LLC

Angel Songs - D. Zolan

YEAR ISSUE	EDITION LIMIT	YEAR RETD.	ISSUE PRICE	*QUOTE U.S.$
1996 Harp Song	200	1997	220.00	220
1996 Love Song	200	1997	220.00	220
1997 Heavenly Song	200	1997	220.00	220

Single Issue - D. Zolan

YEAR ISSUE	EDITION LIMIT	YEAR RETD.	ISSUE PRICE	*QUOTE U.S.$
1997 Country Pumpkins	400	1998	220.00	220
1996 Rained Out	200	1997	220.00	220
1997 Summertime Friends	400	1998	220.00	220

NUTCRACKERS

Christian Ulbricht USA

Christian Ulbricht Collectors' Club - C. Ulbricht

YEAR ISSUE	EDITION LIMIT	YEAR RETD.	ISSUE PRICE	*QUOTE U.S.$
1998 The Lantern Child	Retrd.	1999	Gift	45-50
1998 SnowKing 000501	Retrd.	1999	154.00	200-300
1999 Arabian Knight	Retrd.	2000	Gift	N/A
1999 Teddybear King 000505	Retrd.	2000	154.00	154
2000 Bird Seller Smoker 35-210	5/01		Gift	N/A
2000 Frog King 000508	5/01		154.00	154

Christian Ulbricht Event - C. Ulbricht

YEAR ISSUE	EDITION LIMIT	YEAR RETD.	ISSUE PRICE	*QUOTE U.S.$
1997 Woodpecker 32-450	2,500	1997	49.95	125-150
1998 Penguin 32-451	Yr.Iss.	1998	49.95	65-100
1999 Bluebird 32-453	Yr.Iss.	1999	65.00	65-100
2000 Cardinal 32-455	Yr.Iss.		49.95	50

American Folk Hero/Midwest© - C. Ulbricht

YEAR ISSUE	EDITION LIMIT	YEAR RETD.	ISSUE PRICE	*QUOTE U.S.$
1994 Davy Crockett 12960-9	1,500	1996	160.00	170-229
1994 Johnny Appleseed 12959-3	1,500	1996	160.00	200-229
1995 Paul Bunyan 12800-8	1,500	1996	170.00	170-199
1996 Sacajawea 17018-2	1,000	1996	200.00	185-200
1996 Wyatt Earp 17019-9	1,000	1996	200.00	200-225

A Christmas Carol - C. Ulbricht

YEAR ISSUE	EDITION LIMIT	YEAR RETD.	ISSUE PRICE	*QUOTE U.S.$
1997 Bob Cratchit & Tiny Tim 000145	5,000		236.00	236
1994 Bob Cratchit and Tiny Tim/Midwest© 09577-5	2,500	1996	210.00	275
1996 Ghost of Christmas Past/Midwest© 18299-4	1,500	1996	200.00	275-350
1992 Ghost of Christmas Present/Midwest© 12041-5	1,500	1996	170.00	179-300
2000 Ghost of Christmas Yet to Come 000180	5,000		236.00	236
1996 Ghost of Christmas Yet to Come/Midwest© 17021-2	1,500	1996	190.00	199-300
1999 Marley's Ghost 000170	5,000		236.00	236
1998 Mrs. Cratchit 000149	5,000		230.00	230
1996 Scrooge 000123	5,000		228.00	228
1993 Scrooge/Midwest© 09584-3	2,500	1996	200.00	250

Don Quixote - C. Ulbricht

YEAR ISSUE	EDITION LIMIT	YEAR RETD.	ISSUE PRICE	*QUOTE U.S.$
2000 Don Quixote 000188	5,000		236.00	236
2000 Sancho Pansa 000189	5,000		236.00	236

Great American Inventors - C. Ulbricht

YEAR ISSUE	EDITION LIMIT	YEAR RETD.	ISSUE PRICE	*QUOTE U.S.$
1998 Alexander Graham Bell 000148	1,500	2000	250.00	250-270
1997 Henry Ford 000146	1,500	2000	260.00	260-270
1996 Thomas Edison 000129	1,500	2000	270.00	270

Limited Edition Nutcrackers - C. Ulbricht

YEAR ISSUE	EDITION LIMIT	YEAR RETD.	ISSUE PRICE	*QUOTE U.S.$
1998 Angel 000147	2,500	2000	230.00	230
2000 Artist 000187	2,500		230.00	230
1997 Biker Lady 000124	5,000	1999	198.00	210-220
2000 Country Santa 000183	2,500		230.00	230
1997 Doc Holiday 000137	3,000	2000	222.00	222-229
1999 Dottie Doolittle 000172	5,000		230.00	230
1997 Eagle Dancer 000144	3,000	2000	240.00	240
1996 Elf on Reindeer 000128	5,000	1999	180.00	180
2000 Father Christmas 000184	2,500		230.00	230
2000 Father Time 000191	2,500		236.00	236
1997 Frosty 000143	3,000	2000	117.00	117-119
2000 Hans the Clockmaker 000186	2,500		236.00	236
1997 Jack the Hacker 000135	3,000	2000	240.00	240
2000 James the Golfer 000185	2,500		222.00	222
1999 King Henry VIII 000168	5,000		230.00	230
1998 Lawyer 000149	2,500		222.00	222
1996 Lone Wolf 000107	5,000	2000	209.00	209
2000 Millenium 000200	2,500		236.00	236
1996 Moon & Star Santa 000112	5,000	2000	219.00	219
1994 Mr. Santa Claus/Midwest© 9588-1	2,500	1996	160.00	190-200
1998 Mr. Snowman 000154	2,500	2000	154.00	154-160
1994 Mrs. Santa Claus/Midwest© 9587-4	2,500	1996	160.00	190-200
1998 Mrs. Snowman 000155	2,500	2000	154.00	154-160
1997 Nic Taylor 000134	3,000	2000	240.00	240
1999 Oliver Pickwick 000171	5,000		230.00	230
1998 Santa in Canoe 000163	2,500	2000	230.00	230
1996 Santa in Chimney 000131	5,000		219.00	219
1999 Santa in the Alps 000175	2,500		222.00	222
1997 Santa MacNic 000133	3,000	2000	230.00	230
1997 Santa O'Claus 000132	3,000	2000	230.00	230
1996 Santa on Reindeer 000127	5,000	1999	180.00	180
1998 Santa w/ Long Robe 000161	2,500		222.00	222
1998 Santa w/ Short Robe 000152	2,500		222.00	222
1997 Santa Winterwonderland 000140	3,000	2000	230.00	230
1997 Santa's Ark 000139	3,000	2000	230.00	230
1999 Santa's Coffeetime 000169	2,500		230.00	230
1997 Stars & Stripes Forever 000138	3,000		222.00	222
1998 Summer Wonderland 000153	3,000	2000	230.00	218-230
1999 Sun Face 000174	3,000		240.00	240
1996 Teddybear Maker 000109	500	1996	270.00	600-650
1996 Teddybear Santa 000111	5,000	1998	200.00	225-229
2000 V. Two Sam 000182	2,500		230.00	230
1998 White Buffalo 000157	3,000		240.00	240
1996 White Feather 000108	5,000	2000	209.00	209

Nutcracker Ballet - C. Ulbricht

YEAR ISSUE	EDITION LIMIT	YEAR RETD.	ISSUE PRICE	*QUOTE U.S.$
1996 Clara 000121	5,000		219.00	219
1996 Herr Drosselmeyer 000119	5,000		228.00	228
1996 Mouse King 000120	5,000		228.00	228
1996 Prince 000122	5,000		219.00	219
2000 Sugar Plum Fairy w/Music 000190	5,000		270.00	270
1998 Toy Soldier 000165	5,000		238.00	238

Nutcracker Ballet/Midwest© - C. Ulbricht

YEAR ISSUE	EDITION LIMIT	YEAR RETD.	ISSUE PRICE	*QUOTE U.S.$
1991 Clara 03657-0	Retrd.	1996	124.00	200-220
1991 Herr Drosselmeyer 03656-3	Retrd.	1996	160.00	229-250
1991 Mouse King 04510-7	Retrd.	1996	160.00	225-229
1991 Prince 03665-5	Retrd.	1996	154.00	154-220
1991 Toy Soldier 03666-2	Retrd.	1996	154.00	154-238

Nutcrackers - C. Ulbricht

YEAR ISSUE	EDITION LIMIT	YEAR RETD.	ISSUE PRICE	*QUOTE U.S.$
1993 Red Riding Hood	Retrd.	1996	120.00	165-250

Peter Pan© Disney - C. Ulbricht

YEAR ISSUE	EDITION LIMIT	YEAR RETD.	ISSUE PRICE	*QUOTE U.S.$
1998 Captain Hook 000500	2,500		275.00	275
1999 Peter Pan 000502	2,500		190.00	190
1999 Tinker Bell 000504	2,500		160.00	160

Plays of Shakespeare - C. Ulbricht

YEAR ISSUE	EDITION LIMIT	YEAR RETD.	ISSUE PRICE	*QUOTE U.S.$
1999 Hamlet 000166	5,000		236.00	236
1997 Juliet 000136	5,000		230.00	230
1998 Romeo 000156	5,000		236.00	236
1997 Shakespeare 000142	5,000		236.00	236

Santa Claus/Midwest© - C. Ulbricht

YEAR ISSUE	EDITION LIMIT	YEAR RETD.	ISSUE PRICE	*QUOTE U.S.$
1992 Father Christmas (1st) 07094-9	Retrd.	N/A	210.00	239-350
1993 Toymaker (2nd) 09531-7	2,500	1996	210.00	210-250
1994 Victorian Santa (3rd) 2961-6	2,500	1996	210.00	250
1995 King of Christmas (4th) 13665-2	2,500	1996	210.00	500-750

Snow White© Disney - C. Ulbricht

YEAR ISSUE	EDITION LIMIT	YEAR RETD.	ISSUE PRICE	*QUOTE U.S.$
1999 Bashful 000517	2,500		170.00	170
1999 Doc 000511	2,500		170.00	170
1999 Dopey 000516	2,500		170.00	170
1999 Grumpy 000512	2,500		170.00	170
1999 Happy 000514	2,500		170.00	170
1999 Sleepy 000515	2,500		170.00	170
1999 Sneezy 000513	2,500		170.00	170
1999 Snow White 000510	2,500		209.00	209

Three Musketeers - C. Ulbricht

YEAR ISSUE	EDITION LIMIT	YEAR RETD.	ISSUE PRICE	*QUOTE U.S.$
1996 Portos 000114	5,000		200.00	200

Three Wisemen - C. Ulbricht

YEAR ISSUE	EDITION LIMIT	YEAR RETD.	ISSUE PRICE	*QUOTE U.S.$
1996 Caspar 000115	5,000		209.00	209
1999 Melchior 000176	5,000		209.00	209

Wizard of Oz - C. Ulbricht

YEAR ISSUE	EDITION LIMIT	YEAR RETD.	ISSUE PRICE	*QUOTE U.S.$
1998 Cowardly Lion 000151	5,000		240.00	240
1998 Dorothy 000150	5,000		230.00	230
1999 Scarecrow 000167	5,000		230.00	230
1997 Tin Woodsman 000141	5,000		230.00	230
1999 Wicked Witch 000173	5,000		236.00	236
2000 Wizard of Oz 000181	5,000		236.00	236

Christopher Radko

Nutcrackers - C. Radko

YEAR ISSUE	EDITION LIMIT	YEAR RETD.	ISSUE PRICE	*QUOTE U.S.$
1997 The Bishop 97-K01-00	5,000		485.00	485
1997 Candy Stripe 97-K03-00	5,000		445.00	445
1997 Snow Gent 97-K04-00	5,000		445.00	445
1997 Winter Dream 97-K02-00	5,000		485.00	485

Columbus International

Zuber - N. Zuber

YEAR ISSUE	EDITION LIMIT	YEAR RETD.	ISSUE PRICE	*QUOTE U.S.$
1999 Coal Miner	500		169.00	169
1999 Gutenberg	500		179.00	179
1999 Martin Luther	500		179.00	179
1999 Merlin the Magician	500		179.00	179
1999 Millennium Man	2,000		129.00	129
1999 Pool Shark	500		179.00	179
1999 Rock 'n Roller	500		179.00	179
1999 Wolfgang A. Mozart	500		179.00	179

Zuber Columbus Collection™- N. Zuber

YEAR ISSUE	EDITION LIMIT	YEAR RETD.	ISSUE PRICE	*QUOTE U.S.$
1999 Lunar Landing	500		185.00	185
1999 Millennium 2000	2,000		189.00	189

House of Hatten, Inc.

The Nutcracker - D. Calla

YEAR ISSUE	EDITION LIMIT	YEAR RETD.	ISSUE PRICE	*QUOTE U.S.$
1993 Drosselmeir 14" 32305	Retrd.	1994	70.00	70

Nutcracker - V. & S. Rawson

YEAR ISSUE	EDITION LIMIT	YEAR RETD.	ISSUE PRICE	*QUOTE U.S.$
1998 Clara 33851	Open		10.00	10
1998 Drosselmeier 33853	Open		10.00	10
1998 Mouse King 33852	Open		10.00	10
1998 Mrs. Ginger 33854	Open		10.00	10
1998 Nutcracker 33855	Open		10.00	10
1998 Prince 33850	Open		10.00	10

Kurt S. Adler, Inc.

Jim Henson's Muppet Nutcrackers - KSA/JHP

YEAR ISSUE	EDITION LIMIT	YEAR RETD.	ISSUE PRICE	*QUOTE U.S.$
1993 Kermit The Frog H1223	Retrd.	1995	90.00	90

Nutcracker Suite - KSA Design Team

YEAR ISSUE	EDITION LIMIT	YEAR RETD.	ISSUE PRICE	*QUOTE U.S.$
1998 Clara w/Nutcracker W1904	Open		45.00	45
1998 Drosselmeir W1905	Open		45.00	45
1998 Mouse King W1907	Open		45.00	45
1998 Nutcracker Prince W1906	Open		45.00	45
1998 Sugar Plum Fairy W1918	Retrd.	1999	45.00	45-50

Steinbach Nutcracker Collectors' Club - KSA/Steinbach

YEAR ISSUE	EDITION LIMIT	YEAR RETD.	ISSUE PRICE	*QUOTE U.S.$
1995 Mini Town Crier	Retrd.	1997	Gift	100
1995 King Wenceslaus ES900	Retrd.	1997	225.00	550-650
1997 Mini Chimney Sweep	Retrd.	1998	Gift	55-75
1997 Marek The Royal Guardsman ES856	Retrd.	1998	225.00	400-450
1998 Mini Forester	Retrd.	1999	Gift	50-55
1998 Gustav The Royal Cook ES1824	Retrd.	1999	225.00	420-450
1999 Bavarian Beer Drinker	Retrd.	2000	Gift	N/A
1999 Otto, The Royal Drummer ES1828	Retrd.	2000	250.00	250
2000 Black Forest Clockmaker	4/01		Gift	N/A

YEAR ISSUE	EDITION LIMIT	YEAR RETD.	ISSUE PRICE	*QUOTE U.S.$
2000 Reginald the Beefeater	4/01		250.00	250

Steinbach Nutcracker American Inventor Series - KSA/Steinbach

YEAR ISSUE	EDITION LIMIT	YEAR RETD.	ISSUE PRICE	*QUOTE U.S.$
1993 Ben Franklin ES635	12,000	1996	225.00	450-500

Steinbach Nutcracker American Presidents Series - KSA/Steinbach

YEAR ISSUE	EDITION LIMIT	YEAR RETD.	ISSUE PRICE	*QUOTE U.S.$
1992 Abraham Lincoln ES622	12,000	1995	195.00	450-475
1992 George Washington ES623	12,000	1994	195.00	450-750
1993 Teddy Roosevelt ES644	10,000	1997	225.00	400-450
1996 Thomas Jefferson ES866	7,500	1997	260.00	450

Steinbach Nutcracker Biblical - KSA/Steinbach

YEAR ISSUE	EDITION LIMIT	YEAR RETD.	ISSUE PRICE	*QUOTE U.S.$
1998 Joseph and the Dreamcoat ES1810	7,500		255.00	255
2000 King Solomon ES1811	7,500		275.00	275
1997 Moses ES894	10,000		250.00	250
1996 Noah ES893	10,000	1999	260.00	375-450

Steinbach Nutcracker Camelot Series - KSA/Steinbach

YEAR ISSUE	EDITION LIMIT	YEAR RETD.	ISSUE PRICE	*QUOTE U.S.$
1992 King Arthur ES621	Retrd.	1993	195.00	1200-1500
1991 Merlin The Magician ES610	Retrd.	1991	185.00	4500
1995 Queen Guenevere ES869	10,000	1997	245.00	350-450
1994 Sir Galahad ES862	12,000	1997	225.00	225-450
1993 Sir Lancelot ES638	12,000	1997	225.00	225-450

Steinbach Nutcracker Christmas Carol Series - KSA/Steinbach

YEAR ISSUE	EDITION LIMIT	YEAR RETD.	ISSUE PRICE	*QUOTE U.S.$
1998 Bob Cratchit and Tiny Tim ES1820	7,500		265.00	265
1997 Ebenezer Scrooge ES896	7,500		250.00	275
1999 Marley's Ghost ES1819	7,500		265.00	265

Steinbach Nutcracker Christmas Legends Series - KSA/Steinbach

YEAR ISSUE	EDITION LIMIT	YEAR RETD.	ISSUE PRICE	*QUOTE U.S.$
1995 1930s Santa Claus ES891	7,500	2000	245.00	245-450
1999 Bavarian Santa ES1827	7,500		270.00	270
2000 Duncan Scottish Santa ES1829	7,500		275.00	275
1993 Father Christmas ES645	7,500	1996	225.00	500-750
1997 Grandfather Frost ES895	7,500	1999	250.00	350-750
1998 Père Noel ES1822	7,500	2000	250.00	250-450
1994 St. Nicholas, The Bishop ES865	7,500	1995	225.00	500-750

Steinbach Nutcracker Collection - KSA/Steinbach

YEAR ISSUE	EDITION LIMIT	YEAR RETD.	ISSUE PRICE	*QUOTE U.S.$
1999 Captain Hook ES1826	7,500		270.00	270
1991 Columbus ES697	Retrd.	1992	194.00	229-260
1992 Happy Santa ES601	Retrd.	1998	190.00	199-220
1984 Oil Sheik	Retrd.	1985	100.00	1500-1750

Steinbach Nutcracker Famous Chieftains Series - KSA/Steinbach

YEAR ISSUE	EDITION LIMIT	YEAR RETD.	ISSUE PRICE	*QUOTE U.S.$
1995 Black Hawk ES889	7,500	1996	245.00	375-450
1993 Chief Sitting Bull ES637	8,500	1995	225.00	500-600
1994 Red Cloud ES864	8,500	1996	225.00	229-295

Steinbach Nutcracker Mini Series - KSA/Steinbach

YEAR ISSUE	EDITION LIMIT	YEAR RETD.	ISSUE PRICE	*QUOTE U.S.$
2000 Bavarian Santa ES355	7,500		65.00	65
1999 Bob Cratchit ES358	10,000		66.00	66
1998 Grandfather Frost ES343	10,000	2000	60.00	55-75
2000 Joseph ES353	7,500		65.00	65
1997 King Arthur ES337	15,000		50.00	50
2000 Marley's Ghost ES362	7,500		65.00	65
1996 Merlin ES335	15,000	1999	50.00	55-75
1999 Moses ES359	10,000		66.00	66
1997 Noah and His Ark ES339	10,000		50.00	50
1999 Père Noel ES357	10,000		66.00	66
1996 Robin Hood ES336	10,000		50.00	50
1998 Scrooge ES342	10,000		60.00	60
1999 Sir Galahad ES356	10,000		66.00	66
1998 Sir Lancelot ES344	10,000		60.00	60
1997 St. Nicholas ES338	15,000		50.00	50

Steinbach Nutcracker Peter Pan Series - KSA/Steinbach

YEAR ISSUE	EDITION LIMIT	YEAR RETD.	ISSUE PRICE	*QUOTE U.S.$
2000 Crocodile ES1818	5,000		265.00	265

Steinbach Nutcracker Royalty Series - KSA/Steinbach

YEAR ISSUE	EDITION LIMIT	YEAR RETD.	ISSUE PRICE	*QUOTE U.S.$
1998 King Henry ES1823	7,500		255.00	255

Steinbach Nutcracker Tales of Sherwood Forest - KSA/Steinbach

YEAR ISSUE	EDITION LIMIT	YEAR RETD.	ISSUE PRICE	*QUOTE U.S.$
1995 Friar Tuck ES890	7,500	1997	245.00	450-550
1997 King Richard the Lion-Hearted ES897	7,500	1999	250.00	300-450
1999 Maid Marion ES1825	5,000		260.00	260
1992 Robin Hood ES863	7,500	1996	225.00	500-750
1996 Sherif of Nottingham ES892	7,500	1999	260.00	400

Steinbach Nutcracker Three Musketeers - KSA/Steinbach

YEAR ISSUE	EDITION LIMIT	YEAR RETD.	ISSUE PRICE	*QUOTE U.S.$
1996 Aramis ES722	7,500	1997	130.00	145-175
1998 Athos ES1821	7,500		125.00	125
2000 Porthos ES1815	7,500		180.00	180

Steinbach Nutcracker Wizard of Oz Series - KSA/Warner Brothers

YEAR ISSUE	EDITION LIMIT	YEAR RETD.	ISSUE PRICE	*QUOTE U.S.$
1999 Scarecrow ES961	Open		270.00	270
2000 Tin Man ES960	Open		275.00	275

Zuber Nutcracker Series - KSA/Zuber

YEAR ISSUE	EDITION LIMIT	YEAR RETD.	ISSUE PRICE	*QUOTE U.S.$
1992 The Annapolis Midshipman EK7	5,000	1994	125.00	125
1992 The Bavarian EK16	5,000	1994	130.00	130-139
1992 Bronco Billy The Cowboy EK1	5,000	1994	125.00	125-140
1992 The Chimney Sweep EK6	5,000	1993	125.00	125
1992 The Country Singer EK19	5,000	1993	125.00	125
1992 The Fisherman EK17	5,000	1996	125.00	130-140
1994 The Gardner EK26	2,500	1996	150.00	150
1992 Gepetto, The Toymaker EK9	5,000	1994	125.00	125-139
1992 The Gold Prospector EK18	5,000	1994	125.00	125
1992 The Golfer EK5	5,000	1994	125.00	125-130
1993 Herr Drosselmeir Nutcracker EK21	5,000	1996	150.00	1000-2500
1993 The Ice Cream Vendor EK24	5,000	1996	150.00	150
1992 The Indian EK15	5,000	1994	135.00	135
1994 Jazz Player EK25	2,500	1999	145.00	140-145
1994 Kurt the Traveling Salesman EK28	2,500	1994	155.00	155-159
1994 Mouse King EK31	2,500		150.00	150
1993 Napoleon Bonaparte EK23	5,000	1994	150.00	150
1992 The Nor' Easter Sea Captain EK3	5,000	1999	125.00	125-140
1992 Paul Bunyan The Lumberjack EK2	5,000	1993	125.00	125
1994 Peter Pan EK28	2,500		145.00	145
1992 The Pilgrim EK14	5,000	1994	125.00	125
1993 The Pizzamaker EK22	5,000	1999	150.00	150
1994 Scuba Diver EK27	2,500	1999	150.00	150
1994 Soccer Player EK30	2,500	1999	145.00	145
1992 TheTyrolean EK4	5,000	1994	125.00	125
1992 The West Point Cadet w/Canon EK8	5,000	1994	130.00	130-135

Midwest of Cannon Falls

Americana Nutcracker Collection - Midwest

YEAR ISSUE	EDITION LIMIT	YEAR RETD.	ISSUE PRICE	*QUOTE U.S.$
1997 Uncle Sam 21166-3	500	1998	170.00	170

Cooperstown Collection - Midwest

YEAR ISSUE	EDITION LIMIT	YEAR RETD.	ISSUE PRICE	*QUOTE U.S.$
1997 Chicago Cubs Baseball Player 22868-5	Retrd.	1998	180.00	180
1997 Chicago White Sox Baseball Player 22867-8	Retrd.	1998	180.00	180
1997 New York Yankees Baseball Player 22869-2	Retrd.	1998	180.00	180

Jolly Follies - S. Gore Evans

YEAR ISSUE	EDITION LIMIT	YEAR RETD.	ISSUE PRICE	*QUOTE U.S.$
2000 Snowman 36727-8	250		150.00	150

Ore Mountain "A Christmas Carol" Nutcrackers - Midwest

YEAR ISSUE	EDITION LIMIT	YEAR RETD.	ISSUE PRICE	*QUOTE U.S.$
1993 Bob Cratchit, 09421-1	5,000	1995	120.00	100-130
1994 Ghost of Christmas Future, 10449-1	1,500	1995	116.00	100-125
1994 Ghost of Christmas Past, 10447-7	1,500	1995	116.00	100-125
1994 Ghost of Christmas Present 12041-5	1,500	1996	116.00	100-125
1994 Marley's Ghost, 10448-4	1,500	1995	116.00	100-125
1993 Scrooge, 05522-9	2,500	1995	104.00	100-125

Ore Mountain "Nutcracker Fantasy" Nutcrackers - Midwest

YEAR ISSUE	EDITION LIMIT	YEAR RETD.	ISSUE PRICE	*QUOTE U.S.$
1995 Clara, 12801-5	5,000		125.00	137
1991 Clara, 8" 01254-3	Retrd.	1995	77.00	100
1994 Herr Drosselmeyer, 10456-9	5,000	2000	110.00	137
1988 Herr Drosselmeyer, 14 1/2" 07506-7	Retrd.	1996	75.00	115
1993 The Mouse King, 05350-8	5,000	1997	100.00	120-140
1988 The Mouse King, 10" 07509-8	Retrd.	1997	60.00	85
1994 Nutcracker Prince, 11001-0	5,000	2000	104.00	140
1988 The Prince, 12 3/4" 07507-4	Retrd.	1996	75.00	105
1988 The Toy Soldier, 11" 07508-1	Retrd.	1996	70.00	95
1995 Toy Soldier, 12804-6	5,000		125.00	125

Ore Mountain Easter Nutcrackers - Midwest

YEAR ISSUE	EDITION LIMIT	YEAR RETD.	ISSUE PRICE	*QUOTE U.S.$
1992 Bunny Painter, 06480-1	Retrd.	1993	77.00	80
1991 Bunny with Egg, 00145-5	Retrd.	1993	77.00	80
1984 March Hare, 00312-1	Retrd.	1993	77.00	80

Ore Mountain Nutcracker Collection - Midwest

YEAR ISSUE	EDITION LIMIT	YEAR RETD.	ISSUE PRICE	*QUOTE U.S.$
1995 American Country Santa, 13195-4	Retrd.	1996	165.00	170
1997 Angel w/Horn 21178-6	Retrd.	1998	250.00	250
1996 Angel with Candle 17010-6	Retrd.	1997	220.00	240
1994 Annie Oakley, 10464-4	Retrd.	1995	128.00	130
1996 Attorney 17012-0	Retrd.	1997	120.00	130
1995 August the Strong, 13185-5	Retrd.	1996	190.00	185-190
1997 Ballerina 21180-9	Retrd.	1998	165.00	165-185
1995 Barbeque Dad, 13193-0	Retrd.	1996	176.00	120-176
1994 Baseball Player, 10459-0	Retrd.	1995	111.00	100-120
1995 Basketball Player, 12784-1	Retrd.	1996	135.00	135
1995 Beefeater, 12797-1	Retrd.	1996	175.00	177-197
1998 Bell Body Snow Flake 25940-5	Retrd.	1998	130.00	130
1997 Bell-shaped Hunter 21172-4	Retrd.	1998	130.00	130
1997 Bell-shaped Santa 21169-4	Retrd.	1998	130.00	130
1994 Black Santa, 10460-6	Retrd.	1995	74.00	74
1993 Cat Witch, 09426-6	Retrd.	1995	93.00	93
1994 Cavalier, 12952-4	Retrd.	1998	80.00	110
1994 Cavalier, 12953-1	Retrd.	1998	65.00	90
1994 Cavalier, 12958-6	Retrd.	1998	57.00	77
1996 Chimney Sweep 17043-4	Retrd.	1998	120.00	130
1995 Chimney Sweep, 00326-8	Retrd.	1999	70.00	76
1992 Christopher Columbus, 00152-3	Retrd.	1992	80.00	80
1991 Clown, 03561-0	Retrd.	1994	115.00	118-138
1994 Confederate Soldier, 12837-4	Retrd.	1996	93.00	110
1996 Count Dracula 17050-2	Retrd.	1997	150.00	150
1989 Country Santa, 09326-9	Retrd.	1995	95.00	150
1996 Cow Farmer 17054-0	Retrd.	1997	120.00	145
1992 Cowboy, 00298-8	Retrd.	1995	97.00	150
1997 Doctor 21173-1	Retrd.	1998	75.00	75
1995 Downhill Santa Skier, 13197-8	Retrd.	1997	145.00	150
1996 Drummer 17044-1	Retrd.	1998	120.00	120
1996 East Coast Santa 17047-2	Retrd.	1997	200.00	220
1990 Elf, 04154-3	Retrd.	1993	70.00	73
1996 Emergency Medical Technician 17013-7	Retrd.	1997	140.00	140
1994 Engineer, 10454-5	Retrd.	1995	108.00	108
1992 Farmer, 01109-6	Retrd.	1994	65.00	77
1996 Female Farmer 17011-3	1,000	1997	145.00	180
1997 Fireman 21170-0	Retrd.	1998	75.00	75
1993 Fireman with Dog, 06592-1	Retrd.	1996	134.00	145
1997 Fisherman 21168-7	Open		165.00	165
1989 Fisherman, 09327-6	Retrd.	1995	90.00	100
1996 Frankenstein 17009-0	Retrd.	1997	170.00	190
1997 Gardener 21165-6	Retrd.	1998	160.00	160
1994 Gardening Lady, 10450-7	Retrd.	1996	104.00	112
1993 Gepetto Santa, 09417-4	Retrd.	1995	115.00	115-150
1989 Golfer, 09325-2	Retrd.	1994	85.00	90
1996 Guard 17046-5	Retrd.	1998	120.00	130
1995 Handyman, 12806-0	Retrd.	1996	136.00	137-172
1996 Harlequin Santa 17174-5	Retrd.	1998	150.00	160
1997 Hippie 21184-7	Retrd.	1998	145.00	145
1995 Hockey Player, 12783-4	Retrd.	1996	155.00	155
1995 Hunter Nutcraker 12785-8	Retrd.	1996	136.00	136
1992 Indian, 00195-0	Retrd.	1994	96.00	100
1995 Jack Frost, 12803-9	Retrd.	1997	150.00	150
1997 Jazz Musician 21177-9	Retrd.	1998	200.00	200
1995 Jolly St. Nick with Toys, 13709-3	Retrd.	1996	135.00	135
1995 King Richard the Lionhearted, 12798-8	Retrd.	1996	165.00	165
1996 King with Sceptor 17045-8	Retrd.	1998	120.00	130
1995 Law Scholar, 12789-6	Retrd.	1996	127.00	127
1996 Male Farmer 17015-1	1,000	1997	145.00	145
1990 Merlin the Magician, 04207-6	Retrd.	1995	67.00	75
1994 Miner, 10493-4	Retrd.	1995	110.00	120
1998 Ms. Liberty 25938-2	Retrd.	1998	200.00	200
1994 Nature Lover, 10446-0	Retrd.	1995	112.00	112
1997 Noah 21181-6	Retrd.	1998	150.00	150
1988 Nordic Santa, 08872-2	Retrd.	1995	84.00	110
1996 Northwoods Santa 17048-9	Retrd.	1997	200.00	220
1991 Nutcracker-Maker, 03601-3	Retrd.	1993	62.00	65
1995 Peddler, 12805-3	Retrd.	1996	140.00	140
1995 Pierre Le Chef, 12802-2	Retrd.	1996	147.00	147
1992 Pilgrim, 00188-2	Retrd.	1994	96.00	100
1994 Pinecone Santa, 10461-3	Retrd.	1994	92.00	92
1984 Pinocchio, 00160-8	Retrd.	1996	60.00	68
1995 Pizza Baker, 13194-7	Retrd.	1996	170.00	170
1997 Policeman 21171-7	Retrd.	1998	75.00	75
1997 Portly Carpenter 21287-5	Retrd.	1998	150.00	150
1997 Portly Chef 21163-2	Retrd.	1998	150.00	150
1998 Portly Chimney Sweep 24718-1	Retrd.	1998	150.00	150
1998 Portly Pirate 24436-4	Retrd.	1999	150.00	150
1997 Portly Santa w/Gifts 21164-9	Retrd.	1998	150.00	150
1996 Prince 17038-0	Retrd.	1998	120.00	130
1994 Prince Charming, 10457-6	Retrd.	1995	125.00	130
1994 Pumpkin Head Scarecrow, 10451-1	Retrd.	1996	127.00	140
1994 Regal Prince, 10452-1	Retrd.	1996	140.00	152
1992 Ringmaster, 00196-7	Retrd.	1993	135.00	137-150
1995 Riverboat Gambler, 12787-2	Retrd.	1996	137.00	140
1995 Royal Lion, 13985-1	Retrd.	1996	130.00	140
1995 Santa at Workbench, 13335-4	Retrd.	1996	130.00	140
1998 Santa in Chimney (musical) 24702-0	Retrd.	1998	200.00	200
1994 Santa in Nightshirt, 10462-0	Retrd.	1995	108.00	120
1996 Santa One-Man Band Musical 17051-9	Retrd.	1997	170.00	175
1988 Santa w/Tree & Toys, 07666-8	Retrd.	1993	76.00	87
1993 Santa with Animals, 09424-2	Retrd.	1994	117.00	117
1994 Santa with Basket, 10472-9	Retrd.	1996	80.00	100
1998 Santa with Rudolph 25194-2	Retrd.	1999	200.00	200
1992 Santa with Skis, 01305-2	Retrd.	1994	100.00	110
1990 Sea Captain, 04157-4	Retrd.	1994	86.00	95
1997 Skier 21176-2	Retrd.	1998	180.00	180
1997 Skiing Santa 21252-3	Retrd.	1998	170.00	170
1994 Snow King, 10470-5	Retrd.	1995	108.00	120
1997 Snowman 21183-0	Open		130.00	130
1994 Soccer Player, 10494-1	Retrd.	1995	97.00	107
1994 Sorcerer, 10471-2	Retrd.	1995	100.00	100
1996 Sports Fan 17173-8	Retrd.	1997	120.00	125
1994 Sultan King, 10455-2	Retrd.	1995	130.00	130-145
1995 Teacher, 13196-1	Retrd.	1996	165.00	165
1994 Toy Vendor, 11987-7	Retrd.	1996	124.00	145
1990 Uncle Sam, 04206-9	Retrd.	1993	50.00	62
1994 Union Soldier, 12836-7	Retrd.	1996	93.00	110
1996 Victorian Santa 17172-1	Retrd.	1998	180.00	185
1992 Victorian Santa, 00187-5	Retrd.	1994	130.00	140
1996 Western 17049-6	Retrd.	1997	250.00	250
1997 White Santa with Wreath 21175-5	Retrd.	1998	175.00	175
1993 White Santa, 09533-1	Retrd.	1995	100.00	100
1990 Windsor Club, 04160-4	Retrd.	1994	85.00	87-130
1990 Witch, 04159-8	Retrd.	1995	75.00	76
1990 Woodland Santa, 04191-8	Retrd.	1995	105.00	145-150

San Francisco Music Box Company

Nutcrackers - San Francisco Music Box Company

YEAR ISSUE	EDITION LIMIT	YEAR RETD.	ISSUE PRICE	*QUOTE U.S.$
1998 Alexander the Great	10,000	1998	35.00	35
1999 Father Christmas	10,000	1999	45.00	45
1998 Jolly Ol' St. Nick	10,000	1998	35.00	35
1998 King Arthur	10,000	1998	35.00	35
1999 Prince Charming	10,000	1999	45.00	45
1999 Puss n' Boots	10,000	1999	45.00	45
1999 Sir Galahad	10,000	1999	45.00	45

ORNAMENTS

All God's Children/Miss Martha Originals

Angel Dumpling - M. Root

YEAR ISSUE	EDITION LIMIT	YEAR RETD.	ISSUE PRICE	*QUOTE U.S.$
1993 Eric - 1570	Retrd.	1994	22.50	40-60
1994 Erica - 1578	Retrd.	1995	22.50	39-89
1996 Tia - 1587	Retrd.	1997	23.50	24-60
1997 Tori - 1592	Yr.Iss.	1997	23.00	23-46
1998 Hapi - 1601	Retrd.	1999	24.50	25

*Quotes have been rounded up to nearest dollar

All God's Children/Miss Martha Originals
to Cavanagh Group Intl.

ORNAMENTS

YEAR ISSUE	EDITION LIMIT	YEAR RETD.	ISSUE PRICE	*QUOTE U.S.$

Christmas Ornaments - M. Root

1987 Cameo Ornaments (set of 12) - D1912	Retrd.	1988	144.00	2000-2280
1987 Doll Ornaments (set of 24) - D1924	Retrd.	1988	336.00	3000-3936
1993 Santa with Scooty - 1571	Retrd.	1994	22.50	84-100

American Spirit Collection/Hallmark Keepsake Collections

American Spirit Collection/Hallmark Keepsake Collections

1999 Delaware QMP9400	Open		12.95	15
1999 Pennsylvania QMP9401	Open		12.95	15
1999 New Jersey QMP9402	Open		12.95	15
1999 Georgia QMP9403	Open		12.95	15
1999 Connecticut QMP9404	Open		12.95	15
2000 Massachusetts QMP9423	Open		14.95	15
2000 Maryland QMP9426	Open		14.95	15
2000 South Carolina QMP9429	Open		14.95	15
2000 New Hampshire QMP9432	Open		14.95	15
2000 Virginia QMP9440	Open		14.95	15

Anheuser-Busch, Inc.

A & Eagle Collector Ornament Series - A.-Busch, Inc.

1991 Budweiser Girl-Circa 1890's N3178	Retrd.	N/A	15.00	15-20
1992 1893 Columbian Exposition N3649	Retrd.	N/A	15.00	15-20
1993 Greatest Triumph N4089	Retrd.	N/A	15.00	15-20

Christmas Ornaments - Various

1992 Clydesdales 3 Mini Plate Ornament N3650 - S. Sampson	Retrd.	N/A	23.00	20-28
1993 Budweiser Six-Pack Mini Plate Ornament N4220 - M. Urdahl	Retrd.	1994	10.00	15-30

Annalee Mobilitee Dolls, Inc.

Ornaments - A. Thorndike

1982 Elf Head (green) 7810	Closed	1986	7.00	30
1982 Elf Head (red) 7810	Closed	1986	7.00	30
1982 3" Angel on Cloud (hard) 7820	Closed	1987	13.00	50
1982 3" Angel on Cloud (soft) 7820	Closed	1987	13.00	50
1995 3" Angel Playing Instrument 7819	Closed	1997	16.00	25-35
1986 3" Baby Angel 7820	Closed	1988	12.00	50
1987 3" Baby in Basket 7816	Yr.Iss.	1987	16.00	110
1995 3" Baby in Blue PJ's 7871	Closed	1995	12.00	12-40
1995 3" Baby in Pink PJ's 7872	Closed	1995	12.00	35
1985 3" Baby in Stocking 7870	Yr.Iss.	1985	12.00	60
1985 3" Baby in Stocking 7870	Closed	1988	13.00	50-55
1993 3" Baby Jesus in Manger7881	Closed	1995	18.00	18-45
1987 3" Bear (red ribbon) 7818	Closed	1993	13.00	40
1987 3" Boy & Girl Caroller 7826, 7824	Closed	1988	28.00	75
1986 3" Clown Ornament 7945	Yr.Iss.	1986	12.00	100
1986 3" Drummer Boy 7935	Closed	1989	14.00	18-45
1987 3" Elf (full body) 7822	Closed	1989	14.00	14-45
1993 3" Fishing Santa 7836	Yr.Iss.	1993	25.00	55
1996 3" Gingerbread Boy 7829	Closed	1996	15.00	15-30
1987 3" Girl Caroller 7824	Closed	1988	14.00	40
1995 3" Honey Bear 7817	Closed	1996	14.00	30
1996 3" Just a Jester 7827	Yr.Iss.	1996	21.00	21-25
1987 3" Kid on Sled (sitting) 7812	Closed	1989	17.00	45
1987 3" Kid w/ Snowball 7814	Closed	1989	15.00	45
1987 3" Lovey Bears 7808	Closed	1990	26.00	75
1986 3" Mr & Mrs Victorian Santas 7895, 7900	Closed	1987	28.00	140
1986 3" Mr Victorian Santa 7895	Closed	1987	14.00	65
1987 3" Mrs Santa (logo print) 7838	Closed	1987	13.00	65
1986 3" Mrs Santa 7838	Closed	1986	13.00	60
1984 3" Red Heart (Be Mine) 7855	Closed	1985	4.00	30
1986 3" Skier 7930	Closed	1992	15.00	40
1984 3" Snowman 7845	Closed	1990	15.00	25
1984 3" Star 7850	Closed	1985	7.00	60
1994 3" Sun w/ Santa Hat 7876	Closed	1995	9.00	25
1997 4" When Pigs Fly 7841	Yr.Iss.	1997	17.00	35
1986 5" Elf w/ Stick Horse 7955	Closed	1988	19.00	60
1985 5" Gingerbread Boy 7825	Closed	1986	12.00	35
1991 5" Gingerbread Boy 7825	Closed	1995	18.00	18-30
1994 5" Old World Santa 7800	Closed	1995	24.00	30
1996 5" Old World Santa 7800	Closed	1996	24.00	30
1984 5" Rocking Deer 7840	Closed	1987	14.00	50
1986 5" Stick Horse 7960	Closed	1987	8.00	40
1985 Angel Head 7860	Closed	1986	8.00	40
1994 Annalee Crystal Ornament 7964	Closed	1994	30.00	60
1985 Clown Head 7865	Closed	1986	7.00	55
1980 Deer Head 7815	Closed	1995	11.00	15
1980 Santa Head 7805	Closed	N/A	10.00	10
1991 Snowman Head (green earmuffs) 7830	Closed	1996	13.00	20
1994 Snowman Head (large) 7831	Closed	1994	18.00	75-85
1994 Snowman Head (red earmuffs) 7830	Closed	1996	10.00	30

ANRI

Christmas Eve Series - L. Gaither

1998 First Gift of Christmas, Mr. & Mrs. Santa	500	1998	165.00	165

Disney Four Star Collection - Disney Studios

1989 Maestro Mickey	Yr.Iss.	1989	25.00	75-95
1990 Minnie Mouse	Yr.Iss.	1990	25.00	50

Ferrandiz Message Collection - J. Ferrandiz

1989 Let the Heavens Ring	1,000	1992	215.00	215
1990 Hear The Angels Sing	1,000	1992	225.00	225

Ferrandiz Woodcarvings - J. Ferrandiz

1988 Heavenly Drummer	1,000	1992	175.00	225
1989 Heavenly Strings	1,000	1992	190.00	190

Sarah Kay's First Christmas - S. Kay

1994 Sarah Kay's First Christmas	500	1998	140.00	195
1995 First Xmas Stocking 57502	500	1998	99.00	240
1996 All I Want for Xmas 57503	500	1999	195.00	240
1997 Christmas Puppy	500	1999	295.00	295

Armani

Christmas - G. Armani

1991 Christmas Ornament 779A	Retrd.	1991	11.50	39-175
1992 Christmas Ornament 788F	Retrd.	1992	23.50	39-150
1993 Christmas Ornament 982P	Retrd.	1993	25.00	39-125
1994 Christmas Ornament 801P	Retrd.	1994	25.00	34-68
1995 Christmas Ornament-Gifts & Snow 640P	Retrd.	1995	30.00	39-100
1996 Christmas Ornament-A Sweet Christmas 355P	Retrd.	1996	30.00	100
1997 Christmas Ornament-Christmas Snow 137F	Retrd.	1997	37.50	38-50
1998 Christmas Ornament-Christmas Eve 123F	Retrd.	1998	35.00	70
1999 Christmas Ornament-Cappy 355F	Retrd.	1999	37.50	38-50
2000 Christmas Ornament-Frosty 1327F	Yr.Iss.		35.00	35

Artists of the World

De Grazia Annual Ornaments - T. De Grazia

1986 Pima Indian Drummer Boy	Yr.Iss.	1986	28.00	75-200
1987 White Dove	Yr.Iss.	1987	30.00	75-98
1988 Flower Girl	Yr.Iss.	1988	33.00	75-100
1989 Flower Boy	Yr.Iss.	1989	35.00	65-100
1990 Pink Papoose	Yr.Iss.	1990	35.00	65-100
1990 Merry Little Indian	10,000	1990	88.00	100-175
1991 Christmas Prayer (Red)	Yr.Iss.	1991	50.00	95-110
1992 Bearing Gift	Yr.Iss.	1992	55.00	78-100
1993 Lighting the Way	Yr.Iss.	1993	58.00	80-100
1994 Warm Wishes	Yr.Iss.	1994	65.00	80-100
1995 Little Prayer (White)	Yr.Iss.	1995	49.50	75-80
1995 My Beautiful Rocking Horse	1,995	1995	125.00	125-150
1996 Heavenly Flowers	Yr.Iss.	1995	65.00	65
1997 Oh Holy Night	Yr.Iss.	1997	67.50	75
1998 Christmas Spirit	Yr.Iss	1998	65.00	65
1999 Little Cocopah Indian Girl	Yr.Iss	1999	67.50	68
2000 Love Me	Yr.Iss		72.50	73
2001 Christmas Serenade	Yr.Iss		69.50	70

Bing & Grondahl

Christmas - Various

1985 Christmas Eve at the Farmhouse - E. Jensen	Closed	1985	19.50	30
1986 Silent Night, Holy Night - E. Jensen	Closed	1986	19.50	30
1987 The Snowman's Christmas Eve - E. Jensen	Closed	1987	22.50	23-28
1988 In the King's Garden - E. Jensen	Closed	1988	25.00	27-30
1989 Christmas Anchorage - E. Jensen	Closed	1989	27.00	27-30
1990 Changing of the Guards - E. Jensen	Closed	1990	32.50	33-35
1991 Copenhagen Stock Exchange - E. Jensen	Closed	1991	34.50	35
1992 Christmas at the Rectory - J. Steensen	Closed	1992	36.50	37-39
1993 Father Christmas in Copenhagen - J. Nielsen	Closed	1993	36.50	37
1994 A Day at the Deer Park - J. Nielsen	Closed	1994	36.50	38
1995 The Towers of Copenhagen - J. Nielsen	Closed	1995	37.50	45
1996 Winter at the Old Mill - J. Nielsen	Closed	1996	37.50	32-45
1997 Country Christmas - J. Nielsen	Closed	1998	37.50	32-38
1998 Santa the Storyteller - J. Nielsen	Closed	1998	37.50	32-38
1999 Around the Christmas Tree - J. Nielsen	Closed	1999	39.50	32-40
2000 Ringing at the Bell Tower - J. Nielsen	Annual		39.50	40

Christmas Around the World - H. Hansen

1995 Santa in Greenland	Yr.Iss.	1995	25.00	29-45
1996 Santa in Orient	Yr.Iss.	1996	25.00	30
1997 Santa in Russia	Yr.Iss.	1997	25.00	30
1998 Santa in Australia	Yr.Iss.	1998	25.00	25-29
1999 Santa in Europe	Yr.Iss.	1999	27.50	20-28
2000 Santa in America	Yr.Iss.		27.50	23-28

Christmas In America - J. Woodson

1986 Christmas Eve in Williamsburg	Closed	1986	12.50	126
1987 Christmas Eve at the White House	Closed	1987	15.00	10-21
1988 Christmas Eve at Rockefeller Center	Closed	1988	18.50	10-21
1989 Christmas in New England	Closed	1989	20.00	10-21
1990 Christmas Eve at the Capitol	Closed	1990	20.00	10-45
1991 Independence Hall	Closed	1991	23.50	10-30
1992 Christmas in San Francisco	Closed	1992	25.00	10-30
1993 Coming Home For Christmas	Closed	1993	25.00	10-30
1994 Christmas Eve in Alaska	Closed	1994	25.00	10-30
1995 Christmas Eve in Mississippi	Closed	1995	25.00	10-30

Santa Claus - H. Hansen

1989 Santa's Workshop	Yr.Iss.	1989	20.00	49-54
1990 Santa's Sleigh	Yr.Iss.	1990	20.00	49-54
1991 The Journey	Yr.Iss.	1991	24.00	51-54
1992 Santa's Arrival	Yr.Iss.	1992	25.00	49
1993 Santa's Gifts	Yr.Iss.	1993	25.00	25-49
1994 Christmas Stories	Yr.Iss.	1994	25.00	30-49

Boyds Collection Ltd.

The Bearstone Collection ™ - G.M. Lowenthal

1997 Matthew with Kip (Baby's 1st Christmas) 2508	Retrd.	1997	9.45	22-27
1994 'Charity'-Angel Bear with Star 2502	Retrd.	1996	9.45	38
1994 'Faith'-Angel Bear with Trumpet 2500	Retrd.	1996	9.45	38
1994 'Hope'-Angel Bear with Wreath 2501	Retrd.	1996	9.45	38
1994 'Charity' 2502, 'Faith' 2500, 'Hope' 2501, set/3	Retrd.	1996	28.35	60-94
1995 'Edmund'...Believe 2505	Retrd.	1997	9.45	38
1995 'Elliot with Tree' 2507	Retrd.	1997	9.45	38
1995 'Manheim' the Moose with Wreath 2506	Retrd.	1997	9.45	44
1997 Zoe Starlight Christmas (GCC Exclusive) 25951	Retrd.	1997	21.50	32

The Folkstone Collection ™ - G.M. Lowenthal

1995 Father Christmas 2553	Retrd.	1997	9.45	10-25
1997 Jacques...Starlight Skier 25950	Retrd.	1997	21.00	21-45
1995 Jean Claude & Jacque...the Skiers 2561	Retrd.	1997	9.45	32
1995 Jingles the Snowman with Wreath 2562	Retrd.	1997	9.45	32
1995 Nicholai with Tree 2550	Retrd.	1997	9.45	38
1995 Nicholas the Giftgiver 2551	Retrd.	1997	9.45	32
1995 Olaf...Let it Snow 2560	Retrd.	1997	9.45	38
1995 Sliknick in the Chimney 2552	Retrd.	1997	9.45	32

Calico Kittens/Enesco Group, Inc.

Calico Kittens - P. Hillman

1993 Baby's First Christmas (Boy) 628204	Retrd.	1997	16.00	16
1993 Baby's First Christmas (Girl) 628255	Retrd.	1997	16.00	16
1995 Cat in stocking wearing a red Santa's hat 144304	Yr.Iss.	1995	16.00	16
1993 Cat With Blue Hat 623814	Retrd.	1997	11.00	11
1993 Cat With Green Hat 623814	Retrd.	1997	11.00	11
1993 Cat With Red Hat 623814	Retrd.	1997	11.00	11
2000 Dated Ornament 720771	Yr.Iss.		10.00	10
1994 First Christmas Together 651346	Retrd.	1997	15.00	15
1994 Grey Kitten as Santa 625280	Yr.Iss.	1994	12.50	13
1994 Joy To The World 651354	Retrd.	1997	13.50	14
1998 Kitten in Knitted Mitten 359645	Yr.Iss.	1998	10.00	10
1999 Kitten in Shoe 543489	Yr.Iss.	1999	10.00	10
1996 Kitten in Wreath 178551	Yr.Iss.	1996	10.00	10
1996 Kitty And Me 178543	Retrd.	1996	17.50	18
1996 My Spoiled Kitty 178535	Retrd.	1996	17.50	18
1995 Our First Christmas Together 144282	Retrd.	1999	13.50	14
1994 Peace On Earth 651354	Retrd.	1997	13.50	14
1993 Tan Angel Kitten Reading to a Mouse 627534	Retrd.	1998	12.50	13
1993 White Girl Kitten w/Sewing Basket 628220	Yr.Iss.	1993	12.50	13

Cat in the Act - P. Hillman

1999 Domestic Shorthair 543438	Closed	1999	8.50	9
1999 Himalayan 543373	Closed	1999	8.50	9
1999 Ragdoll 543411	Closed	1999	8.50	9
1999 Scottish Fold 543365	Closed	1999	8.50	9
1999 Siamese 543357	Closed	1999	8.50	9
1999 White Persian 543314	Closed	1999	8.50	9

I Love My Kitty - P. Hillman

1995 Bird-Seed From Kitty 144355	Retrd.	1998	11.00	11
1995 I Love My Cat 144320	Retrd.	1998	11.00	11
1995 To My Cat 144398	Retrd.	1998	11.00	11
1995 To My Kitty 144274	Retrd.	1998	11.00	11

Itty Bitty Kitties - P. Hillman

1998 3 Asst. Itty Bitty Kitty 360260	Retrd.	1999	7.50	8

Cavanagh Group Intl.

Coca-Cola Brand Chrome-Plated Porcelain - CGI

2000 Elf & Penguin on Caboose	Open		9.00	9
2000 Elf & Penguin on Moon	Open		9.00	9
2000 Elf on Locomotive Engine	Open		9.00	9
2000 Mrs. Claus w/Tree on Train Car	Open		9.00	9
2000 Polar B C	Open		9.00	9
2000 Polar Bear on Train Car	Open		9.00	9

Coca-Cola Brand Heritage Collection - Sundblom

1995 Christmas Is Love (polyresin)	Closed	1997	10.00	10
1995 For Me (polyresin)	Closed	1997	10.00	10
1996 Hospitality in Your Refrigerator (porcelain & brass)	10,000	1998	25.00	25
1997 It Will Refresh You Too (polyresin)	Closed	1998	10.00	10
1996 It Will Refresh You, Too (porcelain & brass)	10,000	1998	25.00	25
1996 Please Pause Here (porcelain & brass)	10,000	1998	25.00	25
1997 Ssshh! (polyresin)	Closed	1998	10.00	10
1995 Ssshhh! (polyresin)	Closed	1997	10.00	10
1997 That Extra Something (polyresin)	Closed	1998	10.00	10

Coca-Cola Brand Heritage Collection Polar Bear - CGI

1997 Always Family (polyresin)	Closed	1998	10.00	10
1996 Baby's First Christmas (porcelain)	Closed	1998	12.00	12
1996 Our First Christmas (porcelain)	Closed	1998	12.00	12
1997 A Refreshing Break (polyresin)	Closed	1998	10.00	10
1996 Stocking Stuffers (porcelain)	Closed	1998	12.00	12

YEAR ISSUE	EDITION LIMIT	YEAR RETD.	ISSUE PRICE	*QUOTE U.S.$
1997 Trimming the Tree (polyresin)	Closed	1998	10.00	10

Coca-Cola Brand Historical Building - CGI

YEAR ISSUE	EDITION LIMIT	YEAR RETD.	ISSUE PRICE	*QUOTE U.S.$
1991 1930's Service Station	Closed	1994	10.00	25
1991 Early Coca-Cola Bottling Company	Closed	1994	10.00	25
1991 Jacob's Pharmacy	Closed	1994	10.00	25
1991 The Pemberton House	Closed	1994	10.00	25

Coca-Cola Brand North Pole Bottling Works - CGI

YEAR ISSUE	EDITION LIMIT	YEAR RETD.	ISSUE PRICE	*QUOTE U.S.$
1995 Barrel of Bears	Closed	1996	9.00	12
1993 Blast Off	Closed	1995	9.00	22
1993 Delivery for Santa	Closed	1996	9.00	16
1997 Elf & Walrus	Closed	1998	9.00	9
1997 Elf & Walrus	Closed	1998	9.00	9
1998 Elf & Walrus	Closed	1998	9.00	9
1999 Elf & Walrus	Closed	1999	9.00	9
1999 Elf on Bottle with Opener	Closed	1999	9.00	9
1998 Elf on Carousel Horse	Closed	1999	9.00	9
1993 Fill 'er Up	Closed	1994	9.00	30
1995 Fountain Glass Follies	Closed	1996	9.00	9
1997 Holiday Refreshment	Closed	1998	9.00	9
1993 Ice Sculpting	Closed	1995	9.00	20
1997 A Light in the Window for Santa	Closed	1998	9.00	9
1993 Long Winter's Nap	Closed	1995	9.00	20
1993 North Pole Express	Closed	1994	9.00	35
1995 North Pole Flying School	Closed	1996	9.00	15
1994 Power Drive	Closed	1996	9.00	15
1996 Refreshing Surprise	Closed	1997	9.00	9
1996 Rush Delivery	Closed	1997	9.00	9
1994 Santa's Refreshment	Closed	1995	9.00	15
1994 Seltzer Surprise	Closed	1995	9.00	15
1993 Thirsting for Adventure	Closed	1994	9.00	20-25
1996 To: Mrs. Claus	Closed	1997	9.00	9
1994 Tops Off Refreshment	Closed	1995	9.00	20
1993 Tops On Refreshment	Closed	1995	9.00	15

Coca-Cola Brand Platinum Series - CGI

YEAR ISSUE	EDITION LIMIT	YEAR RETD.	ISSUE PRICE	*QUOTE U.S.$
2000 Bear & Penguin in Truck	Open		12.00	12
2000 Penguin in Helicopter	Open		12.00	12
2000 Reindeer in Airplane	Open		12.00	12
2000 Santa and Reindeer in Car	Open		12.00	12

Coca-Cola Brand Polar Bear - CGI

YEAR ISSUE	EDITION LIMIT	YEAR RETD.	ISSUE PRICE	*QUOTE U.S.$
1996 The Christmas Star	Closed	1998	9.00	9
1997 Double the Fun	Closed	1998	9.00	9-15
1997 Downhill Racers	Open		9.00	9
1994 Downhill Sledder	Closed	1996	9.00	10-15
1996 Hollywood	Closed	1999	9.00	9
1994 North Pole Delivery	Closed	1995	9.00	15
1999 Polar Bear and Cub with Gift	Open		9.00	9
1995 Polar Bear in Bottle Opener	Closed	1997	9.00	10-15
1998 Polar Bear on Fountain Machine	Open		9.00	9
1999 Polar Bear on Jukebox	Open		9.00	9
1998 Polar Bear with Coke Sled	Open		9.00	9
1994 Skating Coca-Cola Polar Bear	Closed	1995	9.00	15
1995 Snowboardin' Bear	Closed	1997	9.00	10-15
1994 Vending Machine Mischief	Closed	1996	9.00	15

Coca-Cola Brand Polar Bear Cubs - CGI

YEAR ISSUE	EDITION LIMIT	YEAR RETD.	ISSUE PRICE	*QUOTE U.S.$
1997 Baby's First Christmas	Closed	1998	8.00	10
1997 Cookies For Santa	Closed	1998	8.00	10
1999 Cub and Penguin on Sled	Closed	1999	8.00	8
1999 Cub with Wreath	Closed	1999	8.00	8
1997 Dreaming of a Magical Christmas	Yr.Iss.	1997	8.00	10
1997 A Refreshing Ice Cold Treat	Closed	1999	8.00	8
1998 Seal on Ball	Closed	1999	8.00	8
1998 Seal on Ice Cube	Closed	1999	8.00	8
1997 Stocking Stuffer Surprise	Yr.Iss.	1997	8.00	10
1997 Twas the Night Before Christmas	Closed	1999	8.00	8

Coca-Cola Brand Trim A Tree Collection - Sundblom

YEAR ISSUE	EDITION LIMIT	YEAR RETD.	ISSUE PRICE	*QUOTE U.S.$
1990 Away with a Tired and Thirsty Face	Closed	1993	10.00	25-30
1994 Busy Man's Pause	Closed	1995	10.00	15-20
1991 Christmas Is Love	Closed	1992	10.00	30
1993 Decorating the Tree	Closed	1994	10.00	25-30
1993 Extra Bright Refreshment	Closed	1994	10.00	15-20
1994 For Sparkling Holidays	Closed	1996	10.00	10-15
1997 Good Boys and Girls	Closed	1997	10.00	10-15
1992 Happy Holidays	Closed	1996	10.00	25-40
1998 Hospitality	Closed	1999	9.00	9
1990 Hospitality	Closed	1993	10.00	15-20
1995 It Will Refresh You Too	Closed	1996	10.00	15
1990 Merry Christmas and a Happy New Year	Closed	1991	10.00	40
1996 The Pause That Refreshes	Closed	1997	10.00	10-15
1995 Please Pause Here	Closed	1997	10.00	10-15
1990 Santa on Stool	Closed	1993	10.00	25-30
1990 Season's Greetings	Closed	1991	10.00	30-40
1992 Sshhh!	Closed	1993	10.00	75-85
1999 That Extra Something	Closed	1999	9.00	9
1996 They Remembered Me	Closed	1997	10.00	10-15
1994 Things Go Better with Coke	Closed	1996	10.00	10-20
1998 Things Go Better with Coke	Closed	1999	9.00	9
1991 A Time to Share	Closed	1993	10.00	25-30
1993 Travel Refreshed	Closed	1995	10.00	20

Harley-Davidson - CGI

YEAR ISSUE	EDITION LIMIT	YEAR RETD.	ISSUE PRICE	*QUOTE U.S.$
1997 Adventures on the Open Road	Yr.Iss.	1997	20.00	20
1998 Chopper (GCC Exclusive)	Yr.Iss.	1998	20.00	20
1998 Elf with Special Delivery	Open		20.00	20
1997 Elves to the Rescue	Closed	1998	20.00	20
1997 King of the Road	Closed	1999	20.00	20
1999 Leader of the Pack	Open		20.00	20
1999 Queen of the Highway	Open		20.00	20
1999 Queen of the Road (GCC Exclusive)	Yr.Iss.	1999	20.00	20
1998 Reindeer on Bad Boy	Closed	1999	20.00	20
2000 Ridin' Cool	Open		20.00	20
1997 Three for the Road	Closed	1998	20.00	20

Humbug - T. Fraley

YEAR ISSUE	EDITION LIMIT	YEAR RETD.	ISSUE PRICE	*QUOTE U.S.$
1998 Midnight Snack	Open		15.00	15
1998 Peek-A-Boo	Open		12.00	12
1998 Ride 'em Cowboy	Open		15.00	15
1998 Sweet Tooth	Open		12.00	12
1998 To Drop or Not to Drop	Open		12.00	12
1998 A Winter's Nap	Open		12.00	12

Charming Tails/Fitz and Floyd Collectibles

Charming Tails Deck The Halls - D. Griff

YEAR ISSUE	EDITION LIMIT	YEAR RETD.	ISSUE PRICE	*QUOTE U.S.$
1991 Sticky Situations (2 pc.) 87/991	Closed	1996	16.00	60
1992 Catching ZZZ's 86/785	Closed	1995	12.00	38-50
1992 Chickadees on Ball 86/787	Closed	1995	13.50	110-150
1992 The Drifters (2 pc.) 86/784	Closed	1996	12.00	35-88
1992 Fresh Fruit (3 pc.) 86/789	Closed	1995	12.00	12-90
1992 Mice/Rabbit Ball (2 pc.) 86/788	Closed	1995	12.00	85-150
1992 Mice in Leaf Sleigh 86/786	Closed	1995	26.00	300-360
1993 Bunny & Mouse Bell (2 pc.) 87/038	Closed	1995	10.50	81
1993 Chick with Bead Garland 86/791	Closed	1995	17.50	86-250
1993 Hang in There (3 pc.) 87/941	Closed	1996	10.00	35
1993 Holiday Wreath (2 pc.) 87/939	Closed	1995	12.00	45-80
1993 Mackenzie Napping 87/940	Closed	1995	12.00	27-45
1993 Maxine Lights a Candle 87/942	Closed	1995	11.00	25-32
1993 Mouse on Snowflake (lighted) 87/037	Closed	1995	11.00	35-47
1993 Mouse w/Apple Candleholder (2 pc.) 87/044	Closed	1995	13.00	160-188
1993 Porcelain Mouse Bell 87/036	Closed	1995	5.00	5
1994 Baby's First Christmas 87/184	Closed	1994	12.00	25-41
1994 Binkey & Reginald on Ice (2 pc.) 87/924	Closed	1994	10.00	88-95
1994 Friends in Flight 87/971	Closed	1994	18.00	126
1994 The Grape Escape (grape) 87/186	Closed	1995	18.00	53-88
1994 The Grape Escape (green) 87/186	Closed	1995	18.00	58-75
1994 High Flying Mackenzie 87/992	Closed	1997	20.00	21-32
1994 Holiday Lights 87/969	Closed	1995	10.00	45-88
1994 Horsin' Around 87/202	Closed	1996	18.00	34-44
1994 Mackenzie and Binkey's Snack (cherry & plum) 87/187	Closed	1994	12.00	120-150
1994 Mackenzie Blowing Bubbles 87/191	Closed	1994	12.00	40-94
1994 Mackenzie on Ice 87/970	Closed	1996	10.00	36-40
1994 Mackenzie's Bubble Ride 87/192	Closed	1996	13.00	35-63
1994 Mackenzie's Snowball (dated) 87/994	Closed	1994	10.00	94-125
1994 Maxine and Mackenzie (2 pc.) 87/185	Closed	1996	12.00	29-88
1994 Reginald's Bubble Ride 87/199	Closed	1994	12.00	41
1994 Reginald On Ice 87/924	Closed	1994	10.00	188
1994 Apple House (lighted) 87/032	Closed	1995	13.00	30-59
1994 Pear House (lighted) 87/027	Closed	1995	13.00	68-94
1994 Mouse on Yellow Bulb (lighted) 87/045	Closed	1995	10.00	88-110
1994 Mouse Star Treetop 87/958	Closed	1995	10.00	50-82
1995 1995 Annual 87/306	Closed	1995	16.00	16-32
1995 Binkey's Poinsettia 87/303	Closed	1997	12.00	13-30
1995 Christmas Cookies (3 pc.) 87/301	Closed	1999	10.00	11
1995 Christmas Flowers 87/304	Open		12.00	13
1995 Holiday Balloon Ride 87/299	Closed	1996	16.00	30-38
1995 Mackenzie's Whirligig 87/300	Closed	1997	20.00	20-44
1995 Peppermint Party (2 pc.) 87/314	Closed	1997	10.00	11-25
1995 Reginald in Leaves (2 pc.) 87/302	Closed	1997	10.00	11-25
1995 Stewart at Play 87/308	Closed	1995	12.00	30-36
1995 Stewart's Winter Fun (2 pc.) 87/307	Closed	1995	10.00	10-36
1996 1996 Annual-All Wrapped Up 87/471	Closed	1996	12.00	12-30
1996 Baby's First Christmas 87/850	Closed	1996	13.00	20-23
1996 Christmas Stamps 87/485	Closed	1997	12.00	13-30
1996 Our First Christmas (dated) 87/532	Closed	1996	18.00	32
1996 Fallen Angel 87/492	Closed	1997	12.00	13-25
1996 Flights of Fancy 87/490	Closed	1997	12.00	13-25
1996 Frequent Flyer 87/491	Closed	1997	12.00	13-25
1996 Letter to Santa 87/486	Closed	1997	12.00	13-37
1996 Stamp Dispenser 87/483	Closed	2000	12.00	13
1996 Weeeeee! 87/493	Closed	1997	12.00	13-25
1997 All Lit Up (lighted) 86/660	Open		11.00	13
1997 Chauncey's First Christmas 86/710	Closed	1997	9.00	9
1997 Mackenzie In Mitten 86/704	Closed	2000	9.00	8-11
1997 Our First Christmas (dated) 86/708	Closed	1997	18.00	32
1997 1997 Annual-Mackenzie's Jack in the Box 86/709	Closed	1997	10.00	10
1997 Maxine's Angel 86/701	Closed	2000	9.00	8-11
1997 Our First Christmas 86/708	Closed	1997	12.50	12-16
1997 A Special Delivery 86/707	Closed	2000	9.00	8-10
1998 Air Mail To Santa 86/652	Closed	2000	13.00	13-14
1998 Our First Christmas Together 86/653	Closed	1998	12.00	12-15
1998 Bundle of Joy - Baby's First Christmas 86/655	Closed	1998	12.00	12-15
1998 Heading For The Slopes 86/656	Open		13.00	13
1998 Ski Jumper 86/657	Closed	2000	13.00	13
1998 Tricycle Built From Treats 86/658	Closed	2000	13.00	13
1998 Pine Cone Predicament 86/659	Closed	1998	11.00	11-20
1993 Chick w/Bead Garland 86/791	Closed	1995	11.50	12
1999 Baby's First Christmas 86/792	Closed	1999	11.50	12
1999 Binkey's Candy Cane Flyer 86/793	Open		11.50	12
1999 A Cup of Christmas Cheer 86/796	Open		11.50	12
1999 Snowbird 86/797	Closed	1999	11.50	12
2000 2000 Annual Snowflakes 86/100	Yr.Iss.		11.50	12
2000 Baby's First (Bootie Baby) 86/101	Closed	2000	11.50	12
2000 Holiday Baking (Mother & Son) 86/102	Open		11.50	12
2000 Our First Christmas 86/103	Closed	2000	11.50	12
2000 Teacher 86/104	Closed	2000	11.50	12
2000 Weeee...Three Kings! 86/105	Open		11.50	12

Charming Tails Easter Basket - D. Griff

YEAR ISSUE	EDITION LIMIT	YEAR RETD.	ISSUE PRICE	*QUOTE U.S.$
1994 Easter Parade 89/615	Closed	1996	10.00	10-27
1994 Peek-a-boo 89/753	Closed	1996	12.00	12-40

Charming Tails Everyday Ornaments- D. Griff

YEAR ISSUE	EDITION LIMIT	YEAR RETD.	ISSUE PRICE	*QUOTE U.S.$
1994 Binkey in the Berry Patch 89/752	Closed	1996	12.00	44-47
1995 Hello, Sweet Pea 87/367	Closed	1997	12.00	13-32
1995 I Am Full 87/365	Closed	1997	15.00	15-30
1995 I'm Berry Happy 87/390	Closed	1997	15.00	16-27
1994 Maxine Pick Strawberries 89/562	Closed	1995	12.00	35-69
1993 Maxine's Butterfly Ride 89/190	Open		16.50	18
1993 Mouse on a Bee 89/191	Closed	1994	16.50	225-360
1993 Mouse on a Dragonfly 89/320	Closed	1994	16.50	400-960
1995 Picking Peppers 87/369	Closed	1997	12.00	13-17
1994 Springtime Showers (3 pc.) 89/563	Closed	1996	10.00	25-36
1995 This Is Hot! 87/366	Closed	1997	15.00	16-20

Cherished Teddies/Enesco Group, Inc.

Across The Seas - P. Hillman

YEAR ISSUE	EDITION LIMIT	YEAR RETD.	ISSUE PRICE	*QUOTE U.S.$
1998 American Boy 451010	Closed	1999	10.00	10
1998 Australian Boy 464120	Closed	1999	10.00	10
1998 Canadian Boy 451053	Closed	1999	10.00	10
1998 Chinese Boy 450960	Closed	1999	10.00	10
1998 Dutch Girl 450995	Closed	1999	10.00	10
1998 English Boy 451045	Closed	1999	10.00	10
1998 French Girl "Joyeux Noel!" 450901	Closed	1999	10.00	10
1998 German Boy 451002	Closed	1999	10.00	10
1998 Indian Girl 450987	Closed	1999	10.00	10
1998 Italian Girl 464112	Closed	1999	10.00	10
1998 Japanese Girl 450936	Closed	1999	10.00	10
1998 Mexican Boy 450952	Closed	1999	10.00	10
1998 Russian Girl 450944	Closed	1999	10.00	10
1998 Scottish Girl 451029	Closed	1999	10.00	10
1998 Spanish Boy 450979	Closed	1999	10.00	10
1998 Swedish Girl 450928	Closed	1999	10.00	10

Cherished Teddies - P. Hillman

YEAR ISSUE	EDITION LIMIT	YEAR RETD.	ISSUE PRICE	*QUOTE U.S.$
1992 Angel 950777	Suspd.		12.50	65-188
1992 Bear In Stocking (dated) 950653	Yr.Iss.	1992	16.00	32-50
1992 Beth On Rocking Reindeer 950793	Suspd.		20.00	38-58
1992 Christmas Sister Bears, 3 asst. 951226	Suspd.		12.50	27-38
1993 Angel, 3 Asst. 912980	Suspd.		12.50	22-60
1993 Baby Boy (dated) 913014	Yr.Iss.	1993	12.50	22-32
1993 Baby Girl (dated) 913006	Yr.Iss.	1993	12.50	25-32
1993 Girl w/Muff (Alice) (dated) 912832	Yr.Iss.	1993	13.50	50-75
1993 Jointed Teddy Bear 914894	Suspd.		12.50	21
1994 Baby in Basket (dated) 617253	Yr.Iss.	1994	15.00	30
1994 Bundled Up For The Holidays "Our First Christmas" (dated) 617229	Yr.Iss.	1994	15.00	28-32
1994 Drummer Boy (dated) 912891	Yr.Iss.	1994	10.00	25-30
1995 Baby Angel on Cloud "Baby's First Christmas" 141240	Open		13.50	14
1995 Elf Bear W/Doll 625434	Suspd.		12.50	13-27
1995 Boy Bear Flying Cupid "Sending You My Heart" 103608	Suspd.		13.00	25-38
1995 Boy/Girl with Banner "Our First Christmas" 141259	Open		13.50	14
1995 Elf Bear W/Stuffed Reindeer 625442	Suspd.		12.50	13-27
1995 Elf Bears/Candy Cane 651389	Suspd.		12.50	13-27
1995 Girl Bear Flying Cupid "Sending You My Heart" 103616	Suspd.		13.00	13-30
1995 Mrs Claus Xmas Holding Tray/Cookies 625426	Suspd.		12.50	13-32
1995 Teddies Santa Bear 651370	Open		12.50	13
1995 Teddy with Ice Skates (dated) 141232	Yr.Iss.	1995	12.50	15-28
1996 Bear w/Dangling Mittens 177768	Open		12.50	13
1996 Toy Soldier (dated) 176052	Yr.Iss.	1996	12.50	20-22
1997 Dangling Snowflake (dated) 272175	Yr.Iss.	1997	12.50	22-25
1998 Bear in Picnic Basket 406627	Closed	1999	12.50	13
1998 Bear in Wagon 400793	Closed	1999	12.50	13
1998 Bear on Kitchen Hutch 406481 (Special Limited Editon)	Closed	1998	12.50	13
1998 Bear on Train 401196	Closed	1999	12.50	13
1998 Bears on Sled 406635	Closed	1999	12.50	13
1998 Gingerbread Bear 352748	Yr.Iss.	1998	12.50	13-16
1998 Two Bears w/Teacup & Saucer 406473	Closed	1999	12.50	13
1999 Eskimo Holding Fish (dated 1999) 534161	Yr.Iss.	1999	25.00	25
2000 Eskimo Holding Fish (dated 2000) 536377	Yr.Iss.		25.00	25
1999 Teddy Bear/Drum 546550	Closed	1999	Gift	N/A
2000 Dated Ornament	Yr.Iss.		12.50	13

Christopher Radko

Christopher Radko Family of Collectors - C. Radko

YEAR ISSUE	EDITION LIMIT	YEAR RETD.	ISSUE PRICE	*QUOTE U.S.$
1993 Angels We Have Heard on High SP1	Retrd.	1993	50.00	195-600
1994 Starbuck Santa SP3	Retrd.	1994	75.00	100-345
1995 Dash Away All SP7	Retrd.	1995	34.00	30-84
1995 Purrfect Present SP8	Retrd.	1995	Gift	36-44
1996 Christmas Magic SP13	Retrd.	1996	50.00	82-192
1996 Frosty Weather SP14	Retrd.	1996	Gift	45-54
1997 Enchanted Evening SP20	Retrd.	1997	55.00	40-70
1997 Li'l Miss Angel SP21	Retrd.	1997	Gift	50
1998 Candy Castle SP36	Retrd.	1998	70.00	70-82
1998 Mouse Wrap SP32	Retrd.	1998	Gift	N/A

*Quotes have been rounded up to nearest dollar

YEAR ISSUE	EDITION LIMIT	YEAR RETD.	ISSUE PRICE	*QUOTE U.S.$
1999 No Time Like The Present 99SP54	Yr.Iss.	1999	Gift	N/A
2000 Starlight Guardian 00-SP-69	Yr.Iss.		Gift	N/A

10 Year Anniversary - C. Radko

YEAR ISSUE	EDITION LIMIT	YEAR RETD.	ISSUE PRICE	*QUOTE U.S.$
1995 On Top of the World SP6	Yr.Iss.	1995	32.00	25-75

Event Only - C. Radko

YEAR ISSUE	EDITION LIMIT	YEAR RETD.	ISSUE PRICE	*QUOTE U.S.$
1993 Littlest Snowman 347S (store & C. Radko event)	Retrd.	1993	15.00	33
1994 Roly Poly 94125E (store & C. Radko event)	Retrd.	1994	22.00	29-65
1995 Forever Lucy 91075E (store & C. Radko event)	Retrd.	1995	32.00	43-60
1996 Poinsettia Elegance 287E (store event)	Retrd.	1996	32.00	32-48
1996 A Job Well Done SP18 (C. Radko event)	Retrd.	1996	30.00	35-60
1997 Little Golden Hood 97-261E (store event)	Retrd.	1997	39.00	39-90
1997 Merry Travelers SP27 (C. Radko event)	Retrd.	1997	44.00	44
1998 Elf Secrets 98-306E (store event)	Retrd.	1998	47.00	47
1999 Mrs. Iceberg 99SP52 (spring event)	Yr.Iss.	1999	30.00	30
1999 Mr. Iceberg 99SP51 (fall event)	Yr.Iss.	1999	30.00	30
2000 Billy Bunny Goes Shopping 00-SP-74 (national rep. Event)	Yr.Iss.		38.00	38
2000 Flower Power 00-SP-67 (spring event)	Yr.Iss.		47.00	47

1986 Holiday Collection - C. Radko

YEAR ISSUE	EDITION LIMIT	YEAR RETD.	ISSUE PRICE	*QUOTE U.S.$
1986 Alpine Flowers 40-0	Retrd.	N/A	16.00	60-125
1986 Big Top 48-1	Retrd.	1988	15.00	75-150
1986 Deep Sea 41-1	Retrd.	N/A	N/A	32-96
1986 Emerald City 17	Retrd.	N/A	N/A	33-90
1986 Golden Alpine 86-040-1	Retrd.	N/A	N/A	48
1986 Long Icicle (red) 6	Retrd.	N/A	N/A	90-174
1986 Midas Touch 49	Retrd.	N/A	N/A	114-120
1986 Roses 115	Retrd.	1988	16.00	125-140
1986 Santa's Cane (pink) 5-1	Retrd.	N/A	N/A	90
1986 Siberian Sleighride 110-1	Retrd.	N/A	N/A	40-48
1986 Three Ribbon Oval 44-0	Retrd.	N/A	N/A	125-150
1986 Three Wise Swans 12	Retrd.	N/A	N/A	72-150

1987 Holiday Collection - C. Radko

YEAR ISSUE	EDITION LIMIT	YEAR RETD.	ISSUE PRICE	*QUOTE U.S.$
1987 Baby Balloons 44	Retrd.	1988	6.00	95
1987 Celestial (red) 21-1	Retrd.	N/A	N/A	48-96
1987 Double Royal Star Reflector 79	Retrd.	N/A	N/A	150
1987 Faberge Ball 34	Retrd.	N/A	N/A	32-84
1987 Four Tier Pendant 50	Retrd.	N/A	N/A	45-50
1987 Granny's Reflector (red)	Retrd.	N/A	N/A	150
1987 Grecian Column (red/gold) 520	Retrd.	N/A	N/A	90-125
1987 Grecian Column (silver) 520	Retrd.	N/A	N/A	125
1987 Kat Koncert 88-067	Retrd.	1994	16.00	49-95
1987 Memphis 18	Retrd.	N/A	15.00	48-95
1987 Neopolitan Angels 14	Retrd.	N/A	N/A	60-72
1987 Ruby Scarlet 10	Retrd.	N/A	N/A	34-48
1987 Serpents 38	Retrd.	N/A	N/A	23-30
1987 Twin Finial 800	Retrd.	N/A	N/A	135
1987 Victorian Lamp 63	Retrd.	N/A	N/A	90

1988 Holiday Collection - C. Radko

YEAR ISSUE	EDITION LIMIT	YEAR RETD.	ISSUE PRICE	*QUOTE U.S.$
1988 Alpine Flowers 8822	Retrd.	N/A	16.00	85-110
1988 Baby Balloon 8832	Retrd.	N/A	7.95	95-110
1988 Birdhouse 8873	Retrd.	1987	10.00	95-120
1988 Blue Rainbow 8863	Retrd.	N/A	16.00	60-150
1988 Buds in Bloom (pink) 8824	Retrd.	N/A	16.00	95-125
1988 Celestial (blue) 884	Retrd.	N/A	15.00	38-65
1988 Celestial 884	Retrd.	N/A	15.00	75
1988 Christmas Fanfare 8850	Retrd.	1988	15.00	72-125
1988 Circle of Santas 11	Retrd.	N/A	14.50	15-50
1988 Circle of Santas 8811	Retrd.	N/A	16.95	54-95
1988 Circus Spikes 75	Retrd.	N/A	9.00	240
1988 Cornucopia/Pear Branch 8839	Retrd.	N/A	15.00	360
1988 Crescent Moon Santa 881	Retrd.	N/A	15.00	95-125
1988 Crown Jewels 8874	Retrd.	1993	15.00	45-60
1988 Double Royal Star 8856	Retrd.	1991	23.00	125
1988 Exclamation Flask 8871	Retrd.	N/A	7.50	25-120
1988 Faberge Oval 883	Retrd.	N/A	15.00	75-110
1988 French Regency 17	Retrd.	N/A	N/A	60-155
1988 Gilded Leaves 8813	Retrd.	N/A	16.00	95-110
1988 Grecian Column 8842	Retrd.	1990	9.95	95
1988 Harlequin 26	Retrd.	N/A	N/A	38
1988 Hot Air Balloon 885	Retrd.	N/A	15.00	125-150
1988 Jumbo Nautilus (gold) 102-1	Retrd.	N/A	N/A	30-36
1988 Kat Koncert 8867	Retrd.	N/A	14.50	48-72
1988 Large Nautilus (gold) 102	Retrd.	N/A	N/A	20-30
1988 Lilac Sparkle 1814	Retrd.	N/A	15.00	140-150
1988 Medium Nautilus 101	Retrd.	N/A	N/A	10-19
1988 Merry Christmas Maiden 52	Retrd.	N/A	14.50	72
1988 Mushroom in Winter 8862	Retrd.	1993	12.00	65-75
1988 Neopolitan Angel 870141	Retrd.	1995	16.00	125-150
1988 Oz Balloon 872	Retrd.	N/A	18.00	78-160
1988 Ripples on Oval 8844	Retrd.	1987	6.00	38-45
1988 Royal Crest Oval 18	Retrd.	N/A	14.50	102
1988 Royal Diadem 8860	Retrd.	1987	25.00	135-240
1988 Royal Porcelain 8812	Retrd.	1991	16.00	125-180
1988 Royal Rooster 70	Retrd.	N/A	14.50	66
1988 Russian St. Nick 8823	Retrd.	N/A	15.00	30-90
1988 Satin Scepter 8847	Retrd.	1987	8.95	50-110
1988 Shiny-Brite 8843	Retrd.	N/A	5.00	36-50
1988 Simply Cartiere 8817	Retrd.	N/A	16.95	65-96
1988 Squiggles 889	Retrd.	N/A	15.00	95-120
1988 Stained Glass 8816	Retrd.	1990	16.00	90-125
1988 Striped Balloon 8877	Retrd.	N/A	16.95	40-96
1988 Tiger 886	Retrd.	N/A	15.00	150-375
1988 Tree on Ball 8864	Retrd.	N/A	9.00	50-75
1988 Twin Finial 8857	Retrd.	N/A	23.50	100-135
1988 Vienna 1900 37	Retrd.	N/A	16.00	96
1988 Zebra 886	Retrd.	N/A	15.00	150

1989 Holiday Collection - C. Radko

YEAR ISSUE	EDITION LIMIT	YEAR RETD.	ISSUE PRICE	*QUOTE U.S.$
1989 Alpine Flowers 9-43	Retrd.	N/A	17.00	30
1989 Baroque Angel 9-11	Retrd.	1989	17.00	125-150
1989 Carmen Miranda 9-40	Retrd.	N/A	17.00	67-95
1989 Charlie Chaplin (blue hat) 9-55	Retrd.	1990	8.50	25-30
1989 Circle of Santas 9-32	Retrd.	1991	17.00	90-95
1989 Clown Snake 60	Retrd.	N/A	9.00	30-40
1989 Clown Snake 60 (signed)	Retrd.	N/A	9.00	96
1989 Double Top 9-71	Retrd.	1989	7.00	40
1989 Drop Reflector 88	Retrd.	N/A	23.00	90
1989 Elf on Ball (matte) 9-62	Retrd.	1990	9.50	45-85
1989 Faberge Finial 106	Retrd.	N/A	36.00	96-116
1989 Fisher Frog 9-65	Retrd.	1991	7.00	75
1989 Fleurs de Provence 30	Retrd.	N/A	17.00	96
1989 Fluted Column (gold) 86	Retrd.	N/A	10.00	120
1989 Friendly Visitor 9-97	Retrd.	N/A	11.00	175
1989 Grecian Urn 9-69	Retrd.	1989	9.00	35
1989 Harlequin Finial (tree topper) 107	Retrd.	N/A	22.00	142-186
1989 Hi-Fi Pink 20	Retrd.	N/A	17.00	240
1989 His Boy Elroy 9-104	Retrd.	1991	8.00	120
1989 The Holly 9-49	Retrd.	N/A	17.00	40-90
1989 Hurricane Lamp 9-67	Retrd.	1989	7.00	45
1989 The Ivy 9-47	Retrd.	N/A	16.50	120
1989 Jester 41	Retrd.	N/A	16.50	120
1989 Joey Clown (light pink) 9-58	Retrd.	1992	9.00	50-96
1989 Kim Ono 9-57	Retrd.	1990	6.50	50-60
1989 King Arthur (Lt. Blue) 9-103	Retrd.	1991	12.00	50-72
1989 Kite Face 64	Retrd.	N/A	8.50	45
1989 Lilac Sparkle 9-7	Retrd.	1989	17.00	75-125
1989 Lucky Fish 9-73	Retrd.	1989	6.50	20-55
1989 Miranda 40	Retrd.	N/A	17.00	48-162
1989 Parachute 9-68	Retrd.	1989	6.50	75-96
1989 Pastel Harlequin 22	Retrd.	N/A	17.00	66
1989 Patchwork 52	Retrd.	N/A	16.50	108
1989 Peppermint Stripes 89	Retrd.	N/A	29.00	300
1989 Royal Rooster 9-18	Retrd.	1993	17.00	95
1989 Royal Star Tree Finial 108	Retrd.	N/A	42.00	95
1989 Santa Claus 15	Retrd.	N/A	16.00	90
1989 Scepter 105	Retrd.	N/A	25.00	144
1989 Seahorse 9-54	Retrd.	1992	10.00	72-150
1989 Serpent 9-72	Retrd.	N/A	7.00	30
1989 Shy Kitten 9-66	Retrd.	N/A	7.00	54-96
1989 Shy Rabbit 9-61	Retrd.	N/A	7.00	48-90
1989 Small Reflector 9-76	Retrd.	N/A	7.50	23-32
1989 Smiling Sun 9-59	Retrd.	N/A	7.00	60
1989 Song Birds 21	Retrd.	N/A	17.50	138-240
1989 Starlight Santa 56	Retrd.	N/A	6.00	72
1989 Tiffany 44	Retrd.	N/A	17.00	500-650
1989 Vineyard 9-51	Retrd.	N/A	17.00	115-200
1989 Walrus 9-63	Retrd.	1990	8.00	120-150
1989 Zebra 9-10	Retrd.	1991	17.50	110

1990 Holiday Collection - C. Radko

YEAR ISSUE	EDITION LIMIT	YEAR RETD.	ISSUE PRICE	*QUOTE U.S.$
1990 Angel on Harp 46	Retrd.	1990	9.00	45-85
1990 Atomic Age 27	Retrd.	N/A	18.00	60
1990 Ballooning Santa 85	Retrd.	1991	20.00	175-200
1990 Bathing Baby 70	Retrd.	N/A	11.00	48-54
1990 Bolero 67	Retrd.	N/A	7.25	72
1990 Boy Clown on Reflector 82	Retrd.	N/A	18.00	36-53
1990 Calla Lilly 38	Retrd.	N/A	7.00	23-30
1990 Candy Trumpet Man (blue) 85-1	Retrd.	N/A	28.00	35-48
1990 Candy Trumpet Man 85-1	Retrd.	N/A	28.00	35-84
1990 Carmen Miranda 18	Retrd.	1991	19.00	95-125
1990 Chimney Sweep Bell 179	Retrd.	N/A	27.00	75-150
1990 Christmas Cardinals 16	Retrd.	1992	18.00	42-90
1990 Classic Column 63	Retrd.	N/A	8.00	90
1990 Comet Reflector 31	Retrd.	N/A	16.00	60
1990 Conch Shell 65	Retrd.	1991	9.00	48-90
1990 Country Church 73	Retrd.	N/A	12.00	36
1990 Crowned Prince 56	Retrd.	1990	14.00	55-64
1990 Deco Floral 29	Retrd.	N/A	19.00	110-120
1990 Double Royal Star Reflector 104	Retrd.	N/A	30.00	150
1990 Dublin Pipe 40	Retrd.	1990	14.00	50
1990 Eagle Medallion 67	Retrd.	1990	9.00	40-60
1990 Early Winter 24	Retrd.	1990	10.00	28-40
1990 Elephant on Ball 94	Retrd.	N/A	20.00	110
1990 Emerald City 92	Retrd.	1990	7.50	33-65
1990 Fat Lady 35	Retrd.	N/A	7.00	36
1990 Father Christmas 76	Retrd.	N/A	7.00	45
1990 Frog Under Balloon 58	Retrd.	1991	14.00	32-60
1990 Frosty 62	Retrd.	N/A	14.00	36-72
1990 Golden Puppy 53	Retrd.	1990	8.00	90-120
1990 Google Eyes 44	Retrd.	1990	9.00	95-100
1990 Gypsy Queen 54	Retrd.	N/A	11.50	54
1990 Happy Gnome 77	Retrd.	1991	8.00	60-75
1990 Hearts & Flowers (ball) 15	Retrd.	N/A	19.00	90
1990 Heritage Santa 9075-2	Retrd.	N/A	24.00	24-36
1990 Holly Ball 4	Retrd.	N/A	19.00	125
1990 Honey Bear 167	Retrd.	N/A	14.00	55
1990 Jester 41	Retrd.	N/A	16.50	120
1990 Joey Clown (red striped) 55	Retrd.	N/A	14.00	28-60
1990 Kim Ono 79	Retrd.	1990	6.00	35-55
1990 King Arthur (Red) 72	Retrd.	N/A	16.00	95-110
1990 Lullaby 47	Retrd.	1990	9.00	25-63
1990 Maracca 94	Retrd.	1990	9.00	45-125
1990 Mediterranean Sunshine 140	Retrd.	N/A	27.00	34-49
1990 Mission Ball 26	Retrd.	N/A	18.00	32-48
1990 Mother Goose (blue bonnet/pink shawl) 52	Retrd.	N/A	10.00	32-58
1990 Nativity 36	Retrd.	1990	6.00	19-50
1990 Olympiad 7	Retrd.	N/A	18.00	48
1990 Peacock (on snowball) 74	Retrd.	N/A	18.00	75-100
1990 Pierre Le Berry	Retrd.	N/A	10.00	48-54
1990 Polish Folk Dance 13	Retrd.	N/A	19.00	120-150
1990 Praying Angel 37	Retrd.	N/A	5.00	27-75
1990 Proud Peacock 74	Retrd.	N/A	18.00	46-84
1990 Pudgy Clown 39	Retrd.	N/A	6.50	25-60
1990 Roly Poly Santa (Red bottom) 69	Retrd.	N/A	13.00	24-72
1990 Rose Lamp 96	Retrd.	1990	14.00	70-180
1990 Santa on Ball 80	Retrd.	1991	16.00	40-59
1990 Silent Movie (black hat) 75	Retrd.	1990	8.50	25-60
1990 Small Nautilus Shell 78	Retrd.	N/A	7.00	22
1990 Smiling Kite 63	Retrd.	1990	14.00	40-85
1990 Snowball Tree 71	Retrd.	1990	17.00	42-114
1990 Snowman on Ball 45	Retrd.	1990	14.00	49-72
1990 Songbirds 6	Retrd.	N/A	19.00	101
1990 Southwest Indian Ball 19	Retrd.	N/A	19.00	240
1990 Spin Top 90	Retrd.	N/A	11.00	36-48
1990 Summer Parasol 88	Retrd.	N/A	7.00	132-156
1990 Sunburst Fish (green/yellow) 68	Retrd.	N/A	13.00	50
1990 Swami 41	Retrd.	N/A	8.00	66
1990 Tabby 42	Retrd.	N/A	7.00	30-36
1990 Tropical Fish 74	Retrd.	N/A	24.00	28-48
1990 Trumpet Player 83	Retrd.	N/A	18.00	100
1990 Tuxedo Penguin 57	Retrd.	1990	8.00	150-250
1990 Walrus 59	Retrd.	1990	8.50	120
1990 Yarn Fight 23	Retrd.	N/A	17.00	125-150

1991 Holiday Collection - C. Radko

YEAR ISSUE	EDITION LIMIT	YEAR RETD.	ISSUE PRICE	*QUOTE U.S.$
1991 All Weather Santa 137	Retrd.	1992	32.00	125-230
1991 Alladin 29	Retrd.	N/A	14.00	28-72
1991 Altar Boy 18	Retrd.	1992	16.00	36-66
1991 Anchor America 65	Retrd.	1992	21.50	52-65
1991 Apache 42	Retrd.	N/A	8.50	22-54
1991 Aspen 76	Retrd.	1992	20.50	60-120
1991 Astro Top (light blue) 168	Retrd.	N/A	11.50	75-168
1991 Aztec 141	Retrd.	1991	21.50	90-104
1991 Aztec Bird 41	Retrd.	1992	20.00	65-162
1991 Ballooning Santa 110	Retrd.	1991	23.00	150-208
1991 Barnum Clown 56	Retrd.	1991	15.00	55-95
1991 Bishop 22	Retrd.	N/A	15.00	30-54
1991 Black Forest Cone 97	Retrd.	N/A	8.00	42
1991 Blue Rainbow 136	Retrd.	1992	21.50	95-100
1991 Bowery Kid 50	Retrd.	1991	14.50	29-48
1991 Butterfly Bouquet 142	Retrd.	N/A	21.50	54
1991 By the Nile 124	Retrd.	1992	21.50	65-72
1991 Cardinal Richelieu 109	Retrd.	N/A	15.50	23-90
1991 Carnival (cloudy) 123	Retrd.	N/A	20.00	15-50
1991 Carousel Stripes 132	Retrd.	N/A	20.50	50
1991 Chance Encounter 104	Retrd.	1992	13.50	60
1991 Chief Sitting Bull 107	Retrd.	1992	16.00	43-90
1991 Chimney Santa 12	Retrd.	N/A	14.50	60-107
1991 Christmas Trim 128	Retrd.	N/A	21.50	75
1991 Clown Drum 33	Retrd.	1991	14.00	10-54
1991 Comet 62	Retrd.	1991	9.00	18-60
1991 Cosette 15	Retrd.	1991	16.00	45-60
1991 Cottage Garden 84	Retrd.	N/A	21.00	60
1991 Country Quilt 140	Retrd.	N/A	21.00	30-60
1991 Cowboy Santa 106	Retrd.	N/A	15.50	32-66
1991 Dapper Shoe 89	Retrd.	1991	10.00	35-42
1991 Dawn & Dusk 34	Retrd.	N/A	14.00	30-36
1991 Deco Floral 133	Retrd.	1991	22.00	75-125
1991 Deco Sparkle 134	Retrd.	1992	21.00	66-96
1991 Deep Sea (pale green, signed) 72	Retrd.	N/A	21.50	72
1991 Dutch Boy 27	Retrd.	1991	11.00	30-55
1991 Dutch Girl 28	Retrd.	1991	11.00	55-75
1991 Edwardian Lace 82	Retrd.	1991	21.50	125
1991 Einstein Kite 98	Retrd.	N/A	20.00	90-125
1991 Elephant on Ball (gold) 115	Retrd.	N/A	23.00	500
1991 Elephant on Ball (striped) 115	Retrd.	N/A	23.00	450-500
1991 Elf Reflector 135	Retrd.	1992	23.00	36-50
1991 Evening Santa 20	Retrd.	N/A	14.50	90
1991 Fanfare 126	Retrd.	1992	21.50	72-98
1991 Fisher Frog 44	Retrd.	1991	11.00	75
1991 Florentine 83	Retrd.	N/A	22.00	66-100
1991 Flower Child 90	Retrd.	1991	13.00	30-40
1991 Forest Santa Reflector 151	Retrd.	N/A	34.50	120-150
1991 Frog Under Balloon 53	Retrd.	N/A	16.00	72
1991 Froggy Child 26	Retrd.	N/A	9.00	18-27
1991 Fruit in Balloon 40	Retrd.	N/A	22.00	95-144
1991 Fu Manchu 11	Retrd.	N/A	15.00	29-75
1991 Galaxy 120	Retrd.	1991	21.50	60-72
1991 Grapefruit Tree 113	Retrd.	N/A	23.00	150-240
1991 Harvest 3	Retrd.	N/A	13.50	22-50
1991 Hatching Duck 35	Retrd.	1991	14.00	40-50
1991 Hearts & Flowers Finial 158	Retrd.	1993	53.00	150-156
1991 Her Majesty 39	Retrd.	1991	21.00	50-96
1991 Her Purse 88	Retrd.	N/A	10.00	20-60
1991 Holly Ball 156	Retrd.	N/A	22.00	49-60
1991 Holly Ribbons Finial 153	Retrd.	N/A	54.00	120
1991 Irish Laddie 10	Retrd.	1991	12.00	55-65
1991 Jemima's Child 111	Retrd.	1991	16.00	45-60
1991 King Arthur (Blue) 95	Retrd.	N/A	18.50	55-85
1991 Lion's Head 31	Retrd.	N/A	16.00	26-36
1991 Lucy's Favorite (gold) 75-1	Retrd.	N/A	10.50	60
1991 Lucy's Favorite (signed) 75	Retrd.	N/A	10.50	42-60
1991 Madeleine's Puppy 25	Retrd.	N/A	11.00	27-36
1991 Madonna & Child 103	Retrd.	N/A	15.00	60-125
1991 Melon Slice 99	Retrd.	N/A	18.00	30-50
1991 Mother Goose 57	Retrd.	N/A	11.00	40

*Quotes have been rounded up to nearest dollar

YEAR ISSUE	EDITION LIMIT	YEAR RETD.	ISSUE PRICE	*QUOTE U.S.$
1991 Ms. Maus 94	Retrd.	N/A	14.00	35-100
1991 Munchkin 91	Retrd.	N/A	8.00	36
1991 Olympiad 125	Retrd.	1992	22.00	43-125
1991 Patrick's Bunny 24	Retrd.	N/A	11.00	35-48
1991 Peruvian 74	Retrd.	1991	21.50	60-100
1991 Pierre Le Berry 2	Retrd.	1993	14.00	66-125
1991 Pink Clown on Ball 32	Retrd.	N/A	14.00	41-60
1991 Pink Elephants 70	Retrd.	N/A	21.50	60-72
1991 Pipe Man 93	Retrd.	N/A	20.00	54-90
1991 Pipe Smoking Monkey 54	Retrd.	1991	11.00	36-48
1991 Polish Folk Art 116	Retrd.	N/A	20.50	48-75
1991 Prince on Ball (pink/blue/green) 51	Retrd.	1991	15.00	36-80
1991 Prince Umbrella 21	Retrd.	1991	15.00	28-60
1991 Proud Peacock 37	Retrd.	N/A	23.00	72-150
1991 Puss N Boots 23	Retrd.	N/A	11.00	19-35
1991 Rainbow Bird 92	Retrd.	1991	16.00	48
1991 Rainbow Cone 105	Retrd.	N/A	10.00	48-84
1991 Rainbow Trout 17	Retrd.	N/A	14.50	22-54
1991 Raspberry & Lime 96	Retrd.	1991	12.00	72-96
1991 Red Star 129	Retrd.	1992	21.50	42-72
1991 Royal Porcelain 71	Retrd.	N/A	21.50	72
1991 Russian Santa (coral) 112-4	Retrd.	N/A	22.00	34-60
1991 Russian Santa (striped) 112	Retrd.	N/A	22.00	34-72
1991 Russian Santa (white) 112	Retrd.	N/A	22.00	36-72
1991 Sally Ann 43	Retrd.	1991	8.00	15-46
1991 Santa Bootie (blue) 55	Retrd.	N/A	10.00	60
1991 Santa Bootie 55	Retrd.	1993	10.00	30-36
1991 Santa in Winter White (red) 112-2	Retrd.	N/A	22.00	100-200
1991 Santa in Winter White (silver) 112-1	Retrd.	N/A	22.00	50
1991 Ship To Shore 122	Retrd.	N/A	20.50	84
1991 Shirley 15	Retrd.	1991	16.00	60-75
1991 Shy Elf 1	Retrd.	1991	10.00	27-60
1991 Silver Bells (signed) 73	Retrd.	N/A	20.50	96
1991 Sitting Bull 107	Retrd.	N/A	16.00	96-240
1991 Sleepy Time Santa (cobalt store exclusive) 52	Retrd.	N/A	15.00	48
1991 Sleepy Time Santa 52	Retrd.	N/A	15.00	48-144
1991 Smitty 9	Retrd.	N/A	15.00	45-60
1991 Snowman Reflector 13	Retrd.	N/A	16.00	66
1991 Star Quilt 139	Retrd.	1991	21.50	66-75
1991 Sunburst Fish 108	Retrd.	N/A	15.00	120
1991 Sunshine 67	Retrd.	N/A	22.00	40-60
1991 Tabby 46	Retrd.	1991	8.00	30-50
1991 Talking Pipe 93	Retrd.	N/A	20.00	84
1991 Tiffany 68	Retrd.	1991	22.00	50
1991 Tiger 5	Retrd.	N/A	15.00	28-42
1991 Timepiece 30	Retrd.	N/A	8.00	42
1991 Trigger 114	Retrd.	1991	15.00	60-102
1991 Tropical Flower (lavender) 61	Retrd.	N/A	14.00	72
1991 Trumpet Man 100	Retrd.	1992	21.00	72
1991 Tulip Fairy 63	Retrd.	1992	16.00	46-72
1991 Vienna 1901 127	Retrd.	1992	21.50	46-72
1991 Villandry 87	Retrd.	1991	21.00	50-75
1991 Winking St. Nick 102	Retrd.	N/A	16.00	96
1991 Woodland Santa 38	Retrd.	N/A	14.00	35-84
1991 Zebra (glittered) 79	Retrd.	1991	22.00	400-500
1992 Holiday Collection - C. Radko				
1992 Alpine Flowers-Tiffany 162	Retrd.	1992	28.00	50-60
1992 Alpine Village 105	Retrd.	N/A	24.00	42-125
1992 Aspen 120	Retrd.	1992	26.00	50
1992 Barbie's Mom 69	Retrd.	1992	18.00	63
1992 Benjamin's Nutcrackers (pr.) 185	Retrd.	N/A	58.00	150-188
1992 Binkie the Clown 168	Retrd.	N/A	12.00	36-60
1992 Blue Santa 65	Retrd.	N/A	18.00	34-48
1992 Butterfly Bouquet 119	Retrd.	1992	26.50	60-125
1992 By the Nile 139	Retrd.	1992	27.00	50-75
1992 Cabaret-Tiffany (see-through) 159	Retrd.	1993	28.00	60
1992 Candy Trumpet Men (pink/blue) 98	Retrd.	N/A	27.00	33-75
1992 Candy Trumpet Men (red) w/ white glitter 98	Retrd.	1992	27.00	33-80
1992 Candy Trumpet Men (red) w/o white glitter 98	Retrd.	N/A	27.00	33-48
1992 Celestial 129	Retrd.	N/A	26.00	100
1992 Cheerful Sun 50	Retrd.	N/A	18.00	40-60
1992 Chevron 160	Retrd.	1992	28.00	40
1992 Chevron-Tiffany 160	Retrd.	N/A	28.00	98
1992 Chimney Sweep Bell 179	Retrd.	N/A	27.00	78-184
1992 Choir Boy 114	Retrd.	1992	24.00	36-50
1992 Christmas Cardinals 123	Retrd.	1992	26.00	42-58
1992 Christmas Rose 143	Retrd.	1992	25.50	48-60
1992 Christmas Spider 212	Retrd.	N/A	22.00	35
1992 Cinderella's Bluebirds 240	Retrd.	N/A	26.00	54
1992 Circus Lady 54	Retrd.	1992	12.00	27
1992 Clown Snake 62	Retrd.	N/A	22.00	22-55
1992 Country Scene 169	Retrd.	N/A	12.00	40-54
1992 Country Star Quilt 176	Retrd.	N/A	12.00	50-100
1992 Cowboy Santa 94	Retrd.	N/A	24.00	48-100
1992 Crescent Moons 189	Retrd.	N/A	26.00	60-72
1992 Dawn & Dusk 96	Retrd.	N/A	19.00	36-48
1992 Delft Design 124	Retrd.	1992	26.50	60-173
1992 Diva 73	Retrd.	1992	17.00	19-65
1992 Dolly Madison 115	Retrd.	1992	17.00	19-60
1992 Down The Chimney 191	Retrd.	N/A	16.50	40-60
1992 Downhill Racer 76	Retrd.	1992	34.00	60-140
1992 Elephant on Parade 141	Retrd.	1992	26.00	70-85
1992 Elephant Reflector 181	Retrd.	N/A	17.00	48-66
1992 Elf Reflectors 136	Retrd.	1992	28.00	48-96
1992 Eveningstar Santa 186	Retrd.	N/A	60.00	144-156
1992 Extravagance Garland 227	Retrd.	N/A	64.00	96
1992 Faberge (pink/lavender) 148	Retrd.	N/A	26.50	45-55
1992 Faith, Hope & Love 183	Retrd.	1992	12.00	17-36
1992 Festive Smitty	Retrd.	N/A	28.95	33-45

YEAR ISSUE	EDITION LIMIT	YEAR RETD.	ISSUE PRICE	*QUOTE U.S.$
1992 Floral Cascade Finial 173	Retrd.	N/A	68.00	102
1992 Floral Cascade Tier Drop 175	Retrd.	1992	64.00	125-400
1992 Florentine 131	Retrd.	N/A	27.00	45-75
1992 Flutter By's 201(Set/4)	Retrd.	N/A	11.00	48-65
1992 Folk Art Set 95	Retrd.	1992	10.00	13
1992 Forest Friends 103	Retrd.	1992	14.00	20-54
1992 French Country 121	Retrd.	N/A	26.00	48-60
1992 Fruit in Balloon 83	Retrd.	N/A	28.00	60-125
1992 Gabriel's Trumpets 188	Retrd.	N/A	20.00	25
1992 Harlequin Ball 196	Retrd.	N/A	27.00	27-48
1992 Harlequin Finial (tree topper) 199	Retrd.	N/A	70.00	120-136
1992 Harlequin Tier Drop 74	Retrd.	1992	36.00	60-90
1992 Harold Lloyd Reflector 218	Retrd.	1992	70.00	200-450
1992 Her Purse 43	Retrd.	N/A	20.00	36-60
1992 Her Slipper 56	Retrd.	1992	17.00	25
1992 Holly Finial 200	Retrd.	N/A	70.00	83
1992 Honey Bear 167	Retrd.	N/A	14.00	34-42
1992 Ice Pear 241	Retrd.	N/A	20.00	36-60
1992 Ice Poppies 127	Retrd.	1992	26.00	48-60
1992 Jester Ball 151	Retrd.	N/A	25.50	66
1992 Jumbo 99	Retrd.	N/A	31.00	45-48
1992 Just Like Grandma's 164	Retrd.	N/A	10.00	25-30
1992 Kewpie 51	Retrd.	N/A	18.00	38-60
1992 King of Prussia 149	Retrd.	1992	27.00	38-48
1992 Kitty Rattle 166	Retrd.	1993	18.00	36-72
1992 Little Eskimo 38	Retrd.	N/A	14.00	20-48
1992 Little League 53	Retrd.	1992	20.00	36-65
1992 The Littlest Snowman (red hat) 67	Retrd.	N/A	14.00	19-36
1992 Littlest Snowman 67	Retrd.	N/A	14.00	42-60
1992 Locomotive Garland 216	Retrd.	N/A	60.00	75-150
1992 Madeline's Puppy 49	Retrd.	N/A	18.00	69
1992 Majestic Reflector 187	Retrd.	N/A	70.00	120
1992 Meditteranean Sunshine 140	Retrd.	N/A	17.00	34-40
1992 Melon Slice 91	Retrd.	N/A	26.00	26-48
1992 Merlin Santa 75	Retrd.	N/A	32.00	84-90
1992 Merry Christmas Maiden 137	Retrd.	1992	26.00	40-48
1992 Mission Ball 153	Retrd.	N/A	27.00	27-48
1992 Mother Goose 37	Retrd.	N/A	15.00	25-48
1992 Mr. & Mrs. Claus 59	Retrd.	N/A	18.00	150-200
1992 Mushroom Elf 87	Retrd.	N/A	18.00	36-60
1992 Neopolitan Angels 152 (Set/3)	Retrd.	1992	27.00	144-300
1992 Norweigian Princess 170	Retrd.	1992	15.00	66
1992 Olympiad 132	Retrd.	N/A	26.00	80
1992 Palace Guard 60	Retrd.	N/A	17.00	26-54
1992 Pierre Winterberry 64	Retrd.	1993	17.00	30-75
1992 Pink Lace Ball (See Through) 158	Retrd.	1992	28.00	60-100
1992 Polar Bear 184	Retrd.	N/A	16.00	22-48
1992 Primary Colors 108	Retrd.	1992	30.00	85-150
1992 Quilted Hearts (Old Salem Museum) 194	Retrd.	N/A	27.50	42-51
1992 Rainbow Parasol 90	Retrd.	1992	30.00	60-100
1992 Royal Scepter 77	Retrd.	1992	36.00	114-120
1992 Ruby Scarlet Finial 198	Retrd.	N/A	70.00	95-156
1992 Russian Imperial 112	Retrd.	1992	25.00	50
1992 Russian Jewel Hearts 146	Retrd.	N/A	27.00	48-100
1992 Russian Star 130	Retrd.	1992	26.00	32-40
1992 Sail Away 215	Retrd.	N/A	22.00	50
1992 Santa Claus Garland 220	Retrd.	N/A	66.00	96-120
1992 Santa in Winter White 106	Retrd.	N/A	28.00	60-65
1992 Santa's Helper 78	Retrd.	N/A	17.00	36-72
1992 Scallop Shell 150	Retrd.	N/A	27.00	30-38
1992 Seafaring Santa 71	Retrd.	N/A	18.00	36-66
1992 Seahorse (pink) 92	Retrd.	1992	20.00	72-86
1992 Serpents of Paradise 97	Retrd.	N/A	13.00	30
1992 Shy Rabbit 40	Retrd.	N/A	14.00	36-72
1992 Siberian Sleigh Ride (pink) 154	Retrd.	N/A	27.00	45-85
1992 Silver Icicle 89	Retrd.	N/A	12.00	48-60
1992 Sitting Bull 93	Retrd.	1992	26.00	43-60
1992 Sleepytime Santa (pink) 81	Retrd.	N/A	18.00	60-95
1992 Sloopy Snowman 328	Retrd.	N/A	19.90	54
1992 Snake Prince 171	Retrd.	N/A	19.00	30
1992 Snowflakes 209	Retrd.	N/A	10.00	30-40
1992 Southern Colonial 142	Retrd.	N/A	27.00	60
1992 Sputniks 134	Retrd.	1992	25.50	72-100
1992 St. Nickcicle 107	Retrd.	N/A	26.00	30-72
1992 Star of Wonder 177	Retrd.	1992	27.00	35-50
1992 Starbursts 214	Retrd.	N/A	12.00	30-48
1992 Stardust Joey 110	Retrd.	1992	16.00	54-150
1992 Starlight Santa (powder blue) 180	Retrd.	N/A	18.00	50
1992 Sterling Silver Garland 204	Retrd.	N/A	12.00	60
1992 Talking Pipe (black stem) 104	Retrd.	N/A	26.00	110
1992 Thunderbolt 178	Retrd.	1993	60.00	186-222
1992 Tiffany Bright Harlequin 161	Retrd.	1992	28.00	48-114
1992 Tiffany Pastel Harlequin 163	Retrd.	N/A	28.00	48-114
1992 Tiffany Pine Lace 158	Retrd.	N/A	28.00	85
1992 To Grandma's House 239	Retrd.	N/A	20.00	58-84
1992 Topiary 117	Retrd.	N/A	30.00	120-250
1992 Tropical Fish 109	Retrd.	N/A	17.00	60
1992 Tulip Fairy 57	Retrd.	1992	18.00	22-45
1992 Tuxedo Santa 88	Retrd.	1993	22.00	25-125
1992 Two Sided Santa Reflector 102	Retrd.	1992	28.00	75
1992 Umbrella Santa 182	Retrd.	N/A	60.00	140-150
1992 Victorian Santa & Angel Balloon 122	Retrd.	1992	68.00	500-600
1992 Vienna 1901 128	Retrd.	1992	27.00	150
1992 Village Carolers 172	Retrd.	N/A	17.00	21-66
1992 Virgin Mary 46	Retrd.	1992	20.00	28-63
1992 Wacko's Brother, Doofus 55	Retrd.	N/A	20.00	36-66
1992 Water Lilies 133	Retrd.	1992	26.00	90-100
1992 Wedding Bells 217	Retrd.	N/A	40.00	165-225
1992 Winking St. Nick 70	Retrd.	N/A	22.00	22-48
1992 Winter Kiss 82	Retrd.	N/A	18.00	48-60
1992 Winter Tree 101	Retrd.	N/A	28.00	48-84

YEAR ISSUE	EDITION LIMIT	YEAR RETD.	ISSUE PRICE	*QUOTE U.S.$
1992 Winter Wonderland 156	Retrd.	1992	26.00	42-96
1992 Woodland Santa 111	Retrd.	N/A	20.00	39-55
1992 Ziegfeld Follies 126	Retrd.	1992	27.00	100-130
1993 Holiday Collection - C. Radko				
1993 1939 World's Fair 149	Retrd.	N/A	26.80	60-100
1993 Accordian Elf 189	Retrd.	N/A	21.00	32-42
1993 Aladdin's Lamp 237	Retrd.	N/A	20.00	39-72
1993 Allegro 179	Retrd.	N/A	26.80	42-108
1993 Alpine Village 420	Retrd.	1993	23.80	125
1993 Alpine Wings 86	Retrd.	N/A	58.00	96
1993 Anassazi 172	Retrd.	N/A	26.60	65-75
1993 Anchor Santa 407	Retrd.	N/A	32.00	54-90
1993 Angel Light 256	Retrd.	N/A	16.00	16-48
1993 Angel of Peace 132	Retrd.	1993	17.00	22-54
1993 Apache 357	Retrd.	1993	13.90	54-75
1993 Auld Lang Syne 246	Retrd.	N/A	15.00	24-60
1993 Away in a Manger 379	Retrd.	N/A	24.00	28-55
1993 Bavarian Santa 335	Retrd.	N/A	23.00	32-66
1993 Beauregard 296	Retrd.	N/A	24.00	29-60
1993 Bedtime Buddy 239	Retrd.	N/A	29.00	102-114
1993 Bell House Boy 291	Retrd.	1993	21.00	48
1993 Bells Are Ringing 268	Retrd.	N/A	18.00	24-36
1993 Bells-Tiffany 334	Retrd.	N/A	8.80	36-45
1993 Beyond the Stars 108	Retrd.	1993	18.50	54-70
1993 Bishop of Myra 327	Retrd.	1993	19.90	25-50
1993 Bishops Cross Garland 79	Retrd.	N/A	48.90	90
1993 Black Forest Clock 360	Retrd.	N/A	20.00	32-48
1993 Blue Top 114	Retrd.	1993	16.00	30-75
1993 Bowzer 228	Retrd.	N/A	22.80	78-125
1993 By Jiminy 285	Retrd.	N/A	16.40	48
1993 Calla Lilly 314	Retrd.	N/A	12.90	15-25
1993 Candied Citrus 278	Retrd.	N/A	9.00	25-42
1993 Candlelight 118	Retrd.	N/A	16.00	22-36
1993 Carnival Rides 303	Retrd.	N/A	18.00	65-75
1993 Cathedral Bells 343	Retrd.	N/A	8.20	54
1993 Celeste 271	Retrd.	N/A	26.00	33-39
1993 Celestial Peacock 197	Retrd.	N/A	27.90	30-75
1993 Celestial Peacock Finial 322	Retrd.	N/A	69.00	200-295
1993 Center Ring (Exclusive) 192	Retrd.	1993	30.80	48-150
1993 Centurian 224	Retrd.	1993	25.50	102-150
1993 Chimney Sweep Bell 294	Retrd.	1993	26.00	180
1993 Christmas Express (Garland) 394	Retrd.	N/A	58.00	32-42
1993 Christmas Goose 129	Retrd.	N/A	14.80	42
1993 Christmas Stars 342	Retrd.	N/A	14.00	20-36
1993 Church Bell 295	Retrd.	N/A	24.00	42-45
1993 Cinderella's Bluebirds 145	Retrd.	1993	25.90	54-120
1993 Circle of Santas Finial 413	Retrd.	N/A	69.00	100
1993 Circus Seal 249	Retrd.	1993	28.00	102-132
1993 Circus Star 358	Retrd.	N/A	24.00	48-90
1993 Class Clown 332	Retrd.	N/A	21.00	35-66
1993 Classic Christmas 408	Retrd.	N/A	29.00	60-126
1993 Cloud Nine 369	Retrd.	N/A	25.00	42-72
1993 Clowning Around 84	Retrd.	N/A	42.50	50-68
1993 Confucius 363	Retrd.	1993	19.00	28
1993 Cool Cat 184	Retrd.	N/A	21.00	100
1993 Copenhagen 166	Retrd.	1993	26.80	100-190
1993 Country Flowers 205	Retrd.	N/A	16.00	30-40
1993 Country Scene 204	Retrd.	N/A	11.90	36-48
1993 Crescent Moons Finial 397	Retrd.	N/A	69.00	69-108
1993 Crocus Blossoms 283	Retrd.	N/A	16.00	54
1993 Crowned Passion 299	Retrd.	1993	23.00	36-48
1993 Crystal Fountain 243	Retrd.	N/A	34.00	114
1993 Crystal Rainbow 308	Retrd.	N/A	29.90	200-300
1993 Dancing Harlequin 232	Retrd.	N/A	36.00	45-84
1993 Daniel Star 211	Retrd.	N/A	26.00	30-54
1993 Dawn & Dusk 318	Retrd.	N/A	18.90	19-36
1993 Deco Snowfall 147	Retrd.	1993	26.80	42-48
1993 Deco Tree Garland 60	Retrd.	N/A	42.00	86-105
1993 Deer Drop 304	Retrd.	N/A	34.00	36-110
1993 Del Monte 219	Retrd.	N/A	23.50	24-54
1993 Devotion 203	Retrd.	N/A	17.00	24-36
1993 Don't Hold Your Breath 92-1	Retrd.	N/A	11.00	50
1993 Downhill Racer 195	Retrd.	1993	30.00	60-108
1993 Dynasty Garland 55	Retrd.	N/A	49.00	78
1993 Eggman 241	Retrd.	N/A	22.50	48-72
1993 Elf Bell 125	Retrd.	N/A	18.00	15-42
1993 Emerald Wizard 279	Retrd.	N/A	18.00	28-51
1993 Emperor's Pet 253	Retrd.	1993	22.00	126
1993 Enchanted Gardens 341	Retrd.	1993	5.50	13
1993 English Kitchen 234	Retrd.	1993	26.00	54-60
1993 Epiphany 421	Retrd.	N/A	29.00	48-90
1993 Eskimo Elves Garland 72	Retrd.	N/A	39.20	78
1993 Eskimo Kitty 281	Retrd.	N/A	14.50	20-36
1993 Evening Star Santa 409	Retrd.	1993	59.00	95
1993 Extravagance Garland 87	Retrd.	N/A	53.00	90
1993 Faberge Egg 257	Retrd.	N/A	17.50	42-45
1993 Fantastia 143	Retrd.	N/A	24.00	55-130
1993 Fantasy Cone 324	Retrd.	N/A	17.90	30-36
1993 Fantasy Garland II 88	Retrd.	N/A	40.40	84
1993 Far Out Santa 138	Retrd.	N/A	39.00	120-150
1993 Fiesta Ball 316	Retrd.	N/A	26.40	48
1993 First Snow 365	Retrd.	N/A	10.00	36
1993 Fleurice 282	Retrd.	N/A	23.50	28-54
1993 Flora Dora 255	Retrd.	N/A	25.00	45-60
1993 Fly Boy 235	Retrd.	N/A	33.00	60-95
1993 Forest Bells 136	Retrd.	N/A	25.00	48-54
1993 Forest Friends 250	Retrd.	1993	28.00	35-100
1993 French Regency Balloon 161	Retrd.	N/A	29.00	44-47
1993 French Rose 152	Retrd.	1993	26.60	48-60
1993 Fruit in Balloon 115	Retrd.	N/A	27.90	80
1993 Geisha Girls 261	Retrd.	1993	11.90	25-60

*Quotes have been rounded up to nearest dollar

YEAR ISSUE	EDITION LIMIT	YEAR RETD.	ISSUE PRICE	*QUOTE U.S.$
1993 Georgian Santa 292	Retrd.	N/A	30.00	48-60
1993 Gerard 252	Retrd.	N/A	26.00	48-96
1993 Gilded Cage 406	Retrd.	N/A	44.00	48-108
1993 Glory on High 116	Retrd.	N/A	17.00	25-72
1993 Gold Fish 158	Retrd.	1993	25.80	75-100
1993 Golden Crescendo Finial 381-1	Retrd.	N/A	50.00	600
1993 Goofy Fruits 367	Retrd.	N/A	14.00	36-66
1993 Goofy Garden (Pickle) 191	Retrd.	N/A	15.00	48
1993 Goofy Garden (Set/4) 191	Retrd.	N/A	60.00	100-150
1993 Grand Monarch 306	Retrd.	N/A	16.00	26-48
1993 Grandpa Bear 260	Retrd.	1993	12.80	30
1993 Grecian Urn 231	Retrd.	1993	23.00	50-60
1993 Guardian Angel 124	Retrd.	N/A	36.00	84-132
1993 Gypsy Girl 371	Retrd.	1993	16.00	16-35
1993 Hansel & Gretel 100	Retrd.	N/A	24.00	25-54
1993 Harvest 354	Retrd.	N/A	19.90	48
1993 Holiday Inn 137	Retrd.	N/A	21.00	54
1993 Holiday Sparkle 144	Retrd.	N/A	16.80	144
1993 Holiday Spice 422	Retrd.	1993	24.00	36-48
1993 Holly Ribbons 415	Retrd.	N/A	24.80	24-36
1993 Honey Bear 352	Retrd.	1993	13.90	20-55
1993 Ice Bear 284	Retrd.	N/A	17.50	36-48
1993 Ice Star Santa 405	Retrd.	1993	38.00	150-250
1993 Injun Joe 102	Retrd.	N/A	24.00	24-48
1993 It's A Small World 96	Retrd.	N/A	17.00	25-42
1993 Jack Frost (blue) 333	Retrd.	N/A	23.00	29-48
1993 Jaques Le Berry 356	Retrd.	N/A	16.90	100-150
1993 Jewel Box 213	Retrd.	N/A	12.00	20-36
1993 Jingle Bells 61	Retrd.	N/A	64.00	145
1993 Joey B. Clown 135	Retrd.	N/A	26.00	45-91
1993 Jumbo Spintops 302	Retrd.	N/A	27.00	45-132
1993 Just Like Grandma's Lg. 200	Retrd.	N/A	7.20	25-50
1993 Just Like Grandma's Sm. 200	Retrd.	N/A	7.20	25-30
1993 King's Ransom 449	Retrd.	N/A	49.00	75
1993 Kissing Cousins (Pair) 245	Retrd.	N/A	30.00	162-180
1993 Kitty Rattle 374	Retrd.	1993	17.80	90
1993 Lamp Light 251	Retrd.	N/A	22.50	50-60
1993 Letter to Santa 188	Retrd.	N/A	22.00	42-48
1993 Light in the Windows 229	Retrd.	1994	24.50	48-55
1993 Little Boy Blue 361	Retrd.	N/A	25.90	60-78
1993 Little Doggie 180	Retrd.	1993	7.00	30-36
1993 Little Eskimo 355	Retrd.	N/A	13.90	22
1993 Little Slugger 187	Retrd.	N/A	22.00	22-36
1993 Lucky Shoe 346	Retrd.	N/A	16.00	54
1993 Majestic Reflector 312	Retrd.	1993	70.00	100
1993 Maxine 240	Retrd.	N/A	10.00	32-84
1993 Mediterranean Sunshine 156	Retrd.	N/A	26.90	75
1993 Midas Touch 162	Retrd.	N/A	27.80	68
1993 Monkey Business 126	Retrd.	N/A	14.80	20-54
1993 Monkey Man 97	Retrd.	1993	16.00	27-42
1993 Monterey 290	Retrd.	1993	15.00	25-36
1993 Moon Dust 128	Retrd.	N/A	15.00	36-78
1993 Moon Jump 423	Retrd.	N/A	29.00	84-120
1993 Mooning Over You 106	Retrd.	N/A	17.00	24
1993 Mountain Christmas 384	Retrd.	N/A	25.50	28-78
1993 Mr. & Mrs. Claus 121	Retrd.	1993	17.90	80-125
1993 Mushroom Elf 267	Retrd.	N/A	17.90	38
1993 Mushroom Santa 212	Retrd.	N/A	28.00	110-156
1993 Nellie (Italian ornament) 225	Retrd.	1993	27.50	132-200
1993 Nesting Stork Finial (red or gold) 380	Retrd.	N/A	50.00	150
1993 Nesting Stork Finial 380	Retrd.	N/A	50.00	216
1993 North Woods 317	Retrd.	1993	26.80	49-120.
1993 Northwind 266	Retrd.	N/A	17.00	22-48
1993 Nuts & Berries (signed) 64	Retrd.	N/A	58.00	120
1993 Nuts & Berries 64	Retrd.	N/A	58.00	50
1993 One Small Leap 222	Retrd.	N/A	26.00	95-175
1993 Pagoda 258	Retrd.	1993	8.00	15-30
1993 Pennsylvania Dutch 146	Retrd.	1993	26.80	42-65
1993 Piggly Wiggly 101	Retrd.	N/A	11.00	54
1993 Pineapple Quilt 150	Retrd.	N/A	26.80	54-65
1993 Pineapple Slice 376	Retrd.	N/A	14.00	15-54
1993 Pinecone Santa 142	Retrd.	N/A	24.00	30-36
1993 Pinocchio 248	Retrd.	N/A	26.00	50-95
1993 Pisces Garland 59	Retrd.	N/A	37.00	72-78
1993 Pixie Santa 186	Retrd.	N/A	16.00	42
1993 Plum 185	Retrd.	N/A	6.40	20
1993 Poinsetta Santa 269	Retrd.	N/A	19.80	65-76
1993 Polar Bears 112A	Retrd.	1993	15.50	16
1993 Pompadour 344	Retrd.	1993	8.80	10-24
1993 President Taft 92	Retrd.	N/A	15.00	24-60
1993 Prince Albert 263	Retrd.	N/A	23.00	30-36
1993 Purse 389	Retrd.	1993	15.60	16
1993 Quartet 392	Retrd.	1993	3.60	11
1993 Radio Monkey 104	Retrd.	N/A	16.20	48
1993 Rainbow Beads 78	Retrd.	N/A	44.00	72-96
1993 Rainbow Reflector 154	Retrd.	1993	26.60	48-96
1993 Rainbow Shark 277	Retrd.	N/A	18.00	65-70
1993 Rainy Day Friend 206	Retrd.	N/A	22.00	30-65
1993 Rambling Rose 148	Retrd.	N/A	16.60	32-52
1993 Regal Rooster 177	Retrd.	N/A	25.80	45-75
1993 Remembrance 151	Retrd.	N/A	16.60	54-72
1993 Rose Pointe Finial 323	Retrd.	1993	34.00	40
1993 Russian Santa (red) 209	Retrd.	N/A	27.90	50
1993 Sail by Starlight 339	Retrd.	1993	11.80	14-19
1993 Sailor Man 238	Retrd.	N/A	22.00	66-95
1993 Santa Baby 112	Retrd.	N/A	18.00	24-36
1993 Santa Hearts Garland 76	Retrd.	N/A	58.00	42-84
1993 Santa in Space 127	Retrd.	N/A	39.00	120-125
1993 Santa in Winter White 300	Retrd.	N/A	27.90	65
1993 Santa Tree 320	Retrd.	N/A	66.00	250-300
1993 Santa's Helper 329	Retrd.	N/A	16.90	20-60
1993 Saraband 140	Retrd.	1993	27.80	75-150

YEAR ISSUE	EDITION LIMIT	YEAR RETD.	ISSUE PRICE	*QUOTE U.S.$
1993 Scotch Pine 167	Retrd.	N/A	26.80	38-48
1993 Serenade Pink 157	Retrd.	1993	26.80	48-60
1993 Shy Rabbit 280	Retrd.	N/A	14.00	75-90
1993 Siberian Sleigh Ride 403	Retrd.	N/A	16.80	60-78
1993 Siegfred 227	Retrd.	1996	25.00	34-90
1993 Silent Night (blue hat) 120	Retrd.	N/A	18.00	75
1993 Silent Night 120	Retrd.	N/A	18.00	48-60
1993 Silver Bells 52	Retrd.	N/A	27.00	90
1993 The Skating Bettinas 242	Retrd.	N/A	29.00	162-200
1993 Ski Baby 99	Retrd.	N/A	21.00	54-100
1993 Sloopy Snowman 328	Retrd.	1993	19.90	37-54
1993 Smitty 378	Retrd.	N/A	17.90	75-90
1993 Snow Dance 247	Retrd.	N/A	29.00	90
1993 Snowday Santa 98	Retrd.	1993	20.00	60-72
1993 Snowman by Candlelight 155	Retrd.	N/A	26.50	42-116
1993 Southern Colonial 171	Retrd.	N/A	26.90	85-135
1993 Special Delivery 91	Retrd.	N/A	17.00	26-36
1993 Spider & the Fly 393	Retrd.	1993	6.40	30
1993 Spintop Santa 288	Retrd.	N/A	22.80	46
1993 Sporty 345	Retrd.	N/A	20.00	36-42
1993 St. Nick's Pipe 330	Retrd.	N/A	4.40	42-54
1993 St. Nickcicle 298	Retrd.	N/A	25.90	35
1993 Star Children 208	Retrd.	1993	18.00	36-60
1993 Star Fire 175	Retrd.	N/A	26.80	40-90
1993 Star Ribbons 377	Retrd.	N/A	16.00	24-102
1993 Starlight Santa 348	Retrd.	N/A	11.90	19
1993 Sterling Reindeer 21	Retrd.	N/A	113.00	540
1993 Stocking Stuffers 236	Retrd.	1993	16.00	30-50
1993 Sugar Plum 185	Retrd.	N/A	6.40	42
1993 Sugar Shack 368	Retrd.	N/A	22.00	40-54
1993 Sunny Side Up 103	Retrd.	N/A	22.00	48-55
1993 Sweetheart 202	Retrd.	1993	16.00	23-60
1993 Talking Pipe 373	Retrd.	N/A	26.00	55
1993 Tannenbaum 273	Retrd.	N/A	24.00	36
1993 Tea & Sympathy 244	Retrd.	N/A	20.00	38-63
1993 Teenage Mermaid 226	Retrd.	N/A	27.50	48
1993 Texas Star 338	Retrd.	1993	7.50	8-15
1993 Thomas Nast Santa 217	Retrd.	N/A	23.00	36-72
1993 Tiffany Bells (cobalt) 334	Retrd.	N/A	9.00	20
1993 Tiger 90	Retrd.	N/A	23.90	24-48
1993 Time Piece 259	Retrd.	N/A	16.50	25-30
1993 Time Will Tell 349	Retrd.	N/A	22.00	30-42
1993 Tutti Fruitti (Carrot) 221	Retrd.	N/A	26.80	50-78
1993 Tuxedo Santa 117	Retrd.	1993	21.90	125-150
1993 Tweeter 94	Retrd.	1993	3.20	36
1993 Twinkle Toes 233	Retrd.	N/A	28.00	52-60
1993 Twinkle Tree 254	Retrd.	N/A	15.50	20-42
1993 Twister 214	Retrd.	N/A	16.80	72-75
1993 U-Boat 353	Retrd.	1993	15.50	34-48
1993 V.I.P. 230	Retrd.	1993	23.00	150-200
1993 Versaille Balloon 176	Retrd.	N/A	29.00	69-90
1993 Victorian Santa Reflector 198	Retrd.	N/A	28.00	60-180
1993 Vintage 67	Retrd.	N/A	49.00	90
1993 Wacko 272	Retrd.	N/A	24.00	35-48
1993 Waddles 95	Retrd.	1993	3.80	30
1993 Wally 223	Retrd.	N/A	26.00	60-75
1993 Will 181	Retrd.	N/A	23.00	30-42
1993 Wings & A Prayer 123	Retrd.	N/A	12.00	18-25
1993 Winter Birds (cloudy) 164	Retrd.	N/A	26.80	38-42
1993 Winterbirds (pr.) 164	Retrd.	1993	26.80	100

1994 Holiday Collection - C. Radko

YEAR ISSUE	EDITION LIMIT	YEAR RETD.	ISSUE PRICE	*QUOTE U.S.$
1994 Accordion Elf 127	Retrd.	N/A	23.00	65
1994 Airplane 315	Retrd.	N/A	56.00	76-150
1994 All Wrapped Up 161	Retrd.	N/A	26.00	28-78
1994 Andy Gump 48	Retrd.	N/A	18.00	36-42
1994 Angel Bounty 208	Retrd.	N/A	44.00	48-60
1994 Angel on Board 310	Retrd.	N/A	37.00	56-228
1994 Angel Song 141	Retrd.	N/A	45.60	40-90
1994 Angel Star 428	Retrd.	N/A	25.00	54-96
1994 Angelique 135	Retrd.	1996	33.30	52-84
1994 Aunt Kitty 183	Retrd.	N/A	26.00	26-42
1994 Autumn Tapestry 203	Retrd.	N/A	29.00	36-66
1994 Baby Booties (pink) 236	Retrd.	N/A	17.00	30-35
1994 Bag of Goodies 56	Retrd.	N/A	26.00	27-78
1994 Batter Up 397	Retrd.	N/A	13.00	25-36
1994 Berry Stripe 454	Retrd.	N/A	48.00	69-95
1994 Bird Bath 272	Retrd.	N/A	76.00	228
1994 Bird Brain 254	Retrd.	N/A	33.00	42-90
1994 Black Berry 340	Retrd.	N/A	14.00	13-27
1994 Bloomers 354	Retrd.	N/A	18.80	19-48
1994 Blue Satin 200	Retrd.	N/A	29.00	48
1994 Bobo 308	Retrd.	N/A	31.00	96
1994 Bow Ties 364	Retrd.	N/A	12.00	15-22
1994 Brazilia 302	Retrd.	N/A	38.00	48-90
1994 Bright Heavens Above 136	Retrd.	N/A	56.00	75-96
1994 Bubbles 267	Retrd.	N/A	42.00	42-72
1994 Bubbly 258	Retrd.	1994	43.00	48-84
1994 Buon Natale 266	Retrd.	N/A	36.00	95
1994 Cabernet 285	Retrd.	N/A	24.00	29-84
1994 Camille 212	Retrd.	N/A	29.00	35-48
1994 Candelabra 303	Retrd.	N/A	33.00	85
1994 Captain 260	Retrd.	N/A	47.20	84-108
1994 Carousel Willie 126	Retrd.	N/A	74.00	74-102
1994 Castanetta 321	Retrd.	N/A	37.00	50-60
1994 Celestial (blue) 408	Retrd.	N/A	28.80	50-63
1994 Checking It Twice 373	Retrd.	N/A	25.90	40-60
1994 Cheeky Santa 311	Retrd.	N/A	22.00	46
1994 Chianti 268	Retrd.	N/A	26.00	46-78
1994 Chic of Araby 220	Retrd.	N/A	17.00	24-30
1994 Chop Suey, set/2 329	Retrd.	N/A	34.00	72-150
1994 Christmas Express 437	Retrd.	N/A	72.00	72-90

YEAR ISSUE	EDITION LIMIT	YEAR RETD.	ISSUE PRICE	*QUOTE U.S.$
1994 Christmas Harlequin 216	Retrd.	N/A	29.00	42-49
1994 Christmas in Camelot 113	Retrd.	N/A	27.00	45
1994 Chubbs & Slim 255	Retrd.	N/A	28.50	45-132
1994 Circus Band 92	Retrd.	1994	33.30	36-60
1994 Circus Delight 446	Retrd.	N/A	64.00	64-90
1994 Circus Star Balloon 201	Retrd.	N/A	29.00	60-90
1994 Classic Christmas 415	Retrd.	N/A	33.90	72-96
1994 Conchita 271	Retrd.	N/A	37.00	48
1994 Concord 342	Retrd.	N/A	16.00	22-31
1994 Cool Cat 219	Retrd.	N/A	26.00	36-100
1994 Corn Husk 336	Retrd.	N/A	13.00	20-36
1994 Cow Poke 284	Retrd.	N/A	42.00	56-84
1994 Crescent Moon Santa 398	Retrd.	N/A	29.00	96
1994 Crescent Moons 195	Retrd.	N/A	29.00	40-75
1994 Crock O'Dile 297	Retrd.	N/A	33.00	75-102
1994 Crown of Thorns 222	Retrd.	N/A	26.00	42-55
1994 Crowned Peacocks 377	Retrd.	N/A	15.00	15-22
1994 Damask Rose 429	Retrd.	N/A	29.00	29-60
1994 Dear-Ring 225	Retrd.	N/A	16.00	46
1994 Deep Sea 425	Retrd.	N/A	29.00	40-55
1994 Deercicle 291	Retrd.	N/A	29.00	48-96
1994 Del Monte 348	Retrd.	N/A	31.00	31-36
1994 Dolly 283	Retrd.	N/A	42.00	60-84
1994 Dolly 283 & Cowpoke 284	Retrd.	N/A	84.00	147
1994 Dutch Maiden 38	Retrd.	N/A	44.00	30-44
1994 Egg Head 166	Retrd.	N/A	19.00	22
1994 Einstein's Kite 375	Retrd.	N/A	29.90	45
1994 Elephant Prince 170	Retrd.	N/A	14.50	25-60
1994 English Santa 55	Retrd.	N/A	26.00	34-78
1994 Epiphany Ball 211	Retrd.	N/A	29.00	48-66
1994 Faberge Finial 417	Retrd.	N/A	78.00	100-142
1994 Fido 50	Retrd.	N/A	20.00	34-42
1994 First Snow 355	Retrd.	N/A	15.00	15-24
1994 Fleet's In 281	Retrd.	N/A	38.00	48-78
1994 Florentine 190	Retrd.	N/A	29.00	48
1994 Forest Holiday 445	Retrd.	N/A	64.00	85-150
1994 Forget Your Troubles 146	Retrd.	N/A	17.00	22-42
1994 Frat Brothers 96	Retrd.	N/A	22.00	66
1994 French Country 192	Retrd.	N/A	29.00	65-95
1994 French Regency Balloon 393	Retrd.	N/A	32.50	35-60
1994 French Regency Finial 388	Retrd.	N/A	78.00	135-156
1994 From a Distance 322	Retrd.	N/A	32.00	75
1994 Gilded Cage 350	Retrd.	N/A	48.00	60-144
1994 Glad Tidings 430	Retrd.	N/A	44.00	114
1994 Glow Worm 275	Retrd.	N/A	32.00	65-78
1994 Golden Alpine 204	Retrd.	N/A	29.00	29-36
1994 Golden Crescendo Finial 384	Retrd.	N/A	42.00	125
1994 Grape Buzz 19	Retrd.	N/A	19.00	19-30
1994 Gretel 500	Retrd.	N/A	70.00	175
1994 H. Dumpty 46	Retrd.	N/A	19.00	24-46
1994 Hansel 501	Retrd.	N/A	70.00	175
1994 Harvest Home 414	Retrd.	N/A	28.80	54-95
1994 Harvest Moon 23	Retrd.	N/A	19.00	35-40
1994 Heavens Above 42	Retrd.	N/A	76.00	150-180
1994 Hieroglyph 194	Retrd.	N/A	29.00	29-54
1994 Holiday Sparkle 426	Retrd.	N/A	29.00	48-95
1994 Holly Heart 402	Retrd.	N/A	24.00	30
1994 Holly Jolly 399	Retrd.	N/A	40.00	54-72
1994 Holly Ribbons Finial 407	Retrd.	N/A	78.00	100
1994 Honey Belle 156	Retrd.	N/A	74.00	90-150
1994 Horse of a Different Color 309	Retrd.	N/A	28.00	60-102
1994 House Sitting Santa 240	Retrd.	N/A	26.00	26
1994 Ice House 98	Retrd.	N/A	14.00	17-23
1994 Ice Man Cometh 63	Retrd.	N/A	22.00	42
1994 Jack Clown 68	Retrd.	N/A	22.00	50
1994 Jean Claude 323	Retrd.	N/A	31.00	44-102
1994 Jockey Pipe 51	Retrd.	N/A	36.00	66-84
1994 Jolly Stripes 210	Retrd.	N/A	28.00	35-120
1994 Jubilee Finial 383-1	Retrd.	N/A	44.00	180
1994 Jumbo Harlequin 379	Retrd.	N/A	48.00	78-85
1994 Just Like Us 324	Retrd.	N/A	29.50	125-192
1994 Kaiser Pipe 134	Retrd.	N/A	32.00	34-60
1994 Kayo 165	Retrd.	N/A	14.00	20-42
1994 Kewpie 292	Retrd.	N/A	22.00	20-40
1994 King of Kings 18	Retrd.	N/A	22.00	22-75
1994 King's Guard 253	Retrd.	N/A	44.00	95
1994 Kissing Cousins (pair) 249	Retrd.	N/A	28.00	200
1994 Kitty Tamer 331	Retrd.	N/A	65.00	195-234
1994 Kosher Dill 338	Retrd.	N/A	12.00	20
1994 Lantern Lights 442	Retrd.	N/A	64.00	84
1994 Leader of the Band 94-915D (wh pants) - signed	Retrd.	1994	25.00	45-100
1994 Leader of the Band 94-915D (wh pants) - unsigned	Retrd.	1994	25.00	50-95
1994 Lemon Twist 28	Retrd.	N/A	14.00	40
1994 Letter to Santa 77	Retrd.	N/A	31.00	55-60
1994 Liberty Ball 172	Retrd.	N/A	26.00	36-66
1994 Liberty Bell 145	Retrd.	N/A	22.00	35-54
1994 Lil' Bo Peep 62	Retrd.	N/A	22.00	39
1994 Little Orphan 47	Retrd.	N/A	18.00	36-42
1994 Little Slugger 95	Retrd.	N/A	26.00	26-48
1994 Lola Ginabridgida 290	Retrd.	N/A	44.00	69-72
1994 The Los Angeles 155	Retrd.	N/A	26.00	54-75
1994 Madonna & Child 177	Retrd.	N/A	24.00	30-35
1994 Major Duck 327	Retrd.	N/A	58.00	198
1994 Mama's Little Angel 175	Retrd.	N/A	23.00	36
1994 Mandolin Angel 76	Retrd.	N/A	46.00	46-66
1994 Martian Holiday 326	Retrd.	N/A	42.00	168
1994 Masquerade 45	Retrd.	N/A	16.00	25-28
1994 Medium Nautilus (gold) 103	Retrd.	N/A	16.00	13-25
1994 Messiah 221	Retrd.	N/A	22.00	48
1994 Metamorphisis 174	Retrd.	N/A	16.00	36-42

*Quotes have been rounded up to nearest dollar

ORNAMENTS

YEAR ISSUE	EDITION LIMIT	YEAR RETD.	ISSUE PRICE	*QUOTE U.S.$
1994 Mexican Hat Dance 307	Retrd.	N/A	32.00	96
1994 Midnight Mass 913	Retrd.	N/A	N/A	32-34
1994 Mission Ball (tree topper) 389	Retrd.	N/A	78.00	78-136
1994 Misty 97	Retrd.	N/A	19.00	25
1994 Mittens For Kittens 21	Retrd.	1994	22.00	35-40
1994 Moon Dust 133	Retrd.	N/A	18.00	36-40
1994 Moon Martian 298	Retrd.	N/A	26.00	140-144
1994 Moon Mullins 230	Retrd.	N/A	18.00	22-28
1994 Moon Ride 60	Retrd.	N/A	28.00	31-46
1994 Mother and Child 83	Retrd.	N/A	28.50	48-78
1994 Mountain Church 86	Retrd.	N/A	42.00	72-126
1994 Mr. Longneck 288	Retrd.	N/A	26.00	84
1994 Mr. Moto 280	Retrd.	N/A	35.60	102
1994 Mr. Smedley Drysdale 37	Retrd.	N/A	44.00	108-120
1994 My Darling 385	Retrd.	N/A	22.00	22-30
1994 My What Big Teeth	Retrd.	N/A	29.00	100-150
1994 New Year's Babe 239	Retrd.	N/A	21.00	48-66
1994 Nicky 316	Retrd.	N/A	24.00	20-60
1994 Nighty Night 299	Retrd.	N/A	36.00	90-120
1994 Oh My Stars 101	Retrd.	N/A	12.00	15-27
1994 Old Sour Puss 256	Retrd.	N/A	34.00	96
1994 Ollie 269	Retrd.	1996	49.50	74-150
1994 On The Run (Spoon/left side) 247	Retrd.	N/A	45.00	72-180
1994 One Small Step 314	Retrd.	N/A	58.00	76-95
1994 Over The Waves 261	Retrd.	N/A	38.00	90
1994 Owl Reflector 40	Retrd.	N/A	54.00	90-96
1994 Papa's Jamboree 427	Retrd.	N/A	29.00	30-45
1994 Partridge Pear Garland 435	Retrd.	N/A	68.00	68-72
1994 Party Hopper 274	Retrd.	N/A	37.00	115-195
1994 Party Time 902	Retrd.	N/A	24.00	24-36
1994 Peas on Earth 227	Retrd.	N/A	16.00	20-22
1994 Peking Santa 102	Retrd.	N/A	18.00	54
1994 Perky Pete 64	Retrd.	N/A	30.00	40-48
1994 Pickled 317	Retrd.	N/A	26.00	46-60
1994 Piggly Wiggly 169	Retrd.	N/A	14.00	40
1994 Piglet 294	Retrd.	N/A	13.00	42-45
1994 Pinecone Santa 118	Retrd.	N/A	29.50	50-100
1994 Pinocchio Gets Hitched 250	Retrd.	N/A	29.50	30-84
1994 Pixie Santa 218	Retrd.	N/A	20.00	28-35
1994 President Taft 74	Retrd.	N/A	18.00	50
1994 Pretty Bird 112	Retrd.	N/A	26.00	39-48
1994 Prince Philip 909	Retrd.	N/A	20.00	150
1994 Princess 286	Retrd.	N/A	18.00	22
1994 Private Eye 163	Retrd.	N/A	18.00	34-48
1994 Purple Plum 347	Retrd.	N/A	15.00	18-48
1994 Queen's Hare 44	Retrd.	N/A	22.00	60
1994 Quick Draw 330	Retrd.	N/A	65.00	220-240
1994 Radiant Birth 75	Retrd.	N/A	76.00	86-144
1994 Rain Dance 282	Retrd.	N/A	34.00	75
1994 Rainbow Snow 361	Retrd.	N/A	15.00	16-36
1994 Rainy Day Smile 54	Retrd.	N/A	22.00	20-30
1994 Rajah 25	Retrd.	N/A	19.00	22-42
1994 Raspberry 339	Retrd.	N/A	12.00	22
1994 Razzle Dazzle 372	Retrd.	N/A	37.90	45-102
1994 Red Cap 24	Retrd.	1996	22.00	33-72
1994 Ring Master 61	Retrd.	N/A	22.00	36-48
1994 Ring Twice 151	Retrd.	N/A	21.00	47-55
1994 Ringing Red Boots 114	Retrd.	N/A	46.00	60-72
1994 Rising Stars 121	Retrd.	N/A	12.90	18
1994 Roly Poly Angel 58	Retrd.	N/A	22.00	28-36
1994 Roly Poly Clown 173	Retrd.	N/A	19.40	45-75
1994 Roly Poly Pinocchio 328	Retrd.	N/A	54.00	110
1994 Rose Cone 31	Retrd.	N/A	25.00	34-36
1994 Rosy Lovebirds 89	Retrd.	N/A	48.00	72-90
1994 Royale Finial 382	Retrd.	N/A	64.00	95
1994 Ruby Reflector 352	Retrd.	N/A	26.00	42-102
1994 Santa Copter 306	Retrd.	N/A	47.00	125-216
1994 Santa Hearts 461	Retrd.	N/A	66.00	96-120
1994 Santa Reflector Finial 381	Retrd.	N/A	92.00	120
1994 Santa's Helper 131	Retrd.	N/A	19.90	35-40
1994 Saturn Rings 458	Retrd.	N/A	64.00	64-72
1994 School's Out 29	Retrd.	N/A	19.00	40-48
1994 Scotch Pine Finial 419	Retrd.	N/A	78.00	110-144
1994 Season's Greetings 41	Retrd.	N/A	42.00	45-60
1994 Serenity 196	Retrd.	N/A	44.00	60-78
1994 Sex Appeal 238	Retrd.	N/A	22.00	78-85
1994 Ships Ahoy 263	Retrd.	N/A	38.00	54
1994 Shivers 262	Retrd.	N/A	25.00	90-150
1994 Shooting The Moon 33	Retrd.	N/A	28.00	96
1994 Siberian Bear 392	Retrd.	N/A	23.90	26-42
1994 Silent Night 129	Retrd.	N/A	27.00	55
1994 Smiley 52	Retrd.	N/A	16.00	60
1994 Snow Bell 237	Retrd.	N/A	13.00	42-48
1994 Snow Dancing 91	Retrd.	N/A	29.00	38-72
1994 Snowy 313	Retrd.	N/A	26.00	50
1994 Soldier Boy 142	Retrd.	N/A	19.00	24-66
1994 Spring Chick 30	Retrd.	1996	27.00	46-84
1994 Squash Man 67	Retrd.	N/A	28.00	28-70
1994 Squiggles 157	Retrd.	N/A	29.90	55
1994 Squirreling Away 39	Retrd.	N/A	26.00	50-54
1994 St. Nick 65	Retrd.	N/A	18.00	30-36
1994 St. Nick's Pipe 235	Retrd.	N/A	12.00	36-42
1994 Stafford Floral 205	Retrd.	N/A	29.00	36-48
1994 Starfire Finial 418	Retrd.	N/A	84.00	95-114
1994 Starry Night 300	Retrd.	N/A	31.00	46-114
1994 Stocking Full 159	Retrd.	N/A	24.00	32-54
1994 Stocking Sam 108	Retrd.	N/A	23.00	42-72
1994 Strawberry 333	Retrd.	N/A	12.00	18-21
1994 Sugar Berry 341	Retrd.	N/A	12.00	13-22
1994 Sugar Cone 413	Retrd.	N/A	46.50	86-120
1994 Sugar Pear 335	Retrd.	N/A	13.00	19
1994 Surf's Up 325	Retrd.	N/A	36.00	84-102

YEAR ISSUE	EDITION LIMIT	YEAR RETD.	ISSUE PRICE	*QUOTE U.S.$
1994 Swami 128	Retrd.	N/A	18.00	25
1994 Swan Fountain 278	Retrd.	N/A	44.00	174
1994 Swan Lake 911	Retrd.	N/A	16.00	65
1994 Sweet Gherkin 343	Retrd.	N/A	12.00	15-18
1994 Sweet Pear 59	Retrd.	N/A	24.00	24-72
1994 Tangerine 332	Retrd.	N/A	12.00	30
1994 Teddy Roosevelt 232	Retrd.	N/A	22.00	22-40
1994 Tee Time 167	Retrd.	N/A	16.00	35
1994 Teenage Mermaid 270	Retrd.	N/A	33.00	58
1994 Terrance 53	Retrd.	N/A	16.00	42-45
1994 Time to Spare 78	Retrd.	N/A	29.00	32-60
1994 Tiny Nautilus (gold) 100	Retrd.	N/A	12.00	15-40
1994 Tiny Ted 49	Retrd.	N/A	15.00	15-21
1994 Tiny Tunes 36	Retrd.	N/A	22.00	72
1994 Tomba 279	Retrd.	N/A	34.00	90
1994 Top Cat 206	Retrd.	N/A	29.00	29-42
1994 Topo 318	Retrd.	N/A	33.00	42-84
1994 Tuxedo Carousel 245	Retrd.	N/A	52.00	70-150
1994 Twinkle Star 360	Retrd.	N/A	13.00	13-36
1994 Uncle Max 66	Retrd.	1994	26.00	42-60
1994 Valcourt 213	Retrd.	N/A	29.00	60-100
1994 Vaudeville Sam 57	Retrd.	N/A	18.00	27-66
1994 Waldo 17	Retrd.	N/A	22.00	28-54
1994 Walnut 337	Retrd.	N/A	11.00	22
1994 Wedded Bliss 94	Retrd.	N/A	88.00	195-216
1994 Wednesday 120	Retrd.	N/A	42.00	45-70
1994 What a Donkey 277	Retrd.	N/A	34.00	46-90
1994 White Nights 197	Retrd.	N/A	26.00	36-48
1994 White Tiger 223	Retrd.	N/A	25.90	45
1994 Wind Swept 188	Retrd.	N/A	28.80	32
1994 Wings and a Snail 301	Retrd.	N/A	32.00	102-110
1994 Wings of Peace 69	Retrd.	N/A	22.00	36-60
1994 Winter Frolic 287	Retrd.	N/A	18.00	36-48
1994 Xenon 304	Retrd.	N/A	38.00	120-195
1994 Yuletide Bells 148	Retrd.	N/A	12.00	66

1995 Holiday Collection - C. Radko

YEAR ISSUE	EDITION LIMIT	YEAR RETD.	ISSUE PRICE	*QUOTE U.S.$
1995 10, 9, 8 139	Retrd.	N/A	22.00	22-36
1995 Al Pine 161	Retrd.	N/A	24.00	30
1995 Aloisius Beer 194	Retrd.	N/A	75.00	125
1995 American Pride 105	Retrd.	N/A	24.00	34
1995 Andrew Jacksons, pair 208	Retrd.	1995	68.00	200-300
1995 Annie 2	Retrd.	N/A	26.00	26-30
1995 Another Fine Mess 160	Retrd.	N/A	16.00	72-80
1995 Aqualina 293	Retrd.	1996	26.00	41-90
1995 Autumn Oak King 23	Retrd.	N/A	28.00	28-38
1995 Away We Go 173	Retrd.	N/A	24.00	28-42
1995 Bailey 283	Retrd.	N/A	46.00	100
1995 Banana Split 246	Retrd.	N/A	24.00	24-27
1995 Be It Ever So Humble 53	Retrd.	N/A	22.00	24-30
1995 Bear Mail 38	Retrd.	1996	28.00	40-107
1995 Bearly Mooning 7	Retrd.	N/A	26.00	36
1995 Beezlebub 94	Retrd.	N/A	14.00	66
1995 Best Friends 130	Retrd.	N/A	22.00	22-65
1995 Bishop (original coloration) 127	Retrd.	N/A	74.00	110-180
1995 Blue Dolphin 238	Retrd.	N/A	22.00	36-48
1995 Blue Lucy Finial 309	Retrd.	N/A	90.00	132
1995 Bordeaux 901	Retrd.	N/A	N/A	24-45
1995 Bringing Home the Bacon 204	Retrd.	N/A	26.00	36-48
1995 Buford T 63	Retrd.	N/A	14.00	30
1995 Bundle of Toys 70	Retrd.	N/A	34.00	34-48
1995 Butcher Sam 190	Retrd.	N/A	22.00	36
1995 Buttons 21	Retrd.	N/A	36.00	34-45
1995 Caribbean Constable 11	Retrd.	N/A	24.00	55-138
1995 Carousel Santa 133	Retrd.	N/A	36.00	36-75
1995 Catch O' Day 93	Retrd.	N/A	13.50	20
1995 Celeste 262	Retrd.	N/A	52.00	72
1995 Cheeky St. Nick 274	Retrd.	N/A	32.00	32-75
1995 Christmas Cake 35	Retrd.	N/A	24.00	25-42
1995 Christmas Joy 33	Retrd.	N/A	42.00	45-60
1995 Christmas Morning 141	Retrd.	N/A	24.00	25-38
1995 Christmas Pie 135	Retrd.	N/A	54.00	54-78
1995 Chubby Decker 3	Retrd.	N/A	36.00	36-54
1995 Claudette 95-017-0	Retrd.	1995	22.00	48-54
1995 Climbing Higher 146	Retrd.	N/A	26.00	30
1995 Clown Rattle 230	Retrd.	N/A	16.00	16-44
1995 Clown Spin 151-1	Retrd.	N/A	38.00	39-60
1995 Cock O' Doodle 91	Retrd.	N/A	19.00	24
1995 Cockle Bell 175	Retrd.	N/A	38.00	34-50
1995 Creole Dancer 275	Retrd.	N/A	52.00	52-90
1995 Curlycue Santa 219	Retrd.	N/A	30.00	35-48
1995 David 56	Retrd.	N/A	28.00	30
1995 Decker 3	Retrd.	N/A	36.00	47
1995 Della Robbia Garland 308	Retrd.	N/A	34.00	48-100
1995 Department Store Santa 131	Retrd.	N/A	36.00	40-60
1995 Dolly For Susie 101	Retrd.	N/A	25.00	42
1995 Drum Major 66	Retrd.	N/A	24.00	24-33
1995 Drummer Santa 149	Retrd.	N/A	38.00	40-48
1995 Dutch Dolls 136	Retrd.	N/A	22.00	30-36
1995 Eagle Eye 104	Retrd.	N/A	26.00	35
1995 Elfin 903	Retrd.	N/A	N/A	24-60
1995 Evening Owl 193	Retrd.	N/A	36.00	36-45
1995 Fairy Dust 253	Retrd.	N/A	72.00	72-110
1995 Farmer Boy 108	Retrd.	N/A	28.00	42-48
1995 Flying High 8	Retrd.	N/A	22.00	50
1995 Forest Cabin 179	Retrd.	N/A	15.00	28-48
1995 French Lace 134	Retrd.	N/A	24.00	24-42
1995 Frog Lady 26	Retrd.	N/A	24.00	42-48
1995 Frosted Santa 143	Retrd.	N/A	25.00	28-62
1995 Fruit Basket 181	Retrd.	N/A	14.00	24
1995 Fruit Kan Chu 267	Retrd.	1995	50.00	60
1995 Fruit Nuts 213	Retrd.	N/A	14.00	20-28

YEAR ISSUE	EDITION LIMIT	YEAR RETD.	ISSUE PRICE	*QUOTE U.S.$
1995 Garden Elves (pink hat) 207	Retrd.	N/A	56.00	56-72
1995 Garden Girls (pair) 39	Retrd.	N/A	18.00	90-108
1995 Gay Blades 272	Retrd.	1996	46.00	46-85
1995 Glad Tidings To All 115	Retrd.	N/A	44.00	44-72
1995 Glorianna 263	Retrd.	N/A	56.00	56-72
1995 Gobbles 203	Retrd.	N/A	52.00	85
1995 Grandpa Jones 144	Retrd.	N/A	22.00	22-40
1995 Gunther 233	Retrd.	N/A	32.00	90-108
1995 Gypsy Bear 908	Retrd.	N/A	N/A	26-30
1995 Having a Ball 126	Retrd.	N/A	26.00	27-47
1995 Heavy Load 19	Retrd.	N/A	42.00	96
1995 Helmut's Bells 28	Retrd.	N/A	18.00	35
1995 Henrietta 217	Retrd.	N/A	24.00	24-40
1995 Here Boy 222	Retrd.	N/A	12.00	30-35
1995 Hi Ho 97	Retrd.	N/A	56.00	56-96
1995 High Flying 8	Retrd.	N/A	22.00	54
1995 Ho Ho Ho 78	Retrd.	N/A	18.00	20-36
1995 Holiday Star Santa 27	Retrd.	N/A	16.00	19-30
1995 Holly Santa 123	Retrd.	N/A	18.00	19-25
1995 Hooty Hoot 24	Retrd.	1996	26.00	30-42
1995 Hot Head 221	Retrd.	N/A	18.00	45
1995 Hubbard's the Name 206	Retrd.	N/A	26.00	34-84
1995 I'm Late, I'm Late 291	Retrd.	N/A	48.00	48-65
1995 Imperial Helmet 240	Retrd.	N/A	22.00	35-42
1995 Jazz Santa 196	Retrd.	N/A	28.00	30-45
1995 Jingles 46	Retrd.	N/A	26.00	39-48
1995 Joy To The World 42	Retrd.	N/A	68.00	40-63
1995 JT Cricket 137	Retrd.	N/A	22.00	22-36
1995 Jumbo Walnut 249	Retrd.	N/A	18.00	35-48
1995 Just A Kiss Away 228	Retrd.	N/A	24.00	63
1995 Kaleidoscope Cone 25	Retrd.	N/A	44.00	48-60
1995 Kitty Claus 225	Retrd.	N/A	22.00	22-40
1995 Kitty Vittles 79	Retrd.	N/A	18.00	18-50
1995 Laugh Til You Cry 236	Retrd.	N/A	24.00	28-45
1995 Lavendar Berry Garland 307	Retrd.	N/A	42.00	72
1995 Lavender Light 157	Retrd.	N/A	28.00	28-75
1995 Lean & Lanky 95	Retrd.	N/A	23.00	23-35
1995 Little Dreamer 159	Retrd.	N/A	16.00	36-51
1995 Little Drummer Bear 37	Retrd.	N/A	22.00	22-30
1995 Little Prince 6	Retrd.	N/A	39.00	125
1995 Little Red 214	Retrd.	N/A	22.00	30-40
1995 Little Toy Maker 167	Retrd.	N/A	26.00	36-48
1995 Midnight Mass 913	Retrd.	N/A	N/A	45-78
1995 Miss Mamie 110	Retrd.	N/A	34.00	45
1995 Mother Mary 98	Retrd.	N/A	24.00	42
1995 Mugsy 183	Retrd.	N/A	22.00	34-48
1995 My Bonnie Lass 170	Retrd.	N/A	24.00	34
1995 My Favorite Chimp 148	Retrd.	N/A	26.00	36-38
1995 My What Big Eyes 910	Retrd.	N/A	N/A	28
1995 Neptune's Charge 113	Retrd.	N/A	36.00	66-90
1995 Nesting Stork 198	Retrd.	N/A	24.00	66
1995 Nibbles 18	Retrd.	N/A	24.00	40-42
1995 O Holy Night 260	Retrd.	N/A	52.00	77
1995 Off to Market 223	Retrd.	N/A	24.00	32-48
1995 Officer Joe 122	Retrd.	N/A	22.00	34-60
1995 On the Court 45	Retrd.	N/A	26.00	26-30
1995 Papa Bear Reflector 292	Retrd.	N/A	52.00	52-56
1995 Party Time 902	Retrd.	N/A	N/A	24.00
1995 Pecky Woodpecker 288	Retrd.	N/A	36.00	36-66
1995 Peek A Boo 212	Retrd.	N/A	18.00	48
1995 Pencil Santa 232	Retrd.	N/A	18.00	18-33
1995 Penelope 197	Retrd.	N/A	26.00	36
1995 Percussion 255	Retrd.	N/A	50.00	50-110
1995 Pere Noel 41	Retrd.	N/A	44.00	33-46
1995 Personal Delivery 116	Retrd.	N/A	36.00	42-48
1995 Pine Tree Santa 912	Retrd.	N/A	N/A	26-46
1995 Pirate Ship 250	Retrd.	N/A	44.00	168-198
1995 Polar Express 76	Retrd.	N/A	24.00	42-45
1995 Pork Chop 231	Retrd.	N/A	22.00	22-40
1995 Prince of Thieves 44	Retrd.	N/A	28.00	40
1995 Punch 172	Retrd.	N/A	22.00	36
1995 Quakers 261	Retrd.	1996	24.00	24-35
1995 Quilted Santa 187	Retrd.	N/A	68.00	40-68
1995 Rainbow Scallop (gold) 9	Retrd.	N/A	16.00	15-42
1995 Rakish Charm 142	Retrd.	N/A	22.00	45
1995 Reflecto 281	Retrd.	N/A	46.00	46-96
1995 Ricky Raccoon 138	Retrd.	N/A	24.00	42
1995 Rockateer 284	Retrd.	N/A	44.00	65
1995 Round About Santa 5	Retrd.	N/A	42.00	42-60
1995 Round Up 1	Retrd.	N/A	26.00	26-30
1995 Royal Tiger 34	Retrd.	N/A	36.00	72
1995 Rummy Tum Tum 168	Retrd.	N/A	44.00	65-72
1995 Santa Fantasy 20	Retrd.	N/A	44.00	95
1995 Santa Maria 286	Retrd.	N/A	64.00	140
1995 Shy Elephant 282	Retrd.	N/A	32.00	85
1995 Siamese Slippers 264	Retrd.	1995	16.00	55
1995 Sister Act-set 140	Retrd.	N/A	18.00	36-48
1995 Skater's Waltz 12	Retrd.	N/A	28.00	38-65
1995 Slim Pickins 114	Retrd.	N/A	22.00	22-55
1995 Snow Ball 100	Retrd.	N/A	28.00	120-240
1995 Snow Song 40	Retrd.	N/A	18.00	20-30
1995 Spellbound 128	Retrd.	N/A	26.00	48
1995 Spring Arrival 82	Retrd.	N/A	44.00	44-65
1995 Springtime Sparrow 119	Retrd.	N/A	14.00	25
1995 St. Peter's Keys 298	Retrd.	N/A	8.00	18
1995 Stork Lantern 241	Retrd.	N/A	18.00	22
1995 Storytime Santa 22	Retrd.	N/A	44.00	44-60
1995 Swan Lake 911	Retrd.	N/A	36.00	58
1995 Sweet Carrot 248	Retrd.	N/A	22.00	29-42
1995 Sweet Dreams 258	Retrd.	N/A	28.00	30-48
1995 Sweet Madame 192	Retrd.	N/A	48.00	150-180
1995 Sweethearts 99	Retrd.	N/A	26.00	34

*Quotes have been rounded up to nearest dollar

ORNAMENTS

YEAR ISSUE	EDITION LIMIT	YEAR RETD.	ISSUE PRICE	*QUOTE U.S.$
1995 Swinging on a Star 183	Retrd.	N/A	44.00	50
1995 Teddy's Tree 156	Retrd.	N/A	22.00	22-45
1995 Tennis Anyone? 14	Retrd.	N/A	18.00	18-36
1995 Time For A Bite 251	Retrd.	N/A	62.00	62-110
1995 Trick or Treat 13	Retrd.	N/A	23.00	30-36
1995 Turtle Bird 121	Retrd.	N/A	22.00	35-35
1995 Very Berry 92	Retrd.	N/A	11.00	15-42
1995 Warm Wishes 112	Retrd.	N/A	22.00	22-36
1995 Washington's (Martha & George) 103	Retrd.	N/A	28.00	28-72
1995 Westminster Santa 189	Retrd.	N/A	24.00	36-48
1995 White Dove 88	Retrd.	N/A	32.00	32-48
1995 Wiggle Men 89	Retrd.	N/A	10.00	15-22
1995 Winter Pooch 163	Retrd.	N/A	22.00	33-35
1995 Winter Sun 145	Retrd.	N/A	31.00	45
1995 Youthful Madonna 259	Retrd.	N/A	28.00	29-42

1996 Holiday Collection - C. Radko

YEAR ISSUE	EDITION LIMIT	YEAR RETD.	ISSUE PRICE	*QUOTE U.S.$
1996 Angel Prayer 135	Retrd.	N/A	22.00	24-36
1996 Astro Pup 36	Retrd.	1996	32.00	30-45
1996 Baby Angel 3	Retrd.	N/A	22.00	22-30
1996 Baby Elephants 277	Retrd.	1996	18.00	30
1996 Bella D. Snowball 160	Retrd.	N/A	26.00	30
1996 Billy Bunny 97	Retrd.	N/A	26.00	30-36
1996 Bottoms Up 148	Retrd.	N/A	26.00	26-40
1996 By The Shore 15	Retrd.	N/A	16.00	16-30
1996 Candy Swirl 299	Retrd.	N/A	24.00	45-50
1996 Caroline 152	Retrd.	N/A	24.00	28-48
1996 Casey 107	Retrd.	N/A	18.00	24-27
1996 Catavarius 84	Retrd.	N/A	38.00	72
1996 Charlie Horse 4	Retrd.	N/A	20.00	21-30
1996 Checkered Past 63	Retrd.	N/A	50.00	50-75
1996 Christmas King 147	Retrd.	N/A	46.00	54-57
1996 Christmas Past 223	Retrd.	N/A	18.00	18-22
1996 Church Window 301	Retrd.	N/A	16.00	16-24
1996 Circus Seal 141	Retrd.	N/A	22.00	33
1996 The Clauses 159	Retrd.	N/A	26.00	48-54
1996 Cookin' Up Christmas 129	Retrd.	N/A	18.00	48
1996 Count Dimitri 145	Retrd.	N/A	24.00	36
1996 Crescent Kringle 40	Retrd.	N/A	36.00	36-67
1996 Croc Cutie 241	Retrd.	N/A	22.00	54
1996 Cycle Santa 114	Retrd.	N/A	26.00	30-35
1996 Czech Express 104	Retrd.	N/A	36.00	39-42
1996 Davey 55	Retrd.	N/A	48.00	48-54
1996 Dreamy 12	Retrd.	N/A	17.00	17-30
1996 Elfcycle 14	Retrd.	N/A	28.00	36-42
1996 English Garden 199	Retrd.	N/A	36.00	54
1996 Eskimo Cheer 157	Retrd.	1996	22.00	30
1996 Every Bead Of My Heart 246	Retrd.	N/A	22.00	32
1996 Festiva (gold) 212	Retrd.	N/A	36.00	44-48
1996 Field Blossom 64	Retrd.	N/A	46.00	48-60
1996 Flying High 257	Retrd.	N/A	42.00	60
1996 For Clara 86	Retrd.	N/A	32.00	48
1996 Frosty Cardinal 215	Retrd.	N/A	32.00	36-45
1996 Frosty Pepper 234	Retrd.	N/A	12.00	28
1996 Full of Joy 134	Retrd.	N/A	12.00	20-25
1996 Gilded Wings (red) 8	Retrd.	N/A	16.00	30
1996 Grape Bouquet 61	Retrd.	N/A	33.00	38-54
1996 Great Gobbles 207	Retrd.	N/A	38.00	48
1996 Heavenly Triumph 185	Retrd.	N/A	22.00	26-36
1996 Hi Ho Trio 56	Retrd.	N/A	47.00	47-60
1996 His Goil 67	Retrd.	N/A	40.00	40-95
1996 His Wizardry 255	Retrd.	N/A	22.00	25-36
1996 Hot n' Frosty 225	Retrd.	N/A	10.00	18
1996 Incantation 105	Retrd.	N/A	24.00	70
1996 Lancer 13	Retrd.	N/A	29.00	30-35
1996 Lemon Guard 233	Retrd.	N/A	22.00	22-28
1996 Lilac Angel 51	Retrd.	N/A	44.00	44-54
1996 Lilac Winter 50	Retrd.	1996	44.00	48
1996 Londonberry 193	Retrd.	N/A	44.00	55-60
1996 Love and Valor (purple) 72	Retrd.	N/A	14.50	24
1996 Love Is In The Air 183	Retrd.	N/A	22.00	24-30
1996 Lucinda 204	Retrd.	N/A	38.00	49
1996 Magic Munchkin 240	Retrd.	N/A	32.00	36-46
1996 Merry Matador 189	Retrd.	N/A	23.95	25-42
1996 Midnight Orchid 285	Retrd.	N/A	32.00	54
1996 Midnight Ride 169	Retrd.	1996	51.00	72-76
1996 Minuet 167	Retrd.	1996	54.00	54-65
1996 Miss Flurry 94	Retrd.	N/A	38.00	150
1996 Monte Carlo 27	Retrd.	1996	52.00	65
1996 Ms. Peanut 42	Retrd.	1996	30.00	100
1996 Night Magic 2	Retrd.	N/A	26.00	26-36
1996 Ocean Call 245	Retrd.	N/A	18.00	18-34
1996 Oh Christmas Tree! 156	Retrd.	N/A	42.00	50-80
1996 Persia 237	Retrd.	N/A	18.00	35
1996 Pineapple Frost 112	Retrd.	N/A	14.00	28
1996 Poinsettia Snow 216	Retrd.	N/A	32.00	36-48
1996 Polar Nights 208	Retrd.	N/A	32.00	32-54
1996 Pookie 187	Retrd.	N/A	16.00	24
1996 Professor Hare 144	Retrd.	N/A	26.00	36
1996 Puff 69	Retrd.	N/A	48.00	57
1996 Pumpkin Eater 203	Retrd.	N/A	34.00	40
1996 Punkin Patch 5	Retrd.	N/A	26.00	42
1996 Ragamuffins 52	Retrd.	N/A	39.00	40-47
1996 Rainbow Drops (set/3) 123	Retrd.	N/A	14.00	72
1996 Rainbow-Tiffany 302	Retrd.	N/A	26.00	26-50
1996 Reach For a Star 209	Retrd.	N/A	32.00	36
1996 Return Engagement 151	Retrd.	N/A	38.00	43
1996 Rocket Santa 38	Retrd.	N/A	48.00	65-84
1996 Rosy Cheek Santa 10	Retrd.	N/A	20.00	21-48
1996 Round Midnight 274	Retrd.	1996	30.00	40
1996 Roxanne 33	Retrd.	N/A	40.00	40-60
1996 Russian Knight 21	Retrd.	N/A	100.00	150
1996 Sapphire Santa 158	Retrd.	N/A	34.00	34-48
1996 Shimmy Down 253	Retrd.	N/A	42.00	51-64
1996 Shining Armour 188	Retrd.	1996	22.00	22
1996 Shoe Shack 140	Retrd.	N/A	44.00	48
1996 Sing We Now 176	Retrd.	N/A	22.00	22
1996 Sleighfull 150	Retrd.	N/A	34.00	46-65
1996 Slim Wizard 115	Retrd.	N/A	18.00	40
1996 Snow Castle 139	Retrd.	1996	12.00	18
1996 Snow Hare 73	Retrd.	N/A	14.00	15-24
1996 Snow Kitties 125	Retrd.	N/A	26.00	32-36
1996 Snowballing 146	Retrd.	N/A	26.00	28-42
1996 Snowday 192	Retrd.	N/A	19.00	24
1996 Snowtem Pole 155	Retrd.	N/A	32.00	40-42
1996 Speed Racer Garland 1	Retrd.	N/A	66.00	195
1996 Star Shot 249	Retrd.	N/A	32.00	32-48
1996 Starscape Santa 143	Retrd.	N/A	44.00	50-85
1996 Starship 113	Retrd.	N/A	28.00	43-60
1996 Strong To The Finish 66	Retrd.	N/A	48.00	50
1996 Sweet Tomato 224	Retrd.	N/A	14.00	34
1996 Tiffany Rainbow 302	Retrd.	N/A	26.00	50
1996 Time Flies 314	Retrd.	1996	28.00	32-46
1996 Topolina 288	Retrd.	1996	42.00	60
1996 Toys For All 153	Retrd.	N/A	44.00	39-44
1996 Twilight Santa Reflector 289	Retrd.	N/A	48.00	79
1996 Under The Sea 313	Retrd.	N/A	17.00	24
1996 Up And Away 286	Retrd.	N/A	42.00	50-60
1996 Village Santa 99	Retrd.	N/A	30.00	36-42
1996 Vintage Classics 222	Retrd.	N/A	24.00	30
1996 Winter Blossom 284	Retrd.	N/A	46.00	46-59
1996 Winter Dream 250	Retrd.	N/A	42.00	40-51
1996 Winter Holiday 62	Retrd.	N/A	44.00	78
1996 Winter Wind 121	Retrd.	N/A	24.00	28-36
1996 Yankee Doodle Santa 251	Retrd.	N/A	34.00	40-52
1996 Yo Ho Ho 53	Retrd.	N/A	48.00	48-50

1997 Holiday Collection - C. Radko

YEAR ISSUE	EDITION LIMIT	YEAR RETD.	ISSUE PRICE	*QUOTE U.S.$
1997 Angel on High 11	Retrd.	N/A	31.00	33-60
1997 Carnivale Garland 453	Retrd.	N/A	68.00	78
1997 Christmas Cloudhoppers 90	Retrd.	N/A	65.00	72-120
1997 Crystal Frost 428	Retrd.	N/A	68.00	73
1997 Dutch Date 137	Retrd.	N/A	56.00	90
1997 Enough For All 209	Retrd.	N/A	76.00	85
1997 Galaxy Frost 59	Retrd.	N/A	65.00	108
1997 Gardening Angels 121	Retrd.	N/A	34.00	60
1997 General Cracker 95	Retrd.	N/A	34.00	41-48
1997 Goodnight Prayer 171	Retrd.	N/A	42.00	45-49
1997 Huggy Bear 161	Retrd.	N/A	50.00	54
1997 Humperdink 328	Retrd.	N/A	24.00	53
1997 Making A List 222	Retrd.	N/A	40.00	42-47
1997 Monster Mash 20	Retrd.	N/A	32.00	44
1997 Nick of Time 289	Retrd.	N/A	70.00	75
1997 Off The Wall Jumbo 356	Retrd.	N/A	60.00	64-84
1997 Pepper's Frost 107	Retrd.	N/A	15.00	21
1997 Rainbow Iris 71	Retrd.	N/A	38.00	66
1997 Roy Rabbit 724	Retrd.	N/A	42.00	44-49
1997 Royal Game 433	Retrd.	N/A	76.00	80
1997 Santa Tree Finial 96	Retrd.	N/A	70.00	96
1997 Star Gazing Finial 81	Retrd.	N/A	100.00	150
1997 Willy Wobble 132	Retrd.	N/A	50.00	53-66
1997 Winter Birds 123	Retrd.	N/A	22.00	30
1997 Winter Skate 341	Retrd.	N/A	54.00	67
1997 Woodland Frost Garland 26	Retrd.	N/A	60.00	96

Aids Awareness - C. Radko

YEAR ISSUE	EDITION LIMIT	YEAR RETD.	ISSUE PRICE	*QUOTE U.S.$
1993 A Shy Rabbit's Heart 462	Retrd.	1993	15.00	50-94
1994 Frosty Cares SP5	Retrd.	1994	25.00	20-50
1995 On Wings of Hope SP10	Retrd.	1995	30.00	30-45
1996 A Winter Bear's Heart SP15	Retrd.	1996	34.00	34-40
1997 A Caring Clown 97-SP-22	Retrd.	1997	36.00	36-50
1998 Sugar Holiday (Elizabeth Taylor Aids Foundation) 98-SP-29	Retrd.	1998	38.00	38-50
1999 Cubby's Rainbow 99-SP-45	Retrd.	1999	36.00	36-40
2000 Sir Elton Claus (Elton John Aids Foundation) 00-SP-59	Yr.Iss.		37.00	37

Alvin And The Chipmunks - C. Radko

YEAR ISSUE	EDITION LIMIT	YEAR RETD.	ISSUE PRICE	*QUOTE U.S.$
1998 Downhill Racer 98-CHP-01	Retrd.	1999	26.00	26
1998 Oh Tannenbaum 98-CHP-02	Retrd.	1999	27.00	27
1998 Winter Fun 98-CHP-03	Retrd.	1999	27.00	27

Animal Related Charities - C. Radko

YEAR ISSUE	EDITION LIMIT	YEAR RETD.	ISSUE PRICE	*QUOTE U.S.$
2000 Pet Pals 00-SP-61	Yr.Iss.		37.00	37

Breast Cancer Research - C. Radko

YEAR ISSUE	EDITION LIMIT	YEAR RETD.	ISSUE PRICE	*QUOTE U.S.$
1998 Felina's Heart 98-SP-31	Retrd.	1998	32.00	32
1999 Bonny Maureen 99-SP-47	Retrd.	1999	32.00	32-40
2000 Bonny Spring 00-SP-60	Yr.Iss.		34.00	34

Carson Pirie Scott - C. Radko

YEAR ISSUE	EDITION LIMIT	YEAR RETD.	ISSUE PRICE	*QUOTE U.S.$
1997 Carson Snowman 97-CPS-01	Retrd.	1997	44.00	44

CBS and Desilu's "I Love Lucy" - C. Radko

YEAR ISSUE	EDITION LIMIT	YEAR RETD.	ISSUE PRICE	*QUOTE U.S.$
1997 Candy Maker 97-LCY-07	Retrd.	1999	42.00	42
1998 Ethel and Fred Heart 98-LCY-03	Open		19.00	19
1997 Ethel's Christmas & Fred's Christmas (pair) 97-LCY-02	Open		80.00	80
1997 I Love Lucy Heart 97-LCY-08	Open		36.00	36
1997 Lucy and Ricky's Christmas 97-LCY-01	Retrd.	1999	45.00	45
1998 Lucy Heart 98-LCY-02	Retrd.	1999	19.00	19
1998 Vitametavegaimin 98-LCY-01	Retrd.	1999	29.00	29

Charlie Chaplin - C. Radko

YEAR ISSUE	EDITION LIMIT	YEAR RETD.	ISSUE PRICE	*QUOTE U.S.$
1997 Charlie Chaplin 97-CAR-01	Open		39.00	39
1999 Modern Times Chaplin 99-CAR-01	Retrd.	1999	34.00	34
1999 Charlie Chaplin Candy Cane 99-CAR-02	Retrd.	1999	28.00	28

A Christmas Carol - C. Radko

YEAR ISSUE	EDITION LIMIT	YEAR RETD.	ISSUE PRICE	*QUOTE U.S.$
1998 Scrooge 98-ACC-1	10,000	1998	62.00	62
1999 Ghost of Christmas Present 99-ACC-2	10,000	1999	62.00	62-65
2000 Bob Crachit & Tiny Tim 00-ACC-3	10,000		49.00	49

The Christopher Radko Foundation for Children Designs - C. Radko

YEAR ISSUE	EDITION LIMIT	YEAR RETD.	ISSUE PRICE	*QUOTE U.S.$
1998 Cozykins 98-SP-28	Retrd.	1998	34.00	34-43
1999 Little Chipper 99-SP-50	Retrd.	1999	34.00	34
2000 Squeakles 00-SP-56	Open		34.00	34

Clara's Beaux - C. Radko

YEAR ISSUE	EDITION LIMIT	YEAR RETD.	ISSUE PRICE	*QUOTE U.S.$
1998 Clara's Beaux 98-NCR-1	10,000	1998	135.00	135
1999 Cracker King 99-NCR-2	10,000	1999	75.00	75
2000 St. Cracker Claus 00-NCR-3	10,000		74.00	74

Disney Art Classics: Hercules - C. Radko

YEAR ISSUE	EDITION LIMIT	YEAR RETD.	ISSUE PRICE	*QUOTE U.S.$
1997 Hercules 97-DIS-79	Retrd.	1998	39.00	39
1997 Pegasus 97-DIS-91	Retrd.	1998	42.00	42

Disney Art Classics: Peter Pan - C. Radko

YEAR ISSUE	EDITION LIMIT	YEAR RETD.	ISSUE PRICE	*QUOTE U.S.$
1998 Captain Hook 98-DIS-20	Retrd.	1999	32.00	32
1998 The Darling Children 98-DIS-19	Retrd.	1999	32.00	32
1998 Peter Pan 98-DIS-18	Retrd.	1999	28.00	28
1998 Peter Pan Boxed Set (includes Pirate Ship 98-DIS-22) 98-DIS-44	Retrd.	1999	149.00	149
1998 Tinker Bell 98-DIS-21	Retrd.	1999	28.00	28

Disney Art Classics: Snow White & the Seven Dwarfs - C. Radko

YEAR ISSUE	EDITION LIMIT	YEAR RETD.	ISSUE PRICE	*QUOTE U.S.$
1997 Snow White 97-DIS-31	Retrd.	1998	46.00	47-84
1997 Bashful 97-DIS-24	Retrd.	1998	38.00	39
1997 Doc 97-DIS-28	Retrd.	1998	38.00	38-45
1997 Dopey 97-DIS-25	Retrd.	1998	38.00	38-45
1997 Grumpy 97-DIS-26	Retrd.	1998	38.00	38-45
1997 Happy 97-DIS-30	Retrd.	1998	38.00	38
1997 Sleepy 97-DIS-27	Retrd.	1998	38.00	38
1997 Sneezy 97-DIS-29	Retrd.	1998	38.00	38
1997 Snow White Boxed Set 98-SW-0	Retrd.	1998	390.00	525-600
1998 The Hag 98-DIS-13	Retrd.	1999	34.00	34
1998 The Queen 98-DIS-14	Retrd.	1999	34.00	34
1998 Snow White Boxed Set (includes Mirror, Mirror 98-DIS-16) 98-DIS-43	Retrd.	1999	94.00	94

Disney Art Classics: The Little Mermaid - C. Radko

YEAR ISSUE	EDITION LIMIT	YEAR RETD.	ISSUE PRICE	*QUOTE U.S.$
1997 Ariel 97-DIS-82	Retrd.	1998	42.00	42
1997 Flounder 97-DIS-84	Retrd.	1998	42.00	42
1997 Sebastian 97-DIS-85	Retrd.	1998	42.00	42
1997 Ursula 97-DIS-83	Retrd.	1998	42.00	42

The Disney Catalog - C. Radko

YEAR ISSUE	EDITION LIMIT	YEAR RETD.	ISSUE PRICE	*QUOTE U.S.$
1997 4th of July Pooh 97-DIS-44	Retrd.	1997	42.00	60-75
1998 Chip and Dale 98-DIS-34	3,500		26.00	26
1997 Christmas Pooh 97-DIS-47	Retrd.	1997	42.00	42
1997 Easter Pooh 97-DIS-16	Retrd.	1997	50.00	50-71
1997 Halloween Pooh 97-DIS-45	Retrd.	1998	42.00	42
1998 Lady and the Tramp 98-DIS-39	3,500		30.00	30
1998 Mickey and Minnie Wedding 98-DIS-30	Open		39.00	39
1998 Pooh Snowman 98-DIS-31	Open		30.00	30
1997 Thanksgiving Pooh 97-DIS-46	Retrd.	1998	42.00	42
1997 Toy Soldier Mickey 97-DIS-77	Open		40.00	40
1997 Toy Soldier Minnie 97-DIS-78	Open		40.00	40
1997 Valentine's Day Pooh 97-DIS-15	Retrd.	1997	45.00	46-65

Disney's Mickey & Co. - C. Radko

YEAR ISSUE	EDITION LIMIT	YEAR RETD.	ISSUE PRICE	*QUOTE U.S.$
1998 Caroler Daisy Duck 98-DIS-09	Retrd.	1999	24.00	24
1999 Caroler Mickey 99-DIS-06	Retrd.	1999	24.00	24
1998 Caroler Minnie Mouse 98-DIS-08	Retrd.	1999	24.00	24
1999 Caroler Pluto 99-DIS-07	Retrd.	1999	24.00	24
1997 Daisy Duck 97-DIS-20	Retrd.	1997	38.00	24-38
1998 Daisy Duck Stocking 98-DIS-06	Retrd.	1999	22.00	22
1999 Disney Petite Set 99-DIS-41	Retrd.	1999	98.00	98
1998 Donald & Daisy Block 98-DIS-11	Open		18.00	18
1998 Down the Chimney 98-DIS-23	Retrd.	1999	28.00	28
1997 Downhill Mickey (Starlight Exclusive) 97-DIS-42	Retrd.	1997	42.00	42
1998 Downhill Minnie 98-DIS-04	Retrd.	1999	26.00	26
1997 Goofy Tree 97-DIS-23	Retrd.	1997	38.00	38
1998 Happy New Year Mickey 98-DIS-01	Open		22.00	22
1998 Happy New Year Pluto 98-DIS-02	Open		22.00	22
1999 Hockey Goofy 99-DIS-12	Retrd.	1999	28.00	28
1998 Mickey & Minnie Block 98-DIS-10	Open		18.00	18
1997 Mickey & Minnie Christmas 97-DIS-34	Retrd.	1997	42.00	42
1998 Mickey Mouse Wreath 98-DIS-03	Retrd.	1999	19.00	19
1998 Mickey Stocking 98-DIS-05	Retrd.	1999	22.00	22
1997 Mickey's Sleigh Ride (Roger's Exclusive) 97-DIS-93	Retrd.	1997	48.00	48
1999 Minnie Mouse Wreath 99-DIS-33	Retrd.	1999	19.00	19
1997 Noel Minnie 97-DIS-21	Retrd.	1997	38.00	38
1998 Pluto & Goofy Block 98-DIS-12	Open		18.00	18
1998 Pluto Stocking 98-DIS-07	Open		22.00	22
1997 Pluto Wreath (Starlight Exclusive) 97-DIS-73	Retrd.	1997	36.00	36-39
1997 Pluto's Dog House 97-DIS-57	Open		39.00	39
1999 Pluto's Snowman 99-DIS-13	Retrd.	1999	29.00	29
1997 Rooftop Mickey 97-DIS-32	Retrd.	1999	40.00	40
1999 Skiing Mickey 99-DIS-08	Retrd.	1999	29.00	29
1999 Skiing Minnie 99-DIS-09	Retrd.	1999	29.00	29
1997 Three Cheers For Mickey 97-DIS-33	Retrd.	1999	44.00	44
1999 Winter Romance 99-DIS-28	Retrd.	1999	33.00	33

*Quotes have been rounded up to nearest dollar

Disneyana - C. Radko

YEAR ISSUE	EDITION LIMIT	YEAR RETD.	ISSUE PRICE	*QUOTE U.S.$
1997 Mistletoe Mickey & Minnie 97-DIS-65	1,500	1997	250.00	350-514
1998 My Best Pal 98-DIS-40	1,000	1998	70.00	121-215
1999 Simba	1,000	1999	50.00	50

Egyptian Series - C. Radko

YEAR ISSUE	EDITION LIMIT	YEAR RETD.	ISSUE PRICE	*QUOTE U.S.$
1997 Ramses 97-EGY-1	15,000	1997	50.00	50-55
1998 Cheops 98-EGY-2	15,000	1998	55.00	55
1999 Eternal Mystery 99-EGY-3	15,000	1999	34.00	34

Event Ornaments - C. Radko

YEAR ISSUE	EDITION LIMIT	YEAR RETD.	ISSUE PRICE	*QUOTE U.S.$
1999 Mr. Iceberg (Fall) 99-SP-51	Retrd.	1999	30.00	30
1999 Mrs. Iceberg (Spring) 99-SP-52	Retrd.	1999	30.00	30

FAO Schwarz - C. Radko

YEAR ISSUE	EDITION LIMIT	YEAR RETD.	ISSUE PRICE	*QUOTE U.S.$
1997 1920 Santa 97-FAO-03	3,000	1997	42.00	42
1998 1929 FAO Santa 98-FAO-02	3,600		38.00	38
1998 FAO Clock Tower 98-FAO-01	5,000		40.00	40
1997 Toy Block Bear 97-FAO-04	3,000	1997	52.00	52-60

Harley-Davidson - C. Radko

YEAR ISSUE	EDITION LIMIT	YEAR RETD.	ISSUE PRICE	*QUOTE U.S.$
1998 Bar & Shield 98-HAR-03	Yr.Iss.	1998	19.00	19
1997 Biker Boot 97-HAR-04	Retrd.	1999	36.00	36-45
1999 Fat Boy 99-HAR-04	Open		38.00	38
1998 Fill-r-up 98-HAR-02	Retrd.	1999	29.00	29
1997 Free Wheeling Santa 97-HAR-01	Retrd.	1999	46.00	46
1998 Harley Santa 98-HAR-01	Open		32.00	32
1999 Mrs. Harley Claus 99-HAR-01	Open		32.00	32
1999 Sidecar Harley Santa 99-HAR-03	Open		38.00	38
1999 Special Delivery Mrs. Claus 99-HAR-02	Open		38.00	38

Harold LLoyd - C. Radko

YEAR ISSUE	EDITION LIMIT	YEAR RETD.	ISSUE PRICE	*QUOTE U.S.$
1997 Harold Lloyd 97-LYD-01	Open		42.00	42
1998 Holiday Reflections 98-LYD-01	Open		75.00	75
1999 Holiday Bounty 99-LYD-02	Retrd.	1999	40.00	40
1999 Millennium Clock 99-LYD-01	Open		40.00	40

Hasbro's Monopoly - C. Radko

YEAR ISSUE	EDITION LIMIT	YEAR RETD.	ISSUE PRICE	*QUOTE U.S.$
1998 Dice Uncle 98-MON-02	Retrd.	1999	26.00	26
1998 High Roller 98-MON-02	Open		26.00	26
1998 Holiday Cheer 98-MON-01	Retrd.	1999	26.00	26
1997 Monopoly Wreath 97-MON-04	Retrd.	1999	36.00	36
1997 Roadster Rich Uncle Pennybags 97-MON-03	Retrd.	1999	39.00	39

Hasbro's Mr. Potato Head - C. Radko

YEAR ISSUE	EDITION LIMIT	YEAR RETD.	ISSUE PRICE	*QUOTE U.S.$
1997 Mr. Potato Head 97-POT-02	Open		39.00	39
1998 Mr. Potato Head Lumberjack 98-POT-01	Open		26.00	26
1997 Mr. Potato Head Santa 97-POT-01	Open		39.00	39
1997 Mrs. Potato Head Santa 97-POT-04	Open		39.00	39
1998 Soldier Potato 98-POT-02	Open		26.00	26

Homes For The Holidays - C. Radko

YEAR ISSUE	EDITION LIMIT	YEAR RETD.	ISSUE PRICE	*QUOTE U.S.$
1997 Sugar Hill 97-HOU-1	10,000	1997	140.00	145-150
1998 Sugar Hill II 98-HOU-2	10,000	1998	190.00	190-200
1999 Candy Land Corner 99-HOU-3	10,000	1999	99.00	99

The Huntington - C. Radko

YEAR ISSUE	EDITION LIMIT	YEAR RETD.	ISSUE PRICE	*QUOTE U.S.$
1997 The Blue Boy 97-HUN-01	5,000		38.00	38
1997 Pinky 97-HUN-02	5,000		38.00	38

International Children's Charity - C. Radko

YEAR ISSUE	EDITION LIMIT	YEAR RETD.	ISSUE PRICE	*QUOTE U.S.$
1999 United We Stand 99-SP-53	Open		44.00	44

It's a Wonder Life - C. Radko

YEAR ISSUE	EDITION LIMIT	YEAR RETD.	ISSUE PRICE	*QUOTE U.S.$
1997 Jimmy Stewart 97-WON-01	Retrd.	1999	42.00	42

Jim Henson's Muppets - C. Radko

YEAR ISSUE	EDITION LIMIT	YEAR RETD.	ISSUE PRICE	*QUOTE U.S.$
1997 Bah Humbug Block 97-MPT-02	Open		38.00	38
1997 Checking It Twice 97-MPT-01	Retrd.	1999	39.00	39
1997 Christmas with Miss Piggy 97-MPT-06	Retrd.	1999	42.00	42
1997 Fozzie & Gonzo Block 97-MPT-04	Open		38.00	38
1997 Fozzie Bear Baker 97-MPT-05	Open		39.00	39
1999 Home For The Holidays 99-MPT-02	Retrd.	1999	32.00	32
1997 Kermit and Miss Piggy Block 97-MPT-03	Open		38.00	38
1998 Kermit and Piggy Snowball 98-MPT-01	Retrd.	1999	30.00	30
1998 Mistletoe Miss Piggy 98-MPT-02	Retrd.	1999	28.00	28
1999 Muppet Bobsled 99-MPT-01	Retrd.	1999	28.00	28
1997 Muppet Totem 97-MPT-09	Retrd.	1999	42.00	42
1998 Nutcracker 98-MPT-03	Retrd.	1999	26.00	26
1997 Play It Again Santa 97-MPT-07	Retrd.	1999	38.00	38
1997 Wocka Wocka Christmas 97-MPT-08	Retrd.	1999	46.00	46

The Kennedy Center - C. Radko

YEAR ISSUE	EDITION LIMIT	YEAR RETD.	ISSUE PRICE	*QUOTE U.S.$
1997 Kennedy Center Honors 97-JFK-03	3,000		36.00	36

Laurel & Hardy - C. Radko

YEAR ISSUE	EDITION LIMIT	YEAR RETD.	ISSUE PRICE	*QUOTE U.S.$
1997 Laurel & Hardy 97-LAH-01	Retrd.	1999	78.00	78
1999 Exit Stage Right 99-LAH-01	Retrd.	1999	34.00	34

Limited Edition Ornaments - C. Radko

YEAR ISSUE	EDITION LIMIT	YEAR RETD.	ISSUE PRICE	*QUOTE U.S.$
1995 And Snowy Makes Eight (set of 8) 169	15,000	1996	125.00	125
1996 Russian Rhapsody RUS (Set/6)	7,500	1996	150.00	150-225
1997 Yippy Yi Yo 97-SP-25	7,000	1997	70.00	70
1998 Cookbook Santas 98-SP-35	10,000		152.00	152
2000 Frosty Carousel 00-SP-75	2,500		180.00	180
2000 N*O*E*L* (set/4) 00-SP-65	7,000		125.00	125
2000 North Pole Express 00-SP-70	10,000		87.00	87
2000 Ring in the Holiday 00-SP-71	7,500		78.00	78
1998 Forest Angel 98-SP-33	7,500	1999	125.00	125
1998 Spring Maidens 98-SP-34	5,000	1999	95.00	95
1998 Sugar Shack Extravaganza 98-SP-37	5,000	1998	178.00	178-210
1999 Peace on Earth 99-SP-41	5,000	1999	58.00	58-60

Lucasfilm's Star Wars - C. Radko

YEAR ISSUE	EDITION LIMIT	YEAR RETD.	ISSUE PRICE	*QUOTE U.S.$
1999 C-3PO & R2D2 99-STW-01	Open		28.00	28
1998 C-3PO 98-STW-03	Open		18.00	18
1998 Chewbacca 98-STW-04	Open		20.00	20
1998 Darth Vader 98-STW-01	Open		20.00	20
1999 Darth Vader 99-STW-02	Open		26.00	26
1999 Darth Vader-The Duel 99-STW-05	7,500		38.00	38
1999 Ewoks 99-STW-06	Open		28.00	28
1998 Storm Tropper 98-STW-05	Open		20.00	20
1998 Yoda 98-STW-02	Open		18.00	18

Make-A-Wish Foundation Charity Design - C. Radko

YEAR ISSUE	EDITION LIMIT	YEAR RETD.	ISSUE PRICE	*QUOTE U.S.$
1997 Well Wishes 97-MAW-01	5,000		64.00	64

Marshall Fields - C. Radko

YEAR ISSUE	EDITION LIMIT	YEAR RETD.	ISSUE PRICE	*QUOTE U.S.$
1997 Marshall Fields Clock 97-MAR-01	Retrd.	1997	38.00	38
1998 Marshall Fields Clock 98-MAR-01	5,000		38.00	38

Matt Berry Memorial Soccer Fund - C. Radko

YEAR ISSUE	EDITION LIMIT	YEAR RETD.	ISSUE PRICE	*QUOTE U.S.$
1995 Matthew's Game 158-0	Open		12.00	12

Mattel's Barbie - C. Radko

YEAR ISSUE	EDITION LIMIT	YEAR RETD.	ISSUE PRICE	*QUOTE U.S.$
1997 Alpine Blush Barbie 97-BAR-03	Retrd.	1999	44.00	44
1998 Barbie Heart 98-BAR-03	Retrd.	1999	15.00	15
1998 Barbie Stocking 98-BAR-02	Open		19.00	19
1998 Elegant Holiday 98-BAR-01	Retrd.	1999	32.00	32
1997 Holiday Barbie 97-BAR-01	Retrd.	1999	50.00	50

Moscow Circus Series - C. Radko

YEAR ISSUE	EDITION LIMIT	YEAR RETD.	ISSUE PRICE	*QUOTE U.S.$
1997 Ivan & Misha 97-CIR-01	10,000	1997	90.00	90
1998 Grand Ring Master 98-CIR-02	10,000	1998	90.00	90-100
1999 Brutus 99-CIR-03	10,000	1999	45.00	45
2000 The Greatest Show on Earth 00-CIR-4	10,000		69.00	69

Musicians Series - C. Radko

YEAR ISSUE	EDITION LIMIT	YEAR RETD.	ISSUE PRICE	*QUOTE U.S.$
1998 Hooked on Classics 98-COM-1	5,000	1998	108.00	108

Nativity Series - C. Radko

YEAR ISSUE	EDITION LIMIT	YEAR RETD.	ISSUE PRICE	*QUOTE U.S.$
1995 Three Wise Men WM (Set/3)	15,000	1996	90.00	90-196
1996 Holy Family HF (Set/3)	15,000	1996	70.00	70-90
1997 Shepherd's Prayer, Gloria 97-NAT-3	15,000	1997	90.00	90

Neiman Marcus - C. Radko

YEAR ISSUE	EDITION LIMIT	YEAR RETD.	ISSUE PRICE	*QUOTE U.S.$
1997 The Original Store 97-NM-01	Retrd.	1997	48.00	48

North American Bears' Muffy Vanderbear - C. Radko

YEAR ISSUE	EDITION LIMIT	YEAR RETD.	ISSUE PRICE	*QUOTE U.S.$
2000 A Christmas Carol: Bearly in Tune Hoppy 00-NAB-02	Yr.Iss.		34.00	34
2000 A Christmas Carol: Bearly in Tune Muffy 00-NAB-01	Yr.Iss.		34.00	34
2000 Czarina Muffina 00-NAB-03	Open		34.00	34
1999 Grand VanderBall Hoppy VanderBear 99-NAB-02	Open		29.00	29
1999 Grand VanderBall Muffy VanderBear 99-NAB-01	Open		29.00	29
1999 Hearts & Flowers Muffy VanderBear 99-NAB-04	Open		29.00	29
1999 Messenger of Love Hoppy VanderBear 99-NAB-03	Open		29.00	29
1998 Muffy Candy C'angel (Roger's Garden Exclusive) 98-NAB-01	Open		29.00	29
1998 Muffy Ginger Bear 98-NAB-02	Retrd.	1999	29.00	29
1998 Muffy Plum Fairy 98-NAB-03	Retrd.	1999	29.00	29
2000 Petite Gingerbear 00-NAB-07	Yr.Iss.		24.00	24
2000 Petite Portrait in Black & White 00-NAB-06	Yr.Iss.		24.00	24
1999 Pickin' Posies Muffy 99-NAB-05	Open		29.00	29
1997 Portrait in Black and White 97-NAB-02	Retrd.	1999	38.00	38
2000 Santa's Workshop Hoppy 00-NAB-05	Yr.Iss.		34.00	34
2000 Santa's Workshop Muffy 00-NAB-04	Yr.Iss.		34.00	34
1997 Sleddin' and Skiddalin' 97-NAB-01	Retrd.	1999	38.00	38

Nutcracker Series - C. Radko

YEAR ISSUE	EDITION LIMIT	YEAR RETD.	ISSUE PRICE	*QUOTE U.S.$
1995 Nutcracker Suite I NC1 (Set/3)	15,000	1996	90.00	90-150
1996 Nutcracker Suite II NC2 (Set/3)	15,000	1997	90.00	90-110
1997 Nutcracker Suite III 97-NC3 (Set/3)	15,000	1997	90.00	90-110

Parkwest - C. Radko

YEAR ISSUE	EDITION LIMIT	YEAR RETD.	ISSUE PRICE	*QUOTE U.S.$
1998 Special Charity Set 98-PW-SPE	Open		140.00	140

Patriots Series - C. Radko

YEAR ISSUE	EDITION LIMIT	YEAR RETD.	ISSUE PRICE	*QUOTE U.S.$
1997 LaFayette 97-PAT-1	7,500	1997	34.00	34
1998 Alexander Hamilton 98-PAT-2	7,500	1998	40.00	40
1999 Paul Revere 99-PAT-3	7,500	1999	28.00	28
2000 Thomas Jefferson 00-PAT-4	7,500	2000	37.00	37

Pediatrics Cancer Research - C. Radko

YEAR ISSUE	EDITION LIMIT	YEAR RETD.	ISSUE PRICE	*QUOTE U.S.$
1994 A Gifted Santa 70	Retrd.	1994	25.00	25-81
1995 Christmas Puppy Love SP11	Retrd.	1995	30.00	30-38
1996 Bearly Awake SP16	Retrd.	1996	34.00	34-54
1997 Kitty Cares 97-SP-23	Retrd.	1997	30.00	30
1998 Elfin Magic 98-SP-30	Retrd.	1998	32.00	32
1999 Dear To My Heart 99-SP-46	Retrd.	1999	28.00	28
2000 Gift of Health 00-SP-73	Yr.Iss.		36.00	36

Polish Children's Home Fund - C. Radko

YEAR ISSUE	EDITION LIMIT	YEAR RETD.	ISSUE PRICE	*QUOTE U.S.$
1997 Watch Over Me 97-SP-26	Retrd.	1997	28.00	28

Rosemont Special - C. Radko

YEAR ISSUE	EDITION LIMIT	YEAR RETD.	ISSUE PRICE	*QUOTE U.S.$
1997 Blue Caroline 96-1521	Retrd.	1997	26.00	44-65

Saks Fifth Avenue - C. Radko

YEAR ISSUE	EDITION LIMIT	YEAR RETD.	ISSUE PRICE	*QUOTE U.S.$
1995 Saks Santa SAK01	2,500	1997	48.00	120-230
1996 Santa Calls 95SAK02	Retrd.	1996	56.00	288-460
1997 Saks Nutcraker 97-SAK-03	5,000	1997	40.00	40
1998 Saks International Santa 98-SAK-01	3,000		36.00	36

South Bend Special - C. Radko

YEAR ISSUE	EDITION LIMIT	YEAR RETD.	ISSUE PRICE	*QUOTE U.S.$
1995 Polar Express (lilac) 95-076SB	Retrd.	1995	24.95	75-85

Special Color Variations - C. Radko

YEAR ISSUE	EDITION LIMIT	YEAR RETD.	ISSUE PRICE	*QUOTE U.S.$
1996 Snowtem Pole (Glass Pheasant) 96155G	Retrd.	1996	33.00	90-100
1996 White Dolphin (Four Seasons) 96238F	Retrd.	1996	25.00	75

Starlight and Rising Star Store Exclusives - C. Radko

YEAR ISSUE	EDITION LIMIT	YEAR RETD.	ISSUE PRICE	*QUOTE U.S.$
1998 Sterling Rider 98-SP-39	2,500	1998	175.00	175
1999 Carousel of Dreams 99-SP-49	2,500	1999	190.00	190
1999 Santa's Shroom 994960	Open		65.00	65
2000 Supreme Santa Finial 00-SP-62	Yr.Iss.		250.00	250

Starlight and Rising Star Store Exclusives/St. Nick Portrait Series - C. Radko

YEAR ISSUE	EDITION LIMIT	YEAR RETD.	ISSUE PRICE	*QUOTE U.S.$
1996 Esquire Santa 96-SP-17	750	1996	150.00	600-650
1997 Regency Santa 97-SP-24	2,500		180.00	180
1998 Moondream 98-SP-38	2,500	1998	186.00	186

Starlight and Rising Star Store Special Colorations - C. Radko

YEAR ISSUE	EDITION LIMIT	YEAR RETD.	ISSUE PRICE	*QUOTE U.S.$
1996 Baby Bear (Christmas Dove) 322-0	N/A		30.00	30
1996 Far Away Places (Christmas Village) 321-0	N/A		40.00	40
1996 Frosty Bear (Christmas House) 326-0	N/A		30.00	30
1996 Kitty Christmas (Tuck's) 323-0	N/A		30.00	30
1996 Little St. Mick (Roger's Gardens) DIS7	N/A	1996	45.00	50-85
1996 On His Way (Geary's) 319-0	N/A		30.00	30
1996 Ruffles (Christmas Attic) 320-0	N/A		30.00	30
1996 Snow Fun (Vinny's) 324-0	N/A		30.00	30
1996 Tweedle Dee (Glass Pheasant) 325-0	N/A		40.00	40
1998 Bergdorf Star (Bergdorf Goodman) 98-BG-01	N/A		90.00	90
1998 Best of Times (Loot N Boot) 98-194-BO	N/A		42.00	42
1998 Bunny Express (FAO Schwarz) 98-378-FA	N/A		50.00	50
1998 Candy Santa (Pine Creek Collectibles) 98-301-PC	N/A		52.00	52
1998 Circle of Cheer (Four Seasons Christmas Shoppe) 98-222-F	N/A		52.00	52
1998 Derby Rocker (Bloomingdales) 98-365-BM	N/A		43.50	44
1998 Ginger Cracker (Christmas Attic) 98-162-CA	N/A		48.00	48
1998 June Buggy (Chatsworth Florist) 98-102-CF	N/A		60.00	60
1998 Lucky Laddie (Borsheim's Jewelry) 98-458-B	N/A		48.00	48
1998 Sleddin' Snowman (Carson Pirie Scott) 98-CPS-01	N/A		44.00	44
1998 Slim Traveler (Margo's Gift Shop) 98-120-M	N/A		38.00	38
1998 Snow Star (Curio Cabinet) 98-129-CC	N/A		36.00	36
1998 Spring Romance (R. Blooms) 98-321-RB	N/A		46.00	46
1998 Stuffings Full (Glass Pheasant) 98-159-GP	N/A		44.00	44
1998 Summertime Santa 98-RG-01	3,000		70.00	70
1998 Teddy Tunes (Christmas Store) 98-256-CS	N/A		42.00	42
1998 Triple Nick (Story Book Kids) 98-150-SK	N/A		36.00	36
1996 Winter Kitten (Margo's) 327-0	N/A		30.00	30
1998 Woodcut Santa (Botanicals on the Park) 98-214-BP	N/A		44.00	44

Sterling Silver Collection - C. Radko

YEAR ISSUE	EDITION LIMIT	YEAR RETD.	ISSUE PRICE	*QUOTE U.S.$
1997 Winter Spirit 97-J01-00	5,000		175.00	175
1998 Regal Reindeer 98-J02-00	5,000		150.00	150

Sunday Brunch - C. Radko

YEAR ISSUE	EDITION LIMIT	YEAR RETD.	ISSUE PRICE	*QUOTE U.S.$
1996 Hansel & Gretel and Witch HG01	7,500	1996	50.00	50
1997 Nibble Nibble 97-HG-02	7,500	1997	58.00	58-60

The Three Stooges - C. Radko

YEAR ISSUE	EDITION LIMIT	YEAR RETD.	ISSUE PRICE	*QUOTE U.S.$
1999 Restless Knights 99-STO-01	Open		28.00	28

Twelve Days of Christmas - C. Radko

YEAR ISSUE	EDITION LIMIT	YEAR RETD.	ISSUE PRICE	*QUOTE U.S.$
1993 Partridge in a Pear Tree SP2	5,000	1993	35.00	960
1994 Two Turtle Doves SP4	10,000	1994	28.00	125-175
1995 Three French Hens SP9	10,000	1995	34.00	90-140
1995 Three French Hens (signed) SP9	Retrd.	1995	34.00	100-175
1996 Four Calling Birds SP12	10,000	1996	44.00	75-125
1997 Five Gold Rings SP19	10,000	1997	60.00	62-125
1998 Six Geese a Laying SP40	10,000	1998	68.00	68-94
1999 Seven Swans a Swimming SP42	10,000	1999	50.00	50-63
2000 Eight Maids a'Milking 00-SP-58	10,000		54.00	54

Universal Studios:Universal and Steven Speilberg's Lost World - C. Radko

YEAR ISSUE	EDITION LIMIT	YEAR RETD.	ISSUE PRICE	*QUOTE U.S.$
1997 Baby T-REX 97-UNI-12	Retrd.	1999	38.00	38
1997 Baby Trike 97-UNI-11	Retrd.	1999	38.00	38
1997 Stegosaurus 97-UNI-15	Open		42.00	42
1997 T-REX 97-UNI-14	Retrd.	1999	42.00	42

Universal Studios:Universal Monsters - C. Radko

YEAR ISSUE	EDITION LIMIT	YEAR RETD.	ISSUE PRICE	*QUOTE U.S.$
1997 Bride of Frankenstein 97-UNI-17	Open		42.00	42
1998 Creature From the Black Lagoon 98-MST-03	Retrd.	1999	22.00	22
1997 Dracula 97-UNI-02	Open		42.00	42

*Quotes have been rounded up to nearest dollar

ORNAMENTS

YEAR ISSUE	EDITION LIMIT	YEAR RETD.	ISSUE PRICE	*QUOTE U.S.$
1997 Frankenstein 97-UNI-03	Retrd.	1999	42.00	42
1998 The Mummy 98-MST-01	Retrd.	1999	21.00	21
1999 Shrunken Heads 99-MST-01	Retrd.	1999	17.00	17
1998 Wolfman 98-MST-02	Open		22.00	22

Universal Studios:Universal's Rocky, Bullwinkle and Friends - C. Radko

YEAR ISSUE	EDITION LIMIT	YEAR RETD.	ISSUE PRICE	*QUOTE U.S.$
1998 Boris & Natasha Block 98-RAB-01	Open		19.00	19
1997 Bullwinkle's Wreath 97-UNI-09	Retrd.	1999	36.00	36-45
1997 Rocky & Bullwinkle Block 97-UNI-06	Open		38.00	38
1997 Rocky's Wreath 97-UNI-08	Retrd.	1999	36.00	36
1998 Sleigh Ride 98-RAB-02	Open		27.00	27
1998 Totem Trouble 98-RAB-03	Retrd.	1999	26.00	26

Virginia Diner Exclusive - C. Radko

YEAR ISSUE	EDITION LIMIT	YEAR RETD.	ISSUE PRICE	*QUOTE U.S.$
1998 Virginia Diner Peanut 98-VAD-01	Open		12.00	12

The Walt Disney Gallery - C. Radko

YEAR ISSUE	EDITION LIMIT	YEAR RETD.	ISSUE PRICE	*QUOTE U.S.$
1997 Bambi 97-DIS-74	5,000		44.00	44
1997 Bambi's Winter Forest (for special boxed set, 4 pc.) 96-273-DG	2,500		N/A	N/A
1997 Bambi, set/4 (signed) 97-DIS-99	1,000		180.00	180
1996 Best Friends DIS10	10,000	1996	60.00	60-72
1996 By Jiminy DIS11	7,500	1996	38.00	54-78
1996 Cruella De Vil DIS13	10,000	1996	55.00	57-110
1998 Disney's Beast 97-DIS-96	5,000		N/A	N/A
1998 Disney's Belle 97-DIS-95	5,000		N/A	N/A
1997 Eeyore 97-DIS-19	5,000		44.00	44
1997 Flower 97-DIS-75	5,000		44.00	44
1996 A Goofy Surprise DIS5	2,500	1996	38.00	49-110
1996 Holiday Skaters DIS8	Retrd.	1996	42.00	54-72
1997 Huey, Louie and Dewey 97-DIS-32	2,500		34.00	34
1996 Lucky DIS14	Retrd.	1996	45.00	65-72
1997 Mickey's Birthday Set, set/5 97-DIS-48	750		N/A	N/A
1995 Mickey's Tree DIS1	2,500	1995	45.00	125-180
1997 Minnie Statue of Liberty (NY City Gallery Only) 97-DIS-94	2,500		38.00	38
1996 Noel Pluto DIS3	2,500	1996	37.00	37-48
1997 Piglet 97-DIS-98	5,000		38.00	38
1996 Pinocchio DIS9	5,000	1996	45.00	78-144
1995 Pooh's Favorite Gift (signed) DIS2	Retrd.	1995	45.00	135-300
1995 Pooh's Favorite Gift DIS2	2,500	1995	45.00	106-180
1997 Puppy Pole 97-DIS-17	2,500		44.00	44
1996 Ready For Sea DIS4	2,500	1996	38.00	55-150
1997 Scrooge McDuck 97-DIS-97	5,000		44.00	44
1997 Snow White Set w/Apple (leather box) 97-DIS-92	500		500.00	500
1997 Thumper 97-DIS-76	5,000		44.00	44
1997 Tigger 97-DIS-18	5,000		42.00	42
1996 Tinker Bell DIS12	10,000	1997	55.00	65-90
1997 Winnie the Pooh 97-DIS-88	5,000		42.00	42
1996 Xmas Eve Mickey DIS06	Retrd.	1996	45.00	40-88

The Walt Disney World - C. Radko

YEAR ISSUE	EDITION LIMIT	YEAR RETD.	ISSUE PRICE	*QUOTE U.S.$
1998 Cinderella Castle 98-DIS-42	Open		39.00	39

Warner Brothers Studio Stores - C. Radko

YEAR ISSUE	EDITION LIMIT	YEAR RETD.	ISSUE PRICE	*QUOTE U.S.$
1997 Alicia Silverstone as Batgirl 97-WB-22	3,000		44.00	44
1997 Arnold Schwarznegger as Mr. Freeze 97-WB-21	3,000		44.00	44
1998 Bugs Bunny Sprite 98-WB-02	5,000		46.00	46
1998 Faberge Tweety 98-WB-01	5,000		38.00	38
1997 George Clooney as Batman 97-WB-20	3,000		44.00	44
1998 Glenda the Good Witch 98-WB-03	10,000		44.00	44
1997 Gossamer 97-WB-17	5,000		44.00	44
1998 Je t'aime Heart 98-WB-04	5,000		36.00	36
1998 K-9 (Warner Bros. Collector's Guild Exclusive) 98-WB-05	2,500		42.00	42
1996 Little Angel Tweety WB10	5,000	1996	45.00	84-96
1997 Marvin the Martian 97-WB-12	5,000		42.00	42
1995 Santa's Bugs Bunny WB1	Retrd.	1995	45.00	38-75
1997 Scooby Doo 97-WB-11	5,000		42.00	42
1998 Scooby Doo Wreath 98-WB-06	5,000		36.00	36
1996 Superman WB7	7,500	1996	48.00	75-94
1997 Sylvester & Tweety Stockings 97-WB-15	5,000		58.00	58
1996 Sylvester Sprite WB9	5,000	1996	45.00	65-88
1996 Taz & Bugs Stockings WB4	5,000	1996	65.00	57-100
1995 Taz Angel WB2	Retrd.	1995	40.00	100-120
1997 Taz Sprite WB13	5,000		46.00	46
1996 Trio Tree Topper 96-WB8	5,000	1997	78.00	150-180
1995 Tweety's Sprite WB3	Retrd.	1995	45.00	100-125
1997 Wizard of Oz Dorothy 97-WB-18	10,000		45.00	45
1998 Wizard of Oz Lion 98-WB-09	10,000		44.00	44
1997 Wizard of Oz Ruby Slippers 97-WB-19	10,000		44.00	44
1998 Wizard of Oz Scarecrow 98-WB-08	10,000		44.00	44
1997 Wizard of Oz Tin Man 97-WB-14	10,000		46.00	46

White Christmas - C. Radko

YEAR ISSUE	EDITION LIMIT	YEAR RETD.	ISSUE PRICE	*QUOTE U.S.$
1999 Bing Crosby as Bob Wallace 99-WHT-03	Open		24.00	24
1999 Danny Kaye as Phil Davis 99-WHT-03	Open		24.00	24
1999 Rosemary Clooney as Betty Haynes 99-WHT-02	Open		24.00	24
1999 Vera-Ellen as Judy Haynes 99-WHT-01	Open		24.00	24
1999 White Christmas, boxed set/4 99-WHT-05	Open		98.00	98

The Wubbulous World of Dr. Seuss - C. Radko

YEAR ISSUE	EDITION LIMIT	YEAR RETD.	ISSUE PRICE	*QUOTE U.S.$
1998 Cat in the Hat and Whozits 98-SUS-01	Retrd.	1999	26.00	26
1997 The Cat-In-The-Hat Wreath 97-SUS-03	Retrd.	1999	36.00	36
1997 The Grinch and Whozits 97-SUS-05	Retrd.	1999	44.00	44
1998 Thidwick and Whozits 98-SUS-03	Open		30.00	30
1998 Up On The Rooftop 98-SUS-02	Retrd.	1999	28.00	28

Coyne's & Company

American Chestnut Folk Art Christmas - P. & D. Bretz

YEAR ISSUE	EDITION LIMIT	YEAR RETD.	ISSUE PRICE	*QUOTE U.S.$
1999 Petey & Friends Candy Cane Ornaments, 4 asst. AM1210	Open		10.00	10
1999 Petey & Friends Wreath Ornaments, 4 asst. AM1209	Open		10.00	10

Ashland Studio Santas - J. McKenna

YEAR ISSUE	EDITION LIMIT	YEAR RETD.	ISSUE PRICE	*QUOTE U.S.$
2000 Santa Ornaments, 3 asst. JM1022	Open		8.00	8

Ashland Studio Snow Angels - J. McKenna

YEAR ISSUE	EDITION LIMIT	YEAR RETD.	ISSUE PRICE	*QUOTE U.S.$
2000 Snow Angel ornaments, 4 asst. JMOR1000	Open		8.00	8

Bavarian Heritage Collection - Coyne's & Company

YEAR ISSUE	EDITION LIMIT	YEAR RETD.	ISSUE PRICE	*QUOTE U.S.$
1999 All Wrapped Up BH1011C	Open		10.00	10
1999 Bastien BH1013	Open		13.00	13
1999 Circle of Peace BH1011D	Open		10.00	10
1999 Humble Walking BH1011E	Open		10.00	10
1999 Joyful Waltzing BH1011F	Open		10.00	10
1999 Light in the Forest BH1011B	Open		10.00	10
1999 Tree of Life BH1011A	Open		10.00	10

David Frykman Christmas Collection - D. Frykman

YEAR ISSUE	EDITION LIMIT	YEAR RETD.	ISSUE PRICE	*QUOTE U.S.$
2000 In The Nick of Time DF2073	Yr.Iss.		13.00	13

Folkwoods Studio Christmas Series - A. Strom

YEAR ISSUE	EDITION LIMIT	YEAR RETD.	ISSUE PRICE	*QUOTE U.S.$
2000 Santa Ornaments, 3 asst. FW1012	Open		17.00	17

Crystal World

Disney Showcase Collection - Various

YEAR ISSUE	EDITION LIMIT	YEAR RETD.	ISSUE PRICE	*QUOTE U.S.$
1999 Tinker Bell - R. Nakai	Yr.Iss.	1999	58.00	58
2000 Sorcerer Mickey - Team	Yr.Iss.		58.00	58

Dave Grossman Creations

Emmett Kelly Sr. - Inspired by E. Kelly Sr.

YEAR ISSUE	EDITION LIMIT	YEAR RETD.	ISSUE PRICE	*QUOTE U.S.$
1986 Christmas Carol EKX-86	Yr.Iss.	1986	12.00	12-16
1987 Christmas Wreath EKX-87	Yr.Iss.	1987	14.00	14
1988 Christmas Dinner EKX-88	Yr.Iss.	1988	15.00	15
1989 Christmas Feast EKX-89	Yr.Iss.	1989	15.00	15
1990 Just What I Needed EKX-90	Yr.Iss.	1990	15.00	15
1991 Emmett The Snowman EKX-91	Yr.Iss.	1991	15.00	15
1992 Christmas Tunes EKX-92	Yr.Iss.	1992	15.00	15
1993 Downhill EKX-93	Yr.Iss.	1993	20.00	20
1994 Holiday Skater EKX-94	Yr.Iss.	1994	20.00	20
1995 Merry Christmas Mr. Scrooge EKX-95	Yr.Iss.	1995	20.00	20
1996 The Christmas Tree EKX-96	Yr.Iss.	1996	20.00	20
1997 Emmett The Santa EKX-97	Yr.Iss.	1997	20.00	20
1998 Bedside Manner EKX-98	Yr.Iss.	1998	20.00	20
1999 A Dog's Life EKX-99	Yr.Iss.	1999	20.00	20
2000 Celebration EKX-00	Yr.Iss.		20.00	20

Gone With the Wind Ornaments - Inspired by Film

YEAR ISSUE	EDITION LIMIT	YEAR RETD.	ISSUE PRICE	*QUOTE U.S.$
1987 Ashley - D. Geenty	Closed	N/A	15.00	45-55
1987 Rhett - D. Geenty	Closed	N/A	15.00	45-75
1987 Scarlett - D. Geenty	Closed	N/A	15.00	45-95
1987 Tara - D. Geenty	Closed	N/A	15.00	45
1988 Rhett and Scarlett - D. Geenty	Closed	N/A	20.00	40-60
1989 Mammy - D. Geenty	Closed	N/A	20.00	20-45
1990 Scarlett (Red Dress) - D. Geenty	Closed	N/A	20.00	45-55
1991 Prissy - Unknown	Closed	N/A	20.00	20-30
1992 Scarlett (Green Dress) - Unknown	Closed	N/A	20.00	20-50
1993 Rhett (White Suit) GWO-93 - Unknown	Closed	N/A	20.00	20-50
1994 Gold Plated GWO-00 - Unknown	Open		13.00	13
1994 Scarlett GWO-94 - Unknown	Closed	N/A	20.00	20
1995 The Kiss GWW-95 - Unknown	Yr.Iss.	1995	25.00	25-50
1994 Scarlett (B-B-Q Dress) GWO-94 - Unknown	Closed	1994	12.00	20-25
1996 Suellen GWO-95 - Unknown	Closed	1996	12.00	12
1996 Scarlett GWO-96 - Unknown	Closed	1996	12.00	12
1996 1996 Ornament GWW-96 - Unknown	Yr.Iss.	1996	25.00	25
1996 Set of 5 Ornaments GWOS-1 - Unknown	Yr.Iss.	1996	100.00	100
1997 Bonnie GWO-97 - Unknown	Retrd.	2000	12.00	12
1997 Scarlett GWW-97 - Unknown	Yr.Iss.	1997	25.00	25

Ornaments - C. Spencer Collin

YEAR ISSUE	EDITION LIMIT	YEAR RETD.	ISSUE PRICE	*QUOTE U.S.$
1996 Cape Hatteras CSC-01	Yr.Iss.	1997	24.00	22-24
1997 Nubble Light CSC-O	Yr.Iss.	1997	24.00	22-24
1998 SF. Lightship CSC-3	Yr.Iss.	1998	24.00	24

Rockwell Collection-Annual Rockwell Ball - Rockwell-Inspired

YEAR ISSUE	EDITION LIMIT	YEAR RETD.	ISSUE PRICE	*QUOTE U.S.$
1975 Santa with Feather Quill NRO-01	Retrd.	N/A	3.50	25-35
1976 Santa at Globe NRO-02	Retrd.	N/A	4.00	25-35
1977 Grandpa on Rocking Horse NRO-03	Retrd.	N/A	4.00	12-20
1978 Santa with Map NRO-04	Retrd.	N/A	4.50	12-20
1979 Santa at Desk with Mail Bag NRO-05	Retrd.	N/A	5.00	12-20
1980 Santa Asleep with Toys NRO-06	Retrd.	N/A	5.00	10-18
1981 Santa with Boy on Finger NRO-07	Retrd.	N/A	5.00	10
1982 Santa Face on Winter Scene NRO-08	Retrd.	N/A	5.00	10
1983 Coachman with Whip NRO-9	Retrd.	N/A	5.00	10
1984 Christmas Bounty Man NRO-10	Retrd.	N/A	5.00	10-18
1985 Old English Trio NRO-11	Retrd.	N/A	5.00	10-15
1986 Tiny Tim on Shoulder NRO-12	Retrd.	N/A	5.00	10
1987 Skating Lesson NRO-13	Retrd.	N/A	5.00	10
1988 Big Moment NRO-14	Retrd.	N/A	5.50	10
1989 Discovery NRO-15	Retrd.	N/A	6.00	10-15
1990 Bringing Home The Tree NRO-16	Retrd.	N/A	6.00	10-15
1991 Downhill Daring NRO-17	Retrd.	N/A	6.00	10-15
1992 On The Ice NRO-18	Retrd.	N/A	6.00	10
1993 Gramps NRO-19	Retrd.	N/A	6.00	10-15
1994 Triple Self Portrait-Commemorative NRO-20	Retrd.	1994	6.00	10
1994 Merry Christmas NRO-94	Retrd.	1994	6.00	7
1995 Young Love NRO-21	Retrd.	N/A	6.00	7
1996 Christmas Feast NRO-22	Retrd.	1996	6.00	7
1997 Lovers NRO-23	Yr.Iss.	1997	6.00	7-11
1998 Merry Christmas NRO-24	Yr.Iss.	1998	6.00	6
1999 Bedside Manner NRO-25	Yr.Iss.	1999	6.00	6
2000 Homecoming NRO-26	Yr.Iss.		6.00	6

Rockwell Collection-Annual Rockwell Figurine Ornaments - Rockwell-Inspired

YEAR ISSUE	EDITION LIMIT	YEAR RETD.	ISSUE PRICE	*QUOTE U.S.$
1978 Caroler NRX-03	Retrd.	N/A	15.00	45
1979 Drum for Tommy NRX-24	Retrd.	N/A	20.00	30-40
1980 Santa's Good Boys NRX-37	Retrd.	N/A	20.00	30-55
1981 Letters to Santa NRX-39	Retrd.	N/A	20.00	55
1982 Cornettist NRX-32	Retrd.	N/A	20.00	30-40
1983 Fiddler NRX-83	Retrd.	N/A	20.00	40
1984 Christmas Bounty NRX-84	Retrd.	N/A	20.00	30-40
1985 Jolly Coachman NRX-85	Retrd.	N/A	20.00	35
1986 Grandpa on Rocking Horse NRX-86	Retrd.	N/A	20.00	35-45
1987 Skating Lesson NRX-87	Retrd.	N/A	20.00	35
1988 Big Moment NRX-88	Retrd.	N/A	20.00	30
1989 Discovery NRX-89	Retrd.	N/A	20.00	30-45
1990 Bringing Home The Tree NRX-90	Retrd.	N/A	20.00	10-30
1991 Downhill Daring B NRX-91	Retrd.	N/A	20.00	30-45
1992 On The Ice	Retrd.	N/A	20.00	30-40
1993 Granps NRX-93	Retrd.	N/A	24.00	10-30
1993 Marriage License First Christmas Together NRX-m1	Retrd.	N/A	30.00	30-50
1994 Merry Christmas NRX-94	Retrd.	N/A	24.00	24
1994 Triple Self-Portrait NRX-TS	Retrd.	N/A	30.00	30-50
1995 Young Love NRX-95	Retrd.	1995	24.00	45-65
1996 Christmas Feast NRX-96	Retrd.	1996	24.00	24-32
1997 Lovers NRX-97	Retrd.	1997	24.00	24
1998 Tiny Tim NRX-98	Retrd.	1998	24.00	24
1999 Bedside Manner NRX-99	Retrd.	1999	24.00	7-24
2000 Homecoming NRX-00	Yr.Iss.		24.00	24

David Winter Cottages/Enesco European Giftware Group

David Winter Ornaments - Various

YEAR ISSUE	EDITION LIMIT	YEAR RETD.	ISSUE PRICE	*QUOTE U.S.$
1991 Christmas Carol - D. Winter	Closed	1991	15.00	13-15
1991 Christmas in Scotland & Hogmanay - D. Winter	Closed	1991	15.00	13-15
1991 Mr. Fezziwig's Emporium - D. Winter	Closed	1991	15.00	13-15
1991 Ebenezer Scrooge's Counting House - D. Winter	Closed	1991	15.00	13-15
1992 Fairytale Castle - D. Winter	Closed	1992	15.00	13-15
1992 Fred's Home - D. Winter	Closed	1992	15.00	13-15
1992 Suffolk House - D. Winter	Closed	1992	15.00	13-15
1992 Tudor Manor - D. Winter	Closed	1992	15.00	13-15
1993 The Grange - J. Hine Studios	Closed	1993	15.00	13-15
1993 Scrooge's School - J. Hine Studios	Closed	1993	15.00	13-15
1993 Tomfool's Cottage - J. Hine Studios	Closed	1993	15.00	13-15
1993 Will-O The Wisp - J. Hine Studios	Closed	1993	15.00	13-15
1994 Old Joe's Beetling Shop - J. Hine Studios	Closed	1994	17.50	13-18
1994 Scrooge's Family Home - J. Hine Studios	Closed	1994	17.50	13-18
1994 What Cottage - J. Hine Studios	Closed	1996	17.50	13-18
1995 Buttercup Cottage - J. Hine Studios	Closed	1996	17.50	13-18
1995 The Flowershop - J. Hine Studios	Closed	1996	17.50	13-.15
1995 Looking for Santa - J. Hine Studios	Closed	1996	17.50	13-18
1995 Miss Belle's Cottage - J. Hine Studios	Closed	1995	17.50	13-15
1995 Robin's Merry Mouse - J. Hine Studios	Closed	1996	17.50	13-15
1995 Porridge Pot Alley Mouse - D. Winter	Closed	1995	Gift	13-30
1995 Season's Greetings - J. Hine Studios	Closed	1996	17.50	13-18
1996 Plough Farmhouse - D. Winter	Closed	1996	17.50	13-18
1996 Tiny Tim - D. Winter	Closed	1996	17.50	13-18
1996 Stocking Mouse - D. Winter	Closed	1996	17.50	13-15
1996 Jolly Roger Mouse - D. Winter	Closed	1996	17.50	13-15
1996 Stable Mouse - D. Winter	Closed	1996	17.50	13-15
1999 Holly Berry Cottage - D. Winter	Closed	1999	30.00	13-30
2000 Mead Cottage - D. Winter	Yr.Iss.		25.00	25

Department 56

Bisque Light-Up, Clip-on Ornaments - Department 56

YEAR ISSUE	EDITION LIMIT	YEAR RETD.	ISSUE PRICE	*QUOTE U.S.$
1986 Angelic Lite-up 8260-0	Closed	1998	4.00	6
1987 Anniversary Love Birds, (pair) w/brass ribbon 8353-4	Closed	1988	4.00	42
1986 Dessert, 4 asst. 3803-4	Closed	1987	5.00	40-96
1990 Owl w/clip 8344-5	Closed	1994	5.00	15-18
1986 Plum Pudding 3803-5	Closed	1987	4.50	42-45
1989 Pond-Frog w/clip 8347-0	Closed	1991	5.00	36-42
1989 Pond-Snail w/clip 8347-0	Closed	1991	5.00	36-58
1988 Rabbit w/clip 8350-0	Open		5.00	4
1987 Shells, set/4 8349-6	Closed	1991	14.00	132-150
1986 Shooting Star 7106-4	Closed	1987	5.50	36-48
1985 Snowbirds, (pair) w/clip 8357-7	Open		5.00	6
1985 Snowbirds, set/6 8367-4	Closed	1988	15.00	15-21
1985 Snowbirds, set/8 8358-5	Closed	1988	20.00	20
1985 Snowmen, 3 asst. 8360-7	Closed	1988	10.50	11
1986 Teddy Bear w/clip 8262-7	Closed	1991	5.00	22
1986 Truffles Sampler, set/4 7102-1	Closed	1987	17.50	42-96
1986 Winged Snowbird 8261-9	Closed	1988	2.50	3-58

*Quotes have been rounded up to nearest dollar

YEAR ISSUE	EDITION LIMIT	YEAR RETD.	ISSUE PRICE	*QUOTE U.S.$
1989 Woodland-Field Mouse w/clip 8348-8	Closed	1991	5.00	30-36
1989 Woodland-Squirrel w/clip 8348-8	Closed	1991	5.00	36-40

CCP Ornaments-Flat - Department 56

YEAR ISSUE	EDITION LIMIT	YEAR RETD.	ISSUE PRICE	*QUOTE U.S.$
1986 Christmas Carol Houses, set/3 (6504-8)	Closed	1989	13.00	35-42
1986 • The Cottage of Bob Cratchit & Tiny Tim	Closed	1989	4.35	7-30
1986 • Fezziwig's Warehouse	Closed	1989	4.35	6-20
1986 • Scrooge and Marley Countinghouse	Closed	1989	4.35	8-20
1986 New England Village, set/7 (6536-6)	Closed	1989	25.00	300
1986 • Apothecary Shop	Closed	1989	3.50	10-25
1986 • Brick Town Hall	Closed	1989	3.50	20-30
1986 • General Store	Closed	1989	3.50	20-55
1986 • Livery Stable & Boot Shop	Closed	1989	3.50	10-20
1986 • Nathaniel Bingham Fabrics	Closed	1989	3.50	10-25
1986 • Red Schoolhouse	Closed	1989	3.50	30-55
1986 • Steeple Church	Closed	1989	3.50	100-150

Christmas Carol Character Ornaments-Flat - Department 56

YEAR ISSUE	EDITION LIMIT	YEAR RETD.	ISSUE PRICE	*QUOTE U.S.$
1986 Christmas Carol Characters, set/3 (6505-6)	Closed	1987	13.00	36-42
1986 • Bob Cratchit & Tiny Tim	Closed	1987	4.35	20
1986 • Poulterer	Closed	1987	4.35	20
1986 • Scrooge	Closed	1987	4.35	20-30

Christmas Carol Ornaments-Face - Department 56

YEAR ISSUE	EDITION LIMIT	YEAR RETD.	ISSUE PRICE	*QUOTE U.S.$
1988 Bob & Mrs. Crachit 5914-5	Closed	1989	18.00	32
1988 Scrooge's Head 5912-9	Closed	1989	12.95	32
1988 Tiny Tim's Head 5913-7	Closed	1989	10.00	24-32

Classic Ornament Series-Christmas in the City - Department 56

YEAR ISSUE	EDITION LIMIT	YEAR RETD.	ISSUE PRICE	*QUOTE U.S.$
1998 Cathedral Church of St. Mark 98759	Open		20.00	20
1998 City Hall 98741	Open		15.00	15
1998 City Hall 98771	Open		20.00	20
1998 Dorothy's Dress Shop 98740	Open		15.00	15
1998 Dorothy's Dress Shop 98770	Closed	1999	20.00	18-20
1999 Hollydale's Department Store (1991-1997) 98782	Open		20.00	20
1998 Red Brick Fire Station 98758	Open		20.00	20

Classic Ornament Series-Dickens' Village - Department 56

YEAR ISSUE	EDITION LIMIT	YEAR RETD.	ISSUE PRICE	*QUOTE U.S.$
1998 Christmas Carol Cottages 98745, set/3	Open		50.00	50
1998 Dickens' Village Church 98737	Open		15.00	15
1998 Dickens' Village Church 98767	Open		20.00	20
1997 Dickens' Village Mill 98733	Open		15.00	15
1998 Dickens' Village Mill 98766	Open		22.50	23
1999 Dickens' Village Victorian Station (1989-1998) 98780	Open		22.50	23
1998 The Old Curiosity Shop 98738	Open		15.00	15
1998 The Old Curiosity Shop 98768	Open		20.00	20

Classic Ornament Series-Heritage Village - Department 56

YEAR ISSUE	EDITION LIMIT	YEAR RETD.	ISSUE PRICE	*QUOTE U.S.$
1999 The Times Tower 98775	Closed	1999	25.00	25-28

Classic Ornament Series-New England - Department 56

YEAR ISSUE	EDITION LIMIT	YEAR RETD.	ISSUE PRICE	*QUOTE U.S.$
1998 Captain's Cottage 98756	Open		20.00	20
1998 Craggy Cove Lighthouse 98739	Open		15.00	15
1998 Craggy Cove Lighthouse 98769	Open		20.00	20
1998 Steeple Church 98757	Open		20.00	20

Classic Ornament Series-North Pole - Department 56

YEAR ISSUE	EDITION LIMIT	YEAR RETD.	ISSUE PRICE	*QUOTE U.S.$
1998 Elf Bunkhouse 98763	Open		20.00	20
1997 North Pole Santa's Workshop 98734	Open		16.50	17
1999 Real Plastic Snow Factory (1998-current) 98781	Open		20.00	20
1998 Reindeer Barn 98762	Open		20.00	20
1998 Santa's Lookout Tower 98742	Open		15.00	15
1998 Santa's Lookout Tower 98773	Open		20.00	20
1998 Santa's Workshop 98772	Open		20.00	20

Classic Ornament Series-The Original Snow Village - Department 56

YEAR ISSUE	EDITION LIMIT	YEAR RETD.	ISSUE PRICE	*QUOTE U.S.$
1998 J. Young's Granary 98632	Open		15.00	15
1998 J. Young's Granary 98644	Open		20.00	20
1999 Jingle Belle Houseboat (1989-1991) 98648	Open		20.00	20
1998 Lighthouse 98635	Open		20.00	20
1998 Nantucket 98630	Open		15.00	15
1998 Nantucket 98642	Open		20.00	20
1998 Pinewood Log Cabin (lighted) 98637	Open		20.00	20
1999 Queen Anne Victorian (1990-1996) 98646	Open		20.00	20
1998 Steepled Church 98631	Open		15.00	15
1998 Steepled Church 98643	Open		20.00	20
1999 Street Car (1982-1984) 98645	Open		20.00	20

Clip On Lite-Up Ornaments - Department 56

YEAR ISSUE	EDITION LIMIT	YEAR RETD.	ISSUE PRICE	*QUOTE U.S.$
1989 Field Mouse 8348-8	Closed	1991	4.50	42
1989 Frog 8347-0	Closed	1991	4.50	54
1990 Owl 8344-5	Closed	1994	5.00	15-18
1989 Snail 8347-0	Closed	1991	4.50	35-58
1989 Squirrel 8348-8	Closed	1991	4.50	48-50

Dickens' Village Signature Series Ornaments - Department 56

YEAR ISSUE	EDITION LIMIT	YEAR RETD.	ISSUE PRICE	*QUOTE U.S.$
1994 Dickens Village Dedlock Arms 9872-8, (porcelain, gift boxed)	Closed	1994	12.50	17-22
1995 Sir John Falstaff 9870-1 (Charles Dickens' Signature Series)	Closed	1995	15.00	19-29
1996 The Grapes Inn 98729	Yr.Iss.	1996	15.00	24-28
1996 Crown & Cricket Inn 98730	Yr.Iss.	1996	15.00	28-40
1996 The Pied Bull Inn 98731	Yr.Iss.	1996	15.00	10-40
1997 Gad's Hill Place 98732	Yr.Iss.	1997	15.00	25-33

Discover Department 56 - Department 56

YEAR ISSUE	EDITION LIMIT	YEAR RETD.	ISSUE PRICE	*QUOTE U.S.$
1999 Ronald McDonald House 98774	Closed	1999	16.50	17
2000 1955 Pink Cadillac 98791	Yr.Iss.		10.00	10
2000 Elvis Presley's Graceland 98790	Yr.Iss.		15.00	15

Home For The Holidays - Department 56

YEAR ISSUE	EDITION LIMIT	YEAR RETD.	ISSUE PRICE	*QUOTE U.S.$
1997 Ronald McDonald House ® 8961	Yr.Iss.	1997	7.50	4-8
1999 The First House That Love Built (25th Anniversary) 98774	Yr.Iss.	1999	16.50	8-17

Merry Makers - Department 56

YEAR ISSUE	EDITION LIMIT	YEAR RETD.	ISSUE PRICE	*QUOTE U.S.$
1994 Burgess The Bell Ringer 9368-8	Closed	1996	13.50	14-18
1993 Horatio The Hornblower 9383-1	Closed	1996	13.50	14-18
1993 Martin The Mandolinist 9383-1	Closed	1996	13.50	14-25
1993 Merry Mountain Chapel 9384-0	Closed	1996	7.50	7-18
1994 Percival/Puddingman, Leopold/Lollipopman, 2 asst. 9396-3	Closed	1996	13.50	14-18
1994 Potter/Peppermint Make, Calvin/Candy Striper, 2 asst. 9397-1	Closed	1996	13.50	14-23
1993 Sinclair The Singer 9383-1	Closed	1996	13.50	19-28
1995 Stanislav The Skier 93977	Closed	1996	13.50	14-24
1995 Stuart The Skater 93978	Closed	1996	13.50	14-24
1992 Tolland The Toller 9369-6	Closed	1995	11.00	8-17

Miscellaneous Ornaments - Department 56

YEAR ISSUE	EDITION LIMIT	YEAR RETD.	ISSUE PRICE	*QUOTE U.S.$
1992 Silver/Gold Ice Skate Ornament 84255	Closed	1992	2.50	20
1983 Snow Village Wood Ornaments, set/6, 5099-7	Closed	1984	30.00	N/A
1983 • Carriage House	Closed	1984	5.00	20-40
1983 • Centennial House	Closed	1984	5.00	30-50
1983 • Countryside Church	Closed	1984	5.00	30-50
1983 • Gabled House	Closed	1984	5.00	50-75
1983 • Pioneer Church	Closed	1984	5.00	50-75
1983 • Swiss Chalet	Closed	1984	5.00	50-75
1984 Dickens 2-sided Tin Ornaments, set/6, 6522-6	Closed	1985	12.00	440
1984 • Abel Beesley Butcher	Closed	1985	2.00	55
1984 • Bean and Son Smithy Shop	Closed	1985	2.00	55
1984 • Crowntree Inn	Closed	1985	2.00	55
1984 • Golden Swan Baker	Closed	1985	2.00	55
1984 • Green Grocer	Closed	1985	2.00	55
1984 • Jones & Co. Brush & Basket Shop	Closed	1985	2.00	55
1986 Cherub on Brass Ribbon, 8248-1	Closed	1988	8.00	72-75
1986 Teddy Bear on Brass Ribbon 8263-5	Closed	1988	7.00	72-94
1988 Balsam Bell Brass Dickens' Candlestick 6244-8	Closed	1989	3.00	15
1988 Christmas Carol- Bob & Mrs. Cratchit 5914-5	Closed	1989	18.00	30-36
1988 Christmas Carol- Scrooge's Head 5912-9	Closed	1989	12.95	25-33
1988 Christmas Carol- Tiny Tim's Head 5913-7	Closed	1989	10.00	20-33

Silhouette Treasures (Winter Silhouette) - Department 56

YEAR ISSUE	EDITION LIMIT	YEAR RETD.	ISSUE PRICE	*QUOTE U.S.$
1995 Angel with Open Arms 78586	Closed	1998	25.00	25-40
1996 Cherub, large 85839	Closed	1998	16.50	17-30
1996 Cherub, small 85820	Closed	1998	8.50	9
1995 Chiming Bell Ornaments 78582, set/3	Closed	1998	36.00	18-36
1999 Christmas Angel 78634	Open		15.00	15
1999 Christmas Drummer 78632	Open		15.00	15
1999 Christmas Skater 78633	Open		15.00	15
1999 Clara & The Nutcracker 78631	Open		15.00	15

Snowbabies Bootiebaby Bisque Ornaments - Department 56

YEAR ISSUE	EDITION LIMIT	YEAR RETD.	ISSUE PRICE	*QUOTE U.S.$
1997 One, Two High Button Shoe 68844	Open		12.50	13
1997 Three, Four, No Room For One More 68845	Open		12.50	13
1998 Five, Six, A Drum With Sticks 68865	Open		13.50	14
1998 Seven, Eight, Time To Skate 68886	Open		12.50	13
1998 Nine, Ten, You're My Best Friend 68900	Open		12.50	13

Snowbabies Mercury Glass Ornaments - Department 56

YEAR ISSUE	EDITION LIMIT	YEAR RETD.	ISSUE PRICE	*QUOTE U.S.$
1997 Snowbaby Atop a Glittered Green Tree 68992	Closed	1998	22.50	23-30
1997 Snowbaby Atop a Glittered Silver Drum 68993	Closed	1998	22.50	23-30
1996 Snowbaby Drummer The Night Before Christmas 68983	Closed	1998	18.00	18-24
1996 Snowbaby in Package The Night Before Christmas 68986	Closed	1998	18.00	18-24
1996 Snowbaby Jinglebaby The Night Before Christmas 68989	Closed	1998	20.00	20-24
1996 Snowbaby on Moon The Night Before Christmas 68988	Closed	1998	18.00	18-24
1996 Snowbaby on Package The Night Before Christmas 68981	Closed	1998	18.00	18-24
1996 Snowbaby on Snowball The Night Before Christmas 68984	Closed	1998	20.00	20-69
1996 Snowbaby Soldier The Night Before Christmas 68982	Closed	1998	18.00	18-24
1996 Snowbaby With Bell The Night Before Christmas 68987	Closed	1998	18.00	18-24
1996 Snowbaby With Sisal Tree The Night Before Christmas 68990	Closed	1998	20.00	20-24
1996 Snowbaby With Star The Night Before Christmas 68991	Closed	1998	18.00	18-24
1996 Snowbaby With Wreath The Night Before Christmas 68980	Closed	1998	18.00	18-24

Snowbabies Miniature Ornaments - Department 56

YEAR ISSUE	EDITION LIMIT	YEAR RETD.	ISSUE PRICE	*QUOTE U.S.$
1999 Best Friends 69038	Open		12.50	13
1998 Celebrate 68902	Open		12.50	13
1998 Give Me A Push 68910	Open		12.50	13
1998 Give Someone A Hug 68905	Open		12.50	13
1998 I Love You 68901	Open		12.50	13
1998 I'll Read You A Story 68907	Open		12.50	13
1998 Let It Snow 68912	Open		12.50	13
1998 Let's Go Skiing 68911	Open		12.50	13
1998 My Gift To You 68909	Open		12.50	13
2000 Pretty As A Picture 69065	Open		12.50	13
1998 Rock-A-Bye-Baby 68908	Open		12.50	13
1998 Shall I Play For You? 68904	Open		12.50	13
1998 Starlight Serenade 68906	Open		12.50	13
1998 Sweet Dreams 68903	Open		12.50	13
1999 They Call Me Joyful 69037	Open		12.50	13
1998 Display Tree 68936	Open		30.00	30

Snowbabies Ornaments - Department 56

YEAR ISSUE	EDITION LIMIT	YEAR RETD.	ISSUE PRICE	*QUOTE U.S.$
1998 Baby's 1st Photo 68913	Open		7.50	9
1996 Baby's 1st Rattle 68828	Closed	1998	15.00	15-30
1994 Be My Baby 6866-7	Closed	1998	15.00	20-30
1998 Candle Light...Season Bright, Clip-On 68864	Open		13.50	14
1986 Crawling, Lite-Up, Clip-On, 7953-7	Closed	1992	7.00	18-35
1994 First Star Jinglebaby, 6858-6	Closed	1997	10.00	8-20
1998 Fly Me To The Moon 68885	Open		16.50	17
1998 Frosty Frolic Friends 68879 (1998 Winter Celebration Event Piece)	Closed	1998	15.00	15-30
1999 Frosty Frolic Friends (1999 Winter Celebration Event Piece) 68950	Closed	1999	15.00	15-27
2000 Frosty Frolic Friends (2000 Winter Celebration Event Piece) 69054	12/00		15.00	15
1994 Gathering Stars in the Sky, 6855-1	Closed	1997	12.50	20-25
1996 Jinglebell Jinglebaby 68826	Closed	1998	11.00	15-20
1995 Joy 68807, set/3	Closed	1999	32.50	33-35
1996 Joy to the World 68829	Closed	1998	16.50	17-25
1994 Juggling Stars in the Sky 6867-5	Closed	1998	15.00	20-30
1994 Just For You Jinglebaby 6869-1	Closed	1998	11.00	9-26
1994 Little Drummer Jinglebaby, 6859-4	Closed	1997	11.00	14-20
1987 Mini, Winged Pair, Lite-Up, Clip-On, 7976-6	Closed	1999	9.00	12
1987 Moon Beams, 7951-0	Closed	1999	7.50	10
1999 Moondreams & Hangin' On 69032	Open		15.00	15
1991 My First Star, 6811-0	Closed	1998	7.00	8-23
1989 Noel, 7988-0	Closed	1998	7.50	18-24
1995 One Little Candle Jinglebaby 68806	Closed	1998	11.00	11-26
1995 Overnight Delivery, 759-5 (Event Piece)	Closed	1995	10.00	35-40
1995 Overnight Delivery, 68808	Open		10.00	10
1990 Penguin, Lite-Up, Clip-On, 7940-5	Closed	1992	5.00	14-30
1990 Polar Bear, Lite-Up, Clip-On, 7941-3	Closed	1992	5.00	18-30
1998 Reach For The Moon 68914, set/2	Open		15.00	15
1990 Rock-A-Bye Baby, 7939-1	Closed	1995	7.00	10-27
1999 Royal Bootiebaby 68951	Open		13.50	14
1986 Sitting, Lite-Up, Clip-On, 7952-9	Closed	1990	7.00	34-58
2000 Sealed With A Kiss 69062	Open		13.50	14
1992 Snowbabies Icicle With Star, 6825-0	Closed	1995	16.00	18-34
1987 Snowbaby Adrift Lite-Up, Clip-On, 7969-3	Closed	1990	8.50	37-157
1996 Snowbaby in my Stocking 68827	Open		10.00	10
1986 Snowbaby on Brass Ribbon, 7961-8	Closed	1989	8.00	147-200
1993 Sprinkling Stars in the Sky, 6848-9	Closed	1997	12.50	15-25
1989 Star Bright, 7990-1	Closed	1999	7.50	9
1996 Starry Pine Jinglebaby 68825	Closed	1998	11.00	12-26
1992 Starry, Starry Night, 6830-6	Open		12.50	13
1994 Stars in My Stocking Jinglebaby 6868-3	Closed	1998	11.00	9-21
1989 Surprise, 7989-8	Closed	1994	12.00	14-42
1991 Swinging On a Star, 6810-1	Open		9.50	10
1988 Twinkle Little Star, 7980-4	Closed	1990	7.00	69-188
1993 Wee...This is Fun!, 6847-0	Closed	1997	13.50	15-20
1986 Winged, Lite-Up, Clip-On, 7954-5	Closed	1990	7.00	50-65

Snowbunnies Ornaments - Department 56

YEAR ISSUE	EDITION LIMIT	YEAR RETD.	ISSUE PRICE	*QUOTE U.S.$
2000 Mini Ornaments, 6 asst. 26335	Open		7.50	8
2000 Ornament Display Tree 26367	Open		25.00	25

Village Light-Up Ornaments - Department 56

YEAR ISSUE	EDITION LIMIT	YEAR RETD.	ISSUE PRICE	*QUOTE U.S.$
1987 Christmas Carol Cottages, set/3 (6513-7)	Closed	1989	17.00	30-72
1987 • The Cottage of Bob Cratchit & Tiny Tim	Closed	1989	6.00	10-30
1987 • Fezziwig's Warehouse	Closed	1989	6.00	10-30
1987 • Scrooge & Marley Countinghouse	Closed	1989	6.00	10-30
1987 Dickens' Village, set/14 (6521-8, 6520-0)	Closed	1989	84.00	400-495
1987 Dickens' Village, set/6 (6520-0)	Closed	1989	36.00	100-150
1987 • Barley Bree Farmhouse	Closed	1989	6.00	10-35
1987 • Blythe Pond Mill House	Closed	1989	6.00	25-40
1987 • Brick Abbey	Closed	1989	6.00	35-75
1987 • Chesterton Manor House	Closed	1989	6.00	35-56
1987 • Kenilworth Castle	Closed	1989	6.00	33-48
1987 • The Old Curiosity Shop	Closed	1989	6.00	32-50
1985 Dickens' Village, set/8 (6521-8)	Closed	1989	48.00	181-200
1985 • Abel Beesley Butcher	Closed	1989	6.00	10-25
1985 • Bean and Son Smithy Shop	Closed	1989	6.00	10-35
1985 • Candle Shop	Closed	1989	6.00	15-30
1985 • Crowntree Inn	Closed	1989	6.00	20-45
1985 • Dickens' Village Church	Closed	1989	6.00	48-50
1985 • Golden Swan Baker	Closed	1989	6.00	10-20
1985 • Green Grocer	Closed	1989	6.00	10-35
1985 • Jones & Co. Brush & Basket Shop	Closed	1989	6.00	20-35
1987 New England Village, set/13 (6533-1, 6534-0)	Closed	1989	78.00	700-750
1987 New England Village, set/6 (6534-0)	Closed	1989	36.00	200-275
1987 • Craggy Cove Lighthouse	Closed	1989	6.00	65-148

*Quotes have been rounded up to nearest dollar

YEAR ISSUE	EDITION LIMIT	YEAR RETD.	ISSUE PRICE	*QUOTE U.S.$
1987 • Jacob Adams Barn	Closed	1989	6.00	20-50
1987 • Jacob Adams Farmhouse	Closed	1989	6.00	20-50
1987 • Smythe Woolen Mill	Closed	1989	6.00	25-115
1987 • Timber Knoll Log Cabin	Closed	1989	6.00	25-105
1987 • Weston Train Station	Closed	1989	6.00	25-65
1986 New England Village, set/7 (6533-1)	Closed	1989	42.00	281-325
1986 • Apothecary Shop	Closed	1989	6.00	10-25
1986 • Brick Town Hall	Closed	1989	6.00	10-40
1986 • General Store	Closed	1989	6.00	10-45
1986 • Livery Stable & Boot Shop	Closed	1989	6.00	10-35
1986 • Nathaniel Bingham Fabrics	Closed	1989	6.00	10-35
1986 • Red Schoolhouse	Closed	1989	6.00	25-90
1986 • Steeple Church	Closed	1989	6.00	65-165

The Encore Group

Santa and Snow Buddies™ - Encore

YEAR ISSUE	EDITION LIMIT	YEAR RETD.	ISSUE PRICE	*QUOTE U.S.$
2000 Santa at Desk	Open		4.00	4
2000 Santa in Sleigh	Open		4.00	4
2000 Santa Skiing with Buddies on Back	Open		4.00	4

Snow Buddies™ - Encore

YEAR ISSUE	EDITION LIMIT	YEAR RETD.	ISSUE PRICE	*QUOTE U.S.$
2000 Blizzy with Box Car	Open		2.50	3
2000 Flurry with Engine	Open		2.50	3
2000 Holding Joy Sign	Open		2.50	3
2000 In Stocking	Open		2.50	3
2000 Knit Cap with 2000 Candy Cane	Yr.Iss.		2.50	3
2000 Knit Cap with 2000 Snowflake	Yr.Iss.		2.50	3
2000 On Candy Cane	Open		2.50	3
2000 Powder with Caboose	Open		2.50	3
1999 Powder with Harp	Retrd.	1999	2.50	3
1999 Powder with Sign	Retrd.	1999	2.50	3
1999 Powder with Tree	Retrd.	1999	2.50	3
1999 Santa & Powder Walking	Retrd.	1999	5.00	5
1999 Santa Holding Powder	Retrd.	1999	5.00	5
1999 Santa with Powder Sitting	Retrd.	1999	5.00	5
2000 Skatin'	Open		2.50	3
1999 The Skier	Open		2.50	3
2000 Sleddin'	Open		2.50	3
2000 Snowboardin'	Open		2.50	3
1999 Special Friend	Open		2.50	3
2000 Tobogganin'	Open		2.50	3
2000 Top Hat with 2000 Sign	Yr.Iss.		2.50	3
2000 Top Hat with 2000 Snowflake	Yr.Iss.		2.50	3

Snow Buddies™ Character Ornaments - Encore

YEAR ISSUE	EDITION LIMIT	YEAR RETD.	ISSUE PRICE	*QUOTE U.S.$
2000 Avalanche	Open		2.50	3
2000 Blizzy	Open		2.50	3
2000 Cousin Slick	Open		2.50	3
2000 Everest	Open		2.50	3
2000 Grandpa Frostbite	Open		2.50	3
2000 Uncle Melty	Open		2.50	3

Fenton Art Glass Company

Christmas Limited Edition - M. Reynolds

YEAR ISSUE	EDITION LIMIT	YEAR RETD.	ISSUE PRICE	*QUOTE U.S.$
1996 Golden Winged Angel, Hndpt. 3 1/2"	2,000	1996	27.50	28-45
1999 Angel, 4 1/2"	Closed	1999	49.00	49

Flambro Imports

Emmett Kelly Jr. Christmas Ornaments - Undisclosed

YEAR ISSUE	EDITION LIMIT	YEAR RETD.	ISSUE PRICE	*QUOTE U.S.$
1989 65th Birthday	Yr.Iss.	1989	24.00	200
1990 30 Years Of Clowning	Yr.Iss.	1990	30.00	75-160
1991 EKJ With Stocking And Toys	Yr.Iss.	1991	30.00	26-50
1992 Home For Christmas	Yr.Iss.	1992	24.00	30-75
1993 Christmas Mail	Yr.Iss.	1993	25.00	30-75
1994 '70 Birthday Commemorative	Yr.Iss.	1994	24.00	70-90
1995 20th Anniversary All Star Circus	Yr.Iss.	1995	25.00	50-70
1996 Christmas Pageant	Yr.Iss.	1996	29.00	75
1997 1997 Dated Ornament	Yr.Iss.	1997	30.00	30
1998 1998 Dated Ornament	Yr.Iss.	1998	20.00	20
1999 1999 Dated Ornament	Yr.Iss.	1999	35.00	35
2000 2000 Dated Ornament	Yr.Iss.		35.00	35

Little Emmett Ornaments - M. Wu

YEAR ISSUE	EDITION LIMIT	YEAR RETD.	ISSUE PRICE	*QUOTE U.S.$
1995 Little Emmett Christmas Wrap	Open		11.50	12
1995 Little Emmett Deck the Neck	Open		11.50	12
1996 Little Emmett Singing Carols	Open		13.00	13
1996 Little Emmett Your Present	Open		13.00	13
1996 Little Emmett Baby 1st Christmas	Open		13.00	13
1996 Little Emmett on Rocking Horse	Open		25.00	25

G. DeBrekht Artistic Studios/Russian Gift & Jewelry

Russkiye Bells - G. DeBrekht Artistic Studios

YEAR ISSUE	EDITION LIMIT	YEAR RETD.	ISSUE PRICE	*QUOTE U.S.$
1999 Angel	Open		19.50	20
1998 Girl	Open		19.50	20
1999 Santa	Open		19.50	20

Russkiye Fantasy and Fairytales - G. DeBrekht Artistic Studios

YEAR ISSUE	EDITION LIMIT	YEAR RETD.	ISSUE PRICE	*QUOTE U.S.$
1999 Fire Bird	Open		59.00	59
1999 Girl-Friends	Open		59.00	59
1999 Meeting	Open		59.00	59
1999 Snow Maiden EO/FT#4	Open		59.00	59
1999 Snow Maiden EO/FT#8	Open		59.00	59
1999 Tea Party	Open		59.00	59
1999 Troika	Open		59.00	59

Russkiye Flowers and Foliage - G. DeBrekht Artistic Studios

YEAR ISSUE	EDITION LIMIT	YEAR RETD.	ISSUE PRICE	*QUOTE U.S.$
1999 Flowers	Open		35.00	35

Russkiye Holiday Traditions - G. DeBrekht Artistic Studios

YEAR ISSUE	EDITION LIMIT	YEAR RETD.	ISSUE PRICE	*QUOTE U.S.$
1998 Boyar Ornament	Open		17.00	17
1998 Cat Fisherman	Open		20.00	20
1998 Czar	Open		39.00	39
1998 Knight"	Open		20.00	20
1998 Ladies #1	Open		20.00	20
1998 Ladies #2	Open		20.00	20
1998 Ladies #3	Open		30.00	30
1998 Ladies #3 with Icons	Open		30.00	30
1998 Peasant Man	Open		20.00	20
1998 Peasant Man Flat	Open		11.00	11
1998 Peasant Musical	Open		20.00	20
1998 Peasant Woman 5PW	Open		20.00	20
1998 Peasant Women 5PW/LE	Open		39.00	39
1998 Priest #3	Open		27.00	27
1998 Snow Maiden	Open		20.00	20
1998 Soldiers 5NS	Open		20.00	20
1998 Soldiers 5VK	Open		20.00	20

Russkiye Roly-Poly - G. DeBrekht Artistic Studios

YEAR ISSUE	EDITION LIMIT	YEAR RETD.	ISSUE PRICE	*QUOTE U.S.$
1998 Angel	Open		20.00	20
1998 Boy RO/B	Open		19.00	19
1998 Bunny	Open		19.00	19
1998 Czar & Czaritsa, set/2	Open		90.00	90
1998 Girl RB/G	Open		20.00	20
1998 Girl RO/G	Open		19.00	19
1998 Santa RB/S	Open		20.00	20
1998 Santa RO/S	Open		19.00	19
1998 Snowmen	Open		35.00	35

Russkiye Santa & Friends - G. DeBrekht Artistic Studios

YEAR ISSUE	EDITION LIMIT	YEAR RETD.	ISSUE PRICE	*QUOTE U.S.$
1998 Bear Ornament	Open		15.00	15
1998 Santa 6ST/2	Open		27.00	27
1998 Santa #1	Open		16.00	16
1998 Santa 6SES	Open		10.00	10
1998 Santa CO/ST	Open		25.00	25
1998 Santa Flat 6ST/F	Open		10.00	10
1998 Santa on Sleigh	Open		20.00	20
1998 Santa with Bag 6ST/3	Open		27.00	27
1998 Santa with Paintings	Open		35.00	35
1998 Santa with Tree	Open		25.00	25
1998 Santa-Bell	Open		15.00	15
1998 Snow Maiden 6SEM	Open		10.00	10
1998 Snow Maiden 6SM/LE	Open		35.00	35
1998 Snow Maiden Flat 6SM/F	Open		10.00	10
1998 Snowman 6SN/2	Open		20.00	20
1998 Snowman S/50MD	Open		50.00	50
1998 Snowman with Bell	Open		16.00	16

Gartlan USA

Jerry Garcia - S. Sun

YEAR ISSUE	EDITION LIMIT	YEAR RETD.	ISSUE PRICE	*QUOTE U.S.$
1997 Jerry Garcia	Yr.Iss.	1997	29.95	30-50

John Lennon - J. Lennon

YEAR ISSUE	EDITION LIMIT	YEAR RETD.	ISSUE PRICE	*QUOTE U.S.$
1997 John Lennon Christmas plate/ornament (3 1/4")	Open		16.95	17

Kiss - Various

YEAR ISSUE	EDITION LIMIT	YEAR RETD.	ISSUE PRICE	*QUOTE U.S.$
1998 Kiss Hanging Figurine - M. Pascucci	Yr.Iss.	1998	50.00	50
1998 Kiss-Mas Hand-Painted Ball - Chase	5,000		80.00	80

Ringo Starr - J. Hoffman

YEAR ISSUE	EDITION LIMIT	YEAR RETD.	ISSUE PRICE	*QUOTE U.S.$
1996 Ringo Starr	Yr.Iss.	1996	19.95	20-40

Geo. Zoltan Lefton Company

Colonial Village Ornaments - Lefton

YEAR ISSUE	EDITION LIMIT	YEAR RETD.	ISSUE PRICE	*QUOTE U.S.$
1987 Charity Chapel	Closed	1990	6.00	18
1987 Church of the Golden Rule	Closed	1990	6.00	18
1987 Lil Red School House	Closed	1990	6.00	18
1987 Nelson House	Closed	1990	6.00	18
1987 Old Stone Church	Closed	1990	6.00	18
1987 Penny House	Closed	1990	6.00	18

The German Doll Company

Kewpie - Staff

YEAR ISSUE	EDITION LIMIT	YEAR RETD.	ISSUE PRICE	*QUOTE U.S.$
1999 Drummer	200	1999	68.00	68

Goebel of North America

Angel Bell 3" - Goebel

YEAR ISSUE	EDITION LIMIT	YEAR RETD.	ISSUE PRICE	*QUOTE U.S.$
1994 Angel w/Clarinet - Red	Closed	1994	17.50	18
1995 Angel w/Harp - Blue	Closed	1995	17.50	18-20
1996 Angel w/Mandolin - Champagne	Closed	1996	18.00	18-20
1997 Angel w/Accordian - Rose	Closed	1997	18.00	18-20
1998 Angel w/Bell - Blue	Closed	1998	20.00	20
1999 Angel w/Violin - Green	Closed	1999	20.00	20

Angel Bells - 3 Asst. Colors - Goebel

YEAR ISSUE	EDITION LIMIT	YEAR RETD.	ISSUE PRICE	*QUOTE U.S.$
1976 Angel Bell w/Clarinet (3 colors)	Closed	1976	8.00	65
1976 Angel Bell w/Clarinet (white bisque)	Closed	1976	6.00	25-50
1977 Angel Bell w/Mandolin (3 colors)	Closed	1977	8.50	55-60
1977 Angel Bell w/Mandolin (white bisque)	Closed	1977	6.50	40-50
1978 Angel Bell w/Harp (3 colors)	Closed	1978	9.00	25-65
1978 Angel Bell w/Harp (white bisque)	Closed	1978	7.00	40-50
1979 Angel Bell w/Accordion (3 colors)	Closed	1979	9.50	55-65
1979 Angel Bell w/Accordion (white bisque)	Closed	1979	7.50	40-50
1980 Angel Bell w/Saxaphone (3 colors)	Closed	1980	10.00	55-65
1980 Angel Bell w/Saxaphone (white bisque)	Closed	1980	8.00	20-50
1981 Angel Bell w/Music (3 colors)	Closed	1981	11.00	55-65
1981 Angel Bell w/Music (white bisque)	Closed	1981	9.00	20-50
1982 Angel Bell w/French Horn (3 colors)	Closed	1982	11.75	55-65
1982 Angel Bell w/French Horn (white bisque)	Closed	1982	9.75	20-50
1983 Angel Bell w/Flute (3 colors)	Closed	1983	12.50	55-65
1983 Angel Bell w/Flute (white bisque)	Closed	1983	10.50	20-50
1984 Angel Bell w/Drum (3 colors)	Closed	1984	14.00	55-65
1984 Angel Bell w/Drum (white bisque)	Closed	1984	12.00	20-50
1985 Angel Bell w/Trumpet (3 colors)	Closed	1985	14.00	20-65
1985 Angel Bell w/Trumpet (white bisque)	Closed	1985	12.00	20-50
1986 Angel Bell w/Bells (3 colors)	Closed	1986	15.00	55-65
1986 Angel Bell w/Bells (white bisque)	Closed	1986	12.50	20-50
1987 Angel Bell w/Conductor (3 colors)	Closed	1987	16.50	55-65
1987 Angel Bell w/Conductor (white bisque)	Closed	1987	13.50	20-50
1988 Angel Bell w/Candle (3 colors)	Closed	1988	17.50	55-65
1988 Angel Bell w/Candle (white bisque)	Closed	1988	15.00	22-50
1989 Angel Bell w/Star (3 colors)	Closed	1989	20.00	55-65
1989 Angel Bell w/Star (white bisque)	Closed	1989	17.50	20-50
1990 Angel Bell w/Lantern (3 colors)	Closed	1990	22.50	55-65
1990 Angel Bell w/Lantern (white bisque)	Closed	1990	20.00	25-50
1991 Angel Bell w/Teddy (3 colors)	Closed	1991	25.00	55-65
1991 Angel Bell w/Teddy (white bisque)	Closed	1991	22.50	40-50
1992 Angel Bell w/Doll (3 colors)	Closed	1992	27.50	55-65
1992 Angel Bell w/Doll (white bisque)	Closed	1992	25.00	40-50
1993 Angel Bell w/Rocking Horse (3 colors)	Closed	1993	30.00	55-65
1993 Angel Bell w/Rocking Horse (white bisque)	Closed	1993	27.50	40-50
1994 Angel Bell w/Clown (3 colors)	Closed	1994	34.50	55-65
1994 Angel Bell w/Clown (white bisque)	Closed	1994	29.50	40-50
1995 Angel Bell w/Train (3 colors)	Closed	1995	37.00	55-65
1995 Angel Bell w/Train (white bisque)	Closed	1995	30.50	31-50
1996 Angel Bell w/Puppy (3 colors)	Closed	1996	40.00	55-65
1996 Angel Bell w/Puppy (white bisque)	Closed	1996	32.00	40-50
1997 Angel Bell w/Kitten (3 colors)	Closed	1997	42.50	55-65
1997 Angel Bell w/Kitten (white bisque)	Closed	1997	32.50	40-50
1998 Angel Bell w/Lamb (3 colors)	Closed	1998	45.00	55-65
1998 Angel Bell w/Lamb (white bisque)	Closed	1998	34.00	40-50
1999 Angel Bell w/Rabbit (3 colors)	Closed	1999	45.00	45
1999 Angel Bell w/Rabbit (white bisque)	Closed	1999	35.00	35

Goebel/M.I. Hummel

M.I. Hummel Annual Figurine Ornaments - M.I. Hummel

YEAR ISSUE	EDITION LIMIT	YEAR RETD.	ISSUE PRICE	*QUOTE U.S.$
1988 Flying High 452	Closed	N/A	75.00	104-300
1989 Love From Above 481	Closed	N/A	75.00	120-156
1990 Peace on Earth 484	Closed	N/A	80.00	65-155
1991 Angelic Guide 571	Closed	N/A	95.00	125-155
1992 Light Up The Night 622	Closed	N/A	100.00	75-155
1993 Herald on High 623	Closed	N/A	155.00	150-200
1997 Boy with Horse 239/C/O	Open		60.00	65-68
1997 Girl with Nosegay 239/A/O	Open		60.00	65-68
1997 Girl with Doll 239/B/O	Open		60.00	65-68
1997 Girl with Fir Tree 239/D/O	10,000		60.00	65-68

M.I. Hummel Collectibles Christmas Bell Ornaments - M.I. Hummel

YEAR ISSUE	EDITION LIMIT	YEAR RETD.	ISSUE PRICE	*QUOTE U.S.$
1989 Ride Into Christmas 775	Closed	1989	35.00	60-195
1990 Letter to Santa Claus 776	Closed	1990	37.50	70-100
1991 Hear Ye, Hear Ye 777	Closed	1991	40.00	60-100
1992 Harmony in Four Parts 778	Closed	1992	50.00	70-80
1993 Celestial Musician 779	Closed	1993	50.00	50-70
1994 Festival Harmony w/Mandolin 780	Closed	1994	50.00	60-70
1995 Festival Harmony w/Flute 781	Closed	1995	55.00	55-70
1996 Christmas Song 782	Closed	1996	65.00	70-75
1997 Thanksgiving Prayer 783	Closed	1997	68.00	70-139
1998 Echoes of Joy 784	Yr.Iss.	1998	70.00	70
1999 Joyful Noise 785	Yr.Iss.	1999	70.00	70
2000 Light The Way 786	Yr.Iss.		70.00	70

M.I. Hummel Collectibles Miniature Ornaments - M.I. Hummel

YEAR ISSUE	EDITION LIMIT	YEAR RETD.	ISSUE PRICE	*QUOTE U.S.$
1993 Celestial Musician 646	Closed	1993	90.00	130
1994 Festival Harmony w/Mandolin 647	Closed	1994	95.00	120-125
1995 Festival Harmony w/Flute 648	Closed	1995	100.00	130
1996 Christmas Song 645	Closed	1996	115.00	130
1997 Thanksgiving Prayer 642	Closed	1997	120.00	130
1998 Echoes of Joy 597	Yr.Iss.	1998	120.00	120-125
1999 Joyful Noise 598	Yr.Iss.	1999	120.00	124
2000 Light The Way 599	Yr.Iss.		120.00	120

Gorham

Annual Crystal Ornaments - Gorham

YEAR ISSUE	EDITION LIMIT	YEAR RETD.	ISSUE PRICE	*QUOTE U.S.$
1985 Crystal Ornament	Closed	1985	22.00	25
1986 Crystal Ornament	Closed	1986	25.00	25
1987 Crystal Ornament	Closed	1987	25.00	25
1988 Crystal Ornament	Closed	1988	28.00	28
1989 Crystal Ornament	Closed	1989	28.00	28
1990 Crystal Ornament	Closed	1990	30.00	30
1991 Crystal Ornament	Closed	1991	35.00	35
1992 Crystal Ornament	Closed	1992	32.50	33
1993 Crystal Ornament	Closed	1993	32.50	33

Annual Snowflake Ornaments - Gorham

YEAR ISSUE	EDITION LIMIT	YEAR RETD.	ISSUE PRICE	*QUOTE U.S.$
1970 Sterling Snowflake	Closed	1970	10.00	240-275
1971 Sterling Snowflake	Closed	1971	10.00	55-108
1972 Sterling Snowflake	Closed	1972	10.00	55-175
1973 Sterling Snowflake	Closed	1973	11.00	46-65
1974 Sterling Snowflake	Closed	1974	18.00	65-100
1975 Sterling Snowflake	Closed	1975	18.00	50-100
1976 Sterling Snowflake	Closed	1976	20.00	95-120
1977 Sterling Snowflake	Closed	1977	23.00	50-95
1978 Sterling Snowflake	Closed	1978	23.00	50-95
1979 Sterling Snowflake	Closed	1979	33.00	80-120

*Quotes have been rounded up to nearest dollar

YEAR ISSUE	EDITION LIMIT	YEAR RETD.	ISSUE PRICE	*QUOTE U.S.$
1980 Silverplated Snowflake	Closed	1980	15.00	150-240
1981 Sterling Snowflake	Closed	1981	50.00	90-125
1982 Sterling Snowflake	Closed	1982	38.00	60-90
1983 Sterling Snowflake	Closed	1983	45.00	90-110
1984 Sterling Snowflake	Closed	1984	45.00	90-110
1985 Sterling Snowflake	Closed	1985	45.00	75-100
1986 Sterling Snowflake	Closed	1986	45.00	70-80
1987 Sterling Snowflake	Closed	1987	50.00	60-90
1988 Sterling Snowflake	Closed	1988	50.00	60-65
1989 Sterling Snowflake	Closed	1989	50.00	40-65
1990 Sterling Snowflake	Closed	1990	50.00	60-80
1991 Sterling Snowflake	Closed	1991	55.00	46-75
1992 Sterling Snowflake	Closed	1992	50.00	50-75
1993 Sterling Snowflake	Closed	1993	50.00	60
1994 Sterling Snowflake	Closed	1994	50.00	50-70
1995 Sterling Snowflake	Closed	1995	50.00	50-65
1996 Sterling Snowflake	Closed	1995	50.00	50-55

Archive Collectible - Gorham

YEAR ISSUE	EDITION LIMIT	YEAR RETD.	ISSUE PRICE	*QUOTE U.S.$
1988 Victorian Heart	Closed	1988	50.00	60-75
1989 Victorian Wreath	Closed	1989	50.00	45-50
1990 Elizabethan Cupid	Closed	1990	60.00	45-60
1991 Baroque Angels	Closed	1991	55.00	45-55
1992 Madonna and Child	Closed	1992	50.00	40-50
1993 Angel With Mandolin	Closed	1993	50.00	45-50

Baby's First Christmas Crystal - Gorham

YEAR ISSUE	EDITION LIMIT	YEAR RETD.	ISSUE PRICE	*QUOTE U.S.$
1991 Baby's First Rocking Horse	Closed	1994	35.00	35

Greenwich Workshop

The Greenwich Workshop Collection - J. Christensen

YEAR ISSUE	EDITION LIMIT	YEAR RETD.	ISSUE PRICE	*QUOTE U.S.$
1995 The Angel's Gift	Yr.Iss.	1995	50.00	95
1996 A Gift of Light	7,500	1996	75.00	75
1997 A Gift of Music	7,500	1997	75.00	75

Pearl Bisque™ - Various

YEAR ISSUE	EDITION LIMIT	YEAR RETD.	ISSUE PRICE	*QUOTE U.S.$
2000 Ancient Angel - J. Christensen	Open		7.50	8
2000 bearing gifts - W. Bullas	Open		6.25	7
2000 The Christmas Angel - J. Christensen	Open		7.50	8
2000 duck tape - W. Bullas	Open		6.25	7
2000 The Fish Walker - J. Christensen	Open		7.50	8
2000 the fool - W. Bullas	Open		6.25	7
2000 The Forest Fishrider - J. Christensen	Open		7.50	8
2000 jingle this - W. Bullas	Open		6.25	7
2000 The Lute Player - J. Christensen	Open		7.50	8
2000 mistle toad - W. Bullas	Open		6.25	7
2000 Olde World Santa - J. Christensen	Open		7.50	8
2000 snow bunny - W. Bullas	Open		6.25	7

Hallmark Galleries

Enchanted Garden - E. Richardson

YEAR ISSUE	EDITION LIMIT	YEAR RETD.	ISSUE PRICE	*QUOTE U.S.$
1992 Neighborhood Dreamer 1500QHG3014	19,500	1994	15.00	15

Hallmark Keepsake Ornaments

1973 Hallmark Keepsake Bell Ornaments - Keepsake

YEAR ISSUE	EDITION LIMIT	YEAR RETD.	ISSUE PRICE	*QUOTE U.S.$
1973 Betsey Clark (1st Ed.) XHD110-2	Yr.Iss.	1973	2.50	61-112
1973 Betsey Clark XHD100-2	Yr.Iss.	1973	2.50	77-85
1973 Christmas Is Love XHD106-2	Yr.Iss.	1973	2.50	64-80
1973 Elves XHD103-5	Yr.Iss.	1973	2.50	60-99
1973 Manger Scene XHD102-2	Yr.Iss.	1973	2.50	95-120
1973 Santa with Elves XHD101-5	Yr.Iss.	1973	2.50	68-85

1973 Keepsake Yarn Ornaments - Keepsake

YEAR ISSUE	EDITION LIMIT	YEAR RETD.	ISSUE PRICE	*QUOTE U.S.$
1973 Angel XHD78-5	Yr.Iss.	1973	1.25	15-23
1973 Blue Girl XHD85-2	Yr.Iss.	1973	1.25	15-23
1973 Boy Caroler XHD83-2	Yr.Iss.	1973	1.25	24-30
1973 Choir Boy XHD80-5	Yr.Iss.	1973	1.25	17-28
1973 Elf XHD79-2	Yr.Iss.	1973	1.25	15-25
1973 Green Girl XHD84-5	Yr.Iss.	1973	1.25	15-21
1973 Little Girl XHD82-5	Yr.Iss.	1973	1.25	15-25
1973 Mr. Santa XHD74-5	Yr.Iss.	1973	1.25	15-25
1973 Mr. Snowman XHD76-5	Yr.Iss.	1973	1.25	15-25
1973 Mrs. Santa XHD75-2	Yr.Iss.	1973	1.25	15-25
1973 Mrs. Snowman XHD77-2	Yr.Iss.	1973	1.25	15-23
1973 Soldier XHD81-2	Yr.Iss.	1973	1.00	15-24

1974 Hallmark Keepsake Bell Ornaments - Keepsake

YEAR ISSUE	EDITION LIMIT	YEAR RETD.	ISSUE PRICE	*QUOTE U.S.$
1974 Angel QX110 -1	Yr.Iss.	1974	2.50	28-75
1974 Betsey Clark (2nd Ed.) QX108-1	Yr.Iss.	1974	2.50	47-85
1974 Buttons & Bo (Set/2) QX113-1	Yr.Iss.	1974	3.50	40-50
1974 Charmers QX109-1	Yr.Iss.	1974	2.50	26-45
1974 Currier & Ives (Set/2) QX112-1	Yr.Iss.	1974	3.50	43-55
1974 Little Miracles (Set/4) QX115-1	Yr.Iss.	1974	4.50	44-55
1974 Norman Rockwell QX106-1	Yr.Iss.	1974	2.50	46-95
1974 Norman Rockwell QX111-1	Yr.Iss.	1974	2.50	68-95
1974 Raggedy Ann and Andy(4/set) QX114-1	Yr.Iss.	1974	4.50	60-75
1974 Snowgoose QX107-1	Yr.Iss.	1974	2.50	50-75

1974 Keepsake Yarn Ornaments - Keepsake

YEAR ISSUE	EDITION LIMIT	YEAR RETD.	ISSUE PRICE	*QUOTE U.S.$
1974 Angel QX103-1	Yr.Iss.	1974	1.50	17-28
1974 Elf QX101-1	Yr.Iss.	1974	1.50	15-23
1974 Mrs. Santa QX100-1	Yr.Iss.	1974	1.50	15-25
1974 Santa QX105-1	Yr.Iss.	1974	1.50	15-25
1974 Snowman QX104-1	Yr.Iss.	1974	1.50	15-23
1974 Soldier QX102-1	Yr.Iss.	1974	1.50	15-23

1975 Handcrafted Ornaments: Adorable - Keepsake

YEAR ISSUE	EDITION LIMIT	YEAR RETD.	ISSUE PRICE	*QUOTE U.S.$
1975 Betsey Clark QX157-1	Yr.Iss.	1975	2.50	180-225
1975 Drummer Boy QX161-1	Yr.Iss.	1975	2.50	180-300
1975 Mrs. Santa QX156-1	Yr.Iss.	1975	2.50	220-275
1975 Raggedy Andy QX160-1	Yr.Iss.	1975	2.50	300-375
1975 Raggedy Ann QX159-1	Yr.Iss.	1975	2.50	236-295
1975 Santa QX155-1	Yr.Iss.	1975	2.50	200-250

1975 Handcrafted Ornaments: Nostalgia - Keepsake

YEAR ISSUE	EDITION LIMIT	YEAR RETD.	ISSUE PRICE	*QUOTE U.S.$
1975 Drummer Boy QX130-1	Yr.Iss.	1975	3.50	92-175
1975 Joy QX132-1	Yr.Iss.	1975	3.50	100-150
1975 Locomotive (dated) QX127-1	Yr.Iss.	1975	3.50	100-175
1975 Peace on Earth (dated) QX131-1	Yr.Iss.	1975	3.50	80-165
1975 Rocking Horse QX128-1	Yr.Iss.	1975	3.50	100-175
1975 Santa & Sleigh QX129-1	Yr.Iss.	1975	3.50	100-125

1975 Keepsake Property Ornaments - Keepsake

YEAR ISSUE	EDITION LIMIT	YEAR RETD.	ISSUE PRICE	*QUOTE U.S.$
1975 Betsey Clark (3rd Ed.) QX133-1	Yr.Iss.	1975	3.00	31-75
1975 Betsey Clark (Set/2) QX167-1	Yr.Iss.	1975	3.50	25-45
1975 Betsey Clark (Set/4) QX168-1	Yr.Iss.	1975	4.50	14-50
1975 Betsey Clark QX163-1	Yr.Iss.	1975	2.50	32-43
1975 Buttons & Bo (Set/4) QX139-1	Yr.Iss.	1975	5.00	40-50
1975 Charmers QX135-1	Yr.Iss.	1975	3.00	24-31
1975 Currier & Ives (Set/2) QX137-1	Yr.Iss.	1975	4.00	32-40
1975 Currier & Ives (Set/2) QX164-1	Yr.Iss.	1975	2.50	28-55
1975 Little Miracles (Set/4) QX140-1	Yr.Iss.	1975	5.00	32-40
1975 Marty Links QX136-1	Yr.Iss.	1975	3.00	48-60
1975 Norman Rockwell QX134-1	Yr.Iss.	1975	3.00	38
1975 Norman Rockwell QX166-1	Yr.Iss.	1975	2.50	45-55
1975 Raggedy Ann and Andy(2/set) QX138-1	Yr.Iss.	1975	4.00	52-65
1975 Raggedy Ann QX165-1	Yr.Iss.	1975	2.50	50-65

1975 Keepsake Yarn Ornaments - Keepsake

YEAR ISSUE	EDITION LIMIT	YEAR RETD.	ISSUE PRICE	*QUOTE U.S.$
1975 Drummer Boy QX123-1	Yr.Iss.	1975	1.75	14-25
1975 Little Girl QX126-1	Yr.Iss.	1975	1.75	14-23
1975 Mrs. Santa QX125-1	Yr.Iss.	1975	1.75	15-22
1975 Raggedy Andy QX122-1	Yr.Iss.	1975	1.75	21-57
1975 Raggedy Ann QX121-1	Yr.Iss.	1975	1.75	18-55
1975 Santa QX124-1	Yr.Iss.	1975	1.75	15-25

1976 Bicentennial Commemoratives - Keepsake

YEAR ISSUE	EDITION LIMIT	YEAR RETD.	ISSUE PRICE	*QUOTE U.S.$
1976 Bicentennial '76 Commemorative QX211-1	Yr.Iss.	1976	2.50	54-60
1976 Bicentennial Charmers QX198-1	Yr.Iss.	1976	3.00	60-95
1976 Colonial Children (Set/2) 4 QX208-1	Yr.Iss.	1976	4.00	52-95

1976 Decorative Ball Ornaments - Keepsake

YEAR ISSUE	EDITION LIMIT	YEAR RETD.	ISSUE PRICE	*QUOTE U.S.$
1976 Cardinals QX205-1	Yr.Iss.	1976	2.30	36-85
1976 Chickadees QX204-1	Yr.Iss.	1976	2.30	40-65

1976 First Commemorative Ornament - Keepsake

YEAR ISSUE	EDITION LIMIT	YEAR RETD.	ISSUE PRICE	*QUOTE U.S.$
1976 Baby's First Christmas QX211-1	Yr.Iss.	1976	2.50	120-150

1976 Handcrafted Ornaments: Nostalgia - Keepsake

YEAR ISSUE	EDITION LIMIT	YEAR RETD.	ISSUE PRICE	*QUOTE U.S.$
1976 Drummer Boy QX130-1	Yr.Iss.	1976	3.50	128-175
1976 Locomotive QX222-1	Yr.Iss.	1976	3.50	160
1976 Peace on Earth QX223-1	Yr.Iss.	1976	3.50	76-175
1976 Rocking Horse QX128-1	Yr.Iss.	1976	3.50	132-165

1976 Handcrafted Ornaments: Tree Treats - Keepsake

YEAR ISSUE	EDITION LIMIT	YEAR RETD.	ISSUE PRICE	*QUOTE U.S.$
1976 Angel QX176-1	Yr.Iss.	1976	3.00	120-195
1976 Reindeer QX 178-1	Yr.Iss.	1976	3.00	92-115
1976 Santa QX177-1	Yr.Iss.	1976	3.00	156-275
1976 Shepherd QX175-1	Yr.Iss.	1976	3.00	115-125

1976 Handcrafted Ornaments: Twirl-Abouts - Keepsake

YEAR ISSUE	EDITION LIMIT	YEAR RETD.	ISSUE PRICE	*QUOTE U.S.$
1976 Angel QX171-1	Yr.Iss.	1976	4.50	117-136
1976 Partridge QX174-1	Yr.Iss.	1976	4.50	156-195
1976 Santa QX172-1	Yr.Iss.	1976	4.50	80-103
1976 Soldier QX173-1	Yr.Iss.	1976	4.50	79-95

1976 Handcrafted Ornaments: Yesteryears - Keepsake

YEAR ISSUE	EDITION LIMIT	YEAR RETD.	ISSUE PRICE	*QUOTE U.S.$
1976 Drummer Boy QX184-1	Yr.Iss.	1976	5.00	98-121
1976 Partridge QX183-1	Yr.Iss.	1976	5.00	83-115
1976 Santa QX182-1	Yr.Iss.	1976	5.00	77-165
1976 Train QX181-1	Yr.Iss.	1976	5.00	100-160

1976 Property Ornaments - Keepsake

YEAR ISSUE	EDITION LIMIT	YEAR RETD.	ISSUE PRICE	*QUOTE U.S.$
1976 Betsey Clark (4th Ed.) QX195-1	Yr.Iss.	1976	3.00	36-125
1976 Betsey Clark (Set/3) QX218-1	Yr.Iss.	1976	4.50	45-65
1976 Betsey Clark QX210-1	Yr.Iss.	1976	2.50	30-68
1976 Charmers (Set/2) QX215-1	Yr.Iss.	1976	3.50	52-95
1976 Currier & Ives QX197-1	Yr.Iss.	1976	3.00	40-50
1976 Currier & Ives QX209-1	Yr.Iss.	1976	2.50	40-50
1976 Happy the Snowman (Set/2) QX216-1	Yr.Iss.	1976	3.50	44-55
1976 Marty Links (Set/2) QX207-1	Yr.Iss.	1976	4.00	36-65
1976 Norman Rockwell QX196-1	Yr.Iss.	1976	3.00	28-85
1976 Raggedy Ann QX212-1	Yr.Iss.	1976	2.50	52-65
1976 Rudolph and Santa QX213-1	Yr.Iss.	1976	2.50	60-95

1976 Yarn Ornaments - Keepsake

YEAR ISSUE	EDITION LIMIT	YEAR RETD.	ISSUE PRICE	*QUOTE U.S.$
1976 Caroler QX126-1	Yr.Iss.	1976	1.75	17-28
1976 Drummer Boy QX123-1	Yr.Iss.	1976	1.75	15-23
1976 Mrs. Santa QX125-1	Yr.Iss.	1976	1.75	15-22
1976 Raggedy Andy QX122-1	Yr.Iss.	1976	1.75	25-40
1976 Raggedy Ann QX121-1	Yr.Iss.	1976	1.75	22-35
1976 Santa QX124-1	Yr.Iss.	1976	1.75	16-24

1977 Christmas Expressions Collection - Keepsake

YEAR ISSUE	EDITION LIMIT	YEAR RETD.	ISSUE PRICE	*QUOTE U.S.$
1977 Bell QX154-2	Yr.Iss.	1977	3.50	28-35
1977 Mandolin QX157-5	Yr.Iss.	1977	3.50	52-65
1977 Ornaments QX155-5	Yr.Iss.	1977	3.50	52-65
1977 Wreath QX156-2	Yr.Iss.	1977	3.50	52-65

1977 Cloth Doll Ornaments - Keepsake

YEAR ISSUE	EDITION LIMIT	YEAR RETD.	ISSUE PRICE	*QUOTE U.S.$
1977 Angel QX220-2	Yr.Iss.	1977	1.75	32-50
1977 Santa QX221-5	Yr.Iss.	1977	1.75	40-80

1977 Colors of Christmas - Keepsake

YEAR ISSUE	EDITION LIMIT	YEAR RETD.	ISSUE PRICE	*QUOTE U.S.$
1977 Bell QX200-2	Yr.Iss.	1977	3.50	36-45
1977 Candle QX203-5	Yr.Iss.	1977	3.50	44-55
1977 Joy QX201-5	Yr.Iss.	1977	3.50	36-45
1977 Wreath QX202-2	Yr.Iss.	1977	3.50	36-65

1977 Commemoratives - Keepsake

YEAR ISSUE	EDITION LIMIT	YEAR RETD.	ISSUE PRICE	*QUOTE U.S.$
1977 Baby's First Christmas QX131-5	Yr.Iss.	1977	3.50	59-75
1977 First Christmas Together QX132-2	Yr.Iss.	1977	3.50	22-45
1977 For Your New Home QX263-5	Yr.Iss.	1977	3.50	96-120
1977 Granddaughter QX208-2	Yr.Iss.	1977	3.50	120-150
1977 Grandmother QX260-2	Yr.Iss.	1977	3.50	120-150
1977 Grandson QX209-5	Yr.Iss.	1977	3.50	120-150
1977 Love QX262-2	Yr.Iss.	1977	3.50	76-95
1977 Mother QX261-5	Yr.Iss.	1977	3.50	60-75

1977 Decorative Ball Ornaments - Keepsake

YEAR ISSUE	EDITION LIMIT	YEAR RETD.	ISSUE PRICE	*QUOTE U.S.$
1977 Christmas Mouse QX134-2	Yr.Iss.	1977	3.50	52-65
1977 Rabbit QX139-5	Yr.Iss.	1977	2.50	76-95
1977 Squirrel QX138-2	Yr.Iss.	1977	2.50	76-95
1977 Stained Glass QX152-2	Yr.Iss.	1977	3.50	32-70

1977 Holiday Highlights - Keepsake

YEAR ISSUE	EDITION LIMIT	YEAR RETD.	ISSUE PRICE	*QUOTE U.S.$
1977 Drummer Boy QX312-2	Yr.Iss.	1977	3.50	30-65
1977 Joy QX310-2	Yr.Iss.	1977	3.50	36-45
1977 Peace on Earth QX311-5	Yr.Iss.	1977	3.50	52-65
1977 Star QX313-5	Yr.Iss.	1977	3.50	40-50

1977 Metal Ornaments - Keepsake

YEAR ISSUE	EDITION LIMIT	YEAR RETD.	ISSUE PRICE	*QUOTE U.S.$
1977 Snowflake Collection (Set/4) QX210-2	Yr.Iss.	1977	5.00	76-95

1977 Nostalgia Collection - Keepsake

YEAR ISSUE	EDITION LIMIT	YEAR RETD.	ISSUE PRICE	*QUOTE U.S.$
1977 Angel QX182-2	Yr.Iss.	1977	5.00	72-125
1977 Antique Car QX180-2	Yr.Iss.	1977	5.00	50-65
1977 Nativity QX181-5	Yr.Iss.	1977	5.00	108-165
1977 Toys QX183-5	Yr.Iss.	1977	5.00	112-155

1977 Peanuts Collection - Keepsake

YEAR ISSUE	EDITION LIMIT	YEAR RETD.	ISSUE PRICE	*QUOTE U.S.$
1977 Peanuts (Set/2) QX163-5	Yr.Iss.	1977	4.00	75
1977 Peanuts QX135-5	Yr.Iss.	1977	3.50	60
1977 Peanuts QX162-2	Yr.Iss.	1977	2.50	60

1977 Property Ornaments - Keepsake

YEAR ISSUE	EDITION LIMIT	YEAR RETD.	ISSUE PRICE	*QUOTE U.S.$
1977 Betsey Clark (5th Ed.) QX264-2	Yr.Iss.	1977	3.50	350-460
1977 Charmers QX153-5	Yr.Iss.	1977	3.50	50-65
1977 Currier & Ives QX130-2	Yr.Iss.	1977	3.50	55
1977 Disney (Set/2) QX137-5	Yr.Iss.	1977	4.00	75
1977 Disney QX133-5	Yr.Iss.	1977	3.50	45-75
1977 Grandma Moses QX150-2	Yr.Iss.	1977	3.50	100-175
1977 Norman Rockwell QX151-5	Yr.Iss.	1977	3.50	35-70

1977 The Beauty of America Collection - Keepsake

YEAR ISSUE	EDITION LIMIT	YEAR RETD.	ISSUE PRICE	*QUOTE U.S.$
1977 Desert QX159-5	Yr.Iss.	1977	2.50	20-25
1977 Mountains QX158-2	Yr.Iss.	1977	2.50	12-15
1977 Seashore QX160-2	Yr.Iss.	1977	2.50	40-50
1977 Wharf QX161-5	Yr.Iss.	1977	2.50	24-50

1977 Twirl-About Collection - Keepsake

YEAR ISSUE	EDITION LIMIT	YEAR RETD.	ISSUE PRICE	*QUOTE U.S.$
1977 Bellringer QX192-2	Yr.Iss.	1977	6.00	45-55
1977 Della Robia Wreath QX193-5	Yr.Iss.	1977	4.50	93-125
1977 Snowman QX190-2	Yr.Iss.	1977	4.50	50-75
1977 Weather House QX191-5	Yr.Iss.	1977	6.00	86-95

1977 Yesteryears Collection - Keepsake

YEAR ISSUE	EDITION LIMIT	YEAR RETD.	ISSUE PRICE	*QUOTE U.S.$
1977 Angel QX172-2	Yr.Iss.	1977	6.00	85-135
1977 House QX170-2	Yr.Iss.	1977	6.00	100-125
1977 Jack-in-the-Box QX171-5	Yr.Iss.	1977	6.00	100-125
1977 Reindeer QX173-5	Yr.Iss.	1977	6.00	106-140

1978 Colors of Christmas - Keepsake

YEAR ISSUE	EDITION LIMIT	YEAR RETD.	ISSUE PRICE	*QUOTE U.S.$
1978 Angel QX354-3	Yr.Iss.	1978	3.50	32-43
1978 Candle QX357-6	Yr.Iss.	1978	3.50	68-85
1978 Locomotive QX356-3	Yr.Iss.	1978	3.50	40-60
1978 Merry Christmas QX355-6	Yr.Iss.	1978	3.50	40-50

1978 Commemoratives - Keepsake

YEAR ISSUE	EDITION LIMIT	YEAR RETD.	ISSUE PRICE	*QUOTE U.S.$
1978 25th Christmas Together QX269-3	Yr.Iss.	1978	3.50	28-35
1978 Baby's First Christmas QX200-3	Yr.Iss.	1978	3.50	52-85
1978 First Christmas Together QX218-3	Yr.Iss.	1978	3.50	36-55
1978 For Your New Home QX217-6	Yr.Iss.	1978	3.50	60-75
1978 Granddaughter QX216-3	Yr.Iss.	1978	3.50	44-55
1978 Grandmother QX267-6	Yr.Iss.	1978	3.50	40-50
1978 Grandson QX215-6	Yr.Iss.	1978	3.50	36-45
1978 Love QX268-3	Yr.Iss.	1978	3.50	44-55
1978 Mother QX266-3	Yr.Iss.	1978	3.50	20-40

1978 Decorative Ball Ornaments - Keepsake

YEAR ISSUE	EDITION LIMIT	YEAR RETD.	ISSUE PRICE	*QUOTE U.S.$
1978 Drummer Boy QX252-3	Yr.Iss.	1978	3.50	28-65
1978 Hallmark's Antique Card Collection Design QX220-3	Yr.Iss.	1978	3.50	32-40
1978 Joy QX254-3	Yr.Iss.	1978	3.50	24-45
1978 Merry Christmas (Santa) QX202-3	Yr.Iss.	1978	3.50	36-55
1978 Nativity QX253-6	Yr.Iss.	1978	3.50	36-150
1978 The Quail QX251-6	Yr.Iss.	1978	3.50	45
1978 Yesterday's Toys QX250-3	Yr.Iss.	1978	3.50	44-55

1978 Handcrafted Ornaments - Keepsake

YEAR ISSUE	EDITION LIMIT	YEAR RETD.	ISSUE PRICE	*QUOTE U.S.$
1978 Angel QX139-6	Yr.Iss.	1981	4.50	68-95
1978 Angels QX150-3	Yr.Iss.	1978	8.00	276-345
1978 Animal Home QX149-6	Yr.Iss.	1978	6.00	113-175
1978 Calico Mouse QX137-6	Yr.Iss.	1978	4.50	120-150
1978 Carrousel Series (1st Ed.) QX146-3	Yr.Iss.	1978	6.00	150-225
1978 Dough Angel QX139-6	Yr.Iss.	1981	5.50	52-95
1978 Dove QX190-3	Yr.Iss.	1978	4.50	62-85

ORNAMENTS

YEAR ISSUE	EDITION LIMIT	YEAR RETD.	ISSUE PRICE	*QUOTE U.S.$
1978 Holly and Poinsettia Ball QX147-6	Yr.Iss.	1978	6.00	68-85
1978 Joy QX138-3	Yr.Iss.	1978	4.50	73-85
1978 Panorama Ball QX145-6	Yr.Iss.	1978	6.00	108-135
1978 Red Cardinal QX144-3	Yr.Iss.	1978	4.50	122-175
1978 Rocking Horse QX148-3	Yr.Iss.	1978	6.00	68-85
1978 Schneeberg Bell QX152-3	Yr.Iss.	1978	8.00	120-190
1978 Skating Raccoon QX142-3	Yr.Iss.	1978	6.00	70-95

1978 Holiday Chimes - Keepsake

YEAR ISSUE	EDITION LIMIT	YEAR RETD.	ISSUE PRICE	*QUOTE U.S.$
1978 Reindeer Chimes QX320-3	Yr.Iss.	1980	4.50	48-60

1978 Holiday Highlights - Keepsake

YEAR ISSUE	EDITION LIMIT	YEAR RETD.	ISSUE PRICE	*QUOTE U.S.$
1978 Dove QX310-3	Yr.Iss.	1978	3.50	77-100
1978 Nativity QX309-6	Yr.Iss.	1978	3.50	28-70
1978 Santa QX307-6	Yr.Iss.	1978	3.50	60-90
1978 Snowflake QX308-3	Yr.Iss.	1978	3.50	52-65

1978 Little Trimmers - Keepsake

YEAR ISSUE	EDITION LIMIT	YEAR RETD.	ISSUE PRICE	*QUOTE U.S.$
1978 Drummer Boy QX136-3	Yr.Iss.	1978	2.50	55-59
1978 Praying Angel QX134-3	Yr.Iss.	1978	2.50	90
1978 Santa QX135-6	Yr.Iss.	1978	2.50	50-59
1978 Set/4 - QX355-6	Yr.Iss.	1978	10.00	400-425
1978 Thimble Series (Mouse) (1st Ed.) QX133-6	Yr.Iss.	1978	2.50	268-295

1978 Peanuts Collection - Keepsake

YEAR ISSUE	EDITION LIMIT	YEAR RETD.	ISSUE PRICE	*QUOTE U.S.$
1978 Peanuts QX203-6	Yr.Iss.	1978	2.50	50
1978 Peanuts QX204-3	Yr.Iss.	1978	2.50	60
1978 Peanuts QX205-6	Yr.Iss.	1978	3.50	65
1978 Peanuts QX206-3	Yr.Iss.	1978	3.50	50

1978 Property Ornaments - Keepsake

YEAR ISSUE	EDITION LIMIT	YEAR RETD.	ISSUE PRICE	*QUOTE U.S.$
1978 Betsey Clark (6th Ed.) QX201-6	Yr.Iss.	1978	3.50	60
1978 Disney QX207-6	Yr.Iss.	1978	3.50	125-150
1978 Joan Walsh Anglund QX221-6	Yr.Iss.	1978	3.50	65
1978 Spencer Sparrow QX219-6	Yr.Iss.	1978	3.50	50

1978 Yarn Collection - Keepsake

YEAR ISSUE	EDITION LIMIT	YEAR RETD.	ISSUE PRICE	*QUOTE U.S.$
1978 Green Boy QX123-1	Yr.Iss.	1979	2.00	27
1978 Green Girl QX126-1	Yr.Iss.	1979	2.00	20
1978 Mr. Claus QX340-3	Yr.Iss.	1979	2.00	25
1978 Mrs. Claus QX125-1	Yr.Iss.	1979	2.00	20-22

1979 Collectible Series - Keepsake

YEAR ISSUE	EDITION LIMIT	YEAR RETD.	ISSUE PRICE	*QUOTE U.S.$
1979 Bellringer (1st Ed.) QX147-9	Yr.Iss.	1979	10.00	320-400
1979 Carousel (2nd Ed.) QX146-7	Yr.Iss.	1979	6.50	150-180
1979 Here Comes Santa (1st Ed.) QX155-9	Yr.Iss.	1979	9.00	340-560
1979 Snoopy and Friends QX141-9	Yr.Iss.	1979	8.00	90-165
1979 Thimble (2nd Ed.) QX131-9	Yr.Iss.	1980	3.00	148-160

1979 Colors of Christmas - Keepsake

YEAR ISSUE	EDITION LIMIT	YEAR RETD.	ISSUE PRICE	*QUOTE U.S.$
1979 Holiday Wreath QX353-9	Yr.Iss.	1979	3.50	29-45
1979 Partridge in a Pear Tree QX351-9	Yr.Iss.	1979	3.50	36-45
1979 Star Over Bethlehem QX352-7	Yr.Iss.	1979	3.50	60-85
1979 Words of Christmas QX350-7	Yr.Iss.	1979	3.50	68-85

1979 Commemoratives - Keepsake

YEAR ISSUE	EDITION LIMIT	YEAR RETD.	ISSUE PRICE	*QUOTE U.S.$
1979 Baby's First Christmas QX154-7	Yr.Iss.	1979	8.00	175
1979 Baby's First Christmas QX208-7	Yr.Iss.	1979	3.50	24-30
1979 Friendship QX203-9	Yr.Iss.	1979	3.50	18
1979 Granddaughter QX211-9	Yr.Iss.	1979	3.50	24-35
1979 Grandmother QX252-7	Yr.Iss.	1979	3.50	10-40
1979 Grandson QX210-7	Yr.Iss.	1979	3.50	35
1979 Love QX258-7	Yr.Iss.	1979	3.50	18-40
1979 Mother QX251-9	Yr.Iss.	1979	3.50	23
1979 New Home QX212-7	Yr.Iss.	1979	3.50	45
1979 Our First Christmas Together QX209-9	Yr.Iss.	1979	3.50	65
1979 Our Twenty-Fifth Anniversary QX250-7	Yr.Iss.	1979	3.50	17-29
1979 Teacher QX213-9	Yr.Iss.	1979	3.50	8-15

1979 Decorative Ball Ornaments - Keepsake

YEAR ISSUE	EDITION LIMIT	YEAR RETD.	ISSUE PRICE	*QUOTE U.S.$
1979 Behold the Star QX255-9	Yr.Iss.	1979	3.50	32-40
1979 Black Angel QX207-9	Yr.Iss.	1979	3.50	20-25
1979 Christmas Chickadees QX204-7	Yr.Iss.	1979	3.50	15-30
1979 Christmas Collage QX257-9	Yr.Iss.	1979	3.50	23-40
1979 Christmas Traditions QX253-9	Yr.Iss.	1979	3.50	28-35
1979 The Light of Christmas QX256-7	Yr.Iss.	1979	3.50	14-30
1979 Night Before Christmas QX214-7	Yr.Iss.	1979	3.50	32-40

1979 Handcrafted Ornaments - Keepsake

YEAR ISSUE	EDITION LIMIT	YEAR RETD.	ISSUE PRICE	*QUOTE U.S.$
1979 Christmas Eve Surprise QX157-9	Yr.Iss.	1979	6.50	52-65
1979 Christmas Heart QX140-7	Yr.Iss.	1979	6.50	104-115
1979 Christmas is for Children QX135-9	Yr.Iss.	1980	5.00	73-75
1979 A Christmas Treat QX134-7	Yr.Iss.	1980	5.00	68-85
1979 The Downhill Run QX145-9	Yr.Iss.	1979	6.50	81-175
1979 The Drummer Boy QX143-9	Yr.Iss.	1979	8.00	90-125
1979 Holiday Scrimshaw QX152-7	Yr.Iss.	1979	4.00	200-270
1979 Outdoor Fun QX150-7	Yr.Iss.	1979	8.00	100-125
1979 Raccoon QX142-3	Yr.Iss.	1979	6.50	68-85
1979 Ready for Christmas QX133-9	Yr.Iss.	1979	6.50	96
1979 Santa's Here QX138-7	Yr.Iss.	1979	5.00	54-75
1979 The Skating Snowman QX139-9	Yr.Iss.	1980	5.00	50-66

1979 Holiday Chimes - Keepsake

YEAR ISSUE	EDITION LIMIT	YEAR RETD.	ISSUE PRICE	*QUOTE U.S.$
1979 Reindeer Chimes QX320-3	Yr.Iss.	1980	4.50	75
1979 Star Chimes QX137-9	Yr.Iss.	1979	4.50	80-86

1979 Holiday Highlights - Keepsake

YEAR ISSUE	EDITION LIMIT	YEAR RETD.	ISSUE PRICE	*QUOTE U.S.$
1979 Christmas Angel QX300-7	Yr.Iss.	1979	3.50	95-150
1979 Christmas Cheer QX303-9	Yr.Iss.	1979	3.50	95
1979 Christmas Tree QX302-7	Yr.Iss.	1979	3.50	75
1979 Love QX304-7	Yr.Iss.	1979	3.50	80-88
1979 Snowflake QX301-9	Yr.Iss.	1979	3.50	40-45

1979 Little Trimmer Collection - Keepsake

YEAR ISSUE	EDITION LIMIT	YEAR RETD.	ISSUE PRICE	*QUOTE U.S.$
1979 Angel Delight QX130-7	Yr.Iss.	1979	3.00	80-95
1979 A Matchless Christmas QX132-7	Yr.Iss.	1979	4.00	67-85
1979 Santa QX135-6	Yr.Iss.	1979	3.00	55
1979 Thimble Series-Mouse QX133-6	Yr.Iss.	1979	3.00	104-225

1979 Property Ornaments - Keepsake

YEAR ISSUE	EDITION LIMIT	YEAR RETD.	ISSUE PRICE	*QUOTE U.S.$
1979 Betsey Clark (7th Ed.) QX201-9	Yr.Iss.	1979	3.50	33-40
1979 Joan Walsh Anglund QX205-9	Yr.Iss.	1979	3.50	35
1979 Mary Hamilton QX254-7	Yr.Iss.	1979	3.50	14-25
1979 Peanuts (Time to Trim) QX202-7	Yr.Iss.	1979	3.50	40
1979 Spencer Sparrow QX200-7	Yr.Iss.	1979	3.50	25-40
1979 Winnie-the-Pooh QX206-7	Yr.Iss.	1979	3.50	40-50

1979 Sewn Trimmers - Keepsake

YEAR ISSUE	EDITION LIMIT	YEAR RETD.	ISSUE PRICE	*QUOTE U.S.$
1979 Angel Music QX343-9	Yr.Iss.	1980	2.00	20
1979 Merry Santa QX342-7	Yr.Iss.	1980	2.00	20
1979 The Rocking Horse QX340-7	Yr.Iss.	1980	2.00	23
1979 Stuffed Full Stocking QX341-9	Yr.Iss.	1980	2.00	18-25

1979 Yarn Collection - Keepsake

YEAR ISSUE	EDITION LIMIT	YEAR RETD.	ISSUE PRICE	*QUOTE U.S.$
1979 Green Boy QX123-1	Yr.Iss.	1979	2.00	20
1979 Green Girl QX126-1	Yr.Iss.	1979	2.00	18
1979 Mr.Claus QX340-3	Yr.Iss.	1979	2.00	20
1979 Mrs.Claus QX125-1	Yr.Iss.	1979	2.00	20

1980 Collectible Series - Keepsake

YEAR ISSUE	EDITION LIMIT	YEAR RETD.	ISSUE PRICE	*QUOTE U.S.$
1980 The Bellringers (2nd Ed.) QX157-4	Yr.Iss.	1980	15.00	50-61
1980 Carrousel (3rd Ed.) QX141-4	Yr.Iss.	1980	7.50	130-165
1980 Frosty Friends (1st Ed.) QX137-4	Yr.Iss.	1980	6.50	550-560
1980 Here Comes Santa (2nd Ed.) QX143-4	Yr.Iss.	1980	12.00	143
1980 Norman Rockwell (1st Ed.) QX306-1	Yr.Iss.	1980	6.50	210
1980 Snoopy & Friends (2nd Ed.) QX154-1	Yr.Iss.	1980	9.00	115-175
1980 Thimble (3rd Ed.) QX132-1	Yr.Iss.	1980	4.00	175-195

1980 Colors of Christmas - Keepsake

YEAR ISSUE	EDITION LIMIT	YEAR RETD.	ISSUE PRICE	*QUOTE U.S.$
1980 Joy QX350-1	Yr.Iss.	1980	4.00	23

1980 Commemoratives - Keepsake

YEAR ISSUE	EDITION LIMIT	YEAR RETD.	ISSUE PRICE	*QUOTE U.S.$
1980 25th Christmas Together QX206-1	Yr.Iss.	1980	4.00	11-22
1980 Baby's First Christmas QX156-1	Yr.Iss.	1980	12.00	40-50
1980 Baby's First Christmas QX200-1	Yr.Iss.	1980	4.00	26-30
1980 Beauty of Friendship QX303-4	Yr.Iss.	1980	4.00	48-65
1980 Black Baby's First Christmas QX229-4	Yr.Iss.	1980	4.00	24-35
1980 Christmas at Home QX210-1	Yr.Iss.	1980	4.00	28-38
1980 Christmas Love QX207-4	Yr.Iss.	1980	4.00	32-40
1980 Dad QX214-1	Yr.Iss.	1980	4.00	7-9
1980 Daughter QX212-1	Yr.Iss.	1980	4.00	24-40
1980 First Christmas Together QX205-4	Yr.Iss.	1980	4.00	30-45
1980 First Christmas Together QX305-4	Yr.Iss.	1980	4.00	24-55
1980 Friendship QX208-1	Yr.Iss.	1980	4.00	10-20
1980 Granddaughter QX202-1	Yr.Iss.	1980	4.00	28-35
1980 Grandfather QX231-4	Yr.Iss.	1980	4.00	8-20
1980 Grandmother QX204-1	Yr.Iss.	1980	4.00	16-20
1980 Grandparents QX213-4	Yr.Iss.	1980	4.00	32-40
1980 Grandson QX201-4	Yr.Iss.	1980	4.00	18-35
1980 Love QX302-1	Yr.Iss.	1980	4.00	52-65
1980 Mother and Dad QX230-1	Yr.Iss.	1980	4.00	11-23
1980 Mother QX203-4	Yr.Iss.	1980	4.00	12-22
1980 Mother QX304-1	Yr.Iss.	1980	4.00	28-35
1980 Son QX211-4	Yr.Iss.	1980	4.00	29-35
1980 Teacher QX209-4	Yr.Iss.	1980	4.00	11-20

1980 Decorative Ball Ornaments - Keepsake

YEAR ISSUE	EDITION LIMIT	YEAR RETD.	ISSUE PRICE	*QUOTE U.S.$
1980 Christmas Cardinals QX224-1	Yr.Iss.	1980	4.00	28-35
1980 Christmas Choir QX228-1	Yr.Iss.	1980	4.00	68-85
1980 Christmas Time QX226-1	Yr.Iss.	1980	4.00	24-30
1980 Happy Christmas QX222-1	Yr.Iss.	1980	4.00	24-30
1980 Jolly Santa QX227-4	Yr.Iss.	1980	4.00	24-30
1980 Nativity QX225-4	Yr.Iss.	1980	4.00	100-125
1980 Santa's Workshop QX223-4	Yr.Iss.	1980	4.00	12-30

1980 Frosted Images - Keepsake

YEAR ISSUE	EDITION LIMIT	YEAR RETD.	ISSUE PRICE	*QUOTE U.S.$
1980 Dove QX308-1	Yr.Iss.	1980	4.00	25-40
1980 Drummer Boy QX309-4	Yr.Iss.	1980	4.00	20-25
1980 Santa QX310-1	Yr.Iss.	1980	4.00	15-25

1980 Handcrafted Ornaments - Keepsake

YEAR ISSUE	EDITION LIMIT	YEAR RETD.	ISSUE PRICE	*QUOTE U.S.$
1980 The Animals' Christmas QX150-1	Yr.Iss.	1980	8.00	62
1980 Caroling Bear QX140-1	Yr.Iss.	1980	7.50	100-113
1980 Christmas is for Children QX135-9	Yr.Iss.	1980	5.50	95
1980 A Christmas Treat QX134-7	Yr.Iss.	1980	5.50	75
1980 A Christmas Vigil QX144-1	Yr.Iss.	1980	9.00	95-185
1980 Drummer Boy QX147-4	Yr.Iss.	1980	5.50	50-85
1980 Elfin Antics QX142-1	Yr.Iss.	1980	9.00	175-210
1980 A Heavenly Nap QX139-4	Yr.Iss.	1981	6.50	41-55
1980 Heavenly Sounds QX152-1	Yr.Iss.	1980	7.50	72-95
1980 Santa 1980 QX146-1	Yr.Iss.	1980	5.50	86
1980 Santa's Flight QX138-1	Yr.Iss.	1980	5.50	102-115
1980 Skating Snowman QX139-9	Yr.Iss.	1980	5.50	80
1980 The Snowflake Swing QX133-4	Yr.Iss.	1980	4.00	41-45
1980 A Spot of Christmas Cheer QX153-4	Yr.Iss.	1980	8.00	149-155

1980 Holiday Chimes - Keepsake

YEAR ISSUE	EDITION LIMIT	YEAR RETD.	ISSUE PRICE	*QUOTE U.S.$
1980 Reindeer Chimes QX320-3	Yr.Iss.	1980	5.50	25
1980 Santa Mobile QX136-1	Yr.Iss.	1981	5.50	25-50
1980 Snowflake Chimes QX165-4	Yr.Iss.	1981	5.50	32

1980 Holiday Highlights - Keepsake

YEAR ISSUE	EDITION LIMIT	YEAR RETD.	ISSUE PRICE	*QUOTE U.S.$
1980 Three Wise Men QX300-1	Yr.Iss.	1980	4.00	30
1980 Wreath QX301-4	Yr.Iss.	1980	4.00	85

1980 Little Trimmers - Keepsake

YEAR ISSUE	EDITION LIMIT	YEAR RETD.	ISSUE PRICE	*QUOTE U.S.$
1980 Christmas Owl QX131-4	Yr.Iss.	1982	4.00	25-40
1980 Christmas Teddy QX135-4	Yr.Iss.	1980	2.50	82-135
1980 Clothespin Soldier QX134-1	Yr.Iss.	1980	3.50	40
1980 Merry Redbird QX160-1	Yr.Iss.	1980	3.50	51-65
1980 Swingin' on a Star QX130-1	Yr.Iss.	1980	4.00	65-85
1980 Thimble Series-A Christmas Salute QX131-9	Yr.Iss.	1980	4.00	175

1980 Old-Fashioned Christmas Collection - Keepsake

YEAR ISSUE	EDITION LIMIT	YEAR RETD.	ISSUE PRICE	*QUOTE U.S.$
1980 In a Nutshell QX469-7	Yr.Iss.	1988	5.50	24-33

1980 Property Ornaments - Keepsake

YEAR ISSUE	EDITION LIMIT	YEAR RETD.	ISSUE PRICE	*QUOTE U.S.$
1980 Betsey Clark (8th Ed.) QX215-4	Yr.Iss.	1980	4.00	25-30
1980 Betsey Clark QX307-4	Yr.Iss.	1980	6.50	54-60
1980 Betsey Clark's Christmas QX194-4	Yr.Iss.	1980	7.50	17-35
1980 Disney QX218-1	Yr.Iss.	1980	4.00	30
1980 Joan Walsh Anglund QX217-4	Yr.Iss.	1980	4.00	20-24
1980 Marty Links QX221-4	Yr.Iss.	1980	4.00	11-23
1980 Mary Hamilton QX219-4	Yr.Iss.	1980	4.00	18-23
1980 Muppets QX220-1	Yr.Iss.	1980	4.00	30-40
1980 Peanuts QX216-1	Yr.Iss.	1980	4.00	40

1980 Sewn Trimmers - Keepsake

YEAR ISSUE	EDITION LIMIT	YEAR RETD.	ISSUE PRICE	*QUOTE U.S.$
1980 Angel Music QX343-9	Yr.Iss.	1980	2.00	20
1980 Merry Santa QX342-7	Yr.Iss.	1980	2.00	20
1980 The Rocking Horse QX340-7	Yr.Iss.	1980	2.00	22
1980 Stuffed Full Stocking QX341-9	Yr.Iss.	1980	2.00	25

1980 Special Editions - Keepsake

YEAR ISSUE	EDITION LIMIT	YEAR RETD.	ISSUE PRICE	*QUOTE U.S.$
1980 Checking it Twice QX158-4	Yr.Iss.	1981	20.00	176
1980 Heavenly Minstrel QX156-7	Yr.Iss.	1980	15.00	325-345

1980 Yarn Ornaments - Keepsake

YEAR ISSUE	EDITION LIMIT	YEAR RETD.	ISSUE PRICE	*QUOTE U.S.$
1980 Angel QX162-1	Yr.Iss.	1981	3.00	10
1980 Santa QX161-4	Yr.Iss.	1981	3.00	9
1980 Snowman QX163-4	Yr.Iss.	1981	3.00	9
1980 Soldier QX164-1	Yr.Iss.	1981	3.00	9

1981 Collectible Series - Keepsake

YEAR ISSUE	EDITION LIMIT	YEAR RETD.	ISSUE PRICE	*QUOTE U.S.$
1981 Bellringer (3rd Ed.) QX441-5	Yr.Iss.	1981	15.00	50-72
1981 Carrousel (4th Ed.) QX427-5	Yr.Iss.	1981	9.00	50-80
1981 Frosty Friends (2nd Ed.) QX433-5	Yr.Iss.	1981	8.00	325-416
1981 Here Comes Santa (3rd Ed.) QX438-2	Yr.Iss.	1981	13.00	219-265
1981 Norman Rockwell (2nd Ed.) QX511-5	Yr.Iss.	1981	8.50	35-50
1981 Rocking Horse (1st Ed.) QX422-2	Yr.Iss.	1981	9.00	585-630
1981 Snoopy and Friends (3rd Ed.) QX436-2	Yr.Iss.	1981	12.00	100-125
1981 Thimble (4th Ed.) QX413-5	Yr.Iss.	1981	4.50	150-155

1981 Commemoratives - Keepsake

YEAR ISSUE	EDITION LIMIT	YEAR RETD.	ISSUE PRICE	*QUOTE U.S.$
1981 25th Christmas Together QX504-2	Yr.Iss.	1981	5.50	10-22
1981 25th Christmas Together QX707-5	Yr.Iss.	1981	4.50	10-22
1981 50th Christmas QX708-2	Yr.Iss.	1981	4.50	6-20
1981 Baby's First Christmas QX440-2	Yr.Iss.	1981	13.00	39-50
1981 Baby's First Christmas QX513-5	Yr.Iss.	1981	8.50	11-20
1981 Baby's First Christmas QX516-5	Yr.Iss.	1981	5.50	24-30
1981 Baby's First Christmas-Black QX602-2	Yr.Iss.	1981	4.50	28
1981 Baby's First Christmas-Boy QX601-5	Yr.Iss.	1981	4.50	20-25
1981 Baby's First Christmas-Girl QX600-2	Yr.Iss.	1981	4.50	15-17
1981 Daughter QX607-5	Yr.Iss.	1981	4.50	21-40
1981 Father QX609-5	Yr.Iss.	1981	4.50	8-20
1981 First Christmas Together QX505-5	Yr.Iss.	1981	5.50	13-25
1981 First Christmas Together QX706-2	Yr.Iss.	1981	4.50	22-33
1981 Friendship QX503-5	Yr.Iss.	1981	5.50	17-30
1981 Friendship QX704-2	Yr.Iss.	1981	4.50	13-30
1981 The Gift of Love QX705-5	Yr.Iss.	1981	4.50	14-25
1981 Godchild QX603-5	Yr.Iss.	1981	4.50	17-23
1981 Granddaughter QX605-5	Yr.Iss.	1981	4.50	13-33
1981 Grandfather QX701-5	Yr.Iss.	1981	4.50	16-20
1981 Grandmother QX702-2	Yr.Iss.	1981	4.50	11-25
1981 Grandparents QX703-5	Yr.Iss.	1981	4.50	11-22
1981 Grandson QX604-2	Yr.Iss.	1981	4.50	13-30
1981 Home QX709-5	Yr.Iss.	1981	4.50	16-20
1981 Love QX502-2	Yr.Iss.	1981	5.50	34-50
1981 Mother and Dad QX700-2	Yr.Iss.	1981	4.50	12-20
1981 Mother QX608-2	Yr.Iss.	1981	4.50	10-20
1981 Son QX606-2	Yr.Iss.	1981	4.50	14-20
1981 Teacher QX800-2	Yr.Iss.	1981	4.50	7-15

1981 Crown Classics - Keepsake

YEAR ISSUE	EDITION LIMIT	YEAR RETD.	ISSUE PRICE	*QUOTE U.S.$
1981 Angel QX507-5	Yr.Iss.	1981	4.50	11-25
1981 Tree Photoholder QX515-5	Yr.Iss.	1981	5.50	17-30
1981 Unicorn QX516-5	Yr.Iss.	1981	8.50	16-28

1981 Decorative Ball Ornaments - Keepsake

YEAR ISSUE	EDITION LIMIT	YEAR RETD.	ISSUE PRICE	*QUOTE U.S.$
1981 Christmas 1981 QX809-5	Yr.Iss.	1981	4.50	9-25
1981 Christmas in the Forest QX813-5	Yr.Iss.	1981	4.50	116-145
1981 Christmas Magic QX810-2	Yr.Iss.	1981	4.50	15-25
1981 Let Us Adore Him QX811-5	Yr.Iss.	1981	4.50	28
1981 Merry Christmas QX814-2	Yr.Iss.	1981	4.50	15-25
1981 Santa's Coming QX812-2	Yr.Iss.	1981	4.50	13-30
1981 Santa's Surprise QX815-5	Yr.Iss.	1981	4.50	14-25
1981 Traditional (Black Santa) QX801-5	Yr.Iss.	1981	4.50	46

1981 Fabric Ornaments - Keepsake

YEAR ISSUE	EDITION LIMIT	YEAR RETD.	ISSUE PRICE	*QUOTE U.S.$
1981 Calico Kitty QX403-5	Yr.Iss.	1981	3.00	20
1981 Cardinal Cutie QX400-2	Yr.Iss.	1981	3.00	9-23
1981 Gingham Dog QX402-2	Yr.Iss.	1981	3.00	15-20
1981 Peppermint Mouse QX401-5	Yr.Iss.	1981	3.00	38

1981 Frosted Images - Keepsake

YEAR ISSUE	EDITION LIMIT	YEAR RETD.	ISSUE PRICE	*QUOTE U.S.$
1981 Angel QX509-5	Yr.Iss.	1981	4.00	50-65
1981 Mouse QX508-2	Yr.Iss.	1981	4.00	28
1981 Snowman QX510-2	Yr.Iss.	1981	4.00	25

*Quotes have been rounded up to nearest dollar

1981 Hand Crafted Ornaments - Keepsake

YEAR ISSUE	EDITION LIMIT	YEAR RETD.	ISSUE PRICE	*QUOTE U.S.$
1981 Candyville Express QX418-2	Yr.Iss.	1981	7.50	55-95
1981 Checking It Twice QX158-4	Yr.Iss.	1981	23.00	195
1981 Christmas Dreams QX437-5	Yr.Iss.	1981	12.00	192-200
1981 Christmas Fantasy QX155-4	Yr.Iss.	1982	13.00	68-85
1981 Dough Angel QX139-6	Yr.Iss.	1981	5.50	36-80
1981 Drummer Boy QX148-1	Yr.Iss.	1981	2.50	36
1981 The Friendly Fiddler QX434-2	Yr.Iss.	1981	8.00	72
1981 A Heavenly Nap QX139-4	Yr.Iss.	1981	6.50	50-80
1981 Ice Fairy QX431-5	Yr.Iss.	1981	6.50	85-100
1981 The Ice Sculptor QX432-2	Yr.Iss.	1982	8.00	70-99
1981 Love and Joy QX425-2	Yr.Iss.	1981	9.00	75-95
1981 Mr. & Mrs. Claus QX448-5	Yr.Iss.	1981	12.00	110-135
1981 Sailing Santa QX439-5	Yr.Iss.	1981	13.00	226-295
1981 Space Santa QX430-2	Yr.Iss.	1981	6.50	88
1981 St. Nicholas QX446-2	Yr.Iss.	1981	5.50	40-50
1981 Star Swing QX421-5	Yr.Iss.	1981	5.50	46-60
1981 Topsy-Turvy Tunes QX429-5	Yr.Iss.	1981	7.50	67
1981 A Well-Stocked Stocking QX154-7	Yr.Iss.	1981	9.00	65-85

1981 Holiday Chimes - Keepsake

YEAR ISSUE	EDITION LIMIT	YEAR RETD.	ISSUE PRICE	*QUOTE U.S.$
1981 Santa Mobile QX136-1	Yr.Iss.	1981	5.50	40
1981 Snowflake Chimes QX165-4	Yr.Iss.	1981	5.50	25
1981 Snowman Chimes QX445-5	Yr.Iss.	1981	5.50	25-30

1981 Holiday Highlights - Keepsake

YEAR ISSUE	EDITION LIMIT	YEAR RETD.	ISSUE PRICE	*QUOTE U.S.$
1981 Christmas Star QX501-5	Yr.Iss.	1981	5.50	17-30
1981 Shepherd Scene QX500-2	Yr.Iss.	1981	5.50	16-30

1981 Little Trimmers - Keepsake

YEAR ISSUE	EDITION LIMIT	YEAR RETD.	ISSUE PRICE	*QUOTE U.S.$
1981 Clothespin Drummer Boy QX408-2	Yr.Iss.	1981	4.50	25-45
1981 Jolly Snowman QX407-5	Yr.Iss.	1981	3.50	25
1981 Perky Penguin QX409-5	Yr.Iss.	1982	3.50	43
1981 Puppy Love QX406-2	Yr.Iss.	1981	3.50	20-25
1981 The Stocking Mouse QX412-2	Yr.Iss.	1981	4.50	82

1981 Plush Animals - Keepsake

YEAR ISSUE	EDITION LIMIT	YEAR RETD.	ISSUE PRICE	*QUOTE U.S.$
1981 Christmas Teddy QX404-2	Yr.Iss.	1981	5.50	24
1981 Raccoon Tunes QX405-5	Yr.Iss.	1981	5.50	15-25

1981 Property Ornaments - Keepsake

YEAR ISSUE	EDITION LIMIT	YEAR RETD.	ISSUE PRICE	*QUOTE U.S.$
1981 Betsey Clark (9th Ed.)QX 802-2	Yr.Iss.	1981	4.50	23-35
1981 Betsey Clark Cameo QX512-2	Yr.Iss.	1981	8.50	20-30
1981 Betsey Clark QX423-5	Yr.Iss.	1981	9.00	40-45
1981 Disney QX805-5	Yr.Iss.	1981	4.50	13-15
1981 The Divine Miss Piggy QX425-5	Yr.Iss.	1982	12.00	75-95
1981 Joan Walsh Anglund QX804-2	Yr.Iss.	1981	4.50	18-30
1981 Kermit the Frog QX424-2	Yr.Iss.	1981	9.00	78-85
1981 Marty Links QX808-2	Yr.Iss.	1981	4.50	19-25
1981 Mary Hamilton QX806-2	Yr.Iss.	1981	4.50	14-24
1981 Muppets QX807-5	Yr.Iss.	1981	4.50	15-35
1981 Peanuts QX803-5	Yr.Iss.	1981	4.50	23-40

1982 Brass Ornaments - Keepsake

YEAR ISSUE	EDITION LIMIT	YEAR RETD.	ISSUE PRICE	*QUOTE U.S.$
1982 Brass Bell QX460-6	Yr.Iss.	1982	12.00	18-25
1982 Santa and Reindeer QX467-6	Yr.Iss.	1982	9.00	40-50
1982 Santa's Sleigh QX478-6	Yr.Iss.	1982	9.00	14-35

1982 Collectible Series - Keepsake

YEAR ISSUE	EDITION LIMIT	YEAR RETD.	ISSUE PRICE	*QUOTE U.S.$
1982 The Bellringer (4th Ed.) QX455-6	Yr.Iss.	1982	15.00	60
1982 Carrousel Series (5th Ed.) QX478-3	Yr.Iss.	1982	10.00	50-95
1982 Clothespin Soldier (1st Ed.) QX458-3	Yr.Iss.	1982	5.00	106-121
1982 Frosty Friends (3rd Ed.) QX452-3	Yr.Iss.	1982	8.00	95-188
1982 Here Comes Santa (4th Ed.) QX464-3	Yr.Iss.	1982	15.00	102-150
1982 Holiday Wildlife (1st Ed.) QX313-3	Yr.Iss.	1982	7.00	360-375
1982 Rocking Horse (2nd Ed.) QX 502-3	Yr.Iss.	1982	10.00	300-450
1982 Snoopy and Friends (4th Ed.) QX478-3	Yr.Iss.	1982	13.00	125-135
1982 Thimble (5th Ed.) QX451-3	Yr.Iss.	1982	5.00	50-62
1982 Tin Locomotive (1st Ed.) QX460-3	Yr.Iss.	1982	13.00	575-600

1982 Colors of Christmas - Keepsake

YEAR ISSUE	EDITION LIMIT	YEAR RETD.	ISSUE PRICE	*QUOTE U.S.$
1982 Nativity QX308-3	Yr.Iss.	1982	4.50	53
1982 Santa's Flight QX308-6	Yr.Iss.	1982	4.50	50

1982 Commemoratives - Keepsake

YEAR ISSUE	EDITION LIMIT	YEAR RETD.	ISSUE PRICE	*QUOTE U.S.$
1982 25th Christmas Together QX211-6	Yr.Iss.	1982	4.50	6-20
1982 50th Christmas Together QX212-3	Yr.Iss.	1982	4.50	6-20
1982 Baby's First Christmas (Boy) QX 216-3	Yr.Iss.	1982	4.50	16-21
1982 Baby's First Christmas (Girl) QX 207-3	Yr.Iss.	1982	4.50	16-22
1982 Baby's First Christmas QX302-3	Yr.Iss.	1982	5.50	19-40
1982 Baby's First Christmas QX455-3	Yr.Iss.	1982	13.00	38-50
1982 Baby's First Christmas-Photoholder QX312-6	Yr.Iss.	1982	6.50	23
1982 Christmas Memories QX311-6	Yr.Iss.	1982	6.50	16-20
1982 Daughter QX204-6	Yr.Iss.	1982	4.50	22
1982 Father QX205-6	Yr.Iss.	1982	4.50	8-20
1982 First Christmas Together QX211-3	Yr.Iss.	1982	4.50	31-39
1982 First Christmas Together QX302-6	Yr.Iss.	1982	5.50	9-23
1982 First Christmas Together QX306-6	Yr.Iss.	1982	8.50	15-45
1982 First Christmas Together-Locket QX456-3	Yr.Iss.	1982	15.00	25-40
1982 Friendship QX208-6	Yr.Iss.	1982	4.50	8-20
1982 Friendship QX304-6	Yr.Iss.	1982	5.50	15-25
1982 Godchild QX222-6	Yr.Iss.	1982	4.50	13-23
1982 Granddaughter QX224-3	Yr.Iss.	1982	4.50	12-30
1982 Grandfather QX207-6	Yr.Iss.	1982	4.50	8-20
1982 Grandmother QX200-3	Yr.Iss.	1982	4.50	8-18
1982 Grandparents QX214-6	Yr.Iss.	1982	4.50	12-18
1982 Grandson QX224-6	Yr.Iss.	1982	4.50	12-30
1982 Love QX209-6	Yr.Iss.	1982	4.50	9-20
1982 Love QX304-3	Yr.Iss.	1982	5.50	16-30
1982 Moments of Love QX209-3	Yr.Iss.	1982	4.50	5-18
1982 Mother and Dad QX222-3	Yr.Iss.	1982	4.50	7-17
1982 Mother QX205-3	Yr.Iss.	1982	4.50	9-19
1982 New Home QX212-6	Yr.Iss.	1982	4.50	10-23
1982 Sister QX208-3	Yr.Iss.	1982	4.50	17-30
1982 Son QX204-3	Yr.Iss.	1982	4.50	14-30
1982 Teacher QX214-3	Yr.Iss.	1982	4.50	8-15
1982 Teacher QX312-3	Yr.Iss.	1982	6.50	11-18
1982 Teacher-Apple QX301-6	Yr.Iss.	1982	5.50	8-14

1982 Decorative Ball Ornaments - Keepsake

YEAR ISSUE	EDITION LIMIT	YEAR RETD.	ISSUE PRICE	*QUOTE U.S.$
1982 Christmas Angel QX220-6	Yr.Iss.	1982	4.50	11-25
1982 Currier & Ives QX201-3	Yr.Iss.	1982	4.50	10-25
1982 Santa QX221-6	Yr.Iss.	1982	4.50	13-20
1982 Season for Caring QX221-3	Yr.Iss.	1982	4.50	18-25

1982 Designer Keepsakes - Keepsake

YEAR ISSUE	EDITION LIMIT	YEAR RETD.	ISSUE PRICE	*QUOTE U.S.$
1982 Merry Christmas QX225-6	Yr.Iss.	1982	4.50	23
1982 Old Fashioned Christmas QX227-6	Yr.Iss.	1982	4.50	59
1982 Old World Angels QX226-3	Yr.Iss.	1982	4.50	25
1982 Patterns of Christmas QX226-6	Yr.Iss.	1982	4.50	15-22
1982 Stained Glass QX228-3	Yr.Iss.	1982	4.50	12-25
1982 Twelve Days of Christmas QX203-6	Yr.Iss.	1982	4.50	30

1982 Handcrafted Ornaments - Keepsake

YEAR ISSUE	EDITION LIMIT	YEAR RETD.	ISSUE PRICE	*QUOTE U.S.$
1982 Baroque Angel QX456-6	Yr.Iss.	1982	15.00	175
1982 Christmas Fantasy QX155-4	Yr.Iss.	1982	13.00	59
1982 Cloisonne Angel QX145-4	Yr.Iss.	1982	12.00	95
1982 Cowboy Snowman QX480-6	Yr.Iss.	1982	8.00	50-55
1982 Cycling Santa QX435-5	Yr.Iss.	1983	20.00	100
1982 Elfin Artist QX457-3	Yr.Iss.	1982	9.00	25-42
1982 Embroidered Tree QX494-6	Yr.Iss.	1982	6.50	40
1982 Ice Sculptor QX432-2	Yr.Iss.	1982	8.00	75
1982 Jogging Santa QX457-6	Yr.Iss.	1982	8.00	32-50
1982 Jolly Christmas Tree QX465-3	Yr.Iss.	1982	6.50	80
1982 Peeking Elf QX419-5	Yr.Iss.	1982	6.50	25-40
1982 Pinecone Home QX461-3	Yr.Iss.	1982	8.00	158-170
1982 Raccoon Surprises QX479-3	Yr.Iss.	1982	9.00	125-130
1982 Santa Bell QX148-7	Yr.Iss.	1982	15.00	59
1982 Santa's Workshop QX450-3	Yr.Iss.	1983	10.00	50-80
1982 The Spirit of Christmas QX452-6	Yr.Iss.	1982	10.00	107-125
1982 Three Kings QX307-3	Yr.Iss.	1982	8.50	17-27
1982 Tin Soldier QX483-6	Yr.Iss.	1982	6.50	33-50

1982 Holiday Chimes - Keepsake

YEAR ISSUE	EDITION LIMIT	YEAR RETD.	ISSUE PRICE	*QUOTE U.S.$
1982 Bell Chimes QX494-3	Yr.Iss.	1982	5.50	21-30
1982 Tree Chimes QX484-6	Yr.Iss.	1982	5.50	50

1982 Holiday Highlights - Keepsake

YEAR ISSUE	EDITION LIMIT	YEAR RETD.	ISSUE PRICE	*QUOTE U.S.$
1982 Angel QX309-6	Yr.Iss.	1982	5.50	16-35
1982 Christmas Magic QX311-3	Yr.Iss.	1982	5.50	22-30
1982 Christmas Sleigh QX309-3	Yr.Iss.	1982	5.50	40-75

1982 Ice Sculptures - Keepsake

YEAR ISSUE	EDITION LIMIT	YEAR RETD.	ISSUE PRICE	*QUOTE U.S.$
1982 Arctic Penguin QX300-3	Yr.Iss.	1982	4.00	10-20
1982 Snowy Seal QX300-6	Yr.Iss.	1982	4.00	14-20

1982 Little Trimmers - Keepsake

YEAR ISSUE	EDITION LIMIT	YEAR RETD.	ISSUE PRICE	*QUOTE U.S.$
1982 Christmas Kitten QX454-3	Yr.Iss.	1983	4.00	34-38
1982 Christmas Owl QX131-4	Yr.Iss.	1982	4.50	35
1982 Cookie Mouse QX454-6	Yr.Iss.	1982	4.50	35-50
1982 Dove Love QX462-3	Yr.Iss.	1982	4.50	32-47
1982 Jingling Teddy QX477-6	Yr.Iss.	1982	4.00	20-23
1982 Merry Moose QX415-5	Yr.Iss.	1982	5.50	50-60
1982 Musical Angel QX459-6	Yr.Iss.	1982	5.50	112-125
1982 Perky Penguin QX409-5	Yr.Iss.	1982	4.00	35

1982 Property Ornaments - Keepsake

YEAR ISSUE	EDITION LIMIT	YEAR RETD.	ISSUE PRICE	*QUOTE U.S.$
1982 Betsey Clark (10th Ed.) QX215-6	Yr.Iss.	1982	4.50	24-34
1982 Betsey Clark QX305-6	Yr.Iss.	1982	8.50	17-25
1982 Disney QX217-3	Yr.Iss.	1982	4.50	22-35
1982 The Divine Miss Piggy QX425-5	Yr.Iss.	1982	12.00	125
1982 Joan Walsh Anglund QX219-3	Yr.Iss.	1982	4.50	10-23
1982 Kermit the Frog QX495-6	Yr.Iss.	1982	11.00	62-95
1982 Mary Hamilton QX217-6	Yr.Iss.	1982	4.50	14-23
1982 Miss Piggy and Kermit QX218-3	Yr.Iss.	1982	4.50	29-35
1982 Muppets Party QX218-6	Yr.Iss.	1982	4.50	31-40
1982 Norman Rockwell (3rd Ed.) QX305-3	Yr.Iss.	1982	8.50	23-26
1982 Norman Rockwell QX202-3	Yr.Iss.	1982	4.50	11-28
1982 Peanuts QX200-6	Yr.Iss.	1982	4.50	22-40

1983 Collectible Series - Keepsake

YEAR ISSUE	EDITION LIMIT	YEAR RETD.	ISSUE PRICE	*QUOTE U.S.$
1983 The Bellringer (5th Ed.) QX 403-9	Yr.Iss.	1983	15.00	80-125
1983 Carrousel (6th Ed.) QX401-9	Yr.Iss.	1983	11.00	35-50
1983 Clothespin Soldier (2nd Ed.) QX402-9	Yr.Iss.	1983	5.00	35-43
1983 Frosty Friends (4th Ed.) QX400-7	Yr.Iss.	1983	8.00	313
1983 Here Comes Santa (5th Ed.) QX403-7	Yr.Iss.	1983	13.00	250-295
1983 Holiday Wildlife (2nd Ed.) QX309-9	Yr.Iss.	1983	7.00	50-53
1983 Porcelain Bear (1st Ed.) QX428-9	Yr.Iss.	1983	7.00	50-74
1983 Rocking Horse (3rd Ed.) QX417-7	Yr.Iss.	1983	10.00	281-300
1983 Snoopy and Friends (5th Ed.) QX416-9	Yr.Iss.	1983	13.00	95
1983 Thimble (6th Ed.) QX401-7	Yr.Iss.	1983	5.00	29-39
1983 Tin Locomotive (2nd Ed.) QX404-9	Yr.Iss.	1983	13.00	200-276

1983 Commemoratives - Keepsake

YEAR ISSUE	EDITION LIMIT	YEAR RETD.	ISSUE PRICE	*QUOTE U.S.$
1983 25th Christmas Together QX224-7	Yr.Iss.	1983	4.50	8-20
1983 Baby's First Christmas QX200-7	Yr.Iss.	1983	4.50	19-30
1983 Baby's First Christmas QX200-9	Yr.Iss.	1983	4.50	24
1983 Baby's First Christmas QX301-9	Yr.Iss.	1983	7.50	9-18
1983 Baby's First Christmas QX302-9	Yr.Iss.	1983	7.00	5-25
1983 Baby's First Christmas QX402-7	Yr.Iss.	1983	14.00	31-40
1983 Baby's Second Christmas QX226-7	Yr.Iss.	1983	4.50	16-35
1983 Child's Third Christmas QX226-9	Yr.Iss.	1983	4.50	20-25
1983 Daughter QX203-7	Yr.Iss.	1983	4.50	28
1983 First Christmas Together QX208-9	Yr.Iss.	1983	4.50	17-35
1983 First Christmas Together QX301-7	Yr.Iss.	1983	7.50	9-25
1983 First Christmas Together QX306-9	Yr.Iss.	1983	6.00	17-23
1983 First Christmas Together QX310-7	Yr.Iss.	1983	6.00	31-40
1983 First Christmas Together-Brass Locket QX432-9	Yr.Iss.	1983	15.00	20-40
1983 Friendship QX207-7	Yr.Iss.	1983	4.50	8-15
1983 Friendship QX305-9	Yr.Iss.	1983	6.00	6-20
1983 Godchild QX201-7	Yr.Iss.	1983	4.50	19-23
1983 Grandchild's First Christmas QX312-9	Yr.Iss.	1983	6.00	19-25
1983 Grandchild's First Christmas QX430-9	Yr.Iss.	1983	14.00	21-30
1983 Granddaughter QX202-7	Yr.Iss.	1983	4.50	24-30
1983 Grandmother QX205-7	Yr.Iss.	1983	4.50	10-24
1983 Grandparents QX429-9	Yr.Iss.	1983	6.50	11-22
1983 Grandson QX201-9	Yr.Iss.	1983	4.50	12-30
1983 Love Is a Song QX223-9	Yr.Iss.	1983	4.50	8-30
1983 Love QX207-9	Yr.Iss.	1983	4.50	34-70
1983 Love QX305-7	Yr.Iss.	1983	6.00	10-20
1983 Love QX310-9	Yr.Iss.	1983	6.00	32-40
1983 Love QX422-7	Yr.Iss.	1983	13.00	12-40
1983 Mom and Dad QX429-7	Yr.Iss.	1983	6.50	14-24
1983 Mother QX306-7	Yr.Iss.	1983	6.00	12-20
1983 New Home QX210-7	Yr.Iss.	1983	4.50	12-32
1983 Sister QX206-9	Yr.Iss.	1983	4.50	16-23
1983 Son QX202-9	Yr.Iss.	1983	4.50	32-40
1983 Teacher QX224-9	Yr.Iss.	1983	4.50	8-17
1983 Teacher QX304-9	Yr.Iss.	1983	6.00	11-15
1983 Tenth Christmas Together QX430-7	Yr.Iss.	1983	6.50	12-24

1983 Crown Classics - Keepsake

YEAR ISSUE	EDITION LIMIT	YEAR RETD.	ISSUE PRICE	*QUOTE U.S.$
1983 Enameled Christmas Wreath QX311-9	Yr.Iss.	1983	9.00	8-15
1983 Memories to Treasure QX303-7	Yr.Iss.	1983	7.00	19-40
1983 Mother and Child QX302-7	Yr.Iss.	1983	7.50	18-30

1983 Decorative Ball Ornaments - Keepsake

YEAR ISSUE	EDITION LIMIT	YEAR RETD.	ISSUE PRICE	*QUOTE U.S.$
1983 1983 QX220-9	Yr.Iss.	1983	4.50	13-30
1983 Angels QX219-7	Yr.Iss.	1983	5.00	17-24
1983 The Annunciation QX216-7	Yr.Iss.	1983	4.50	24-30
1983 Christmas Joy QX216-9	Yr.Iss.	1983	4.50	12-30
1983 Christmas Wonderland QX221-9	Yr.Iss.	1983	4.50	76-125
1983 Currier & Ives QX215-9	Yr.Iss.	1983	4.50	6-25
1983 Here Comes Santa QX217-7	Yr.Iss.	1983	4.50	30-43
1983 An Old Fashioned Christmas QX2217-9	Yr.Iss.	1983	4.50	29-35
1983 Oriental Butterflies QX218-7	Yr.Iss.	1983	4.50	24-30
1983 Season's Greeting QX219-9	Yr.Iss.	1983	4.50	10-22
1983 The Wise Men QX220-7	Yr.Iss.	1983	4.50	43-59

1983 Handcrafted Ornaments - Keepsake

YEAR ISSUE	EDITION LIMIT	YEAR RETD.	ISSUE PRICE	*QUOTE U.S.$
1983 Angel Messenger QX408-7	Yr.Iss.	1983	6.50	89-95
1983 Baroque Angels QX422-9	Yr.Iss.	1983	13.00	130
1983 Bell Wreath QX420-9	Yr.Iss.	1983	6.50	35
1983 Brass Santa QX423-9	Yr.Iss.	1983	9.00	23
1983 Caroling Owl QX411-7	Yr.Iss.	1983	4.50	25
1983 Christmas Kitten QX454-3	Yr.Iss.	1983	4.00	35
1983 Christmas Koala QX419-9	Yr.Iss.	1983	4.00	20-33
1983 Cycling Santa QX435-5	Yr.Iss.	1983	20.00	195
1983 Embroidered Heart QX421-7	Yr.Iss.	1983	6.50	25
1983 Embroidered Stocking QX479-6	Yr.Iss.	1983	6.50	9-27
1983 Hitchhiking Santa QX424-7	Yr.Iss.	1983	8.00	33-40
1983 Holiday Puppy QX412-7	Yr.Iss.	1983	3.50	16
1983 Jack Frost QX407-9	Yr.Iss.	1983	9.00	60
1983 Jolly Santa QX425-9	Yr.Iss.	1983	3.50	21-25
1983 Madonna and Child QX428-7	Yr.Iss.	1983	12.00	27-45
1983 Mailbox Kitten QX415-7	Yr.Iss.	1983	6.50	40
1983 Mountain Climbing Santa QX407-7	Yr.Iss.	1984	6.50	15-23
1983 Mouse in Bell QX419-7	Yr.Iss.	1983	10.00	30-65
1983 Mouse on Cheese QX413-7	Yr.Iss.	1983	6.50	25-45
1983 Old-Fashioned Santa QX409-9	Yr.Iss.	1983	11.00	42-65
1983 Peppermint Penguin QX408-9	Yr.Iss.	1983	6.50	20-29
1983 Porcelain Doll, Diana QX423-7	Yr.Iss.	1983	9.00	18-30
1983 Rainbow Angel QX416-7	Yr.Iss.	1983	5.50	113
1983 Santa's Many Faces QX311-6	Yr.Iss.	1983	6.00	30
1983 Santa's on His Way QX426-9	Yr.Iss.	1983	10.00	20-35
1983 Santa's Workshop QX450-3	Yr.Iss.	1983	10.00	60
1983 Scrimshaw Reindeer QX424-9	Yr.Iss.	1983	8.00	17-35
1983 Skating Rabbit QX409-7	Yr.Iss.	1983	8.00	47-55
1983 Ski Lift Santa QX418-7	Yr.Iss.	1983	8.00	60
1983 Skiing Fox QX420-7	Yr.Iss.	1983	8.00	31-40
1983 Sneaker Mouse QX400-9	Yr.Iss.	1983	4.50	20-24
1983 Tin Rocking Horse QX414-9	Yr.Iss.	1983	6.50	45-50
1983 Unicorn QX426-7	Yr.Iss.	1983	10.00	55

1983 Holiday Highlights - Keepsake

YEAR ISSUE	EDITION LIMIT	YEAR RETD.	ISSUE PRICE	*QUOTE U.S.$
1983 Christmas Stocking QX303-9	Yr.Iss.	1983	6.00	14
1983 Star of Peace QX304-7	Yr.Iss.	1983	6.00	15-20
1983 Time for Sharing QX307-7	Yr.Iss.	1983	6.00	40

1983 Holiday Sculptures - Keepsake

YEAR ISSUE	EDITION LIMIT	YEAR RETD.	ISSUE PRICE	*QUOTE U.S.$
1983 Heart QX307-9	Yr.Iss.	1983	4.00	45-50
1983 Santa QX308-7	Yr.Iss.	1983	4.00	17-35

1983 Property Ornaments - Keepsake

YEAR ISSUE	EDITION LIMIT	YEAR RETD.	ISSUE PRICE	*QUOTE U.S.$
1983 Betsey Clark (11th Ed.) QX211-9	Yr.Iss.	1983	4.50	33
1983 Betsey Clark QX404-7	Yr.Iss.	1983	6.50	31-35
1983 Betsey Clark QX440-1	Yr.Iss.	1983	9.00	31-35
1983 Disney QX212-9	Yr.Iss.	1983	4.50	45-95
1983 Kermit the Frog QX495-6	Yr.Iss.	1983	11.00	35
1983 Mary Hamilton QX213-7	Yr.Iss.	1983	4.50	68-75
1983 Miss Piggy QX405-7	Yr.Iss.	1983	13.00	225

*Quotes have been rounded up to nearest dollar

ORNAMENTS

YEAR ISSUE	EDITION LIMIT	YEAR RETD.	ISSUE PRICE	*QUOTE U.S.$
1983 The Muppets QX214-7	Yr.Iss.	1983	4.50	39-50
1983 Norman Rockwell (4th Ed.) QX300-7	Yr.Iss.	1983	7.50	35
1983 Norman Rockwell QX215-7	Yr.Iss.	1983	4.50	32-50
1983 Peanuts QX212-7	Yr.Iss.	1983	4.50	24-40
1983 Shirt Tales QX214-9	Yr.Iss.	1983	4.50	25

1984 Collectible Series - Keepsake

YEAR ISSUE	EDITION LIMIT	YEAR RETD.	ISSUE PRICE	*QUOTE U.S.$
1984 Art Masterpiece (1st Ed.) QX349-4	Yr.Iss.	1984	6.50	16
1984 The Bellringer (6th & Final Ed.) QX438-4	Yr.Iss.	1984	15.00	34-50
1984 Betsey Clark (12th Ed.) QX249-4	Yr.Iss.	1984	5.00	25-33
1984 Clothespin Soldier (3rd Ed.) QX447-1	Yr.Iss.	1984	5.00	22-30
1984 Frosty Friends (5th Ed.) QX437-1	Yr.Iss.	1984	8.00	63-70
1984 Here Comes Santa (6th Ed.) QX438-4	Yr.Iss.	1984	13.00	63-90
1984 Holiday Wildlife (3rd Ed.) QX347-4	Yr.Iss.	1984	7.25	21
1984 Norman Rockwell (5th Ed.) QX341-1	Yr.Iss.	1984	7.50	24-35
1984 Nostalgic Houses and Shops (1st Ed.) QX448-1	Yr.Iss.	1984	13.00	133-215
1984 Porcelain Bear (2nd Ed.) QX454-1	Yr.Iss.	1984	7.00	34-50
1984 Rocking Horse (4th Ed.) QX435-4	Yr.Iss.	1984	10.00	50-77
1984 Thimble (7th Ed.) QX430-4	Yr.Iss.	1984	5.00	42-60
1984 Tin Locomotive (3rd Ed.) QX440-4	Yr.Iss.	1984	14.00	65-75
1984 The Twelve Days of Christmas (1st Ed.) QX3484	Yr.Iss.	1984	6.00	200-260
1984 Wood Childhood Ornaments (1st Ed.) QX439-4	Yr.Iss.	1984	6.50	25-41

1984 Commemoratives - Keepsake

YEAR ISSUE	EDITION LIMIT	YEAR RETD.	ISSUE PRICE	*QUOTE U.S.$
1984 Baby's First Christmas QX300-1	Yr.Iss.	1984	7.00	9-20
1984 Baby's First Christmas QX340-1	Yr.Iss.	1984	6.00	24-40
1984 Baby's First Christmas QX438-1	Yr.Iss.	1984	14.00	38-50
1984 Baby's First Christmas QX904-1	Yr.Iss.	1984	16.00	40-50
1984 Baby's First Christmas-Boy QX240-4	Yr.Iss.	1984	4.50	20-23
1984 Baby's First Christmas-Girl QX340-1	Yr.Iss.	1984	4.50	21
1984 Baby's Second Christmas QX241-1	Yr.Iss.	1984	4.50	17-40
1984 Baby-sitter QX253-1	Yr.Iss.	1984	4.50	6-14
1984 Child's Third Christmas QX261-1	Yr.Iss.	1984	4.50	15-25
1984 Daughter QX244-4	Yr.Iss.	1984	4.50	20-33
1984 Father QX257-1	Yr.Iss.	1984	6.00	15-20
1984 First Christmas Together QX245-1	Yr.Iss.	1984	4.50	13-30
1984 First Christmas Together QX340-4	Yr.Iss.	1984	7.50	12-30
1984 First Christmas Together QX342-1	Yr.Iss.	1984	6.00	11-23
1984 First Christmas Together QX436-4	Yr.Iss.	1984	15.00	12-40
1984 First Christmas Together QX904-4	Yr.Iss.	1984	16.00	32-41
1984 Friendship QX248-1	Yr.Iss.	1984	4.50	14-23
1984 From Our Home to Yours QX248-4	Yr.Iss.	1984	4.50	40-50
1984 The Fun of Friendship QX343-1	Yr.Iss.	1984	6.00	8-35
1984 A Gift of Friendship QX260-4	Yr.Iss.	1984	4.50	19-25
1984 Godchild QX242-1	Yr.Iss.	1984	4.50	20-25
1984 Grandchild's First Christmas QX257-4	Yr.Iss.	1984	4.50	7-17
1984 Grandchild's First Christmas QX460-1	Yr.Iss.	1984	11.00	20-30
1984 Granddaughter QX243-1	Yr.Iss.	1984	4.50	24-30
1984 Grandmother QX244-1	Yr.Iss.	1984	4.50	13-23
1984 Grandparents QX256-1	Yr.Iss.	1984	4.50	14-20
1984 Grandson QX242-4	Yr.Iss.	1984	4.50	18-30
1984 Gratitude QX344-4	Yr.Iss.	1984	6.00	8-12
1984 Heartful of Love QX443-4	Yr.Iss.	1984	10.00	36-45
1984 Love QX255-4	Yr.Iss.	1984	4.50	16-25
1984 Love...the Spirit of Christmas QX247-4	Yr.Iss.	1984	4.50	15-43
1984 The Miracle of Love QX342-4	Yr.Iss.	1984	6.00	25-33
1984 Mother and Dad QX258-1	Yr.Iss.	1984	6.50	13-25
1984 Mother QX343-4	Yr.Iss.	1984	6.00	14-18
1984 New Home QX245-4	Yr.Iss.	1984	4.50	68-85
1984 Sister QX259-4	Yr.Iss.	1984	6.50	20-32
1984 Son QX243-4	Yr.Iss.	1984	4.50	8-30
1984 Teacher QX249-1	Yr.Iss.	1984	4.50	13
1984 Ten Years Together QX258-4	Yr.Iss.	1984	6.50	11-25
1984 Twenty-Five Years Together QX259-1	Yr.Iss.	1984	6.50	15-20

1984 Holiday Humor - Keepsake

YEAR ISSUE	EDITION LIMIT	YEAR RETD.	ISSUE PRICE	*QUOTE U.S.$
1984 Bell Ringer Squirrel QX443-1	Yr.Iss.	1984	10.00	20-40
1984 Christmas Owl QX444-1	Yr.Iss.	1984	6.00	20-33
1984 A Christmas Prayer QX246-1	Yr.Iss.	1984	4.50	24
1984 Flights of Fantasy QX256-4	Yr.Iss.	1984	4.50	20
1984 Fortune Cookie Elf QX452-4	Yr.Iss.	1984	4.50	28-36
1984 Frisbee Puppy QX444-4	Yr.Iss.	1984	5.00	45-50
1984 Marathon Santa QX456-4	Yr.Iss.	1984	8.00	39-43
1984 Mountain Climbing Santa QX407-7	Yr.Iss.	1984	6.50	35
1984 Musical Angel QX434-4	Yr.Iss.	1984	5.50	70
1984 Napping Mouse QX435-1	Yr.Iss.	1984	5.50	38-50
1984 Peppermint 1984 QX452-1	Yr.Iss.	1984	4.50	45
1984 Polar Bear Drummer QX430-1	Yr.Iss.	1984	4.50	30
1984 Raccoon's Christmas QX447-7	Yr.Iss.	1984	9.00	30-36
1984 Reindeer Racetrack QX254-4	Yr.Iss.	1984	4.50	10-25
1984 Roller Skating Rabbit QX457-1	Yr.Iss.	1985	5.00	18-30
1984 Santa Mouse QX433-4	Yr.Iss.	1984	4.50	40-50
1984 Santa Star QX450-4	Yr.Iss.	1984	5.50	33-40
1984 Snowmobile Santa QX431-4	Yr.Iss.	1984	6.50	36-40
1984 Snowshoe Penguin QX453-1	Yr.Iss.	1984	6.50	50-61
1984 Snowy Seal QX450-1	Yr.Iss.	1985	4.00	13-24
1984 Three Kittens in a Mitten QX431-1	Yr.Iss.	1985	8.00	32-60

1984 Keepsake Magic Ornaments - Keepsake

YEAR ISSUE	EDITION LIMIT	YEAR RETD.	ISSUE PRICE	*QUOTE U.S.$
1984 All Are Precious QLX704-1	Yr.Iss.	1985	8.00	10-25
1984 Brass Carrousel QLX707-1	Yr.Iss.	1984	9.00	76-95
1984 Christmas in the Forest QLX703-4	Yr.Iss.	1984	8.00	12-20
1984 City Lights QLX701-4	Yr.Iss.	1984	10.00	34-54
1984 Nativity QLX700-1	Yr.Iss.	1985	12.00	20-30
1984 Santa's Arrival QLX702-4	Yr.Iss.	1984	13.00	47-65
1984 Santa's Workshop QLX700-4	Yr.Iss.	1985	13.00	47-62
1984 Stained Glass QLX703-1	Yr.Iss.	1984	8.00	16-20
1984 Sugarplum Cottage QLX701-1	Yr.Iss.	1986	11.00	36-45
1984 Village Church QLX702-1	Yr.Iss.	1985	15.00	37-45

1984 Limited Edition - Keepsake

YEAR ISSUE	EDITION LIMIT	YEAR RETD.	ISSUE PRICE	*QUOTE U.S.$
1984 Classical Angel QX459-1	Yr.Iss.	1984	28.00	50-61

1984 Property Ornaments - Keepsake

YEAR ISSUE	EDITION LIMIT	YEAR RETD.	ISSUE PRICE	*QUOTE U.S.$
1984 Betsey Clark Angel QX462-4	Yr.Iss.	1984	9.00	19-35
1984 Currier & Ives QX250-1	Yr.Iss.	1984	4.50	23
1984 Disney QX250-4	Yr.Iss.	1984	4.50	23-43
1984 Katybeth QX463-1	Yr.Iss.	1984	9.00	17-33
1984 Kit QX453-4	Yr.Iss.	1984	5.50	28
1984 Muffin QX442-1	Yr.Iss.	1984	5.50	25-33
1984 The Muppets QX251-4	Yr.Iss.	1984	4.50	20-35
1984 Norman Rockwell QX251-4	Yr.Iss.	1984	4.50	35
1984 Peanuts QX252-1	Yr.Iss.	1984	4.50	33-40
1984 Shirt Tales QX252-4	Yr.Iss.	1984	4.50	8-20
1984 Snoopy and Woodstock QX439-1	Yr.Iss.	1984	7.50	95

1984 Traditional Ornaments - Keepsake

YEAR ISSUE	EDITION LIMIT	YEAR RETD.	ISSUE PRICE	*QUOTE U.S.$
1984 Alpine Elf QX452-1	Yr.Iss.	1984	6.00	32-40
1984 Amanda QX432-1	Yr.Iss.	1984	9.00	14-25
1984 Chickadee QX451-4	Yr.Iss.	1984	6.00	33-40
1984 Christmas Memories Photoholder QX300-4	Yr.Iss.	1984	6.50	25
1984 Cuckoo Clock QX455-1	Yr.Iss.	1984	10.00	45
1984 Gift of Music QX451-1	Yr.Iss.	1984	15.00	63-95
1984 Holiday Friendship QX445-1	Yr.Iss.	1984	13.00	20-30
1984 Holiday Jester QX437-4	Yr.Iss.	1984	11.00	20-30
1984 Holiday Starburst QX253-4	Yr.Iss.	1984	5.00	25
1984 Madonna and Child QX344-1	Yr.Iss.	1984	6.00	50
1984 Needlepoint Wreath QX459-4	Yr.Iss.	1984	6.50	5-15
1984 Nostalgic Sled QX442-4	Yr.Iss.	1984	6.00	13-15
1984 Old Fashioned Rocking Horse QX346-4	Yr.Iss.	1984	7.50	10-20
1984 Peace on Earth QX341-4	Yr.Iss.	1984	7.50	10-30
1984 Santa QX458-4	Yr.Iss.	1984	7.50	9-20
1984 Santa Sulky Driver QX436-1	Yr.Iss.	1984	9.00	18-35
1984 A Savior is Born QX254-1	Yr.Iss.	1984	4.50	33
1984 Twelve Days of Christmas QX415-9	Yr.Iss.	1984	15.00	100-125
1984 Uncle Sam QX449-1	Yr.Iss.	1984	6.00	42-50
1984 White Christmas QX905-1	Yr.Iss.	1984	16.00	71-95

1985 Collectible Series - Keepsake

YEAR ISSUE	EDITION LIMIT	YEAR RETD.	ISSUE PRICE	*QUOTE U.S.$
1985 Art Masterpiece (2nd Ed.) QX377-2	Yr.Iss.	1985	6.75	12-16
1985 Betsey Clark (13th & final Ed.) QX263-2	Yr.Iss.	1985	5.00	24-50
1985 Clothespin Soldier (4th Ed.) QX471-5	Yr.Iss.	1985	5.50	21-30
1985 Frosty Friends (6th Ed.) QX482-2	Yr.Iss.	1985	8.50	35-55
1985 Here Comes Santa (7th Ed.) QX496-5	Yr.Iss.	1985	14.00	45-53
1985 Holiday Wildlife (4th Ed.) QX376-5	Yr.Iss.	1985	7.50	22-30
1985 Miniature Creche (1st Ed.) QX482-5	Yr.Iss.	1985	8.75	20-35
1985 Norman Rockwell (6th Ed.) QX374-5	Yr.Iss.	1985	7.50	22-30
1985 Nostalgic Houses and Shops (2nd Ed.) QX497-5	Yr.Iss.	1985	13.75	113-165
1985 Porcelain Bear (3rd Ed.) QX479-2	Yr.Iss.	1985	7.50	36-60
1985 Rocking Horse (5th Ed.) QX493-2	Yr.Iss.	1985	10.75	59-77
1985 Thimble (8th Ed.) QX472-5	Yr.Iss.	1985	5.50	20-33
1985 Tin Locomotive (4th Ed.) QX497-2	Yr.Iss.	1985	14.75	58-80
1985 Twelve Days of Christmas (2nd Ed.) QX371-2	Yr.Iss.	1985	6.50	53-70
1985 Windows of the World (1st Ed.) QX490-2	Yr.Iss.	1985	9.75	75-77
1985 Wood Childhood Ornaments (2nd Ed.) QX472-2	Yr.Iss.	1985	7.00	30-34

1985 Commemoratives - Keepsake

YEAR ISSUE	EDITION LIMIT	YEAR RETD.	ISSUE PRICE	*QUOTE U.S.$
1985 Baby Locket QX401-2	Yr.Iss.	1985	16.00	15-30
1985 Baby's First Christmas QX260-2	Yr.Iss.	1985	5.00	20-25
1985 Baby's First Christmas QX370-2	Yr.Iss.	1985	5.75	12-22
1985 Baby's First Christmas QX478-2	Yr.Iss.	1985	7.00	5-18
1985 Baby's First Christmas QX499-2	Yr.Iss.	1985	15.00	45-49
1985 Baby's First Christmas QX499-5	Yr.Iss.	1985	16.00	23-45
1985 Baby's Second Christmas QX478-5	Yr.Iss.	1985	6.00	24-37
1985 Baby-sitter QX264-2	Yr.Iss.	1985	4.75	5-13
1985 Child's Third Christmas QX475-5	Yr.Iss.	1985	6.00	25-33
1985 Daughter QX503-2	Yr.Iss.	1985	5.50	21-30
1985 Father QX376-2	Yr.Iss.	1985	6.50	3-13
1985 First Christmas Together QX261-2	Yr.Iss.	1985	4.75	13-25
1985 First Christmas Together QX370-5	Yr.Iss.	1985	6.75	4-20
1985 First Christmas Together QX400-5	Yr.Iss.	1985	16.75	7-30
1985 First Christmas Together QX493-5	Yr.Iss.	1985	13.00	15-26
1985 First Christmas Together QX507-2	Yr.Iss.	1985	8.00	4-18
1985 Friendship QX378-5	Yr.Iss.	1985	6.75	12-20
1985 Friendship QX506-2	Yr.Iss.	1985	7.75	3-15
1985 From Our House to Yours QX520-2	Yr.Iss.	1985	7.75	12-15
1985 Godchild QX380-2	Yr.Iss.	1985	6.75	12-25
1985 Good Friends QX265-2	Yr.Iss.	1985	4.75	15-30
1985 Grandchild's First Christmas QX260-5	Yr.Iss.	1985	5.00	12-15
1985 Grandchild's First Christmas QX495-5	Yr.Iss.	1985	11.00	11-24
1985 Granddaughter QX263-5	Yr.Iss.	1985	4.75	24-30
1985 Grandmother QX262-5	Yr.Iss.	1985	4.75	12-20
1985 Grandparents QX380-5	Yr.Iss.	1985	7.00	7-15
1985 Grandson QX262-2	Yr.Iss.	1985	4.75	27-30
1985 Heart Full of Love QX378-2	Yr.Iss.	1985	6.75	5-20
1985 Holiday Heart QX498-2	Yr.Iss.	1985	8.00	18-29
1985 Love at Christmas QX371-5	Yr.Iss.	1985	5.75	20-40
1985 Mother and Dad QX509-2	Yr.Iss.	1985	7.75	10-25
1985 Mother QX372-2	Yr.Iss.	1985	6.75	3-5
1985 New Home QX269-5	Yr.Iss.	1985	4.75	24-30
1985 Niece QX520-5	Yr.Iss.	1985	5.75	7-11
1985 Sister QX506-5	Yr.Iss.	1985	7.25	7-25
1985 Son QX502-5	Yr.Iss.	1985	5.50	36-50
1985 Special Friends QX372-5	Yr.Iss.	1985	5.75	7-10
1985 Teacher QX505-2	Yr.Iss.	1985	6.00	8-20
1985 Twenty-Five Years Together QX500-5	Yr.Iss.	1985	8.00	5-20
1985 With Appreciation QX375-2	Yr.Iss.	1985	6.75	7-10

1985 Country Christmas Collection - Keepsake

YEAR ISSUE	EDITION LIMIT	YEAR RETD.	ISSUE PRICE	*QUOTE U.S.$
1985 Country Goose QX518-5	Yr.Iss.	1985	7.75	4-14
1985 Old-Fashioned Doll QX519-5	Yr.Iss.	1985	15.00	40
1985 Rocking Horse Memories QX518-2	Yr.Iss.	1985	10.00	6-15
1985 Sheep at Christmas QX517-5	Yr.Iss.	1985	8.25	14-29
1985 Whirligig Santa QX519-2	Yr.Iss.	1985	13.00	13-30

1985 Heirloom Christmas Collection - Keepsake

YEAR ISSUE	EDITION LIMIT	YEAR RETD.	ISSUE PRICE	*QUOTE U.S.$
1985 Charming Angel QX512-5	Yr.Iss.	1985	9.75	6-25
1985 Keepsake Basket QX514-5	Yr.Iss.	1985	15.00	14-20
1985 Lacy Heart QX511-2	Yr.Iss.	1985	8.75	24-27
1985 Snowflake QX510-5	Yr.Iss.	1985	6.50	7-23
1985 Victorian Lady QX513-2	Yr.Iss.	1985	9.50	25

1985 Holiday Humor - Keepsake

YEAR ISSUE	EDITION LIMIT	YEAR RETD.	ISSUE PRICE	*QUOTE U.S.$
1985 Baker Elf QX491-2	Yr.Iss.	1985	5.75	30
1985 Beary Smooth Ride QX480-5	Yr.Iss.	1986	6.50	13-25
1985 Bottlecap Fun Bunnies QX481-5	Yr.Iss.	1985	7.75	12-24
1985 Candy Apple Mouse QX470-5	Yr.Iss.	1985	6.50	65
1985 Children in the Shoe QX490-5	Yr.Iss.	1985	9.50	33-50
1985 Dapper Penguin QX477-2	Yr.Iss.	1985	5.00	30
1985 Do Not Disturb Bear QX481-2	Yr.Iss.	1986	7.75	16-30
1985 Doggy in a Stocking QX474-2	Yr.Iss.	1985	5.50	24-40
1985 Engineering Mouse QX473-5	Yr.Iss.	1985	5.50	15-25
1985 Ice-Skating Owl QX476-5	Yr.Iss.	1985	5.00	17-25
1985 Kitty Mischief QX474-5	Yr.Iss.	1986	5.00	14-25
1985 Lamb in Legwarmers QX480-2	Yr.Iss.	1985	7.00	14-25
1985 Merry Mouse QX403-2	Yr.Iss.	1986	4.50	18-30
1985 Mouse Wagon QX476-2	Yr.Iss.	1985	5.75	38-58
1985 Nativity Scene QX264-5	Yr.Iss.	1985	4.75	30
1985 Night Before Christmas QX449-4	Yr.Iss.	1985	13.00	14-45
1985 Roller Skating Rabbit QX457-1	Yr.Iss.	1985	5.00	19
1985 Santa's Ski Trip QX496-2	Yr.Iss.	1985	12.00	43-60
1985 Skateboard Raccoon QX473-2	Yr.Iss.	1986	6.50	25-43
1985 Snow-Pitching Snowman QX470-2	Yr.Iss.	1986	4.50	21-25
1985 Snowy Seal QX450-1	Yr.Iss.	1985	4.00	16
1985 Soccer Beaver QX477-5	Yr.Iss.	1986	6.50	10-14
1985 Stardust Angel QX475-2	Yr.Iss.	1985	5.75	22-27
1985 Sun and Fun Santa QX492-2	Yr.Iss.	1985	7.75	40
1985 Swinging Angel Bell QX492-5	Yr.Iss.	1985	11.00	17-40
1985 Three Kittens in a Mitten QX431-1	Yr.Iss.	1985	8.00	35
1985 Trumpet Panda QX471-2	Yr.Iss.	1985	4.50	13-25

1985 Keepsake Magic Ornaments - Keepsake

YEAR ISSUE	EDITION LIMIT	YEAR RETD.	ISSUE PRICE	*QUOTE U.S.$
1985 All Are Precious QLX704-1	Yr.Iss.	1985	8.00	25-30
1985 Baby's First Christmas QLX700-5	Yr.Iss.	1985	17.00	25-40
1985 Chris Mouse-1st Ed.) QLX703-2	Yr.Iss.	1985	13.00	74-89
1985 Christmas Eve Visit QLX710-5	Yr.Iss.	1985	12.00	26-33
1985 Katybeth QLX710-2	Yr.Iss.	1985	10.75	30-43
1985 Little Red Schoolhouse QLX711-2	Yr.Iss.	1985	15.75	71-95
1985 Love Wreath QLX702-5	Yr.Iss.	1985	8.50	19-30
1985 Mr. and Mrs. Santa QLX705-2	Yr.Iss.	1986	15.00	55-68
1985 Nativity QLX700-1	Yr.Iss.	1985	12.00	18-30
1985 Santa's Workshop QLX700-4	Yr.Iss.	1985	13.00	58
1985 Season of Beauty QLX712-2	Yr.Iss.	1985	8.00	19-36
1985 Sugarplum Cottage QLX701-1	Yr.Iss.	1985	11.00	45
1985 Swiss Cheese Lane QLX706-5	Yr.Iss.	1985	13.00	34-50
1985 Village Church QLX702-1	Yr.Iss.	1985	15.00	35-50

1985 Limited Edition - Keepsake

YEAR ISSUE	EDITION LIMIT	YEAR RETD.	ISSUE PRICE	*QUOTE U.S.$
1985 Heavenly Trumpeter QX405-2	Yr.Iss.	1985	28.00	69-75

1985 Property Ornaments - Keepsake

YEAR ISSUE	EDITION LIMIT	YEAR RETD.	ISSUE PRICE	*QUOTE U.S.$
1985 Betsey Clark QX508-5	Yr.Iss.	1985	8.50	30
1985 A Disney Christmas QX271-2	Yr.Iss.	1985	4.75	30
1985 Fraggle Rock Holiday QX265-5	Yr.Iss.	1985	4.75	23-30
1985 Hugga Bunch QX271-5	Yr.Iss.	1985	5.00	15-30
1985 Kit the Shepherd QX484-5	Yr.Iss.	1985	5.75	24
1985 Merry Shirt Tales QX267-2	Yr.Iss.	1985	4.75	20
1985 Muffin the Angel QX483-5	Yr.Iss.	1985	5.75	24
1985 Norman Rockwell QX266-2	Yr.Iss.	1985	4.75	28
1985 Peanuts QX266-5	Yr.Iss.	1985	4.75	36
1985 Rainbow Brite and Friends QX268-2	Yr.Iss.	1985	4.75	25
1985 Snoopy and Woodstock QX491-5	Yr.Iss.	1985	7.50	65-80

1985 Traditional Ornaments - Keepsake

YEAR ISSUE	EDITION LIMIT	YEAR RETD.	ISSUE PRICE	*QUOTE U.S.$
1985 Candle Cameo QX374-2	Yr.Iss.	1985	6.75	15
1985 Christmas Treats QX507-5	Yr.Iss.	1985	5.50	18
1985 Nostalgic Sled QX442-4	Yr.Iss.	1985	6.00	20
1985 Old-Fashioned Wreath QX373-5	Yr.Iss.	1985	7.50	25
1985 Peaceful Kingdom QX373-2	Yr.Iss.	1985	5.75	20-30
1985 Porcelain Bird QX479-5	Yr.Iss.	1985	6.50	25-40
1985 Santa Pipe QX494-2	Yr.Iss.	1985	9.50	10-15
1985 Sewn Photoholder QX379-5	Yr.Iss.	1985	7.00	25-35
1985 The Spirit of Santa Claus (Special Ed.) QX498-5	Yr.Iss.	1985	23.00	72-95

1986 Christmas Medley Collection - Keepsake

YEAR ISSUE	EDITION LIMIT	YEAR RETD.	ISSUE PRICE	*QUOTE U.S.$
1986 Christmas Guitar QX512-6	Yr.Iss.	1986	7.00	13-25
1986 Favorite Tin Drum QX514-3	Yr.Iss.	1986	8.50	30
1986 Festive Treble Clef QX513-3	Yr.Iss.	1986	8.75	9-28
1986 Holiday Horn QX514-6	Yr.Iss.	1986	8.00	17-33
1986 Joyful Carolers QX513-6	Yr.Iss.	1986	9.75	21-36

1986 Collectible Series - Keepsake

YEAR ISSUE	EDITION LIMIT	YEAR RETD.	ISSUE PRICE	*QUOTE U.S.$
1986 Art Masterpiece (3rd & Final Ed.) QX350-6	Yr.Iss.	1986	6.75	20-32

*Quotes have been rounded up to nearest dollar

YEAR ISSUE	EDITION LIMIT	YEAR RETD.	ISSUE PRICE	*QUOTE U.S.$
1986 Betsey Clark: Home for Christmas (1st Ed.) QX277-6	Yr.Iss.	1986	5.00	32-35
1986 Clothespin Soldier (5th Ed.) QX406-3	Yr.Iss.	1986	5.50	21-29
1986 Frosty Friends (7th Ed.) QX405-3	Yr.Iss.	1986	8.50	64-75
1986 Here Comes Santa (8th Ed.) QX404-3	Yr.Iss.	1986	14.00	50-75
1986 Holiday Wildlife (5th Ed.) QX321-6	Yr.Iss.	1986	7.50	21-30
1986 Miniature Creche (2nd Ed.) QX407-6	Yr.Iss.	1986	9.00	45-59
1986 Mr. and Mrs. Claus (1st Ed.) QX402-6	Yr.Iss.	1986	13.00	90-105
1986 Norman Rockwell (7th Ed.) QX321-3	Yr.Iss.	1986	7.75	20-30
1986 Nostalgic Houses and Shops (3rd Ed.) QX403-3	Yr.Iss.	1986	13.75	294-320
1986 Porcelain Bear (4th Ed.) QX405-6	Yr.Iss.	1986	7.75	28-45
1986 Reindeer Champs (1st Ed.) QX422-3	Yr.Iss.	1986	7.50	100-145
1986 Rocking Horse (6th Ed.) QX401-6	Yr.Iss.	1986	10.75	57-90
1986 Thimble (9th Ed.) QX406-6	Yr.Iss.	1986	5.75	20-30
1986 Tin Locomotive (5th Ed.) QX403-6	Yr.Iss.	1986	14.75	54-80
1986 Twelve Days of Christmas (3rd Ed.) QX378-6	Yr.Iss.	1986	6.50	35-45
1986 Windows of the World (2nd Ed.) QX408-3	Yr.Iss.	1986	10.00	23-41
1986 Wood Childhood Ornaments (3rd Ed.) QX407-3	Yr.Iss.	1986	7.50	21-30

1986 Commemoratives - Keepsake

YEAR ISSUE	EDITION LIMIT	YEAR RETD.	ISSUE PRICE	*QUOTE U.S.$
1986 Baby Locket QX412-3	Yr.Iss.	1986	16.00	24-27
1986 Baby's First Christmas Photoholder QX379-2	Yr.Iss.	1986	8.00	14-25
1986 Baby's First Christmas QX271-3	Yr.Iss.	1986	5.50	20-30
1986 Baby's First Christmas QX380-3	Yr.Iss.	1986	6.00	16-25
1986 Baby's First Christmas QX412-6	Yr.Iss.	1986	9.00	31-40
1986 Baby's Second Christmas QX413-3	Yr.Iss.	1986	6.50	23-30
1986 Baby-Sitter QX275-6	Yr.Iss.	1986	4.75	7-12
1986 Child's Third Christmas QX413-6	Yr.Iss.	1986	6.50	20-27
1986 Daughter QX430-6	Yr.Iss.	1986	5.75	28-40
1986 Father QX431-3	Yr.Iss.	1986	6.50	5-15
1986 Fifty Years Together QX400-6	Yr.Iss.	1986	10.00	5-16
1986 First Christmas Together QX270-3	Yr.Iss.	1986	4.75	12-30
1986 First Christmas Together QX379-3	Yr.Iss.	1986	7.00	17-35
1986 First Christmas Together QX400-3	Yr.Iss.	1986	16.00	12-17
1986 First Christmas Together QX409-6	Yr.Iss.	1986	12.00	32-38
1986 Friends Are Fun QX272-3	Yr.Iss.	1986	4.75	32-40
1986 Friendship Greeting QX427-3	Yr.Iss.	1986	8.00	5-15
1986 Friendship's Gift QX381-6	Yr.Iss.	1986	6.00	12-15
1986 From Our Home to Yours QX383-3	Yr.Iss.	1986	6.00	10-15
1986 Godchild QX271-6	Yr.Iss.	1986	4.75	12-20
1986 Grandchild's First Christmas QX411-6	Yr.Iss.	1986	10.00	7
1986 Granddaughter QX273-6	Yr.Iss.	1986	4.75	20-33
1986 Grandmother QX274-3	Yr.Iss.	1986	4.75	8-16
1986 Grandparents QX432-3	Yr.Iss.	1986	7.50	9-25
1986 Grandson QX273-3	Yr.Iss.	1986	4.75	20-40
1986 Gratitude QX432-6	Yr.Iss.	1986	6.00	9
1986 Husband QX383-6	Yr.Iss.	1986	8.00	10-20
1986 Joy of Friends QX382-3	Yr.Iss.	1986	6.75	14-18
1986 Loving Memories QX409-3	Yr.Iss.	1986	9.00	15-35
1986 Mother and Dad QX431-6	Yr.Iss.	1986	7.50	12-28
1986 Mother QX382-6	Yr.Iss.	1986	7.00	11-25
1986 Nephew QX381-3	Yr.Iss.	1986	6.25	12-15
1986 New Home QX274-6	Yr.Iss.	1986	4.75	52-65
1986 Niece QX426-6	Yr.Iss.	1986	6.00	7-11
1986 Season of the Heart QX270-6	Yr.Iss.	1986	4.75	6-18
1986 Sister QX380-6	Yr.Iss.	1986	6.75	12-18
1986 Son QX430-3	Yr.Iss.	1986	5.75	28-39
1986 Sweetheart QX408-6	Yr.Iss.	1986	11.00	63-70
1986 Teacher QX275-3	Yr.Iss.	1986	4.75	5-12
1986 Ten Years Together QX401-3	Yr.Iss.	1986	7.50	20-25
1986 Timeless Love QX379-6	Yr.Iss.	1986	6.00	17-40
1986 Twenty-Five Years Together QX410-3	Yr.Iss.	1986	8.00	20-25

1986 Country Treasures Collection - Keepsake

YEAR ISSUE	EDITION LIMIT	YEAR RETD.	ISSUE PRICE	*QUOTE U.S.$
1986 Country Sleigh QX511-3	Yr.Iss.	1986	10.00	14-29
1986 Little Drummers QX511-6	Yr.Iss.	1986	12.50	17-35
1986 Nutcracker Santa QX512-3	Yr.Iss.	1986	10.00	25-50
1986 Remembering Christmas QX510-6	Yr.Iss.	1986	8.75	30
1986 Welcome, Christmas QX510-3	Yr.Iss.	1986	8.25	20-35

1986 Holiday Humor - Keepsake

YEAR ISSUE	EDITION LIMIT	YEAR RETD.	ISSUE PRICE	*QUOTE U.S.$
1986 Acorn Inn QX424-3	Yr.Iss.	1986	8.50	25-30
1986 Beary Smooth Ride QX480-5	Yr.Iss.	1986	6.50	20
1986 Chatty Penguin QX417-6	Yr.Iss.	1986	5.75	13-25
1986 Cookies for Santa QX414-6	Yr.Iss.	1986	4.50	19-30
1986 Do Not Disturb Bear QX481-2	Yr.Iss.	1986	7.75	15-25
1986 Happy Christmas to Owl QX418-3	Yr.Iss.	1986	6.00	14-25
1986 Heavenly Dreamer QX417-3	Yr.Iss.	1986	5.75	22-35
1986 Jolly Hiker QX483-2	Yr.Iss.	1987	5.00	16-30
1986 Kitty Mischief QX474-5	Yr.Iss.	1986	5.00	25
1986 Li'l Jingler QX419-3	Yr.Iss.	1987	6.75	22-40
1986 Merry Koala QX415-3	Yr.Iss.	1987	5.00	17-23
1986 Merry Mouse QX403-2	Yr.Iss.	1986	4.50	22
1986 Mouse in the Moon QX416-6	Yr.Iss.	1987	5.50	30
1986 Open Me First QX422-6	Yr.Iss.	1986	7.25	35
1986 Playful Possum QX425-3	Yr.Iss.	1986	11.00	35
1986 Popcorn Mouse QX421-3	Yr.Iss.	1986	6.75	42-50
1986 Puppy's Best Friend QX420-3	Yr.Iss.	1986	6.50	17-30
1986 Rah Rah Rabbit QX421-6	Yr.Iss.	1986	7.00	40
1986 Santa's Hot Tub QX426-3	Yr.Iss.	1986	12.00	55-60
1986 Skateboard Raccoon QX473-2	Yr.Iss.	1986	6.50	40
1986 Ski Tripper QX420-6	Yr.Iss.	1986	6.75	12-22
1986 Snow Buddies QX423-6	Yr.Iss.	1986	8.00	38
1986 Snow-Pitching Snowman QX470-2	Yr.Iss.	1986	4.50	23
1986 Soccer Beaver QX477-5	Yr.Iss.	1986	6.50	25
1986 Special Delivery QX415-6	Yr.Iss.	1986	5.00	17-30
1986 Tipping the Scales QX418-6	Yr.Iss.	1986	6.75	15-30
1986 Touchdown Santa QX423-3	Yr.Iss.	1986	8.00	42
1986 Treetop Trio QX424-6	Yr.Iss.	1987	11.00	18-33
1986 Walnut Shell Rider QX419-6	Yr.Iss.	1987	6.00	17-30
1986 Wynken, Blynken and Nod QX424-6	Yr.Iss.	1986	9.75	20-39

1986 Lighted Ornament Collection - Keepsake

YEAR ISSUE	EDITION LIMIT	YEAR RETD.	ISSUE PRICE	*QUOTE U.S.$
1986 Baby's First Christmas QLX710-3	Yr.Iss.	1986	19.50	45
1986 Chris Mouse (2nd Ed.) QLX705-6	Yr.Iss.	1986	13.00	66-75
1986 Christmas Classics (1st Ed.) QLX704-3	Yr.Iss.	1986	17.50	65-80
1986 Christmas Sleigh Ride QLX701-2	Yr.Iss.	1986	24.50	120-145
1986 First Christmas Together QLX707-3	Yr.Iss.	1986	14.00	43
1986 General Store QLX705-3	Yr.Iss.	1986	15.75	43-60
1986 Gentle Blessings QLX708-3	Yr.Iss.	1986	15.00	110-175
1986 Keep on Glowin' QLX707-6	Yr.Iss.	1987	10.00	37-50
1986 Merry Christmas Bell QLX709-3	Yr.Iss.	1986	8.50	10-16
1986 Mr. and Mrs. Santa QLX705-2	Yr.Iss.	1986	14.50	83-100
1986 Santa and Sparky (1st Ed.) QLX703-3	Yr.Iss.	1986	22.00	97
1986 Santa's On His Way QLX711-5	Yr.Iss.	1986	15.00	63-75
1986 Santa's Snack QLX706-6	Yr.Iss.	1986	10.00	58
1986 Sharing Friendship QLX706-3	Yr.Iss.	1986	8.50	15-20
1986 Sugarplum Cottage QLX701-1	Yr.Iss.	1986	11.00	45
1986 Village Express QLX707-2	Yr.Iss.	1987	24.50	89-125

1986 Limited Edition - Keepsake

YEAR ISSUE	EDITION LIMIT	YEAR RETD.	ISSUE PRICE	*QUOTE U.S.$
1986 Magical Unicorn QX429-3	Yr.Iss.	1986	27.50	75

1986 Property Ornaments - Keepsake

YEAR ISSUE	EDITION LIMIT	YEAR RETD.	ISSUE PRICE	*QUOTE U.S.$
1986 Heathcliff QX436-3	Yr.Iss.	1986	7.50	21-33
1986 Katybeth QX435-3	Yr.Iss.	1986	7.00	25
1986 Norman Rockwell QX276-3	Yr.Iss.	1986	4.75	30
1986 Paddington Bear QX435-6	Yr.Iss.	1986	6.00	38-40
1986 Peanuts QX276-6	Yr.Iss.	1986	4.75	30
1986 Shirt Tales Parade QX277-3	Yr.Iss.	1986	4.75	18
1986 Snoopy and Woodstock QX434-6	Yr.Iss.	1986	8.00	55-60
1986 The Statue of Liberty QX384-3	Yr.Iss.	1986	6.00	8-26

1986 Special Edition - Keepsake

YEAR ISSUE	EDITION LIMIT	YEAR RETD.	ISSUE PRICE	*QUOTE U.S.$
1986 Jolly St. Nick QX429-6	Yr.Iss.	1986	22.50	48-75

1986 Traditional Ornaments - Keepsake

YEAR ISSUE	EDITION LIMIT	YEAR RETD.	ISSUE PRICE	*QUOTE U.S.$
1986 Bluebird QX428-3	Yr.Iss.	1986	7.25	54
1986 Christmas Beauty QX322-3	Yr.Iss.	1986	6.00	3-10
1986 Glowing Christmas Tree QX428-6	Yr.Iss.	1986	7.00	15
1986 Heirloom Snowflake QX515-3	Yr.Iss.	1986	6.75	32-47
1986 Holiday Jingle Bell QX404-6	Yr.Iss.	1986	16.00	32-55
1986 The Magi QX272-6	Yr.Iss.	1986	4.75	23
1986 Mary Emmerling:American Country Collection QX275-2	Yr.Iss.	1986	7.95	25
1986 Memories to Cherish QX427-6	Yr.Iss.	1986	7.50	25
1986 Star Brighteners QX322-6	Yr.Iss.	1986	6.00	20

1987 Artists' Favorites - Keepsake

YEAR ISSUE	EDITION LIMIT	YEAR RETD.	ISSUE PRICE	*QUOTE U.S.$
1987 Beary Special QX455-7	Yr.Iss.	1987	4.75	16-30
1987 December Showers QX448-7	Yr.Iss.	1987	5.50	24-38
1987 Three Men in a Tub QX454-7	Yr.Iss.	1987	8.00	18-30
1987 Wee Chimney Sweep QX451-9	Yr.Iss.	1987	6.25	16-25

1987 Christmas Pizzazz Collection - Keepsake

YEAR ISSUE	EDITION LIMIT	YEAR RETD.	ISSUE PRICE	*QUOTE U.S.$
1987 Christmas Fun Puzzle QX467-9	Yr.Iss.	1987	8.00	30
1987 Doc Holiday QX467-7	Yr.Iss.	1987	8.00	43
1987 Happy Holidata QX471-7	Yr.Iss.	1988	6.50	15-30
1987 Holiday Hourglass QX470-7	Yr.Iss.	1987	8.00	23-25
1987 Jolly Follies QX466-9	Yr.Iss.	1987	8.50	35
1987 Mistletoad QX468-7	Yr.Iss.	1988	7.00	23-30
1987 St. Louie Nick QX453-9	Yr.Iss.	1988	7.75	17-30

1987 Collectible Series - Keepsake

YEAR ISSUE	EDITION LIMIT	YEAR RETD.	ISSUE PRICE	*QUOTE U.S.$
1987 Betsey Clark:Home for Christmas (2nd Ed.) QX272-7	Yr.Iss.	1987	5.00	17-25
1987 Clothespin Soldier (6th & Final Ed.) QX480-7	Yr.Iss.	1987	5.50	20-30
1987 Collector's Plate (1st Ed.) QX481-7	Yr.Iss.	1987	8.00	64-79
1987 Frosty Friends (8th Ed.) QX440-9	Yr.Iss.	1987	8.50	45-60
1987 Here Comes Santa (9th Ed.) QX484-7	Yr.Iss.	1987	14.00	63-95
1987 Holiday Heirloom (1st Ed./limited Ed.) QX485-7	Yr.Iss.	1987	25.00	25-48
1987 Holiday Wildlife (6th Ed.) QX371-7	Yr.Iss.	1987	7.50	18-27
1987 Miniature Creche (3rd Ed.) QX481-9	Yr.Iss.	1987	9.00	25-40
1987 Mr. and Mrs. Claus (2nd Ed.) QX483-7	Yr.Iss.	1987	13.25	47-69
1987 Norman Rockwell (8th Ed.) QX370-7	Yr.Iss.	1987	7.75	16-25
1987 Nostalgic Houses and Shops (4th Ed.) QX483-9	Yr.Iss.	1987	14.00	62-80
1987 Porcelain Bear (5th Ed.) QX442-7	Yr.Iss.	1987	7.75	26-40
1987 Porcelain Bear (5th Ed.) QX442-7	Yr.Iss.	1987	7.75	26-35
1987 Reindeer Champs (2nd Ed.) QX480-9	Yr.Iss.	1987	7.50	36-41
1987 Rocking Horse (7th Ed.) QX482-9	Yr.Iss.	1987	10.75	58-80
1987 Thimble (10th Ed.) QX441-9	Yr.Iss.	1987	5.75	21-30
1987 Tin Locomotive (6th Ed.) QX484-9	Yr.Iss.	1987	14.75	48-65
1987 Twelve Days of Christmas (4th Ed.) QX370-9	Yr.Iss.	1987	6.50	28-40
1987 Windows of the World (3rd Ed.) QX482-7	Yr.Iss.	1987	10.00	26-30
1987 Wood Childhood Ornaments (4th Ed.) QX441-7	Yr.Iss.	1987	7.50	18-27

1987 Commemoratives - Keepsake

YEAR ISSUE	EDITION LIMIT	YEAR RETD.	ISSUE PRICE	*QUOTE U.S.$
1987 Baby Locket QX461-7	Yr.Iss.	1987	15.00	24-30
1987 Baby's First Christmas Photoholder QX4661-9	Yr.Iss.	1987	7.50	24-30
1987 Baby's First Christmas QX372-9	Yr.Iss.	1987	6.00	20-25
1987 Baby's First Christmas QX411-3	Yr.Iss.	1987	9.75	23-30
1987 Baby's First Christmas-Baby Boy QX274-9	Yr.Iss.	1987	4.75	20-30
1987 Baby's First Christmas-Baby Girl QX274-7	Yr.Iss.	1987	4.75	20-28
1987 Baby's Second Christmas QX460-7	Yr.Iss.	1987	5.75	27-33
1987 Babysitter QX279-7	Yr.Iss.	1987	4.75	12-20
1987 Child's Third Christmas QX459-9	Yr.Iss.	1987	5.75	23-30
1987 Dad QX462-9	Yr.Iss.	1987	6.00	29-40
1987 Daughter QX463-7	Yr.Iss.	1987	5.75	21-36
1987 Fifty Years Together QX443-7	Yr.Iss.	1987	8.00	20-25
1987 First Christmas Together QX272-9	Yr.Iss.	1987	4.75	21-30
1987 First Christmas Together QX371-9	Yr.Iss.	1987	6.50	6-20
1987 First Christmas Together QX445-9	Yr.Iss.	1987	8.00	19-38
1987 First Christmas Together QX446-7	Yr.Iss.	1987	9.50	19-30
1987 First Christmas Together QX446-9	Yr.Iss.	1987	15.00	24-30
1987 From Our Home to Yours QX279-9	Yr.Iss.	1987	4.75	40-50
1987 Godchild QX276-7	Yr.Iss.	1987	4.75	16-25
1987 Grandchild's First Christmas QX460-9	Yr.Iss.	1987	9.00	16-28
1987 Granddaughter QX374-7	Yr.Iss.	1987	6.00	23-27
1987 Grandmother QX277-9	Yr.Iss.	1987	4.75	12-18
1987 Grandparents QX277-7	Yr.Iss.	1987	4.75	15-20
1987 Grandson QX276-9	Yr.Iss.	1987	4.75	24-30
1987 Heart in Blossom QX372-7	Yr.Iss.	1987	6.00	20-25
1987 Holiday Greetings QX375-7	Yr.Iss.	1987	6.00	5-13
1987 Husband QX373-9	Yr.Iss.	1987	7.00	9-12
1987 Love is Everywhere QX278-7	Yr.Iss.	1987	4.75	25-28
1987 Mother and Dad QX462-7	Yr.Iss.	1987	7.00	20-25
1987 Mother QX373-7	Yr.Iss.	1987	6.50	16-20
1987 New Home QX376-7	Yr.Iss.	1987	6.00	24-30
1987 Niece QX275-9	Yr.Iss.	1987	4.75	9-13
1987 Sister QX474-7	Yr.Iss.	1987	6.00	12-15
1987 Son QX463-9	Yr.Iss.	1987	5.75	12-45
1987 Sweetheart QX447-9	Yr.Iss.	1987	11.00	18-30
1987 Teacher QX466-7	Yr.Iss.	1987	5.75	16-21
1987 Ten Years Together QX444-7	Yr.Iss.	1987	7.00	20-25
1987 Time for Friends QX280-7	Yr.Iss.	1987	4.75	18-22
1987 Twenty-Five Years Together QX443-9	Yr.Iss.	1987	7.50	6-30
1987 Warmth of Friendship QX375-9	Yr.Iss.	1987	6.00	9-12
1987 Word of Love QX447-7	Yr.Iss.	1987	8.00	8-25

1987 Holiday Humor - Keepsake

YEAR ISSUE	EDITION LIMIT	YEAR RETD.	ISSUE PRICE	*QUOTE U.S.$
1987 Bright Christmas Dreams QX440-7	Yr.Iss.	1987	7.25	27-80
1987 Chocolate Chipmunk QX456-7	Yr.Iss.	1987	6.00	46-50
1987 Christmas Cuddle QX453-7	Yr.Iss.	1987	5.75	19-35
1987 Dr. Seuss:The Grinch's Christmas QX278-3	Yr.Iss.	1987	4.75	95
1987 Fudge Forever QX449-7	Yr.Iss.	1987	5.00	23-40
1987 Happy Santa QX456-9	Yr.Iss.	1987	4.75	28-30
1987 Hot Dogger QX471-9	Yr.Iss.	1987	6.50	21-30
1987 Icy Treat QX450-9	Yr.Iss.	1987	4.50	21-30
1987 Jack Frosting QX449-9	Yr.Iss.	1987	7.00	29-50
1987 Jammie Pies QX283-9	Yr.Iss.	1987	4.75	16-18
1987 Jogging Through the Snow QX457-7	Yr.Iss.	1987	7.25	22-40
1987 Jolly Hiker QX483-2	Yr.Iss.	1987	5.00	18
1987 Joy Ride QX440-7	Yr.Iss.	1987	11.50	56-75
1987 Let It Snow QX458-9	Yr.Iss.	1987	6.50	12-30
1987 Li'l Jingler QX419-3	Yr.Iss.	1987	6.75	22-36
1987 Merry Koala QX415-3	Yr.Iss.	1987	5.00	17
1987 Mouse in the Moon QX416-6	Yr.Iss.	1987	5.50	21
1987 Nature's Decorations QX273-9	Yr.Iss.	1987	4.75	35
1987 Night Before Christmas QX451-7	Yr.Iss.	1988	6.50	20-33
1987 Owliday Wish QX455-9	Yr.Iss.	1988	6.50	14-25
1987 Peanuts QX281-9	Yr.Iss.	1987	4.75	28-40
1987 Pretty Kitten QX448-9	Yr.Iss.	1987	11.00	35
1987 Raccoon Biker QX458-7	Yr.Iss.	1987	7.00	16-30
1987 Reindoggy QX452-7	Yr.Iss.	1988	5.75	20-35
1987 Santa at the Bat QX457-9	Yr.Iss.	1987	7.75	19-30
1987 Seasoned Greetings QX454-9	Yr.Iss.	1987	6.25	16-30
1987 Sleepy Santa QX450-7	Yr.Iss.	1987	6.25	30
1987 Snoopy and Woodstock QX472-9	Yr.Iss.	1987	7.25	45-50
1987 Spots 'n Stripes QX452-9	Yr.Iss.	1987	5.50	25
1987 Treetop Dreams QX459-7	Yr.Iss.	1988	6.75	16-30
1987 Treetop Trio QX425-6	Yr.Iss.	1987	11.00	25
1987 Walnut Shell Rider QX419-6	Yr.Iss.	1987	6.00	18

1987 Keepsake Collector's Club - Keepsake

YEAR ISSUE	EDITION LIMIT	YEAR RETD.	ISSUE PRICE	*QUOTE U.S.$
1987 Carousel Reindeer QXC580-7	Yr.Iss.	1987	8.00	43-56
1987 Wreath of Memories QXC580-9	Yr.Iss.	1988	Gift	25-48

1987 Keepsake Magic Ornaments - Keepsake

YEAR ISSUE	EDITION LIMIT	YEAR RETD.	ISSUE PRICE	*QUOTE U.S.$
1987 Angelic Messengers QLX711-3	Yr.Iss.	1987	18.75	42-54
1987 Baby's First Christmas QLX704-9	Yr.Iss.	1987	13.50	30-40
1987 Bright Noel QLX705-9	Yr.Iss.	1987	7.00	18-33
1987 Chris Mouse (3rd Ed.) QLX705-7	Yr.Iss.	1987	11.00	48-60
1987 Christmas Classics (2nd Ed.) QLX702-9	Yr.Iss.	1987	16.00	40-75
1987 Christmas Morning QLX701-3	Yr.Iss.	1988	24.50	35-50
1987 First Christmas Together QLX708-7	Yr.Iss.	1987	11.50	40-50
1987 Good Cheer Blimp QLX704-6	Yr.Iss.	1987	16.00	48-59
1987 Keeping Cozy QLX704-7	Yr.Iss.	1987	11.75	24-37
1987 Lacy Brass Snowflake QLX709-7	Yr.Iss.	1987	11.50	16-30
1987 Loving Holiday QLX701-6	Yr.Iss.	1987	22.00	38-55
1987 Memories are Forever Photoholder QLX706-7	Yr.Iss.	1987	8.50	33-42
1987 Meowy Christmas QLX708-9	Yr.Iss.	1987	10.00	50-63
1987 Santa and Sparky (2nd Ed.) QLX701-9	Yr.Iss.	1987	19.50	65-75
1987 Season for Friendship QLX706-9	Yr.Iss.	1987	8.50	16-20
1987 Train Station QLX703-9	Yr.Iss.	1987	12.75	40-50

1987 Lighted Ornament Collection - Keepsake

YEAR ISSUE	EDITION LIMIT	YEAR RETD.	ISSUE PRICE	*QUOTE U.S.$
1987 Keep on Glowin' QLX707-6	Yr.Iss.	1987	10.00	37
1987 Village Express QLX707-2	Yr.Iss.	1987	24.50	87-120

*Quotes have been rounded up to nearest dollar

1987 Limited Edition - Keepsake

YEAR ISSUE	EDITION LIMIT	YEAR RETD.	ISSUE PRICE	*QUOTE U.S.$
1987 Christmas is Gentle QX444-9	Yr.Iss.	1987	17.50	58-75
1987 Christmas Time Mime QX442-9	Yr.Iss.	1987	27.50	40-46

1987 Old-Fashioned Christmas Collection - Keepsake

YEAR ISSUE	EDITION LIMIT	YEAR RETD.	ISSUE PRICE	*QUOTE U.S.$
1987 Country Wreath QX470-9	Yr.Iss.	1987	5.75	30
1987 Folk Art Santa QX474-9	Yr.Iss.	1987	5.25	20-35
1987 In a Nutshell QX469-7	Yr.Iss.	1988	5.50	24-35
1987 Little Whittler QX469-9	Yr.Iss.	1987	6.00	25-33
1987 Nostalgic Rocker QX468-9	Yr.Iss.	1987	6.50	27-33

1987 Special Edition - Keepsake

YEAR ISSUE	EDITION LIMIT	YEAR RETD.	ISSUE PRICE	*QUOTE U.S.$
1987 Favorite Santa QX445-7	Yr.Iss.	1987	22.50	32-45

1987 Traditional Ornaments - Keepsake

YEAR ISSUE	EDITION LIMIT	YEAR RETD.	ISSUE PRICE	*QUOTE U.S.$
1987 Christmas Keys QX473-9	Yr.Iss.	1987	5.75	30
1987 Currier & Ives: American Farm Scene QX282-9	Yr.Iss.	1987	4.75	30
1987 Goldfinch QX464-9	Yr.Iss.	1987	7.00	46-61
1987 Heavenly Harmony QX465-9	Yr.Iss.	1987	15.00	20-35
1987 I Remember Santa QX278-9	Yr.Iss.	1987	4.75	33
1987 Joyous Angels QX465-7	Yr.Iss.	1987	7.75	22-25
1987 Norman Rockwell:Christmas Scenes QX282-7	Yr.Iss.	1987	4.75	30
1987 Promise of Peace QX374-9	Yr.Iss.	1987	6.50	25
1987 Special Memories Photoholder QX464-7	Yr.Iss.	1987	6.75	27

1988 Artist Favorites - Keepsake

YEAR ISSUE	EDITION LIMIT	YEAR RETD.	ISSUE PRICE	*QUOTE U.S.$
1988 Baby Redbird QX410-1	Yr.Iss.	1988	5.00	18-20
1988 Cymbals of Christmas QX411-1	Yr.Iss.	1988	5.50	18-30
1988 Little Jack Horner QX408-1	Yr.Iss.	1988	8.00	16-25
1988 Merry-Mint Unicorn QX423-4	Yr.Iss.	1988	8.50	12-23
1988 Midnight Snack QX410-4	Yr.Iss.	1988	6.00	21-23
1988 Very Strawbeary QX409-1	Yr.Iss.	1988	4.75	14-23

1988 Christmas Pizzazz Collection - Keepsake

YEAR ISSUE	EDITION LIMIT	YEAR RETD.	ISSUE PRICE	*QUOTE U.S.$
1988 Happy Holidata QX471-7	Yr.Iss.	1988	6.50	15-30
1988 Mistletoad QX468-7	Yr.Iss.	1988	7.00	22-30
1988 St. Louie Nick QX453-9	Yr.Iss.	1988	7.75	17-22

1988 Collectible Series - Keepsake

YEAR ISSUE	EDITION LIMIT	YEAR RETD.	ISSUE PRICE	*QUOTE U.S.$
1988 Betsey Clark: Home for Christmas (3rd Ed.) QX271-4	Yr.Iss.	1988	5.00	18-25
1988 Collector's Plate (2nd Ed.) QX406-1	Yr.Iss.	1988	8.00	35-50
1988 Five Golden Rings (5th Ed.) QX371-4	Yr.Iss.	1988	6.50	18-30
1988 Frosty Friends (9th Ed.) QX403-1	Yr.Iss.	1988	8.75	45-65
1988 Here Comes Santa (10th Ed.) QX400-1	Yr.Iss.	1988	14.00	34-50
1988 Holiday Heirloom (2nd Ed.) QX406-4	Yr.Iss.	1988	25.00	24-30
1988 Holiday Wildlife (7th Ed.) QX371-1	Yr.Iss.	1988	7.75	18-30
1988 Mary's Angels (1st Ed.) QX407-4	Yr.Iss.	1988	5.00	40-53
1988 Miniature Creche (4th Ed.) QX403-4	Yr.Iss.	1988	8.50	22-35
1988 Mr. and Mrs. Claus (3rd Ed.) QX401-1	Yr.Iss.	1988	13.00	43-58
1988 Norman Rockwell (9th Ed.) QX370-4	Yr.Iss.	1988	7.75	14-23
1988 Nostalgic Houses and Shops (5th Ed.) QX401-4	Yr.Iss.	1988	14.50	44-65
1988 Porcelain Bear (6th Ed.) QX404-4	Yr.Iss.	1988	8.00	26-40
1988 Reindeer Champs (3rd Ed.) QX405-1	Yr.Iss.	1988	7.50	28-40
1988 Rocking Horse (8th Ed.) QX402-4	Yr.Iss.	1988	10.75	56-70
1988 Thimble (11th Ed.) QX405-4	Yr.Iss.	1988	5.75	18-25
1988 Tin Locomotive (7th Ed.) QX400-4	Yr.Iss.	1988	14.75	40-60
1988 Windows of the World (4th Ed.) QX402-1	Yr.Iss.	1988	10.00	22-30
1988 Wood Childhood (5th Ed.) QX404-1	Yr.Iss.	1988	7.50	20-23

1988 Commemoratives - Keepsake

YEAR ISSUE	EDITION LIMIT	YEAR RETD.	ISSUE PRICE	*QUOTE U.S.$
1988 Baby's First Christmas (Boy) QX272-1	Yr.Iss.	1988	4.75	20-25
1988 Baby's First Christmas (Girl) QX272-4	Yr.Iss.	1988	4.75	20-30
1988 Baby's First Christmas QX372-1	Yr.Iss.	1988	6.00	20-23
1988 Baby's First Christmas QX470-1	Yr.Iss.	1988	9.75	33-40
1988 Baby's First Christmas QX470-4	Yr.Iss.	1988	7.50	24-30
1988 Baby's Second Christmas QX471-1	Yr.Iss.	1988	6.00	20-33
1988 Babysitter QX279-1	Yr.Iss.	1988	4.75	5-11
1988 Child's Third Christmas QX471-4	Yr.Iss.	1988	6.00	24-30
1988 Dad QX414-1	Yr.Iss.	1988	7.00	20-25
1988 Daughter QX415-1	Yr.Iss.	1988	5.75	52-65
1988 Fifty Years Together QX374-1	Yr.Iss.	1988	6.75	8-20
1988 First Christmas Together QX274-1	Yr.Iss.	1988	4.75	22-28
1988 First Christmas Together QX373-1	Yr.Iss.	1988	6.75	12-23
1988 First Christmas Together QX489-4	Yr.Iss.	1988	9.00	22-40
1988 Five Years Together QX274-4	Yr.Iss.	1988	4.75	7-23
1988 From Our Home to Yours QX279-4	Yr.Iss.	1988	4.75	14-18
1988 Godchild QX278-4	Yr.Iss.	1988	4.75	16-20
1988 Granddaughter QX277-4	Yr.Iss.	1988	4.75	40-50
1988 Grandmother QX276-4	Yr.Iss.	1988	4.75	16-23
1988 Grandparents QX277-1	Yr.Iss.	1988	4.75	16-20
1988 Grandson QX278-1	Yr.Iss.	1988	4.75	20-40
1988 Gratitude QX375-4	Yr.Iss.	1988	6.00	9-12
1988 Love Fills the Heart QX374-4	Yr.Iss.	1988	6.00	18-25
1988 Love Grows QX275-4	Yr.Iss.	1988	4.75	26-32
1988 Mother and Dad QX414-4	Yr.Iss.	1988	8.00	20-25
1988 Mother QX375-1	Yr.Iss.	1988	6.50	16-23
1988 New Home QX376-1	Yr.Iss.	1988	6.00	20-25
1988 Sister QX499-4	Yr.Iss.	1988	8.00	26-33
1988 Son QX415-4	Yr.Iss.	1988	5.75	33-40
1988 Spirit of Christmas QX276-1	Yr.Iss.	1988	4.75	18-23
1988 Sweetheart QX490-1	Yr.Iss.	1988	9.75	14-30
1988 Teacher QX417-1	Yr.Iss.	1988	6.25	14-30
1988 Ten Years Together QX275-1	Yr.Iss.	1988	4.75	9-23
1988 Twenty-Five Years Together QX373-4	Yr.Iss.	1988	6.75	4-19

YEAR ISSUE	EDITION LIMIT	YEAR RETD.	ISSUE PRICE	*QUOTE U.S.$
1988 Year to Remember QX416-4	Yr.Iss.	1988	7.00	20-25

1988 Hallmark Handcrafted Ornaments - Keepsake

YEAR ISSUE	EDITION LIMIT	YEAR RETD.	ISSUE PRICE	*QUOTE U.S.$
1988 Americana Drum QX488-1	Yr.Iss.	1988	7.75	19-34
1988 Arctic Tenor QX472-1	Yr.Iss.	1988	4.00	11-19
1988 Christmas Cardinal QX494-1	Yr.Iss.	1988	4.75	9-20
1988 Christmas Cuckoo QX480-1	Yr.Iss.	1988	8.00	40
1988 Christmas Memories QX372-4	Yr.Iss.	1988	6.50	25
1988 Christmas Scenes QX273-1	Yr.Iss.	1988	4.75	24
1988 Cool Juggler QX487-4	Yr.Iss.	1988	6.50	20
1988 Feliz Navidad QX416-1	Yr.Iss.	1988	6.75	22-35
1988 Filled with Fudge QX419-1	Yr.Iss.	1988	4.75	18-33
1988 Glowing Wreath QX492-1	Yr.Iss.	1988	6.00	14
1988 Go For The Gold QX417-4	Yr.Iss.	1988	8.00	17-30
1988 Goin' Cross-Country QX476-4	Yr.Iss.	1988	8.50	14-29
1988 Gone Fishing QX479-4	Yr.Iss.	1989	5.00	16-19
1988 Hoe-Hoe-Hoe QX422-1	Yr.Iss.	1988	5.00	11-20
1988 Holiday Hero QX423-1	Yr.Iss.	1988	5.00	20
1988 Jingle Bell Clown QX477-4	Yr.Iss.	1988	15.00	21-30
1988 Jolly Walrus QX473-1	Yr.Iss.	1988	4.50	24-30
1988 Kiss from Santa QX482-1	Yr.Iss.	1989	4.50	10-30
1988 Kiss the Claus QX486-1	Yr.Iss.	1988	5.00	10-19
1988 Kringle Moon QX495-1	Yr.Iss.	1988	5.00	35
1988 Kringle Portrait QX496-1	Yr.Iss.	1988	7.50	22-40
1988 Kringle Tree QX495-4	Yr.Iss.	1988	6.50	21-40
1988 Love Santa QX486-4	Yr.Iss.	1988	5.00	20
1988 Loving Bear QX493-4	Yr.Iss.	1988	4.75	10-20
1988 Nick the Kick QX422-4	Yr.Iss.	1988	5.00	25
1988 Noah's Ark QX490-4	Yr.Iss.	1988	8.50	40
1988 Old-Fashioned Church QX498-1	Yr.Iss.	1988	4.00	25
1988 Old-Fashioned School House QX497-1	Yr.Iss.	1988	4.00	23
1988 Oreo QX481-4	Yr.Iss.	1989	4.00	13-20
1988 Par for Santa QX479-1	Yr.Iss.	1988	5.00	20
1988 Party Line QX476-1	Yr.Iss.	1989	8.75	22-30
1988 Peanuts QX280-1	Yr.Iss.	1988	4.75	50
1988 Peek-a-boo Kittens QX487-1	Yr.Iss.	1989	7.50	23
1988 Polar Bowler QX478-4	Yr.Iss.	1989	5.00	11-20
1988 Purrfect Snuggle QX474-4	Yr.Iss.	1988	6.25	16-30
1988 Sailing! Sailing! QX491-1	Yr.Iss.	1988	8.50	20-25
1988 Santa Flamingo QX483-4	Yr.Iss.	1988	4.75	25-31
1988 Shiny Sleigh QX492-4	Yr.Iss.	1988	5.75	20
1988 Slipper Spaniel QX472-4	Yr.Iss.	1988	4.50	11-20
1988 Snoopy and Woodstock QX474-1	Yr.Iss.	1988	6.00	43-47
1988 Soft Landing QX475-1	Yr.Iss.	1988	7.00	13-25
1988 Sparkling Tree QX483-1	Yr.Iss.	1988	6.00	19
1988 Squeaky Clean QX475-4	Yr.Iss.	1988	6.75	13-25
1988 Starry Angel QX494-4	Yr.Iss.	1988	4.75	20
1988 Sweet Star QX418-4	Yr.Iss.	1988	5.00	21-33
1988 Teeny Taster QX418-1	Yr.Iss.	1989	4.75	25-30
1988 The Town Crier QX473-4	Yr.Iss.	1988	5.50	14-20
1988 Travels with Santa QX477-1	Yr.Iss.	1988	10.00	27-40
1988 Uncle Sam Nutcracker QX488-4	Yr.Iss.	1988	7.00	27-30
1988 Winter Fun QX478-1	Yr.Iss.	1988	8.50	17-25

1988 Hallmark Keepsake Ornament Collector's Club - Keepsake

YEAR ISSUE	EDITION LIMIT	YEAR RETD.	ISSUE PRICE	*QUOTE U.S.$
1988 Angelic Minstrel QXC408-4	Yr.Iss.	1988	27.50	40-53
1988 Christmas is Sharing QXC407-1	Yr.Iss.	1988	17.50	31-50
1988 Hold on Tight QXC570-4	Yr.Iss.	1988	Gift	30-77
1988 Holiday Heirloom (2nd Ed.) QXC406-4	Yr.Iss.	1988	25.00	24
1988 Our Clubhouse QXC580-4	Yr.Iss.	1988	Gift	20-33
1988 Sleighful of Dreams QC580-1	Yr.Iss.	1988	8.00	28-55

1988 Holiday Humor - Keepsake

YEAR ISSUE	EDITION LIMIT	YEAR RETD.	ISSUE PRICE	*QUOTE U.S.$
1988 Night Before Christmas QX451-7	Yr.Iss.	1988	6.50	31-44
1988 Owliday Wish QX455-9	Yr.Iss.	1988	6.50	14-25
1988 Reindoggy QX452-7	Yr.Iss.	1988	5.75	20-25
1988 Treetop Dreams QX459-7	Yr.Iss.	1988	6.75	15-25

1988 Keepsake Magic Ornaments - Keepsake

YEAR ISSUE	EDITION LIMIT	YEAR RETD.	ISSUE PRICE	*QUOTE U.S.$
1988 Baby's First Christmas QLX718-4	Yr.Iss.	1988	24.00	45-60
1988 Bearly Reaching QLX715-1	Yr.Iss.	1988	9.50	26-41
1988 Chris Mouse (4th Ed.) QLX715-4	Yr.Iss.	1988	8.75	43-60
1988 Christmas Classics (3rd Ed.) QLX716-1	Yr.Iss.	1988	15.00	31-45
1988 Christmas is Magic QLX717-1	Yr.Iss.	1988	12.00	35-55
1988 Christmas Morning QLX701-3	Yr.Iss.	1988	24.50	33-50
1988 Circling the Globe QLX712-4	Yr.Iss.	1988	10.50	36-47
1988 Country Express QLX721-1	Yr.Iss.	1988	24.50	40-75
1988 Festive Feeder QLX720-4	Yr.Iss.	1988	11.50	44-50
1988 First Christmas Together QLX702-7	Yr.Iss.	1988	12.00	37-40
1988 Heavenly Glow QLX711-4	Yr.Iss.	1988	11.75	19-30
1988 Kitty Capers QLX716-4	Yr.Iss.	1988	13.00	36-40
1988 Kringle's Toy Shop QLX701-7	Yr.Iss.	1988	25.00	32-39
1988 Last-Minute Hug QLX718-1	Yr.Iss.	1988	19.50	16-49
1988 Moonlit Nap QLX713-4	Yr.Iss.	1988	8.75	22-30
1988 Parade of the Toys QLX719-4	Yr.Iss.	1988	22.00	37-52
1988 Radiant Tree QLX712-1	Yr.Iss.	1988	11.75	22-28
1988 Santa and Sparky (3rd Ed.) QLX719-1	Yr.Iss.	1988	19.50	31-43
1988 Skater's Waltz QLX720-1	Yr.Iss.	1988	19.50	38-63
1988 Song of Christmas QLX711-1	Yr.Iss.	1988	8.50	14-30
1988 Tree of Friendship QLX710-4	Yr.Iss.	1988	8.50	20-25

1988 Keepsake Miniature Ornaments - Keepsake

YEAR ISSUE	EDITION LIMIT	YEAR RETD.	ISSUE PRICE	*QUOTE U.S.$
1988 Baby's First Christmas	Yr.Iss.	1988	6.00	12
1988 Brass Angel	Yr.Iss.	1988	1.50	13
1988 Brass Star	Yr.Iss.	1988	1.50	13
1988 Brass Tree	Yr.Iss.	1988	1.50	9-19
1988 Candy Cane Elf	Yr.Iss.	1988	3.00	10-21
1988 Country Wreath	Yr.Iss.	1988	4.00	12
1988 Family Home (1st Ed.)	Yr.Iss.	1988	8.50	11-31
1988 First Christmas Together	Yr.Iss.	1988	4.00	9-25
1988 Folk Art Lamb	Yr.Iss.	1988	2.50	14-23
1988 Folk Art Reindeer	Yr.Iss.	1988	2.50	14-20
1988 Friends Share Joy	Yr.Iss.	1988	2.00	10-16
1988 Gentle Angel	Yr.Iss.	1988	2.00	16-20
1988 Happy Santa	Yr.Iss.	1988	4.50	19-21
1988 Holy Family	Yr.Iss.	1988	8.50	12
1988 Jolly St. Nick	Yr.Iss.	1988	8.00	31
1988 Joyous Heart	Yr.Iss.	1988	3.50	24-30
1988 Kittens in Toyland (1st Ed.)	Yr.Iss.	1988	5.00	19-26
1988 Little Drummer Boy	Yr.Iss.	1988	4.50	21-27
1988 Love is Forever	Yr.Iss.	1988	2.00	15
1988 Mother	Yr.Iss.	1988	3.00	14
1988 Penguin Pal (1st Ed.)	Yr.Iss.	1988	3.75	16-28
1988 Rocking Horse (1st Ed.)	Yr.Iss.	1988	4.50	31-45
1988 Skater's Waltz	Yr.Iss.	1988	7.00	15
1988 Sneaker Mouse	Yr.Iss.	1988	4.00	14-20
1988 Snuggly Skater	Yr.Iss.	1988	4.50	29
1988 Sweet Dreams	Yr.Iss.	1988	7.00	16-23
1988 Three Little Kitties	Yr.Iss.	1988	6.00	13-19

1988 Old Fashioned Christmas Collection - Keepsake

YEAR ISSUE	EDITION LIMIT	YEAR RETD.	ISSUE PRICE	*QUOTE U.S.$
1988 In A Nutshell QX469-7	Yr.Iss.	1988	5.50	24-33

1988 Special Edition - Keepsake

YEAR ISSUE	EDITION LIMIT	YEAR RETD.	ISSUE PRICE	*QUOTE U.S.$
1988 The Wonderful Santacycle QX411-4	Yr.Iss.	1988	22.50	37-40

1989 Artists' Favorites - Keepsake

YEAR ISSUE	EDITION LIMIT	YEAR RETD.	ISSUE PRICE	*QUOTE U.S.$
1989 Baby Partridge QX452-5	Yr.Iss.	1989	6.75	10-15
1989 Bear-i-Tone QX454-2	Yr.Iss.	1989	4.75	11-20
1989 Carousel Zebra QX451-5	Yr.Iss.	1989	9.25	16-31
1989 Cherry Jubilee QX453-2	Yr.Iss.	1989	5.00	16-20
1989 Mail Call QX452-2	Yr.Iss.	1989	8.75	16-20
1989 Merry-Go-Round Unicorn QX447-2	Yr.Iss.	1989	10.75	16-25
1989 Playful Angel QX453-5	Yr.Iss.	1989	6.75	17-25

1989 Collectible Series - Keepsake

YEAR ISSUE	EDITION LIMIT	YEAR RETD.	ISSUE PRICE	*QUOTE U.S.$
1989 Betsey Clark:Home for Christmas (4th Ed.) QX230-2	Yr.Iss.	1989	5.00	19-29
1989 Christmas Kitty (1st Ed.) QX544-5	Yr.Iss.	1989	14.75	15-26
1989 Collector's Plate (3rd Ed.) QX461-2	Yr.Iss.	1989	8.25	21-28
1989 Crayola Crayon (1st Ed.) QX435-2	Yr.Iss.	1989	8.75	30-69
1989 Frosty Friends (10th Ed.) QX457-2	Yr.Iss.	1989	9.25	44-70
1989 The Gift Bringers (1st Ed.) QX279-5	Yr.Iss.	1989	5.00	21-25
1989 Hark! It's Herald (1st Ed.) QX455-5	Yr.Iss.	1989	6.75	16-25
1989 Here Comes Santa (11th Ed.) QX458-5	Yr.Iss.	1989	14.75	34-49
1989 Mary's Angels (2nd Ed.) QX454-5	Yr.Iss.	1989	5.75	90-95
1989 Miniature Creche (5th Ed.) QX459-2	Yr.Iss.	1989	9.25	15-23
1989 Mr. and Mrs. Claus (4th Ed.) QX457-5	Yr.Iss.	1989	13.25	33-60
1989 Nostalgic Houses and Shops (6th Ed.) QX458-2	Yr.Iss.	1989	14.25	63-70
1989 Porcelain Bear (7th Ed.) QX461-5	Yr.Iss.	1989	8.75	21-40
1989 Reindeer Champs (4th Ed.) QX456-2	Yr.Iss.	1989	7.75	17-20
1989 Rocking Horse (9th Ed.) QX462-2	Yr.Iss.	1989	10.75	54-70
1989 Thimble (12th Ed.) QX455-2	Yr.Iss.	1989	5.75	18-27
1989 Tin Locomotive (8th Ed.) QX460-2	Yr.Iss.	1989	14.75	33-60
1989 Twelve Days of Christmas (6th Ed.) QX381-2	Yr.Iss.	1989	6.75	18-28
1989 Windows of the World (5th Ed.) QX462-5	Yr.Iss.	1989	10.75	22-30
1989 Winter Surprise (1st Ed.) QX427-2	Yr.Iss.	1989	10.75	27
1989 Wood Childhood Ornaments (6th Ed.) QX459-5	Yr.Iss.	1989	7.75	15-20

1989 Commemoratives - Keepsake

YEAR ISSUE	EDITION LIMIT	YEAR RETD.	ISSUE PRICE	*QUOTE U.S.$
1989 Baby's Fifth Christmas QX543-5	Yr.Iss.	1989	6.75	16-20
1989 Baby's First Christmas Photoholder QX468-2	Yr.Iss.	1989	6.25	40-50
1989 Baby's First Christmas QX381-5	Yr.Iss.	1989	6.75	10-18
1989 Baby's First Christmas QX449-2	Yr.Iss.	1989	7.25	66-85
1989 Baby's First Christmas-Baby Boy QX272-5	Yr.Iss.	1989	4.75	17-23
1989 Baby's First Christmas-Baby Girl QX272-2	Yr.Iss.	1989	4.75	20-65
1989 Baby's Fourth Christmas QX543-2	Yr.Iss.	1989	6.75	15-20
1989 Baby's Second Christmas QX449-5	Yr.Iss.	1989	6.75	26-35
1989 Baby's Third Christmas QX469-5	Yr.Iss.	1989	6.75	13-28
1989 Brother QX445-2	Yr.Iss.	1989	6.25	18-23
1989 Dad QX442-5	Yr.Iss.	1989	7.25	12-15
1989 Daughter QX443-2	Yr.Iss.	1989	6.25	18-33
1989 Festive Year QX384-2	Yr.Iss.	1989	7.75	10-25
1989 Fifty Years Together Photoholder QX486-2	Yr.Iss.	1989	8.75	13-20
1989 First Christmas Together QX273-2	Yr.Iss.	1989	4.75	25-30
1989 First Christmas Together QX383-2	Yr.Iss.	1989	6.75	18-25
1989 First Christmas Together QX485-2	Yr.Iss.	1989	9.75	18-25
1989 Five Years Together QX273-5	Yr.Iss.	1989	4.75	18-23
1989 Forty Years Together Photoholder QX545-2	Yr.Iss.	1989	8.75	12-18
1989 Friendship Time QX413-2	Yr.Iss.	1989	9.75	25-33
1989 From Our Home to Yours QX384-5	Yr.Iss.	1989	6.25	12-15
1989 Godchild QX311-2	Yr.Iss.	1989	6.25	14-20
1989 Granddaughter QX278	Yr.Iss.	1989	4.75	7-27
1989 Granddaughter's First Christmas QX382-2	Yr.Iss.	1989	6.75	7-9
1989 Grandmother QX277-5	Yr.Iss.	1989	4.75	16-20
1989 Grandparents QX277-2	Yr.Iss.	1989	4.75	14-20
1989 Grandson QX278-5	Yr.Iss.	1989	4.75	15-25
1989 Grandson's First Christmas QX382-5	Yr.Iss.	1989	6.75	9-18
1989 Gratitude QX385-2	Yr.Iss.	1989	6.75	11-14
1989 Language of Love QX383-5	Yr.Iss.	1989	6.25	20-25
1989 Mom and Dad QX442-5	Yr.Iss.	1989	9.75	19-24
1989 Mother QX440-5	Yr.Iss.	1989	9.75	28-30
1989 New Home QX275-5	Yr.Iss.	1989	4.75	16-20

*Quotes have been rounded up to nearest dollar

YEAR ISSUE	EDITION LIMIT	YEAR RETD.	ISSUE PRICE	*QUOTE U.S.$
1989 Sister QX279-2	Yr.Iss.	1989	4.75	16-20
1989 Son QX444-5	Yr.Iss.	1989	6.25	20-35
1989 Sweetheart QX486-5	Yr.Iss.	1989	9.75	22-33
1989 Teacher QX412-5	Yr.Iss.	1989	5.75	14-25
1989 Ten Years Together QX274-2	Yr.Iss.	1989	4.75	24-30
1989 Twenty-five Years Together Photoholder QX485-5	Yr.Iss.	1989	8.75	14-18
1989 World of Love QX274-5	Yr.Iss.	1989	4.75	28-35

1989 Hallmark Handcrafted Ornaments - Keepsake

YEAR ISSUE	EDITION LIMIT	YEAR RETD.	ISSUE PRICE	*QUOTE U.S.$
1989 Peek-a-boo Kittens QX487-1	Yr.Iss.	1989	7.50	21

1989 Hallmark Keepsake Ornament Collector's Club - Keepsake

YEAR ISSUE	EDITION LIMIT	YEAR RETD.	ISSUE PRICE	*QUOTE U.S.$
1989 Christmas is Peaceful QXC451-2	Yr.Iss.	1989	18.50	30-45
1989 Collect a Dream QXC428-5	Yr.Iss.	1989	9.00	44-59
1989 Holiday Heirloom (3rd Ed.) QXC460-5	Yr.Iss.	1989	25.00	29
1989 Noelle QXC448-3	Yr.Iss.	1989	19.75	39-50
1989 Sitting Purrty QXC581-2	Yr.Iss.	1989	Gift	32-44
1989 Visit from Santa QXC580-2	Yr.Iss.	1989	Gift	39

1989 Holiday Traditions - Keepsake

YEAR ISSUE	EDITION LIMIT	YEAR RETD.	ISSUE PRICE	*QUOTE U.S.$
1989 Camera Claus QX546-5	Yr.Iss.	1989	5.75	13-23
1989 A Charlie Brown Christmas QX276-5	Yr.Iss.	1989	4.75	35-40
1989 Cranberry Bunny QX426-2	Yr.Iss.	1989	5.75	11-18
1989 Deer Disguise QX426-5	Yr.Iss.	1989	5.75	17-25
1989 Feliz Navidad QX439-2	Yr.Iss.	1989	6.75	20-30
1989 The First Christmas QX547-5	Yr.Iss.	1989	7.75	14-18
1989 Gentle Fawn QX548-5	Yr.Iss.	1989	7.75	15-20
1989 George Washington Bicentennial QX386-2	Yr.Iss.	1989	6.75	9-20
1989 Gone Fishing QX479-4	Yr.Iss.	1989	5.75	17
1989 Gym Dandy QX418-5	Yr.Iss.	1989	5.75	12-20
1989 Hang in There QX430-5	Yr.Iss.	1989	5.25	23-27
1989 Here's the Pitch QX545-5	Yr.Iss.	1989	5.75	12-20
1989 Hoppy Holidays QX469-2	Yr.Iss.	1989	7.75	14-25
1989 Joyful Trio QX437-2	Yr.Iss.	1989	9.75	15-20
1989 A Kiss™ From Santa QX482-1	Yr.Iss.	1989	4.50	20
1989 Kristy Claus QX424-5	Yr.Iss.	1989	5.75	10-15
1989 Norman Rockwell QX276-2	Yr.Iss.	1989	4.75	20-25
1989 North Pole Jogger QX546-2	Yr.Iss.	1989	5.75	12-23
1989 Old-World Gnome QX434-5	Yr.Iss.	1989	7.75	16-30
1989 On the Links QX419-2	Yr.Iss.	1989	5.75	16-23
1989 Oreo® Chocolate Sandwich Cookies QX481-4	Yr.Iss.	1989	4.00	15
1989 Owliday Greetings QX436-5	Yr.Iss.	1989	4.00	13-23
1989 Paddington Bear QX429-2	Yr.Iss.	1989	5.75	16-27
1989 Party Line QX476-1	Yr.Iss.	1989	8.75	27
1989 Peek-a-Boo Kitties QX487-1	Yr.Iss.	1989	7.50	16-22
1989 Polar Bowler QX478-4	Yr.Iss.	1989	5.75	17
1989 Sea Santa QX415-2	Yr.Iss.	1989	5.75	14-30
1989 Snoopy and Woodstock QX433-2	Yr.Iss.	1989	6.75	23-40
1989 Snowplow Santa QX420-5	Yr.Iss.	1989	5.75	12-23
1989 Special Delivery QX432-5	Yr.Iss.	1989	5.25	13-25
1989 Spencer Sparrow, Esq. QX431-2	Yr.Iss.	1990	6.75	16-28
1989 Stocking Kitten QX456-5	Yr.Iss.	1990	6.75	13-23
1989 Sweet Memories Photoholder QX438-5	Yr.Iss.	1989	6.75	25
1989 Teeny Taster QX418-1	Yr.Iss.	1989	4.75	17

1989 Keepsake Magic Collection - Keepsake

YEAR ISSUE	EDITION LIMIT	YEAR RETD.	ISSUE PRICE	*QUOTE U.S.$
1989 Angel Melody QLX720-2	Yr.Iss.	1989	9.50	20-25
1989 The Animals Speak QLX723-2	Yr.Iss.	1989	13.50	78
1989 Baby's First Christmas QLX727-2	Yr.Iss.	1989	30.00	47-55
1989 Backstage Bear QLX721-5	Yr.Iss.	1989	13.50	15-27
1989 Busy Beaver QLX724-5	Yr.Iss.	1989	17.50	36-50
1989 Chris Mouse (5th Ed.) QLX722-5	Yr.Iss.	1989	9.50	40-58
1989 Christmas Classics (4th Ed.) QLX724-2	Yr.Iss.	1989	13.50	27-43
1989 First Christmas Together QLX734-2	Yr.Iss.	1989	17.50	33-45
1989 Forest Frolics (1st Ed.) QLX728-2	Yr.Iss.	1989	24.50	83-95
1989 Holiday Bell QLX722-2	Yr.Iss.	1989	17.50	20-35
1989 Joyous Carolers QLX729-5	Yr.Iss.	1989	30.00	47-70
1989 Kringle's Toy Shop QLX701-7	Yr.Iss.	1989	24.50	60
1989 Loving Spoonful QLX726-2	Yr.Iss.	1989	19.50	32-38
1989 Metro Express QLX727-5	Yr.Iss.	1989	28.00	35-80
1989 Moonlit Nap QLX713-4	Yr.Iss.	1989	8.75	73-80
1989 Rudolph the Red-Nosed Reindeer QLX725-2	Yr.Iss.	1989	19.50	63-70
1989 Spirit of St. Nick QLX728-5	Yr.Iss.	1989	24.50	39-75
1989 Tiny Tinker QLX717-4	Yr.Iss.	1989	19.50	52-60
1989 Unicorn Fantasy QLX723-5	Yr.Iss.	1989	9.50	13-17

1989 Keepsake Miniature Ornaments - Keepsake

YEAR ISSUE	EDITION LIMIT	YEAR RETD.	ISSUE PRICE	*QUOTE U.S.$
1989 Acorn Squirrel QXM568-2	Yr.Iss.	1989	4.50	9
1989 Baby's First Christmas QXM573-2	Yr.Iss.	1989	6.00	8-12
1989 Brass Partridge QXM572-5	Yr.Iss.	1989	3.00	10-12
1989 Brass Snowflake QXM570-2	Yr.Iss.	1989	4.50	14
1989 Bunny Hug QXM577-5	Yr.Iss.	1989	3.00	8-11
1989 Country Wreath QXM573-1	Yr.Iss.	1989	4.50	12
1989 Cozy Skater QXM573-5	Yr.Iss.	1989	4.50	12
1989 First Christmas Together QXM564-2	Yr.Iss.	1989	8.50	8-12
1989 Folk Art Bunny QXM569-2	Yr.Iss.	1989	4.50	10
1989 Happy Bluebird QXM566-2	Yr.Iss.	1989	4.50	12-15
1989 Holiday Deer QXM577-2	Yr.Iss.	1989	3.00	12
1989 Holy Family QXM561-1	Yr.Iss.	1989	8.50	15
1989 Kittens in Toyland (2nd Ed.) QXM561-2	Yr.Iss.	1989	4.50	15-20
1989 Kitty Cart QXM572-2	Yr.Iss.	1989	3.00	7
1989 The Kringles (1st Ed.) QXM562-2	Yr.Iss.	1989	6.00	20-26
1989 Little Soldier QXM567-5	Yr.Iss.	1989	4.50	9-24
1989 Little Star Bringer QXM562-2	Yr.Iss.	1989	6.00	17-27
1989 Load of Cheer QXM574-5	Yr.Iss.	1989	6.00	12-20
1989 Lovebirds QXM563-5	Yr.Iss.	1989	6.00	10-14

YEAR ISSUE	EDITION LIMIT	YEAR RETD.	ISSUE PRICE	*QUOTE U.S.$
1989 Merry Seal QXM575-5	Yr.Iss.	1989	6.00	13-15
1989 Mother QXM564-5	Yr.Iss.	1989	6.00	9-15
1989 Noel R.R. (1st Ed.) QXM576-2	Yr.Iss.	1989	8.50	37
1989 Old English Village (2nd Ed.) QXM561-5	Yr.Iss.	1989	8.50	29
1989 Old-World Santa QXM569-5	Yr.Iss.	1989	3.00	7-16
1989 Penguin Pal (2nd Ed.) QXM560-2	Yr.Iss.	1989	4.50	16-20
1989 Pinecone Basket QXM573-4	Yr.Iss.	1989	4.50	7-10
1989 Puppy Cart QXM571-5	Yr.Iss.	1989	3.00	7-22
1989 Rejoice QXM578-2	Yr.Iss.	1989	3.00	10
1989 Rocking Horse (2nd Ed.) QXM560-5	Yr.Iss.	1989	4.50	26
1989 Roly-Poly Pig QXM571-2	Yr.Iss.	1989	3.00	13-18
1989 Roly-Poly Ram QXM570-5	Yr.Iss.	1989	3.00	13-18
1989 Santa's Magic Ride QXM563-2	Yr.Iss.	1989	8.50	17-20
1989 Santa's Roadster QXM566-5	Yr.Iss.	1989	6.00	12-15
1989 Scrimshaw Reindeer QXM568-5	Yr.Iss.	1989	4.50	7-10
1989 Sharing a Ride QXM576-5	Yr.Iss.	1989	8.50	12-17
1989 Slow Motion QXM575-2	Yr.Iss.	1989	6.00	13-17
1989 Special Friend QXM565-2	Yr.Iss.	1989	4.50	12-14
1989 Starlit Mouse QXM565-5	Yr.Iss.	1989	4.50	12-16
1989 Stocking Pal QXM567-2	Yr.Iss.	1989	4.50	11
1989 Strollin' Snowman QXM574-2	Yr.Iss.	1989	4.50	13-18
1989 Three Little Kitties QXM569-4	Yr.Iss.	1989	6.00	19

1989 New Attractions - Keepsake

YEAR ISSUE	EDITION LIMIT	YEAR RETD.	ISSUE PRICE	*QUOTE U.S.$
1989 Balancing Elf QX489-5	Yr.Iss.	1989	6.75	21
1989 Cactus Cowboy QX411-2	Yr.Iss.	1989	6.75	30-33
1989 Claus Construction QX488-5	Yr.Iss.	1990	7.75	19-40
1989 Cool Swing QX487-5	Yr.Iss.	1989	6.25	30-35
1989 Country Cat QX467-2	Yr.Iss.	1989	6.25	16-20
1989 Festive Angel QX463-5	Yr.Iss.	1989	6.75	13-27
1989 Goin' South QX410-5	Yr.Iss.	1989	4.25	18-20
1989 Graceful Swan QX464-2	Yr.Iss.	1989	6.75	16-20
1989 Horse Weathervane QX463-2	Yr.Iss.	1989	5.75	16-18
1989 Let's Play QX488-2	Yr.Iss.	1989	7.25	27-30
1989 Nostalgic Lamb QX466-5	Yr.Iss.	1989	6.75	10-20
1989 Nutshell Dreams QX465-5	Yr.Iss.	1989	5.75	14-23
1989 Nutshell Holiday QX465-2	Yr.Iss.	1990	5.75	17-27
1989 Nutshell Workshop QX487-2	Yr.Iss.	1989	5.75	23
1989 Peppermint Clown QX450-5	Yr.Iss.	1989	24.75	23-35
1989 Rodney Reindeer QX407-2	Yr.Iss.	1989	6.75	10-15
1989 Rooster Weathervane QX467-5	Yr.Iss.	1989	5.75	25
1989 Sparkling Snowflake QX547-2	Yr.Iss.	1989	7.75	22-25
1989 TV Break QX409-2	Yr.Iss.	1989	6.25	16-20
1989 Wiggly Snowman QX489-2	Yr.Iss.	1989	6.75	21-36

1989 Special Edition - Keepsake

YEAR ISSUE	EDITION LIMIT	YEAR RETD.	ISSUE PRICE	*QUOTE U.S.$
1989 The Ornament Express QX580-5	Yr.Iss.	1989	22.00	35-50

1990 Artists' Favorites - Keepsake

YEAR ISSUE	EDITION LIMIT	YEAR RETD.	ISSUE PRICE	*QUOTE U.S.$
1990 Angel Kitty QX4746	Yr.Iss.	1990	8.75	16-25
1990 Donder's Diner QX4823	Yr.Iss.	1990	13.75	11-23
1990 Gentle Dreamers QX4756	Yr.Iss.	1990	8.75	21-30
1990 Happy Woodcutter QX4763	Yr.Iss.	1990	9.75	18-23
1990 Mouseboat QX4753	Yr.Iss.	1990	7.75	13-20
1990 Welcome, Santa QX4773	Yr.Iss.	1990	11.75	19-34

1990 Collectible Series - Keepsake

YEAR ISSUE	EDITION LIMIT	YEAR RETD.	ISSUE PRICE	*QUOTE U.S.$
1990 Betsey Clark: Home for Christmas (5th Ed.) QX2033	Yr.Iss.	1990	5.00	16-25
1990 Christmas Kitty (2nd Ed.) QX4506	Yr.Iss.	1990	14.75	18-22
1990 Cinnamon Bear (8th Ed.) QX4426	Yr.Iss.	1990	8.75	22-35
1990 Cookies for Santa (4th Ed.) QX4436	Yr.Iss.	1990	8.75	22-35
1990 CRAYOLA Crayon-Bright Moving Colors (2nd Ed.) QX4586	Yr.Iss.	1990	8.75	40-50
1990 Fabulous Decade (1st Ed.) QX4466	Yr.Iss.	1990	7.75	20-40
1990 Festive Surrey (12th Ed.) QX4923	Yr.Iss.	1990	14.75	32-43
1990 Frosty Friends (11th Ed.) QX4396	Yr.Iss.	1990	9.75	25-34
1990 The Gift Bringers-St. Lucia (2nd Ed.) QX2803	Yr.Iss.	1990	5.00	15-25
1990 Greatest Story (1st Ed.) QX4656	Yr.Iss.	1990	12.75	20-26
1990 Hark! It's Herald (2nd Ed.) QX4463	Yr.Iss.	1990	6.75	10-17
1990 Heart of Christmas (1st Ed.) QX4726	Yr.Iss.	1990	13.75	65-80
1990 Holiday Home (7th Ed.) QX4696	Yr.Iss.	1990	14.75	78
1990 Irish (6th Ed.) QX4636	Yr.Iss.	1990	10.75	21
1990 Mary's Angels-Rosebud (3rd Ed.) QX4423	Yr.Iss.	1990	5.75	29-40
1990 Merry Olde Santa (1st Ed.) QX4736	Yr.Iss.	1990	14.75	50-73
1990 Popcorn Party (5th Ed.) QX4393	Yr.Iss.	1990	13.75	38-58
1990 Reindeer Champs-Comet (5th Ed.) QX4433	Yr.Iss.	1990	7.75	22-30
1990 Rocking Horse (10th Ed.) QX4646	Yr.Iss.	1990	10.75	89-100
1990 Seven Swans A-Swimming (7th Ed.) QX3033	Yr.Iss.	1990	6.75	21-33
1990 Winter Surprise (2nd Ed.) QX4443	Yr.Iss.	1990	10.75	19

1990 Commemoratives - Keepsake

YEAR ISSUE	EDITION LIMIT	YEAR RETD.	ISSUE PRICE	*QUOTE U.S.$
1990 Across The Miles QX3173	Yr.Iss.	1990	6.75	14-18
1990 Baby's First Christmas QX3036	Yr.Iss.	1990	6.75	11-23
1990 Baby's First Christmas QX4853	Yr.Iss.	1990	9.75	19
1990 Baby's First Christmas QX4856	Yr.Iss.	1990	7.75	33-40
1990 Baby's First Christmas-Baby Boy QX2063	Yr.Iss.	1990	4.75	16-20
1990 Baby's First Christmas-Baby Girl QX2066	Yr.Iss.	1990	4.75	16-19
1990 Baby's First Christmas-Photo Holder QX4843	Yr.Iss.	1990	7.75	21-30
1990 Baby's Second Christmas QX4683	Yr.Iss.	1990	6.75	27-34
1990 Brother QX4493	Yr.Iss.	1990	5.75	10-15
1990 Child Care Giver QX3166	Yr.Iss.	1990	6.75	11-14
1990 Child's Fifth Christmas QX4876	Yr.Iss.	1990	6.75	15-20
1990 Child's Fourth Christmas QX4873	Yr.Iss.	1990	6.75	15-25
1990 Child's Third Christmas QX4866	Yr.Iss.	1990	6.75	19-30
1990 Copy of Cheer QX4486	Yr.Iss.	1990	7.75	16-20

YEAR ISSUE	EDITION LIMIT	YEAR RETD.	ISSUE PRICE	*QUOTE U.S.$
1990 Dad QX4533	Yr.Iss.	1990	6.75	12-15
1990 Dad-to-Be QX4913	Yr.Iss.	1990	5.75	17-23
1990 Daughter QX4496	Yr.Iss.	1990	5.75	19-25
1990 Fifty Years Together QX4906	Yr.Iss.	1990	9.75	16-20
1990 Five Years Together QX2103	Yr.Iss.	1990	4.75	18-25
1990 Forty Years Together QX4903	Yr.Iss.	1990	9.75	16-20
1990 Friendship Kitten QX4142	Yr.Iss.	1990	6.75	17-23
1990 From Our Home to Yours QX2166	Yr.Iss.	1990	4.75	9-20
1990 Godchild QX3167	Yr.Iss.	1990	6.75	11-20
1990 Granddaughter QX2286	Yr.Iss.	1990	4.75	16-30
1990 Granddaughter's First Christmas QX3106	Yr.Iss.	1990	6.75	18-23
1990 Grandmother QX2236	Yr.Iss.	1990	4.75	16-20
1990 Grandparents QX2253	Yr.Iss.	1990	4.75	16-20
1990 Grandson QX2293	Yr.Iss.	1990	4.75	21-28
1990 Grandson's First Christmas QX3063	Yr.Iss.	1990	6.75	17-20
1990 Jesus Loves Me QX3156	Yr.Iss.	1990	6.75	11-14
1990 Mom and Dad QX4593	Yr.Iss.	1990	8.75	17-30
1990 Mom-to-Be QX4916	Yr.Iss.	1990	5.75	25-33
1990 Mother QX4536	Yr.Iss.	1990	8.75	24-30
1990 New Home QX4343	Yr.Iss.	1990	6.75	26-30
1990 Our First Christmas Together QX2136	Yr.Iss.	1990	4.75	20-27
1990 Our First Christmas Together QX3146	Yr.Iss.	1990	6.75	13-25
1990 Our First Christmas Together QX4883	Yr.Iss.	1990	9.75	16-30
1990 Our First Christmas Together-Photo Holder Ornament QX4886	Yr.Iss.	1990	7.75	16-20
1990 Peaceful Kingdom QX2106	Yr.Iss.	1990	4.75	18-23
1990 Sister QX2273	Yr.Iss.	1990	4.75	14-23
1990 Son QX4516	Yr.Iss.	1990	5.75	16-23
1990 Sweetheart QX4893	Yr.Iss.	1990	11.75	19-30
1990 Teacher QX4483	Yr.Iss.	1990	7.75	14-17
1990 Ten Years Together QX2153	Yr.Iss.	1990	4.75	18-23
1990 Time for Love QX2133	Yr.Iss.	1990	4.75	20-25
1990 Twenty-Five Years Together QX4896	Yr.Iss.	1990	9.75	18-24

1990 Holiday Traditions - Keepsake

YEAR ISSUE	EDITION LIMIT	YEAR RETD.	ISSUE PRICE	*QUOTE U.S.$
1990 Spencer Sparrow, Esq. QX431-2	Yr.Iss.	1990	6.75	12-15
1990 Stocking Kitten QX456-5	Yr.Iss.	1990	6.75	8-15

1990 Keepsake Collector's Club - Keepsake

YEAR ISSUE	EDITION LIMIT	YEAR RETD.	ISSUE PRICE	*QUOTE U.S.$
1990 Armful of Joy QXC445-3	Yr.Iss.	1990	8.00	20-41
1990 Christmas Limited 1975 QXC476-6	38,700	1990	19.75	75-80
1990 Club Hollow QXC445-6	Yr.Iss.	1990	Gift	20-36
1990 Crown Prince QXC560-3	Yr.Iss.	1990	Gift	10-39
1990 Dove of Peace QXC447-6	25,400	1990	24.75	50-65
1990 Sugar Plum Fairy QXC447-3	25,400	1990	27.75	35-50

1990 Keepsake Magic Ornaments - Keepsake

YEAR ISSUE	EDITION LIMIT	YEAR RETD.	ISSUE PRICE	*QUOTE U.S.$
1990 Baby's First Christmas QLX7246	Yr.Iss.	1990	28.00	50-65
1990 Beary Short Nap QLX7326	Yr.Iss.	1990	10.00	24-33
1990 Blessings of Love QLX7363	Yr.Iss.	1990	14.00	44-50
1990 Children's Express QLX7243	Yr.Iss.	1990	28.00	44-66
1990 Chris Mouse Wreath QLX7296	Yr.Iss.	1990	10.00	31-35
1990 Christmas Memories QLX7276	Yr.Iss.	1990	25.00	38-95
1990 Deer Crossing QLX7213	Yr.Iss.	1990	18.00	41-50
1990 Elf of the Year QLX7356	Yr.Iss.	1990	10.00	16-25
1990 Elfin Whittler QLX7265	Yr.Iss.	1990	20.00	37-55
1990 Forest Frolics QLX7236	Yr.Iss.	1990	25.00	49-55
1990 Holiday Flash QLX7333	Yr.Iss.	1990	18.00	26-40
1990 Hop 'N Pop Popper QLX7353	Yr.Iss.	1990	20.00	89-95
1990 Letter to Santa QLX7226	Yr.Iss.	1990	14.00	28-40
1990 The Littlest Angel QLX7303	Yr.Iss.	1990	14.00	31-50
1990 Mrs. Santa's Kitchen QLX7263	Yr.Iss.	1990	25.00	65-90
1990 Our First Christmas Together QLX7255	Yr.Iss.	1990	18.00	30-50
1990 Partridges in a Pear QLX7212	Yr.Iss.	1990	14.00	22-35
1990 Santa's Ho-Ho-Hoedown QLX7256	Yr.Iss.	1990	25.00	50-90
1990 Song and Dance QLX7253	Yr.Iss.	1990	20.00	59-95
1990 Starlight Angel QLX7306	Yr.Iss.	1990	14.00	27-38
1990 Starship Christmas QLX7336	Yr.Iss.	1990	18.00	38-49

1990 Keepsake Miniature Ornaments - Keepsake

YEAR ISSUE	EDITION LIMIT	YEAR RETD.	ISSUE PRICE	*QUOTE U.S.$
1990 Acorn Wreath QXM5686	Yr.Iss.	1990	6.00	9-12
1990 Air Santa QXM5656	Yr.Iss.	1990	4.50	10-13
1990 Baby's First Christmas QXM5703	Yr.Iss.	1990	8.50	15-20
1990 Basket Buddy QXM5696	Yr.Iss.	1990	6.00	9-12
1990 Bear Hug QXM5633	Yr.Iss.	1990	6.00	10-14
1990 Brass Bouquet 600QMX5776	Yr.Iss.	1990	6.00	5-7
1990 Brass Horn QXM5793	Yr.Iss.	1990	3.00	5-10
1990 Brass Peace QXM5796	Yr.Iss.	1990	3.00	5-10
1990 Brass Santa QXM5786	Yr.Iss.	1990	3.00	6-9
1990 Brass Year QXM5833	Yr.Iss.	1990	3.00	5-8
1990 Busy Carver QXM5673	Yr.Iss.	1990	4.50	10
1990 Christmas Dove QXM5636	Yr.Iss.	1990	4.50	13
1990 Cloisonne Poinsettia QMX5533	Yr.Iss.	1990	10.75	13-25
1990 Coal Car QXM5756	Yr.Iss.	1990	8.50	21-28
1990 Country Heart QXM5693	Yr.Iss.	1990	4.50	6-9
1990 First Christmas Together QXM5536	Yr.Iss.	1990	6.00	11-15
1990 Going Sledding QXM5683	Yr.Iss.	1990	4.50	11-15
1990 Grandchild's First Christmas QXM5723	Yr.Iss.	1990	6.00	10-12
1990 Holiday Cardinal QXM5526	Yr.Iss.	1990	3.00	8-11
1990 Kittens in Toyland QXM5736	Yr.Iss.	1990	4.50	12-17
1990 The Kringles (2nd Ed.) QXM5753	Yr.Iss.	1990	6.00	12-24
1990 Lion and Lamb QXM5676	Yr.Iss.	1990	4.50	7-12
1990 Loving Hearts QXM5523	Yr.Iss.	1990	3.00	8-10
1990 Madonna and Child QXM5643	Yr.Iss.	1990	6.00	11

*Quotes have been rounded up to nearest dollar

YEAR ISSUE	EDITION LIMIT	YEAR RETD.	ISSUE PRICE	*QUOTE U.S.$
1990 Mother QXM5716	Yr.Iss.	1990	4.50	9-13
1990 Nativity QXM5706	Yr.Iss.	1990	4.50	9-14
1990 Nature's Angels QMX5733	Yr.Iss.	1990	4.50	16-28
1990 Panda's Surprise QXM5616	Yr.Iss.	1990	4.50	11
1990 Penguin Pal QXM5746	Yr.Iss.	1990	4.50	14-20
1990 Perfect Fit QXM5516	Yr.Iss.	1990	4.50	10-13
1990 Puppy Love QXM5666	Yr.Iss.	1990	6.00	11-15
1990 Rocking Horse QXM5743	Yr.Iss.	1990	4.50	21
1990 Ruby Reindeer QXM5816	Yr.Iss.	1990	6.00	10-12
1990 Santa's Journey QXM5826	Yr.Iss.	1990	8.50	13-18
1990 Santa's Streetcar QXM5766	Yr.Iss.	1990	8.50	13-20
1990 School QXM5763	Yr.Iss.	1990	8.50	19-21
1990 Snow Angel QXM5773	Yr.Iss.	1990	6.00	11-15
1990 Special Friends QXM5726	Yr.Iss.	1990	6.00	11-13
1990 Stamp Collector QXM5623	Yr.Iss.	1990	4.50	8
1990 Stringing Along QXM5606	Yr.Iss.	1990	8.50	15-18
1990 Sweet Slumber QXM5663	Yr.Iss.	1990	4.50	11
1990 Teacher QXM5653	Yr.Iss.	1990	4.50	7
1990 Thimble Bells QXM5543	Yr.Iss.	1990	6.00	15-20
1990 Type of Joy QXM5646	Yr.Iss.	1990	4.50	7-10
1990 Warm Memories QXM5713	Yr.Iss.	1990	4.50	9
1990 Wee Nutcracker QXM5843	Yr.Iss.	1990	8.50	12-15

1990 New Attractions - Keepsake

YEAR ISSUE	EDITION LIMIT	YEAR RETD.	ISSUE PRICE	*QUOTE U.S.$
1990 Baby Unicorn QX5486	Yr.Iss.	1990	9.75	12-25
1990 Bearback Rider QX5483	Yr.Iss.	1990	9.75	13-32
1990 Beary Good Deal QX4733	Yr.Iss.	1990	6.75	8-17
1990 Billboard Bunny QX5196	Yr.Iss.	1990	7.75	13-20
1990 Born to Dance QX5043	Yr.Iss.	1990	7.75	15-25
1990 Chiming In QX4366	Yr.Iss.	1990	9.75	20-25
1990 Christmas Croc QX4373	Yr.Iss.	1990	7.75	13-28
1990 Christmas Partridge QX5246	Yr.Iss.	1990	7.75	10-23
1990 Claus Construction QX4885	Yr.Iss.	1990	7.75	12-20
1990 Country Angel QX5046	Yr.Iss.	1990	6.75	76
1990 Coyote Carols QX4993	Yr.Iss.	1990	8.75	17-20
1990 Cozy Goose QX4966	Yr.Iss.	1990	5.75	10-14
1990 Feliz Navidad QX5173	Yr.Iss.	1990	6.75	18-30
1990 Garfield QX2303	Yr.Iss.	1990	4.75	13-25
1990 Gingerbread Elf QX5033	Yr.Iss.	1990	5.75	15-23
1990 Goose Cart QX5236	Yr.Iss.	1990	7.75	14-18
1990 Hang in There QX4713	Yr.Iss.	1990	6.75	15-23
1990 Happy Voices QX4645	Yr.Iss.	1990	6.75	14-18
1990 Holiday Cardinals QX5243	Yr.Iss.	1990	7.75	16-23
1990 Home for the Owlidays QX5183	Yr.Iss.	1990	6.75	11-18
1990 Hot Dogger QX4976	Yr.Iss.	1990	7.75	15-20
1990 Jolly Dolphin QX4683	Yr.Iss.	1990	6.75	16-21
1990 Joy is in the Air QX5503	Yr.Iss.	1990	7.75	15-20
1990 King Klaus QX4106	Yr.Iss.	1990	7.75	13-25
1990 Kitty's Best Pal QX4716	Yr.Iss.	1990	6.75	16-20
1990 Little Drummer Boy QX5233	Yr.Iss.	1990	7.75	19-30
1990 Long Winter's Nap QX4703	Yr.Iss.	1990	6.75	15-25
1990 Lovable Dears QX5476	Yr.Iss.	1990	8.75	14-19
1990 Meow Mart QX4446	Yr.Iss.	1990	7.75	17-30
1990 Mooy Christmas QX4933	Yr.Iss.	1990	6.75	26-33
1990 Norman Rockwell Art QX2296	Yr.Iss.	1990	4.75	10-25
1990 Nutshell Chat QX5193	Yr.Iss.	1990	6.75	16-258
1990 Nutshell Holiday QX465-2	Yr.Iss.	1990	5.75	13-28
1990 Peanuts QX2233	Yr.Iss.	1990	4.75	27-30
1990 Pepperoni Mouse QX4973	Yr.Iss.	1990	6.75	14-20
1990 Perfect Catch QX4693	Yr.Iss.	1990	7.75	12-20
1990 Polar Jogger QX4666	Yr.Iss.	1990	5.75	9-20
1990 Polar Pair QX4626	Yr.Iss.	1990	5.75	15-30
1990 Polar Sport QX5156	Yr.Iss.	1990	7.75	12-25
1990 Polar TV QX5166	Yr.Iss.	1990	7.75	12-20
1990 Polar V.I.P. QX4663	Yr.Iss.	1990	5.75	12-20
1990 Polar Video QX4633	Yr.Iss.	1990	5.75	9-24
1990 Poolside Walrus QX4986	Yr.Iss.	1990	7.75	14-30
1990 S. Claus Taxi QX4686	Yr.Iss.	1990	11.75	25-30
1990 Santa Schnoz QX4983	Yr.Iss.	1990	6.75	32-40
1990 Snoopy and Woodstock QX4723	Yr.Iss.	1990	6.75	28-43
1990 Spoon Rider QX5496	Yr.Iss.	1990	9.75	10-14
1990 Stitches of Joy QX5186	Yr.Iss.	1990	7.75	16-23
1990 Stocking Kitten QX456-5	Yr.Iss.	1990	6.75	7
1990 Stocking Pals QX5493	Yr.Iss.	1990	10.75	20-25
1990 Three Little Piggies QX4996	Yr.Iss.	1990	7.75	15-25
1990 Two Peas in a Pod QX4926	Yr.Iss.	1990	4.75	26

1990 Special Edition - Keepsake

YEAR ISSUE	EDITION LIMIT	YEAR RETD.	ISSUE PRICE	*QUOTE U.S.$
1990 Dickens Caroler Bell-Mr. Ashbourne QX5056	Yr.Iss.	1990	21.75	42-55

1991 Artists' Favorites - Keepsake

YEAR ISSUE	EDITION LIMIT	YEAR RETD.	ISSUE PRICE	*QUOTE U.S.$
1991 Fiddlin' Around QX4387	Yr.Iss.	1991	7.75	16-20
1991 Hooked on Santa QX4109	Yr.Iss.	1991	7.75	20-25
1991 Noah's Ark QX4867	Yr.Iss.	1991	13.75	28-50
1991 Polar Circus Wagon QX4399	Yr.Iss.	1991	13.75	25-30
1991 Santa Sailor QX4389	Yr.Iss.	1991	9.75	19-27
1991 Tramp and Laddie QX4397	Yr.Iss.	1991	7.75	21-50

1991 Club Limited Editions - Keepsake

YEAR ISSUE	EDITION LIMIT	YEAR RETD.	ISSUE PRICE	*QUOTE U.S.$
1991 Galloping Into Christmas QXC4779	28,400	1991	19.75	99-101
1991 Secrets for Santa QXC4797	28,700	1991	23.75	50

1991 Collectible Series - Keepsake

YEAR ISSUE	EDITION LIMIT	YEAR RETD.	ISSUE PRICE	*QUOTE U.S.$
1991 1957 Corvette (1st Ed.) QX4319	Yr.Iss.	1991	12.75	135-190
1991 Betsey Clark: Home for Christmas (6th Ed.) QX2109	Yr.Iss.	1991	5.00	19-30
1991 Checking His List (6th Ed.) QX4339	Yr.Iss.	1991	13.75	31-50
1991 Christmas Kitty (3rd Ed.) QX4377	Yr.Iss.	1991	14.75	17-27
1991 CRAYOLA CRAYON-Bright Vibrant Carols (3rd Ed.) QX4219	Yr.Iss.	1991	9.75	29-40
1991 Eight Maids A-Milking (8th Ed.) QX3089	Yr.Iss.	1991	6.75	20-30
1991 Fabulous Decade (2nd Ed.) QX4119	Yr.Iss.	1991	7.75	32-40
1991 Fire Station (8th Ed.) QX4139	Yr.Iss.	1991	14.75	44-70
1991 Frosty Friends (12th Ed.) QX4327	Yr.Iss.	1991	9.75	30-40
1991 The Gift Bringers-Christkind (3rd Ed.) QX2117	Yr.Iss.	1991	5.00	20-25
1991 Greatest Story (2nd Ed.) QX4129	Yr.Iss.	1991	12.75	24-30
1991 Hark! It's Herald (3rd Ed.) QX4379	Yr.Iss.	1991	6.75	19-24
1991 Heart of Christmas (2nd Ed.) QX4357	Yr.Iss.	1991	13.75	27-30
1991 Heavenly Angels (1st Ed.) QX4367	Yr.Iss.	1991	7.75	30
1991 Let It Snow! (5th Ed.) QX4369	Yr.Iss.	1991	8.75	19-30
1991 Mary's Angels-Iris (4th Ed.) QX4279	Yr.Iss.	1991	6.75	35-40
1991 Merry Olde Santa (2nd Ed.) QX4359	Yr.Iss.	1991	14.75	54-83
1991 Peace on Earth-Italy (1st Ed.) QX5129	Yr.Iss.	1991	11.75	12-27
1991 Puppy Love (1st Ed.) QX5379	Yr.Iss.	1991	7.75	60-69
1991 Reindeer Champ-Cupid (6th Ed.) QX4347	Yr.Iss.	1991	7.75	20-30
1991 Rocking Horse (11th Ed.) QX4147	Yr.Iss.	1991	10.75	42-60
1991 Santa's Antique Car (13th Ed.) QX4349	Yr.Iss.	1991	14.75	40-60
1991 Winter Surprise (3rd Ed.) QX4277	Yr.Iss.	1991	10.75	18-23

1991 Commemoratives - Keepsake

YEAR ISSUE	EDITION LIMIT	YEAR RETD.	ISSUE PRICE	*QUOTE U.S.$
1991 Across the Miles QX3157	Yr.Iss.	1991	6.75	13-15
1991 Baby's First Christmas QX4889	Yr.Iss.	1991	7.75	10-31
1991 Baby's First Christmas QX5107	Yr.Iss.	1991	17.75	33-45
1991 Baby's First Christmas-Baby Boy QX2217	Yr.Iss.	1991	4.75	16-20
1991 Baby's First Christmas-Baby Girl QX2227	Yr.Iss.	1991	4.75	16-20
1991 Baby's First Christmas-Photo Holder QX4869	Yr.Iss.	1991	7.75	22
1991 Baby's Second Christmas QX4897	Yr.Iss.	1991	6.75	25-31
1991 The Big Cheese QX5327	Yr.Iss.	1991	6.75	18-20
1991 Brother QX5479	Yr.Iss.	1991	6.75	11-18
1991 A Child's Christmas QX4887	Yr.Iss.	1991	9.75	14-18
1991 Child's Fifth Christmas QX4909	Yr.Iss.	1991	6.75	15-20
1991 Child's Fourth Christmas QX4907	Yr.Iss.	1991	6.75	16-25
1991 Child's Third Christmas QX4899	Yr.Iss.	1991	6.75	21
1991 Dad QX5127	Yr.Iss.	1991	7.75	19
1991 Dad-to-Be QX4879	Yr.Iss.	1991	5.75	13-18
1991 Daughter QX5477	Yr.Iss.	1991	5.75	40-50
1991 Extra-Special Friends QX2279	Yr.Iss.	1991	4.75	12-18
1991 Fifty Years Together QX4947	Yr.Iss.	1991	8.75	18
1991 Five Years Together QX4927	Yr.Iss.	1991	7.75	12-16
1991 Forty Years Together QX4939	Yr.Iss.	1991	7.75	18
1991 Friends Are Fun QX5289	Yr.Iss.	1991	9.75	18-23
1991 From Our Home to Yours QX2287	Yr.Iss.	1991	4.75	15-23
1991 Gift of Joy QX5319	Yr.Iss.	1991	8.75	19-25
1991 Godchild QX5489	Yr.Iss.	1991	6.75	18-20
1991 Granddaughter QX2299	Yr.Iss.	1991	4.75	25-30
1991 Granddaughter's First Christmas QX5119	Yr.Iss.	1991	6.75	15-25
1991 Grandmother QX2307	Yr.Iss.	1991	4.75	16-20
1991 Grandparents QX2309	Yr.Iss.	1991	4.75	14-17
1991 Grandson QX2297	Yr.Iss.	1991	4.75	19-25
1991 Grandson's First Christmas QX5117	Yr.Iss.	1991	6.75	14-27
1991 Jesus Loves Me QX3147	Yr.Iss.	1991	7.75	14
1991 Mom and Dad QX5467	Yr.Iss.	1991	9.75	22
1991 Mom-to-Be QX4877	Yr.Iss.	1991	5.75	20-27
1991 Mother QX5457	Yr.Iss.	1991	9.75	25-33
1991 New Home QX5449	Yr.Iss.	1991	6.75	20-30
1991 Our First Christmas Together QX2229	Yr.Iss.	1991	4.75	14-20
1991 Our First Christmas Together QX3139	Yr.Iss.	1991	6.75	20-30
1991 Our First Christmas Together QX4919	Yr.Iss.	1991	8.75	18-28
1991 Our First Christmas Together-Photo Holder QX4917	Yr.Iss.	1991	8.75	24-30
1991 Sister QX5487	Yr.Iss.	1991	6.75	16-20
1991 Son QX5469	Yr.Iss.	1991	5.75	16-23
1991 Sweetheart QX4957	Yr.Iss.	1991	9.75	18-25
1991 Teacher QX2289	Yr.Iss.	1991	4.75	9-12
1991 Ten Years Together QX4929	Yr.Iss.	1991	7.75	15-23
1991 Terrific Teacher QX5309	Yr.Iss.	1991	6.75	13-15
1991 Twenty -Five Years Together QX4937	Yr.Iss.	1991	8.75	16-20
1991 Under the Mistletoe QX4949	Yr.Iss.	1991	8.75	19

1991 Keepsake Collector's Club - Keepsake

YEAR ISSUE	EDITION LIMIT	YEAR RETD.	ISSUE PRICE	*QUOTE U.S.$
1991 Beary Artistic QXC7259	Yr.Iss.	1991	10.00	32-40
1991 Hidden Treasure/Li'l Keeper QXC4769	Yr.Iss.	1991	15.00	37-40

1991 Keepsake Magic Ornaments - Keepsake

YEAR ISSUE	EDITION LIMIT	YEAR RETD.	ISSUE PRICE	*QUOTE U.S.$
1991 Angel of Light QLT7239	Yr.Iss.	1991	30.00	48-60
1991 Arctic Dome QLX7117	Yr.Iss.	1991	25.00	46-55
1991 Baby's First Christmas QLX7247	Yr.Iss.	1991	30.00	90-99
1991 Bringing Home the Tree-QLX7249	Yr.Iss.	1991	28.00	51-58
1991 Chris Mouse Mail QLX7207	Yr.Iss.	1991	10.00	25-40
1991 Elfin Engineer QLX7209	Yr.Iss.	1991	10.00	20-25
1991 Father Christmas QLX7147	Yr.Iss.	1991	14.00	29-40
1991 Festive Brass Church QLX7179	Yr.Iss.	1991	14.00	26-33
1991 Forest Frolics QLX7219	Yr.Iss.	1991	25.00	56-70
1991 Friendship Tree QLX7169	Yr.Iss.	1991	10.00	23-25
1991 Holiday Glow QLX7177	Yr.Iss.	1991	14.00	24-30
1991 It's A Wonderful Life QLX7237	Yr.Iss.	1991	20.00	62-75
1991 Jingle Bears QLX7323	Yr.Iss.	1991	25.00	45-58
1991 Kringles's Bumper Cars-QLX7119	Yr.Iss.	1991	25.00	38-55
1991 Mole Family Home QLX7149	Yr.Iss.	1991	20.00	37-50
1991 Our First Christmas Together QXL7137	Yr.Iss.	1991	25.00	50-60
1991 PEANUTS QLX7229	Yr.Iss.	1991	18.00	32-75
1991 Salvation Army Band QLX7273	Yr.Iss.	1991	30.00	64-80
1991 Santa Special QLX7167	Yr.Iss.	1992	40.00	57-80
1991 Santa's Hot Line QLX7159	Yr.Iss.	1991	18.00	33-45
1991 Ski Trip QLX7266	Yr.Iss.	1991	28.00	50-60
1991 Sparkling Angel QLX7157	Yr.Iss.	1991	18.00	27-38
1991 Toyland Tower QLX7129	Yr.Iss.	1991	20.00	37-45

1991 Keepsake Miniature Ornaments - Keepsake

YEAR ISSUE	EDITION LIMIT	YEAR RETD.	ISSUE PRICE	*QUOTE U.S.$
1991 All Aboard QXM5869	Yr.Iss.	1991	4.50	17
1991 Baby's First Christmas QXM5799	Yr.Iss.	1991	6.00	18-23
1991 Brass Church QXM5979	Yr.Iss.	1991	3.00	9
1991 Brass Soldier QXM5987	Yr.Iss.	1991	3.00	9
1991 Bright Boxers QXM5877	Yr.Iss.	1991	4.50	6-16
1991 Busy Bear QXM5939	Yr.Iss.	1991	4.50	12
1991 Cardinal Cameo QXM5957	Yr.Iss.	1991	6.00	17
1991 Caring Shepherd QXM5949	Yr.Iss.	1991	6.00	18
1991 Cool 'n' Sweet QXM5867	Yr.Iss.	1991	4.50	25
1991 Country Sleigh QXM5999	Yr.Iss.	1991	4.50	13-15
1991 Courier Turtle QXM5857	Yr.Iss.	1991	4.50	14
1991 Fancy Wreath QXM5917	Yr.Iss.	1991	4.50	13
1991 Feliz Navidad QXM5887	Yr.Iss.	1991	6.00	14-22
1991 Fly By QXM5859	Yr.Iss.	1991	4.50	13-18
1991 Friendly Fawn QXM5947	Yr.Iss.	1991	6.00	13-17
1991 Grandchild's First Christmas QXM5697	Yr.Iss.	1991	4.50	13
1991 Heavenly Minstrel QXM5687	Yr.Iss.	1991	9.75	22
1991 Holiday Snowflake QXM5997	Yr.Iss.	1991	3.00	12
1991 Inn (4th Ed.) QXM5627	Yr.Iss.	1991	8.50	23-30
1991 Key to Love QXM5689	Yr.Iss.	1991	4.50	17
1991 Kittens in Toyland (4th Ed.) QXM5639	Yr.Iss.	1991	4.50	15-20
1991 Kitty in a Mitty QXM5879	Yr.Iss.	1991	4.50	14
1991 The Kringles (3rd Ed.) QXM5647	Yr.Iss.	1991	6.00	15-21
1991 Li'l Popper QXM5897	Yr.Iss.	1991	4.50	17
1991 Love Is Born QXM5959	Yr.Iss.	1991	6.00	18
1991 Lulu & Family QXM5677	Yr.Iss.	1991	6.00	21
1991 Mom QXM5699	Yr.Iss.	1991	6.00	17
1991 N. Pole Buddy QXM5927	Yr.Iss.	1991	4.50	18
1991 Nature's Angels (2nd Ed.) QXM5657	Yr.Iss.	1991	4.50	13-21
1991 Noel QXM5989	Yr.Iss.	1991	3.00	12
1991 Our First Christmas Together QXM5819	Yr.Iss.	1991	6.00	17
1991 Passenger Car (3rd Ed.) QXM5649	Yr.Iss.	1991	8.50	38-50
1991 Penquin Pal (4th Ed.) QXM5629	Yr.Iss.	1991	4.50	16
1991 Ring-A-Ding Elf QXM5669	Yr.Iss.	1991	8.50	18
1991 Rocking Horse (4th Ed.) QXM5637	Yr.Iss.	1991	4.50	24-26
1991 Seaside Otter QXM5909	Yr.Iss.	1991	4.50	15
1991 Silvery Santa QXM5679	Yr.Iss.	1991	9.75	22
1991 Special Friends QXM5797	Yr.Iss.	1991	8.50	18
1991 Thimble Bells (2nd Ed.) QXM5659	Yr.Iss.	1991	6.00	10
1991 Tiny Tea Party (set/6) QXM5827	Yr.Iss.	1991	29.00	145-165
1991 Top Hatter QXM5889	Yr.Iss.	1991	6.00	11-16
1991 Treeland Trio QXM5899	Yr.Iss.	1991	8.50	16
1991 Upbeat Bear QXM5907	Yr.Iss.	1991	6.00	16
1991 Vision of Santa QXM5937	Yr.Iss.	1991	4.50	13
1991 Wee Toymaker QXM5967	Yr.Iss.	1991	8.50	6-16
1991 Woodland Babies QXM5667	Yr.Iss.	1991	6.00	12-24

1991 New Attractions - Keepsake

YEAR ISSUE	EDITION LIMIT	YEAR RETD.	ISSUE PRICE	*QUOTE U.S.$
1991 All-Star QX5329	Yr.Iss.	1991	6.75	17-23
1991 Basket Bell Players QX5377	Yr.Iss.	1991	7.75	21-28
1991 Bob Cratchit QX4997	Yr.Iss.	1991	13.75	22-35
1991 Chilly Chap QX5339	Yr.Iss.	1991	6.75	14-17
1991 Christmas Welcome QX5299	Yr.Iss.	1991	9.75	21-25
1991 Christopher Robin QX5579	Yr.Iss.	1991	9.75	32-38
1991 Cuddly Lamb QX5199	Yr.Iss.	1991	6.75	16-20
1991 Dinoclaus QX5277	Yr.Iss.	1991	7.75	17-27
1991 Ebenezer Scrooge QX4989	Yr.Iss.	1991	13.75	28-45
1991 Evergreen Inn QX5389	Yr.Iss.	1991	8.75	15-18
1991 Fanfare Bear QX5337	Yr.Iss.	1991	8.75	18
1991 Feliz Navidad QX5279	Yr.Iss.	1991	6.75	16-28
1991 Folk Art Reindeer QX5359	Yr.Iss.	1991	8.75	14-20
1991 GARFIELD QX5177	Yr.Iss.	1991	7.75	27-30
1991 Glee Club Bears QX4969	Yr.Iss.	1991	8.75	12-18
1991 Holiday Cafe QX5399	Yr.Iss.	1991	8.75	10-14
1991 Jolly Wolly Santa QX5419	Yr.Iss.	1991	7.75	10-23
1991 Jolly Wolly Snowman QX5427	Yr.Iss.	1991	7.75	10-21
1991 Jolly Wolly Soldier QX5429'	Yr.Iss.	1991	7.75	18-20
1991 Joyous Memories-Photoholder QX5369	Yr.Iss.	1991	6.75	16-28
1991 Kanga and Roo QX5617	Yr.Iss.	1991	9.75	35-48
1991 Look Out Below QX4959	Yr.Iss.	1991	8.75	18-20
1991 Loving Stitches QX4987	Yr.Iss.	1991	8.75	23-29
1991 Mary Engelbreit QX2237	Yr.Iss.	1991	4.75	22-27
1991 Merry Carolers QX4799	Yr.Iss.	1991	29.75	75-95
1991 Mrs. Cratchit QX4999	Yr.Iss.	1991	13.75	28-33
1991 Night Before Christmas QX5307	Yr.Iss.	1991	9.75	13-25
1991 Norman Rockwell Art QX2259	Yr.Iss.	1991	5.00	10-30
1991 Notes of Cheer QX5357	Yr.Iss.	1991	5.75	12-14
1991 Nutshell Nativity QX5176	Yr.Iss.	1991	6.75	19-27
1991 Nutty Squirrel QX4833	Yr.Iss.	1991	5.75	10-13
1991 Old-Fashioned Sled QX4317	Yr.Iss.	1991	8.75	16-20
1991 On a Roll QX5347	Yr.Iss.	1991	6.75	16-22
1991 Partridge in a Pear Tree QX5297	Yr.Iss.	1991	9.75	10-18
1991 PEANUTS QX2257	Yr.Iss.	1991	5.00	14-23
1991 Piglet and Eeyore QX5577	Yr.Iss.	1991	9.75	30-50
1991 Plum Delightful QX4977	Yr.Iss.	1991	8.75	18-22
1991 Polar Classic QX5287	Yr.Iss.	1991	6.75	15-23
1991 Rabbit QX5607	Yr.Iss.	1991	9.75	30-33
1991 Santa's Studio QX5397	Yr.Iss.	1991	8.75	14-20
1991 Ski Lift Bunny QX5447	Yr.Iss.	1991	6.75	14-23
1991 Snoopy and Woodstock QX5197	Yr.Iss.	1991	6.75	28-40
1991 Snow Twins QX4979	Yr.Iss.	1991	8.75	11-20
1991 Snowy Owl QX5269	Yr.Iss.	1991	7.75	18
1991 Sweet Talk QX5367	Yr.Iss.	1991	8.75	14-18
1991 Tigger QX5609	Yr.Iss.	1991	9.75	76-130

*Quotes have been rounded up to nearest dollar

YEAR ISSUE	EDITION LIMIT	YEAR RETD.	ISSUE PRICE	*QUOTE U.S.$
1991 Tiny Tim QX5037	Yr.Iss.	1991	10.75	24-40
1991 Up 'N'Down Journey QX5047	Yr.Iss.	1991	9.75	22-28
1991 Winnie-the Pooh QX5569	Yr.Iss.	1991	9.75	40-55
1991 Yule Logger QX4967	Yr.Iss.	1991	8.75	19-22

1991 Special Edition - Keepsake

YEAR ISSUE	EDITION LIMIT	YEAR RETD.	ISSUE PRICE	*QUOTE U.S.$
1991 Dickens Caroler Bell-Mrs. Beaumont QX5039	Yr.Iss.	1991	21.75	41-43
1991 Starship Enterprise QLX7199	Yr.Iss.	1991	20.00	195-348

1992 Artists' Favorites - Keepsake

YEAR ISSUE	EDITION LIMIT	YEAR RETD.	ISSUE PRICE	*QUOTE U.S.$
1992 Elfin Marionette QX5931	Yr.Iss.	1992	11.75	22-25
1992 Mother Goose QX4984	Yr.Iss.	1992	13.75	27-30
1992 Polar Post QX4914	Yr.Iss.	1992	8.75	20
1992 Stocked With Joy QX5934	Yr.Iss.	1992	7.75	12-17
1992 Turtle Dreams QX4991	Yr.Iss.	1992	8.75	20-28
1992 Uncle Art's Ice Cream QX5001	Yr.Iss.	1992	8.75	12-23

1992 Collectible Series - Keepsake

YEAR ISSUE	EDITION LIMIT	YEAR RETD.	ISSUE PRICE	*QUOTE U.S.$
1992 1966 Mustang (2nd Ed.) QX4284	Yr.Iss.	1992	12.75	25-55
1992 Betsey's Country Christmas (1st Ed.) QX2104	Yr.Iss.	1992	5.00	24-30
1992 CRAYOLA CRAYON-Bright Colors (4th Ed.) QX4264	Yr.Iss.	1992	9.75	25-34
1992 Fabulous Decade (3rd Ed.) QX4244	Yr.Iss.	1992	7.75	31-50
1992 Five-and-Ten-Cent Store (9th Ed.) QX4254	Yr.Iss.	1992	14.75	29-45
1992 Frosty Friends (13th Ed.) QX4291	Yr.Iss.	1992	9.75	29-35
1992 The Gift Bringers-Kolyada (4th Ed.) QX2124	Yr.Iss.	1992	5.00	14-23
1992 Gift Exchange (7th Ed.) QX4294	Yr.Iss.	1992	14.75	30-45
1992 Greatest Story (3rd Ed.) QX4251	Yr.Iss.	1992	12.75	15-25
1992 Hark! It's Herald (4th Ed.) QX4464	Yr.Iss.	1992	7.75	18-20
1992 Heart of Christmas (3rd Ed.) QX4411	Yr.Iss.	1992	13.75	16-31
1992 Heavenly Angels (2nd Ed.) QX4454	Yr.Iss.	1992	7.75	21-30
1992 Kringle Tours (14th Ed.) QX4341	Yr.Iss.	1992	14.75	28-39
1992 Mary's Angels-Lily (5th Ed.) QX4274	Yr.Iss.	1992	6.75	41-52
1992 Merry Olde Santa (3rd Ed.) QX4414	Yr.Iss.	1992	14.75	35-40
1992 Nine Ladies Dancing (9th Ed.) QX3031	Yr.Iss.	1992	6.75	19-25
1992 Owliver (1st Ed.) QX4544	Yr.Iss.	1992	7.75	19
1992 Peace On Earth-Spain (2nd Ed.) QX5174	Yr.Iss.	1992	11.75	10-21
1992 Puppy Love (2nd Ed.) QX4484	Yr.Iss.	1992	7.75	25-44
1992 Reindeer Champs-Donder (7th Ed.) QX5284	Yr.Iss.	1992	8.75	27-35
1992 Rocking Horse (12th Ed.) QX4261	Yr.Iss.	1992	10.75	35-50
1992 Sweet Holiday Harmony (6th Ed.) QX4461	Yr.Iss.	1992	8.75	19-25
1992 Tobin Fraley Carousel (1st Ed.) QX4891	Yr.Iss.	1992	28.00	20-62
1992 Winter Surprise (4th Ed.) QX4271	Yr.Iss.	1992	11.75	22-27

1992 Collectors' Club - Keepsake

YEAR ISSUE	EDITION LIMIT	YEAR RETD.	ISSUE PRICE	*QUOTE U.S.$
1992 Chipmunk Parcel Service QXC5194	Yr.Iss.	1992	6.75	21
1992 Rodney Takes Flight QXC5081	Yr.Iss.	1992	9.75	15-21
1992 Santa's Club List QXC7291	Yr.Iss.	1992	15.00	36-40

1992 Commemoratives - Keepsake

YEAR ISSUE	EDITION LIMIT	YEAR RETD.	ISSUE PRICE	*QUOTE U.S.$
1992 Across the Miles QX3044	Yr.Iss.	1992	6.75	10-14
1992 Anniversary Year QX4851	Yr.Iss.	1992	9.75	18-27
1992 Baby's First Christmas QX4641	Yr.Iss.	1992	7.75	20-25
1992 Baby's First Christmas QX4644	Yr.Iss.	1992	7.75	27-30
1992 Baby's First Christmas-Baby Boy QX2191	Yr.Iss.	1992	4.75	16-20
1992 Baby's First Christmas-Baby Girl QX2204	Yr.Iss.	1992	4.75	16-25
1992 Baby's First ChristmasQX4581	Yr.Iss.	1992	18.75	38-40
1992 Baby's Second Christmas QX4651	Yr.Iss.	1992	6.75	21-23
1992 Brother QX4684	Yr.Iss.	1992	6.75	13-16
1992 A Child's Christmas QX4574	Yr.Iss.	1992	9.75	19
1992 Child's Fifth Christmas QX4664	Yr.Iss.	1992	6.75	17-23
1992 Child's Fourth Christmas QX4661	Yr.Iss.	1992	6.75	20-25
1992 Child's Third Christmas QX4654	Yr.Iss.	1992	6.75	20-25
1992 Dad QX4674	Yr.Iss.	1992	7.75	18-23
1992 Dad-to-Be QX4611	Yr.Iss.	1992	6.75	10-17
1992 Daughter QX5031	Yr.Iss.	1992	6.75	8-20
1992 For My Grandma QX5184	Yr.Iss.	1992	7.75	10-14
1992 For The One I Love QX4884	Yr.Iss.	1992	9.75	20
1992 Friendly Greetings QX5041	Yr.Iss.	1992	7.75	10-14
1992 Friendship Line QX5034	Yr.Iss.	1992	9.75	23-29
1992 From Our Home To Yours QX2131	Yr.Iss.	1992	4.75	13-17
1992 Godchild QX5941	Yr.Iss.	1992	6.75	19
1992 Grandaughter QX5604	Yr.Iss.	1992	6.75	13-25
1992 Grandaughter's First Christmas QX4634	Yr.Iss.	1992	6.75	14-20
1992 Grandmother QX2011	Yr.Iss.	1992	4.75	16-20
1992 Grandparents QX2004	Yr.Iss.	1992	4.75	13-17
1992 Grandson QX5611	Yr.Iss.	1992	6.75	19-25
1992 Grandson's First Christmas QX4621	Yr.Iss.	1992	6.75	16-23
1992 Holiday Memo QX5044	Yr.Iss.	1992	7.75	15
1992 Love To Skate QX4841	Yr.Iss.	1992	8.75	10-20
1992 Mom and Dad QX4671	Yr.Iss.	1992	9.75	21-37
1992 Mom QX5164	Yr.Iss.	1992	7.75	19
1992 Mom-to-Be QX4614	Yr.Iss.	1992	6.75	16-20
1992 New Home QX5191	Yr.Iss.	1992	8.75	20
1992 Our First Christmas Together QX4694	Yr.Iss.	1992	8.75	20-25
1992 Our First Christmas Together QX3011	Yr.Iss.	1992	6.75	17
1992 Our First Christmas Together QX5061	Yr.Iss.	1992	9.75	19
1992 Secret Pal QX5424	Yr.Iss.	1992	7.75	14
1992 Sister QX4681	Yr.Iss.	1992	6.75	14
1992 Son QX5024	Yr.Iss.	1992	6.75	21-27
1992 Special Cat QX5414	Yr.Iss.	1992	7.75	14-17
1992 Special Dog QX5421	Yr.Iss.	1992	7.75	10-30
1992 Teacher QX2264	Yr.Iss.	1992	4.75	13-17
1992 V. P. of Important Stuff QX5051	Yr.Iss.	1992	6.75	12-15
1992 World-Class Teacher QX5054	Yr.Iss.	1992	7.75	10-20

1992 Easter Ornaments - Keepsake

YEAR ISSUE	EDITION LIMIT	YEAR RETD.	ISSUE PRICE	*QUOTE U.S.$
1992 Easter Parade (1st Ed.) 675QEO8301	Yr.Iss.	1992	6.75	19-26
1992 Egg in Sports (1st Ed.) 675QEO9341	Yr.Iss.	1992	6.75	24-35

1992 Limited Edition Ornaments - Keepsake

YEAR ISSUE	EDITION LIMIT	YEAR RETD.	ISSUE PRICE	*QUOTE U.S.$
1992 Christmas Treasures QXC5464	15,500	1992	22.00	110-122
1992 Victorian Skater (w/ base) QXC4067	14,700	1992	25.00	50-75

1992 Magic Ornaments - Keepsake

YEAR ISSUE	EDITION LIMIT	YEAR RETD.	ISSUE PRICE	*QUOTE U.S.$
1992 Angel Of Light QLT7239	Yr.Iss.	1992	30.00	30
1992 Baby's First Christmas QLX7281	Yr.Iss.	1992	22.00	72-110
1992 Chris Mouse Tales (8th Ed.) QLX7074	Yr.Iss.	1992	12.00	18-25
1992 Christmas Parade QLX7271	Yr.Iss.	1992	30.00	55-60
1992 Continental Express QLX7264	Yr.Iss.	1992	32.00	61-75
1992 The Dancing Nutcracker QLX7261	Yr.Iss.	1992	30.00	54-60
1992 Enchanted Clock QLX7274	Yr.Iss.	1992	30.00	48-60
1992 Feathered Friends QLX7091	Yr.Iss.	1992	14.00	28-30
1992 Forest Frolics (4th Ed.) QLX7254	Yr.Iss.	1992	28.00	52-65
1992 Good Sledding Ahead QLX7244	Yr.Iss.	1992	28.00	42-58
1992 Lighting the Way QLX7231	Yr.Iss.	1992	18.00	31-50
1992 Look! It's Santa QLX7094	Yr.Iss.	1992	14.00	30-50
1992 Nut Sweet Nut QLX7081	Yr.Iss.	1992	10.00	21
1992 Out First Christmas Together QLX7221	Yr.Iss.	1992	20.00	39-45
1992 PEANUTS (2nd Ed.) QLX7214	Yr.Iss.	1992	18.00	49-64
1992 Santa Special QLX7167	Yr.Iss.	1992	40.00	80
1992 Santa Sub QLX7321	Yr.Iss.	1992	18.00	34-40
1992 Santa's Answering Machine QLX7241	Yr.Iss.	1992	22.00	41-44
1992 Under Construction QLX7324	Yr.Iss.	1992	18.00	36-40
1992 Watch Owls QLX7084	Yr.Iss.	1992	12.00	25-30
1992 Yuletide Rider QLX7314	Yr.Iss.	1992	28.00	53-60

1992 Miniature Ornaments - Keepsake

YEAR ISSUE	EDITION LIMIT	YEAR RETD.	ISSUE PRICE	*QUOTE U.S.$
1992 A+ Teacher QXM5511	Yr.Iss.	1992	3.75	5-8
1992 Angelic Harpist QXM5524	Yr.Iss.	1992	4.50	12-15
1992 Baby's First Christmas QXM5494	Yr.Iss.	1992	4.50	17-20
1992 The Bearymores(1st Ed.) QXM5544	Yr.Iss.	1992	5.75	10-18
1992 Black-Capped Chickadee QXM5484	Yr.Iss.	1992	3.00	12-15
1992 Box Car (4th Ed.) Noel R.R. QXM5441	Yr.Iss.	1992	7.00	14-24
1992 Bright Stringers QXM5841	Yr.Iss.	1992	3.75	12-15
1992 Buck-A-Roo QXM5814	Yr.Iss.	1992	4.50	6-11
1992 Christmas Bonus QXM5811	Yr.Iss.	1992	3.00	5-8
1992 Christmas Copter QXM5844	Yr.Iss.	1992	5.75	14
1992 Church (5th Ed.) Old English V. QXM5384	Yr.Iss.	1992	7.00	24-35
1992 Coca-Cola Santa QXM5884	Yr.Iss.	1992	5.75	7-17
1992 Cool Uncle Sam QXM5561	Yr.Iss.	1992	3.00	15-18
1992 Cozy Kayak QXM5551	Yr.Iss.	1992	3.75	10-14
1992 Fast Finish QXM5301	Yr.Iss.	1992	3.75	12
1992 Feeding Time QXM5481	Yr.Iss.	1992	5.75	12-15
1992 Friendly Tin Soldier QXM5874	Yr.Iss.	1992	4.50	14-18
1992 Friends Are Tops QXM5521	Yr.Iss.	1992	4.50	10-12
1992 Gerbil Inc. QXM5924	Yr.Iss.	1992	3.75	8-11
1992 Going Places QXM5871	Yr.Iss.	1992	3.75	9
1992 Grandchild's First Christmas QXM5501	Yr.Iss.	1992	5.75	12-15
1992 Grandma QXM5514	Yr.Iss.	1992	4.50	3-15
1992 Harmony Trio-Set/3 QXM5471	Yr.Iss.	1992	11.75	12-21
1992 Hickory, Dickory, Dock QXM5861	Yr.Iss.	1992	3.75	13-15
1992 Holiday Holly QXM5364	Yr.Iss.	1992	9.75	15-21
1992 Holiday Splash QXM5834	Yr.Iss.	1992	5.75	12
1992 Hoop It Up QXM5831	Yr.Iss.	1992	4.50	5-13
1992 Inside Story QXM5881	Yr.Iss.	1992	7.25	14-19
1992 Kittens in Toyland (5th Ed.) QXM5391	Yr.Iss.	1992	4.50	14-18
1992 The Kringles (4th Ed.) QXM5381	Yr.Iss.	1992	6.00	16-19
1992 Little Town of Bethlehem QXM5864	Yr.Iss.	1992	3.00	17-23
1992 Minted For Santa QXM5854	Yr.Iss.	1992	3.75	12-15
1992 Mom QXM5504	Yr.Iss.	1992	4.50	12-15
1992 Nature's Angels (3rd Ed.) QXM5451	Yr.Iss.	1992	4.50	13-20
1992 The Night Before Christmas QXM5541	Yr.Iss.	1992	13.75	28
1992 Perfect Balance QXM5571	Yr.Iss.	1992	3.00	10-14
1992 Polar Polka QXM5534	Yr.Iss.	1992	4.50	14
1992 Puppet Show QXM5574	Yr.Iss.	1992	3.00	10-13
1992 Rocking Horse (5th Ed.) QXM5454	Yr.Iss.	1992	4.50	16-19
1992 Sew Sew Tiny (set/6) QXM5794	Yr.Iss.	1992	29.00	35-65
1992 Ski For Two QXM5821	Yr.Iss.	1992	4.50	10-15
1992 Snowshoe Bunny QXM5564	Yr.Iss.	1992	3.75	13
1992 Snug Kitty QXM5554	Yr.Iss.	1992	3.75	5-14
1992 Spunky Monkey QXM5921	Yr.Iss.	1992	3.00	12-15
1992 Thimble Bells (3rd Ed.) QXM5461	Yr.Iss.	1992	6.00	15-18
1992 Visions Of Acorns QXM5851	Yr.Iss.	1992	4.50	12-15
1992 Wee Three Kings QXM5531	Yr.Iss.	1992	5.75	17-23
1992 Woodland Babies (2nd Ed.) QXM5444	Yr.Iss.	1992	6.00	16

1992 New Attractions - Keepsake

YEAR ISSUE	EDITION LIMIT	YEAR RETD.	ISSUE PRICE	*QUOTE U.S.$
1992 Bear Bell Champ QX5071	Yr.Iss.	1992	7.75	16-30
1992 Caboose QX5321	Yr.Iss.	1992	9.75	19
1992 Cheerful Santa QX5154	Yr.Iss.	1992	9.75	8-29
1992 Coal Car QX5401	Yr.Iss.	1992	9.75	19
1992 Cool Fliers QX5474	Yr.Iss.	1992	10.75	20-25
1992 Deck the Hogs QX5204	Yr.Iss.	1992	8.75	17-22
1992 Down-Under Holiday QX5144	Yr.Iss.	1992	7.75	18-23
1992 Egg Nog Nest QX5121	Yr.Iss.	1992	7.75	14-18
1992 Eric the Baker QX5244	Yr.Iss.	1992	8.75	8-18
1992 Feliz Navidad QX5181	Yr.Iss.	1992	6.75	17-23
1992 Franz the Artist QX5261	Yr.Iss.	1992	8.75	19-25
1992 Freida the Animals' Friend QX5264	Yr.Iss.	1992	8.75	8-19
1992 Fun on a Big Scale QX5134	Yr.Iss.	1992	10.75	22-24
1992 GARFIELD QX5374	Yr.Iss.	1992	7.75	15-25
1992 Genius at Work QX5371	Yr.Iss.	1992	10.75	20-22
1992 Golf's a Ball QX5984	Yr.Iss.	1992	6.75	27-30
1992 Gone Wishin' QX5171	Yr.Iss.	1992	8.75	19
1992 Green Thumb Santa QX5101	Yr.Iss.	1992	7.75	15-18
1992 Hello-Ho-Ho QX5141	Yr.Iss.	1992	9.75	17-23
1992 Holiday Teatime QX5431	Yr.Iss.	1992	14.75	27-30
1992 Holiday Wishes QX5131	Yr.Iss.	1992	7.75	17
1992 Honest George QX5064	Yr.Iss.	1992	7.75	12-16
1992 Jesus Loves Me QX3024	Yr.Iss.	1992	7.75	12-14
1992 Locomotive QX5311	Yr.Iss.	1992	9.75	25-40
1992 Loving Shepherd QX5151	Yr.Iss.	1992	7.75	14-17
1992 Ludwig the Musician QX5281	Yr.Iss.	1992	8.75	19-23
1992 Mary Engelbreit Santa Jolly Wolly QX5224	Yr.Iss.	1992	7.75	5-8
1992 Max the Tailor QX5251	Yr.Iss.	1992	8.75	20-23
1992 Memories to Cherish QX5161	Yr.Iss.	1992	10.75	20
1992 Merry "Swiss" Mouse QX5114	Yr.Iss.	1992	7.75	14-16
1992 Norman Rockwell Art QX2224	Yr.Iss.	1992	5.00	17-25
1992 North Pole Fire Fighter QX5104	Yr.Iss.	1992	9.75	21
1992 Otto the Carpenter QX5254	Yr.Iss.	1992	8.75	19-23
1992 Owl QX5614	Yr.Iss.	1992	9.75	15-28
1992 Partridge In a Pear Tree QX5234	Yr.Iss.	1992	8.75	18
1992 PEANUTS® QX2244	Yr.Iss.	1992	5.00	10-23
1992 Please Pause Here QX5291	Yr.Iss.	1992	14.75	20-32
1992 Rapid Delivery QX5094	Yr.Iss.	1992	8.75	20-25
1992 Santa's Hook Shot QX5434	Yr.Iss.	1992	12.75	28
1992 Santa's Roundup QX5084	Yr.Iss.	1992	8.75	20-25
1992 A Santa-Full! QX5991	Yr.Iss.	1992	9.75	32-40
1992 Silver Star QX5324	Yr.Iss.	1992	28.00	55-68
1992 Skiing 'Round QX5214	Yr.Iss.	1992	8.75	15-19
1992 SNOOPY®and WOODSTOCK QX5954	Yr.Iss.	1992	8.75	25-50
1992 Spirit of Christmas Stress QX5231	Yr.Iss.	1992	8.75	10-18
1992 Stock Car QX5314	Yr.Iss.	1992	9.75	19-25
1992 Tasty Christmas QX5994	Yr.Iss.	1992	9.75	19-25
1992 Toboggan Tail QX5459	Yr.Iss.	1992	7.75	15-20
1992 Tread Bear QX5091	Yr.Iss.	1992	8.75	22-25

1992 Special Edition - Keepsake

YEAR ISSUE	EDITION LIMIT	YEAR RETD.	ISSUE PRICE	*QUOTE U.S.$
1992 Dickens Caroler Bell-Lord Chadwick (3rd Ed.) QX4554	Yr.Iss.	1992	21.75	38-45

1992 Special Issues - Keepsake

YEAR ISSUE	EDITION LIMIT	YEAR RETD.	ISSUE PRICE	*QUOTE U.S.$
1992 Elvis QX562-4	Yr.Iss.	1992	14.75	15-31
1992 Santa Maria QX5074	Yr.Iss.	1992	12.75	10-27
1992 Shuttlecraft Galileo 2400QLX733-1	Yr.Iss.	1992	24.00	47-51

1993 Anniversary Edition - Keepsake

YEAR ISSUE	EDITION LIMIT	YEAR RETD.	ISSUE PRICE	*QUOTE U.S.$
1993 Frosty Friends QX5682	Yr.Iss.	1993	20.00	28-47
1993 Glowing Pewter Wreath QX5302	Yr.Iss.	1993	18.75	22-31
1993 Shopping With Santa QX5675	Yr.Iss.	1993	24.00	32-45
1993 Tannenbaum's Dept. Store QX5612	Yr.Iss.	1993	26.00	25-55

1993 Artists' Favorites - Keepsake

YEAR ISSUE	EDITION LIMIT	YEAR RETD.	ISSUE PRICE	*QUOTE U.S.$
1993 Bird Watcher QX5252	Yr.Iss.	1993	9.75	19
1993 Howling Good Time QX5255	Yr.Iss.	1993	9.75	19-23
1993 On Her Toes QX5265	Yr.Iss.	1993	8.75	18
1993 Peek-a-Boo Tree QX5245	Yr.Iss.	1993	10.75	22
1993 Wake-Up Call QX5262	Yr.Iss.	1993	8.75	8-18

1993 Collectible Series - Keepsake

YEAR ISSUE	EDITION LIMIT	YEAR RETD.	ISSUE PRICE	*QUOTE U.S.$
1993 1956 Ford Thunderbird (3rd Ed.) QX5275	Yr.Iss.	1993	12.75	20-40
1993 Betsey's Country Christmas (2nd Ed.) QX2062	Yr.Iss.	1993	5.00	15-21
1993 Cozy Home (10th Ed.) QX4175	Yr.Iss.	1993	14.75	34-53
1993 CRAYOLA CRAYON-Bright Shining Castle (5th Ed.) QX4422	Yr.Iss.	1993	11.00	28-33
1993 Fabulous Decade (4th Ed.) QX4475	Yr.Iss.	1993	7.75	8-17
1993 A Fitting Moment (8th Ed.) QX4202	Yr.Iss.	1993	14.75	28-45
1993 Frosty Friends (14th Ed.) QX4142	Yr.Iss.	1993	9.75	26-40
1993 The Gift Bringers-The Magi (5th Ed.) QX2065	Yr.Iss.	1993	5.00	17-20
1993 Happy Haul-idays (15th Ed.) QX4102	Yr.Iss.	1993	14.75	28-40
1993 Heart Of Christmas (4th Ed.) QX4482	Yr.Iss.	1993	14.75	27-30
1993 Heavenly Angels (3rd Ed.) QX4945	Yr.Iss.	1993	7.75	18
1993 Humpty-Dumpty (1st Ed.) QX5282	Yr.Iss.	1993	13.75	39-54
1993 Mary's Angels-Ivy (6th Ed.) QX4282	Yr.Iss.	1993	6.75	19-30
1993 Merry Olde Santa (4th Ed.) QX4842	Yr.Iss.	1993	14.75	28-40
1993 Owliver (2nd Ed.) QX5425	Yr.Iss.	1993	7.75	5-16
1993 Peace On Earth-Poland (3rd Ed.) QX5242	Yr.Iss.	1993	11.75	21-25
1993 Peanuts (1st Ed.) QX5315	Yr.Iss.	1993	9.75	30-63
1993 Puppy Love (3rd Ed.) QX5045	Yr.Iss.	1993	7.75	28-30
1993 Reindeer Champs-Blitzen (8th Ed.) QX4331	Yr.Iss.	1993	8.75	21-30
1993 Rocking Horse (13th Ed.) QX4162	Yr.Iss.	1993	10.75	41-50
1993 Ten Lords A-Leaping (10th Ed.) QX3012	Yr.Iss.	1993	6.75	15-25
1993 Tobin Fraley Carousel (2nd Ed.) QX5502	Yr.Iss.	1993	28.00	41-56

*Quotes have been rounded up to nearest dollar

YEAR ISSUE	EDITION LIMIT	YEAR RETD.	ISSUE PRICE	*QUOTE U.S.$
1993 U.S. Christmas Stamps (1st Ed.) QX5292	Yr.Iss.	1993	10.75	29-44

1993 Commemoratives - Keepsake

YEAR ISSUE	EDITION LIMIT	YEAR RETD.	ISSUE PRICE	*QUOTE U.S.$
1993 Across the Miles QX5912	Yr.Iss.	1993	8.75	16-20
1993 Anniversary Year QX5972	Yr.Iss.	1993	9.75	18
1993 Apple for Teacher QX5902	Yr.Iss.	1993	7.75	12-16
1993 Baby's First Christmas QX5512	Yr.Iss.	1993	18.75	36-40
1993 Baby's First Christmas QX5515	Yr.Iss.	1993	10.75	21-23
1993 Baby's First Christmas QX5522	Yr.Iss.	1993	7.75	20-25
1993 Baby's First Christmas QX5525	Yr.Iss.	1993	7.75	26-32
1993 Baby's First Christmas-Baby Boy QX2105	Yr.Iss.	1993	4.75	16-20
1993 Baby's First Christmas-Baby Girl QX2092	Yr.Iss.	1993	4.75	12-16
1993 Baby's Second Christmas QX5992	Yr.Iss.	1993	6.75	21-23
1993 Brother QX5542	Yr.Iss.	1993	6.75	13
1993 A Child's Christmas QX5882	Yr.Iss.	1993	9.75	20
1993 Child's Fifth Christmas QX5222	Yr.Iss.	1993	6.75	18-20
1993 Child's Fourth Christmas QX5215	Yr.Iss.	1993	6.75	15-20
1993 Child's Third Christmas QX5995	Yr.Iss.	1993	6.75	17-20
1993 Coach QX5935	Yr.Iss.	1993	6.75	14
1993 Dad QX5855	Yr.Iss.	1993	7.75	17
1993 Dad-to-Be QX5532	Yr.Iss.	1993	6.75	5-16
1993 Daughter QX5872	Yr.Iss.	1993	6.75	9-21
1993 Godchild QX5875	Yr.Iss.	1993	8.75	5-18
1993 Grandchild's First Christmas QX5552	Yr.Iss.	1993	6.75	13
1993 Granddaughter QX5635	Yr.Iss.	1993	6.75	18-23
1993 Grandmother QX5665	Yr.Iss.	1993	6.75	13-20
1993 Grandparents QX2085	Yr.Iss.	1993	4.75	10-18
1993 Grandson QX5632	Yr.Iss.	1993	6.75	19-22
1993 Mom and Dad QX5845	Yr.Iss.	1993	9.75	18
1993 Mom QX5852	Yr.Iss.	1993	7.75	17-20
1993 Mom-to-Be QX5535	Yr.Iss.	1993	6.75	15-18
1993 Nephew QX5735	Yr.Iss.	1993	6.75	13
1993 New Home QX5905	Yr.Iss.	1993	7.75	40-50
1993 Niece QX5732	Yr.Iss.	1993	6.75	13
1993 Our Christmas Together QX5942	Yr.Iss.	1993	10.75	12-23
1993 Our Family QX5892	Yr.Iss.	1993	7.75	17-20
1993 Our First Christmas Together QX3015	Yr.Iss.	1993	6.75	17
1993 Our First Christmas Together QX5642	Yr.Iss.	1993	9.75	15-25
1993 Our First Christmas Together QX5952	Yr.Iss.	1993	8.75	16-25
1993 Our First Christmas Together QX5955	Yr.Iss.	1993	18.75	34-38
1993 People Friendly QX5932	Yr.Iss.	1993	8.75	16-18
1993 Sister QX5545	Yr.Iss.	1993	6.75	19-25
1993 Sister to Sister QX5885	Yr.Iss.	1993	9.75	48-50
1993 Son QX5865	Yr.Iss.	1993	6.75	9-18
1993 Special Cat QX5235	Yr.Iss.	1993	7.75	14
1993 Special Dog QX5962	Yr.Iss.	1993	7.75	15-18
1993 Star Teacher QX5645	Yr.Iss.	1993	5.75	13
1993 Strange and Wonderful Love QX5965	Yr.Iss.	1993	8.75	5-16
1993 To My Grandma QX5555	Yr.Iss.	1993	7.75	16
1993 Top Banana QX5925	Yr.Iss.	1993	7.75	18-20
1993 Warm and Special Friends QX5895	Yr.Iss.	1993	10.75	16-23

1993 Easter Ornaments - Keepsake

YEAR ISSUE	EDITION LIMIT	YEAR RETD.	ISSUE PRICE	*QUOTE U.S.$
1993 Easter Parade (2nd Ed.) QEO8325	Yr.Iss.	1993	6.75	10-17
1993 Egg in Sports (2nd Ed.) QEO8332	Yr.Iss.	1993	6.75	6-18
1993 Springtime Bonnets (1st Ed.) QEO8322	Yr.Iss.	1993	7.75	16-26

1993 Keepsake Collector's Club - Keepsake

YEAR ISSUE	EDITION LIMIT	YEAR RETD.	ISSUE PRICE	*QUOTE U.S.$
1993 It's In The Mail QXC5272	Yr.Iss.	1993	10.00	21
1993 Trimmed With Memories QXC5432	Yr.Iss.	1993	12.00	30-38

1993 Keepsake Magic Ornaments - Keepsake

YEAR ISSUE	EDITION LIMIT	YEAR RETD.	ISSUE PRICE	*QUOTE U.S.$
1993 Baby's First Christmas QLX7365	Yr.Iss.	1993	22.00	41-45
1993 Bells Are Ringing QLX7402	Yr.Iss.	1993	28.00	33-65
1993 Chris Mouse Flight (9th Ed.) QLX7152	Yr.Iss.	1993	12.00	27-38
1993 Dog's Best Friend QLX7172	Yr.Iss.	1993	12.00	22-25
1993 Dollhouse Dreams QLX7372	Yr.Iss.	1993	22.00	46-50
1993 Forest Frolics (5th Ed.) QLX7165	Yr.Iss.	1993	25.00	48-53
1993 Home On The Range QLX7395	Yr.Iss.	1993	32.00	63-75
1993 The Lamplighter QLX7192	Yr.Iss.	1993	18.00	36-43
1993 Last-Minute Shopping QLX7385	Yr.Iss.	1993	28.00	41-60
1993 North Pole Merrython QLX7392	Yr.Iss.	1993	25.00	46-50
1993 Our First Christmas Together QLX7355	Yr.Iss.	1993	20.00	39-43
1993 PEANUTS (3rd Ed.) QLX7155	Yr.Iss.	1993	18.00	40-50
1993 Radio News Flash QLX7362	Yr.Iss.	1993	22.00	41-44
1993 Raiding The Fridge QLX7185	Yr.Iss.	1993	16.00	28-41
1993 Road Runner and Wile E. Coyote QLX7415	Yr.Iss.	1993	30.00	54-68
1993 Santa's Snow-Getter QLX7352	Yr.Iss.	1993	18.00	39
1993 Santa's Workshop QLX7375	Yr.Iss.	1993	28.00	48-60
1993 Song Of The Chimes QLX7405	Yr.Iss.	1993	25.00	50-55
1993 Winnie The Pooh QLX7422	Yr.Iss.	1993	24.00	23-51

1993 Limited Edition Ornaments - Keepsake

YEAR ISSUE	EDITION LIMIT	YEAR RETD.	ISSUE PRICE	*QUOTE U.S.$
1993 Gentle Tidings QXC5442	17,500	1993	25.00	40-47
1993 Sharing Christmas QXC5435	16,500	1993	20.00	30-41

1993 Miniature Ornaments - Keepsake

YEAR ISSUE	EDITION LIMIT	YEAR RETD.	ISSUE PRICE	*QUOTE U.S.$
1993 'Round The Mountain QXM4025	Yr.Iss.	1993	7.25	17
1993 Baby's First Christmas QXM5145	Yr.Iss.	1993	5.75	10-15
1993 The Bearymores (2nd Ed.) QXM5125	Yr.Iss.	1993	5.75	14-17
1993 Cheese Please QXM4072	Yr.Iss.	1993	3.75	8
1993 Christmas Castle QXM4085	Yr.Iss.	1993	5.75	9-13
1993 Cloisonne Snowflake QXM4012	Yr.Iss.	1993	9.75	15-20
1993 Country Fiddling QXM4062	Yr.Iss.	1993	3.75	10
1993 Crystal Angel QXM4015	Yr.Iss.	1993	9.75	30-54
1993 Ears To Pals QXM4075	Yr.Iss.	1993	3.75	7-9
1993 Flatbed Car (5th Ed.) QXM5105	Yr.Iss.	1993	7.00	20-25
1993 Grandma QXM5162	Yr.Iss.	1993	4.50	10-13
1993 I Dream Of Santa QXM4055	Yr.Iss.	1993	3.75	6-11
1993 Into The Woods QXM4045	Yr.Iss.	1993	3.75	6-8
1993 The Kringles (5th Ed.) QXM5135	Yr.Iss.	1993	5.75	8-14
1993 Learning To Skate QXM4122	Yr.Iss.	1993	3.00	8-11
1993 Lighting A Path QXM4115	Yr.Iss.	1993	3.00	7-9
1993 March Of The Teddy Bears (1st Ed.) QX2403	Yr.Iss.	1993	4.50	13-15
1993 Merry Mascot QXM4042	Yr.Iss.	1993	3.75	7-9
1993 Mom QXM5155	Yr.Iss.	1993	4.50	5-11
1993 Monkey Melody QXM4092	Yr.Iss.	1993	5.75	13
1993 Nature's Angels (4th Ed.) QXM5122	Yr.Iss.	1993	4.50	14-20
1993 The Night Before Christmas (2nd Ed.) QXM5115	Yr.Iss.	1993	4.50	8-16
1993 North Pole Fire Truck QXM4105	Yr.Iss.	1993	4.75	6-11
1993 On The Road (1st Ed.) QXM4002	Yr.Iss.	1993	5.75	10-18
1993 Pear-Shaped Tones QXM4052	Yr.Iss.	1993	3.75	5-8
1993 Pull Out A Plum QXM4095	Yr.Iss.	1993	5.75	10-13
1993 Refreshing Flight QXM4112	Yr.Iss.	1993	5.75	13
1993 Rocking Horse (6th Ed.) QXM5112	Yr.Iss.	1993	4.50	10-14
1993 Secret Pals QXM5172	Yr.Iss.	1993	3.75	8-10
1993 Snuggle Birds QXM5182	Yr.Iss.	1993	5.75	10-14
1993 Special Friends QXM5165	Yr.Iss.	1993	4.50	9-14
1993 Thimble Bells (4th Ed.) QXM5142	Yr.Iss.	1993	5.75	39-54
1993 Tiny Green Thumbs, set/6, QXM4032	Yr.Iss.	1993	29.00	32-54
1993 Toy Shop (6th Ed.) QXM5132	Yr.Iss.	1993	7.00	16-22
1993 Visions Of Sugarplums QXM4022	Yr.Iss.	1993	7.25	15
1993 Woodland Babies (3rd Ed.) QXM5102	Yr.Iss.	1993	5.75	6-14

1993 New Attractions - Keepsake

YEAR ISSUE	EDITION LIMIT	YEAR RETD.	ISSUE PRICE	*QUOTE U.S.$
1993 Beary Gifted QX5762	Yr.Iss.	1993	7.75	15-18
1993 Big on Gardening QX5842	Yr.Iss.	1993	9.75	18
1993 Big Roller QX5352	Yr.Iss.	1993	8.75	16-19
1993 Bowling For ZZZ's QX5565	Yr.Iss.	1993	7.75	18
1993 Bugs Bunny QX5412	Yr.Iss.	1993	8.75	15-24
1993 Caring Nurse QX5785	Yr.Iss.	1993	6.75	12-18
1993 Christmas Break QX5825	Yr.Iss.	1993	7.75	18-25
1993 Clever Cookie QX5662	Yr.Iss.	1993	7.75	16-30
1993 Curly 'n' Kingly QX5285	Yr.Iss.	1993	10.75	20-25
1993 Dunkin' Roo QX5575	Yr.Iss.	1993	7.75	15
1993 Eeyore QX5712	Yr.Iss.	1993	9.75	18-21
1993 Elmer Fudd QX5495	Yr.Iss.	1993	8.75	12-19
1993 Faithful Fire Fighter QX5782	Yr.Iss.	1993	7.75	18-20
1993 Feliz Navidad QX5365	Yr.Iss.	1993	9.75	17-25
1993 Fills the Bill QX5572	Yr.Iss.	1993	8.75	17
1993 Great Connections QX5402	Yr.Iss.	1993	10.75	18-23
1993 He Is Born QX5362	Yr.Iss.	1993	9.75	36-40
1993 High Top-Purr QX5332	Yr.Iss.	1993	8.75	24
1993 Home For Christmas QX5562	Yr.Iss.	1993	7.75	15-18
1993 Icicle Bicycle QX5835	Yr.Iss.	1993	9.75	15-18
1993 Kanga and Roo QX5672	Yr.Iss.	1993	9.75	10-22
1993 Little Drummer Boy QX5372	Yr.Iss.	1993	8.75	22-25
1993 Look For Wonder QX5685	Yr.Iss.	1993	12.75	25-28
1993 Lou Rankin Polar Bear QX5745	Yr.Iss.	1993	9.75	15-22
1993 Makin' Music QX5325	Yr.Iss.	1993	9.75	15-18
1993 Making Waves QX5775	Yr.Iss.	1993	9.75	22-27
1993 Mary Engelbreit QX2075	Yr.Iss.	1993	5.00	14-18
1993 Maxine QX5385	Yr.Iss.	1993	8.75	23-30
1993 One-Elf Marching Band QX5342	Yr.Iss.	1993	12.75	25-28
1993 Owl QX5695	Yr.Iss.	1993	9.75	20-23
1993 PEANUTS QX2072	Yr.Iss.	1993	5.00	15-30
1993 Peep Inside QX5322	Yr.Iss.	1993	13.75	25-30
1993 Perfect Match QX5772	Yr.Iss.	1993	8.75	5-18
1993 The Pink Panther QX5755	Yr.Iss.	1993	12.75	25-29
1993 Playful Pals QX5742	Yr.Iss.	1993	14.75	27-30
1993 Popping Good Times QX5392	Yr.Iss.	1993	14.75	27-30
1993 Porky Pig QX5652	Yr.Iss.	1993	8.75	12-20
1993 Putt-Putt Penguin QX5795	Yr.Iss.	1993	9.75	18-24
1993 Quick As A Fox QX5792	Yr.Iss.	1993	8.75	10-17
1993 Rabbit QX5702	Yr.Iss.	1993	9.75	15-20
1993 Ready For Fun QX5124	Yr.Iss.	1993	7.75	16-20
1993 Room For One More QX5382	Yr.Iss.	1993	8.75	38-48
1993 Silvery Noel QX5305	Yr.Iss.	1993	12.75	19-35
1993 Smile! It's Christmas QX5335	Yr.Iss.	1993	9.75	18
1993 Snow Bear Angel QX5355	Yr.Iss.	1993	7.75	16
1993 Snowbird QX5765	Yr.Iss.	1993	7.75	5-17
1993 Snowy Hideaway QX5312	Yr.Iss.	1993	9.75	18
1993 Star Of Wonder QX5982	Yr.Iss.	1993	6.75	25-32
1993 Superman QX5752	Yr.Iss.	1993	12.75	15-47
1993 The Swat Team QX5395	Yr.Iss.	1993	12.75	22-30
1993 Sylvester and Tweety QX5405	Yr.Iss.	1993	9.75	25-34
1993 That's Entertainment QX5345	Yr.Iss.	1993	8.75	18-20
1993 Tigger and Piglet QX5705	Yr.Iss.	1993	9.75	28-50
1993 Tin Airplane QX5622	Yr.Iss.	1993	7.75	28-30
1993 Tin Blimp QX5625	Yr.Iss.	1993	7.75	16
1993 Tin Hot Air Balloon QX5615	Yr.Iss.	1993	7.75	17-25
1993 Water Bed Snooze QX5375	Yr.Iss.	1993	9.75	15-21
1993 Winnie the Pooh QX5715	Yr.Iss.	1993	9.75	25-30

1993 Showcase Folk Art Americana - Keepsake

YEAR ISSUE	EDITION LIMIT	YEAR RETD.	ISSUE PRICE	*QUOTE U.S.$
1993 Angel in Flight QK1052	Yr.Iss.	1993	15.75	15-50
1993 Polar Bear Adventure QK1055	Yr.Iss.	1993	15.00	50-65
1993 Riding in the Woods QK1065	Yr.Iss.	1993	15.75	60-75
1993 Riding the Wind QK1045	Yr.Iss.	1993	15.75	50-65
1993 Santa Claus QK1072	Yr.Iss.	1993	16.75	180-225

1993 Showcase Holiday Enchantment - Keepsake

YEAR ISSUE	EDITION LIMIT	YEAR RETD.	ISSUE PRICE	*QUOTE U.S.$
1993 Angelic Messengers QK1032	Yr.Iss.	1993	13.75	16-30
1993 Bringing Home the Tree QK1042	Yr.Iss.	1993	13.75	16-25
1993 Journey to the Forest QK1012	Yr.Iss.	1993	13.75	16-33
1993 The Magi QK1025	Yr.Iss.	1993	13.75	16-30
1993 Visions of Sugarplums QK1005	Yr.Iss.	1993	13.75	16-35

1993 Showcase Old-World Silver - Keepsake

YEAR ISSUE	EDITION LIMIT	YEAR RETD.	ISSUE PRICE	*QUOTE U.S.$
1993 Silver Dove of Peace QK1075	Yr.Iss.	1993	24.75	25-35
1993 Silver Santa QK1092	Yr.Iss.	1993	24.75	25-50
1993 Silver Sleigh QK1082	Yr.Iss.	1993	24.75	32-60
1993 Silver Stars and Holly QK1085	Yr.Iss.	1993	24.75	32-35

1993 Showcase Portraits in Bisque - Keepsake

YEAR ISSUE	EDITION LIMIT	YEAR RETD.	ISSUE PRICE	*QUOTE U.S.$
1993 Christmas Feast QK1152	Yr.Iss.	1993	15.75	25-31
1993 Joy of Sharing QK1142	Yr.Iss.	1993	15.75	25-32
1993 Mistletoe Kiss QK1145	Yr.Iss.	1993	15.75	20-30
1993 Norman Rockwell-Filling the Stockings QK1155	Yr.Iss.	1993	15.75	27-35
1993 Norman Rockwell-Jolly Postman QK1142	Yr.Iss.	1993	15.75	27-33

1993 Special Editions - Keepsake

YEAR ISSUE	EDITION LIMIT	YEAR RETD.	ISSUE PRICE	*QUOTE U.S.$
1993 Dickens Caroler Bell-Lady Daphne (4th Ed.) QX5505	Yr.Iss.	1993	21.75	32-41
1993 Julianne and Teddy QX5295	Yr.Iss.	1993	21.75	45-55

1993 Special Issues - Keepsake

YEAR ISSUE	EDITION LIMIT	YEAR RETD.	ISSUE PRICE	*QUOTE U.S.$
1993 Holiday Barbie (1st Ed.) QX572-5	Yr.Iss.	1993	14.75	95-176
1993 Messages of Christmas QLX747-6	Yr.Iss.	1993	35.00	46-58
1993 Star Trek® The Next Generation QLX741-2	Yr.Iss.	1993	24.00	61-75

1994 Artists' Favorites - Keepsake

YEAR ISSUE	EDITION LIMIT	YEAR RETD.	ISSUE PRICE	*QUOTE U.S.$
1994 Cock-a-Doodle Christmas QX5396	Yr.Iss.	1994	8.95	10-30
1994 Happy Birthday Jesus QX5423	Yr.Iss.	1994	12.95	16-20
1994 Keep on Mowin' QX5413	Yr.Iss.	1994	8.95	15-30
1994 Kitty's Catamaran QX5416	Yr.Iss.	1994	10.95	17-24
1994 Making It Bright QX5403	Yr.Iss.	1994	8.95	14-20

1994 Collectible Series - Keepsake

YEAR ISSUE	EDITION LIMIT	YEAR RETD.	ISSUE PRICE	*QUOTE U.S.$
1994 1957 Chevy (4th Ed.) QX5422	Yr.Iss.	1994	12.95	20-33
1994 Baseball Heroes-Babe Ruth (1st Ed.) QX5323	Yr.Iss.	1994	12.95	20-50
1994 Betsey's Country Christmas (3rd Ed.) QX2403	Yr.Iss.	1994	5.00	13-17
1994 Cat Naps (1st Ed.) QX5313	Yr.Iss.	1994	7.95	40-50
1994 CRAYOLA CRAYON-Bright Playful Colors (6th Ed.) QX5273	Yr.Iss.	1994	10.95	24-30
1994 Fabulous Decade (5th Ed.) QX5263	Yr.Iss.	1994	7.95	11-24
1994 Frosty Friends (15th Ed.) QX5293	Yr.Iss.	1994	9.95	24-40
1994 Handwarming Present (9th Ed.) QX5283	Yr.Iss.	1994	14.95	28-40
1994 Heart of Christmas (5th Ed.) QX5266	Yr.Iss.	1994	14.95	27-30
1994 Hey Diddle Diddle (2nd Ed.) QX5213	Yr.Iss.	1994	13.95	20-47
1994 Makin' Tractor Tracks (16th Ed.) QX5296	Yr.Iss.	1994	14.95	50-55
1994 Mary's Angels-Jasmine (7th Ed.) QX5276	Yr.Iss.	1994	6.95	21-25
1994 Merry Olde Santa (5th Ed.) QX5256	Yr.Iss.	1994	14.95	33-35
1994 Murray Blue Champion (1st Ed.) QX5426	Yr.Iss.	1994	13.95	45-66
1994 Neighborhood Drugstore (11th Ed.) QX5286	Yr.Iss.	1994	14.95	31-40
1994 Owliver (3rd Ed.) QX5226	Yr.Iss.	1994	7.95	18
1994 PEANUTS-Lucy (2nd Ed.) QX5203	Yr.Iss.	1994	9.95	10-30
1994 Pipers Piping (11th Ed.) QX3183	Yr.Iss.	1994	6.95	16-23
1994 Puppy Love (4th Ed.) QX5253	Yr.Iss.	1994	7.95	19-25
1994 Rocking Horse (14th Ed.) QX5016	Yr.Iss.	1994	10.95	24-35
1994 Tobin Fraley Carousel (3rd Ed.) QX5223	Yr.Iss.	1994	28.00	56-60
1994 Xmas Stamp (2nd Ed.) QX5206	Yr.Iss.	1994	10.95	10-23
1994 Yuletide Central (1st Ed.) QX5316	Yr.Iss.	1994	18.95	30-53

1994 Commemoratives - Keepsake

YEAR ISSUE	EDITION LIMIT	YEAR RETD.	ISSUE PRICE	*QUOTE U.S.$
1994 Across the Miles QX5656	Yr.Iss.	1994	8.95	17
1994 Anniversary Year QX5683	Yr.Iss.	1994	10.95	16-20
1994 Baby's First Christmas Photo QX5636	Yr.Iss.	1994	7.95	16-19
1994 Baby's First Christmas QX5633	Yr.Iss.	1994	18.95	25-40
1994 Baby's First Christmas QX5713	Yr.Iss.	1994	7.95	21-28
1994 Baby's First Christmas QX5743	Yr.Iss.	1994	12.95	22-27
1994 Baby's First Christmas-Baby Boy QX2436	Yr.Iss.	1994	5.00	13
1994 Baby's First Christmas-Baby Girl QX2433	Yr.Iss.	1994	5.00	12-14
1994 Baby's Second Christmas QX5716	Yr.Iss.	1994	7.95	21
1994 Brother QX5516	Yr.Iss.	1994	6.95	15
1994 Child's Fifth Christmas QX5733	Yr.Iss.	1994	6.95	17-22
1994 Child's Fourth Christmas QX5726	Yr.Iss.	1994	6.95	17-23
1994 Child's Third Christmas QX5723	Yr.Iss.	1994	6.95	17-21
1994 Dad QX5463	Yr.Iss.	1994	7.95	17
1994 Dad-To-Be QX5473	Yr.Iss.	1994	7.95	17-20
1994 Daughter QX5623	Yr.Iss.	1994	6.95	10-16
1994 Friendly Push QX5686	Yr.Iss.	1994	8.95	14-18
1994 Godchild QX4453	Yr.Iss.	1994	8.95	21-25
1994 Godparents QX2423	Yr.Iss.	1994	5.00	16-23
1994 Grandchild's First Christmas QX5676	Yr.Iss.	1994	7.95	13-18
1994 Granddaughter QX5523	Yr.Iss.	1994	6.95	18-22
1994 Grandma Photo QX5613	Yr.Iss.	1994	6.95	15
1994 Grandmother QX5673	Yr.Iss.	1994	7.95	18-20
1994 Grandpa QX5616	Yr.Iss.	1994	7.95	17-20
1994 Grandparents QX2426	Yr.Iss.	1994	5.00	12-17
1994 Grandson QX5526	Yr.Iss.	1994	6.95	17-22
1994 Mom and Dad QX5666	Yr.Iss.	1994	9.95	21-25
1994 Mom QX5466	Yr.Iss.	1994	7.95	12-17
1994 Mom-To-Be QX5506	Yr.Iss.	1994	7.95	14-18
1994 Nephew QX5546	Yr.Iss.	1994	7.95	15-17
1994 New Home QX5663	Yr.Iss.	1994	8.95	18-20

*Quotes have been rounded up to nearest dollar

YEAR ISSUE	EDITION LIMIT	YEAR RETD.	ISSUE PRICE	*QUOTE U.S.$
1994 Niece QX5543	Yr.Iss.	1994	7.95	12-16
1994 Our Family QX5576	Yr.Iss.	1994	7.95	16-20
1994 Our First Christmas Together Photo QX5653	Yr.Iss.	1994	8.95	18-20
1994 Our First Christmas Together QX3186	Yr.Iss.	1994	6.95	13-17
1994 Our First Christmas Together QX4816	Yr.Iss.	1994	9.95	18-20
1994 Our First Christmas Together QX5643	Yr.Iss.	1994	9.95	18-25
1994 Our First Christmas Together QX5706	Yr.Iss.	1994	18.95	36-40
1994 Secret Santa QX5736	Yr.Iss.	1994	7.95	14-18
1994 Sister QX5513	Yr.Iss.	1994	6.95	16-20
1994 Sister to Sister QX5533	Yr.Iss.	1994	9.95	16-25
1994 Son QX5626	Yr.Iss.	1994	6.95	15-18
1994 Special Cat QX5606	Yr.Iss.	1994	7.95	12-16
1994 Special Dog QX5603	Yr.Iss.	1994	7.95	7-16
1994 Thick 'N' Thin QX5693	Yr.Iss.	1994	10.95	13-23
1994 Tou Can Love QX5646	Yr.Iss.	1994	8.95	14-18

1994 Easter Ornaments - Keepsake

YEAR ISSUE	EDITION LIMIT	YEAR RETD.	ISSUE PRICE	*QUOTE U.S.$
1994 Baby's First Easter QEO8153	Yr.Iss.	1994	6.75	8-18
1994 Carrot Trimmers QEO8226	Yr.Iss.	1994	5.00	5-20
1994 CRAYOLA CRAYON-Colorful Spring QEO8166	Yr.Iss.	1994	7.75	18-28
1994 Daughter QEO8156	Yr.Iss.	1994	5.75	6-15
1994 Divine Duet QEO8183	Yr.Iss.	1994	6.75	16
1994 Easter Art Show QEO8193	Yr.Iss.	1994	7.75	17
1994 Egg Car (1st Ed.) QEO8093	Yr.Iss.	1994	7.75	30-35
1994 Golf (3rd Ed.) QEO8133	Yr.Iss.	1994	6.75	15-19
1994 Horn (3rd Ed.) QEO8136	Yr.Iss.	1994	6.75	19
1994 Joyful Lamb QEO8206	Yr.Iss.	1994	5.75	15
1994 PEANUTS QEO8176	Yr.Iss.	1994	7.75	20-50
1994 Peeping Out QEO8203	Yr.Iss.	1994	6.75	16
1994 Riding a Breeze QEO8213	Yr.Iss.	1994	5.75	15
1994 Son QEO8163	Yr.Iss.	1994	5.75	6-14
1994 Springtime Bonnets (2nd Ed.) QEO8096	Yr.Iss.	1994	7.75	15-25
1994 Sunny Bunny Garden, (Set/3) QEO8146	Yr.Iss.	1994	15.00	15-28
1994 Sweet as Sugar QEO8086	Yr.Iss.	1994	8.75	8-20
1994 Sweet Easter Wishes Tender Touches QEO8196	Yr.Iss.	1994	8.75	22-25
1994 Treetop Cottage QEO8186	Yr.Iss.	1994	9.75	19
1994 Yummy Recipe QEO8143	Yr.Iss.	1994	7.75	6-19

1994 Keepsake Collector's Club - Keepsake

YEAR ISSUE	EDITION LIMIT	YEAR RETD.	ISSUE PRICE	*QUOTE U.S.$
1994 First Hello QXC4846	Yr.Iss.	1994	5.00	22-27
1994 Happy Collecting QXC4803	Yr.Iss.	1994	3.00	20-25
1994 Holiday Pursuit QXC4823	Yr.Iss.	1994	11.75	12-22
1994 Mrs. Claus' Cupboard QXC4843	Yr.Iss.	1994	55.00	100-210
1994 On Cloud Nine QXC4853	Yr.Iss.	1994	12.00	17-27
1994 Sweet Bouquet QXC4806	Yr.Iss.	1994	8.50	12-22
1994 Tilling Time QXC8256	Yr.Iss.	1994	5.00	20-68

1994 Keepsake Magic Ornaments - Keepsake

YEAR ISSUE	EDITION LIMIT	YEAR RETD.	ISSUE PRICE	*QUOTE U.S.$
1994 Away in a Manager QLX7383	Yr.Iss.	1994	16.00	36-40
1994 Baby's First Christmas QLX7466	Yr.Iss.	1994	20.00	39-45
1994 Candy Cane Lookout QLX7376	Yr.Iss.	1994	18.00	60-95
1994 Chris Mouse Jelly (10th Ed.) QLX7393	Yr.Iss.	1994	12.00	10-16
1994 Conversations With Santa QLX7426	Yr.Iss.	1994	28.00	15-52
1994 Country Showtime QLX7416	Yr.Iss.	1994	22.00	36-45
1994 The Eagle Has Landed QLX7486	Yr.Iss.	1994	24.00	36-46
1994 Feliz Navidad QLX7433	Yr.Iss.	1994	28.00	51-75
1994 Forest Frolics (6th Ed.) QLX7436	Yr.Iss.	1994	28.00	54-60
1994 Gingerbread Fantasy (Sp. Ed.) QLX7382	Yr.Iss.	1994	44.00	45-97
1994 Kringle Trolley QLX7413	Yr.Iss.	1994	20.00	20-48
1994 Maxine QLX7503	Yr.Iss.	1994	20.00	42-50
1994 PEANUTS (4th Ed.) QLX7406	Yr.Iss.	1994	20.00	40-43
1994 Peekaboo Pup QLX7423	Yr.Iss.	1994	20.00	34-43
1994 Rock Candy Miner QLX7403	Yr.Iss.	1994	20.00	10-36
1994 Santa's Sing-Along QLX7473	Yr.Iss.	1994	24.00	47-59
1994 Tobin Fraley (1st Ed.) QLX7496	Yr.Iss.	1994	32.00	68-75
1994 Very Merry Minutes QLX7443	Yr.Iss.	1994	24.00	43-48
1994 White Christmas QLX7463	Yr.Iss.	1994	28.00	54-75
1994 Winnie the Pooh Parade QLX7493	Yr.Iss.	1994	32.00	45-65

1994 Limited Editions - Keepsake

YEAR ISSUE	EDITION LIMIT	YEAR RETD.	ISSUE PRICE	*QUOTE U.S.$
1994 Jolly Holly Santa QXC4833	N/A	1994	22.00	35-45
1994 Majestic Deer QXC4836	N/A	1994	25.00	35-45

1994 Miniature Ornaments - Keepsake

YEAR ISSUE	EDITION LIMIT	YEAR RETD.	ISSUE PRICE	*QUOTE U.S.$
1994 Babs Bunny QXM4116	Yr.Iss.	1994	5.75	5-12
1994 Baby's First Christmas QXM4003	Yr.Iss.	1994	5.75	5-13
1994 Baking Tiny Treats, (Set/6) QXM4033	Yr.Iss.	1994	29.00	44-60
1994 Beary Perfect Tree QXM4076	Yr.Iss.	1994	4.75	9
1994 The Bearymores (3rd Ed.) QXM5133	Yr.Iss.	1994	5.75	13-17
1994 Buster Bunny QXM5163	Yr.Iss.	1994	5.75	6-12
1994 Centuries of Santa (1st Ed.) QXM5153	Yr.Iss.	1994	6.00	22-25
1994 Corny Elf QXM4063	Yr.Iss.	1994	4.50	6-9
1994 Cute as a Button QXM4103	Yr.Iss.	1994	3.75	12-15
1994 Dazzling Reindeer (Pr. Ed.) QXM4026	Yr.Iss.	1994	9.75	18
1994 Dizzy Devil QXM4133	Yr.Iss.	1994	5.75	5-13
1994 Friends Need Hugs QXM4016	Yr.Iss.	1994	4.50	13-15
1994 Graceful Carousel QXM4056	Yr.Iss.	1994	7.75	10-17
1994 Hamton QXM4126	Yr.Iss.	1994	5.75	9-12
1994 Hat Shop (7th Ed.) QXM5143	Yr.Iss.	1994	7.00	7-17
1994 Have a Cookie QXM5166	Yr.Iss.	1994	5.75	15-20
1994 Hearts A-Sail QXM4006	Yr.Iss.	1994	5.75	10-13
1994 Jolly Visitor QXM4053	Yr.Iss.	1994	5.75	8-16
1994 Jolly Wolly Snowman QXM4093	Yr.Iss.	1994	3.75	12-15
1994 Journey to Bethlehem QXM4036	Yr.Iss.	1994	5.75	14-18
1994 Just My Size QXM4086	Yr.Iss.	1994	3.75	9-12
1994 Love Was Born QXM4043	Yr.Iss.	1994	4.50	13
1994 March of the Teddy Bears (2nd Ed.) QXM5106	Yr.Iss.	1994	4.50	13-14
1994 Melodic Cherub QXM4066	Yr.Iss.	1994	3.75	6-10
1994 A Merry Flight QXM4073	Yr.Iss.	1994	5.75	6-12
1994 Mom QXM4013	Yr.Iss.	1994	4.50	5-9
1994 Nature's Angels (5th Ed.) QXM5126	Yr.Iss.	1994	4.50	6-12
1994 Night Before Christmas (3rd Ed.) QXM5123	Yr.Iss.	1994	4.50	7-13
1994 Noah's Ark (Sp. Ed.) QXM4106	Yr.Iss.	1994	24.50	45-56
1994 Nutcracker Guild (1st Ed.) QXM5146	Yr.Iss.	1994	5.75	18-23
1994 On the Road (2nd Ed.) QXM5103	Yr.Iss.	1994	5.75	6-14
1994 Plucky Duck QXM4123	Yr.Iss.	1994	5.75	5-12
1994 Pour Some More QXM5156	Yr.Iss.	1994	5.75	6-12
1994 Rocking Horse (7th Ed.) QXM5116	Yr.Iss.	1994	4.50	12
1994 Scooting Along QXM5173	Yr.Iss.	1994	6.75	5-14
1994 Stock Car (6th Ed.) QXM5113	Yr.Iss.	1994	7.00	17-22
1994 Sweet Dreams QXM4096	Yr.Iss.	1994	3.00	13
1994 Tea With Teddy QXM4046	Yr.Iss.	1994	7.25	8-15

1994 New Attractions - Keepsake

YEAR ISSUE	EDITION LIMIT	YEAR RETD.	ISSUE PRICE	*QUOTE U.S.$
1994 All Pumped Up QX5923	Yr.Iss.	1994	8.95	18
1994 Angel Hare QX5896	Yr.Iss.	1994	8.95	18-27
1994 Batman QX5853	Yr.Iss.	1994	12.95	30-35
1994 Beatles Gift Set QX5373	Yr.Iss.	1994	48.00	40-100
1994 BEATRIX POTTER The Tale of Peter Rabbit QX2443	Yr.Iss.	1994	5.00	16-23
1994 Big Shot QX5873	Yr.Iss.	1994	7.95	17
1994 Busy Batter QX5876	Yr.Iss.	1994	7.95	1620
1994 Candy Caper QX5776	Yr.Iss.	1994	8.95	12-19
1994 Caring Doctor QX5823	Yr.Iss.	1994	8.95	5-18
1994 Champion Teacher QX5836	Yr.Iss.	1994	6.95	13-16
1994 Cheers to You! QX5796	Yr.Iss.	1994	10.95	15-23
1994 Cheery Cyclists QX5786	Yr.Iss.	1994	12.95	15-27
1994 Child Care Giver QX5906	Yr.Iss.	1994	7.95	15-18
1994 Coach QX5933	Yr.Iss.	1994	7.95	16
1994 Colors of Joy QX5893	Yr.Iss.	1994	7.95	10-18
1994 Cowardly Lion QX5446	Yr.Iss.	1994	9.95	51-55
1994 Daffy Duck QX5415	Yr.Iss.	1994	8.95	16-19
1994 Daisy Days QX5986	Yr.Iss.	1994	9.95	5-16
1994 Deer Santa Mouse (2) QX5806	Yr.Iss.	1994	14.95	27-30
1994 Dorothy and Toto QX5433	Yr.Iss.	1994	10.95	68-85
1994 Extra-Special Delivery QX5833	Yr.Iss.	1994	7.95	13-17
1994 Feelin' Groovy QX5953	Yr.Iss.	1994	7.95	21
1994 A Feline of Christmas QX5816	Yr.Iss.	1994	8.95	24-30
1994 Feliz Navidad QX5793	Yr.Iss.	1994	8.95	21-23
1994 Follow the Sun QX5846	Yr.Iss.	1994	8.95	14-18
1994 Fred and Barney QX5003	Yr.Iss.	1994	14.95	15-29
1994 Friendship Sundae QX4766	Yr.Iss.	1994	10.95	24-29
1994 GARFIELD QX5753	Yr.Iss.	1994	12.95	26-30
1994 Gentle Nurse QX5973	Yr.Iss.	1994	6.95	18-20
1994 Harvest Joy QX5993	Yr.Iss.	1994	9.95	17-25
1994 Hearts in Harmony QX4406	Yr.Iss.	1994	10.95	21-23
1994 Helpful Shepherd QX5536	Yr.Iss.	1994	8.95	18-20
1994 Holiday Patrol QX5826	Yr.Iss.	1994	8.95	18-20
1994 Ice Show QX5946	Yr.Iss.	1994	7.95	5-17
1994 In the Pink QX5763	Yr.Iss.	1994	9.95	8-21
1994 It's a Strike QX5856	Yr.Iss.	1994	8.95	18-20
1994 Jingle Bell Band QX5783	Yr.Iss.	1994	10.95	25-30
1994 Joyous Song QX4473	Yr.Iss.	1994	8.95	18-20
1994 Jump-along Jackalope QX5756	Yr.Iss.	1994	8.95	17-23
1994 Kickin' Roo QX5916	Yr.Iss.	1994	7.95	16-20
1994 Kringle's Kayak QX5886	Yr.Iss.	1994	7.95	17-22
1994 LEGO'S QX5453	Yr.Iss.	1994	10.95	12-23
1994 Lou Rankin Seal QX5456	Yr.Iss.	1994	9.95	16-21
1994 Magic Carpet Ride QX5883	Yr.Iss.	1994	7.95	17-25
1994 Mary Engelbreit QX2416	Yr.Iss.	1994	5.00	14-20
1994 Merry Fishmas QX5913	Yr.Iss.	1994	8.95	12-23
1994 Mistletoe Surprise (2)QX5996	Yr.Iss.	1994	12.95	26-33
1994 Norman Rockwell QX2413	Yr.Iss.	1994	5.00	13-20
1994 Open-and-Shut Holiday QX5696	Yr.Iss.	1994	9.95	20-22
1994 Out of This World Teacher QX5766	Yr.Iss.	1994	7.95	14-19
1994 Practice Makes Perfect QX5863	Yr.Iss.	1994	7.95	17-20
1994 Red Hot Holiday QX5843	Yr.Iss.	1994	7.95	17-20
1994 Reindeer Pro QX5926	Yr.Iss.	1994	7.95	5-20
1994 Relaxing Moment QX5356	Yr.Iss.	1994	14.95	15-30
1994 Road Runner and Wile E. Coyote QX5602	Yr.Iss.	1994	12.95	15-30
1994 Scarecrow QX5436	Yr.Iss.	1994	9.95	51-60
1994 A Sharp Flat QX5773	Yr.Iss.	1994	10.95	20-25
1994 Speedy Gonzales QX5343	Yr.Iss.	1994	8.95	10-21
1994 Stamp of Approval QX5703	Yr.Iss.	1994	7.95	16-18
1994 Sweet Greeting (2) QX5803	Yr.Iss.	1994	10.95	21-23
1994 Tasmanian Devil QX5605	Yr.Iss.	1994	8.95	58-60
1994 Thrill a Minute QX5866	Yr.Iss.	1994	8.95	14-20
1994 Time of Peace QX5813	Yr.Iss.	1994	7.95	5-15
1994 Tin Man QX5443	Yr.Iss.	1994	9.95	52-55
1994 Tulip Time QX5983	Yr.Iss.	1994	9.95	16-25
1994 Winnie the Pooh/Tigger QX5746	Yr.Iss.	1994	12.95	24-30
1994 Yosemite Sam QX5346	Yr.Iss.	1994	8.95	12-21
1994 Yuletide Cheer QX5976	Yr.Iss.	1994	9.95	16-25

1994 Personalized Ornaments - Keepsake

YEAR ISSUE	EDITION LIMIT	YEAR RETD.	ISSUE PRICE	*QUOTE U.S.$
1994 Baby Block QP6035	Yr.Iss.	1994	14.95	12-15
1994 Computer Cat 'N' Mouse QP6046	Yr.Iss.	1994	12.95	9-13
1994 Cookie Time QP6073	Yr.Iss.	1994	12.95	9-13
1994 Etch-A-Sketch QP6006	Yr.Iss.	1994	12.95	9-13
1994 Festive Album QP6025	Yr.Iss.	1994	12.95	9-26
1994 From the Heart QP6036	Yr.Iss.	1994	14.95	10-15
1994 Goin' Fishin' QP6023	Yr.Iss.	1994	14.95	10-15
1994 Goin' Golfin' QP6012	Yr.Iss.	1994	12.95	9-13
1994 Holiday Hello QXR6116	Yr.Iss.	1994	24.95	17-25
1994 Mailbox Delivery QP6015	Yr.Iss.	1994	14.95	10-15
1994 Novel Idea QP6066	Yr.Iss.	1994	12.95	9-13
1994 On the Billboard QP6022	Yr.Iss.	1994	12.95	9-13
1994 Playing Ball QP6032	Yr.Iss.	1994	12.95	9-13
1994 Reindeer Rooters QP6056	Yr.Iss.	1994	12.95	9-13
1994 Santa Says QP6005	Yr.Iss.	1994	14.95	10-15

1994 Premiere Event - Keepsake

YEAR ISSUE	EDITION LIMIT	YEAR RETD.	ISSUE PRICE	*QUOTE U.S.$
1994 Eager for Christmas QX5336	Yr.Iss.	1994	15.00	12-28

1994 Showcase Christmas Lights - Keepsake

YEAR ISSUE	EDITION LIMIT	YEAR RETD.	ISSUE PRICE	*QUOTE U.S.$
1994 Home for the Holidays QK1123	Yr.Iss.	1994	15.75	25-32
1994 Moonbeams QK1116	Yr.Iss.	1994	15.75	13-16
1994 Mother and Child QK1126	Yr.Iss.	1994	15.75	13-16
1994 Peaceful Village QK1106	Yr.Iss.	1994	15.75	13-20

1994 Showcase Folk Art Americana Collection - Keepsake

YEAR ISSUE	EDITION LIMIT	YEAR RETD.	ISSUE PRICE	*QUOTE U.S.$
1994 Catching 40 Winks QK1183	Yr.Iss.	1994	16.75	28-38
1994 Going to Town QK1166	Yr.Iss.	1994	15.75	28-35
1994 Racing Through the Snow QK1173	Yr.Iss.	1994	15.75	40-50
1994 Rarin' to Go QK1193	Yr.Iss.	1994	15.75	28-38
1994 Roundup Time QK1176	Yr.Iss.	1994	16.75	28-43

1994 Showcase Holiday Favorites - Keepsake

YEAR ISSUE	EDITION LIMIT	YEAR RETD.	ISSUE PRICE	*QUOTE U.S.$
1994 Dapper Snowman QK1053	Yr.Iss.	1994	13.75	11-14
1994 Graceful Fawn QK1033	Yr.Iss.	1994	11.75	19-24
1994 Jolly Santa QK1046	Yr.Iss.	1994	13.75	12-28
1994 Joyful Lamb QK1036	Yr.Iss.	1994	11.75	9-24
1994 Peaceful Dove QK1043	Yr.Iss.	1994	11.75	19-24

1994 Showcase Old World Silver Collection - Keepsake

YEAR ISSUE	EDITION LIMIT	YEAR RETD.	ISSUE PRICE	*QUOTE U.S.$
1994 Silver Bells QK1026	Yr.Iss.	1994	24.75	32-40
1994 Silver Bows QK1023	Yr.Iss.	1994	24.75	32-40
1994 Silver Poinsettias QK1006	Yr.Iss.	1994	24.75	32-40
1994 Silver Snowflakes QK1016	Yr.Iss.	1994	24.75	32-40

1994 Special Edition - Keepsake

YEAR ISSUE	EDITION LIMIT	YEAR RETD.	ISSUE PRICE	*QUOTE U.S.$
1994 Lucinda and Teddy QX4813	Yr.Iss.	1994	21.75	18-24

1994 Special Issues - Keepsake

YEAR ISSUE	EDITION LIMIT	YEAR RETD.	ISSUE PRICE	*QUOTE U.S.$
1994 Barney QLX7506	Yr.Iss.	1994	24.00	45-50
1994 Barney QX5966	Yr.Iss.	1994	9.95	22-25
1994 Holiday Barbie™ (2nd Ed.) QX5216	Yr.Iss.	1994	14.95	36-55
1994 Klingon Bird of Prey™ QLX7386	Yr.Iss.	1994	24.00	28-40
1994 Mufasa/Simba-Lion King QX5406	Yr.Iss.	1994	14.95	12-32
1994 Nostalgic-Barbie™ (1st Ed.) QX5006	Yr.Iss.	1994	14.95	28-51
1994 Simba/Nala-Lion King (2) QX5303	Yr.Iss.	1994	12.95	15-32
1994 Simba/Sarabi/Mufasa the Lion King QLX7513	Yr.Iss.	1994	32.00	41-52
1994 Simba/Sarabi/Mufasa the Lion King QLX7513	Yr.Iss.	1994	20.00	66-81
1994 Timon/Pumbaa-Lion King QX5366	Yr.Iss.	1994	8.95	15-27

1995 Anniversary Edition - Keepsake

YEAR ISSUE	EDITION LIMIT	YEAR RETD.	ISSUE PRICE	*QUOTE U.S.$
1995 Pewter Rocking Horse QX6167	Yr.Iss.	1995	20.00	31-46

1995 Artists' Favorite - Keepsake

YEAR ISSUE	EDITION LIMIT	YEAR RETD.	ISSUE PRICE	*QUOTE U.S.$
1995 Barrel-Back Rider QX5189	Yr.Iss.	1995	9.95	25-30
1995 Our Little Blessings QX5209	Yr.Iss.	1995	12.95	24-36

1995 Collectible Series - Keepsake

YEAR ISSUE	EDITION LIMIT	YEAR RETD.	ISSUE PRICE	*QUOTE U.S.$
1995 1956 Ford Truck (1st Ed.) QX5527	Yr.Iss.	1995	13.95	20-35
1995 1969 Chevrolet Camaro (5th Ed.) QX5239	Yr.Iss.	1995	12.95	18-23
1995 Bright 'n' Sunny Tepee (7th Ed.) QX5247	Yr.Iss.	1995	10.95	19-35
1995 Camellia - Mary's Angels (8th Ed.) QX5149	Yr.Iss.	1995	6.95	17-23
1995 Cat Naps (2nd Ed.) QX5097	Yr.Iss.	1995	7.95	21-30
1995 A Celebration of Angels (1st Ed.) QX5077	Yr.Iss.	1995	12.95	26
1995 Christmas Eve Kiss (10th Ed.) QX5157	Yr.Iss.	1995	14.95	27-33
1995 Fabulous Decade (6th Ed.) QX5147	Yr.Iss.	1995	7.95	17-22
1995 Frosty Friends (16th Ed.) QX5169	Yr.Iss.	1995	10.95	22-30
1995 Jack and Jill (3rd Ed.) QX5099	Yr.Iss.	1995	13.95	25-30
1995 Lou Gehrig (2nd Ed.) QX5029	Yr.Iss.	1995	12.95	5-22
1995 Merry Olde Santa (6th Ed.) QX5139	Yr.Iss.	1995	14.95	13-20
1995 Murray® Fire Truck (2nd Ed.) QX5027	Yr.Iss.	1995	13.95	18-35
1995 The PEANUTS® Gang (3rd Ed.) QX5059	Yr.Iss.	1995	9.95	15-22
1995 Puppy Love (5th Ed.) QX5137	Yr.Iss.	1995	7.95	20-25
1995 Rocking Horse (15th Ed.) QX5167	Yr.Iss.	1995	10.95	26-30
1995 Santa's Roadster (17th Ed.) QX5179	Yr.Iss.	1995	14.95	18-25
1995 St. Nicholas (1st Ed.) QX5087	Yr.Iss.	1995	14.95	15-28
1995 Tobin Fraley Carousel (4th Ed.) QX5069	Yr.Iss.	1995	28.00	25-50
1995 Town Church (12th Ed.) QX5159	Yr.Iss.	1995	14.95	20-39
1995 Twelve Drummers Drumming (12th Ed.) QX3009	Yr.Iss.	1995	6.95	15-18
1995 U.S. Christmas Stamps (3rd Ed.) QX5067	Yr.Iss.	1995	10.95	10-22
1995 Yuletide Central (2nd Ed.) QX5079	Yr.Iss.	1995	18.95	15-27

1995 Commemoratives - Keepsake

YEAR ISSUE	EDITION LIMIT	YEAR RETD.	ISSUE PRICE	*QUOTE U.S.$
1995 Across the Miles QX5847	Yr.Iss.	1995	8.95	18-20
1995 Air Express QX5977	Yr.Iss.	1995	7.95	12-18
1995 Anniversary Year QX5819	Yr.Iss.	1995	8.95	14-20
1995 Baby's First Christmas QX5547	Yr.Iss.	1995	18.95	17-32
1995 Baby's First Christmas QX5549	Yr.Iss.	1995	7.95	16-21
1995 Baby's First Christmas QX5557	Yr.Iss.	1995	9.95	13-20

*Quotes have been rounded up to nearest dollar

ORNAMENTS

YEAR ISSUE	EDITION LIMIT	YEAR RETD.	ISSUE PRICE	*QUOTE U.S.$
1995 Baby's First Christmas QX5559	Yr.Iss.	1995	7.95	20-22
1995 Baby's First Christmas-Baby Boy QX2319	Yr.Iss.	1995	5.00	12-45
1995 Baby's First Christmas-Baby Girl QX2317	Yr.Iss.	1995	5.00	14
1995 Baby's Second Christmas QX5567	Yr.Iss.	1995	7.95	20-25
1995 Brother QX5679	Yr.Iss.	1995	6.95	13
1995 Child's Fifth Christmas QX5637	Yr.Iss.	1995	6.95	15-18
1995 Child's Fourth Christmas QX5629	Yr.Iss.	1995	6.95	19
1995 Child's Third Christmas QX5627	Yr.Iss.	1995	7.95	18-22
1995 Christmas Fever QX5967	Yr.Iss.	1995	7.95	16-20
1995 Christmas Patrol QX5959	Yr.Iss.	1995	7.95	17-20
1995 Dad QX5649	Yr.Iss.	1995	7.95	14-18
1995 Dad-to-Be QX5667	Yr.Iss.	1995	7.95	12-16
1995 Daughter QX5677	Yr.Iss.	1995	6.95	10-19
1995 For My Grandma QX5729	Yr.Iss.	1995	6.95	14-16
1995 Friendly Boost QX5827	Yr.Iss.	1995	8.95	17-22
1995 Godchild QX5707	Yr.Iss.	1995	7.95	18-25
1995 Godparent QX2417	Yr.Iss.	1995	5.00	10-17
1995 Grandchild's First Christmas QX5777	Yr.Iss.	1995	7.95	15
1995 Granddaughter QX5779	Yr.Iss.	1995	6.95	18-20
1995 Grandmother QX5767	Yr.Iss.	1995	7.95	25-28
1995 Grandpa QX5769	Yr.Iss.	1995	8.95	12-16
1995 Grandparents QX2419	Yr.Iss.	1995	5.00	9-13
1995 Grandson QX5787	Yr.Iss.	1995	6.95	12-17
1995 Important Memo QX5947	Yr.Iss.	1995	8.95	18-20
1995 In a Heartbeat QX5817	Yr.Iss.	1995	8.95	18-23
1995 Mom and Dad QX5657	Yr.Iss.	1995	9.95	17-23
1995 Mom QX5647	Yr.Iss.	1995	7.95	14-19
1995 Mom-to-Be QX5659	Yr.Iss.	1995	7.95	12-15
1995 New Home QX5839	Yr.Iss.	1995	8.95	17
1995 North Pole 911 QX5957	Yr.Iss.	1995	10.95	22-25
1995 Number One Teacher QX5949	Yr.Iss.	1995	7.95	16
1995 Our Christmas Together QX5809	Yr.Iss.	1995	9.95	16-20
1995 Our Family QX5709	Yr.Iss.	1995	7.95	16-19
1995 Our First Christmas Together QX3177	Yr.Iss.	1995	6.95	12-20
1995 Our First Christmas Together QX5797	Yr.Iss.	1995	16.95	31-35
1995 Our First Christmas Together QX5799	Yr.Iss.	1995	8.95	18-20
1995 Our First Christmas Together QX5807	Yr.Iss.	1995	8.95	18-20
1995 Packed With Memories QX5639	Yr.Iss.	1995	7.95	17-20
1995 Sister QX5687	Yr.Iss.	1995	6.95	10-13
1995 Sister to Sister QX5689	Yr.Iss.	1995	8.95	18-20
1995 Son QX5669	Yr.Iss.	1995	6.95	10-16
1995 Special Cat QX5717	Yr.Iss.	1995	7.95	13-17
1995 Special Dog QX5719	Yr.Iss.	1995	7.95	13-17
1995 Two for Tea QX5829	Yr.Iss.	1995	9.95	23-32

1995 Easter Ornaments - Keepsake

YEAR ISSUE	EDITION LIMIT	YEAR RETD.	ISSUE PRICE	*QUOTE U.S.$
1995 3 Flowerpot Friends 1495QEO8229	Yr.Iss.	1995	14.95	16-23
1995 Baby's First Easter QEO8237	Yr.Iss.	1995	7.95	13-17
1995 Bugs Bunny (Looney Tunes) QEO8279	Yr.Iss.	1995	8.95	19
1995 Bunny w/Crayons (Crayola) QEO8249	Yr.Iss.	1995	7.95	18-22
1995 Bunny w/Seed Packets (Tender Touches) QEO8259	Yr.Iss.	1995	8.95	19-22
1995 Bunny w/Water Bucket QEO8253	Yr.Iss.	1995	6.95	10-13
1995 Collector's Plate (2nd Ed.) QEO8219	Yr.Iss.	1995	7.95	12-19
1995 Daughter Duck QEO8239	Yr.Iss.	1995	5.95	12
1995 Easter Beagle (Peanuts) QEO8257	Yr.Iss.	1995	7.95	15-20
1995 Easter Egg Cottages (1st Ed.) QEO8207	Yr.Iss.	1995	8.95	23-25
1995 Garden Club (1st Ed.) QEO8209	Yr.Iss.	1995	7.95	11-19
1995 Ham n Eggs QEO8277	Yr.Iss.	1995	7.95	11-15
1995 Here Comes Easter (2nd Ed.) QEO8217	Yr.Iss.	1995	7.95	12-20
1995 Lily (Religious) QEO8267	Yr.Iss.	1995	6.95	8-12
1995 Miniature Train QEO8269	Yr.Iss.	1995	4.95	13-15
1995 Son Duck QEO8247	Yr.Iss.	1995	5.95	16-18
1995 Springtime Barbie™ (1st Ed.) QEO8069	Yr.Iss.	1995	12.95	17-45
1995 Springtime Bonnets (3rd Ed.) QEO8227	Yr.Iss.	1995	7.95	18-23

1995 Keepsake Collector's Club - Keepsake

YEAR ISSUE	EDITION LIMIT	YEAR RETD.	ISSUE PRICE	*QUOTE U.S.$
1995 1958 Ford Edsel Citation Convertible QXC4167	Yr.Iss.	1995	12.95	50-68
1995 Brunette Debut-1959 QXC5397	Yr.Iss.	1995	14.95	35-68
1995 Christmas Eve Bake-Off QXC4049	Yr.Iss.	1995	55.00	170
1995 Cinderella's Stepsisters QXC4159	Yr.Iss.	1995	3.75	4
1995 Collecting Memories QXC4117	Yr.Iss.	1995	12.00	10-32
1995 Cool Santa QXC4457	Yr.Iss.	1995	5.75	8-13
1995 Cozy Christmas QXC4119	Yr.Iss.	1995	8.50	15
1995 Fishing for Fun QXC5207	Yr.Iss.	1995	10.95	8-17
1995 A Gift From Rodney QXC4129	Yr.Iss.	1995	5.00	8-10
1995 Home From the Woods QXC1059	Yr.Iss.	1995	15.95	30-41
1995 May Flower QXC8246	Yr.Iss.	1995	4.95	25-47

1995 Keepsake Magic Ornaments - Keepsake

YEAR ISSUE	EDITION LIMIT	YEAR RETD.	ISSUE PRICE	*QUOTE U.S.$
1995 Baby's First Christmas QLX7317	Yr.Iss.	1995	22.00	42-45
1995 Chris Mouse Tree (11th Ed.) QLX7307	Yr.Iss.	1995	12.50	24-30
1995 Coming to See Santa QLX7369	Yr.Iss.	1995	32.00	52-65
1995 Forest Frolics (7th Ed.) QLX7299	Yr.Iss.	1995	28.00	40-56
1995 Fred and Dino QLX7289	Yr.Iss.	1995	28.00	48-60
1995 Friends Share Fun QLX7349	Yr.Iss.	1995	16.50	34-38
1995 Goody Gumballs! QLX7367	Yr.Iss.	1995	12.50	30-33
1995 Headin' Home QLX7327	Yr.Iss.	1995	22.00	45-50
1995 Holiday Swim QLX7319	Yr.Iss.	1995	18.50	27-35
1995 Jukebox Party QLX7339	Yr.Iss.	1995	24.50	18-25
1995 Jumping for Joy QLX7347	Yr.Iss.	1995	28.00	48-60
1995 My First HOT WHEELS™ QLX7279	Yr.Iss.	1995	28.00	25-60
1995 PEANUTS® (5th Ed.) QLX7277	Yr.Iss.	1995	24.50	18-50
1995 Santa's Diner QLX7337	Yr.Iss.	1995	24.50	24-35
1995 Space Shuttle QLX7396	Yr.Iss.	1995	24.50	41-50
1995 Superman™ QLX7309	Yr.Iss.	1995	28.00	31-50
1995 Tobin Fraley Holiday Carousel (2nd Ed.) QLX7269	Yr.Iss.	1995	32.00	48-60
1995 Victorian Toy Box (Special Ed.) QLX7357	Yr.Iss.	1995	42.00	47-67
1995 Wee Little Christmas QLX7329	Yr.Iss.	1995	22.00	41-45
1995 Winnie the Pooh Too Much Hunny QLX7297	Yr.Iss.	1995	24.50	40-50

1995 Miniature Ornaments - Keepsake

YEAR ISSUE	EDITION LIMIT	YEAR RETD.	ISSUE PRICE	*QUOTE U.S.$
1995 Alice in Wonderland (1st Ed.) QXM4777	Yr.Iss.	1995	6.75	9-13
1995 Baby's First Christmas QXM4027	Yr.Iss.	1995	4.75	11-14
1995 Calamity Coyote QXM4467	Yr.Iss.	1995	6.75	12-16
1995 Centuries of Santa (2nd Ed.) QXM4789	Yr.Iss.	1995	5.75	8-15
1995 Christmas Bells (1st Ed.) QXM4007	Yr.Iss.	1995	4.75	12-26
1995 Christmas Wishes QXM4087	Yr.Iss.	1995	3.75	5-14
1995 Cloisonne Partridge QXM4017	Yr.Iss.	1995	9.75	18
1995 Downhill Double QXM4837	Yr.Iss.	1995	4.75	12
1995 Friendship Duet QXM4019	Yr.Iss.	1995	4.75	13
1995 Furrball QXM4459	Yr.Iss.	1995	5.75	12-16
1995 Grandpa's Gift QXM4829	Yr.Iss.	1995	5.75	10-13
1995 Heavenly Praises QXM4037	Yr.Iss.	1995	5.75	10-15
1995 Joyful Santa QXM4089	Yr.Iss.	1995	4.75	11-13
1995 Little Beeper QXM4469	Yr.Iss.	1995	5.75	12-16
1995 March of the Teddy Bears (3rd Ed.) QXM4799	Yr.Iss.	1995	4.75	10-13
1995 Merry Walruses QXM4057	Yr.Iss.	1995	5.75	19
1995 Milk Tank Car (7th Ed.) QXM4817	Yr.Iss.	1995	6.75	17-19
1995 Miniature Clothespin Soldier (1st Ed.) QXM4097	Yr.Iss.	1995	3.75	9-14
1995 A Moustershire Christmas QXM4839	Yr.Iss.	1995	24.50	28-44
1995 Murray® "Champion" (1st Ed.) QXM4079	Yr.Iss.	1995	5.75	7-20
1995 Nature's Angels (6th Ed.) QXM4809	Yr.Iss.	1995	4.75	14-20
1995 The Night Before Christmas (4th Ed.) QXM4807	Yr.Iss.	1995	4.75	12-18
1995 Nutcracker Guild (2nd Ed.) QXM4787	Yr.Iss.	1995	5.75	8-16
1995 On the Road (3rd Ed.) QXM4797	Yr.Iss.	1995	5.75	14-17
1995 Pebbles and Bamm-Bamm QXM4757	Yr.Iss.	1995	9.75	14-22
1995 Playful Penguins QXM4059	Yr.Iss.	1995	5.75	10-23
1995 Precious Creations QXM4077	Yr.Iss.	1995	9.75	18-20
1995 Rocking Horse (8th Ed.) QXM4827	Yr.Iss.	1995	4.75	11-14
1995 Santa's Little Big Top (1st Ed.) QXM4779	Yr.Iss.	1995	6.75	15-20
1995 Santa's Visit QXM4047	Yr.Iss.	1995	7.75	16-18
1995 Starlit Nativity QXM4039	Yr.Iss.	1995	7.75	18-20
1995 Sugarplum Dreams QXM4099	Yr.Iss.	1995	4.75	10-15
1995 Tiny Treasures (set of 6) QXM4009	Yr.Iss.	1995	29.00	44-45
1995 Tudor House- (8th Ed.) QXM4819	Yr.Iss.	1995	6.75	15-25
1995 Tunnel of Love QXM4029	Yr.Iss.	1995	4.75	12

1995 New Attractions - Keepsake

YEAR ISSUE	EDITION LIMIT	YEAR RETD.	ISSUE PRICE	*QUOTE U.S.$
1995 Acorn 500 QX5929	Yr.Iss.	1995	10.95	18-20
1995 Batmobile QX5739	Yr.Iss.	1995	14.95	15-30
1995 Betty and Wilma QX5417	Yr.Iss.	1995	14.95	12-27
1995 Bingo Bear QX5919	Yr.Iss.	1995	7.95	18-20
1995 Bobbin' Along QX5879	Yr.Iss.	1995	8.95	28-40
1995 Bugs Bunny QX5019	Yr.Iss.	1995	8.95	12-16
1995 Catch the Spirit QX5899	Yr.Iss.	1995	7.95	18-20
1995 Christmas Morning QX5997	Yr.Iss.	1995	10.95	12-16
1995 Colorful World QX5519	Yr.Iss.	1995	10.95	20-23
1995 Cows of Bali QX5999	Yr.Iss.	1995	8.95	18-20
1995 Delivering Kisses QX4107	Yr.Iss.	1995	10.95	15-23
1995 Dream On QX6007	Yr.Iss.	1995	10.95	21-24
1995 Dudley the Dragon QX6209	Yr.Iss.	1995	10.95	16-23
1995 Faithful Fan QX5897	Yr.Iss.	1995	8.95	18
1995 Feliz Navidad QX5869	Yr.Iss.	1995	7.95	8-19
1995 Forever Friends Bear QX5258	Yr.Iss.	1995	8.95	10-21
1995 GARFIELD QX5007	Yr.Iss.	1995	10.95	23-25
1995 Glinda, Witch of the North QX5749	Yr.Iss.	1995	13.95	25-32
1995 Gopher Fun QX5887	Yr.Iss.	1995	9.95	20-25
1995 Happy Wrappers QX6037	Yr.Iss.	1995	10.95	20-23
1995 Heaven's Gift QX6057	Yr.Iss.	1995	20.00	24-50
1995 Hockey Pup QX5917	Yr.Iss.	1995	9.95	18-23
1995 In Time With Christmas QX6049	Yr.Iss.	1995	12.95	25-30
1995 Joy to the World QX5867	Yr.Iss.	1995	8.95	19
1995 LEGO® Fireplace With Santa QX4769	Yr.Iss.	1995	10.95	15-23
1995 Lou Rankin Bear QX4069	Yr.Iss.	1995	9.95	19-23
1995 The Magic School Bus™ QX5849	Yr.Iss.	1995	10.95	22
1995 Mary Engelbreit QX2409	Yr.Iss.	1995	5.00	18
1995 Merry RV QX6027	Yr.Iss.	1995	12.95	25-30
1995 Muletide Greetings QX6009	Yr.Iss.	1995	7.95	8-16
1995 The Olympic Spirit QX3169	Yr.Iss.	1995	7.95	15-20
1995 On the Ice QX6047	Yr.Iss.	1995	7.95	21-23
1995 Perfect Balance QX5927	Yr.Iss.	1995	7.95	16-18
1995 PEZ® Santa QX5267	Yr.Iss.	1995	7.95	19-22
1995 Polar Coaster QX6117	Yr.Iss.	1995	8.95	22-30
1995 Popeye® QX5257	Yr.Iss.	1995	10.95	12-23
1995 Refreshing Gift QX4067	Yr.Iss.	1995	14.95	29
1995 Rejoice! QX5987	Yr.Iss.	1995	10.95	23
1995 Roller Whiz QX5937	Yr.Iss.	1995	7.95	17-20
1995 Santa in Paris QX5877	Yr.Iss.	1995	8.95	24-30
1995 Santa's Serenade QX6017	Yr.Iss.	1995	8.95	18-20
1995 Santa's Visitors QX2407	Yr.Iss.	1995	5.00	14-20
1995 Simba, Pumbaa and Timon QX6159	Yr.Iss.	1995	12.95	20
1995 Ski Hound QX5909	Yr.Iss.	1995	8.95	18-20
1995 Surfin' Santa QX6019	Yr.Iss.	1995	9.95	15-28
1995 Sylvester and Tweety QX5017	Yr.Iss.	1995	13.95	24-27
1995 Takin' a Hike QX6029	Yr.Iss.	1995	7.95	18-20
1995 Tennis, Anyone? QX5907	Yr.Iss.	1995	7.95	18-20
1995 Thomas the Tank Engine-No. 1 QX5857	Yr.Iss.	1995	9.95	24-35
1995 Three Wishes QX5979	Yr.Iss.	1995	7.95	18-20
1995 Vera the Mouse QX5537	Yr.Iss.	1995	8.95	17-19
1995 Waiting Up for Santa QX6106	Yr.Iss.	1995	8.95	18-20
1995 Water Sports QX6039	Yr.Iss.	1995	14.95	29-35
1995 Wheel of Fortune® QX6187	Yr.Iss.	1995	12.95	12-21
1995 Winnie the Pooh and Tigger QX5009	Yr.Iss.	1995	12.95	29
1995 The Winning Play QX5889	Yr.Iss.	1995	7.95	18-23

1995 Personalized Ornaments - Keepsake

YEAR ISSUE	EDITION LIMIT	YEAR RETD.	ISSUE PRICE	*QUOTE U.S.$
1995 Baby Bear QP6157	Yr.Iss.	1995	12.95	9-13
1995 The Champ QP6127	Yr.Iss.	1995	12.95	9-13
1995 Computer Cat 'n' Mouse QP6046	Yr.Iss.	1995	12.95	9-13
1995 Cookie Time QP6073	Yr.Iss.	1995	12.95	9-27
1995 Etch-A-Sketch® QP6006	Yr.Iss.	1995	12.95	9-13
1995 From the Heart QP6036	Yr.Iss.	1995	14.95	10-15
1995 Key Note QP6149	Yr.Iss.	1995	12.95	9-13
1995 Mailbox Delivery QP6015	Yr.Iss.	1995	12.95	9-13
1995 Novel Idea QP6066	Yr.Iss.	1995	12.95	9-13
1995 On the Billboard QP6022	Yr.Iss.	1995	12.95	9-13
1995 Playing Ball QP6032	Yr.Iss.	1995	12.95	9-13
1995 Reindeer Rooters QP6056	Yr.Iss.	1995	14.95	10-15

1995 Premiere Event - Keepsake

YEAR ISSUE	EDITION LIMIT	YEAR RETD.	ISSUE PRICE	*QUOTE U.S.$
1995 Wish List QX5859	Yr.Iss.	1995	15.00	15-30

1995 Showcase All Is Bright Collection - Keepsake

YEAR ISSUE	EDITION LIMIT	YEAR RETD.	ISSUE PRICE	*QUOTE U.S.$
1995 Angel of Light QK1159	Yr.Iss.	1995	11.95	15-23
1995 Gentle Lullaby QK1157	Yr.Iss.	1995	11.95	15-23

1995 Showcase Angel Bells Collection - Keepsake

YEAR ISSUE	EDITION LIMIT	YEAR RETD.	ISSUE PRICE	*QUOTE U.S.$
1995 Carole QK1147	Yr.Iss.	1995	12.95	24
1995 Joy QK1137	Yr.Iss.	1995	12.95	22-25
1995 Noelle QK1139	Yr.Iss.	1995	12.95	24

1995 Showcase Folk Art Americana Collection - Keepsake

YEAR ISSUE	EDITION LIMIT	YEAR RETD.	ISSUE PRICE	*QUOTE U.S.$
1995 Fetching the Firewood QK1057	Yr.Iss.	1995	15.95	24-32
1995 Fishing Party QK1039	Yr.Iss.	1995	15.95	24-32
1995 Guiding Santa QK1037	Yr.Iss.	1995	18.95	33-44
1995 Learning to Skate QK1047	Yr.Iss.	1995	14.95	25-35

1995 Showcase Holiday Enchantment Collection - Keepsake

YEAR ISSUE	EDITION LIMIT	YEAR RETD.	ISSUE PRICE	*QUOTE U.S.$
1995 Away in a Manger QK1097	Yr.Iss.	1995	13.95	22-25
1995 Following the Star QK1099	Yr.Iss.	1995	13.95	22-25

1995 Showcase Invitation to Tea Collection - Keepsake

YEAR ISSUE	EDITION LIMIT	YEAR RETD.	ISSUE PRICE	*QUOTE U.S.$
1995 Cozy Cottage Teapot QK1127	Yr.Iss.	1995	15.95	24-30
1995 European Castle Teapot QK1129	Yr.Iss.	1995	15.95	24-30
1995 Victorian Home Teapot QK1119	Yr.Iss.	1995	15.95	24-32

1995 Showcase Nature's Sketchbook Collection - Keepsake

YEAR ISSUE	EDITION LIMIT	YEAR RETD.	ISSUE PRICE	*QUOTE U.S.$
1995 Backyard Orchard QK1069	Yr.Iss.	1995	18.95	24-30
1995 Christmas Cardinal QK1077	Yr.Iss.	1995	18.95	32-41
1995 Raising a Family QK1067	Yr.Iss.	1995	18.95	24-31
1995 Snowy Garden QX8284	Yr.Iss.		13.95	30
1995 Violets and Butterflies QK1079	Yr.Iss.	1995	16.95	24-31

1995 Showcase Symbols of Christmas Collection - Keepsake

YEAR ISSUE	EDITION LIMIT	YEAR RETD.	ISSUE PRICE	*QUOTE U.S.$
1995 Jolly Santa QK1087	Yr.Iss.	1995	15.95	16-28
1995 Sweet Song QK1089	Yr.Iss.	1995	15.95	16-28

1995 Showcase Turn-of-the-Century Parade - Keepsake

YEAR ISSUE	EDITION LIMIT	YEAR RETD.	ISSUE PRICE	*QUOTE U.S.$
1995 The Fireman QK1027	Yr.Iss.	1995	16.95	36-40

1995 Special Edition - Keepsake

YEAR ISSUE	EDITION LIMIT	YEAR RETD.	ISSUE PRICE	*QUOTE U.S.$
1995 Beverly and Teddy QX5259	Yr.Iss.	1995	21.75	29

1995 Special Issues - Keepsake

YEAR ISSUE	EDITION LIMIT	YEAR RETD.	ISSUE PRICE	*QUOTE U.S.$
1995 Captain James T. Kirk QXI5539	Yr.Iss.	1995	13.95	21-25
1995 Captain Jean-Luc Picard QXI5737	Yr.Iss.	1995	13.95	15-21
1995 Captain John Smith and Meeko QXI6169	Yr.Iss.	1995	12.95	23
1995 Holiday Barbie™ (3rd Ed.) QXI5057	Yr.Iss.	1995	14.95	15-35
1995 Hoop Stars (1st Ed.) QXI5517	Yr.Iss.	1995	14.95	22-41
1995 Joe Montana (1st Ed.) QXI5759	Yr.Iss.	1995	14.95	41-98
1995 Percy, Flit and Meeko QXI6179	Yr.Iss.	1995	9.95	17
1995 Pocahontas and Captain John Smith QXI6197	Yr.Iss.	1995	14.95	23
1995 Pocahontas QXI6177	Yr.Iss.	1995	12.95	18
1995 Romulan Warbird™ QXI7267	Yr.Iss.	1995	24.00	36-40
1995 The Ships of Star Trek® QXI4109	Yr.Iss.	1995	19.95	20-23
1995 Solo in the Spotlight-Barbie™ (2nd Ed.) QXI5049	Yr.Iss.	1995	14.95	21-54

1995 Special Offer - Keepsake

YEAR ISSUE	EDITION LIMIT	YEAR RETD.	ISSUE PRICE	*QUOTE U.S.$
1995 Charlie Brown QRP4207	Yr.Iss.	1995	3.95	36
1995 Linus QRP4217	Yr.Iss.	1995	3.95	25
1995 Lucy QRP4209	Yr.Iss.	1995	3.95	25
1995 SNOOPY QRP4219	Yr.Iss.	1995	3.95	35
1995 Snow Scene QRP4227	Yr.Iss.	1995	3.95	25
1995 5-Pc. Set	Yr.Iss.	1995	19.95	50-60

1996 Collectible Series - Keepsake

YEAR ISSUE	EDITION LIMIT	YEAR RETD.	ISSUE PRICE	*QUOTE U.S.$
1996 1955 Chevrolet Camero (2nd Ed.) QX5241	Yr.Iss.	1996	13.95	15-30
1996 1959 Cadillac De Ville (6th Ed.) QX5384	Yr.Iss.	1996	12.95	15-28
1996 700E Hudson Steam Locomotive (1st Ed.) QX5531	Yr.Iss.	1996	18.95	22-100

*Quotes have been rounded up to nearest dollar

YEAR ISSUE	EDITION LIMIT	YEAR RETD.	ISSUE PRICE	*QUOTE U.S.$
1996 Bright Flying Colors (8th Ed.) QX5391	Yr.Iss.	1996	10.95	22-25
1996 Cat Naps (3rd Ed.) QX5641	Yr.Iss.	1996	7.95	22
1996 A Celebration of Angels (2nd Ed.) QX5634	Yr.Iss.	1996	12.95	28
1996 Christkind (2nd Ed.) QX5631	Yr.Iss.	1996	14.95	12-27
1996 Christy-All God's Children-Martha Holcombe (1st Ed.) QX5564	Yr.Iss.	1996	12.95	23-28
1996 Cinderella-1995 (1st Ed.) QX6311	Yr.Iss.	1996	14.95	26-46
1996 Evergreen Santa (Special Ed.) QX5714	Yr.Iss.	1996	22.00	36-44
1996 Fabulous Decade (7th Ed.) QX5661	Yr.Iss.	1996	7.95	18-20
1996 Frosty Friends (17th Ed.) QX5681	Yr.Iss.	1996	10.95	23-30
1996 Mary Had a Little Lamb (4th Ed.) QX5644	Yr.Iss.	1996	13.95	10-25
1996 Merry Olde Santa (7th Ed.) QX5654	Yr.Iss.	1996	14.95	28-30
1996 Murray Airplane (3rd Ed.) QX5364	Yr.Iss.	1996	13.95	12-26
1996 Native American Barbie™ (1st Ed.) QX5561	Yr.Iss.	1996	14.95	21-31
1996 The PEANUTS Gang (4th Ed.) QX5381	Yr.Iss.	1996	9.95	10-21
1996 Puppy Love (6th Ed.) QX5651	Yr.Iss.	1996	7.95	10-19
1996 Rocking Horse (16th Ed.) QX5674	Yr.Iss.	1996	10.95	30-34
1996 Santa's 4X4 (18th Ed.) QX5684	Yr.Iss.	1996	14.95	31-33
1996 Satchel Paige (3rd Ed.) QX5304	Yr.Iss.	1996	12.95	8-23
1996 Victorian Painted Lady (13th Ed.) QX5671	Yr.Iss.	1996	14.95	27-30
1996 Violet-Mary's Angels (9th Ed.) QX5664	Yr.Iss.	1996	6.95	17-20
1996 Yuletide Central (3rd Ed.) QX5011	Yr.Iss.	1996	18.95	23-40

1996 Commemoratives - Keepsake

YEAR ISSUE	EDITION LIMIT	YEAR RETD.	ISSUE PRICE	*QUOTE U.S.$
1996 Baby's First Christmas QX5754	Yr.Iss.	1996	9.95	10-17
1996 Baby's First Christmas-Beatrix Potter QX5744	Yr.Iss.	1996	18.95	25-29
1996 Baby's First Christmas-Bessie Pease Gutmann QX5751	Yr.Iss.	1996	10.95	13-25
1996 Baby's First Christmas-Child's Age Collection QX5764	Yr.Iss.	1996	7.95	19-25
1996 Baby's First Christmas-Photo Holder QX5761	Yr.Iss.	1996	7.95	14-25
1996 Baby's Second Christmas-Child's Age Collection QX5771	Yr.Iss.	1996	7.95	20-22
1996 Child's Fifth Christmas-Child's Age Collection QX5784	Yr.Iss.	1996	6.95	12-18
1996 Child's Fourth Christmas-Child's Age Collection QX5781	Yr.Iss.	1996	7.95	14-19
1996 Child's Third Christmas-Child's Age Collection QX5774	Yr.Iss.	1996	7.95	18-20
1996 Close-Knit Friends QX5874	Yr.Iss.	1996	9.95	7-20
1996 Dad QX5831	Yr.Iss.	1996	7.95	15-17
1996 Daughter QX6077	Yr.Iss.	1996	8.95	19
1996 Godchild QX5841	Yr.Iss.	1996	8.95	18-20
1996 Granddaughter QX5697	Yr.Iss.	1996	7.95	15-20
1996 Grandma QX5844	Yr.Iss.	1996	8.95	7-23
1996 Grandpa QX5851	Yr.Iss.	1996	8.95	7-18
1996 Grandson QX5699	Yr.Iss.	1996	7.95	17-19
1996 Hearts Full of Love QX5814	Yr.Iss.	1996	9.95	16-19
1996 Mom and Dad QX5821	Yr.Iss.	1996	9.95	14-30
1996 Mom QX5824	Yr.Iss.	1996	7.95	18-20
1996 Mom-to-Be QX5791	Yr.Iss.	1996	7.95	16-20
1996 New Home QX5881	Yr.Iss.	1996	8.95	19
1996 On My Way-Photo Holder QX5861	Yr.Iss.	1996	7.95	12-15
1996 Our Christmas Together QX5794	Yr.Iss.	1996	18.95	31-40
1996 Our Christmas Together-Photo Holder QX5804	Yr.Iss.	1996	8.95	21-28
1996 Our First Christmas Together QX5811	Yr.Iss.	1996	9.95	18-20
1996 Our First Christmas Together-Acrylic QX3051	Yr.Iss.	1996	6.95	21
1996 Our First Christmas Together-Collector's Plate QX5801	Yr.Iss.	1996	10.95	8-21
1996 Sister to Sister QX5834	Yr.Iss.	1996	9.95	15-19
1996 Son QX6079	Yr.Iss.	1996	8.95	7-18
1996 Special Dog Photo Holder QX5864	Yr.Iss.	1996	7.95	6-8
1996 Thank You, Santa-Photo Holder QX5854	Yr.Iss.	1996	7.95	6-18

1996 Keepsake Collector's Club - Keepsake

YEAR ISSUE	EDITION LIMIT	YEAR RETD.	ISSUE PRICE	*QUOTE U.S.$
1996 1937 Steelcraft Auburn by Murray® QXC4174	Yr.Iss.	1996	15.95	35-56
1996 1988 Happy Holidays® Barbie™ Doll QXC4181	Yr.Iss.	1996	14.95	40-77
1996 Airmail for Santa QXC4194	Yr.Iss.	1996	8.95	15
1996 Rudolph the Red-Nosed Reindeer® QXC7341	Yr.Iss.	1996	N/A	15-29
1996 Rudolph®'s Helper QXC4171	Yr.Iss.	1996	N/A	8-13
1996 Santa QXC4164	Yr.Iss.	1996	N/A	10-20
1996 Santa's Club Soda #4 QXC4191	Yr.Iss.	1996	8.50	12-15
1996 Santa's Toy Shop QXC4201	Yr.Iss.	1996	60.00	50-125
1996 The Wizard of Oz QXC4161	Yr.Iss.	1996	12.95	35-67

1996 Keepsake Magic Ornaments - Keepsake

YEAR ISSUE	EDITION LIMIT	YEAR RETD.	ISSUE PRICE	*QUOTE U.S.$
1996 Baby's First Christmas QLX7404	Yr.Iss.	1996	22.00	42-45
1996 Chicken Coop Chorus QLX7491	Yr.Iss.	1996	24.50	25-41
1996 Chris Mouse Inn (12th Ed.) QLX7371	Yr.Iss.	1996	14.50	27-30
1996 Father Time QLX7391	Yr.Iss.	1996	24.50	50
1996 Freedom 7 (1st Ed.) QLX7524	Yr.Iss.	1996	24.00	54-65
1996 THE JETSONS QLX7411	Yr.Iss.	1996	28.00	20-38
1996 Jukebox Party QLX7339	Yr.Iss.	1996	24.50	51-56
1996 Let Us Adore Him QLX7381	Yr.Iss.	1996	16.50	27-45
1996 North Pole Volunteers (Special Ed.) QLX7471	Yr.Iss.	1996	42.00	52-91
1996 Over the Rooftops QLX7374	Yr.Iss.	1996	14.50	10-30
1996 PEANUTS-Lucy and Schroeder QLX7394	Yr.Iss.	1996	18.50	28-36
1996 Pinball Wonder QLX7451	Yr.Iss.	1996	28.00	20-60
1996 Sharing a Soda QLX7424	Yr.Iss.	1996	24.50	28-49
1996 Slippery Day QLX7414	Yr.Iss.	1996	24.50	45-50
1996 STAR WARS-Millennium Falcon QLX7474	Yr.Iss.	1996	24.00	35-61
1996 The Statue of Liberty QLX7421	Yr.Iss.	1996	24.50	28-50
1996 Tobin Fraley Holiday Carousel (3rd Ed.) QLX7461	Yr.Iss.	1996	32.00	44-55
1996 Treasured Memories QLX7384	Yr.Iss.	1996	18.50	36-40
1996 Video Party QLX7431	Yr.Iss.	1996	28.00	20-59
1996 THE WIZARD OF OZ-Emerald City QLX7454	Yr.Iss.	1996	32.00	40-65

1996 Miniature Ornaments - Keepsake

YEAR ISSUE	EDITION LIMIT	YEAR RETD.	ISSUE PRICE	*QUOTE U.S.$
1996 African Elephants QXM4224	Yr.Iss.	1996	5.75	19-35
1996 Centuries of Santa (3rd Ed.) QXM4091	Yr.Iss.	1996	5.75	8-15
1996 A Child's Gifts QXM4234	Yr.Iss.	1996	6.75	9-13
1996 Christmas Bear QXM4241	Yr.Iss.	1996	4.75	12-14
1996 Christmas Bells (2nd Ed.) QXM4071	Yr.Iss.	1996	4.75	13-15
1996 Cookie Car (8th Ed.) QXM4114	Yr.Iss.	1996	6.75	10-18
1996 Cool Delivery Coca-Cola QXM4021	Yr.Iss.	1996	5.75	14
1996 GONE WITH THE WIND QXM4211	Yr.Iss.	1996	19.95	20-29
1996 Hattie Chapeau QXM4251	Yr.Iss.	1996	4.75	6-12
1996 Joyous Angel QXM4231	Yr.Iss.	1996	4.75	9-14
1996 Long Winter's Nap QXM4244	Yr.Iss.	1996	5.75	12-14
1996 Loony Tunes Lovables Baby Sylvester QXM4154	Yr.Iss.	1996	5.75	9-14
1996 Loony Tunes Lovables Baby Tweety QXM4014	Yr.Iss.	1996	5.75	21-23
1996 Mad Hatter (2nd Ed.) QXM4074	Yr.Iss.	1996	6.75	12-17
1996 March of the Teddy Bears (4th Ed.) QXM4094	Yr.Iss.	1996	4.75	9-12
1996 Message for Santa QXM4254	Yr.Iss.	1996	6.75	10-16
1996 Miniature Clothespin Soldier (2nd Ed.) QXM4144	Yr.Iss.	1996	4.75	11-13
1996 Murray "Fire Truck" (2nd Ed.) QXM4031	Yr.Iss.	1996	6.75	8-19
1996 Nature's Angels (7th Ed.) QXM4111	Yr.Iss.	1996	4.75	6-12
1996 The Night Before Christmas (5th Ed.) QXM4104	Yr.Iss.	1996	5.75	10-13
1996 The Nutcracker Ballet (1st Ed.) QXM4064	Yr.Iss.	1996	14.75	15-27
1996 Nutcracker Guild (3rd Ed.) QXM4084	Yr.Iss.	1996	5.75	15-17
1996 O Holy Night (Special Ed.) QXM4204	Yr.Iss.	1996	24.50	24-36
1996 On the Road (4th Ed.) QXM4101	Yr.Iss.	1996	5.75	7-13
1996 Peaceful Christmas QXM4214	Yr.Iss.	1996	4.75	12-15
1996 Rocking Horse (9th Ed.) QXM4121	Yr.Iss.	1996	4.75	9-15
1996 Santa's Little Big Top (2nd Ed.) QXM4081	Yr.Iss.	1996	6.75	8-15
1996 Sparkling Crystal Angel (Precious Ed.) QXM4264	Yr.Iss.	1996	9.75	10-24
1996 Tiny Christmas Helpers QXM4261	Yr.Iss.	1996	29.00	53-58
1996 A Tree for WOODSTOCK QXM4767	Yr.Iss.	1996	5.75	10-15
1996 The Vehicles of STAR WARS QXM4024	Yr.Iss.	1996	19.95	28-40
1996 Village Mill (9th Ed.) QXM4124	Yr.Iss.	1996	6.75	10-15
1996 Winnie the Pooh and Tigger QXM4044	Yr.Iss.	1996	9.75	12-21

1996 New Attractions - Keepsake

YEAR ISSUE	EDITION LIMIT	YEAR RETD.	ISSUE PRICE	*QUOTE U.S.$
1996 Antlers Aweigh! QX5901	Yr.Iss.	1996	9.95	20-24
1996 Apple for Teacher QX6121	Yr.Iss.	1996	7.95	6-16
1996 Bounce Pass QX6031	Yr.Iss.	1996	7.95	15-18
1996 Bowl 'em Over QX6014	Yr.Iss.	1996	7.95	13-20
1996 BOY SCOUTS OF AMERICA Growth of a Leader QX5541	Yr.Iss.	1996	9.95	7-24
1996 Child Care Giver QX6071	Yr.Iss.	1996	8.95	7-15
1996 Christmas Joy QX6241	Yr.Iss.	1996	14.95	27-30
1996 Christmas Snowman QX6214	Yr.Iss.	1996	9.95	21-23
1996 Come All Ye Faithful QX6244	Yr.Iss.	1996	12.95	22-28
1996 Fan-tastic Season QX5924	Yr.Iss.	1996	9.95	7-20
1996 Feliz Navidad QX6304	Yr.Iss.	1996	9.95	10-18
1996 Glad Tidings QX6231	Yr.Iss.	1996	14.95	27-30
1996 Goal Line Glory QX6001	Yr.Iss.	1996	12.95	25-33
1996 Happy Holi-doze QX5904	Yr.Iss.	1996	9.95	7-20
1996 High Style QX6064	Yr.Iss.	1996	8.95	13-19
1996 Hillside Express QX6134	Yr.Iss.	1996	12.95	25-28
1996 Holiday Haul QX6201	Yr.Iss.	1996	14.95	33-35
1996 Hurrying Downstairs QX6074	Yr.Iss.	1996	8.95	13-17
1996 I Dig Golf QX5891	Yr.Iss.	1996	10.95	21-24
1996 Jackpot Jingle QX5911	Yr.Iss.	1996	9.95	12-20
1996 Jolly Wolly Ark QX6221	Yr.Iss.	1996	12.95	10-23
1996 Kindly Shepherd QX6274	Yr.Iss.	1996	12.95	21-30
1996 Lighting the Way QX6124	Yr.Iss.	1996	12.95	10-30
1996 A Little Song and Dance QX6211	Yr.Iss.	1996	9.95	7-20
1996 Little Spooners QX5504	Yr.Iss.	1996	12.95	23-27
1996 LOONEY TUNES Foghorn Leghorn and Henery Hawk QX5444	Yr.Iss.	1996	13.95	12-26
1996 LOONEY TUNES Marvin the Martian QX5451	Yr.Iss.	1996	10.95	21-25
1996 Madonna & Child QX6324	Yr.Iss.	1996	12.95	5-24
1996 Making His Rounds QX6271	Yr.Iss.	1996	14.95	11-30
1996 Matchless Memories QX6061	Yr.Iss.	1996	9.95	7-20
1996 Maxine QX6224	Yr.Iss.	1996	9.95	15-29
1996 Merry Carpoolers QX5884	Yr.Iss.	1996	14.95	15-27
1996 Olive Oyl and Swee' Pea QX5481	Yr.Iss.	1996	10.95	17-22
1996 Peppermint Surprise QX6234	Yr.Iss.	1996	7.95	8-16
1996 Percy the Small Engine-No. 6 QX6314	Yr.Iss.	1996	9.95	18-20
1996 PEZ® Snowman QX6534	Yr.Iss.	1996	7.95	19
1996 Polar Cycle QX6034	Yr.Iss.	1996	12.95	12-27
1996 Prayer for Peace QX6261	Yr.Iss.	1996	7.95	14-16
1996 Precious Child QX6251	Yr.Iss.	1996	8.95	6-18
1996 Pup-Tenting QX6011	Yr.Iss.	1996	7.95	8-18
1996 Regal Cardinal QX6204	Yr.Iss.	1996	9.95	21-23
1996 Sew Sweet QX5921	Yr.Iss.	1996	8.95	10-20
1996 SPIDER-MAN QX5757	Yr.Iss.	1996	12.95	21-30
1996 Star of the Show QX6004	Yr.Iss.	1996	8.95	16-20
1996 Tamika QX6301	Yr.Iss.	1996	7.95	10-15
1996 Tender Lovin' Care QX6114	Yr.Iss.	1996	7.95	15
1996 This Big! QX5914	Yr.Iss.	1996	9.95	18-20
1996 Time for a Treat QX5464	Yr.Iss.	1996	11.95	10-22
1996 Tonka Mighty Dump Truck QX6321	Yr.Iss.	1996	13.95	20-35
1996 A Tree for SNOOPY QX5507	Yr.Iss.	1996	8.95	12-22
1996 Welcome Guest QX5394	Yr.Iss.	1996	14.95	11-30
1996 Welcome Him QX6264	Yr.Iss.	1996	8.95	16-18
1996 Winnie the Pooh and Piglet QX5454	Yr.Iss.	1996	12.95	20-28
1996 THE WIZARD OF OZ Witch of the West QX5554	Yr.Iss.	1996	13.95	20-30
1996 WONDER WOMAN QX5941	Yr.Iss.	1996	12.95	26-30
1996 Woodland Santa QX6131	Yr.Iss.	1996	12.95	10-24
1996 Yogi Bear and Boo Boo QX5521	Yr.Iss.	1996	12.95	15-27
1996 Yuletide Cheer QX6054	Yr.Iss.	1996	7.95	6-18
1996 Ziggy QX6524	Yr.Iss.	1996	9.95	15-25

1996 NFL Ornaments - Keepsake

YEAR ISSUE	EDITION LIMIT	YEAR RETD.	ISSUE PRICE	*QUOTE U.S.$
1996 Arizona Cardinals QSR6484	Yr.Iss.	1996	9.95	14
1996 Atlanta Falcons QSR6364	Yr.Iss.	1996	9.95	14
1996 Browns QSR6391	Yr.Iss.	1996	9.95	10-20
1996 Buffalo Bills QSR6371	Yr.Iss.	1996	9.95	10-14
1996 Carolina Panthers QSR6374	Yr.Iss.	1996	9.95	10-20
1996 Chicago Bears QSR6381	Yr.Iss.	1996	9.95	14
1996 Cincinnati Bengals QSR6384	Yr.Iss.	1996	9.95	14-20
1996 Dallas Cowboys QSR6394	Yr.Iss.	1996	9.95	14-20
1996 Denver Broncos QSR6411	Yr.Iss.	1996	9.95	14
1996 Detroit Lions QSR6414	Yr.Iss.	1996	9.95	14-20
1996 Green Bay Packers QSR6421	Yr.Iss.	1996	9.95	50
1996 Indianapolis Colts QSR6431	Yr.Iss.	1996	9.95	14
1996 Jacksonville Jaguars QSR6434	Yr.Iss.	1996	9.95	14-20
1996 Kansas City Chiefs QSR6361	Yr.Iss.	1996	9.95	14
1996 Miami Dolphins QSR6451	Yr.Iss.	1996	9.95	10-20
1996 Minnesota Vikings QSR6454	Yr.Iss.	1996	9.95	10-20
1996 New England Patriots QSR6461	Yr.Iss.	1996	9.95	15-23
1996 New Orleans Saints QSR6464	Yr.Iss.	1996	9.95	14-20
1996 New York Giants QSR6471	Yr.Iss.	1996	9.95	14-20
1996 New York Jets QSR6474	Yr.Iss.	1996	9.95	14-20
1996 Oakland Raiders QSR6441	Yr.Iss.	1996	9.95	10
1996 Oilers QSR6424	Yr.Iss.	1996	9.95	14
1996 Philadelphi Eagles QSR6481	Yr.Iss.	1996	9.95	14-20
1996 Pittsburgh Steelers QSR6491	Yr.Iss.	1996	9.95	10
1996 San Diego Chargers QSR6494	Yr.Iss.	1996	9.95	14
1996 San Francisco 49ers QSR6501	Yr.Iss.	1996	9.95	14-20
1996 Seattle Seahawks QSR6504	Yr.Iss.	1996	9.95	14-20
1996 St.Louis Rams QSR6444	Yr.Iss.	1996	9.95	10-15
1996 Tampa Bay Buccaneers QSR6511	Yr.Iss.	1996	9.95	14
1996 Washington Redskins QSR6514	Yr.Iss.	1996	9.95	10-20

1996 Premiere Event - Keepsake

YEAR ISSUE	EDITION LIMIT	YEAR RETD.	ISSUE PRICE	*QUOTE U.S.$
1996 Bashful Mistletoe-Merry Minatures QFM8054	Yr.Iss.	1996	12.95	9-13
1996 Welcome Sign-Tender Touches QX6331	Yr.Iss.	1996	15.00	10-30

1996 Showcase Cookie Jar Friends Collection - Keepsake

YEAR ISSUE	EDITION LIMIT	YEAR RETD.	ISSUE PRICE	*QUOTE U.S.$
1996 Carmen QK1164	Yr.Iss.	1996	15.95	27-30
1996 Clyde QK1161	Yr.Iss.	1996	15.95	20-27

1996 Showcase Folk Art Americana Collection - Keepsake

YEAR ISSUE	EDITION LIMIT	YEAR RETD.	ISSUE PRICE	*QUOTE U.S.$
1996 Caroling Angel QK1134	Yr.Iss.	1996	16.95	27-30
1996 Mrs. Claus QK1204	Yr.Iss.	1996	18.95	27-30
1996 Santa's Gifts QK1124	Yr.Iss.	1996	18.95	37-40

1996 Showcase Magi Bells Collection - Keepsake

YEAR ISSUE	EDITION LIMIT	YEAR RETD.	ISSUE PRICE	*QUOTE U.S.$
1996 Balthasar (Frankincense) QK1174	Yr.Iss.	1996	13.95	14-26
1996 Caspar (Myrrh) QK1184	Yr.Iss.	1996	13.95	14-26
1996 Melchior (Gold) QK1181	Yr.Iss.	1996	13.95	14-26

1996 Showcase Nature's Sketchbook Collection - Keepsake

YEAR ISSUE	EDITION LIMIT	YEAR RETD.	ISSUE PRICE	*QUOTE U.S.$
1996 The Birds' Christmas Tree QK1114	Yr.Iss.	1996	18.95	35-45
1996 Christmas Bunny QK1104	Yr.Iss.	1996	18.95	30
1996 The Holly Basket QK1094	Yr.Iss.	1996	18.95	19-30

1996 Showcase Sacred Masterworks Collection - Keepsake

YEAR ISSUE	EDITION LIMIT	YEAR RETD.	ISSUE PRICE	*QUOTE U.S.$
1996 Madonna and Child QK1144	Yr.Iss.	1996	15.95	16-30
1996 Praying Madonna QK1154	Yr.Iss.	1996	15.95	16-30

1996 Showcase The Language of Flowers Collection - Keepsake

YEAR ISSUE	EDITION LIMIT	YEAR RETD.	ISSUE PRICE	*QUOTE U.S.$
1996 Pansy (1st Ed.) QK1171	Yr.Iss.	1996	15.95	40-65

1996 Showcase Turn-of-the-Century Parade Collection - Keepsake

YEAR ISSUE	EDITION LIMIT	YEAR RETD.	ISSUE PRICE	*QUOTE U.S.$
1996 Uncle Sam (2nd Ed.) QK1084	Yr.Iss.	1996	16.95	17-32

1996 Special Issues - Keepsake

YEAR ISSUE	EDITION LIMIT	YEAR RETD.	ISSUE PRICE	*QUOTE U.S.$
1996 101 Dalmatians-Collector's Plate QXI6544	Yr.Iss.	1996	12.95	9-20
1996 Featuring the Enchanted Evening -Barbie™ Doll (3rd Ed.) QXI6541	Yr.Iss.	1996	14.95	10-31
1996 Holiday Barbie™ (4th Ed.) QXI5371	Yr.Iss.	1996	14.95	33-35
1996 HUNCHBACK OF NOTRE DAME -Esmeralda and Djali QXI6351	Yr.Iss.	1996	14.95	18-27
1996 HUNCHBACK OF NOTRE DAME -Laverne, Victor and Hugo QXI6354	Yr.Iss.	1996	12.95	13-26

*Quotes have been rounded up to nearest dollar

YEAR ISSUE	EDITION LIMIT	YEAR RETD.	ISSUE PRICE	*QUOTE U.S.$
1996 THE HUNCHBACK OF NOTRE DAME-Quasimodo QXI6341	Yr.Iss.	1996	9.95	13-19
1996 It's A Wonderful Life™ (Anniversay Ed.) QXI6531	Yr.Iss.	1996	14.95	29-40
1996 Larry Bird-Hoop Stars (2nd Ed.) QXI5014	Yr.Iss.	1996	14.95	20-30
1996 Nolan Ryan-At the Ballpark (1st Ed.) QXI5711	Yr.Iss.	1996	14.95	26-52
1996 OLYMIC-Parade of Nations-Collector's Plate QXE5741	Yr.Iss.	1996	10.95	7-11
1996 OLYMPIC-Cloisonne Medallion QXE4041	Yr.Iss.	1996	9.75	7-20
1996 OLYMPIC-Invitation to the Games QXE5511	Yr.Iss.	1996	14.95	24-29
1996 OLYMPIC-IZZY-The Mascot QXE5724	Yr.Iss.	1996	9.95	7-20
1996 OLYMPIC-Lighting the Flame QXE7444	Yr.Iss.	1996	28.00	20-55
1996 OLYMPIC-Olympic Triumph QXE5731	Yr.Iss.	1996	10.95	10-22
1996 STAR TREK® THE NEXT GENERATION-Commander William T. Riker QXI5551	Yr.Iss.	1996	14.95	29-33
1996 STAR TREK®-30 Years QXI7534	Yr.Iss.	1996	45.00	50-77
1996 STAR TREK®-Mr. Spock QXI5544	Yr.Iss.	1996	14.95	29-33
1996 STAR TREK®-U.S.S.Voyager QXI7544	Yr.Iss.	1996	24.00	36-47
1996 Troy Aikman-Football Legends (2nd Ed.) QXI5021	Yr.Iss.	1996	14.95	15-27

1996 Spring Ornaments - Keepsake

YEAR ISSUE	EDITION LIMIT	YEAR RETD.	ISSUE PRICE	*QUOTE U.S.$
1996 Apple Blossom Lane QEO8084	Yr.Iss.	1996	8.95	12-16
1996 Collector's Plate QEO8221	Yr.Iss.	1996	7.95	15-18
1996 Daffy Duck, LOONEY TUNES QEO8154	Yr.Iss.	1996	8.95	11-16
1996 Easter Morning QEO8164	Yr.Iss.	1996	7.95	17
1996 Eggstra Special Surprise, Tender Touches QEO8161	Yr.Iss.	1996	8.95	13-18
1996 Garden Club QEO8091	Yr.Iss.	1996	7.95	11-17
1996 Here Comes Easter QEO8094	Yr.Iss.	1996	7.95	10-17
1996 Hippity-Hop Delivery, CRAYOLA® Crayon QEO8144	Yr.Iss.	1996	7.95	13-17
1996 Joyful Angels QEO8184	Yr.Iss.	1996	9.95	13-30
1996 Locomotive, Cottontail Express QEO8074	Yr.Iss.	1996	8.95	15-43
1996 Look What I Found! QEO8181	Yr.Iss.	1996	7.95	13-15
1996 Parade Pals, PEANUTS® QEO8151	Yr.Iss.	1996	7.95	16
1996 Peter Rabbit™ Beatrix Potter™ QEO8071	Yr.Iss.	1996	8.95	60-85
1996 Pork 'n Beans QEO8174	Yr.Iss.	1996	7.95	14
1996 Springtime Barbie™ QEO8081	Yr.Iss.	1996	12.95	25-28
1996 Springtime Bonnets QEO8134	Yr.Iss.	1996	7.95	26-30
1996 Strawberry Patch QEO8171	Yr.Iss.	1996	6.95	11-14
1996 Strike Up the Band! QEO8141	Yr.Iss.	1996	14.95	20-23

1997 Collectible Series - Keepsake

YEAR ISSUE	EDITION LIMIT	YEAR RETD.	ISSUE PRICE	*QUOTE U.S.$
1997 1950 Santa Fe F3 Diesel Locomotive (2nd Ed.) QX6145	Yr.Iss.	1997	18.95	25-43
1997 1953 GMC (3rd Ed.) QX6105	Yr.Iss.	1997	13.95	14-27
1997 1969 Hurst Oldsmobile 442 (7th Ed.) QX6102	Yr.Iss.	1997	13.95	14-28
1997 Bright Rocking Colors (8th Ed.) QX6235	Yr.Iss.	1997	12.95	26-44
1997 Cafe (14th Ed.) QX6245	Yr.Iss.	1997	16.95	32-35
1997 Cat Naps (4th Ed.) QX6205	Yr.Iss.	1997	8.95	16-19
1997 A Celebration of Angels (3rd Ed.) QX6175	Yr.Iss.	1997	13.95	28-30
1997 Chinese Barbie™ (2nd Ed.) QX6162	Yr.Iss.	1997	14.95	27-30
1997 The Claus-Mobile (19th Ed.) QX6262	Yr.Iss.	1997	14.95	18-27
1997 The Clauses on Vacation (1st Ed.) QX6112	Yr.Iss.	1997	14.95	15-41
1997 Daisy-Mary's Angels (10th Ed.) QX6242	Yr.Iss.	1997	7.95	8-16
1997 Fabulous Decade (8th Ed.) QX6232	Yr.Iss.	1997	7.95	10-16
1997 The Flight at Kitty Hawk (1st Ed.) QX5574	Yr.Iss.	1997	14.95	26-32
1997 Frosty Friends (18th Ed.) QX6255	Yr.Iss.	1997	10.95	15-20
1997 Jackie Robinson (4th Ed.) QX6202	Yr.Iss.	1997	12.95	24-28
1997 Kolyada (3rd Ed.) QX6172	Yr.Iss.	1997	14.95	10-27
1997 Little Boy Blue (5th Ed.) QX6215	Yr.Iss.	1997	13.95	14-30
1997 Little Red Riding Hood-1991 (2nd Ed.) QX6155	Yr.Iss.	1997	14.95	22-33
1997 Marilyn Monroe (1st Ed.) QX5704	Yr.Iss.	1997	14.95	20-30
1997 Merry Olde Santa (8th Ed.) QX6225	Yr.Iss.	1997	14.95	18-28
1997 Murray Dump Truck (4th Ed.) QX6195	Yr.Iss.	1997	13.95	15-25
1997 Nikki-All God's Children®-Martha Root (2nd Ed.) QX6142	Yr.Iss.	1997	12.95	24-26
1997 Puppy Love (7th Ed.) QX6222	Yr.Iss.	1997	7.95	10-23
1997 Scarlett O'Hara (1st Ed.) QX6125	Yr.Iss.	1997	14.95	22-36
1997 Snowshoe Rabbits in Winter-Mark Newman (1st Ed.) QX5694	Yr.Iss.	1997	12.95	23-30
1997 Yuletide Central (4th Ed.) QX5812	Yr.Iss.	1997	18.95	20-36

1997 Commemoratives - Keepsake

YEAR ISSUE	EDITION LIMIT	YEAR RETD.	ISSUE PRICE	*QUOTE U.S.$
1997 Baby's First Christmas QX6485	Yr.Iss.	1997	9.95	16-32
1997 Baby's First Christmas QX6492	Yr.Iss.	1997	9.95	5-21
1997 Baby's First Christmas QX6495	Yr.Iss.	1997	7.95	16-18
1997 Baby's First Christmas QX6535	Yr.Iss.	1997	14.95	18-25
1997 Baby's First Christmas-Photo Holder QX6482	Yr.Iss.	1997	7.95	16-27
1997 Baby's Second Christmas QX6502	Yr.Iss.	1997	7.95	16
1997 Book of the Year-Photo Holder QX6645	Yr.Iss.	1997	7.95	8-20
1997 Child's Fifth Christmas QX6515	Yr.Iss.	1997	7.95	12-20
1997 Child's Fourth Christmas QX6512	Yr.Iss.	1997	7.95	5-18
1997 Child's Third Christmas QX6505	Yr.Iss.	1997	7.95	16-20
1997 Dad QX6532	Yr.Iss.	1997	8.95	7-16
1997 Daughter QX6612	Yr.Iss.	1997	7.95	16
1997 Friendship Blend QX6655	Yr.Iss.	1997	9.95	19
1997 Godchild QX6662	Yr.Iss.	1997	7.95	15-17
1997 Granddaughter QX6622	Yr.Iss.	1997	7.95	17-20
1997 Grandma QX6625	Yr.Iss.	1997	8.95	7-20
1997 Grandson QX6615	Yr.Iss.	1997	7.95	6-16
1997 Mom and Dad QX6522	Yr.Iss.	1997	9.95	20-22
1997 Mom QX6525	Yr.Iss.	1997	8.95	19
1997 New Home QX6652	Yr.Iss.	1997	8.95	3-19
1997 Our Christmas Together QX6475	Yr.Iss.	1997	16.95	5-32
1997 Our First Christmas Together QX6465	Yr.Iss.	1997	10.95	5-20
1997 Our First Christmas Together-Acrylic QX3182	Yr.Iss.	1997	7.95	5-15
1997 Our First Christmas Together-Photo Holder QX6472	Yr.Iss.	1997	8.95	17-25
1997 Sister to Sister QX6635	Yr.Iss.	1997	9.95	7-21
1997 Son QX6605	Yr.Iss.	1997	7.95	16-20
1997 Special Dog-Photo Holder QX6632	Yr.Iss.	1997	7.95	8-17

1997 Disney Ornaments - Keepsake

YEAR ISSUE	EDITION LIMIT	YEAR RETD.	ISSUE PRICE	*QUOTE U.S.$
1997 Ariel QX14072	Yr.Iss.	1997	12.95	24-26
1997 Bandleader Mickey (1st Ed.) QXD4022	Yr.Iss.	1997	13.95	12-24
1997 Cinderella (1st Ed.) QXD4045	Yr.Iss.	1997	14.95	18-30
1997 Donald's Surprising Gift (1st Ed.) QXD4025	Yr.Iss.	1997	12.95	12-40
1997 Esmeralda & Phoebus QXD6344	Yr.Iss.	1997	14.95	8-24
1997 Goofy's Ski Adventure QXD4042	Yr.Iss.	1997	12.95	17-24
1997 Gus & Jaq QXD4052	Yr.Iss.	1997	12.95	13-30
1997 Hercules QXI4005	Yr.Iss.	1997	12.95	10-26
1997 Honey of a Gift (Miniature) QXD4255	Yr.Iss.	1997	6.95	7-15
1997 Jasmine & Aladdin QXD4062	Yr.Iss.	1997	14.95	8-27
1997 Megara and Pegasus QXI4012	Yr.Iss.	1997	16.95	31-34
1997 Mickey Snow Angel QXD4035	Yr.Iss.	1997	9.95	8-18
1997 Mickey's Long Shot QXD6412	Yr.Iss.	1997	10.95	7-28
1997 New Pair of Skates QXD4032	Yr.Iss.	1997	13.95	25-28
1997 Snow White (Anniversary Ed.) QXD4055	Yr.Iss.	1997	16.95	16-31
1997 Timon & Pumbaa QXD4065	Yr.Iss.	1997	12.95	13-26
1997 Two Tone QXD4015	Yr.Iss.	1997	9.95	10-18
1997 Waitin' on Santa QXD6365	Yr.Iss.	1997	12.95	8-26
1997 Winnie the Pooh Plate QXE6835	Yr.Iss.	1997	12.95	13-24

1997 Keepsake Collector's Club - Keepsake

YEAR ISSUE	EDITION LIMIT	YEAR RETD.	ISSUE PRICE	*QUOTE U.S.$
1997 1937 Steelcraft Airflow by Murray® QXC5185	Yr.Iss.	1997	15.95	32-50
1997 1989 Happy Holidays® Barbie™ Doll QXC5162	Yr.Iss.	1997	15.95	25-52
1997 Away to the Window QXC5135	Yr.Iss.	1997	N/A	14
1997 Farmer's Market, Tender Touches QXC5182	Yr.Iss.	1997	15.00	20-36
1997 Happy Christmas to All! QXC5132	Yr.Iss.	1997	N/A	16-18
1997 Jolly Old Santa QXC5145	Yr.Iss.	1997	N/A	9-14
1997 Mrs. Claus (Artist on Tour) QXC5192	Yr.Iss.	1997	14.95	10-26
1997 Ready for Santa QXC5142	Yr.Iss.	1997	N/A	9-12
1997 Trimming Santa's Tree (Artist on Tour) QXC5175	Yr.Iss.	1997	60.00	40-76

1997 Keepsake Magic Ornaments - Keepsake

YEAR ISSUE	EDITION LIMIT	YEAR RETD.	ISSUE PRICE	*QUOTE U.S.$
1997 Chris Mouse Luminaria (13th Ed.) QLX7525	Yr.Iss.	1997	14.95	27-30
1997 Decorator Taz QLX7502	Yr.Iss.	1997	30.00	20-60
1997 Friendship 7 (2nd Ed.) QLX7532	Yr.Iss.	1997	24.00	18-51
1997 Glowing Angel QLX7435	Yr.Iss.	1997	18.95	14-39
1997 Holiday Serenade QLX7485	Yr.Iss.	1997	24.00	43-48
1997 Joy to the World QLX7512	Yr.Iss.	1997	14.95	12-30
1997 Lighthouse Greetings (1st Ed.) QLX7442	Yr.Iss.	1997	24.00	45-75
1997 The Lincoln Memorial QLX7522	Yr.Iss.	1997	24.00	43-48
1997 Madonna & Child QLX7425	Yr.Iss.	1997	19.95	36-50
1997 Motorcycle Chums QLX7495	Yr.Iss.	1997	24.00	41-45
1997 Santa's Secret Gift QLX7455	Yr.Iss.	1997	24.00	43-48
1997 Santa's Showboat (Special Ed.) QLX7465	Yr.Iss.	1997	42.00	77-85
1997 SNOOPY Plays Santa QLX7475	Yr.Iss.	1997	22.00	16-44
1997 Teapot Party QLX7482	Yr.Iss.	1997	18.95	34-38

1997 Miniature Ornaments - Keepsake

YEAR ISSUE	EDITION LIMIT	YEAR RETD.	ISSUE PRICE	*QUOTE U.S.$
1997 Antique Tractors (1st Ed.) QXM4185	Yr.Iss.	1997	6.95	10-23
1997 Candy Car (9th Ed.) QXM4175	Yr.Iss.	1997	6.95	7-15
1997 Casablanca, set/3 QXM4272	Yr.Iss.	1997	19.95	18-36
1997 Centuries of Santa (4th Ed.) QXM4295	Yr.Iss.	1997	5.95	12
1997 Christmas Bells (3rd Ed.) QXM4162	Yr.Iss.	1997	4.95	13-20
1997 Clothespin Soldier (3rd Ed.) QXM4155	Yr.Iss.	1997	4.95	4-11
1997 Future Star QXM4232	Yr.Iss.	1997	5.95	4-12
1997 Gentle Giraffes QXM4221	Yr.Iss.	1997	5.95	6-15
1997 He Is Born QXM4235	Yr.Iss.	1997	7.95	6-15
1997 Heavenly Music QXM4292	Yr.Iss.	1997	5.95	4-12
1997 Herr Drosselmeyer (2nd Ed.) QXM4135	Yr.Iss.	1997	5.95	12-15
1997 Home Sweet Home QXM4222	Yr.Iss.	1997	5.95	5-13
1997 Ice Cold Coca-Cola® QXM4252	Yr.Iss.	1997	6.95	14-16
1997 King of the Forest QXM4262	Yr.Iss.	1997	24.00	25-45
1997 Murray "Pursuit" Airplane (3rd Ed.) QXM4132	Yr.Iss.	1997	6.95	6-14
1997 Nutcracker Guild (4th Ed.) QXM4165	Yr.Iss.	1997	6.95	6-16
1997 On The Road (5th Ed.) QXM4172	Yr.Iss.	1997	5.95	5-12
1997 Our Lady of Guadalupe (Precious Ed.) QXM4275	Yr.Iss.	1997	8.95	17-19
1997 Peppermint Painter QXM4312	Yr.Iss.	1997	4.95	5-12
1997 Polar Buddies QXM4332	Yr.Iss.	1997	4.95	5-12
1997 Rocking Horse (10th Ed.) QXM4302	Yr.Iss.	1997	4.95	5-15
1997 Santa's Little Big Top (3rd Ed.) QXM4152	Yr.Iss.	1997	6.95	14
1997 Seeds of Joy QXM4242	Yr.Iss.	1997	6.95	5-14
1997 Sew Talented QXM4195	Yr.Iss.	1997	5.95	5-14
1997 Shutterbug QXM4212	Yr.Iss.	1997	5.95	5-14
1997 Snowboard Bunny QXM4315	Yr.Iss.	1997	4.95	4-12
1997 Snowflake Ballet (1st Ed.) QXM4192	Yr.Iss.	1997	5.95	6-14
1997 Teddy-Bear Style (1st Ed.) QXM4215	Yr.Iss.	1997	5.95	3-15
1997 Tiny Home Improvers,set/6 QXM4282	Yr.Iss.	1997	29.00	31-44
1997 Victorian Skater QXM4305	Yr.Iss.	1997	5.95	4-12
1997 Village Depot (10th Ed.) QXM4182	Yr.Iss.	1997	6.95	7-15
1997 Welcome Friends, set/4 (1st Ed.) QXM4205	Yr.Iss.	1997	6.95	15-20
1997 White Rabbit (3rd Ed.) QXM4142	Yr.Iss.	1997	6.95	8-17

1997 NBA Collection - Keepsake

YEAR ISSUE	EDITION LIMIT	YEAR RETD.	ISSUE PRICE	*QUOTE U.S.$
1997 Charlotte Hornets QSR1222	Yr.Iss.	1997	9.95	10
1997 Chicago Bulls QSR1232	Yr.Iss.	1997	9.95	20
1997 Detroit Pistons QSR1242	Yr.Iss.	1997	9.95	10
1997 Houston Rockets QSR1245	Yr.Iss.	1997	9.95	10
1997 Indiana Pacers QSR1252	Yr.Iss.	1997	9.95	18-20
1997 Los Angeles Lakers QSR1262	Yr.Iss.	1997	9.95	10
1997 New York Knickerbockers QSR1272	Yr.Iss.	1997	9.95	10
1997 Orlando Magic QSR1282	Yr.Iss.	1997	9.95	10
1997 Phoenix Suns QSR1292	Yr.Iss.	1997	9.95	10
1997 Seattle Supersonics QSR1295	Yr.Iss.	1997	9.95	10

1997 New Attractions - Keepsake

YEAR ISSUE	EDITION LIMIT	YEAR RETD.	ISSUE PRICE	*QUOTE U.S.$
1997 All-Round Sports Fan QX6392	Yr.Iss.	1997	8.95	9-30
1997 All-Weather Walker QX6415	Yr.Iss.	1997	8.95	16-18
1997 Angel Friend (Archive Collection) QX6762	Yr.Iss.	1997	14.95	29-32
1997 Biking Buddies QX6682	Yr.Iss.	1997	12.95	5-23
1997 Breezin' Along QX6722	Yr.Iss.	1997	8.95	6-17
1997 Bucket Brigade QX6382	Yr.Iss.	1997	8.95	5-16
1997 Catch of the Day QX6712	Yr.Iss.	1997	9.95	5-18
1997 Christmas Checkup QX6385	Yr.Iss.	1997	7.95	8-16
1997 Classic Cross QX6805	Yr.Iss.	1997	13.95	14
1997 Clever Camper QX6445	Yr.Iss.	1997	7.95	8-15
1997 Cycling Santa QX6425	Yr.Iss.	1997	14.95	27-30
1997 Downhill Run QX6705	Yr.Iss.	1997	9.95	18-20
1997 Elegance on Ice QX6432	Yr.Iss.	1997	9.95	19-21
1997 Expressly for Teacher QX6375	Yr.Iss.	1997	7.95	8-16
1997 Feliz Navidad QX6665	Yr.Iss.	1997	8.95	28-30
1997 God's Gift of Love QX6792	Yr.Iss.	1997	16.95	31-34
1997 Heavenly Song (Archive Collection) QX6795	Yr.Iss.	1997	12.95	26
1997 Howdy Doody (Anniversary Ed.) QX6272	Yr.Iss.	1997	12.95	13-24
1997 The Incredible Hulk QX5471	Yr.Iss.	1997	12.95	20-26
1997 Jingle Bell Jester QX6695	Yr.Iss.	1997	9.95	18-20
1997 Juggling Stars QX6595	Yr.Iss.	1997	9.95	6-20
1997 King Noor-First King QX6552	Yr.Iss.	1997	12.95	40-45
1997 Lion and Lamb QX6602	Yr.Iss.	1997	7.95	16-18
1997 The Lone Ranger QX6265	Yr.Iss.	1997	12.95	20-38
1997 Love to Sew QX6435	Yr.Iss.	1997	7.95	8-17
1997 Madonna del Rosario QX6545	Yr.Iss.	1997	12.95	24-26
1997 Marbles Champion QX6342	Yr.Iss.	1997	10.95	4-22
1997 Meadow Snowman QX6715	Yr.Iss.	1997	12.95	30-33
1997 Michigan J. Frog QX6332	Yr.Iss.	1997	9.95	10-20
1997 Miss Gulch QX6372	Yr.Iss.	1997	13.95	28-30
1997 Mr. Potato Head QX6335	Yr.Iss.	1997	10.95	24
1997 Nativity Tree QX6575	Yr.Iss.	1997	14.95	29-32
1997 The Night Before Christmas -Collector's Choice QX5721	Yr.Iss.	1997	24.00	24-55
1997 Playful Shepherd QX6592	Yr.Iss.	1997	9.95	18-20
1997 Porcelain Hinged Box QX6772	Yr.Iss.	1997	14.95	15-27
1997 Praise Him QX6542	Yr.Iss.	1997	8.95	9-18
1997 Prize Topiary QX6675	Yr.Iss.	1997	14.95	15-30
1997 Sailor Bear QX6765	Yr.Iss.	1997	14.95	27-30
1997 Santa Mail QX6702	Yr.Iss.	1997	10.95	11-23
1997 Santa's Friend QX6685	Yr.Iss.	1997	12.95	24-27
1997 Santa's Magical Sleigh QX6672	Yr.Iss.	1997	24.00	43-48
1997 Santa's Polar Friend (Archive Collection) QX6755	Yr.Iss.	1997	16.95	32-35
1997 Santa's Ski Adventure QX6422	Yr.Iss.	1997	12.95	13-27
1997 Snow Bowling QX6395	Yr.Iss.	1997	6.95	7-15
1997 Snow Girl QX6562	Yr.Iss.	1997	7.95	4-17
1997 The Spirit of Christmas-Collector's Plate QX6585	Yr.Iss.	1997	9.95	27
1997 Stealing a Kiss QX6555	Yr.Iss.	1997	14.95	27-30
1997 Sweet Discovery QX6325	Yr.Iss.	1997	11.95	22-24
1997 Sweet Dreamer QX6732	Yr.Iss.	1997	6.95	7-15
1997 Swinging in the Snow QX6775	Yr.Iss.	1997	12.95	13-26
1997 Taking a Break QX6305	Yr.Iss.	1997	14.95	25-30
1997 Tomorrow's Leader QX6452	Yr.Iss.	1997	9.95	10
1997 Tonka® Mighty Front Loader QX6362	Yr.Iss.	1997	13.95	28-30
1997 What a Deal! QX6442	Yr.Iss.	1997	8.95	5-18

1997 NFL Ornaments - Keepsake

YEAR ISSUE	EDITION LIMIT	YEAR RETD.	ISSUE PRICE	*QUOTE U.S.$
1997 Arizona Cardinals QSR5505	Yr.Iss.	1997	9.95	10
1997 Atlanta Falcons QSR5305	Yr.Iss.	1997	9.95	10
1997 Baltimore Ravens QSR5352	Yr.Iss.	1997	9.95	10-20
1997 Buffalo Bills QSR5312	Yr.Iss.	1997	9.95	10
1997 Carolina Panthers QSR5315	Yr.Iss.	1997	9.95	10-20
1997 Chicago Bears QSR5322	Yr.Iss.	1997	9.95	10-20

*Quotes have been rounded up to nearest dollar

YEAR ISSUE	EDITION LIMIT	YEAR RETD.	ISSUE PRICE	*QUOTE U.S.$
1997 Cincinnati Bengals QSR5325	Yr.Iss.	1997	9.95	10
1997 Dallas Cowboys QSR5355	Yr.Iss.	1997	9.95	10-20
1997 Denver Broncos QSR5362	Yr.Iss.	1997	9.95	10-30
1997 Detroit Lions QSR5365	Yr.Iss.	1997	9.95	10
1997 Green Bay Packers QSR5372	Yr.Iss.	1997	9.95	22-25
1997 Houston Oilers QSR5375	Yr.Iss.	1997	9.95	10-18
1997 Indianapolis Colts QSR5411	Yr.Iss.	1997	9.95	10
1997 Jacksonville Jaquars QSR5415	Yr.Iss.	1997	9.95	10-20
1997 Kansas City Chiefs QSR5502	Yr.Iss.	1997	9.95	10-20
1997 Miami Dolphins QSR5472	Yr.Iss.	1997	9.95	10-20
1997 Minnesota Vikings QSR5475	Yr.Iss.	1997	9.95	10-20
1997 New England Patriots QSR5482	Yr.Iss.	1997	9.95	10-18
1997 New Orleans Saints QSR5485	Yr.Iss.	1997	9.95	10
1997 New York Giants QSR5492	Yr.Iss.	1997	9.95	10
1997 New York Jets QSR5495	Yr.Iss.	1997	9.95	10
1997 Oakland Raiders QSR5422	Yr.Iss.	1997	9.95	10-20
1997 Philadelphia Eagles QSR5502	Yr.Iss.	1997	9.95	10
1997 Pittsburgh Steelers QSR5512	Yr.Iss.	1997	9.95	10-20
1997 San Diego Chargers QSR5515	Yr.Iss.	1997	9.95	10-20
1997 San Francisco 49ers QSR5522	Yr.Iss.	1997	9.95	4-20
1997 Seattle Seahawks QSR5525	Yr.Iss.	1997	9.95	10
1997 St. Louis Rams QSR5425	Yr.Iss.	1997	9.95	10
1997 Tampa Bay Buccaneers QSR5532	Yr.Iss.	1997	9.95	10
1997 Washington Redskins QSR5535	Yr.Iss.	1997	9.95	10

1997 Premiere Event - Keepsake

YEAR ISSUE	EDITION LIMIT	YEAR RETD.	ISSUE PRICE	*QUOTE U.S.$
1997 The Perfect Tree-Tender Touches QX6572	Yr.Iss.	1997	15.00	27-30

1997 Showcase Folk Art Americana Collection - Keepsake

YEAR ISSUE	EDITION LIMIT	YEAR RETD.	ISSUE PRICE	*QUOTE U.S.$
1997 Leading the Way QX6782	Yr.Iss.	1997	16.95	17-35
1997 Santa's Merry Path QX6785	Yr.Iss.	1997	16.95	33-36

1997 Showcase Nature's Sketchbook Collection - Keepsake

YEAR ISSUE	EDITION LIMIT	YEAR RETD.	ISSUE PRICE	*QUOTE U.S.$
1997 Garden Bouquet QX6752	Yr.Iss.	1997	14.95	15-30
1997 Garden Bunnies QEO8702	Yr.Iss.	1997	14.95	18-30
1997 Honored Guest QX6745	Yr.Iss.	1997	14.95	30-33

1997 Showcase The Language of Flowers Collection - Keepsake

YEAR ISSUE	EDITION LIMIT	YEAR RETD.	ISSUE PRICE	*QUOTE U.S.$
1997 Snowdrop Angel (2nd Ed.) QX1095	Yr.Iss.	1997	15.95	15-31

1997 Showcase Turn-of-the-Century Parade Collection - Keepsake

YEAR ISSUE	EDITION LIMIT	YEAR RETD.	ISSUE PRICE	*QUOTE U.S.$
1997 Santa Claus (3rd Ed.) QX1215	Yr.Iss.	1997	16.95	15-31

1997 Special Issues - Keepsake

YEAR ISSUE	EDITION LIMIT	YEAR RETD.	ISSUE PRICE	*QUOTE U.S.$
1997 1997 Corvette Miniature QXI4322	Yr.Iss.	1997	6.95	12-14
1997 1997 Corvette QXI6455	Yr.Iss.	1997	13.95	8-25
1997 Ariel QXI4072	Yr.Iss.	1997	12.95	18-26
1997 Barbie™ And Ken Wedding Day QXI6815	Yr.Iss.	1997	35.00	51-55
1997 Barbie™ Wedding Day-1959-1962 (4th Ed.) QXI6812	Yr.Iss.	1997	15.95	30-32
1997 C-3PO & R2-D2 QXI4265	Yr.Iss.	1997	12.95	13-28
1997 Commander Data QXI6345	Yr.Iss.	1997	14.95	21-30
1997 Darth Vader QXI7531	Yr.Iss.	1997	24.00	45-48
1997 Dr. Leonard H. McCoy QXI6352	Yr.Iss.	1997	14.95	29-32
1997 Hank Aaron (2nd Ed.) QXI6152	Yr.Iss.	1997	14.95	15-27
1997 Holiday Barbie™(5th Ed.) QXI6212	Yr.Iss.	1997	15.95	29-32
1997 Jeff Gordon (1st Ed.) QXI6165	Yr.Iss.	1997	15.95	25-50
1997 Joe Namath (3rd Ed.) QXI6182	Yr.Iss.	1997	14.95	15-28
1997 Luke Skywalker (1st Ed.) QXI5484	Yr.Iss.	1997	13.95	20-32
1997 Magic Johnson (3rd Ed.) QXI6832	Yr.Iss.	1997	14.95	15-27
1997 U.S.S. Defiant QXI7481	Yr.Iss.	1997	24.00	44-48
1997 Victorian Christmas-Thomas Kinkade (1st Ed.) QXI6135	Yr.Iss.	1997	10.95	26-30
1997 The Warmth of Home QXI7545	Yr.Iss.	1997	18.95	20-37
1997 Wayne Gretzky (1st Ed.) QXI6275	Yr.Iss.	1997	15.95	26-33
1997 Yoda QXI6355	Yr.Iss.	1997	9.95	20-40

1997 Spring Ornaments - Keepsake

YEAR ISSUE	EDITION LIMIT	YEAR RETD.	ISSUE PRICE	*QUOTE U.S.$
1997 1935 Steelcraft Streamline Velocipede by Murray® (1st Ed.) QEO8632	Yr.Iss.	1997	12.95	16-29
1997 Apple Blossom Lane QEO8662	Yr.Iss.	1997	8.95	11-16
1997 Barbie™ as Rapunzel Doll (1st Ed.) QEO8635	Yr.Iss.	1997	14.95	9-32
1997 Bumper Crop, Tender Touches QEO8735	Yr.Iss.	1997	14.95	18-27
1997 Collector's Plate QEO8675	Yr.Iss.	1997	7.95	8-15
1997 Colorful Coal Car (2nd Ed.) QEO8652	Yr.Iss.	1997	8.95	12-18
1997 Digging In QEO8712	Yr.Iss.	1997	7.95	10-16
1997 Eggs-pert Artist QEO8695	Yr.Iss.	1997	8.95	19
1997 Garden Club QEO8665	Yr.Iss.	1997	7.95	16-18
1997 Gentle Guardian QEO8732	Yr.Iss.	1997	6.95	14-16
1997 Here Comes Easter QEO8682	Yr.Iss.	1997	7.95	15-18
1997 Jemima Puddle-Duck (2nd Ed.) QEO8645	Yr.Iss.	1997	8.95	10-26
1997 Joyful Angels QEO8655	Yr.Iss.	1997	10.95	15-22
1997 A Purr-fect Princess QEO8715	Yr.Iss.	1997	7.95	11-16
1997 Springtime Barbie™ QEO8642	Yr.Iss.	1997	12.95	14-25
1997 Springtime Bonnets QEO8672	Yr.Iss.	1997	7.95	16-18
1997 Swing-Time QEO8705	Yr.Iss.	1997	7.95	15-17
1997 Victorian Cross QEO8725	Yr.Iss.	1997	8.95	11-19

1998 25th Anniversary - Keepsake

YEAR ISSUE	EDITION LIMIT	YEAR RETD.	ISSUE PRICE	*QUOTE U.S.$
1998 Angelic Flight QXI4146	25,000	1998	85.00	85-125
1998 Halls Station QX6833	Yr.Iss.	1998	25.00	45-50
1998 Joyful Messenger QXI4146	Yr.Iss.	1998	18.95	36-40
1998 Tin Locomotive QX6826	Yr.Iss.	1998	25.00	45-50

1998 Collectible Series - Keepsake

YEAR ISSUE	EDITION LIMIT	YEAR RETD.	ISSUE PRICE	*QUOTE U.S.$
1998 1917 Curtiss JN-4D "Jenny" (2nd Ed.) QX6286	Yr.Iss.	1998	14.95	21-28
1998 1937 Ford V-8 (4th Ed.) QX6263	Yr.Iss.	1998	13.95	21-24
1998 1955 Murray® Tractor and Trailer (5th Ed.) QX6376	Yr.Iss.	1998	16.95	20-26
1998 1970 Plymouth Hemi 'Cuda (8th Ed.) QX6256	Yr.Iss.	1998	13.95	18-27
1998 Bright Sledding Colors (10th Ed.) QX6166	Yr.Iss.	1998	12.95	18-23
1998 Cat Naps (5th Ed.) QX6383	Yr.Iss.	1998	8.95	12-18
1998 A Celebration of Angels (4th Ed.) QX6366	Yr.Iss.	1998	13.95	14-26
1998 The Clauses on Vacation (2nd Ed.) QX6276	Yr.Iss.	1998	14.95	18-20
1998 Daphne-Mary's Angels (11th Ed.) QX6153	Yr.Iss.	1998	7.95	12-16
1998 Fabulous Decade (9th Ed.) QX6393	Yr.Iss.	1998	7.95	20-30
1998 Frosty Friends (19th Ed.) QX6226	Yr.Iss.	1998	10.95	15-33
1998 Glorious Angel (1st Ed.) QX6493	Yr.Iss.	1998	14.95	18-27
1998 Grocery Store (15th Ed.) QX6266	Yr.Iss.	1998	16.95	27-30
1998 Joe Cool (1st Ed.) QX6453	Yr.Iss.	1998	9.95	20-22
1998 Marilyn Monroe (2nd Ed.) QX6333	Yr.Iss.	1998	14.95	15-27
1998 Merry Olde Santa (9th Ed.) QX6386	Yr.Iss.	1998	15.95	16-30
1998 Mexican Barbie™ (3rd Ed.) QX6356	Yr.Iss.	1998	14.95	27-30
1998 Mop Top Wendy (3rd Ed.) QX6353	Yr.Iss.	1998	14.95	20-25
1998 Pennsylvania GG-1 Locomotive (3rd Ed.) QX6346	Yr.Iss.	1998	18.95	28-35
1998 Pony Express Rider (1st Ed.) QX6323	Yr.Iss.	1998	13.95	20-27
1998 A Pony for Christmas (1st Ed.) QX6316	Yr.Iss.	1998	10.95	28-30
1998 Puppy Love (8th Ed.) QX6163	Yr.Iss.	1998	7.95	12-15
1998 Ricky-All God's Children®-Martha Root (3rd Ed.) QX6363	Yr.Iss.	1998	12.95	23
1998 Santa's Bumper Car (20th Ed.) QX6283	Yr.Iss.	1998	14.95	27-30
1998 Scarlett O'Hara (2nd Ed.) QX6336	Yr.Iss.	1998	14.95	21-27
1998 Snow Buddies (1st Ed.) QX6853	Yr.Iss.	1998	7.95	20-27
1998 Timber Wolves at Play-Mark Newman (2nd Ed.) QX6273	Yr.Iss.	1998	12.95	15-28
1998 A Visit From Piglet (1st Ed.) QXD4086	Yr.Iss.	1998	13.95	14-28
1998 Yuletide Central (5th Ed.) QX6373	Yr.Iss.	1998	18.95	32-50

1998 Collegiate Ornaments - Keepsake

YEAR ISSUE	EDITION LIMIT	YEAR RETD.	ISSUE PRICE	*QUOTE U.S.$
1998 Florida State Seminoles™ QSR2316	Yr.Iss.	1998	9.95	10
1998 Michigan Wolverines™ QSR2323	Yr.Iss.	1998	9.95	10
1998 North Carolina Tar Heels™ QSR2333	Yr.Iss.	1998	9.95	10
1998 Notre Dame® Fighting Irish™ QSR2313	Yr.Iss.	1998	9.95	10-14
1998 Penn State Nittany Lions™ QSR2326	Yr.Iss.	1998	9.95	10

1998 Commemoratives - Keepsake

YEAR ISSUE	EDITION LIMIT	YEAR RETD.	ISSUE PRICE	*QUOTE U.S.$
1998 #1 Student QX6646	Yr.Iss.	1998	7.95	6-17
1998 Baby's Fifth Christmas QX6623	Yr.Iss.	1998	7.95	16
1998 Baby's First Christmas QX6233	Yr.Iss.	1998	9.95	18-20
1998 Baby's First Christmas QX6586	Yr.Iss.	1998	9.95	19
1998 Baby's First Christmas QX6596	Yr.Iss.	1998	8.95	7-20
1998 Baby's First Christmas QX6603	Yr.Iss.	1998	7.95	16-25
1998 Baby's Fourth Christmas QX6616	Yr.Iss.	1998	7.95	16
1998 Baby's Second Christmas QX6606	Yr.Iss.	1998	7.95	16-18
1998 Baby's Third Christmas QX6613	Yr.Iss.	1998	7.95	16-20
1998 Chatty Chipmunk QX6716	Yr.Iss.	1998	9.95	8-22
1998 Dad QX6663	Yr.Iss.	1998	8.95	17
1998 Daughter QX6673	Yr.Iss.	1998	8.95	16
1998 Forever Friends Bear QX6303	Yr.Iss.	1998	8.95	16-18
1998 Friend of My Heart QX6723	Yr.Iss.	1998	14.95	27-30
1998 Godchild QX6703	Yr.Iss.	1998	7.95	6-17
1998 Granddaughter QX6683	Yr.Iss.	1998	7.95	14-16
1998 Grandma's Memories QX6686	Yr.Iss.	1998	8.95	7-18
1998 Grandson QX6676	Yr.Iss.	1998	7.95	15
1998 Mom and Dad QX6653	Yr.Iss.	1998	9.95	8-20
1998 Mom QX6656	Yr.Iss.	1998	8.95	17
1998 Mother and Daughter QX6696	Yr.Iss.	1998	8.95	7-25
1998 New Arrival QX6306	Yr.Iss.	1998	18.95	14-30
1998 New Home QX6713	Yr.Iss.	1998	9.95	8-23
1998 Our First Christmas Together QX3193	Yr.Iss.	1998	7.95	15-20
1998 Our First Christmas Together QX6636	Yr.Iss.	1998	8.95	7-20
1998 Our First Christmas Together QX6643	Yr.Iss.	1998	18.95	33-36
1998 A Perfect Match QX6633	Yr.Iss.	1998	10.95	8-22
1998 Sister to Sister QX6693	Yr.Iss.	1998	8.95	17
1998 Son QX6666	Yr.Iss.	1998	8.95	16
1998 Special Dog QX6606	Yr.Iss.	1998	7.95	6-16

1998 Crown Reflections - Keepsake

YEAR ISSUE	EDITION LIMIT	YEAR RETD.	ISSUE PRICE	*QUOTE U.S.$
1998 1955 Murray® Fire Truck QBG6909	Yr.Iss.	1998	35.00	41-48
1998 Festive Locomotive QBG6903	Yr.Iss.	1998	35.00	29-32
1998 Frankincense QBG6896	2-Yr.		22.00	22
1998 Frosty Friends, set/2 QBG6907	Yr.Iss.	1998	48.00	55-60
1998 Gold QBG6836	2-Yr.		22.00	22
1998 Myrrh QBG6893	2-Yr.		22.00	22
1998 Pink Poinsettias QBG6926	Yr.Iss.	1998	25.00	32-35
1998 Red Poinsettias (1st) QBG6906	Yr.Iss.	1998	35.00	43-48
1998 Sugarplum Cottage QBG6917	Yr.Iss.	1998	35.00	41-45
1998 Sweet Memories, set/8 QBG6933	Yr.Iss.	1998	45.00	45-60
1998 White Poinsettias QBG6923	Yr.Iss.	1998	25.00	32-35

1998 Disney Ornaments - Keepsake

YEAR ISSUE	EDITION LIMIT	YEAR RETD.	ISSUE PRICE	*QUOTE U.S.$
1998 Bouncy Baby-sitter QXD4096	Yr.Iss.	1998	12.95	14-24
1998 Building a Snowman QXD4133	Yr.Iss.	1998	14.95	25-28
1998 Buzz Lightyear QXD4066	Yr.Iss.	1998	14.95	29
1998 Cinderella's Coach QXD4083	Yr.Iss.	1998	14.95	21-28
1998 Cruella de Vil (1st Ed.) QXD4063	Yr.Iss.	1998	14.95	18-24
1998 Daydreams QXD4136	Yr.Iss.	1998	13.95	27-30
1998 Donald and Daisy in Venice (1st Ed.) QXD4103	Yr.Iss.	1998	14.95	18-26
1998 Flik QXD4153	Yr.Iss.	1998	12.95	27-30
1998 Goofy Soccer Star QXD4123	Yr.Iss.	1998	10.95	21-23
1998 Iago, Abu amd the Genie QXD4076	Yr.Iss.	1998	12.95	25
1998 Make-Believe Boat QXD4113	Yr.Iss.	1998	12.95	13-25
1998 The Mickey and Minnie Handcar QXD4116	Yr.Iss.	1998	14.95	22-26
1998 Mickey's Favorite Reindeer QXD4013	Yr.Iss.	1998	13.95	25-28
1998 Minnie Plays the Flute (2nd Ed.) QXD4106	Yr.Iss.	1998	13.95	14-22
1998 Mulan, Mushu and Cri-Kee QXD4156	Yr.Iss.	1998	14.95	29
1998 Princess Aurora QXD4126	Yr.Iss.	1998	12.95	15-27
1998 Ready For Christmas (2nd Ed.) QXD4006	Yr.Iss.	1998	12.95	15-23
1998 Runaway Toboggan QXD4003	Yr.Iss.	1998	16.95	17-33
1998 Simba & Nala QXD4073	Yr.Iss.	1998	13.95	14-28
1998 Tree Trimmin' Time,set/3 QXD4236	Yr.Iss.	1998	19.95	20-39
1998 A Visit From Piglet QXD4086	Yr.Iss.	1998	13.95	16-24
1998 Walt Disney's Snow White (2nd Ed.) QXD4056	Yr.Iss.	1998	14.95	17-26
1998 Woody the Sheriff QXD4163	Yr.Iss.	1998	14.95	18-27

1998 Holiday Traditions - Keepsake

YEAR ISSUE	EDITION LIMIT	YEAR RETD.	ISSUE PRICE	*QUOTE U.S.$
1998 A Child Is Born QX6176	Yr.Iss.	1998	12.95	13-23
1998 A Christmas Eve Story QX6873	Yr.Iss.	1998	13.95	14-24
1998 Christmas Request QX6193	Yr.Iss.	1998	14.95	15-21
1998 Christmas Sleigh Ride QX6556	Yr.Iss.	1998	12.95	13-26
1998 Cross of Peace QX6856	Yr.Iss.	1998	9.95	10-20
1998 Cruising Into Christmas QX6196	Yr.Iss.	1998	16.95	30-33
1998 Fancy Footwork QX6536	Yr.Iss.	1998	8.95	16
1998 Feliz Navidad QX6173	Yr.Iss.	1998	8.95	17
1998 Guardian Friend QX6543	Yr.Iss.	1998	8.95	9-18
1998 Heavenly Melody (Archive Collection) QX6576	Yr.Iss.	1998	18.95	19-40
1998 Holiday Decorator QX6566	Yr.Iss.	1998	13.95	14-21
1998 The Holy Family, set/3 QX6523	3-Yr.		25.00	25
1998 Journey To Bethlehem (Collector's Choice) QX6223	Yr.Iss.	1998	16.95	27-30
1998 King Kharoof-Second King QX6186	Yr.Iss.	1998	12.95	26
1998 Madonna and Child QX6516	Yr.Iss.	1998	12.95	27
1998 Memories of Christmas QX2406	Yr.Iss.	1998	5.95	12
1998 Merry Chime QX6692	Yr.Iss.	1998	9.95	20-23
1998 Miracle in Bethlehem QX6513	Yr.Iss.	1998	12.95	30-34
1998 Mistletoe Fairy QX6216	Yr.Iss.	1998	12.95	29
1998 Nick's Wish List QX6863	Yr.Iss.	1998	8.95	9-18
1998 Night Watch QX6725	Yr.Iss.	1998	9.95	10-20
1998 Our Song QX6183	Yr.Iss.	1998	9.95	18
1998 Peekaboo Bears QX6563	Yr.Iss.	1998	12.95	15-29
1998 Purr-fect Little Deer QX6526	Yr.Iss.	1998	7.95	8-15
1998 Santa's Deer Friend QX6583	Yr.Iss.	1998	24.00	56
1998 Santa's Flying Machine QX6573	Yr.Iss.	1998	16.95	34-38
1998 Santa's Hidden Surprise QX6913	Yr.Iss.	1998	14.95	27-30
1998 Sweet Rememberings QX6876	Yr.Iss.	1998	8.95	9-18
1998 Treetop Choir QX6506	Yr.Iss.	1998	9.95	10-20
1998 Warm and Cozy QX6866	Yr.Iss.	1998	8.95	9-19
1998 Watchful Shepherd QX6496	Yr.Iss.	1998	8.95	18
1998 Writing to Santa QX6533	Yr.Iss.	1998	7.95	8-16

1998 Keepsake Collector's Club - Keepsake

YEAR ISSUE	EDITION LIMIT	YEAR RETD.	ISSUE PRICE	*QUOTE U.S.$
1998 1935 Steelcraft by Murray®	Yr.Iss.	1998	15.95	25-54
1998 1990 Happy Holidays® Barbie™ Doll	Yr.Iss.	1998	15.95	25-38
1998 Follow The Leader, set/2	Yr.Iss.	1998	16.95	32
1998 Kringle Bells	Yr.Iss.	1998	N/A	13
1998 Making His Way	Yr.Iss.	1998	N/A	21
1998 New Christmas Friend	Yr.Iss.	1998	N/A	14

1998 Keepsake Magic Ornaments - Keepsake

YEAR ISSUE	EDITION LIMIT	YEAR RETD.	ISSUE PRICE	*QUOTE U.S.$
1998 1998 Corvette® QLX7605	Yr.Iss.	1998	24.00	47
1998 Apollo Lunar Module (3rd Ed.) QLX7543	Yr.Iss.	1998	24.00	30-49
1998 Cinderella at the Ball QXD7576	Yr.Iss.	1998	24.00	19-52
1998 Lighthouse Greetings (2nd Ed.) QLX7536	Yr.Iss.	1998	24.00	35-50
1998 Mickey's Comet QXD7586	Yr.Iss.	1998	24.00	24-48
1998 Santa's Show 'n' Tell QLX7566	Yr.Iss.	1998	18.95	19-40
1998 Santa's Spin Top QLX7573	Yr.Iss.	1998	22.00	43
1998 St. Nicholas Circle QXI7556	Yr.Iss.	1998	18.95	28-40
1998 The Stone Church (1st Ed.) QLX7636	Yr.Iss.	1998	18.95	35-48
1998 U.S.S. Enterprise™ NCC-1701-E QXI7633	Yr.Iss.	1998	24.00	36-45
1998 The Washington Monument QLX7553	Yr.Iss.	1998	24.00	25-45
1998 X-wing Starfighter™ QXI7596	Yr.Iss.	1998	24.00	30-39

1998 Lifestyles & Occupations - Keepsake

YEAR ISSUE	EDITION LIMIT	YEAR RETD.	ISSUE PRICE	*QUOTE U.S.$
1998 Catch of the Season QX6786	Yr.Iss.	1998	14.95	27-30
1998 Checking Santa's Files QX6806	Yr.Iss.	1998	8.95	9-18
1998 Compact Skater QX6766	Yr.Iss.	1998	9.95	19-21
1998 Downhill Dash QX6776	Yr.Iss.	1998	13.95	14-30
1998 Future Ballerina QX6756	Yr.Iss.	1998	7.95	8-16
1998 Gifted Gardener QX6736	Yr.Iss.	1998	7.95	14-16
1998 Good Luck Dice QX6813	Yr.Iss.	1998	9.95	10-20
1998 Holiday Camper QX6783	Yr.Iss.	1998	12.95	13-25
1998 National Salute QX6293	Yr.Iss.	1998	8.95	9-16
1998 North Pole Reserve QX6803	Yr.Iss.	1998	10.95	18-20
1998 Polar Bowler QX6746	Yr.Iss.	1998	7.95	8-16
1998 Puttin' Around QX6763	Yr.Iss.	1998	8.95	17
1998 Rocket to Success QX6793	Yr.Iss.	1998	8.95	9-18
1998 Sew Gifted QX6743	Yr.Iss.	1998	7.95	18-20
1998 Spoonful of Love QX6796	Yr.Iss.	1998	8.95	16-18
1998 Surprise Catch QX6753	Yr.Iss.	1998	7.95	15

*Quotes have been rounded up to nearest dollar

1998 Miniature Ornaments - Keepsake

YEAR ISSUE	EDITION LIMIT	YEAR RETD.	ISSUE PRICE	*QUOTE U.S.$
1998 1937 Steelcraft Auburn (1st Ed.) QXM4143	Yr.Iss.	1998	6.95	14-20
1998 Angel Chime (Precious Ed.) QXM4283	Yr.Iss.	1998	8.95	16-18
1998 Antique Tractors (2nd Ed.) QXM4166	Yr.Iss.	1998	6.95	9-18
1998 Betsey's Prayer QXM4263	Yr.Iss.	1998	4.95	10
1998 Caboose (10th Ed.) QXM4216	Yr.Iss.	1998	6.95	14
1998 Centuries of Santa (5th Ed.) QXM4206	Yr.Iss.	1998	5.95	6-12
1998 Cheshire Cat (4th Ed.) QXM4186	Yr.Iss.	1998	6.95	10-13
1998 Christmas Bells (4th Ed.) QXM4196	Yr.Iss.	1998	4.95	8-11
1998 Coca-Cola Time QXM4296	Yr.Iss.	1998	6.95	7-15
1998 Fishy Surprise QXM4276	Yr.Iss.	1998	6.95	7-14
1998 Glinda, The Good Witch™, The Wicked Witch of the West™ QXM4233	Yr.Iss.	1998	14.95	25-28
1998 Holly-Jolly Jig QXM4266	Yr.Iss.	1998	6.95	13
1998 Miniature Clothespin Soldier (4th Ed.) QXM4193	Yr.Iss.	1998	4.95	9
1998 Murray Inc.® Dump Truck (4th Ed.) QXM4183	Yr.Iss.	1998	6.95	12
1998 The Nativity (1st Ed.) QXM4156	Yr.Iss.	1998	9.95	13-25
1998 Noel R.R. Locomotive (Anniversary Ed.)1989-1998 QXM4286	Yr.Iss.	1998	10.95	15-18
1998 Nutcracker (3rd Ed.) QXM4146	Yr.Iss.	1998	5.95	14-20
1998 Nutcracker Guild (5th Ed.) QXM4203	Yr.Iss.	1998	6.95	14
1998 On the Road (6th Ed.) QXM4213	Yr.Iss.	1998	5.95	10
1998 Peaceful Pandas QXM4253	Yr.Iss.	1998	5.95	10
1998 Pixie Parachute QXM4256	Yr.Iss.	1998	4.95	5-9
1998 Sharing Joy QXM4273	Yr.Iss.	1998	4.95	10
1998 Singin' in the Rain™ QXM4303	Yr.Iss.	1998	10.95	11-20
1998 Snowflake Ballet (2nd Ed.) QXM4173	Yr.Iss.	1998	5.95	12
1998 SUPERMAN™ QXM4313	Yr.Iss.	1998	10.95	16-20
1998 Teddy-Bear Style (2nd Ed.) QXM4176	Yr.Iss.	1998	5.95	11
1998 Welcome Friends (2nd Ed.) QXM4153	Yr.Iss.	1998	6.95	11-15
1998 Winter Fun With SNOOPY® (1st Ed.) QXM4243	Yr.Iss.	1998	6.95	10-14

1998 NBA Ornaments - Keepsake

YEAR ISSUE	EDITION LIMIT	YEAR RETD.	ISSUE PRICE	*QUOTE U.S.$
1998 Charlotte Hornets QSR1033	Yr.Iss.	1998	9.95	10
1998 Chicago Bulls QSR1036	Yr.Iss.	1998	9.95	18
1998 Detroit Pistons QSR1043	Yr.Iss.	1998	9.95	10
1998 Houston Rockets QSR1046	Yr.Iss.	1998	9.95	10
1998 Indiana Pacers QSR1053	Yr.Iss.	1998	9.95	18
1998 Los Angeles Lakers QSR1056	Yr.Iss.	1998	9.95	10
1998 New York Knickerbockers QSR1063	Yr.Iss.	1998	9.95	10
1998 Orlando Magic QSR1066	Yr.Iss.	1998	9.95	10
1998 Seattle Supersonics QSR1076	Yr.Iss.	1998	9.95	10
1998 Utah Jazz QSR1083	Yr.Iss.	1998	9.95	10

1998 NFL Ornaments - Keepsake

YEAR ISSUE	EDITION LIMIT	YEAR RETD.	ISSUE PRICE	*QUOTE U.S.$
1998 Carolina Panthers™ QSR5026	Yr.Iss.	1998	9.95	10-18
1998 Chicago Bears™ QSR5033	Yr.Iss.	1998	9.95	10-18
1998 Dallas Cowboys™ QSR5046	Yr.Iss.	1998	9.95	14
1998 Denver Broncos™ QSR5053	Yr.Iss.	1998	9.95	23-30
1998 Green Bay Packers™ QSR5063	Yr.Iss.	1998	9.95	14-18
1998 Kansas City Chiefs™ QSR5013	Yr.Iss.	1998	9.95	10-18
1998 Miami Dolphins™ QSR5096	Yr.Iss.	1998	9.95	10
1998 Minnesota Vikings™ QSR5126	Yr.Iss.	1998	9.95	10-20
1998 New York Giants™ QSR5143	Yr.Iss.	1998	9.95	10-18
1998 Oakland Raiders™ QSR5086	Yr.Iss.	1998	9.95	10-13
1998 Philadelphia Eagles™ QSR5153	Yr.Iss.	1998	9.95	10-18
1998 Pittsburgh Steelers™ QSR5163	Yr.Iss.	1998	9.95	10
1998 San Francisco 49ers™ QSR5173	Yr.Iss.	1998	9.95	10
1998 St. Louis Rams™ QSR5093	Yr.Iss.	1998	9.95	10-18
1998 Washington Redskins™ QSR5186	Yr.Iss.	1998	9.95	13-18

1998 Pop Culture Icons - Keepsake

YEAR ISSUE	EDITION LIMIT	YEAR RETD.	ISSUE PRICE	*QUOTE U.S.$
1998 1998 Corvette® Convertible QX6416	Yr.Iss.	1998	13.95	14-26
1998 Bugs Bunny-LOONEY TUNES QX6443	Yr.Iss.	1998	13.95	14-24
1998 Decorating Maxine-Style	Yr.Iss.	1998	10.95	19-22
1998 Hot Wheels™ QX6436	Yr.Iss.	1998	13.95	25-28
1998 Larry, Moe, and Curly-The Three Stooges™ QX6503	Yr.Iss.	1998	27.00	48-73
1998 Maxine QX6446	Yr.Iss.	1998	9.95	19-21
1998 Mrs. Potato Head® QX6886	Yr.Iss.	1998	10.95	21-23
1998 Munchkinland™ Mayor and Cornoner QX6463	Yr.Iss.	1998	13.95	15-28
1998 Superman™ QX6423	Yr.Iss.	1998	12.95	14-24
1998 Sweet Treat HERSHEY'S™ QX6433	Yr.Iss.	1998	10.95	20-35
1998 Tonka® Road Grader QX6483	Yr.Iss.	1998	13.95	27

1998 Premiere Event - Keepsake

YEAR ISSUE	EDITION LIMIT	YEAR RETD.	ISSUE PRICE	*QUOTE U.S.$
1998 Santa's Merry Workshop QX6816	Yr.Iss.	1998	32.00	32-56

1998 Showcase Folk Art Americana Collection - Keepsake

YEAR ISSUE	EDITION LIMIT	YEAR RETD.	ISSUE PRICE	*QUOTE U.S.$
1998 Soaring With Angels QX6213	Yr.Iss.	1998	16.95	25-39

1998 Showcase Nature's Sketchbook Collection - Keepsake

YEAR ISSUE	EDITION LIMIT	YEAR RETD.	ISSUE PRICE	*QUOTE U.S.$
1998 Country Home QX5172	Yr.Iss.	1998	10.95	22

1998 Showcase The Language of Flowers Collection - Keepsake

YEAR ISSUE	EDITION LIMIT	YEAR RETD.	ISSUE PRICE	*QUOTE U.S.$
1998 Iris Angel (3rd Ed.) QX6156	Yr.Iss.	1998	15.95	24-27

1998 Special Issues - Keepsake

YEAR ISSUE	EDITION LIMIT	YEAR RETD.	ISSUE PRICE	*QUOTE U.S.$
1998 Barbie™Silken Flame (5th Ed.) QXI4043	Yr.Iss.	1998	15.95	21-27
1998 Boba Fett™ QXI4053	Yr.Iss.	1998	14.95	20-32
1998 Cal Ripken Jr. (3rd) QXI4033	Yr.Iss.	1998	14.95	20-27
1998 Captain Kathryn Janeway™ QXI4046	Yr.Iss.	1998	14.95	27-30
1998 Emmitt Smith (4th) QXI4036	Yr.Iss.	1998	14.95	20-27
1998 Ewoks™ QXI4223	Yr.Iss.	1998	16.95	27-31
1998 Grant Hill (4th) QXI6846	Yr.Iss.	1998	14.95	18-28
1998 The Grinch QXI6466	Yr.Iss.	1998	13.95	50-65
1998 Holiday Barbie™(6th Ed.) QXI4023	Yr.Iss.	1998	15.95	30-34
1998 Holiday Barbie™- African American (1st Ed.) QX6936	Yr.Iss.	1998	15.95	27-30
1998 Joe Montana-Notre Dame QXI6843	Yr.Iss.	1998	14.95	24-26
1998 Mario Lemieux (2nd) QXI6476	Yr.Iss.	1998	15.95	20-27
1998 Princess Leia™ (2nd Ed.) QXI4026	Yr.Iss.	1998	13.95	14-28
1998 Richard Petty (2nd) QXI4143	Yr.Iss.	1998	15.95	18-27
1998 Victorian Christmas II-Thomas Kinkade (2nd Ed.) QX6343	Yr.Iss.	1998	10.95	23-25

1998 Spring Ornaments - Keepsake

YEAR ISSUE	EDITION LIMIT	YEAR RETD.	ISSUE PRICE	*QUOTE U.S.$
1998 1931 Ford Model A Roadster (1st Ed.) QEO8416	Yr.Iss.	1998	14.95	15-27
1998 1939 Mobo Horse (2nd Ed.) QEO8393	Yr.Iss.	1998	12.95	12-29
1998 Barbie™ as Little Bo Peep Doll (2nd Ed.) QEO8373	Yr.Iss.	1998	14.95	9-27
1998 Bashful Gift QEO8446	Yr.Iss.	1998	11.95	22-24
1998 Benjamin Bunny™ Beatrix Potter™ (3rd Ed.) QEO8383	Yr.Iss.	1998	8.95	8-20
1998 Bouquet of Memories QEO8456	Yr.Iss.	1998	7.95	15
1998 Forever Friends QEO8423	Yr.Iss.	1998	9.95	10-20
1998 Garden Club (4th Ed.)	Yr.Iss.	1998	7.95	8-17
1998 The Garden of Piglet and Pooh QEO8396	Yr.Iss.	1998	10.95	13-24
1998 Going Up? Charlie Brown-PEANUTS® QEO8433	Yr.Iss.	1998	9.95	10-21
1998 Happy Diploma Day! QEO8476	Yr.Iss.	1998	7.95	8
1998 Joyful Angels (3rd Ed.) QEO8386	Yr.Iss.	1998	10.95	13-22
1998 Midge™-35th Anniversary QEO8413	Yr.Iss.	1998	14.95	9-27
1998 Passenger Car (3rd Ed.) QEO8376	Yr.Iss.	1998	9.95	10-23
1998 Practice Swing-Donald Duck QEO8396	Yr.Iss.	1998	10.95	11-21
1998 Precious Baby QEO8463	Yr.Iss.	1998	9.95	10-18
1998 Special Friends QEO8523	Yr.Iss.	1998	12.95	13
1998 Star Wars™ QEO8406	Yr.Iss.	1998	12.95	18-100
1998 Sweet Birthday QEO8473	Yr.Iss.	1998	7.95	8-15
1998 Tigger in the Garden QEO8436	Closed	1998	9.95	10-18
1998 Victorian Cross QEO8453	Yr.Iss.	1998	8.95	9-18
1998 Wedding Memories QEO8466	Yr.Iss.	1998	9.95	10
1998 What's Your Name QEO8443	Yr.Iss.	1998	7.95	8-16

1999 Collectible Series - Keepsake

YEAR ISSUE	EDITION LIMIT	YEAR RETD.	ISSUE PRICE	*QUOTE U.S.$
1999 1955 Chevrolet® Nomad® Wagon (9th Ed.) QX6367	Yr.Iss.	1999	13.95	20-40
1999 1957 Dodge® Sweptside D100 (5th Ed.) QX6269	Yr.Iss.	1999	13.95	18-21
1999 1968 Murray® Jolly Roger Flagship (6th Ed.) QX6279	Yr.Iss.	1999	13.95	16
1999 746 Norfolk and Western Steam Locomotive (4th Ed.) QX6377	Yr.Iss.	1999	18.95	25-32
1999 Angel of the Nativity (2nd Ed.) QX6419	Yr.Iss.	1999	14.95	28-30
1999 Bill Elliott (3rd Ed.) QXI4039	Yr.Iss.	1999	15.95	29-44
1999 The Cat in the Hat (1st Ed.) QXI6457	Yr.Iss.	1999	14.95	20-41
1999 The Clauses on Vacation (3rd Ed.) QX6399	Yr.Iss.	1999	14.95	15
1999 Colonial Church (2nd Ed.) QLX7387	Yr.Iss.	1999	18.95	19-39
1999 Curious Raccoons (3rd Ed.) QX6287	Yr.Iss.	1999	12.95	15-26
1999 Curtiss R3C-2 Seaplane (3rd Ed.) QX6387	Yr.Iss.	1999	14.95	16-24
1999 Dan Marino (5th Ed.) QXI4029	Yr.Iss.	1999	14.95	15
1999 David and Goliath (1st Ed.) QX6447	Yr.Iss.	1999	13.95	15-25
1999 Donald Plays the Cymbals (3rd Ed.) QXD4057	Yr.Iss.	1999	13.95	14
1999 Fabulous Decade (10th Ed.) QX6357	Yr.Iss.	1999	7.95	25
1999 Famous Flying Ace (2nd Ed.) QX6409	Yr.Iss.	1999	9.95	15-18
1999 Farm House (1st Ed.) QX6439	Yr.Iss.	1999	15.95	24-39
1999 Frosty Friends (20th Ed.) QX6297	Yr.Iss.	1999	12.95	25-33
1999 Gay Parisienne™ (6th Ed.) QXI5301	Yr.Iss.	1999	15.95	21-32
1999 Gift Bearers (1st Ed.) QX6437	Yr.Iss.	1999	12.95	16-23
1999 Gordie Howe® (3rd Ed.) QXI4047	Yr.Iss.	1999	15.95	16
1999 Han Solo™ (3rd Ed.) QXI4007	Yr.Iss.	1999	13.95	15-26
1999 Heather - Mary's Angels (12th Ed.) QX6329	Yr.Iss.	1999	7.95	16
1999 Heritage Springer® (1st Ed.) QXI8007	Yr.Iss.	1999	14.95	25-30
1999 Honey Time (2nd Ed.) QXD4129	Yr.Iss.	1999	13.95	14
1999 House on Holly Lane (16th Ed.) QX6349	Yr.Iss.	1999	16.95	17-29
1999 Joyful Santa (1st Ed.) QX6949	Yr.Iss.	1999	14.95	15-29
1999 Ken Griffey Jr. (4th Ed.) QXI4037	Yr.Iss.	1999	14.95	15-25
1999 Lighthouse Greetings (3rd Ed.) QLX7379	Yr.Iss.	1999	24.00	24-40
1999 Lunar Rover Vehicle (4th Ed.) QLX7377	Yr.Iss.	1999	24.00	24-35
1999 Marilyn Monroe (3rd Ed.) QX6389	Yr.Iss.	1999	14.95	20-26
1999 Merry Olde Santa (10th Ed.) QX6359	Yr.Iss.	1999	15.95	16-29
1999 Mickey and Minnie in Paradise (2nd Ed.) QXD4049	Yr.Iss.	1999	14.95	15
1999 Minnie Trims the Tree (3rd Ed.) QXD4059	Yr.Iss.	1999	12.95	13
1999 Mischievous Kittens (1st Ed.) QX6427	Yr.Iss.	1999	9.95	20-24
1999 Playing With Pooh (1st Ed.) QXD4197	Yr.Iss.	1999	13.95	14
1999 A Pony for Christmas (2nd Ed.) QX6299	Yr.Iss.	1999	10.95	11-22
1999 Prospector (2nd Ed.) QX6317	Yr.Iss.	1999	13.95	14-27
1999 Puppy Love (9th Ed.) QX6327	Yr.Iss.	1999	7.95	12-17
1999 Red Queen - Alice in Wonderland (4th Ed.) QX6379	Yr.Iss.	1999	14.95	15-18
1999 Rose Angel (4th Ed.) QX6289	Yr.Iss.	1999	15.95	16
1999 Russian BARBIE™ (4th Ed.) QX6369	Yr.Iss.	1999	14.95	21-28
1999 Santa's Golf Cart (21st Ed.) QX6337	Yr.Iss.	1999	14.95	15-29
1999 Scarlett O'Hara™ (3rd Ed.) QX6397	Yr.Iss.	1999	14.95	15-27
1999 Scottie Pippen (5th Ed.) QXI4177	Yr.Iss.	1999	14.95	15
1999 Snow Buddies (2nd Ed.) QX6319	Yr.Iss.	1999	7.95	12-18
1999 Snow White's Jealous Queen (2nd Ed.) QXD4089	Yr.Iss.	1999	14.95	15-28
1999 Victorian Christmas III (3rd Ed.) QX6407	Yr.Iss.	1999	10.95	11-20
1999 Walt Disney's Sleeping Beauty (3rd Ed.) QXD4097	Yr.Iss.	1999	14.95	15-21

1999 Collegiate Ornaments - Keepsake

YEAR ISSUE	EDITION LIMIT	YEAR RETD.	ISSUE PRICE	*QUOTE U.S.$
1999 Arizona Wildcats QSR2429	Yr.Iss.	1999	9.95	10
1999 Duke Blue Devils QSR2437	Yr.Iss.	1999	9.95	10
1999 Florida State® Seminoles® QSR2439	Yr.Iss.	1999	9.95	10
1999 Georgetown Hoyas QSR2447	Yr.Iss.	1999	9.95	10
1999 Kentucky Wildcats QSR2449	Yr.Iss.	1999	9.95	10
1999 Michigan Wolverines QSR2457	Yr.Iss.	1999	9.95	10
1999 Nebraska Cornhuskers QSR2459	Yr.Iss.	1999	9.95	10
1999 North Carolina Tar Heels® QSR2467	Yr.Iss.	1999	9.95	10
1999 Notre Dame® Fighting Irish® QSR2427	Yr.Iss.	1999	9.95	10
1999 Penn State® Nittany Lions® QSR2469	Yr.Iss.	1999	9.95	10

1999 Commemoratives - Keepsake

YEAR ISSUE	EDITION LIMIT	YEAR RETD.	ISSUE PRICE	*QUOTE U.S.$
1999 Baby's First Christmas QX6647	Yr.Iss.	1999	18.95	19-38
1999 Baby's First Christmas QX6649	Yr.Iss.	1999	7.95	8-17
1999 Baby's First Christmas QX6657	Yr.Iss.	1999	8.95	9-17
1999 Baby's First Christmas QX6659	Yr.Iss.	1999	9.95	10
1999 Baby's First Christmas QX6667	Yr.Iss.	1999	7.95	16-22
1999 Baby's Second Christmas QX6669	Yr.Iss.	1999	7.95	16-18
1999 Child's Fifth Christmas QX6679	Yr.Iss.	1999	7.95	16
1999 Child's Fourth Christmas QX6687	Yr.Iss.	1999	7.95	8-21
1999 Child's Third Christmas QX6677	Yr.Iss.	1999	7.95	8-16
1999 Counting on Success QX6707	Yr.Iss.	1999	7.95	8
1999 Dad QX6719	Yr.Iss.	1999	8.95	9-17
1999 Daughter QX6729	Yr.Iss.	1999	8.95	16-21
1999 For My Grandma QX6747	Yr.Iss.	1999	8.95	9
1999 Godchild QX6759	Yr.Iss.	1999	7.95	8-16
1999 Granddaughter QX6739	Yr.Iss.	1999	8.95	9-15
1999 Grandson QX6737	Yr.Iss.	1999	8.95	9-19
1999 Handled With Care QX6769	Yr.Iss.	1999	8.95	9-16
1999 Hello, Hello QX6777	Yr.Iss.	1999	14.95	15-20
1999 Mom and Dad QX6709	Yr.Iss.	1999	9.95	10-20
1999 Mom QX6717	Yr.Iss.	1999	8.95	9-18
1999 Mother and Daugher QX6757	Yr.Iss.	1999	9.95	10
1999 My Sister, My Friend QX6749	Yr.Iss.	1999	7.95	8-21
1999 New Home QX6347	Yr.Iss.	1999	9.95	10-19
1999 Our Christmas Together QX6689	Yr.Iss.	1999	9.95	10
1999 Our First Christmas Together QX3207	Yr.Iss.	1999	7.95	8-17
1999 Our First Christmas Together QX6697	Yr.Iss.	1999	8.95	9
1999 Our First Christmas Together QX6699	Yr.Iss.	1999	22.00	22
1999 Son QX6727	Yr.Iss.	1999	8.95	9-16
1999 Special Dog QX6767	Yr.Iss.	1999	7.95	8
1999 Sweet Friendship QX6779	Yr.Iss.	1999	9.95	10

1999 Crown Reflections - Keepsake

YEAR ISSUE	EDITION LIMIT	YEAR RETD.	ISSUE PRICE	*QUOTE U.S.$
1999 1950 LIONEL® Santa Fe F3 Diesel Locomotive QBG6119	Yr.Iss.	1999	35.00	45-48
1999 1955 Murray® Ranch Wagon QBG6077	Yr.Iss.	1999	35.00	35-38
1999 Childhood Treasures QBG4237	Yr.Iss.	1999	30.00	30
1999 Festival of Fruit (2nd Ed.) QBG6069	Yr.Iss.	1999	35.00	35
1999 Frosty Friends QBG6067	Yr.Iss.	1999	35.00	35-58
1999 Harvest of Grapes QBG6047	Yr.Iss.	1999	25.00	25
1999 The Holy Family QBG6127	Yr.Iss.	1999	30.00	30
1999 Jolly Snowman QBG6059	Yr.Iss.	1999	20.00	20
1999 U.S.S. Enterprise™ NCC-1701 QBG6117	Yr.Iss.	1999	25.00	36-59
1999 Village Church QBG6057	Yr.Iss.	1999	30.00	30
1999 Yummy Memories QBG6049	Yr.Iss.	1999	45.00	45-58

1999 Disney Ornaments - Keepsake

YEAR ISSUE	EDITION LIMIT	YEAR RETD.	ISSUE PRICE	*QUOTE U.S.$
1999 Baby Mickey's Sweet Dreams QXD4087	Yr.Iss.	1999	10.95	11
1999 Donald Plays the Cymbals (3rd Ed.) QXD4057	Yr.Iss.	1999	13.95	14-20
1999 Dumbo's First Flight QXD4117	Yr.Iss.	1999	13.95	16-27
1999 The Family Portrait QXD4149	Yr.Iss.	1999	14.95	15-28
1999 Girl Talk QXD4069	Yr.Iss.	1999	12.95	13
1999 Goofy As Santa's Helper QXD4079	Yr.Iss.	1999	12.95	13-23
1999 Honey Time (2nd Ed.) QXD4129	Yr.Iss.	1999	13.95	15-27
1999 Mickey and Minnie in Paradise (2nd Ed.) QXD4049	Yr.Iss.	1999	14.95	20-28
1999 Minnie Trims the Tree (3rd Ed.) QXD4059	Yr.Iss.	1999	12.95	13-15
1999 Piano Player Mickey QXD7389	Yr.Iss.	1999	24.00	24
1999 Pinocchio and Geppetto QXD4107	Yr.Iss.	1999	16.95	17-30
1999 Playing With Pooh QXD4197	Yr.Iss.	1999	13.95	15-28
1999 Presents From Pooh QXD4093	Yr.Iss.	1999	14.95	15-18
1999 Skating With Pooh QXD4127	Yr.Iss.	1999	6.95	7
1999 Snow White's Jealous Queen (2nd Ed.) QXD4089	Yr.Iss.	1999	14.95	20-28
1999 Tigger Plays Soccer QXD4119	Yr.Iss.	1999	10.95	11-19

*Quotes have been rounded up to nearest dollar

YEAR ISSUE	EDITION LIMIT	YEAR RETD.	ISSUE PRICE	*QUOTE U.S.$
1999 Walt Disney's Sleeping Beauty (3rd Ed.) QXD4097	Yr.Iss.	1999	14.95	15
1999 Woody's Roundup Walt Disney's Toy Story 2	Yr.Iss.	1999	13.95	20-27

1999 Holiday Traditions - Keepsake

YEAR ISSUE	EDITION LIMIT	YEAR RETD.	ISSUE PRICE	*QUOTE U.S.$
1999 All Sooted Up QX6837	Yr.Iss.	1999	9.95	10-19
1999 Angel of Hope QXI6339	Yr.Iss.	1999	14.95	15-28
1999 Angel Song QX6939	Yr.Iss.	1999	18.95	19
1999 Balthasar-The Magi QX8037	2-Yr.		12.95	13
1999 Best Pals QX6879	2-Yr.		18.95	19
1999 Caspar-The Magi QX8039	2-Yr.		12.95	13
1999 Child of Wonder QX6817	Yr.Iss.	1999	14.95	15-29
1999 The Christmas Story QX6897	Yr.Iss.	1999	22.00	22
1999 Cross of Hope QX6557	Yr.Iss.	1999	9.95	10
1999 Feliz Navidad - Santa QX6999	Yr.Iss.	1999	8.95	9-17
1999 Forecast for Fun QX6869	Yr.Iss.	1999	14.95	15
1999 In The Workshop QX6979	Yr.Iss.	1999	9.95	10
1999 Jazzy Jalopy QX6549	Yr.Iss.	1999	24.00	24-40
1999 Jolly Locomotive QX6859	Yr.Iss.	1999	14.95	15-28
1999 Joyous Angel QX6787	Yr.Iss.	1999	8.95	9
1999 A Joyous Christmas QX6827	Yr.Iss.	1999	5.95	6-18
1999 King Malh-Third King QX6797	Yr.Iss.	1999	13.95	14-27
1999 Kringle's Whirligig QX6847	Yr.Iss.	1999	12.95	13-25
1999 Let It Snow! QLX7427	Yr.Iss.	1999	18.95	19-31
1999 Little Cloud Keeper QX6877	Yr.Iss.	1999	16.95	17-25
1999 Mary's Bears QX5569	Yr.Iss.	1999	12.95	13-26
1999 Melchior-The Magi QX6819	2-Yr.		12.95	13
1999 Milk 'n' Cookies Express QX6839	Yr.Iss.	1999	8.95	9-15
1999 Millennium Snowman QX8059	Yr.Iss.	1999	8.95	64-75
1999 Noah's Ark QX6809	Yr.Iss.	1999	12.95	25-28
1999 Playful Snowman QX6867	Yr.Iss.	1999	12.95	13-18
1999 Praise the Day QX6799	Yr.Iss.	1999	14.95	15-27
1999 Red Barn QX6947	Yr.Iss.	1999	15.95	16-24
1999 Sleddin' Buddies QX6849	Yr.Iss.	1999	9.95	10
1999 Snowmen of Mitford QXI8587	Yr.Iss.	1999	15.95	35-39
1999 Spellin' Santa QX6857	Yr.Iss.	1999	9.95	10-16
1999 A Time of Peace QX6807	Yr.Iss.	1999	8.95	9
1999 Warm Welcome QLX7417	Yr.Iss.	1999	16.95	17
1999 Welcome to 2000 QX6829	Yr.Iss.	1999	10.95	25-94
1999 Wintertime Treat QX6989	Yr.Iss.	1999	12.95	13-25

1999 Keepsake Collector's Club - Keepsake

YEAR ISSUE	EDITION LIMIT	YEAR RETD.	ISSUE PRICE	*QUOTE U.S.$
1999 1939 GARTON® Ford Station Wagon QXC4509	Yr.Iss.	1999	15.95	16
1999 1991 Happy Holidays® BARBIE® Doll QXC4507	Yr.Iss.	1999	15.95	35-41
1999 Arctic Artist QXC4527A	Yr.Iss.	1999	N/A	N/A
1999 Hollow Log Café QXC4667A	Yr.Iss.	1999	14.95	15
1999 Noel R.R.-gold plated	Yr.Iss.	1999	10.95	11
1999 North Pole Pond QXC4677A	Yr.Iss.	1999	40.00	40
1999 Snowy Days-PEANUTS® QXC4517	Yr.Iss.	1999	18.95	19
1999 Snowy Plaza QXC4669A	Yr.Iss.	1999	35.00	35
1999 Snowy Surprise QXC4529A	Yr.Iss.	1999	N/A	N/A
1999 The Toymaker's Gift QXC4519A	Yr.Iss.	1999	N/A	N/A
1999 Waiting for a Hug QXC4537A	Yr.Iss.	1999	N/A	N/A

1999 Laser Creations - Keepsake

YEAR ISSUE	EDITION LIMIT	YEAR RETD.	ISSUE PRICE	*QUOTE U.S.$
1999 Angelic Messenger QLZ4287	Yr.Iss.	1999	7.95	8
1999 Christmas in Bloom QLZ4257	Yr.Iss.	1999	8.95	9
1999 Don't Open Till 2000 QLZ4289	Yr.Iss.	1999	8.95	9-18
1999 Inside Santa's Workshop QLZ4239	Yr.Iss.	1999	8.95	9
1999 Ringing in Christmas QLZ4277	Yr.Iss.	1999	6.95	7
1999 A Visit From St. Nicholas QLZ4229	Yr.Iss.	1999	5.95	6-17
1999 A Wish for Peace QLZ4249	Yr.Iss.	1999	6.95	7
1999 Yuletide Charm QLZ4269	Yr.Iss.	1999	5.95	6

1999 Lifestyles & Occupations - Keepsake

YEAR ISSUE	EDITION LIMIT	YEAR RETD.	ISSUE PRICE	*QUOTE U.S.$
1999 Adding the Best Part QX6569	Yr.Iss.	1999	7.95	8
1999 Angel in Disguise QX6629	Yr.Iss.	1999	8.95	9
1999 Bowling's a Ball QX6577	Yr.Iss.	1999	7.95	8
1999 Dance for the Season QX6587	Yr.Iss.	1999	9.95	10
1999 Flame-Fighting Friends QX6619	Yr.Iss.	1999	14.95	15-23
1999 Merry Motorcycle QX6637	Yr.Iss.	1999	8.95	9-18
1999 Military on Parade QX6639	Yr.Iss.	1999	10.95	11-22
1999 A Musician of Note QX6567	Yr.Iss.	1999	7.95	8-16
1999 North Pole Star QX6589	Yr.Iss.	1999	8.95	9
1999 Outstanding Teacher QX6627	Yr.Iss.	1999	8.95	9
1999 Reel Fun QX6609	Yr.Iss.	1999	10.95	11-19
1999 Sew Handy QX6597	Yr.Iss.	1999	8.95	9-26
1999 Sprinkling Stars QX6599	Yr.Iss.	1999	9.95	10
1999 Sundae Golfer QX6617	Yr.Iss.	1999	12.95	13-19
1999 Surfin' the Net QX6607	Yr.Iss.	1999	9.95	10-19
1999 Sweet Skater QX6579	Yr.Iss.	1999	7.95	8

1999 Miniature Ornaments - Keepsake

YEAR ISSUE	EDITION LIMIT	YEAR RETD.	ISSUE PRICE	*QUOTE U.S.$
1999 1937 Steelcraft Airflow by Murray® (2nd Ed.) QXM4477	Yr.Iss.	1999	6.95	7-16
1999 1955 Murray® Tractor and Trailer (5th Ed.) QXM4479	Yr.Iss.	1999	6.95	7-15
1999 Antique Tractors (3rd Ed.) QXM4567	Yr.Iss.	1999	6.95	8-14
1999 Betsey's Perfect 10 QXM4609	Yr.Iss.	1999	4.95	5-12
1999 Celestial Kitty QXM4639	Yr.Iss.	1999	6.95	7
1999 Centuries of Santa (6th Ed.) QXM4589	Yr.Iss.	1999	5.95	6-13
1999 Christmas Bells (5th Ed.) QXM4489	Yr.Iss.	1999	4.95	5-8
1999 Classic Batman™ and Robin™ QXM4659	Yr.Iss.	1999	12.95	15-25
1999 Crystal Claus QXM4637	Yr.Iss.	1999	9.95	15-19
1999 Dorothy's Ruby Slippers (1st Ed.) QXM4599	Yr.Iss.	1999	5.95	25-35
1999 Electric Glide (2nd Ed.) QXI6137	Yr.Iss.	1999	7.95	10-16
1999 Holiday Flurries (1st Ed.) QXM4547	Yr.Iss.	1999	6.95	7-15
1999 Locomotive and Tender (1st Ed.) QXM4549	Yr.Iss.	1999	10.95	15-25
1999 Love to Share QXM4557	Yr.Iss.	1999	6.95	7
1999 Marvin The Martian QXM4657	Yr.Iss.	1999	8.95	9-10
1999 Merry Grinch-mas! QXI4627	Yr.Iss.	1999	19.95	25-35
1999 Miniature Clothespin Soldier (5th Ed.) QXM4579	Yr.Iss.	1999	4.95	5-10
1999 Mouse King (4th Ed.) QXM4487	Yr.Iss.	1999	5.95	6-13
1999 The Nativity (2nd Ed.) QXM4497	Yr.Iss.	1999	9.95	10-18
1999 Nutcracker Guild (6th Ed.) QXM4587	Yr.Iss.	1999	6.95	7-12
1999 Roll-a-Bear QXM4629	Yr.Iss.	1999	6.95	7
1999 Santa Time QXM4647	Yr.Iss.	1999	7.95	8
1999 Seaside Scenes (1st Ed.) QXM4649	Yr.Iss.	1999	7.95	8-17
1999 Snowflake Ballet (3rd Ed.) QXM4569	Yr.Iss.	1999	5.95	6-12
1999 Taz and the She-Devil QXM4619	Yr.Iss.	1999	8.95	10-18
1999 Teddy-Bear Style (3rd Ed.) QXM4499	Yr.Iss.	1999	5.95	6-12
1999 Trusty Reindeer QXM4617	Yr.Iss.	1999	5.95	8-13
1999 Welcome Friends (3rd Ed.) QXM4577	Yr.Iss.	1999	6.95	7-15
1999 Winter Fun With SNOOPY® (2nd Ed.) QXM4559	Yr.Iss.	1999	6.95	10-19

1999 NBA Ornaments - Keepsake

YEAR ISSUE	EDITION LIMIT	YEAR RETD.	ISSUE PRICE	*QUOTE U.S.$
1999 Charlotte Hornets™ QSR1057	Yr.Iss.	1999	10.95	11
1999 Chicago Bulls™ QSR1019	Yr.Iss.	1999	10.95	11
1999 Detroit Pistons™ QSR1027	Yr.Iss.	1999	10.95	11
1999 Houston Rockets™ QSR1029	Yr.Iss.	1999	10.95	11
1999 Indiana Pacers™ QSR1037	Yr.Iss.	1999	10.95	11
1999 Los Angeles Lakers™ QSR1039	Yr.Iss.	1999	10.95	11
1999 New York Knicks™ QSR1047	Yr.Iss.	1999	10.95	11
1999 Orlando Magic™ QSR1059	Yr.Iss.	1999	10.95	11
1999 Seattle Supersonics™ QSR1067	Yr.Iss.	1999	10.95	11
1999 Utah Jazz™ QSR1069	Yr.Iss.	1999	10.95	11

1999 NFL Ornaments - Keepsake

YEAR ISSUE	EDITION LIMIT	YEAR RETD.	ISSUE PRICE	*QUOTE U.S.$
1999 Carolina Panthers™ QSR5217	Yr.Iss.	1999	10.95	11
1999 Chicago Bears™ QSR5219	Yr.Iss.	1999	10.95	11
1999 Cleveland Browns™	Yr.Iss.	1999	10.95	11
1999 Dallas Cowboys™ QSR5227	Yr.Iss.	1999	10.95	11
1999 Denver Broncos™ QSR5229	Yr.Iss.	1999	10.95	11
1999 Green Bay Packers™ QSR5237	Yr.Iss.	1999	10.95	11
1999 Kansas City Chiefs™ QSR5197	Yr.Iss.	1999	10.95	11
1999 Miami Dolphins™ QSR5239	Yr.Iss.	1999	10.95	11
1999 Minnesota Vikings™ QSR5247	Yr.Iss.	1999	10.95	11
1999 New England Patriots™ QSR5279	Yr.Iss.	1999	10.95	11
1999 New York Giants™ QSR5249	Yr.Iss.	1999	10.95	11
1999 Oakland Raiders™ QSR5257	Yr.Iss.	1999	10.95	11
1999 Philadelphia Eagles™ QSR5259	Yr.Iss.	1999	10.95	11
1999 Pittsburgh Steelers™ QSR5267	Yr.Iss.	1999	10.95	11
1999 San Francisco 49ers™ QSR5269	Yr.Iss.	1999	10.95	11
1999 Washington Redskins™ QSR5277	Yr.Iss.	1999	10.95	11

1999 Pop Culture Icons - Keepsake

YEAR ISSUE	EDITION LIMIT	YEAR RETD.	ISSUE PRICE	*QUOTE U.S.$
1999 1949 Cadillac® Coupe deVille QX6429	Yr.Iss.	1999	14.95	18-29
1999 Clownin' Around QX6487	Yr.Iss.	1999	10.95	11-20
1999 Cocoa Break HERSHEY'S™ QX8009	Yr.Iss.	1999	10.95	11-20
1999 Dorothy and Glinda, The Good Witch™ QX6509	Yr.Iss.	1999	24.00	30-40
1999 The Flash™ QX6469	Yr.Iss.	1999	12.95	13-20
1999 G.I. Joe®, Action Soldier™ QX6537	Yr.Iss.	1999	13.95	14-26
1999 Howdy Doody™ QX6519	Yr.Iss.	1999	14.95	18-23
1999 Jet Threat™ Car With Case QX6527	Yr.Iss.	1999	12.95	16-22
1999 Larry, Moe, and Curly QX6499	Yr.Iss.	1999	30.00	41-56
1999 The Lollipop Guild™ QX8029	Yr.Iss.	1999	19.95	26-34
1999 Lucy Gets in Pictures QX6547	Yr.Iss.	1999	13.95	18-26
1999 North Pole Mr. Potato Head™ QX8027	Yr.Iss.	1999	10.95	11-17
1999 On Thin Ice QX6489	Yr.Iss.	1999	10.95	11-20
1999 Pepé Le Pew and Penelope QX6507	Yr.Iss.	1999	12.95	20-24
1999 The Poky Little Puppy QX6479	Yr.Iss.	1999	11.95	16-23
1999 Rhett Butler™ QX6467	Yr.Iss.	1999	12.95	17-23
1999 Scooby Doo™ QX6997	Yr.Iss.	1999	14.95	20-24
1999 The Tender QX6497	Yr.Iss.	1999	14.95	18-29
1999 Tonka® 1956 Suburban Pumper No. 5 QX6459	Yr.Iss.	1999	13.95	22-25

1999 Premiere Event - Keepsake

YEAR ISSUE	EDITION LIMIT	YEAR RETD.	ISSUE PRICE	*QUOTE U.S.$
1999 Zebra Fantasy QX6559	Yr.Iss.	1999	14.95	20-31

1999 Special Issues - Keepsake

YEAR ISSUE	EDITION LIMIT	YEAR RETD.	ISSUE PRICE	*QUOTE U.S.$
1999 40th Anniversary Barbie™ QXI8049	Yr.Iss.	1999	15.95	16-45
1999 African-American Millennium Princess Barbie™ QXI6449	Yr.Iss.	1999	15.95	16-38
1999 Barbie™Gay Parisienne (6th Ed.) QXI5301	Yr.Iss.	1999	15.95	16-26
1999 Chewbacca™ QXI4009	Yr.Iss.	1999	14.95	16-43
1999 Darth Vader's TIE Fighter QXI7399	Yr.Iss.	1999	24.00	26-33
1999 Dream House® Playhouse QXI8047	Yr.Iss.	1999	14.95	15-30
1999 Han Solo™ (3rd Ed.) QXI4007	Yr.Iss.	1999	13.95	14
1999 Lieutenant Commander Worf™ QXI4139	Yr.Iss.	1999	14.95	20-28
1999 Max Rebo Band™ QXI4597	Yr.Iss.	1999	19.95	25-30
1999 Millennium Princess Barbie™ QXI4019	Yr.Iss.	1999	15.95	45-48
1999 Muhammed Ali QXI4147	Yr.Iss.	1999	14.95	15-25
1999 Runabout-U.S.S. Rio Grande QXI7593	Yr.Iss.	1999	24.00	30-40
1999 Star Wars Figural-Star Wars™ QXI4187	Yr.Iss.	1999	14.95	15-28
1999 Starship-Star Wars™ QXI7613	Yr.Iss.	1999	18.95	20-50
1999 Travel Case and Barbie™ QXI6129	Yr.Iss.	1999	12.95	13

1999 Spring Ornaments - Keepsake

YEAR ISSUE	EDITION LIMIT	YEAR RETD.	ISSUE PRICE	*QUOTE U.S.$
1999 1932 Chevrolet Standard Sports Roadster (2nd Ed.) QEO8379	Yr.Iss.	1999	14.95	15-27
1999 1950 GARTON® Delivery Cycle (3rd Ed.) QEO8367	Yr.Iss.	1999	12.95	13-23
1999 1956 GARTON® Hot Rod Racer QEO8479	Yr.Iss.	1999	13.95	14-26
1999 Barbie™ Anniversary Edition QEO8399	Yr.Iss.	1999	12.95	13-23
1999 Barbie® as Cinderella Doll (3rd Ed.) QEO8327	Yr.Iss.	1999	14.95	15-27
1999 Batter Up! QEO8389	Yr.Iss.	1999	12.95	13-23
1999 Birthday Celebration QEO8409	Yr.Iss.	1999	8.95	9
1999 Cross of Faith QEO8467	Yr.Iss.	1999	13.95	14
1999 Easter Egg Nest QEO8427	Yr.Iss.	1999	7.95	8
1999 Easter Egg Surprise QEO8377	Yr.Iss.	1999	14.95	15
1999 Eastern Bluebird (1st) QEO8451	Yr.Iss.	1999	9.95	10
1999 Final Putt - Minnie Mouse QEO8349	Yr.Iss.	1999	10.95	11
1999 Flatbed Car (4th Ed.) QEO8387	Yr.Iss.	1999	9.95	10
1999 Friendly Delivery - Mary's Bears QEO8419	Yr.Iss.	1999	12.95	13-22
1999 Happy Bubble Blower QEO8437	Yr.Iss.	1999	7.95	8
1999 Happy Diploma Day! QEO8357	Yr.Iss.	1999	10.95	11
1999 Inspirational Angel QEO8347	Yr.Iss.	1999	12.95	13
1999 Mop Top Billy, Madame Alexander® QEO8337	Yr.Iss.	1999	14.95	16-29
1999 Precious Baby QEO8417	Yr.Iss.	1999	9.95	10
1999 Spring Chick QEO8469	Yr.Iss.	1999	22.00	22
1999 Springtime Harvest QEO8429	Yr.Iss.	1999	7.95	8
1999 Strawberry QEO8369	Yr.Iss.	1999	9.95	12-18
1999 The Tale of Peter Rabbit™-Beatrix Potter™ QEO8397	Yr.Iss.	1999	19.95	25-36
1999 Tiggerific Easter Delivery QEO8359	Yr.Iss.	1999	10.95	12-20
1999 Tom Kitten™ (4th Ed.) QEO8329	Yr.Iss.	1999	8.95	10-18
1999 Wedding Memories QEO8407	Yr.Iss.	1999	9.95	10

2000 American Spirit Collection - Keepsake

YEAR ISSUE	EDITION LIMIT	YEAR RETD.	ISSUE PRICE	*QUOTE U.S.$
2000 Connecticut Ornament QMP9404	Yr.Iss.		12.95	13
2000 Delaware Ornament QMP9400	Yr.Iss.		12.95	13
2000 Georgia Ornament QMP9403	Yr.Iss.		12.95	13
2000 Maryland Ornament QMP9426	Yr.Iss.		12.95	13
2000 Massachusetts Ornament QMP9423	Yr.Iss.		12.95	13
2000 New Hampshire Ornament QMP9432	Yr.Iss.		12.95	13
2000 New Jersey Ornament QMP9402	Yr.Iss.		12.95	13
2000 Pennsylvania Ornament QMP9401	Yr.Iss.		12.95	13
2000 South Carolina Ornament QMP9429	Yr.Iss.		12.95	13

2000 Collectible Series - Keepsake

YEAR ISSUE	EDITION LIMIT	YEAR RETD.	ISSUE PRICE	*QUOTE U.S.$
2000 1924 Toledo Fire Engine #6 (7th Ed.) QX6691	Yr.Iss.		13.95	14
2000 1969 Pontiac® GTO™–The Judge™ (10th Ed.) QX6584	Yr.Iss.		13.95	14
2000 1978 Dodge® Li'l Red Express Truck (6th Ed.) QX6581	Yr.Iss.		13.95	14
2000 Adobe Church (3rd Ed.) LX7334	Yr.Iss.		18.95	19
2000 Bait Shop With Boat (2nd Ed.) QX6631	Yr.Iss.		15.95	16
2000 Baton Twirler Daisy (4th Ed.) QXD4034	Yr.Iss.		13.95	14
2000 A Blustery Day (3rd Ed.) QXD4021	Yr.Iss.		13.95	14
2000 Christmas Holly (5th Ed.) QX6611	Yr.Iss.		14.95	15
2000 Commuter Set™ (7th Ed.) QX6814	Yr.Iss.		15.95	16
2000 Cool Decade QX6764	Yr.Iss.		7.95	8
2000 The Detective (3rd Ed.) QX6564	Yr.Iss.		9.95	10
2000 Donald & Daisy at Lover's Lodge (3rd Ed.) QXD4031	Yr.Iss.		14.95	15
2000 Eric Lindros (4th Ed.) QXI6801	Yr.Iss.		15.95	16
2000 Fashion Afoot QX8341	Yr.Iss.		14.95	15
2000 Fat Boy® (2nd Ed.) QXI6774	Yr.Iss.		14.95	15
2000 Foxes in the Forest (4th Ed.) QX6794	Yr.Iss.		12.95	13
2000 Frosty Friends (21st Ed.) QX6601	Yr.Iss.		10.95	11
2000 Gift Bearers (2nd Ed.) QX6651	Yr.Iss.		12.95	13
2000 John Elway (6th Ed.) QXI6811	Yr.Iss.		14.95	15
2000 Jonah and the Great Fish (2nd Ed.) QX6701	Yr.Iss.		13.95	14
2000 Joyful Santa (2nd Ed.) QX6784	Yr.Iss.		14.95	15
2000 Karl Malone (6th Ed.) QXI6901	Yr.Iss.		14.95	15
2000 Lighthouse Greetings (4th Ed.) QLX7344	Yr.Iss.		24.00	24
2000 LIONEL® General Steam Locomotive (5th Ed.) QX6684	Yr.Iss.		18.95	19
2000 Marguerite-Mary's Angels (13th Ed.) QX6571	Yr.Iss.		7.95	8
2000 Mark McGwire (5th Ed.) QXI5361	Yr.Iss.		14.95	15
2000 Mischievous Kittens (2nd Ed.) QX6641	Yr.Iss.		9.95	10
2000 Mountain Man (3rd Ed.) QX6594	Yr.Iss.		15.95	16
2000 Obi-Wan Kenobi™ (4th Ed.) QXI6704	Yr.Iss.		14.95	15
2000 One Fish Two Fish Red Fish Blue Fish™ (2nd Ed.) QX6781	Yr.Iss.		14.95	15
2000 A Pony for Christmas (3rd Ed.) QX6624	Yr.Iss.		12.95	13
2000 Puppy Love (10th Ed.) QX6554	Yr.Iss.		7.95	8
2000 Robot Parade QX6771	Yr.Iss.		14.95	15
2000 Scarlett O'Hara™ (4th Ed.) QX6671	Yr.Iss.		14.95	15
2000 Schoolhouse (17th Ed.) QX6591	Yr.Iss.		14.95	15
2000 Sleeping Beauty's Maleficent (3rd Ed.) QXD4001	Yr.Iss.		14.95	15
2000 Sleigh X-2000 (22nd Ed.) QX6824	Yr.Iss.		14.95	15
2000 Snow Buddies (3rd Ed.) QX6654	Yr.Iss.		7.95	8
2000 Spirit of St. Louis (4th Ed.) QX6634	Yr.Iss.		14.95	15
2000 Story Time With Pooh (2nd Ed.) QXD4024	Yr.Iss.		13.95	14
2000 Toymaker Santa QX6751	Yr.Iss.		14.95	15

*Quotes have been rounded up to nearest dollar

YEAR ISSUE	EDITION LIMIT	YEAR RETD.	ISSUE PRICE	*QUOTE U.S.$
2000 Twilight Angel (3rd Ed.) QX6614	Yr.Iss.		14.95	15

2000 Collegiate Ornaments - Keepsake

YEAR ISSUE	EDITION LIMIT	YEAR RETD.	ISSUE PRICE	*QUOTE U.S.$
2000 Alabama® Crimson Tide® QSR2344	Yr.Iss.		9.95	10
2000 Florida Gators® QSR2324	Yr.Iss.		9.95	10
2000 Florida State® Seminoles® QSR2341	Yr.Iss.		9.95	10
2000 Michigan Wolverines™ QSR2271	Yr.Iss.		9.95	10
2000 Nebraska Cornhuskers™ QSR2321	Yr.Iss.		9.95	10
2000 North Carolina® Tar Heels® QSR2304	Yr.Iss.		9.95	10
2000 Notre Dame® Fighting Irish™ QSR2284	Yr.Iss.		9.95	10
2000 Penn State® Nittany Lions® QSR2311	Yr.Iss.		9.95	10
2000 Tennessee Volunteers® QSR2334	Yr.Iss.		9.95	10
2000 The University Of Kentucky® Wildcats™ QSR2291	Yr.Iss.		9.95	10

2000 Commemoratives - Keepsake

YEAR ISSUE	EDITION LIMIT	YEAR RETD.	ISSUE PRICE	*QUOTE U.S.$
2000 Baby's First Christmas QX6914	Yr.Iss.		7.95	8
2000 Baby's First Christmas QX8031	Yr.Iss.		8.95	9
2000 Baby's First Christmas QX8034	Yr.Iss.		10.95	11
2000 Baby's First Christmas QX8041	Yr.Iss.		18.95	19
2000 Baby's Second Christmas QX6921	Yr.Iss.		7.95	8
2000 Child's Fifth Christmas QX6934	Yr.Iss.		7.95	8
2000 Child's Fourth Christmas QX6931	Yr.Iss.		7.95	8
2000 Child's Third Christmas QX6924	Yr.Iss.		7.95	8
2000 A Class Act QX8074	Yr.Iss.		7.95	8
2000 Close-Knit Friends QX8204	Yr.Iss.		14.95	15
2000 Dad QX8071	Yr.Iss.		8.95	9
2000 Daughter QX8081	Yr.Iss.		8.95	9
2000 Friendly Greeting QX8174	Yr.Iss.		9.95	10
2000 Godchild QX8161	Yr.Iss.		7.95	8
2000 Granddaughter QX8091	Yr.Iss.		8.95	9
2000 Grandma's House QX8141	Yr.Iss.		10.95	11
2000 Grandson QX8094	Yr.Iss.		8.95	9
2000 Mom and Dad QX8061	Yr.Iss.		9.95	10
2000 Mom QX8064	Yr.Iss.		8.95	9
2000 Mother and Daughter QX8154	Yr.Iss.		9.95	10
2000 New Home QX8171	Yr.Iss.		8.95	9
2000 New Millennium Baby QX8581	Yr.Iss.		10.95	11
2000 Our Christmas Together QX8054	Yr.Iss.		9.95	10
2000 Our Family QX8211	Yr.Iss.		7.95	8
2000 Our First Christmas Together QX3104	Yr.Iss.		7.95	8
2000 Our First Christmas Together QX8051	Yr.Iss.		8.95	9
2000 Our First Christmas Together QX8701	Yr.Iss.		10.95	11
2000 Sister to Sister QX8144	Yr.Iss.		12.95	13
2000 Son QX8084	Yr.Iss.		8.95	9

2000 Crown Reflections - Keepsake

YEAR ISSUE	EDITION LIMIT	YEAR RETD.	ISSUE PRICE	*QUOTE U.S.$
2000 1955 Murray® Dump Truck QBG4081	Yr.Iss.		35.00	35
2000 Backpack Bear QBG4071	Yr.Iss.		30.00	30
2000 Christmas Rose QBG4054	Yr.Iss.		35.00	35
2000 Frosty Friends QBG4094	Yr.Iss.		40.00	40
2000 Li'l Apple QBG4261	Yr.Iss.		7.95	8
2000 Li'l Cascade-Red (Tri-Color) QBG4241	Yr.Iss.		7.95	8
2000 Li'l Cascade-White (Tri-Color) QBG4244	Yr.Iss.		7.95	8
2000 Li'l Christmas Tree QBG4361	Yr.Iss.		7.95	8
2000 Li'l Gift-Green Bow QBG4344	Yr.Iss.		7.95	8
2000 Li'l Gift-Red Bow QBG4341	Yr.Iss.		7.95	8
2000 Li'l Grapes QBG4141	Yr.Iss.		7.95	8
2000 Li'l Jack-in-the-Box QBG4274	Yr.Iss.		7.95	8
2000 Li'l Mr. Claus QBG4364	Yr.Iss.		7.95	8
2000 Li'l Mrs. Claus QBG4371	Yr.Iss.		7.95	8
2000 Li'l Partridge QBG4374	Yr.Iss.		7.95	8
2000 Li'l Pear QBG4254	Yr.Iss.		7.95	8
2000 Li'l Pineapple QBG4251	Yr.Iss.		7.95	8
2000 Li'l Robot QBG4271	Yr.Iss.		7.95	8
2000 Li'l Roly-Poly Penguin QBG4281	Yr.Iss.		7.95	8
2000 Li'l Roly-Poly Santa QBG4161	Yr.Iss.		7.95	8
2000 Li'l Roly-Poly Snowman QBG4284	Yr.Iss.		7.95	8
2000 Li'l Santa-Traditional QBG4354	Yr.Iss.		7.95	8
2000 Li'l Snowman-Traditional QBG4351	Yr.Iss.		7.95	8
2000 Li'l Stars-Metallic Look QBG4221	Yr.Iss.		9.95	10
2000 Li'l Stars-Patriotic QBG4214	Yr.Iss.		9.95	10
2000 Li'l Stars-Traditional QBG4224	Yr.Iss.		9.95	10
2000 Li'l Swirl-Green QBG4234	Yr.Iss.		7.95	8
2000 Li'l Swirl-Red QBG4231	Yr.Iss.		7.95	8
2000 Li'l Teddy Bear QBG4264	Yr.Iss.		7.95	8
2000 Lieutenant Commander Worf™ QBG4064	Yr.Iss.		30.00	30
2000 LIONEL® 4501 Southern Mikado Steam Locomotive QBG4074	Yr.Iss.		35.00	35
2000 Thimble Soldier QBG4061	Yr.Iss.		22.00	22

2000 Disney Ornaments - Keepsake

YEAR ISSUE	EDITION LIMIT	YEAR RETD.	ISSUE PRICE	*QUOTE U.S.$
2000 Alice Meets the Cheshire Cat QXD4011	Yr.Iss.		14.95	15
2000 Baton Twirler Daisy (4th) QXD4034	Yr.Iss.		13.95	14
2000 A Blustery Day (3rd Ed.) QXD4021	Yr.Iss.		13.95	14
2000 Dog Dish Dilemma QXD4044	Yr.Iss.		12.95	13
2000 Donald and Daisy at Lovers' Lodge (3rd Ed.) QXD4031	Yr.Iss.		14.95	15
2000 Dressing Cinderella QXD4109	Yr.Iss.		12.95	13
2000 Mickey and Minnie Mouse QXD4041	Yr.Iss.		12.95	13
2000 Mickey's Bedtime Reading QXD4077	Yr.Iss.		10.95	11
2000 Mickey's Sky Rider QXD4159	Yr.Iss.		18.95	19
2000 The Newborn Prince QXD4194	Yr.Iss.		13.95	14
2000 Off To Neverland! QXD4004	Yr.Iss.		12.95	13
2000 Piglet's Jack-in-the-Box QXD4187	Yr.Iss.		14.95	15
2000 Pooh Chooses the Tree QXD4157	Yr.Iss.		12.95	13
2000 Sleeping Beauty's Maleficent (3rd Ed.) QXD4001	Yr.Iss.		14.95	15
2000 Story Time With Pooh (2nd Ed.) QXD4024	Yr.Iss.		13.95	14
2000 Tigger-ific Tidings to Pooh QXD4014	Yr.Iss.		8.95	9

2000 Holiday Traditions - Keepsake

YEAR ISSUE	EDITION LIMIT	YEAR RETD.	ISSUE PRICE	*QUOTE U.S.$
2000 All Things Beautiful QX8351	Yr.Iss.		13.95	14
2000 Angel-Blessed Tree QX8241	Yr.Iss.		8.95	9
2000 Angelic Trio QX8234	Yr.Iss.		10.95	11
2000 Blue Glass Angel QX8381	Yr.Iss.		7.95	8
2000 Bringing Her Gift QX8334	Yr.Iss.		10.95	11
2000 Caroler's Best Friend QX8354	Yr.Iss.		12.95	13
2000 Celebrate His Birth! QX2464	Yr.Iss.		6.95	7
2000 The Christmas Belle QX8311	Yr.Iss.		10.95	11
2000 Christmas Tree Surprise QX8321	Yr.Iss.		16.95	17
2000 Cool Character QX8271	Yr.Iss.		12.95	13
2000 Feliz Navidad QX8214	Yr.Iss.		8.95	9
2000 Gingerbread Church QX8244	Yr.Iss.		9.95	10
2000 The Good Book QX8254	Yr.Iss.		13.95	14
2000 Graceful Glory QX8304	Yr.Iss.		18.95	19
2000 A Holiday Gathering QX8561	Yr.Iss.		10.95	11
2000 Holly Berry Bell QX8291	Yr.Iss.		14.95	15
2000 The Holy Family QX6523	Yr.Iss.		25.00	25
2000 Hooray for the U.S.A. QX8281	Yr.Iss.		9.95	10
2000 Max QX8584	Yr.Iss.		7.95	8
2000 Memories of Christmas QX8264	Yr.Iss.		12.95	13
2000 Merry Ballooning QX8384	Yr.Iss.		16.95	17
2000 Millennium Time Capsule QX8044	Yr.Iss.		10.95	11
2000 Northern Art Bear QX8294	Yr.Iss.		8.95	9
2000 Our Lady of Guadalupe QX8231	Yr.Iss.		12.95	13
2000 Safe in Noah's Ark QX8514	Yr.Iss.		10.95	11
2000 Santa's Chair QX8314	Yr.Iss.		12.95	13
2000 The Shepherds QX8361	Yr.Iss.		25.00	25
2000 Snow Girl QX8274	Yr.Iss.		9.95	10
2000 Toy Shop Serenade QX8301	Yr.Iss.		16.95	17
2000 A Visit From St. Nicholas QX8344	Yr.Iss.		10.95	11
2000 Warmed by Candleglow QX2471	Yr.Iss.		6.95	7
2000 Winterberry Santa QXI4331	Yr.Iss.		14.95	15

2000 Keepsake Collector's Club - Keepsake

YEAR ISSUE	EDITION LIMIT	YEAR RETD.	ISSUE PRICE	*QUOTE U.S.$
2000 1938 GARTON® Lincoln Zephyr QXC4501	Yr.Iss.		15.95	16
2000 1992 Happy Holidays® BARBIE® Doll QXC4494	Yr.Iss.		15.95	16
2000 Angelic Bell QXC4504	Yr.Iss.		16.95	17
2000 Bell-Bearing Elf QXC4514A	Yr.Iss.		N/A	N/A
2000 A Friend Chimes In QXC4491A	Yr.Iss.		N/A	N/A
2000 Jingle Bell Kringle QXC4481A	Yr.Iss.		N/A	N/A
2000 Ringing Reindeer QXC4484A	Yr.Iss.		N/A	N/A

2000 Keepsake Magic Ornaments - Keepsake

YEAR ISSUE	EDITION LIMIT	YEAR RETD.	ISSUE PRICE	*QUOTE U.S.$
2000 Angels Over Bethlehem QLX7563	Yr.Iss.		18.95	19
2000 The Blessed Family QLX7564	Yr.Iss.		18.95	19
2000 Mary's Angels QLX7561	Yr.Iss.		18.95	19
2000 Millennium Express QLX7364	Yr.Iss.		42.00	42
2000 Time for Joy QX6904	Yr.Iss.		24.00	24

2000 Laser Ornaments - Keepsake

YEAR ISSUE	EDITION LIMIT	YEAR RETD.	ISSUE PRICE	*QUOTE U.S.$
2000 Angel Light QLZ4311	Yr.Iss.		7.95	8
2000 Dove QLZ4294	Yr.Iss.		7.95	8
2000 Fun-Stuffed Stocking QLZ4291	Yr.Iss.		5.95	6
2000 Heavenly Peace QLZ4314	Yr.Iss.		6.95	7
2000 Jack-in-the-Box QLZ4321	Yr.Iss.		8.95	9
2000 Nativity QLZ4301	Yr.Iss.		8.95	9
2000 The Nutcracker QLZ4284	Yr.Iss.		5.95	6
2000 Window View into a Home QLZ4281	Yr.Iss.		8.95	9

2000 Lifestyles & Occupations - Keepsake

YEAR ISSUE	EDITION LIMIT	YEAR RETD.	ISSUE PRICE	*QUOTE U.S.$
2000 Busy Bee Shopper QX6964	Yr.Iss.		7.95	8
2000 Dancin' In Christmas QX6971	Yr.Iss.		7.95	8
2000 Dousin' Dalmatian QX8024	Yr.Iss.		9.95	10
2000 The Fishing Hole QX6984	Yr.Iss.		12.95	13
2000 Friends in Harmony QX8001	Yr.Iss.		9.95	10
2000 Gold-Star Teacher QX6951	Yr.Iss.		7.95	8
2000 Golfer Supreme QX6991	Yr.Iss.		10.95	11
2000 Kris "Cross-Country" Kringle QX6954	Yr.Iss.		12.95	13
2000 Loggin' On to Santa QX8224	Yr.Iss.		8.95	9
2000 Mrs. Claus's Holiday QX8011	Yr.Iss.		9.95	10
2000 North Pole Network QX6994	Yr.Iss.		10.95	11
2000 A Reader to the Core QX6974	Yr.Iss.		9.95	10
2000 Stroll Round the Pole QX8164	Yr.Iss.		10.95	11
2000 Tending Her Topiary QX8004	Yr.Iss.		9.95	10
2000 Together We Serve QX8021	Yr.Iss.		9.95	10
2000 Tree Guy QX6961	Yr.Iss.		8.95	9
2000 Warm Kindness QX8014	Yr.Iss.		8.95	9
2000 Yule Tide Runner QX6981	Yr.Iss.		9.95	10

2000 Miniature Ornaments - Keepsake

YEAR ISSUE	EDITION LIMIT	YEAR RETD.	ISSUE PRICE	*QUOTE U.S.$
2000 1935 Steelcraft by Murray® (3rd Ed.) QXM5951	Yr.Iss.		6.95	7
2000 1968 Murray® Jolly Roger Flagship (6th Ed.) QXM5944	Yr.Iss.		6.95	7
2000 Antique Tractors (4th Ed.) QXM5994	Yr.Iss.		6.95	7
2000 Bugs Bunny and Elmer Fudd QXM5934	Yr.Iss.		9.95	10
2000 Catwoman QXM6021	Yr.Iss.		9.95	10
2000 Celestial Bunny QXM6641	Yr.Iss.		6.95	7
2000 Christmas Bells (6th Ed.) QXM5964	Yr.Iss.		4.95	5
2000 Devoted Donkey QXM6044	Yr.Iss.		6.95	7
2000 Green Eggs and Ham™ Dr. Seuss™ set/3 QXM6034	Yr.Iss.		19.95	20
2000 Holiday Flurries (2nd Ed.) QXM5311	Yr.Iss.		6.95	7
2000 Horse Car and Milk Car (2nd Ed.) QXM5971	Yr.Iss.		12.95	13
2000 Ice Block Buddies (1st Ed.) QXM6011	Yr.Iss.		5.95	6
2000 Kindly Lions QXM5314	Yr.Iss.		5.95	6
2000 Loyal Elephant QXM6041	Yr.Iss.		6.95	7
2000 Mr. Potato Head™ QXM6014	Yr.Iss.		5.95	6
2000 The Nativity (3rd Ed.) QXM5961	Yr.Iss.		9.95	10
2000 Nutcracker Guild (7th Ed.) QXM5991	Yr.Iss.		6.95	7
2000 Precious Penguin (Precious Ed.) QXM6104	Yr.Iss.		9.95	10
2000 Sack of Money (1st Ed.) QXM5341	Yr.Iss.		8.95	9
2000 Sailor (6th Ed.) QXM5334	Yr.Iss.		4.95	5
2000 Santa's Journey Begins QXM6004	Yr.Iss.		9.95	10
2000 Seaside Scenes (2nd Ed.) QXM5974	Yr.Iss.		7.95	8
2000 Silken Flame™ BARBIE™ Ornament and Travel Case QXM6031	Yr.Iss.		12.95	13
2000 Star Fairy QXM6101	Yr.Iss.		4.95	5
2000 Sugarplum Fairy (5th Ed.) QXM5984	Yr.Iss.		5.95	6
2000 Teddy-Bear Style (4th Ed.) QXM5954	Yr.Iss.		5.95	6
2000 The Tin Man's Heart (2nd Ed.) QXM5981	Yr.Iss.		5.95	6
2000 Welcoming Angel QXM5321	Yr.Iss.		5.95	6
2000 Winter Fun With SNOOPY® (3rd Ed.) QXM5324	Yr.Iss.		6.95	7

2000 Nature's Sketchbook - Keepsake

YEAR ISSUE	EDITION LIMIT	YEAR RETD.	ISSUE PRICE	*QUOTE U.S.$
2000 Snowy Garden QX8284	Yr.Iss.		13.95	14

2000 NFL Ornaments - Keepsake

YEAR ISSUE	EDITION LIMIT	YEAR RETD.	ISSUE PRICE	*QUOTE U.S.$
2000 Cleveland Browns QSR5161	Yr.Iss.		9.95	10
2000 Dallas Cowboys QSR5121	Yr.Iss.		9.95	10
2000 Denver Broncos QSR5111	Yr.Iss.		9.95	10
2000 Green Bay Packers QSR5114	Yr.Iss.		9.95	10
2000 Kansas City Chiefs QSR5131	Yr.Iss.		9.95	10
2000 Miami Dolphins QSR5144	Yr.Iss.		9.95	10
2000 Minnesota Vikings QSR5164	Yr.Iss.		9.95	10
2000 Pittsburgh Steelers QSR5124	Yr.Iss.		9.95	10
2000 San Francisco 49ers QSR5134	Yr.Iss.		9.95	10
2000 Washington Redskins QSR5151	Yr.Iss.		9.95	10

2000 Pop Culture Icons - Keepsake

YEAR ISSUE	EDITION LIMIT	YEAR RETD.	ISSUE PRICE	*QUOTE U.S.$
2000 1962 BARBIE™ Hatbox Doll Case QX6791	Yr.Iss.		9.95	10
2000 1968 DEORA™ QXI6891	Yr.Iss.		14.95	15
2000 Blue's Clues QXI8391	Yr.Iss.		10.95	11
2000 Bob the Tomato™ and Larry the Cucumber™ QXI4334	Yr.Iss.		9.95	10
2000 Borg™ Cube QLX7354	Yr.Iss.		24.00	24
2000 Bugs Bunny and Gossamer QX6574	Yr.Iss.		12.95	13
2000 G.I. Joe® Action Pilot QX6734	Yr.Iss.		13.95	14
2000 The Great Oz QLX7361	Yr.Iss.		32.00	32
2000 Hopalong Cassidy™ QX6714	Yr.Iss.		14.95	15
2000 I Love Lucy™ "Lucy Is Enciente" QX6884	Yr.Iss.		15.95	16
2000 Jeannie the Genie QXI8564	Yr.Iss.		14.95	15
2000 King of the Ring QX6864	Yr.Iss.		10.95	11
2000 Larry, Moe & Curly QX6851	Yr.Iss.		30.00	30
2000 The Lone Ranger™ QX6941	Yr.Iss.		15.95	16
2000 The Lullabye League QX6604	Yr.Iss.		19.95	20
2000 Mr. Monopoly™ QX8101	Yr.Iss.		10.95	11
2000 Rhett Butler™ QX6674	Yr.Iss.		12.95	13
2000 Scooby-Doo™ QXI8394	Yr.Iss.		12.95	13
2000 Scuffy The Tugboat QX6871	Yr.Iss.		11.95	12
2000 Self-Portrait Maxine QX6644	Yr.Iss.		10.95	11
2000 Seven of Nine™ QX6844	Yr.Iss.		14.95	15
2000 Super Friends™ QX6724	Yr.Iss.		14.95	15
2000 The Tender QX6834	Yr.Iss.		13.95	14
2000 Tonka Dump Truck® QX6681	Yr.Iss.		13.95	14
2000 The Yellow Submarine QXI6841	Yr.Iss.		13.95	14

2000 Premiere Event - Keepsake

YEAR ISSUE	EDITION LIMIT	YEAR RETD.	ISSUE PRICE	*QUOTE U.S.$
2000 Frosty Friends QX8524	Yr.Iss.		18.95	19
2000 Little Red Riding Hood – 1991 QFM7062	Yr.Iss.		6.95	7

2000 Snoopy Christmas - Keepsake

YEAR ISSUE	EDITION LIMIT	YEAR RETD.	ISSUE PRICE	*QUOTE U.S.$
2000 Charlie Brown QRP4191	Yr.Iss.		4.95	5
2000 Linus QRP4204	Yr.Iss.		4.95	5
2000 Lucy QRP4174	Yr.Iss.		4.95	5
2000 Snoopy QRP4184	Yr.Iss.		4.95	5
2000 Woodstock on Doghouse QRP4211	Yr.Iss.		4.95	5

2000 Special Issues - Keepsake

YEAR ISSUE	EDITION LIMIT	YEAR RETD.	ISSUE PRICE	*QUOTE U.S.$
2000 102 Dalmatians QXI5231	Yr.Iss.		12.95	13
2000 1962 Duo-Glide™ (2nd Ed.) QXI6001	Yr.Iss.		7.95	8
2000 Angel of Promise QXI4144	Yr.Iss.		14.95	15
2000 Arnold Palmer QXI4324	Yr.Iss.		14.95	15
2000 BARBIE™ Angel of Joy™ QXI6861	Yr.Iss.		14.95	15
2000 BARBIE™ QXI6821	Yr.Iss.		15.95	16

*Quotes have been rounded up to nearest dollar

YEAR ISSUE	EDITION LIMIT	YEAR RETD.	ISSUE PRICE	*QUOTE U.S.$
2000 Big Twin Evolution® Engine Harley-Davidson® Motorcycles QXI7571	Yr.Iss.		24.00	24
2000 Dale Earnhardt QXI6754	Yr.Iss.		14.95	15
2000 Darth Maul™ QXI6885	Yr.Iss.		14.95	15
2000 Eric Lindros (4th Ed.) QXI6801	Yr.Iss.		15.95	16
2000 Fat Boy® (2nd Ed.) QXI6774	Yr.Iss.		14.95	15
2000 THE GRINCH QXI5344	Yr.Iss.		12.95	13
2000 Gungan™ Submarine QXI7351	Yr.Iss.		24.00	24
2000 Harley-Davidson® BARBIE™ QXI8554	Yr.Iss.		14.95	15
2000 Imperial Stormtrooper™ QXI6711	Yr.Iss.		14.95	15
2000 Jedi Council Members: Saesee Tinn, Yoda and Ki-Ad-Mundi QXI6744	Yr.Iss.		19.95	20
2000 John Elway (6th Ed.) QXI6811	Yr.Iss.		14.95	15
2000 Karl Malone (6th Ed.) QXI6901	Yr.Iss.		14.95	15
2000 Kristi Yamaguchi QXI6854	Yr.Iss.		13.95	14
2000 Mark McGwire (5th Ed.) QXI5361	Yr.Iss.		14.95	15
2000 Obi-Wan Kenobi™ (4th Ed.) QXI6704	Yr.Iss.		14.95	15
2000 Qui-Gon Jinn™ QXI6741	Yr.Iss.		14.95	15
2000 Toy Story II-Space Ranger QXI5234	Yr.Iss.		14.95	15
2000 Winter Fun With BARBIE™ and KELLY™ QXI6561	Yr.Iss.		15.95	16

2000 Spring Ornaments - Keepsake

YEAR ISSUE	EDITION LIMIT	YEAR RETD.	ISSUE PRICE	*QUOTE U.S.$
2000 1935 Auburn Speedster (3rd Ed.) QEO8401	Yr.Iss.		14.95	15
2000 1940 GARTON® "Red Hot" Roadster (2nd in Winner's Circle) QEO8404	Yr.Iss.		13.95	14
2000 Alice in Wonderland QEO8421	Yr.Iss.		14.95	15
2000 Ballerina Barbie™ QEO8471	Yr.Iss.		12.95	13
2000 Bar and Shield QEO8544	Yr.Iss.		13.95	14
2000 Blueberry (2nd) QEO8454	Yr.Iss.		9.95	10
2000 Bugs Bunny QEO8524	Yr.Iss.		10.95	11
2000 Caboose (5th Ed.) QEO8464	Yr.Iss.		9.95	10
2000 Eastern Bluebird QEO8485	Yr.Iss.		9.95	10
2000 Frolicking Friends Bambi, Thumper, and Flower QEO8434	Yr.Iss.		14.95	15
2000 Happy Diploma Day! QEO8431	Yr.Iss.		10.95	11
2000 Hopalong Cassidy™ Velocipede (4th Ed.) QEO8411	Yr.Iss.		12.95	13
2000 Mr. Jeremy Fisher™ Beatrix Potter™ (5th Ed.) QEO8441	Yr.Iss.		8.95	9
2000 Peanuts® QEO8444	Yr.Iss.		14.95	15
2000 Rabbit (2nd Ed.) QEO8461	Yr.Iss.		14.95	15
2000 A Snug Hug QEO8424	Yr.Iss.		9.95	10
2000 A Swing With Friends QEO8414	Yr.Iss.		14.95	15
2000 Time in the Garden QEO8511	Yr.Iss.		10.95	11

Hamilton Collection

Christmas Angels - S. Kuck

YEAR ISSUE	EDITION LIMIT	YEAR RETD.	ISSUE PRICE	*QUOTE U.S.$
1994 Angel of Charity	Open		19.50	20
1995 Angel of Joy	Open		19.50	20
1995 Angel of Grace	Open		19.50	20
1995 Angel of Faith	Open		19.50	20
1995 Angel of Patience	Open		19.50	20
1995 Angel of Glory	Open		19.50	20
1996 Angel of Gladness	Open		19.50	20
1996 Angel of Innocence	Open		19.50	20
1996 Angel of Beauty	Open		19.50	20
1996 Angel of Purity	Open		19.50	20
1996 Angel of Charm	Open		19.50	20
1996 Angel of Kindness	Open		19.50	20

Derek Darlings - N/A

YEAR ISSUE	EDITION LIMIT	YEAR RETD.	ISSUE PRICE	*QUOTE U.S.$
1995 Jessica, Sara, Chelsea (set)	Open		29.85	30

Dreamsicles Joy of Christmas Suncatcher - N/A

YEAR ISSUE	EDITION LIMIT	YEAR RETD.	ISSUE PRICE	*QUOTE U.S.$
1997 Bearing Gifts	Open		14.95	15
1997 Open Me First	Open		14.95	15
1997 Snowflake Magic	Open		14.95	15
1997 Under The Mistletoe	Open		14.95	15

Dreamsicles Suncatchers - K. Haynes

YEAR ISSUE	EDITION LIMIT	YEAR RETD.	ISSUE PRICE	*QUOTE U.S.$
1996 Stolen Kiss	Open		19.95	20
1996 Sharing Hearts	Open		19.95	20
1996 Love Letters	Open		19.95	20
1996 I Love You	Open		19.95	20
1996 Daisies and Dreamsicles	Open		19.95	20
1997 First Love	Open		19.95	20
1997 Perfect Match	Open		19.95	20
1997 Hand in Hand	Open		19.95	20

Earnhardt Ornaments - S. Bass

YEAR ISSUE	EDITION LIMIT	YEAR RETD.	ISSUE PRICE	*QUOTE U.S.$
2000 Black Attack	Open		12.95	13
2000 Champion's Choice!	Open		12.95	13
2000 Fade To Black!	Open		12.95	13
2000 Finally First!	Open		12.95	13
2000 Hooked Up!	Open		12.95	13
2000 The Intimidator!	Open		12.95	13
1999 Look of a Winner	Open		12.95	13
2000 The Magnificent Seven!	Open		12.95	13
1999 Man On A Mission!	Open		12.95	13
1999 Ready!	Open		12.95	13
2000 Rising Son!	Open		12.95	13
2000 Silver Select!	Open		12.95	13

Little Messengers - P. Parkins

YEAR ISSUE	EDITION LIMIT	YEAR RETD.	ISSUE PRICE	*QUOTE U.S.$
1997 Ice Skater, Christmas Lights, Gingerbreadman, set/3	Open		29.90	30
1997 Shining Star, Candle, Mistletoe, set/3	Open		29.90	30
1997 Snowflake, Wreath, Choirbook, set/3	Open		29.90	30
1997 Stocking, Harp, Kitten, set/3	Open		29.90	30

Harbour Lights

Christmas Ornaments - Harbour Lights

YEAR ISSUE	EDITION LIMIT	YEAR RETD.	ISSUE PRICE	*QUOTE U.S.$
1996 Big Bay Pt. MI 7040	Closed	1996	15.00	14-30
1996 Burrows Island WA 7043	Closed	1996	15.00	14-30
1996 Holland MI 7041	Closed	1999	15.00	14-15
1996 Sand Island WI 7042	Closed	1996	15.00	14-30
1996 Set of 4 702	Closed	1999	60.00	60
1996 30 Mile Pt. NY 7044	Closed	1996	15.00	14-30
1996 Cape Neddick ME 7047	Closed	1999	15.00	14-15
1996 New London Ledge CT 7046	Closed	1999	15.00	15
1996 S.E. Block Island RI 7045	Closed	1999	15.00	14-15
1996 Set of 4 703	Closed	1999	60.00	56-60
1997 Cape Hatteras NC 7048	Closed	1999	15.00	14-15
1997 Saugerties NY 7049	Closed	1999	15.00	14-15
1997 Thomas Point MD 7050	Closed	1999	15.00	14-15
1997 Colchester Reef VI 7051	Closed	1999	15.00	15
1997 Set of 4 705	Closed	1999	60.00	60
1998 Montauk NY 7052	Open		15.00	15
1998 Middle Bay AL 7053	Open		15.00	15
1998 White Shoal MI 7054	Open		15.00	15
1998 Alcatraz CA 7055	Open		15.00	15
1998 Set of 4 706	Open		60.00	60
1999 Barnegat NJ 7056	Open		15.00	15
1999 Gay Head MA 7057	Open		15.00	15
1999 West Quoddy ME 7058	Open		15.00	15
1999 Old Field NY 7059	Open		15.00	15
1999 Set of 4 709	Open		60.00	60
2000 Old Mackinac MI 7060	Open		15.00	15
2000 Cape Elizabeth ME 7061	Open		15.00	15
2000 Hudson-Athens NY 7062	Open		15.00	15
2000 East Quoddy Canada 7063	Open		15.00	15
2000 Set of 4 711	Open		60.00	60

Harmony Kingdom

Holiday Edition - Martin Perry Studios

YEAR ISSUE	EDITION LIMIT	YEAR RETD.	ISSUE PRICE	*QUOTE U.S.$
1998 Holiday Ornaments, set/4	10,000		100.00	100

House of Hatten, Inc.

Angels Triumphant - D. Calla

YEAR ISSUE	EDITION LIMIT	YEAR RETD.	ISSUE PRICE	*QUOTE U.S.$
1998 Heavenly Flyer Angel 39856	Open		24.00	24
1998 Noel Angel 39860	Retrd.	1999	14.00	14
1998 Star Keeper Angel 39858	Retrd.	1999	60.00	60
1998 Star Rider Angel 39857	Open		25.00	25

The Bittersweets Harvest Collection - D. Calla

YEAR ISSUE	EDITION LIMIT	YEAR RETD.	ISSUE PRICE	*QUOTE U.S.$
2000 Bittersweet Riding Broom 4" 50010	Open		12.00	12
2000 Harvest Moon 3" 50006	Open		12.00	12

A Christmas Alphabet - V. & S. Rawson

YEAR ISSUE	EDITION LIMIT	YEAR RETD.	ISSUE PRICE	*QUOTE U.S.$
1998 "A" Angel Block 33808	Retrd.	1999	8.00	8
1998 "C" Candle Block 33801	Retrd.	1999	8.00	8
1998 "H" Holly Elf Block 33802	Retrd.	1999	8.00	8
1998 "I" Ice Skates Block 33804	Retrd.	1999	8.00	8
1998 "M" Manger Block 33807	Retrd.	1999	8.00	8
1998 "R" Reindeer Block 33803	Retrd.	1999	8.00	8
1998 "S" Santa Block 33805	Retrd.	1999	8.00	8
1998 "S" Sleigh Block 33809	Retrd.	1999	8.00	8
1998 "T" Tree Block 33806	Retrd.	1999	8.00	8
1998 Christmas Block Ornaments Set/9 33810	Open		72.00	72
1999 Merry Block Ornaments Set/5 26905	Open		40.00	40

Christmas Messengers - V. & S. Rawson

YEAR ISSUE	EDITION LIMIT	YEAR RETD.	ISSUE PRICE	*QUOTE U.S.$
1999 Ark Santa-Green Coat 26951	Open		18.00	18
1999 Ark Santa-Red Coat 26952	Open		14.00	14
1999 Ark Santa-White Coat 26950	Open		18.00	18
1997 Flying Santa 32763	Retrd.	1999	22.00	22
1997 Noah's Ark Santa 32764	Retrd.	1998	26.50	27
1996 Santa on Goat 22605	Open		29.00	29
1998 Santa on Goose 32852	Open		10.00	10
1996 Santa on Hog 22612	Open		24.00	24
1998 Santa on Pull Toy 32853	Open		10.00	10
1998 Santa on Rabbit 32851	Open		10.00	10
1996 Santa on Reindeer 22601	Open		30.00	30
1997 Santa on Whale 32765	Retrd.	1997	26.50	27
1996 Santa Over Moon 22618	Retrd.	1999	28.00	28
1996 Santa with Pull Toy 22616	Retrd.	1999	20.00	20
1996 Santa with Toys 22614	Open		24.00	24
1998 Santa, Snowman and Sled 32854	Open		10.00	10
2000 Santa/Bell 7.5" 27335	Open		9.00	9
2000 Santa/Chimney 3.5" 27332	Open		8.00	8
2000 Santa/Lantern 4" 27334	Open		8.00	8
2000 Santa/Moon 4" 27330	Open		8.00	8
2000 Santa/Stars 3.5" 27333	Open		8.00	8
2000 Santa/Tree 4" 27331	Open		8.00	8
1998 Skating Santa 32855	Open		10.00	10

Cupboard Keepers - D. Calla

YEAR ISSUE	EDITION LIMIT	YEAR RETD.	ISSUE PRICE	*QUOTE U.S.$
1990 Little Boy Cupboard Fairy 33003	Open		29.00	29
1990 Little Girl Cupboard Fairy 33004	Open		29.00	29

December's Bouquet - D. Calla

YEAR ISSUE	EDITION LIMIT	YEAR RETD.	ISSUE PRICE	*QUOTE U.S.$
2000 Ceramic Acorn 2" 27566	Open		7.00	7
2000 Ceramic Dove 1.5" 27564	Open		7.00	7
2000 Ceramic Partridge Bell 3.5" 27567	Open		8.00	8
2000 Ceramic Pear 2" 27565	Open		7.00	7
2000 Ceramic Santa/Toys Bell 3.5" 27569	Open		8.00	8
2000 Ceramic Santa/Tree Bell 3.5" 27568	Open		8.00	8

Enchanted Forest - D. Calla

YEAR ISSUE	EDITION LIMIT	YEAR RETD.	ISSUE PRICE	*QUOTE U.S.$
1991 Christmas Herald Elf 31198	Retrd.	1994	27.00	27
1988 Elf 31853	Open		15.00	15
1989 Elf with Doves 31959	Retrd.	1992	23.00	23
1989 Elf with Forest Fawn 31960	Retrd.	1996	21.00	21
1989 Elf with Lantern 31961	Retrd.	1996	19.00	19
1993 Forest Elf 31358	Retrd.	1995	19.00	19
1993 Forest Elf with Dove 31359	Retrd.	1997	21.00	21
1989 Forest Fawn, lg. 31957	Retrd.	1993	13.00	13
1989 Forest Fawn, sm. 31964	Retrd.	1996	8.00	8
1991 Girl Elf 31199	Retrd.	1994	24.00	24
1989 Mini St. Nick with Goose 31963	Retrd.	1999	8.00	8
1989 Mini St. Nick with Stars 31962	Retrd.	1999	8.00	8
1989 St. Nicholas Messenger 31954	Retrd.	1991	27.00	27

Enchanted Forest in Glass - D. Calla

YEAR ISSUE	EDITION LIMIT	YEAR RETD.	ISSUE PRICE	*QUOTE U.S.$
1998 Angel with Gold Wings 39877	Retrd.	1999	26.00	26
1998 Angel with White Wings 39876	Retrd.	1999	26.00	26
1998 Blue Santa Head 39881	Retrd.	1999	24.00	24
1998 Elf With Stars 39878	Retrd.	1999	26.00	26
1998 Green and Gold Santa Icicle 39883	Retrd.	1999	24.00	24
1998 Green Santa Head 39880	Retrd.	1999	24.00	24
1998 House 39875	Retrd.	1999	38.00	38
1998 Peace Santa 39879	Retrd.	1999	26.00	26
1998 Red and Green Santa Icicle 39884	Retrd.	1999	24.00	24
1998 Snowman 39882	Retrd.	1999	26.00	26

Fire & Ice - D. Calla

YEAR ISSUE	EDITION LIMIT	YEAR RETD.	ISSUE PRICE	*QUOTE U.S.$
1999 Fire & Ice Bear 26461	Open		6.00	6
1999 Fire & Ice Candy Cane 26463	Open		5.00	5
1999 Fire & Ice Sleigh 26462	Open		6.00	6
1999 Fire & Ice Snowman 26460	Open		6.00	6
1999 Jack Frost Flying 26452	Open		52.00	52
1999 Santa Snowflake 26471	Open		12.00	12
1999 Snowman Snowflake 26472	Open		12.00	12
1999 Tiny Jack Frost 26473	Open		12.00	12

From Out of the North - R. Leeseberg

YEAR ISSUE	EDITION LIMIT	YEAR RETD.	ISSUE PRICE	*QUOTE U.S.$
2000 Bear Angel 4.5" 27188	Retrd.	2000	16.00	16
2000 Beaver Angel 6" 27191	Retrd.	2000	16.00	16
2000 Fox Angel 5" 27187	Retrd.	2000	16.00	16
2000 Moose Angel 5" 27186	Retrd.	2000	16.00	16
2000 Nativity Ornament 4" 27192	Retrd.	2000	12.00	12
2000 Rabbit Angel 5.5" 27190	Retrd.	2000	16.00	16
2000 Racoon Angel 4.5" 27189	Retrd.	2000	16.00	16
1998 Santa and Hummingbird 34862	Retrd.	2000	5.00	5
1999 Santa on Swing 26546	Retrd.	2000	20.00	20
1999 Santa w/Butterfly 26550	Retrd.	2000	8.00	8

Glad Tidings - D. Calla

YEAR ISSUE	EDITION LIMIT	YEAR RETD.	ISSUE PRICE	*QUOTE U.S.$
1999 "Gift Givers" Gift Box, set/7 26422	Open		80.00	80
1999 "Home Keepers" Gift Box, set/7 26415	Open		80.00	80
1999 "The Christmas Box" Gift Box, set/4 26428	Open		70.00	70

Good Cheer - D. Calla

YEAR ISSUE	EDITION LIMIT	YEAR RETD.	ISSUE PRICE	*QUOTE U.S.$
1998 Eggy Santa 39814	Open		13.00	13
1998 Santa Bird Skier 39815	Open		21.00	21
1998 Santa Collector Elf 39817	Open		19.00	19
1998 St. Nick Christmas Toy 39813	Retrd.	1999	50.00	50
1998 Swing Home For the Holidays 39816	Open		19.00	19
1998 Telluride Snowman 39812	Open		22.00	22

Grand Finale - P. Herrick

YEAR ISSUE	EDITION LIMIT	YEAR RETD.	ISSUE PRICE	*QUOTE U.S.$
1998 Bear 38825	Retrd.	1998	24.00	24
1998 Bear Tassel 38835	Open		26.00	26
1998 Black and White Striped Ball 38833	Open		11.00	11
1998 Black Stocking 38802	Retrd.	1998	36.00	36
1998 Deer 38826	Retrd.	1998	24.00	24
1998 Deer Tassel 38836	Open		26.00	26
1998 Floral Striped Finial 38817	Open		24.00	24
1998 Floral Zigzag Finial 38818	Open		24.00	24
1998 Fox 38828	Retrd.	1998	24.00	24
1998 Fox Tassel 38838	Open		26.00	26
1998 Green and Peach Leaves Finial 38821	Retrd.	1998	18.00	18
1998 Green Leaves Finial 38820	Retrd.	1998	18.00	18
1998 Rabbit 38827	Retrd.	1998	24.00	24
1998 Rabbit Tassel 38837	Open		26.00	26
1998 Red and Gold Check Ball 38831	Open		11.00	11
1998 Red and Gold Check Finial 38819	Retrd.	1998	18.00	18
1998 Red and Green Swirl Ball 38832	Retrd.	1998	11.00	11
1998 Rose Ball 38830	Open		11.00	11
1998 Santa Head 38823	Open		20.00	20
1998 Santa Tassel 38834	Open		26.00	26
1998 Snowman 38824	Open		20.00	20
1998 Sun, Moon, Stars 38822	Open		20.00	20
1998 White Stocking 38801	Retrd.	1998	36.00	36

Halloween - D. Calla

YEAR ISSUE	EDITION LIMIT	YEAR RETD.	ISSUE PRICE	*QUOTE U.S.$
1993 Broomhilda 11" 50350	Retrd.	1999	35.00	35

Halloween - J. Crvich

YEAR ISSUE	EDITION LIMIT	YEAR RETD.	ISSUE PRICE	*QUOTE U.S.$
1996 Witch Seated on Moon 51601	Retrd.	1998	43.00	43

Honey Bees - D. Calla

YEAR ISSUE	EDITION LIMIT	YEAR RETD.	ISSUE PRICE	*QUOTE U.S.$
2000 Dragonfly w/"Dewdrop" in Basket 5" 27078	Open		18.00	18
2000 Honey Bee "Baby Bee" 2" 27080	Open		7.00	7
2000 Honey Bee Flying Garden Faery 3.75" 27075	Open		10.00	10

*Quotes have been rounded up to nearest dollar

YEAR ISSUE	EDITION LIMIT	YEAR RETD.	ISSUE PRICE	*QUOTE U.S.$
2000 "Estrelle" Flying Buzzy Bee 4" 27081	Open		12.00	12
2000 "Zelda" Dragonfly 3.5" 27079	Open		7.00	7

The Magic of Christmas - V. & S. Rawson

YEAR ISSUE	EDITION LIMIT	YEAR RETD.	ISSUE PRICE	*QUOTE U.S.$
1998 Elf Holding Lightbulb 32814	Open		7.00	7
1998 Elf Holding Ornament 32811	Open		7.00	7
1998 Elf with Boxes 32815	Open		7.00	7
1998 Elf with List 32812	Open		7.00	7
1998 Elf with Presents 32816	Open		7.00	7
1998 Elf Wrapping Package 32813	Retrd.	1999	7.00	7
1998 Seated Elf 32810	Open		7.00	7

Nursery Rhyming - V. & S. Rawson

YEAR ISSUE	EDITION LIMIT	YEAR RETD.	ISSUE PRICE	*QUOTE U.S.$
1999 Bo Peep 26927	Retrd.	1999	12.00	12
1999 Cow Over Moon 26923	Retrd.	1999	10.00	10
1999 Hickory Dickory Dock 26926	Retrd.	1999	12.00	12
1999 Humpty Dumpty 26928	Retrd.	1999	10.00	10
1999 Jack Be Nimble 26924	Retrd.	1999	10.00	10
1999 Man in the Moon 26920	Retrd.	1999	10.00	10
1999 Old Woman in the Shoe 26921	Retrd.	1999	10.00	10
1999 Peter Pumpkin Eater 26922	Retrd.	1999	10.00	10
1999 Sing/Song Sixpence 26925	Retrd.	1999	14.00	14

The Nutcracker - D. Calla

YEAR ISSUE	EDITION LIMIT	YEAR RETD.	ISSUE PRICE	*QUOTE U.S.$
1993 Drosselmeir 9" 32307	Retrd.	1994	27.00	27
1993 Fritz 7" 32311	Retrd.	1994	25.00	25
1993 Marie 7" 32310	Retrd.	1994	25.00	25
1993 Mouse King 9" 32308	Retrd.	1994	27.00	27
1993 Soldier 10" 32309	Retrd.	1994	27.00	27
1993 Soldier/Owl/Candy Cane, set/3 32313	Retrd.	1994	18.00	18
1993 Stick Horse 7" 32312	Retrd.	1994	11.00	11
1993 Sugar Plum Fairy 10" 32306	Retrd.	1994	27.00	27

Paul Bolinger Collection - P. Bolinger

YEAR ISSUE	EDITION LIMIT	YEAR RETD.	ISSUE PRICE	*QUOTE U.S.$
2000 Jester/Snowman 5.25" 27235	Open		6.00	6
2000 Snowman w/Purple Hat 5.5" 27233	Open		6.00	6
2000 Snowman w/Red Hat 6" 27234	Open		6.00	6

Peace on Earth - D. Calla

YEAR ISSUE	EDITION LIMIT	YEAR RETD.	ISSUE PRICE	*QUOTE U.S.$
1993 Doves, set/2 32356	Open		16.00	16

River Road - D. Calla

YEAR ISSUE	EDITION LIMIT	YEAR RETD.	ISSUE PRICE	*QUOTE U.S.$
2000 Blue Jay Bird 3" 27542	Open		8.00	8
2000 Cardinal Bird 3" 27541	Open		8.00	8
2000 Chickadee Bird 3" 27543	Open		8.00	8
2000 Cranberry Faery 4" 27538	Open		12.00	12
2000 Cranberry Faery Flying holding Acorn 4" 27540	Open		11.00	11
2000 Cranberry Faery Riding Chickadee Bird 5" 27537	Open		16.00	16
2000 Cranberry Faery Swinging on Acorn 5" 27539	Open		14.00	14
2000 Mini Santa/Bells 3" 27509	Open		10.00	10
2000 Mini Santa/Snowman 3" 27511	Open		10.00	10
2000 Mini Santa/Star 3" 27510	Open		10.00	10
2000 Mini Santa/Tree 3" 27508	Open		10.00	10
2000 NOEL Gift Box w/Ornaments Set/5 9" 27506	Open		85.00	85
2000 NOEL Ornaments, set/4 4.5" 27507	Open		50.00	50
2000 O Snow Sled 4.5" 27524	Open		12.00	12
2000 Santa/Deer Flying 7.5" 27503	Open		38.00	38
2000 Sitting Bear 4" 27527	Open		12.00	12
2000 Snowman 4" 27525	Open		9.00	9
2000 Wiggly Santa 4" 27526	Open		10.00	10

Santa's Kingdom - S. Smith

YEAR ISSUE	EDITION LIMIT	YEAR RETD.	ISSUE PRICE	*QUOTE U.S.$
2000 Flying Pig 3.5" 27306	Open		4.00	4
2000 Hare 4" 27305	Open		4.00	4
2000 Skating Bear 4.5" 27303	Open		4.00	4
2000 Tortoise 4" 27304	Open		4.00	4

SnowMa'am - D. Calla

YEAR ISSUE	EDITION LIMIT	YEAR RETD.	ISSUE PRICE	*QUOTE U.S.$
1997 Flutter By Flying Santa with green Coat 30754	Open		44.00	44
1997 Flutter By Santa with Star 30753	Open		44.00	44
1997 Flutter By Santa with Tree 30755	Open		44.00	44
1997 SnowMa'am on Sled 30757	Retrd.	1999	28.00	28
1997 Snowman Candy Cane Hanger 30756	Retrd.	1999	28.00	28
1997 Winged Snowman with Tree 30758	Open		28.00	28

Ten Christmas - D. Calla

YEAR ISSUE	EDITION LIMIT	YEAR RETD.	ISSUE PRICE	*QUOTE U.S.$
1997 2D Goose in Basket with Greeting 30778	Retrd.	1998	14.00	14
1997 Father Christmas 30781	Open		14.00	14
1997 Folk Art Santa with Hood 30779	Open		14.00	14
1997 Goose in Basket 30789	Retrd.	1998	9.00	9
1997 Merry Christmas Snowman 30793	Open		12.00	12
1997 North Star Bear 30795	Retrd.	1999	9.00	9
1997 Our House Santa 30791	Retrd.	1999	12.00	12
1997 Santa with Cap 30780	Retrd.	1999	14.00	14
1997 Simple Gifts Dove with Heart 30792	Retrd.	1999	7.00	7
1997 Star/Moon 30788	Retrd.	1998	5.50	6
1997 Ten Christmas Santa 30797	Retrd.	1998	8.00	8
1997 Twelve Days Partridge 30790	Retrd.	1999	9.00	9
1997 Two By Two Ark 30794	Retrd.	1998	10.00	10
1997 Wings of Light Angel 30796	Retrd.	1999	8.00	8

Twelve Days of Christmas - D. Calla

YEAR ISSUE	EDITION LIMIT	YEAR RETD.	ISSUE PRICE	*QUOTE U.S.$
1990 Partridge on Pear 32004	Open		12.00	12
1990 Turtle Doves 32005	Open		12.00	12
1990 French Hen 32006	Open		9.00	9
1990 Calling Bird 32007	Open		9.00	9
1990 Golden Rings 32008	Open		12.00	12
1990 Goose-A-Laying 32009	Open		12.00	12
1990 Swan-A-Swimming 32010	Open		13.00	13
1990 Maid-A-Milking 32011	Open		18.00	18
1990 Lady Dancing 32014	Open		18.00	18
1990 Lord-A-Leaping 32015	Open		18.00	18
1990 Piper Piping 32013	Open		18.00	18
1990 Drummer Drumming 32012	Open		18.00	18

Twelve Days of Christmas - V. & S. Rawson

YEAR ISSUE	EDITION LIMIT	YEAR RETD.	ISSUE PRICE	*QUOTE U.S.$
1997 Partridge on Pear 32701	Retrd.	1999	26.00	26
1997 Turtle Doves 32702	Retrd.	1999	20.00	20
1997 French Hen 32703	Retrd.	1999	20.00	20
1997 Calling Bird 32704	Retrd.	1999	20.00	20
1997 Golden Rings 32705	Retrd.	1999	18.00	18
1997 Goose-A-Laying 32706	Retrd.	1999	20.00	20
1997 Swan-A-Swimming 32707	Retrd.	1999	20.00	20
1997 Maid-A-Milking 32708	Retrd.	1999	22.00	22
1997 Lady Dancing 32711	Retrd.	1999	22.00	22
1997 Lord-A-Leaping 32712	Retrd.	1999	22.00	22
1997 Piper Piping 32710	Retrd.	1999	22.00	22
1997 Drummer Drumming 32709	Retrd.	1999	22.00	22
1997 Twelve Days of Christmas Ornaments Set/12 32720	Open		254.00	254

Twelve Days of Christmas Anniversary Collection - D. Calla

YEAR ISSUE	EDITION LIMIT	YEAR RETD.	ISSUE PRICE	*QUOTE U.S.$
1999 Miniature Partridge on Pear 2.5" 27016	Open		7.00	7
1999 Miniature Turtle Doves 1.75" 27017	Open		7.00	7
1999 Miniature French Hen 2.5" 27018	Open		7.00	7
1999 Miniature Calling Bird 2.75" 27019	Open		7.00	7
1999 Miniature Golden Rings 3" 27020	Open		6.00	6
1999 Miniature Goose-a-Laying 2.25" 27021	Open		7.00	7
1999 Miniature Swan-a-Swimming 2.5" 27022	Open		7.00	7
1999 Miniature Maid-a-Milking 3" 27023	Open		8.00	8
1999 Miniature Drummer Drumming 3" 27024	Open		8.00	8
1999 Miniature Piper Piping 3" 27025	Open		8.00	8
1999 Miniature Lady Dancing 3" 27026	Open		8.00	8
1999 Miniature Lord-a-Leaping 3" 27027	Open		8.00	8
1999 Miniature Twelve Days of Christmas Ornaments, set/12 27028	Open		88.00	88
1999 The Twelve Days of Christmas Gift Box and Ornaments, set/13 10" 27015	Open		117.00	117

Ye Olde Santa Maker - D. Gann

YEAR ISSUE	EDITION LIMIT	YEAR RETD.	ISSUE PRICE	*QUOTE U.S.$
2000 Santa Ornament - Tartan Plaid 12" 27108	Open		36.00	36
2000 Victorian Santa Orn. - Burgundy Coat 12" 27106	Open		44.00	44
2000 Victorian Santa Orn. - Red/Black Coat 12" 27106	Open		44.00	44

Islandia International

International Fatcats - G. Pitt

YEAR ISSUE	EDITION LIMIT	YEAR RETD.	ISSUE PRICE	*QUOTE U.S.$
1998 Scotland	Numbrd.		10.00	10
1998 Ireland	Numbrd.		10.00	10
1998 Great Britain	Numbrd.		10.00	10

Sonshine Promises - G. Clasby

YEAR ISSUE	EDITION LIMIT	YEAR RETD.	ISSUE PRICE	*QUOTE U.S.$
1998 Baby's First Christmas 8003	Open		12.50	13
1998 Friends Are Tied Together with Ribbons of Love 8005	Open		11.00	11
1998 A Joyful Wish - Christmas 1998 8000	Yr.Iss.	1998	13.50	14
1998 Let Your Light Shine 8001	Open		11.00	11
1998 Love From the Heart 8007	Open		11.00	11
1999 Sonny - Singing to You Makes My Heart Shine 8020	Yr.Iss.	1999	13.50	14
1998 You're an Angel to Me 8006	Open		11.00	11
1998 You're One in a Million to Me 8004	Open		11.00	11
1998 Your Friendship is a Timeless Treasure 8002	Open		11.00	11
1999 Sonshine Carolers, set/8 8021	Open		55.00	55
1999 Cuddly - My Favorite Thing is Cuddling You	Open		set	set
1999 Downy - Sing With Me and We'll Never Be Down	Open		set	set
1999 Happy - I'm So Happy You're Here	Open		set	set
1999 Printzy - You Are My Prince	Open		set	set
1999 Roary - I Roar Everytime I See You	Open		set	set
1999 Sonny - Singing to You Makes My Heart Shine	Yr.Iss.	1999	set	set
1999 Toughy - It's Tough Not Being With You	Open		set	set
1999 Wooly - I Wooly Wooly Miss You	Open		set	set
1999 Faith For The Future	2-Yr.		10.00	10
2000 Together We're Going Places 8077	Open		12.50	13

June McKenna Collectibles, Inc.

Flatback Ornaments - J. McKenna

YEAR ISSUE	EDITION LIMIT	YEAR RETD.	ISSUE PRICE	*QUOTE U.S.$
1988 1776 Santa	Closed	1991	17.00	50-75
1986 Amish Boy, blue	Closed	1989	13.00	85-100
1986 Amish Boy, pink	Closed	1986	13.00	135-200
1986 Amish Girl, blue	Closed	1989	13.00	100
1986 Amish Girl, pink	Closed	1986	13.00	300
1985 Amish Man	Closed	1989	13.00	105
1985 Amish Woman	Closed	1989	13.00	100-145
1993 Angel of Peace, white or pink	Closed	1994	30.00	55-75
1984 Angel with Horn	Closed	1988	14.00	150
1995 Angel with Teddy	Closed	1997	30.00	35-55
1982 Angel With Toys	Closed	1988	14.00	150
1995 Angel, Guiding Light, pink, green & white	Closed	1996	30.00	35-50
1983 Baby Bear in Vest, 5 colors	Closed	1988	11.00	85
1982 Baby Bear, Teeshirt	Closed	1984	11.00	125-175
1985 Baby Pig	Closed	1988	11.00	100-125
1983 Baby, blue trim	Closed	1988	11.00	110
1983 Baby, pink trim	Closed	1988	11.00	110-150
1991 Boy Angel, white	Closed	1992	20.00	100-125
1982 Candy Cane	Closed	1984	10.00	320-375
1993 Christmas Treat, blue	Closed	1996	30.00	60
1982 Colonial Man, 3 colors	Closed	1984	12.00	175
1982 Colonial Woman, 3 colors	Closed	1984	12.00	100-150
1984 Country Boy, 2 colors	Closed	1988	12.00	65-100
1984 Country Girl, 2 colors	Closed	1988	12.00	65-100
1993 Elf Bernie	Closed	1994	30.00	45-65
1995 Elf Danny	Closed	1997	30.00	45-65
1990 Elf Jeffrey	Closed	1992	17.00	50-65
1991 Elf Joey	Closed	1993	20.00	50-65
1994 Elf Ricky	Closed	1995	30.00	45-65
1992 Elf Scotty	Closed	1993	25.00	45-65
1994 Elf Tammy	Closed	1995	30.00	35-65
1988 Elizabeth, sill sitter	Closed	1989	20.00	150-175
1983 Father Bear in Suit, 3 colors	Closed	1988	12.00	100
1985 Father Pig	Closed	1988	12.00	100
1993 Final Notes	Closed	1994	30.00	55-65
1991 Girl Angel, white	Closed	1993	20.00	100-125
1983 Gloria Angel	Closed	1984	14.00	400-500
1989 Glorious Angel	Closed	1992	17.00	75-85
1983 Grandma, 4 colors	Closed	1988	12.00	75-100
1983 Grandpa, 4 colors	Closed	1988	12.00	75-100
1988 Guardian Angel	Closed	1991	16.00	40
1990 Harvest Santa	Closed	1992	17.00	65-75
1990 Ho Ho Ho	Closed	1992	17.00	65-75
1982 Kate Greenaway Boy, 3 colors	Closed	1983	12.00	155-310
1982 Kate Greenaway Girl, 3 colors	Closed	1983	12.00	125-200
1982 Mama Bear, Blue Cape	Closed	1984	12.00	100-175
1983 Mother Bear in Dress, 3 colors	Closed	1988	12.00	75-85
1985 Mother Pig	Closed	1988	12.00	100-125
1984 Mr. Claus	Closed	1988	14.00	75
1984 Mrs. Claus	Closed	1988	14.00	75
1994 Mrs. Klaus	Closed	1997	30.00	50-65
1992 Northpole News	Closed	1993	25.00	55-75
1994 Nutcracker	Closed	1995	30.00	40
1993 Old Lamplighter	Closed	1994	30.00	55-65
1984 Old World Santa, 3 colors	Closed	1989	14.00	185-220
1984 Old World Santa, gold	Closed	1986	14.00	300
1982 Papa Bear, Red Cape	Closed	1984	12.00	100-175
1992 Praying Angel	Closed	1993	25.00	30-45
1985 Primitive Santa	Closed	1989	17.00	175
1983 Raggedy Andy, 2 colors	Closed	1983	12.00	220-250
1983 Raggedy Ann, 2 colors	Closed	1983	12.00	300-325
1994 Ringing in Christmas	Closed	1995	30.00	45-65
1995 Santa Nutcracker	Closed	1997	30.00	40
1986 Santa with Bag	Closed	1989	16.00	75-85
1991 Santa with Banner	Closed	1992	20.00	50-75
1992 Santa with Basket	Closed	1993	25.00	50-75
1986 Santa with Bear	Closed	1991	14.00	75-85
1986 Santa with Bells, blue	Closed	1989	14.00	75
1986 Santa with Bells, green	Closed	1987	14.00	300-500
1988 Santa with Book, blue & red	Closed	1988	17.00	300-360
1991 Santa with Lights, black or white	Closed	1992	20.00	75-100
1994 Santa with Pipe	Closed	1997	30.00	45-50
1992 Santa with Sack	Closed	1993	25.00	45-65
1989 Santa with Staff	Closed	1991	17.00	75-85
1982 Santa with Toys	Closed	1988	14.00	150-200
1988 Santa with Toys	Closed	1991	17.00	50-100
1989 Santa with Tree	Closed	1991	17.00	50-75
1988 Santa with Wreath	Closed	1991	17.00	40-75
1995 Santa's Lil' Helper, brown	Closed	1996	30.00	50-65
1996 Santa's Lil' Helper, white	Closed	1997	30.00	30-55
1994 Snow Showers	Closed	1997	30.00	50-55
1983 St. Nick with Lantern (wooden)	Closed	1988	14.00	65-75
1995 Who's This Frosty?	Closed	1997	30.00	50-60
1989 Winking Santa	Closed	1991	17.00	75

Kurt S. Adler, Inc.

Children's Hour - J. Mostrom

YEAR ISSUE	EDITION LIMIT	YEAR RETD.	ISSUE PRICE	*QUOTE U.S.$
1995 Alice in Wonderland J5751	Retrd.	1996	22.50	23
1995 Bow Peep J5753	Retrd.	1997	27.00	27
1995 Cinderella J5752	Retrd.	1996	28.00	28
1995 Little Boy Blue J5755	Retrd.	1995	18.00	18
1995 Miss Muffet J5753	Retrd.	1997	27.00	27
1995 Mother Goose J5754	Retrd.	1996	27.00	27
1995 Red Riding Hood J5751	Retrd.	1996	22.50	23

Christmas in Chelsea Collection - J. Mostrom

YEAR ISSUE	EDITION LIMIT	YEAR RETD.	ISSUE PRICE	*QUOTE U.S.$
1994 Alice, Marguerite W2973	Retrd.	1996	28.00	28
1992 Allison Sitting in Chair W2812	Retrd.	1994	25.50	26
1992 Allison W2729	Retrd.	1993	21.00	21
1992 Amanda W2709	Retrd.	1994	21.00	21
1992 Amy W2729	Retrd.	1993	21.00	21
1992 Christina W2812	Retrd.	1994	25.50	26
1992 Christopher W2709	Retrd.	1994	21.00	21
1992 Delphinium W2728	Retrd.	1997	20.00	20
1995 Edmond With Violin W3078	Retrd.	1996	32.00	32
1994 Guardian Angel With Baby W2974	Retrd.	1995	31.00	31
1992 Holly Hock W2728	Retrd.	1997	20.00	20
1992 Holly W2709	Retrd.	1994	21.00	21
1995 Jose With Violin W3078	Retrd.	1996	32.00	32
1995 Pauline With Violin W3078	Retrd.	1996	32.00	32
1992 Peony W2728	Retrd.	1997	20.00	20

*Quotes have been rounded up to nearest dollar

YEAR ISSUE	EDITION LIMIT	YEAR RETRD.	ISSUE PRICE	*QUOTE U.S.$
1992 Rose W2728	Retrd.	1997	20.00	20
Cornhusk Mice Ornament Series - M. Rothenberg				
1994 3" Father Christmas W2976	Retrd.	1998	18.00	18
1994 9" Father Christmas W2982	Retrd.	1997	25.00	25
1995 Angel Mice W3088	Retrd.	1997	10.00	10
1995 Baby's First Mouse W3087	Retrd.	1998	10.00	10
1993 Ballerina Cornhusk Mice W2700	Retrd.	1994	13.50	14
1994 Clara, Prince W2948	Retrd.	1997	16.00	16
1994 Cowboy W2951	Retrd.	1996	18.00	18
1994 Drosselmeir Fairy, Mouse King W2949	Retrd.	1997	16.00	16
1994 Little Pocahontas, Indian Brave W2950	Retrd.	1997	18.00	18
1995 Miss Tammie Mouse W3086	Retrd.	1996	17.00	17
1995 Mr. Jamie Mouse W3086	Retrd.	1996	17.00	17
1995 Mrs. Molly Mouse W3086	Retrd.	1996	17.00	17
1993 Nutcracker Suite Fantasy Cornhusk Mice W2885	Retrd.	1994	15.50	16
Fabriché™ Ornament Series - KS. Adler, unless otherwise noted				
1994 All Star Santa W1665	Retrd.	1996	27.00	27
1992 An Apron Full of Love W1594 - M. Rothenberg	Retrd.	1996	27.00	27
1995 Captain Claus W1711	Retrd.	1998	25.00	25
1994 Checking His List W1634	Retrd.	1996	23.50	24
1992 Christmas in the Air W1593	Retrd.	1996	35.50	36
1994 Cookies For Santa W1639	Retrd.	1996	28.00	28
1994 Firefighting Friends W1668	Retrd.	1996	28.00	28
1992 Hello Little One! W1561	Retrd.	1996	22.00	22
1994 Holiday Flight W1637 - Smithsonian	Retrd.	1996	40.00	40
1993 Homeward Bound W1596	Retrd.	1996	27.00	27
1992 Hugs And Kisses W1560	Retrd.	1996	22.00	22
1993 Master Toymaker W1595	Retrd.	1996	27.00	27
1992 Merry Chrismouse W1565	Retrd.	1994	10.00	10
1992 Not a Creature Was Stirring W1563	Retrd.	1996	22.00	22
1992 Par For the Claus W1625	Retrd.	1997	27.00	27
1993 Santa With List W1510	Retrd.	1996	20.00	20
1994 Santa's Fishtales W1666	Retrd.	1996	29.00	29
1995 Strike Up The Band W1710	Retrd.	1996	25.00	25
Fabriché™ Vatican Library Collection - Vatican Library				
1998 Vatican Angels in Flight (2 asst.) V34/A	Retrd.	1999	29.00	29
1998 Vatican Angels in Flight (gold) V34/GO	Retrd.	1999	29.00	29
International Christmas - J. Mostrom				
1994 Cathy, Johnny W2945	Retrd.	1996	24.00	24
1994 Eskimo-Atom, Ukpik W2967	Retrd.	1996	28.00	28
1994 Germany-Katerina, Hans W2969	Retrd.	1996	27.00	27
1994 Native American-White Dove, Little Wolf W2970	Retrd.	1994	28.00	28
1994 Poland-Marissa, Hedwig W2965	Retrd.	1997	27.00	27
1994 Scotland-Bonnie, Douglas W2966	Retrd.	1997	27.00	27
1994 Spain-Maria, Miguel W2968	Retrd.	1997	27.00	27
Little Dickens - J. Mostrom				
1994 Little Bob Crachit W2961	Retrd.	1996	30.00	30
1994 Little Marley's Ghost W2964	Retrd.	1996	33.50	34
1994 Little Mrs. Crachit W2962	Retrd.	1997	27.00	27
1994 Little Scrooge in Bathrobe W2959	Retrd.	1997	30.00	30
1994 Little Scrooge in Overcoat W2960	Retrd.	1997	30.00	30
1994 Little Tiny Tim W2963	Retrd.	1997	22.50	23
Polonaise™ - KSA/Komozja, unless otherwise noted				
2000 2000 Global Santa AP1144	Open		30.00	30
1999 2000 Ornament AP1119	Open		17.95	18
1994 Acorn AP342	Retrd.	1995	11.00	60-150
1999 Adoring Santa, 6 1/2" AP955 - I. Wiszniewska	Retrd.	1999	39.95	40-45
1995 African-American Santa AP389/A	Retrd.	1998	22.50	28
1995 Alarm Clock AP452	Retrd.	1996	25.00	25
1997 Alice Collection 4 pc set AP548	Open		150.00	150
1997 Alice Collection 5 pc set AP547	7,500	1998	175.00	175-190
1997 Alice in Wonderland AP692	Open		29.95	30
1997 Alice in Wonderland, 4 asst. AP692/356	Open		29.95	30
1994 Angel AP309	Retrd.	1996	18.00	20
1999 Angel Tree Top AP1042	Retrd.	1999	80.00	80
1994 Angel w/Bear AP396	Retrd.	1996	20.00	30-45
1998 Ann & Andy on the Moon AP887	Retrd.	1999	39.95	40
1999 Annunciation Box (Artist Series) AP201	Open		70.00	70
1996 Antique Cars boxed set AP522	Retrd.	1999	120.00	120-135
1995 Antique Cars, 4 asst. AP429	Retrd.		22.50	23
1994 Apple AP339	Retrd.	1995	11.00	15-25
1999 Arabian Nights 3 pc. AP582	Open		120.00	120
1999 Arabian Nights 3/Asst, 6 1/2" AP982/34	Open		34.95	35
1997 Babar Elephant, 5" AP817 - Clifford Ross/Nelrana	Retrd.	1999	37.50	40
1998 Babe Ruth AP914	Open		39.95	40
2000 Babe Ruth Bust AP1203	Open		36.00	36
1999 Baby's 1st Christmas AP985/BF	Open		24.95	25
2000 Baby's First Christmas Elephant AP1200	Open		22.50	23
2000 Bear and Bull AP1231	Open		33.00	33
2000 Bear in Stocking AP1096	Open		35.00	35
2000 Beefeater AP1258	Open		33.00	33
1994 Beer Glass AP366	Retrd.	1999	15.95	18
1999 Behold, the Lamb of God AP971 - I. Wiszniewska	Retrd.	1999	34.95	35-40
1998 Believe Santa AP890 - M. Engelbreit	Open		37.50	38
1999 Best Friends Cat and Dog, 4 1/2" AP980	Open		29.95	30
1999 Betty Boop "2000" AP1165	Open		37.50	38

YEAR ISSUE	EDITION LIMIT	YEAR RETRD.	ISSUE PRICE	*QUOTE U.S.$
1996 Betty Boop AP624 - King Features	Retrd.	1999	34.95	35-45
1996 Betty Boop as Mae West AP876	Retrd.	2000	39.95	40
1999 Betty Boop in Bubble Bath AP1038	Open		39.95	40
2000 Betty Boop w/Toys AP1253	Open		40.00	40
1998 Bi-Plane, green AP896	Retrd.	2000	45.00	45
1999 Bi-Plane, red AP896/2R	Open		45.00	45
1997 The Bible AP841 - I. Wiszniewska	Open		34.95	35
1997 Big Bird AP699	Retrd.	1999	34.95	36
1998 Bishop AP856	Retrd.	2000	34.95	35
2000 Black Holly Bearie AP827/BLK - H. Adler	Open		29.95	30
1999 Black Piano, AP1018 BLK	Open		29.95	30
1995 Blessed Mother AP413	Retrd.	1997	19.95	25
1998 Bob Cratchit w/Tiny Tim AP885	Open		39.95	40
1994 Boot w/Gifts AP375	Retrd.	1999	19.95	20
1995 Caesar AP422	Retrd.	1998	19.95	20-25
1997 Calvary, Gunner, Drummer AP645	Open		29.95	30
2000 Campbell Chicken Soup AP877/CH	Open		33.00	33
1998 Campbell Soup Can-Tomato AP877	Open		34.95	35
1999 Campbell Soup Kid, 6 1/2" AP975	Open		29.95	30
1999 Campbell Soup Kids AP1187	Open		40.00	40
1996 Candleholder AP450	Retrd.	1997	17.95	20
1995 Cardinal AP473 - Stefan	Retrd.	1999	29.95	30-33
1994 Cardinal on Pine Cone AP420	Retrd.	1995	18.00	33
1999 Carousel, 5 1/2" AP998	Retrd.	2000	34.50	35
1999 Casablanca 3 pc. boxed set AP589	Open		170.00	170
1999 Casablanca Disc AP1065	Open		39.95	40
1995 Cat in Boot AP478 - Rothenberg	Retrd.	1999	29.95	30-33
1994 Cat w/Ball AP390	Retrd.	1995	18.00	50
1995 Cat w/Bow AP443	Retrd.	1999	22.50	24
2000 Celebrate Millennium 3 pc. Set AP1230	Open		120.00	120
2000 Charlie Brown as Santa AP1212	Open		36.00	36
1997 Charlie Brown Peanuts, 5 1/2" AP824	Retrd.	1999	34.95	35-40
1998 Charlie Brown with Gifts AP917	Retrd.	2000	39.95	40
1994 Cherubs AP845/67	Retrd.	1999	19.95	20
2000 Chimney Sweeper AP1111	Open		25.00	25
1999 Chiquita Banana AP1037	Open		37.50	38
1997 Christ Child AP414	Retrd.	1997	17.95	20
1999 Christmas Carol Book, 6 1/2" AP973 - I. Wiszniewska	Open		34.95	35
1998 Christmas Carol, 4 asst. AP832/4	Open		37.50	38
1997 Christmas in Poland 4pc set AP534	Retrd.	1999	150.00	150-165
1995 Christmas Tree AP461	Retrd.	1999	24.95	25-45
1997 Church AP369	Retrd.	1997	15.95	20
1999 Cigar Store Indian AP1026	Open		29.95	30
1996 Cinderella 4 pc boxed set AP512	Retrd.	1998	130.00	135
1996 Cinderella 6 pc boxed set AP511	7,500	1996	190.00	250
1996 Cinderella AP488	Retrd.	1996	27.50	28-31
1996 Cinderella Coach AP487	Retrd.	1999	34.95	37-40
1997 Circus Collection 5 pc set AP545	Open		180.00	180
1997 Circus Ring Master AP691	Open		32.50	35
1997 Circus Seal AP688	Retrd.	2000	29.95	30
1997 Circus Strongman AP690	Open		32.50	35
1995 Clara AP408	Retrd.	2000	19.95	20
2000 Cleopatra's Boat-Egyptian Boat AP1084	Open		35.00	35
1999 Climbing Santa, 5 1/2" AP1004	Retrd.	1999	34.95	36
1994 Clown 4" AP301	Retrd.	1995	13.50	45
1994 Clown 6" AP303	Retrd.	1995	22.50	40
1994 Clown Head 4.5" AP460	Retrd.	1997	22.50	30-40
1994 Clown on Ball 6.5" AP302	Retrd.	1995	22.50	35
2000 Clown, 4 asst. AP1126	Open		30.00	30
1994 Clowns 3 asst. AP682	Retrd.	1999	34.95	35
1997 Coca-Cola 3 pc AP553	Open		130.00	130
1995 Coca-Cola 4 pc boxed set AP517	Retrd.	1998	135.00	135
1996 Coca-Cola 6 Pack AP803	Retrd.	1999	34.95	40-45
1999 Coca-Cola 8 Wheeler, 8" AP1040	Open		37.50	38
1998 Coca-Cola Balloon AP939	Open		45.00	45
1996 Coca-Cola Bear AP630	Retrd.	1999	34.95	37-40
1997 Coca-Cola Bear Skiing AP801	Retrd.	2000	34.95	35-40
1997 Coca-Cola Bear Snowmobile AP802	Retrd.		34.95	35-40
1997 Coca-Cola Bottle (golden) AP800	Retrd.	1999	34.95	35-40
1996 Coca-Cola Bottle AP631	Retrd.	1999	29.95	35-40
1996 Coca-Cola Bottle Cap AP633	Retrd.	1999	24.95	27-30
2000 Coca-Cola Bottle, green AP631/GB	Open		32.50	33
1998 Coca-Cola Bottles 4 pc. AP567	Open		150.00	150
1999 Coca-Cola Can, 4" AP1014	Open		34.95	35
2000 Coca-Cola Carousel Bear AP1239	Open		40.00	40
1996 Coca-Cola Disk AP632	Retrd.	1998	24.95	40-45
1998 Coca-Cola Disk w/Santa Hat AP842	Open		29.95	30
1999 Coca-Cola Ho-Ho-Ho 2 pc. boxed set AP585	Open		120.00	120
2000 Coca-Cola Millenium Bear AP1238	Open		40.00	40
1997 Coca-Cola Old Delivery Truck AP804	Retrd.	2000	37.50	38-40
1997 Coca-Cola Roly Poly Santa AP867	Open		45.00	40
2000 Coca-Cola Sign AP1221	Open		33.00	33
2000 Coca-Cola Soda Fountain AP1076	Open		34.95	35
2000 Coca-Cola Soda Fountain AP1076	Open		34.95	35
2000 Coca-Cola Soda Fountain AP1076	Open		34.95	35
2000 Coca-Cola Soda Fountain AP1076	Open		34.95	35
2000 Coca-Cola Soda Fountain AP1076	Open		34.95	35
2000 Coca-Cola Soda Fountain AP1076	Open		34.95	35
2000 Coca-Cola Soda Fountain AP1076	Open		34.95	35
2000 Coca-Cola Soda Fountain AP1076	Open		34.95	35
2000 Coca-Cola Soda Fountain AP1076	Open		34.95	35
1997 Coca-Cola Train 4 pc AP572	Retrd.	1999	110.00	110
1996 Coca-Cola Vending Machine AP634	Retrd.	1999	34.95	36-51
2000 Coke Can-Diet AP1014DC	Open		33.00	33
1999 Coke Locomotive AP444	Retrd.	1999	25.00	25

YEAR ISSUE	EDITION LIMIT	YEAR RETRD.	ISSUE PRICE	*QUOTE U.S.$
1998 Coke Roly Santa AP867	Open		45.00	45
1999 Coke Signature Ball AP1064	Open		29.95	30
1999 Columbus Flotilla 3 asst. AP1051/23	Open		32.50	33
1999 Columbus Flotilla 3 pc. boxed set AP587	Open		130.00	130
2000 Confederate Soldier AP1122	Open		27.50	28
1998 Cookie Monster AP923	Open		37.50	38
1996 Cossack AP604	Retrd.	1998	34.95	35-39
1999 Couch Cat AP1045 - Stefan	Open		37.50	38
2000 Cow Over the Moon AP1233 - Stefan	Open		37.00	37
1999 Cow, 5 1/2" AP961	Open		27.50	28
1995 Cowboy Head AP462	Retrd.	1998	29.95	33-45
1998 Cowboy Head, black hat AP462/BH	Open		29.95	30
2000 Cracker Jack Bear AP1204	Open		36.00	36
1999 Cracker Jack Box AP1020	Open		39.95	40
1999 Creche AP458 - Stefan	Retrd.	1999	27.50	28
1995 Crocodile AP468	Retrd.	1996	28.00	30
1999 Dec. 1999 & Jan. 2000 Calendars, 2 asst. AP1140/1	Retrd.	2000	20.00	20
2000 December Santa-Santa of the Month AP1178	Open		37.50	38
1996 Dice boxed set AP509	Retrd.	1997	55.00	60
1994 Dinosaurs 2 asst. green AP397	Retrd.	1996	22.50	24-60
1994 Dinosaurs-brown AP397	Retrd.	1995	22.50	55-60
2000 Divine Love AP1250 - I. Wiszniewska	Open		39.00	39
1999 Dog in Tub, 5" AP981	Retrd.	1999	29.95	30
1994 Doll AP377	Retrd.	1995	13.50	35
1999 Doll, 5 1/2" AP1003	Retrd.	2000	17.95	18
2000 Don Quixote 3 pc. boxed set AP215	Open		130.00	130
2000 Dorothy w/Rainbow-Oz AP1214	Open		30.00	30
1999 Dorothy-Full Body AP1060	Open		39.95	40
1995 Dove on Ball AP472 - Stefan	Retrd.	1996	29.95	30
1998 Down the Chimney Santa AP860	Open		29.95	30
1997 Dr. Watson AP813	Retrd.	1999	29.95	30-36
2000 Drum "Beating The Drums" AP1108	Open		25.00	25
1995 Eagle AP453	Retrd.	1999	29.95	30
1997 Ebenezer Scrooge AP832	Open		37.50	38
1994 Egyptian (12 pc boxed set) AP500	Retrd.	1995	214.00	214-360
1997 Egyptian 4 pc set AP515	Retrd.	1999	150.00	150
1996 Egyptian Architecture AP1083	Open		34.95	35
1996 Egyptian Cat AP351	Open		27.50	30
1996 Egyptian II boxed set AP510	Retrd.	1999	150.00	150-170
1998 Egyptian Princess AP482	Retrd.	1999	34.95	33-35
1995 Egyptian set 4 pc. boxed AP500/4	Retrd.	1997	100.00	110-120
1998 Elegant Santa, burgundy AP857/BURG	Open		32.50	33
1998 Elegant Santa, gold AP857/GD	Retrd.	1999	32.50	33
1998 Elegant Santa, purple AP857/PURP	Retrd.	1999	32.50	33
1998 Elegant Santa, white AP857/W	Retrd.	1999	32.50	33
1998 Elegant Santas, 4 asst. AP857	Retrd.	2000	32.50	33
1995 Elephant AP 464	Retrd.	1999	27.50	25-28
2000 Elephant AP1219 - WWF	Open		30.00	30
1997 Elmo AP843	Open		37.50	38
1996 Elves AP611/23	Retrd.	1999	29.95	30
2000 Elvis Name AP1205	Open		36.00	36
2000 Elvis with Guitar AP1207	Open		50.00	50
1996 Emerald City AP623	Retrd.	1998	29.95	30-37
1998 English Barrister AP831	Open		29.95	30
1997 English Bobbie AP814	Retrd.	1999	29.95	30-36
1999 Ermine Santa, 6 1/2" AP945	Open		34.95	35
1999 Ernie AP1049	Open		37.50	38
1997 The Evolution of Polonaise™ Kit (boxed set) AP564	Open		50.00	50
2000 Farm Horse "Stable Mate" AP1112	Open		25.00	25
1999 Fearful Lion AP1063	Open		39.95	40
2000 Fire Engine "To The Rescue" AP1197	Open		35.00	35
1996 Fire Engine AP605	Retrd.	1999	29.95	30-40
1995 Fish 4 pc. boxed AP506	Retrd.	1998	110.00	120-125
2000 Fish, 4 asst. AP1125	Open		22.50	23
1998 Five Golden Rings AP899 - Stefan	Open		37.50	38
1999 Flight Into Egypt (Artist Series) AP597	Open		70.00	70
1998 Flying Angels, 3 asst. AP881	Open		45.00	45
2000 Flying Man "Up & Away" AP1085	Open		37.50	38
1999 Flying Monkey-Oz AP1054	Open		39.95	40
1998 Ford Mustang, red AP929	Open		39.95	40
1998 Ford Truck w/Christmas Tree AP937	Open		39.95	40
1997 Four Calling Birds AP828	Open		37.50	38
1996 French Boots AP1115 - L. Nicole	Open		29.95	30
1996 French Hen AP626 - Stefan	Open		36.00	36
1998 Friendly Ghost AP834	Retrd.	1999	29.95	25-30
1999 Frog King AP1000	Open		37.50	38
1998 Garfield AP891	Open		37.50	38
1999 Garfield Santa w/Gifts AP1073	Open		37.50	38
2000 Gentleman Golfer AP1232	Open		37.00	37
1999 Gepetto, 7 1/2" AP947	Open		37.50	38
1996 Gift Boxes AP614	Retrd.	1999	24.95	25
1997 Gingerbread House AP664	Retrd.	1999	29.95	30-36
2000 Giraffe-World Wild Fund AP1130	Open		25.00	25
1995 Girl with Bear, 6 1/2" AP989	Retrd.	1999	24.95	25
1995 Glinda Good Witch-Oz AP621	Retrd.	1998	34.95	35-40
1998 Glinda the Good Witch AP920	Open		37.50	38
2000 Glinda The Good Witch-Oz AP1189	Open		37.50	38
1994 Gnome AP347	Retrd.	1995	18.00	35
1994 Golden Cherub Head AP372	Retrd.	1994	18.00	60-75
1994 Golden Rocking Horse AP355	Retrd.	1994	22.50	60-65
1999 Gone With The Wind 2 pc. boxed set AP590	Open		135.00	135

ORNAMENTS

YEAR ISSUE	EDITION LIMIT	YEAR RETD.	ISSUE PRICE	*QUOTE U.S.$
1997 Gone With The Wind 3 pc boxed set AP557	Retrd.	1999	150.00	150-175
1998 Gone with the Wind Heart AP925	Retrd.	1999	39.95	40
1997 Gone With The Wind Rhett Butler AP815	Retrd.	1999	37.50	38-45
1997 Gone With The Wind Scarlett O'Hara AP805	Retrd.	1999	39.95	40-45
1997 Gone With The Wind Tara AP816	Open		37.50	38
1999 Good Humor Truck AP1068	Open		39.95	40
1995 Goose w/Wreath AP475 - Stefan	Retrd.	1999	29.95	30-33
1996 Gramophone AP446	Retrd.	1996	22.50	23
1997 Grand Father Frost AP810COL	Retrd.	1999	50.00	50
2000 Halloween Cat AP1223	Open		25.00	25
1999 Handyman Teddy Bear, 6" AP958	Retrd.	1999	34.95	35
1997 Hansel & Gretel AP662	Open		29.95	30
1997 Hansel/Gretel 4 pc set AP538	Retrd.	2000	150.00	135-150
1999 Happy Easter Snoopy AP1164	Open		35.00	35
2000 Happy Holiday 2000/2001 Ball AP1227	Open		30.00	30
1997 Hat Boxes AP620	Retrd.	1999	27.50	28
1997 Herald Rabbit AP693	Open		32.50	35
1995 Herr Drosselmeir AP465 - Rothenberg	Retrd.	1999	29.95	30-35
1999 Hockey Player, 6" AP1013	Open		34.95	35
1997 Holly Bear AP827	Retrd.	2000	29.95	35-38
2000 The Holy Family 1 pc. boxed set AP200	Open		70.00	70
1995 Holy Family 3 pc. AP504	Retrd.	1997	80.00	60-84
1998 Holy Family 3 pc. boxed set AP576	Open		100.00	100
2000 The Holy Family AP1148	Open		27.50	28
1994 Holy Family AP371	Retrd.	1998	27.50	28-30
1998 Holy Family AP898	Retrd.	1999	37.50	38
1998 Holy Family, 3 asst. AP861/23	Open		29.95	30
1998 Honey Bear AP900	Retrd.	1999	29.95	30
2000 Honey Bee & Wasp, 2 asst. AP1080/81	Open		27.50	28
1996 Horus AP484	Retrd.	1998	34.95	30-35
1995 Houses (2 asst.) AP455	Retrd.	1996	25.00	30
1999 Howdy Doody AP968	Open		39.95	40
1998 Hummingbirds, 2 asst. AP893	Open		37.50	38
1999 Humphrey Bogart AP1048	Open		39.95	40
1995 Humpty Dumpty AP477 - Stefan	Retrd.	1999	29.95	30-33
1997 Hunter AP667	Open		29.95	30
1995 Icicle Santa AP474 - Stefan	Retrd.	1995	25.00	40-45
1995 Indian Chief AP463	Retrd.	1999	29.95	30-33
1998 Indian Motorcycle AP940	Open		39.95	40
1999 Ingrid Bergman AP1047	Open		39.95	40
2000 Irish Santa-Santa of the Month Series AP1193	Open		35.00	35
1999 Isis AP1041	Open		32.50	33
1998 It's a Wonderful Life AP910	Retrd.	2000	45.00	45
2000 Jack O'Lantern AP897/NW	Open		19.95	20
1999 James Dean, 7" AP995	Open		39.95	40
1998 Jazz Band 4 pc. AP569	Retrd.	1999	150.00	150
1998 Jazz Musicians, 4 asst. AP851/04	Retrd.	1999	29.95	30
1997 Jewelry Boxes AP637	Retrd.	1999	15.95	16
1998 Joseph AP862	Open		29.95	30
2000 Journey to Egypt 3 pc. boxed set AP208	Open		120.00	120
1999 Just Married 2 pc. boxed set AP584	Open		90.00	90
1997 Just Married AP829	Open		22.50	23
1996 King Balthazar AP607	Retrd.	1997	29.95	31
1998 King Kong AP918	Retrd.	2000	39.95	40
2000 King Kong II AP1183	Open		37.50	38
1996 King Neptune AP496	Retrd.	1999	34.95	35
2000 King Richard-Shakespearean Collection AP1185	Open		35.00	35
1994 Knight's Helmet AP304	Retrd.	1995	18.00	22-26
1995 Knight's Horse AP640	Retrd.	1999	34.95	35
1997 Krakow Castle AP670	Retrd.	1999	34.95	33-35
1997 Krakow Man AP674	Retrd.	1999	29.95	30-38
1998 Large Churches, 3 asst. AP880/03	Open		29.95	30
1998 Let It Rain AP901	Retrd.	2000	29.95	30
1996 Light Bulb AP449	Retrd.	1996	20.00	20
2000 Lion-Oz AP1215	Open		30.00	30
1998 Little Elfers AP935	Retrd.	1999	37.50	38-44
1995 The Little Mermaid 5 pc. boxed set AP513	Retrd.	1998	165.00	165-175
1996 Little Mermaid AP492	Retrd.	1997	27.50	28-31
1998 Little Mermaid, 2 asst. AP492/NW	Retrd.	1999	27.50	28
1997 Little Red Riding Hood 3 pc. AP544	Retrd.	1999	110.00	110
1997 Little Red Riding Hood 4 pc set AP539	Yr.Iss.	1997	140.00	135-150
1997 Little Red Riding Hood 5 1/2" AP665	Open		29.95	30
1994 Locomotive AP353	Retrd.	1998	19.95	20-24
1995 Locomotive AP447	Retrd.	1999	27.50	28-30
1998 London Bus AP686	Retrd.	2000	29.95	30
1998 London Phone Booth AP698	Open		27.50	28
1997 Lucy Peanuts AP825	Retrd.	1999	34.95	35
1997 Mad Hatter AP696	Open		32.50	35
1998 Madeline AP922	Open		37.50	38
1999 Madeline by Eiffel Tower AP1069	Open		39.95	40
1998 Madonna & Child AP861	Open		29.95	30
1994 Madonna w/Child AP370	Retrd.	1997	22.50	25
1999 Magic Fish, 4" AP963	Open		17.95	18
1997 Magician's Hat AP689	Retrd.	1999	34.95	35-39
1998 Mammy-GWW AP924	Open		39.95	40
2000 Man of the Hour AP1175 - M. Engelbriet	Open		40.00	40
1997 Marilyn Monroe AP818	Open		37.50	38
2000 Marilyn Monroe Bust AP1210 - CMG	Open		39.00	39
1999 Marilyn Monroe II, 7" AP992	Open		37.50	38
1998 Marley's Ghost AP886	Open		34.95	35
1996 Medieval boxed set AP519	Retrd.	1998	150.00	100-170
1996 Medieval Dragon AP642	Retrd.	1999	34.95	35
1996 Medieval Knight AP641	Retrd.	1999	34.95	35
1996 Medieval Lady AP643	Retrd.	1998	34.95	35
1994 Merlin AP373	Retrd.	1995	20.00	30-42
2000 Merlin The Magician AP1194	Open		30.00	30
1997 MGM Cowardly Lion AP821	Open		39.95	40
1997 MGM Dorothy AP819	Open		39.95	40
1997 MGM Scarecrow AP822	Open		39.95	40
1997 MGM Tin Man AP820	Open		39.95	40
1997 MGM Wizard of Oz 4 pc. boxed set AP555	Open		180.00	180
1995 Mickey Mouse AP392	Retrd.	1995	33.00	30-100
1995 Mickey Mouse AP392 & Minnie Mouse (pr.) AP391,set	Retrd.	1995	66.00	90-125
1999 Millenium 3 pc. boxed set AP595	Retrd.	1999	100.00	100
2000 Millenium Tree AP1235	Open		22.50	23
1999 Millennium Santa on Moon, 6 1/2" (Santa of the Month Series) AP1012	Open		37.50	38
1995 Minnie Mouse AP391	Retrd.	1995	33.00	36-82
1999 Monk with Cask, 5 1/2" AP986	Retrd.	2000	27.50	28
1999 Motorcycles 2 asst., 6 1/2" AP993/4	Open		34.50	35
1994 Mouse King AP406	Retrd.	1999	19.95	20-25
1999 Mr. & Mrs. Claus Decorating 2 pc. AP580/DN	Retrd.	1999	100.00	100
1999 Mr. & Mrs. Claus-Chair 2 asst., 7" AP1010/1	Retrd.	1999	37.50	38
2000 Mr. Peanut "Everybody Loves Nut" AP1188	Open		37.50	38
1998 Mr. Peanut AP938	Open		37.50	38
1998 Mrs. Cratchit AP884	Retrd.	1999	34.95	35
1996 Mummy AP483	Retrd.	1999	34.95	30-35
2000 The Munchkin Mayor-Oz AP1191	Open		25.00	25
2000 Mushroom with Elf AP1092	Open		25.00	25
2000 Musical Quartet 4 pc. boxed set AP214	Open		130.00	130
1999 Muskateers 4 pc. AP579	7,500		150.00	150
2000 Mustang Convertible, white AP929/W	Open		39.95	40
1997 Napoleonic Soldier AP543	Retrd.	2000	150.00	150
2000 Nativity Ball AP1173 - Stefan	Open		35.00	35
1996 Nefertiti 96 AP485	Open		34.95	35
1994 Nefertiti AP349	Retrd.	1996	24.95	40-45
1999 New Christmas Tree, 6" AP997	Open		45.00	45
1999 New Locomotive, 6" AP1032	Open		34.95	35
1998 New Scarlett AP928	Retrd.	1999	39.95	40
1994 Night & Day AP307	Retrd.	1997	19.95	20-23
2000 Night Before Christmas Book AP1225 - I. Wiszniewska	Open		36.00	36
2000 Noah And His Ark AP1196	Open		35.00	35
1995 Noah's Ark AP469	Retrd.	2000	27.50	30-35
2000 North & South 4 pc. boxed set AP596	Open		120.00	120
1999 North Pole Exoress 3 pc. boxed set AP586	Open		110.00	110
1999 North Star Santa, 10 1/2" AP1039	Open		37.50	38
1998 Northwind Santa AP878 - Stefan	Open		29.95	30
1994 Nutcracker AP404	Retrd.	1999	19.95	20-22
1995 Nutcracker Suite 4 pc. boxed AP507	Retrd.	1999	125.00	120-125
1997 NY Ball 5/asst. AP677	Open		27.50	28
1994 Old Fashioned Car AP380	Retrd.	1999	22.50	25-29
2000 The Old West 2 pc. boxed set AP578	Open		90.00	90
2000 Ole' King Cole AP1149 - Stefan	Open		35.00	35
1998 Oma & Opa AP870/1	Retrd.	2000	27.50	28
1998 Our New Home AP933	Retrd.	1999	29.95	30
1995 Owl (gold) AP328	Retrd.	1999	17.50	18-20
1994 Owl AP328	Retrd.	1998	17.50	23
1998 Paddington Bear AP915	Retrd.	1999	37.50	38-40
2000 Paddington Bear AP915/BL	Open		34.50	35
1998 Paddington Bear, red coat AP915/R	Open		37.50	38
2000 Parrot "Jungle Fever" AP1091	Open		25.00	25
1994 Parrot AP332	Retrd.	1995	15.50	40-48
1995 Partridge in a Pear Tree AP467 - Stefan	Retrd.	1999	34.95	40-45
2000 Party Elephant "Party Time" AP1113	Open		27.50	28
1998 Peace on Angel AP888	Retrd.	1999	39.95	40-45
2000 Peace on Earth 2 pc. boxed set (dealers only) AP232 - KSA/Wiszniewska	Open		100.00	100
1994 Peacock 5" AP324	Retrd.	1996	18.00	25
1994 Peacock on Ball 7.5" AP323	Retrd.	1996	28.00	28
1997 Peanuts 3 pc boxed set AP556	Open		135.00	135
1998 Peanuts 3 pc. boxed set AP575	Retrd.	1999	150.00	150
2000 Peanuts 50th Anniversary AP1177	Open		40.00	40
2000 Peanuts Ball AP1211	Open		37.00	37
1999 Peanuts Gang on Toboggan AP1027	Open		39.95	40
1998 Peanuts, 3 asst. AP879/79	Retrd.	2000	39.95	40
2000 Penguin "Dressed To The Nines" AP1128	Open		22.50	23
1995 Peter Pan 4 pc. boxed set AP503	Retrd.	1997	125.00	94-125
1995 Peter Pan AP419	Retrd.	1998	19.95	23
2000 Phantom of the Opera AP1179	Open		35.00	35
1999 Phantom of the Opera, 6" AP1016	Open		39.95	40
1996 Pharaoh AP481	Retrd.	1999	34.95	32-35
1994 Pierrot Clown AP405	Retrd.	1995	18.00	35-40
1998 Pillsbury Doughboy AP916	Retrd.	1999	37.50	38
2000 Pillsbury Doughboy w/Candy Cane AP1171	Open		37.50	38
1998 Pink Panther AP889	Retrd.	2000	39.95	40
1999 Pinocchio 3 pc. AP583	Open		140.00	140
1999 Pinocchio, 6 1/2" AP946	Open		34.95	35
2000 Playtime Santa-Swinging Santa AP944	Open		34.95	35
1997 Polish Mountain Man AP675	Retrd.	1999	29.95	30-38
1999 Pony 3 asst. AP985/123	Open		24.95	25
1998 Popeye the Sailor AP907	Retrd.	2000	37.50	38
1996 Prince Charming AP489	Retrd.	1997	27.50	28-31
1998 Pumpkin AP897	Retrd.	2000	22.50	23
1999 Puppeteer, 7" AP948	Retrd.	2000	39.95	40
1994 Puppy (gold) AP333	Retrd.	1994	13.50	35
2000 Puss 'N Boots AP1151 - Stefan	Open		35.00	35
1994 Pyramid AP352	Retrd.	1998	21.95	22
2000 Queen Elizabeth Shakespearean Collection AP1186	Open		35.00	35
1997 Queen of Hearts AP695	Open		32.50	35
1997 Raggedy Andy AP322	Open		24.95	25
2000 Raggedy Ann & Andy on Rocking Horse AP1213	Open		40.00	40
1996 Raggedy Ann AP321	Open		27.50	28
1999 Raggedy Ann on Cushion, 5 1/2" AP1024	Open		37.50	38
1997 Raggedy Ann/Andy AP550	Open		80.00	80
1998 Red & White Santa AP858	Retrd.	1999	24.95	25
1995 Red Dice AP363/R	Retrd.	1999	17.50	14-18
2000 Rhett and Scarlett Embraced AP1209	Open		36.00	36
1999 Rhett Butler Bust AP1067	Open		39.95	40
1998 Riverboat AP855	Retrd.	2000	29.95	30
2000 Rocking Horse "Holiday Rocker" AP1136	Open		25.00	25
1994 Rocking Horse 5" AP356	Retrd.	1999	22.50	25
1999 Rocking Pony 3/Asst, 4 1/2" AP985/123	Open		24.95	25
1994 Roly-Poly Santa AP317	Retrd.	1999	21.95	22
1995 Roman 4 pc. boxed set AP502/4	Retrd.	1995	110.00	140-150
1995 Roman 7 pc. boxed set AP502	Retrd.	1995	164.00	165-195
1995 Roman Centurion AP427	Retrd.	1998	19.95	23
1997 Royal Suite 4 pc set AP552	Retrd.	1999	140.00	140-155
1997 Royal Suite 4/asst. AP806	Retrd.	2000	29.95	30
1998 Ruby Slippers-Oz AP838	Open		29.95	30
1996 Russian 5 pc boxed set AP514	Retrd.	1998	180.00	190
1996 Russian Bishop AP603	Retrd.	1998	34.95	35-39
1996 Russian Woman AP602	Retrd.	1998	34.95	35-39
1998 Sabrina Snow Girl AP859/BL	Retrd.	1999	19.95	20
1995 Sailing Ship AP415	Retrd.	1999	29.95	30
1994 Saint Nick AP316	Retrd.	1998	24.95	30
1998 San Francisco Ball AP927/SF	Open		29.95	30
1998 San Francisco Trolley Car AP911/SF	Open		34.95	35
1995 Santa AP317	Retrd.	1999	22.50	24-28
1995 Santa AP389	Retrd.	1998	22.50	25-28
2000 Santa Bringing Gifts AP1201	Open		30.00	30
2000 Santa Bringing Toys AP1174 - Giordand	Open		40.00	40
1999 Santa Cowboy, 5 1/2" AP1023	Open		29.95	30
2000 Santa Dollar Bill "On the Dollar" AP1087	Open		27.50	28
1999 Santa Drinking Coke, 6 1/2" AP1031	Open		37.50	38
1999 Santa Golfer, 6 1/2" AP1025	Open		29.95	30
1994 Santa Head 4" AP315	Retrd.	1995	13.50	25
1994 Santa Head 4.5" AP374	Retrd.	1996	19.00	25
2000 Santa Head w/Wreath AP1226	Open		30.00	30
1997 Santa Heart AP811	Retrd.	1999	22.50	23
1996 Santa in Airplane AP365	Retrd.	1999	34.95	40-45
2000 Santa in Car AP1228	Open		33.00	33
1996 Santa in Car AP367	Retrd.	2000	34.95	30-35
1995 Santa Moon AP454 - Stefan	Retrd.	1999	27.50	28-30
1995 Santa on Goose on Sled AP479	Retrd.	1999	29.95	30-32
2000 Santa on Locomotive AP1220	Open		33.00	33
1998 Santa on Motorcycle AP931	Retrd.	1999	34.95	35
2000 Santa on Skateboard AP1202	Open		30.00	30
2000 Santa on Spaceship AP1230	Open		33.00	33
1999 Santa Sleeping Under Tree, 5 1/2" AP943	Retrd.	1999	34.95	35
2000 Santa Turtle "Slow Poke" AP1134	Open		22.50	23
1995 Santa w/Puppy AP442	Retrd.	1999	22.50	25-28
1999 Scarecrow Leaning on Fence AP1062	Open		39.95	40
2000 Scarecrow w/Diploma AP1216	Open		30.00	30
2000 Scarlett O'Hara "Riches to Rags" AP1195	Open		35.00	35
1999 Scarlett O'Hara Bust AP1066	Open		39.95	40
2000 Scrooge "Bah Humbug!" AP1180	Open		35.00	35
1996 Sea Horse AP494	Retrd.	1998	24.95	25-38
1997 Seven Dwarfs AP611	Retrd.	2000	29.95	30-38
2000 Seven Swans Swimming AP1167 - Stefan	Open		35.00	35
2000 Shakespeare 3 pc. boxed set AP599	1,000		135.00	135
1995 Shark AP417	Retrd.	1996	18.00	25
1998 Shepherd AP863	Open		29.95	30
1997 Sherlock Holmes 3 pc set AP551	Retrd.	1999	125.00	125-135
1997 Sherlock Holmes AP812	Retrd.	1999	29.95	30-36
1999 Singing in the Rain AP1070	Open		37.50	38
1999 Sir Bones, 6 1/2" AP934	Open		27.50	28
1998 Sir Hogmas AP902	Retrd.	1999	24.95	25
1999 Six Geese AP1075 - Stefan	Open		39.95	40
1996 Slipper AP490	Retrd.	1997	19.95	20-25
1997 Smithsonian Astronaut AP826	Retrd.	1999	34.95	35
2000 Smithsonian Locomotive Phantom AP1181	Open		40.00	40
1998 Smithsonian Montgolfier Balloon AP908	Retrd.	1999	39.95	40
2000 Smithsonian Santa in Hot Air Balloon AP1237	Open		33.00	33
1997 Smithsonian Space Capsule AP839	Retrd.	1999	34.95	35
1999 Smokey Bear, 6 1/2" AP1007	Open		37.50	38
1999 Snoopy Dracula on Pumpkin AP1057	Open		37.50	38

510 Collectors' Information Bureau

*Quotes have been rounded up to nearest dollar

YEAR ISSUE	EDITION LIMIT	YEAR RETD.	ISSUE PRICE	*QUOTE U.S.$
1998 Snoopy on the Doghouse AP879	Open		39.95	40
1997 Snoopy Peanuts AP823	Retrd.	1999	34.95	35-40
1999 Snoopy Santa AP1046	Open		37.50	38
1998 Snow Bearie AP827/S	Retrd.	1999	29.95	30
1997 Snow White & 7 Dwarfs 8 pc boxed set AP558	Open		290.00	290
1997 Snow White AP660	Retrd.	2000	29.95	30
1998 Snowgirl AP859/BL	Retrd.	1999	19.50	20
1999 Snowman Family AP1077	Open		34.95	35
1999 Snowman w/Coke Bottle, 6 1/2" AP1028	Open		39.95	40
1994 Snowman w/Parcel AP313	Retrd.	1999	21.95	22
1994 Snowman w/Specs AP312	Retrd.	1995	20.00	35
1999 Snowman, 6" AP991	Open		19.95	20
2000 Snowtown Snowman AP1078 - M. Stoebner	Open		27.50	28
1994 Soldier AP407	Retrd.	1995	15.50	175
1998 Songbirds AP894	Retrd.	1999	34.95	35-38
1994 Sparrow AP329	Retrd.	1995	15.50	20
1994 Sphinx AP350	Retrd.	1995	22.50	60-65
1996 Sphinx AP480	Retrd.	1999	29.95	30
1994 Spinner Top AP359	Retrd.	1995	9.00	28
1996 St. Basils Cathedral AP600	Retrd.	1999	34.95	35-39
1995 St. Joseph AP412	Retrd.	1996	22.50	23
2000 St. Nick on Horseback AP1154 - Stefan	Open		35.00	35
1998 Standing Angels, 3 asst. AP882	Retrd.	1999	55.00	55
1997 Star 3/asst. AP671	Retrd.	1999	19.95	20
1997 Star Boy AP676	Retrd.	2000	34.95	35
1995 Star Santa AP470 - Stefan	Retrd.	1999	27.50	30-35
1997 Star Santa, blue AP470/BL - Stefan	Retrd.	1999	27.50	28
1996 Star Snowman AP625 - Stefan	Retrd.	1999	29.95	33-45
1997 Star Snowman AP625/BL - Stefan	Retrd.	1999	29.95	30-35
1999 Starlight Angel AP1092	Open		35.00	35
1998 Statue of Liberty AP942	Open		39.95	40
1998 Statue of Liberty Ball AP677/SL	Open		27.50	28
1996 Sting Ray AP495	Retrd.	1996	28.00	28-44
1999 Sunface, 4 1/2" AP967	Retrd.	1999	19.95	20
1994 Swan AP325	Retrd.	1997	17.50	20
1997 Tatar Prince AP672	Retrd.	1999	34.95	35
2000 Teapot "Tea For Two" AP1169 - M. Engelbriet	Open		40.00	40
1999 Teapot AP1043 - M. Engelbreit	Open		44.95	45
1994 Teddy Bear (gold) AP338	Retrd.	1994	13.50	25-40
1999 Teddy Bear in Chair, 6" AP959	Retrd.	2000	34.95	35-37
1999 Teddy Bear with Balloons, 6 1/2" AP987	Retrd.	1999	24.95	25
1995 Telephone AP448	Retrd.	1996	25.00	25
1999 Texaco Pump, 6 1/2" AP1030	Open		34.95	35
2000 Three Kings Ball AP1166 - Stefan	Open		35.00	35
1996 Three Kings boxed set AP516	Open		125.00	144
1995 Three Kings, 3 asst. AP609	Retrd.	1999	29.95	30
1999 Three Musketeers 3/Asst, 6 1/2" AP950/12	Open		37.50	38
2000 Thunderbird, red AP930/R	Open		39.95	40
2000 Tiger-World Wild Fund AP1131	Open		25.00	25
1999 Tin Man Sitting on Stump AP1061	Open		39.95	40
2000 Tin Man w/Heart AP1217	Open		30.00	30
1998 Titanic AP941	Open		45.00	45
1999 Toucan, 7" AP1009	Retrd.	1999	19.95	20-22
1994 Train Coaches AP354	Retrd.	1999	14.95	15
1994 Train Set (boxed) AP501	Retrd.	1999	100.00	100-110
1995 Treasure Chest AP416	Retrd.	1996	20.00	20
1998 Trolley Car AP911	Open		34.95	35
1994 Tropical Fish (4 asst.) AP409	Retrd.	1997	22.50	25-35
2000 Tropical Fish 4 pc. boxed set AP598	Open		120.00	120
1997 Tropical Fish AP410	Retrd.	1999	22.50	28
1997 Tropical Fish AP554	Retrd.	1999	110.00	110
1994 Tropical Fish boxed set AP506	Retrd.	1997	110.00	110-135
1996 Tsar Ivan AP601	Retrd.	1998	34.95	39
1994 Turkey AP326	Retrd.	1996	20.00	20
1995 Turtle Doves AP471 - Stefan	Open		34.95	35
1996 Tutenkhamen #2 AP476	Open		32.50	35
1994 Tutenkhamen AP348	Retrd.	1996	28.00	33
1999 Two Little Pigs, 4" AP962	Open		24.95	25
1998 Uncle Sam AP869	Open		34.95	35
2000 Union Soldier AP1121	Open		27.50	28
2000 United States of Santa 3 pc. boxed set AP210	Open		100.00	100
1998 Vintage Ford 3 asst. AP937/09	Retrd.	1999	39.95	40
2000 Wedding Cake AP1199	Open		35.00	35
1998 Wedding Couple AP868	Open		34.95	35
1999 Wheel of Fortune AP1071	Open		29.95	30
1994 White Dice (original-square) AP363	Retrd.	1994	18.00	42-66
1999 White Piano AP1018/W	Retrd.	1999	29.95	33-40
1996 Wicked Witch AP606	Open		29.95	30
2000 The Wicked Witch of the West-Oz AP1190	Open		37.50	38
1998 Wicked Witch-Oz AP921	Open		39.95	40
1996 Winter Boy AP615	Retrd.	1998	19.95	20-22
1996 Winter Girl AP615	Retrd.	1998	19.95	20-22
1997 Witch-Hanzel & Gretel, 7" AP661	Retrd.	1999	34.95	36-38
1996 Wizard in Balloon AP622	Open		34.95	35
1998 Wizard of Oz 3 pc. boxed set AP573	Open		150.00	150
1999 Wizard of Oz 4 asst. AP1060/123	Open		39.95	40
1995 Wizard of Oz 4 pc. boxed AP505	Open		125.00	125
1999 Wizard of Oz 4 pc. boxed set AP591	Open		190.00	190
1995 Wizard of Oz 6 pc. boxed AP508	5,000	1995	170.00	120-180
1999 Wizard of Oz Book AP1050	Open		37.50	38
1995 Wizard of Oz Dorothy AP434	Open		22.50	25
1996 Wizard of Oz II boxed set AP518	Open		150.00	164
1995 Wizard of Oz Lion AP433	Open		22.50	23
1995 Wizard of Oz Scarecrow AP435	Open		22.50	23
1995 Wizard of Oz Tinman AP436	Open		22.50	23
1999 Wizard of Oz Under Rainbow AP1074	Open		44.95	45
1997 Wizard of Oz, 4 asst. AP819/4	Open		39.95	40
1997 Wolf AP666	Open		32.50	35
1998 Woodstock on Candy Cane AP919	Retrd.	2000	37.50	38
1998 Yellow Taxi Cab AP909	Open		34.95	35
2000 Zebra-World Wild Fund AP1129	Open		25.00	25
1998 Zeppelin Dirigible AP913	Retrd.	1999	27.50	28
1994 Zodiac Sun AP381	Retrd.	1995	22.50	52-55

The Polonaise™ Collector's Guild - KSA/Komozja, unless otherwise noted

YEAR ISSUE	EDITION LIMIT	YEAR RETD.	ISSUE PRICE	*QUOTE U.S.$
1997 Grandfather Frost AP810/COL	Retrd.	1998	Gift	60-65
1999 Carousel Horse AP972/COL	Retrd.	1999	Gift	50
2000 Peace Angel AP1224/CLB	Yr.Iss.		Gift	N/A

Polonaise™ Event Signing Collection - KSA/Komozja

YEAR ISSUE	EDITION LIMIT	YEAR RETD.	ISSUE PRICE	*QUOTE U.S.$
1996 Szlachcic AP673/SIG	Yr.Iss.	1996	35.50	35-65
1997 Szlachcianka AP840	Yr.Iss.	1997	34.95	35
1998 Patriarch Alexis AP926/SIG	Yr.Iss.	1998	35.95	36-45
1999 Just In Time Santa AP1035/SIG	Yr.Iss.	1999	35.95	36-45
2000 Coming Down The Chimney AP1234/SIG	Yr.Iss.		35.00	35

Polonaise™ Pedestals - KSA/Komozja, unless otherwise noted

YEAR ISSUE	EDITION LIMIT	YEAR RETD.	ISSUE PRICE	*QUOTE U.S.$
2000 Angel APD882	Open		60.00	60
2000 Babe Ruth APD914	Open		45.00	45
2000 Baby's 1st Christmas APD1200	Open		27.00	27
2000 Believe Santa APD890 - M. Engelbreight	Open		45.00	45
2000 Betty Boop APD876	Open		45.00	45
2000 Black Piano APD1018/BLK	Open		35.00	35
2000 Christmas Tree II APD997	Open		50.00	50
2000 English Barrister APD831	Open		30.00	30
2000 Garfield APD891	Open		45.00	45
2000 Just Married APD829	Open		30.00	30
2000 King Kong APD918	Open		45.00	45
2000 Madonna & Child APD653	Open		40.00	40
2000 Nativity APD458	Open		33.00	33
2000 Phantom of the Opera APD1016	Open		50.00	50
2000 Raggedy Ann APD321	Open		33.00	33
2000 Santa Bringing Gifts APD1201	Open		40.00	40
2000 Smithsonian Astronaut APD826	Open		40.00	40
2000 Snoopy Easter Beagle APD1164/E	Open		40.00	40
2000 Statue of Liberty APD942	Open		40.00	40
2000 Titanic APD941	Open		45.00	45
2000 Trolley APD911	Open		36.00	36
2000 Tutentkhamen APD476	Open		36.00	36
2000 Wedding Cake APD1199	Open		40.00	40
2000 Wedding Couple APD868	Open		40.00	40
2000 Yellow Cab Taxi APD909	Open		40.00	40

Polonaise™ Vatican Library Collection - Vatican Library

YEAR ISSUE	EDITION LIMIT	YEAR RETD.	ISSUE PRICE	*QUOTE U.S.$
1995 Cherub AP650	Retrd.	1999	37.50	38-40
1996 Cherub Bust Glass AP651	Retrd.	1999	34.95	35
1996 Cherubum boxed set, AP 521	Retrd.	1999	150.00	160-175
1996 Dancing Cherubs on Ball AP652	Retrd.	1998	34.95	40
1995 Eggs AP656	Retrd.	1999	29.50	30
1996 Full Body Cherub AP 650	Retrd.	1999	34.95	40
1996 Garden of Mary boxed set, AP 520	Retrd.	1998	135.00	150
1996 Lily Glass AP655	Retrd.	1998	34.95	35-37
1996 Madonna & Child AP653	Retrd.	1999	34.95	35-37
1996 Rose Glass Pink/Ivory Rose AP654/PIV	Retrd.	1999	34.95	37
1996 Rose Glass Red Rose AP654/R	Retrd.	1999	34.95	37
1999 Vatican Angels AP1058	Open		39.95	40
1999 Vatican Cross w/Jewels AP1059	Retrd.	1999	40.00	40-45
1995 Vatican Egg "Noel" AP658	Retrd.	2000	32.50	33
1995 Vatican Egg-Cherub AP657	Retrd.	2000	32.00	32
2000 Vatican Madonna Foligno AP1245	Open		39.00	39
1997 Vatican Madonna w/Child Egg AP830	Retrd.	1998	37.50	38

Royal Heritage Collection - J. Mostrom

YEAR ISSUE	EDITION LIMIT	YEAR RETD.	ISSUE PRICE	*QUOTE U.S.$
1993 Anastasia W2922	Retrd.	1994	28.00	28
1996 Angelique Angel Baby W3278	Retrd.	1996	25.00	25
1995 Benjamin J5756	Retrd.	1996	24.50	25
1995 Blythe J5756	Retrd.	1996	24.50	25
1996 Brianna Ivory W7663	Retrd.	1999	25.00	25
1996 Brianna Pink W7663	Retrd.	1999	25.00	25
1993 Caroline W2924	Retrd.	1995	25.50	26
1993 Charles W2924	Retrd.	1995	25.50	26
1993 Elizabeth W2924	Retrd.	1995	25.50	26
1996 Etoile Angel Baby W3278	Retrd.	1996	25.00	25
1996 Francis Winter Boy W3279	Retrd.	1997	28.00	28
1996 Gabrielle in Pink Coat W3276	Retrd.	1999	28.00	28
1996 Giselle w/Bow W3277	Retrd.	1997	28.00	28
1996 Giselle Winter Girl w/Package W3279	Retrd.	1997	28.00	28
1994 Ice Fairy, Winter Fairy W2972	Retrd.	1996	25.50	26
1993 Joella W2979	Retrd.	1993	27.00	27
1993 Kelly W2979	Retrd.	1993	27.00	27
1996 Lady Colette in Sled W3301	Retrd.	1997	32.00	32
1996 Laurielle Lady Skater W3281	Retrd.	1997	36.00	36
1996 Miniotte w/Muff W3279	Retrd.	1997	28.00	28
1996 Monique w/Hat Box W3277	Retrd.	1999	28.00	28
1993 Nicholas W2923	Retrd.	1996	25.50	26
1996 Nicole w/Balloon W3277	Retrd.	1999	28.00	28
1993 Patina W2923	Retrd.	1996	25.50	26
1996 Rene Victorian Lady W3280	Retrd.	1997	36.00	36
1993 Sasha W2923	Retrd.	1996	25.50	26
1994 Snow Princess W2971	Retrd.	1996	28.00	28

Smithsonian Museum Carousel - KSA/Smithsonian

YEAR ISSUE	EDITION LIMIT	YEAR RETD.	ISSUE PRICE	*QUOTE U.S.$
1987 Antique Bunny S3027/2	Retrd.	1992	14.50	15-22
1992 Antique Camel S3027/12	Retrd.	1996	15.00	15-22
1989 Antique Cat S3027/6	Retrd.	1995	14.50	15
1992 Antique Elephant S3027/11	Retrd.	1996	14.50	15-22
1995 Antique Frog S3027/18	Retrd.	1999	15.50	16
1988 Antique Giraffe S3027/4	Retrd.	1993	14.50	15
1987 Antique Goat S3027/1	Retrd.	1992	14.50	15
1991 Antique Horse S3027/10	Retrd.	1996	14.50	15-22
1993 Antique Horse S3027/14	Retrd.	1998	15.00	15-22
1988 Antique Horse S3027/3	Retrd.	1993	14.50	15
1989 Antique Lion S3027/5	Retrd.	1994	14.50	15
1994 Antique Pig S3027/16	Retrd.	1998	15.50	16-22
1994 Antique Reindeer S3027/15	Retrd.	1999	15.50	16
1991 Antique Rooster S3027/9	Retrd.	1994	14.50	15
1990 Antique Seahorse S3027/8	Retrd.	1999	14.50	15

Larry Fraga Designs

Larry Fraga Designs Collectors' Club - L. Fraga

YEAR ISSUE	EDITION LIMIT	YEAR RETD.	ISSUE PRICE	*QUOTE U.S.$
2000 Christmas I Bring	1,000		45.00	45

1995 Limited Edition - L. Fraga

YEAR ISSUE	EDITION LIMIT	YEAR RETD.	ISSUE PRICE	*QUOTE U.S.$
1995 Brown Buffalo	5,000	1997	22.00	22
1995 Pickle	5,000	1996	18.00	18
1995 Rainbow Garlands	5,000	1998	28.00	28

1996 Christmas Edition - L. Fraga

YEAR ISSUE	EDITION LIMIT	YEAR RETD.	ISSUE PRICE	*QUOTE U.S.$
1996 Mr. Blackface	2,500	1998	37.00	275-305

1996 Limited Edition - L. Fraga

YEAR ISSUE	EDITION LIMIT	YEAR RETD.	ISSUE PRICE	*QUOTE U.S.$
1996 Big M Mouse	5,000	1999	32.00	32-75
1996 Blimp	5,000	1997	30.00	30-32
1996 Santa on a Shell	5,000	1997	34.00	34-90
1996 Victorian Angel	5,000	1997	35.00	35-80
1996 Victorian Fantasy	5,000	1997	45.00	45-115
1996 Victorian Lyre	5,000	1997	35.00	35-83
1996 Victorian Ship	5,000	1998	45.00	45-125
1996 Wire Zeppelin w/Basket	5,000	1997	37.00	37-142
1996 The Wizard	1,500	1996	88.00	88-97

1997 Christmas Edition - L. Fraga

YEAR ISSUE	EDITION LIMIT	YEAR RETD.	ISSUE PRICE	*QUOTE U.S.$
1997 50's Kitty	300	1998	22.00	22
1997 Accordion	300	1998	49.00	49
1997 African Face	100	1997	33.00	33
1997 Angel Face	300	1998	29.00	29
1997 Angel Fish	120	1998	30.00	30
1997 Angel Light	5,000	1997	67.00	67-76
1997 Angel on Flower	500	1998	25.00	25-57
1997 Aviator Duck	300	1998	28.00	28
1997 Barn Owl	600	1998	42.00	42
1997 Beach Ball Bear	500	1998	30.00	30
1997 Bi-Centennial Owl	500	1998	30.00	30
1997 Blowfish	500	1998	30.00	30
1997 Candle on Clip	1,000	1998	15.00	15
1997 Choo Choo	1,000	1998	22.00	22
1997 Clown on the Moon	500	1998	29.00	29
1997 Crane on Ball	100	1998	30.00	30
1997 Dresden Dove, white	1,000	1998	15.00	15
1997 Duck with Toys	5,000	1997	35.00	35-75
1997 Eskimo	450	1998	38.00	38
1997 Fireplace Stocking	500	1998	23.00	23
1997 Forever Christmas	125	1998	40.00	40-175
1997 Forget Me Knots	5,000	1998	22.00	22
1997 Freeform Santa	400	1998	38.00	38
1997 Gambler's Luck	500	1998	32.00	32-83
1997 Glitter Nutcracker	500	1998	26.00	26
1997 Glitz & Glitter - Fantasy Santa	5,000	1999	37.00	37-135
1997 Grandma Nana	300	1998	24.00	24
1997 Harp	250	1998	30.00	30
1997 Ho Ho Santa	500	1998	29.00	29
1997 Hot Air Balloon	5,000	1997	32.00	32-175
1997 Jennifer	900	1998	45.00	45
1997 Lover's Christmas	900	1998	42.00	42-145
1997 Madonna	200	1998	33.00	42-46
1997 Mardi Gras Magic	700	1998	68.00	68
1997 Masked Moon	500	1998	32.00	32
1997 Mixed Fruit, small, set/12	1,500	1998	42.00	42
1997 Mr. Fabulous	800	1998	38.00	125-335
1997 Nativity Set, set/8	300	1998	125.00	125
1997 Nutcracker	1,000	1998	19.00	19
1997 Nutcracker on Ball	500	1998	42.00	42
1997 Nutcracker, large	500	1998	42.00	42
1997 Nutcracker, small	500	1998	33.00	33
1997 Old Fashioned Santa	500	1998	29.00	29
1997 Owl on Indent	300	1998	60.00	60
1997 Panda Bear	350	1998	30.00	30
1997 Penguin	450	1998	35.00	35
1997 Penguin on Ball	300	1998	43.00	43
1997 Polly	400	1998	28.00	28
1997 Pumpkin Face	500	1998	47.00	47-104
1997 Razzle Dazzle	5,000	1997	35.00	35-83
1997 Rooster	500	1998	22.00	22
1997 Rooster on Egg	500	1998	32.00	32
1997 Russian Woman	1,900	1998	45.00	45
1997 Santa on a Heart	900	1998	47.00	47-57
1997 Santa on Ball	500	1998	45.00	45
1997 Santa on Horse	1,000	1998	22.50	23
1997 Santa on Icicle	250	1998	45.00	45
1997 Santa's List	1,500	1997	60.00	60
1997 Santa's Moon Ride	600	1998	62.00	138
1997 Shaker Basket	500	1998	47.00	47
1997 Shoemaker	500	1998	33.00	33
1997 Shy Kitten	600	1998	37.00	37
1997 Snow Princess	500	1998	42.00	42
1997 Snowman	1,000	1998	15.00	15

*Quotes have been rounded up to nearest dollar

ORNAMENTS

YEAR ISSUE	EDITION LIMIT	YEAR RETD.	ISSUE PRICE	*QUOTE U.S.$
1997 Swan on Clip	1,000	1998	30.00	30
1997 Waiting for a Prince	500	1998	42.00	42
1997 Wire Boat	1,000	1998	23.00	23
1997 Wrapped-In-A-Rainbow, round	300	1998	25.00	25
1997 Yogi Bear	700	1998	43.00	43

1997 Limited Edition - L. Fraga

YEAR ISSUE	EDITION LIMIT	YEAR RETD.	ISSUE PRICE	*QUOTE U.S.$
1997 Santa's List	1,500	1998	85.00	85
1997 Santa's Scooter Ride	1,500	1998	68.00	68

1998 Christmas Edition - L. Fraga

YEAR ISSUE	EDITION LIMIT	YEAR RETD.	ISSUE PRICE	*QUOTE U.S.$
1998 Christmas Music	120	1998	40.00	40
1998 Chubby Santa	120	1998	45.00	45
1998 Hollie Bear	5,000	1998	45.00	45-50
1998 Mommy, He's Here	5,000	1999	34.00	34-105
1998 Moon Struck	5,000	1998	37.00	37
1998 Mrs. Claus	5,000	1998	35.00	35
1998 Sparkle Eyes	5,000	1997	30.00	30-42
1998 Teardrop	40	1998	65.00	65

1998 Glitter Series - L. Fraga

YEAR ISSUE	EDITION LIMIT	YEAR RETD.	ISSUE PRICE	*QUOTE U.S.$
1998 Baranaby	120	1998	41.00	41
1998 Queen's Guard	120	1998	41.00	41
1998 Santa in the Chimney	120	1998	48.00	48
1998 Sparkle Snowman	120	1998	33.00	33

1999 Exclusives - L. Fraga

YEAR ISSUE	EDITION LIMIT	YEAR RETD.	ISSUE PRICE	*QUOTE U.S.$
1999 Classic Santa (Joyeaux)	54	1999	50.00	50
1999 Collector's Spirit (Glass Links-Internet Only)	54	1999	54.00	54
1999 Cool Breeze (Recollections)	54	1999	N/A	N/A
1999 The Gift of Giving (East Bay Nursery)	54	1999	N/A	N/A
1999 Mr. & Mrs. Claus (Tickled Pink)	350	1999	N/A	175
1999 Oregon's Finest (Ludeman's)	54	1999	46.00	46
1999 Santa's at the Cottage (Christmas Cottage)	54	1999	50.00	50
1999 Sapphire Santa (Holiday Treasures)	54	1999	N/A	42
1999 Silent Night Santa (Patioworld)	54	1999	44.00	44
1999 Silver Lining (Baltimore Park)	54	1999	N/A	N/A
1999 St. Nickals (Lyal Nickals)	54	1999	N/A	N/A
1999 Sterling Santa (Christmas in Seattle)	54	1999	N/A	N/A
1999 Winter Royal (Christmas in Seattle)	54	1999	N/A	N/A

1999 Glitter Series - L. Fraga

YEAR ISSUE	EDITION LIMIT	YEAR RETD.	ISSUE PRICE	*QUOTE U.S.$
1999 "25 Cents - 3 Plays"	300	1999	49.00	49
1999 Blue Hawaii	300	1999	30.00	30
1999 Blue Snowman	300	1999	23.00	23
1999 Bubbles	300	1999	52.00	52
1999 Carnival Nights	300	1999	37.00	37
1999 Chartreuse Sparkler	300	1999	46.00	46
1999 Child's Play	300	1999	36.00	36
1999 Christmas 2000	300	1999	53.00	53
1999 Christmas Bridesmaid	300	1999	45.00	45
1999 Christmas Quackers	300	1999	36.00	36
1999 Christmas Spirit	300	1999	52.00	52-135
1999 Constable	300	1999	26.00	26
1999 Fireball	300	1999	46.00	46
1999 Freedom	300	1999	38.00	38
1999 Getting Ready	300	1999	52.00	52
1999 The Ghost That Stole the Pumpkin	300	1999	46.00	46-145
1999 Halloween Santa	300	1999	46.00	46
1999 Ho Ho Hum	300	1999	37.00	37
1999 Hope	300	1999	40.00	40
1999 Kris Kringle	300	1999	52.00	52
1999 Midnight He Comes	300	1999	46.00	46-225
1999 Moon & Stars	300	1999	52.00	52
1999 A Night to Remember	300	1999	50.00	50
1999 Passion	300	1999	18.00	18
1999 Playing the Blues	300	1999	46.00	46-110
1999 Poinsettia Ball	300	1999	35.00	35
1999 Pop Up	300	1999	28.00	28-80
1999 Purple Heart	300	1999	18.00	18
1999 Purrfect	300	1999	40.00	40
1999 The Rainbow Glitters On	100	1999	56.00	56
1999 Renaissance Santa	300	1999	40.00	40
1999 Rojo Santa	300	1999	46.00	46
1999 Roosevelt Teddy	108	1999	64.00	64
1999 Royal Grizzly	150	1999	55.00	55
1999 Sabrina's Stocking	300	1999	22.00	22
1999 Santa Baby	300	1999	49.00	49
1999 Santa in Concert	300	1999	46.00	46
1999 Santa's Helper	300	1999	24.00	24
1999 Settling In	300	1999	52.00	52-175
1999 Shades of Royal	300	1999	46.00	46
1999 Sleighride	300	1999	30.00	30
1999 Spinner	300	1999	36.00	36
1999 Storytime	300	1999	52.00	52
1999 Toy Soldier	300	1999	28.00	28
1999 Victoria	300	1999	48.00	48
1999 Winter Mint	300	1999	46.00	46
1999 Winter Snowflake	300	1999	46.00	46

2000 Exclusives - L. Fraga

YEAR ISSUE	EDITION LIMIT	YEAR RETD.	ISSUE PRICE	*QUOTE U.S.$
2000 Gracing us Gracefully (Christmas In Seattle)	42		52.00	52
2000 Katherine's Santa (Tickled Pink Gift Shop)	64		48.00	48
2000 Misty Blue (Christmas Cottage)	54		34.00	34

2000 Glitter Series - L. Fraga

YEAR ISSUE	EDITION LIMIT	YEAR RETD.	ISSUE PRICE	*QUOTE U.S.$
2000 Abracadabra!	8,000		39.00	39
2000 Airborne Santa	8,000		38.00	38
2000 Alien Pumpkin	8,000		41.00	41
2000 American Santa	8,000		56.00	56
2000 Amor	8,000		19.00	19
2000 Around The World	8,000		41.00	41
2000 Autumn Leaves	8,000		30.00	30
2000 Balancing Act	1,500		56.00	56
2000 Balloon For You	1,500	2000	52.00	52
2000 The Beat Goes On	8,000		38.00	38
2000 Blessing	8,000		38.00	38
2000 Blooming Star	8,000		61.00	61
2000 Blue Dot Boo Boo	8,000		38.00	38
2000 Boooo!	8,000		45.00	45
2000 Bursting With Pride	8,000		41.00	41
2000 Busy As A Bee	8,000		13.00	13
2000 The Butler Did It	8,000	2000	38.00	38
2000 Bzzz	8,000		41.00	41
2000 Century Santa	1,500		51.00	51
2000 Charlotte	8,000		41.00	41
2000 Christmas Eve	1,200		51.00	51
2000 Christmas Night	8,000		51.00	51
2000 Churchill	8,000		51.00	51
2000 Cloud Jumping	1,200		42.00	42
2000 Dancing Monkey	8,000		40.00	40
2000 Devil Beware	8,000		45.00	45
2000 Double Jump	8,000		38.00	38
2000 Drumming Santa	8,000		38.00	38
2000 Elizabeth	8,000		41.00	41
2000 Empress	54	2000	51.00	51
2000 Falling Snowflakes	54	2000	46.00	46
2000 Fan Dancer	1,500		49.00	49
2000 First Love	8,000		45.00	45
2000 Florida's Best	8,000		38.00	38
2000 Free Ride	8,000		42.00	42
2000 Frosty Blue	8,000		41.00	41
2000 Got One!	8,000		41.00	41
2000 Harmony	1,500		56.00	56
2000 Hat Parade	1,200		58.00	58
2000 Heart For The Tin Man	8,000		26.00	26
2000 Hydrangea	8,000		30.00	30
2000 I'll Get You!	8,000		45.00	45
2000 Icicle Santa	8,000		31.00	31
2000 Jolly Friendly	8,000		38.00	38
2000 Jolly Holly	8,000		41.00	41
2000 Jungle King	1,200		46.00	46
2000 Just About Midnight	8,000		41.00	41
2000 Just For Me	1,200		38.00	38
2000 Lady Bug Johnson	8,000		46.00	46
2000 Lady in Blue	54	2000	51.00	51
2000 Lavender Lady	8,000		41.00	41
2000 Lavender Plum	8,000		41.00	41
2000 Little Red Ho Ho	8,000	2000	20.00	20
2000 Lucky Charm	8,000		47.00	47
2000 Magic Fairy, purple	8,000		39.00	39
2000 Magic Fairy, red	8,000		39.00	39
2000 Magic Ride	1,200		53.00	53
2000 Marigold	8,000		38.00	38
2000 Marshmallow Dream	8,000		45.00	45
2000 Midnight Snowman	1,500		45.00	45
2000 Monet	8,000	2000	30.00	30
2000 Moonlight Love	1,200		45.00	45
2000 Mr. Washington	8,000		41.00	41
2000 Multiflora	8,000		41.00	41
2000 Nathan	8,000		41.00	41
2000 Nicholas	8,000		26.00	26
2000 Night Watch	1,200		51.00	51
2000 No Fire Please!	1,200		45.00	45
2000 Nose So Bright	8,000		45.00	45
2000 Political Joe	8,000		41.00	41
2000 Polka Dot Boo Boo	8,000	2000	38.00	38
2000 Ready To Go	1,200		52.00	52
2000 Robotican	8,000		41.00	41
2000 Rodeo Santa	8,000		41.00	41
2000 Rolling in the Snow	54	2000	43.00	43
2000 Royal Russian	8,000		38.00	38
2000 Royal Swirl	8,000	2000	46.00	46
2000 Rudolph	8,000		41.00	41
2000 Santa Express	1,200		53.00	53
2000 Santa in Bloom	1,200		57.00	57
2000 Santa's Big Heart	1,200		45.00	45
2000 Santa's Delight	8,000		38.00	38
2000 Senorita	8,000		46.00	46
2000 Silver Spirit	8,000	2000	46.00	46
2000 Sleigh Bells Ring, set/4	8,000		128.00	128
2000 Snowflake Santa	8,000	2000	46.00	46
2000 Special Delivery	8,000		38.00	38
2000 Spring Pop Up	8,000		30.00	30
2000 Springtime Bouquet	1,200		49.00	49
2000 Springtime Gold	8,000		30.00	30
2000 Starry Night	1,200		38.00	38
2000 Striding Pride	8,000		45.00	45
2000 Sugar Sweet Santa	8,000		41.00	41
2000 Summertime Bloom	8,000		30.00	30
2000 Surprise!	8,000		41.00	41
2000 Swan Ride	8,000		57.00	57
2000 Tail Dancing	8,000		19.00	19
2000 Three Kings	1,200		58.00	58
2000 Tick Tock	8,000		41.00	41
2000 Tiger Lily	8,000		30.00	30
2000 Tree Delivery	8,000		41.00	41
2000 Tricky Sticky Piggy	8,000		38.00	38
2000 U.S.A. Low Rider	8,000		38.00	38
2000 Waiting For Rudolph	8,000		66.00	66
2000 Where Are The Cookies?	8,000		38.00	38
2000 Where's The Cheese?	8,000		41.00	41
2000 Winter Stroll	8,000	2000	46.00	46

Charity Design Ornaments - L. Fraga

YEAR ISSUE	EDITION LIMIT	YEAR RETD.	ISSUE PRICE	*QUOTE U.S.$
1997 Red Ribbon Ball (AIDS)	Open		14.00	14
1998 Angel of Hope (Breast Cancer)	Open		35.00	35
1999 Purple Heart (Veterans)	Open		18.00	18
2000 Angel in Flight (Breast Cancer)	66		80.00	80
2000 Flamingo Fling (Seeing Eye Dog)	N/A		47.00	47

Father Christmas Series - L. Fraga

YEAR ISSUE	EDITION LIMIT	YEAR RETD.	ISSUE PRICE	*QUOTE U.S.$
1997 Father Christmas, black/pink	600	1998	43.00	140-165

Lyal Nickals Exclusive - L. Fraga

YEAR ISSUE	EDITION LIMIT	YEAR RETD.	ISSUE PRICE	*QUOTE U.S.$
1998 Purple Moon Child	120	1998	47.50	48
1998 Springtime Flowers for Deb	120	1998	65.00	65

Marshall Fields Exclusive - L. Fraga

YEAR ISSUE	EDITION LIMIT	YEAR RETD.	ISSUE PRICE	*QUOTE U.S.$
1998 June's Tradition	240	1998	75.00	75

Prototypes - L. Fraga

YEAR ISSUE	EDITION LIMIT	YEAR RETD.	ISSUE PRICE	*QUOTE U.S.$
1999 Jumping Reindeer	8	1999	38.00	38-71
1999 Larry's Personal Palette	8	1999	32.00	32
1999 Southward Bound	10	1999	44.00	44-63
1999 White House Cigar	8	1999	28.00	28

Signing Event - L. Fraga

YEAR ISSUE	EDITION LIMIT	YEAR RETD.	ISSUE PRICE	*QUOTE U.S.$
1998 Joey	120	1998	55.00	55-79
1998 Midnight Sparkler	120	1998	55.00	55
1999 Rustic Santa (Tickled Pink Gift Shop)	12	1999	48.00	48
1999 Wistful Santa	48	1999	48.00	48
1999 Silver Spirit (Christmas Cottage)	12	1999	48.00	48
1999 Aquamarine Santa (Christmas in Seattle)	12	1999	48.00	48
2000 Rolling in the Snow	120		50.00	50

Tickled Pink Exclusives - L. Fraga

YEAR ISSUE	EDITION LIMIT	YEAR RETD.	ISSUE PRICE	*QUOTE U.S.$
2000 Blue Spruce	17		48.00	48
2000 Deliver Christmas	18		48.00	48
2000 Harvest Moon	5		43.00	43
2000 Night Watch	6		38.00	38
2000 Opulence	18		29.00	29
2000 Russian Woman	24		43.00	43
2000 Shiny & New	8		40.00	40
2000 Sunshine Santa	12		48.00	48
2000 Thanksgiving Plenty	10		43.00	43
2000 Time Marches On	6		38.00	38
2000 Time Out	9		35.00	35
2000 Twilight Angel	12		38.00	38

Lenox China

Annual Ornaments - Lenox

YEAR ISSUE	EDITION LIMIT	YEAR RETD.	ISSUE PRICE	*QUOTE U.S.$
1982 1982 Ball	Yr.Iss.	1983	30.00	55-70
1983 1983 Teardrop Shape	Yr.Iss.	1984	35.00	75
1984 1984 Starburst	Yr.Iss.	1985	38.00	65
1985 1985 Bell	Yr.Iss.	1986	37.50	60
1986 1986 The Three Magi	Yr.Iss.	1987	38.50	50
1987 1987 Dickens Village	Yr.Iss.	1988	39.00	40-45
1988 1988 Ball	Yr.Iss.	1989	39.00	45
1989 1989 Faberge Egg	Yr.Iss.	1990	39.00	39
1990 1990 Bell	Yr.Iss.	1991	42.00	42
1991 1991 Ornament	Yr.Iss.	1992	39.00	39
1992 1992 Ball	Yr.Iss.	1993	42.00	42
1993 1993 Lantern	Yr.Iss.	1994	45.00	45
1994 1994 Star	Yr.Iss.	1995	39.00	39
1995 1995 Santa	Yr.Iss.	1996	46.50	47
1996 1996 Traditional Ball	Yr.Iss.		46.50	47

Yuletide - Lenox

YEAR ISSUE	EDITION LIMIT	YEAR RETD.	ISSUE PRICE	*QUOTE U.S.$
1994 Cat	Open		19.50	20
1995 Candle	Open		19.95	20
1996 Christmas Angel™	Open		21.00	21

Lenox Classics

Lenox Classics-China Ivory Snowman - Lenox

YEAR ISSUE	EDITION LIMIT	YEAR RETD.	ISSUE PRICE	*QUOTE U.S.$
2000 Joyful Tidings	Open		25.00	25

Lenox Classics-China Ornaments - Lenox

YEAR ISSUE	EDITION LIMIT	YEAR RETD.	ISSUE PRICE	*QUOTE U.S.$
2000 Millennium Drummer	12/00		25.00	25
2000 Santa's Special Delivery	12/00		25.00	25
2000 Teddy's Millennium Wish	12/00		25.00	25

Lenox Classics-Crystal Ornaments - Lenox

YEAR ISSUE	EDITION LIMIT	YEAR RETD.	ISSUE PRICE	*QUOTE U.S.$
1999 Heavenly Messenger (Angel)	Open		45.00	45
1999 Eternal Peace (Dove)	Open		60.00	60

Lenox Classics-Little Graces - Lenox

YEAR ISSUE	EDITION LIMIT	YEAR RETD.	ISSUE PRICE	*QUOTE U.S.$
1997 Little Surprise	5,000		45.00	45
1998 Little Hope (Cherub wStar)	5,000	1999	45.00	45
2000 Little Trumpeter	5,000		45.00	45

Lilliput Lane Ltd./Enesco European Giftware Group

Christmas Ornaments - Lilliput Lane

YEAR ISSUE	EDITION LIMIT	YEAR RETD.	ISSUE PRICE	*QUOTE U.S.$
1992 Mistletoe Cottage	Retrd.	1992	27.50	35-40
1993 Robin Cottage	Retrd.	1993	35.00	35-45
1994 Ivy House	Retrd.	1994	35.00	8-25
1995 Plum Cottage	Retrd.	1995	30.00	30-40
1996 Fir Tree Cottage	Retrd.	1996	30.00	25-30
1997 Evergreens	Retrd.	1997	30.00	20-30
1998 Great Expectations	Retrd.	1998	35.00	25-35
1999 Jingle Bells	Retrd.	1999	32.00	32
2000 Silent Night	Yr.Iss.		35.00	35

*Quotes have been rounded up to nearest dollar

Ray Day/Coca Cola Country - R. Day

YEAR ISSUE	EDITION LIMIT	YEAR RETD.	ISSUE PRICE	*QUOTE U.S.$
1996 Santa's Corner	19,960	1999	35.00	25-35

Little Angel Publishing

Delicate Blessings - D. Gelsinger

YEAR ISSUE	EDITION LIMIT	YEAR RETD.	ISSUE PRICE	*QUOTE U.S.$
1999 Tree Topper	Open		39.95	40

Heaven's Little Angels - D. Gelsinger

YEAR ISSUE	EDITION LIMIT	YEAR RETD.	ISSUE PRICE	*QUOTE U.S.$
1999 Angel's Guidance, Angel's Tenderness, Nature's Guardian	95-day		29.97	30
1998 Gentle Guardian, Gentle Miracle, Loving Kindness, set #1	95-day		29.97	30
1999 Nature's Beauty, Devine Guardian, Heavenly Innocence	95-day		29.97	30
1998 Nature's Blessings, Garden Beauty, Gentle Hugs, set #2	95-day		29.97	30
1999 Precious Devotion, Angel's Spirit, Delicate Blessings	95-day		29.97	30

Lladró

Angels - Lladró

YEAR ISSUE	EDITION LIMIT	YEAR RETD.	ISSUE PRICE	*QUOTE U.S.$
1994 Joyful Offering L6125G	Yr.Iss.	1994	245.00	245-300
1995 Angel of the Stars L6132G	Yr.Iss.	1995	195.00	195-250
1996 Rejoice L6321G	Yr.Iss.	1996	220.00	220-240

Annual Ornaments - Lladró

YEAR ISSUE	EDITION LIMIT	YEAR RETD.	ISSUE PRICE	*QUOTE U.S.$
1988 Christmas Ball-L1603M	Yr.Iss.	1988	60.00	75-104
1989 Christmas Ball-L5656M	Yr.Iss.	1989	65.00	45-75
1990 Christmas Ball-L5730M	Yr Iss.	1990	70.00	45-75
1991 Christmas Ball-L5829M	Yr.Iss.	1991	52.00	40-52
1992 Christmas Ball-L5914M	Yr.Iss.	1992	52.00	45-52
1993 Christmas Ball-L6009M	Yr.Iss.	1993	54.00	54-78
1994 Christmas Ball-L6105M	Yr.Iss.	1994	55.00	55
1995 Christmas Ball-L6207M	Yr.Iss.	1995	55.00	45-55
1996 Christmas Ball-L6298M	Yr.Iss.	1996	55.00	55-65
1997 Christmas Ball-L6442M	Yr.Iss.	1997	55.00	55-65
1998 Christmas Ball-01016561	Yr.Iss.	1998	55.00	55-60
1999 Christmas Ball-01016637	Yr.Iss.	1999	55.00	55-60
2000 Christmas Ball-01016699	Yr.Iss.		60.00	60

Miniature Ornaments - Lladró

YEAR ISSUE	EDITION LIMIT	YEAR RETD.	ISSUE PRICE	*QUOTE U.S.$
1988 Miniature Angels-L1604G, Set/3	Yr.Iss.	1988	75.00	200-225
1989 Holy Family-L5657G, Set/3	Yr.Iss.	1990	79.50	143-225
1990 Three Kings-L5729G, Set/3	Yr Iss.	1991	87.50	125
1991 Holy Shepherds-L5809G	Yr.Iss.	1991	97.50	150-175
1993 Nativity Trio-L6095G	Yr.Iss.	1993	115.00	175-260

Ornaments - Lladró

YEAR ISSUE	EDITION LIMIT	YEAR RETD.	ISSUE PRICE	*QUOTE U.S.$
1995 Christmas Tree L6261G	Open		75.00	75
1995 Landing Dove L6266G	Closed	1998	49.00	43-50
1995 Surprised Cherub L6253G	Closed	1998	120.00	102-120
1995 Flying Dove L6267G	Closed	1998	49.00	43-50
1995 Playing Cherub L6254G	Closed	1998	120.00	102-120
1995 Rocking Horse L6262G	Closed	1998	69.00	75-80
1995 Doll L6263G	Closed	1998	69.00	75
1995 Thinking Cherub L6255G	Closed	1998	120.00	102-120
1995 Train L6264G	Closed	1998	69.00	49-92
1991 Our First-1991-L5840G	Closed	1991	50.00	65-75
1992 Snowman-L5841G	Closed	1994	50.00	79-125
1992 Santa-L5842G	Closed	1994	55.00	79-125
1992 Baby's First-1992-L5922G	Closed	1992	55.00	55
1992 Our First-1992-L5923G	Closed	1992	50.00	52-59
1992 Elf Ornament-L5938G	Closed	1994	50.00	79-300
1992 Mrs. Claus-L5939G	Closed	1994	55.00	45-59
1992 Christmas Morning-L5940G	Closed	1992	97.50	125-200
1993 Nativity Lamb-L5969G	Closed	1994	85.00	85
1993 Baby's First 1993-L6037G	Closed	1993	57.00	57
1993 Our First-L6038G	Closed	1993	52.00	57-75
1996 Santa's Journey-L6265	Closed	1997	49.00	49
1996 Welcome Home-L6335	Closed	1998	85.00	85-100
1996 King Melchior-L6341	Closed	1998	75.00	75-90
1996 Seraph With Bells-L6342	Closed	1998	79.00	79
1996 Little Aviator-L6343	Closed	1998	79.00	79
1996 Teddy Bear-L6344	Closed	1998	67.00	67
1996 Toy Soldier-L6345	Closed	1998	90.00	90-95
1996 Heavenly Tenor-L6372	Closed	1998	98.00	98-105
1998 Seraph with Bow-01006445	Closed	1999	79.00	80
1998 Heavenly Musician-01006498	Closed	1999	98.00	98-100
1998 King Balthaser-01006509	Closed	1999	75.00	75
1998 Our Winter Home-01006519	Closed	1999	85.00	85
1998 Baby's First Christmas-1998 01016588	Closed	1998	55.00	55
1999 Baby's First Christmas-1999 01016694	Closed	1999	55.00	55
2000 Baby's First Christmas-2000 01016697	Yr.Iss.		65.00	65
2000 Our First Christmas-2000 01016716	Yr.Iss.		65.00	65

Tree Topper Ornaments - Lladró

YEAR ISSUE	EDITION LIMIT	YEAR RETD.	ISSUE PRICE	*QUOTE U.S.$
1990 Angel Tree Topper-L5719G-Blue	Yr.Iss.	1990	100.00	200-325
1991 Angel Tree Topper-L5831G-Pink	Yr.Iss.	1991	115.00	175-250
1992 Angel Tree Topper-L5875G-Green	Yr.Iss.	1992	120.00	160-195
1993 Angel Tree Topper -L5962G-Lavender	Yr.Iss.	1993	125.00	143-195
1997 Angel of Light-01006501	Closed	1997	175.00	149-175
1998 Message of Peace-01006587	Closed	1998	150.00	125-150
1999 Message of Love-01006643	Yr.Iss.	1999	150.00	150
2000 A Celestial Christmas-01006747	Yr.Iss.		270.00	270

Margaret Furlong Designs

Margaret Furlong Collector's Club - M. Furlong

YEAR ISSUE	EDITION LIMIT	YEAR RETD.	ISSUE PRICE	*QUOTE U.S.$
1999 1999 Collector's Club Kit	Closed	2000	49.50	40-60
1999 Hummingbird Box	Closed	2000	20.00	15-25
2000 2000 Collector's Club Kit	12/00		49.95	50

National Event - M. Furlong

YEAR ISSUE	EDITION LIMIT	YEAR RETD.	ISSUE PRICE	*QUOTE U.S.$
1999 3 1/2" Nestling Quail Angel	Yr.Iss.	1999	13.50	15
2000 3 1/2" Trio of New Life Angel	Yr.Iss.		15.00	15

Annual Ornaments - M. Furlong

YEAR ISSUE	EDITION LIMIT	YEAR RETD.	ISSUE PRICE	*QUOTE U.S.$
1980 3" Trumpeter Angel	Closed	1994	12.00	74-125
1980 4" Trumpeter Angel	Closed	1994	21.00	125-150
1982 3" Star Angel	Closed	1994	12.00	92-150
1982 4" Star Angel	Closed	1994	21.00	150-175
1983 3" Holly Angel	Closed	1998	14.00	14-45
1983 4" Holly Angel	Closed	1998	23.00	20-45
1984 3" Dove Angel	Closed	1995	12.00	40-87
1984 4" Dove Angel	Closed	1995	21.00	100-116
1985 3" Wreath Angel	12/00		14.00	14
1985 4" Wreath Angel	12/00		23.00	23
1986 3" Heart Angel	Open		14.00	14
1986 4" Heart Angel	Open		23.00	23
1987 3" Bouquet Angel	12/00		14.00	14
1987 4" Bouquet Angel	12/00		23.00	23
1988 3" Butterfly Angel	Closed	1996	12.00	40-65
1988 4" Butterfly Angel	Closed	1996	21.00	35-76
1989 3" Snowflake Angel	Open		14.00	14
1989 4" Snowflake Angel	Open		23.00	23
1990 3" Christmas Tree Angel	Open		14.00	14
1990 4" Christmas Tree Angel	Open		23.00	23
1991 3" Gift Angel	Open		14.00	14
1991 4" Gift Angel	Open		23.00	23
1992 3" Noel Angel	Closed	1997	12.00	14-37
1992 4" Noel Angel	Closed	1997	21.00	25-42
1993 2" Miniature Celestial Angel	Open		12.00	12
1993 3" Cross Angel	Open		14.00	14
1993 4" Cross Angel	Open		23.00	23
1994 2" Miniature Heart Angel	Open		12.00	12
1994 3" Sun Angel	Closed	1999	14.00	15-39
1994 4" Sun Angel	Closed	1999	23.00	21-46
1995 2" Miniature Wreath Angel	12/00		12.00	12
1995 3" Flower Garland Angel	Open		14.00	14
1995 4" Flower Garland Angel	Open		23.00	23
1996 2" Miniature Daisy Angel	12/00		12.00	12
1996 3" Morning Glory Angel	12/00		14.00	14
1997 2" Miniature Viola Angel	Open		12.00	12
1997 3" Dogwood Angel	Open		14.00	14
1997 1 1/2" Tea For Two Angel	Open		22.00	22
1998 3" Wild Rose Angel	Open		14.00	14
1998 2" Shamrock Angel	Open		12.00	12
1998 1 1/2" Gardening Friends	Open		22.00	22
1999 2" Flower Basket Angel	Open		11.50	12
1999 3" Coneflower and Goldfinch Angel	Open		13.50	14
1999 1 1/2" Celebration Angels	Open		22.00	22
1999 1 1/2" Love Tokens Heart	Open		18.00	18
2000 3" Gifts From the Sea Angel	Open		14.00	14
2000 2 1/4" Token of My Love Heart	Open		8.00	8
2000 2" New Heart of Faith Angel	Open		12.00	12

Crosses - M. Furlong

YEAR ISSUE	EDITION LIMIT	YEAR RETD.	ISSUE PRICE	*QUOTE U.S.$
1998 Blooms of Hope, 3"	Open		8.00	8
1999 Everlasting Hope, 3"	Open		8.00	8
2000 4 1/2" New Hope for the Millennium Cross	Open		10.00	10

Flora Angelica - M. Furlong

YEAR ISSUE	EDITION LIMIT	YEAR RETD.	ISSUE PRICE	*QUOTE U.S.$
1995 Faith Angel	10,000	1995	45.00	80-145
1996 Hope Angel	10,000	1996	45.00	115
1997 Charity Angel	10,000	1997	50.00	67-80
1998 Grace Angel	10,000	1998	50.00	50-65
1999 Angel of Love	10,000	1999	54.00	50-65

Gifts from God - M. Furlong

YEAR ISSUE	EDITION LIMIT	YEAR RETD.	ISSUE PRICE	*QUOTE U.S.$
1985 1985 The Charis Angel	3,000	1985	45.00	625-650
1986 1986 The Hallelujah Angel	3,000	1986	45.00	690-725
1987 1987 The Angel of Light	3,000	1987	45.00	465-805
1988 1988 The Celestial Angel	3,000	1988	45.00	300-800
1989 1989 Coronation Angel	3,000	1989	45.00	450-475

Gold Leaf Porcelain - M. Furlong

YEAR ISSUE	EDITION LIMIT	YEAR RETD.	ISSUE PRICE	*QUOTE U.S.$
1993 Catch a Falling Star 2" (gold)	Closed	1998	11.00	18-20
1992 Evening Star 5" (gold)	Closed	1998	16.00	23-25
1992 Morning Star 3" (gold)	Closed	1998	13.00	13-20
1996 Oak and Acorn Wreath 3" (gold)	Closed	1998	16.00	17-30
1992 A Star in the Night 2 1/2" (gold)	Closed	1998	11.00	18-20
1993 Sunshell 2" (gold)	Closed	1998	11.00	12-35
1995 Tree Top Finial 7" (gold)	Closed	1998	24.00	12-45

Hearts - M. Furlong

YEAR ISSUE	EDITION LIMIT	YEAR RETD.	ISSUE PRICE	*QUOTE U.S.$
1998 Blossoming Love, 2 1/2"	12/00		8.00	8
1997 From the Heart, 2 1/2"	Open		8.00	8
1981 Lattice Heart, 3 1/4"	300	1982	24.00	1150-1600
1999 Love Song, 2 1/2"	Open		8.00	8
1987 Oh Sweetest Heart, 2"	12/00		6.00	6
1996 Wings of Love, 2 1/2"	Open		7.00	7

Joyeux Noel - M. Furlong

YEAR ISSUE	EDITION LIMIT	YEAR RETD.	ISSUE PRICE	*QUOTE U.S.$
1990 1990 Celebration Angel	10,000	1994	45.00	180-185
1991 1991 Thanksgiving Angel	10,000	1994	45.00	145-200
1992 1992 Joyeux Noel Angel	10,000	1994	45.00	120-135
1993 1993 Star of Bethlehem Angel	10,000	1994	45.00	130-174
1994 1994 Messiah Angel	10,000	1994	45.00	265-400

Madonna and Child - M. Furlong

YEAR ISSUE	EDITION LIMIT	YEAR RETD.	ISSUE PRICE	*QUOTE U.S.$
1996 Madonna of the Cross	20,000		80.00	80
1997 Madonna of the Flowers	20,000		80.00	80
1998 Madonna of the Heavens	20,000		80.00	80

Musical Series - M. Furlong

YEAR ISSUE	EDITION LIMIT	YEAR RETD.	ISSUE PRICE	*QUOTE U.S.$
1980 1980 The Caroler	3,000	1980	50.00	465-600
1981 1981 The Lyrist	3,000	1981	45.00	650-800
1982 1982 The Lutist	3,000	1982	45.00	650-900
1983 1983 The Concertinist	3,000	1983	45.00	250-575
1984 1984 The Herald Angel	3,000	1984	45.00	460-600

Seasons of a New Millennium - M. Furlong

YEAR ISSUE	EDITION LIMIT	YEAR RETD.	ISSUE PRICE	*QUOTE U.S.$
2000 Spring Angel, 5"	15,000		54.00	54

Special Edition - M. Furlong

YEAR ISSUE	EDITION LIMIT	YEAR RETD.	ISSUE PRICE	*QUOTE U.S.$
1996 4" Sunflower Angel	Yr.Iss.	1996	21.00	31-75
1997 4" Iris Angel	Yr.Iss.	1997	23.00	23-28
1998 4" Tulip Angel	Yr.Iss.	1998	23.00	23-50
1999 4" Hummingbird Angel	Yr.Iss.	1999	24.00	24-30
1999 3" Millennium Angel	12/00		15.00	15
2000 4" Song of New Life Angel	Yr.Iss.		24.00	24

Stars - M. Furlong

YEAR ISSUE	EDITION LIMIT	YEAR RETD.	ISSUE PRICE	*QUOTE U.S.$
1980 Catch a Falling Star, 2"	Open		6.00	6
1980 Evening Star, 5"	12/00		10.00	10
1980 Morning Star, 3"	Open		7.00	7
1980 A Star in the Night, 2 1/2"	Open		6.00	6

Tassels - M. Furlong

YEAR ISSUE	EDITION LIMIT	YEAR RETD.	ISSUE PRICE	*QUOTE U.S.$
1995 Coral Tassel Copper-foil, 5"	Retrd.	1997	24.00	18-35
1995 Coral Tassel Gold-foil, 5"	Retrd.	1997	24.00	18-35
1995 Coral Tassel, 5"	Retrd.	1997	16.00	23-25
1994 Shell Tassel Gold-foil, 5"	Retrd.	1997	24.00	25-27
1994 Shell Tassel, 5"	Retrd.	1997	16.00	25-27

Tree Toppers - M. Furlong

YEAR ISSUE	EDITION LIMIT	YEAR RETD.	ISSUE PRICE	*QUOTE U.S.$
1984 Tree Top Star, 6 1/2"	Retrd.	1996	30.00	95-158

Various Ornaments - M. Furlong

YEAR ISSUE	EDITION LIMIT	YEAR RETD.	ISSUE PRICE	*QUOTE U.S.$
1996 Acorn, 5"	Open		15.00	15
2000 Heaven & Earth Roundel, 4"	Open		20.00	20
1995 Icicle, 4 1/2"	Retrd.	1997	12.00	20-36
1995 Icicle, Copper-foil, 4 1/2"	Retrd.	1997	18.00	24-36
1995 Icicle, Gold-foil, 4 1/2"	Retrd.	1997	18.00	23-36
1995 Icicle, Silver-foil, 4 1/2"	Retrd.	1997	18.00	23-36
1994 Shell Fish Gold-foil, 4"	Retrd.	1997	19.00	20-25
1994 Shell Fish, 4"	Retrd.	1997	11.00	11
1988 Stars by the Yard (Ivory, Red, and Gold), 1 1/2"	Retrd.	1995	20.00	20-69
1993 Sunshell Gold-foil, 2"	Retrd.	1998	11.00	14-19
1993 Sunshell, 2"	Open		6.00	6
1989 A Winter Jewel, Snowflake, 2"	Open		6.00	6

Victoria - M. Furlong

YEAR ISSUE	EDITION LIMIT	YEAR RETD.	ISSUE PRICE	*QUOTE U.S.$
1994 Victoria Heart Angel	10,000	1994	24.95	85-200
1995 Victoria Lily of the Valley Angel	30,000	1995	25.00	25-55

Wreaths - M. Furlong

YEAR ISSUE	EDITION LIMIT	YEAR RETD.	ISSUE PRICE	*QUOTE U.S.$
1986 Heart Wreath, 4"	Retrd.	1996	20.00	40-51
1996 Oak and Acorn Wreath, 3"	Open		8.00	8
1981 Shell Wreath, 8"	Retrd.	1995	95.00	95

Matchbox Collectibles/Mattel

Christmas Themes - Mattel

YEAR ISSUE	EDITION LIMIT	YEAR RETD.	ISSUE PRICE	*QUOTE U.S.$
1994 MBC Christmas Ornaments (Set of 4) YCC01	Retrd.	1996	27.50	28
1995 MBC Christmas Ornaments (Set of 4) YCC02	Open		29.95	30
1996 MBC Christmas Ornaments (Set of 4) YCC03-M	Open		19.95	20

Memories of Yesterday/Enesco Group, Inc.

Memories of Yesterday Society Member's Only - M. Attwell

YEAR ISSUE	EDITION LIMIT	YEAR RETD.	ISSUE PRICE	*QUOTE U.S.$
1992 With Luck And A Friend, I's In Heaven MY922	Yr.Iss.	1992	16.00	20
1993 I'm Bringing Good Luck-Wherever You Are	Yr.Iss.	1993	16.00	22

Memories of Yesterday - M. Attwell

YEAR ISSUE	EDITION LIMIT	YEAR RETD.	ISSUE PRICE	*QUOTE U.S.$
1997 Angel w/Holder 264709	Retrd.	1999	17.50	18
1997 Sharing Gingerbread Blessings 271721	Yr.Iss.	1999	17.50	18-39
1988 Baby's First Christmas 1988 520373	Yr.Iss.	1988	13.50	40-60
1988 Special Delivery! 1988 520381	Yr.Iss.	1988	13.50	25-35
1989 Baby's First Christmas 522465	Retrd.	1996	15.00	15-20
1989 A Surprise for Santa 522473 (1989)	Yr.Iss.	1989	13.50	15-28
1989 Christmas Together 522562	Retrd.	1999	15.00	15-25
1995 Happy Landings (Dated 1995) 522619	Yr.Iss.	1995	16.00	16
1990 Time For Bed 524638	Yr.Iss.	1990	15.00	15-30
1990 New Moon 524646	Retrd.	1999	15.00	15-25
1994 Just Dreaming of You 524786	Retrd.	1999	16.00	16
1990 Moonstruck 524794	Retrd.	1992	15.00	25
1991 Just Watchin' Over You 525421	Retrd.	1994	17.50	25
1991 Lucky Me 525448	Retrd.	1993	16.00	22
1993 Wish I Could Fly To You 525790 (dated)	Yr.Iss.	1993	16.00	16
1992 I'll Fly Along To See You Soon 525804 (1992 Dated Bisque)	Yr.Iss.	1992	16.00	16-25
1991 Star Fishin' 525820	Retrd.	1999	16.00	16
1991 Lucky You 525847	Retrd.	1993	16.00	16
1995 Now I Lay Me Down to Sleep 527009	Retrd.	1999	15.00	15
1995 I Pray the Lord My Soul to Keep 527017	Retrd.	1999	15.00	15

*Quotes have been rounded up to nearest dollar

YEAR ISSUE	EDITION LIMIT	YEAR RETD.	ISSUE PRICE	*QUOTE U.S.$
1992 Mommy, I Teared It 527041 (Five Year Anniversary Limited Edition)	Yr.Iss.	1992	15.00	20
1991 S'no Use Lookin' Back Now! 527181(dated)	Yr.Iss.	1991	17.50	28
1992 Merry Christmas, Little Boo-Boo 528803	Retrd.	1999	37.50	38
1993 May All Your Finest Dreams Come True 528811	Retrd.	1999	16.00	16
1992 Star Light. Star Bright 528838	Retrd.	1999	16.00	16
1994 Give Yourself a Hug From Me! 529109 ('94 Dated)	Yr. Iss.	1994	17.50	18
1998 God Bless And Merry Christmas! 531731 ('98 Dated)	Yr. Iss.	1998	17.50	18
1992 Swinging Together 580481(1992 Dated Artplas)	Yr.Iss.	1992	17.50	22
1992 Sailin' With My Friends 587575 (Artplas)	Retrd.	1999	25.00	25
1993 Bringing Good Wishes Your Way 592846 (Artplas)	Retrd.	1999	25.00	25
1994 Bout Time I Came Along to See You 592854 (Artplas)	Retrd.	1999	17.50	18

Event Item Only - Enesco

YEAR ISSUE	EDITION LIMIT	YEAR RETD.	ISSUE PRICE	*QUOTE U.S.$
1993 How 'Bout A Little Kiss? 527068	Closed	1993	16.50	50
1996 Hoping To See You Soon 527033	Yr.Iss.	1996	15.00	15

Friendship - Enesco

YEAR ISSUE	EDITION LIMIT	YEAR RETD.	ISSUE PRICE	*QUOTE U.S.$
1996 I Love You This Much! 185809	Retrd.	1999	13.50	14

Peter Pan - Enesco

YEAR ISSUE	EDITION LIMIT	YEAR RETD.	ISSUE PRICE	*QUOTE U.S.$
1996 Tinkerbell 164682	Retrd.	1999	17.50	20

Midwest of Cannon Falls

Eddie Walker Collection - E. Walker

YEAR ISSUE	EDITION LIMIT	YEAR RETD.	ISSUE PRICE	*QUOTE U.S.$
1999 Santa and Clock, dated 1999 32351-9	Yr.Iss.	1999	8.00	8
1997 Santa Holding Reindeer, dated 1997 22284-3	Yr.Iss.	1997	10.00	10
1998 Santa, dated 1998 25193-5	Yr.Iss.	1998	15.00	15
1998 Mini Stocking, dated 1998 26471-3	Yr.Iss.	1998	8.00	8
1999 Santa and Shooting Star, set/2 32953-5	Yr.Iss.	1999	15.00	15
1999 Santa with Pets, dated 1999 33656-4	Yr.Iss.	1999	15.00	15
1999 Santa, 2 asst., dated 1999/2000 31714-3	Yr.Iss.	1999	20.00	20
2000 Brilliant Christmas, dated 2000 36937-1	Yr.Iss.	2000	10.00	10

Heaven and Nature Sings Millennium Edition Angel Ornaments - Midwest

YEAR ISSUE	EDITION LIMIT	YEAR RETD.	ISSUE PRICE	*QUOTE U.S.$
2000 Angel with Instrument, 3 asst. 37966-0	Open		120.00	120

Jolly Follies - S. Gore Evans

YEAR ISSUE	EDITION LIMIT	YEAR RETD.	ISSUE PRICE	*QUOTE U.S.$
1999 "Oh My 1999" Snowman 32709-8	Yr.Iss.	1999	8.00	8
2000 Swinging on a Star, dated 2000 36806-0	Yr.Iss.		10.00	10

Leo R. Smith III Collection - L.R. Smith

YEAR ISSUE	EDITION LIMIT	YEAR RETD.	ISSUE PRICE	*QUOTE U.S.$
1994 Flying Woodsman Santa 11921-1	2,500	1994	35.00	250-300
1995 Angel of Love 16123-4	3,500	1996	32.00	40-45
1995 Angel of Peace 16199-9	3,500	1996	32.00	45-50
1995 Angel of Dreams 16130-2	3,500	1996	32.00	35-50
1995 Partridge Angel 13994-3	3,500	1996	30.00	30-35
1995 Santa on Reindeer 13780-2	3,500	1996	35.00	80-100
1996 Angel of Dependability 19218-4	Retrd.	1996	37.00	37
1996 Angel of Adventure 19219-1	Retrd.	1996	37.00	37
1996 Angel of Nurturing 19220-7	Retrd.	1996	37.00	37
1996 Angel of Generosity 19221-4	Retrd.	1996	37.00	37
1996 Angel of Knowledge 19222-1	Retrd.	1996	37.00	37
1996 Angel of Sharing 19223-8	Retrd.	1996	37.00	37
1996 Angel of Guidance 19224-5	Retrd.	1996	37.00	37
1996 Angel of Pride 19225-2	Retrd.	1996	37.00	37
1996 Angel of Heaven and Earth 18396-0	3,500	1999	33.00	33
1996 Angel of Light 18076-1	4,000	1999	33.00	33
1996 Angel of Music 18073-4	3,500	1999	33.00	33
1996 Everyday Angel Ornament Stand 19554-3	Retrd.	1996	25.00	25
1996 Belsnickle Santa 18074-7	4,000	1996	39.00	39-100
1997 Santa Riding Bird 19928-2	3,000	1999	35.00	35
1997 Stars & Stripes Santa 19929-9	3,000	1999	35.00	35
1998 Santa with Gifts, dated 1998 25144-7	1,500	1999	40.00	40

Miss Martha's Collection/Enesco Group, Inc.

Miss Martha's Collection - M. Holcombe

YEAR ISSUE	EDITION LIMIT	YEAR RETD.	ISSUE PRICE	*QUOTE U.S.$
1993 Caroline - Always Someone Watching Over Me 350532	Closed	1994	25.00	50
1993 Arianna - Heavenly Sounds 350567	Closed	1994	25.00	50-55
1992 Baby in Basket 369454	Closed	1994	25.00	50-75
1992 Baby In Swing 421480	Retrd.	1993	25.00	50-75
1992 Girl Holding Stocking DTD 1992 421499	Closed	1994	25.00	45-55
1992 Girl/Bell In Hand 421502	Retrd.	1993	25.00	50

Possible Dreams

Crinkle Claus - Staff

YEAR ISSUE	EDITION LIMIT	YEAR RETD.	ISSUE PRICE	*QUOTE U.S.$
1996 Bishop of Maya-659702	Retrd.	1998	7.80	8
1996 Black Forest Santa-659706	Open		7.80	8
1999 Blazing Crinkle 659720	Open		9.20	10
1999 Cardinal Crinkle 659730	Open		9.20	10
1999 Choo-Choo Crinkle 659719	Open		6.90	7
1999 Christmas Crinkle 659718	Open		6.90	7
1999 Crinkle Jester 659725	Open		9.40	10
1999 Crinkle on the Chimney 659717	Open		6.90	7
1999 Crinkle on the Links 659722	Open		9.40	10
1999 Crinkle on the Moon 659723	Open		9.20	10
1999 Crinkle Star 659727	Open		9.20	10
1999 Crinkle Tree 659715	Open		6.90	7
2000 Crinkle World Peace 659733	Open		16.00	16
1999 Crinkle Wreath 659721	Open		9.40	10
1999 Diamond Crinkle 659724	Open		9.20	10
1996 Father Christmas-659703	Open		7.80	8
1999 Fire Fighting Crinkle 659728	Open		9.20	10
1996 German Santa-659701	Retrd.	1998	7.80	8
1999 Irish Crinkle Shepherd 659732	Open		8.00	8
1999 Leaping Crinkle 659729	Open		9.20	10
1996 Pere Noel Santa-659705	Open		7.80	8
1999 Quarter Moon Crinkle 659716	Open		6.90	7
1999 Red Bow Crinkle 659726	Open		9.20	10
1997 Slavic Crinkle 659713	Retrd.	1998	7.80	10
1996 St. Nicholas-659704	Retrd.	1998	7.80	8
1999 Traveling Crinkle 659731	Open		9.20	10

Garfield® Ornaments - Staff

YEAR ISSUE	EDITION LIMIT	YEAR RETD.	ISSUE PRICE	*QUOTE U.S.$
1997 Frostbite Feline 275103	Open		20.50	21
1997 Here Comes Santa Paws 275102	Open		25.50	26
1997 Wake Me When It's Christmas 275101	Open		25.50	26

Splanglers Realm® - R. Splangler

YEAR ISSUE	EDITION LIMIT	YEAR RETD.	ISSUE PRICE	*QUOTE U.S.$
1997 The Stowaway 191052	Open		8.40	9
1997 Tied To Perfection 191051	Open		9.30	10
1997 Twinkle, Twinkle, Little Dragon 191050	Open		7.90	8

Stebleton Folk Art - B. Stebleton

YEAR ISSUE	EDITION LIMIT	YEAR RETD.	ISSUE PRICE	*QUOTE U.S.$
1998 Ball & Cone Shaped Santa 194012	Open		6.80	7
1998 Bell Shaped Santa 194007	Open		6.30	7
1998 Big Ball Shaped Santa 194009	Open		6.30	7
1998 Big Top Shaped Santa 194010	Open		5.90	6
1998 Candle Shaped 194011	Open		4.40	5
1998 Egg Shaped Santa 194003	Open		5.90	6
1998 Funnel Shaped Santa 194006	Open		7.00	7
1998 Oval Shaped Santa 194002	Open		5.20	6
1998 Pear Shaped Santa 194013	Open		6.30	7
1998 Pencil Shaped Santa 194008	Open		5.90	6
1998 Santas, bell shaped, wood, set/6 194001	Open		19.50	20
1998 Tall Cone Shaped Santa 194004	Open		6.90	7
1998 Tiny Top Shaped Santa 194005	Open		4.80	5

Stebleton's Cagey Critters - B. Stebleton

YEAR ISSUE	EDITION LIMIT	YEAR RETD.	ISSUE PRICE	*QUOTE U.S.$
2000 Beach Belly 194510	Open		9.00	9
2000 Curly Q 194500	Open		8.00	8
2000 Derby Day Duo 194508	Open		10.00	10
2000 Dream Team 194507	Open		9.00	9
2000 Finger Food 194501	Open		10.00	10
2000 Furry Yellow Fellow 194502	Open		8.00	8
2000 Hearts and Whiskers 194145	Open		16.00	16
2000 Kitty Court Jester 194512	Open		9.00	9
2000 Lunch is on Me 194505	Open		10.00	10
2000 Randolph the Red Nose 194509	Open		9.00	9
2000 Simply Red 194506	Open		8.00	8
2000 Skateboard Buddies 194503	Open		10.00	10
2000 Sushi Cat 194511	Open		10.00	10
2000 Yokes on You 194504	Open		10.00	10

The Thickets at Sweetbriar® - B. Ross

YEAR ISSUE	EDITION LIMIT	YEAR RETD.	ISSUE PRICE	*QUOTE U.S.$
1995 Christmas Whiskers 350400	Retrd.	1996	11.50	12
1995 Jingle Bells 350407	Retrd.	1996	12.00	12
1996 Snuggles 350416	Open		11.70	12
2000 Nibbley-Do 350415	Open		10.50	11
2000 Twinkle Tails 350415	Retrd.	1996	11.50	12

Precious Moments/Enesco Group, Inc.

Precious Moments - S. Butcher

YEAR ISSUE	EDITION LIMIT	YEAR RETD.	ISSUE PRICE	*QUOTE U.S.$
1983 Surround Us With Joy E-0513	Yr.Iss.	1983	9.00	50-88
1983 Mother Sew Dear E-0514	Open		9.00	16-38
1983 To A Special Dad E-0515	Suspd.		9.00	46-82
1983 The Purr-fect Grandma E-0516	Open		9.00	16-50
1983 The Perfect Grandpa E-0517	Suspd.		9.00	39-50
1983 Blessed Are The Pure In Heart E-0518	Yr.Iss.	1983	9.00	25-50
1983 O Come All Ye Faithful E-0531	Suspd.		10.00	40-69
1983 Let Heaven And Nature Sing E-0532	Retrd.	1986	9.00	28-35
1983 Tell Me The Story Of Jesus E-0533	Suspd.		9.00	36-47
1983 To Thee With Love E-0534	Retrd.	1989	9.00	28-37
1984 Love Is Patient E-0535	Suspd.		9.00	40-92
1984 Love Is Patient E-0536	Suspd.		9.00	35-55
1983 Jesus Is The Light That Shines E-0537	Suspd.		9.00	62-75
1982 Joy To The World E-2343	Suspd.		9.00	38-60
1982 I'll Play My Drum For Him E-2359	Yr.Iss.	1982	9.00	57-119
1982 Baby's First Christmas E-2362	Suspd.		9.00	50-57
1982 The First Noel E-2367	Suspd.		9.00	12-78
1982 The First Noel E-2368	Retrd.	1984	9.00	25-70
1982 Dropping In For Christmas E-2369	Retrd.	1986	9.00	27-60
1982 Unicorn E-2371	Retrd.	1988	10.00	32-63
1982 Baby's First Christmas E-2372	Suspd.		9.00	20-57
1982 Dropping Over For Christmas E-2376	Retrd.	1985	9.00	29-55
1982 Mouse With Cheese E-2381	Suspd.		9.00	112-130
1982 Our First Christmas Together E-2385	Suspd.		10.00	20-52
1982 Camel, Donkey & Cow (3 pc. set) E-2386	Suspd.		25.00	69-95
1984 Wishing You A Merry Christmas E-5387	Yr.Iss.	1984	10.00	28-40
1984 Joy To The World E-5388	Retrd.	1987	10.00	26-60
1984 Peace On Earth E-5389	Suspd.		10.00	35-52
1984 May God Bless You With A Perfect Holiday Season E-5390	Suspd.		10.00	22-50
1984 Love Is Kind E-5391	Suspd.		10.00	29-48
1984 Blessed Are The Pure In Heart E-5392	Yr.Iss.	1984	10.00	14-36
1981 But Love Goes On Forever E-5627	Suspd.		6.00	94-132
1981 But Love Goes On Forever E-5628	Suspd.		6.00	72-115
1981 Let The Heavens Rejoice E-5629	Yr.Iss.	1981	6.00	232-288
1981 Unto Us A Child Is Born E-5630	Suspd.		6.00	39-75
1981 Baby's First Christmas E-5631	Suspd.		6.00	50-68
1981 Baby's First Christmas E-5632	Suspd.		6.00	48-68
1981 Come Let Us Adore Him (4pc. set) E-5633	Suspd.		22.00	145-182
1981 Wee Three Kings (3pc. set) E-5634	Suspd.		19.00	113-175
1981 We Have Seen His Star E-6120	Retrd.	1984	6.00	25-75
1991 Sharing The Good News Together PM-37	Retrd.	1991	N/A	64-95
1986 Birds Of A Feather Collect Together PM-864	Retrd.	1986	N/A	113-200
1990 My Happiness PM-904	Retrd.	1990	N/A	68-95
1985 Have A Heavenly Christmas 12416	Suspd.		12.00	17-34
1985 God Sent His Love 15768	Yr.Iss.	1985	10.00	23-40
1985 May Your Christmas Be Happy 15822	Suspd.		10.00	28-40
1985 Happiness Is The Lord 15830	Suspd.		10.00	20-34
1985 May Your Christmas Be Delightful 15849	Suspd.		10.00	22-38
1999 May Your Christmas Be Delightful 15849R	Open		20.00	15-20
1985 Honk If You Love Jesus 15857	Suspd.		10.00	23-35
1985 Baby's First Christmas 15903	Yr.Iss.	1985	10.00	25-38
1985 Baby's First Christmas 15911	Yr.Iss.	1985	10.00	30-40
1986 Shepherd of Love 102288	Suspd.		10.00	18-48
1986 Wishing You A Cozy Christmas 102326	Yr.Iss.	1986	10.00	30-42
1986 Our First Christmas Together 102350	Yr.Iss.	1986	10.00	18-40
1986 Trust And Obey 102377	Open		10.00	16-35
1986 Love Rescued Me 102385	Open		10.00	16-32
1986 Angel Of Mercy 102407	Open		10.00	16-35
1986 It's A Perfect Boy 102415	Suspd.		10.00	19-43
1986 Lord Keep Me On My Toes 102423	Retrd.	1990	10.00	20-48
1986 Serve With A Smile 102431	Suspd.		10.00	17-40
1986 Serve With A Smile 102458	Suspd.		10.00	22-40
1986 Reindeer 102466	Yr.Iss.	1986	11.00	125-185
1986 Rocking Horse 102474	Suspd.		10.00	14-35
1986 Baby's First Christmas 102504	Yr.Iss.	1986	10.00	19-40
1986 Baby's First Christmas 102512	Yr.Iss.	1986	10.00	17-35
1987 Bear The Good News Of Christmas 104515	Yr.Iss.	1987	12.50	18-24
1987 Baby's First Christmas 109401	Yr.Iss.	1987	12.00	37-63
1987 Baby's First Christmas 109428	Yr.Iss.	1987	12.00	30-60
1987 Love Is The Best Gift Of All 109770	Yr.Iss.	1987	11.00	32-63
1987 I'm A Possibility 111120	Suspd.		11.00	27-48
1987 You Have Touched So Many Hearts 112356	Retrd.	1996	11.00	16-42
1987 Waddle I Do Without You 112364	Retrd.	1999	11.00	16-30
1987 I'm Sending You A White Christmas 112372	Suspd.		11.00	20-36
1987 He Cleansed My Soul 112380	Retrd.	1999	12.00	16-30
1987 Our First Christmas Together 112399	Yr.Iss.	1987	11.00	21-47
1988 To My Forever Friend 113956	Retrd.	1999	16.00	17-38
1988 Smile Along The Way 113964	Suspd.		15.00	21-45
1988 God Sent You Just In Time 113972	Suspd.		13.50	24-40
1988 Rejoice O Earth 113980	Retrd.	1991	13.50	19-45
1988 Cheers To The Leader 113999	Suspd.		13.50	23-45
1988 My Love Will Never Let You Go 114006	Suspd.		13.50	27-35
1988 Baby's First Christmas 115282	Yr.Iss.	1988	15.00	28-31
1988 Time To Wish You A Merry Christmas 115320	Yr.Iss.	1988	13.00	27-42
1996 Owl Be Home For Christmas 128708	Yr.Iss.	1996	18.50	16-25
1995 Lighting The Way To A Happy Holiday (Chapel Exclusive) 129275	Open		20.00	20
1995 He Covers The Earth With His Beauty 142662	Yr.Iss.	1995	17.00	20-45
1995 He Covers The Earth With His Beauty (ball) 142689	Yr.Iss.	1995	30.00	26-40
1995 Our First Christmas Together 142700	Yr.Iss.	1995	18.50	17-20
1995 Baby's First Christmas 142719	Yr.Iss.	1995	17.50	16-20
1995 Baby's First Christmas 142727	Yr.Iss.	1995	17.50	16-24
1995 Joy From Head To Mistletoe 150126	Open		18.50	15-19
1995 You're "A" Number One In My Book, Teacher 150142	Open		18.50	15-22
1995 Personalized House 150231	Open		19.95	20-68
1995 Joy To The World (trumpet) 150320	Retrd.	1999	20.00	18-25
1996 Joy To The World (flute) 153338	Retrd.	1999	20.00	18-20
1995 Peace On Earth (Century Circle) 177091	15,000	1995	25.00	26-38
1996 Peace On Earth...Anyway (Ball) 183350	Yr.Iss.	1996	30.00	26-30
1996 Peace On Earth...Anyway 183369	Yr.Iss.	1996	18.50	17-30
1996 God's Precious Gift 183881	Open		20.00	18-20
1996 When The Skating's Ruff, Try Prayer 183903	Open		18.50	17-19
1996 Our First Christmas Together 183911	Yr.Iss.	1996	22.50	21-33
1996 Baby's First Christmas 183938	Yr.Iss.	1996	17.50	16-25
1996 Baby's First Christmas 183946	Yr.Iss.	1996	17.50	16-20
1996 Your Precious Spirit Comes Shining Through 212563	Yr.Iss.	1996	30.00	122
1998 In God's Beautiful Garden Of Love 261599	Open		50.00	50-73

*Quotes have been rounded up to nearest dollar

YEAR ISSUE	EDITION LIMIT	YEAR RETD.	ISSUE PRICE	*QUOTE U.S.$
1997 Joy To The World (harp) 272566	Retrd.	1999	20.00	18-20
1997 Cane You Join Us For A Merry Christmas 272671	Yr.Iss.	1997	18.50	17-32
1997 Cane You Join Us For A Merry Christmas 272728	Yr.Iss.	1997	18.50	26
1997 Our First Christmas Together 272736	Yr.Iss.	1997	20.00	20-25
1997 Baby's First Christmas (Girl) 272744	Yr.Iss.	1997	18.50	17-19
1997 Baby's First Christmas (Boy) 272752	Yr.Iss.	1997	18.50	17-19
1997 Slow Down For The Holidays 272760	Yr.Iss.	1997	18.50	17-19
1997 Puppies With Sled 272892	Open		18.50	17-19
1997 My Love/Keep You 272965	Retrd.	N/A	20.00	16-20
1998 I'm Sending You A Merry Christmas 455628	Yr.Iss.	1998	18.50	19-25
1998 Our First Christmas Together 455636	Yr.Iss.	1998	25.00	21-28
1998 Baby's First Christmas (Girl) 455644	Yr.Iss.	1998	18.50	16-22
1998 Baby's First Christmas (Boy) 455652	Yr.Iss.	1998	18.50	16-22
1998 I'll Be Dog-ged It's That Season Again 455660	Yr.Iss.	1998	18.50	16-19
1998 I'm Just Nutty About The Holidays 455776	Open		17.50	17-19
1988 Our First Christmas Together 520233	Yr.Iss.	1988	13.00	13-35
1988 Baby's First Christmas 520241	Yr.Iss.	1988	15.00	20-38
1988 You Are My Gift Come True 520276	Yr.Iss.	1988	12.50	15-29
1988 Hang On For The Holly Days 520292	Yr.Iss.	1988	13.00	21-33
1988 A Growing Love 520349	Yr.Iss.	1988	N/A	68
1992 I'm Nuts About You 520411	Yr.Iss.	1992	15.00	15-32
1995 Hippo Holy Days 520403	Yr.Iss.	1995	17.00	26-40
1991 Sno-Bunny Falls For You Like I Do 520438	Yr.Iss.	1991	15.00	25-31
1998 Happy Holi-daze 520454	Open		17.50	17-19
1989 Christmas is Ruff Without You 520462	Yr.Iss.	1989	13.00	28-36
1993 Slow Down & Enjoy The Holidays 520489	Yr.Iss.	1993	16.00	28-36
1990 Wishing You A Purr-fect Holiday 520497	Yr.Iss.	1990	15.00	25-40
1989 May All Your Christmases Be White 521302 (dated)	Suspd.		15.00	20-50
1999 May All Your Christmases Be White 521302R	Open		20.00	16-20
1989 Our First Christmas Together 521558	Yr.Iss.	1989	17.50	25-30
1990 Glide Through the Holidays 521566	Retrd.	1992	13.50	20-40
1990 Dashing Through the Snow 521574	Suspd.		15.00	18-35
1990 Don't Let the Holidays Get You Down 521590	Retrd.	1994	15.00	20-32
1989 Oh Holy Night 522848	Yr.Iss.	1989	13.50	21-30
1989 Make A Joyful Noise 522910	Suspd.		15.00	16-31
1989 Love One Another 522929	Open		17.50	20-25
1990 Friends Never Drift Apart 522937	Retrd.	1995	17.50	27-53
1991 Our First Christmas Together 522945	Yr.Iss.	1991	17.50	17-28
1989 I Believe In The Old Rugged Cross 522953	Suspd.		15.00	18-53
1989 Always Room For One More 522961	Retrd.	1989	N/A	83
1989 Peace On Earth 523062	Yr.Iss.	1989	25.00	39-69
1989 Baby's First Christmas 523194	Yr.Iss.	1989	15.00	19-35
1989 Baby's First Christmas 523208	Yr.Iss.	1989	15.00	19-25
1991 Happy Trails Is Trusting Jesus 523224	Suspd.		15.00	18-45
1990 May Your Christmas Be A Happy Home 523704	Yr.Iss.	1990	27.50	24-30
1990 Baby's First Christmas 523798	Yr.Iss.	1990	15.00	14-35
1990 Baby's First Christmas 523771	Yr.Iss.	1990	15.00	14-35
1990 Once Upon A Holy Night 523852	Yr.Iss.	1990	15.00	17-30
1992 Good Friends Are For Always 524131	Retrd.	1996	15.00	28-50
1991 May Your Christmas Be Merry 524174	Yr.Iss.	1991	15.00	28-38
1990 Bundles of Joy 525057	Yr.Iss.	1990	15.00	24-31
1990 Our First Christmas Together 525324	Yr.Iss.	1990	17.50	16-35
1993 Lord, Keep Me On My Toes 525332	Open		15.00	19-50
1991 May Your Christmas Be Merry (on Base) 526940	Yr.Iss.	1991	30.00	30-45
1991 Baby's First Christmas (Boy) 527084	Yr.Iss.	1991	15.00	15-30
1991 Baby's First Christmas (Girl) 527092	Yr.Iss.	1991	15.00	15-40
1991 The Good Lord Always Delivers 527165	Suspd.		15.00	26-42
1993 Share in The Warmth of Christmas 527211	Open		15.00	16-19
1994 Onward Christmas Soldiers 527327	Open		16.00	15-19
1992 Baby's First Christmas 527475	Yr.Iss.	1992	15.00	30-39
1992 Baby's First Christmas 527483	Yr.Iss.	1992	15.00	25-40
1992 But The Greatest of These Is Love 527696	Yr.Iss.	1992	15.00	25-45
1992 But The Greatest of These Is Love 527734 (on Base)	Yr.Iss.	1992	30.00	19-50
1992 There's A Christian Welcome Here (Chapel Exclusive) 528021	Open		22.50	15-31
1994 Sending You A White Christmas 528218	Open		16.00	19-35
1994 Bringing You A Merry Christmas 528226	Retrd.	1998	16.00	15-20
1993 It's So Uplifting to Have a Friend Like You 528846	Retrd.	1999	16.00	16-30
1992 Our First Christmas Together 528870	Yr.Iss.	1992	17.50	30-40
1994 Our 1st Christmas Together 529206	Yr.Iss.	1994	18.50	30-35
1993 Wishing You the Sweetest Christmas 530190	Yr.Iss.	1993	30.00	40-63
1993 Wishing You the Sweetest Christmas 530212	Yr.Iss.	1993	15.00	35-45
1994 Baby's First Christmas 530255	Yr.Iss.	1994	16.00	15-78
1994 Baby's First Christmas 530263	Yr.Iss.	1994	16.00	19-36
1994 You're As Pretty As A Christmas Tree 530387	Yr.Iss.	1994	30.00	37-57
1994 You're As Pretty As A Christmas Tree 530395	Yr.Iss.	1994	16.00	30-50
1993 Our First Christmas Together 530506	Yr.Iss.	1993	17.50	25-36
1993 Baby's First Christmas 530859	Yr.Iss.	1993	15.00	14-25
1993 Baby's First Christmas 530867	Yr.Iss.	1993	15.00	14-30
1994 You Are Always In My Heart 530972	Yr.Iss.	1994	16.00	25-35
1993 Surrounded With Joy 531685	Open		17.50	18-30
1994 Death Can't Keep Him In The Ground (Chapel Exclusive) 531928	Open		30.00	30-36
1994 You Are Always In My Heart (Chapel Exclusive) 532088	Retrd.	1995	17.50	29
1999 Slide Into The Next Millenium with Joy 587788	Open		20.00	20
1999 Our First Christmas Together 587796	Open		25.00	20-25
1999 May Your Wishes For Peace Take Wing 587818	Open		20.00	20
1999 Baby's First Christmas 587826	Open		18.50	15-19
1999 Baby's First Christmas 587834	Open		18.50	19
1999 May Your Christmas Be Delightful 587931	Open		20.00	16-20
1999 Pretty As A Princess 587958	Open		20.00	16-20
1999 The Future Is In Our Hands 730076	Yr.Iss.		19.00	19
2000 Our First Christmas Together 730084	Yr.Iss.		25.00	25
2000 Baby's First Christmas 730092	Yr.Iss.		19.00	19
2000 Baby's First Christmas 730106	Yr.Iss.		19.00	19
2000 One Good Turn Deserves Another 737569	Open		20.00	20
2000 Let's Keep Our Eyes On The Goal (Canadian Exclusive) 802557	Open		20.00	20

Precious Moments Club 15th Anniversary Commemorative Edition - S. Butcher

YEAR ISSUE	EDITION LIMIT	YEAR RETD.	ISSUE PRICE	*QUOTE U.S.$
1993 15 Years Tweet Music Together 530840	Yr.Iss.	1993	15.00	24-40

Precious Moments Club 20th Anniversary Commemorative Edition - S. Butcher

YEAR ISSUE	EDITION LIMIT	YEAR RETD.	ISSUE PRICE	*QUOTE U.S.$
1998 20 Years And The Vision's Still The Same 451312	Yr.Iss.	1998	22.50	19-23
1998 How Can Two Work Together Except They Agree	Yr.Iss.	1998	25.00	25

Christmas Remembered - S. Butcher

YEAR ISSUE	EDITION LIMIT	YEAR RETD.	ISSUE PRICE	*QUOTE U.S.$
2000 One Good Turn Deserves Another 737569	Open		20.00	20

DSR Open House Weekend Ornaments - S. Butcher

YEAR ISSUE	EDITION LIMIT	YEAR RETD.	ISSUE PRICE	*QUOTE U.S.$
1992 The Magic Starts With You 529648	Yr.Iss.	1992	16.00	15-35
1993 An Event For All Seasons 529974	Yr.Iss.	1993	15.00	14-40
1994 Take A Bow Cuz You're My Christmas Star 520470	Yr.Iss.	1994	16.00	15-42
1995 Merry Chrismoose 150134	Yr.Iss.	1995	17.00	20-45
1996 Wishing You a Bearie Merry Christmas 531200	Yr.Iss.	1996	17.50	16-30
1997 Pack Your Trunk For The Holidays 272949	Yr.Iss.	1997	20.00	18-25
1999 Merry Giftness 532223	Yr.Iss.	1999	20.00	16-20

Easter Seal Commemorative Ornaments - S. Butcher

YEAR ISSUE	EDITION LIMIT	YEAR RETD.	ISSUE PRICE	*QUOTE U.S.$
1990 Always In His Care 225290	Yr.Iss.	1990	8.00	7
1991 Sharing A Gift Of Love 233196	Yr.Iss.	1991	8.00	7
1994 It's No Secret What God Can Do 244570	Yr.Iss.	1994	6.50	7
1995 Take Time To Smell The Flowers 128899	Yr.Iss.	1995	7.50	8
1996 You Can Always Count on Me 152579	Yr.Iss.	1996	6.50	7
1997 Give Ability A Chance 192384	Yr.Iss.	1997	6.50	7
1998 Somebody Cares 272922	Yr.Iss.	1998	6.50	7
1999 Heaven Bless You 475076	Yr.Iss.	1999	6.50	7
2000 Give Your Whole Heart 634751	Yr.Iss.		9.50	10

Members' Only - S. Butcher

YEAR ISSUE	EDITION LIMIT	YEAR RETD.	ISSUE PRICE	*QUOTE U.S.$
1992 The Club That's Out Of This World PM-38	Yr.Iss.	1992	N/A	60-84
1990 Blessed Are The Poor In Spirit, For Theirs Is The Kingdom of Heaven PM-190	Yr.Iss.	1990	15.00	15
1990 Blessed Are They That Mourn, For They Shall Be Comforted PM-290	Yr.Iss.	1990	15.00	15
1990 Blessed Are The Meek, For They Shall Inherit The Earth PM-390	Yr.Iss.	1990	15.00	15
1990 Blessed Are They That Hunger And Thirst, For They Shall Be Filled PM-490	Yr.Iss.	1990	15.00	15
1990 Blessed Are The Merciful, For They Shall Obtain Mercy PM-590	Yr.Iss.	1990	15.00	15
1990 Blessed Are The Pure In Heart, For They Shall See God PM-690	Yr.Iss.	1990	15.00	15
1990 Blessed Are The Peacemakers, For They Shall Be Called Sons of God PM-790	Yr.Iss.	1990	15.00	15
1990 Set of 7 PM-890	Yr.Iss.	1990	105.00	88-105

Special Edition Members' Only - S. Butcher

YEAR ISSUE	EDITION LIMIT	YEAR RETD.	ISSUE PRICE	*QUOTE U.S.$
1993 Loving, Caring And Sharing Along The Way PM-040 (Club Appreciation)	Yr.Iss.	1993	12.50	25-35
1994 You Are The End of My Rainbow PM-041	Yr.Iss.	1994	15.00	22-35

Sugartown - S. Butcher

YEAR ISSUE	EDITION LIMIT	YEAR RETD.	ISSUE PRICE	*QUOTE U.S.$
1993 Sugartown Chapel Ornament 530484	Yr.Iss.	1993	17.50	28-35
1994 Sam's House 530468	Yr.Iss.	1994	17.50	20-38
1995 Dr. Sugar's Office 530441	Yr.Iss.	1995	17.50	16-30
1996 Train Station 18a101	Yr.Iss.	1996	18.50	17-35

Twelve Days Of Christmas - S. Butcher

YEAR ISSUE	EDITION LIMIT	YEAR RETD.	ISSUE PRICE	*QUOTE U.S.$
1998 My True Love Gave To Me - Day 1 455989	Yr.Iss.	1998	20.00	20
1998 We're Two' Of A Kind - Day 2 455997	Yr.Iss.	1998	20.00	20
1998 Saying 'Oui' To Our Love - Day 3 456004	Yr.Iss.	1998	20.00	20-24
1998 Ringing In The Season - Day 4 456012	Yr.Iss.	1998	20.00	20
1999 The Golden Rings of Friendship - Day 5 456020	Yr.Iss.	1999	20.00	20
1999 Hatching The Perfect Holiday - Day 6 456039	Yr.Iss.	1999	20.00	20
1999 Swimming Into Your Heart - Day 7 456047	Yr.Iss.	1999	20.00	20
1999 Eight Mice A Milking - Day 8 456055	Yr.Iss.	1999	20.00	20
2000 Nine Ladies Dancing w/Joy - Day 9 456063	Yr.Iss.		20.00	20
2000 Leaping Into The Holidays - Day 10 456071	Yr.Iss.		20.00	20
2000 Piping in Perfect Harmony - Day 11 456098	Yr.Iss.		20.00	20
2000 Twelve Drummers Drumming Fun - Day 12 456101	Yr.Iss.		20.00	20

Prizm, Inc./Pipka

Pipka's Earth Angel Ornaments - Pipka

YEAR ISSUE	EDITION LIMIT	YEAR RETD.	ISSUE PRICE	*QUOTE U.S.$
1999 Angel of Hearts 11500	Open		15.00	15
1999 Angel of Roses 11502	Open		15.00	15
1999 Celeste-Angel of Stars 11505	Open		15.00	15
1999 Christine-The Christmas Angel 11504	Open		15.00	15
2000 Cottage Angel 11508	Open		15.00	15
1999 Elizabeth-Forget-Me-Not Angel 11506	Open		15.00	15
1999 Gardening Angel 11507	Open		15.00	15
1999 Guardian Angel 11503	Open		15.00	15
1999 Messenger Angel 11501	Open		15.00	15
2000 Michele The Snow Angel 11509	Open		15.00	15
2000 Pauline- The Poinsettia Angel 11513	Open		15.00	15
2000 Sang-The Teddy Bear Angel 11510	Open		15.00	15
2000 Sylvia- The Song Angel 11511	Open		15.00	15
2000 Whitney- The Wedding Angel 11512	Open		15.00	15

Pipka's Stories of Christmas - Pipka

YEAR ISSUE	EDITION LIMIT	YEAR RETD.	ISSUE PRICE	*QUOTE U.S.$
1999 Amish County Santa 11416	Open		15.00	15
1997 Aussie Santa 11404	4,000	1999	15.00	15
1999 Better Watch Out 11420	Open		15.00	15
2000 The Christmas Traveler 11429	Open		15.00	15
1997 Czechoslovakian Santa 11401	4,000	1999	15.00	15
2000 Dear Santa 11426	Open		15.00	15
2000 The Door County Santa 11427	Open		15.00	15
1998 Father Christmas 11412	Open		15.00	15
1999 German St. Nick 11424	Open		15.00	15
1999 Gingerbread Santa 11422	Open		15.00	15
1999 Good News Santa 11417	Open		15.00	15
1999 Irish Santa 11423	Open		15.00	15
1997 Midnight Visitor 11400	4,000	1999	15.00	15
1998 Norwegian/Julenisse Santa 11407	3,680	2000	15.00	15
1998 Peace Maker 11413	Open		15.00	15
1998 Polish Father Christmas 11408	Open		15.00	15
1999 Russian Santa 11421	Open		15.00	15
1998 San Nicolas 11415	Open		15.00	15
2000 Santa & Snow Friend 11430	Open		15.00	15
1998 Santa's Spotted Grey 11411	Open		15.00	15
1998 St. Nicholas 11409	Open		15.00	15
1997 Star Catcher Santa 11403	4,000	1999	15.00	15
1997 Starcoat Santa 11402	4,000	1999	15.00	15
1998 Storytime Santa 11410	Open		15.00	15
2000 Swedish Father Christmas 11431	Open		15.00	15
1998 Teddy Bear Santa 11414	Open		15.00	15
1997 Ukrainian Santa 11405	4,000	1999	15.00	15
1998 Where's Rudolph? 11406	Open		15.00	15
2000 The Winterman 11428	Open		15.00	15
1999 Yes Virginia 11425	Open		15.00	15

Reco International

Heaven Sent - S. Kuck

YEAR ISSUE	EDITION LIMIT	YEAR RETD.	ISSUE PRICE	*QUOTE U.S.$
1999 Angelic Moments	95-day		9.99	10
1999 Dreamy Days	95-day		9.99	10
1999 Heavenly Thoughts	95-day		9.99	10
2000 Heavens Blossom	95-day		9.99	10
2000 Gracious Blessing	95-day		9.99	10
2000 Precious Wonder	95-day		9.99	10
2000 Innocent Spirit	95-day		9.99	10
2000 Sweetest Devotion	95-day		9.99	10
2000 Graceful Touch	95-day		9.99	10

Sugar & Spice - S. Kuck

YEAR ISSUE	EDITION LIMIT	YEAR RETD.	ISSUE PRICE	*QUOTE U.S.$
1999 Best Friends	95-day		9.99	10
1999 Special Day	95-day		9.99	10
1999 Tea Party	95-day		9.99	10

Reed & Barton

12 Days of Christmas Sterling and Lead Crystal - Reed & Barton

YEAR ISSUE	EDITION LIMIT	YEAR RETD.	ISSUE PRICE	*QUOTE U.S.$
1988 Partridge in a Pear Tree	Yr.Iss.	1988	25.00	30-40

*Quotes have been rounded up to nearest dollar

ORNAMENTS

YEAR ISSUE	EDITION LIMIT	YEAR RETD.	ISSUE PRICE	*QUOTE U.S.$
1989 Two Turtle Doves	Yr.Iss.	1989	25.00	30-40
1990 Three French Hens	Yr.Iss.	1990	27.50	30-40
1991 Four Colly birds	Yr.Iss.	1991	27.50	30-40
1992 Five Golden Rings	Yr.Iss.	1992	27.50	30-40
1993 Six Geese A Laying	Yr.Iss.	1993	27.50	30-40
1994 Seven Swans A 'Swimming	Yr.Iss.	1994	27.50	30-40
1995 Eight Maids A Milking	Yr.Iss.	1995	30.00	30-40
1996 Nine Ladies Dancing	Yr.Iss.	1996	30.00	30-40
1997 Ten Lords a-Leaping	Yr.Iss.	1997	32.50	33-40
1998 Eleven Pipers Piping	Yr.Iss.	1998	32.50	33-40
1999 Twelve Drummers Drumming	Yr.Iss.		35.00	35

Christmas Cross - Reed & Barton

YEAR ISSUE	EDITION LIMIT	YEAR RETD.	ISSUE PRICE	*QUOTE U.S.$
1971 Sterling Silver-1971	Closed	1971	10.00	150-175
1971 24Kt. Gold over Sterling-V1971	Closed	1971	17.50	120-300
1972 Sterling Silver-1972	Closed	1972	10.00	60-125
1972 24Kt. Gold over Sterling-V1972	Closed	1972	17.50	75
1973 Sterling Silver-1973	Closed	1973	10.00	60-85
1973 24Kt. Gold over Sterling-V1973	Closed	1973	17.50	60-85
1974 Sterling Silver-1974	Closed	1974	12.95	75-90
1974 24Kt. Gold over Sterling-V1974	Closed	1974	20.00	60
1975 Sterling Silver-1975	Closed	1975	12.95	35-75
1975 24Kt. Gold over Sterling-V1975	Closed	1975	20.00	50-60
1976 Sterling Silver-1976	Closed	1976	13.95	60
1976 24Kt. Gold over Sterling-V1976	Closed	1976	19.95	45-50
1977 Sterling Silver-1977	Closed	1977	15.00	60
1977 24Kt. Gold over Sterling-V1977	Closed	1977	18.50	45-50
1978 Sterling Silver-1978	Closed	1978	16.00	60
1978 24Kt. Gold over Sterling-V1978	Closed	1978	20.00	50
1979 Sterling Silver-1979	Closed	1979	20.00	50-60
1979 24Kt. Gold over Sterling-V1979	Closed	1979	24.00	45
1980 Sterling Silver-1980	Closed	1980	35.00	50-60
1980 24Kt. Gold over Sterling-V1980	Closed	1980	40.00	45-50
1981 Sterling Silver-1981	Closed	1981	35.00	45-60
1981 24Kt. Gold over Sterling-V1981	Closed	1981	40.00	45-50
1982 Sterling Silver-1982	Closed	1982	35.00	60-65
1982 24Kt. Gold over Sterling-V1982	Closed	1982	40.00	45-50
1983 Sterling Silver-1983	Closed	1983	35.00	60
1983 24Kt. Gold over Sterling-V1983	Closed	1983	40.00	45-50
1984 Sterling Silver-1984	Closed	1984	35.00	45-60
1984 24Kt. Gold over Sterling-V1984	Closed	1984	45.00	50
1985 Sterling Silver-1985	Closed	1985	35.00	60-80
1985 24Kt. Gold over Sterling-V1985	Closed	1985	40.00	40-50
1986 Sterling Silver-1986	Closed	1986	38.50	45-60
1986 24Kt. Gold over Sterling-V1986	Closed	1986	40.00	40-50
1987 Sterling Silver-1987	Closed	1987	35.00	60
1987 24Kt. Gold over Sterling-V1987	Closed	1987	40.00	40-50
1988 Sterling Silver-1988	Closed	1988	35.00	60
1988 24Kt. Gold over Sterling-V1988	Closed	1988	40.00	40-50
1989 Sterling Silver-1989	Closed	1989	35.00	45-50
1989 24Kt. Gold over Sterling-V1989	Closed	1989	40.00	40
1990 Sterling Silver-1990	Closed	1990	40.00	50
1990 24Kt. Gold over Sterling-1990	Closed	1990	45.00	40-45
1991 Sterling Silver-1991	Closed	1991	40.00	50
1991 24Kt. Gold over Sterling-1991	Closed	1991	45.00	40-45
1992 Sterling Silver-1992	Closed	1992	40.00	40-50
1992 24Kt. Gold over Sterling-1992	Closed	1992	45.00	40-45
1993 Sterling Silver-1993	Closed	1993	40.00	40
1993 24Kt. Gold over Sterling-1993	Closed	1993	45.00	35-45
1994 Sterling Silver-1994	Closed	1994	40.00	40
1994 24Kt. Gold over Sterling-1994	Closed	1994	45.00	35-45
1995 Sterling Silver-1995	Closed	1995	40.00	40-45
1995 24Kt. Gold over Sterling-1995	Closed	1995	45.00	35-45
1996 Sterling Silver-1996	Closed	1996	40.00	35-45
1996 Gold Vermiel-1996	Closed	1996	45.00	35-45
1997 Sterling Silver-1997	Closed	1997	40.00	35-40
1997 24Kt. Gold over Sterling-1997	Closed	1997	45.00	35-45
1998 Sterling Silver-1998	Closed	1998	40.00	30-40
1998 24Kt. Gold over Sterling-1998	Closed	1998	45.00	35-45
1999 Sterling Silver-1999	Closed	1999	40.00	40
1999 Vermeil-1999	Closed	1999	45.00	45
2000 Sterling Silver-2000	Yr.Iss.		45.00	45
2000 24 Kt. Vermeil-2000	Yr.Iss.		50.00	50

Holly Ball/Bell - Reed & Barton

YEAR ISSUE	EDITION LIMIT	YEAR RETD.	ISSUE PRICE	*QUOTE U.S.$
1976 1976 Ball	Closed	1976	14.00	26-40
1977 1977 Ball	Closed	1977	15.00	15-26
1978 1978 Ball	Closed	1978	15.00	15-26
1979 1979 Ball	Closed	1979	15.00	15-26
1980 1980 Bell	Closed	1980	22.50	26-35
1980 Bell, gold plate, V1980	Closed	1980	25.00	26-45
1981 1981 Bell	Closed	1981	22.50	26-30
1981 Bell, gold plate, V1981	Closed	1981	27.50	26-35
1982 1982 Bell	Closed	1982	22.50	26-35
1982 Bell, gold plate, V1982	Closed	1982	27.50	26-50
1983 1983 Bell	Closed	1983	23.50	26-45
1983 Bell, gold plate, V1983	Closed	1983	30.00	26-30
1984 1984 Bell	Closed	1984	25.00	26-35
1984 Bell, gold plate, V1984	Closed	1984	28.50	26-50
1985 1985 Bell	Closed	1985	25.00	26-80
1985 Bell, gold plate, V1985	Closed	1985	28.50	26-50
1986 1986 Bell	Closed	1986	25.00	26-75
1986 Bell, gold plate, V1986	Closed	1986	28.50	26-50
1987 1987 Bell	Closed	1987	27.50	26-70
1987 Bell, gold plate, V1987	Closed	1987	30.00	26-50
1988 1988 Bell	Closed	1988	27.50	26-40
1988 Bell, gold plate, V1988	Closed	1988	30.00	26-30
1989 1989 Bell	Closed	1989	27.50	26-55
1989 Bell, gold plate, V1989	Closed	1989	30.00	26-30
1990 Bell, gold plate, V1990	Closed	1990	30.00	26-30
1990 1990 Bell	Closed	1990	27.50	26-55
1991 Bell, gold plate, V1991	Closed	1991	30.00	26-30
1991 1991 Bell	Closed	1991	27.50	26-50
1992 Bell, gold plate, V1992	Closed	1992	30.00	26-30
1992 Bell, silver plate, 1992	Closed	1992	27.50	26-50
1993 Bell, gold plate, V1993	Closed	1993	27.50	28
1993 Bell, silver plate, 1993	Closed	1993	30.00	26-50
1994 Bell, gold plate, 1994	Closed	1994	30.00	26-30
1994 Bell, silver plate, 1994	Closed	1994	27.50	26-30
1995 Bell, gold plate, 1995	Closed	1995	30.00	26-30
1995 Bell, silver plate, 1995	Closed	1995	27.50	26-30
1996 Bell, gold plate, 1996	Closed	1996	35.00	26-35
1996 Bell, silver plate, 1996	Closed	1996	30.00	26-35
1997 Bell, 24Kt. gold plate, 1997	Closed	1997	35.00	26-35
1997 Bell, silver plate, 1997	Closed	1997	30.00	26-30
1998 Bell, 24Kt. gold plate, 1998	Closed	1998	35.00	26-35
1998 Bell, silver plate, 1998	Closed	1998	30.00	26-30
1999 Bell, Sterling, 1999	Closed	1999	50.00	50
1999 Bell, Engraved, 1999	Closed	1999	55.00	55

Roman, Inc.

Animal Kingdom - D. Griff

YEAR ISSUE	EDITION LIMIT	YEAR RETD.	ISSUE PRICE	*QUOTE U.S.$
1994 3 Kittens Sleeping in Basket	Closed	N/A	9.00	9
1994 Bear Cub on Ball	Closed	N/A	10.00	10
1994 Bear Juggling Ball	Closed	N/A	8.00	8
1994 Bear Taking Bath	Closed	N/A	13.50	14
1994 Bear with Bubble on Nose	Closed	N/A	6.50	7
1994 Cat Holding on Ball	Closed	N/A	12.00	12
1994 Cat in Bubbles Jar	Closed	N/A	8.00	8
1994 Cat on Bubble Wand	Closed	N/A	10.00	10
1994 Cat w/Dangling Bubbles	Closed	N/A	9.00	9
1994 Cat w/Mouse on Tail	Closed	N/A	13.50	14
1994 Cat w/Paw on Bubble	Closed	N/A	9.00	9
1994 Chipmunk Blowing Bubble	Closed	N/A	9.50	10
1994 Chipmunk Hangs From Bubble	Closed	N/A	9.00	9
1994 Chipmunk w/Bubble	Closed	N/A	6.50	7
1994 Lounging Cat	Closed	N/A	9.00	10
1994 Mice on Bubble	Closed	N/A	4.00	4
1994 Raccoon Opens Walnut	Closed	N/A	9.00	9
1995 Skunk with Bubble on Tail	Closed	N/A	7.00	7
1995 Squirrel with Bubble	Closed	N/A	4.00	4
1995 Two Chickadees w/Metal Bow	Closed	N/A	17.50	18

Cat-tastrophes - G. Talbott-Boassy

YEAR ISSUE	EDITION LIMIT	YEAR RETD.	ISSUE PRICE	*QUOTE U.S.$
2000 ...better be good for goodness sake	Open		17.50	18
2000 Deck the Halls	Open		8.50	9
2000 The Purr-fect Present	Open		12.00	12
2000 Uh-Oh Christmas Tree	Open		12.00	12
2000 Wrapped Up in the Spirit of the Season	Open		12.00	12

Fontanini Limited Edition Ornaments - E. Simonetti

YEAR ISSUE	EDITION LIMIT	YEAR RETD.	ISSUE PRICE	*QUOTE U.S.$
1995 The Annunciation	20,000	N/A	20.00	20
1996 Journey to Bethlehem	20,000	N/A	20.00	20
1997 Gloria Angel	Yr.Iss.	1997	20.00	20-40

Fontanini Tour Exclusive - E. Simonetti

YEAR ISSUE	EDITION LIMIT	YEAR RETD.	ISSUE PRICE	*QUOTE U.S.$
2000 2000 Fontanini Tour Ornament	Yr.Iss.		20.00	20

Goin' Places Bears - G. Talbott-Boassy

YEAR ISSUE	EDITION LIMIT	YEAR RETD.	ISSUE PRICE	*QUOTE U.S.$
2000 Goin' Crazy	Open		10.00	10
2000 Goin' East	Open		10.00	10
2000 Goin' Home	Open		10.00	10
2000 Goin' North	Open		10.00	10
2000 Goin' South	Open		10.00	10
2000 Goin' to College	Open		10.00	10
2000 Goin' to Grandmas	Open		10.00	10
2000 Goin' to School	Open		10.00	10
2000 Goin' to the Chapel	Open		10.00	10
2000 Goin' West	Open		10.00	10

Holiday Traditions Collection - Roman, Inc.

YEAR ISSUE	EDITION LIMIT	YEAR RETD.	ISSUE PRICE	*QUOTE U.S.$
1998 Bee of Prosperity	Open		12.00	12
1998 Candle in the Window	Retrd.	1998	10.00	10
1997 Christmas Cardinal	Open		5.00	5
1998 Christmas Cheer	Retrd.	1999	12.00	12
1997 Christmas Pickle	Open		7.50	8
1998 Christmas S'mores	Retrd.	1999	7.50	8
1998 A Christmas Treasure	Retrd.	1998	25.00	25
1997 Christmas Wine Bottle	Open		10.00	10
1998 Friendship	Open		12.00	12
2000 Gift of the Magi	Open		12.00	12
1998 Gingerbread House	Retrd.	1999	12.00	12
1997 Golden Nest	Open		7.50	8
1997 Hospitality Pineapple	Retrd.	1999	7.50	8
1999 Ivy Leaf	Retrd.	1999	10.00	10
1998 Jingle Bell Acorn	Retrd.	1999	10.00	10
2000 Legend of Las Posadas	Open		7.50	8
1999 Legend of Mistletoe	Open		10.00	10
1999 Legend of the Amaryllis	Open		12.00	12
2000 Legend of the Church Bell	Open		10.00	10
1999 Legend of the Holly	Open		15.00	15
2000 Legend of the Reindeer	Open		15.00	15
1999 Legend of the Sand Dollar	Open		10.00	10
2000 Light of the World	Open		7.50	8
2000 Lucky Ladybug	Open		9.00	9
1998 Miracle of the Fruit Tree	Retrd.	1999	7.50	8
1999 Moravian Star	Open		5.00	5
1998 Nightingale's Song	Retrd.	1998	10.00	10
1999 Nutcracker	Open		5.00	5
1997 Partridge in a Pear	Open		20.00	20
2000 Peppermint Pig	Open		10.00	10
2000 Quaking Aspen Leaf Wind Chime	Open		15.00	15
1998 Silent Night Feather	Open		6.50	7
1998 Sock Monkey	Open		10.00	10
1998 St. Francis Wreath	Open		14.00	14
2000 Tradition of the Christmas Tree	Open		10.00	10
1998 Wishing Well	Retrd.	1998	12.00	12

Magic of Christmas - D. Morgan

YEAR ISSUE	EDITION LIMIT	YEAR RETD.	ISSUE PRICE	*QUOTE U.S.$
2000 Magic of Christmas figural	Open		18.00	18
2000 Magic of Christmas glass ball	Open		40.00	40
2000 Magic of Giving figural	Open		18.00	18
2000 Magic of Giving glass ball	Open		40.00	40
2000 Santa's Magic Figural	Open		18.00	18
2000 Santa's Magic glass ball	Open		40.00	40

The Millenium™ Collection - Sr. Mary Jean Dorcy

YEAR ISSUE	EDITION LIMIT	YEAR RETD.	ISSUE PRICE	*QUOTE U.S.$
1992 Silent Night	20,000	1992	20.00	20-100
1993 The Annunciation	20,000	1993	20.00	20-75
1994 Peace On Earth	20,000	1994	20.00	20-66
1995 Cause of Our Joy	20,000	1995	20.00	20
1996 Prince of Peace	30,000	1996	20.00	20-55
1997 Gentle Love	Yr.Iss.	1997	20.00	20
1998 Rejoice	Yr.Iss.	1998	20.00	20
1999 Heaven's Blessing	Yr.Iss.	1999	20.00	20
1999 Joyful Promise	2-Yr.		20.00	20

Seraphim Classics® Club Exclusive Dimensional Ornaments - G. Ho

YEAR ISSUE	EDITION LIMIT	YEAR RETD.	ISSUE PRICE	*QUOTE U.S.$
2000 Cassidy - Blessings From Above	Yr.Iss.		19.50	20

Seraphim Classics® Tour Exclusive Ornaments - G. Ho

YEAR ISSUE	EDITION LIMIT	YEAR RETD.	ISSUE PRICE	*QUOTE U.S.$
2000 Laurel - Nature's Harmony	Yr.Iss.		15.00	15

Seraphim Classics® Dimensional Ornaments - G. Ho

YEAR ISSUE	EDITION LIMIT	YEAR RETD.	ISSUE PRICE	*QUOTE U.S.$
1999 Annalisa - Celebrating The Millennium	2-Yr.		20.00	20
2000 Celeste - Light of the World	Open		19.50	20
1999 Hope-Light in the Distance	Open		20.00	20
1999 Joy-Gift of Heaven	Open		19.50	20
1998 Noelle - Giving Spirit	Open		19.50	20

Seraphim Classics® Faro Collection - Faro Studios

YEAR ISSUE	EDITION LIMIT	YEAR RETD.	ISSUE PRICE	*QUOTE U.S.$
1994 Rosalyn, Rarest of Heaven	20,000	1995	25.00	25-125
1995 Helena, Heaven's Herald	20,000	1996	25.00	25-70
1996 Flora, Flower of Heaven	20,000	1997	25.00	25-60
1997 Emily, Heaven's Treasure	Yr.Iss.	1997	25.00	25-55
1998 Elise - Heaven's Glory	Yr.Iss.	1998	25.00	25-55
1999 Gwydolyn-Heaven's Triumph	Yr.Iss.	1999	25.00	25-65

Seraphim Classics® Heaven Sent Collection - Seraphim Studios

YEAR ISSUE	EDITION LIMIT	YEAR RETD.	ISSUE PRICE	*QUOTE U.S.$
1997 Hope Eternal	Open		30.00	30
1997 Loving Spirit	Open		30.00	30
1997 Pure At Heart	Open		30.00	30

Seraphim Classics® Wafer Ornaments - G. Ho

YEAR ISSUE	EDITION LIMIT	YEAR RETD.	ISSUE PRICE	*QUOTE U.S.$
1995 Isabel - Gentle Spirit	Retrd.	1999	15.00	15
1995 Iris - Rainbow's End	Retrd.	2000	15.00	15
1995 Lydia - Winged Poet	Retrd.	1997	15.00	15-55
1995 Cymbeline - Peacemaker	Retrd.	1997	15.00	15-20
1995 Ophelia - Heart Seeker	Retrd.	1997	15.00	15-20
1995 Evangeline - Angel of Mercy	Retrd.	1997	15.00	15-20
1996 Laurice - Wisdom's Child	Retrd.	1997	15.00	15-20
1996 Felicia - Adoring Maiden	Retrd.	1997	15.00	15-20
1996 Priscilla - Benevolent Guide	Retrd.	1997	15.00	15-20
1996 Seraphina - Heaven's Helper	Retrd.	1997	15.00	15
1997 Celine - The Morning Star	Open		15.00	15
1997 Francesca - Loving Guardian	Open		15.00	15
1997 Gabriel - Celestial Messenger	Retrd.	2000	15.00	15
1997 Mariah - Heavenly Joy	Retrd.	2000	15.00	15
1997 Rosalie - Nature's Delight	Open		15.00	15
1997 Serena - Angel of Peace	Retrd.	2000	15.00	15
1998 Chelsea - Summer's Delight	Retrd.	2000	15.00	15
1998 Melody - Heaven's Song	Open		15.00	15
1998 Harmony - Love's Guardian	Retrd.	2000	15.00	15
1998 Tamara - Blessed Guardian	Retrd.	2000	15.00	15
1998 Rachel - Children's Joy	Open		15.00	15
1999 Diana-Heaven's Rose	Retrd.	2000	15.00	15
1999 Grace-Born Anew	Open		15.00	15
1999 Hannah-Always Near	Open		15.00	15
1999 Heather-Autumn Beauty	Retrd.	2000	15.00	15
1999 Samantha-Blessed at Birth	Open		15.00	15
2000 Audra - Embraced by Love	Open		15.00	15
2000 Naomi - Nurturing Spirit	Open		15.00	15

Timeless Teddies Collection - Roman, Inc.

YEAR ISSUE	EDITION LIMIT	YEAR RETD.	ISSUE PRICE	*QUOTE U.S.$
2000 1903 Teddy	Open		12.00	12
2000 1905 Buttons	Open		12.00	12
2000 1908 Britt	Open		12.00	12
2000 1909 Bing	Open		12.00	12
2000 1910 General Barnum	Open		12.00	12
2000 1920 Jacques	Open		12.00	12

Royal Doulton

Bunnykins - Royal Doulton, unless otherwise noted

YEAR ISSUE	EDITION LIMIT	YEAR RETD.	ISSUE PRICE	*QUOTE U.S.$
1991 Santa Bunny - D. Lyttleton	Yr.Iss.	1991	19.00	19
1992 Caroling - D. Lyttleton	Yr.Iss.	1992	19.00	19
1994 Trimming the Tree	Yr.Iss.	1994	20.00	20
1995 Fun in the Snow	Yr.Iss.	1995	20.00	20
1996 Christmas Morn	Yr.Iss.	1996	20.00	20
1997 Home for the Holidays	Yr.Iss.		20.00	20

Christmas Ornaments - Various

YEAR ISSUE	EDITION LIMIT	YEAR RETD.	ISSUE PRICE	*QUOTE U.S.$
1993 Royal Doulton-Together For Christmas - J. James	Yr.Iss.	1993	20.00	20
1993 Royal Albert-Sleighride - N/A	Yr.Iss.	1993	20.00	20

*Quotes have been rounded up to nearest dollar

YEAR ISSUE	EDITION LIMIT	YEAR RETD.	ISSUE PRICE	*QUOTE U.S.$
1994 Royal Doulton-Home For Christmas - J. James	Yr.Iss.	1994	20.00	20
1994 Royal Albert-Coaching Inn - N/A	Yr.Iss.	1994	20.00	20
1995 Royal Doulton-Season's Greetings - J. James	Yr.Iss.	1995	20.00	20
1995 Royal Albert-Skating Pond - N/A	Yr.Iss.	1995	20.00	20
1996 Royal Doulton-Night Before Christmas - J. James	Yr.Iss.	1996	20.00	20
1996 Royal Albert-Gathering Winter Fuel - N/A	Yr.Iss.	1996	20.00	20

Merry Wreath Ornaments - Royal Doulton

YEAR ISSUE	EDITION LIMIT	YEAR RETD.	ISSUE PRICE	*QUOTE U.S.$
1998 Angels	Retrd.	1998	17.50	18
1998 Candy Cane	Retrd.	1998	17.50	18
1998 Toyland	Retrd.	1998	17.50	18
1998 Winter Wonderland	Retrd.	1998	17.50	18

Santa Bell Ornaments - V. Heilbron

YEAR ISSUE	EDITION LIMIT	YEAR RETD.	ISSUE PRICE	*QUOTE U.S.$
1998 Father Christmas	Retrd.	1998	25.00	25
1998 Pere Noel	Retrd.	1998	25.00	25
1998 Santa Claus	Retrd.	1998	25.00	25
1998 St. Nicholas	Retrd.	1998	25.00	25

Victorian Card Ornaments - Royal Doulton

YEAR ISSUE	EDITION LIMIT	YEAR RETD.	ISSUE PRICE	*QUOTE U.S.$
1998 Joy	Retrd.	1998	15.00	15
1998 Merry Christmas	Retrd.	1998	15.00	15
1998 Noel	Retrd.	1998	15.00	15
1998 Peace on Earth	Retrd.	1998	15.00	15

San Francisco Music Box Company

Boyds Bears Musical Bearstone - G.M. Lowenthal

YEAR ISSUE	EDITION LIMIT	YEAR RETD.	ISSUE PRICE	*QUOTE U.S.$
1999 Home Sweet Home	Closed	1999	18.00	18
1999 Peace on Earth	Open		18.00	18
1999 Two Hearts	Open		18.00	18

Boyds Bears Musicals - G. M. Lowenthal

YEAR ISSUE	EDITION LIMIT	YEAR RETD.	ISSUE PRICE	*QUOTE U.S.$
1999 Angelina Cat	Open		10.00	10
1999 Galaxy Bear	Closed	1999	15.00	15
1998 Juliette Bear	Open		10.00	10

Cloissone - San Francisco Music Box Company

YEAR ISSUE	EDITION LIMIT	YEAR RETD.	ISSUE PRICE	*QUOTE U.S.$
1999 Bell	2,500	1999	35.00	35

Santa -Harley Davidson

YEAR ISSUE	EDITION LIMIT	YEAR RETD.	ISSUE PRICE	*QUOTE U.S.$
1998 King of the Road Santa	10,000		25.00	25

Slavic Treasures

Treasure Hunters Club - G. Lewis

YEAR ISSUE	EDITION LIMIT	YEAR RETD.	ISSUE PRICE	*QUOTE U.S.$
2000 2000 Treasures 00-CLUB	Yr.Iss.		45.00	45

1998 Animal Collages - G. Lewis

YEAR ISSUE	EDITION LIMIT	YEAR RETD.	ISSUE PRICE	*QUOTE U.S.$
1998 Elephant Ball PG-088	Closed	1998	34.00	35
1998 Kitten Ball PG-087	Closed	1998	34.00	34
1998 Rabbit Ball PG-086	Closed	1998	34.00	35

1998 Christmas Icons - G. Lewis

YEAR ISSUE	EDITION LIMIT	YEAR RETD.	ISSUE PRICE	*QUOTE U.S.$
1998 Bunches O' Santa Ball PG-092	Closed	1998	34.00	35
1998 Christmas Candy Ball PG-093	Closed	1998	34.00	35
1998 Holiday Fancy Ball PG-094	Closed	1998	34.00	35

1998 Christmas Nostalgia - G. Lewis

YEAR ISSUE	EDITION LIMIT	YEAR RETD.	ISSUE PRICE	*QUOTE U.S.$
1998 Ania's Dollhouse PG-030	Closed	1998	32.00	33
1998 Aunt Betty's Cookies PG-032	Closed	1998	33.00	34
1998 Deck the Halls PG-031	Closed	1998	33.00	33-46
1998 Tomek's Train PG-029	Closed	1998	32.00	33

1998 Classic Christmas - G. Lewis

YEAR ISSUE	EDITION LIMIT	YEAR RETD.	ISSUE PRICE	*QUOTE U.S.$
1998 Cheerful Cherubs PG-011	Closed	1998	33.00	34
1998 Chest O' Fun PG-072	Closed	1998	31.00	31
1998 Four Hands Required PG-013	Closed	1998	33.00	33-42
1998 Fresh Delivery PG-012	Closed	1998	33.00	33-38
1998 Heavenly Harpist PG-010	Closed	1998	31.00	31-38
1998 Heavenly Light PG-059	Closed	1998	31.00	32
1998 Heavenly Package PG-058	Closed	1998	31.00	31
1998 Heavenly Prayer PG-009	Closed	1998	31.00	31
1998 Heavenly Star-catcher PG-057	Closed	1998	31.00	32
1998 Holiday Hard Drive PG-074	Closed	1998	32.00	33
1998 Hot Doggin' PG-054	Closed	1998	35.00	36-48
1998 King with Frankincense PG-006	Closed	1998	31.00	31
1998 King with Gold PG-005	Closed	1998	31.00	31
1998 King with Myrrh PG-007	Closed	1998	31.00	31
1998 Oh, Tannenbaum PG-008	Closed	1998	31.00	31
1998 Stately Dazzler PG-055	Closed	1998	33.00	33
1998 Totem Elf Cane PG-061	Closed	1998	40.00	40
1998 Totem Santa Cane PG-075	Closed	1998	40.00	40
1998 Totem Santa Icicle PG-076	Closed	1998	40.00	40
1998 Toy Soldier Cane PG-062	Closed	1998	40.00	40
1998 Wrap Me Up PG-014	Closed	1998	32.00	32

1998 Elegant Birds - G. Lewis

YEAR ISSUE	EDITION LIMIT	YEAR RETD.	ISSUE PRICE	*QUOTE U.S.$
1998 Feather-Crown Jewel Peacock FB-016	Closed	1998	37.00	37-48
1998 Fine Feathers - Blue Band FB-029	Closed	1998	37.00	37-56
1998 Fine Feathers - Feather Top FB-027	Closed	1998	37.00	37
1998 Fine Feathers - Gold Band FB-030	Closed	1998	37.00	37
1998 Fine Feathers - White Band FB-028	Closed	1998	37.00	37
1998 Rainbow Peacock FB-026	Closed	1998	37.00	37
1998 Winter Peacock FB-015	Closed	1998	37.00	37

1998 Fresh Fruits - G. Lewis

YEAR ISSUE	EDITION LIMIT	YEAR RETD.	ISSUE PRICE	*QUOTE U.S.$
1998 Fruit and Leaves Ball PG-089	Closed	1998	34.00	34-40
1998 Fruit Bowl Ball PG-090	Closed	1998	34.00	34
1998 Fruit Slice Ball PG-091	Closed	1998	34.00	34

1998 Frog Ballet/Orchestra Series - G. Lewis

YEAR ISSUE	EDITION LIMIT	YEAR RETD.	ISSUE PRICE	*QUOTE U.S.$
1998 Bow-Tie Bullfrog FB-007	Closed	1998	37.00	37
1998 Frog Astaire FB-006	Closed	1998	37.00	38
1998 Frog King FB-008	Closed	1998	37.00	37-42
1998 Green Kelley FB-014	Closed	1998	37.00	37
1998 Maestro FB-009	Closed	1998	37.00	38
1998 Pretty Prancer FB-031	Closed	1998	37.00	37
1998 Tutu Toad FB-005	Closed	1998	37.00	38
1998 Twinkle Toes FB-004	Closed	1998	37.00	37

1998 Full Bloom Series - G. Lewis

YEAR ISSUE	EDITION LIMIT	YEAR RETD.	ISSUE PRICE	*QUOTE U.S.$
1998 Full Bloom Daisies PG-080	Closed	1998	32.00	33
1998 Full Bloom Irises PG-081	Closed	1998	32.00	33
1998 Full Bloom Mixed Roses PG-085	Closed	1998	32.00	33
1998 Full Bloom Red Roses PG-084	Closed	1998	32.00	33
1998 Full Bloom Sunflowers PG-082	Closed	1998	32.00	33
1998 Full Bloom Tiger Lillies PG-083	Closed	1998	32.00	33

1998 Holiday Critters - G. Lewis

YEAR ISSUE	EDITION LIMIT	YEAR RETD.	ISSUE PRICE	*QUOTE U.S.$
1998 Acrobatic Tree-trimmers PG-017	Closed	1998	32.00	33
1998 Beary Much Love PG-018	Closed	1998	32.00	32
1998 Geoffrey Giraffe PG-020	Closed	1998	33.00	33-38
1998 It's YOU, Daddy! PG-015	Closed	1998	33.00	33-38
1998 Kelly Kitty PG-019	Closed	1998	33.00	33
1998 Mama's Safe Arms PG-016	Closed	1998	32.00	32
1998 Zeke Zebra PG-021	Closed	1998	33.00	33-38

1998 Jolly Roger Pirates - G. Lewis

YEAR ISSUE	EDITION LIMIT	YEAR RETD.	ISSUE PRICE	*QUOTE U.S.$
1998 Captain Christmas PG-038	Closed	1998	32.00	32
1998 Jolly Roger PG-041	Closed	1998	32.00	32
1998 Lucky's Loot PG-040	Closed	1998	32.00	32
1998 One-Eyed Pete PG-039	Closed	1998	32.00	32

1998 Lamps - G. Lewis

YEAR ISSUE	EDITION LIMIT	YEAR RETD.	ISSUE PRICE	*QUOTE U.S.$
1998 Orange Ball Tiffany FB-021	Closed	1998	33.00	33
1998 Pink Ridge Tiffany FB-022	Closed	1998	33.00	33
1998 White Point Tiffany FB-023	Closed	1998	33.00	33

1998 Modern Art - G. Lewis

YEAR ISSUE	EDITION LIMIT	YEAR RETD.	ISSUE PRICE	*QUOTE U.S.$
1998 Cocoon PG-065	Closed	1998	32.00	32
1998 Infinity PG-064	Closed	1998	32.00	32

1998 Officially Licensed Grateful Dead Designs - G. Lewis

YEAR ISSUE	EDITION LIMIT	YEAR RETD.	ISSUE PRICE	*QUOTE U.S.$
1998 At The Show GG-001	Open		25.00	27
1998 Bearly Dancin' GG-005	Open		25.00	27
1998 Bearly Jammin' GG-007	Open		25.00	27
1998 Bearly Shufflin' GG-006	Open		25.00	27
1998 Chorus Line GG-002	Open		25.00	27
1998 Love Our Earth GG-008	Open		25.00	27
1998 Skull and Roses GG-009	Open		25.00	27
1998 Steal Your Face GG-003	Open		25.00	27
1998 Steal Your Tree GG-004	Open		25.00	27

1998 Old McDonald - G. Lewis

YEAR ISSUE	EDITION LIMIT	YEAR RETD.	ISSUE PRICE	*QUOTE U.S.$
1998 ... There Was A Dog PG-035	Closed	1998	32.00	33
1998 ... There Was A Horse PG-034	Closed	1998	32.00	33
1998 ... There Was A Pig PG-036	Closed	1998	30.00	30-32
1998 ... There Was A Sheep PG-037	Closed	1998	30.00	30-32
1998 Old McDonald PG-033	Closed	1998	33.00	33

1998 Retailer Designs - G. Lewis

YEAR ISSUE	EDITION LIMIT	YEAR RETD.	ISSUE PRICE	*QUOTE U.S.$
1998 Gleam Team I - Diamond RT-03	500	1998	34.00	34
1998 Gleam Team I - Emerald RT-01	500	1998	34.00	34
1998 Gleam Team I - Ruby RT-02	500	1998	34.00	34

1998 Saint Nicholas - G. Lewis

YEAR ISSUE	EDITION LIMIT	YEAR RETD.	ISSUE PRICE	*QUOTE U.S.$
1998 Blue-bell Santa PG-004	Closed	1998	33.00	34
1998 Classic Claus PG-005	Closed	1998	28.50	29-34
1998 Golden Santa PG-003	Closed	1998	33.00	33-42
1998 Regal Santa PG-002	Closed	1998	33.00	34-40
1998 Santa in the Hood PG-006	Closed	1998	33.00	29-33
1998 Toy Bundle PG-001	Closed	1998	33.00	33

1998 SETS - Grecian, Urns, and Neptune - G. Lewis

YEAR ISSUE	EDITION LIMIT	YEAR RETD.	ISSUE PRICE	*QUOTE U.S.$
1998 Black and White Urns FB-033	Closed	1998	60.00	60
1998 Grecian Tabletop FB-032	Closed	1998	96.00	96
1998 Neptune Set - 5 pcs. FB-034	Closed	1998	56.00	56

1998 Singing Moons - G. Lewis

YEAR ISSUE	EDITION LIMIT	YEAR RETD.	ISSUE PRICE	*QUOTE U.S.$
1998 Crescent Crooner FB-036	Closed	1998	37.00	37
1998 Moonlight Melody FB-035	Closed	1998	37.00	37
1998 Moonlight Serenade FB-024	Closed	1998	37.00	37

1998 Small Wonders - G. Lewis

YEAR ISSUE	EDITION LIMIT	YEAR RETD.	ISSUE PRICE	*QUOTE U.S.$
1998 Angel of Peace PG-049	Closed	1998	13.00	13
1998 Bonzo PG-050	Closed	1998	10.50	11
1998 Cross-legged Kringle PG-044	Closed	1998	14.00	14
1998 Gold Fish - "Make A Wish" PG-053	Closed	1998	10.50	11
1998 Gold Star Santa PG-063	Closed	1998	12.50	13
1998 Harold Bear PG-067	Closed	1998	12.50	13
1998 King's Court Clown PG-051	Closed	1998	10.50	11
1998 Load of Goodies PG-042	Closed	1998	15.50	16
1998 Madonna and Child PG-048	Closed	1998	13.00	13
1998 The Santa Express PG-043	Closed	1998	14.00	14-20
1998 Smiling Moon PG-066	Closed	1998	10.50	11
1998 Teddy Loves Presents PG-046	Closed	1998	12.50	13
1998 Teddy's Ice Cream PG-073	Closed	1998	12.50	13
1998 Teddy's Toy PG-045	Closed	1998	12.50	13
1998 Winter Bunny PG-052	Closed	1998	10.50	11
1998 Winter Warm-up PG-047	Closed	1998	13.00	13

1998 Special Event/Commemorative Designs - G. Lewis

YEAR ISSUE	EDITION LIMIT	YEAR RETD.	ISSUE PRICE	*QUOTE U.S.$
1998 Autumn Antics SE-003	250	1998	34.00	34
1998 Beach-Bum Santa SE-004	150	1998	34.00	34
1998 First Year Fanfare SE-001	1,500	1998	34.00	34
1998 Hawaiian Holiday SE-010	15	1998	Gift	40
1998 Lobster Limbo SE-008	250	1998	34.00	34
1998 Patriotic Santa SE-007	250	1998	34.00	34-47
1998 Peach Pal SE-002	250	1998	34.00	34
1998 Reardon Hearts SE-009	350	1998	25.00	25
1998 Regal Santa in Green SE-006	250	1998	34.00	34
1998 Seaside Santa SE-005	250	1998	34.00	34
1998 Six-Shootin' Santa SE-011	15	1998	Gift	N/A

1998 The L.E. Phant Family - G. Lewis

YEAR ISSUE	EDITION LIMIT	YEAR RETD.	ISSUE PRICE	*QUOTE U.S.$
1998 Junior FB-003	Closed	1998	37.00	37
1998 Momma's Girl FB-025	Closed	1998	37.00	37
1998 Mr. L.E. Phant FB-001	Closed	1998	37.00	37
1998 Mrs. Phant FB-002	Closed	1998	37.00	37

1998 Tree-toppers and Coordinating Balls - G. Lewis

YEAR ISSUE	EDITION LIMIT	YEAR RETD.	ISSUE PRICE	*QUOTE U.S.$
1998 Holiday Reflections Ball PG-095	Closed	1998	31.00	31
1998 Holiday Reflections Dazzler PG-096	Closed	1998	33.00	33
1998 Holiday Reflections Tree-Topper TT-001	Closed	1998	56.00	56

1998 Vases - G. Lewis

YEAR ISSUE	EDITION LIMIT	YEAR RETD.	ISSUE PRICE	*QUOTE U.S.$
1998 Black Vase FB-019	Closed	1998	33.00	33
1998 Blue Vase FB-018	Closed	1998	33.00	33
1998 Coffee Mug FB-020	Closed	1998	26.00	26
1998 White Vase FB-017	Closed	1998	33.00	33

1998 Way-Out Bugs and Such - G. Lewis

YEAR ISSUE	EDITION LIMIT	YEAR RETD.	ISSUE PRICE	*QUOTE U.S.$
1998 Gentleman Ant FB-011	Closed	1998	37.00	37
1998 Green "Kootie" FB-013	Closed	1998	37.00	37
1998 Jeepers Creepers FB-010	Closed	1998	37.00	37
1998 Queen Bee FB-012	Closed	1998	37.00	37

1998 World Wildlife Series - G. Lewis

YEAR ISSUE	EDITION LIMIT	YEAR RETD.	ISSUE PRICE	*QUOTE U.S.$
1998 African Elephant PG-023	Closed	1998	33.00	33-42
1998 Bengal Tiger PG-024	Closed	1998	32.00	32-42
1998 Black Rhino PG-025	Closed	1998	33.00	33-42
1998 Lion PG-026	Closed	1998	32.00	32-40
1998 Monkey PG-027	Closed	1998	32.00	33
1998 Zebra PG-028	Closed	1998	32.00	32-40

1999 Aliens - G. Lewis

YEAR ISSUE	EDITION LIMIT	YEAR RETD.	ISSUE PRICE	*QUOTE U.S.$
1999 Star-Belly 99-159-A-FB	300	1999	48.00	49

1999 Allyson's Corner - Limited Edition Sculpted Orbs - B. Lewis

YEAR ISSUE	EDITION LIMIT	YEAR RETD.	ISSUE PRICE	*QUOTE U.S.$
1999 Butterfly Ball 99-086-A	1,000	1999	85.00	86
1999 Fantasy Bird Ball 99-089-A	1,000	1999	68.00	68
1999 Fish and Coral Ball 99-090-A	1,000	1999	74.00	74
1999 Flamingo Ball 99-088-A	1,000	1999	68.00	68
1999 Hummingbird Ball 99-087-A	1,000	1999	85.00	86
1999 Winter Cardinal Ball 99-091-A	1,000	1999	68.00	69

1999 Angel Series - G. Lewis

YEAR ISSUE	EDITION LIMIT	YEAR RETD.	ISSUE PRICE	*QUOTE U.S.$
1999 Heavenly Light - Glitter '99 98-059-B	Closed	1999	38.00	38
1999 Millennium Angel 99-033-A	Closed	1999	38.00	38

1999 Animal Collage Series - G. Lewis

YEAR ISSUE	EDITION LIMIT	YEAR RETD.	ISSUE PRICE	*QUOTE U.S.$
1999 Elephant Ball 98-088-B	Closed	1999	42.00	35-43
1999 Jurassic Ball 99-074-A	Open		42.00	42
1999 Kitten Ball 98-087-B	Closed	1999	42.00	43
1999 Puppy Ball 99-073-A	Closed	1999	42.00	43
1999 Rabbit Ball 98-086-B	Open		42.00	42

1999 Beary Merry Christmas - G. Lewis

YEAR ISSUE	EDITION LIMIT	YEAR RETD.	ISSUE PRICE	*QUOTE U.S.$
1999 It's YOU, Daddy! 98-015-B	Closed	1999	38.00	39
1999 Mama's Safe Arms 98-016-B	Closed	1999	36.00	36-37
1999 Roll Away (With You) 99-036-A	Closed	1999	36.00	36-37

1999 Bugs - G. Lewis

YEAR ISSUE	EDITION LIMIT	YEAR RETD.	ISSUE PRICE	*QUOTE U.S.$
1999 Fly Guy 99-155-A-FB	300	1999	85.00	85
1999 Gentleman Ant - Glitter 99 98-111-B-FB	600	1999	48.00	48
1999 Goldstinger 99-156-A-FB	150	1999	135.00	135
1999 Jeepers Baby 99-153-A-FB	600	1999	48.00	48
1999 Jeepers Daddy - '99 98-110-D-FB	600	1999	48.00	49
1999 Jeepers Momma 99-152-A-FB	600	1999	48.00	49
1999 The Lady's A Bug 99-157-A-FB	1,000		48.00	48
1999 Rainbow "Kootie" - '99 98-113-B-FB	600	1999	48.00	49
1999 Whopper Hopper 99-154-A-FB	1,000		44.00	44

1999 Cat Breeds - G. Lewis

YEAR ISSUE	EDITION LIMIT	YEAR RETD.	ISSUE PRICE	*QUOTE U.S.$
1999 Flame-Point Himalayan 99-063-A	Open		38.00	40
1999 Tin Roof Prowler 99-062-A	Open		38.00	40

1999 Christmas At The Zoo Series - G. Lewis

YEAR ISSUE	EDITION LIMIT	YEAR RETD.	ISSUE PRICE	*QUOTE U.S.$
1999 Charlie Chimp 99-046-A	Open		38.00	38
1999 Emily Elephant 99-045-A	Open		38.00	38
1999 Geoffrey Giraffe - Glitter '99 98-020-B	Open		38.00	38
1999 Zeke Zebra - Glitter '99 98-021-B	Open		38.00	38

1999 Christmas Canes - G. Lewis

YEAR ISSUE	EDITION LIMIT	YEAR RETD.	ISSUE PRICE	*QUOTE U.S.$
1999 Fruit Cane 99-114-A	Closed	1999	56.00	57
1999 Kitten Cane 99-113-A	Closed	1999	56.00	56
1999 Totem Santa Cane Glitter 98-075-C	Closed	1999	56.00	57

1999 Christmas Icon Series - G. Lewis

YEAR ISSUE	EDITION LIMIT	YEAR RETD.	ISSUE PRICE	*QUOTE U.S.$
1999 Bunches O' Santa Ball 98-092-B	Closed	1999	40.00	40
1999 Christmas Candy Ball 98-093-B	Closed	1999	40.00	40
1999 Holiday Fancy Ball 98-094-B	Closed	1999	40.00	40

1999 Classic Christmas Series - G. Lewis

YEAR ISSUE	EDITION LIMIT	YEAR RETD.	ISSUE PRICE	*QUOTE U.S.$
1999 Best Friends 99-025-A	Open		32.00	34
1999 Gift-Wrapped 99-026-A	Open		38.00	40
1999 Hear Them Ring 99-028-A	Closed	1999	32.00	33

*Quotes have been rounded up to nearest dollar

ORNAMENTS

Year Issue	Edition Limit	Year Retd.	Issue Price	*Quote U.S.$
1999 Hot Doggin' - Glitter 98-054-C	Closed	1999	48.00	49
1999 Polar Pals 99-024-A	Open		36.00	38
1999 Ski Bear 99-023-A	Closed	1999	48.00	48
1999 Tannenbaum 98-008-B	Closed	1999	36.00	37
1999 Two of a Feather 99-177-A	Open		38.00	40
1999 Woody 99-027-A	Open		38.00	40

1999 Cosmic Collection - G. Lewis

Year Issue	Edition Limit	Year Retd.	Issue Price	*Quote U.S.$
1999 Big Head and Spot 99-082-A	Open		40.00	40
1999 Big's Cruiser 99-083-A	Open		36.00	36
1999 Rocket Ride 99-081-A	Open		38.00	38
1999 Space Cadet 99-080-A	Open		42.00	42

1999 Crystal Kringles - Series I - G. Lewis

Year Issue	Edition Limit	Year Retd.	Issue Price	*Quote U.S.$
1999 Amber Santa 99-013-A	Open		47.00	47
1999 Amethyst Santa 99-014-A	Open		47.00	47
1999 Malachite Santa 99-015-A	Open		47.00	47
1999 Rose Quartz Santa 99-016-A	Open		47.00	47

1999 Dog Breeds - G. Lewis

Year Issue	Edition Limit	Year Retd.	Issue Price	*Quote U.S.$
1999 Black Lab 99-060-A	Open		38.00	40
1999 Dalmation 99-059-A	Open		40.00	42
1999 English Bulldog 99-058-A	Open		38.00	40
1999 Yellow Lab 99-061-A	Open		38.00	40
1999 Yorkshire Terrier 99-057-A	Open		36.00	38

1999 Easter Designs - G. Lewis

Year Issue	Edition Limit	Year Retd.	Issue Price	*Quote U.S.$
1999 Goose Party 99-128-A	Open		40.00	40
1999 Just Hatched 99-124-A	Open		32.00	32
1999 Robert Rabbit 99-125-A	Open		34.00	34
1999 Rose and Roxy Rabbit 99-126-A	Open		34.00	34
1999 Spring Parade 99-127-A	Open		38.00	34

1999 Elegant Birds - G. Lewis

Year Issue	Edition Limit	Year Retd.	Issue Price	*Quote U.S.$
1999 Feather-Crown Jewel Peacock 98-116-B-FB	300		48.00	48
1999 Fine Feathers - Blue Band 98-129-B-FB	300	1999	56.00	56

1999 Frog Series - 1st in Series of 3 - G. Lewis

Year Issue	Edition Limit	Year Retd.	Issue Price	*Quote U.S.$
1999 Mr. Saxy 99-151-A-FB	150	1999	90.00	90
1999 Number 3 99-150-A-FB	300	1999	56.00	56

1999 Frogs - G. Lewis

Year Issue	Edition Limit	Year Retd.	Issue Price	*Quote U.S.$
1999 Frog Astaire - Glitter Boy 99 98-106-B-FB	600	1999	48.00	49
1999 Frog King - Purple Robe 99 98-108-B-FB	600	1999	48.00	49
1999 Maestro - White Tux 99 98-109-B-FB	600	1999	48.00	49
1999 Mr. Happy Hoppy 99-146-A-FB	1,000	1999	44.00	45
1999 Mrs. Happy Hoppy 99-147-A-FB	1,000	1999	44.00	44
1999 Pea Green - The Spotted Toad 99-148-A-FB	150	1999	48.00	48

1999 Fruit and Vegetable "Clusters" Series - G. Lewis

Year Issue	Edition Limit	Year Retd.	Issue Price	*Quote U.S.$
1999 Fruit and Leaves Ball 98-089-B	Open		40.00	40
1999 Fruit Cluster I - Watermelon 99-037-A	Open		38.00	38
1999 Fruit Cluster II - Banana 99-038-A	Open		38.00	38
1999 Pairs of Pears 99-039-A	Open		38.00	38
1999 Sun Kissed 99-040-A	Open		38.00	38
1999 Veggie Cluster I - Corn 99-041-A	Open		38.00	38
1999 Veggie Cluster II - Tomato 99-042-A	Open		38.00	38

1999 Full Bloom Series - G. Lewis

Year Issue	Edition Limit	Year Retd.	Issue Price	*Quote U.S.$
1999 Flower Cluster I 99-072-A	Open		38.00	40
1999 Full Bloom Irises 98-081-B	Open		40.00	42
1999 Full Bloom Poinsettias 99-071-A	Open		40.00	42
1999 Full Bloom Red Roses 98-084-B	Open		40.00	42
1999 Full Bloom Sunflowers 98-082-B	Open		40.00	42
1999 Sugar Magnolia - Blossoms Bloomin' 99-070-A	Closed	1999	40.00	40-42

1999 Garlands - G. Lewis

Year Issue	Edition Limit	Year Retd.	Issue Price	*Quote U.S.$
1999 Halloween Collection Garland I 99-120-A	Closed	1999	115.00	116
1999 Holiday Travel Garland 99-119-A	Closed	1999	115.00	115
1999 Santa and Packages Garland 99-118-A	Closed	1999	115.00	116
1999 Santa Bell Garland 99-117-A	Closed	1999	115.00	115

1999 Ghosts - G. Lewis

Year Issue	Edition Limit	Year Retd.	Issue Price	*Quote U.S.$
1999 Polter Gal 99-164-A-FB	600		48.00	48
1999 Polter Guy 99-165-A-FB	600		48.00	48
1999 Pumpkin Haid 99-166-A-FB	150		135.00	135

1999 Halloween Goodies - G. Lewis

Year Issue	Edition Limit	Year Retd.	Issue Price	*Quote U.S.$
1999 The A. P. Reeshun Family 99-138-A	Closed	1999	38.00	38-40
1999 Blue Boo 99-134-A	Closed	1999	36.00	37
1999 Funny Phantom 99-135-A	Open		36.00	36
1999 Perry Normal 99-140-A	Open		40.00	40
1999 Pinkie Poltergeist 99-133-A	Closed	1999	36.00	37
1999 Scary Airy 99-137-A	Open		36.00	36
1999 Skeleton Sam 99-141-A	Closed	1999	34.00	35
1999 Spooky Specter 99-136-A	Open		36.00	36
1999 Witchy's Kitty 99-139-A	Open		40.00	40

1999 Just For Fun - G. Lewis

Year Issue	Edition Limit	Year Retd.	Issue Price	*Quote U.S.$
1999 America's Cup 99-084-A	Closed	1999	38.00	39
1999 Holiday Hard-drive 98-074-B	Closed	1999	38.00	38
1999 Sour Grapes 99-085-A	Open		42.00	42

1999 Nostalgia Series - G. Lewis

Year Issue	Edition Limit	Year Retd.	Issue Price	*Quote U.S.$
1999 Ania's Dollhouse 98-030-B	Closed	1999	38.00	39
1999 Deck the Halls - Glitter 98-031-B	Open		46.00	46
1999 Happy First 99-035-A	Closed	1999	44.00	45
1999 A Teddy From Mama 99-034-A	Closed	1999	44.00	45

1999 Pedestal Designs - Annealed Glass Stands - G. Lewis

Year Issue	Edition Limit	Year Retd.	Issue Price	*Quote U.S.$
1999 Royal Crown Egg 99-170-A-PD	150	1999	135.00	136
1999 Santa Sleigh Egg 99-169-A-PD	150	1999	135.00	136
1999 Standing Figurine - Amber Santa 99-173-A-PD	300	1999	135.00	136
1999 Standing Figurine - Deck The Halls 99-171-A-PD	300	1999	110.00	111
1999 Standing Figurine - White Whistler 99-176-A-PD	300	1999	110.00	111
1999 Standing Figurine - Woodland Santa 99-172-A-PD	300	1999	110.00	111

1999 Retailer Designs - G. Lewis

Year Issue	Edition Limit	Year Retd.	Issue Price	*Quote U.S.$
1999 Gleam Team II - Elf with Diamond 99-180-C	600		38.00	38
1999 Gleam Team II - Elf with Emerald 99-180-A	600		38.00	38
1999 Gleam Team II - Elf with Ruby 99-180-B	600		38.00	38

1999 Saint Nicholas - G. Lewis

Year Issue	Edition Limit	Year Retd.	Issue Price	*Quote U.S.$
1999 Beach-Bum Santa 99-010-B	Closed	1999	38.00	39
1999 Checking It Twice 99-001-A	Closed	1999	38.00	39
1999 Christmas Carp 99-005-A	Closed	1999	40.00	40
1999 Classic Claus in Red 98-056-B	Open		32.00	32
1999 Ebony Santa 99-006-A	Open		38.00	40
1999 Golden Flame Santa 98-003-B	Open		40.00	40
1999 Leader of the Band 99-008-A	Open		38.00	40
1999 Patriotic Santa 99-009-B	Open		42.00	44
1999 Pause For St. Nick 99-003-A	Open		40.00	42
1999 Regal Santa in Red 98-002-C	Open		38.00	38
1999 Santa's Secret (Behind His Back) 99-002-A	Open		42.00	44
1999 Seaside Santa 99-011-B	Open		38.00	40
1999 Silver-bell Santa in Blue 98-004-B	Closed	1999	38.00	39
1999 Six-Shootin' Santa 99-012-C	Open		40.00	42
1999 Toy Bundle 98-001-B	Closed	1999	38.00	39
1999 Winter Winks - cobalt blue 99-007-B	Closed	1999	32.00	32-34
1999 Winter Winks - purple 99-007-C	Open		32.00	34
1999 Winter Winks - red 99-007-A	Open		32.00	34
1999 Woodland Santa 99-004-A	Open		42.00	44

1999 Santa's Elves - G. Lewis

Year Issue	Edition Limit	Year Retd.	Issue Price	*Quote U.S.$
1999 Autumn Antics 99-018-C	Open		38.00	40
1999 Four Hands Required 98-013-B	Closed	1999	42.00	42
1999 Fresh Delivered Ornament 98-012-B	Closed	1999	38.00	39
1999 Hangin' On 99-022-A	Open		42.00	42
1999 Joyful Noises 99-020-A	Open		32.00	34
1999 Peach Pal 99-017-C	Closed	1999	38.00	38-39
1999 Pepper Meant Elf 99-021-A	Open		30.00	32
1999 Pining For Christmas 99-019-B	Open		40.00	42

1999 Seashell Clusters - G. Lewis

Year Issue	Edition Limit	Year Retd.	Issue Price	*Quote U.S.$
1999 Seashell Cluster I - Sanddollar 99-043-A	Open		40.00	40
1999 Seashell Cluster II - Conch 99-044-A	Open		40.00	40

1999 Seasonal Egg Designs - G. Lewis

Year Issue	Edition Limit	Year Retd.	Issue Price	*Quote U.S.$
1999 Autumn Egg - Harvest 99-132-A	Open		36.00	38
1999 Spring Egg - Blossom 99-131-A	Open		36.00	38
1999 Summer Egg - Fire 99-129-A	Open		36.00	38
1999 Winter Egg - Ice 99-130-A	Open		36.00	38

1999 Small Wonders Series (Smaller Size) - G. Lewis

Year Issue	Edition Limit	Year Retd.	Issue Price	*Quote U.S.$
1999 Bats-'n-Spiders Santa 99-107-A	Closed	1999	24.00	25
1999 Chilly Charlie 99-092-A	Open		25.00	25
1999 Christmas Morn Surprise 99-099-A	Open		28.00	28
1999 Cobalt Santa Head 99-100-A	Closed	1999	24.00	25
1999 Enchantress 99-105-A	Open		26.00	26
1999 Fruit Cluster - Mini 99-104-A	Closed	1999	26.00	27
1999 Hall Decker 99-101-A	Closed	1999	30.00	30
1999 Harold Bear - Glitter 98-067-B	Closed	1999	20.00	20
1999 Ice Rink Cutie 99-093-A	Closed	1999	28.00	29
1999 Lion Head - Mini 99-103-A	Open		30.00	30
1999 Little Nicholas 99-096-A	Open		25.00	25
1999 Littlest Golf Pro 99-097-A	Open		25.00	25
1999 Pint-Size Specter 99-108-A	Open		22.00	22
1999 Purple Fish 98-053-B	Closed	1999	20.00	20
1999 Rock-A-Billy 99-098-A	Open		25.00	25
1999 Ski Boy 99-094-A	Open		25.00	25
1999 Super Kid 99-106-A	Open		26.00	26
1999 Sweet Susie 99-095-A	Open		25.00	25
1999 Tiger Head - Mini 99-102-A	Open		30.00	30

1999 Small-Size Santas - G. Lewis

Year Issue	Edition Limit	Year Retd.	Issue Price	*Quote U.S.$
1999 Lighten Your Holiday 99-110-A	Open		30.00	30
1999 North Wind Santa 99-111-A	Open		30.00	30
1999 Old World Wanderer 99-112-A	Open		30.00	30
1999 Santa's Tree 99-109-A	Open		30.00	30

1999 Snowmen/Snowwomen - G. Lewis

Year Issue	Edition Limit	Year Retd.	Issue Price	*Quote U.S.$
1999 Polar Postage 99-032-A	Open		38.00	40
1999 Snowman Santa 99-030-A	Open		38.00	40
1999 White Whistler 99-029-A	Open		38.00	40
1999 Wintry Woman 99-031-A	Closed	1999	38.00	38-39

1999 Special Event/Commemorative Designs - G. Lewis

Year Issue	Edition Limit	Year Retd.	Issue Price	*Quote U.S.$
1999 Second Year Santa 99-144-A	1,500	1999	40.00	40

1999 St. Patrick's - G. Lewis

Year Issue	Edition Limit	Year Retd.	Issue Price	*Quote U.S.$
1999 Catch Lucky! 99-123-A	Open		36.00	36

1999 Stocking Stuffers - G. Lewis

Year Issue	Edition Limit	Year Retd.	Issue Price	*Quote U.S.$
1999 Kyle Kitty 98-019-B	Closed	1999	38.00	38-39
1999 Paulie Puppy 99-047-A	Closed	1999	38.00	38-39
1999 Peggy Pig 99-048-A	Open		38.00	38

1999 Thanksgiving Designs - G. Lewis

Year Issue	Edition Limit	Year Retd.	Issue Price	*Quote U.S.$
1999 Giving Thanks 99-143-A	Open		40.00	40
1999 Pilgrim's Bounty 99-142-A	Open		38.00	38

1999 The Night Before Christmas - (Boxed, Numbered, Tagged Set) First In Series - G. Lewis

Year Issue	Edition Limit	Year Retd.	Issue Price	*Quote U.S.$
1999 Night Before Christmas I - 3 pcs. 99-145-A	2,800	1999	280.00	280

1999 Tree-Toppers - G. Lewis

Year Issue	Edition Limit	Year Retd.	Issue Price	*Quote U.S.$
1999 Heading For Christmas 99-115-A	Open		76.00	76
1999 Two Better Than One 99-116-A	Open		76.00	76

1999 Tropical Fish - G. Lewis

Year Issue	Edition Limit	Year Retd.	Issue Price	*Quote U.S.$
1999 Deep Sea I - Blue/Navy/Yellow 99-064-A	Open		38.00	38
1999 Deep Sea II - Black/White 99-065-A	Open		38.00	38
1999 Deep Sea III - Orange/White 99-066-A	Open		38.00	38
1999 Deep Sea IV - Blue/Orange 99-067-A	Open		38.00	38
1999 Deep Sea V - Black 99-068-A	Open		38.00	38
1999 Deep Sea VI - Pearl 99-069-A	Open		38.00	38

1999 Veterans Memorial - G. Lewis

Year Issue	Edition Limit	Year Retd.	Issue Price	*Quote U.S.$
1999 All You Can Be 99-075-A	Open		40.00	40
1999 Anchors Aweigh 99-077-A	Open		40.00	40
1999 The Few and Proud 99-076-A	Open		40.00	40
1999 High-Flying Hero 99-078-A	Open		40.00	40
1999 M*A*S*H Nurse 99-079-A	Open		40.00	40

1999 Wedded Bliss - G. Lewis

Year Issue	Edition Limit	Year Retd.	Issue Price	*Quote U.S.$
1999 Across The Threshold 99-122-A	Open		36.00	38
1999 Just Married 99-121-A	Open		36.00	40

1999 World Wildlife Series - G. Lewis

Year Issue	Edition Limit	Year Retd.	Issue Price	*Quote U.S.$
1999 African Elephant 98-023-A	Closed	1999	42.00	43
1999 Bengal Tiger 98-024-B	Closed	1999	38.00	38-40
1999 Black Rhino 98-025-B	Closed	1999	42.00	43
1999 Cheetah 99-049-A	Open		40.00	42
1999 Chimpanzee (Monkey - '99) 98-027-B	Open		40.00	42
1999 Giraffe 99-053-A	Open		42.00	44
1999 Gorilla 99-051-A	Open		38.00	40
1999 Hippo 99-054-A	Open		38.00	40
1999 Lion 98-026-B	Open		38.00	40
1999 Panda 99-050-A	Open		38.00	40
1999 Parrot - Blue Macaw 99-052-A	Closed	1999	42.00	42
1999 Polar Bear 99-055-A	Open		38.00	40
1999 White-Tail Deer 99-056-A	150	1999	48.00	48
1999 Zebra 98-028-B	Open		38.00	40

2000 4th of July - G. Lewis

Year Issue	Edition Limit	Year Retd.	Issue Price	*Quote U.S.$
2000 Miss Stars-N'-Stripes 00-189-A	Open		40.00	40

2000 Allyson's Corner - G. Lewis

Year Issue	Edition Limit	Year Retd.	Issue Price	*Quote U.S.$
2000 Butterfly Ball - 2000 99-086-B	1,000		85.00	85
2000 Flamingo Ball - 2000 99-088-B	1,000		68.00	68
2000 Hummingbird Ball - 2000 99-087-B	1,000		85.00	85
2000 Winter Cardinal Ball - 2000 99-091-B	1,000		68.00	68

2000 Angel Series - G. Lewis

Year Issue	Edition Limit	Year Retd.	Issue Price	*Quote U.S.$
2000 Angelic Mandolin 00-246-A	Open		38.00	38
2000 Heard on High 00-245-A	Open		38.00	38
2000 Millennium Angel 99-033-B	Open		38.00	38

2000 Animal Collage Series - G. Lewis

Year Issue	Edition Limit	Year Retd.	Issue Price	*Quote U.S.$
2000 Kitten Ball 98-087-C	Open		42.00	42
2000 Puppy Ball 99-073-B	Open		42.00	42

2000 Animal Theme - G. Lewis

Year Issue	Edition Limit	Year Retd.	Issue Price	*Quote U.S.$
2000 Cheetah Pattern 00-305-A	Open		28.00	28
2000 Dalmation Pattern 00-310-A	Open		28.00	28
2000 Elephant Pattern 00-308-A	Open		28.00	28
2000 Giraffe Pattern 00-309-A	Open		28.00	28
2000 Tiger Pattern 00-306-A	Open		28.00	28
2000 Zebra Pattern 00-307-A	Open		28.00	28

2000 Bugs - G. Lewis

Year Issue	Edition Limit	Year Retd.	Issue Price	*Quote U.S.$
2000 Bloodsucker 00-407-A-FB	450		48.00	48
2000 Flying Dragon 00-409-A-FB	150		77.00	77
2000 The Lady's A Bug 99-157-B-FB	750		48.00	48
2000 Lightning Flasher 00-412-A-FB	225		48.00	48
2000 Mantis Man 00-410-A-FB	225		64.00	64
2000 Nat the Gnat 00-411-A-FB	750		40.00	40
2000 Web Weaver 00-408-A-FB	450		56.00	56
2000 Whopper Hopper 99-154-B-FB	750		44.00	44

2000 Cat Breeds - G. Lewis

Year Issue	Edition Limit	Year Retd.	Issue Price	*Quote U.S.$
2000 Midnite 00-207-A	Open		40.00	40
2000 Patches 00-208-A	Open		40.00	40
2000 Salt and Pepper 00-206-A	Open		40.00	40
2000 Siamese 00-205-A	Open		40.00	40

2000 Chess Set - G. Lewis

Year Issue	Edition Limit	Year Retd.	Issue Price	*Quote U.S.$
2000 Bishop 00-265-A	Open		40.00	40
2000 King 00-267-A	Open		42.00	42
2000 Knight 00-264-A	Open		38.00	38
2000 Pawn 00-262-A	Open		36.00	36
2000 Queen 00-266-A	Open		40.00	40
2000 Rook 00-263-A	Open		38.00	38

2000 Christmas Canes - G. Lewis

Year Issue	Edition Limit	Year Retd.	Issue Price	*Quote U.S.$
2000 Kitten Cane 99-113-A	300		56.00	56

*Quotes have been rounded up to nearest dollar

YEAR ISSUE	EDITION LIMIT	YEAR RETD.	ISSUE PRICE	*QUOTE U.S.$
2000 Christmas Icon Series - G. Lewis				
2000 Bunches O' Santa Ball 98-092-C	150		70.00	70
2000 Christmas Candy Ball 98-093-C	150		70.00	70
2000 Christmas Memory Balls - G. Lewis				
2000 Double Dazzle 00-333-A	Open		33.00	33
2000 Ice Drop 00-332-A	Open		33.00	33
2000 Party Ball 00-334-A	Open		30.00	30
2000 Snow Blanket 00-331-A	Open		30.00	30
2000 Star Bright 00-335-A	Open		30.00	30
2000 Winter Woods Walk 00-330-A	Open		30.00	30
2000 Classic Christmas Series - G. Lewis				
2000 Christmas is for Lovers 00-233-A	Open		34.00	34
2000 Gift For A Friend 00-238-A	Open		38.00	38
2000 Ginger Boy 00-234-A	Open		40.00	40
2000 Ginger Girl 00-235-A	Open		40.00	40
2000 Hound-dog Holiday 00-239-A	Open		34.00	34
2000 Kitty Christmas 00-240-A	Open		34.00	34
2000 Season's Greetings 00-236-A	Open		34.00	34
2000 Together We Shine 00-237-A	Open		40.00	40
2000 Crystal Kringles - Series I - G. Lewis				
2000 Agate Santa 00-230-A	Open		47.00	47
2000 Citrine Santa 00-231-A	Open		47.00	47
2000 Dog Breeds - G. Lewis				
2000 Chocolate Lab 00-288-A	Open		40.00	40
2000 Cocker Spaniel 00-200-A	Open		40.00	40
2000 Golden Retriever 00-204-A	Open		40.00	40
2000 Pekinese 00-203-A	Open		38.00	38
2000 Saint Bernhard 00-199-A	Open		42.00	42
2000 Shar-pei 00-202-A	Open		42.00	42
2000 Sheepdog 00-201-A	Open		42.00	42
2000 Easter Designs - G. Lewis				
2000 Bunny Boy 00-184-A	Open		38.00	38
2000 Crusin' For Chicks 00-185-A	Open		42.00	42
2000 Easter Morning 00-187-A	Open		40.00	40
2000 Eggspressive 00-183-A	Open		38.00	38
2000 Topper 00-186-A	Open		38.00	38
2000 Flower Balls - G. Lewis				
2000 Gerbers 00-313-A	Open		28.00	28
2000 Hydrangea 00-315-A	Open		28.00	28
2000 Irises 00-311-A	Open		28.00	28
2000 Pansies 00-316-A	Open		28.00	28
2000 Roses 00-312-A	Open		28.00	28
2000 Tulips 00-314-A	Open		28.00	28
2000 Frog Series - 2nd in Series of 3 - G. Lewis				
2000 Number 5 00-405-A-FB	225		56.00	56
2000 Tune Jumper 00-406-A-FB	150		72.00	72
2000 Frogs - G. Lewis				
2000 Chief Big Croak 00-401-A-FB	750		48.00	48
2000 Flambe Froggy 00-404-A-FB	750		48.00	48
2000 High-Wire Honey 00-403-A-FB	750		48.00	48
2000 Jumping Jester 00-402-A-FB	750		48.00	48
2000 Mr. Happy Hoppy 99-146-A-FB	750		44.00	44
2000 Mrs. Happy Hoppy 99-147-E-FB	750		44.00	44
2000 Rootin' Tootin' Toad 00-400-A-FB	450		48.00	48
2000 Full Bloom Flower Clusters - G. Lewis				
2000 Flower Cluster II 00-188-A	Open		40.00	40
2000 Sugar Magnolia - Blossoms Bloomin' 99-070-B	Open		42.00	42
2000 Garlands - G. Lewis				
2000 Halloween Collection Garland 99-120-A	125		115.00	115
2000 Santa and Packages Garland 99-118-A	125		115.00	115
2000 Santa Bell Garland 99-117-A	125		115.00	115
2000 Ghosts - G. Lewis				
2000 Pumpkin Daid 99-165-B-FB	150		135.00	135
2000 Glitter Balls - G. Lewis				
2000 Burgundy Glitter 00-318-A	Open		15.00	15
2000 Gold Glitter 00-320-A	Open		15.00	15
2000 Opal Glitter 00-323-A	Open		15.00	15
2000 Orange Glitter 00-322-A	Open		15.00	15
2000 Pink/Salmon Glitter 00-321-A	Open		15.00	15
2000 Purple Glitter 00-319-A	Open		15.00	15
2000 Red & Gold Glitter Mix 00-324-A	Open		15.00	15
2000 Red Glitter 00-317-A	Open		15.00	15
2000 Glitter Swirls - G. Lewis				
2000 Blue & White 00-336-A	Open		19.00	19
2000 Purple & Gold 00-340-A	Open		19.00	19
2000 Purple & Orange 00-339-A	Open		19.00	19
2000 Red & Gold 00-337-A	Open		19.00	19
2000 Red & White 00-338-A	Open		19.00	19
2000 Halloween Goodies - G. Lewis				
2000 (I've Got My) Eye On You 00-271-A	Open		40.00	40
2000 Bone Pile 00-277-A	Open		40.00	40
2000 Count Pumpkula 00-275-A	Open		24.00	24
2000 Howling Goblin 00-269-A	Open		24.00	24
2000 Jack's Bat 00-270-A	Open		38.00	38
2000 Moonlight Goblin 00-268-A	Open		28.00	28
2000 Scare D. Cat 00-274-A	Open		40.00	40
2000 Spiderella 00-276-A	Open		38.00	38
2000 Who's Afraid? 00-273-A	Open		38.00	38
2000 Zelda and the Raven 00-272-A	Open		40.00	40

YEAR ISSUE	EDITION LIMIT	YEAR RETD.	ISSUE PRICE	*QUOTE U.S.$
2000 Hermitage Museum Series - G. Lewis				
2000 Amber Ball 00-304-A	Open		37.00	37
2000 Burgandy Court Ball 00-302-A	Open		37.00	37
2000 Burgandy Court Icicle 00-303-A	Open		42.00	42
2000 Enamel Motif Ball 00-325-A	Open		37.00	37
2000 Enamel Motif Double Orb 00-326-A	Open		52.00	52
2000 Gilded Facet Ball 00-327-A	Open		37.00	37
2000 Regal Green Ball 00-301-A	Open		37.00	37
2000 Royal Blue Ball 00-300-A	Open		37.00	37
2000 Just For Fun - G. Lewis				
2000 Formerly Known As Prince 00-278-A	Open		34.00	34
2000 Green With Envy 00-280-A	Open		42.00	42
2000 Holiday Cheer 00-279-A	Open		42.00	42
2000 Mother's/Father's Day - G. Lewis				
2000 Gift For Dad 00-191-A	Open		40.00	40
2000 Mom's Bouquet 00-190-A	Open		40.00	40
2000 Nostalgia Series - G. Lewis				
2000 Newborn Miracle 00-248-A	Open		38.00	38
2000 Terrific Twos 00-247-A	Open		42.00	42
2000 Officially Licensed Bozo The Clown - G. Lewis				
2000 Bozo Santa BZ-001	Open		29.00	29
2000 Here's Bozo! BZ-003	Open		29.00	29
2000 Top Hat Bozo BZ-002	Open		29.00	29
2000 Officially Licensed Nancy & Sluggo - G. Lewis				
2000 Nancy UM-001	Open		29.00	29
2000 Sluggo UM-002	Open		29.00	29
2000 Officially Licensed Ziggy & Friends - G. Lewis				
2000 Purr-fect Pets UM-005	Open		29.00	29
2000 Ziggy Santa UM-003	Open		29.00	29
2000 Ziggy's Best Friend UM-004	Open		29.00	29
2000 Retailer Designs - G. Lewis				
2000 Gleam Santa - Diamond 00-286-A	600		42.00	42
2000 Gleam Santa - Emerald 00-284-A	600		42.00	42
2000 Gleam Santa - Ruby 00-285-A	600		42.00	42
2000 Saint Nicholas - G. Lewis				
2000 Christmas for Rover 00-223-A	Open		38.00	38
2000 Fireworks Santa 00-228-A	Open		38.00	38
2000 Flight Plan 00-224-A	Open		40.00	40
2000 Frosty Holiday 00-225-A	Open		38.00	38
2000 Golden Holly Santa 98-003-C	Open		42.00	42
2000 Holiday Heart Santa 00-227-A	Open		38.00	38
2000 Jolly Old Elf 00-292-A	Open		44.00	44
2000 Patriotic Santa 99-009-B	Open		44.00	44
2000 Regal Santa in Red 98-002-C	Open		40.00	40
2000 Reindeer Wreath 00-221-A	Open		38.00	38
2000 Santa's Secret (Behind His Back) 99-002-B	Open		44.00	44
2000 Seaside Santa 99-011-B	Open		40.00	40
2000 Six-Shootin' Santa 99-012-C	Open		42.00	42
2000 Toy Maker Santa 00-222-A	Open		40.00	40
2000 Twist-Top Santa 00-226-A	Open		34.00	34
2000 Winter Winks - green 00-229-A	Open		34.00	34
2000 Santa's Elves - G. Lewis				
2000 Lobster Limbo 00-232-B	Open		40.00	40
2000 Small Wonders Series (Smaller Size) - G. Lewis				
2000 Captain Jack 00-260-A	Open		24.00	24
2000 Childlike Glow 00-254-A	Open		24.00	24
2000 Christmas Moon 00-252-A	Open		24.00	24
2000 Downhill Dasher 00-253-A	Open		24.00	24
2000 Little Engineer 00-259-A	Open		24.00	24
2000 Panda Head - Mini 00-290-A	Open		28.00	28
2000 Polar Bear Head - Mini 00-291-A	Open		28.00	28
2000 Snow Bunny 00-249-A	Open		17.00	17
2000 Snowball Attack! 00-258-A	Open		24.00	24
2000 Snowfort Architect 00-257-A	Open		24.00	24
2000 Snowman Planned 00-256-A	Open		24.00	24
2000 Summer - Winter 00-251-A	Open		24.00	24
2000 Thanksgiving Catch 00-255-A	Open		21.00	21
2000 Twinkle, Twinkle - (Set of 3 pcs.) 00-250-A	Open		33.00	33
2000 Small-Size Santas - G. Lewis				
2000 Satchel Santa 00-261-A	Open		28.00	28
2000 Snowmen/Snowwomen - G. Lewis				
2000 Blizzard Boomer 00-244-A	Open		24.00	24
2000 Cool Rhythm 00-242-A	Open		24.00	24
2000 Deep Freeze Diva 00-241-A	Open		24.00	24
2000 Squeezebox Snowdude 00-243-A	Open		24.00	24
2000 Special Event/Commemorative Designs - G. Lewis				
2000 Third Year Thrills 00-287-A	1,500		42.00	42
2000 Twisted Toads SP-01-A/B/C/D	350		30.00	30
2000 St. Patrick's Day - G. Lewis				
2000 Golden Clover 00-182-A	Open		38.00	38
2000 Stocking Stuffers - G. Lewis				
2000 Kevin Kitty 98-019-C	Open		38.00	38
2000 Peter Puppy 99-047-B	Open		38.00	38
2000 The Night Before Christmas II - Second In Series - G. Lewis				
2000 I In My Cap 00-281-A	2,800		120.00	120
2000 Snug In Their Beds 00-281-A	2,800		120.00	120
2000 Sugar Plum Visions 00-281-A	2,800		120.00	120

YEAR ISSUE	EDITION LIMIT	YEAR RETD.	ISSUE PRICE	*QUOTE U.S.$
2000 Theme Compostions - G. Lewis				
2000 Beach Party 00-218-A	Open		42.00	42
2000 Catch of the Day 00-219-A	Open		42.00	42
2000 Octopus' Garden 00-217-A	Open		42.00	42
2000 Santa's Golf Bag 00-220-A	Open		42.00	42
2000 Sports Nut 00-216-A	Open		42.00	42
2000 Valentine's Day - G. Lewis				
2000 Puppy Love 00-181-A	Open		40.00	40
2000 Woodland Animals - G. Lewis				
2000 Black Bear 00-193-A	Open		42.00	42
2000 Falcon 00-198-A	Open		40.00	40
2000 Gray Squirrel 00-194-A	Open		38.00	38
2000 Owl 00-197-A	Open		38.00	38
2000 Raccoon 00-196-A	Open		38.00	38
2000 Skunk 00-195-A	Open		38.00	38
2000 Timber Wolf 00-192-A	Open		40.00	40
2000 World Wildlife - G. Lewis				
2000 African Elephant II 00-289-A	Open		40.00	40
2000 Bald Eagle 00-215-A	Open		42.00	42
2000 Bengal Tiger - white 98-024-C	Open		40.00	40
2000 Emperor Penguin 00-213-A	Open		40.00	40
2000 Kangaroo 00-209-A	Open		38.00	38
2000 Koala 00-210-A	Open		38.00	38
2000 Lioness 00-211-A	Open		40.00	40
2000 Lynx 00-212-A	Open		42.00	42
2000 Parrot - Scarlet Macaw 99-052-B	Open		44.00	44
2000 Walrus 00-214-A	Open		42.00	42
Glasscots University Mascots-Atlantic Coast Conference - G. Lewis				
1999 Clemson Tiger - Full Figure GM-090	Open		25.00	29
1998 Clemson Tigers GM-001	Open		25.00	25
2000 Duke Blue Devils - Basketball GM-127	Open		29.00	29
1999 Duke Blue Devils - Full Figure GM-003	Open		25.00	33
1999 Duke Blue Devils - Head Only GM-002	Open		25.00	29
1998 Florida State Seminoles GM-004	Open		25.00	29
1998 Georgia Tech Yellow Jackets GM-005	Open		25.00	29
1998 Maryland Terrapins GM-006	Open		25.00	29
1998 NCSU Wolfpack - Full Figure GM-054	Open		25.00	29
1998 NCSU Wolfpack - Head Only GM-053	Open		25.00	29
2000 North Carolina Tar Heels - Basketball GM-131	Open		33.00	33
1998 North Carolina Tar Heels - Full Figure GM-008	Open		25.00	29
1998 North Carolina Tar Heels - Head Only GM-007	Open		25.00	29
1999 Virginia Cavaliers - Cav Head GM-091	Open		25.00	29
1998 Virginia Cavaliers GM-055	Open		25.00	29
1999 Wake Forest Deacons - Full Figure GM-057	Open		25.00	29
1998 Wake Forest Deacons - Head Only GM-056	Open		25.00	29
Glasscots University Mascots-Big 10 Conference - G. Lewis				
1998 Illinois Fighting Illini GM-022	Open		25.00	29
1998 Indiana Hoosiers GM-023	Open		25.00	25
1998 Iowa Hawkeyes GM-024	Open		25.00	25
2000 Michigan State Spartans - Basketball GM-130	Open		33.00	33
1998 Michigan State Spartans GM-075	Open		27.00	29
2000 Michigan Wolverines Block "M" GM-123	Open		25.00	25
1998 Michigan Wolverines GM-025	Open		27.00	29
1998 Minnesota Gophers GM-026	Open		25.00	29
1998 Northwestern Wildcats GM-027	Open		25.00	25
2000 Ohio State Buckeyes - Basketball GM-132	Open		33.00	33
1998 Ohio State Buckeyes GM-028	Open		25.00	29
1998 Penn State Nittany Lions GM-029	Open		27.00	29
1998 Purdue Boilermakers GM-030	Open		27.00	29
1998 Wisconsin Badgers GM-031	Open		25.00	29
Glasscots University Mascots-Big East Conference - G. Lewis				
1998 Boston College Eagles GM-061	Open		25.00	29
2000 Connecticut Huskies - Basketball GM-125	Open		33.00	33
1998 Connecticut Huskies GM-043	Open		25.00	29
1998 Georgetown Hoyas GM-044	Open		25.00	29
1999 Miami Hurricanes GM-045	Open		27.00	29
1998 Pittsburgh Panthers GM-047	Open		25.00	29
1999 St. John's Red Storm GM-100	Open		25.00	29
1998 Syracuse University Orangemen GM-086	Open		25.00	29
1998 Temple University Owls GM-074	Open		25.00	29
1998 Villanova Wildcats GM-058	Open		25.00	29
1998 Virginia Tech Hokies GM-049	Open		25.00	25
1998 West Virginia Mountaineers GM-048	Open		25.00	25
2000 West Virginia Mountaineers GM-119	Open		29.00	29
Glasscots University Mascots-Big Twelve Conference - G. Lewis				
1998 Baylor Bears GM-078	Open		27.00	29

*Quotes have been rounded up to nearest dollar

YEAR ISSUE	EDITION LIMIT	YEAR RETD.	ISSUE PRICE	*QUOTE U.S.$
1998 Colorado Buffs GM-077	Open		25.00	29
1998 Iowa State Cyclones GM-079	Open		25.00	29
2000 Kansas Jayhawks - Basketball GM-128	Open		33.00	33
1998 Kansas Jayhawks GM-041	Open		27.00	29
2000 Kansas State - "Power Cat" GM-124	Open		29.00	29
1998 Kansas State Wildcats GM-040	Open		25.00	29
1998 Missouri Tigers GM-080	Open		25.00	29
1999 Nebraska Cornhuskers GM-038	Open		25.00	29
1998 Oklahoma Sooners GM-081	Open		27.00	29
1998 Oklahoma State Cowboys GM-039	Open		25.00	29
1999 Texas - Football Figure GM-099	Open		27.00	29
1998 Texas A&M Aggies GM-082	Open		27.00	29
1998 Texas Longhorns GM-042	Open		25.00	25
1998 Texas Tech Red Raiders GM-083	Open		25.00	29

Glasscots University Mascots-Conference USA - G. Lewis

YEAR ISSUE	EDITION LIMIT	YEAR RETD.	ISSUE PRICE	*QUOTE U.S.$
1999 Army Black Knights GM-101	Open		25.00	29
2000 Cincinnati Bearcats - Basketball GM-126	Open		33.00	33
1998 Cincinnati Bearcats GM-050	Open		25.00	29
1998 East Carolina Pirates GM-051	Open		25.00	29
1998 Memphis Tigers GM-066	Open		25.00	29
1998 Univ. of Ala. at Birmingham Blazers GM-060	Open		27.00	29

Glasscots University Mascots-Miscellaneous - G. Lewis

YEAR ISSUE	EDITION LIMIT	YEAR RETD.	ISSUE PRICE	*QUOTE U.S.$
1998 Boston University Terriers GM-062	Open		25.00	29
2000 The Citadel Bulldogs GM-116	Open		29.00	29
1999 Delaware Fightin' Blue Hens GM-102	Open		25.00	29
2000 Harvard GM-121	Open		29.00	29
1998 James Madison University - JMU GM-073	Open		25.00	29
1998 Maine Black Bears GM-072	Open		25.00	29
1999 Marshall Thundering Herd GM-059	Open		27.00	29
1999 Naval Academy Midshipmen - (Navy) GM-103	Open		25.00	29
1998 North Dakota Fighting Sioux GM-070	Open		25.00	25
1999 Rhode Island Rams GM-104	Open		25.00	29
2000 SMS - Southwest Missouri State GM-120	Open		29.00	29
2000 Southern Mississippi GM-118	Open		29.00	29
2000 Yale Bulldogs GM-122	Open		29.00	29

Glasscots University Mascots-Pacific Ten Conference - G. Lewis

YEAR ISSUE	EDITION LIMIT	YEAR RETD.	ISSUE PRICE	*QUOTE U.S.$
1998 Arizona State Sun Devils GM-089	Open		25.00	29
1998 Arizona Wildcats GM-032	Open		25.00	29
1998 California Bears GM-033	Open		25.00	29
1998 Oregon Ducks GM-087	Open		25.00	25
1998 Oregon State Beavers GM-088	Open		25.00	29
1998 Stanford University Cardinal GM-085	Open		25.00	29
1998 UCLA Bruins GM-034	Open		27.00	29
1998 USC Trojans - Disk Logo GM-035	Open		25.00	29
1998 Washington Huskies GM-036	Open		25.00	29
1998 Washington State Cougars GM-037	Open		25.00	29

Glasscots University Mascots-Southeastern Conference - G. Lewis

YEAR ISSUE	EDITION LIMIT	YEAR RETD.	ISSUE PRICE	*QUOTE U.S.$
1999 Alabama - Elephant Figure GM-092	Open		27.00	29
1998 Alabama Crimson Tide GM-009	Open		25.00	29
1998 Arkansas Razorbacks GM-010	Open		25.00	29
1999 Auburn Disk - Tiger Eyes GM-093	Open		25.00	29
1998 Auburn Tigers GM-011	Open		25.00	29
1998 Florida Gators - Disk Logo GM-012	Open		25.00	29
1998 Florida Gators - Gator Full Figure GM-076	Open		27.00	29
2000 Georgia "Uga" with Football GM-117	Open		29.00	29
1998 Georgia Bulldogs - Full Figure GM-014	Open		25.00	29
1998 Georgia Bulldogs - Head Only GM-013	Open		25.00	29
2000 Kentucky Wildcats - Basketball GM-129	Open		33.00	33
1998 Kentucky Wildcats GM-015	Open		25.00	29
1998 Louisiana State Tigers GM-016	Open		25.00	29
1998 Mississippi State Bulldogs GM-017	Open		25.00	29
1999 Ole Miss Rebels GM-018	Open		25.00	29
1998 South Carolina Gamecocks GM-019	Open		25.00	29
1999 Tennessee - Smokey with Football GM-094	Open		27.00	29
1998 Tennessee Volunteers GM-020	Open		25.00	29
1999 Vanderbilt Commodores GM-021	Open		25.00	29

Glasscots University Mascots-Western Athletic Conference - G. Lewis

YEAR ISSUE	EDITION LIMIT	YEAR RETD.	ISSUE PRICE	*QUOTE U.S.$
1999 Air Force Academy Falcons GM-095	Open		25.00	29
1998 Brigham Young Cougars GM-065	Open		25.00	29
1998 Colorado State Rams GM-067	Open		25.00	29
1998 New Mexico Lobos GM-068	Open		25.00	29
1999 San Diego State Aztecs GM-096	Open		25.00	29
1999 Southern Methodist Mustangs GM-097	Open		27.00	29
1999 Texas Christian Horned Frogs GM-098	Open		25.00	29
1999 UNLV Rebels GM-052	Open		25.00	29
1998 Utah Utes GM-063	Open		25.00	29

Santa Football Helmets - G. Lewis

YEAR ISSUE	EDITION LIMIT	YEAR RETD.	ISSUE PRICE	*QUOTE U.S.$
1999 Alabama Crimson Tide GM-105	1,000		40.00	40
1999 Arkansas Razorbacks GM-106	1,000		40.00	40
1999 Clemson Tigers GM-107	1,000		40.00	40
1999 Florida State Seminoles GM-108	1,000		40.00	40
2000 Michigan State Spartans GM-136	1,000		40.00	40
1999 Michigan Wolverines GM-109	1,000		40.00	40
1999 Nebraska Cornhuskers GM-110	1,000		40.00	40
1999 Ohio State Buckeyes GM-111	1,000		40.00	40
1999 Penn State Nittany Lions GM-112	1,000		40.00	40
1999 Syracuse Orangemen GM-113	1,000		40.00	40
1999 Tennessee Volunteers GM-114	1,000		40.00	40
2000 Texas Longhorns GM-134	1,000		40.00	40
1999 UCLA Bruins GM-115	1,000		40.00	40
1999 USC Trojans - Santa Wearing Helmet GM-084	1,000		40.00	40
2000 Washington Huskies GM-135	1,000		40.00	40
2000 Wisconsin Badgers GM-133	1,000		40.00	40

Swarovski Consumer Goods Ltd.

Christmas Ornaments - Swarovski

YEAR ISSUE	EDITION LIMIT	YEAR RETD.	ISSUE PRICE	*QUOTE U.S.$
1981 1981 Snowflake 7563NR35	Yr.Iss.	1981	30.00	422-500
1986 1986 Holiday Ornament 92086	Yr.Iss.	1986	N/A	170-429
1987 1987 Holiday Etching-Candle	Yr.Iss.	1987	20.00	210-240
1988 1988 Holiday Etching-Wreath	Yr.Iss.	1988	25.00	85-120
1989 1989 Holiday Etching-Dove	Yr.Iss.	1989	35.00	240-360
1990 1990 Holiday Etching-Merry Christmas	Yr.Iss.	1990	25.00	210-270
1991 1991 Holiday Ornament-Star (U.S. Version, silver cap)	Yr.Iss.	1991	35.00	285-375
1991 1991 Holiday Ornament-Star (European Version, gold cap)	Yr.Iss.	1991	35.00	210-240
1992 1992 Holiday Ornament-Star	Yr.Iss.	1992	37.50	120-200
1993 1993 Holiday Ornament-Star	Yr.Iss.	1993	37.50	145-213
1993 1993 Holiday Ornament-Season's Greetings 94004	Yr.Iss.	1993	25.00	135-150
1994 1994 Holiday Ornament-Star	Yr.Iss.	1994	37.50	110-195
1995 1995 Holiday Ornament-Star	Yr.Iss.	1995	40.00	90-181
1996 1996 Holiday Ornament-Snowflake	Yr.Iss.	1996	45.00	45-125
1997 1997 Holiday Ornament-Star	Yr.Iss.	1997	45.00	45-100
1998 1998 Christmas Ornament - Snowflake	Yr.Iss.	1998	49.50	50-85
1999 1999 Christmas Ornament	Yr.Iss.	1999	55.00	55-155
2000 2000 Christmas Ornament	Yr.Iss.		65.00	65

Swarovski Crystal Memories Ornaments

YEAR ISSUE	EDITION LIMIT	YEAR RETD.	ISSUE PRICE	*QUOTE U.S.$
2000 Angel	Open		85.00	85
1996 Bells	Open		45.00	45
1996 Boot	Open		45.00	45
1997 Candy Cane	Open		45.00	45
1998 Christmas Tree	Open		45.00	45
1999 Drum	Open		45.00	45
1998 Gingerbread House	Open		45.00	45
1999 Harp	Open		55.00	55
1996 Holly	Open		45.00	45
1997 Icicles	Open		45.00	45
1998 Locomotive	Open		45.00	45
1996 Moon	Open		45.00	45
1997 Pine Cone	Open		45.00	45
1996 Sun	Open		45.00	45
1999 Violin	Open		45.00	45
1996 Wreath	Open		45.00	45

Swarovski Crystal Memories-Annual Edition Angels

YEAR ISSUE	EDITION LIMIT	YEAR RETD.	ISSUE PRICE	*QUOTE U.S.$
1996 1996 Annual Edition Angel 9443NR960001	Retrd.	1996	75.00	75-240
1997 1997 Annual Edition Angel 9443NR970001	Retrd.	1997	75.00	50-115
1998 1998 Annual Edition Angel 9443NR980001	Retrd.	1998	75.00	45-96
1999 1999 Annual Edition Angel 9443NR990001	Retrd.	1999	75.00	45-75

Towle Silversmiths

Christmas Angel Medallions - Towle

YEAR ISSUE	EDITION LIMIT	YEAR RETD.	ISSUE PRICE	*QUOTE U.S.$
1991 1991 Angel	Closed	1991	45.00	70
1992 1992 Angel	Closed	1992	45.00	70
1993 1993 Angel	Closed	1993	45.00	55-70
1994 1994 Angel	Closed	1994	50.00	50-60
1995 1995 Angel	Closed	1995	50.00	50-55
1996 1996 Angel	Closed	1996	50.00	40-50
1997 1997 Angel	Closed	1997	50.00	50
1998 1998 Angel	Closed	1998	50.00	50
1999 1999 Angel	Closed	1999	50.00	50

Christmas Star - Towle

YEAR ISSUE	EDITION LIMIT	YEAR RETD.	ISSUE PRICE	*QUOTE U.S.$
1997 1997 Star	Closed	1997	50.00	50
1998 1998 Star	Closed	1998	50.00	50
1999 1999 Star	Closed	1999	50.00	50

Millennium 2000 Ornament - Towle

YEAR ISSUE	EDITION LIMIT	YEAR RETD.	ISSUE PRICE	*QUOTE U.S.$
1999 Millennium Ornament	Closed	1999	45.00	45

Remembrance Collection - Towle

YEAR ISSUE	EDITION LIMIT	YEAR RETD.	ISSUE PRICE	*QUOTE U.S.$
1990 1990 - Old Master Snowflake	Closed	1990	40.00	70
1991 1991 - Old Master Snowflake	Closed	1991	40.00	60
1992 1992 - Old Master Snowflake	Closed	1992	40.00	40-60
1993 1993 - Old Master Snowflake	Closed	1993	40.00	45-60
1994 1994 - Old Master Snowflake	Closed	1994	50.00	60
1995 1995 - Old Master Snowflake	Closed	1995	50.00	40-60
1996 1996 - Old Master Snowflake	Closed	1995	50.00	40-60
1997 1997 - Old Master Snowflake	Closed	1997	50.00	35-50
1998 1998 - Old Master Snowflake	Closed	1998	50.00	50
1999 1999 - Old Master Snowflake	Closed	1999	50.00	50

Songs of Christmas Medallions - Towle

YEAR ISSUE	EDITION LIMIT	YEAR RETD.	ISSUE PRICE	*QUOTE U.S.$
1978 Silent Night Medallion	Closed	1978	35.00	60
1979 Deck The Halls	Closed	1979	35.00	60
1980 Jingle Bells	Closed	1980	53.00	60
1981 Hark the Hearld Angels Sing	Closed	1981	53.00	60-125
1982 O Christmas Tree	Closed	1982	35.00	60-100
1983 Silver Bells	Closed	1983	40.00	60-65
1984 Let It Snow	Closed	1984	30.00	60
1985 Chestnuts Roasting on Open Fire	Closed	1985	35.00	60-70
1986 It Came Upon a Midnight Clear	Closed	1986	35.00	60-70
1987 White Christmas	Closed	1987	35.00	60-100

Sterling Cross - Towle

YEAR ISSUE	EDITION LIMIT	YEAR RETD.	ISSUE PRICE	*QUOTE U.S.$
1994 Sterling Cross	Closed	1994	50.00	60
1995 Christmas Cross	Closed	1995	50.00	40-60
1996 1996 Cross	Closed	1996	50.00	40-50
1997 1997 Cross	Closed	1997	50.00	40-50
1998 1998 Cross	Closed	1998	50.00	50
1999 1999 Cross	Closed	1999	50.00	50

Sterling Floral Medallions - Towle

YEAR ISSUE	EDITION LIMIT	YEAR RETD.	ISSUE PRICE	*QUOTE U.S.$
1983 Christmas Rose	Closed	1983	40.00	40
1984 Hawthorn/Glastonbury Thorn	Closed	1984	40.00	40
1985 Poinsettia	Closed	1985	35.00	40-50
1986 Laurel Bay	Closed	1986	35.00	40-45
1987 Mistletoe	Closed	1987	35.00	40-45
1988 Holly	Closed	1988	40.00	50-95
1989 Ivy	Closed	1989	35.00	50-95
1990 Christmas Cactus	Closed	1990	40.00	50-95
1991 Chrysanthemum	Closed	1991	40.00	40-55
1992 Star of Bethlehem	Closed	1992	40.00	40-50

Sterling Nativity Medallions - Towle

YEAR ISSUE	EDITION LIMIT	YEAR RETD.	ISSUE PRICE	*QUOTE U.S.$
1988 The Angel Appeared	Closed	1988	40.00	60
1989 The Journey	Closed	1989	40.00	60
1990 No Room at the Inn	Closed	1990	40.00	60
1991 Tidings of Joy	Closed	1991	40.00	60
1992 Star of Bethlehem	Closed	1992	40.00	60
1993 Mother and Child	Closed	1993	40.00	60
1994 Three Wisemen	Closed	1994	40.00	50
1995 Newborn King	Closed	1995	40.00	50

Sterling Twelve Days of Christmas Medallions - Towle

YEAR ISSUE	EDITION LIMIT	YEAR RETD.	ISSUE PRICE	*QUOTE U.S.$
1971 Partridge in A Pear Tree	Closed	1971	10.00	300
1972 Two Turtle Doves	Closed	1972	10.00	125-250
1973 Three French Hens	Closed	1973	10.00	75
1974 Four Colly Birds	Closed	1974	30.00	75-90
1975 Five Gold Rings	Closed	1975	30.00	60
1975 Five Gold Rings (vermeil)	Closed	1975	30.00	60
1976 Six Geese-a-Laying	Closed	1976	30.00	60
1977 Seven Swans-a-Swimming	Closed	1977	35.00	60
1977 Seven Swans-a-Swimming (turquoise)	Closed	1977	35.00	50
1978 Eight Maids-a-Milking	Closed	1978	37.00	60
1979 Nine Ladies Dancing	Closed	1979	37.00	60
1980 Ten Lords-a-Leaping	Closed	1980	76.00	60
1981 Eleven Pipers Piping	Closed	1981	50.00	60
1982 Twelve Drummers Drumming	Closed	1982	35.00	60

Twelve Days of Christmas - Towle

YEAR ISSUE	EDITION LIMIT	YEAR RETD.	ISSUE PRICE	*QUOTE U.S.$
1991 Partridge in A Pear Tree In A Wreath	Closed	1991	50.00	55-75
1992 Two Turtle Doves In A Wreath	Closed	1992	50.00	50-60
1993 Three French Hens In A Wreath	Closed	1993	50.00	40-50
1994 Four Colly Birds In A Wreath	Closed	1995	50.00	40-60
1996 Five Gold Rings In A Wreath	Closed	1996	50.00	40-50
1996 Six Geese A Laying In A Wreath	Closed	1996	50.00	40-50
1997 Seven Swans A Swimming	Closed	1997	50.00	35-50
1998 Eight Maids-a-Milking	Closed	1998	50.00	50
1999 Nine Ladies Dancing	Closed	1999	50.00	50

Treasury Masterpiece Editions/Enesco Group, Inc.

Treasury Ornaments Collectors' Club (formerly known as Enesco Treasury of Christmas Ornaments Collectors' Club) - Enesco, unless otherwise noted

YEAR ISSUE	EDITION LIMIT	YEAR RETD.	ISSUE PRICE	*QUOTE U.S.$
1993 The Treasury Card T0001 - Gilmore	Yr.Iss.	1993	Gift	20
1993 Together We Can Shoot For The Stars TR931 - Hahn	Yr.Iss.	1993	17.50	35
1993 Can't Weights For The Holidays TR932	Yr.Iss.	1993	18.50	35
1994 Seedlings Greetings TR933 - Hahn	Yr.Iss.	1994	22.50	23
1994 Spry Fry (Club) TR934	Yr.Iss.	1994	15.00	15
1995 You're the Perfect Fit T0002 - Hahn	Yr.Iss.	1995	Gift	20
1995 You're the Perfect Fit T0102 (Charter Members) - Hahn	Yr.Iss.	1995	Gift	20
1995 Things Go Better With Coke™ TR951	Yr.Iss.	1995	15.00	15
1995 Buttoning Up Our Holiday Best TR952 - Gilmore	Yr.Iss.	1995	22.50	23
1995 Holiday High-Light TR953 - Gilmore	Yr.Iss.	1995	15.00	15
1995 First Class Christmas TR954 - Gilmore	Yr.Iss.	1995	22.50	23
1996 Yo Ho Holidays T0003	Yr.Iss.	1996	Gift	20
1996 Yo Ho Holidays T0103 (Charter Members)	Yr.Iss.	1996	Gift	20
1996 Coca Cola® Choo Choo TR961	Yr.Iss.	1996	35.00	35
1996 Friends Are Tea-riffic TR962	Yr.Iss.	1996	25.00	25
1996 On Track With Coke™ TR963	Yr.Iss.	1996	25.00	25
1996 Riding High TR964 - Hahn	Yr.Iss.	1996	20.00	20
1997 Advent-ures In Ornament Collecting T0004 - Hahn	Yr.Iss.	1997	Gift	N/A
1997 Advent-ures In Ornament Collecting T0104 (Charter Members) - Hahn	Yr.Iss.	1997	Gift	N/A
1997 Coca Cola® Caboose TR971	Yr.Iss.	1997	25.00	25-59
1997 The Sweetest Nativity TR972 - Hahn	Yr.Iss.	1997	20.00	20

*Quotes have been rounded up to nearest dollar

Treasury Masterpiece Editions (formerly known as Enesco Treasury of Christmas Ornaments) - Enesco, unless otherwise noted

YEAR ISSUE	EDITION LIMIT	YEAR RETD.	ISSUE PRICE	*QUOTE U.S.$
1983 Wide Open Throttle E-0242	3-Yr.	1985	12.00	35
1983 Baby's First Christmas E-0271	Yr.Iss.	1983	6.00	N/A
1983 Grandchild's First Christmas E-0272	Yr.Iss.	1983	5.00	N/A
1983 Baby's First Christmas E-0273	3-Yr.	1985	9.00	N/A
1983 Toy Drum Teddy E-0274	4-Yr.	1986	9.00	N/A
1983 Watching At The Window E-0275	3-Yr.	1985	13.00	N/A
1983 To A Special Teacher E-0276	7-Yr.	1989	5.00	15
1983 Toy Shop E-0277	7-Yr.	1989	8.00	50
1983 Merry Christmas Carousel Horse E-0278	7-Yr.	1989	9.00	20
1981 Look Out Below E-6135	2-Yr.	1982	6.00	N/A
1982 Flyin' Santa Christmas Special 1982 E-6136	Yr.Iss.	1982	9.00	75
1981 Flyin' Santa Christmas Special 1981 E-6136	Yr.Iss.	1981	9.00	N/A
1981 Sawin' Elf Helper E-6138	2-Yr.	1982	6.00	40
1981 Snow Shoe-In Santa E-6139	2-Yr.	1982	6.00	35
1981 Baby's First Christmas 1981 E-6145	Yr.Iss.	1981	6.00	N/A
1981 Our Hero E-6146	2-Yr.	1982	4.00	N/A
1981 Whoops E-6147	2-Yr.	1982	3.50	N/A
1981 Whoops, It's 1981 E-6148	Yr.Iss.	1981	7.50	75
1981 Not A Creature Was Stirring E-6149	2-Yr.	1982	4.00	25
1984 Joy To The World E-6209	2-Yr.	1985	9.00	35
1984 Letter To Santa E-6210	2-Yr.	1985	5.00	30
1984 Lucy & Me Someone Special Photo Frame E-6211	3-Yr.	1986	5.00	N/A
1984 Lucy & Me Special Friend Photo Frame E-6211	3-Yr.	1986	5.00	N/A
1984 Lucy & Me Teacher Photo Frame E-6211	3-Yr.	1986	5.00	N/A
1984 Lucy & Me Grandma Photo Frame E-6211	3-Yr.	1986	5.00	N/A
1984 Lucy & Me For Baby Photo Frame E-6211	3-Yr.	1986	5.00	N/A
1984 Lucy & Me Grandpa Photo Frame E-6211	3-Yr.	1986	5.00	N/A
1984 Baby's First Christmas 1984 E-6212 - Gilmore	Yr.Iss.	1984	10.00	30
1984 Merry Christmas Mother E-6213	3-Yr.	1986	10.00	30
1984 Baby's First Christmas 1984 E-6215	Yr.Iss.	1984	6.00	N/A
1984 Ferris Wheel Mice E-6216	2-Yr.	1985	9.00	30
1984 Cuckoo Clock E-6217	2-Yr.	1985	8.00	40
1984 Muppet Babies Baby's First Christmas E-6222 - J. Henson	Yr.Iss.	1984	10.00	45
1984 Muppet Babies Baby's First Christmas E-6223 -J. Henson	Yr.Iss.	1984	10.00	45
1984 Garfield Hark! The Herald Angel E-6224 - J. Davis	2-Yr.	1985	7.50	35
1984 Fun in Santa's Sleigh E-6225 - J. Davis	2-Yr.	1985	12.00	35
1984 Deer! Odie E-6226 -J. Davis	2-Yr.	1985	6.00	30
1984 Garfield The Snow Cat E-6227 - J. Davis	2-Yr.	1985	12.00	35
1984 Peek-A-Bear Baby's First Christmas E-6228	3-Yr.	1986	10.00	N/A
1984 Peek-A-Bear Baby's First Christmas E-6229	3-Yr.	1986	9.00	N/A
1984 Owl Be Home For Christmas E-6230	2-Yr.	1985	8.00	23
1984 Santa's Trolley E-6231	3-Yr.	1986	11.00	40
1984 Holiday Penguin E-6240	3-Yr.	1986	1.50	15-20
1984 Little Drummer E-6241	5-Yr.	1988	2.00	N/A
1984 Happy Holidays E-6248	2-Yr.	1985	2.00	5
1984 Christmas Nest E-6249	2-Yr.	1985	3.00	25
1984 Bunny's Christmas Stocking E-6251	Yr.Iss.	1984	2.00	15
1984 Santa On Ice E-6252	3-Yr.	1986	2.50	25
1984 Treasured Memories The New Sled E-6256	2-Yr.	1985	7.00	N/A
1984 Penguins On Ice E-6280	2-Yr.	1985	7.50	N/A
1984 Up On The House Top E-6281	6-Yr.	1989	9.00	N/A
1984 Grandchild's First Christmas (pink) 1984 E-6286	Yr.Iss.	1984	5.00	N/A
1984 Grandchild's First Christmas (blue) 1984 E-6286	Yr.Iss.	1984	5.00	N/A
1984 Godchild's First Christmas E-6287	3-Yr.	1986	7.00	N/A
1984 Santa In The Box E-6292	2-Yr.	1985	6.00	N/A
1984 Carousel Horse E-6913	2-Yr.	1985	1.50	N/A
1983 Arctic Charmer E-6945	2-Yr.	1984	7.00	N/A
1982 Victorian Sleigh E-6946	4-Yr.	1985	9.00	15
1983 Wing-A-Ding Angel E-6948	3-Yr.	1985	7.00	50
1982 A Saviour Is Born This Day E-6949	8-Yr.	1989	4.00	18
1982 Crescent Santa E-6950 - Gilmore	4-Yr.	1985	10.00	50
1982 Baby's First Christmas 1982 E-6952	Yr.Iss.	1982	10.00	N/A
1982 Polar Bear Fun Whoops, It's 1982 E-6953	Yr.Iss.	1982	10.00	75
1982 Holiday Skier E-6954 - J. Davis	5-Yr.	1986	7.00	N/A
1982 Toy Soldier 1982 E-6957	Yr.Iss.	1982	6.50	N/A
1982 Carousel Horses E-6958	3-Yr.	1984	8.00	20-40
1982 Dear Santa E-6959 - Gilmore	8-Yr.	1989	10.00	25
1982 Merry Christmas Grandma E-6975	3-Yr.	1984	5.00	N/A
1982 Penguin Power E-6977	2-Yr.	1983	6.00	15
1982 Bunny Winter Playground 1982 E-6978	Yr.Iss.	1982	10.00	N/A
1982 Baby's First Christmas 1982 E-6979	Yr.Iss.	1982	10.00	N/A
1983 Carousel Horses E-6980	4-Yr.	1986	8.00	N/A
1982 Grandchild's First Christmas 1982 E-6983	Yr.Iss.	1982	5.00	73
1982 Merry Christmas Teacher E-6984	4-Yr.	1985	7.00	N/A
1983 Garfield Cuts The Ice E-8771 - J. Davis	3-Yr.	1985	6.00	45

YEAR ISSUE	EDITION LIMIT	YEAR RETD.	ISSUE PRICE	*QUOTE U.S.$
1984 A Stocking Full For 1984 E-8773 - J. Davis	Yr.Iss.	1984	6.00	N/A
1983 Stocking Full For 1983 E-8773 - J. Davis	Yr.Iss.	1983	6.00	N/A
1985 Santa Claus Balloon 55794	Yr.Iss.	1985	8.50	20
1985 Carousel Reindeer 55808	4-Yr.	1988	12.00	33
1985 Angel In Flight 55816	4-Yr.	1988	8.00	23
1985 Christmas Penguin 55824	4-Yr.	1988	7.50	43
1985 Merry Christmas Godchild 55832 - Gilmore	5-Yr.	1989	8.00	N/A
1985 Baby's First Christmas 55840	2-Yr.	1986	15.00	N/A
1985 Old Fashioned Rocking Horse 55859	2-Yr.	1986	10.00	15
1985 Child's Second Christmas 55867	5-Yr.	1989	11.00	N/A
1985 Fishing For Stars 55875	5-Yr.	1989	9.00	25
1985 Baby Blocks 55883	2-Yr.	1986	12.00	N/A
1985 Christmas Toy Chest 55891	5-Yr.	1989	10.00	N/A
1985 Grandchild's First Christmas 55921	5-Yr.	1989	7.00	30
1985 Joy Photo Frame 55956	Yr.Iss.	1985	6.00	N/A
1985 We Three Kings 55964	Yr.Iss.	1985	4.50	20
1985 The Night Before Christmas 55972	2-Yr.	1986	5.00	N/A
1985 Baby's First Christmas 1985 55980	Yr.Iss.	1985	6.00	N/A
1985 Baby Rattle Photo Frame 56006	2-Yr.	1986	5.00	N/A
1985 Baby's First Christmas 1985 56014 - Gilmore	Yr.Iss.	1985	10.00	N/A
1985 Christmas Plane Ride 56049 - L. Rigg	6-Yr.	1990	10.00	N/A
1985 Scottie Celebrating Christmas 56065	5-Yr.	1989	7.50	25
1985 North Pole Native 56073	2-Yr.	1986	9.00	N/A
1985 Skating Walrus 56081	2-Yr.	1986	9.00	20
1985 Ski Time 56111 - J. Davis	Yr.Iss.	1985	13.00	N/A
1985 North Pole Express 56138 - J. Davis	Yr.Iss.	1985	12.00	N/A
1985 Merry Christmas Mother 56146 - J. Davis	Yr.Iss.	1985	8.50	N/A
1985 Hoppy Christmas 56154 - J. Davis	Yr.Iss.	1985	8.50	N/A
1985 Merry Christmas Teacher 56170 - J. Davis	Yr.Iss.	1985	6.00	N/A
1985 Garfield-In-The-Box 56189 - J. Davis	Yr.Iss.	1985	6.50	25
1985 Merry Christmas Grandma 56197	Yr.Iss.	1985	7.00	N/A
1985 Christmas Lights 56200	2-Yr.	1986	8.00	N/A
1985 Victorian Doll House 56251	Yr.Iss.	1985	13.00	40
1985 Tobaoggan Ride 56286	4-Yr.	1988	6.00	15
1985 St. Nicholas Circa 1910 56359	5-Yr.	1989	6.00	15
1985 Look Out Below 56375	Yr.Iss.	1985	8.50	40
1985 Flying Santa Christmas Special 56383	2-Yr.	1986	10.00	N/A
1985 Sawin Elf Helper 56391	Yr.Iss.	1985	8.00	N/A
1985 Snow Shoe-In Santa 56405	Yr.Iss.	1985	8.00	50
1985 Our Hero 56413	Yr.Iss.	1985	5.50	N/A
1985 Not A Creature Was Stirring 56421	2-Yr.	1986	4.00	N/A
1985 Merry Christmas Teacher 56448	Yr.Iss.	1985	9.00	N/A
1985 A Stocking Full For 1985 56464 - J. Davis	Yr.Iss.	1985	6.00	25
1985 Christmas Tree Photo Frame 56871	4-Yr.	1988	10.00	N/A
1995 How...Do I Love Thee 104949	Yr.Iss.	1995	22.50	23
1995 Swishing You Sweet Greetings 105201	Yr.Iss.	1995	20.00	20
1995 Planely Delicious 109665	Yr.Iss.	1996	20.00	20
1996 Spice Up The Season 111724	Yr. Iss.	1996	20.00	20
1995 Home For The Howl-i-days 111732	Yr.Iss.	1995	20.00	20
1995 Time For Refreshment 111872	Yr.Iss.	1995	20.00	20
1995 Holiday Bike Hike 111937	Yr.Iss.	1995	20.00	20
1996 Santa's Sacks 111945 - Hahn	Yr. Iss.	1996	15.00	18
1995 Ho, Ho, Hole in One! 111953	Yr.Iss.	1995	20.00	20
1995 No Time To Spare at Christmas 111961	Yr.Iss.	1995	20.00	20
1995 Hustling Up Some Cheer 112038	Yr.Iss.	1995	20.00	20
1995 Scoring Big at Christmas 112046	Yr.Iss.	1995	20.00	20
1995 Serving Up the Best 112054	Yr.Iss.	1995	17.50	18
1995 Sea-sons Greetings, Teacher 112070 - Gilmore	Yr.Iss.	1996	17.50	18
1995 Siesta Santa 112089 - Gilmore	Yr.Iss.	1995	25.00	25
1995 We've Shared Sew Much 112097 - Gilmore	Yr.Iss.	1995	25.00	25
1995 Toys To Treasure 112119	Yr.Iss.	1995	20.00	20
1995 To Santa, Post Haste 112151 - Gilmore	Yr.Iss.	1995	15.00	15
1995 Yule Logon For Christmas Cheer 122513	Yr.Iss.	1995	20.00	20
1995 Pretty Up For The Holidays 125830 - Butcher	Yr.Iss.	1995	20.00	20
1995 You Bring The Love to Christmas 125849 - Butcher	Yr.Iss.	1995	15.00	15
1995 Happy Birthday Jesus 125857 - Butcher	Yr.Iss.	1995	15.00	15
1995 Let's Snuggle Together For Christmas 125865 - Butcher	Yr.Iss.	1995	15.00	15
1995 I'm In A Spin Over You 125873 - Butcher	Yr.Iss.	1995	15.00	15
1995 Our First Christmas Together 125881 - Butcher	Yr.Iss.	1995	22.50	23
1995 Twinkle, Twinkle Christmas Star 125903 - Butcher	Yr.Iss.	1995	17.50	18
1995 Bringing Holiday Wishes To You 125911 - Butcher	Yr.Iss.	1995	22.50	23
1995 You Pull The Strings To My Heart 125938 - Butcher	Yr.Iss.	1995	20.00	20
1995 Baby's First Christmas 125946 - Butcher	Yr.Iss.	1995	15.00	15
1995 Baby's First Christmas 125954 - Butcher	Yr.Iss.	1995	15.00	15
1995 Friends Are The Greatest Treasure 125962 - Butcher	20,000	1995	25.00	25
1995 4-Alarm Christmas 128767 - Gilmore	Yr.Iss.	1995	17.50	18

YEAR ISSUE	EDITION LIMIT	YEAR RETD.	ISSUE PRICE	*QUOTE U.S.$
1995 Truckin'/1956 Ford F-100 Truck 128813	Yr.Iss.	1995	25.00	20-25
1995 1955 Red Ford Thunderbird 128821	19,550	1995	20.00	28
1995 57 HVN/1957 Chevy Bel Air 128848	Yr.Iss.	1995	20.00	20-29
1995 1965 Chevrolet Corvette Stingray 128856	Yr.Iss.	1995	20.00	20
1995 Mom's Taxi/Dodge Caravan 128872	Yr.Iss.	1995	25.00	25
1995 Choc Full of Wishes 128945	Yr.Iss.	1995	20.00	20
1995 Have a Coke and a Smile™ 128953	Yr.Iss.	1995	22.50	23
1995 Trunk Full of Treasures 128961	20,000	1995	25.00	25
1995 Make Mine a Coke™ 128988	Yr.Iss.	1995	25.00	25
1995 Dashing Through the Snow 128996	Yr.Iss.	1995	20.00	20
1995 Happy Yuleglide 129003	Yr.Iss.	1995	17.50	18
1995 Santa's Speedway 129011	Yr.Iss.	1995	20.00	20
1995 You're My Cup of Tea 129038	Yr.Iss.	1996	20.00	20
1995 Crackin' a Smile 129046	Yr.Iss.	1995	17.50	18
1995 Rx:Mas Greetings 129054	Yr.Iss.	1995	17.50	18
1996 Special Bear-Livery 129062	Yr.Iss.	1996	15.00	15
1995 Merry McMeal 129070	Yr.Iss.	1995	17.50	18
1995 Above the Crowd 129089	Yr.Iss.	1995	20.00	20
1995 Mickey at the Helm 132063	Yr.Iss.	1995	17.50	18
1995 1959 Cadillac Eldorado 132705	Yr.Iss.	1995	20.00	20
1996 Catch Of The Holiday 132888 - Hahn	Yr.Iss.	1996	20.00	20
1995 Jackpot Joy! 132896 - Hahn	Yr.Iss.	1995	17.50	18
1995 Get in the Spirit...Recycle 132918 - Hahn	Yr.Iss.	1996	17.50	18
1995 Miss Merry's Secret 132934 - Hahn	Yr.Iss.	1995	20.00	20
1995 ...Good Will Toward Men 132942 - Hahn	19,450	1995	25.00	25
1995 Friendships Bloom Through All Seasons 132950 - Hahn	Yr.Iss.	1995	22.50	23
1995 Merry Monopoly 132969	Yr.Iss.	1996	22.50	23
1995 The Night B 4 Christmas 134848 - Hahn	Yr.Iss.	1995	20.00	20
1996 A Cup Of Cheer 135070 - Gilmore	Yr.Iss.	1996	25.00	25
1995 Bubblin' With Joy 136581	Yr.Iss.	1995	15.00	15
1996 Steppin' With Minnie 136603	Yr.Iss.	1996	13.50	14
1995 Minnie's Merry Christmas 136611	Yr.Iss.	1995	20.00	20
1996 Motorcycle Mickey 136654	Yr.Iss.	1996	25.00	25
1995 Makin' Tracks With Mickey 136662	Yr.Iss.	1995	20.00	20
1995 Mickey's Airmail 136670	Yr.Iss.	1996	20.00	20
1995 Holiday Bound 136689	Yr.Iss.	1996	20.00	20
1995 Goofed-Up! 136697	Yr.Iss.	1996	20.00	20
1995 On The Ball At Christmas 136700	Yr.Iss.	1996	15.00	15
1995 Sweet on You 136719	Yr.Iss.	1995	22.50	23
1995 Nutty About Christmas 137030	Yr.Iss.	1995	22.50	23
1995 Tinkertoy Joy 137049	Yr.Iss.	1996	20.00	20
1995 Starring Roll At Christmas 137057	Yr.Iss.	1995	17.50	18
1995 A Thimble of the Season 137243 - Gilmore	Yr.Iss.	1996	22.50	23
1995 A Little Something Extra...Extra 137251	10,000	1995	25.00	25
1995 The Maze Of Our Lives 139599 - Hahn	Yr.Iss.	1995	17.50	18
1995 A Sip For Good Measure 139610	Yr.Iss.	1995	17.50	18
1995 Christmas Fishes, Dad 139629 - Hahn	Yr.Iss.	1996	17.50	18
1995 Christmas Is In The Bag 139645	Yr.Iss.	1995	17.50	18
1995 Gotta Have a Clue 139653	Yr.Iss.	1995	20.00	20
1995 Fun In Hand 139661	Yr.Iss.	1995	17.50	18
1995 Christmas Cuddle 139688	Yr.Iss.	1996	20.00	20
1995 Dreaming Of the One I Love 139696	Yr.Iss.	1996	25.00	25
1995 Sneaking a Peek 139718	Yr.Iss.	1996	22.50	23
1995 Christmas Eve Mischief 139726	Yr.Iss.	1995	17.50	18
1995 All Tucked In 139734	Yr.Iss.	1995	15.00	15
1995 Merry Christmas To Me 139742	Yr.Iss.	1995	20.00	20
1995 Looking Our Holiday Best 139750	Yr.Iss.	1995	25.00	25
1995 Christmas Vacation 142158	Yr.Iss.	1996	20.00	20
1995 Just Fore Christmas 142174	Yr.Iss.	1996	15.00	15
1995 Christmas Belle 142182	Yr.Iss.	1996	20.00	20
1995 Tail Waggin' Wishes 142190	Yr.Iss.	1995	17.50	18
1995 Holiday Ride 142204	Yr.Iss.	1995	17.50	18
1995 A Carousel For Ariel 142212	Yr.Iss.	1995	17.50	18
1995 On The Move At Christmas 142220 - Hahn	Yr.Iss.	1995	17.50	18
1995 T-Bird 146838	Yr.Iss.	1995	20.00	20
1996 Swinging On A Star 166642	Yr.Iss.	1996	20.00	20
1996 A-Joy Matie, Throw Me A Lifesavers 166677	Yr.Iss.	1996	20.00	20
1996 It's Plane To See...Coke Is It 166723	Yr.Iss.	1996	25.00	25
1996 A Century Of Good Taste 166774	Yr.Iss.	1996	25.00	25
1996 Servin' Up Joy 166847	Yr.Iss.	1996	20.00	20
1996 In-Line To Help Santa 166855	Yr.Iss.	1996	20.00	10-20
1996 I Love My Daughter 166863	Yr.Iss.	1996	9.00	9
1996 I Love Grandma 166898	Yr.Iss.	1996	9.00	9
1996 I Love Dad 166901	Yr.Iss.	1996	9.00	9
1996 I Love Mom 166928	Yr.Iss.	1996	9.00	9
1996 I Love My Godchild 166936	Yr.Iss.	1996	9.00	9
1996 Baby's 1st Christmas 166944	Yr.Iss.	1996	9.00	9
1996 A Boot Full Of Cheer 166952	Yr.Iss.	1996	20.00	20
1996 Summons For A Merry Christmas 166960	Yr.Iss.	1996	22.50	23
1996 An Appointment With Santa 166979	Yr.Iss.	1996	20.00	20
1996 Play It Again, Nick 166987	Yr.Iss.	1996	17.50	18
1996 Holiday Tinkertoy Tree 166995	Yr.Iss.	1996	17.50	18
1996 A Picture Perfect Pair 167002	Yr.Iss.	1996	25.00	25
1996 Santa's On The Line 167037	Yr.Iss.	1996	25.00	18-25
1996 Downhill Delivery 167053	Yr.Iss.	1996	25.00	25
1996 On A Roll With Diet Coke 167061	Yr.Iss.	1996	20.00	20
1996 Hold On, Santa! 167088	Yr.Iss.	1996	25.00	25
1996 There's A Friendship Brewing 167096 - Hahn	Yr.Iss.	1996	25.00	25
1996 Tails A' Waggin' 167126	Yr.Iss.	1996	20.00	20

*Quotes have been rounded up to nearest dollar

Treasury Masterpiece Editions/Enesco Group, Inc. to Treasury Masterpiece Editions/Enesco Group, Inc.

ORNAMENTS

YEAR ISSUE	EDITION LIMIT	YEAR RETD.	ISSUE PRICE	*QUOTE U.S.$
1996 In Store For More 167134	15,000	1996	25.00	25
1996 Jeep Grand Cherokee 167215	Yr.Iss.	1996	22.50	15-23
1996 Chevy Blazer 167223	Yr.Iss.	1996	22.50	23
1996 Ford Explorer 167231	Yr.Iss.	1996	22.50	23
1996 Dodge Ram Truck 167258	Yr.Iss.	1996	22.50	23
1996 Trees To Please 168378	Yr.Iss.	1996	25.00	25
1996 Plane Crazy 168386	Yr.Iss.	1996	22.50	23
1996 I Love My Son 168432	Yr.Iss.	1996	9.00	9
1996 #1 Coach 168440	Yr.Iss.	1996	9.00	9
1996 Goin' Fishin' 168459	Yr.Iss.	1996	22.50	23
1996 Gifts From Mickey 168467	Yr.Iss.	1996	20.00	20
1996 All Fired Up For Christmas 168475	Yr.Iss.	1996	25.00	25
1996 Minnie's Mall Haul 168491	Yr.Iss.	1996	25.00	25
1996 A Magic Moment 172197	Yr.Iss.	1996	17.50	18
1996 Happy's Holiday 172200	Yr.Iss.	1996	17.50	18
1996 Sitting Pretty 172219	Yr.Iss.	1996	17.50	18
1996 Life's Sweet Choices 172634	Yr.Iss.	1996	25.00	25
1996 Holiday In Bloom 172669	Yr.Iss.	1996	25.00	25
1996 Have A Cracker Jack Christmas 172979	Yr.Iss.	1996	25.00	20
1996 Hair's The Place 173029 - Hahn	Yr.Iss.	1996	25.00	25
1996 Merry Manicure 173339 - Hahn	Yr.Iss.	1996	25.00	25
1996 100 Years...And Still On A Roll 173770	19,960	1996	17.50	18
1996 Tracking Reindeer Pause 173789 - Hahn	Yr.Iss.	1996	25.00	25
1996 Holiday Dreams Of Green 173797 - Hahn	Yr.Iss.	1996	15.00	15
1996 1965 Ford Mustang 173800	Yr.Iss.	1996	22.50	23
1996 Toyland, Joyland 173878	Yr.Iss.	1996	20.00	20
1996 Tobin's Debut Dancer 173886 - Fraley	20,000	1996	20.00	20
1996 Thou Art My Lamp, O Lord 173894 - Hahn	Yr.Iss.	1996	25.00	25
1996 'Tis The Season To Be Nutty 175234	Yr.Iss.	1996	17.50	18
1996 1956 Chevy Corvette 175269	19,560	1996	22.50	23
1996 A World Of Good Taste 175420	18,600	1996	20.00	20
1996 It's Time For Christmas 175455	Yr.Iss.	1996	25.00	25
1996 15 Years Of Hits 175463	10,000	1996	25.00	25
1996 Sew Darn Cute 176761 - Hahn	Yr.Iss.	1996	25.00	25
1996 Decked Out For Christmas 176796 - Hahn	Yr.Iss.	1996	25.00	10-25
1996 Campaign For Christmas 176818	19,960	1996	17.50	15-18
1996 Delivering Holiday Cheers 177318	Yr.Iss.	1996	25.00	25
1996 A Splash Of Cool Yule 213713	Yr.Iss.	1996	20.00	20
1997 100 Years of Soup-erb Good Taste! 265586	Yr.Iss.	1997	20.00	20
1997 Tobin's Graceful Steed 265594 - Fraley	Yr.Iss.	1997	20.00	20
1997 Movin' And Groovin' 270482	Yr.Iss.	1997	22.50	23
1997 Twist And Shout, "Have A Coke!" 277398	Yr.Iss.	1997	25.00	25
1997 Cracker Jack...The Home Run Snack 277401	Yr.Iss.	1997	25.00	25
1997 I'm So Glad I Fondue As A Friend 277428 - Hahn	Yr.Iss.	1997	20.00	20
1997 Workin' 'Round The Clock 277436	Yr.Iss.	1997	22.50	23
1997 WWW.HappyHolidays!.Com 277444	Yr.Iss.	1997	25.00	25
1997 Always Cool With Coke 277967	Yr.Iss.	1997	22.50	23
1997 The Forecast Calls For Coke 277983	Yr.Iss.	1997	20.00	20
1997 Stockin' Up For The Holidays 277991	Yr.Iss.	1997	22.50	23
1997 Home Sweet Home 278017	Yr.Iss.	1997	25.00	25
1997 Ordering Up A Merry Christmas 278068	Yr.Iss.	1997	25.00	25
1997 Best Bet's A 'Vette 278092	Yr.Iss.	1997	22.50	23
1997 Deere Santa 278106	Yr.Iss.	1997	25.00	25
1997 On Track With Santa 278114	Yr.Iss.	1997	20.00	20
1997 Prepare For Battle 278122	Yr.Iss.	1997	25.00	25
1997 Have Your Cake & Bake It, Too 278130	Yr.Iss.	1997	20.00	20
1997 G.I. Joe Loves Christmas 278149	Yr.Iss.	1997	20.00	20
1997 Primping Iron 278165 - Hahn	Yr.Iss.	1997	20.00	20
1997 On Course With Santa 278394 - Hahn	Yr.Iss.	1997	20.00	20
1997 Ice Cream Of The Crop 278408	Yr.Iss.	1997	20.00	20
1997 50 Years Of Miracles 278432	Yr.Iss.	1997	20.00	20
1997 Beep Me Up! 278440	Yr.Iss.	1997	20.00	20
1997 Bubbling With Cheer 278467 - Hahn	Yr.Iss.	1997	20.00	20
1997 Fired Up For Christmas 278491 - Hahn	Yr.Iss.	1997	22.50	23
1997 Spare Time For Christmas Fun 280291 - Hahn	Yr.Iss.	1997	25.00	25
1997 Everyone Knows It's Slinky 280992	Yr.Iss.	1997	22.50	23
1997 Cherish The Joy 281263 - Hillman	Yr.Iss.	1997	25.00	25-30
1997 Ho, Ho, Ho, A Grilling We Will Go! 281301	Yr.Iss.	1997	20.00	20
1997 Hula Hoop Holidays 281336	Yr.Iss.	1997	20.00	20
1997 Howl-A-Day Pet Shoppe 286192 - Hahn	Yr.Iss.	1997	25.00	25
1997 Heading 4-Wheel Merry Christmas 287059	Yr.Iss.	1997	22.50	23
1997 For All You Do, Merry Christmas To You 290858	Yr.Iss.	1997	25.00	25
1997 Play It Again, Santa 295256	Yr.Iss.	1997	20.00	20
1988 Making A Point 489212 - G.G. Santiago	3-Yr.	1990	10.00	N/A
1988 Mouse Upon A Pipe 489220 - G.G. Santiago	2-Yr.	1989	10.00	12
1988 North Pole Deadline 489387	3-Yr.	1990	13.50	25
1988 Christmas Pin-Up 489409	2-Yr.	1989	11.00	30
1988 Airmail For Teacher 489425 - Gilmore	3-Yr.	1990	13.50	N/A
1994 Sending You A Season's Greetings 550140 - Butcher	Yr.Iss.	1994	25.00	25
1994 Goofy Delivery 550639	Yr.Iss.	1994	22.50	23
1994 Happy Howl-idays 550647	Yr.Iss.	1994	22.50	23
1994 Christmas Crusin' 550655	Yr.Iss.	1994	22.50	23
1994 Holiday Honeys 550663	Yr.Iss.	1994	20.00	20
1994 May Your Holiday Be Brightened With Love 550698 - Butcher	Yr.Iss.	1994	15.00	15
1994 May All Your Wishes Come True 550701 - Butcher	Yr.Iss.	1994	20.00	20
1994 Baby's First Christmas 550728 - Butcher	Yr.Iss.	1994	20.00	20
1994 Baby's First Christmas 550736 - Butcher	Yr.Iss.	1994	20.00	20
1994 Our First Christmas Together 550744 - Butcher	Yr.Iss.	1994	25.00	25
1994 Drumming Up A Season Of Joy 550752 - Butcher	Yr.Iss.	1994	18.50	19
1994 Friendships Warm The Holidays 550760 - Butcher	Yr.Iss.	1994	20.00	20
1994 Dropping In For The Holidays 550779 - Butcher	Yr.Iss.	1994	20.00	20
1994 Ringing Up Holiday Wishes 550787 - Butcher	Yr.Iss.	1994	18.50	19
1994 A Child Is Born 550795 - Butcher	Yr.Iss.	1995	25.00	25
1994 Tis The Season To Go Shopping 550817 - Butcher	Yr.Iss.	1994	22.50	23
1994 The Way To A Mouse's Heart 550922	Yr.Iss.	1994	15.00	15
1994 Teed-Off Donald 550930	Yr.Iss.	1994	15.00	15
1994 Holiday Show-Stopper 550949	Yr.Iss.	1995	15.00	15
1994 Answering Christmas Wishes 551023	Yr.Iss.	1994	17.50	18
1994 Pure Christmas Pleasure 551066	Yr.Iss.	1995	20.00	20
1986 First Christmas Together 1986 551171	Yr.Iss.	1986	9.00	15-35
1986 Elf Stringing Popcorn 551198	4-Yr.	1989	10.00	20-30
1986 Christmas Scottie 551201	4-Yr.	1989	7.00	15-30
1986 Santa and Child 551236	4-Yr.	1989	13.50	25-50
1986 The Christmas Angel 551244	4-Yr.	1989	22.50	75
1986 Peace, Love, Joy Carousel Unicorn 551252 - Gilmore	4-Yr.	1989	12.00	38
1986 Have a Heavenly Holiday 551260	4-Yr.	1989	9.00	N/A
1986 Siamese Kitten 551279	4-Yr.	1989	9.00	36
1986 Old Fashioned Doll House 551287	4-Yr.	1989	15.00	N/A
1986 Holiday Fisherman 551309	3-Yr.	1988	8.00	40
1986 Antique Toy 551317	3-Yr.	1988	9.00	10
1986 Time For Christmas 551325 - Gilmore	4-Yr.	1989	13.00	N/A
1986 Christmas Calendar 551333	2-Yr.	1987	7.00	12
1994 Good Tidings, Tidings, Tidings, Tidings 551333	Yr.Iss.	1995	20.00	15-20
1986 Merry Christmas 551341 - Gilmore	3-Yr.	1988	8.00	40-50
1994 From Our House To Yours 551384 - Gilmore	Yr.Iss.	1994	25.00	25
1994 Sugar 'N' Spice For Someone Nice 551406 - Gilmore	Yr.Iss.	1994	30.00	30
1994 Picture Perfect Christmas 551465	Yr.Iss.	1994	15.00	15
1994 Toodles 551503 - Zimnicki	Yr.Iss.	1994	25.00	25
1994 A Bough For Belle! 551554	Yr.Iss.	1995	18.50	15-19
1986 The Santa Claus Shoppe Circa 1905 551562 - J. Grossman	4-Yr.	1989	8.00	15
1994 Ariel's Christmas Surprise! 551570	Yr.Iss.	1994	20.00	20
1994 Merry Little Two-Step 551589	Yr.Iss.	1995	12.50	13
1994 Sweets For My Sweetie 551600	Yr.Iss.	1994	15.00	15
1994 Friends Are The Spice of Life - 551619 - Hahn	Yr.Iss.	1995	20.00	20
1994 Cool Cruise/1964 1/2 Ford Mustang 551635	19,640	1994	20.00	20
1986 Baby Bear Sleigh 551651 - Gilmore	3-Yr.	1988	9.00	30
1994 Special Delivery 561657	Yr.Iss.	1994	20.00	20
1986 Baby's First Christmas 1986 551678 - Gilmore	Yr.Iss.	1986	10.00	20
1986 First Christmas Together 551708	3-Yr.	1988	6.00	10
1986 Baby's First Christmas 551716	3-Yr.	1988	5.50	10
1986 Baby's First Christmas 1986 551724	Yr.Iss.	1986	6.50	30
1994 A Christmas Tail 551759	Yr.Iss.	1995	20.00	20
1994 Merry Mischief- 551767	Yr.Iss.	1994	15.00	15
1994 L'il Stocking Stuffer 551791	Yr.Iss.	1994	17.50	18
1994 Once Upon A Time 551805	Yr.Iss.	1994	15.00	15
1994 Wishing Upon A Star 551813	Yr.Iss.	1994	18.50	19
1994 A Real Boy For Christmas 551821	Yr.Iss.	1995	15.00	15
1986 Peek-A-Bear Grandchild's First Christmas	Yr.Iss.	1986	6.00	23
1986 Peek-A-Bear in Stocking Present 552089	4-Yr.	1989	2.50	N/A
1986 Peek-A-Bear in Box Present 552089	4-Yr.	1989	2.50	N/A
1986 Peek-A-Bear in Shopping Bag Present 552089	4-Yr.	1989	2.50	N/A
1986 Peek-A-Bear in Cloth Bag Present 552089	4-Yr.	1989	2.50	N/A
1986 Merry Christmas (Boy) 552186 - L. Rigg	Yr.Iss.	1986	8.00	N/A
1994 Minnie's Holiday Treasure 552216	Yr.Iss.	1994	12.00	12
1994 Sweet Holidays 552259 - Butcher	Yr.Iss.	1994	12.00	12
1986 Merry Christmas (Girl) 552534 - L. Rigg	Yr.Iss.	1986	8.00	N/A
1986 Lucy & Me Christmas Tree 552542 - L. Rigg	3-Yr.	1988	7.00	25
1986 Santa's Helpers 552607	3-Yr.	1988	2.50	N/A
1986 My Special Friend 552615	3-Yr.	1988	6.00	10
1986 Christmas Wishes From Panda 552623	3-Yr.	1988	6.00	N/A
1986 Lucy & Me Ski Time 552658 - L. Rigg	2-Yr.	1987	6.50	30
1986 Merry Christmas Teacher 552666	3-Yr.	1988	6.50	N/A
1986 Country Cousins Merry Christmas, Mom (Girl on Skates) 552704	3-Yr.	1988	7.00	23
1986 Country Cousins Merry Christmas, Dad (Girl on Skates) 552704	3-Yr.	1988	7.00	23
1986 Country Cousins Merry Christmas, Mom (Boy w/Kite) 552712	4-Yr.	1989	7.00	23
1986 Country Cousins Merry Christmas, Dad (Boy w/Kite) 552712	4-Yr.	1989	7.00	25
1986 Grandmother's Little Angel 552747	4-Yr.	1989	8.00	N/A
1988 Puppy's 1st Christmas 552909	Yr.Iss.	1988	4.00	N/A
1988 Kitty's 1st Christmas 552917	Yr.Iss.	1988	4.00	25
1988 Kitty's 1st Christmas 552917	Yr.Iss.	1988	4.00	25
1988 Merry Christmas Puppy 552925	Yr.Iss.	1988	3.50	N/A
1988 Merry Christmas Kitty 552933	Yr.Iss.	1988	3.50	N/A
1986 I Love My Grandparents 553263	Yr.Iss.	1986	6.00	N/A
1986 Merry Christmas Mom & Dad 553271	Yr.Iss.	1986	6.00	N/A
1986 Hollycopter 553344	4-Yr.	1989	13.50	35
1986 From Our House To Your House 553360	3-Yr.	1988	15.00	40
1986 Christmas Rattle 553379	3-Yr.	1988	8.00	35
1986 Bah, Humbug! 553387	4-Yr.	1989	9.00	N/A
1986 God Bless Us Everyone 553395	4-Yr.	1989	10.00	15
1987 Carousel Mobile 553409	3-Yr.	1989	15.00	50
1986 Holiday Train 553417	4-Yr.	1989	10.00	N/A
1986 Lighten Up! 553603 - J. Davis	5-Yr.	1990	10.00	N/A
1986 Gift Wrap Odie 553611 - J. Davis	Yr.Iss.	1986	7.00	20
1986 Merry Christmas 553646	4-Yr.	1989	8.00	N/A
1987 M.V.B. (Most Valuable Bear) Golfing 554219	2-Yr.	1988	3.00	N/A
1987 M.V.B. (Most Valuable Bear) Ice Hockey 554219	2-Yr.	1988	3.00	N/A
1987 M.V.B. (Most Valuable Bear) Skiing 554219	2-Yr.	1988	3.00	N/A
1987 M.V.B. (Most Valuable Bear) Bowling 554219	2-Yr.	1988	3.00	N/A
1988 1st Christmas Together 554537 - Gilmore	3-Yr.	1990	15.00	N/A
1988 An Eye On Christmas 554545 - Gilmore	3-Yr.	1990	22.50	60
1988 A Mouse Check 554553 - Gilmore	3-Yr.	1990	13.50	45
1988 Merry Christmas Engine 554561	2-Yr.	1989	22.50	35
1989 Sardine Express 554588 - Gilmore	2-Yr.	1990	17.50	30
1988 1st Christmas Together 1988 554596	Yr.Iss.	1988	10.00	N/A
1988 Forever Friends 554626 - Gilmore	2-Yr.	1989	12.00	27
1988 Santa's Survey 554642	2-Yr.	1989	35.00	75-100
1989 Old Town Church 554871 - Gilmore	2-Yr.	1990	17.50	20
1988 Christmas Is Coming 554901	3-Yr.	1990	12.00	12
1988 Baby's First Christmas 1988 554928	Yr.Iss.	1988	7.50	N/A
1988 Baby's First Christmas 1988 554936 - Gilmore	Yr.Iss.	1988	10.00	25
1988 The Christmas Train 554944	3-Yr.	1990	15.00	N/A
1988 Li'l Drummer Bear 554952 - Gilmore	3-Yr.	1990	12.00	12
1987 Baby's First Christmas 555061	3-Yr.	1989	12.00	N/A
1987 Baby's First Christmas 555088	3-Yr.	1989	7.50	N/A
1987 Baby's First Christmas 555118	3-Yr.	1989	6.00	N/A
1988 Sugar Plum Bearies 555193	Yr.Iss.	1988	4.50	N/A
1987 Garfield Merry Kissmas 555215 - J. Davis	3-Yr.	1989	8.50	30
1988 Sleigh Away 555401	2-Yr.	1989	12.00	N/A
1987 Merry Christmas (Boy) 555428 - L. Rigg	Yr.Iss.	1987	8.00	N/A
1987 Merry Christmas (Girl) 555436 - L. Rigg	Yr.Iss.	1987	8.00	N/A
1987 Lucy & Me Storybook Bear 555444 - L. Rigg	3-Yr.	1989	6.50	N/A
1987 Time For Christmas 555452 - L. Rigg	3-Yr.	1989	12.00	20
1987 Lucy & Me Angel On A Cloud 555487 - L. Rigg	3-Yr.	1989	8.00	35
1987 Teddy's Stocking 555940 - Gilmore	3-Yr.	1989	10.00	N/A
1987 Kitty's Jack-In-The-Box 555959	3-Yr.	1989	11.00	30
1987 Merry Christmas Teacher 555967	3-Yr.	1989	7.50	N/A
1987 Mouse In A Mitten 555975	3-Yr.	1989	7.50	N/A
1987 Boy On A Rocking Horse 555983	3-Yr.	1989	12.00	18
1987 Peek-A-Bear Letter To Santa 555991	2-Yr.	1988	8.00	30
1987 Garfield Sugar Plum Fairy 556009 - J. Davis	3-Yr.	1989	8.50	12
1987 Garfield The Nutcracker 556017 - J. Davis	4-Yr.	1990	8.50	10-20
1987 Joy To The World Carousel Lion 556025 - Gilmore	3-Yr.	1989	12.00	25
1988 Home Sweet Home 556033 - Gilmore	2-Yr.	1989	15.00	40
1988 Baby's First Christmas 556041	3-Yr.	1990	10.00	20
1988 Little Sailor Elf 556068	2-Yr.	1989	10.00	12-20
1987 Carousel Goose 556076	3-Yr.	1989	17.00	40
1988 Night Caps Mom 556084	Yr.Iss.	1988	5.50	N/A
1988 Night Caps Dad 556084	Yr.Iss.	1988	5.50	N/A
1988 Night Caps Grandpa 556084	Yr.Iss.	1988	5.50	N/A
1988 Night Caps Grandma 556084	Yr.Iss.	1988	5.50	N/A
1988 Rocking Horse Past Joys 556157	2-Yr.	1989	10.00	20
1987 Partridge In A Pear Tree 556173 - Gilmore	3-Yr.	1989	9.00	35
1987 Skating Santa 1987 556211	Yr.Iss.	1987	13.50	75
1987 Baby's First Christmas 1987 556238 - Gilmore	Yr.Iss.	1987	10.00	25
1987 Baby's First Christmas 1987 556254	Yr.Iss.	1987	7.00	25
1988 Teddy's Suspenders 556262	3-Yr.	1990	8.50	22
1987 Baby's First Christmas (boy) 1987 556297	Yr.Iss.	1987	2.00	N/A
1987 Baby's First Christmas (girl) 1987 556297	Yr.Iss.	1987	2.00	N/A
1987 Beary Christmas Family (Grandma) 556300	2-Yr.	1988	2.00	N/A
1987 Beary Christmas Family (Grandpa) 556300	2-Yr.	1988	2.00	N/A

522 Collectors' Information Bureau

*Quotes have been rounded up to nearest dollar

YEAR ISSUE	EDITION LIMIT	YEAR RETD.	ISSUE PRICE	*QUOTE U.S.$
1987 Beary Christmas Family (Mom) 556300	2-Yr.	1988	2.00	N/A
1987 Beary Christmas Family (Dad) 556300	2-Yr.	1988	2.00	N/A
1987 Beary Christmas Family (Brother) 556300	2-Yr.	1988	2.00	N/A
1987 Beary Christmas Family (Sister)556300	2-Yr.	1988	2.00	N/A
1987 Merry Christmas Teacher (Boy) 556319	2-Yr.	1988	2.00	N/A
1987 Merry Christmas Teacher (Girl) 556319	2-Yr.	1988	2.00	N/A
1987 1st Christmas Together 1987 556335	Yr.Iss.	1987	9.00	18
1987 Katie Goes Ice Skating 556378	3-Yr.	1989	8.00	30
1987 Scooter Snowman 556386	3-Yr.	1989	8.00	30
1987 Santa's List 556394	3-Yr.	1989	7.00	23
1988 Kitty's Bed 556408	3-Yr.	1989	12.00	30
1988 Grandchild's First Christmas 556416	2-Yr.	1989	10.00	N/A
1987 Two Turtledoves 556432 - Gilmore	2-Yr.	1989	9.00	30
1987 Three French Hens 556440 - Gilmore	3-Yr.	1989	9.00	30
1988 Four Calling Birds 556459 - Gilmore	3-Yr.	1990	11.00	30
1988 Teddy Takes A Spin 556467	3-Yr.	1990	13.00	35
1987 Tiny Toy Thimble Mobile 556475	2-Yr.	1988	12.00	35
1987 Bucket O'Love (Puppy's 1st Christmas) 556491	2-Yr.	1988	2.50	N/A
1987 Bucket O'Love (Kitty's 1st Christmas) 556491	2-Yr.	1988	2.50	N/A
1987 Bucket O'Love (Christmas Kitty) 556491	2-Yr.	1988	2.50	N/A
1987 Bucket O'Love (Christmas Puppy) 556491	2-Yr.	1988	2.50	N/A
1987 Puppy Love 556505	3-Yr.	1989	6.00	N/A
1987 Peek-A-Bear My Special Friend 556513	4-Yr.	1990	6.00	30
1987 Our First Christmas Together 556548	3-Yr.	1989	13.00	20
1987 Three Little Bears 556556	3-Yr.	1989	7.50	15
1988 Lucy & Me Mailbox Bear 556564 - L. Rigg	3-Yr.	1990	3.00	N/A
1987 Twinkle Bear 556572 - Gilmore	3-Yr.	1989	8.00	N/A
1988 I'm Dreaming Of A Bright Christmas 556602	Yr.Iss.	1988	2.50	N/A
1988 Christmas Train 557196	2-Yr.	1989	10.00	N/A
1988 Dairy Christmas 557501 - M. Cook	2-Yr.	1989	10.00	30
1988 Merry Christmas (Boy) 557595 - L. Rigg	Yr.Iss.	1988	10.00	N/A
1988 Merry Christmas (Girl) 557609 - L. Rigg	Yr.Iss.	1988	10.00	N/A
1988 Toy Chest Keepsake 558206 - L. Rigg	3-Yr.	1990	12.50	30
1988 Teddy Bear Greetings 558214 - L. Rigg	3-Yr.	1990	8.00	30
1988 Jester Bear 558222 - L. Rigg	2-Yr.	1989	8.00	N/A
1988 Night-Watch Cat 558362 - J. Davis	3-Yr.	1990	13.00	35
1988 Christmas Thim-bell Mouse 558389	Yr.Iss.	1988	4.00	30
1988 Christmas Thim-bell Snowman 558389	Yr.Iss.	1988	4.00	N/A
1988 Christmas Thim-bell Bear 558389	Yr.Iss.	1988	4.00	N/A
1988 Christmas Thim-bell Santa 558389	Yr.Iss.	1988	4.00	N/A
1988 Baby's First Christmas 558397 - D. Parker	3-Yr.	1990	16.00	30
1988 Christmas Tradition 558400 - Gilmore	2-Yr.	1989	10.00	25
1988 Stocking Story 558419 - G.G. Santiago	3-Yr.	1990	10.00	23
1988 Winter Tale 558427 - G.G. Santiago	2-Yr.	1989	6.00	N/A
1988 Party Mouse 558435 - G.G. Santiago	3-Yr.	1990	12.00	30
1988 Christmas Watch 558443 - G.G. Santiago	2-Yr.	1989	11.00	32
1988 Christmas Vacation 558451 - G.G. Santiago	3-Yr.	1990	8.00	23
1988 Sweet Cherub 558478 - G.G. Santiago	3-Yr.	1990	7.00	8
1988 Time Out 558486 - G.G. Santiago	2-Yr.	1989	11.00	N/A
1988 The Ice Fairy 558516 - G.G. Santiago	3-Yr.	1990	23.00	45-55
1988 Santa Turtle 558559	2-Yr.	1989	10.00	35
1988 The Teddy Bear Ball 558567	3-Yr.	1990	10.00	25
1988 Turtle Greetings 558583	2-Yr.	1989	8.50	25
1988 Happy Howladays 558605	Yr.Iss.	1988	7.00	15
1988 Special Delivery 558699 - J. Davis	3-Yr.	1990	9.00	30
1988 Deer Garfield 558702 - J. Davis	3-Yr.	1990	12.00	30
1988 Garfield Bags O' Fun 558761 - J. Davis	Yr.Iss.	1988	3.30	N/A
1988 Gramophone Keepsake 558818	2-Yr.	1989	13.00	20
1988 North Pole Lineman 558834 - Gilmore	2-Yr.	1989	10.00	50
1988 Five Golden Rings 559121 - Gilmore	3-Yr.	1990	11.00	25
1988 Six Geese A-Laying 559148 - Gilmore	3-Yr.	1990	11.00	25
1988 Pretty Baby 559156 - R. Morehead	3-Yr.	1990	12.50	25
1988 Old Fashioned Angel 559164 - R. Morehead	3-Yr.	1990	12.50	20
1988 Two For Tea 559776 - Gilmore	3-Yr.	1990	20.00	35-40
1988 Merry Christmas Grandpa 560065	3-Yr.	1990	8.00	N/A
1990 Reeling In The Holidays 560405 - M. Cook	2-Yr.	1991	8.00	15
1991 Walkin' With My Baby 561029 - M. Cook	2-Yr.	1992	10.00	N/A
1989 Scrub-A-Dub Chipmunk 561037 - M. Cook	2-Yr.	1990	8.00	20
1989 Christmas Cook-Out 561045 - M. Cook	2-Yr.	1990	9.00	20
1989 Bunkie 561835 - S. Zimnicki	3-Yr.	1991	22.50	30
1989 Sparkles 561843 - S. Zimnicki	3-Yr.	1991	17.50	25-28
1992 Sparky & Buffer 561851 - S. Zimnicki	3-Yr.	1994	25.00	25
1989 Popper 561878 - S. Zimnicki	3-Yr.	1991	12.00	25
1989 Seven Swans A-Swimming 562742 - Gilmore	3-Yr.	1991	12.00	23

YEAR ISSUE	EDITION LIMIT	YEAR RETD.	ISSUE PRICE	*QUOTE U.S.$
1989 Eight Maids A-Milking 562750 - Gilmore	3-Yr.	1991	12.00	23
1989 Nine Ladies Dancing 562769 - Gilmore	3-Yr.	1991	15.00	23
1989 Baby's First Christmas 1989 562807	Yr.Iss.	1989	8.00	20
1989 Baby's First Christmas 1989 562815 - Gilmore	Yr.Iss.	1989	10.00	N/A
1989 First Christmas Together 1989 562823	Yr.Iss.	1989	11.00	N/A
1989 Travelin' Trike 562882 - Gilmore	3-Yr.	1991	15.00	15
1989 Victorian Sleigh Ride 562890	3-Yr.	1991	22.50	23
1991 Santa Delivers Love 562904 - Gilmore	2-Yr.	1992	17.50	18
1989 Chestnut Roastin' 562912 - Gilmore	2-Yr.	1990	13.00	13
1990 Th-Ink-In' Of You 562920 - Gilmore	2-Yr.	1991	20.00	30
1989 Ye Olde Puppet Show 562939	2-Yr.	1990	17.50	34
1989 Static In The Attic 562947	2-Yr.	1990	13.00	25
1989 Mistle-Toast 1989 562963 - Gilmore	Yr.Iss.	1989	15.00	25
1989 Merry Christmas Pops 562971 - Gilmore	3-Yr.	1991	12.00	12
1990 North Pole Or Bust 562998 - Gilmore	2-Yr.	1991	25.00	25
1989 By The Light Of The Moon 563005 - Gilmore	3-Yr.	1991	12.00	24
1989 Stickin' To It 563013 - Gilmore	2-Yr.	1990	10.00	12
1989 Christmas Cookin' 563048 - Gilmore	3-Yr.	1991	22.50	25
1989 All Set For Santa 563080 -Gilmore	3-Yr.	1991	17.50	25
1990 Santa's Sweets 563196 - Gilmore	2-Yr.	1991	20.00	20
1990 Purr-Fect Pals 563218	2-Yr.	1991	8.00	8
1989 The Pause That Refreshes 563226	3-Yr.	1991	15.00	75
1989 Ho-Ho Holiday Scrooge 563234 - J. Davis	3-Yr.	1991	13.50	30
1989 God Bless Us Everyone 563242 - J. Davis	3-Yr.	1991	13.50	20
1989 Scrooge With The Spirit 563250 - J. Davis	3-Yr.	1991	13.50	30
1989 A Chains Of Pace For Odie 563269 - J. Davis	3-Yr.	1991	12.00	25
1990 Jingle Bell Rock 1990 563390 - G. Armgardt	Yr.Iss.	1990	13.50	30
1989 Joy Ridin' 563463 - J. Davis	2-Yr.	1990	15.00	30
1989 Just What I Wanted 563668 - M. Peters	3-Yr.	1991	13.50	14
1990 Pucker Up! 563676 - M. Peters	3-Yr.	1992	11.00	11
1989 What's The Bright Idea 563684 - M. Peters	3-Yr.	1991	13.50	14
1990 Fleas Navidad 563978 - M. Peters	3-Yr.	1992	13.50	25
1990 Tweet Greetings 564044 - J. Davis	2-Yr.	1991	15.00	12-20
1990 Trouble On 3 Wheels 564052 - J. Davis	3-Yr.	1992	20.00	25
1989 Mine, All Mine! 564079 - J. Davis	Yr.Iss.	1989	15.00	25
1989 Star of Stars 564389 - J. Jonik	3-Yr.	1991	9.00	15
1990 Hang Onto Your Hat 564397 - J. Jonik	3-Yr.	1992	8.00	15
1990 Fireplace Frolic 564435 - N. Teiber	2-Yr.	1991	25.00	32
1994 Merry Miss Merry 564508 - Hahn	Yr.Iss.	1994	12.00	12
1994 Santa Delivers 564567	Yr.Iss.	1994	12.00	12
1989 Hoe! Hoe! Hoe! 564761	Yr.Iss.	1989	20.00	35
1991 Double Scoop Snowmouse 564796 - M. Cook	3-Yr.	1993	13.50	14
1990 Christmas Is Magic 564826 - M. Cook	2-Yr.	1991	10.00	10
1990 Lighting Up Christmas 564834 - M. Cook	2-Yr.	1991	10.00	10
1989 Feliz Navidad! 1989 564842 - M. Cook	Yr.Iss.	1989	11.00	40
1989 Spreading Christmas Joy 564850 - M. Cook	3-Yr.	1991	10.00	10
1989 Yuletide Tree House 564915 - J. Jonik	3-Yr.	1991	20.00	20
1990 Brewing Warm Wishes 564974	2-Yr.	1991	10.00	10
1990 Yippie-I-Yuletide 564982 - Hahn	3-Yr.	1992	15.00	15
1990 Coffee Break 564990 - Hahn	3-Yr.	1992	15.00	15
1990 You're Sew Special 565008 - Hahn	Yr.Iss.	1990	20.00	35
1989 Full House Mouse 565016 - Hahn	2-Yr.	1990	13.50	75
1989 I Feel Pretty 565024 - Hahn	3-Yr.	1991	20.00	30
1990 Warmest Wishes 565032 - Hahn	3-Yr.	1992	15.00	15
1990 Baby's Christmas Feast 565040 - Hahn	3-Yr.	1992	13.50	14
1990 Bumper Car Santa 565083 - G.G. Santiago	Yr.Iss.	1990	20.00	40
1989 Special Delivery (Proof Ed.) 565091 - G.G. Santiago	Yr.Iss.	1989	12.00	15
1990 Ho! Ho! Yo-Yo! (Proof Ed.) 565105 - G.G. Santiago	Yr.Iss.	1990	12.00	15
1989 Weightin' For Santa 565148 - G.G. Santiago	3-Yr.	1991	7.50	8
1989 Holly Fairy 565199 - C.M. Baker	Yr.Iss.	1989	15.00	45
1990 The Christmas Tree Fairy 565202 - C.M. Baker	Yr.Iss.	1990	15.00	40
1989 Merry Christmas (Boy) 565210 - L. Rigg	Yr.Iss.	1989	12.00	38
1989 Top Of The Class 565237 - L. Rigg	3-Yr.	1991	11.00	11
1989 Deck The Hogs 565490 - M. Cook	2-Yr.	1990	12.00	14
1989 Pinata Ridin' 565504 - M. Cook	2-Yr.	1990	11.00	N/A
1989 Hangin' In There 1989 565598 - K. Wise	Yr.Iss.	1989	10.00	20
1990 Meow-y Christmas 1990 565601 - K. Wise	Yr.Iss.	1990	10.00	25
1990 Seaman's Greetings 566047	2-Yr.	1991	11.00	24
1990 Hang In There 566055	3-Yr.	1992	13.50	14
1990 Deck The Halls 566063	3-Yr.	1992	12.50	N/A
1991 Pedal Pushin' Santa 566071	Yr.Iss.	1991	20.00	30
1990 Merry Christmas Teacher 566098	2-Yr.	1991	11.00	11
1990 Festive Flight 566101	2-Yr.	1991	11.00	11
1993 I'm Dreaming of a White-Out Christmas 566144	2-Yr.	1994	22.50	23
1990 Santa's Suitcase 566160	3-Yr.	1992	25.00	25
1989 The Purr-Fect Fit! 566462	3-Yr.	1991	15.00	35
1990 Tumbles 1990 566519 - S. Zimnicki	Yr.Iss.	1990	16.00	25
1990 Twiddles 566551 - S. Zimnicki	3-Yr.	1992	15.00	30

YEAR ISSUE	EDITION LIMIT	YEAR RETD.	ISSUE PRICE	*QUOTE U.S.$
1991 Snuffy 566578 - S. Zimnicki	3-Yr.	1993	17.50	18
1990 All Aboard 567671 - Gilmore	2-Yr.	1991	17.50	18
1989 Gone With The Wind 567698	Yr.Iss.	1989	13.50	30
1989 Dorothy 567760	Yr.Iss.	1989	12.00	35
1989 The Tin Man 567779	Yr.Iss.	1989	12.00	12
1989 The Cowardly Lion 567787	Yr.Iss.	1989	12.00	12
1989 The Scarecrow 567795	Yr.Iss.	1989	12.00	12
1990 Happy Holiday Readings 568104	2-Yr.	1991	8.00	8
1989 Merry Christmas (Girl) 568325 - L. Rigg	Yr.Iss.	1989	12.00	N/A
1991 Holidays Ahoy 568368	2-Yr.	1992	12.50	13
1990 Christmas Countdown 568376	3-Yr.	1992	20.00	20
1989 Clara 568406	Yr.Iss.	1989	12.50	20
1990 The Nutcracker 568414	Yr.Iss.	1990	12.50	30
1991 Clara's Prince 568422	Yr.Iss.	1991	12.50	18
1989 Santa's Little Reindear 568430	2-Yr.	1990	15.00	25
1991 Tuba Totin' Teddy 568449	3-Yr.	1993	15.00	15
1990 A Calling Home At Christmas 568457	2-Yr.	1991	15.00	15
1991 Love Is The Secret Ingredient 568562 - L. Rigg	2-Yr.	1992	15.00	15
1990 A Spoonful of Love 568570 - L. Rigg	2-Yr.	1991	10.00	10
1990 Merry Christmas (Boy) 568597 - L. Rigg	Yr.Iss.	1990	13.00	N/A
1990 Merry Christmas (Girl) 568600 - L. Rigg	Yr.Iss.	1990	13.00	N/A
1990 Bearing Holiday Wishes 568619 - L. Rigg	3-Yr.	1992	22.50	23
1992 Moonlight Swing 568627 - L. Rigg	3-Yr.	1994	15.00	15
1990 Smitch 570184 - S. Zimnicki	3-Yr.	1992	22.50	23
1992 Carver 570192 - S. Zimnicki	Yr.Iss.	1992	17.50	18
1991 Twinkle & Sprinkle 570206 - S. Zimnicki	3-Yr.	1993	22.50	23
1990 Blinkie 570214 - S. Zimnicki	3-Yr.	1992	15.00	15
1990 Have A Coke And A Smile™ 571512	3-Yr.	1992	15.00	55
1990 Fleece Navidad 571903 - M. Cook	2-Yr.	1991	13.50	25
1990 Have a Navaho-Ho-Ho 1990 571970 - M. Cook	Yr.Iss.	1990	15.00	35
1990 Cheers 1990 572411 - T. Wilson	Yr.Iss.	1990	13.50	22
1990 A Night Before Christmas 572438 - T. Wilson	2-Yr.	1991	17.50	18
1990 Merry Kissmas 572446 - T. Wilson	2-Yr.	1991	10.00	30
1992 A Rockin' GARFIELD Christmas 572527 - J. Davis	2-Yr.	1993	17.50	18
1991 Here Comes Santa Paws 572535 - J. Davis	3-Yr.	1993	20.00	20
1990 Frosty Garfield 1990 572551 - J. Davis	Yr.Iss.	1990	13.50	35
1990 Pop Goes The Odie 572578 - J. Davis	2-Yr.	1991	15.00	30
1991 Sweet Beams 572586 - J. Davis	2-Yr.	1992	13.50	14
1990 An Apple A Day 572594 - J. Davis	2-Yr.	1991	12.00	12
1990 Dear Santa 572608 - J. Davis	3-Yr.	1992	17.00	17
1991 Have A Ball This Christmas 572616 - J. Davis	Yr.Iss.	1991	15.00	15
1990 Oh Shoosh! 572624 - J. Davis	3-Yr.	1992	17.00	17
1990 Little Red Riding Cat 572632 - J. Davis	Yr.Iss.	1990	13.50	33
1991 All Decked Out 572659 - J. Davis	2-Yr.	1992	13.50	14
1990 Over The Rooftops 572721 - J. Davis	2-Yr.	1991	17.50	28-35
1990 Garfield NFL Los Angeles Rams 572764 - J. Davis	2-Yr.	1991	12.50	13
1993 Born To Shop 572942	Yr.Iss.	1993	26.50	35
1990 Garfield NFL Cincinnati Bengals 573000 - J. Davis	2-Yr.	1991	12.50	13
1990 Garfield NFL Cleveland Browns 573019 - J. Davis	2-Yr.	1991	12.50	13
1990 Garfield NFL Houston Oiliers 573027 - J. Davis	2-Yr.	1991	12.50	13
1990 Garfield NFL Pittsburg Steelers 573035 - J. Davis	2-Yr.	1991	12.50	13
1990 Garfield NFL Denver Broncos 573043 - J. Davis	2-Yr.	1991	12.50	13
1990 Garfield NFL Kansas City Chiefs 573051 - J. Davis	2-Yr.	1991	12.50	13
1990 Garfield NFL Los Angeles Raiders 573078 - J. Davis	2-Yr.	1991	12.50	13
1990 Garfield NFL San Diego Chargers 573086 - J. Davis	2-Yr.	1991	12.50	13
1990 Garfield NFL Seattle Seahawks 573094 - J. Davis	2-Yr.	1991	12.50	13
1990 Garfield NFL Buffalo Bills 573108 - J. Davis	2-Yr.	1991	12.50	13
1990 Garfield NFL Indianapolis Colts 573116 - J. Davis	2-Yr.	1991	12.50	13
1990 Garfield NFL Miami Dolphins 573124 - J. Davis	2-Yr.	1991	12.50	13
1990 Garfield NFL New England Patriots 573132 - J. Davis	2-Yr.	1991	12.50	13
1990 Garfield NFL New York Jets 573140 - J. Davis	2-Yr.	1991	12.50	13
1990 Garfield NFL Atlanta Falcons 573159 - J. Davis	2-Yr.	1991	12.50	13
1990 Garfield NFL New Orleans Saints 573167 - J. Davis	2-Yr.	1991	12.50	13
1990 Garfield NFL San Francisco 49ers 573175 - J. Davis	2-Yr.	1991	12.50	13
1990 Garfield NFL Dallas Cowboys 573183 - J. Davis	2-Yr.	1991	12.50	13
1990 Garfield NFL New York Giants 573191 - J. Davis	2-Yr.	1991	12.50	13
1990 Garfield NFL Philadelphia Eagles 573205 - J. Davis	2-Yr.	1991	12.50	13
1990 Garfield NFL Phoenix Cardinals 573213 - J. Davis	2-Yr.	1991	12.50	13

*Quotes have been rounded up to nearest dollar

Treasury Masterpiece Editions/Enesco Group, Inc.
to Treasury Masterpiece Editions/Enesco Group, Inc.

ORNAMENTS

YEAR ISSUE	EDITION LIMIT	YEAR RETD.	ISSUE PRICE	*QUOTE U.S.$
1990 Garfield NFL Washington Redskins 573221 - J. Davis	2-Yr.	1991	12.50	13
1990 Garfield NFL Chicago Bears 573248 - J. Davis	2-Yr.	1991	12.50	13
1990 Garfield NFL Detroit Lions 573256 - J. Davis	2-Yr.	1991	12.50	13
1990 Garfield NFL Green Bay Packers 573264 - J. Davis	2-Yr.	1991	12.50	13
1990 Garfield NFL Minnesota Vikings 573272 - J. Davis	2-Yr.	1991	12.50	13
1990 Garfield NFL Tampa Bay Buccaneers 573280 - J. Davis	2-Yr.	1991	12.50	13
1991 Tea For Two 573299 - Hahn	3-Yr.	1993	30.00	50
1991 Hot Stuff Santa 573523	Yr.Iss.	1991	25.00	30
1990 Merry Moustronauts 573558 - M. Cook	3-Yr.	1992	20.00	40
1991 Santa Wings It 573612 - J. Jonik	3-Yr.	1993	13.00	13
1990 All Eye Want For Christmas 573647 - Gilmore	3-Yr.	1992	27.50	32
1990 Stuck On You 573655 - Gilmore	2-Yr.	1991	12.50	13
1990 Professor Michael Bear, The One Bear Band 573663 - Gilmore	3-Yr.	1992	22.50	28
1990 A Caroling Wee Go 573671 - Gilmore	3-Yr.	1992	12.00	12
1990 Merry Mailman 573698 - Gilmore	2-Yr.	1991	15.00	30
1990 Deck The Halls 573701 - Gilmore	3-Yr.	1992	22.50	30
1992 Sundae Ride 583707	2-Yr.	1993	20.00	20
1990 You're Wheel Special 573728 - Gilmore	3-Yr.	1992	15.00	15
1991 Come Let Us Adore Him 573736 - Gilmore	2-Yr.	1992	9.00	9
1991 Moon Beam Dreams 573760 - Gilmore	3-Yr.	1993	12.00	12
1991 A Song For Santa 573779 - Gilmore	3-Yr.	1993	25.00	25
1990 Warmest Wishes 573825 - Gilmore	Yr.Iss.	1990	17.50	25
1991 Kurious Kitty 573868 - Gilmore	3-Yr.	1993	17.50	18
1990 Old Mother Mouse 573922 - Gilmore	2-Yr.	1991	17.50	20-32
1990 Railroad Repairs 573930 - Gilmore	2-Yr.	1991	12.50	25
1990 Ten Lords A-Leaping 573949 - Gilmore	3-Yr.	1992	15.00	25
1990 Eleven Drummers Drumming 573957 - Gilmore	3-Yr.	1992	15.00	25
1990 Twelve Pipers Piping 573965 - Gilmore	3-Yr.	1992	15.00	25
1990 Baby's First Christmas 1990 573973 - Gilmore	Yr.Iss.	1990	10.00	N/A
1990 Baby's First Christmas 1990 573981 - Gilmore	Yr.Iss.	1990	12.00	N/A
1991 Peter, Peter Pumpkin Eater 574015 - Gilmore	2-Yr.	1992	20.00	30
1992 The Nutcracker 574023 - Gilmore	3-Yr.	1994	25.00	25
1990 Little Jack Horner 574058 - Gilmore	2-Yr.	1991	17.50	35
1991 Mary, Mary Quite Contrary 574066 - Gilmore	2-Yr.	1992	22.50	33
1992 Humpty Dumpty 574244 - Gilmore	2-Yr.	1993	25.00	25
1991 Through The Years 574252 - Gilmore	Yr.Iss.	1991	17.50	18
1991 Holiday Wing Ding 574333	3-Yr.	1993	22.50	23
1991 North Pole Here I Come 574597	3-Yr.	1993	10.00	10
1991 Christmas Caboose 574856 - Gilmore	2-Yr.	1992	25.00	30
1990 Bubble Trouble 575038 - Hahn	3-Yr.	1992	20.00	35
1991 Merry Mother-To-Be 575046 - Hahn	3-Yr.	1993	13.50	14
1990 A Holiday 'Scent' Sation 575054 - Hahn	3-Yr.	1992	15.00	30
1990 Catch Of The Day 575070 - Hahn	3-Yr.	1992	25.00	25
1990 Don't Open 'Til Christmas 575089 - Hahn	3-Yr.	1992	17.50	18
1990 I Can't Weight 'Til Christmas 575119 - Hahn	3-Yr.	1992	16.50	30
1991 Deck The Halls 575127 - Hahn	2-Yr.	1992	15.00	25
1992 Music Mice-Tro! 575143	2-Yr.	1993	12.00	12
1990 Mouse House 575186	3-Yr.	1992	16.00	16
1991 Dream A Little Dream 575593	2-Yr.	1992	17.50	18
1991 Christmas Two-gether 575615 - L. Rigg	3-Yr.	1993	22.50	23
1992 On Target Two-Gether 575623	Yr.Iss.	1992	17.00	17
1991 Christmas Trimmings 575631	2-Yr.	1992	17.00	17
1991 Gumball Wizard 575658 - Gilmore	2-Yr.	1992	13.00	13
1991 Crystal Ball Christmas 575666 - Gilmore	2-Yr.	1992	22.50	23
1990 Old King Cole 575682 - Gilmore	2-Yr.	1991	20.00	29
1991 Tom, Tom The Piper's Son 575690 - Gilmore	2-Yr.	1992	15.00	33
1992 Rock-A-Bye Baby 575704 - Gilmore	2-Yr.	1993	13.50	14
1992 Queen of Hearts 575712 - Gilmore	2-Yr.	1992	17.50	18
1993 Toy To The World 575763	2-Yr.	1994	25.00	25
1992 Tasty Tidings 575836 - L. Rigg	Yr.Iss.	1992	13.50	14
1991 Tire-d Little Bear 575852 - L. Rigg	Yr.Iss.	1991	12.50	13
1990 Baby Bear Christmas 1990 575860 - L. Rigg	Yr.Iss.	1990	12.00	28
1991 Crank Up The Carols 575887 - L. Rigg	2-Yr.	1992	17.50	18
1990 Beary Christmas 1990 576158 - L. Rigg	Yr.Iss.	1990	12.00	12
1991 Merry Christmas (Boy) 576166 - L. Rigg	Yr.Iss.	1991	13.00	13
1991 Merry Christmas (Girl) 576174 - L. Rigg	Yr.Iss.	1991	13.00	13
1991 Christmas Cutie 576182	3-Yr.	1993	13.50	14
1991 Meow Mates 576220	3-Yr.	1993	12.00	12
1991 Frosty The Snowmant 576425	3-Yr.	1993	15.00	15
1991 Ris-ski Business 576719 - T. Wilson	2-Yr.	1992	10.00	10
1991 Pinocchio 577391 - J. Davis	3-Yr.	1993	15.00	15
1990 Yuletide Ride 1990 577502 - Gilmore	Yr.Iss.	1990	13.50	50
1990 Tons of Toys 577510	Yr.Iss.	1990	13.00	30
1990 McHappy Holidays 577529	2-Yr.	1991	17.50	25
1990 Heading For Happy Holidays 577537	3-Yr.	1992	17.50	18
1990 'Twas The Night Before Christmas 577545	3-Yr.	1992	17.50	18
1990 Over One Million Holiday Wishes! 577553	Yr.Iss.	1990	17.50	30
1990 You Malt My Heart 577596	2-Yr.	1991	25.00	25
1991 All I Want For Christmas 577618	2-Yr.	1992	20.00	20
1992 Bearly Sleepy 578029 - Gilmore	Yr.Iss.	1992	17.50	18
1994 Buttons 'N' Bow Boutique 578363 - Gilmore	Yr.Iss.	1995	22.50	23
1992 Spreading Sweet Joy 580465	Yr.Iss.	1992	13.50	14
1991 Things Go Better With Coke™ 580597	3-Yr.	1993	17.00	25
1991 Christmas To Go 580600 - M. Cook	Yr.Iss.	1991	22.50	23
1991 Have A Mariachi Christmas 580619 - M. Cook	2-Yr.	1992	13.50	14
1993 Bearly Balanced 580724	Yr.Iss.	1993	15.00	15
1992 Ring My Bell 580740 - J. Davis	Yr.Iss.	1992	13.50	14
1992 4 x 4 Holiday Fun 580783 - J. Davis	2-Yr.	1993	20.00	20
1991 Christmas Is In The Air 581453	Yr.Iss.	1991	15.00	15
1991 Holiday Treats 581542	Yr.Iss.	1991	17.50	18
1991 Christmas Is My Goal 581550	2-Yr.	1992	17.50	12-18
1991 A Quarter Pounder With Cheer® 581569	3-Yr.	1993	20.00	20
1992 The Holidays Are A Hit 581577	2-Yr.	1993	17.50	18
1991 From The Same Mold 581798 - Gilmore	3-Yr.	1993	17.00	17
1991 The Glow Of Christmas 581801	2-Yr.	1992	20.00	20
1992 Tip Top Tidings 581828	2-Yr.	1993	13.00	13
1994 A Sign of Peace 581992	Yr.Iss.	1994	18.50	19
1992 Christmas Lifts The Spirits 582018	2-Yr.	1993	25.00	25
1993 Joyeux Noel 582026	2-Yr.	1994	24.50	25
1992 A Pound Of Good Cheers 582034	2-Yr.	1993	17.50	18
1994 Wishing You Well At Christmas 582050	Yr.Iss.	1994	25.00	25
1994 Ahoy Joy! 582085	Yr.Iss.	1994	20.00	20
1993 Holiday Mew-Sic 582107	2-Yr.	1994	20.00	20
1993 Santa's Magic Ride 582115	2-Yr.	1994	24.00	24
1994 Santa...Phone Home 582166	Yr.Iss.	1994	25.00	25
1993 Warm And Hearty Wishes 582344	Yr.Iss.	1993	17.50	18
1993 Cool Yule 582352	Yr.Iss.	1993	12.00	12
1994 Christmas Swishes 582379	Yr.Iss.	1994	17.50	18
1993 Have A Holly Jell-O Christmas 582387	Yr.Iss.	1993	14.50	45
1994 The Latest Scoop From Santa 582395 - Gilmore	Yr.Iss.	1994	18.50	19
1994 Chiminy Cheer 582409 - Gilmore	Yr.Iss.	1994	22.50	23
1994 Cozy Candlelight Dinner 582417 - Gilmore	Yr.Iss.	1994	25.00	25
1994 Fine Feathered Festivities 582425 - Gilmore	Yr.Iss.	1994	22.50	23
1994 Joy From Head To Hose 582433 - Gilmore	Yr.Iss.	1994	15.00	15
1993 Festive Firemen 582565 - Gilmore	2-Yr.	1994	17.00	17
1991 Lights..Camera..Kissmas! 583626 - Gilmore	Yr.Iss.	1991	15.00	35
1991 All Caught Up In Christmas 583537	2-Yr.	1992	10.00	10
1991 Sweet Steed 583634 - Gilmore	3-Yr.	1993	15.00	15
1992 Sweet as Cane Be 583642 - Gilmore	3-Yr.	1994	15.00	15
1991 Dreamin' Of A White Christmas 583669 - Gilmore	2-Yr.	1992	15.00	15
1991 Merry Millimeters 583677 - Gilmore	3-Yr.	1993	17.00	17
1991 Here's The Scoop 583693	2-Yr.	1992	13.50	20
1991 Happy Meal® On Wheels 583715	3-Yr.	1993	22.50	23
1991 Christmas Kayak 583723	2-Yr.	1992	13.50	14
1993 Light Up Your Holidays With Coke 583758	Yr.Iss.	1993	27.50	28
1992 The Cold, Crisp Taste Of Coke 583766	3-Yr.	1994	17.00	17
1991 Marilyn Monroe 583774	Yr.Iss.	1991	20.00	20
1992 Sew Christmasy 583820	3-Yr.	1994	25.00	25
1991 A Christmas Carol 583928 - Gilmore	3-Yr.	1993	22.50	23
1991 Checking It Twice 583936	2-Yr.	1992	25.00	25
1992 Catch A Falling Star 583944 - Gilmore	2-Yr.	1993	15.00	15
1992 Swingin' Christmas 584096	2-Yr.	1993	15.00	15
1994 Yuletide Yummies 584835 - Gilmore	Yr.Iss.	1994	20.00	20
1993 Pool Hall-idays 584851	2-Yr.	1994	19.00	20
1994 Merry Christmas Tool You, Dad 584886	Yr.Iss.	1994	22.50	23
1994 Exercising Good Taste 584967	Yr.Iss.	1994	17.50	18
1994 Holiday Chew-Chew 584983 - Gilmore	Yr.Iss.	1994	22.50	23
1992 Mc Ho, Ho, Ho 585181	3-Yr.	1994	22.50	23
1991 Merry Christmas Go-Round 585203 - J. Davis	3-Yr.	1993	20.00	20
1992 Holiday On Ice 585254 - J. Davis	3-Yr.	1994	17.50	18
1991 Holiday Hideout 585270 - J. Davis	2-Yr.	1992	15.00	15
1992 Fast Track Cat 585289 - J. Davis	3-Yr.	1994	17.50	18
1992 Holiday Cat Napping 585319 - J. Davis	2-Yr.	1993	20.00	20
1993 Bah Humbug 585394 - Davis	Yr.Iss.	1993	15.00	15
1992 The Finishing Touches 585610 - T. Wilson	2-Yr.	1993	17.50	18
1992 Jolly Ol' Gent 585645 - J. Jonik	3-Yr.	1994	13.50	14
1991 Our Most Precious Gift 585726	Yr.Iss.	1991	17.50	18
1991 Christmas Cheer 585769	2-Yr.	1992	13.50	14
1993 Chimer 585777 - Zimnicki	Yr.Iss.	1993	25.00	10-25
1993 Sweet Whiskered Wishes 585807	Yr.Iss.	1993	17.00	17
1993 Grade "A" Wishes From Garfield 585823 - Davis	2-Yr.	1994	20.00	20
1992 A Child's Christmas 586358	3-Yr.	1994	25.00	25
1992 Festive Fiddlers 586501	Yr.Iss.	1992	20.00	25
1992 La Luminaria 586579 - M. Cook	2-Yr.	1993	13.50	14
1991 Fired Up For Christmas 586587 - Gilmore	2-Yr.	1992	32.50	33
1991 One Foggy Christmas Eve 586625 - Gilmore	3-Yr.	1993	30.00	30
1991 For A Purr-fect Mom 586641 - Gilmore	Yr.Iss.	1991	12.00	12
1991 For A Special Dad 586668 - Gilmore	Yr.Iss.	1991	17.50	18
1991 With Love 586676 - Gilmore	Yr.Iss.	1991	13.00	13
1991 For A Purr-fect Aunt 586692 - Gilmore	Yr.Iss.	1991	12.00	12
1991 For A Dog-Gone Great Uncle 586706 - Gilmore	Yr.Iss.	1991	12.00	12
1991 Peddling Fun 586714 - Gilmore	Yr.Iss.	1991	16.00	16
1991 Special Keepsakes 586722 - Gilmore	Yr.Iss.	1991	13.50	14
1992 Cozy Chrismas Carriage 586730 - Gilmore	2-Yr.	1993	22.50	23
1992 Small Fry's First Christmas 586749	2-Yr.	1993	17.00	17
1991 Hats Off To Christmas 586757 - Hahn	Yr.Iss.	1991	22.50	23
1992 Friendships Preserved 586765 - Hahn	Yr.Iss.	1992	22.50	23
1995 Sweet Harmony 586773 - Gilmore	Yr.Iss.	1995	17.50	18
1993 Tree For Two 586781 - Gilmore	2-Yr.	1994	17.50	18
1993 A Bright Idea 586803 - Gilmore	2-Yr.	1994	22.50	23
1992 Window Wish List 586854 - Gilmore	2-Yr.	1993	30.00	30
1992 Through The Years 586862 - Gilmore	Yr.Iss.	1992	17.50	18
1993 Baby's First Christmas 1993 586870 - Gilmore	Yr.Iss.	1993	17.50	18
1993 My Special Christmas 586900 - Gilmore	Yr.Iss.	1993	17.50	18
1991 Baby's First Christmas 1991 586935	Yr.Iss.	1991	12.50	13
1992 Baby's First Christmas 1992 586943	Yr.Iss.	1992	12.50	13
1992 Firehouse Friends 586951 - Gilmore	Yr.Iss.	1992	22.50	23
1992 Bubble Buddy 586978 - Gilmore	2-Yr	1993	13.50	14
1992 The Warmth Of The Season 586994	2-Yr.	1993	20.00	20
1993 Baby's First Christmas Dinner 587001	Yr.Iss.	1993	12.00	12
1991 Jugglin' The Holidays 587028	2-Yr.	1992	13.00	13
1991 Santa's Steed 587044	Yr.Iss.	1991	15.00	15
1991 A Decade of Treasures 587052 - Gilmore	Yr.Iss.	1991	37.50	75
1992 It's A Go For Christmas 587095 - Gilmore	2-Yr.	1993	15.00	15
1991 Mr. Mailmouse 587109 - Gilmore	2-Yr.	1992	17.00	17
1992 Post-Mouster General 587117 - Gilmore	2-Yr.	1993	20.00	20
1992 To A Deer Baby 587168	Yr.Iss.	1992	18.50	19
1991 Starry Eyed Santa 587176	2-Yr.	1992	15.00	15
1992 Moon Watch 587184	2-Yr.	1993	20.00	20
1992 Guten Cheers 587192	Yr.Iss.	1992	22.50	23
1992 Put On A Happy Face 588237	2-Yr.	1993	15.00	15
1992 Beginning To Look A Lot Like Christmas 588253	2-Yr.	1993	15.00	15
1992 A Christmas Toast 588261	2-Yr.	1993	20.00	20
1992 Merry Mistle-Toad 588288	2-Yr.	1993	15.00	15
1992 Tic-Tac-Mistle-Toe 588296	3-Yr.	1994	23.00	23
1993 A Pause For Claus 588318	2-Yr.	1994	22.50	23
1992 Heaven Sent 588423 - J. Penchoff	2-Yr.	1993	12.50	13
1992 Holiday Happenings 588555 - Gilmore	3-Yr.	1994	30.00	30
1993 Not A Creature Was Stirring... 588563 - Gilmore	2-Yr.	1994	27.50	28
1992 Seed-son's Greetings 588571 - Gilmore	3-Yr.	1994	27.00	27
1992 Santa's Midnight Snack 588598 - Gilmore	2-Yr.	1993	20.00	20
1992 Trunk Of Treasures 588636	Yr.Iss.	1992	20.00	20
1993 Terrific Toys 588644	Yr.Iss.	1993	20.00	20
1993 Christmas Dancer 588652	Yr.Iss.	1993	15.00	15
1995 Yule Tide Prancer 588660	Yr.Iss.	1995	15.00	15
1994 To The Sweetest Baby 588725 - Gilmore	Yr.Iss.	1994	18.50	19
1995 Baby's Sweet Feast 588733 - Gilmore	Yr.Iss.	1995	17.50	19
1991 Lighting The Way 588776	2-Yr.	1992	20.00	20
1991 Rudolph 588784	2-Yr.	1992	17.50	18
1992 Festive Newsflash 588792	2-Yr.	1993	17.50	18
1992 A-B-C-Son's Greetings 588806	2-Yr.	1993	16.50	17
1992 Hoppy Holidays 588814	Yr.Iss.	1992	13.50	14
1992 Fireside Friends 588830	2-Yr.	1993	20.00	20
1992 Christmas Eve-mergency 588849	2-Yr.	1993	27.00	27
1992 A Sure Sign Of Christmas 588857	2-Yr.	1993	22.50	23
1992 Holidays Give Me A Lift 588865	2-Yr.	1993	30.00	30
1992 Yule Tide Together 588903	2-Yr.	1993	20.00	20
1992 Have A Soup-er Christmas 588911	2-Yr.	1993	17.50	18
1992 Christmas Cure-Alls 588938	2-Yr.	1993	20.00	20
1993 Countin' On A Merry Christmas 588954	2-Yr.	1994	22.50	23
1994 Rockin' Ranger 588970	Yr.Iss.	1994	25.00	25
1994 Peace On Earthworm 588989	Yr.Iss.	1994	20.00	20
1993 To My Gem 589004	Yr.Iss.	1993	27.50	28
1993 Christmas Mail Call 589012	2-Yr.	1994	20.00	20
1993 Spreading Joy 589047	2-Yr.	1994	27.50	28
1993 Pitter-Patter Post Office 589055	2-Yr.	1994	20.00	20
1994 Good Things Crop Up At Christmas 589071	Yr.Iss.	1994	25.00	25
1993 Happy Haul-idays 589098	2-Yr.	1994	30.00	30
1994 Christmas Crossroads 589128	Yr.Iss.	1994	20.00	20
1993 Hot Off The Press 589292	2-Yr.	1994	27.50	28
1993 Designed With You In Mind 589306	2-Yr.	1994	16.00	16
1992 Dial 'S' For Santa 589373	2-Yr.	1993	25.00	25
1993 Seeing Is Believing 589381 - Gilmore	2-Yr.	1994	20.00	20
1992 Joy To The Whirled 589551 - Hahn	2-Yr.	1993	20.00	20
1992 Merry Make-Over 589586 - Hahn	3-Yr.	1994	20.00	20
1992 Campin' Companions 590282 - Hahn	3-Yr.	1994	20.00	20
1994 Have A Ball At Christmas 590673	Yr.Iss.	1994	15.00	15
1992 Fur-Ever Friends 590797 - Gilmore	2-Yr.	1993	13.50	14
1993 Roundin' Up Christmas Together 590800	Yr.Iss.	1993	25.00	25
1994 Have A Totem-ly Terrific Christmas 590819	Yr.Iss.	1994	30.00	30
1992 Tee-rific Holidays 590827	3-Yr.	1994	25.00	25

*Quotes have been rounded up to nearest dollar

YEAR ISSUE	EDITION LIMIT	YEAR RETD.	ISSUE PRICE	*QUOTE U.S.$
1992 Spinning Christmas Dreams 590908 - Hahn	3-Yr.	1994	22.50	23
1992 Christmas Trimmin' 590932	3-Yr.	1994	17.00	12-17
1993 Toasty Tidings 590940	2-Yr.	1994	20.00	20
1993 Focusing On Christmas 590983 - Gilmore	2-Yr.	1994	27.50	28
1993 Dunk The Halls 591009	2-Yr.	1994	18.50	19
1993 Mice Capades 591386 - Hahn	2-Yr.	1994	26.50	27
1993 25 Points For Christmas 591750	Yr.Iss.	1993	25.00	25
1994 Cocoa 'N' Kisses For Santa- 591939	Yr.Iss.	1995	22.50	23
1994 On The Road With Coke™ 592528	Yr.Iss.	1995	25.00	25
1993 Carving Christmas Wishes 592625 - Gilmore	2-Yr.	1994	25.00	25
1995 A Well, Balanced Meal For Santa 592633	Yr.Iss.	1995	17.50	18
1994 What's Shakin' For Christmas 592668	Yr.Iss.	1994	18.50	19
1994 "A" For Santa 592676	Yr.Iss.	1994	17.50	18
1993 Celebrating With A Splash 592692	Yr.Iss.	1993	17.00	17
1994 Christmas Fly-By 592714	Yr.Iss.	1994	15.00	15
1993 Slimmin' Santa 592722	Yr.Iss.	1993	18.50	24
1993 Plane Ol' Holiday Fun 592773	Yr.Iss.	1993	27.50	28
1995 Salute 593133	Yr.Iss.	1995	22.50	23
1992 Wrappin' Up Warm Wishes 593141	Yr.Iss.	1992	17.50	18
1992 Christmas Biz 593168	2-Yr.	1993	22.50	23
1993 Smooth Move, Mom 593176	Yr.Iss.	1993	20.00	20
1993 Tool Time, Yule Time 593192	Yr.Iss.	1993	18.50	15-19
1993 Speedy 593370 - Zimnicki	2-Yr.	1994	25.00	25
1992 Holiday Take-Out 593508	Yr.Iss.	1992	17.50	18
1992 A Christmas Yarn 593516 - Gilmore	Yr.Iss.	1992	20.00	20
1993 On Your Mark, Set, Is That To Go? 593524	Yr.Iss.	1993	13.50	14
1993 Do Not Open 'Til Christmas 593737 - Hahn	2-Yr.	1994	15.00	15
1993 Greetings In Stereo 593745 - Hahn	Yr.Iss.	1993	19.50	20
1994 Santa...You're The Pops! 593761	Yr.Iss.	1994	22.50	23
1992 Treasure The Earth 593826 - Hahn	2-Yr.	1993	25.00	25
1994 Purdy Packages, Pardner! 593834	Yr.Iss.	1994	20.00	20
1994 Handle With Care 593842	Yr.Iss.	1994	20.00	20
1994 To Coin A Phrase, Merry Christmas 593877	Yr.Iss.	1994	20.00	20
1994 Featured Presentation 593885	Yr.Iss.	1994	20.00	20
1994 Christmas Fishes From Santa Paws 593893	Yr.Iss.	1994	18.50	19
1993 Tangled Up For Christmas 593974	2-Yr.	1994	14.50	15
1992 Toyful' Rudolph 593982	2-Yr.	1993	22.50	23
1992 Take A Chance On The Holidays 594075	3-Yr.	1994	20.00	20
1993 Sweet Season's Eatings 594202	Yr.Iss.	1993	22.50	23
1993 Have A Darn Good Christmas 594229 - Gilmore	2-Yr.	1994	21.00	21
1994 You Melt My Heart 594237 - Gilmore	Yr.Iss.	1994	15.00	15
1993 The Sweetest Ride 594253 - Gilmore	2-Yr.	1994	18.50	19
1994 Finishing First 594342 - Gilmore	Yr.Iss.	1994	20.00	20
1992 Lights..Camera..Christmas! 594369	2-Yr.	1993	20.00	20
1994 Yule Fuel 594385	Yr.Iss.	1994	20.00	20
1992 Spirited Stallion 594407	Yr.Iss.	1992	15.00	15
1993 Have A Cheery Christmas, Sister 594687	Yr.Iss.	1993	13.50	14
1993 Say Cheese 594962 - Gilmore	2-Yr.	1994	13.50	14
1993 Christmas Kicks 594989	Yr.Iss.	1993	17.50	18
1993 Time For Santa 594997 - Gilmore	2-Yr.	1994	17.50	18
1993 Holiday Orders 595004	Yr.Iss.	1993	20.00	20
1993 'Twas The Night Before Christmas 595012	Yr.Iss.	1993	22.50	23
1995 Filled To The Brim 595039 - Gilmore	Yr.Iss.	1995	25.00	25
1994 Toy Tinker Topper 595047 - Gilmore	Yr.Iss.	1994	20.00	20
1993 Sugar Chef Shoppe 595055 - Gilmore	2-Yr.	1994	23.50	24
1993 Merry Mc-Choo-Choo 595063	Yr.Iss.	1993	30.00	30
1993 Merry Christmas, Daughter 595098	Yr.Iss.	1993	20.00	20
1993 Rockin' With Santa 595195	2-Yr.	1994	13.50	14
1994 Santa Claus Is Comin' 595209	Yr.Iss.	1994	20.00	20
1993 Christmas-To-Go 595217	Yr.Iss.	1993	25.50	12-26
1994 Seasoned With Love 595268	Yr.Iss.	1994	22.50	23
1993 Sleddin' Mr. Snowman 595276	2-Yr.	1994	13.00	13
1993 A Kick Out Of Christmas 595373	2-Yr.	1994	10.00	10
1993 Friends Through Thick And Thin 595381	2-Yr.	1994	10.00	10
1993 See-Saw Sweethearts 595403	2-Yr.	1994	10.00	10
1993 Special Delivery For Santa 595411	2-Yr.	1994	10.00	10
1993 Top Marks For Teacher 595438	2-Yr.	1994	10.00	10
1993 Home Tweet Home 595446	2-Yr.	1994	10.00	10
1993 Clownin' Around 595454	2-Yr.	1994	10.00	10
1993 Heart Filled Dreams 595462	2-Yr.	1994	10.00	10
1993 Merry Christmas Baby 595470	2-Yr.	1994	10.00	10
1994 Sweet Dreams 595489	Yr.Iss.	1994	12.50	13
1994 Peace On Earth 595497	Yr.Iss.	1994	12.50	13
1994 Christmas Two-gether 595500	Yr.Iss.	1994	12.50	13
1994 Santa's L'il Helper 595519	Yr.Iss.	1994	12.50	13
1994 Expecting Joy 595527 - Hahn	Yr.Iss.	1994	12.50	13
1993 Your A Hit With Me, Brother 595535 - Hahn	Yr.Iss.	1993	10.00	10
1993 For A Sharp Uncle 595543	Yr.Iss.	1993	10.00	10
1993 Paint Your Holidays Bright 595551 - Hahn	2-Yr.	1994	10.00	10
1994 Sweet Greetings 595578	Yr.Iss.	1994	12.50	13
1994 Ring In The Holidays 595586 - Hahn	Yr.Iss.	1994	12.50	13
1994 Grandmas Are Sew Special 595594	Yr.Iss.	1994	12.50	13
1994 Holiday Catch 595608 - Hahn	Yr.Iss.	1994	12.50	13
1994 Bubblin' with Joy 595616	Yr.Iss.	1994	12.50	13
1992 A Watchful Eye 595713	Yr.Iss.	1992	15.00	15
1992 Good Catch 595721	Yr.Iss.	1992	12.50	13
1992 Squirrelin' It Away 595748 - Hahn	Yr.Iss.	1992	12.00	12
1992 Checkin' His List 595756	Yr.Iss.	1992	12.50	13
1992 Christmas Cat Nappin' 595764	Yr.Iss.	1992	12.00	12
1992 Bless Our Home 595772	Yr.Iss.	1992	12.00	12
1992 Salute the Season 595780 - Hahn	Yr.Iss.	1992	12.00	12
1992 Fired Up For Christmas 595799	Yr.Iss.	1992	12.00	12
1992 Speedin' Mr. Snowman 595802 - M. Rhyner-Nadig	Yr.Iss.	1992	12.00	12
1992 Merry Christmas Mother Earth 595810 - Hahn	Yr.Iss.	1992	11.00	11
1994 Mine, Mine, Mine 585815 - Davis	Yr.Iss.	1994	20.00	20
1992 Wear The Season With A Smile 595829	Yr.Iss.	1992	10.00	10
1992 Jesus Loves Me 595837 - Hahn	Yr.Iss.	1992	10.00	10
1994 Good Friends Are Forever 595950 - Gilmore	Yr.Iss.	1994	13.50	14
1993 Treasure The Holidays, Man! 596051	Yr.Iss.	1993	22.50	23
1993 Ariel's Under-The-Sea Tree 596078	Yr.Iss.	1993	20.00	20
1993 Here Comes Santa Claws 596086	Yr.Iss.	1993	22.50	35
1993 A Spot of Love 596094	Yr.Iss.	1993	17.50	18
1993 Hearts Aglow 596108	Yr.Iss.	1993	18.50	35
1993 Love's Sweet Dance 596116	Yr.Iss.	1993	25.00	25
1993 Holiday Wishes 596124	Yr.Iss.	1993	15.00	15
1993 Hangin Out For The Holidays 596132	Yr.Iss.	1993	15.00	35
1993 Magic Carpet Ride 596140	Yr.Iss.	1993	20.00	20
1993 Holiday Treasures 596159	Yr.Iss.	1993	18.50	35
1993 Happily Ever After 596167	Yr.Iss.	1993	22.50	23
1993 The Fairest Of Them All 596175	Yr.Iss.	1993	18.50	19
1994 Christmas Tee Time 596256	Yr.Iss.	1995	25.00	25
1994 Have a Merry Dairy Christmas 596264	Yr.Iss.	1994	22.50	23
1994 Happy Holi-date 596272 - Hahn	Yr.Iss.	1995	22.50	23
1994 O' Come All Ye Faithful 596280 - Hahn	Yr.Iss.	1994	15.00	15-75
1994 One Small Step... 596299 - Hahn	19,690	1994	25.00	45
1994 To My Favorite V.I.P. 596698	Yr.Iss.	1994	20.00	20
1993 December 25...Dear Diary 596809 - Hahn	2-Yr.	1994	10.00	10
1994 Building Memories 596876 - Hahn	Yr.Iss.	1994	25.00	25
1994 Open For Business 596906 - Hahn	Yr.Iss.	1994	17.50	18
1993 Wheel Merry Wishes 596930 - Hahn	2-Yr.	1994	15.00	15
1993 Good Grounds For Christmas 596957 - Hahn	Yr.Iss.	1993	24.50	25
1993 Ducking The Season's Rush 597597	Yr.Iss.	1993	17.50	18
1994 Twas The Nite Before Christmas 597643 - Gilmore	Yr.Iss.	1994	18.50	19
1993 Here Comes Rudolph® 597686	2-Yr.	1994	17.50	18
1993 It's Beginning To Look A Lot Like Christmas 597694	Yr.Iss.	1993	22.50	23
1993 Christmas In The Making 597716	Yr.Iss.	1993	20.00	20
1994 I Can Bear-ly Wait For A Coke™ 597724	Yr.Iss.	1995	18.50	19
1993 Mickey's Holiday Treasure 597759	Yr.Iss.	1993	12.00	12
1993 Dream Wheels/1953 Chevrolet Corvette 597856	Yr.Iss.	1993	29.50	50-75
1994 Gallant Greeting- 598313	Yr.Iss.	1994	15.00	20
1994 Merry Menage 598321	Yr.Iss.	1994	20.00	20
1993 All You Add Is Love 598429	Yr.Iss.	1993	18.50	19
1993 Goofy About Skiing 598631	Yr.Iss.	1993	22.50	23
1994 Ski-son's Greetings 599069	Yr.Iss.	1994	20.00	20
1994 Bundle Of Joy 598992	Yr.Iss.	1994	10.00	12-15
1994 Bundle Of Joy 599018	Yr.Iss.	1994	10.00	10
1994 Have A Dino-mite Christmas 599026 - Hahn	Yr.Iss.	1994	18.50	19
1994 Good Fortune To You 599034	Yr.Iss.	1994	25.00	25
1994 Building a Sew-man 599042	Yr.Iss.	1994	18.50	19
1994 Merry Memo-ries 599050	Yr.Iss.	1994	22.50	23
1994 Holiday Freezer Teaser 599085 - Gilmore	Yr.Iss.	1994	25.00	25
1994 Almost Time For Santa 599093 - Gilmore	Yr.Iss.	1994	25.00	25
1994 Santa's Secret Test Drive 599107 - Gilmore	Yr.Iss.	1994	20.00	20
1994 You're A Wheel Cool Brother 599115 - Gilmore	Yr.Iss.	1994	22.50	23
1994 Hand-Tossed Tidings 599166	Yr.Iss.	1994	17.50	18
1994 Tasty Take Off 599174	Yr.Iss.	1994	20.00	20
1994 Formula For Love 599530 - Olsen	Yr.Iss.	1994	10.00	10
1994 Santa's Ginger-bred Doe 599697 - Gilmore	Yr.Iss.	1994	15.00	15
1994 Nutcracker Sweetheart 599700	Yr.Iss.	1994	15.00	15
1994 Merry Reindeer Ride 599719	Yr.Iss.	1994	20.00	20
1994 Santa's Sing-A-Long 599727 - Gilmore	Yr.Iss.	1994	20.00	20
1994 A Holiday Opportunity 599735	Yr.Iss.	1995	20.00	20
1994 Holiday Stars 599743	Yr.Iss.	1994	20.00	20
1994 The Latest Mews From Home 653977	Yr.Iss.	1994	16.00	16
1989 Tea For Two 693758 - N. Teiber	2-Yr.	1990	12.50	30
1990 Holiday Tea Toast 694770 - N. Teiber	2-Yr.	1991	13.50	14
1991 It's Tea-lightful 694789	2-Yr.	1992	13.50	14
1989 Tea Time 694797 - N. Teiber	2-Yr.	1990	12.50	30
1989 Bottom's Up 1989 830003	Yr.Iss.	1989	11.00	32
1990 Sweetest Greetings 1990 830011 - Gilmore	Yr.Iss.	1990	10.00	27
1990 First Class Christmas 830038 - Gilmore	3-Yr.	1992	10.00	10
1989 Caught In The Act 830046 - Gilmore	3-Yr.	1991	12.50	13
1989 Readin' & Ridin' 830054 - Gilmore	3-Yr.	1991	13.50	34
1991 Beary Merry Mailman 830151 - L. Rigg	3-Yr.	1993	13.50	14
1990 Here's Looking at You! 830259 - Gilmore	2-Yr.	1991	17.50	18
1991 Stamper 830267 - S. Zimnicki	Yr.Iss.	1991	13.50	14
1991 Santa's Key Man 830461 - Gilmore	2-Yr.	1992	11.00	11
1991 Tie-dings Of Joy 830488 - Gilmore	Yr.Iss.	1991	12.00	12
1990 Have a Cool Yule 830496 - Gilmore	3-Yr.	1992	12.00	27
1990 Slots of Luck 830518 - Hahn	2-Yr.	1991	13.50	45-60
1991 Straight To Santa 830534 - J. Davis	2-Yr.	1992	13.50	14
1993 A Toast Ladled With Love 830828 - Hahn	2-Yr.	1994	15.00	15
1991 Letters To Santa 830925 - Gilmore	2-Yr.	1992	15.00	15
1991 Sneaking Santa's Snack 830933 - Gilmore	3-Yr.	1993	13.00	13
1991 Aiming For The Holidays 830941 - Gilmore	2-Yr.	1992	12.00	12
1991 Ode To Joy 830968 - Gilmore	3-Yr.	1993	10.00	10
1991 Fittin' Mittens 830976 - Gilmore	3-Yr.	1993	12.00	12
1992 Merry Kisses 831166	2-Yr.	1993	17.50	18
1992 Christmas Is In The Air 831174	2-Yr.	1993	25.00	25
1992 To The Point 831182	2-Yr.	1993	13.50	14
1992 Poppin' Hoppin' Holidays 831263 - Gilmore	Yr.Iss.	1992	25.00	25
1992 Tankful Tidings 831271 - Gilmore	2-Yr.	1993	30.00	30
1991 The Finishing Touch 831530 - Gilmore	Yr.Iss.	1991	10.00	10
1992 Ginger-Bred Greetings 831581 - Gilmore	Yr.Iss.	1992	12.00	10-12
1991 A Real Classic 831603 - Gilmore	Yr.Iss.	1991	10.00	10
1993 Delivered to The Nick In Time 831808 - Gilmore	2-Yr.	1994	13.50	14
1993 Sneaking A Peek 831840 - Gilmore	2-Yr.	1994	10.00	10
1993 Jewel Box Ballet 831859 - Hahn	2-Yr.	1994	20.00	20
1993 A Mistle-Tow 831867 - Gilmore	2-Yr.	1994	15.00	15
1991 Christmas Fills The Air 831921 - Gilmore	3-Yr.	1993	12.00	12
1992 A Gold Star For Teacher 831948 - Gilmore	3-Yr.	1994	15.00	15
1992 A Tall Order 832758 - Gilmore	3-Yr.	1994	12.00	12
1992 Candlelight Serenade 832766 - Gilmore	2-Yr.	1993	12.00	12
1992 Holiday Glow Puppet Show 832774 - Gilmore	3-Yr.	1994	15.00	15
1992 Christopher Columouse 832782 - Gilmore	Yr.Iss.	1992	12.00	12
1992 Cartin' Home Holiday Treats 832790	2-Yr.	1993	13.50	14
1992 Making Tracks To Santa 832804 - Gilmore	2-Yr.	1993	15.00	15
1992 Special Delivery 832812	2-Yr.	1993	12.00	12
1992 A Mug Full Of Love 832928 - Gilmore	Yr.Iss.	1992	13.50	14
1993 Grandma's Liddle Griddle 832936 - Gilmore	Yr.Iss.	1993	10.00	10
1992 Have A Cool Christmas 832944 - Gilmore	Yr.Iss.	1992	13.50	14
1992 Knittin' Kittens 832952 - Gilmore	Yr.Iss.	1992	17.50	18
1992 Holiday Honors 833029 - Gilmore	Yr.Iss.	1992	15.00	15
1993 To A Grade "A" Teacher 833037 - Gilmore	2-Yr.	1994	10.00	10
1992 Christmas Nite Cap 834424 - Gilmore	3-Yr.	1994	13.50	14
1993 Have A Cool Christmas 834467 - Gilmore	2-Yr.	1994	10.00	10
1993 For A Star Aunt 834556 - Gilmore	Yr.Iss.	1993	12.00	12
1994 You're A Winner Son! 834564 - Gilmore	Yr.Iss.	1994	18.50	19
1994 Especially For You 834580 - Gilmore	Yr.Iss.	1994	27.50	28
1992 North Pole Peppermint Patrol 840157 - Gilmore	2-Yr.	1993	25.00	25
1992 A Boot-iful Christmas 840165 - Gilmore	Yr.Iss.	1992	20.00	20
1994 Watching For Santa 840432	2-Yr.	1994	25.00	30
1992 Special Delivery 840440	Yr.Iss.	1992	22.50	23
1991 Deck The Halls 860573 - M. Peters	3-Yr.	1993	12.00	12
1991 Bathing Beauty 860581 - Hahn	3-Yr.	1993	13.50	35

United Design Corp.

Angels Collection-Tree Ornaments™ - P.J. Jonas, unless otherwise noted

YEAR ISSUE	EDITION LIMIT	YEAR RETD.	ISSUE PRICE	*QUOTE U.S.$
1992 Angel and Tambourine IBO-422 - S. Bradford	Retrd.	1997	20.00	20
1992 Angel and Tambourine, ivory IBO-425 - S. Bradford	Retrd.	1997	20.00	20
1993 Angel Baby w/ Bunny IBO-426 - D. Newburn	Retrd.	1996	23.00	24
1996 Angel w/Doves on Cloud IBO-472	Retrd.	1998	25.00	25
1996 Angel w/Doves on Cloud, blue IBO-473	Retrd.	1998	25.00	25
1991 Angel Waif, ivory IBO-411	Retrd.	1998	15.00	20
1993 Angel Waif, plum IBO-437	Retrd.	1996	20.00	20
1995 Autumn's Bounty IBO-460	Retrd.	1997	32.00	32
1995 Autumn's Bounty, light IBO-454	Retrd.	1997	32.00	32
1995 Birds of a Feather IBO-457	Retrd.	1998	27.00	27
1990 Crystal Angel IBO-401	Retrd.	1993	20.00	20
1993 Crystal Angel, emerald IBO-446	Retrd.	1997	20.00	20
1990 Crystal Angel, ivory IBO-405	Retrd.	1997	20.00	20
1991 Fra Angelico Drummer, blue IBO-414 - S. Bradford	Retrd.	1997	20.00	20
1991 Fra Angelico Drummer, ivory IBO-420 - S. Bradford	Retrd.	1997	20.00	20
1991 Girl Cupid w/Rose, ivory IBO-413 - S. Bradford	Retrd.	1997	15.00	20
1995 Heavenly Blossoms IBO-458	Retrd.	1997	27.00	27
1993 Heavenly Harmony IBO-428	Retrd.	1997	25.00	30
1993 Heavenly Harmony, crimson IBO-433	Retrd.	1998	22.00	30
1993 Little Angel IBO-430 - D. Newburn	Retrd.	1998	18.00	20
1993 Little Angel, crimson IBO-445 - D. Newburn	Retrd.	1996	18.00	20
1992 Mary and Dove IBO-424 - S. Bradford	Retrd.	1997	20.00	20
1994 Music and Grace IBO-448	Retrd.	1998	24.00	25
1994 Music and Grace, crimson IBO-449	Retrd.	1997	24.00	24
1994 Musical Flight IBO-450	Retrd.	1997	28.00	28
1994 Musical Flight, crimson IBO-451	Retrd.	1997	28.00	28

*Quotes have been rounded up to nearest dollar

United Design Corp.
to Walt Disney

ORNAMENTS

YEAR ISSUE	EDITION LIMIT	YEAR RETD.	ISSUE PRICE	*QUOTE U.S.$
1991 Peace Descending, ivory IBO-412	Retrd.	1997	20.00	20
1993 Peace Descending, crimson IBO-436	Retrd.	1997	20.00	20
1993 Renaissance Angel IBO-429	Retrd.	1997	24.00	24
1993 Renaissance Angel, crimson IBO-431	Retrd.	1997	24.00	24
1990 Rose of Sharon IBO-402	Retrd.	1993	20.00	20
1993 Rose of Sharon, crimson IBO-439	Retrd.	1997	20.00	20
1990 Rose of Sharon, ivory IBO-406	Retrd.	1998	20.00	20
1993 Rosetti Angel, crimson IBO-434	Retrd.	1997	20.00	24
1991 Rosetti Angel, ivory IBO-410	Retrd.	1998	20.00	24
1995 Special Wishes IBO-456 - D. Newburn	Retrd.	1998	27.00	27
1995 Spring's Rebirth IBO-452	Retrd.	1998	32.00	32
1996 Spring's Rebirth, green IBO-474	Retrd.	1998	25.00	25
1992 St. Francis and Critters IBO-423 - S. Bradford	Retrd.	1997	20.00	20
1994 Star Flight IBO-447	Retrd.	1998	20.00	20
1996 Star Flight, sapphire IBO-475	Retrd.	1998	20.00	20
1990 Star Glory IBO-403	Retrd.	1993	15.00	15
1993 Star Glory, crimson IBO-438	Retrd.	1997	20.00	20
1990 Star Glory, ivory IBO-407	Retrd.	1997	15.00	20
1993 Stars & Lace IBO-427	Retrd.	1998	18.00	20
1993 Stars & Lace, emerald IBO-432	Retrd.	1998	18.00	20
1995 Summer's Glory IBO-453	Retrd.	1998	32.00	32
1996 Summer's Glory, green IBO-476	Retrd.	1998	25.00	25
1995 Tender Time IBO-459	Retrd.	1997	27.00	27
1990 Victorian Angel IBO-404	Retrd.	1993	15.00	15
1990 Victorian Angel, ivory IBO-408	Retrd.	1997	15.00	20
1993 Victorian Angel, plum IBO-435	Retrd.	1997	18.00	20
1993 Victorian Cupid, crimson IBO-440	Retrd.	1998	15.00	20
1991 Victorian Cupid, ivory IBO-409	Retrd.	1998	15.00	20
1995 Winter's Light IBO-455	Retrd.	1997	32.00	32
1996 Wooden Angel IBO-461 - M. Ramsey	Retrd.	1998	20.00	20

Teddy Angels™ - P.J. Jonas

YEAR ISSUE	EDITION LIMIT	YEAR RETD.	ISSUE PRICE	*QUOTE U.S.$
1995 Casey "You're a bright & shining star." BA-017	Retrd.	1998	13.00	13
1995 Ivy "Enchantment glows in winter snows." BA-018	Retrd.	1998	13.00	13

Wallace Silversmiths

Annual Pewter Bells - Wallace

YEAR ISSUE	EDITION LIMIT	YEAR RETD.	ISSUE PRICE	*QUOTE U.S.$
1992 Angel	Closed	1992	25.00	20-40
1993 Santa Holding List	Closed	1993	25.00	20-25
1994 Large Santa Bell	Closed	1994	25.00	20-25
1995 Santa Bell	Closed	1995	25.00	25
1996 Santa Bell (North Pole)	Closed	1996	25.00	20-25
1997 Santa Bell	Closed	1997	25.00	20-25
1998 Santa Bell Workshop	Closed	1998	30.00	30
1999 Santa Bell Sleigh	Closed	1999	30.00	30
2000 Santa Decorating Tree	Yr.Iss.		30.00	30

Annual Silverplated Sleigh Bells - Wallace

YEAR ISSUE	EDITION LIMIT	YEAR RETD.	ISSUE PRICE	*QUOTE U.S.$
1971 1st Edition Sleigh Bell	Closed	1971	12.95	600-1000
1972 2nd Edition Sleigh Bell	Closed	1972	12.95	400-600
1973 3rd Edition Sleigh Bell	Closed	1973	12.95	300-400
1974 4th Edition Sleigh Bell	Closed	1974	13.95	175-400
1975 5th Edition Sleigh Bell	Closed	1975	13.95	200-275
1976 6th Edition Sleigh Bell	Closed	1976	13.95	200-275
1977 7th Edition Sleigh Bell	Closed	1977	14.95	150-240
1978 8th Edition Sleigh Bell	Closed	1978	14.95	40-45
1979 9th Edition Sleigh Bell	Closed	1979	15.95	40-45
1980 10th Edition Sleigh Bell	Closed	1980	18.95	40-50
1981 11th Edition Sleigh Bell	Closed	1981	18.95	40-50
1982 12th Edition Sleigh Bell	Closed	1982	19.95	50-100
1983 13th Edition Sleigh Bell	Closed	1983	19.95	50-74
1984 14th Edition Sleigh Bell	Closed	1984	21.95	50-60
1985 15th Edition Sleigh Bell	Closed	1985	21.95	50-77
1986 16th Edition Sleigh Bell	Closed	1986	21.95	40-50
1987 17th Edition Sleigh Bell	Closed	1987	21.99	40-50
1988 18th Edition Sleigh Bell	Closed	1988	21.99	40-50
1989 19th Edition Sleigh Bell	Closed	1989	24.99	44-60
1990 20th Edition Sleigh Bell	Closed	1990	25.00	36-40
1990 Special Edition Sleigh Bell, gold	Closed	1990	35.00	40-60
1991 21st Edition Sleigh Bell	Closed	1991	25.00	40-50
1992 22nd Edition Sleigh Bell	Closed	1992	25.00	40-45
1993 23rd Edition Sleigh Bell	Closed	1993	25.00	40
1994 24th Edition Sleigh Bell	Closed	1994	25.00	40-42
1994 Sleigh Bell, gold	Closed	1994	35.00	35-45
1995 25th Edition Sleigh Bell	Closed	1995	30.00	30-40
1995 Sleigh Bell, gold	Closed	1995	35.00	30-40
1996 26th Edition Sleigh Bell	Closed	1996	30.00	35-45
1996 Sleigh Bell, gold	Closed	1996	35.00	35-40
1997 27th Edition Sleigh Bell	Closed	1997	30.00	25-30
1997 Sleigh Bell, gold	Closed	1997	35.00	30-35
1998 28th Edition Sleigh Bell	Closed	1998	30.00	30
1998 Sleigh Bell, gold	Closed	1998	35.00	35
1999 29th Edition Sleigh Bell	Closed	1999	30.00	30
1999 Sleigh Bell, gold	Closed	1999	35.00	35
2000 30th Edition Sleigh Bell	Yr.Iss.		35.00	35
2000 Sleigh Bell, gold	Yr.Iss.		40.00	40

Candy Canes - Wallace

YEAR ISSUE	EDITION LIMIT	YEAR RETD.	ISSUE PRICE	*QUOTE U.S.$
1981 Peppermint	Closed	1981	8.95	120-300
1982 Wintergreen	Closed	1982	9.95	83-95
1983 Cinnamon	Closed	1983	10.95	70-110
1984 Clove	Closed	1984	10.95	60-110
1985 Dove Motif	Closed	1985	11.95	50-59
1986 Bell Motif	Closed	1986	11.95	30-120
1987 Teddy Bear Motif	Closed	1987	12.95	75-135
1988 Christmas Rose	Closed	1988	13.99	60-76
1989 Christmas Candle	Closed	1989	14.99	30-40
1990 Reindeer	Closed	1990	16.00	30-35
1991 Christmas Goose	Closed	1991	16.00	15-30
1992 Angel	Closed	1992	16.00	30-38
1993 Snowmen	Closed	1993	16.00	25-30
1994 Canes	Closed	1994	17.00	15-20
1995 Santa	Closed	1995	18.00	20-38
1996 Soldiers	Closed	1996	18.00	21
1997 Candy Cane	Closed	1997	18.00	18-20
1998 Snowman	Closed	1998	18.00	18
1999 Reindeer	Closed	1999	18.00	18
2000 Bells and Ribbons	Yr.Iss.		18.00	18

Cathedral Ornaments - Wallace

YEAR ISSUE	EDITION LIMIT	YEAR RETD.	ISSUE PRICE	*QUOTE U.S.$
1988 1988-1st Edition	Closed	1988	24.99	15-45
1989 1989-2nd Edition	Closed	1989	24.99	15-30
1990 1990-3rd Edition	Closed	1990	25.00	15-25

Grande Baroque 12 Day Series - Wallace

YEAR ISSUE	EDITION LIMIT	YEAR RETD.	ISSUE PRICE	*QUOTE U.S.$
1988 Partridge	Closed	1988	39.99	40-65
1989 Two Turtle Doves	Closed	1989	39.99	65-80
1990 Three French Hens	Closed	1990	40.00	60
1991 Four Colly Birds	Closed	1991	40.00	55-75
1992 Five Golden Rings	Closed	1992	40.00	50
1993 Six Geese-a-Laying	Closed	1993	40.00	50
1994 Seven Swans-a-Swimming	Closed	1994	40.00	32-50
1995 Eight Maids-a-Milking	Closed	1995	40.00	32-45
1996 Nine Ladies Dancing	Closed	1996	40.00	45
1997 Ten Lords Aleaping	Closed	1997	40.00	40-45
1998 Eleven Pipers Piping	Closed	1998	40.00	40
1999 Twelve Drummers Drumming	Closed	1999	40.00	40

Walnut Ridge Collectibles

Gossamer Wings - K. Bejma

YEAR ISSUE	EDITION LIMIT	YEAR RETD.	ISSUE PRICE	*QUOTE U.S.$
1996 Charity Piece - Glimmer of Hope I	Yr.Iss.	1996	40.00	40
1997 Charity Piece - Glimmer of Hope II	Yr.Iss.	1997	40.00	46
1998 Charity Piece - Glimmer of Hope III	Yr.Iss.	1998	36.00	36
1999 Charity Piece - Glimmer of Hope IV	Yr.Iss.	1999	36.00	36

Limited Edition Christmas Ornament - K. Bejma

YEAR ISSUE	EDITION LIMIT	YEAR RETD.	ISSUE PRICE	*QUOTE U.S.$
1996 Snowy, Snowy Night 703	Yr.Iss.	1996	56.00	56

Ornament Collection - K. Bejma

YEAR ISSUE	EDITION LIMIT	YEAR RETD.	ISSUE PRICE	*QUOTE U.S.$
1997 Acorn 68	Retrd.	1999	22.00	24
1997 Angel 84	Retrd.	1999	30.00	30
1999 Angel Bell T-12	Open		36.00	36
1994 Angel Bunny 21	Retrd.	1997	26.00	30
1995 Angel Donkey 24	Open		26.00	30
1995 Angel Elephant 23	Open		26.00	30
1996 Angel Frog 40	Open		22.00	24
1997 Angel Holding Child 52	Open		30.00	36
1993 Angel Icicle 9	Retrd.	1996	22.00	22
1994 Angel Kitty 20	Retrd.	1997	26.00	30
1999 Angel on Shooting Star T-13	Open		34.00	34
1998 Angel on World T-5	Retrd.	1999	36.00	36
1997 Angel Penguin 82	Open		30.00	30
1994 Angel Pig 22	Open		26.00	30
1996 Angel w/Star on Wand 35	Retrd.	1999	24.00	30
1997 Angel with 2 Children 53	Open		30.00	36
1997 Angel with Doves 51	Retrd.	1998	30.00	36
2000 Angel with Muff T20	Open		34.00	34
1994 Angels, set/3 15	Retrd.	1997	66.00	76
1995 Angels, set/3 18	Retrd.	1997	66.00	72
1998 Angels, set/3 94	Open		76.00	76
1997 Artichoke 67	Retrd.	1999	22.00	24
1997 Asparagus 66	Retrd.	1999	22.00	24
1997 Baby on Crescent Moon 50	Open		30.00	36
1993 Baby Snowman Icicle 12	Retrd.	1996	22.00	22
1996 Baby's First 33	Retrd.	1999	30.00	36
1998 Basket 78	Open		26.00	26
1997 Bear Angel 61	Open		26.00	30
1996 Black and White Bunny 28	Open		26.00	30
2000 Black Cat T22	Open		24.00	24
1999 Black Lab Angel T-16	Open		30.00	30
1997 Blue Father Xmas 56	Open		22.00	24
2000 Buffalo Angel T22	Open		34.00	34
1996 Calico Cat 27	Open		26.00	32
1998 Candy Cane Santa 91	Open		36.00	36
2000 Candy Stripe Snowman (Gold Star Dealers) T29	Yr.Iss.		30.00	30
1995 Carrot-cicle 17	Retrd.	1999	22.00	30
1998 Carrots, set/12 79	Open		48.00	48
1996 Cat-cicle 36	Retrd.	1999	22.00	28
1996 Cat-cicle w/Stocking 37	Retrd.	1999	22.00	26
1998 Celestial Santa 92	Open		36.00	36
1999 Charity IV T-6	Retrd.	1999	36.00	36
2000 Charity V T24	Open		36.00	36
1993 Cherub Icicle 8	Retrd.	1996	22.00	22
1997 Cherubs, set/3 83	Open		54.00	54
1998 Chicks, set/3 74	Open		44.00	44
2000 Chihuahua Angel T37	Open		30.00	30
1997 Chili Pepper 62	Retrd.	1999	22.00	24
1997 Christmas Tree 89	Open		26.00	26
2000 Collie Angel T36	Open		30.00	30
1997 Corkscrew Santa 58	Open		22.00	24
1997 Corn 65	Retrd.	1999	22.00	24
2000 Crescent Moon Santa T26	Open		38.00	38
1996 Crescent Santa 29	Retrd.	1999	28.00	36
1998 Dog Angel 97	Open		30.00	30
1997 Dolphin Angel 86	Open		30.00	30
1997 Eggplant 64	Retrd.	1999	22.00	24
1993 Father Christmas Icicle 13	Retrd.	1996	22.00	22
1994 Father Christmas, set/3 16	Retrd.	1997	66.00	80
1993 Father Snowman Icicle 10	Retrd.	1996	22.00	22
1997 Giraffe Angel 41	Open		28.00	36
1996 Golden Father Christmas 38	Open		24.00	30
1997 Golden Top Father Xmas 57	Open		22.00	24
1997 Green Pepper 63	Retrd.	1999	22.00	24
1997 Ice Top Santa 55	Retrd.	1999	24.00	26
2000 Icicle Santa Head T28	Open		34.00	34
1997 Kangaroo Angel 43	Open		26.00	30
1996 Kitty Angel 34	Retrd.	1999	24.00	30
1998 Lace Egg, oblong 76	Open		26.00	26
1998 Lace Egg, upright 75	Open		26.00	26
1998 Lacy Eggs, set/6 81	Open		64.00	64
1998 Lacy Hearts, set/5 77	Open		60.00	60
1999 Lamb Angel T-15	Open		26.00	26
1993 Mother Snowman Icicle 11	Retrd.	1996	22.00	24
1994 Nutcracker 30	Retrd.	1997	22.00	24
1995 Nutcracker 31	Retrd.	1997	22.00	24
1996 Nutcracker 32	Retrd.	1997	22.00	24
1998 Ostrich Angel 99	Open		36.00	36
1999 Patriotic Santa T-8	Open		28.00	28
1997 Peach 69	Retrd.	1999	22.00	22
1998 Pegasus Angel 98	Open		36.00	36
1998 Pinecone with Holly 93	Open		24.00	24
1998 Pinecone, lg. T 2	Open		24.00	24
1997 Pinetree Santa 54	Retrd.	1999	24.00	26
1997 Polar Bear Angel 42	Open		26.00	30
1999 Pumpkin Basket T-18	Open		20.00	20
2000 Pumpkin Face T31	Open		24.00	24
2000 Pumpkin Man T32	Open		24.00	24
1995 Reindeer 26	Retrd.	1999	22.00	30
1997 Reindeer Angel 88	Open		30.00	30
1999 Rooster Angel T-17	Open		30.00	30
1997 Santa Bell 59	Open		30.00	40
1997 Santa Face, lg. 45	Open		30.00	34
1993 Santa Icicle 14	Retrd.	1996	22.00	25
1999 Santa Star T-10	Open		26.00	26
1998 Santa's Heads, set/3 T-1	Open		78.00	78
2000 Scottie Angel T35	Open		30.00	30
2000 Seal Angel T25	Open		30.00	30
1995 Snow Family, set/3 19	Retrd.	1997	66.00	80
1999 Snowangel T-7	Open		26.00	26
1998 Snowbaby T-4	Open		24.00	24
2000 Snowflake Santa Head T27	12/00		40.00	40
1999 Snowgirl Angel T-14	Open		28.00	28
1999 Snowgirl with Candle T-19	Open		30.00	30
1997 Snowman Face 48	Open		24.00	26
1997 Snowman Icicle/Stocking Hat 47	Retrd.	1999	24.00	26
1997 Snowman Icicle/Top Hat 46	Retrd.	1999	24.00	26
1997 Snowman with Cane 49	Open		26.00	30
1996 Snowman, set/2 39	Retrd.	1999	44.00	54
2000 Spiral Angel (Gold Star Dealers) T30	Yr.Iss.		38.00	38
1998 Spiral Snowman T-3	Open		26.00	26
1997 Spring Bunnies, set/2 90	Open		60.00	60
2000 Stork with Baby T21	Open		40.00	40
1995 Tabby/Holly Bunch 25	Retrd.	1999	30.00	30
1998 Tiger Angel 95	Open		36.00	36
1997 Tricolor Pinecones, set/3 44	Retrd.	2000	48.00	50
1997 Turtle Angel 60	Open		24.00	26
1998 Victorian Ball, oblong 73	Open		24.00	24
1998 Victorian Ball, round 72	Open		24.00	24
1998 Victorian Ball/1 Cherub 71	Open		28.00	28
1998 Victorian Ball/4 Cherubs 70	Open		30.00	30
1999 Victorian Santa Face T-9	Open		24.00	24
1997 Whale Angel 87	Open		30.00	30
2000 Whimsical Snowman T23	Open		34.00	34
2000 White Santa Head T34	Open		28.00	28
1999 Windblown Santa T-11	Open		24.00	24
1998 Zebra Angel 96	Open		36.00	36

Walt Disney

Annual Ball Ornaments - Disney Studios

YEAR ISSUE	EDITION LIMIT	YEAR RETD.	ISSUE PRICE	*QUOTE U.S.$
1999 On Ice 1200909	Closed	1999	40.00	40
2000 Pluto's Xmas Tree 1210003	Yr.Iss.		40.00	40

Boxed Ornament Set- Disney Studios

YEAR ISSUE	EDITION LIMIT	YEAR RETD.	ISSUE PRICE	*QUOTE U.S.$
1999 Snow White & The Seven Dwarfs 1204380	5,000		395.00	395
2000 Pinocchio 1209687	5,000		375.00	375

Disney's Enchanted Castles - Disney Studios

YEAR ISSUE	EDITION LIMIT	YEAR RETD.	ISSUE PRICE	*QUOTE U.S.$
1998 A Castle for Cinderella 41293	Open		45.00	45
1998 The Beast's Castle 41294	Open		45.00	45
1999 Sleeping Beauty Castle 41391	Open		45.00	45
2000 Snow White Castle 1209689	Open		45.00	45

Disney's Enchanted Places - Disney Studios

YEAR ISSUE	EDITION LIMIT	YEAR RETD.	ISSUE PRICE	*QUOTE U.S.$
1997 Cruella's Car 41245	Retrd.	1999	45.00	45
1997 An Elegant Coach for Cinderella 41244	Retrd.	1999	45.00	45
1996 Grandpa's House from Peter & The Wolf 41222	Closed	1996	35.00	35
1997 The Jolly Roger 41243	Retrd.	1999	45.00	45

Mickey's Christmas Carol - Disney Studios

YEAR ISSUE	EDITION LIMIT	YEAR RETD.	ISSUE PRICE	*QUOTE U.S.$
1998 Jiminy Cricket: "Ghost of Christmas Past" 41251	Retrd.	1999	50.00	50
1997 Mickey Mouse: "And a Merry Christmas to you..." 41144	Retrd.	1999	50.00	50
1997 Minnie Mouse: Mrs. Crachit 41145	Retrd.	1999	50.00	50
1997 Scrooge: "Bah-humbug!" 41146	Retrd.	1999	50.00	50

Walt Disney Classics Collection-Holiday Series - Disney Studios

YEAR ISSUE	EDITION LIMIT	YEAR RETD.	ISSUE PRICE	*QUOTE U.S.$
1995 Mickey Mouse: "Presents for My Pals" 41087	Closed	1995	40.00	25-75

526 Collectors' Information Bureau

*Quotes have been rounded up to nearest dollar

YEAR ISSUE	EDITION LIMIT	YEAR RETD.	ISSUE PRICE	*QUOTE U.S.$
1996 Pluto: Pluto Helps Decorate 41113	Closed	1996	50.00	29-50
1997 Chip 'n Dale: Little Mischief Makers 41190	Closed	1997	50.00	30-60
1998 Minnie Mouse: Caroler Minnie 41311	Closed	1998	50.00	50
1999 Goofy: "Tis the Season to Be Jolly" 41368	Closed	1999	50.00	50
2000 Donald Duck: "Fa La La..." 1207742	Yr.Iss.		50.00	50

Walt Disney Classics Special Events - Disney Studios

1998 Simba 41256	Closed	1998	49.00	44-55
1998 Dumbo 41283	Closed	1998	50.00	50-55

Willitts Designs

Orna Magic™ Lighted Motion - Willitts Designs

1999 Angel	Open		15.99	16
1999 Ballerina	Open		15.99	16
1999 Christmas Tree	Open		15.99	16
1999 Colorful Bell	Open		15.99	16
1999 Fireplace	Open		15.99	16
1999 Jack-in-the-Box	Open		15.99	16
1999 Ornaments	Open		15.99	16
1999 Santa and Reindeer	Open		15.99	16
1999 Santa Down Chimney	Open		15.99	16
1999 Snowman	Open		15.99	16

Rainbow Babies - A. Blackshear

1998 Flutterby	Retrd.	1999	28.50	29

Thomas Blackshear's Ebony Visions - T. Blackshear

1997 Little Blue Wings	17,200	1997	28.50	183-200
1998 On Wings of Praise	23,200	1998	29.50	62-95
1999 Peace on Earth	24,200	1999	29.50	41-55
2000 Joy To The World	Yr.Iss.	2000	27.50	28

Woodland Winds/Christopher Radko

Woodland Winds Glass Ornaments - C. Radko

1998 Balancing Act 98-820-0	Retrd.	1999	47.00	47
1999 Balancing Act Jr. 99-924-0	Open		26.00	26
1998 Bearly Napping 98-715-0	Retrd.	1999	36.00	36
1998 Blizzard Baron 98-822-0	Retrd.	1999	42.00	42
1998 Blizzard Santa 98-811-0	Retrd.	1999	45.00	45
1999 Blizzard Snow Angel 99-811-0	Retrd.	1999	36.00	36
1998 Blizzard's Tree 98-818-0	Retrd.	1999	39.00	39
1998 Bunny Drifter 98-714-0	Retrd.	1999	36.00	36
1999 Carlton 'cicle 99-714-0	Retrd.	1999	42.00	42
1998 Carlton The Snowman 98-712-0	Retrd.	1999	42.00	42
1998 Deer Friends Wreath 98-815-0	Retrd.	1999	39.00	39
1998 Emerald Nuts & Berries 98-717-0	Open		80.00	80
1998 Flying Squirrel 98-716-0	Retrd.	1999	36.00	36
1999 Frosty Leaf Jr. 99-715-0	Open		26.00	26
1998 Frosty Leaf Santa 98-711-0	Retrd.	1999	47.00	47
1998 Guardian Angel 98-821-0	Retrd.	1999	42.00	42
1998 Maple Frost 98-489-0	Open		26.00	26
1998 Mini Maple Frost 98-148-0	Open		18.00	18
1998 Mini Oak Frost 98-164-0	Open		18.00	18
1999 Nana Leaf 99-713-0	Open		42.00	42
1998 Oak Frost 98-490-0	Open		26.50	27
1999 Pinecone Perch 99-817-0	Retrd.	1999	38.00	38
1999 Santa 'cicle 99-712-0	Retrd.	1999	34.00	34
1998 Santa's Leaf Ride 98-713-0	Retrd.	1999	45.00	45
1998 Scarlet Nuts & Berries 98-718-0	Open		80.00	80
1998 Snow Bunny 98-813-0	Retrd.	1999	45.00	45
1998 Snow Racer 98-814-0	Retrd.	1999	39.00	39
1998 Snow Tunes 98-812-0	Retrd.	1999	45.00	45
1999 Some Bunnies In Love 99-810-0	Retrd.	1999	38.00	38
1998 Stardust Santa 98-817-0	Retrd.	1999	47.00	47
1999 StarDust Santa Jr. 99-926-0	Open		28.00	28
1998 Stardust Snowflake 98-816-0	Retrd.	1999	47.00	47
1999 Stardust Tree Topper 99-815-0	Retrd.	1999	65.00	65
1999 Stardust World 99-813-0	Retrd.	1999	38.00	38
1999 Stuck In A Snowball 99-812-0	Retrd.	1999	28.00	28
1998 Surrounded by Friends 98-819-0	Retrd.	1999	49.00	49

Woodland Winds Porcelain Ornaments - C. Radko

1998 Balancing Act 98-837-0	Retrd.	1999	14.00	14
1998 Bearly Drifting 98-732-0	Open		12.00	12
1998 Bunny Drifter 98-733-0	Retrd.	1999	12.00	12
2000 Burl's Gift Giving 00-835-0	Open		15.00	15
1999 Carlton 'cicle 99-725-0	Open		16.00	16
2000 Carlton Bell 00-735-0	Open		15.00	15
2000 Carlton Charm Leaf 00-743-0	Open		12.50	13
1998 Carlton The Snowman 98-729-0	Open		20.00	20
2000 Carved Bear 00-747-0	Open		8.00	8
2000 Carved Bunny 00-748-0	Open		8.00	8
2000 Carved Fox 00-746-0	Open		8.00	8
2000 Carved Squirrel 00-749-0	Open		8.00	8
2000 Carved Wooden Snowflake 00-737-0	Open		4.50	5
1999 Chickadee Snowflake 99-729-0	Open		10.00	10
1998 Close To My Heart 98-832-0	Retrd.	1999	12.00	12
2000 Country Cottage 00-740-0	Open		12.50	13
2000 Crystal Ride 00-842-0	Open		15.00	15
2000 Crystal Sleeping 00-841-0	Open		15.00	15
1999 Dream 'cicle 99-827-0	Open		16.00	16
1999 Floating Fun 99-726-0	Open		16.00	16
1998 Floating Leaf Santa 98-725-0	Open		16.00	16
1999 Frosty Leaf In Love 99-736-0	Open		17.00	17
1998 Frosty Leaf Santa 98-726-0	Open		22.50	23
1998 Frosty Leaf Santa 98-728-0	Retrd.	1999	20.00	20
2000 Frosty Leaf Santa Bell 00-736-0	Open		15.00	15
2000 Frosty Leaf Santa Charm Leaf 00-742-0	Open		12.50	13
1998 Frosty Leaf Santa w/Bear 98-730-0	Retrd.	1999	16.00	16
2000 Frosty Love Wreath 00-741-0	Open		15.00	15
1998 Good Catch 98-838-0	Retrd.	1999	12.00	12
1998 Gotcha 98-835-0	Retrd.	1999	12.00	12
1998 Guardian Angel 98-836-0	Open		12.00	12
1999 Hale On Snowflake 99-829-0	Open		15.00	15
2000 Hale Snowflake Ring 00-845-0	Open		15.00	15
2000 Hang on Hudson! 00-738-0	Open		12.50	13
1998 High Flying 98-827-0	Retrd.	1999	12.00	12
1999 Holiday Swing 99-734-0	Open		18.00	18
2000 Hudson Wreath 00-739-0	Open		12.50	13
1998 Jingle Bell Ride 98-833-0	Open		12.00	12
1998 Leaf Acorn Snowflake 98-736-0	Open		10.00	10
1998 Leaf Bunnies 98-731-0	Open		14.00	14
1998 Look What I Found 98-830-0	Retrd.	1999	14.00	14
2000 Madison Snowflake 00-844-0	Open		15.00	15
2000 Mini Carlton 00-743-0	Open		10.00	10
2000 Mini Frosty Leaf Santa 00-743-0	Open		10.00	10
1999 Nana In Leaf 99-727-0	Open		18.00	18
1999 Nana Leaf 99-735-0	Open		22.50	23
1998 Peppermint Twist 98-829-0	Retrd.	1999	14.00	14
1999 Pinecone Perch 99-834-0	Open		16.00	16
1998 Sailing The North Wind 98-831-0	Open		12.00	12
1999 Santa 'cicle 99-731-0	Open		16.00	16
1998 Santa Leaf Ride 98-734-0	Open		16.00	16
1998 Santa w/Banner-1998 98-727-0	Yr.Iss.	1998	20.00	20
1999 Shootin The Breeze 99-733-0	5,000	1999	15.00	15
1998 Sleeping Teddy 98-735-0	Open		12.00	12
1998 Snow Flight 98-828-0	Retrd.	1999	14.00	14
2000 Snow Sailors 00-850-0	Open		15.00	15
1998 Snowfall 98-826-0	Retrd.	1999	12.00	12
1999 Somebunnies In Love 99-828-0	Open		18.00	18
2000 Stardust Santa Snowflake 00-849-0	Open		15.00	15
1999 Stardust Waving 99-825-0	Open		17.00	17
2000 Stormy Snow Shoes 00-843-0	Open		12.00	12
2000 Stormy Snowflake 00-848-0	Open		15.00	15
1999 Tiny Totem Trio 99-833-0	Open		15.00	15

PLATES/PLAQUES

American Artists

The Best of Fred Stone-Mares & Foals Series (6 1/2") - F. Stone

1991 Patience	19,500		25.00	30
1992 Water Trough	19,500		25.00	30
1992 Pasture Pest	19,500		25.00	30
1992 Kidnapped Mare	19,500		25.00	30
1993 Contentment	19,500		25.00	30
1993 Arabian Mare & Foal	19,500		25.00	30
1994 Diamond in the Rough	19,500		25.00	30
1995 The First Day	19,500		25.00	30

Famous Fillies Series - F. Stone

1987 Lady's Secret	9,500		65.00	70-75
1988 Ruffian	9,500		65.00	75-80
1988 Genuine Risk	9,500		65.00	70
1992 Go For The Wand	9,500		65.00	70-80

Fred Stone Classic Series - F. Stone

1986 The Shoe-8,000 Wins	9,500		75.00	75
1986 The Eternal Legacy	9,500		75.00	95-99
1988 Forever Friends	9,500		75.00	85-125
1989 Alysheba	9,500		75.00	75-85

Gold Signature Series - F. Stone

1990 Secretariat Final Tribute, signed	4,500		150.00	450-500
1990 Secretariat Final Tribute, unsigned	7,500		75.00	75-150
1991 Old Warriors, signed	4,500		150.00	425-500
1991 Old Warriors, unsigned	7,500		75.00	100

Gold Signature Series II - F. Stone

1991 Northern Dancer, double signature	1,500		175.00	250-350
1991 Northern Dancer, single signature	3,000		150.00	150-199
1991 Northern Dancer, unsigned	7,500		75.00	75-99
1991 Kelso, double signature	1,500		175.00	250
1991 Kelso, single signature	3,000		150.00	150-199
1991 Kelso, unsigned	7,500		75.00	65-75

Gold Signature Series III - F. Stone

1992 Dance Smartly-Pat Day, Up, double signature	1,500		175.00	175
1992 Dance Smartly-Pat Day, Up, single signature	3,000		150.00	150
1992 Dance Smartly-Pat Day, Up, unsigned	7,500		75.00	75
1993 American Triple Crown-1937-1946, signed	2,500		195.00	200-250
1993 American Triple Crown-1937-1946, unsigned	7,500		75.00	75-95
1993 American Triple Crown-1948-1978, signed	2,500		195.00	200-250
1993 American Triple Crown-1948-1978, unsigned	7,500		75.00	75-175
1994 American Triple Crown-1919-1935, signed	2,500		95.00	80-95
1994 American Triple Crown-1919-1935, unsigned	7,500		75.00	70-75

Gold Signature Series IV - F. Stone

1995 Julie Krone - Colonial Affair	7,500		75.00	75
1995 Julie Krone - Colonial Affair, signed	2,500		150.00	150

The Horses of Fred Stone - F. Stone

1982 Patience	9,500		55.00	95-125
1982 Arabian Mare and Foal	9,500		55.00	125-149
1982 Safe and Sound	9,500		55.00	95
1983 Contentment	9,500		55.00	95-125

Mare and Foal Series - F. Stone

1986 Water Trough	12,500		49.50	149-175
1986 Tranquility	12,500		49.50	95-149
1986 Pasture Pest	12,500		49.50	125-149
1987 The Arabians	12,500		49.50	95-125

Mare and Foal Series II - F. Stone

1989 The First Day	Open		35.00	35
1989 Diamond in the Rough	Retrd.		35.00	35

Racing Legends - F. Stone

1989 Phar Lap	9,500		75.00	75
1989 Sunday Silence	9,500		75.00	75
1990 John Henry-Shoemaker	9,500		75.00	75

Sport of Kings Series - F. Stone

1984 Man O'War	9,500		65.00	149-175
1984 Secretariat	9,500		65.00	125-200
1985 John Henry	9,500		65.00	70-85
1986 Seattle Slew	9,500		65.00	70-85

The Stallion Series - F. Stone

1983 Black Stallion	19,500		49.50	75-125
1983 Andalusian	19,500		49.50	75-120

Anheuser-Busch, Inc.

1992 Olympic Team Series - A-Busch, Inc.

1991 1992 Olympic Team Winter N3180	Retrd.	1994	35.00	20-25
1992 1992 Olympic Team Summer N3122	Retrd.	1994	35.00	20-25

Archives Plate Series - D. Langeneckert

1992 1893 Columbian Exposition N3477	25-day	1996	27.50	25-30
1992 Ganymede N4004	25-day	1996	27.50	20-35
1995 Budweiser's Greatest Triumph N5195	25-day	1996	27.50	25-35
1995 Mirror of Truth N5196	25-day	1997	27.50	25-35

Budweiser Holiday Plate Series - Various

1989 Winters Day N2295 - B. Kemper	25-day	N/A	30.00	55-85
1990 An American Tradition N2767 - S. Sampson	25-day	N/A	30.00	35-125
1991 The Season's Best N3034 - S. Sampson	25-day	N/A	30.00	25-30
1992 A Perfect Christmas N3440 - S. Sampson	25-day	N/A	27.50	25-30
1993 Special Delivery N4002 - N. Koerber	25-day	1994	27.50	35-135
1994 Hometown Holiday N4572 - B. Kemper	25-day	N/A	27.50	25-30
1995 Lighting the Way Home N5215 - T. Jester	25-day	1998	27.50	25-45
1996 Budweiser Clydesdales N5778 - J. Raedeke	25-day	2000	27.50	25-28
1997 Home For The Holidays N5779 - H. Droog	25-day		27.50	25-28
1998 Grant's Farm Holiday N5780 - E. Kastaris	25-day		28.00	25-28
1999 A Century of Tradition N5998 - G. Ciccarelli	25-day		30.00	30-60
2000 Holiday In The Mountains N5999 - E. Kastaris	25-day		30.00	30

Civil War Series - D. Langeneckert

1992 General Grant N3478	Retrd.	1994	45.00	20-30
1993 General Robert E. Lee N3590	Retrd.	1994	45.00	25-28
1993 President Abraham Lincoln N3591	Retrd.	1994	45.00	25-28

Collector Edition Series - M. Urdahl

1995 "This Bud's For You" N4945	25-day		27.50	25-30

Man's Best Friend Series - M. Urdahl

1990 Buddies N2615	25-day	N/A	30.00	55-100
1990 Six Pack N3005	25-day	1992	30.00	35-75
1992 Something's Brewing N3147	25-day	1994	30.00	25-30
1993 Outstanding in Their Field N4003	25-day	1995	27.50	25-30

ANRI

ANRI Father's Day - Unknown

1972 Alpine Father & Children	Closed	1972	35.00	100
1973 Alpine Father & Children	Closed	1973	40.00	100-149
1974 Cliff Gazing	Closed	1974	50.00	100
1975 Sailing	Closed	1975	60.00	90

ANRI Mother's Day - Unknown

1972 Alpine Mother & Children	Closed	1972	35.00	50
1973 Alpine Mother & Children	Closed	1973	40.00	50
1974 Alpine Mother & Children	Closed	1974	50.00	55
1975 Alpine Stroll	Closed	1975	60.00	65
1976 Knitting	Closed	1976	60.00	65

Christmas - J. Malfertheiner, unless otherwise noted

1971 St. Jakob in Groden	6,000	1971	37.50	65
1972 Pipers at Alberobello	6,000	1972	45.00	75-156
1973 Alpine Horn	6,000	1973	45.00	395
1974 Young Man and Girl	6,000	1974	50.00	95
1975 Christmas in Ireland	6,000	1975	60.00	60
1976 Alpine Christmas	6,000	1976	65.00	190

*Quotes have been rounded up to nearest dollar

PLATES/PLAQUES

YEAR ISSUE	EDITION LIMIT	YEAR RETD.	ISSUE PRICE	*QUOTE U.S.$
1977 Legend of Heligenblut	6,000	1977	65.00	91
1978 Klockler Singers	6,000	1978	80.00	90
1979 Moss Gatherers - Unknown	6,000	1979	135.00	177
1980 Wintry Churchgoing - Unknown	6,000	1980	165.00	165
1981 Santa Claus in Tyrol - Unknown	6,000	1981	165.00	200
1982 The Star Singers - Unknown	6,000	1982	165.00	165
1983 Unto Us a Child is Born - Unknown	6,000	1983	165.00	310
1984 Yuletide in the Valley - Unknown	6,000	1984	165.00	170
1985 Good Morning, Good Cheer	6,000	1985	165.00	165
1986 A Groden Christmas	6,000	1986	165.00	200
1987 Down From the Alps	6,000	1987	195.00	250
1988 Christkindl Markt	6,000	1988	220.00	230
1989 Flight Into Egypt	6,000	1989	275.00	275
1990 Holy Night	6,000	1990	300.00	300

Disney Four Star Collection - Disney Studios

YEAR ISSUE	EDITION LIMIT	YEAR RETD.	ISSUE PRICE	*QUOTE U.S.$
1989 Mickey Mini Plate	5,000	1989	40.00	65-125
1990 Minnie Mini Plate	5,000	1990	40.00	95-125
1991 Donald Mini Plate	5,000	1991	50.00	95-175

Ferrandiz Christmas - J. Ferrandiz

YEAR ISSUE	EDITION LIMIT	YEAR RETD.	ISSUE PRICE	*QUOTE U.S.$
1972 Christ In The Manger	4,000	1972	35.00	163-200
1973 Christmas	4,000	1973	40.00	225-275
1974 Holy Night	4,000	1974	50.00	100
1975 Flight into Egypt	4,000	1975	60.00	95
1976 Tree of Life	4,000	1976	60.00	85
1977 Girl with Flowers	4,000	1977	65.00	185-234
1978 Leading the Way	4,000	1978	77.50	143-180
1979 The Drummer	4,000	1979	120.00	78-175
1980 Rejoice	4,000	1980	150.00	160
1981 Spreading the Word	4,000	1981	150.00	150-195
1982 The Shepherd Family	4,000	1982	150.00	150-195
1983 Peace Attend Thee	4,000	1983	150.00	150-195

Ferrandiz Mother's Day Series - J. Ferrandiz

YEAR ISSUE	EDITION LIMIT	YEAR RETD.	ISSUE PRICE	*QUOTE U.S.$
1972 Mother Sewing	3,000	1972	35.00	200
1973 Alpine Mother & Child	3,000	1973	40.00	150
1974 Mother Holding Child	3,000	1974	50.00	150
1975 Dove Girl	3,000	1975	60.00	150
1976 Mother Knitting	3,000	1976	60.00	200
1977 Alpine Stroll	3,000	1977	65.00	125
1978 The Beginning	3,000	1978	75.00	78-100
1979 All Hearts	3,000	1979	120.00	78-120
1980 Spring Arrivals	3,000	1980	150.00	165
1981 Harmony	3,000	1981	150.00	150
1982 With Love	3,000	1982	150.00	150

Ferrandiz Wooden Birthday Plates - J. Ferrandiz

YEAR ISSUE	EDITION LIMIT	YEAR RETD.	ISSUE PRICE	*QUOTE U.S.$
1972 Boy	Unkn.	1972	15.00	100-125
1972 Girl	Unkn.	1972	15.00	160
1973 Boy	Unkn.	1973	20.00	200
1973 Girl	Unkn.	1973	20.00	150
1974 Boy	Unkn.	1974	22.00	160
1974 Girl	Unkn.	1974	22.00	160

Ferrandiz Wooden Wedding Plates - J. Ferrandiz

YEAR ISSUE	EDITION LIMIT	YEAR RETD.	ISSUE PRICE	*QUOTE U.S.$
1972 Boy and Girl Embracing	Closed	1972	40.00	100-125
1973 Wedding Scene	Closed	1973	40.00	104-150
1974 Wedding	Closed	1974	48.00	150
1976 Wedding	Closed	1976	60.00	90-150
1975 Wedding	Closed	1975	60.00	150

Gunther Granget Animals - G. Granget

YEAR ISSUE	EDITION LIMIT	YEAR RETD.	ISSUE PRICE	*QUOTE U.S.$
1974 Great Horned Owl Family (plaque)	Closed	1976	550.00	550
1974 Great Horned Owl Family (plaque)	Closed	1976	800.00	800
1974 Great Horned Owl Family (plaque)	Closed	1976	2500.00	2500
1974 Mallard Family (plaque)	Closed	1976	550.00	550
1974 Mallard Family (plaque)	Closed	1976	800.00	800
1974 Mallard Family (plaque)	Closed	1976	2500.00	2500

Armstrong's

Commemorative Issues - R. Skelton

YEAR ISSUE	EDITION LIMIT	YEAR RETD.	ISSUE PRICE	*QUOTE U.S.$
1983 70 Years Young (10 1/2")	15,000		85.00	100-155
1984 Freddie the Torchbearer (8 1/2")	15,000		62.50	50-65
1994 Red & His Friends (12 1/4")	165	1994	700.00	1000-3500

Freedom Collection of Red Skelton - R. Skelton

YEAR ISSUE	EDITION LIMIT	YEAR RETD.	ISSUE PRICE	*QUOTE U.S.$
1990 The All American, (signed)	1,000	1990	195.00	400-600
1990 The All American	9,000		62.50	50-75
1991 Independence Day? (signed)	1,000	1991	195.00	250-375
1991 Independence Day?	9,000		62.50	50-65
1992 Let Freedom Ring, (signed)	1,000	1992	195.00	250-350
1992 Let Freedom Ring	9,000		62.50	50-75
1993 Freddie's Gift of Life, (signed)	1,000	1993	195.00	250-350
1993 Freddie's Gift of Life	9,000		62.50	50-60

The Golden Memories - R. Skelton

YEAR ISSUE	EDITION LIMIT	YEAR RETD.	ISSUE PRICE	*QUOTE U.S.$
1995 The Donut Dunker (signed)	1,000	1995	375.00	525-800
1996 Clem & Clementine (signed)	1,000	1996	385.00	420-600
1996 San Fernando Red (signed)	1,000	1996	385.00	375-500
1997 Jr., The Mean Widdle Kid (signed)	1,000	1997	385.00	375-500
1997 Cauliflower McPugg	1,000		295.00	295

Happy Art Series - W. Lantz

YEAR ISSUE	EDITION LIMIT	YEAR RETD.	ISSUE PRICE	*QUOTE U.S.$
1981 Woody's Triple Self-Portrait, (signed)	1,000		100.00	200
1981 Woody's Triple Self-Portrait	9,000		39.50	40
1983 Gothic Woody, (signed)	1,000	N/A	100.00	200
1983 Gothic Woody	9,000		39.50	40
1984 Blue Boy Woody, (signed)	1,000	N/A	100.00	200
1984 Blue Boy Woody	9,000	1992	39.50	40-50

Pro Autographed Ceramic Baseball Card Plaque - Unknown

YEAR ISSUE	EDITION LIMIT	YEAR RETD.	ISSUE PRICE	*QUOTE U.S.$
1985 Brett, Garvey, Jackson, Rose, Seaver, auto, 3-1/4X5	1,000	N/A	150.00	150-250

The Red Skelton Porcelain Plaque - R. Skelton

YEAR ISSUE	EDITION LIMIT	YEAR RETD.	ISSUE PRICE	*QUOTE U.S.$
1991 All American	1,500	1993	495.00	1000-1500
1994 Another Day	1,994	N/A	675.00	750-1000
1992 Independance Day?	1,500	1997	525.00	575-685
1993 Red & Freddie Both Turned 80	1,993	1993	595.00	1000-1500

The Signature Collection - R. Skelton

YEAR ISSUE	EDITION LIMIT	YEAR RETD.	ISSUE PRICE	*QUOTE U.S.$
1986 Anyone for Tennis?	9,000	N/A	62.50	85-125
1986 Anyone for Tennis? (signed)	1,000	1986	125.00	500-850
1987 Ironing the Waves	9,000	N/A	62.50	90-125
1987 Ironing the Waves (signed)	1,000	1987	125.00	200-500
1988 The Cliffhanger	9,000	N/A	62.50	65-100
1988 The Cliffhanger (signed)	1,000	1988	150.00	350
1988 Hooked on Freddie	9,000	N/A	62.50	65-95
1988 Hooked on Freddie (signed)	1,000	1988	175.00	350

Sports - Schenken

YEAR ISSUE	EDITION LIMIT	YEAR RETD.	ISSUE PRICE	*QUOTE U.S.$
1985 Pete Rose h/s (10 1/4")	1,000	N/A	100.00	295-395
1985 Pete Rose u/s (10 1/4")	10,000	N/A	45.00	75-99

Armstrong's/Crown Parian

Freddie The Freeloader - R. Skelton

YEAR ISSUE	EDITION LIMIT	YEAR RETD.	ISSUE PRICE	*QUOTE U.S.$
1979 Freddie in the Bathtub	10,000	N/A	55.00	144-200
1980 Freddie's Shack	10,000	N/A	55.00	83-175
1981 Freddie on the Green	10,000	N/A	60.00	50-150
1982 Love that Freddie	10,000	N/A	60.00	25-89

Freddie's Adventures - R. Skelton

YEAR ISSUE	EDITION LIMIT	YEAR RETD.	ISSUE PRICE	*QUOTE U.S.$
1982 Captain Freddie	15,000	N/A	60.00	25-89
1982 Bronco Freddie	15,000		62.50	30-75
1983 Sir Freddie	15,000		62.50	60-95
1984 Gertrude and Heathcliffe	15,000		62.50	80

Armstrong's/Fairmont

Famous Clown Collection - R. Skelton

YEAR ISSUE	EDITION LIMIT	YEAR RETD.	ISSUE PRICE	*QUOTE U.S.$
1976 Freddie the Freeloader	10,000	N/A	55.00	320-600
1977 W. C. Fields	10,000	N/A	55.00	75-150
1978 Happy	10,000	N/A	55.00	143-150
1979 The Pledge	10,000	N/A	55.00	115-150

Artaffects

Club Member Limited Edition Redemption Offerings - G. Perillo

YEAR ISSUE	EDITION LIMIT	YEAR RETD.	ISSUE PRICE	*QUOTE U.S.$
1992 The Pencil	Yr. Iss.	1992	35.00	75-150
1992 Studies in Black and White (Set of 4)	Yr. Iss.	1992	75.00	100-149
1993 Watcher of the Wilderness	Yr. Iss.	1993	60.00	60

America's Indian Heritage - G. Perillo

YEAR ISSUE	EDITION LIMIT	YEAR RETD.	ISSUE PRICE	*QUOTE U.S.$
1987 Cheyenne Nation	Closed	N/A	24.50	65-75
1988 Arapaho Nation	Closed	N/A	24.50	65-75
1988 Kiowa Nation	Closed	N/A	24.50	65-75
1988 Sioux Nation	Closed	N/A	24.50	65-75
1988 Chippewa Nation	Closed	N/A	24.50	65-75
1988 Crow Nation	Closed	N/A	24.50	65-75
1988 Nez Perce Nation	Closed	N/A	24.50	65-75
1988 Blackfoot Nation	Closed	N/A	24.50	65-75

Chieftains I - G. Perillo

YEAR ISSUE	EDITION LIMIT	YEAR RETD.	ISSUE PRICE	*QUOTE U.S.$
1979 Chief Sitting Bull	7,500	N/A	65.00	275-349
1979 Chief Joseph	7,500	N/A	65.00	90-150
1980 Chief Red Cloud	7,500	N/A	65.00	112-149
1980 Chief Geronimo	7,500	N/A	65.00	70-149
1981 Chief Crazy Horse	7,500	N/A	65.00	69-149

Chieftains II - G. Perillo

YEAR ISSUE	EDITION LIMIT	YEAR RETD.	ISSUE PRICE	*QUOTE U.S.$
1983 Chief Pontiac	7,500	N/A	70.00	85-149
1983 Chief Victorio	7,500	N/A	70.00	150
1984 Chief Tecumseh	7,500	N/A	70.00	150
1984 Chief Cochise	7,500	N/A	70.00	80-150
1984 Chief Black Kettle	7,500	N/A	70.00	150

The Colts - G. Perillo

YEAR ISSUE	EDITION LIMIT	YEAR RETD.	ISSUE PRICE	*QUOTE U.S.$
1985 Appaloosa	5,000	N/A	40.00	40
1985 Pinto	5,000	N/A	40.00	56
1985 Arabian	5,000	N/A	40.00	56
1985 Thoroughbred	5,000	N/A	40.00	56

Council of Nations - G. Perillo

YEAR ISSUE	EDITION LIMIT	YEAR RETD.	ISSUE PRICE	*QUOTE U.S.$
1992 Strength of the Sioux	Closed	N/A	29.50	45-55
1992 Pride of the Cheyenne	Closed	N/A	29.50	40-55
1992 Dignity of the Nez Perce	Closed	N/A	29.50	40-49
1992 Courage of the Arapaho	Closed	N/A	29.50	40-49
1992 Power of the Blackfoot	Closed	N/A	29.50	40-60
1992 Nobility of the Algonquin	Closed	N/A	29.50	40
1992 Wisdom of the Cherokee	Closed	N/A	29.50	40-55
1992 Boldness of the Seneca	Closed	N/A	29.50	40

Indian Bridal - G. Perillo

YEAR ISSUE	EDITION LIMIT	YEAR RETD.	ISSUE PRICE	*QUOTE U.S.$
1990 Yellow Bird (6 1/2")	Closed	N/A	25.00	39-49
1990 Autumn Blossom (6 1/2")	Closed	N/A	25.00	39-45
1990 Misty Waters (6 1/2")	Closed	N/A	25.00	30
1990 Sunny Skies (6 1/2")	Closed	N/A	25.00	30

Indian Nations - G. Perillo

YEAR ISSUE	EDITION LIMIT	YEAR RETD.	ISSUE PRICE	*QUOTE U.S.$
1983 Blackfoot	7,500	N/A	140.00	350
1983 Cheyenne	7,500	N/A	set	Set
1983 Apache	7,500	N/A	set	Set
1983 Sioux	7,500	N/A	set	Set

March of Dimes: Our Children - G. Perillo

YEAR ISSUE	EDITION LIMIT	YEAR RETD.	ISSUE PRICE	*QUOTE U.S.$
1989 A Time to Be Born	7,500	N/A	29.00	15-29

Mother's Love - G. Perillo

YEAR ISSUE	EDITION LIMIT	YEAR RETD.	ISSUE PRICE	*QUOTE U.S.$
1988 Feelings	Yr.Iss.	1988	35.00	75-125
1989 Moonlight	Yr.Iss.	1989	35.00	65-100
1990 Pride & Joy	Yr.Iss.	1990	39.50	95-100
1991 Little Shadow	Yr.Iss.	1991	39.50	55-100

Motherhood Series - G. Perillo

YEAR ISSUE	EDITION LIMIT	YEAR RETD.	ISSUE PRICE	*QUOTE U.S.$
1983 Madre	10,000	N/A	50.00	75
1984 Madonna of the Plains	3,500	N/A	50.00	75-85
1985 Abuela	3,500	N/A	50.00	75
1986 Nap Time	3,500	N/A	50.00	75-85

Native American Christmas - G. Perillo

YEAR ISSUE	EDITION LIMIT	YEAR RETD.	ISSUE PRICE	*QUOTE U.S.$
1993 The Little Shepherd	Yr.Iss.	1993	35.00	55-65
1994 Joy to the World	Yr.Iss.	1994	45.00	45-55

Nature's Harmony - G. Perillo

YEAR ISSUE	EDITION LIMIT	YEAR RETD.	ISSUE PRICE	*QUOTE U.S.$
1982 The Peaceable Kingdom	12,500	N/A	100.00	125-299
1982 Zebra	12,500	N/A	50.00	50
1982 Bengal Tiger	12,500	N/A	50.00	60
1983 Black Panther	12,500	N/A	50.00	70
1983 Elephant	12,500	N/A	50.00	95-125

North American Wildlife - G. Perillo

YEAR ISSUE	EDITION LIMIT	YEAR RETD.	ISSUE PRICE	*QUOTE U.S.$
1989 Mustang	Closed	N/A	29.50	35-55
1989 White-Tailed Deer	Closed	N/A	29.50	30-50
1989 Mountain Lion	Closed	N/A	29.50	30-50
1990 American Bald Eagle	Closed	N/A	29.50	35-65
1990 Timber Wolf	Closed	N/A	29.50	35-55
1990 Polar Bear	Closed	N/A	29.50	30
1990 Buffalo	Closed	N/A	29.50	35-55
1990 Bighorn Sheep	Closed	N/A	29.50	30-50

Perillo Christmas - G. Perillo

YEAR ISSUE	EDITION LIMIT	YEAR RETD.	ISSUE PRICE	*QUOTE U.S.$
1987 Shining Star	Yr.Iss.	1987	29.50	70-85
1988 Silent Light	Yr.Iss.	1988	35.00	80-100
1989 Snow Flake	Yr.Iss.	1989	35.00	75-100
1990 Bundle Up	Yr.Iss.	1990	39.50	75-100
1991 Christmas Journey	Yr.Iss.	1991	39.50	50-100

Portraits of American Brides - R. Sauber

YEAR ISSUE	EDITION LIMIT	YEAR RETD.	ISSUE PRICE	*QUOTE U.S.$
1986 Caroline	Closed	N/A	29.50	45-150
1986 Jacqueline	Closed	N/A	29.50	30-95
1987 Elizabeth	Closed	N/A	29.50	60-85
1987 Emily	Closed	N/A	29.50	75-85
1987 Meredith	Closed	N/A	29.50	75
1987 Laura	Closed	N/A	29.50	45
1987 Sarah	Closed	N/A	29.50	45
1987 Rebecca	Closed	N/A	29.50	65

Pride of America's Indians - G. Perillo

YEAR ISSUE	EDITION LIMIT	YEAR RETD.	ISSUE PRICE	*QUOTE U.S.$
1986 Brave and Free	Closed	N/A	24.50	45-85
1986 Dark-Eyed Friends	Closed	N/A	24.50	25-65
1986 Noble Companions	Closed	N/A	24.50	25-55
1987 Kindred Spirits	Closed	N/A	24.50	25-55
1987 Loyal Alliance	Closed	N/A	24.50	42-93
1987 Small and Wise	Closed	N/A	24.50	25-55
1987 Winter Scouts	Closed	N/A	24.50	25-55
1987 Peaceful Comrades	Closed	N/A	24.50	25-75

The Princesses - G. Perillo

YEAR ISSUE	EDITION LIMIT	YEAR RETD.	ISSUE PRICE	*QUOTE U.S.$
1982 Lily of the Mohawks	7,500	N/A	50.00	175
1982 Pocahontas	7,500	N/A	50.00	100
1982 Minnehaha	7,500	N/A	50.00	100
1982 Sacajawea	7,500	N/A	50.00	100

Proud Young Spirits - G. Perillo

YEAR ISSUE	EDITION LIMIT	YEAR RETD.	ISSUE PRICE	*QUOTE U.S.$
1990 Protector of the Plains	Closed	N/A	29.50	75-100
1990 Watchful Eyes	Closed	N/A	29.50	55-65
1990 Freedom's Watch	Closed	N/A	29.50	45-65
1990 Woodland Scouts	Closed	N/A	29.50	35-45
1990 Fast Friends	Closed	N/A	29.50	35-45
1990 Birds of a Feather	Closed	N/A	29.50	30
1990 Prairie Pals	Closed	N/A	29.50	35-45
1990 Loyal Guardian	Closed	N/A	29.50	30

Special Issue - G. Perillo

YEAR ISSUE	EDITION LIMIT	YEAR RETD.	ISSUE PRICE	*QUOTE U.S.$
1981 Apache Boy	5,000	N/A	95.00	175-399
1983 Papoose	3,000	N/A	100.00	125
1983 Indian Style	17,500	N/A	50.00	50
1984 The Lovers	Closed	N/A	50.00	100
1984 Navajo Girl	3,500	N/A	95.00	175-250
1986 Navajo Boy	3,500	N/A	95.00	175-250

The Thoroughbreds - G. Perillo

YEAR ISSUE	EDITION LIMIT	YEAR RETD.	ISSUE PRICE	*QUOTE U.S.$
1984 Whirlaway	9,500	N/A	50.00	250-399
1984 Secretariat	9,500	N/A	50.00	350-499
1984 Man o' War	9,500	N/A	50.00	150-250
1984 Seabiscuit	9,500	N/A	50.00	150

War Ponies of the Plains - G. Perillo

YEAR ISSUE	EDITION LIMIT	YEAR RETD.	ISSUE PRICE	*QUOTE U.S.$
1992 Nightshadow	Closed	N/A	27.00	27-40
1992 Windcatcher	Closed	N/A	27.00	27
1992 Prairie Prancer	Closed	N/A	27.00	27
1992 Thunderfoot	Closed	N/A	27.00	27-40
1992 Proud Companion	Closed	N/A	27.00	27-40
1992 Sun Dancer	Closed	N/A	27.00	27-40
1992 Free Spirit	Closed	N/A	27.00	27-33
1992 Gentle Warrior	Closed	N/A	27.00	27

The Young Chieftains - G. Perillo

YEAR ISSUE	EDITION LIMIT	YEAR RETD.	ISSUE PRICE	*QUOTE U.S.$
1985 Young Sitting Bull	5,000	N/A	50.00	100-250
1985 Young Joseph	5,000	N/A	50.00	75-150
1986 Young Red Cloud	5,000	N/A	50.00	75-125
1986 Young Geronimo	5,000	N/A	50.00	75-150

*Quotes have been rounded up to nearest dollar

YEAR ISSUE	EDITION LIMIT	YEAR RETD.	ISSUE PRICE	*QUOTE U.S.$
1986 Young Crazy Horse	5,000	N/A	50.00	75-150

Artists of the World

Celebration Series - T. DeGrazia

YEAR ISSUE	EDITION LIMIT	YEAR RETD.	ISSUE PRICE	*QUOTE U.S.$
1993 The Lord's Candle	5,000		39.50	45-75
1993 Pinata Party	5,000		39.50	45-75
1993 Holiday Lullaby	5,000	1995	39.50	45-75
1993 Caroling	5,000	1995	39.50	45-75

Children (Signed) - T. DeGrazia

YEAR ISSUE	EDITION LIMIT	YEAR RETD.	ISSUE PRICE	*QUOTE U.S.$
1978 Los Ninos	500		100.00	1500-2200
1978 White Dove	500		100.00	450-700
1978 Flower Girl	500		100.00	450-700
1979 Flower Boy	500		100.00	450-700
1980 Little Cocopah Girl	500		100.00	299-450
1981 Beautiful Burden	500		100.00	299-450
1981 Merry Little Indian	500		100.00	299-450

Children - T. DeGrazia

YEAR ISSUE	EDITION LIMIT	YEAR RETD.	ISSUE PRICE	*QUOTE U.S.$
1976 Los Ninos	5,000		35.00	1000
1977 White Dove	5,000		40.00	60-150
1978 Flower Girl	9,500		45.00	43-150
1979 Flower Boy	9,500		45.00	40-150
1980 Little Cocopah	9,500		50.00	53-100
1981 Beautiful Burden	9,500		50.00	52-60
1982 Merry Little Indian	9,500		55.00	60-80
1983 Wondering	10,000		60.00	43-250
1984 Pink Papoose	10,000		65.00	59-150
1985 Sunflower Boy	10,000		65.00	59-150

Children at Play - T. DeGrazia

YEAR ISSUE	EDITION LIMIT	YEAR RETD.	ISSUE PRICE	*QUOTE U.S.$
1985 My First Horse	15,000		65.00	140-299
1986 Girl With Sewing Machine	15,000		65.00	100-275
1987 Love Me	15,000		65.00	90-100
1988 Merrily, Merrily, Merrily	15,000		65.00	85-100
1989 My First Arrow	15,000		65.00	100-250
1990 Away With My Kite	15,000		65.00	100-250

Children Mini-Plates - T. DeGrazia

YEAR ISSUE	EDITION LIMIT	YEAR RETD.	ISSUE PRICE	*QUOTE U.S.$
1980 Los Ninos	5,000		15.00	300-475
1981 White Dove	5,000		15.00	100-149
1982 Flower Girl	5,000		15.00	120
1982 Flower Boy	5,000		15.00	100-149
1983 Little Cocopah Indian Girl	5,000		15.00	75-149
1983 Beautiful Burden	5,000		20.00	75-149
1984 Merry Little Indian	5,000		20.00	120
1984 Wondering	5,000		20.00	120
1985 Pink Papoose	5,000		20.00	75-149
1985 Sunflower Boy	5,000		20.00	100-149

Children of the Sun - T. DeGrazia

YEAR ISSUE	EDITION LIMIT	YEAR RETD.	ISSUE PRICE	*QUOTE U.S.$
1987 Spring Blossoms	150-day		34.50	80-100
1987 My Little Pink Bird	150-day		34.50	55-100
1987 Bright Flowers of the Desert	150-day		37.90	65-149
1988 Gifts from the Sun	150-day		37.90	50-149
1988 Growing Glory	150-day		37.90	50-149
1988 The Gentle White Dove	150-day		37.90	55-100
1988 Sunflower Maiden	150-day		39.90	65-149
1989 Sun Showers	150-day		39.90	60-100

Floral Fiesta - T. DeGrazia

YEAR ISSUE	EDITION LIMIT	YEAR RETD.	ISSUE PRICE	*QUOTE U.S.$
1994 Little Flower Vendor	5,000		39.50	40-75
1994 Flowers For Mother	5,000		39.50	40-75
1995 Floral Innocence	5,000		39.50	40-75
1995 Floral Bouquet	5,000		39.50	40-75
1996 Floral Celebration	5,000		39.50	40-75
1996 Floral Fiesta	5,000		39.50	40-75

Holiday (Signed) - T. DeGrazia

YEAR ISSUE	EDITION LIMIT	YEAR RETD.	ISSUE PRICE	*QUOTE U.S.$
1976 Festival of Lights	500		100.00	100-300
1977 Bell of Hope	500		100.00	299-450
1978 Little Madonna	500		100.00	100-450
1979 The Nativity	500		100.00	75-100
1980 Little Pima Drummer	500		100.00	100-450
1981 A Little Prayer	500		100.00	275-450
1982 Blue Boy	96		100.00	275-500

Holiday - T. DeGrazia

YEAR ISSUE	EDITION LIMIT	YEAR RETD.	ISSUE PRICE	*QUOTE U.S.$
1976 Festival of Lights	9,500		45.00	100-150
1977 Bell of Hope	9,500		45.00	38-175
1978 Little Madonna	9,500		45.00	53-65
1979 The Nativity	9,500		50.00	75
1980 Little Pima Drummer	9,500		50.00	35-50
1981 A Little Prayer	9,500		55.00	44-55
1982 Blue Boy	10,000		60.00	38-60
1983 Heavenly Blessings	10,000		65.00	15-65
1984 Navajo Madonna	10,000		65.00	53
1985 Saguaro Dance	10,000		65.00	65-125

Holiday Mini-Plates - T. DeGrazia

YEAR ISSUE	EDITION LIMIT	YEAR RETD.	ISSUE PRICE	*QUOTE U.S.$
1980 Festival of Lights	5,000		15.00	200-350
1981 Bell of Hope	5,000		15.00	75-150
1982 Little Madonna	5,000		15.00	80-100
1982 The Nativity	5,000		15.00	75-150
1983 Little Pima Drummer	5,000		15.00	25-75
1983 Little Prayer	5,000		20.00	25-75
1984 Blue Boy	5,000		20.00	25-75
1984 Heavenly Blessings	5,000		20.00	25-75
1985 Navajo Madonna	5,000		20.00	50-125
1985 Saguaro Dance	5,000		20.00	20-125

Special Release - T. DeGrazia

YEAR ISSUE	EDITION LIMIT	YEAR RETD.	ISSUE PRICE	*QUOTE U.S.$
1996 Wedding Party	5,000		49.50	50-60

Western - T. DeGrazia

YEAR ISSUE	EDITION LIMIT	YEAR RETD.	ISSUE PRICE	*QUOTE U.S.$
1986 Morning Ride	5,000		65.00	95-150
1987 Bronco	5,000		65.00	100-275
1988 Apache Scout	5,000		65.00	175-275
1989 Alone	5,000		65.00	100-275

BARBIE Collectibles by Hallmark/Hallmark Keepsake Collections

Holiday Homecoming Collection

YEAR ISSUE	EDITION LIMIT	YEAR RETD.	ISSUE PRICE	*QUOTE U.S.$
1997 Holiday Traditions™ Barbie® QHB6003	24,500	1998	30.00	30
1998 Holiday Voyage™ Barbie® QHB6018	24,500	1999	30.00	30

Victorian Christmas Collection

YEAR ISSUE	EDITION LIMIT	YEAR RETD.	ISSUE PRICE	*QUOTE U.S.$
1997 Victorian Elegance™ Barbie® QHB6005	24,500	1998	30.00	30
1998 Holiday Memories™ Barbie® QHB6021	24,500	1999	30.00	30

Barbie/Enesco Group, Inc.

Bob Mackie - Enesco

YEAR ISSUE	EDITION LIMIT	YEAR RETD.	ISSUE PRICE	*QUOTE U.S.$
1996 Queen of Hearts Barbie 157678	Open		25.00	25
1997 Goddess of the Sun 260215	7,500		35.00	35
1997 Moon Goddess 260231	7,500		35.00	35

Bob Mackie JC Penney Exclusive - Enesco

YEAR ISSUE	EDITION LIMIT	YEAR RETD.	ISSUE PRICE	*QUOTE U.S.$
1995 Queen of Hearts Barbie J1276	7,500	1995	30.00	30
1996 Goddess of the Sun J8768	7,500		30.00	30
1997 Moon Goddess 260266	5,000		30.00	30

Elite Dealer Exclusive - Enesco

YEAR ISSUE	EDITION LIMIT	YEAR RETD.	ISSUE PRICE	*QUOTE U.S.$
1997 Goddess of the Sun/Moon Goddess Set 270539	2,500		125.00	125
1997 Barbie as Dorothy/Ken as Lion/Ken as the Scarecrow/Ken as the Tin Man 284335	2,500		150.00	150

FAO Schwarz Exclusive - Enesco

YEAR ISSUE	EDITION LIMIT	YEAR RETD.	ISSUE PRICE	*QUOTE U.S.$
1994 Silver Screen Barbie 128805	3,600	1995	30.00	30
1995 Circus Star Barbie 150339	3,600	1995	30.00	30

Glamour - Enesco

YEAR ISSUE	EDITION LIMIT	YEAR RETD.	ISSUE PRICE	*QUOTE U.S.$
1994 35th Anniversary Barbie 655112	5,000	1994	30.00	30-40
1995 Barbie Solo In The Spotlight, 1959 114383	5,000	1995	30.00	45-55
1995 Barbie Enchanted Evening, 1960 175587	10,000		30.00	30
1996 Here Comes The Bride, 1966 170984	Open		30.00	30
1996 Holiday Dance, 1965 188794	10,000		30.00	30
1997 Wedding Day, 1959 260282	7,500		30.00	30

Great Eras - Enesco

YEAR ISSUE	EDITION LIMIT	YEAR RETD.	ISSUE PRICE	*QUOTE U.S.$
1996 Gibson Girl Barbie 174769	10,000		30.00	30
1996 1920's Flapper Barbie 174777	10,000		30.00	30
1997 1850's Southern Belle 174785	7,500		30.00	30
1997 Egyptian Queen 174793	7,500		30.00	30
1997 Elizabethan Queen Barbie 174815	7,500		30.00	30
1997 Medieval Lady Barbie 174807	7,500	1997	30.00	30

Happy Holidays - Enesco

YEAR ISSUE	EDITION LIMIT	YEAR RETD.	ISSUE PRICE	*QUOTE U.S.$
1994 Happy Holidays Barbie, 1994 115088	5,000	1994	30.00	75-100
1995 Happy Holidays Barbie, 1995 143154	Yr.Iss.	1995	30.00	30
1995 Happy Holidays Barbie, 1988 154180	Yr.Iss.	1995	30.00	30
1996 Happy Holidays Barbie, 1989 188859	Yr.Iss.	1996	30.00	30
1996 Happy Holidays Barbie, 1996 188816	Yr.Iss.	1996	30.00	30
1997 Happy Holidays Barbie, 1997 274259	Yr.Iss.	1997	30.00	30
1997 Happy Holidays Barbie, 1990 274232	Yr.Iss.	1997	30.00	30

Hollywood Legends - Enesco

YEAR ISSUE	EDITION LIMIT	YEAR RETD.	ISSUE PRICE	*QUOTE U.S.$
1996 Barbie As Scarlett O'Hara in Green Velvet 171085	10,000	1996	35.00	30-35
1997 Barbie As Scarlett O'Hara in Red Velvet 260169	7,500		35.00	35
1997 Barbie As Dorothy 260193	7,500		35.00	35
1997 Barbie As Dorothy/Ken as the Lion/Ken as the Scarecrow/Ken as the Tin Man 284327	5,000		35.00	35
1997 Barbie As Glinda the Good Witch 274275	7,500	1997	35.00	35

My Fair Lady - Enesco

YEAR ISSUE	EDITION LIMIT	YEAR RETD.	ISSUE PRICE	*QUOTE U.S.$
1997 Barbie As Eliza Doolittle At Ascot 270512	7,500		30.00	30
1997 Barbie As Eliza Doolittle At Embassy Ball 274291	7,500		35.00	35

Bing & Grondahl

American Christmas Heritage Collection - C. Magadini

YEAR ISSUE	EDITION LIMIT	YEAR RETD.	ISSUE PRICE	*QUOTE U.S.$
1996 The Statue of Liberty	Yr.Iss.	1996	47.50	48-69
1997 Christmas Eve at The Lincoln Memorial	Yr.Iss.	1997	47.50	29-69
1998 Chicago Water Tower	Yr.Iss.	1998	34.50	29-79
1999 At Mount Rushmore	Yr.Iss.	1999	37.50	29-69
2000 Christmas at the Alamo	Yr.Iss.		39.50	40

Centennial Anniversary Commemoratives - Various

YEAR ISSUE	EDITION LIMIT	YEAR RETD.	ISSUE PRICE	*QUOTE U.S.$
1995 Centennial Plaquettes: Series of 10-5" plates featuring B&G motifs: 1895, 1905, 1919, 1927, 1932, 1945, 1954, 1967, 1974, 1982	Yr.Iss.	1995	250.00	240-300
1995 Centennial Plate: Behind the Frozen Window - F.A. Hallin	10,000	1995	39.50	39-45
1995 Centennial Platter: Towers of Copenhagen - J. Nielsen	7,500	1995	195.00	195

Centennial Collection - Various

YEAR ISSUE	EDITION LIMIT	YEAR RETD.	ISSUE PRICE	*QUOTE U.S.$
1991 Crows Enjoying Christmas - D. Jensen	Annual	1991	59.50	60-90
1992 Copenhagen Christmas - H. Vlugenring	Annual	1992	59.50	60-90
1993 Christmas Elf - H. Thelander	Annual	1993	59.50	63-72
1994 Christmas in Church - H. Thelander	Annual	1994	59.50	63-90
1995 Behind The Frozen Window - A. Hallin	Annual	1995	59.50	30-60

Children's Day Plate Series - S. Vestergaard, unless otherwise noted

YEAR ISSUE	EDITION LIMIT	YEAR RETD.	ISSUE PRICE	*QUOTE U.S.$
1985 The Magical Tea Party - C. Roller	Annual	1985	24.50	25-28
1986 A Joyful Flight - C. Roller	Annual	1986	26.50	48-54
1986 The Little Gardeners - C. Roller	Annual	1987	29.50	25-74
1988 Wash Day - C. Roller	Annual	1988	34.50	30-48
1989 Bedtime - C. Roller	Annual	1989	37.00	30-79
1990 My Favorite Dress	Annual	1990	37.00	31-75
1991 Fun on the Beach	Annual	1991	45.00	38-60
1992 A Summer Day in the Meadow	Annual	1992	45.00	35-64
1993 The Carousel	Annual	1993	45.00	45-105
1994 The Little Fisherman	Annual	1994	45.00	44-67
1995 My First Book	Annual	1995	45.00	60-144
1996 The Little Racers	Annual	1996	45.00	45-60
1997 Bath Time	Annual	1997	45.00	47-56
1998 Little Vendors	Annual	1998	34.50	32-75
1999 The Little Concert	Annual	1999	37.50	32-45
2000 Don't Tell	Annual		39.50	40

Christmas - Various

YEAR ISSUE	EDITION LIMIT	YEAR RETD.	ISSUE PRICE	*QUOTE U.S.$
1895 Behind The Frozen Window - F.A. Hallin	Annual	1895	.50	4750-7200
1896 New Moon - F.A. Hallin	Annual	1896	.50	1950-3183
1897 Sparrows - F.A. Hallin	Annual	1897	.75	975-1872
1898 Roses and Star - F. Garde	Annual	1898	.75	799-966
1899 Crows - F. Garde	Annual	1899	.75	950-2247
1900 Church Bells - F. Garde	Annual	1900	.75	950-1425
1901 Three Wise Men - S. Sabra	Annual	1901	1.00	450-663
1902 Gothic Church Interior - D. Jensen	Annual	1902	1.00	444-570
1903 Expectant Children - M. Hyldahl	Annual	1903	1.00	395-426
1904 Fredericksberg Hill - C. Olsen	Annual	1904	1.00	140-219
1905 Christmas Night - D. Jensen	Annual	1905	1.00	145-219
1906 Sleighing to Church - D. Jensen	Annual	1906	1.00	100-144
1907 Little Match Girl - E. Plockross	Annual	1907	1.00	133-150
1908 St. Petri Church - P. Jorgensen	Annual	1908	1.00	85-125
1909 Yule Tree - Aarestrup	Annual	1909	1.50	80-123
1910 The Old Organist - C. Ersgaard	Annual	1910	1.50	75-120
1911 Angels and Shepherds - H. Moltke	Annual	1911	1.50	99-105
1912 Going to Church - E. Hansen	Annual	1912	1.50	75-99
1913 Bringing Home the Tree - T. Larsen	Annual	1913	1.50	99-105
1914 Amalienborg Castle - T. Larsen	Annual	1914	1.50	80-105
1915 Dog Outside Window - D. Jensen	Annual	1915	1.50	139-165
1916 Sparrows at Christmas - P. Jorgensen	Annual	1916	1.50	54-90
1917 Christmas Boat - A. Friis	Annual	1917	1.50	89-105
1918 Fishing Boat - A. Friis	Annual	1918	1.50	90-99
1919 Outside Lighted Window - A. Friis	Annual	1919	2.00	75-90
1920 Hare in the Snow - A. Friis	Annual	1920	2.00	75-96
1921 Pigeons - A. Friis	Annual	1921	2.00	60-82
1922 Star of Bethlehem - A. Friis	Annual	1922	2.00	59-87
1923 The Ermitage - A. Friis	Annual	1923	2.00	50-79
1924 Lighthouse - A. Friis	Annual	1924	2.50	72-90
1925 Child's Christmas - A. Friis	Annual	1925	2.50	70-96
1926 Churchgoers - A. Friis	Annual	1926	2.50	70-90
1927 Skating Couple - A. Friis	Annual	1927	2.50	70-114
1928 Eskimos - A. Friis	Annual	1928	2.50	69-84
1929 Fox Outside Farm - A. Friis	Annual	1929	2.50	70-100
1930 Town Hall Square - H. Flugenring	Annual	1930	2.50	90-108
1931 Christmas Train - A. Friis	Annual	1931	2.50	80-96
1932 Life Boat - H. Flugenring	Annual	1932	2.50	75-109
1933 Korsor-Nyborg Ferry - H. Flugenring	Annual	1933	3.00	70-96
1934 Church Bell in Tower - H. Flugenring	Annual	1934	3.00	90-107
1935 Lillebelt Bridge - O. Larson	Annual	1935	3.00	75-122
1936 Royal Guard - O. Larson	Annual	1936	3.00	75-90
1937 Arrival of Christmas Guests - O. Larson	Annual	1937	3.00	79-165
1938 Lighting the Candles - I. Tjerne	Annual	1938	3.00	99-201
1939 Old Lock-Eye, The Sandman - I. Tjerne	Annual	1939	3.00	149-230
1940 Christmas Letters - O. Larson	Annual	1940	4.00	164-222
1941 Horses Enjoying Meal - O. Larson	Annual	1941	4.00	243-310
1942 Danish Farm - O. Larson	Annual	1942	4.00	174-290
1943 Ribe Cathedral - O. Larson	Annual	1943	5.00	174-237
1944 Sorgenfri Castle - O. Larson	Annual	1944	5.00	99-134
1945 The Old Water Mill - O. Larson	Annual	1945	5.00	119-225
1946 Commemoration Cross - M. Hyldahl	Annual	1946	5.00	79-105
1947 Dybbol Mill - M. Hyldahl	Annual	1947	5.00	99-170
1948 Watchman - M. Hyldahl	Annual	1948	5.50	73-215
1949 Landsoldaten - M. Hyldahl	Annual	1949	5.50	73-148
1950 Kronborg Castle - M. Hyldahl	Annual	1950	5.50	100-150
1951 Jens Bang - M. Hyldahl	Annual	1951	6.00	93-132
1952 Thorsvaldsen Museum - B. Pramvig	Annual	1952	6.00	79-120
1953 Snowman - B. Pramvig	Annual	1953	7.50	79-120

*Quotes have been rounded up to nearest dollar

YEAR ISSUE	EDITION LIMIT	YEAR RETD.	ISSUE PRICE	*QUOTE U.S.$
1954 Royal Boat - K. Bonfils	Annual	1954	7.00	89-115
1955 Kaulundorg Church - K. Bonfils	Annual	1955	8.00	89-128
1956 Christmas in Copenhagen - K. Bonfils	Annual	1956	8.50	123-235
1957 Christmas Candles - K. Bonfils	Annual	1957	9.00	139-195
1958 Santa Claus - K. Bonfils	Annual	1958	9.50	105-130
1959 Christmas Eve - K. Bonfils	Annual	1959	10.00	129-165
1960 Village Church - K. Bonfils	Annual	1960	10.00	128-210
1961 Winter Harmony - K. Bonfils	Annual	1961	10.50	98-135
1962 Winter Night - K. Bonfils	Annual	1962	11.00	74-90
1963 The Christmas Elf - H. Thelander	Annual	1963	11.00	58-165
1964 The Fir Tree and Hare - H. Thelander	Annual	1964	11.50	24-64
1965 Bringing Home the Tree - H. Thelander	Annual	1965	12.00	33-69
1966 Home for Christmas - H. Thelander	Annual	1966	12.00	19-63
1967 Sharing the Joy - H. Thelander	Annual	1967	13.00	20-65
1968 Christmas in Church - H. Thelander	Annual	1968	14.00	20-45
1969 Arrival of Guests - H. Thelander	Annual	1969	14.00	12-38
1970 Pheasants in Snow - H. Thelander	Annual	1970	14.50	10-55
1971 Christmas at Home - H. Thelander	Annual	1971	15.00	9-30
1972 Christmas in Greenland - H. Thelander	Annual	1972	16.50	10-27
1973 Country Christmas - H. Thelander	Annual	1973	19.50	16-45
1974 Christmas in the Village - H. Thelander	Annual	1974	22.00	18-27
1975 Old Water Mill - H. Thelander	Annual	1975	27.50	20-39
1976 Christmas Welcome - H. Thelander	Annual	1976	27.50	19-36
1977 Copenhagen Christmas - H. Thelander	Annual	1977	29.50	15-39
1978 Christmas Tale - H. Thelander	Annual	1978	32.00	20-49
1979 White Christmas - H. Thelander	Annual	1979	36.50	20-49
1980 Christmas in Woods - H. Thelander	Annual	1980	42.50	23-50
1981 Christmas Peace - H. Thelander	Annual	1981	49.50	18-50
1982 Christmas Tree - H. Thelander	Annual	1982	54.50	20-60
1983 Christmas in Old Town - H. Thelander	Annual	1983	54.50	20-55
1984 The Christmas Letter - E. Jensen	Annual	1984	54.50	20-75
1985 Christmas Eve at the Farmhouse - E. Jensen	Annual	1985	54.50	25-77
1986 Silent Night, Holy Night - E. Jensen	Annual	1986	54.50	25-75
1987 The Snowman's Christmas Eve - E. Jensen	Annual	1987	59.50	40-77
1988 In the Kings Garden - E. Jensen	Annual	1988	64.50	40-77
1989 Christmas Anchorage - E. Jensen	Annual	1989	59.50	50-75
1990 Changing of the Guards - E. Jensen	Annual	1990	64.50	65-105
1991 Copenhagen Stock Exchange - E. Jensen	Annual	1991	69.50	49-90
1992 Christmas At the Rectory - J. Steensen	Annual	1992	69.50	70-120
1993 Father Christmas in Copenhagen - J. Nielsen	Annual	1993	69.50	68-96
1994 A Day At The Deer Park - J. Nielsen	Annual	1994	72.50	59-96
1995 The Towers of Copenhagen - J. Nielsen	Annual	1995	72.50	59-105
1996 Winter at the Old Mill - J. Nielsen	Annual	1996	74.50	48-85
1997 Country Christmas - J. Nielsen	Annual	1997	69.50	68-90
1998 Santa the Storyteller - J. Nielsen	Annual	1998	69.50	65-105
1999 Around the Christmas Tree - J. Nielsen	Annual	1999	72.50	73-150
2000 Ringing at the Bell Tower - J. Nielsen	Annual		72.50	73

Christmas Around the World - H. Hansen

YEAR ISSUE	EDITION LIMIT	YEAR RETD.	ISSUE PRICE	*QUOTE U.S.$
1995 Santa in Greenland	Yr.Iss.	1995	74.50	50-95
1996 Santa in Orient	Yr.Iss.	1996	74.50	59-90
1997 Santa in Russia	Yr.Iss.	1997	74.50	59-75
1998 Santa in Australia	Yr.Iss.	1998	69.50	59-70
1999 Santa in Europe	Yr.Iss.	1999	72.50	59-73
2000 Santa in America	Yr.Iss.		72.50	73

Christmas In America - J. Woodson

YEAR ISSUE	EDITION LIMIT	YEAR RETD.	ISSUE PRICE	*QUOTE U.S.$
1986 Christmas Eve in Williamsburg	Annual	1986	29.50	39-150
1987 Christmas Eve at the White House	Annual	1987	34.50	10-75
1988 Christmas Eve at Rockefeller Center	Annual	1988	34.50	10-68
1989 Christmas In New England	Annual	1989	37.00	20-59
1990 Christmas Eve at the Capitol	Annual	1990	39.50	20-57
1991 Christmas Eve at Independence Hall	Annual	1991	45.00	30-90
1992 Christmas in San Francisco	Annual	1992	47.50	10-60
1993 Coming Home For Christmas	Annual	1993	47.50	10-75
1994 Christmas Eve In Alaska	Annual	1994	47.50	40-79
1995 Christmas Eve in Mississippi	Annual	1995	47.50	39-48

Christmas in America Anniversary Plate - J. Woodson

YEAR ISSUE	EDITION LIMIT	YEAR RETD.	ISSUE PRICE	*QUOTE U.S.$
1991 Christmas Eve in Williamsburg	Annual	1991	69.50	73-100
1995 The Capitol	Annual	1995	74.50	75

Jubilee-5 Year Cycle - Various

YEAR ISSUE	EDITION LIMIT	YEAR RETD.	ISSUE PRICE	*QUOTE U.S.$
1915 Frozen Window - F.A. Hallin	Annual	1915	Unkn.	199-250
1920 Church Bells - F. Garde	Annual	1920	Unkn.	99-149
1925 Dog Outside Window - D. Jensen	Annual	1925	Unkn.	180-300
1930 The Old Organist - C. Ersgaard	Annual	1930	Unkn.	210-275
1935 Little Match Girl - E. Plockross	Annual	1935	Unkn.	450-900
1940 Three Wise Men - S. Sabra	Annual	1940	Unkn.	1795-2400
1945 Amalienborg Castle - T. Larsen	Annual	1945	Unkn.	90-249
1950 Eskimos - A. Friis	Annual	1950	Unkn.	90-259
1955 Dybbol Mill - M. Hyldahl	Annual	1955	Unkn.	195-259
1960 Kronborg Castle - M. Hyldahl	Annual	1960	25.00	90-199
1965 Chruchgoers - A. Friis	Annual	1965	25.00	59-75
1970 Amalienborg Castle - T. Larsen	Annual	1970	30.00	15-30
1975 Horses Enjoying Meal - O. Larson	Annual	1975	40.00	18-69
1980 Yule Tree - Aarestrup	Annual	1980	60.00	48-60
1985 Lifeboat at Work - H. Flugenring	Annual	1985	65.00	75-89
1990 The Royal Yacht Dannebrog - J. Bonfils	Annual	1990	95.00	85-125
1995 Centennial Platter - J. Nielsen	7,500	1995	195.00	125-199
1996 Lifeboat at Work (released a year late) - H. Flugenring	1,000	1996	95.00	89-95
2000 Star of Bethlehem - J. Achton Friis	Annual		100.00	100

Mother's Day - Various

YEAR ISSUE	EDITION LIMIT	YEAR RETD.	ISSUE PRICE	*QUOTE U.S.$
1969 Dogs and Puppies - H. Thelander	Annual	1969	9.75	250-450
1970 Bird and Chicks - H. Thelander	Annual	1970	10.00	17-30
1971 Cat and Kitten - H. Thelander	Annual	1971	11.00	10-23
1972 Mare and Foal - H. Thelander	Annual	1972	12.00	10-23
1973 Duck and Ducklings - H. Thelander	Annual	1973	13.00	12-22
1974 Bear and Cubs - H. Thelander	Annual	1974	16.50	10-23
1975 Doe and Fawns - H. Thelander	Annual	1975	19.50	10-22
1976 Swan Family - H. Thelander	Annual	1976	22.50	9-25
1977 Squirrel and Young - H. Thelander	Annual	1977	23.50	19-34
1978 Heron and Young - H. Thelander	Annual	1978	24.50	15-23
1979 Fox and Cubs - H. Thelander	Annual	1979	27.50	15-28
1980 Woodpecker and Young - H. Thelander	Annual	1980	29.50	25-60
1981 Hare and Young - H. Thelander	Annual	1981	36.50	25-37
1982 Lioness and Cubs - H. Thelander	Annual	1982	39.50	22-45
1983 Raccoon and Young - H. Thelander	Annual	1983	39.50	25-50
1984 Stork and Nestlings - H. Thelander	Annual	1984	39.50	25-50
1985 Bear and Cubs - H. Thelander	Annual	1985	39.50	29-60
1986 Elephant with Calf - H. Thelander	Annual	1986	39.50	40-59
1987 Sheep with Lambs - H. Thelander	Annual	1987	42.50	55-89
1988 Crested Plover and Young - H. Thelander	Annual	1988	47.50	63-95
1988 Lapwing Mother with Chicks - H. Thelander	Annual	1988	49.50	63-90
1989 Cow With Calf - H. Thelander	Annual	1989	49.50	44-85
1990 Hen with Chicks - L. Jensen	Annual	1990	52.50	64-120
1991 The Nanny Goat and her Two Frisky Kids - L. Jensen	Annual	1991	54.50	49-90
1992 Panda With Cubs - L. Jensen	Annual	1992	59.50	74-120
1993 St. Bernard Dog and Puppies - A. Therkelsen	Annual	1993	59.50	75-120
1994 Cat with Kittens - A. Therkelsen	Annual	1994	59.50	58-120
1995 Hedgehog with Young - A. Therkelsen	Annual	1995	59.50	46-90
1996 Koala with Young - A. Therkelsen	Annual	1996	59.50	56-90
1997 Goose with Gooslings - L. Didier	Annual	1997	59.50	60-133
1998 Penguin With Young - L. Didier	Annual	1998	49.50	50-64
1999 Rabbit - F. Clausen	Annual	1999	49.50	49-68
2000 Dolphin with Calf - F. Clausen	Yr.Iss.		54.50	55

Mother's Day Jubilee-5 Year Cycle - Thelander, unless otherwise noted

YEAR ISSUE	EDITION LIMIT	YEAR RETD.	ISSUE PRICE	*QUOTE U.S.$
1979 Dog & Puppies	Yr.Iss.	1979	55.00	42-89
1984 Swan Family	Yr.Iss.	1984	65.00	65-100
1989 Mare & Colt	Yr.Iss.	1989	95.00	89-112
1994 Woodpecker & Young	Yr.Iss.	1994	95.00	89-95
1999 Panther with Cubs - L. Jensen	Yr.Iss.	1999	95.00	70-95

Olympic - Unknown

YEAR ISSUE	EDITION LIMIT	YEAR RETD.	ISSUE PRICE	*QUOTE U.S.$
1972 Munich, Germany	Closed	1972	20.00	10-30
1976 Montreal, Canada	Closed	1976	29.50	57-59
1980 Moscow, Russia	Closed	1980	43.00	79-87
1984 Los Angeles, USA	Closed	1984	45.00	250-359
1988 Seoul, Korea	Closed	1988	60.00	49-87
1992 Barcelona, Spain	Closed	1992	74.50	59-87

Santa Claus Collection - H. Hansen

YEAR ISSUE	EDITION LIMIT	YEAR RETD.	ISSUE PRICE	*QUOTE U.S.$
1989 Santa's Workshop	Annual	1989	59.50	59-120
1990 Santa's Sleigh	Annual	1990	59.50	59-80
1991 Santa's Journey	Annual	1991	69.50	59-120
1992 Santa's Arrival	Annual	1992	74.50	59-90
1993 Santa's Gifts	Annual	1993	74.50	59-75
1994 Christmas Stories	Annual	1994	74.50	59-90

Statue of Liberty - Unknown

YEAR ISSUE	EDITION LIMIT	YEAR RETD.	ISSUE PRICE	*QUOTE U.S.$
1985 Statue of Liberty	10,000	1985	60.00	49-100

The Bradford Exchange/Canada

Big League Dreams

YEAR ISSUE	EDITION LIMIT	YEAR RETD.	ISSUE PRICE	*QUOTE U.S.$
1993 Hey, Batter Batter	Closed		29.90	50-58
1994 The Wind Up	Closed		29.90	57
1994 Safe!!!	Closed		32.90	90-99
1994 A Difference of Opinion	Closed		32.90	100
1994 I Got It, I Got It!	Closed		32.90	80
1994 Victory	Closed		32.90	69

The Bradford Exchange/China

Dream of the Red Chamber

YEAR ISSUE	EDITION LIMIT	YEAR RETD.	ISSUE PRICE	*QUOTE U.S.$
1994 Pao-Choi: Precious Clasp	Closed		29.90	35-65
1994 Hsiang-Yun: Little Cloud	Closed		29.90	38-45
1994 Yuan-Chun: Beginning of Spring	Closed		29.90	36
1994 Hsi-Feng: Phoenix	Closed		29.90	100
1994 Tai-Yu: Black Jade	Closed		29.90	45-100
1994 Tan-Chun: Taste of Spring	Closed		29.90	69

The Bradford Exchange/Russia

The Nutcracker - N. Zaitseva

YEAR ISSUE	EDITION LIMIT	YEAR RETD.	ISSUE PRICE	*QUOTE U.S.$
1993 Marie's Magical Gift	Closed		39.87	40-45
1993 Dance of Sugar Plum Fairy	Closed		39.87	45-52
1994 Waltz of the Flowers	Closed		39.87	50-69
1994 Battle With the Mice King	Closed		39.87	48-50

Songs of Angels - Vladimirdvich

YEAR ISSUE	EDITION LIMIT	YEAR RETD.	ISSUE PRICE	*QUOTE U.S.$
1994 Heavenly Hearalds	Closed		29.87	30
1994 Divine Chorus	Closed		29.87	30
1995 Springtime Duet	Closed		32.87	33
1995 Mystical Chimes	Closed		32.87	33

The Bradford Exchange/United States

101 Dalmatians - Disney Studios

YEAR ISSUE	EDITION LIMIT	YEAR RETD.	ISSUE PRICE	*QUOTE U.S.$
1993 Watch Dogs	95-day		29.90	30
1994 A Happy Reunion	95-day		29.90	30
1994 Hello Darlings	95-day		32.90	33
1994 Sergeant Tibs Saves the Day	95-day		32.90	33
1994 Halfway Home	95-day		32.90	33
1994 True Love	95-day		32.90	33
1995 Bedtime	95-day		34.90	35
1995 A Messy Good Time	95-day		34.90	35

Aladdin - Disney Studios

YEAR ISSUE	EDITION LIMIT	YEAR RETD.	ISSUE PRICE	*QUOTE U.S.$
1993 Magic Carpet Ride	Closed		29.90	66
1993 A Friend Like Me	Closed		29.90	30-35
1994 Aladdin in Love	Closed		29.90	30-35
1994 Traveling Companions	Closed		29.90	45
1994 Make Way for Prince Ali	Closed		29.90	31-36
1994 Aladdin's Wish	Closed		29.90	49
1995 Bee Yourself	Closed		29.90	33-35
1995 Group Hug	Closed		29.90	35-39

Alice in Wonderland - S. Gustafson

YEAR ISSUE	EDITION LIMIT	YEAR RETD.	ISSUE PRICE	*QUOTE U.S.$
1993 The Mad Tea Party	Closed		29.90	39-47
1993 The Cheshire Cat	Closed		29.90	69-75
1994 Croquet with the Queen	Closed		29.90	69-73
1994 Advice from a Caterpillar	Closed		29.90	65-71

America's Famous Fairways - D. Day

YEAR ISSUE	EDITION LIMIT	YEAR RETD.	ISSUE PRICE	*QUOTE U.S.$
1995 Pebble Beach	Closed		34.95	50
1995 Augusta Beach	Closed		34.95	65
1995 Cypress Course	Closed		34.95	150-300
1995 Medinah Course	Closed		34.95	60-64

America's Triumph in Space - R. Schaar

YEAR ISSUE	EDITION LIMIT	YEAR RETD.	ISSUE PRICE	*QUOTE U.S.$
1993 The Eagle Has Landed	Closed		29.90	27
1993 The March Toward Destiny	Closed		29.90	24-27
1994 Flight of Glory	Closed		32.90	42-45
1994 Beyond the Bounds of Earth	Closed		32.90	63
1994 Conquering the New Frontier	Closed		32.90	40-44
1994 Rendezvous With Victory	Closed		34.90	67
1994 The New Explorers	Closed		34.90	65
1994 Triumphant Finale	Closed		34.90	55-58

Ancient Seasons - M. Silversmith

YEAR ISSUE	EDITION LIMIT	YEAR RETD.	ISSUE PRICE	*QUOTE U.S.$
1995 Edge of Night	Closed		29.90	30
1995 Journey of Midnight	95-day		29.90	30
1995 Winter Sojurn	95-day		29.90	30
1995 Mid Winter	95-day		29.90	30

Autumn Encounters - C. Fisher

YEAR ISSUE	EDITION LIMIT	YEAR RETD.	ISSUE PRICE	*QUOTE U.S.$
1995 Woodland Innocents	95-day		29.90	30

Babe Ruth Centennial - P. Heffernan

YEAR ISSUE	EDITION LIMIT	YEAR RETD.	ISSUE PRICE	*QUOTE U.S.$
1994 The 60th Homer	Closed		34.90	48
1995 Ruth's Pitching Debut	Closed		29.90	52-60
1995 The Final Home Run	Closed		29.90	53-90
1995 Barnstorming Days	Closed		34.90	69

Baskets of Love - A. Isakov

YEAR ISSUE	EDITION LIMIT	YEAR RETD.	ISSUE PRICE	*QUOTE U.S.$
1993 Andrew and Abbey	Closed		29.90	26-32
1993 Cody and Courtney	Closed		29.90	30-41
1993 Emily and Elliott	Closed		32.90	64
1993 Heather and Hannah	Closed		32.90	35
1993 Justin and Jessica	Closed		32.90	40
1993 Katie and Kelly	Closed		34.90	44
1994 Louie and Libby	Closed		34.90	89
1994 Sammy and Sarah	Closed		34.90	35-79

Battles of American Civil War - J. Griffin

YEAR ISSUE	EDITION LIMIT	YEAR RETD.	ISSUE PRICE	*QUOTE U.S.$
1994 Gettysburg	95-day		29.90	30
1995 Vicksburg	95-day		29.90	30

Beary Merry Christmas - S. Sherwood

YEAR ISSUE	EDITION LIMIT	YEAR RETD.	ISSUE PRICE	*QUOTE U.S.$
1995 Loving Tradition	Closed		29.95	30-55
1995 Moment/Treasure	Closed		29.95	30
1995 Romantic Ride	Closed		29.95	30
1995 Wreath of Love	Closed		29.95	30
1995 Topping on the Tree	Closed		29.95	30
1995 Under the Mistletoe	Closed		29.95	30

The Bunny Workshop - J. Maday

YEAR ISSUE	EDITION LIMIT	YEAR RETD.	ISSUE PRICE	*QUOTE U.S.$
1995 Make Today Eggstra Special	Closed		19.95	20

By Gone Days - L. Dubin

YEAR ISSUE	EDITION LIMIT	YEAR RETD.	ISSUE PRICE	*QUOTE U.S.$
1994 Soda Fountain	Closed		29.90	60-63
1995 Sam's Grocery Store	Closed		29.90	45-59
1995 Saturday Matinee	Closed		29.90	45
1995 The Corner News Stand	Closed		29.90	45
1995 Main Street Splendor	Closed		29.90	32-45
1995 The Barber Shop	Closed		29.90	50

Cabins of Comfort River - F. Buchwitz

YEAR ISSUE	EDITION LIMIT	YEAR RETD.	ISSUE PRICE	*QUOTE U.S.$
1995 Comfort by Camplights Fire	Closed		29.95	30
1995 Lantern Light	Closed		29.95	30-40
1995 Reflections in the Moonlight	Closed		29.95	30
1995 Tranquility	95-day		29.95	30

Carousel Daydreams - N/A, unless otherwise noted

YEAR ISSUE	EDITION LIMIT	YEAR RETD.	ISSUE PRICE	*QUOTE U.S.$
1994 Swept Away - Mr. Tseng	Closed		39.90	79-85
1995 When I Grow Up	Closed		39.90	137-200
1995 All Aboard	Closed		44.90	85-100
1995 Hold Onto Your Dreams	Closed		44.90	125-149
1995 Flight of Fancy	Closed		44.90	170-194
1995 Big Hopes, Bright Dreams	Closed		49.90	60-145

*Quotes have been rounded up to nearest dollar

YEAR ISSUE	EDITION LIMIT	YEAR RETD.	ISSUE PRICE	*QUOTE U.S.$
1995 Victorian Reverie	Closed		49.90	119-200
1995 Wishful Thinking	Closed		49.90	125-175
1995 Dreams of Destiny	Closed		49.90	125-130
1995 My Favorite Memory	Closed		49.90	100-195

Charles Wysocki's American Frontier - C. Wysocki

YEAR ISSUE	EDITION LIMIT	YEAR RETD.	ISSUE PRICE	*QUOTE U.S.$
1993 Timberline Jack's Trading Post	Closed		29.90	30-75
1994 Dr. Livingwell's Medicine Show	Closed		29.90	28-42
1994 Bustling Boomtown	Closed		29.90	28-48
1994 Kirbyville	Closed		29.90	30-35
1994 Hearty Homesteaders	Closed		29.90	40
1994 Oklahoma or Bust	Closed		29.90	55

Charles Wysocki's Hometown Memories - C. Wysocki

YEAR ISSUE	EDITION LIMIT	YEAR RETD.	ISSUE PRICE	*QUOTE U.S.$
1994 Small Talk at Birdie's Perch	Closed		29.90	60-73
1995 Tranquil Days/Ravenswhip Cove	Closed		29.90	60-260
1995 Summer Delights	Closed		29.90	50-150
1995 Capturing the Moment	Closed		29.90	55-60
1995 A Farewell Kiss	Closed		29.90	54
1995 Jason Sparkin the Lighthouse Keeper's Daughter	Closed		29.90	55-150

Charles Wysocki's Peppercricket Grove - C. Wysocki

YEAR ISSUE	EDITION LIMIT	YEAR RETD.	ISSUE PRICE	*QUOTE U.S.$
1993 Peppercricket Farms	Closed		24.90	45-48
1993 Gingernut Valley Inn	Closed		24.90	50-54
1993 Budzen's Fruits and Vegetables	Closed		24.90	47-49
1993 Virginia's Market	Closed		24.90	45-50
1993 Pumpkin Hollow Emporium	Closed		24.90	55
1993 Liberty Star Farms	Closed		24.90	48-50
1993 Overflow Antique Market	Closed		24.90	48-50
1993 Black Crow Antique Shoppe	Closed		24.90	54

Cherished Traditions - M. Lasher

YEAR ISSUE	EDITION LIMIT	YEAR RETD.	ISSUE PRICE	*QUOTE U.S.$
1995 The Wedding Ring	Closed		29.90	68-71
1995 The Star	Closed		29.90	50
1995 Log Cabin	Closed		29.90	49
1995 Ocean Wave	Closed		29.90	50-60
1995 Dresden	Closed		29.90	50-70
1995 Goose on the Pond	Closed		29.90	71-80
1995 Starburst	Closed		29.90	74-80
1995 Grandmothers Flower	Closed		29.90	80-85

Cherubs of Innocence - Various

YEAR ISSUE	EDITION LIMIT	YEAR RETD.	ISSUE PRICE	*QUOTE U.S.$
1994 The First Kiss	Closed		29.90	35-74
1995 Love at Rest	Closed		29.90	30-45
1995 Thoughts of Love	Closed		32.90	35
1995 Loving Gaze	Closed		32.90	35-57

Choir of Angels - Toole, unless otherwise noted

YEAR ISSUE	EDITION LIMIT	YEAR RETD.	ISSUE PRICE	*QUOTE U.S.$
1995 Song of Joy - Unknown	Closed		34.95	35
1995 Song of Peace	Closed		34.95	35
1995 Song of Hope	Closed		34.95	35
1995 Song of Harmony	95-day		34.95	35

Chosen Messengers - G. Running Wolf

YEAR ISSUE	EDITION LIMIT	YEAR RETD.	ISSUE PRICE	*QUOTE U.S.$
1994 The Pathfinders	Closed		29.90	21
1994 The Overseers	Closed		29.90	22
1994 The Providers	Closed		32.90	48-50
1994 The Surveyors	Closed		32.90	50-53

A Christmas Carol - L. Garrison

YEAR ISSUE	EDITION LIMIT	YEAR RETD.	ISSUE PRICE	*QUOTE U.S.$
1993 God Bless Us Everyone	Closed		29.90	58
1993 Ghost of Christmas Present	Closed		29.90	66-69
1994 A Merry Christmas to All	Closed		29.90	50-59
1994 A Visit From Marley's Ghost	Closed		29.90	77-89
1994 Remembering Christmas Past	Closed		29.90	62
1994 A Spirit's Warning	Closed		29.90	96
1994 The True Spirit of Christmas	Closed		29.90	87
1994 Merry Christmas, Bob	Closed		29.90	58

Christmas in the Village - R. McGinnis

YEAR ISSUE	EDITION LIMIT	YEAR RETD.	ISSUE PRICE	*QUOTE U.S.$
1995 The Village Toy Shop	Closed		29.95	27-50
1995 Little Church in the Vale	Closed		29.95	30-38
1995 The Village Confectionary	Closed		29.95	52
1996 The Village Inn	Closed		29.95	30-55
1996 Goodnight Dear Friends	Closed		29.95	55-65
1996 A New Fallen Snow	Closed		29.95	55-65

Christmas Memories - J. Tanton

YEAR ISSUE	EDITION LIMIT	YEAR RETD.	ISSUE PRICE	*QUOTE U.S.$
1993 A Winter's Tale	Closed		29.90	25-35
1993 Finishing Touch	Closed		29.90	43
1993 Welcome to Our Home	Closed		29.90	59
1993 A Christmas Celebration	Closed		29.90	57

Classic Cars - D. Everhart

YEAR ISSUE	EDITION LIMIT	YEAR RETD.	ISSUE PRICE	*QUOTE U.S.$
1993 1957 Corvette	Closed		54.00	55
1993 1956 Thunderbird	Closed		54.00	55
1994 1957 Bel Air	Closed		54.00	103
1994 1965 Mustang	Closed		54.00	100

Classic Melodies from the "Sound of Music" - M. Hampshire

YEAR ISSUE	EDITION LIMIT	YEAR RETD.	ISSUE PRICE	*QUOTE U.S.$
1995 Sing Along with Maria	Closed		29.90	47
1995 A Drop of Golden Sun	Closed		29.90	60
1995 The Von Trapp Family Singers	Closed		29.90	70
1995 Alpine Refuge	Closed		29.90	50

Classic Roses - L. Moser

YEAR ISSUE	EDITION LIMIT	YEAR RETD.	ISSUE PRICE	*QUOTE U.S.$
1995 Beauty in Bloom	Closed		34.95	35-100
1995 Pretty in Pink	Closed		34.95	35
1995 Precious Purple	95-day		37.95	38
1995 Magic/Mauve	95-day		37.95	38

Classic Waterfowl - J. Hautman

YEAR ISSUE	EDITION LIMIT	YEAR RETD.	ISSUE PRICE	*QUOTE U.S.$
1995 Mallards	Closed		29.90	30-55
1995 Black Bellied	Closed		29.90	30-45
1995 Wood Ducks	Closed		29.90	30-45
1995 American Wigeon	Closed		29.90	30-45
1995 Canvasbacks	Closed		29.90	30-45
1995 Blue Wing Teals	Closed		29.90	30-45
1995 Mergansers	Closed		29.90	30
1995 Golden Eye	Closed		29.90	30-35

The Costuming of A Legend: Dressing Gone With The Wind - D. Klauba

YEAR ISSUE	EDITION LIMIT	YEAR RETD.	ISSUE PRICE	*QUOTE U.S.$
1993 The Red Dress	Closed		29.90	30-60
1993 The Green Drapery Dress	Closed		29.90	50
1994 The Green Sprigged Dress	Closed		29.90	32-40
1994 Black & White Bengaline Dress	Closed		29.90	41-45
1994 Widow's Weeds	Closed		29.90	45-49
1994 The Country Walking Dress	Closed		29.90	45-48
1994 Plaid Business Attire	Closed		29.90	35-48
1994 Orchid Percale Dress	Closed		29.90	35-42
1994 The Mourning Gown	Closed		29.90	75
1994 Final Outtake:The Green Muslin Dress	Closed		29.90	75

A Country Wonderland - W. Goebel

YEAR ISSUE	EDITION LIMIT	YEAR RETD.	ISSUE PRICE	*QUOTE U.S.$
1995 The Quiet Hour	Closed		29.90	30
1995 First Blush	Closed		29.90	30
1995 Sunrise Serenade	Closed		32.90	33
1995 Dawns Early Light	95-day		32.90	33
1995 Soft Morning	95-day		32.90	33
1995 Dawns Golden Warmth	95-day		32.90	33

Cow-Hide - P. Casey

YEAR ISSUE	EDITION LIMIT	YEAR RETD.	ISSUE PRICE	*QUOTE U.S.$
1995 Incowspicuous	Closed		34.95	35-65
1995 Incowgnito	Closed		34.95	35-45
1995 Cowmooflage	Closed		34.95	35-75
1995 Cowpanions	Closed		34.95	35-50

Currier and Ives Christmas Collection - Currier & Ives

YEAR ISSUE	EDITION LIMIT	YEAR RETD.	ISSUE PRICE	*QUOTE U.S.$
1995 Early Winter	Closed		34.95	35-45
1995 American Homestead	Closed		34.95	35-50
1995 American Winter	Closed		34.95	35-45
1995 Winter Morn	Closed		34.95	35

Deer Friends at Christmas - J. Thornbrugh

YEAR ISSUE	EDITION LIMIT	YEAR RETD.	ISSUE PRICE	*QUOTE U.S.$
1994 All a Glow	Closed		29.90	38-42
1994 A Glistening Season	Closed		29.90	30-32
1994 Holiday Sparkle	Closed		29.90	30-34
1995 Woodland Splendor	Closed		29.90	35
1995 Starry Night	Closed		29.90	32-44
1995 Radiant Countryside	Closed		29.90	30

Desert Rhythms - M. Cowdery

YEAR ISSUE	EDITION LIMIT	YEAR RETD.	ISSUE PRICE	*QUOTE U.S.$
1994 Partner With A Breeze	Closed		29.90	30
1994 Wind Dancer	95-day		29.90	30
1994 Riding On Air	95-day		29.90	30
1994 Wilderness	95-day		29.90	30

Diana: Queen of Our Hearts - J. Monti

YEAR ISSUE	EDITION LIMIT	YEAR RETD.	ISSUE PRICE	*QUOTE U.S.$
1997 The People's Princess	95-day		29.95	30

Divine Light - Stained Glass Windows by Causland Studio

YEAR ISSUE	EDITION LIMIT	YEAR RETD.	ISSUE PRICE	*QUOTE U.S.$
1996 Savior/Born	Closed		34.95	35-55
1996 Blessed/Child	Closed		34.95	35
1996 Birth of a King	Closed		34.95	35
1996 Praise Him	Closed		34.95	35

Dog Days - J. Gadamus

YEAR ISSUE	EDITION LIMIT	YEAR RETD.	ISSUE PRICE	*QUOTE U.S.$
1993 Sweet Dreams	Closed		29.90	63-110
1993 Pier Group	Closed		29.90	59
1993 Wagon Train	Closed		32.90	65
1993 First Flush	Closed		32.90	50-60
1993 Little Rascals	Closed		32.90	125
1993 Where'd He Go	Closed		32.90	90

Dreams Come True: The Tale of Snow White - Disney Artists

YEAR ISSUE	EDITION LIMIT	YEAR RETD.	ISSUE PRICE	*QUOTE U.S.$
1995 Wish Come True	Closed		49.95	50

Elvis: Young & Wild - B. Emmett

YEAR ISSUE	EDITION LIMIT	YEAR RETD.	ISSUE PRICE	*QUOTE U.S.$
1993 The King of Creole	95-day		29.90	55
1993 King of the Road	95-day		29.90	50
1994 Tough But Tender	95-day		32.90	33
1994 With Love, Elvis	95-day		32.90	33
1994 The Picture of Cool	95-day		32.90	33
1994 Kissing Elvis	95-day		34.90	35
1994 The Perfect Take	95-day		34.90	35
1994 The Rockin' Rebel	95-day		34.90	35

Enchanted Charms of Oz - M. Dudash

YEAR ISSUE	EDITION LIMIT	YEAR RETD.	ISSUE PRICE	*QUOTE U.S.$
1995 No Place	Closed		34.95	35-65
1995 Wonderland Wizard	Closed		34.95	35
1995 Can't/Scarecrow	Closed		37.95	38
1995 Fresh/Brush Up	Closed		37.95	38

Faces of the Wild - D. Parker

YEAR ISSUE	EDITION LIMIT	YEAR RETD.	ISSUE PRICE	*QUOTE U.S.$
1995 The Wolf	Closed		39.90	140
1995 The White Wolf	Closed		39.90	148
1995 The Cougar	Closed		44.90	97-100
1995 The Bobcat	Closed		44.90	130
1995 The Bear	Closed		44.90	125
1995 The Fox	Closed		44.90	75-139
1995 The Bison	Closed		44.90	88
1995 The Lynx	Closed		44.90	150-200

Fairyland - M. Jobe

YEAR ISSUE	EDITION LIMIT	YEAR RETD.	ISSUE PRICE	*QUOTE U.S.$
1994 Trails of Starlight	95-day		29.90	30
1994 Twilight Trio	95-day		29.90	30
1994 Forest Enchantment	95-day		32.90	33
1995 Silvery Splasher	95-day		32.90	33
1995 Magical Mischief	95-day		32.90	33
1995 Farewell to the Night	95-day		34.90	35

A Family Affair - C. Brenders

YEAR ISSUE	EDITION LIMIT	YEAR RETD.	ISSUE PRICE	*QUOTE U.S.$
1994 Den Mother	Closed		29.90	75-118
1994 Rocky Camp	Closed		29.90	47
1994 Watchful Eye	Closed		29.90	49
1994 Close to Mom	Closed		29.90	40-50
1994 Mother of Pearls	Closed		29.90	30-49
1994 Shadows in the Grass	Closed		29.90	30-59

Family Circles - R. Rust

YEAR ISSUE	EDITION LIMIT	YEAR RETD.	ISSUE PRICE	*QUOTE U.S.$
1993 Great Gray Owl Family	Closed		29.90	28-36
1994 Great Horned Owl Family	Closed		29.90	50
1994 Barred Owl Family	Closed		29.90	40
1994 Spotted Owl Family	Closed		29.90	50

Field Pup Follies - C. Jackson

YEAR ISSUE	EDITION LIMIT	YEAR RETD.	ISSUE PRICE	*QUOTE U.S.$
1994 Sleeping on the Job	Closed		29.90	26-35
1994 Hat Check	Closed		29.90	107
1994 Fowl Play	Closed		29.90	40
1994 Tackling Lunch	Closed		29.90	125

Fierce and Free: Big Cats - G. Beecham

YEAR ISSUE	EDITION LIMIT	YEAR RETD.	ISSUE PRICE	*QUOTE U.S.$
1995 Snow Leopard	Closed		39.90	75
1995 Cougar	Closed		39.90	40-74
1995 Jaquar	Closed		39.90	40-66
1995 Black Leopard	Closed		39.90	54-75
1995 Tiger	Closed		39.90	75-90
1995 African Lion	Closed		39.90	75-150

Fleeting Encounters - M. Budden

YEAR ISSUE	EDITION LIMIT	YEAR RETD.	ISSUE PRICE	*QUOTE U.S.$
1995 Autumn Retreat	95-day		29.90	30

Floral Frolics - G. Kurz

YEAR ISSUE	EDITION LIMIT	YEAR RETD.	ISSUE PRICE	*QUOTE U.S.$
1994 Spring Surprises	Closed		29.90	34
1994 Bee Careful	Closed		29.90	50
1995 Fuzzy Fun	Closed		32.90	48
1995 Sunny Hideout	Closed		32.90	50

Floral Greetings - L. Liu

YEAR ISSUE	EDITION LIMIT	YEAR RETD.	ISSUE PRICE	*QUOTE U.S.$
1994 Circle of Love	Closed		29.90	30-40
1994 Circle of Elegance	95-day		29.90	30
1994 Circle of Harmony	95-day		32.90	33
1994 Circle of Joy	95-day		32.90	33
1994 Circle of Romance	95-day		34.90	35
1995 Circle of Inspiration	95-day		34.90	35
1995 Circle of Delight	95-day		34.90	35

Footsteps of the Brave - H. Schaare

YEAR ISSUE	EDITION LIMIT	YEAR RETD.	ISSUE PRICE	*QUOTE U.S.$
1993 Noble Quest	Closed		24.90	13-24
1993 At Storm's Passage	Closed		24.90	37-42
1993 With Boundless Vision	Closed		27.90	24-32
1993 Horizons of Destiny	Closed		27.90	31-40
1993 Path of His Forefathers	Closed		27.90	30-46
1993 Soulful Reflection	Closed		29.90	32-44
1993 The Reverent Trail	Closed		29.90	25-44
1994 At Journey's End	Closed		34.90	45-49

Forever Glamorous Barbie - C. Falberg

YEAR ISSUE	EDITION LIMIT	YEAR RETD.	ISSUE PRICE	*QUOTE U.S.$
1995 Enchanted Evening	Closed		49.90	34
1995 Sophisticated Lady	Closed		49.90	45
1995 Solo in the Spotlight	Closed		49.90	55
1995 Midnight Blue	Closed		49.90	80

Fracé's Kingdom of the Great Cats:Signature Collection - C. Fracé

YEAR ISSUE	EDITION LIMIT	YEAR RETD.	ISSUE PRICE	*QUOTE U.S.$
1994 Mystic Realm	Closed		39.90	39
1994 Snow Leopard	Closed		39.90	50
1994 Emperor of Siberia	Closed		39.90	75
1994 His Domain	Closed		39.90	50
1994 American Monarch	Closed		39.90	40
1995 A Radiant Moment	Closed		39.90	40

Freshwater Game Fish of North America - E. Totten

YEAR ISSUE	EDITION LIMIT	YEAR RETD.	ISSUE PRICE	*QUOTE U.S.$
1994 Rainbow Trout	Closed		29.90	48-52
1995 Largemouth Bass	Closed		29.90	55-69
1995 Blue Gills	Closed		32.90	69
1995 Northern Pike	Closed		32.90	68-85
1995 Brown Trout	Closed		32.90	80-90
1995 Smallmouth Bass	Closed		34.90	45-125
1995 Walleye	Closed		34.90	65-78
1995 Brook Trout	Closed		34.90	74-125

Friendship in Bloom - L. Chang

YEAR ISSUE	EDITION LIMIT	YEAR RETD.	ISSUE PRICE	*QUOTE U.S.$
1994 Paws in the Posies	Closed		34.90	37-40
1995 Cozy Petunia Patch	Closed		34.90	40-85
1995 Patience & Impatience	Closed		34.90	40
1995 Primrose Playmates	Closed		34.90	70

Gallant Men of Civil War - J. P. Strain

YEAR ISSUE	EDITION LIMIT	YEAR RETD.	ISSUE PRICE	*QUOTE U.S.$
1994 Robert E. Lee	95-day		29.90	30-45
1995 Stonewall Jackson	95-day		29.90	30
1995 Nathan Bedford Forest	95-day		29.90	30
1995 Joshua Chamberlain	95-day		29.90	30
1995 John Hunt Morgan	95-day		29.90	30
1996 Turner Ashby	95-day		29.90	30
1996 John C. Breckenridge	95-day		29.90	30
1996 Ben Hardin Holm	95-day		29.90	30

Gardens of Innocence - D. Richardson

YEAR ISSUE	EDITION LIMIT	YEAR RETD.	ISSUE PRICE	*QUOTE U.S.$
1994 Hope	95-day		29.90	30
1994 Charity	95-day		29.90	30
1994 Joy	95-day		32.90	33
1994 Faith	95-day		32.90	33
1994 Grace	95-day		32.90	33
1995 Serenity	95-day		34.90	35

*Quotes have been rounded up to nearest dollar

YEAR ISSUE	EDITION LIMIT	YEAR RETD.	ISSUE PRICE	*QUOTE U.S.$
1995 Peace	95-day		34.90	35
1995 Patience	95-day		34.90	35
1995 Kindness	95-day		36.90	37

Getting Away From It All - D. Rust

YEAR ISSUE	EDITION LIMIT	YEAR RETD.	ISSUE PRICE	*QUOTE U.S.$
1995 Mountain Hideaway	Closed		34.90	35
1995 Riverside	Closed		34.90	35
1995 Mountain Escape	Closed		34.90	35
1995 Weekend Refuge	95-day		34.90	35
1995 Homeward Bound	95-day		34.90	35
1995 Evenings Glow	95-day		34.90	35

The Glory of Christ - R. Barrett

YEAR ISSUE	EDITION LIMIT	YEAR RETD.	ISSUE PRICE	*QUOTE U.S.$
1995 Ascension	Closed		29.90	30
1995 Walks on Water	Closed		29.90	30
1995 Christ Feeds	Closed		29.90	30
1995 Wedding at Cana	Closed		29.90	30
1995 Christ and the Apostles	95-day		29.90	30
1995 Raising of Lazarus	95-day		29.90	30

Gone With The Wind: A Portrait in Stained Glass - M. Phalen

YEAR ISSUE	EDITION LIMIT	YEAR RETD.	ISSUE PRICE	*QUOTE U.S.$
1995 Scarlett Radiance	Closed		39.90	49-54
1995 Rhett's Bright Promise	Closed		39.90	80
1995 Ashley's Smoldering Fire	Closed		39.90	150
1995 Melanie Lights His World	Closed		39.90	120

Gone With The Wind: Musical Treasures - A. Jenks

YEAR ISSUE	EDITION LIMIT	YEAR RETD.	ISSUE PRICE	*QUOTE U.S.$
1994 Tara: Scarlett's True Love	95-day		29.90	30
1994 Scarlett: Belle of/12 Oaks BBQ	95-day		29.90	30
1995 Charity Bazaar	95-day		32.90	33
1995 The Proposal	95-day		32.90	33

Great Moments in Baseball - S. Gardner

YEAR ISSUE	EDITION LIMIT	YEAR RETD.	ISSUE PRICE	*QUOTE U.S.$
1993 Joe DiMaggio: The Streak	Closed		29.90	110-124
1993 Stan Musial: 5 Homer Double Header	Closed		29.90	28
1994 Bobby Thomson: Shot Heard Round the World	Closed		32.90	20-24
1994 Bill Mazeroski: Winning Home Run	Closed		32.90	26-28
1994 Don Larsen: Perfect Series Game	Closed		32.90	29
1994 J. Robinson: Saved Pennant	Closed		34.90	39-55
1994 Satchel Paige: Greatest Games	Closed		34.90	30
1994 Billy Martin: The Rescue Catch	Closed		34.90	73-75
1994 Dizzy Dean: The World Series Shutout	Closed		34.90	47-50
1995 Carl Hubbell: The 1934 All State	Closed		36.90	50-60
1995 Ralph Kiner	Closed		36.90	65
1995 Enos Slaughter	Closed		36.90	65

Great Superbowl Quarterbacks - R. Brown

YEAR ISSUE	EDITION LIMIT	YEAR RETD.	ISSUE PRICE	*QUOTE U.S.$
1995 Joe Montana: King of Comeback	95-day		29.90	30

Guardians of the Wild

YEAR ISSUE	EDITION LIMIT	YEAR RETD.	ISSUE PRICE	*QUOTE U.S.$
1996 Jaguar	Closed		34.95	35
1996 Tiger	Closed		34.95	35
1996 Black Jaguar	Closed		34.95	35
1996 Leopard	Closed		34.95	35

Guidance From Above - B. Jaxon

YEAR ISSUE	EDITION LIMIT	YEAR RETD.	ISSUE PRICE	*QUOTE U.S.$
1994 Prayer to the Storm	Closed		29.90	50
1995 Appeal to Thunder	Closed		29.90	50
1995 Blessing the Future	Closed		32.90	50
1995 Sharing the Wisdom	Closed		32.90	50

Happy Hearts - J. Daly

YEAR ISSUE	EDITION LIMIT	YEAR RETD.	ISSUE PRICE	*QUOTE U.S.$
1995 Contentment	Closed		29.90	35
1995 Playmates	Closed		29.90	30-85
1995 Childhood Friends	Closed		32.90	35
1995 Favorite Gift	Closed		32.90	40-45
1995 Good Company	Closed		32.90	40
1995 Secret Place	Closed		34.90	40-44

Heart to Heart - Various

YEAR ISSUE	EDITION LIMIT	YEAR RETD.	ISSUE PRICE	*QUOTE U.S.$
1995 Thinking of You	Closed		29.90	30-70
1995 Speaking of Love	Closed		29.90	30
1995 Whispers in Romance	95-day		29.90	30
1995 Tales of Fancy	95-day		29.90	30
1995 Affection	95-day		29.90	30
1995 Feelings of Endearment	95-day		29.90	30

Heaven on Earth - T. Kinkade

YEAR ISSUE	EDITION LIMIT	YEAR RETD.	ISSUE PRICE	*QUOTE U.S.$
1994 I Am the Light of/World	Closed		29.90	38-50
1995 I Am the Way	Closed		29.90	38-55
1995 Thy Word is a Lamp	Closed		29.90	38-60
1995 For Thou Art My Lamp	Closed		29.90	38-55
1995 In Him Was Life	Closed		29.90	38
1995 But The Path of Just	Closed		29.90	38-75
1995 For With Thee	Closed		29.90	38-100
1995 Let Your Light so Shine	Closed		29.90	38-74

Heaven Sent - L. Bogle

YEAR ISSUE	EDITION LIMIT	YEAR RETD.	ISSUE PRICE	*QUOTE U.S.$
1994 Sweet Dreams	Closed		29.90	94-125
1994 Puppy Dog Tails	Closed		29.90	98-100
1994 Timeless Treasure	Closed		32.90	40-48
1995 Precious Gift	Closed		32.90	33-85

Heavenly Chorus - R. Akers

YEAR ISSUE	EDITION LIMIT	YEAR RETD.	ISSUE PRICE	*QUOTE U.S.$
1994 Hark the Herald Angels Sing	Closed		39.90	40-55
1994 Angels We Have Heard on High	Closed		39.90	40
1994 Joy to the World	Closed		39.90	40
1994 First Noel	Closed		39.90	40
1994 Come All Ye Faithful	Closed		39.90	40
1994 Little Town of Bethlehem	Closed		39.90	40

Heirloom Memories - A. Pech

YEAR ISSUE	EDITION LIMIT	YEAR RETD.	ISSUE PRICE	*QUOTE U.S.$
1994 Porcelain Treasure	Closed		29.90	149
1994 Rhythms in Lace	Closed		29.90	65

YEAR ISSUE	EDITION LIMIT	YEAR RETD.	ISSUE PRICE	*QUOTE U.S.$
1994 Pink Lemonade Roses	Closed		29.90	75-80
1994 Victorian Romance	Closed		29.90	69
1994 Teatime Tulips	Closed		29.90	75
1994 Touch of the Irish	Closed		29.90	75

A Hidden Garden - T. Clausnitzer

YEAR ISSUE	EDITION LIMIT	YEAR RETD.	ISSUE PRICE	*QUOTE U.S.$
1993 Curious Kittens	Closed		29.90	45
1994 Through the Eyes of Blue	Closed		29.90	39
1994 Amber Gaze	Closed		29.90	38-45
1994 Fascinating Find	Closed		29.90	34

A Hidden World - R. Rust

YEAR ISSUE	EDITION LIMIT	YEAR RETD.	ISSUE PRICE	*QUOTE U.S.$
1993 Two by Night, Two by Light	Closed		29.90	48-50
1993 Two by Steam, Two in Dream	Closed		29.90	36-55
1993 Two on Sly, Two Watch Nearby	Closed		32.90	38-40
1993 Hunter Growls, Spirits Prowl	Closed		32.90	35-50
1993 In Moonglow One Drinks	Closed		32.90	64
1993 Sings at the Moon, Spirits Sing in Tune	Closed		34.90	63-70
1994 Two Cubs Play As Spirits Show the Way	Closed		34.90	55-70
1994 Young Ones Hold on Tight As Spirits Stay in Sight	Closed		34.90	80-105

Hideaway Lake - R. Rust

YEAR ISSUE	EDITION LIMIT	YEAR RETD.	ISSUE PRICE	*QUOTE U.S.$
1993 Rusty's Retreat	Closed		34.90	21
1993 Fishing For Dreams	Closed		34.90	38
1993 Sunset Cabin	Closed		34.90	36
1993 Echoes of Morning	Closed		34.90	50
1994 Great Grey Owl	Closed		29.90	28
1994 Great Horned Owl	Closed		29.90	50
1994 Barred Owl	Closed		29.90	40
1994 Spotted Owl	Closed		29.90	50

Historic Home Runs

YEAR ISSUE	EDITION LIMIT	YEAR RETD.	ISSUE PRICE	*QUOTE U.S.$
1995 Carlton Fisk	Closed		49.95	125

Home in the Heartland - M. Levne

YEAR ISSUE	EDITION LIMIT	YEAR RETD.	ISSUE PRICE	*QUOTE U.S.$
1995 Barn Raising	Closed		34.95	38
1995 Auction	Closed		34.95	35
1995 Apple Blossom	Closed		34.95	35-50
1995 Country Fair	Closed		34.95	35-60

Hunchback of Notre Dame - Disney Artists

YEAR ISSUE	EDITION LIMIT	YEAR RETD.	ISSUE PRICE	*QUOTE U.S.$
1996 Touched by Love	Closed		34.95	35
1996 Topsy Turvy	95-day		34.95	35
1996 Dance/Enchantment	95-day		34.95	35
1996 Good Day to Fly	95-day		34.95	35

Hunters of the Spirit - R. Docken

YEAR ISSUE	EDITION LIMIT	YEAR RETD.	ISSUE PRICE	*QUOTE U.S.$
1995 Provider	Closed		29.90	30-45
1995 Seekers	Closed		29.90	30-48
1995 Gatherers	Closed		29.90	30-45
1995 Defender	Closed		29.90	30
1995 Hunter	Closed		29.90	30
1995 Keeper	Closed		29.90	30

Illusions of Nature - M. Bierlinski

YEAR ISSUE	EDITION LIMIT	YEAR RETD.	ISSUE PRICE	*QUOTE U.S.$
1995 A Trio of Wolves	Closed		29.90	43
1995 Running Deer	Closed		29.90	30-34

Immortals of the Diamond - C. Jackson

YEAR ISSUE	EDITION LIMIT	YEAR RETD.	ISSUE PRICE	*QUOTE U.S.$
1994 Babe Ruth: The Sultan of Swat	Closed		39.90	67
1994 Lou Gehrig: Pride of the Yankees	Closed		39.90	67
1995 Ty Cobb: The Georgia Peach	Closed		39.90	75
1995 Cy Young: The Winningest Pitcher	Closed		39.90	90

Kalendar Kitties - Higgins Bond

YEAR ISSUE	EDITION LIMIT	YEAR RETD.	ISSUE PRICE	*QUOTE U.S.$
1995 Oct/Nov/Dec	Closed		44.95	45-85
1996 Jan/Feb/Mar	Closed		44.95	45
1996 April/May/June	Closed		44.95	45
1996 Jul/Aug/Sep	Closed		44.95	45-100

Keepsakes of the Heart - C. Layton

YEAR ISSUE	EDITION LIMIT	YEAR RETD.	ISSUE PRICE	*QUOTE U.S.$
1993 Forever Friends	Closed		29.90	30-32
1993 Afternoon Tea	Closed		29.90	32-36
1993 Riding Companions	Closed		29.90	35-40
1994 Sentimental Sweethearts	Closed		29.90	38

Kindred Moments - C. Poulin

YEAR ISSUE	EDITION LIMIT	YEAR RETD.	ISSUE PRICE	*QUOTE U.S.$
1996 Forever Friends	95-day		29.90	30
1995 Sisters Are Blossoms	95-day		29.90	30

Kindred Spirits - D. Casey

YEAR ISSUE	EDITION LIMIT	YEAR RETD.	ISSUE PRICE	*QUOTE U.S.$
1995 Eyes of the Wolf	Closed		29.95	30
1995 Spirit of the Wolf	Closed		29.95	30
1995 Songs of the Wolf	Closed		29.95	30
1995 Prayer of the Wolf	Closed		29.95	30
1995 Guardian of the Wolf	Closed		29.95	30
1995 Quest of the Wolf	Closed		29.95	30
1995 Memory of the Wolf	Closed		29.95	30
1995 Hope of the Wolf	Closed		29.95	30

Kingdom of the Unicorn - M. Ferraro

YEAR ISSUE	EDITION LIMIT	YEAR RETD.	ISSUE PRICE	*QUOTE U.S.$
1993 The Magic Begins	Closed		29.90	30-34
1993 In Crystal Waters	Closed		29.90	41-47
1993 Chasing a Dream	Closed		29.90	60-65
1993 The Fountain of Youth	Closed		29.90	50

Land of Oz: A New Dimension

YEAR ISSUE	EDITION LIMIT	YEAR RETD.	ISSUE PRICE	*QUOTE U.S.$
1984 Emerald City	Closed		39.90	40

Legend of the White Buffalo - D. Stanley

YEAR ISSUE	EDITION LIMIT	YEAR RETD.	ISSUE PRICE	*QUOTE U.S.$
1995 Mystic Spirit	Closed		29.90	30-35
1995 Call of the Clouds	95-day		29.90	30
1995 Valley of the Sacred	95-day		29.90	30
1995 Spirit of the Buffalo	95-day		29.90	30
1995 Buffalo Spirit	95-day		29.90	30
1995 White Buffalo Calf	95-day		29.90	30

Lena Liu's Beautiful Gardens - Inspired by L. Liu

YEAR ISSUE	EDITION LIMIT	YEAR RETD.	ISSUE PRICE	*QUOTE U.S.$
1994 Iris Garden	Closed		34.00	34-74
1994 Peony Garden	Closed		34.00	66
1994 The Rose Garden	Closed		39.00	109-125
1995 Lily Garden	Closed		39.00	99
1995 Tulip Garden	Closed		39.00	99
1995 Orchid Garden	Closed		44.00	109
1995 The Poppy Garden	Closed		44.00	80
1995 Calla Lily Garden	Closed		44.00	135
1995 The Morning Glory Garden	Closed		44.00	90
1995 The Hibiscus Garden	Closed		47.00	99
1995 The Clematis Garden	Closed		47.00	70
1995 The Gladiola Garden	Closed		47.00	73

Lena Liu's Holiday Angels - L. Liu

YEAR ISSUE	EDITION LIMIT	YEAR RETD.	ISSUE PRICE	*QUOTE U.S.$
1995 Rejoice	Closed		29.95	30
1996 Glad Tidings	Closed		29.95	30
1996 Celebrations	Closed		32.95	33
1996 Yuletide	Closed		32.95	33
1996 Noel	95-day		32.95	33
1996 Jubilee	95-day		32.95	33

The Life of Christ - R. Barrett

YEAR ISSUE	EDITION LIMIT	YEAR RETD.	ISSUE PRICE	*QUOTE U.S.$
1994 The Passion in the Garden	Closed		29.90	49-54
1994 Jesus Enters Jerusalem	Closed		29.90	46-50
1994 Jesus Calms the Waters	Closed		32.90	56
1994 Sermon on the Mount	Closed		32.90	55-66
1994 The Last Supper	Closed		32.90	57
1994 The Ascension	Closed		34.90	60-80
1994 The Resurrection	Closed		34.90	69
1994 The Crucifixion	Closed		34.90	66

The Light of the World - C. Nick

YEAR ISSUE	EDITION LIMIT	YEAR RETD.	ISSUE PRICE	*QUOTE U.S.$
1995 The Last Supper	Closed		29.90	30
1995 Betrayal in the Garden	Closed		29.90	30
1995 Facing the Accusers	Closed		29.90	30-40
1995 Prayer in the Garden	Closed		29.90	30
1995 Jesus and Pilate	Closed		29.90	30
1995 Way of the Cross	Closed		29.90	30-35

Lincoln's Portraits of Valor - B. Maguire

YEAR ISSUE	EDITION LIMIT	YEAR RETD.	ISSUE PRICE	*QUOTE U.S.$
1993 The Gettysburg Address	Closed		29.90	30-60
1993 Emancipation Proclamation	Closed		29.90	49
1993 The Lincoln-Douglas Debates	Closed		29.90	35
1993 The Second Inaugural Address	Closed		29.90	60

The Lion King - Disney Studios

YEAR ISSUE	EDITION LIMIT	YEAR RETD.	ISSUE PRICE	*QUOTE U.S.$
1994 The Circle of Life	95-day		29.90	30
1995 Like Father, Like Son	95-day		29.90	30
1995 A Crunchy Feast	95-day		32.90	33

Little Bandits - C. Jagodits

YEAR ISSUE	EDITION LIMIT	YEAR RETD.	ISSUE PRICE	*QUOTE U.S.$
1993 Handle With Care	Closed		29.90	57
1993 All Tied Up	Closed		29.90	60
1993 Everything's Coming Up Daisies	Closed		32.90	43-50
1993 Out of Hand	Closed		32.90	43
1993 Pupsicles	Closed		32.90	58
1993 Unexpected Guests	Closed		32.90	28

Lords of Forest & Canyon - G. Beecham

YEAR ISSUE	EDITION LIMIT	YEAR RETD.	ISSUE PRICE	*QUOTE U.S.$
1994 Mountain Majesty	Closed		29.90	45
1995 Proud Legacy	Closed		29.90	27-32
1995 Golden Monarch	Closed		32.90	35
1995 Forest Emperor	Closed		32.90	48
1995 Grand Domain	Closed		32.90	50
1995 Canyon Master	Closed		34.90	40

Loving Hearts

YEAR ISSUE	EDITION LIMIT	YEAR RETD.	ISSUE PRICE	*QUOTE U.S.$
1995 Patient/Kind	Closed		29.95	30
1995 Beauty/Splendor	Closed		29.95	30-75
1995 Unselfish/Giving	Closed		29.95	30-50
1995 God's Gift Divine	Closed		29.95	30-50

Lullabears - M. Scott

YEAR ISSUE	EDITION LIMIT	YEAR RETD.	ISSUE PRICE	*QUOTE U.S.$
1995 Sweet Dreamin	Closed		29.90	30
1995 Rock a Bye Read	95-day		29.90	30
1995 Story Tellin	95-day		29.90	30
1995 Wishin on a Star	95-day		29.90	30

Marilyn: Golden Collection - M. Deas/C. Notarile

YEAR ISSUE	EDITION LIMIT	YEAR RETD.	ISSUE PRICE	*QUOTE U.S.$
1995 Sultry/Regal	Closed		29.90	39
1995 Graceful Beauty	95-day		29.90	30
1995 Essence/Glamour	95-day		29.90	30
1995 Sweet Sizzle	95-day		32.90	33
1995 Fire/Ice	95-day		32.90	33
1995 Satin/Cream	95-day		34.90	35
1995 Shimmer/Chiffon	95-day		34.90	35
1997 Frankly Feminine	95-day		34.90	35
1997 Forever Radiant	95-day		34.90	35
1997 Radiant/Red	95-day		34.90	35

Me & My Shadow - J. Welty

YEAR ISSUE	EDITION LIMIT	YEAR RETD.	ISSUE PRICE	*QUOTE U.S.$
1994 Easter Parade	Closed		29.90	40
1994 A Golden Moment	Closed		29.90	35
1994 Perfect Timing	Closed		29.90	45
1995 Giddyup	Closed		29.90	39

Mewsic For The Holidays - Spangler

YEAR ISSUE	EDITION LIMIT	YEAR RETD.	ISSUE PRICE	*QUOTE U.S.$
1996 Purrfect Harmony	Closed		34.95	30-35
1996 Kitten Tree	Closed		34.95	35
1996 Frosty the Snow Cat	Closed		34.95	35

*Quotes have been rounded up to nearest dollar

YEAR ISSUE	EDITION LIMIT	YEAR RETD.	ISSUE PRICE	*QUOTE U.S.$
1996 Santa Claws is Coming to Town	Closed		34.95	35
Michael Jordan: A Legend for all Time - A. Katzman				
1995 Soaring Star	Closed		79.95	550-625
1996 Rim Rocker	Closed		79.95	97-99
1997 Slam Jammer	95-day		79.95	80
1998 High Flyer	95-day		79.95	80
Michael Jordon Collection - C. Gillies				
1994 91 Championship	Closed		29.90	94-120
1994 Comeback	Closed		29.90	30
1994 92 Champions	Closed		32.90	33-150
1994 82 NCAA	Closed		32.90	33
1995 93 Champions	95-day		32.90	33
1995 88 Slam Dunk	95-day		34.90	35
1995 86 Playoffs	95-day		34.90	35
1996 Rookie Year	95-day		34.90	35
1996 Shot	95-day		34.90	35
1997 91 Eastern Finals	95-day		34.90	35
1997 Record 23/Row	95-day		34.90	35
1997 Career High 69	95-day		34.90	35
Mickey and Minnie's Through the Years - Disney Studios				
1995 Mickey's Birthday Party 1942	95-day		29.90	30-55
1995 Brave Little Tailor	95-day		29.90	30
1996 Steamboat Willie	95-day		29.90	30
1996 Mickey's Gala Premiere	95-day		32.90	33
1996 The Mickey Mouse Club	95-day		32.90	33
1996 Mickey's 65th Birthday	95-day		34.90	35
Mickey Mantle All American Legend				
1997 Triple Crown King	Closed		79.95	120
Miracle of Christmas - J. Welty				
1995 Little Drummer	Closed		34.95	35-45
1995 Holy Night	Closed		34.95	35-68
1995 Angelic Serenade	Closed		34.95	35
1995 Shepherd of Love	Closed		34.95	35
Moments in the Garden - C. Fisher				
1995 Ruby Treasures	Closed		29.95	30
1995 Shimmering Splendor	95-day		29.95	30
1995 Radiant Gems	95-day		32.95	33
1995 Luminous Jewels	95-day		32.95	33
1995 Precious Beauty	95-day		34.95	35
1995 Lustrous Sapphire	95-day		34.95	35
A Mother's Love - J. Anderson				
1995 Remembrance	Closed		29.90	30
1995 Patience	Closed		29.90	30
1995 Thoughtfulness	95-day		29.90	30
1995 Kindness	95-day		29.90	30
Musical Tribute to Elvis the King - B. Emmett				
1994 Rockin' Blue Suede Shoes	95-day		29.90	75
1994 Hound Dog Bop	95-day		29.90	30
1995 Red, White & GI Blues	95-day		32.90	33
1995 American Dream	95-day		32.90	33
Mysterious Case of Fowl Play - H. Bond				
1994 Inspector Clawseau	Closed		29.90	40
1994 Glamourpuss	Closed		29.90	55
1994 Sophisicat	Closed		29.90	50-75
1994 Kool Cat	Closed		29.90	75
1994 Sneakers & High-Top	Closed		29.90	125-140
1995 Tuxedo	Closed		29.90	125
Mystic Guardians - S. Hill				
1993 Soul Mates	Closed		29.90	30-34
1993 Majestic Messenger	Closed		29.90	25-28
1993 Companion Spirits	Closed		32.90	38
1994 Faithful Fellowship	Closed		32.90	35-38
1994 Spiritual Harmony	Closed		32.90	35-60
1994 Royal Unity	Closed		34.90	38
Mystic Spirits - V. Crandell				
1995 Moon Shadows	95-day		29.90	30
1995 Midnight Snow	95-day		29.90	30
1995 Arctic Nights	95-day		32.90	33
Native American Legends: Chiefs of Destiny - C. Jackson				
1994 Sitting Bull	Closed		39.90	45-64
1994 Chief Joseph	Closed		39.90	40-64
1995 Red Cloud	Closed		44.90	57
1995 Crazy Horse	Closed		44.90	240
1995 Geronimo	Closed		44.90	175
1996 Tecumseh	Closed		44.90	149
Native Beauty - L. Bogle				
1994 The Promise	95-day		29.90	30
1994 Afterglow	95-day		29.90	30
1994 White Feather	95-day		29.90	30
1995 First glance	95-day		29.90	30
1995 Morning Star	95-day		29.90	30
1995 Quiet Time	95-day		29.90	30
1995 Warm Thoughts	95-day		29.90	30
Native Visions - J. Cole				
1994 Bringers of the Storm	Closed		29.90	72
1994 Water Vision	Closed		29.90	44
1994 Brother to the Moon	Closed		29.90	45
1995 Son of the Sun	Closed		29.90	45
1995 Man Who Sees Far	Closed		29.90	45
1995 Listening	Closed		29.90	35
1996 The Red Shield	Closed		29.90	45-53
1996 Toponas	Closed		29.90	35

YEAR ISSUE	EDITION LIMIT	YEAR RETD.	ISSUE PRICE	*QUOTE U.S.$
Nature's Little Treasures - L. Martin				
1993 Garden Whispers	Closed		29.90	58-60
1994 Wings of Grace	Closed		29.90	69-98
1994 Delicate Splendor	Closed		32.90	73-80
1994 Perfect Jewels	Closed		32.90	59
1994 Miniature Glory	Closed		32.90	60-85
1994 Precious Beauties	Closed		34.90	56
1994 Minute Enchantment	Closed		34.90	94-100
1994 Rare Perfection	Closed		34.90	65
1995 Misty Morning	Closed		36.90	35-95
1995 Whisper in the Wind	Closed		36.90	39-85
Nature's Nobility				
1995 Buck	Closed		39.95	40-82
1995 Pronghorn	95-day		39.95	40
1995 Dall Sheep	95-day		44.95	45
1995 Mule Deer	95-day		44.95	45
1995 Big Horn Sheep	95-day		44.95	45
1995 Mountain Goat	95-day		44.95	45
New Horizons - R. Copple				
1993 Building For a New Generation	Closed		29.90	19-30
1993 The Power of Gold	Closed		29.90	28-30
1994 Wings of Snowy Grandeur	Closed		32.90	30-33
1994 Master of the Chase	Closed		32.90	34
1995 Coastal Domain	Closed		32.90	38
1995 Majestic Wings	Closed		32.90	33
Nightsongs: The Loon - J. Hansel				
1994 Moonlight Echoes	Closed		29.90	64
1994 Evening Mist	Closed		29.90	58
1994 Nocturnal Glow	Closed		32.90	65
1994 Tranquil Reflections	Closed		32.90	40
1994 Peaceful Waters	Closed		32.90	75
1994 Silently Nestled	Closed		34.90	85
1994 Night Light	Closed		34.90	69
1995 Peaceful Homestead	Closed		34.90	57
1995 Silent Passage	Closed		34.90	70
1995 Tranquil Refuge	Closed		36.90	80
1995 Serene Sanctuary	Closed		36.90	60
1995 Moonlight Cruise	Closed		36.90	64
Nightwatch: The Wolf - D. Ningewance				
1994 Moonlight Serenade	Closed		29.90	30-52
1994 Midnight Guard	Closed		29.90	35-39
1994 Snowy Lookout	Closed		29.90	30
1994 Silent Sentries	Closed		29.90	40
1994 Song to the Night	Closed		29.90	47
1994 Winter Passage	Closed		29.90	45
Northern Companions - K. Weisberg				
1995 Midnight Harmony	95-day		29.90	30
Northwoods Spirit - D. Wenzel				
1994 Timeless Watch	Closed		29.90	48
1994 Woodland Retreat	Closed		29.90	40
1995 Forest Echo	Closed		29.90	42-45
1995 Timberland Gaze	Closed		29.90	40-48
1995 Evening Respite	Closed		29.90	50
1995 Fleeting	Closed		29.90	50
Nosy Neighbors - P. Weirs				
1994 Cat Nap	Closed		29.90	50-75
1994 Special Delivery	95-day		29.90	30
1995 House Sitting	95-day		29.90	30
1995 Observation Deck	95-day		32.90	33
1995 Surprise Visit	95-day		32.90	33
1995 Room With a View	95-day		32.90	33
1995 Bird Watchers	95-day		34.90	35
1995 Board Meeting	95-day		34.90	35
1995 Lifeguard	95-day		34.90	35
1995 Full House	95-day		34.90	35
Notorious Disney Villains - Disney Studios				
1993 The Evil Queen	Closed		29.90	40
1994 Maleficent	Closed		29.90	50-61
1994 Ursella	Closed		29.90	45
1994 Cruella De Vil	Closed		29.90	38
Old Fashioned Christmas with Thomas Kinkade - T. Kinkade				
1993 All Friends Are Welcome	Closed		29.90	38-65
1993 Winters Memories	Closed		29.90	38-110
1993 A Holiday Gathering	Closed		32.90	41-50
1994 Christmas Tree Cottage	Closed		32.90	41-75
1995 The Best Tradition	Closed		32.90	41-124
1995 Stonehearth Hutch	Closed		32.90	41-99
Our Heavenly Mother - H. Garrido				
1995 Adoration	Closed		34.90	35-40
1995 Devotion	Closed		34.90	35
1995 Faithfulness	Closed		34.90	35
1995 Constancy	95-day		34.90	35
1995 Purity	95-day		34.90	35
1995 Love	95-day		34.90	35
Panda Bear Hugs - W. Nelson				
1993 Rock-A-Bye	Closed		39.90	60
1993 Loving Advice	Closed		39.90	60
1993 A Playful Interlude	Closed		39.90	60
1993 A Taste of Life	Closed		39.90	60
Pathways of the Heart - J. Barnes				
1993 October Radiance	Closed		29.90	40-50
1993 Daybreak	Closed		29.90	75-80
1994 Harmony with Nature	Closed		29.90	56

YEAR ISSUE	EDITION LIMIT	YEAR RETD.	ISSUE PRICE	*QUOTE U.S.$
1994 Distant Lights	Closed		29.90	75
1994 A Night to Remember	Closed		29.90	50
1994 Peaceful Evening	Closed		29.90	50
Paws in Action - M. Rien				
1995 Playful Dreams	Closed		34.95	35
1995 Sweet Slumber	Closed		34.95	35
1995 Nestled Wrestled	Closed		34.95	35
1995 Rise and Shine	Closed		34.95	35
Paws in Play - M. Rien				
1995 Cuddle Buddies	Closed		34.95	35
1995 Bedtime Tails	Closed		34.95	35
1995 Break Time	Closed		34.95	35
1995 Wake up Call	Closed		34.95	35
Peace on Earth - D. Geisness				
1993 Winter Lullaby	Closed		29.90	35-52
1994 Heavenly Slumber	Closed		29.90	48
1994 Sweet Embrace	Closed		32.90	75
1994 Woodland Dreams	Closed		32.90	50
1994 Snowy Silence	Closed		32.90	48
1994 Dreamy Whispers	Closed		32.90	40
Picked from an English Garden - W. Von Schwarzbek				
1994 Inspired by Romance	Closed		32.90	50
1995 Lasting Treasures	Closed		32.90	39
1995 Nature's Wonders	Closed		32.90	125
1995 Summer Rhapsody	Closed		32.90	100-125
Pinegrove's Winter Cardinals - S. Timm				
1994 Evening in Pinegrove	95-day		29.90	30
1994 Pinegrove's Sunset	95-day		29.90	30
1994 Pinegrove's Twilight	95-day		29.90	30
1994 Daybreak in Pinegrove	95-day		29.90	30
1994 Pinegrove's Morning	95-day		29.90	30
1994 Afternoon in Pinegrove	95-day		29.90	30
1994 Midnight in Pinegrove	95-day		29.90	30
1994 At Home in Pinegrove	95-day		29.90	30
Pocohontas - Disney Artists				
1995 Loves Embrace	Closed		29.95	30
1995 Just Around the Corner	Closed		29.95	30-38
1995 Moment/Touch	Closed		32.95	33-40
1995 Listen/Heart	Closed		32.95	33
1995 Fathers Love	95-day		32.95	33
1995 Best/Friends	95-day		34.95	35
Portraits of Majesty - Various				
1994 Snowy Monarch	Closed		29.90	41
1995 Reflections of Kings	Closed		29.90	44
1995 Emperor of His Realm	Closed		29.90	48
1995 Solemn Sovereign	Closed		29.90	48
Postcards from Thomas Kinkade - T. Kinkade				
1995 San Francisco-California Street	Closed		34.90	55-68
1995 Paris	Closed		34.90	47
1995 New York City	Closed		34.90	47-50
1995 Boston	Closed		34.90	44-50
1995 Carmel	Closed		34.90	50
1995 Market Street	Closed		34.90	56-76
Practice Makes Perfect - L. Kaatz				
1994 What's a Mother to Do?	Closed		29.90	52
1994 The Ones That Got Away	Closed		29.90	30
1994 Pointed in the Wrong Direction	Closed		32.90	54
1994 Fishing for Compliments	Closed		32.90	55-60
1994 A Dandy Distraction	Closed		32.90	48-50
1995 More Than a Mouthful	Closed		34.90	60
1995 On The Right Track	Closed		34.90	67
1995 Missing the Point	Closed		34.90	55-59
Precious Visions - J. Grande				
1994 Brilliant Moment	Closed		29.90	30
1995 Brief Interlude	Closed		29.90	30
1995 Timeless Radiance	95-day		29.90	30
1995 Enduring Elegance	95-day		32.90	33
1995 Infinite Splendor	95-day		32.90	33
1995 Everlasting Beauty	95-day		34.90	35
1995 Shining Instant	95-day		34.90	35
1995 Eternal Glory	95-day		34.90	35
Promise of a Savior - Various				
1993 An Angel's Message	Closed		29.90	48
1993 Gifts to Jesus	Closed		29.90	56-58
1993 The Heavenly King	Closed		29.90	40-45
1993 Angels Were Watching	Closed		29.90	61
1993 Holy Mother and Child	Closed		29.90	44
1994 A Child is Born	Closed		29.90	52-58
Proud Heritage - M. Amerman				
1994 Mystic Warrior: Medicine Crow	Closed		34.90	27-30
1994 Great Chief: Sitting Bull	Closed		34.90	35
1994 Brave Leader: Geronimo	Closed		34.90	40
1995 Peaceful Defender: Chief Joseph	Closed		34.90	35
Purrfectly at Home - M. Roderick				
1995 Home Sweet Home	Closed		39.95	40-45
1995 Kitty Corner	Closed		39.95	40
1995 Cozy Kitchen	Closed		39.95	59-66
1995 Sweet Solice	Closed		39.95	70
Quiet Moments - K. Daniel				
1994 Time for Tea	Closed		29.90	37-46
1995 A Loving Hand	Closed		29.90	27
1995 Kept with Care	Closed		29.90	27-45

*Quotes have been rounded up to nearest dollar

YEAR ISSUE	EDITION LIMIT	YEAR RETD.	ISSUE PRICE	*QUOTE U.S.$
1995 Puppy Love	Closed		29.90	28-45

Radiant Messengers - L. Martin

YEAR ISSUE	EDITION LIMIT	YEAR RETD.	ISSUE PRICE	*QUOTE U.S.$
1994 Peace	Closed		29.90	30
1994 Hope	Closed		29.90	30
1994 Beauty	Closed		29.90	30
1994 Inspiration	Closed		29.90	30

Rainbow of Irises - S. Rickert

YEAR ISSUE	EDITION LIMIT	YEAR RETD.	ISSUE PRICE	*QUOTE U.S.$
1995 Alluring Amethyst	Closed		34.90	35-50
1995 Pink Pastoral	Closed		34.90	35
1995 Polonaise	Closed		34.90	35
1995 Lyrical Lavender	Closed		34.90	35
1995 Violet Vision	95-day		34.90	35
1995 Perfect Peach	95-day		34.90	35

Realm of the Wolf - K. Daniel

YEAR ISSUE	EDITION LIMIT	YEAR RETD.	ISSUE PRICE	*QUOTE U.S.$
1996 Midnight Harmony	Closed		29.95	30-50
1996 Night Watch	Closed		29.95	30
1996 Evening Song	95-day		29.95	30
1996 Night Sentries	95-day		29.95	30
1996 Moon Shadow	95-day		29.95	30
1996 Moonlit Phantom	95-day		29.95	30
1996 Shadow Spirit	95-day		29.95	30
1996 Moonglow	95-day		29.95	30

Reflections of Marilyn - C. Notarile

YEAR ISSUE	EDITION LIMIT	YEAR RETD.	ISSUE PRICE	*QUOTE U.S.$
1994 All That Glitters	95-day		29.90	30
1994 Shimmering Heat	95-day		29.90	30
1994 Million Dollar Star	95-day		29.90	30
1995 A Twinkle in Her Eye	95-day		29.90	30

Remembering Elvis - N. Giorgio

YEAR ISSUE	EDITION LIMIT	YEAR RETD.	ISSUE PRICE	*QUOTE U.S.$
1994 The King	95-day		29.90	30
1995 The Legend	95-day		29.90	30

Royal Enchantments - J. Penchoff

YEAR ISSUE	EDITION LIMIT	YEAR RETD.	ISSUE PRICE	*QUOTE U.S.$
1994 The Gift	Closed		39.90	75
1995 The Courtship	Closed		39.90	60
1995 The Promise	Closed		39.90	75
1995 The Embrace	Closed		39.90	80

Sacred Circle - K. Randle

YEAR ISSUE	EDITION LIMIT	YEAR RETD.	ISSUE PRICE	*QUOTE U.S.$
1993 Before the Hunt	Closed		29.90	38-42
1993 Spiritual Guardian	Closed		29.90	59
1993 Ghost Dance	Closed		32.90	50
1994 Deer Dance	Closed		32.90	70
1994 The Wolf Dance	Closed		32.90	50
1994 The Painted Horse	Closed		34.90	50-56
1994 Transformation Dance	Closed		34.90	49-65
1994 Elk Dance	Closed		34.90	55

Santa's Little Helpers - B. Higgins Bond

YEAR ISSUE	EDITION LIMIT	YEAR RETD.	ISSUE PRICE	*QUOTE U.S.$
1994 Stocking Stuffers	Closed		24.90	30
1994 Wrapping Up the Holidays	Closed		24.90	40
1994 Not a Creature Was Stirring	Closed		24.90	35
1995 Cozy Kittens	Closed		24.90	60
1995 Holiday Mischief	Closed		24.90	35
1995 Treats For Santa	Closed		24.90	29

Santa's On His Way - S. Gustafson

YEAR ISSUE	EDITION LIMIT	YEAR RETD.	ISSUE PRICE	*QUOTE U.S.$
1994 Checking It Twice	Closed		29.90	48-50
1994 Up, Up & Away	Closed		29.90	55
1995 Santa's First Stop	Closed		32.90	75
1995 Gifts for One and All	Closed		32.90	80
1995 A Warm Send-off	Closed		32.90	80
1995 Santa's Reward	Closed		34.90	110

Seasons on the Open Range - Zabel

YEAR ISSUE	EDITION LIMIT	YEAR RETD.	ISSUE PRICE	*QUOTE U.S.$
1995 Dog Tired	Closed		29.95	30-60
1995 September Bulls	Closed		29.95	30-38
1995 Outfitters	Closed		29.95	30
1995 Season/Gold	Closed		29.95	30

Signs of Spring - J. Thornbrugh

YEAR ISSUE	EDITION LIMIT	YEAR RETD.	ISSUE PRICE	*QUOTE U.S.$
1994 A Family Feast	95-day		29.90	30
1995 How Fast They Grow	95-day		29.90	30
1995 Our First Home	95-day		29.90	30
1995 Awaiting New Arrivals	95-day		29.90	30

Silent Journey - D. Casey

YEAR ISSUE	EDITION LIMIT	YEAR RETD.	ISSUE PRICE	*QUOTE U.S.$
1994 Where Paths Cross	95-day		29.90	30
1994 On Eagle's Wings	95-day		29.90	30
1994 Seeing the Unseen	95-day		29.90	30
1995 Where the Buffalo Roam	95-day		29.90	30
1995 Unbridled Majesty	95-day		29.90	30
1995 Wisdom Seeker	95-day		29.90	30
1995 Journey of the Wild	95-day		29.90	30

Sitting Pretty - K. Murray

YEAR ISSUE	EDITION LIMIT	YEAR RETD.	ISSUE PRICE	*QUOTE U.S.$
1995 Cats Make a House	Closed		34.95	35-39
1995 Cats Add Love	Closed		34.95	35-50
1995 Little Paws	Closed		34.95	35
1995 Home/Cat	Closed		34.95	35

Soft Elegance - R. Iverson

YEAR ISSUE	EDITION LIMIT	YEAR RETD.	ISSUE PRICE	*QUOTE U.S.$
1994 Priscilla in Pearls	Closed		29.90	45-50
1995 Tabitha on Taffeta	Closed		29.90	50-52
1995 Emily in Emeralds	Closed		29.90	45
1995 Alexandra in Amethysts	Closed		29.90	49

Some Beary Nice Places - J. Tanton

YEAR ISSUE	EDITION LIMIT	YEAR RETD.	ISSUE PRICE	*QUOTE U.S.$
1994 Welcome to the Libeary	Closed		29.90	37-40
1994 Welcome to Our Country Kitchen	Closed		29.90	55
1995 Bearennial Garden	Closed		32.90	35

YEAR ISSUE	EDITION LIMIT	YEAR RETD.	ISSUE PRICE	*QUOTE U.S.$
1995 Welcome to Our Music Conserbeartory	Closed		32.90	46

Soul Mates - L. Bogle

YEAR ISSUE	EDITION LIMIT	YEAR RETD.	ISSUE PRICE	*QUOTE U.S.$
1995 The Lovers	Closed		29.90	30-125
1995 The Awakening	95-day		29.90	30
1996 The Embrace	95-day		29.90	30
1996 Warm Interlude	95-day		29.90	30

Soul of the Wilderness

YEAR ISSUE	EDITION LIMIT	YEAR RETD.	ISSUE PRICE	*QUOTE U.S.$
1996 One Last Look	Closed		34.95	29-35
1996 Silent Watch	Closed		34.95	35
1996 Chance/Flurries	Closed		34.95	35
1996 Winter Solstice	Closed		34.95	35-60
1996 Storm Runner	Closed		34.95	35-60
1996 Winter Whites	Closed		34.95	35

Sovereigns of the Sky - G. Dieckhoner

YEAR ISSUE	EDITION LIMIT	YEAR RETD.	ISSUE PRICE	*QUOTE U.S.$
1994 Spirit of Freedom	Closed		39.00	30
1994 Spirit of Pride	Closed		39.00	70
1994 Spirit of Valor	Closed		44.00	54
1994 Spirit of Majesty	Closed		44.00	65
1995 Spirit of Glory	Closed		44.00	75
1995 Spirit of Courage	Closed		49.00	60
1995 Spirit of Bravery	Closed		49.00	60
1995 Spirit of Honor	Closed		49.00	90

Sovereigns of the Wild - D. Grant

YEAR ISSUE	EDITION LIMIT	YEAR RETD.	ISSUE PRICE	*QUOTE U.S.$
1993 The Snow Queen	Closed		29.90	37
1994 Let Us Survive	Closed		29.90	36
1994 Cool Cats	Closed		29.90	49
1994 Siberian Snow Tigers	Closed		29.90	30
1994 African Evening	Closed		29.90	31-45
1994 First Outing	Closed		29.90	30-34

Star of Hope - H. Garrido

YEAR ISSUE	EDITION LIMIT	YEAR RETD.	ISSUE PRICE	*QUOTE U.S.$
1995 Most Precious	Closed		34.95	35
1995 Gifts of the Magi	Closed		34.95	35-50
1995 Adoration of the Shepherds	Closed		34.95	35
1995 Rest/Flight	Closed		34.95	35

Star Trek Ships of the Galaxy

YEAR ISSUE	EDITION LIMIT	YEAR RETD.	ISSUE PRICE	*QUOTE U.S.$
1995 Enterprise	Closed		59.95	70-95
1995 Klingon Battle	Closed		59.95	90
1995 Romulan	Closed		59.95	80-100
1995 Shuttlecraft	Closed		59.95	100

Study of a Champion - B. Langton

YEAR ISSUE	EDITION LIMIT	YEAR RETD.	ISSUE PRICE	*QUOTE U.S.$
1995 Loyal Companion	Closed		29.90	30-55
1995 Trusted Friend	Closed		29.90	30-50
1995 Devoted Partner	Closed		29.90	30-45
1995 Faithful Buddy	Closed		29.90	30

Superstars of Baseball - T. Sizemore

YEAR ISSUE	EDITION LIMIT	YEAR RETD.	ISSUE PRICE	*QUOTE U.S.$
1994 Willie "Say Hey" Mays	Closed		29.90	45-59
1995 Carl "Yaz" Yastrzemski	Closed		29.90	50
1995 Frank "Robby" Robinson	Closed		32.90	59
1995 Bob Gibson	Closed		32.90	54
1995 Harmon Killebrew	Closed		32.90	49-60
1995 Don Drysdale	Closed		34.90	74
1995 Al Kaline	Closed		34.90	74
1995 Maury Wills	Closed		34.90	100

Superstars of Country Music - N. Giorgio

YEAR ISSUE	EDITION LIMIT	YEAR RETD.	ISSUE PRICE	*QUOTE U.S.$
1993 Dolly Parton: I Will Always Love You	Closed		29.90	34
1993 Kenny Rogers: Sweet Music Man	Closed		29.90	29
1994 Barbara Mandrell	Closed		32.90	33
1994 Glen Campbell: Rhinestone Cowboy	Closed		32.90	24

Tale of Peter Rabbit & Benjamin Bunny - R. Akers

YEAR ISSUE	EDITION LIMIT	YEAR RETD.	ISSUE PRICE	*QUOTE U.S.$
1994 A Pocket Full of Onions	Closed		39.00	80
1994 Beside His Cousin	Closed		39.00	58-80
1995 Round that Corner	Closed		39.00	50-99
1995 Safely Home	Closed		44.00	75-88
1995 Mr. McGregor's Garden	Closed		44.00	50-150
1995 Rosemary Tea and Lavender	Closed		44.00	60-129
1995 Amongst the Flowerpots	Closed		44.00	90-100
1995 Upon the Scarecrow	Closed		44.00	150

Teddy Bear Dreams - D. Parker

YEAR ISSUE	EDITION LIMIT	YEAR RETD.	ISSUE PRICE	*QUOTE U.S.$
1995 Catch a Falling Star	Closed		49.95	69-86
1995 Thank Heaven	Closed		49.95	60-90
1995 Let Me Be Teddy	Closed		49.95	50
1995 Fly Me To The Moon	Closed		49.95	50

Terry Redlin's America the Beautiful - T. Redlin

YEAR ISSUE	EDITION LIMIT	YEAR RETD.	ISSUE PRICE	*QUOTE U.S.$
1995 Oh Beautiful	Closed		34.95	35
1995 Amber Waves	Closed		34.95	35
1995 Purple Mountain	Closed		34.95	35
1995 Fruited Plain	Closed		34.95	35
1995 America	Closed		34.95	35
1995 God Shed His Grace	Closed		34.95	35

That's What Friends Are For - A. Isakov

YEAR ISSUE	EDITION LIMIT	YEAR RETD.	ISSUE PRICE	*QUOTE U.S.$
1994 Friends Are Forever	Closed		29.90	40-48
1994 Friends Are Comfort	Closed		29.90	75
1994 Friends Are Loving	Closed		29.90	45-48
1995 Friends Are For Fun	Closed		29.90	65

Thomas Kinkade's Illuminated Cottages - T. Kinkade

YEAR ISSUE	EDITION LIMIT	YEAR RETD.	ISSUE PRICE	*QUOTE U.S.$
1994 The Flagstone Path	Closed		34.90	43-105
1995 The Garden Walk	Closed		34.90	43-105
1995 Cherry Blossom Hideaway	Closed		37.90	46-125
1995 The Lighted Gate	Closed		37.90	46-250

Thomas Kinkade's Lamplight Village - T. Kinkade

YEAR ISSUE	EDITION LIMIT	YEAR RETD.	ISSUE PRICE	*QUOTE U.S.$
1995 Lamplight Brooke	Closed		29.90	38-80
1995 Lamplight Lane	Closed		29.90	38-50
1995 Lamplight Inn	Closed		29.90	38-50
1995 Lamplight Country	Closed		29.90	38-50
1995 Lamplight Glen	Closed		29.90	34-38
1995 Lamplight Bridge	Closed		29.90	38-50
1995 Lamplight Mill	Closed		29.90	38-79
1995 Lamplight Farm	Closed		29.90	35-38

Those Who Guide Us - H. Garrido

YEAR ISSUE	EDITION LIMIT	YEAR RETD.	ISSUE PRICE	*QUOTE U.S.$
1996 St. Francis	Closed		29.90	30-42
1996 St. Joseph	Closed		29.90	30-45
1996 St. Jude	Closed		29.90	30
1996 St. Anthony	Closed		29.90	30

Through a Child's Eyes - K. Noles

YEAR ISSUE	EDITION LIMIT	YEAR RETD.	ISSUE PRICE	*QUOTE U.S.$
1994 Little Butterfly	Closed		29.90	65
1995 Woodland Rose	Closed		29.90	45-50
1995 Treetop Wonder	Closed		29.90	35-50
1995 Little Red Squirrel	Closed		32.90	60-65
1995 Water Lily	Closed		32.90	65
1995 Prairie Song	Closed		34.90	65-70

Thunder in the Sky

YEAR ISSUE	EDITION LIMIT	YEAR RETD.	ISSUE PRICE	*QUOTE U.S.$
1995 Mighty 8th Coming	Closed		34.95	35
1995 D-Day	Closed		34.95	35
1995 Home/Dusk	Closed		34.95	35
1995 Winters Welcome	Closed		34.95	35

Thundering Waters - F. Miller

YEAR ISSUE	EDITION LIMIT	YEAR RETD.	ISSUE PRICE	*QUOTE U.S.$
1994 Niagara Falls	Closed		34.90	30
1994 Lower Falls, Yellowstone	Closed		34.90	61
1994 Bridal Veil Falls	Closed		34.90	60
1995 Havasu Falls	Closed		29.90	55

Timberland Secrets - L. Daniels

YEAR ISSUE	EDITION LIMIT	YEAR RETD.	ISSUE PRICE	*QUOTE U.S.$
1995 Sweet Dreams	Closed		29.90	30
1995 Gentle Awakening	Closed		29.90	30
1995 Good Day to Play	Closed		29.90	30
1995 Wintry Watch	Closed		29.90	30
1995 Moments Pause	Closed		29.90	30
1995 Tranquil Retreat	Closed		29.90	30

To Soar With Eagles - P. Clayton Weirs

YEAR ISSUE	EDITION LIMIT	YEAR RETD.	ISSUE PRICE	*QUOTE U.S.$
1995 Cascading Inspiration	Closed		32.95	33-38
1995 Crystal Mist	Closed		32.95	33-50
1995 Turbulent Tide	Closed		32.95	33-50
1995 Soaring/Greater	Closed		32.95	33

Trains of the Great West - K. Randle

YEAR ISSUE	EDITION LIMIT	YEAR RETD.	ISSUE PRICE	*QUOTE U.S.$
1993 Moonlit Journey	Closed		29.90	31-36
1993 Mountain Hideaway	Closed		29.90	45-50
1993 Early Morning Arrival	Closed		29.90	48-52
1994 The Snowy Pass	Closed		29.90	43-48

Tribute to Selena - B. Emmett

YEAR ISSUE	EDITION LIMIT	YEAR RETD.	ISSUE PRICE	*QUOTE U.S.$
1996 Selena Forever	Closed		29.95	250

Tribute to the Armed Forces - B. Dodge

YEAR ISSUE	EDITION LIMIT	YEAR RETD.	ISSUE PRICE	*QUOTE U.S.$
1995 Proud/Serve	Closed		34.95	58

Triumph in the Air - H. Krebs

YEAR ISSUE	EDITION LIMIT	YEAR RETD.	ISSUE PRICE	*QUOTE U.S.$
1994 Checkmate!	Closed		34.90	59
1994 One Heck of a Deflection Shot	Closed		34.90	38
1994 Hunting Fever	Closed		34.90	89
1995 Thunderbolt	Closed		34.90	65-74

Twilight Memories - J. Barnes

YEAR ISSUE	EDITION LIMIT	YEAR RETD.	ISSUE PRICE	*QUOTE U.S.$
1995 Winter's Twilight	95-day		29.90	30

Two's Company - S. Eide

YEAR ISSUE	EDITION LIMIT	YEAR RETD.	ISSUE PRICE	*QUOTE U.S.$
1994 Golden Harvest	Closed		29.90	90
1995 Brotherly Love	Closed		29.90	88
1995 Seeing Double	Closed		29.90	88
1995 Spring Spaniels	Closed		29.90	110

Under A Snowy Veil - C. Sams

YEAR ISSUE	EDITION LIMIT	YEAR RETD.	ISSUE PRICE	*QUOTE U.S.$
1995 Winter's Warmth	Closed		29.90	30
1995 Snow Mates	Closed		29.90	27
1995 Winter's Dawn	Closed		29.90	30
1995 First Snow	Closed		29.90	30-50

Under the Northern Lights - D. McCaffery

YEAR ISSUE	EDITION LIMIT	YEAR RETD.	ISSUE PRICE	*QUOTE U.S.$
1995 Running/Light	Closed		29.90	30
1995 River of Light	Closed		29.90	30
1995 Monarchs Light	Closed		29.90	30
1995 Catching the Light	Closed		29.90	30

Untamed Spirits - P. Weirs

YEAR ISSUE	EDITION LIMIT	YEAR RETD.	ISSUE PRICE	*QUOTE U.S.$
1993 Wild Hearts	Closed		29.90	39
1994 Breakaway	Closed		29.90	50
1994 Forever Free	Closed		29.90	33-49
1994 Distant Thunder	Closed		29.90	70

Untamed Wilderness - P. Weirs

YEAR ISSUE	EDITION LIMIT	YEAR RETD.	ISSUE PRICE	*QUOTE U.S.$
1995 Unexpected Encounter	95-day		29.90	30

Vanishing Paradises - G. Dieckhoner

YEAR ISSUE	EDITION LIMIT	YEAR RETD.	ISSUE PRICE	*QUOTE U.S.$
1994 The Rainforest	Closed		29.90	40
1994 The Panda's World	Closed		29.90	70
1994 Splendors of India	Closed		29.90	60
1994 An African Safari	Closed		29.90	79

Visions from Eagle Ridge - D. Casey

YEAR ISSUE	EDITION LIMIT	YEAR RETD.	ISSUE PRICE	*QUOTE U.S.$
1995 Assembly of Pride	Closed		29.90	30

534

Collectors' Information Bureau

*Quotes have been rounded up to nearest dollar

YEAR ISSUE	EDITION LIMIT	YEAR RETD.	ISSUE PRICE	*QUOTE U.S.$
1995 Generation	Closed		29.90	30
1995 Freedom	Closed		29.90	30
1995 Stately Summit	Closed		29.90	30
1995 Wings of Honor	Closed		29.90	30
1995 Legacy/Liberty	Closed		29.90	30

Visions of Glory - D. Cook

YEAR ISSUE	EDITION LIMIT	YEAR RETD.	ISSUE PRICE	*QUOTE U.S.$
1995 Iwo Jima	Closed		29.90	57
1995 Freeing of Paris	Closed		29.90	98

Visions of Our Lady - H. Garrido

YEAR ISSUE	EDITION LIMIT	YEAR RETD.	ISSUE PRICE	*QUOTE U.S.$
1994 Our Lady of Lourdes	Closed		29.90	37
1994 Our Lady of Medjugorje	Closed		29.90	57
1994 Our Lady of Fatima	Closed		29.90	47-50
1994 Our Lady of Guadeloupe	Closed		29.90	54-63
1994 Our Lady of Grace	Closed		29.90	30-35
1994 Our Lady of Mt. Carmel	Closed		29.90	70-74
1994 Our Lady of La Salette	95-day		29.90	30
1994 Virgin of the Poor	95-day		29.90	30
1994 Virgin of the Golden Heart	95-day		29.90	30
1994 Our Lady of Hope	95-day		29.90	30
1994 Our Lady of Silence	95-day		29.90	30
1994 Our Lady of Snow	95-day		29.90	30

Visions of the Sacred - D. Stanley

YEAR ISSUE	EDITION LIMIT	YEAR RETD.	ISSUE PRICE	*QUOTE U.S.$
1994 Snow Rider	95-day		29.90	30
1994 Spring's Messenger	95-day		29.90	30
1994 The Cheyenne Prophet	95-day		32.90	33
1995 Buffalo Caller	95-day		32.90	33
1995 Journey of Harmony	95-day		32.90	33

A Visit from St. Nick - C. Jackson

YEAR ISSUE	EDITION LIMIT	YEAR RETD.	ISSUE PRICE	*QUOTE U.S.$
1995 Twas the Night Before Christmas	Closed		49.00	61-65
1995 Up to the Housetop	Closed		49.00	65-67
1995 A Bundle of Toys	Closed		54.00	65
1995 The Stockings Were Filled	Closed		54.00	55
1995 Visions of Sugarplums	Closed		54.00	65-75
1995 To My Wondering Eyes	Closed		59.00	65
1995 A Wink of His Eye	Closed		59.00	75
1995 Happy Christmas To All	Closed		59.00	75

A Visit to Brambly Hedge - J. Barklem

YEAR ISSUE	EDITION LIMIT	YEAR RETD.	ISSUE PRICE	*QUOTE U.S.$
1994 Summer Story	Closed		39.90	70
1994 Spring Story	Closed		39.90	68
1994 Autumn Story	Closed		39.90	90
1995 Winter Story	Closed		39.90	90

Warm Country Moments - M.A. Lasher

YEAR ISSUE	EDITION LIMIT	YEAR RETD.	ISSUE PRICE	*QUOTE U.S.$
1994 Mabel's Sunny Retreat	95-day		29.90	30
1994 Annebelle's Simple Pleasures	95-day		29.90	30
1994 Harriet's Loving Touch	95-day		29.90	30
1994 Emily and Alice in a Jam	95-day		29.90	30
1995 Hanna's Secret Garden	95-day		29.90	30
1995 Mabel's Summer Retreat	95-day		29.90	30
1995 Harriet's Loving Touch	95-day		29.90	30
1995 Emily & Alice in a Jam	95-day		29.90	30

Welcome to the Neighborhood - B. Mock

YEAR ISSUE	EDITION LIMIT	YEAR RETD.	ISSUE PRICE	*QUOTE U.S.$
1994 Ivy Lane	Closed		29.90	52
1994 Daffodil Drive	Closed		29.90	50
1995 Lilac Lane	Closed		34.90	50
1995 Tulip Terrace	Closed		34.90	50

When All Hearts Come Home - J. Barnes

YEAR ISSUE	EDITION LIMIT	YEAR RETD.	ISSUE PRICE	*QUOTE U.S.$
1993 Oh Christmas Tree	Closed		29.90	60
1993 Night Before Christmas	Closed		29.90	70-73
1993 Comfort and Joy	Closed		29.90	69
1993 Grandpa's Farm	Closed		29.90	78
1993 Peace on Earth	Closed		29.90	77
1993 Night Departure	Closed		29.90	72
1993 Supper and Small Talk	Closed		29.90	60-63
1993 Christmas Wish	Closed		29.90	60-65

When Dreams Blossom - R. McGinnis

YEAR ISSUE	EDITION LIMIT	YEAR RETD.	ISSUE PRICE	*QUOTE U.S.$
1994 Dreams to Gather	Closed		29.90	30
1994 Where Friends Dream	Closed		29.90	32
1994 The Sweetest of Dreams	95-day		32.90	33
1994 Dreams of Poetry	95-day		32.90	33
1995 A Place to Dream	95-day		32.90	33
1995 Dreaming of You	95-day		32.90	33

Where Eagles Soar - F. Mittelstadt

YEAR ISSUE	EDITION LIMIT	YEAR RETD.	ISSUE PRICE	*QUOTE U.S.$
1994 On Freedom's Wing	Closed		29.90	32-35
1994 Allegiance with the Wind	Closed		29.90	30
1995 Pride of the Sky	Closed		29.90	50
1995 Windward Majesty	Closed		29.90	32
1995 Noble Legacy	Closed		29.90	35
1995 Pristine Domains	Closed		29.90	40
1995 Splendor in Flight	Closed		29.90	32-60
1995 Royal Ascent	Closed		29.90	30

Whispers on the Wind - K. O'Malley

YEAR ISSUE	EDITION LIMIT	YEAR RETD.	ISSUE PRICE	*QUOTE U.S.$
1995 Ruby Throated	Closed		44.90	45
1995 Annas	Closed		44.90	45
1995 Allen	95-day		44.90	45
1996 Broad Billed	95-day		44.90	45
1996 Rufous	95-day		44.90	45
1996 Blue Throated	95-day		44.90	45

Wild Pagentry - F. Mittelstadt

YEAR ISSUE	EDITION LIMIT	YEAR RETD.	ISSUE PRICE	*QUOTE U.S.$
1995 Flight of the Pheasant	Closed		49.90	50

Windows on a World of Song - K. Daniel

YEAR ISSUE	EDITION LIMIT	YEAR RETD.	ISSUE PRICE	*QUOTE U.S.$
1993 The Library: Cardinals	Closed		34.90	5757
1993 The Den: Black-Capped Chickadees	Closed		34.90	32
1993 The Bedroom: Bluebirds	Closed		34.90	31
1994 The Kitchen: Goldfinches	Closed		34.90	52

Wings of Glory - J. Spurlock

YEAR ISSUE	EDITION LIMIT	YEAR RETD.	ISSUE PRICE	*QUOTE U.S.$
1995 Pride of America	Closed		32.90	34
1995 Spirit of Freedom	Closed		32.90	38
1996 Portrait of Liberty	Closed		32.90	34-42
1996 Paragon of Courage	Closed		32.90	34-40

Wings of Love - L. Liu

YEAR ISSUE	EDITION LIMIT	YEAR RETD.	ISSUE PRICE	*QUOTE U.S.$
1997 Tender Hearts	Closed		29.95	30-50
1997 Precious Gift	Closed		29.95	30
1997 Tender Hearts	Closed		29.95	30
1997 Sacred Promise	Closed		29.95	30
1997 Sweet Dreams	Closed		29.95	30
1997 Bright/Light	Closed		29.95	30

Winnie the Pooh and Friends - C. Jackson

YEAR ISSUE	EDITION LIMIT	YEAR RETD.	ISSUE PRICE	*QUOTE U.S.$
1995 Time For a Little Something	Closed		39.90	350-393
1995 Bouncing's/Tiggers do Best	Closed		39.90	90
1995 You're a Real Friend	Closed		44.90	37-48
1995 Silly Old Bear	Closed		44.90	42-49
1995 Rumbly in my Tummy	Closed		44.90	44-49
1995 Many Happy Returns of the Day	Closed		49.90	60-64
1996 T is For Tigger	Closed		49.90	69
1996 Nobody Uncheered w/Balloons	Closed		49.90	93
1996 Do You Think It's a Woozle?	Closed		49.90	71-75
1996 Fine Day to Buzz with the Bees	Closed		49.90	50-69
1996 Pooh Sticks	Closed		49.90	50-70
1996 Three Cheers For Pooh	Closed		49.90	65-80

Winter Evening Reflections

YEAR ISSUE	EDITION LIMIT	YEAR RETD.	ISSUE PRICE	*QUOTE U.S.$
1995 Twilight Falls	Closed		39.95	40
1995 Down by the Stream	Closed		39.95	40
1995 Shadows Grow	Closed		39.95	40
1995 Day Fades	Closed		39.95	40

Winter Garlands - S. Timm

YEAR ISSUE	EDITION LIMIT	YEAR RETD.	ISSUE PRICE	*QUOTE U.S.$
1995 Winter Spirits	Closed		34.95	35-39
1996 Jewel in the Snow	Closed		34.95	35-45
1996 Crisp Morning	Closed		34.95	35
1996 Frosty Season	Closed		34.95	35

Winter Shadows - Various

YEAR ISSUE	EDITION LIMIT	YEAR RETD.	ISSUE PRICE	*QUOTE U.S.$
1995 Canyon Moon	Closed		29.90	30-38
1995 Shadows of Gray	95-day		29.90	30
1995 December Watch	95-day		29.90	30
1995 Broken Silence	95-day		29.90	30
1995 Vigilant Companion	95-day		29.90	30
1995 Moonlight	95-day		29.90	30
1995 Trackers	95-day		29.90	30
1995 Icy Dawn	95-day		29.90	30

Wish You Were Here - T. Kinkade

YEAR ISSUE	EDITION LIMIT	YEAR RETD.	ISSUE PRICE	*QUOTE U.S.$
1994 End of a Perfect Day	Closed		29.90	38-60
1994 A Quiet Evening/Riverlodge	Closed		29.90	38-125
1994 Soft Morning Light	Closed		32.90	41-85
1994 Forest Lake	Closed		32.90	41-75
1994 Evening in the Forest	Closed		32.90	41-75
1994 Simpler Times	Closed		32.90	41-90

Wolf Pups Young Faces of the Wilderness - L. Daniels

YEAR ISSUE	EDITION LIMIT	YEAR RETD.	ISSUE PRICE	*QUOTE U.S.$
1995 Tomorrow's Pride	Closed		29.95	30-42
1995 New Adventure	Closed		29.95	30
1995 Morning Innocence	95-day		29.95	30
1995 Call/Future	95-day		29.95	30
1995 Early Aspiration	95-day		29.95	30
1995 Rosy Beginnings	95-day		29.95	30

Woodland Tranquility - G. Alexander

YEAR ISSUE	EDITION LIMIT	YEAR RETD.	ISSUE PRICE	*QUOTE U.S.$
1994 Winter's Calm	95-day		29.90	30
1995 Frosty Morn	95-day		29.90	30
1995 Crossing Boundaries	95-day		29.90	30

Woodland Wings - J. Hansel

YEAR ISSUE	EDITION LIMIT	YEAR RETD.	ISSUE PRICE	*QUOTE U.S.$
1994 Twilight Flight	Closed		34.90	55
1994 Gliding on Gilded Skies	Closed		34.90	80
1994 Sunset Voyage	Closed		34.90	60
1995 Peaceful Journey	Closed		34.90	35-75

The World Beneath the Waves - D. Terbush

YEAR ISSUE	EDITION LIMIT	YEAR RETD.	ISSUE PRICE	*QUOTE U.S.$
1995 Sea of Light	Closed		29.90	50-100
1995 All God's Children	Closed		29.90	70
1995 Circle of Light	Closed		29.90	45-58
1995 Reach/Dreams	Closed		29.90	50-65
1995 Share the Love	Closed		29.90	30-59
1995 Follow Your Heart	Closed		29.90	60
1995 Long Before Man	95-day		29.90	30
1995 Miracles of the Sea	95-day		29.90	30

The World of the Eagle - J. Hansel

YEAR ISSUE	EDITION LIMIT	YEAR RETD.	ISSUE PRICE	*QUOTE U.S.$
1993 Sentinel of the Night	Closed		29.90	34
1994 Silent Guard	Closed		29.90	48
1994 Night Flyer	Closed		32.90	50
1995 Midnight Duty	Closed		32.90	81

A World of Wildlife: Celebrating Earth Day - T. Clausnitzer

YEAR ISSUE	EDITION LIMIT	YEAR RETD.	ISSUE PRICE	*QUOTE U.S.$
1995 A Delicate Balance	Closed		29.90	29
1995 Europe	Closed		29.90	89
1995 Africa	Closed		29.90	40
1995 South America	Closed		29.90	50

WWII: A Remembrance - J. Griffin

YEAR ISSUE	EDITION LIMIT	YEAR RETD.	ISSUE PRICE	*QUOTE U.S.$
1994 D-Day	Closed		29.90	30
1994 The Battle of Midway	Closed		29.90	39
1994 The Battle of The Bulge	Closed		32.90	47
1995 Battle of the Philippines	Closed		32.90	58
1995 Doolittle's Raid Over Tokyo	Closed		32.90	50
1995 Operation Torch	Closed		34.90	68-71
1995 Italian Campaign	Closed		34.90	68-80
1995 Liberation of France	Closed		34.90	90-105

Cavanagh Group Intl.

Coca-Cola Brand Heritage Collection - Various

YEAR ISSUE	EDITION LIMIT	YEAR RETD.	ISSUE PRICE	*QUOTE U.S.$
1995 Boy Fishing - N. Rockwell	5,000	1997	60.00	70
1995 Good Boys and Girls - Sundblom	2,500	1995	60.00	60-70
1995 Hilda Clark with Roses - CGI	5,000	1997	60.00	65-75
1996 Travel Refreshed - Sundblom	Closed	1998	60.00	60-80

Prince of Egypt - Dreamworks

YEAR ISSUE	EDITION LIMIT	YEAR RETD.	ISSUE PRICE	*QUOTE U.S.$
1998 Chariot Race	5,000		35.00	35
1998 Exodos Scene	5,000		35.00	35
1998 New Beginnings	5,000		35.00	35

Cherished Teddies/Enesco Group, Inc.

The Cherished Seasons - P. Hillman

YEAR ISSUE	EDITION LIMIT	YEAR RETD.	ISSUE PRICE	*QUOTE U.S.$
1997 Spring-"Spring Brings A Season of Beauty" 203386	Open		35.00	35
1997 Summer-"Summer Brings A Season of Warmth" 203394	Open		35.00	35
1997 Autumn-"Autumn Brings A Season of Thanksgiving" 203408	Open		35.00	35
1997 Winter "Winter Brings A Season of Joy" 203416	Open		35.00	35

Cherished Teddies - P. Hillman

YEAR ISSUE	EDITION LIMIT	YEAR RETD.	ISSUE PRICE	*QUOTE U.S.$
1997 We Bear Thanks 272426	Closed	1999	35.00	38-40
1999 Eskimo Holding Stars 534196	Yr.Iss.	1999	37.50	38
1995 Sculpted Irish Plaque "A Cherished Irish Blessing" 110981	Closed	N/A	13.50	14
1992 Signage Plaque (Hamilton) 951005	Closed	N/A	15.00	24-50
1992 Signage Plaque 951005	Open		15.00	15

Cherished Teddies Mini Plates - P. Hillman

YEAR ISSUE	EDITION LIMIT	YEAR RETD.	ISSUE PRICE	*QUOTE U.S.$
1997 Joann "Cup Full Of Love" 269840	Retrd.	2000	25.00	25
1997 Jordan "Cup Full Of Joy" 269832	Retrd.	2000	25.00	25

Christmas - P. Hillman

YEAR ISSUE	EDITION LIMIT	YEAR RETD.	ISSUE PRICE	*QUOTE U.S.$
1995 "The Season of Joy" Dtd 95 141550	Yr.Iss.	1995	35.00	44-50
1996 "The Season of Peace" Dtd 96 176060	Yr.Iss.	1996	35.00	28-35
1997 "The Season to Believe" Dtd 97 272183	Yr.Iss.	1997	35.00	35
1998 "The Season of Magic" Dtd 98 352764	Yr.Iss.	1998	35.00	35
1999 Christmas Dtd 99 534196	Yr.Iss.	1999	37.50	38

Easter - P. Hillman

YEAR ISSUE	EDITION LIMIT	YEAR RETD.	ISSUE PRICE	*QUOTE U.S.$
1996 "Some Bunny Loves You" Dtd 96 156590	Yr.Iss.	1996	35.00	44-80
1997 Springtime Happiness Dtd 97 203009	Yr.Iss.	1997	35.00	35

Mother's Day - P. Hillman

YEAR ISSUE	EDITION LIMIT	YEAR RETD.	ISSUE PRICE	*QUOTE U.S.$
1996 "A Mother's Heart is Full of Love" Dtd 96 156493	Yr.Iss.	1996	35.00	35-65
1997 Our Love Is Ever-Blooming Dtd 97 203025	Yr.Iss.	1997	35.00	35
1998 Mom-Maker of Miracles 303046	Closed	1999	35.00	35

Nursery Rhymes - P. Hillman

YEAR ISSUE	EDITION LIMIT	YEAR RETD.	ISSUE PRICE	*QUOTE U.S.$
1995 Jack/Jill "Our Friendship Will Never Tumble" 114901	Closed		35.00	35
1995 Mary/Lamb "I'll Always Be By Your Side" 128902	Closed		35.00	35
1995 Old King Cole "You Wear Your Kindness Like a Crown" 135437	Closed		35.00	35
1996 Mother Goose & Friends "Happily Ever After With Friends" 170968	Closed		35.00	35
1996 Little Miss Muffet "I'm Never Afraid With You At My Side" 145033	Closed		35.00	35
1996 Little Jack Horner "I'm Plum Happy You're My Friend" 151998	Closed		35.00	35
1996 Wee Willie Winkie "Good Night, Sleep Tight" 170941	Closed		35.00	35
1996 Little Bo Peep "Looking For A Friend Like You" 164658	Closed		35.00	35

Dave Grossman Creations

Emmett Kelly Commemorative Plate - B. Leighton-Jones

YEAR ISSUE	EDITION LIMIT	YEAR RETD.	ISSUE PRICE	*QUOTE U.S.$
1990 Commemorative Plate EKPC-01	Retrd.	1992	25.00	25

Emmett Kelly Plates - B. Leighton-Jones

YEAR ISSUE	EDITION LIMIT	YEAR RETD.	ISSUE PRICE	*QUOTE U.S.$
1986 Christmas Carol EKP-86	Yr.Iss.	1986	20.00	400
1987 Christmas Wreath EKP-87	Yr.Iss.	1987	20.00	225
1988 Christmas Dinner EKP-88	Yr.Iss.	1988	20.00	135
1989 Christmas Feast EKP-89	Yr.Iss.	1989	20.00	125
1990 Just What I Needed EKP-90	Yr.Iss.	1990	24.00	125
1991 Emmett The Snowman EKP-91	Yr.Iss.	1991	25.00	75-95
1992 Christmas Tunes EKP-92	Yr.Iss.	1992	25.00	60-75
1993 Downhill EKP-93	Yr.Iss.	1993	30.00	55-65
1994 Holiday Skater EKP-94	Yr.Iss.	1994	30.00	50-60
1995 Merry Christmas Mr. Scrooge EKP-95	Yr.Iss.	1995	30.00	50-65

*Quotes have been rounded up to nearest dollar

Legacy Series - T. Snyder

YEAR ISSUE	EDITION LIMIT	YEAR RETD.	ISSUE PRICE	*QUOTE U.S.$
1998 African Kings (wall plaque) LS-4522W	Open		24.00	24
1998 African Queens (wall plaque) LS-4523W	Open		24.00	24
1998 Jungle Beauty (wall plaque) LS-4552W	Open		24.00	24
1998 Jungle Eyes (wall plaque) LS-4551W	Open		24.00	24
1998 Royal Family (wall plaque) LS-4508W	Open		20.00	20
1998 Twilight Gathering (wall plaque) LS-4509W	Open		20.00	20
1998 Watchful Guardians (wall plaque) LS-4507W	Open		20.00	20

Norman Rockwell Collection - Rockwell-Inspired

YEAR ISSUE	EDITION LIMIT	YEAR RETD.	ISSUE PRICE	*QUOTE U.S.$
1982 American Mother RGP-42	Retrd.		45.00	55
1980 Back To School RMP-80	Retrd.		24.00	24
1984 Big Moment RMP-84	Retrd.		27.00	27
1979 Butterboy RP-01	Retrd.		40.00	40
1983 Christmas Chores RXP-83	Retrd.		75.00	75
1980 Christmas Trio RXP-80	Retrd.		75.00	75
1983 Circus NRP-83	Retrd.		65.00	65
1982 Doctor and Doll NRP-82	Retrd.		65.00	95
1983 Doctor and Doll RMP-83	Retrd.		27.00	27
1983 Dreamboat RGP-83	Retrd.		24.00	30
1981 Dreams of Long Ago NRP-81	Retrd.		60.00	60
1982 Faces of Christmas RXP-82	Retrd.		75.00	75
1979 Leapfrog NRP-79	Retrd.		50.00	50
1982 Love Letter RMP-82	Retrd.		27.00	30
1980 Lovers NRP-80	Retrd.		60.00	60
1998 Marriage License NRP-ML	Open		30.00	30
1981 No Swimming RMP-81	Retrd.		25.00	25
1981 Santa's Good Boys RXP-81	Retrd.		75.00	75
1984 Tiny Tim RXP-84	Retrd.		75.00	75
1984 Visit With Rockwell NRP-84	Retrd.		65.00	65
1978 Young Doctor RDP-26	Retrd.		50.00	65

Norman Rockwell Collection-Boy Scout Plates - Rockwell-Inspired

YEAR ISSUE	EDITION LIMIT	YEAR RETD.	ISSUE PRICE	*QUOTE U.S.$
1981 Can't Wait BSP-01	Retrd.		30.00	45
1982 Guiding Hand BSP-02	Retrd.		30.00	35-65
1983 Tomorrow's Leader BSP-03	Retrd.		30.00	45-65

Norman Rockwell Collection-Huck Finn Plates - Rockwell-Inspired

YEAR ISSUE	EDITION LIMIT	YEAR RETD.	ISSUE PRICE	*QUOTE U.S.$
1979 Secret HFP-01	Retrd.		40.00	65-75
1980 Listening HFP-02	Retrd.		40.00	65-75
1980 No Kings HFP-03	Retrd.		40.00	65-75
1981 Snake Escapes HFP-04	Retrd.		40.00	65-75

Norman Rockwell Collection-Tom Sawyer Plates - Rockwell-Inspired

YEAR ISSUE	EDITION LIMIT	YEAR RETD.	ISSUE PRICE	*QUOTE U.S.$
1975 Whitewashing the Fence TSP-01	Retrd.		26.00	50-75
1976 First Smoke TSP-02	Retrd.		26.00	50-75
1977 Take Your Medicine TSP-03	Retrd.		26.00	30-75
1978 Lost in Cave TSP-04	Retrd.		26.00	45-50

The Original Emmett Kelly Circus Collection - B. Leighton-Jones

YEAR ISSUE	EDITION LIMIT	YEAR RETD.	ISSUE PRICE	*QUOTE U.S.$
1993 Downhill Daring	Yr.Iss.	1993	30.00	30
1994 Holiday Skater	Yr.Iss.	1994	30.00	30
1995 Merry Christmas Mr. Scrooge	Yr.Iss.	1995	30.00	30

Saturday Evening Post Collection - Rockwell-Inspired

YEAR ISSUE	EDITION LIMIT	YEAR RETD.	ISSUE PRICE	*QUOTE U.S.$
1991 Downhill Daring BRP-91	Yr.Iss.	1991	25.00	35
1991 Missed BRP-101	Yr.Iss.	1991	25.00	25-30
1992 Choosin Up BRP-102	Yr.Iss.	1992	25.00	30

David Winter Cottages/Enesco European Giftware Group

David Winter Plate Collection - M. Fisher

YEAR ISSUE	EDITION LIMIT	YEAR RETD.	ISSUE PRICE	*QUOTE U.S.$
1991 A Christmas Carol	10,000	1993	30.00	30-35
1991 Cotswold Village Plate	10,000	1993	30.00	30-54
1992 Chichester Cross Plate	10,000	1993	30.00	34
1992 Little Mill Plate	10,000	1993	30.00	30
1992 Old Curiosity Shop	10,000	1993	30.00	30
1992 Scrooge's Counting House	10,000	1993	30.00	30
1993 Dove Cottage	10,000	1996	30.00	35
1993 Little Forge	10,000	1996	30.00	35

Delphi

The Beatles Collection - N. Giorgio

YEAR ISSUE	EDITION LIMIT	YEAR RETD.	ISSUE PRICE	*QUOTE U.S.$
1991 The Beatles, Live In Concert	Closed		24.75	35-37
1991 Hello America	Closed		24.75	54
1991 A Hard Day's Night	Closed		27.75	45-59
1992 Beatles '65	Closed		27.75	69
1992 Help	Closed		27.75	94
1992 The Beatles at Shea Stadium	Closed		29.75	45-48
1992 Rubber Soul	Closed		29.75	47-79
1992 Yesterday and Today	Closed		29.75	48

Commemorating The King - M. Stutzman

YEAR ISSUE	EDITION LIMIT	YEAR RETD.	ISSUE PRICE	*QUOTE U.S.$
1993 The Rock and Roll Legend	Closed		29.75	40-55
1993 Las Vegas, Live	Closed		29.75	35-40
1993 Blues and Black Leather	Closed		29.75	29-52
1993 Private Presley	Closed		29.75	34
1993 Golden Boy	Closed		29.75	27
1993 Screen Idol	Closed		29.75	32
1993 Outstanding Young Man	Closed		29.75	29
1993 The Tiger: Faith, Spirit & Discipline	Closed		29.75	35

Dream Machines - P. Palma

YEAR ISSUE	EDITION LIMIT	YEAR RETD.	ISSUE PRICE	*QUOTE U.S.$
1988 '56 T-Bird	Closed		24.75	13-50
1988 '57 'Vette	Closed		24.75	14-50
1989 '58 Biarritz	Closed		27.75	19-35
1989 '56 Continental	Closed		27.75	21-35
1989 '57 Bel Air	Closed		27.75	25-50
1989 '57 Chrysler 300C	Closed		27.75	22-35

Elvis on the Big Screen - B. Emmett

YEAR ISSUE	EDITION LIMIT	YEAR RETD.	ISSUE PRICE	*QUOTE U.S.$
1992 Elvis in Loving You	Closed		29.75	54
1992 Elvis in G.I. Blues	Closed		29.75	70
1992 Viva Las Vegas	Closed		32.75	90
1993 Elvis in Blue Hawaii	Closed		32.75	38
1993 Elvis in Jailhouse Rock	Closed		32.75	38
1993 Elvis in Spinout	Closed		34.75	30
1993 Elvis in Speedway	Closed		34.75	30-32
1993 Elvis in Harum Scarum	Closed		34.75	22

The Elvis Presley Hit Parade - N. Giorgio

YEAR ISSUE	EDITION LIMIT	YEAR RETD.	ISSUE PRICE	*QUOTE U.S.$
1992 Heartbreak Hotel	150-day		29.75	30-35
1992 Blue Suede Shoes	150-day		29.75	35
1992 Hound Dog	150-day		32.75	35
1992 Blue Christmas	150-day		32.75	33-35
1992 Return to Sender	150-day		32.75	35
1993 Teddy Bear	150-day		34.75	35
1993 Always on My Mind	150-day		34.75	35
1993 Mystery Train	150-day		34.75	35
1993 Blue Moon of Kentucky	150-day		34.75	35
1993 Wear My Ring Around Your Neck	150-day		36.75	35
1993 Suspicious Minds	150-day		36.75	37
1993 Peace in the Valley	150-day		36.75	37

Elvis Presley: In Performance - B. Emmett

YEAR ISSUE	EDITION LIMIT	YEAR RETD.	ISSUE PRICE	*QUOTE U.S.$
1990 '68 Comeback Special	Closed		24.75	33-75
1991 King of Las Vegas	Closed		24.75	45-85
1991 Aloha From Hawaii	Closed		27.75	43-46
1991 Back in Tupelo, 1956	Closed		27.75	41-44
1991 If I Can Dream	Closed		27.75	50-59
1991 Benefit for the USS Arizona	Closed		29.75	39-52
1991 Madison Square Garden, 1972	Closed		29.75	65-67
1991 Tampa, 1955	Closed		29.75	50-60
1991 Concert in Baton Rouge, 1974	Closed		29.75	80-85
1992 On Stage in Wichita, 1974	Closed		31.75	65-67
1992 In the Spotlight: Hawaii, '72	Closed		31.75	36-38
1992 Tour Finale: Indianapolis 1977	Closed		31.75	32

Elvis Presley: Looking At A Legend - B. Emmett

YEAR ISSUE	EDITION LIMIT	YEAR RETD.	ISSUE PRICE	*QUOTE U.S.$
1988 Elvis at/Gates of Graceland	Closed		24.75	42-44
1989 Jailhouse Rock	Closed		24.75	42-55
1989 The Memphis Flash	Closed		27.75	27-45
1989 Homecoming	Closed		27.75	44-55
1990 Elvis and Gladys	Closed		27.75	34-55
1990 A Studio Session	Closed		27.75	26-47
1990 Elvis in Hollywood	Closed		29.75	30-35
1990 Elvis on His Harley	Closed		29.75	55
1990 Stage Door Autographs	Closed		29.75	25-36
1991 Christmas at Graceland	Closed		32.75	50
1991 Entering Sun Studio	Closed		32.75	40-44
1991 Going for the Black Belt	Closed		32.75	32-35
1991 His Hand in Mine	Closed		32.75	45-50
1991 Letters From Fans	Closed		32.75	43
1991 Closing the Deal	Closed		34.75	45-55
1992 Elvis Returns to the Stage	Closed		34.75	63-74

Fabulous Cars of the '50's - G. Angelini

YEAR ISSUE	EDITION LIMIT	YEAR RETD.	ISSUE PRICE	*QUOTE U.S.$
1993 '57 Red Corvette	Closed		24.75	31
1993 '57 White T-Bird	Closed		24.75	52
1993 '57 Blue Belair	Closed		27.75	40-42
1993 '59 Cadillac	Closed		27.75	45
1994 '56 Lincoln Premier	Closed		27.75	44
1994 '59 Red Ford Fairlane	Closed		27.75	42

In the Footsteps of the King - D. Sivavec

YEAR ISSUE	EDITION LIMIT	YEAR RETD.	ISSUE PRICE	*QUOTE U.S.$
1993 Graceland: Memphis, Tenn.	Closed		29.75	29
1994 Elvis' Birthplace: Tupelo, Miss	Closed		29.75	43-46
1994 Day Job: Memphis, Tenn.	Closed		32.75	30-39
1994 Flying Circle G. Ranch: Walls, Miss.	Closed		32.75	28-30
1994 The Lauderdale Courts	Closed		32.75	29
1994 Patriotic Soldier: Bad Nauheim, W. Germany	Closed		34.75	47-50

Indiana Jones - V. Gadino

YEAR ISSUE	EDITION LIMIT	YEAR RETD.	ISSUE PRICE	*QUOTE U.S.$
1989 Indiana Jones	Closed		24.75	14-18
1989 Indiana Jones and his Dad	Closed		24.75	35
1990 Indiana Jones/Dr. Schneider	Closed		27.75	20-23
1990 A Family Discussion	Closed		27.75	23-25
1990 Young Indiana Jones	Closed		27.75	33
1991 Indiana Jones/The Holy Grail	Closed		27.75	57

The Magic of Marilyn - C. Notarile

YEAR ISSUE	EDITION LIMIT	YEAR RETD.	ISSUE PRICE	*QUOTE U.S.$
1992 For Our Boys in Korea, 1954	Closed		24.75	40-50
1992 Opening Night	Closed		24.75	40
1993 Rising Star	Closed		27.75	45
1993 Stopping Traffic	Closed		27.75	55
1992 Strasberg's Student	Closed		27.75	60-80
1993 Photo Opportunity	Closed		29.75	27-29
1993 Shining Star	Closed		29.75	25
1993 Curtain Call	Closed		29.75	27

The Marilyn Monroe Collection - C. Notarile

YEAR ISSUE	EDITION LIMIT	YEAR RETD.	ISSUE PRICE	*QUOTE U.S.$
1989 Marilyn Monroe/7 Year Itch	Closed		24.75	40-53
1990 Diamonds/Girls Best Friend	Closed		24.75	50-54
1991 Marilyn Monroe/River of No Return	Closed		27.75	65-74
1992 How to Marry a Millionaire	Closed		27.75	57-70
1992 There's No Business/Show Business	Closed		27.75	50-58
1992 Marilyn Monroe in Niagra	Closed		29.75	59-63
1992 My Heart Belongs to Daddy	Closed		29.75	56-64
1992 Marilyn Monroe as Cherie in Bus Stop	Closed		29.75	42-49
1992 Marilyn Monroe in All About Eve	Closed		29.75	44-50
1992 Marilyn Monroe in Monkey Business	Closed		31.75	41-49
1992 Marilyn Monroe in Don't Bother to Knock	Closed		31.75	50-58
1992 Marilyn Monroe in We're Not Married	Closed		31.75	44-50

Portraits of the King - D. Zwierz

YEAR ISSUE	EDITION LIMIT	YEAR RETD.	ISSUE PRICE	*QUOTE U.S.$
1991 Love Me Tender	Closed		27.75	30-45
1991 Are You Lonesome Tonight?	Closed		27.75	59
1991 I'm Yours	Closed		30.75	47-41
1991 Treat Me Nice	Closed		30.75	60
1992 The Wonder of You	Closed		30.75	35
1992 You're a Heartbreaker	Closed		32.75	35-37
1992 Just Because	Closed		32.75	35
1992 Follow That Dream	Closed		32.75	40

Department 56

A Christmas Carol - R. Innocenti

YEAR ISSUE	EDITION LIMIT	YEAR RETD.	ISSUE PRICE	*QUOTE U.S.$
1991 The Cratchit's Christmas Pudding 5706-1	18,000	1991	60.00	42-58
1992 Marley's Ghost Appears To Scrooge 5721-5	18,000	1992	60.00	42-65
1993 The Spirit of Christmas Present 5722-3	18,000	1993	60.00	40-42
1994 Visions of Christmas Past 5723-1	18,000	1994	60.00	68-72

Duncan Royale

History of Santa Claus I - S. Morton

YEAR ISSUE	EDITION LIMIT	YEAR RETD.	ISSUE PRICE	*QUOTE U.S.$
1985 Medieval	Retrd.	1993	40.00	75
1985 Kris Kringle	Retrd.	1993	40.00	75
1985 Pioneer	10,000	1993	40.00	40
1986 Russian	Retrd.	1993	40.00	65
1986 Soda Pop	Retrd.	1993	40.00	75
1986 Civil War	10,000	1993	40.00	40
1986 Nast	Retrd.	1993	40.00	75
1987 St. Nicholas	Retrd.	1993	40.00	75
1987 Dedt Moroz	10,000	1993	40.00	45
1987 Black Peter	10,000	1993	40.00	60
1987 Victorian	Retrd.	1993	40.00	45
1987 Wassail	Retrd.	1993	40.00	45
XX Collection of 12 Plates	Retrd.	1993	480.00	480

Edna Hibel Studios

Allegro - E. Hibel

YEAR ISSUE	EDITION LIMIT	YEAR RETD.	ISSUE PRICE	*QUOTE U.S.$
1978 Plate & Book	7,500		120.00	95-150

Arte Ovale - E. Hibel

YEAR ISSUE	EDITION LIMIT	YEAR RETD.	ISSUE PRICE	*QUOTE U.S.$
1980 Takara, gold	300		1000.00	4200
1980 Takara, blanco	700		450.00	1200
1980 Takara, cobalt blue	1,000		595.00	2350
1984 Taro-kun, gold	300		1000.00	2700
1984 Taro-kun, blanco	700		450.00	825
1984 Taro-kun, cobalt blue	1,000		995.00	1050-1555

Christmas Annual - E. Hibel

YEAR ISSUE	EDITION LIMIT	YEAR RETD.	ISSUE PRICE	*QUOTE U.S.$
1985 The Angels' Message	Yr.Iss.		45.00	28-89
1986 Gift of the Magi	Yr.Iss.		45.00	52
1987 Flight Into Egypt	Yr.Iss.		49.00	59
1988 Adoration of the Shepherds	Yr.Iss.		49.00	75
1989 Peaceful Kingdom	Yr.Iss.		49.00	40
1990 The Nativity	Yr.Iss.		49.00	123

David Series - E. Hibel

YEAR ISSUE	EDITION LIMIT	YEAR RETD.	ISSUE PRICE	*QUOTE U.S.$
1979 Wedding of David & Bathsheba	5,000		250.00	650
1980 David, Bathsheba & Solomon	5,000		275.00	125-425
1982 David the King	5,000		275.00	150-295
1982 David the King, cobalt A/P	25		275.00	150-275
1984 Bathsheba	5,000		275.00	150-295
1984 Bathsheba, cobalt A/P	100		275.00	1200

Edna Hibel Holiday - E. Hibel

YEAR ISSUE	EDITION LIMIT	YEAR RETD.	ISSUE PRICE	*QUOTE U.S.$
1991 The First Holiday	Yr.Iss.		49.00	40
1991 The First Holiday, gold	1,000		99.00	110-150
1992 The Christmas Rose	Yr.Iss.		49.00	65
1992 The Christmas Rose, gold	1,000		99.00	125

Eroica - E. Hibel

YEAR ISSUE	EDITION LIMIT	YEAR RETD.	ISSUE PRICE	*QUOTE U.S.$
1990 Compassion	10,000		49.50	65-100
1992 Darya	10,000		49.50	95-149

Famous Women & Children - E. Hibel

YEAR ISSUE	EDITION LIMIT	YEAR RETD.	ISSUE PRICE	*QUOTE U.S.$
1980 Pharaoh's Daughter & Moses, gold	2,500		350.00	625-750
1980 Pharaoh's Daughter & Moses, cobalt blue	500		350.00	1350
1982 Cornelia & Her Jewels, gold	2,500		350.00	495-575
1982 Cornelia & Her Jewels, cobalt blue	500		350.00	350
1982 Anna & The Children of the King of Siam, gold	2,500		350.00	495-575
1982 Anna & The Children of the King of Siam, colbalt blue	500		350.00	1350
1984 Mozart & The Empress Marie Theresa, gold	2,500		350.00	395-495
1984 Mozart & The Empress Marie Theresa, cobalt blue	500		350.00	975

Flower Girl Annual - E. Hibel

YEAR ISSUE	EDITION LIMIT	YEAR RETD.	ISSUE PRICE	*QUOTE U.S.$
1985 Lily	15,000		79.00	200-300
1986 Iris	15,000		79.00	200-300
1987 Rose	15,000		79.00	200-300

*Quotes have been rounded up to nearest dollar

YEAR ISSUE	EDITION LIMIT	YEAR RETD.	ISSUE PRICE	*QUOTE U.S.$
1988 Camellia	15,000		79.00	200-395
1989 Peony	15,000		79.00	90
1992 Wisteria	15,000		79.00	229

International Mother Love French - E. Hibel

YEAR ISSUE	EDITION LIMIT	YEAR RETD.	ISSUE PRICE	*QUOTE U.S.$
1985 Yvette Avec Ses Enfants	5,000		125.00	140-195
1991 Liberte, Egalite, Fraternite	5,000		95.00	95

International Mother Love German - E. Hibel

YEAR ISSUE	EDITION LIMIT	YEAR RETD.	ISSUE PRICE	*QUOTE U.S.$
1982 Gesa Und Kinder	5,000		195.00	195
1983 Alexandra Und Kinder	5,000		195.00	195

March of Dimes: Our Children Our Future - E. Hibel

YEAR ISSUE	EDITION LIMIT	YEAR RETD.	ISSUE PRICE	*QUOTE U.S.$
1990 A Time To Embrace	150-day		29.00	22-35

Mother and Child - E. Hibel

YEAR ISSUE	EDITION LIMIT	YEAR RETD.	ISSUE PRICE	*QUOTE U.S.$
1973 Colette & Child	15,000		40.00	425-450
1974 Sayuri & Child	15,000		40.00	425
1975 Kristina & Child	15,000		50.00	100-250
1976 Marilyn & Child	15,000		55.00	100-400
1977 Lucia & Child	15,000		60.00	100-200
1981 Kathleen & Child	15,000		85.00	275

Mother's Day - E. Hibel

YEAR ISSUE	EDITION LIMIT	YEAR RETD.	ISSUE PRICE	*QUOTE U.S.$
1992 Molly & Annie	Yr.Iss.		39.00	39
1992 Molly & Annie, gold	2,500		95.00	150
1992 Molly & Annie, platinum	500		275.00	275

Mother's Day Annual - E. Hibel

YEAR ISSUE	EDITION LIMIT	YEAR RETD.	ISSUE PRICE	*QUOTE U.S.$
1984 Abby & Lisa	Yr.Iss.		29.50	20
1985 Erica & Jamie	Yr.Iss.		29.50	20
1986 Emily & Jennifer	Yr.Iss.		29.50	38-40
1987 Catherine & Heather	Yr.Iss.		34.50	40
1988 Sarah & Tess	Yr.Iss.		34.90	25
1989 Jessica & Kate	Yr.Iss.		34.90	27
1990 Elizabeth, Jorday & Janie	Yr.Iss.		36.90	55
1991 Michele & Anna	Yr.Iss.		36.90	47
1992 Olivia & Hildy	Yr.Iss.		39.90	300-400

Museum Commemorative - E. Hibel

YEAR ISSUE	EDITION LIMIT	YEAR RETD.	ISSUE PRICE	*QUOTE U.S.$
1977 Flower Girl of Provence	12,750		175.00	425
1980 Diana	3,000		350.00	395-495

Nobility Of Children - E. Hibel

YEAR ISSUE	EDITION LIMIT	YEAR RETD.	ISSUE PRICE	*QUOTE U.S.$
1976 La Contessa Isabella	12,750		120.00	150-425
1977 Le Marquis Maurice Pierre	12,750		120.00	150-225
1978 Baronesse Johanna-Maryke Van Vollendam Tot Marken	12,750		130.00	150-175
1979 Chief Red Feather	12,750		140.00	180-200

Nordic Families - E. Hibel

YEAR ISSUE	EDITION LIMIT	YEAR RETD.	ISSUE PRICE	*QUOTE U.S.$
1987 A Tender Moment	7,500		79.00	95

Oriental Gold - E. Hibel

YEAR ISSUE	EDITION LIMIT	YEAR RETD.	ISSUE PRICE	*QUOTE U.S.$
1975 Yasuko	2,000		275.00	3000
1976 Mr. Obata	2,000		275.00	235-900
1978 Sakura	2,000		295.00	1800
1979 Michio	2,000		325.00	235-595

Scandinavian Mother & Child - E. Hibel

YEAR ISSUE	EDITION LIMIT	YEAR RETD.	ISSUE PRICE	*QUOTE U.S.$
1987 Pearl & Flowers	7,500		55.00	225
1989 Anemone & Violet	7,500		75.00	95
1990 Holly & Talia	7,500		75.00	85

To Life Annual - E. Hibel

YEAR ISSUE	EDITION LIMIT	YEAR RETD.	ISSUE PRICE	*QUOTE U.S.$
1986 Golden's Child	5,000		99.00	200-275
1987 Triumph! Everyone A Winner	19,500		55.00	49
1988 The Whole Earth Bloomed as a Sacred Place	15,000		85.00	45
1989 Lovers of the Summer Palace	5,000		65.00	75
1992 People of the Fields	5,000		49.00	49

Tribute To All Children - E. Hibel

YEAR ISSUE	EDITION LIMIT	YEAR RETD.	ISSUE PRICE	*QUOTE U.S.$
1984 Giselle	19,500		55.00	95
1984 Gerard	19,500		55.00	95
1985 Wendy	19,500		55.00	125
1986 Todd	19,500		55.00	125

The World I Love - E. Hibel

YEAR ISSUE	EDITION LIMIT	YEAR RETD.	ISSUE PRICE	*QUOTE U.S.$
1981 Leah's Family	17,500		85.00	150-265
1982 Kaylin	17,500		85.00	300-415
1983 Edna's Music	17,500		85.00	80-195
1983 O' Hana	17,500		85.00	195-235

Edwin M. Knowles

Aesop's Fables - M. Hampshire

YEAR ISSUE	EDITION LIMIT	YEAR RETD.	ISSUE PRICE	*QUOTE U.S.$
1988 The Goose That Laid the Golden Egg	Closed		27.90	9-28
1988 The Hare and the Tortoise	Closed		27.90	12-25
1988 The Fox and the Grapes	Closed		30.90	18-28
1989 The Lion And The Mouse	Closed		30.90	21-32
1989 The Milk Maid And Her Pail	Closed		30.90	27-30
1989 The Jay And The Peacock	Closed		30.90	27-30

American Innocents - Marsten/Mandrajji

YEAR ISSUE	EDITION LIMIT	YEAR RETD.	ISSUE PRICE	*QUOTE U.S.$
1986 Abigail in the Rose Garden	Closed		19.50	13-18
1986 Ann by the Terrace	Closed		19.50	20
1986 Ellen and John in the Parlor	Closed		19.50	13-20
1986 William on the Rocking Horse	Closed		19.50	24-27

The American Journey - M. Kunstler

YEAR ISSUE	EDITION LIMIT	YEAR RETD.	ISSUE PRICE	*QUOTE U.S.$
1987 Westward Ho	Closed		29.90	20
1988 Kitchen With a View	Closed		29.90	8-11
1988 Crossing the River	Closed		29.90	25
1988 Christmas at the New Cabin	Closed		29.90	11-22

Americana Holidays - D. Spaulding

YEAR ISSUE	EDITION LIMIT	YEAR RETD.	ISSUE PRICE	*QUOTE U.S.$
1978 Fourth of July	Closed		26.00	10-25
1979 Thanksgiving	Closed		26.00	10-26
1980 Easter	Closed		26.00	10-26
1981 Valentine's Day	Closed		26.00	13-26
1982 Father's Day	Closed		26.00	10-35
1983 Christmas	Closed		26.00	12-33
1984 Mother's Day	Closed		26.00	12-30

Amy Brackenbury's Cat Tales - A. Brackenbury

YEAR ISSUE	EDITION LIMIT	YEAR RETD.	ISSUE PRICE	*QUOTE U.S.$
1987 A Chance Meeting: White American Shorthairs	Closed		21.50	14
1987 Gone Fishing: Maine Coons	Closed		21.50	26
1988 Strawberries and Cream: Cream Persians	Closed		24.90	43
1988 Flower Bed: British Shorthairs	Closed		24.90	14
1988 Kittens and Mittens: Silver Tabbies	Closed		24.90	15
1988 All Wrapped Up: Himalayans	Closed		24.90	36

Annie - W. Chambers

YEAR ISSUE	EDITION LIMIT	YEAR RETD.	ISSUE PRICE	*QUOTE U.S.$
1983 Annie and Sandy	Closed		19.00	15
1983 Daddy Warbucks	Closed		19.00	8-10
1983 Annie and Grace	Closed		19.00	8-10
1984 Annie and the Orphans	Closed		21.00	24
1985 Tomorrow	Closed		21.00	10-12
1986 Annie and Miss Hannigan	Closed		21.00	11-14
1986 Annie, Lily and Rooster	Closed		24.00	17-19
1986 Grand Finale	Closed		24.00	10-17

Baby Owls of North America - J. Thornbrugh

YEAR ISSUE	EDITION LIMIT	YEAR RETD.	ISSUE PRICE	*QUOTE U.S.$
1991 Peek-A-Whoo: Screech Owls	Closed		27.90	23
1991 Forty Winks: Saw-Whet Owls	Closed		29.90	27
1991 The Tree House: Northern Pygmy Owls	Closed		30.90	28
1991 Three of a Kind: Great Horned Owls	Closed		30.90	25
1991 Out on a Limb: Great Gray Owls	Closed		30.90	19
1991 Beginning to Explore: Boreal Owls	Closed		32.90	45
1992 Three's Company: Long Eared Owls	Closed		32.90	42
1992 Whoo's There: Barred Owl	Closed		32.90	54

Backyard Harmony - J. Thornbrugh

YEAR ISSUE	EDITION LIMIT	YEAR RETD.	ISSUE PRICE	*QUOTE U.S.$
1991 The Singing Lesson	Closed		27.90	27
1991 Welcoming a New Day	Closed		27.90	32
1991 Announcing Spring	Closed		30.90	49
1992 The Morning Harvest	Closed		30.90	42
1992 Spring Time Pride	Closed		30.90	45
1992 Treetop Serenade	Closed		32.90	60
1992 At The Peep Of Day	Closed		32.90	42-45
1992 Today's Discoveries	Closed		32.90	43-45

Bambi - Disney Studios

YEAR ISSUE	EDITION LIMIT	YEAR RETD.	ISSUE PRICE	*QUOTE U.S.$
1992 Bashful Bambi	Closed		34.90	35
1992 Bambi's New Friends	Closed		34.90	50
1992 Hello Little Prince	Closed		37.90	50
1992 Bambi's Morning Greetings	Closed		37.90	39
1992 Bambi's Skating Lesson	Closed		37.90	55-59
1993 What's Up Possums?	Closed		37.90	60

Biblical Mothers - E. Licea

YEAR ISSUE	EDITION LIMIT	YEAR RETD.	ISSUE PRICE	*QUOTE U.S.$
1983 Bathsheba and Solomon	Closed		39.50	22-25
1984 Judgment of Solomon	Closed		39.50	23-25
1984 Pharaoh's Daughter and Moses	Closed		39.50	25
1985 Mary and Jesus	Closed		39.50	28-40
1985 Sarah and Isaac	Closed		44.50	37-40
1986 Rebekah, Jacob and Esau	Closed		44.50	35

Birds of the Seasons - S. Timm

YEAR ISSUE	EDITION LIMIT	YEAR RETD.	ISSUE PRICE	*QUOTE U.S.$
1990 Cardinals In Winter	Closed		24.90	43-55
1990 Bluebirds In Spring	Closed		24.90	39-55
1991 Nuthatches In Fall	Closed		27.90	20-35
1991 Baltimore Orioles In Summer	Closed		27.90	17-40
1991 Blue Jays In Early Fall	Closed		27.90	31-40
1991 Robins In Early Spring	Closed		27.90	20-35
1991 Cedar Waxwings in Fall	Closed		29.90	34-40
1991 Chickadees in Winter	Closed		29.90	35-55

Call of the Wilderness - K. Daniel

YEAR ISSUE	EDITION LIMIT	YEAR RETD.	ISSUE PRICE	*QUOTE U.S.$
1991 First Outing	Closed		29.90	33-53
1991 Howling Lesson	Closed		29.90	54-95
1991 Silent Watch	Closed		32.90	39
1991 Winter Travelers	Closed		32.90	33-35
1992 Ahead of the Pack	Closed		32.90	34
1992 Northern Spirits	Closed		34.90	39
1992 Twilight Friends	Closed		34.90	35-44
1992 A New Future	Closed		34.90	35-44
1992 Morning Mist	Closed		36.90	37-44
1992 The Silent One	Closed		36.90	37-46

Carousel - D. Brown

YEAR ISSUE	EDITION LIMIT	YEAR RETD.	ISSUE PRICE	*QUOTE U.S.$
1987 If I Loved You	Closed		24.90	10
1988 Mr. Snow	Closed		24.90	10
1988 The Carousel Waltz	Closed		24.90	11
1988 You'll Never Walk Alone	Closed		24.90	12-20

Casablanca - J. Griffin

YEAR ISSUE	EDITION LIMIT	YEAR RETD.	ISSUE PRICE	*QUOTE U.S.$
1990 Here's Looking At You, Kid	Closed		34.90	16-20
1990 We'll Always Have Paris	Closed		34.90	23-27
1991 We Loved Each Other Once	Closed		37.90	23-25
1991 Rick's Cafe American	Closed		37.90	30
1991 A Franc For Your Thoughts	Closed		37.90	31-34
1991 Play it Sam	Closed		37.90	40

Castari Grandparent - J. Castari

YEAR ISSUE	EDITION LIMIT	YEAR RETD.	ISSUE PRICE	*QUOTE U.S.$
1980 Bedtime Story	Closed		18.00	20
1981 The Skating Lesson	Closed		20.00	10
1982 The Cookie Tasting	Closed		20.00	10
1983 The Swinger	Closed		20.00	5-29
1984 The Skating Queen	Closed		22.00	10-25
1985 The Patriot's Parade	Closed		22.00	16-22
1986 The Home Run	Closed		22.00	14-22
1987 The Sneak Preview	Closed		22.00	10

China's Natural Treasures - T.C. Chiu

YEAR ISSUE	EDITION LIMIT	YEAR RETD.	ISSUE PRICE	*QUOTE U.S.$
1992 The Siberian Tiger	Closed		29.90	13
1992 The Snow Leopard	Closed		29.90	22
1992 The Giant Panda	Closed		32.90	38
1992 The Tibetan Brown Bear	Closed		32.90	30
1992 The Asian Elephant	Closed		32.90	58
1992 The Golden Monkey	Closed		34.90	45

Christmas in the City - A. Leimanis

YEAR ISSUE	EDITION LIMIT	YEAR RETD.	ISSUE PRICE	*QUOTE U.S.$
1992 A Christmas Snowfall	Closed		34.90	37
1992 Yuletide Celebration	Closed		34.90	50
1993 Holiday Cheer	Closed		34.90	60
1993 The Magic of Christmas	Closed		34.90	53-55

Cinderella - Disney Studios

YEAR ISSUE	EDITION LIMIT	YEAR RETD.	ISSUE PRICE	*QUOTE U.S.$
1988 Bibbidi, Bobbidi, Boo	Closed		29.90	35-65
1988 A Dream Is A Wish Your Heart Makes	Closed		29.90	36-43
1989 Oh Sing Sweet Nightingale	Closed		32.90	42-45
1989 A Dress For Cinderelly	Closed		32.90	45-58
1989 So This Is Love	Closed		32.90	47-50
1990 At The Stroke Of Midnight	Closed		32.90	43-53
1990 If The Shoe Fits	Closed		34.90	45-54
1990 Happily Ever After	Closed		34.90	34

Classic Fairy Tales - S. Gustafson

YEAR ISSUE	EDITION LIMIT	YEAR RETD.	ISSUE PRICE	*QUOTE U.S.$
1991 Goldilocks and the Three Bears	Closed		29.90	30
1991 Little Red Riding Hood	Closed		29.90	40
1991 The Three Little Pigs	Closed		32.90	42
1991 The Frog Prince	Closed		32.90	50
1992 Jack and the Beanstalk	Closed		32.90	47
1992 Hansel and Gretel	Closed		34.90	70
1992 Puss in Boots	Closed		34.90	48
1992 Tom Thumb	Closed		34.90	45

Classic Mother Goose - S. Gustafson

YEAR ISSUE	EDITION LIMIT	YEAR RETD.	ISSUE PRICE	*QUOTE U.S.$
1992 Little Miss Muffet	Closed		29.90	19
1992 Mary had a Little Lamb	Closed		29.90	39
1992 Mary, Mary, Quite Contrary	Closed		29.90	38
1992 Little Bo Peep	Closed		29.90	34

The Comforts of Home - H. Hollister Ingmire

YEAR ISSUE	EDITION LIMIT	YEAR RETD.	ISSUE PRICE	*QUOTE U.S.$
1992 Sleepyheads	Closed		24.90	34-38
1992 Curious Pair	Closed		24.90	25-32
1993 Mother's Retreat	Closed		27.90	32-35
1993 Welcome Friends	Closed		27.90	26-35
1993 Playtime	Closed		27.90	36-50
1993 Feline Frolic	Closed		29.90	35-40
1993 Washday Helpers	Closed		29.90	35-40
1993 A Cozy Fireside	Closed		29.90	42-50

Cozy Country Corners - H. H. Ingmire

YEAR ISSUE	EDITION LIMIT	YEAR RETD.	ISSUE PRICE	*QUOTE U.S.$
1990 Lazy Morning	Closed		24.90	50
1990 Warm Retreat	Closed		24.90	32-36
1991 A Sunny Spot	Closed		27.90	30-34
1991 Attic Afternoon	Closed		27.90	40-45
1991 Mirror Mischief	Closed		27.90	40-46
1991 Hide and Seek	Closed		29.90	33-40
1991 Apple Antics	Closed		29.90	54-62
1991 Table Trouble	Closed		29.90	52

The Disney Treasured Moments Collection - Disney Studios

YEAR ISSUE	EDITION LIMIT	YEAR RETD.	ISSUE PRICE	*QUOTE U.S.$
1992 Cinderella	Closed		29.90	38-45
1992 Snow White and the Seven Dwarves	Closed		29.90	45-48
1993 Alice in Wonderland	Closed		32.90	45-49
1993 Sleeping Beauty	Closed		32.90	40-47
1993 Peter Pan	Closed		32.90	43-54
1993 Pinocchio	Closed		34.90	58-64
1993 The Jungle Book	Closed		34.90	38-45
1994 Beauty & The Beast	Closed		34.90	45-50

Ency. Brit. Birds of Your Garden - K. Daniel

YEAR ISSUE	EDITION LIMIT	YEAR RETD.	ISSUE PRICE	*QUOTE U.S.$
1985 Cardinal	Closed		19.50	15
1985 Blue Jay	Closed		19.50	13-15
1985 Oriole	Closed		22.50	13-15
1986 Bluebird	Closed		22.50	15
1986 Robin	Closed		22.50	15
1986 Hummingbird	Closed		24.50	20-25
1987 Goldfinch	Closed		24.50	18
1987 Downy Woodpecker	Closed		24.50	19
1987 Cedar Waxwing	Closed		24.90	16-19

Eve Licea Christmas - E. Licea

YEAR ISSUE	EDITION LIMIT	YEAR RETD.	ISSUE PRICE	*QUOTE U.S.$
1987 The Annunciation	Closed		44.90	25
1988 The Nativity	Closed		44.90	35
1989 Adoration Of The Shepherds	Closed		49.90	46
1990 Journey Of The Magi	Closed		49.90	45
1991 Gifts Of The Magi	Closed		49.90	50
1992 Rest on the Flight into Egypt	Closed		49.90	65

Fantasia: (The Sorcerer's Apprentice) Golden Anniversary - Disney Studios

YEAR ISSUE	EDITION LIMIT	YEAR RETD.	ISSUE PRICE	*QUOTE U.S.$
1990 The Apprentice's Dream	Closed		29.90	45-48
1990 Mischievous Apprentice	Closed		29.90	86-90
1991 Dreams of Power	Closed		32.90	28-70
1991 Mickey's Magical Whirlpool	Closed		32.90	35
1991 Wizardry Gone Wild	Closed		32.90	28

YEAR ISSUE	EDITION LIMIT	YEAR RETD.	ISSUE PRICE	*QUOTE U.S.$
1991 Mickey Makes Magic	Closed		34.90	35
1991 The Penitent Apprentice	Closed		34.90	19
1992 An Apprentice Again	Closed		34.90	23

Father's Love - B. Bradley

YEAR ISSUE	EDITION LIMIT	YEAR RETD.	ISSUE PRICE	*QUOTE U.S.$
1984 Open Wide	Closed		19.50	10
1984 Batter Up	Closed		19.50	10
1985 Little Shaver	Closed		19.50	10-29
1985 Swing Time	Closed		22.50	19-29

Field Puppies - L. Kaatz

YEAR ISSUE	EDITION LIMIT	YEAR RETD.	ISSUE PRICE	*QUOTE U.S.$
1987 Dog Tired-The Springer Spaniel	Closed		24.90	33-40
1987 Caught in the Act-The Golden Retriever	Closed		24.90	25
1988 Missing/Point/Irish Setter	Closed		27.90	21
1988 A Perfect Set-Labrador	Closed		27.90	18-34
1988 Fritz's Folly-German Shorthaired Pointer	Closed		27.90	18
1988 Shirt Tales: Cocker Spaniel	Closed		27.90	15
1989 Fine Feathered Friends-English Setter	Closed		29.90	20
1989 Command Performance/ Wiemaraner	Closed		29.90	15-30

Field Trips - L. Kaatz

YEAR ISSUE	EDITION LIMIT	YEAR RETD.	ISSUE PRICE	*QUOTE U.S.$
1990 Gone Fishing	Closed		24.90	18
1991 Ducking Duty	Closed		24.90	20
1991 Boxed In	Closed		27.90	16
1991 Pups 'N Boots	Closed		27.90	20
1991 Puppy Tales	Closed		27.90	15
1991 Pail Pals	Closed		29.90	29-32
1991 Chesapeake Bay Retrievers	Closed		29.90	25
1991 Hat Trick	Closed		29.90	23-25

First Impressions - J. Giordano

YEAR ISSUE	EDITION LIMIT	YEAR RETD.	ISSUE PRICE	*QUOTE U.S.$
1991 Taking a Gander	Closed		29.90	29-39
1991 Two's Company	Closed		29.90	30
1991 Fine Feathered Friends	Closed		32.90	35
1991 What's Up?	Closed		32.90	42-44
1991 All Ears	Closed		32.90	48
1992 Between Friends	Closed		32.90	35

The Four Ancient Elements - G. Lambert

YEAR ISSUE	EDITION LIMIT	YEAR RETD.	ISSUE PRICE	*QUOTE U.S.$
1984 Earth	Closed		27.50	19-28
1984 Water	Closed		27.50	30
1985 Air	Closed		29.50	27-30
1985 Fire	Closed		29.50	30-59

Frances Hook Legacy - F. Hook

YEAR ISSUE	EDITION LIMIT	YEAR RETD.	ISSUE PRICE	*QUOTE U.S.$
1985 Fascination	Closed		19.50	5-45
1985 Daydreaming	Closed		19.50	5-40
1986 Discovery	Closed		22.50	5-40
1986 Disappointment	Closed		22.50	5-40
1986 Wonderment	Closed		22.50	5-40
1987 Expectation	Closed		22.50	5-40

Free as the Wind - M. Budden

YEAR ISSUE	EDITION LIMIT	YEAR RETD.	ISSUE PRICE	*QUOTE U.S.$
1992 Skyward	Closed		29.90	40-50
1992 Aloft	Closed		29.90	50-55
1992 Airborne	Closed		32.90	35-50
1993 Flight	Closed		32.90	45-50
1993 Ascent	Closed		32.90	40-50
1993 Heavenward	Closed		32.90	45-69

Friends of the Forest - K. Daniel

YEAR ISSUE	EDITION LIMIT	YEAR RETD.	ISSUE PRICE	*QUOTE U.S.$
1987 The Rabbit	Closed		24.50	15-41
1987 The Raccoon	Closed		24.50	25-29
1987 The Squirrel	Closed		27.90	15
1988 The Chipmunk	Closed		27.90	15
1988 The Fox	Closed		27.90	14
1988 The Otter	Closed		27.90	11-14

Garden Secrets - B. Higgins Bond

YEAR ISSUE	EDITION LIMIT	YEAR RETD.	ISSUE PRICE	*QUOTE U.S.$
1993 Nine Lives	Closed		24.90	38-55
1993 Floral Purr-fume	Closed		24.90	38-53
1993 Bloomin' Kitties	Closed		24.90	44-47
1993 Kitty Corner	Closed		24.90	50
1993 Flower Fanciers	Closed		24.90	49-55
1993 Meadow Mischief	Closed		24.90	56-60
1993 Pussycat Potpourri	Closed		24.90	48-70
1993 Frisky Business	Closed		24.90	40-55

Gone with the Wind - R. Kursar

YEAR ISSUE	EDITION LIMIT	YEAR RETD.	ISSUE PRICE	*QUOTE U.S.$
1978 Scarlett	Closed		21.50	100
1979 Ashley	Closed		21.50	59
1980 Melanie	Closed		21.50	25-40
1981 Rhett	Closed		23.50	24
1982 Mammy Lacing Scarlett	Closed		23.50	32
1983 Melanie Gives Birth	Closed		23.50	35
1984 Scarlet's Green Dress	Closed		25.50	25-31
1985 Rhett and Bonnie	Closed		25.50	39-44
1985 Scarlett and Rhett: The Finale	Closed		29.50	35-37

Great Cats Of The Americas - L. Cable

YEAR ISSUE	EDITION LIMIT	YEAR RETD.	ISSUE PRICE	*QUOTE U.S.$
1989 The Jaguar	Closed		29.90	38
1989 The Cougar	Closed		29.90	35-38
1989 The Lynx	Closed		32.90	37-39
1990 The Ocelot	Closed		32.90	16-23
1990 The Bobcat	Closed		32.90	13-15
1990 The Jaguarundi	Closed		32.90	17
1990 The Margay	Closed		34.90	15
1991 The Pampas Cat	Closed		34.90	14-16

Heirlooms and Lace - C. Layton

YEAR ISSUE	EDITION LIMIT	YEAR RETD.	ISSUE PRICE	*QUOTE U.S.$
1989 Anna	Closed		34.90	24
1989 Victoria	Closed		34.90	30
1990 Tess	Closed		37.90	43-45
1990 Olivia	Closed		37.90	80
1991 Bridget	Closed		37.90	62
1991 Rebecca	Closed		37.90	63

Hibel Christmas - E. Hibel

YEAR ISSUE	EDITION LIMIT	YEAR RETD.	ISSUE PRICE	*QUOTE U.S.$
1985 The Angel's Message	Closed		45.00	26-28
1986 The Gifts of the Magi	Closed		45.00	48-52
1987 The Flight Into Egypt	Closed		49.00	47-59
1988 Adoration of the Shepherd	Closed		49.00	45-75
1989 Peaceful Kingdom	Closed		49.00	40
1990 Nativity	Closed		49.00	119-123

Home Sweet Home - R. McGinnis

YEAR ISSUE	EDITION LIMIT	YEAR RETD.	ISSUE PRICE	*QUOTE U.S.$
1989 The Victorian	Closed		39.90	28
1989 The Greek Revival	Closed		39.90	27
1989 The Georgian	Closed		39.90	18
1990 The Mission	Closed		39.90	23

It's a Dog's Life - L. Kaatz

YEAR ISSUE	EDITION LIMIT	YEAR RETD.	ISSUE PRICE	*QUOTE U.S.$
1992 We've Been Spotted	Closed		29.90	29
1992 Literary Labs	Closed		29.90	28
1993 Retrieving Our Dignity	Closed		32.90	50
1993 Lodging a Complaint	Closed		32.90	44
1993 Barreling Along	Closed		32.90	50
1993 Play Ball	Closed		34.90	34
1993 Dogs and Suds	Closed		34.90	32
1993 Paws for a Picnic	Closed		34.90	34

J. W. Smith Childhood Holidays - J. W. Smith

YEAR ISSUE	EDITION LIMIT	YEAR RETD.	ISSUE PRICE	*QUOTE U.S.$
1986 Easter	Closed		19.50	8-20
1986 Thanksgiving	Closed		19.50	11-22
1986 Christmas	Closed		19.50	10-22
1986 Valentine's Day	Closed		22.50	15-25
1987 Mother's Day	Closed		22.50	10-16
1987 Fourth of July	Closed		22.50	13-25

Jeanne Down's Friends I Remember - J. Down

YEAR ISSUE	EDITION LIMIT	YEAR RETD.	ISSUE PRICE	*QUOTE U.S.$
1983 Fish Story	Closed		17.50	5-29
1984 Office Hours	Closed		17.50	7-29
1985 A Coat of Paint	Closed		17.50	5-29
1985 Here Comes the Bride	Closed		19.50	10-20
1985 Fringe Benefits	Closed		19.50	7-20
1986 High Society	Closed		19.50	10-29
1986 Flower Arrangement	Closed		21.50	7-29
1986 Taste Test	Closed		21.50	7-29

Jerner's Less Traveled Road - B. Jerner

YEAR ISSUE	EDITION LIMIT	YEAR RETD.	ISSUE PRICE	*QUOTE U.S.$
1988 The Weathered Barn	Closed		29.90	10
1988 The Murmuring Stream	Closed		29.90	10-14
1988 The Covered Bridge	Closed		32.90	19
1989 Winter's Peace	Closed		32.90	22
1989 The Flowering Meadow	Closed		32.90	22
1989 The Hidden Waterfall	Closed		32.90	23

Jewels of the Flowers - T.C. Chiu

YEAR ISSUE	EDITION LIMIT	YEAR RETD.	ISSUE PRICE	*QUOTE U.S.$
1991 Sapphire Wings	Closed		29.90	18
1991 Topaz Beauties	Closed		29.90	42
1991 Amethyst Flight	Closed		32.90	19-21
1991 Ruby Elegance	Closed		32.90	24
1991 Emerald Pair	Closed		32.90	36-39
1991 Opal Splendor	Closed		34.90	29
1992 Pearl Luster	Closed		34.90	47-51
1992 Aquamarine Glimmer	Closed		34.90	28-30

Keepsake Rhymes - S. Gustafson

YEAR ISSUE	EDITION LIMIT	YEAR RETD.	ISSUE PRICE	*QUOTE U.S.$
1992 Humpty Dumpty	Closed		29.90	29-35
1993 Peter Pumpkin Eater	Closed		29.90	50-59
1993 Pat-a-Cake	Closed		29.90	60-68
1993 Old King Cole	Closed		29.90	73

The King and I - W. Chambers

YEAR ISSUE	EDITION LIMIT	YEAR RETD.	ISSUE PRICE	*QUOTE U.S.$
1984 A Puzzlement	Closed		19.50	7
1985 Shall We Dance?	Closed		19.50	8
1985 Getting to Know You	Closed		19.50	7
1985 We Kiss in a Shadow	Closed		19.50	7

Lady and the Tramp - Disney Studios

YEAR ISSUE	EDITION LIMIT	YEAR RETD.	ISSUE PRICE	*QUOTE U.S.$
1992 First Date	Closed		34.90	40-59
1992 Puppy Love	Closed		34.90	50
1992 Dog Pound Blues	Closed		37.90	32-35
1993 Merry Christmas To All	Closed		37.90	47
1993 Double Siamese Trouble	Closed		37.90	35-37
1993 Ruff House	Closed		39.90	30-34
1993 Telling Tails	Closed		39.90	65
1993 Moonlight Romance	Closed		39.90	99-125

Lincoln, Man of America - M. Kunstler

YEAR ISSUE	EDITION LIMIT	YEAR RETD.	ISSUE PRICE	*QUOTE U.S.$
1986 The Gettysburg Address	Closed		24.50	9
1987 The Inauguration	Closed		24.50	10
1987 The Lincoln-Douglas Debates	Closed		27.50	12-18
1987 Beginnings in New Salem	Closed		27.90	25
1988 The Family Man	Closed		27.90	25
1988 Emancipation Proclamation	Closed		27.90	19

The Little Mermaid - Disney Studio Artists

YEAR ISSUE	EDITION LIMIT	YEAR RETD.	ISSUE PRICE	*QUOTE U.S.$
1993 A Song From the Sea	Closed		29.90	34-36
1993 A Visit to the Surface	Closed		29.90	38-40
1993 Daddy's Girl	Closed		32.90	29
1993 Underwater Buddies	Closed		32.90	47-50
1994 Ariel's Treasured Collection	Closed		32.90	50
1994 Kiss the Girl	Closed		32.90	143
1994 Fireworks at First Sight	Closed		34.90	53
1994 Forever Love	Closed		34.90	50-53

Living with Nature-Jerner's Ducks - B. Jerner

YEAR ISSUE	EDITION LIMIT	YEAR RETD.	ISSUE PRICE	*QUOTE U.S.$
1986 The Pintail	Closed		19.50	23
1986 The Mallard	Closed		19.50	23
1987 The Wood Duck	Closed		22.50	25
1987 The Green-Winged Teal	Closed		22.50	25-27
1987 The Northern Shoveler	Closed		22.90	27-35
1987 The American Widgeon	Closed		22.90	20
1987 The Gadwall	Closed		24.90	27-30
1988 The Blue-Winged Teal	Closed		24.90	30

Majestic Birds of North America - D. Smith

YEAR ISSUE	EDITION LIMIT	YEAR RETD.	ISSUE PRICE	*QUOTE U.S.$
1988 The Bald Eagle	Closed		29.90	9
1988 Peregrine Falcon	Closed		29.90	10
1988 The Great Horned Owl	Closed		32.90	10-12
1989 The Red-Tailed Hawk	Closed		32.90	10
1989 The White Gyrfalcon	Closed		32.90	10
1989 The American Kestral	Closed		32.90	15
1990 The Osprey	Closed		34.90	13
1990 The Golden Eagle	Closed		34.90	20-27

Mary Poppins - M. Hampshire

YEAR ISSUE	EDITION LIMIT	YEAR RETD.	ISSUE PRICE	*QUOTE U.S.$
1989 Mary Poppins	Closed		29.90	39-44
1989 A Spoonful of Sugar	Closed		29.90	25
1990 A Jolly Holiday With Mary	Closed		32.90	23
1990 We Love To Laugh	Closed		32.90	30
1991 Chim Chim Cher-ee	Closed		32.90	20
1991 Tuppence a Bag	Closed		32.90	35

Mickey's Christmas Carol - Disney Studios

YEAR ISSUE	EDITION LIMIT	YEAR RETD.	ISSUE PRICE	*QUOTE U.S.$
1992 Bah Humbug!	Closed		29.90	28-30
1992 What's So Merry About Christmas?	Closed		29.90	39
1993 God Bless Us Every One	Closed		32.90	35
1993 A Christmas Surprise	Closed		32.90	35
1993 Yuletide Greetings	Closed		32.90	27
1993 Marley's Warning	Closed		34.90	45-50
1993 A Cozy Christmas	Closed		34.90	59
1993 A Christmas Feast	Closed		34.90	54

Musical Moments From the Wizard of Oz - K. Milnazik

YEAR ISSUE	EDITION LIMIT	YEAR RETD.	ISSUE PRICE	*QUOTE U.S.$
1993 Over the Rainbow	Closed		29.90	60-64
1993 We're Off to See the Wizard	Closed		29.90	77-80
1993 Munchkin Land	Closed		29.90	43-45
1994 If I Only Had a Brain	Closed		29.90	68-76
1994 Ding Dong The Witch is Dead	Closed		29.90	95-129
1993 The Lullabye League	Closed		29.90	69
1994 If I Were King of the Forest	Closed		29.90	50-60
1994 Merry Old Land of Oz	Closed		29.90	66-69

My Fair Lady - W. Chambers

YEAR ISSUE	EDITION LIMIT	YEAR RETD.	ISSUE PRICE	*QUOTE U.S.$
1989 Opening Day at Ascot	Closed		24.90	10
1989 I Could Have Danced All Night	Closed		24.90	10
1989 The Rain in Spain	Closed		27.90	15-20
1989 Show Me	Closed		27.90	17-23
1990 Get Me To/Church On Time	Closed		27.90	15-18
1990 I've Grown Accustomed/Face	Closed		27.90	30-48

Nature's Child - M. Jobe

YEAR ISSUE	EDITION LIMIT	YEAR RETD.	ISSUE PRICE	*QUOTE U.S.$
1990 Sharing	Closed		29.90	21-30
1990 The Lost Lamb	Closed		29.90	30
1990 Seems Like Yesterday	Closed		32.90	34
1990 Faithful Friends	Closed		32.90	42-45
1990 Trusted Companion	Closed		32.90	47-50
1991 Hand in Hand	Closed		32.90	45-50

Nature's Nursery - J. Thornbrugh

YEAR ISSUE	EDITION LIMIT	YEAR RETD.	ISSUE PRICE	*QUOTE U.S.$
1992 Testing the Waters	Closed		29.90	45-50
1993 Taking the Plunge	Closed		29.90	45-49
1993 Race Ya Mom	Closed		29.90	44-46
1993 Time to Wake Up	Closed		29.90	38-45
1993 Hide and Seek	Closed		29.90	40-45
1993 Piggyback Ride	Closed		29.90	30

Not So Long Ago - J. W. Smith

YEAR ISSUE	EDITION LIMIT	YEAR RETD.	ISSUE PRICE	*QUOTE U.S.$
1988 Story Time	Closed		24.90	16-25
1988 Wash Day for Dolly	Closed		24.90	15-25
1988 Suppertime for Kitty	Closed		24.90	26
1988 Mother's Little Helper	Closed		24.90	20-25

Oklahoma! - M. Kunstler

YEAR ISSUE	EDITION LIMIT	YEAR RETD.	ISSUE PRICE	*QUOTE U.S.$
1985 Oh, What a Beautiful Mornin'	Closed		19.50	5-9
1986 Surrey with the Fringe on Top'	Closed		19.50	10-35
1986 I Cain't Say No	Closed		19.50	15-20
1986 Oklahoma!	Closed		19.50	11-35

The Old Mill Stream - C. Tennant

YEAR ISSUE	EDITION LIMIT	YEAR RETD.	ISSUE PRICE	*QUOTE U.S.$
1991 New London Grist Mill	Closed		39.90	24-40
1991 Wayside Inn Grist Mill	Closed		39.90	31-40
1991 The Red Mill	Closed		39.90	30-40
1991 Glade Creek Grist Mill	Closed		39.90	40-50

Old-Fashioned Favorites - M. Weber

YEAR ISSUE	EDITION LIMIT	YEAR RETD.	ISSUE PRICE	*QUOTE U.S.$
1991 Apple Crisp	Closed		29.90	74
1991 Blueberry Muffins	Closed		29.90	75
1991 Peach Cobbler	Closed		29.90	105
1991 Chocolate Chip Oatmeal Cookies	Closed		29.90	188

Once Upon a Time - K. Pritchett

YEAR ISSUE	EDITION LIMIT	YEAR RETD.	ISSUE PRICE	*QUOTE U.S.$
1988 Little Red Riding Hood	Closed		24.90	14
1988 Rapunzel	Closed		24.90	10
1988 Three Little Pigs	Closed		27.90	19
1989 The Princess and the Pea	Closed		27.90	11-17
1989 Goldilocks and the Three Bears	Closed		27.90	37-39
1989 Beauty and the Beast	Closed		27.90	32

*Quotes have been rounded up to nearest dollar

YEAR ISSUE	EDITION LIMIT	YEAR RETD.	ISSUE PRICE	*QUOTE U.S.$
Pinocchio - Disney Studios				
1989 Gepetto Creates Pinocchio	Closed		29.90	34-41
1990 Pinocchio And The Blue Fairy	Closed		29.90	47-75
1990 It's an Actor's Life For Me	Closed		32.90	38
1990 I've Got No Strings On Me	Closed		32.90	24-45
1991 Pleasure Island	Closed		32.90	23-45
1991 A Real Boy	Closed		32.90	36
Portraits of Motherhood - W. Chambers				
1987 Mother's Here	Closed		29.50	15-30
1988 First Touch	Closed		29.50	30
Precious Little Ones - M. T. Fangel				
1988 Little Red Robins	Closed		29.90	13-30
1988 Little Fledglings	Closed		29.90	22-30
1988 Saturday Night Bath	Closed		29.90	27-39
1988 Peek-A-Boo	Closed		29.90	28-32
Proud Sentinels of the American West - N. Glazier				
1993 Youngblood	Closed		29.50	49-55
1993 Cat Nap	Closed		29.90	67-70
1993 Desert Bighorn Mormon Ridge	Closed		32.90	45-50
1993 Crown Prince	Closed		32.90	60-63
Purrfect Point of View - J. Giordano				
1992 Unexpected Visitors	Closed		29.90	24-30
1992 Wistful Morning	Closed		29.90	39-45
1992 Afternoon Catnap	Closed		29.90	41-50
1992 Cozy Company	Closed		29.90	33-35
Pussyfooting Around - C. Wilson				
1991 Fish Tales	Closed		24.90	22-25
1991 Teatime Tabbies	Closed		24.90	20-25
1991 Yarn Spinners	Closed		24.90	20-25
1991 Two Maestros	Closed		24.90	25-30
Romantic Age of Steam - R.B. Pierce				
1992 The Empire Builder	Closed		29.90	23
1992 The Broadway Limited	Closed		29.90	32
1992 Twentieth Century Limited	Closed		32.90	40
1992 The Chief	Closed		32.90	60
1992 The Crescent Limited	Closed		32.90	73
1993 The Overland Limited	Closed		34.90	48
1993 The Jupiter	Closed		34.90	59
1993 The Daylight	Closed		34.90	54
Santa's Christmas - T. Browning				
1991 Santa's Love	Closed		29.90	333
1991 Santa's Cheer	Closed		29.90	33-36
1991 Santa's Promise	Closed		32.90	65
1991 Santa's Gift	Closed		32.90	45
1992 Santa's Surprise	Closed		32.90	60
1992 Santa's Magic	Closed		32.90	54
Season For Song - M. Jobe				
1991 Winter Concert	Closed		34.90	42
1991 Snowy Symphony	Closed		34.90	40-45
1991 Frosty Chorus	Closed		34.90	50-60
1991 Silver Serenade	Closed		34.90	55-63
Season of Splendor - K. Randle				
1992 Autumn's Grandeur	Closed		29.90	38
1992 School Days	Closed		29.90	38
1992 Woodland Mill Stream	Closed		32.90	59-63
1992 Harvest Memories	Closed		32.90	50-55
1992 A Country Weekend	Closed		32.90	60-75
1993 Indian Summer	Closed		32.90	59-70
Shadows and Light: Winter's Wildlife - N. Glazier				
1993 Winter's Children	Closed		29.90	39-42
1993 Cub Scouts	Closed		29.90	50
1993 Little Snowman	Closed		29.90	45-50
1993 The Snow Cave	Closed		29.90	36-40
Singin' In The Rain - M. Skolsky				
1990 Singin' In The Rain	Closed		32.90	35-52
1990 Good Morning	Closed		32.90	23
1991 Broadway Melody	Closed		32.90	32-37
1991 We're Happy Again	Closed		32.90	50
Sleeping Beauty - Disney Studios				
1991 Once Upon A Dream	Closed		39.90	25-39
1991 Awakened by a Kiss	Closed		39.90	64
1991 Happy Birthday Briar Rose	Closed		42.90	35
1992 Together At Last	Closed		42.90	40
Small Blessings - C. Layton				
1992 Now I Lay Me Down to Sleep	Closed		29.90	24
1992 Bless Us O Lord For These, Thy Gifts	Closed		29.90	27-34
1992 Jesus Loves Me, This I Know	Closed		32.90	32
1992 This Little Light of Mine	Closed		32.90	28-30
1992 Blessed Are The Pure In Heart	Closed		32.90	37
1993 Bless Our Home	Closed		32.90	35
Snow White and the Seven Dwarfs - Disney Studios				
1991 The Dance of Snow White/Seven Dwarfs	Closed		29.90	33-65
1991 With a Smile and a Song	Closed		29.90	29-36
1991 A Special Treat	Closed		32.90	31-40
1992 A Kiss for Dopey	Closed		32.90	42-45
1992 The Poison Apple	Closed		32.90	46
1992 Fireside Love Story	Closed		34.90	38-45
1992 Stubborn Grumpy	Closed		34.90	29
1992 A Wish Come True	Closed		34.90	47-57

YEAR ISSUE	EDITION LIMIT	YEAR RETD.	ISSUE PRICE	*QUOTE U.S.$
1993 Time To Tidy Up	Closed		34.50	43-48
1993 May I Have This Dance?	Closed		36.90	44-46
1993 A Surprise in the Clearing	Closed		36.50	40-49
1993 Happy Ending	Closed		36.90	50-63
Songs of the American Spirit - H. Bond				
1991 The Star Spangled Banner	Closed		29.90	19
1991 Battle Hymn of the Republic	Closed		29.90	20-39
1991 America the Beautiful	Closed		29.90	31
1991 My Country 'Tis of Thee	Closed		29.90	60
Sound of Music - T. Crnkovich				
1986 Sound of Music	Closed		19.50	7
1986 Do-Re-Mi	Closed		19.50	10-12
1986 My Favorite Things	Closed		22.50	13
1986 Laendler Waltz	Closed		22.50	13-15
1987 Edelweiss	Closed		22.50	19-24
1987 I Have Confidence	Closed		22.50	15-17
1987 Maria	Closed		24.90	19
1987 Climb Ev'ry Mountain	Closed		24.90	19
South Pacific - E. Gignilliat				
1987 Some Enchanted Evening	Closed		24.50	7-25
1987 Happy Talk	Closed		24.50	10-25
1987 Dites Moi	Closed		24.90	9-25
1988 Honey Bun	Closed		24.90	9-25
Stately Owls - J. Beaudoin				
1989 The Snowy Owl	Closed		29.90	12-14
1989 The Great Horned Owl	Closed		29.90	28
1990 The Barn Owl	Closed		32.90	15
1990 The Screech Owl	Closed		32.90	15-22
1990 The Short-Eared Owl	Closed		32.90	19
1990 The Barred Owl	Closed		32.90	16-24
1990 The Great Grey Owl	Closed		34.90	27
1991 The Saw-Whet Owl	Closed		34.90	25-29
Sundblom Santas - H. Sundblom				
1989 Santa By The Fire	Closed		27.90	12-15
1990 Christmas Vigil	Closed		27.90	15-24
1991 To All A Good Night	Closed		32.90	40
1992 Santa's on His Way	Closed		32.90	40
A Swan is Born - L. Roberts				
1987 Hopes and Dreams	Closed		24.50	25
1987 At the Barre	Closed		24.50	23-25
1987 In Position	Closed		24.50	30
1988 Just For Size	Closed		24.50	40
Sweetness and Grace - J. Welty				
1992 God Bless Teddy	Closed		34.90	35
1992 Sunshine and Smiles	Closed		34.90	35-47
1992 Favorite Buddy	Closed		34.90	45
1992 Sweet Dreams	Closed		34.90	60
Thomas Kinkade's Enchanted Cottages - T. Kinkade				
1993 Fallbrooke Cottage	Closed		29.90	75-90
1993 Julianne's Cottage	Closed		29.90	35-95
1993 Seaside Cottage	Closed		29.90	59-64
1993 Sweetheart Cottage	Closed		29.90	88-90
1993 Weathervane Cottage	Closed		29.90	72-74
1993 Rose Garden Cottage	Closed		29.90	85
Thomas Kinkade's Garden Cottages of England - T. Kinkade				
1991 Chandler's Cottage	Closed		27.90	50
1991 Cedar Nook Cottage	Closed		27.90	47
1991 Candlelit Cottage	Closed		30.90	57
1991 Open Gate Cottage	Closed		30.90	36
1991 McKenna's Cottage	Closed		30.90	44
1992 Woodsman's Thatch Cottage	Closed		32.90	44
1992 Merritt's Cottage	Closed		32.90	60
1992 Stonegate Cottage	Closed		32.90	60
Thomas Kinkade's Home for the Holidays - T. Kinkade				
1991 Sleigh Ride Home	Closed		29.90	44
1991 Home to Grandma's	Closed		29.90	35-37
1991 Home Before Christmas	Closed		32.90	44
1992 The Warmth of Home	Closed		32.90	41
1992 Homespun Holiday	Closed		32.90	42
1992 Hometime Yuletide	Closed		34.90	38-47
1992 Home Away From Home	Closed		34.90	49
1992 The Journey Home	Closed		34.90	45
Thomas Kinkade's Home is Where the Heart Is - T. Kinkade				
1992 Home Sweet Home	Closed		29.90	50-69
1992 A Warm Welcome Home	Closed		29.90	44
1992 A Carriage Ride Home	Closed		32.90	48
1993 Amber Afternoon	Closed		32.90	40-56
1993 Country Memories	Closed		32.90	55-78
1993 The Twilight Cafe	Closed		34.90	43-54
1993 Our Summer Home	Closed		34.90	60
1993 Hometown Hospitality	Closed		34.90	65
Thomas Kinkade's Thomashire - T. Kinkade				
1992 Olde Porterfield Tea Room	Closed		29.90	35
1992 Olde Thomashire Mill	Closed		29.90	24-46
1992 Swanbrook Cottage	Closed		32.90	80
1992 Pye Corner Cottage	Closed		32.90	40-44
1993 Blossom Hill Church	Closed		32.90	55
1993 Olde Garden Cottage	Closed		32.90	48-58
Thomas Kinkade's Yuletide Memories - T. Kinkade				
1992 The Magic of Christmas	Closed		29.90	100
1992 A Beacon of Faith	Closed		29.90	45
1993 Moonlit Sleighride	Closed		29.90	30

YEAR ISSUE	EDITION LIMIT	YEAR RETD.	ISSUE PRICE	*QUOTE U.S.$
1993 Silent Night	Closed		29.90	75
1993 Olde Porterfield Gift Shoppe	Closed		29.90	45
1993 The Wonder of the Season	Closed		29.90	52
1993 A Winter's Walk	Closed		29.90	55
1993 Skater's Delight	Closed		32.90	52
Tom Sawyer - W. Chambers				
1987 Whitewashing the Fence	Closed		27.50	25-35
1987 Tom and Becky	Closed		27.90	25-35
1987 Tom Sawyer the Pirate	Closed		27.90	25-35
1988 First Pipes	Closed		27.90	23-35
Under Mother's Wing - J. Beaudoin				
1992 Arctic Spring: Snowy Owls	Closed		29.90	38
1992 Forest's Edge: Great Gray Owls	Closed		29.90	35-40
1992 Treetop Trio: Long-Eared Owls	Closed		32.90	45-50
1992 Woodland Watch: Spotted Owls	Closed		32.90	55
1992 Vast View: Saw Whet Owls	Closed		32.90	50
1992 Lofty-Limb: Great Horned Owl	Closed		34.90	50-55
1993 Perfect Perch: Barred Owls	Closed		34.90	45
1993 Happy Home: Short-Eared Owl	Closed		34.90	50
Upland Birds of North America - W. Anderson				
1986 The Pheasant	Closed		24.50	10
1986 The Grouse	Closed		24.50	7
1987 The Quail	Closed		27.50	8-10
1987 The Wild Turkey	Closed		27.50	14-28
1987 The Gray Partridge	Closed		27.50	10-14
1987 The Woodcock	Closed		27.90	14
Windows of Glory - J. Welty				
1993 King of Kings	Closed		29.90	30-51
1993 Prince of Peace	Closed		29.90	74
1993 The Messiah	Closed		32.90	33-73
1993 The Good Shepherd	Closed		32.90	33-59
1994 The Light of the World	Closed		32.90	33-75
1994 The Everlasting Father	Closed		32.90	33
Wizard of Oz - J. Auckland				
1977 Over the Rainbow	Closed		19.00	35-40
1978 If I Only Had a Brain	Closed		19.00	30-35
1978 If I Only Had a Heart	Closed		19.00	38
1978 If I Were King of the Forest	Closed		19.00	40-48
1979 Wicked Witch of the West	Closed		19.00	40-56
1979 Follow the Yellow Brick Road	Closed		19.00	56-59
1979 Wonderful Wizard of Oz	Closed		19.00	50-52
1980 The Grand Finale	Closed		24.00	54-60
Wizard of Oz: A National Treasure - R. Laslo				
1991 Yellow Brick Road	Closed		29.90	31
1992 I Haven't Got a Brain	Closed		29.90	35
1992 I'm a Little Rusty Yet	Closed		32.90	40-44
1992 I Even Scare Myself	Closed		32.90	52-55
1992 We're Off To See the Wizard	Closed		32.90	80-100
1992 I'll Never Get Home	Closed		34.90	59
1992 I'm Melting	Closed		34.90	83
1992 There's No Place Like Home	Closed		34.90	68
Yesterday's Innocents - J. Wilcox Smith				
1992 My First Book	Closed		29.90	44-50
1992 Time to Smell the Roses	Closed		29.90	48-55
1993 Hush, Baby's Sleeping	Closed		32.90	38
1993 Ready and Waiting	Closed		32.90	50-60
Enchantica				
Retired Enchantica Collection - J. Woodward				
1992 Winter Dragon-Grawlfang-2200	15,000	1993	50.00	75-165
1992 Spring Dragon-Gorgoyle-2201	15,000	1993	50.00	80-165
1993 Summer Dragon-Arangast-2202	15,000	1993	50.00	75
1993 Autumn Dragon-Snarlgard-2203	15,000	1993	50.00	165
Ernst Enterprises/Porter & Price, Inc.				
A Beautiful World - S. Morton				
1981 Tahitian Dreamer	Retrd.	1987	27.50	30
1982 Flirtation	Retrd.	1987	27.50	30
1984 Elke of Oslo	Retrd.	1987	27.50	30
Classy Cars - S. Kuhnly				
1982 The 26T	Retrd.	1990	24.50	40
1982 The 31A	Retrd.	1990	24.50	40
1983 The Pickup	Retrd.	1990	24.50	40
1984 Panel Van	Retrd.	1990	24.50	40-85
Commemoratives - S. Morton				
1981 John Lennon	Retrd.	1988	39.50	145
1982 Elvis Presley	Retrd.	1988	39.50	90-120
1982 Marilyn Monroe	Retrd.	1988	39.50	125
1983 Judy Garland	Retrd.	1988	39.50	65-120
1984 John Wayne	Retrd.	1988	39.50	110
Elvira - S. Morton				
1988 Night Rose	Retrd.		29.50	45
1988 Red Velvet	Retrd.		29.50	35
1988 Mistress of the Dark	Retrd.		29.50	35
Elvis Presley - S. Morton				
1987 The King	Retrd.	1991	39.50	125-139
1987 Loving You	Retrd.	1991	39.50	95-149
1987 Early Years	Retrd.	1991	39.50	75-110
1987 Tenderly	Retrd.	1991	39.50	95-139
1988 Forever Yours	Retrd.	1991	39.50	75-195
1988 Rockin in the Moonlight	Retrd.	1991	39.50	95-145

*Quotes have been rounded up to nearest dollar

YEAR ISSUE	EDITION LIMIT	YEAR RETD.	ISSUE PRICE	*QUOTE U.S.$
1988 Moody Blues	Retrd.	1991	39.50	75-90
1988 Elvis Presley	Retrd.	1991	39.50	90-175
1989 Elvis Presley-Special Request	Retrd.	1991	150.00	95-225

Elvis Remembered - S. Morton

YEAR ISSUE	EDITION LIMIT	YEAR RETD.	ISSUE PRICE	*QUOTE U.S.$
1989 Loving You	90-day		37.50	100-175
1989 Early Years	90-day		37.50	195-210
1989 Tenderly	90-day		37.50	125-200
1989 The King	90-day		37.50	175
1989 Forever Yours	90-day		37.50	70-195
1989 Rockin in the Moonlight	90-day		37.50	70-195
1989 Moody Blues	90-day		37.50	70-195
1989 Elvis Presley	90-day		37.50	70-200

Hollywood Greats - S. Morton

YEAR ISSUE	EDITION LIMIT	YEAR RETD.	ISSUE PRICE	*QUOTE U.S.$
1981 Henry Fonda	Retrd.	1988	29.95	55
1981 John Wayne	Retrd.	1988	29.95	38-100
1981 Gary Cooper	Retrd.	1988	29.95	40-65
1982 Clark Gable	Retrd.	1988	29.95	65
1984 Alan Ladd	Retrd.	1988	29.95	60

Hollywood Walk of Fame - S. Morton

YEAR ISSUE	EDITION LIMIT	YEAR RETD.	ISSUE PRICE	*QUOTE U.S.$
1989 Jimmy Stewart	Retrd.	1992	39.50	50-125
1989 Elizabeth Taylor	Retrd.	1992	39.50	125
1989 Tom Selleck	Retrd.	1992	39.50	45
1989 Joan Collins	Retrd.	1992	39.50	125
1990 Burt Reynolds	Retrd.	1992	39.50	125
1990 Sylvester Stallone	Retrd.	1992	39.50	45

The Republic Pictures Library - S. Morton

YEAR ISSUE	EDITION LIMIT	YEAR RETD.	ISSUE PRICE	*QUOTE U.S.$
1991 Showdown With Laredo	Retrd.		37.50	38-45
1991 The Ride Home	Retrd.		37.50	38
1991 Attack at Tarawa	Retrd.		37.50	45
1991 Thoughts of Angelique	Retrd.		37.50	38-45
1992 War of the Wildcats	Retrd.		37.50	55-60
1992 The Fighting Seabees	Retrd.		37.50	40
1992 The Quiet Man	Retrd.		37.50	40-45
1992 Angel and the Badman	Retrd.		37.50	45-50
1993 Sands of Iwo Jima	Retrd.		37.50	50
1993 Flying Tigers	Retrd.		37.50	65-70
1993 The Tribute (12")	Retrd.		97.50	98
1994 The Tribute (8 1/4") AP	9,500		35.00	35

Seems Like Yesterday - R. Money

YEAR ISSUE	EDITION LIMIT	YEAR RETD.	ISSUE PRICE	*QUOTE U.S.$
1981 Stop & Smell the Roses	Retrd.	1988	24.50	59
1982 Home by Lunch	Retrd.	1988	24.50	35
1982 Lisa's Creek	Retrd.	1988	24.50	25
1983 It's Got My Name on It	Retrd.	1988	24.50	30
1983 My Magic Hat	Retrd.	1988	24.50	52
1984 Little Prince	Retrd.	1988	24.50	25

Star Trek - S. Morton

YEAR ISSUE	EDITION LIMIT	YEAR RETD.	ISSUE PRICE	*QUOTE U.S.$
1984 Mr. Spock	Retrd.	1989	29.50	200-295
1985 Dr. McCoy	Retrd.	1989	29.50	125-285
1985 Sulu	Retrd.	1989	29.50	100-195
1985 Scotty	Retrd.	1989	29.50	225-275
1985 Uhura	Retrd.	1989	29.50	100-225
1985 Chekov	Retrd.	1989	29.50	100-195
1985 Captain Kirk	Retrd.	1989	29.50	120-295
1985 Beam Us Down Scotty	Retrd.	1989	29.50	100-235
1985 The Enterprise	Retrd.	1989	39.50	180-295

Star Trek: Commemorative Collection - S. Morton

YEAR ISSUE	EDITION LIMIT	YEAR RETD.	ISSUE PRICE	*QUOTE U.S.$
1987 The Trouble With Tribbles	Retrd.	1989	29.50	225
1987 Mirror, Mirror	Retrd.	1989	29.50	225
1987 A Piece of the Action	Retrd.	1989	29.50	225
1987 The Devil in the Dark	Retrd.	1989	29.50	225
1987 Amok Time	Retrd.	1989	29.50	225
1987 The City on the Edge of Forever	Retrd.	1989	29.50	225
1987 Journey to Babel	Retrd.	1989	29.50	225
1987 The Menagerie	Retrd.	1989	29.50	225

Turn of The Century - R. Money

YEAR ISSUE	EDITION LIMIT	YEAR RETD.	ISSUE PRICE	*QUOTE U.S.$
1981 Riverboat Honeymoon	Retrd.	1987	35.00	20-40
1982 Children's Carousel	Retrd.	1987	35.00	20-35
1984 Flower Market	Retrd.	1987	35.00	20-35
1985 Balloon Race	Retrd.	1987	35.00	20-35

Women of the West - D. Putnam

YEAR ISSUE	EDITION LIMIT	YEAR RETD.	ISSUE PRICE	*QUOTE U.S.$
1979 Expectations	Retrd.	1986	39.50	10-40
1981 Silver Dollar Sal	Retrd.	1986	39.50	15-40
1982 School Marm	Retrd.	1986	39.50	10-40
1983 Dolly	Retrd.	1986	39.50	10-40

Fenton Art Glass Company

American Classic Series - M. Dickinson

YEAR ISSUE	EDITION LIMIT	YEAR RETD.	ISSUE PRICE	*QUOTE U.S.$
1986 Jupiter Train on Opal Satin	5,000	1986	75.00	75
1986 Studebaker-Garford Car on Opal Satin	5,000	1986	75.00	75

American Craftsman Carnival - Fenton

YEAR ISSUE	EDITION LIMIT	YEAR RETD.	ISSUE PRICE	*QUOTE U.S.$
1970 Glassmaker	Closed	1970	10.00	20-60
1971 Printer	Closed	1971	10.00	20-60
1972 Blacksmith	Closed	1972	10.00	20-60
1973 Shoemaker	Closed	1973	10.00	20-60
1974 Pioneer Cooper	Closed	1974	11.00	20-60
1975 Paul Revere (Patriot & Silversmith)	Closed	1975	12.50	20-60
1976 Gunsmith	Closed	1976	13.50	20-60
1977 Potter	Closed	1977	15.00	20-60
1978 Wheelwright	Closed	1978	15.00	20-60
1979 Cabinetmaker	Closed	1979	15.00	20-60
1980 Tanner	Closed	1980	16.50	20-60
1981 Housewright	Closed	1981	17.50	20-60

Christmas - Various

YEAR ISSUE	EDITION LIMIT	YEAR RETD.	ISSUE PRICE	*QUOTE U.S.$
1979 Nature's Christmas - K. Cunningham	Yr.Iss.	1979	35.00	35
1980 Going Home - D. Johnson	Yr.Iss.	1980	38.50	40
1981 All Is Calm - D. Johnson	Yr.Iss.	1981	42.50	43-45
1982 Country Christmas - R. Spindler	Yr.Iss.	1982	42.50	43-45
1983 Anticipation - D. Johnson	7,500	1983	45.00	45
1984 Expectation - D. Johnson	7,500	1984	50.00	50
1985 Heart's Desire - D. Johnson	7,500	1986	50.00	50
1987 Sharing The Spirit - L. Everson	Yr.Iss.	1987	50.00	50
1987 Cardinal in the Churchyard - D. Johnson	4,500	1987	39.50	40-45
1988 A Chickadee Ballet - D. Johnson	4,500	1988	39.50	40-45
1989 Downy Pecker - Chisled Song - D. Johnson	4,500	1989	39.50	40-45
1990 A Blue Bird in Snowfall - D. Johnson	4,500	1990	39.50	40-45
1990 Sleigh Ride - F. Burton	3,500	1990	45.00	45
1991 Christmas Eve - F. Burton	3,500	1991	45.00	45
1992 Family Tradition - F. Burton	3,500	1992	49.00	49
1993 Family Holiday - F. Burton	3,500	1993	49.00	49
1994 Silent Night - F. Burton	1,500	1994	65.00	65-95
1995 Our Home Is Blessed - F. Burton	1,500	1995	65.00	65
1996 Star of Wonder - F. Burton	1,750	1996	65.00	65
1997 The Way Home - F. Burton	1,750	1997	85.00	85
1998 The Arrival - F. Burton	2,500	1998	75.00	75
1999 The Announcement - F. Burton	2,500	1999	79.00	79
2000 The Journey - F. Burton	2,500		85.00	85

Easter Series - Various

YEAR ISSUE	EDITION LIMIT	YEAR RETD.	ISSUE PRICE	*QUOTE U.S.$
1995 Covered Hen & Egg Opal Irid. Hndpt. - M. Reynolds	950	1995	95.00	95-120
1997 Covered Hen & Egg Opal Irid. Hndpt. - R. Spindler	950	1997	115.00	115

Mary Gregory - M. Reynolds

YEAR ISSUE	EDITION LIMIT	YEAR RETD.	ISSUE PRICE	*QUOTE U.S.$
1994 Plate w/stand, 9"	Closed	1994	65.00	65-75
1995 Plate w/stand, 9"	Closed	1995	65.00	65-75

Flambro Imports

Emmett Kelly Jr. Plates - D. Rust, unless otherwise noted

YEAR ISSUE	EDITION LIMIT	YEAR RETD.	ISSUE PRICE	*QUOTE U.S.$
1983 Why Me? Plate I - C. Kelly	10,000	N/A	40.00	215-400
1984 Balloons For Sale Plate II - C. Kelly	10,000	N/A	40.00	215-275
1985 Big Business Plate III - C. Kelly	10,000	N/A	40.00	215-250
1986 And God Bless America IV - C. Kelly	10,000	N/A	40.00	100-200
1988 Tis the Season	10,000	N/A	50.00	120-175
1989 Looking Back- 65th Birthday	6,500	N/A	50.00	250
1991 Winter	10,000	1996	30.00	35-175
1992 Spring	10,000	1996	30.00	35-99
1992 Summer	10,000	1996	30.00	35-99
1992 Autumn	10,000	1996	30.00	35-85
1993 Santa's Stowaway	5,000	1996	30.00	30-90
1994 70th Birthday Commemorative	5,000	1996	30.00	90-150
1995 All Wrapped Up in Christmas	5,000	1996	30.00	30-65

Fountainhead

As Free As The Wind - M. Fernandez

YEAR ISSUE	EDITION LIMIT	YEAR RETD.	ISSUE PRICE	*QUOTE U.S.$
1989 As Free As The Wind	Unkn.		295.00	670-775

The Wings of Freedom - M. Fernandez

YEAR ISSUE	EDITION LIMIT	YEAR RETD.	ISSUE PRICE	*QUOTE U.S.$
1985 Courtship Flight	2,500		250.00	1300-1500
1986 Wings of Freedom	2,500		250.00	1300-1500

Gartlan USA

Club Gift - M. Taylor, unless otherwise noted

YEAR ISSUE	EDITION LIMIT	YEAR RETD.	ISSUE PRICE	*QUOTE U.S.$
1989 Pete Rose (8 1/2") - B. Forbes	Closed	1990	Gift	290-349
1990 Al Barlick (8 1/2")	Closed	1991	Gift	175-249
1991 Joe Montana (8 1/2")	Closed	1992	Gift	75-175
1992 Ken Griffey Jr. (8 1/2")	Closed	1993	Gift	69-95
1993 Gordie Howe (8 1/2")	Closed	1994	Gift	150
1994 Shaquille O'Neal (8 1/2")	Closed	1995	Gift	60-250
1996 Ringo Starr (8 1/2")	Closed	1996	Gift	30-50
1997 Jerry Garcia (8 1/8")	Yr.Iss.	1997	Gift	30-40
1998 John Lennon Self Portrait (8 1/4") - J. Lennon	1,000	1998	Gift	30-50
1999 The Beatles - Yellow Submarine (8 1/8")	1,000		Gift	35

Bob Cousy - M. Taylor

YEAR ISSUE	EDITION LIMIT	YEAR RETD.	ISSUE PRICE	*QUOTE U.S.$
1994 Signed Plate (10 1/4")	950	1995	175.00	100-175
1994 Plate (8 1/2")	10,000		30.00	35
1994 Plate (3 1/4")	Open		15.00	17

Brett & Bobby Hull - M. Taylor

YEAR ISSUE	EDITION LIMIT	YEAR RETD.	ISSUE PRICE	*QUOTE U.S.$
1992 Hockey's Golden Boys (10 1/4") signed by both	950	1995	250.00	150-250
1992 Hockey's Golden Boys (10 1/4") A/P, signed by both	300	1995	350.00	100-350
1992 Hockey's Golden Boys (8 1/2")	10,000	1999	30.00	35-65
1992 Hockey's Golden Boys (3 1/4")	Open		15.00	17

Carl Yastrzemski - M. Taylor

YEAR ISSUE	EDITION LIMIT	YEAR RETD.	ISSUE PRICE	*QUOTE U.S.$
1993 Signed Plate (10 1/4")	950	1995	175.00	150-175
1993 Plate (8 1/2")	10,000		30.00	35
1993 Plate (3 1/4")	Open		15.00	17

Carlton Fisk - M. Taylor

YEAR ISSUE	EDITION LIMIT	YEAR RETD.	ISSUE PRICE	*QUOTE U.S.$
1993 Signed Plate (10 1/4")	950	1995	175.00	150-175
1993 Plate (8 1/2")	5,000		30.00	35
1993 Plate (3 1/4")	Open		15.00	17

Darryl Strawberry - M. Taylor

YEAR ISSUE	EDITION LIMIT	YEAR RETD.	ISSUE PRICE	*QUOTE U.S.$
1991 Signed Plate (10 1/4")	2,500	1995	150.00	50-150
1991 Plate (8 1/2")	10,000	1995	40.00	30-40
1991 Plate (3 1/4")	Retrd.	1995	15.00	17

George Brett Gold Crown Collection - J. Martin

YEAR ISSUE	EDITION LIMIT	YEAR RETD.	ISSUE PRICE	*QUOTE U.S.$
1986 George Brett "Baseball's All Star" (3 1/4")	Open		15.00	17
1986 George Brett "Baseball's All Star" (10 1/4") signed	2,000	1988	100.00	350-375
1986 George Brett "Baseball's All Star" (10 1/4"), A/P signed	24	1988	225.00	N/A

Gordie Howe - M. Taylor

YEAR ISSUE	EDITION LIMIT	YEAR RETD.	ISSUE PRICE	*QUOTE U.S.$
1993 Signed Plate (10 1/4")	2,358	1995	150.00	150
1993 Signed Plate (8 1/2")	10,000		30.00	35
1993 Signed Plate (3 1/4")	Open		15.00	17

Jerry Garcia - M. Taylor

YEAR ISSUE	EDITION LIMIT	YEAR RETD.	ISSUE PRICE	*QUOTE U.S.$
1997 Jerry Garcia (10 1/4")	1,995		125.00	125
1997 Jerry Garcia (10 1/4") A/P	300		225.00	225
1997 Jerry Garcia (8 1/4")	10,000		30.00	35
1997 Jerry Garcia plate/ornament (3 1/4")	Open		15.00	17

Joe Montana - M. Taylor

YEAR ISSUE	EDITION LIMIT	YEAR RETD.	ISSUE PRICE	*QUOTE U.S.$
1991 Signed Plate (10 1/4")	2,250	1991	125.00	275-495
1991 Signed Plate (10 1/4") A/P	250	1991	195.00	395-475
1991 Plate (8 1/2")	10,000	1995	30.00	30-50
1991 Plate (3 1/4")	Open		15.00	17

John Lennon - J. Lennon

YEAR ISSUE	EDITION LIMIT	YEAR RETD.	ISSUE PRICE	*QUOTE U.S.$
1999 Baby Grand (8")	10,000		35.00	35
1997 Christmas plate (8 1/8")	10,000		30.00	35
1997 Christmas plate/ornament (3 1/4")	Open		16.95	17
1998 Borrowed Time (8 1/8")	10,000		30.00	35
1998 Borrowed Time plate/ornament (3 1/4")	Open		16.95	17
1998 Family Tree (8 1/8")	10,000		30.00	35
1998 Family Tree (3 1/4")	Open		16.95	17
1998 Imagine (8 1/8")	10,000		30.00	35
1998 Imagine (3 1/4")	Open		16.95	17
1998 Peace Brother (8 1/8")	10,000		30.00	35
1998 Peace Brother plate/ornament (3 1/4")	Open		16.95	17
1998 Self Portrait plate/ornament (3 1/4")	Open		16.95	17
1998 4 mini plate framed ensemble	Open		150.00	150
1999 Baby Grand plate/ornament (3")	Open		17.00	17
1999 Feeling Good (8")	10,000		35.00	35
1999 Feeling Good plate/ornament (3")	Open		17.00	17
1999 Looking Back (8")	10,000		35.00	35
1999 Looking Back plate/ornament (3")	Open		17.00	17
1999 Self Portrait '99 (8")	10,000		35.00	35
1999 Self Portrait '99 plate/ornament (3")	Open		17.00	17
1999 Why Not? (8")	10,000		35.00	35
1999 Why Not? plate/ornament (3")	Open		17.00	17
2000 Why Not? 4 mini plate framed ensemble	Open		165.00	165

John Wooden - M. Taylor

YEAR ISSUE	EDITION LIMIT	YEAR RETD.	ISSUE PRICE	*QUOTE U.S.$
1990 Signed Plate (10 1/4")	1,975	1995	150.00	150
1990 Plate (8 1/2")	10,000	1995	30.00	35
1990 Plate (3 1/4")	Retrd.	1995	15.00	17

Johnny Bench - M. Taylor

YEAR ISSUE	EDITION LIMIT	YEAR RETD.	ISSUE PRICE	*QUOTE U.S.$
1989 Signed Plate (10 1/4")	1,989	1991	100.00	125-300
1989 Plate (3 1/4")	Closed	1998	15.00	15

Kareem Abdul-Jabbar Sky-Hook Collection - M. Taylor

YEAR ISSUE	EDITION LIMIT	YEAR RETD.	ISSUE PRICE	*QUOTE U.S.$
1989 Kareem Abdul-Jabbar "Path of Glory" (10 1/4"), signed	1,989	1991	100.00	195-395
1989 Plate (3 1/4")	Closed	1993	16.00	15-30

Ken Griffey Jr. - M. Taylor

YEAR ISSUE	EDITION LIMIT	YEAR RETD.	ISSUE PRICE	*QUOTE U.S.$
1992 Signed Plate (10 1/4")	1,989	1995	150.00	150-300
1992 Plate (8 1/2")	10,000		30.00	35
1992 Plate (3 1/4")	Open		15.00	17

Kiss "Psycho-Circus" - R. Hollis

YEAR ISSUE	EDITION LIMIT	YEAR RETD.	ISSUE PRICE	*QUOTE U.S.$
1998 Plate (3 1/4")	Open		17.00	17
1998 Plate (8 1/8")	10,000		35.00	35

Kiss - M. Pascucci

YEAR ISSUE	EDITION LIMIT	YEAR RETD.	ISSUE PRICE	*QUOTE U.S.$
1998 Kiss Bas Relief 8" Plate	5,000		95.00	95

Kiss - M. Taylor

YEAR ISSUE	EDITION LIMIT	YEAR RETD.	ISSUE PRICE	*QUOTE U.S.$
1997 Kiss plate/ornament (3 1/4")	Open		15.00	17
1997 Plate (10 1/4"), A/P signed	250		495.00	495
1997 Plate (8 1/4")	10,000		30.00	35
1997 Signed Plate (10 1/4")	1,000		275.00	275

Kiss - R. Hollis

YEAR ISSUE	EDITION LIMIT	YEAR RETD.	ISSUE PRICE	*QUOTE U.S.$
1999 KISSmas (8")	10,000		35.00	35
1999 KISSmas plate/ornament (3")	Open		17.00	17

Kristi Yamaguchi - M. Taylor

YEAR ISSUE	EDITION LIMIT	YEAR RETD.	ISSUE PRICE	*QUOTE U.S.$
1993 Signed Plate (10 1/4")	950	1995	150.00	375-444
1993 Plate (8 1/2")	5,000	1999	30.00	50
1993 Plate (3 1/4")	Open		15.00	17

Leave It To Beaver - M. Taylor

YEAR ISSUE	EDITION LIMIT	YEAR RETD.	ISSUE PRICE	*QUOTE U.S.$
1995 Jerry Mathers (10 1/4") signed	1,963		125.00	125
1995 Jerry Mathers (8 1/4")	10,000		39.95	40
1995 Jerry Mathers plate/ornament (3 1/4")	Open		14.95	17

Luis Aparicio - M. Taylor

YEAR ISSUE	EDITION LIMIT	YEAR RETD.	ISSUE PRICE	*QUOTE U.S.$
1991 Signed Plate (10 1/4")	1,984	1995	150.00	250-300
1991 Plate (8 1/2")	10,000	1998	30.00	35
1991 Plate (3 1/4")	Closed	1998	15.00	17

*Quotes have been rounded up to nearest dollar

Magic Johnson Gold Rim Collection - R. Winslow

Year Issue	Edition Limit	Year Retd.	Issue Price	*Quote U.S.$
1987 Magic Johnson "The Magic Show" (10 1/4"), signed	1,987	1988	100.00	350-495
1987 Magic Johnson "The Magic Show" (3 1/4")	Closed	1993	14.50	15-25

Mike Schmidt "500th" Home Run Edition - C. Paluso

Year Issue	Edition Limit	Year Retd.	Issue Price	*Quote U.S.$
1987 Mike Schmidt "Power at the Plate" (10 1/4"), signed	1,987	1988	100.00	325-350
1987 Mike Schmidt "Power at the Plate" (3 1/4")	Open		14.50	19
1987 Mike Schmidt A/P, signed & dated	56	1988	150.00	595

Neil Diamond - M. Taylor

Year Issue	Edition Limit	Year Retd.	Issue Price	*Quote U.S.$
1998 Signed Plate (10 1/4")	1,000		225.00	225
1998 Neil Diamond (10 1/4") A/P signed	250		325.00	325
1998 Neil Diamond (8 1/8")	5,000		30.00	35
1998 Neil Diamond plate/ornament (3 1/4")	5,000		16.95	17

Ozzy Osbourne - M. Taylor

Year Issue	Edition Limit	Year Retd.	Issue Price	*Quote U.S.$
1999 Ozzy Osbourne, (10 1/4") signed	1,999		175.00	175
1999 Ozzy Osbourne (10 1/4") A/P signed	250		275.00	275
1999 Ozzy Osbourne (8")	10,000		35.00	35
1999 Ozzy Osbourne plate/ornament (3")	Open		17.00	17

Pete Rose Diamond Collection - Forbes

Year Issue	Edition Limit	Year Retd.	Issue Price	*Quote U.S.$
1988 Pete Rose "The Reigning Legend" (10 1/4"), signed	950	1989	195.00	250-295
1988 Pete Rose "The Reigning Legend" (10 1/4"), A/P signed	50	1989	300.00	350-395
1988 Pete Rose "The Reigning Legend"(3 1/4")	Open		14.50	19

Pete Rose Platinum Edition - T. Sizemore

Year Issue	Edition Limit	Year Retd.	Issue Price	*Quote U.S.$
1985 Pete Rose "The Best of Baseball" (3 1/4")	Open		12.95	15-20
1985 Pete Rose "The Best of Baseball"(10 1/4")	4,192	1988	100.00	275

Plaques - Various

Year Issue	Edition Limit	Year Retd.	Issue Price	*Quote U.S.$
1986 George Brett-"Royalty in Motion", signed - J. Martin	2,000	1987	75.00	250-300
1987 Mike Schmidt-"Only Perfect", A/P - Paluso	20	1988	200.00	450-550
1987 Mike Schmidt-"Only Perfect", signed - Paluso	500	1988	150.00	350-400
1985 Pete Rose-"Desire to Win", signed - T. Sizemore	4,192	1986	75.00	325-350
1986 Reggie Jackson A/P-The Roundtripper, signed - J. Martin	44	1987	175.00	475-550
1986 Reggie Jackson-"The Roundtripper" signed - J. Martin	500	1987	150.00	350-400
1987 Roger Staubach, signed - C. Soileau	1,979	1988	85.00	325-350

Ringo Starr - M. Taylor

Year Issue	Edition Limit	Year Retd.	Issue Price	*Quote U.S.$
1996 Ringo Starr, (10 1/4") signed	1,000	1996	225.00	250-390
1996 Ringo Starr (10 1/4") A/P signed	250		400.00	400
1996 Ringo Starr (8 1/4")	10,000		29.95	35
1996 Ringo Starr plate/ornament (3 1/4")	Open		14.95	17

Rod Carew - M. Taylor

Year Issue	Edition Limit	Year Retd.	Issue Price	*Quote U.S.$
1992 Signed Plate (10 1/4")	950	1995	150.00	100-150
1992 Plate (8 1/2")	10,000	1999	30.00	35
1992 Plate (3 1/4")	Open		15.00	17

Roger Staubach Sterling Collection - C. Soileau

Year Issue	Edition Limit	Year Retd.	Issue Price	*Quote U.S.$
1987 Roger Staubach (3 1/4" diameter)	Closed	1998	12.95	20
1987 Roger Staubach (10 1/4" diameter) signed	1,979	1990	100.00	300

Sam Snead - M. Taylor

Year Issue	Edition Limit	Year Retd.	Issue Price	*Quote U.S.$
1994 Signed Plate (10 1/4")	950	1995	100.00	100-200
1994 Plate (8 1/2")	5,000		30.00	35
1994 Plate (3 1/4")	Open		15.00	17

Tom Seaver - M. Taylor

Year Issue	Edition Limit	Year Retd.	Issue Price	*Quote U.S.$
1993 Signed Plate (10 1/4")	1,992	1995	150.00	350-495
1993 Plate (8 1/2")	10,000		30.00	35
1993 Plate (3 1/4")	Open		15.00	17

Troy Aikman - M. Taylor

Year Issue	Edition Limit	Year Retd.	Issue Price	*Quote U.S.$
1994 Signed Plate (10 1/4")	1,993	1995	225.00	250-300
1994 Plate (8 1/2")	10,000		30.00	35
1994 Plate (3 1/4")	Open		14.95	17

Wayne Gretzky - M. Taylor

Year Issue	Edition Limit	Year Retd.	Issue Price	*Quote U.S.$
1989 Plate (10 1/4"), signed by Gretzky and Howe	1,851	1989	225.00	325-495
1989 Plate (10 1/4") A/P, signed by Gretzky and Howe	300	1989	300.00	400-450
1989 Plate (8 1/2")	10,000	1989	30.00	50-75
1989 Plate (3 1/4")	Open		15.00	17

Whitey Ford - M. Taylor

Year Issue	Edition Limit	Year Retd.	Issue Price	*Quote U.S.$
1991 Signed Plate (10 1/4")	2,360	1995	150.00	150-349
1991 Plate (8 1/2")	10,000		30.00	35
1991 Plate (3 1/4")	Retrd.	1995	15.00	25-39

Yellow Submarine - M. Nardi

Year Issue	Edition Limit	Year Retd.	Issue Price	*Quote U.S.$
1999 All Together Now, (8")	9,000		35.00	35
1999 Pepperland plate/ornament (3")	Open		17.00	17
1999 All Together Now plate/ornament (3")	Open		17.00	17

Yogi Berra - M. Taylor

Year Issue	Edition Limit	Year Retd.	Issue Price	*Quote U.S.$
1991 Signed Plate (10 1/4")	2,150	1995	150.00	225-349
1991 Plate (8 1/2")	10,000		30.00	35
1991 Plate (3 1/4")	Open		15.00	17
1991 Signed Plate (10 1/4") A/P	250	1995	250.00	250

Goebel of North America

Pocket Dragons - R. Musgrave

Year Issue	Edition Limit	Year Retd.	Issue Price	*Quote U.S.$
1997 The Astronomy Lesson	1,250	1998	35.00	35
1997 Bedtime	1,250	1998	35.00	35

Goebel/M.I. Hummel

Century Collection Mini Plates - M.I. Hummel

Year Issue	Edition Limit	Year Retd.	Issue Price	*Quote U.S.$
1999 Chapel Time (1986)	Open		30.00	30
1999 Pleasant Journey (1987)	Open		30.00	30
1999 Call To Worship (1988)	Open		30.00	30
1999 Harmony in Four Parts (1989)	Open		30.00	30
1999 Let's Tell The World (1990)	Open		30.00	30
1999 We Wish You The Best (1991)	Open		30.00	30
1999 On Our Way (1992)	Open		30.00	30
1999 Welcome Spring (1993)	Open		30.00	30
1999 Rock-A-Bye (1994)	Open		30.00	30
1999 Strike Up The Band (1995)	Open		30.00	30
1999 Love's Bounty (1996)	Open		30.00	30
1999 Fond Goodbye (1997)	Open		30.00	30
1999 Here's My Heart (1998)	Open		30.00	30
1999 Fanfare (1999)	Open		30.00	30

M.I. Hummel Annual Figural Christmas Plates - M.I. Hummel

Year Issue	Edition Limit	Year Retd.	Issue Price	*Quote U.S.$
1995 Festival Harmony w/Flute 693	Closed	1995	125.00	100-150
1996 Christmas Song 692	Closed	1996	130.00	98-150
1997 Thanksgiving Prayer 694	Closed	1997	140.00	140-150
1998 Echoes of Joy 695	Closed	1998	145.00	145-150
1999 Joyful Noise 696	Closed	1999	145.00	145

M.I. Hummel Annual Plates - M.I. Hummel

Year Issue	Edition Limit	Year Retd.	Issue Price	*Quote U.S.$
2000 Garden Splendor 921	Yr.Iss.		198.00	198

M.I. Hummel Club Exclusive Celebration - M.I. Hummel

Year Issue	Edition Limit	Year Retd.	Issue Price	*Quote U.S.$
1986 Valentine Gift (Hum 738)	Closed		90.00	149-195
1987 Valentine Joy (Hum 737)	Closed		98.00	149-195
1988 Daisies Don't Tell (Hum 736)	Closed		115.00	139-195
1989 It's Cold (Hum 735)	Closed		120.00	149-195

M.I. Hummel Collectibles Anniversary Plates - M.I. Hummel

Year Issue	Edition Limit	Year Retd.	Issue Price	*Quote U.S.$
1975 Stormy Weather 280	Closed		100.00	55-295
1980 Spring Dance 281	Closed		225.00	120-245
1985 Auf Wiedersehen 282	Closed		225.00	105-295

M.I. Hummel Collectibles Annual Plates - M.I. Hummel

Year Issue	Edition Limit	Year Retd.	Issue Price	*Quote U.S.$
1971 Heavenly Angel 264	Closed		25.00	425-1300
1972 Hear Ye, Hear Ye 265	Closed		30.00	32-275
1973 Globe Trotter 266	Closed		32.50	57-395
1974 Goose Girl 267	Closed		40.00	37-175
1975 Ride into Christmas 268	Closed		50.00	47-175
1976 Apple Tree Girl 269	Closed		50.00	42-155
1977 Apple Tree Boy 270	Closed		52.50	43-295
1978 Happy Pastime 271	Closed		65.00	30-175
1979 Singing Lesson 272	Closed		90.00	20-125
1980 School Girl 273	Closed		100.00	35-125
1981 Umbrella Boy 274	Closed		100.00	40-135
1982 Umbrella Girl 275	Closed		100.00	84-225
1983 The Postman 276	Closed		108.00	137-850
1984 Little Helper 277	Closed		108.00	40-195
1985 Chick Girl 278	Closed		110.00	65-215
1986 Playmates 279	Closed		125.00	126-245
1987 Feeding Time 283	Closed		135.00	175-324
1988 Little Goat Herder 284	Closed		145.00	91-225
1989 Farm Boy 285	Closed		160.00	137-275
1990 Shepherd's Boy 286	Closed		170.00	245-275
1991 Just Resting 287	Closed		196.00	130-275
1992 Wayside Harmony 288	Closed		210.00	188-275
1993 Doll Bath 289	Closed		210.00	197-250
1994 Doctor 290	Closed		225.00	163-350
1995 Come Back Soon 291	Closed		250.00	190-350
1998 Echoes of Joy 695	Closed		145.00	109-145
1999 Joyful Noise 696	Closed		145.00	145
2000 Light The Way 697	Yr.Iss.		145.00	145

M.I. Hummel Four Seasons - M.I. Hummel

Year Issue	Edition Limit	Year Retd.	Issue Price	*Quote U.S.$
1996 Winter Melody 296	Yr.Iss.	1996	195.00	195
1997 Springtime Serenade 297	Yr.Iss.	1997	195.00	195
1998 Summertime Stroll 298	Yr.Iss.	1998	195.00	195
1999 Autumn Glory 299	Yr.Iss.	1999	195.00	146-195

M.I. Hummel Friends Forever - M.I. Hummel

Year Issue	Edition Limit	Year Retd.	Issue Price	*Quote U.S.$
1992 Meditation 292	Closed	N/A	180.00	195
1993 For Father 293	Closed	N/A	195.00	195
1994 Sweet Greetings 294	Closed	N/A	205.00	163-205
1995 Surprise 295	Closed	N/A	210.00	163-210

M.I. Hummel Little Music Makers - M.I. Hummel

Year Issue	Edition Limit	Year Retd.	Issue Price	*Quote U.S.$
1984 Little Fiddler 744	Closed		30.00	39-125
1985 Serenade 741	Closed		30.00	33-125
1986 Soloist 743	Closed		35.00	39-125
1987 Band Leader 742	Closed		40.00	46-125

M.I. Hummel Special Millennium Edition - M.I. Hummel

Year Issue	Edition Limit	Year Retd.	Issue Price	*Quote U.S.$
2000 Star Gazer 920	Yr.Iss.		198.00	198

M.I. Hummel The Little Homemakers - M.I. Hummel

Year Issue	Edition Limit	Year Retd.	Issue Price	*Quote U.S.$
1988 Little Sweeper (Hum 745)	Closed		45.00	75-125
1989 Wash Day (Hum 746)	Closed		50.00	75-125
1990 A Stitch in Time (Hum 747)	Closed		50.00	125
1991 Chicken LIttle (Hum 747)	Closed		70.00	125

Gorham

(Four Seasons) A Boy and His Dog Plates - N. Rockwell

Year Issue	Edition Limit	Year Retd.	Issue Price	*Quote U.S.$
1971 Boy Meets His Dog	Annual	1971	50.00	215-425
1971 Adventures Between Adventures	Annual	1971	Set	Set
1971 The Mysterious Malady	Annual	1971	Set	Set
1971 Pride of Parenthood	Annual	1971	Set	Set

(Four Seasons) A Helping Hand Plates - N. Rockwell

Year Issue	Edition Limit	Year Retd.	Issue Price	*Quote U.S.$
1979 Year End Court	Annual	1979	100.00	94-200
1979 Closed for Business	Annual	1979	Set	Set
1979 Swatter's Rights	Annual	1979	Set	Set
1979 Coal Season's Coming	Annual	1979	Set	Set

(Four Seasons) Dad's Boys Plates - N. Rockwell

Year Issue	Edition Limit	Year Retd.	Issue Price	*Quote U.S.$
1980 Ski Skills	Annual	1980	135.00	80-225
1980 In His Spirits	Annual	1980	Set	Set
1980 Trout Dinner	Annual	1980	Set	Set
1980 Careful Aim	Annual	1980	Set	Set

(Four Seasons) Four Ages of Love - N. Rockwell

Year Issue	Edition Limit	Year Retd.	Issue Price	*Quote U.S.$
1973 Gaily Sharing Vintage Time	Annual	1973	60.00	175-195
1973 Flowers in Tender Bloom	Annual	1973	Set	Set
1973 Sweet Song So Young	Annual	1973	Set	Set
1973 Fondly We Do Remember	Annual	1973	Set	Set

(Four Seasons) Going on Sixteen Plates - N. Rockwell

Year Issue	Edition Limit	Year Retd.	Issue Price	*Quote U.S.$
1977 Chilling Chore	Annual	1977	75.00	100
1977 Sweet Serenade	Annual	1977	Set	Set
1977 Shear Agony	Annual	1977	Set	Set
1977 Pilgrimage	Annual	1977	Set	Set

(Four Seasons) Grand Pals Four Plates - N. Rockwell

Year Issue	Edition Limit	Year Retd.	Issue Price	*Quote U.S.$
1976 Snow Sculpturing	Annual	1976	70.00	150
1976 Soaring Spirits	Annual	1976	Set	Set
1976 Fish Finders	Annual	1976	Set	Set
1976 Ghostly Gourds	Annual	1976	Set	Set

(Four Seasons) Grandpa and Me Plates - N. Rockwell

Year Issue	Edition Limit	Year Retd.	Issue Price	*Quote U.S.$
1974 Gay Blades	Annual	1974	60.00	145-150
1974 Day Dreamers	Annual	1974	Set	Set
1974 Goin' Fishing	Annual	1974	Set	Set
1974 Pensive Pals	Annual	1974	Set	Set

(Four Seasons) Life with Father Plates - N. Rockwell

Year Issue	Edition Limit	Year Retd.	Issue Price	*Quote U.S.$
1982 Big Decision	Annual	1982	100.00	100
1982 Blasting Out	Annual	1982	Set	Set
1982 Cheering the Champs	Annual	1982	Set	Set
1982 A Tough One	Annual	1982	Set	Set

(Four Seasons) Me and My Pals Plates - N. Rockwell

Year Issue	Edition Limit	Year Retd.	Issue Price	*Quote U.S.$
1975 A Lickin' Good Bath	Annual	1975	70.00	91
1975 Young Man's Fancy	Annual	1975	Set	Set
1975 Fisherman's Paradise	Annual	1975	Set	Set
1975 Disastrous Daring	Annual	1975	Set	Set

(Four Seasons) Old Buddies Plates - N. Rockwell

Year Issue	Edition Limit	Year Retd.	Issue Price	*Quote U.S.$
1983 Shared Success	Annual	1983	115.00	150
1983 Endless Debate	Annual	1983	Set	Set
1983 Hasty Retreat	Annual	1983	Set	Set
1983 Final Speech	Annual	1983	Set	Set

(Four Seasons) Old Timers Plates - N. Rockwell

Year Issue	Edition Limit	Year Retd.	Issue Price	*Quote U.S.$
1981 Canine Solo	Annual	1981	100.00	125
1981 Sweet Surprise	Annual	1981	Set	Set
1981 Lazy Days	Annual	1981	Set	Set
1981 Fancy Footwork	Annual	1981	Set	Set

(Four Seasons) Tender Years Plates - N. Rockwell

Year Issue	Edition Limit	Year Retd.	Issue Price	*Quote U.S.$
1978 New Year Look	Annual	1978	100.00	87-225
1978 Spring Tonic	Annual	1978	Set	Set
1978 Cool Aid	Annual	1978	Set	Set
1978 Chilly Reception	Annual	1978	Set	Set

(Four Seasons) Young Love Plates - N. Rockwell

Year Issue	Edition Limit	Year Retd.	Issue Price	*Quote U.S.$
1972 Downhill Daring	Annual	1972	60.00	145-180
1972 Beguiling Buttercup	Annual	1972	Set	Set
1972 Flying High	Annual	1972	Set	Set
1972 A Scholarly Pace	Annual	1972	Set	Set

American Artist - R. Donnelly

Year Issue	Edition Limit	Year Retd.	Issue Price	*Quote U.S.$
1976 Apache Mother & Child	9,800	1980	25.00	35-56

American Landscapes - N. Rockwell

Year Issue	Edition Limit	Year Retd.	Issue Price	*Quote U.S.$
1980 Summer Respite	Annual	1980	45.00	80
1981 Autumn Reflection	Annual	1981	45.00	65
1982 Winter Delight	Annual	1982	50.00	70
1983 Spring Recess	Annual	1983	60.00	75

Barrymore - Barrymore

Year Issue	Edition Limit	Year Retd.	Issue Price	*Quote U.S.$
1971 Quiet Waters	15,000	1980	25.00	25
1972 San Pedro Harbor	15,000	1980	25.00	25
1972 Nantucket, Sterling	1,000	1972	100.00	100
1972 Little Boatyard, Sterling	1,000	1972	100.00	145

Bas Relief - N. Rockwell

Year Issue	Edition Limit	Year Retd.	Issue Price	*Quote U.S.$
1981 Sweet Song So Young	Undis.	1984	100.00	100
1981 Beguiling Buttercup	Undis.	1984	62.50	70
1982 Flowers in Tender Bloom	Undis.	1984	100.00	100
1982 Flying High	Undis.	1984	62.50	65

Boy Scout Plates - N. Rockwell

Year Issue	Edition Limit	Year Retd.	Issue Price	*Quote U.S.$
1975 Our Heritage	18,500	1980	19.50	80
1976 A Scout is Loyal	18,500	1990	19.50	55-75
1977 The Scoutmaster	18,500	1990	19.50	80

*Quotes have been rounded up to nearest dollar

PLATES/PLAQUES

YEAR ISSUE	EDITION LIMIT	YEAR RETD.	ISSUE PRICE	*QUOTE U.S.$
1977 A Good Sign	18,500	1990	19.50	50-75
1978 Pointing the Way	18,500	1990	19.50	50-75
1978 Campfire Story	18,500	1990	19.50	25-75
1980 Beyond the Easel	18,500	1990	45.00	45-75

Charles Russell - C. Russell

YEAR ISSUE	EDITION LIMIT	YEAR RETD.	ISSUE PRICE	*QUOTE U.S.$
1980 In Without Knocking	9,800	1990	38.00	65-75
1981 Bronc to Breakfast	9,800	1990	38.00	75
1982 When Ignorance is Bliss	9,800	1990	45.00	75-95
1983 Cowboy Life	9,800	1990	45.00	95-100

China Bicentennial - Gorham

YEAR ISSUE	EDITION LIMIT	YEAR RETD.	ISSUE PRICE	*QUOTE U.S.$
1972 1776 Plate	18,500	1980	17.50	35
1976 1776 Bicentennial	8,000	1980	17.50	35

Christmas - N. Rockwell

YEAR ISSUE	EDITION LIMIT	YEAR RETD.	ISSUE PRICE	*QUOTE U.S.$
1974 Tiny Tim	Annual	1974	12.50	45
1975 Good Deeds	Annual	1975	17.50	50
1976 Christmas Trio	Annual	1976	19.50	30
1977 Yuletide Reckoning	Annual	1977	19.50	45
1978 Planning Christmas Visit	Annual	1978	24.50	30
1979 Santa's Helpers	Annual	1979	24.50	30
1980 Letter to Santa	Annual	1980	27.50	32
1981 Santa Plans His Visit	Annual	1981	29.50	30
1982 Jolly Coachman	Annual	1982	29.50	30
1983 Christmas Dancers	Annual	1983	29.50	35
1984 Christmas Medley	17,500	1984	29.95	30
1985 Home For The Holidays	17,500	1985	29.95	30
1986 Merry Christmas Grandma	17,500	1986	29.95	65
1987 The Homecoming	17,500	1987	35.00	45
1988 Discovery	17,500	1988	37.50	45

Christmas/Children's Television Workshop - Unknown

YEAR ISSUE	EDITION LIMIT	YEAR RETD.	ISSUE PRICE	*QUOTE U.S.$
1981 Sesame Street Christmas	Annual	1981	17.50	18
1982 Sesame Street Christmas	Annual	1982	17.50	18
1983 Sesame Street Christmas	Annual	1983	19.50	20

Encounters, Survival and Celebrations - J. Clymer

YEAR ISSUE	EDITION LIMIT	YEAR RETD.	ISSUE PRICE	*QUOTE U.S.$
1982 A Fine Welcome	7,500	1983	50.00	80
1983 Winter Trail	7,500	1984	50.00	80
1983 Alouette	7,500	1984	62.50	80
1983 The Trader	7,500	1984	62.50	63
1983 Winter Camp	7,500	1984	62.50	75
1983 The Trapper Takes a Wife	7,500	1984	62.50	63

Gallery of Masters - Various

YEAR ISSUE	EDITION LIMIT	YEAR RETD.	ISSUE PRICE	*QUOTE U.S.$
1971 Man with a Gilt Helmet - Rembrandt	10,000	1975	50.00	50
1972 Self Portrait with Saskia - Rembrandt	10,000	1975	50.00	50
1973 The Honorable Mrs. Graham - Gainsborough	7,500	1975	50.00	50

Gorham Museum Doll Plates - Gorham

YEAR ISSUE	EDITION LIMIT	YEAR RETD.	ISSUE PRICE	*QUOTE U.S.$
1984 Lydia	5,000	1984	29.00	79
1984 Belton Bebe	5,000	1984	29.00	65
1984 Christmas Lady	7,500	1984	32.50	33-50
1985 Lucille	5,000	1985	29.00	35-50
1985 Jumeau	5,000	1985	29.00	65

Julian Ritter - J. Ritter

YEAR ISSUE	EDITION LIMIT	YEAR RETD.	ISSUE PRICE	*QUOTE U.S.$
1977 Christmas Visit	9,800	1977	24.50	29
1978 Valentine, Fluttering Heart	7,500	1978	45.00	45

Julian Ritter, Fall In Love - J. Ritter

YEAR ISSUE	EDITION LIMIT	YEAR RETD.	ISSUE PRICE	*QUOTE U.S.$
1977 Enchantment	5,000	1977	100.00	100
1977 Frolic	5,000	1977	set	Set
1977 Gutsy Gal	5,000	1977	set	Set
1977 Lonely Chill	5,000	1977	set	Set

Julian Ritter, To Love a Clown - J. Ritter

YEAR ISSUE	EDITION LIMIT	YEAR RETD.	ISSUE PRICE	*QUOTE U.S.$
1978 Awaited Reunion	5,000	1978	120.00	120
1978 Twosome Time	5,000	1978	120.00	120
1978 Showtime Beckons	5,000	1978	120.00	120
1978 Together in Memories	5,000	1978	120.00	120

Leyendecker Annual Christmas Plates - J. C. Leyendecker

YEAR ISSUE	EDITION LIMIT	YEAR RETD.	ISSUE PRICE	*QUOTE U.S.$
1988 Christmas Hug	10,000	1988	37.50	30-50

Moppet Plates-Anniversary - Unknown

YEAR ISSUE	EDITION LIMIT	YEAR RETD.	ISSUE PRICE	*QUOTE U.S.$
1976 Anniversary	20,000	1977	13.00	13

Moppet Plates-Christmas - Unknown

YEAR ISSUE	EDITION LIMIT	YEAR RETD.	ISSUE PRICE	*QUOTE U.S.$
1973 Christmas	Annual	1973	10.00	35
1974 Christmas	Annual	1974	12.00	12
1975 Christmas	Annual	1975	13.00	13
1976 Christmas	Annual	1976	13.00	10-15
1977 Christmas	Annual	1977	13.00	14
1978 Christmas	Annual	1978	10.00	10
1979 Christmas	Annual	1979	12.00	12
1980 Christmas	Annual	1980	12.00	12
1981 Christmas	Annual	1981	12.00	12
1982 Christmas	Annual	1982	12.00	12
1983 Christmas	Annual	1983	12.00	12

Moppet Plates-Mother's Day - Unknown

YEAR ISSUE	EDITION LIMIT	YEAR RETD.	ISSUE PRICE	*QUOTE U.S.$
1973 Mother's Day	Annual	1973	10.00	30
1974 Mother's Day	Annual	1974	12.00	20
1975 Mother's Day	Annual	1975	13.00	15
1976 Mother's Day	Annual	1976	13.00	15
1977 Mother's Day	Annual	1977	13.00	15
1978 Mother's Day	Annual	1978	10.00	10

Pastoral Symphony - B. Felder

YEAR ISSUE	EDITION LIMIT	YEAR RETD.	ISSUE PRICE	*QUOTE U.S.$
1982 When I Was a Child	7,500	1983	42.50	20-50
1982 Gather the Children	7,500	1983	42.50	20-50
1984 Sugar and Spice	7,500	1985	42.50	20-50
XX He Loves Me	7,500	1985	42.50	20-50

Pewter Bicentennial - R. Pailthorpe

YEAR ISSUE	EDITION LIMIT	YEAR RETD.	ISSUE PRICE	*QUOTE U.S.$
1971 Burning of the Gaspee	5,000	1971	35.00	35
1972 Boston Tea Party	5,000	1972	35.00	35

Presidential - N. Rockwell

YEAR ISSUE	EDITION LIMIT	YEAR RETD.	ISSUE PRICE	*QUOTE U.S.$
1976 John F. Kennedy	9,800	1976	30.00	65
1976 Dwight D. Eisenhower	9,800	1976	30.00	35

Remington Western - F. Remington

YEAR ISSUE	EDITION LIMIT	YEAR RETD.	ISSUE PRICE	*QUOTE U.S.$
1973 A New Year on the Cimarron	Annual	1973	25.00	35-50
1973 Aiding a Comrade	Annual	1973	25.00	30-125
1973 The Flight	Annual	1973	25.00	30-95
1973 The Fight for the Water Hole	Annual	1973	25.00	30-125
1975 Old Ramond	Annual	1975	20.00	35-60
1975 A Breed	Annual	1975	20.00	35-65
1976 Cavalry Officer	5,000	1976	37.50	60-75
1976 A Trapper	5,000	1976	37.50	60-75

Silver Bicentennial - Various

YEAR ISSUE	EDITION LIMIT	YEAR RETD.	ISSUE PRICE	*QUOTE U.S.$
1972 1776 Plate - Gorham	500	1972	500.00	500
1972 Burning of the Gaspee - R. Pailthorpe	750	1972	500.00	500
1973 Boston Tea Party - R. Pailthorpe	750	1973	550.00	575

Single Release - F. Quagon

YEAR ISSUE	EDITION LIMIT	YEAR RETD.	ISSUE PRICE	*QUOTE U.S.$
1976 The Black Regiment 1778	7,500	1978	25.00	58

Single Release - N. Rockwell

YEAR ISSUE	EDITION LIMIT	YEAR RETD.	ISSUE PRICE	*QUOTE U.S.$
1974 Weighing In	Annual	1974	12.50	75-150
1974 The Golden Rule	Annual	1974	12.50	30-40
1975 Ben Franklin	Annual	1975	19.50	35
1976 The Marriage License	Numbrd	1985	37.50	79-95
1978 Triple Self Portrait Memorial	Annual	1978	37.50	50-95
1980 The Annual Visit	Annual	1980	32.50	50-70
1981 Day in Life of Boy	Annual	1981	50.00	50-80
1981 Day in Life of Girl	Annual	1981	50.00	50-125

Time Machine Teddies Plates - B. Port

YEAR ISSUE	EDITION LIMIT	YEAR RETD.	ISSUE PRICE	*QUOTE U.S.$
1986 Miss Emily, Bearing Up	5,000	1986	32.50	35-50
1987 Big Bear, The Toy Collector	5,000	1987	32.50	35-45
1988 Hunny Munny	5,000	1988	37.50	35-45

Vermeil Bicentennial - Gorham

YEAR ISSUE	EDITION LIMIT	YEAR RETD.	ISSUE PRICE	*QUOTE U.S.$
1972 1776 Plate	250	1972	750.00	300-800

Gzhel USA/Russian Gift & Jewelry

Churches of Russia - Moskovskaya

YEAR ISSUE	EDITION LIMIT	YEAR RETD.	ISSUE PRICE	*QUOTE U.S.$
1998 Church of Christ 60200	Open		990.00	990
1996 Saint Basil 60400	Open		200.00	200

Floral - Nekrasova

YEAR ISSUE	EDITION LIMIT	YEAR RETD.	ISSUE PRICE	*QUOTE U.S.$
1996 Floral Elegance 60300	Open		175.00	175

Russian Life - Podgornaya

YEAR ISSUE	EDITION LIMIT	YEAR RETD.	ISSUE PRICE	*QUOTE U.S.$
1998 Village Celebrations 61000	500		770.00	770

Hackett American

Sports - Various

YEAR ISSUE	EDITION LIMIT	YEAR RETD.	ISSUE PRICE	*QUOTE U.S.$
1981 Reggie Jackson (Mr. Oct.) h/s - Paluso	Retrd.	N/A	100.00	695-750
1983 Steve Garvey h/s - Paluso	Retrd.	N/A	100.00	150-175
1983 Nolan Ryan h/s - Paluso	Retrd.	N/A	100.00	595-750
1983 Tom Seaver h/s - Paluso	3,272	N/A	100.00	200-300
1984 Steve Carlton h/s - Paluso	Retrd.	N/A	100.00	200-250
1985 Willie Mays h/s - Paluso	Retrd.	N/A	125.00	395
1985 Whitey Ford h/s - Paluso	Retrd.	N/A	125.00	200-250
1985 Hank Aaron h/s - Paluso	Retrd.	N/A	125.00	375-395
1985 Sandy Koufax h/s - Paluso	1,000	N/A	125.00	450
1985 H. Killebrew d/s - Paluso	Retrd.	N/A	125.00	275
1985 E. Mathews d/s - Paluso	Retrd.	N/A	125.00	275
1986 T. Seaver 300 d/s - Paluso	1,200	N/A	125.00	200-250
1986 Roger Clemens (great events) d/s - Paluso	Retrd.	N/A	125.00	595-750
1986 Reggie Jackson (great events) d/s - Paluso	Retrd.	N/A	125.00	200-250
1986 Wally Joyner (great events) d/s - Paluso	Retrd.	N/A	125.00	200-250
1986 Don Sutton d/s (great events)- Paluso	300	N/A	125.00	200-250
XX Gary Carter d/s - Simon	Retrd.	N/A	125.00	50-150
1985 Dwight Gooden 8 1/2" u/s - Simon	Retrd.	N/A	55.00	40-55
XX Arnold Palmer h/s - Alexander	Retrd.	N/A	125.00	200
XX Gary Player h/s - Alexander	Retrd.	N/A	125.00	200
1983 Reggie Jackson (500 HRs) h/s - Alexander	Retrd.	N/A	125.00	200-500
1983 Reggie Jackson (500 HRs), proof - Alexander	Retrd.	N/A	250.00	1000
1986 Joe Montana d/s - Alexander	Retrd.	N/A	125.00	600

Hadley House

American Memories Series - T. Redlin

YEAR ISSUE	EDITION LIMIT	YEAR RETD.	ISSUE PRICE	*QUOTE U.S.$
1987 Coming Home	9,500	1998	85.00	85
1988 Lights of Home	9,500	1994	85.00	125
1989 Homeward Bound	9,500	1996	85.00	85
1991 Family Traditions	9,500	1998	85.00	85

Annual Christmas Series - T. Redlin

YEAR ISSUE	EDITION LIMIT	YEAR RETD.	ISSUE PRICE	*QUOTE U.S.$
1991 Heading Home	9,500	1994	65.00	225
1992 Pleasures Of Winter	19,500		65.00	125
1993 Winter Wonderland	19,500		65.00	125
1994 Almost Home	19,500		65.00	125
1995 Sharing the Evening	45-day		29.95	30

YEAR ISSUE	EDITION LIMIT	YEAR RETD.	ISSUE PRICE	*QUOTE U.S.$
1996 Night on the Town	45-day		29.95	30
1998 Racing Home	45-day		29.95	30

Country Doctor Collection - T. Redlin

YEAR ISSUE	EDITION LIMIT	YEAR RETD.	ISSUE PRICE	*QUOTE U.S.$
1995 Wednesday Afternoon	45-day		29.95	30
1995 Office Hours	45-day		29.95	30
1995 House Calls	45-day		29.95	30
1995 Morning Rounds	45-day		29.95	30

Glow Series - T. Redlin

YEAR ISSUE	EDITION LIMIT	YEAR RETD.	ISSUE PRICE	*QUOTE U.S.$
1985 Evening Glow	5,000	1986	55.00	250-325
1985 Morning Glow	5,000	1986	55.00	130-150
1985 Twilight Glow	5,000	1988	55.00	130-388
1988 Afternoon Glow	5,000	1989	55.00	100-129

Lovers Collection - O. Franca

YEAR ISSUE	EDITION LIMIT	YEAR RETD.	ISSUE PRICE	*QUOTE U.S.$
1992 Lovers	9,500	1997	50.00	50

Navajo Visions Suite - O. Franca

YEAR ISSUE	EDITION LIMIT	YEAR RETD.	ISSUE PRICE	*QUOTE U.S.$
1993 Navajo Fantasy	9,500	1998	50.00	50
1993 Young Warrior	9,500	1998	50.00	50

Navajo Woman Series - O. Franca

YEAR ISSUE	EDITION LIMIT	YEAR RETD.	ISSUE PRICE	*QUOTE U.S.$
1990 Feathered Hair Ties	5,000	1994	50.00	50
1991 Navajo Summer	5,000	1998	50.00	50
1992 Turquoise Necklace	5,000	1998	50.00	50
1993 Pink Navajo	5,000	1998	50.00	50

Retreat Series - T. Redlin

YEAR ISSUE	EDITION LIMIT	YEAR RETD.	ISSUE PRICE	*QUOTE U.S.$
1987 Morning Retreat	9,500	1988	65.00	160
1987 Evening Retreat	9,500	1989	65.00	175
1988 Golden Retreat	9,500	1989	65.00	150
1989 Moonlight Retreat	9,500	1993	65.00	110

Seasons - T. Redlin

YEAR ISSUE	EDITION LIMIT	YEAR RETD.	ISSUE PRICE	*QUOTE U.S.$
1994 Autumn Evening	45-day		29.95	30
1995 Spring Fever	45-day		29.95	30
1995 Summertime	45-day		29.95	30
1995 Wintertime	45-day		29.95	30

That Special Time - T. Redlin

YEAR ISSUE	EDITION LIMIT	YEAR RETD.	ISSUE PRICE	*QUOTE U.S.$
1991 Evening Solitude	9,500	1994	65.00	95-103
1991 That Special Time	9,500	1993	65.00	95
1992 Aroma of Fall	9,500	1994	65.00	95-112
1993 Welcome To Paradise	9,500	1997	65.00	65

Tranquility - O. Franca

YEAR ISSUE	EDITION LIMIT	YEAR RETD.	ISSUE PRICE	*QUOTE U.S.$
1994 Blue Navajo	9,500	1997	50.00	50
1994 Blue Tranquility	9,500	1997	50.00	50
1994 Navajo Meditating	9,500		50.00	50
1995 Navajo Reflection	9,500		50.00	50

Wildlife Memories - T. Redlin

YEAR ISSUE	EDITION LIMIT	YEAR RETD.	ISSUE PRICE	*QUOTE U.S.$
1994 Best Friends	19,500		65.00	65
1994 Comforts of Home	19,500		65.00	65
1994 Pure Contentment	19,500		65.00	65
1994 Sharing in the Solitude	19,500		65.00	65

Windows to the Wild - T. Redlin

YEAR ISSUE	EDITION LIMIT	YEAR RETD.	ISSUE PRICE	*QUOTE U.S.$
1990 Master's Domain	9,500		65.00	65
1991 Winter Windbreak	9,500		65.00	65
1992 Evening Company	9,500		65.00	65
1994 Night Mapling	9,500		65.00	65

Hallmark Galleries

Days to Remember-The Art of Norman Rockwell - Rockwell-Inspired

YEAR ISSUE	EDITION LIMIT	YEAR RETD.	ISSUE PRICE	*QUOTE U.S.$
1992 A Boy Meets His Dog (pewter medallion) QHG9715	9,500	1994	45.00	45
1992 Sweet Song So Young (pewter medallion) QHG9716	9,500	1994	45.00	45
1992 Fisherman's Paradise (pewter medallion) QHG9717	9,500	1994	45.00	45
1992 Sleeping Children (pewter medallion) QHG9718	9,500	1994	45.00	45
1993 Breaking Home Ties QHG9723	9,500	1995	35.00	35
1994 Growing Years QHG9724	9,500	1995	35.00	35

Easter Plate - L. Votruba

YEAR ISSUE	EDITION LIMIT	YEAR RETD.	ISSUE PRICE	*QUOTE U.S.$
1994 Collector's Plate-(1st Ed.) QEO8233	Yr.Iss.	1995	7.75	25

Enchanted Garden - E. Richardson

YEAR ISSUE	EDITION LIMIT	YEAR RETD.	ISSUE PRICE	*QUOTE U.S.$
1992 Neighborhood Dreamer QHG3001	9,500	1994	45.00	45
1992 Swan Lake (tile) QHG3010	9,500	1994	35.00	35
1992 Fairy Bunny Tale: The Beginning (tile) QHG3011	14,500	1994	25.00	25
1992 Fairy Bunny Tale: Beginning II (tile) QHG3015	14,500	1994	35.00	35

Innocent Wonders - T. Blackshear

YEAR ISSUE	EDITION LIMIT	YEAR RETD.	ISSUE PRICE	*QUOTE U.S.$
1992 Pinkie Poo QHG4017	9,500	1995	35.00	35
1992 Dinky Toot QHG4019	9,500	1995	35.00	35
1993 Pockets QHG4022	9,500	1995	35.00	35
1994 Twinky Wink QHG4023	9,500	1995	35.00	35

Majestic Wilderness - M. Englebreit

YEAR ISSUE	EDITION LIMIT	YEAR RETD.	ISSUE PRICE	*QUOTE U.S.$
1994 Golden Rule (tile) QHG5010	14,500	1995	30.00	30
1994 Recipe for Happiness (tile) QHG5011	14,500	1995	30.00	30

Majestic Wilderness - M. Newman

YEAR ISSUE	EDITION LIMIT	YEAR RETD.	ISSUE PRICE	*QUOTE U.S.$
1992 Timber Wolves (porcelain) QHG2012	9,500	1995	35.00	35
1992 Vixen & Kits QHG2018	9,500	1995	35.00	35
1994 White Tail Buck QHG2030	9,500	1995	35.00	35

*Quotes have been rounded up to nearest dollar

Hamilton Collection

All in a Day's Work - J. Lamb

YEAR ISSUE	EDITION LIMIT	YEAR RETD.	ISSUE PRICE	*QUOTE U.S.$
1994 Where's the Fire?	28-day	1994	29.50	30
1994 Lunch Break	28-day	1994	29.50	30
1994 Puppy Patrol	28-day	1994	29.50	30
1994 Decoy Delivery	28-day	1994	29.50	30
1994 Budding Artist	28-day	1994	29.50	30
1994 Garden Guards	28-day	1994	29.50	30
1994 Saddling Up	28-day	1994	29.50	30
1995 Taking the Lead	28-day	1994	29.50	30

All Star Memories - D. Spindel

YEAR ISSUE	EDITION LIMIT	YEAR RETD.	ISSUE PRICE	*QUOTE U.S.$
1995 The Mantle Story	28-day		35.00	35-39
1996 Momentos of the Mick	28-day		35.00	35
1996 Mantle Appreciation Day	28-day		35.00	35
1996 Life of a Legend	28-day		35.00	35
1996 Yankee Pride	28-day		35.00	35-39
1996 A World Series Tribute	28-day		35.00	35
1996 The Ultimate All Star	28-day		35.00	35
1997 Triple Crown	28-day		35.00	35-45

America's Greatest Sailing Ships - T. Freeman

YEAR ISSUE	EDITION LIMIT	YEAR RETD.	ISSUE PRICE	*QUOTE U.S.$
1988 USS Constitution	14-day	1991	29.50	55
1988 Great Republic	14-day	1991	29.50	55
1988 America	14-day	1991	29.50	55
1988 Charles W. Morgan	14-day	1991	29.50	27-95
1988 Eagle	14-day	1991	29.50	27-50
1988 Bonhomme Richard	14-day	1991	29.50	50-55
1988 Gertrude L. Thebaud	14-day	1991	29.50	45-50
1988 Enterprise	14-day	1991	29.50	50-65

The American Civil War - D. Prechtel

YEAR ISSUE	EDITION LIMIT	YEAR RETD.	ISSUE PRICE	*QUOTE U.S.$
1990 General Robert E. Lee	14-day		37.50	65-75
1990 Generals Grant and Lee At Appomattox	14-day		37.50	50-75
1990 General Thomas "Stonewall" Jackson	14-day		37.50	50-75
1990 Abraham Lincoln	14-day		37.50	50-60
1991 General J.E.B. Stuart	14-day		37.50	50-59
1991 General Philip Sheridan	14-day		37.50	50-60
1991 A Letter from Home	14-day		37.50	50-60
1991 Going Home	14-day		37.50	45-50
1992 Assembling The Troop	14-day		37.50	50-75
1992 Standing Watch	14-day		37.50	80-85

American Water Birds - R. Lawrence

YEAR ISSUE	EDITION LIMIT	YEAR RETD.	ISSUE PRICE	*QUOTE U.S.$
1988 Wood Ducks	14-day		37.50	40-54
1988 Hooded Mergansers	14-day		37.50	40-54
1988 Pintail	14-day		37.50	40-45
1988 Canada Geese	14-day		37.50	45-50
1988 American Widgeons	14-day		37.50	50
1988 Canvasbacks	14-day		37.50	40-54
1988 Mallard Pair	14-day		37.50	50-60
1988 Snow Geese	14-day		37.50	40-45

The American Wilderness - M. Richter

YEAR ISSUE	EDITION LIMIT	YEAR RETD.	ISSUE PRICE	*QUOTE U.S.$
1995 Gray Wolf	28-day		29.95	27-45
1995 Silent Watch	28-day		29.95	30
1995 Moon Song	28-day		29.95	27
1995 Silent Pursuit	28-day		29.95	30
1996 Still of the Night	28-day		29.95	27
1996 Nighttime Serenity	28-day		29.95	30
1996 Autumn Solitude	28-day		29.95	30
1996 Arctic Wolf	28-day		29.95	30-45

Andy Griffith - R. Tanenbaum

YEAR ISSUE	EDITION LIMIT	YEAR RETD.	ISSUE PRICE	*QUOTE U.S.$
1992 Sheriff Andy Taylor	28-day	1994	29.50	95-100
1992 A Startling Conclusion	28-day	1994	29.50	45-90
1993 Mayberry Sing-a-long	28-day	1994	29.50	85-90
1993 Aunt Bee's Kitchen	28-day	1994	29.50	90-95
1993 Surprise! Surprise!	28-day	1994	29.50	75-85
1993 An Explosive Situation	28-day	1994	29.50	45-110
1993 Meeting Aunt Bee	28-day	1994	29.50	75-85
1993 Opie's Big Catch	28-day	1994	29.50	45-75

The Angler's Prize - M. Susinno

YEAR ISSUE	EDITION LIMIT	YEAR RETD.	ISSUE PRICE	*QUOTE U.S.$
1991 Trophy Bass	14-day		29.50	55-85
1991 Blue Ribbon Trout	14-day		29.50	33
1991 Sun Dancers	14-day		29.50	30
1991 Freshwater Barracuda	14-day		29.50	30-36
1991 Bronzeback Fighter	14-day		29.50	30-36
1991 Autumn Beauty	14-day		29.50	30-40
1992 Old Mooneyes	14-day		29.50	30-36
1992 Silver King	14-day		29.50	33

Beauty Of Winter - N/A

YEAR ISSUE	EDITION LIMIT	YEAR RETD.	ISSUE PRICE	*QUOTE U.S.$
1992 Silent Night	28-day		29.50	30
1993 Moonlight Sleighride	28-day		29.50	30

The Best Of Baseball - R. Tanenbaum

YEAR ISSUE	EDITION LIMIT	YEAR RETD.	ISSUE PRICE	*QUOTE U.S.$
1993 The Legendary Mickey Mantle	28-day		29.50	55-65
1993 The Immortal Babe Ruth	28-day		29.50	38-45
1993 The Great Willie Mays	28-day		29.50	42-55
1993 The Unbeatable Duke Snider	28-day		29.50	25-45
1993 The Extraordinary Lou Gehrig	28-day		29.50	30-42
1993 The Phenomenal Roberto Clemente	28-day		29.50	30-42
1993 The Remarkable Johnny Bench	28-day		29.50	30-42
1993 The Incredible Nolan Ryan	28-day		29.50	30-59
1993 The Exceptional Brooks Robinson	28-day		29.50	30-42
1993 The Unforgettable Phil Rizzuto	28-day		29.50	30-42
1995 The Incomparable Reggie Jackson	28-day		29.50	30-42

Bialosky® & Friends - P./A.Bialosky

YEAR ISSUE	EDITION LIMIT	YEAR RETD.	ISSUE PRICE	*QUOTE U.S.$
1992 Family Addition	28-day		29.50	33
1993 Sweetheart	28-day		29.50	30-36
1993 Let's Go Fishing	28-day		29.50	30-36
1993 U.S. Mail	28-day		29.50	30-45
1993 Sleigh Ride	28-day		29.50	30
1993 Honey For Sale	28-day		29.50	30
1993 Breakfast In Bed	28-day		29.50	30-36
1993 My First Two-Wheeler	28-day		29.50	30

Big Cats of the World - D. Manning

YEAR ISSUE	EDITION LIMIT	YEAR RETD.	ISSUE PRICE	*QUOTE U.S.$
1989 African Shade	14-day		29.50	42
1989 View from Above	14-day		29.50	40
1990 On The Prowl	14-day		29.50	30
1990 Deep In The Jungle	14-day		29.50	30
1990 Spirit Of The Mountain	14-day		29.50	30
1990 Spotted Sentinel	14-day		29.50	30
1990 Above the Treetops	14-day		29.50	30
1990 Mountain Dweller	14-day		29.50	30
1992 Jungle Habitat	14-day		29.50	30
1992 Solitary Sentry	14-day		29.50	30

Bundles of Joy - B. P. Gutmann

YEAR ISSUE	EDITION LIMIT	YEAR RETD.	ISSUE PRICE	*QUOTE U.S.$
1988 Awakening	14-day	1991	24.50	90-95
1988 Happy Dreams	14-day	1991	24.50	90
1988 Tasting	14-day	1991	24.50	45-95
1988 Sweet Innocence	14-day	1991	24.50	60
1988 Tommy	14-day	1991	24.50	80
1988 A Little Bit of Heaven	14-day	1991	24.50	75-99
1988 Billy	14-day	1991	24.50	60-65
1988 Sun Kissed	14-day	1991	24.50	90

Butterfly Garden - P. Sweany

YEAR ISSUE	EDITION LIMIT	YEAR RETD.	ISSUE PRICE	*QUOTE U.S.$
1987 Spicebush Swallowtail	14-day		29.50	30-55
1987 Common Blue	14-day		29.50	30-55
1987 Orange Sulphur	14-day		29.50	30-55
1987 Monarch	14-day		29.50	30-55
1987 Tiger Swallowtail	14-day		29.50	30-55
1987 Crimson Patched Longwing	14-day		29.50	30-55
1988 Morning Cloak	14-day		29.50	30-55
1988 Red Admiral	14-day		29.50	30-55

The Call of the North - J. Tift

YEAR ISSUE	EDITION LIMIT	YEAR RETD.	ISSUE PRICE	*QUOTE U.S.$
1993 Winter's Dawn	28-day		29.50	30
1994 Evening Silence	28-day		29.50	30
1994 Moonlit Wilderness	28-day		29.50	30-39
1994 Silent Snowfall	28-day		29.50	30
1994 Snowy Watch	28-day		29.50	30-40
1994 Sentinels of the Summit	28-day		29.50	30
1994 Arctic Seclusion	28-day		29.50	30
1994 Forest Twilight	28-day		29.50	30
1994 Mountain Explorer	28-day		29.50	30
1994 The Cry of Winter	28-day		29.50	30

Call to Adventure - R. Cross

YEAR ISSUE	EDITION LIMIT	YEAR RETD.	ISSUE PRICE	*QUOTE U.S.$
1993 USS Constitution	28-day		29.50	30-35
1993 The Bounty	28-day		29.50	30
1994 Bonhomme Richard	28-day		29.50	30
1994 Old Nantucket	28-day		29.50	30
1994 Golden West	28-day		29.50	30
1994 Boston	28-day		29.50	30
1994 Hannah	28-day		29.50	30
1994 Improvement	28-day		29.50	30
1995 Anglo-American	28-day		29.50	30
1995 Challenge	28-day		29.50	30

Cameo Kittens - Q. Lemonds

YEAR ISSUE	EDITION LIMIT	YEAR RETD.	ISSUE PRICE	*QUOTE U.S.$
1993 Ginger Snap	28-day		29.50	30
1993 Cat Tails	28-day		29.50	30
1993 Lady Blue	28-day		29.50	59
1993 Tiny Heart Stealer	28-day		29.50	49
1993 Blossom	28-day		29.50	30
1994 Whisker Antics	28-day		29.50	30
1994 Tiger's Temptation	28-day		29.50	30
1994 Scout	28-day		29.50	30
1995 Timid Tabby	28-day		29.50	30
1995 All Wrapped Up	28-day		29.50	30-55

A Child's Best Friend - B. P. Gutmann

YEAR ISSUE	EDITION LIMIT	YEAR RETD.	ISSUE PRICE	*QUOTE U.S.$
1985 In Disgrace	14-day	1990	24.50	90-125
1985 The Reward	14-day	1990	24.50	90-110
1985 Who's Sleepy	14-day	1990	24.50	45-125
1985 Good Morning	14-day	1990	24.50	70-99
1985 Sympathy	14-day	1990	24.50	60-95
1985 On the Up and Up	14-day	1990	24.50	60-85
1985 Mine	14-day	1990	24.50	60-99
1985 Going to Town	14-day	1990	24.50	65-120

A Child's Christmas - J. Ferrandiz

YEAR ISSUE	EDITION LIMIT	YEAR RETD.	ISSUE PRICE	*QUOTE U.S.$
1995 Asleep in the Hay	28-day		29.95	30
1995 Merry Little Friends	28-day		29.95	30
1995 Love is Warm All Over	28-day		29.95	30
1995 Little Shepard Family	28-day		29.95	30
1995 Life's Little Blessings	28-day		29.95	30
1995 Happiness is Being Loved	28-day		29.95	30
1995 My Heart Belongs to You	28-day		29.95	30
1996 Lil' Dreamers	28-day		29.95	30

Childhood Reflections - B.P. Gutmann

YEAR ISSUE	EDITION LIMIT	YEAR RETD.	ISSUE PRICE	*QUOTE U.S.$
1991 Harmony	14-day	1990	29.50	60
1991 Kitty's Breakfast	14-day	1990	29.50	60
1991 Friendly Enemies	14-day	1990	29.50	35-80
1991 Smile, Smile, Smile	14-day	1990	29.50	35-95
1991 Lullaby	14-day	1990	29.50	60
1991 Oh! Oh! A Bunny	14-day	1990	29.50	60
1991 Little Mother	14-day	1990	29.50	35-85
1991 Thank You, God	14-day	1990	29.50	35-65

Children of the American Frontier - D. Crook

YEAR ISSUE	EDITION LIMIT	YEAR RETD.	ISSUE PRICE	*QUOTE U.S.$
1986 In Trouble Again	10-day		24.50	45
1986 Tubs and Suds	10-day		24.50	45
1986 A Lady Needs a Little Privacy	10-day		24.50	45
1986 The Desperadoes	10-day		24.50	28-40
1986 Riders Wanted	10-day		24.50	45
1987 A Cowboy's Downfall	10-day		24.50	28-40
1987 Runaway Blues	10-day		24.50	28-40
1987 A Special Patient	10-day		24.50	35-40

Civil War Generals - M. Gnatek

YEAR ISSUE	EDITION LIMIT	YEAR RETD.	ISSUE PRICE	*QUOTE U.S.$
1994 Robert E. Lee	28-day		29.50	35-45
1994 J.E.B. Stewart	28-day		29.50	40
1994 Joshua L. Chamberlain	28-day		29.50	40
1994 George Armstrong Custer	28-day		29.50	40
1994 Nathan Bedford Forrest	28-day		29.50	40-50
1994 James Longstreet	28-day		29.50	40-75
1995 Thomas "Stonewall" Jackson	28-day		29.50	40-45
1995 Confederate Heroes	28-day		29.50	36-40

Classic American Santas - G. Hinke

YEAR ISSUE	EDITION LIMIT	YEAR RETD.	ISSUE PRICE	*QUOTE U.S.$
1993 A Christmas Eve Visitor	28-day		29.50	30-36
1994 Up on the Rooftop	28-day		29.50	30-35
1994 Santa's Candy Kitchen	28-day		29.50	35-55
1994 A Christmas Chorus	28-day		29.50	30-35
1994 An Exciting Christmas Eve	28-day		29.50	30-75
1994 Rest Ye Merry Gentlemen	28-day		29.50	30-35
1994 Preparing the Sleigh	28-day		29.50	35-55
1994 The Reindeer's Stable	28-day		29.50	33-35
1994 He's Checking His List	28-day		29.50	30-35

Classic Corvettes - M. Lacourciere

YEAR ISSUE	EDITION LIMIT	YEAR RETD.	ISSUE PRICE	*QUOTE U.S.$
1994 1957 Corvette	28-day		29.50	89
1994 1963 Corvette	28-day		29.50	30
1994 1968 Corvette	28-day		29.50	89
1994 1986 Corvette	28-day		29.50	30
1995 1967 Corvette	28-day		29.50	30
1995 1953 Corvette	28-day		29.50	30
1995 1962 Corvette	28-day		29.50	30
1995 1990 Corvette	28-day		29.50	30

Classic Sporting Dogs - B. Christie

YEAR ISSUE	EDITION LIMIT	YEAR RETD.	ISSUE PRICE	*QUOTE U.S.$
1989 Golden Retrievers	14-day		24.50	50-75
1989 Labrador Retrievers	14-day		24.50	50-60
1989 Beagles	14-day		24.50	30-60
1989 Pointers	14-day		24.50	50-60
1989 Springer Spaniels	14-day		24.50	50
1990 German Short-Haired Pointers	14-day		24.50	50-60
1990 Irish Setters	14-day		24.50	40-60
1990 Brittany Spaniels	14-day		24.50	48-60

Classic TV Westerns - K. Milnazik

YEAR ISSUE	EDITION LIMIT	YEAR RETD.	ISSUE PRICE	*QUOTE U.S.$
1990 The Lone Ranger and Tonto	14-day		29.50	95-100
1990 Bonanza™	14-day		29.50	60-99
1990 Roy Rogers and Dale Evans	14-day		29.50	45-55
1991 Rawhide	14-day		29.50	50-85
1991 Wild Wild West	14-day		29.50	50-110
1991 Have Gun, Will Travel	14-day		29.50	45-50
1991 The Virginian	14-day		29.50	50-85
1991 Hopalong Cassidy	14-day		29.50	75-85

Cloak of Visions - A. Farley

YEAR ISSUE	EDITION LIMIT	YEAR RETD.	ISSUE PRICE	*QUOTE U.S.$
1994 Visions in a Full Moon	28-day		29.50	30-55
1994 Protector of the Child	28-day		29.50	30
1995 Spirits of the Canyon	28-day		29.50	30-55
1995 Freedom Soars	28-day		29.50	30
1995 Mystic Reflections	28-day		29.50	55
1995 Staff of Life	28-day		29.50	30-55
1995 Springtime Hunters	28-day		29.50	30-55
1996 Moonlit Solace	28-day		29.50	30-55

Close Up Collection #24 - M. Lacourciere

YEAR ISSUE	EDITION LIMIT	YEAR RETD.	ISSUE PRICE	*QUOTE U.S.$
1998 Champion's Ride	Open		35.00	35
1998 Practice Makes Perfect	Open		35.00	35
1998 Rainbow Rocket	Open		35.00	35
1998 The Champ!	Open		35.00	35

Close Up Collection #3 - M. Lacourciere

YEAR ISSUE	EDITION LIMIT	YEAR RETD.	ISSUE PRICE	*QUOTE U.S.$
1997 Ready To Race	Open		35.00	35
1997 Like Clockwork	Open		35.00	35
1997 Black at Light Speed	Open		35.00	35
1997 Lightning Quick	Open		35.00	35
1997 Night Ride	Open		35.00	35
1997 Reflections	Open		35.00	35

Close Up Collection #94 - M. Lacourciere

YEAR ISSUE	EDITION LIMIT	YEAR RETD.	ISSUE PRICE	*QUOTE U.S.$
1999 Burnin' Up The Track!	Open		35.00	35

Comical Dalmations - Landmark

YEAR ISSUE	EDITION LIMIT	YEAR RETD.	ISSUE PRICE	*QUOTE U.S.$
1996 I Will Not Bark In Class	28-day		29.95	30-40
1996 The Master	28-day		29.95	30
1996 Spot At Play	28-day		29.95	30
1996 A Dalmation's Dream	28-day		29.95	30
1996 To The Rescue	28-day		29.95	30
1996 Maid For A Day	28-day		29.95	30
1996 Dalmation Celebration	28-day		29.95	30
1996 Concert in D-Minor	28-day		29.95	30

Coral Paradise - H. Bond

YEAR ISSUE	EDITION LIMIT	YEAR RETD.	ISSUE PRICE	*QUOTE U.S.$
1989 The Living Oasis	14-day		29.50	40
1990 Riches of the Coral Sea	14-day		29.50	40

*Quotes have been rounded up to nearest dollar

PLATES/PLAQUES

YEAR ISSUE	EDITION LIMIT	YEAR RETD.	ISSUE PRICE	*QUOTE U.S.$
1990 Tropical Pageantry	14-day		29.50	40
1990 Caribbean Spectacle	14-day		29.50	40
1990 Undersea Village	14-day		29.50	40
1990 Shimmering Reef Dwellers	14-day		29.50	40
1990 Mysteries of the Galapagos	14-day		29.50	40
1990 Forest Beneath the Sea	14-day		29.50	40

Cottage Puppies - K. George

YEAR ISSUE	EDITION LIMIT	YEAR RETD.	ISSUE PRICE	*QUOTE U.S.$
1993 Little Gardeners	28-day		29.50	30-35
1993 Springtime Fancy	28-day		29.50	30
1993 Endearing Innocence	28-day		29.50	30
1994 Picnic Playtime	28-day		29.50	30
1994 Lazy Afternoon	28-day		29.50	30-40
1994 Summertime Pals	28-day		29.50	30
1994 A Gardening Trio	28-day		29.50	30
1994 Taking a Break	28-day		29.50	30

Council Of Nations - G. Perillo

YEAR ISSUE	EDITION LIMIT	YEAR RETD.	ISSUE PRICE	*QUOTE U.S.$
1992 Strength of the Sioux	14-day		29.50	45-55
1992 Pride of the Cheyenne	14-day		29.50	40-55
1992 Dignity of the Nez Parce	14-day		29.50	40-49
1992 Courage of the Arapaho	14-day		29.50	40-49
1992 Power of the Blackfoot	14-day		29.50	40-60
1992 Nobility of the Algonqui	14-day		29.50	40
1992 Wisdom of the Cherokee	14-day		29.50	40-55
1992 Boldness of the Seneca	14-day		29.50	40

Country Garden Cottages - E. Dertner

YEAR ISSUE	EDITION LIMIT	YEAR RETD.	ISSUE PRICE	*QUOTE U.S.$
1992 Riverbank Cottage	28-day		29.50	30-36
1992 Sunday Outing	28-day		29.50	30
1992 Shepherd's Cottage	28-day		29.50	30
1993 Daydream Cottage	28-day		29.50	30
1993 Garden Glorious	28-day		29.50	30
1993 This Side of Heaven	28-day		29.50	30
1993 Summer Symphony	28-day		29.50	30
1993 April Cottage	28-day		29.50	30

Country Kitties - G. Gerardi

YEAR ISSUE	EDITION LIMIT	YEAR RETD.	ISSUE PRICE	*QUOTE U.S.$
1989 Mischief Makers	14-day		24.50	55-75
1989 Table Manners	14-day		24.50	55-75
1989 Attic Attack	14-day		24.50	35-75
1989 Rock and Rollers	14-day		24.50	40
1989 Just For the Fern of It	14-day		24.50	48-65
1989 All Washed Up	14-day		24.50	45-75
1989 Stroller Derby	14-day		24.50	50
1989 Captive Audience	14-day		24.50	45-65

A Country Season of Horses - J.M. Vass

YEAR ISSUE	EDITION LIMIT	YEAR RETD.	ISSUE PRICE	*QUOTE U.S.$
1990 First Day of Spring	14-day		29.50	30-55
1990 Summer Splendor	14-day		29.50	30-55
1990 A Winter's Walk	14-day		29.50	30-55
1990 Autumn Grandeur	14-day		29.50	30-55
1990 Cliffside Beauty	14-day		29.50	30-55
1990 Frosty Morning	14-day		29.50	30-55
1990 Crisp Country Morning	14-day		29.50	30-55
1990 River Retreat	14-day		29.50	30-55

A Country Summer - N. Noel

YEAR ISSUE	EDITION LIMIT	YEAR RETD.	ISSUE PRICE	*QUOTE U.S.$
1985 Butterfly Beauty	10-day		29.50	30-36
1985 The Golden Puppy	10-day		29.50	30
1986 The Rocking Chair	10-day		29.50	30-36
1986 My Bunny	10-day		29.50	30-33
1988 The Piglet	10-day		29.50	30
1988 Teammates	10-day		29.50	30

Curious Kittens - B. Harrison

YEAR ISSUE	EDITION LIMIT	YEAR RETD.	ISSUE PRICE	*QUOTE U.S.$
1990 Rainy Day Friends	14-day		29.50	30-55
1990 Keeping in Step	14-day		29.50	30-55
1991 Delightful Discovery	14-day		29.50	30-55
1991 Chance Meeting	14-day		29.50	30-55
1991 All Wound Up	14-day		29.50	30-55
1991 Making Tracks	14-day		29.50	30-55
1991 Playing Cat and Mouse	14-day		29.50	30-55
1991 A Paw's in the Action	14-day		29.50	30-55
1992 Little Scholar	14-day		29.50	30-75
1992 Cat Burglar	14-day		29.50	30-55

Dale Earnhardt - Various

YEAR ISSUE	EDITION LIMIT	YEAR RETD.	ISSUE PRICE	*QUOTE U.S.$
1996 The Intimidator - S. Bass	28-day		35.00	35
1996 The Man in Black - R. Tanenbaum	28-day		35.00	35-45
1996 Silver Select - S. Bass	28-day		35.00	35-45
1996 Back in Black - R. Tanenbaum	28-day		35.00	35
1996 Ready to Rumble - R. Tanenbaum	28-day		35.00	35-45
1996 Always a Champion - R. Tanenbaum	28-day		35.00	35
1996 Look of a Winner - S. Bass	28-day		35.00	35
1996 Black Attack! - S. Bass	28-day		35.00	35

Dale Earnhardt II "The Future Is Now!" - Panorama Plates - S. Bass

YEAR ISSUE	EDITION LIMIT	YEAR RETD.	ISSUE PRICE	*QUOTE U.S.$
1999 Red Rocket!	28-day		39.95	40
1999 Black Bullet!	28-day		39.95	40
2000 New Journey!	28-day		39.95	40
2000 Leading The Way!	28-day		39.95	40
2000 A Heart On Fire!	28-day		39.95	40
2000 A Heart Of A Legend!	28-day		39.95	40

Dale Earnhardt II - S. Bass

YEAR ISSUE	EDITION LIMIT	YEAR RETD.	ISSUE PRICE	*QUOTE U.S.$
1998 Rising Son!	28-day		35.00	35
1998 Hooked Up!	28-day		35.00	35
1998 Finally First!	28-day		35.00	35
1999 Man On A Mission	28-day		35.00	35

Dale Earnhardt, Jr. - Various

YEAR ISSUE	EDITION LIMIT	YEAR RETD.	ISSUE PRICE	*QUOTE U.S.$
1999 A Tradition Begins - B. Tanenbaum	Open		35.00	35
1999 Finishing First! - M. Lacourciere	Open		35.00	35
1999 Red Hot Ride! - B. Tanenbaum	Open		35.00	35
1999 Born On 5/30/99! - M. Lacourciere	Open		35.00	35

Daughters Of The Sun - K. Thayer

YEAR ISSUE	EDITION LIMIT	YEAR RETD.	ISSUE PRICE	*QUOTE U.S.$
1993 Sun Dancer	28-day		29.50	36-45
1993 Shining Feather	28-day		29.50	30
1993 Delighted Dancer	28-day		29.50	30
1993 Evening Dancer	28-day		29.50	30
1993 A Secret Glance	28-day		29.50	30
1993 Chippewa Charmer	28-day		29.50	30
1994 Pride of the Yakima	28-day		29.50	30
1994 Radiant Beauty	28-day		29.50	30

Dear to My Heart - J. Hagara

YEAR ISSUE	EDITION LIMIT	YEAR RETD.	ISSUE PRICE	*QUOTE U.S.$
1990 Cathy	14-day		29.50	30-50
1990 Addie	14-day		29.50	30-50
1990 Jimmy	14-day		29.50	30-65
1990 Dacy	14-day		29.50	30-50
1990 Paul	14-day		29.50	30-50
1991 Shelly	14-day		29.50	30-50
1991 Jenny	14-day		29.50	30-50
1991 Joy	14-day		29.50	30-50

Dolphin Discovery - D. Queen

YEAR ISSUE	EDITION LIMIT	YEAR RETD.	ISSUE PRICE	*QUOTE U.S.$
1995 Sunrise Reverie	28-day		29.50	30
1995 Dolphin's Paradise	28-day		29.50	30
1995 Coral Cove	28-day		29.50	30
1995 Undersea Journey	28-day		29.50	30
1995 Dolphin Canyon	28-day		29.50	30
1995 Coral Garden	28-day		29.50	30
1996 Dolphin Duo	28-day		29.50	30
1996 Underwater Tranquility	28-day		29.50	30

Dreamsicles - K. Haynes

YEAR ISSUE	EDITION LIMIT	YEAR RETD.	ISSUE PRICE	*QUOTE U.S.$
1994 The Flying Lesson	28-day		19.50	20-35
1995 By the Light of the Moon	28-day		19.50	25-29
1995 The Recital	28-day		19.50	30
1995 Heavenly Pirouettes	28-day		19.50	40
1995 Blossoms and Butterflies	28-day		19.50	30
1995 Love's Shy Glance	28-day		19.50	20-30
1996 Wishing Upon a Star	28-day		19.50	20
1996 Rainy Day Friends	28-day		19.50	20-22
1996 Starboats Ahoy!	28-day		19.50	40
1996 Teeter Tots	28-day		19.50	30
1996 Star Magic	28-day		19.50	20
1996 Heavenly Tea Party	28-day		19.50	22-30

Dreamsicles Christmas Annual Sculptural - K. Haynes

YEAR ISSUE	EDITION LIMIT	YEAR RETD.	ISSUE PRICE	*QUOTE U.S.$
1996 The Finishing Touches	Closed	1997	39.95	40-50

Dreamsicles Heaven Sent - N/A

YEAR ISSUE	EDITION LIMIT	YEAR RETD.	ISSUE PRICE	*QUOTE U.S.$
1996 Quiet Blessings	28-day		29.95	30
1996 A Heartfelt Embrace	28-day		29.95	30
1996 Earth's Blessings	28-day		29.95	30
1996 A Moment In Dreamland	28-day		29.95	30
1996 Sew Cuddly	28-day		29.95	30
1996 Homemade With Love	28-day		29.95	30
1996 A Sweet Treat	28-day		29.95	30
1996 Pampered And Pretty	28-day		29.95	30

Dreamsicles Home Sweet Home Sculptural - K. Haynes

YEAR ISSUE	EDITION LIMIT	YEAR RETD.	ISSUE PRICE	*QUOTE U.S.$
1997 We Love Gardening	Open		39.95	40
1998 Homemade From the Heart	Open		39.95	40
1998 Love Is the Thread of Life	Open		39.95	40
1998 We Love Sharing	Open		39.95	40

Dreamsicles Life's Little Blessings - K. Haynes

YEAR ISSUE	EDITION LIMIT	YEAR RETD.	ISSUE PRICE	*QUOTE U.S.$
1995 Happiness	28-day		29.95	30
1996 Peace	28-day		29.95	30
1996 Love	28-day		29.95	30
1996 Creativity	28-day		29.95	30
1996 Friendship	28-day		29.95	30
1996 Knowledge	28-day		29.95	30
1996 Hope	28-day		29.95	30
1996 Faith	28-day		29.95	30

Dreamsicles Love & Lace - N/A

YEAR ISSUE	EDITION LIMIT	YEAR RETD.	ISSUE PRICE	*QUOTE U.S.$
1997 Stolen Kiss	Open		19.95	20
1997 Sharing Hearts	Open		19.95	20
1997 Love Letters	Open		19.95	20
1997 I Love You	Open		19.95	20
1997 Daisies & Dreamsicles	Open		19.95	20
1997 First Love	Open		19.95	20
1997 Perfect Match	Open		19.95	20
1997 Hand In Hand	Open		19.95	20

Dreamsicles Ornamental Mini Plates - K. Haynes

YEAR ISSUE	EDITION LIMIT	YEAR RETD.	ISSUE PRICE	*QUOTE U.S.$
1996 The Flying Lesson	28-day		19.95	20
1996 By The Light of the Moon	28-day		set	set
1996 The Recital	28-day		19.95	20
1996 Heavenly Pirouettes	28-day		set	set
1997 Blossoms and Butterflies	28-day		19.95	20
1997 Love's Shy Glance	28-day		set	set
1997 Wishing on a Star	28-day		19.95	20
1997 Rainy Day Friends	28-day		set	set
1997 Starboats Ahoy	28-day		19.95	20
1997 Teeter Tots	28-day		set	set
1997 Star Magic	28-day		19.95	20
1997 A Heavenly Tea Party	28-day		set	set

Dreamsicles Sculptural - N/A

YEAR ISSUE	EDITION LIMIT	YEAR RETD.	ISSUE PRICE	*QUOTE U.S.$
1995 The Flying Lesson	Open		37.50	38
1996 By The Light of the Moon	Open		37.50	38
1996 The Recital	Open		37.50	38
1996 Teeter Tots	Open		37.50	38
1996 Poetry In Motion	Open		37.50	38
1996 Rock-A-Bye Dreamsicles	Open		37.50	38
1996 The Birth Certificate	Open		37.50	38
1996 Sharing Hearts	Open		37.50	38

Dreamsicles Special Friends - K. Haynes

YEAR ISSUE	EDITION LIMIT	YEAR RETD.	ISSUE PRICE	*QUOTE U.S.$
1995 A Hug From the Heart	28-day		29.95	30
1995 Heaven's Little Helper	28-day		29.95	30
1995 Bless Us All	28-day		29.95	30
1996 Love's Gentle Touch	28-day		29.95	30
1996 The Best Gift of All	28-day		29.95	30
1996 A Heavenly Hoorah!	28-day		29.95	30
1996 A Love Like No Other	28-day		29.95	30
1996 Cuddle Up	28-day		29.95	30

Dreamsicles Special Friends Sculptural - K. Haynes

YEAR ISSUE	EDITION LIMIT	YEAR RETD.	ISSUE PRICE	*QUOTE U.S.$
1995 Heaven's Little Helper	Open		37.50	38
1996 A Hug From The Heart	Open		37.50	38
1996 Bless Us All	Open		37.50	38
1996 The Best Gift of All	Open		37.50	38
1996 A Heavenly Hoorah!	Open		37.50	38
1996 A Love Like No Other	Open		37.50	38
1997 Cuddle Up	Open		45.00	45
1997 Love's Gentle Touch	Open		45.00	45

Dreamsicles Sweethearts - K. Haynes

YEAR ISSUE	EDITION LIMIT	YEAR RETD.	ISSUE PRICE	*QUOTE U.S.$
1996 Stolen Kiss	28-day		35.00	35
1996 Sharing Hearts	28-day		35.00	35
1996 Love Letters	28-day		35.00	35
1996 I Love You	28-day		35.00	35
1996 Daisies & Dreamsicles	28-day		35.00	35
1997 First Love	28-day		35.00	35
1997 Perfect Match	28-day		35.00	35
1997 Hand in Hand	28-day		35.00	35

Drivers of Victory Lane - R. Tanenbaum

YEAR ISSUE	EDITION LIMIT	YEAR RETD.	ISSUE PRICE	*QUOTE U.S.$
1994 Bill Elliott #11	28-day		29.50	40-55
1994 Jeff Gordon #24	28-day		29.50	30-40
1994 Rusty Wallace #2	28-day		29.50	30-40
1995 Geoff Bodine #7	28-day		29.50	26-40
1995 Dale Earnhardt #3	28-day		29.50	30-40
1996 Sterling Martin #4	28-day		29.50	30-40
1996 Terry Labonte #5	28-day		29.50	26-40
1996 Ken Scharder #25	28-day		29.50	30-40
1996 Jeff Gordon #24	28-day		29.50	30-40
1996 Bill Elliott #94	28-day		29.50	40-55
1996 Rusty Wallace #2	28-day		29.50	30-40
1996 Mark Martin #6	28-day		29.50	30-40
1996 Dale Earnhardt #3	28-day		29.50	30-40

Earnhardt Championship Plates - S. Bass

YEAR ISSUE	EDITION LIMIT	YEAR RETD.	ISSUE PRICE	*QUOTE U.S.$
1999 The Magnificent Seven!	Open		37.50	38

Easyrider Close Up - M. Lacourciere

YEAR ISSUE	EDITION LIMIT	YEAR RETD.	ISSUE PRICE	*QUOTE U.S.$
1997 Brotherhood of Honor	28-day		35.00	35
1997 Sounds of Freedom	28-day		35.00	35
1997 Alamo Sundown	28-day		35.00	35
1997 We The People	28-day		35.00	35
1997 Dawn's Early Light	28-day		35.00	35
1997 Harvest Cruise	28-day		35.00	35
1997 Gambler's Ride	28-day		35.00	35
1997 Brother To Brother	28-day		35.00	35

Easyrider Mini Plates - D. Mann

YEAR ISSUE	EDITION LIMIT	YEAR RETD.	ISSUE PRICE	*QUOTE U.S.$
1998 Brotherhood of Biking	Open		12.95	13
1998 Ghost of the West	Open		12.95	13
1998 Ghost of the Round Table	Open		12.95	13
1998 Ghost of the North	Open		12.95	13
1998 Ghost of the Moutain Man	Open		12.95	13
1998 Ghost of the Sea	Open		12.95	13
1998 Ghost From the Past	Open		12.95	13
1998 Easyriders 25th Anniversary	Open		12.95	13
1998 Silver Anniversary Tribute	Open		12.95	13
1998 Ghost of the Saloon	Open		12.95	13

Easyriders - M. Lacourciere

YEAR ISSUE	EDITION LIMIT	YEAR RETD.	ISSUE PRICE	*QUOTE U.S.$
1995 American Classic	28-day		29.95	30-65
1995 Symbols of Freedom	28-day		29.95	30-55
1996 Patriot's Pride	28-day		29.95	40-55
1996 The Way of the West	28-day		29.95	30-55
1996 Revival of an Era	28-day		29.95	30-55
1996 Hollywood Style	28-day		29.95	30-55
1996 Vietnam Express	28-day		29.95	30-55
1996 Las Vegas	28-day		29.95	40-60
1996 Beach Cruising	28-day		29.95	30-55
1996 New Orleans Scene	28-day		29.95	30-60

Enchanted Seascapes - J. Enright

YEAR ISSUE	EDITION LIMIT	YEAR RETD.	ISSUE PRICE	*QUOTE U.S.$
1993 Sanctuary of the Dolphin	28-day		29.50	50-57
1994 Rhapsody of Hope	28-day		29.50	30-55
1994 Oasis of the Gods	28-day		29.50	30
1994 Sphere of Life	28-day		29.50	30
1994 Edge of Time	28-day		29.50	30
1994 Sea of Light	28-day		29.50	30
1994 Lost Beneath the Blue	28-day		29.50	30
1994 Blue Paradise	28-day		29.50	30-100
1995 Morning Odyssey	28-day		29.50	30
1995 Paradise Cove	28-day		29.50	30-100

English Country Cottages - M. Bell

YEAR ISSUE	EDITION LIMIT	YEAR RETD.	ISSUE PRICE	*QUOTE U.S.$
1990 Periwinkle Tea Room	14-day		29.50	60-75
1991 Gamekeeper's Cottage	14-day		29.50	60-75
1991 Ginger Cottage	14-day		29.50	60
1991 Larkspur Cottage	14-day		29.50	45-60
1991 The Chaplain's Garden	14-day		29.50	33-60

*Quotes have been rounded up to nearest dollar

YEAR ISSUE	EDITION LIMIT	YEAR RETD.	ISSUE PRICE	*QUOTE U.S.$
1991 Lorna Doone Cottage	14-day		29.50	45-60
1991 Murrle Cottage	14-day		29.50	36-60
1991 Lullabye Cottage	14-day		29.50	30-60

Eternal Wishes of Good Fortune - Shuho

YEAR ISSUE	EDITION LIMIT	YEAR RETD.	ISSUE PRICE	*QUOTE U.S.$
1983 Friendship	10-day		34.95	35-50
1983 Purity and Perfection	10-day		34.95	35-50
1983 Illustrious Offspring	10-day		34.95	35-50
1983 Longevity	10-day		34.95	35-50
1983 Youth	10-day		34.95	35-50
1983 Immortality	10-day		34.95	35-50
1983 Marital Bliss	10-day		34.95	35-50
1983 Love	10-day		34.95	35-50
1983 Peace	10-day		34.95	35-50
1983 Beauty	10-day		34.95	35-50
1983 Fertility	10-day		34.95	35-50
1983 Fortitude	10-day		34.95	35-50

Exotic Tigers of Asia - K. Ottinger

YEAR ISSUE	EDITION LIMIT	YEAR RETD.	ISSUE PRICE	*QUOTE U.S.$
1995 Lord of the Rainforest	28-day		29.50	30-40
1995 Snow King	28-day		29.50	30-40
1995 Ruler of the Wetlands	28-day		29.50	30-40
1996 Majestic Vigil	28-day		29.50	30-40
1996 Keeper of the Jungle	28-day		29.50	30-40
1996 Eyes of the Jungle	28-day		29.50	30-40
1996 Sovereign Ruler	28-day		29.50	30-40
1996 Lord of the Lowlands	28-day		29.50	30-40

Familiar Spirits - D. Wright

YEAR ISSUE	EDITION LIMIT	YEAR RETD.	ISSUE PRICE	*QUOTE U.S.$
1996 Faithful Guardians	28-day		29.95	30
1996 Sharing Nature's Innocence	28-day		29.95	30
1996 Trusted Friend	28-day		29.95	30
1996 A Friendship Begins	28-day		29.95	30
1996 Winter Homage	28-day		29.95	30
1996 The Blessing	28-day		29.95	30
1996 Healing Powers	28-day		29.95	30

Farmyard Friends - J. Lamb

YEAR ISSUE	EDITION LIMIT	YEAR RETD.	ISSUE PRICE	*QUOTE U.S.$
1992 Mistaken Identity	28-day	1994	29.50	30-40
1992 Little Cowhands	28-day	1994	29.50	30
1993 Shreading the Evidence	28-day	1994	29.50	30
1993 Partners in Crime	28-day	1994	29.50	30
1993 Fowl Play	28-day	1994	29.50	30
1993 Follow The Leader	28-day	1994	29.50	36-40
1993 Pony Tales	28-day	1994	29.50	30
1993 An Apple A Day	28-day	1994	29.50	30-40

Favorite American Songbirds - D. O'Driscoll

YEAR ISSUE	EDITION LIMIT	YEAR RETD.	ISSUE PRICE	*QUOTE U.S.$
1989 Blue Jays of Spring	14-day		29.50	40-55
1989 Red Cardinals of Winter	14-day		29.50	40-55
1989 Robins & Apple Blossoms	14-day		29.50	40-55
1989 Goldfinches of Summer	14-day		29.50	40-55
1990 Autumn Chickadees	14-day		29.50	40-55
1990 Bluebirds and Morning Glories	14-day		29.50	40-55
1990 Tufted Titmouse and Holly	14-day		29.50	40-55
1991 Carolina Wrens of Spring	14-day		29.50	40-55

Favorite Old Testament Stories - S. Butcher

YEAR ISSUE	EDITION LIMIT	YEAR RETD.	ISSUE PRICE	*QUOTE U.S.$
1994 Jacob's Dream	28-day		35.00	35
1995 The Baby Moses	28-day		35.00	35
1995 Esther's Gift To Her People	28-day		35.00	35-75
1995 A Prayer For Victory	28-day		35.00	35
1995 Where You Go, I Will Go	28-day		35.00	35-75
1995 A Prayer Answered, A Promise Kept	28-day		35.00	35
1996 Joseph Sold Into Slavery	28-day		35.00	35
1996 Daniel In the Lion's Den	28-day		35.00	35
1996 Noah And The Ark	28-day		35.00	35

The Fierce And The Free - F. McCarthy

YEAR ISSUE	EDITION LIMIT	YEAR RETD.	ISSUE PRICE	*QUOTE U.S.$
1992 Big Medicine	28-day		29.50	30-45
1993 Land of the Winter Hawk	28-day		29.50	30
1993 Warrior of Savage Splendor	28-day		29.50	30-85
1994 War Party	28-day		29.50	30
1994 The Challenge	28-day		29.50	30
1994 Out of the Rising Mist	28-day		29.50	30-45
1994 The Ambush	28-day		29.50	30-35
1994 Dangerous Crossing	28-day		29.50	30

Flower Festivals of Japan - N. Hara

YEAR ISSUE	EDITION LIMIT	YEAR RETD.	ISSUE PRICE	*QUOTE U.S.$
1985 Chrysanthemum	10-day		45.00	45
1985 Hollyhock	10-day		45.00	45
1985 Plum Blossom	10-day		45.00	45
1985 Morning Glory	10-day		45.00	45
1985 Cherry Blossom	10-day		45.00	45
1985 Iris	10-day		45.00	45
1985 Lily	10-day		45.00	45
1985 Peach Blossom	10-day		45.00	45

Forging New Frontiers - J. Deneen

YEAR ISSUE	EDITION LIMIT	YEAR RETD.	ISSUE PRICE	*QUOTE U.S.$
1994 The Race is On	28-day		29.50	30-39
1994 Big Boy	28-day		29.50	30-39
1994 Cresting the Summit	28-day		29.50	30-36
1994 Spring Roundup	28-day		29.50	30-35
1994 Winter in the Rockies	28-day		29.50	30
1994 High Country Logging	28-day		29.50	30
1994 Confrontation	28-day		29.50	30
1994 A Welcome Sight	28-day		29.50	30

Four Seasons of the Eagle - S. Hardock

YEAR ISSUE	EDITION LIMIT	YEAR RETD.	ISSUE PRICE	*QUOTE U.S.$
1997 Winter Solstice	Open		39.95	40
1997 Spring Awakening	Open		39.95	40
1997 Summer's Glory	Open		39.95	40
1997 Autumn Bounty	Open		39.95	40
1998 Winter's Flight	Open		39.95	40
1998 Spring's Journey	Open		39.95	40
1998 Summer's Splendor	Open		39.95	40
1998 Autumn Nesting	Open		39.95	40

A Garden Song - M. Hanson

YEAR ISSUE	EDITION LIMIT	YEAR RETD.	ISSUE PRICE	*QUOTE U.S.$
1994 Winter's Splendor	28-day		29.50	30
1994 In Full Bloom	28-day		29.50	30
1994 Golden Glories	28-day		29.50	30
1995 Autumn's Elegance	28-day		29.50	30
1995 First Snowfall	28-day		29.50	30
1995 Robins in Spring	28-day		29.50	30
1995 Summer's Glow	28-day		29.50	30
1995 Fall's Serenade	28-day		29.50	30
1996 Sounds of Winter	28-day		29.50	30
1996 Springtime Haven	28-day		29.50	30

Gardens of the Orient - S. Suetomi

YEAR ISSUE	EDITION LIMIT	YEAR RETD.	ISSUE PRICE	*QUOTE U.S.$
1983 Flowering of Spring	10-day		19.50	20
1983 Festival of May	10-day		19.50	20
1983 Cherry Blossom Brocade	10-day		19.50	20
1983 Winter's Repose	10-day		19.50	20
1983 Garden Sanctuary	10-day		19.50	20
1983 Summer's Glory	10-day		19.50	20
1983 June's Creation	10-day		19.50	20
1983 New Year's Dawn	10-day		19.50	20
1983 Autumn Serenity	10-day		19.50	20
1983 Harvest Morning	10-day		19.50	20
1983 Tranquil Pond	10-day		19.50	20
1983 Morning Song	10-day		19.50	20

Glory of Christ - C. Micarelli

YEAR ISSUE	EDITION LIMIT	YEAR RETD.	ISSUE PRICE	*QUOTE U.S.$
1992 The Ascension	48-day		29.50	50-75
1992 Jesus Teaching	48-day		29.50	30
1993 Last Supper	48-day		29.50	30
1993 The Nativity	48-day		29.50	30
1993 The Baptism of Christ	48-day		29.50	30
1993 Jesus Heals the Sick	48-day		29.50	30
1994 Jesus Walks on Water	48-day		29.50	30
1994 Descent From the Cross	48-day		29.50	30

Glory of the Game - T. Fogarty

YEAR ISSUE	EDITION LIMIT	YEAR RETD.	ISSUE PRICE	*QUOTE U.S.$
1994 "Hank Aaron's Record-Breaking Home Run"	28-day		29.50	30
1994 "Bobby Thomson's Shot Heard 'Round the World"	28-day		29.50	30
1994 1969 Miracle Mets	28-day		29.50	30
1995 Reggie Jackson: Mr. October	28-day		29.50	30
1995 Don Larsen's Perfect World	28-day		29.50	30
1995 Babe Ruth's Called Shot	28-day		29.50	30-39
1995 Wille Mays: Greatest Catch	28-day		29.50	30
1995 Bill Mazeroski's Series	28-day		29.50	30
1996 Mickey Mantle's Tape Measure Home Run	28-day		29.50	30-35

The Golden Age of American Railroads - T. Xaras

YEAR ISSUE	EDITION LIMIT	YEAR RETD.	ISSUE PRICE	*QUOTE U.S.$
1991 The Blue Comet	14-day		29.50	50-80
1991 The Morning Local	14-day		29.50	60-75
1991 The Pennsylvania K-4	14-day		29.50	70-75
1991 Above the Canyon	14-day		29.50	62-65
1991 Portrait in Steam	14-day		29.50	62-80
1991 The Santa Fe Super Chief	14-day		29.50	84-100
1991 The Big Boy	14-day		29.50	60-100
1991 The Empire Builder	14-day		29.50	75-84
1992 An American Classic	14-day		29.50	60-75
1992 Final Destination	14-day		29.50	60-75

Golden Discoveries - L. Budge

YEAR ISSUE	EDITION LIMIT	YEAR RETD.	ISSUE PRICE	*QUOTE U.S.$
1995 Boot Bandits	28-day		29.95	30
1995 Hiding the Evidence	28-day		29.95	30
1995 Decoy Dilemma	28-day		29.95	30
1995 Fishing for Dinner	28-day		29.95	30
1996 Lunchtime Companions	28-day		29.95	30
1996 Friend or Foe?	28-day		29.95	30

Golden Puppy Portraits - P. Braun

YEAR ISSUE	EDITION LIMIT	YEAR RETD.	ISSUE PRICE	*QUOTE U.S.$
1994 Do Not Disturb!	28-day		29.50	30-39
1995 Teething Time	28-day		29.50	30-35
1995 Table Manners	28-day		29.50	30-75
1995 A Golden Bouquet	28-day		29.50	30-35
1995 Time For Bed	28-day		29.50	30-35
1995 Bathtime Blues	28-day		29.50	30-35
1996 Spinning a Yarn	28-day		29.50	30-35
1996 Partytime Puppy	28-day		29.50	30-35

Good Sports - J. Lamb

YEAR ISSUE	EDITION LIMIT	YEAR RETD.	ISSUE PRICE	*QUOTE U.S.$
1990 Wide Retriever	14-day	1994	29.50	45-50
1990 Double Play	14-day	1994	29.50	50-59
1990 Hole in One	14-day	1994	29.50	45
1990 The Bass Masters	14-day	1994	29.50	45-75
1990 Spotted on the Sideline	14-day	1994	29.50	40-45
1990 Slap Shot	14-day	1994	29.50	40-45
1991 Net Play	14-day	1994	29.50	34-45
1991 Bassetball	14-day	1994	29.50	40-52
1992 Boxer Rebellion	14-day	1994	29.50	33-40
1992 Great Try	14-day	1994	29.50	40

Grateful Dead Album Covers - S. Mouse

YEAR ISSUE	EDITION LIMIT	YEAR RETD.	ISSUE PRICE	*QUOTE U.S.$
1999 Cats Under The Stars	28-day		35.00	35
1999 Cyclops	28-day		35.00	35
1999 Terrapin Station	28-day		35.00	35
1999 Mars Hotel (part 1)	28-day		35.00	35
1999 Ice Cream Kid	28-day		35.00	35
1999 Mars Hotel (part 2)	28-day		35.00	35
1999 Rainbow Foot	28-day		35.00	35

The Grateful Dead Art by Stanley Mouse - S. Mouse

YEAR ISSUE	EDITION LIMIT	YEAR RETD.	ISSUE PRICE	*QUOTE U.S.$
1997 One More Saturday Night	28-day		29.95	30-49
1997 The Grateful Dead Family Album	28-day		29.95	30-49
1998 Sunset Jester	28-day		29.95	30-55
1998 Lightning Rose	28-day		29.95	30-55
1998 Europe 81	28-day		29.95	30-49
1998 Timeless	28-day		29.95	30-49
1998 Dancing Jester	28-day		29.95	30-100
1998 Rose Photographer	28-day		29.95	30-100

Graveriders - D. Mann

YEAR ISSUE	EDITION LIMIT	YEAR RETD.	ISSUE PRICE	*QUOTE U.S.$
1999 Flyin' Flamin' Phantom	Open		35.00	35
1999 Skull Rider	Open		35.00	35
1999 Dead Mann's Hand	Open		35.00	35
1999 Dem Bones Dem Bones	Open		35.00	35
1999 Breath of Death	Open		35.00	35
1999 Skeleton Tatoo	Open		35.00	35

Great Fighter Planes Of World War II - R. Waddey

YEAR ISSUE	EDITION LIMIT	YEAR RETD.	ISSUE PRICE	*QUOTE U.S.$
1992 Old Crow	14-day		29.50	40-48
1992 Big Hog	14-day		29.50	40-48
1992 P-47 Thunderbolt	14-day		29.50	30-35
1992 P-40 Flying Tiger	14-day		29.50	30-38
1992 F4F Wildcat	14-day		29.50	30-35
1992 P-38F Lightning	14-day		29.50	30-40
1993 F6F Hellcat	14-day		29.50	35-40
1993 P-39M Airacobra	14-day		29.50	30-35
1995 Memphis Belle	14-day		29.50	30-35
1995 The Dragon and His Tail	14-day		29.50	30-43
1995 Big Beautiful Doll	14-day		29.50	30-75
1995 Bats Out of Hell	14-day		29.50	30-75

Great Mammals of the Sea - Wyland

YEAR ISSUE	EDITION LIMIT	YEAR RETD.	ISSUE PRICE	*QUOTE U.S.$
1991 Orca Trio	14-day		35.00	40-65
1991 Hawaii Dolphins	14-day		35.00	45-55
1991 Orca Journey	14-day		35.00	40
1991 Dolphin Paradise	14-day		35.00	45-49
1991 Children of the Sea	14-day		35.00	45-60
1991 Kissing Dolphins	14-day		35.00	50-85
1991 Islands	14-day		35.00	45-60
1991 Orcas	14-day		35.00	45-50

The Greatest Show on Earth - F. Moody

YEAR ISSUE	EDITION LIMIT	YEAR RETD.	ISSUE PRICE	*QUOTE U.S.$
1981 Clowns	10-day		30.00	35-45
1981 Elephants	10-day		30.00	30-45
1981 Aerialists	10-day		30.00	39
1981 Great Parade	10-day		30.00	30-45
1981 Midway	10-day		30.00	30-55
1981 Equestrians	10-day		30.00	30-55
1982 Lion Tamer	10-day		30.00	30-45
1982 Grande Finale	10-day		30.00	30-45

Growing Up Together - P. Brooks

YEAR ISSUE	EDITION LIMIT	YEAR RETD.	ISSUE PRICE	*QUOTE U.S.$
1990 My Very Best Friends	14-day		29.50	30-36
1990 Tea for Two	14-day		29.50	30-35
1990 Tender Loving Care	14-day		29.50	30-36
1990 Picnic Pals	14-day		29.50	30
1991 Newfound Friends	14-day		29.50	30
1991 Kitten Caboodle	14-day		29.50	30
1991 Fishing Buddies	14-day		29.50	30-39
1991 Bedtime Blessings	14-day		29.50	30

The Historic Railways - T. Xaras

YEAR ISSUE	EDITION LIMIT	YEAR RETD.	ISSUE PRICE	*QUOTE U.S.$
1995 Harper's Ferry	28-day		29.95	30-45
1995 Horseshoe Curve	28-day		29.95	30-45
1995 Kentucky's Red River	28-day		29.95	30-45
1995 Sherman Hill Challenger	28-day		29.95	30-45
1996 New York Central's 4-6-4 Hudson	28-day		29.95	30-45
1996 Rails By The Seashore	28-day		29.95	30-45
1996 Steam in the High Sierras	28-day		29.95	30-45
1996 Evening Departure	28-day		29.95	30-45

The I Love Lucy Plate Collection - J. Kritz

YEAR ISSUE	EDITION LIMIT	YEAR RETD.	ISSUE PRICE	*QUOTE U.S.$
1989 California, Here We Come	14-day	1992	29.50	120-225
1989 It's Just Like Candy	14-day	1992	29.50	195-275
1990 The Big Squeeze	14-day	1992	29.50	165-250
1990 Eating the Evidence	14-day	1992	29.50	200-295
1990 Two of a Kind	14-day	1992	29.50	200-275
1991 Queen of the Gypsies	14-day	1992	29.50	195-269
1992 Night at the Copa	14-day	1992	29.50	150-200
1992 A Rising Problem	14-day	1992	29.50	130-225

James Dean Commemorative Issue - T. Blackshear

YEAR ISSUE	EDITION LIMIT	YEAR RETD.	ISSUE PRICE	*QUOTE U.S.$
1991 James Dean	14-day		37.50	100

James Dean The Legend - M. Weistling

YEAR ISSUE	EDITION LIMIT	YEAR RETD.	ISSUE PRICE	*QUOTE U.S.$
1992 Unforgotten Rebel	28-day		29.50	100

Japanese Floral Calendar - Shuho/Kage

YEAR ISSUE	EDITION LIMIT	YEAR RETD.	ISSUE PRICE	*QUOTE U.S.$
1981 New Year's Day	10-day		32.50	33-40
1982 Early Spring	10-day		32.50	33-40
1982 Spring	10-day		32.50	33-40
1982 Girl's Doll Day Festival	10-day		32.50	33-40
1982 Buddha's Birthday	10-day		32.50	33-40
1982 Early Summer	10-day		32.50	33-40
1982 Boy's Doll Day Festival	10-day		32.50	33-40
1982 Summer	10-day		32.50	33-40
1982 Autumn	10-day		32.50	33-40
1983 Festival of the Full Moon	10-day		32.50	33-40
1983 Late Autumn	10-day		32.50	33-40
1983 Winter	10-day		32.50	33-65

Jeff Gordon - Various

YEAR ISSUE	EDITION LIMIT	YEAR RETD.	ISSUE PRICE	*QUOTE U.S.$
1996 On The Warpath - S. Bass	28-day		35.00	35

*Quotes have been rounded up to nearest dollar

PLATES/PLAQUES

YEAR ISSUE	EDITION LIMIT	YEAR RETD.	ISSUE PRICE	*QUOTE U.S.$
1996 Headed to Victory Lane - R. Tanenbaum	28-day		35.00	35-45
1996 Gordon Takes the Title - S. Bass	28-day		35.00	35
1996 From Winner to Champion - R. Tanenbaum	28-day		35.00	35-45

Jeff Gordon Championship Plate - R. Tanenbaum

YEAR ISSUE	EDITION LIMIT	YEAR RETD.	ISSUE PRICE	*QUOTE U.S.$
1998 A Champion's Year	Open		35.00	35

Jeff Gordon Panorama - B. Tanenbaum

YEAR ISSUE	EDITION LIMIT	YEAR RETD.	ISSUE PRICE	*QUOTE U.S.$
1999 Look of a Warrior	Open		39.95	40
1999 Heart of a Warrior	Open		39.95	40
1999 A Warrior's Ride	Open		39.95	40
1999 Foundation of a Warrior	Open		39.95	40

The Jeweled Hummingbirds - J. Landenberger

YEAR ISSUE	EDITION LIMIT	YEAR RETD.	ISSUE PRICE	*QUOTE U.S.$
1989 Ruby-throated Hummingbirds	14-day		37.50	45-50
1989 Great Sapphire Wing Hummingbirds	14-day		37.50	45-50
1989 Ruby-Topaz Hummingbirds	14-day		37.50	45-50
1989 Andean Emerald Hummingbirds	14-day		37.50	45-50
1989 Garnet-throated Hummingbirds	14-day		37.50	45-50
1989 Blue-Headed Sapphire Hummingbirds	14-day		37.50	45-50
1989 Pearl Coronet Hummingbirds	14-day		37.50	45-50
1989 Amethyst-throated Sunangels	14-day		37.50	35-45

Joe Montana - Various

YEAR ISSUE	EDITION LIMIT	YEAR RETD.	ISSUE PRICE	*QUOTE U.S.$
1996 40,000 Yards - R. Tanenbaum	28-day		35.00	35-45
1996 Finding a Way to Win - A. Catalano	28-day		35.00	35-45
1996 Comeback Kid - A. Catalano	28-day		35.00	35-55
1996 Chief on the Field - Petronella	28-day		35.00	35-45

Kitten Classics - P. Cooper

YEAR ISSUE	EDITION LIMIT	YEAR RETD.	ISSUE PRICE	*QUOTE U.S.$
1985 Cat Nap	14-day		29.50	30
1985 Purrfect Treasure	14-day		29.50	30-55
1985 Wild Flower	14-day		29.50	30-45
1985 Birdwatcher	14-day		29.50	30-45
1985 Tiger's Fancy	14-day		29.50	33-55
1985 Country Kitty	14-day		29.50	33-55
1985 Little Rascal	14-day		29.50	30-45
1985 First Prize	14-day		29.50	30-55

Knick Knack Kitty Cat Sculptural - L. Yencho

YEAR ISSUE	EDITION LIMIT	YEAR RETD.	ISSUE PRICE	*QUOTE U.S.$
1996 Kittens in the Cupboard	Open		39.95	40
1996 Kittens in the Cushion	Open		39.95	40
1996 Kittens in the Plant	Open		39.95	40
1996 Kittens in the Yarn	Open		39.95	40

The Last Warriors - C. Ren

YEAR ISSUE	EDITION LIMIT	YEAR RETD.	ISSUE PRICE	*QUOTE U.S.$
1993 Winter of '41	28-day		29.50	35-45
1993 Morning of Reckoning	28-day		29.50	35
1993 Twilights Last Gleaming	28-day		29.50	35
1993 Lone Winter Journey	28-day		29.50	35-45
1994 Victory's Reward	28-day		29.50	30-35
1994 Solitary Hunter	28-day		29.50	35
1994 Solemn Reflection	28-day		29.50	35
1994 Confronting Danger	28-day		29.50	35
1995 Moment of Contemplation	28-day		29.50	35-60
1995 The Last Sunset	28-day		29.50	35

The Legend of Father Christmas - V. Dezerin

YEAR ISSUE	EDITION LIMIT	YEAR RETD.	ISSUE PRICE	*QUOTE U.S.$
1994 The Return of Father Christmas	28-day		29.50	30
1994 Gifts From Father Christmas	28-day		29.50	30
1994 The Feast of the Holiday	28-day		29.50	30
1995 Christmas Day Visitors	28-day		29.50	30
1995 Decorating the Tree	28-day		29.50	30
1995 The Snow Sculpture	28-day		29.50	30
1995 Skating on the Pond	28-day		29.50	30
1995 Holy Night	28-day		29.50	30

Legendary Warriors - M. Gentry

YEAR ISSUE	EDITION LIMIT	YEAR RETD.	ISSUE PRICE	*QUOTE U.S.$
1995 White Quiver and Scout	28-day		29.95	30
1995 Lakota Rendezvous	28-day		29.95	30
1995 Crazy Horse	28-day		29.95	30
1995 Sitting Bull's Vision	28-day		29.95	30
1996 Crazy Horse	28-day		29.95	30
1996 Sitting Bull's Vision	28-day		29.95	30
1996 Noble Surrender	28-day		29.95	30
1996 Sioux Thunder	28-day		29.95	30
1996 Eagle Dancer	28-day		29.95	30
1996 The Trap	28-day		29.95	30

Let Freedom Ring (Landscapes) - S. Hardock

YEAR ISSUE	EDITION LIMIT	YEAR RETD.	ISSUE PRICE	*QUOTE U.S.$
1999 Land of Liberty	95-day		39.95	40
1999 Land of Reverence	95-day		39.95	40
1999 Land of Independence	95-day		39.95	40

Let Freedom Ring (Monuments) - S. Hardock

YEAR ISSUE	EDITION LIMIT	YEAR RETD.	ISSUE PRICE	*QUOTE U.S.$
1999 Liberty	95-day		39.95	40
1999 Reverence	95-day		39.95	40

A Lisi Martin Christmas - L. Martin

YEAR ISSUE	EDITION LIMIT	YEAR RETD.	ISSUE PRICE	*QUOTE U.S.$
1992 Santa's Littlest Reindeer	28-day		29.50	35-49
1993 Not A Creature Was Stirring	28-day		29.50	35-55
1993 Christmas Dreams	28-day		29.50	35-55
1993 The Christmas Story	28-day		29.50	35-55
1993 Trimming The Tree	28-day		29.50	35-55
1993 A Taste Of The Holidays	28-day		29.50	35-49
1993 The Night Before Christmas	28-day		29.50	35-55
1993 Christmas Watch	28-day		29.50	35-55
1995 Christmas Presence	28-day		29.50	35-55
1995 Nose to Nose	28-day		29.50	35-49

Little Fawns of the Forest - R. Manning

YEAR ISSUE	EDITION LIMIT	YEAR RETD.	ISSUE PRICE	*QUOTE U.S.$
1995 In the Morning Light	28-day		29.95	30
1995 Cool Reflections	28-day		29.95	30
1995 Nature's Lesson	28-day		29.95	30
1996 A Friendship Blossoms	28-day		29.95	30
1996 Innocent Companions	28-day		29.95	30
1996 New Life, New Day	28-day		29.95	30

Little House on the Prairie - E. Christopherson

YEAR ISSUE	EDITION LIMIT	YEAR RETD.	ISSUE PRICE	*QUOTE U.S.$
1986 Founder's Day Picnic	10-day		29.50	60
1986 The Woman's Harvest	10-day		29.50	60
1986 The Medicine Show	10-day		29.50	60
1986 Caroline's Eggs	10-day		29.50	65-75
1986 Mary's Gift	10-day		29.50	60
1986 Bell For Walnut Grove	10-day		29.50	60
1986 Ingalls Family Christmas	10-day		29.50	60
1986 Sweetheart Tree	10-day		29.50	60

Little Ladies - M.H. Bogart

YEAR ISSUE	EDITION LIMIT	YEAR RETD.	ISSUE PRICE	*QUOTE U.S.$
1989 Playing Bridesmaid	14-day	1991	29.50	45-85
1990 The Seamstress	14-day	1991	29.50	45-60
1990 Little Captive	14-day	1991	29.50	45-55
1990 Playing Mama	14-day	1991	29.50	45-55
1990 Susanna	14-day	1991	29.50	45-55
1990 Kitty's Bath	14-day	1991	29.50	45-49
1990 A Day in the Country	14-day	1991	29.50	45
1991 Sarah	14-day	1991	29.50	45-80
1991 First Party	14-day	1991	29.50	45-55
1991 The Magic Kitten	14-day	1991	29.50	45-48

The Little Rascals - Unknown

YEAR ISSUE	EDITION LIMIT	YEAR RETD.	ISSUE PRICE	*QUOTE U.S.$
1985 Three for the Show	10-day	1989	24.50	30-49
1985 My Gal	10-day	1989	24.50	25-49
1985 Skeleton Crew	10-day	1989	24.50	25-49
1985 Roughin' It	10-day	1989	24.50	25-49
1985 Spanky's Pranks	10-day	1989	24.50	25-49
1985 Butch's Challenge	10-day	1989	24.50	25-49
1985 Darla's Debut	10-day	1989	24.50	25-49
1985 Pete's Pal	10-day	1989	24.50	25-40

Little Shopkeepers - G. Gerardi

YEAR ISSUE	EDITION LIMIT	YEAR RETD.	ISSUE PRICE	*QUOTE U.S.$
1990 Sew Tired	14-day	1989	29.50	45
1991 Break Time	14-day	1989	29.50	30-40
1991 Purrfect Fit	14-day	1989	29.50	30-40
1991 Toying Around	14-day	1989	29.50	35
1991 Chain Reaction	14-day	1989	29.50	40-45
1991 Inferior Decorators	14-day	1989	29.50	45
1991 Tulip Tag	14-day	1989	29.50	36-40
1991 Candy Capers	14-day	1989	29.50	36-40

Lore Of The West - L. Danielle

YEAR ISSUE	EDITION LIMIT	YEAR RETD.	ISSUE PRICE	*QUOTE U.S.$
1993 A Mile In His Mocassins	28-day		29.50	30
1993 Path of Honor	28-day		29.50	30
1993 A Chief's Pride	28-day		29.50	30-39
1994 Pathways of the Pueblo	28-day		29.50	30
1994 In Her Seps	28-day		29.50	30
1994 Growing Up Brave	28-day		29.50	30
1994 Nomads of the Southwest	28-day		29.50	30
1994 Sacred Spirit of the Plains	28-day		29.50	30
1994 We'll Fight No More	28-day		29.50	30
1994 The End of the Trail	28-day		29.50	30-42

Love's Messengers - J. Grossman

YEAR ISSUE	EDITION LIMIT	YEAR RETD.	ISSUE PRICE	*QUOTE U.S.$
1995 To My Love	28-day	1994	29.50	40-45
1995 Cupid's Arrow	28-day	1994	29.50	40-45
1995 Love's Melody	28-day	1994	29.50	40
1995 A Token of Love	28-day	1994	29.50	40
1995 Harmony of Love	28-day	1994	29.50	40-45
1996 True Love's Offering	28-day	1994	29.95	40
1996 Love's In Bloom	28-day	1994	29.95	40-45
1996 To My Sweetheart	28-day	1994	29.95	40

Loving Lucy - M. Weistling

YEAR ISSUE	EDITION LIMIT	YEAR RETD.	ISSUE PRICE	*QUOTE U.S.$
1997 We're Having a Baby	28-day	1999	29.95	30-50
1997 Soaking Up the Local Color	28-day	1999	35.00	30-50
1998 Million Dollar Idea	28-day	1999	29.95	30-50
1997 Chatter Box Ricardo	28-day	1999	35.00	30-50
1998 Wanted: 'Sperienced Chicken Farmer	28-day	1999	29.95	30-50
1998 Caught in the Act	28-day	1999	29.95	30-50
1999 Parisian Potato Sacks	28-day	1999	29.95	30-50
1999 Lucy Chills Out	28-day	1999	29.95	30-50

The Lucille Ball (Official) Commemorative Plate - M. Weistling

YEAR ISSUE	EDITION LIMIT	YEAR RETD.	ISSUE PRICE	*QUOTE U.S.$
1993 Lucy	28-day	1994	37.50	175-250

Lucy Meets The Stars - M. Weistling

YEAR ISSUE	EDITION LIMIT	YEAR RETD.	ISSUE PRICE	*QUOTE U.S.$
1997 L.A. at Last!	28-day	1999	35.00	35-79
1997 Tennessee Ernie Ford Visits	28-day	1999	35.00	35-79
1997 Lucy Meets Harpo Marx	28-day	1999	35.00	35-85
1998 Lucy Meets Orson Wells	28-day	1999	35.00	35-75
1999 Lucy Meets Red Skelton	28-day	1999	35.00	55-95

Madonna And Child - Various

YEAR ISSUE	EDITION LIMIT	YEAR RETD.	ISSUE PRICE	*QUOTE U.S.$
1992 Madonna Della Sedia - R. Sanzio	28-day		37.50	38
1992 Virgin of the Rocks - L. DaVinci	28-day		37.50	38
1993 Madonna of Rosary - B. E. Murillo	28-day		37.50	38
1993 Sistine Madonna - R. Sanzio	28-day		37.50	38
1993 Virgin Adoring Christ Child - A. Correggio	28-day		37.50	38
1993 Virgin of the Grape - P. Mignard	28-day		37.50	38
1993 Madonna del Magnificat - S. Botticelli	28-day		37.50	38
1993 Madonna col Bambino - S. Botticelli	28-day		37.50	38

The Magical World of Legends & Myths - J. Shalatain

YEAR ISSUE	EDITION LIMIT	YEAR RETD.	ISSUE PRICE	*QUOTE U.S.$
1993 A Mother's Love	28-day	1994	35.00	35-55
1993 Dreams of Pegasus	28-day	1994	35.00	35-45
1994 Flight of the Pegasus	28-day	1994	35.00	35-45
1994 The Awakening	28-day	1994	35.00	35-45
1994 Once Upon a Dream	28-day	1994	35.00	35-45
1994 The Dawn of Romance	28-day	1994	35.00	35-45
1994 The Astral Unicorn	28-day	1994	35.00	35-45
1994 Flight into Paradise	28-day	1994	35.00	35
1995 Pegasus in the Stars	28-day	1994	35.00	35-45
1995 Unicorn of the Sea	28-day	1994	35.00	35

Majestic Birds of Prey - C.F. Riley

YEAR ISSUE	EDITION LIMIT	YEAR RETD.	ISSUE PRICE	*QUOTE U.S.$
1983 Golden Eagle	12,500		55.00	55-85
1983 Coopers Hawk	12,500		55.00	55-60
1983 Great Horned Owl	12,500		55.00	55-60
1983 Bald Eagle	12,500		55.00	55-60
1983 Barred Owl	12,500		55.00	55-60
1983 Sparrow Hawk	12,500		55.00	55-60
1983 Peregrine Falcon	12,500		55.00	55-60
1983 Osprey	12,500		55.00	55-60

Majesty of Flight - T. Hirata

YEAR ISSUE	EDITION LIMIT	YEAR RETD.	ISSUE PRICE	*QUOTE U.S.$
1989 The Eagle Soars	14-day		37.50	60-65
1989 Realm of the Red-Tail	14-day		37.50	40
1989 Coastal Journey	14-day		37.50	38-45
1989 Sentry of the North	14-day		37.50	38-48
1989 Commanding the Marsh	14-day		37.50	38
1990 The Vantage Point	14-day		29.50	38-45
1990 Silent Watch	14-day		29.50	48-65
1990 Fierce and Free	14-day		29.50	38-45

Man's Best Friend - L. Picken

YEAR ISSUE	EDITION LIMIT	YEAR RETD.	ISSUE PRICE	*QUOTE U.S.$
1992 Special Delivery	28-day		29.50	30
1992 Making Waves	28-day		29.50	30
1992 Good Catch	28-day		29.50	30
1993 Time For a Walk	28-day		29.50	30-45
1993 Faithful Friend	28-day		29.50	30-45
1993 Let's Play Ball	28-day		29.50	30-36
1993 Sitting Pretty	28-day		29.50	30
1993 Bedtime Story	28-day		29.50	30
1993 Trusted Companion	28-day		29.50	30

Mickey Mantle - R. Tanenbaum

YEAR ISSUE	EDITION LIMIT	YEAR RETD.	ISSUE PRICE	*QUOTE U.S.$
1996 The Mick	28-day		35.00	50
1996 536 Home Runs	28-day		35.00	45
1996 2,401 Games	28-day		35.00	45
1996 Switch Hitter	28-day		35.00	30-52
1996 16 Time All Star	28-day		35.00	45
1996 18 World Series Home Runs	28-day		35.00	45
1997 1956-A Crowning Year	28-day		35.00	45
1997 Remembering a Legendary Yankee	28-day		35.00	45

Mike Schmidt - R. Tanenbaum

YEAR ISSUE	EDITION LIMIT	YEAR RETD.	ISSUE PRICE	*QUOTE U.S.$
1994 The Ultimate Competitor: Mike Schmidt	28-day		29.50	30
1995 A Homerun King	28-day		29.50	30
1995 An All Time, All Star	28-day		29.50	30
1995 A Career Retrospective	28-day		29.50	30

Milestones in Space - D. Dixon

YEAR ISSUE	EDITION LIMIT	YEAR RETD.	ISSUE PRICE	*QUOTE U.S.$
1994 Moon Landing	28-day		29.50	45
1995 Space Lab	28-day		29.50	30
1995 Maiden Flight of Columbia	28-day		29.50	30
1995 Free Walk in Space	28-day		29.50	30
1995 Lunar Rover	28-day		29.50	30
1995 Handshake in Space	28-day		29.50	30
1995 First Landing on Mars	28-day		29.50	30
1995 Voyager's Exploration	28-day		29.50	30

Mixed Company - P. Cooper

YEAR ISSUE	EDITION LIMIT	YEAR RETD.	ISSUE PRICE	*QUOTE U.S.$
1990 Two Against One	14-day		29.50	36-55
1990 A Sticky Situation	14-day		29.50	35-45
1990 What's Up	14-day		29.50	30-45
1990 All Wrapped Up	14-day		29.50	35-45
1990 Picture Perfect	14-day		29.50	30-45
1991 A Moment to Unwind	14-day		29.50	33-45
1991 Ole	14-day		29.50	33-45
1991 Picnic Prowlers	14-day		29.50	35-45

Murals From The Precious Moments Chapel - S. Butcher

YEAR ISSUE	EDITION LIMIT	YEAR RETD.	ISSUE PRICE	*QUOTE U.S.$
1995 The Pearl of Great Price	28-day		35.00	35
1995 The Good Samaritan	28-day		35.00	35
1996 The Prodigal Son	28-day		35.00	35
1996 The Good Shepherd	28-day		35.00	35

Mystic Warrior Shield Collection - C. Ren

YEAR ISSUE	EDITION LIMIT	YEAR RETD.	ISSUE PRICE	*QUOTE U.S.$
1996 Deliverance	28-day		39.95	40-45
1996 Blue Thunder	28-day		39.95	40
1997 Mystic Warrior	28-day		39.95	40-49
1997 Windrider	28-day		39.95	40
1999 Morning of Reckoning	28-day		39.95	40
1999 Winter of '41	28-day		39.95	40-52
1999 Sun Seeker	28-day		39.95	40
1999 Peacemaker	28-day		39.95	40

Mystic Warriors - C. Ren

YEAR ISSUE	EDITION LIMIT	YEAR RETD.	ISSUE PRICE	*QUOTE U.S.$
1992 Deliverance	28-day		29.50	65-75
1992 Mystic Warrior	28-day		29.50	40-75
1992 Sun Seeker	28-day		29.50	40-75
1992 Top Gun	28-day		29.50	40-85
1992 Man Who Walks Alone	28-day		29.50	40-75
1992 Windrider	28-day		29.50	45-75
1992 Spirit of the Plains	28-day		29.50	40-75
1993 Blue Thunder	28-day		29.50	40-75
1993 Sun Glow	28-day		29.50	40-75
1993 Peace Maker	28-day		29.50	45-75

*Quotes have been rounded up to nearest dollar

Native American Legends - A. Biffignandi

YEAR ISSUE	EDITION LIMIT	YEAR RETD.	ISSUE PRICE	*QUOTE U.S.$
1996 Peace Pipe	28-day		29.95	30
1996 Feather-Woman	28-day		29.95	30
1996 Spirit of Serenity	28-day		29.95	30
1996 Enchanted Warrior	28-day		29.95	30
1996 Mystical Serenade	28-day		29.95	30
1996 Legend of Bridal Veil	28-day		29.95	30-40
1996 Seasons of Love	28-day		29.95	30
1996 A Bashful Courtship	28-day		29.95	30-39

Nature's Majestic Cats - M. Richter

YEAR ISSUE	EDITION LIMIT	YEAR RETD.	ISSUE PRICE	*QUOTE U.S.$
1993 Siberian Tiger	28-day		29.50	40
1993 Himalayan Snow Leopard	28-day		29.50	30-39
1993 African Lion	28-day		29.50	30-35
1994 Asian Clouded Leopard	28-day		29.50	30-35
1994 American Cougar	28-day		29.50	30-42
1994 East African Leopard	28-day		29.50	30-39
1994 African Cheetah	28-day		29.50	30-39
1994 Canadian Lynx	28-day		29.50	30-40

Nature's Nighttime Realm - G. Murray

YEAR ISSUE	EDITION LIMIT	YEAR RETD.	ISSUE PRICE	*QUOTE U.S.$
1992 Bobcat	28-day		29.50	30
1992 Cougar	28-day		29.50	30
1993 Jaguar	28-day		29.50	30
1993 White Tiger	28-day		29.50	30-40
1993 Lynx	28-day		29.50	30
1993 Lion	28-day		29.50	30
1993 Snow Leopard	28-day		29.50	30-50
1993 Cheetah	28-day		29.50	30-35

Nature's Quiet Moments - R. Parker

YEAR ISSUE	EDITION LIMIT	YEAR RETD.	ISSUE PRICE	*QUOTE U.S.$
1988 A Curious Pair	14-day		37.50	47-60
1988 Northern Morning	14-day		37.50	40-55
1988 Just Resting	14-day		37.50	40-50
1989 Waiting Out the Storm	14-day		37.50	38
1989 Creekside	14-day		37.50	38
1989 Autumn Foraging	14-day		37.50	38
1989 Old Man of the Mountain	14-day		37.50	38
1989 Mountain Blooms	14-day		37.50	38

Newsom Santa Takes a Break - T. Newsom

YEAR ISSUE	EDITION LIMIT	YEAR RETD.	ISSUE PRICE	*QUOTE U.S.$
1995 Santa's Last Stop	28-day		29.95	30
1996 Santa's Railroad	28-day		29.95	30
1996 A Jolly Good Catch	28-day		29.95	30
1996 Simple Pleasures	28-day		29.95	30
1996 Skating On Penguin Pond	28-day		29.95	30
1996 Santa's Sing-along	28-day		29.95	30
1996 Sledding Adventures	28-day		29.95	30
1997 Santa's Sweet Treats	28-day		29.95	30

Noble American Indian Women - D. Wright

YEAR ISSUE	EDITION LIMIT	YEAR RETD.	ISSUE PRICE	*QUOTE U.S.$
1989 Sacajawea	14-day		29.50	50-90
1990 Pocahontas	14-day		29.50	40-95
1990 Minnehaha	14-day		29.50	65
1990 Pine Leaf	14-day		29.50	65
1990 Lily of the Mohawk	14-day		29.50	60
1990 White Rose	14-day		29.50	55-69
1991 Lozen	14-day		29.50	55
1991 Falling Star	14-day		29.50	55-65

Noble Owls of America - J. Seerey-Lester

YEAR ISSUE	EDITION LIMIT	YEAR RETD.	ISSUE PRICE	*QUOTE U.S.$
1986 Morning Mist	15,000		55.00	45-65
1987 Prairie Sundown	15,000		55.00	55-60
1987 Winter Vigil	15,000		55.00	55-60
1987 Autumn Mist	15,000		75.00	60-75
1987 Dawn in the Willows	15,000		55.00	55-60
1987 Snowy Watch	15,000		60.00	60
1988 Hiding Place	15,000		55.00	55-60
1988 Waiting for Dusk	15,000		55.00	55-60

Nolan Ryan - R. Tanenbaum

YEAR ISSUE	EDITION LIMIT	YEAR RETD.	ISSUE PRICE	*QUOTE U.S.$
1994 The Strikeout Express	28-day		29.50	50-69
1994 Birth of a Legend	28-day		29.50	25-35
1994 Mr. Fastball	28-day		29.50	25-35
1994 Million-Dollar Player	28-day		29.50	25-35
1994 27 Seasons	28-day		29.50	25-35
1994 Farewell	28-day		29.50	25-35
1994 The Ryan Express	28-day		29.50	25-50

Norman Rockwell's Saturday Evening Post Baseball - N. Rockwell

YEAR ISSUE	EDITION LIMIT	YEAR RETD.	ISSUE PRICE	*QUOTE U.S.$
1992 100th Year of Baseball	Open		19.50	20
1993 The Rookie	Open		19.50	20
1993 The Dugout	Open		19.50	20
1993 Bottom of the Sixth	Open		19.50	20

North American Ducks - R. Lawrence

YEAR ISSUE	EDITION LIMIT	YEAR RETD.	ISSUE PRICE	*QUOTE U.S.$
1991 Autumn Flight	14-day		29.50	30-36
1991 The Resting Place	14-day		29.50	30
1991 Twin Flight	14-day		29.50	30
1992 Misty Morning	14-day		29.50	30
1992 Springtime Thaw	14-day		29.50	30
1992 Summer Retreat	14-day		29.50	30
1992 Overcast	14-day		29.50	30
1992 Perfect Pintails	14-day		29.50	30

North American Gamebirds - J. Killen

YEAR ISSUE	EDITION LIMIT	YEAR RETD.	ISSUE PRICE	*QUOTE U.S.$
1990 Ring-necked Pheasant	14-day		37.50	75
1990 Bobwhite Quail	14-day		37.50	80-100
1990 Ruffed Grouse	14-day		37.50	75
1990 Gambel Quail	14-day		37.50	38-42
1990 Mourning Dove	14-day		37.50	38-45
1990 Woodcock	14-day		37.50	38-45
1991 Chukar Partridge	14-day		37.50	38-45
1991 Wild Turkey	14-day		37.50	38-45

North American Waterbirds - R. Lawrence

YEAR ISSUE	EDITION LIMIT	YEAR RETD.	ISSUE PRICE	*QUOTE U.S.$
1988 Wood Ducks	14-day		37.50	45
1988 Hooded Mergansers	14-day		37.50	50
1988 Pintails	14-day		37.50	40-45
1988 Canada Geese	14-day		37.50	40-45
1989 American Widgeons	14-day		37.50	45-55
1989 Canvasbacks	14-day		37.50	45-55
1989 Mallard Pair	14-day		37.50	45-60
1989 Snow Geese	14-day		37.50	45

The Nutcracker Ballet - S. Fisher

YEAR ISSUE	EDITION LIMIT	YEAR RETD.	ISSUE PRICE	*QUOTE U.S.$
1978 Clara	28-day		19.50	36-50
1979 Godfather	28-day		19.50	15-25
1979 Sugar Plum Fairy	28-day		19.50	45-70
1979 Snow Queen and King	28-day		19.50	25-40
1980 Waltz of the Flowers	28-day		19.50	20-25
1980 Clara and the Prince	28-day		19.50	25-45

Official Honeymooner's Commemorative Plate - D. Bobnick

YEAR ISSUE	EDITION LIMIT	YEAR RETD.	ISSUE PRICE	*QUOTE U.S.$
1993 The Official Honeymooner's Commemorative Plate	28-day		37.50	135-290

The Official Honeymooners Plate Collection - D. Kilmer

YEAR ISSUE	EDITION LIMIT	YEAR RETD.	ISSUE PRICE	*QUOTE U.S.$
1987 The Honeymooners	14-day		24.50	160-225
1987 The Hucklebuck	14-day		24.50	160-200
1987 Baby, You're the Greatest	14-day		24.50	170-225
1988 The Golfer	14-day		24.50	150-225
1988 The TV Chefs	14-day		24.50	125-225
1988 Bang! Zoom!	14-day		24.50	150-225
1988 The Only Way to Travel	14-day		24.50	150-225
1988 The Honeymoon Express	14-day		24.50	200-235

On Wings of Eagles - J. Pitcher

YEAR ISSUE	EDITION LIMIT	YEAR RETD.	ISSUE PRICE	*QUOTE U.S.$
1994 "By Dawn's Early Light"	28-day		29.50	30-39
1994 Winter's Majestic Flight	28-day		29.50	30-35
1994 Over the Land of the Free	28-day		29.50	30
1994 Changing of the Guard	28-day		29.50	30
1995 Free Flight	28-day		29.50	30
1995 Morning Majesty	28-day		29.50	30
1995 Soaring Free	28-day		29.50	30
1994 Majestic Heights	28-day		29.50	30

Once In A Lifetime - Earnhardt & Jr. Panorama Plates - B. Tanenbaum

YEAR ISSUE	EDITION LIMIT	YEAR RETD.	ISSUE PRICE	*QUOTE U.S.$
1999 The Mentor	Open		39.95	40
1999 Classic Red	Open		39.95	40
1999 First Black	Open		39.95	40
1999 The Protégé	Open		39.95	40

Our Cherished Seas - S. Barlowe

YEAR ISSUE	EDITION LIMIT	YEAR RETD.	ISSUE PRICE	*QUOTE U.S.$
1992 Whale Song	48-day		37.50	38
1992 Lions of the Sea	48-day		37.50	38
1992 Flight of the Dolphins	48-day		37.50	38-42
1992 Palace of the Seals	48-day		37.50	38
1993 Orca Ballet	48-day		37.50	38
1993 Emperors of the Ice	48-day		37.50	38
1993 Sea Turtles	48-day		37.50	38
1993 Splendor of the Sea	48-day		37.50	38

Petals and Purrs - B. Harrison

YEAR ISSUE	EDITION LIMIT	YEAR RETD.	ISSUE PRICE	*QUOTE U.S.$
1988 Blushing Beauties	14-day		24.50	55
1988 Spring Fever	14-day		24.50	38-55
1988 Morning Glories	14-day		24.50	45-55
1988 Forget-Me-Not	14-day		24.50	36-55
1989 Golden Fancy	14-day		24.50	30-55
1989 Pink Lillies	14-day		24.50	30-55
1989 Summer Sunshine	14-day		24.50	55
1989 Siamese Summer	14-day		24.50	55

Pillars of Baseball - A. Hicks

YEAR ISSUE	EDITION LIMIT	YEAR RETD.	ISSUE PRICE	*QUOTE U.S.$
1995 Babe Ruth	28-day		29.95	30-35
1995 Lou Gehrig	28-day		29.95	30
1995 Ty Cobb	28-day		29.95	30
1996 Cy Young	28-day		29.95	30
1996 Honus Wagner	28-day		29.95	30
1996 Rogers Hornsby	28-day		29.95	30
1996 Dizzy Dean	28-day		29.95	30
1996 Christy Mathewson	28-day		29.95	30

Portraits of Childhood - T. Utz

YEAR ISSUE	EDITION LIMIT	YEAR RETD.	ISSUE PRICE	*QUOTE U.S.$
1981 Butterfly Magic	28-day		24.95	14-40
1981 Sweet Dreams	28-day		24.95	25-40
1981 Turtle Talk	28-day		24.95	36-40
1981 Friends Forever	28-day		24.95	35-40

Portraits of Jesus - W. Sallman

YEAR ISSUE	EDITION LIMIT	YEAR RETD.	ISSUE PRICE	*QUOTE U.S.$
1994 Jesus, The Good Shepherd	28-day		29.50	30-39
1994 Jesus in the Garden	28-day		29.50	30
1994 Jesus, Children's Friend	28-day		29.50	30
1994 The Lord's Supper	28-day		29.50	30-35
1994 Christ at Dawn	28-day		29.50	30
1994 Christ at Heart's Door	28-day		29.50	30
1994 Portrait of Christ	28-day		29.50	30
1994 Madonna and Christ Child	28-day		29.50	30-40

Portraits of the Bald Eagle - J. Pitcher

YEAR ISSUE	EDITION LIMIT	YEAR RETD.	ISSUE PRICE	*QUOTE U.S.$
1993 Ruler of the Sky	28-day		37.50	40-45
1993 In Bold Defiance	28-day		37.50	40
1993 Master Of The Summer Skies	28-day		37.50	40
1993 Spring's Sentinel	28-day		37.50	40

Portraits of the Wild - J. Meger

YEAR ISSUE	EDITION LIMIT	YEAR RETD.	ISSUE PRICE	*QUOTE U.S.$
1994 Interlude	28-day		29.50	30-35
1994 Winter Solitude	28-day		29.50	30-75
1994 Devoted Protector	28-day		29.50	30
1994 Call of Autumn	28-day		29.50	30
1994 Watchful Eyes	28-day		29.50	30
1994 Babies of Spring	28-day		29.50	30
1994 Rocky Mountain Grandeur	28-day		29.50	30
1995 Unbridled Power	28-day		29.50	30
1995 Moonlight Vigil	28-day		29.50	30
1995 Monarch of the Plains	28-day		29.50	30-35
1995 Tender Courtship	28-day		29.50	30-40

Precious Moments Bible Story - S. Butcher

YEAR ISSUE	EDITION LIMIT	YEAR RETD.	ISSUE PRICE	*QUOTE U.S.$
1990 Come Let Us Adore Him	28-day		29.50	30
1992 They Followed The Star	28-day		29.50	30
1992 The Flight Into Egypt	28-day		29.50	30
1992 The Carpenter Shop	28-day		29.50	30
1992 Jesus In The Temple	28-day		29.50	30
1992 The Crucifixion	28-day		29.50	30-65
1993 He Is Not Here	28-day		29.50	30-65

Precious Moments Classics - S. Butcher

YEAR ISSUE	EDITION LIMIT	YEAR RETD.	ISSUE PRICE	*QUOTE U.S.$
1993 God Loveth A Cheerful Giver	28-day		35.00	35
1993 Make A Joyful Noise	28-day		35.00	35
1994 Love One Another	28-day		35.00	35
1994 You Have Touched So Many Hearts	28-day		35.00	35
1994 Praise the Lord Anyhow	28-day		35.00	35
1994 I Believe in Miracles	28-day		35.00	35
1994 Good Friends Are Forever	28-day		35.00	35
1994 Jesus Loves Me	28-day		35.00	35
1995 Friendship Hits the Spot	28-day		35.00	35
1995 To My Deer Friend	28-day		35.00	35

Precious Moments of Childhood Plates - T. Utz

YEAR ISSUE	EDITION LIMIT	YEAR RETD.	ISSUE PRICE	*QUOTE U.S.$
1979 Friend in the Sky	28-day		21.50	50-70
1980 Sand in her Shoe	28-day		21.50	15-35
1980 Snow Bunny	28-day		21.50	20-35
1980 Seashells	28-day		21.50	38-55
1981 Dawn	28-day		21.50	15-35
1982 My Kitty	28-day		21.50	36-55

Precious Moments Words of Love - S. Butcher

YEAR ISSUE	EDITION LIMIT	YEAR RETD.	ISSUE PRICE	*QUOTE U.S.$
1995 Your Friendship Is Soda-licious	28-day		35.00	35
1996 Your Love Is So Uplifting	28-day		35.00	35
1996 Love Is From Above	28-day		35.00	35
1996 Love Lifted Me	28-day		35.00	35

Precious Portraits - B. P. Gutmann

YEAR ISSUE	EDITION LIMIT	YEAR RETD.	ISSUE PRICE	*QUOTE U.S.$
1987 Sunbeam	14-day	1991	24.50	60
1987 Mischief	14-day	1991	24.50	60
1987 Peach Blossom	14-day	1991	24.50	55
1987 Goldilocks	14-day	1991	24.50	55-95
1987 Fairy Gold	14-day	1991	24.50	40-50
1987 Bunny	14-day	1991	24.50	30-95

The Prideful Ones - C. DeHaan

YEAR ISSUE	EDITION LIMIT	YEAR RETD.	ISSUE PRICE	*QUOTE U.S.$
1994 Village Markers	28-day		29.50	30
1994 His Pride	28-day		29.50	30
1994 Appeasing the Water People	28-day		29.50	30
1994 Tribal Guardian	28-day		29.50	30
1994 Autumn Passage	28-day		29.50	30
1994 Winter Hunter	28-day		29.50	30
1994 Silent Trail Break	28-day		29.50	30
1994 Water Breaking	28-day		29.50	30
1994 Crossing at the Big Trees	28-day		29.50	30
1995 Winter Songsinger	28-day		29.50	30

Princesses of the Plains - D. Wright

YEAR ISSUE	EDITION LIMIT	YEAR RETD.	ISSUE PRICE	*QUOTE U.S.$
1993 Prairie Flower	28-day		29.50	32-38
1993 Snow Princess	28-day		29.50	40-65
1993 Wild Flower	28-day		29.50	30-40
1993 Noble Beauty	28-day		29.50	35-40
1993 Winter's Rose	28-day		29.50	30-40
1993 Gentle Beauty	28-day		29.50	30-40
1994 Nature's Guardian	28-day		29.50	40-45
1994 Mountain Princess	28-day		29.50	30-40
1995 Proud Dreamer	28-day		29.50	40-45
1995 Spring Maiden	28-day		29.50	30-40

Proud Chieftains - N. Rose

YEAR ISSUE	EDITION LIMIT	YEAR RETD.	ISSUE PRICE	*QUOTE U.S.$
1999 Spirit Quest	28-day		39.95	40
1999 Sacred Journey	28-day		39.95	40

Proud Indian Families - K. Freeman

YEAR ISSUE	EDITION LIMIT	YEAR RETD.	ISSUE PRICE	*QUOTE U.S.$
1991 The Storyteller	14-day		29.50	40-45
1991 The Power of the Basket	14-day		29.50	30-36
1991 The Naming Ceremony	14-day		29.50	30
1992 Playing With Tradition	14-day		29.50	30
1992 Preparing the Berry Harvest	14-day		29.50	30
1992 Ceremonial Dress	14-day		29.50	30
1992 Sounds of the Forest	14-day		29.50	30
1992 The Marriage Ceremony	14-day		29.50	30-39
1993 The Jewelry Maker	14-day		29.50	30
1993 Beautiful Creations	14-day		29.50	30

Proud Innocence - J. Schmidt

YEAR ISSUE	EDITION LIMIT	YEAR RETD.	ISSUE PRICE	*QUOTE U.S.$
1994 Desert Bloom	28-day		29.50	30
1994 Little Drummer	28-day		29.50	30
1995 Young Archer	28-day		29.50	30-36
1995 Morning Child	28-day		29.50	30
1995 Wise One	28-day		29.50	30
1995 Sun Blossom	28-day		29.50	30
1995 Laughing Heart	28-day		29.50	30
1995 Gentle Flower	28-day		29.50	30

The Proud Nation - R. Swanson

YEAR ISSUE	EDITION LIMIT	YEAR RETD.	ISSUE PRICE	*QUOTE U.S.$
1989 Navajo Little One	14-day		24.50	65-75
1989 In a Big Land	14-day		24.50	35-60
1989 Out with Mama's Flock	14-day		24.50	40-50
1989 Newest Little Sheepherder	14-day		24.50	50-65
1989 Dressed Up for the Powwow	14-day		24.50	35-45
1989 Just a Few Days Old	14-day		24.50	60-65
1989 Autumn Treat	14-day		24.50	30-45
1989 Up in the Red Rocks	14-day		24.50	60

Puppy Playtime - J. Lamb

YEAR ISSUE	EDITION LIMIT	YEAR RETD.	ISSUE PRICE	*QUOTE U.S.$
1987 Double Take-Cocker Spaniels	14-day		24.50	60-80
1987 Catch of the Day-Golden Retrievers	14-day		24.50	50-80
1987 Cabin Fever-Black Labradors	14-day		24.50	40-60
1987 Weekend Gardener-Lhasa Apsos	14-day		24.50	35-45
1987 Getting Acquainted-Beagles	14-day		24.50	30-36
1987 Hanging Out-German Shepherd	14-day		24.50	40-45
1987 New Leash on Life-Mini Schnauzer	14-day		24.50	45-59
1987 Fun and Games-Poodle	14-day		24.50	30-45

Quiet Moments Of Childhood - D. Green

YEAR ISSUE	EDITION LIMIT	YEAR RETD.	ISSUE PRICE	*QUOTE U.S.$
1991 Elizabeth's Afternoon Tea	14-day		29.50	45
1991 Christina's Secret Garden	14-day		29.50	36
1991 Eric & Erin's Storytime	14-day		29.50	30
1992 Jessica's Tea Party	14-day		29.50	33
1992 Megan & Monique's Bakery	14-day		29.50	36
1992 Children's Day By The Sea	14-day		29.50	30
1992 Jordan's Playful Pups	14-day		29.50	33
1992 Daniel's Morning Playtime	14-day		29.50	30

The Quilted Countryside: A Signature Collection by Mel Steele - M. Steele

YEAR ISSUE	EDITION LIMIT	YEAR RETD.	ISSUE PRICE	*QUOTE U.S.$
1991 The Old Country Store	14-day		29.50	36
1991 Winter's End	14-day		29.50	36
1991 The Quilter's Cabin	14-day		29.50	45
1991 Spring Cleaning	14-day		29.50	36
1991 Summer Harvest	14-day		29.50	30
1991 The Country Merchant	14-day		29.50	36
1992 Wash Day	14-day		29.50	30
1992 The Antiques Store	14-day		29.50	33

Realm of the Majestic Eagle - Rigby

YEAR ISSUE	EDITION LIMIT	YEAR RETD.	ISSUE PRICE	*QUOTE U.S.$
1997 Winter Watch & Winter's Call	28-day		70.00	70
1997 Spring Flight & Spring Pursuit	28-day		70.00	70
1997 Summer Guard & Mother's Nest	28-day		70.00	70
1997 Autumn Soar & Autumn Splendor	28-day		70.00	70

Realm of the Wolf - A. Agnew

YEAR ISSUE	EDITION LIMIT	YEAR RETD.	ISSUE PRICE	*QUOTE U.S.$
1997 Midnight Serenade	Open		39.95	40
1997 Free as the Wind	Open		39.95	40
1997 Guardians of the High Country	Open		39.95	40
1997 Lords of the Tundra	Open		39.95	40

Remembering Norma Jeane - F. Accornero

YEAR ISSUE	EDITION LIMIT	YEAR RETD.	ISSUE PRICE	*QUOTE U.S.$
1994 The Girl Next Door	28-day		29.50	50-70
1994 Her Day in the Sun	28-day		29.50	50-65
1994 A Star is Born	28-day		29.50	45-70
1994 Beauty Secrets	28-day		29.50	50-70
1995 In the Spotlight	28-day		29.50	50-65
1995 Bathing Beauty	28-day		29.50	45-60
1995 Young & Carefree	28-day		29.50	45-50
1995 Free Spirit	28-day		29.50	50-55
1995 A Country Girl at Heart	28-day		29.50	45-55
1996 Hometown Girl	28-day		29.50	50

The Renaissance Angels - L. Bywaters

YEAR ISSUE	EDITION LIMIT	YEAR RETD.	ISSUE PRICE	*QUOTE U.S.$
1994 Doves of Peace	28-day		29.50	30-65
1994 Angelic Innocence	28-day		29.50	36-65
1994 Joy to the World	28-day		29.50	30-65
1995 Angel of Faith	28-day		29.50	30-65
1995 The Christmas Star	28-day		29.50	30-65
1995 Trumpeter's Call	28-day		29.50	30-65
1995 Harmonious Heavens	28-day		29.50	30-65
1995 The Angels Sing	28-day		29.50	30-65

Rockwell Home of the Brave - N. Rockwell

YEAR ISSUE	EDITION LIMIT	YEAR RETD.	ISSUE PRICE	*QUOTE U.S.$
1981 Reminiscing	18,000		35.00	55
1981 Hero's Welcome	18,000		35.00	55
1981 Back to his Old Job	18,000		35.00	55
1981 War Hero	18,000		35.00	35-55
1982 Willie Gillis in Church	18,000		35.00	55
1982 War Bond	18,000		35.00	35-55
1982 Uncle Sam Takes Wings	18,000		35.00	55-75
1982 Taking Mother over the Top	18,000		35.00	35-55

Romance of the Rails - D. Tutwiler

YEAR ISSUE	EDITION LIMIT	YEAR RETD.	ISSUE PRICE	*QUOTE U.S.$
1994 Starlight Limited	28-day		29.50	30-50
1994 Portland Rose	28-day		29.50	30-50
1994 Orange Blossom Special	28-day		29.50	40
1994 Morning Star	28-day		29.50	30-50
1994 Crescent Limited	28-day		29.50	30-50
1994 Sunset Limited	28-day		29.50	30-50
1994 Western Star	28-day		29.50	30-50
1994 Sunrise Limited	28-day		29.50	30-50
1995 The Blue Bonnett	28-day		29.50	30-50
1995 The Pine Tree Limited	28-day		29.50	30-50

Romantic Castles of Europe - D. Sweet

YEAR ISSUE	EDITION LIMIT	YEAR RETD.	ISSUE PRICE	*QUOTE U.S.$
1990 Ludwig's Castle	19,500		55.00	55
1991 Palace of the Moors	19,500		55.00	55
1991 Swiss Isle Fortress	19,500		55.00	55-75
1991 The Legendary Castle of Leeds	19,500		55.00	55-65
1991 Davinci's Chambord	19,500		55.00	55-65
1991 Eilean Donan	19,500		55.00	55
1992 Eltz Castle	19,500		55.00	55
1992 Kylemore Abbey	19,500		55.00	55

Romantic Flights of Fancy - Q. Lemonds

YEAR ISSUE	EDITION LIMIT	YEAR RETD.	ISSUE PRICE	*QUOTE U.S.$
1994 Sunlit Waltz	28-day		29.50	30
1994 Morning Minuet	28-day		29.50	30
1994 Evening Solo	28-day		29.50	30
1994 Summer Sonata	28-day		29.50	30
1995 Twilight Tango	28-day		29.50	30
1995 Sunset Ballet	28-day		29.50	30-35
1995 Exotic Interlude	28-day		29.50	30-36
1995 Sunrise Samba	28-day		29.50	30

Romantic Victorian Keepsake - J. Grossman

YEAR ISSUE	EDITION LIMIT	YEAR RETD.	ISSUE PRICE	*QUOTE U.S.$
1992 Dearest Kiss	28-day		35.00	40-58
1992 First Love	28-day		35.00	52
1992 As Fair as a Rose	28-day		35.00	50
1992 Springtime Beauty	28-day		35.00	35-55
1992 Summertime Fancy	28-day		35.00	40-50
1992 Bonnie Blue Eyes	28-day		35.00	40
1992 Precious Friends	28-day		35.00	50
1994 Bonnets and Bouquets	28-day		35.00	35-55
1994 My Beloved Teddy	28-day		35.00	50
1994 A Sweet Romance	28-day		35.00	40-50

A Salute to Mickey Mantle - T. Fogarty

YEAR ISSUE	EDITION LIMIT	YEAR RETD.	ISSUE PRICE	*QUOTE U.S.$
1996 1961 Home Run Duel	28-day		35.00	35
1996 Power at the Plate	28-day		35.00	35
1996 Saluting a Magnificent Yankee	28-day		35.00	35
1996 Triple Crown Achievement	28-day		35.00	35
1996 1953 Grand Slam	28-day		35.00	35
1997 1963's Famous Facade Homer	28-day		35.00	35
1997 Mickey as a Rookie	28-day		35.00	35
1997 A Look Back	28-day		35.00	35

Santa Takes a Break - T. Newsom

YEAR ISSUE	EDITION LIMIT	YEAR RETD.	ISSUE PRICE	*QUOTE U.S.$
1995 Santa's Last Stop	28-day		29.95	30
1995 Santa's Railroad	28-day		29.95	30
1995 A Jolly Good Catch	28-day		29.95	30
1995 Simple Pleasures	28-day		29.95	30
1996 Skating On Penquin Pond	28-day		29.95	30
1996 Santa's Sing Along	28-day		29.95	30
1996 Sledding Adventures	28-day		29.95	30
1996 Santa's Sweet Treats	28-day		29.95	30

The Saturday Evening Post - N. Rockwell

YEAR ISSUE	EDITION LIMIT	YEAR RETD.	ISSUE PRICE	*QUOTE U.S.$
1989 The Wonders of Radio	14-day		35.00	45-50
1989 Easter Morning	14-day		35.00	60
1989 The Facts of Life	14-day		35.00	35-45
1990 The Window Washer	14-day		35.00	45
1990 First Flight	14-day		35.00	54-60
1990 Traveling Companion	14-day		35.00	35-60
1990 Jury Room	14-day		35.00	35-50
1990 Furlough	14-day		35.00	50-55

Scenes of An American Christmas - B. Perry

YEAR ISSUE	EDITION LIMIT	YEAR RETD.	ISSUE PRICE	*QUOTE U.S.$
1994 I'll Be Home for Christmas	28-day		29.50	30-35
1994 Christmas Eve Worship	28-day		29.50	30-35
1994 A Holiday Happening	28-day		29.50	30-35
1994 A Long Winter's Night	28-day		29.50	30-35
1994 The Sounds of Christmas	28-day		29.50	30-35
1994 Dear Santa	28-day		29.50	30-35
1995 An Afternoon Outing	28-day		29.50	30-35
1995 Winter Worship	28-day		29.50	30-35

Seasons of the Bald Eagle - J. Pitcher

YEAR ISSUE	EDITION LIMIT	YEAR RETD.	ISSUE PRICE	*QUOTE U.S.$
1991 Autumn in the Mountains	14-day		37.50	55-63
1991 Winter in the Valley	14-day		37.50	55-63
1991 Spring on the River	14-day		37.50	63
1991 Summer on the Seacoast	14-day		37.50	63-70

Serenity At Sea Sculptural - A. Jones

YEAR ISSUE	EDITION LIMIT	YEAR RETD.	ISSUE PRICE	*QUOTE U.S.$
1998 Graceful Duet	Open		39.95	40
1998 Morning Majesty	Open		39.95	40
1998 Peaceful Journey	Open		39.95	40
1998 Sealife At Sunset	Open		39.95	40
1998 Sunset Splash	Open		39.95	40

Serenity of the Sea - A. Jones

YEAR ISSUE	EDITION LIMIT	YEAR RETD.	ISSUE PRICE	*QUOTE U.S.$
1998 Sunset Ballet	N/A		39.95	40
1998 Peaceful Journey	N/A		39.95	40
1999 Graceful Duet	N/A		39.95	40
1999 Morning Majesty	N/A		39.95	40
1999 Sunset Splash	N/A		39.95	40
1999 Riding the Waves	N/A		39.95	40
1999 Journey Home	N/A		39.95	40
1999 Moonlight Splendor	N/A		39.95	40

Sharing Life's Most Precious Memories - S. Butcher

YEAR ISSUE	EDITION LIMIT	YEAR RETD.	ISSUE PRICE	*QUOTE U.S.$
1995 Thee I Love	28-day		35.00	35
1995 The Joy of the Lord Is My Strength	28-day		35.00	35
1995 May Your Every Wish Come True	28-day		35.00	35
1996 I'm So Glad That God	28-day		35.00	35
1996 Heaven Bless You	28-day		35.00	35

Sharing the Moments - S. Butcher

YEAR ISSUE	EDITION LIMIT	YEAR RETD.	ISSUE PRICE	*QUOTE U.S.$
1995 You Have Touched So Many Hearts	28-day		35.00	35
1996 Friendship Hits The Spot	28-day		35.00	35
1996 Jesus Love Me	28-day		35.00	35

Single Issues - T. Utz

YEAR ISSUE	EDITION LIMIT	YEAR RETD.	ISSUE PRICE	*QUOTE U.S.$
1983 Princess Grace	21-day		39.50	50-79

Small Wonders of the Wild - C. Frace

YEAR ISSUE	EDITION LIMIT	YEAR RETD.	ISSUE PRICE	*QUOTE U.S.$
1989 Hideaway	14-day		29.50	35-56
1990 Young Explorers	14-day		29.50	35-48
1990 Three of a Kind	14-day		29.50	40-62
1990 Quiet Morning	14-day		29.50	35
1990 Eyes of Wonder	14-day		29.50	35
1990 Ready for Adventure	14-day		29.50	35
1990 Uno	14-day		29.50	35-42
1990 Exploring a New World	14-day		29.50	35

Soaring Spirits Shield Collection - J. Pitcher

YEAR ISSUE	EDITION LIMIT	YEAR RETD.	ISSUE PRICE	*QUOTE U.S.$
1999 Majestic Sunrise	N/A		39.95	40
1999 Watchful Eye	N/A		39.95	40
1999 Royal Flight	N/A		39.95	40
1999 Riding the Wing	N/A		39.95	40

Space, The Final Frontier - D. Ward

YEAR ISSUE	EDITION LIMIT	YEAR RETD.	ISSUE PRICE	*QUOTE U.S.$
1996 To Boldly Go...	28-day	1998	37.50	45-85
1996 Second Star From The Right	28-day	1998	37.50	40-75
1996 Signs of Intelligence	28-day	1998	37.50	40-59
1996 Preparing To Cloak	28-day	1998	37.50	40-65
1997 Distant Worlds	28-day	1998	37.50	40-60
1997 Where No One Has Gone Before	28-day	1998	37.50	40-62
1997 Beyond the Neutral Zone	28-day	1998	37.50	40-78
1997 We Are Borg	28-day	1998	37.50	40-45
1997 Cataloging Gascous Anomalies	28-day	1998	37.50	38
1997 Searching the Galaxy	28-day	1998	37.50	38

Spirit of the Mustang - C. DeHaan

YEAR ISSUE	EDITION LIMIT	YEAR RETD.	ISSUE PRICE	*QUOTE U.S.$
1995 Winter's Thunder	28-day		29.95	30-35
1995 Moonlit Run	28-day		29.95	30-35
1995 Morning Reverie	28-day		29.95	30-42
1995 Autumn Respite	28-day		29.95	35-40
1996 Spring Frolic	28-day		29.95	30-35
1996 Dueling Mustangs	28-day		29.95	35-48
1996 Tranquil Waters	28-day		29.95	30-35
1996 Summer Squall	28-day		29.95	30-40

Sporting Generation - J. Lamb

YEAR ISSUE	EDITION LIMIT	YEAR RETD.	ISSUE PRICE	*QUOTE U.S.$
1991 Like Father, Like Son	14-day		29.50	40-75
1991 Golden Moments	14-day		29.50	48
1991 The Lookout	14-day		29.50	40-48
1992 Picking Up The Scent	14-day		29.50	48
1992 First Time Out	14-day		29.50	42
1992 Who's Tracking Who	14-day		29.50	40-55
1992 Springing Into Action	14-day		29.50	35-55
1992 Point of Interest	14-day		29.50	35-55

STAR TREK® : 25th Anniversary Commemorative - T. Blackshear

YEAR ISSUE	EDITION LIMIT	YEAR RETD.	ISSUE PRICE	*QUOTE U.S.$
1991 STAR TREK 25th Anniversary Commemorative Plate	14-day	1998	37.50	250-325
1991 SPOCK	14-day	1998	35.00	95-235
1991 Kirk	14-day	1998	35.00	125-265
1992 McCoy	14-day	1998	35.00	90-210
1992 Uhura	14-day	1998	35.00	130-155
1992 Scotty	14-day	1998	35.00	90-175
1993 Sulu	14-day	1998	35.00	90-175
1993 Chekov	14-day	1998	35.00	90-155
1994 U.S.S. Enterprise NCC-1701	14-day	1998	35.00	125-200

STAR TREK® : 30 Years - T. Treadway

YEAR ISSUE	EDITION LIMIT	YEAR RETD.	ISSUE PRICE	*QUOTE U.S.$
1997 Captain's Tribute	28-day	1998	37.50	50-98
1997 Second in Command	28-day	1998	37.50	45-84
1997 Starfleet Doctors	28-day	1998	37.50	45-85
1998 Starfleet Navigators	28-day	1998	37.50	38-85
1998 Starfleet Security	28-day	1998	37.50	45-89
1998 Women of Star Trek	28-day	1998	37.50	50-92
1998 Engineers Tribute	28-day	1998	37.50	45-90

STAR TREK® : Captain James T. Kirk Autographed Wall Plaque - N/A

YEAR ISSUE	EDITION LIMIT	YEAR RETD.	ISSUE PRICE	*QUOTE U.S.$
1995 Captain James T. Kirk	5,000		195.00	195

STAR TREK® : Captain Jean-Luc Picard Autographed Wall Plaque - N/A

YEAR ISSUE	EDITION LIMIT	YEAR RETD.	ISSUE PRICE	*QUOTE U.S.$
1994 Captain Jean-Luc Picard	5,000		195.00	175-200

STAR TREK® : Deep Space 9 - M. Weistling

YEAR ISSUE	EDITION LIMIT	YEAR RETD.	ISSUE PRICE	*QUOTE U.S.$
1994 Commander Benjamin Sisko	28-day	1998	35.00	50-69
1994 Security Chief Odo	28-day	1998	35.00	50-68
1994 Major Kira Nerys	28-day	1998	35.00	75-92
1994 Space Station	28-day	1998	35.00	68-75
1994 Proprietor Quark	28-day	1998	35.00	50-68
1995 Doctor Julian Bashir	28-day	1998	35.00	50-68
1995 Lieutenant Jadzia Dax	28-day	1998	35.00	75-92
1995 Chief Miles O'Brien	28-day	1998	35.00	50-68

STAR TREK® : Deep Space 9 The Episodes - D. Blair

YEAR ISSUE	EDITION LIMIT	YEAR RETD.	ISSUE PRICE	*QUOTE U.S.$
1997 The Way of the Warrior	28-day	1998	39.95	40
1997 Emissary	28-day	1998	39.95	40

STAR TREK® : First Contact Sculptural Plate - J. Eaves

YEAR ISSUE	EDITION LIMIT	YEAR RETD.	ISSUE PRICE	*QUOTE U.S.$
1998 Maiden Voyage	28-day		49.95	50
1998 Resistance Is Futile	28-day		49.95	50

STAR TREK® : First Contact: A New Dimension - J. Eaves

YEAR ISSUE	EDITION LIMIT	YEAR RETD.	ISSUE PRICE	*QUOTE U.S.$
1998 Borg Cube	28-day		55.00	55
1998 U.S.S. Enterprise NCC-1701-E	28-day		55.00	55

STAR TREK® : First Contact: The Battle Begins - M. D. Ward

YEAR ISSUE	EDITION LIMIT	YEAR RETD.	ISSUE PRICE	*QUOTE U.S.$
1998 U.S.S. Defiant	28-day		39.95	40-50
1998 Borg Cube	28-day		39.95	40-50
1998 U.S.S. Enterprise NCC-1701-E	28-day		39.95	40-50
1998 Borg Sphere	28-day		39.95	40-150

STAR TREK® : First Contact: The Collective - K. Birdsong

YEAR ISSUE	EDITION LIMIT	YEAR RETD.	ISSUE PRICE	*QUOTE U.S.$
1998 Duty vs. Desire	Closed	1998	19.95	20

*Quotes have been rounded up to nearest dollar

YEAR ISSUE	EDITION LIMIT	YEAR RETD.	ISSUE PRICE	*QUOTE U.S.$
1998 The Borg are Back	Closed	1998	19.95	20
1998 Locutus of Borg	Closed	1998	19.95	20
1998 First Contact	Closed	1998	19.95	20
1998 Forward to the Past	Closed	1998	19.95	20
1998 Klingon Honor	Closed	1998	19.95	20
1998 Remember the Prime Directive	Closed	1998	19.95	20

STAR TREK® : First Contact: The Fourth Dimension - S. Wurmser

YEAR ISSUE	EDITION LIMIT	YEAR RETD.	ISSUE PRICE	*QUOTE U.S.$
1998 The Queen of the Hive	Closed	1998	45.00	45
1998 The Collective	Closed	1998	45.00	45

STAR TREK® : First Officer Spock® Autographed Wall Plaque - N/A

YEAR ISSUE	EDITION LIMIT	YEAR RETD.	ISSUE PRICE	*QUOTE U.S.$
1994 First Officer Spock®	2,500		195.00	195

STAR TREK® : Generations - K. Birdsong

YEAR ISSUE	EDITION LIMIT	YEAR RETD.	ISSUE PRICE	*QUOTE U.S.$
1996 The Ultimate Confrontation	28-day	1998	35.00	50-75
1996 Kirk's Final Voyage	28-day	1998	35.00	50-75
1996 Meeting In The Nexus	28-day	1998	35.00	50
1996 Picard's Christmas In The Nexus	28-day	1998	35.00	50
1996 Worf's Ceremony	28-day	1998	35.00	50
1996 The Final Plot/Duras Sisters	28-day	1998	35.00	50
1997 Stellar Cartography	28-day	1998	35.00	50
1997 Act of Courage	28-day	1998	35.00	50-82

STAR TREK® : Life of Spock - S. Stanley

YEAR ISSUE	EDITION LIMIT	YEAR RETD.	ISSUE PRICE	*QUOTE U.S.$
1997 Spock Reborn	28-day	1998	35.00	35-99
1997 Amok Time	28-day	1998	35.00	35-99
1997 Voyage Home	28-day	1998	35.00	35-49
1997 Wrath of Khan	28-day	1998	35.00	35-45
1997 Unification	28-day	1998	35.00	35-55

STAR TREK® : Ships in Motion - N/A

YEAR ISSUE	EDITION LIMIT	YEAR RETD.	ISSUE PRICE	*QUOTE U.S.$
1997 Full Impulse	Closed	1998	49.95	75-80
1997 Set a Course - Warp 5	Closed	1998	49.95	50-95
1997 Warp Speed	Closed	1998	49.95	50-59
1997 Maiden Voyage	Closed	1998	49.95	50-59

STAR TREK® : Starships Mini Plates - K. Birdsong

YEAR ISSUE	EDITION LIMIT	YEAR RETD.	ISSUE PRICE	*QUOTE U.S.$
1997 U.S.S. Enterprise NCC-1701	28-day	1998	25.90	26-35
1997 Klingon Battlecruiser	28-day	1998	set	32
1997 U.S.S. Enterprise NCC-1701 D	28-day	1998	set	32
1997 Romulan Warbird	28-day	1998	set	35
1997 U.S.S. Enterprise NCC-1701 A	28-day	1998	set	set
1997 Ferengei Marauder	28-day	1998	set	35
1997 Klingon Bird of Prey	28-day	1998	set	set
1997 Cardassian Galor Warship	28-day	1998	set	set
1997 Triple Nacelled U.S.S. Enterprise	28-day	1998	set	39
1997 U.S.S. Excelsior	28-day	1998	set	set
1997 U.S.S. Defiant NX-74205	28-day	1998	set	set
1997 U.S.S. Voyager NCC-74656	28-day	1998	set	set

STAR TREK® : The Movies - M. Weistling

YEAR ISSUE	EDITION LIMIT	YEAR RETD.	ISSUE PRICE	*QUOTE U.S.$
1994 STAR TREK IV: The Voyage Home	28-day	1998	35.00	75-90
1994 STAR TREK II: The Wrath of Khan	28-day	1998	35.00	75-92
1994 STAR TREK VI: The Undiscovered Country	28-day	1998	35.00	75-90
1995 STAR TREK III: The Search For Spock	28-day	1998	35.00	75-100
1995 STAR TREK V: The Final Frontier	28-day	1998	35.00	75
1996 Triumphant Return	28-day	1998	35.00	75
1996 Destruction of the Reliant	28-day	1998	35.00	75
1996 STAR TREK I: The Motion Picture	28-day	1998	35.00	75-85

STAR TREK® : The Next Generation - T. Blackshear

YEAR ISSUE	EDITION LIMIT	YEAR RETD.	ISSUE PRICE	*QUOTE U.S.$
1993 Captain Jean-Luc Picard	28-day	1998	35.00	100-180
1993 Commander William T. Riker	28-day	1998	35.00	75-130
1994 Lieutenant Commander Data	28-day	1998	35.00	75-120
1994 Lieutenant Worf	28-day	1998	35.00	75-98
1994 Counselor Deanna Troi	28-day	1998	35.00	75-120
1995 Dr. Beverly Crusher	28-day	1998	35.00	75-95
1995 Lieutenant Commander Laforge	28-day	1998	35.00	35-95
1996 Ensign W. Crusher	28-day	1998	35.00	35-95

STAR TREK® : The Next Generation 10th Anniversary Mini Plates - N/A

YEAR ISSUE	EDITION LIMIT	YEAR RETD.	ISSUE PRICE	*QUOTE U.S.$
1997 Captain Jean-Luc Picard	28-day	1998	25.90	30
1997 Commander William T. Riker	28-day	1998	set	75

STAR TREK® : The Next Generation 5th Anniversary - M. Weistling

YEAR ISSUE	EDITION LIMIT	YEAR RETD.	ISSUE PRICE	*QUOTE U.S.$
1997 Guinan	28-day	1998	35.00	55

STAR TREK® : The Next Generation Mini Plates - T. Blackshear/ K. Birdsong

YEAR ISSUE	EDITION LIMIT	YEAR RETD.	ISSUE PRICE	*QUOTE U.S.$
1997 Counselor Deanna Troi	28-day	1998	25.50	26
1997 Dr. Beverly Crusher	28-day	1998	set	set
1997 Lieutenant Commander Data	28-day	1998	set	set
1997 Lieutenant Worf	28-day	1998	set	set
1997 Best of Both Worlds	28-day	1998	set	set
1997 Encounter at Far Point	28-day	1998	set	set
1997 Lieutenant Commander Geordi Laforge	28-day	1998	set	set
1997 Ensign Wesley Crusher	28-day	1998	set	set
1997 All Good Things	28-day	1998	set	set
1997 Yesterday's Enterprise	28-day	1998	set	set

STAR TREK® : The Next Generation The Episodes - K. Birdsong

YEAR ISSUE	EDITION LIMIT	YEAR RETD.	ISSUE PRICE	*QUOTE U.S.$
1994 The Best of Both Worlds	28-day	1998	35.00	50-80
1994 Encounter at Far Point	28-day	1998	35.00	50-80
1995 Unification	28-day	1998	35.00	50-80
1995 Yesterday's Enterprise	28-day	1998	35.00	50
1995 All Good Things	28-day	1998	35.00	50
1995 Descent	28-day	1998	35.00	50
1996 Relics	28-day	1998	35.00	50
1996 Redemption	28-day	1998	35.00	50
1996 The Big Goodbye	28-day	1998	35.00	50
1996 The Inner Light	28-day	1998	35.00	50

STAR TREK® : The Original Episodes - J. Martin

YEAR ISSUE	EDITION LIMIT	YEAR RETD.	ISSUE PRICE	*QUOTE U.S.$
1996 The Tholian Web	28-day	1998	35.00	50-75
1996 Space Seed	28-day	1998	35.00	50
1996 The Menagerie	28-day	1998	35.00	50
1996 City on the Edge	28-day	1998	35.00	50
1996 Journel to Babel	28-day	1998	35.00	50
1996 Trouble With Tribbles	28-day	1998	35.00	50-65
1996 Where No Man Has Gone	28-day	1998	35.00	50-125
1996 Devil in the Dark	28-day	1998	35.00	50

STAR TREK® : The Power of Command - K. Birdsong

YEAR ISSUE	EDITION LIMIT	YEAR RETD.	ISSUE PRICE	*QUOTE U.S.$
1996 Captain Picard	28-day	1998	35.00	75-150
1996 Admiral Kirk	28-day	1998	35.00	75-120
1996 Captain Sisko	28-day	1998	35.00	50-110
1996 Captain Sulu	28-day	1998	35.00	50
1996 Janeway	28-day	1998	35.00	50-140
1996 Khan	28-day	1998	35.00	50
1996 General Chang	28-day	1998	35.00	50
1996 Dukat	28-day	1998	35.00	50-59
1997 Captain Kirk and the U.S.S. Enterprise NCC-1701	28-day	1998	35.00	75-125
1997 The Borg Queen and the Borg Sphere	28-day	1998	35.00	50-97

STAR TREK® : The Spock® Commemorative Wall Plaque - N/A

YEAR ISSUE	EDITION LIMIT	YEAR RETD.	ISSUE PRICE	*QUOTE U.S.$
1993 Spock®/STAR TREK VI The Undiscovered Country	2,500		195.00	195

STAR TREK® : The Voyagers - K. Birdsong

YEAR ISSUE	EDITION LIMIT	YEAR RETD.	ISSUE PRICE	*QUOTE U.S.$
1994 U.S.S. Enterprise NCC-1701	28-day	1998	35.00	100-120
1994 U.S.S. Enterprise NCC-1701-D	28-day	1998	35.00	75-120
1994 Klingon Battlecruiser	28-day	1998	35.00	75-95
1994 Romulan Warbird	28-day	1998	35.00	75-95
1994 U.S.S. Enterprise NCC-1701-A	28-day	1998	35.00	50-120
1995 Ferengi Marauder	28-day	1998	35.00	35-95
1995 Klingon Bird of Prey	28-day	1998	35.00	50-95
1995 Triple Nacelled U.S.S. Enterprise	28-day	1998	35.00	50
1995 Cardassian Galor Warship	28-day	1998	35.00	50
1995 U.S.S. Excelsior	28-day	1998	35.00	50

STAR TREK® : Voyager - D. Curry

YEAR ISSUE	EDITION LIMIT	YEAR RETD.	ISSUE PRICE	*QUOTE U.S.$
1996 The Voyage Begins	28-day	1998	35.00	50
1996 Bonds of Friendship	28-day	1998	35.00	50
1996 Life Signs	28-day	1998	35.00	50
1996 The Vidiians	28-day	1998	35.00	50
1997 New Beginnings	28-day	1998	35.00	50
1997 Basics	28-day	1998	35.00	50

Star Wars 10th Anniversary Commemorative - T. Blackshear

YEAR ISSUE	EDITION LIMIT	YEAR RETD.	ISSUE PRICE	*QUOTE U.S.$
1990 Star Wars 10th Anniversary Commemorative Plates	14-day	1998	39.50	175-200

Star Wars Heros and Villains - K. Birdsong

YEAR ISSUE	EDITION LIMIT	YEAR RETD.	ISSUE PRICE	*QUOTE U.S.$
1997 Luke Skywalker	28-day	1999	35.00	35-49
1997 Han Solo	28-day	1999	35.00	35-49
1997 Darth Vader	28-day	1999	35.00	35-49
1997 Princess Leia	28-day	1999	35.00	35-50
1997 Obi-Wan Kenobi	28-day	1999	35.00	35-49
1998 Boba Fett	28-day	1999	35.00	35-49
1998 Yoda I	28-day	1999	35.00	35-49
1999 Emperor Palpatine	28-day	1999	35.00	35-49

Star Wars Heros and Villains - Treadway

YEAR ISSUE	EDITION LIMIT	YEAR RETD.	ISSUE PRICE	*QUOTE U.S.$
1999 R2-D2	28-day	1999	35.00	35-49
1999 Chewbacca	28-day	1999	35.00	35-49
1999 Jabba the Hutt	28-day	1999	35.00	35-60
1999 Lando Calrissian	28-day	1999	35.00	35-55

Star Wars Plate Collection - T. Blackshear

YEAR ISSUE	EDITION LIMIT	YEAR RETD.	ISSUE PRICE	*QUOTE U.S.$
1987 Hans Solo	14-day	1999	29.50	190-250
1987 R2-D2 and Wicket	14-day	1999	29.50	190-250
1987 Luke Skywalker and Darth Vader	14-day	1999	29.50	150-250
1987 Princess Leia	14-day	1999	29.50	130-275
1987 The Imperial Walkers	14-day	1999	29.50	160-200
1987 Luke and Yoda	14-day	1999	29.50	180-200
1988 Space Battle	14-day	1999	29.50	210-250
1988 Crew in Cockpit	14-day	1999	29.50	225-250

Star Wars Space Vehicles - S. Hillios

YEAR ISSUE	EDITION LIMIT	YEAR RETD.	ISSUE PRICE	*QUOTE U.S.$
1995 Millenium Falcon	28-day	1999	35.00	46-75
1995 TIE Fighters	28-day	1999	35.00	50-65
1995 Red Five X-Wing Fighters	28-day	1999	35.00	50-65
1995 Imperial Shuttle	28-day	1999	35.00	50-65
1995 STAR Destroyer	28-day	1999	35.00	50-65
1996 Snow Speeders	28-day	1999	35.00	50-58
1996 B-Wing Fighter	28-day	1999	35.00	35-58
1996 The Slave I	28-day	1999	35.00	50-58
1996 Medical Frigate	28-day	1999	35.00	50-65
1996 Jabba's Sail Barge	28-day	1999	35.00	60-75
1997 Y-Wing Fighter	28-day	1999	35.00	50-69
1997 Death Star	28-day	1999	35.00	50-69

Star Wars Trilogy - M. Weistling

YEAR ISSUE	EDITION LIMIT	YEAR RETD.	ISSUE PRICE	*QUOTE U.S.$
1993 Star Wars	28-day		37.50	115-250
1993 The Empire Strikes Back	28-day		37.50	115-255
1993 Return Of The Jedi	28-day		37.50	115-255

Starships of the Next Generation - B. Eggleton

YEAR ISSUE	EDITION LIMIT	YEAR RETD.	ISSUE PRICE	*QUOTE U.S.$
1996 Engage	28-day	1998	39.95	85
1997 Enterprise of the Future	28-day	1998	39.95	40-75
1997 Resistance is Futile	28-day	1998	39.95	40-90
1997 All Good Things	28-day	1998	39.95	40-75
1997 Klingon Defense Force	28-day	1998	39.95	40-90
1997 Unexpected Confrontation	28-day	1998	39.95	40-95
1997 Searching the Galaxy	28-day	1998	39.95	40-75
1997 Shields Up	28-day	1998	39.95	40-75
1997 Yesterday's Enterprise	28-day	1998	39.95	40-75
1997 Earth's Last Stand	28-day	1998	39.95	40-75

Summer Days of Childhood - T. Utz

YEAR ISSUE	EDITION LIMIT	YEAR RETD.	ISSUE PRICE	*QUOTE U.S.$
1983 Mountain Friends	10-day		29.50	30-35
1983 Garden Magic	10-day		29.50	30
1983 Little Beachcombers	10-day		29.50	30
1983 Blowing Bubbles	10-day		29.50	30
1983 Birthday Party	10-day		29.50	30
1983 Playing Doctor	10-day		29.50	30
1983 Stolen Kiss	10-day		29.50	30
1983 Kitty's Bathtime	10-day		29.50	30
1983 Cooling Off	10-day		29.50	30
1983 First Cucumber	10-day		29.50	30
1983 A Jumping Contest	10-day		29.50	30
1983 Balloon Carnival	10-day		29.50	30

Symphony of the Sea - R. Koni

YEAR ISSUE	EDITION LIMIT	YEAR RETD.	ISSUE PRICE	*QUOTE U.S.$
1995 Fluid Grace	28-day		29.95	30-35
1995 Dolphin's Dance	28-day		29.95	30-35
1995 Orca Ballet	28-day		29.95	30-39
1995 Moonlit Minuet	28-day		29.95	30-39
1995 Sailfish Serenade	28-day		29.95	30-35
1995 Starlit Waltz	28-day		29.95	30-35
1995 Sunset Splendor	28-day		29.95	30-35
1995 Coral Chorus	28-day		29.95	30-35

Those Delightful Dalmations - N/A

YEAR ISSUE	EDITION LIMIT	YEAR RETD.	ISSUE PRICE	*QUOTE U.S.$
1995 You Missed a Spot	28-day		29.95	25-30
1995 Here's a Good Spot	28-day		29.95	25-30
1996 The Best Spot	28-day		29.95	25-30
1996 Spotted In the Headlines	28-day		29.95	25-30
1996 A Spot In My Heart	28-day		29.95	25-30
1996 Sweet Spots	28-day		29.95	25-30
1996 Naptime Already?	28-day		29.95	25-30
1996 He's In My Spot	28-day		29.95	25-30
1996 The Serious Studying Spot	28-day		29.95	25-30
1996 Check Out My Spots	28-day		29.95	25-30

Timeless Expressions of the Orient - M. Tsang

YEAR ISSUE	EDITION LIMIT	YEAR RETD.	ISSUE PRICE	*QUOTE U.S.$
1990 Fidelity	15,000		75.00	95
1991 Femininity	15,000		75.00	75
1991 Longevity	15,000		75.00	75
1991 Beauty	15,000		55.00	55
1992 Courage	15,000		55.00	55

Treasured Days - H. Bond

YEAR ISSUE	EDITION LIMIT	YEAR RETD.	ISSUE PRICE	*QUOTE U.S.$
1987 Ashley	14-day		29.50	70-90
1987 Christopher	14-day		24.50	35-40
1987 Sara	14-day		24.50	40-45
1987 Jeremy	14-day		24.50	29-40
1987 Amanda	14-day		24.50	35-45
1988 Nicholas	14-day		24.50	40-45
1988 Lindsay	14-day		24.50	29-40
1988 Justin	14-day		24.50	40-50

A Treasury of Cherished Teddies - P. Hillman

YEAR ISSUE	EDITION LIMIT	YEAR RETD.	ISSUE PRICE	*QUOTE U.S.$
1994 Happy Holidays, Friend	28-day		29.50	30
1995 A New Year with Old Friends	28-day		29.50	30
1995 Valentines For You	28-day		29.50	30
1995 Friendship is in the Air	28-day		29.50	30
1995 Showers of Friendship	28-day		29.50	30
1996 Friendship is in Bloom	28-day		29.50	30
1996 Planting the Seeds of Friendship	28-day		29.50	30
1996 A Day in the Park	28-day		29.50	30
1996 Smooth Sailing	28-day		29.50	30
1996 School Days	28-day		29.50	30
1996 Holiday Harvest	28-day		29.50	30
1996 Thanks For Friends	28-day		29.50	30

Unbridled Spirit - C. DeHaan

YEAR ISSUE	EDITION LIMIT	YEAR RETD.	ISSUE PRICE	*QUOTE U.S.$
1992 Surf Dancer	28-day		29.50	30-45
1992 Winter Renegade	28-day		29.50	30-50
1992 Desert Shadows	28-day		29.50	30-45
1993 Painted Sunrise	28-day		29.50	30-50
1993 Desert Duel	28-day		29.50	30-40
1993 Midnight Run	28-day		29.50	30-45
1993 Moonlight Majesty	28-day		29.50	30-45
1993 Autumn Reverie	28-day		29.50	30-39
1993 Blizzard's Peril	28-day		29.50	30-50
1993 Sunrise Surprise	28-day		29.50	30-40

Under the Sea - C. Bragg

YEAR ISSUE	EDITION LIMIT	YEAR RETD.	ISSUE PRICE	*QUOTE U.S.$
1993 Tales of Tavarua	28-day		29.50	40-48
1993 Water's Edge	28-day		29.50	40-45
1994 Beauty of the Reef	28-day		29.50	40-45
1994 Rainbow Reef	28-day		29.50	40-45
1994 Orca Odyssey	28-day		29.50	30-40
1994 Rescue the Reef	28-day		29.50	36-40
1994 Underwater Dance	28-day		29.50	36-40
1994 Gentle Giants	28-day		29.50	30-40
1995 Undersea Enchantment	28-day		29.50	30-40
1995 Penguin Paradise	28-day		29.50	30-40

*Quotes have been rounded up to nearest dollar

PLATES/PLAQUES

Undersea Visions - J. Enright

Year Issue	Edition Limit	Year Retd.	Issue Price	*Quote U.S.$
1995 Secret Sanctuary	28-day		29.95	30-45
1995 Temple of Treasures	28-day		29.95	40-45
1996 Temple Beneath the Sea	28-day		29.95	40-45
1996 Lost Kingdom	28-day		29.95	30-40
1996 Mysterious Ruins	28-day		29.95	30-40
1996 Last Journey	28-day		29.95	30-40
1996 Egyptian Dreamscape	28-day		29.95	30-40
1996 Lost Galleon	28-day		29.95	30-40

Utz Mother's Day - T. Utz

Year Issue	Edition Limit	Year Retd.	Issue Price	*Quote U.S.$
1983 A Gift of Love	N/A		27.50	35-38
1983 Mother's Helping Hand	N/A		27.50	28-35
1983 Mother's Angel	N/A		27.50	28-35

Vanishing Rural America - J. Harrison

Year Issue	Edition Limit	Year Retd.	Issue Price	*Quote U.S.$
1991 Quiet Reflections	14-day		29.50	40-45
1991 Autumn's Passage	14-day		29.50	40-45
1991 Storefront Memories	14-day		29.50	30-40
1991 Country Path	14-day		29.50	36-40
1991 When the Circus Came To Town	14-day		29.50	36-40
1991 Covered in Fall	14-day		29.50	40-45
1991 America's Heartland	14-day		29.50	33-40
1991 Rural Delivery	14-day		29.50	33-40

Victorian Christmas Memories - J. Grossman

Year Issue	Edition Limit	Year Retd.	Issue Price	*Quote U.S.$
1992 A Visit from St. Nicholas	28-day		29.50	35-42
1993 Christmas Delivery	28-day		29.50	40-51
1993 Christmas Angels	28-day		29.50	30-35
1992 With Visions of Sugar Plums	28-day		29.50	30-65
1993 Merry Olde Kris Kringle	28-day		29.50	35-65
1993 Grandfather Frost	28-day		29.50	30-35
1993 Joyous Noel	28-day		29.50	35-45
1993 Christmas Innocence	28-day		29.50	35-80
1993 Dreaming of Santa	28-day		29.50	40
1993 Mistletoe & Holly	28-day		29.50	35-40

Victorian Playtime - M. H. Bogart

Year Issue	Edition Limit	Year Retd.	Issue Price	*Quote U.S.$
1991 A Busy Day	14-day		29.50	45-65
1992 Little Masterpiece	14-day		29.50	45-65
1992 Playing Bride	14-day		29.50	85-90
1992 Waiting for a Nibble	14-day		29.50	45-65
1992 Tea and Gossip	14-day		29.50	55-65
1992 Cleaning House	14-day		29.50	45-65
1992 A Little Persuasion	14-day		29.50	45-65
1992 Peek-a-Boo	14-day		29.50	45-65

Voyages of the Starship Enterprise - K. Birdsong

Year Issue	Edition Limit	Year Retd.	Issue Price	*Quote U.S.$
1997 NCC-1701-E	Closed		24.95	50
1997 NCC-1701-D	Closed		24.95	50
1997 NCC-1701-Refit	Closed		24.95	50
1997 NCC-1701	Closed		24.95	50

Warrior's Pride - C. DeHaan

Year Issue	Edition Limit	Year Retd.	Issue Price	*Quote U.S.$
1994 Crow War Pony	28-day		29.50	30-35
1994 Running Free	28-day		29.50	30-35
1994 Blackfoot War Pony	28-day		29.50	30-35
1994 Southern Cheyenne	28-day		29.50	30-35
1995 Shoshoni War Ponies	28-day		29.50	30-35
1995 A Champion's Revelry	28-day		29.50	30-35
1995 Battle Colors	28-day		29.50	30-35
1995 Call of the Drums	28-day		29.50	30-35

WCW Sting Plate Collection - N/A

Year Issue	Edition Limit	Year Retd.	Issue Price	*Quote U.S.$
1998 Sting	Open		35.00	35
1998 The Stinger!	Open		35.00	35
1998 The White Knight	Open		35.00	35
1998 Mystery Man	Open		35.00	35

The West of Frank McCarthy - F. McCarthy

Year Issue	Edition Limit	Year Retd.	Issue Price	*Quote U.S.$
1991 Attacking the Iron Horse	14-day		37.50	60-65
1991 Attempt on the Stage	14-day		37.50	45-55
1991 The Prayer	14-day		37.50	55
1991 On the Old North Trail	14-day		37.50	55
1991 The Hostile Threat	14-day		37.50	45
1991 Bringing Out the Furs	14-day		37.50	45
1991 Kiowa Raider	14-day		37.50	45
1991 Headed North	14-day		37.50	39-45

Wilderness Spirits - P. Koni

Year Issue	Edition Limit	Year Retd.	Issue Price	*Quote U.S.$
1994 Eyes of the Night	28-day		29.95	30
1995 Howl of Innocence	28-day		29.95	30
1995 Midnight Call	28-day		29.95	30
1995 Breaking the Silence	28-day		29.95	30
1995 Moonlight Run	28-day		29.95	30
1995 Sunset Vigil	28-day		29.95	30
1995 Sunrise Spirit	28-day		29.95	30
1996 Valley of the Wolf	28-day		29.95	30

Winged Reflections - R. Parker

Year Issue	Edition Limit	Year Retd.	Issue Price	*Quote U.S.$
1989 Following Mama	14-day		37.50	38
1989 Above the Breakers	14-day		37.50	38
1989 Among the Reeds	14-day		37.50	38
1989 Freeze Up	14-day		37.50	38
1989 Wings Above the Water	14-day		37.50	38
1990 Summer Loon	14-day		29.50	30
1990 Early Spring	14-day		29.50	30
1990 At The Water's Edge	14-day		29.50	30

Wings of Freedom - S. Hardock

Year Issue	Edition Limit	Year Retd.	Issue Price	*Quote U.S.$
1999 Coming Home	28-day		39.95	40
1999 Noble Watch	28-day		39.95	40
1999 Glorious Flight	28-day		39.95	40
1999 Regal Sanctuary	28-day		39.95	40
2000 Windswept Return	28-day		39.95	40

Winter Rails - T. Xaras

Year Issue	Edition Limit	Year Retd.	Issue Price	*Quote U.S.$
1992 Winter Crossing	28-day		29.50	45
1993 Coal Country	28-day		29.50	30-65
1993 Daylight Run	28-day		29.50	30-65
1993 By Sea or Rail	28-day		29.50	30-65
1993 Country Crossroads	28-day		29.50	30-65
1993 Timber Line	28-day		29.50	60
1993 The Long Haul	28-day		29.50	30-65
1993 Darby Crossing	28-day		29.50	30-65
1995 East Broad Top	28-day		29.50	30-65
1995 Landsdowne Station	28-day		29.50	30-65

Winter Wildlife - J. Seerey-Lester

Year Issue	Edition Limit	Year Retd.	Issue Price	*Quote U.S.$
1989 Close Encounters	15,000		55.00	55-60
1989 Among the Cattails	15,000		55.00	55-60
1989 The Refuge	15,000		55.00	55-60
1989 Out of the Blizzard	15,000		55.00	55-60
1989 First Snow	15,000		55.00	55-60
1989 Lying In Wait	15,000		55.00	55-60
1989 Winter Hiding	15,000		55.00	55-60
1989 Early Snow	15,000		55.00	55-60

Wizard of Oz Commemorative - T. Blackshear

Year Issue	Edition Limit	Year Retd.	Issue Price	*Quote U.S.$
1988 We're Off to See the Wizard	14-day		24.50	150-210
1988 Dorothy Meets the Scarecrow	14-day		24.50	150-210
1989 The Tin Man Speaks	14-day		24.50	90-210
1989 A Glimpse of the Munchkins	14-day		24.50	150-200
1989 The Witch Casts A Spell	14-day		24.50	150-250
1989 If I Were King Of The Forest	14-day		24.50	125-200
1989 The Great and Powerful Oz	14-day		24.50	150-200
1989 There's No Place Like Home	14-day		24.50	150-250

Wizard of Oz-Fifty Years of Oz - T. Blackshear

Year Issue	Edition Limit	Year Retd.	Issue Price	*Quote U.S.$
1989 Fifty Years of Oz	14-day		37.50	175-300

Wizard of Oz-Portraits From Oz - T. Blackshear

Year Issue	Edition Limit	Year Retd.	Issue Price	*Quote U.S.$
1989 Dorothy	14-day		29.50	200-325
1989 Scarecrow	14-day		29.50	200-265
1989 Tin Man	14-day		29.50	200-249
1990 Cowardly Lion	14-day		29.50	200-249
1990 Glinda	14-day		29.50	200-270
1990 Wizard	14-day		29.50	95-225
1990 Wicked Witch	14-day		29.50	175-290
1990 Toto	14-day		29.50	275-350

The Wonder Of Christmas - J. McClelland

Year Issue	Edition Limit	Year Retd.	Issue Price	*Quote U.S.$
1991 Santa's Secret	28-day		29.50	30
1991 My Favorite Ornament	28-day		29.50	30
1991 Waiting For Santa	28-day		29.50	30
1993 The Caroler	28-day		29.50	30

A World of Puppy Adventures - J. Ren

Year Issue	Edition Limit	Year Retd.	Issue Price	*Quote U.S.$
1995 The Water's Fine	28-day		29.95	30-55
1996 Swimming Lessons	28-day		29.95	30
1996 Breakfast Is Served	28-day		29.95	30
1996 Laundry Tug O' War	28-day		29.95	30
1996 Did I Do That?	28-day		29.95	30
1996 DeCoy Dismay	28-day		29.95	30
1996 Puppy Picnic	28-day		29.95	30
1996 Sweet Terrors	28-day		29.95	30

The World Of Zolan - D. Zolan

Year Issue	Edition Limit	Year Retd.	Issue Price	*Quote U.S.$
1992 First Kiss	28-day		29.50	30-100
1992 Morning Discovery	28-day		29.50	30-35
1993 The Little Fisherman	28-day		29.50	30-75
1993 Letter to Grandma	28-day		29.50	30-85
1993 Twilight Prayer	28-day		29.50	30-85
1993 Flowers for Mother	28-day		29.50	55-80

Year Of The Wolf - A. Agnew

Year Issue	Edition Limit	Year Retd.	Issue Price	*Quote U.S.$
1993 Broken Silence	28-day		29.50	30-55
1993 Leader of the Pack	28-day		29.50	30-35
1993 Solitude	28-day		29.50	30-35
1994 Tundra Light	28-day		29.50	30-35
1994 Guardians of the High Country	28-day		29.50	30-35
1994 A Second Glance	28-day		29.50	27-55
1994 Free as the Wind	28-day		29.50	30-35
1994 Song of the Wolf	28-day		29.50	27-30
1995 Lords of the Tundra	28-day		29.50	27-30
1995 Wilderness Companions	28-day		29.50	30-35

Young Lords of The Wild - M. Richter

Year Issue	Edition Limit	Year Retd.	Issue Price	*Quote U.S.$
1994 Siberian Tiger Club	28-day		29.95	30-45
1995 Snow Leopard Cub	28-day		29.95	30-45
1995 Lion Cub	28-day		29.95	30
1995 Clouded Leopard Cub	28-day		29.95	30
1995 Cougar Cub	28-day		29.95	30
1995 Leopard Cub	28-day		29.95	30
1995 Cheetah Cub	28-day		29.95	30
1996 Canadian Lynx Cub	28-day		29.95	30

Hamilton/Boehm

Award Winning Roses - Boehm

Year Issue	Edition Limit	Year Retd.	Issue Price	*Quote U.S.$
1979 Peace Rose	15,000		45.00	100
1979 White Masterpiece Rose	15,000		45.00	75
1979 Tropicana Rose	15,000		45.00	63
1979 Elegance Rose	15,000		45.00	63
1979 Queen Elizabeth Rose	15,000		45.00	63
1979 Royal Highness Rose	15,000		45.00	63
1979 Angel Face Rose	15,000		45.00	63
1979 Mr. Lincoln Rose	15,000		45.00	63

Gamebirds of North America - Boehm

Year Issue	Edition Limit	Year Retd.	Issue Price	*Quote U.S.$
1984 Ring-Necked Pheasant	15,000		62.50	63
1984 Bob White Quail	15,000		62.50	63
1984 American Woodcock	15,000		62.50	63
1984 California Quail	15,000		62.50	63
1984 Ruffed Grouse	15,000		62.50	63
1984 Wild Turkey	15,000		62.50	63
1984 Willow Partridge	15,000		62.50	63
1984 Prairie Grouse	15,000		62.50	63

Hummingbird Collection - Boehm

Year Issue	Edition Limit	Year Retd.	Issue Price	*Quote U.S.$
1980 Calliope	15,000		62.50	80
1980 Broadbilled	15,000		62.50	63
1980 Rufous Flame Bearer	15,000		62.50	80
1980 Broadtail	15,000		62.50	63
1980 Streamertail	15,000		62.50	80
1980 Blue Throated	15,000		62.50	80
1980 Crimson Topaz	15,000		62.50	63
1980 Brazilian Ruby	15,000		62.50	80

Owl Collection - Boehm

Year Issue	Edition Limit	Year Retd.	Issue Price	*Quote U.S.$
1980 Boreal Owl	15,000		45.00	95
1980 Snowy Owl	15,000		45.00	95
1980 Barn Owl	15,000		45.00	80
1980 Saw Whet Owl	15,000		45.00	75
1980 Great Horned Owl	15,000		45.00	60-75
1980 Screech Owl	15,000		45.00	75
1980 Short Eared Owl	15,000		45.00	75
1980 Barred Owl	15,000		45.00	60-75

Water Birds - Boehm

Year Issue	Edition Limit	Year Retd.	Issue Price	*Quote U.S.$
1981 Canada Geese	15,000		62.50	65
1981 Wood Ducks	15,000		62.50	65
1981 Hooded Merganser	15,000		62.50	65
1981 Ross's Geese	15,000		62.50	65
1981 Common Mallard	15,000		62.50	65
1981 Canvas Back	15,000		62.50	65
1981 Green Winged Teal	15,000		62.50	65
1981 American Pintail	15,000		62.50	65

Haviland

Twelve Days of Christmas - R. Hetreau

Year Issue	Edition Limit	Year Retd.	Issue Price	*Quote U.S.$
1970 Partridge	30,000		25.00	80
1971 Two Turtle Doves	30,000		25.00	30
1972 Three French Hens	30,000		27.50	30
1973 Four Calling Birds	30,000		28.50	30
1974 Five Golden Rings	30,000		30.00	30
1975 Six Geese a'laying	30,000		32.50	33
1976 Seven Swans	30,000		38.00	38
1977 Eight Maids	30,000		40.00	40
1978 Nine Ladies Dancing	30,000		45.00	45
1979 Ten Lord's a'leaping	30,000		50.00	50
1980 Eleven Pipers Piping	30,000		55.00	55
1981 Twelve Drummers	30,000		60.00	60

Haviland & Parlon

Christmas Madonnas - Various

Year Issue	Edition Limit	Year Retd.	Issue Price	*Quote U.S.$
1972 By Raphael - Raphael	5,000		35.00	42
1973 By Feruzzi - Feruzzi	5,000		40.00	78
1974 By Raphael - Raphael	5,000		42.50	43
1975 By Murillo - Murillo	7,500		42.50	43
1976 By Botticelli - Botticelli	7,500		45.00	45
1977 By Bellini - Bellini	7,500		48.00	48
1978 By Lippi - Lippi	7,500		48.00	53
1979 Madonna of The Eucharist - Botticelli	7,500		49.50	112

House of Hatten, Inc.

River Road - D. Calla

Year Issue	Edition Limit	Year Retd.	Issue Price	*Quote U.S.$
2000 Santa/Basket Plaque 19" x 10" 27501	Open		78.00	78
2000 Santa/Deer Plaque 20" x 15" 27500	Open		98.00	98

Hutschenreuther

The Glory of Christmas - W./C. Hallett

Year Issue	Edition Limit	Year Retd.	Issue Price	*Quote U.S.$
1982 The Nativity	25,000		80.00	125
1983 The Annunciation	25,000		80.00	115
1984 The Shepherds	25,000		80.00	100
1985 The Wiseman	25,000		80.00	100

Gunther Granget - G. Granget

Year Issue	Edition Limit	Year Retd.	Issue Price	*Quote U.S.$
1972 American Sparrows	5,000		50.00	75-100
1972 European Sparrows	5,000		30.00	65
1973 American Kildeer	2,250		75.00	75
1973 American Squirrel	2,500		75.00	75
1973 European Squirrel	2,500		35.00	50
1974 American Partridge	2,500		75.00	90
1975 American Rabbits	2,500		90.00	90
1976 Freedom in Flight	5,000		100.00	100
1976 Wrens	2,500		100.00	110
1976 Freedom in Flight, Gold	200		200.00	200
1977 Bears	2,500		100.00	100
1978 Foxes' Spring Journey	1,000		125.00	200

*Quotes have been rounded up to nearest dollar

Imperial Ching-te Chen

Beauties of the Red Mansion - Z. HuiMin

YEAR ISSUE	EDITION LIMIT	YEAR RETD.	ISSUE PRICE	*QUOTE U.S.$
1986 Pao-chai	115-day		27.92	12-30
1986 Yuan-chun	115-day		27.92	14-30
1987 Hsi-feng	115-day		30.92	15-35
1987 Hsi-chun	115-day		30.92	15-35
1988 Miao-yu	115-day		30.92	15-35
1988 Ying-chun	115-day		30.92	15-35
1988 Tai-yu	115-day		32.92	21-35
1988 Li-wan	115-day		32.92	21-35
1988 Ko-Ching	115-day		32.92	24-35
1988 Hsiang-yun	115-day		34.92	24-35
1989 Tan-Chun	115-day		34.92	24-35
1989 Chiao-chieh	115-day		34.92	15-35

Blessings From a Chinese Garden - Z. Song Mao

YEAR ISSUE	EDITION LIMIT	YEAR RETD.	ISSUE PRICE	*QUOTE U.S.$
1988 The Gift of Purity	175-day		39.92	19-40
1989 The Gift of Grace	175-day		39.92	20-40
1989 The Gift of Beauty	175-day		42.92	17-43
1989 The Gift of Happiness	175-day		42.92	28-43
1990 The Gift of Truth	175-day		42.92	35
1990 The Gift of Joy	175-day		42.92	23-30

Flower Goddesses of China - Z. HuiMin

YEAR ISSUE	EDITION LIMIT	YEAR RETD.	ISSUE PRICE	*QUOTE U.S.$
1991 The Lotus Goddess	175-day		34.92	15-35
1991 The Chrysanthemum Goddess	175-day		34.92	19-35
1991 The Plum Blossom Goddess	175-day		37.92	27-38
1991 The Peony Goddess	175-day		37.92	25-38
1991 The Narcissus Goddess	175-day		37.92	37-50
1991 The Camellia Goddess	175-day		37.92	26-38

The Forbidden City - S. Fu

YEAR ISSUE	EDITION LIMIT	YEAR RETD.	ISSUE PRICE	*QUOTE U.S.$
1990 Pavilion of 10,000 Springs	150-day		39.92	10-40
1990 Flying Kites/Spring Day	150-day		39.92	25-40
1990 Pavilion/Floating Jade Green	150-day		42.92	21-43
1991 The Lantern Festival	150-day		42.92	17-43
1991 Nine Dragon Screen	150-day		42.92	18-43
1991 The Hall of the Cultivating Mind	150-day		42.92	22-43
1991 Dressing the Empress	150-day		45.92	33-46
1991 Pavilion of Floating Cups	150-day		45.92	30-46

Garden of Satin Wings - J. Xue-Bing

YEAR ISSUE	EDITION LIMIT	YEAR RETD.	ISSUE PRICE	*QUOTE U.S.$
1992 A Morning Dream	115-day		29.92	30-35
1993 An Evening Mist	115-day		29.92	28-36
1993 A Garden Whisper	115-day		29.92	36-40
1993 An Enchanting Interlude	115-day		29.92	34-40

Legends of West Lake - J. Xue-Bing

YEAR ISSUE	EDITION LIMIT	YEAR RETD.	ISSUE PRICE	*QUOTE U.S.$
1989 Lady White	175-day		29.92	19-30
1990 Lady Silkworm	175-day		29.92	29-50
1990 Laurel Peak	175-day		29.92	32
1990 Rising Sun Terrace	175-day		32.92	32
1990 The Apricot Fairy	175-day		32.92	15-33
1990 Bright Pearl	175-day		32.92	17-33
1990 Thread of Sky	175-day		34.92	14-35
1991 Phoenix Mountain	175-day		34.92	17-35
1991 Ancestors of Tea	175-day		34.92	18-35
1991 Three Pools Mirroring/Moon	175-day		36.92	23-37
1991 Fly-In Peak	175-day		36.92	23-40
1991 The Case of the Folding Fans	175-day		36.92	40-48

Maidens of the Folding Sky - J. Xue-Bing

YEAR ISSUE	EDITION LIMIT	YEAR RETD.	ISSUE PRICE	*QUOTE U.S.$
1992 Lady Lu	175-day		29.92	34-38
1992 Mistress Yang	175-day		29.92	35-58
1992 Bride Yen Chun	175-day		32.92	40-65
1993 Parrot Maiden	175-day		32.92	70

Scenes from the Summer Palace - Z. Song Mao

YEAR ISSUE	EDITION LIMIT	YEAR RETD.	ISSUE PRICE	*QUOTE U.S.$
1988 The Marble Boat	175-day		29.92	12-35
1988 Jade Belt Bridge	175-day		29.92	15-35
1989 Hall that Dispels the Clouds	175-day		32.92	25-33
1989 The Long Promenade	175-day		32.92	20-39
1989 Garden/Harmonious Pleasure	175-day		32.92	23-33
1989 The Great Stage	175-day		32.92	26-33
1989 Seventeen Arch Bridge	175-day		34.92	18-35
1989 Boaters on Kumming Lake	175-day		34.92	16-35

International Silver

Bicentennial - M. Deoliveira

YEAR ISSUE	EDITION LIMIT	YEAR RETD.	ISSUE PRICE	*QUOTE U.S.$
1972 Signing Declaration	7,500		40.00	310
1973 Paul Revere	7,500		40.00	160
1974 Concord Bridge	7,500		40.00	115
1975 Crossing Delaware	7,500		50.00	80
1976 Valley Forge	7,500		50.00	65
1977 Surrender at Yorktown	7,500		50.00	60

Islandia International

African Wildlife - T. Swanson

YEAR ISSUE	EDITION LIMIT	YEAR RETD.	ISSUE PRICE	*QUOTE U.S.$
1997 Elephant	Numbrd.		30.00	33
1997 Lion	Numbrd.		30.00	33
1997 Giraffe	Numbrd.		30.00	33
1997 Zebra	Numbrd.		30.00	33

Birds of Prey - T. Swanson

YEAR ISSUE	EDITION LIMIT	YEAR RETD.	ISSUE PRICE	*QUOTE U.S.$
2000 Monarchs of the Sky - Bald Eagle	30-day		32.50	33

Celebration of Christmas - K. Dowd

YEAR ISSUE	EDITION LIMIT	YEAR RETD.	ISSUE PRICE	*QUOTE U.S.$
1997 Checking His List	Numbrd.		30.00	33
1997 Christmas Party	Numbrd.		30.00	33
1997 Harvesting Wood For Toys	Numbrd.		30.00	33
1997 The First Christmas Tree	Numbrd.		30.00	33

Chiefs of Nations - Jonnié Chardonn

YEAR ISSUE	EDITION LIMIT	YEAR RETD.	ISSUE PRICE	*QUOTE U.S.$
1999 Pautiwa	10,000		39.95	40
1999 Titichakyo	10,000		39.95	40

Coming Home - C. Hayes

YEAR ISSUE	EDITION LIMIT	YEAR RETD.	ISSUE PRICE	*QUOTE U.S.$
1997 The American Air Force	Numbrd.		30.00	33
1997 The American Army (White Male)	Numbrd.		30.00	33
1997 The American Navy	Numbrd.		30.00	33
1997 The American Marines	Numbrd.		30.00	33
1997 The American Army (African-American)	Numbrd.		30.00	33
1997 The American Army (White Female)	Numbrd.		30.00	33

Creation & Emergence - Jonnié Chardonn

YEAR ISSUE	EDITION LIMIT	YEAR RETD.	ISSUE PRICE	*QUOTE U.S.$
1999 First White Hactcin Female Dream	10,000		39.95	40
1999 First Black Hactcin Female Dream	10,000		39.95	40

Feathered Friends - S. Etem

YEAR ISSUE	EDITION LIMIT	YEAR RETD.	ISSUE PRICE	*QUOTE U.S.$
1998 Bluebird of Happiness	30-day		30.00	33
1998 Reach For Your Dreams	30-day		30.00	33

Festival of Life - W. A. Still

YEAR ISSUE	EDITION LIMIT	YEAR RETD.	ISSUE PRICE	*QUOTE U.S.$
1998 "Blessed Day" - Wedding	30-day		30.00	33
1998 "Blessed Event" - New Baby	30-day		30.00	33
1998 "Blessed Holiday" - Christmas	30-day		30.00	33

Fine Art of Gretchen Clasby - G. Clasby

YEAR ISSUE	EDITION LIMIT	YEAR RETD.	ISSUE PRICE	*QUOTE U.S.$
1999 Dogwood Days	30-day		32.50	33
1999 Garden Party	30-day		32.50	33
2000 Dogwood Delight	30-day		32.50	33
2000 Garden Gaiety	30-day		32.50	33

Gift of Love - S. Etem

YEAR ISSUE	EDITION LIMIT	YEAR RETD.	ISSUE PRICE	*QUOTE U.S.$
1998 The Miracle of Life	30-day		30.00	33
1998 Miracle of Friends	30-day		30.00	33

Great Bears of the World - T. Swanson

YEAR ISSUE	EDITION LIMIT	YEAR RETD.	ISSUE PRICE	*QUOTE U.S.$
1998 The Black Bear	Numbrd.		30.00	33
1998 The Grizzly Bear	Numbrd.		30.00	33
1998 The Koala Bear	Numbrd.		30.00	33
1998 The Panda Bear	Numbrd.		30.00	33
1998 The Polar Bear	Numbrd.		30.00	33

International Fatcats - G. Pitt

YEAR ISSUE	EDITION LIMIT	YEAR RETD.	ISSUE PRICE	*QUOTE U.S.$
1997 USA	Numbrd.		30.00	33
1997 Switzerland	Numbrd.		30.00	33
1997 Spain	Numbrd.		30.00	33
1997 Russia	Numbrd.		30.00	33
1997 Mexico	Numbrd.		30.00	33
1997 Japan	Numbrd.		30.00	33
1997 Italy	Numbrd.		30.00	33
1997 Israel	Numbrd.		30.00	33
1997 India	Numbrd.		30.00	33
1997 Greece	Numbrd.		30.00	33
1997 Great Britain	Numbrd.		30.00	33
1997 Germany	Numbrd.		30.00	33
1997 France	Numbrd.		30.00	33
1997 China	Numbrd.		30.00	33
1997 Canada	Numbrd.		30.00	33
1997 Australia	Numbrd.		30.00	33
1999 Poland	Numbrd.		32.50	33
1999 Ireland	Numbrd.		32.50	33

Kat Kapers - K. Swanson

YEAR ISSUE	EDITION LIMIT	YEAR RETD.	ISSUE PRICE	*QUOTE U.S.$
2000 King of the Sill	30-day		32.50	33

Large Cats of North America - T. Swanson

YEAR ISSUE	EDITION LIMIT	YEAR RETD.	ISSUE PRICE	*QUOTE U.S.$
1999 Keeping An Eye Out	30-day		32.50	33
1999 King of the Mountain	30-day		32.50	33
1999 Descending Grace	30-day		32.50	33
1999 The King of His Throne	30-day		32.50	33

Mocking Bird - Jonnié Chardonn

YEAR ISSUE	EDITION LIMIT	YEAR RETD.	ISSUE PRICE	*QUOTE U.S.$
1999 Hethuska	10,000		39.95	40
1999 Shadamgeah	10,000		39.95	40

Moon of the Sun - Jonnié Chardonn

YEAR ISSUE	EDITION LIMIT	YEAR RETD.	ISSUE PRICE	*QUOTE U.S.$
1999 Tcu-Unnyikita	10,000		39.95	40
1999 Uwashil	10,000		39.95	40

North American Wildlife - T. Swanson

YEAR ISSUE	EDITION LIMIT	YEAR RETD.	ISSUE PRICE	*QUOTE U.S.$
1998 Big Horn Sheep - "Mountain Gathering"	Numbrd.		30.00	33
1998 Whitetail Deer - "Regal Solitude"	Numbrd.		30.00	33
1998 Buffalo - "Roaming The Plains"	Numbrd.		30.00	33
1998 Wolves - "Mist Morning Hunters"	Numbrd.		30.00	33
1998 Mule Deer - "Trouble Ahead"	Numbrd.		30.00	33
1998 Mountain Goat - "Chilly Heights"	Numbrd.		30.00	33
1998 Red Fox - "Prey in Sight"	Numbrd.		30.00	33
1998 Gamble Quail - "Family Gathering"	Numbrd.		30.00	33

People of Africa - W. A. Still

YEAR ISSUE	EDITION LIMIT	YEAR RETD.	ISSUE PRICE	*QUOTE U.S.$
1997 Maasai Warrior and Lion	Numbrd.		35.00	40
1997 Bororo Man and Camels	Numbrd.		35.00	40
1997 African Elephant and Bush Woman	Numbrd.		35.00	40
1997 Nigerian Woman and Giraffe	Numbrd.		35.00	40
1997 Rendille Woman and Crowned Crane	Numbrd.		35.00	40
1997 Samburu Warrior and Cheetah	Numbrd.		35.00	40
1997 Muslim Musicians and Pelicans	Numbrd.		35.00	40
1997 Peul Woman and Zebras	Numbrd.		35.00	40

Powers of Commitment - Jonnié Chardonn

YEAR ISSUE	EDITION LIMIT	YEAR RETD.	ISSUE PRICE	*QUOTE U.S.$
1999 Wazi and Kanka	10,000		39.95	40
1999 Linkan and Waupee	10,000		39.95	40

Rocky Mountain Wildlife - T. Swanson

YEAR ISSUE	EDITION LIMIT	YEAR RETD.	ISSUE PRICE	*QUOTE U.S.$
1997 Elk - "Storm King"	Numbrd.		30.00	33
1997 Moose - "Evening Solitude"	Numbrd.		30.00	33
1997 Grizzly Bear - "Fishing in Still Water"	Numbrd.		30.00	33
1997 Mountain Lion - "Dangers Approach"	Numbrd.		30.00	33

Seasonal Winds - Jonnié Chardonn

YEAR ISSUE	EDITION LIMIT	YEAR RETD.	ISSUE PRICE	*QUOTE U.S.$
1999 Seneca	10,000		39.95	40
1999 Bmola	10,000		39.95	40

Single Issue - G. Clasby

YEAR ISSUE	EDITION LIMIT	YEAR RETD.	ISSUE PRICE	*QUOTE U.S.$
1998 Snowy Day	30-day		30.00	33
1998 The Flowers of the Fields	30-day		30.00	33

Single Issue - R. Tanenbaum

YEAR ISSUE	EDITION LIMIT	YEAR RETD.	ISSUE PRICE	*QUOTE U.S.$
1997 "England's Rose" - Princess Diana	30-day	1997	30.00	33
1998 Mother Teresa	30-day		30.00	33

Single Issue - S. Etem

YEAR ISSUE	EDITION LIMIT	YEAR RETD.	ISSUE PRICE	*QUOTE U.S.$
1998 The Winner	30-day		30.00	33
1998 Second Place	30-day		30.00	33
1998 The Winner & Second Place, set	30-day		60.00	65

Single Issue - T. Swanson

YEAR ISSUE	EDITION LIMIT	YEAR RETD.	ISSUE PRICE	*QUOTE U.S.$
1999 Regal Pair - Elk	30-day		49.50	50
2000 Moorland Meander - Antelope	30-day		49.50	50

Single Issue - W. Christensen

YEAR ISSUE	EDITION LIMIT	YEAR RETD.	ISSUE PRICE	*QUOTE U.S.$
1997 Christmas Surprise	Numbrd.		30.00	33

Single Issue - W.A. Still

YEAR ISSUE	EDITION LIMIT	YEAR RETD.	ISSUE PRICE	*QUOTE U.S.$
1998 Vietnam Memorial	30-day		30.00	33

The Sporting Hound Series by Kimberly Swanson - K. Swanson

YEAR ISSUE	EDITION LIMIT	YEAR RETD.	ISSUE PRICE	*QUOTE U.S.$
1999 Badger - Golden Retriever	30-day		32.50	33
1999 Gopher - Labrador Retriever	30-day		32.50	33

Stars & Spirits - Jonnié Chardonn

YEAR ISSUE	EDITION LIMIT	YEAR RETD.	ISSUE PRICE	*QUOTE U.S.$
1999 Ganegware	10,000		39.95	40
1999 Wani-Sapa	10,000		39.95	40

To Have And To Hold - R. Tanenbaum

YEAR ISSUE	EDITION LIMIT	YEAR RETD.	ISSUE PRICE	*QUOTE U.S.$
1997 The Engagement	Numbrd.		30.00	33
1997 The Bridal Shower	Numbrd.		30.00	33
1997 The Wedding Ceremony	Numbrd.		30.00	33
1997 The First Dance	Numbrd.		30.00	33
1997 The Wedding Reception	Numbrd.		30.00	33
1997 The Honeymoon	Numbrd.		30.00	33

Trevor's Farm Friends - T. Swanson

YEAR ISSUE	EDITION LIMIT	YEAR RETD.	ISSUE PRICE	*QUOTE U.S.$
1997 Paulie The Pig	Numbrd.		30.00	33
1997 Rollie The Rooster	Numbrd.		30.00	33
1997 Catie The Cow	Numbrd.		30.00	33
1997 Gerrie The Goat	Numbrd.		30.00	33

Wildlife Art of Trevor Swanson - T. Swanson

YEAR ISSUE	EDITION LIMIT	YEAR RETD.	ISSUE PRICE	*QUOTE U.S.$
1999 Regal Pair	15,000		32.50	33
1999 Life in the Antarctic	15,000		32.50	33
1999 Life in the Arctic	15,000		32.50	33
1999 The Little Investigators	30-day		32.50	33
1999 Looking For Trouble	30-day		32.50	33
1999 Mischief Makers	30-day		32.50	33

Wolves - Dusk To Dawn - T. Swanson

YEAR ISSUE	EDITION LIMIT	YEAR RETD.	ISSUE PRICE	*QUOTE U.S.$
1997 Winter Hunt	Numbrd.		30.00	33
1997 Wolves of Dawn	Numbrd.		30.00	33
1997 Distant Danger	Numbrd.		30.00	33
1997 Midnight Challenge	Numbrd.		30.00	33
1997 Close to Home	Numbrd.		30.00	33

World's Greatest - C. Hayes

YEAR ISSUE	EDITION LIMIT	YEAR RETD.	ISSUE PRICE	*QUOTE U.S.$
1998 Teacher	Numbrd.		30.00	33
1998 Nurse	Numbrd.		30.00	33
1998 Attorney	Numbrd.		30.00	33
1998 Firewoman	Numbrd.		30.00	33
1998 Policewoman	Numbrd.		30.00	33
1998 Secretary	Numbrd.		30.00	33

Jan Hagara Collectables

Christmas Series - J. Hagara

YEAR ISSUE	EDITION LIMIT	YEAR RETD.	ISSUE PRICE	*QUOTE U.S.$
1983 Carol	15,000	1983	45.00	150
1984 Chris	15,000	1984	45.00	100
1985 Noel	15,000	1985	45.00	100
1986 Nikki	15,000	1986	45.00	100

Country Series - J. Hagara

YEAR ISSUE	EDITION LIMIT	YEAR RETD.	ISSUE PRICE	*QUOTE U.S.$
1984 Cristina	20,000	1986	42.50	150
1985 Laurel	20,000	1987	42.50	50
1986 Leslie	20,000	1987	42.50	45
1987 Mary Ann & Molly	20,000	1988	42.50	45

Fall in Love Again - J. Hagara

YEAR ISSUE	EDITION LIMIT	YEAR RETD.	ISSUE PRICE	*QUOTE U.S.$
1994 Tammy	7,500	1997	39.00	39

Hamilton Collection - J. Hagara

YEAR ISSUE	EDITION LIMIT	YEAR RETD.	ISSUE PRICE	*QUOTE U.S.$
1990 Cathy	14-day	1991	29.50	30-50
1990 Paul	14-day	1991	29.50	30-50
1990 Addie	14-day	1991	29.50	30-50
1990 Shelley	14-day	1991	29.50	30-50
1990 Dacy	14-day	1991	29.50	30-50
1990 Jenny	14-day	1991	29.50	30-50
1990 Jimmy	14-day	1991	29.50	30-65

*Quotes have been rounded up to nearest dollar

PLATES/PLAQUES

YEAR ISSUE	EDITION LIMIT	YEAR RETD.	ISSUE PRICE	*QUOTE U.S.$
1990 Joy	14-day	1991	29.50	30-50

Heart Series - J. Hagara

YEAR ISSUE	EDITION LIMIT	YEAR RETD.	ISSUE PRICE	*QUOTE U.S.$
1980 My Heart Desire (Cara)	Yr.Iss.	1981	24.50	125
1981 Hearts & Flowers	Yr.Iss.	1982	24.50	100-125
1982 Hearty Sailor	Yr.Iss.	1983	24.50	50-100
1983 Shannon's Sweetheart	Yr.Iss.	1984	24.50	70-100

Mother's Day Series - J. Hagara

YEAR ISSUE	EDITION LIMIT	YEAR RETD.	ISSUE PRICE	*QUOTE U.S.$
1979 Daisies From Mary Beth	Yr.Iss.	1980	37.50	125
1980 Daisies From Jimmy	Yr.Iss.	1981	37.50	125-150
1981 Daisies From Meg	Yr.Iss.	1982	37.50	125
1982 Daisies From Mommie	Yr.Iss.	1983	37.50	125

Romantic Designer - J. Hagara

YEAR ISSUE	EDITION LIMIT	YEAR RETD.	ISSUE PRICE	*QUOTE U.S.$
1988 Hannah 8 1/2"	5,000	1989	50.00	150-195
1988 Hannah 4 1/2"	15,000	1989	22.50	35-75
1990 Jamie 8 1/2"	5,000	1992	50.00	50-75
1991 Jamie 4 1/2"	15,000	1991	22.50	23
1991 David 8 1/2"	5,000	1993	50.00	50-75
1991 David 4 1/2"	15,000	1993	22.50	23
1991 Violet 8 1/2"	5,000	1994	50.00	50-90
1991 Violet 4 1/2"	15,000	1994	22.50	23

Yesterday's Children - J. Hagara

YEAR ISSUE	EDITION LIMIT	YEAR RETD.	ISSUE PRICE	*QUOTE U.S.$
1979 Lisa & Jumeau Doll	5,000	1980	60.00	80-200
1980 Adrianne & the Bye Lo Doll	5,000	1981	60.00	250
1981 Lydia & Shirley Temple	5,000	1982	60.00	200
1982 Melanie & Scarlett O'Hara	5,000	1983	60.00	85-185

Lalique Society of America

Annual - M. Lalique

YEAR ISSUE	EDITION LIMIT	YEAR RETD.	ISSUE PRICE	*QUOTE U.S.$
1965 Deux Oiseaux (Two Birds)	2,000		25.00	1250
1966 Rose de Songerie (Dream Rose)	5,000		25.00	75
1967 Ballet de Poisson (Fish Ballet)	5,000		25.00	95
1968 Gazelle Fantaisie (Gazelle Fantasy)	5,000		25.00	67-75
1969 Papillon (Butterfly)	5,000		30.00	50-55
1970 Paon (Peacock)	5,000		30.00	70
1971 Hibou (Owl)	5,000		35.00	50-75
1972 Coquillage (Shell)	5,000		40.00	73-75
1973 Petit Geai (Jayling)	5,000		42.50	100
1974 Sous d'Argent (Silver Pennies)	5,000		47.50	95
1975 Duo de Poisson (Fish Duet)	5,000		50.00	139
1976 Aigle (Eagle)	5,000		60.00	87-100

Lenox China

Colonial Christmas Wreath - Unknown

YEAR ISSUE	EDITION LIMIT	YEAR RETD.	ISSUE PRICE	*QUOTE U.S.$
1981 Colonial Virginia	Yr.Iss.	1982	65.00	76-110
1982 Massachusetts	Yr.Iss.	1983	70.00	93
1983 Maryland	Yr.Iss.	1984	70.00	135-185
1984 Rhode Island	Yr.Iss.	1985	70.00	82
1985 Connecticut	Yr.Iss.	1986	70.00	75-95
1986 New Hampshire	Yr.Iss.	1987	70.00	75
1987 Pennsylvania	Yr.Iss.	1988	70.00	75
1988 Delaware	Yr.Iss.	1989	70.00	140-155
1989 New York	Yr.Iss.	1990	75.00	155
1990 New Jersey	Yr.Iss.	1991	75.00	78
1991 South Carolina	Yr.Iss.	1992	75.00	75
1992 North Carolina	Yr.Iss.	1993	75.00	155
1993 Georgia	Yr.Iss.	1994	75.00	155

Lenox Collections

Boehm Birds - E. Boehm

YEAR ISSUE	EDITION LIMIT	YEAR RETD.	ISSUE PRICE	*QUOTE U.S.$
1970 Wood Thrush	Yr.Iss.	1970	35.00	94-130
1971 Goldfinch	Yr.Iss.	1971	35.00	35-50
1972 Mountain Bluebird	Yr.Iss.	1972	37.50	40-50
1973 Meadowlark	Yr.Iss.	1973	50.00	24-45
1974 Rufous Hummingbird	Yr.Iss.	1974	45.00	39-68
1975 American Redstart	Yr.Iss.	1975	50.00	27-50
1976 Cardinals	Yr.Iss.	1976	53.00	39
1977 Robins	Yr.Iss.	1977	55.00	39-49
1978 Mockingbirds	Yr.Iss.	1978	58.00	35-55
1979 Golden-Crowned Kinglets	Yr.Iss.	1979	65.00	73-80
1980 Black-Throated Blue Warblers	Yr.Iss.	1980	80.00	75-80
1981 Eastern Phoebes	Yr.Iss.	1981	92.50	80

Boehm Woodland Wildlife - E. Boehm

YEAR ISSUE	EDITION LIMIT	YEAR RETD.	ISSUE PRICE	*QUOTE U.S.$
1973 Racoons	Yr.Iss.	1973	50.00	75
1974 Red Foxes	Yr.Iss.	1974	52.50	70-75
1975 Cottontail Rabbits	Yr.Iss.	1975	58.50	60-75
1976 Eastern Chipmunks	Yr.Iss.	1976	62.50	75
1977 Beaver	Yr.Iss.	1977	67.50	75
1978 Whitetail Deer	Yr.Iss.	1978	70.00	60-75
1979 Squirrels	Yr.Iss.	1979	76.00	46-75
1980 Bobcats	Yr.Iss.	1980	82.50	83
1981 Martens	Yr.Iss.	1981	100.00	100
1982 River Otters	Yr.Iss.	1982	100.00	100

Lightpost Publishing

Kinkade-Thomas Kinkade Signature Collection - T. Kinkade

YEAR ISSUE	EDITION LIMIT	YEAR RETD.	ISSUE PRICE	*QUOTE U.S.$
1991 Cedar Nook	2,500		49.95	50-75
1991 Chandler's Cottage	2,500		49.95	50-75
1991 Home to Grandma's	2,500		49.95	50-75
1991 Sleigh Ride Home	2,500		49.95	50-75

Lilliput Lane Ltd./Enesco European Giftware Group

American Landmarks Collection - R. Day

YEAR ISSUE	EDITION LIMIT	YEAR RETD.	ISSUE PRICE	*QUOTE U.S.$
1990 Country Church	5,000	1996	35.00	35
1990 Riverside Chapel	5,000	1996	35.00	30-35

Countryside Scene Plaques - D. Simpson

YEAR ISSUE	EDITION LIMIT	YEAR RETD.	ISSUE PRICE	*QUOTE U.S.$
1989 Bottle Kiln	Retrd.	1991	49.50	25-50
1989 Cornish Tin Mine	Retrd.	1991	49.50	25-50
1989 Country Inn	Retrd.	1991	49.50	25-50
1989 Cumbrian Farmhouse	Retrd.	1991	49.50	25-50
1989 Lighthouse	Retrd.	1991	49.50	25-50
1989 Norfolk Windmill	Retrd.	1991	49.50	25-50
1989 Oasthouse	Retrd.	1991	49.50	25-50
1989 Old Smithy	Retrd.	1991	49.50	25-50
1989 Parish Church	Retrd.	1991	49.50	25-50
1989 Post Office	Retrd.	1991	49.50	25-50
1989 Village School	Retrd.	1991	49.50	25-50
1989 Watermill	Retrd.	1991	49.50	25-50

Framed English Plaques - D. Tate

YEAR ISSUE	EDITION LIMIT	YEAR RETD.	ISSUE PRICE	*QUOTE U.S.$
1990 Ashdown Hall	Retrd.	1991	59.50	30-60
1990 Battleview	Retrd.	1991	59.50	30-70
1990 Cat Slide Cottage	Retrd.	1991	59.50	30-70
1990 Coombe Cot	Retrd.	1991	59.50	30-70
1990 Fell View	Retrd.	1991	59.50	30-70
1990 Flint Fields	Retrd.	1991	59.50	30-70
1990 Huntingdon House	Retrd.	1991	59.50	30-70
1990 Jubilee Lodge	Retrd.	1991	59.50	30-70
1990 Stowside	Retrd.	1991	59.50	30-70
1990 Trevan Cove	Retrd.	1991	59.50	30-70

Framed Irish Plaques - D. Tate

YEAR ISSUE	EDITION LIMIT	YEAR RETD.	ISSUE PRICE	*QUOTE U.S.$
1990 Ballyteag House	Retrd.	1991	59.50	30-70
1990 Crockuna Croft	Retrd.	1991	59.50	30-70
1990 Pearses Cottages	Retrd.	1991	59.50	30-70
1990 Shannons Bank	Retrd.	1991	59.50	30-70

Framed Scottish Plaques - D. Tate

YEAR ISSUE	EDITION LIMIT	YEAR RETD.	ISSUE PRICE	*QUOTE U.S.$
1990 Barra Black House	Retrd.	1991	59.50	30-70
1990 Fife Ness	Retrd.	1991	59.50	30-70
1990 Kyle Point	Retrd.	1991	59.50	30-70
1990 Preston Oat Mill	Retrd.	1991	59.50	30-70

Heritage Gallery - Lilliput Lane

YEAR ISSUE	EDITION LIMIT	YEAR RETD.	ISSUE PRICE	*QUOTE U.S.$
2000 Big Ben Plaque	Open		50.00	50
2000 Buckingham Palace Plaque	Open		50.00	50
2000 Tower Bridge Plaque	Open		50.00	50
2000 Tower of London Plaque	Open		50.00	50

Lakeland Bridge Plaques - D. Simpson

YEAR ISSUE	EDITION LIMIT	YEAR RETD.	ISSUE PRICE	*QUOTE U.S.$
1989 Aira Force	Retrd.	1991	35.00	18-35
1989 Ashness Bridge	Retrd.	1991	35.00	18-35
1989 Birks Bridge	Retrd.	1991	35.00	18-35
1989 Bridge House	Retrd.	1991	35.00	18-35
1989 Hartsop Packhorse	Retrd.	1991	35.00	18-35
1989 Stockley Bridge	Retrd.	1991	35.00	18-35

London Plaques - D. Simpson

YEAR ISSUE	EDITION LIMIT	YEAR RETD.	ISSUE PRICE	*QUOTE U.S.$
1989 Big Ben	Retrd.	1991	39.50	20-40
1989 Buckingham Palace	Retrd.	1991	39.50	20-40
1989 Piccadilly Circus	Retrd.	1991	39.50	20-40
1989 Tower Bridge	Retrd.	1991	39.50	20-40
1989 Tower of London	Retrd.	1991	39.50	20-40
1989 Trafalgar Square	Retrd.	1991	39.50	20-40

Ray Day/Coca Cola Country - R. Day

YEAR ISSUE	EDITION LIMIT	YEAR RETD.	ISSUE PRICE	*QUOTE U.S.$
1998 Catch of the Day (3-D)	Open		40.00	40
1998 Ice Cold Coke (3-D)	Open		40.00	40
1998 Spring Has Sprung (3-D)	Open		40.00	40
1998 When I Was Your Age... (3-D)	Open		40.00	40
1999 Dixie Bottling Company (3-D)	Open		40.00	40

Specials - Various

YEAR ISSUE	EDITION LIMIT	YEAR RETD.	ISSUE PRICE	*QUOTE U.S.$
1996 Honeysuckle Plaque (with doves) - Lilliput Lane	Retrd.	1996	N/A	90
1996 Honeysuckle Plaque (without doves) - Lilliput Lane	Retrd.	1996	N/A	N/A

Unframed Plaques - D. Tate

YEAR ISSUE	EDITION LIMIT	YEAR RETD.	ISSUE PRICE	*QUOTE U.S.$
1989 Large Lower Brockhampton	Retrd.	1991	120.00	120-150
1989 Large Somerset Springtime	Retrd.	1991	130.00	130-135
1989 Medium Cobble Combe Cottage	Retrd.	1991	68.00	68
1989 Medium Wishing Well	Retrd.	1991	75.00	75
1989 Small Stoney Wall Lea	Retrd.	1991	47.50	48
1989 Small Woodside Farm	Retrd.	1991	47.50	48

Little Angel Publishing

All God's Treasures - D. Gelsinger

YEAR ISSUE	EDITION LIMIT	YEAR RETD.	ISSUE PRICE	*QUOTE U.S.$
1999 All Things Bright and Beautiful	95-day		39.95	40

An Angel's Light - D. Gelsinger

YEAR ISSUE	EDITION LIMIT	YEAR RETD.	ISSUE PRICE	*QUOTE U.S.$
1998 A Little Hope Lights the Way	95-day		29.95	30
1998 A Little Love Lights The Heart	95-day		29.95	30
1998 A Little Faith Shines From Within	95-day		29.95	30
1998 A Little Kindness Shines Through	95-day		29.95	30
1998 A Little Joy Lights Your World	95-day		29.95	30
1999 A Little Tenderness Enlightens The Soul	95-day		29.95	30
1999 A Little Harmony Lights The Day	95-day		29.95	30
1999 A Little Joy Shines Within	95-day		29.95	30

Garden Blessings - D. Gelsinger

YEAR ISSUE	EDITION LIMIT	YEAR RETD.	ISSUE PRICE	*QUOTE U.S.$
1996 An Angel's Touch	95-day		29.95	30
1996 An Angel's Guidance	95-day		29.95	30
1996 An Angel's Gift	95-day		29.95	30
1996 An Angel's Care	95-day		29.95	30
1996 An Angel's Warmth	95-day		29.95	30
1997 An Angel's Spirit	95-day		29.95	30
1997 An Angel's Tenderness	95-day		29.95	30
1997 An Angel's Grace	95-day		29.95	30
1997 An Angel's Gentleness	95-day		29.95	30
1997 An Angel's Love	95-day		29.95	30

Nature's Heavenly Guardians - D. Gelsinger

YEAR ISSUE	EDITION LIMIT	YEAR RETD.	ISSUE PRICE	*QUOTE U.S.$
1997 Gentle Guidance	95-day		29.95	30
1997 A Wondrous Discovery	95-day		29.95	30
1997 Making New Friends	95-day		29.95	30
1997 A Gift of Love	95-day		29.95	30

Our Loving Guardians - D. Gelsinger

YEAR ISSUE	EDITION LIMIT	YEAR RETD.	ISSUE PRICE	*QUOTE U.S.$
1998 Someone to Guide The Way	295-day		39.95	40
1998 Her Perpetual Embrace	295-day		39.95	40
1999 Her Blessed Gift	295-day		39.95	40
1999 Heaven's Helping Hand	295-day		39.95	40
1999 Heaven's Little Wonders	295-day		39.95	40

Prayers For Little Hearts - D. Gelsinger

YEAR ISSUE	EDITION LIMIT	YEAR RETD.	ISSUE PRICE	*QUOTE U.S.$
2000 Joyful in Hope	95-day		29.95	30

Lladró

Lladró Plate Collection - Lladró

YEAR ISSUE	EDITION LIMIT	YEAR RETD.	ISSUE PRICE	*QUOTE U.S.$
1993 The Great Voyage L5964G	Closed	1995	50.00	50
1993 Looking Out L5998G	Closed	1998	38.00	38
1993 Swinging L5999G	Closed	1998	38.00	38
1993 Duck Plate L6000G	Closed	1998	38.00	38
1994 Friends L6158	Closed	1998	32.00	32
1994 Apple Picking L6159M	Closed	1998	32.00	32
1994 Turtledove L6160	Closed	1998	32.00	32
1994 Flamingo L6161M	Closed	1998	32.00	32

Lowell Davis Farm Club

Davis Cat Tales Plates. - L. Davis

YEAR ISSUE	EDITION LIMIT	YEAR RETD.	ISSUE PRICE	*QUOTE U.S.$
1982 Right Church, Wrong Pew	12,500	1986	37.50	55-100
1982 Company's Coming	12,500	1986	37.50	100-195
1982 On the Move	12,500	1986	37.50	55-100
1982 Flew the Coop	12,500	1986	37.50	55-100

Davis Christmas Plates - L. Davis

YEAR ISSUE	EDITION LIMIT	YEAR RETD.	ISSUE PRICE	*QUOTE U.S.$
1983 Hooker at Mailbox With Present 224-100	7,500	1984	45.00	130-163
1984 Country Christmas 224-101	7,500	1985	45.00	104-125
1985 Christmas at Foxfire Farm 224-102	7,500	1986	45.00	150
1986 Christmas at Red Oak 224-103	7,500	1987	45.00	85-150
1987 Blossom's Gift 224-104	7,500	1988	47.50	52-100
1988 Cutting the Family Christmas Tree 224-105	7,500	1989	47.50	75-100
1989 Peter and the Wren	7,500	1990	47.50	52-75
1990 Wintering Deer	7,500	1991	47.50	52
1991 Christmas at Red Oak II	7,500	1992	55.00	39-98
1992 Born On A Starry Night	7,500	1993	55.00	55
1993 Waiting For Mr. Lowell	5,000	1994	55.00	55
1994 Visions of Sugarplums	5,000	1995	55.00	55
1995 Bah Humbug	5,000		55.00	55

Davis Country Pride Plates - L. Davis

YEAR ISSUE	EDITION LIMIT	YEAR RETD.	ISSUE PRICE	*QUOTE U.S.$
1981 Surprise in the Cellar	7,500	1983	35.00	195-325
1981 Plum Tuckered Out	7,500	1983	35.00	115-150
1981 Duke's Mixture	7,500	1983	35.00	190-200
1982 Bustin' with Pride	7,500	1983	35.00	100-150

Davis Pen Pals - L. Davis

YEAR ISSUE	EDITION LIMIT	YEAR RETD.	ISSUE PRICE	*QUOTE U.S.$
1993 The Old Home Place 25800	Closed	1995	50.00	50

Davis Red Oak Sampler - L. Davis

YEAR ISSUE	EDITION LIMIT	YEAR RETD.	ISSUE PRICE	*QUOTE U.S.$
1986 General Store	5,000	1987	45.00	100-110
1987 Country Wedding	5,000	1988	45.00	125-150
1989 Country School	5,000	1990	45.00	110
1990 Blacksmith Shop	5,000	1991	52.50	25-50

Davis Special Edition Plates - L. Davis

YEAR ISSUE	EDITION LIMIT	YEAR RETD.	ISSUE PRICE	*QUOTE U.S.$
1983 The Critics	12,500	1985	45.00	95
1984 Good Ole Days Privy Set 2	5,000	1986	60.00	185
1986 Home From Market	7,500	1988	55.00	145

March of Dimes

Our Children, Our Future - Various

YEAR ISSUE	EDITION LIMIT	YEAR RETD.	ISSUE PRICE	*QUOTE U.S.$
1989 A Time for Peace - D. Zolan	150-day		29.00	10-15
1989 A Time To Love - S. Kuck	150-day		29.00	30
1989 A Time To Plant - J. McClelland	150-day		29.00	12-29
1989 A Time To Be Born - G. Perillo	150-day		29.00	15-29
1990 A Time To Embrace - E. Hibel	150-day		29.00	22-35
1990 A Time To Laugh - A. Williams	150-day		29.00	14-29

Marigold

Sport - Carreno

YEAR ISSUE	EDITION LIMIT	YEAR RETD.	ISSUE PRICE	*QUOTE U.S.$
1983 Mickey Mantle-handsigned	1,000		100.00	695-895
1983 Mickey Mantle-unsigned	1,000		60.00	195
1984 Joe DiMaggio-handsigned	325		100.00	1495-1795
1984 Joe DiMaggio f/s (blue sig.)	10,000		60.00	250
1984 Joe DiMaggio AP-handsigned	25		N/A	2900-3900

*Quotes have been rounded up to nearest dollar

Maruri USA

Eagle Plate Series - W. Gaither

YEAR ISSUE	EDITION LIMIT	YEAR RETD.	ISSUE PRICE	*QUOTE U.S.$
1984 Free Flight	995	1993	150.00	150-198

Four Seasons - Maruri Studios

YEAR ISSUE	EDITION LIMIT	YEAR RETD.	ISSUE PRICE	*QUOTE U.S.$
1999 Autumn - Cedar Waxwing w/Berries FS-9953	Open		45.00	45
1999 Spring - Bluebird w/Iris FS-9951	Open		45.00	45
1999 Summer - Goldfinch w/Sunflowers FS-9952	Open		45.00	45
1999 Winter - Cardinal w/Pine FS-9954	Open		45.00	45

Treasures of the Sky - Maruri Studios

YEAR ISSUE	EDITION LIMIT	YEAR RETD.	ISSUE PRICE	*QUOTE U.S.$
1998 Anna's w/Lily HP-9801	Open		39.95	40
1998 Allen's w/Hibiscus HP-9802	Open		39.95	40
1998 Ruby-throated w/Trumpet HP-9803	Open		39.95	40

Memories of Yesterday/Enesco Group, Inc.

Dated Plate Series - Various

YEAR ISSUE	EDITION LIMIT	YEAR RETD.	ISSUE PRICE	*QUOTE U.S.$
1993 Look Out-Something Good Is Coming Your Way! 530298 - S. Butcher	Yr.Iss.	1993	50.00	50
1994 Pleasant Dreams and Sweet Repose 528102 - M. Atwell	Yr.Iss.	1994	50.00	50
1995 Join Me For a Little Song 134880 - M. Attwell	Yr.Iss.	1995	50.00	50

Museum Collections, Inc.

American Family I - N. Rockwell

YEAR ISSUE	EDITION LIMIT	YEAR RETD.	ISSUE PRICE	*QUOTE U.S.$
1979 Baby's First Step	9,900		28.50	48
1979 Happy Birthday Dear Mother	9,900		28.50	45
1979 Sweet Sixteen	9,900		28.50	35-45
1979 First Haircut	9,900		28.50	45
1979 First Prom	9,900		28.50	35
1979 Wrapping Christmas Presents	9,900		28.50	35
1979 The Student	9,900		28.50	35
1979 Birthday Party	9,900		28.50	35-45
1979 Little Mother	9,900		28.50	35
1979 Washing Our Dog	9,900		28.50	45
1979 Mother's Little Helpers	9,900		28.50	45
1979 Bride and Groom	9,900		28.50	35

American Family II - N. Rockwell

YEAR ISSUE	EDITION LIMIT	YEAR RETD.	ISSUE PRICE	*QUOTE U.S.$
1980 New Arrival	22,500		35.00	45-50
1980 Sweet Dreams	22,500		35.00	38-45
1980 Little Shaver	22,500		35.00	40
1980 We Missed You Daddy	22,500		35.00	38-45
1980 Home Run Slugger	22,500		35.00	45
1980 Giving Thanks	22,500		35.00	55
1980 Space Pioneers	22,500		35.00	35
1980 Little Salesman	22,500		35.00	45
1980 Almost Grown up	22,500		35.00	45
1980 Courageous Hero	22,500		35.00	38-45
1981 At the Circus	22,500		35.00	38
1981 Good Food, Good Friends	22,500		35.00	38-45

Christmas - N. Rockwell

YEAR ISSUE	EDITION LIMIT	YEAR RETD.	ISSUE PRICE	*QUOTE U.S.$
1979 Day After Christmas	Yr.Iss		75.00	75
1980 Checking His List	Yr.Iss		75.00	75
1981 Ringing in Good Cheer	Yr.Iss		75.00	75
1982 Waiting for Santa	Yr.Iss		75.00	75
1983 High Hopes	Yr.Iss		75.00	75
1984 Space Age Santa	Yr.Iss		55.00	55

Norman Rockwell Gallery

Norman Rockwell Centennial - Rockwell Inspired

YEAR ISSUE	EDITION LIMIT	YEAR RETD.	ISSUE PRICE	*QUOTE U.S.$
1993 The Toymaker	Closed		39.90	60-65
1993 The Cobbler	Closed		39.90	45-70

Rockwell's Christmas Legacy - Rockwell Inspired

YEAR ISSUE	EDITION LIMIT	YEAR RETD.	ISSUE PRICE	*QUOTE U.S.$
1992 Santa's Workshop	Closed		49.90	51-60
1993 Making a List	Closed		49.90	65-84
1993 While Santa Slumbers	Closed		54.90	60-85
1993 Visions of Santa	Closed		54.90	60-110

Pemberton & Oakes

Adventures of Childhood Collection - D. Zolan

YEAR ISSUE	EDITION LIMIT	YEAR RETD.	ISSUE PRICE	*QUOTE U.S.$
1989 Almost Home	Retrd.	1989	19.60	12-35
1989 Crystal's Creek	Retrd.	1989	19.60	12-20
1989 Summer Suds	Retrd.	1990	22.00	16-25
1990 Snowy Adventure	Retrd.	1990	22.00	14-24
1991 Forests & Fairy Tales	Retrd.	1991	24.40	16-30

The Best of Zolan in Miniature - D. Zolan

YEAR ISSUE	EDITION LIMIT	YEAR RETD.	ISSUE PRICE	*QUOTE U.S.$
1985 Sabina	Retrd.	1985	12.50	110-120
1986 Erik and Dandelion	Retrd.	1986	12.50	85-90
1986 Tender Moment	Retrd.	1986	12.50	68-95
1986 Touching the Sky	Retrd.	1987	12.50	59-75
1987 A Gift for Laurie	Retrd.	1987	12.50	25-55
1987 Small Wonder	Retrd.	1987	12.50	55-85

Childhood Discoveries (Miniature) - D. Zolan

YEAR ISSUE	EDITION LIMIT	YEAR RETD.	ISSUE PRICE	*QUOTE U.S.$
1990 Colors of Spring	Retrd.	1990	14.40	28-33
1990 Autumn Leaves	Retrd.	1990	14.40	23-32
1991 Enchanted Forest	Retrd.	1991	16.60	23-75
1991 Just Ducky	Retrd.	1991	16.60	23-65
1991 Rainy Day Pals	Retrd.	1991	16.60	59-65
1992 Double Trouble	Retrd.	1992	16.60	23-65
1990 First Kiss	Retrd.	1990	14.40	46-85
1993 Peppermint Kiss	Retrd.	1993	16.60	23-85
1995 Tender Hearts	Retrd.	1995	16.60	29-65

Childhood Friendship Collection - D. Zolan

YEAR ISSUE	EDITION LIMIT	YEAR RETD.	ISSUE PRICE	*QUOTE U.S.$
1986 Beach Break	Retrd.	1987	19.00	38-69
1987 Little Engineers	Retrd.	1987	19.00	45-66
1988 Tiny Treasures	Retrd.	1988	19.00	18-43
1988 Sharing Secrets	Retrd.	1988	19.00	60-85
1988 Dozens of Daisies	Retrd.	1989	19.00	20-30
1990 Country Walk	Retrd.	1989	19.00	30-75

Children and Pets - D. Zolan

YEAR ISSUE	EDITION LIMIT	YEAR RETD.	ISSUE PRICE	*QUOTE U.S.$
1984 Tender Moment	Retrd.	1984	19.00	35-80
1984 Golden Moment	Retrd.	1984	19.00	15-25
1985 Making Friends	Retrd.	1985	19.00	25-45
1985 Tender Beginning	Retrd.	1985	19.00	15-45
1986 Backyard Discovery	Retrd.	1986	19.00	17-39
1986 Waiting to Play	Retrd.	1986	19.00	20-35

Children at Christmas - D. Zolan

YEAR ISSUE	EDITION LIMIT	YEAR RETD.	ISSUE PRICE	*QUOTE U.S.$
1981 A Gift for Laurie	Retrd.	1981	48.00	55-75
1982 Christmas Prayer	Retrd.	1982	48.00	60-90
1983 Erik's Delight	Retrd.	1983	48.00	65-70
1984 Christmas Secret	Retrd.	1984	48.00	55-66
1985 Christmas Kitten	Retrd.	1985	48.00	50-65
1986 Laurie and the Creche	Retrd.	1986	48.00	50-80

Christmas (Miniature) - D. Zolan

YEAR ISSUE	EDITION LIMIT	YEAR RETD.	ISSUE PRICE	*QUOTE U.S.$
1993 Snowy Adventure	Retrd.	1993	16.60	14-23
1994 Candlelight Magic	Retrd.	1994	16.60	15-23
1995 Laurie and Creche	Retrd.	1995	16.60	15-23

Christmas - D. Zolan

YEAR ISSUE	EDITION LIMIT	YEAR RETD.	ISSUE PRICE	*QUOTE U.S.$
1991 Candlelight Magic	Retrd.	1991	24.80	25-95

Companion to Brotherly Love - D. Zolan

YEAR ISSUE	EDITION LIMIT	YEAR RETD.	ISSUE PRICE	*QUOTE U.S.$
1989 Sisterly Love	Retrd.		22.00	35-42

Easter (Miniature) - D. Zolan

YEAR ISSUE	EDITION LIMIT	YEAR RETD.	ISSUE PRICE	*QUOTE U.S.$
1991 Easter Morning	Retrd.		16.60	23-32

Father's Day (Miniature) - D. Zolan

YEAR ISSUE	EDITION LIMIT	YEAR RETD.	ISSUE PRICE	*QUOTE U.S.$
1994 Two of a Kind	Retrd.		16.60	40-125

Father's Day - D. Zolan

YEAR ISSUE	EDITION LIMIT	YEAR RETD.	ISSUE PRICE	*QUOTE U.S.$
1986 Daddy's Home	Retrd.		19.00	40-50

Grandparent's Day (Miniature) - D. Zolan

YEAR ISSUE	EDITION LIMIT	YEAR RETD.	ISSUE PRICE	*QUOTE U.S.$
1995 Lap of Love	Retrd.	1996	16.60	25-55

Grandparent's Day - D. Zolan

YEAR ISSUE	EDITION LIMIT	YEAR RETD.	ISSUE PRICE	*QUOTE U.S.$
1990 It's Grandma & Grandpa	Retrd.		24.40	38-75
1993 Grandpa's Fence	Retrd.		24.40	45-52

Heirloom Ovals - D. Zolan

YEAR ISSUE	EDITION LIMIT	YEAR RETD.	ISSUE PRICE	*QUOTE U.S.$
1992 My Kitty	Retrd.		18.80	36-50

March of Dimes: Our Children, Our Future - D. Zolan

YEAR ISSUE	EDITION LIMIT	YEAR RETD.	ISSUE PRICE	*QUOTE U.S.$
1989 A Time for Peace	Retrd.		29.00	10-15

Members Only Single Issue (Miniature) - D. Zolan

YEAR ISSUE	EDITION LIMIT	YEAR RETD.	ISSUE PRICE	*QUOTE U.S.$
1990 By Myself	Retrd.		14.40	59-68
1993 Summer's Child	Retrd.		16.60	35-44
1994 Little Slugger	Retrd.		16.60	52-65

Membership (Miniature) - D. Zolan

YEAR ISSUE	EDITION LIMIT	YEAR RETD.	ISSUE PRICE	*QUOTE U.S.$
1987 For You	Retrd.		12.50	90-130
1988 Making Friends	Retrd.		12.50	63-100
1989 Grandma's Garden	Retrd.		12.50	40-75
1990 A Christmas Prayer	Retrd.		14.40	36-59
1991 Golden Moment	Retrd.		15.00	36-75
1992 Brotherly Love	Retrd.		15.00	76-100
1993 New Shoes	Retrd.		16.60	23-75
1994 My Kitty	Retrd.		Gift	23-75

Mini Plates by Donald Zolan - D. Zolan

YEAR ISSUE	EDITION LIMIT	YEAR RETD.	ISSUE PRICE	*QUOTE U.S.$
1995 Golden Harvest	Retrd.		16.60	23-37
1995 My New Kitten	Retrd.	1996	16.60	18-37
1995 Reflections	Retrd.	1996	16.60	18
1995 Secret Friends	Retrd.	1996	16.60	18-23

Miniatures - D. Zolan

YEAR ISSUE	EDITION LIMIT	YEAR RETD.	ISSUE PRICE	*QUOTE U.S.$
1995 Lap of Love	Retrd.	1996	16.60	24-55

Moments To Remember (Miniature) - D. Zolan

YEAR ISSUE	EDITION LIMIT	YEAR RETD.	ISSUE PRICE	*QUOTE U.S.$
1992 Just We Two	Retrd.		16.60	23-65
1992 Almost Home	Retrd.		16.60	23-75
1993 Tiny Treasures	Retrd.		16.60	35-65
1993 Forest Friends	Retrd.		16.60	27-75

Mother's Day (Miniature) - D. Zolan

YEAR ISSUE	EDITION LIMIT	YEAR RETD.	ISSUE PRICE	*QUOTE U.S.$
1990 Flowers for Mother	Retrd.		14.40	23-52
1992 Twilight Prayer	Retrd.		16.60	23-80
1993 Jessica's Field	Retrd.		16.60	23-65
1994 One Summer Day	Retrd.		16.60	23-75
1995 Little Ballerina	Retrd.		16.60	20-65

Mother's Day - D. Zolan

YEAR ISSUE	EDITION LIMIT	YEAR RETD.	ISSUE PRICE	*QUOTE U.S.$
1988 Mother's Angels	Retrd.		19.00	75-125

Nutcracker II - Various

YEAR ISSUE	EDITION LIMIT	YEAR RETD.	ISSUE PRICE	*QUOTE U.S.$
1981 Grand Finale - S. Fisher	Retrd.		24.40	36
1982 Arabian Dancers - S. Fisher	Retrd.		24.40	39-68
1983 Dew Drop Fairy - S. Fisher	Retrd.		24.40	36
1984 Clara's Delight - S. Fisher	Retrd.		24.40	42-65
1985 Bedtime for Nutcracker - S. Fisher	Retrd.		24.40	45
1986 The Crowning of Clara - S. Fisher	Retrd.		24.40	36
1987 Dance of the Snowflakes - D. Zolan	Retrd.		24.40	38-75
1988 The Royal Welcome - R. Anderson	Retrd.		24.40	33
1989 The Spanish Dancer - M. Vickers	Retrd.		24.40	45-75

Plaques - D. Zolan

YEAR ISSUE	EDITION LIMIT	YEAR RETD.	ISSUE PRICE	*QUOTE U.S.$
1991 New Shoes	Retrd.		18.80	40-85
1992 Grandma's Garden	Retrd.		18.80	30-65
1992 Small Wonder	Retrd.		18.80	20-30
1992 Easter Morning	Retrd.		18.80	20-30

Plaques-Single Issues - D. Zolan

YEAR ISSUE	EDITION LIMIT	YEAR RETD.	ISSUE PRICE	*QUOTE U.S.$
1991 Flowers for Mother	Retrd.		16.80	65

Single Issue - D. Zolan

YEAR ISSUE	EDITION LIMIT	YEAR RETD.	ISSUE PRICE	*QUOTE U.S.$
1993 Winter Friends	Retrd.		18.80	45-65

Single Issue Day to Day Spode - D. Zolan

YEAR ISSUE	EDITION LIMIT	YEAR RETD.	ISSUE PRICE	*QUOTE U.S.$
1991 Daisy Days	Retrd.		48.00	43-79

Single Issues (Miniature) - D. Zolan

YEAR ISSUE	EDITION LIMIT	YEAR RETD.	ISSUE PRICE	*QUOTE U.S.$
1986 Backyard Discovery	Retrd.		12.50	90
1986 Daddy's Home	Retrd.		12.50	820
1989 Sunny Surprise	Retrd.		12.50	49-65
1989 My Pumpkin	Retrd.		14.40	55-125
1991 Backyard Buddies	Retrd.		16.60	23-40
1991 The Thinker	Retrd.		16.60	45-49
1993 Quiet Time	Retrd.		16.60	20-66
1994 Little Fisherman	Retrd.		16.60	23-80

Single Issues Bone China (Miniature) - D. Zolan

YEAR ISSUE	EDITION LIMIT	YEAR RETD.	ISSUE PRICE	*QUOTE U.S.$
1992 Window of Dreams	Retrd.		18.80	23-70
1995 Little Splasher	Retrd.		16.60	23-26

Special Moments of Childhood Collection - D. Zolan

YEAR ISSUE	EDITION LIMIT	YEAR RETD.	ISSUE PRICE	*QUOTE U.S.$
1988 Brotherly Love	Retrd.		19.00	25-50
1988 Sunny Surprise	Retrd.		19.00	10-50
1989 Summer's Child	Retrd.		22.00	16-45
1990 Meadow Magic	Retrd.		22.00	14
1990 Cone For Two	Retrd.		24.60	14-25
1990 Rodeo Girl	Retrd.		24.60	14-25

Tenth Anniversary - D. Zolan

YEAR ISSUE	EDITION LIMIT	YEAR RETD.	ISSUE PRICE	*QUOTE U.S.$
1988 Ribbons and Roses	Retrd.		24.40	55-85

Thanksgiving (Miniature) - D. Zolan

YEAR ISSUE	EDITION LIMIT	YEAR RETD.	ISSUE PRICE	*QUOTE U.S.$
1993 I'm Thankful Too	Retrd.		16.60	23-40

Thanksgiving - D. Zolan

YEAR ISSUE	EDITION LIMIT	YEAR RETD.	ISSUE PRICE	*QUOTE U.S.$
1981 I'm Thankful Too	Retrd.		19.00	68-125

Times To Treasure Bone China (Miniature) - D. Zolan

YEAR ISSUE	EDITION LIMIT	YEAR RETD.	ISSUE PRICE	*QUOTE U.S.$
1993 Little Traveler	Retrd.		16.60	23-65
1993 Garden Swing	Retrd.		16.60	23-55
1994 Summer Garden	Retrd.		16.60	23-30
1994 September Girl	Retrd.		16.60	23-28

Wonder of Childhood - D. Zolan

YEAR ISSUE	EDITION LIMIT	YEAR RETD.	ISSUE PRICE	*QUOTE U.S.$
1982 Touching the Sky	Retrd.		19.00	35-65
1983 Spring Innocence	Retrd.		19.00	45-65
1984 Winter Angel	Retrd.		22.00	42-75
1985 Small Wonder	Retrd.		22.00	25-45
1986 Grandma's Garden	Retrd.		22.00	48-75
1987 Day Dreamer	Retrd.		22.00	30-36

Yesterday's Children (Miniature) - D. Zolan

YEAR ISSUE	EDITION LIMIT	YEAR RETD.	ISSUE PRICE	*QUOTE U.S.$
1994 Little Friends	Retrd.		16.60	23-40
1994 Seaside Treasures	Retrd.		16.60	23-65

Zolan's Children - D. Zolan

YEAR ISSUE	EDITION LIMIT	YEAR RETD.	ISSUE PRICE	*QUOTE U.S.$
1978 Erik and Dandelion	Retrd.		19.00	35-185
1979 Sabina in the Grass	Retrd.		22.00	50-75
1980 By Myself	Retrd.		24.00	9-14
1981 For You	Retrd.		24.00	8-15

Porterfield's

Rob Anders Collectors Society - R. Anders

YEAR ISSUE	EDITION LIMIT	YEAR RETD.	ISSUE PRICE	*QUOTE U.S.$
1997 Short Stories	Yr.Iss.	1997	19.00	60-110
1998 Cuddling Up	Yr.Iss.	1998	19.00	26-40
1999 First Look	Yr.Iss.	1999	19.00	19-26

Memories of Childhood - R. Anders

YEAR ISSUE	EDITION LIMIT	YEAR RETD.	ISSUE PRICE	*QUOTE U.S.$
1999 Swimming Lessons	10-day		16.60	17
1999 Tickled Pink	10-day		16.60	17
1999 Tiny Ballerina	10-day		16.60	17

Moments of Wonder - R. Anders

YEAR ISSUE	EDITION LIMIT	YEAR RETD.	ISSUE PRICE	*QUOTE U.S.$
1996 First Love	44-day	1996	16.60	45-84
1996 Time Out	19-day	1997	16.60	64-82
1996 Safe Harbor	19-day	1997	16.60	28-39
1996 Digging In	19-day	1997	16.60	35-41
1997 Two Bites To Go	19-day	1998	16.60	28-41
1997 Sweet Dreams	19-day	1998	16.60	17-32

Single Issues - R. Anders

YEAR ISSUE	EDITION LIMIT	YEAR RETD.	ISSUE PRICE	*QUOTE U.S.$
1997 Cookies For Daddy (Father's Day, 1997)	19-day	1998	16.60	35-56
1997 Spooky Stories (Halloween, 1997)	10-day	1998	16.60	37
1998 Tucked In (Mother's Day, 1998)	10-day		16.60	17
1998 A Visit to Santa (Christmas, 1998)	10-day	1998	16.60	17-36
1999 Just Like Mommy (Mother's Day, 1999)	10-day		16.60	17
1999 Trimming The Tree (Christmas, 1999)	10-day		16.60	17
2000 My New Bunny (Easter, 2000)	10-day		16.60	17

*Quotes have been rounded up to nearest dollar

YEAR ISSUE	EDITION LIMIT	YEAR RETD.	ISSUE PRICE	*QUOTE U.S.$
2000 Eskimo Kisses (Mother's Day, 2000)	10-day		16.60	17

Treasures of the Heart - R. Anders

YEAR ISSUE	EDITION LIMIT	YEAR RETD.	ISSUE PRICE	*QUOTE U.S.$
1997 In Good Hands	10-day	1998	16.60	17-36
1998 Bubbles Away	10-day	1998	16.60	17-34
1998 Mr. Muscles	10-day	1999	16.60	17-28
1998 Lazy Days	10-day	1999	16.60	17-22
1998 Picture Perfect	10-day	1999	16.60	17
1999 Teddy & Me	10-day		16.60	17

Precious Moments/Enesco Group, Inc.

Beauty of Christmas Collection - S. Butcher

YEAR ISSUE	EDITION LIMIT	YEAR RETD.	ISSUE PRICE	*QUOTE U.S.$
1994 You're as Pretty as a Christmas Tree 530409	Yr.Iss.		50.00	42-50
1995 He Covers the Earth With His Beauty 142670	Yr.Iss.		50.00	42-50
1996 Peace On Earth...Anyway 183377	Yr.Iss.		50.00	42-50
1997 Cane You Join Us For A Merry Christmas 272701	Yr.Iss.		50.00	42-50
1998 I'm Sending You a Merry Christmas 469327	Yr.Iss.		50.00	50

Christmas Blessings - S. Butcher

YEAR ISSUE	EDITION LIMIT	YEAR RETD.	ISSUE PRICE	*QUOTE U.S.$
1990 Wishing You A Yummy Christmas 523801	Yr.Iss.		50.00	50
1991 Blessings From Me To Thee 523860	Yr.Iss.		50.00	50-85
1992 But The Greatest of These Is Love 527742	Yr.Iss.		50.00	42-50
1993 Wishing You the Sweetest Christmas 530204	Yr.Iss.		50.00	42-50

Christmas Collection - S. Butcher

YEAR ISSUE	EDITION LIMIT	YEAR RETD.	ISSUE PRICE	*QUOTE U.S.$
1981 Come Let Us Adore Him E-5646	15,000		40.00	34-42
1982 Let Heaven and Nature Sing E-2347	15,000		40.00	38-45
1983 Wee Three Kings-E-0538	15,000		40.00	38-45
1984 Unto Us a Child Is Born E-5395	15,000		40.00	34-40

Christmas Love Series - S. Butcher

YEAR ISSUE	EDITION LIMIT	YEAR RETD.	ISSUE PRICE	*QUOTE U.S.$
1986 I'm Sending You a White Christmas 101834	Yr.Iss.		45.00	57-85
1987 My Peace I Give Unto Thee 102954	Yr.Iss.		45.00	73-85
1988 Merry Christmas Deer 520284	Yr.Iss.		50.00	50-85
1989 May Your Christmas Be A Happy Home 523003	Yr.Iss.		50.00	48-85

The Four Seasons Series - S. Butcher

YEAR ISSUE	EDITION LIMIT	YEAR RETD.	ISSUE PRICE	*QUOTE U.S.$
1985 The Voice of Spring 12106	Yr.Iss.		40.00	60
1985 Summer's Joy 12114	Yr.Iss.		40.00	57-75
1986 Autumn's Praise 12122	Yr.Iss.		40.00	37-44
1986 Winter's Song 12130	Yr.Iss.		40.00	37-44

Inspired Thoughts Series - S. Butcher

YEAR ISSUE	EDITION LIMIT	YEAR RETD.	ISSUE PRICE	*QUOTE U.S.$
1981 Love One Another E-5215	15,000		40.00	34-40
1982 Make a Joyful Noise E-7174	15,000		40.00	34-40
1983 I Believe In Miracles E-9257	15,000		40.00	34-40
1984 Love is Kind E-2847	15,000		40.00	34-40

Joy of Christmas Series - S. Butcher

YEAR ISSUE	EDITION LIMIT	YEAR RETD.	ISSUE PRICE	*QUOTE U.S.$
1982 I'll Play My Drum For Him E-2357	Yr.Iss.		40.00	60
1983 Christmastime is for Sharing E-0505	Yr.Iss.		40.00	63
1984 The Wonder of Christmas E-5396	Yr.Iss.		40.00	40
1985 Tell Me the Story of Jesus 15237	Yr.Iss.		40.00	86

Mother's Day Series - S. Butcher

YEAR ISSUE	EDITION LIMIT	YEAR RETD.	ISSUE PRICE	*QUOTE U.S.$
1981 Mother Sew Dear E-5217	15,000		40.00	34-40
1982 The Purr-fect Grandma E-7173	15,000		40.00	34-40
1983 The Hand that Rocks the Future E-9256	15,000		40.00	34-40
1984 Loving Thy Neighbor E-2848	15,000		40.00	34-40
1994 Thinking of You Is What I Really Like to Do 531766	Yr.Iss.		50.00	42-50
1996 Of All The Mothers I Have Known There's None As Precious As My Own 163716	Yr.Iss.		50.00	50

Open Editions - S. Butcher

YEAR ISSUE	EDITION LIMIT	YEAR RETD.	ISSUE PRICE	*QUOTE U.S.$
1982 Our First Christmas Together E-2378	Suspd.		30.00	30-45
1981 The Lord Bless You and Keep You E-5216	Suspd.		30.00	28-38
1982 Rejoicing with You E-7172	Suspd.		30.00	30-40
1983 Jesus Loves Me E-9275	Suspd.		30.00	30-40
1983 Jesus Loves Me E-9276	Suspd.		30.00	30-40
1994 Bring The Little Ones To Jesus 531359	Yr.Iss.		50.00	42-50

Precious Moments - S. Butcher

YEAR ISSUE	EDITION LIMIT	YEAR RETD.	ISSUE PRICE	*QUOTE U.S.$
1995 He Hath Made Everything Beautiful in His Time 129151	Open		50.00	42-50
1997 Love One Another 186406	Open		35.00	30-35

Reco International

Alan Maley's Past Impressions - A. Maley

YEAR ISSUE	EDITION LIMIT	YEAR RETD.	ISSUE PRICE	*QUOTE U.S.$
1997 Festive Occasion	95-day		29.90	30
1997 Sleigh Bells	95-day		29.90	30
1997 Summer Elegance	95-day		29.90	30
1997 The Recital	95-day		29.90	30
1999 Summer Romance	95-day		29.90	30
1999 Elegant Affair	95-day		29.90	30
1999 Romantic Engagement	95-day		29.90	30
1999 Secret Thoughts	95-day		29.90	30

Always With You Calendar - S. Kuck

YEAR ISSUE	EDITION LIMIT	YEAR RETD.	ISSUE PRICE	*QUOTE U.S.$
1999 January	95-day		29.95	30
2000 February	95-day		29.95	30
2000 March	95-day		29.95	30
2000 April	95-day		29.95	30
2000 May	95-day		29.95	30
2000 June	95-day		29.95	30
2000 July	95-day		29.95	30
2000 August	95-day		29.95	30
2000 September	95-day		29.95	30
2000 October	95-day		29.95	30
2000 November	95-day		29.95	30
2000 December	95-day		29.95	30

Amish Traditions - B. Farnsworth

YEAR ISSUE	EDITION LIMIT	YEAR RETD.	ISSUE PRICE	*QUOTE U.S.$
1994 Golden Harvest	95-day		29.50	30
1994 Family Outing	95-day		29.50	30
1994 The Quilting Bee	95-day		29.50	30
1995 Last Day of School	95-day	1998	29.50	30

Barefoot Children - S. Kuck

YEAR ISSUE	EDITION LIMIT	YEAR RETD.	ISSUE PRICE	*QUOTE U.S.$
1987 Night-Time Story	Retrd.	1994	29.50	54-60
1987 Golden Afternoon	Retrd.	1996	29.50	36-55
1988 Little Sweethearts	Retrd.	1995	29.50	39-50
1988 Carousel Magic	Retrd.	1996	29.50	65-70
1988 Under the Apple Tree	Retrd.	1995	29.50	50
1988 The Rehearsal	Retrd.	1995	29.50	60-85
1988 Pretty as a Picture	Retrd.	1993	29.50	65-70
1988 Grandma's Trunk	Retrd.	1993	29.50	50-70

Birds of the Hidden Forest - G. Ratnavira

YEAR ISSUE	EDITION LIMIT	YEAR RETD.	ISSUE PRICE	*QUOTE U.S.$
1994 Macaw Waterfall	96-day		29.50	30
1994 Paradise Valley	96-day		29.50	30
1995 Toucan Treasure	96-day		29.50	30

Bohemian Annuals - Factory Artist

YEAR ISSUE	EDITION LIMIT	YEAR RETD.	ISSUE PRICE	*QUOTE U.S.$
1974 1974	Retrd.	1975	130.00	155
1975 1975	Retrd.	1976	140.00	160
1976 1976	Retrd.	1978	150.00	160

Carnival Collection - R. Lee

YEAR ISSUE	EDITION LIMIT	YEAR RETD.	ISSUE PRICE	*QUOTE U.S.$
1998 Wheelin'	2,500		29.90	30
1998 Clown-Air	2,500		29.90	30
1998 Runaway Train	2,500		29.90	30
1998 Horsin'	2,500		29.90	30

Castles & Dreams - J. Bergsma

YEAR ISSUE	EDITION LIMIT	YEAR RETD.	ISSUE PRICE	*QUOTE U.S.$
1992 The Birth of a Dream	48-day		29.50	30
1992 Dreams Come True	48-day		29.50	30
1993 Believe In Your Dreams	48-day		29.50	30
1994 Follow Your Dreams	48-day		29.50	30

A Childhood Almanac - S. Kuck

YEAR ISSUE	EDITION LIMIT	YEAR RETD.	ISSUE PRICE	*QUOTE U.S.$
1985 Fireside Dreams-January	Retrd.	1991	29.50	35-59
1985 Be Mine-February	Retrd.	1992	29.50	45-59
1986 Winds of March-March	Retrd.	1994	29.50	59
1985 Easter Morning-April	Retrd.	1992	29.50	60
1985 For Mom-May	Retrd.	1992	29.50	35-59
1985 Just Dreaming-June	Retrd.	1992	29.50	60-65
1985 Star Spangled Sky-July	Retrd.	1995	29.50	60
1985 Summer Secrets-August	Retrd.	1991	29.50	65
1985 School Days-September	Retrd.	1991	29.50	59-75
1986 Indian Summer-October	Retrd.	1991	29.50	60-65
1986 Giving Thanks-November	Retrd.	1995	29.50	59-70
1985 Christmas Magic-December	Retrd.	1995	35.00	68-75

Children of the Sun - V. Di Fate

YEAR ISSUE	EDITION LIMIT	YEAR RETD.	ISSUE PRICE	*QUOTE U.S.$
1998 Mars The Red Planet	95-day	2000	29.90	30
1998 The Bright Rings of Saturn	95-day	2000	29.90	30

A Children's Christmas Pageant - S. Kuck

YEAR ISSUE	EDITION LIMIT	YEAR RETD.	ISSUE PRICE	*QUOTE U.S.$
1986 Silent Night	Retrd.	1987	32.50	75-90
1987 Hark the Herald Angels Sing	Retrd.	1988	32.50	65-69
1988 While Shepherds Watched...	Retrd.	1990	32.50	39-55
1989 We Three Kings	Retrd.	N/A	32.50	55-59

Christening Gift - S. Kuck

YEAR ISSUE	EDITION LIMIT	YEAR RETD.	ISSUE PRICE	*QUOTE U.S.$
1995 God's Gift	Open		29.90	30

The Christmas Series - J. Bergsma

YEAR ISSUE	EDITION LIMIT	YEAR RETD.	ISSUE PRICE	*QUOTE U.S.$
1990 Down The Glistening Lane	Retrd.	1996	35.00	35
1991 A Child Is Born	Retrd.	1996	35.00	35
1992 Christmas Day	Retrd.	1996	35.00	35
1993 I Wish You An Angel	Retrd.	1996	35.00	35

Christmas Wishes - J. Bergsma

YEAR ISSUE	EDITION LIMIT	YEAR RETD.	ISSUE PRICE	*QUOTE U.S.$
1994 I Wish You Love	75-day	1998	29.50	30-35
1995 I Wish You Joy	75-day	1998	29.50	30-35
1996 I Wish You Peace	75-day	1998	29.50	30

Clowning Around - R. Lee

YEAR ISSUE	EDITION LIMIT	YEAR RETD.	ISSUE PRICE	*QUOTE U.S.$
1998 Beware of Snakes	5,000		29.90	30
1998 Duck Crossing	5,000		29.90	30
1998 On The Edge	5,000		29.90	30
1998 Almost There	5,000		29.90	30

Days Gone By - S. Kuck

YEAR ISSUE	EDITION LIMIT	YEAR RETD.	ISSUE PRICE	*QUOTE U.S.$
1983 Sunday Best	Retrd.	1984	29.50	49-60
1983 Amy's Magic Horse	Retrd.	1985	29.50	23-50
1984 Little Anglers	Retrd.	1985	29.50	70
1984 Afternoon Recital	Retrd.	1985	29.50	70
1984 Little Tutor	Retrd.	1985	29.50	20-55
1985 Easter at Grandma's	Retrd.	1985	29.50	60
1985 Morning Song	Retrd.	1986	29.50	40-45
1985 The Surrey Ride	Retrd.	1987	29.50	60

Dresden Christmas - Factory Artist

YEAR ISSUE	EDITION LIMIT	YEAR RETD.	ISSUE PRICE	*QUOTE U.S.$
1971 Shepherd Scene	Retrd.	1978	15.00	50
1972 Niklas Church	Retrd.	1978	15.00	25
1973 Schwanstein Church	Retrd.	1978	18.00	35
1974 Village Scene	Retrd.	1978	20.00	30
1975 Rothenburg Scene	Retrd.	1978	24.00	30
1976 Village Church	Retrd.	1978	26.00	35
1977 Old Mill	Retrd.	1978	28.00	30

Dresden Mother's Day - Factory Artist

YEAR ISSUE	EDITION LIMIT	YEAR RETD.	ISSUE PRICE	*QUOTE U.S.$
1972 Doe and Fawn	Retrd.	1979	15.00	20
1973 Mare and Colt	Retrd.	1979	16.00	25
1974 Tiger and Cub	Retrd.	1979	20.00	23
1975 Dachshunds	Retrd.	1979	24.00	28
1976 Owl and Offspring	Retrd.	1979	26.00	30
1977 Chamois	Retrd.	1979	28.00	30

Eagle of America - S. Barlowe

YEAR ISSUE	EDITION LIMIT	YEAR RETD.	ISSUE PRICE	*QUOTE U.S.$
1996 Land of The Free	96-day	1998	29.90	30

Enchanted Gardens - S. Kuck

YEAR ISSUE	EDITION LIMIT	YEAR RETD.	ISSUE PRICE	*QUOTE U.S.$
1998 Tea For Three	95-day		32.95	33
1998 Sweetest Delights	95-day		32.95	33
1998 Wildflowers of Love	95-day		32.95	33
1998 Innocence Shared	95-day		32.95	33

Everlasing Friends - S. Kuck

YEAR ISSUE	EDITION LIMIT	YEAR RETD.	ISSUE PRICE	*QUOTE U.S.$
1996 Sharing Secrets	95-day		29.95	30
1996 Sharing Dreams	95-day		29.95	30
1997 Sharing Beauty	95-day		29.95	30
1997 Sharing Love	95-day		29.95	30
1998 Sharing Harmony	95-day		29.95	30
1998 Sharing Stories	95-day		29.95	30

Everyday Heroes - B. Brown

YEAR ISSUE	EDITION LIMIT	YEAR RETD.	ISSUE PRICE	*QUOTE U.S.$
1998 Out of the Blaze	95-day		29.90	30

Fishtales - R. Manning

YEAR ISSUE	EDITION LIMIT	YEAR RETD.	ISSUE PRICE	*QUOTE U.S.$
1997 Rainbow River	76-day		29.90	30

Four Seasons - J. Poluszynski

YEAR ISSUE	EDITION LIMIT	YEAR RETD.	ISSUE PRICE	*QUOTE U.S.$
1973 Spring	Retrd.	1975	50.00	75
1973 Summer	Retrd.	1975	50.00	75
1973 Fall	Retrd.	1975	50.00	75
1973 Winter	Retrd.	1975	50.00	75

Friends For Keeps - S. Kuck

YEAR ISSUE	EDITION LIMIT	YEAR RETD.	ISSUE PRICE	*QUOTE U.S.$
1996 Puppy Love	95-day		29.95	30
1996 Gone Fishing	95-day		29.95	30
1997 Golden Days	95-day		29.95	30
1997 Take Me Home	95-day		29.95	30

Furstenberg Christmas - Factory Artist

YEAR ISSUE	EDITION LIMIT	YEAR RETD.	ISSUE PRICE	*QUOTE U.S.$
1971 Rabbits	Retrd.	1977	15.00	30
1972 Snowy Village	Retrd.	1977	15.00	20
1973 Christmas Eve	Retrd.	1977	18.00	35
1974 Sparrows	Retrd.	1977	20.00	30
1975 Deer Family	Retrd.	1977	22.00	30
1976 Winter Birds	Retrd.	1977	25.00	25

Furstenberg Easter - Factory Artist

YEAR ISSUE	EDITION LIMIT	YEAR RETD.	ISSUE PRICE	*QUOTE U.S.$
1971 Sheep	Retrd.	1973	15.00	25-100
1972 Chicks	Retrd.	1975	15.00	60
1973 Bunnies	Retrd.	1976	16.00	80
1974 Pussywillow	Retrd.	1976	20.00	33
1975 Easter Window	Retrd.	1977	22.00	30
1976 Flower Collecting	Retrd.	1977	25.00	25

Furstenberg Mother's Day - Factory Artist

YEAR ISSUE	EDITION LIMIT	YEAR RETD.	ISSUE PRICE	*QUOTE U.S.$
1972 Hummingbirds, Fe	Retrd.	1974	15.00	45
1973 Hedgehogs	Retrd.	1974	16.00	40
1974 Doe and Fawn	Retrd.	1974	20.00	30
1975 Swans	Retrd.	1976	22.00	23
1976 Koala Bears	Retrd.	1976	25.00	30

Furstenberg Olympic - J. Poluszynski

YEAR ISSUE	EDITION LIMIT	YEAR RETD.	ISSUE PRICE	*QUOTE U.S.$
1972 Munich	Retrd.	1972	20.00	75
1976 Montreal	Retrd.	1976	37.50	38

Games Children Play - S. Kuck

YEAR ISSUE	EDITION LIMIT	YEAR RETD.	ISSUE PRICE	*QUOTE U.S.$
1979 Me First	Retrd.	1983	45.00	50-75
1980 Forever Bubbles	Retrd.	1983	45.00	48-65
1981 Skating Pals	Retrd.	1983	45.00	48-65
1982 Join Me	10,000	1998	45.00	45

Gardens of Innocence - S. Kuck

YEAR ISSUE	EDITION LIMIT	YEAR RETD.	ISSUE PRICE	*QUOTE U.S.$
1997 Heavenly Hideaway	95-day		32.95	33
1997 Sweetly Swinging	95-day		32.95	33
1998 Gently Giving	95-day		32.95	33
1998 Precious Party	95-day		32.95	33
1998 Highest Harmony	95-day		32.95	33
1999 Perfect Place	95-day		32.95	33
1999 Peaceful Prayers	95-day		32.95	33
1999 Heaven's Blossoms	95-day		32.95	33

Generations - B. Brown

YEAR ISSUE	EDITION LIMIT	YEAR RETD.	ISSUE PRICE	*QUOTE U.S.$
1997 Passing On The Faith	95-day		29.90	30
1998 Guiding the Way	95-day		29.90	30
1998 Learning To Imagine	95-day		29.90	30
1998 Loving Time	95-day		29.90	30

Gift of Love Mother's Day Collection - S. Kuck

YEAR ISSUE	EDITION LIMIT	YEAR RETD.	ISSUE PRICE	*QUOTE U.S.$
1993 Morning Glory	Retrd.	1994	65.00	75-85
1994 Memories From The Heart	Retrd.	1994	65.00	75-85

*Quotes have been rounded up to nearest dollar

The Glory Of Christ - C. Micarelli

YEAR ISSUE	EDITION LIMIT	YEAR RETD.	ISSUE PRICE	*QUOTE U.S.$
1992 The Ascension	48-day		29.50	30
1993 Jesus Teaching	48-day		29.50	30
1993 The Last Supper	48-day	1999	29.50	30
1993 The Nativity	48-day		29.50	30
1993 The Baptism Of Christ	48-day		29.50	30
1993 Jesus Heals The Sick	48-day		29.50	30
1994 Jesus Walks On Water	48-day		29.50	30
1994 Descent From The Cross	48-day		29.50	30

Great Stories from the Bible - G. Katz

YEAR ISSUE	EDITION LIMIT	YEAR RETD.	ISSUE PRICE	*QUOTE U.S.$
1987 Moses in the Bulrushes	Retrd.	1994	29.50	30-45
1987 King Saul & David	Retrd.	1994	29.50	30-45
1987 Moses and the Ten Commandments	Retrd.	1994	29.50	38-45
1987 Joseph's Coat of Many Colors	Retrd.	1994	29.50	30-45
1988 Rebekah at the Well	Retrd.	1994	29.50	35-45
1988 Daniel Reads the Writing on the Wall	Retrd.	1994	29.50	45-65
1988 The Story of Ruth	Retrd.	1994	29.50	35-45
1988 King Solomon	Retrd.	1994	29.50	35-45

Guardian Angel Collection Plaques - C. Lael

YEAR ISSUE	EDITION LIMIT	YEAR RETD.	ISSUE PRICE	*QUOTE U.S.$
2000 Angel of Goodness - January	Open		20.00	20
2000 Angel of Peace & Tranquility - February	Open		20.00	20
2000 Angel of Comfort - March	Open		20.00	20
2000 Angel of Power - April	Open		20.00	20
2000 Angel of Loveliness - May	Open		20.00	20
2000 Angel of Wisdom - June	Open		20.00	20
2000 Angel of Protection - July	Open		20.00	20
2000 Angel of Praise - August	Open		20.00	20
2000 Angel of Light - September	Open		20.00	20
2000 Angel of Healing - October	Open		20.00	20
2000 Guardian Angel - November	Open		20.00	20
2000 Angel of Wonder - December	Open		20.00	20

Guardians Of The Kingdom - J. Bergsma

YEAR ISSUE	EDITION LIMIT	YEAR RETD.	ISSUE PRICE	*QUOTE U.S.$
1990 Rainbow To Ride On	Retrd.	1993	35.00	40
1990 Special Friends Are Few	17,500	1998	35.00	35
1990 Guardians Of The Innocent Children	17,500	1998	35.00	35
1990 The Miracle Of Love	17,500	1998	35.00	35
1991 The Magic Of Love	17,500	1998	35.00	35
1991 Only With The Heart	17,500	1998	35.00	35
1991 To Fly Without Wings	17,500	1998	35.00	35
1991 In Faith I Am Free	17,500	1998	35.00	35

Guiding Lights - D Hahlbohm

YEAR ISSUE	EDITION LIMIT	YEAR RETD.	ISSUE PRICE	*QUOTE U.S.$
1996 Robbins Reef	96-day		29.90	30
1996 Cape Hateras	96-day		29.90	30
1997 Cape Neddick	96-day		29.90	30
1998 Split Rock, MN	96-day		29.90	30

Haven of the Hunters - H. Roe

YEAR ISSUE	EDITION LIMIT	YEAR RETD.	ISSUE PRICE	*QUOTE U.S.$
1994 Eagle's Castle	Retrd.	1996	29.50	30
1994 Sanctuary of the Hawk	Retrd.	1996	29.50	30

Hearts And Flowers - S. Kuck

YEAR ISSUE	EDITION LIMIT	YEAR RETD.	ISSUE PRICE	*QUOTE U.S.$
1991 Patience	Retrd.	1999	29.50	33-55
1991 Tea Party	Retrd.	1999	29.50	33-55
1992 Cat's In The Cradle	Retrd.	1999	32.50	40-45
1992 Carousel of Dreams	Retrd.	1999	32.50	23-33
1992 Storybook Memories	120-day	1998	32.50	35
1993 Delightful Bundle	120-day		34.50	35
1993 Easter Morning Visitor	120-day		34.50	35
1993 Me and My Pony	120-day		34.50	40

Heavenly Kingdom - C. Micarelli

YEAR ISSUE	EDITION LIMIT	YEAR RETD.	ISSUE PRICE	*QUOTE U.S.$
1997 The Blessed Child	95-day		29.90	30

Imaginary Gardens - S. Somerville

YEAR ISSUE	EDITION LIMIT	YEAR RETD.	ISSUE PRICE	*QUOTE U.S.$
1996 Pussywillows	76-day		29.90	30
1996 Dogwood	76-day		29.90	30
1997 Cowslip	76-day		29.90	30

In The Eye of The Storm - W. Lowe

YEAR ISSUE	EDITION LIMIT	YEAR RETD.	ISSUE PRICE	*QUOTE U.S.$
1991 First Strike	Retrd.	1996	29.50	30
1992 Night Force	Retrd.	1996	29.50	30
1992 Tracks Across The Sand	Retrd.	1996	29.50	30
1992 The Storm Has Landed	Retrd.	1996	29.50	30

J. Bergsma Mother's Day Series - J. Bergsma

YEAR ISSUE	EDITION LIMIT	YEAR RETD.	ISSUE PRICE	*QUOTE U.S.$
1990 The Beauty Of Life	Retrd.	1996	35.00	35-38
1992 Life's Blessing	Retrd.	1996	35.00	35-38
1993 My Greatest Treasures	Retrd.	1996	35.00	35-38
1994 Forever In My Heart	Retrd.	1996	35.00	35-38

Jesus And The Children - N. Mc Naulty

YEAR ISSUE	EDITION LIMIT	YEAR RETD.	ISSUE PRICE	*QUOTE U.S.$
1998 Come Unto Me	96-day		29.90	30

King's Flowers - A. Falchi

YEAR ISSUE	EDITION LIMIT	YEAR RETD.	ISSUE PRICE	*QUOTE U.S.$
1973 Carnation	Retrd.	1974	85.00	130
1974 Red Rose	Retrd.	1975	100.00	145
1975 Yellow Dahlia	Retrd.	1976	110.00	162
1976 Bluebells	Retrd.	1977	130.00	165
1977 Anemones	Retrd.	1979	130.00	175

King's Mother's Day - Merli

YEAR ISSUE	EDITION LIMIT	YEAR RETD.	ISSUE PRICE	*QUOTE U.S.$
1973 Dancing Girl	Retrd.	1974	100.00	225
1974 Dancing Boy	Retrd.	1975	115.00	250
1975 Motherly Love	Retrd.	1976	140.00	225
1976 Maiden	Retrd.	1978	180.00	200

Life's Little Celebrations - C. Tait

YEAR ISSUE	EDITION LIMIT	YEAR RETD.	ISSUE PRICE	*QUOTE U.S.$
1997 The New Baby	96-day		29.90	30
1997 An Apple For The Teacher	96-day		29.90	30
1997 School Bell	96-day		29.90	30
1997 Graduation Smile	96-day		29.90	30
1997 Celebration of Love	96-day		29.90	30
1997 I Love You	96-day		29.90	30

Little Angel Plate Collection - S. Kuck

YEAR ISSUE	EDITION LIMIT	YEAR RETD.	ISSUE PRICE	*QUOTE U.S.$
1994 Angel of Charity	95-day		29.50	30
1994 Angel of Joy	95-day		29.50	30

Little Professionals - S. Kuck

YEAR ISSUE	EDITION LIMIT	YEAR RETD.	ISSUE PRICE	*QUOTE U.S.$
1982 All is Well	Retrd.	1983	39.50	65-95
1983 Tender Loving Care	Retrd.	1985	39.50	55-70
1984 Lost and Found	Retrd.	1995	39.50	45-65
1985 Reading, Writing and...	Retrd.	1989	39.50	50-65

Little Wonders - A. Grant

YEAR ISSUE	EDITION LIMIT	YEAR RETD.	ISSUE PRICE	*QUOTE U.S.$
1998 Safely Through The Night	95-day		29.90	30
1998 First Friend	95-day		29.90	30
1998 Cherished Toys	95-day		29.90	30
1998 Tender Moments	95-day		29.90	30

Magic Companions - J. Bergsma

YEAR ISSUE	EDITION LIMIT	YEAR RETD.	ISSUE PRICE	*QUOTE U.S.$
1994 Believe in Love	48-day		29.50	30
1994 Imagine Peace	48-day		29.50	30
1995 Live in Harmony	48-day		29.50	30
1995 Trust in Magic	48-day		29.50	30

Majestic Spirits - G. Perillo

YEAR ISSUE	EDITION LIMIT	YEAR RETD.	ISSUE PRICE	*QUOTE U.S.$
1999 Nature's Might	5,000		29.90	30
1999 Noble Spirit	5,000		35.00	35
1999 Freedom's Thunder	5,000		29.90	30

March of Dimes: Our Children, Our Future - Various

YEAR ISSUE	EDITION LIMIT	YEAR RETD.	ISSUE PRICE	*QUOTE U.S.$
1989 A Time to Love (2nd in Series) - S. Kuck	Retrd.	1993	29.00	30
1989 A Time to Plant (3rd in Series) - J. McClelland	150-day	1993	29.00	12-29

Marmot Christmas - Factory Artist

YEAR ISSUE	EDITION LIMIT	YEAR RETD.	ISSUE PRICE	*QUOTE U.S.$
1970 Polar Bear, Fe	Retrd.	1971	13.00	20-60
1971 Buffalo Bill	Retrd.	1972	16.00	55
1972 Boy and Grandfather	Retrd.	1973	20.00	50
1971 American Buffalo	Retrd.	1973	14.50	35
1973 Snowman	Retrd.	1974	22.00	45
1974 Dancing	Retrd.	1975	24.00	30
1975 Quail	Retrd.	1976	30.00	40
1976 Windmill	Retrd.	1978	40.00	40

Marmot Father's Day - Factory Artist

YEAR ISSUE	EDITION LIMIT	YEAR RETD.	ISSUE PRICE	*QUOTE U.S.$
1970 Stag	Retrd.	1970	12.00	40-70
1971 Horse	Retrd.	1972	12.50	40

Marmot Mother's Day - Factory Artist

YEAR ISSUE	EDITION LIMIT	YEAR RETD.	ISSUE PRICE	*QUOTE U.S.$
1972 Seal	Retrd.	1973	16.00	60
1973 Bear with Cub	Retrd.	1974	20.00	140
1974 Penguins	Retrd.	1975	24.00	50
1975 Raccoons	Retrd.	1976	30.00	45
1976 Ducks	Retrd.	1977	40.00	40

Memories of Childhood - C. Getz

YEAR ISSUE	EDITION LIMIT	YEAR RETD.	ISSUE PRICE	*QUOTE U.S.$
1994 Teatime with Teddy	75-day		29.50	30
1995 Bases Loaded	75-day		29.50	30
1996 Mommy's Little Helper	75-day		29.50	30

Moments At Home - S. Kuck

YEAR ISSUE	EDITION LIMIT	YEAR RETD.	ISSUE PRICE	*QUOTE U.S.$
1995 Moments of Caring	95-day		29.90	30
1995 Moments of Tenderness	95-day		29.90	30
1995 Moments of Friendship	95-day		29.90	30
1995 Moments of Sharing	95-day		29.90	30
1995 Moments of Love	95-day		29.90	30
1996 Moments of Reflection	95-day		29.90	30

Moser Christmas - Factory Artist

YEAR ISSUE	EDITION LIMIT	YEAR RETD.	ISSUE PRICE	*QUOTE U.S.$
1970 Hradcany Castle	Retrd.	1971	75.00	170
1971 Karlstein Castle	Retrd.	1972	75.00	80
1972 Old Town Hall	Retrd.	1973	85.00	85
1973 Karlovy Vary Castle	Retrd.	1974	90.00	100

Moser Mother's Day - Factory Artist

YEAR ISSUE	EDITION LIMIT	YEAR RETD.	ISSUE PRICE	*QUOTE U.S.$
1971 Peacocks	Retrd.	1971	75.00	100
1972 Butterflies	Retrd.	1972	85.00	90
1973 Squirrels	Retrd.	1973	90.00	95

Mother Goose - J. McClelland

YEAR ISSUE	EDITION LIMIT	YEAR RETD.	ISSUE PRICE	*QUOTE U.S.$
1979 Mary, Mary	Retrd.	1979	22.50	69
1980 Little Boy Blue	Retrd.	1980	22.50	35
1981 Little Miss Muffet	Retrd.	1981	24.50	25-30
1982 Little Jack Horner	Retrd.	1982	24.50	10-45
1983 Little Bo Peep	Retrd.	1983	24.50	30-38
1984 Diddle, Diddle Dumpling	Retrd.	1984	24.50	40-45
1985 Mary Had a Little Lamb	Retrd.	1985	27.50	20-30
1986 Jack and Jill	Retrd.	1988	27.50	23

Mother's Day Collection - S. Kuck

YEAR ISSUE	EDITION LIMIT	YEAR RETD.	ISSUE PRICE	*QUOTE U.S.$
1985 Once Upon a Time	Retrd.	1987	29.50	60-65
1986 Times Remembered	Retrd.	1988	29.50	45-60
1987 A Cherished Time	Retrd.	1987	29.50	60-70
1988 A Time Together	Retrd.	1988	29.50	60-70

Noble and Free - Kelly

YEAR ISSUE	EDITION LIMIT	YEAR RETD.	ISSUE PRICE	*QUOTE U.S.$
1994 Gathering Storm	95-day	1998	29.50	30
1994 Protected Journey	95-day	1998	29.50	30
1994 Moonlight Run	95-day	1998	29.50	30

The Nutcracker Ballet - C. Micarelli

YEAR ISSUE	EDITION LIMIT	YEAR RETD.	ISSUE PRICE	*QUOTE U.S.$
1989 Christmas Eve Party	Retrd.	1994	35.00	30-35
1990 Clara And Her Prince	Retrd.	1999	35.00	35
1990 The Dream Begins	Retrd.	1999	35.00	35
1991 Dance of the Snow Fairies	Retrd.	1994	35.00	35
1992 The Land of Sweets	Retrd.	1999	35.00	35
1992 The Sugar Plum Fairy	Retrd.	1999	35.00	35

On Angels Wings - S. Kuck

YEAR ISSUE	EDITION LIMIT	YEAR RETD.	ISSUE PRICE	*QUOTE U.S.$
1999 Angel Kisses	95-day		29.95	30
2000 Wings of Wonder	95-day		29.95	30
2000 Heaven's Secrets	95-day		29.95	30
2000 Blossoms of Love	95-day		29.95	30
2000 Heaven's Gentle Touch	95-day		29.95	30

Oscar & Bertie's Edwardian Holiday - P.D. Jackson

YEAR ISSUE	EDITION LIMIT	YEAR RETD.	ISSUE PRICE	*QUOTE U.S.$
1991 Snapshot	Retrd.	1996	29.50	30
1992 Early Rise	Retrd.	1996	29.50	30
1992 All Aboard	Retrd.	1996	29.50	30
1992 Learning To Swim	Retrd.	1996	29.50	30

Our Cherished Seas - S. Barlowe

YEAR ISSUE	EDITION LIMIT	YEAR RETD.	ISSUE PRICE	*QUOTE U.S.$
1991 Whale Song	48-day		37.50	38
1991 Lions of the Sea	48-day		37.50	38
1991 Flight of the Dolphins	48-day	1999	37.50	38
1992 Palace of the Seals	48-day		37.50	38
1992 Orca Ballet	48-day		37.50	38
1993 Emperors of the Ice	48-day		37.50	38
1993 Turtle Treasure	48-day		37.50	38
1993 Splendor of the Sea	48-day		37.50	38

Out of The Wild - S. Barlowe

YEAR ISSUE	EDITION LIMIT	YEAR RETD.	ISSUE PRICE	*QUOTE U.S.$
1996 The Pride	76-day		29.90	30
1997 Graceful Giants	76-day		29.90	30

Plate Of The Month Collection - S. Kuck

YEAR ISSUE	EDITION LIMIT	YEAR RETD.	ISSUE PRICE	*QUOTE U.S.$
1990 January	Retrd.	1996	25.00	28-50
1990 February	Retrd.	1996	25.00	28-50
1990 March	Retrd.	1996	25.00	28-50
1990 April	Retrd.	1996	25.00	28-50
1990 May	Retrd.	1996	25.00	28-50
1990 June	Retrd.	1996	25.00	28-50
1990 July	Retrd.	1996	25.00	28-50
1990 August	Retrd.	1996	25.00	28-50
1990 September	Retrd.	1996	25.00	28-50
1990 October	Retrd.	1996	25.00	28-50
1990 November	Retrd.	1996	25.00	28-50
1990 December	Retrd.	1996	25.00	28-50

Precious Angels - S. Kuck

YEAR ISSUE	EDITION LIMIT	YEAR RETD.	ISSUE PRICE	*QUOTE U.S.$
1995 Angel of Grace	95-day		29.90	30
1995 Angel of Happiness	95-day		29.90	30
1995 Angel of Hope	95-day		29.90	30
1995 Angel of Laughter	95-day		29.90	30
1995 Angel of Love	95-day		29.90	30
1995 Angel of Peace	95-day		29.90	30
1995 Angel of Sharing	95-day		29.90	30
1995 Angel of Sunshine	95-day		29.90	30

Premier Collection - S. Kuck

YEAR ISSUE	EDITION LIMIT	YEAR RETD.	ISSUE PRICE	*QUOTE U.S.$
1991 Puppy	Retrd.	1993	95.00	125-200
1991 Kitten	Retrd.	1992	95.00	145-300
1992 La Belle	7,500	1996	95.00	95
1992 Le Beau	7,500	1996	95.00	95

Protectors of the Wild - M. Wood

YEAR ISSUE	EDITION LIMIT	YEAR RETD.	ISSUE PRICE	*QUOTE U.S.$
1998 Moon Song	95-day		29.90	30

Protectors of the Wild - R. Frentner

YEAR ISSUE	EDITION LIMIT	YEAR RETD.	ISSUE PRICE	*QUOTE U.S.$
1998 Genesis	95-day		29.90	30

Quinceañera - C. Micarelli

YEAR ISSUE	EDITION LIMIT	YEAR RETD.	ISSUE PRICE	*QUOTE U.S.$
1999 Quinceañera	Open		30.00	30

Reflection of Love - S. Kuck

YEAR ISSUE	EDITION LIMIT	YEAR RETD.	ISSUE PRICE	*QUOTE U.S.$
1999 Mother's Love	95-day		35.00	35
2000 Mother's Gentle Touch	95-day		35.00	35

Romantic Gardens - S. Kuck

YEAR ISSUE	EDITION LIMIT	YEAR RETD.	ISSUE PRICE	*QUOTE U.S.$
1997 Emma	95-day		35.00	35
1997 Alexandra	95-day		35.00	35

Royal Mother's Day - Factory Artist

YEAR ISSUE	EDITION LIMIT	YEAR RETD.	ISSUE PRICE	*QUOTE U.S.$
1970 Swan and Young	Retrd.	1971	12.00	80
1971 Doe and Fawn	Retrd.	1972	13.00	55
1972 Rabbits	Retrd.	1973	16.00	40
1973 Owl Family	Retrd.	1974	18.00	40
1974 Duck and Young	Retrd.	1975	22.00	40
1975 Lynx and Cubs	Retrd.	1976	26.00	40
1976 Woodcock and Young	Retrd.	1978	27.50	33
1977 Koala Bear	Retrd.	1978	30.00	30

Royale - Factory Artist

YEAR ISSUE	EDITION LIMIT	YEAR RETD.	ISSUE PRICE	*QUOTE U.S.$
1969 Apollo Moon Landing	Retrd.	1969	30.00	80

Royale Christmas - Factory Artist

YEAR ISSUE	EDITION LIMIT	YEAR RETD.	ISSUE PRICE	*QUOTE U.S.$
1969 Christmas Fair	Retrd.	1970	12.00	125
1970 Vigil Mass	Retrd.	1971	13.00	110
1971 Christmas Night	Retrd.	1972	16.00	50
1972 Elks	Retrd.	1973	16.00	45
1973 Christmas Down	Retrd.	1974	20.00	38
1974 Village Christmas	Retrd.	1975	22.00	60
1975 Feeding Time	Retrd.	1976	26.00	35
1976 Seaport Christmas	Retrd.	1977	27.50	30
1977 Sledding	Retrd.	1978	30.00	30

Royale Father's Day - Factory Artist

YEAR ISSUE	EDITION LIMIT	YEAR RETD.	ISSUE PRICE	*QUOTE U.S.$
1970 Frigate Constitution	Retrd.	1971	13.00	80

*Quotes have been rounded up to nearest dollar

YEAR ISSUE	EDITION LIMIT	YEAR RETD.	ISSUE PRICE	*QUOTE U.S.$
1971 Man Fishing	Retrd.	1972	13.00	35
1972 Mountaineer	Retrd.	1973	16.00	55
1973 Camping	Retrd.	1974	18.00	45
1974 Eagle	Retrd.	1975	22.00	35
1975 Regatta	Retrd.	1976	26.00	35
1976 Hunting	Retrd.	1977	27.50	33
1977 Fishing	Retrd.	1978	30.00	30

Royale Game Plates - Various

YEAR ISSUE	EDITION LIMIT	YEAR RETD.	ISSUE PRICE	*QUOTE U.S.$
1972 Setters - J. Poluszynski	Retrd.	1974	180.00	200
1973 Fox - J. Poluszynski	Retrd.	1975	200.00	250
1974 Osprey - W. Schiener	Retrd.	1976	250.00	250
1975 California Quail - W. Schiener	Retrd.	1976	265.00	265

Royale Germania Christmas Annual - Factory Artist

YEAR ISSUE	EDITION LIMIT	YEAR RETD.	ISSUE PRICE	*QUOTE U.S.$
1970 Orchid	Retrd.	1971	200.00	650
1971 Cyclamen	Retrd.	1972	200.00	325
1972 Silver Thistle	Retrd.	1973	250.00	290
1973 Tulips	Retrd.	1974	275.00	310
1974 Sunflowers	Retrd.	1975	300.00	320
1975 Snowdrops	Retrd.	1976	450.00	500

Royale Germania Crystal Mother's Day - Factory Artist

YEAR ISSUE	EDITION LIMIT	YEAR RETD.	ISSUE PRICE	*QUOTE U.S.$
1971 Roses	Retrd.	1971	135.00	650
1972 Elephant and Youngster	Retrd.	1972	180.00	250
1973 Koala Bear and Cub	Retrd.	1973	200.00	225
1974 Squirrels	Retrd.	1974	240.00	250
1975 Swan and Young	Retrd.	1975	350.00	360

Sandra Kuck Fan Collection - S. Kuck

YEAR ISSUE	EDITION LIMIT	YEAR RETD.	ISSUE PRICE	*QUOTE U.S.$
2000 Summer Outing	65-day		30.00	30

Sandra Kuck Mothers' Day - S. Kuck

YEAR ISSUE	EDITION LIMIT	YEAR RETD.	ISSUE PRICE	*QUOTE U.S.$
1995 Home is Where the Heart Is	Retrd.	1999	35.00	35-50
1996 Dear To The Heart	Retrd.	1998	35.00	40-50
1997 Welcome Home	Retrd.	2000	35.00	35
1998 Wings of Love	Retrd.	2000	35.00	35

Sculpted Heirlooms - S. Kuck

YEAR ISSUE	EDITION LIMIT	YEAR RETD.	ISSUE PRICE	*QUOTE U.S.$
1996 Best Friends (sculpted plate)	24-mo.		29.95	30
1996 Tea Party (sculpted plate)	24-mo.		29.90	30
1996 Storybook Memories (sculpted plate)	24-mo.		29.90	30
1996 Patience (sculpted plate)	24-mo.		29.90	30

Single Issue - T. Gronland

YEAR ISSUE	EDITION LIMIT	YEAR RETD.	ISSUE PRICE	*QUOTE U.S.$
1997 Happiness In Heaven	95-day	1998	29.90	30

Sisters Love Forever - S. Kuck

YEAR ISSUE	EDITION LIMIT	YEAR RETD.	ISSUE PRICE	*QUOTE U.S.$
2000 Sister's Touch	95-day		29.95	30

Songs From The Garden - G. Ratnavira

YEAR ISSUE	EDITION LIMIT	YEAR RETD.	ISSUE PRICE	*QUOTE U.S.$
1996 Love Song	76-day		29.90	30
1996 Rhapsody In Blue	76-day		29.90	30
1997 Hummingbirds In Harmony	76-day		29.90	30
1997 Golden Melody	76-day		29.90	30
1997 Spring Serenade	76-day		29.90	30
1998 Ode To The Oriole	76-day		29.90	30

The Sophisticated Ladies Collection - A. Fazio

YEAR ISSUE	EDITION LIMIT	YEAR RETD.	ISSUE PRICE	*QUOTE U.S.$
1985 Felicia	21-day	1997	29.50	30-45
1985 Samantha	21-day	1994	29.50	35
1985 Phoebe	21-day	1994	29.50	33-45
1985 Cleo	21-day	1998	29.50	30
1986 Cerissa	21-day	1994	29.50	33-45
1986 Natasha	21-day	1994	29.50	33-45
1986 Bianka	21-day	1994	29.50	33-45
1986 Chelsea	21-day	1994	29.50	33-45

Special Occasions by Reco - S. Kuck

YEAR ISSUE	EDITION LIMIT	YEAR RETD.	ISSUE PRICE	*QUOTE U.S.$
1988 The Wedding	Open		35.00	35
1989 Wedding Day (6 1/2")	Retrd.	1996	25.00	25-45
1990 The Special Day	Retrd.	1996	25.00	25

Sugar and Spice - S. Kuck

YEAR ISSUE	EDITION LIMIT	YEAR RETD.	ISSUE PRICE	*QUOTE U.S.$
1993 Best Friends	95-day		29.90	30
1993 Sisters	95-day		29.90	30
1994 Little One	95-day		32.90	33
1994 Teddy Bear Tales	95-day		32.90	33
1994 Morning Prayers	95-day		32.90	33
1995 First Snow	95-day		34.90	35
1994 Garden of Sunshine	95-day		34.90	35
1995 A Special Day	95-day		34.90	35

Tidings Of Joy - S. Kuck

YEAR ISSUE	EDITION LIMIT	YEAR RETD.	ISSUE PRICE	*QUOTE U.S.$
1992 Peace on Earth	Retrd.	1995	35.00	35-55
1993 Rejoice	Retrd.	1996	35.00	35-55
1994 Noel	Retrd.	1995	35.00	65-100

Totems of the West - J. Bergsma

YEAR ISSUE	EDITION LIMIT	YEAR RETD.	ISSUE PRICE	*QUOTE U.S.$
1994 The Watchmen	96-day		29.50	30
1995 Peace At Last	96-day		29.50	30
1995 Never Alone	96-day		35.00	35

Town And Country Dogs - S. Barlowe

YEAR ISSUE	EDITION LIMIT	YEAR RETD.	ISSUE PRICE	*QUOTE U.S.$
1990 Fox Hunt	36-day		35.00	35
1991 The Retrieval	36-day		35.00	35
1991 Golden Fields (Golden Retriever)	36-day		35.00	35
1993 Faithful Companions (Cocker Spaniel)	36-day		35.00	35

Treasured Songs of Childhood - J. McClelland

YEAR ISSUE	EDITION LIMIT	YEAR RETD.	ISSUE PRICE	*QUOTE U.S.$
1987 Twinkle, Twinkle, Little Star	Retrd.	1990	29.50	38-49
1988 A Tisket, A Tasket	Retrd.	1991	29.50	38-45
1988 Baa, Baa, Black Sheep	Retrd.	1991	32.90	38-45
1989 Round The Mulberry Bush	150-day	1998	32.90	33
1989 Rain, Rain Go Away	Retrd.	1993	32.90	38-50
1989 I'm A Little Teapot	Retrd.	1993	32.90	38-45
1989 Pat-A-Cake	150-day	1998	34.90	35
1990 Hush Little Baby	150-day	1998	34.90	35

Up, Up And Away - P. Alexander

YEAR ISSUE	EDITION LIMIT	YEAR RETD.	ISSUE PRICE	*QUOTE U.S.$
1996 Rally At The Grand Canyon	76-day		29.90	30
1996 Gateway To Heaven	76-day		29.90	30
1997 Boston Balloon Party	76-day		29.90	30
1998 Through The Golden Gates	76-day		29.90	30

Vanishing Animal Kingdoms - S. Barlowe

YEAR ISSUE	EDITION LIMIT	YEAR RETD.	ISSUE PRICE	*QUOTE U.S.$
1986 Rama the Tiger	21,500	1996	35.00	35
1986 Olepi the Buffalo	21,500	1996	35.00	35
1987 Coolibah the Koala	21,500	1996	35.00	35
1987 Ortwin the Deer	21,500	1996	35.00	35
1987 Yen-Poh the Panda	21,500	1996	35.00	35
1988 Mamakuu the Elephant	21,500	1996	35.00	35

Victorian Christmas - S. Kuck

YEAR ISSUE	EDITION LIMIT	YEAR RETD.	ISSUE PRICE	*QUOTE U.S.$
1995 Dear Santa	72-day		35.00	35
1996 Night Before Christmas	72-day		35.00	35
1997 Wrapped With Love	72-day		35.00	35
1998 Christmas Day Joy	72-day	1999	35.00	35

Victorian Mother's Day - S. Kuck

YEAR ISSUE	EDITION LIMIT	YEAR RETD.	ISSUE PRICE	*QUOTE U.S.$
1989 Mother's Sunshine	Retrd.	1990	35.00	85-95
1990 Reflection Of Love	Retrd.	1991	35.00	90-95
1991 A Precious Time	Retrd.	1992	35.00	80-90
1992 Loving Touch	Retrd.	1993	35.00	75-90

Western - E. Berke

YEAR ISSUE	EDITION LIMIT	YEAR RETD.	ISSUE PRICE	*QUOTE U.S.$
1974 Mountain Man	Retrd.		165.00	165

The Wings of Nature Collection - W. Mumm

YEAR ISSUE	EDITION LIMIT	YEAR RETD.	ISSUE PRICE	*QUOTE U.S.$
1999 Royal Courtship	95-day		29.90	30

Winter Wonderland - S. Kuck

YEAR ISSUE	EDITION LIMIT	YEAR RETD.	ISSUE PRICE	*QUOTE U.S.$
1999 Magic Sleighride	95-day		35.00	35

Women of the Plains - C. Corcilius

YEAR ISSUE	EDITION LIMIT	YEAR RETD.	ISSUE PRICE	*QUOTE U.S.$
1994 Pride of a Maiden	36-day	1999	29.50	30
1995 No Boundaries	36-day	1998	29.50	30
1995 Silent Companions	36-day		35.00	35

The World of Children - J. McClelland

YEAR ISSUE	EDITION LIMIT	YEAR RETD.	ISSUE PRICE	*QUOTE U.S.$
1977 Rainy Day Fun	10,000	1977	50.00	55-75
1978 When I Grow Up	15,000	1978	50.00	55-75
1979 You're Invited	15,000	1979	50.00	55-75
1980 Kittens for Sale	15,000	1980	50.00	55-85

River Shore

Baby Animals - R. Brown

YEAR ISSUE	EDITION LIMIT	YEAR RETD.	ISSUE PRICE	*QUOTE U.S.$
1979 Akiku	20,000		50.00	50-80
1980 Roosevelt	20,000		50.00	50-90
1981 Clover	20,000		50.00	50-65
1982 Zuela	20,000		50.00	50-65

Famous Americans - Rockwell-Brown

YEAR ISSUE	EDITION LIMIT	YEAR RETD.	ISSUE PRICE	*QUOTE U.S.$
1976 Brown's Lincoln	9,500		40.00	40-75
1977 Rockwell's Triple Self-Portrait	9,500		45.00	45-75
1978 Peace Corps	9,500		45.00	45-75
1979 Spirit of Lindbergh	9,500		50.00	50-70

Little House on the Prairie - E. Christopherson

YEAR ISSUE	EDITION LIMIT	YEAR RETD.	ISSUE PRICE	*QUOTE U.S.$
1985 Founder's Day Picnic	10-day		29.50	45-100
1985 Women's Harvest	10-day		29.50	45-65
1985 Medicine Show	10-day		29.50	45-65
1985 Caroline's Eggs	10-day		29.50	45-65
1985 Mary's Gift	10-day		29.50	45-65
1985 A Bell for Walnut Grove	10-day		29.50	45-65
1985 Ingall's Family	10-day		29.50	45-65
1985 The Sweetheart Tree	10-day		29.50	45-65

Norman Rockwell Single Issue - N. Rockwell

YEAR ISSUE	EDITION LIMIT	YEAR RETD.	ISSUE PRICE	*QUOTE U.S.$
1979 Spring Flowers	17,000		75.00	125-145
1980 Looking Out to Sea	17,000		75.00	175-195
1982 Grandpa's Guardian	17,000		80.00	75-80
1982 Grandpa's Treasures	17,000		80.00	75-80

Puppy Playtime - J. Lamb

YEAR ISSUE	EDITION LIMIT	YEAR RETD.	ISSUE PRICE	*QUOTE U.S.$
1987 Double Take	14-day		24.50	35-45
1988 Catch of the Day	14-day		24.50	25-35
1988 Cabin Fever	14-day		24.50	25-35
1988 Weekend Gardener	14-day		24.50	25-35
1988 Getting Acquainted	14-day		24.50	25-35
1988 Hanging Out	14-day		24.50	25-35
1988 A New Leash On Life	14-day		24.50	30-35
1987 Fun and Games	14-day		24.50	30-35

Rockwell Four Freedoms - N. Rockwell

YEAR ISSUE	EDITION LIMIT	YEAR RETD.	ISSUE PRICE	*QUOTE U.S.$
1981 Freedom of Speech	17,000		65.00	100-149
1982 Freedom of Worship	17,000		65.00	100-125
1982 Freedom from Fear	17,000		65.00	100-200
1982 Freedom from Want	17,000		65.00	200-425

Rockwell Society

Christmas - N. Rockwell

YEAR ISSUE	EDITION LIMIT	YEAR RETD.	ISSUE PRICE	*QUOTE U.S.$
1974 Scotty Gets His Tree	Yr.Iss.		24.50	88-140
1975 Angel with Black Eye	Yr.Iss.		24.50	34-65
1976 Golden Christmas	Yr.Iss.		24.50	30-40
1977 Toy Shop Window	Yr.Iss.		24.50	21-40
1978 Christmas Dream	Yr.Iss.		24.50	15-45
1979 Somebody's Up There	Yr.Iss.		24.50	10-45
1980 Scotty Plays Santa	Yr.Iss.		24.50	10-50
1981 Wrapped Up in Christmas	Yr.Iss.		25.50	9-26
1982 Christmas Courtship	Yr.Iss.		25.50	8-30
1983 Santa in the Subway	Yr.Iss.		25.50	10-50
1984 Santa in the Workshop	Yr.Iss.		27.50	11-45
1985 Grandpa Plays Santa	Yr.Iss.		27.90	11-45
1986 Dear Santy Claus	Yr.Iss.		27.90	13-45
1987 Santa's Golden Gift	Yr.Iss.		27.90	12-45
1988 Santa Claus	Yr.Iss.		29.90	12-45
1989 Jolly Old St. Nick	Yr.Iss.		29.90	12-40
1990 A Christmas Prayer	Yr.Iss.		29.90	16-50
1991 Santa's Helpers	Yr.Iss.		32.90	13-35
1992 The Christmas Surprise	Yr.Iss.		32.90	20-35
1993 The Tree Brigade	Yr.Iss.		32.90	18-33
1994 Christmas Marvel	Yr.Iss.		32.90	25-45
1995 Filling The Stockings	Yr.Iss.		32.90	44-54
1996 Christmas	Yr.Iss.		32.90	44-49

Colonials-The Rarest Rockwells - N. Rockwell

YEAR ISSUE	EDITION LIMIT	YEAR RETD.	ISSUE PRICE	*QUOTE U.S.$
1985 Unexpected Proposal	150-day		27.90	6-28
1986 Words of Comfort	150-day		27.90	8-28
1986 Light for the Winter	150-day		30.90	7-31
1987 Portrait for a Bridegroom	150-day		30.90	8-31
1987 The Journey Home	150-day		30.90	10-31
1987 Clinching the Deal	150-day		30.90	9-31
1988 Sign of the Times	150-day		32.90	12-47
1988 Ye Glutton	150-day		32.90	9-15

Coming Of Age - N. Rockwell

YEAR ISSUE	EDITION LIMIT	YEAR RETD.	ISSUE PRICE	*QUOTE U.S.$
1990 Back To School	150-day		29.90	10-55
1990 Home From Camp	150-day		29.90	21-55
1990 Her First Formal	150-day		32.90	25-75
1990 The Muscleman	150-day		32.90	33-40
1990 A New Look	150-day		32.90	31-55
1991 A Balcony Seat	150-day		32.90	12-33
1991 Men About Town	150-day		34.90	13-35
1991 Paths of Glory	150-day		34.90	17-55
1991 Doorway to the Past	150-day		34.90	20-35
1991 School's Out!	150-day		34.90	28-30

Heritage - N. Rockwell

YEAR ISSUE	EDITION LIMIT	YEAR RETD.	ISSUE PRICE	*QUOTE U.S.$
1977 Toy Maker	Yr.Iss.		14.50	45-125
1978 Cobbler	Yr.Iss.		19.50	34-70
1979 Lighthouse Keeper's Daughter	Yr.Iss.		19.50	13-50
1980 Ship Builder	Yr.Iss.		19.50	8-45
1981 Music maker	Yr.Iss.		19.50	7-55
1982 Tycoon	Yr.Iss.		19.50	6-45
1983 Painter	Yr.Iss.		19.50	7-45
1984 Storyteller	Yr.Iss.		19.50	9-45
1985 Gourmet	Yr.Iss.		19.50	8-40
1986 Professor	Yr.Iss.		22.90	9-40
1987 Shadow Artist	Yr.Iss.		22.90	11-23
1988 The Veteran	Yr.Iss.		22.90	21-47
1988 The Banjo Player	Yr.Iss.		22.90	25-40
1990 The Old Scout	Yr.Iss.		24.90	30-45
1991 The Young Scholar	Yr.Iss.		24.90	19-35
1992 The Family Doctor	Yr.Iss.		27.90	40-52
1993 The Jeweler	Yr.Iss.		27.90	27-30
1994 Halloween Frolic	Yr.Iss.		27.90	35-40
1995 The Apprentice	Yr.Iss.		29.90	35-38
1996 Master Violinist	Yr.Iss.		29.90	60-73

Innocence and Experience - N. Rockwell

YEAR ISSUE	EDITION LIMIT	YEAR RETD.	ISSUE PRICE	*QUOTE U.S.$
1991 The Sea Captain	150-day		29.90	14-30
1991 The Radio Operator	150-day		29.90	22-30
1991 The Magician	150-day		32.90	49-51
1992 The American Heroes	150-day		32.90	19-35

A Mind of Her Own - N. Rockwell

YEAR ISSUE	EDITION LIMIT	YEAR RETD.	ISSUE PRICE	*QUOTE U.S.$
1986 Sitting Pretty	150-day		24.90	12-26
1987 Serious Business	150-day		24.90	15-35
1987 Breaking the Rules	150-day		24.90	21-23
1987 Good Intentions	150-day		27.90	27-40
1988 Second Thoughts	150-day		27.90	35-37
1988 World's Away	150-day		27.90	35-37
1988 Kiss and Tell	150-day		29.90	13-30
1988 On My Honor	150-day		29.90	38-40

Mother's Day - N. Rockwell

YEAR ISSUE	EDITION LIMIT	YEAR RETD.	ISSUE PRICE	*QUOTE U.S.$
1976 A Mother's Love	Yr.Iss.		24.50	40-70
1977 Faith	Yr.Iss.		24.50	35-50
1978 Bedtime	Yr.Iss.		24.50	25-34
1979 Reflections	Yr.Iss.		24.50	10-25
1980 A Mother's Pride	Yr.Iss.		24.50	11-30
1981 After the Party	Yr.Iss.		24.50	9-25
1982 The Cooking Lesson	Yr.Iss.		24.50	10-29
1983 Add Two Cups and Love	Yr.Iss.		25.50	12-30
1984 Grandma's Courting Dress	Yr.Iss.		25.50	10-26
1985 Mending Time	Yr.Iss.		27.50	11-35
1986 Pantry Raid	Yr.Iss.		27.90	13-28
1987 Grandma's Surprise	Yr.Iss.		29.90	11-30
1988 My Mother	Yr.Iss.		29.90	14-24
1989 Sunday Dinner	Yr.Iss.		29.90	23-30
1990 Evening Prayers	Yr.Iss.		29.90	10-45
1991 Building Our Future	Yr.Iss.		32.90	9-33
1991 Gentle Reassurance	Yr.Iss.		32.90	17-33
1992 A Special Delivery	Yr.Iss.		32.90	7-35

Rockwell Commemorative Stamps - N. Rockwell

YEAR ISSUE	EDITION LIMIT	YEAR RETD.	ISSUE PRICE	*QUOTE U.S.$
1994 Triple Self Portrait	95-day		29.90	44-56
1994 Freedom From Want	95-day		29.90	109-120
1994 Freedom From Fear	95-day		29.90	40-50
1995 Freedom of Speech	95-day		29.90	35-65
1995 Freedom of Worship	95-day		29.90	45-56

*Quotes have been rounded up to nearest dollar

Rockwell on Tour - N. Rockwell

YEAR ISSUE	EDITION LIMIT	YEAR RETD.	ISSUE PRICE	*QUOTE U.S.$
1983 Walking Through Merrie Englande	150-day		16.00	6-16
1983 Promenade a Paris	150-day		16.00	30
1983 When in Rome	150-day		16.00	7-16
1984 Die Walk am Rhein	150-day		16.00	7-16

Rockwell's American Dream - N. Rockwell

YEAR ISSUE	EDITION LIMIT	YEAR RETD.	ISSUE PRICE	*QUOTE U.S.$
1985 A Young Girl's Dream	150-day		19.90	10-40
1985 A Couple's Commitment	150-day		19.90	16-40
1985 A Family's Full Measure	150-day		22.90	15-40
1986 A Mother's Welcome	150-day		22.90	14-23
1986 A Young Man's Dream	150-day		22.90	14-40
1986 The Musician's Magic	150-day		22.90	14-40
1987 An Orphan's Hope	150-day		24.90	20-40
1987 Love's Reward	150-day		24.90	20-27

Rockwell's Golden Moments - N. Rockwell

YEAR ISSUE	EDITION LIMIT	YEAR RETD.	ISSUE PRICE	*QUOTE U.S.$
1987 Grandpa's Gift	150-day		19.90	10-40
1987 Grandma's Love	150-day		19.90	20
1988 End of day	150-day		22.90	20-30
1988 Best Friends	150-day		22.90	25
1989 Love Letters	150-day		22.90	27
1989 Newfound Worlds	150-day		22.90	12-23
1989 Keeping Company	150-day		24.90	12-40
1989 Evening's Repose	150-day		24.90	10-25

Rockwell's Light Campaign - N. Rockwell

YEAR ISSUE	EDITION LIMIT	YEAR RETD.	ISSUE PRICE	*QUOTE U.S.$
1983 This is the Room that Light Made	150-day		19.50	9-55
1984 Grandpa's Treasure Chest	150-day		19.50	9-50
1984 Father's Help	150-day		19.50	9-45
1984 Evening's Ease	150-day		19.50	9-40
1984 Close Harmony	150-day		21.50	8-45
1984 The Birthday Wish	150-day		21.50	7-55

Rockwell's Rediscovered Women - N. Rockwell

YEAR ISSUE	EDITION LIMIT	YEAR RETD.	ISSUE PRICE	*QUOTE U.S.$
1984 Dreaming in the Attic	100-day		19.50	7-45
1984 Waiting on the Shore	100-day		22.50	8-45
1984 Pondering on the Porch	100-day		22.50	10-45
1984 Making Believe at the Mirror	100-day		22.50	18-25
1984 Waiting at the Dance	100-day		22.50	15-40
1984 Gossiping in the Alcove	100-day		22.50	15-25
1984 Standing in the Doorway	100-day		22.50	10-40
1984 Flirting in the Parlor	100-day		22.50	14-40
1984 Working in the Kitchen	100-day		22.50	14-40
1984 Meeting on the Path	100-day		22.50	15-45
1984 Confiding in the Den	100-day		22.50	22-45
1984 Reminiscing in the Quiet	100-day		22.50	30-38
XX Complete Collection	100-day		267.00	267

Rockwell's The Ones We Love - N. Rockwell

YEAR ISSUE	EDITION LIMIT	YEAR RETD.	ISSUE PRICE	*QUOTE U.S.$
1988 Tender Loving Care	150-day		19.90	11-45
1989 A Time to Keep	150-day		19.90	14-17
1989 The Inventor And The Judge	150-day		22.90	20-29
1989 Ready For The World	150-day		22.90	15-23
1989 Growing Strong	150-day		22.90	18-25
1990 The Story Hour	150-day		22.90	20-30
1990 The Country Doctor	150-day		24.90	12-25
1990 Our Love of Country	150-day		24.90	12-25
1990 The Homecoming	150-day		24.90	18-48
1991 A Helping Hand	150-day		24.90	15-25

Rockwell's Treasured Memories - N. Rockwell

YEAR ISSUE	EDITION LIMIT	YEAR RETD.	ISSUE PRICE	*QUOTE U.S.$
1991 Quiet Reflections	150-day		29.90	17-30
1991 Romantic Reverie	150-day		29.90	27-30
1991 Tender Romance	150-day		32.90	18-33
1991 Evening Passage	150-day		32.90	15-33
1991 Heavenly Dreams	150-day		32.90	25-33
1991 Sentimental Shores	150-day		32.90	22-33

Roman, Inc.

A Child's Play - F. Hook

YEAR ISSUE	EDITION LIMIT	YEAR RETD.	ISSUE PRICE	*QUOTE U.S.$
1982 Breezy Day	30-day	N/A	29.95	39
1982 Kite Flying	30-day	N/A	29.95	39
1984 Bathtub Sailor	30-day	N/A	29.95	35
1984 The First Snow	30-day	N/A	29.95	35

A Child's World - F. Hook

YEAR ISSUE	EDITION LIMIT	YEAR RETD.	ISSUE PRICE	*QUOTE U.S.$
1980 Little Children, Come to Me	15,000	N/A	45.00	49

Fontanini Annual Christmas Plate - E. Simonetti

YEAR ISSUE	EDITION LIMIT	YEAR RETD.	ISSUE PRICE	*QUOTE U.S.$
1986 A King Is Born	Yr.Iss.	1986	60.00	60
1987 O Come, Let Us Adore Him	Yr.Iss.	1987	60.00	65
1988 Adoration of the Magi	Yr.Iss.	1988	70.00	75
1989 Flight Into Egypt	Yr.Iss.	1989	75.00	85

Frances Hook Collection-Set I - F. Hook

YEAR ISSUE	EDITION LIMIT	YEAR RETD.	ISSUE PRICE	*QUOTE U.S.$
1982 I Wish, I Wish	15,000	N/A	24.95	75-85
1982 Baby Blossoms	15,000	N/A	24.95	39-45
1982 Daisy Dreamer	15,000	N/A	24.95	39-55
1982 Trees So Tall	15,000	N/A	24.95	39-55

Frances Hook Collection-Set II - F. Hook

YEAR ISSUE	EDITION LIMIT	YEAR RETD.	ISSUE PRICE	*QUOTE U.S.$
1983 Caught It Myself	15,000	N/A	24.95	25
1983 Winter Wrappings	15,000	N/A	24.95	25
1983 So Cuddly	15,000	N/A	24.95	25
1983 Can I Keep Him?	15,000	N/A	24.95	25

Frances Hook Legacy - F. Hook

YEAR ISSUE	EDITION LIMIT	YEAR RETD.	ISSUE PRICE	*QUOTE U.S.$
1985 Fascination	100-day	N/A	19.50	39-49
1985 Daydreaming	100-day	N/A	19.50	39-49
1985 Discovery	100-day	N/A	22.50	39-49
1985 Disappointment	100-day	N/A	22.50	39-49
1985 Wonderment	100-day	N/A	22.50	39-49
1985 Expectation	100-day	N/A	22.50	39-49

March of Dimes: Our Children, Our Future - A. Williams

YEAR ISSUE	EDITION LIMIT	YEAR RETD.	ISSUE PRICE	*QUOTE U.S.$
1990 A Time To Laugh	150-day	N/A	29.00	14-29

The Masterpiece Collection - Various

YEAR ISSUE	EDITION LIMIT	YEAR RETD.	ISSUE PRICE	*QUOTE U.S.$
1979 Adoration - F. Lippe	5,000	N/A	65.00	65
1980 Madonna with Grapes - P. Mignard	5,000	N/A	87.50	88
1981 The Holy Family - G. Delle Notti	5,000	N/A	95.00	95
1982 Madonna of the Streets - R. Ferruzzi	5,000	N/A	85.00	85

The Millenium™ Collection - Sr. Mary Jean Dorcy

YEAR ISSUE	EDITION LIMIT	YEAR RETD.	ISSUE PRICE	*QUOTE U.S.$
1992 Silent Night	2,000	1992	49.50	80-175
1993 The Annunciation	5,000	1993	49.50	100-150
1994 Peace On Earth	5,000	1994	49.50	75-110
1995 Cause of Our Joy	7,500	1995	49.50	50
1996 Prince of Peace	15,000	1996	49.50	50
1997 Gentle Love	Yr.Iss.	1997	49.50	50
1998 Rejoice	Yr.Iss.	1998	48.50	49
1999 Heaven's Blessing	Yr.Iss.		48.50	49
1999 Joyful Promise	2-Yr.		48.50	49

Roman Memorial - F. Hook

YEAR ISSUE	EDITION LIMIT	YEAR RETD.	ISSUE PRICE	*QUOTE U.S.$
1984 The Carpenter	Closed	1984	100.00	135

Seraphim Classics® Faro Collection - Faro Studios

YEAR ISSUE	EDITION LIMIT	YEAR RETD.	ISSUE PRICE	*QUOTE U.S.$
1994 Rosalyn - Rarest of Heaven	7,200	1994	65.00	65-175
1995 Helena - Heaven's Herald	7,200	1995	65.00	65-125
1996 Flora - Flower of Heaven	7,200	1996	65.00	65-110
1997 Emily - Heaven's Treasure	Yr.Iss.	1997	65.00	65-90
1998 Elise - Heaven's Glory	Yr.Iss.	1998	65.00	65-85
1999 Gwydolyn-Heaven's Triumph	Yr.Iss.		65.00	65

Seraphim Classics® Oval Plate - Seraphim Studios

YEAR ISSUE	EDITION LIMIT	YEAR RETD.	ISSUE PRICE	*QUOTE U.S.$
1996 Cymbeline - Peacemaker	2-Yr.	1998	49.95	50
1996 Isabel - Gentle Spirit	2-Yr.	1998	49.95	50
1996 Lydia - Winged Poet	2-Yr.	1998	49.95	50
1996 Priscilla - Benevolent Guide	2-Yr.	1998	49.95	50

Single Releases - A. Williams

YEAR ISSUE	EDITION LIMIT	YEAR RETD.	ISSUE PRICE	*QUOTE U.S.$
1987 The Christening	Open		29.50	30
1990 The Dedication	Open		29.50	30
1990 The Baptism	Open		29.50	30

Ron Lee's World of Clowns

Ron Lee Plate Collection - R. Lee

YEAR ISSUE	EDITION LIMIT	YEAR RETD.	ISSUE PRICE	*QUOTE U.S.$
1982 Christmas RLP400	10,000	1997	42.50	150-300
1999 Clown-Air RLP40000	2,500		29.95	30
1980 Do Not Disturb RLP100	10,000	1997	42.50	150-300
1999 Ducks/Crossing RLP7000	5,000		29.95	30
1982 Hold the Onions RLP200	10,000	1997	42.50	150-300
1999 Horsin RLP3000	2,500		29.95	30
1982 No Camping, No Fishing RLP300	10,000	1997	42.50	150-300
1999 Runaway Train RLP2000	2,500		29.95	30
1999 Three for Par/Almost There RLP8000	5,000		29.95	30
1980 Traveling in Style RLP500	10,000	1997	42.50	150-300
1999 Up a Tree/On The Edge RLP5000	5,000		29.95	30
1999 Water Trap/Beware of Snakes RLP6000	5,000		29.95	30
1999 Wheelin RLP1000	2,500		29.95	30

Rosenthal

Christmas - Unknown

YEAR ISSUE	EDITION LIMIT	YEAR RETD.	ISSUE PRICE	*QUOTE U.S.$
1910 Winter Peace	Annual		Unkn.	550
1911 Three Wise Men	Annual		Unkn.	325
1912 Stardust	Annual		Unkn.	255
1913 Christmas Lights	Annual		Unkn.	235
1914 Christmas Song	Annual		Unkn.	350
1915 Walking to Church	Annual		Unkn.	180
1916 Christmas During War	Annual		Unkn.	240
1917 Angel of Peace	Annual		Unkn.	200
1918 Peace on Earth	Annual		Unkn.	200
1919 St. Christopher with Christ Child	Annual		Unkn.	225
1920 Manger in Bethlehem	Annual		Unkn.	325
1921 Christmas in Mountains	Annual		Unkn.	200
1922 Advent Branch	Annual		Unkn.	200
1923 Children in Winter Woods	Annual		Unkn.	200
1924 Deer in the Woods	Annual		Unkn.	200
1925 Three Wise Men	Annual		Unkn.	200
1926 Christmas in Mountains	Annual		Unkn.	195
1927 Station on the Way	Annual		Unkn.	135-175
1928 Chalet Christmas	Annual		Unkn.	185
1929 Christmas in Alps	Annual		Unkn.	225
1930 Group of Deer Under Pines	Annual		Unkn.	225
1931 Path of the Magi	Annual		Unkn.	225
1932 Christ Child	Annual		Unkn.	185
1933 Thru the Night to Light	Annual		Unkn.	190
1934 Christmas Peace	Annual		Unkn.	190
1935 Christmas by the Sea	Annual		Unkn.	190
1936 Nurnberg Angel	Annual		Unkn.	175-200
1937 Berchtesgaden	Annual		Unkn.	195
1938 Christmas in the Alps	Annual		Unkn.	195
1939 Schneekoppe Mountain	Annual		Unkn.	195
1940 Marien Chruch(girl) in Danzig	Annual		Unkn.	200-225
1941 Strassburg Cathedral	Annual		Unkn.	200-225
1942 Marianburg Castle	Annual		Unkn.	300
1943 Winter Idyll	Annual		Unkn.	300
1944 Wood Scape	Annual		Unkn.	300
1945 Christmas Peace	Annual		Unkn.	400
1946 Christmas in an Alpine Valley	Annual		Unkn.	240
1947 Dillingen Madonna	Annual		Unkn.	985
1948 Message to the Shepherds	Annual		Unkn.	875
1949 The Holy Family	Annual		Unkn.	185
1950 Christmas in the Forest	Annual		Unkn.	185
1951 Star of Bethlehem	Annual		Unkn.	450
1952 Christmas in the Alps	Annual		Unkn.	195
1953 The Holy Light	Annual		Unkn.	195
1954 Christmas Eve	Annual		Unkn.	195
1955 Christmas in a Village	Annual		Unkn.	195
1956 Christmas in the Alps	Annual		Unkn.	195
1957 Christmas by the Sea	Annual		Unkn.	195
1958 Christmas Eve	Annual		Unkn.	195
1959 Midnight Mass	Annual		Unkn.	75-125
1960 Christmas in a Small Village	Annual		Unkn.	195
1961 Solitary Christmas	Annual		Unkn.	100-200
1962 Christmas Eve	Annual		Unkn.	75-150
1963 Silent Night	Annual		Unkn.	75-150
1964 Christmas Market in Nurnberg	Annual		Unkn.	225
1965 Christmas Munich	Annual		Unkn.	185
1966 Christmas in Ulm	Annual		Unkn.	275
1967 Christmas in Reginburg	Annual		Unkn.	185
1968 Christmas in Bremen	Annual		Unkn.	195
1969 Christmas in Rothenburg	Annual		Unkn.	175-220
1970 Christmas in Cologne	Annual		Unkn.	175
1971 Christmas in Garmisch	Annual		42.00	100
1972 Christmas in Franconia	Annual		50.00	95
1973 Lubeck-Holstein	Annual		77.00	105
1974 Christmas in Wurzburg	Annual		85.00	90-100

Nobility of Children - E. Hibel

YEAR ISSUE	EDITION LIMIT	YEAR RETD.	ISSUE PRICE	*QUOTE U.S.$
1976 La Contessa Isabella	12,750		120.00	120
1977 La Marquis Maurice-Pierre	12,750		120.00	120
1978 Baronesse Johanna	12,750		130.00	140
1979 Chief Red Feather	12,750		140.00	180

Wiinblad Christmas - B. Wiinblad

YEAR ISSUE	EDITION LIMIT	YEAR RETD.	ISSUE PRICE	*QUOTE U.S.$
1971 Maria & Child	Undis.		100.00	750
1972 Caspar	Undis.		100.00	290
1973 Melchior	Undis.		125.00	335
1974 Balthazar	Undis.		125.00	300
1975 The Annunciation	Undis.		195.00	195
1976 Angel with Trumpet	Undis.		195.00	195
1977 Adoration of Shepherds	Undis.		225.00	225
1978 Angel with Harp	Undis.		275.00	295
1979 Exodus from Egypt	Undis.		310.00	310
1980 Angel with Glockenspiel	Undis.		360.00	360
1981 Christ Child Visits Temple	Undis.		375.00	375
1982 Christening of Christ	Undis.		375.00	375

Royal Copenhagen

Christmas - Various

YEAR ISSUE	EDITION LIMIT	YEAR RETD.	ISSUE PRICE	*QUOTE U.S.$
1908 Madonna and Child - C. Thomsen	Annual	1908	1.00	2750-6000
1909 Danish Landscape - S. Ussing	Annual	1909	1.00	192-360
1910 The Magi - C. Thomsen	Annual	1910	1.00	130-285
1911 Danish Landscape - O. Jensen	Annual	1911	1.00	144-259
1912 Christmas Tree - C. Thomsen	Annual	1912	1.00	199-264
1913 Frederik Church Spire - A. Boesen	Annual	1913	1.50	147-207
1914 Holy Spirit Church - A. Boesen	Annual	1914	1.50	165-249
1915 Danish Landscape - A. Krog	Annual	1915	1.50	180-205
1916 Shepherd at Christmas - R. Bocher	Annual	1916	1.50	128-150
1917 Our Savior Church - O. Jensen	Annual	1917	2.00	109-147
1918 Sheep and Shepherds - O. Jensen	Annual	1918	2.00	109-147
1919 In the Park - O. Jensen	Annual	1919	2.00	85-147
1920 Mary and Child Jesus - G. Rode	Annual	1920	2.00	85-147
1921 Aabenraa Marketplace - O. Jensen	Annual	1921	2.00	80-135
1922 Three Singing Angels - E. Selschau	Annual	1922	2.00	80-118
1923 Danish Landscape - O. Jensen	Annual	1923	2.00	80-99
1924 Sailing Ship - B. Olsen	Annual	1924	2.00	115-184
1925 Christianshavn - O. Jensen	Annual	1925	2.00	105-162
1926 Christianshavn Canal - R. Bocher	Annual	1926	2.00	94-162
1927 Ship's Boy at Tiller - B. Olsen	Annual	1927	2.00	135-213
1928 Vicar's Family - G. Rode	Annual	1928	2.00	98-147
1929 Grundtvig Church - O. Jensen	Annual	1929	2.00	98-141
1930 Fishing Boats - B. Olsen	Annual	1930	2.50	134-150
1931 Mother and Child - G. Rode	Annual	1931	2.50	134-184
1932 Frederiksberg Gardens - O. Jensen	Annual	1932	2.50	113-157
1933 Ferry and the Great Belt - B. Olsen	Annual	1933	2.50	188-213
1934 The Hermitage Castle - O. Jensen	Annual	1934	2.50	240-299
1935 Kronborg Castle - B. Olsen	Annual	1935	2.50	240-425
1936 Roskilde Cathedral - R. Bocher	Annual	1936	2.50	254-349
1937 Main Street Copenhagen - N. Thorsson	Annual	1937	2.50	250-395
1938 Round Church in Osterlars - H. Nielsen	Annual	1938	3.00	425-507
1939 Greenland Pack-Ice - S. Nielsen	Annual	1939	3.00	525-699
1940 The Good Shepherd - K. Lange	Annual	1940	3.00	525-575
1941 Danish Village Church - T. Kjolner	Annual	1941	3.00	540-597
1942 Bell Tower - N. Thorsson	Annual	1942	4.00	300-822
1943 Flight into Egypt - N. Thorsson	Annual	1943	4.00	625-999
1944 Danish Village Scene - V. Olson	Annual	1944	4.00	350-498
1945 A Peaceful Motif - R. Bocher	Annual	1945	4.00	475-810
1946 Zealand Village Church - N. Thorsson	Annual	1946	4.00	270-375
1947 The Good Shepherd - K. Lange	Annual	1947	4.50	190-414
1948 Nodebo Church - T. Kjolner	Annual	1948	4.50	300-499
1949 Our Lady's Cathedral - H. Hansen	Annual	1949	5.00	250-399
1950 Boeslunde Church - V. Olson	Annual	1950	5.00	225-395
1951 Christmas Angel - R. Bocher	Annual	1951	5.00	310-630
1952 Christmas in the Forest - K. Lange	Annual	1952	5.00	159-219
1953 Frederiksborg Castle - T. Kjolner	Annual	1953	6.00	159-213
1954 Amalienborg Palace - K. Lange	Annual	1954	6.00	178-240

*Quotes have been rounded up to nearest dollar

YEAR ISSUE	EDITION LIMIT	YEAR RETD.	ISSUE PRICE	*QUOTE U.S.$
1955 Fano Girl - K. Lange	Annual	1955	7.00	229-270
1956 Rosenborg Castle - K. Lange	Annual	1956	7.00	175-294
1957 The Good Shepherd - H. Hansen	Annual	1957	8.00	120-155
1958 Sunshine over Greenland - H. Hansen	Annual	1958	9.00	134-234
1959 Christmas Night - H. Hansen	Annual	1959	9.00	150-225
1960 The Stag - H. Hansen	Annual	1960	10.00	96-261
1961 Training Ship - K. Lange	Annual	1961	10.00	157-231
1962 The Little Mermaid - Unknown	Annual	1962	11.00	199-465
1963 Hojsager Mill - K. Lange	Annual	1963	11.00	85-90
1964 Fetching the Tree - K. Lange	Annual	1964	11.00	36-90
1965 Little Skaters - K. Lange	Annual	1965	12.00	33-84
1966 Blackbird - K. Lange	Annual	1966	12.00	30-55
1967 The Royal Oak - K. Lange	Annual	1967	13.00	22-55
1968 The Last Umiak - K. Lange	Annual	1968	13.00	18-42
1969 The Old Farmyard - K. Lange	Annual	1969	14.00	20-48
1970 Christmas Rose and Cat - K. Lange	Annual	1970	14.00	31-120
1971 Hare In Winter - K. Lange	Annual	1971	15.00	19-116
1972 In the Desert - K. Lange	Annual	1972	16.00	17-116
1973 Train Homeward Bound - K. Lange	Annual	1973	22.00	25-36
1974 Winter Twilight - K. Lange	Annual	1974	22.00	18-105
1975 Queen's Palace - K. Lange	Annual	1975	27.50	15-105
1976 Danish Watermill - S. Vestergaard	Annual	1976	27.50	30-36
1977 Immervad Bridge - K. Lange	Annual	1977	32.00	15-33
1978 Greenland Scenery - K. Lange	Annual	1978	35.00	27-39
1979 Choosing Christmas Tree - K. Lange	Annual	1979	42.50	40-96
1980 Bringing Home the Tree - K. Lange	Annual	1980	49.50	28-45
1981 Admiring Christmas Tree - K. Lange	Annual	1981	52.50	18-60
1982 Waiting for Christmas - K. Lange	Annual	1982	54.50	68-90
1983 Merry Christmas - K. Lange	Annual	1983	54.50	49-90
1984 Jingle Bells - K. Lange	Annual	1984	54.50	49-66
1985 Snowman - K. Lange	Annual	1985	54.50	97-129
1986 Christmas Vacation - K. Lange	Annual	1986	54.50	60-96
1987 Winter Birds - S. Vestergaard	Annual	1987	59.50	70-120
1988 Christmas Eve in Copenhagen - S. Vestergaard	Annual	1988	59.50	90-120
1989 The Old Skating Pond - S. Vestergaard	Annual	1989	59.50	98-157
1990 Christmas at Tivoli - S. Vestergaard	Annual	1990	64.50	200-255
1991 The Festival of Santa Lucia - S. Vestergaard	Annual	1991	69.50	125-205
1992 The Queen's Carriage - S. Vestergaard	Annual	1992	69.50	95-135
1993 Christmas Guests - S. Vestergaard	Annual	1993	69.50	190-450
1994 Christmas Shopping - S. Vestergaard	Annual	1994	72.50	74-120
1995 Christmas at the Manor House - S. Vestergaard	Annual	1995	72.50	250-600
1996 Lighting the Street Lamps - S. Vestergaard	Annual	1996	74.50	69-127
1997 Roskilde Cathedral - S. Vestergaard	Annual	1997	69.50	72-95
1998 Coming Home For Christmas - S. Vestergaard	Annual	1998	69.50	70-225
1999 The Sleigh Ride - S. Vestergaard	Annual	1999	72.50	73-113
2000 Decorating The Tree - S. Vestergaard	Annual		72.50	73

Royal Doulton

All God's Children - L. DeWinne

YEAR ISSUE	EDITION LIMIT	YEAR RETD.	ISSUE PRICE	*QUOTE U.S.$
1978 A Brighter Day	10,000	1984	75.00	75-100
1980 Village Children	10,000	1984	65.00	65
1981 Noble Heritage	10,000	1984	85.00	85
1982 Buddies	10,000	1984	85.00	85
1983 My Little Brother	10,000	1984	95.00	95

American Tapestries - C.A. Brown

YEAR ISSUE	EDITION LIMIT	YEAR RETD.	ISSUE PRICE	*QUOTE U.S.$
1978 Sleigh Bells	15,000	1983	70.00	70
1979 Pumpkin Patch	15,000	1983	70.00	70
1981 General Store	10,000	1983	95.00	95
1982 Fourth of July	10,000	1983	95.00	95

Behind the Painted Mask - B. Black

YEAR ISSUE	EDITION LIMIT	YEAR RETD.	ISSUE PRICE	*QUOTE U.S.$
1982 Painted Feelings	10,000	1986	95.00	175-200
1983 Make Me Laugh	10,000	1986	95.00	175-200
1984 Minstrel Serenade	10,000	1986	95.00	175-200
1985 Pleasing Performance	10,000	1986	95.00	175-200

Celebration of Faith - J. Woods

YEAR ISSUE	EDITION LIMIT	YEAR RETD.	ISSUE PRICE	*QUOTE U.S.$
1982 Rosh Hashanah	7,500	1986	250.00	300-400
1983 Yom Kippur	7,500	1986	250.00	250
1984 Passover	7,500	1986	250.00	250
1985 Chanukah	7,500	1986	250.00	250

Character Plates - N/A

YEAR ISSUE	EDITION LIMIT	YEAR RETD.	ISSUE PRICE	*QUOTE U.S.$
1979 Old Balloon Seller	Closed	1983	100.00	120-125
1980 Balloon Man	Closed	1983	125.00	125
1981 Silks and Ribbons	Closed	1983	125.00	140
1982 Biddy Penny Farthing	Closed	1983	125.00	125

Charles Dickens Plates - N/A

YEAR ISSUE	EDITION LIMIT	YEAR RETD.	ISSUE PRICE	*QUOTE U.S.$
1980 Artful Dodger	Closed	1984	65.00	65
1980 Barkis	Closed	1984	80.00	80-95
1980 Cap'n Cuttle	Closed	1984	80.00	80
1980 Fagin	Closed	1984	65.00	65
1980 Fat Boy	Closed	1984	65.00	65
1980 Mr. Micawber	Closed	1984	80.00	80
1980 Mr. Pickwick	Closed	1984	80.00	80-95
1980 Old Peggoty	Closed	1984	65.00	65
1980 Poor Jo	Closed	1984	80.00	80
1980 Sairey Gamp	Closed	1984	80.00	80
1980 Sam Weller	Closed	1984	65.00	65
1980 Sergeant Buz Fuz	Closed	1984	80.00	80
1980 Tony Weller	Closed	1984	65.00	65

Childhood Christmas - N/A

YEAR ISSUE	EDITION LIMIT	YEAR RETD.	ISSUE PRICE	*QUOTE U.S.$
1983 Silent Night	Yr.Iss.	1983	35.00	75
1984 While Shepherds Watched	Yr.Iss.	1984	39.95	75
1985 Oh Little Town of Bethlehem	Yr.Iss.	1985	39.95	40
1986 We Saw 3 Ships A-Sailing	Yr.Iss.	1986	39.95	40
1987 The Holly and the Ivy	Yr.Iss.	1987	39.95	40

Children of the Pueblo - M. Jungbluth

YEAR ISSUE	EDITION LIMIT	YEAR RETD.	ISSUE PRICE	*QUOTE U.S.$
1983 Apple Flower	15,000	1985	60.00	150-195
1984 Morning Star	15,000	1985	60.00	150-195

Christmas Around the World - N/A

YEAR ISSUE	EDITION LIMIT	YEAR RETD.	ISSUE PRICE	*QUOTE U.S.$
1972 Old England	15,000	1979	35.00	35-80
1973 Mexico	15,000	1979	37.50	38
1974 Bulgaria	15,000	1979	37.50	38
1975 Norway	15,000	1979	45.00	45-80
1976 Holland	15,000	1979	50.00	50
1977 Poland	15,000	1979	50.00	50-80
1978 America	15,000	1979	55.00	55

Christmas Plates - Various

YEAR ISSUE	EDITION LIMIT	YEAR RETD.	ISSUE PRICE	*QUOTE U.S.$
1993 Royal Doulton-Together For Christmas - J. James	Yr.Iss.	1993	45.00	50
1993 Royal Albert-Sleighride - N/A	Yr.Iss.	1993	45.00	45
1994 Royal Doulton-Home For Christmas - J. James	Yr.Iss.	1994	45.00	45
1994 Royal Albert-Coaching Inn - N/A	Yr.Iss.	1994	45.00	45
1995 Royal Doulton-Season's Greetings - J. James	Yr.Iss.	1995	45.00	45
1995 Royal Albert-Skating Pond - N/A	Yr.Iss.	1995	45.00	45
1996 Royal Doulton-Night Before Christmas - J. James	Yr.Iss.	1996	45.00	45
1996 Royal Albert-Gathering Winter Fuel - N/A	Yr.Iss.	1996	45.00	45

Commedia Dell Arte - L. Neiman

YEAR ISSUE	EDITION LIMIT	YEAR RETD.	ISSUE PRICE	*QUOTE U.S.$
1974 Harlequin	15,000	1979	100.00	125-195
1975 Pierrot	15,000	1979	90.00	125-145
1977 Columbine	15,000	1979	80.00	80-95
1978 Punchinello	15,000	1979	75.00	75-80

Family Christmas Plates - N/A

YEAR ISSUE	EDITION LIMIT	YEAR RETD.	ISSUE PRICE	*QUOTE U.S.$
1991 Dad Plays Santa	Closed	1991	60.00	60

Festival Children of the World - B. Burke

YEAR ISSUE	EDITION LIMIT	YEAR RETD.	ISSUE PRICE	*QUOTE U.S.$
1983 Mariana (Balinese)	15,000	1986	65.00	35-65
1984 Magdalena (Mexico)	15,000	1986	65.00	35-65
1985 Michiko (Japanese)	15,000	1986	65.00	35-65

Flower Garden - H. Vidal

YEAR ISSUE	EDITION LIMIT	YEAR RETD.	ISSUE PRICE	*QUOTE U.S.$
1975 Spring Harmony	15,000	1981	80.00	80
1976 Dreaming Lotus	15,000	1981	90.00	90
1977 From the Poet's Garden	15,000	1981	75.00	75
1978 Country Bouquet	15,000	1981	75.00	75
1979 From My Mother's Garden	15,000	1981	85.00	90

The Grandest Gift - Mago

YEAR ISSUE	EDITION LIMIT	YEAR RETD.	ISSUE PRICE	*QUOTE U.S.$
1985 Reunion	10,000	1986	75.00	100-150
1985 Storytime	10,000	1986	75.00	100

Grandparents - Mago

YEAR ISSUE	EDITION LIMIT	YEAR RETD.	ISSUE PRICE	*QUOTE U.S.$
1984 Grandfather and Children	15,000	1985	95.00	200-250

I Remember America - E. Sloane

YEAR ISSUE	EDITION LIMIT	YEAR RETD.	ISSUE PRICE	*QUOTE U.S.$
1977 Pennsylvania Pastorale	15,000	1982	90.00	90
1978 Lovejoy Bridge	15,000	1982	80.00	80
1979 Four Corners	15,000	1982	75.00	75
1981 Marshland	15,000	1982	95.00	95

Jungle Fantasy - G. Novoa

YEAR ISSUE	EDITION LIMIT	YEAR RETD.	ISSUE PRICE	*QUOTE U.S.$
1979 The Ark	10,000	1984	75.00	75
1981 Compassion	10,000	1984	95.00	95
1982 Patience	10,000	1984	95.00	95
1983 Refuge	10,000	1984	95.00	95

Log of the Dashing Wave - J. Stobart

YEAR ISSUE	EDITION LIMIT	YEAR RETD.	ISSUE PRICE	*QUOTE U.S.$
1976 Sailing With the Tide	15,000	1983	115.00	115
1977 Running Free	15,000	1983	110.00	120-150
1978 Rounding the Horn	15,000	1983	85.00	85-95
1979 Hong Kong	15,000	1983	75.00	75
1981 Bora Bora	15,000	1983	95.00	95
1982 Journey's End	15,000	1983	95.00	150

Mother and Child - E. Hibel

YEAR ISSUE	EDITION LIMIT	YEAR RETD.	ISSUE PRICE	*QUOTE U.S.$
1973 Colette and Child	15,000	1982	500.00	500
1974 Sayuri and Child	15,000	1982	175.00	150
1975 Kristina and Child	15,000	1982	125.00	150-195
1976 Marilyn and Child	15,000	1982	110.00	140-195
1977 Lucia and Child	15,000	1982	90.00	90
1981 Kathleen and Child	15,000	1982	85.00	150-195

Portraits of Innocence - F. Masseria

YEAR ISSUE	EDITION LIMIT	YEAR RETD.	ISSUE PRICE	*QUOTE U.S.$
1980 Panchito	15,000	1987	65.00	95-250
1981 Adrien	15,000	1987	85.00	65-120
1982 Angelica	15,000	1987	95.00	65-120
1983 Juliana	15,000	1987	95.00	75-120
1985 Gabriella	15,000	1987	95.00	75-120
1986 Francesca	15,000	1987	95.00	195-210

Ports of Call - D. Kingman

YEAR ISSUE	EDITION LIMIT	YEAR RETD.	ISSUE PRICE	*QUOTE U.S.$
1975 San Francisco, Fisherman's Wharf	15,000	1979	90.00	90
1976 New Orleans, Royal Street	15,000	1979	80.00	80
1977 Venice, Grand Canal	15,000	1979	65.00	65
1978 Paris, Montmartre	15,000	1979	70.00	70

Reflections of China - C. Chi

YEAR ISSUE	EDITION LIMIT	YEAR RETD.	ISSUE PRICE	*QUOTE U.S.$
1976 Garden of Tranquility	15,000	1981	90.00	90
1977 Imperial Palace	15,000	1981	80.00	80
1978 Temple of Heaven	15,000	1981	75.00	75
1980 Lake of Mists	15,000	1981	85.00	85

Victorian Era Christmas - N/A

YEAR ISSUE	EDITION LIMIT	YEAR RETD.	ISSUE PRICE	*QUOTE U.S.$
1977 Winter Fun	Yr.Iss.	1977	55.00	55
1978 Christmas Day	Yr.Iss.	1978	55.00	55
1979 Christmas	Yr.Iss.	1979	25.00	25
1980 Santa's Visit	Yr.Iss.	1980	30.00	30
1981 Christmas Carolers	Yr.Iss.	1981	37.50	38
1982 Santa on Bicycle	Yr.Iss.	1982	39.95	40

Victorian Era Valentines - N/A

YEAR ISSUE	EDITION LIMIT	YEAR RETD.	ISSUE PRICE	*QUOTE U.S.$
1976 Victorian Boy and Girl	Yr.Iss.	1976	65.00	65-75
1977 My Sweetest Friend	Yr.Iss.	1977	40.00	40-65
1978 If I Loved You	Yr.Iss.	1978	40.00	40
1979 My Valentine	Yr.Iss.	1979	35.00	35
1980 Valentine	Yr.Iss.	1980	33.00	33
1981 Valentine Boy and Girl	Yr.Iss.	1981	35.00	35
1982 Angel with Mandolin	Yr.Iss.	1982	39.95	40
1985 My Valentine	Yr.Iss.	1985	39.95	40

Seymour Mann, Inc.

Connoisseur Christmas Collection™ - Bernini™

YEAR ISSUE	EDITION LIMIT	YEAR RETD.	ISSUE PRICE	*QUOTE U.S.$
1996 Cardinals CLT-310	25,000	1998	50.00	75
1996 Chickadees CLT-300	25,000		50.00	75
1996 Doves CLT-305	25,000		50.00	75

Connoisseur Collection™ - Bernini™

YEAR ISSUE	EDITION LIMIT	YEAR RETD.	ISSUE PRICE	*QUOTE U.S.$
1997 Anna's Hummingbird CLT-440	25,000		50.00	75
1997 Blue Butterfly CLT-450	25,000		50.00	75
1995 Bluebird CLT-13	25,000	1996	50.00	75
1997 Bluebird/Lily CLT-390	25,000		50.00	75
1996 Butterfly/Lily CLT-330	25,000		50.00	75
1995 Canary CLT-10	25,000	1997	50.00	75
1995 Cardinal CLT-7	25,000	1997	50.00	75
1997 Cardinal/Dogwood CLT-405	25,000		50.00	50
1998 Costa's Hummingbird CLT-470	25,000		40.00	48
1995 Dove Duo CLT-1	25,000	1997	50.00	75
1995 Dove/Magnolia CLT-350	25,000		50.00	75
1995 Hummingbird Duo CLT-4	25,000		50.00	75
1995 Hummingbirds, Morning Glory, blue CLT-320B	25,000		50.00	75
1995 Hummingbirds, Morning Glory, pink CLT-320	25,000		50.00	75
1997 Love Doves/Roses CLT-420	25,000		50.00	75
1995 Magnolia CLT-76	25,000		50.00	75
1995 Pink Rose CLT-70	25,000		50.00	75
1995 Robin CLT-16	25,000		50.00	75
1996 Roses/Forget-Me-Not CLT-340	25,000		50.00	75
1998 Ruby Hummingbird Chicks CLT-460	25,000		40.00	48
1997 Star Gazer Lily CLT-430	25,000		50.00	80
1995 Swan Duo CLT-50	25,000		50.00	75
1997 Violet Crowned Hummingbird CLT-440B	25,000		50.00	75

Sports Impressions/Enesco Group, Inc.

Gold Edition Plates - Various

YEAR ISSUE	EDITION LIMIT	YEAR RETD.	ISSUE PRICE	*QUOTE U.S.$
XX A's Jose Canseco Gold (10 1/4") 1028-04 - J. Canseco	2,500	N/A	125.00	100-125
1990 Andre Dawson - R. Lewis	Closed	N/A	150.00	100-150
1987 Brooks Robinson F/S - R. Simon	1,000	N/A	125.00	125-150
1988 Brooks Robinson, signed - R. Simon	Closed	N/A	125.00	150-250
1987 Carl Yastrzemski, signed - R. Simon	1,500	N/A	125.00	100-150
1992 Chicago Bulls '92 World Champions - C. Hayes	Closed	N/A	150.00	150
1993 Chicago Bulls 1993 World Championship Gold (10 1/4") 4062-04 - B. Vann	1,993	1994	150.00	100-150
1987 Darryl Strawberry #1 - R. Simon	Closed	N/A	125.00	100-125
1989 Darryl Strawberry #2 - T. Fogerty	Closed	N/A	125.00	100-125
1986 Don Mattingly - B. Johnson	Closed	N/A	125.00	125-150
1991 Dream Team (1st Ten Chosen) - L. Salk	Closed	N/A	150.00	495-750
1992 Dream Team 1992 Gold (101/4") 5509-04 - R. Tanenbaum	1,992	1994	150.00	150-200
1992 Dream Team 1992 Platinum (8 1/2") 5507-03 - C. Hayes	7,500	1994	60.00	95
1991 Hawks Dominique Wilkins - J. Catalano	Closed	N/A	150.00	150-195
1990 Joe Montana 49ers Gold (10 1/4") 3000-04 - J. Catalano	1,990	1991	150.00	195-250
1986 Keith Hernandez - R. Simon	Closed	N/A	125.00	150-175
1991 Larry Bird - J. Catalano	Closed	N/A	150.00	195
1988 Larry Bird - R. Simon	Closed	N/A	125.00	275
1990 Living Triple Crown - R. Lewis	Closed	N/A	150.00	150
1993 Magic Johnson - T. Fogerty	Closed	N/A	150.00	150
1991 Magic Johnson Lakers Gold (10 1/4") 4007-04 - C.W. Mundy	1,991	1991	150.00	225
1992 Magic Johnson Lakers Gold (10 1/4") 4042-04 - R. Tanenbaum	1,992	1994	150.00	175
1991 Magic Johnson Lakers Platinum (8 1/2") 4007-03 - M. Petronella	5,000	1992	60.00	75
1989 Mantle Switch Hitter - J. Catalano	Closed	N/A	150.00	225-275
1992 Michael Jordan Bulls (10 1/4") 4032-04 - R. Tanenbaum	1,991	1992	150.00	225

*Quotes have been rounded up to nearest dollar

PLATES/PLAQUES

Sports Impressions/Enesco Group, Inc. to W.S. George

YEAR ISSUE	EDITION LIMIT	YEAR RETD.	ISSUE PRICE	*QUOTE U.S.$
1993 Michael Jordan Bulls Gold (10 1/4") 4046-04 - T. Fogarty	2,500	1993	150.00	150-175
1991 Michael Jordan Gold (10 1/4") 4002-04 - J. Catalano	1,991	1992	150.00	200
1991 Michael Jordan Platinum (8 1/2") 4002-03 - M. Petronella	1,991	1993	60.00	95
1995 Mickey Mantle "My Greatest Year 1956" 1229-04 - B. Vann	1,956	N/A	100.00	100-195
1991 Mickey Mantle 7 - B. Simon	Closed	N/A	150.00	150-195
1986 Mickey Mantle At Night (signed) - R. Simon	Closed	N/A	125.00	250-395
1995 Mickey Mantle double plate set, Platinum (8 1/2") 176923 - T. Treadway	2,401		75.00	75
1987 Mickey, Willie, & Duke (signed) - R. Simon	1,500	N/A	150.00	195-395
1988 Mickey, Willie, & Duke, (signed) 1041-59 - R. Simon	2,500		150.00	150
1992 NBA 1st Ten Chosen Platinum (8 1/2") (blue) 5502-03 - J. Catalano	7,500	1993	60.00	95
1992 NBA 1st Ten Chosen Platinum (8 1/2") (red) 5503-03 - C.W. Mundy	7,500	1993	60.00	95
1990 Nolan Ryan 300 Gold 1091-04 - T. Fogarty	1,990	1992	150.00	150
1990 Nolan Ryan 5,000 K's - J. Catalano	1,990		150.00	150
1995 Profiles in Courage Mickey Mantle Platinum (8 1/2") 1231-03 - M. Petronella	Open		30.00	30
1990 Rickey Henderson - R. Lewis	Closed	N/A	150.00	125-150
XX Roberto Clemente 1090-03 - R. Lewis	10,000	N/A	75.00	75
1993 Shaquille O'Neal Gold (10 1/4") 4047-04 - T. Fogarty	2,500	1994	150.00	150-195
1994 Shaquille O'Neal, Rookie of the Year - N/A	Open		100.00	100
1987 Ted Williams (signed) - R. Simon	Closed	N/A	125.00	450-495
1990 Tom Seaver - R. Lewis	Closed	N/A	150.00	150-200
1986 Wade Bogg (signed) - B. Johnson	Closed	N/A	125.00	150-175
1989 Will Clark - J. Catalano	Closed	N/A	125.00	100-150
1988 Yankee Tradition - J. Catalano	Closed	N/A	150.00	195-200

V-Palekh Art Studios

Russian Legends - Various

YEAR ISSUE	EDITION LIMIT	YEAR RETD.	ISSUE PRICE	*QUOTE U.S.$
1988 Ruslan and Ludmilla - G. Lubimov	195-day		29.87	12-30
1988 The Princess/Seven Bogatyrs - A. Kovalev	195-day		29.87	15-30
1988 The Golden Cockerel - V. Vleshko	195-day		32.87	15-33
1988 Lukomorya - R. Belousov	195-day		32.87	18-33
1989 Fisherman and the Magic Fish - N. Lopatin	195-day		32.87	15-33
1989 Tsar Saltan - G. Zhiryakova	195-day		32.87	15-33
1989 The Priest and His Servant - O. An	195-day		34.87	20-35
1990 Stone Flower - V. Bolshakova	195-day		34.87	28-35
1990 Sadko - E. Populor	195-day		34.87	30-40
1990 The Twelve Months - N. Lopatin	195-day		36.87	40-48
1990 Silver Hoof - S. Adeyanor	195-day		36.87	47-55
1990 Morozko - N. Lopatin	195-day		36.87	61-70

Villeroy & Boch

Flower Fairy - C. Barker

YEAR ISSUE	EDITION LIMIT	YEAR RETD.	ISSUE PRICE	*QUOTE U.S.$
1979 Lavender	21-day		35.00	125
1980 Sweet Pea	21-day		35.00	125
1980 Candytuft	21-day		35.00	89
1981 Heliotrope	21-day		35.00	75
1981 Blackthorn	21-day		35.00	75
1981 Appleblossom	21-day		35.00	95

Russian Fairytales Maria Morevna - B. Zvorykin

YEAR ISSUE	EDITION LIMIT	YEAR RETD.	ISSUE PRICE	*QUOTE U.S.$
1983 Maria Morevna and Tsarevich Ivan	27,500		70.00	70-140
1983 Koshchey Carries Off Maria Morevna	27,500		70.00	70-150
1983 Tsarevich Ivan and the Beautiful Castle	27,500		70.00	70-125

Russian Fairytales The Firebird - B. Zvorykin

YEAR ISSUE	EDITION LIMIT	YEAR RETD.	ISSUE PRICE	*QUOTE U.S.$
1982 In Search of the Firebird	27,500		70.00	88-100
1982 Ivan and Tsarevna on the Grey Wolf	27,500		70.00	90-118
1982 The Wedding of Tsarevna Elena the Fair	27,500		70.00	100-200

Russian Fairytales The Red Knight - B. Zvorykin

YEAR ISSUE	EDITION LIMIT	YEAR RETD.	ISSUE PRICE	*QUOTE U.S.$
1981 The Red Knight	27,500		70.00	30-66
1981 Vassilissa and Her Stepsisters	27,500		70.00	40-50
1981 Vassilissa is Presented to the Tsar	27,500		70.00	45-71

Villeroy & Boch - B. Zvorykin

YEAR ISSUE	EDITION LIMIT	YEAR RETD.	ISSUE PRICE	*QUOTE U.S.$
1980 The Snow Maiden	27,500		70.00	75-100
1980 Snegurochka at the Court of Tsar Berendei	27,500		70.00	80-97
1980 Snegurochka and Lei, the Shepherd Boy	27,500		70.00	100-200

W.S. George

Alaska: The Last Frontier - H. Lambson

YEAR ISSUE	EDITION LIMIT	YEAR RETD.	ISSUE PRICE	*QUOTE U.S.$
1991 Icy Majesty	Closed		34.50	19-35
1991 Autumn Grandeur	Closed		34.50	23-27
1992 Mountain Monarch	Closed		37.50	30-39
1992 Down the Trail	Closed		37.50	35-39
1992 Moonlight Lookout	Closed		37.50	48-52
1992 Graceful Passage	Closed		39.50	59-60
1992 Arctic Journey	Closed		39.50	55
1992 Summit Domain	Closed		39.50	45-60

Along an English Lane - M. Harvey

YEAR ISSUE	EDITION LIMIT	YEAR RETD.	ISSUE PRICE	*QUOTE U.S.$
1993 Summer's Bright Welcome	Closed		29.50	41-50
1993 Greeting the Day	Closed		29.50	53-60
1993 Friends and Flowers	Closed		29.50	60
1993 Cottage Around the Bend	Closed		29.50	53

America the Beautiful - H. Johnson

YEAR ISSUE	EDITION LIMIT	YEAR RETD.	ISSUE PRICE	*QUOTE U.S.$
1988 Yosemite Falls	Closed		34.50	26-29
1989 The Grand Canyon	Closed		34.50	16-29
1989 Yellowstone River	Closed		37.50	18-30
1989 The Great Smokey Mountains	Closed		37.50	18-30
1990 The Everglades	Closed		37.50	19-42
1990 Acadia	Closed		37.50	15-20
1990 The Grand Tetons	Closed		39.50	25-32
1990 Crater Lake	Closed		39.50	10-28

America's Pride - R. Richert

YEAR ISSUE	EDITION LIMIT	YEAR RETD.	ISSUE PRICE	*QUOTE U.S.$
1992 Misty Fjords	Closed		29.50	38
1992 Rugged Shores	Closed		29.50	30-36
1992 Mighty Summit	Closed		32.50	37-45
1993 Lofty Reflections	Closed		32.50	60
1993 Tranquil Waters	Closed		32.50	33-50
1993 Mountain Majesty	Closed		34.50	33
1993 Canyon Climb	Closed		34.50	49
1993 Golden Vista	Closed		34.50	35

Art Deco - M. McDonald

YEAR ISSUE	EDITION LIMIT	YEAR RETD.	ISSUE PRICE	*QUOTE U.S.$
1989 A Flapper With Greyhounds	Closed		39.50	40-42
1990 Tango Dancers	Closed		39.50	48-50
1990 Arriving in Style	Closed		39.50	47-50
1990 On the Town	Closed		39.50	48-56

Baby Cats of the Wild - C. Fracé

YEAR ISSUE	EDITION LIMIT	YEAR RETD.	ISSUE PRICE	*QUOTE U.S.$
1992 Morning Mischief	Closed		29.50	41
1993 Togetherness	Closed		29.50	42
1993 The Buddy System	Closed		32.50	59
1993 Nap Time	Closed		32.50	50-65

Bear Tracks - J. Seerey-Lester

YEAR ISSUE	EDITION LIMIT	YEAR RETD.	ISSUE PRICE	*QUOTE U.S.$
1992 Denali Family	Closed		29.50	30
1993 Their First Season	Closed		29.50	30
1993 High Country Champion	Closed		29.50	30
1993 Heavy Going	Closed		29.50	30
1993 Breaking Cover	Closed		29.50	30
1993 Along the Ice Flow	Closed		29.50	30

Beloved Hymns of Childhood - C. Barker

YEAR ISSUE	EDITION LIMIT	YEAR RETD.	ISSUE PRICE	*QUOTE U.S.$
1988 The Lord's My Shepherd	Closed		29.50	35-39
1988 Away In a Manger	Closed		29.50	23-45
1989 Now Thank We All Our God	Closed		32.50	21-29
1989 Love Divine	Closed		32.50	22-26
1989 I Love to Hear the Story	Closed		32.50	17-21
1989 All Glory, Laud and Honour	Closed		32.50	23-29
1990 All People on Earth Do Dwell	Closed		34.50	25-35
1990 Loving Shepherd of Thy Sheep	Closed		34.50	25-35

A Black Tie Affair: The Penguin - C. Jagodits

YEAR ISSUE	EDITION LIMIT	YEAR RETD.	ISSUE PRICE	*QUOTE U.S.$
1992 Little Explorer	Closed		29.50	40-50
1992 Penguin Parade	Closed		29.50	45-49
1992 Baby-Sitters	Closed		29.50	50-60
1993 Belly Flopping	Closed		29.50	53

Blessed Are The Children - W. Rane

YEAR ISSUE	EDITION LIMIT	YEAR RETD.	ISSUE PRICE	*QUOTE U.S.$
1990 Let the/Children Come To Me	Closed		29.50	39-45
1990 I Am the Good Shepherd	Closed		29.50	29-33
1991 Whoever Welcomes/Child	Closed		32.50	29-32
1991 Hosanna in the Highest	Closed		32.50	34-40
1991 Jesus Had Compassion on Them	Closed		32.50	40-45
1991 Blessed are the Peacemakers	Closed		34.50	52
1991 I am the Vine, You are the Branches	Closed		34.50	41-45
1991 Seek and You Will Find	Closed		34.50	35-45

Bonds of Love - B. Burke

YEAR ISSUE	EDITION LIMIT	YEAR RETD.	ISSUE PRICE	*QUOTE U.S.$
1989 Precious Embrace	Closed		29.50	23-30
1990 Cherished Moment	Closed		29.50	25-30
1991 Tender Caress	Closed		32.50	35-51
1992 Loving Touch	Closed		32.50	25-33
1992 Treasured Kisses	Closed		32.50	32-40
1994 Endearing Whispers	Closed		32.50	34-45

Charles Vickery's Romantic Harbors - C. Vickery

YEAR ISSUE	EDITION LIMIT	YEAR RETD.	ISSUE PRICE	*QUOTE U.S.$
1993 Advent of the Golden Bough	Closed		34.50	42
1993 Christmas Tree Schooner	Closed		34.50	50-60
1993 Prelude to the Journey	Closed		37.50	55-68
1993 Shimmering Light of Dusk	Closed		37.50	150-160

The Christmas Story - H. Garrido

YEAR ISSUE	EDITION LIMIT	YEAR RETD.	ISSUE PRICE	*QUOTE U.S.$
1992 Gifts of the Magi	Closed		29.50	37-45
1993 Rest on the Flight into Egypt	Closed		29.50	50
1993 Journey of the Magi	Closed		29.50	30-43
1993 The Nativity	Closed		29.50	50
1993 The Annunciation	Closed		29.50	30-51
1993 Adoration of the Shepherds	Closed		29.50	50

Classic Waterfowl: The Ducks Unlimited - L. Kaatz

YEAR ISSUE	EDITION LIMIT	YEAR RETD.	ISSUE PRICE	*QUOTE U.S.$
1988 Mallards at Sunrise	Closed		36.50	18-39
1988 Geese in the Autumn Fields	Closed		36.50	42-50
1989 Green Wings/Morning Marsh	Closed		39.50	42
1989 Canvasbacks, Breaking Away	Closed		39.50	42
1989 Pintails in Indian Summer	Closed		39.50	42
1990 Wood Ducks Taking Flight	Closed		39.50	23-42
1990 Snow Geese Against November Skies	Closed		41.50	30-45
1990 Bluebills Coming In	Closed		41.50	42

Columbus Discovers America: The 500th Anniversary - J. Penalva

YEAR ISSUE	EDITION LIMIT	YEAR RETD.	ISSUE PRICE	*QUOTE U.S.$
1991 Under Full Sail	Closed		29.50	30
1992 Ashore at Dawn	Closed		29.50	20-35
1992 Columbus Raises the Flag	Closed		32.50	24-30
1992 Bringing Together Two Cultures	Closed		32.50	34-39
1992 The Queen's Approval	Closed		32.50	25-33
1992 Treasures From The New World	Closed		32.50	35-50

Country Bouquets - G. Kurz

YEAR ISSUE	EDITION LIMIT	YEAR RETD.	ISSUE PRICE	*QUOTE U.S.$
1991 Morning Sunshine	Closed		29.50	47
1991 Summer Perfume	Closed		29.50	31-35
1992 Warm Welcome	Closed		32.50	44-47
1992 Garden's Bounty	Closed		32.50	44-48

Country Nostalgia - M. Harvey

YEAR ISSUE	EDITION LIMIT	YEAR RETD.	ISSUE PRICE	*QUOTE U.S.$
1989 The Spring Buggy	Closed		29.50	15-20
1989 The Apple Cider Press	Closed		29.50	20-28
1989 The Vintage Seed Planter	Closed		29.50	29-55
1989 The Old Hand Pump	Closed		32.50	43-50
1990 The Wooden Butter Churn	Closed		32.50	30-40
1990 The Dairy Cans	Closed		32.50	23-28
1990 The Forgotten Plow	Closed		34.50	19-21
1990 The Antique Spinning Wheel	Closed		34.50	20-24

Critic's Choice: Gone With The Wind - P. Jennis

YEAR ISSUE	EDITION LIMIT	YEAR RETD.	ISSUE PRICE	*QUOTE U.S.$
1991 Marry Me, Scarlett	Closed		27.50	36-60
1991 Waiting for Rhett	Closed		27.50	44-60
1991 A Declaration of Love	Closed		30.50	43-55
1991 The Paris Hat	Closed		30.50	35-79
1991 Scarlett Asks a Favor	Closed		30.50	45
1992 Scarlett Gets Her Way	Closed		32.50	39
1992 The Smitten Suitor	Closed		32.50	48-55
1992 Scarlett's Shopping Spree	Closed		32.50	40-50
1992 The Buggy Ride	Closed		32.50	65-69
1992 Scarlett Gets Down to Business	Closed		34.50	39-45
1993 Scarlett's Heart is with Tara	Closed		34.50	50-75
1993 At Cross Purposes	Closed		34.50	50-65

A Delicate Balance: Vanishing Wildlife - G. Beecham

YEAR ISSUE	EDITION LIMIT	YEAR RETD.	ISSUE PRICE	*QUOTE U.S.$
1992 Tomorrow's Hope	Closed		29.50	33
1993 Today's Future	Closed		29.50	43
1993 Present Dreams	Closed		32.50	30-35
1993 Eyes on the New Day	Closed		32.50	21-35

Dr. Zhivago - G. Bush

YEAR ISSUE	EDITION LIMIT	YEAR RETD.	ISSUE PRICE	*QUOTE U.S.$
1990 Zhivago and Lara	Closed		39.50	22-40
1991 Love Poems For Lara	Closed		39.50	30-40
1991 Zhivago Says Farewell	Closed		39.50	38-45
1991 Lara's Love	Closed		39.50	45-50

The Elegant Birds - J. Faulkner

YEAR ISSUE	EDITION LIMIT	YEAR RETD.	ISSUE PRICE	*QUOTE U.S.$
1988 The Swan	Closed		32.50	35
1988 Great Blue Heron	Closed		32.50	20-28
1989 Snowy Egret	Closed		32.50	17-21
1989 The Anhinga	Closed		35.50	36
1989 The Flamingo	Closed		35.50	24-27
1990 Sandhill and Whooping Crane	Closed		35.50	23

Enchanted Garden - E. Antonaccio

YEAR ISSUE	EDITION LIMIT	YEAR RETD.	ISSUE PRICE	*QUOTE U.S.$
1993 A Peaceful Retreat	Closed		24.50	25-40
1993 Pleasant Pathways	Closed		24.50	53
1993 A Place to Dream	Closed		24.50	25
1993 Tranquil Hideaway	Closed		24.50	25

Eyes of the Wild - D. Pierce

YEAR ISSUE	EDITION LIMIT	YEAR RETD.	ISSUE PRICE	*QUOTE U.S.$
1993 Eyes in the Mist	Closed		29.50	50-57
1993 Eyes in the Pines	Closed		29.50	30
1993 Eyes on the Sly	Closed		29.50	45-51
1993 Eyes of Gold	Closed		29.50	30
1993 Eyes of Silence	Closed		29.50	30-40
1993 Eyes in the Snow	Closed		29.50	30-95
1993 Eyes of Wonder	Closed		29.50	30
1994 Eyes of Strength	Closed		29.50	30-50

The Faces of Nature - J. Kramer Cole

YEAR ISSUE	EDITION LIMIT	YEAR RETD.	ISSUE PRICE	*QUOTE U.S.$
1992 Canyon of the Cat	Closed		29.50	45
1992 Wolf Ridge	Closed		29.50	45
1993 Trail of the Talisman	Closed		29.50	45
1993 Wolfpack of the Ancients	Closed		29.50	45
1993 Two Bears Camp	Closed		29.50	45
1993 Wintering With the Wapiti	Closed		29.50	40-45
1993 Within Sunrise	Closed		29.50	45
1993 Wambli Okiye	Closed		29.50	40-45

The Federal Duck Stamp Plate Collection - Various

YEAR ISSUE	EDITION LIMIT	YEAR RETD.	ISSUE PRICE	*QUOTE U.S.$
1990 The Lesser Scaup	Closed		27.50	15-28
1990 The Mallard	Closed		27.50	26-33
1990 The Ruddy Ducks	Closed		30.50	19-23
1990 Canvasbacks	Closed		30.50	19-31
1991 Pintails	Closed		30.50	24-29
1991 Wigeons	Closed		30.50	24-29
1991 Cinnamon Teal	Closed		32.50	25-33
1991 Fulvous Wistling Duck	Closed		32.50	36-44
1991 The Redheads	Closed		32.50	45-54
1991 Snow Goose	Closed		32.50	33-39

Feline Fancy - H. Ronner

YEAR ISSUE	EDITION LIMIT	YEAR RETD.	ISSUE PRICE	*QUOTE U.S.$
1993 Globetrotters	Closed		34.50	32
1993 Little Athletes	Closed		34.50	49
1993 Young Adventurers	Closed		34.50	45
1993 The Geographers	Closed		34.50	50-65

*Quotes have been rounded up to nearest dollar

Field Birds of North America - D. Bush

YEAR ISSUE	EDITION LIMIT	YEAR RETD.	ISSUE PRICE	*QUOTE U.S.$
1991 Winter Colors: Ring-Necked Pheasant	Closed		39.50	41
1991 In Display: Ruffed Grouse	Closed		39.50	31-40
1991 Morning Light: Bobwhite Quail	Closed		42.50	43-46
1991 Misty Clearing: Wild Turkey	Closed		42.50	65-74
1992 Autumn Moment: American Woodcock	Closed		42.50	48-50
1992 Season's End: Willow Ptarmigan	Closed		42.50	50-54

Floral Fancies - C. Callog

YEAR ISSUE	EDITION LIMIT	YEAR RETD.	ISSUE PRICE	*QUOTE U.S.$
1993 Sitting Softly	Closed		34.50	45
1993 Sitting Pretty	Closed		34.50	46-65
1993 Sitting Sunny	Closed		34.50	65-79
1993 Sitting Pink	Closed		34.50	45-58

Flowers From Grandma's Garden - G. Kurz

YEAR ISSUE	EDITION LIMIT	YEAR RETD.	ISSUE PRICE	*QUOTE U.S.$
1990 Country Cuttings	Closed		24.50	33-40
1990 The Morning Bouquet	Closed		24.50	29-35
1991 Homespun Beauty	Closed		27.50	30-35
1991 Harvest in the Meadow	Closed		27.50	35-37
1991 Gardener's Delight	Closed		27.50	40
1991 Nature's Bounty	Closed		27.50	40-44
1991 A Country Welcome	Closed		29.50	45-55
1991 The Springtime Arrangement	Closed		29.50	42-50

Flowers of Your Garden - V. Morley

YEAR ISSUE	EDITION LIMIT	YEAR RETD.	ISSUE PRICE	*QUOTE U.S.$
1988 Roses	Closed		24.50	20-25
1988 Lilacs	Closed		24.50	44-59
1988 Daisies	Closed		27.50	18-35
1988 Peonies	Closed		27.50	18-35
1988 Chrysanthemums	Closed		27.50	10-39
1989 Daffodils	Closed		27.50	22-28
1989 Tulips	Closed		29.50	15-30
1989 Irises	Closed		29.50	30-34

Garden of the Lord - C. Gillies

YEAR ISSUE	EDITION LIMIT	YEAR RETD.	ISSUE PRICE	*QUOTE U.S.$
1992 Love One Another	Closed		29.50	37
1992 Perfect Peace	Closed		29.50	32-38
1992 Trust In the Lord	Closed		32.50	33-46
1992 The Lord's Love	Closed		32.50	33-43
1992 The Lord Bless You	Closed		32.50	33-45
1992 Ask In Prayer	Closed		34.50	35
1993 Peace Be With You	Closed		34.50	35-45
1993 Give Thanks To The Lord	Closed		34.50	35

Gardens of Paradise - L. Chang

YEAR ISSUE	EDITION LIMIT	YEAR RETD.	ISSUE PRICE	*QUOTE U.S.$
1992 Tranquility	Closed		29.50	37
1992 Serenity	Closed		29.50	33-40
1993 Splendor	Closed		32.50	40-64
1993 Harmony	Closed		32.50	55-66
1993 Beauty	Closed		32.50	40-56
1993 Elegance	Closed		32.50	50-56
1993 Grandeur	Closed		32.50	65
1993 Majesty	Closed		32.50	50-60

Gentle Beginnings - W. Nelson

YEAR ISSUE	EDITION LIMIT	YEAR RETD.	ISSUE PRICE	*QUOTE U.S.$
1991 Tender Loving Care	Closed		34.50	27-40
1991 A Touch of Love	Closed		34.50	39-43
1991 Under Watchful Eyes	Closed		37.50	71-76
1991 Lap of Love	Closed		37.50	43-49
1992 Happy Together	Closed		37.50	63-68
1992 First Steps	Closed		37.50	40-93

Glorious Songbirds - R. Cobane

YEAR ISSUE	EDITION LIMIT	YEAR RETD.	ISSUE PRICE	*QUOTE U.S.$
1991 Cardinals on a Snowy Branch	Closed		29.50	15-18
1991 Indigo Buntings and/Blossoms	Closed		29.50	14-18
1991 Chickadees Among The Lilacs	Closed		32.50	18-20
1991 Goldfinches in/Thistle	Closed		32.50	15-23
1991 Cedar Waxwing/Winter Berries	Closed		32.50	22-44
1991 Bluebirds in a Blueberry Bush	Closed		34.50	30-40
1991 Baltimore Orioles/Autumn Leaves	Closed		34.50	42-60
1991 Robins with Dogwood in Bloom	Closed		34.50	33-45

The Golden Age of the Clipper Ships - C. Vickery

YEAR ISSUE	EDITION LIMIT	YEAR RETD.	ISSUE PRICE	*QUOTE U.S.$
1989 The Twilight Under Full Sail	Closed		29.50	15-30
1989 The Blue Jacket at Sunset	Closed		29.50	15-30
1989 Young America, Homeward	Closed		32.50	17-33
1990 Flying Cloud	Closed		32.50	24-30
1990 Davy Crocket at Daybreak	Closed		32.50	21-35
1990 Golden Eagle Conquers Wind	Closed		32.50	27-33
1990 The Lightning in Lifting Fog	Closed		34.50	30-35
1990 Sea Witch, Mistress/Oceans	Closed		34.50	35-40

Gone With the Wind: Golden Anniversary - H. Rogers

YEAR ISSUE	EDITION LIMIT	YEAR RETD.	ISSUE PRICE	*QUOTE U.S.$
1988 Scarlett and Her Suitors	Closed		24.50	25-75
1988 The Burning of Atlanta	Closed		24.50	25-75
1988 Scarlett and Ashley After the War	Closed		27.50	25-75
1988 The Proposal	Closed		27.50	40-89
1989 Home to Tara	Closed		27.50	24-50
1989 Strolling in Atlanta	Closed		27.50	26-55
1989 A Question of Honor	Closed		29.50	24-65
1989 Scarlett's Resolve	Closed		29.50	31-90
1989 Frankly My Dear	Closed		29.50	33-85
1989 Melane and Ashley	Closed		32.50	20-55
1990 A Toast to Bonnie Blue	Closed		32.50	30-65
1990 Scarlett and Rhett's Honeymoon	Closed		32.50	30-80

Gone With the Wind: The Passions of Scarlett O'Hara - P. Jennis

YEAR ISSUE	EDITION LIMIT	YEAR RETD.	ISSUE PRICE	*QUOTE U.S.$
1992 Fiery Embrace	Closed		29.50	35-50
1992 Pride and Passion	Closed		29.50	48
1992 Dreams of Ashley	Closed		32.50	50
1992 The Fond Farewell	Closed		32.50	42-50
1992 The Waltz	Closed		32.50	60-63
1992 As God Is My Witness	Closed		34.50	74-79
1993 Brave Scarlett	Closed		34.50	44-69
1993 Nightmare	Closed		34.50	35-65
1993 Evening Prayers	Closed		34.50	50
1993 Naptime	Closed		36.50	49-55
1993 Dangerous Attraction	Closed		36.50	70
1994 The End of An Era	Closed		36.50	48-50

Grand Safari: Images of Africa - C. Fracé

YEAR ISSUE	EDITION LIMIT	YEAR RETD.	ISSUE PRICE	*QUOTE U.S.$
1992 A Moment's Rest	Closed		34.50	30-35
1992 Elephant's of Kilimanjaro	Closed		34.50	47
1992 Undivided Attention	Closed		37.50	42
1993 Quiet Time in Samburu	Closed		37.50	38-49
1993 Lone Hunter	Closed		37.50	35-38
1993 The Greater Kudo	Closed		37.50	25-38

Heart of the Wild - G. Beecham

YEAR ISSUE	EDITION LIMIT	YEAR RETD.	ISSUE PRICE	*QUOTE U.S.$
1992 A Gentle Touch	Closed		29.50	18-30
1992 Mother's Pride	Closed		29.50	37
1992 An Afternoon Together	Closed		32.50	46-50
1993 Quiet Time?	Closed		32.50	33-50

Hollywood's Glamour Girls - E. Dzenis

YEAR ISSUE	EDITION LIMIT	YEAR RETD.	ISSUE PRICE	*QUOTE U.S.$
1989 Jean Harlow-Dinner at Eight	Closed		24.50	35-55
1990 Lana Turner-Postman Ring Twice	Closed		29.50	30-50
1990 Carol Lombard-The Gay Bride	Closed		29.50	18-30
1990 Greta Garbo-In Grand Hotel	Closed		29.50	26-45

Hometown Memories - H.T. Becker

YEAR ISSUE	EDITION LIMIT	YEAR RETD.	ISSUE PRICE	*QUOTE U.S.$
1993 Moonlight Skaters	Closed		29.50	23-30
1993 Mountain Sleigh Ride	Closed		29.50	39
1993 Heading Home	Closed		29.50	54
1993 A Winter Ride	Closed		29.50	50

Last of Their Kind: The Endangered Species - W. Nelson

YEAR ISSUE	EDITION LIMIT	YEAR RETD.	ISSUE PRICE	*QUOTE U.S.$
1988 The Panda	Closed		27.50	17-50
1989 The Snow Leopard	Closed		27.50	17-40
1989 The Red Wolf	Closed		30.50	13-31
1989 The Asian Elephant	Closed		30.50	18-35
1990 The Slender-Horned Gazelle	Closed		30.50	11-31
1990 The Bridled Wallaby	Closed		30.50	14-31
1990 The Black-Footed Ferret	Closed		33.50	21-34
1990 The Siberian Tiger	Closed		33.50	21-34
1991 The Vicuna	Closed		33.50	17-34
1991 Przewalski's Horse	Closed		33.50	19-32

Lena Liu's Basket Bouquets - L. Liu

YEAR ISSUE	EDITION LIMIT	YEAR RETD.	ISSUE PRICE	*QUOTE U.S.$
1992 Roses	Closed		29.50	30-39
1992 Pansies	Closed		29.50	48-50
1992 Tulips and Lilacs	Closed		32.50	50-55
1992 Irises	Closed		32.50	41-46
1992 Lilies	Closed		32.50	35-39
1992 Parrot Tulips	Closed		32.50	36-40
1992 Peonies	Closed		32.50	38-45
1993 Begonias	Closed		32.50	55-67
1993 Magnolias	Closed		32.50	40-95
1993 Calla Lilies	Closed		32.50	49-57
1993 Orchids	Closed		32.50	44-59
1993 Hydrangeas	Closed		32.50	49-53

Lena Liu's Flower Fairies - L. Liu

YEAR ISSUE	EDITION LIMIT	YEAR RETD.	ISSUE PRICE	*QUOTE U.S.$
1993 Magic Makers	Closed		29.50	48
1993 Petal Playmates	Closed		29.50	45-65
1993 Delicate Dancers	Closed		32.50	55-70
1993 Mischief Masters	Closed		32.50	84
1993 Amorous Angels	Closed		32.50	60-65
1993 Winged Wonders	Closed		34.50	60-75
1993 Miniature Mermaids	Closed		34.50	60-90
1993 Fanciful Fairies	Closed		34.50	85

Lena Liu's Hummingbird Treasury - L. Liu

YEAR ISSUE	EDITION LIMIT	YEAR RETD.	ISSUE PRICE	*QUOTE U.S.$
1992 Ruby-Throated Hummingbird	Closed		29.50	40-50
1992 Anna's Hummingbird	Closed		29.50	55-65
1992 Violet-Crowned Hummingbird	Closed		32.50	75-80
1993 Rufous Hummingbird	Closed		32.50	74
1993 White-Eared Hummingbird	Closed		32.50	68-75
1993 Broad-Billed Hummingbird	Closed		34.50	60-84
1993 Calliope Hummingbird	Closed		34.50	60-80
1993 The Allen's Hummingbird	Closed		34.50	80-100

Little Angels - B. Burke

YEAR ISSUE	EDITION LIMIT	YEAR RETD.	ISSUE PRICE	*QUOTE U.S.$
1992 Angels We Have Heard on High	Closed		29.50	39-55
1992 O Tannenbaum	Closed		29.50	60
1993 Joy to the World	Closed		32.50	50-64
1993 Hark the Herald Angels Sing	Closed		32.50	55-65
1993 It Came Upon a Midnight Clear	Closed		32.50	50
1993 The First Noel	Closed		32.50	45-60

A Loving Look: Duck Families - B. Langton

YEAR ISSUE	EDITION LIMIT	YEAR RETD.	ISSUE PRICE	*QUOTE U.S.$
1990 Family Outing	Closed		34.50	19-35
1991 Sleepy Start	Closed		34.50	20-35
1991 Quiet Moment	Closed		37.50	22-43
1991 Safe and Sound	Closed		37.50	29-40
1991 Spring Arrivals	Closed		37.50	34-38
1991 The Family Tree	Closed		37.50	36-50

The Majestic Horse - P. Wildermuth

YEAR ISSUE	EDITION LIMIT	YEAR RETD.	ISSUE PRICE	*QUOTE U.S.$
1992 Classic Beauty: Thoroughbred	Closed		34.50	35
1992 American Gold: The Quarterhorse	Closed		34.50	45-50
1992 Regal Spirit: The Arabian	Closed		34.50	60
1992 Western Favorite: American Paint Horse	Closed		34.50	54

Melodies in the Mist - A. Sakhavarz

YEAR ISSUE	EDITION LIMIT	YEAR RETD.	ISSUE PRICE	*QUOTE U.S.$
1993 Early Morning Rain	Closed		34.50	39
1993 Among the Dewdrops	Closed		34.50	34
1993 Feeding Time	Closed		37.50	36
1994 Garden Party	Closed		37.50	55
1994 Unpleasant Surprise	Closed		37.50	40
1994 Spring Rain	Closed		37.50	40

Memories of a Victorian Childhood - Unknown

YEAR ISSUE	EDITION LIMIT	YEAR RETD.	ISSUE PRICE	*QUOTE U.S.$
1992 You'd Better Not Pout	Closed		29.50	30-33
1992 Sweet Slumber	Closed		29.50	35-41
1992 Through Thick and Thin	Closed		32.50	31-34
1992 An Armful of Treasures	Closed		32.50	52-57
1993 A Trio of Bookworms	Closed		32.50	52-57
1993 Pugnacious Playmate	Closed		32.50	55-60

Nature's Legacy - J. Sias

YEAR ISSUE	EDITION LIMIT	YEAR RETD.	ISSUE PRICE	*QUOTE U.S.$
1990 Blue Snow at Half Dome	Closed		24.50	10-12
1991 Misty Morning/Mt. McKinley	Closed		24.50	13-18
1991 Twilight Reflections on Mount Ranier	Closed		27.50	20-30
1991 Redwalls of Havasu Canyon	Closed		27.50	16-20
1991 Autumn Splendor in the Smoky Mts.	Closed		27.50	18-28
1991 Winter Peace in Yellowstone Park	Closed		29.50	24-30
1991 Golden Majesty/Rocky Mountains	Closed		29.50	25-27
1991 Radiant Sunset Over the Everglades	Closed		29.50	31-35

Nature's Lovables - C. Fracé

YEAR ISSUE	EDITION LIMIT	YEAR RETD.	ISSUE PRICE	*QUOTE U.S.$
1990 The Koala Bear	Closed		27.50	30
1991 New Arrival	Closed		27.50	16-30
1991 Chinese Treasure	Closed		27.50	35
1991 Baby Harp Seal	Closed		30.50	26-31
1991 Bobcat: Nature's Dawn	Closed		30.50	22-31
1991 Clouded Leopard	Closed		32.50	24-33
1991 Zebra Foal	Closed		32.50	30-33
1991 Bandit	Closed		32.50	35

Nature's Playmates - C. Fracé

YEAR ISSUE	EDITION LIMIT	YEAR RETD.	ISSUE PRICE	*QUOTE U.S.$
1991 Partners	Closed		29.50	24-30
1991 Secret Heights	Closed		29.50	21-30
1991 Recess	Closed		32.50	20-33
1991 Double Trouble	Closed		32.50	18-33
1991 Pals	Closed		32.50	20-33
1992 Curious Trio	Closed		34.50	35
1992 Playmates	Closed		34.50	31-35
1992 Surprise	Closed		34.50	24-35
1992 Peace On Ice	Closed		36.50	40-44
1992 Ambassadors	Closed		36.50	35-40

Nature's Poetry - L. Liu

YEAR ISSUE	EDITION LIMIT	YEAR RETD.	ISSUE PRICE	*QUOTE U.S.$
1989 Morning Serenade	Closed		24.50	10-55
1989 Song of Promise	Closed		24.50	24-55
1990 Tender Lullaby	Closed		27.50	28-55
1990 Nature's Harmony	Closed		27.50	29-55
1990 Gentle Refrain	Closed		27.50	21-55
1990 Morning Chorus	Closed		27.50	32-55
1990 Melody at Daybreak	Closed		29.50	21-55
1991 Delicate Accord	Closed		29.50	20-55
1991 Lyrical Beginnings	Closed		29.50	30-55
1991 Song of Spring	Closed		32.50	27-55
1991 Mother's Melody	Closed		32.50	33-55
1991 Cherub Chorale	Closed		32.50	44-55

On Golden Wings - W. Goebel

YEAR ISSUE	EDITION LIMIT	YEAR RETD.	ISSUE PRICE	*QUOTE U.S.$
1993 Morning Light	Closed		29.50	38
1993 Early Risers	Closed		29.50	44
1993 As Day Breaks	Closed		32.50	45
1993 Daylight Flight	Closed		32.50	45-62
1993 Winter Dawn	Closed		32.50	33
1994 First Light	Closed		34.50	50

On Gossamer Wings - L. Liu

YEAR ISSUE	EDITION LIMIT	YEAR RETD.	ISSUE PRICE	*QUOTE U.S.$
1988 Monarch Butterflies	Closed		24.50	21-30
1988 Western Tiger Swallowtails	Closed		24.50	28-45
1988 Red-Spotted Purple	Closed		27.50	30-35
1988 Malachites	Closed		27.50	18-20
1988 White Peacocks	Closed		27.50	20-30
1989 Eastern Tailed Blues	Closed		27.50	16-30
1989 Zebra Swallowtails	Closed		29.50	19-22
1989 Red Admirals	Closed		29.50	18-30

On the Wing - T. Humphrey

YEAR ISSUE	EDITION LIMIT	YEAR RETD.	ISSUE PRICE	*QUOTE U.S.$
1992 Winged Splendor	Closed		29.50	19-29
1992 Rising Mallard	Closed		29.50	28
1992 Glorious Ascent	Closed		32.50	33
1992 Taking Wing	Closed		32.50	40
1992 Upward Bound	Closed		32.50	40
1993 Wondrous Motion	Closed		34.50	40-48
1993 Springing Forth	Closed		34.50	55-60
1993 On The Wing	Closed		34.50	65

On Wings of Snow - L. Liu

YEAR ISSUE	EDITION LIMIT	YEAR RETD.	ISSUE PRICE	*QUOTE U.S.$
1991 The Swans	Closed		34.50	23-35
1991 The Doves	Closed		34.50	35-40
1991 The Peacocks	Closed		37.50	34-40
1991 The Egrets	Closed		37.50	38-49
1991 The Cockatoos	Closed		37.50	25-36
1992 The Herons	Closed		37.50	38

Our Woodland Friends - C. Brenders

YEAR ISSUE	EDITION LIMIT	YEAR RETD.	ISSUE PRICE	*QUOTE U.S.$
1989 Fascination	Closed		29.00	15-30
1990 Beneath the Pines	Closed		29.50	20-30
1990 High Adventure	Closed		32.50	20-33
1990 Shy Explorers	Closed		32.50	29-33

*Quotes have been rounded up to nearest dollar

YEAR ISSUE	EDITION LIMIT	YEAR RETD.	ISSUE PRICE	*QUOTE U.S.$
1991 Golden Season: Gray Squirrel	Closed		32.50	25-33
1991 Full House: Fox Family	Closed		32.50	33-45
1991 A Jump Into Life: Spring Fawn	Closed		34.50	27-35
1991 Forest Sentinel: Bobcat	Closed		34.50	22-34

Petal Pals - L. Chang

YEAR ISSUE	EDITION LIMIT	YEAR RETD.	ISSUE PRICE	*QUOTE U.S.$
1992 Garden Discovery	Closed		24.50	40-44
1992 Flowering Fascination	Closed		24.50	45-48
1993 Alluring Lilies	Closed		24.50	25-37
1993 Springtime Oasis	Closed		24.50	25-30
1993 Blossoming Adventure	Closed		24.50	38-40
1993 Dancing Daffodils	Closed		24.50	25-30
1993 Summer Surprise	Closed		24.50	30
1993 Morning Melody	Closed		24.50	31

Poetic Cottages - C. Valente

YEAR ISSUE	EDITION LIMIT	YEAR RETD.	ISSUE PRICE	*QUOTE U.S.$
1992 Garden Paths of Oxfordshire	Closed		29.50	32-35
1992 Twilight at Woodgreen Pond	Closed		29.50	70
1992 Stonewall Brook Blossoms	Closed		32.50	53-65
1992 Bedfordshire Evening Sky	Closed		32.50	41
1993 Wisteria Summer	Closed		32.50	48
1993 Wiltshire Rose Arbor	Closed		32.50	48
1993 Alderbury Gardens	Closed		32.50	56
1993 Hampshire Spring Splendor	Closed		32.50	59

Portraits of Christ - J. Salamanca

YEAR ISSUE	EDITION LIMIT	YEAR RETD.	ISSUE PRICE	*QUOTE U.S.$
1991 Father, Forgive Them	Closed		29.50	80-83
1991 Thy Will Be Done	Closed		29.50	50-56
1991 This is My Beloved Son	Closed		32.50	45-54
1991 Lo, I Am With You	Closed		32.50	44-49
1991 Become as Little Children	Closed		32.50	30-49
1992 Peace I Leave With You	Closed		34.50	40-45
1992 For God So Loved the World	Closed		34.50	35-42
1992 I Am the Way, the Truth and the Life	Closed		34.50	35-42
1992 Weep Not For Me	Closed		34.50	55-58
1992 Follow Me	Closed		34.50	60-65

Portraits of Exquisite Birds - C. Brenders

YEAR ISSUE	EDITION LIMIT	YEAR RETD.	ISSUE PRICE	*QUOTE U.S.$
1990 Backyard Treasure/Chickadee	Closed		29.50	20-30
1990 The Beautiful Bluebird	Closed		29.50	18-30
1991 Summer Gold: The Robin	Closed		32.50	19-33
1991 The Meadowlark's Song	Closed		32.50	25-33
1991 Ivory-Billed Woodpecker	Closed		32.50	25-33
1991 Red-Winged Blackbird	Closed		32.50	19-35

Purebred Horses of the Americas - D. Schwartz

YEAR ISSUE	EDITION LIMIT	YEAR RETD.	ISSUE PRICE	*QUOTE U.S.$
1989 The Appalosa	Closed		34.50	14-20
1989 The Tenessee Walker	Closed		34.50	22-27
1990 The Quarterhorse	Closed		37.50	37-39
1990 The Saddlebred	Closed		37.50	20-38
1990 The Mustang	Closed		37.50	33-38
1990 The Morgan	Closed		37.50	25-33

Rare Encounters - J. Seerey-Lester

YEAR ISSUE	EDITION LIMIT	YEAR RETD.	ISSUE PRICE	*QUOTE U.S.$
1993 Softly, Softly	Closed		29.50	35
1993 Black Magic	Closed		29.50	43
1993 Future Song	Closed		32.50	55-60
1993 High and Mighty	Closed		32.50	50
1993 Last Sanctuary	Closed		32.50	30-40
1993 Something Stirred	Closed		34.50	35-50

Romantic Gardens - C. Smith

YEAR ISSUE	EDITION LIMIT	YEAR RETD.	ISSUE PRICE	*QUOTE U.S.$
1989 The Woodland Garden	Closed		29.50	23-30
1989 The Plantation Garden	Closed		29.50	20-30
1990 The Cottage Garden	Closed		32.50	25-33
1990 The Colonial Garden	Closed		32.50	22-33

Scenes of Christmas Past - L. Garrison

YEAR ISSUE	EDITION LIMIT	YEAR RETD.	ISSUE PRICE	*QUOTE U.S.$
1987 Holiday Skaters	Closed		27.50	18-24
1988 Christmas Eve	Closed		27.50	21-30
1989 The Homecoming	Closed		30.50	17-30
1990 The Toy Store	Closed		30.50	30-40
1991 The Carollers	Closed		30.50	30-40
1992 Family Traditions	Closed		32.50	28-30
1993 Holiday Past	Closed		32.50	57-62
1994 A Gathering of Faith	Closed		32.50	50-58

The Secret World Of The Panda - J. Bridgett

YEAR ISSUE	EDITION LIMIT	YEAR RETD.	ISSUE PRICE	*QUOTE U.S.$
1990 A Mother's Care	Closed		27.50	18-30
1991 A Frolic in the Snow	Closed		27.50	20-30
1991 Lazy Afternoon	Closed		30.50	18-31
1991 A Day of Exploring	Closed		30.50	30
1991 A Gentle Hug	Closed		32.50	35
1991 A Bamboo Feast	Closed		32.50	50

Soaring Majesty - C. Fracé

YEAR ISSUE	EDITION LIMIT	YEAR RETD.	ISSUE PRICE	*QUOTE U.S.$
1991 Freedom	Closed		29.50	10-30
1991 The Northern Goshhawk	Closed		29.50	17-30
1991 Peregrine Falcon	Closed		32.50	21-33
1991 Red-Tailed Hawk	Closed		32.50	20-33
1991 The Osprey	Closed		32.50	20-33
1991 The Gyrfalcon	Closed		34.50	30-35
1991 The Golden Eagle	Closed		34.50	27-35
1992 Red-Shouldered Hawk	Closed		34.50	24-35

Sonnets in Flowers - G. Kurz

YEAR ISSUE	EDITION LIMIT	YEAR RETD.	ISSUE PRICE	*QUOTE U.S.$
1992 Sonnet of Beauty	Closed		29.50	30-34
1992 Sonnet of Happiness	Closed		34.50	40-60
1992 Sonnet of Love	Closed		34.50	35-55
1992 Sonnet of Peace	Closed		34.50	55

The Sound of Music: Silver Anniversary - V. Gadino

YEAR ISSUE	EDITION LIMIT	YEAR RETD.	ISSUE PRICE	*QUOTE U.S.$
1991 The Hills are Alive	Closed		29.50	20-23
1992 Let's Start at the Very Beginning	Closed		29.50	20-25
1992 Something Good	Closed		32.50	40

YEAR ISSUE	EDITION LIMIT	YEAR RETD.	ISSUE PRICE	*QUOTE U.S.$
1992 Maria's Wedding Day	Closed		32.50	40-54

Spirit of Christmas - J. Sias

YEAR ISSUE	EDITION LIMIT	YEAR RETD.	ISSUE PRICE	*QUOTE U.S.$
1990 Silent Night	Closed		29.50	15-30
1991 Jingle Bells	Closed		29.50	21-30
1991 Deck The Halls	Closed		32.50	28-33
1991 I'll Be Home For Christmas	Closed		32.50	30-38
1991 Winter Wonderland	Closed		32.50	24-33
1991 O Christmas Tree	Closed		32.50	33-35

Spirits of the Sky - C. Fisher

YEAR ISSUE	EDITION LIMIT	YEAR RETD.	ISSUE PRICE	*QUOTE U.S.$
1992 Twilight Glow	Closed		29.50	30-40
1992 First Light	Closed		29.50	60
1992 Evening Glimmer	Closed		32.50	74
1992 Golden Dusk	Closed		32.50	35
1993 Sunset Splendor	Closed		32.50	33-45
1993 Amber Flight	Closed		34.50	42-75
1993 Winged Radiance	Closed		34.50	49
1993 Day's End	Closed		34.50	35-75

A Splash of Cats - J. Seerey-Lester

YEAR ISSUE	EDITION LIMIT	YEAR RETD.	ISSUE PRICE	*QUOTE U.S.$
1992 Moonlight Chase: Cougar	Closed		29.50	30

Symphony of Shimmering Beauties - L. Liu

YEAR ISSUE	EDITION LIMIT	YEAR RETD.	ISSUE PRICE	*QUOTE U.S.$
1991 Iris Quartet	Closed		29.50	41-48
1991 Tulip Ensemble	Closed		29.50	39-45
1991 Poppy Pastorale	Closed		32.50	45-50
1991 Lily Concerto	Closed		32.50	44-48
1991 Peony Prelude	Closed		32.50	38-48
1991 Rose Fantasy	Closed		34.50	45-47
1991 Hibiscus Medley	Closed		34.50	36-45
1992 Dahlia Melody	Closed		34.50	37-40
1992 Hollyhock March	Closed		34.50	33-35
1992 Carnation Serenade	Closed		36.50	40-45
1992 Gladiolus Romance	Closed		36.50	52
1992 Zinnia Finale	Closed		36.50	40-50

Tis the Season - J. Sias

YEAR ISSUE	EDITION LIMIT	YEAR RETD.	ISSUE PRICE	*QUOTE U.S.$
1993 World Dressed in Snow	Closed		29.50	26-35
1993 A Time for Tradition	Closed		29.50	34
1993 We Shall Come Rejoining	Closed		29.50	30-40
1993 Our Family Tree	Closed		29.50	35-40

Tomorrow's Promise - W. Nelson

YEAR ISSUE	EDITION LIMIT	YEAR RETD.	ISSUE PRICE	*QUOTE U.S.$
1992 Curiosity: Asian Elephants	Closed		29.50	39
1992 Playtime Pandas	Closed		29.50	38
1992 Innocence: Rhinos	Closed		32.50	59
1992 Friskiness: Kit Foxes	Closed		32.50	36-39

Touching the Spirit - J. Kramer Cole

YEAR ISSUE	EDITION LIMIT	YEAR RETD.	ISSUE PRICE	*QUOTE U.S.$
1993 Running With the Wind	Closed		29.50	48-60
1993 Kindred Spirits	Closed		29.50	34
1993 The Marking Tree	Closed		29.50	43-46
1993 Wakan Tanka	Closed		29.50	30-63
1993 He Who Watches	Closed		29.50	47-50
1994 Twice Traveled Trail	Closed		29.50	41-43
1994 Keeper of the Secret	Closed		29.50	46-48
1994 Camp of the Sacred Dogs	Closed		29.50	70-84

A Treasury of Songbirds - R. Stine

YEAR ISSUE	EDITION LIMIT	YEAR RETD.	ISSUE PRICE	*QUOTE U.S.$
1992 Springtime Splendor	Closed		29.50	33-39
1992 Morning's Glory	Closed		29.50	37
1992 Golden Daybreak	Closed		32.50	41-51
1992 Afternoon Calm	Closed		32.50	39-45
1992 Dawn's Radiance	Closed		32.50	45
1993 Scarlet Sunrise	Closed		34.50	55-60
1993 Sapphire Dawn	Closed		34.50	50
1995 Alluring Daylight	Closed		34.50	65

The Vanishing Gentle Giants - A. Casay

YEAR ISSUE	EDITION LIMIT	YEAR RETD.	ISSUE PRICE	*QUOTE U.S.$
1991 Jumping For Joy	Closed		32.50	20-33
1991 Song of the Humpback	Closed		32.50	25-33
1991 Monarch of the Deep	Closed		35.50	28-36
1991 Travelers of the Sea	Closed		35.50	40
1991 White Whale of the North	Closed		35.50	39-45
1991 Unicorn of the Sea	Closed		35.50	38

The Victorian Cat - H. Bonner

YEAR ISSUE	EDITION LIMIT	YEAR RETD.	ISSUE PRICE	*QUOTE U.S.$
1990 Mischief With The Hatbox	Closed		24.50	23-30
1991 String Quartet	Closed		24.50	24-34
1991 Daydreams	Closed		27.50	30-35
1991 Frisky Felines	Closed		27.50	36-49
1991 Kittens at Play	Closed		27.50	30-50
1991 Playing in the Parlor	Closed		29.50	60
1991 Perfectly Poised	Closed		29.50	49-80
1992 Midday Repose	Closed		29.50	50

Victorian Cat Capers - Various

YEAR ISSUE	EDITION LIMIT	YEAR RETD.	ISSUE PRICE	*QUOTE U.S.$
1992 Who's the Fairest of Them All? - F. Paton	Closed		24.50	40-44
1992 Puss in Boots - Unknown	Closed		24.50	28-39
1992 My Bowl is Empty - W. Hepple	Closed		27.50	28-34
1992 A Curious Kitty - C. Van den Eycken	Closed		27.50	22-29
1992 Vanity Fair - C. Van den Eycken	Closed		27.50	22-29
1992 Forbidden Fruit - H. Blain	Closed		29.50	41-50
1993 The Purr-fect Pen Pal - A. Tucker	Closed		29.50	30-40
1993 The Kitten Express - L. Huber	Closed		29.50	50-60

Vieonne Morley's Romantic Roses - V. Morley

YEAR ISSUE	EDITION LIMIT	YEAR RETD.	ISSUE PRICE	*QUOTE U.S.$
1993 Victorian Beauty	Closed		29.50	30-40
1993 Old-Fashioned Grace	Closed		29.50	30
1993 Country Charm	Closed		32.50	65
1993 Summer Romance	Closed		32.50	35
1993 Pastoral Delight	Closed		32.50	38-45
1993 Springtime Elegance	Closed		34.50	49-60

YEAR ISSUE	EDITION LIMIT	YEAR RETD.	ISSUE PRICE	*QUOTE U.S.$
1993 Vintage Splendor	Closed		34.50	45-55
1994 Heavenly Perfection	Closed		34.50	35-49

Wild Innocents - C. Fracé

YEAR ISSUE	EDITION LIMIT	YEAR RETD.	ISSUE PRICE	*QUOTE U.S.$
1993 Reflections	Closed		29.50	32-35
1993 Spiritual Heir	Closed		29.50	30-43
1993 Lion Cub	Closed		29.50	43
1993 Sunny Spot	Closed		29.50	44

Wild Spirits - T. Hirata

YEAR ISSUE	EDITION LIMIT	YEAR RETD.	ISSUE PRICE	*QUOTE U.S.$
1992 Solitary Watch	Closed		29.50	32
1992 Timber Ghost	Closed		29.50	35-50
1992 Mountain Magic	Closed		32.50	32-35
1993 Silent Guard	Closed		32.50	35-45
1993 Sly Eyes	Closed		32.50	49
1993 Mighty Presence	Closed		34.50	30-35
1993 Quiet Vigil	Closed		34.50	50
1993 Lone Vanguard	Closed		34.50	32-35

Wings of Winter - D. Rust

YEAR ISSUE	EDITION LIMIT	YEAR RETD.	ISSUE PRICE	*QUOTE U.S.$
1992 Moonlight Retreat	Closed		29.50	30-35
1993 Twilight Serenade	Closed		29.50	33-40
1993 Silent Sunset	Closed		29.50	36-40
1993 Night Lights	Closed		29.50	30-40
1993 Winter Haven	Closed		29.50	47
1993 Full Moon Companions	Closed		29.50	30-48
1993 White Night	Closed		29.50	30-50
1993 Winter Reflections	150-day		29.50	30-35

Winter's Majesty - C. Fracé

YEAR ISSUE	EDITION LIMIT	YEAR RETD.	ISSUE PRICE	*QUOTE U.S.$
1992 The Quest	Closed		34.50	26-35
1992 The Chase	Closed		34.50	29-35
1993 Alaskan Friend	Closed		34.50	35
1993 American Cougar	Closed		34.50	30-35
1993 On Watch	Closed		34.50	43
1993 Solitude	Closed		34.50	48

Wonders Of The Sea - R. Harm

YEAR ISSUE	EDITION LIMIT	YEAR RETD.	ISSUE PRICE	*QUOTE U.S.$
1991 Stand By Me	Closed		34.50	31-35
1991 Heart to Heart	Closed		34.50	25-35
1991 Warm Embrace	Closed		34.50	37
1991 A Family Affair	Closed		34.50	31-34

The World's Most Magnificent Cats - C. Fracé

YEAR ISSUE	EDITION LIMIT	YEAR RETD.	ISSUE PRICE	*QUOTE U.S.$
1991 Fleeting Encounter	Closed		24.50	31-40
1991 Cougar	Closed		24.50	30-35
1991 Royal Bengal	Closed		27.50	25-30
1991 Powerful Presence	Closed		27.50	23-30
1991 Jaguar	Closed		27.50	25-35
1991 The Clouded Leopard	Closed		29.50	20-30
1991 The African Leopard	Closed		29.50	17-30
1991 Mighty Warrior	Closed		29.50	30-45
1992 The Cheetah	Closed		31.50	35
1992 Siberian Tiger	Closed		31.50	35-40

Waterford Wedgwood USA

Bicentennial - Unknown

YEAR ISSUE	EDITION LIMIT	YEAR RETD.	ISSUE PRICE	*QUOTE U.S.$
1972 Boston Tea Party	Annual		40.00	40
1973 Paul Revere's Ride	Annual		40.00	115
1974 Battle of Concord	Annual		40.00	55
1975 Across the Delaware	Annual		40.00	105
1975 Victory at Yorktown	Annual		45.00	53
1976 Declaration Signed	Annual		45.00	45

Wedgwood Christmas - Various

YEAR ISSUE	EDITION LIMIT	YEAR RETD.	ISSUE PRICE	*QUOTE U.S.$
1969 Windsor Castle - T. Harper	Annual		25.00	95-125
1970 Trafalgar Square - T. Harper	Annual		30.00	15-35
1971 Picadilly Circus - T. Harper	Annual		30.00	19-30
1972 St. Paul's Cathedral - T. Harper	Annual		35.00	35-45
1973 Tower of London - T. Harper	Annual		40.00	60-90
1974 Houses of Parliament - T. Harper	Annual		40.00	40-45
1975 Tower Bridge - T. Harper	Annual		45.00	40-45
1976 Hampton Court - T. Harper	Annual		50.00	35-40
1977 Westminister Abbey - T. Harper	Annual		55.00	35-40
1978 Horse Guards - T. Harper	Annual		60.00	40-60
1979 Buckingham Palace - Unknown	Annual		65.00	40-65
1980 St. James Palace - Unknown	Annual		70.00	59-70
1981 Marble Arch - Unknown	Annual		75.00	75
1982 Lambeth Palace - Unknown	Annual		80.00	80-90
1983 All Souls, Langham Palace - Unknown	Annual		80.00	80
1984 Constitution Hill - Unknown	Annual		80.00	80
1985 The Tate Gallery - Unknown	Annual		80.00	80-150
1986 The Albert Memorial - Unknown	Annual		80.00	80
1987 Guildhall - Unknown	Annual		80.00	200
1988 The Observatory/Greenwich - Unknown	Annual		80.00	90
1989 Winchester Cathedral - Unknown	Annual		88.00	88

Willitts Designs

Our Song - B. Joysmith

YEAR ISSUE	EDITION LIMIT	YEAR RETD.	ISSUE PRICE	*QUOTE U.S.$
1999 Madonna with Flowers (Bas Relief)	9,500		45.00	45
2000 Time Honored (Bas Relief)	9,500		37.50	38

Thomas Blackshear's Ebony Visions - T. Blackshear

YEAR ISSUE	EDITION LIMIT	YEAR RETD.	ISSUE PRICE	*QUOTE U.S.$
1997 The Madonna	7,500		35.00	35-75
1997 The Protector	7,500		35.00	35-75
1998 The Storyteller	7,500		45.00	45-85
1999 The Guardian	7,500		50.00	45-50

*Quotes have been rounded up to nearest dollar

Zolan Fine Arts, LLC

The Donald Zolan Society (3 5/8") - D. Zolan

YEAR ISSUE	EDITION LIMIT	YEAR RETD.	ISSUE PRICE	*QUOTE U.S.$
1997 A Child's Faith	Yr.Iss.	1997	Gift	35
1997 Rained Out	Yr.Iss.	1997	19.90	30-35
1998 Reach For The Sky	Yr.Iss.	1998	Gift	28-35
1998 Summer Thunder	3,000	1998	19.90	20-35
1999 Field of Dreams	Yr.Iss.	1999	Gift	N/A
1999 Wait Your Turn	15-day	2000	19.90	20
1999 A Child's Prayer	3,000	2000	19.90	20
1999 My Little Snowman	3,000	2000	19.90	20

Angel Songs (3 5/8") - D. Zolan

YEAR ISSUE	EDITION LIMIT	YEAR RETD.	ISSUE PRICE	*QUOTE U.S.$
1997 Harp Song	15-day	2000	19.90	20
1997 Love Song	15-day	2000	19.90	20
1997 Heavenly Song	15-day	2000	19.90	20

Companions (8 1/4") - D. Zolan

YEAR ISSUE	EDITION LIMIT	YEAR RETD.	ISSUE PRICE	*QUOTE U.S.$
1998 Cuddly Companion	75-day	2000	29.90	30
1998 Mommy's Little Helpers	75-day	2000	29.90	30
1998 Feeding Time	75-day	2000	29.90	30
1998 Giggles & Wiggles	75-day	2000	29.90	30
1998 Little Gardener	75-day	2000	29.90	30
1998 Horsing Around	75-day	2000	29.90	30
1998 Tender Loving Care	75-day	2000	29.90	30
1998 A Special Bond	75-day	2000	29.90	30

Country Friends (3 5/8") - D. Zolan

YEAR ISSUE	EDITION LIMIT	YEAR RETD.	ISSUE PRICE	*QUOTE U.S.$
1998 Little Gardener	15-day	2000	19.90	20
1998 Giggles and Wiggles	15-day	2000	19.90	20
1998 Let's Play	15-day	2000	19.90	20
1998 Two In A Tree	15-day	2000	19.90	20

Little Boys' Big Dreams (3 5/8") - D. Zolan

YEAR ISSUE	EDITION LIMIT	YEAR RETD.	ISSUE PRICE	*QUOTE U.S.$
1999 Family Treasures	15-day	2000	19.90	20
1999 Suds and Shine	15-day	2000	19.90	20
1999 Puppy's Palace	15-day	2000	19.90	20
1999 Finishing Touches	15-day	2000	19.90	20

Little Farmlands (8 1/4") - D. Zolan

YEAR ISSUE	EDITION LIMIT	YEAR RETD.	ISSUE PRICE	*QUOTE U.S.$
1997 Tractor Ride	75-day	2000	29.90	30
1997 Clean and Shiny	75-day	2000	29.90	30
1997 Pitching In	75-day	2000	29.90	30
1997 Bumper Crop	75-day	2000	29.90	30
1997 Morning Song	75-day	2000	29.90	30
1997 Tug O' War	75-day	2000	29.90	30
1998 Too Busy To Play	75-day	2000	29.90	30
1998 Piglet Roundup	75-day	2000	29.90	30

Single Issue (3 5/8") - D. Zolan

YEAR ISSUE	EDITION LIMIT	YEAR RETD.	ISSUE PRICE	*QUOTE U.S.$
2000 Bedtime Prayer	2,000	2000	19.90	20
1998 Downhill Delight	15-day	2000	19.90	20
2000 Spring Bouquet	2,000	2000	19.90	20
1999 Spring Breezes	15-day	2000	19.90	20

Single Issue (8 1/4") - D. Zolan

YEAR ISSUE	EDITION LIMIT	YEAR RETD.	ISSUE PRICE	*QUOTE U.S.$
1996 Harp Song	2,000	1996	29.90	45-48

Symphony of Seasons (3 5/8") - D. Zolan

YEAR ISSUE	EDITION LIMIT	YEAR RETD.	ISSUE PRICE	*QUOTE U.S.$
1997 Winter Wonder	15-day	1999	19.90	20-23
1997 Puddles 'n Splashes	15-day	1999	19.90	20
1997 Summertime Friends	15-day	1999	19.90	20
1997 Country Pumpkins	15-day	1999	19.90	20

STEINS/JUGS

Anheuser-Busch, Inc.

Anheuser-Busch Collectors Club - Various

YEAR ISSUE	EDITION LIMIT	YEAR RETD.	ISSUE PRICE	*QUOTE U.S.$
1995 Budweiser Clydesdales at the Bauernhof CB1 - A. Leon	Yr.Iss.	1996	Gift	75-230
1995 The Brew House Clock Tower CB2 - D. Thompson	Retrd.	1996	150.00	210-795
1996 The World's Largest Brewer CB3 - A. Leon	Yr.Iss.	1996	Gift	60-150
1996 King - A Regal Spirit CB4 - D. Thompson	Retrd.	1997	100.00	195-275
1997 Pride & Tradition CB5 - J. Turgeon	Yr.Iss.	1997	Gift	35-150
1997 The Budweiser Girls-Historical Reflections CB6 - D. Curran	Retrd.	1998	100.00	100-200
1998 Old World Heritage CB7 - J. Turgeon	Yr.Iss.	1998	Gift	35-150
1998 Early Delivery Days CB8 - D. Curran	Retrd.	1999	100.00	100-200
1999 The Golden Age of Brewing, Circa 1898 CB10 - J. Turgeon	Yr.Iss.	1999	Gift	40-200
1999 The Anheuser-Busch Collectors Club 5th Anniversary Stein CB13 - A-Busch, Inc.	Retrd.	2000	40.00	40-50
1999 The Anheuser-Busch Collectors Club 5th Anniversary Stein Charter Member CB13C - A-Busch, Inc.	Retrd.	2000	40.00	40-80
1999 Clydesdale Stable CB11 - D. Curran	Retrd.	2000	100.00	90-125
2000 Born To Greatness CB14 - J. Wainwright	Yr.Iss.		Gift	30-40
2000 A Celebration of Anheuser-Busch Achievements CB15 - D. Thompson	4/01		125.00	125

Anheuser-Busch Collectors Club-Anheuser-Busch Heritage Series - A-Busch, Inc.

YEAR ISSUE	EDITION LIMIT	YEAR RETD.	ISSUE PRICE	*QUOTE U.S.$
1998 Bevo Mill CB9	Retrd.	1999	120.00	110-200
1999 The Bauernhof CB12	Retrd.	2000	120.00	95-130
2000 The Brew House CB16	4/01		120.00	95-130

A & Eagle Historical Trademark Series-Giftware Edition - Various

YEAR ISSUE	EDITION LIMIT	YEAR RETD.	ISSUE PRICE	*QUOTE U.S.$
1992 A & Eagle Trademark I (1872) CS201, tin	Retrd.	1993	31.00	75-130
1993 A & Eagle Trademark I (1872) CS191, boxed	Retrd.	1993	22.00	25-60
1993 A & Eagle Trademark II (1890s) CS218, tin	Retrd.	N/A	24.00	50-85
1994 A & Eagle Trademark II (1890s) CS219, boxed	Retrd.	1994	24.00	35-60
1994 A & Eagle Trademark III (1900s) CS238, tin	20,000	1994	28.00	49-80
1995 A & Eagle Trademark III (1900s) CS240, boxed	30,000	1995	25.00	30-45
1995 A & Eagle Trademark IV (1930s) CS255, tin	20,000	1996	30.00	35-60
1996 A & Eagle Trademark IV (1930s) CS271, boxed	30,000		27.00	27

America The Beautiful Series-Collector Edition - Various

YEAR ISSUE	EDITION LIMIT	YEAR RETD.	ISSUE PRICE	*QUOTE U.S.$
1997 Smoky Mountains CS297 - A-Busch, Inc.	50,000		39.95	40
1998 Grand Canyon CS334 - H. Droog	50,000	2000	39.95	40
1999 Yellowstone CS376 - H. Droog	50,000		39.95	40
2000 Everglades CS420 - H. Droog	50,000		39.95	40

American Bald Eagle Series - Collector Edition - B. Kemper

YEAR ISSUE	EDITION LIMIT	YEAR RETD.	ISSUE PRICE	*QUOTE U.S.$
1999 Winter CS293	50,000		35.00	35
2000 Spring CS365	50,000		35.00	35

American Originals Series-Collector Edition - A-Busch, Inc.

YEAR ISSUE	EDITION LIMIT	YEAR RETD.	ISSUE PRICE	*QUOTE U.S.$
1997 Black & Tan CS314	5,000	1997	75.00	75-350
1997 Faust CS330	5,000	1997	75.00	75-300

Anheuser-Busch Founder Series-Premier Collection - A-Busch, Inc.

YEAR ISSUE	EDITION LIMIT	YEAR RETD.	ISSUE PRICE	*QUOTE U.S.$
1993 Adophus Busch CS216	10,000	1996	180.00	125-189
1994 August A. Busch, Sr. CS229	10,000	1996	220.00	160-189
1995 Adolphus Busch III CS265	10,000		220.00	220
1996 August A. Busch, Jr. CS286	10,000		220.00	220

Animal Families Series-Collector Edition - C. Brenders

YEAR ISSUE	EDITION LIMIT	YEAR RETD.	ISSUE PRICE	*QUOTE U.S.$
1998 Fox Family Den CS366	25,000		45.00	45
1999 Wolf Family Lair CS368	25,000		45.00	45
2000 Bear Family Cave CS369	25,000		45.00	45

Animals of the Seven Continents Series-Collector Edition - J. Turgeon

YEAR ISSUE	EDITION LIMIT	YEAR RETD.	ISSUE PRICE	*QUOTE U.S.$
1997 Africa CS308	100,000		49.00	49
1998 Australia CS339	100,000		49.00	49
1999 Asia CS349	100,000		49.00	49
2000 Antartica CS377	100,000		49.00	49

Archives Series-Collector Edition - D. Langeneckert

YEAR ISSUE	EDITION LIMIT	YEAR RETD.	ISSUE PRICE	*QUOTE U.S.$
1992 1893 Columbian Exposition CS169	75,000	1995	35.00	28-95
1993 Ganymede CS190	Retrd.	1995	35.00	95-200
1994 Budweiser's Greatest Triumph CS222	75,000	1996	35.00	40-80
1995 Mirror of Truth CS252	75,000		35.00	35

Birds of Prey Series-Premier Edition - P. Ford

YEAR ISSUE	EDITION LIMIT	YEAR RETD.	ISSUE PRICE	*QUOTE U.S.$
1991 American Bald Eagle CS164	25,000	1995	125.00	115-175
1992 Peregrine Falcon CS183	25,000	1996	125.00	99-175
1994 Osprey CS212	Retrd.	1994	135.00	675-950
1995 Great Horned Owl CS264	25,000	1997	137.00	99-175

Bud Label Series-Giftware Edition - A-Busch, Inc.

YEAR ISSUE	EDITION LIMIT	YEAR RETD.	ISSUE PRICE	*QUOTE U.S.$
1989 Budweiser Label CS101	Retrd.	1995	14.00	14-40
1990 Antique Label II CS127	Retrd.	1994	14.00	20-35
1991 Bottled Beer III CS136	Retrd.	1995	15.00	20-50
1995 Budweiser Label CS282	Open		19.50	20
2000 Budweiser Millennium Label CS423	Open		23.00	23

Budweiser Anglers Edition Series-Giftware Edition - D. Kueker

YEAR ISSUE	EDITION LIMIT	YEAR RETD.	ISSUE PRICE	*QUOTE U.S.$
1998 Largemouth Bass CS270	Open		24.95	25
1999 Rainbow Trout CS338	Open		24.95	25
2000 Crappie CS412	Open		24.95	25

Budweiser Classic Car Series-Collector Edition - M. Watts

YEAR ISSUE	EDITION LIMIT	YEAR RETD.	ISSUE PRICE	*QUOTE U.S.$
1998 1957 Chevolet Bel Air CS304	50,000		49.00	49
1999 1957 Chevy Corvette CS340	50,000		49.00	49
1999 '59 Cadillac Eldorado CS403	50,000		49.00	49
2000 '48 Buick Roadmaster CS418	50,000		49.00	49

Budweiser Holiday Series - Various

YEAR ISSUE	EDITION LIMIT	YEAR RETD.	ISSUE PRICE	*QUOTE U.S.$
1980 1st-Budweiser Champion Clydesdales CS19 - A-Busch, Inc.	Retrd.	N/A	9.95	95-185
1981 1st-Budweiser Champion Clydesdales CS19A - A-Busch, Inc.	Retrd.	N/A	N/A	175-250
1981 2nd-Snowy Woodland CS50 - A-Busch, Inc.	Retrd.	N/A	9.95	175-325
1982 3rd-50th Anniversary CS57 - A-Busch, Inc.	Retrd.	N/A	9.95	60-100
1983 4th-Cameo Wheatland CS58 - A-Busch, Inc.	Retrd.	N/A	9.95	29-50
1984 5th-Covered Bridge CS62 - A-Busch, Inc.	Retrd.	N/A	9.95	15-49
1985 6th-Snow Capped Mountains CS63 - A-Busch, Inc.	Retrd.	N/A	9.95	15-49
1986 7th-Traditional Horses CS66 - A-Busch, Inc.	Retrd.	N/A	9.95	25-49
1987 8th-Grant's Farm Gates CS70 - A-Busch, Inc.	Retrd.	N/A	9.95	18-60
1988 9th-Cobblestone Passage CS88 - A-Busch, Inc.	Retrd.	N/A	9.95	20-39
1989 10th-Winter Evening CS89 - A-Busch, Inc.	Retrd.	N/A	12.95	10-30
1990 11th-An American Tradition, CS112, 1990 - S. Sampson	Retrd.	N/A	13.50	9-30
1990 11th-An American Tradition, CS112-SE, 1990 - S. Sampson	Retrd.	N/A	50.00	29-69
1991 12th-The Season's Best, CS133, 1991 - S. Sampson	Retrd.	N/A	14.50	9-30
1991 12th-The Season's Best, CS133-SE Signature Edition, 1991 - S. Sampson	Retrd.	N/A	50.00	29-69
1992 13th-The Perfect Christmas, CS167, 1992 - S. Sampson	Retrd.	N/A	14.50	12-30
1992 13th-The Perfect Christmas, CS167-SE Signature Edition, 1992 - S. Sampson	10,000	N/A	50.00	29-69
1993 14th-Special Delivery, CS192, 1993 - N. Koerber	Retrd.	N/A	15.00	15-59
1993 14th-Special Delivery, CS192-SE Signature Edition, 1993 - N. Koerber	10,000	N/A	60.00	95-140
1994 15th-Hometown Holiday, CS211, 1994 - B. Kemper	Retrd.	1994	14.00	10-25
1994 15th-Hometown Holiday, CS211 -SE Signature Edition, 1994 - B. Kemper	10,000	1994	65.00	85-140
1995 16th-Lighting the Way Home, CS263 - T. Jester	Retrd.	1997	17.00	10-25
1995 16th-Lighting the Way Home, CS263-SE Signature Edition - T. Jester	10,000	1995	75.00	75-125
1996 17th-Budweiser Clydesdales, CS273 - J. Raedeke	Retrd.	1998	17.00	13-20
1996 17th-Budweiser Clydesdales, CS273-SE Signature Edition - J. Raedeke	10,000	1996	75.00	75-100
1997 18th-Home For The Holidays, CS313 - H. Droog	Retrd.	1999	19.00	15-25
1997 18th-Home For The Holidays, CS313-SE Signature Edition - H. Droog	20,000		75.00	58-75
1998 19th-Grant's Farm Holiday, CS343 - E. Kastaris	Retrd.	1999	19.00	14-22
1998 19th-Grant's Farm Holiday, CS343SE Signature Edition - E. Kastaris	15,000		75.00	58-75
1999 20th-A Century of Tradition, CS389 - G. Ciccarelli	Retrd.	2000	19.00	18-20
1999 20th-A Century of Tradition, CS389SE Signature Edition - G. Ciccarelli	15,000	2000	75.00	64-150
2000 21st-Holiday In The Mountains CS416- E. Kastaris	Open		19.00	19
2000 21st-Holiday In The Mountains CS416SE Signature Edition - E. Kastaris	10,000		75.00	75

Budweiser Military Series-Giftware Edition - M. Watts

YEAR ISSUE	EDITION LIMIT	YEAR RETD.	ISSUE PRICE	*QUOTE U.S.$
1994 Army CS224	Retrd.	1995	19.00	45-155
1994 Air Force CS228	Retrd.	1997	19.00	20-69
1995 Budweiser Salutes the Navy CS243	Retrd.	1997	19.50	20-69
1995 Marines CS256	Retrd.	1997	22.00	22-60
1997 Coast Guard CS294	Retrd.	1999	22.00	22-55

Budweiser Opera Card Series-Premier Collection - A-Busch, Inc.

YEAR ISSUE	EDITION LIMIT	YEAR RETD.	ISSUE PRICE	*QUOTE U.S.$
1997 "Martha" CS300	5,000		169.00	169
1998 "The Hugenhots" CS331	5,000		169.00	169
1999 "Siegfried" CS373	5,000		169.00	169

Budweiser Racing Series - H. Droog

YEAR ISSUE	EDITION LIMIT	YEAR RETD.	ISSUE PRICE	*QUOTE U.S.$
1993 Budweiser Racing Team CS194	Retrd.	1995	19.00	19-35
1993 Bill Elliott CS196	25,000	1995	150.00	110-150
1993 Bill Elliott, Signature Edition, CS196SE	1,500	1995	295.00	175-275

Budweiser Salutes The Fire Fighters Series-Giftware Edition - A-Busch, Inc.

YEAR ISSUE	EDITION LIMIT	YEAR RETD.	ISSUE PRICE	*QUOTE U.S.$
1997 Fire Fighter's Boot CS321	Open		32.00	32

Century In Review Series-Premier Collection - A-Busch, Inc., unless otherwise noted

YEAR ISSUE	EDITION LIMIT	YEAR RETD.	ISSUE PRICE	*QUOTE U.S.$
1997 1900-1919 CS311	5,000	1999	279.00	237-280
1998 1920-1939 CS335	5,000	1999	279.00	237-280
1999 1940-1959 CS342	5,000	2000	279.00	237-300
2000 1960-1979 CS383	5,000		279.00	279

Civil War Series-Premier Edition - D. Langeneckert

YEAR ISSUE	EDITION LIMIT	YEAR RETD.	ISSUE PRICE	*QUOTE U.S.$
1992 General Grant CS181	25,000	1995	150.00	95-200
1993 General Robert E. Lee CS188	25,000	1995	150.00	135-200
1993 President Abraham Lincoln CS189	25,000	1995	150.00	135-200

Classic Series - A-Busch, Inc.

YEAR ISSUE	EDITION LIMIT	YEAR RETD.	ISSUE PRICE	*QUOTE U.S.$
1988 1st Edition CS93	Retrd.	N/A	34.95	149-189
1989 2nd Edition CS104	Retrd.	N/A	54.95	95-170
1990 3rd Edition CS113	Retrd.	N/A	65.00	45-95
1991 4th Edition CS130	Retrd.	1994	75.00	45-105

Clydesdales Series-Giftware Edition - A-Busch, Inc., unless otherwise noted

YEAR ISSUE	EDITION LIMIT	YEAR RETD.	ISSUE PRICE	*QUOTE U.S.$
1987 World Famous Clydesdales CS74	Retrd.	N/A	9.95	25-45
1988 Mare & Foal CS90	Retrd.	N/A	11.50	40-85
1989 Parade Dress CS99	Retrd.	N/A	11.50	65-100
1991 Training Hitch CS131	Retrd.	1993	13.00	20-45
1992 Clydesdales on Parade CS161	Retrd.	1994	16.00	25-55
1994 Proud and Free CS223	Retrd.	1997	17.00	15-45
1996 Budweiser Clydesdale Hitch CS292	Retrd.	2000	22.50	20-32
1999 Clydesdales At Home CS386 - J. Wainright	Open		28.00	28

*Quotes have been rounded up to nearest dollar

Collector Edition - A-Busch, Inc., unless otherwise noted

YEAR ISSUE	EDITION LIMIT	YEAR RETD.	ISSUE PRICE	*QUOTE U.S.$
1994 Budweiser World Cup CS230 - J. Tull	25,000	1994	40.00	50-95
1997 The Official 1998 Olympic Winter Games CS350	Retrd.	1998	50.00	45-55
1998 Bald Eagle Character CS326	50,000		99.00	50-100
1998 NASCAR 50th Anniversary CS360 - J. Wainright	25,000	1998	60.00	50-125
1998 Ohio University CS363 - D. Thompson	Open		59.95	60
1999 Celebrating The Millennium CS414 - D. Curran	10,000		150.00	150
1999 Kenny Bernstein Anniversary CS406 - C. Hayes	20,000		50.00	50
2000 Separated at Birth CS421 - H. Droog	25,000		40.00	40
2000 Dale Earnhardt Jr. CS450 - J. Wainwright	25,000		75.00	75

Discover America Series-Collector Edition - A-Busch, Inc.

YEAR ISSUE	EDITION LIMIT	YEAR RETD.	ISSUE PRICE	*QUOTE U.S.$
1990 Nina CS107	100,000	1995	40.00	35-42
1991 Pinta CS129	100,000	1995	40.00	35-75
1992 Santa Maria CS138	100,000	1995	40.00	35-75

Ducks Unlimited, Waterfowl Flyway Series-Collector Edition - A. LaMay

YEAR ISSUE	EDITION LIMIT	YEAR RETD.	ISSUE PRICE	*QUOTE U.S.$
1999 Mississippi Flyway CS384	25,000		50.00	50
1999 Pacific Flyway CS397	25,000		50.00	50
2000 Central Flyway CS410	25,000		50.00	50
2000 Atlanta Flyway CS429	25,000		50.00	50

Endangered Species Series-Collector Edition - B. Kemper

YEAR ISSUE	EDITION LIMIT	YEAR RETD.	ISSUE PRICE	*QUOTE U.S.$
1989 Bald Eagle CS106 (First)	100,000	N/A	24.95	245-600
1990 Asian Tiger CS126 (Second)	100,000	1993	27.50	100-139
1991 African Elephant CS135 (Third)	100,000	1995	29.00	35-75
1992 Giant Panda CS173 (Fourth)	100,000	1996	29.00	50-70
1993 Grizzly CS199 (Fifth)	100,000	1996	29.50	30-60
1994 Gray Wolf CS226 (Sixth)	100,000	1997	29.50	24-60
1995 Cougar CS253 (Seventh)	100,000		32.00	32
1996 Gorilla CS283 (Eighth)	100,000		32.00	32

German Holiday Series-Premier Collection - A-Busch, Inc.

YEAR ISSUE	EDITION LIMIT	YEAR RETD.	ISSUE PRICE	*QUOTE U.S.$
1999 St. Nicholas CS413	5,000		150.00	150

Giftware Edition - A-Busch, Inc.

YEAR ISSUE	EDITION LIMIT	YEAR RETD.	ISSUE PRICE	*QUOTE U.S.$
1992 1992 Rodeo CS184	Retrd.	N/A	18.00	16-29
1993 Bud Man Character CS213	Retrd.	1996	45.00	50-150
1994 "Fore!" Budweiser Golf Bag CS225	Retrd.	1995	16.00	16-40
1994 "Walking Tall" Budweiser Cowboy Boot CS251	Retrd.	1998	17.50	18-29
1995 "Play Ball" Baseball Mitt CS244	Open		18.00	18
1995 Billiards CS278	Open		24.00	24
1995 Bud K. Schrader N5054	Retrd.	1997	25.00	25-39
1996 BUD-WEIS-ER Frog CS289	Retrd.	2000	27.95	28-35
1996 Indianapolis 500 N6003	Retrd.	1999	25.00	25-39
1996 "STRIKE" Bowling CS288	Open		24.50	25
1997 Budweiser Salutes Dad CS298	Open		19.95	20
1997 "Let Freedom Ring" CS305	Open		24.95	25
1997 Budweiser Tool Belt CS320	Open		29.95	30
1997 Budweiser Boxing Glove CS322	Open		35.00	35
1998 Budweiser Black Cowboy Boot CS347	Open		20.00	20
1998 Budweiser Golf Bag II CS362	Retrd.	1999	24.95	23-25
1998 The Budweiser Lizards Louie & Frank CS372	Open		29.50	30
2000 Ferret Takes Center Stage CS422	Open		29.50	30

Great Cities of Germany Series-Premier Collection - A-Busch, Inc.

YEAR ISSUE	EDITION LIMIT	YEAR RETD.	ISSUE PRICE	*QUOTE U.S.$
1997 Berlin CS328	5,000		139.00	139
1998 Munich CS346	5,000		139.00	139
1999 Cologne CS388	5,000		139.00	139

Historic Budweiser Advertising-Giftware Edition - A. Busch, Inc.

YEAR ISSUE	EDITION LIMIT	YEAR RETD.	ISSUE PRICE	*QUOTE U.S.$
1998 Stein and Tin I CS359	Open		36.00	36
1999 Stein and Tin II CS390	Open		36.00	36
2000 Stein and Tin III CS408	Open		36.00	36

Historical Landmark Series - A-Busch, Inc.

YEAR ISSUE	EDITION LIMIT	YEAR RETD.	ISSUE PRICE	*QUOTE U.S.$
1986 Brew House CS67 (First)	Retrd.	N/A	19.95	35-75
1987 Stables CS73 (Second)	Retrd.	1992	19.95	30-75
1988 Grant Cabin CS83 (Third)	Retrd.	N/A	19.95	20-125
1988 Old School House CS84 (Fourth)	Retrd.	1992	19.95	25-75

Honoring Tradition & Courage Series-Collector Edition - C. Hayes

YEAR ISSUE	EDITION LIMIT	YEAR RETD.	ISSUE PRICE	*QUOTE U.S.$
1999 Army CS357	50,000		35.00	35
1999 Air Force CS378	50,000		35.00	35
2000 Navy CS381	50,000		35.00	35
2000 Marines CS398	50,000		35.00	35

Horseshoe Series - A-Busch, Inc.

YEAR ISSUE	EDITION LIMIT	YEAR RETD.	ISSUE PRICE	*QUOTE U.S.$
1986 Horseshoe CS68	Retrd.	N/A	14.95	45-75
1987 Horsehead CS76	Retrd.	N/A	16.00	35-78
1987 Horseshoe CS77	Retrd.	N/A	16.00	35-70
1987 Horsehead CS78	Retrd.	N/A	14.95	50-79
1988 Harness CS94	Retrd.	N/A	16.00	60-110

Hunter's Companion Series-Collector Edition - Various

YEAR ISSUE	EDITION LIMIT	YEAR RETD.	ISSUE PRICE	*QUOTE U.S.$
1993 Labrador Retriever CS195 - L. Freeman	50,000	1996	32.50	49-150
1994 The Setter CS205 - S. Ryan	50,000	1996	32.50	35-75
1995 The Golden Retreiver CS248 - S. Ryan	50,000	1998	34.00	35-60
1996 Beagle CS272 - S. Ryan	50,000		35.00	35
1997 Springer Spaniel CS296 - S. Ryan	50,000		35.00	35

Limited Edition Series - A-Busch, Inc.

YEAR ISSUE	EDITION LIMIT	YEAR RETD.	ISSUE PRICE	*QUOTE U.S.$
1985 Ltd. Ed. I Brewing & Fermenting CS64	Retrd.	N/A	29.95	125-195
1986 Ltd. Ed. II Aging & Cooperage CS65	Retrd.	N/A	29.95	50-100
1987 Ltd. Ed. III Transportation CS71	Retrd.	N/A	29.95	50-75
1988 Ltd. Ed. IV Taverns & Public Houses CS75	Retrd.	1994	29.95	30-75
1989 Ltd. Ed.V Festival Scene CS98	Retrd.	1994	34.95	39-55

Logo Series Steins-Giftware Edition - A-Busch, Inc.

YEAR ISSUE	EDITION LIMIT	YEAR RETD.	ISSUE PRICE	*QUOTE U.S.$
1990 Budweiser CS143	Retrd.	N/A	16.00	10-20
1990 Bud Light CS144	Retrd.	N/A	16.00	10-20
1990 Michelob CS145	Retrd.	1993	16.00	10-20
1990 Michelob Dry CS146	Retrd.	1994	16.00	10-20
1990 Busch CS147	Retrd.	N/A	16.00	10-20
1990 A&Eagle CS148	Retrd.	N/A	16.00	10-20
1990 Bud Dry CS156	Retrd.	N/A	16.00	10-20

Man's Best Friend Series-Collector Edition - S. Ryan

YEAR ISSUE	EDITION LIMIT	YEAR RETD.	ISSUE PRICE	*QUOTE U.S.$
2000 Labrador CS379	25,000		45.00	45

Marine Conservation Series-Collector Edition - B. Kemper

YEAR ISSUE	EDITION LIMIT	YEAR RETD.	ISSUE PRICE	*QUOTE U.S.$
1994 Manatee CS203	25,000	1997	33.50	35-75
1995 Great White Shark CS247	25,000	1999	39.50	36-50
1996 Dolphin CS284	25,000		39.50	40

Michelob PGA Tour Series-Collector Edition - A. Leon

YEAR ISSUE	EDITION LIMIT	YEAR RETD.	ISSUE PRICE	*QUOTE U.S.$
1997 TPC at Sawgrass CS299	10,000		59.95	60
1998 TPC of Scottsdale CS329	10,000		59.95	60
1999 TPC of Tampa Bay CS380	10,000		59.95	60

NHL Team Steins - A-Busch, Inc.

YEAR ISSUE	EDITION LIMIT	YEAR RETD.	ISSUE PRICE	*QUOTE U.S.$
1998 Boston Bruins CS382BOS	50,000		42.00	42
1998 Chicago Blackhawks CS382CHI	50,000		42.00	42
1998 Detroit Red Wings CS382DET	50,000		42.00	42
1998 Florida Panthers CS382FLA	50,000		42.00	42
1998 New York Islanders CS382NYI	50,000		42.00	42
1998 New York Rangers CS382NYR	50,000		42.00	42
1998 Philadelphia Flyers CS382PHI	50,000		42.00	42
1998 Pittsburgh Penguins CS382PIT	50,000		42.00	42
1998 St. Louis Blues CS382STL	50,000		42.00	42
1998 Tampa Bay Lightning CS382TBL	50,000		42.00	42

Oktoberfest Series-Giftware Edition - A-Busch, Inc.

YEAR ISSUE	EDITION LIMIT	YEAR RETD.	ISSUE PRICE	*QUOTE U.S.$
1991 1991 Oktoberfest N3286	25,000	N/A	19.00	25-35
1992 1992 Oktoberfest CS185	35,000	1996	16.00	16-30
1993 1993 Oktoberfest CS202	35,000	1995	18.00	19-49
1996 1996 Oktoberfest CS291	Open		24.95	25

Olympic Centennial Collection - A-Busch, Inc.

YEAR ISSUE	EDITION LIMIT	YEAR RETD.	ISSUE PRICE	*QUOTE U.S.$
1995 1996 U.S. Olympic Team "Gymnastics" CS262	10,000	1998	85.00	50-85
1995 1996 U.S. Olympic Team "Track & Field" CS246	10,000	1998	85.00	50-85
1995 Bud Atlanta 1996 CS249	Retrd.	N/A	17.00	13-25
1995 Centennial Olympic Games Giftware CS266	Retrd.	1997	25.00	15-25
1995 Centennial Olympic Games Premier Edition 22" CS267	1,996	1996	500.00	850-1000
1995 Collector's Edition Official Centennial Olympic Games CS259	Retrd.	1996	50.00	45-75

Olympic Team Series 1992-Collector Edition - A-Busch, Inc.

YEAR ISSUE	EDITION LIMIT	YEAR RETD.	ISSUE PRICE	*QUOTE U.S.$
1991 1992 Winter Olympic CS162	25,000	N/A	85.00	30-75
1992 1992 Summer Olympic CS163	Retrd.	1994	85.00	40-75
1992 1992 U.S.Olympic CS168	50,000	N/A	16.00	10-20

Porcelain Heritage Series-Premier Edition - Various

YEAR ISSUE	EDITION LIMIT	YEAR RETD.	ISSUE PRICE	*QUOTE U.S.$
1990 Berninghaus CS105 - Berninghaus	Retrd.	1994	75.00	75-85
1991 After The Hunt CS155 - A-Busch, Inc.	Retrd.	1994	100.00	65-85
1992 Cherub CS182 - D. Langeneckert	25,000	1996	100.00	75-150

Post Convention Series - A-Busch, Inc.

YEAR ISSUE	EDITION LIMIT	YEAR RETD.	ISSUE PRICE	*QUOTE U.S.$
1982 1st Post Convention Olympic CS53	23,000	1982	N/A	100-185
1982 2nd Post Convention Olympic CS54	23,000	1982	N/A	75-175
1982 3rd Post Convention Olympic CS55	23,000	1982	N/A	100-195
1988 1st Post Convention Heritage CS87	25,000	1988	N/A	50-125
1988 2nd Post Convention Heritage CS102	25,000	1988	N/A	50-125
1989 3rd Post Convention Heritage CS114	25,000	1989	N/A	50-125
1990 4th Post Convention Heritage CS141	25,000	1990	N/A	50-125
1991 5th/Final Post Convention Heritage CS174	25,000	1991	N/A	25-125
1992 1st Advertising Through the Decades 1879-1912 N3989	29,000	1992	N/A	45-75
1994 2nd Advertising Through the Decades 1905-1914 N3990	31,106	1993	N/A	45-75
1995 3rd Advertising Through the Decades 1911-1915 SO85203	31,000	1994	N/A	35-75
1996 4th Advertising Through the Decades 1918-1922 SO95150	31,000	1995	N/A	35-75
1997 5th Advertising Through the Decades 1933-1938 SO95248	31,000	1996	N/A	75-95

Premier Collection - A-Busch, Inc., unless otherwise noted

YEAR ISSUE	EDITION LIMIT	YEAR RETD.	ISSUE PRICE	*QUOTE U.S.$
1997 Bud Ice Penguin Character CS315	10,000		199.00	199
1997 Budweiser Frog Character CS301	10,000	2000	219.00	185-219
1997 Louie The Lizard Character CS344	25,000	1999	99.00	84-109
1998 World Cup Soccer CS351	10,000	1999	99.00	65-125
1999 Frankenstein™ Character CS323	10,000		125.00	125
1999 Bud Man 30th Anniversary Character CS401	25,000		100.00	100
1999 Dalmatian Character CS324	10,000		220.00	220
1999 One Thousand Years of Progress, 2000 A.D. - J. Wainwright	2,000	1999	800.00	795-900

Sea World Series-Collector Edition - A-Busch, Inc.

YEAR ISSUE	EDITION LIMIT	YEAR RETD.	ISSUE PRICE	*QUOTE U.S.$
1992 Killer Whale CS186	25,000	1996	100.00	85-100
1992 Dolphin CS187	22,500	1996	90.00	65-85

Specialty Steins - A-Busch, Inc.

YEAR ISSUE	EDITION LIMIT	YEAR RETD.	ISSUE PRICE	*QUOTE U.S.$
1975 Bud Man CS1	Retrd.	N/A	N/A	400-630
1976 A&Eagle CS2	Retrd.	N/A	N/A	125-150
1976 A&Eagle Lidded CSL2 (Reference CS28)	Retrd.	N/A	N/A	176-225
1976 Katakombe CS3	Retrd.	N/A	N/A	225-259
1976 Katakombe Lidded CSL3	Retrd.	N/A	N/A	295-350
1976 German Tavern Scene Lidded CS4	Retrd.	N/A	N/A	49-75
1975 Senior Grande Lidded CSL4	Retrd.	N/A	N/A	650-790
1975 German Pilique CS5	Retrd.	N/A	N/A	350-450
1976 German Pilique Lidded CSL5	Retrd.	N/A	N/A	400-550
1976 Senior Grande CS6	Retrd.	N/A	N/A	500-650
1975 German Tavern Scene CSL6	Retrd.	N/A	N/A	195-250
1975 Miniature Bavarian CS7	Retrd.	N/A	N/A	200-695
1976 Budweiser Centennial Lidded CSL7	Retrd.	N/A	N/A	295-395
1976 U.S. Bicentennial Lidded CSL8	Retrd.	N/A	N/A	325-395
1976 Natural Light CS9	Retrd.	N/A	N/A	200-300
1976 Clydesdales Hofbrau Lidded CSL9	Retrd.	N/A	N/A	179-249
1976 Blue Delft CS11	Retrd.	N/A	N/A	1200-1520
1976 Clydesdales CS12	Retrd.	N/A	N/A	300
1976 Budweiser Centennial CS13	Retrd.	N/A	N/A	225-350
1976 U.S. Bicentennial CS14	Retrd.	N/A	N/A	300-350
1976 Clydesdales Grants Farm CS15	Retrd.	N/A	N/A	145-215
1976 German Cities (6 assorted) CS16	Retrd.	N/A	N/A	1410-1500
1976 Americana CS17	Retrd.	N/A	N/A	225-300
1976 Budweiser Label CS18	Retrd.	N/A	N/A	450-595
1980 Budweiser Ladies (4 assorted) CS20	Retrd.	N/A	N/A	1200-1308
1977 Budweiser Girl CS21	Retrd.	N/A	N/A	350-375
1976 Budweiser Centennial CS22	Retrd.	N/A	N/A	245-285
1977 A&Eagle CS24	Retrd.	N/A	N/A	360-395
1976 A&Eagle Barrel CS26	Retrd.	N/A	N/A	95-125
1976 Michelob CS27	Retrd.	N/A	N/A	139-150
1976 A&Eagle Lidded CS28 (Reference CSL2)	Retrd.	N/A	N/A	195-200
1976 Clydesdales Lidded CS29	Retrd.	N/A	N/A	175-225
1976 Coracao Decanter Set (7 piece) CS31	Retrd.	N/A	N/A	492-500
1976 German Wine Set (7 piece) CS32	Retrd.	N/A	N/A	450-550
1976 Clydesdales Decanter CS33	Retrd.	N/A	N/A	980-1600
1976 Holanda Brown Decanter Set (7 piece) CS34	Retrd.	N/A	N/A	1012-1250
1976 Holanda Blue Decanter Set (7 piece) CS35	Retrd.	N/A	N/A	415-750
1976 Canteen Decanter Set (7 piece) CS36	Retrd.	N/A	N/A	500-890
1976 St. Louis Decanter CS37	Retrd.	N/A	N/A	275-300
1976 St. Louis Decanter Set (7 piece) CS38	Retrd.	N/A	N/A	900-1022
1980 Wurzburger Hofbrau CS39	Retrd.	N/A	N/A	275-300
1980 Budweiser Chicago Skyline CS40	Retrd.	N/A	N/A	79-149
1978 Busch Gardens CS41	Retrd.	N/A	N/A	195-219
1980 Oktoberfest - "The Old Country" CS42	Retrd.	N/A	N/A	175-250
1980 Natural Light Label CS43	Retrd.	N/A	N/A	225-300
1980 Busch Label CS44	Retrd.	N/A	N/A	225-250
1980 Michelob Label CS45	Retrd.	N/A	N/A	45-69
1980 Budweiser Label CS46	Retrd.	N/A	N/A	60-100
1981 Budweiser Chicagoland CS51	Retrd.	N/A	N/A	29-75
1981 Budweiser Texas CS52	Retrd.	N/A	N/A	39-60
1981 Budweiser California CS56	Retrd.	N/A	N/A	39-60
1983 Budweiser San Francisco CS59	Retrd.	N/A	N/A	150-195
1984 Budweiser 1984 Summer Olympic Games CS60	Retrd.	N/A	N/A	10-19
1983 Bud Light Baron CS61	Retrd.	N/A	N/A	30-55
1987 Santa Claus CS79	Retrd.	N/A	N/A	50-125
1987 King Cobra CS80	Retrd.	N/A	N/A	105-395
1987 Winter Olympic Games, Lidded CS81	Retrd.	N/A	49.95	30-105
1988 Budweiser Winter Olympic Games CS85	Retrd.	N/A	24.95	10-25
1988 Summer Olympic Games, Lidded CS91	Retrd.	N/A	54.95	18-80
1988 Budweiser Summer Olympic Games CS92	Retrd.	N/A	54.95	20-40
1988 Budweiser/ Field&Stream Set (4 piece) CS95	Retrd.	N/A	69.95	225-295
1989 Bud Man CS100	Retrd.	1993	29.95	65-125
1990 Baseball Cardinal CS125	Retrd.	N/A	30.00	45-75
1991 Bevo Fox Stein CS160	Retrd.	1994	250.00	180-279
1992 Budweiser Racing-Elliot/Johnson N3553 - M. Watts	Retrd.	1995	19.00	15-35

Sports Action Series-Giftware Edition - J. Whitney

YEAR ISSUE	EDITION LIMIT	YEAR RETD.	ISSUE PRICE	*QUOTE U.S.$
1997 "Play Ball" Budweiser Baseball CS295	Open		29.00	29
1998 "Touchdown!" Budweiser Football CS325	Retrd.	1999	29.00	25-29
1998 "Swish!" Basketball CS333	Open		29.00	29

Sports History Series-Giftware Edition - A-Busch, Inc.

YEAR ISSUE	EDITION LIMIT	YEAR RETD.	ISSUE PRICE	*QUOTE U.S.$
1990 Baseball, America's Favorite Pastime CS124	100,000	1992	20.00	15-40
1990 Football, Gridiron Legacy CS128	100,000	1994	20.00	15-40
1991 Auto Racing, Chasing The Checkered Flag CS132	100,000	1995	22.00	15-40
1991 Basketball, Heroes of the Hardwood CS134	100,000	1995	22.00	12-40
1992 Golf, Par For The Course CS165	100,000	1995	22.00	15-65
1993 Hockey, Center Ice CS209	100,000	N/A	22.00	15-36

*Quotes have been rounded up to nearest dollar

STEINS/JUGS

Sports Legend Series-Collector Edition - Various

YEAR ISSUE	EDITION LIMIT	YEAR RETD.	ISSUE PRICE	*QUOTE U.S.$
1991 Babe Ruth CS142 - A-Busch	50,000	1995	85.00	70-95
1992 Jim Thorpe CS171 - M. Caito	50,000	1995	85.00	70-95
1993 Joe Louis CS206 - M. Caito	Retrd.	1994	85.00	85-155

St. Patrick's Day Series-Giftware Edition - A-Busch, Inc., unless otherwise noted

YEAR ISSUE	EDITION LIMIT	YEAR RETD.	ISSUE PRICE	*QUOTE U.S.$
1991 1991 St. Patrick's Day CS109	Retrd.	N/A	15.00	55-75
1992 1992 St. Patrick's Day CS166	100,000	N/A	15.00	15-39
1993 1993 St. Patrick's Day CS193	Retrd.	N/A	15.30	20-65
1994 Luck O' The Irish CS210	Retrd.	1995	18.00	15-45
1995 1995 St. Patrick's Day CS242	Retrd.	1995	19.00	15-45
1996 "Horseshoe" 1996 St. Patrick's Day CS269	Open		19.50	20
1997 Luck O' The Longneck 1997 St. Patrick's Day CS287	Open		21.95	22
1998 Erin Go Budweiser 1998 St. Patrick's Day CS332	Open		22.95	23
1999 "The Bud That Got Away" 1999 St. Patrick's Day CS385	Open		24.00	24
2000 "Leapin' Leprechauns" 2000 St. Patrick's Day CS411 - T. Buttner	Open		24.00	24

Upland Game Birds Series-Collector Edition - P. Ford

YEAR ISSUE	EDITION LIMIT	YEAR RETD.	ISSUE PRICE	*QUOTE U.S.$
1997 Ruffed Grouse CS316	5,000	1997	75.00	64-149
1997 Pheasant CS319	5,000	1997	75.00	68-149
1998 Turkey CS327	5,000	1998	75.00	80-149
1998 Prairie Chicken CS337	5,000	1998	75.00	80-110

Working America Series-Premier Collection - A-Busch, Inc.

YEAR ISSUE	EDITION LIMIT	YEAR RETD.	ISSUE PRICE	*QUOTE U.S.$
1997 The American Worker I CS318	10,000		209.00	209
1998 The American Worker II CS336	10,000		209.00	209
1999 The American Worker III CS353	10,000		209.00	209

Anheuser-Busch, Inc./Meisterwerke Collection

American Heritage Collection - Gerz

YEAR ISSUE	EDITION LIMIT	YEAR RETD.	ISSUE PRICE	*QUOTE U.S.$
1993 John F. Kennedy GM4	10,000		220.00	220

Animals of the Prairie Series - N. Glazier

YEAR ISSUE	EDITION LIMIT	YEAR RETD.	ISSUE PRICE	*QUOTE U.S.$
1997 Buffalo GL11	5,000	1997	149.00	118-175
1998 Wild Mustang GL15	5,000	1998	149.00	139-160
1999 Mule Deer GL19	5,000		149.00	149
2000 Elk GL20	5,000		149.00	149

Collectorwerke - Various

YEAR ISSUE	EDITION LIMIT	YEAR RETD.	ISSUE PRICE	*QUOTE U.S.$
1993 The Dugout Stein GL1 - A-Busch, Inc.	10,000		110.00	110
1994 Winchester Stein GL2 - A-Busch, Inc.	10,000	1995	120.00	95-150
1995 "Saturday Evening Post" Christmas #1 GL5 - J.C. Leyendecker	5,000	1999	105.00	90-105
1996 "Saturday Evening Post" Christmas #2 GL6 - A-Busch, Inc.	5,000	1997	105.00	89-139
1997 "Saturday Evening Post" Christmas #3 GL13 - J.C. Leyendecker	5,000		105.00	105

Collectorwerke-Call of the Wild Series - J. Rideout

YEAR ISSUE	EDITION LIMIT	YEAR RETD.	ISSUE PRICE	*QUOTE U.S.$
1996 Wolf GL9	10,000		139.00	139
1997 Grizzly GL12	10,000	1999	139.00	108-139
1998 Mountain Lion GL17	10,000		139.00	139

Meisterwerke Collection - A-Busch, Inc.

YEAR ISSUE	EDITION LIMIT	YEAR RETD.	ISSUE PRICE	*QUOTE U.S.$
1994 Norman Rockwell-Triple Self Portrait GM6	5,000	1997	250.00	189-250
1994 Mallard Stein GM7	5,000	1996	220.00	129-250
1994 Winchester "Model 94" Centennial GM10	5,000	2000	150.00	135-175
1995 Giant Panda GM8	3,500	1997	210.00	129-250
1995 Rosie the Riveter GM9	5,000	1997	165.00	125-175
1997 Norman Rockwell-Do Unto Others GM21	7,500		189.00	189

Meisterwerke-Early Transporation Series - T. MacDonald

YEAR ISSUE	EDITION LIMIT	YEAR RETD.	ISSUE PRICE	*QUOTE U.S.$
1997 Train GM28	5,000	1999	179.00	145-179
1998 Train II GM29	5,000	1999	179.00	145-179
2000 Train III GM30	5,000		179.00	179

Meisterwerke-First Hunt Series - P. Ford

YEAR ISSUE	EDITION LIMIT	YEAR RETD.	ISSUE PRICE	*QUOTE U.S.$
1992 Golden Retriever GM2	10,000	1999	150.00	79-190
1994 Springer Spaniel GM5	10,000		190.00	190
1995 Pointer GM16	10,000	1997	190.00	125-190
1995 Labrador GM17	10,000	1998	190.00	125-190

Meisterwerke-Holidays Through the Decades - A-Busch, Inc.

YEAR ISSUE	EDITION LIMIT	YEAR RETD.	ISSUE PRICE	*QUOTE U.S.$
1996 Holidays: Decade of the 30's GM18	3,500	1997	169.00	115-169
1997 Holidays: Decade of the 40's GM23	3,500		169.00	169
1998 Holidays: Decade of the 50's GM26	3,500	1999	169.00	135-169

Meisterwerke-Winchester Hunt Series - A-Busch, Inc.

YEAR ISSUE	EDITION LIMIT	YEAR RETD.	ISSUE PRICE	*QUOTE U.S.$
1996 Pheasant Hunt GM20	3,500	1997	215.00	150-225
1997 Duck Hunt GM24	3,500		215.00	215
1998 Quail Hunt GM27	3,500		215.00	215

Meisterwerke-Winchester Rodeo Series - A-Busch, Inc.

YEAR ISSUE	EDITION LIMIT	YEAR RETD.	ISSUE PRICE	*QUOTE U.S.$
1996 Rodeo Calf Roping GM19	5,000		179.00	179
1997 Rodeo Bull Riding GM22	5,000	1998	179.00	152-185
1998 Saddle Bronc Riding GM25	5,000		179.00	179

Saturday Evening Post Collection - J.C. Leyendecker

YEAR ISSUE	EDITION LIMIT	YEAR RETD.	ISSUE PRICE	*QUOTE U.S.$
1993 Santa's Mailbag GM1	Retrd.	1993	195.00	180-249
1993 Santa's Helper GM3	7,500		200.00	200
1994 "All I Want For Christmas" GM13	5,000	1997	220.00	149-160
1995 Fourth of July GM15	5,000	1998	180.00	125-180

Anheuser-Busch, Promotional Products Group/Licensed

Coca Cola - Various

YEAR ISSUE	EDITION LIMIT	YEAR RETD.	ISSUE PRICE	*QUOTE U.S.$
1999 COKE on Ice CS393 - D. Curran	Open		30.00	30
1999 Vintage Holiday Vending Machine CS392 - D. Curran	25,000		60.00	60
1999 Santa Character CS394	10,000		270.00	270

Coca Cola Early Illustrators Series - Various

YEAR ISSUE	EDITION LIMIT	YEAR RETD.	ISSUE PRICE	*QUOTE U.S.$
2000 First Edition CS400	25,000		55.00	55

Coca Cola Historical Slogans Series - Various

YEAR ISSUE	EDITION LIMIT	YEAR RETD.	ISSUE PRICE	*QUOTE U.S.$
2000 First Edition CS399	25,000		65.00	65
2000 Second Edition CS451	25,000		65.00	65

Coca Cola Holiday Series - Various

YEAR ISSUE	EDITION LIMIT	YEAR RETD.	ISSUE PRICE	*QUOTE U.S.$
1998 Candy Cane CS391 - J. Turgeon	25,000	1999	50.00	43-75
1999 Santa's Reward CS402	25,000		50.00	50

Elvis Presley - Various

YEAR ISSUE	EDITION LIMIT	YEAR RETD.	ISSUE PRICE	*QUOTE U.S.$
1999 '68 Comeback Special Collector Edition CS375	25,000		65.00	65
1999 '68 Comeback Special Giftware Edition CS374	Open		30.00	30
2000 Elvis Jukebox CS396	25,000		65.00	65

Cavanagh Group Intl.

Harley-Davidson - CGI

YEAR ISSUE	EDITION LIMIT	YEAR RETD.	ISSUE PRICE	*QUOTE U.S.$
1998 The American Dream	Open		60.00	60
1998 Engineer of the Road	Open		40.00	40
1998 Evolution	15,000		150.00	150
1998 Live to Ride, Ride to Live	Yr.Iss.	1998	90.00	90

Dave Grossman Creations

Emmett Kelly Sr. Mugs - Inspired by Emmett Kelly Sr.

YEAR ISSUE	EDITION LIMIT	YEAR RETD.	ISSUE PRICE	*QUOTE U.S.$
1986 I Don't Get No Respect EKM-1	Closed	1988	5.50	6
1986 I Love You EKM-2	Closed	1988	5.50	6
1986 The Tycoon EKM-3	Closed	1988	5.50	6
1986 You Look Marvelous EKM-4	Closed	1988	5.50	6

Three Stooges Collection - Dave Grossman Creations

YEAR ISSUE	EDITION LIMIT	YEAR RETD.	ISSUE PRICE	*QUOTE U.S.$
1998 Curly TSMUG-2	Closed	2000	15.00	15
199 Larry TSMUG-1	Closed	2000	15.00	15
1998 Moe TSMUG-3	Closed	2000	15.00	15

Hamilton Collection

Mickey Mantle - R. Tanenbaum

YEAR ISSUE	EDITION LIMIT	YEAR RETD.	ISSUE PRICE	*QUOTE U.S.$
1996 The Legendary Mickey Mantle	Open		39.95	40

The STAR TREK® Tankard Collection - T. Blackshear

YEAR ISSUE	EDITION LIMIT	YEAR RETD.	ISSUE PRICE	*QUOTE U.S.$
1995 U.S.S. Enterprise NCC-1701	Closed	1998	49.50	50
1994 SPOCK	Closed	1998	49.50	50
1995 Kirk	Closed	1998	49.50	50
1995 McCoy	Closed	1998	49.50	50
1995 Uhura	Closed	1998	49.50	50
1995 Scotty	Closed	1998	49.50	50
1995 Sulu	Closed	1998	49.50	50
1995 Chekov	Closed	1998	49.50	50

Warriors of the Plains Tankards - G. Stewart

YEAR ISSUE	EDITION LIMIT	YEAR RETD.	ISSUE PRICE	*QUOTE U.S.$
1995 Battle Grounds	Open		125.00	125
1992 Thundering Hooves	Open		125.00	125
1992 Warrior's Choice	Open		125.00	125
1992 Healing Spirits	Open		125.00	125

Royal Doulton

Character Jug of the Year - Various

YEAR ISSUE	EDITION LIMIT	YEAR RETD.	ISSUE PRICE	*QUOTE U.S.$
1991 Fortune Teller D6824 - S. Taylor	Closed	1991	130.00	225-350
1992 Winston Churchill D6907 - S. Taylor	Closed	1992	195.00	195-225
1993 Vice-Admiral Lord Nelson D6932 - S. Taylor	Closed	1993	225.00	225
1994 Captain Hook - M. Alcock	Closed	1994	235.00	235-525
1995 Captain Bligh D6967 - S. Taylor	Closed	1995	200.00	140-275
1996 Jesse Owens, lg. D7019 - S. Taylor	Closed	1996	225.00	225-255
1997 Count Dracula, lg. D7053 - D. Biggs	Closed	1997	235.00	250
1998 Lewis Carroll - D. Biggs	Closed	1998	195.00	195
1999 Shakespeare, lg. D7136 - R. Tabbenor	Yr.Iss.	1999	205.00	205-209
2000 Oscar Wilde, lg. D7146 - D. Biggs	Yr.Iss.		245.00	245

Character Jugs - Various

YEAR ISSUE	EDITION LIMIT	YEAR RETD.	ISSUE PRICE	*QUOTE U.S.$
1993 Abraham Lincoln - M. Alcock	2,500	1994	190.00	230-295
1991 Airman, sm. - W. Harper	Retrd.	1996	75.00	75-115
1996 Albert Einstein, lg.- S. Taylor	Retrd.	1996	225.00	250
1995 Alfred Hitchcock D6987 - D. Biggs	Retrd.	1997	200.00	238
1997 Angler, sm. - D. Biggs	Open		132.50	133
1990 Angler, sm. - S. Taylor	Retrd.	1995	82.50	83
1947 Beefeater, lg. - H. Fenton	Retrd.	1996	137.50	145-200
1947 Beefeater, sm. - H. Fenton	Retrd.	1996	75.00	40-138
1998 Captain Scott - D. Biggs	Retrd.	2000	195.00	195
1975 Catherine of Aragon, lg. D6643 - A. Maslankowski	Retrd.	1981	N/A	90-200
1981 Catherine Parr, lg. D6664 - M. Abberley	Retrd.	1989	N/A	175-195
1995 Charles Dickens D6939 - W. Harper	2,500	1997	500.00	500
1989 Clown, lg.- S. Taylor	Retrd.	1995	205.00	300-370
1991 Columbus, lg. 6891 - S. Taylor	Retrd.	1997	137.50	138-145
1995 Cyrano de Bergerac, lg. 7004 - D. Biggs	Retrd.	1997	200.00	210
1983 D'Artagnan, lg.- S. Taylor	Retrd.	1995	150.00	200
1983 D'Artagnan, sm.- S. Taylor	Retrd.	1995	82.50	149-175
1995 Dennis and Gnasher, lg.- S. Ward	Retrd.	1999	212.50	235
1995 Deperate Dan, lg.- S. Ward	Retrd.	1999	212.50	235
1991 Equestrian, sm.- S. Taylor	Retrd.	1995	82.50	83
1997 General Custer, lg.- S. Taylor	Retrd.	1999	237.50	238
1995 George Washington - M. Alcock	2,500	1995	200.00	225
1982 George Washington, lg. - S. Taylor	Retrd.	1994	150.00	140-195
1994 Glenn Miller - M. Alcock	Retrd.	1998	270.00	210-335
1971 Golfer, lg. - D. Biggs	Retrd.	1995	150.00	250
1997 Golfer, sm. - D. Biggs	Retrd.	1999	132.50	133
1993 Graduate-Male, sm.- S. Taylor	Retrd.	1995	85.00	85
1986 Guardsman, lg.- S. Taylor	Retrd.	1999	137.50	125-155
1986 Gurardsman, sm.- S. Taylor	Retrd.	1999	75.00	65-85
1990 Guy Fawkes, lg. - W. Harper	Retrd.	1996	137.50	125-138
1975 Henry VIII, lg. - E. Griffiths	Retrd.	2000	137.50	155
1975 Henry VIII, sm. - E. Griffiths	Retrd.	1999	75.00	85-115
1991 Jockey, sm.- S. Taylor	Retrd.	1995	82.50	83
1995 Judge and Thief Toby D6988 - S. Taylor	Retrd.	1998	185.00	225
1959 Lawyer, lg. - M. Henk	Retrd.	1996	137.50	175
1959 Lawyer, sm. - M. Henk	Retrd.	1996	75.00	50-90
1990 Leprechaun, lg. - W. Harper	Retrd.	1996	205.00	210-225
1990 Leprechaun, sm. - W. Harper	Retrd.	1996	75.00	85
1986 London Bobby, lg.- S. Taylor	Open		137.50	155
1986 London Bobby, sm.- S. Taylor	Open		75.00	85
1952 Long John Silver, lg. - M. Henk	Open		137.50	155
1952 Long John Silver, sm. - M. Henk	Open		75.00	85
2000 Lord Kitchner D7148 - D. Biggs	Open		310.00	310
1965 Mad Hatter, sm. D6602 - M. Henk	Retrd.	1983	N/A	100-195
1989 March Hare, lg. D6776 - W. Harper	Retrd.	1991	N/A	100-195
1960 Merlin, lg. - G. Sharpe	Retrd.	1998	137.50	145-150
1960 Merlin, sm. - G. Sharpe	Retrd.	1998	75.00	50-105
1990 Modern Golfer, sm.- S. Taylor	Retrd.	1999	75.00	83
1961 Old Salt, lg.- G. Sharpe	Open		137.50	155
1961 Old Salt, sm.- G. Sharpe	Open		75.00	85
1955 Rip Van Winkle, lg. - M. Henk	Retrd.	1995	150.00	125-150
1955 Rip Van Winkle, sm. - M. Henk	Retrd.	1995	82.50	55-90
1991 Sailor, sm. - W. Harper	Retrd.	1996	75.00	83
1984 Santa Claus, lg. - M. Abberley	Retrd.	2000	137.50	155
1984 Santa Claus, sm. - M. Abberley	Open		75.00	85
1993 Shakespeare, sm. - W. Harper	Open		99.00	120
1973 The Sleuth, lg.- A. Moore	Retrd.	1996	137.50	249-275
1973 The Sleuth, sm. - A. Moore	Retrd.	1996	75.00	55-120
1991 Snooker Player, sm.- S. Taylor	Retrd.	1995	82.50	70-90
1991 Soldier, sm. - W. Harper	Retrd.	1996	75.00	75
1994 Thomas Jefferson - M. Alcock	2,500	1995	200.00	175-225
1991 Town Crier, lg. - S. Taylor	Retrd.	1994	170.00	130-210
1993 Winston Churchill, sm.- S. Taylor	Open		99.00	120
1990 Wizard, lg.- S. Taylor- S. Taylor	Retrd.	1996	175.00	225
1990 Wizard, sm.- S. Taylor	Retrd.	1999	75.00	85
1991 Yeoman of the Guard, lg. 6873 - S. Taylor	Retrd.	1997	137.50	145

Great Artists - D. Biggs

YEAR ISSUE	EDITION LIMIT	YEAR RETD.	ISSUE PRICE	*QUOTE U.S.$
2000 Monet, lg. D7150	Open		205.00	205
2000 Van Goch, lg. D7151	Open		205.00	205

Great Composers - S. Taylor

YEAR ISSUE	EDITION LIMIT	YEAR RETD.	ISSUE PRICE	*QUOTE U.S.$
1996 Beethoven, lg. D7021	Open		225.00	250
1996 Chopin, lg. D7030	Open		225.00	250
1999 Elgar, lg. D7118	Open		195.00	195
1997 Handel, lg.	Open		237.50	238
1996 Mozart, lg. D7031	Open		225.00	250
1997 Schubert, lg. D7056	Open		225.00	250
1996 Tchaikovsky, lg. D7022	Open		225.00	250

Limited Edition Character Jugs - Various

YEAR ISSUE	EDITION LIMIT	YEAR RETD.	ISSUE PRICE	*QUOTE U.S.$
1992 Abraham Lincoln D6936 - S. Taylor	2,500	1994	190.00	295
1994 Aladdin's Genie D6971 - D. Biggs	1,500	1994	335.00	395
1996 Angel Miniature - M. Alcock	2,500	1996	77.50	78
1993 Clown Toby - S. Taylor	3,000	1996	175.00	225-250
1993 Elf Miniature D6942 - W. Harper	2,500	1994	55.00	75-110
1997 Explorer Tinies, set/6 - S. Taylor	2,500	1997	495.00	495
1993 Father Christmas Toby - W. Harper	3,500	1996	125.00	125
1996 Geoffrey Chaucer, lg. - R. Tabbenor	1,500	1996	800.00	850
1995 George Washington, lg. - M. Alcock	2,500	1996	200.00	200
1990 Henry VIII - N/A	Open		150.00	150
1991 Henry VIII - W. Harper	1,991	1992	395.00	1200-1400
1991 Jester - S. Taylor	2,500	1996	125.00	150-185
1994 King & Queen of Diamonds D6969 - J. Taylor	2,500	1994	260.00	260-275
1996 King and Queen of Hearts Toby - S. Taylor	2,500	1997	275.00	275-295
1997 King and Queen of Spades Toby - S. Taylor	2,500	1998	275.00	275
1997 King Arthur, lg. D7055 - R. Tabbenor	1,500	1997	350.00	380
1992 King Charles I D6917 - W. Harper	2,500	1995	450.00	495
1994 Leprechaun Toby - S. Taylor	2,500	1996	150.00	150
1999 Merlin, lg. D7117 - R. Tabbenor	1,500	2000	310.00	310
1992 Mrs. Claus Miniature D6922 - S. Taylor	2,500	1994	50.00	95-125
1993 Napoleon, lg. D6941 - S. Taylor	2,000	1994	225.00	225
1994 Oliver Cromwell D6968 - W. Harper	2,500	1994	475.00	475
1996 Pharoah Flambe, lg. - R. Tabbenor	1,500	1996	500.00	500
1991 Santa Claus Miniature D6900 - M. Abberley	5,000	1993	50.00	75-100
1988 Sir Francis Drake D6805 - P. Gee	Open		N/A	100
1997 Sir Henry Doulton, lg. D7054 - W. Harper	1,997	1997	285.00	285
1992 Snake Charmer - S. Taylor	2,500	1992	210.00	250-275
1994 Thomas Jefferson - S. Taylor	2,500	1996	200.00	225
1992 Town Crier D6895 - S. Taylor	2,500	1995	175.00	175-200
1992 William Shakespeare D6933 - W. Harper	2,500	1994	625.00	625

*Quotes have been rounded up to nearest dollar

DIRECTORY TO SECONDARY MARKET DEALERS

The CIB *Directory to Secondary Market Dealers* is designed to put you in touch with secondary market experts who are in the business of making it easier for you to buy and sell retired collectibles. Together, they have a wealth of knowledge about the field of collectibles and are eager to help you enjoy your hobby even more.

HOW TO USE THIS DIRECTORY

We've organized this directory to make it easy for you to find the dealer you need. Each dealer is listed alphabetically by state. They are also listed in the Index to Dealer Directory by Specialty on pages D2-D3.

LOCATING DEALERS BY THEIR SPECIALTY

Each dealer has been assigned a locator number in the top right-hand corner of their listing. This number will come in handy when you are looking for a dealer who is an expert in a particular line or company. For example, if you are looking for a dealer to help you buy or sell a Department 56 piece, just turn to the index and look up the Department 56 listing. The numbers you find next to the listing are the locator numbers of the dealers who specialize in Department 56. Once you've found the numbers, look over the individual dealer listings and begin contacting the dealers who most appeal to you.

LOCATING DEALERS BY STATE

Though most dealers are accustomed to doing business on a national basis, you may want to start by contacting dealers closer to home. That's why we've also organized the dealers by state. Within each state listing, dealers are organized in alphabetical order by business name.

LET'S GET STARTED!

Now that you know how to use the directory, you may want to take a moment or two to turn to pages 266-267 and learn the answers to the "10 MOST FREQUENTLY ASKED QUESTIONS ABOUT BUYING AND SELLING LIMITED EDITION COLLECTIBLES." These questions have come to us from collectors like you who want to know more about buying and selling on the secondary market. We've gathered the answers from our panel of secondary market experts. Hopefully, they'll give you the background you need to make the most out of your secondary market transactions!

ABBREVIATIONS

B&G = Bing & Grondahl	MO = Money Order
Byers' = Byers' Choice	MOY = Memories of Yesterday
CT = Cherished Teddies	PM = Precious Moments
D56 or Dept. 56 = Department 56	RC = Royal Copenhagen
EKJ = Emmett Kelly, Jr.	WFF = Wee Forest Folk
Ltd. = Limited	

Locating Secondary Market Dealers

Secondary market dealers have been indexed by their specialties. To find a dealer for a particular product:

1. Use the index below to find the name of the line or manufacturer that produced the collectible(s) you're seeking.

2. The numbers listed after the line or manufacturer's name represent the dealer locator numbers. THESE ARE NOT PAGE NUMBERS. Dealer locator numbers correspond to the numbers found in the upper right-hand corner of the dealer listings presented between pages D4-D20.

3. Turn to the listings indicated by the dealer locator numbers and contact the dealer that you choose to work with.

EXAMPLE

One of the dealers specializing in *Ebony Visions* can be found by finding the dealer listing that has the number "10" in the upper right hand corner. The dealer in this example is Rystad's Limited Editions, found on page D6.

Rystad's Limited Editions since 1967

1013 Lincoln Avenue, San Jose, CA 95125
Phone: (408) 279-1960
Fax: (408) 279-196_
Hours: Tues-Sat 10-5, Mon by Appt.
Services: Buy outright. Lists welcome.

Specialties: Red Skelton, Rockwell, Hamilton, M.I. Hummel, David Winter, Ashton-Drake, Harmony Kingdom, Nortake, Lenox, All God's Children, Bradford, Snowbabies, Disney Classics, Pooh n' Friends, Royal Copenhagen, B&G, Ebony Visions, Sass 'N Class, Christmas ornaments (Radko, Adler, Dresden Dove, Midwest).

Noteworthy: Dean Rystad started in the collectibles mail order business in 1967. In 1978, Rystad opened a store, which today features over 7,000 collector plates and many figurines. Rystad specializes in locating back issues of collectibles, and has an excellent track record. Rystad's is a Redemption Center for most collector clubs. A new gallery was added recently to feature the artwork of Red Skelton, Thomas Kinkade, Buddy Ebsen, Sandra Kuck, Jack Terry, Donald Zolan and Tom Dubois.

Directory to Secondary Market Dealers

AZ | **1**

CRYSTAL WORLD
5750 East Broadway
Tucson, AZ 85719-3108

Phone: (520) 745-5991
Fax: (520) 745-5991
Hours: Tues-Fri: 10:30-6, Sat: 11-3

Services: Buy/sell, appraise, engrave, design and repair crystal. Brokerage fee applicable. Visa, MasterCard and checks accepted.

Secondary: Authorized Swarovski/SCS retailer, Authorized Crystal World Disney Showcase Dealer, Austrian Faceted figurines, Abelman Art Glass Ltd. Edition Clowns.

Noteworthy: In business for over 25 years, Crystal World specializes in cut glass, paperweights, custom engraving on wedding and anniversary gifts, corporate presentation awards and trophies expertly created. Attention Swarovski collectors: Crystal World pays your membership fee. Now you can purchase your investment collectibles with confidence. All crystal professionally inspected, evaluated and graded for mint condition by William Threm, master glass engraver. Complete crystal showroom of exquisite cut glass and art glass from around the world.

Repairs on Steuben, Baccarat, Lalique, Waterford, Swarovski, etc. Appraisal services and expert advice on future crystal investments.

SECONDARY MARKET SPECIALIST CIB 2000-2001

AZ | **2**

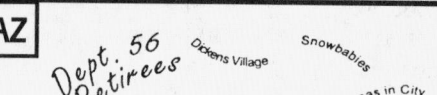

DEPARTMENT 56 RETIREES
Harry & June McGowan
1415 McCulloch Island Townhouse #101
Lake Havasu City, AZ 86403

Phone: (520) 505-5655
Fax: (520) 505-3709
Website: www.dept56retirees.com
Hours: Flexible.

Services: Buy outright, "What's on our price list is in our possession" creating fast delivery. Price list always available on the Internet at www.dept56retirees.com. No added commission. Visa, MasterCard, Discover and American Express accepted. Daily UPS shipping year-round. Free shipping over $500.

Secondary: Department 56 (Dickens Village, Disney Village, Christmas in the City, New England, Alpine, North Pole and some Snow Village, Snowbabies, Snowbunnies, Merry Makers, Winter Silhouettes, All Through the House), Disney Classics.

SECONDARY MARKET SPECIALIST CIB 2000-2001

AZ | **3**

SÁNCHEZ
COLLECTIBLES
SECONDARY MARKET SPECIALISTS IN
SWAROVSKI & LLADRÓ

1555 East Glendale Avenue • Phoenix, Arizona 85020 USA

Phone: (602) 395-9974   7 AM - 9 PM 7 DAYS
FAX: (602) 241-0702   24 HOURS / 7 DAYS
Email: sanchcol@primenet.com
Web Page: www.primenet.com/~sanchcol
Visits by Appointment Only

Services: BUY & SELL retired **SWAROVSKI** and **LLADRÓ**. Free locator service is available. Deal only in retired or sold-out pieces that can no longer be purchased on the primary market. Dealer and insurance replacement inquires are welcomed. NOT a Broker: Everything shipped from on-hand inventory.

Lines: SWAROVSKI and LLADRÓ.

Other: SANCHEZ COLLECTIBLES is 99.9% telephone, email, and mail order and only handles retired and sold-out pieces. They specialize in the Collector's Society or 'club' pieces but offer a good selection of other pieces as well. Every Fall owner Charlotte Sanchez edits and mails a newsletter and an updated listing of pieces and prices. This is sent FREE to all interested collectors. She also participates in several collectibles shows around the country every year. A free copy of the latest product listings and show schedule is available upon request.

SECONDARY MARKET SPECIALIST CIB 2000-2001

CA | **4**

City Lights
Year Round Christmas & Collectibles Emporium
1202 Morena Blvd., San Diego, CA 92110
EVERYTHING SHIPS FREE

Phone & Fax: (800) 262-5335
E-mail: D56heaven@aol.com
Website: www.citylightscollectibles.com
Hours: Open 7 Days

Services: Full website: www.citylightscollectibles.com Layaway available. Visa, MasterCard, Discover, American Express accepted.

Secondary: Department 56 (all Villages, Snowbabies, Snowbunnies, All Through The House, Winter Silhouette), Byers' Choice Carolers, Annalee, Fontanini, Cottontail Lane, Creepy Hollow, Margaret Furlong, Christopher Radko, Polonaise, Old World Christmas, Birgits Collections, Seraphim Angels, Harbour Lights, Shelia's, Possible Dreams, David Winter, Britains, Pipkas, Charming Tails.

Noteworthy: City Lights is a 6,000 square foot store with award-winning permanent displays. Everything listed **ships free.** Enormous inventory of both current and retired pieces. Department 56 "Gold Key" dealer, Byers' Choice "Preferred Dealer," Annalee "Doll Society" store, Fontanini "Guild" store, Polonaise "Listed" dealer, Old World Christmas "Collector's Club" store. Knowledgeable staff and friendly efficient service.

Directory to Secondary Market Dealers

CA **5**

Crystal Reef

is your primary source
on the secondary market for:

**Pocket Dragons • WeeForest • Swarovski
Disney Classics • Disneyana • Waterford
Tom Clark • Lilliput Lane • Gene
Land of Legend • Armani • Animation Art
Charming Tails • Lladro • Steiff • Radko
Harmony Kingdom and R. John Wright**

Crystal Reef is one of the largest secondary market
exchanges in North America for retired and limited
edition collectibles, offering very competitive "True"
secondary market values on listed pieces. We do the
work of locating and brokering your fine collectibles.

With Crystal Reef, there are no membership,
subscription or listing fees, and we provide free
secondary market price lists on any of the lines
which we represent.

Call us today for a free secondary market price list.

© R. John Wright

© Walt Disney Co.

© Annette Peterson

Crystal Reef

Visa * Mastercard * AMEX

(925) 778-8146

e-mail: reef@sirius.com

Visit our Web Site at **www.crystal-reef.com**

© RM

SECONDARY MARKET SPECIALIST
CIB
2000-2001

CA **6**

FLASH

Collectibles

560 N.Moorpark Road, PMB 287, Thousand Oaks, CA 91360

Phone: (800) 266-2337 (805) 499-9222
Fax: (805) 376-5541
E-Mail: flashcoll@aol.com
Website: www.flashcollectibles.com
Hours: Mon-Fri: 10-5, 24-Hour Answering Service

Services: Buy outright. Consignment & trades. Search service.

Secondary: Budweiser, Anheuser-Busch, Strohs, Old Style,
Miller, Hamms, Pabst, Coors, steins and plates. New stein
importers catalog shows over 1,000 steins in full color.
Features traditional German steins, pewter, character, fire
fighters, flasks, Rockwell, Looney Tunes, Superman,
Coca-Cola, and Corona.

Noteworthy: Flash Collectibles started as a part-time
business in 1971. By 1973, owners Doug and Natalie Marks
were totally consumed by the antiques and collectibles "bug"
and opened their first store called The Antique Co. In 1984, the
Marks discovered the Anheuser-Busch collectible steins. In 1986,
the firm moved to their current location and changed their name
to Flash Collectibles. Specializing in mail order beer steins, they
offer a free brochure listing their current stock of over 1,000
beer steins. Also featured are movie stills, and an exceptionally
large collection of full-color original fruit and vegetable
labels.

CA **7**

THE FRAME GALLERY

305 Third Avenue
Chula Vista, CA 91910

Phone: (619) 422-1700
Fax: (619) 422-5860
Hours: Mon-Fri: 10-5:30
Sat: 10-5

Services: Specializes in searching for hard-to-find
collectibles. Does not buy outright. Call for details.
All major credit cards accepted.

Secondary: All collector plates. Also prints, figurines,
crystal, and pewter, including Snowbabies, Perillo, Disney
Classics Sericels, Lenox Classics, Enesco, Hamilton,
Beanies, Swarovski, M.I. Hummel, Rockwell, Kevin
Francis, Mill Pond Press, Hadley House, Somerset House,
and autographed celebrity photos, etc.

Noteworthy: The Frame Gallery began as a framing shop,
but soon collectors began coming to the store for advice
on the art of framing different collectibles. Before long,
mother-daughter team Margaret and Jan introduced
collectibles to their store. Today, they are a Redemption
Center for Disney Classics, Lilliput, Krystonia,
Pocket Dragons, Myth & Magic, Hantel
Miniatures, Swarovski and Snowbabies.

SECONDARY MARKET SPECIALIST
CIB
2000-2001

CA **8**

THE GOLDEN SWANN

881 Lincoln Way
Auburn, CA 95603

Phone: (800) 272-7926
(530) 823-7739
Fax: (530) 823-1945
Hours: Daily: 10-5:30-7 days a week

Services: Buy/Sell outright. Layaway plan available. Visa,
MasterCard, American Express and Discover accepted.

Secondary: Lladró, Swarovski, Armani, David Winter
Cottages, M.I. Hummel, Caithness Paperweights and all
retired collectibles.

Noteworthy: With 25 years of business expertise,
The Golden Swann has become the largest dealer in
Northern California for current and retired pieces of Lladró,
Swarovski, Armani, Disney Classics, Mark Hopkins,
Country Artists, M.I. Hummel, Maruri, and Genesis.
Free membership for Swarovski and Armani Collectors
Clubs, call for further details. Redemption Center.
CALL FOR THE BEST PRICES ON RETIRED ITEMS.

Directory to Secondary Market Dealers

CA — 9 — JULIET'S COLLECTIBLES AND WEDDING GARDENS

44060 Margarita Road, Temecula, CA 92592-2746

Phone: (909) 302-0208
Fax: (909) 302-0210
Hours: Wed-Sat: 9:30-5:30, Sun: 10-4
Evenings by Appointment

Services: Buy outright, consignment, 90 day layaway. Free shipping in the continental U.S.

Secondary: All God's Children, M.I. Hummel, Sarah's Attic, Wee Forest Folk, Kinkade, Lena Liu, Sandra Kuck, D. Zolan, G. Harvey, Alan Maley, Fenton Art Glass.

Noteworthy: Juliet's Collectibles was opened in 1967 by Juliet Anne Boysen. The store has one of the largest selections of All God's Children retired pieces to be found in California, including most of the Father Christmas pieces, and a large selection of Sarah's Attic. They are a Redemption Center for Fenton Art Glass, Sarah's Attic, and Hummel. They print a quarterly newsletter which collectors can receive just by calling the store. Open houses are hosted when either an artist or a representative comes to the store. Customer service is a most important part of Juliet Anne Boysen's policy. The Wedding Garden, three acres of paradise, is now open. It features gazebos, romantic gardens and over 1,000 beautiful plants.

CA — 10 — Rystad's Limited Editions since 1967

1013 Lincoln Avenue, San Jose, CA 95125

Phone: (408) 279-1960
Fax: (408) 279-1960
Hours: Tues-Sat: 10-5, Mon by Appt.

Services: Buy outright. Lists welcome.

Secondary: Red Skelton, Rockwell, Hamilton, M.I. Hummel, David Winter, Ashton-Drake, Harmony Kingdom, Noritake, Lenox, All God's Children, Bradford, Snowbabies, Disney Classics, Pooh n' Friends, Royal Copenhagen, B&G, Ebony Visions, Sass 'N Class, Christmas ornaments (Radko, Adler, Dresden Dove, Midwest).

Noteworthy: Dean Rystad started in the collectibles mail order business in 1967. In 1978, Rystad opened a store, which today features over 7,000 collector plates and many figurines. Rystad specializes in locating back issues of collectibles, and has an excellent track record. Rystad's is a Redemption Center for most collector clubs. A new gallery was added recently to feature the artwork of Red Skelton, Thomas Kinkade, Buddy Ebsen, Sandra Kuck, Jack Terry, Donald Zolan and Tom Dubois.

CIB SECONDARY MARKET SPECIALIST 2000-2001

CA — 11 — SUGARBUSH GIFT GALLERY

1921 W. San Marcos Blvd. #105
San Marcos, CA 92069

Phone: (800) 771-9945 (760) 599-9945
Fax: (760) 599-9945
Hours: Mon-Fri: 10:30-6, Sat: 10:30-4

Services: Primary/Secondary Market. Mail your list with asking price. Visa, MasterCard, Discover and American Express accepted. Checks and money orders also accepted. 90-day layaway plan available. Ship insured.

Secondary: Primary and Secondary for Thomas Kinkade, Dona Gelsinger, Boyds (PAW), Cherished Teddies, Maruri, Charming Tails, Harbour Lights, Seraphim Angels, Harmony Kingdom (Queen Empress), Country Artists, Fenton, Richard Simmons Dolls, and Santa's World Travels. Retired Lilliput and David Winter.

Noteworthy: Sugarbush Gift Gallery is a primary and secondary source of marketable collectibles, with a knowledgeable and service orientated staff on hand.

CA — 12 — SWAN SEEKERS NETWORK

9740 Campo Road, Suite 134
Spring Valley, CA 91977

Phone: (619) 462-2333
Fax: (619) 462-5517
E-mail: jimer@swanseekers.com or
marilyn@swanseekers.com
Website: www.swanseekers.com
Hours: Mon-Thurs: 9-5 PST

Services: Retired Swarovski Crystal Brokerage specialists. We offer a full color newsletter, published 3 times a year and the "Crystal Gallery" (a 'For Sale' retired items list) updated and issued every 2 months *all year round*. 'Express Sidewalk Sale' by E-mail, sent out weekly free of charge. We accept MasterCard, Visa and Discover.

Secondary: *Exclusively* Swarovski Crystal

Noteworthy: Swan Seekers Network, established in 1989, is the *FIRST* strictly Swarovski Crystal Brokerage service. Listing your retired items for sale is *free of charge.* We offer UNBIASED information to any interested Swarovski collector. Keep up with what's new and what's happening. Give us a call. We may have what you're looking for.

CIB SECONDARY MARKET SPECIALIST 2000-2001

Directory to Secondary Market Dealers

Directory to Secondary Market Dealers

Directory to Secondary Market Dealers

FL | HEIRLOOM COLLECTIBLES | 21

2516c McMullen Booth Rd
Clearwater, Florida 33761
1-800-929-4567
fax: 1-727-669-8052
Online: www.heirloomcollectibles.com

Lines: Lladro, Armani, Swarovski, Boyds
Precious Moments, Department 56, Annalee
Tom Clark Gnomes, Charming Tails,
Harbor Lights, Cherished Teddies and others.

Services: All major Credit Cards Accepted.
We are a retail store for all the above lines and more
and also buy, sell and broker secondary items. We
ship insured UPS unless other arrangements are
desired. Layaways available.

Noteworthy: Established in 1993, we have built a
strong reputation for quality service. Our staff is
knowledgeable and helpful. The owners, Margie and
Al are experienced collectors who
understand the joy of finding
that special something you
have been searching for.

FL | HEIRLOOMS OF TOMORROW | 22

750 N.E. 125th Street
North Miami, FL 33161

Phone: (305) 899-0920
Fax: (305) 899-2877
Hours: Mon-Wed & Fri: 10-6, Thurs: 10-8,
Sat: 9-5

Services: Commission. Collectors send a typed list divided
into buy and sell.

Secondary: ANRI, Hibel, Lladró, Goebel Miniatures,
David Winter, M.I. Hummel, Armani, Swarovski,
Department 56, Cabbage Patch, Legends, Bradford,
Krystonia, Sarah's Attic, Precious Moments, Chilmark,
Disney Classics, Lilliput Lane, Lowell Davis, Caithness,
Ashton-Drake dolls, Thomas Kinkade, Olszewski,
Sandra Kuck, Beanie Babies.

Noteworthy: With over 20 years of experience and literally
thousands of items, Heirlooms of Tomorrow is considered
one of South Florida's foremost one-stop collectible shops.
Family owned and operated since 1980, they have a
booming mail order business. Care is taken to ensure that
collectibles will arrive safely, as they are shipped
worldwide.

FL | KATHY'S HALLMARK | 23

7709 Seminole Mall
Seminole, FL 33772

Phone: (727) 392-2459
Hours: Mon-Sat: 10-9, Sun: 12-5

Services: Buy and sell outright. Visa, MasterCard,
American Express and Discover accepted. Ship via UPS.

Secondary: Swarovski, Collector Plates, Precious Moments,
Cherished Teddies, Hallmark Ornaments and
Kiddie Car Classics, Snowbabies, Barbie, Dreamsicles,
Star Wars, and Star Trek.

Noteworthy: Kathy's Hallmark is a Redemption Center
for Swarovski, Precious Moments, Cherished Teddies,
Dreamsicles, and Hallmark. Many past year ornaments
and some 5-piece Christmas promotion sets are available
(i.e. Santa and Reindeer, Snoopy, Bearinger Bears).
Call or write for specifics.

FL | | 24

 VIKING

**WORLD SPECIALIST IN BING & GRONDAHL
AND ROYAL COPENHAGEN COLLECTIBLES**

If you want to buy or sell previous year's
RC or B&G collectibles, call Viking first! We
have been buying and selling RC and B&G
since 1948 and have a large inventory, plus
a nationwide network of sources. We buy
outright, or list your RC and B&G collectibles
on our active "Videx" exchange.

**CALL US FOR A CURRENT PRICE LIST ON
RC AND B&G COLLECTIBLES**

**We also carry many of
the other fine collectibles you love:**

Swarovski	Kaiser
Hummel	Wedgwood
Bradford	Edna Hibel
Maruri	Berlin Design

And Many Other Lines

VIKING IMPORT HOUSE, INC.
690 N. E. 13th St., Ft. Lauderdale, FL 33304
CALL US TOLL-FREE (800) 327-2297

Directory to Secondary Market Dealers

ID | 25

 **Donna's Place**

200 Main Street
P.O. Box 520
Idaho City ID 83631

Phone: (208) 392-6000
(800) 574-8714
Fax: (208) 392-6006
E-mail: dplac2@juno.com
Website: www.donnas-place.com
Hours: Seven Days a Week: 10-7

Services: Buy/Sell/Trade. Locator Service. MasterCard, Visa, American Express, Discover accepted. Worldwide shipping.

Secondary: Anheuser-Busch, Michelob, Corona, Budweiser, Bud Light steins and related collectibles. Coca-Cola products, Ertl and Spec Cast collector trucks and banks.

Noteworthy: Donna's Place has been owned and operated by Skip and Donna Myers since 1992. An avid beer stein collector for 10 years, Skip brings enthusiasm and knowledge to his collectors. His retail store carries over 5,000 steins in stock, both retail and secondary. Authorized dealer and Redemption Center for Anheuser-Busch. Skip also runs a gift shop carrying collectible dolls and other gift items. Visit their website for more information.

CIB SECONDARY MARKET SPECIALIST 2000-2001

IL | 26

C.A. Jensen JEWELERS

709 First Street, LaSalle, IL 61301

Phone: (815) 223-0377 (800) 499-5977
Website: www.cajensenjewelers.com
Hours: Mon-Fri: 9:30-5:30, Sat: 9:30-5

Services: All of their many fine retired collectible lines including china, crystal and silver are new. Checks and credit cards accepted.

Secondary: Figurines: Cybis, Boehm, Royal Copenhagen, Bing & Grondahl, Lladró, M.I. Hummel, Goebel, Ispanky, Lalique, Baccarrat, Waterford, Lowell Davis, Lilliput Lane, Lenox, ANRI, and Rockwell. Dolls: Gorham musical. Ornaments: Lunt, Kirk Stieff, Wallace, as well as other sterling, wood, and crystal lines. Collector Plates: Many discontinued and obscure plates in stock including B&G, Royal Copenhagen, Bradford, M.I. Hummel, and much more.

Noteworthy: C.A. Jensen Jewelers has been in business for 80 years and is second generation family owned and operated. They house a huge inventory in their 8,000 square foot warehouse and offer many fine collectible lines in their 6,500 square foot store. There are over 3,000 plates on display, of which many are discontinued. Come see for yourself!

IL | 27

 **The Crystal Connection Ltd.**

8510 N. Knoxville Avenue, PMB 218
Peoria • IL 61615-2034 • USA
"SWAROVSKI crystal specialist"

Phone: (309) 692-2221 / (800) 692-0708 order
Fax: (309) 692-2221 (24 hours)
E-mail: crystalconnection@att.net
Web: www.crystal.org

CIB SECONDARY MARKET SPECIALIST 2000-2001

Services: • Secondary market buy & sell listing brokerage
• *Crystal News* newsletter • Appraisals for insurance and claims
• VISA, MasterCard, American Express and checks accepted
• Worldwide operations with offices in US, Europe and Australia

Lines: SWAROVSKI crystal

Noteworthy: *Crystal Connection* established in 1991 is operated by Robin Yaw, the world's leading authority on Swarovski. He has appeared on the Swarovski's *"Ask the Experts"* shows and CIB's secondary market seminars. He's a full accredited member of the International Society of Appraisers and the world's *first* appraiser to specialize in Swarovski. He authors the very popular *Crystal News*, a newsletter for Swarovski collectors worldwide. *Crystal Connection* is also renowned worldwide for its exclusive XYZ inspection technique that guarantees perfect pieces every shipment. No other brokerages can come close to what *Crystal Connection* offers. Both *Crystal Europe* and *Crystal Connection Australia* are affiliated with *The Crystal Connection Ltd.*

IL | 28

EILENE'S TREASURES
P.O. Box 285
Virden, IL 62690

Phone: (217) 965-3648
Cell Phone: (217) 652-2773
E-mail: eekgak9@ctllc.com
Hours: 9-8 daily

Services: Buy/Sell. Layaways available. Fair prices. Satisfaction guaranteed. Large inventory in stock. MasterCard and Visa accepted. Locator service available.

Secondary: Precious Moments (suspended and retired figurines, bells, ornaments, plates), Memories of Yesterday figurines and ornaments, Hallmark Ornaments, Enesco Treasury Ornaments, Beanie Babies.

Noteworthy: Eilene Kruse is an expert on Precious Moments marks, purchasing many early pieces with original marks. She has expanded her business to include other Enesco lines and Hallmark ornaments. Eilene attends three to four ornament and collectible shows in the Illinois area and publishes a price list which is available upon request.

Directory to Secondary Market Dealers

IL **EUROPEAN IMPORTS & GIFTS** **29**

7900 N. Milwaukee Avenue
Niles, IL 60714

Phone: (800) 227-8670   (847) 967-5253
Fax: (847) 967-0133
E-mail: ei-collectibles@worldnet.att.net
Website: www.europeanimports.com
Hours: Mon-Fri: 10-8, Sat: 10-5:30, Sun: 12-5

Services: No consignments. Buy outright. Mail complete listing. Free shipping in the U.S. with purchases over $75. Visa, MasterCard, American Express and Discover accepted.

Secondary: Annalee, ANRI, Armani, Byers' Choice, Department 56, Disney Classics, Animation Art, M.I. Hummel, EKJ, Krystonia, Lilliput Lane, Lladró, All God's Children, Precious Moments, Swarovski, Wee Forest Folk, David Winter, Madame Alexander Dolls, Cherished Teddies, Radko, Ebony Visions, Dreamsicles, Harmony Kingdom, Goebel Looney Tunes, Seraphim Classics, Just The Right Shoe.

Noteworthy: Established in 1966, European Imports & Gifts is one of the largest dealers in the Midwest. Year-round Christmas village.

CIB SECONDARY MARKET SPECIALIST 2000-2001

IL *CIB SECONDARY MARKET SPECIALIST 2000-2001*  **Gift MUSIC MINISTRY** **30**

GIFT MUSIC, BOOK & COLLECTIBLES SHOPPE

Phone: (708) 877-7099 - 24 hrs. Fax: (208)275-5014
E-mail: jntschulte@rocketmail.com (want list only)
Website: www.tias.com/stores/gift (current specials)

Secondary: Seraphim Angels, **Precious Moments**, Memories of Yesterday, M.I Hummel, All God's Children, D. Winter, ANRI, T. Clark, Lladró, Cherished Teddies, Beanie Babies, Sports Impressions, D-56, EKJ, Lilliput, **Fontanini**, **Hallmark**, Enesco, Lenox and **Carlton** ornaments, Rockwell, Kurt S. Adler, Remington Bronze, Midwest, **Swarovski**, Schmid, Ron Lee, Seymour Mann, Wedgwood, **Roman**, Armani, Disney, CUI, Possible Dreams, Royal Doulton, Harmony Kingdom, Reco, Anheuser, Budweiser, Steinbach, Hamilton, Gartlan, Lenox, Caithness, Goebel, Grossman, Hibel, Royal Copenhagen, Halcyon Days, B & G, Svend Jensen, toys, games, Bibles, plates, dolls, instruments, sheet music, steins and books-1800s to current.

Noteworthy: Joe and Terri Schulte recently lost their store in an uninsured fire. However, they are trading on the secondary market, doing insurance appraisals and offer a worldwide locator service. Because they operate a **501(c)3 non-profit** religious organization, they offer a full current value tax deduction for all donations of collections. Their goal is to bring quality religious and inspirational items into homes, and to bring people of various cultures and backgrounds together. Visit their website for current specials.

IN **GRAHAM'S CRACKERS** **31**

5981 E. 86th Street
Indianapolis, IN 46250

Phone: (800) 442-5727
         (317) 842-5727
Fax: (317) 577-7777
Hours: Mon-Sat: 9-9, Sun: 11-5

Services: We buy retired Department 56 pieces outright, or will trade for new merchandise. Please call for details. We host many artist appearances throughout the year. SPECIAL ORDERS ARE OUR SPECIALTY. We also offer layaway.

Secondary: The only line that we purchase outright is Dept. 56. We are a GOLD KEY DEALER. However, we carry a large amount of other retired pieces, in particular: GERMAN NUTCRACKERS, Harmony Kingdom, PM, Christopher Radko, Byers' Choice, Looney Tunes, Shelia's and North American Bear. We currently represent over 200 LINES!

Noteworthy: Opened in 1986, Graham's Crackers is a collector's paradise. We also have a year-round CHRISTMAS STORE. Combined, both stores have over 26,000 square feet. We have a great, new REWARDS PROGRAM that makes shopping with us a breeze! Call for details and also to have your name included on our mailing list.

LA **DICKENS' EXCHANGE, INC.** **32**

5150 Highway 22, Suite C-16
Mandeville, LA 70471

Phone: (504) 845-1954
         (888) 337-7486
Fax: (504) 845-1873
Hours: Mon-Fri: 9-5:30, Sat: 10-2

Services: 10% commission paid by purchaser on consignment listings. Exchange sells outright-no commissions. Call for details.

Secondary: Department 56: Snow Village, Dickens Village, Christmas in the City, New England, Alpine, Disney Parks Village, Little Town of Bethlehem, North Pole, Cold Cast Porcelains, Snowbabies, all accessories, as well as other Department 56 collectibles.

Noteworthy: Lynda Blankenship began as a collector of Department 56 collectibles. Eventually, this led to the publishing of *The Dickens' Exchange*, a reliable source for Department 56 news and a thriving exchange. Today, Lynda publishes a 52-page newsletter. She describes her newsletter as a place for collectors to meet and share their hobby. She is also the author of "Willage Mania," a 442-page color book for Department 56 collectors, and co-author of "Display Mania."

CIB SECONDARY MARKET SPECIALIST 2000-2001

Directory to Secondary Market Dealers

MA | 33

Linda's Originals & The Yankee Craftsmen

220 Rt. 6A Brewster MA 02631
Summer 9-9 (Seven Days) Winter 9-5 (Seven Days)
Toll Free Order Line 1-800-385-4758

Services: Buy Out Right, Consignment for Byers' Choice, Swarovski and Harbour Lights. On-Line Classified also available.

Lines: Annalee, Armani, Boyds Bears, Byers' Choice, Cats Meow, Cherished Teddies, Department 56, Disney Classics, Harmony Kingdom, Harbour Lights, Lladró, Lizzie High, Radko, Snow Babies, Spencer Collin, Swarovski, Thomas Kinkade, Wee Forest Folk.

Join our Free Collectible Clubs with your First Purchase.

Visit Our On-Line Catalog
at www.capecodcollectibles.com

SECONDARY MARKET SPECIALIST
CIB
2000-2001

MI | 34

RETIRED FIGURINE EXCHANGE INC.
Where the 'Hard to Find' is EASY!

8170 Cooley Lake Road, White Lake, MI 48386

Phone: (800) 893-4494   (248) 360-4155
Fax: (248) 363-1360
E-mail: stewart@retiredfigurine.com
Website: www.retiredfigurine.com
Hours: Mon-Tues: 10-6, Wed: 10-8, Thurs-Sat: 10-6

Services: Have large stock of items in store. Some consignments accepted. Buy outright. **Exchange and locator service.**

Secondary: Cherished Teddies, Disney Classics, Dreamsicles, Harmony Kingdom, **Lladró**, **M.I. Hummel**, PenDelfin, Precious Moments, **Royal Doulton**, **Swarovski**, **Department 56**, **Possible Dreams**, Prizm/Pipka Santas, Snowbabies, Creepy Hollow, Crinkle Claus, **Muffy Vanderbear**, Harbour Lights, Wee Forest Folk.

Noteworthy: Owners Stewart and Arlene Richardson have been dealing in collectibles for 12 years. They have an extensive background in Royal Doulton, M.I. Hummel, Precious Moments, Possible Dreams, and Department 56. In 1993, the Richardsons opened a showroom which stocks over 5,000 figurines.
Visit their website at www.retiredfigurine.com.

MO | 35

C AND N SOUTH 5 STEINS

324 S. Hwy 5
Camdenton, MO 65020

Phone: (573) 346-6307 Toll Free: (877) 346-6307
Fax: (573) 346-4248
Hours: 7 am- 7 pm: 7 days a week

Services: Personal checks, money orders and all major credit cards accepted. Layaway available. Buy single steins or whole collections outright. Redemption Center for Anheuser-Busch collectors clubs and Clydesdales collection.

Secondary: Anheuser-Busch, Miller, Coors, Pabst, Corona, NASCAR Steins and related beer items - figurines, neons, and mirrors.

Noteworthy: Started in 1997, C and N South 5 Steins has become one of the biggest stein dealers in the Midwest. They are also a locator of hard-to-find steins.

MO | 36

Tra-Art, Ltd.
Your One Stop Collectibles Shop
421 West Miller Street
Jefferson City, MO 65101

Phone: (573) 635-8278
Hours: Tues-Fri: 10-6, Sat: 10-5
Phone: (573) 893-3779
          (By appointment - Mon-Sat: 10-6)
E-mail: tra-art@socket.net

Services: Primary & secondary market. From stock or consignment. Occasionally buy outright. Layaway, Discover, Visa and MasterCard accepted. Insured shipping available.
Secondary: Primary and secondary market for Anheuser-Busch, Anna Perenna, Ashton-Drake, Bergsma, Bing & Grondahl, Bradford, Hadley House, Hamilton, Hibel, Knowles, Sandra Kuck, Lilliput, Moss, Old World Christmas, Possible Dreams, Pipka, Reco, Redlin, Rockwell, Roman, Shelia's, Spencer Collin, Tudor Mint, Zolan...More!
Noteworthy: Collecting since the early '70s, owners Don and Joyce Trabue have more than 25 years of experience in the collectible business. In 1980, they formed Tra-Art, Ltd. and expanded to a second location in 1993. They carry many older collectibles and have an inventory of over 9,000 collector plates. Club Redemption Center for many lines. Member of NALED. Personalized Service!

SECONDARY MARKET SPECIALIST
CIB
2000-2001

Directory to Secondary Market Dealers

NC | CALLAHAN'S OF CALABASH | 37

9973 Beach Drive
Calabash, NC 28467

Phone: (800) 344-3816
Fax: (910) 579-7209
Website: www.callahansgifts.com
Hours: Daily: 9am-10pm (Summer)
Daily: 9am-9pm (Winter)

Services: Price list available. Items taken on consignment with 15% commission fee added to the selling price.

Secondary: As a Department 56 "Gold Key" Dealer, Callahan's specialty is Department 56 Villages, accessories and Snowbabies. They also offer a secondary market for Wee Forest Folk and a growing Christopher Radko market.

Noteworthy: Come visit their 30,000 sq. ft. shopping extravaganza, featuring the 2,000 sq. ft. award-winning Department 56 room. In 1996, as a Rising Star Dealer, they proudly introduced their Christopher Radko Room. Gold-Wing Seraphim Angel dealer. Visit their website at www.callahansgifts.com.

NJ | MORTON'S CRYSTAL, INC. | 38

600 Harbor Blvd.
Weehawken, NJ 07087

Phone: (201) 865-7777
Fax: (201) 865-7777
Website: www.mortonscrystal.com
www.crystal-auction.com
Hours: Mon-Sat: 9-9 EST

Services: Listing service for Swarovski Crystal - Retired and Limited Edition pieces. Free listing service for sellers. Free electronic newsletter. Buy/Sell/Consignment.

Secondary: Limited to Swarovski crystal only.

Noteworthy: Tony and Cindy Morton have developed an extensive website of information for Swarovski collectors including For Sale Listings, Special Sale Items, Event Calendar, Repairs, Insurance, Books, Links to Other Sites, Retirements, Introductions, News and Information, Display Cabinets, Trimlite Gallery, Bulletin Board, Chat Room, and much much more. Their website has won awards, and they are active secondary market panelists for CIB.

Visit Morton's Crystal at
www.mortonscrystal.com
www.crystal-auction.com

NJ | PRESTIGE COLLECTIONS | 39

The Mall at Short Hills, Short Hills, NJ 07078
Bridgewater Commons, Bridgewater, NJ 08807
The Westchester, White Plains, NY 10601
Garden State Plaza, Paramus, NJ 07652

Phone: (800) 227-7979 Fax: (973) 597-9408
Hours: Mon-Sat: 10-9:30, Sun: 11-6

Services: Mail your list with asking price, buy outright. In-home or office shows. Layaway, gift wrapping, special orders, and delivery available. Visa, MC, Amex, Discover.

Secondary: Millenium Lladró, Armani, Swarovski, Department 56, Snowbabies, Precious Moments, Disney Classics, Lalique, Daum, Caithness, Waterford, Lenox Classics, Boehm, Lilliput, Limoges Boxes, M.I. Hummel, GiftStar (Déjà Vu), Harbour Lights, Radko, Kinkade, Cherished Teddies, Halcyon Days, and much more.

Noteworthy: Established in 1977, Prestige Collections has grown to four locations in the finest regional malls in New Jersey and New York. They are a service oriented business that sells fine gifts and collectibles from $5.00-$25,000. Prestige has some of the finest selections of the best brand name collectibles. A Redemption Center for most major collectibles. NALED member. Artists and collector events throughout the year. They can help you with corporate and personal shopping. JUST CALL!

NY | Collectibly Yours | 40

80 E Route 59
Spring Valley, NY 10977

Phone: (800) 863-7227 (out of NY)
(914) 425-9244
Hours: Tues-Sat: 10-6, Sun. by chance.
Holiday hours.

Services: Retail store and mail order. Visa, MasterCard, Discover accepted. NO APPRAISALS.

Secondary: Swarovski, Precious Moments, Lladró, Ebony Visions, M.I. Hummel, Wee Forest Folk, Memories of Yesterday, Cherished Teddies, All God's Children, Collector's plates, Disney Classics, Thomas Kinkade, Lowell Davis, Lilliput Lane, David Winter, Sports Impressions, Department 56 (all Villages, accessories, Snowbabies, Merry Makers). Dolls: Yolanda Bello, Annette Himstedt, Ashton-Drake, Cabbage Patch, Robin Woods, Dolls by Jerri, Gorham, Susan Wakeen, Georgetown, Hamilton, North American Bear, Virginia Turner, Wendy Lawton.

Noteworthy: Extensive selection of dolls. Department 56 Gold Key dealer, Kinkade Premier Center, NALED, GCC (Gift Creation Concepts) retailer. In collectible business since 1978.

Directory to Secondary Market Dealers

NY Glorious Treasures Ltd. 41

Mail: 1467 East 70th Street; Brooklyn, N.Y. 11234
Phone: 718-241-8185   **Fax:** 718-241-8184

Visit our Web Site.....

Glorious Treasures ONLINE
http://www.glorioustreasures.com/

E-Mail: inquiry@glorioustreasures.com

Services: A worldwide virtual dealer of beautiful and rare collectible and gift items from around the world. Item search and find. Collection and estate appraisals and sales. Items bought and traded as needed. Sales by personal check, money orders, and all major credit cards. All transactions in US funds and instruments only. Sales tax as required by law & shipping extra.

Lines: OLD & NEW: Hamilton and Bradford plates. Ashton-Drake dolls, Hummel, Disney, Schmid, Royal-Doulton, Donald Zolan, Sandra Kuck, Edna Hibel, Gregory Perillo, Francis Hook, Red Skelton, Dave Grossman, Gorham, Norman Rockwell, Anna Perenna, Lowell Davis, Bessie Pease Gutmann, ANRI, Jan Hagara, Maud Humphrey Bogart, Ted DeGrazia, Enesco, Lladro, Goebel, Olszewski and Sebastian miniatures, Emmett Kelly Jr., Fred Stone, Pat Buckley Moss, Terry Redlin, Donald Polland, John McClelland and Cabbage Patch.

Noteworthy: Established 1977. THEMES: Star Trek, Beatles, Elvis, GWW, Lucy, Honeymooners, Barbie, Wizard of Oz, popular television /movie subjs. RELIGIOUS: Roman. Used records/memorabilia. SPORTS: Sports Impressions, Gartlan, Hackett. Budweiser & beer stuff. Rare stamps and coins.

AmericanExpress,M/C,Visa,Discover

CIB SECONDARY MARKET SPECIALIST 2000-2001

NY 42

Main St., PO Box 201, Essex, NY 12936

Phone: (800) 898-6098   (518) 963-4347
Website: www.discoverhk.com
Hours: 10-5 (seven days per week)

Services: Retail store. Worldwide web access for 24 hr. on-line shopping and secondary market services. Flat fee for shipping and free shipping once total purchases reach $300. Personal checks, money orders, Discover, Visa, MasterCard and Amex accepted. Enjoy the _personalized service_ your collection deserves.

Secondary: Harmony Kingdom. Queens Empress Dealer with over 800 pieces in stock.

Noteworthy: For six years, Natural Goods & Finery has specialized in Harmony Kingdom collectibles, sharing their knowledge about new, rare and retired pieces with their loyal customers. They have one of the largest selections in both current and retired Harmony Kingdom pieces. Also offering Debbee Thibaults American Collectibles.

CIB SECONDARY MARKET SPECIALIST 2000-2001

NY Village Collectors 43

12 Hart Place
Dix Hills, N.Y. 11746

Phone: (631) 242-2457
Fax: (631) 243-4607
E-Mail: dcrupi@villagecollectors.com
Website: www.villagecollectors.com
Hours: M-F Days: Answering Service
Evenings: 5:30 - 9:00 EST
Weekends: 11:00 - 9:00 EST

Services: Offering a complete secondary market service. Including a free listing service, consignments, or outright buying of your Department 56 secondary market collectibles, UPS insured shipping, an inspection period, layaways, gift certficates, & gift wrapping. Our commission on listings or consignments is 15% , which is included in our selling price. A FREE price quote or listing is only a call away! Find our current listing at **www.villagecollectors.com**. We accept Visa, MasterCard, Discover, American Express, & checks.

Lines: All Department 56 Retired or Limited Edition collectibles. Including Villages, Snowbabies & Giftware.

Noteworthy: We started collecting D56 during Christmas of '89 and have been helping collectors find the piece of their dreams since 1992. As my husband always says, "Donna collects the little white D56 sticker."

OH Collectible Exchange, Inc.™ 44

Retired & Limited Edition Collectibles

Phone: (800) 752-3208
Fax: (330) 542-9644
E-Mail: INFO@colexch.com
www.colexch.com
Hours: M-F 9:00 a.m. - 8:00 p.m.
Sat: 10:00 a.m. - 4:00 p.m.

CIB SECONDARY MARKET SPECIALIST 2000-2001

Services: International Secondary Market Listing Service. Serving individuals and dealers. No cost no obligation listing service. Personal check, money order, Visa, MasterCard, Discover or American Express accepted. Toll Free 800 Service.

Lines: Boyds Bears, Byers' Choice, Charming Tails, Cherished Teddies, Department 56, Disney Classics, Dreamsicles, Hallmark, Harbour Lights, Hummel, Jan Hagara, Kiddie Car Classics, Krystonia, Lefton, Lilliput, Lowell Davis, Maud Humphrey, Memories of Yesterday, Midwest, Olszewski, Precious Moments, Shellia's, Swarovski Crystal, Wee Forest Folk and Wysocki.

Noteworthy: Started in 1989 as the first Independent Nationwide Secondary Service. Has grown to a large scale International Service trading over $2 million annually. Member of original CIB Panel. Referred by many major collectible manufactures.

Directory to Secondary Market Dealers

OH — 45

Colonial House of Collectibles & Santa's North Pole World

182 Front Street, Berea, OH 44017

Phone: (440) 826-4169   (800) 344-9299
Fax: (440) 826-0839
E-mail: yworrey@aol.com
Hours: Mon-Fri: 9-6, Sat: 10-5

Services: Buy/Sell/Trade/Appraise. MasterCard, Visa, Discover and American Express accepted.

Secondary: Royal Doulton, Department 56, M.I. Hummel, Lladró, David Winter, Lilliput Lane, Wee Forest Folk, Disney Classics, Swarovski, Precious Moments, Bing & Grondahl, Royal Copenhagen, Cherished Teddies, Harmony Kingdom, Harbour Lights, Franklin Mint Die Cast Cars, Looney Tunes Spotlight Collection, Lenox Classics, Beanie Babies.

Noteworthy: Colonial House of Collectibles has been in business for over 24 years. For the past 12 years, they have been located in an 1873 house in the southwest suburb of Cleveland. A year-round Christmas room is always on display. They are a Redemption Center for collector club pieces.

OH — 46

 **Gift Garden**

SINCE 1970

House of Fine Gifts & Collectibles
624 Great Northern Mall
N. Olmsted, OH 44070

Phone: (440) 777-0116   (800) 777-4802
Fax: (440) 777-0116
E-mail: dgupta@giftgarden.com
Website: www.giftgarden.com
Hours: Mon-Sat: 10-9, Sun: 11-6

Services: Visa, MasterCard, Discover and American Express accepted. Free Layaway and 90 days same as cash (w/AC). Frequent buyer program available.

Secondary: Armani, ANRI, Anheuser-Busch, Enchantica, Disney Classics, M.I. Hummel, Swarovski, Waterford, Lenox Classics China & Crystal, Robert Olszewski, Emmett Kelly Jr., Ron Lee, PM, Royal Doulton, Cherished Teddies, Collector Plates, Polonaise, Christopher Radko, Chilmark, Legends, Krystonia, Seraphim Classics Angels, Norman Rockwell, Department 56, Snowbuddies, and Steinbach.

Noteworthy: Gift Garden has been in business since 1970, serving collectors all over the country. Gift Garden showcases the best artists and creations of fine collectibles in the world. Call for further information on their artist events throughout the year. Will pay your collector club dues. Call for details on your club.

OH — 47

 **Little Red Gift House**

"a unique treasure of a gift shop"
State Route 113, Birmingham, OH 44816

Phone: (440) 965-5420
Hours: Tues-Sat: 10-6, Sun: 12-5 (Sept.-Dec. only)
Closed Mon (except Dec.)

Services: Specialist in Norman Rockwell figurines and plates. Occasionally buy Rockwell collections or individual pieces. No consignments. Free appraisals for insurance. Ship UPS daily. Visa and MasterCard accepted.

Secondary: Norman Rockwell figurines and plates.

Noteworthy: Little Red Gift House has become known nationwide as a major source of Norman Rockwell collectibles, both new and older pieces. In stock is a large inventory of retired, discontinued, and limited edition Rockwell figurines. Listing of in-stock Rockwell items is available upon request. Little Red Gift House also carries M.I. Hummel, Precious Moments, Thomas Kinkade, Department 56, Collector Plates, Cherished Teddies, Sports Collectibles, Ray Day, Memories of Yesterday, Seraphim Angels, Possible Dreams Santas, Bradford, Anheuser-Busch Steins, Emmett Kelly, Amish Heritage, Jan Hagara, Pretty As A Picture, Snowbabies and Snowbunnies.

 **CIB** SECONDARY MARKET SPECIALIST 2000-2001

OH — 48

Your Link To The Best
Swarovski *at the lowest possible prices...*

THE

CRYSTAL BROKERAGE

* **Thousands of listings**
* **Knowledgeable Brokers**
* **Shop Online @**
  www.millershallmark.com
* **Or simply call 1-800-89-CRYSTAL**
  (1-800-892-7978)
* **Shop online or by phone with the country's leading Swarovski Silver Crystal Dealer**

The Crystal Brokerage
owned and operated by

MILLER'S HALLMARK

1322 North Barron Street
Eaton, OH 45320
Ph. 937-456-4151   Fax 937-456-7851

CIB SECONDARY MARKET SPECIALIST 2000-2001

Directory to Secondary Market Dealers

OH   **49**

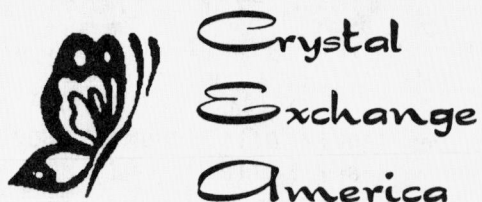

Crystal Exchange America

Swarovski Specialists for the Secondary Market

TEL: 513.423.5272
FAX: 513.423.8318

Internet: www.CrystalExchange.com
Email: Angie@CrystalExchange.com

Listing & Selling - There is no fee to list or sell. The buyer pays our commission. We can give sellers assistance on pricing based on current market trends.

Buying - You can receive free copies of our listings. We professionally inspect all items in your order at no additional charge before shipping. Domestic and worldwide delivery using FedEx. Visa / MC / Discover / personal checks accepted.

We are **Exclusively Swarovski Brokers**. Whether you want to buy or sell, we will be happy to answer any question you may have about your collection and our brokerage service. Visit our web site to view current listings and see details on the Listing, Selling and Buying policies. We also have secure online listing and ordering at our web site!

Crystal Exchange Ltd. is our sister operation in the United Kingdom. They have listings on the internet: **www.crystalexchange.co.uk** and CrystalWise newsletter 3 times a year.

SECONDARY MARKET SPECIALIST
CIB
2000-2001

OH   **50**

WARNER'S BLUE RIBBON BOOKS

on *Swarovski Crystal*

7163 W. Fred-Garland Rd.
Union, Ohio 45322-9621

Phone: 937.698.4508
Fax: 937.698.5408

Web site: www.wbrb.com
Email: jane@wbrb.com

Warner's Blue Ribbon Books on *Swarovski* make collecting and keeping track of your *Swarovski* more enjoyable.

We currently have four books, each containing photographic illustrations, designer names, physical dimensions, and other information on *Swarovski* items.

Our original book, Warner's Blue Ribbon Book on *Swarovski Silver Crystal*, is a comprehensive reference guide that includes information on retired and current, European and U.S., crystal pieces from 1976 to present. It also includes the *SCS* Annual Edition member pieces.

All books are updated and republished every year to reflect new pieces, new retirements and current Estimated Replacement Values (for insurance purposes).

Place your order online, using our SECURE order form!

Recognized Worldwide!

"The *Swarovski* Guides written *for* Collectors *by* Collectors."

Directory to Secondary Market Dealers

OK 51

PICTORIAL TREASURES

Your Limited Edition Art Print Specialist

SECONDARY MARKET SPECIALIST CIB 2000-2001

Current and Sold-out Prints for over 100 Artists such as Kinkade, Doolittle, Lyman, Wysocki, Moss

Pictorial Treasures

is the largest secondary market Ltd. Edition Art Exchange open to both the retail dealer and private collector.
"For Sale" listings always accepted.

Free price quotes available for over 3,000 art prints.
All art prints are inspected and come with certificates.

Call 918 287-2668
today for friendly, reliable service.

Thomas Kinkade Online e-newsletter

Information on what's new, what's sold out, seasonal and collector print favorites....
Want to know what's hot? E-mail to subscribe!

Online Gallery: http://www.artontheweb.com
E-mail: staff@artontheweb.com
Fax: 603-925-5639

P.O. Box 1586 - Pawhuska, OK

OK 52

SHIRLEY'S COLLECTIBLE EXCHANGE
1500 Ward Rd.
Ardmore, OK 73401

Phone: (580) 226-6228
Hours: Daily: 9-9

Services: Locate/Sell/Occasionally Buy.

Secondary: Mattel Barbies, Disney Classics, Swarovski, Hallmark & Carlton Ornaments, Lefton Colonial Village, Norman Rockwell, M.I. Hummel, Department 56, Cherished Teddies, Boyds Bears, Precious Moments, Madame Alexander, Tom Clark, Tim Wolfe, Lee Sievers, Armani, All God's Children, Margaret Furlong, Dreamsicles, Seraphim Angels, Fontanini, Lladró, Chilmark, and more!

Noteworthy: Shirley and Bob Fast owned and operated Shirley's Gifts Inc. for over 17 years. Their store specialized in both primary and secondary market for most major collectible lines. Shirley recently retired to concentrate solely on the secondary market. Her customers can be assured that she will continue to provide that personal touch and knowledge for which she is known.

SECONDARY MARKET SPECIALIST CIB 2000-2001

OK 53

WINTER IMAGES
3008 Hilltop, Muskogee, OK 74403

Phone: (918) 683-3488
Fax: (918) 683-2325 (24 hrs.)
E-mail: jeanine@intellex.com
Hours: Weekends and after 4pm weekdays

Services: Secondary market exchange, listing retired pieces to buy or sell. Major credit cards accepted. If paying by check, prefer money order or certified check. Order is held for one week if paid by personal check.

Secondary: Collectible lines including: David Winter, Precious Moments, Hallmark, Swarovski, Lladró, DeGrazia, Disney, Department 56, Lilliput Lane, Enesco, Lucy and Me, ANRI, Cherished Teddies, Boyds, Armani, Charming Tails, and others.

Noteworthy: Jeanine Barrett and her children, Jamie and Kirk Brown, began their business in 1992, specializing in David Winter. The business has expanded to a secondary market exchange, helping customers buy and sell in all collectible lines. Winter Images prides itself on personalized service, including insurance appraisals.

PA 54

BOB LAMSON BEER STEINS, INC.
509 N. 22nd Street
Allentown, PA 18104

Phone: (800) 435-8611
(610) 435-8611
Fax: (610) 435-8188
Website: www.lamsonsteins.com
Hours: Mon-Fri: 8am-7pm
Sat: 8am-2pm
Other Hours by appointment

Services: Buy/Sell/Trade. Terms available upon request for larger purchases. Please inquire.

Secondary: Anheuser-Busch, Michelob, Budweiser, Bud Light, Coors, Strohs, Miller, steins and related collectibles with beer affiliations, i.e. neons, lights, clocks, signs, tap knobs, mirrors, plates, figurines.

Noteworthy: Incorporated in 1990, Bob Lamson Beer Steins, Inc. is owned and operated solely by the Lamson family. The company has a retail store located in Allentown, Pennsylvania, and also ships orders to every state in the nation and to Canada. Collectors should call with any additional questions they have regarding the company. Bob Lamson Beer Steins is an Anheuser-Busch Collectors Club Redemption Center.

Directory to Secondary Market Dealers

PA — CRAYON SOUP — 55

King of Prussia Plaza, King of Prussia, PA 19406

Phone: (610) 265-0458   (800) 552-3760
Fax: (610) 265-2979
Hours: Mon-Sat: 10-9:30,
       Sun: 11-6

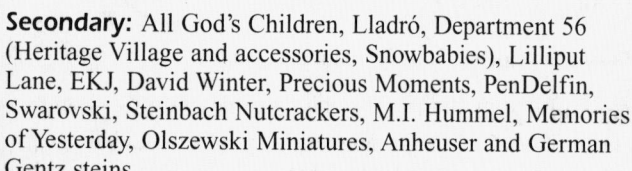

Services: Buy outright.

Secondary: All God's Children, Lladró, Department 56 (Heritage Village and accessories, Snowbabies), Lilliput Lane, EKJ, David Winter, Precious Moments, PenDelfin, Swarovski, Steinbach Nutcrackers, M.I. Hummel, Memories of Yesterday, Olszewski Miniatures, Anheuser and German Gentz steins.

Noteworthy: The formation of Crayon Soup in 1982 was a natural, considering that owners Joe and Trish Zawislack had already been collecting for 30 years! The store started in a mall kiosk, with the couple selling stickers and novelties geared toward children. Eventually, the Zawislacks entered the collectibles market. The name, Crayon Soup, was the brainchild of Trish, who formulated the name, thinking the couple would start an educational store for children. Today, the store is a Redemption Center for several collectible lines. Hummel enthusiasts will be delighted to view over 400 Hummels in stock. Crayon Soup hosts 40 collector events including artist appearances, and organizes in-store collector clubs. Information on new and retired products and collectors clubs is available free of charge.

PA — SAM'S STEINS & COLLECTIBLES — 56

2207 Lincoln Highway East RT 30
Lancaster, PA 17602

Phone: (717) 394-6404
E-mail: samssteins@msn.com
Website: www.samssteins.com
Hours: Mon-Wed & Sat: 10-6
       Thurs & Fri: 10-8, Sun: 11-5
       Closed Sun & Mon (Jan-Mar)

Services: Buy outright. Mail order catalog available, send two $.33 stamps.

Secondary: Specializes in beer steins (Anheuser-Busch, Miller, Coors, Strohs, Pabst, Hamm's, Yuengling, large selection of German beer steins) and brewery advertising items (steins, neons, signs, tap markers and mirrors). Authorized Anheuser-Busch Dealer. Sam also carries Cavanagh Coca-Cola Cubs, Ande Rooney porcelain signs, First Gear, ERTL, and Spec cast collector trucks and banks.

Noteworthy: Sam's Steins & Collectibles, located 1/8 mile from Dutch Wonderland, has been in business since 1967. A collector himself, owner Sam May houses one of the largest displays of beer memorabilia in the United States. Over 900 different U.S. and German steins are on display, including the stein in the Guinness Book of Records -- 4' tall which holds 8.45 gallons of beer.

PA — WORLDWIDE COLLECTIBLES AND GIFTS — 57

P.O. Box 158, 2 Lakeside Avenue
Berwyn, PA 19312-0158

Phone: (800) 222-1613   (610) 644-2442
Fax: (610) 889-9549
Website: www.worldwidecollectibles.com
Hours: Mon-Sat: 10-5, order desk open 24 hrs.

Services: A 64-page mail order catalog available free, upon request. Call for specific quotes. Prompt payment on all items purchased. Prompt delivery on items ordered.

Secondary: Swarovski, Lladró, Department 56, Disney Classics, M.I. Hummel, David Winter, Duncan Royale, Steiff, collector plates, bells, collector club pieces and many others.

Noteworthy: Worldwide Collectibles is a full service company established in 1975. They deal in current and secondary market pieces and maintain a large inventory on all lines carried. The Worldwide staff is actively involved with major insurers for replacement and estimate valuation purposes. Appraisals and references are available upon request.

SC — 58

1370 Broughton Street, Orangeburg, SC 29115

Phone: (803) 536-4176   (800) 822-5556 (orders only)
Fax: (803) 531-2007
Hours: Mon-Fri: 9-6, Sat: 9-5,
       Sun: 1:30-5:30 (Nov. & Dec. only)

Services: Buy/Sell. Visa, MasterCard, Discover and American Express accepted. Shipping available.

Secondary: Department 56 (Snow Village, Dickens Village, New England Village, Alpine Village, North Pole, Christmas in the City, Disney Parks Village, Snowbabies, Snowbunnies, All Through the House, Winter Silhouettes, Merry Makers), Harbour Lights, Shelia's, Keepers, Byers' Choice, Seraphim Classics, and Margaret Furlong.

Noteworthy: Broughton Christmas Shoppe, in business since 1983, is a family run business, catering to their customers' collectible needs. All staff members are collectors themselves, and offer friendly, knowledgeable service. Broughton's is a Gold Key Dealer for Department 56, a Platinum Dealer for Shelia's (3 exclusive custom designs) and an Earn Your Wings Dealer for Roman, Inc.

Directory to Secondary Market Dealers

TN | BARBARA'S GATLINBURG SHOPS | 59

Barbara's Elegants, The John Cody Gallery
The Gatlinburg Shop
511,716,963 Parkway, Gatlinburg, TN 37738

Phone: (800) 433-1132
E-mail: shop@barbarashops.com
Web site: www.barbarashops.com
Hours: Daily: 9-9

Services: As a service to their customers, Barbara's Gatlinburg Shops try to help both the buyer and the seller. They keep an up-to-date listing of collectibles that customers are interested in selling or buying. Call if you are interested in more information. There is no charge for the listing. A 25% commission is charged if a sale is made.
Secondary: All God's Children, Armani, Byers' Choice, Boyds Bearstone Bears, Cades Cove Cabin, Cairn Gnomes, Chilmark, Dept. 56, D. Winter, Disney Classics, Harmony Kingdom, Hudson, John Cody Prints, Legends, Mickey & Co., Sandicast, Swarovski, Wee Forest Folk, plus many more exciting lines!
Noteworthy: Barbara's started in 1977 as a small retailer. They have now grown to three shops with a large mailing list composed of customers from 49 states and several foreign countries. Barbara's ships daily, provides appraisals, and mails brochures and catalogs to customers interested in a particular line. "Our sales consultants are committed to you!"

SECONDARY MARKET SPECIALIST CIB 2000-2001

TX | AMANDA'S FINE GIFTS | 60

265 Central Park Mall
San Antonio, TX 78216-5506

Phone: (800) 441-4458
(210) 525-0412
Hours: Mon-Sat: 10-9, Sun: 12-6

Services: 10-month layaway. Consignments. Buy outright when needed. Redemption Center for Lladró, Disney, Swarovski, Armani, M.I. Hummel and Lalique Collectors Club. Appraisal service for insurance purposes.

Secondary: Lladró, Swarovski, M.I. Hummel, Ron Lee, Armani, Chilmark, Disney.

Noteworthy: Barry Harris developed a deep appreciation for Lladró artwork, which eventually led to the purchase of Amanda's Fine Gifts in 1983. Realizing the great potential for offering Lladró artwork and information to collectors, Barry and his staff have become known as experts in the field. The largest Lladró dealer in the southwest, Amanda's has welcomed Lladró family members to the store for artist appearances. Other guests have included Don Polland, Ron Lee, Michael Boyett, M.I. Hummel representatives and Armani artists.

TX | | 61

Cheryl M. McCants
(877) 519-5609

*Secondary Market Dealer
for
Halcyon Days
and
Bilston & Battersea Enamels
Buying - Selling*

SECONDARY MARKET SPECIALIST CIB 2000-2001

*140 Clearwater W.
Montgomery, TX 77356*
www.mccantsenamels.com
cmccants@mccantsenamels.com

TX | | 62

GARY'S COLLECTABLES

*Specializing in
Secondary Collectables
for...*
**Armani ♦ Beanie Babies
Cherished Teddies ♦ Harbour Lights
Lladro ♦ Snowbabies
Swarovski Crystal ♦ and more!**

*1217 Trinity Drive
Benbrook, Texas 76126-4209*

887-343-GARY or (817) 249-2741
Fax: (817) 249-6639
E-mail: gary@garyscollectables.com
www.gary@garyscollectables.com

Directory to Secondary Market Dealers

Collectible Inventory Record

Item Name: _____

Manufacturer's Name: _____ Artist's Name: _____

Series Name/Number: _____

Special Markings: _____

Year of Issue: _____ Edition Limit: _____

Purchase Price: _____ Date of Purchase: _____

Purchased From: _____

Address: _____ Phone: _____

Secondary Market Price: _____

Additional Information: _____

Item Name: _____

Manufacturer's Name: _____ Artist's Name: _____

Series Name/Number: _____

Special Markings: _____

Year of Issue: _____ Edition Limit: _____

Purchase Price: _____ Date of Purchase: _____

Purchased From: _____

Address: _____ Phone: _____

Secondary Market Price: _____

Additional Information: _____

Item Name: _____

Manufacturer's Name: _____ Artist's Name: _____

Series Name/Number: _____

Special Markings: _____

Year of Issue: _____ Edition Limit: _____

Purchase Price: _____ Date of Purchase: _____

Purchased From: _____

Address: _____ Phone: _____

Secondary Market Price: _____

Additional Information: _____

Item Name:

Manufacturer's Name: Artist's Name:

Series Name/Number:

Special Markings:

Year of Issue: Edition Limit:

Purchase Price: Date of Purchase:

Purchased From:

Address: Phone:

Secondary Market Price:

Additional Information:

Item Name:

Manufacturer's Name: Artist's Name:

Series Name/Number:

Special Markings:

Year of Issue: Edition Limit:

Purchase Price: Date of Purchase:

Purchased From:

Address: Phone:

Secondary Market Price:

Additional Information:

Item Name:

Manufacturer's Name: Artist's Name:

Series Name/Number:

Special Markings:

Year of Issue: Edition Limit:

Purchase Price: Date of Purchase:

Purchased From:

Address: Phone:

Secondary Market Price:

Additional Information:

Collectible Inventory Record

Item Name:

Manufacturer's Name: _____ Artist's Name:

Series Name/Number:

Special Markings:

Year of Issue: _____ Edition Limit:

Purchase Price: _____ Date of Purchase:

Purchased From:

Address: _____ Phone:

Secondary Market Price:

Additional Information:

Item Name:

Manufacturer's Name: _____ Artist's Name:

Series Name/Number:

Special Markings:

Year of Issue: _____ Edition Limit:

Purchase Price: _____ Date of Purchase:

Purchased From:

Address: _____ Phone:

Secondary Market Price:

Additional Information:

Item Name:

Manufacturer's Name: _____ Artist's Name:

Series Name/Number:

Special Markings:

Year of Issue: _____ Edition Limit:

Purchase Price: _____ Date of Purchase:

Purchased From:

Address: _____ Phone:

Secondary Market Price:

Additional Information:

Item Name:

Manufacturer's Name: Artist's Name:

Series Name/Number:

Special Markings:

Year of Issue: Edition Limit:

Purchase Price: Date of Purchase:

Purchased From:

Address: Phone:

Secondary Market Price:

Additional Information:

Item Name:

Manufacturer's Name: Artist's Name:

Series Name/Number:

Special Markings:

Year of Issue: Edition Limit:

Purchase Price: Date of Purchase:

Purchased From:

Address: Phone:

Secondary Market Price:

Additional Information:

Item Name:

Manufacturer's Name: Artist's Name:

Series Name/Number:

Special Markings:

Year of Issue: Edition Limit:

Purchase Price: Date of Purchase:

Purchased From:

Address: Phone:

Secondary Market Price:

Additional Information:

Editorial Index